編集主幹

清水　護

成田成寿

講談社学術文庫

●編集主幹

東京女子大学教授――清水　護

東京教育大学名誉教授――成田成寿

●編集委員

国際基督教大学教授――小林栄智

共立女子大学教授――中村義勝

東京学芸大学名誉教授――細川泉二郎

共立女子大学教授――吉田正俊

●編集参与

英語教育協議会英語研修所主任講師―Edmund C. Wilkes

共立女子大学講師――Glyndon Townhill

国際基督教大学教授――Noah S. Brannen

はしがき

本辞典は，種々の工夫をこらした，最新の，ユニークな書きおろしの和英辞典である。ひらがな見出しで引きやすいと同時に，最近の言葉や表現までも精選した語数5万語は，比較的初歩の英語学習者はもとより，高校生から大学生までの学習と，一般社会人の実用にじゅうぶん役立つことと確信する。

本辞典は手頃な大きさで，英語の語感，文体，慣用語法，米英の風俗習慣，会話までじゅうぶんに考慮をはらった，文例中心主義の活用英作文辞典としても広く役立つものである。書くときばかりでなく会話の際にも応用できるであろう。日本語を英語に訳すのには，多少のぎごちなさが伴いがちなものであるが，本辞典はできるだけ自然な英語になるように努力した。具体的方法として，

(1) 見出し語は「講談社国語辞典」に準拠して，さらにそれに大幅に新しい用語を加え，現代国語を中心に選定した。見出し語の順序は，五十音順にすることとした。

(2) 語義の分類にあたっては，日本語を英語で表現する立場から検索の便を考慮して，慎重に独自の工夫を加えた。

(3) 訳語だけ与えられても実際の運用にはふじゅうぶんであるので，見出し語の訳語はおもに名詞だけに限り，かつ煩瑣を避けるため代表的訳語にしぼった。また類似の意味をもった語句を列記する必要があるときは，その意味の差異などもできる限り解説した。

(4) 文例は平明簡潔を旨とした。収めた文例は6万に及び，応用範囲は広く，教室から実際社会までの要求にじゅうぶん応えうる，清新な和英辞典である。また表現を豊かにするため同じ原文を二通り，または三通りの英文にも言い換えた例もある。

(5) 文例中の見出し語に相当する個所，または見出し語に相当する英語を含む慣用語法は原則として斜字体にして判別を容易にした。

(6) 語法，語感，文体上の注意（文語的とか，口語的とか），米語と英語の区別，米英との風俗習慣の相違に関する英訳上の周到な解説，また発音の指示も適宜加えてある。

(7) C（可算名詞），U（非可算名詞）等の記号はとくに用いなかったが，可算名詞 (Countable) には見出し語の名詞に a，または an を付してこの区別をも示すように配慮をした。

(8) つづりは米式つづりを優先させ，米英で異なる場合は，原則として米式のみを採用した。

(9) 米英人との共同作業。問題のない英文を示すためには，米英の雑誌や諸文献に使われている文例に頼るのも一方法であろうが，日本語としては英語にない特殊な言い方もあるわけで，これらもできるだけ分かりやすい英語に言い

表わす工夫をすべきである。こういう場合はもちろん，全般にわたって自然で明快な英文を例示するため，日本語に堪能な米英人の協力を得ることができたのは本辞典の大きな特色である。

これに関して，別記の編集参与の諸氏のほか共立女子大学の Patricia H. Massy 氏，元国際基督教大学の Anatole A. Gorshkoff 氏をはじめ，多くの教職にある米英人の助言に負うところが多い。

最後に，これまで編集，原稿の作成，ないしは校閲にご協力いただいた下記の諸氏，その他いちいちお名前はあげない多数の方々に厚く謝意を表したい。

赤祖父哲二	新井　廸之	池谷　　彰	石黒さえ子
岩淵　育男	氏家　文昭	木野　嘉明	倉持　三郎
小島　義郎	小林　祐子	四宮　　満	柴田　又吉
清水　阿や	高橋　俊昭	田部　　滋	土屋　晴子
中島　　知	野村　行信	宮尾　洋子	横山　幸三
吉岡　元子	吉沢　　貞	吉田　正治	和仁　恒夫

（五十音順）

またこの長い年月のあいだ，隠忍してくださった出版社の方々の寛容と好意に深謝し，直接仕事を担当された方々の労をねぎらうしだいである。

なお本辞典につきお気付きの点はご教示いただき，将来内容の改善をはかることができれば幸である。

1976年 8 月

清　水　護

成　田　成　寿

この辞書を利用する人のために

I．見出し語

(1) 見出し語は，ひらがな見出しを採用し，現代かなづかいで示し，五十音順に配列，相当する漢字を【　】で囲んで示した。漢字は当用漢字には限らない。
　外来語はカタカナで表記した。

(2) 配列は清音，濁音，半濁音の順とし，接頭辞，接尾辞はその後とした。
　はは【母】
　はば【幅】

(3) 促音の「っ」，拗(ょう)音の「ゃ」，「ゅ」，「ょ」はそれぞれ「つ」，「や」，「ゆ」，「よ」の前に配列した。
　みょう【妙】
　みよう【見様】

(4) 外来語は国語の後に置き，長音は―で示し，「あ行」に置き換えた位置に配列した。
　アパート（アパアトの位置においた）　**データ**（デエタの位置に置いた）

(5) 見出し語に相当する漢字表記には，送りがなは省略しない法をとった。
　ふるま·う【振る舞う】

(6) 見出し語が動詞，形容詞で，語幹と語尾とに分けられるときは，その間に「·」を入れた。
　か·く【書く】　**わか·い【若い】**

(7) 接頭辞・接尾辞はそれぞれ結びつく語の位置を - で示した。

(8) 合成語は見出し語の部分を―で表わし，用例のあとに改行して示した。

II．訳　語

(1) 訳語，訳文のつづりは米式を優先させた。

(2) 訳語は主として代表訳語に限り，訳語を併記する必要があるときは，その意味，用法の差などを《　》で囲み解説した。
　しゅうぜん【修繕】 repair; mending《mend は「構造の簡単な小さなもの」の修繕に用い，repair は「家などの大きなものや，自動車・テレビ・時計などの複雑なもの」の修繕に用いることが多い。またアメリカの口語では，repair, mend のかわりに，しばしば fix〔up〕が用いられる》

(3) 訳語をその意味によって分類する必要がなくても，用例が豊富な項目では，見やすさをはかるため，助詞などによって用例を整理した。
　ひつよう【必要】

1〖必要だ〗…………………………	**4**〖必要はない〗……………………
2〖必要を〗…………………………	**5**〖必要な〗…………………………
3〖必要がある〗……………………	…………………………………………

III．つづり，用例，語法

(1) つづり，用例，語法は米式を優先させ，とくに必要なときは，㊊，㊎の記号あるいは《　》で囲み解説によってその相違を示した。
　めいよ【名誉】 honor.
　はいいろ【灰色】 ㊊ gray; ㊎ grey.
　エレベーター ㊊ an elevator; ㊎ a lift.
　まど【窓】 ぼんやりとバスの～から外を見ていた I was looking out〔of〕the *window* of the bus absent-mindedly.《of を省くのは米語法》

(2) 用例の日本語の中で，見出し語に相当する箇所は～で示した。この場合，動詞，形容詞などのように活用があって語幹と語尾を「・」でわけたものは，語幹だけを～で示した。

はいかん【拝観】 ¶その国宝を～に行った

は・える【生える】 ¶庭に雑草が～えだした

(3) 用例中の見出し語に相当する英語，またそれを含む慣用語法のうち注意すべき部分は原則としては斜字体で示した。

うみ【海】 the sea. そのホテルは～に面している The hotel faces on *the sea.* 辺り一面，火の～であった There was *a sea of* flames all around.

(4) 日本文のことわざに相当する英文のことわざは，《諺》として斜字体で示した。

かえる【蛙】 ～の子は～《諺》*Like father, like son.*

(5) 用例中の英語表現が他の英語表現と交換可能なときは，≒の記号のあとにその表現を添えて丸かっこで囲んだ。

うまみ【うま味】 ～のある文体 a *charming* (≒*pleasing*) style.

はいたつ【配達】 この手紙はまちがって～された This letter *has been wrongly delivered* (≒*was miscarried*).

(6) ひとつの日本語の用例に英訳がふたつ以上あるときは，例句は ;（セミコロン）で区切って示し，例文は /（斜線）で区切って示した。

はな・つ【放つ】 芳香を～つ *smell* sweet; *emit* (≒*give out*) a sweet smell.

は【歯】 この問題は～が立たない This problem is too hard for me. / This problem is beyond me.

(7) つねに定冠詞 the とともに用いられる語は the を付けて示した。

たいよう【大洋】 the ocean.

(8) 訳語の名詞が「可算名詞」(Countable) のときは，不定冠詞 a（または an）をつけ，「非可算名詞」(Uncountable) との区別を示した。

ほん【本】 a book.　**りんご【林檎】** an apple.　**みず【水】** water.

(9) 訳語の名詞が「加算名詞」(Countable) にも，「非加算名詞」(Uncountable) にも用いられるときは a（または an）を〔 〕に入れて示した。

いのり【祈り】〔a〕prayer.

(10) 名詞の訳語で複数形が不規則なもの，誤りやすいものはかっこの中に示した。

げんしょう【現象】 a phenomenon (複 phenomena).

は【葉】 a leaf (複 leaves).

(11) 用例中の一般的な「人」を示すばあい，主語と同じ「人」は，*one, one's* を用い，主語と異なる「人」は *a person, a person's* を用い，すべて斜字体で示した。また一般的な「物」を示すばあいは，*something* または *a thing* を用い，斜字体で示した。

(12) 適当な英訳ができない日本語の名詞は，ローマ字の斜字体で示した。

さけ【酒】 *sake*; (酒類) alcoholic drinks.

IV. 専門語の表記

専門語については〘鳥〙のような略表記を用いず，〘鳥類〙とした。

はやぶさ【隼】〘鳥類〙　**はんおん【半音】**〘音楽〙

V. 記号

(　)	語義分類；単数形，複数形；男性形，女性形	⇒	参照
(≒　)	交換可能	〔 〕	省略可能
《　》	語法，文体，発音，風物などの解説	〘 〙	専門語
米	米語	英	英語
単	単数形	複	複数形
;	語句の区切り	/	例文の区切り

あ

あ Ah! / Oh! / Oh (≒ O) God! / Heavens! / Dear me! ¶ ～, きみか *Why,* it's you.

ああ ¶ この子どもは～言えばこう言うから小憎らしい This child always *talks back to* me, and this is why I hate him. 彼が～おくびょうだとは思わなかった I did not think he was *so* timid. ～忙しくては休む暇もないはずだ *Such* a busy man as he cannot have any spare time. ～暗い所で読書すると目を痛める You will strain your eyes if you read in *such* a dark place. ～無礼な男は初めてだ He is the most impolite man I have ever met. ～がみがみ言わなくともいいのに He need not scold us *so* violently. ～言うには言ったが, 実のところ半信半疑なんだ Although I did say *such* a thing, I am really not quite sure of it. / I said *that,* but I am really not quite sure of it.

ああ【嗚呼】¶ ～, きれいな景色だ *What* a beautiful sight! ～, 寒い *How* cold it is! ～, わかった *Oh,* I see! ～忙しい I am *exceedingly* busy. ～びっくりした *Ah,* what a shock. 「この本はきみのかね」「～そうだ」"Is this book yours?" "*Yes,* it is." ～なるほど *Oh,* I see! ～痛い *Ouch!*

ああいう ¶ ～所はきらいだ I dislike *such* a place. ～ことはやめてほしい I want you not to do it. ～しゃべり方はだれに教わったのですか Who has taught you to talk *like that?*

アーケード an arcade.

アース〔無電〕英 an earth; 米 a ground.

アーチ an arch. ¶ ～式のダム an arch 〔dam〕.

ああでもない ¶ どんな計画を立てても, 彼はいつでも～こうでもないと言って反対する He always *raises objections* to whatever plan I make. ～こうでもないと言わないで, 私の言うとおりにしてください Do as I say without *objecting* (≒ *raising objections*) *this way or that.*

アートし【アート紙】art paper.

アートシアター an art theater.

アーメン〔キリスト教〕Amen!

アーモンド an almond.

アール (面積の単位) an are. ¶ 1～の土地 an *are* of land.

あい【愛】love. ¶ ～は惜しみなく奪う *Love* is a plunderer. ～は死よりも強し *Love* is stronger than death. (Love is stronger as death (聖書のことば)). ～のささやき whispers of *love.* ～のない結婚 a *loveless* marriage. 彼の～をすなおに受け入れた I accepted his *love* meekly. / I was willing to accept his *love.* ～におぼれて子どもを甘やかしすぎた I *doted on* my child and spoiled him. この子は親の～に飢えている This child is starving for parental *love.* 命をかけてあなたを～します I *love* you with all my life. 私は私なりに国を～している I *love* my country in my own way. 彼はなかなか稚気～すべき人だ He is a nice fellow of a childish disposition.

あい【藍】indigo (形容詞としても使われる). ¶ 窓ガラスは～色がかっていた The window pane was *bluish.* その布地は～色に染められていた The cloth was dyed *indigo.* ～より出でて～より青し(諺) A disciple sometimes outshines his master.

あいあいがさ【相合い傘】¶ ふたりは～で歩いていた The two walked in the rain *under an umbrella.*

あいいく【愛育】¶ 子どもを～する *bring up* a child *with tender care.*

あいいれな・い【相容れない】¶ 彼の教育方針は時勢と～い His principles of education *are out of harmony with* the times. 私の考えは彼らの考えと～い My idea *runs counter to* theirs. 両者の主張はどうしても～い The assertions of both parties *are* quite *incompatible.* この二つの方策は～いところがある These two plans *conflict with each other.*

アイ エム エフ IMF (<the *I*nternational *M*onetary *F*und 国際通貨基金).

アイ エル オー ILO (<the *I*nternational *L*abor *O*rganization 国際労働機構).

あいえんか【愛煙家】a heavy (≒ habitual; an addicted) smoker.

アイ オー シー IOC (<the *I*nternational *O*lympic *C*ommittee 国際オリンピック委員会).

あいか【哀歌】a sad (≒ plaintive) song; an elegy; a dirge.

あいかぎ【合い鍵】¶ この～はきかない This *master key* doesn't work. これの～を作ってください Make *a duplicate* of this key.

あいかわらず【相変わらず】¶ あの人はいつも～だ He *is* always *the same.* ～忙しい He *is* 〔*as*〕 busy *as usual.* 彼は～減らず口をたたいた He made a sarcastic retort *as usual.* 彼は～こつこつ勉強した He studied *as* hard *as ever.*

あいかん【哀歓】joys and sorrows.

あいがん【哀願】entreaty. ¶ われわれは彼に彼女の助命を～した We *appealed* to him for sparing her life. / We *begged* him to spare her life. 彼女は～するかのように私に話しかけた She spoke to me *imploringly.*

あいがん【愛玩】¶ 彼女は小犬を～している She *makes a pet of* a puppy. これは私の～用のチンだ This is my *pet* Pekingese.

あ

—動物 *one's* pet. —物 *one's* prized article.

あいぎ【合い着】 a spring (≒ an autumn) suit (≒ wear).

あいきゃく【相客】 a fellow lodger. ¶ 宿屋でひとりの老人と〜になった I *shared a room with* an old man at the inn.

あいきょう【愛郷】 ¶ 彼は〜心がある He *loves his home town* (≒ *native place*).

あいきょう【愛敬・愛嬌】 a charm. ¶ 彼女は器量はよくないが〜がある She is homely but *amiable*. なんと〜のある顔だろう What a *charming* face! 彼女は目に〜がある She has *a charm* in her eyes. 彼はだれにでも〜を振りまく He tries to *please* everybody. 彼の失敗はご〜だった He failed only to *please* those around him. あのウエートレスはいつも〜のない返事をする That waitress always makes a *blunt* answer.
—者 ¶ あの子は〜者だ That child *is jolly and charming*.

あいくぎ【合釘】 a dowel; a double-pointed nail.

あいくち【合口・匕首】 a dagger; a knife.

あいくるし・い【愛くるしい】 cute; lovely.

あいけん【愛犬】 ¶ ジョンは彼の〜だ John is his *pet dog*.
—家 a lover of dogs. ¶ あの人は〜家なのにネコはきらいだ He *loves dogs* so much, and yet hates cats. / He *loves dogs* as much as hates cats.

あいこ【相子】 a tie. ¶ 勝負は〜になった The game ended in *a tie*. きみとぼくはこれで〜(恨みっこなし)だ Now you *are even with* me. これで〜になったわけだ Now we *are* all *square*.

あいこ【愛顧】 patronage. ¶ ご〜のほどお願いします We solicit your *patronage*. 当店をご〜のほどを Please *patronize* our store.

あいご【愛護】 protection. ¶ 動物〜協会 the Society for the Prevention of Cruelty to Animals (S.P.C.A. と略して呼ぶことがある).

あいこう【愛好】 ¶ 彼は音楽を〜する He *loves* (≒ *is fond of*; *adores*) music. / He is *a lover* of music. 日本人は平和を〜する国民です The Japanese are a peace-*loving* nation.
—家(者) a lover; (動・植物の) a fancier; (芸術などの) a devotee; (スポーツなどの) a fan.

あいこうしん【愛校心】 love of *one's* school; love of *one's* alma mater. ¶ 彼は〜に燃えている He *is* deeply *attached to his school*. / He *loves his school* dearly.

あいこく【愛国】 ¶ 彼は〜の熱情に燃えている He *loves his own country* passionately. / He *is patriotic*.
—者 a patriot. —心 patriotism; love of *one's* country.

あいことば【合い言葉】 a password. ¶ おたがいに〜を言うことにしよう Let's give the *password* to each other.

あいさい【愛妻】 *one's* [beloved] wife.
—家 a devoted (≒ loving) husband.

あいさつ【挨拶】 greeting; salutation.
¶ 彼らは初対面の〜を交わした They *introduced themselves to* each other. あなたがたは毎日〜を交わしますか Do you exchange *greetings* every day? ひと言ご〜申し上げます Allow me to say a word of *greeting*. 先生に〜もせず帰る子どもたちもいた Some children went home without *saying good-by*[*e*] to their teachers. 帽子を取って私に〜したのはだれだろう I wonder who it was that raised his hat to me. 「おはようございます」とまず彼に〜した "Good morning, sir," I *greeted* him before everything else.

あいし【哀史】 a sad (≒ pathetic) history.

あいし【哀詩】 an elegy.

あいじ【愛児】 *one's* dear child (複 children).

あいしゃ【愛車】 *one's* own car.

アイシャドー eye shadow. ¶ 彼女は〜をつけている She wears *eye shadow*.

あいしゅう【哀愁】 sorrow. ¶ 彼の話は皆の〜をそそった His story made us *feel sad*. このシャンソン歌手がうたうと歌は一種の〜を帯びる Songs, when sung by this chanson singer, take on a peculiar *pathetic* note.

あいしょう【相性】 affinity. ¶ あのふたりは〜がいい(悪い)ようだ It seems they *are* (not) *made for* each other. / It seems the two *are* (not) *congenial*. 彼女との結婚の〜を易者に見てもらった I consulted a fortuneteller if she and I would be a happy pair.

あいしょう【愛称】 a pet name. ¶ 彼女を〜で呼ぶ call her by her *pet name*. ジョンは妻をシュガー(砂糖)という〜で呼ぶ John's pet name for his wife is "Sugar." / John calls his wife by the pet name of "Sugar."

あいしょう【愛唱】 ¶ これは私の〜する歌だ This is my favorite song.
—歌集 a songbook.

あいしょう【愛誦】 ¶ 彼はよくゲーテの詩を〜する He often *recites* Goethe's poems *admiringly*.

あいじょう【愛情】 love; affection. ¶ 彼はその娘に〜をいだきはじめた He began to feel *affection* for the girl. あの人は〜の深い人だ He is a man of strong *affection*. 手紙は彼に対する〜にあふれていた The letter was full of *affection* for him. きみは彼女の〜をかち得るだろう You will win her *heart*. 彼は自分の仕事に〜を持っている He *is attached to* his own work. 彼女の〜のこもった手紙に感動した I was moved by her *affectionate* letter. 〜のない結婚は罪悪だ A *loveless* marriage is a sin.

あいじょう【愛嬢】 *one's* beloved (≒ dear) daughter.

あいしょか【愛書家】 a booklover; a bibliophile.

あいじん【愛人】 (男性) a lover; (女性) a love; (男・女) a sweetheart.

あいず【合図】 a signal. ¶ まだ仕事を始める〜はない The *signal* for us to begin our work has not been given. 〜の鐘が鳴っている The *signal* bell is ringing. 彼女は目で彼に〜した She *made a sign to* him with the eye. 〜が出るとすぐ彼らは席に着いた They took their seats *at a given signal*. 手を上げて出発の〜を

してください Raise your hand for us to start.

アイスクリーム〔an〕ice cream; 囲 an ice.

アイスコーヒー iced coffee.

アイススケート〔ice〕skating.

アイスホッケー ice hockey.

アイスランド Iceland.
—語 Icelandic. —人 an Icelander.

あい・する【愛する】⇒あい

あいせき【哀惜】 grief. ¶ご尊父ご他界の悲報に接し～の念に耐えません The news of your father's death has filled me with deepest *grief*.

アイゼン〘登山〙 climbing irons.

あいそ【哀訴】 a petition.

あいそ【愛想】 ¶～のよい agreeable; amiable; affable. ～のない(冷たい) cold; (ぶっきらぼうな) blunt. 彼は目上の者には～がいい He makes himself *agreeable* to his elders. あの店の者は客にあまり～がよくない They are not very *civil* (≒ *obliging*) to their customers at that store. 彼女は～よくもてなしてくれた She received me *warmly*. 彼は子どもたちにいいお子さんたちだと～を言った He said *nice things* about my children. 彼にはまったく～が尽きた I *am* quite *disgusted with* him. 彼は息子に～をつかしている He *is out of patience with* his son. 彼は彼女に～をつかされた He *was given up* (≒ *was abandoned*) by her. / He *lost* (≒ *killed*) *her affection*. 長居して～をつかされないように注意しなさい Be careful not to *overstay your welcome*.

あいそう【愛想】⇒あいそ

あいぞう【愛憎】 love and hatred (≒ hate).

あいぞう【愛蔵】 ¶～の書 *one's cherished* books. ～の骨董(こっとう)品 *one's treasured* antiques.

アイソトープ【物理】 an isotope (ふつう radioisotope を指す).

あいた【愛他】 —主義 altruism. —主義者 an altruist.

あいた【開いた・空いた】 ¶～窓 an *open* window. ～部屋 a *vacant* room. ～席がありますか Is there any seat still *vacant*? ～室がありますか Is there any *vacancy*? 彼はびっくりして～口がふさがらなかった He was so frightened that he kept his mouth wide *open*.

あいた【あ痛】 Ouch!

あいだ【間】1〘時間〙 ¶1時と2時の～に来てください Please come〔to see me〕*between* one and two.

彼とは長い～会っていない I have not seen him *for a long time*.

しばらくの～彼は黙って立っていた He kept standing without uttering a word *for a little while*.

当分の～はじっとしていなさい Keep quiet *for the time being* (≒ *for some time*).

夏の～軽井沢にいた I stayed at Karuizawa *during* the summer.

留守の～にだれか来たらしい Somebody seems to have come *during my absence* (≒ *while I was out*).

元気な～は彼のめんどうを見てやれる I can look after him *as long as* I am in good health.

そうしている～に彼は病気になった *In the meantime* (≒ *Meanwhile*) he fell ill.

授乳と授乳との～をもっとあけなさい Suckle the baby *at longer intervals*.

15分ずつ～をおいてけいれんがあった I had a convulsive fit *at fifteen minute intervals* (≒ *every fifteen minutes*).

2〘場所〙 ¶名古屋は東京と大阪の～にある Nagoya lies *between* Tokyo and Osaka. / Nagoya is nearly *halfway between* Tokyo and Osaka.

木々の～では小鳥がさえずっていた There were small birds singing *in* the trees.

何マイルもの～人影を見なかった Not a soul was to be seen *for* many miles.

10メートルの～をおいてくいを打った I drove in a stake *at ten meter intervals*.

～をあけて通してあげなさい *Make way* and let him pass.

この列とこの列の～を1歩詰めなさい Please *close* these two lines a step. / Make the space *between* these two rows a bit closer.

列の～に割り込まぬこと Don't squeeze yourself *into* the line.

戸の～に指をはさまれた I had one of my fingers caught *in* the door. / Some of my fingers were pinched *between* the doors.

3〘関係〙 ¶ふたりの～で話し合ってほしい I want you to talk *with each other* about it. / Please discuss the matter *between* you.

われわれの～では彼女の評判は芳しくない She is not well spoken of *among* us.

われわれの～にはなんのやましいところはない We have nothing to be ashamed of *between* us.

ふたりの～はどうもうまくいかないようだ It seems they don't get on well *with each other*.

なんでも言ってくれよ，きみとぼくとの～じゃないか Speak out your mind. You should not stand on ceremony *with* me.

だれかふたりの～に立ってくれる人はないかね Don't you know of somebody who will be kind enough to mediate *between* them?

あいたい・する【相対する】 ¶両軍は川をはさんで～した Both armies *faced* (≒ *confronted*) *each other* across the river.

あいだがら【間柄】 relation. ¶きみと彼とはどういう～か What *relation* is he to you? 彼とは親しい～だ I am on friendly *terms* with him.

あいたずさえて【相携えて】 ¶夫婦～旅に出た The couple started on a journey *together*. ふたり～私のところに来た They came to see me *together*.

あいちゃく【愛着】 attachment; love (*for*). ¶彼は故郷の山々に～を感じている He *is attached to* the mountains around his native place. 母校に～を覚えるようになった I became *attached to* my alma mater. 彼は海に深い～を持っている He has *a passionate love* for the sea.

あいちょう【哀調】 ¶～を帯びた歌 a *plaintive*

あ

song. ～を帯びたメロディー a *sad* melody. ～を帯びた朗読ぶりだった He recited the poem in a *plaintive* manner.

あいちょう【愛鳥】 ―家 a bird fancier; a lover of birds. ―週間 the Bird Week.

あいつ【彼奴】 ¶ 女をだますなんて～はとんでもないやつだ What *a fellow* to cheat a woman! ～にやれるならぼくだってやれるさ If *he* can, I can. ～どこの馬の骨かわからんが, おうへいなやつだ I don't know where *that guy* comes from, but I think he holds his head very high.

あいついで【相次いで】 ¶ 一行全員～倒れた All the members of the party fell down *one after another*. 編隊は～飛び立っていった *One* formation *after another* took off. いろいろやっかいなことが～起きた Many troubles happened *in succession*. われわれの間に～病人が出た Many of us were taken ill *one after another*.

あいづち【相槌】 ¶ 彼らは私の言うことに～を打った They *chimed in with* what I remarked.

あいて【相手】 a companion. ¶ テニスの～はだれですか Who is your *partner* in playing tennis? 彼がピンポンの～をしてくれた He *played against* me at table tennis. 彼にあなたの～をしてもらおう I will let him *keep company with* you. ボーリングで彼の～になる者はこのグループにはいない No one in this group can *be a match for* him in bowling. 彼女を～にして英語の会話を練習するといいだろう It will be nice for you to practice English conversation *on* her. だれも～にしてくれなくなった Now I have no one to *have anything to do with* me. しばらくお客の～をしていてほしい I want you to *bear* the guest *company* for a while. いつも私が彼の将棋の～をする I always play a game of Japanese chess *with* him. 話す～を捜しているらしい He seems to be seeking for *a person to talk to*. 彼は～として不足はなかった No other person *is a better match for* me than he. けんかをするなら私が～になろう I will *have a quarrel with* you if you want to have one. 遊び― a playmate. 競争― a rival. 相談― an adviser. 話し― a person to talk to.

アイディア an idea. ¶ それはすばらしい～だ That's *a* splendid *idea*! 会の進め方についてなにかいい～があったら聞かせてください Please give us any good *idea* about the procedure of the meeting.

あいでし【相弟子】 a fellow pupil (≒ disciple).

あいとう【哀悼】 sorrow. ¶ 謹んで～の意を表します I respectfully express my *condolence* to you. われわれは彼の不慮の死に～の意を表した We expressed our *regret* over his sudden death.
―式 a memorial service.

あいどく【愛読】 ¶ 彼は若いころその書を～した He used to *read* the book *with great pleasure* when young. 私はマーク＝トウェインを～している Mark Twain is *my favorite author*. その小説は家庭の主婦に～されている The novel is *very popular* (≒ *a favorite*) among housewives.
―者 ¶ その雑誌は～者が多い The magazine has a large circle of *readers*. 私はデーリーエクスプレス紙の～者だ I am *a regular reader* of the Daily Express. ―書 *one's* favorite book.

アイドル an idol. ¶ 民衆の～ *a* popular *idol*.

あいにく unfortunately; unluckily. ¶ ～雨が降りだした *Unfortunately* it began to rain. ～彼は不在だった *To my disappointment*, he was not at home. ～だがほかに約束がある *I am sorry* I have another engagement. それは～だね That's *too bad*. お～さま I'm sorry.

アイヌ (アイヌ人) an Ainu; (全体) the Ainus.
―語 Ainu.

あいのこ【合いの子・間の子】 ¶ 白人と黒人の～ a mulatto. ヨーロッパ人とアジア人の～ a Eurasian. 白人とアメリカインディアンの～ a half-breed. 彼は日本人とフランス人の～だ He was born of Japanese and French parentage. 彼女は父はアメリカ人, 母は日本人の～だ She was born of an American father and a Japanese mother.

あいのて【合いの手・間の手】 ¶ 彼が歌うと聴衆は手拍子の～を入れた When he started singing, the audience *beat time* with their hands.

あいのり【相乗り】 ¶ タクシーに彼と～した I *went* in the same taxi *with* him.

あいば【愛馬】 *one's* favorite horse.

アイバンク an eye bank.

あいはん・する【相反する】 ¶ ふたりは～する意見を持っている The two have *antagonistic* views against each other. 会員の利益は～している The interests of the members of the club *run counter to* each other.

あいびき【逢い引き】 a date. ¶ ふたりは公園で～した The two lovers *met secretly* in the park. / The two lovers *had a date secretly* in the park.

あいぶ【愛撫】 caress. ¶ 彼女はしばらくぶりで会ったわが子を抱いて～した She embraced her child whom she had not seen for a long time and *caressed* her.

あいふく【合い服】 ¶ きょうは～がよかろう You had better wear your *spring clothes* today.

あいふだ【合い札】 a check.

あいべつ【哀別】 a sad parting.

あいべや【相部屋】 ¶ ～で彼と同じ宿屋に部屋をとった I *shared* the hotel *room* with him.

あいぼ【愛慕】 attachment; love; affection.

あいぼう【相棒】 *one's* mate; *one's* fellow. ¶ A君とB君は～だ A and B are *partners*.

あいま【合間】 an interval. ¶ 仕事の～にテレビを見た I watched television *between* work.

あいまい【曖昧】 ¶ ～な vague. その答えは～だ The answer *is not clear*. ～な説明をする give an *ambiguous* explanation; explain *ambiguously*. 彼はいつも～な態度をとる He always takes an *undecisive* attitude. この記事は～だ This news *is of doubtful authority*. / This report *is not definite*. 何もかも～もことしている Everything *is in hazy vagueness*. /

Nothing *is distinct*. 彼の返事は～もことしている His answer *is vague* (≒ *ambiguous*; *equivocal*).

あいまって【相まって】 ¶ 両者～効果をあげている The two *go hand in hand to* be effective. 精神と肉体が～人間性を形づくる Mind and body *combine to* form humanity.

あいみたがい【相身互い】 ¶ 武士は～ (諺) It is a *samurai's* duty to help his kind.

あいよう【愛用】 ¶ もっと国産品を～すべきだ We should buy more domestic products. これが彼の～のカメラだ This is his *favorite* camera.

あいよく【愛欲】 love [and lust]; passion. ¶ 彼は～のとりことなった He became a slave to *passion*.

あいらし・い【愛らしい】 ¶ なんと～い少女だろう What a *pretty* girl she is! リスは～い目をしている A squirrel has *charming* eyes. この人形は口もとが～い This doll has *lovely* lips.

アイルランド Ireland.
—語 Irish. —人 an Irishman. —共和国 the Irish Republic; the Republic of Ireland; Eire.

あいろ【隘路】 a bottleneck. ¶ 生産の～を打開する break the *bottleneck in* production. 労働力不足が～になっている A labor shortage is the *bottleneck*.

アイロン an iron. ¶ ズボンに～をかける *iron* trousers. ～をかけてワイシャツのしわをとる *iron out* the wrinkles in a shirt.

あいわ【哀話】 a sad (≒ pathetic) story.

あ・う【合う】 **1** 〖寸法が一致する〗 fit. ¶ その服は彼女の体にぴったり～った The dress *fitted* her neatly.
その手袋はぼくの手に～わぬ Those gloves don't *fit* me.
その絵は額の大きさに～う The picture *fits* the frame.
寸法の～わぬ箱を持ってきた They have brought me a box made of *wrong* measurements.
2 〖証言・報告などが一致する〗 agree with. ¶ 彼の言っていることは事実と～わぬ His testimony does not *agree with* the facts.
二つの証言はぴったりと～っている The two testimonies *coincide* perfectly with each other.
3 〖意見・気質・調子などが〗 agree (*with*).
¶ ふたりの意見は～わなかった The two didn't *agree*. / They were of *different* opinions.
息の～った仲だった We *got on well* with each other. / We *hit it off* together.
ふたりは性格が～わず離婚した As they were of *conflicting* characters, they were divorced.
テンポが～わぬので困った It was difficult for me to *adjust myself to* the tempo.
彼の考えに～うように計画を立てなさい Make your plan *on* his ideas.
4 〖時刻・勘定・答えなどが〗 ¶ きみの時計は～っていますか *Is* your watch *right* (≒ *correct*)? / Do you have the *correct* time? / Are you sure your watch *is right*?
眼鏡の度が～わない My glasses *are* not *correct*.
ピアノは音階が～っていない The piano *is not in tune* (≒ *is out of tune*).
収支の勘定が～わない The accounts do not *balance*.
答えは～っている The answer *is correct*. / You *are right*.
5 〖制度・慣習に合致する〗 ¶ そんなことはわが家の家風に～わぬ Such a thing *is* not *in harmony with* the ways of our family.
大家族制は日本の現状に～わぬ The large family system *is* not *suited to* the present social conditions of Japan.
6 〖体質・味覚などに〗 agree. ¶ 日本酒はぼくの体質に～わない *Sake* does not *agree with* me.
山より海の気候がぼくの体に～っている The climate of the seaside *suits* me better than that of the highlands.
お口に～いますかどうか I wonder if you *like* it.
7 〖性格・能力・趣味など〗 ¶ そういうもうけ仕事は彼の性分に～わぬ He *is* not *suited for* such a profitable venture.
ジャズはぼくの趣味に～わない Jazz does not *suit* my taste.
8 〖色彩・食品などが〗 ¶ この料理には白ぶどう酒がよく～う White wine *goes* very *well with* this dish.
甘いものと酒とは私の口に～わぬ Sweet things and *sake* do not *suit* my taste.
壁の色と敷物の色とが～っていない The walls and the carpet do not *match* in color.
どの色とどの色とがよく～うか What colors *match* well *with* each other?
このネクタイとこの背広とはよく～う This tie and the lounge coat *match* well. / This tie *goes well with* the suit.
9 〖人に似合う〗 ¶ 紺がきみによく～う The blue color *becomes* you. / Blue *looks good on* you.
この柄はきみに～う This pattern *looks* very *good on* you.
10 〖引き合う〗 ¶ これではとても～った話じゃない It doesn't *pay* at all. / It's anything but a *paying* business.

あ・う【会う】 see; meet. **1** 〖面会する〗 ¶ 久しく彼女には～っていない I *have* not *seen* her for quite a while.
この前お～いしたのはいつでしたかしら When did I *see* you last? / When was it that I *saw* you last?
またお～いしたいと思います I hope we can *get together* again.
またあとでお～いします I will *see* you later. / (口語で) *See* you later.
一度お～いしてゆっくりとお話しいたしたいと思います I should like to *see* you one of these days and have a long talk.
あなたにお～いしたいと言って, 先程からどなたか事務所でお待ちです Someone (≒ Some gentleman; Some lady) has been waiting in the office hoping to *see* you for some time.
だれか～いに来たら留守だと言ってくれ If anyone comes to *see* me, tell him I am not in.
5時に有楽町で～いましょう Let's *meet* at Yurakucho at five. / I will *look out for*

あ

you at Yurakucho at five.
彼女に〜ったらよろしく If you *meet* her, please remember me to her.
一度彼に〜ってやってくれませんか Will you be so kind as to *see* him one of these days?
2 〖偶然出会う〗¶ 駅でばったり彼に〜った I *happened to see* him (≒ *came across* him; *chanced upon* him) at the station.
まずい所で彼に〜ったな It's very awkward for me to *see* him here. / Damn it! I little expected to *see* him here.
汽車に乗り遅れたのでその事故に〜わずにすんだ Failing to catch the train, I took the next one and escaped *involvement in* the accident.
目と目が〜った Our eyes *met*.
3 〖雨・事件・災難などに会う〗 ¶ 帰りに夕立に〜った On my way home I *was caught in* a shower.
彼はひどい災難に〜ったものだ It is a pity that he *met with* such a terrible disaster.
もう一度やったらひどい目に〜うぞ If you should do it again, you shall *regret it*.
彼女はいろいろ不幸な目に〜っている She *has met with* a variety of misfortune. / She *has gone through* many misfortunes.
あそこにいたころはいろいろな目に〜った I *had* a lot of bitter experiences there.
そのマンション建設計画は近隣の人々の大反対に〜った Their project of building an apartment house there *met with* the bitterest opposition of the neighboring inhabitants.

アウト 〖野球〗 out. ¶ バッターは〜だ The batter *is out*. 彼は二塁塁上で〜になった He *was tagged out* on the second base.
アウトカーブ an outcurve.
アウトサイダー an outsider.
アウトドロップ an outdrop.
アウトライン an outline. ¶ 日本史の〜を述べよ Give *an outline* of Japanese History. / *Outline* Japanese History. その企画の〜はこうです The *general idea* of the plan is ....
あえ・ぐ 【喘ぐ】 ¶ 彼は〜ぎながらしゃべった He *gasped out* the news. 男は丘を登って〜ぎながら話をした Coming up the hill, the man *panted out* his story. 犬が〜ぎながら走った The dog ran *panting*. 国民は重税に〜いでいる The people *are groaning under* the heavy taxation.
あえて 【敢えて】 ¶ 〜彼を訪ねるには及ばない You need not *take the trouble to* call on him. 彼は彼女の招待を〜断わろうとはしなかった He *dared* not decline her invitation. 彼はまちがっていると私は〜言う I *insist* that he is wrong. 彼は訴訟も〜辞せずと言っている He says that he *is even ready to* take legal procedures.
あえな・い 【敢え無い】 ¶ 彼は〜い最期を遂げた He died a *tragic* death.
あえん 【亜鉛】 〖化学〗 zinc. ¶銅板に〜でめっきした I coated the copper board with *zinc*. —板 a zinc sheet.
あお 【青】 blue. ¶ 信号は〜だ The light is *green*. 彼は〜くなった He turned *pale* (≒ *white*).
あおあお 【青青】 ¶ 〜とした blue (日本語では green (緑)を指すことが多い). 〜とした芝生が続いている The lawn is spreading *lush*. ここの草は〜としている The grass here is *luxuriant*.
あおい 【葵】 〖植物〗 a hollyhock.
あお・い 【青い】 blue. ¶ 〜い空 a (≒ the) *blue* sky. 〜い目をした少女 a *blue-eyed* girl. このりんごはまだ〜い This apple *is* still *green*. 彼は顔色が〜い He looks *pale*. 海は〜みがかった灰色であった The sea *is bluish* gray.
あおいき 【青息】 ¶ 彼は〜吐息だ He *is in great distress*. こんな不景気では〜吐息だ This depression *has* us *at a loss*.
あおいろしんこく 【青色申告】 a blue return. ¶ 〜を提出する file *a blue return*.
あおうめ 【青梅】 an unripe plum.
あおうなばら 【青海原】 a blue expanse of water; blue water.
あおがえる 【青蛙】 a green frog.
あおかび 【青かび】 a green mould. ¶ もちに〜が生えた A *green mould* has formed on the rice cake.
あおき 【青木】 a green tree; (みずき科の一種) a Japanese laurel.
あお・ぐ 【仰ぐ】 ¶ 空を〜ぐ *look up at* the sky. 彼はその学者を師と〜いでいた He *looked up to* the scholar as a teacher. 彼はすべての人から人格者と〜がれている He *is looked up to* by everybody as a man of character. 〜げば尊し師の恩 We should remember our teachers with respect and gratitude. 彼の援助を〜いでもだめだ It is no use *looking to* him *for* help. きみは会社の補助を〜ぐべきだった You ought to *have sought* the assistance on the part of the company. 石油の供給を海外に〜ぐべきだ We should *rely on* foreign countries *for* the supply of oil.
あお・ぐ 【扇ぐ】 ¶ 火を〜ぐ *fan* a fire. 扇子で〜ぐ *fan oneself*. 〜いで火を起こした I *fanned* the fire into flame. 〜いではえを追い払った I *fanned* away the fly.
あおくさ・い 【青臭い】 ¶ 生野菜は〜い Fresh vegetables have *a greenish smell*. なんという〜い議論だ How *unskilled* that argument is!
あおぐろ・い 【青黒い】 pale and dark.
あおざ・める 【青ざめる】 ¶ 〜めた顔をしている He looks *pale*. 知らせを聞いて土のように〜めた He *turned* ashy *pale* at hearing the news.
あおじゃしん 【青写真】 a blueprint. ¶ 新築の家の〜を作らせよう I shall order *blueprints* drawn up for the new house.
あおじろ・い 【青白い】 ¶ 彼はなんて〜い顔だろう How *pale* he looks! 〜いインテリ *pale-faced* intellectuals.
あおしんごう 【青信号】 a green light. ¶ 〜だ The light is on for "Go." 〜で渡りなさい Cross the road when the light is *green*.
あおすじ 【青筋】 ¶ 彼は〜を立てて怒った He *turned purple* with rage. 〜が立った The

veins stood out. 別に～を立てるほどでもなかろう There is no need to argue about this.

あおぞら【青空】 a (≒ the) blue sky. ¶ 久しぶりの～だ This is the first time we have seen such *a blue sky* in a long time.

あおた【青田】 (青々とした田) green rice-fields; (まだ実っていない田) unripe rice-fields.
—買い ¶ ～買いをする buy rice before the harvest; make a crop-trade on green rice-fields; (求人で) make contracts of employment with undergraduates far ahead of their graduation.

あおだいしょう【青大将】 a blue-green snake; a common harmless snake.

あおてんじょう【青天井】 the blue vault of heaven.

あおな【青菜】 greens. ¶ 彼は自分の名が載っていないのを見たときは, ～に塩だった Not finding his name on the list, he *was quite disheartened* (≒ *was crest-fallen*).

あおにさい【青二才】 a greenhorn; a novice. ¶ ～になにができる What can *an inexperienced stripling* do?

あおば【青葉】 green leaves (≒ foliage); verdure. ¶ ～の頃 the season of *verdure*.

あおばえ【青蠅】 a bluebottle 〔fly〕; a blowfly.

あおびょうたん【青瓢箪】 a green gourd; (顔色の悪い人) a pale-faced fellow.

あおまめ【青豆】 green beans (≒ peas).

あおみ【青味】 greens.

あおむ·く【仰向く】 look up.

あおむけ【仰向け】 ¶ 私は～に寝た I lay *on my back*. / I lay *face up*. 彼は～になった He turned over *on his back*. 彼はカメを～にした He turned the tortoise *upside down*.

あおむし【青虫】 a green caterpillar.

あおもの【青物】 greens.
—市場 a greengrocery market.

あおり【煽り】 flapping; (風の) a blast; gust; (そばづえ) by-blow. ¶ 突進する車の～で木がゆれた The tree swayed, caught *in the blast of* a rushing car. 風の～で戸がぱっと開いた *Fanned* by the wind, the door flung open. 不景気の～をくって会社はつぶれた The company failed *as a result of* (≒ *in the wake of*) a business recession.

あおりどめ【煽り止め】 a doorstop.

あお·る【呷る】 ¶ ぐいぐいと酒を～る *gulp down* cup after cup of *sake*.

あお·る【煽る】 ¶ 強風に～られて火は町一帯に広がった *Fanned* by a strong wind, the fire spread all over the town. 鎧戸が風に～られている The shutters *are flapping* in the wind. 彼は反米感情を～った He *stirred up* anti-American feelings.

あか【赤】 **1** 〘色〙 red; (深紅) crimson; (緋) scarlet.
2 〘共産主義者〙 a Communist; a Red.
3 〘まったくの〙 utter; sheer. ¶ 彼は～の他人にも親切である He is kind even to an *utter* (≒ a *total*) stranger.

あか【垢】 dirt; filth. ¶ あなたの手は～だらけだ Your hand is covered with *dirt*. ～のついたシャツ *dirty* shirts. えりに～がついた. 落とさなくちゃ The collar *has become dirty*. I must wash off the *dirt*.

あかあかと【赤赤と】 ¶ 西の空に～夕日が沈む The sun is setting *aglow* (≒ *glowing*) in the western sky.

あかあかと【明明と】 ¶ 広間は～燈がともっていた The hall was *brightly* lit up.

あか·い【赤い】 red. ¶ ～い広場 the *Red* Square. ～い羽根募金運動 a "*Red* Feather" collection campaign. 彼は～い He is a *Red*. / He is a *communist*. ～作家 a *communistic* writer.

あかえい【赤鱏】 〘魚類〙 a stingray.

あかがい【赤貝】 〘貝類〙 an ark-shell.

あかがえる【赤蛙】 a brown frog.

あかがね【銅】 copper. ¶ ～色の copper-colored; (日焼けした) sunburnt; tanned.

あがき【足掻き】 ¶ ～がとれない I *am in a fix*. 借金で～がつかない I *am up to my neck in debt*. 彼は逃げようと最後の～を試みた He made the last *struggle* to escape.

あかぎれ【皹】 chaps; cracks. ¶ 足に～ができた I *had* my feet *chapped*. / I'*ve got chapped* feet. / My feet *got chapped*. 寒いとすぐ～がきれる My skin *chaps* easily in cold weather.

あが·く【足掻く】 ¶ この期(ご)に及んで～いてもむだだ It's no use *struggling* now. ～けば～くほど損をする The more you *struggle*, the less you will gain.

あかぐろ·い【赤黒い】 dark-red.

あかげ【赤毛】 red hair. ¶ ～の少女 a *red-haired* girl.

あかゲット【赤ゲット】 a red blanket.

あかご【赤子】 ⇒あかんぼう

あかざ【藜】 〘植物〙 a goosefoot; wild spin-「ach.

あかさびびょう【赤錆病】 red rust.

あかし【証】 witness; evidence; proof. ¶ 彼は身の～を立てた He *proved* his innocence.

あかじ【赤字】 deficit. ¶ 事業は～だ The business *is in* 〔*the*〕 *red*. 今月は1,000ドルの～だ We *have gone* 1,000 dollars *into the red* this month. ～を出さないくふうはないものか Is there any good way to *keep out of the red*?
—公債 a "red-ink" bond. —経営 deficit operation. —財政 deficit finance. —予算 an unbalanced budget.

あかじ【赤地】 ¶ その旗は～に白の十字を抜いてある The flag has a white cross on *a red background*.

アカシア 〘植物〙 an acacia.

あかしお【赤潮】 a red water; a red (≒ reddish brown) tide.

あかしんごう【赤信号】 a red (≒ danger) signal; a red light. ¶ ～では必ず止まりなさい You must stop for (≒ on) the *red signal*.

あか·す【明かす】 ¶ われわれは山小屋で一夜を～した We *passed* a night at (≒ in) a mountain hut. われわれは寝ずに夜を～した We *sat up* all night. ある者は飲み～し, ある者は語り～した

あ

Some *made a night of it,* and others *talked till dawn.* きみに秘密を〜そう I'll *tell* you the secret. / I'll *let* you *into my secret.* 今までだれにもこれを〜さなかった I *have kept* this *to myself.*

あか·せる【飽かせる】¶ 彼は金に〜して絵を買った He bought pictures *regardless of expense.*

あかちゃ·ける【赤茶ける】turn reddish-brown.

あかちゃん【赤ちゃん】a baby. ⇒あかんぼう

あかチン【赤チン】〘薬品〙mercurochrome.

あかつき【暁】(夜明け) dawn; daybreak.
¶ ダム完成の〜には *on* the completion of the dam. 成人の〜には必ずご恩返しをいたします I will repay your kindness *when* I am a man.

あがったり【上がったり】¶ 雨の日はお客が来ないので商売は〜だ As we have few customers on a rainy day, we *have little business.* こう不景気では商売は〜だ If such a severe depression continues, our *business* will *be ruined* before long.

あかつち【赤土】red clay (≒ earth).

アカデミー an academy.
—賞〘映画〙the Oscar.

アカデミック academic.

あかでんわ【赤電話】a 〔red-colored〕 public telephone.

あかとんぼ【赤とんぼ】a red dragonfly.

あかぬ·ける【垢抜ける】¶ 〜けた態度 *refined* manners. 〜けない趣味 *unrefined* taste. 〜けた青年 an *elegant* young man. 彼の趣味は〜けている He *is refined in* taste.

あかね【茜】〘植物〙a 〔Bengal〕 madder.
—色 madder-red. ¶ 〜色の空 the *glowing* (≒ *rosy*) sky; the *purpling* sky.

あかはじ【赤恥】¶ 私は〜をかいた I *was put* (≒*was brought*) *to shame.* 彼は人前で〜をかかされた He *was brought* (≒ *was put*) *to shame* in public.

あかはた【赤旗】a red flag.

あかはだか【赤裸】⇒はだか

あかふだ【赤札】(特価品の) a red label of clearance goods; (売約済みの) a red label of sold goods.

あかぼう【赤帽】a red cap; (駅の) 米 a redcap; a baggage porter.

あかまつ【赤松】a 〔Japanese〕 red pine.

あかみ【赤み】¶ 〜がかった reddish; rosy. 〜がさす become *red-shot*; turn *reddish.* 空が〜を帯びている The sky *is tinged with rose* (≒ *red*).

あかみ【赤身】(肉の) lean meat; (木材の) heart-wood.

あが·める【崇める】¶ 人々は彼を偉大な指導者として〜めた People *looked up to* him as a great leader. 彼は死後神として〜められた He *was deified* after his death.

あからがお【赤ら顔】a ruddy face. ¶ 〜の男 a *ruddy-faced* man.

あからさま ¶ 〜な (あきらかな) clear; plain; (率直な) frank; open; candid. 〜に frankly; candidly; without reserve. 〜に言えば私は野球がきらいです *Frankly speaking,* I don't like baseball. 〜に言えば，彼は不正直だ *Frankly speaking* (≒ *To be frank with you*), he is dishonest.

あから·める【赤らめる】¶ 彼女はその知らせを聞いて顔を〜めた She *blushed* to hear the news.

あかり【明かり】a light. ¶ 電気の〜 an electric *light.* ランプの〜 lamplight. 〜をつける(消す) turn on (off) the *light.* 部屋は〜が暗かった(明るかった) The room *was* dimly (brightly) *lit up.* 薄暗い〜で本を読む read in *a* poor *light.*
—窓 a skylight. 雪— the gleam of snow.

あがり【上がり】¶ このごろの物価の〜方はひどい Prices *have* recently *risen* amazingly. 月にどのくらいの〜があるか How much do you *earn* in a month? この絵は色の〜がよくない The colors of this picture *have* not *come out* well.
—口 the doorway. —下がり ups and downs. —高 (売り上げ高) the proceeds. —段 steps; door-steps. —場 (船着き場) a landing place. —目 almond (≒ slanting) eyes.

あが·る【上がる】**1**〘自然に上昇する〙rise; go up. ¶ 太陽は東から〜る The sun *rises* in the east.
たこが空高く〜っている A kite *is flying* high up in the sky.
1発花火が〜った *Up went* a firework.
合図ののろしが〜った The signal rocket *was fired.*
(劇の)幕が〜った The curtain *rose.*
2〘人が登る〙go up. ¶ 私は屋上に〜った I *went up* on the roof.
この階段をお〜りください *Go up* these stairs, please.
3〘家に〙¶ 彼はずかずかと家に〜ってきた He *walked* right *into* the house.
どうぞお〜りください Please *come* 〔*on*〕 in. (on を入れるのは米口語).
いつお宅に〜ったらよろしいでしょうか When shall I *come* to your house? / When will it be convenient for you to see me at your house?
4〘学校に〙¶ 彼は7歳で小学校に〜った He *entered* an elementary school at 〔the age of〕 seven.
5〘値段·温度など〙rise. ¶ あすは気温は3度ほど〜るでしょう The temperature will probably *rise* about 3 degrees tomorrow.
円の価値が〜った The exchange rate of the yen *has risen.*
給料がちょっと〜った My salary *has been raised* a little.
野菜の値がまた〜った The vegetables *have gone up* in price again.
6〘地位が〙¶ 彼の地位は大いに〜った His position *has been* greatly *raised.*
彼は階級が一つ〜った He *was promoted* one grade in rank.
7〘発生する〙break out. ¶ 火の手が一度に3か

所から〜った A fire *broke out* in three quarters at once.
歓声が〜った A shout of joy *was heard* (≒ *was given*).
この処置に対して反対の声が〜った There were some outcries against this decision.
8〖場所から出てくる〗¶ 今ふろから〜ったばかりだ I *have* just *come out of* the bath.
早くプールから〜りなさい *Get out of* the swimming pool quickly.
船から〜ったばかりで，まだ船酔いぎみです As I *have* just *come ashore*, I still feel a bit seasick.
9〖終了・完成する〗¶ やっと梅雨が〜った At last the rainy season *is over*.
雨が〜った It *has stopped* raining.
この仕事は年内には〜りません This job will not *be finished* before the end of the year.
はい，いっちょう〜ったよ There! *It's done*.
(すごろくで)ぼくがいちばん先に〜りそうだ I'll be the first to *finish* the game.
10〖費用がすむ〗¶ 10万円じゃとてもこの仕事は〜らない It'll be impossible to do this job for less than 100,000 yen.
5,000円でなんとか〜らないかな Won't you try to *finish* it for 5,000 yen?
11〖向上する〗¶ 営業成績が〜らない Our business *is* not *improving*. / We *aren't doing better* in our business.
彼は学業成績が〜った He *has made good progress in* his studies.
きみの書道の腕は確かに〜った You *have* certainly *made some progress in* calligraphy.
さっぱり効果は〜らない This *is* quite *fruitless*. / It *has no effect* at all.
12〖風采(ふうさい)・名が〗¶ その身なりでは風采が〜らない You *are plain-looking* in these clothes.
そのことで彼の名が〜った That *made* him *famous*.
13〖興奮する〗¶ 大ぜいの前で歌うので〜った I *felt stage fright* singing before a large audience.
試験場で〜らないようにするにはどうしたらいいだろう I wonder what I must do in order not to *lose my cool* (≒ *be nervous*) in the examination room.
〜りっぱなしだった I *remained too excited* to feel relaxed.
われわれは意気が大いに〜った We *were in high spirits*.
14〖神仏に供えられる〗¶ 墓前には菊の花が1輪〜っていた There was a chrysanthemum *offered* at the gravestone.
燈明がまだ〜っていない The sacred lights (≒ candles) *have* not *been offered* yet before the altar.
15〖食べる〗¶ クッキーを一つお〜りになってみてください Please *help yourself to* the cookies.
朝食になにをお〜りになりますか What will you *have* for breakfast?
16〖犯人・証拠など〗¶ 犯人はまだ〜らないのか *Is* the criminal still *at large*?
証拠が〜らない以上，彼がやったとは断定できぬ Without sufficient evidence, we cannot blame the crime upon him.
17〖その他〗¶ その事業から月に10万円ほど利益が〜ってくる I *make a profit of* 100,000 yen on that business every month.
商売〜ったりだ *It's all up with* my business.
バッテリーが〜った The battery *has run down*.
てんぷらが〜った The *tempura is ready*.

あが·る【揚がる】¶ 旗が〜っている The flag *is* 〔*put*〕 *up*. 野菜はすぐに〜る（てんぷらなど）Vegetables *are fried* in oil quickly.

あかる·い【明るい】**1**〖光〗¶ シャンデリアが煌煌(こうこう)として部屋は〜かった The room was *brightly* lit up with brilliant chandeliers.
街路はネオンの輝きで〜い The streets *are lighted up* with neon lights.
この電燈は〜い This electric lamp *gives a good light*.
太陽は〜く照っていた The sun was shining *bright*〔*ly*〕.
夏は4時前に〜くなる In summer it *gets light* before four o'clock.
まだ外は〜い It *is light* outdoors yet.
〜い夜だった It was a *clear* night.
空は〜くなってきた The sky *is brightening*. / The sky *is clearing up*.
〜いうちに帰宅しなさい Come home while *it is light*. / Come home before it gets dark.
日ざしのよい〜いへや a *bright* sunlit room.
もっと照明を〜くしてください Make lighting more effective.
2〖色彩〗¶ 〜い色 *bright* colors.
この絵の色は全体に〜い The coloring of the painting *is* on the whole *bright*.
3〖明朗な〗¶ 彼は生まれつき〜いたちだ He *is cheerful* by nature. / He is of a *cheerful* disposition.
この吉報で彼女の顔は〜くなった At the good news her face *brightened up*. / Hearing the good news, she *looked cheerful*.
〜い政治 *clean* politics.
4〖見通しが〗¶ 彼はその計画に〜い見通しを立てていた His outlook for the project *was bright*.
本年度の外国貿易の見通しは〜い There is a *good* outlook on foreign trade this year.
きみの将来は〜い You have a *bright* future before you.
見込みは〜い We have a *good* prospect.
5〖精通している〗¶ 彼はその辺の事情に〜い He *is well acquainted with* the affairs. / He *is familiar with* the situation.
彼は日本の歴史に〜い He *is well versed in* Japanese history.
この土地に〜い者がやったに相違ない The offender must *know* this place.

あかるさ【明るさ】(光の) light; brightness; (心の) cheerfulness.

あかるみ【明るみ】¶ 〜に出す bring (a matter) to light; bring (a matter) before the public; make known; make public. 〜に出る come to light; become known. ついに彼はそのことを

あ

〜に出した At last he *made* it *known to the public*. まもなくそれは〜に出るだろう It will soon *be known to the public*.

あかんたい【亜寒帯】〖気象〗the subarctic zone.

あかんぼう【赤ん坊】a baby. ¶男(女)の〜 a *baby* boy (girl). 〜は男の子だった The *baby* was *a* boy. ぼくを〜扱いするな Don't treat me as a *baby*. 夫はまるで大きな〜です My husband is, as it were, *a* grown-up *baby*. 〜のお守をしてくれませんか Would you please take care of the *baby*? / Won't you please *baby-sit*? 〜の子守 *baby*-sitting.

あき【秋】autumn; 米 fall (autumn はアメリカでも用いられる). ¶〜の空 the *autumn* sky. 当地もだいぶ〜めいてきた *Autumn* seems to be on its way here. / It has become quite *autumnlike* here.

あき【飽き】¶仕事に〜がくる *lose interest in one's* work; *get* (≒ *become; grow*) *tired of one's* work.

あき【明き・空き】(すきま) a gap; an opening; room; (余白) a space; a blank; (余地) room; space (冠詞はつけない); (欠員) a vacancy; (空席) a vacant seat. ¶会社に〜がある There is *a vacancy* in our firm. 時間の〜がない I have no *time to spare*.

あきあき【飽き飽き】¶もう雨には〜だ We *are fed up with* rain. 彼のいつもの愚痴には〜だ I *am* thoroughly *sick of* his old complaints. 毎日同じ仕事ではだれだって〜する Anybody will *be sick and tired of* doing the same work every day. 〜だ It *is boring*.

あきうえ【秋植え】autumn planting.

あきかん【空き罐】an empty can (≒ 英 tin).

あきぐち【秋口】early autumn.

あきさめ【秋雨】an autumn rain.

あきしょう【飽き性】fickle nature.

あきす【空き巣】a sneak thief; a snooper. ¶昨夜〜に入られた Last night our house *was broken into* (≒ *was robbed*) while we were away.

あきたりな・い【飽き足りない】(人が主語で) be not contented (*with*); (物が主語で) be not satisfactory. ¶われわれはその計画には〜い We *are not contented* (≒ *satisfied*) *with* the plan. / The plan *is not satisfactory to* us.

あきち【空き地】a vacant lot; vacant land; (広場) an open space.

あきっぽ・い【飽きっぽい】¶〜い人 a *capricious* man. 彼はなにをしても〜い He *is apt to get tired of* anything. / He *sticks to nothing*.

あきない【商い】business; trade. ¶よい〜をする do *a* good *business*. 〜を広げる expand the *business*.

あきな・う【商う】sell; deal (≒ trade) (*in* building materials). ¶本を〜う *deal in* books.

あきばれ【秋晴れ】¶きょうは〜のいい天気だ Today is *a fine day of autumn*.

あきびん【空きびん】an empty bottle. ¶牛乳の〜 *an empty* milk *bottle*. 〜を集める gather *empty bottles*.

あきま【空き間】a vacant room; (貸し間) a room for rent.

あきや【空き家】a vacant (≒ an unoccupied) house; (貸家) a house for rent (≒ 英 to let).

あきらか【明らか】¶〜な事実 a *plain* fact. 〜な証拠 a *clear* evidence; an *evident* proof. 火を見るより〜だった It was as *clear* as day. 〜にきみのまちがいだ It is *plain* (≒ *obvious*) that you are mistaken. / *Obviously* you are mistaken. どこの何者かは〜でない He *is* not *identified*. どうして彼が家出したのかは〜でない It *is* not *known* yet why he ran away from home. 彼は自分の立場を〜にした He *made* his position *clear*. いつか事の真相は〜になるだろう Some day the truth will *be made known* (≒ *be revealed*).

あきらめ【諦め】resignation. ¶何事も〜がたいせつだ *Resignation* is the first lesson of life. 彼は自分の失敗に〜がつかない He can't *get over* his failure. 彼は〜がいい(悪い) He is a good (bad) loser. これで彼女もいくらか〜がつくだろう This will be some *consolation* (≒ *comfort*) to her.

あきら・める【諦める】1〖断念する〗¶彼は留学を〜めた He *gave up* the idea of studying abroad.

最後までけっしてそれを〜めない I'll never *give* it *up* to the last.

あんな男は〜めなさい *Think no more of* him.

2〖観念する〗¶彼をもう死んだものと〜めるほかはなかった We had to *give* him *up for lost*.

私は父の病気回復を〜めた I *gave up* any hope of my father's recovery. / I *despaired of* my father's recovery.

彼女は運命と〜めた She *resigned herself* (≒ *was resigned*) *to* her fate.

母親は息子の死を〜めきれない The mother can't *get over* her son's death.

あ・きる【飽きる】1〖いやになる〗¶彼は勉強に〜きて散歩に出た *Tired of* studying, he went out for a walk.

私はサラリーマンの生活にすっかり〜きた I *am* very *tired of* a salaried man's life.

彼女は息子の話になると〜きることがない She never *gets tired of* talking about her son.

2〖食傷する〗¶甘い物は〜きるほど食べた I *have had enough of* sweets.

あの人の話に〜きた I *was bored* by his talk. / His talk *bored* me.

彼の長話に子どもたちは〜きた The children *got tired of* his long talk.

アキレスけん【アキレス腱】Achilles tendon.

あき・れる【呆れる】1〖驚く〗¶彼の態度にはほとほと〜れる I *am* greatly *astonished at* his behavior.

〜れて物が言えない I *am* too *amazed* to speak.

2〖あいそが尽きる〗¶〜れた政治家 a *disgusting* politician.

〜れた値段 an *absurd* (≒ a *fabulous*) price.

忘れっぽいのにわれながら〜れる I *am disgusted at* my poor memory. / I *am disgusted with* myself for my poor memory.

あく【灰汁】lye;(野菜などの) a harsh taste. ¶ ~を抜く get rid of *lye*. ~の強い人 an *egoistic* man; a man *with a strong ego*.

あく【悪】(一般的に悪い) badness;(不正, 道徳的に悪い) evil;〔a〕sin;(悪い行為・習慣)〔a〕vice. ¶ ~の生活 an *evil* life.

あ・く【空く】**1**『場所などが』¶ 席が~いた The seat *became vacant*.
その箱は~いている The box *is empty*.
2『ひま』¶ 彼は午後はたいてい~いている He *is* usually *free* in the afternoon.
手が~いていますか Do you *have your hands free*? / *Are* you *free*?
3『用済み』¶ 新聞が~いたら貸してください Lend me the paper if you *have done with* (≒ *have finished*) it.

あ・く【開く】¶ このドアは内側に~く The door *opens* inwards. びんは~かない I can't *uncap* (≒ *uncork*) the bottle. この店は日曜日は~かない This store does not *open* on Sundays. / This store *is closed* on Sundays. 銀行は3時まで~いている The bank *is open* till three o'clock. 5時に幕が~きます The curtain *rises* at five.

あくい【悪意】ill will; malice. ¶ 彼は私に~を持っている He harbors *malice* (≒ *ill will*) against me. ~あってのことではない I meant no *harm* (≒ *offense*). ~があってしたのではない I didn't do it *out of malice*. 彼の言っていることには~はない There is no *malice* in what he says.

あくうん【悪運】¶ 彼は~が強い He *has the devil's luck*. 彼もついに~尽きた At last he *has come to the end of his devil's luck*. かわいそうにあの女はいつも~につきまとわれている The poor woman is always pursued by *bad fortune*.

あくえき【悪疫】a plague. ¶ ~流行地域 an *infected* area; a *plague* spot. ~が流行している *A plague* is prevalent.

あくかんじょう【悪感情】an ill feeling. ¶ 彼は私に~をいだいている He has *an ill feeling* toward me. 彼女は人に~を与える She gives *an unfavorable feeling* on others. / She *impresses* others *unfavorably*.

あくぎゃく【悪逆】¶ ~非道の行ない a *brutal* act; an *atrocious* act; an atrocity. ~の徒 a traitor.

あくぎょう【悪行】wrong doing; an evil act.

あくきりゅう【悪気流】a treacherous air current.

あくじ【悪事】evil; wrongdoing. ¶ ~を働く do *wrong* (≒ *evil*); commit *a crime*. ~を重ねる commit one *crime* after another. ~をたくらむ plot *evil* (≒ *wrong*) (*against a person*). ~千里を走る(諺) *Ill news runs apace*.

あくしつ【悪疾】a malignant disease.

あくしつ【悪質】(質の劣悪) bad (≒ inferior) quality;(たちのよくない) evil nature. ¶ ~な詐欺 a *vicious* fraud. ~な業者 a *wicked* (≒ *vicious*) trader. ~な契約違反 a *vicious* violation of the contract.

あくしゅ【握手】〔a〕handshake. ¶ 私は彼と~した I *shook hands with* him. 彼は~を求めた He *offered his hand*. 両会社は~した The two companies *have joined hands with* each other.

あくしゅう【悪臭】a bad smell; an ill odor. ¶ ~が鼻をついた *A bad smell* greeted my nose. この魚は~を放つ This fish *stinks* (≒ *smells bad*).

あくしゅう【悪習】a bad habit. ¶ ~は身につきやすい We are apt to fall into *bad habits*.

あくしゅみ【悪趣味】¶ 彼女のヘアスタイルは~だ Her hair style is *in bad taste*.

あくじゅんかん【悪循環】a vicious circle. ¶ ~を起こす cause *a vicious circle*. 物価と賃銀の~を断ち切る break *a vicious circle* of prices and wages.

あくじょうけん【悪条件】a bad condition. ¶ ~ももののかわ in spite of *unfavorable conditions*. このような~では研究を続けられない We can't continue the study any longer under these *bad conditions*.

あくしん【悪心】an evil intention.

あくせい【悪声】a bad voice. ¶ ~を張り上げて歌をうたった I sang at the top of my *bad voice*.

あくせい【悪政】misgovernment. ¶ ~に苦しむ suffer from *misgovernment*.

あくせい【悪性】¶ ~の風邪 a *bad* cold.
—インフレ vicious inflation. —腫瘍(しゅよう) a malignant tumor.

あくぜい【悪税】¶ ~に苦しむ suffer from *bad taxes*; groan under *bad taxation*.

あくせく ¶ ~する be busy (*about*). 彼は~働いている He works *hard*. 彼は金もうけに~している He *is very eager to* make money. 小事に~するな Don't *worry about* trifles.

アクセサリー an accessory. ¶ ~をつける wear *accessories* (複数形が普通).

アクセル an accelerator. ¶ ~を踏む step on the *accelerator*.

あくせん【悪戦】¶ ~苦闘の末やっと成功した After *a desperate effort* we managed to succeed. 彼は選挙で~苦闘した He had *a close contest* in the election. 彼らは強敵に~苦闘した They *struggled hard against* the powerful enemy.

あくせん【悪銭】¶ ~身につかず(諺) *Ill-gotten money is soon spent*. / *Easily got, easily gone*. / *Ill got, ill spent*.

アクセント an accent; a stress; an emphasis. ¶ ~は第3シラブルにある The *accent* is on the third syllable. ポケットに~をつけたら(ポケットを目だたせたら)いかがでしょう How about *accenting* the pockets?

あくそう【悪僧】a vicious priest.

あくた【芥】dirt; rubbish; refuse; trash.

あくたい【悪態】¶ 彼はぼくに~をついた He *used bad* (≒ *abusive*) *language* to me. / He *called* me *names*.

あくだま【悪玉】a rogue; a scoundrel.

あくたれ【悪たれ】—小僧 a naughty boy; a

あ

mischievous urchin.

あくてんこう【悪天候】bad(≒(やや形式ばって) inclement) weather (冠詞はつかない). ¶ ～を冒して出発した We started in spite of *bad* (≒ *rough*) *weather*. ～のため出発を延ばした Because of *bad weather* I put off the departure.

あくど・い ¶ ～いいたずらをする play a *nasty* trick on *a person*. ～い冗談を言う make an *excessive* joke.

あくとう【悪党】a bad man; a wicked man; a villain; a rogue; a rascal.

あくどう【悪童】a bad boy; a naughty boy.

あくとく【悪徳】〔a〕vice. ¶ きつ煙は～だ Smoking is *a vice*.

—業者 a wicked dealer (≒ merchant). —政治家 a corrupt politician.

あくな・き【飽くなき】¶ ～き野望 an *insatiable* ambition.

あくにん【悪人】a bad man; a wicked man; a knave; a rogue; a villain; a rascal.

あくび【欠伸】a yawn. ¶ 彼は人前で口に手をあてずに～をした He *yawned* before others without covering his mouth. / He *gave a yawn* before others. 大～をした I *yawned* heavily. / I *gave a* heavy *yawn*. ～をかみ殺した I *stifled* (≒ *suppressed*) *a yawn*.

あくひつ【悪筆】¶ 彼は～である He writes *a bad* (≒ *poor*) *hand*. / He is *a bad* (≒ *poor*) *penman*.

あくひょう【悪評】a bad reputation; ill fame. ¶ ～の高い人 a *notorious* person; a person *of ill repute*. 彼女には～が絶えない She is a constant subject of *scandal*. あまり彼に～を加えるな Don't *criticize* him too *severely*.

あくふう【悪風】a bad custom. ¶ 彼は世間の～に染まっていない He is not infected with *the evil ways* of the world.

あくぶん【悪文】a bad style; poor writing.

あくへい【悪弊】evil practices; abuses. ¶ 積年の～を打破する do away with *an evil* of long standing.

あくへき【悪癖】a bad habit.

あくほう【悪法】a bad law.

あくま【悪魔】an evil spirit; a devil; a demon. ¶ ～のような devilish; demoniac; fiendish. ～を払う drive out *evil spirits*.

—主義 diabolism; diabolical principle.

あくまでも【飽く迄も】¶ 彼は～やると言った He said he would *do his best*. 彼は～意見を主張した He *persisted in* his opinion. ～戦い抜くつもりだ We will fight it out *to the bitter end*. ～初志を貫徹する I'll carry out my original intention *in spite of anything*.

あくむ【悪夢】a bad dream; a nightmare. ¶ ～に襲われた I had *a bad dream* (≒ *a nightmare*). / I was troubled *by* (≒ *with*) *nightmare*. ～から覚めた I started from *a nightmare*. / (本心に立ち返る) I *came to my senses*.

あぐ・む【倦む】grow weary of; get tired of; get sick of.

あくめい【悪名】a bad name (≒ reputation); notoriety. ¶ ～が高い be *notorious* (*for*).

あくやく【悪役】a villain's part. ¶ ～をやる play *a villain's part*.

あくゆう【悪友】a bad friend; (総称) bad company. ¶ 彼は～とつきあっている He *keeps bad company*. 先生は私たちに～と交際しないように忠告した Our teacher advised us not to *get into bad company*.

あくよう【悪用】misuse; abuse. ¶ 権力を～する *abuse one's* authority; *make an ill use of one's* power.

あぐら【趺坐・胡座】¶ ～をかく *sit cross-legged*; *sit with one's legs crossed*. …の上に～をかいている take advantage of ….

あくらつ【悪辣】¶ 彼はぼくに～なことをした He played me a *dirty* (≒*nasty*; *mean*) trick.

あくりょう【悪霊】¶ 彼は～に取りつかれている He is possessed by *an evil spirit*.

あくりょく【握力】¶ 彼は～が強い He has *a* strong *grip*.

—計 a hand-dynamometer.

あくる【明くる】¶ ～朝〔on〕the *next* (≒ *following*) morning. ～日〔on〕the *next* (≒ *following*) day. 事故の～日彼は警察に届けた *On the day after* the accident he reported the matter to the police.

あくれい【悪例】a bad example; (前例) a bad precedent. ¶ ～を残す set (≒ form; establish) *a bad precedent*.

あくろ【悪路】a bad road; a rough way.

アクロバット (人) an acrobat; (曲芸) acrobatics.

—ダンス an acrobatic dance.

あけ【明け】¶ ～の明星 the morning star; Venus. 休会～の国会 the Diet *after* the recess. 梅雨～ *the end of* the rainy season.

あけ【朱】¶ 彼は～に染まって倒れた He *was covered with blood* and fell.

あげ【揚げ】(着物の) a tuck. ¶ スカートに～をする *shorten* the skirt; *hem up* the skirt. ～をおろす take out *a tuck*; *let down* the hem〔of the skirt〕.

あげあし【揚げ足】¶ 彼の～を取ることはできない It is impossible to *trip* him *up*. / It is impossible to *take up him on a slip of the tongue*.

あげおろし【上げ下ろし】taking up and down; raising and lowering; (積荷の) loading and unloading. ¶ 船荷の～をする *load and unload* a vessel (≒ a ship). 彼女ははしの～にも小言をいう She finds fault with everything I do.

あけがた【明け方】dawn; daybreak. ¶ ～に at *dawn*. ～近く地震があった There was an earthquake *toward daybreak*.

あげく【揚げ句】¶ ～の果てに in the end; finally. 迷った～に *after* wavering choice. 考え抜いた～に *after* hard thinking.

あけくれ【明け暮れ】day and night. ¶ 家庭の

雑用に～する *spend busy days over* small domestic jobs.

あげさげ【上げ下げ】 putting up and down; (抑揚) intonations.

あげしお【上げ潮】 the rising tide. ¶ ～どきに at *high tide*.

あけすけ ¶ ～な意見 a *candid* (≒ *frank*) opinion. ～に言うと to be frank with you. ～に物を言う人だ He is quite *outspoken*.

あげぞこ【上げ底】 ¶ この箱は～だ This box has *a false bottom*.

あけたて【開け閉て】 ¶ 戸の～に注意しなさい Don't slam the door.

あけっぱなし【開けっ放し】 ¶ 戸を～にするな Don't leave the door *open*. 彼はだれとでも～でつきあう He *is free and open with* everybody.

あげて【挙げて】 ¶ 全力を～ with all *one's* might; with might and main. 全力を～の戦い an *all-out* fight. 町を～彼らを出迎えた The *whole* town turned out to welcome them.

あけてもくれても【明けても暮れても】 day in, day out; from morning till night. ¶ ～彼は小説ばかり読んでいる He does nothing but read novels *from morning till night*. ～彼は家にじっとしている He stays at home *day in, day out*.

あげなべ【揚げ鍋】 a frying pan; a fry pan.

あげはちょう【揚げ羽蝶】〘虫類〙a swallowtail.

あけぼの【曙】 (文語) dawn; daybreak.

あげまく【揚げ幕】 a curtain.

あげまど【揚げ窓】 a push-up window.

あげもの【揚げ物】 fried food.

あ・ける【明ける】 ¶ 夜がほのぼのと～けた Day was beginning to *break*. / The first signs of *dawn* appeared. / It was early *dawn*. 年が～けた The New Year *has come*. / The New Year's Day *dawned*. その子は～けて6歳になります The child will be six years old *next year*. ～けましておめでとう A Happy *New Year* 〔to you〕! / I wish you a Happy *New Year*. 梅雨が～けた The rainy (≒ wet) season *is over*. やっと年季が～けた I *am through with* my apprenticeship now. / My term of service *is up* at last.

あ・ける【空ける】 **1**〘容器をからにする〙 ¶ はちの水を～けてください Please *pour out* the water in the bowl. / *Empty* the bowl *of* its water, please.

彼はバケツにその水を～けた He *poured* (≒ *emptied*) the water into the bucket.

たちまちのうちに彼は1升びんを～けてしまった He *drank up* a one-*sho* bottle of *sake* in a little while.

2〘場所・余白を〙 ¶ 通り道を～けてくれませんか Will you please *make way for* me?

彼女が来るからそこに席を一つ～けておきなさい Please *reserve the seat for* her; she will be here soon.

1行ずつ～けて書きなさい Write on every other (≒ second) line. / Write double spacing.

そこは2ページ～けておきなさい Leave the two pages *blank*.

左を10センチほど～けて書きはじめなさい Begin to write, *leaving a* 10 centimeter *blank space* on the left side 〔of the sheet of paper〕.

3〘穴を〙 ¶ 板に直径5センチの穴を～ける *make a hole* 5 centimeters in diameter through a board.

彼らはへいに小さな穴を～けてのぞきこんだ They *bored a* small *hole* in the fence and peeped through it.

彼は帳簿に大穴を～けた He *made a* big *hole* in his accounts.

4〘家を〙 ¶ 彼女は日曜日にはよく家を～ける She often *stays away from home* on Sundays.

5〘とっておく〙 ¶ 会をするからこの次の土曜の午後は～けておいてください We must have a meeting. Please *keep* next Saturday afternoon *open* for it. / Please *keep* next Saturday afternoon *free* for our party.

あ・ける【開ける】 **1**〘戸・窓・包み・本など〙 open. ¶ 私は窓を～けた I *opened* the window〔s〕.

門を～けてください Please *open* the gate.

彼女は玄関の戸を～けたままにしておいた She *left* the front door *open*.

その小包を～けたら中身はいたんでいた I *undid* the package and found the contents damaged.

びんのせんを～ける *uncap* (≒ *uncork*) a bottle.

本の32ページを～けなさい Please *turn* to page 32. / *Open* your book〔s〕 at page 32.

ひどいほこりで目を～けていられなかった I could not *keep* my eyes *open* as the air was filled with dust. / It was so dusty that I could hardly *keep* my eyes *open*.

口を大きく～けて「アー」と言ってごらん Just say "ah" with your mouth wide *open*.

2〘始める〙 ¶ お店は10時までは～けません We don't *open* our store before ten o'clock.

巨人・中日戦でリーグ戦の幕を～けた The baseball league tournament *started with* a game between the Giants and the Dragons. / The opener of the baseball league series was played between the Giants and the Dragons.

あ・げる【上げる・挙げる】 **1**〘物を上にあげる〙 ¶ 風でたこを～げる *fly* a kite.

左手を～げなさい *Raise* your left hand.

わかった人は手を～げなさい Those who understand it, *raise* your hands. / Show me your hands if you understand.

恥ずかしくて顔が～げられなかった I was not able to *look up* with shame.

海岸で花火を～げよう Let's *set off* fireworks on the seaside, shall we?

この箱をそのたなの上に～げてください *Put* this box *up* on the shelf, please.

この荷物を2階に～げてください *Carry* this baggage upstairs, please.

2〘家に〙 ¶ うちにお～げしなさい *Show* him *in*.

先日はお～げもしないで失礼しました Sorry I didn't

あ

ask you to come on in the other day.

3 〖学校に〗 ¶ ふたりの娘を大学に～げておくのは容易でない It is not easy to *send* two daughters *to college*. / I can hardly afford to *have* two daughters *at college*.

4 〖値段・給料・地位などを〗 ¶ 給料を～げてもらわねば食べていかれない I cannot make both ends meet unless I *get a raise*.

会社はぼくの月給を10パーセント～げてくれた The company *raised* my salary 10 percent.

またタクシー料金を～げようとする動きが業者の間にある The taxi companies are likely to *raise* the taxi fares again.

教員の社会的地位を～げる *raise* teacher's status in society.

5 〖名声を〗 ¶ その作品で彼は一躍名を～げた He *sprang to fame* through that work. / That work *brought* him *fame*.

彼は詩人として名を～げた He *became famous* as a poet.

6 〖温度・速度・生産量・能率を〗 ¶ ここでは時速100キロ以上に車の速度を～げてはいけない Speeds of over 100 kph are not allowed here.

その製品の生産量を２倍に～げよう We will *double* the output of the goods.

もっと能率を～げるにはどうしたらよいか What should we do in order to *increase* efficiency?

部屋の温度を５度～げてください *Raise* the temperature of the room five more degrees, please.

7 〖声を〗 ¶ 彼は突然大声を～げた Suddenly, he *shouted*. / Suddenly he *raised his voice loud*.

金切り声を～げて彼女は助けを求めた She *shrieked* for help.

歓声を～げて子どもたちは彼女を迎え入れた The children welcomed her *with cries of welcome*.

学生はみな戦争反対の声を～げているのがきみには聞こえないのか I wonder why you turn a deaf ear to the students' *outcry against* war.

8 〖費用で済ませる〗 ¶ この仕事を１万円で～げてほしい Please *do* this work for 10,000 yen.

この仕事を百万円で～げようたって無理だ It is impossible to *finish up* this work for one million yen.

忘年会を安く～げる方法はないかね Do you happen to know how we can have an inexpensive year-end party?

9 〖完了する〗 ¶ せめてピアノの教則本１冊ぐらいは～げたい I want to *finish* practicing at least one piano lesson-book.

１月かかって謡を１曲～げた It took me a month to *master* 〔the recitation of〕 a *no* text.

10 〖例・証拠を〗 ¶ 実例を二, 三～げましょう Let me *give* a few examples.

あなたが不在であった証拠が～げられますか Can you *prove* your alibi?

その場にいた人の名を～げなさい *Name* those who were on the spot.

その理由を～げなさい *Give* the reasons for it.

11 〖成果・収穫をおさめる〗 ¶ 彼は当社の社員としてりっぱな成績を～げた He *made a great showing* (≒ *has done well*) as a clerk of our company.

12 〖犯人を〗 ¶ 主犯はまだ～げられていない The principal offender *is* still *at large*.

～げられたのは小物ばかりだ Those *arrested* are only petty hooligans.

13 〖差し上げる〗 give. ¶ ごほうびになにを～げようか How shall I *reward* you?

これを記念に～げましょう I'll *give* this to you as a memento.

御仏前にお明かりを～げてください Please *offer* sacred lights to the altar. / Please *light* the candles for the altar.

14 〖式を〗 ¶ いつごろ〔結婚〕式をお～げになりますか When will you *have* your wedding ceremony?

２月１日に式を～げます We are going to *get married* on February 1.

15 〖…してあげる〗 ¶ なにを買って～げようか What shall I *buy for* you?

きみのためならなんでもして～げる I will *do* anything I can *for* you.

彼にその手紙を読んで～げなさい Read him the letter. / Read the letter for him.

16 〖慣用的表現〗 ¶ そんなに～げたり下げたりするな Don't *flatter* me so much.

寝床を～げなさい *Put away* your bedding and mattress.

一同杯を～げてふたりの前途を祝した We *drank a toast* to wish success to the two.

彼は重い腰をやっと～げて, 一肌脱ごうと言った After much hesitation, he promised to work for us at last.

われわれは全力を～げて勝利へと邁進(まいしん)します We will strive for victory *as hard as we can* (≒ *with all our power*).

彼は現政権打倒の兵を～げた He *rose up* 〔*in arms*〕 against the present regime.

一旗～げたいのだが資金がない I wish I could *make a name for myself* but I'm out of funds.

彼は碁の腕を大いに～げた He *has made* great *progress in go* play.

あけわた·す 【明け渡す】 ¶ 敵に城を～す *surrender* the castle to the enemy. 家を人に～す move out of the house and *turn* it *over to a person*; *transfer the ownership* of the house to *a person*.

あご 【顎】 a jaw; (おとがい) a chin. ¶ ～が落ちるほどおいしい食事 a dinner that is *out of this world*. 彼は助手を～で使う He *orders* his assistant *around*. ～が干上がる go broke; be down and out. 過労で～を出す *be run-down* from overwork.

—ひげ a beard. **—ひも(帽子の)** a chin strap.

アコーディオン an accordion.

—奏者 an accordionist; an accordion player. **—ドア** an accordion door. **—プリーツのスカート** an *accordion* pleated skirt.

あこがれ 【憧れ】 (行為) 〔a〕 longing; a thirst;

a yearning ; (対象) an idol ; an ideal.

あこが·れる【憧れる】long (*for* a thing ; *to* do) ; yearn (≒ hanker) (*for* a thing ; *to* do) ; thirst (*for*) ; have a longing (*for*) (long ; yearn, hanker のあとに物がくる時, for のかわりに after を使うこともあるが古風な使い方. 動詞が来るときは to ＋不定詞のかたちをとる) ; (崇拝する) adore ; revere.

¶ 海に〜れている I *have a* 〔great〕 *longing for* the sea. 彼女は演劇に〜れている She *is stage-struck*. 彼は華やかな都会生活に〜れている He *feels attracted* by the bright lights of a city. 彼は名声に〜れている He *longs for* (≒ *longs after*) fame.

あこやがい【阿古屋貝】〘貝類〙 a mother-of-pearl ; a pearl oyster.

あさ【麻】〘植物〙 (大麻) hemp ; (亜麻) flax ; (黄麻) jute. ¶ 天下が〜のごとく乱れている The country is in *turmoil* (≒ *utter chaos*).

—糸 flax (≒ hemp) thread. **—なわ** a hempen rope. **—布** hemp cloth. **—袋** a gunny (≒ hemp) sack.

あさ【朝】morning. ¶ 〜のうちに in the *morning*. 〜から晩まで from *morning* till night. 〜の間じゅう all 〔the〕 *morning*. ある〜 one *morning*. あすの〜 tomorrow *morning* (one morning, tomorrow morning などは副詞句に扱って前置詞をつけない. 15日の朝という場合は on the morning of the 15 th と on をつけるのが普通. なお「朝のうちに」の場合, *in* the morning だったものが, 何月何日の朝, 何曜の朝には on に前置詞がかわる). 彼は〜が早い(遅い) He gets up *early* (*late*) *in the morning*.

—がた ¶ 〜がた雪になりだした It began to snow *toward morning*. **—露** the morning dew. **—なぎ** a morning calm. **—もや** the morning mists. **—焼け** the morning glow.

あざ【字】a 〔village〕 section. ¶ 南村〜中丸 1097 1097 Nakamaru, Minamimura.

あざ【痣】(生来の) a birthmark ; a mole ; (打撲の) a bruise. ¶ 全身〜だらけだ I am covered with *bruises*. 打たれて腕に〜ができた The blow *bruised* my arm.

あさ·い【浅い】 **1** 〘水が〙 shallow. ¶ この池は〜い This pond *is shallow*.

水の〜い所で泳いだ I swam in *shallow* waters.

2 〘容器が〙 shallow ; flat (浅いなべには a pan, 深なべには a pot という独立の単語がある). ¶ 〜いさら a *shallow* dish.

3 〘傷が〙 slight ; superficial. ¶ 〜い切り傷 a *slight* cut ; (内部に及ばぬ)〜い傷 a *flesh* wound.

彼の傷は〜かった He was *slightly* wounded. / He had a *slight* wound.

4 〘眠りが〙 ¶ 私は眠りが〜いほうだ I'm *a light sleeper*.

5 〘色が〙 light ; pale ; faint.

6 〘日が〙 ¶ 私たちは知り合ってから日が〜い We haven't known each other long. / We've just met.

春はまだ〜い It is still *early* spring.

退院後日が〜い It has been (≒ is) only a short time since I got out of the hospital.

本校は創立以来日が浅く, ほんの数年しか過っていない Our school *is* quite *young yet*, with a history of only a few years.

7 〘関係が〙 slight ; not close. ¶ 彼らは〜からぬ関係にある They are bound 〔up〕 by *close* ties.

ぼくらは関係が〜い We are *slightly* connected with each other.

8 〘思慮·知識が〙 superficial ; shallow. ¶ 彼は思慮が〜い He'*s imprudent*.

その問題にはごく〜い知識しか持っていない I have only a *superficial* knowledge of that subject.

あさがお【朝顔】〘植物〙 a morning-glory.

あさぎ【浅黄】light yellow.

あさく【浅く】¶ 本を〜読む read *cursorily* ; *skim* a book.

あさぐろ·い【浅黒い】(生まれつきの膚が) dark-skinned ; (日焼けした膚が) tanned. ¶ 〜い顔の人 a *dark-skinned* (≒ *swarthy*) man ; a man with a *dark* complexion (単に He's dark. と言えば髪の毛が黒い意になる). 彼は〜く日焼けした He *got* 〔deeply〕 *tanned*.

あざけり【嘲り】 scoff ; sneer ; derision ; mockery. ¶ 〜のまと an object of *derision*.

あざけ·る【嘲る】 ¶ 彼らは私を〜った They *laughed scornfully at* me. 馬鹿馬鹿しいと〜る *laugh at* (*a thing*) as ridiculous.

あさせ【浅瀬】a shoal ; shallows (通常複数形) ; a ford. ¶ 〜を渡る cross (a river) *by a ford*. 船は〜に乗り上げた The boat *ran aground*.

あさって【明後日】the day after tomorrow.

¶ 〜の朝 the morning *after next*.

あさっぱら【朝っぱら】¶ 〜からなんの騒ぎだ What has happened at this *unearthly hour*?

あさね【朝寝】late rising. ¶ 〜する rise (≒ get up) late ; sleep late ; lie in bed late in the morning ; (寝過ごす) oversleep *oneself*. けさは〜をした I *got up* (≒ *rose*) *late* this morning.

あさねぼう【朝寝坊】a late riser ; a sleepy-head ; a lie-abed.

あさはか【浅墓】¶ 〜な人 a *shallow-brained* (≒ *thoughtless*) person. 彼は〜にも私を欺こうとした He was *thoughtless* enough to try to deceive me.

あさばん【朝晩】morning and evening.

¶ 〜かなり涼しくなった We have much cooler *mornings and evenings* now. / It has become quite cool *in the mornings and evenings*. 息子の無事を〜祈りつづけた She prayed for the safety of her son *day in and day out*.

あさひ【朝日】the morning (≒ rising) sun.

¶ 〜を浴びる bask (≒ be bathed) in *the morning sunshine*. 〜が山の向こうから昇る *The sun* rises from behind the mountain.

—影 morning sunshine.

あさまし·い【浅間敷い】(みじめな) wretched ; miserable ; (卑しい) base ; mean ; despicable ; (恥ずべき) shameful ; ignoble.

あ

¶〜い考え a *base* idea. 〜い行為 a *shameful* conduct. なんという〜い世の中だ What a *miserable* world we live in! 彼はなんとも〜い姿をしていた He was a picture of *misery*. こんなことをしてわれながら〜い I *am ashamed of my self* for having done such a thing. 〜い! It is *a shame*!

あざみ【薊】〔植物〕a thistle. ¶〜の花もひと盛り (諺) *Every dog has his day.*

あさみどり【浅緑】 light green.

あざむ・く【欺く】 ¶自己を〜くな Don't *deceive* yourself. / Be honest to yourself. 彼女は花を〜く美人だった She was *as fair as a May rose* (≒ *pretty as a picture; lovely as the day*). 庭は昼を〜くように明るかった It was *as bright as day* in the garden.

あさめし【朝飯】 breakfast. ¶〜を食べた I *had* (≒ *took*) *breakfast*.

—前 ¶そんなことは〜前さ That's quite easy (≒ simple). / That's nothing〔to me〕.

あざやか【鮮やか】 ¶その印象は今もなお〜だ The impression remains *vivid* in my mind. 観客はその〜な演技に見とれた The audience watched the *neat* (≒ *splendid*) performance with admiration. 花は〜な赤い色をしていた The flower was of a *bright* red color. 〜に clearly; vividly; (みごとに) admirably; neatly.

あさゆう【朝夕】 morning and evening; every day.

あざらし【海豹】〔動物〕a seal.

あさり【浅蜊】〔貝類〕a short-necked clam.

あさ・る【漁る】 ¶犬がごみ箱を〜っている Dogs *are rummaging* the garbage can. 珍本を〜る *search for* rare books.

あざわら・う【あざ笑う】 ¶彼らは私を〜った They *laughed scornfully at* (≒ *mocked at*) me. 〜うように mockingly; scornfully.

あし【足・脚】 **1**〖足〗 ¶犬(ネコ)の〜 a dog's (cat's) *paw*.

タコの8本〜 the eight *arms* of an octopus.

〜の甲 the instep of *a foot*.

〜の裏 the sole of *a foot*.

テーブルの〜 the *legs* of a table.

彼女は〜がほっそりしている She has slender *legs*.

あの人は〜が悪い He *is lame*.

〜がしびれた My *feet* are asleep.

〜ががくがく震えた My *legs* trembled. / My knees knocked together.

彼は左〜を折った He broke his left *leg*. / He had his left *leg* broken.

私は〜を波にさらわれた I had my *feet* carried off by the waves. / I lost my *footing* in the waves.

彼は相手の〜をとって倒した Grasping him by the *leg*, he threw the opponent down.

彼は〜をそろえて跳んだ He jumped with both *legs*.

ふたりは〜をそろえて歩いた The two walked *in step*. / They walked *keeping pace* with each other.

両〜を十分に開きなさい Spread out your *legs*.

右〜を踏まれた I had my right *foot* trodden upon.

〜を棒にして職を捜した I went hunting for a job till my *legs* got stiff.

彼は〜を組んで腰かけた He sat down with his *legs* crossed.

階段から〜を踏みはずした I lost my *footing* on the stairs.

左〜にまめができた I have got a blister on my left *foot*.

ぼくは左〜でうまく球がけれない I can't kick a ball well with my left *leg*.

片〜で立っていた I was standing on one *leg*.

後ろ〜で砂をかけるようなことをするな Refrain from doing anything *ungrateful* on parting with a person.

左〜から1歩踏み出しなさい Take a step forward with your left *leg*.

老人は〜から衰える Old people grow weak in the *legs* first.

〜の先から頭のてっぺんまでじろじろ見られた I was stared at from head to *toe*.

〜のおもむくままに市内を散歩した I walked about the city *as fancy led me*.

私の〜に合うくつがなかった I couldn't get well-fitting shoes.

2〖歩行・行程〗 ¶あの人は〜が達者だ He is *a good walker*.

彼は〜が速い He *walks fast*. / He is quick on his *feet*.

ここまで来たからには四国まで〜をのばそう Since we have come this far, let's *extend our journey* as far as Shikoku.

きみの〜じゃそこまで行けば日暮れになる *At your pace* it will be dark when you get there.

彼女は〜を速めてその場に近づいていった Quickening her *pace*, she approached the scene.

その〜で駅へ友人を迎えに行った I went *right away* to the station to meet my friend.

3〖訪問・往来〗 ¶このような所にまでわざわざ〜をお運びいただき恐縮です I am very much obliged to you for your kindness in *coming* all the way to see me.

彼女のもとに彼はしげしげ〜を運んだ He *frequented* her house.

彼は彼女からしだいに〜が遠のいていった He began to *keep away* from her.

4〖交通手段〗 ¶国鉄ストで100万人の〜が奪われた On account of the walkout of the National Railway workers, no less than one million passengers were deprived of any *means of transportation*.

5〖慣用的表現〗 ¶彼はやくざ稼業(かぎょう)から〜を洗った He *washed his hands* of the gambling business.

盗品から〜がついて捕えられた The criminal *was traced by* the stolen goods and arrested.

参会者が少なく費用に〜が出た There being only a small attendance, the fees *did not cover* the expenses.

彼のやることは〜が地についてない He isn't *steady* in his conduct. / He ignores reality in everything he does.

人の〜を引っ張るようなことはするな Don't try to *trip up* (≒ *drag down*) others.

ばかの大〜 A fool has big *feet*.

あし【葦】〘植物〙a reed ; a rush.

―笛 a reed pipe.

アジ agitation.

―演説 an agitation speech. ―ビラ an agitation bill.

あじ【味】1〘食物の〙(味覚)taste ; (風味) flavor. ¶この薬はにがい〜がする This medicine *tastes* bitter.

この薬はなんの〜もしない This medicine has hardly any *taste*.

ニンニクの〜がする It *tastes* (≒ *savors*) *of* garlic. / There is some *taste* of garlic in the food.

「どんな〜がしますか」「甘い〜がします」"What does it *taste* like? (≒ How does it *taste*?)" "It *tastes* sweet."

けっこうな〜です It *tastes* nice.

塩の〜が足りない It isn't salty enough. / It has too little salt in it.

〜がすっかり抜けてしまった It has utterly lost its *flavor*. / It has become quite *flat*.

長く置いといたので〜が変わった Having been kept long, it has *got stale*.

〜がよくないね It *tastes* bad, doesn't it?

ちょっとこの〜をみてくれませんか Will you just *taste* this? / Will you just try its *flavor*?

これは〜のつけすぎだ. もう少し薄〜のほうがいい This is too *strong*. I would like it a little *weaker*. / This dish is too highly *seasoned*. Please *season* it more lightly.

2〘趣味・妙味〙¶彼はなかなか〜のあることを言った His remarks *are* much *to the point*. / He made a *significant* remark.

〜なことをするね You *are smart*. / You *have played your part quite well*.

そのことばはかみしめればかみしめるほど〜が出てくる The more we digest the remark, the more *significant* it becomes.

つきあえばつきあうほど彼は〜が出てくる人です The longer you know him, the more you *will be charmed by him*.

そう言ってしまえば, 〜もそっけもない If you put it [in] that way, it is *quite dry and dull* (≒ *just dry as dust*).

3〘経験〙¶貧乏の〜などきみにわかるものか You don't *know* poverty at all. / You don't *know* at all what it is to be poor.

彼は競馬でもうけた〜が忘れられない Once he has made money on the turf, he cannot leave off betting on horse races.

そんなことで〜をしめるな You should not *be elated by* such a petty success.

あじ【鯵】〘魚類〙a horse-mackerel.

あしあと【足跡】a footprint; a footmark. ¶雪の上に彼の〜を発見した We found his *footprints* in the snow.

あしおと【足音】a footfall; a footstep. ¶あわただしい〜が聞こえた I heard hurried *footsteps*.

あしか【海驢】〘動物〙a sea-lion.

あしがかり【足掛かり】a foothold. ¶これで〜ができた By this I could *secure a footing* (≒ *get a foothold*).

あしかけ【足掛け】¶ここへ来てから〜3年になる This is my third year here.

あしかせ【足枷】fetters; leg irons. ¶彼に〜をかけろ Put him in *fetters*.

あしがため【足固め】(下準備) preparation.

あしからず【悪しからず】¶〜思ってください I hope you will understand. 〜ご了承ください I beg you to understand my position. / Please understand.

あしがる【足軽】a footman.

あしくせ【足癖】a gait.

あしくび【足首】an ankle.

あしげ【葦毛】(馬) a gray horse.

あしげ【足蹴】¶彼はみんなから〜にされてもがまんした He suffered them to *kick* him.

あじけな・い【味気ない】dull; wearisome; dreary; wretched. ¶人世が〜くなった I *have grown weary of* life. / I have *got sick of* every day life. なんて〜い人世だ What a *dull*, *insipid* life!

あしこし【足腰】¶〜の立たぬ病人 a *crippled* invalid. 〜が立たない I *am crippled*. / I am unable to get about. 年老いて〜が立たなくなってきた I am not strong enough to get about with age.

あじさい【紫陽花】〘植物〙a hydrangea.

あしざまに【悪し様に】¶友人を〜言うな Don't *speak ill of* your friend. / Don't *call* your friend *names*.

あししげく【足繁く】¶彼は図書館に〜通った He *frequently* visited the library.

あした【明日】tomorrow.

あしだ【足駄】high clogs; rain-clogs.

あしだい【足台】a stool; a step.

あしだい【足代】¶〜もばかにならぬ *Transportation* costs a lot.

あしつき【足つき】¶彼は危ない〜だ He walks with unsteady *steps*.

あしでまとい【足手まとい】¶逃げるとき婦女子が〜になった Women and children were *a burden* on them when they took to flight.

〜になるからついてくるな Don't follow me, for you will be *a burden* on me.

アジト an agitating point; (口語) a hide-out.

あしどめ【足止め】detention. ¶〜をくう *be pinned* in one place. 豪雨のため半日駅に〜された The heavy rain *detained* us at the station for half a day.

あしどり【足取り】a step. ¶私たちは軽い〜で山道を登った We climbed up the mountain path with light *steps*. その後の彼の〜はわからない His *movements* (≒ *whereabouts*) after that are unknown. (whereabouts は is (ときに are) で受ける).

あしなみ【足並み】¶ふたりは〜をそろえて歩いている The two are walking *in step* with each other. 隊の〜がそろわない The platoon is *out of step*.

あしならし【足慣らし】¶〜に二, 三分歩いた I

walked for a few minutes *for practice*. きょうは〜をしてみよう I am going to *practice walking* today.

あしば【足場】 a footing. ¶ 〜を得る secure *a footing*. 〜を失う lose *one's footing*. どこに〜を掛けたらいいだろう Where shall I *scaffold* the building?

あしばや【足早・足速】 ¶ 〜な swift-footed. 〜に at a rapid pace. 男は〜に走り去った The man ran away *rapidly*.

あしびょうし【足拍子】 ¶ 彼女は〜をとって踊っていた She was dancing, *keeping time with her feet*.

あしぶみ【足踏み】 ¶ 〜する march in place; (体操) mark time. 景気は〜している The market is *at a standstill*. もうこの家には〜するな Don't ever show your face at this house!

あしもと【足元】 1 ¶ 〜に気をつけなさい Watch your steps.
〜の明るいうちに帰りましょう Let's go back home while it is light.
2 〖比喩的に〗 ¶ 〜から鳥が立つように出ていった He went away *abruptly*.
クラスのだれも彼の〜にも及ばない No one in his class can *compare with* him.
私はとても彼の〜にも寄りつけない I cannot *be compared with* him at all.

あしゅら【阿修羅】 (梵語) *Asura*. ¶ 〜のように暴れた He was wild *with rage*. 〜のような場面となった The place became *like a battlefield*.

あしよわ【足弱】 (人) a poor walker.

あしらい treatment; reception; entertainment.

あしら・う ¶ 彼はいいかげんに〜っておけばいい There is no need to *deal with* him seriously. ジャガイモにはパセリを刻んで〜ってあった The boiled potatoes *were garnished with* chopped parsley.

アジ・る ¶ 彼らは群衆を〜って暴動を起こした They *inflamed* the crowd to riot.

あじわい【味わい】 ¶ 〜の深いことば a *significant* remark. 彼の短い話にはえも言われぬ〜がある There is something peculiarly *suggestive* in his little talk.

あじわ・う【味わう】 ¶ この料理はよく〜ってほしい I hope you will *enjoy* this dish *with relish*. さまざまの苦労を〜った I *tasted* every bitter experience of life. 幾多の困難を〜った I *went through* (≒ *experienced*) every hardship. まさに〜うべきことばだ It is indeed a *significant* remark.

あしわざ【足技】 footwork. ¶ 〜は彼の得意だ He has marvelous *footwork* in *judo*.

あす【明日】 tomorrow. ¶ 〜の朝 *tomorrow* morning. 〜は〜の風が吹く *Tomorrow* will take care of itself.

あずかり【預かり】 ¶ 勝負は〜となった The match ended in *a draw*.
—金 money on deposit. —証 a deposit receipt. —物 an article left in *one's* charge.

あずか・る【預かる】 ¶ 取りに来るまでこの荷物を〜ってください Please *keep* this parcel till I call for it. その時計は彼が〜っている He *is entrusted with* the watch. 彼は1年級を〜っている He *is in charge of* the first-year class. 親類の子を〜っている We *are taking care of* our relative's child. この家では学生をひとり〜っている They *are boarding* a student in this house.

あずか・る【与る】 ¶ それは私の〜り知るところではない I *have nothing to do with* it. 収益の配当には〜らなかった I did not *have a share in* the profits. 事業の成功には彼の尽力が〜って力があった His exertions *did much toward* the success in the enterprise. 私が相談に〜りましょう I shall *be consulted*. お招きに〜りましてありがたく存じます I am much obliged to you for your kind invitation.

あずき【小豆】 a red bean. ¶ 〜色の花 a *reddish brown* flower.

あず・ける【預ける】 ¶ 金はだれに〜けたのですか Whom did you *leave* the money *with*? かばんは彼に〜けた I *have entrusted* the briefcase *with* him. 銀行に金を〜けるのはきらいだ I don't like to *deposit* my money *in* a bank. 赤ん坊は知らない人には〜けられない We cannot *leave* our baby *in the care of* a stranger. 貴重品はフロントに〜けたほうがいい You had better *entrust* valuables *at* the hotel front.

アスパラガス 〔an〕 asparagus. ¶ 〜の茎は食用になる The young stalks of *asparagus* are used as (≒ are good for) food.

アスピリン aspirin. ¶ 〜を2錠飲む take two *aspirins* (≒ *aspirin tablets*).

アスファルト asphalt. ¶ 〜の道 an *asphalt* road. この道路は〜が敷かれている This road is paved with *asphalt*.

あずまや【東屋・四阿】 an arbor. ¶ あの〜で一ぷくしよう Let's have a rest in that *arbor*.

あせ【汗】 sweat (sweat が普通だが, 品位のある語として perspiration を用いることもある).
1 〖汗が〗 ¶ 〜が盛んに出ている He *is sweating* profusely.
背中を〜がだらだら流れている I *am dripping* (≒ *am beaded*) *with sweat* along the back.
〜が流れた *Sweat* streamed down.
2 〖汗を〗 ¶ 〜をうっすらかいているね You have a thin film of *sweat*, haven't you?
顔の〜をふきなさい Wipe the *perspiration* from your face.
絞るほど〜をかいている He is wringing wet with *perspiration*.
わきの下に〜をかいている *Sweat* is coming from under my armpits.
〜をたくさんかくと風邪は治るそうだ It is said that a good *sweat* cures a cold.
額に玉のような〜をかいていた Beads of *perspiration* stood on his forehead.
3 〖その他〗 ¶ 彼は〜だくになって畑仕事をしている He is at work on the farm, *dripping* (≒ *drenched*) *with sweat*.
額に〜してこつこつ働いた I worked continuou-

sly *by the sweat of my brow*.
手に～握って見守っている They are watching *breathlessly*.

アセチレン acetylene.
—ランプ an acetylene torch.

アセテート acetate.

あせば·む【汗ばむ】¶きょうは～むような感じだ It is warm enough to make us slightly *sweaty* today.

あせび【馬酔木】〔植物〕a Japanese andromeda ; an andromeda.

あせみず【汗水】¶彼は日夜～流して働いている He toils and sweats day and night.

あぜみち【畦道】a footpath between rice fields.

あせも【汗疹】〔a〕heat rash. ¶この赤ん坊は～ができない This baby has no *heat rash*.

あせ·る【焦る】¶あの男はけっして～らない He *is* never *in a hurry*. 成功を～っているようすが見える He seems *too eager* for success. ～るな Take your time.

あ·せる【褪せる】¶この色は～せない This color does not *fade*. この革は日に当たって色が～せた The sun *has burnt the color out of* this piece of leather.

あぜん【啞然】¶彼の大胆さに～とした I *was* 〔quite〕*stunned by* his boldness. 彼は～として黙って立っていた He was standing speechless *with astonishment*.

あそこ ¶～に見えるのがかの有名なホテルです The building seen *over there* is the famous hotel. ～の丘まで行くのにどのくらいかかりますか How long does it take to get to the hill *over there*?

あそば·す【遊ばす】¶陛下は野球場においで～された His Majesty *was pleased to pay* (≒ *graciously paid*) a visit to the baseball field. どうぞたばこをおのみ～せ Won't you please smoke?

あそば·せる【遊ばせる】¶子どもを～せてほしい I want you to *look after* the child. 彼は娘を～せている He *leaves* his daughter *idle*. 金を～せておくのはもったいない How wasteful it is to *have* your money *idle*!

あそび【遊び】play ; amusement ; recreation. ¶ゴルフは金持ちの～だ Golf is a rich man's *amusement*. ～半分に勉強してはいけない Never study *in a half-hearted way*. この子は～ざかりだ This child is in his *playful* (≒ *sportive*) age. 彼は～好きだ He is a *pleasure* hunter. 子どもたちは～に夢中だ The children are absorbed in *pleasure*. ～がてら横浜に行った We made a trip to Yokohama *for pleasure*.
—道具 a plaything. **—**仲間 a playmate.
—人(ばくち打ち) a gambler ; (道楽者) a playboy. ¶彼は～人といわれてもしかたがない He may well be called *a man of pleasure* (≒ *a pleasure hunter ; a playboy*). **—**場 a playground.

あそ·ぶ【遊ぶ】 **1**〘好きなことをして楽しむ〙play. ¶かるたをして～んだ We *played* 〔at〕 cards. 子どもたちは鬼ごっこをして～んだ The children *played* tag. なにかこの子の～べるおもちゃがないかしら Do you have any toy for the child to *play* with? 庭で～ぼう Let's *play* in the garden. / Let's *have* some *fun* in the garden.
2〘仕事·勉強をしない〙¶そんなに～んでばかりいてはいけません Don't *be idle* all the time, neglecting your lessons. きのうは一日じゅう～んでしまった Yesterday I *idled away* the whole day. / I *loafed about* all day yesterday. ～んで暮らせる身分じゃない I cannot afford to live *idle*. 彼は今～んでいる(職がない) He *is out of work* now.
3〘役にたっていない〙¶不景気で設備の半分が～んでいる Half of our facilities *are not in use* owing to the depression.
4〘行楽をする〙¶彼はフランスに～んだ He *went on a pleasure trip to* France. / He *visited* France. 正月をハワイで～んでこようと思います I am going to *make a trip to* Hawaii to spend the New Year.
5〘酒色にふける〙¶彼は若いときにはずいぶんと～んだものだ He *led a dissipated life* in his youth.

あだ【婀娜】charming. ¶～な charming ; coquettish.

あだ【仇】¶ハムレットは父の～としておじを討った Hamlet *revenged himself upon* his uncle for the murder of his father. 彼は親の～を討った He *avenged* his father. 恩を～で返すのはよくない It is not good to return *evil* for good. まじめさがかえって身の～となった His faithfulness *brought ruin to him*.

あたい【価·値】price. ¶この品は10万円の～がある This article *is worth* a hundred thousand yen. この本は一読に～するということだ They say this book *is worth* reading. 彼の行動はまさに賞賛に～する His behavior *is* really *worthy of* praise. 彼の言動は処罰に～する His speech and action *deserves* punishment. 私はこんなことに～しない I don't *deserve* such a thing.

あだうち【仇討ち】vengeance.

あた·える【与える】give. ¶もう一度チャンスを～えてほしい I want to *be given* one more chance. 彼の行動は私に好印象を～えた His conduct *gave* me a good impression. 子どもひとりに2個ずつりんごを～えなさい *Allot* two apples to each child. 彼は子どもに衣食を～えた He *provided* the child *with* food and clothes. 豪雨はこの地方に少なからぬ損害を～えた The heavy rain *caused* (≒ *inflicted*) not a little damage to this district. このバスは付近の住民に便宜を～えている This bus *serves* the neighborhood. 解答は～えられた紙面に記しなさい Write your answers in the space *at your disposal*. 先生はクラスにめったに宿題を～えない The teacher seldom *assigns* homework to the class. 名誉教授の称号が彼に～え

あ

られた The title of honorary professor *was bestowed* upon him. ～えられた一線上の～えられた一点 a *given* point in a *given* line.

あだおろそか【徒疎か】¶ 私は彼の親切を～には思いません I *appreciate* his kindness *very much*. 彼は1円も～にしなかった He made every penny count.

あたかも【恰も】¶ 彼は～なんでも知っているような口ぶりだ He talks *as if* he knew (≒ knows) everything. 彼は～おとなの赤ん坊だ He is, *as it were*, a grown-up baby.

あたたか·い【暖かい·温かい】warm. ¶ ことしは～い冬になりそうだ It seems we are going to have a *mild* winter. 陽気が～くなった It *has become warmer* (≒ *warm*). 日一日と～くなる It *is getting warmer* day by day. ～い心 a *warm* heart. ～い家庭 a *happy* home. ～い援助 *friendly* help. 彼は心の～い人です He has a *warm* heart. / He is *warm*-hearted. ～くしていなさい Keep yourself *warm*. 彼らはいたるところで～く迎えられた They received a *warm* welcome everywhere they went. きょうはふところが～いらしい He seems to *have a fat purse* today.

あたたかみ【暖かみ·温かみ】warmth. ¶ あの人は～がある He is a *warm-hearted* man. 彼には人間的な～がある He has something of human *warmth* in him.

あたたま·る【暖まる·温まる】¶ ふろで～った We took a bath to *get warm*. 心～る歓迎ぶりだった It was a *heart-warming* reception (≒ welcome). たき火で～った We *warmed ourselves* at a fire.

あたた·める【暖める·温める】¶ スープを～めた We *warmed* (≒ *heated*) *up* the soup. 私たちは旧交を～めた We *renewed* our old friendship. その計画はしばらく～めておいたほうがいい You had better *keep* the idea *in mind*.

あだな【綽名·渾名】a nickname. ¶ 彼は「ペンギン」という～をつけられた He *was nicknamed* "Penguin." みんなはその背の高い少年に「のっぽ」と～をつけた Everybody *nicknamed* the tall boy "Lamppost." その先生はたちまち～をつけられた The teacher was immediately given *a nickname*.

あたふた ¶ 彼が～と駆けてくる He *is rushing* toward us.

あたま【頭】**1**〘頭部〙a head. ¶ 彼はていねいに～を下げた He bowed his *head* deeply. / He *bowed* politely.
彼は深く～を下げてあいさつした He greeted me with *a* deep *bow*.
～を上げて彼を見すえた Raising my *head*, I stared at him.
～を壁にぶつけてこぶをつくった I knocked my *head* against the wall and got a bump.
彼は～を垂れてしおれていた He was dejected and his *head* hung 〔down〕.
～から先に川に跳び込んだ I jumped *headlong* (≒ *head foremost*) into the river.
彼は～のてっぺんから足のつま先までじろじろと私を見た He looked hard at me *from top to toe*.
きょうは風邪をひいて～が痛い Today *I have a headache* (≒ *my head aches*) with a cold.
～が重い気分です I feel heavy in the *head*.
それは～隠してしり隠さずだ It's an *ostrich* attitude.
2〘頭髪〙¶ きのう床屋で～を刈ってもらった Yesterday I had my *hair* cut at the barber's.
3〘頭脳〙a head; a brain. ¶ きみはなかなか～がいい You have *a* very clear *head*.
彼女は～が少しおかしい She is rather queer in the *head*. / She is a little off her *head*.
彼は哲学の～がある He has *a* 〔good〕 *head* for philosophy.
これはかなり～のいる仕事だ It requires a good deal of *brain* work.
～が痛い話だ It makes me heavy in the *head*. / I *am* really *worried* over it.
彼は～がかたい He *is* quite *obstinate*.
きみの～は古い You cherish outworn *ideas*.
彼は～の回転が早い He is a *quick-witted* fellow.
～の悪いやつだ He is a *dull-witted* fellow. / He has *a* thick *head*.
～を使えよ，そんなことやさしいことだ Use your *brains*! It's quite easy, isn't it?
その考えが私の～を悩ませた I racked my *brains* over it. / I bothered my *head* about it.
きみ少し～を冷やしたほうがいいよ You had better cool your *head* for a while.
この説明は難しくて～に入らない The explanation is too difficult for me to *understand*. / The explanation doesn't *go down with me*, for it's rather difficult.
いい考えが～に浮かんだ A good idea *came into my head* (≒ *occurred to me*).
4〘慣用的表現〙¶ 彼はそのことを～から否定した He denied it *flatly*. / He gave a *flat* denial to it.
ぼくは～から彼女にばかにされた She made a fool of me *completely*. / She treated me with contempt *mercilessly*.
彼女には～が上がらない I cannot hold up my *head* before her.
～を下げて頼むよ Please do it for me.
あまりそのことに～を突っ込まないほうがいい You will do well *not to be too much involved in the affair* (≒ *not to poke your nose into the matter*).
いっぺん彼の～を押えつけないと増長する If we don't *bring* him *under control* once, he will grow more and more wayward.
彼はだんだん～をもたげてきた He began to *gain strength* (≒ *get influential*).

あたまうち【頭打ち】¶ 給料が～になってしまった The pay has reached the *upper limit*.
—値段 the ceiling list.

あたまかず【頭数】¶ ～を数えたら11人だった They counted eleven *members*. ～が足りない They are lacking in *number*. 子ども達は～をそろえてやってきた All the children came. / The children *made up the members*.

あたまかぶ【頭株】a leader; a boss; (会社な

どの) an executive.

あたまきん【頭金】〔a〕down payment. ¶ テレビを買うのに～を２万円払った I made *a down payment* of 20,000 yen for the television set.

あたまごなし【頭ごなし】¶ ～にしかられた I was scolded *unsparingly*. いきなり～に言われるとは驚いた I was surprised to be scolded *without a chance to defend myself*.

あたまでっかち【頭でっかち】¶ あの人は～に見える He looks *top-heavy*. ～しりすぼみだ It's *an anticlimax*.

あたまわり【頭割り】¶ 勘定は～にしよう Expenses shall *be shared equally*. / (口) Let's *go Dutch*. 費用は各自～で払った Each of us *paid his share* of the expenses.

あだやおろそかに ¶ ～彼の名を口にすべきではない We should not mention his name *lightly*. ～そんなことをすべきではない You should never do such a thing *thoughtlessly*.

あたら【可惜】¶ ～チャンスをのがした *Much to our regret*, we missed a golden opportunity. ～生命を失った He lost his *precious* life.

あたらし・い【新しい】new. ¶ ～い家 a *new* house. 向こうに見える～い家はホワイト先生の家です The *new* house〔seen〕over there is Mr. White's. ～い研究によってこの民族の起源が明らかになった *Recent* studies have made the origin of this race clear. ～く家を建てた I had a house *newly* built. ほんの最近～く仕事を始めたばかりだ He started a *new* business just recently.

あたらしがりや【新しがり屋】¶ 彼は～だ He *is fond of novelty* (≒ *new things*).

あたらな・い【当たらない】¶ そういう言い方は～い That is *not* the *proper* word for it. これは驚くに～い This is not a matter for surprise. 彼を人格者というのは～い He *does not deserve* to be called a man of character. 彼を賞賛するのは～い Words of praise *are not suitable* for him.

あたり【当たり】¶ 彼の一打はすごい～だった The ball he hit was *a smash hit*. 芝居は大～だった The play was *a great success*. 彼みたいに～のよい人は少ない Few people are as *affable* as he. 費用はひとり～3,000円だ The expenses will cost three thousand yen *per head*. この仕事は～はずれがある This sort of work is sometimes *risky*.

あたり【辺り】¶ この～はよく知らない I do not know this *neighborhood* well. / I am quite a stranger *here*. ～にはだれもいなかった No one was *about*. ～を見まわした I looked *around*. ～は急に暗くなってきた It began to grow dark quickly. 今度の日曜日～に彼が来そうだ He is likely to come next Sunday.

あたりさわり【当たり障り】¶ ～のない noncommittal. あの人はいつも～のないことを言う He is always talking *harmlessly*. これなら～はあるまい This won't be *offensive* to anybody. ～のないように返事しておいた I gave a *noncommittal* answer to him.

あたりちら・す【当たり散らす】¶ 彼は周囲のだれかれとなく～した He *was cross with* everybody around him. 彼は私に～した He *turned his anger upon* me.

あたりどし【当たり年】¶ ことしは米の～になりそうだ This seems to be *a bumper* (≒ *lucky*) *year* for the rice crop. / We are likely to have a *bumper* crop of rice this year. (bumper はとくに豊作の場合に用いる). ぶどうの～だ It is a *vintage year*.

あたりまえ【当たりまえ】¶ ～の(自然な) natural; (普通の) ordinary; (当然の) proper; right; (合理的) reasonable. それは～だ It is *a matter of course*. / That must *be expected*. 彼が断わるのは～だ He *may well* decline it. 彼が怒るのは～だ It is *natural* that he〔should〕be angry. 知っている人に会ったらあいさつするのは～だ It is *only natural* for you to exchange greetings〔with each other〕when you meet an acquaintance. あの男が罰せられるのは～だ He *deserves* to be punished. ～のことを～にやるのはやさしいようで難しい It seems easy but in reality difficult to do a *simple* thing in an *ordinary* way.

あた・る【当たる】**1**〖命中する〗¶ 矢が的に～った The arrow *hit* the target.

大きな石が頭に～って重傷を負った A big stone *hit* me on the head, and I was seriously injured.

波が岩に～って砕けた The waves *broke* on the rocks.

きょうはバットにうまく球が～る Today I can *hit* balls very naturally.

犬も歩けば棒に～る (諺) *Every dog has his day.*

2〖適中する〗¶ ぼくの推量が～った I *have guessed right*!

くじに～った The lot *fell upon* me.

～るも八卦(はっけ)～らぬも八卦 There is no saying how〔a〕prediction may *turn out*.

計画が図に～った My plan *had the desired effect*.

商売が～った I *made a hit* in my business.

ことしはミカンが～った *This is a good* (≒ *lucky*) *year for* tangerine oranges.

3〖該当する〗¶ ことしのクリスマスは水曜に～る This year's Christmas Day *falls on* Wednesday.

彼は私のおじに～る He *is* my uncle.

10日は父の命日に～ります The anniversary of my father's death *falls on* the tenth.

それは刑法15条に～る It *is stipulated in* Article 15 of the criminal law.

その誹謗(ひぼう)は彼には～らない He does not *deserve* the reprobation.

そんなことをすれば失礼に～る It *is impolite of you* to do such a thing.

そんなことを言うと罰が～る Heaven will *punish* you for what you say.

この方角が南に～る This direction *points to* the south.

この語に～るうまい訳語はない There is no appropriate Japanese *equivalent* (≒ *coun-*

あ

terpart) for this word.

4 〖担当する〗 ¶ その交渉には彼が〜っている He *takes it upon himself* to conduct the negotiations. / He *is responsible for* the negotiations.

だれがきょうの日直に〜っているのか Who *is on* day duty today?

この次はきっときみが〜るよ. よく下調べをしておいたほうがいい Next time you will surely *be called upon* to do the work. You had better prepare well for it.

5 〖探索する・交渉〗 ¶ あちこち〜ってみたがだめだった I *contacted* a few places with no result.

彼にじかに〜ってみなさい I suggest that you *make* direct *negotiations with* him.

値段を〜ってみてください *Feel* the price, please.

原文に〜って確かめてみなさい Make sure by *checking* the original.

6 〖いじめる〗 ¶ ぼくにそんなに〜るな Don't *be* so *hard on* me.

彼はネコにまで〜りちらしている He *works off his bad temper* even *on* his cat.

彼女は嫁につらく〜った She *treated* her daughter-in-law *very harshly*.

7 〖日光・雨・風など〗 ¶ この部屋は日がよく〜る The sun *streams* into this room.

雨が〜らないようにしておきなさい You'd better see that it *is* not *exposed to* rain.

どうぞ火にお〜りください Please *warm yourself at* the fire.

8 〖中毒する・やられる〗 ¶ お昼に食べた魚に〜った The fish I ate at lunch *disagreed with* me.

なにかに〜ったに相違ない Something I ate must *have upset* my stomach.

彼女は暑さに〜った She *was affected by* the summer heat.

9 〖直面する〗 ¶ 会を始めるに〜って一言申し上げます *Before* beginning this meeting, let me say a few words of greetings.

出発に〜っていま一度皆に注意したい *At this time* of our departure, I want to call your special attention once more.

10 〖対抗する〗 ¶ 一致団結してこの強敵に〜ろう Let's *be united against* this formidable enemy.

〜って砕けろ Do or die.

彼の勢い〜るべからず He is *in roaring spirits*.

11 〖その他〗 ¶ ひげを〜ってくれ I want to *get myself shaved*.

〜るを幸い敵をなぎ倒した He struck down everything that *came in his way*.

くつが指に〜って痛い These shoes pinch me at the toes.

あちこち here and there. ¶ 〜30分ほど歩きまわった I walked *up and down* for about half an hour. 数人の人が並んで通りを〜歩いていた Several persons were walking side by side *up and down* the street. 京都を〜旅をした We traveled *from place to place* around Kyoto. カモメが〜飛びまわっている Gulls are flying *here and there* in the sky.

あちら ¶ どうぞ〜へ Please go *that way*. 〜は雪がないそうです They have no snow *over there*, I hear. 〜の建物はおじの家です The (≒ That) building *over there* is my uncle's. 〜の国では今なにが流行していますか What is in fashion in *that* country? 〜からもこちらからも賞賛の声があった Praises came *from all quarters*.

あっ ¶ 〜, わかった *Oh*, I see! 〜, カメラを家に忘れた *Dear me!* I've left my camera at home! 〜, 危ない. 自動車だ *Oh*, look out! A car is coming!

あつ・い 【厚い】 thick. ¶ 〜い板 a *thick* board. 〜い本 a *thick* book.

あつ・い 【暑い】 hot; warmer. ¶ 〜くならぬうちに出かけよう Let's go before the *heat* of the day. うだるように〜い It is scorching *hot*. 日ましに〜くなっている It is getting *warmer* day by day. 〜いのは苦手だ *Heat* is hard for me to put up with. きょうも〜そうだ It's going to be another *hot* day!

あつ・い 【熱い】 hot. ¶ 〜いコーヒーを1杯いかがですか Won't you have a cup of *hot* coffee? お茶の〜いのをください May I have a cup of *hot* tea? この牛乳は〜くて赤ん坊には無理だ This milk is too *hot* for a baby to drink. 夏に〜い飲み物も悪くない A *hot* drink in summer is not bad. ふたりはお〜いらしい They seem to be *deeply in love* with each other.

あつ・い 【篤い】 ¶ 彼は病いが〜いということだ He is rumored to be *seriously* ill. 彼はなんと友情に〜い人だろう How *loyal* (≒ *faithful*) he is to his friends!

あついた (厚板) a thick board; (ガラス) a plate (≒ glass); (金属) a plate.

あつえん 【圧延】 rolling. ¶ 〜する roll.

—工場 a rolling mill.

あっか 【悪化】 ¶ 事態はますます〜した The situation *grew* even *worse*. 彼の病状は急に〜した His condition *took a* sudden *turn for the worse*. この地域での風紀の〜は著しいものがある There is much *corruption* (≒ *deterioration*) in public morals in this district.

あっか 【悪貨】 a bad coin. ¶ 〜は良貨を駆逐する *Evil* (≒ *Bad*) *money* drives out good.

あつかい 【扱い】 treatment. ¶ 彼女は息子を子ども〜する She *treats* her grown sons like children. 現地ではひどい〜を受けた He *was* cruelly *treated* there. このホテルは客〜がよい (悪い) This hotel gives good (poor) *service* to guests. 彼は道具の〜が不器用だ He is awkward with tools.

あつか・う 【扱う】 ¶ 客を丁重に〜う *treat one's* guests politely. この機械は〜いにくい This machine is hard to *handle*. こういう人は〜いやすい This sort of person is easy to *deal with*. この道具をそんなに乱暴に〜っては困る Don't *use* this tool so roughly! こちらでは小包を〜っていますか Do you *handle* parcels here? 彼はこの会社の事務を〜っている He is working as a clerk in this office.

あつかまし・い 【厚かましい】 impudent.

¶ 〜さ impudence. 〜いお願いですが留守に泊まり

にきていただけませんか I am afraid *I am asking too much*, but won't you come and stay at our home while I am away? そんなことをするとはなんと～い男だ How *impudent* he is to do such a thing! ～くも家に上がり込んだ He was *impudent* enough to barge into my house.

あつがみ【厚紙】cardboard.

あつが·る【暑がる】¶こんな日に～るなんて I am surprised that he should *feel* so *hot* on such a day.

—り屋 a person who is sensitive to heat. ¶彼はたいへんな～り屋だ He *is* very *sensitive to heat*.

あっかん【圧巻】¶当日の～はチンパンジーのショーだった The *highlight* of the day was the show by the chimpanzees. この場面はその劇の～だ This scene is *the best part* of the drama. この小説は現代小説の～といわれている This novel is said to be one of *the greatest masterpieces* of modern fiction.

あっかん【悪漢】a villain.

あつかん【熱燗】¶～で出してほしい Serve me some *heated sake*. ～で出してくれた He served *sake hot*.

あっき【悪鬼】a devil; a demon.

あつぎ【厚着】¶～する be thickly dressed. 幼児には～させないほうがいい You had better not *clothe* babies too *heavily*.

あつく【厚く】**1**〖ていねいに〗¶～もてなす receive *a person warmly*; (ごちそうする) entertain *a person hospitably*.

～礼を言う thank *a person cordially*.

2〖厚さ〗¶～切る cut (a thing) *thick*.

あつくるし·い【暑苦しい】¶今晩は～い It is *sultry* this evening. この室内は～くてどうにもならない This room is too *stuffy* for me.

あっけ【呆気】¶～にとられた I *was taken aback*. 彼は～にとられて物も言えなかった He *was struck dumb* (≒ *was dumfounded*) *with amazement*.

あっけい【悪計】an evil design; a plot; a dirty trick.

あつげしょう【厚化粧】¶～の女 a woman with *a thick make-up*. 彼女はよく～する She often wears *a heavy make-up*. 彼女は～をしている She *is heavily* (≒ *thickly*) *painted*.

あっけな·い【呆気ない】¶まったく～い死に方だった He died *so suddenly* (≒ *abruptly*). 夏休みは～く終わった The summer vacation has come to an end *too quickly* (≒ *too soon*). 余興は～く終わった The entertainment was over *before we knew it*. あまりにも～い話だ The story is 〔all〕 *too short*.

あっこう【悪口】abuse. ¶彼は～雑言の限りをつくした He *used* all sorts of *abuse* (≒ *bad names*).

あつさ【厚さ】thickness. ¶この板の～はどのくらいですか How *thick* is this board? ここの氷は～5インチです The ice here is five inches *thick*.

あつさ【暑さ】heat. ¶この～では外に出ることもできない We cannot even go out in this *heat*. この～に耐えられますか Can you stand this *heat*? 彼は～にはだめだということだ He is said to be sensitive to *heat*. ～を避けて南房総に出かけた We went to south Boso to avoid *the heat*.

あっさく【圧搾】compression. ¶ガスを～してボンベの中に入れる *compress* gas into a cylinder.

—機 a compressor. **—空気** compressed air.

あっさり ¶彼は～した気性だ He is of a *frank* disposition. 彼は～した食物が好きだ He likes *plain* food. 申し出を～断わった I refused the offer *flatly*. 彼女はいつも～した色のドレスを着ている She always wears a *plain*-colored dress. なんという～した返事だろう What a *brief* answer!

あっし【圧死】¶彼は地震のため～した An earthquake *crushed him to death*.

あっしゅく【圧縮】¶この一節を二,三行に～してほしい I want this paragraph to *be condensed* (≒ *be shortened*) into a few lines. 空気を～する *compress* air.

—器 a compressor; a press.

あっしょう【圧勝】an overwhelming victory. ¶知事選では革新が～した In the gubernatorial election the reformist party *won an overwhelming* (≒ *landslide*) *victory* over the conservatives.

アッシリア Assyria.

—人 an Assyrian. **—語** Assyrian.

あっ·する【圧する】¶一同は彼の威厳に～せられた All those present *were overawed* by his dignity. 多勢に～せられて声も出なかった *Overwhelmed* by the superior numbers, he was speechless.

あっせい【圧制】oppression; tyranny.

¶王の～に苦しんでいた人民は反逆した The people who groaned under the *tyranny* of the king rebelled against him. 人々は独裁者の～に苦しんできた People have been suffering from the dictator's *oppression*.

—者 a tyrant; an oppressor.

あっせん【斡旋】(世話) good (≒ kind) offices; (調停) mediation. ¶A氏の～で by (≒ through) the *good offices* of Mr. A. 彼はいろいろ～してくれた He did me many *good offices*. / He was very kind to me. 彼は就職を～してくれた He helped me find a job. 彼に就職の～を頼んだ I asked him to find a job for me.

—者 an arbitrator; a mediator.

あっち that; (向こうの方) 〔over〕 there; that way. ¶～へ行け Go *away*! / Get out!

あつで【厚手】¶～のノート a *thick* notebook. ～の板 a *thick* piece of board.

あっと ¶彼は～いう間にいなくなった He was gone *in an instance*. それは～いう間の出来事だった It happened *in a moment*. ジェット機は～いう間に姿が見えなくなった The jet plane disappeared *in a split-second*. 彼が突然現われて皆～驚いた Everyone *was startled at* his sudden appearance. 私はその知らせに～驚いた I *was taken aback* at the news. 彼は世間を～いわせる発明をした He made an invention that *astonished* the world.

あっとう【圧倒】¶ われわれのチームは技では相手を～する Our team *overwhelms* the opponent in technique. 市場では舶来品が国産品を～する Foreign imports will *drive out* domestic goods from the market. アメリカ合衆国は石油の生産では他の国を～する The United States of America *excels* all other countries in the production of oil. 彼は～的多数で当選した He obtained a *sweeping* (≒ *landslide*) victory in the vote.

あっぱく【圧迫】pressure; oppression; suppression. ¶ 圧力団体は政府を～する The pressure groups *oppress* the government. 政府は世論の～に屈服した The government yielded to the *pressure* of public opinion. 官憲の～に耐える bear the official *pressure*.

あっぱれ【天晴れ】¶ これは～な記録だ This is a *splendid* (≒ *impressive*) record. 彼女のピアノは～な出来栄えだった She performed *brilliantly* on the piano. 敵ながら～ Our enemy fought *bravely*, we must admit. ～! Bravo! / Well done!

アップ ¶ 彼女は髪を～にした She did *up* her hair.

あつまり【集まり】(会合) a meeting; a gathering; (社交的) a party; (教会の) a congregation; (群衆) a crowd. ¶ 会の～はよかった(悪かった) There was *a* large (small) *attendance*. / The *attendance* was large (small). 寄付金の～がよくない The *collection* (≒ *sum collected*) is meager.

あつま・る【集まる】**1**〖人・生物が〗¶ たくさんの人がその会に～った A lot of people *attended* the meeting.

上野駅に午前7時までに～ってください I want all of you to *meet* (≒ *assemble*) at Ueno Station by seven o'clock in the morning.

みんなで～って相談しよう Let's *gather together* and talk about it.

彼のまわりに～った者はみな志を同じくした者であった Those who *gathered around* him had the same mind.

2〖無生物が〗¶ みんなの視線が彼女に～った All eyes *were turned on* her.

多くの票がこの候補者に～るだろう This candidate will probably *get* a majority of the votes.

たくさんの寄付金が～った A lot of subscriptions *have been collected*.

まだその件に関する資料が十分に～っていないのでなんとも言えない We can't answer definitely, since sufficient information *is* not *coming* about that matter.

多大の同情が彼に～った Great sympathy *was shown* to him. / Great sympathy *was centered* on him. (centered... はほかの人よりとくに集中した意).

あつみ【厚み】thickness. ¶ 板の～は5インチある The board is five inches *thick*. / The board has *a thickness* of five inches. 壁の～はいくらありますか How *thick* is the wall? / What is the *thickness* of the wall?

あつ・める【集める】collect; gather. ¶ 切手を～める *collect* postage stamps. 資料を～める *gather* data. 友だちを～める *summon* friends. 彼の新しい提案はわれわれの注目を～めた His new proposal *attracted* our attention.

あつらえ【誂え】an order. ¶ このくつは～だ I *had* this pair of shoes *made to order*. この服は～だ These are *made-to-order* (≒*custom-made*) suits./The suit *was made to measure*.

あつらえむき【誂え向き】¶ この人形はお土産に～だ This doll *is* just *suitable for* a souvenir. これは～だ This is *the very thing that I have wanted*. その役柄には彼は～だ He *fits* the role *very well*. きょうはハイキングには～の天気だ This is an *ideal* day for hiking.

あつら・える【誂える】¶ 上着を3万円で～えた I *have ordered* a coat at 30,000 yen. 服を～える *order one's* clothes.

あつりょく【圧力】pressure; stress. ¶ このタイヤには20ポンドの～がかかっている The *pressure* of this tire is 20 pounds to the inch. 彼に～をかけて従わせた I *pressured* him *into* obedience.

—釜(がま) a pressure cooker. **—計** a pressure gauge; a manometer. **—団体** a pressure group.

あつれき【軋轢】friction; discord. ¶ その2国間の～は容易には解消しないだろう The *friction* between the two nations will not be reduced soon. 意見の相違でしばしば～が生じる A difference of opinions often causes *discord*. あのふたりの間に～が起こっている Those two have fallen out.

あて【当て】(目的) an object; an aim; (期待) anticipation; expectation; (信頼) dependence.

¶ 彼に会う～はない I have no *anticipation* of meeting him. ～のない生活は耐えがたい I can't afford to live without any *object*. 昇給を～にしている I *am expecting* a raise in my salary. ～がはずれた I was quite disappointed in my *expectation*. 彼は～にできません We can't *put* any *dependence* (≒ *count*) *on* him. 彼の約束は～にならない We can't *count on* (≒ *place* any *reliance on*) his promise. このごろの天気は～にならない The weather *has been changeable* these days. 彼らは～もなく町をぶらついた They walked about the street *at random*.

あて【宛】¶ 私～の手紙はありませんか Is there any letter 〔*addressed*〕 *to* me? / Is there any letter *for* me? 私書箱56号～お尋ねください *Address* your questions *to* P.O. box 56. あなた～に手形を切りました I have drawn a check *in your favor*. 彼に自宅～に手紙を書いた I wrote him *at his home*. 子ども達はひとり～100円与えられた The children were given 100 yen *each*.

あてがいぶち【宛がい扶持】a fixed allowance.

あてが・う【宛がう】¶ 私は彼に月10ドルの小づかいを〜う I *allow* him $ 10 a month for spending (≒ pocket) money. 私は睡眠に8時間〜う I *allot* eight hours to sleep. すてきな部屋が〜われた I *was assigned* a nice room.

あてこす・る【当て擦る】hint (*at*); insinuate. ¶ 彼は実は私に〜っているのだ He *is* really *talking at* me. それは私への〜りだ That is *an indirect cut at* me.

あてこ・む【当て込む】count upon; expect; anticipate. ¶ 彼らはクリスマスを〜んで多量に注文した They ordered many goods *in expectation of* the sales at Christmas. 歳末売り出しを〜んでひともうけしよう We'll make a big profit *in anticipation of* the year-end sale.

あてさき【宛先】an address. ¶ この小包の〜はどこですか What is the *destination* of this package? 〜ははっきり書いてください Write the *address* clearly. 私の手紙は〜不明で戻ってきた My letter was sent back labeled "*blind*" (≒ "*adress unclear*").

あてじ【当て字】a makeshift spelling; a false substitute character. ¶ この作文には〜が多い This composition contains many *makeshift spellings*.

あてずいりょう【当て推量】a guess. ¶ それはとんでもない〜だ It is *a* wild *guess*. 〜だけで物を言うな Don't talk from mere *guesses*. きみは〜を言っている You *are* merely *guessing*.

あてずっぽう【当てずっぽう】a guess. ¶ 質問に〜で答えたらうまく当たった I took a lucky shot at the question. 〜でぼくの体重がわかりますか Can you *tell* my weight?

あてつけがまし・い【当て付けがましい】¶ 彼は〜く笑った He gave me an *insinuating* smile at me. / He smiled at me *insinuatingly*. 彼は〜い声で私にたずねた He asked me in an *insinuating* voice.

あてど【当て所】¶ 兵隊たちは〜なく密林をさまよった The soldiers wandered through the jungle *not knowing where to go*.

あてな【宛名】an address. ¶ この手紙の〜はまちがっている This letter bears *a* wrong *address*. / The letter *is* wrongly *addressed*. / The letter *is addressed to* a wrong house.

あてはずれ【当て外れ】a disappointment. ¶ その映画はまったく〜だった The film was quite *a disappointment* to me. 彼の講義は〜だった His lecture *disappointed* me. あなたの仕事は〜だ Your work is *disappointing*.

あてはま・る【当てはまる】¶ 同じ規則がここにも〜る The same rule *applies* (≒ *holds good*) here. 彼の行為は第10条の規則に〜る His conduct *comes under* Article 10 of the Regulations. 彼の理論は事実に〜る His theory *fits in with* the fact.

あては・める【当てはめる】¶ 理論は事実に〜めてみることがたいせつだ It is important to try to *apply* our theory to facts. この規則をその場合に〜めることはできない We can't *apply* this rule to the case.

あてみ【当て身】a body attack; a K. O. punch. ¶ 彼は〜をくらって倒れた He was knocked down by the force of his physical attacker. ボクサーは相手に〜を食わした The boxer stunned the opponent by striking *a K. O. punch*.

あでやか【艶やか】¶ 〜に着飾った婦人 a lady *charmingly* (≒ *attractively*) dressed up.

あてら・れる【当てられる】¶ 彼らの仲のよさに〜れた I *was embarrassed* by their free love-making.

あ・てる【当てる】¶ 的にうまく〜てる *make a* good *hit* at a target. 株で〜てた I *made a* big *hit* in the stock market. その芝居は〜てた The performance *was a hit*. 私がなにを思っているか〜てられますか Can you *guess* what I am thinking of? 試験でうまく山を〜てた I *made a lucky shot* (≒ *guess*) at the examination. この品物は日に〜てないでください Don't *expose* this article *to* the sun. どうぞ座布団をお〜てください Please *sit on a cushion*.

あ・てる【充てる】¶ 公園の一部を遊び場に〜てる計画を立てている We are planning to *allot* part of the park *for* a playground. 睡眠に何時間〜てますか How many hours do you *allot for* sleep? 夜を勉強に〜ている I *allot* (≒ *devote*) evening hours to study. 収入の20パーセントを家賃に〜ている We *allow* 20 percent of our income *for* the rent. 水曜日を会議に〜ている We *set aside* Wednesday *for* the meeting. 5階は事務所に〜てられている The fifth floor *is given over to* offices.

あと【跡】(痕跡) a mark; (人・車・動物などの通った跡) a track; a trace.

¶ 雪の上にウサギの〜があった We saw *traces* of rabbits on the snow.

強盗はなにも〜を残さなかった The thief left no *traces*.

彼には英語の進歩の〜が見えない He shows no *sign* of progress in English.

城は昔の栄華の〜を少しもとどめていない The castle keeps no *vestiges* (≒ *traces*) of its former glory.

探検隊は昔の都市の〜を見つけた The explorers found *traces* (≒ *remains*) of an ancient city.

彼の手には犬にかまれた〜があった His hand bore *a scar* from a dog bite.

本に指の〜を残してはいけない Be careful not to leave your *fingerprints* in a book.

これは古戦場の〜だ This is the *site* of an ancient battle.

船の通った〜は白い波が立つ After the *wake* of a ship white waves run high.

何事にも〜を濁さぬように Be careful not to leave any bad impressions *behind you*.

〜をくらます disappear; cover up *one's tracks*.

〜をつける follow (≒ shadow) (*a person*).

この種の物事は〜を絶たない There *is no end to* troubles of this kind.

彼の商売の〜を継ぐ者がいない There is no one

あ

to *succeed* his business.

あと【後】 1 〖時間〗 ¶ ～で後悔しますよ You will be sorry for it *later*.
私は～から参ります I will come *afterward*. / I will come *later*.
詳しいことは～でお話します I will tell you about the details *later on*.
雨の降った～で道はぬれていた The roads were wet *after* the rain.
きみが立ち去った～すぐ彼女が来た She came just *after* you left.
列車が出るまで～二, 三分しかない There are only two or three minutes *more* before the train starts.
それから～はどうなったか思い出せない I can't remember how the matter ended.
～10分すれば彼も帰ってくる He will return *in* about ten minutes.
～10年たてばぼくの言うこともわかる You will understand me ten years *after*.
～10日でお正月だ New Year's Day will come ten days *hence*.
～のたたりが恐ろしいぞ It will cost you dearly.
下衆(げす)の知恵は～から出る (諺) Afterwit is a fool's wit.
それから二, 三日～で彼に会った I met him two or three days *after* that day.
2 〖後方〗 ¶ そんなに～から押さないでください Don't push me so hard *from behind*.
今はまったく～に引けない立場なんだ I *can't yield an inch* now.
子どもは母の～を追った The child *ran after* its mother.
彼女は黙って私の～についてきた She *followed* me without a word.
彼ひとり～に残された He *was left behind* alone.
3 〖順序〗 ¶ それは～にまわしましょう It can wait. / We will leave the matter till *later on*.
彼女はいちばん～から会に出席した She was *the last* who attended the meeting. / She was *the last* to attend (≒ come to) the meeting.
4 〖残余〗 ¶ そう言って彼は～を濁した Saying that he evaded the point.
彼女はそう言っただけで～はなにも言わなかった She said nothing *more* about it.
～は言わなくてもわかるでしょう You can well understand *the rest*, can't you? / You know what I mean even if I don't explain it *further*.
～はわけなくできる *The rest* will easily be done.
5 〖後事〗 ¶ (留守中)～を頼む Please look after my affairs *while I am away*.
～のことは引き受けた I will answer for *the consequences*.
～のことなどかまっていられるか I don't care what will *become of* it.
～は野となれ山となれ (諺) I don't care what follows. / *After us* (≒ *me*) *the deluge*.
～がこわい You will pay dearly for it.
6 〖死後〗 ¶ ～に残った家族は悲惨だった The *surviving* family were miserable.
両親の急死で～には 3 歳の幼児が残された The parents died suddenly *leaving* a three-year-old child.
～が絶えた As there was no heir, he was the last person of his family line.
7 〖その他〗 ¶ 南京豆は～を引く Once we start eating peanuts there seems no end to it.

あとあし【後足】 a hind leg. ¶ その音に驚いて馬は～で立った The horse stood on its *hind legs* at the noise. そんな～で砂をかけるようなまねはよせ Don't *be* so *ungrateful* when you leave.

あとあじ【後味】 ¶ ～がわるかった It left a bad taste in my mouth. その事件は国民全体にいやな～を残した The event left a gloomy *impression* on all the nation.

あとあと【後後】 ¶ 彼は～のことまで考える人だ He *is far-sighted*. / He always figures *ahead*. そんな～のことまで考えられません I cannot afford to think of such *distant future*. そんなことをすると～までたたるよ You will rue the consequences if you take such a step.

あとおし【後押し】 ¶ われわれはその車の～をした We *pushed* the car *from behind*. だれかが彼の～をしているにちがいない I am sure somebody *is backing* him *up*.

あとがき【後書き】 a postscript (P.S. と略す).

あとかた【跡形】 ¶ 今はそのお寺の～もない *Nothing remains* (≒ *There is nothing left*) of the temple now.

あとかたづけ【後かたづけ・跡かたづけ】 ¶ パーティーの～をする *put* things *in order* after the party. 食事の～をする(食卓) clear the table; (さら洗い) do the dishes. ～がたいへんだった(事後の処置) It was a lot of trouble to *get* everything *straightened up*.

あとがま【後釜】 a successor. ¶ 彼が社長となってA氏の～にすわった He *has succeeded* Mr. A (≒ *has taken* Mr. A's *place*) as president. 彼らは彼をA氏の～にすえるだろう They will *put* him *in* Mr. A's *place*.

あとくされ【後腐れ】 ¶ ～のないようにしろよ Take care so that there may *be no trouble left behind*. ～のないように始末してくれ Please settle the matter so that there may *be no trouble left behind*.

あとくち【後口】 ¶ それは～に回そう That can wait. / Let's deal with it later on.

あどけな・い ¶ ～い顔をしているがなかなかずるがしこい His seemingly *innocent* face covers his craftiness. きみは～いことを言う You talk *like a child*. 彼には子どものような～さがある He has *the naivety of a child*. / He has *something innocent about him*.

あとさき【後先】 ¶ 彼は～を考えずに家を出た He left home without thinking of *what it might cause*. ～を考えてものを言いなさい Think well before you speak. 話が～になったが… I should have told you this first, but....

あとざん【後産】the afterbirth.

あとしまつ【後始末】¶ やっと事件の～をつけた I *have settled* the whole matter at last. 息子の借金の～をするのがたいへんだった It was a lot of trouble to *settle* my son's debt.

あとずさり【後退り】¶ 彼は二, 三歩～した He *stepped backward* (≒ *drew back*) a few paces.

あとつぎ【跡継ぎ】(男) an heir; (女) an heiress; a successor. ¶ 昔は長兄が父の財産の～となった The oldest brother used to *succeed to* his father's estates.

あととり【跡取り】⇒あとつぎ

あとのまつり【後の祭り】¶ 今更後悔しても～だ *It's too late* now to repent. ～さ It's "*a day after the fair*."

あとばらい【後払い】¶ ～で買う buy (*something*) *on credit*.

アドバルーン an ad〔vertising〕balloon.

あとまわし【後回し】¶ われわれはとかくめんどうなことを～にしがちになる We are inclined to *put off* (≒ *postpone*) what seems troublesome to us. それは～にしてよい That can *wait*.

あとめ【跡目】¶ ～相続でうんともめた We had a lot of trouble as to who should *inherit* (≒ *succeed to*) the family property. 父の～を継ぐ *succeed one's* father at the head of the family. おじの～を継いで２代め社長となった I *succeeded* my uncle as the second president of the company.

あともどり【後戻り】¶ 一, 二歩～した I *stepped back* a pace or two. 彼は途中で～した He *turned back* on the way.

アトラクション an attraction

アトリエ an atelier; a studio.

アドリブ ad-lib. (名詞・動詞・形容詞に使われる). ¶ 彼は～で映画の音楽を吹き込んだ He *ad-libbed* music in the film.

あな【穴】**1** a hole. ¶ 板に～をあける make *a hole* on a board.
地面に～を掘る dig *a hole* in the ground.
この道は～だらけだ This road is full of *holes*.
くつ下の～がだんだん大きくなってきた *A hole* in my socks has grown larger and larger.
この虫歯の～は詰めたほうがいい This *hole* in the decayed tooth had better be stopped up.
虫に食われてセーターが～だらけになった My sweater *was eaten* by worms *into holes*.
人をのろわば～二つ(諺) *Curses are sure to come home to roost*.
2〖比喩的に〗彼の議論は～だらけだ His argument *is* too *full of holes* to hold water.
彼女は家計簿に～をあけた She made *a hole* in her family budget.
人の顔をそんなに～のあくほど見詰めないでください Please don't *stare* so *hard at* me.
～があったら入りたい気持ちだ I wish I could *sink through the floor*.

アナーキスト an anarchist.

あなうめ【穴埋め】¶ 虫歯の～をした I had my decayed tooth *filled up*. ～をせよ(試験問題で) *Fill*〔*in*〕the blanks. どうして欠損の～をしようか How shall we *make up for* the loss?

アナウンサー an announcer; (女の) a woman (≒ lady) announcer. ¶ ラジオ(テレビ)の～ *a* radio (TV) *announcer*.

アナウンス an announcement.

あながち【強ち】¶ ～そうとはかぎらない That's *not always* (≒ *not necessarily*) the case. ～彼の言ったことはまちがってはいない He is *not altogether* wrong.

あなぐま【穴熊】〖動物〗a badger.

あなぐら【穴蔵】a cellar. ¶ その～には燃料が貯蔵されていた The *cellar* stored fuel.

あなご【穴子】〖魚類〗a conger.

あなた【彼方】¶ 山の～のなお遠く away *beyond* the mountain.

あなた【貴方・貴女】you; (夫婦・恋人間の呼びかけ) my dear; my darling. ¶ (他人への呼びかけ)もしもし～ Excuse me, *sir* (≒ *ma'am*). / I say. そんな～任せのやり方ではだめだ Don't do it in such a *happy-go-lucky* manner.

あなどり【侮り】contempt; scorn. ¶ 他人の～を受けるようなことはするな Don't do anything which invites *scorn* from others. 彼らはすべての外国人を～のまなざしで見た They *looked down on* all foreigners.

あなど・る【侮る】¶ ～りがたい敵 a *formidable* enemy. ～がたい学者 *no mean* scholar. ～りがたい問題 *no easy* matter. 彼の実力を～るな Never *make light of* his ability. 相手が弱いとみて～るな You mustn't *despise* him because he seems weak. 貧乏だからといって人を～るべきではない You should not *despise* a man because he is poor. みすぼらしい身なりをしていたので皆に～られた I *was scorned* (≒ *was looked down upon*) because of my shabby clothes.

あに【兄】an older brother; a big brother; 英 an elder brother (英米では, ふつう brother だけで, 話の内容から兄か弟かわかる場合など, 一般に older とか elder をつけない).
¶ いちばん上の～ the oldest brother. 義理の～ a brother-in-law.
―嫁 a sister-in-law. ―弟子 a senior disciple.

あに【豈】¶ ～図らんや to *one's* surprise; contrary to *one's* expectations.

アニリン〖化学〗anilin〔e〕.
―染料 aniline dye.

あね【姉】an older sister; a big sister; 英 an elder sister. ⇒あに
―娘 an older (≒ 英 elder) daughter.
―さん女房 a wife older than her husband.

あねったい【亜熱帯】the subtropics; the subtropical zones.

アネモネ〖植物〗an anemone.

あの【彼の】¶ ～人 *that* man; *that* woman; he; she. ～人たち *those* people; they. ～ころは in *those* days; at *that* time.

あの〔う〕 ¶ ～ね山田君 *I say*, Yamada. ～失礼ですが… *Excuse me*, but.... ～, えーっと *Well*, let me see. / Let's see. 出来ますか―～出来そうもありません Can you do that? ―*Well*, I'm afraid not.

あ

あのてこのて【あの手この手】¶ ～を使って彼を説き伏せようとした I tried to persuade him *by every possible means*.
あのね say ; well.
あのよ【あの世】¶ 彼はもうとっくに～の人となっています He passed away (≒ died) long ago.
アノラック an anorak.
アパート（建物のとき）㊮ an apartment house ; ㊫ a flat ; flats ;（一室のとき）㊮ an apartment ; ㊫ a flat（アメリカではいわゆる日本のアパートのことを an apartment または an apartment house といい，イギリスでは共同住宅またはその一部を a flat, a block of flats を用いる）.
あば・く【暴く】¶ 陰謀を～く *expose* a plot. 秘密を～く *unearth* a secret. 墓を～く *dig* (≒ *break*) a grave *open* ;（検屍などのため）exhume (a dead body). 正体を～く *reveal a person's* true character ; *show a person* in his true colors.
あばずれ a saucy woman (≒ girl) ; a jade.
あばた【痘痕】a pockmark ; a pit. ¶ ～もえくぼ（諺）Love blinds us to all imperfections.
—面 a pitted face. ¶ 彼は天然痘で～面だ His face *is pitted* with smallpox.
あばら〔ぼね〕【肋〔骨〕】ribs. ¶ ～骨を折る break *a rib*.
あばらや【あばら屋】a tumble-down house ; ㊮ a shabby shack. ¶ ～になる become dilapidated ; fall into dilapidation.
あば・れる【暴れる】¶ 彼は部屋に～れ込んだ He *broke* into the room. 暴徒の群れは大いに～れた The mob *rioted*. 彼は警察の手から逃れようとして～れに～れた He *struggled* hard to escape from the police.
あびきょうかん【阿鼻叫喚】¶ ～のちまた an agonizing scene ; a confusing scene. 街は～のちまたと化した The town turned into a babel of *agonies and cries*.
あひさん【亜砒酸】〔化学〕arsenious (≒ arsenic) acid ; arsenic.
あび・せる【浴びせる】¶ 水を～せる *throw* (≒ *dash* ; *pour*) water on (*a person*). 質問を～せる *rain* questions on (a speaker). 悪口を～せる *shower* (≒ *heap*) abuse on (*a person*).
あひる【家鴨】a duck. ¶ ～の子 a duckling. ～が鳴く *A duck* quacks. ～の火事見舞い（諺）*A duck's* wobble.
あ・びる【浴びる】¶ 川で水を～びる *have a bathe* in a river. ほこりを～びる *be covered with* dust. 非難を～びる *be exposed to* criticism. 嘲笑(ちょうしょう)を～びる *be ridiculed* (≒ *be laughed at*) (*by* others). 彼は～びるように酒を飲んだ He drank *sake like a fish*.
あぶ【虻】a horsefly ; a gadfly.
あぶく【泡】a bubble.
—銭 ill-gotten wealth ; unearned money ; undeserving money.
アブサン absinthe.
アブストラクト abstract.
—芸術 abstract art.
アフターケア aftercare.
アフターサービス after-sales service.
あぶな・い【危ない】**1**〘危険〙¶ その古い橋を渡るのは～い It *is dangerous* to cross the old bridge.
彼の命は度々～かった His life *was in danger* many times.
その商売は～いものだ The business *is risky* (≒ *is not safe*).
その患者は～い The patient *is seriously* (≒ *critically* ; *dangerously*) *ill*. / The patient's condition *is critical*.
私は～いところを助かった I *had a narrow escape*.
彼に大金を預けるのは～い We *cannot trust* him *with* a large sum of money.
夜間窓を開けておくと～い It *is not safe* to leave the windows open at night.
～い! わきによけなさい *Look out !* Step aside.
～い空もようだ It *looks like rain*. / Black clouds *threaten rain*.
2〘当てにならない〙¶ 彼が来るかどうか～い It *is doubtful* whether he will come or not.
彼の約束は～い His promises *are unreliable* (≒ *are untrustworthy*).
3〘すんでのことに〙¶ 船が出帆するという～いところだった The ship was on the point of setting sail.
私は～いところで死を免れた I *narrowly* escaped death.
あぶなく【危なく】¶ ～命拾いした I had a *narrow* escape from death. ～おぼれるところだった I *narrowly* escaped drowning. ～まちがえるところだった I *nearly* made a mistake. ～遅れるところだった I *came near* being late.
あぶなげ【危なげ】¶ ～のない sound ; safe ; sure. 彼の演技はまったく～がない His performance *leaves nothing to be desired*. ～な clumsy ; awkward.
あぶはち【虻蜂】¶ 二つのことを同時にやろうとすると，結局～取らずになる Try to do two things at the same time, and you will end up *falling between two stools*. きみは～取らずに終わるよ You would *fall between two stools*.
あぶみ【鐙】stirrups (㊞ a stirrup). ¶ ～に足をかける rest *one's* feet on the *stirrups*.
あぶら【油】**1** oil. ¶ 野菜を～でいためる fry vegetables（英語ではいためるのも揚げるのも fry である）.
時計に～をさす *oil* a watch.
この機械は～が切れている This machine needs *oiling*.
—揚げ 〔a piece of〕 fried 〔soy〕 bean. **—汗** greasy sweat. **—紙** oilpaper. **—かん** an oilcan. **—差し** an oiler. **—菜** a rape ; a cole. **—虫** a cockroach. **—気** ¶ ～気のない髪の毛 *unoiled* (≒ *oilless* ; *dry*) hair.
2〘慣用的表現〙¶ 彼は勤務時間中に～を売ってばかりいる He *is* always *idling away his time* while on duty.
怠けて彼から～を絞られた I was called to task by him for my laziness.
あぶら【脂】¶ 彼は～がのっている（働き盛り）He is in the prime of life.
—身 fat ; fatty meat.
あぶらえ【油絵】an oil painting. ¶ 彼女はしば

しば～を描く She often paints *in oils*.

あぶらっこ・い【脂っこい】oily; greasy; fatty. ¶～い食物 *greasy* food. ～いベーコン *fatty* bacon.

あぶりだし【炙り出し】a thermotype.

あぶ・る【炙る・焙る】(肉・魚を) roast; broil; (海苔などを) heat. ¶火で手を～る *warm one's* hands over the fire.

アフレコ (映画・テレビの) post-recording; after-recording.

あふ・れる【溢れる】¶川が～れた The river *overflowed* [its banks]. 競技場に観客が～れた The stadium *was crowded* (≒ *packed*) *with* spectators. / Spectators *overflowed* the stadium. 群衆は廊下に～れ出た The crowd *overflowed into* the hall. 涙が～れている His eyes *are filled with* tears. 室内には人が～れるばかりだ The room *is full of* (≒ *is filled with*) people. 彼は元気～れんばかりだ He *is brimming over with* high spirits.

あぶ・れる【溢れる】¶彼はこの1年間仕事に～れている He *has been out of* a job for a year.

あべこべ ¶きみの言うことはみな～だ What you say *is* all *contrary* to the truth. 絵を上下～にかけた I hung the picture *upside down*. 怒ってやろうと思って行ったら, ～に彼に怒られた I went to scold him, but I myself was scolded *instead*.

アベック a couple; a boy and a girl in a couple (フランス語 avec (≒ with) から). ¶～で出かける go out *together*.

アベマリア〔キリスト教〕Ave Maria.

あへん【阿片】opium. ¶～を吸う smoke *opium*.

—戦争 the Opium War. **—**吸引者 an opium smoker. **—**常用者 an opium eater. **—**窟(くつ) an opium den.

あほう【阿呆】a fool.

あほうどり【信天翁】〔鳥類〕an albatross.

アポロ Apollo.

—計画 the Apollo space program.

あま【尼】a nun; a Buddhist nun. ¶～になる enter a convent.

—寺 a nunnery; a convent.

あま【海女】a woman diver; a fisherwoman (男の海人(あま)は a fisher または a fisherman という).

あま【亜麻】flax.

あまあし【雨足】¶～が速い The *rain* is approaching fast. 夏の夕立は～が速い A summer shower comes on fast. ～が激しくなった The *rain* became heavier.

あま・い【甘い】¶砂糖は～い Sugar tastes *sweet*. ～いことば *sugared* words; *honeyed* words. ～い小説 a *sentimental* novel. あの先生は点が～い That teacher *is generous* with his marks. 彼は子どもに～い He *is indulgent* to his children. きみは考え方が～い Your way of thinking *is* too *easy going* (≒ *is* too *optimistic*).

あま・える【甘える】¶あの子は親に～えている The child *plays the baby to* his parents. ご好意に～えてもう一晩ごやっかいになります I will *take advantage of* your kindness to stay another night with you.

あまおおい【雨覆い】a rain-cover; (船のデッキ・窓の外などに取り付ける) an awning.

あまがえる【雨蛙】a tree toad; a tree frog.

あまがき【甘柿】a sweet persimmon.

あまがさ【雨傘】an umbrella.

あまがっぱ【雨合羽】a raincoat; a waterproof.

あまぐ【雨具】(総称) rain wear; (傘) an umbrella; (レーンコート) a raincoat; a waterproof; (くつ) rainshoes.

あまくだり【天下り】¶多くの高級官僚は定年に達する前にコネをきかせる～人事で会社の要職についてしまう Many high-ranking Government officials assume an important post in a private firm by [using] their influence.

あまくち【甘口】¶～の酒 *light* (≒ *sweet*) wine. ～のたばこ *mild* tobacco.

あまぐつ【雨靴】rain shoes; galoshes; (おもに米) rubbers.

あまぐも【雨雲】a rain cloud; 〔気象〕a nimbus (複 nimbi).

あまぐもり【雨曇り】cloudy (≒ dull) weather. ¶～する be (≒ get) *cloudy*. 今日は～だ It's *cloudy* today. / The sky *is overcast* today.

あまぐり【甘栗】sweet roast chestnuts.

あまごい【雨乞い】¶～する pray for rain; offer prayers for rain.

あまざけ【甘酒】a sweet drink made from fermented rice.

あまざらし【雨曝し】¶～の weather-beaten; weathered. ～になる be exposed to rain. ～にする expose (*a thing*) to rain.

あまじたく【雨支度】¶～をする prepare for rain; dress [*oneself*] against rain.

あま・す【余す】¶金を～さず使う spend *all one's* money; spend *one's* money *to the last penny*. 旅費を少し～す *save* something from *one's* travel expenses. ことしも～すところ1週間しかない We have only one week left before New Year. / There *remains* only one week before New Year. ～すところなく報告する give a *full* account.

あまた【数多・許多】¶～の(数) many; a large (≒ great) number of; a lot of; (量) much; a good (≒ great) deal of; a lot of.

あまだれ【雨垂れ】raindrops; eavesdrops; drips from the roofs. ¶～の音 the patter of *raindrops*. ～石をうがつ(諺) Falling drops [at last] will hole (≒ wear) a stone.

あまちゃ【甘茶】(飲み物) tea of heaven; hydrangea tea; sweet tea.

アマチュア an amateur. ¶～らしい amateurish.

—無線士 a radio ham.

あまちょろ・い【甘ちょろい】¶きみの考え方はあまりにも～い You *take too optimistic a view of* the world. / You *take* things too *easy*.

あまつさえ【剰え】besides; moreover; in addition; into the bargain. ⇒そのうえ

あまったる·い【甘ったるい】too sweet; sugary; honeyed. ¶ 彼女は～い口調で話す She talks in *honeyed* tones.
あまったれ【甘ったれ】¶ あの子は～だ He is *a spoilt child*./ He *is spoiled*.
あまでら【尼寺】a nunnery; a convent.
あまど【雨戸】a sliding door; storm windows.
あまとう【甘党】¶ 彼は～だ He *has a sweet tooth*. / He *likes sweets*. / He *has a weakness for sweets*.
あまなっとう【甘納豆】sugared beans.
あまにゆ【亜麻仁油】linseed oil.
あまねく【普く·遍く】¶ 彼の名前は～知れ渡っている His name is *widely* known. 彼は世界を～旅行している He has traveled *throughout* (≒ *all over*) the world.
あまのがわ【天の川】the Milky Way; the Galaxy.
あまのじゃく【天の邪鬼】(性質) perversity; self-will; (人) a perverse (≒an obstinate) person.
あまみ【甘味】a sweet taste; sweetness. ¶ ～がある have *a sweet taste*; be *sweet*. この丸薬は砂糖で～がついている This pill *is sweetened* with sugar. / This pill *is sugar-coated*.
あまみず【雨水】rain water.
あまもよう【雨模様】⇒あめもよう
あまもり【雨漏り】¶ ～を修理する stop *a leak*; repair *a leaky place*. ひどく～がする The roof *leaks* badly. 屋根に～の穴がある There is *a leak* in the roof.
あまやか·す【甘やかす】¶ 子どもを～して育てる bring up a child *indulgently* (≒ *with indulgence*). ～すと子どもはだめになる(諺) *Spare the rod, and spoil the child.*
あまやどり【雨宿り】¶ ～した I *took shelter from the rain*. 雨がやむまで木の下で～した I *sheltered* under a tree till the rain was over.
あまり【余り】the remainder. ¶ ～はいくつですか How many *are left*? ～はもうない There is not anything *left* now. 15から7を引くと～はいくらですか If you take 7 from 15, what *remains*? 給料の～は貯金しなさい Save what *is left of* your salary. ～のリンゴはこの箱に入れてください Please put the *remaining* apples into this box. 弁当の～は捨てた I threw away the *leftover* lunch.
あまり ¶ ～心配しないでいい You don't have to worry *too much*. ライスカレーは～好きでない I don't like curry and rice *so much* (≒ *too well*). ～飲みすぎぬよう Never drink *too much*. 野球には～興味がない I am *not very* interested in baseball. ～勉強しないでよい You need not study *too hard*. 時間は～残っていない There is *only a little* time *left*. ～歩いたので疲れた I walked *so long* a time *that* I got tired. この箱は～に大きすぎる This box is *too* big. 目的地に着くのが～遅くならないようにしなさい Don't be *too* late in arriving at your destination. ～驚いたのでことばも出なかった I was *so* surprised *that* I could not utter a word. ～眠りすぎて体の調子がおかしい I have slept *too much*, *so* I feel unwell now. 彼女は～丈夫ではない She is *not very* healthy. 彼はすぐれた学者だが, ～有名ではない He is a great scholar but is *not so* well-known.
-あまり【-余り】¶ 1時間～も for *over* an hour. この本箱には100冊～の本がある There are *more than* one hundred books in this bookcase.
あまりある【余りある】¶ 彼のみごとな出来栄えは失敗を補って～ His wonderful achievement *has done more than* offset his failure.
あまりもの【余り物】remains. ¶ 食事の～ the *remains* (≒ *remnants*) of the dinner.
アマリリス〔植物〕an amaryllis.
あま·る【余る】**1**〚物などが〛¶ 給料はどのくらい～っていますか How much of your salary *is left*?
費用は5,000円～った Five thousand yen *is left of* the expenses.
リンゴはどのくらい～っていますか How many apples *are left over*?
1枚～っている写真 a *spare* photo.
50から3を引くと47～る Three from fifty *leaves* forty-seven.
～ったエンピツはきみにあげよう You shall have the *leftover* pencils.
2〚慣用的表現〛¶ 最近の彼の行動は目に～る His conduct these days *is unpardonable*.
身に～る光栄に存じます This is the honor that *is more than I deserve*.
彼の生活がどれほど苦しかったかは想像に～るものがある We *can hardly imagine* how bitter his life was.
アマルガム amalgam.
あまん·ずる【甘んずる】¶ 彼はこの安い給料に～じている He *is contented with* this small salary. 現在の運命に～じていてはいけない Never *be contented with* your present lot. 彼は獄中で1か月もの間冷遇に～じていた He *was submitting tamely to* cold treatment in the prison for a month. 彼は～じて屈辱に耐える人である He *eats humble pie*. 世人の軽べつを～じて受けた He *submitted himself to* people's insult.
あみ【網】a net; (引き網) a seine; a dragnet. ¶ ～を打つ cast (≒ shoot) *a net*. ～を張る stretch *a net*; (テニスなどの) put up *a net*; (捜査の) spread *a dragnet*; be on the lookout; lie in wait for. (捜査の)～にかかる be caught in the 〔*drag*〕*net*. (捜査の)～をくぐる escape *a* 〔drag〕*net*.
あみあげ【編み上げ】**—ぐつ** lace-shoes; 米 high shoes; 英 boots.
アミーバ ⇒アメーバ
あみがさ【網笠】a braiden hat.
あみシャツ【網シャツ】a netted shirt; a gauze shirt.
あみだ【阿弥陀】*Amitabha*. ¶ 彼は帽子を～にかぶった He *tilted* his hat *backward*. ～くじ

をやる have a pool by drawing lots.
あみだ·す【編み出す】¶彼は新しい画法を～した He *originated* a new style of painting.
あみだな【網棚】a [baggage] rack.
あみど【網戸】a window screen; a mosquito gauze (≒ screen).
アミノさん【アミノ酸】〘化学〙amino acid.
あみばり【編み針】a knitting-needle.
あみばん【網版】〘印刷〙a halftone; a halftone plate.
あみぼう【編み棒】a knitting needle; (クロッシェ編みかぎ針) a crochet hook (≒ needle).
あみめ【網目】a mesh [of a net]. ¶この～は半インチである This net has half-inch *meshes*.
あみめ【編み目】a stitch. ¶もっと～を細かくして編んでください Knit with smaller *sticthes*.
あみもと【網元】a fishermen's boss.
あみもの【編み物】knitting; (クロッシェ編みの) crochet. ¶～をする knit. 彼女は朝から晩まで～をしている She *knits* from morning till night. 彼女は～を下に置いた She laid her *knitting* down.
あ·む【編む】¶くつ下を～む *knit* a pair of socks. かぎ針で～む crochet. 髪をお下げに～む *plait one's* hair. 花を輪に～む *make* a wreath; *weave* flowers *into a wreath*. むしろを～む *make* a straw-mat. 町史を～む *compile* a history of a town.
あめ【飴】wheat gluten; [a] candy; 英 sweets; (棒の先についた) a lollipop.
—玉 米 a taffy; 英 a toffee. ¶～玉をしゃぶらせる(甘やかす) cajole; give (*a person*) an initial advantage to put him off his guard.
—屋 a candy store.
あめ【雨】rain. ¶どしゃぶりの～ *a* pouring *rain*.
～になったぞ Here comes the *rain*.
ひどい～だった It *rained* very hard.
～降って地固まる After *rain* comes fair weather.
～が降りそうだ It is likely to *rain*. / It looks like *rain*.
今にも～が降りだしそうだ It threatens to *rain* at any moment.
～が降りだした It started *raining*. / The *rain* began to fall.
午前中～が降った It *was raining* (≒ *rained*) in the morning.
～がやんだ It stopped *raining*.
この～はやみそうにない The *rain* does not seem to be passing over.
～が小やみになった The *rain* is letting up a little.
長～が降りつづいている We have had a long spell of *rainy* weather.
～が降ったりやんだりしている It *is raining on and off*.
ことしは今のところ～が少ない We have had little *rain* this year.
当地はいつも今ごろ～が多い At this time of the year we usually have a lot of *rain* here.
今月になって4度～が降りました We have had four *rainy* days this month.
～の日はたいてい家にこもっています On *rainy* days I usually stay at home.
～にぬれて木の葉の緑が鮮やかだった The leaves of the trees were showed in fresh green in the *rain*.
～に会ってずぶぬれになった I was caught in the *rain* and got wet to the skin.
～をついて出発した We started in spite of the [heavy] *rain*.
試合は～で中止になった The game *was rained out* (≒ *was washed out*).
～の場合は延期になる It will be put off in case of *rain*.
あめあがり【雨上がり】¶きのう～に美しいにじが出た Yesterday a beautiful rainbow appeared *after the rain*.
あめあられ【雨霰】¶～と降りかかる弾丸 *a rain of* bullets.
あめいろ【飴色】amber; light brown.
アメーバ an amoeba (複 amoebas; amoebae).
—赤痢 amoebic dysentery.
あめがち【雨勝ち】¶今月は～だった We have had many rainy days this month.
あめつづき【雨続き】¶当地ではこのところ～だ It *has been raining* here of late.
あめふり【雨降り】¶～に出歩くな Don't go out *in the rain*.
あめもよう【雨模様】¶～の空 a *threatening* sky. ～だ *It looks like rain.* / *It threatens rain.*
アメリカ America.
—インディアン an American Indian. —英語 American English. —合衆国 the United States of America (U.S. または U.S.A. と略す); the States (外国にいるアメリカ人が自国についていうとき用いる). —軍 the U.S. Armed Forces. —語法 Americanism. —州 the Americas (北·中·南アメリカの総称). —人 an American; (全体) the Americans. —政府 the United States Government. 北(南; ラテン)— North (South; Latin) America.
アメリカンフットボール American football.
アメリシウム〘化学〙americium.
あめんぼ【水黽】〘虫類〙a water strider; a pond skater.
あや【文】¶一つのことばにもいろいろの意味の～がある A word has many *shades* of meaning.
あやうく【危うく】¶彼は～助かった He *had a narrow escape*. ～おぼれるところだった I was *nearly* drowned. ～車にひかれるところだった I was *almost* run over by a car.
あやおり【綾織り】twill; figured stuff; diagonal cloth.
あやか·る【肖る】¶きみに～りたい I wish to be as lucky as you. 彼に～って息子に太郎という名をつけた I named my son Taro *after* him.
あやし·い【怪しい】**1**〖(道徳的に)嫌疑がかかる·うさんくさい〗suspicious.
¶どうも彼が～い I cannot help *suspecting*

あ

him. / I am rather *suspicious* of him.
あのふたりの仲は～い I *suspect* they are carrying on with each other.
～げな格好の男 a *suspicious-looking* man.
そういえば彼の挙動は～い Well, his behavior arouses my *suspicion*. / I see, his actions seem to me quite *suspicious*.
2 〖信用できぬ・疑わしい〗 ¶ 彼は～げな商売をしている He is engaged in *dubious* business.
その薬の効果は～い The efficacy of the medicine *is doubtful*.
そいつは～げな話だな It's an *incredible* story.
その前置詞の使い方は～い The use of the preposition *is questionable* (≒ *may be wrong*).
これが大観の真筆だって？ ～いものだ Can it be a Taikan? *I am quite doubtful* [*of* it].
あすの天気は～い Tomorrow's weather *is unpromising*. / *I am afraid* we will have rain tomorrow.
空もようが～くなってきた *It threatens to rain*. / The look of the sky *threatens rain*.
それがほんとうかどうかは～い *I doubt* if it can be true.
彼の商売があたるかどうか～い His success in business *is doubtful*. / It *is* quite *doubtful* if he will make a hit in business.
そう問い詰められるとこっちも～くなる My *confidence is shaken* when I am questioned so closely.
3 〖不器用な・拙劣な〗 ¶ 彼女のピアノの腕前なんて～いものだ I wonder if she is a good pianist.
彼の英語は～いものだ His English *is* rather *shaky*.
彼女は～げな手つきで裁断をしはじめた She began to cut a dress with a *clumsy* hand.
4 〖変な・気味悪い〗 ¶ それらの調度品がこの部屋に一種の～いふんい気を醸し出していた The pieces of furniture created an *uncanny* atmosphere in the room.
～い物音が階上から伝わってきた A *queer* (≒ *strange*) sound came from upstairs.

あやし・む 【怪しむ】 ¶ 彼が来なかったとて～むにたりない *It is no* (≒ *small*; *little*) *wonder* that he didn't come. 彼は盗みをしたのではないかと～まれた He *was suspected of* theft.

あや・す ¶ 赤ん坊を～す *dandle* (≒ *fondle*) a baby. 子どもを～す(きげんをとる) *humor* a small child.

あやつり 【操り】 **—**人形 a puppet; a marionette. **—**人形芝居 a puppet (≒ marionette) show.

あやつ・る 【操る】 ¶ 人形を～る *manipulate* a puppet. 舟を巧みに～る *manage* (≒ *handle*) a boat skillfully. 櫓(ろ)を～る *pull* (≒ *row*) an oar. 彼は大ぜいの人をうまく～った He *handled* a lot of people *at his will*. だれかがあの政治家を～っているにちがいない I'm sure somebody *has* that politician *on a string*. 彼女は巧みにことばを～って彼をだました She deceived him *with honeyed words*. 彼は3か国語を自由に～る He *has a good command of* three languages.

あやとり 【綾取り】 ¶ ～をしましょう Let's play *cat's cradle*.

あやぶ・む 【危ぶむ】 ¶ 彼は私の成功を～んだ He *was doubtful of* my success. 天候が～まれる The weather *looks* very *doubtful*. 彼の容体が～まれた The condition of his health *caused anxiety*. 彼はまた失敗するのではなかろうかと～んだ He *feared* (≒ *was afraid*) [that] he would fail again.

あやふや ¶ ～なことを言う speak *ambiguously*; equivocate. ～な態度をとる take an *uncertain* attitude. ～に答える give a *vague* answer.

あやまち 【過ち】 a fault; an error. ¶ ～をおかす commit *a fault* (≒ *an error*). ～を改める amend *one's fault*. ～を改むるにはばかるなかれ(諺) *It is never too late to mend*.

あやまり 【誤り】 an error; a mistake. ¶ 筆の～ *a slip of* the pen. 文法上の～ *a* grammatical *mistake*. 印刷の～ a misprint. つづりの～ a misspelling. 計算の～ *an error* in calculation; a miscalculation. だれでもときには～を犯す Everyone *makes a mistake* (≒ *commits an error*) now and then. ～があれば正しなさい Correct *errors* if any. きみの手紙には～が多い(ない) Your letter is full of (free from) *mistakes*.

あやま・る 【誤る】 ¶ 彼は職業の選択を～った He *made a wrong choice* for a profession. 私は進路を～った I *took the wrong course*. そんな生活を続けたらきみは一生を～る You will *make a failure* of your life if you continue to live such a life. 世間を～る宣伝がある Some advertisements *mislead* the world. 判断を～って彼をひきょう者だと思った I *mistook* him *for* a coward. / I *made an error in* judgment that he was a coward.

あやま・る 【謝る】 ¶ すぐにあの人に～りなさい *Say sorry to* him at once. / *Apologize to* him at once. 彼は不始末を平謝りに～った He *made* profuse *apologies for* his misconduct. 手紙の返事が遅れたことを～った I *apologized* for my delay in replying to his letter.

あやめ 【菖蒲】 〖植物〗 a sweet flag; an iris (複 irises; irides).

あやめ 【文目】 ¶ ～も分かぬ真のやみ a pitch-dark (≒ pitch-black) night.

あゆ 【鮎】 〖魚類〗 an *ayu*.

あゆみ 【歩み】 ¶ ～を早める(緩める) quicken (slacken) *one's pace*. ～を止める stop [walking]; come to a halt. ～がのろい(速い) walk at a slow (quick) pace. 過去1年のわが国経済の～ the *performance* of our economy in the past year. 日米文化交流100年の～ the hundred-year *history* of cultural exchange between the United States and Japan.

あゆみより 【歩み寄り】 a concession. ¶ ～の精神で in a *conciliatory* spirit. 双方の～で妥協が成立した A compromise was reached by mutual *concession*[*s*].

あゆみよ・る 【歩み寄る】 walk up to; ap-

proach; (譲歩する) compromise; meet (*a person*) halfway; split the difference.
¶ 彼は～ることに同意した He agreed to *compromise*.

あら【粗】(欠点) a fault; a defect; (魚の) offal; the bony parts [of a fish]. ¶ 彼の議論には～が目だつ There are a lot of *flaws* in his arguments.

あら Oh! / Oh dear! / My goodness! ¶ ～, もう4時だわ *My goodness!* It's already four now. ～, 困ったわ *Oh dear!* What shall I do? ～, ひどいわ *Oh,* you are so mean.

あらあらし·い【荒荒しい】¶ ～い気性の人 a man of a *violent* temper. ～い語調で in a *harsh* tone. ～い態度で in a *rude* manner. ～く席を立った He *flung out* of the room.

あらい【洗い】¶ シャツを～に出す *send* a shirt *to the laundry*. 背広は～に出ている The suit *is at the cleaner's*. そのブラウスは～がきく That blouse *is washable*.
—おけ a washing tub. **—髪** newly washed hair.

あら·い【荒い】¶ ～い海 a *rough* sea. 波が～い Waves *are running high*. 彼は息遣いが～い He is breathing *hard*. 彼は人使いが～い He works people *too hard*. 彼は金使いが～い He *is too free with* his money. / He spends money *lavishly* (≒ *extravagantly*). 彼はだれにたいしても鼻息が～い He *is haughty* to everybody.

あら·い【粗い】¶ 地の～い切れ *coarse* fabric. 織り目の～い布地 cloth of *loose* texture. きめの～い膚 a *rough* skin. ～い格子じまの着物 a *kimono* with a *large* plaid pattern. ～い針目で縫う sew in *large* stitches.

あらいぐま〘動物〙a raccoon.

あらいざらい【洗い浚い】¶ 彼は何もかも～打ち明けた He made a clean breast of *everything*. 彼は私の有り金を～持ってにげた He made off with *all* my money.

あらいざらし【洗い晒し】¶ ～の worn-out; threadbare. ～の服 *worn-out* clothes.

あらいそ【荒磯】a rock-strewn beach; a rugged shore.

あらいたて【洗いたて】¶ ～のシーツ a *freshly laundered* sheet. ～のズボン *freshly washed* trousers.

あらいた·てる【洗い立てる】¶ 新聞は彼の暗い過去を～てた The newspaper *raked up* his shady past.

あらいはり【洗い張り】a Japanese *kimono* laundry. ¶ ～に出す send (*something*) to a fuller.

あらいもの【洗い物】¶ きょうはたくさん～がある We have a lot of *washing* to do today. 夕食後の～をする *wash up* after supper.

あら·う【洗う】wash; cleanse (発音は [klenz]). ¶ 顔を～っていらっしゃい Go and *wash yourself*. 食事の前には手をよく～いなさい *Have* (≒ *Get*) *a* good *wash* before meals. きょうはこの車をよく～いなさい *Give* this car *a* good *wash* today. 彼は水で目を～った He *bathed* his eyes in water. 牛乳びんを～ってから返してください *Cleanse* milk bottles before you return them, please. このきゅうすを～いましたか *Have* you *rinsed* this teapot? 1週間に1度髪を～う I *shampoo my hair* (≒ *give my hair a wash*) once a week. このしみは～えば落ちる This stain will come out *in the wash*. 刑事は加害者の素性を～った The detective *inquired into* the assaulter's past life.

あらうみ【荒海】a high (≒ rough) sea.

あらかじめ【予め】¶ ～知らせる give *advance* notice. ～許可を取っておく secure permission *in advance*. 万事～打ちあわせた通りに進んだ Everything proceeded by a *preconcerted* arrangement. ～知っていればよかった I should have known it *beforehand*.

あらかせぎ【荒稼ぎ】¶ 彼は競馬で～をした He *made quick money* in a horse race. ～をしていた男(どろぼうをしていた)が捕まった The man who had committed *burglary* (≒ *robbery*) was arrested.

あらかた【粗方】¶ 準備は～できている The preparation is *practically* (≒ *almost*) complete. きみの論文は～いい Your paper is good *on the whole*.

あらかべ【粗壁】an unfinished (≒ a rough-coated) wall. ¶ ～を塗る give a rough coat of plaster.

あらぎょう【荒行】¶ 彼は山中で～に励んだ He devoted himself to *austere discipline* in the mountain.

あらくれおとこ【荒くれ男】a rough fellow (≒ man); a rowdy.

あらけずり【荒削り·粗削り】¶ ～の板 a *rough-planed* (≒ *rough-hewn*) board. ～の作風 a *rough* (≒ an *unpolished*; an *unrefined*) style.

あらさがし【粗捜し】faultfinding. ¶ 彼はいつも他人の～ばかりしている He *is* always *finding fault with* others.

あらし【嵐】a storm. ¶ 私は～にあった I was caught in *a storm*. ～が来そうだ We are going to have *a storm*. / It is likely to *storm*. ～が吹きすさぶ(やむ) *A storm* rages (calms down). ～のような拍手が起こった There was *a storm of* applause. それは～の前の静けさであった It was the calm before *a storm*.

あらしごと【荒仕事】¶ 炭坑夫の仕事は～だ Miners do *hard manual labor*. 盗賊たちは～でかせいだ The gang of robbers earned their living *by violence*.

あら·す【荒らす】¶ 侵略者たちが国土を～した The aggressors *ravaged* (≒ *devastated*; *ruined*) the country. / The aggressors *laid* the country *waste*. 企業の進出が農村を～していく The advances of industry into the countryside *are doing damage to* the farm villages. ネズミが作物を～す Rats *damage* the crops. 銀行を～しまわっていた一味が捕まった A group of bank *robbers* were arrested.

アラスカ Alaska. ¶ ～の Alaskan.

あ

あらすじ【粗筋】¶話の～を述べなさい Give the *outline* (≒ *plot*) of the story. これが事件の～だ This is the *long and short* (≒ *gist*) of the matter.

あらずもがな ¶それは～の蛇足(だそく)だ That is quite *unnecessary to add.* / We can *do without* saying it. / That may quite well (≒ much better) be left out. / That is [like putting] a fifth wheel to the coach.

あらせいとう 〖植物〗a stock.

あらそい【争い】(論争) a dispute; an argument; (けんか) a quarrel; (競争) a competition; a contest; (不和) a discord; a strife. ¶～が起こる *A dispute* arises. 遺産相続のことで兄弟の間に～が起きた *A quarrel* arose between the brothers about inherited property. 内輪の～ *a* family *trouble*. 学問上の～ academic *controversies*. ～の種 the apple of *discord*.

あらそ・う【争う】(論争する) dispute; argue; (けんかする) quarrel; (口論する) argue; (競争する) compete; contend.
¶正々堂々と勝敗を～う *contend* for victory fairly. 7人が国会の1議席を～った Seven *contested* one seat in Parliament. 一刻を～うときだ There is *no time to lose*. 朝はみんなが席を取ろうと先を～って列車に乗り込む People *rush into* the train for seats in the morning. 住民たちは日照権のことで役所と激しく～った The inhabitants *had a violent dispute with* the Office concerning the right of light.

あらそわれな・い【争われない】¶～い事実 an *undeniable* (≒ *indisputable*) fact. 空気の汚染がますますひどくなってきたのは～い事実だ *There is no denying* the fact that the air has become more and more polluted. 年(血筋)は～い Age (Blood) *will tell* (≒ *will be out*).

あらた【新た】¶きみの便りは学校時代の記憶を～にさせた Your letter *refreshed* my memory about our schooldays. 気持ちを～にして勉強に励みます *Recreating my mind* (≒ *Refreshing myself*), I will work hard. 彼は～に店を開いた He opened a shop *newly*. / He opened a *new* shop. 彼は郊外の～に建ったアパートに引っ越した He moved to a *newly* built apartment house in the suburbs.

あらたか【灼】¶このお札は霊験～だ This amulet *is miraculous* (≒ *is wonder-working*). この地蔵様は霊験～だ This *Jizo is* wonderfully *responsive* to prayers. ～な miraculous; wonder-working.

あらだ・つ【荒だつ】¶そんなことを言えば事が～つだけだ Saying such a thing will only *aggravate the matters* (≒ *make the matters worse*).

あらだ・てる【荒だてる】¶事を～てないように Try to *hush up* the matter. / Try not to *make* the matter *worse*. 声を～てるな Don't talk *in an excited* (≒ *agitated*) voice.

あらたま・る【改まる】¶年が～った The old year has gone and *we are now in the new year*. 仲間の忠告で彼の素行が～った He *mended his ways* (≒ *reformed himself*) on his friends' advice. 彼が会長になって会はすっかり面目が～った After he became the president, the association *has improved* a lot (≒ *has* completely *changed*). 彼の病状は急に～った He suddenly *grew worse*. / His condition suddenly *took a serious turn*. ～った口調で in a *serious* tone; in a *formal* way.

あらためて【改めて】¶また日を～お伺いします I will be back *some other time*. このことは～別の機会にお話ししたい I would like to discuss this *again* on another occasion. この機会に～(正式に)お礼を申し上げたい I would like to take this opportunity to express my appreciation [to you]. ～言うこともない I have nothing *special* (≒ *particular*) to say. ～電話します I will call you *later*.

あらた・める【改める】¶計画を～める *change* (≒ *revise*) *one's* plan. 服装を～める *change one's* clothes; (身なりを整える) dress *oneself* properly. 悪習を～める *reform* (≒ *amend*; *mend*) a bad habit. 行ないを～める *mend one's* ways; *reform one's* conduct. 誤りを～める *correct* an error. 規則を～める *revise* regulations. きみは勉強法を～める必要がある You need to *improve* your way of studying. おつりをお～めください Please *check* the change.

あらっぽ・い【荒っぽい】¶～い仕事 [a] *rough* work. ～い態度 *rough* manners. ～い若者 a *rough* young man. ～いことば *violent* (≒ *rough*; *rude*) language. その子は子ネコを～く扱った The child handled the kitten *roughly*.

あらて【新手】¶敵は～を繰り出してきた The enemy sent out *fresh troops* against us. ～の詐欺にご用心 Beware of *the new type of* swindling!

あらなみ【荒波】¶船は～にもまれた The ship was tossed about by *angry waves*. 人生の～に船出する embark upon *a troubled sea* of life. 人生の～にもまれる labor through *the turbulent sea* of life.

あらなわ【荒縄】a thick straw rope.

あらぬ ¶彼は盗みの～疑いをかけられた He was *falsely* suspected of [a] theft. 彼に声をかけたが,～方をながめて耳に入らぬようだった I spoke to him, but he had a *faraway* look and didn't seem to hear me.

アラビア Arabia.
—語 Arabic. **—**人 an Arabian; an Arab. **—**馬 an Arab horse. **—**ゴム gum arabic. **—**数字 Arabic figures (≒ numerals). **—**夜話 the Arabian Nights' Entertainments. **—**文化 Arabic culture.

アラベスク an arabesque.

あらまし (概略) an outline; (ほとんど) nearly.
¶計画の～をお話ししましょう Let me give you *an outline* of the plan. / I am going to *outline* the plan. 仕事は～終わりました The work is

nearly (≒ *almost*) finished.

あらむしゃ【荒武者】a fierce warrior.

あらめ【荒布】〘植物〙an edible seaweed.

あらもの【荒物】kitchenware; (雑貨) sundries.

—屋(人) a kitchenware dealer; (店) a kitchenware store; (雑貨店)米 a general store; 英 a general shop.

あらゆる【有らゆる】all; every (単数名詞について単数扱い). ¶ ~機会を利用する make use of *every* opportunity (*for*). ~手段を講じる try *every* possible means. ~種類の伝達機関 *all sorts* (≒ *kinds*) *of* communication sources.

あらら·げる【荒らげる】¶ 父親は声を~げて息子をしかった The father scolded his son *in a rough voice*.

あらりょうじ【荒療治】(療治) a desperate treatment; (処置) a drastic measure. ¶ 医者はけが人に~を施した The doctor gave *a desperate treatment* to the injured. 彼に政界の腐敗を正す~を望みたい We want him to *take drastic measures* to correct political corruption.

あられ【霰】hail; a hailstone. ¶ ~が降る It *hails*. 弾丸が雨~と降ってきた Bullets came *thick and fast* (≒ *in hail storms*). ジャガイモを2センチ角の~に切る cut potatoes into two centimeter *cubes*.

あられもな·い ¶ 彼女はすっかり取り乱して~い姿で泣き叫んだ She was so distracted that she cried *ungraciously* (≒ *in an unladylike fashion; in an unbecoming way*).

あらわ【露】¶ 彼女は怒りも~に声を震わせた Her voice trembled in anger. 膚も~なビキニスタイルが目につく The bikini style *exposing* (≒ *revealing*) women's *bare skin* catches our eyes.

あらわ·す【表わす·現わす】**1**〘明らかに見せる〙¶ 彼はその席には姿を~さなかった He did not *appear* in the meeting. / He failed to *turn up* on the occasion.

彼女が舞台にその姿を~すと, 聴衆は熱狂して拍手した When she *appeared* on the stage, the audience greeted her with wild applause. / *At her appearance* on the stage, she won the warm applause of the audience.

怒りをおもてに~すな You must not *show* your anger. / Don't *betray* your anger. / Try to disguise your wrath.

彼はとうとう馬脚を~した Finally he *betrayed* himself. / In the end he *showed* the cloven foot.

彼はついに正体を~した Finally he *showed himself* in his true colors. / Eventually he *gave himself away*.

彼女は英会話ではクラスで断然頭角を~していた She *was distinguished* (≒ *distinguished herself*) in speaking English among her classmates. / She *stood at the top of* her class in speaking English.

その仕事で彼はおのれの手腕を~した In carrying out the task, he *showed* his talent.

2〘象徴する〙¶ 白は純潔を~す White *stands for* purity. / White *symbolizes* chastity.

ハトの図案は平和を~している The design of a dove *symbolizes* (≒ *represents*) peace.

この絵はなにを~しているのか What does this picture *represent*?

3〘意味する〙¶ この a. m. という字はなにを~しているのか What do the letters 'a. m.' *stand for* (≒ *signify*)?

m²は平方メートルを~す The sign 'm²' *stands for* square meter.

4〘表現する〙¶ 思っていることを英語で正確に~すのは私には難しい I cannot *express myself* well in correct English. / It is difficult to *make myself understood* in correct English.

その悲惨な光景はとてもことばでは~せぬ The pitiable scene is beyond all *description*. / The sight is too miserable to *put into* words.

誠実さを態度で~せ *Put* your sincerity *into* actions. / *Show* your honesty *in* your behavior.

そこに加わる風圧は次の数式で~される The wind pressure on it *is represented* by means of this expression.

この事実は彼の人格の高潔なことを~している The fact *proves* the nobility of his character.

あらわ·す【著わす】¶ 彼はこれまでに50冊以上の本を~した He *has written* (≒ *has published*) more than fifty books. / He *is the author of* more than fifty books.

あらわれ【現われ】an expression; a sign. ¶ 愛国心の~ *an expression* of patriotism. それは彼の温かい愛情の~だ It shows *a sign* of his affection.

あらわ·れる【現われる】**1**〘人の姿が〙¶ 彼女はその会には~れなかった She failed to *show up* at the meeting.

突然彼はわれわれの会に~れた Unexpectedly he *put in an appearance* (≒ *showed up; turned up*) at our meeting.

警官が~れると, 不良どもはみな逃げだした The moment a policeman *was on the scene*, all the hooligans took flight.

夜ごとに亡霊があそこに~れるとのことだ They say that a ghost *haunts* the place night after night.

2〘物の姿が〙¶ 月が雲間から~れた The moon *has come out* through a break in the clouds.

水平線上に1せきの船が~れた A ship *came in sight* on the horizon.

3〘感情·性質などが〙¶ 彼女の一挙一動には悲しみが~れていた Sorrow *showed itself* in her every act. / Everything she did *showed* how sad she was. / She *looked* sorrowful in her every act.

彼の顔には疲労の色がありありと~れていた Fatigue *could be* vividly *seen* on his face. / Fatigue *was written* on his face. / He *seemed* very tired.

あ

弱音をはかないで通すところはいかにも彼らしさが〜れている It is just like him to stand firm without complaining.

4〖効き目・事実などが〗¶ 薬の効き目はまもなく〜れた The medicine *worked* on me very soon.

いつかはがんの特効薬も〜れるだろう Some day a specific for cancer will *be found* (≒ *come out*), too.

いくつかの興味ある事実が〜れた A number of interesting facts *have been brought to light*.

5〖評判・流行などが〗¶ 彼の業績が世に〜れずに埋もれてしまうのは惜しいことだ It is regrettable that his achievements should remain in obscurity.

きみの名がこの発明ですぐ世に〜れるだろう This invention of yours will *make* you *famous* very soon.

女性の服装にはまた新しい流行が〜れた Another new style in dress *has come into vogue*.

あらんかぎり【有らん限り】¶ 彼はその競技に勝つために〜の力を出した He *tried as hard as he could* to win the race. / He *did his utmost* to win the race. 彼は〜の声を上げて「オオカミだ.オオカミだ」と叫んだ He shouted *at the top of his voice*, "Wolf! Wolf!" 命の〜あなたをお助けしましょう I will help you *as long as* I live.

あり【蟻】an ant. ¶ 集会場は満員で〜のはい出す透きもなかった The hall *was crowded* (≒ *full*) *to the doors*. 千丈の堤も〜の一穴から壊る (諺) *A little leak will sink a great ship*. 〜の無言にしてよく働くを師とせよ Nothing preaches better than *the ant*, which says nothing.

雄— a male ant. 女王— a queen ant. 働き— a worker ant.

アリア〔音楽〕an aria.

ありあま・る【有り余る】¶ 彼は〜るほど金がある He has *more* money *than he can spend*. / He has *enough* money *and more to spare*. / He has money *enough and to spare*. 商店には〜るほどいろんな品物が並んでいる The stores *are overflowing with* various goods.

ありありと ¶ 困惑が〜彼の顔に浮かんだ Perplexity was *plainly* seen in his face. その美しい光景が〜目に浮かぶ I have a *vivid* recollection of the beautiful scene.

ありあわせ【有り合わせ】¶ 〜の金は十分じゃない I have not sufficient money *in* (≒ *on*) *hand*. 〜の食事ですが食べにいらしてください Please come and take *potluck* with us.

ありうる【有り得る】¶ それは〜ことだ That's *possible*. / That *may well be*. そんなことは〜ことではない That's *impossible*. / How *can* it *be*? / It *cannot be* true. 彼が成功する見込は〜 *It is possible that* he will succeed.

ありか【在り処】whereabouts. ¶ 彼女の〜を突き止めた I found out *her whereabouts* (≒ *where she was*). / I *located* her. 彼は宝の〜を何年間も捜しつづけている He has been trying to find out *the place where* the treasure is kept.

ありかた【在り方】¶ 大学教育の〜が論議されている They are discussing what university education *should be*. 少なからぬ人々が政治の今の〜に批判的である Not a few people are critical about *the present state* of politics.

ありがた・い【有り難い】¶ この本は私には〜い This book is *a blessing to* me. 彼の家へ行っていただけると〜いのですが I should *be* very much *obliged to* you if you would visit his house for me. お便り〜く存じます *Many thanks for* your letter. 3日続きの休日は〜い Three consecutive holidays *are welcome*. 健康でいることを〜いと思いなさい *Be thankful* that you are in good health. / I hope you *appreciate* your good health. 彼があす来てくれると〜い I shall *be obliged* if he will come tomorrow. ご協力願えれば〜いのですが Your cooperation would *be appreciated*. 今の雨は〜 Rain *is* now *welcome*. この機械はまことに〜い How *convenient* this machine *is*! 〜いことに当日は一点の雲もない青空だった *Fortunately* the sky was blue and cloudless that day.

ありがたが・る【有り難がる】¶ 被災者たちは見舞いの品々をとても〜った The sufferers *were* very *thankful* (≒ *grateful*) *for* those gifts to them. / The sufferers received those gifts [to them] *with deep appreciation*. 彼はあなたの援助を大いに〜るだろう He will greatly *appreciate* your help.

ありがたさ【有り難さ】⇒ありがたみ

ありがたなみだ【有り難涙】¶ 〜をこぼした I shed *tears of gratitude*. / I *wept for gratitude*.

ありがたみ【有り難み】¶ 金の〜 *the value* of money. 健康の〜 *the blessing* of good health. 私は家庭の〜を知っている I know what *a blessing* it is to have home. 妻を失って初めて〜がわかった I could not appreciate *the blessing* of having a good wife until I lost her.

ありがためいわく【有り難迷惑】¶ それは〜なことだ That is *too much of a good thing*. きみ,それは〜だよ Thank you (≒ Thanks) for nothing. / No thanks!

ありがち【有り勝ち】¶ それはだれにも〜な過ちだ That's a fault *common* to everybody. そういう事故は〜だ Such accidents *are apt to happen*. この病気は老人には〜だ The old *are subject to* this disease. 共働きの妻には〜なことだが,彼女は過労で体をこわした She worked so hard that she broke down, *as is often the case with* such working wives.

ありがとう【有り難う】¶ どうも〜 *Thank you* very much. / *Many thanks*. ご親切〜ございます *Thank you* very much for your kindness. / I *appreciate* your kindness. 晩餐(ばんさん)にお招きいただいて〜ございます *It's very kind of you to* invite us to dinner. 彼は〜と言ってその

本を私に返してくれた He returned the book to me with *thanks*. おいでくださって～ *Thank you* for coming.

ありがね【有り金】¶これで～全部だ This is *all the money I have*. ～をはたいてカメラを買った I spent (≒ used) *all my money* on (≒ for) a camera. / I bought a camera with *what money I had*.

ありきたり【在り来たり】¶～の方法 an *ordinary* method. ～のお世辞なんかよしてくれ Don't flatter me.

ありさま【有り様】(a) condition ; a spectacle. ¶現在のような～では落ち着いていられない I cannot be at ease *under the present condition* (≒ *circumstances*). / I can't be at ease *as things are now*. 彼は空襲の～を語った He *gave a* terrible *account* of the air raid. 街はいたるところ惨憺(さん)たる～だった The town presented *a* fearful *spectacle* (≒ *scene*) everywhere.

ありじごく【蟻地獄】〘虫類〙(a larva of) an ant lion.

ありしひ【在りし日】old days. ¶～の思い出 the memories *of old days*; *old* memories. ～の父をしのぶ recall *the memories of one's* father. 彼の顔には～の面影がかすかに認められた I could see in his visage just *the traces of his youthful features*. ～の彼の面影が浮かんだ I was reminded of his appearance *while in life*./His image *while alive* flashed across my mind.

ありそう【有りそう】¶それはいかにも～な話だ It is quite *probable*. / It is quite *a likely story*. (もっともらしいが信用できない話)・そんなことはまず～にもない Such a thing seems quite *improbable* (≒ *impossible*). 一雨～だ *It is likely to* rain. / A shower *seems probable*. ～もないことを言って脅かすな Don't scare us by talking about things which *are unlikely to happen* (≒ *seem impossible*).

ありた・い【有りたい】¶いつも健康で～い *I hope to be* always in good health (≒ healthy). だれもが正直で～い Every man *ought to be* honest.

ありだか【有り高】(手元の現金) the cash in (≒ on) hand ; (在庫品) the goods in stock.

ありづか【蟻塚】an ant hill.

ありつ・く【有り付く】 ¶いい職に～きましたか *Have* you *found* a good job? 小づかい銭に～いた I *got* some pocket money. 彼の家でごちそうに～いた We *got treated* at his home.

ありったけ all (that *one* has); the whole. ¶彼は～の財産をなくした He lost *all* the fortune that he had. 彼は～の力を出した He put forth *all* his strength. ～の声で叫んだ I cried *at the top of* my voice. 彼は～の力で走った He ran *as* fast *as* he *could*. ～の知恵をふりしぼった I racked (≒ cudgeled) my brains *as hard as* I *could*.

ありてい【有り体】¶～に申せばあなたには賛成できません *To be frank with you*, I can't agree with you. その件については～にすべてを告白しました I *frankly* confessed everything (≒ the whole truth) about the matter.

ありとあらゆる ¶彼は火事で～財産をなくした He lost *all* his fortune in the fire. ～ことはした I have done *all that I can do*. ～点であなたに賛成します I agree with you *in all respects*. 博物館の～ものが私に興味を与えました *Everything* in the museum interested me.

ありのまま【有りの儘】¶～に事実を述べなさい Tell the facts *as they happened*. これは～の事実だ This is a *naked* fact. 彼のことばを～受け入れた I believed every word he said.

アリバイ an alibi. ¶彼には～があった He had *an alibi*. 彼は～を証明した He proved (≒ established) his *alibi*. / His *alibi* was proved. 彼の～をくずした We broke his *alibi*.

ありふれた【有り触れた】 ¶～名前 a *common* name. ～光景 a *habitual* sight. 宇宙旅行はいずれまったく～ことになるだろう The space travel will be quite *a commonplace* before long.

ありもしない【有りもしない】¶彼は～報告をした He made a *false* report.

ありゅう【亜流】a follower. ¶彼はディケンズの～だ He is *a follower* of Dickens. / He *imitates* Dickens.

ありゅうさんガス【亜硫酸ガス】〘化学〙sulfurous acid gas.

ありんさん【亜燐酸】〘化学〙phosphorous acid.

あ・る【有る・在る】**1**〖存在・所在する〗¶まだ汽車が出るまでたっぷり時間が～る We still *have* plenty of time before the train leaves. / *There is* still plenty of time before the train leaves.

卓上にはテレビが～る *There is* a television (set) on the desk. / A TV set *stands* on the table.

その本どこに～った. 私の机の上に～った Where did you find the book? I *found* it on my desk.

神が～るときみは思うか Do you think God *exists*? / Do you *believe in* God?

金は～るところには～るものだ Some people *have* more money than they can spend. / Some people *have* money enough and to spare.

彼の事務所は市の中心街に～る His office *is* in the central part of the city. / He *has* his office on the main street of the city.

きみの家はどこに～るのか Where *is* your house?

当市の人口は100万～る This city *has* a population of a million inhabitants.

全部で120種類～る *There are* 120 kinds of them in all. / They are divided into 120 species altogether.

彼女は～ることないこと言いふらした She spread a *groundless* story.

～りもしないことを言うな Don't tell a lie. / That's impossible. / How can that *be*?

どこの店にも～るというのとは質が違う You cannot *get* an article of such fine quality at a common store.

この薬品はたいていの薬屋に～る You can *get*

あ

this medicine at a common drugstore.

2 〖あり方〗 ¶ わが校の教育の～り方はこれでよいのか Is the education of our students what it ought to *be*? 異性との交際はこう～ってほしい This is what relationship between men and women should *be*. 今～るがままの姿をお目にかけましょう I will let you see it *as it really is* (≒ *in its true colors*). ～るがままに物事をみるのは難しい It is not easy to see things as they *are*.

3 〖所有・所持〗 ¶ 金と暇が～ればヨーロッパに旅行したい If I *had* time and money to spare, I would go on a tour of Europe. 彼の家はなかなか財産が～る He is a very rich man. / He belongs to a wealthy family. 金は～れば～るだけ欲しくなる The more money you *have*, the more you want. ～るだけ使ってしまいなさい Spend all you have. 彼は経営の腕が～る He *has* business ability. / He *has* ability in management. なかなか目がお～りですね You *have* an eye for it. / You are an accomplished expert. / You are a good judge. きょうは風邪ぎみで少し熱が～る Today I am feverish on account of a cold. きみに言いたいことが山ほど～る I *have* lots of things to tell you. / I *have* a lot of complaints to make against you. / You deserve a long lecture from me. 彼にも言い分が～る He *has* his say, too. / Let him *have* his say, too. 「お子さんが～りますか」「はい, ふたり～ります」 "Do you *have* any children?" "Yes, I *have* two." 同情する気持ちが～るのなら, 彼を助けてやれ You should help him, if you do feel for him. きみには借りが～る(借金) I owe you money. / I am in debt to you. / (恩義) I owe you a debt of gratitude.

4 〖生起する〗 ¶ なにか～ったなと彼女の顔を見て思った Taking a glance at her face, I thought something *had happened* to her. 昨夜気味の悪いことが～って寝られなかった Last night I *had* an uncanny experience and could not sleep. 会議でなにか変わったことでも～りましたか Did anything particular *happen* at the conference? 早朝強い地震が～った We *had* a severe earthquake early this morning. あの踏切ではよく自動車事故が～る Motoring accidents often *happen* at the crossing. そういうことはよく～る We often *have* such an experience. / It often *happens*. よく～るミスだ It is a *common* mistake. よく～る話だ It's an *everyday* affair. ふたりがけんかするなんて～りえない *It's impossible* that the two should fall out with each other. ここへ来たことが～るか Have you ever been here?

5 〖行なわれる〗 ¶ 2時間めに英語の試験が～る We *have* an examination in English at the second period. 3時から総会が～る The general meeting *begins* at three o'clock. 特別な催しは～りません We will *have* no special gathering for the occasion. 機会が～り次第参ります I will come on the first occasion.

6 〖数・度量衡〗 ¶ その箱は縦・横・高さそれぞれ8・5・3メートル～る The box *is* eight meters long, five meters wide, and three meters high. 塔の高さは120メートル～る The tower *is* 120 meters high (≒ in height). 校庭の面積は約4万平方メートル～る The schoolyard *has* an area of about 40,000 square meters. 川幅はどのくらい～るか How wide *is* the river? きみはどのくらい目方が～るか How much do you *weigh*? その高さはこのビルの2倍～る It *is* twice as tall as this building. この池の深さは3メートル～る This pond *is* three meters deep.

7 〖…に存する〗 ¶ 幸福は満足に～る Happiness *consists* (≒ *lies*) *in* contentment. 成功は勤勉に～る Success *lies in* industry. 最大の難点はそこに～るのだ (困難な点) That *is* the most difficult point of the affair. / (よくない点) That *is* the worst point of it. 非はむしろ彼女のほうに～る It is she who is to blame for it. / The blame should *be placed upon* her.

ある【或】 ¶ ～日彼は散歩に出かけた *One day* he went out for a walk. ～朝彼女はいつもより早く目がさめた *One morning* she woke up earlier than usual. その村に～金持ちが住んでいた *A certain* rich man lived in the village. ゆうべ～人があなたをたずねて来た *A certain* man called on you yesterday evening. なにか～一つのことを一生懸命やりなさい Be intent on *something or other*. ～人からこの話を聞いた I was told the story by *a certain* person. そのころ彼は～仕事を持っていた At the time he was engaged in *some sort of* work.

あるいは【或いは】 ¶ 彼は～生きているかもしれない He *may* be alive. 彼は～来るかもしれないし来ないかもしれない He *may or may not* come. 私たちは～負けないとも限らない We *might possibly* be defeated.

アルカリ 〘化学〙 alkali. ¶ ～性 alkalinity. ～性の alkaline. この水は～性だ This water *is alkaline*. ～反応 *alkaline* reaction.

アルカロイド 〘化学〙 alkaloid.

ある・く【歩く】 walk. ¶「駅まで～いていきますか, バスに乗りますか」「～きましょう」 "Shall we go to the station *on foot* or by bus?" "Let's *walk*." そこまで～いたとてたいしたことはない It won't take

so long to *walk* there.
学校まで～いて10分かかる It takes ten minutes to *walk* to school. (go on foot はさける). / It is ten minutes' *walk* [from my home] to the school.
彼は疲れた手足を引きずって～いた He was so tired that he *dragged himself along*.
一日じゅう足を棒にして～いたがうまい職は見つからなかった I *walked* myself lame, but found no profitable job.
ひとりとぼとぼ～いていく彼の姿はあわれだった I took pity on him *plodding* along by himself.
彼に大またで～かれると,こちらは小走りになる When he *walks* with long strides, I must trot along to keep up with him.
どこを～きまわっていたんだ Where *have* you *been wandering about*?
彼は部屋の中を～きまわって,考えをまとめようとした He tried to get his ideas into shape, *pacing* up and down the room.
きょうは～き疲れた I am tired from *walking* today.
この打者は～かせたほうがいい *Walk* the batter.
犬も～けば棒に当たる(諺) *Every dog has his day*.

アルコール alcohol.
—飲料 alcoholic drinks. —中毒 alcoholism. —中毒患者 an alcoholic. —ランプ an alcohol (≒ a spirit) lamp.

アルゴン〘化学〙argon.

あるじ【主】a master. ¶その家の～ the *master* of the house. 私がこの店の～です I am the *proprietor* of this store.

アルゼンチン Argentina; the Argentine Republic.
—人 an Argentine.

アルト〘音楽〙alto.
—歌手 an alto [singer].

アルバイト a job (job は臨時の仕事の意味もあるから a side job という必要はない). ¶彼は～に小学生を教えている He teaches an elementary schoolboy *on the side*. 彼は～に家庭教師をした He tutored for his school expenses. 私は～をして大学を出た I *worked my way through college*. ～学生 a *working* student.

アルパカ〘動物〙an alpaca.

アルバム an album.

アルファ alpha. ¶労働組合は給料3か月分プラス～のボーナスを要求した The labor union demanded a bonus equivalent to three months' pay plus *something*.

アルファベット the alphabet. ¶～順に in *alphabetical* order; alphabetically. ロシア語は～も知らない I don't know *the ABC of* Russian.

アルプス the Alps. ¶～の植物 *alpine* plants. 日本— the Japan Alps. —登山家 an alpinist.

アルマイト alumite. ¶～のやかん an *alumite* kettle. ～のなべ an *alumite* pan.

あるまじき【有るまじき】¶学生に～言動は慎みなさい Keep from speech and conduct *unbecoming to* a student. ～振舞いだ It's a highly *objectionable* behavior. / Such conduct *is unworthy of* you. そんなことをしたとは彼に～ことだ *It is unworthy of* him to have done such a thing.

アルミニウム 米 aluminum; 英 aluminium.
—線 alminum wire. —製品 aluminum ware.

あれ【荒れ】¶このクリームは皮膚の～によい This cream is good for *chapped* skin. この建物は～ほうだいになっている This building is left to run *waste*.

あれい【亜鈴】a dumbbell (しばしば [a pair of] dumbbells).
—体操 dumbbell exercise.

あれくる・う【荒れ狂う】¶～う波 *raging* waves. 昨夜台風が九州地方を～った A typhoon *raged* (≒ *swept*) about the Kyushu area last night.

アレグレット〘音楽〙allegretto.

アレグロ〘音楽〙allegro.

あれこれ ¶～と考える *take* all things *together*. ～と考えた末きみが彼に会うのがいちばんよいと思う *All things considered*, I think it is best for you to see him. ～考えたがいい案は浮かばなかった Even after *a great deal of thinking*, I got no good idea. 彼はいつも～と職を変えている He is always changing *this* job *or that*. ～と着てみてください Please try on *one* clothes *after another*.

あれしき ¶～のことに騒ぎたてるな Don't make a fuss about *such a trifling matter*. ～のことに思い惑う必要はない You don't have to worry about *such a trifle*. ～のことには腹を立てない I won't get angry at *a trivial matter like that*.

あれしょう【荒れ性】¶～の皮膚 a *chappy* skin.

あれち【荒れ地】a wasteland; a waste. ¶～を耕す till *the wilderness*. そのあき地は～になっている The vacant lot *lies waste*.

あれっきり ¶彼は～音さたがない He hasn't dropped me a line *since* [*then*]. / I have not heard from him *since then*. ～彼に会わない I haven't seen any more of him *since*. 彼は～なにも言わなかった He said nothing *beyond that*. ～しか金を持ってなかった That was all money I had then. 彼は～の男です He is worth no more than what he looks.

あれの【荒れ野】waste (≒ desert) land; a wilderness; the wilds.

あれは・てる【荒れ果てる】¶寺はまったく～てていた The temple *was* utterly *ruined* (≒ *desolate*). 庭は手入れする者もなく～てていた There being nobody to tend it, the garden *was overgrown with weeds*. / The garden *was* awfully *neglected*.

あれほど【あれ程】¶～の学問がありながら with all *one's* learning. ～英語が話せたらいいのですが I wish I could speak English *that much*. 彼は～一生懸命努力したのに試験に落第した He failed the exams *in spite of all his efforts*. ～がんこな男に会ったことがない He is *the most* obstinate man *I have ever seen*. ～言ったのに彼は山に出かけた He went mountain-climbing *after all my warnings*.

あれもよう【荒れ模様】 ¶ きょうは～だ It *looks like a storm* today. 山の天候は～だ The weather in the mountains *looks wild*.

あれやこれや ¶ ～とたいへん忙しい I am very busy with *one thing or another*. ～と思いあぐんでもしかたがない It's no use worrying about *this and that matter*. ～と考えたあげく東京に行くことにした *After fully considering the matter*, I have determined to go to Tokyo.

あ·れる【荒れる】 **1**〖天候が〗¶ 北部山岳地方は一日じゅう～れるでしょう The weather will *be stormy* all day in the northern mountainous areas.
海は～れていた The sea *was running high* (≒ *rough*).
一日じゅう激しい北の風が吹き～れた A strong northerly wind *was raging* all day.
2〖荒廃〗¶ 農民は離村し, 田畑は～れるにまかされた As the farmers had deserted the village, the fields were left to *run waste*.
3〖膚が〗¶ 彼女の手は水仕事で～れていた Her hands *were rough* with kitchen work and washing.
膚の～れるのを防ぐにはこのクリームがよく効く This cream is the best prevention for a *rough* skin.
舌が～れていますね Your tongue has become *rough*.
4〖生活·感情が〗¶ そんなに～れるな Don't *lose your temper* (≒ *blow your top*; *lose restraint*) like that.
きみの生活は～れている You *lead a wild* (≒ *dissolute*; *dissipated*) *life*.

アレルギー〘医学〙allergy. ¶ 私は～体質で困る I suffer from an *allergic* constitution.
ぼくは牛乳を飲むと～反応を起こす I *am allergic to* milk. ～の allergic.

-あろうに ¶ 人も～彼が私の悪口を言ったなんて信じられない I can't believe that he, *of all persons*, has said bad things about me.

アロハ シャツ an aloha shirt.

あわ【泡】 **1** (波·口の) foam; (ビールなどの) froth; (せっけんの) lather.
¶ ～の多いビール *frothy* beer.
ビールはコップにつぐと～が立つ Beer *froths* when it is poured out into a glass.
このせっけんはよく～が立つ This soap *lathers* well.
2〖転義〗¶ われわれの努力もすべて水の～となった All our efforts *have come to nothing*.
～をくった I *was upset*. / I *was confounded*.
彼は私に～をふかせた He *gave me fits*.
口角～を飛ばして議論した We argued *sputteringly*.

あわ【粟】 millet.

あわ·い【淡い】 ¶ ～い光 〔a〕*faint* light. ～い恋 *transitory* (≒ *fleeting*) love. ～い望みをいだく have a *faint* hope (*in*).

あわせめ【合わせ目】 a joint; a seam.

あわ·せる【合わせる】 **1**〖結合させる〗¶ 彼女は両手を～せて仏像を拝んだ With her hands *joined* (≒ *clasped*; *folded*) in prayer, she bowed before the image of Buddha.
その壁板は2枚の板を～せたものだ The partition is made up of two boards *put together*.
彼は両派を～せて一党を結成した He *united* the two parties into a new party.
2〖合計する〗¶ 全部～せていくらですか (総額) How much is it *altogether*? / (総数) How many are they *in all*? / (重さ) What is the *total* weight?
～せて50万円です The total *amounts to* 500,000 yen. / It *sums up to* 500,000 yen.
反対者は全部～せて10人いた The dissenters *totaled* 10.
みんなで声を～せて助けてと叫んだ We cried for help *in one voice*.
3〖一致させる〗¶ 目覚まし時計を7時に～せた I *set* my alarm clock *for* seven o'clock.
毎朝ぼくは時計をテレビの時報に～せる Every morning I *set* (≒ *check*) my watch *by* the television time signal.
話のつじつまを～せなきゃまずい We should try to *make* our story *consistent*.
ふたりで口うらを～せて彼をごまかした We two deceived him by telling the story which *had been arranged* between us. / Both of us *chimed in* trying to deceive him.
4〖照合する〗¶ このふたをあの箱と～せてみたが合わなかった I tried to *fit* this lid to the box, but I couldn't.
きみの答えとぼくの答えを～せてみよう Let me *compare* (≒ *check*) my answers *with* yours. / Let's *compare* our papers.
原文と訳文とを～せてみた I *compared* the translation *with* the original.
5〖適合させる〗¶ この絵の大きさに～せて額を作ってください Please make a frame to *fit* this picture.
その寸法に～せてこの布地を裁断しなさい Cut the cloth *according to* the measurements.
壁の色に～せて床の塗料も考えましょう It will be better to *match* the colors of the walls and floor.
6〖調子を〗¶ 私たちはバンドの演奏に～せて踊った We danced *to* the accompaniment of the band.
彼女はその曲に～せて美しく氷を滑った She skated gracefully over the ice *to* the tune.
彼女のバイオリンに～せて彼はピアノをひいた He *accompanied* her violin on the piano.
ぼくは一生懸命彼のきげんをうかがって調子を～せようとした I tried very hard to please him and *chime in* with him.
7〖面会〗¶ あのふたりを～せましょうか Shall I *bring* them *together*?
きみには～す顔がない I am deeply ashamed of myself. / I feel deeply ashamed to *see* you.

あわただし·い【慌ただしい】 ¶ 彼は～く2階へ駆け上がった He ran upstairs *in a hurry*. ことしも～く暮れた This year passed *all too* *quickly*. 都会の〜い生活にも慣れた I am accustomed to a *busy* life in the city.

あわだ·つ【泡立つ】foam. ¶ 波が〜ちながら浜辺におしよせていた Waves *were foaming* along the beach.

あわだ·てる【泡立てる】froth. ¶ 卵を〜てる *froth* eggs. 狂犬はときどき口を〜てる A mad dog sometimes *froths* at the mouth.

あわてもの【慌て者】a hasty person; a careless person.

あわ·てる【慌てる】¶ そんなに〜てるな Never *be* so *hasty*. / *Take your time*. /(とくに㊩) *Take it easy*. 彼は少しも〜てなかった He remained quite calm. ひどく〜てて走っていった He ran away *in a* great *hurry*. 〜てて失敗しないよう気をつけなさい Be careful not to make *hasty* mistakes. 〜てたためにかさをバスの中に置き忘れた I left my umbrella in the bus *in my hurry*.

あわび【鮑】an ear shell; a sea-ear. ¶ 彼の恋は〜の片思いだった His love was one-sided (≒ not returned).

あわや ¶ 私は〜おぼれそうになった I *was very near* being drowned. その子は〜車にひかれるところだった The child *was within an ace of* being run over by a car. 〜大惨事かと思う瞬間汽車は急停車した *In the instant of* causing a big tragic disaster, the train was brought to a sudden stop.

あわゆき【沫雪】light snow.

あわよくば ¶ 〜成功するかもしれない *With good luck*, I might succeed.

あわれ【哀れ】¶ 彼はなんて〜な男だ What a *poor* fellow he is! なんて〜な一生なんだ What a *wretched* life! 〜な話に心を打たれた I was moved by the *sad* story. 彼らは死んだ友を〜に思った They thought *sorrowfully* of their dead friend. 〜にもその子どもは洪水で両親を亡くした The *poor* child lost his parents in the flood. 彼はたいへん〜な暮らしをしている He lives *in* great *misery*. 物の〜(日本文学の) *the pensive beauty* of things.

あわれみ【哀れみ】pity. ¶ 見捨てられた子どもは〜をかう The deserted children deserve our *pity*. あんなやつに〜をかけるな Don't take *pity* on such a fellow. 彼女はたいへん〜深い She *is* very *compassionate* (≒ *sympathetic*). 彼は〜深い顔付きをしていた He put on *sad* looks on the face.

あわれ·む【哀れむ】¶ その病気の子どもを〜んだ We *took pity on* the sick child. 彼を〜まずにはいられなかった I couldn't but *pity* him. 彼女は彼の身の上を〜んで泣いた She wept *in pity of* his fate. 同病相〜む(諺) *Misery loves company*.

あん【案】a plan. ¶ 〜を立てる make (≒ form) *a plan*. それはすばらしい〜だ That's *a* splendid (≒ ㊩ cute) *idea*. 彼のブラジル移住の〜に不賛成だ I am opposed to his *plan* to emigrate to Brazil. 〜に相違して彼は私の依頼を断わった *Contrary to my expectation*, he declined my request.

あん【餡】bean jam; bean paste. ¶ 〜でくるむ cover a cake with *bean jam*.

—もち a rice-cake stuffed with bean paste.

あんあんり【暗暗裏】¶ 彼はその提案に〜に同意を示した He gave a *tacit* consent to the proposal. 〜に事を運ぶ do something *in secret*. 〜に会合を開いた We held a meeting *in secret*.

あんい【安易】¶ 人生を〜に考えてはいけない Don't *take* life *too easy*. 〜な生活は怠惰を招く An *easy-going* way of life induces idleness. 物事はいつも〜に運ぶとはかぎらない Everything can't always be done *with ease*.

あんいつ【安逸】¶ 〜に過ごす spend time *in idleness*; pass *one's* days *in indolence*. 〜はすべての悪の源である *Idleness* is the source of all vice. 〜な生活から脱することはむずかしい It is difficult to get away from a life of *ease*.

あんえい【暗影】a gloom; a shadow. ¶ 彼の死は世界に〜を投じた His death cast *a gloom* over the world. 前途は〜に覆われているようだった Our future loomed *dark*. 世界の危機に〜を感じる I *feel gloomy about* the crisis of the world.

あんか【安価】cheapness. ¶ 〜な娯楽を追い求める hunt (≒ seek) *cheap* amusements. 現金なら〜にします I'll sell them *cheap* for cash.

あんか【行火】a foot warmer; a bed-warmer.

あんがい【案外】¶ 結果は〜だった The results *were unexpected*. 問題は〜やさしかった The problem was easier *than* [*I had*] *expected*. 彼の病気は〜重い He is more seriously ill *than he has been first imagined*. 〜なことに彼は私の言うことを信じようとしなかった I *was surprised to* know he would not believe me.

あんかん【安閑】¶ 〜としてはおれない This is no time for *idling*. 青春を〜として過ごすな Don't *idle away* your youth.

あんき【安危】welfare. ¶ その内戦は国の〜にもかかわる The civil war will affect the *welfare* of the nation. 彼は自分の〜も返り見ず溺れる子を助けに流れに飛びこんだ He jumped into the current to help a drowning child regardless of his *safety*.

あんき【暗記】memorization. ¶ 〜は英語の学習に大いに役だつ *Memorizing* is very helpful for the study of English. この課を全部〜した I *learned* the whole lesson *by heart*. 私はこの詩を〜している I *know* this poem *by heart*. 彼は月日をよく〜している He *has a good head for* dates.

あんぎゃ【行脚】a pilgrimage. ¶ その僧は諸国を〜している The priest *is making pilgrimages* to various parts of the country.

—僧 an itinerant priest (≒ monk); a priest on a pilgrimage.

あんきょ【暗渠】an underdrain; a culvert; a blind ditch.

—式 a conduit system. **—排水** underdrainage; drainage by a culvert.

あんぐり ¶ 彼は驚いて口を〜開けていた He was

agape with surprise.

アングロサクソン the Anglo-Saxon.
—語 Anglo-Saxon. —民族 the Anglo-Saxons; the Anglo-Saxon race.

アンケート a questionnaire (アンケートはフランス語の enquête から). ¶ ～をとる send out *questionnaires*. その情報は50人の大学生に出された～をもとにして得られた The information was obtained through *questionnaires* sent to fifty university students.

あんけん【案件】 an issue. ¶ その重要～は次回に討論される The important *issue* will be discussed in the next meeting. ～は午後1時までに提出すること *Affairs* (≒ *Topics*) to discuss are to be handed in by 1 : 00 p. m.

あんこう【鮟鱇】〖魚類〗an angler.

あんごう【暗号】 a code; a cipher. ¶ ～を解読する decipher (≒ decode) *a message in cipher*. 彼の文字はまるで～みたいだ His handwriting is, as it were, *a puzzle*.
—帳 a code book. —電報 a cipher telegram; a telegram cipher (≒ in code). —文字 a code word.

あんごう【暗合】〔a〕coincidence. ¶ ～する coincide (*with something*); happen to agree (*with something*).

アンコール an encore. ¶ 聴衆は～を求めた The audience called for *an encore*. 彼は～に答えて歌った He sang for his *encore*. 彼女は続けて3回～に答えた She gave us three *encores* on end.

あんこく【暗黒】 darkness. ¶ 社会の～面 *the dark side* of society.
—街 dark quarters. —時代(中世ヨーロッパの) the Dark Ages; (一般の) a dark age. —大陸 the Dark Continent.

アンゴラ (ウサギ) an Angora rabbit.

あんさつ【暗殺】〔an〕assassination. ¶ ～する murder (≒ assassinate) (*a person*).
—者 an assassin; a murderer.

あんざん【安産】 ¶ 妻は男の子を～した My wife *gave an easy birth* (≒ *delivery*) *to* a boy.

あんざん【暗算】 mental calculation. ¶ 彼はその等式を～で解いた He answered the equation by *mental calculation*. 彼は4けたの～をその場でやった He did *mental calculation* of four figures on the spot.

アンサンブル an ensemble.

あんじ【暗示】 a hint; a suggestion; a cue. ¶ この事実は将来の政治の方向を～している This fact *suggests* the direction of the future politics. 彼は～にかかりやすい He *is suggestible*./ He is easily subjected to *suggestion*. 彼はその光景から～を得てその曲を書いた He composed the tune *suggested* by the sight. この絵は詩的なものを～させる This picture *is suggestive of* something poetic.
—療法 a suggestive medicine (≒ cure). 自己— an autosuggestion.

あんしつ【暗室】 (写真の) a darkroom.

あんじゅう【安住】 ¶ 彼らは～の地を求めてこの土地までやってきた They have come here for *peaceful living*. 彼女は宗教に～の境地を見いだした She found *relief* in religion. いつまでもこんな生活に～してはいられない I shouldn't keep living like this so long.

あんしゅつ【案出】 (くふう) contrivance; (発明) invention. ¶ ある計画を～する *think out* a plan.
—者 an inventor; an originator.

あんしょう【暗唱】 recitation. ¶ 詩を～する *recite* a poem.

あんしょう【暗礁】 a reef; a sunken (≒ submerged) rock. ¶ このあたりは～が多い There are lots of *reefs* around here. 船は下田沖で～に乗り上げた The ship *went* (≒ *ran*) *on a rock* off the coast of Shimoda. 3者首脳会談は完全に～に乗り上げた The big-three conference *has come to a* complete *deadlock*.

あん·じる【案じる】 ⇒あんずる

あんしん【安心】 ¶ その知らせを聞いて～した I *was relieved at* the news. 会社の将来については～してよいだろう We may *feel easy* about the future of the firm. まだ～はできない I cannot *be sure* yet. 患者はもう～だ The patient *is out of danger*. 彼はあすは帰るから～してください You can *rest assured* that he will be back tomorrow. 彼は定刻に来ると思って～してください Please *be confident* of his coming here punctually. その件についてはまだ～できない I cannot *set my mind at ease* as yet about that. あの人に～して仕事を頼めるのか不安だ I cannot *be sure* whether he can do the work for me. もう危険はないから～してよい You may *feel relieved* (≒ *feel relief*; *breathe freely*) since the danger is gone. 今晩は～して眠れる I can sleep *soundly* tonight.

あんず【杏】〖植物〗an apricot.

あん·ずる【案ずる】 ¶ 私は彼の将来を～じている I *am anxious about* his future. ～ずるより生むがやすし(諺) *Fear is greater than the danger*. 一計を～ずる *think* (≒ *work*) *out* a plan.

あんせい【安静】 rest. ¶ 医者は彼に絶対～を命じた The doctor prescribed *an* absolute *rest* for him. 十分～にしていればすぐ治るでしょう Have *a* good *rest in bed*, and you will be better soon.
—療法 a rest cure.

あんぜん【安全】 safety; security. ¶ ～な場所 a *safe* place. この品物をもっと～な場所に置きなさい Put this article in a *safer* place. ～第一(標語) *Safety first*. われわれは彼の生命財産の～を保障する We *secure* his life and property. 彼は無事～に帰るだろう He will return *safe and sound*. 彼はいつも身の～だけを図る He always looks to his own *safety*.
—運転 safety drive. ¶ ～運転を心がけよう Let's drive *safely* (≒ *safe*). —運動 a safety campaign. —かみそり a safety razor. —週間 a safety week. —性 safety. —操業 safety operation. —装置(鉄砲の) a safety bolt (≒ lock). —地帯 a safety zone; (街路の) an island; a safety island. —燈 a safety lamp. —ピン a safety pin. —ベルト

a safety belt. ━弁 a safety valve. ━保障条約 the Security Pact. ━保障理事会(国連の) the Security Council. 集団━保障 collective security.

あんぜん【暗然】¶ ～として gloomily; melancholily; sadly. ～たる未来 a *gloomy* future. 彼は～とした面持ちであった He looked *blue* (≒ *melancholy*).

あんそく【安息】rest; repose.
━日 the day of rest; (ユダヤ教・キリスト教の) the Sabbath [day]. ¶ ～日を守る keep (≒ observe) *the Sabbath*.

あんそっこう【安息香】〔化学〕benzoin.

アンソロジー an anthology.

あんだ【安打】〔野球〕a hit; (単打) a single. ¶ センターに～する *hit* to center. 相手チームを5～散発に封ずる hold the other team to five scattered *hits*. 無～に封ずる hold batters *hitless*. 彼はきょう2～した He made two *hits* (≒ *singles*) today.

アンダーウエア underwear.

アンダーシャツ an undershirt.

アンダースロー 〔野球〕an underhand throw (≒ pitch).

アンダーライン an underline. ¶ 語に～を引く *underline* a word.

あんたい【安泰】¶ 国家の～ *peace and security* of the nation. 彼の地位は～だ His position *is secured*.

あんたん【暗澹】¶ ～たる前途 *gloomy* prospects. 彼の前途は～たるものだ His future looks *gloomy*.

アンダンテ 〔音楽〕andante.

あんち【安置】¶ 仏像を～する *enshrine* a Buddhist image. 遺骸(いがい)を～する *lay a person's* body *in state*.

アンチック 〔印刷〕antique.

アンチテーゼ 〔論理〕antithesis.

アンチピリン 〔薬品〕antipyrin[e].

アンチモニー 〔化学〕antimony.

あんちゃく【安着】¶ ご送付の品昨日～いたしました We *received* your goods *in good condition* yesterday.

あんちゅうもさく【暗中模索】¶ 秘密を解くかぎを～した I *groped for* a clue to the mystery.

あんちょく【安直】¶ ～な料理(簡単な) a *simple* dish; (料理が楽な) food *easy to cook*; (値が安い) a *cheap* dish. ～な解決 an *easy-going* solution. その仕事を～にやろうと思うな Don't try to finish the work *easily*.

アンツーカー ¶ ～のテニス コート an *en-tout-cas* tennis court.

あんてい【安定】stability; stabilization; (均衡) balance. ¶ ～を保つ(失う) keep (lose) *balance*. 物価の～を図る strive for price *stability*. まず生活の～を図らねばならない We should *secure* our living first. 彼は情緒の～を欠いている He lacks emotional *stability*. その国の事情は前よりずっと～している Things are now much *stabler* in that country than before.
━感 a sense of stability. ━経済 stabilized economy. ━勢力 a stabilizing power.

アンテナ an antenna (複 antennas). ¶ ～を立てる set up *an antenna*.

あんてん【暗転】〔演劇〕a dark change.

あんど【安堵】relief. ¶ ～の胸をなでおろす give a sigh of *relief*.

あんとう【暗闘】a secret strife. ¶ 両家には代々～が絶えなかった The two families *have been at feud* with each other for many generations.

あんな ¶ ～人 *such* a man. ～に正直な人 *such* an honest man [as he]. ～に才能のある人 *such* an able man; a man of *such* ability. ～に愉快なことはなかった I've never had *such* a good time. ～に走らなくてもいいのに He doesn't have to run *so* fast.

あんない【案内】**1**〖導く〗¶ 彼は町じゅう～してくれた He *showed* me round (≒ all over) the town.
私は京都の史跡を彼のため～してまわった I *showed* him round the historic sites in Kyoto.
彼は工場の中をくまなく～してくれた He *showed* me all round the factory.
途中までご～いたしましょうか Shall I *set* you *on* your *way*? / Shall I go part of the way with you?
彼は私どもの先に立って夜道を駅まで～してくれた He *led* us to the station at night.
だれか事件の現場に～してくれませんか Will anyone *take* us to the spot of the accident (≒ disaster)?
旅館の女中は私を一室へ～した At the hotel a waitress *showed* me into a room.
2〖招待〗¶ 晩餐(ばんさん)会にご出席いただきたくご～申し上げます We *request the pleasure of your company* at dinner.
卒業式は3月10日午前10時より行なわれます. ご来臨の栄を得たくご～申し上げます We *request the honor of your presense* at the graduation ceremony on the tenth of March, at ten in the morning.
3〖通知〗¶ 会は10日にあるとのことだが, ぼくのところにはなんの～も来ない I have heard the meeting is to take place on the tenth, but I haven't got any *notice* of it.
かねてご～申し上げましたとおり, 今月の10日には開店いたします As we *have notified* you previously, we will open our store on the tenth of this month.
4〖承知〗¶ ご～のとおりの現下の不況故今期の売り上げははかばかしくありません As you *know*, owing to the present business depression, the sales for this session have fallen off considerably.
この土地は不～です I am *a stranger* here [(myself)].
5〖取り次ぎ〗¶ 玄関に立って～を請うた At the entrance I *knocked on* (≒ *at*) the door.
不作法にも彼は～なしにずかずか家に上がり込んだ It was very rude of him to enter the house without *knocking* (≒ *unannounced*). / He came into the house *unreservedly*.
━係 a guide; a clerk at the information

い

desk; an usher; (受付け) a receptionist; (劇場などの女の) an usherette. ―所 an information bureau; an inquiry office. ―書 a guide[book]. ―図 an information map. ―役 a clerk for guidance; a receptionist. ―人 a guide. 演劇― theater news. 観光― a sightseeing guide; a sightseers' guide. 娯楽― an entertainment guide. 道― a guidance; (人) a guide; (掲示板) a guidepost; a road sign.

あんに【暗に】 ¶ この論説は～彼の政策を非難している This article *indirectly* blames his policy. 彼は～引退をほのめかした He *hinted at* his retirement. / He *suggested* that he might retire. 彼女は～その計画を承認した She gave her *tacit* consent to the plan.

あんねい【安寧】 public peace. ¶ ついにその国の～秩序は回復された *Peace* and order were finally restored in the country.

あんのじょう【案の定】 ¶ ～彼女は病気だった *Sure enough*, she was ill. ～彼は遅れてやってきた *As usual*, he didn't appear in time.

あんのん【安穏】 ¶ ～な生活 a *peaceful* life. ～に暮らす live *in peace*. 彼はひたすら～無事を願っている He prays only for his *safety*.

あんば【鞍馬】〘体操〙a side horse.

あんばい【案配】 ¶ 仕事を～する *assign* (≒ *arrange*) work.

あんばい【塩梅・按排】 ¶ いい～に right; luckily; fortunately. スープの～をみる taste the soup. ふろの～をみる see how the bath is. 体の～はどうかね How do you feel today? どういう～に並べようか How shall we arrange them? この～ではあすは雨だろう It looks like rain tomorrow, I'm afraid.

アンパイア an umpire; (フットボール, ボクシング) a referee.

アンバランス unbalance; imbalance. ¶ 支出と収入が～だ The expenditure *does not balance* with the income.

あんぴ【安否】 ¶ ～を気遣っている I worry (≒ am anxious) about his *safety*. 彼の～(健康)を尋ねた I *inquired* (≒ *asked*) *after* him. 遭難者の～が気遣われている The *safety* of the victims is apprehended. 彼の～を知らせてくれ Let me know *how he is*.

あんぶ【鞍部】 (山の) a col; a saddle.

あんぷ【暗譜】 ¶ ～でピアノを弾く *play* the piano *from memory*.

アンプ〘電気〙an amplifier.

アンプル〘薬学〙an ampule.

あんぶん【案文】 a draft.

あんぶん【案分】 ¶ 利益金を～する *divide* (≒ *distribute*) the profit *proportionally*.
―比例 ¶ ～比例で予算を分ける *divide* the budget *in proportion*.

アンペア〘電気〙an ampere.

アンペラ a bulrush mat.

あんぽう【罨法】〘医学〙fomentation.

あんま【按摩】 massage; (人) a massager; a massagist. ¶ ～する massage (*a person*). ～してもらう have *oneself massaged*.

あんまり【余り】 ¶ そりゃ～だ That's too much. / How cruel (≒ heartless; cold) of you!

あんみん【安眠】 a sound (≒ good; peaceful) sleep. ¶ 昨夜は～できた I could *sleep well* last night. / I *had a good* (≒ *sound*) *sleep* last night. 風の音で一晩じゅう～できなかった The noise of the wind *kept* me *awake* all night. 他人の～を妨害するな Don't disturb others' *sleep*.

あんもく【暗黙】 ¶ ～の了解 a *tacit* (≒ an *implicit*) understanding. ～のうちに彼らの和解が成立した They have come to terms *tacitly* (≒ *by a tacit understanding*).

アンモニア〘化学〙ammonia.
―水 liquid ammonia.

アンモニウム〘化学〙ammonium.

あんや【暗夜】 a dark night. ¶ ～に乗じて taking advantage of *a dark night*.

あんやく【暗躍】 ¶ ～する act secretly; engage in secret maneuvers. ～して彼らを仲間割れさせた I *maneuvered* them out of union.

あんらく【安楽】 ¶ ～に暮らす live *comfortably* (≒ *in comfort*).
―いす an easy chair; an armchair. ―死 euthanasia; (おもに子どもに対し) mercy killing.

あんりゅう【暗流】 an undercurrent.

あんるい【暗涙】 ¶ ～にむせぶ weep in silence.

い

い【医】 medicine. ¶ ～を業とする practice *medicine*; be a physician. ～は仁術なり *Medicine* is a benevolent art.

い【胃】 the stomach. ¶ ～が弱い (じょうぶだ) I have *a* weak (strong) *stomach*. ～が悪い I have *stomach* trouble. ～が痛む I have *a stomachache*. それは～に悪い It is bad for the *stomach*. それは～にもたれる It will lie on your *stomach*. 食べすぎて～をこわした I injured my *stomach* by eating too much.
―液 gastric juice. ―炎 gastritis. ―潰瘍(かいよう) a gastric ulcer. ―拡張 gastric dilation. ―下垂 gastroptosis. ―カタル gastric catarrh. ―カメラ a gastrocamera.

—がん a stomach cancer. —酸過多 acid dyspepsia. —病 a stomach disease.

い【異】 ¶ ～を立てる(変わったことを言う) say something uncommon; (反対する) take objection (*to*). これは～なことをおっしゃる I can't understand you. そんなことは～とするに足らぬ You don't have to even understand.

い【意】 **1** 〚考え・好み〛 an opinion; a mind; a liking. ¶ きみの意見はわが～にかなっている Your opinion agrees with mine.

それはわが～にかなっている(好みに合う) It is to my *liking*.

～のあるところをくんでください Please consider well *what I mean*.

彼はついに～を決した He *made up his mind* at last.

わが～を得たり That's it. / That's exactly *what I mean*!

万事～のごとくいった Everything turned out *as I wished*.

彼の～を受けて彼女を訪ねた I called on her in compliance with his *will*.

きみは～を尽くして説明しなければならない You must explain *fully* what you have in mind.

2 〚意志〛 〔a〕 will. ¶ 何事においてもきみの～のままにふるまうというわけにはいかない You cannot *have your own way* in everything.

彼は両親の～に背いて彼女と結婚した He married her against the *will* of his parents.

3 〚心・気持ち〛 ¶ 遺憾の～を表明する express *one's* regret; say that *one* is sorry.

それを聞いて～を強くした I *was encouraged* to hear it.

4 〚注意〛 attention. ¶ ～を用いる pay *attention* (*to*); be careful about.

彼らがなんと言おうとぼくはまったく～に介さぬ I don't *care* at all what they say.

5 〚意義〛 a meaning; a sense.

い【威】 (威厳) dignity; (権威) authority. ¶ ～のある imposing; dignified. ～をふるう exercise *one's authority* (*over*). ～あって猛(たけ)からず He *is dignified* but not imposing. とらの～をかるきつね(諺) the ass in the lion's skin.

-い【-位】 ¶ 上～3チーム the three best teams. 第1(2)～を占める take first (second) *place*; *rank* first (second). その地方はダイヤモンドの産額では世界第1～を占めている The district ranks first in the world as regards the output of diamond. 彼は3～に落ちた He dropped to the third 〔place〕.

いあつ【威圧】 overpowering; coercion. ¶ 彼に～された I *was overpowered* by him.

いあわ・せる【居合わせる】 ¶ たまたまその場に～せた I *happened to be* there. / I *was* there *by chance*. ～せた人々はみな深く感動した All those *present* were deeply moved.

いあん【慰安】 (慰め) comfort; consolation; (気晴らし) 〔a〕 recreation. ¶ 店員を～する give *comfort* to *one's* employees.

—旅行 a recreation trip (この種の旅行は英米では行なわれない). —会 a recreation meeting. —設備 recreation facilities.

いい【良い・善い・好い】 **1** 〚善い〛 good; nice. ¶ その行ないは～いとはいえぬ That conduct cannot be said to *be good* (≒ *be acceptable*).

ふだんの行ないが～いからね It's because I know how to behave.

～いお友だちをお持ちですね You have a *nice* friend. / You are lucky to have such a *good* friend.

坊やは～い子だから，おとなしくしてね That's a *good* boy. Keep still, won't you?

2 〚優秀な〛 good. ¶ これは品が～い This is of *good* quality.

彼は頭が～い He *is* 〔quite〕 *smart*.

ぼくは今学期は～い成績をとった I *did well* at school this term.

坊やは聞き分けが～いね Aren't you a *good* boy? / My! You're a *good* boy.

彼女は気立てが～い She is of *loving* disposition.

3 〚美しい・快適な〛 beautiful; fine; pleasant. ¶ きょうは～い天気だ It's a *beautiful* (≒ *fine*) day today.

～い湯だな The bath *is* just *fine*.

バラの香りが～い The roses smell *sweet*.

久しぶりに旅に出て～い気分だった It *was pleasant* to take a trip after such a long time.

彼女は器量が～い She is *good*-looking. / She is *a beauty*.

彼は男前が～い He *is handsome*.

4 〚時機・状況に適している〛 good; right. ¶ どうすれば～いんだ What should I do? / What am I supposed to do?

こうやれば～いのだ This is the way to do it.

～い考えがある I have a *good* idea.

なにか～い知恵はないかね Can't you give me some *good* advice?

そいつは～いや That'll *be splendid*. / That'll *be* just *fine*.

ちょうど～いところに来てくれた You came just at the *right* moment.

つごうの～いとき来てください Please come when it'*s convenient to* (≒ *for*) you.

～い土地を見つけた I've found a *good* piece of land.

答えはこれで～いのか How is this answer? / *Will* this answer *do*?

5 〚…するがいい〛 ¶ 若いうちに苦労するが～い You *should* experience hardships when young. / It *is good* for you to experience hardships when young.

ぐっすり眠るが～い Have a good sleep.

6 〚…したほうがいい〛 ¶ きみはすぐ医者に行ったほうが～い You *had better* see a doctor at once.

そんなことはよしたほうが～い Don't do such a thing.

きみは体に気をつけたほうが～い You *ought to* take good care of yourself.

7 〚好む〛 ¶ ぼくはこっちのほうが～いな I *would rather* have this one.

どっちが～いかしら Which do you think is

better?
〜いようにしなさい Do as you like.
彼に〜いようにされたよ He did what he liked of me. / I was made a fool of [by him].
8 〚親しい〛 ¶ あの兄弟はみな仲が〜い The brothers *are* very much *attached* (≒ *close*) *to* one another.
9 〚十分な〛 enough. ¶ もう〜い, なにも言うな That'*s enough*. Keep quiet.
たったこれだけの金額で〜いのか Will this much money *be enough*?
そんなことで〜いのかな Is that *all right* (≒ 米 *O.K.*)?
もう支度は〜いか *Are* you *ready*?
10 〚役だつ〛 good; useful. ¶ 早起きは健康に〜い It'*s good for* the health to rise early.
マッサージは疲れをとるのに〜い A massage *helps* you recover from fatigue.
このフィルムは暗い場所を撮るのに〜い This film *is fine for* taking pictures in the dark.
この本は初歩の英語学習に〜い This book *is useful for* beginners of English.
〜いお話を伺いました. これで心も落ち着きます I'm glad to hear that. Now I feel relieved.
11 〚健康である〛 well. ¶ もうすっかり〜いのですか *Are* you quite *well* now?
きょうは体の調子が〜い I *feel well* today.
きょうは顔色も〜い You *look* (≒ *are looking*) *well* today. / You have a *good* complexion today.
元気の〜いお子さんですね What a *lively* boy [he is]!
12 〚めでたい〛 lucky; auspicious. ¶ きみは運が〜い You *are lucky* (≒ *are fortunate*).
これは縁起の〜い番号だ This is a *lucky* number.
ふたりは〜い日を選んで式を挙げた They chose an *auspicious* day for their wedding.
13 〚経済的にいい〛 ¶ 彼は景気が〜い He *is* doing very *well*.
ばかに景気が〜いようだね(比喩的) You look quite *prosperous*.
彼は近ごろはぶりが〜い He *is influential* these days. / He is now an *important* person.
彼はこのごろ金まわりが〜い Recently he *is well off*.
14 〚…しやすい〛 easy. ¶ この文章はわかり〜い It has an *easy* style.
飲み〜い薬です This medicine *is easy* to take.
15 〚差し支えない〛 ¶ ここでたばこを吸っても〜いのですか *May* (≒ *Can*) I smoke here?
ほんとに〜いのかね Are you sure *you don't mind* (≒ *it's all right*)? / Is it really *good*?
「そんなことをしても〜いのか」「ああ, 〜いとも」 "*Can* you do such a thing?" "Yes, sure."
いつ来ても〜いよ You *can* come any time [you like].
これは彼の最高の作といっても〜い This *could* be called his masterpiece.
そんなにまでしないでも〜い You *needn't* do that much.
金はすぐに返さなくても〜い You *don't have to* return the money immediately.
そんなにびくびくしなくても〜い You *needn't* be so nervous.
16 〚かまわない〛 ¶ どうなっても〜いんだ I *don't care* what happens. / Who cares what may happen?
なんと言われたって〜い I *don't care* what they say.
久しぶりだ. 〜いじゃないか, 一杯やろう It's a long time since we met last. *Come on*. Let's have a drink.
17 〚納得・承知する〛 ¶ それでほんとに〜いんだね You *are* quite *satisfied with* it, aren't you?
彼はそれでは〜いとは言うまい He won't *agree to* that. / He won't *say yes* for that.
18 〚…できればいいのだが〛 ¶ もっと金があれば〜いのだが *I wish I had* more money. / *I wish we had* more capital.
お助けできると〜いのですが *I wish I could* be of your help. / *I wish I could* help you.
もっと早く来れば〜いのに Why don't you come earlier?
19 〚その他〛 ¶ 〜いか, よく聞けよ *Now*, listen to me.
〜いとこ10万円に売れたらと思ってる I hope to get a hundred thousand yen for it *at best*.
ていの〜いことを言うな None of your lip service!
〜いご身分だね You are in *comfortable* (≒ *easy*) circumstances, aren't you?

いい 【唯唯】 ¶ 彼の援助が必要になったとき〜諾々として助けてくれた He *readily* came to my aid when I needed him.

いいあい 【言い合い】 a dispute; a quarrel. ¶ 彼は彼女と〜をした He *had a quarrel with* her. 境界線のことで隣の人と〜をした I *disputed* with neighbors over a boundary.

いいあ・う 【言い合う】 ¶ 政治について何時間も〜った We *disputed* over politics for hours.

いいあやまり 【言い誤り】 a slip of the tongue.

いいあらそ・う 【言い争う】 ¶ 私はそのことで彼女と〜った I *quarreled* with her about it.

いいあらわ・す 【言い表わす】 ¶ 〜し方 how to *express*. 自分の考えを〜す *express oneself*. 自分の考えをはっきりと〜しなさい *Express* your ideas clearly. / *Speak* your mind. 景色の美しさは〜すことができないほどである The scenery is beautiful beyond *description*.

いいあわ・せる 【言い合わせる】 make previous arrangements; arrange beforehand. ¶ 〜せたように as if by common consent.

いいえ ¶ 「あなたは車の運転ができますか」「〜, できません」 "Can you drive a car?" "*No*, I can't." (答えの文が肯定文のときは, 質問の文がどうであっても答えは Yes, 否定の場合は No を用いる). 「ゴルフはお好きではありませんか」「〜, 好きです」 "Don't you like golf?" "*Yes*, I like it." 「お茶をもう1杯いかがですか」「〜, もうけっこうです」 "Won't you have another cup of tea?" "*No*, thank you."「ありがとう」「〜」"Thank you". "You are quite welcome (≒ 圏 Don't mention it. / Not at all)."

いいお·く【言い置く】¶ 彼はぼくになにか〜いていきましたか Did he *leave* any *message* for me?

いいおく·る【言い送る】send word; send a message; write to (*a person*).

いいおとし【言い落とし】¶ なにか〜がないかしら *Have* I *left* anything *unsaid*?

いいおと·す【言い落とす】forget to say (≒ mention); leave unsaid.

いいがい【言い甲斐】¶ きみも〜があったわけだ You haven't talked in vain after all. 彼は〜のないやつだ He is a coward.

いいかえ·す【言い返す】¶ みんなが彼をなじったら, 彼はすぐ〜した He *retorted* quickly when they blamed him. 私のあとについて〜しなさい Please *repeat* these words after me.

いいか·える【言い替える】say in other words; put (*it*) in another way; change the wording. ¶ 〜えれば in other words; that is [to say].

いいかお【いい顔】(美貌) good-looking; (きげんのよい顔) a joyful (≒ cheerful) look; (顔がきく) a man of influence. ¶ 彼女は私の忠告を聞いて〜をしなかった She didn't *welcome* my advice.

いいがかり【言い掛かり】a false charge; a pretext. ¶ 〜をつけるな Don't *bring a false charge against* me. / Don't *accuse* me *falsely*. 彼はちょっとしたことにも〜をつけてけんかした He picked a quarrel on the slightest *pretext*.

いいかげん【好い加減】¶ 〜なことを言うな Don't *talk nonsense*. もう〜くたびれた I'm *pretty* tired. 彼はなんでも〜にしておく He leaves everything *half done*. 〜な返事をするな Don't give *irresponsible* answers. 冗談も〜にしてほしい None of your nonsense!

いいかた【言い方】¶ うまい〜 *a* good *expression*; *a* happy *way of expressing* an idea. 彼はものの〜を知らない He does not know the proper *way of speaking*. / He has no manners. ものの〜を慎みなさい Be careful in *speaking*. ぼくの〜が誤解の種だった My *way of saying* it was the cause of misunderstanding.

いいか·ねる【言い兼ねる】¶ なんとも〜ねる I don't know what to say.

いいかわ·す【言い交わす】¶ また会おうと〜して別れた We *promised* to meet again and parted. 彼らは〜した仲だ They *are* (≒ *have become*) *engaged* (≒ *plighted lovers*). / They *have plighted themselves to* each other.

いいき【いい気】self-complacency. ¶ 〜な(呑気な) easygoing; light-hearted; (得意) proud; vain; self-conceited. 彼が黙っているのにつけあがって〜になるな Don't *presume upon* his tolerance. そんなに〜になるな Don't *be* so *cheeky* (≒ *complacent*)! みんなに拍手されて彼は〜になった Their applause *puffed* him *up*.

いいきか·せる【言い聞かせる】¶ そんな赤ん坊に〜せようたってむだだ It is useless to *reason with* such an infant. 休みをとるよう彼に〜せた I *persuaded* him to take a holiday. 心配ないと彼に〜せた I *reasoned* him out of his fears. 彼は生徒に遅刻しないように〜せた He *told* (≒ *admonished*) the boys not to be late.

いいきみ【いい気味】¶ 〜だ That serves you (≒ him) right!

いいき·る【言い切る】¶ どっちとも〜れないな I couldn't say which is better (≒ more advisable).

いいぐさ【言いぐさ】(ことば) words; remarks; (口実) an excuse. ¶ 彼の〜ではないが to borrow his favorite *phrase*. 彼の〜が気に入らない I don't like *his words*. なんという〜だ How can you say so?

いいくる·める【言いくるめる】¶ 油断してはいけない. 彼は〜めるのがじょうずだから You must always be on the alert. He is such *a clever talker*.

いいこ【いい子】a good boy (≒ girl). ¶ 自分だけ〜になる gain credit at others' expense. 〜だから静かにしなさい Be quiet, that's (≒ there's) *a good boy* (≒ *girl*). 子どもたちは一日じゅう〜でした The children have been *good* all day.

いいこ·める【言い込める】¶ 〜められてたまるものか I won't *be talked down*. 彼は〜められて黙った He *was argued into* silence.

イージー ¶ 非常に〜な人間 a man who takes things too *easy*. 〜な考え *wishful* thinking; an *optimistic* view.

イージーオーダー semi-custom-made.

イージーペイメント payment by installment.

いいしぶ·る【言い渋る】hesitate to say; falter.

いいしれない【言い知れない】unspeakable; inexpressible; indescribable. ¶ 〜喜び *unspeakable* joy.

いいす·ぎる【言い過ぎる】¶ …と言っても〜ぎることはない *It is not too much* (≒ *no exaggeration*) *to say* that.... ちょっと〜ぎて悪かった I am sorry I *have put* it *too strong*.

いいす·てる【言い捨てる】¶ そう〜てて彼は部屋を出ていった So saying (≒ With these words), he went out of the room without waiting for an answer.

イースト yeast. ¶ 固形〜 *yeast* cake.

イーゼル an easel.

いいそこない【言い損い】a slip of the tongue.

いいそび·れる【言いそびれる】¶ 言うつもりだったが〜れた I intended to tell him, but I *hadn't the heart to* do so.

いい·たす【言い足す】add; make an additional remark.

いいだ·す【言い出す】¶ 彼がそう〜したのだ He *was the first to say* so. 私についてそんな悪口を〜したのは彼だ He *started talking* that sort of scandal about me. 彼女はその計画を変えようと〜した She *proposed* to change the plan.

～した以上あとには引けない I cannot withdraw now that I have said it. 彼がまずその言いにくいことをあえて～した He *broke the ice* in the delicate matter. そのことを～すのは気がひけた I found it hard to *broach* the matter.

いいた·てる【言い立てる】¶ 囚人は無罪であると～てた The prisoner *asserted* (≒ *declared*) that he was innocent. / The prisoner *pleaded* not guilty. 盗んだ女性は貧乏であるからと～てた The woman who stole *pleaded* poverty.

いいちが·える【言い違える】¶ 彼は～えた He *made a slip of the tongue*.

いいちら·す【言い散らす】¶ 彼女はいつも好きかってなことを～す She always *makes irresponsible remarks*.

いいつく·す【言い尽くす】¶ ～せない喜び *unspeakable* joy. ～せない苦しみ *indescribable* suffering. 彼は知っていることを～した He *told all* he knew. ご親切はことばでは～せません I have no words to *express* my gratitude. それは一言では～せない It cannot *be summed up* in a word. 英語では思っていることが～せない I cannot *express myself fully* in English.

いいつくろ·う【言い繕う】¶ 失敗を～う *gloss over* (≒ *explain away*) a mistake.

いいつけ【言いつけ】an order; orders (ふつう複数形で用いられる). ¶ 目上の者の～に従いなさい Obey your elders' *orders*.

いいつ·ける【言い付ける】¶ ～けられたとおりにせよ Do as you *are told*. ぼくにああしろこうしろと～けるな Don't *tell* me what to do. 彼はそのことを彼女に～けた He *told* her about it.

いいつた·える【言い伝える】¶ 真夜中になると幽霊がそこに出ると～えられている Tradition *says* (≒ *runs*) that a ghost appears there at midnight. これがその地方で昔から～えられている伝説だ This is the legend *handed down by word of mouth* in that province since old days. そう彼に～えてください Please *tell* him so. よろしく彼女に～えてください *Give my best regards to* her. すぐ行くと彼に～えてください *Send* him *word* that I will be there soon.

いいとお·す【言い通す】¶ そのことについてはなにも知らないとあくまで～した I *insisted* that I did not know anything about it.

いいとし【いい年】¶ 彼は～だ He *is pretty old*. / He *is well advanced in years*. 彼は～をしてなんということか He ought to know better *at his age*. ～を(幸福な新年を)〔I wish you〕A Happy New Year!

いいなお·す【言い直す】(訂正する) correct; (再び言う, 換言する) restate.

いいなか【いい仲】(親しい交友関係) on good (≒ intimate) terms; (愛し合う) in love. ¶ 彼は私の妹と～だ He *is in love with* my sister.

いいなずけ【許嫁】*one's* betrothed; (男) *one's* fiancé; (女) *one's* fiancée. ¶ 彼女は私の～である She *is engaged to* me.

いいならわし【言い習わし】(言い伝え) tradition; a common saying; (慣用)〔a〕usage; an idiom. ¶ …という～がある It is traditionally said that....

いいなり【言いなり】¶ ～になる人 a *yes* man. 人の～になる at *a person's* beck and call; under *a person's* thumb. 彼の～になる秘書がいる He has a secretary *at his beck and call*.

いいにく·い【言いにくい】¶ ～いことだが言いましょう I must tell you this, though I find it *hard to bring* it *up*. みんなの前では～い話だ It is a matter *too delicate* (≒ *awkward*) *to discuss* in public. 彼女は～そうに話を切りだした She began to talk about it *hesitatingly*.

いいぬけ【言い抜け】an excuse. ¶ 彼は～がうまい He is good at *making excuses*.

いいぬ·ける【言い抜ける】¶ こんな失敗を～けることができると思うか Can you *make any excuse for* (≒ *explain away*) such an error? 私はこの苦境を～けられた I could *talk myself out of* the difficulty.

いいね【言い値】¶ ～でそれを買いましょう I will pay the price you ask for it.

いいのが·れる【言い逃れる】¶ この場をどう～れたものかな What *excuse* shall I *make* to get over the difficulty?

いいのこ·す【言い残す】¶ 彼はそう～して立ち去った *Leaving a message* to that effect, he went away. 彼はまたそれを～した He *left* it *untold* again.

いいはな·つ【言い放つ】¶ やるならやってみろと彼は～った He *spoke boldly*, "Do it if you dare!"

いいは·る【言い張る】insist. ¶ 彼は無罪だと～っていた He *insisted* that he was innocent. 彼はひとりでそこへ行くと～っている He *insists on* going there alone.

いいひと【いい人】(りっぱな人物) a good man; (好人物) a good-natured man; (恋人) a lover (単数のとき男); a love (主として女, ときには男); a sweet-heart (女). ¶ 彼女には～ができた She has〔won〕*a lover*.

いいひらき【言い開き】vindication; justification; an excuse.

いいひろ·める【言い広める】¶ うわさを～める *spread* a rumor.

いいふく·める【言い含める】¶ 前もって十分～めておかないと彼はなにを言いだすかわからない He may speak anything, if we don't *give* him *full instructions* beforehand. もうそのことは彼に～めてありますからご心配はありません You need not worry, since I *have carefully told* him about it already. そのことは十分注意するようにと～めておいた I *gave* him *an instruction* to be very cautious of it. / I *instructed* him to be very cautious of it.

いいふら·す【言いふらす】spread. ¶ 彼はそのニュースを～した He *spread* the news. 彼は新しい学校がここに建てられるというわさを～した He *spread* (≒ *started*) the rumor that a new school would be built here.

いいふるした【言い古した】old; hackneyed; worn-out; stale.

いいふる·す【言い古す】¶ …と昔から～されている *It is proverbially said* that.... ～されたことば

a *worn-out* saying ; a *hackneyed* phrase.

いいぶん【言い分】(不平) a complaint ; (主張) *one's* say. ¶ 遅れたことに対するきみの～を聞こう Give me your *excuses* (≒ *account*) for being late. 彼の～を聞こう Let him have *his say*. 双方に相当の～がある There is *much to be said* on both sides. ～のない(満足な) perfect ; faultless.

いいまか・す【言い負かす】¶ 彼女の議論に～された I *was talked down* by her argument.

いいまぎら・す【言い紛らす】¶ その話をする際彼は自分の行動について～した In reporting the event, he didn't refer to his actions clearly.

いいまわし【言い回し】an expression. ¶ うまい～が思いつかない I can't think of any suitable *expression* for this. ぼくの～が誤解を生んだ My *manner of speaking* caused misunderstanding.

いいもら・す【言い漏らす】¶ なにか～したことはありませんか Is there anything you *have left unsaid*? 一つたいせつなことを～していた I *forgot to mention* an important matter.

いいよう【言い様】¶ それはきみの～が悪いからだ That is all because you are careless in *speech*. ものも～で角が立つ (諺) Smooth words make smooth ways.

いいよ・る【言い寄る】woo (*a person*) ; make amorous advances (*to a person*).

いいわけ【言い訳】**1** 〖弁解〗〔an〕excuse. ¶ 彼が学校へ遅刻した～は目覚ましが鳴らなかったということだ His *excuse* for coming late to school is that the alarm did not go off.
彼は失敗してもけっして～をしない Though he fails, he never *explains*.
きみのそのまちがいをなんと～するね How do you *explain* your mistake?
それは苦しい～だね That's *a* poor *excuse*.
彼のなした過ちは～がたたない The error he made *is* not *excusable*.
ぼくにはなんとも～がたたない I cannot *defend myself*. / I have no *excuse* for it.
彼は病気だったという～をした He *pleaded* illness.
～がましいからぼくはなにも言わなかった I didn't say anything, for it would have sounded *a* poor *excuse*.
2 〖謝罪〗an apology. ¶ 別に～をする必要はありません There is no need to *apologize* for it.

いいわたし【言い渡し】(命令) an order ; a command ; (通告) an announcement ; (判決) a sentence.
¶ 彼は窃盗により5年の刑の～を受けた He *was sentenced to* five years in prison for theft. / The judge passed *sentence* of five years in prison upon him for theft.

いいわた・す【言い渡す】¶ 裁判官は彼に5年の懲役を～した The judge *sentenced* him to five years in prison. / The judge *passed sentence* of five years in prison upon him. 彼は死刑を～された He *was sentenced* to death. 医者は彼に寝ているように～した The doctor *ordered* (≒ *told*) him to stay in bed.

いいん【医院】a doctor's office ; 英 a surgery. ¶ 清水～ *Dr*. Shimizu's *Office*.

いいん【委員】a member of a committee ; a committeeman ; (政府任命の) a commissioner. ¶ ～に選ばれる(任命される) be elected (≒ appointed) *a member of a committee*.
～をつとめている sit (≒ be) on *a committee*.
～会を通過する pass through the *committee*.
～付託の案件 a bill referred (≒ submitted) to *a committee*.
—長 the chairman of a committee. 運営**—**会 a steering committee. 執行**—**会 an executive committee. 常任**—**会 a standing committee. 政府**—** a government commissioner (committee はふつう単数に扱われるが, 委員会の構成員を中心に考えるときは複数とみなされる).

い・う【言う】**1** 〖言う・告げる〗say ; tell. ¶ そんなことは～うな Don't *say* such a thing.
だれがそんなことを～った Who *said* such a thing?
彼は来月結婚すると～った He *said* that he was going to be married next month.
彼はぼくのことをうそつきと～った He *called* me a liar.
そんなことはよせと彼はぼくに～った He *told* me not to do such a thing.
ぼくの～ったとおりにしたか Did you do as I *told* you?
彼にも～うに～われぬ悩みがあったのだ He too suffered *inexpressibly*.
きみがぼくに先日～った店はこの店か Is this the shop you *told* me of the other day?
それは～わないでおきたまえ You had better leave it *unsaid*.
きみの気持ちは～わないでもわかっている I understand your feeling without your *telling* me.
～うだけやぼだ It goes without *saying*. / It is needless to *say*.
～うはやすく行なうはかたし Easier *said* than done.
あいまいなことを～わず真実を～え *Tell* the truth without *speaking* ambiguously.
2 〖表現する・描写する〗¶「おはよう」を英語ではなんと～うか What is the English for "Ohayo"?
なんとも～えぬいい香りがした There was an *inexpressibly* sweet smell.
よく～えば変人, 悪く～えば狂人だ To *put* it mildly he is an odd fellow ; to *put* it harshly he is a mad man.
3 〖主張する・意見や本心を言う〗¶ ～いたいだけ～ってさっぱりした Now I *have had my say*, I feel the easier for it.
彼は一度～いだしたらあとへ引かない He does not yield an inch, if he *has* once *declared* his intention.
ぼくにもひと言～わせてもらいたい Let me *say* a word.
今となってはなにも～うことはない It is now too late to *say* anything.
そのことについては～いたいことはいくらでもある There

are a lot of things I want to *say* about it.

とてもそんなことを～える義理じゃない I could never bring myself to *say* such a thing.

彼もなかなか～うね Just listen to him. / What a thing to say?

いったいきみはなにを～いたいのだ What on earth do you want to *say*?

断わると～うのか Am I to understand that you refuse?

4 〖忠告する・議論する・批判する・非難する〗 ¶ 彼にこれ以上～ってもむだだ It is no use *giving* him more *advice*.

だからそう～ったじゃないか That is why I *said* so.

いくら～っても彼はきかない It is no use *advising* him (≒ *giving* him *advice*).

彼はぼくの～うことをすなおに受け入れた He followed my *advice* obediently.

なかなか～うことをきかぬ子だね The child *is* very *independent*.

今更ああだこうだ～ってもどうにもならぬ It is no longer of any use to *talk* about it.

別に～うことはない，りっぱな成績だ There is nothing to *complain of* in particular; it is an excellent school record.

5 〖仲介する〗 ¶ そのことについてひと言きみから彼に～ってもらうと助かるのだが A single word from you [to him] about it will be of great help to me.

きみのことはぼくから彼に～ってあげよう I will *put in a good word* to him for you (≒ on your behalf).

6 〖うわさをする〗 ¶ だれも彼のことはよく～う(悪く～う) Everybody *speaks well* (*ill*) *of* him.

世間では彼の今度の作品をなんと～うだろう What will people *say* about his new work?

近く大地震があると～われている *People say* (≒ *It is said*) that there will be a great earthquake before long.

7 〖呼称する〗 ¶ その本の題名はなんと～いますか What is the title of the book?

留守中に田中さんと～う人が来た A Mr. Tanaka called on you while you were out.

日本は東洋のイギリスと～われる Japan *is called* the England of the East.

彼は学者と～うより教育者だ He is not so much a scholar as an educator. / He is more [of] an educator than a scholar. / He is an educator rather than a scholar. (「学者」らしくないという意味がかなり強く感じられる).

8 〖慣用的表現〗 ¶ 窓と～う窓から皆手を振って彼の帰還を歓迎した They gave him a welcome on his return, waving their hands out of *every* window.

～うまでもないがこれは秘密だ It is needless to *say* that this is a secret.

皆が反対したのは～うまでもない *It goes without saying* (≒ *It need scarcely be said*) that all disagreed.

彼の名は国内は～うに及ばず世界じゅうに知られている His name is known *not only* at home, *but also* abroad. / His name is known abroad *as well as* at home.

ぼくをまぬけだと～わんばかりの口ぶりだった He *talked* to me *as if* I were stupid.

もう年で体が～うことをきかない I am helpless, as I have grown old.

そう～えばぼくにも思いあたるふしがある That reminds me of something I heard.

野球と～えば彼のことを思い出す *Talking of* baseball, I think of him.

～うなればぼくがばかだった You *might say* I was a fool.

～ってみれば彼にだまされたわけだ If one might so *put* it (≒ As one might *say*), I was cheated by him.

～われてみればもっともだ I admit the truth of what you *say*.

9 〖譲歩…とはいえ〗 ¶ そうは～っても今更計画を変更できない Even if you *say* so, it is now too late to change the plan.

年はとったとは～え，まだそれぐらいの仕事はできる I may have grown old, but I am still equal to that sort of work.

そうは～うものの，ぼくもびくびくしていた I was, however, afraid.

10時だと～うのにまだ彼は出社していない It is already ten and he still has not come to the office.

そう～ったってぼくにできないものはできない Still, what I can't do, I can't do.

10 〖同格…という〗 ¶ 彼が当日欠席したと～う事実にまちがいはない There is no mistake in the fact *that* he was absent on that day.

結局はよそうと～うことになった After all we have decided to give up.

別にこれと～った決まりはない There is no particular rule.

試合に負けたからと～って，別にどうと～うことはない Even if we lose the game it doesn't matter.

ガチャンと～う音がしてガラス戸が壊れた A glass door broke with a crash.

11 〖…といい…といい〗 ¶ 学識と～い人物と～い彼は申し分ない He is perfect *both* in learning *and* character.

図案と～い色彩と～いみごとなものだ It is splendid *both* in the design *and* the color.

いえ【家】 a house. **1** 〖家屋〗 a house. ¶ かわらぶきの～ *a* tile-roofed *house*.

鉄筋２階建ての～ *a* ferroconcrete two-story *house*.

建て売りの～を買った I bought *a* ready-built *house*.

彼は郊外に～を建てた He had *a house* built in the suburbs.

その～を月３万円で借りている I rent the *house* for 30,000 yen a month.

2 〖自宅・家庭・家族・一家〗 ¶ ～に帰る途中で彼女に会った I met her on my way *home*.

彼の～にやっかいになっています I live on his hospitality. / I live (≒ lodge) under his care.

彼女はその～に住み込み，家事見習いをしている She lives in the *house* learning household affairs.

ぼくは彼の〜に長いこと居候をしていた I used to be dependent on him for a long time.

〜に２匹ペルシア ネコを飼っています We keep two Persian cats *at home*.

寒いので〜にこもりがちだ I *stay at home* most of the time as it is so cold. / I'm inclined to *stay indoors* because of the cold. / I am apt to *be confined to my house* on account of the cold weather.

〜に帰ってゆっくり休みなさい *Go home* and take (≒ have) a good rest.

きょうは午前中は〜におります Today I will *be at home* in the morning.

彼女はいつも〜をあけている She *is* always *out*. / She *is* hardly ever *at home*.

彼は去年３月〜を持った He *got married and settled down* last March.

彼は20歳のとき〜を飛び出した He *ran away from home* (≒ *left home*) at the age of twenty.

彼は事業に失敗し〜を畳んで故郷に帰った As he failed in his business, he shut up his *house* to return to his hometown.

ぼくの〜の留守をしてくれないか Will you look after the *house* while I'm out?

きょうは〜の者はだれもおりません None of my *folks* are in (≒ at home) today.

〜の者はみな元気でおります All my *family* are quite well.

あの人の〜ではいつもなにかごたごたがある His *family* is constantly (≒ continually) in trouble. / He is always in trouble *at home*.

その間彼は〜から一歩も出なかった During that time he never stepped out of the *house*.

3 〘家系〙 a family. ¶あの人の〜は代々お医者です His *family* have been doctors for generations.

そんなことをすると〜の名を汚すことになる Such behavior will be a disgrace to our *family*.

彼は貧しい〜の出だ He is of *a* poor *family*. / He comes from *a* poor *family*.

いえ no.

いえがら【家柄】birth. ¶彼は〜がよい(悪い) He *is of* good (humble) *birth*. 彼女は〜のよいのを自慢している She is proud of her good *birth*.

いえじ【家路】a homeward trip; *one's* way home. ¶ぼくらは連れだって〜をたどった We *made our way homeward* together.

イエス yes. ¶この計画についてきみは彼の〜は取ってあるのか Do you have his *yes* to this plan? 答えは〜かノーかだ The answer is a plain "yes" or "no."

イエス=キリスト Jesus Christ.

イエスマン a yes man.

いえつき【家付き】¶〜の娘 an heiress; a daughter of the house.

いえで【家出】¶〜する leave home; run away from home.

—人 a runaway [person].

いえども【雖も】¶老いたりと〜彼は相変わらず元気だ *Though* he is old, he is as strong as ever. 愚か者と〜そのくらいはわかる *Even* a fool knows that. 当たらずと〜遠からず Your guess is not quite right, nor is it wide of the mark. / It is not very far from the mark.

千万人と〜われ行かん I am determined to fight against any powerful enemy.

いえのころうどう【家の子郎等】*one's* followers.

いえもと【家元】(芸能の宗家) the head master (of a school); (実家) *one's* parents' home. ¶藤間流の〜 *the head master* of the 'Fujima' school of Japanese dancing.

いえやしき【家屋敷】*one's* house and lot.

い·える【癒える】get well.

いおう【硫黄】〘化学〙 sulfur; sulphur. ¶この水は〜くさい The water smells of *sulfur*.

—華 flowers of sulfur. —泉 a sulfur spring.

いおと·す【射落とす】shoot down (a bird).

いおり【庵】a hermitage; a hut. ¶〜を結ぶ build *a hermitage*; live in *a hut* in solitude; (世を避ける) seclude *one*self.

イオン 〘化学〙 ion. ¶〜化する ionize.

陰— anion; a negative ion. 陽— cation; a positive ion.

いか【以下】**1** 〘より下位〙 ¶０度〜になってもその液体は凍らなかった The liquid didn't freeze even *below* zero.

室温を５度〜に保ちなさい Keep the temperature of the room *below* five degrees.

山腹の1,000メートル〜は原生林でおおわれている The mountainside *below* 1,000 meters is thick (≒ is covered) with wild forests.

３階〜はエレベーターが止まりません The elevator doesn't stop *below* the third floor.

３けた〜の数は四捨五入すること The figure should be rounded to three units.

50点〜は不合格 Those *below* 50 marks are disqualified.

この病気は10歳〜の児童がかかりやすい Children *under* ten are liable to suffer from this disease.

隊長〜一兵卒に至るまで自決した All men *from* the captain *down to* the private killed themselves.

2 〘それよりあと〙 ¶〜同文 Same as above.

〜10ページに続く Continued on page 10.

〜次号 To be continued.

〜省略 *Rest* [is] omitted.

〜は補足的説明です *Below* is a supplementary explanation.

詳しくは52ページ〜を参照 For further details refer to page 52 *and on*.

応募手続きは〜のとおり Application procedures are *as follows*.

いか【烏賊】a cuttlefish; (ヤリイカ) a squid (集合的にはいずれも単複同形). ¶〜は襲われると墨を吐く *A cuttlefish* sends out black liquid when attacked.

いか【医科】the medical department; the school (≒ department) of medicine. ¶〜の学生 a *medical* student.

い

—大学 a medical college.

いかい【位階】 rank; court rank.

—勲等 court ranks and honors.

いがい【以外】1〚以外に〛 except; besides; save; but; excepting.

¶ 日曜日～にご在宅の日はおありでしょうか Are you at home any other day *besides* Sunday?

これ～に手の打ちようがありません There is nothing else to be done *than* (≒ *besides*) this. / There is no other means *but* this.

これ～になにか本日の議題はありますか Is there *anything else* to discuss today?

事故の原因はそれ～に考えられない We can't think of anything *besides* that as the cause of the accident. / The cause of the accident cannot be thought of *anything else* than that.

それ～にもまだまだ言いたいことがあったんだ I had other things I wanted to tell you *besides* that.

彼～にはそんなことをする人は思いあたらない I can't think of anyone *except* (≒ *but*) him who would do such a thing.

彼はその土地～にもあちこちに不動産を持っている *In addition to* that land, he has other real property in many places.

2〚以外の〛 ¶ 規則に定められた～のことはするな Don't do anything *except* what the rule permits you to do. / Nothing should be done against the regulations.

まだまだそれ～のぼくに言えぬ秘密があるんだろう You still have lots of other things to keep secret from me, don't you?

本学学生教職員～の無断入館お断わり No admittance without leave *except* faculty and students of this school.

関係者～の立入禁止 No trespassing *except* persons concerned.

いがい【意外】 ¶ ～な unexpected; surprising. ～に unexpectedly; contrary to *one's* expectation. その知らせはまったく～だ The news *is* quite *unexpected to* me. あの人が約束を破るとは～だ I *little expected* that he should break his promise. あそこで彼女に会うとは～だった She was the last person I [had] expected to see there. ～な結果に終わった The result *was* quite *contrary to my expectation*. 彼の到着は～に早いだろう He will arrive *earlier than is expected*. ～にも彼は失敗した *To my surprise* he failed. 事の～さに驚いた This is quite a *surprising* event.

いがい【遺骸】 remains; a dead body; a corpse. ¶ 彼の～はきのう近所の寺院に運ばれた His *corpse* was carried to a near-by temple yesterday.

いかが【如何】1〚どのように〛(相手の意向・感情・健康等を尋ねて) ¶ ～いたしましょうか *What* shall I do with this? / *What* shall be done about this?

～とりはからいましょうか *How* shall I deal with this? / *How* shall I manage this?

お芝居は～でした *How* did you like the play?

東京の印象は～です *What* is your impression of Tokyo?

その後～お暮らしですか *How* are you getting along? / *How* have you been?

2〚相手にすすめる〛 ¶ もう一つお茶を～ですか *How* would you like to have another cup of tea?

明日そこへお出かけになっては～ですか *How about* going there tomorrow? / *Would*[*n't*] it suit you to go there tomorrow? / Why not go there tomorrow?

いかがわし・い ¶ ～い人物 a *dubious* character. ～い場所 a *disreputable* place. ～い歌 an *indecent* song.

いかく【威嚇】 a threat; [a] menace. ¶ ～的なことば *threatening* words. 彼の態度にはどことなく～的なところがある He has something *overbearing* in his manner. 彼らはピストルで～された They *were menaced* with a revolver.

—射撃 ¶ 彼に～射撃をした I *fired warning shots* at him.

いがく【医学】 medical science; medicine.

—界 the medical world. **—士** Bachelor of Medicine (M.B.). **—博士** Doctor of Medicine (M.D.). **—部** the department of medicine.

いかさま (偽物) a fraud; a swindle; (不良品) worthless goods.

—師 a swindler. **—ばくち** a prearranged gambling.

いか・す ¶ 彼は～す格好で現われた He appeared *stylishly* dressed. 彼は自分では～しているつもりなんだ He looks on himself as *a dandy*. まったく～すね How *wonderful*!

いか・す【生かす】 ¶ 彼はお金を～して使うすべを知らない He does not know how to *make good use of* his money. 彼は経営学の知識を～して使えない He cannot *put* his knowledge of industrial administration *to practical use*. そのこん虫は10日以上～しておくことはできない We cannot *keep* the insect *alive* more than ten days.

いかぞく【遺家族】 a bereaved family.

いかだ【筏】 a raft. ¶ ～で運ぶ carry (something) on *a raft*. ～で流れを下る(渡る) go down (cross) the stream on *a raft*.

いがた【鋳型】 a mold; 英 a mould. ¶ 学生を一つの～にはめるのは感心できない We do not think it right to *mold* students *into* one and the same pattern.

—師 a caster; a molder.

いかつ・い【厳い】 (いかめしい) stern; grave; (ぶこつな) rough; rude. ¶ ～い顔つき *stern* looks. ～い(ぶこつな)態度 *rough* manners.

いかなる【如何なる】 ⇒どんな

いかに【如何に】 ¶ この問題を～解決すべきか I wonder *how* we should solve this problem. ～努力しても彼の成功は無理だ *However* hard he tries, he will never succeed.

いかにも【如何にも】1〚なるほど〛 ¶ それは～彼が言いそうなことだ It's *just* like him to say so.

〜彼は年は若いが思慮は深い *Indeed* (≒ *It is true*) he is young, *but* he is prudent.

2 〚あたかも〛 ¶ 彼は〜事件の真相を知っているような口ぶりだ He speaks *as if* he knew the actual state of the affair.

3 〚ほんとうに〛 ¶ おおせ〜(まったく)ごもっともです You are right, *indeed*.

その事故は〜お気の毒です I'm *heartily* sorry for the accident.

いかほど【如何程】¶ それは〜ですか *How much* is it? 〜努力しても彼の成功はおぼつかない *However hard* he may try, he cannot hope for success.

いがみあ･う【いがみ合う】¶ 彼らはいつも〜っている They *are* always *quarreling with* each other. あの夫婦はどうしていつも〜ってばかりいるのだろう I wonder why that couple *are* always *quarreling*. あの3人の女性たちはまた〜いを始めた Those three women began to *quarrel* again.

いかめし･い【厳しい】¶ なんという〜い顔つきだろう How *stern* (≒ *severe*) he looks!

いかもの【如何物】a false article; a fake; a sham; (米俗語) a phony.

―食い a gross feeder; a man of eccentric (≒ abnormal) taste in food.

いから･せる【怒らせる】¶ ぐれん隊が肩を〜せて通りを歩いていた Hooligans *were swaggering* about the street.

いかり【怒り】anger; (激怒) rage; fury; (義憤) indignation. ¶ 〜に燃えて in *a rage* (≒ *fury*). 彼は〜を抑えることができなかった He was unable to restrain his *anger*. 彼女は〜を顔に表わさなかった Her face did not show any *anger*. 彼は〜にわれを忘れた He was beside himself with *anger*. 〜のあまり彼は花びんをぶちこわした In his *fury* he broke the vase. 彼の声は〜で震えていた His voice was trembling with *rage*. 〜肩の女 a square-shouldered woman.

いかり【錨・碇】an anchor. ¶ 〜をおろす drop *anchor*. 〜をあげる weigh *anchor*. 船は〜をおろしている(停泊している) The ship *is at anchor*. / The ship *is lying at anchor*.

いか･れる ¶ 〜れたやつ a *frivolous* fellow. あいつは頭が少し〜れているようだ He *is* a little *touched* in the head. あの男はどことなく〜れている There is something *flippant* about him.

いかん【移管】transfer. ¶ われわれの部〔の仕事〕は教育部に〜された Our department *was transferred to* the care of the department of education.

いかん【偉観】a grand sight; a magnificent view; a fine spectacle. ¶ すばらしい〜だ What *a grand* (≒ *great*) *sight*! 邸宅はすばらしい〜を呈している That mansion presents *a grand sight*.

いかん【遺憾】〔a〕regret. ¶ 彼が来られないのは〜なことだ *It is a matter for regret that* (≒ *It is to be regretted that*) he should not come. 〜の意を表します I heartily express my *regret*. 〜ながら彼は失敗しました *To my regret* he failed. 〜ながらそれは事実として認めざるをえない I cannot but admit, *though with much regret*, that it is a fact. 彼は〜なく実力を発揮した He used his ability *to the fullest extent*.

いかん【如何】¶ それは〜ともしがたい It can't be helped. / There's no help for it. それは方法〜による It depends upon how to do it. 結果〜は予測できない I cannot foretell what the result will be. 〜せん金がない *To my regret*, I have no money.

いがん【依願】¶ 彼は〜免官となった He was dismissed *at his own request*.

いき【域】¶ その案はまだ試験の〜を脱していない The plan is still in the trial (≒ experimental) *stage*. その計画は実行の〜に達した The plan has now reached the *stage* to be carried out. 彼のゴルフはプロの〜に達している He has a professional's skill in golf. 彼の権力は前人未踏の〜に達した He won an uncharted noman's land of power.

いき【息】**1** 〚呼吸〛 breath. ¶ バスが超満員で〜が詰まりそうだった I *was* almost *suffocated* in the overcrowded bus.

首を絞められ〜ができなかった I was choked and couldn't *breathe*.

病人は〜が苦しそうだった The sick person looked *short of breath*.

赤ん坊は高熱で〜が荒い The baby *is breathing hard* with a high fever.

速く走ったので〜が切れた I ran so fast that I was *out of breath*.

彼女の〜はもはやとだえていた She *was* no longer *breathing*.

救助されたときには彼はまだかすかに〜がかよっていた When he was rescued, he *was* still *breathing* faintly.

冷気で人の〜が白く見えた We saw a steam of *breath* in the cold.

虫歯で〜がくさい He has bad *breath* from a decayed tooth.

深く〜を吸って大きく吐く. 深呼吸始め *Breathe* in deeply and *breathe* out fully. Now begin.

彼はハアハア肩で〜をしていた He *was gasping* (≒ *was panting*) hard.

彼は酒くさい〜を吹きかけた He *breathed out* an alcoholic *breath on* me.

〜を凝らして隣室のようすをうかがった He *held his breath* and tried to find out the situation in the next room.

あまりのことに思わず〜をのんだ It was so shocking that it *took my breath away*.

1時間後に子どもは〜を吹き返した An hour later the child recovered its *breath*.

つい10分前に彼は〜を引き取った He *breathed his last* only ten minutes ago.

〜をころしてできるだけ長く水中に潜れ Keep (≒ Hold) your *breath*, and stay under water as long as possible.

〜を切らして彼はしゃべった He *gasped out* his words.

この英文を読むのにどこで～をついだらいいのですか Where should I *pause* in this English sentence?

～もつかずにビールを飲み干した He drank the beer *in one breath* (≒ *at a draft*).

～もつかずに彼はしゃべりまくった He talked and talked without *pausing for breath*.

～も絶え絶えに彼女は泣いた She cried *gasping for breath*.

2 〖慣用的表現〗 ¶ 忙しくて～つく暇もない I'm too busy to *take a rest*. / I'm so busy that I have hardly any *breathing spell*.

彼には社長の～がかかっている He *is backed up by* the president.

ふたりの～がぴったり合った They *were* simply *congenial with* each other.

あのふたりは～が合う The two are in *congenial* spirit.

ずいぶんと～の長い話だね What a slow business!

いき【粋】 ¶ ～な男(しゃれた服装の) a *chic* man. 彼女には～なところがある There is something *chic* about her. 彼はしきりに～がっている He is anxious to be thought a nice guy.

いき【意気】 ¶ その～, その～, おれがついてるぞ Go it! I'll help you. あの男の～には打たれた I was deeply moved by his firm *resolution*. 彼は～軒昂(けんこう)である He *is in high spirits*. 彼は～消沈している He *is in low spirits*. / He *is depressed*. 彼らは～投合している They *are in congenial spirits*. 彼らは～揚々と家路についた They left for home *triumphantly*.

いき【遺棄】 abandonment. ¶ 彼らは死体を～して逃げた *Leaving* the body *behind*, they ran away.

―死体 an abandoned corpse.

いき【生き】 ¶ ～のいい魚 a *fresh* fish.

いぎ【威儀】 dignity; solemnity. ¶ ～ある風貌 *dignified* appearance. ～を正して in a *dignified* manner.

いぎ【異議】(反対意見) an objection; (抗議) a protest; (不賛成) dissent.

¶ ～なく(満場一致で) without any *objection*; unanimously; with one accord. ～あり I have *an objection*. ～なし I have no *objection*. / No *objection*. 彼はその提案に～を申し立てた He took *objection* to the proposal.

いぎ【意義】 significance; meaning.

¶ ～のある significant. ～のない meaningless. その運動には政治的～はまったくない The movement has no political *significance*. 大学生活の～を考えたことがありますか Have you ever thought of the *significance* of your college life?

いきいきと【生き生きと】 ¶ 今は万物が～する季節だ This is the season when everything *becomes full of life*. 彼の顔つきは～している He looks *lively*. 彼女はその小説で彼女の故郷を～描き出した She gave a *vivid* description of her hometown in the novel. 彼は夜が明けると～してくる He *is refreshed* when day breaks. 彼の想像力は～している He has a *vivid* (≒ *lively*) imagination.

いきうつし【生き写し】 ¶ あの少女はまったく母親に～だ The girl *is the very picture of* her mother. この肖像画は彼に～だ This portrait of him *is true to the life*. / This portrait represents him *to the life*. / This is a *life-like* portrait of him.

いきうま【生き馬】 ¶ 彼は～の目を抜くような男だ He is a very cunning fellow. 東京は～の目を抜くような所だ Tokyo has a lot of shrewd operators.

いきうめ【生き埋め】 ¶ ～になる be buried alive. 雪崩で一行は～になった The snowslide *has buried* the party *alive*.

いきおい【勢い】 **1** 〖物理的な力〗 ¶ 水が～よくほとばしり出た Water *gushed out*. / Water flowed out *with a gush*.

風の～が弱まった The wind *has abated*.

潮の～が強く舟は沖へと流された The strong tide drifted the boat off the coast.

彼は猛烈な～でぼくに体当たりした He flung himself against me *furiously*. / He dashed against me *furiously*.

～余ってすってんころり I fell right down from spending too much *energy*. / I slipped right over from an excess of *energy*.

山道を駆けおりはじめたら～がついて止まらなくなった I began rushing down the mountain path and couldn't stop *with increased speed*.

2 〖元気・気力〗 ¶ ばかに～がいいね You are exceedingly *energetic* (≒ *lively*; *spirited*), aren't you?

もっと～よく声を張り上げろ Louder *with more spirit*! / Shout with a louder voice!

彼女のことばに～を得て彼は気を取り直して仕事に立ち向かった *Encouraged* by her words, he pulled himself together and set to work.

始めの～もどこへやら, こそこそ彼は逃げ去った Losing his initial *enthusiasm*, he sneaked away.

3 〖威勢・人を圧する力〗 ¶ 敵の～は侮りがたい We should not underrate the *force* of the enemy.

彼の運はまさに日の出の～だ Fortune favors him ungrudgingly. / He is lucky, one luck following another.

4 〖弾み・調子・なりゆき〗 ¶ 酔った～でついくだらぬことを言った Just because I was drunk, I talked nonsense.

その～でやれば1日でかたづく If you work at it so *hard* (≒ *energetically*), you'll be through in a day.

～のおもむくところいかなる事態になるか測りがたい Things are such that there is no telling what they will come to.

～に乗じて一挙に勝負をつけてしまえ Take advantage of the chance and fight it out at once.

これが事の～というものだ I would say this is the way things go.

いうなれば騎虎の～止むをえない Since we have made headway so far, there is no way but to go ahead.

い

いきおいこ·む【勢い込む】¶彼は～んでぼくの家に飛び込んできた He *dashed into* my house. 彼は～んで駆けつけた He *came dashing into* the room. ～んでいったいなんだ What happened that you should *be in such a hurry*?

いきがい【生き甲斐】¶～のある人生を送りたい I want to lead a life *worth living*. / I want to live a *worthy life*. 生活に～がない I have nothing to live for./ My life is not *worth living*. これこそ私の～だ This is what I live for.

いきかえ·る【生き返る】¶人工呼吸をしたら彼は～った By artificial respiration he *came to life* (≒ *was brought to life*). 水につければその花は～るだろう The flowers will *revive* in water. どんな名医でも死者を～らせることはできない No skilled physician can *bring* the dead *to life again*. ぼくは～った思いがした I *felt refreshed*.

いきぎれ【息切れ】¶太った人は～がする Fat men *pant for breath*. 彼女は～がひどいので腰をおろしてしまった She *was* so *out* (≒ *short*) *of breath* that she sat down.

いきぐるし·い【息苦しい】¶暑くて～かった It *was* hot and *stuffy*. 会議の～いふんい気に耐えられなかった I could not stand the *stuffy* atmosphere of the meeting. むっとする空気で～くなった The oppressive air *stifled* me. ～い沈黙が続いた A *suffocating* silence continued.

いきごみ【意気込み】(熱意) eagerness; enthusiasm; (決意) determination.
¶彼の～はたいへんなものだ He *is* firmly *determined* to do that. 彼はなにがなんでも行くのだとたいへんな～だ He *has determined* that nothing shall prevent him from going. 物すごい～で仕事にとりかかった He set to work *with unusual* (≒ *unusually great*) *enthusiasm*. 勝つ見込みもないのに，～だけはたいしたものだ He is unlikely to win, but he *is* amazingly *determined* to win.

いきご·む【意気込む】¶自分ひとりでやるんだと～んでいる He *is determined* to do it for himself. 彼は～んでいる He *is determined*. / He *is firmly resolved*.

いきさつ ¶事件の～はだれも知らない Nobody knows the *particulars* of the case. そのけんかには深い～がある There are some serious *causes* behind the quarrel.

いきじびき【生き字引】a walking dictionary.
¶彼はこの村の～だ He knows every place and thing of this village. 彼は～だ He is *a walking dictionary*. / He is *an encyclopedia*.

いきせきき·る【息せき切る】¶走者は～ってゴールに入った The runner reached the goal *breathlessly* (≒ *panting for breath*).

いきづかい【息遣い】¶患者は荒い～をしていた The patient *was breathing* hard (≒ short).

いきづま·る【息詰まる】¶蒸し暑い熱気で～りそうだ I *was smothering* in the sultry heat. / The sultry heat *was stifling* (≒*was smothering*) ～る試合 a *breath-taking* close game. 重苦しい空気で彼女は～る思いがした The oppressive air *stifled* her.

いきどお·る【憤る】¶彼はその不正に対して～った He *grew indignant at* the injustice.

いきとしいけるもの【生きとし生けるもの】all living things; all living creatures.

いきながら·える【生き長らえる】¶彼は90歳まで～えた He *lived* to be ninety. ～えて恥をかくより死んだほうがましだ I would rather die than *live* in shame.

いきなり suddenly; abruptly.

いきぬき【息抜き】¶～に散歩しましょう Let's take a walk *for a change*.

いきぬ·く【生き抜く】¶彼は明治，大正，昭和の3代を～いてきた He *lived through* the three periods of Meiji, Taisho, and Showa. / He is a man who *has outlived* the three periods of Meiji, Taisho, and Showa.

いきのこり【生き残り】a survivor. ¶彼は大戦～の兵士です He is a soldier who *survived* the great war.

いきのこ·る【生き残る】¶難船して，～った船員はたった10名だった Only ten of the crew *survived* the shipwreck. 船客中～った者はわずか5名だった There *were* only five passengers *left alive*. / Only five passengers *remained alive*.

いきのね【息の根】¶彼の～を止めてやるぞ I'll *kill* him.

いきの·びる【生き延びる】¶彼女は80歳まで～びた She *lived to* be eighty. 彼は妻よりも何年も～びた He *survived* his wife [for] many years.

いきはじ【生き恥】¶～をさらすくらいなら死んだほうがましだ I would die rather than *live in disgrace*. 彼は～をさらした He *lived* his life *disgraced*.

いきぼとけ【生き仏】a living Buddha.

いきま·く【息巻く】¶彼は彼女を殺すと～いた He *threatened* to kill her.

いきもの【生き物】a living thing; (動物) an animal; (総称) a creature.

いきょう【異境·異郷】a foreign country; a strange land. ¶～の土となる die in *a foreign country*.

いきょう【異教】paganism; heathenism; heresy. ¶～の pagan; heathen.
—徒 a pagan; a heathen; a heretic.

いぎょう【偉業】a great work. ¶～を成す achieve *a great work*.

いぎょう【遺業】¶彼は父の～を継いだ He took up his father's *unfinished work*.

いきょく【医局】a medical office; a dispensary.
—長 a chief of dispensary.

いきょく【委曲】¶～を尽くす explain in *detail*; give *a full account* of.

イギリス England; [Great] Britain (England は Scotland, Wales などに対してイギリス中央部だけを指すので，イギリス全体のことをいうときは，

い

Britainという場合が少なくない); (Great Britainとその全属領を含んで) Greater Britain; the United Kingdom (Great BritainとNorthern Irelandをいい, 略してU.K., 公式にはThe United Kingdom of Great Britain and Northern Ireland. 特に旅券などではこの形が用いられる. ほかに正式名に, the British Commonwealth of Nationsがあって, U. K.と全属領を指し, 簡単にthe Commonwealthともいう).
¶ ～の English; British. ～製の made in England; English made.
—人 an Englishman (≒ Englishwoman); a Briton; 米 a Britisher; (総称的) the English; the British. —語 English; the English language. —教会 the Church of England; the English Church. —国旗 the Union Jack. —ぎらい Anglophobia; (人) an Anglophobe. —びいき Anglophilia; (人) an Anglophile. —文学 English literature.

いきりた·つ【いきり立つ】be excited; be enraged.

い·きる【生きる】**1**〖生存する〗¶ ～きた魚 a *live* fish.
～きた英語 *living* English.
～けるしかばね a *living* corpse.
彼は100まで～きた He *lived* to be 100.
～きて再び会えるとは思わぬ I'm afraid I'll not *survive* to meet you again. / I don't think I shall *be alive* to see you again. / We shall never meet again.
どうやって～きていこうか I am at a loss how to *live*.
あと10年はとても～きていられまい I will not be able to *live* another ten years. / I probably won't *last* ten years.
彼はまだ～きているはずだ He must *be* still *alive*.
そんなものばかり食べてよく～きていられたね I wonder how you'*ve survived on* such kind of food.
この島の土人はイモを食べて～きている The natives of this island *live on* potatoes.
あの当時の先生で今～きいている人は少ない Few of those teachers *are alive* today.
ぼくにとっては～きるか死ぬかの問題だ For me it's *a matter of life and death*.
～きる望みをなくした I've given up all hope of *life*.
～きているのがいやになった I'm tired of *life*.
そんなことをして～きているより死んだほうがましだ I would rather die than *live* that way.
どっこい彼は～きていた To our surprise, he *was alive*.
私の～きている間はおまえに不自由はさせぬ I'll support you in comfort, as long as I *live*.
2〖有効である〗¶ こんな法律が～きているとは思わなかった I did not know such a law *was* still *valid*.
もっと～きた金の使い方をしたら Why don't you use your money more *effectively*?
(マージャンで)このパイはまだ～きている This piece *is* still *safe*.
3〖生き生きする〗¶ この1語で全文が～きてくる This very word makes the sentence *come alive*.
この色で全体の柄が～きている This color *sets off* the whole pattern *to advantage*.
4〖野球で〗¶ 滑りこんで二塁に走者は～きた The runner slid into the second base in time.

いきわかれ【生き別れ】¶ 戦争のために私は両親と～になった During the war I *parted from* my parents never *to see them again*.

い·く【行く】⇒ゆく

いく-【幾-】¶ ～日も for *some* (≒ *many*) days. ～百人 hundreds of men. ～人 *how many* people. ～十となく by dozens; by scores.

いくえ【幾重】¶ ～にもおわびいたします I beg you *thousand* pardons. わが軍は～にも取り囲まれた Our troops were *thickly* surrounded on all sides.

いくえい【育英】—資金 a scholarship〔fund〕.
—会 a scholarship association (≒ society).

いくさ【戦】(戦争) a war; warfare; (戦闘) a battle; a fight; an action.

いくじ【育児】nursing; childcare; upbringing of a child.
—室 a nursery. —院 a nursery house (≒ home); (孤児の) an orphanage.

いくじ【意気地】¶ ～のない spiritless; weak-hearted.
—なし a coward.

いくせい【育成】¶ ～する bring up; rear; nurse; nurture; cultivate; (助成する) foster.

いくたび【幾度】how often; how many times. ⇒いくど

いくつ【幾つ】¶ リンゴは1,000円で～買えますか *How many* apples can I get for 1,000 yen? あなたはお～ですか *How old* are you? トマトを～かあげましょう You shall have *some* (≒ *several*) tomatoes. ～でも欲しいだけ取りなさい Take as *many*〔ones〕as you like.

いくど【幾度】¶ きみは～アメリカへ行きましたか *How often* have you been in America?
～やっても失敗した *However often* he might try, he failed. / Every time he tried, he failed. ～も many times; often. ～も～も over and over again; again and again. ～となく many times.

いくどうおん【異口同音】unanimously.
¶ ～に彼らは叫んだ They cried *with one voice* (≒ *unanimously*).

いくとおり【幾通り】¶ ～もの many kinds (≒ sorts) of; a variety of; various. ～にも in several ways.

いくにち【幾日】how many days; how long.
¶ ～も for days; for many days. 東京に～ご滞在でしたか *How long* did you stay in Tokyo? ロンドンへ行くのに～かかりますか *How many days* does it take to go to London? きょうは～ですか *What day of the month* is this? ～にきみの友だちは出発ですか *When* is your friend starting?

いくび【猪首】a bull neck ; a short and thick neck.

いくぶん【幾分】¶ 彼はきょう～気分がいいようだ He seems to be *a little* better today. 寒さが～和らいだ The cold has *somewhat* softened. 彼は～か芸術家はだのところがある He has *something of* an artist in him. 給料の～かを貯金しなさい Save *something* from your pay. 彼女には～変わったところがある There is *something* strange about her.

イクラ salmon roe.

いくら【幾ら】 **1**〚金額〛 ¶ ～ですか. 500円です *How much* is it? It is 500 yen.

このバターは1ポンド～ですか *How much* is this butter by the pound?

この机を～で買ったのですか *How much* did you pay for this desk?

1日～で働いてくれるか *How much* will you work for by the day?

この給料は1時間～で支払われる The salary is paid by the hour.

～もするものじゃないから買いなさい It's not so expensive. Go ahead and buy it.

2〚数・量〛 ¶ この箱の容量は～ですか. 10リットルです *What* is the capacity of this box? It's 10 liters.

この自動車の積載量は～ですか *What* load can this car carry?

この小包の目方は～ありますか *How much* does this parcel weigh?

入学志願者の数が～になるか見当がつかない We can't guess *how many* students apply for admission to our school.

そんな人は～もいる There are 〔so〕 *many* people like this.

3〚距離・時間〛 ¶ ここから駅までは～もない It is not so far from here to the station.

向こう岸まで距離は～ぐらいでしょう *How far* is it to the other side of the river?

退職後～もしないうちに彼は死んだ He died *soon* after he retired from office.

開演まで時間は～もなかった It did not take *long* before the performance began.

4〚いくら…でも〛 ¶ ～なんでもあんまりだ That's going too far. / That's too much, to say the least 〔of it〕.

～おどかしたって, 怖くはない *However much* you may threaten me, I will not be frightened. ～ばかでもそのくらいのことはわかるだろう *Even* a fool knows better.

～考えてもいい知恵が浮かばなかった *However hard* I might try, I did not hit upon a good idea.

～うまいといっても彼の英語は日本人の英語だ *Indeed* he speaks very fluently, *but* his English is Japanese English.

～欠点があっても, 私は彼女が好きだった *With all* her faults, I still liked her. / *For all* faults and all, I adored her.

～悪くても60点ぐらいはとれそうだ I can possibly get sixty points *at* 〔*the*〕 *worst*.

～なんでも1万円はくれるだろう I hope he will give me *at least* 10,000 yen.

～遅くても, もう着いている He will have arrived there by now *at the latest*.

～よくてもわれわれは2回戦どまりだ I wonder if we'll be able to go on the second round *at best*. / I guess we will go as far as the second inning *at best*.

いくらか【幾らか】¶ ～寒気が和らいだ It has become *a little* less cold. / It has got *a little* milder. / It has got milder *a bit*. ～彼女の容体は持ち直したようだ She seems to have made a *slight* recovery. 私は～後ろめたいところがあった I felt guilty *to some extent* (≒ *a little bit*).

いくらでも ¶ あの絵を手に入れるためなら, 彼に金は～出すつもりだ I would be ready to pay *as much money as he demands* for that picture. 酒なら～ある. どんどん飲んでくれ We have *a lot of sake*. Drink as much as you want. さあ, お好きなものを～とってください Help yourself to *as much* of everything *as you want* 〔*to*〕.

いくん【偉勲】a great service (≒ deed); a brilliant exploit; a distinguished achievement. ¶ ～をたてる accomplish *a great service*.

いくん【遺訓】*one's* last teachings (≒ instructions).

いけ【池】a pond; a pool.

いけい【畏敬】reverence. ¶ ～する revere; hold (*a person*) in awe.

いけいれん【胃痙攣】stomach convulsion. ¶ ～を起こす have *the cramp in the stomach*.

いけがき【生け垣】a hedge; a live fence. ¶ 庭に～を巡らす *hedge* a garden.

いけす【生け簀】a fish preserve; a fishpond; (浅瀬の) a crawl.

いけすかな・い【いけ好かない】disgusting; disagreeable; nasty.

いけどり【生け捕り】¶ ノウサギを～にする *catch* a hare *alive*.

いけど・る【生け捕る】¶ われわれは逃げたサルをやっと～った We finally *caught* the runaway monkey. 敵将を～った We *took* the enemy's general *prisoner* (≒ *captive*).

いけな・い **1**〚禁止・必要〛¶ この部屋に入っては～い You *must not* enter this room. / *No* admittance.

～いと言ったら～い Oh, *no*, you *must not*, I tell you.

他人の権利を無視しては～いと言われた I *was told not* to ignore another's rights.

今すぐ行かなければ～いのですか *Must* you go so soon?

どうしてもきょうでなければ～いのですか *Must* it be today?

2〚悪い・まちがっている〛¶ ～い子だね What a *naughty* boy you are!

そんなことをするのは～いね You *must not* do such a thing. / You ought to know better.

～いのはきみのほうだ It's you that *are to blame*.

い

3 〖欠点がある・不備または不十分である〗 ¶ この計画のどこが～いかわかりますか Can you see what *is wrong* with this plan?
ぼくの言うことのどこが～いのだ What do you find *wrong* in my explanation?
真空管が～い The tube *is no good*.
これでは～い, もっと上質の紙が欲しい This *won't do*. I want better quality paper.
4 〖望みなし・不成功〗 ¶ 医者に「もう～い」と言われた The doctor told me that *there was no hope* at all.
どうやったって～いな. ぼくの負けだ All further effort *is useless*. I am beaten.
9回2死となってもう～いと思った I thought the team would lose the game when two were out in the ninth inning.
～かった(うまくいかなかった)とは残念 I am sorry it *did not go well* as expected.
5 〖…だといけない〗 ¶ なにかあると～いから, 少し余分にお金を持っていきなさい Take some extra money with you *in case* some accident *should* happen.
雨が降ると～いと思ってかさを持って出かけた I took my umbrella *in case* it *should* rain.
まちがえると～から, 持ち物に名札をつけなさい Attach a name tag to your belongings *so that* you won't lose them.
6 〖まずい〗 ¶ それは～いね Oh, that's too *bad*.
しまった. これは～い Oh, dear! / Confound it!
そのうえ～いことに, 彼の説明が不十分だった *What was even worse*, his explanation was not sufficient.

いけにえ【生け贄】 a sacrifice; a victim. ¶ ～をささげる offer *a sacrifice* to.

いけばな【生け花】 flower arrangement; (生けた花) flowers arranged in a vase.

い・ける【生ける】 ¶ 花を～ける *arrange* flowers *in a vase*.

い・ける【行ける】 1 〖行くことができる〗 ¶ 大阪は〔東京から〕3時間で～ける Osaka *can be reached* in three hours 〔from Tokyo〕.
2 〖味がいい〗 ¶ この酒は～ける This *sake is good*.
3 〖飲める〗 ¶ あなたは～ける口ですね You are *a drinker*, aren't you?
4 〖できる〗 ¶ フランス語ならちょっと～ける I *am good at* French.

いけん【意見】 1 〖考え・見解〗 〔an〕 opinion.
¶ きみの～は Have you any *opinions* about it? / Have you anything to say about it?
ご～を伺いたい I want to have your *comment on* it.
ひとりひとり～を聞いた I asked each person's *opinion*.
そのことについて～を求められた I was asked my own *views* about the matter.
～を忌憚(きたん)なく述べてください Will you please state your *opinion* without reserve? / Will you please let us hear your frank *opinion*?
私の～を申し上げます I'm going to express my *opinion*.
二, 三～を申し述べさせていただきたい I would like to express some *opinions*.
このことについては別にはっきりした～は持っていない I have no definite *opinion* on this point.
腹蔵なく皆で～を交換し合った We have exchanged our *views* very frankly.
まったくきみと同～だ I completely *agree with* you.
その～には反対だ I disagree with that *opinion*.
皆の～はまちまちだった They were divided in *opinion* on that question.
なかなか～がまとまらない We have not arrived at *a* definite *opinion*.
ついにふたりの間では～の一致をみなかった No *agreement* was reached between the two till the end.
要するに～の相違だ In other words it is a difference of *opinions*.
ふたりは～を異にした They *disagreed with* each other.
きみとは～が合わぬ I differ from you in *opinion*.
2 〖忠告・小言〗 advice. ¶ 彼はぼくの～を受け入れた He took my *advice*.
彼に～したとてむだだ It is 〔of〕 no use *reasoning with* him. / It's a waste of time to *reason with* him.
思いとどまるようにと彼女に～しておいた I *advised* her to change her mind.
彼は親の～を聞こうとしなかった He would not obey (≒ listen to) his parents.

いけん【違憲】 unconstitutionality; 〔a〕 violation of the constitution.

いげん【威厳】 dignity; majesty. ¶ そんなことばを使うとあなたの～にかかわる Such language would be beneath your *dignity*. あの政治家にはどことなく～がある There is *something dignified* (≒ *majestic*) *about* that politician.

いご【以後】 ¶ 10時～に帰ってこないように You must not come back *after* ten in the evening. バス料金は4月1日～に上がるそうだ I hear the bus fare will be raised *from* April 1. ～健康にもっと気をつけなさい Be more careful of your health *from now on*. ～こんなことはやめてほしい I don't want you to do this *again*.

いご【囲碁】 the play of *go*; *go* play.

いこい【憩い】 〔a〕 rest; repose. ¶ ～のひととき a moment of *rest*.

いこう【以降】 on and after. ¶ 9日～ *on and after* the 9th; *from* the 9th *on*.

いこう【威光】 authority; power; influence. ¶ 親の～で through the *influence* of *one's* parent.

いこう【移項】 〖数学〗 transposition. ¶ ～する transpose.

いこう【移行】 ¶ ～する switch over (*to*).

いこう【意向】 an intention; a disposition; (考え) an idea; a mind. ¶ 彼にはそうする～はなかった He had no *intention* of doing so. 彼は自分の～を漏らしたがらなかった He was unwilling to tell his *mind*. 私は彼の～を探ってみた I tried to sound his *opinion* (≒ *view*). 彼の～を確かめたか Have you ascertained his *mind*?

いこう【遺稿】*one's* posthumous works.

いこ・う【憩う】rest; take (≒ have) a rest.

イコール equal. ¶5プラス4～9 Five and four *equal*[*s*] nine. / Five and four *is* (≒ *are*) nine. 5マイナス4～1 Five minus four (≒ Four from five) *is* (≒ *leaves*) one. 5掛ける4～20 Five times four *is* (≒ *are*) twenty. 6割る3～2 Three into six goes twice. / Six divided by three gives two.

いこく【異国】a foreign country (≒ land). ¶～の人 a foreigner (≒ stranger).
―情緒 an exotic mood (≒ atmosphere).
―趣味 exoticism.

いごこち【居心地】¶そのホテルは～がよかった(悪かった) I *felt comfortable* (*uncomfortable*) at the hotel. ここはとても～がいい I *feel* quite *at home* here. / This is a very *comfortable* place to live in.

いこじ【依怙地】obstinacy; stubbornness; perversity. ¶そう～になるな Don't *be* so *obstinate*! 彼はたぶん～になってそうしたのだろう Probably he did it *out of spite* (≒ *out of perversity*).

いこつ【遺骨】*one's* ashes (≒ remains). ¶この墓の下に彼の～が葬ってある His *ashes* rest under this tomb. (ashes と複数形であることに注意).

いこ・む【鋳込む】¶鉛を鋳型に～む *cast* lead in a mold.

いこん【遺恨】a grudge. ¶彼女は私に～をいだいている She has *a grudge* against me. / She bears me *a grudge*. 彼らは敵に～を晴らした They *revenged themselves on* their enemy. / They *paid off* their *old scores* with their enemy. ふたりの間につのる～の気持 a growing ill will between the two persons.

いざ ¶故国よ～さらば Good-by, my native country. ～出発だ Let's start *now*. ～となれば実力が出るものだ One can show one's full ability *at a moment of crisis*. ～というときの覚悟はできていますか Are you prepared *for the worst*? 人は～知らず私はそれはいやだ *As far as I am concerned*, I don't care for it.

いさい【委細】details. ¶～は12月号参照 For *further details* see the December issue [of the magazine]. 私は～かまわずしゃべりつづけた I went on talking *regardless of consequences*. ～承知した All right! / It's OK by me! お申し越しの件～承知しました Everything you proposed is OK by me. ことの～を聞きたい Let me have a full account of the matter. ～面談(広告文) *Details* to be arranged personally. イサイフミ(電文) Letter follows.

いさい【異彩】¶彼は文壇で～を放つ存在だ He *cuts a brilliant figure* in the literary circles. 彼の語学の才は同輩間で～を放っていた He *was conspicuous* (≒ *distinguished himself*) for his linguistic ability among his comrades.

いさい【偉才】a genius; a great talent; an extraordinary man.

いさかい【諍い】a quarrel; a dispute. ¶そんなことで彼と～するな Don't *quarrel with* him *about* such a thing.

いざかや【居酒屋】㊍a saloon; ㊇a public house; ㊇(口語) a pub.

いさぎよ・い【潔い】(男らしい) manly; brave; (潔白な) pure; chaste; clean.
¶彼は～く死んだ He died *like a* [*brave*] *man*. 彼は～く負けた He *was a good loser*. 彼は～く白状した He made a *manly* confession. 彼は～く大学進学をあきらめた He *readily* gave up the idea of going to college.

いさく【遺作】¶これは彼の～の一つだ This is one of his *posthumous works*.

いさぎよしとしない【潔しとしない】¶うそをつくことを～ He *is above* telling lies. あの男は物ごいをするのを～ He *is too proud to* beg. 彼らは降伏するのを～で, 自決した *Ashamed* (≒ [*Being*] *Too proud*) to surrender, they killed themselves.

いざこざ a quarrel; [a] trouble. ¶～の種 the cause[s] of *a quarrel*. 彼女はいつも彼と～を起こしている She *is* always *making trouble* with him. 彼の家ではいつも～が絶えない There is no end of *trouble* in his house.

いささか【些か】¶この詩は私には～難しい This poem is *a bit* too hard for me. きみの答えは～見当違いだ Your answer is *somewhat* beside the mark. その知らせを聞いて～驚いた I was *a little* surprised at the news. そのことには～の疑いもない There is not *the slightest* doubt about it. 私には～の蓄えがある I have *a little* saving. 私は～てれくさかった I felt *a little* awkward. われわれは～のちゅうちょもしないで敵に向かって突進した We rushed at the enemy without *the least* hesitation.

いさまし・い【勇ましい】¶～い人 a *brave* (≒ *courageous*) man. ～い歌 a *stirring* song. ～い物語 a *heroic* tale.

いさみあし【勇み足】¶今度の事件は彼の～だ I feel that in this matter he *jumped the gun*.

いさみはだ【勇み肌】¶～の男 a *dashing* man.

いさ・む【勇む】¶彼らは～んで外出した They went out *in high spirits*. 彼らはその知らせを聞いて～み立った *Their spirits rose* at the news. / They *were encouraged* when they heard the news.

いさ・める【諫める】¶愚行を～めておいた I *remonstrated with* him *about* (≒ *against*) his foolish behavior.

いざり【躄】a cripple.

いざ・る【躄る】¶彼らの方に～り寄った I *crept up toward* them. 足がしびれて～りながら席を替えた I changed my seat *creeping along on my knees* as my feet were numb.

いさん【胃酸】〔医学〕acid in the stomach.
―過多症〔医学〕acid dyspepsia.

いさん【遺産】an inheritance. ¶彼は妻子にか

い

なりの～を残した He left *a* considerable *fortune* (⇆ *estate*) *to* his widow and children. 彼はおじの～を相続した He *inherited* (⇆ *succeeded to*) his uncle's *property*. / He *inherited* (⇆ *came into*) *a fortune from* his uncle. 彼には相当の～がある He has *a* large *fortune* left to him. 彼は～として1億円受け取った He received one hundred million yen *by inheritance*.

—相続 succession to property. —相続人 an inheritor; (男) an heir; (女) an heiress.

いし【石】 **1** [a] stone; (宝石) a precious stone; a jewel. ¶～造りの家 a house [made] of *stone*; a *stone* building.

～ころだらけの道 a road covered with *pebbles*; a *stony* (⇆ *pebbly*) path.

2 〚慣用的表現〛 ¶私は～にかじりついても目的を果たすつもりだ I will manage to effect my purpose *at any cost* (⇆ *by any means*).

～の上にも三年(諺) Perseverance brings success.

いし【医師】 a doctor; a physician.

—会 a medical association. —国家試験 the National Examination for Medical Practitioners.

いし【意志】 will. ¶彼は～が強い He is a man of strong *will*. / He has an iron *will*. ～の弱い人だ He is a man of weak *will*. / He is a weak-*willed* man. 私は自分の～に反した行動をとってしまった I conducted myself *against my will*. 彼は自分の～でそうした He did so *of his own will* (⇆ *accord*). 彼はたいてい自分の～を通す He usually *has his will*. 彼には自分の～というものがない He has no *will of his own*. するしないは各人の自由～に任せた I left it to each person's *free will* whether he did it or not. 女性側の両親の～を踏みにじって彼らは結婚した They married against the *will* of her parents. 彼にはそれをする～もない He has no *intention* of doing it. / He has no *mind* to do it.

いし【意思】 an intention. ¶私は～を貫徹した I carried out my *intention*. / I accomplished my *purpose*. われわれはもっと～の疎通を図るべきだ We should *understand each other* much better. われわれは～の疎通が欠けている There is a lack of *understanding* between us. その会に出席する～はない I have no *intention* of attending the party. 賛成の～表示をした I expressed my *will* of approval. われわれの～を明らかにする必要がある It is necessary for us to *speak up* (⇆ *speak our mind*).

いし【遺志】 *one's* last wishes. ¶彼は父の～を継いで医者になった He became a doctor according to (⇆ because of) his father's *last wishes*. 亡父の～を果したいと思います I hope I will carry out the *intention* (⇆ *will*) of my deceased father.

いじ【意地】 (根性) nature; (強情) obstinacy. ¶あの人は～が悪い He is an ill-*natured* (⇆ a cross-*tempered*) perosn. 友だちに～の悪いことをしてはいけません Never *be unkind to* your friends. 出かけようとしたら～悪く人が来た We were about to go out, when *unluckily* (⇆ *unfortunately*) we had a visitor. 彼はあくまで～を通すつもりだ He will have his *will* (⇆ have his own *way*). 彼は～になってその計画に反対した He opposed the scheme *obstinately* (⇆ *doggedly*). 菓子には～ぎたないほうです I *am* so *greedy for* cakes and candies. / I *can't resist* sweets.

いじ【維持】 maintenance. ¶世界の平和を～する *maintain* (⇆ *keep*) the peace of the world. 健康～のために適度の運動をやっている I take moderate exercise to *keep me in good health*. 運動をして健康を～しよう Let's *keep* (⇆ *preserve*) our health by exercise. 政府は現状～の政策をとった The government pursued the policy of *maintaining* the present condition.

—費 ¶車の～費に1か月どれくらいかかりますか How much does it cost a month to *keep up* your car?

いじ【遺児】 an orphan.

いしあたま【石頭】 ¶彼は～だ He *is as obstinate as a mule*. あの～にはとてもわかるまい Such *a thickheaded person* could not possibly understand it.

いしがき【石垣】 a stone wall.

いしき【意識】 consciousness; the will. ¶彼は頭をなぐられて～を失った He lost his *consciousness* when he was struck on the head. そのうち～を回復するだろう He will *regain consciousness* (⇆ *come to himself*) soon. あの子どもたちは罪の～がまるでない Those children have no *sense of* guilt whatever. 死ぬまで彼の～は確かだった His *mind* remained clear to the last. ～的に努力しないでも人間はみな呼吸する We all breathe without any *conscious* efforts. 彼は～的に私に会わないらしい I feel that he is avoiding me *on purpose*.

—不明 ¶彼は路上で～不明になって倒れた He fell *senseless* on the street.

いじ・ける ¶～けた少年(おどおどした) a *timid* boy; (ひねくれた) a *perverse* boy. 1回の失敗で～けるな Don't *be daunted* by your only failure.

いしころ【石ころ】 a piece of stone.

—道 a stony road.

いしずえ【礎】 the foundation. ¶その国の～を築いたのは彼だ It was he who *laid* (⇆ *built*) *the foundation* of the country. 城の～だけが残っている There remains only the *foundation stone* (⇆ *cornerstone*) of the castle.

いしだたみ【石畳】 a stone pavement.

いしだん【石段】 a flight of stone steps.

いしつ【異質】 heterogeneity. ¶～の文化 culture *of a different nature*.

—分子 heterogeneous elements.

いしつ【遺失】 loss.

—物 lost articles. —物取扱所 the lost and the found. —届 a report on lost property.

いじっぱり【意地っ張り】 obstinacy. ¶彼女は

～だ She is quite an *obstinate* woman. / She *persists in her own opinion*. 彼はなかなか～だ He *is* rather *obstinate* (≒ *stubborn*).

いしばし【石橋】 a stone bridge. ¶ 彼は～をたたいて渡るタイプの人間だ He *is overcautious* indeed. / He is the kind of person who *makes assurance doubly sure*.

いじ・める【虐める】 ¶ 弱い者を～めてはいけない Don't *bully* the weaker. 動物を～めてはいけません You must not *be cruel to* animals. どうかそんなにわれわれを～めないでください Don't *be so hard on* us, please.

いしゃ【医者】 a doctor; (内科医) a physician; (外科医) a surgeon. (歯科医) a dentist; (眼科医) an eye doctor; (一般開業医) a general practitioner.

¶ かかりつけの～ *a* family *doctor*. ～を開業する set up as *a doctor*. ～を呼ぶ call in *a doctor*. ～に診てもらう consult (≒ see) *a doctor*. ～にかかっている I *am* now *under medical treatment*. / I *am under the doctor*. 彼はもうすっかり～の手を離れた He has completely recovered his health.

いしゃ【慰謝】 ―料 consolation money. ¶ ～料を請求する demand *compensation* for.

いしゅ【異種】 a different kind; a variety; a different species.

いしゅ【意趣】 malice; grudge. ¶ ～を含む bear (*a person*) a grudge.

―返し revenge. ¶ ～返しをする *revenge oneself* on (*a person*).

いしゅう【異臭】 a nasty smell; a foul smell; an offensive smell. ¶ 死体が～を放っていた The dead body gave out *a nasty smell* (≒ *foul smell*). 現場には～が漂っていた All over the scene there hung *an offensive smell*.

いじゅう【移住】 migration; (外国への) emigration; (外国からの) immigration; (移転) [a] removal.

¶ それらの鳥は冬になると南へ～する Those birds *migrate* southward in the winter. 彼は3年前にブラジルに～した He *emigrated to* Brazil three years ago. あの家は韓国(かんこく)から東京に～してきた That family *immigrated into* Tokyo from Korea.

―民 a settler; (外国への) an emigrant; (外国からの) an immigrant. ―地 a settlement.

いしゅく【畏縮】 ¶ 大ぜいの前で～して声も出なかった I *cowered* (≒ *quailed*) before many people and lost my voice.

いじゅつ【医術】 the medical art; medicine.

いしょ【遺書】 a will; a note left behind by a deceased person. ¶ 彼は～も書かずに死んだ He died without making *a will*. 死後彼の～が発見された After his death his *last will and testament* was found.

いしょう【衣装】 dresses; (舞台など) [a] costume. ¶ 彼女はたいへんな～持ちだ She has a lot of *dresses*. / She has a very large *wardrobe*. 馬子にも～(諺) Clothes make the man.

いしょう【意匠】 a design. ¶ 上品な～の門 the gate of elegant *design*.

―権 copyright in registered designs. ―登録 registration of designs.

いじょう【以上】 **1** 〖数・量・程度の比較〗 more than. ¶ 列車は30分～も遅れた The train was *more than* thirty minutes behind time.

高速道路は時速60キロ～で走らねばならぬ One should drive at *more than* 60 kilometers per hour on the expressway.

この小屋には10人～泊まれない This cottage can not accommodate *more than* ten persons.

定数の3分の2～の出席がないと総会は成立しない The general meeting is not valid unless two-thirds of the members are present. / The general meeting is not valid until there is a quorum of two-thirds of the members.

船は定員～に客を乗せた The ship was overloaded.

本大会に出場できる者は15歳～18歳までの高校女子に限る Those who can take part in this meeting are limited to the high-school girls between the ages of 15 and 18.

新車は予想～の売れ行きだった The new cars sold well *beyond* our expectation[s].

想像していた～の雄大な景色だった It was a sight *far more* splendid than I had expected.

覚悟していた～に激しくぼくは非難された I was criticized *more* severely *than* I had been prepared for.

実力～のことをしようとしたとて無理だ It is no use trying to do *beyond* your ability.

収入～の暮らしをするな Don't live *beyond* your income (≒ means).

これ～のことは申し上げられない I have nothing *further* to say.

これ～のご要求には応じかねます We cannot comply with *further* requests.

2 〖上述・上記〗 ¶ ～をもって報告を終わります *This much* is all I have to say as the report. / Well, I'm going to close my report *with this*.

～が事件のあらましです *The above* is the outline of this case.

～の理由で本計画には賛成しかねます For the reasons *mentioned above*, I cannot approve this plan.

3 〖…からには〗 now that... ¶ やると言った～やりたまえ Do the job thoroughly, *now that* you have promised to do it.

こうなった～あとにはひけぬ *Now that* things have come to this (≒ such a pass), there is no going back.

彼の世話になっている～彼にあまり不平も言えないのだ *So long as* I am under his care, I cannot say even a word of complaint to him.

いやだという～無理に頼むな *Since* he has refused it, don't ask him any more.

いじょう【委譲】 ¶ 権限を彼に～した We *transferred* our rights *to* him.

いじょう【異状】 something wrong. ¶ エンジ

い

ンに～があった Something *was wrong* (≒ *the matter*) *with* the engine. / The engine *was out of order*. なにも～なし Everything *is all right*. / Nothing *is the matter*. 途中～はなかった We had no *accident* on the way. 留守中～はなかったろうね There wasn't any *change* in the house when I was out, was there? 彼は体の～を訴えた He complained of *indisposition*. 彼は精神に～をきたしている He *is* mentally *deranged*. / He *is out of his mind*.

いじょう【異常】 ¶～なふんい気だった The atmosphere *was extraordinary* (≒ *unusual*). 彼は～な性格の持ち主だった He was a man of *abnormal* character. 彼はそのことに～な熱意を示した He showed an *uncommon* interest in it. 彼は～な進歩をしたHe mede *remarkable* progress.

いじょうふ【偉丈夫】 a great man. ¶彼は～ぶりを発揮した He showed himself *a hero*. / Great *heroism* was shown by him.

いしょく【衣食】 ¶彼は～には事欠かない収入がある He has an income enough to support himself. 彼は～に窮した He found it hard to *make a living*.

—住 food, clothing and shelter.

いしょく【委嘱】 commission. ¶委員を～された I *was commissioned* to be a member of the committee. 彼に設計を～した I *committed* the plan *to* him. / I *entrusted* him *with* the plan.

いしょく【異色】 ¶彼は学界でも～ある存在として認められている He is recognized as *unique* in academic circles.

—作品 a rare work.

いしょく【移植】 transplantation.

角膜(心臓)**—** transplantation of the cornea (heart).

いじらし·い pitiful; touching. ¶病気の母親の手伝いをしている子どもが～かった I *was touched with pity* (≒ I *felt pity*) for the child helping her mother ill in bed.

いじ·る【弄る】 ¶このおもちゃの自動車を～るな Don't *finger* this toy car. 子どもはおもちゃを～って遊んでいた The child *was playing with* toys. 彼は錠を～りまわしていた He *was fumbling at* (≒ *with*) a lock.

いしわた【石綿】 asbestos.

いじわる【意地悪】 ¶人に～なことをするな Don't *be unkind to* others. ～そうな顔つきの男だ He looks *malicious* (≒ *cross-tempered*). 彼は～そうに笑った He laughed *maliciously*. あんな～な娘に会ったことがない I have never seen such an *ill-natured* girl.

いしん【威信】 dignity. ¶そんなことをすると親の～にかかわる It will injure your parents' *honor* to do such a thing. 政府の～も地に落ちた The government lost its *prestige* (≒ *authority*). 一国の～にかかわる事柄 a question affecting national *prestige*. 国家の～を高める enhance national *prestige*.

いしん【維新】 the Restoration. ¶明治～ the Meiji *Restoration*.

いじん【偉人】 a great man.

—伝 the life of a great mind.

いしんでんしん【以心伝心】 telepathy. ¶あなたの思っていることは～わかっている I understand *instinctively* what you have in mind.

いす【椅子】 **1**〖腰かけ〗 a chair; (ひじかけ) an armchair; (安楽いす) an easy chair; (寝いす) a couch; (揺りいす) a rocking chair; (折り畳みいす) a folding chair; (背のない) a stool. ¶～の腕(脚,背,座部) the arms (legs, back, seat) of *a chair*.

～から立ち上がる rise from *a chair*.

この～は座り心地がいい This *chair* is comfortable to sit in (≒ on). (ひじのあるいすには sit in, ひじのないいすには sit on を用いることが多い).

部屋には座る～がない There is no *chair* to sit on (≒ in) in the room.

2〖地位〗 a position; a post. ¶代議士はだれでも大臣の～に座りたがる Any dietman is eager to take (≒ hold) *a seat* in the Cabinet. 彼はその～をねらっていた He had an eye to the *post*.

いずまい【居住まい】 a sitting posture. ¶～を正して話を聞きなさい *Sit up straight* to listen to me. いつも～を正しくしておかなければならない We should always *keep straight*. / We should always *straighten ourselves*.

いずみ【泉】 a spring; a fountain. ¶知識の～ the *spring* (≒ *fountain*) of knowledge.

～の水がこんこんとわき出ている The *fountain* is gushing out.

イスラエル Israel.

—人 an Israeli.

イスラムきょう【イスラム教】 Islam.

いずれ【何れ】 **1**〖近いうち〗 ¶～詳しく申し上げます I will tell you about it in detail *sometime*.

～そのうち伺います I'll come to see you *some day soon*.

2〖やがては〗 ¶～はぼくの言うこともわかってくれるだろう Give me time and you will understand what I mean.

～は知れてしまうよ *Sooner or later* it will come out in the open.

～またのことにしよう Let's talk it over *some other time*.

～はきみもぼくも死ぬ身だ Both you and I are determined to die *some day*.

3〖とにかく·結局〗 ¶～にせよよくないことだ *At any rate*, it is not good.

～にしても無理だ It can't be done *any way*.

～にしてもおかしな話だ *Anyhow* it is an odd story.

～にせよ彼が無実であることにかわりはない *In any case*, it still means that he is innocent.

4〖どちら〗 ¶～の案を採るにせよ相当の損失は免れない *Whichever* plan we choose, we can't help suffering a considerable loss.

きみたちの～かがしたことに違いない *One* of you must have done it.

5〖どれ〗 ¶これらの案は～もみなどこかに難点がある

All of these plans have some weaknesses. 双方～も欲張りすぎている *Both* of them want too much.
この理論は～の場合にもあてはまる This theory applies well in *all* cases.
みなさま方のご意見は～もごもっともです There is something in *all* your opinions.
剣にかけては～劣らぬ者ばかりであった They were *all* equally excellent in fencing.
6 〚どこ〛 ¶ 彼は～ともなく立ち去った He disappeared *no one knows where*.
～を見ても私の知らぬ者ばかりだった Everyone around me was a stranger to me.

いすわ·る【居座る】¶ 現内閣は～ることになるだろう The present Cabinet will *remain in power*. 彼はまだリーダーとして～るだろう He intends to *remain* a leader.

いせい【以西】¶ 関東地方～にはその鳥はめったに見られない The bird is rarely found *west of* the Kanto area.

いせい【威勢】(勢力) power; influence; (元気) spirits. ¶ 彼はいつも～のいいことを言っている He *is* always *bragging* (≒ *boasting*). 彼は～のいい男だ He is a *dashing* man. さあ, ～よくやろう Let's cheer up. 彼らは～よく出発した They started *in good* (≒ *high*) *spirits*.

いせい【異性】the opposite (≒ other) sex.

いせい【為政】government.
—者 a statesman; a ruler.

いせえび【伊勢蝦】〔動物〕a lobster.

いせき【移籍】transfer of the register. ¶ 彼は昨年巨人軍に～した He *was transferred to* the Giants last year.

いせき【遺跡】ruins; remains. ¶ われわれはきのう古代ローマの～を訪れた Yesterday we visited the *ruins* of ancient Rome.

いせつ【異説】a different opinion. ¶ 彼はそれに関して～を唱えている He has *a different opinion* on it.

いせん【緯線】a parallel [of latitude].

いぜん【以前】¶ ～のご住所をお知らせください Please tell me your *former* address. ～にたった1回だけ彼に会っている I have seen him only once *before*. ～は怠け者だった *In the old days* he was idle. / He used to be idle *long ago*. あの人は～とはすっかり人が変わったようだ He has become quite another (≒ a changed) man. ここは～ほど寒くはない It is not so cold here as it used to be *before*. お名前は～からお聞きしていました I have known you by name *for some time*. 医者になることが～から私の願いだった It was my *long-cherished* wish to become a doctor. 彼はこのごろ～ほど病弱でなくなった He is not so weak as he used to be. もう～の彼ではない He is quite a changed man.

いぜん【依然】¶ 彼らは～としてその計画に反対だ They are *still* against the plan. 波は～として高い The waves are *as* high *as ever*.

いそ【磯】a beach; a shore. ¶ ～伝いに歩く walk along the *beach*.

いそいそと cheerfully; lightheartedly. ¶ 彼女は～デートに出かけた She went on a date *lightheartedly*. 彼女は～とデパートへ出かけた She went out *happily* to the department store. 彼女は台所で～働いている She is working *cheerfully* in the kitchen.

いそう【位相】〔電気〕〔天文〕phase. ¶ 金星にはいろいろな～がある Venus goes through various *phases*.
—差 phase difference. **—速度**〔物理〕phase velocity. **—変調**〔電気〕phase modulation.

いそう【移送】removal; transference. ¶ 彼らは別の収容所に～された They *were transferred to* another camp. その件を高裁に～した The case *was transferred* to a higher court.

いそうがい【意想外】¶ 彼の失敗はまったく～だ His failure is *a surprise* to me. ～の結果であった It was an *unexpected* result. / The result was *more than we expected*.

いそうろう【居候】a hanger-on (複 hangers-on); a dependent. ¶ 彼は親戚に～している He *lives on* his relative. ～は肩身がせまい *A dependent* feels small.

いそがし·い【忙しい】busy (busy のあとが動詞のときは busy *doing*. 名詞のときは busy with *something*. busy *in doing* はやや古体). ¶ 彼は仕事で～かった He *was busy with* his work. 出発準備で～い I'*m busy* preparing for the departure. 彼は～い日程から時間をさいてくれた He took time off his *heavy schedule*. ～くて読書する暇がない I *am* too *busy* to read. 商売で～くて手がはなせない I *have my hands full with* business. / I *am tied down to* my business. 彼はいつも～く働いている He is always working *busily*. 彼は～そうに出て行った He went out in a *hurried* manner.

いそが·す【急がす】¶ 仕事を～せるな Don't *press* me to do the work. 彼に道を～せた I *hurried* him *up* on his way. 会におくれないよう車を～せた I *hurried* the car to be in time for the meeting. 彼は妻の化粧を～せた He *hurried up* his wife's make-up.

いそぎ【急ぎ】¶ ～の用で on an *urgent* business. ～足で with a *quick* pace.

いそぎんちゃく〔動物〕a sea anemone.

いそ·ぐ【急ぐ】hurry; make haste (「急げ」のような命令文ではしばしば Hurry up! という). ¶ 彼は学校へ～いだ He *hurried to* school. 私たちは帰りの道を～いだ We *hurried* on the way home. お～ぎですか *Are* you *in a hurry*? 彼は仕事を～いだ He *hurried* (≒ *speeded up*) his work. ～がば回れ(諺) *The more haste, the less speed*. 成功を～いではいけない Don't *be in a hurry* for success.

いぞく【遺族】a bereaved family. ¶ 彼の～は妻とふたりの息子である He is survived by his wife and two sons. 政府は戦争～を援助すべきだ The government ought to help *the war bereaved*.
—年金 a survivor's pension. **—扶助料** an allowance to a surviving family.

い

いそづり【磯釣り】¶ ～する fish on the beach.

いそん【依存】dependence. ¶ きみは他人に～しすぎる You *depend* too much *on* others. わが国は外国貿易に大いに～している This country *depends* chiefly *upon* foreign trade. この条約は相互～を目的としている This treaty aims at the *interdependence*.

いぞん【異存】an objection. ¶ 私はそのことには～ありません I have no *objection* to it.

いた【板】a board; (厚い木の) a plank; (金属の) a plate; (金属の薄い) a sheet. ¶ 厚さ3センチの～ *a board* three centimeters thick. 床には～が張り詰めてあった The floor *was boarded* over. そこは～で塀をしてあった It was fenced with *board*. 彼の議長ぶりもなかなか～についてきた He *is* now quite *at home* as a chairman. 彼の仕事ぶりはまだ～についていない He *is* still *green at* his job. この脚本は～にのる(上演できる) This play will *stage* well.

—金 a metal plate. —紙 cardboard. —ガラス plate glass. —チョコ a chocolate bar. トタン— sheet zinc. —べい a wooden wall; a board fence.

いたい【遺体】a 〔dead〕 body; a corpse (corps「部隊」との違いに注意). ¶ 彼らは～を棺におさめた They put the 〔*dead*〕 *body* in a coffin.

いた・い【痛い】**1** 〖肉体的に〗 ¶ 歯が～い I *have a toothache*.

頭が～い I *have a headache*.

目が～い I *feel a pain* in my eye.

胃が～い I *have a stomachache*. / I *have a pain* in the stomach.

背中が～い I *feel a pain* in the back.

のどが～い I *have a sore throat*.

体じゅう～い My whole body *aches*.

足の皮がむけてひりひり～い The scratch on my foot still *smarts*.

切り傷がずきずき～い I *feel a* bad *pain* in my cut.

風邪で骨の節々が～い I've got a cold and *feel a pain* in every joint.

深呼吸をすると胸が～い It *pains* me to take deep breaths.

あまりの緊張で胸が～くなった The strain brought about a bellyache.

慣れぬ仕事をしたので右腕の筋が～い The unaccustomed work *has pained* the muscle of my right arm.

歩き疲れて足が～い I *have a sore foot* from the long walk.

～い足を引きずって歩いた He dragged himself along with *sore* feet.

転んで打ったところがまだときどき～い A bruise I got when I tumbled still *hurts* me sometimes.

まだ～いですか. もう～くはありません Do you still *feel any pain*? No, I don't *feel any pain* at all.

どこが～いのですか Where is the *pain*?

注射は～くてきらいだ I hate injections because of the *pain*.

あ, ～い Oh! *Ouch!*

(なにかで体などが痛むとき) ～いよ It *hurts* 〔*me*〕.

その手術は～いかしら I wonder if the operation *is painful*. / I wonder if the operation will *hurt*.

～くないお産ができるそうだ I hear *painless* delivery is now carried out.

2 〖慣用的表現〗 ¶ 頭の～くなる話ばかりで参った It's one problem after another.

耳の～いことを言うね What you say *sounds disagreeable* (≒ *harsh*) *to my ear*.

～いところをついてくるね Your remark *touches* me *to the quick*. / That *hurts*.

あんまり～いところに触れてくれるな Don't *touch on* a *painful* subject.

なにを言われたって～くもかゆくもない You can say whatever you like. You can't *hurt* me.

～くもない腹を探られた I'*ve had unwarranted suspicion* directed against me.

いまにみろ, ～い目に会わせてやる I'll *get back at you* for this one day.

そんなことをすると～い目に会うよ You'll only *get hurt* if you do such a thing.

その悲しい知らせを聞いて胸が～んだ I *grieved at* the sad news.

あそこでエラーが出たのが～かった It *hurt* to have an error at that moment.

交通ストで出荷が遅れたのが～かった *To our regret*, a traffic strike delayed the forwarding of goods.

1,000円ぐらいの損だってぼくには～い Even the loss of a thousand yen *hurts* me.

いだい【偉大】greatness. ¶ ～な人物 a *great* man. 彼の～さに並ぶ者はない His *greatness* can't be matched. / Nothing can beat his *greatness*. ～さ greatness; mightiness.

いたいけ ¶ ～な子 a *lovely* (≒ *tender*) child.

いたいたし・い【痛痛しい】pitiful; painful. ¶ ～しげに; ～しく painfully; pitifully. 見るのも～い光景だった It was a *pitiful* scene to see. その子は～いほどやせていた The child was *painfully* thin. ～い話だった It was a *touching* (≒ *pathetic*) story.

いたく【委託】trust. ¶ この仕事は彼に～した We *entrusted* him *with* this task. / We *entrusted* this task *to* him. その商品の販売を会社に～した They *consigned* the goods to a firm. 彼らは品物を～で発送した They sent goods *on consignment*.

—金 trust money. —販売 consignment sale; sale on consignment. —手数料 a consignment fee. —品 consignment goods; goods consigned. —学生 a scholarship student.

いだ・く【抱く】**1** 〖うでの中に〗 ¶ 彼女は子どもをしっかりと～いていた She *held* her child tightly in her arms.

2 〖不安・疑いなどを〗 ¶ 彼は私に恨みを～いている He *has* a grudge against me. / He *bears* me a grudge.

彼はつまらぬ考えを～いている He *has* (≒ *holds*) a silly idea in mind.

いたけだか【居丈高】¶ 彼の～な態度にがまんならない I can't bear his *arrogant* behavior.
～になって arrogantly; high-handedly.

いたさ【痛さ】pain. ¶ あまりの～に彼は思わず叫び声をあげた He was in such *pain* that he cried out in spite of himself. ⇒いたい(痛い)

いたしかた【致し方】¶ ～なく unwillingly; against *one's* will. どうにも～がなかった It couldn't be helped. / There was *no help for it*. 彼の意見に～なく同意した I agreed to his opinion *against my will*.

いたしかゆし【痛し痒し】¶ 私たちには～である We *are in a dilemma*. / We *are in a fix*.
それは私には～の問題である It is a *delicate* matter to me.

いた・す【致す】¶ いかが～しましょうか What shall I *do*? / What do you want me to *do*? どう～しまして You are welcome. / Not at all.
そのように～したく思います I'd like to *do* so. なにに～しましょうか What can I *do* for you? / Can I help you? これはみな不徳の～すところです This is all my fault.

いたずら【徒】¶ ～に時を過ごす人が多い Many people *waste* time. ～に英語の勉強をしているのでない I don't study English *without purpose*. 私たちは～に苦労をしたことになる We have taken pains *in vain*.

いたずら【悪戯】mischief. ¶ 男の子は～をするのが好きだ Boys like to *play tricks*. 彼は友だちによく～をする He often *plays a trick on* his friends. ～をしないように子どもたちに言った I told the children to *keep out of mischief*. 彼はまた～をたくらんでいる He is *up to mischief* again. ～にも程がある You *play a trick* (≒ *joke*) too far.
―半分 ¶ ～半分にそれをした I just did it *for fun*. **―書き** ¶ 黒板に～書きするな Don't scribble on the blackboard. **―っ子** ¶ おまえはほんとに～っ子だね What *a naughty boy* [you are]!

いただき【頂】**1**〖頂上〗the top; the peak; the summit. ¶ 山の～ a mountaintop.
2 ¶ その勝負は～だ We'll win the race by all means.

いただきもの【頂き物】a present; a gift.

いただ・く【頂く】**1**〖…していただく〗¶ いろいろ教えて～きたいことがあります I have lots of things to ask of you for advice. / I want your advice on several things.
ぜひまた来て～きたい I very much want you to come again.
ゆっくりとご歓談～きたい Please *make yourself at home*.
そうして～ければ大いに助かります I'll be very obliged (≒ grateful) to you if you can do that.
このことは世間に漏らさないで～きたい Please keep the matter to yourself. / I would appreciate it if you would keep the matter to yourself.
そのようなことはしないで～きたい Please don't do that. / You needn't do such things. / Please leave me alone.
2〖もらう〗¶ 記念にこの写真を～けませんか Can I *have* (≒ *keep*) this photograph as a happy memory?
今月中にご返事を～ければ幸いです It will be appreciated if we can *have* your answer in the course of this month.
ご祝詞を～きたく存じます We would like to *have* your congratulatory address, if you don't mind.
お送りのお金～きました I *have* just *received* the money.
3〖飲食する〗¶ ～きましょう Let's start.
もうじゅうぶん～きました. これ以上は～けません I *have had* enough. I can't *eat* any more.
遠慮なく～きます(物を食べる) I'll *help myself*, thank you. / (物をもらう) I'll *accept* it with pleasure.
～きます(食事の時など英語ではこの習慣がないので, たとえば Doesn't this look good? (「おいしそうだ」など).
4〖上にのせる・かぶる〗¶ 山々は雪を～いていた The mountains *were crowned* (≒ *covered*) with snow.

いたたまらな・い ¶ 部屋が暑くて, ～かった The room was too warm (≒ hot) for me [to stay in]. 彼女は彼の仕打ちに～かった She *couldn't bear* his behavior. 彼を～いようにしてやる I'll make things *too warm for* him.
彼女の泣いているのを見て, その場に～かった I *couldn't remain* there when I saw her crying.

いたち【鼬】〔動物〕a weasel; a skunk.
¶ 物価と賃金が～ごっこしている Prices and wages are *in a vicious circle*.

いたって【至って】very; greatly; exceedingly. ¶ 彼は～元気です He is *very* well.

いたで【痛手】(傷など) a severe wound; (打撃) a heavy blow. ¶ 彼は～を負っている He *is severely wounded* (≒ *injured*). 彼女の死は両親にとって大きな～であった Her death was *a hard blow* to her parents. 彼らは敵に～を負わせた They gave the enemy *a heavy* (≒ *hard*) *blow*. / The enemy *was* hard *hit*.

いたのま【板の間】(床) a wooden floor; (部屋) a room with a wooden floor.

いたばさみ【板ばさみ】¶ 彼らふたりの～になっている I'm *in a dilemma* (≒ *in a fix*) between them both.

いたばり【板張り】boarding; planking. ¶ 床は～になっている The floor *is boarded over*.

いたまえ【板前】a cook.

いたまし・い【痛ましい】¶ ～いありさまだった It was a *horrible* sight. あまりの～さにみな涙を流した It was such a *pathetic* sight that it brought tears to everyone's eyes.

いたみ【痛み】[a] pain. ¶ ときどき目に激しい～がある I sometimes feel *a* severe *pain* in my eyes. 頭に軽い～がある I have *a* slight *headache*. 急に手の指にひどい～を感じた Suddenly I felt *an* acute *pain* in my fingers. 薬で～を鎮めた I took medicine to relieve my *pain*.

い

歯の一はどうですか How is your *pain* in your tooth?
―止め an anodyne.

いたみい・る【痛み入る】¶ご親切～ります *Many thanks* (≒ *I do thank you*) for your kindness.

いた・む【痛む・傷む】**1**〖肉体的に〗¶酒を飲むと胃が～む My stomach *aches* whenever I drink *sake*.
歯がずきずき～んでよく眠れなかった I could not sleep well because I *had a bad toothache*.
まだ手術したところが～みます I *feel a pain* even now in the place where I underwent the operation.
そこが～む It *hurts* there.
2〖心が〗¶子を亡くした母を思うと胸の～む思いがする I *feel very sad* when I think of the mother who lost her child.
心を～ませ目をおおわせる光景であった It was a sight too *sad and miserable* to look at.
3〖品物が損傷する〗¶このバナナは～んでいる This banana *is bruised*.
生鮮食品は夏はすぐ～む Fresh foodstuffs easily *become bad* in summer.
アルカリ洗剤を使うと純毛製品は～む The alkaline cleanser *damages* wool material.
地震で壁が～んだ The walls of the room *were damaged* by the earthquake.
古い家でだいぶあちらこちら～んでいる My house is so old that it *needs repairs* here and there.

いた・む【悼む】grieve; mourn. ¶彼の死を～む I *grieved over* his death. 全世界の人がその国の大統領の死を～んだ All the world *mourned over* the death of the president of the country.

いためつ・ける【痛めつける】¶彼はすっかり～けられている He *has gone through an ordeal*. 弱い者を～けてはいけない Don't *be a bully*.

いた・める【痛める・傷める】¶太陽を見ると目を～める You will *hurt* (≒ *ruin*) your eyes if you look at the sun. のどを～めている I *have a sore throat*. サッカーをやっている間に右ひじを～めた While playing soccer, I *hurt* my right elbow. 子どもの教育のことで心を～めている I *am worried about* the education of my children.

いた・める【炒める】¶野菜を油で～める *fry* vegetables in oil.

いたらぬ【至らぬ】¶みんな私の～せいです It is all due to my *carelessness*. / It is all my *faults*. ～ことばかりで申しわけありません I'm sorry for all my *faults*. 私には～ところがたくさんある I have a lot of *faults*. なにもかも～者ですが I have no experience in everything.

いたり【至り】¶光栄の～です It is my greatest honor. ご成功の由慶賀の～です I offer my heartiest (≒ sincerest) congratulations to you on your success. 若げの～でした I was all too young and rash〔when I did that〕.

イタリア Italy.
―語 Italian. ―人 an Italian.

イタリック（活字） italics; italic letters. ¶～にする italicize; print *in italics*. ～は私のものである *Italics* are mine. (引用文の個所などに用いる).

いた・る【至る】**1**〖行き着く・達する〗¶この道はAを経てB市に～る This road *leads to* B City via A.
東京から名古屋に～る高速道路が完成した The superhighway (≒ 英 motorway) from Tokyo to Nagoya has been constructed.
今に～るも彼の消息は不明 *So far* (≒ *As yet*) nothing has been heard of him. / *As yet* no news of him.
今日に～るまで彼からはなんの音さたもない We have not heard anything from him *yet*.
(道路標識)～浦和10 km Urawa City 10 km.
2〖及ぶ〗¶わが国では小学生から高校生に～るまでみな受験勉強で悩まされる In this country *from* high school students *down to* primary school pupils all are worried about the preparations for their entrance examinations.
全国津々浦々に～るまで彼の名は知れ渡っている His name is known *all over* (≒ *throughout*) the country.
子を思う情は犬猫(いぬねこ)に～るまで変わらない *Even* cats and dogs have an affection for their young.
3〖…になる〗¶事ここに～っては手の施しようがない Now〔that〕things *have come to* this, there is no help for it.
大事に～らないでよかった Luckily it did not *become* serious.
大事に～らないうちに火を消し止めた The fire was put out before it *got* serious.
それ以後彼は神を信ずるに～った After that he *came to* believe in God.
悪天候のため大会は中止のやむなきに～った Owing to the bad weather, the general meeting is inevitably called off.
酒と女で彼は身を滅ぼすに～った He gave himself up to wine and women and ruined himself. / Indulgence in wine and women *led* to the ruin.
4〖来る〗¶悲喜こもごも～る We *have* a mixed feeling of joy and sorrow. / We *have* joy and sorrow all together.

いたるところ【至る所】everywhere; all over. ¶私たちは～で歓迎された We were welcomed *wherever* we went. 米は国じゅう～でできる Rice is grown *throughout* (≒ *all over*) the country. その銀行はほとんど～に支店がある That bank has its branches in almost *all parts of* the country.

いたれりつくせり【至れり尽くせり】¶このホテルの設備は～だ The accommodation at this hotel *is perfect* (≒ *is satisfactory*). ～のもてなしを受けた We were given *the most gracious* hospitality. / We were given *the most hospitable* welcome.

いたわし・い【労しい】feel sorry (*for*); feel pity (*for*). ¶ほんとにお～いことです I *am* very *sorry for* you. / I *feel a* great *pity for* you.

いたわり【労り】pity; sympathy. ¶彼は他人に対して～の心を欠いている He is lacking in *sympathy* for others.

いたわ・る【労る】(同情する) pity; sympathize; (世話する) care for. ¶老人を～らなくてはならない We must *be kind to* the old. 彼女は病気の母を～った She *took good care of* her sick mother.

いたん【異端】〔a〕heresy. ¶私はまわりの人すべてから～視された I *was looked coldly upon* by everybody around me.

―者 a heretic.

いち【一】one; (第1) the first.

¶私の父は～英語教師だ My father is a teacher of English. ～かばちかやってみよう I'll run a risk. / I'll take my chances. 彼は～から十まで知っていた He knew *everything* about it. / He knew it *from A to Z*. 彼女は彼の要求を～も二もなく拒否した She refused his demand *flatly*. 私はその計画に～も二もなく賛成した I agreed to the plan *readily* (≒ *without thinking twice*). その少年は～を聞いて十を知る One word is enough (≒ sufficient) for that wise boy. / The boy is very quick to understand. 彼女は知力では～といって二と下がらない In intelligence she is second to none.

いち【市】a market; a fair. ¶金曜日には～が立つ *A fair* is opened on Friday. ～の立つ日には大ぜい人が出る There is a crowd on *a market day*.

国際見本― an international trade fair. 青物― a vegetable market.

いち【位置】〔a〕position; a location. ¶この本だなの～は変えたほうがいい We must change the *position* of this bookshelf. 3人の警官が門の前に～を占めた Three policemen took their *stand* in front of the gate. この郵便局は～がよい This post office *is* favorably *situated*.

いちい【一位】¶第～になる take 〔*the*〕 *first rank*; rank (≒ stand) *first*; be placed *first*. 彼はクラスで第～だ He *is at the top of* his class. がんが死因の第～になるだろう Cancer will *take* 〔*the*〕 *first rank* as the cause of death.

いちいせんしん【一意専心】¶彼は～科学の研究に没頭している He *devotes himself to* the study of science. / He *is deeply absorbed in* the study of science.

いちいち【一一】¶彼は宝石を～拡大鏡で調べた He examined the gems *one by one* with a magnifying glass. ぼくのすることに～難癖をつけるな Don't find fault with *everything* I do. きみはそのことを～説明する必要はない You needn't explain it *in detail*.

いちいん【一員】a member.

いちいんせい【一院制】the single-chamber system.

いちえん【一円】¶関東～に *all over* the Kanto district (≒ area).

いちおう【一応】¶～両親とも相談のうえ決めたい Let me decide after consulting with my parents. 報告書には～目を通した I have glanced over the report. 彼の言うことは～もっともだ What he says sounds reasonable *in a way*. これで～よかろう That will do *for the time being*.

いちがいに【一概に】¶～そうとは言えない We cannot *always* say so. ～彼をけなすのはまちがいだ It's wrong to blame him *indiscriminately*.

いちがつ【一月】January. ¶～に in *January*.

いちぐう【一隅】a corner; a nook.

いちげき【一撃】a blow; a stroke. ¶～で at (≒ with) *a blow*. 彼の頭に～を加えた I struck (≒ gave) him *a blow* on the head.

いちげん【一元】¶～化 unification; centralization. ～化する unify. ～的(論の) unitary.

―論 monism. **―論者** a monist. **―一次方程式**〔数学〕a simple equation.

いちげん【一言】¶彼は～居士だ He has something to say about everything. ⇒いちごん

いちげん【一見】¶～の客(初対面の客) a *chance* customer.

いちご【苺】〔植物〕a strawberry.

―畑 a strawberry-bed. **―クリーム** strawberry and cream.

いちご【一期】¶～の思い出に as the last chance *in one's life*; for the last time on earth. 彼は60歳を～としてこの世を去った He died at the age of sixty. ～一会(いちえ) the only chance *in one's life*. ～の不覚 the greatest failure *in one's life*.

いちご【一語】¶～～word for word. ～も聞き漏らすまいと彼の演説に耳を澄ませた During his speech I was all ears.

いちごう【一号】No. 1; Number One.

いちごうめ【一合目】the first tenth of the distance up the hill; the first milestone on the way to the summit.

いちごん【一言】¶～も弁解の余地はない I have not *a word* to say in excuse. 彼はその申し出を～のもとに断わった He refused the offer flatly. 彼は～のあいさつもなく立ち去った He left without saying *a single word* of greeting. ドイツ語は～半句もわからない I don't understand German at all.

いちざ【一座】¶～を見渡す glance over *those present*. ～を組織する organize *a troupe*. 菊五郎～ Kikugoro and his *company*.

いちじ【一次】¶～試験 a *primary* examination.

―方程式〔数学〕a simple equation.

いちじ【一事】¶～が万事 He that will steal a pin will steal an ox.

いちじ【一時】**1**〖かつて〗¶そのヘアスタイルは～ほどはやらなくなった The hair style is not so much in fashion as it *once* was.

～彼は金にひどく困っていた *Once* he was hard up for money.

私は～釣りに夢中になった *Once* I was crazy about angling. / I *used to* be very keen on

い

(≒ about) angling.
その作家は～は人気があった The writer was popular *at one time*.
2 〚しばらくの間〛 for a while. ¶ 試合は～雨で中断された The game was interrupted by the rain *for some time*.
～休憩しよう Let's take a *short* rest. / Let's rest *for a while*.
最近の輸出の不振は～的な現象だ The recent decrease in exports *is temporary*. / The recent depression in exportation is only a *temporary* phenomenon.
家電業界は～的には不況に見舞われた The household electric machinery industry suffered a *transitory* (≒ *temporary*) depression.
会場は混乱し～はどうなることかと思われた The meeting place was thrown into confusion *for a while*, and we could not tell how it would end up.
—預かり所 a checkroom; a cloakroom.
—しのぎ ¶ そんなのは～しのぎの策にしかすぎぬ Such 〔a thing〕 is *a* mere *makeshift*. **—**逃れ ¶ 彼は～逃れの弁解をしている He is making an *evasive* excuse. **—**預け ¶ 荷物は駅で～預けにしよう I will have my baggage *checked* at the station. / I will leave my baggage at the station locker.
3 〚同時に・一度に〛 ¶ そんなにたくさん～にやれと言ったって無理だ It is too much to ask me to do so many things *at a time*. / You must not ask me to do so many things *at a time*.
—払い ¶ 工費は完成後1週間以内に～払いという約束になっている We have made a contract to *pay* the cost of construction *in a lump sum* within a week after its completion.
—金 ¶ 彼は～金をもらって退職した He retired on *a lump sum*.

いちじいっく【一字一句】 ¶ 彼は～もゆるがせにしない He carefully weighs *every word and phrase*.

いちじく【無花果】 〘植物〙 (実) a fig; (木) a fig tree.

いちじつ【一日】 ¶ 英語教育にかけては彼はきみより～の長がある He *is a little more experienced than* you *in* teaching English. 彼は十年～のごとくがんの研究に専念している He has devoted himself to the study of cancer *for a long time*.

いちじゅういっさい【一汁一菜】 (かんたんな食事) a simple meal.

いちじゅん【一巡】 a tour. ¶ 彼は災害地を～した He *made a tour of* the damaged areas. 巡査は彼の受け持ち区域を～した The policeman *patrolled his beat*.

いちじょ【一助】 a help; an aid. ¶ 外国貿易振興の～として as *a help* to 〔the〕 promotion of foreign trade.

いちじょう【一条】 ¶ ～のいなずま *a streak of* lightning. 第～ Article (≒ Art.) 1.

いちじるし・い【著しい】 ¶ 彼は近ごろ英語の勉強に～い進歩をみせた He has recently made *remarkable* progress in the study of English. 原子科学は～く発達した Atomic science has *strikingly* developed. 野菜の値が～く下落した Vegetables have *considerably* fallen in prices.

いちじん【一陣】 ¶ ～の風が起こった *A gust* (≒ *blast*) *of wind* rose.

いちず【一途】 ¶ 彼の～な願いも退けられた His *earnest* request was refused. 彼の～な気持ちに引かされてぼくは申し出に同意した Being touched by his *eagerness*, I agreed to the proposal. 彼はぼくがまちがっていると～に思い込んでいる He *is quite sure* that I am wrong. 彼女は～に彼のことを思いつめている She *is mad* (≒ *crazy*) *about* him. 彼の～さに深く打たれた I was deeply moved by his *eagerness*.

いちぞく【一族】 (一家族) *one's* whole family; (親類たち) relatives; kinsmen.
—郎党 all *one's* family and followers.

いちぞん【一存】 *one's* own will. ¶ そのことは私の～では決められない I cannot decide it *on my own responsibility*.

いちだい【一代】 (世代) a generation; (一生) *one's* lifetime; *one's* whole life; (治世) one dynasty.
¶ ～の英雄 the *greatest* hero *of the age*. 彼の～の不覚 the *greatest* mistake *in his life*. 人は～, 名は末代 (諺) Man *is mortal* but fame is immortal. 彼は～で富を築いた He made a big fortune *in his lifetime*.
—記 a biography; a life.

いちだいじ【一大事】 a serious matter; a great matter. ¶ それはぼくらにとって～だ It is *a vital matter to* us. 彼の身にもしものことがあったら～だ What if anything should happen to him!

いちだん【一団】 ¶ ～となって in a group; in a body. それぞれ～となって in groups. ～の子どもたち *a group of* children. 彼はヨーロッパ旅行の～をつくった He formed *a party* to go to Europe.

いちだん【一段】 (階段) one step; (文章) a paragraph; a passage.

いちだんと【一段と】 ¶ ～声を張り上げて *more* loudly. それは～おもしろそうだ It seems *more* interesting. そのスカーフだとあなたはまた～おきれいです The scarf *adds to* your beauty.

いちだんらく【一段落】 ¶ これでこの仕事も～だ We *have completed the first stage of* the work. / The work *has been brought to an end for the present*.

いちど【一度】 ¶ 北海道には～行ったことがある I have been to Hokkaido *once*. ～見たいものだ I want to have a look at it. この祭りは1年に～行なわれる This festival is held *once* a year. もう～言ってください Please say *once* more. もう～おっしゃってください(相手のことばが聞きとれなかったとき) I beg your pardon. (文尾を上がり調子に). / (かんたんに) Pardon. ふたりは～に帰ってきた The two returned *at the same time*. この仕事を～に仕上げるのは難しい It is not possible to complete the work *at a* *stretch*. 鎌倉は～ならず訪れた I have visited Kamakura more than *once*. その博物館には～も行ったことがない I have never visited the museum.

いちどう【一同】all; everyone. ¶ 家内～ *all one's* family. われわれ～ *all* of us; we *all*. ～を代表して on behalf of *the company*.

いちどう【一堂】a hall. ¶ ～に会す gather together; meet together.

いちどく【一読】¶ その本は～の価値がある The book is worth *reading*.

いちなん【一難】one misfortune; a disaster. ¶ ～去ってまた～(諺) One misfortune follows〔close on the heels of〕another. / Hills peep o'er hills, and Alps on Alps arise. (Alexander Pope の詩より).

いちに【一二】¶ 彼は数学ではクラスで～を争うほどだ Almost no one in his class can match (≒ touch) him in mathematics. / His classmates can hardly match him in mathematics.

いちにち【一日】(日数) a day; (その日) the day; (終日) all day. ¶ 第～ (*on*) the first day. ～の仕事 *a day's* work. ～働く work *all day*. ～休む have *a day* off. ～か2日で in *a day* or two. ～おきに every other day. ～に3回 three times *a day*. ～かかる It takes *a whole day*. ～延ばしに延ばす keep on putting off (something) *from day to day*. ～～と春が近づく Spring is coming nearer *day by day*. 交通事故のない日は～もない Not *a day* passes without some traffic accidents.

いちにん【一任】¶ そのことはきみに～しよう I'll *leave* the matter *to* you. / I'll *leave* the matter *in* your hands.

いちにんまえ【一人前】(食物の) one portion; (年齢が) an adult. ¶ ～になる(成人する) become *an adult*; (独立する) become independent. すき焼き～ *one portion of sukiyaki*. 上ずしは～800円です A better *sushi* costs eight hundred yen *for one person*.
彼には～の仕事はできない He cannot do *one man's* work.

いちねん【一年】**1**〚年月の〛a year. ¶ ～は365日だ *A year* has 365 days.
彼は～おきに海外に行く He goes abroad *every other year*.
あの山の頂上は～じゅう雪に覆われている The top of the mountain is covered with snow *all the year round*.
子どもは～～大きくなる Children grow bigger *year after year*.
2〚学校の〛¶ 彼の息子は高校～だ His son is a high school freshman. (freshman は女生徒にも用いる).
私の弟は小学校～だ My brother is *a first grader*. / My brother is *in the first grade*. (小中学校には grade を用いる).

いちねん【一念】¶ 彼は～発起して禁煙した He *is* firmly *determined to* give up (≒ quit) smoking.

いちば【市場】a market〔place〕. ¶ 野菜～ a vegetable market.

いちはやく【逸早く】at once; quickly. ¶ 救急車は～現場に向かった The ambulance hurried to the spot *at once*.

いちばん【一番】**1**〚番号〛¶ 受験番号～から50番の方は～教室で受験する The examinees whose numbers are between *1* and 50 (≒ with numbers *1*-50) are to sit in the schoolroom *One*.
「あなたの番号は何番ですか」「～です」 "Your number, please?" "It's *One*."
2〚順位〛¶ 彼はクラスの～で卒業した He graduated〔*at*〕*the top of* the class.
今学期は成績が～だけ上がった This term I jumped over *one place*.
100メートル競走で～になった I *won* a 100 meter race (≒ dash).
競技会で～になった I *got the first place in* the contest.
健康が～だ Health *is everything*. / *Nothing is more important* than health.
そうするのが～だ You *had best* do so, I'm sure. / It is *the best* to do so.
あす～列車に乗るつもりだ Tomorrow I will take *the first* train.
彼はいの～に投票した He was *the very first person to* vote. / He voted *first of all*.
彼はその町の～街に店を出している He keeps a store on *the main street* in the town.
その列車は～線に到着します The train is due on *Track One*.
もう～茶が出るころだ It is about time for *the first* pick of tea to be ready for sale.
現場に～乗りをしたのはわが社の記者だ Our pressman was *the first to* arrive at the spot.
彼は村～の人気者だ He is *the most* popular person with the village. / He is a lion among the villagers.
彼女の家は上町5丁目～地2号にある Her house is at Lot 2, *No. 1*, Kamimachi 5 chome.
だれが～打者か Who is *the first* (≒ *lead-off*) batter?
3〚なによりも・だれよりも〛¶ 彼の忠告が～こたえた His advice came home to me *more than anything else*.
～印象に残ったのは主役の演技だった *The most* impressive was the performance of the leading man. / I was impressed *most* with the performance of the star player.
～よく働いたのは彼だ It was he that worked *hardest*.
彼に会えなかったのが～心残りだ That I couldn't see him was *the most* regrettable. / I regret it *most deeply* that I could not see him.
最後の問題が～難しかった The last question was *the hardest*.
彼が家じゅうで～背が高い He is *the tallest* of all the family.
そこへ行くには地下鉄が～速い The subway will be *the fastest* to get there by. / You will make the best time there by subway.
4〚ひと勝負〛¶ 将棋を～指そう Shall we have

い

a game of Japanese chess?

いちぶ【一分】 ¶ 彼女は～の隙もない身なりで外出した She went out, *fully dressed up*.

いちぶ【一部】 (部分) 〔a〕 part; (1冊) a copy. ¶ ～は in part; partly. ～の人々 *some* people. 借金の～を支払う pay 〔a〕 *part of* the debt. 委員会は～は使用者～は労働者から成る The committee is made up *partly* of the employers and *partly* of the workers. (本が)～1,000円です It costs a thousand yen *a copy*. ～始終を聞かせてください Tell me the whole story 〔of it〕.

いちぶいちりん【一分一厘】 ¶ これはあれと～も違わない This is *exactly* the same as that.

いちぶぶん【一部分】 〔a〕 part (*of something*).

いちべつ【一別】 ¶ ～以来7年にもなります It is seven long years since *I saw you last* (≒ *we last met*). / It has been already seven years since *we met last*

いちべつ【一瞥】 a glance. ¶ ～してどちらが正しいかわかった I knew *at a glance* which was right. 彼は～もせずその場を去った He went away without 〔casting〕 *a glance*.

いちぼう【一望】 ¶ 晴れた日にはそこからは富士の全景が～のうちにおさめられる On a nice day it *commands a complete view of* Mt. Fuji. ～千里の海原 *an unlimited expanse of* waters.; *a vast stretch of* waters.

いちまい【一枚】 ¶ ～の紙 *a sheet of* paper. きみの写真を～ください Please give me *a picture* of you. 彼のほうがきみよりなにをやっても役者が～上だ He is a little better than you in everything.

—看板 the shining star.

いちまつ【一抹】 ¶ ～の不安 *a touch* (≒ *a shadow*) *of* uneasiness. 彼女には～の哀愁がある There is *a touch of* sadness about her.

いちまつ【市松】 checks; plaid.

いちみ【一味】 (陰謀などの) fellow conspirators; (ギャングの) a gang. ¶ 陰謀の～に加わる take part in the conspiracy. ギャングの～は残らず検挙された The whole gang was arrested.

いちみゃく【一脈】 ¶ あのふたりの間には，なにか～相通ずるものがあるにちがいない Those two must have something in common.

いちめい【一名】 (ひとり) a person; (別名) another name. ¶ ～1,000円 a thousand yen *a person*. イギリスの警官は～ボビーと呼ばれる Bobby is *another name* for the policeman in England.

いちめん【一面】 ¶ 彼は問題の～だけしか知らぬ He knows only *one side* (≒ *one phase*) of the problem. それはアメリカの社会の明るい～を表わしている It shows the brighter *side* of American society. 彼女のことばにも～の真理がある There is *some* truth in her words. この子は頭はいいが，～そそっかしいところもある This boy is bright, but *on the other hand* he is careless. 空～に雲が垂れ込めていた The cloud hung *all over* the sky. 家は～火の海と化していた The whole house was in flames. 辺り～銀世界だった The whole place was covered with snow.

いちめんしき【一面識】 ¶ 彼とは～もない He is a 〔perfect〕 stranger to me. / I have never met him before.

いちもうさく【一毛作】〘農業〙 a single crop.

いちもうだじん【一網打尽】 a wholesale arrest. ¶ 盗賊たちを～にする *make a wholesale arrest of* all the robbers.

いちもく【一目】 ¶ 英語ではぼくは彼に～置いている I *admit that he is superior to* me in English. 彼も彼女には～置いている He *admits his inferiority to* her. それは～瞭然(りょうぜん)だ It is 〔as〕 clear as day (≒ daylight).

いちもくさんに【一目散に】 ¶ 彼は～逃げ去った He ran off *at full speed*.

いちもつ【一物】 ¶ ～も取らずに without stealing *a thing*. 彼は胸に～ありそうだ I suspect 〔that〕 he *has some plot* in his mind. / I suspect he *has an axe to grind*.

いちもん【一文】 a penny; a farthing. ¶ それは～の値うちもない It's not worth *a farthing*. 彼は～なしになった He *has become penniless*. / He *is broke*. ～惜しみの百失い (諺) *Penny-wise and pound-foolish*.

いちもん【一門】 (一家・一族) a family; a clan; (同門) a fellow pupil (≒ student); (同じ宗派の者) one who belongs to the same religious party.

いちもんいっとう【一問一答】 questions and answers; a dialogue. ¶ ～する give an immediate answer to each question.

いちもんじ【一文字】 ¶ 口を～に結んで with *one's* lips tightly pressed. ～に in a straight; in a beeline.

いちや【一夜】 a night; one night. ¶ ～を過ごす spend (≒ pass) *a night*; stay *overnight* (*in*; *at*). 不安な～を過ごす spend *an* uneasy *night*. 眠られない～を過ごす spend *a* sleepless *night*. ～で有名になる become famous *in a night*; leap into fame.

—づけ(つけ物) pickles salted only overnight; (試験勉強) cramming for an examination; (知識) a hastily acquired knowledge.

いちやく【一躍】 ¶ 彼は直木賞を取り，～人気作家になった He got the *Naoki* Prize and became *suddenly* a popular writer.

いちゃつ・く ¶ 女と～く *flirt with* a woman. ～き合う *flirt with* each other.

いちゅう【意中】 *one's* mind; *one's* heart. ¶ 彼の～の女 his sweetheart. 彼女の～の男 her lover. 彼の後継者として彼の～の人物 the man he wants to choose as his successor. ～を明かす speak 〔out〕 *one's mind*. ～を読む read *a person's mind*. ～を探る sound *a person* out about (≒ on) his *idea*.

いちょ【遺著】 a posthumous work.

いちょう【銀杏】〘植物〙 a maidenhair tree; a ginkgo; a gingko.

いちょう【医長】 the head physician (*of a*

department).

いちょう【胃腸】 ¶ 私は～が弱い I have a poor digestion. 夏にはよく～をこわす I often suffer from indigestion in summer.

―病 a disorder of digestion. **―病院** a hospital for stomach and intestines.

いちよう【一様】 ¶ ～の(同一の) 〔the〕 same; (似ている) alike; similar. ～に alike; similarly. それらは大きさが～ではない They are not *of a size*. 子どもは～には扱えない Children cannot be treated *all alike*.

いちらん【一卵】 **―性双生児** an identical twin.

いちらん【一覧】 (閲覧) a look; an inspection; (概要) a summary. ¶ カタログをご～ください Please *have a look at* the catalog. ご～のうえお返しください Please return it after *looking through* it.

―払い為替手形 a bill payable at sight. **―表** a catalog; a list.

いちり【一理】 some truth. ¶ 彼らの言い分にも～ある There is *some truth* in what they say.

いちりいちがい【一利一害】 advantages and disadvantages; merits and demerits.

¶ それには～ある It has its *advantages and disadvantages*.

いちりつ【一律】 ¶ それらは～には論じられない We cannot *apply the same rule to* them. 老若～にはいかぬ The old and the young do not go *uniformly*.

いちりゅう【一流】 **1**〖第一級の〗 first class. ¶ この辺には～ホテルが並んでいる There stand *first-class* hotels around here.

彼は実業界における～の人物だ He is one of *the foremost* men in the business circles.

2〖独特の〗 ¶ この本の中には彼～の機知に富んだ発言が随所に見られる The witty remarks *characteristic of* him are 〔to be found〕 on almost every page.

この本は彼～の文体で書かれている This book is written in a style *of his own*.

いちりん【一輪】 (花の) a 〔single〕 flower.

¶ 梅が～二輪と咲きはじめた The plum-blossoms are coming out one after another.

―差し a single-stalk flower vase; a small flower vase.

いちる【一縷】 ¶ かくて～の望みも絶えた Thus went down our *last* hope. ～の望みを天候の変化に託した We hung our *last* hope on the change of weather.

いちるい【一塁】 〘野球〙 〔the〕 first base. ¶ 彼は四球で～に出た He walked to *first base* 〔on four balls〕.

―手 〔the〕 first baseman.

いちれい【一例】 an example. ¶ ～として as an example. 彼は～をあげた He gave *an example*. これは数々ある中の～にすぎない This is only *one instance* out of many. ～をあげれば (物なら) for example; (事なら) for instance.

いちれい【一礼】 a bow (〔bau〕 と発音する).

¶ 彼は私にていねいに～した He *bowed* to me politely. / He made *a* polite *bow to* me.

いちれんたくしょう【一蓮托生】 ¶ われわれはみな～だ We share our fortunes, good or bad. / We *are in the same boat*.

いちろ【一路】 ¶ 船は～シアトルに向かっていた The ship was sailing *straight* (≒ *direct*) for Seattle. ～平安を祈る *Good luck!* / *Bon voyage!* / *I wish you a very nice trip*.

いつ【何時】 ¶ ～お出かけですか *When* (≒ *What time*) will you leave? ～ここに引っ越したのですか *When* did you move here? ～横浜に行ったのか忘れた I forgot *when* I visited Yokohama. ～私がそんなことを言った *When* did I say such a thing?

いっか【一家】 **1**〖家庭・家族〗 a family.

¶ ～こぞってブラジルに移住した *The whole family* emigrated to Brazil.

～そろって海に出かけます *All my family* are going to the seaside.

彼女の細腕で～を支えるのは容易ではなかった It was no easy task for her to support her *family* on her limited means.

久しぶりに～だんらんの楽しみを味わった After a long time I enjoyed the pleasure of *a happy home*. / I enjoyed relaxing with *the whole family* after a long time.

彼もようやく～を構えるようになった At length he also has got *a home of his own*.

～のあるじともなれば彼も責任を感じるだろう As the head of *a family*, he will feel responsible.

2〖独自の流派〗 ¶ 木彫のほうで彼は既に～をなしている He *has* already *established a reputation as* a wood carver.

彼女は現代書道で～をなしている She *has developed a style of her own in* modern calligraphy. / She *has established a school of her own as* a modern calligrapher.

いつか【何時か】 ¶ ～は彼も後悔するだろう *Some day* he will repent 〔of〕 it. ～またお目にかかりましょう I'll see you *sometime* again. 夏休み中～北海道にいらっしゃいませんか Will you please come over to Hokkaido *sometime* during the summer vacation? 私たちは～は別れるのだ We are to part *sooner or later*. 正しい者は～は勝つ The righteous will win *in the long run*. ～お目にかかりましたね I think I've met you *before*. ～彼に通りで会った I *once* met him on the street. この方が～お話したスミス氏です This is Mr. Smith I spoke of *the other day*. ～のお話はどうなったの What has become of the matter we spoke of *the other day*? そのうち～そこへ連れてってあげるよ I'll take you there *one of these days*. ～春になった Spring has come *before we are aware of it*. 歩いているうちに～暗くなった While I was walking I found it had got dark.

いっかい【一介】 ¶ 私は～のサラリーマンにすぎない I am a *mere* salaried man.

いっかい【一回】 (1度) once; one time; (勝負の) a round; a game; (野球の) the first inning〔s〕. ¶ 週に～ *once* a week. もう～ *once* more. 彼は～で成功した He succeeded

い

at his first attempt.

いっかい【一階】㊍ the first floor; ㊎ the ground floor.

いっかく【一角】¶ 天の〜を見詰めた I looked into *a corner* of the sky.

—獣 a unicorn.

いっかくせんきん【一攫千金】¶ 彼はいつも〜を夢みている He is always attempting to *become wealthy at a single bound*. / He is always attempting to *get rich quick*.

いっかげん【一家言】*one's* own opinion.

いっかつ【一括】¶ それらの法案は〜して審議された Those bills were discussed *en bloc*. 〜して購入するのが得だ It is more economical to buy it *in bulk*. これらの家具を〜して売りたい I want to sell the furniture *in one lot*.

いっかつ【一喝】¶ 彼に〜を食らわした I *gave* him *a good scolding*.

いつから【何時から】¶ 〜待っていたのですか *How long* have you been waiting? 〜上京していらっしゃるのですか *When* did you come to Tokyo? / *Since when* have you been staying in Tokyo?

いっかん【一貫】¶ 党には〜した政策がない The party has no *consistent* policy. あの人の話は〜していなかった His talk *was incoherent*. きみの説明は〜していない Your explanation lacks *coherence*. 彼は終始〜して画道に専念した He was devoted to the art of painting *throughout his life*. 彼は〜した主張を通している He *is consistent in* his opinions.

いっかん【一環】a link. ¶ これが彼の政策の〜をなしている This forms *a part* of his policy. これは事実の〜だ This is *a link* in a chain of facts.

いっき【一気】¶ 〜に読み終えた I read the book *at a sitting*. 彼は〜に1時間以上も走った He ran more than an hour *without a rest*. 彼は〜に3時間も働きつづけた He continued to work for three hours *at a stretch*. ひとびんを〜に飲み干した I emptied the bottle *at a draft*.

いっき【一騎】a [single] horseman. ¶ 彼らは〜打ちに及んだ The horsemen *fought in a single combat*. / (歩兵の場合) They *fought man to man*. 〜当千のつわものぞろいだった Each of the soldiers was *a match for a thousand*.

いっき【一揆】a riot. ¶ 〜が起こった *A revolt* broke out.

百姓— a peasants' uprising.

いっきいちゆう【一喜一憂】¶ ニュースの入るたびごとに私どもは〜した As the news came in, we *felt now joyous, now depressed*.

いっきゅう【一級】the first class. ¶ 彼の腕前は〜だ His skill is *excellent* (≒ *first-class*). このぶどう酒は〜品だ This wine is of *the first class*.

いっきょ【一挙】¶ 〜に仕事をやり終えた I finished the work *at a stretch*. 〜に敵を破った We defeated the enemy *by one charge*. 彼女の〜一動を見守った I watched her *every movement*. それは〜両得だ It serves two ends. 〜に事を決しよう Let's decide the issue *by one effort*.

いっきょう【一興】fun. ¶ それも〜だろう It would be *fun* to do so.

いっきょう【一驚】¶ まさに〜に値する事件だった The incident was *surprising* enough.

いっきょしゅいっとうそく【一挙手一投足】¶ 観衆はみんな彼の〜を見守った All the spectators watched *every movement* of his performance.

いつ·く【居つく】¶ あの家にはお手伝いさんが〜かない Maids won't *stay long* in that family. 息子が家に〜かない My son *seldom stays* at home. ここに〜いてもう10年になる It is ten years since I *settled down* here.

いつくしみ【慈しみ】love; affection; loving-kindness. ¶ 彼らはその子に〜深いまなざしを向けた They cast *loving* glances upon the child. 彼は〜深い性格だ He is a man of great *benevolence*.

いつくし·む【慈しむ】¶ 王は民を〜んだ The king *loved* the people. 動物を〜む *be kind to* animals.

いっけい【一計】a plan. ¶ そこで彼は〜を案じた Then he devised *a plan*.

いっけん【一見】¶ 問題は〜やさしそうだった *At first sight* the problem seemed easy. そのすりは〜紳士風だった The pickpocket *looked* like a gentleman *to all appearance*. 彼は〜健康そうだが,体が弱いということだ He *looks* healthy, but he is said to be weak.

いっけん【一件】a case; a matter. ¶ あの〜はもみ消されてしまった That *case* has been covered up. 例の〜はかたづきましたか Is everything settled about *the affair*?

いっこ【一戸】a house; (世帯) a household. ¶ 郊外に〜を構えた I have got *a home of my own* in the suburbs. 〜当たり200円の寄付を仰いだ Two hundred yen per *household* was asked for as the contribution.

いっこ【一己】oneself. ¶ 私〜の考えでやったことです I did it *on my own responsibility*.

いっこ【一個】one; a piece. ¶ 〜100円のリンゴ apples one hundred yen *each* (≒ *a piece*). 〜ずつ数えなさい Count them *one by one*.

いっこ【一顧】¶ この映画は〜の価値もない This film *is quite worthless*. そんな議論は〜にもあたいしない Such a discussion *is beneath our notice*. それは〜の価値がある It *deserves an examination*.

いっこう【一行】a party. ¶ 〜は全部で14名であった *The party* was fourteen in all. われわれ〜に加わりませんか Will you join our *party*? 首相の〜はその工場を視察した The Premier and *his suite* inspected the plant.

いっこう【一考】¶ どうぞご〜を願います I ask you to *think of* the matter. / Please give your *consideration to* the matter. この件に関してご〜くださればありがたく存じます Thank you for your *consideration* in this matter. (手紙のきまり文句). 〜を要する問題だ This is a matter for *consideration*. それにはなお～の余地がある It leaves room for *consideration*.

いっこう〔に〕【一向〔に〕】 ¶～に存じません I know *nothing* of it. / I *don't* know *at all*. ～にかまいません I *don't* mind *a bit*. / I *don't* care *a damn*. 彼はそんなことは～にとんじゃくしない He is *absolutely* indifferent to such a matter.

いっこく【一刻】 ¶～の猶予もできません Not *a moment* is to be lost. / We cannot afford to lose *a moment* now. ～を争う問題です It is a *burning* question. ～も早くおいでください Come 〔over〕 *at once* (≒ *as soon as you can*). 彼を～も早く入院させねばならない We must send him to 〔the〕 hospital *without a moment's delay*.

いっこく【一国】 ¶これでも～一城のあるじだ I have a home of my own, be it ever so humble.

いっこくもの【一刻者】 an obstinate person. ¶彼は～だ He *is stubborn* (≒ *is obdurate*).

いつごろ【何時頃】 ¶～おいでくださいますか *When* will you come? ここでは～桜が満開になりますか Tell me *about what time* cherry blossoms are in full bloom here.

いっさい【一切】 ¶この事件に私は～無関係です I *have nothing at all to do with* this affair. それについては～知らない I know *nothing* about it. 彼とは～つきあわないことにした I made up my mind *not to have anything to do with* him. 彼は自分の過去について～忘れたということだ He is said to have forgotten *everything* about his past.

いつざい【逸材】 a man of talent.

いっさく-【一昨-】 ¶～日 the day before yesterday. ～夜 the night before last. ～年 the year before last. ～昨年 three years ago.

いっさつ【一札】(書きつけ) a written statement; (借用証) an I.O.U.(I owe you. の短縮形). ¶彼に金を貸すときは必ず～を取っておきなさい Be sure to get *an I.O.U.* from him when you lend him money. 後日のために～を入れておきましょう I will give you *a written statement* for future reference.

いっさんかたんそ【一酸化炭素】〖化学〗 carbon monoxide.

いっさんに【一散に】 ¶どろぼうは～逃げだした The thief took to his heels *at the top of his speed* (≒ *for his life*).

いっし【一糸】 ¶彼らは～乱れず進軍した They marched on *in perfect order*. 彼女は身に～もまとわない死体で発見された She was found dead *without a strip of clothing on*.

いっし【一矢】 ¶彼の悪意ある批評になんとかして～報わねばならぬ I must *make a retort to* his malicious criticism.

いっしき【一式】 ¶茶道具～ *a* 〔*complete*〕 *set of* tea things. 家具～ *a suit of* furniture. キャンプ用具～ *an outfit for* a camping trip.

いっしそうでん【一子相伝】 ¶これは～の秘薬だ This is the secret medicine *handed down from our ancestors*.

いっしゃせんり【一瀉千里】 ¶彼らは～に森を馬で駆け抜けた They rode through the forest *at full gallop*. 彼は～に脚本を書き上げた He *dashed off* a play. / He *wrote off* a play *at a stretch*.

いっしゅ【一首】 ¶その場で～作った I composed *a poem* offhand.

いっしゅ【一種】 a kind; a variety. ¶キルトは～のスカートだ A kilt is *a kind* (≒ *sort*) of skirt. これはサボテンの～だ This is *a variety* of cactus. この種の果物は～独特な味がする This *kind* of fruit has a taste all its own. 会場は～異様なふんい気に包まれていた An *indescribable* atmosphere filled the meeting place.

いっしゅう【一周】 ¶月は地球を約28日で～する The moon *goes* (≒ *revolves*) *round* the earth in about 28 days. 世界～旅行をする *travel round* the world. 伊豆七島を～する *make a circuit of* the Islands of Izu.

―忌 the first anniversary of *a person's* death.

いっしゅう【一週】 a week. ¶～間に3回の英語の授業 three English classes *a week*. ～間以内に within *a week*. ～いくらで by the *week*. ～間の休暇 *a week's* holiday. この～間どこに行っていたのか Where have you been *all this week*?

いっしゅう【一蹴】 ¶彼はわれわれの要求を～した He *refused* (≒ *turned down*) our request *flatly*. わがチームは敵を軽く～した Our team *beat* the opponent very *easily*.

いっしゅん【一瞬】 a moment. ¶それはほんの～の間の出来事であった All this happened *for an instant*. 彼は～気を失ったような感じがした He felt as if he were unconscious *for a moment*. 彼は～の透きをつかれた He was attacked at *an* unguarded *moment*.

いっしょ【一緒】 ¶夕食後私たちは～に散歩した We took a walk *together* after supper. きみはだれかに～に行ってもらいなさい Ask someone to go along *with* you. 水と油は～にならない Water and oil cannot *mix*. 2か月分の給料を～にもらった I received two months' pay *in a lump*. きみも～に行かないか Why not *join* us? 私たちは～になって彼を助けた We all helped him *together*. 彼らは大学を卒業したらすぐ～になろうと誓いあった They pledged themselves to *get married* soon after graduating from the university. あんなやつと～にされちゃ大変だ I don't want to *be lumped with* such a fellow.

いっしょう【一生】 a lifetime; *one's* life. ¶彼は～孤独だった He was lonely *all his life*. 彼は医学の研究に～をささげた He devoted *his life* to the study of medicine. ～に1度のチャンスだ Such an opportunity will never come again in our *lifetime*. それを～の仕事にしている That is his lifework. 彼が～を棒に振ったのは悲しいことだ It is a pity that he made a failure of *his life*. あなたの恩は～忘れません I will never forget your kindness. 九死に

い

～を得た He had a narrow escape. 彼は新聞記者として～を送った He spent *all his life* as a pressman.

いっしょう【一笑】 ¶ 彼はぼくの懸念を～に付した He *laughed away* my fears. / He *dismissed* my fears *with a laugh*.

いっしょうけんめい【一生懸命】 ¶ 彼は～勉強した He studied *very hard*. 彼は～走った He ran *as fast as he could*. 彼は～(命からがら)逃げた He ran *for his life*. なにをするにも～にやりなさい *Do your best* in 〔doing〕 anything. 彼は～に働いた He worked *with all his might*. 彼は息子の教育に～だ He *is very earnest over* his son's education.

いっしょくそくはつ【一触即発】 ¶ 2国間の関係は～の様相を呈していた The relationship between the two countries *was strained to the breaking point*. / The two countries faced each other in a *touch-and-go* situation.

いっしょけんめい【一所懸命】 ⇒いっしょうけんめい

いっしん【一心】 ¶ 彼は～に勉強していた He *was absorbed in* his studies. 彼は日本に帰りたい～で金をためた He saved money because he *was so eager* to return to Japan. 彼らは～同体だ They *are of one mind*.

いっしん【一身】 ¶ 彼は～上のつごうで辞職した He resigned for some *personal* reasons.

いっしん【一審】 the first trial. ¶ 彼は～で無罪となった He was found not guilty *at the first trial*.

いっしん【一新】 ¶ 面目を～する assume a new aspect. 生活を～する begin a new life.

いっしんいったい【一進一退】 ¶ ～の接戦だった It was a *seesaw* (≒ *close*) game. 彼の病状は～を続けている His condition still *hangs in the balance*.

いっしんきょう【一神教】 〔宗教〕 monotheism.
—徒 a monotheist.

いっすい【一睡】 ¶ 昨夜は～もしなかった I could not *get a wink of sleep* last night.

いっ·する【逸する】 ¶ 彼は絶好の機会を～した He *let* the chance of a lifetime *go by*. 彼の行動は常規を～している His conduct *is very eccentric* (≒ *abnormal*).

いっすん【一寸】 ¶ 暗くて～先も見えなかった It was so dark that we could not see *an inch ahead*. ～の光陰軽んずべからず Not *a moment* 〔of time〕 may be wasted. ～の虫にも五分の魂(諺) *Even a worm will turn*.
—法師 a dwarf; a midget.

いっせい【一世】 (移民などの) an 'issei' (日本語の「一世」から). ¶ エリザベス～ Elizabeth I (the first と読む). ～の雄 the greatest hero of *the age*. ～を風靡(ふうび)した流行ももうすたれた The fashion which *has swept the whole world* has gone.

いっせい【一声】 a voice. ¶ 首相の帰国後の第～ the prime minister's *first statement* after his homecoming.

いっせい【一斉】 ¶ ～射撃 volley-firing. ランナーは～にスタートを切った All the runners started *at the same time*. 彼らは～に彼女の方を振り向いた They turned toward her *all at once*. 全国～の中学生学力テストがあす行なわれる The *nation-wide* achievement tests for junior high school students will be held tomorrow. 本誌は10日に全国～に発売になります The magazine will be issued on the 10th *throughout* the country. きのう交通の～取り締まりが行なわれた The traffic regulation was *simultaneously* held yesterday.

いっせいき【一世紀】 a century.

いっせいちだい【一世一代】 ¶ その企てで彼は～の大成功を収めた The undertaking turned out *the greatest* success *in his life*.

いっせき【一席】 ¶ ～ぶつ make a speech. ～設ける give (≒ hold) a party.

いっせき【一石】 ¶ ～二鳥(諺) *Killing two birds with one stone*.

いっせき【一夕】 one evening.

いっせつ【一節】 (文章の) a paragraph; a passage; (音節) a section; (聖書の) a verse.

いっせん【一線】 ¶ 両者の間にはっきり～を画するのは困難だ We find it hard to *draw the line* between the two. 正邪の間に明確な～を画せ Draw *a* definite *line* between right and wrong. ～級の投手 〔one of〕 the first-line pitchers.

いっせん【一戦】 a battle; a fight. ¶ そのためにはだれとでも～を辞しません We are ready to *fight* (≒ *wage war*) *against* anybody for the cause. われわれは正義を守るためにはだれとでも～を交えよう We will *fight against* anybody for the cause of our righteousness.

いっそ ¶ ～のことやめたほうがいい You *had better* give up. 屈服するぐらいなら～死んだほうがましだ I *would rather* die *than* submit.

いっそう【一掃】 ¶ 敵軍は町から～された The enemy force in the town *was wiped out*. 市当局はスラム街を～する計画を立てた The city authorities made a plan to *sweep away* its slum areas. 彼は適時打を放ってランナーを～した He made a timely hit to *clean* the bases.

いっそう【一層】 more; still more. ¶ 彼女は前より～美しくなった She has become still *more* beautiful than before. その子は両親もなかったので～ふびんに思われた I took pity on the child *all the more* because he was an orphan. ～のご援助をお願いします I am looking forward to *further* assistance from you.

いっそく【一足】 a pair (*of* shoes).

いっそくとび【一足飛び】 ¶ 彼は平社員から～に社長になった From a mere clerk he became president of the company *at a bound*. その子は～に第6学年に編入された The child was admitted into the sixth grade *at a leap*.

いつぞや【何時ぞや】 the other day. ¶ ～はお世話になりました Thank you for your kind help *the other day*. ～お話の本を貸していただけますか Will you lend me the book you talked of *the other day*?

いったい【一体】 ¶ ～彼がそんなことを口にするのがおかしい He has no right *whatever* to say such things. ～だれがそれをこわしたんだ Who *ever* broke it? ～きみはなにを言おうというのだ What *on earth* do you mean? ～ぜんたいぼくにどうしろっていうんだ What *the hell* do you want me to do? 日本人は～に英語を話すのがへただ *Generally speaking*, the Japanese are poor speakers of English.

いったい【一帯】 ¶ 九州～は大雨だ It is raining heavily *all over* Kyushu. その辺～にくわしい I am familiar with the *whole* neighborhood.

いつだつ【逸脱】 deviation. ¶ それは本校の生徒の本分を～した行為である This is conduct *unbecoming to* the students in our school. それでは本来の目的から～している That is not what was originally intended. 労働協約を～した行為を見逃すわけにはいかない We cannot overlook any *deviation* from the labor agreement.

いったん【一端】 (片端) one end; (一部) a part; (大体) an outline. ¶ これでその～がうかがわれる This gives us some idea of the matter. これで彼の性格の～がうかがえる This reveals *part* of his character.

いったん【一旦】 ¶ ～決めたからには変えるべきではない *Once* you have made up your mind, you should not change it. 赤の点滅信号は～停止を表わす The red blinking light is a signal for drivers to stop *for a moment*. ～は思いとどまったのだが… *For a moment* I held myself back, but....

いっち【一致】 agreement. ¶ ふたりの意見は完全に～している The two *are in* perfect *agreement*. / The two *agree with* each other one hundred percent. 彼と私は意見が～してる I *agree with* him. 彼の言うこととすることは～していない His acts *are contrary to* his words. ふたりの間にさほど～点は見いだせない We cannot find very much *agreement* between the two. 彼らはその報告を全員～で承認した They *were unanimous in* their approval of the report. / They approved the report *unanimously*. 彼は全員～で議長に選ばれた He was elected chairman *unanimously* (≒ *by a unanimous vote*).

いっちゃく【一着】 (競技の) the first [in the race]; (衣服の) a suit of clothes ¶ その馬が～になった The horse *came in first* (≒ *won the first place*). 彼は新調したての三つぞろいを～に及んだ He *was dressed in* his new three-piece suit.

いっちょう【一朝】 ¶ ～一夕に in a [single] day; in a short period of time. ～事あるときは in case of emergency.

いっちょういったん【一長一短】 merits and demerits; virtues and faults; advantages and disadvantages. ¶ それも～だ It has its *merits and demerits*.

いっちょうら【一張羅】 (晴れ着) *one's* best; *one's* best (≒ Sunday) clothes; (1枚きりの着物) *one's* only suit [of clothes]. ¶ 彼は～を着込んでいた He was dressed in *his best*.

いっちょくせん【一直線】 a straight line. ¶ ～に straight; in a straight line. ここから～に行って5マイルだ It is five miles, *as the crow flies*, from here. / It's 5 miles *straight* ahead. ～に進む go *as the crow flies*.

いっつい【一対】 a pair (*of*); a couple (*of*).

いっつう【一通】 a copy (*of*); (手紙) a letter. 写しを～ください Give me *a copy of* the original.

いって【一手】 **1** ¶ その仕事を～に引き受けた I took the task upon myself *single-handed*. 押しの～でいこう Let's push on.

—販売店 the sole agency. **—販売** ¶ ～販売をする make *an exclusive sale* (*of something*).

2 〖将棋などの〗 a move.

いってい【一定】 ¶ 彼には～の収入がない He does not have any *regular* income. われわれはある～の規準で製品の品質を検査している We examine the quality of the products by a *certain* standard. 自動車部品の規格は～している The parts of an automobile *are standardized*. 履歴書には～の書式がある There is a *fixed* form of writing a personal record. このホールは収容人数が～している The hall holds a *set* number of people. われわれは～の場所に集まることにした We decided to meet at a *certain* place.

いってき【一滴】 a drop. ¶ もう酒は～も飲むまい I won't touch another *drop* of alcohol. われわれはその町を～の血も流さず占領した We captured the town without shedding *a drop* of blood.

いってつ【一徹】 obstinacy. ¶ あの老いの～には参った I was embarrassed by the *obstinacy* of that old man.

いつでも【何時でも】 ¶ ～よい *Any time* will do. ～好きなときに来なさい Come *whenever* you like (≒ *any time* that suits you). 彼は～文句ばかり言う He is *always* complaining. ～こううまくいくとはかぎらない You cannot expect to succeed so well *every time*.

いってん【一点】 a point; a spot. ¶ 空には～の雲もなかった There was not *a speck of* cloud in the sky. / Not *a* cloud was to be seen in the sky. 彼の無実には～の疑いもない There is *no* doubt *whatever* that he is innocent. ジャイアンツが～先取した The Giants got the first run.

いってん【一転】 ¶ 敵は～して攻勢に移った The enemy *turned to* the offensive. 飛行機は～して飛行場にもどってきた The plane *made a turn* and came back to the airfield. 彼は心機～して別人のように働いた *With a fresh determination* he worked hard as if he were quite another.

いってんばり【一点張り】 ¶ 彼は知らぬ存ぜぬの～だった He *persisted in* denying his knowledge of it.

い

いっと【一途】¶病状は悪化の〜をたどった His condition grew worse and worse.

いっとう【一党】 a party. ¶〜一派に偏する be partial to *a* specific *party*.
—独裁 one-party dictatorship.

いっとう【一等】¶それが〜よい That is *the best*. 〜で旅行する travel *first-class*; (海上) travel *in the first cabin*.
—国 a first-class power. **—車** a first-class car (≒ carriage). **—乗客** a first-class passenger. **—親**〚法律〛a relation of the first degree. **—星**〚天文〛a star of the first magnitude. **—地** ¶これがこの町の〜地です This place is among *the first rate* districts of the town. **—賞** the first prize. ¶〜賞を得る win *first prize*.

いっとう【一頭】¶彼は同僚の中で〜地を抜いていた He *cut a conspicuous figure* among his comrades.

いっとうりょうだん【一刀両断】¶〜する(文字通りに) cut into two by a single hit; (比喩的に) take a drastic measure; cut the Gordian knot.

いっとき【一時】¶〜の休む余裕もない I have no *time* for rest.

いつなんどき【いつ何時】〔at〕any moment. ¶われわれは〜事故に会うかもわからない We may have an accident *at any moment*.

いつに【一に】 solely; entirely; wholly. ¶日本の将来は〜かかって青少年の双肩にある The future of Japan rests *wholly* upon the shoulders of the young generation.

いつのまにか【何時の間にか】 before *one* knows; unnoticed. ¶〜10年が過ぎた Ten years have passed *in a twinkling*. 彼女の姿は〜見えなくなった She disappeared *unnoticed*. 彼女は〜悪に染まっていた She had sunk in vice *before she was aware of it*.

いっぱ【一派】 a group; (党派) a party; a faction; (流派) a school; (宗派) a sect; a denomination. ¶〜をなす found *a school* of *one's* own.

いっぱい【一杯】1〚分量〛¶茶さじ〜分の塩 *a teaspoonful of* salt.
大さじ〜分の砂糖 *a tablespoonful of* sugar.
コップ〜の水 *a glass of* water.
コーヒー〜いかがですか Won't you have *a cup of* coffee?
もう〜いかが〔Won't you have〕Another *cup* (≒ *glass*)? / Another helping, please.
つめたい水を〜頂けますか May I trouble you for *a glass of* cold water? / Can I have *a glass of* water?
2〚酒〛¶〜やろうか. よかろう What about *a drink*? A good idea.
近いうちに〜やろう Let's *have a drink* sometime soon. / Won't you *have a drink* sometime soon?
彼は〜きげんで帰ってきた He came home *warm with a drink*. / He was back *under the influence of liquor*.
彼は〜きげんでいい気なものだ He is quite elated *with a drink*. / He *has taken a pull* and is quite optimistic.
3〚充満〛¶このおけに水を〜にしてください *Fill* this pail *with* water〔*to the full*〕, please.
お米をこの袋に〜に入れてください Please *pack up* this bag *with* rice.
彼女はお土産を〜持ってきた She brought *a lot of* presents.
会場は人で〜だった The hall *was crowded* (≒ *was packed*) *with* people.
行楽地はどこも〜の人出だった Every pleasure resort *was crowded with* people.
きみに言いたいことが〜ある I have *a lot* to tell you. / I have several bones to pick with you. (文句の場合).
胸が〜でなにも言えない My heart *is* too *full* for words.
彼は彼女のことで頭が〜だ He *is crazy about* her. / He *has lost his head over* her.
子どもたちは腹〜食べた The children ate their *fill*. / The children have had *enough*.
彼女は目に涙を〜ためていた Her eyes *were filled with* tears.
4〚全部〛¶これでも精〜やったつもりだ This is *the best* I can do, I assure you. / I have done *everything* in my power.
仕事は今月〜かかる The work will take *all* this month.
力〜押したが戸は開かなかった I pushed the door with *all* my strength, but it would not open.
5〚だます〛¶彼には〜食った I *was* fairly *taken in* by him.
なんとかして仕返しに彼に〜食わせてやりたい I will *play a trick on* him by hook or by crook to get even with him.

いっぱい【一敗】¶4勝〜 four wins and *one defeat*. 今のところわれわれのチームは〜してるだけだ Up to now our team *has lost only one game*. われわれは〜地にまみれた We *suffered a* complete *defeat*.

いっぱく【一泊】 a night's lodging. ¶伊東へ〜旅行をする make an *overnight* trip to Ito. 今夜は箱根で〜する I am going to *stop* at Hakone tonight. その晩は市内のホテルに〜した I *stayed* (≒ *put up*) at a hotel in the city *for the night*.

いっぱし【一端】¶あの子は〜の大人のような口をきく That boy talks like a *regular* grown-up man. 彼も〜の音楽家になった He has become a *pretty good* musician.

いっぱつ【一発】 a shot. ¶その鳥をねらって〜撃った I fired *a shot* at the bird. 銃声が〜聞こえた *A* loud *report* of a gun was heard. 彼は〜必中の腕前だ He never fails to hit the mark with *a single shot*.

いっぱん【一般】¶〜の人々 people *in general*. 食後にお茶を飲むのは日本では〜の習慣だ It is a *general* custom in Japan to have tea after a meal. 彼の小説の文章は〜に難解だ The sentences in his novels are, *for the most part*, difficult to understand. 〜に人は批評

されるのをきらう People *generally* dislike being criticized.

—会計 general account.

いっぱん【一斑】(一部) a part; a section. ¶～を見て全豹(ぜんぴょう)を卜(ぼく)す judge the whole by a part.

いっぱん【一版】 an edition.

いっぴき【一匹】 ¶ウサギ～ *a* rabbit. ～のサル *a* monkey.

—おおかみ a lone wolf.

いっぴつ【一筆】 ¶彼からその件に関し～書き送ってきた He sent me *a note* about the affair.

いっぴん【一品】 1 〖品物〗 an article.

2 〖料理〗 a dish; a course.

—料理 an *à la carte* dinner. ¶～料理を食べる eat *à la carte*.

3 〖すぐれた〗 unique, superb. ¶彼女の歌は天下～だ Her singing is *superb*.

いっぴん【逸品】 an excellent article; a rarity; a masterpiece.

いっぷいっぷせい【一夫一婦制】 monogamy.

いっぷう【一封】 an enclosure. ¶人々は感謝のしるしに彼に金～を贈った They made him a gift of money as a token of gratitude.

いっぷう【一風】 ¶あの人は～変わっている He is *quite* a character. / He is *a little bit* eccentric. / There is *something* queer about him. これは～変わった小説だ This novel is *quite* unconventional.

いっぷく【一幅】 a scroll. ¶～の名画 a notable painting.

いっぷく【一服】(薬) a dose; (たばこ) a smoke. ¶彼は～毒を盛られて死んだ He *was poisoned* to death. 食前にこの薬を～お飲みください Take *a dose* of this medicine before each meal. 食後の～ほど楽しいものはない Nothing compares with the pleasure of *a smoke* after a meal. ちょっと～しましょう(休みましょう) Let's *take a rest* for a while. / (たばこをのみましょう) Let's *have a smoke*.

いっぷたさい【一夫多妻】 polygamy.

—主義者 a polygamist.

いっぺん【一片】 a piece; a bit; a slice (*of* cake). ¶彼には～の良心もない He does not have *an ounce of* conscience. / He is an unscrupulous rogue.

いっぺん【一変】 a complete change. ¶事態は～した The situation *has completely changed*. そのこと以来彼の性格は～した The incident left him a changed man.

いっぺん【一編】(詩などの) a piece (*of* poetry); (詩) a poem.

いっぺん【一遍】 ¶彼はその本を～に100ページも読んだ He read a hundred pages of the book *at a sitting*. 彼はここに一週～来る He comes here *once* a week. もう～やらせてくれ Give me *another chance* to try.

いっぺんとう【一辺倒】 ¶今の政府はアメリカ～だ The present government supports American policies in every respect. / The present administration takes thoroughly pro-American policies.

いっぽ【一歩】 a step. ¶～～ step by step. ～進む(退く) take *a step* forward (backward). 疲れてもう～も歩けない I'm so tired that I cannot walk *any* (≒ *a step*) farther. ～誤ればおしまいだ Take *one* false *step* and I am lost. 彼は言いだしたら～も譲らぬ He won't yield *a point*, once he starts an argument. ～譲ってきみの言うとおりだとしてもやはりきみがまちがっていると思う Admitting what you say, I still believe you are wrong. 百里の道も～から A hundred miles' journey begins with *a step* forward.

いっぽう【一方】(片側) one side; (相手) one party; the other party. ¶物価は上がる～だ Prices *keep* rising. 寒くなる～だ It is getting colder and colder. まじめな人がいる～, いいかげんな人もいる There are serious people, *while on the other hand* there are also careless people. 医者は～では治療し, ～では研究しなければならない Doctors have to treat sick persons *on one hand* and study *on the other*. それは例によって彼の～的意見だ It is, as usual, his *one-sided* view (≒ opinion).

—通行道路 a one-way street.

いっぽう【一報】 ¶ご来京の節はご～ください *Let me know* when you come to Tokyo. ご～次第カタログ進呈 We shall send you a catalog immediately *on receipt of your notice*.

いっぽん【一本】 ¶鉛筆～ a pencil. チョーク～ *a piece of* chalk. 彼はその試合で～も取らなかった He didn't score *a point* in the match. これは～参った That's one on me.

—気 ¶～気な男 a *single-minded* man. **—立ち** ¶彼は～立ちすることにした He decided to become *independent*. **—調子** ¶彼は～調子な話し方をする He speaks in a *monotonous* way. **—道** ¶～道だから駅はすぐわかります You'll soon find the station, as the road has no turning. **—やり** ¶彼は常に正直～やりだ Honesty is always his only policy.

いつまで【何時まで】 how long; till when. ¶この寒さは～続くだろうか *How long* will this cold spell last? ～待っても彼は来なかった He did not come, *no matter how long* I waited. きみは～寝ているんだ You've been sleeping long enough. ～でも好きなだけここにいてよろしい You may stay here *as long as* you like. 私は～もこの町を忘れないだろう I shall never forget this town.

いつも【何時も】 ¶このごろは～天気がいい It has *always* been nice recently. ～6時に起きる I *usually* get up at six. 彼は～不平ばかり言っている He is *always* complaining. (always はしばしば進行形とともに用いる). 彼を訪ねると～留守だ He is out *whenever* (≒ *every time*) I go to see him. ～の所でお待ちします I'll be expecting you at the *usual* place. 彼の遅刻は～のことだ(習慣) He is a *habitual* late-comer. / (おくれてきたとき) He came late *as usual*. 彼は～のとおりバスで行った He went by bus *as usual*. 私は～より30分早く出勤した I

い

went to work half an hour earlier than *usual*.

いつらく【逸楽】pleasure. ¶ 〜にふける Give *one*self up to *pleasure*.

いつわ【逸話】an anecdote.

いつわ·る【偽る】¶ 彼は病気と〜って仕事を休んだ He *pretended* to be ill and stayed away from work. 週刊誌は真相を〜って伝えた The weekly magazine gave a *false* report of the fact. 彼女は大学出だと〜っている She *passes herself off as* a college graduate.

イデア〘哲学〙an idea.

イディオム an idiom.

イデオロギー an ideology; *one's* way of thinking.

いでたち【出で立ち】dress; attire; an outfit.

いてん【移転】a move; 〔a〕removal. ¶ 私たちは来週新居に〜します We *move to* a new house next week. 事務所は横浜に〜した The office *was removed to* Yokohama.
—先 *one's* new address (≒ house). —通知 a removal notice.

いでん【遺伝】heredity. ¶ 彼の目の色は母からの〜だ He *inherited* the color of his eyes from his mother.
—学〔a study of〕heredity; genetics. —子 a gene.

いと【糸】(縫い糸)〔a〕thread; (織り糸·編み糸) yarn; (ひも·楽器の弦) a string; (釣り糸) a line. ¶ 〜を垂れる cast *a line* 〔for fishing〕; angle. 彼が陰で〜を引いている He *is pulling the wires*. そのけんかは何年も〜を引いた The quarrel lasted for years.

いと【意図】an intention; a purpose. ¶ 彼らは新会社の設立を〜している They *aim at* establishing a new company. われわれの〜したところと違う結果になった The result was cross to our *purpose*.

いど【井戸】a well. ¶ 〜を掘る dig *a well*. 〜がかれた The *well* dried up.
—端会議〔a〕women's gossip.

いど【緯度】latitude (緯度の読み方. 北緯42度13分 Lat. 42°13′ N. = latitude forty-two degrees thirteen minutes north). ¶ この町はワシントンと同〜にある This city is situated at the same *latitude* as Washington, D. C.

いとう【以東】¶ 名古屋〜に(の·は) east of Nagoya.

いと·う【厭う】¶ 彼は費用を〜わずに仕事を続けた He continued the work *regardless of* expenses. お体をお〜いください *Take good care of* yourself. (病人にのみ用いる).

いどう【異同】〔a〕difference.

いどう【異動】〔personnel〕changes; a reshuffle. ¶ あの会社では人事〜を行なった They made *changes* in the staff at that company.

いどう【移動】〔a〕removal; (民族の)〔a〕migration. ¶ 風に乗って〜する草の種子もある Some grass seeds *travel* on the wind.
—証明 a certificate of *one's* removal. —大使 a roving ambassador. —図書館 a traveling library; 米 a bookmobile.

いときりば【糸切り歯】an eyetooth.

いとく【威徳】virtue and influence.

いとく【遺徳】posthumous influence.

いとぐち【糸口】(端緒) a clue. ¶ それが彼の出世の〜となった That became *the first step* to his success in life.

いとけな·い【幼い·稚い】very young; childish.

いとこ【従兄弟·従姉妹】a 〔first〕cousin. またー a second cousin.

いどころ【居所】(住所) *one's* address; (行方) *one's* whereabouts (通例単数扱い). ¶ 彼の〜を教えてくれ Tell me *where he is*.

いとざくら【糸桜】a drooping cherry tree.

いとし·い【愛しい】¶ だれでもわが子は〜い Everybody *loves* his child.

いとすぎ【糸杉】〘植物〙a cypress 〔tree〕.

いとなみ【営み】(仕事) work; 〔an〕occupation; (営業) business; management.

いとな·む【営む】¶ 彼らは幸福な家庭を〜んでいる They *keep* a happy home. 彼は文筆で生計を〜んでいる He *earns his living* by writing. 彼は農業を〜んでいる He is a farmer. / He *carries on* agriculture.

いとま【暇】(休暇) leave of absence; (解雇) dismissal; (別れ) leave-taking.
¶ もうお〜いたします I must say good-by now. / I must be going now. / It is time I went. 彼は友人に〜を告げた He said good-by to his friend. 10日間の〜をもらった I have 10 days' *leave*. その例は枚挙に〜がないほど多い The instances are too many to mention.

いとまき【糸巻き】a spool; a bobbin; a reel; (弦楽器の) a peg.

いとまごい【暇乞い】leave-taking. ¶ 彼は〜もそこそこにそこを去った He left the place, bidding *farewell* in haste.

いど·む【挑む】¶ ドイツは5か国に対して戦いを〜んだ Germany *forced war upon* five countries. 彼は見知らぬ男にけんかを〜んだ He *picked a quarrel with* a stranger.

いとめ【糸目】¶ 彼は金に〜をつけずに家を新築した He built a new house, *regardless of* expenses.

いと·める【射止める】¶ 彼は100万ドルの賞金を〜めた He *won* the prize of a million dollars. 彼は彼女の愛を〜めた He *won* the heart of the girl.

いとわし·い【厭わしい】disgusting; disagreeable; hateful.

いな【鯔】〘魚類〙a grey mullet.

いな【否】¶ 〜とは言わせぬ I will have no *denial*. / I won't take *no* for an answer.

いな【異な】¶ それは〜ことを承る That sounds *strange* (≒ *funny*).

いない【以内】**1**〘時間〙¶ 学校は私の家から歩いて10分〜の所にある My school is *within* ten minutes' walk of my house.
彼は1週間〜に来る He will be here *within* (≒ *in less than*) a week. (in a week は「1週間後に」の意味で使われることが多い).
2〘金銭〙¶ 旅行の費用は5,000円〜だろう The

expense for the trip will *not exceed* five thousand yen.
収入〜で生活するのは難しい It is hard to live *within* our income.

いなお·る【居直る】 assume a threatening (≒ strong) attitude; change *one's* attitude.

いなか【田舎】 the country; a rural district; 英 the provinces; (故郷) *one's* home 〔country〕; 米 *one's* home town (農村や大都会の場合にも使う).
¶ 〜くさい countrified; rustic; boorish. 〜へ行く go 〔out〕 into *the country*. 〜(故郷)へ帰る go home; go back to *one's* home town. 〜はどこですか What part of *the country* are you from? / Where are you from?
—者(男) a countryman; (女) a countrywoman; (軽べつ的) a 〔country〕 bumpkin. —暮らし country life. —町 a country town.

いながらにして【居乍らにして】 ¶ テレビのおかげで〜世界中の出来事が見られる Thanks to television, we can watch (≒ enjoy) the events around the world *as they happen*.

いなご【蝗】〔昆虫〕 a locust.

いなさく【稲作】 a rice crop.

いなずま【稲妻】 〔a flash of〕 lightning.
¶ 〜形の zigzag; in a *zigzag* line.

いなせな dashing; dapper; gallant.

いなだ〔魚類〕 a yellowtail.

いなな·く【嘶く】 neigh; whinny; (ロバが) bray. ¶ 馬は一声高く〜いた The horse *gave a* loud *neigh*.

いなびかり【稲光】 〔a flash of〕 lightning.
¶ 〜がする The *lightning* flashes.

いなほ【稲穂】 an ear of a rice plant.

いな·む【否む】 ¶ この事実は〜めない There is no *denying* this fact. / This fact *is undeniable*.

いなむら【稲叢】 a stack (≒ rick) 〔of rice straw〕.

いなや【否や】 ¶ 彼はぼくの顔を見るや〜逃げ出した *As soon as* (≒ *The moment*) he saw me, he ran away. そのニュースを聞くや〜出発した *On* hearing the news, I started out.

いなら·ぶ【居並ぶ】 ¶ 〜ぶ人々 all the people present; the whole company.

いなり【稲荷】 the god of cereals.

いなん【以南】 ¶ 青森〜に (の·は) south of Aomori.

イニシアチブ an initiative. ¶ 彼はその運動で〜をとった He took the *initiative* in the movement.

イニシアル *one's* initials.

いにしえ【古】 ancient times; old times; antiquity. ¶ 〜の ancient; old. 〜は in old times.

いにゅう【移入】 import. ¶ 〜する import; introduce; bring in.

いにん【委任】 ¶ 彼は私に全権を〜した He *entrusted* me *with* full powers.
—状 a letter of attorney; a procuration.
—投票 a proxy vote.

イニング an inning; 英 innings (単数扱い).

いぬ【犬】 a dog; (雌犬) a bitch; (子犬) a puppy; (猟犬) a hound; (スパイ) a spy.
¶ 〜も歩けば棒に当たる(諺) Every dog has his day. 警察の〜 a police spy.
—小屋 a kennel. —猫病院 a pets' hospital; an animal hospital; a veterinary hospital.

いぬかき【犬掻き】 (水泳) dog paddle. ¶ 〜で泳ぐ dog-paddle.

いぬき【居抜き】 ¶ 店を〜で買う buy a store with stocks and all.

いぬくぎ【犬釘】 a 〔dog〕 spike.

いぬじに【犬死に】 ¶ 〜する die in vain; die to no purpose; die a dog's death; die like a dog.

いね【稲】 ¶ 〜を刈る reap (≒ cut down) the *rice* 〔*plant*〕.

いねむり【居眠り】 a doze. ¶ 〜運転をする drive 〔a car〕 *half sleeping*. 彼女は仕事をしながら〜した She *dozed over* her work. 彼が〜しているのを見つけた I caught him *nodding*.

いのいちばん【いの一番】 first of all.

いのこり【居残り】 ¶ 彼は(罰として)放課後〜させられた He *was kept in* after school. 〜で仕事をした He worked *overtime*.

いのこ·る【居残る】 stay (≒ remain) behind; (残業する) work overtime.

いのしし【猪】〔動物〕 a wild boar.
—武者 a foolhardy warrior; an impetuous warrior; a hotspur.

いのち【命】 life. ¶ 〜のある(ない)もの an animate (inanimate) thing. 〜の綱 the staff of *life*. 〜のあるかぎりあなたのことを忘れません I shall never forget you *so long as I live*. / I shall remember you *all my life*. あなたの〜が危ない Your *life* is in peril. 彼は〜から2番めにたいせつなものをなくした He lost something next to his *life*. それは私にとって〜にかかわることだ It is a matter of *life* and death to me. 病人は〜を取り留めた The patient escaped death. 彼は交通事故で〜を落とした He lost his *life* in a traffic accident. 〜にかけて誓います I swear *upon my life*. 彼の〜に別条はない He is out of danger 〔of losing his *life*〕. 〜あっての物種(諺) *Where there is life, there is hope*. 〜の洗たくをした I *have refreshed myself*. 彼は〜からがら逃げ出した He *had a narrow escape*.

いのちがけ【命がけ】 ¶ 〜の努力をする make a *desperate* effort. 彼は〜で大洋を横断した He *staked his life on* sailing across the ocean.

いのちごい【命乞い】 ¶ 〜をする ask for *one's* life.

いのちしらず【命知らず】 ¶ 〜のならず者 a desperado. 彼の〜の運転 his *reckless* driving.

いのちづな【命綱】 a life line.

いのちとり【命取り】 ¶ その失敗は彼の〜になった The failure proved *fatal* to him.

いのちびろい【命拾い】 ¶ 彼はあやうく〜をした

い

He *escaped death* by a hair's breadth.

いのり【祈り】〔a〕prayer；〔a〕supplication；(食前の)〔a〕grace. ¶ 朝の～ the morning *prayer*; matins. 夕べの～ the evening *prayer*; vespers. ～をささげる offer *a prayer*；(食事の前後) say〔a〕*grace*. 私の～は聞き入れられた My *prayer* was heard.

いの・る【祈る】 pray；supplicate；(望む) wish. ¶ 彼女は息子の無事を神に～った She *prayed to* God for her son's being safe. 彼らは戦争が始まらぬよう～った They *prayed* that the war might not break out. ご成功を～る I *wish* you success. ご幸運を～る Good luck〔to you〕! / I *wish* you good luck.

いはい【位牌】 a〔Buddhist〕mortuary (≒ memorial) tablet.

いはつ【遺髪】 the hair of the deceased.

いはつ【衣鉢】 ¶ 彼は師の～を継いだ He is heir to his master's mantle.

いばら【茨】 a thorn；a bramble. ¶ ～の道を歩む tread a *thorny* path.

いば・る【威張る】 ¶ 彼は～って歩く He *swaggers*. 彼は～ったようすをしている He *puts on airs*. あの人は部下に～り散らす He *puts on airs with* his men. / He *lords it over* his subordinates. ちゃんとした職があれば～って世の中が渡れる You can get through the world *respectably* if you have a decent occupation.

いはん【違反】 a breach；〔a〕violation. ¶ それは法律～だ It is *a violation* of the law. それは規則～だ It is *against* the rule. 法律に～してはならない You must not *violate* the law. 彼は選挙法～のかどで逮捕された He was arrested on charges of the election law *violation*.

―者 a violator；an offender.

いびき【鼾】 a snore. ¶ 彼は～をかく He snores.

いびつ【歪】 ¶ ～な円 a *distorted* circle；(長円) an oval. ～になる get out of shape. ～な鏡は顔を～にする An *uneven* mirror *distorts* the features.

いひょう【意表】 ¶ 彼はよく人の～に出るようなことをした He often took us by surprise. 彼の新しい計画はわれわれの～をつくものだった His new plan was something we had never expected.

いびょう【胃病】 a stomach trouble (≒ disorder)；〖医学〗dyspepsia.

いび・る ¶ 男の子はよく妹を～って泣かせる Little boys often *tease* their sisters and make them cry. あの継母は子どもを～る The stepmother *is hard on* the child.

いひん【遺品】 an article left behind；the bequeathed articles.

いふ【異父】 a stepfather.

―兄弟 a brother by a different father；a half brother.

いふ【畏怖】 awe. ¶ 自然の崇高な力は人間に～の念を起こさせる The sublime power of nature *awes* (≒ *arouses awe in*) human beings.

イブ **1**〖前夜〗an eve. ¶ 12月24日はクリスマス～です December 24th is Christmas *Eve*.
2〖聖書〗¶ アダムと～ Adam and *Eve*.

いふう【威風】 a majestic air；〔a〕dignified bearing. ¶ 彼の～はあたりを払った Everybody was overawed by his *imposing air*. 彼は～堂々としている He is a man of *commanding* appearance.

いぶかし・い【訝しい】 ¶ 彼女は彼を～そうに見た She gave him a *suspicious* look. 彼は～そうな顔をした He *looked suspicious* (≒ *looked dubious*). 彼の行動は～い His actions *are suspicious* (≒ *are dubious*).

いぶか・る【訝る】 ¶ 彼は私をだましているのではないかと～った I *suspected* that he was deceiving me. 彼は私の報告の真実性を～った He *doubted* (≒ *wondered about*) the truth of my report.

いぶき【息吹き】 breath. ¶ 春の～を感じた I felt the *breath* of spring.

いふく【衣服】 clothes；a dress (dress は一般に外部に着る衣服, clothing はいろいろな衣服の総称, clothes は着る物を意味する一般的な語でつねに複数扱い).

いぶくろ【胃袋】 the stomach；(動物の) a craw.

いぶ・す【燻す】 ¶ 蚊を～し出す *smoke out* mosquitoes.

―し銀 oxidized silver.

いぶつ【異物】 an alien substance；foreign matter；a foreign substance. ¶ 体から～を摘出する take *an alien substance* out of the body.

いぶつ【遺物】 a relic；remains. ¶ その博物館には昔の～がたくさんある The museum contains many *relics* of the past. ここから古代の～が掘り出された The *remains* of the ancient times were dug out here.

イブニング〔ドレス〕 an evening dress.

いぶ・る【燻る】 ¶ 薪が～った The wood *smoldered*. たばこの～る煙がきらいだ I hate the *smoldering* smell of cigarets.

いぶんし【異分子】 a foreign element；an outsider. ¶ 彼は～だ He is *an outsider*. ～を党から追い出そう Let's get rid of every *alien element* from our party.

いへき【胃壁】 the wall of the stomach.

いへん【異変】 an accident；an emergency. ¶ ことしは暖冬異変だ Winter is *unusually* mild this year. 政界の～が伝えられている *A disturbance* in political circles is reported.

いぼ【疣】 a wart. ¶ ～ができる have *a wart* grown；*A wart* grows.

―痔(じ) blind piles. **―がえる** a toad.

いぼ【異母】 a stepmother.

―兄弟 a brother by a different mother；a half brother.

いほう【違法】 illegality；unlawfulness. ¶ 免許証なしに運転するのは～だ It is *illegal* (≒ *against the law*) to drive a car without a license.

いほう【異邦】 a strange (≒ foreign) country.

いほうじん【異邦人】 a foreigner；an alien；

〖聖書〗 a Gentile.

いまく【以北】¶ 東京〜(の,に) north of Tokyo. 関東〜には雨が降っています It is raining *north of* Kanto District.

いま【今】1〖現在〗now. ¶ 〜何時ですか What time is it *now*?

彼は〜席をはずしております He is not at his seat (≒ desk), I'm afraid.

やるなら〜だ *Now* is the chance. / It's *now or never*.

〜手元に金がない I don't have any money with me *now*.

〜はやりのがらです It is a pattern of *the latest* fashion. / It is a pattern of *the newest* model.

〜は原子力が日常生活に利用される時代だ *This* is a time in which atomic power is used in daily life.

〜がたいせつなときだ *The present moment* is the most important.

〜となっては手の打ちようがない We can do nothing about it *now*.

〜は冬でもイチゴが食べられる時代だ *In this age* we can eat strawberries even in winter.

〜は言えません I'm afraid I cannot tell you *at present*.

〜だからこそそんなことが言えるのだ You would not have dared to say such a thing once.

〜でもときどきそのことは夢にみる I *still* dream about it now and then.

彼女のことは〜なお忘れられない Her image is *still* (≒ *even now*) present in my mind.

〜のうちに身辺の整理をしておきたまえ Put your house in order *when you have time*. / *Before it is too late*, you must adjust your household affairs.

〜のうちに休養をとっておきなさい Take this chance and have a rest.

〜の若い者は根性がない Young people *today* lack grit.

そんな言い分は〜の社会では通用しない Such ideas will not be accepted *nowadays*.

〜のところこれからさきどうなるのか見当がつかない *As matters stand*, I have not the least idea of the future.

〜のところはようすを見ているだけだ(事態を) *For the present* I am only watching how things will turn out. / (病状を) *For the present* we can only see how the patient is progressing.

〜のところ金には不自由していない *For the time being* I am not hard up for money.

2〖たった今〗¶ 〜彼に会ったばかりだ I have *just* seen him.

彼女は〜出ていった She went out *just a moment ago*.

3〖今すぐに〗¶ 〜やる, 〜やると言って, いったいいつやるのか You often said you would do it *right away*. But when will you really start?

〜行きます I am coming *in a moment*.

〜彼はもどってくる He will be back *in no time* (≒ *very soon*).

4〖助詞などとの組み合わせ〗¶ 〜か〜かと彼の帰りを待ちうけた I was expecting him to return *every moment*.

〜から行きます I am *just* leaving.

〜からでも遅くない It is not too late *yet*.

〜から1時間後にここを出る I am leaving here *in* an hour.

〜こそと奮い立った I roused myself saying, "*Now or never*." / Firmly resolved, I braced myself up.

〜しばらくお待ちください Kindly wait *a little longer*. / (略式で) *A moment*, please.

〜一度彼に掛け合ってみよう I will negotiate with him *once more* (≒ *again*).

〜までなにをしていたのですか What have you been doing *all this while*?

〜まで3年ここに住んでいる I have lived here for 3 years. (「いままで」は現在完了形そのものに意味されていて, いちいち訳すに及ばないこともある).

〜までちっとも気がつかなかった I haven't noticed it *until now*.

〜までにもこんな誤りをしたことがありますか Have you made any mistake like this *before*?

〜までのところは故障がなかった It has worked well *as yet*.

〜までのところはみんなよくやっている Everyone has worked well *so far*.

〜まで25年間ずっと英語を教えています I have been teaching English these 25 years.

いま【居間】 a living room; 英 a sitting room. ¶ 彼を〜に通しなさい Show him into the *living room*.

いまいまし·い【忌忌しい】¶ えい, 〜い How *provoking* (≒ *vexatious; disgusting*)! バスに乗り損って〜かった It *was annoying* to miss the bus. 彼に先を越されて〜く思った I *was vexed at* being forestalled by him. 彼らは〜げに曇り空をながめた They looked up at the cloudy sky *with vexation*. 〜いやつだ What an *aggravating* fellow!

いまごろ【今頃】 about this time; at this time. ¶ 毎年〜は雨が多い Every year *about this time* we have a great deal of rain. 彼らは〜奈良に着いているにちがいない They must have arrived at Nara *by this time*. 夜だというのに〜どこに行くつもりですか Where are you going *at this time* of night? 彼は来年の〜はアメリカにいるでしょう He shall be in the United States *by this time* next year.

いまさら【今更】 now; at this time. ¶ 〜どうしようもない Nothing can be done *now*. / It can't be helped *now*. 〜言うまでもありません It is *hardly necessary* to say that.... 〜とりかえしはつきません I can't be irrecoverable *now*.

いましがた【今し方】¶ 彼は〜出かけた He went out *a moment ago*.

いまじぶん【今時分】¶ あすの〜は帰っている I will be home *by now* tomorrow. 彼は〜は忙しいでしょう He will be busy *just now* (≒ *at this time*).

い

いましめ【戒め】a lesson;〔a〕caution;〔a〕warning. ¶ 彼の例がわれわれにはよい〜だ His example is *a* good *lesson* to us.

いましめ【縛め】binding; bonds; bondage. ¶ 彼は〜の身となっている(とらわれている) He is in *bonds*.

いまし·める【戒める】¶ そういうことはしてはならぬと厳に〜められている We *are given a* strict *warning* not to do it.

いまだ【未だ】¶ 彼は〜事態の重大性に気づいていない He hasn't *yet* realized the seriousness of the situation. その件は〜に解決していない The matter is *still* unsettled. 〜に彼は自説を固執している He *still* holds fast to his views.

いまどき【今時】nowadays; the present day; these days. ¶ 〜の若者 young people *now* (≒ *of today*). そんな誠実な人は〜珍しい Such a sincere man is rather rare *nowadays*.

いまに【今に】¶ 彼は〜よい作家になるだろう He will be a good writer *some day*. 〜水中で生活できるようになるだろう We will be able to live in the water *in future*. 〜きみだって結婚するさ *Sooner or later*, you also will be married. 〜わかるよ Wait and see. 〜みろ See what I will do. / You shall smart for this. 〜なってみればうそだとわかる We *now* know that it was a lie. 〜「テレビ電話」が発明されるだろう *Some day in the near future* "the TV telephone" will be invented.

いまにも【今にも】¶ 木は〜も倒れそうだ The tree *is about to* fall. 〜も降りだしそうだ *It is threatening to* rain. / It may rain *at any moment*.

いまひとつ【今一つ】¶ 〜のヒントを与えます I will give you *another* hint. 〜質問します I will ask you *one more* question. 〜注文があります I have *another* order to give. / (要求) I have *another* request to make.

いまもって【今もって】yet; as yet; still. ¶ その世界記録は〜破られていない The world record is not broken *yet*. 〜彼からの音信がない I have not heard from him *yet*.

いまや【今や】now. ¶ 〜一刻の猶予もできない There is no time to be lost *now*. 〜危急存亡のとき We are *now* facing a crisis.

いまわ【今際】¶ 〜の際に on *one's* deathbed.

いまわし·い【忌まわしい】¶ 過去の〜い思い出など忘れなさい Forget the *unpleasant* memories of the past. 彼女のような年はもゆかぬ娘を誘惑するなんて〜い話だ It is quite *ignoble* (≒ *disgusting*) to seduce a young girl like her.

いみ【意味】〔a〕meaning. ¶ この語の〜を教えてください Please tell me the *meaning* of this word. 彼の言うことの〜がわからない I don't understand him. / I don't understand what his remarks *mean*. / I can't make out what he *means*. それはどういう〜ですか What do you *mean* by that? / What does that *mean*? ある〜で彼は大きな赤ん坊だ *In a sense* he is a grown-up baby. 彼女は〜深長にウインクした She gave me a *significant* wink.

いみ【忌み】mourning. ¶ 〜が明ける go out of mourning.

いみきら·う【忌み嫌う】¶ ヘビを〜う人が多い Many people *hate* (≒ *shudder to see*) snakes. 彼は毛虫のごとく〜われた He *was hated* like a serpent.

いみことば【忌み言葉】a taboo; a tabooed word.

いみじくも excellently; admirably. ¶ 文は剣に勝るとは〜いったものだ It is *excellently* stated that the pen is mightier than the sword.

イミテーション〔an〕imitation. ¶ 〜の真珠 an *imitation* (≒ *artificial*) pearl.

いみはばか·る【忌み憚る】fear; abhor; dread.

いみょう【異名】¶ その盗人は昭和のねずみ小僧と〜をとっていた The thief *was nicknamed* (≒ *was called*) a Nezumikozo in Showa Era.

いみん【移民】(外国へ) emigration; (外国から) immigration; (移入民) an immigrant; (移出民) an emigrant.
¶ アメリカはヨーロッパからの〜が多い The United States has a great number of *immigrants* from Europe. 海外〜の数が増えている The *emigrants* overseas are increasing in number. 彼は一家を挙げてブラジルに〜した All his family *emigrated* to Brazil.
—官 an immigration officer. —法 an immigration law.

いむ【医務】medical affairs.
—室 a dispensary.

い·む【忌む】(きらう) dislike; (避ける) avoid.
¶ 〜むべき行為 an *abominable* behavior.

いめい【威名】fame; renown.

イメージ an image. ¶ 私には父の〜が浮かばない I cannot recall *what my father was like*. このことばからどんな〜をきみは持つか What *image* do you call up when you hear the word?

いも【芋】(ジャガイモ) a potato (複 potatoes); (サツマイモ) a sweet potato; (ヤマノイモ) a yam; (サトイモ) a taro. ¶ 〜を洗うような雑踏 a crowd packed like sardines.

いもうと【妹】a younger sister (younger は大てい省略する); *one's* little sister.
—婿 a younger sister's husband.

いもづる【芋蔓】sweet-potato vines. ¶ スパイの一味は〜式に逮捕された The group of spies were arrested *one after another*.

いもの【鋳物】a casting; cast metal; a molding.
—工場 a foundry. —工 a founder; a caster.

いもむし【芋虫】a green caterpillar.

いもり【井守】a newt; a water lizard.

いもん【慰問】consolation. ¶ 彼女は傷病兵の〜に野戦病院を訪れた She visited the field hospital to *console* the sick and wounded soldiers. 水害地の人に〜の手紙を送った We sent letters of *sympathy* to the people of the flooded district.
—状 a consolatory〔letter〕; a letter of sympathy. —品 comforts.

いや【嫌・厭】 a dislike; 〔an〕 aversion. ¶ なんという～なやつだ What a *disgusting* (⇐ *disagreeable*) fellow he is! こういう小説は～だ I *don't like* this sort of novel. そう言ったら彼は～な顔をした When I said so, he *looked displeased*. もう彼の話は～だ I *am fed up with* his speech. / (うわさの意ならば) I *don't want to* hear another word about him. ～な笑い方をする人だ He laughs quite an *ugly* laugh. 貧乏は～だから働きたい I want to work to stay out of poverty. 考えれば考えるほど世の中が～になった The more I thought of the world, the more I *disliked* it. 結婚するのが～になった I *have become reluctant to* marry.

いや【否】 no. ¶「これはあなたの本ですか」「～違います」 "Is this your book?" "*No*, it isn't." なにがなんでも～です I *say no*, once for all. ～とは言わせない I won't take *no* for an answer. ～が応でも試験は受けねばならない You must take the examination *whether* 〔*you are*〕 *willing or not*.

イヤーブック a yearbook.

いやいや【嫌嫌・厭厭】 reluctantly. ¶ 私は～その申し入れを受け入れた I *was reluctant to* accept the offer. 彼は～同意した He gave an *unwilling* consent. 彼は～外出した He went out *against his will*.

いやおう【否応】 yes or no. ¶ 彼は私に～なしに署名させた He *forced* me *to* sign a paper.

いやがうえにも【弥が上にも】 all the more. ¶ ～闘志がわく I have become full of fight (⇐ My blood is up) *all the more*.

いやがらせ【嫌がらせ】 ¶ ～をするな Don't *annoy* me. 彼女はよく～を言う She often says *disagreeable things*.

いやが・る【嫌がる】 dislike; abhor; hate. ¶ 彼女はネコを～る She *hates* cats. 彼は薬を飲むのを～る He *abhors* taking medicine. 赤ん坊はふろに入るのを～る The baby *dislikes* taking a bath.

いやき【嫌気】 a dislike; 〔an〕 disgust; aversion. ¶ 都会生活に～がさしてきた I begin to *feel aversion to* city life. 彼は勉強に～がさしてきた He began to *feel aversion to* hard study.

いやく【医薬】 (薬) medicine; (医療) medical treatment.

—品 medical supplies. **—分業** separation of dispensary from medical practice.

いやく【意訳】 a free translation. ¶ ～する make *a free translation*. この訳は～にすぎる This translation is too free.

いやく【違約】 a breach of promise (⇐contract). ¶ 彼はけっして～しない He never *breaks his promise*. / He is faithful to his promise.

—金 a penalty; an indemnity.

いやけ【嫌気】 ⇒ いやき

いやし・い【卑しい】 ¶ 世の中には～い職業などない No occupation *is mean*, if it is legitimate. 彼はお金に～い He *is stingy* (⇐ *is mean*) about money. 品性の～い人だ He is a man of *mean* character. ～からぬ身なりをしている He is *decently* dressed. 彼はことば遣いが～い He *is vulgar* in speech.

いやしくも【苟も】 ¶ ～やる以上はきちんとやりなさい Do it well if you do it *at all*. ～学生ならばそんなことはしない Such a behavior is unbecoming to any student worthy of the name. ～良識ある者はそんなことはしない No man with any good sense would do it.

いやし・める【卑しめる】 ¶ 彼はみずからわが身を～めている He *makes himself despised* by what he does. 自分の職業を～めるな Don't *make* your profession *cheap*.

いや・す【癒やす】 ¶ 時はすべての悲しみを～す Time *heals* all sorrows. のどの渇きは～された My thirst *was quenched*.

いやに ¶ ～寒いですね It is *terribly* cold, isn't it? ～のどが渇く I feel *terribly* thirsty. ～じめじめしますね It's *unpleasantly* damp, isn't it? ～急いでいるじゃないか Why are you in *such* a hurry? 地下の穴倉は～暗かった The cellar was *uncannily* dark. けさは～冷える It is *exceedingly* cold this morning.

いやはや ¶ ～驚きました *Well*, I am surprised. ～困りました *Oh dear!* I can't help it. ～まったくおかしな話ですよ *Heavens!* It is quite a strange story.

イヤホーン an earphone; a headphone (2語ともふつう複数形で用いる).

いやみ【嫌味・厭味】 (皮肉) sarcasm; irony; (きざ) 〔an〕 affectation. ¶ 彼は～たっぷりにしゃべる He speaks with much *irony*. 彼女の言うことにはなんの～(皮肉)も感じられなかった I didn't sense any *sarcasm* in what she said. 彼は彼女の服装について彼女に～を言った He made *sarcastic remarks* to her on her dress. おまえはずるいやつだと～を言われた I *was insinuated* that I evaded my duty. 彼女はなんの～もない人だ She doesn't *put on airs*. 彼の話しぶりにはなんとなく～がある He has somewhat *an affected way* of speech. このがらには～がない This design looks quite *refined*.

いやらし・い【嫌(厭)らしい】 ¶ まあ, ～い How *indecent* (⇐ *embarrassing*)! 彼は～い目つきで彼女を見た He *leered at* her. 彼は～いほどていねいだった He was *disagreeably* (⇐ *embarrassingly*) polite. 女性に～いことを言うな Don't say *improper* things to a woman. (improper は obscene (みだらな)という語のえん曲な言い方).

イヤリング 〔a pair of〕 earrings.

いゆう【畏友】 a respected friend.

いよいよ ¶ ～春だ Spring has come *at last*. どちらかに決めるときが～きた *There has come the time when* we must choose between the two. 雨は～激しく降った It rained *harder and harder*. 物価は～上昇している Prices are rising *higher and higher*.

いよう【異様】 ¶ 彼の声は～に聞こえた His voice sounded *strange*. 彼女の態度は～に見えた Her manners struck me as *strange*. 一種～なふんい気が醸されていた A *strange* (⇐ An *awkward*) situation was created.

いよく【意欲】 〔a〕 will; 〔a〕 desire. ¶ 彼には出

世しようなどという～はあまりない He has no strong *will* to rise in the world. 彼は新技術の開発に～的だ He *is eager to* develop a new technique. それは～的な作品だ It is a very *ambitious* work. 彼はその仕事に～的に取り組んだ He grappled with the task *with a will*.

いらい【以来】¶ それ～彼から便りがない I have not heard from him *since* [*then*]. 先週の月曜～ずっと雨が降っている It has been raining *since* last Monday. 彼が死んで～10年になる He has been dead for ten years. / Ten years have passed (≒ It is ten years) *since* he died. (上例のように since... を含む文の主節では現在完了, since... の節では過去形が多く用いられる. ただし He has been getting better since *he has been here*. のような例もある).

いらい【依頼】a request ; (委任) trust ; commission. ¶ ご～したいことがあります I have a favor to *ask of* you. このことについては弁護士に～するのがいちばんいい In regard to this, nothing is better than to *leave* it *to* a lawyer. 彼の～により会社へ電話した I telephoned his office *at his request*. きみには～心が強すぎる You *rely* too much *upon* others.
—者 a client. —状 a written request.

いらいら【苛苛】¶ ～しながらバスを待った I was waiting for the bus *impatiently* (≒ *with impatience*). 彼ののんきなのに～した I *became impatient with* his idleness. その答えは私を～させた The answer *irritated* me. 彼女はすぐに～する She *is* very *irritable*.

イラク Iraq. ¶ ～の Iraqi.
—人 an Iraqi. —語 Iraqi.

いらくさ【刺草】〖植物〗a nettle.

いらだたし·い【苛立たしい】¶ 彼の話を聞いていると～くなった I *got irritated with* his talk. ～い顔つきで彼は私を見た He turned to me with an *irritable* look.

いらだ·つ【苛立つ】⇒いらいら

いらっしゃい (こちらへ来なさい) Come here. / (お入りなさい) Come in. (米口語ではしばしば Come on in.) / (ようこそ) Hello, Bill (Peter など人名)! / Welcome! / (店頭で) May (≒ Can) I help you? / What can I do for you? ¶ また～ませ Please come again. スミスさんは～ますか Is Mr. Smith in (≒ at home)? / May I see Mr. Smith? (パーティーなどで)よく～ました Welcome! / I'm glad you came (≒ could come).

いらぬ needless ; unnecessary. ¶ ～おせっかいをするな It's none of your business. / Mind your own business. ～詮議(せんぎ)だ It's an *unnecessary* (≒ a *useless*) inquiry.

イラン Iran.
—人 an Iranian. —語 Iranian.

いり【入り】**1**〖入ること〗¶ 彼はプロ～した He *entered* the professional world. / He *was registered* as a professional.
2〖入場者〗¶ 今夜は劇場の～がいい The house *is full* this evening. / We *have a good house* this evening. 彼の講演会はいつも聴衆の～がいい His lecture always *attracts a large audience*.
3〖容量〗¶ 10万円～のかばん a bag *containing* 100,000 yen.
2リットル～のびん a two-liter bottle.
10立方メートル～のタンク a tank *with a capacity of* ten cubic meters.
4〖始め〗¶ 梅雨の～はいつですか When does the rainy season *start* (≒ *set in*)?

いりあい【入り相】¶ ～の鐘 the *evening* (≒ *vesper*) bell tolling at a Buddhism temple.

いりうみ【入り海】a bay ; an inlet.

いりえ【入り江】an inlet ; a creek.

いりかわり【入り代わり】⇒いれかわる

いりかわる【入り代わる】⇒いれかわる

いりくち【入り口】an entrance ; a way in.
¶ 港の～ the *mouth of* (≒ *entrance to*) a harbor. 公園の～ *a* park *gate*. トンネルの～ *a* tunnel *entrance*. どうぞ～に立たないでください Please do not stand *in the doorway*. 私は～で彼らを迎えた I welcomed them *at the threshold*. ～はおわかりでしょうね I trust you will be able to find your *way in*.

いりく·む【入り組む】¶ ～んだ事件 an *intricate* case. 彼の説明はとても～んでいる His explanation *is* very *involved*. これにはいろいろと事情が～んでいる Various things *have been mixed up* in this affair. 彼は～んだ通りで道にまよった He was lost *in the tangle of* streets.

いりこ·む【入り込む】enter into. ¶ 海が陸地の奥深く～んでいる The sea *reaches far into* the land.

イリジウム〖化学〗iridium.

いりつ·ける【煎り付ける】(太陽が) sizzle.

いりたまご【炒り卵】scrambled eggs.

いりに【入り荷】arrivals ; goods received.

いりひ【入り日】the setting sun.

いりびた·る【入り浸る】¶ 彼は妻の実家に妻と～っている He often *stays long* at his wife's parents' [home] with his wife.

いりふね【入り船】an incoming ship.
出船— ships coming in and going out.

いりまじ·る【入り交じる】¶ 私は彼の死を聞いたときはいろいろな感情が～っていた I heard the news of his death *with mixed* (≒ *mingled*) *feelings*.

いりまめ【炒り豆】 parched (≒ roast[ed]) peas.

いりみだ·れる【入り乱れる】¶ 敵味方～れての戦いとなった Both sides fought *in great confusion* (≒ *in a melee*).

いりむこ【入り婿】a husband married to an heiress. ¶ ～になる marry *an heiress*. (英語では妻の姓を名のる習慣がないので,「婿になる」という日本的感じがない).

いりゅう【慰留】¶ 彼に現在の職にとどまるよう～した I *persuaded* him *to stay* in his present position. 彼に辞職しないように～した I tried to *prevent* him *from resigning*.

いりゅうひん【遺留品】(忘れ物) a lost property ; (死後に残された物) properties (≒ articles) left behind.

いりよう【入り用】⇒ひつよう
いりょう【衣料】(総称的) clothing; clothes. —費 clothing expenses.
いりょう【医療】medical treatment. ¶ ～を受ける get (≒ undergo) *medical treatment*.
—器械 medical instruments. —機関 a medical institution. —施設 medical facilities. —品 medical supplies. —扶助 medical care aid. —用(アルコールなど) for medical use.
いりょく【意力】will; will power.
いりょく【威力】power; authority. ¶ 新型爆弾が～を発揮した The new-type bomb *has proved powerful*. 彼のカウンターブローは～があった His counterblow *was powerful*.
い·る【要る】(必要) need; (欲しい) want; (時間·金·手数などがかかる) take. ¶ 今すぐ 1,000 円～る I *want* 1,000 yen right now. この本はもう～らない I *have done with* this book. 電話の返事は～りません No answer to this telephone *is needed*. この仕事をするのに何日ぐらい日数が～りますか How many days does it *take* to do this work? 家を建てるにはたいへんな金が～る It *costs* a huge fortune to build a house. この箱が～るなら持っていきなさい You may take this box if you *need* it.
い·る【煎る·炒る】¶ 豆を～る *parch* beans.
いる【射る】¶ 矢を射る *shoot* an arrow. 的を射る *shoot* at a target. 彼は射るような目で私を見た He looked at me with *piercing* eyes.
いる【鋳る】¶ その像は青銅で鋳られている The statue *is cast* in bronze.
いる【居る】**1**〖在宅·居住·滞在する〗be at home; stay. ¶ご主人はいますか *Is* your husband *in* (≒ *at home*)?
きょうは一日じゅう家にいます Today I will *be* [*at*] *home* all day long.
おばの家にいます I *am staying with* my aunt. / I *am staying at* my aunt's.
今学校にいる. あと20分したらもどる I *am in* (≒ *am at*) school now, I will be back in twenty minutes.
いまどこにいるのですか. 東京の郊外の小金井市にいます Where do you *live* now? I *live* in Koganei City in the suburbs of Tokyo.
あと三, 四日ロンドンにいるつもりだ I *am going to stay* (≒ *am staying*) in London for a few days more.
日本に何年おいでですか. 10年います How long *have* you *been* in Japan? Ten years.
2〖存在する〗¶ 神がいるとは信じられぬ I do not *believe in* God. / I don't believe in the *existence* of God.
きみがいなくてもそのくらいのことはできる I will be able to do that much *without* you.
昔々ひとりのおばあさんがいました Once upon a time there *lived* an old woman.
今どきそんなやぼなことを言う人はいない Nobody would *be* so silly these days.
その動物は日本にだけいる The animal *is found* in Japan alone.
その事実に気づいた人はひとりもいなかった Nobody noticed the fact.
戸口の所にだれかいる Someone *is* at the door.
3〖居合わせる〗¶ きみがあのときその場にいたらなあ If you had happened to *be* there at that time! / If you *had been* there!
折あしく彼を助けてやれる人がいなかった Unfortunately no one *was present* there to help him. / As ill luck would have it, nobody *happened to be* by to save him.
ぼくのいるところでよくもそんなことが言えるね How dare you speak like that *in my presence*.
彼女のいないうちに, 早くそれをかたづけろ Put it straight quickly while she *is away*.
そういうことは本人のいる前で言わなければだめだ You should say this much *in the presence of* the person in question.
鬼のいぬまにせんたく When the cat's *away*, the mice will play.
4〖所有する〗¶ 彼には娘がふたりいた He *had* two daughters.
彼にはいい弟子がたくさんいる He *has* a number of good followers.
5〖動作の継続·完了·状態〗¶ なにをしているの What *are* you *doing*? / What *are* you *about*? / What *are* you *working* at?
宿題をやっているところだ I *am doing* my homework.
赤ん坊はすやすや眠っていた The baby *was sleeping* calmly.
彼の来るのを待っている I *am waiting* for him to come.
仕事がなくてぶらぶらしている [Because I am] Out of employment, I *idle* my time *away*.
私は大きな犬を飼っている I *have* a big dog.
6〖いられない〗¶ じっとしていられない I cannot *sit still* (≒ *keep quiet*).
もう黙ってはいられない I cannot *hold my tongue* (≒ *keep silent*) any longer.
そんなのんきなことを言っていられない We *cannot afford to* indulge in such an idle talk. / We *cannot remain* so easygoing.
きみにあわずにいられようか I am dying to see you. / I miss you dreadfully.
いても立ってもいられない I am quite restless. / I am really impatient.
いるい【衣類】(総称的) clothing; clothes.
いるか【海豚】〘動物〙a dolphin; a porpoise.
いるす【居留守】¶ 彼は～を使った He *pretended to be out*.
イルミネーション illumination. ¶ その通りはきれいに～がついている The street *is* beautifully *illuminated*.
いれい【威令】authority. ¶ 彼の～はよく行き渡っている He has a great hold all over. / He has a strong *influence* all over. 彼の～に服さないものはない There is nobody who does not submit himself to his *authority*.
いれい【異例】¶ ～の処置 an *unprecedented* treatment. ～の昇進 an *exceptional* promotion. ～の昇進で課長になった His promotion to the chief of the section was *exceptional*

for his age.

いれい【慰霊】―祭 a memorial service for the dead. ―塔 a memorial 〔tower〕.

いれかえ【入れ替え】replacement.
―線〖鉄道〗a sidetrack.

いれか・える【入れ替える】¶ われわれはその窓ガラスを～えた We have new glass put in the window. お茶を～えましょう Let me make fresh tea. 気分を～えて仕事に取りかかった I set to work with a *renewed* heart. 彼は心を～えた He *has turned over a new leaf*.

いれかわり【入れ替わり】¶ 彼女が出ていくと～に彼が入ってきた *Just as* (≒ *The moment*) she went out, he came in. 皆が～立ち替わり彼を祝福した Everybody congratulated him *one after another*.

いれかわ・る【入れ替わる】¶ 彼と席を～ってください *Change* seats with him, please. 劇の配役が～った There was *a change* in the cast of the play.

イレギュラー ―バウンド〖野球〗an irregular bound. ¶ 球が～バウンドした The ball bounced *irregularly*.

いれげ【入れ毛】false (≒ artificial) hair.

いれずみ【入れ墨】a tattoo. ¶ 彼の右腕にヘビの～があった A snake *was tattooed* on his right arm.

いれぢえ【入れ知恵】(与える側からみて) a suggestion; (受け取る側からみて) a borrowed idea.
¶ だれかが～したにちがいない Somebody must have *put the idea into* his head. だれの～だ Who *suggested* the idea to you?

いれちがい【入れ違い】¶ 彼と～に彼女がやってきた She came in as he went out. ～になって彼女に会えなかった I didn't meet her, because she came in while I was out.

いれちが・える【入れ違える】misplace; place (*a thing*) in the wrong place. ¶ この薬のびんを～えないでください Don't *put* this bottle of medicine *in the wrong place*.

いれば【入れ歯】a false (≒ an artificial) tooth. ¶ ～をする have *a false tooth* put in. 歯医者で総～にしてもらった I had a full set of *false teeth* put in at the dentist's.

いれめ【入れ目】a false (≒ an artificial) eye.
¶ 彼の右目は～だ His right eye is artificial (≒ is false).

いれもの【入れ物】a container; (カップ・ポット・びんなど) a vessel; (箱・ケースなど) a case; a receptacle.

い・れる【入れる・容れる】**1**〖中に人・物を入れる〗
¶ この箱になにを～れようか What shall I *keep* in this box?
このかごにリンゴを10個～れてください Please *put* ten apples in this basket.
窓を開けて新鮮な空気を～れなさい Open the window(s) to *let* fresh air *in*.
彼はズボンのポケットに手を～れた He *put* his hands *into* his trouser pocket.
(部屋の)中に～れてあげなさい *Let* him *into* the room. / *Let* him *in*.
関係者以外はだれも部屋に～れるな *Admit* nobody *into* the room except the persons concerned.

2〖挿入する・はめ込む〗¶ 彼女はダイヤを～れた時計をしていた She wore a watch *set with* diamonds.
この時計にはいくつの石が～れてありますか How many jewels *are set* in this watch?
その項目は「雑」の部に～れるがよい You must *put* this item under "Miscellaneous."
先日歯を～れたところがまだ痛む Some days ago I *had* a false tooth *put in*, but it still hurts (≒ pains) me.

3〖加入させる・送り込む〗¶ きみたちの仲間に～れてくれ Let me *join* your party.
資格不十分でその会には～れてもらえなかった I was not qualified enough to *be a member of* (≒ *be admitted to*) the society.
娘は近所の幼稚園に～れた I *sent* my little daughter *to* a nearby kindergarten.
すぐ彼を病院に～れなさい *Send* him *to* hospital without delay.
あの学校に～れると金がかかる Education at that school is expensive.

4〖収容する〗¶ この講堂は2,000人～れることができる This hall *accommodates* two thousand 〔persons〕.
まだ2階席なら20人ぐらいは～れられる The second floor will *seat* about twenty persons more.
そんな大きな家具はこの部屋には～れられない Such an article of furniture *is too large for* this room.

5〖含める〗¶ 雑費まで～れて旅行はひとり約2万円かかる The trip (≒ tour) costs about twenty thousand yen for each person, *inclusive of* sundry expenses.
発起人に彼の名を～れた I *put* his name in the list of promoters.

6〖念頭にとどめる〗¶ そういうことも計算に～れておくほうがいい You must *take* that kind of thing *into account*, too.
こういう計画もあるということも頭に～れておいてください Please *keep* it *in your mind* that we have such a plan.
ちょっとお耳に～れておきたいことがあります I have something to *tell* you. / (内緒の話) Just a word in *your ear*.

7〖容認する〗¶ 使用者側は賃上げ要求を～れようとはしなかった The employers would not *accede to* the demand for a wage increase.
彼はなかなか他人の説を～れようとはしない He will not *listen to* others' opinions. / He *sticks to* his own opinion.
両者の説は互いに相～れない The opinions of the two *are incompatible with* each other.

8〖納入する〗pay. ¶ 家賃をふた月も～れてない I *have* not *paid* the house rent for two months.
少しは食事代ぐらい～れてくれ *Pay* for your board at least.
その金は当分銀行に～れておく I will *deposit* the

money in a bank for some time.

9 〖注意を集中する〗 ¶ 彼はその商売に身を〜れる気はしなかった He was not inclined to *put his heart into* the trade.

彼はその仕事に力を〜れはじめた He began to *throw his energy into* the work.

いろ【色】 **1** 〖赤・青などの色〗 color. ¶ 壁の〜はなに色にしようか What shall be the *color* of the wall? / What *color* shall we paint the wall?

このカラー写真は〜がぼやけている This color photo *has faded.* / This color photo *is blurred.*

〜あせた服 a *discolored* dress.

ひなたに長く置いたので絵の〜が変わった Left in the sun for a long time, the picture has changed *color*.

若者たちは〜とりどりの上着を着ていた The young people wore coats of various *colors*.

壁画の〜が落ちないようにする方法はないか Isn't there any way to prevent the *color* of the wall painting from fading?

2 〖顔色〗 ¶ 彼は憤然として〜をなした He *turned red* with indignation.

彼女は〜が白い She has *a* fair *complexion*. / She *is fair-skinned*.

彼女はろうばいの〜を隠すことができなかった She could not keep from showing *signs* of confusion on her face. / She betrayed confusion in her *looks*.

彼の顔には苦悩の〜がにじみ出ていた *A look* of anguish came over his face.

彼は悲しみの〜をおもてにあらわすまいとした He tried hard not to show his sorrow.

敗北の報に一同〜を失った We all *turned pale* at the news of the defeat.

彼は目の〜を変えてぼくに詰め寄った *Looking furious*, he drew closer to me.

日に焼けて〜が黒くなった I have got a good *tan*.

3 〖趣・様相〗 ¶ 秋の〜が濃くなった Autumnal *tints* have grown glorious.

4 〖おまけ〗 ¶ もうすこし〜よい返事を期待していたのだが I have expected a little more *favorable* answer.

すこしは〜をつけてくれよ(金を出す) Come down a little. / (値引きする) Just lower it a little.

5 〖情事〗 ¶ 英雄〜を好む Heroes are amorous.

〜におぼれたのが運のつきだった His indulgence in women sealed his fate.

いろあい【色合い】 (配色の仕方) coloring; (濃淡の度合い) shades. ¶ 〜といい柄といいあなたにぴったりです Its *coloring* and design suit you well. あたりの風景の緑にはいろいろの〜がある There are so many *shades* in the landscape.

いろいろ【色色】 ¶ 本にも〜ある There are *various kinds of* books. 〜な料理道具 *a variety of* cooking utensils. その問題について〜な人と話し合った We talked with *a lot of* people about the subject. 〜な犬を飼っている I have *various sorts of* dogs. とにかく〜やってみよう Anyway I will try *every* means. 〜考えてみた I *carefully* weighed the problems.

いろう【遺漏】 ¶ 万事〜なくやりなさい Take care (≒ See) that everything is done *well* (≒ *right*). なんの〜もないと思います I think there is nothing *left omitted*.

いろう【慰労】 ¶ 社長は社員〜の会を開いた The president held a party for his employees *in appreciation of their services*. 大いに彼を〜してやれ *Reward* him well *for his services*.

—金 a gratuity.

いろえんぴつ【色鉛筆】 a colored pencil.

いろおとこ【色男】 (情夫) a lover; a beau; (好男子) a dandy; a lady-killer.

いろおんな【色女】 (愛人) a sweetheart; a mistress.

いろか【色香】 ¶ 女の〜に迷う be charmed by a woman's *beauty*; be smitten with a woman's *charms*.

いろがみ【色紙】 colored paper.

いろガラス【色ガラス】 colored glass; (教会などの) stained glass.

いろがわり【色変わり】 ¶ この服は1年の間にひどく〜をした This dress *has been* much *discolored* within a year.

いろけ【色気】 **1** 〖性的な〗 ¶ 彼女はお〜たっぷりだ She *is* very *sexy* (≒ *coquettish*).

そろそろこの子も〜が出てくる年ごろだ Pretty soon she will reach *the age of puberty*.

あの子は最近〜づいてきた(性に目覚めた) The girl *has become sexually awakened* lately. / (色っぽくなる) The girl has *become coquettish* lately.

彼女はまだ〜がない She *is* still quite *innocent* (≒ *naive*).

〜のない話だね It's a very *prosaic* story.

2 〖意欲〗 ¶ 私にはそんなことをやってみようという〜などない I *am* not *interested in* making such an attempt.

彼はその地位に〜があった He *was ambitious for* the position.

彼はそれをやることに〜たっぷりだ He *has a good mind to* do it.

いろけし【色消し】 **1** 〖物理〗 achromatism.

—レンズ an achromatic lens.

2 〖無粋〗 bad taste; (人) a kill-joy.

いろごと【色事】 a love affair; an amour.

いろじかけ【色仕掛け】 ¶ 女に〜で金を巻き上げられた I was cleaned out by her *tricks of love*.

いろずり【色刷り】 color printing. ¶ 〜にする print (a picture) *in colors*. 〜のさし絵 an illustration *in colors*.

いろづ・く【色づく】 ¶ 谷間の木々は秋に赤く〜く The trees in the valley *turn red* in fall. 木の葉はみな真っ赤に〜いていた All the leaves have become *tinged with* bright red.

いろっぽ・い【色っぽい】 ¶ 〜い女 a *coquettish* (≒ *sexy*) girl. 〜い身なり a *sexy* style.

い

いろつや【色艶】(顔色) complexion;(光沢) luster. ¶ 顔の～がいい look well (≒ healthy; fresh). 顔の～が悪い look pale (≒ sallow; sick). 病人は～もよくなっている The patient has improved his *complexion*. / The patient has a better *complexion*. / The patient looks far better in *complexion*.

いろどり【色どり・彩り】coloring; a color scheme. ¶ この居間の色調は～がまずい The *color scheme* of the living room is not well integrated.

いろど・る【色どる・彩る】¶ 紅葉に～られた山々 the mountains beautifully *colored* with red and yellow leaves. 室内がいろいろの光で～られていた The room *was decorated* with lights of various colors.

いろなおし【色直し】(結婚式後ひろう宴で衣服を替える習慣は欧米にはない. 英語で説明すれば) a traditional Japanese custom of a bride changing to other costumes for variety during her wedding party.

いろは the Japanese alphabet. ¶ 彼は～のいの字も知らぬ He *is* completely *illiterate*. ～順に名前を書いてくれ Write down the names *in* 〔*Japanese*〕 *alphabetical order*. まずこの商売の～を教えてください Please initiate me first into *the ABC* of this business.

いろめ【色目】¶ 彼女はその紳士に～を使った She cast an amorous glance at the gentleman.

いろめがね【色眼鏡】colored glasses. ¶ 彼は～をかけている He wears a pair of *sunglasses*. つまらないことを言ったので近所の人は私を～で見るようになった My careless remarks *prejudiced* my neighbors *against* me.

いろめ・く【色めく】¶ その知らせに記者たちは～きたった The news *caused a stir* among the reporters. / The reporters *became active* at the news.

いろもの【色物】(織物の) colored fabrics.

いろよい【色よい】¶ ～返事を聞かせてください Give me a *favorable* answer.

いろり【囲炉裏】a hearth; a fireplace.

いろわけ【色分け】classification. ¶ 敵味方をどうして～できるか How can you *tell* our friends *from* our enemies?

いろん【異論】an objection. ¶ その問題に関しては人々の間に～がある People *differ in opinion* about the problem. 彼が行くことには～がない I have no *objection* to his going. なにか～がありますか Have you any *objection* to it?

いわ【岩】a rock. ¶ ～の多い rocky.

いわい【祝い】(ことばで祝う) congratulations; (祝典・祝賀) celebration; (祝祭) a festival. ¶ 結婚のお～をする give *a* wedding *gift*. お～に乾杯しよう Let's have a toast *in honor of the occasion*.

—酒 a drink in honor of...; *sake* to drink in celebration of....

いわ・う【祝う】¶ 友だちを呼んで娘の誕生日を～った We *celebrated* our daughter's birthday, inviting her friends. 私どもはクリスマスをツリーと贈り物で～う We *celebrate* Christmas with a tree and presents. 試験合格をお～いいたします Please accept *congratulations on* your success in the examination. (congratulations と複数にすること). きみの成功を心からお～い申し上げます I *congratulate* you on your success. / I *offer* (≒ *extend*) my hearty *congratulations to* you *on* success (形式ばった形). ご結婚をお～いいたします I *congratulate* you *on* your marriage. (ただしこれは男性に向かってのみ用いる. 女性には congratulate, congratulations は用いず, I wish you every happiness. / I hope you'll be very happy. などという. 女王などのお祝いのときは Felicitations).

いわく【曰く】¶ どうも～がありそうだ There seems to be something more than meets the eye. ～つきの男 a man of unsavory reputation. ～きの女 a woman with a past. これは～つきの時計だ This watch has a story connected with it.

—因縁 a complicated story. ¶ ～を聞かされた I was told about its *history* (≒ *origin*)./ I was told how it had come about.

いわし【鰯】〘魚類〙a sardine.

—雲 white, fleecy clouds; mackerel clouds.

いわず【言わず】¶ ～語らずに tacitly; implicitly. ～語らずのうちに互いに相手の気持がわかった Each *had a tacit understanding* of how the other party felt. ～もがなのことを言ってしまった I said something I shouldn't have. 山と～谷と～, つつじが咲き乱れている Everything—mountains and valleys—is covered with azaleas.

いわたおび【岩田帯】a maternity binding.

いわな【岩魚】〘魚類〙a char.

いわぬがはな【言わぬが花】Things are often better left unsaid.

いわば【言わば】so to speak; as it were; in other words.

いわゆる【所謂】what is called; what they (≒ we; you) 〔might〕 call; so-called. ¶ これが～一石二鳥だ This is *what you might call* "killing two birds with one stone."

いわれ【謂れ】(わけ) a reason; a cause; (由来) an origin; a story; (来歴) a history. ¶ ～なき反抗 a rebel *without cause*. ～のない非難 an *uncalled-for* (≒ *undue*) criticism. なんの～があって彼はそんなことを口にしたのか *Why on earth* he said that?

いん【印】a stamp; a seal. ¶ この書類にあなたの～を押してください Please put your *seal* to this document.

いん【因】a cause; a factor. ¶ 成功の～をなす form *a source for* success; constitute *a factor in* success.

いん【陰】¶ 彼女はすぐに～にこもるほうだ She is inclined to *take* things too much *to heart*. 彼は私を～に陽に助けてくれた He backed me up *directly and indirectly*.

いん【韻】a rhyme. ¶ Find と Mind は～を踏

む "Find" *is a rhyme for* "Mind." / "Find" rhymes with "Mind." / "Find" and "Mind" rhyme.

いんいん【殷殷】 ¶ ～たる砲声 the *booming* of guns. 夜更けに砲声が～ととどろき渡った *A roar of* guns *resounded* in the dead of night.

いんうつ【陰鬱】 ¶ ～な場所 a *depressing* (≒ *dismal*) place. ～な天気 *gloomy* (≒ *dull*) weather. ～な話 *dismal* talk. ～な顔つきをしている look *depressed* (≒ *sullen*).

いんえい【陰影】 shadow ; the shade.

いんか【引火】 ignition. ¶ ベンジンは～しやすい Benzine *is* highly *combustible*. / Benzine is easy to *catch fire*.

―点 the flash point.

インカ Inca.

―族 the Incas. **―帝国** the Inca Empire.

いんが【因果】 (原因と結果) cause and effect ; (不幸) misfortune. ¶ 彼にはよく～を含めた I explained to him the inevitableness of the circumstances. ～とあきらめた I *resigned myself to my destiny*. 親の～が子に報いる The child *is doomed to suffer for what his father has done*. / The sins of the father are visited upon his children. ～は巡る小車 The wheel of *fortune* keeps spinning around and around.

―応報 retribution; nemesis. **―関係** causal relation ; causality. **―律** the law of cause and effect ; causality.

いんが【印画】〘写真〙 a print.

―紙 printing paper.

いんが【陰画】〘写真〙 a negative [picture].

インカーブ〘野球〙 an incurve.

いんがい【院外】 **―勢力** outside influences. **―活動** lobbying. ¶ ～活動をする lobby. **―団**(ひとり) a lobbyist ; (団体) the lobby.

いんかしょくぶつ【隠花植物】〘植物〙 a cryptogam ; (総称) the Cryptogamia.

いんかん【印鑑】 a seal.

―証明 ¶ ～証明をもらう have *one's personalized stamp* notarized. **―届** ¶ ～届けを出す have *one's seal impression* registered.

いんき【陰気】 gloominess. ¶ ～な人 a *gloomy* person. ～な天気 *depressing* (≒ *sulky*) weather. じめじめして～な部屋 a damp, *dreary* room. ～な顔つきをしている look *sullen* (≒ *gloomy*).

いんぎ【院議】 a Congressional (≒ 英 a Parliamentary) decision ; (日本の) a decision of the Diet.

いんきくさい【陰気くさい】 gloomy. ⇒いんき

いんきょ【隠居】 retirement ; (人) a retired person. ¶ ～する *retire from* active life.

―仕事 ¶ ～仕事にこれをやっています I do this work to keep myself occupied in my *retirement*. **楽―** ¶ 彼は楽～ができる身だ He can look forward to a comfortable life in *retirement*.

いんきょく【陰極】〘電気〙 the negative pole ; the cathode.

―管 a cathode ray tube. **―線** cathode rays.

いんぎん【慇懃】 courtesy ; civility. ¶ ～にあいさつする greet *a person warmly* (≒ *cordially*). ～にお辞儀をする make a *courteous* bow to *a person*. 彼のわれわれに対する態度には～無礼なところがある He *is* a little *too polite* to us.

インク ink. ¶ ～で書く write *in ink*. (「インクで」の「で」に当たる前置詞はふつう in を使う. ただし「ペンとインクで書く」というときは, 慣用句的に write *with* pen and ink という). ～をこぼす spill *ink*. ～のしみは落ちない *Ink* stains don't come off. ～を入れる *fill* a pen.

―消し ink eradicator. **―スタンド** an inkstand. **―つぼ** an inkwell ; 英 an inkpot. **―びん** an ink bottle.

いんけい【陰茎】〘解剖〙 the penis (複 penes).

いんけん【引見】 an interview ; an audience. ¶ 皇帝は彼らを～した The emperor *granted* (≒ *gave*) *an interview* (≒ *an audience*) *to* them.

―室 a reception room ; an audience chamber.

いんけん【隠見】 appearance and disappearance. ¶ 湖は木々の間に～している The lake briefly *appears and disappears* through the trees. / We can *catch glimpses* of the lake through the trees.

いんけん【陰険】 ¶ ～なたくらみ an *insidious* scheme. ～な手段を使う use a *crafty* means. 彼は～な目つきをしている He has a *sinister* look. 彼は～な人だ He is *an old* (≒ *a sly*) *fox*.

いんげんまめ【隠元豆】 a kidney bean.

いんこ【鸚哥】〘鳥類〙 a parakeet ; a macaw.

いんご【隠語】 secret language ; a jargon ; a cant.

いんこう【咽喉】 ⇒のど

いんごう【因業】 ¶ ～[な]おやじ a *hard* (≒ *mean*) old man.

いんさつ【印刷】 (状態) print ; (技術) printing. ¶ 詩を～する *put one's* poem into *print*. ～の誤り a *typographical* error ; a misprint. ～中 be *in* [*the*] *press*. ～が仕上がる be *off the press*. ～になっている be [available] in print. 太字(細字)の～ in large (small) *print*. 原稿を～に回す *send one's* manuscript to *the printer* (≒ *press*). この小説の初版は2,000部～された This novel had a first *printing* of two thousand copies. 本は～に回っている The book *has gone to press*.

―インク printing ink. **―機** 米 a [printing] press ; 英 a printing machine. **―業者** a printer. **―工** a pressman. **―所** 米 a print shop ; a printing office (≒ house). **―物** printed matter. **―用紙** printing paper. **―物在中**(郵便物に記す) Printed matter [only].

いんさん【陰惨】 ¶ ～な光景 a *ghastly* scene.

いんし【因子】〘数学〙〘生物〙 a factor.

―型 a genotype. **遺伝―** a gene ; a factor.

いんし【印紙】 a stamp. ¶ ～をはる put *a stamp*

(*on*); affix *a stamp* (*to*). ～で納める pay in *stamps*.

—税 stamp duty. 収入— a revenue stamp.

いんじゃ【隠者】a hermit.

いんしゅ【飲酒】drinking. ¶ 過度の～ excessive *drinking*. ～にふける take to *drink*.

—家 a drinker.

いんしゅう【因習】convention; a long-established custom. ¶ ～を打破する break the *long-established conventions* (≒ *customs*). 社会的～にとらわれるのはばかばかしい It is silly to be a slave to social *conventions*. / It is absurd to be fettered by *tradition*.

インシュート〔野球〕an inshoot.

インシュリン〔薬学〕insulin.

いんじゅん【因循】¶ ～姑息(こそく)な手段 a makeshift; a faltering half measure.

いんしょう【引証】quotation. ¶ ～する quote (a passage *from* a book).

いんしょう【印章】a seal; a stamp.

いんしょう【印象】〔an〕impression.

¶ ～的な光景 an *impressive* scene. 良い(悪い)～を与える *impress* (*a person*) favorably (unfavorably); leave a favorable (an unfavorable) *impression* (*on a person*). 強い～を受ける *be* deeply *impressed* (*by*). …の～を強める confirm the *impression* (*that*...). 彼はまじめな好青年という～を与えた He *impressed* us as a sincere young man. / *It struck* us that he was a decent young man. 日本の第一～はいかがですか What is your first *impression* of Japan? 面接ではぜひともいい～を与えるようにしよう I'll certainly try to give *a* good *impression* at the interview. あの人は親切だという～だ *I am under the impression that* he is a kind man.

—主義(派) impressionism. —主義者 an impressionist. —派絵画 an impressionist painting.

いんしょく【飲食】food and drink; eating and drinking.

—店 an eating house (大衆的な店); a restaurant. —物 food and drink.

いんしん【殷賑】prosperity. ¶ ～を窮める be prosperous.

いんしん【陰唇】〔解剖学〕the labium (複 labia).

いんすう【因数】〔数学〕a factor. ¶ ～に分解する resolve into *factors*; factorize.

—分解 resolution into factors; factorization.

いんずう【員数】¶ ～は確かめたか Did you ascertain *the number*? 彼は～外だ He *is not included*.

インスタントコーヒー instant coffee.

いん・する【印する】¶ 彼がその島に最初の第一歩を～した He was the first to *set* foot on the island.

いんせい【陰性】〔電気〕negative; 〔医学〕negative; (性質が) gloomy (名詞はgloominess); melancholy.

¶ ツベルクリン反応の結果は～と判明した The tuberculin test turned out to be *negative*.

—元素 negative element. —電気 negative electricity.

いんぜい【印税】a royalty. ¶ 著者に～を払う pay the author *a royalty* (*on* his work). 本の定価に対し1割の～を払う pay *a* ten percent *royalty* on the retail price of the book.

いんせき【引責】¶ 彼はその事件で～辞職した He *took the blame for* the incident and resigned.

いんせき【姻戚】¶ 彼とは～関係にある I *am related to* him *by marriage*.

いんせき【隕石】a meteorite.

—学 astrolithology.

いんぜん【隠然】¶ 彼は財界に～たる勢力を持っている He wields *great* power in the financial circles.

いんそつ【引率】¶ 学生を～して美術館に行った I *took* a group of students to the art museum. / I *visited* (≒ *went to*) the art gallery *with* a group of students.

—者 a leader; a commander.

インターカレッジ intercollegiate; intercollege.

インターナショナル international. ¶ 第3～ the Third 〔Communist〕International; the Comintern.

インターフェア〔競技〕interference.

インターホン an interphone; the intercom (intercommunication system の略).

インターン (病院実習医学生) an intern〔e〕; (実習) internship. ¶ 市立病院で～をやる serve *one's internship* at the city hospital.

いんたい【引退】retirement. ¶ 第一線(政界)から～する *retire from* active life (politics). ～生活をする live in *retirement*.

—選手 a retired player.

インタビュー an interview. ¶ ～する interview (*a person*); have *an interview* (*with a person*). ～に応じる give *an interview* to (*a person*).

インチ【吋】an inch (しばしば in. と略す). ¶ 2フィート5～ two feet five *inches*; 2 ft. 5 *in.*; 2′5″. 彼は5フィート2～ある He is five foot (≒ feet) two 〔*inches*〕.

いんちき trickery. ¶ ～な訳 a *false* translation. ～なやつ a fake. ～会社 a *bogus* company. 商売で～をする *cheat* in trade.

いんちょう【院長】(病院の) the director of a hospital; (学院の) a president; a principal.

インディアペーパー India paper.

インディアン an American (≒ a Red) Indian; an Indian.

いんてつ【隕鉄】meteoric iron.

インテリ〔ゲンチャ〕the intelligentsia (among the intelligentsia のように, 集合的にのみ用いられる. 個々の知識人を指す場合は an intellectual を使う).

いんでんき【陰電気】〔電気〕negative electricity.

いんでんし【陰電子】〔電気〕an electron; a

negatron.

インド【印度】India.
—共和国 the Republic of India. —語 an Indian language; (公用語) Hindi. —人 an Indian. —哲学 Hindu (≒ Indian) philosophy. —洋 the Indian Ocean. —教 Hinduism.

インドア indoor. ¶ ～ゲーム an *indoor* game.

いんとう【咽頭】〔解剖学〕the pharynx (複 pharynxes; pharynges).

いんとう【淫蕩】dissipation. ¶ ～な生活をする lead a *dissolute* life.

いんどう【引導】¶ 僧が死者に～を渡した The priest *read the last service to the dead*. あの男に～を渡してやる I'll *tell* him *to prepare for the worst*. 社長は彼に～を渡した The president *gave* him *a notice of dismissal*.

いんとく【隠匿】concealment. ¶ ～する hide; conceal.

イントネーション〔音声〕intonation.

インドネシア Indonesia. ¶ ～の Indonesian.
—人 an Indonesian.

インドロップ〔野球〕an in-drop.

いんとん【隠遁】retirement; seclusion.
—生活 a retired life. ¶ 彼は～生活を送った He *lived in seclusion*. / He *secluded himself from society*. —者 a retired man; a hermit.

いんない【院内】—活動 〔the〕 activities in the Diet; 〔the〕 activities as a Dietman.
—総務 米 the floor leader; 英 the leader of the House.

いんにく【印肉】an ink pad; stampink.

いんにん【隠忍】patience; endurance.
¶ 彼はあらゆる侮辱に～自重した He *put up with* every kind of insult. われわれは～して時の至るのを待った We waited for the opportunity *with patience*. もう～できない I am now out of *patience*. / I've come to the end of my *endurance*.

いんねん【因縁】(運命) fate; (縁) connection; (由来) origin; (言いがかり) a pretext.
¶ ～だとあきらめた I resigned myself to my *fate*. きみといっしょに(夫婦に)なったのもなにかの～だ Perhaps you and I *are predestined* to become man and wife. 中国と日本とは浅からぬ～がある There is *a* close *connection* between Japan and China. 彼はすぐに～をつける He is ready to *invent a pretext* for quarreling.

いんび【隠微】obscurity; mystery. ¶ ～な obscure; (玄妙な) occult.

いんび【淫靡】obscenity; lasciviousness.
¶ ～な obscene; indecent.

いんぶ【陰部】the private parts; genitals.

インフェリオリティーコンプレックス inferiority complex.

インフルエンザ influenza; (俗語) flu〔e〕.

インフレ〔ーション〕〔経済〕inflation. ¶ ～を抑える(おこす) curb (cause) *inflation*.
—傾向 an inflationary tendency. —政策 an inflationary policy. —対策 anti-inflation measures.

いんぶん【韻文】verse (散文 prose と対に).
¶ ～で書く write in *verse*.

いんぺい【隠蔽】concealment; hiding; coverture. ¶ 彼はその事実を～した He *covered up* the fact. / He *suppressed* the fact.
—者 a suppressor.

インボイス〔商〕an invoice.

いんぼう【陰謀】a plot; a conspiracy.
¶ 彼らは政府転覆の～を企てた They *plotted* to overthrow the government. 彼らは首相暗殺の～を企てた They *plotted against* the Premier's life.
—家 a schemer; a mischief maker. —者 a plotter. —団 a cabal.

インポテンツ〔医学〕impotent (これは形容詞。形で, 名詞は impotence; かな書き「インポテンツ」はドイツ語 Impotenz から).

いんぽん【淫奔】lewdness. ¶ ～な女 a *wanton* woman.

いんめつ【隠滅】(故意の) destruction; (自然の) extinction. ¶ 彼は証拠を～した He *destroyed* (≒ *suppressed*) the evidence.

いんもう【陰毛】pubic hair; pubes.

いんもん【陰門】the vulva; the vagina.

いんゆ【引喩】〔修辞〕an allusion.

いんゆ【隠喩】〔修辞〕a metaphor. ¶ ～の metaphorical.

いんよう【引用】a quotation; citation. ¶ 聖書からの～ *a quotation* from the Bible. 漱石からこの文を～した I *quoted* this passage from Soseki. 彼女はよく先生のことばを～する She often *quotes* her teacher. 聖書からの～だと思う I think it is *a quotation* from the Bible.
—文 a quotation. —符 quotation marks. —書 reference books; books referred to. —書目 a list of works consulted in the preparation of a book.

いんよう【飲用】¶ この水は～に適する This water is *good to drink*.
—水(掲示) Fit to drink.

いんらん【淫乱】lewdness; lasciviousness.
¶ ～な女 a *lewd* (≒ *wanton*) woman.

いんりつ【韻律】meter; a metric system; a rhythm. ¶ ～的な rhythmical; metrical.

いんりょう【飲料】¶ この水は～に適する This water *is good* (≒ *fit*) *to drink*.
—水 drinking water; water to drink; (掲示) Fit to drink. 清涼— soft drinks.

いんりょく【引力】〔物理〕(宇宙・天体の) gravitation; (物体間の) attraction; (磁気の) magnetism. ¶ ～の法則 the law of *gravitation*.
—説 the theory of gravitation. 地球— gravity; terrestrial gravitation. 万有— universal gravitation.

いんれい【引例】(文章の) a quotation. ¶ この～の出典はなんですか Where *is* this *quoted from*?

いんれき【陰暦】the lunar calendar. ¶ ～8月 August according to *the lunar calendar*.

いんわい【淫猥】obscenity.

う

う【鵜】〘鳥類〙 a cormorant. ¶ 彼は～の目たかの目で獲物を捜した He searched for his victim *with sharp eyes*. ～のまねをするな〘諺〙 You'll ruin yourself if you try to ape your better.

ウイークエンド a weekend. ¶ 楽しく～をお過ごしください Have *a* nice *weekend*.

ウイークデー a weekday. ¶ ～はいつも忙しい I am always busy *on weekdays*.

ウイークポイント a weak point. ¶ 彼の～をついた I attacked his *weak point*. そこが彼の議論の～だった That was the *weak point* of his argument.

ウィーン Vienna ([viénə] と発音する. ドイツ語では Wien). ¶ ～の Viennese.
—人 a Viennese.

ういういし・い【初初しい】 innocent; naive. ¶ ～い花嫁姿に打たれた I was charmed with the *young, modest* bride.

ういざん【初産】 *one's* first childbirth.

ういじん【初陣】 *one's* first campaign.

ウイスキー whisky; whiskey. ¶ ～を生(き)で飲む drink *whisky* neat (≒ straight).
—ソーダ whisky and soda. 水割り— a whisky and water.

ういた【浮いた】 ¶ 彼女には～話はない We have never heard any *scandal* about her.

ウイニングショット〘野球〙〘テニス〙 a winning shot.

ウイニングボール a winning ball.

ういまご【初孫】 *one's* first grandchild.

ウインク a wink. ¶ 彼女は私の方に～した She *winked at* me.

ウインター winter.
—スポーツ winter sports.

ウインナソーセージ Vienna sausage; 米 wiener.

ウーステッド worsted.

ウール wool.

うえ【上】 **1**〘上部〙 ¶ 頭の～からつま先までじろじろ見られた I was stared at *from head to foot* (≒ *from top to toe*).
そのビルの～から見ると町全体が見える The *roof* of the building overlooks the whole town. / On the *roof* (≒ *top*) of the building you can get a complete view of the city. / The *top* of the building commands the whole view of the town.
ページの～から4行めのところが文字がはっきりしない The fourth line from the *top* of this page is not printed clearly.
山の～に行くにつれ, 木が少なくなる *The higher* we go *up* the mountain, the fewer trees we see.
塔の～に月が出ていた The moon had risen *above* the tower.
その丘の～に彼女の家があった Her house stood on the *top* of the hill.
～にだれか人がいる(階上に) Somebody is in the room *overhead*. / Someone is *upstairs*.
もっと～の方を見てごらん Look up *higher*. / Just raise your eyes *higher*.
2〘表面〙 ¶ 海の～に油が一面に浮かんでいた Oil floated *all over* the sea.
テーブルの～をふいてください Please wipe the *surface* of the table.
机の～の本を持ってきてくれ Bring me the book(s) *on* the desk.
3〘地位・年齢・能力などがまさっていること〙 ¶ ～には～があるものだ Anybody has somebody *above* him. / There is no limit to *one's* cunning. / Diamond cut diamond. (毒をもって毒を制すの意味もある). / There is no limit to *excellence*. / *Superiority* is comparative.
英語を書く能力はきみのほうが～だ You *are superior to* me in writing English. / You can write English *better* than I.
彼女は私より年が三つ～だ She *is* three years *older* than I. / She *is* my *senior* by three years. / She *is* three years my *senior*.
いちばん～の兄は大学をことし出た My *oldest* (≒ *eldest*) brother graduated from a university this year.
～の子は高校に, 下の子は中学に行っている The *older* (≒ *elder*) one attends a senior high school, while the younger one attends a junior high school.
18歳より～の人でないと入場できない Persons of eighteen years of age and *onward* only are admitted. / Admission to persons *above* eighteen only.
そんなことをしては人の～には立てない If you do such a thing, you cannot hope to *command people* (≒ *be a leader of men*).
彼は会社ではぼくより地位が～だ He is *above* me in the company. / He is *higher* in position than I in the company.
これは～からの命令だ This is an order from *above*.
そんなことには～も下もない Rank has nothing to do with such a matter. / Such a thing is irrespective of rank.
4〘その上〙 ¶ この品は値段が安い～に品質もよい This article is low in price and *what is more*, of good quality. / This article is

moderate in price and good in quality *as well*.

彼女は頭がいい～に美人だ *Besides* being blessed with a clear head, she is a beauty. / She is *not only* clearheaded, *but* beautiful.

日本の夏は暑い～に湿気が多い Summers are hot in Japan and *what is worse*, there is high humidity.

この～まだ要求するとはきみもあつかましい What [a] cheek to demand *more than* that! / How dare you make *another* impudent demand!

5 〖…に関すること〗 ¶ この程度の近眼なら仕事の～では支障はない Such a degree of shortsightedness will not interfere *with* your work.

6 〖…の結果〗 ¶ 彼とよく相談した～でご返事します I will give you an answer *after* much consultation with him.

至急調査の～ご報告します *On* urgent investigation into the matter, we will send you a report on it. / *After* looking into the matter without delay, we will give you an account of it.

こうなった～はしかたない *Now* [*that*] things have come to this, there is no help for it.

酒の～のことではすまされぬ You cannot get away with it, though you did it *under the influence of liquor*.

7 〖その他〗 ¶ ～を下への大騒動が持ち上がった There arose a *dreadful* confusion. / All was in *utter* confusion.

うえ【飢え】 hunger; starvation. ¶ 彼らは～で死んだ They died of (≒ from) *hunger*. / They *were starved* to death. 彼は水を飲んで～をしのいだ He drank water to stay his *hunger*. 子どもたちは～で苦しんでいた The children were suffering from *hunger*. われわれには～が迫っていた We were hard pressed for food.

ウエート weight. ¶ それに～をおいた（重点を）I laid *emphasis* on it.

—リフティング weight lifting.

ウエートレス a waitress.

ウエーブ a wave. ¶ 彼女の髪は天然の～をしている She has *a* natural *wave* in her hair. 彼女の髪の～は美しい Her hair *waves* in beautiful curves.

うえき【植木】（庭木）a garden plant; (鉢植え) a pot plant; (一般に) a plant.

—ばち a flower pot. **—**屋(庭師) a gardener; (苗木商) a nurseryman.

うえこみ【植え込み】（やぶの）a thicket; (低木の) a shrubbery.

¶ 庭にバラの～をした I *planted* the garden *with* roses. / I *planted* roses in the garden.

うえした【上下】 ¶ それは～〔逆〕になっている It is *upside down*.

うえじに【飢え死に】 starvation. ¶ 多くの人が～した Many people *died of hunger*. / Many people *were starved to death*.

ウエスト ¶ 彼女は～が60センチだ She is sixty centimeters round the *waist*. 彼女の～は細い She has *a* slim *waist*.

—ライン the waistline. ¶ 彼女の～ラインはきれいだ She has *a* neat *waistline*.

うえつけ【植え付け】 ¶ 彼らは稲の～をした They *did* rice *planting*. / They *planted* rice.

うえつ·ける【植え付ける】 **1** 〖植物を〗 ¶ 庭に松を～けた I *planted* the garden *with* a pine.

2 〖思想を〗 ¶ 彼は子どもの心に高い理想を～けた He *implanted* high ideals in children.

偏見が彼らの心深く～けられている Prejudice *is deeply fixed in* them.

彼は学生の間に不満の種を～けた He *sowed* seeds of discontent among the students.

ウエット sentimental. ¶ ～な少女 a *sentimental* girl.

ウェディング [a] wedding.

—ケーキ a wedding cake. **—**ドレス a wedding dress. **—**マーチ a wedding march.

ウエハース wafers (単 a wafer).

う·える【飢える】 be hungry; starve. ¶ 彼は～えた顔をしていた He *looked hungry*. その少年は愛情に～えていた The boy *was hungry for* affection. 彼は知識に～えていた He *had a thirst for* knowledge.

う·える【植える】 ¶ 庭にバラを～えた I *planted* the garden *with* roses. / I *planted* roses in the garden. 今年は大麦を～えなかった We didn't *sow* barley this year.

ウエルターきゅう【ウエルター級】〖ボクシング〗 welterweight. ¶ ～のボクサー a welterweight [boxer].

うえん【迂遠】 ¶ そんな～なやり方はごめんだ I don't like such a *roundabout* way of doing things. 彼はいつも～な言い方をする He always talks in a *roundabout* way. / He always *beats about the bush*.

うお【魚】 fish.

—市場 a fish market. **—**河岸 a riverside fish market.

うおうさおう【右往左往】 in all directions; this way and that. ¶ 彼らは～していた They went *this way and that* in confusion. / They *went pellmell*.

ウオーキートーキー a walkie-talkie.

ウオーター water.

—シュート a water chute. **—**プルーフ waterproof (形容詞に使う). **—**ポロ water polo.

ウオーミングアップ warming-up. ¶ ～する余裕もほとんどなく彼はマウンドに立たされた He had to stand on the mound before he could find enough time to *warm up*. ピッチャーは～を始めた The pitcher began to *warm up*.

うおごころ【魚心】 ¶ ～あれば水心（諺）*Roll my log and I'll roll yours*.

ウオツカ vodka.

うおのめ【魚の目】 a corn.

うかい【鵜飼い】 fishing with cormorants; cormorant fishing; (人) a cormorant fisher. ¶ 私たちは～見物をした We saw the fishermen *fish with cormorants*.

うかい【迂回】 a detour. ¶ ～する make *a de-*

う

tour; take *a roundabout way*. その通りが通行止めだったので～しなければならなかった As the street was blocked, we had to *make a detour* (≒ *take a roundabout way*).
一路 a detour.

うがい ¶～する gargle; rinse out the mouth.
一薬 a gargle.

うかうか〔と〕 (軽率に) carelessly; thoughtlessly; (ぼんやりと) absent-mindedly. ¶～と彼の手に乗った I believed him *carelessly* (≒ *thoughtlessly*). / I was taken in by him. ～と時を過ごすな Don't *idle away* your time.

うかがい【伺い】 (訪問) a visit; (見舞い) an inquiry (*after a person*); (質問) a question. ¶彼のごきげん～をした I *paid a visit to* him. 彼に～をたててみてくれ Please *ask for* his instructions. いつお～したらよろしいでしょうか When shall I *call on* you? ちょっとお～しますが, 郵便局はどこでしょうか *Excuse me, but* could you tell me where the post office is?

うかが·う【伺う】 ¶人物が～われるね We could easily *imagine* his character. 明日～います I will *call on* you tomorrow. 彼から～いましたが, ご入院中だったそうですね *I've heard* from him that you were in the hospital.

うかが·う【窺う】 ¶彼は逃げる機会を～っていた He *was watching for* an opportunity to run away. しばらく形勢を～うことにしよう Let's *see* how things go on for some time. じっと目をこらしてすきを～った I *looked for* an opportunity, straining my eyes.

うかさ·れる【浮かされる】 ¶彼は熱に～れてあんなたわごとを言っているらしい He seems to be talking such nonsense *in the delirium of fever*.

うか·す【浮かす】 ¶舟を川に～す *float* a ship down a river.

うかつ【迂濶】 ¶～な人 a *careless* (≒ *thoughtless*) man. まったく～なことをしてしまった It was very *careless of* me. / How *silly* of me to have done it! ～にものは言えない We could not be too careful of what to say.

うが·つ【穿つ】 ¶穴を～つ *dig* (≒ *make*) a hole. 雨だれ石を～つ (諺) A falling drop at last will *carve* a stone. / Constant dropping *wears* the stone. 彼はよく～ったことを言う He often makes a *penetrating* remark. それは～ちすぎた冗談だ It is a *cynical* joke.

うかぬかお【浮かぬ顔】 ¶彼は～をしている He *looks gloomy* (≒ *looks depressed*). / He *pulls a long face*. (a longish face (長い顔) との違いに注意).

うかば·れる【浮かばれる】 ¶これでようやく～れる Then I *can rest safely* (≒ *can rest in peace*)! そうなれば彼の霊もようやく～れるだろう Then his soul *could rest in peace*.

うかびあが·る【浮かび上がる】 ¶1匹の大きな魚が水面に～った A big fish *rose to the surface* of water. 潜水艦が～った The submarine *has broken the surface*.

うか·ぶ【浮かぶ】 **1**〖水や空に〗¶白い雲が二つ三つ青空に～んでいた A few white clouds *were floating* across the blue sky.
入り江には釣り舟がたくさん～んでいた In the inlet there were a good many fishing boats *floating* on the water.
白鳥が水に～んでいる A swan *is floating* on the water.
あそこになにか～んでいる Something *is floating* (≒ *is afloat*) over there. / I see something *floating* over there.
川面に水死体が～んでいた A drowned body *was floating* on the river.
石は水に～ばない The stone does not *float* on the water.
2〖現われる〗¶思わず目に涙が～んだ In spite of myself, I felt tears *gathering* in my eyes.
彼の顔に不快の色が～んだ A look of displeasure *passed* over his face. / He *looked* displeased.
彼女の口もとにほほ笑みが～んだ A faint smile *came to* (≒ *played about*) her lips.
3〖心に〗¶なかなかその文句が～んでこなかった The phrase would not *come into my mind*. / I tried to *hit upon* (≒ *call to mind*) the phrase in vain.
なにも名案が～ばないで困っている I am at a loss for a good idea. / I am sorry I cannot *think of* any capital idea.
彼の助けを得られるかもしれぬという考えが心に～んできた *It occurred to me* that I might obtain his assistance.
母の姿がまぶたに～んだ I *saw* my mother *in my mind's eye*.
4〖出世する〗¶そんなことをしてると一生～ばれない If you keep on doing such a thing, you will have no chance to *get on in the world*. / If you go on like this, you will *be ruined for life*.
身を捨ててこそ～ぶ瀬もあれ (諺) *Burn the bridge behind you and you may conquer*. / *Risk all and gain all*. / *Nothing venture, nothing have*.
今度こそぼくも～ばれるかな This time I wish to *rise from obscurity*. / Now *luck may turn in my favor*.

うか·べる【浮かべる】 **1**〖水に〗¶子どもはおもちゃの船を池に～べた The child *set* a toy boat *afloat* on the pond.
2〖現わす〗¶彼女は満面に笑みを～べて応対した She received me *all smiles*. / She received me, *smiling* all over her face.
彼は目に涙を～べていた Tears *stood* in his eyes. / He *had* his eyes *filled* with tears.
婦人は目に涙を～べて亡夫のことを語った The lady told me of her late husband *with* tears in her eyes.
彼は不満の色を顔に～べた He *looked* dissatisfied.
その話を聞くと彼は失望の色を顔に～べた He *looked* disappointed at the news.
3〖心に〗¶亡き母の面影を胸に～べた I *pictured to myself* my departed mother's

countenance. / My deceased mother's face *came across my mind.* / My deceased mother's face *flashed across my mind.*

学生時代を思い～べた I *looked back* on my school days.

うか・る【受かる】¶ 彼は試験に～った He *passed* (≒ *succeeded in*) the examination.

うか・れる【浮かれる】¶ 彼らは酒を飲んで～れている They *are making merry* over their cups.

うき【浮き】(釣りの) a float ; (浮標) a buoy.

うき【雨季・雨期】the rainy season ; (熱帯地方の) the rains. ¶ ～に入った *The rainy* (≒ *The wet*) *season* has set in (≒ has begun).

うきあしだ・つ【浮き足立つ】¶ 彼は～っている He *is ready to run away.*

うきうき〔と〕【浮き浮き〔と〕】¶ きみは～している You *look light-hearted.* 彼は～した顔つきをしている He *looks cheerful.*

うきくさ【浮き草】〘植物〙 duckweed.

—稼業(かぎょう) an unstable occupation.

うきぐも【浮き雲】a floating cloud ; a drifting cloud.

うきしずみ【浮き沈み】ups and downs ; rise and fall. ¶ 彼にも運の～はあった He had his *ups and downs* of fortune.

うきしま【浮き島】a floating island.

うきた・つ【浮き立つ】¶ 彼らは心が～っている They *are buoyed* (≒ *are cheered*) *up.*

うき・でる【浮き出る】¶ 高い塔は青空に～出ているようだ The tall tower *is standing* 〔*out*〕 *in bold relief* against the blue sky. 丘は朝空を背景に～出ていた The hills *stood out in sharp relief* against the morning sky.

うきドック【浮きドック】a floating dock.

うきな【浮き名】a scandal. ¶ 彼女は～を流した Her love affairs were much rumored.

うきぼり【浮き彫り】relief. ¶ それは～にしたキューピッドの像だった It was a figure of Cupid *in relief.* その塔は青空にくっきりと～にされていた The spire stood out *in strong relief* against the blue sky.

うきみ【憂き身】¶ 彼はなにに～をやつしているのか What does he *devote himself to*? 彼は恋に～をやつしている He *is being a slave to* love.

うきみ【浮き身】(水泳) floating on *one's* back.

うきめ【憂き目】misery ; misfortune ; a bitter experience. ¶ ～を見る have *a bitter experience.* 私はどうしてこんな～を見たのだろうか Why did I meet with such *hardships*?

うきよ【浮き世】life ; the world. ¶ それが～の習いというものだ It is *the way of the world.* 彼は～を捨てて孤独に暮らしている He has retired from *the world* and lives a solitary life. 彼は～の荒波にもまれた He has gone through the storms of *life.* / He has been tossed about in the storms of *the world.* ～はままならぬもの *Life* is full of vexations.

—離れ ¶ 彼は～離れのした生活を送っている He leads *an unworldly life.*

うきよえ【浮世絵】an *ukiyo-e* print.

う・く【浮く】¶ 白い雲が青い空に～いている A white cloud *is floating* in the blue sky. 木の葉が2枚池に～いている Two leaves *are floating* on the surface of the pond. 月に1万円は～くようにしたい I want to *save* ten thousand yen a month.

うぐいす【鶯】〘鳥類〙 a 〔Japanese〕 nightingale (イギリスの nightingale は夜鳴くので日本のと違う. なおアメリカにはいない).

—茶 greenish brown.

ウクレレ a ukulele.

うけ【受け】**1** 〘評判〙 popularity. ¶ 彼は同僚の間に～がいい He *is popular* among his colleagues.

この映画は世間の～がよくない This movie *is* not *in public favor.*

この小説は批評家の～がいい This novel *is well received* by the critics.

彼は先輩たちに～がいい He *stands high in the favor* (≒ *eyes*) *of* his superiors.

2 〘防御〙 ¶ 彼の将棋は～にまわると強い In playing a game of Japanese chess he is strong when he *is on the defensive.*

うけ【有卦】¶ 彼らは～に入っている Luck is with them. / Fortune is smiling upon them.

うけあ・う【請け合う】¶ 彼はどんなことでもすぐ～う He *undertakes* every job that is offered. 彼の身元は私が～う I *vouch for* him. 彼が正直なことは私が～う I *assure* you *of* his honesty. / I *assure* you that he is honest. 彼の支払能力は～う I *vouch for* his ability to pay. 彼は私にその仕事は土曜日までに終わらせると～った He *promised* me that the work would be done before Saturday.

うけい【右傾】¶ 国民は～(右翼化)しつつある The people *are turning to the right.*

うけいれ【受け入れ】¶ 移民の～計画 an immigration *induction* program. 彼をクラブに入れるための～態勢はととのっている We are quite ready for *receiving* him *into* the club.

うけい・れる【受け入れる】¶ 彼はすぐに私の要求を～れた He readily *complied with* my request. きみはその説明を事実として～れることができるか Can you *accept* the explanation *as* a fact?

うけうり【受け売り】(小売り) retail ; (人の説を自分の説のように述べること) secondhand knowledge (≒ information).

¶ 彼の話は～だ What he says is *secondhand information.* / What he says is *parrot-learning.* 彼は有名な学者の意見を～している He *tells* eminent scholars' views *at second hand.*

うけおい【請負】undertaking ; a contract. ¶ その仕事は～でやらせよう I will have the work done *by contract.* それを～に出す予定だ It is to *be put out to contract.* そのビルは～で造られたものだ The building was built *by contract.*

—業 〔the〕 contracting business. **—**仕事 contract work. **—**人 a contractor. **—**値段 a contract price.

うけお・う【請け負う】¶ その家の建築を～うつもり

う

だ I am going to *undertake* to build the house. 会社はそのビルを5億円で〜った The company *contracted for* the building at five hundred million yen.

うけこたえ【受け答え】a reply; an answer. ¶ 彼は口べたなので適当な〜はできない He is such a poor talker that he cannot *give an* appropriate *answer*. / He is too poor a talker to *give an* appropriate *answer*. なんの〜もなかった There is no *response*.

うけざら【受け皿】a saucer.

うけだ・す【請け出す】¶ (質に入れてある)時計を〜した I *got* my watch *out of pawn*. / I *redeemed* my pawned watch.

うけだち【受け太刀】¶ 彼は〜になって(たじろいで)いる He *is* (≒ *stands*) *on the defensive*.

うけたまわ・る【承る】¶ 〜ればお父上はご病床にある由 *I am told* [*that*] your father is ill in bed.

うけつ・ぐ【受け継ぐ】¶ 息子が彼の財産を〜ぐことになっている His son is to *be heir to* (≒ *succeed to*) his property. 王位を〜ぐ *succeed to* the throne. 彼は父の事業を〜いだ He *succeeded to* his father's business. 彼は父の性質を〜いでいる He *has inherited* part of his father's disposition.

うけつけ【受け付け】¶ ホテルのフロントの〜に電話した I telephoned to *the information desk* in the front hall of the hotel. その会社の〜で聞いてごらんなさい Please ask at *the inquiry office* of the company. 彼はそのホテルの〜[係]だ He is one of *the reception clerks* of the hotel. 彼女はその会社の〜[係]として勤めている She works as one of *the receptionists* in the company. 願書の〜期限 the time for application.

―番号 a receipt number.

うけつ・ける【受け付ける】¶ 申し込みは3月2日から〜ける Applications are to *be accepted* on and after the 2nd of March. 彼は人の意見を〜けない He won't *listen to* others. 彼はわれわれの申し出を〜けなかった He did not *accept* (≒ *receive*) our proposal.

うけと・める【受け止める】¶ 彼はボールを帽子で〜めた He *caught* the ball in his cap. その考えをどう〜めるか What is your *reaction* to the idea? / How should we *respond* to the idea?

うけとり【受け取り】a receipt. ¶ 〜をください Give me the *receipt for* it.

―人 a receiver; (物品・金銭の) a recipient; (荷物などの) a consignee.

うけと・る【受け取る】¶ 彼から1通の手紙を〜った I *received* a letter from him. 品物を〜りしだい代金を支払います(商業文として) I will pay the money *on receipt of* the goods. お〜りの際はご一報ください(商業文として) Kindly acknowledge [your] *receipt*. 金10万円まさに〜りました(商業文として) *Received* the sum of a hundred thousand yen. 彼はどうしても私の贈り物を〜ろうとしなかった He would not *accept* my present. そのことばはそのままには〜れない Those words cannot *be taken* to be true. 彼の説はふた通りに〜れる His explanation *admits* of two different interpretations.

うけはらい【受け払い】receipts and payments.

うけみ【受け身】**1**〖態度〗a passive state; a passive condition. ¶ 〜になる be passive.

〜の読書 *passive* reading.

彼は〜の立場にある He is *in a passive position*.

〜の態勢にある We are *on the defensive*.

2〖柔道の〗*judo's* way of falling.

3〖文法〗the passive voice.

―形(受動態) the passive voice.

うけもち【受け持ち】¶ 彼が私たちの〜の先生だ He is our *class teacher* (≒ 英 *form master*). / He *is in charge of* our class. 彼は3年の〜だ He *is in charge of* the third-year class. あの少年は彼の〜の生徒のひとりだ That boy is one of the students *under his charge*. その課は彼の〜だ He *is responsible for* the department. 警官はそれぞれ〜の区域がある Every policeman has his *beat*. 郵便配達人は〜の区域を回り終わった The postman has finished his *round*.

うけも・つ【受け持つ】¶ 彼はこの学校で英文法の授業を〜っている He *teaches* us English grammar at this school. その仕事は彼に〜たせるべきだ The task ought to *be assigned to* him.

う・ける【受ける】**1**〖受けとめる〗¶ 素手でボールを〜けた I *caught* the ball with my bare hand[s].

雨垂れをバケツで〜けてためておいた I *stored* the falling raindrops in the bucket.

草花は春の太陽の光を〜けてすくすくとのびた The flowering plants grew up rapidly *in* the spring sunshine.

2〖接する〗¶ 彼から一身上の相談を〜けた I *was consulted* by him about his personal affairs. / I *was requested* to give my opinion about his personal affairs.

まだそのような知らせは〜けていない We *have* not *received* such news yet.

そんな注文は〜けたことがない We *have* never *received* (≒ *accepted*) such an order.

だれがこの電話を〜けたのか Who *answered* the phone?

私は突然彼の訪問を〜けた Unexpectedly I *had* a visit from him. / Unexpectedly I *received* a call from him. / Without notice he paid me a visit.

3〖受諾する〗¶ ご厚意をありがたくお〜けいたします I *accept* your favor with thanks.

4〖与えられる〗¶ 彼はイギリスで小学校教育を〜けた He *received* his elementary school education in England.

人から〜けた恩を忘れるな Never forget the kindness you *received* from others.

氏はノーベル文学賞を〜けた He *was awarded* the Nobel Prize for literature.

5〖もらう〗¶ まだ許可を〜けていない I *have* not *been given* leave yet.

老人は国からもっと手厚い保護を～けるべきだ Old people should *be given* more cordial protection of the state. / The aged should *be taken* care of more warmly by the government.

6〖こうむる〗¶ 畑作は洪水で多大の損害を～けた The dry field crops *suffered* serious damage from the flood.

彼の演説は多くの批判を～けた His address *invited* a lot of criticism. / His speech *was subjected to* severe criticisms. / There were endless criticisms on his speech. / His speech *gave rise* to a great deal of criticism.

7〖みずから進んで接する〗¶ 来年東大文学部を～けるつもりだ Next year I am going to *take* the entrance examination to the department of literature of Tokyo University.

あす盲腸の手術を～ける Tomorrow I *undergo* an operation for appendicitis.

健康診断を～けなさい You should *undergo* (≒ *have*) a medical examination. (undergo はいやいや受ける場合にも言える).

8〖評判を取る〗¶ その芝居は大いに～けた The play *was a great success*. / The play *won great popularity*. / The performance *was very well received*.

この映画は若い女性に～けるだろう This picture will *be* very *popular with* young women. / The movie will *take the fancy of* young ladies. / This motion picture seems to *make a big hit with* young women.

あの政治家は大衆に～ける The politician is *popular* with the masses.

9〖信ずる〗¶ そんなこと，真に～けないほうがいい You had better not *take* it seriously. / You should not *believe* it to be true.

10〖前の語句に応じる〗¶ この語は前行のあの語を～けている This word *refers to* that in the preceding line. / This word is used instead of that word in the preceding line. / This word is used as a substitute for that word in the preceding line. / This word is related to that word in the preceding line.

11〖対抗する〗¶ 彼がそう言うのなら私も～けて立とう If he means it, I will *accept* his challenge.

うけわたし【受け渡し】 delivery.
—日 the delivery day. —条件 terms of delivery.

うげん【右舷】〖航海術〗starboard. ¶ 船は～に傾いた The ship listed to the *starboard*. 船は～の方向に針路を変えた The ship altered its course to *starboard*.

うご【雨後】 ¶ 戦後～の竹の子のように新興宗教が現われた After the war new religions have appeared *like so many mushrooms*.

うごうのしゅう【烏合の衆】 a disorderly crowd; a rabble; a mob.

うごか·す【動かす】 **1**〖物を移動させる〗move. ¶ その机の位置をもう少し左へ～してください Please *move* the desk a little farther to the left.

部屋の中の物を～されたのでどこになにがあるのやらわからない As I have had the things in my room *moved*, I cannot tell where they are.

石は重くて～せなかった The stone was too heavy for me to *move*. / The stone was so heavy that I could not *budge* it.

強風が木の枝を揺り～している The gale is swaying the branches. / The tree is swaying in the wind.

2〖地位・職場を移動させる〗¶ 彼はあの地位に適任だから～せない As he is just the man for the position, we cannot *change his post*. / Being well-fitted for the post, he cannot *be transferred*.

3〖体を運動させる〗¶ 左足を上下に～してごらんなさい Just *move* your left foot up and down. / Try to *move* your left foot upward and downward.

球をけるときの体の～し方がまずい Your *motion* in kicking a ball is awkward (≒ clumsy). / You are awkward in kicking a ball.

その話を聞いても彼はまゆ一つ～さなかった He *was calm and self-possessed*, hearing the report. / He did not *turn a hair* at the news.

4〖機械を作動させる〗¶ この機械の～し方を知っていますか Do you know how to *work* this machine?

蒸気の力で機械を～そうという考えは古くからあった People had long been thinking of *setting* a machine *in motion* by the power of steam.

5〖行動をとらせる〗¶ そんなわずかな金でぼくを～そうとしたとてだめだ You cannot *influence* me with such a small sum of money. / It's no use trying to *influence* me with such a pittance.

彼は日本の政界を～している陰の男だ He *controls* in secret the political world of Japan. / He is the very man who *pulls the wires* in political circles in this country.

今の社会を～すものは若人の熱と力である It is the enthusiasm and power of the young that *move* the world of today.

6〖感動させる〗¶ 彼女の話は聞く人々の心を～した Her talk *stirred* (≒ *moved*) the hearts of the hearers. / Her story *moved* the audience. / The audience *was moved* by her speech.

そんなことでは人の心を～せない You will never be able to *stir* the hearts of people in your way (≒ in that manner). / You cannot *work on* the minds of people with anything like that. / That is not the proper way to *stir* the hearts of people.

7〖変更する〗¶ 彼の決意は～しがたい It is hard to *shake* his resolution. / He will hardly *be shaken* in his resolution. / He is firmly determined. / He sticks to his decision. / He has formed a firm resolution.

それについては～しがたい証拠がある There is a *positive* (≒ an *indisputable*) proof of it.

う

これは何人も〜すことのできぬ事実だ This is a fact none can *deny*. / This is an *undeniable* (≒ *incontestable*) fact. / We have an *indisputable* evidence of it.

うごき【動き】1〖運動〗movement. ¶ 彼は〜が鈍い He is slow in *action*.
彼は60歳だが〜が敏捷(びんしょう)だ Though he is sixty, he is quick.
道路は車でいっぱいのため, 私の車は〜がとれなかった Owing to the flood of cars along the road, my car *was caught* (≒ *tied up*) in the traffic.
2〖状勢. 動勢〗¶ 彼らは借金で〜がとれない They *are over head and ears* (≒ *up to the ears*) *in debt*.
彼は世界の〜に絶えず注意している He always pays attention to the *trends* of the world.

うご·く【動く】1〖場所を移動する〗¶ 彼はその場を〜こうとはしなかった He would not *move* (≒ *budge*) from his place. / He would not *quit* his post.
〜くな. じっとしていろ Don't *stir*. Keep quiet.
新駅の位置は現在より南へ約 300 メートル〜きます The site of the new station is to *be removed* about three hundred meters south of the present one.
彼らはみんな職場を〜きたがっている They are all eager for *a change* of post. / All of them are eager to *change* employment.
2〖機械が作動する〗¶ この時計は〜いていない This watch *is* not *going* (≒ *working*; *running*). / The clock *has stopped going* (≒ *has run down*).
バッテリーが故障して自動車が〜かなくなった Something being wrong with the battery, the car *has come to a standstill*. / The battery went wrong and the car *broke down*.
突然機械が全部〜かなくなった On a sudden the whole machinery stopped *going* (≒ *working*).
ストライキできょうは電車が〜いていない Owing to the traffic strike, the trains *are* not *running* today.
3〖策動する〗¶ この一件をかぎつけて警察が〜きだした Having got scent of the case, the police *got into action*.
その事件には陰で〜いている者がいるに相違ない There must be somebody secretly *active* in the affair.
4〖変心する〗¶ ついに彼の心は〜いた At length his heart *was touched*. / After all he *changed his mind*.
彼は強情でてこでも〜かぬ He *stands firm in his opinion*. / He *is as stubborn as a mule*.
5〖変化する〗¶ 世の中はいつも〜いている The world *is* constantly *changing* (≒ *moving*).
6〖確かな〗¶ それに関しては〜かぬ証拠がある We have got an *incontestable* proof of it.
彼女の優勝はまず〜くまい *It is* almost *certain* that she will win 〔the victory〕. / She *is* almost *sure* to secure the championship. / *We are* pretty *confident* of her championship.

うごめか·す【蠢かす】¶ 彼は得意の鼻を〜している He *is* 〔*as*〕 *proud as a peacock*.

うごめ·く【蠢く】¶ 虫が〜いている A worm *is squirming*.

うさ【憂さ】¶ 彼は酒で〜をまぎらわしている He is drowning his *sorrows* in drink.
—晴らし ¶ 〜晴らしに映画を見にいった I went to the movies *for diversion*.

うさぎ【兎】(飼いウサギ) a rabbit; (ノウサギ) a hare.

うさんくさ·い【胡散臭い】¶ 〜い男 a *suspicious*〔*-looking*〕 man. 彼は〜そうに私をながめた He looked at me *suspiciously*. その犬は〜そうに私の足をかいだ The dog gave a *suspicious* sniff at my leg.

うし【牛】(雌牛) a cow; (雄牛) a bull; (去勢した雄牛) an ox; (子牛) a calf; (総称的) cattle (冠詞はつけない).
¶ 仕事の進みぐあいは〜の歩みのようだ The work progresses *at a snail's pace*. (「かたつむりの歩み」という言い方に注意). 彼は「〜に引かれて善光寺参り」といったところだ He is "making a virtue of necessity." 〜は〜づれ鳥は鳥づれ(諺) *Birds of a feather flock together*.

うじ【氏】(家柄) birth; (家名) a family name.
¶ 〜より育ち Breeding is better than *birth*.

うじ【蛆】a maggot; a worm. ¶ この魚には〜がわいている(物が主語) This fish is infested with *maggots*. / (うじが主語) *Maggots* have bred in this fish. 男やもめに〜がわく(諺) A widower is proverbially untidy.

うじうじ ¶ なにを〜しているのだ Why *are* you so *bashful*? 彼は〜しているように見えた He seemed to *be hesitating*.

うしお【潮】a tide. ¶ 群衆は〜のごとく門に向かって殺到した The crowd *surged* toward the gate. 〜のごとく寄せる敵軍を撃退することはできなかった We could not drive back the *surging* enemy.

うしかい【牛飼い】a cowherd; 困 a cowboy.

うじがみ【氏神】a tutelar god; a tutelary deity.

うじこ【氏子】a *protégé* of a tutelary god.
—総代 a parish representative.

うじすじょう【氏素性】¶ 今は〜など要らない時代だ *Birth* counts for nothing nowadays.

うしな·う【失う】¶ 彼女はまったく望みを〜った She *lost* all her hope. 彼はその知らせを聞くと色を〜った He *lost color* (≒ *turned pale*) to hear the news. 彼は仕事に興味を〜った He *lost* interest in his work. 最後のチャンスを〜った I *missed* the last chance. 彼は視力(聴力)を〜った He *lost* his sight (hearing). / He *was deprived of* his sight (hearing).

うしみつどき【丑三つ時】¶ 草木も眠る〜に at the witching time of night.

うしろ【後ろ】the back. ¶ あなたの〜に立っているのはだれですか Who is it standing *behind* you? 学校の〜に杉の大木があった There was a big cedar at *the back* of the school. だれかが

〜から呼んでいるようだ I seem to hear someone calling me from *behind*. 3歩進んで2歩〜へさがりなさい Take three steps forward and then two steps *backward*. 私は犬の〜からついていった I *followed* the dog.

うしろあし【後ろ足】a hind leg. ¶ 〜で立つ stand on *its hind legs*.

うしろがみ【後ろ髪】the back hair. ¶ 〜を引かれる思いがする be loath to part from (*a person*); feel as if *one's* heart were left behind.

うしろぐら・い【後ろ暗い】¶ 私には〜いことはない I have a clear conscience. それにはなにか〜いところがある There is something *underhand* about it.

うしろめた・い【後ろめたい】feel uneasy; feel guilty; have a bad conscience.

うしろゆび【後ろ指】¶ 〜を指されないようにしなさい Keep yourself above suspicion.

うす【臼】a mortar; (ひきうす) a hand mill.

うず【渦】a maelstrom; a whirl 〔pool〕; an eddy. ¶ 興奮の〜 *a firestorm* of excitement. 川が〜を巻いていた The river *whirled* around. 群衆の〜の中に巻き込まれた I was drawn into *a vortex* of people.

うすあかり【薄明かり】dim light; glimmer; (たそがれ) twilight; (夜明け) the morning twilight. ¶ 〜で in the twilight; (ともしびの) in the dim light.

うすあかる・い【薄明るい】dim; half-lighted. ¶ 〜い部屋 a *dimly-lit* room; a room *in half-light*.

うすい【雨水】rain water.

うす・い【薄い】thin. ¶ この雑誌は〜い This magazine *is thin*. この牛乳は〜い This milk *is watery*. この紅茶は〜すぎる This tea *is* too *weak*. チーズを〜く切ってください Please cut the cheese into *thin* slices. この病人は回復の望みが〜い There is *little* hope for this patient to get well.

うすいた【薄板】a thin board; (はがねの) a sheet steel.

うすいろ【薄色】a light color. ¶ 〜の light-colored; pale.

うすうす【薄薄】a little; slightly; dimly; hazily. ¶ 〜感づく become *vaguely* aware (*of*); *get an inkling of* (*something*).

うずうず ¶ 〜する be impatient (*to* do); be burning with a desire (*to* do); have an itch (*to* do).

うすがみ【薄紙】thin paper; tissue paper. ¶ 〜をはがすようによくなる get better *very gradually* (≒ *bit by bit*).

うすかわ【薄皮】a thin skin; a film; (層) a thin coating (≒ layer); (膜) a membrane.

うすぎ【薄着】thin clothing; a light dress. ¶ 私は〜だ I am in the habit of *being dressed lightly*.

うすぎたな・い【薄汚い】dirty; untidy; filthy; slovenly.

うすぎぬ【薄絹】thin (≒ light) silk.

うすきみわる・い【薄気味悪い】weird; uncanny; eerie.

うず・く【疼く】ache; tingle; throb with pain. ¶ 心に〜く *rankle* in *one's* mind.

うすくち【薄口】a light, weak taste. ¶ 〜のしょうゆ *light* soy.

うずくま・る【蹲る】crouch; squat down.

うすぐもり【薄曇り】¶ きょうは〜だ It is *a little* (≒ *a bit*) *cloudy* today.

うすぐら・い【薄暗い】¶ 〜くなる It gets *dark*. 〜いランプの明かりで読書する read in the *dim* light of a lamp. この部屋は〜い This room *is poorly lighted*. 〜くて見えない It is invisible *in the dusk*.

うすくらがり【薄暗がり】dim light; gloom; (朝夕の) twilight.

うすくれない【薄紅】light pink.

うすげしょう【薄化粧】a light toilet; 〔a〕 light make-up. ¶ 〜する *powder one's* face *lightly*; do *a little make-up*. 山々が初雪で〜していた I found the mountains *slightly powdered* with the first snow of the year.

うすごおり【薄氷】¶ 池に〜が張った The pond was covered with *thin ice*.

うすさ【薄さ】thinness. ¶ このパンはなんという〜だ How *thin* these slices of bread are! 彼の髪の〜には驚いた I am surprised to see his *thinning* hair.

うすじお【薄塩】¶ 〜の slightly salted.

うずしお【渦潮】whirling waves; an eddying current.

うずたかく【堆く】high in a heap. ¶ 落ち葉を〜積む *pile up* the fallen leaves.

うすっぺら【薄っぺら】(薄い) thin; (浅薄な) shallow; superficial; (軽薄な) frivolous; flimsy. ¶ 〜な議論 a *flimsy* argument.

うすで【薄手】**1** 〘厚さ〙 ¶ 〜の of thin-make. **—**焼き eggshell china.
2 〘浅い傷〙 a slight cut; a slight wound. ¶ 〜を負う get (≒ received) *a slight wound*; be *slightly* wounded.

うすのろ【薄のろ】a fool; a simpleton; a stupid fellow. ¶ 〜な stupid; dumb. 彼は〜だ He *is half-witted*. / He *is slow-witted*.

うすばか【薄馬鹿】a fool; a simpleton; a blockhead; a dunce. ¶ 彼女は〜だ She *is weak in the head*.

うすび【薄日】¶ 〜が雲間から漏れてきた *A little sunlight* came through the clouds.

うすべり【薄縁】a thin, bordered mat 〔usually used for covering *tatami* in Japanese houses〕.

うずまき【渦巻き】a whirlpool; a vortex (複 vortexes, vortices); (小さい) an eddy; (大きい) a maelstrom.

うずま・く【渦巻く】(水が) whirl; eddy; (煙が) curl.

うすめ【薄め】comparative thinness (≒ lightness). ¶ 〜のコーヒー *weak* coffee.

うすめ【薄目】¶ 〜をあけて見る look (*at* something) *with half-closed eyes*.

うす・める【薄める】make thin; weaken; dilute; (水で) water down. ¶ 〜めた牛乳

う

watered milk.

うず·める【埋める】 bury; inter. ¶ 彼女は彼の胸に顔を～めて泣いた She *hid* her face in his breast and cried.

うすもの【薄物】 light stuff; thin silk. ¶ ～のカーテン a *flimsy* curtain. ～の衣類 garments of [a] *lighter texture*.

うずも·れる【埋もれる】 ¶ 彼はしばらく田舎に～れていた For a time he *led an obscure* (≒ *a retired*) *life* in the country.

うずら【鶉】〘鳥類〙a quail.
—豆 mottled kidney beans.

うすら·ぐ【薄らぐ】 ¶ 痛みが少し～いだ The pain *has mitigated* a little. その問題についてますます興味が～いでいく My interest in the subject *is flagging* more and more.

うすらさむ·い【薄ら寒い】 chilly; slightly cold. ¶ きょうは～い日だ This is a *chilly* day. / It *is chilly* today.

うす·れる【薄れる】(色が) fade; (光が) become dim (≒ faint).

うすわらい【薄笑い】 a faint smile; a half smile. ¶ ～を口もとに浮かべて with *a faint smile* about *one's* lips.

うせつ【右折】 right turn. ¶ ～する turn to the right.
—禁止(掲示) No Right Turn.

う·せる【失せる】 ¶ 出て～せろ Get out. 彼女には娘かたぎがまだ～せていない There still remains something girlish about her. 彼女は色香が～せた Her beauty *has faded away*.

うそ【嘘】 a lie. ¶ 彼は時たま～をつく He sometimes *tells lies*. 彼の言うことに～はないと思う He seems to be telling the truth. もっともらしい～をつく人が多い Many people *tell* plausible *lies*. 彼は～八百を並べたてた He *told* all sorts of *lies*. それは真っ赤な～だった It was *a* downright (≒ *an* out and out) *lie*. 彼は見えすいた～をつく He *tells* obvious *lies*.
—発見器 a lie detector.

うぞうむぞう【有象無象】 the rabble; the mob. ¶ ～の寄り集まりだ There's a motley crowd of worthless fellows.

うそつき【嘘吐き】 a liar.
大— a big liar.

うそぶ·く【嘯く】(大言する) talk big; boast; (大きな動物が) roar; howl. ¶ 彼は何食わぬ顔で～いている(とぼけている) He assumes an air of ignorance.

うた【歌】(詩) a poem; (総称) poetry; (歌謡) a song; (民謡) a ballad; (和歌) a *waka* (英語で説明すれば a 31 syllable Japanese poem). ¶ ～を歌う sing *a song*. ～を詠む write (≒ compose) *a poem*. あの人は～も少しは詠める He is also something of a poet.

うたい【謡】 an *utai*; chanting a *no* drama text. ¶ ～をうたう recite [from] *a no drama*.

うたいあ·げる【歌い上げる】(情感を込めて歌う) chant (≒ set forth) (*one's* emotion) in song; (終わりまで歌う) sing a song to the end.

うたいて【歌い手】 a singer; a vocalist; (独唱家) a soloist.

うたいもんく【歌い文句】 a catchword; a catch phrase. ¶ それを売り込みの～にしよう Let's use it as *a catchword* for sales campaign.

うた·う【歌う】 sing. ¶ オルガンに合わせて～う *sing* to the organ. 低い声で～う *sing* in a low voice. 子守歌を～って赤ん坊を寝かせる *lullaby* a baby to sleep.

うた·う【謳う】 ¶ 彼はイギリス最大の詩人として～われている He *has the reputation of* being the best poet in England. 憲法は宗教の自由を～っている The Constitution *declares* freedom of religion.

うたがい【疑い】(嫌疑) [a] suspicion; (疑念) [a] doubt.

1〖疑いが〗¶ 他殺の～が十分にある Murder *is* strongly *suspected*. / We *suspect* it to be a case of murder.
安全性に～がある We *are doubtful about* its safety. / Its security *is doubtful*.

2〖疑いを〗¶ 私は盗作の～をかけられた I *was suspected of* plagiarism. / I *came under suspicion of* piracy.
試験で不正をしたと～を受けた I *was suspected of* cheating in the examination.
その話はうそではないかと～をいだいた I *suspected* that the story might be false. / I *suspected* the news to be a fiction.
どうしたらこの～を晴らすことができよう How could I clear myself of the *suspicion*? / How can I remove this *doubt*? / How could I *acquit myself* [*of* this doubt]?
人から～を招く行為は慎んだほうがいい You had better be discreet in your action so as not to incur others' *suspicions*. / You should refrain from doing *suspicious* acts. / You should always act above *suspicion*.
彼の死因に私は～をいだいている I *am doubtful of* the cause of his death. / I have some *doubts* about the cause of his death.

3〖疑いの〗¶ 皆から～のまなこで見られるのがつらかった It was hard for me to be looked at with *doubtful* (≒ *suspicious*) eyes. / I felt it painful to be seen with *suspicious* eyes.
彼女が金持ちであることに～の余地はない There is no room for *doubt* that she is rich. / There is no *doubt* that she is wealthy.

4〖疑いで〗¶ 彼はコレラの～で入院させられた He was sent to hospital with *a suspected case* of cholera.
彼は詐欺の～で逮捕された He was arrested *on suspicion of* (≒ *on a charge of*) fraud.

5〖疑いは〗¶ あの工場が汚水源だとの～は十分にある There is *a* strong *suspicion* that the factory is responsible for the pollution of the water there. / The factory is responsible for discharging the pollutants which caused the foul water.
きみのいだくその～は根拠があるのか Do you have any ground for that *suspicion* you have?
それについて～はいささかもない There is not a

shadow of *doubt* about it. / I haven't the least *doubt* in regard to that. / It admits of no *doubt* whatever. / It is above *suspicion*.

6 〖疑いなく・疑いない〗 ¶ ～なく天平時代の作品だ *No doubt* this is a work of art of the Tenpyo period. / *It is unquestionable* that this is a piece of work made in the Tenpyo period.

～なく彼は当選する(選挙に) *It is certain* that he will be elected. / He *is sure to* be returned. / (入賞する) He *is sure to* win the prize.

彼がそこで死んだことには～ない *There is* no *doubt* that he died there.

それは～ない事実だ It is an *undeniable* fact. / *There is no denying* the fact.

うたがいぶか・い【疑い深い】¶ 彼は～い He *is distrustful of* others. / He is of a *suspicious* nature. そんな～いことを言うな Don't *be* so *distrustful* (≒ *suspicious*).

うたが・う【疑う】**1** 〖嫌疑をかける〗 ¶ 人をみだりに～うな Don't *be distrustful* (≒ *suspicious*) *of* others without good reason.

彼が盗んだのだろうと皆が～った They all *suspected* him *of* the theft.

人に～われるようなことはするな Never do anything that will excite others' *suspicion*.

2 〖疑念・不信をいだく〗 ¶ その話を聞いてぼくは自分の耳を～った Hearing the news, I could *hardly believe my ears*.

彼がその作者であることは～う余地がない There is no room for *doubt* about his authorship of the work. / We have no *doubt* that he is the author of the work. / We have no *doubt* that it is his work. / We *are sure* he was the artist that created the work.

彼の言うことを少しも～わずに真に受けた I took his words seriously without the least *doubt*.

ぼくは彼の成功を信じて～わなかった I *was sure of* his success.

これだけ言ってもぼくをまだ～うつもりか Will you *distrust* (≒ *doubt*) me for all my words?

こんな失敗をするとは彼の手腕を～いたくなる I am inclined to *doubt* his ability, seeing that he has made such a failure.

うたがわし・い【疑わしい】¶ 彼がはたして来るかどうか～い *I doubt* if he will come. そのうわさの真偽は～い *It is doubtful* whether the rumor is true or not. 彼の行動には～い点がある There is something *questionable* in his actions. 単語の意味が～いときは辞書で調べなさい When *in doubt* about the meaning of some word, consult your dictionary.

うたげ【宴】a banquet; a feast; a party. ¶ 宮中で～が催された *A feast* was given at Court.

うたた【転】(ますます) more and more; (はなはだしく) deeply; keenly; indeed; (なんとなく) in some way; somehow. ¶ ～今昔の感に耐えぬ I am *deeply* impressed with the change of times.

うたたね【うたた寝】a nap; a doze. ¶ ～する take (≒ fall into) *a nap*; nap; doze.

うだつ【梲】¶ ～が上がらない cannot get on (≒ rise) in the world. ぼくは～が上がらない I have little hope of advancement.

うだ・る【茹る】¶ ～るような暑さ the *sweltering* heat.

うち【内】**1** 〖内部〗 〔the〕 inside. ¶ 官邸は～も外も警官で固められていた The official residence was guarded by the police both *inside* and outside.

部屋の～も外も真っ暗やみだった It was pitch-dark *inside* and outside the room.

この戸に～からもかぎのかかるようにしてくれ Please fit the door with a lock 〔so〕 that it can be locked from *within* and without (≒ on the *inside* and the outside).

胸の～を打ち明けたい Just allow me to speak my mind. / I'd like to say just a word to express my true feeling.

2 〖範囲・範疇〗 ¶ あれでも学者の～に入るのかね How can a man like him be a learned man? / Can he be counted *among* our scholars? / Can he be a scholar worthy of the name?

その費用も必要経費の～にかぞえておくべきだ The cost is to be included *in* the necessary expenses, too.

それらの～から適当なものを選びなさい Choose what is suitable for you *from among* them.

きみたちの～でだれがいちばん背が高いのか Who is the tallest *of* you all?

10問の～8問は答えられた I answered eight questions *out of* ten.

今までつきあった外国人の～で彼ほど日本語のうまい人はいない *Of* all the foreigners that I have known, no one speaks Japanese so well as he. (読むとき well に強勢がある).

3 〖時間〗 ¶ いずれその～に伺います I'll come and see you *one of these days*. / I'd like to call on you *before long*.

今の～に宿題をやっておきなさい Do your homework *while* there is yet time. / Prepare your assignment *before* it is too late.

若い～が花だ Youth is a treasure. / Youth is the springtime of life. / You have your best days (≒ the prime of life) *in youth*.

二,三日の～に桜も咲きます The cherry blossoms will come out *within* a few days. / I think the cherry trees will blossom *in the course of* a few days.

暗くならない～に帰宅しなさい Come (≒ Go) home *before dark*.

知らない～にぼくは眠っていた I fell asleep *before* I knew. / Sleep fell upon me *before* I was aware. (形式ばった形).

忘れない～にきみに言っておく I will tell you of it now *before* (≒ *in case*) I forget it. / I tell you to do it now *before* it escapes my memory.

あれこれ考えている～にふときみの姿が心に浮かんだ

う

While I was thinking of one thing or another, I happened to think about you. / Your image flashed across my mind *while* I was thinking of this and that.
きみが謝らない〜は,ぼくも手の出しようがない *If* you don't apologize, I can't do anything for the matter.
ぼくの目の黒い〜は,そんなことはやらせない I won't have you do such a thing *while* I live. / You shall do it only over my dead body. (気どった言い方) / You shall not do it *so long as* I am alive.
4〖自分〗¶ 〜の会社は今とても忙しい We are very busy at *our* company now.
〜の子どもは絵がへただ *My* child is poor at drawing. / *Our* child cannot draw very well.
〜の人がなんと申しますか I wonder what *my husband* will say about it.

うち【家】**1**〖建築物〗a house. ¶ 最近近所にたくさん〜が建った Recently a large number of *houses* have been built in my neighborhood.
彼女は去年郊外に〜を買った She bought *a house* in the suburbs last year.
家族が増えて〜が手狭になった My *house* is now too small for my large family.
来週新しい〜に移ります Next week I〔am going to〕move to my new *house*.
2〖自分の家庭・家〗〔a〕home. ¶ この次の日曜は一日じゅう〜にいます Next Sunday I am going to *stay* 〔*at*〕 *home* (≒ (米口語) *be home*) all day〔long〕.
早く〜に帰ったほうがいい You will do well to *come home* early. / You'd better *go home* soon. (強い表現).
〜にすぐ知らせなさい Let your *family* know it right away. / Inform your *people at home* of the matter at once. (形式ばった形) / Break the news to your *family* instantly.
長い間〜をあけてしまった I have stayed away from *home* for a long time.
彼はいつも〜を外にしている He is usually away from *home*.
この子は〜ではいばるが外へ行くと意気地なしです The boy is haughty *at home*, but quite timid abroad. / This child is a lion *at home*, but a mouse abroad.
〜のことは妻に任せてある I leave all my *household affairs* to my wife. / I have entrusted my wife with all the *household affairs*. (形式ばった形) / My wife keeps *house* for me. / My wife manages my *household*.
彼は去年4月に〜を持った He *set up home* (≒ *settled down*) in April last year. / (結婚した) He *married* in April last year.
どうも彼のところでは年中〜の中でごたごたが絶えないらしい I have heard he has always some trouble or other *at home*. / He seems to be worried about *domestic* troubles all the time.

うちあい【打ち合い・撃ち合い】(射撃) an exchange of shots; (ボクシング・テニス) a rally.

うちあ・う【打ち合う・撃ち合う】exchange blows (≒ shots); shoot each other; fight; (テニス・ボクシング) rally.

うちあげ【打ち上げ】(ロケット) launching (an artificial satellite; a space rocket); (芝居) the close (of a run of performance).
—花火 a sky rocket.

うちあけばなし【打ち明け話】a confidential talk. ¶ 〜をする talk confidentially; (互いに) exchange *confidences*.

うちあ・ける【打ち明ける】¶ 〜けて言えば *to be frank with you*. 心を〜ける *unbosom oneself* (*to*); *open one's* heart (*to*); *speak one's* mind. 胸中を〜ける *open one's* heart (*to a person*); *speak one's* mind *frankly*. 心を〜けない *conceal one's* heart. 彼は彼女に希望を〜けた He *confided* all his hopes *to* her. 私は妻になんでも〜ける I always *keep nothing from* my wife.

うちあ・げる【打ち上げる】**1**〖上方に〗¶ 人工衛星を〜げる *launch* an artificial satellite.
内野フライを〜げる *hit* (≒ *pop*) an infield fly.
花火を〜げる *shoot up* (≒ *set off*) fireworks.
2〖岸に〗¶ 波が岸に〜げている Waves *are dashing* against the coast.
難破船が岸に〜げられた A wreck *was cast up* on the shore.
3〖興行・芝居〗finish; close (the performance).

うちあわせ【打ち合わせ】a previous arrangement; (会う約束) an appointment.
—会 a preliminary meeting; a consultation.

うちあわ・せる【打ち合わせる】¶ その旅行について彼と〜せた I *made arrangements with* him for the trip. 日程を〜せる *arrange* the schedule.

うちいり【討ち入り】a raid. ¶ 四十七士の〜 the *raid* by the 47 *ronin*.

うちいわい【内祝い】(病気回復の) a get-well gift; (結婚の) gifts from a wedding shower; (赤ん坊誕生の) gifts from a baby shower.

うちうち【内内】¶ 〜のこと a *family* (≒ *private*) affair. 葬式を〜に済ませた We held the funeral *within our family circle*.

うちうみ【内海】an inland sea.

うちおと・す【打ち落とす・撃ち落とす】(たたき落とす) strike (≒ knock) down; (切り落とす) cut off; behead; (鉄砲などで) shoot (≒ bring) down (a plane).

うちかえ・す【打ち返す】strike (≒ beat; hit) back; return a blow; (テニス) return (the ball).

うちかか・る【打ち掛かる】strike at (*a person*); (不意に) pounce (*upon a person*). ¶ 敵が不意に彼らに〜った The enemy *fell on* them suddenly.

うちかた【打ち方・撃ち方】¶ 〜始め Begin *firing*! / *Fire*!

うちか・つ【打ち勝つ】¶ 困難に〜つ *overcome* obstacles; *get over* difficulties. 誘惑に〜つ *resist* a temptation. 〜ちがたい invincible;

unconquerable ; insurmountable.

うちがわ【内側】the inside ; the inner part.
¶ ～のポケット an *inner* pocket. ～のコースを走る have the *inside* track. ドアは～へだけ開く The door opens only *inward*. ドアは～からかぎがかかっていた The door was locked from (≒ on) the *inside*. ナプキンは汚れた方を～にしてたたみなさい Fold the napkin with the soiled part *inside*.

うちき【内気】¶ ～な人 a *shy* person. ～な娘 a *modest* girl. 彼は～で討論に参加できない He *is* too *timid* to take part in the discussion.

うちきず【打ち傷】a bruise.

うちきり【打ち切り】¶ 交渉が～となった The negotiation *has come to an end* (≒ *has come to a close*).

うちき・る【打ち切る】terminate ; put an end (*to* a matter). ¶ 討論を～る *close* a debate.

うちきん【内金】money paid on account ; partial payment. ¶ ～として５万円受け取った I received fifty thousand yen *on account* (≒ *as partial payment*).

うちけし【打ち消し】〔a〕denial ; negation.
¶ ～の文 a *negative* sentence.

うちけ・す【打ち消す】¶ うわさを～す *deny* the rumor.

うちこ・む【打ち込む】¶ 壁にくぎを～む *drive* a nail *into* the wall. 彼はその仕事に真剣に～んだ He *devoted himself to* the work. 彼は外野席に盛んにボールを～んだ He *swatted* one ball after another *into* the bleachers. 彼はその仕事に全力を～んだ He *put* his heart and soul *into* the work.

うちころ・す【打ち殺す・撃ち殺す】(なぐり殺す) beat (*a person*) to death ; strike (*a person*) dead ; (射殺する) shoot (*a person*) dead.

うちじゅう【家中】(家族) all〔members of〕the family ; the whole family ; (家の中) all over the house.
¶ ～が大騒ぎをした There was an excitement *all over the house*.

うちそこな・う【打ち損う・撃ち損う】fail to hit ; miss (the mark).

うちだし【打ち出し】(芝居の) the end (≒ closing) of the show ; (すもうの) a drum to announce closing.
¶ 芝居の～は10時半だった The theater *closed* at 10 : 30 p.m.
―細工 embossment ; embossed work.

うちだ・す【打ち出す】(物を打ち始める) begin to beat (≒ strike) ; (案出する) hammer out ; (芝居が) close ; (型・模様などを打って出す) strike out ; emboss.
¶ 新しい政策を～す *hammer out* (≒ *set forth*) a new policy.

うちた・てる【打ち立てる】¶ 新しい学説を～てる *start* (≒ *begin* ; *found*) a new theory ; *come up with* a new theory. (口語).

うちつ・ける【打ち付ける】¶ 板をへいに～ける *nail* a plate *on* the wall. 板を柱に～ける *nail* a board *to* a post. 雨が窓に～けている The rain *is dashing against* the window. 頭を柱に～けた I *bumped* (≒ *struck*) my head *against* a post.

うちつづ・く【打ち続く】¶ ～く不幸 *a series of* misfortunes. ～く干天 *a long spell of* drought.

うちづら【内面】¶ 彼は～が悪い He *is always sullen at home*.

うちつ・れる【打ち連れる】¶ みんなは～れて散歩に出かけた They went out for a walk all *together*.

うちでし【内弟子】a home (≒ private) pupil ; an apprentice.

うちでのこづち【打ち出の小槌】a mallet of luck (近似語は Aladdin's lamp).

うちと・ける【打ち解ける】open *one's* heart (*to a person*) ; throw off reserve.
¶ ～けた態度で in a *familiar* way ; in a *friendly* manner. ～けない人 a *reserved* person. 彼らはじきに～けた They soon *made friends with each other*. 私たちは～けて話をした We had a *heart-to-heart* talk. イギリス人は初対面の人に～けない性質がある The English have an *uncommunicative* disposition toward strangers.

うちと・る【討ち取る】(殺す) kill ; put (*a person*) to death ; murder ; slay ; (射殺) shoot (*a person*) dead ; (負かす) outdo ; beat.
¶ 打者を三振に～る *strike* a batter *out*.

うちぬ・く【打ち抜く】(穴など) punch (a hole) ; pierce ; penetrate ; (弾丸が) shoot through ; (型で) stamp out (a coin).
¶ 金属板に穴を～く *punch* holes in a sheet of metal. 金属板から輪型を～く *stamp out* rings from a sheet of metal. 弾が壁を～いた A bullet *shot through* the wall.

うちのめ・す【打ちのめす】¶ 徹底的に彼を～した I completely *knocked* him *down*. 彼女は悲しみに～されている She *is overwhelmed with* grief.

うちのり【内法】inside measure ; inside measurement. ¶ その廊下は～が３メートルある The corridor is three meters *wide*.

うちぶ【打ち歩】〘商業〙 premium. ¶ 12パーセントの～で売る sell at *a premium* of 12 percent.

うちぶところ【内懐】(洋服) an inner breast-pocket ; (内心) *one's*〔inmost〕bosom ; (胸部) the breast.
¶ ～を見透かされる have *one's design* seen through. 相手の～に飛び込む hurl *one*self at the adversary.

うちべんけい【内弁慶】a lion at home, a mouse abroad.

うちまく【内幕】the inside〔facts〕; inner workings (of a business). ¶ ～をのぞく see (≒ peep) *behind the scenes* (≒ *screen*). ～を暴く expose *a secret* (*of*). ～を知っている be familiar with *the situation*.
―話 an inside story (≒ account) ; inside information.

うちまた【内股】the inner side of the thigh ; the inner part of the thigh. ¶ ～に歩く

う

walk *pigeon-toed*. 「dealer.
—こうやく double-dealing; (人) a double-
うちみ【打ち身】a bruise.
うちみず【打ち水】¶ 庭に～をする *water* (≒ *sprinkle water in*) the garden.
うちもの【打ち物】(鋳物) cast metal; wrought work; (武器) a weapon; (刀) a sword.
¶ 彼は～取っては後れをとらぬ He is second to none *in swordsmanship*.
—師 a swordsmith.
うちやぶ·る【打ち破る】(破壊する) break; (負かす) defeat (the enemy). ¶ 城門を～る *break down* the castle gate.
うちゅう【宇宙】the universe; the cosmos; space. ¶ ～の universal; cosmic.
—医学 space medicine. —引力 universal gravitation. —空間 space. —国際法 the international law of the universe. —ステーション a space station. —船 a spaceship; a spacecraft. —速度 space velocity. —飛行士 a cosmonaut; a space pilot. —旅行 a space travel. —ロケット a space rocket. —開発 space activities. —犬 a space dog. —観 a cosmic view.
うちょうてん【有頂天】¶ ～になる be *beside oneself with joy*; fall into *raptures*; be in *an ecstasy of joy*.
うちわ【内輪】**1**〘控えめ〙¶ ～に見積もっても100万円はかかる It costs (≒ The cost is) one million yen *at a moderate estimate*.
控えめに～に暮らしなさい You had better live *moderately* (≒ *within your means*).
2〘内密〙¶ これは～の話だ This is a *private* affair. / This is *between ourselves*.
3〘内部·家族·親しい者〙¶ ～の恥をさらすものではない You must not *wash your dirty linen in public*.
そんなことは～どうしで話し合いなさい Discuss such a thing *among yourselves*.
その事件は～で済ますことができるはずだ I am sure you can settle the matter *among yourselves* (≒ *without outside intermediation*).
そんな～のことにぼくは関知しない I have nothing to do with such a *private* affair.
なにか～もめがあるらしい There seems to be some *internal* trouble.
結婚式は～の者だけでいたします We are going to hold a *simple family* wedding.
～げんかをしたってしようがない What is the use of quarreling *among ourselves*?
～の事情を知っていると, なにも言えない I don't dare make any comments since I know the *inside* story.
うちわ【団扇】a fan. ¶ ～であおぐ fan; (自分を) fan *oneself*. ～をあげる(すもうで勝者を宣する) declare (*a person*) winner; decide in favor of (*a person*).
左— ¶ 左～で暮らす live in ease and luxury.
うちわけ【内訳】an accounting; the items (*of* an account); details; (会計報告) an accounting.
¶ ～をする state the items (*of* an account); set down (an account) by items. ～はどうですか Give me the *details* of it. / What's the *breakdown* of it?
—書 a statement of items.
う·つ【打つ·討つ·撃つ】**1**〘力を入れてたたく〙¶ ここにくぎを1本～ってください *Drive in* a nail here, please. / *Hammer* (≒ *Drive*; *Knock*), please.
彼は手を～って喜んだ He *clapped* his hands with joy.
合図の太鼓を～った I *beat* a drum as a signal.
くいを～って地境をはっきりさせた We *drove in* stakes to fix the boundaries.
鉄は熱いうちに～て *Strike* while the iron is hot.
カーブをねらって～て Wait for a curve.
あの投手の速球は～ちにくい It is hard to *hit* the fast (≒ speed) ball of that pitcher.
2〘ほかのものに強く当たる〙¶ 転んで床に頭を～った I fell down and *hit* my head *against* the floor.
激しい雨が軒を～っていた The rain *was* heavily *beating* the eaves.
高波が岸壁に～ち寄せた The high waves *dashed against* the quay.
3〘たたくような動作であることをする〙¶ 彼女は英文タイプを早く～てる She can *type* fast on an English typewriter.
時計は6時を～った The clock *struck* six.
列車の窓から畑を～つ農夫の姿が見られた From the window of the train we could see farmers *tilling* the soil.
4〘電報·注射·その他〙¶ すぐ彼に合格の電報を～ってやった I immediately *wired* to him congratulating him on his success in the examination.
庭に水を～って涼を求めた I *watered* the garden to stimulate a cool breeze.
医者は痛みどめの注射を～ってくれた The doctor *gave* me *an injection* to stop the pain.
碁を～とう Let's *play* 〔a game of〕 *go*.
5〘感動を与える〙¶ そのことばに胸を～たれた I *was moved* (≒ *was touched*) by the words.
彼のひたむきな努力が私の心を～った I *was impressed* by his assiduous efforts.
6〘ある方法を行なう〙¶ そんな芝居を～ったってごまかされない It is no use *trying* that trick on me. / I know a trick worth two of that.
これよりほかに～つ手がない This is my last card.
手金を～ってください Please pay a down payment.
7〘リズミカルな動きをする〙¶ 脈の～ち方がおかしい The pulse is irregular.
8〘襲う〙¶ ぼくは不意を～たれてあわてた I *was* utterly *taken aback*.
敵は不意を～たれて逃げだした The enemy *was taken by surprise* and routed.
相手を～ち倒すかこちらが死ぬかどちらかだ Either I *defeat* the opponent or I die.
このあだはどうしても～つ I will *take revenge for*

this insult at any cost.

9 〚弾を撃つ〛 ¶ ～て *Fire!*

その鳥は～ってはいけない Don't *shoot* the bird.

彼はライフル銃で～たれて死んだ He *was shot to death* (≒ *was shot dead*) with a rifle.

10発～ったが一つも的に当たらなかった I *fired* (≒ *let go*) ten shots, but all missed the mark.

彼は～つぞとピストルでぼくをおどかした He threatened to *fire* a pistol at me (≒ to *shoot* me with a pistol).

敵はロケット砲を～ってきた The enemy attacked us with rocket guns.

うつうつ【鬱鬱】 melancholy; sadness; gloom; pessimism. ¶ ～たる unhappy; gloomy; depressed. 当時私ははまったく～たる毎日だった I *was* terribly *depressed* in those days.

うっかり (不注意に) carelessly; thoughtlessly; by mistake; (ぼんやりして) absent-mindedly; (われ知らず) in spite of *one*self; unconsciously; (気を許して) in *one's* unguarded moment.

¶ ～しているうちに before *one* is aware of it. ～していた I was forgetting. ～できない I must *be careful* (≒ *on my guard*). ～してバスをまちがえた I took a wrong bus *by mistake*. ～して定期券を家に忘れてきた I was so *careless* as to leave my season ticket at home. 彼は～秘密を漏らした He gave away the secret *in an unguarded moment*.

うつくし·い【美しい】 pretty; beautiful; lovely; (特に人物) good-looking; (特に女性) charming; attractive; fair; (男性, ときには物) handsome; (声) sweet; (心) noble〔-minded〕; (風景) fine; picturesque (最初の3語は以下の分類と関係なくわりに広く用いられる).

¶ 少女は声が～かった The girl had a *sweet* (≒ *charming*) voice. 会場は花で～く飾られていた The hall was decorated *beautifully* with flowers. / The hall was decorated with *beautiful* flowers. その家の庭は～い The house has a *beautiful* (≒ *handsome*) garden.

¶ ～く beautifully. ～しくする beautify.

うっけつ【鬱血】〘医学〙〔blood〕 congestion. ¶ ～する suffer from *blood congestion*; be congested with blood.

うつし【写し】 a copy; a facsimile; a transcript. ¶ ～をとる copy; make *a copy* (*of*).

うつ·す【写す·映す】 **1** 〚模写·筆写する〛 copy. ¶ あなたのノートを～させてください Let me *copy* your notebook.

このページを全部複写機で～しとってください *Copy* the whole page by mimeograph, please.

2 〚写真を撮る〛 take. ¶ 皆で写真を～そう Let's *take* our picture. / (写してもらう) Let us *have* our picture *taken*.

この景色を～そう I'll *take a photograph* (≒ *a picture*) *of* this scene.

暗くて写真は～せなかった I could not *take a photograph* since it was dark.

ぼくがテニスのサーブをするところを～してください *Take a picture of* me, when I am serving a ball in the tennis game.

3 〚投影する〛 ¶ 旅行で撮ったスライドを～してあげよう I'll *show* you the slides I took during the travel.

周囲の山々は湖面にその姿を～していた The surrounding mountains *were casting* their shadows on the lake.

鏡にきみの姿を～してごらんなさい *Look at* (≒ *See*) yourself *in a mirror*.

4 〚描写する〛 express. ¶ 絵はよくその凄惨(せいさん)な場面を～している The picture well *expresses* the ghastly scene.

うつ·す【移す】 **1** 〚移動〛 ¶ 彼は最近住居を東京から横浜へ～した He *moved* from Tokyo to Yokohama quite recently.

問題は小委員会に～された The matter *was referred to* the sub-committee for discussion.

事務所を5階に～す予定だ We are to *move* our office *to* the fifth floor.

バケツからたらいに水を～してほしい I want the water in the bucket to be emptied into the tub.

右手のコップを左手に～した He *shifted* the glass from his right hand to his left.

2 〚病気を〛 ¶ 彼に風邪を～された He gave me his cold.

うっすらと【薄らと】 slightly; faintly; (ぼんやりと) dimly. ¶ 地面に雪が～積もっている The ground is *slightly* white with snow (≒ is covered with *slight* snow).

うっせき【鬱積】 congestion. ¶ ～する be pent up. ～した怒り a *pent-up* fury.

うっそう【鬱蒼】 ¶ ～とした森 a *dense* forest. ～とした樹木の繁茂 the *luxuriant* growth of trees.

うったえ【訴え】 a lawsuit. ¶ 彼は加害者に～を起こした He brought *a suit against* the man who had committed an act of violence against him. 損害賠償の～は退けられた My *action for* damages was rejected. 被害者の～によってその問題の審議が行なわれた The problem was discussed on 〔the〕 *complaint* of the injured.

うった·える【訴える】 **1** 〚告訴·告発する〛 ¶ こうなれば裁判に～えるよりほかにない There is nothing for it but to *bring* the matter *to trial*.

彼女は離婚訴訟を家庭裁判所に～えた She *sued for* a divorce at the family court.

彼は国を相手どって損害賠償を～えた He *demanded* damages from the government.

いつまでもここに駐車しておくと警察に～えます I will *report* you to the police office if you keep parking here all 〔the〕 time.

暴行を加えられたと彼は警察に～えた He *reported* to the police that he had suffered violence.

彼女は約束不履行で～えられた She *was sued for* 〔a〕 breach of promise.

彼は詐欺で～えられた He *was accused of* (≒ *was charged with*) fraud.

ぼくは借金を返さないので彼を～えた I *sued* him,

as he did not pay back the money.

2〖手段に頼る〗¶ 腕力に～えるのはよせ Don't *resort to* force (≒ violence).

国際間の紛争を武力に～えて解決する settle international disputes by *resorting to* military power.

3〖感覚に働きかける〗¶ 大気汚染の惨害を世論に～えよう Let's *appeal to* the public opinion concerning the horrors of air pollution.

テレビは目と耳とに同時に強く～える Television *appeals to* the eye and ear at the same time.

この絵はなにを～えようとしているのかわからない I can't understand what this picture is supposed to *express*.

そういうことをしてよいかどうかきみの良心に～えるがよい *Ask* your own conscience if it is right to do such a thing.

4〖告げる〗¶ 子どもは突然腹痛を～えた The child suddenly *complained of* a stomachache.

彼らは彼女のやり口に不平不満を～えた They *expressed* dissatisfaction with her doings.

うっちゃらか・す【打っちゃらかす】¶ 彼女は家事を～した She *neglected* (≒ *laid aside*) her household work.

うっちゃり【打遣り】reversal; inversion; (すもう) the trick of leaning back and carrying round the opponent out of the ring. ¶ ～を食わす(すもうで) throw the opponent down at the edge of the ring; (比喩的) betray (≒ beat) (*a person*) at the last moment.

うっちゃ・る【打遣る】¶ ～っておいてください Let me alone. / Forget 〔it〕. 彼がなにをしたってかまうものか, ～っておけ Never mind what he does. *Leave* him *alone*.

うつつ【現】(現実) reality; the actual. ¶ 彼は彼女に～を抜かしていた He *was madly in love with* her.

うって【討っ手】pursuers. ¶ ～を向ける send *a force* (*against*).

うってかわ・る【打って変わる】¶ 彼は昔とは～った人になった He is *quite* a *different* man from what he was. きのうとは～った寒さだ It is far colder than 〔it was〕 yesterday.

うってつけ【打って付け】¶ 隠れるには～の場所だ This is *the best* place for hiding ourselves. きみには～の仕事だ This is the work *best fitted for* you. / This is *just* the work *for* you. その役には～の人だ He is *just* the man *for* the position.

うって・でる【打って出る】¶ 総選挙に～出る *stand for* the Diet at the general election. 政界に～出る *enter upon* a political career.

うっとうし・い【鬱陶しい】¶ ～い空もよう a *dull* (≒ *gloomy*) sky. ～い雨 a *disagreeable* rain. ～い天気 *nasty* (≒ *depressing*) weather. 彼は～げにぼくの顔を見た He looked at me *with annoyance*.

うっとり (ぼんやりして) absent-mindedly; (恍惚として) absorbedly. ¶ 彼女の歌に～と聞きほれていた I was listening to her song *with rapture*. 彼女のしとやかな物腰に～と見とれていた I *was enchanted by* her elegant manner. 彼女は～したまなざしで彼を見た She cast her *rapt eyes* on him. / She looked at him *with rapt attention*.

うつぶせ【俯せ】¶ ～になる lie on *one's* face. ～に倒れる fall on *one's* face.

うっぷん【鬱憤】anger. ¶ 彼はわれわれに当たって～を晴らした He *worked off* his *anger* on us. 日ごろの～を彼にぶちまけた I *vented* my *pent-up anger on* him. ～を抑えることができなかった I could not *check* my *anger*.

うつぼ【鱓】〔魚類〕a moray.

うつぼつ【鬱勃】¶ ～たる野心 a *burning* ambition. ～として aspiringly; luxuriantly; ambitiously.

うつむき【俯き】¶ ～に prone; face downward. ～に倒れる fall on *one's* face.

うつむ・く【俯く】¶ 恥ずかしくて～く *hang* (≒ *bend*) *one's head* for shame.

うつむ・ける【俯ける】(物を) turn (*something*) upside down; (顔を) drop (*one's* head).

うつり【写り】reflection. ¶ この写真は～がよい This photo is well taken. 彼女は写真～がよい She always comes out well. この子はいつも写真～が悪い This child is not photogenic.

うつりが【移り香】a lingering scent.

うつりかわり【移り変わり】a change; 〔a〕 transformation. ¶ 季節の～ *changes* of the seasons.

うつ・る【映る・写る】**1**〖反射・反映する〗¶ 私は鏡に～った自分のやせた姿に驚いた I was surprised to see myself worn to a shadow in a mirror.

照明塔の光が水面に～ってまぶしい The light of the illumination tower *is* dazzlingly *reflected* on the surface of the water.

カーテンに人影が～った The shadow of a man *fell* on the curtain.

2〖配合する〗¶ この色はあなたによく～ります This color *suits* (≒ *becomes*) you admirably.

そのハンドバッグはこの服には～らない The handbag does not *match* this dress.

3〖写真に撮られる〗¶ 実物以上によく～っている You *look* better *in pictures*.

富士山がきれいに～っている Mt. Fuji *looks* beautiful *in the picture*.

この写真はみんながよく～っている All of us *look* fine *in this picture*.

ニュースできみの姿がテレビに～った I saw you on the TV news program.

4〖写真を撮る〗¶ 部屋が暗くて写真がよく～らないと思う The room is very dark, so I'm afraid the photograph won't *come out* well.

このカメラは小さいがよく～る This camera is small, but *works* well.

うつ・る【移る】**1**〖人や物の位置が変わる〗move. ¶ 今いるうちを～ろうと思う I am thinking of *moving* out of my house.

本社は4月から大阪に～る The head office is to *be transferred* to Osaka in April. / The head office will *be moved to* Osaka in April.

彼は営業部に〜った He *has been transferred to* the business department.

その土地は人手に〜った The land *passed into* another's hands.

隣に〜ってきた者です I *have moved to* the next door.

その問題は司直の手に〜った The arm of law *has reached* the affair.

2〖心・話題が〗¶ 彼女は気が〜りやすい She is a *fickle* woman. / She *is full of whims*.

話はそれからそれへと〜っていった The conversation *drifted* from one subject to another.

ふたりの話は戦争中の苦労に〜っていった The conversation of the two *turned on* their hardships during the war.

3〖時が過ぎる〗 ¶ 時は〜って平和の世となった Times *have changed*. Now we live in peace.

時代が〜るにつれ風俗は変わってゆく Manners and customs *change* with the times.

4〖病気や火が伝わる〗 ¶ その病気は〜りやすい The disease *is contagious*.

その病気は〜りますか *Is* the disease *infectious* (≒ *catching*)? (contagious は接触感染による場合, infectious は間接伝染の場合).

はしかが〜った He *has been infected with* the measles. / He *has caught* (≒ *has got*) the measles.

風邪が〜るといけないから, お子さんを連れてこないでください Don't bring your children, lest they should *catch* cold.

火が隣の家に〜った The fire *spread to* the neighboring house. / The neighboring house *caught* fire.

火がわらに〜って納屋が焼けた The flames *spread to* the straw and the barn was burnt down.

5〖色・においが他の物にしみつく〗 ¶ いっしょに洗たくしたのでワイシャツにくつ下の色が〜った The color of the socks *has soaked into* the shirt, because I washed them together.

まだそのにおいが手に〜ってとれない The scent *has soaked into* my hands and won't wear off.

うつろ【空・虚】hollow; void. ¶ 〜な目 *vacant* eyes. 〜に笑う give a *hollow* laugh; laugh *without mirth*.

うつわ【器】(容器) a vessel; a receptacle; ¶ 彼は経営者の〜ではない He *is* not *suitable to* be an administrator. / He *is incompetent as* an administrator. 私はその〜でない I *am* not *equal to* it. / I *am* not *qualified for* it.

うで【腕】**1**〖手首から肩の間の部分〗 the arm. ¶ 両〜を前に伸ばしなさい Stretch your *arms* forward.

彼女は左〜を折った She had her left *arm* broken.

彼は〜を組んで考え込んだ He was lost in thought with his *arms* folded. / He was lost in thought with folded *arms*.

子どもは母親の〜にすがりついた The child clung to its mother's *arm*.

彼の〜は太い He has big (≒ brawny) *arms*.

彼は〜をまくって傷あとを見せた He rolled (≒ tucked; turned) up his *sleeve* and showed the scar. / He bared his *arm* and showed the scar.

〜をまくってさあこいと身構えた With his *sleeves* rolled up, he pulled himself up in a fighting posture.

彼は赤ん坊を〜に抱きかかえた He took up the baby in his *arms*.

彼は〜をこまぬいてふたりの論争を見ているだけだった He did nothing but look on unconcernedly at the dispute between the two.

2〖仕事をする能力・技量〗 talent; ability. ¶ きみの〜をふるう機会だ This is a good opportunity for exercising your *talent*.

彼は会社の再建に縦横の〜をふるった He freely exercised his *talent* to reconstruct the company.

彼の〜は確かだから, 任せておけ Leave it to him, because he is *a man of ability*. / Leave it to him, because he *is quite capable*.

このごろゴルフの〜が急に上がった Recently I *have improved* my golf in quick order.

それを1日でかたづけるとはたいした〜だ What *an able man* you are to finish it in a day!

あの人はいい〜がありながらそれを生かそうとしない Although he has great *ability*, he won't make the best use of it.

あの医者は〜がいい He is a *competent* physician.

給料はきみの〜しだいだ The salary depends upon your *ability*.

彼はその名工のもとで〜をみがいた He improved his *skill* under the guidance of the master.

これは彼女が〜によりをかけて作ったケーキだ This is the cake that she made with her utmost *skill*.

ぼくの〜には狂いはない I have an unerring *skill*.

英語の翻訳ならぼくも少し〜に覚えがある I am somewhat confident of my *ability*, so far as the translation of English is concerned.

そういう話を聞くときみも〜がむずむずするだろう Your *fingers* must be itching when you hear such a story.

あまり練習していないのでゴルフの〜がさがった Since I am out of practice, I have fallen off in my *skill* in golf.

あの人から100万円出資させるとは彼もすごい〜だ He is a man of amazing persuasion to have talked him into investing one million yen.

うでぎ【腕木】(屋根・橋などの) a truss; (たな・軒などの) a bracket.

うできき【腕利き】an able man; a skillful man. ¶ 〜の刑事 a *competent* detective.

うでぐみ【腕組み】¶ 〜をする fold *one's* arms. 彼は〜して座っていた He sat *with his arms folded*.

うでくらべ【腕比べ】a competition; a contest (of skill). ¶ 私は彼とチェスの〜をした I

う

competed with him in chess.

うでずく【腕ずく】¶ ～でもそれを取ってみせる I'll take it *by force*.

うでずもう【腕相撲】¶ ～する wrestle with *one's* arms.

うでたてふせ【腕立て伏せ】push-up. ¶ ～をする do push-ups.

うでだめし【腕試し】a trial (*of* skill). ¶ 私はそのタイピストの～をした I *tried* the typist's *skill*. ～にその試験を受けた I took the examination *to try my ability*.

うでっぷし【腕っぷし】¶ ～の強い男 a *strong* man; a man *of great strength*.

うでどけい【腕時計】a 〔wrist〕 watch.

うてな【台】〘植物〙a calyx (複 calyxes, calyces); (像の) a pedestal.

うでまえ【腕前】ability. ¶ あの外科医はなかなかの～だ That surgeon *is* very *skillful*. きみの～では無理だ It is beyond your *ability*. 彼はその仕事で～を発揮した He showed his *ability* in the work. / He demonstrated his *talent* in the work. たいした～だね I admire your *ability*.

う·でる【茹でる】boil (eggs).

うでわ【腕輪】a bracelet.

うてん【雨天】rainy weather; a rainy day. ¶ ～ならば in case of *rain*; if it *rains*. もう1週間～続きだ *It has been wet* for a week. ～続きのため不作だった We had a bad crop because of a spell of *rain*. 運動会は～順延だ In case of *rain*, the athletic meet is to be put off till the first fine day.

—体操場 a gymnasium; a gym.

うど〘植物〙an *udo* 〔plant〕; Aralia cordata. ¶ ～の大木 a big, useless fellow.

西洋**—** asparagus.

うと·い【疎い】¶ 私たちは世事に～い We *know little about* the world. 彼は法律に～い He *is ignorant of* law. 去る者は日々に～し(諺) *Out of sight, out of mind*.

うとうと ¶ ～している間に財布を盗まれた I had my wallet stolen while *dozing*. 彼は授業の間～していた He *was dozing off* during the lesson.

うどん noodles.

—粉 〔wheat〕 flour. **—屋** a noodle shop.

うとん·ずる【疎んずる】¶ 彼は世間に～じられている He *is neglected* by the world. 彼は友だちに～じられている He *is treated coldly* by his friends.

うなが·す【促す】¶ 彼は私にその返答を～した He *urged* (≒ *pressed*) me *to* answer it. / He *pressed* me *for* the answer. 父は娘に帰郷を～した The father *suggested* that his daughter 〔*should*〕 return home. 私は彼に借金の返済を～した I *pressed* him *to* pay the debt back.

うなぎ【鰻】an eel. ¶ ～のかば焼き broiled *eels*.

—どんぶり a bowl of eel and rice. **—登り** ¶ 物価が～登りだ Prices *are rising rapidly*.

うなさ·れる【魘される】¶ 昨夜は～れた I *had a nightmare* (≒ *bad dreams*) last night.

うなじ【項】the nape.

うなずき【頷き】a nod.

うなず·く【頷く·肯く】**1** nod. ¶ 彼は私の方にちょっと～いた He *gave* me *a* slight *nod*. 彼は彼女の方によく来たと～いた He *nodded* a welcome to her. 彼は通り過ぎながら私の方に～いた He *nodded to* (≒ *at*) me as he passed. 彼は彼女の説明にもっともだと～いた He *gave* her *a nod* of approval when she explained.

2 〚納得する〛¶ 彼がそう言うのも～ける I can *understand* why he says so. その問題に対する彼の態度には～けないところがある I can't quite *agree with* his attitude toward the problem.

うなだ·れる【項垂れる】¶ 彼は悲しそうに～れた He *drooped his head* sadly. 彼女は恥ずかしさのあまり～れた She *hung her head* for shame. (hang の過去·過去分詞形は hung で hanged ではない).

ウナでん【ウナ電】an urgent telegram. ¶ 彼は彼女に～を打った He sent *an urgent telegram* to her.

うなばら【海原】the sea; the ocean; the wide expanse of waters.

うなり【唸り】a groan; (猛獣の) a roar; (オオカミ·犬などの) a growl; a howl; (風の) a howl. ¶ 犬が～声をあげながら飛びかかってきた A dog jumped at me with *a growl*. 彼は苦しくて～声をあげた He gave *a groan* of pain. ライオンが急に～声をあげた A lion *roared* suddenly. 矢が～をあげて飛んでいった An arrow *whizzed* past.

うな·る【唸る】groan; roar. ¶ 彼は苦痛で～った He *groaned* with pain. 戸外では風が～っていた The wind *was howling* outdoors. 矢が～って飛んでいった An arrow *whizzed* past. 彼の演奏は聴衆を～らせた(感嘆させた) His performance *moved* the audience *deeply*.

うに【海胆·雲丹】(動物の) a sea urchin; (食物の) seasoned sea urchins.

うぬぼれ【己惚れ·自惚れ】〔self-〕conceit; vanity. ¶ 彼女は～が強い She *is full of conceit*. / She *thinks highly of herself*.

うぬぼ·れる【己惚れる·自惚れる】¶ あまり～れるな Don't *flatter yourself* too much. 彼女は美人であると～れている She *is vain of* her beauty. / She *fancies herself* beautiful. 彼は頭がよいと～れている He *has a conceit* that he is bright. / He is bright *in his own conceit*.

うね【畝】(畑の) a ridge (in the field); a furrow; (織物の) a rib. ¶ ～をうつ make *furrows*; form *ridges*.

うねうね ¶ ～とした流れ a *meandering* stream. 山の道は～している The paths on the mountain *are winding*.

うねり (波の) a swell; (丘の) undulation. ¶ あらしのあとひどい～がある There is *a* heavy *swell* after the storm.

うね·る wind ([waind] と発音); (土地が) undulate ; (波が) roll ; swell.

¶ 丘は～っている The hills *are undulating*. あらしのあとは波は～る The waves *are high* after the storm. その小道は～りくねっている The path *is winding*.

うのみ【鵜呑み】¶ 彼は食物をかまないで～にする He *swallows* food without chewing. 彼女はどんな話でも～にする She will *swallow* any story. 彼の話を～にするな Don't *swallow* his story. / Don't *believe* his story *too easily*.

うは【右派】the right wing ; the rightists.

うば【乳母】a nurse.

―車 a baby carriage ; a perambulator (略 pram).

うばいあい【奪い合い】a scramble (*for*). ¶ 子どもたちはボールの～をした The children *scrambled for* the ball. 彼らは席の～をした They *scrambled* to get the seats. 彼らはみな予算の～をした They all *bade for* bigger shares in the budget.

うば・う【奪う】**1**〘物を〙 ¶ 人のものを～ってはいけない You must not *take* another's thing *away*.

彼は帰り道に時計を～われた He *was robbed of* his watch on his way home.

強盗は彼女のハンドバッグを～った The robber *robbed* her *of* her handbag.

2〘心など〙 ¶ 突然彼らは楽しみを一挙に～われた All of a sudden, they *were deprived of* their joy.

彼は推理小説に心を～われている He *is fascinated by* detective stories.

彼は狩猟に心を～われている He *is absorbed in* hunting.

うばざくら【姥桜】a faded beauty ; a matron 〔of forty〕. ¶ 彼女はもう～だ She is past her prime. / (米俗) She is a has-been.

うぶ【初】naive ; simple ; inexperienced.

¶ ～な少女 an *innocent* (≒ *inexperienced*) girl. こんなことをするとはきみも～だ You must *be* very *simple* to do such a thing.

うぶぎ【産着】baby clothes ; clothes for a newborn baby. ¶ 彼女は生まれる子の～をつくっている She is sewing up for the coming baby.

うぶげ【産毛】downy hair (*of* a baby).

¶ ～の生えた downy.

うぶごえ【産声】the first cry of a newborn baby. ¶ わが社が～をあげてから20年になる It is 20 years since our firm *was established*.

うぶゆ【産湯】¶ 彼女が赤ん坊に～をつかわせた She *bathed* my newborn baby.

うま【馬】**1** a horse ; (雌馬) a mare ; (小馬) a pony ; (子馬) a colt.

¶ ～に乗る ride 〔on〕 *a horse*.

～から落ちる fall from (≒ be thrown off) *a horse*.

～に乗って on *horseback*.

～で行く ride *horseback*.

～をさくにつなぐ fasten (≒ hitch) *a horse* to a fence.

2〘慣用的表現〙 ¶ それは～を牛に乗り換えたようなもの It is a change for the worse.

彼はどこの～の骨だかわからない He came from no one knows where. / He is a man of doubtful origin.

私の忠告なんか彼には～の耳に念仏だった He was deaf to my advice. / He would not listen to my advice.

私は彼と～が合う I get on well with him.

～は～づれ (諺) *Birds of a feather flock together*.

うま・い【上手い・巧い・甘い・旨い】**1**〘よい・優れている・じょうずだ〙 ¶ あの先生は教え方が～い He is a *good* teacher. / That teacher *has tact in* teach*ing*.

そりゃ～い考えだ That's a *cute* (≒ *good*) idea.

彼女は絵が～い She draws *well*. / She is a *good* painter. / She *is good at* drawing.

彼はテニスが～い He plays tennis *well*. / He is a *good* tennis player.

彼女は琴が非常に～い She is a *good* player of *koto*. (日常ききなれぬ楽器の場合は a *koto* player はさける).

あのアメリカ人は日本語が～い That American is a *good* speaker of Japanese.

きみのほうが私より～い You are a *better* player 〔than I〕.

あの人はいつも～いことばかり言っている He *is* always *flattering* people.

2〘味がよい〙 ¶ このリンゴは～い This apple *tastes sweet*.

これは～いビフテキだ This beefsteak *tastes nice*!

なにか～そうなにおいがする It smells of something *delicious*.

こういうふうに料理すると～い味になる This style of cooking brings out the flavor.

腹がへればなんでも～い Everything *tastes good* when you are hungry. / (諺) *Hunger is the best sauce*.

3〘自分に好都合だ〙 ¶ それでは話が～すぎる The news *is* too *good* to be true. / That job *sounds* too *good*.

～い話があるんだ. 一口乗らないか Won't you be interested in a *good* deal?

彼は自分だけ～い汁を吸っている He *is taking the lion's share*. / He *is squeezing the orange all to himself*.

そんな～い話に乗ってはいけない Don't take share in too *good* a scheme like that.

うまかた【馬方】a 〔packhorse〕 driver.

うまく【上手く】**1**〘じょうずに〙 ¶ もっと～書きなさい Write more *neatly*.

英語が～しゃべれない I cannot speak English *well*. / I am not a *good* English speaker. / I am a poor speaker of English.

この絵は～くかけている This is a *good* picture.

英語が～くなるにはどうしたらいいでしょうか What shall I do to *improve* my English?

彼に～ごまをすっておいた I flattered him. / I polished his apple.

2〘好都合に〙 ¶ 仕事は～いっている I am doing *well* in my job.

～いけばいいのだが I hope it *comes off satis-*

factorily.
彼の商売は〜いっていないようだ He does not seem to *be getting on well* in his business.
すべては〜いっている Everything *is getting on well*.
世の中は〜いかないこともある Things sometimes do not *come off well*.
ふたりの結婚生活は〜いっていないらしい It seems that their married life *is* not *working out well*.
万事〜いきました Everything *went well*. / Everything *went off smoothly*.

うまごやし 〖植物〗 a clover.

うまさ 【上手さ・旨さ】 ¶ 彼の話の〜は定評がある He is established as a *good* speaker. 彼の文章の〜はよく知られている It is well known that he writes a *very good* style. この菓子の〜を知らない人は気の毒に思う I feel sorry for those who do not know the *taste* of this cake.

うまずたゆまず 【倦まず弛まず】 ¶ 彼は〜努力した He made *untiring* efforts.

うまずめ 【産まず女】 a childless woman; a barren woman.

うまづら 【馬面】 ¶ 彼は〜だ He *is horse-faced*.

うまに 【甘煮・旨煮】 meat and vegetables boiled in soy with sugar.

うまのり 【馬乗り】 〔horse〕 riding. ¶ 彼はその少年に〜になった He *sat astride* 〔*of*〕 the boy. 彼は〜が得意だ He is good at *riding* 〔*a horse*〕.

うまみ 【うま味】 (味のよさ) 〔a〕 taste; 〔a〕 flavor; (妙味) a charm; beauty. ¶ 〜のある文体 a *charming* (≒ *pleasing*) style. 〜のない文体 a *dry* (≒ *dull*) style. これはなかなか〜のある文章である This passage is 〔written〕 in a style with *a* peculiar *charm*. その契約にはあまり〜がない(条件が悪い) We can't do a fat job on the contract. ウイスキーの〜がわかってきた I have got *a taste* for whisky. / I can appreciate the *taste* of whisky now.

うまや 【馬屋・厩】 a stable; (特に 米) a barn.

うま・る 【埋まる】 be buried; be filled.
¶ 子どもが砂の中に〜った A child *was buried* in the sand. 庭が落ち葉で〜った The garden *was covered* 〔*up*〕 with fallen leaves. 席が全部見物人で〜った The seats *were* all *filled up* with spectators. 赤字は〜らない The deficit (≒ loss) can't *be covered*.

うまれ 【生まれ】 ¶ お〜はどちらですか Where do you *come from*? 彼は東京〜だ He *was born* in Tokyo. / His *home town* is Tokyo. 彼は名門の〜だ He *comes of* a noble family. / He is a man of noble *birth*. 彼は〜からいうとアメリカ人だ He is an American *by birth*.
—変わり(再生) rebirth; (化身) a reincarnation (*of*). —故郷 *one's* home town; *one's* birthplace.

うまれかわ・る 【生まれ変わる】 ¶ 彼はまったく〜ったように見える He *looks quite like another person*. / He *looks quite like a stranger*. 〜ったらやはり医者になりたい If I *were born again*, I would be a doctor again. 〜った気持ちになった I *felt like another man*. 人間は精神的に〜ることができる A man can *be reborn* (≒ *be regenerated*) spiritually.

うまれつき 【生まれつき】 ¶ 彼は〜怠け者だ He is lazy *by nature*. 彼は〜体がじょうぶである He is *naturally* strong. 彼は〜体が弱い He is delicate *by birth*. 〜の饒舌(じょうぜつ)家だ He *was born* talkative.

うまれつ・く 【生まれつく】 ¶ 彼は詩人に〜いている He is a *born* (≒ *natural*) poet. 彼は幸運に〜いている He *was born* under a lucky star.

うまれながら 【生まれながら】 ¶ 彼は〜の画家だ He is a *born* painter. 〜の才人はいない No man *is born* with ability.

うま・れる 【生まれる】 **1** 〖人が〗 ¶ 私は1938年3月15日神戸で〜れた I *was born* in Kobe on March 15, 1938.
彼は金持ちの家に〜れた He *was born* rich.
この子どもは〜れてこのかた病気をしたことがない The child has never been sick *since his birth*.
そのとき〜れて初めて飛行機に乗った On that occasion, I took an airplane for the first time in my life. / That was the first air trip in my life.
来月彼女に子どもが〜れる予定だ She is going to *have a baby* next month.
2 〖事物が〗 ¶ 新聞はどうして〜れたか知っていますか Do you happen to know how a newspaper *came into existence*.

うみ 【生み・産み】 ¶ 〜の苦しみ *birth* (≒ *labor*) pains; travail. 〜の親より育ての親 The foster parent is dearer to one than the *real* parent.

うみ 【海】 **1** the sea; the ocean (慣用的な言い方を除き通常 the をつける). ¶ 〜の家(海水浴用の) a *sea* cottage.
〜の生活 a *sea* life; life *on the sea*.
彼はいま〜に出ている He is at *sea*. / He is out on *the sea*.
〜の風 a *sea* breeze.
わが国は四方〜に取り囲まれている This country is surrounded by *the sea* on all sides.
そのホテルは〜に面している The hotel faces on *the sea*.
夏は〜に出かける I go to the *seaside* in summer.
〜でひと泳ぎしよう Let's have a swim in *the ocean*. (米語では sea より ocean が口語的).
〜が荒れている(穏やかだ) *The sea* is rough (calm).
—ガメ a turtle. —鳥 a sea bird. —ネコ a sea gull. —ヘビ a sea snake. —坊主 a sea monster.
2 〖比喩的・慣用的表現〗 ¶ 辺り一面火の〜であった There was *a sea of* flames all around.
結果は〜のものとも山のものともわからない The result can't be predicted yet.
彼は〜千山千だ He is an old stager (≒ hand).

うみ 【膿】 pus. ¶ 傷が〜をもつ *Pus* is formed

(≒ gathered) in the wound. はれものが～を吹き切った The *swelling* has burst. 傷口から～を出した I pressed *pus* from out of the wound. 傷が～を出す The wound discharges *pus*.

うみおと·す【生み落とす】give birth to (a baby).

うみだ·す【生み出す・産み出す】¶ 彼は新しい方法を～した He *invented* a new method.

うみたて【生みたて】¶ ～の卵 a *newly laid* egg; a *fresh* egg.

うみなり【海鳴り】rumbling of the sea. ¶ ～がする The sea *rumbles*.

うみびらき【海開き】the opening of the swimming season (at Kamakura). ¶ 6月25日から～する *The sea opens* to swimmers on June 25.

うみべ【海辺】¶ ～を on (≒ along) *the beach* (≒ *seaside*; *seashore*). 私たちは～を歩いた We walked *on* (≒ *along*) *the sea*.

うむ【有無】¶ 彼女に～を言わさず承諾させた I *forced* her *to* agree to it. 彼らは～を言わさず彼を連れていった They took him out *by force*. 欠員の～を知らせてほしい Let me know whether there is any *vacancy or not*. ご出席の～をお知らせください Please let me know whether you will *attend or not*.

う·む【産む・生む】**1**〘出産する〙 bear; give birth to.

¶ 彼女は双子を～んだ She *gave birth to* twins.

彼女はきのう男の赤ん坊を～んだ She *gave birth to* a [baby-]boy yesterday.

彼女は彼との間に5人の子どもを～んだ She *bore* five children *to* him.

うちの犬は昨夜3匹子を～んだ Our dog *had* three pups last night.

この鶏はよく卵を～む This hen *lays* many eggs. / This hen *lays* well.

案ずるより～むがやすい Fear often exaggerates danger.

2〘生じる〙 ¶ そのことがあらぬうわさを～んだ It *gave rise to* a groundless rumor.

そういうことをすると疑惑を～みやすい Such conduct is apt to *excite* (≒ *arouse*) suspicions.

ただ金をくれたってよい結果を～むとはかぎらない The mere contribution of money does not always *produce* good results.

利が利を～んで思わぬ金額になった Interest *has borne* interest, and it has amounted to an unexpected sum.

彼女は日本の～んだ最高のバイオリニストです She is the greatest violinist that Japan has ever *had* (≒ *produced*).

う·む【倦む】be tired of; be sick of. ¶ ～まずたゆまず働いた I worked *tirelessly*. 彼は～まずたゆまず研究を続けた He pursued his study *with untiring zeal*.

う·む【膿む】¶ 傷口が～んだ The wound *formed pus*. / The wound *festered*. できものが～んだ The boil *is ripe*.

うめ【梅】〖植物〗(木) an *ume* tree; a plum tree; (実) a plum; a Japanese apricot; (花) plum blossoms.

うめあわせ【埋め合わせ】compensation. ¶ 損失の～ができない I can't *make up for* the loss. 長く待たせた～にその子にチョコレートをやった I gave the child a chocolate to *make up for* his long waiting.

うめき【呻き】a groan; a moan. ¶ 彼は～声をあげながらそこに横たわっていた He lay there *moaning* (≒ *groaning*).

うめ·く【呻く】groan; moan. ¶ 負傷者は～きながら横になっていた The injured lay *groaning*. 彼は苦しみで～いていた He *moaned* with pain.

うめくさ【埋め草】padding; a [space] filler. ¶ この記事を～に書いた I wrote this article *to fill up the space*.

うめしゅ【梅酒】plum liquor.

うめず【梅酢】salted plum juice [used for pickling].

うめたて【埋め立て・埋立】reclamation. ―工事 reclaiming work. ―地 a reclaimed land.

うめた·てる【埋め立てる】fill up (a pond); reclaim (marshy land; wilds). ¶ 海を～てる *reclaim* land from the sea. 沼地を～てる *reclaim* marshy land. その池は～てられた The pond *was filled up with earth*. あの土地は海を～てた所だ That is the land *reclaimed* from the sea.

うめぼし【梅干し】pickled plums (ふつう複数形). ―ばばあ a crone; a withered old woman.

う·める【埋める】(地中に) bury; (埋め立てる) reclaim; fill up. ¶ 余白を～める *fill* [*in*] a blank (in は副詞). 赤字を～める *make up* the deficit.

うもれぎ【埋もれ木】(炭化した木) bogwood; (不遇) [an] obscure life. ¶ きょうの授賞で～に花が咲いた Having won the prize this time, I could rise out of obscurity. ―細工 bogwood work.

うやうやし·い【恭しい】¶ ～く一礼する make a *respectful* bow; bow *reverently*.

うやま·う【敬う】¶ 父母を～う *respect one's* parents; *honor* thy father and thy mother (聖書の文句). 子どもは目上の人を～うべきだ Children should *show respect to* their superiors. 彼は神を～う心があつい He *is* very *pious*. 彼らはわれわれとは違う神を～っている They *worship* a god different from ours.

うやむや ¶ 彼はその問題を～にしておいた He *has left* the matter *undecided*. 話は～に終わった The talk yielded *no definite* results. 彼は万事～にしてごまかす He shuffles through by *leaving* everything *vague*. 彼らは問題を～にしてしまった They *hugger-muggered* the matter.

うようよ ¶ ～する(場所を主語として) swarm (*with*); team (*with*); be crowded (*with*). 池に魚が～している The pond *swarms with* fish. / Fish *swarm* in the pond. カエルが～池から上がってきた Frogs came out of the pond *in swarms*.

うよきょくせつ【紆余曲折】 ¶ 幾多の～を経て after many *turns and twists*. ～があった There were many *complications*.

うよく【右翼】 (つばさ・列などの) the right wing ; (野球の) the right field ; (思想の) the right wing ; (その思想をいだく人) a rightist ; (保守の人) a conservative ; (極右派の人) an ultra-conservative.

—思想 right-wing thought. **—**手(野球) a right fielder. **—**団体 a right-wing organization.

うら【浦】 (海辺) the seashore ; (入り江) a bay ; an inlet ; a creek.

うら【裏】 **1** 〚表面と反対の側〛 the back.

¶ 手の～ the palm.

足の～ the sole 〔of *one's* foot〕.

答案を～に返してください *Turn* your paper *over*.

書ききれなければ～に書きなさい If the space is exhausted, write on *the opposite side* of the paper.

～を見てください See *the overleaf*. /Please *turn over*. (略 p. t. o.) / (米) Over.

この紙はどちらが表でどちらが～かわからない I cannot tell the right from *the wrong side* of the paper.

きみは50円貨の～と表がわかりますか Can you tell me the head and *tail* of 50 yen coin?

レコードの～もかけてください Play *the reverse side* of the record, too.

2 〚裏布地〛 the lining. ¶ 夏服だから～はいりません I don't need *the lining*, because this is a summer suit.

～にはどんな布地をつけましょうか What kind of cloth shall I use for *the lining*?

3 〚家などの背後の所〛 ¶ ～の戸を開けてください Open the *back* door, please.

～にまわってください Go round to *the back door*, please.

彼は～の畑にいる He is in the field at the *back* of the house.

この家の～は林になっている There is a wood at the *back* of this house.

どろぼうは～から入ったらしい It seems that the thief broke into the house from *the back door*.

4 〚表に出ない事情〛 ¶ ～には～があるんだ, この事件には There are *secrets within secrets* in this matter.

彼がそう言う～の意味をくんでやれ Consider *the hidden implications* of his words.

彼は政界の～をよく知っている He is familiar with *the seamy* (≒ *shady*) *side* of the political world.

この話の～を知っていますか Do you know *the hidden side* of this story?

この事件を～から見てみる必要がある We must view the matter from *the other side*.

彼の心の～を見抜けないようではきみも甘い You have a lot to learn if you can't see through his heart.

うらうち【裏打ち】 lining ; backing.

¶ やぶけた地図を厚紙で～した I *backed* the torn map *with* cardboard. / I *mounted* the torn map *on* cardboard. そのコートは絹の～がしてあった The coat *was lined with* silk. 世論に～される be backed by public opinion.

うらおもて【裏表】 (裏と表) the right and the wrong sides.

¶ 紙の～ *both sides* of the paper. 事件の～を知る know *the ins and outs* (≒ *the in and outside*) of the affair. ～のある人 a double-dealer. きみの寝巻きは～になっている Your pajamas are *wrong side out*. パリの～ *in and out* of Paris. 硬貨の～ *the head and tail* of a coin.

うらがえし【裏返し】 ¶ くつ下を～にはく put on *one's* socks *inside out*. ～に置く put (examination papers) *face down*. それは～だ That's *wrong side out*.

うらがえ・す【裏返す】 turn (*a thing*) over.

うらがき【裏書き】 (小切手の) 〔an〕 endorsement ; (証明) 〔a〕 proof ; (旅券の) a visa ; a visé ([vi:zei] と発音).

¶ 小切手に～する *endorse* a check 〔with a signature〕; *endorse one's* name on a check. ～する(証明する) prove ; confirm.

うらかた【裏方】 (芝居の) a stagehand ; (貴人の妻) the lady consort. ¶ 本願寺～は皇室の出である *The Lady Abbess of* Honganji comes of Imperial Household.

うらぎり【裏切り】 〔a〕 betrayal ; 〔a〕 treachery.

¶ 労働者への～行為 an act of *treachery* against the working masses.

—者 a betrayer ; a traitor ; (密告者) an informer ; (スト破り) a strikebreaker.

うらぎ・る【裏切る】 ¶ 彼は親友〔の信頼〕を～った He *betrayed* 〔the confidence of〕 his best friend. 結果はわれわれの期待を～った The result *disappointed* us. 彼は部下に～られて敵手に落ちた He fell into the hands of the enemy by his men's *treachery*. きみが～ったから彼は怒ったんだ He got angry because you *played* him *false*.

うらぐち【裏口】 the back door. ¶ ～から入る enter by the *back door*.

—営業 backdoor (≒ illegal) business.

—入学 ¶ ～入学する obtain a *backdoor* admission to a school.

うらごえ【裏声】 ¶ ～で歌う sing 〔*in*〕 *falsetto*.

うらごし【裏漉し】 (道具) a strainer. ¶ じゃがいもを～する *strain* potatoes.

うらさく【裏作】 the second crop.

うらじ【裏地】 lining 〔cloth〕.

うらづけ【裏付け】 ¶ 警察は～となる証拠がとれなかった The police had no *proof*. きみの主張には事実の～がない Your argument *is* not *based on* facts.

うらづ・ける【裏付ける】 ¶ 彼には主張を～ける資料がない He has no data to *support* his argument. どうしてきみの主張を～けるか How can you *prove* (≒ *substantiate*) your statement? 事件を～けるもうひとつの証拠がある We have another evidence which *corroborates* the case. 義務に～けられない権利などはない There is no right *unaccompanied* by duty.

うらて【裏手】¶ わが家の～はすぐ山だ Just *at the back of* my house there is a hill.

うらどおり【裏通り】a back street (ふつう main street と平行); a side street (ふつう main street と直角); an alley (ふつう狭い back street); a lane (ひじょうに狭い道).

うらない【占い】fortunetelling; (易者) a fortuneteller; (手相占い師) a palmist. ¶ ～に見てもらう consult *a fortuneteller*.

うらな・う【占う】¶ トランプで人の運勢を～う *tell a person's fortune* with cards. 商売の成否を～ってもらう *have one's fortune told* about *one's* business.

うらながや【裏長屋】a tenement house in an alley.

うらなり【末成り】(なり物) a fruit grown near the top end of the vine; (人) a pale, weakly person.

ウラニウム〖化学〗uranium. ⇒ウラン

うらにほん【裏日本】districts along the coast of the Japan Sea.

うらにわ【裏庭】a back yard.

うらばなし【裏話】¶ これには～がある There is *a hidden side* to the information.

うらはら【裏腹】the contrary. ¶ 彼は言うことと行なうことが～だ He does *the reverse* of what he says. / He acts *contrary to* his words.

うらぶ・れる ¶ 彼は～れた姿で現われた He turned up *in a shabby appearance*. / He turned up *down at* [the] *heel*[s]. 彼は～れていた He *was reduced to poverty*. / He *was down and out*. 彼は～れたわびずまいをしていた He lived lonely in a *dilapidated* house.

うらまち【裏町】a back street; an alley. ⇒うらどおり

うらみ【恨み】**1**〖怨恨〗a grudge; [an] enmity. ¶ 私は彼に～がある I *have* (≒ *bear*) *a grudge against* him.

彼は人々の～を買った He *incurred enmity from* many people.

彼らはその男に対して～を晴らした They *took revenge on* him. / They *revenged themselves on* him.

あの人には～骨髄に徹している I *bear* him *a* deep *grudge*.

なにも彼に～がましいことを言うな Don't say anything *reproachful against* him.

2〖残念なこと〗¶ チャンスを生かしきれなかった～がある I *regret* that I haven't made full use of the opportunity.

うらみごと【恨み言】a grudge; a grievance.

うらみち【裏道】a back lane (≒ street); a by-path.

うら・む【恨む】bear (≒ have) a grudge (*against a person*). ¶ 彼は私を～んでいる He *has* (≒ *bears*) *a grudge against* me. / He *is bitter against* me. 人を～むな Don't *blame* (≒ *think ill of*) others. 彼の若死にが～まれる We *regret* that he died young.

うらめし・い【恨めしい】¶ 彼女は彼が～かった She *was* (≒ *felt*) *bitter against* him. 彼女は～そうに私を見た She cast a *reproachful* look at me.

うらもん【裏門】a back (≒ rear) gate.

うらやまし・い【羨ましい】envy. ¶ きみが～い I *envy* you. きみの成功が～い I *am envious of* your success. ～いご身分だ You are in *enviable* circumstances. みんな彼の美しい妻を～がった Everybody *envied* him his beautiful wife. 子どもは友のおもちゃを～そうに見た The child looked *enviously* (≒ *with envy*) at his friend's toy.

うらや・む【羨む】envy; be envious (*of*); be jealous (*of*). ¶ きみの成功を～む I *envy* [you] your success. / I *am envious of* your success. 彼は人の～むような職を得た He got an *enviable* job. 他人の成功なんか～むことはない Don't *be jealous* (≒ *envious*) *of* others' success.

うららか【麗らか】¶ ～な日 a *beautiful* (≒ *nice; lovely*) day. 日が～に照っている The sun is shining *bright*.

うらわか・い【うら若い】young; youthful; youngish.

ウラン〖化学〗uranium.

—鉱 uranium ore. **濃縮—** enriched uranium.

うり【瓜】a melon. ¶ あの双生児は～ふたつだ The twins *are just alike*. / The twins *are as like as two peas*. ～のつるにはなすびはならぬ (諺) An onion will not produce a rose.

うり【売り】(販売) sale; selling. ¶ 彼は自分の浮世絵のコレクションを～に出した He *put* his collection of *ukiyoe to sale*. 展覧会にはピカソの作品が2点～に出ている Two pieces by Picasso *are on* (≒ *for*) *sale* at the exhibition. 彼の家は～に出されている His house *is on the market*.

うりあげ【売り上げ・売上】**—金(高)** sales; proceeds. **—伝票** a sales slip.

うりいそ・ぐ【売り急ぐ】¶ 相場が下がったからといって～ぐことはない You need not *sell in haste* because of the bearish market.

うりおし・む【売り惜しむ】¶ 値上がりを見越して～んだ They *were unwilling to sell* the goods in expectation of better price. 彼らは品不足を見込んで～んだ They *restricted the sale of* these articles in anticipation of the shortage.

うりかけ【売り掛け・売掛】credit sales.

—代金 accounts; a bill.

うりかた【売り方】(販売法) a way of selling; (売り手) a seller; 〖株式〗a bear (≒ short).

うりき・る【売り切る】¶ 在庫品を全部～った We *sold out* all the stock on hand.

うりきれ【売り切れ】a sellout; (掲示) Sold Out. (切符などが) / Out of Stock (商品が).

う

うりき·れる【売り切れる】¶ その本は発売後２日で～れた All the copies *were sold out* within two days of the publication. その品は～れた The article *is out of stock* now. / We *have no stock of* the article now.

うりこ【売り子】(男) a salesman; a clerk; (女) a saleswoman; a shopgirl; (駅などの) a seller; a vendor.

うりごえ【売り声】a peddler's (≒ seller's) cry. ¶ 行商人の～ street cries.

うりことば【売り言葉】¶ ～に買いことばでそう言った I said so as a retort.

うりこみ【売り込み】sale.

うりこ·む【売り込む】¶ 彼女は文房具をその学校に～んでいる She *sells* stationery materials *to* the school. わが社の小型車をインドに～もうと計画中である We are planning to *find a market for* our compact car in India. その製品はアメリカなら～める The product will *find a market* in America. その地位につきたいのならきみはもっと自分を～まなきゃだめだ You must *advertise yourself* more if you want to get the position.

うりざねがお【瓜実顔】an oval face.

うりさば·く【売り捌く】sell. ¶ 彼はその本を１日のうちに500部～いた He *sold* five hundred copies of the book in a day. この種の商品を～くには多年の経験がいる It requires many years' experience to *sell* this kind of articles.

うりだし【売り出し】(安売り) a bargain sale. ¶ 年末～ *a* special year-end *sale*. 彼は今～の歌手です He is a *rising* singer.
大— (掲示) Sale!

うりだ·す【売り出す】¶ その歌手はこの歌で～した The singer *became popular* by this song. / The singer *gained his reputation* by this song. / The song *won* the singer *a reputation*. この新型車は近く～される The new style car will soon *come into the market*.

うりつ·ける【売りつける】¶ 彼は私に偽物を～けた He *imposed* an imitation *on* me. とうとうその絵を～けられた I *was persuaded to buy* the painting in the end. 店員はおせじを言って彼女にくつを～けた The clerk *sold* a pair of shoes *to* her by flattery.

うりて【売り手】a seller; 〖株式〗 a bear.
—市場 a sellers' market.

うりとば·す【売り飛ばす】¶ 彼は家宝を二束三文で～した He *sold off* the family treasure at a wretched price.

うりね【売り値】a sale (≒ selling) price.

うりば【売り場】a counter.
切符— a ticket (≒ booking) office.

うりはら·う【売り払う】sell out; sell off. ¶ 不要な家財道具を～った We *sold out* all our belongings in disuse.

うりもの【売り物】an article for (≒ on) sale; (掲示) For Sale. ¶ ～に出す offer (≒ put up) for *sale*. あの店はサービスが～だ They attract customers by good service at that store.

うりや【売り家】a house for (≒ on) sale.

うりょう【雨量】rainfall; the amount of precipitation. ¶ 先週の～は10ミリだった We had ten millimeters of rain last week.
—計 a rain gauge.

うりわた·す【売り渡す】sell (*a thing*) 〔over〕 (*to*). ¶ 彼はその土地を千万円で土地ブローカーに～した He *sold* the estate *to* a realtor for ten million yen.

う·る【売る】**1** 〖品物を売る〗 sell. ¶ これをいくらで～るのですか What (≒ How much) are you asking for it?
1,000円で～れば100円もうかる If we *sell* it for one thousand yen, we can gain one hundred yen.
もっと安く～れないか Can't you *sell* it a bit cheaper? / Can't you *sell* it at a lower price?
損をしてまで～るつもりはありません I am not going to *sell* at a loss.
このハンカチは１ダースなら2,000円，１枚なら200円で～ります These handkerchieves *sell* at two thousand yen a dozen or two hundred yen apiece.
この品は１ポンドいくらで～ります This article *is sold* by the pound.
それはどこで～っていますか Where can I buy it? / Where is it available?
全国の主要デパートで～っています You can buy it at major department stores in all parts of the country. / It is procurable from the main department stores all over the country.
あちこち捜したがどこにも～ってなかった I searched in this store or that, but couldn't find it anywhere.
あの店に行けば日用雑貨はなんでも～っている You can buy everything you need for daily use in that store. / You can buy all daily necessities in that store.
2 〖世の中に広める〗 ¶ 彼はテレビ，ラジオにたびたび出たので名が～れてきた He appeared on the television and radio programs so often that he *became well-known*.
彼は度胸のよさで男を～った He *became famous* on account of his courage. / He *built up a reputation* on account of his courage.
あの歌手は美貌(ぼう)と若さで～っている The singer *is famous for* her beauty and youthfulness.
今度新しく出る週刊誌は記事の正確さで～ろうとしている The new weekly intends to *sell* the accuracy of articles.
3 〖裏切る·背く〗 betray. ¶ 私は友を～るようなことはしない I would never *betray* a friend.
彼は外交の機密を漏らし国を～ったと非難された He was censured for *having betrayed* the diplomatic secrets of his country.

うるう【閏】intercalation. ¶ ～の intercalary.
—年 a leap (≒ intercalary) year.

うるおい【潤い】(湿気) moisture; (情味) charm; (利益) profit; (繁盛) prosperity.

¶ 彼女は〜のあるまなざしで私を見た She looked at me with *liquid* eyes. 長い間〜のない生活を送った I led a *dreary* life for many years. 都会生活は〜がない There is nothing *charming* in city life.

うるお・う【潤う】 ¶ 観光客の落とす金で町は〜っている The town *is prosperous* owing to the tourists who spend a lot of money for sight-seeing. このことでぼくの懐も少しは〜った I *have profited* a little by this. この雨で田畑は〜った This rain *is welcome* to the fields.

うるお・す【潤す】 ¶ 昨夜の雨が畑を〜した The fields *are wet* after the rain last night. 彼は谷間の水でのどを〜した He *quenched his thirst* by drinking water from a streamlet in the valley.

うるさ・い【煩い】 noisy. ¶ 〜い! Shut up! この子どもたちはほんとうに〜い These children *are noisy*, indeed. ハエは〜いものだ Flies *are a nuisance*. 彼は〜いやつだ He *is a disturbing* fellow. 世間の口は〜い People will talk. 食べ物については彼はかなり〜いほうだ He *is* very *particular about* food. 生徒が〜く質問した The students *troubled* me with questions.

うるさがた【煩型】 a fastidious person; a faultfinder.

うるさが・る【煩がる】 feel annoyed; (人・物を) consider (*a person; a matter*) annoying.

うるし【漆】 lacquer; (木) a lacquer tree. ¶ 箱は黒い〜が塗られている The box *is lacquered* in black. 〜にかぶれやすい I am easily poisoned by *lacquer*.

ウルトラ ultra.

うる・む【潤む】 ¶ 〜んだ目 *dim* eyes. 彼女の目は涙で〜んでいた Her eyes *were dim* with tears.

うるめ〔魚類〕 a round herring.

うるわし・い【麗しい】 sweet; beautiful. ¶ ごきげん〜き由なによりのことと存じます I am very glad to hear that *you are in good health*. 彼女の声は〜い Her voice *is sweet*. 〜い音楽に魅せられた We were charmed by the *beautiful* music.

うれあし【売れ足】 sale; demand. ¶ 〜が速い sell quickly.

うれい【憂い】 trouble; worry; distress; grief. ¶ 知らせを聞いて人々は〜に包まれた People were filled with *concern* when the news came. 彼の顔は〜に包まれていた He wore *a sad look*. 彼には後顧の〜はない He has no *care* about his home.

うれ・える【憂える】 ¶ 国の将来を大いに〜えている I *am* much *concerned* about the future of our country. 交通事故が跡を絶たないのは〜うべきことだ *It is deplorable* that there is no end to traffic accidents.

うれくち【売れ口】 a market; demand; sale. ¶ 卒業生は〜がいい There is *a* good *demand* for the graduates. 大学卒業生も来年は〜が減るだろう University graduates will be *in* less *demand* next year.

うれし・い【嬉しい】 glad; happy. ¶ 彼に会えて〜かった I *was glad to* see him. その吉報に接して彼は〜そうだ He *looks pleased at* the good news. その本が手に入って〜い I *am delighted to* be able to get the book. 会においでいただければたいへん〜く思います We shall *be* very *happy* if you could be present at the party. 〜いことに彼は来てくれた I *was glad* he came to see me. / I *was delighted* when he came to see me. 晴れた日に釣りに出かけることほど〜いことはない Nothing gives me so much *pleasure* as going fishing on a nice day.

うれしが・る【嬉しがる】 ¶ そのニュースを聞いてその場に居合わせた人はみな〜った All the people present *were glad to* hear the news. 両親は息子の無事を知って〜った The parents *were delighted to* hear of their son's safety.

うれしさ【嬉しさ】 joy. ¶ 〜でとびあがった I jumped for *joy*.

うれしなき【嬉し泣き】 cry for (≒ with) joy. ¶ 少女は試験に合格したとわかって〜に泣いていた The girl *was crying with joy* to know that she had passed the examination.

うれしなみだ【嬉し涙】 tears for joy. ¶ 彼らは〜にむせんだ They were choked with *tears of joy*.

うれっこ【売れっ子】 a favorite; a popular person. ¶ 彼はテレビの〜だ He is *a favorite* as a TV talent. 彼は文壇の〜だ He is *a popular writer*.

うれのこり【売れ残り】 remainders; unsold goods. ¶ あの店では〜を安く売っている *Remainders* are sold cheap at the store. きょうは〜がたくさん出た We have many *goods unsold* today. 彼女は〜だ She is *an old maid*.

うれのこ・る【売れ残る】 ¶ 多くの品物が〜っている Many articles *remain unsold*. 〜ったきっぷがありますか Are there any tickets which *remain unsold*?

うれゆき【売れ行き】 sale; demand. ¶ その雑誌は〜がよい The magazine *is enjoying a wide circulation*. その品は〜が悪い(よい) The article *is in poor* (*great*) *demand*. この本がいちばん〜がよい This book is *a best seller*. テニスボールは夏がいちばん〜がよい Tennis balls *sell* best in summer.

う・れる【売れる】 **1**〖買われる〗sell. ¶ 新製品は飛ぶように〜れた The new products *sold* like wildfire (≒ like hot cakes).

この型の洗たく機がよく〜れている Washing machines of this type *sell well*. / Washing machines of this type *are in great demand*.

今ではこのカメラはあまり〜れていない Nowadays this type of camera is slow to *unload*.

値段を下げればきっと〜れる It will surely *sell* at a lower price.

2〖売ることができる〗sell. ¶ あの中古車はいい値に〜れた That used car *was sold* for a good price.

この絵は〜れても〜れなくてもいい,慰みにかいたのだから I don't care if this picture may *sell* or not. I have painted it for my own pleasure.

この土地は売れません・先祖代々のものです I cannot *sell* this land, as it is a hereditary property.

3 〚広く知られる〛 ¶ 彼は芸能界では顔が〜れている He *is popular* (≒ *widely known*) *in* the entertainment world.

彼女はまだ踊り手としては名があまり〜れていない She *is* not yet *known* as a dancer.

う・れる【熟れる】ripen.

うろうろ・する ¶ 知らない男が通りを〜していた A stranger *was hanging about* in the street. 知らせを聞いて彼はなすすべもなく〜していた He *was confused* when he heard the news.

うろおぼえ【うろ覚え】a faint memory. ¶ 私は母を〜に覚えている I *have a faint memory of* my mother.

うろこ【鱗】a scale. ¶ ナイフで魚の〜を落とした I *scaled* the fish with a knife. 目から〜の落ちる思いがする have *one's* eyes opened; *Scale* fall from *one's* eyes. (聖書の文句).

—雲 a cirrocumulus. **—**模様 imbrication.

うろた・える【狼狽える】¶ 彼は息子の事故を聞いて〜えた The news of his son's accident completely *upset* him. 彼は〜えて一瞬口もきけなかった For a moment he could not say anything *in confusion*. 彼は終始〜えずにいた He *kept calm* throughout.

うろつ・く【彷徨く】¶ ショーウインドーをながめながら町を〜いた I *loitered* along the street, browsing in the stores. 野良犬が食べ物を求めて〜いていた A stray dog *was prowling* for food.

うろん【胡乱】¶ 〜な男 a *suspicious-looking* man.

うわあご【上顎】the upper jaw.

うわがき【上書き】an address; a superscription. ¶ 手紙の〜を書く *address* a letter. 封筒の〜を書く write *an address* on an envelope.

うわき【浮気】fickleness; inconsistency. ¶ 彼は〜な男だ He is *a flirt*. (flirt は男女ともに用いる). 彼女は〜な女だ She is *a wanton*. (wanton は女性に用い a wanton woman として形容詞用法もある). 彼女は〜な夫に思い悩んでいる She is worried about her husband's *fickleness*. あの奥さんは〜などしない She *is true to her husband*. 彼には〜のうわさなどない He has never given rise to *scandal*.

—者 a flirt; (女) a fickle woman.

うわぎ【上着】a coat; a jacket.

うわぐすり【上薬】glaze. ¶ 〜を塗った茶わん a *glazed* cup.

うわくちびる【上唇】the upper lip. ¶ 彼は〜をかむ癖がある He has a habit of biting *the upper lip*.

うわごと delirious talk; talking in delirium; (たわごと) nonsense. ¶ 彼は高熱に浮かされ 2 日も〜を言った He kept *talking in delirium* in a high fever for two days.

うわさ【噂】〔a〕rumor. ¶ きのうきみの〜をした We *talked about* you yesterday. / *Were your ears burning* yesterday? 彼らの〜をしていた We *were talking about* them. 彼がつかまったというのは〜にすぎない The news that he was arrested is *a* mere *rumor*. 彼が山の中でひとり暮らしをしているという〜はほんとうだった The *rumor* that he lived alone in the mountains turned out to be true. 〜をすれば影(諺) *Speak of the devil and he will appear*. その後の彼の〜を聞いていますか *Have* you *heard* anything *of* him since then?

うわすべり【上滑り】¶ 〜な読み方は益がない A *superficial* way of reading is of little value.

うわずみ【上澄み】top; supernatant fluid. ¶ ミルクの〜をとる *skim* milk.

うわず・る【上ずる】¶ 〜った声で in an *excited* voice; in a *hollow-sounding* voice.

うわつ・く【浮つく】¶ 彼には〜いた話もない There has never been any rumor that he *is fickle*. 〜いた flippant; flighty; restless.

うわっちょうし【上っ調子】¶ 〜な答え a *flippant* answer.

うわっぱり【上っ張り】(画家・婦人・子どもなどの) a smock; (作業用の) overalls; ㊥ a wrapper (㊥ では婦人の化粧着).

うわづみ【上積み】the upper load. ¶ 壊れやすい物は〜にしなさい *Load* the fragile articles *on the top*.

うわつら【上面】an appearance. ¶ 〜だけで人は判断できない We can't judge people by *appearances*. 彼はいつも物事の〜だけしか見ない He always looks only at the *surface* of things.

うわて【上手】¶ きみはスポーツでは私より〜だ You are my *senior* in sports. テニスは彼のほうがぼくより〜だ He is a *better* tennis player than I. 歴史では私のほうが〜だ I am *better* than you in history.

うわぬり【上塗り】¶ 机にはニスの〜がしてある The desk *is coated with* varnish. それこそ恥の〜だ This is *the more* shameful.

うわのそら【上の空】¶ 彼はぼくの質問には〜で答えた He answered me *absent-mindedly* (≒ *in an absent way*). 私の講義を〜で聞いていたのでは、わからないのがあたりまえだ Because you *are inattentive to* my lecture, it is natural that you should not understand it. 彼は〜の返事をした He gave a *half-hearted* answer.

うわべ【上辺】an appearance; a surface. ¶ それは〜はまったく革そっくりだ It has all the *appearance* of leather. 〜で人を判断するな Don't judge a man *by* (≒ *from*) *his appearance*. 彼の親切は〜だけのものだ His kindness is *on the surface*. / He is kind *on the surface*. 彼は〜を飾っているだけだ He only *keeps up appearances*. 確かにそれは〜は非常に美しい Indeed it presents a very attractive *appearance*.

うわまえ【上前】a commission. ¶ 彼は彼らが売った売り上げから 10 パーセントの〜をはねる He *takes a commission of* ten percent on all sales they make.

うわまわ·る【上回る】¶ことしの収穫は予想を〜った This year's crop *has exceeded* the expected amount. 彼の体力は私を〜る He *exceeds* me *in* physical strength. 東京の人口はニューヨークより〜る Tokyo *exceeds* New York *in* population. 彼の車は制限速度を〜った He drove *far above* the speed limit.

うわむき【上向き】¶物価は〜だ Prices *are rising* (≒ *are on the rise*). 景気は〜になっている Business *is looking up*. きみの成績は徐々に〜になっている Your grade *is* slowly *going upward*.

うわめ【上目】an upward look. ¶〜を使って人を見るのはよしなさい Don't look at others *from under your eyebrows*.

うわやく【上役】*one's* superior.

うわ·る【植わる】¶稲の苗が水田にきれいに〜っている Rice plants *are* beautifully *planted* in the paddy. 種が花壇にきちんと〜っている Seeds *are* neatly *planted* in the flower bed.

うん【運】fate; luck. ¶〜よく fortunately. 〜悪く unfortunately. なんと〜のいい男だ What a *lucky* man he is! ぼくにも〜が向いてきたようだ *Fortune* seems to be smiling upon me. きのうは〜が悪かった I *was out of luck* yesterday. 〜よく助かった I was saved *by mere luck*. 〜を天に任せてそれを実行した I carried it out, trusting everything to *Providence*. けがひとつしないで〜がよかった We *were* very *fortunate* to escape without being injured. 〜よく明るいうちに駅に着いた I *was fortunate* enough to reach the railroad station before dark. 何事にも〜不運がある *Luck* effects everything.

うん ¶〜と言いなさい Say *yes*. / Give your *consent*. 彼を〜と言わせるのはほねだ It is hard to obtain his *consent*. 〜, まったくだ *Yes*, you are quite right. 〜, そんなら好きなようにしたまえ *Well then*, please yourself about it. 〜ともすんとも言わなかった He did not say even a word.

うんえい【運営】management; operation; administration. ¶彼は会議の〜がうまい He is good at *managing* a meeting.

—委員会 a steering committee. **—規則** managerial regulations. **—資金** working funds. **—費** cost of operation; operation expenses.

うんおう【蘊奥】⇒うんのう

うんか【浮塵子】〘虫類〙a rice insect; a leaf hopper.

うんか【雲霞】¶〜のごとき敵軍が押し寄せてきた The enemy advanced against us *in swarms*. 〜のごとき大軍 a *great* host.

うんが【運河】a canal. ¶〜が閉鎖された The *canal* was blocked. その土地に〜を切り開く案を立てた We made a plan to cut (≒ build) *a canal* through the land.

—地帯 a canal zone. **—通行料** canal tolls. パナマ(スエズ)**—** the Panama (Suez) Canal. 水閘(こう)式**—** a lock canal. 海平式**—** a sea level canal.

うんきゅう【運休】¶東海道新幹線は雪がひどいとよく〜する The New Tokaido Line *is* often *blocked* by heavy snowfall. 中央線は踏切事故で〜している The train service *has been suspended* on the Chuo Line because of a traffic accident at a crossing. 機械は全部〜している The machinery *lies idle*.

うんこう【運行】movement; revolution. ¶天体の〜 the *movement* of heavenly bodies. 惑星は軌道を〜する The planets *revolve* on their courses.

うんこう【運航】operation. ¶青森と函館の間を〜している連絡船 a ferryboat that *runs* between Aomori and Hakodate.

うんざり ¶彼には〜している I *am disgusted with* him. 彼の長話には〜した I *was sick of* hear*ing* his endless talk. 毎日彼女にコロッケばかり食べさせられて〜している I *have had enough of* her croquettes day after day.

うんさん【雲散】¶長い間の疑問が〜霧消した The question which has haunted me for a long time now *vanished* like a mist.

うんざん【運算】calculation; operation. ¶〜する operate; calculate; do sums; figure out. やさしい〜は頭の中でできる I can *do* easy *sums* in my head.

うんすい【雲水】an itinerant priest.

うんせい【運勢】fortune; luck; *one's* star (星が人の運勢を支配するとされることから). ¶易者に〜をみてもらった I had a fortuneteller tell my *fortune*. 彼の〜は上り坂だ His *star* is in the ascendant. / His *fortunes* are improving. 私は〜が悪い I was born under an unlucky *star*. 私は〜が良い I was born under a lucky *star*.

うんそう【運送】conveyance; transportation; (貨物の) shipping. ¶鉄道便で〜する *transport* by rail. この列車は旅客と貨物を〜する This train *conveys* both passengers and goods.

—業 the carrying trade; transportation business. **—業者** a shipper; a shipping agent. **—船** a transport; a cargo boat. **—人** a carrier; a porter. **—費** shipping expenses; a cost of transport. **—料** freight. 貨物**—** shipment; 圏goods transport. 海上**—** transportation by sea. 陸上**—** transportation by land. 旅客**—** passenger traffic.

うんだめし【運試し】¶もう一度〜にやってごらん *Take* your *chance* and do it again. 〜のつもりで試験を受けた I sat for the exam, *leaving the result to fate*.

うんちく【蘊蓄】erudition; *one's* vast stock of knowledge. ¶これは彼が〜を傾けた論文だ This is a thesis to which he applied all he had learned.

うんちん【運賃】freight〔rates〕; carriage; (旅客の) a〔passenger〕fare. ¶バスの〜が上がった The bus *fare* has been raised.

—表 a tariff; a freight list. **—率** freight rates.

うんでい【雲泥】 ¶品物は同じ材料で作られているが出来上がりに～の差がある There is *a great difference* among the articles in their workmanship, though they are made of the same material.

うんてん【運転】 operation; working; (運用) employment; (回転) revolution. ¶機械を～する *operate* a machine. 自動車を～する *drive* a car. ゆっくり注意して～しなさい *Drive* slowly and carefully. 彼は酔っていて車の～はだめだ He is too drunk to *drive* a car. 日曜日には特別列車が～される Special trains *are run* on Sundays. 9時の列車は～休止となった The 9:00 train *was canceled*. この電車は10分間隔で～されている This train *runs* every ten minutes. 大みそかなので, 電車は終夜～する Since this is New Year's Eve, the trains are to *run* all night.
—系統(バスなどの) a route. —資金 working funds. —手(自動車の) a driver; (電車の) a motorman. —台(自動車の) a driver's seat; (電車の) a motorman's platform. —免許証 a driver's license.

うんと (強く) hard; severely; (たくさん) much; a great deal of; a lot of. ¶彼を～しかってください Give him a *good* scolding. アイスクリームを～食べたい I want to eat my *fill* of ice cream. 彼は結婚に～金を使った He spent *a lot of* money for (≒ on) his marriage. 若いうちに本を～読みなさい Read *as many* books *as you can* while you are young.

うんどう【運動】 1〖身体の〗 exercise; (競技) sports; athletics; (体操) gymnastics.
¶日ごろどんな～をしていますか What kind of *exercise* do you take usually?
どんな～が好きですか What kind of *sports* do you like?
～して体を鍛えなさい Train yourself by taking *exercise*. / Build up your constitution by *exercise*.
きょうは犬に～させましたか Did you *exercise* the dog today? / Did you take the dog for a walk today?
このごろ少し～不足だ Recently I lack *exercise*.
老人には散歩がいい～になる For old people, taking a walk is one of the best forms of *exercise*.
医者に軽い～なら差し支えないと言われた The doctor told me that I might take light *exercise*.
—会 an athletic meet. —界 sporting circles. —器具 sporting goods. —記事(記者) a sports news (writer). —ぐつ athletic shoes. —具店 a sporting goods store. —場 sports ground; field. —神経 reflex action. ¶彼は—神経が発達している He has quick control of his muscles. —選手 an athlete. —部 a sport club. —欄 a sports column. 陸上— field and track. 屋内—場 a gymnasium; (口語) a gym.
2〖目的への努力〗 an effort; (団体としての) a movement; a campaign; a drive; (選挙の) a campaign; 图 electioneering.
¶交通安全～が今週行なわれている *A* traffic safety *campaign* is being carried out this week.
公害防止の～が各地に広まっている The public pollution prevention *movement* is spreading out in various parts of the country.
政界浄化の～を盛り上げよう Let's push forward the *movement* for the purification of the political world.
反米～を政府は弾圧するかに見える It seems that the Government intends to suppress anti-American *movements*.
彼らは校長排斥～を起こした They started *an agitation* to expel the principal.
市当局は大学誘致の猛～をした The city authorities eagerly *campaigned* for the foundation of a new university.
裏にまわって変な～はするな Don't try anything funny behind my back.
彼は今からもう選挙の～をしている He has already started election *campaign activities*.
就職～する make an effort to obtain a position.
住民はマンション建設反対の～をした The residents conducted *a* protest *movement* against a high-rise apartment building.
—員 a canvasser. —費 running expenses. 労働— labor movement. 学生— student movement. 政治— political activities. 大衆— a mass movement.
3〖物体の〗 motion. ¶ニュートンは物体の～に関する法則を発見した Newton discovered the law of the *motion* of bodies.
この条件のもとでは, その物体はどのような～を起こすか In what way do bodies *move* under this condition?
—量〔物理〕 momentum. ¶～量保存の法則 the law of conservation of *momentum*.

うんぬん【云云】 and so on; and so forth. ¶～する comment (*on*); criticize. 最近たばこは害がある～という意見がある Of late the opinion is heard that smoking is harmful to the health *and so on*. われわれの決定について～しないでもらいたい Please don't *make* any *comment on* our decision.

うんのう【蘊奥】 profundity; (奥義) mysteries. ¶彼は生物学の～をきわめた He *has made a profound research of* biology. 彼の学問の～は計り知れない His *depth of learning* is unfathomable.

うんぱん【運搬】 conveyance; transportation; carriage. ¶荷物をトラックで～する *transport* parcels by truck. 新築の家に家具を～する *carry* the furniture to a newly-built house.
—費 carriage; portage; cartage. —車 a cart; a truck; a wagon; a lorry. —人 a carrier; (人夫) a porter.

うんまかせ【運任せ】 ¶すべて～です I *submit* everything *to fate*. / I *leave myself to fate*.

うんめい【運命】 fate ; fortune.
1〖運命を〗¶ きみと～をともにするよ I will cast 〔in〕 my *lot* with you.
船長は船と～をともにした The captain went down with the ship. / The captain shared the *fate* of the vessel.
われわれは自分から～を切り開いてゆかねばならぬ We must seek our *fortune* for ourselves. / We should carve 〔out〕 our own *fortune*.
死か生かいよいよ～を決するときがきた The *fatal* hour has come at last.
これは国の～を左右するほどの大事件だ This is a serious problem which will decide the *fate* of the country.
2〖運命に〗¶ 彼は異国でひとり死ぬ～にあった He *was destined* (≒ *fated*) to die alone in a foreign land.
するだけのことはしたから，あとは～に任せよう We have done our best. Let's leave the rest to *fate*.
3〖運命は〗¶ 生まれる前から人の～は定められているのか Is your *destiny* determined before you are born?
人間の～はわからぬものだ No one can foretell his *destiny*. / No one can tell what will happen to us tomorrow. / Our *destiny* is a sealed book to us.
4〖運命と〗¶ こうなるのも～とあきらめるな Don't submit to *fate*.
これも～とあきらめなさい You must resign yourself to your *fate*.
5〖運命の〗¶ 自己の～の支配者となれ Be the master of your *destiny*. / Control your own *destiny*.
～のいたずらか愛しあっているふたりはついに結ばれなかった Perhaps it was *the irony of fate* that prevented the lovers from getting married.
～の女神は彼にほほえみかけていた *Fortune* smiled on him.
彼は～の寵児(ちょうじ)といってよい *Lady Luck* seems to be smiling at him.
—論 fatalism. **—論者** a fatalist.
うんも【雲母】〖鉱物〗 mica.
うんゆ【運輸】 transportation ; conveyance ; traffic 〔service〕.
—会社 a transportation company ; a shipping agency. **—機関** transportation facilities ; means of transportation. **—省(大臣)** the Ministry (Minister) of Transport. **鉄道—** railway transportation ; (業務) railway traffic. **陸上—** overland transportation.
うんよう【運用】（適用） application ; (実施) practical use ; (投資) investment.
¶ 彼は規則の～の仕方を知らない He does not know how to *apply* the rules. 資金はどう～するつもりですか How are you going to *employ* the funds? 日本人は概して英語の～能力に欠ける The Japanese people, in general, lack *practical ability* in English.

え

え【絵】（一般的） a picture ; (鉛筆・クレヨン画) a drawing ; (水彩・油彩) a painting ; (下絵・写生画) a sketch ; (さし絵) an illustration.
¶ ターナーの～ a Turner. ～のような(美しい)景色 a *picturesque* scenery. ～の本(画集) a *picture* book. 彼は～がじょうずだ He is good at *painting*. / He *draws* well. / He is *a good painter*. ～が好きだ I like *painting*. ネコの～をかく *draw* (≒ *make*) *a picture of* a cat. この雑誌は～が多い This magazine has a lot of *pictures* in it. / This magazine is illustrated with many *pictures*. 壁に～を掛ける hang *a picture* on the wall. 彼がこの～をかいた He did this *painting*. 彼女は～にかいたような美人だ She is *a picture of* beauty.
え【柄】 a handle. ¶ 金づちの～ the *handle* of a hammer. ナイフの～ the *haft* of a knife. おのの～ the *shaft* of an ax. ほうきの～ a broomstick. ～の長いひしゃく a long-*handled* ladle.
え【餌】 ⇒えさ
エアターミナル an air terminal.
エアブレーキ an air brake.
エアポケット an air pocket.
エアメール air mail.
えい【栄】 honor ; distinction.
えい【頴】〖植物〗 an arista ; an awn.
えい【嬰】〖音楽〗 a sharp. ¶ ～ロ短調 B *sharp* minor.
えいい【鋭意】 vigorously ; whole-heartedly.
えいえい【営々】 ¶ 彼は～と働いた He worked *hard*. 彼は～と商売を築き上げた He built up the (≒ his) business *tirelessly* (≒ *with unceasing effort*).
えいえん【永遠】 eternity. ¶ ～の女性 an *eternal* woman. 彼は～の眠りについた He passed away. / He entered into *eternal* sleep. それは～に解けないなぞだろう It will remain a riddle *for ever*. 彼の作品の中に偉大な芸術の～の美を見いだす We see the *timeless* beauty of great art in his work.
えいか【英貨】 British currency ; British money ; sterling. ¶ ～5ポンド five pounds

え

sterling. この本は〜でいくらになりますか How much would this book be *in English currency*?

えいが【映画】 a movie; a [motion] picture; a film; (集合的に) the movies; the screen; 英 the cinema.

¶ 〜に行く go to *the movies* (特定の映画でない場合は the movies という). 〜を撮影する shoot *a film*. 小説を〜化する make *a movie* based on a novel; bring a novel to *the screen*. その〜はどこでやっていますか Where is that *movie* on? 〜は好きですか Are you interested in the *movies*? ここでおもしろい〜をやっている *An* interesting *movie* is showing here. (showing は映画にのみ用いる). その〜は近く封切られる予定だ The *movie* is soon to be released. この小説は〜に向く(向かない) This novel *films* well (ill). 彼の劇が〜用に脚色された His play was adapted for *the screen*.

—界 the motion picture world (≒ business); the filmdom; 米 the screendom. —館 a motion picture theater; (口語) a movie house (米でも映画館名にはしばしば Theatre とつづる). —祭 a film festival. —スター a movie star. —俳優(女優) a movie actor (actress). —評論家 a film critic. —ファン a movie fan; a movie goer. 教育— an educational film. 記録— a documentary. 天然色— a technicolor film (商標名). ニュース— a newsreel.

えいが【栄華】 (繁栄) glory; splendor; prosperities; (ぜいたく) luxury. ¶ 〜の生活を送る live an *extravagant* (≒ a *sumptuous*) life; live in *luxury* (≒ *grand style*).

えいかいわ【英会話】 English conversation.

えいかく【鋭角】〔数学〕an acute angle.

¶ 〜をなす make *an acute angle* (*with*).

—三角形 an acute-angled triangle.

えいがく【英学】 the study of English.

えいかん【栄冠】 ¶ 彼の頭上に勝利の〜は輝くであろう He will *glory* in victory.

えいき【英気】 vigor; strength. ¶ 〜を養う build up *one's strength* (≒ *energy*).

えいきゅう【永久】 permanence; permanency. ¶ 〜に戦争を放棄する renounce war *forever*. 〜の愛 *everlasting* love. 霊魂は〜に不滅である The soul *is immortal*.

—運動 perpetual motion. —歯 a permanent tooth.

えいきょう【影響】 influence; an effect.

¶ 人心に深い〜を与える produce *a* powerful *effect* on the mind of people. 戦争の〜はいまだに生活のあちこちで感じられる The *influences* (≒ *repercussions*) of the last war are still felt in every aspect of our life. 多くの人が彼から深い〜を受けた There are many people who *were* deeply *influenced by* him. 母親は子どもの人格形成に強い〜力を持っている Mothers *have* strong *influence on* the character development of their children.

えいぎょう【営業】 business. ¶ 日曜日でも〜していますか Are they open on Sundays too? 日曜日は〜していない They are closed on Sundays. あの店は4月に〜を始めた The store opened in April.

—時間 business (≒ office) hours. —所 a place of business. —停止 suspension of an operating license. —費 operating costs. —品目 a line of business. —妨害 interference with business.

えいけつ【英傑】 a great man; a hero; a master mind.

えいこ【栄枯】 ¶ 〜盛衰は世の習い Life has many *vicissitudes*.

えいご【英語】 English; the English language. ¶ じょうずな〜 excellent (≒ perfect) *English*. へたな〜 broken (≒ poor) *English*. 〜の先生 an *English* teacher (teacher に強勢をおくと「イギリス人の教師」となる). 〜の試験 an examination in *English*. 〜の教科書 an *English* textbook. 〜を話す speak *English*. 〜で話す speak in *English*. この花は〜でなんというか What is this flower called in *English*? 日本語の「渋い」にあたる〜はない There is no *English* equivalent for the Japanese "shibui." 彼は〜がへただ(うまい) He is poor (good) at *English*.

—国民 an English-speaking people. アメリカ— American English. 現代— present-day English. 商業— business English. 標準— standard English; 英 Queen's (≒ King's) English.

えいこう【栄光】 glory; honor. ¶ 神の〜をたたえる *glorify* God.

えいこう【曳航】 ¶ 船を港に〜する *tow* a ship into a harbor.

えいごう【永劫】 ¶ 地球の回転は未来〜に続くであろう The rotation of the earth will continue *throughout all eternity*.

えいこうだん【曳光弾】 a tracer bullet.

えいこく【英国】 England; [Great] Britain; the United Kingdom (略して U.K.).

えいさい【英才】 (才能) unusual talent; (人) a man of great talent.

—教育 special education for gifted children.

えいさくぶん【英作文】 (学課) English composition; (書いたもの) an English composition.

えいし【英詩】 (詩の1編) an English poem; (総称) English poetry.

えいじ【英字】 an English letter.

—新聞 an English [language] newspaper; a newspaper in English.

えいじ【嬰児】 an infant; a baby.

えいしゃ【映射】 reflection.

えいしゃ【映写】 projection. ¶ 8ミリを〜しよう Let's *project* the 8 mm film *on* the screen.

—機 a [film] projector. —技師 a projectionist. —時間 the running time (*for* a film). —室 a projection booth.

えいじゅう【永住】 ¶ こんな所に〜したくない I don't want to *settle down* in such a place.

—権 the right of permanent residence.

—地 a place of permanent residence.

えいしょ【英書】an English book.

えいしょう【詠唱】〘音楽〙an aria.

えいしょう【栄称】an honorable title.

えいしょく【栄職】a high (≒ an honorable) position (≒ post).

えい·ずる【映ずる】¶ 夕日が雲に〜じて美しいながめだ What a beautiful view with clouds *reflecting* the setting sun! 湖畔の山影が水面に〜じている The hills by the lake *are reflected* in the water. 日本はそのアメリカ人にどう〜じただろう I wonder how Japan *struck* (≒ *impressed*) the American.

えいせい【永世】—中立 permanent neutrality. —中立国 a permanently neutral country.

えいせい【衛生】sanitation; hygiene; health. ¶ 不〜な生活状態 *insanitary* (≒ *unsanitary*) living conditions. 彼らは〜観念がない They have no sense of *hygiene* (≒ *sanitation*). 〜状態を改善する improve *sanitary* conditions.

—学 hygiene. —学者 a sanitarian. —管理 health control. —工学 sanitary engineering. —試験所 a hygienic laboratory. —設備 health facilities. 公衆— public health. 精神— mental hygiene.

えいせい【衛星】a satellite.

—国 a satellite country. —都市 a satellite city. 人工— a man-made satellite; an artificial satellite. 通信— a communications satellite.

えいそう【営倉】a guardhouse. ¶ 彼は〜に入れられた He was confined in the *guardhouse*.

えいぞう【営造】¶ 〜する build; construct.

—物 a building; a structure.

えいぞう【映像】¶ テレビの〜 *an image* (≒ *a picture*) on a TV screen. このテレビの〜は鮮明だ This television set gives *a* clear *picture*.

えいぞく【永続】perpetuity; permanence. ¶ こんな状態は〜しないだろう This situation will not *last long*.

えいたい【永代】permanence. ¶ 〜の permanent; perpetual.

—借地権〘法律〙a perpetual lease. —所有権〘法律〙perpetuity; perpetual ownership.

えいたつ【栄達】advancement. ¶ 今私は一身の〜など考える余裕はない I have no time to be concerned with my own personal *advancement*.

えいたん【詠嘆】exclamation.

えいだん【英断】resolution; decisive judgment; (処置) a drastic measure. ¶ 彼の〜を待つ We await his *wise decision*. 〜を下す take *a decisive measure*. 〜に欠く waver in making *the decision*.

えいだん【営団】a corporation.

えいち【英知】wisdom. ¶ 非凡な〜を必要とする require unusual *acumen*. 彼は〜に輝いていた He was endowed with *wisdom* (≒ *a brilliant mind*).

えいてん【栄典】(儀式) a ceremony; (位階·勲章など) honors. ¶ 〜制度は廃止された *Decorations of honor* have been discarded.

えいてん【栄転】promotion; preferment. ¶ 彼は〜のチャンスを逃がした He missed a chance of *promotion*. 彼は地方支店の支店長から本社の総務部長に〜した He *was promoted from* the manager of a local branch *to* the general manager of the head office.

えいトン【英トン·英噸】an English (≒ a long) ton.

えいねん【永年】—勤続者 a long-time employee.

えいびん【鋭敏】sharpness; keenness; (知力の) acumen. ¶ 犬は耳が〜だ A dog has *sharp* (≒ *keen*) ears. / A dog has a *keen* sense of hearing. 彼女には〜な美的感覚がある She has a *fine* sense of beauty. 犬は〜な臭覚で犯人の跡をつけた The dog followed the criminal with *the sharp sense of smell* (≒ *its good nose*).

えいぶん【英文】English〔writing〕; an English sentence. ¶ 〜の手紙 a letter〔*written*〕*in English*. 〜からの引用 quotations from *English writings*. 〜のリポートを書く write a report *in English*. 達者な〜を書く write *English* well.

—科 the department of English〔literature〕. —タイプ (器具) an English typewriter; (学科目) typing (typewriting としない).

—和訳 English-Japanese translation; translation from English into Japanese. ¶ 〜和訳せよ Put the *English* into Japanese.

えいぶんがく【英文学】English literature (冠詞なし).

—概説 a survey of (≒ an introduction to) English literature. —教師 a professor of English. —史 a history of English literature. —者 a scholar of English literature.

えいぶんぽう【英文法】English grammar.

えいべい【英米】England and America.

—人 the English and Americans.

えいべつ【永別】parting forever; the last parting.

えいほう【英法】British (≒ English) law.

えいほう【鋭鋒】¶ 敵の〜をくじく repel the *brunt* of the enemy's attack. 敵の〜をまともに受ける be in the *brunt* of the enemy's attack.

えいまい【英邁】¶ 〜な君主 a *bright, magnanimous* ruler.

えいみん【永眠】¶ 彼はパリで〜した He *passed away* in Paris. スイスが彼の〜の地となった Switzerland was his final resting place.

えいやく【英訳】an English translation.

¶「羅生門」の〜 *an English translation* (≒ *version*) of the "Rashomon." 小説を〜する *put* (≒ *translate*) a novel *into English*.

えいゆう【英雄】a hero. ¶ 〜的行為 a *heroic* conduct; heroism. 〜視する make *a hero*

え

of (*a person*).
—崇拝 hero worship. 国民的— a national hero.

えいよ【栄誉】honor; glory.

えいよう【栄養】nourishment; nutrition.
¶ ~に富む食物 *nutritious* (≒ *nourishing*) food; nutriment. この食物にはあまり~がない This food is low in *nourishment*.
—価 nutritive value. —学 dietetics. —士 a dietitian; a dietician. —失調 malnutrition. —素 a nutrient. —不良 undernourishment. ¶ ~不良の赤ちゃん an *undernourished* baby. —物 nourishment; nutritious food. ¶ ~物をとる take *nourishment*.

えいり【営利】moneymaking. ¶ 非~的な団体 a *nonprofit* organization. あの学校は~的すぎる That school *is* too *commercialized*.
—事業(会社) a commercial enterprise. —主義 commercialism.

えいり【鋭利】sharpness; keenness. ¶ ~なかみそりの刃 a *sharp* razor blade. ~な頭脳 a *keen* mind.

えいりょう【英領】a British territory; (イギリス直轄植民地) a 〔British〕 Crown Colony. ¶ この島は~だ This island is *a British territory*.

えいりん【営林】forest management.
—局 the Forest Service. —署 a forest service station; a forest service field office.

えいれい【英霊】the spirit of the deceased.

えいれんぽう【英連邦】the British Commonwealth 〔of Nations〕.

えいわ【英和】—辞典 an English-Japanese dictionary.

ええ (肯定) yes; (問い返し) What?; (ためらい) Well / Let me see. / Let's see. (くだけた形).
¶ ~そうなの? Really? / Is that so?

エーカー an acre.

エース an ace. ¶ 彼はジャイアンツの~(主戦投手)だ He is *an ace pitcher* in the Giants.

エーテル 〖化学〗ether. ¶ ~〔性〕の ethereal.

エービーシー【ABC】(アルファベット) the alphabet; (初歩) the elements; the ABC.
¶ 彼は英語は~も知らない He doesn't know even *the ABC* of English. ~順に in *alphabetical* order; alphabetically.

エープリルフール (その日) April Fools' Day; (人) an April fool.

エール a yell. ¶ われわれは試合後~を交換した We exchanged *yells* after the game.

えがお【笑顔】a smiling face (≒ look); a smile. ¶ 優しい~ *a* kindly *smile*. かわいらしい~ *a* lovely *smile*. ~で with *a smile*; smilingly. 彼女はぼくに~を見せた She *smiled at* me. 彼は~でわれわれを迎えてくれた He greeted us with *a smile*. 彼女は無理に~を見せた She forced *a smile* on her face.

えかき【絵かき】a painter; an artist.

えが・く【描く】¶ その小説は当時の社会を鮮やかに~いている The novel vividly *describes* (≒ *depicts*) the society of those days. 彼女は子どもたちが芝生で遊んでいる姿を胸に~いた She *imagined* (≒ *pictured to herself*) her children playing out on the lawn.

えがた・い【得難い】¶ またと~い品 a very *rare* (≒ *valuable*) article. 外遊できる~いチャンスを逸した I missed a *very good* chance to go abroad. この種の本は近ごろではなかなか~い This kind of book *is* very *hard to get* nowadays. 彼はまったく~い人物だ He is *one in a thousand*.

えき【易】fortunetelling; divination.
¶ ~を見てもらった I had my *fortune* told.
—学 the science of fortunetelling.

えき【益】use; good. ¶ 彼らと議論してもなんの~もない It's *useless* (≒ 〔*of*〕 *no use*) to argue with them. その発明は世に~するところが多いだろう The invention will *be* very *useful* (≒ *do* much *good*) *to* the world. それは~より害が多いでしょう It will do more harm than *good*. 彼に会ってなんの~があるのか What's *the use* of seeing him?

えき【液】(果実の) juice; (液体) a liquid; (溶液) 〔a〕 solution.

えき【駅】a railroad (≒ 英 railway) station; 米 a depot. ¶ 東京~ Tokyo *Station* (冠詞はつかない).
貨物— a freight station. 終着— 米 a terminal 〔station〕; 英 a terminus. 中央— the central station. 乗換— a transfer station. 発(着)— a departing (an arrival) station.

えきいん【駅員】a station employee.

えきか【液化】liquefaction. ¶ ~する liquefy. アンモニアが~される Ammonia *is changed into a liquid*.
—ガス liquefied gas.

エキジビション an exhibition.
—ゲーム an exhibition game.

えきしゃ【易者】a fortuneteller.

エキス extract. ¶ 牛肉の~ beef *extract*.

エキストラ an extra.

エキスパート an expert.

エキゾチック ¶ ~な exotic. 彼女には~なところがある There is something *exotic* about her.

えきたい【液体】〔a〕 liquid; fluid.
—空気 liquid air. —酸素 liquid oxygen. —燃料 liquid fuel.

えきちゅう【益虫】a useful insect.

えきちょう【益鳥】a useful bird.

えきちょう【駅長】a station agent; 英 a stationmaster.

えきでん【駅伝】a long-distance relay race.

えきばしゃ【駅馬車】a stagecoach.

えきびょう【疫病】(伝染病) an epidemic; (ペストなど) a pestilence; a plague.
¶ ~を撲滅する stamp out *an epidemic*. いろいろな~が蔓延(まんえん)している *Pestilences* are spreading out.

えきべん【駅弁】a lunch 〔sold on a railroad platform〕.

えきむ【役務】labor; services.
—賠償 reparation in labor.

えきり【疫痢】〖医学〗children's dysentery.
えくぼ【笑窪】a dimple. ¶ 彼女は笑うと～ができた A smile *dimpled* her face. / Her cheeks *dimpled* with smiles.
えぐ・る【抉る】 ¶ 河岸が洪水で～りとられた The river bank *was hollowed out* by the flood. 木をのみで～った I *gouged* the wood *out* with a chisel. それを聞いて胸を～られる思いがした I felt as if my heart were breaking to hear that.
エクレア〔an〕éclair.（フランス語から）.
えげつない（あくどい）nasty;（下品な）mean; dirty;（いやらしい）disagreeable.
エゴ ego.
エゴイスト an egoist; egotist.
エゴイズム egoism; egotism.
えこう【回向】 ¶ ～する hold a memorial service〔*for the dead*〕.
—料 the fee for a memorial service.
エコー an echo.
えごころ【絵心】¶ 彼には～がある（絵がうまい）He is good at painting. /（絵がわかる）He has a taste for painting.
えこじ【依怙地】obstinacy. ¶ ～な人 a *stubborn* man. ～になって obstinately.
えこひいき【依怙贔屓】partiality. ¶ ～の partial; unfair. あの先生は生徒に～する The teacher *is partial to* some of his pupils. 彼は私たちを～なしに扱ってくれた He treated us *fairly*.
えさ【餌】（魚・鳥の） food; feed;（釣りの）a bait;（人を誘いこむための）a bait; a lure.
¶ 魚に～をやる *feed* the fish. 釣り針に～をつける *bait* a hook. ～に食いつく take *a bait*. 人を～で釣る lure *a person* with *a bait*.
えさがし【絵捜し】a picture-puzzle.
えじき【餌食】a prey; a victim. ¶ そのシカはライオンの～になった The deer fell *a prey* to a lion.
エジプト Egypt.
—学 Egyptology. —人 an Egyptian.
えしゃく【会釈】a nod. ¶ 通り過ぎるときに彼の方に～した I *nodded to* him as I passed.
エスオーエス an SOS. ¶ 難破船が～を発信した The wrecked ship sent *an SOS* by radio.
えすがた【絵姿】a portrait; a picture.
エスカレーター an escalator.
エスカレート escalate. ¶ それは戦争を～することになろう It would *escalate* a war.
エスキモー an Eskimo.
エスケープ ¶ 彼は～した He *cut a lecture*（≒ *class*）.（学生用語）.
エスペラント Esperanto.
えせしんし【似非紳士】a specious gentleman.
えそ【壊疽】〖医学〗gangrene.
えぞぎく【蝦夷菊】〖植物〗a China aster.
えぞまつ【蝦夷松】〖植物〗a silver fir.
えそらごと【絵空事】an illusion; an imaginary thing.
えだ【枝】a branch;（小枝）a twig;（大枝）a bough. ¶ 植木屋は～をおろした The gardener cut off *branches*. その木は大きな～を張っていた The tree was spreading out big *boughs*.
えたい【得体】 ¶ ～の知れない男 a *mysterious* man. ～の知れない病気 *nondescripted* disease.
えだは【枝葉】（樹木の）branches and leaves;（物事の）digression. ¶ ～の問題にこだわるな Don't stick to *a side issue*.
えだぶり【枝ぶり】the shape of a tree. ¶ この松の～はよい This pine tree has a beautiful shape.
えだまめ【枝豆】green soybeans.
えたり【得たり】¶ ～賢しと（～や応と）その申し出に飛びついた I jumped at the offer *with avidity*. 彼は～とばかりその男を投げつけた He *lost no time in* throwing the man down.
エタン〖化学〗ethane.
エチオピア Ethiopia.
—人 an Ethiopian.
エチケット etiquette. ¶ 彼女は～をよく心得ている She knows *etiquette* very well. それは～に反している It is against *etiquette*.
エチル〖化学〗ethyl.
—アルコール ethyl alcohol.
エチレン〖化学〗ethylene.
えっ（驚き）Oh! / Eh! / Well!（疑問）What!
えつ【悦】 ¶ 彼女はひとり～に入っている She is pleased with herself.
えっきょう【越境】 ¶ 彼はついに～してスイスに入ることができた He could at last *cross the border* into Switzerland. 彼は息子を～入学させた He made his son enter a school outside his school district.
エックス X; x.
—線 x-rays; X-rays; Roentgen rays. —線検査 an x-ray examination.
えっけん【越権】arrogation. ¶ そんなことをするのは～だ It is *beyond your right* to do such a thing.
—行為 an act of arrogation.
えっけん【謁見】an audience. ¶ 彼は王の～をたまわった The king granted him *an audience*.
エッセイ an essay.
エッセイスト an essayist.
エッセンス essence. ¶ レモンの～ lemon *essence*.
エッチング〔an〕etching（an をつければ作品）.
えっとう【越冬】¶ 彼は南極で～している He *is passing the winter* in the Antarctic.
—資金 a winter allowance. —隊 a wintering party.
えつどく【閲読】careful reading;（文語）perusal. ¶ ～する read carefully; peruse.
えつねん【越年】¶ ～する pass the year-end.
—資金 a year-end allowance. —生植物 a biennial plant.
えっぺい【閲兵】inspection of troops.
¶ ～する *review*（≒ *inspect*）troops.
—式 a review of troops.
えつらん【閲覧】reading; perusal. ¶ ～する read; peruse.

え

—室 a reading room; a browsing room. —者 a reader; a visitor.

えて【得手】 ¶ ～不得手 *one's* strong and weak points.

エディプスコンプレックス 〔精神分析〕 Oedipus complex.

えてかって【得手勝手】 ¶ ～な男 a *selfish* (≒ an *egoistic*) man. ～なことを言うな Don't say a *selfish* thing. 彼は～なことをする He *acts selfishly* (≒ *has his own way*) in everything.

えてして ¶ ああいう男は～誤りを犯しがちだ Such a man *is apt* (≒ *is liable*) *to* make mistakes. 不平をこぼす者は～義務を実行しないものだ A grumbling person *is likely to* fail to do his duty. 私たちは～他の人々のことを考えないものだ We *have a tendency to* ignore the others.

エデン 〔聖書〕 Eden. ¶ ～の園 the Garden of *Eden*.

えど【江戸】 *Edo*; *Yedo*.
—時代 the *Edo* period. —文学 the literature of the *Edo* period. —趣味 the flavor of *Edo*.

えとく【会得】 ¶ 商売のこつを～するのは容易ではない It is not easy to *learn* how to handle business.

えどっこ【江戸っ子】 a person born and bred (≒ brought up) in Tokyo. ¶ 彼は生粋の～だ He is *an Edokko* to the backbone.

えな【胞衣】 〔解剖学〕 a placenta.

エナメル enamel.
—皮 enameled leather.

エネルギー energy. ¶ その仕事で彼は～を使い果たしてしまった The work has sapped his *energy*. / He *is* quite *exhausted* by (≒ from) the work. ～不滅の法則 the principle of the conservation of *energy*.
核— nuclear energy. 原子— atomic energy. 太陽— the sun's energy.

エネルギッシュ ¶ ～な男 an *energetic* man. ～に働く work *energetically*.

えのき【榎】 〔植物〕 a hackberry.

えのぐ【絵の具】 colors; paints; pigments. ¶ ～をぬる paint. ～を溶く dissolve *colors*. ～でかく paint in *colors*.
—ざら a palette. —ばけ a paintbrush. —箱 a paintbox. 油— oil colors; oils. 水彩— water color.

えはがき【絵葉書】 a postcard; a picture postcard. ¶ そこに着いたら～を送ります When I get there I will send you some *picture postcards*. ～ありがとう Thank you very much for sending me beautiful *picture postcards*.

えび【蝦・海老】 (イセエビ) a [spiny] lobster; (クルマエビ) a prawn; (小エビ) a shrimp.
¶ ～でタイを釣る throw a sprat to catch a mackerel (≒ whale).

えびす【恵比寿】 —顔 a smiling face.

エピソード an episode. ¶ 彼は数々のこっけいな～の持ち主だ He has many humorous *episodes*.

えびちゃ【海老茶】 ¶ ～のコート a *reddish brown* coat.

エフエム【FM】 〔電子工学〕 FM; F.M. (< *frequency modulation*). ¶ このラジオで～放送が聞けますか Can you tune this radio in to the *FM* program? ～で音楽を聞きたい I'd like to listen to music broadcast on the *FM* program.

エプロン an apron. ¶ 彼女は～をしたまま買い物に出かけた She went shopping *in an apron*.

えへん ¶ 彼は彼女の注意を引くために～とせき払いした He made a noise of "*Ahem!*" to call her attention.

エポック an epoch. ¶ 明治維新はわが国の歴史でひとつの～を画した The Meiji Restoration was *an epoch* in the history of our country.

エボナイト ebonite.

エホバ 〔聖書〕 Jehovah.

えほん【絵本】 a picture book; (さし絵入りの本) an illustrated book. ¶ この子は～を見るのが好きだ This child likes to look at *picture books*. ～は幼児教育にはたいせつだ *Illustrated books* are important for children's education.

えま【絵馬】 a votive picture (≒ tablet).
—堂 an *ex voto* gallery.

えまきもの【絵巻物】 a picture scroll. ¶ この小説は～をほうふつさせる This novel makes us visualize *a picture scroll*.

えみ【笑み】 a smile. ¶ 彼女は～を浮かべて私に話しかけた She spoke to me *with a smile*.

エメラルド 〔鉱物〕 emerald. ¶ 彼女は～の指輪をしている She wears an *emerald* ring.

えもいわれぬ【えも言われぬ】 ¶ この花は～いい香りがする This flower smells *indescribably* sweet. その景色は～ほど美しい The scenery is beautiful *beyond description*. / The scenery is *indescribably* beautiful.

えもの【得物】 a weapon. ¶ 彼らはてんでに～を持ってかけ出していった They went running with *a weapon* in their hands. これは手ごろの～だ This is *a* ready *weapon*.

えもの【獲物】 (狩猟の) game (集合名詞で単数扱い); (捕獲高) a bag; (分捕り品) a spoil. ¶ きょうは猟の～はなかった I did not get any *game* today. ～はカモが5羽だった I had *a bag* of five ducks.

えもん【衣紋】 ¶ ～を繕う adjust *one's kimono*.
—掛け a coat (≒ dress) hanger.

えら【鰓】 the gill[s] (*of* a fish).

エラー 〔野球〕 an error. ¶ 名選手だってときには～はする Even the best player sometimes *makes an error*. われわれのチームは～が多くて負けた Our team lost the game by many *errors*.

えら・い【偉い】 **1** 〘偉大な〙 great. ¶ ～い人 a *great* man.
外交官として彼は～い人物だ He is *great* as a diplomat.
～い人もいるものだ I did not expect to find such a *great* man.

だれもが彼を〜いといってほめる Everybody *makes much of* him.

将来この子は〜くなるだろう This child will *make a conspicuous figure* in the future.

彼は文部省の〜い役人だ He is an official *of high rank* in the Education Ministry.

それがこの紳士の〜いところだ That is where this gentleman's *greatness* lies.

彼は自分で〜いと思っている He thinks himself 〔*a*〕 *somebody*.

2 〖ひどい〗 ¶ 〜い暑さだった It was *awfully* hot.

きのうは〜い目に会った Yesterday I *had a hard time of it*.

〜い高いものを買った I bought something *far too* expensive.

〜い仕事を引き受けてしまった I agreed to take on an *extraordinary* job.

競馬で〜い損をした I lost *a lot* on a horse-race.

えら·ぶ 【選ぶ】 **1** 〖選択する〗 choose. ¶ 友だちは慎重に〜ぶべきだ You should *choose* your friends very carefully.

彼はその中でいちばん厚い本を〜んだ He *selected* the thickest book of them all.

自分の仕事は慎重に〜ばないと, あとで後悔する Unless you *decide* your own job carefully, you will repent of it later.

彼はよい〜び方をしたと思う I think he *made a good choice*.

この中から1冊〜びなさい *Choose* one book *from* among these.

フランス語かドイツ語のどちらかを〜びなさい You are required to *choose between* French and German.

このふたつの方法のうちよい方を〜んでほしい I want you to *choose* the better method of the two.

彼は金より愛を〜んだ He *chose* love *over* money.

彼女は彼にすばらしい贈り物を〜んだ She *chose* a nice present for him.

皆は彼を会計係に〜んだ Everybody *elected* him accountant.

これは彼女が自分で〜んだネックレスだ This is the necklace she *chose* herself.

2 〖選出する〗 ¶ 彼は委員のひとりに〜ばれた He *was selected* as a member of the committee.

彼はたったひとり〜ばれて会に参加した He *was singled out* for participation in the meeting.

彼は主将に〜ばれた He *was chosen* 〔*as*〕 captain.

3 〖より好む〗 prefer. ¶ 彼は学問より富のほうを〜んだ He *preferred* wealth *to* learning.

えらぶつ 【偉物】 (偉人) a great man; a respectable man.

えり 【襟】 (洋服の) a collar; (和服の) a neckband. ¶ 風が寒かったのでコートの〜を立てた The wind was so cold that I turned my coat *collar* up. 私たちは天皇陛下のおことばを〜を正して聞いた We listened to our Emperor's speech *with sincerity*.

えりあし 【襟足】 the nape of the neck. ¶ 彼女は〜が美しい She has *a* charming *nape*.

エリート the elite (複数扱い). ¶ 知的〜 *an* intellectual *elite*. 彼は〜だ He is *an elitist*. 彼にはいささか〜意識がある He has a touch of *elitism*.

えりがみ 【襟髪】 ¶ 彼女の〜をつかんだ I *took* her *by the back hair*. (定冠詞 the に注意).

えりくび 【襟首】 ¶ 彼はネコの〜をつかまえて外にほうり出した He seized the cat by *the scruff of the neck* and threw it out of the house.

えりごのみ 【選り好み】 ¶ 彼女は食べ物の〜が激しい She *is* very *particular about* her food. 〜する暇はありません You have no time to *pick and choose*.

えりしょう 【襟章】 a collar badge. ¶ クラスをはっきりさせるために〜をつける We wear *collar badges* to show our classes.

えりまき 【襟巻き】 a muffler; a scarf (複 米 scarfs; 英 scarves).

えりもと 【襟元】 ¶ 〜が寒い I feel cold *at the neck*. 〜はよごれやすい The *neck* is easily soiled.

える 【得る】 (獲得する) gain; earn; (好意を) win; (見つける) find. ¶ 彼のおかげで私は仕事を得ることができた I was able to *find* work thanks to him.

その発明によって彼は名声を得た He *gained* fame by the invention.

努力の結果彼は富と地位を得た As a result of his efforts he *acquired* wealth and position.

彼の話から大いに得るところがあった I *learned* a lot of things from his speech.

知識は主として本から得られる Knowledge *is acquired* chiefly through books.

彼はまだ賞を得たことがない He *has* never *won* a prize.

彼らのチームが勝利を得たのは当然だった It was natural that their team should *have won* the victory.

仕事の成功で彼は力を得た He *was encouraged* by his success in his work.

彼が現在の地位を得たのは最近だ He *has obtained* this position only recently.

エルピー an LP 〔record〕 (複 LPs; LP's) (LP は a *long-playing* record から作った登録商標).

エレガンス elegance.

エレガント ¶ 〜なお嬢さん an *elegant* young girl. 彼女の服装は〜だ She *is elegant in* dress.

エレクトロニクス electronics.

エレクトロン 〖物理〗 an electron.

エレジー an elegy.

エレベーター 米 an elevator; 英 a lift. ¶ この〜は上へ行きますか Is this *elevator* going up?

エロ eroticism. ¶ 〜な人 an *erotic* person.

—本 (集合的) erotica; pornography; (1冊の) an *obscene* book.

エロチシズム eroticism.

えん 【円】 **1** 〖円い輪〗 a circle. ¶ ジェット機が空で〜を描いて飛んでいる A jet plane *is circling*

え

in the sky. ～を作って踊る *make a circle* and have a dance.

2 〖貨幣〗 a yen (記号は¥). ¶ それは500～で買った I bought it for five hundred *yen*.

えん【宴】 a feast; a banquet. ¶ ～を催す give (⇆ hold) *a banquet*. ～はいまが盛りです The *banquet* is at its highest now.

えん【縁】 **1** 〖血縁の結びつき〗 ¶ 親子の～を切るわけにはいかぬ A parent and a child cannot be strangers.

彼と義兄弟の～を結んだ He became my sworn brother.

彼女とは遠い～続きだ She is remotely related to me.

2 〖夫婦の結びつき〗 ¶ ～は異なものだ There is no telling which two will make a couple.

夫婦の～を結んだからにはそう簡単には別れられない Once tied, the nuptial *knot* cannot be easily untied.

3 〖縁談〗 ¶ よい～があったら娘に世話してください If you happen to know *a* good *match* for my daughter, will you kindly let us know?

4 〖運命の引き合わせ〗 ¶ これも前世の～でしょう(悪いことを前提としている場合) Perhaps, this is a debt I owe to *fate* (⇆ *destiny*).

またどんなご～でお会いできるかわかりません I hope *fate* will bring us together again some day.

これをご～にどうぞよろしく I hope to see more of you.

不思議な～でふたりは結ばれた The couple were united by a kind of miracle.

娘は～あってアメリカ人と結婚した My daughter married an American by *a* happy *chance*.

この縁談はご～がなかったものとあきらめてください May I ask you to forget this marriage talk?

～なき衆生は度しがたい A lost soul is given to the devil. / A lost soul is beyond redemption / A lost soul is hard to be saved.

5 〖かかわりあい・関係〗 ¶ ぼくは金に～がないらしい Money seems to fly away from me.

そんな人とは～もゆかりもありません I have nothing to do with such a man.

その話はぼくには～もゆかりもないことだ That's none of my business. / That has nothing to do with me at all.

金の切れ目が～の切れ目 Poverty drives love away. / When poverty comes in at the door, love flies away out of the window.

6 〖縁がわ〗 ¶ 彼は～から落ちてけがをした He fell from the 〔side〕 *veranda* and hurt himself.

～の端まで出て月をながめた I walked out to the edge of the *veranda* to gaze at the moon.

～の下でなにか音がする A strange noise comes from *under the floor*.

彼は～の下の力持ちばかりやらされている He is always forced to work *in the backstage* (⇆ *background*). / His *portion is* always *a thankless job* (⇆ *task*).

えんいん【延引】 delay; postponement.

えんいん【遠因】 an indirect cause. ¶ 洪水の～ *a remote cause* of a flood. 毎日の努力が最後の成功の～となる Daily efforts will be *an indirect cause* of a final success.

えんえい【遠泳】 a long-distance swim; endurance swimming. ¶ ～する have *a long-distance swim*.

えんえき【演繹】〔論理〕 deduction. ¶ ～する deduce.

—法 the deductive method.

えんえん【延延】 ¶ ～長蛇(ちょうだ)の列をなして in a *long* queue. 試合は～4時間も続いた The game lasted *as long as* four hours.

えんえん【炎炎】 ¶ キャンプファイアが～と燃えさかっていた The camp fire *was blazing up*. 消防隊がきたとき建物は～と燃えていた When the fire company arrived, the building was *in flames*.

えんか【塩化】〔化学〕 —カリウム potassium chloride. —ナトリウム sodium chloride. —物 a chloride.

えんかい【沿海】 the coast.

えんかい【宴会】 a banquet; a feast; a dinner party. ¶ 非常に盛大な～ *a* most magnificent *banquet*. ～を催す give (⇆ hold) *a banquet*.

—場 a banquet hall.

えんがい【煙害】 injury from smoke; air pollution.

えんがい【塩害】 damage from salt water.

えんがい【円蓋】〔建築〕 a dome; a cupola.

えんかく【沿革】 outline; history; origin and development. ¶ 学校の～を簡単に教えてください Please tell me the *history* of your school in brief.

えんかく【遠隔】 ¶ ～の地に住む live in a *remote* place.

—制御(操縦)〔電気〕〔通信〕 remote control.

えんかし【演歌師】 a street singer.

えんかつ【円滑】 smoothness. ¶ 議長は議事を～に運んだ The chairman expedited the proceedings *smoothly*. すべて～にいった Everything went on *smoothly*.

えんがわ【縁側】 a veranda; a verandah. ⇒ えん(縁)

えんかん【鉛管】 a lead pipe.

えんがん【沿岸】 the coast; the shore. ¶ 私の郷里は新潟の日本海の～にある My hometown lies *on the coast of* the Japan Sea in Niigata Prefecture.

—漁業 coastal fishery; inshore fishing. **—**航路 coasting service. **—**線 a coastline.

えんき【延期】 postponement; (会合の) adjournment. ¶ 出発を土曜日まで～した I *put off* my departure till Saturday. 試合は雨で～された The game *was postponed* because of rain. / The game *was washed off*. 調査は1か月間～された The inquiry *was adjourned* for a month. ～で計画が狂った The *delay* upset my plans.

えんき【塩基】〔化学〕 a base.

—性塩 basic salt. **—類** basic salts. 有機— an organic base.

えんぎ【演技】 a performance. ¶ 彼女のすばらしい～にはまったく感心した I was deeply moved (≒ touched) by her splendid *performance*. 監督は俳優たちに～のしかたを教えていた The director was instructing the actors how to *act*.

えんぎ【縁起】 ¶ きょうは～がよさそうだ Today is going to be my *lucky* day! / Fortune seems to smile on me today. ～でもない It would bring *bad luck*. 私は～などかつがない I never believe in *omens*. / I *am* not *superstitious*. ～直しに一杯やろう Let's have a drink in order to change the *luck*.

えんきょく【婉曲】 ¶ 彼は私を～にほめた He praised me *in a roundabout way* (≒ *in euphemistic expressions*). 私は指名を～にことわった I refused my nomination in an *indirect* expression.

えんきょり【遠距離】 a long distance. ¶ そんな～をわざわざ訪ねてくださいましてありがとうございます It is very kind of you to come over *from* such *a distant place*.
—弾道弾 a long-range ballistic missile.

えんきり【縁切り】 dissolution of a tie; separation.

えんきん【遠近】 ¶ ～を問わず regardless of *distance*. 片目で見ると～がよくわからない With one eye closed we can't see things *in the right perspective*.
—法 perspective.

えんぐみ【縁組み】 (結婚) [a] marriage; (養子の) [an] adoption.

えんぐん【援軍】 a reinforcement. ¶ 前線に～を送らねばならない We must send *reinforcements* to the front.

えんけい【円形】 a circle.
—校舎 a circular school building; a rotunda (一般に丸屋根のある円形の建物をいう).
—劇場 an amphitheater.

えんけい【遠景】 a distant view.

えんげい【園芸】 gardening; horticulture.
—家 a gardener; a horticulturist. **—用具** a gardening tool.

えんげい【演芸】 an entertainment; a variety show; 米 vaudeville.
—場 an entertainment hall; (よせ) a variety hall; a music hall.

エンゲージリング an engagement ring.

えんげき【演劇】 a play; the drama.
—批評家 a dramatic critic. **—界** the theatrical world.

エンゲル —係数 〘経済〙 Engel's coefficient.

えんこ【円弧】 an arc.

えんこ【塩湖】 a salt lake.

えんこ【縁故】 (縁続き) relation; connection; (人) a relative. ¶ 彼は～を頼って就職した He got a job through his *relative*. 私たちの間にはなんの～もない There is no *family connection* between us. あの方とどういうご～がおありですか How *are* you *connected with* him?

えんご【援護】 protection; help. ¶ 砲兵は彼らの上陸を～した The artillery *covered* their landing.

えんこう【鉛鉱】 lead mine.

えんこ・する ¶ バスが～した The bus *broke down*. 坊や, そんな所に～しちゃだめ You won't *sit down* there, baby.

えんこん【怨恨】 a grudge; ill will.

えんさ【怨嗟】 ¶ 彼は国民～の的となった He became the object of *resentment* all over the country.

えんざい【冤罪】 a false charge. ¶ 彼は～をそそぎたかった He wanted to prove his innocence.

えんさん【塩酸】 〘化学〙 hydrochloric acid.
—ガス hydrochloric acid gas.

えんざん【演算】 ⇒うんざん

えんし【遠視】 far-sightedness. ¶ ～の眼鏡 *far-sight* glasses. 彼は～である He *is far-sighted*.

えんじ【園児】 a kindergarten child.

えんじ【臙脂】 dark red.

エンジェル an angel.

えんじつてん【遠日点】 〘天文〙 the aphelion (複 aphelia).

エンジニア an engineer.

えんじゃ【縁者】 a relative; a relation.

えんしゅう【円周】 [a] circumference.
¶ ～2メートルの円 a circle two meters *round* (≒ *in circumference*).
—率 pi [pai] (記号 π).

えんしゅう【演習】 a practice; (ゼミナール) a seminar. ¶ 陸軍が大～をした The army held great *maneuvers*. 英文法の～をした We did *exercises* in English grammar.
射撃— a rifle training (≒ practice). **英文学—** a seminar in English literature. **代数問題—** exercises in algebra. **予行—** a rehearsal. ¶ 予行～をしておこう Let's have *a rehearsal*, shall we?

えんじゅく【円熟】 maturity. ¶ 彼の芸は30で～の境に達した His art reached *maturity* at thirty. 人は年齢と経験を積んで～してくる We *mature* by age and experience. 彼は性格が～している He has a *mellow* character.

えんしゅつ【演出】 production. ¶ この劇はA氏の～である This play *is produced by* Mr. A. 彼はみずからこの事件を～した He *directed* (≒ *cooked*) this case himself.
—家 米 a [stage] director; 英 a producer.

えんしょ【炎暑】 ¶ 夏の～には耐えられない I can't stand *the extreme heat* of summer days.

えんじょ【援助】 help; assistance. ¶ その子どもに～の手を差し伸べた I gave the child a *helping* hand. ～を申し出た I offered *help*. できるかぎりのご～をいたします I will give you all the *help* in my power. 彼は乏しい収入をさいて両親を～している He *helps* his parents out of his small income. 彼に財政的～を頼んだ I asked him for financial *assistance*.

えんしょう【延焼】 ¶ 火事はまわりに～している The fire *is spreading* around. 私の家は～を

え

免れた My house escaped catching fire from next door.

えんしょう【炎症】〖医学〗inflammation. ¶ 目はほこりで～を起こしている The eyes *are inflamed with* dust. 体のその部分は～を起こしやすい That part of the body is easy to *inflame*. 傷口が～を起こさないように注意した I took care to keep the wound from *inflammation*. ～性の inflammatory.

えんじょう【炎上】¶ ～する be burnt down; be destroyed by fire.

えんしん【円心】the center of a circle.

えんしん【遠心】—分離機 a centrifugal machine. —ポンプ a centrifugal pump. —力 centrifugal force.

エンジン an engine. ¶ ～を動かす start the *engine*. ～を止める stop the *engine*. やっと～がかかった The *engine* started at last. ～がこわれた The *engine* broke down.

ディーゼル— a Diesel engine.

えんじん【円陣】a circle. ¶ ～を作る form *a circle*.

えんじん【猿人】〖人類学〗a pithecanthrope.

えんすい【円錐】a cone.

—曲線 conic [section]; a conic. —花序〖植物〗a panicle. —火山 a conical volcano.

えんすい【塩水】salt water.

—湖 a salt-water lake; a saline lake.

えんずい【延髄】〖解剖〗the medulla oblongata.

えん·ずる【演ずる】¶ 彼女はシンデレラの役を～じた She *played* (⇆ *performed*) the part of Cinderella. 彼はそのことに重要な役割を～じた He *played* an important part in it. 人前で醜態を～じた I *made a fool of myself* in company.

えんせい【遠征】an expedition. ¶ 彼らは～の途についた They started on the *expedition*. 彼らはペルシアまで～した They made their *expedition* as far as Persia. われわれは～の試合に勝った We won in *the away game*. われわれは京都のA校へ～に出かけた We *visited* A school in Kyoto *for a game*.

—軍 an expeditionary force; (スポーツ) a visiting team; the visitors.

えんせい【厭世】pessimism. ¶ 彼の人生観はかなり～的なものであった His view of life *was* very *pessimistic*. 彼女は～自殺をした She killed herself because she lost all hope in life.

えんせき【宴席】a [dinner] party. ¶ ～に出る attend *a banquet* (⇆ *a party*).

えんぜつ【演説】[a] speech. ¶ 彼は短い～をした He made *a* short *speech*. 彼は映画の歴史についてわれわれに～した He *addressed* us on the history of movies. 原稿を見ながら～してもいいですか May I make *a speech* from notes?

えんせん【沿線】¶ 私の家は鉄道の～にある My house is *on the railway* (⇆ *railroad*) *line*.

えんせん【厭戦】war-weariness. ¶ 彼らは～気分になっている They *are sick of war*.

えんそ【塩素】〖化学〗chlorine.

えんそう【演奏】performance. ¶ 彼女のピアノの～はとてもすばらしかった She *played* the piano wonderfully well. きょうオーケストラの～がある We'll have *a concert* by the orchestra today.

—会 a concert; (個人の) a recital. —曲目 a program[me]. —者 a player.

えんそく【遠足】a hike; a picnic; an excursion. ¶ ～に行く go on *a hike* (⇆ *picnic*); make (⇆ go on) *an excursion*. ～で山に行った I went to the hill *on a hike*.

えんそくせん【鉛測線】a sounding line.

えんたい【延滞】delay (*in* payment). ¶ 彼らは家賃を～している They *are behind* (⇆ *are in arrears*) *with* their rent.

—利子 overdue interest. —金 arrears.

えんだい【遠大】greatness; grandeur. ¶ ～な計画を立てる make a *long-ranged* (⇆ *farseeing*) plan. ～な志 a *great* ambition.

えんだい【演台】a platform.

えんだい【演題】the subject (of a speech); the theme.

えんだい【縁台】a bench.

えんたく【円卓】a round table. ¶ ～につく sit at *a round table*.

—会議 a round table conference.

えんだん【演壇】a platform.

えんだん【縁談】an offer of marriage. ¶ 彼女には～がたくさんある She has many *offers of marriage*. ～がまとまった The *marriage* has been arranged. 彼からの～を断わった I declined his *proposal*.

えんちゃく【延着】delay. ¶ 列車は1時間～した The train *arrived* an hour *late* (⇆ *behind schedule*). / The train *was delayed* [for] an hour.

えんちゅう【円柱】a column. ¶ ～の columnar (発音は [kəlʌ́mnər]).

えんちょう【延長】extension. ¶ 期間が3日間～された The term *was prolonged* (⇆ *was extended*) for three days. 道路がその橋まで～された The road *was extended to* the bridge. 休暇を二·三日～してよいですか May I *prolong* (⇆ *extend*) my holidays for a few days?

えんちょう【園長】the head (*of*). ¶ 動物園～ *the head* of a zoo. 幼稚園～ *the head* (⇆ *chief*) of a kindergarten.

えんちょく【鉛直】¶ ～の(な) perpendicular; vertical; upright.

—線 a plumb line.

えんづ·く【縁づく】¶ 彼の娘はもう～いている His daughter *is married*. 彼女の年ごろにはもう私は～いていた I *had* already *got married* at her age.

えんつづき【縁続き】¶ 彼とは遠い～である He is *a* distant *relation* of mine. 彼とは～ではない I'*m* not *related to* him. 彼は結婚によってその家と～になった He *was connected* with the

family by marriage.
えんてい【園丁】a gardener; a park-keeper.
えんてん【炎天】¶～下に働く work *in the scorching heat*; work *under the scorching sun*.
えんでん【塩田】a salt pan (≒ plot); a saltern.
えんとう【円筒】a cylinder.
えんどう【沿道】(道筋) the route; (道路) the street. ¶～で多くの人が待っていた A lot of people were waiting *by the roadside*.
えんどう【豌豆】〘植物〙a pea.
えんどお·い【縁遠い】¶その問題は私には～い I *have little relation to* the problem. 彼女は～い She *has few opportunities of* marriage.
えんどく【鉛毒】〘医学〙lead poisoning.
えんとつ【煙突】a chimney; a smokestack. ¶～のすすを払う sweep soot from *a chimney*.
—掃除 a chimney-sweep; (人) a chimney-sweeper.
えんにち【縁日】a fair.
えんねつ【炎熱】¶～下に働く work *in the intense heat*; work *under the scorching sun*.
えんのう【延納】¶税務署に税金の～を願い出た I made a petition to the taxation office for *deferred payment*. 代金を～せざるをえなかった I had to *put off paying* the money for it.
えんのした【縁の下】⇒えん(縁)
えんばく【燕麦】oats.
えんばん【円盤】a disc (≒ disk); (競技用の) a discus.
—投げ the discus throw. 空飛ぶ— a flying disc.
えんばん【鉛版】a stereotype.
えんぴつ【鉛筆】a pencil. ¶～を削る sharpen *a pencil*. ～で書く write *in pencil* (≒ *with a pencil*).
—入れ a pencil case. —削り a pencil sharpener. 色— a colored pencil.
えんびふく【燕尾服】a swallow-tailed coat.
えんぶきょく【円舞曲】a waltz.
えんぶじょう【演舞場】a playhouse.
えんぶん【塩分】salt. ¶～のある salty. ～をいくらか含む contain some *salt*.
えんぶん【艶聞】a romance; a love affair. ¶彼には～がある He has *a romance*.
えんぼう【遠謀】foresight; a long-sighted plan. ¶～深慮に富む政治家 a *far-sighted* (≒ *foresighted*) statesman.
えんぽう【遠方】(距離) a long way; a long distance; (遠い所) a distant place. ¶～に人影が見えた I saw a figure *in the distance*. 友あり～より来たる, また楽しからずや How delightful to have old friends coming *a long way* to see us!
えんま【閻魔】*Yama*; the King of Hell.
—帳(学校の) a mark (≒ grade) book.
えんまく【煙幕】a smoke screen. ¶敵は～を張って逃げた The enemy laid down (≒ hid behind) *a smoke screen* and ran away.
えんまん【円満】¶～な家庭 a *happy* home; a *harmonious* family. ～な性質 an *amicable* disposition. 彼女は～な人だ She is an *amiable* (≒ *affable*) woman. 彼らは夫婦仲が～だ They are living *happily* together as man and wife. 労働争議は～に解決した The labor dispute has been brought to an *amicable* settlement.
えんむ【煙霧】mist; smog; haze.
えんむすび【縁結び】matchmaking. ¶～の神 the god of *marriage*.
えんゆうかい【園遊会】a garden party.
えんよう【援用】¶ピタゴラスの定理を～する *invoke* Pythagorean proposition 〔theorem〕. 弁護士は「言論の自由の権利」を～して被告の無罪を主張した The lawyer maintained that the defendant was innocent, *quoting* the right of free speech.
えんよう【遠洋】(大洋) an ocean; (深海) a deep sea.
—漁業 deep-sea fishing (≒ fishery). —航海 ocean navigation (≒ voyage). —航路 an ocean lane (≒ route).
えんらい【遠来】¶～の客 a visitor *from afar*; a visitor *from a distant place*.
えんらい【遠雷】distant thunder. ¶砲声が～のようにとどろく The distant boom of cannons sounds like *thunder*.
えんりょ【遠慮】**1**〘差し控える〙reserve. ¶駐車ご～ください No parking, please. / Please *refrain from* parking.
車内でのおたばこはご～ください (掲示) No smoking in the car. / (口頭で) I must remind you that smoking is prohibited in the car.
風邪をひいていたので, 行くのを～した I *declined* the invitation because I had a cold.
ふたりだけで話したいので, ちょっと～してくれませんか Would you kindly leave us two alone for a few moments for a confidential talk?
そんなに会費が高いなら, ぼくは～する I will *abstain from* joining; the membership fee is much too high.
2〘気兼ね〙constrain; deference. ¶このパンフレットを1部頂けますか. どうぞご～なく Can I have a copy of this pamphlet? Yes, of course. (≒ Please go ahead!)
では～なく頂きます (食事のとき) Thank you, I will help myself. / (贈り物などのとき) It is very kind of you 〔to give me this present〕.
～なく思っていることを言ってください You must *feel free* to tell us what you have in mind.
～なく意見を言いたまえ Tell me your opinion *without reserve*.
～なくご用を申しつけください Don't *hesitate* to tell me if there is anything I can do for you.
～のないとこ, 彼女の絵をどう思う *Honestly*, what do you think about her painting?
～のないとこ, きみの英文はなってない *Frankly*, you cannot write English 〔at all〕.

～のないご批評を願います I welcome your *honest* (≒ *frank*) criticism.
彼に～してぼくはほんとうのことは言わなかった In order not to embarrass him, I did not tell the truth.
先輩に～してあえて反対はしなかった *Out of deference to* my senior, I refrained from opposing him.
ぼくなんかに～することはない Don't let me stand in your way.
この際～は無用, だれでもいい案があったら言ってください Now I hope everybody will speak up if he has a good idea.
～も時によりけりだ. 彼が悪いとはっきり言ってやれ *Modesty* is not always good. So tell him frankly that he is mistaken.
～しないで楽にしてください Make yourself at home. / Please feel right at home.
～なんかしないで飲んで歌って愉快にやってくれ *Feel free* to eat, drink and make merry.
彼は～がちに言った He spoke with some *hesitation*.
3 〖遠慮深い・けんそんな〗 modesty ; humility. ¶ 日本人は～深くて困る The Japanese *are* too *self-conscious* (≒ *modest*).
彼女はずいぶん～深い人だ I am afraid she *keeps herself too much* to *herself* (≒ she *is* too *shy*).
そんなに～したら損をする. もっと自分を売り込まねばだめだ Too much *modesty* will do you no good. You must make yourself known.
あんなことを言うとは無～にも程がある He knows no *modesty* to say such a thing.
彼は～勝ちな人だ He is a *reserved* man.
4 〖深謀〗 foresight. ¶ 深謀～の計略が図に当たった His *thoughtful* plan brought about the success.

えんるい【塩類】 salts.
えんるい【遠類】 a connection ; a relation ; a relative.
えんれい【艶麗】 beauty ; charm. ¶ ～な女 a *glamo*(*u*)*r* girl. ～な姿 a *glamorous* figure. ～な筆(文体) an *ornate* style.
えんろ【遠路】 a long distance ; (長旅) a long journey. ¶ ～ご苦労さまでした It's very kind of you to come *all the way* to see us.

お

お【尾】 a tail ; (キツネなどの毛のふさふさした尾) a brush ; (ウサギ・シカなどの短い尾) a scut ; (クジャクなどの) a train ; (すい星などの) a trail.
¶ 犬が～を振る The dog wags its *tail*. 牛が～を振る The cow swishes its *tail*.
お【緒】 a cord ; a string ; (皮の) a thong.
おあいそ【お愛想】 a compliment. ¶ 彼女はだれにでも～を言う She pays *a compliment* to everyone. ～してください(勘定する) Bring me the bill.
オアシス an oasis (複 oases). ¶ 人生の～ *an oasis* in life. この公園は都会生活者の～だ This park is *an oasis* for the city dwellers.
おあずけ【お預け】 ¶ 彼の病気のため家族旅行は当分～だ Our family trip *has been postponed* for the present owing to his illness. ポチ, ～ *Wait for it*, Pochi.
おい【老い】 ¶ ～も若きもその競技を楽しんだ Both young and *old* enjoyed the game. ～の一徹で with the stubbornness of *the aged*.
おい【甥】 a nephew. ¶ 彼はA氏の～に当たる He is *a nephew of* (≒ *to*) Mr. A.
おい (感) Hello! / Say. / I say. / Hey. / Look. / Look here. ¶ ～きみたち You there! / *Hey*, you! ～, いいかい *Say*, are you ready? ～, ちょっと待て *Hey*, wait a minute!
おいうち【追い打ち】 ¶ 敵に～をかけた We *followed up* our attack. / They attacked the routed enemy.
おいえ【御家】 ━騒動 a family trouble (≒ quarrel). ━芸 a specialty ; 英 a speciality.
おいおい【追い追い】 ¶ 私の病気も～よくなっている I am getting better [*little by little*]. 真相が～わかってきた The truth has *gradually* dawned upon me.
おいおい ¶ 彼女は～泣いた She cried *bitterly*. / She *cried her heart out*.
おいかえ·す【追い返す】 ¶ しつこい押し売りを～した I *repelled* the importunate peddler.
おいか·ける【追いかける】 run after (*a person*). ¶ 犬がネコを～ける The dog *runs after* the cat. 毎日仕事に～けられている I am very busy with work every day. その品を～けて注文した I gave another order for the article *immediately after*.
おいかぜ【追い風】 a tail wind ; a fair wind. ¶ 風は～だった The wind *was fair* (≒ *was favorable*).
おいこし【追い越し】 ━禁止(掲示) No passing. ━禁止区域 a no-passing zone.
おいこ·す【追い越す】 ¶ 学校へ行く途中彼女を～した I *passed* her on my way to school. 競走でウサギがカメに～された The hare *was outstripped* by the tortoise in the race. 私の乗ったタクシーが大型バスを～した My taxi *got ahead of* a large bus.
おいこみ【追い込み】 the last spurt. ¶ 選挙戦も～に入った The election campaign has got

to *the final stage*. / They have gone into *the final stage* of the election campaign. 彼は受験勉強に最後の～をかけた He *put the last spurt on* the preparation for the entrance examination.

おいこ·む【老い込む】¶ 彼は退職後急に～んだ After retirement he *aged* rapidly. ～むには早い You are not so old as to *dote*. / It is too early to *think yourself an old man*.

おいこ·む【追い込む】¶ 鶏を小屋へ～んでおくれ *Get* the hens *into* the coop. 彼女の追及が彼を窮地に～んだ She *cornered* him. / She *drove* him *into a corner*.

おいさき【老い先】¶ ～短い老人を悩ませたくない I don't want to worry an old man who *has not many years to live* (≒ *is not long for this world*).

おいし·い【美味しい】delicious ; nice.
¶ この魚料理はとても～い This fish dish *is* very *nice* (≒ *delicious*). / This fish dish *tastes good*. このお菓子は～い This cake *tastes sweet*. ごちそうを～く頂きました The dinner *was wonderful*. / I enjoyed the nice dinner.

おいしげ·る【生い茂る】grow thick. ¶ 空き地に雑草が～っている The vacant lot *is overgrown* (≒ *is rank*) *with* weeds.

おいすが·る【追い縋る】run after (*a person*) closely. ¶ ～る敵を振り切って逃げた We ran away from the *pursuing* enemy.

おいそれと (すぐに) at a moment's notice ; readily ; (かんたんに) easily ; readily. ¶ 彼の申し込みを～受け入れるわけにはいかない I cannot accept his proposal so *readily*. ～は決めかねる I cannot decide *offhand*.

おいだ·す【追い出す】¶ 借家人を～す *eject* (≒ *evict*) a tenant. 彼は暴力をふるったために学校を～された He *was expelled* from school for violence.

おいたち【生い立ち】(成長) bringing up ; (幼年時代) *one's* childhood ; *one's* early days ; (経歴) *one's* personal history.
¶ 彼女は～を話してくれた She told me the story of her childhood.
—の記 a story of *one's* childhood ; a memoir of *one's* early life.

おいたて【追い立て】¶ 間借人は5か月部屋代を払わなかったので～を食った The lodger *was ejected* (≒ *was evicted*) because he had not paid his rent for five months. 彼は1か月以内に立ち退くよう～を食っている He has been given *a* one-month *notice to move out*.

おいた·てる【追い立てる】¶ 家主が借家人を～てた The houseowner *evicted* his tenant from the house. 子どもたちを～ててはいけない Don't *hurry* (≒ *rush*) the children.

おいちら·す【追い散らす】¶ 警官がやじうまを～した The police *scattered* the mob. 敵を～して大勝利を収めた We *put* the enemy *to rout* and gained a great victory.

おいつ·く【追い付く】overtake. ¶ 走って彼に～きなさい Run to *catch up with* him. / Run to *catch* him *up*. 今更悔やんでも～かない *It is too late for* regrets.

おいつ·める【追い詰める】¶ 群衆は強盗を袋小路に～めた The crowd *pressed* the robber *into* a blind alley. その借金が彼を～めた That debt *cornered* him.

おいて【追い風】¶ 船は～に帆を上げて走った The ship sailed *before the wind*. / The ship sailed *with a fair wind*.

おいて【於て】¶ 銀座に～ *at* Ginza. 日本に～ *in* Japan. プラットホームに～ *on* the platform. ここに～ hereupon ; upon this.

おいて【措いて】¶ 彼を～ほかにできる者はいない No one can do it *except* him.

おいで【御出で】**1**〖来訪・来ること〗¶ お客様が～になりました The guests have come.
ようこそ～くださいました I am very glad (≒ pleased) to see you.
どうぞまた～ください I hope you will *call* again soon.
～をお待ちしています I shall be waiting for you.
どうぞこちらへ～ください *Come* this way, please.
坊や, こっちへ～ *Come*, little boy, *come* here.
2〖在宅〗¶ ご主人はお宅に～ですか Is your husband in?

おいてきぼり ¶ 友だちに～を食った I *was left behind* by a friend of mine.

おいぬ·く【追い抜く】⇒おいこす

おいはぎ【追い剝ぎ】(おもに馬に乗った) a highwayman ; (徒歩の) a footpad ; (米俗語) a holdup [man].

おいはら·う【追い払う】¶ この人たちをみんな～ってください Please *send* all these people *away*. 風が雲を～った The wind *dispersed* the cloud.

おいぼれ【老いぼれ】(人) a dotard ; a silly old man ; (状態) old age ; dotage. ¶ 彼は年のわりには～て見える He *looks decrepit* for his age. 母はもう～ています My mother *is in her dotage* now.

おいまわ·す【追い回す】¶ ひよこを～す *run after* chickens. その子はいつも母親を～している The child *is always following* its mother.

おいや·る【追いやる】¶ 彼は僻地(へきち)へ～られた He *was ordered off to* a remote corner of the country.

おいらく【老いらく】¶ ～の恋 love *in old age* ; an *old man's* (≒ *woman's*) love affair.

オイル oil ; gasoline.
—シャンプー oil shampoo. —タンク an oil tank. —ストーブ a kerosene stove. —スキン skin oil. サラダ— salad oil.

お·いる【老いる】grow old ; age. ¶ 彼は～いてますます盛んだ He enjoys a green old age. / He *is* still *hale and hearty*. ～いては子に従え Be guided by your children *when you are old*.

おう【王】a king ; (巨頭) a magnate.
¶ ライオンは百獣の～だ The lion is the *king* of beasts. 彼は「石油～」と呼ばれた He was called "the oil *magnate*." 彼は～の位についた He ascended (≒ came to) the throne.

お

打点── a king of batters. 発明── a king of inventors.

おう【翁】an old (≒ aged) man.

お·う【負う】**1**〖背負う〗carry on *one's* back. ¶重いリュックを～って朝早く出発した I started early in the morning *with* a heavy rucksack *on my back*.

2〖手に負えない〗¶この子は手に～えないいたずらっ子だ This child *is naughty and unmanageable*.

あの男の子は母親の手に～えない That boy is *a handful* for his mother.

この仕事はとてもぼくの手に～えない This task is quite *beyond me*.

3〖引き受ける〗¶だれがこの責任を～うのか Who is to *take the responsibility for* this?

このことで責任を～っていただかなくてもけっこうです You don't have to *feel responsible for* it.

彼は監督不行き届きの責めを～って辞職した He resigned from his post *holding himself responsible for* want of control over the matter.

多大の借金を～ったまま彼は死んだ He died leaving a great amount of debts behind him.

そんな義務まで～わされるのか Do I have to *assume* (≒ *take on myself*) such a responsibility?

4〖傷を受ける〗¶彼女は自動車事故で重傷を～った She *was* seriously *injured* in a car accident.

彼は重い手傷を～ってそこに倒れていた He was lying on the spot *with a severe wound* (≒ *seriously wounded*).

5〖おかげをこうむる〗¶戦後の目覚ましい復興は国民の勤勉に～うところが多い The remarkable postwar reconstruction of this country *is* mainly *due to* the diligence of the people.

このコンピューターの完成は彼の研究に～うところが多い The completion of this computer *owes* much *to* his research.

お·う【追う】**1**〖追いかける〗¶子どもは母の跡を～って走った The child *ran after* its mother.

彼女は亡き夫の跡を～って自殺した She committed suicide and *followed* her husband in death.

～いつ～われつの大接戦だった It was *a seesaw game*. / It was *a very close game*. / It was *a neck and neck race*.

2〖犯人·獲物を追跡する〗¶友人とどろぼうを～ったが街頭で見失った I *pursued* the thief with a friend of mine, but we lost sight of him in the street.

彼は警察に～われる身であった He *was wanted by* the police.

望遠レンズでロケットの航跡を～った I *followed* the track of the rocket through a telephoto lens.

3〖追い払う〗¶いくら～ってもハエがたかる Flies come back as often as they *are driven away*.

4〖時間·仕事に追われる〗¶時間に～われてそのことを深く考える余裕がなかった I could not give it much thought, as I *was pressed for* time.

このところずっと仕事に～われている I have been very busy all these days.

5〖追求する〗¶きみは夢ばかり～っている You *are* always *pursuing* (≒ *are* always *running after*) dreams. / You *are* always *chasing* rainbows. / You are a dreamer.

理想を～うのはけっこうだが，実現の手段も考えてほしい It is all right to *pursue* an ideal, but you should think about how to realize it.

まだ若いのだから流行を～うのも無理はない You may well *follow* the fashion, as you are young.

6〖家畜を追う〗¶少年は牛を～って牧舎に戻った *Driving* the cattle, the boy returned to the farmhouse.

7〖追放する〗¶彼は国を～われてイタリアに行った He *was exiled from* his country and went to Italy.

彼は汚職のかどでその地位を～われた He *was ousted from* his post on account of corruption.

彼は郷里を～われて東京に出た *Expelled from* his hometown, he came up to Tokyo.

8〖従う〗¶順序を～って事の次第をお話しいたします I will tell you how it happened *in due order*.

その仕事は日を～って忙しくなった The job kept me increasingly busy *every day*.

年を～ってその効果が現われてきた The effect was manifested *as the years went by*.

9〖その他〗¶自分の頭のハエを～え Mind your own business.

おうあ【欧亜】Europe and Asia.
──大陸 Eurasia; the Eurasian Continent.
──混血児 a Eurasian〔child〕.

おうい【王位】the crown; the throne.
¶アレクサンダー大王は13年間～にあった Alexander the Great was on *the throne* for thirteen years. 彼は紀元前336年に～についた He came to the *throne* in 336 B.C. だれが～をついだか Who succeeded *the throne*?

おういつ【横溢】¶彼は元気～して外国から帰ってきた He returned home from abroad〔*being*〕*full of* vigor. 街は群衆で活気が～している The streets are lively with the crowd.

おういん【押韻】〖詩〗rhyming;〔a〕rhyme.

おうえん【応援】(援助) assistance; aid; help; (支持) support; (競技の声援) cheering; 米 rooting. ¶私たちはみんなきみのチームを～する We all are going to *cheer* (≒ *root for*) your team. あの候補者を～して当選させよう Let us *support* the candidate and help him win the election.
──演説 (make) a campaign speech (*for*). ──団 米 rooters; a cheering party. ──団長 米 a head rooter; a cheer leader. ──旗 a rooter's pennant.

おうおう【往往】(時折) sometimes; now and then; (しばしば) often; frequently; not infrequently.

¶ そんなことは～あることだ Such things *are not uncommon*. 疲れていると～にして誤りをおかす We *are apt to* make mistakes when we are tired. 子どもには～あることだ It is *often* the case with children.

おうか【欧化】Europeanization; westernization. ¶ 日本人の生活様式は明治以来～されてきた The living modes of Japanese people have been *westernized* since the Meiji era.
―主義 Europeanism; Westernism.

おうか【謳歌】praise; glorification.
¶ 彼は青春を～する He sings the praises of youth. / He rejoices in the blessings of youth. 私たちは人生を～する We sing the joys of life.

おうかくまく【横隔膜】〘解剖学〙the diaphragm.

おうかん【王冠】a crown; (びんの) a crown cap (≒ cork).

おうぎ【扇】a 〔folding〕 fan. ¶ ～を使う *fan oneself*. ここで三角州が～形に広がる Here a delta is formed in the shape of *an* unfolded *fan*.

おうぎ【奥義】⇒おくぎ

おうきゅう【応急】¶ ～処置をとる take an *emergency* measure. 負傷者に～手当をした We *gave first aid to* the wounded man.

おうぎょく【黄玉】〘鉱物〙topaz.

おうけ【王家】a royal family.

おうけん【王権】royal authority; sovereign powers (≒ rights).
―神授説 the divine rights of kings.

おうこう【王侯】kings and princes. ¶ 彼は～のような暮らしをしている He lives like *a prince*.

おうこう【横行】¶ この町の盛り場には不良が～している The busiest quarters of this city *are infested with* (≒ *are overrun by*) delinquents. 役人の間に汚職が～していた Corruption *was rampant* among officers.

おうこく【王国】a kingdom; a monarchy.
¶ 野獣の～ *a kingdom* of beasts.

おうごん【黄金】(金) gold; (貨幣) money.
―時代 the golden age. ―分割 the golden section.

おうざ【王座】**1** the throne. ¶ 彼は～についた He mounted (≒ came to) *the throne*.
2 〘第一人者〙 ¶ 彼が依然～を占めている He continues to hold *the premier position*.
彼と～を争った I contended with him for *the premier position*.
彼は再び世界の～についた(世界選手権を獲得した) He regained *the world's championship*.

おうし【雄牛】a bull; an ox (複 oxen) (後者は食用に去勢したものを示す).

おうじ【王子・皇子】a prince; a royal prince.

おうじ【往時】old times; old days; former times; former days.
¶ ～をしのぶ look back on *the past*.

おうしつ【王室】the royal family (≒ house).

おうじて【応じて】¶ あなたがたは収入に～暮らすのがよい You will do well to live *within* your means. 収入に～お使いなさい Please spend *according to* your income. 仕事は能力に～やればよい You have only to do your work *according to* your ability. 君がもらう金高は年齢に～決まる The amount of money you get *depends upon* your age. 多くの人の要求に～その作品は再版されることになった The work was to be reprinted *in compliance with* the requests of a lot of people. 必要に～この用紙を使いなさい Use this form *if it is necessary*. 勤務年数に～じて退職金を出す A retirement allowance is to be paid *depending on* the length of service. 手当は勤務年数に～違う The allowance varies *in proportion to* the length of service. 金は必要に～じて出す Money will be given as the occasion demands.

おうじゃ【王者】(王様) a king; a monarch; (第一人者) the champion.

おうしゅう【応酬】(返答) an answer; a reply; a response; (交換) an exchange; (返礼) a return. ¶ やじの～ *an exchange* of heckling.

おうしゅう【欧州】Europe.
―経済協力機構 the Organization for European Economic Co-operation (OEEC).
―経済共同体 the European Economic Community (EEC). ―共同市場 the European Common Market (ECM).

おうしゅう【押収】confiscation. ¶ 警官は彼のピストルを～した The policeman *confiscated* his pistol.

おうじょ【王女・皇女】a princess; a royal princess.

おうしょう【王将】〘将棋〙the king of chess.

おうしょう【応召】¶ 彼は～して陸軍に入隊した He *was drafted into* the army.

おうじょう【往生】¶ 彼も大～を遂げた He *died in peace*. 彼にはまったく～する He is *a regular pest*. どうしたらよいのかまったく～した I *was* quite *at a loss* what to do.
―ぎわ ¶ 彼は～ぎわが悪い He is *a bad loser*.

おうしょく【黄色】yellow.
―人種 the yellow race.

おうしん【往診】a 〔doctor's〕 visit. ¶ 先生は～中だ The doctor *is away on his round of visits*.
―料 a doctor's fee for a visit. ―時間 hours for visiting patients.

おう・ずる【応ずる】**1** 〘答える〙 ¶ ひととおりお話をさせていただいたあとで, みなさんの質問に～じます I will *answer* your questions after I have finished my speech.
だれもその呼びかけに～ずる者はいなかった There was nobody who *responded* to the call.
2 〘相手になる〙 ¶ 喜んでご相談に～じます I will be happy to give you advice, if necessary.
いつでも挑戦に～じる I am ready to *accept* your challenge any time.
3 〘「うん」と言う〙 ¶ 彼はわれわれとの話し合いに～じようとはしなかった He refused to have a talk with us.
そういう条件では～じられない We cannot *accept*

お

お

your proposal on such conditions.
そんな懇請には～じてはいけない You should not *accept* such a solicitation.
この招待に～じたものかどうか I wonder if I have to *accept* this invitation or not.
4 〘かなうようにする〙 ¶ その要求に～じるわけにはいかない We cannot possibly *meet* the demand. すべての学生の希望に～じることはできない It is impossible to *meet* (≒ *satisfy*) the wishes of all the students.
とてもそのような大量の注文には～じきれません We can hardly *accept* such a large order.
時代の要求に～じて女子の入会も認めるべきだ Women should also be invited to membership *meeting* the requirement of the times.
5 〘かなう・適する〙 ¶ 生徒の学力に～じた問題とはいえぬ This question *is* not *appropriate* to test the ability of the students.
収入に～じた暮らしを考えなさい Adjust your living to your income.

おうせい【王政】 the Imperial (≒ Royal) rule (≒ regime).
—復古 the restoration of the imperial regime; 〘歴史〙 the Restoration.

おうせい【旺盛】 ¶ 彼は元気～だ He *is full of vigor*. 彼らの士気は～であった They *were in high spirits*. 食欲は～である I have a *good* appetite. 彼女は知識欲が～である She has a *keen* appetite for knowledge.

おうせつ【応接】 an interview; reception. ¶ 客の～に忙しかった I was busy with visitors. いろいろな事が起こって～にいとまがない Things happen one after another with a bewildering rapidity.
—係 a receptionist. —間 米 a parlor; 英 a drawing room.

おうせん【応戦】 ¶ 彼らは勇敢に～した They *fought back* bravely.

おうせん【横線】 a horizontal line.
—小切手 a crossed cheque.

おうたい【応対】 (応接) reception; (会見) meeting. ¶ ～のじょうずな(へたな)人 a man of *good* (*awkward*) *address*. 書斎で客に～した I *received* my guest in my study. 早くあのお客様に～してください Please *wait on* that customer quickly.

おうたい【横隊】 a line; a rank. ¶ 2列～になる form *a* double *line*.

おうたいホルモン【黄体ホルモン】〘生化学〙 progesterone.

おうだく【応諾】 consent; agreement.
¶ ～する say yes; give *one's* consent (*to*); agree *with* (*a person*); agree *to* (a plan).

おうだん【横断】 crossing; intersection.
¶ 彼は通りを～中自動車にはねられた When he *was crossing* the street, he was hit by a car. ジャンボジェット機で太平洋を～した I *flew across* the Pacific in a jumbo jet. 彼はただひとりで，ヨットで太平洋を～した He *sailed across* the Pacific in a yacht by himself. 彼女はイギリス海峡を泳いで～した She *swam across* the English Channel.
—歩道 a pedestrian crossing; a zebra crossing.

おうだん【黄疸】〘医学〙 jaundice.

おうちゃく【横着】 ¶ ～な男(無精な) a lazy man; (ずるい) a cunning man; (怠慢な) a neglectful man.

おうちょう【王朝】 a dynasty.

おうて【王手】〘将棋〙 a check. ¶ ～! Check! ～をかけた I *checked* the king.

おうてん【横転】 a lateral turning. ¶ 彼の車は～した His car *turned sideways*.

おうと【嘔吐】 vomiting. ¶ ～を催させるようなにおい a *nasty* (≒ *disgusting*) smell. ～を催しはじめてきた I began to *feel sick*.

おうとう【応答】 a response; an answer.
¶ 無線の呼び出しに間もなく～があった The wireless calls *were* soon *responded to*.

おうどう【王道】 ¶ 学問に～なし (諺) *There is no royal road to learning*.

おうとつ【凹凸】 unevenness; ruggedness.
¶ ～のある uneven; rugged; irregular.

おうねつびょう【黄熱病】〘医学〙 yellow fever.

おうねん【往年】 the past; the former years; the years gone by. ¶ 彼は～の名ピッチャーだ He was *formerly* a star pitcher. 彼女にはもう～の人気はない She is not so popular *as she used to be*.

おうひ【王妃】 a queen; an empress.

おうふう【欧風】 ¶ ～の建築 a building *in European* (≒ *Western*) *style*.

おうふく【往復】 a return trip; (手紙の) communication; correspondence. ¶ 駅まで～してどのくらい時間がかかりますか How long does it take to *go to* the station *and back*? 彼は週2回東京大阪間を～している He *goes back and forth* between Tokyo and Osaka twice a week. 演奏会場へは～ともバスが便利だ It is convenient for you to *go to and from* the concert hall by bus. そのコースを～すると3時間以上かかる It takes more than three hours to *go* along that course *and back*. 彼は練習のため何回もプールを～して泳ぐ He swims *several lengths* of the swimming pool for practice.
～の運賃はいくらですか How much is the *roundtrip* (≒ *return*) fare?
—切符 a round-trip ticket; 英 a return ticket. —はがき a return postcard.

おうぶん【応分】 ¶ ～の寄付 contribution *according to one's means*.

おうぶん【欧文】 European languages (≒ writing).
—タイプライター a Roman typewriter.

おうへい【横柄】 ¶ ～な顔で with a *haughty* (≒ an *insolent*) look. 彼はなんて～な男なんだ What an *arrogant* (≒ a *haughty*) fellow he is! 彼女はだれに対しても～だ She *is insolent to* anyone.

おうべい【欧米】 Europe and America.
¶ ～の風習 *Western* customs. ～を旅して歩く make a tour of *Europe and America*.
—人 Europeans and Americans.

おうぼ【応募】(予約) subscription;(志願) application;(募兵に) enlistment. ¶ 彼女はその会社のタイピスト募集に～した She *applied for* a position as a typist in the company. 公債募集に～した I *subscribed for* government bonds.

—者(入学・就職などの) an applicant;(株式などの) a subscriber.

おうぼう【横暴】¶ ～な政策 a *high-handed* (≒ an *oppressive*) policy. 彼はまったく～な男だ He is *a tyrant*.

おうむ【鸚鵡】a parrot. ¶ ～返しに答える repeat another's words.

おうめんきょう【凹面鏡】a concave mirror.

おうよう【応用】application. ¶ その理論は広く～がきく The theory has wide *application*. 科学を実際に～することが必要だ It is necessary to *put* science *to practical use*.

—化学 applied chemistry. —力学 applied dynamics. —問題 exercises.

おうよう【鷹揚】¶ 彼は～にうなずいた He nodded in a *lordly* manner. 彼はいつも～に構えている He always assumes a *lordly* manner. 彼女は～に育った She was brought up *in easy* (≒ *comfortable*) *circumstances*. 彼は～な態度でにっこりした He smiled in a *generous* manner.

おうらい【往来】(通行) traffic;(道路) a street. ¶ この通りは昼間は～が激しい The *traffic* on this road is busy during the daytime. 夜になると人の～が絶える The road *is deserted* after dark. ～は車でいっぱいだった The *street* was full of cars. このあたりは車の～がはげしすぎる Motor *traffic* is too heavy in this part of the street. 今ごろの時間は～が少ない There is little *traffic* here about this time.

おうりょう【横領】seizure;(金銭の) embezzlement. ¶ 彼は公金を～した He *embezzled* public money. 彼はおいの金を～した He *embezzled* money *from* his nephew.

—罪 ¶ 彼は～罪で訴えられた He was accused of *embezzlement*.

おうりょくしょく【黄緑色】yellow green.

おうりん【黄燐】〖化学〗yellow phosphor.

おうレンズ【凹レンズ】a concave lens.

おうろ【往路】an outward trip.

おえつ【嗚咽】a sob. ¶ ～する sob; give a sob. ～しながら話す talk *between sobs*.

おえらがた【お偉方】〔one of〕the dignitaries (≒ betters);(軽蔑的に) panjandrum.

お・える【終える】¶ きょうの仕事は～えた I *have finished* today's work. この小説はまだ読み～えていない I *have* not *finished* reading this novel yet. 夕食を～えたら散歩に出かけよう I will go out for a walk *after* supper. 彼女はこの春高等学校を～えた She *finished* the senior high school course last spring.

おお O! / Oh.

おおあじ【大味】¶ ～な savorless; tasteless; flat.

おおあたり【大当たり】a big hit; a great success. ¶ その映画は記録破りの～だった The film made *a* record-breaking *hit*.

おおあな【大穴】¶ 彼は使い込みで会社の帳簿に～をあけた He *embezzled* a large amount of money *from* the company. ダービーで～を当てた I *made a lucky hit* in the Derby.

おおあめ【大雨】a heavy rain. ¶ ～が降った There was *a heavy rain*. / It *rained heavily* (≒ *hard*).

おおあれ【大荒れ】(嵐) a heavy storm; a tempest. ¶ ～する(人が) act violently.

おおい【覆い】a cover; a covering;(光よけ) a shade. ¶ いすの～ *a* chair *cover*. その～を取りはずしなさい Take off the *cover*.

おお・い【多い】(数が) many; a good (≒ great) many; a large (≒ great) number of; numerous;(口語) quite a few;(量が) much; a good (≒ great) deal of;(数量ともに) a lot (≒ lots) of; plenty of (肯定では a lot of か plenty of でも否定では not many; not much とすることが多い);(豊富) abundant;(頻度が) frequent.

¶ 彼にはよい友だちが～い He has *many* good friends.

彼は欠点が～い He has *a lot of* faults.

ことしは雪が～かった We have had *plenty of* snow this winter.

夏は冬より雨が～い We have *more* rain in summer than in winter.

日本は地震が～い Earthquakes *are frequent* in Japan.

この国には不思議な伝説が～い This country *is rich in* strange traditions. / This country has an *abundance* of strange traditions.

野球の好きな人が～い *Many* people are fond of baseball.

約束の時間に遅れることが～い I am *often* late for the appointed time.

彼はポカをやることが～い He *is apt to* make careless mistakes.

彼女はひとりきりでいることが～い She *mostly* keeps alone.

おおい(呼び声) Hello! / Hullo! / 米 Hi!

おおいそぎ【大急ぎ】a great hurry. ¶ 彼は～部屋を出た He went out of the room *in a great hurry* (≒*in great haste*). ～で川岸を進んだ We *rushed our way* along the river. 彼女は～の用事で外出した She went out *on urgent business*. ～で昼食をすませた I *rushed through* my lunch.

おおいに【大いに】¶ 彼はその知らせを聞いて～喜んだ He was *very* glad at the news. / He was *much* delighted at the news. ぼくも～勉強しよう I will study *very hard*. 彼女は英語が～上達した She has made *great* progress in English. 今夜は～飲もう Let's drink *heartily* (≒ *heavily*) this evening. ～がんばりましょう Let's *do our best*.

おおいぬざ【大犬座】〖天文〗the Great Dog.

おおいばり【大威張り】¶ 彼は～で帰ってきた He came back *triumphantly*.

おおいり【大入り】¶ 彼の講演は～だった His lecture *had a crowded audience*. 劇場は～だっ

お

た The theater *was filled with spectators.* / The theater *was filled to capacity.* そのミュージカルは～だった There was *a packed audience* at the musical.
—袋 a full house bonus. —満員(掲示) House Full.

おお·う【覆う】 cover. ¶ 彼女はハンカチで顔を～った She *covered* her face with a handkerchief. 悲しい知らせを聞くと，彼女は顔を手で～って立ち去った When she heard the sad news, she went away *with her face buried in her hands.* 建物はツタで～われている The building *is overgrown with* ivy. 山の頂はまだ雪で～われている The top of the mountain *is* still *covered with* snow. 谷は霧で～われている The valley *is enveloped in* mist. 空は黒雲で～われている The sky *is overspread with* black clouds. 木々はまもなく緑で～われるだろう The trees will soon *be green.*

おおうけ【大受け】 a great success; a great popularity. ¶ 芝居は～だった The play *was astonishingly successful.* / The play was *a great hit* (≒ *a brilliant success*).

おおうつし【大写し】〖映画〗a close-up. ¶ ～をする take *a close-up.*

おおうなばら【大海原】 the ocean; the deep; the vast expanse of waters.

おおうりだし【大売り出し】 a great (≒ bargain; special) sale.

おおおじ【大叔父·大伯父】 a granduncle; a great-uncle.

おおおとこ【大男】 a big man. ¶ ～総身に知恵が回りかね(諺) *Big head, little wit.*

おおおば【大叔母·大伯母】 a grandaunt; a great-aunt.

おおがかり【大がかり】 ¶ ～な密輸 a *large scale* smuggling; smuggling *on a large scale.* それには～な調査が必要だ It needs a *large scale* investigation.

おおかぜ【大風】 a strong wind; a violent wind. ¶ 昨夜は～が吹いた It *blew very hard* last night. / There was *a violent wind* last night.

おおかた【大方】 ¶ その件については～の意見が入れられた The *general* opinion on the subject was accepted. 仕事は～終わった The work is *nearly* finished. 建物は～完成した The building has *almost* been completed. 今晩は～雨だろう It will *probably* rain tonight. 彼は～明日は来ないだろう He *is* not *likely to* come tomorrow.

おおがた【大形·大型】 ¶ ～バス a *large* bus. ～の台風 a *large scale* typhoon.

おおかみ【狼】〖動物〗a wolf.

おおがら【大柄】 ¶ ～の女 a woman *of big build.* 選手はみんな～だ All the players *are of big build.*

おおかれすくなかれ【多かれ少なかれ】 more or less. ¶ 人は多く～エゴイストだ Most people tend to be *more or less* egotistic. 人は～失敗の経験がある Most people have *more or less* an experience of failure.

おおき·い【大きい】 big; large (big は「大きい」の意味で広く用いられる口語. large は特に面積·容積の大きいことを表わす. 主として big は感情を伴った表現. large は感情を伴わない表現).
¶ 日本でいちばん～い都市 *the biggest* city in Japan. ～い動物 a *large* animal. ～いニュース a *big* piece of news. ～な地震 a *big* earthquake. 強風は作物に～い損害を与えた The strong wind did *serious* damage to the crops. もう一度～い声で言ってください Please say it again in a *loud* voice. その知らせを聞いて彼の喜びは～かった He was *much* delighted at the news. 彼はまったく～い人間だ He is indeed a *great* man. 彼は～いことばかり言って実行が伴わない He always *talks big* and yet he does not put it into practice at all. 彼は心の～いことだけがとりえだ His only merit is that he has a *big* heart. そんな～い数字は実感がない I cannot really grasp such an *enormous* number.

おおきく【大きく】 ¶ この村は最近～なった This village has grown *big* recently. どの新聞もそのニュースを～報道した Every newspaper gave a prominent report of the news. 店を～することを考えている I intend to *extend* my business. 問題は～なった The problem has grown *serious.* 火事は瞬く間に～なった The fire *spread* in a moment. 彼はその町で～商売をしている He is engaged in business *on a large scale* in the town. 彼は北海道で生まれ，青森で～なった He *was* born in Hokkaido and *brought up* in Aomori. できるだけ～口を開けなさい Open your mouth as *wide* as possible. 彼は口を～開けてあくびをした He gave a *big* yawn.

おおきさ【大きさ】 size. ¶ このスーツケースは持ち運びに手ごろな～だ This suitcase is just the right *size* for carrying about. あなたのくつ下の～はどのくらいですか What *size* do you take in socks? この紙の～は縦10センチ，横15センチだ This sheet of paper *measures* fifteen by ten centimeters.

おおきめ【大きめ】 ¶ この写真を～にのばしてください I'd like *a rather big* enlargement of this photo.

おおく【多く】（たくさん）in plenty;（主として）chiefly; mainly; for the most part.
¶ 彼女は～の欠点がある She has *lots of* defects. この町の人口は最近とみに～なった The population of this town *has increased* rapidly in recent years. この1節に誤りは～て三つだ There are *not more than* three mistakes in this paragraph. そんなに～の本はない There are not so *many* books. そんなに～の金は必要でない We don't need so *much* money. 事故のため乗客の～は死亡した *Most* of the passengers were killed in the accident.

おおぐち【大口】 ¶ ～を開けて笑う laugh *with one's mouth open.* 彼は寺に～の寄付をした He made a *big* donation to the temple. 彼は～をたたく He *talks big.* ～の売れ口が多い There is much demand for *big lots.*

おおくまざ【大熊座】the Great Bear; the Big Dipper; Ursa Major.

おおくらしょう【大蔵省】the Ministry of Finance; the Finance Ministry; 米 the Treasury; 英 the Exchequer.

おおくらだいじん【大蔵大臣】the Minister of Finance; the Finance Minister; 英 the Chancellor of the Exchequer.

オーケー an O. K. (複 O.K.'s); all right. ¶～する O. K. (過去分詞 O. K.ed; 現在分詞 O. K.'ing). 上司は私の提案に～した The boss *okayed* my proposal. これで万事～だ Everything *is all right* now.

おおげさ【大袈裟】¶あなたの説明は少し～だ Your explanation *is* somewhat *exaggerated*. 彼は～にわれわれに手を振って挨拶を返した He waved back to us in an *exaggerated* way. 彼は自分の見たものを話すときはいつも～に話す He always *talks big* when he tells about things he has seen. 彼女は少しのけがも～にする She *makes too much of* a slight injury. 週刊誌はとかく～に書きたてる Weekly magazines often *play up* an affair.

オーケストラ an orchestra.

おおごえ【大声】a loud voice. ¶彼は～を出して叫んだ He cried in *a loud voice*. / He gave *a loud cry*. 彼らは～をあげてわめきたてた They shouted *at the top of their voice*.

おおごしょ【大御所】a magnate. ¶財界の～ *a* financial *magnate*. 文壇の～ *a great figure* of the literary world.

おおざけ【大酒】¶～を飲む drink *heavily*. ━飲み a heavy (≒ good) drinker.

おおざっぱ【大雑把】¶～に言えば roughly speaking. ～に見積もっても多額の費用がかかる Even a *rough* estimate of the expense shows it will cost us a lot of money.

おおし・い【雄雄しい】¶彼らは～く最後まで戦った They fought *heroically* (≒ *bravely*) to the last. 彼は～く仕事に立ち向かった He confronted the task in a very *manly* way. 彼の～さにほれた I was attracted by his *manliness*.

おおしお【大潮】the flood tide; the spring tide. ¶あすは～だ *The spring tide* comes tomorrow.

おおじかけ【大仕掛け】a large scale. ¶地すべりを調査するため～な実験をした They made an experiment *on a large scale* to examine the causes of a landslide. ～のダム工事を始めた We started *a large scale* construction of the dam. その映画の製作は～のセットが必要だった The production of the film required *a large scale* set.

おおじだい【大時代】¶～の of old fashion; antiquated. 彼は～の演説口調で演説した He made a speech in an *old-fashioned* oratorical tone.

おおすじ【大筋】¶話の～ *an outline* of the story. 事件の～はこうだ *A summary* of the event is this.

オーストラリア Australia. ¶～の Australian. ━人 an Australian.

オーストリア Austria. ¶～の Austrian. ━人 an Austrian.

おおせ【仰せ】what you say; (命令) an order (しばしば複数で用いる). ¶お上の～によって by *order* of the authorities. あなたの～に従います I will obey your *orders*. / I will do *as you say*. ～のとおりです You're right. / Yes, indeed.

おおぜい【大勢】a large number. ¶～の人々 *a large number of* people. ～の家族 a *big* family. ～の前で話す speak *in public*. 敵は～で攻めてきた The enemy attacked us *in great numbers*.

おおぜき【大関】〚相撲〛the second highest rank of *sumo*; (比喩的) a champion.

おおせつか・る【仰せつかる】¶彼は海外出張を～った He *was ordered* abroad on official business. 私は議長の役を～った I *was appointed* chairman.

おおせつ・ける【仰せつける】¶私でできることがありましたら何なりと遠慮なく～けてください Please let me know if there is anything I can do for you.

おおそうじ【大掃除】general house cleaning. ¶年に2度～する We carry out *general house cleaning* twice a year.

オーソドックス ¶彼の理論は～なものとは言いかねる His theory can hardly be regarded as *orthodox*.

おおぞら【大空】the sky.

オーソリティ an authority; an expert; a specialist. ¶人口問題の～ *an authority* on a population problem.

オーダー order.

オーダーメード ¶～の背広 a *made-to-order* suit; 米 a *custom* suit. この外とうは～だ I *had* this coat *made to order*.

おおだてもの【大立て者】¶文壇の～ *a great* (≒ *colossal*) *figure* of the literary world. 歌舞伎界の～ *a shining star* of the *kabuki*.

おおちがい【大違い】(差異) a great difference; (見当はずれ) a gross mistake. ¶そう考えるのはまったく～だ It's *a gross mistake* for you to think so. 見ると聞くとは～だった There was *a world of difference* between what I was told and what I actually saw.

おおっぴら【大っぴら】¶こんにちわれわれは～にものを言えるが数十年前は～にものも言えなかった Nowadays we can *openly* speak our mind, but several decades ago we were not permitted to speak *freely* in public.

おおづめ【大詰め】(終わり) the end; (劇などの) the last act; (特に悲劇の) the catastrophe. ¶選挙戦もいよいよ～に近づいた The election campaign is now very close to *the end*.

おおて【大手】(大会社) a big corporation; a big business organization. ¶私鉄～7社 the seven *big* private railroad *companies*.

おおで【大手】¶～を広げて with *one's* arms extended. このあたりは不良が～を振ってまかり通る場所だ The area around here is swarming

お

with swaggering hooligans.

オーディション an audition. ¶ ～をうける take *an audition*. 彼らは5人の若い女性に～を行った They gave *an audition* to five girls./ They *auditioned* five girls.

おおでき【大出来】 ¶ 今晩は～でした You were *a great success* this evening. / You *were at your best* this evening. 彼にしては～だ For him, it was a good job. / He did far better than we 〔had〕 expected.

オート ―三輪車 an auto-tricycle; a three-wheeled motor van. ―バイ an autocycle; a motorbike; 米 a motorcycle. ―レース an auto race.

おおどうぐ【大道具】 stage setting; a set scene; (人) a scene man; a scene shifter.

おおどおり【大通り】 a main street; an avenue.

おおどころ【大所】 ¶ 財界の～が集まった *Leading figures* of the financial world met together.

オードブル 〔料理〕 hors d'oeuvre (フランス語から).

オートマチック automatic.

オートミール oatmeal.

オートメーション automation. ¶ 生産コストは～によって節約される The production cost is saved by *automation*.

オーナー ¶ プロ野球の～ *the owner* of a professional baseball team.

―ドライバー an owner driver.

おおなた【大鉈】 ¶ 大蔵大臣は来年度予算に～をふるった The Minister of Finance *made a drastic cut* in the budget of the next fiscal year. 会社は大量の人員整理に～をふるった The company *weeded out* the employees on a large scale.

おおなみ【大波】 a high wave.

―小波 high and low waves.

オーバー ¶ あなたの話は少し～だ Your story *is* somewhat *exaggerated*. 会費は3,000円を～しそうだ The fee will *exceed* three thousand yen.

オーバー〔コート〕 an overcoat; a heavy coat.

オーバースロー 〔野球〕 an overhand throw.

オーバータイム overtime. ¶ 彼は毎日～で働く He works *overtime* every day.

オーバーホール overhaul. ¶ このタイプライターは～しなければならない This typewriter needs *overhauling*. 車のエンジンを～してもらった I *had* the engine of my car *overhauled*.

オーバーラップ overlap.

おおばこ【車前草】 〔植物〕 a plantain.

おおはば【大幅】 ¶ ～な減税 a *big* reduction in taxes. ～な人員整理 a *wholesale* discharge. 旅客運賃が～に値上げされた Passengers' fares have been raised *sharply*. ～な人事異動がうわさされている A *wholesale* personnel change is talked of.

―物(きれの) broadcloth.

おおばん【大判】 ¶ ～のグラフ用紙 〔a sheet of〕 *large-sized* graph paper.

オービー an O. B.; an old boy; an alumnus (複 alumni). ¶ 早慶～サッカー戦 a soccer game between the Waseda and Keio *old boys*.

おおひろま【大広間】 a 〔grand〕 hall.

おおぶね【大船】 a large ship. ¶ もう～に乗った気でいなさい Set your mind at rest now.

おおぶり【大降り】 a heavy rain. ¶ ～になった It began to *rain heavily*. この～に出かけるのはよしなさい You had better not go out in this *heavy rain*.

おおぶろしき【大風呂敷】 (大きな風呂敷) a big cloth wrapper; (大言) a big talk; a tall talk; big words.

¶ 彼の～にはうんざりした I was bored with his *big talk*. 彼は～を広げる He *talks big*.

オーブン an oven ([ʌvn] と発音する). ¶ パンを～で焼く bake bread in *an oven*.

オープン open. ¶ プールは6月に～する The swimming pool will *open* in June.

オープンカー (たためるほろ付き自動車) a convertible; (無蓋車) an open car.

オーボエ 〔音楽〕 an oboe. ¶ ～吹奏者 an oboist.

おおまか ¶ ～に言って *roughly* speaking. ～な計画でけっこうです A *rough* plan will do. ～な考えを言ってください Please tell us *the outline* of your idea. 彼はお金には～だ He *is liberal of* (≒ *with*) his money.

おおまけ【大負け】 ¶ 彼は選挙で～に負けた He *was completely defeated* in the election. ～に負けても1,000円です We cannot reduce the price to less than a thousand yen. / We will come down as far as a thousand yen.

おおまた【大股】 a long stride. ¶ ～で歩く walk with *long strides*.

おおまちがい【大間違い】 a great (≒ serious; gross) mistake; a blunder. ¶ ～をしでかす commit *a gross error*. 計算で～をする make *a serious mistake* in calculation. そう思うのは～だ It would be *a great mistake* to think so.

おおまわり【大回り】 ¶ ～したので時間に遅れた As I took *a roundabout route*, I was behind time.

おおみえ【大見得】 ¶ 彼は～を切って話した He used *proud* (≒ *magnificent*) *gestures* in his speech.

おおみず【大水】 a flood. ¶ その地方に～が出た There was *an inundation* (≒ *a deluge*) in the district.

おおみそか【大晦日】 New Year's Eve; the last day of the year.

おおみだし【大見出し】 a big headline; a banner 〔headline〕 (banner は一面トップ抜きの見出し).

¶ そのニュースは～で報道されている The news is reported *in a big headline*.

オーム 〔電気〕 an ohm. ¶ ～の法則 Ohm's law.

おおむかし【大昔】 ¶ ～は a long time ago. ～の人々 people of *old days*.

おおむぎ【大麦】barley.

おおむこう【大向こう】(芝居の天上さじきの見物人) the gallery; (大衆) the mass.

おおむね【概ね】generally; on the whole; roughly; almost; mostly.

おおめ【大目】¶ 彼は私の無礼を～に見てくれた He *overlooked* my imprudence. 彼らの規則違反を～に見ることはできない We can't *connive at* their violation of the regulations. 今度だけは～に見てあげよう I will *shut my eyes* to your behavior this time.

おおめ【大目】¶ 水をもうちょっと～に加えてください Add some *more* water.

おおめだま【大目玉】(大きな目玉) a big eye; (こごと) a good scolding. ¶ 窓をこわして彼から～を食った He *scolded* me *severely* because I broke the window.

おおもじ【大文字】a capital letter; 〘印刷〙 an upper-case letter. ¶ 文頭の語の第一字は～で書かなくてはならない The first letter of the word at the beginning of a sentence must be written *in a capital letter*.

おおもて【大持て】¶ その歌手は女子学生に～だ The singer *is very popular among* girl students. その作家はどこへ行っても～だった The writer *was lionized* everywhere.

おおもと【大元・大本】¶ 民主主義の～ *the principles* of democracy.

おおもの【大物】a very important person; (口語で) a VIP (VIP は very important person から).
¶ 政界の～ *a VIP* (≒ *a big shot*) of the political world; *a very influential person* of the political world.

おおや【大家・大屋】(男の) a landlord; (女の) a landlady.

おおやけ【公】¶ 真実が～になった The fact *was brought before the public*. / The fact *was made public*. / The fact *was made known to the public*. ～の金は私事のためにつかわれてはならない *Public* money must not be spent for private affairs.

おおやすうり【大安売り】a bargain 〔sale〕. ¶ デパートで特選品を～している They *are selling* choice articles *at bottom* (≒ *at bargain*) *prices* at the department store.

おおゆき【大雪】a heavy (≒ big) snow. ¶ ～になった It *is snowing hard* (≒ *heavily*). 20年来の大雪だ This is *the biggest snowfall* that we have had for these twenty years.

おおよう【大様】¶ 彼はお金には～だ He *is liberal of* (≒ *with*) his money. 彼は～な人だ He *is generous* (≒ *is broad-minded*).

おおよそ【大凡】⇒およそ

オーライ all right; O.K.

おおらか ¶ もっと～さが欲しい More *broad-mindedness* is needed. あの人は～な人だ He *is broad-minded* (≒ *is liberal*).

オール an oar. ¶ 上手に～でこぐ pull *a* good *oar*.

オールスター ━戦(野球) the All Star Baseball Game. ━キャスト an all-star cast.

オールドミス an old maid; a spinster (オールドミスは和製英語).

オールバック ¶ 彼は頭を～にしている He wears his hair straight back.

オーレオマイシン 〘薬品〙 aureomycin.

オーロラ an aurora.

おおわらい【大笑い】a good laugh. ¶ 彼らは～した They had *a good* (≒ *hearty*) *laugh*. / They *burst into laughter*.

おおわらわ【大童】¶ ～で働いた I worked *busily* (≒ *desperately*). 彼は～のていである He seems *extremely busy*.

おか【丘】a hill.

おか【陸】land. ¶ 彼は～に上がったかっぱだ He *is a fish out of water*. / He *is* now *out of his element*.

おかあさん【御母さん】mother (家庭内では無冠詞. 大文字で Mother); (口語) mom; (子どもが母を呼ぶとき) mam〔m〕a; mummy.

おかえし【御返し】(返礼) return; (返事) an answer; (復しゅう) revenge. ¶ ～はなにもいりません I want nothing *in return*. 彼はきっと～(仕返し)をするにちがいない He is sure to *have* (≒ *take*) *his revenge*.

おかかえ【御抱え】¶ ～の運転手 *one's* chauffeur.

おがくず【大鋸屑】sawdust.

おかげ【御陰】(好意) favor; (力づくし) efforts; good offices; (助け) assistance. ¶ ～でうまくいきました I *owe* my success *to* you. あの人の援助の～で成功した I *am indebted to* him *for* my success. 「お元気ですか」「はい, ～さまで」"How are you?" "I am very well, *thank you.*" きみの～でまたしかられたよ *Thanks to* you, I was scolded again.

おかし・い【可笑しい】¶ 彼はなんとなく～い He *is* somehow *funny*. 彼の話はいつも～くて笑ってしまう What he says *is* always so *amusing* that I laugh in spite of myself. なにがそんなに君には～いのか私にはわからない I cannot see what *makes* you *laugh* so much. それはまったく～い It strikes me as quite *funny*. 彼はやることなすことなんとなく～い Whatever he does *is* somehow *queer*. これだけしか金が残っていないとは～い *I wonder why* there is so little money left. ～な話だが, 夢で会った人ときのう実際に会った *Strange to say*, yesterday I really met the man who had appeared in a dream. 彼がまだ来ないのは～い *It is strange that* he should not have come yet.

おかしがた・い【犯し難い】¶ ～い威厳 inaccessible dignity.

おかしが・る【可笑しがる】¶ 皆は彼の姿を見て～った Everybody *was amused to* see him. 彼は私がなにをやっても～る He *laughs at* whatever I try to do. どうして答えが合わないのか彼は～った He *wondered why* he had the wrong answer.

おかしさ【可笑しさ】amusement. ¶ この話の～がわからない I cannot understand the *humor* of this story. ～が自然に込み上げてきた *Laugh-*

お

ter rose within me before I was aware of it.

おかしらつき【尾頭付き】 a whole fish; (お祝いのタイの) a sea bream with its head and tail.

¶タイの～で祝う celebrate (an anniversary) with a sea bream, head and all.

おか·す【犯す】 ¶(法律上の)罪を～す *commit* a crime; (宗教·道徳の) *commit* a sin. 法を～す *violate* a law. 禁を～す *violate* the ban. 校則を～す *break* the school regulations. 私のプライバシーを～す *infringe on* my privacy. ～すべからざる権利 an *inviolable* right. 他人の権利を～す *encroach upon* other's rights.

おか·す【侵す】(侵入する) ¶国土を～す *invade* a country.

おか·す【冒す】(危険を) risk; face; (病気が) attack; affect. ¶ある程度の危険は～すつもりだ I am going to *run* some *risk*. 彼は生命の危険を～した He *ran the risk of* his life. 風雨を～して出発した I started *in spite of* the storm. 彼は肝臓が～されている His liver *is affected*. / He *has some trouble in* the liver. 万難を～してもやってみます I will try *in the face of* all the difficulties.

おかず a dish; a side dish. ¶今晩の～はなんですか What are we having for dinner this evening?

おかた【御方】 ¶あの～をご存じですか Do you know who he (≒ she) is? (英語ではこのような敬称は普通用いない. he または she などでよい).

おかっぱ【お河童】 a bob. ¶～の女の子 a girl *with her hair bobbed*.

—頭 bobbed hair. ¶彼女は～頭になった She *had* her hair *bobbed*.

おかどちがい【お門違い】 ¶そんな苦情は～だ Such a complaint *has nothing to do with* me. / You are complaining to *the wrong* man. ぼくのところに(頼みに)来るなんて～だ You have come to *the wrong shop*.

おかぶ【お株】 ¶彼に歌の～を奪われた He *outshone* me *in* my favorite song.

おかぼ【陸稲】 upland rice〔plant〕; dryland rice〔plant〕.

おかまい【お構い】 ¶どうぞ～なく Please don't bother. (人が帰るとき)～もせず失礼しました(英語では内容によって) Thank you for coming. / Very glad to have met you.

おかみ【御上】(当局者) the authorities; (政府) the government; (天皇) the Emperor; His Majesty; (主君) *one's* lord. ¶～のご用で on *official* business.

おがみたお·す【拝み倒す】(人に頼みこむ) win (*a person*) over by entreaty; entreat (*a person*) into consent. ¶とうとう彼に～された At last I had to consent to his repeated entreaties.

おが·む【拝む】 worship; pray. ¶かしわ手を打って神を～んだ We clapped our hands to *worship* the god. 手を合わせて～む *pray* with *one's* hands folded. ～むから助けてくれ I *beg* (≒ *entreat*) you *for* your help.

おかめはちもく【傍目八目】 The outsider sees the best of the game. / Lookers-on see more than the players.

おかやき【傍焼き】 jealousy〔entertained by the third party〕. ¶彼は私に～している He *is jealous of* me. / He *is envious of* me.

おから【雪花菜】 bean-curd refuse.

おかわり【お代わり】 a second helping; another helping; another cup; another glass. ¶～をどうぞ Will you please have (≒ take) *helping*? お茶の～をどうぞ Won't you have *another* cup of tea?

おかん【悪寒】 a chill. ¶ひどく～がする I *feel* badly *chilly*. / I *feel a* severe *chill*.

おかんむり【お冠】 displeasure; sullenness. ¶ひどく～だ He *is* very *displeased*. その発言に彼は～だ He *is displeased with* the remark. 彼は～でものも言わない He *is* too *cross* to speak.

おき【沖】 the offing. ¶2マイル～に two miles *off the shore*. ～にこぎ出そう Let's pull out to *sea*.

-おき【-置き】 ¶1日～に *every* other day. 3日～に *every* four days; *every* fourth day. 1行～に on *every* other line. 1時間～に at intervals of an hour. 2メートル～に two meters apart.

おぎ【荻】〔植物〕 a common reed.

おきあい【沖合い】 ¶～に停泊する cast anchor *off the coast*.

おきあがりこぼうし【起き上がり小法師】 a tumbling *Dharma* toy.

おきあが·る【起き上がる】 get up; rise. ¶この子は転んでもすぐ～る The child *rises* as soon as he tumbles down.

おきか·える【置き換える】 ¶部屋の中の家具を～える *rearrange* the furniture in the room. 石炭ストーブをガスストーブに～える *replace* a potbellied stove *with* a gas heater.

おきざり【置き去り】 ¶彼はただひとり～にされた He *was deserted* (≒ *was left*) alone. 子どもを～にして彼は立ち去った He went away *leaving his child*〔*behind*〕.

オキシフル〔薬品〕 Oxyful (商品名).

おきちが·える【置き違える】 misplace; put (*a thing*) in the wrong way.

おきづり【沖釣り】 offshore angling (≒ fishing).

おきて【掟】 a law; a rule; a regulation. ¶～を守る keep the *rule*; observe the *law*; stick to the *rule*. ～を破る break the *law*.

おきてがみ【置き手紙】 a letter left behind. ¶彼は～をして出かけていった He went out of doors *leaving a letter at home*. ～がしてある. 何事だろう *A note* is left here. What has happened to him?

おきどけい【置き時計】 a table (≒ desk; mantel) clock.

おきどころ【置き所】 ¶身の～もない I have no place to rest my head in the world. 自動車を買いたいが～がない I want to buy a car, but have no place to park it.

おぎない【補い】a supplement.

おぎな·う【補う】supplement; make up (*for*); make good; (埋め合わせをする) compensate. ¶ 損失を～う *make up for* the loss. 健康の損失は～えない Nothing can *compensate for* the loss of our health. 彼は本を書いて収入を～っている He *supplements* his income *by* writing books.

おきなお·る【起き直る】sit up.

おきなかし【沖仲士】a stevedore.

おきにいり【お気に入り】*one's* favorite; a pet. ¶ ～の favorite. 彼はおじさんの～だ He is *a favorite with* his uncle. / He is his uncle's *favorite*. 彼女は先生の～だ She is the teacher's *pet*.

おきぬけ【起き抜け】¶ ～に庭へ出た I went out into the garden *as soon as I got up*. 明朝～にお電話します I'll telephone you 〔*the*〕 *first thing in the morning*.

おきば【置き場】¶ これらの本の～がない I can find no *room for* these books. これらの物の～はどこですか Where do these things belong? (答えは belong *in* the bookcase などとなる).
木材— a lumberyard (英 timberyard); a woodshed. 石炭— a coal shed. 自転車— a bicycle shed.

おきまり【お決まり】¶ ～の文句 a *stock* phrase; *habitual* words; a cliché; *one's favorite* expression. それは彼の～だ That *is usual with* him.

おきみやげ【置き土産】¶ その研究を～にして世を去った He passed away, leaving the research behind as *a parting present* to the world.

おきもの【置物】¶ 床の間の～ *an ornament* for the alcove.

おぎゃあ ¶ 赤ん坊が～と泣く A baby *mewls*.

お·きる【起きる】**1**〖起床する·目を覚ます〗get up. ¶ 私は5時に～きる I *get up* at five.
もう～きなさい. 学校に遅れますよ *Wake up*, or you will be late for school.
冬は暖かいベッドから～きるのがつらい In winter, it is hard to *get out of* the warm bed.
2〖眠らないでいる〗¶ 昨夜は遅くまで～きてテレビを見ていた I *sat up* late last night watching television.
とても眠くて～きていられない I am too sleepy to *keep awake*.
家の中は真っ暗でだれも～きているようすはなかった It was dark and no one seemed to *be stirring* in the house.
3〖起き上がる〗¶ 子どもは転んで～きてまた走りだした The child fell, *got up* and then started to run again.
病人は寝たり～きたりの状態です The patient is not exactly confined to bed but cannot move around too much.
頭が痛くて～きていられなかった I had such a bad headache that I could not *be up*.
もう～きてもいいと医者は言った The doctor said that I might *leave my bed*.
4〖発生する〗¶ いったいなにが～きたんだ Whatever (≒ Whatever) *has happened*?
困ったことが～きた Trouble *has arisen*. / Something difficult *has happened*.
まったく私の不注意から～きたことです Everything *started* from my carelessness.
騒動が～きそうだ A riot is likely to *break out*.

お·きる【熾きる】¶ 火ばちの火が～きましたか *Have* you *fixed* fire in the brazier?

おきわすれる【置き忘れる】leave (場所を示す語句とともに); forget (場所を示す語句がないとき). ¶ 机の上に本を～れた I *have left* the book on the desk. 手紙をどこかに～れた I *have mislaid* the letter somewhere. かさを～れぬように Be careful not to *leave* your umbrella *behind*. バスにかばんを～れた I *lost* my bag in the bus. 財布を～れて取りに戻った I *forgot* my wallet and went back for it.

おく【億】a (≒ one) hundred million〔s〕. ¶ 10～ 米 a billion; 英 a thousand million〔s〕.

おく【奥】(入り口から離れた所) the inner part; the recesses; (深い所, 奥底) the depth. ¶ 山の～ *the heart* of a mountain. 心の～ *the depth* of *one's* heart. そのほら穴の～に in *the innermost part* of the cave. ～にお通ししなさい Show him into *the drawing room*.

お·く【置く】**1**〖物を〗put. ¶ どこにこれを～きましょうか Where shall I *put* this?
たなの上に～いてください *Put* it on the shelf, please.
こんなにたくさんの荷物は～く場所がない There is no room to *put away* so many things.
この品物はそっと～いてください *Put* this article *down* carefully.
逆さに～くと壊れるから注意してください Be sure to *place* it right side up, otherwise it will be broken.
2〖残しておく〗leave. ¶ 彼は郷里に家族を～いて東京に出た He went to Tokyo, *leaving* his family at home.
彼女は手紙を～いて立ち去った She has gone *with* a message *left behind*. / She has gone *leaving* a letter *behind*.
ぜひお金を少し～いていってください Be sure to *leave* some money for me.
3〖…のままにする〗¶ 窓を開け放しにして～いた I *left* the window open.
ほうって～くとだめになります It will spoil, if *left there* (≒ *uncared for*).
彼のなすがままにさせて～いた I *let* him do it as he wanted to.
4〖ある状態に保つ〗keep. ¶ ビールを冷やして～くのを忘れないで Be sure to *keep* the beer cold.
今のうちにお金をためて～きなさい Save your money while you can.
彼はその絵を食堂の壁に掛けて～いた He *kept* the picture hanging on the wall of the dining room.
5〖人をある状態に置く〗¶ あなたは不利な立場に～かれている You *are placed* in a disadvantageous situation.
彼をそのような環境に～いておくわけにはゆかぬ We

お

cannot *leave* him in such an environment. われわれは今きわめて困難な状況に～かれている We *are put* in a very difficult situation.

6 〖貯蔵する〗 keep. ¶ この魚は(そんなに)長く～いておけない This fish cannot *be kept* for a long time.

これは暗い湿気のない所に～いておきなさい *Keep* this in a dark, dry place.

7 〖陳列する〗 ¶ あの書店には洋書は～いてない That bookstore does not *stock* (≒ 米 *carry*) foreign books.

8 〖召使・下宿人を〗 ¶ とてもお手伝いさんを～く余裕はありません We cannot *afford* 〔*to keep*〕 a maid.

彼女は下宿人を～いて生計の足しにしている She *takes in* some boarders to supplement her income.

9 〖設置する〗 ¶ 当会社は全国主要都市に支店を～いております This company *has* branch offices in major cities of the country.

10 〖駐在させる・任命する〗 ¶ 当社はこの度ペキンに特派員を～くことになった Our company decided on *sending* a new correspondent to Peking.

ご旅行中はだれか代理を～いていってください *Appoint* someone to take your place, while you are away on a trip.

11 〖隔てる〗 ¶ それから 3 日～いて彼女は再びぼくのところに来た She came to me again four days *afterward*.

お·く 【措く】 ¶ そのことはしばらく～くとして *laying* this *aside* for a moment. この難事業をやってのけるのは彼を～いてほかにはない No one *except* (≒ *but*) him are equal to this difficult enterprise. きみを～いてはほかにだれも考えられぬ I cannot count on anybody *except* you. 彼女を～いてほかに適任者はない Nobody *but* her qualifies for the position. 感嘆～くあたわざるものあり I *cannot help* admiring it. 冗談はさて～ききみの本心はどうなのだ Joking *aside*, what do you really mean?

おくがい 【屋外】 the outdoors.
—競技 outdoor games. **—スポーツ** outdoor (≒ open-air) sports.

おくがた 【奥方】 a lady; the wife of a nobleman.

おくぎ 【奥義】 the mystery; the secret.
¶ ～をきわめる master *the secret*〔*s*〕 (*of*); see into *the heart* (*of*). ～を授ける initiate (*a person*) into *the secrets* (*of*).

おくざしき 【奥座敷】 an inner room.

おくさま 【奥様】 (人の妻) *a person's* wife; a married lady; (呼びかけ) Mrs....
¶ あの方はどなたの～ですか Whose *wife* is she? / Who is that *lady*? ～, Aさんからお電話でございます Miss A is on the phone, *ma'am*.

おくじょう 【屋上】 the roof. ¶ ～屋を架すようなものだ This is like *carrying coals to Newcastle*.

おく·する 【臆する】 ¶ おめず～せず without *hesitation*. 彼はその恐ろしい光景を見ても～さなかった He *was undaunted* at the horrible sight.

彼はどこにいても～することはない He never *gets nervous* wherever he may be.

おくそく 【憶測】 a guess; a conjecture.
¶ それは～にすぎない That is *a mere guess* (≒ *conjecture*). 私の～は当たっていた My *guess* was right. / I *guessed* right. あなたの～は外れている Your *guess* is wrong. / You *guess* wrong. 彼の知識はたいしたものではないと私は～した I *suspected* his knowledge did not amount to very much.

おくそこ 【奥底】 the depth. ¶ 心の～では安心している I am relieved *at the bottom of* my heart. 彼は心の～から感謝している He is grateful *from the bottom of* his heart.

オクターブ 〔音楽〕 an octave. ¶ 1～声を高くする raise *one's* voice *an octave* higher. 1～低くする drop *one's* voice *an octave* lower.

オクタンか 【オクタン価】 octane number.
¶ ～の高いガソリン high-*octane* gasoline.

おくづけ 【奥付け】 a colophon.

おくて 【奥手・晩生】 (米) a late variety of rice; (野菜・果実) late crops.
¶ この子は～だ The child *is late maturing*. / This child *is backward*.

おくない 【屋内】 ¶ ～のスポーツ *indoor* sports. ～で遊ぶ play *indoors*.
—競技 indoor games. **—競技場** a gymnasium.

おくに 【御国】 (相手の故郷) your home town; (相手の人の国家) your country. ¶ ～はどちらですか Where do you come from? / Where are you from? / Where is your *home town*? (大都会でも村でもよい). 彼はよく～自慢をする He often talks proudly about his own *home* (≒ *country*).
—ことば the dialect of *one's* home.

おくのて 【奥の手】 (最後の手段) the last resort.
¶ ～を出す play *one's best card*. きみにそんな～があるとは知らなかった I never imagined you held such *a trump*.

おくば 【奥歯】 (臼歯) a molar; a back tooth.
¶ ～に物がはさまったような言い方だった He talked as if he was (≒ were) concealing something. / He seemed to hold back something in his talk.

おくび 【噯気】 belching. ¶ 彼はそんなことは～にも出さなかった He did not show the slightest sign of it. / He just kept silent about it.

おくびょう 【臆病】 cowardice; timidity.
¶ 彼はなんて～なんだ How *cowardly* he *is*! / What *a coward* he is!
—風 ¶ 彼は～風に吹かれた He *lost his nerve*. / He *became timid*. **—者** a coward.

おくふか·い 【奥深い】 ¶ ～い洞窟 a *deep* cave. ～い原理 a *profound* doctrine. その動物は～い山中に住む The animal lives *far back* in the mountains.

おくま·った 【奥まった】 ¶ ～った部屋 an *inner* room. ～った所(人里離れた) a *secluded* place.

おくめん 【臆面】 ¶ 彼は～もなく金を貸せと言った He asked me *impudently* for a loan of money.

おくゆかし·い【奥ゆかしい】¶ ～い女性 a *graceful* lady. ～い生活 an *elegant* life. ～いことば *refined* words.

おくゆき【奥行き】depth ; length. ¶ 彼の学問は～がない His knowledge *is not profound*. ～3メートルの所に three meters *inside* from the front.

おくら·せる【遅らせる】¶ 時計を10分～せる *turn* (⇐ *set*) *back* the watch ten minutes.

おくりじょう【送り状】an invoice ([ínvɔis] と発音する).

おくりだ·す【送り出す】¶ この包みはすぐ～してください Will you please *send off* this package at once? 彼をバス停まで～した I *saw* him *to* the bus stop.

おくりな【おくり名·諡】a posthumous name (⇐ title).

おくりむかえ【送り迎え】¶ 子どもの～は彼に頼んだ I asked him to *take* my child *to and from* school.

おくりもの【贈り物】a present ; a gift. ¶ 彼女にネックレスの～をした I *made* her *a present of* a necklace. / I *presented* her *with* a necklace.

おく·る【送る】**1**〖物を発送する〗send. ¶ 荷物は車で～ります The baggage will *be sent* by car.

～った小包は届いたでしょうか Have you received the package I *sent to* you? / I wonder if you received the package I *sent to* you.

代金は為替で～ります The money will *be sent* by money order.

鉄道で～ったほうがトラックで～るより安い It is cheaper to *send* it by rail than by truck.

世界各国から救援物資が～られてきた Relief goods *were sent* from various countries of the world.

彼から感謝の手紙が～られてきた A letter of gratitude *was sent to* me from him.

2〖送り届ける〗¶ お宅まで車でお～りします I will *drive* you *home*. / Let me *take* you *home* by car.

このお方を駅までお～りしなさい *See* this gentleman *to* the station.

3〖見送る〗¶ 駅には彼を～る人がたくさん来ていた A lot of people were at the station to *see* him *off*.

彼は私をわざわざ門まで～ってきた He took the trouble to *see* me *to* the gate.

4〖過ごす〗spend. ¶ 彼は余生を郷里の村で～った He *spent* the rest of his life in his home village.

彼はなすことなく日を～った He *idled away* his time.

平和で豊かな生活を～ることが国民ひとりひとりの願いである *Living a* happy and prosperous *life* is what each person wishes for.

そのひと月というものは毎日毎日の大半を寄付金集めに～った I *spent* most of the time raising funds during that month.

おく·る【贈る】make (*a person*) a present (*of something*); (授与する) confer (*something on a person*). ¶ 彼女に指輪を～った I *made* her *a present of* a ring. 私はその女の子にお別れのしるしとして人形を～った I *gave* a doll *to* the girl as a souvenir. 彼に博士号が～られた A doctor's degree *was conferred on* him. 彼は女王から MBE 勲位を～られた He *was awarded* the MBE by the Queen.

おくれ【後れ·遅れ】¶ 彼に～をとった I *was outstripped by* him. どんなことでも人には～をとるな Never *drop behind* other people in anything. ようやく仕事の～を取り戻した I *have caught up with* my work at last.

おく·れる【遅れる·後れる】**1**〖時計が〗¶ この時計は2分～れている This clock *is* two minutes *slow*.

この時計は日に3分～れる This clock *loses* three minutes a day.

2〖定刻に〗¶ この列車は～れている This train *is late*.

列車は事故のため1時間～れた The train *was* one hour *late* because of an accident. / The train *was delayed* one hour because of an accident.

けさは学校に～れた I *was late for* school this morning.

彼は～れて会合にやってきた He arrived *late for* the meeting.

彼女は約束の時間に10分～れてきた She *was* ten minutes *late for* the appointment.

運転手は～れた時間を取り戻そうとつとめた The driver tried to make up for the *lost* time.

ことしは春の来方が～れている Spring *comes late* this year.

その会社の支払が～れて困っている We are troubled by the *delayed* payment from the company.

次のマラソン走者は100メートルほど～れて競技場に入ってきた The next runner came into the stadium about one hundred meters *behind*.

3〖文化·学業·発育などが〗¶ そんなことをしていると時勢に～れる You will *be behind the times*, if you keep doing that.

時勢に～れないようにニュース番組をよく見る In order to *keep up with the times*, I very often watch TV news programs.

この国は重工業の発達が～れている This country *is slow in* developing its heavy industries.

彼は勉強が～れている He *is backward in* his studies.

未熟児だったので知能の発達が～れている The baby *is slow in* intellectual development, because he was born prematurely.

病気で1か月休んだので勉強が人より～れてしまった I am *behind* the others in my studies, because I have been sick in bed for a month.

ことしは苗の発育が～れている The growth of seedlings *is slow* this year.

工事は予定よりはるかに～れている The construction work *is* far *behind* the schedule.

いなかは都会に比べると文化が～れている The rural areas *are* culturally *behind* the urban areas.

おけ【桶】(洗たく用) a tub; (手おけ) a pail.

おけら【螻蛄】〖虫類〗a mole cricket; (俗語) (一文なし) a penniless man.

おこえがかり【お声掛かり】¶社長の～で彼を採用した We engaged him on the president's *recommendation*.

おこがまし·い【烏滸がましい】¶そいつは～い(ばかばかしい)話だ That's a *laughable* (≒ *ridiculous*) story. 自分で言うのも～いがそんな仕事ならばやってみせる I *flatter myself* that I am equal to the task. ～いやつだ(出過ぎた) He is a *forward* fellow.

おこ·す【熾す】¶彼はいろりに火を～した He *built* (≒ *made*) a fire in the hearth. 炭火を～す *make* fire with charcoal.

おこ·す【起こす】1〖倒れたものを〗¶あらしで倒れた庭の木を～しているところだ I *am* just *setting up* the tree the storm knocked down.

転んで泣いている子を助け～してやった A child had fallen down and was crying, and I *helped* him *to his feet*.

2〖眠っている人を〗¶彼はいくら～しても起きなかった I *called* him again and again, but he did not wake up.

母が6時に私を～してくれた My mother *woke* me *up* at six.

3〖発生させる〗¶雨の日は事故を～しやすいから注意しなさい Take special care on rainy days, as accidents are likely to *occur*.

彼は発作を～して倒れた He *had a fit* and fell down.

ささいなことが口論を～すもととなった A small matter *caused* the disputes. / The disputes *arose* out of a trifle.

そういうことを言うと各方面に摩擦を～しやすいからよしてくれ Don't say it; it would *cause* trouble all over.

そんなことでねたみ心を～すな Don't be jealous over such a thing.

彼はわざわざ平地に波瀾(らん)を～したがる He likes to *raise* troubles where there is no cause.

4〖やりはじめる〗¶彼は会社を相手どって訴訟を～した He *sued* the company. / He *brought a lawsuit against* the company.

食糧不足のため市民は暴動を～した A shortage of food *drove* the citizens *to* riot.

運賃値上げ反対運動を～す *start* a campaign *against* the raise in fares.

新しく事業を～すので,助けていただきたいのです We need your help in *starting* a new enterprise. / Could you help us *start* a new business?

おこ·す【興す】¶彼は破産した家を再び～した He *restored* his ruined house *to* its former prosperity. 彼は貧しい境遇から身を～した He *rose* from the gutter.

おごそか【厳か】¶～な儀式 a *solemn* ceremony. ～に in a *solemn* (≒ *grave*) tone.

おこたりがち【怠り勝ち】¶野球が好きで勉強を～だ I like playing baseball so much that I *am* often *neglectful of* my study.

おこた·る【怠る】neglect; be lazy; (怠ける) be idle. ¶彼は職務を～った He *was neglectful of* his duties. / He *neglected* his duties.

おこない【行ない】an action. ¶きみのそういう～はとがめられるべきだ You are to blame for such *conduct*. 彼は～がいい He *is* good-*mannered*. そういう～は慎んだほうがいい You must refrain from that sort of *behavior*. 彼は～を改めようとしない He won't mend his *ways*. 彼女がそんな～をしたとは驚いた I was surprised that she should *have acted* like that. 彼のその～は賞賛に値する That *conduct* of his is worthy of praise.

おこな·う【行なう】¶悪事を～う人はだれからもきらわれる Those who *do* wrong are hated by everybody. 言うはやすく～うはかたし(諺) It is easier to preach than to *practice*. / *Easier said than done*. その試験は明後日に～う The examination will *be given* the day after tomorrow.

おこなわ·れる【行なわれる】¶その試験はあす～れる The examination will *be given* tomorrow. 式典は晴雨にかかわらず～れる The ceremony will *be held* whether it rains or not. この島ではいろいろ変わった祭式が～れる Various strange rites *are observed* on this island.

おこら·せる【怒らせる】make (*a person*) angry. ¶彼はよく友だちを～せる He often *gives offense to* his friends. なにが彼女を～せたのだ What *has put* her *out of temper*? 彼を～せたらたいへんだ If you *offend* him, the situation will become serious.

おこり【起こり】the origin. ¶事の～は今から50年前です It *originated* fifty years ago. 事の～はこんなぐあいだった This is how it happened to *start*. この習慣の～はインドだ This custom *is of* Indian *origin*.

おごり【奢り】(ぜいたく) luxury; extravagance; (ご馳走) a treat. ¶彼女の生活は～をきわめている She lives in [the lap of] *luxury*. この一杯はぼくの～だ This drink is my *treat*. 今夜はぼくの～だ You're my guest this evening.

おこ·る【起こる】(事故などが) happen; occur. ¶事故はいつ～ったのか When did the accident *take place*? その事件は今から2年前に～った The incident *occurred* two years ago. なにかが彼の身の上に～ったのかもしれない Something may *have happened* to him. やっかいなことが～った A trouble *arose*. 雨の日は交通事故が～りがちだ Traffic accidents are likely to *occur* on rainy days. 物を摩擦すると電気が～る Friction *generates* electricity.

おこ·る【興る】¶原子力産業が～った Atomic industry *has sprung up*. アジアの未開発国が最近～ってきた Underdeveloped countries in Asia *have come to prosper* lately.

おこ·る【怒る】¶彼は私に対して～っている He *gets angry with* me. こんなことに～ってはならない You mustn't *get angry at* such a thing. なにをそんなに～っているのだ What *makes* you so *angry*? 彼の～っているのを見たことがない I have never seen him *out of temper*. 彼は簡単には～らない He is slow to *take offense*. ～りやすいのが彼の唯一の欠点だ His only defect is that he *gets irritable* easily. 彼は不当な扱いを受けて～っている He *is offended at* being badly treated. 彼の～った顔は見ものだ His *angry* look is a sight to see. 彼女は～って部屋を出ていった She went out of the room *in anger*.

おこ・る【熾る】 ¶ いろりに火が～った A fire *is made* in the hearth.

おご・る【奢る】 ¶ 彼は～った暮らしをしていた He lived *in luxury*. 晩飯を～ろう I'll *stand* you a dinner this evening. じゃ～ってもらおうか Then, let me feel guilty. きょうはきみが～る番だ It is your *treat* today. 彼は口が～っている He *keeps a good table*.

おご・る【驕る・傲る】 ¶ ～る者久しからず (諺) *Pride goes before a fall*. 彼のわれわれに対する態度は～り高ぶったものだ He *is arrogant with* us.

おさえ【押さえ・抑え】 ¶ この書類には～(文鎮)が必要だ We want *a paperweight* for these documents. 彼は部下の～がきかない He cannot *control* his men.

おさえがた・い【抑え難い】 uncontrollable. ¶ ～い欲望が彼を襲った He was prompted by an *irresistible* temptation. 彼の独立したいという気持ちは～かった His desire for independence *was uncontrollable*.

おさ・える【押さえる・抑える】 **1**〖動かぬようにする〗 hold. ¶ はしごをしっかりと～えていてください *Hold* the ladder tight, please.

紙が飛ばないようにこれで～えておきなさい Put this on the paper, so that it cannot be blown off.

彼が入ってこないように戸を～えた I *held* the door *shut* to prevent his coming in.

飛びつかないように犬を～えていてくれ *Hold* the dog *down* so that it may not jump on me.

笑いを見せまいと手で口を～えた She *held* a hand *over* her mouth to cover her smile.

彼はぼくの手を～えて引き止めた *Taking hold of* my hand, he did not let me go.

2〖感情を〗 ¶ ぼくははやる気持ちを～えた I *restrained* my passion.

彼は怒りを～えて相手の言うことを聞いていた He *repressed* his anger, and listened to the other party.

彼女はその知らせを聞いて涙を～えることができなかった When she heard the news, she could not *keep* her tears *back*.

～えつけられていた欲求不満が一気に爆発した His *suppressed* frustration suddenly broke out.

3〖確保する〗 ¶ すべての通信機関は反乱軍の手に～えられた All the information facilities *have* now *fallen into* the hands of the rebel army.

動かぬ証拠物件を～えてある We *got hold of* an undeniable evidence.

4〖捕らえる〗 ¶ すりを現場で～えた A pickpocket *was caught* in the act.

5〖費用を食い止める・見積もる〗 ¶ 生産費1個1,000円以下に～えることはできないか Can't you *hold* the production cost below one thousand yen a piece?

物価の上昇を～えることは難しい It is difficult to *check* the rise in prices.

接待費を～えないと赤字になる You will go into red unless you *cut down* the entertainment expenses.

6〖抑圧する〗 ¶ 味方の打撃はすっかりあの投手に～えられた All the batting of our nine *was held down* by his pitching.

警察には暴動を～えるだけの力はなかった The police did not have enough power to *suppress* the rioters.

彼は女房に～えられて頭が上がらない He *is* completely *under his wife's thumb*. // He *is a henpecked husband*.

上の兄弟に～えられてあの子はいつも小さくなっている He is always timid, because he *is bossed by* his older brothers.

あの人のわがままを～える人がいないので困っている The pity is that there is no one who can *check* his selfishness.

安打2本に～えられてはどうしようもない We can't do anything with only two hits.

あの足の速いウイングを～えなければ勝ち味はない We have no chance, unless we *check* that swift wing.

7〖没収する〗 ¶ 借金不払いの故に給料全額を～えることは違法である It is against the law to *seize* a man's whole salary on account of unpaid debts.

おさがり【お下がり】 hand-me-downs; old (≒ used) clothes handed down from *one's* father or *one's* brother.

おさき【お先】 ¶ ～に失礼(中途で退席する) Excuse me for leaving now. / (相手より先に出る) Excuse me for going first. ～にどうぞ Go ahead. / After you. ～真っ暗だ I don't have any bright *future*.

おさきぼう【お先棒】 ¶ その件では彼は～を担いだ He *was willingly made a cat's-paw in* that affair.

おさげ【お下げ】 a plait; a pigtail. ¶ ～にしている She wears her hair in *a plait*. / She has her *hair hanging down the shoulder*.

おさつ【お札】 a bill; a bank note; paper money. ¶ 1,000円の～ *a* thousand yen *bill*.

おさと【お里】 (実家) *one's* parents' house; (素性) *one's* origin. ¶ 彼女のあの身なりでは～が知れる Her dress betrays her *origin* (≒ *character*).

おさな・い【幼い】 very young; infant; (子どもっぽい) childish; (幼稚な) infantile. ¶ 彼はまだ～い He *is very young*. / (子どもっぽい) He *is childish*.

おさながお【幼顔】 *one's* baby (≒ childhood) face. ¶ 彼にはまだ～が残っている He still retains some of his *infant features*.

おさなごころ【幼心】 a child's mind; *one's*

お

innocent heart. ¶ ～にもなんだか変に思えた It seemed a little strange even to my *childish mind*.

おさなともだち【幼友だち】a childhood friend.

おさななじみ【幼馴染み】a friend of *one's* infancy (≒ childhood). ¶ 彼らは～だ They have known one another since they were children.

おざなり【お座なり】¶ ～を言ってごまかした I evaded the real issue, saying *common-places* just to suit the occasion. 彼は～のやり方でその仕事を済ませた He did the work in a *perfunctory* manner.

おさまり【納まり】¶ その事件はまだ～がつかない The affair *has* not *been settled* yet. この事件はなかなか～がつきそうにない This affair is not likely to *be brought to an end* in the near future.

おさま・る【収まる・納まる】¶ この箱にリンゴは全部～るだろう All the apples will *go in* this box. そのケースにこの扇風機は～らない This fan won't *go in* that case. そんな回答で私は～らない I *am* not *satisfied with* such an answer.

おさま・る【治まる】(静かになる) calm down; (平和になる) be at peace.
¶ その国はうまく～っている The nation *is at peace*. 暴動はまだ～らない The riot *has* not *been suppressed*. 風は～りそうにない The wind shows no sign of *dropping*. 雨は急に～った The rain *stopped* suddenly. 1日たっても痛みはまだ～らない Though a day has passed since then, the pain *has* not *gone* yet. 苦痛は～っている The pain *has passed*. 戦争はやっと～った The war *came to an end* at last.

おさま・る【修まる】¶ どうも彼は素行が～らない I am afraid he won't *mend his ways*. / He seems unable to *mend his ways*.

おさ・める【収める・納める】**1**〚中に入れる・しまう〛put. ¶ 彼は金を数えてかばんに～めた He counted the money and *stowed* it *away* in his bag. 証書は金庫に～めてあるはずだ I am sure the bond *is kept* in the safe. この小説は彼の全集に～められていない This novel *is* not *included* in his collected works. これはあなただけの胸に～めておいてください Please *keep* this *to yourself*.
2〚納入する〛¶ ご注文の品は今月末までにはお～めいたします The goods you kindly ordered from us will *be delivered to* you by the end of this month. / We expect to *supply* your orders by the end of this month. 当社は都内小中学校に手広く机・いすを～めている We are extensively engaged in the business of *serving* elementary and junior high schools in the city *with* desks and chairs. 税金をまだ～めていない I *have* not *paid* my taxes yet. 入学金をいくら～めましたか How much entrance fee *have* you *paid*?
3〚獲得する〛¶ 彼は為替変動を利用してばく大な利益を～めた He took advantage of the fluctuations in exchange, and *made* an enormous profit. その国は武力によって同地方の石油資源を手中に～めた The country *took possession of* the oil resources in the area by force of arms.

おさ・める【治める】¶ 国王は国を～める A king *rules over* the country. 家を～めるのは主人だ The master *manages* his household. 彼には騒ぎを～める責任があった He had the responsibility for *suppressing* the uprising. そのごたごたを丸く～めることはむずかしい It is difficult to *settle* the trouble amicably.

おさ・める【修める】(修業) pursue; study; (修養) cultivate. ¶ 生け花について一通りのことは～めた I *have acquired* a general knowledge of the art of flower arrangement. 彼は大学で中世文学を～めた He *has completed* his studies of medieval literature at a university.

おさらい【お浚い】(復習) a review; (けいこ) a rehearsal. ¶ 習ったところを～しましょう Let's *review* what we have learned so far.

おさらば Good-bye!; Farewell!; Adieu.
¶ 彼は～をきめこんだ He *absconded*.

おさん【お産】childbirth; a delivery. ¶ 彼女の～は軽かった She had *an* easy *delivery*. 彼女はけさ～した She *had* a baby this morning. / She *gave birth to* a baby this morning.

おし【押し】a push; (ずうずうしさ) audacity.
¶ 彼は～が強い He *is aggressive*. / He *has got lots of nevers*. 彼は～が弱い He *is fainthearted*. ～の一手でいこう Let's *push forward*.

おし【唖】a dumb person.

おじ【叔父・伯父】an uncle.

おしあ・う【押し合う】push one another. ¶ 群衆は～いへし合いで駅へ入った The crowd *jostled into* the station. どうか～わないでください Please don't *jostle one another*.

おし・い【惜しい】regrettable. ¶ 今は一刻も～い *There is not a moment to lose* now. この本は捨てるには～い This book *is too good to* be thrown away. テレビを見るのに時間を使うのは～い Time *is* too *valuable* to spend in watching television. 彼の夭折(ようせつ)は国家にとって～い His early death *is a* great *loss to* the nation. 命はだれでも～い Life *is precious to* every one of us. このチャンスをものにできなかったことは～い *It is a pity that* I should have failed to grasp this opportunity. ～いところで負けた I lost the game I had nearly won. ～いことに彼は今東京にはいない *It is a pity that* he should not be in Tokyo now. たいへん～いことをした It *was a great pity*. 歌手になれるならなにをやっても～くない I *would give anything to* be able to become a singer. 彼に会えるなら10万円を犠牲にしても～くない I *would give* ten thousand yen to meet him.

おじいさん【お祖父さん】a grandfather; (小児語) a grandpa.

おじいさん【お爺さん】an old man.

おしい·る【押し入る】¶ 昨夜どろぼうが隣家に～った A burglar *broke into* my neighbor's house last night.

おしいれ【押し入れ】a closet.

おしうり【押し売り】forcing sale; (人) an importunate peddler. ¶ ～する force (≒ press) (*a person*) to buy; force a sale on (*a person*).

おしえ【教え】teaching. ¶ 中学校では彼に～を受けた During my junior high school days, I *was taught* by him. 両親の～に従うのは当然だ It is natural to follow the *precepts* of our parents. 私は個人的に彼に英語の～を受けた I was given personal *instruction* in English by him.

おしえこ·む【教え込む】¶ 礼儀作法は子どものころ～むのがよい Training in good manners *is* best *given* in *one's* childhood.

おし·える【教える】teach. ¶ 外国語を～える *teach* a foreign language. 泳ぎ方を～える *teach* how to swim. バス停へ行く道を～えてください Could you *tell* me the way to the bus stop? / Please *direct* me to the bus stop. この問題の解き方を～えていただきたいのですが Would you mind *showing* me how to solve this problem? 彼は近所の子どもたちに個人的に数学を～えている He *teaches* mathematics privately to the children in his neighborhood. / He *tutors* the children in the neighborhood *in* mathematics. 彼はバイオリンを彼女に～えている He *gives* her violin *lessons*. 彼にこの機械の使い方を～えてもらおう I want him to *give* me *instructions* for using this machine.

おしかえ·す【押し返す】¶ 警官は群衆を～した The police *pushed back* the crowd.

おしかけにょうぼう【押しかけ女房】a self-claimed wife.

おしか·ける【押しかける】visit; go uninvited; (大ぜいで) throng. ¶ 大ぜいの人がその映画を見ようと～けた A lot of people *thronged* to see the movie. 1日じゅう学生たちに～けられた I *was visited* by the students all day.

おしかり【お叱り】a scolding.

おじぎ【お辞儀】a bow. ¶ 彼は深く～をした He made *a* low *bow*. 彼は私の方にちょっと～をした He *bowed* slightly to me. / He *nodded to* me. 彼は帽子にちょっと手をあてて～をした He touched his hat.

おしきせ【お仕着せ】〔a〕livery.

おじぎそう【含羞草】〖植物〗a mimosa.

おしき·る【押し切る】¶ われわれはあらゆる反対を～った We *have overcome* all opposition. この法案を圧倒的多数の力で～るつもりだ We will *carry* the bill *through* by an overwhelming majority.

おしくも【惜しくも】to *one's* regret; to *one's* disappointment. ¶ 彼は～優勝を逸した He was defeated *by a narrow margin* in the championship tournament.

おしげ【惜しげ】¶ 彼はお金を～もなく困っている人に与える He gives money *freely* to the needy. / He *lavishes* money *on* poor people. 彼女は～もなく長い美しい髪を切った She cut her long beautiful hair *without the least regret*.

おじけづ·く【怖じ気づく】¶ 人の前に出ると～く I *become timid* (≒ *become nervous*) before others. 聴衆の前に出ると～いてしまう When I face the audience, I *have stage fright*. ～いて口がきけなかった I *was* too *scared* to speak. 子どもたちはその音に～いた The children *were frightened at* the sound.

おしこみ【押し込み】—強盗 a burglar.

おしこ·む【押し込む】¶ 彼女は部屋に～められた She *was shut up in* the room. / (文字どおり押し込める) She *was pushed into* the room. 大ぜいが部屋に～められた(詰めこまれた) A crowd *was jammed* (≒ *was crammed*) *into* the room.

おしこ·める【押し込める】⇒おしこむ

おじさん【伯父さん·叔父さん·小父さん】(叔父さん) an uncle; (小父さん) a gentleman. ¶ ～! (呼びかけ) Mister; Uncle. よその～ *a* strange *gentleman*.

おしすす·める【押し進める】¶ 計画を～める *go ahead with* a plan; *push on with* a plan.

おしたお·す【押し倒す】¶ 後ろから～された I *was pushed down* from behind.

おしだし【押し出し】**1**〖風采〗¶ 彼はまったく～がよい He *looks* quite *presentable*. 彼の～は堂々としている His *appearance* is imposing. 彼の～はりっぱだ He *has a* dignified *appearance*. **2**〖野球〗¶ ～で1点とった We got a point by *forcing*.

おしだ·す【押し出す】¶ 彼を部屋から～した I *pushed* him *out of* the room.

おした·てる【押し立てる】¶ われわれは彼を前面に～てた We *put* him *at the front*. 彼らは旗を～てて進んだ They marched with a flag *hoisted* (≒ *put up*).

おしつけがまし·い【押しつけがましい】¶ ～いことを言うね You *are imposing too much on* me, aren't you?

おしつ·ける【押しつける】¶ 彼を壁に～けた I *pressed* (≒ *pushed*) him *against* the wall. 彼はその仕事を私に～けた He *forced* (≒ *thrust*) the work *on* me. 学校は寄付金を父兄に～けた The school authorities *forced* the parents of the students *to* make a contribution. 彼は無理にその品物を私に～けた He *forced* the article *upon* me. 私は偽物を～けられた I *had* a false article *palmed off upon* me.

おしつぶ·す【押し潰す】crush.

おしつま·る【押し詰まる】¶ ことしも～ってきた The end of the year *is drawing near*.

おして【押して】¶ 彼は病気を～出かけた He went out *in spite of* his illness.

おして【推して】¶ このことからも～知るべし You can *infer from* this.

おしとお·す【押し通す】¶ 彼は自分の信念を～した He *persisted in* his beliefs. 彼は自分

の計画を～す気構えだ He is resolved to *go through with* his plan. その男は無罪の主張を～した The man *insisted on* his innocence.

おしどり【鴛鴦】〔鳥類〕a mandarin duck.
―夫婦 a loving couple.

おしなが·す【押し流す】¶ 多くの家が洪水で～された Many houses *were swept* (≒ *were washed*) *away* by the flood.

おしなべて【押し並べて】as a whole ; on the whole ; generally. ¶ この人たちは～親切だ These people are *generally* kind.

おしの·ける【押し退ける】¶ 私は彼を～けようとした I tried to *push* him *aside*. 群衆を～けながら進んだ I *pushed* (≒ *elbowed*) *my way* through the crowd.

おしのび【お忍び】¶ 王子が～で旅行した The prince traveled *incognito*.

おしはか·る【推し測る·推し量る】¶ 私には彼の心中が～れない I cannot *guess* how he feels.

おしばな【押し花】a dried (≒ pressed) flower.

おしべ【雄蕊】〔植物〕a stamen (複 stamens ; stamina).

おしボタン【押しボタン】a push button.

おしぼり【お絞り】a moist towelette.

おしまずに【惜しまずに】¶ 彼は骨身を～働いた He *spared no* pains. / He worked *as hard as possible*. 彼らは命を～戦った They fought desperately *in defiance of* death. 彼女はお客に～親切の限りを尽くした She *lavished* kindness *on* her guests.

おしみな·い【惜しみない】¶ ～い拍手を送った We gave him a storm of handclaps. / We did the storm of hand clapping.

おし·む【惜しむ】**1**〘たいせつにする〙 ¶ 彼は寸暇を～んで勉強した He worked hard *making the most of his spare moments*.

2〘残念に思う〙 ¶ 彼は学園からすべての者に～まれて去った He left the school *to the deep regret of* all.

～むらくは，彼にはよき助言者がいなかった *It is a pity that* he did not have an able counselor.

その軽率な行為がなかったならばとわれわれは彼のために～む *It is to be regretted that* he behaved in such a thoughtless manner.

才ありながら若くしていった彼女の死を～む I *feel* deep *regret at* her untimely death. She was so young and gifted.

駅の近くの喫茶店で彼との別れを～んだ By way of leave-taking, I spent some time with him at a tea shop near the station.

3〘けちけちする〙 ¶ スポーツ振興のためなら費用は～まない In order to promote the developments of sports, I *grudge* (≒ *spare*) no expense.

彼のすばらしい業績にはだれも賛辞を～まなかった Nobody *was sparing of* his praise for his remarkable achievement.

おしめ【襁褓】a diaper.

おしめり【お湿り】¶ いい～だ It is *a* grateful *rain*.

おしもおされもしない【押しも押されもしない】¶ 彼は日本では～科学者だ He is the Japan's *best-known* scientist. / He *is known as the best* scientist in Japan.

おしもど·す【押し戻す】¶ 警官は群衆を～した The police *pushed back* the crowd.

おしもんどう【押し問答】an argument. ¶ 彼は～の末それを受け入れた He accepted it after *an argument*.

おしゃかさま【御釈迦様】¶ ～でもご存じあるまい *God* knows.

おしゃく【御酌】¶ ～をしましょう Let me *serve* you. (イギリス·アメリカでは給仕人以外，客にお酌をする風習はない).

おしやぶ·る【押し破る】¶ 戸を～る *burst* a door *open*.

おしゃべり【お喋り】a chat ; (人) a chatterbox ; (おしゃべり女) a gossip. ¶ 彼女と長く～をした I *had a* long *chat with* her. / I *chatted with* her for hours. 彼女は～だ She is *a gossip*.

おしゃま a precocious child.

おしや·る【押し遣る】¶ 本をわきに～る *push* a book *aside*.

おしゃれ【御洒落】¶ 彼はなかなか～だ He is quite *a dandy*. 彼女はパーティーに出るためすっかり～をした She *is* all *dressed up* for the party. 彼女はとても～だ She *is* very *careful of her appearance*. きょうはとても～な格好をしているね You *look* very *spruce* (≒ *smart*) today.

おじゃん ¶ すべての計画が～になった All the plans *have failed*. / All the plans *have come to nothing*.

おしょう【和尚】a 〔Buddhist〕 priest.

おじょうさん【お嬢さん】a daughter ; a young lady. ¶ ～育ち a young girl who knows little of the world. ～，おはようございます (目上の人の娘への呼びかけで) Good morning, *miss*.

おしょく【汚職】corruption ; official corruption. ¶ ～の役人 a *corrupt* official. 最近役人の～が多い There have been many cases of *corruption* among officials recently. 彼は～の疑いをかけられている He is suspected of *having taken the bribe*.
―事件 a case of corruption.

おじょく【汚辱】shame ; disgrace ; dishonor.

おしよ·せる【押し寄せる】¶ 敵軍が～せてきた The enemy *advanced against* us. / The enemy *rushed toward* us. 高波が～せてきた High waves *came surging*. 大ぜいの人がその店に～せた A lot of people *stormed* the store. 人々はその女優を見ようと劇場に～せた People *thronged* the theater to see the actress.

おしろい【白粉】〔face〕 powder. ¶ ～をつける *powder one's* face.

オシログラフ〔物理〕an oscillograph.

おしわ·ける【押し分ける】¶ 彼は群衆を～けながら進んだ He *pushed* (≒ *elbowed*) *his way through* the crowd.

おす【雄】a male. ¶ ～のヤギ a he-goat. ～のネ

コ a he-cat; a tomcat. ～の牛 a bull; (去勢牛) an ox. ～の馬 a horse; (種馬) a stallion.

お·す【押す】¶この呼びりんを～してください Please *push* this call button. そんなに～さないでください Don't *push* so much. / (米口語) Take it easy! 人を～して車内に入った I *pushed my way into* the train. 駅のプラットホームは～すな～すなの混雑だった The platform of the station *was jammed with* people.

お·す【推す】**1**〖推察〗infer. ¶彼の話から～すと彼は今東京にはいないらしい I *infer from* what he says that he is now away from Tokyo.
あなたの言うことから～すと彼には罪がない *Judging from* what you say, he is innocent.
彼の服装から～すと彼はあまり裕福ではなさそうだ *From* his dress, he does not seem to be very well off.
2〖推挙〗recommend. ¶彼は皆に～されて議長になった He *was proposed* by everyone *for* chairman.

おすい【汚水】polluted water. ¶工場の～を処理する treat *waste liquids* from factories.
—処理場 a sewage disposal plant.

おずおず【怖ず怖ず】¶彼は～と教員室に入っていった He went into the faculty room *timidly*.

おすそわけ【お裾分け】shared gifts. ¶そのもらいものを彼に～した I *gave* him *a portion of* the gift. / I *shared* the gift *with* him.

おせじ【お世辞】a compliment. ¶～はよせ Stop *flattering*. それは～でしょう Oh, you *flatter* me. ～がうまいね You *are* very *diplomatic*. 私は～が言えない I can't make *compliments*. ～にも彼女は美人とは言えない I couldn't say she is beautiful *even in compliment*.
—笑い a simper.

おせっかい【お節介】¶きみはいつも～をやいている You *are* always *meddling*. ～をやいてくれるな Mind your own business. / Don't *meddle in* my affairs. よけいな～だ It's none of your business. 彼女はすぐ～をやく She is quite ready to *put her nose into* others' business. / She *is* very *nosy*.
—焼き a meddler; a busybody.

おせん【汚染】pollution; contamination.
¶川は工場の廃液で～されている The rivers *are polluted* by waste liquids from factories. 空気は煤煙(ばいえん)で～されている The air *is polluted* with smoke.
海洋**—** sea pollution. 大気**—** air pollution.

おぜんだて【お膳立て】arrangement; preparation. ¶彼が私のためになにもかも～してくれた He *has arranged* everything for me. 会議の～がすっかりできている All *preparations* are made for the conference. それに対する～をした I *have prepared the way* 〔for it〕.

おそ·い【遅い】**1**〖朝·夜が〗late. ¶きょうは帰りが～くなる I will *be late* coming home today.
もう夜が～いから寝なさい It *is* already *late*. You must go to bed.
もう～くなるから帰ります It'*s getting late*. I've got to be going now. / It'*s getting late*. I'd better be going now.
会議は夜～くまでかかった We had the conference far into the night.
朝～く朝食をとったので昼はなにも食べなかった Because I had a *late* breakfast, I skipped lunch.
このごろ帰りが～いね You *have* often *been late* coming home lately.
2〖より遅い〗¶きょうから10分学校の始まるのが～くなる From today school begins ten minutes *later*.
きみの来るのが一足～かった. 彼女にあげた You just missed your chance. I have given it to her.
3〖予定より遅い〗slow. ¶ことしは春の来るのが～い This year spring *is slow in* coming. 稲の発育が～い The rice shoots *are slow in* growing.
ご返事が～くなってすみません I must apologize to you for *being late* in answering. / I'm sorry to have left your letter unanswered for a long time. / I ought to have answered your letter sooner.
4〖まにあわぬ〗¶そんなことを言ったってもう～い It is no use to say that now. It'*s too late*.
今からでも～くない It *is* not *too late* even now.
5〖速度がにぶい〗slow. ¶この電車はずいぶん～い How *slow* this streetcar *is*!
老人は歩くのが～い Old people are *slow* walkers. / Old people *are slow of* foot.
彼は頭のめぐりが～い He is *slow*-witted.

おそ·う【襲う】**1** (攻撃) attack; raid; (災害が) hit; visit. ¶昨夜強盗に～われた A burglar *broke into* my house last night.
四国地方は暴風雨に～われた The Shikoku area *was hit* (≒ *was swept*) by storms.
2〖継承〗¶彼は父の仕事を～った He *succeeded to* his father's occupation.

おそうまれ【遅生まれ】a child born between April 2 and December 31.

おそかれはやかれ【遅かれ早かれ】sooner or later.

おそく〔と〕も【遅く〔と〕も】¶～5時までには帰る I'll be back by five *at* 〔*the*〕 *latest*.

おそざき【遅咲き】¶～の桜 a *late-blooming* cherry tree.

おそなえ【お供え】an offering.

おそばん【遅番】a late turn (≒ shift).

おそまき【遅蒔き】¶～ながらやってみましょう I'll try *though it may be too late*. いささか～のきらいがある I am afraid we *have missed the chance*.

おそらくは【恐らくは】perhaps; probably.

おそるおそる【恐る恐る】(おくびょうに) timidly; (うやうやしく) humbly.

おそるべき【恐るべき】¶～才能 a *wonderful* (≒ *prodigious*) talent. ～光景 a *dreadful* scene. ～量の麻薬 an *enormous* amount of narcotics.

お

おそれ【恐れ】fear. ¶この子どもは～を知らない This child knows no *fear*. あの男の心臓の強さにはみな～をなしている Everyone *stands in awe of* his brazen face. 彼は何物にも～を感じない He *is afraid of* nothing.

おそれ【虞】¶彼が仕事に失敗する～はまったくない There is not the slightest *danger* of his failing in his work. 彼は病気になる～がある I am afraid he *is in danger of* getting sick. 失敗に対する～からその試みをちゅうちょした I hesitated to attempt it *for fear of* failure.

おそれい·る【恐れ入る】¶まことに～ります I am much obliged to you. ～りますが,ご住所を教えていただけませんか *I am sorry to trouble you*, but will you please tell me your address? ～りますが,その絵を見せてください Will you show me the picture, *if you please*? わざわざおいでくださって～ります *It's very kind of you to* have come to see me. ごやっかいをおかけいたしまして～ります *I am sorry* I have troubled you. ご援助～りました *I am very grateful for* your help. ご親切～ります *Thank you very much for* your kindness. 彼は～って引きさがった He withdrew *with* great *humility*. 彼が弁舌さわやかなのには～った *I am astonished at* his eloquence. 彼の話の長いのに～った He talked too much for me. I'*m fed up*.

おそれおお·い【畏多い】awful; reverend; gracious; venerable. ¶陛下より～いおことばを頂いた His Majesty *graciously* spoke to me. 申すも～いことながら *with due respect* I may say...; it is *with deep respect* that I say ...; it is awful to relate that....

おそれおのの·く【恐れ戦く】¶彼女は～き声もたてられなかった She *trembled with fear* and couldn't utter a word.

おそ·れる【恐れる】fear; dread; stand in fear of; be afraid of. ¶私は雷を～れる I *have a horror of* thunder. 子どもの将来を～れる I'm *apprehensive of* my son's future. 神を～れる We *stand in awe of* God.

おそろい【お揃い】¶姉妹は～の着物で踊った The sisters danced in Japanese clothes made with *the same cloth*. みなさん～でどちらへ Where are all of you going *in a body*?

おそろし·い【恐ろしい】**1**〚怖い〛fierce; horrible. ¶彼は～い目つきでぼくをにらんだ He looked at me with a *fierce* look. / He glared in anger at me.
見るも～い事故現場であった The scene of the accident *was* simply *horrible*.
あの先生は～い I *am afraid of* the teacher.
夜道で～い目に会った I *got the fright of my life* on a dark street.
戦争は～いものだ The *horrors* of warfare! / War *is* truly *terrible*. / Nothing in the world *is* so *horrible* as war.
都会は～いところだ A city is really a *horrible* place.
2〚恐れる〛be afraid of. ¶あんなやつが～いのか You should not *be afraid of* a man like him.
私はそのような手術を受けるのは～い I *am afraid of* undergoing such an operation.
3〚非常な〛awfully; terribly. ¶けさは～く寒い It is *very* cold this morning. (very の代わりに awfully, terribly を用いるのは女性の場合に多い).
彼女は～いおしゃべりだ She is an *awful* chatterbox.

おそろしが·る【恐ろしがる】¶子どもは暗やみを～る Children *are afraid of* darkness. そんなに～るな Don't *be* so *afraid* (≒ *scared*). / Don't *fear* so much. そんなものを～ることはない You must not *fear* such a thing. / You need not *be scared at* such a thing.

おそわ·る【教わる】¶田中先生から英語を～った I *was taught* English by Mr. Tanaka. / I *learned* English from Mr. Tanaka.

オゾン〘化学〙ozone.

おたか·い【お高い】¶そんなに～く留まるな Don't *be* so *proud*. 彼はいつも～く留まっている He always *puts on airs*.

おたけび【雄叫】¶～をあげる give (≒ raise) *a battle cry*.

おたずねもの【お尋ね者】a suspect.

おだて【煽て】flattery. ¶そんな～には乗らないよ I won't yield to such *flattery*. 彼の～に乗ってつい「うん」と言った I was so pleased with his *flattery* that I finally gave my consent.

おだ·てる【煽てる】¶彼は～てられてそれをする気になった He *was flattered to* do it. そんなに～てるな Don't *flatter* (≒ *favor upon*) me so.

おたふく【阿多福】a moon-faced woman (≒ girl); (不美人) a homely (≒ plain) woman.
—風邪〘医学〙mumps.

おだぶつ【御陀仏】¶～になる(死ぬ) die. とうとうぼくも～だ(絶望だ) My time has come at last. / Everything is hopeless with me now.

おだまき【苧環】〘植物〙a columbine.

おたまじゃくし【お玉じゃくし】〘動物〙a tadpole; (音符) a note.

おだやか【穏やか】¶～な一日だった It was a *calm* day. このところ～な天気が続いている We have had a spell of *calm* weather recently. なんと～な海だろう What a *quiet* sea! どうかできるだけ～にお話しください Would you mind speaking as *quietly* as possible? 彼は心中～ならぬものを感じた He did not *feel at ease* in his heart. あなたがその申し出を拒むことは～でない It would be *improper* of you to refuse the offer. 彼の～な話しぶりに安心した I was relieved at his *gentle* way of speaking.

おだわらひょうじょう【小田原評定】a fruitless discussion; an inconclusive conference. ¶こんな～はもうやめよう Let's stop this *fruitless discussion*.

おち【落ち】¶そんな計画は損失を受けるのが～だ Such a plan will *result in* a loss. ～はないだろうな Is everything fully prepared? この計画に～はないだろうな Are you sure nothing *is missing* in this plan? 冗談の～がわからない I don't see *the point* of the joke.

おちあ·う【落ち合う】 ¶ 空港で10時に～いましょう Let's *meet* at the airport at ten.

おちい·る【陥る】 ¶ 危篤に～る *get* critically ill. 混乱に～る *fall into* confusion. 敵の重囲に～る *be* closely *besieged by* the enemy.

おちうど【落人】 a refugee ; a fugitive.

おちおち ¶ ～してはいられない I can't afford to *feel at ease* now. 昨夜は心配で～眠れなかった Last night I didn't sleep well with anxiety. / I passed a bad night with anxiety last night.

おちつき【落ち着き】 presence of mind. ¶ 彼はどんなことがあっても～を失わない Whatever may happen to him, he never loses his *presence of mind*. 知らせを聞いて彼は～を失った He *became restless at* the news. 彼はようやく～を取り戻した He recovered his *presence of mind* at last. 彼の表情には～の色が認められた His expression seemed very *calm*. 事件は彼に～を失わせた The incident disconcerted him.

おちつきはら·う【落ち着き払う】 ¶ 難局に当たって彼は～って行動した He acted *with serenity*, though he was in a difficult situation. 彼は自信があったので～っていた He has so much self-confidence that he *showed great presence of mind*. 世間の非難を浴びても彼は～っていた He *remained calm and serene* even when he was exposed to public censure.

おちつ·く【落ち着く】 **1** 〖気持ちが静まる〗 ¶ ～かない男だ He *is nervous*.
もっと～け *Calm* yourself.
試験の前でなんとなく～かない As the examination is near at hand, I cannot help *feeling uneasy* (≒ *nervous*).
よく～いてどちらがいいか考えてごらん *Keep* perfectly *cool* and consider which you will prefer.
～いて勉強しなさい You must *settle down to* your studies.
彼も年をとって～いてきた He *has got quieter* with age.
2 〖物事が安定する〗 ¶ 戦争が終わり世の中が～いてきた The war has come to an end and the general confusion seems to *be settling down*.
台風が去って天気も～いてきた The typhoon has gone. We will have *good* weather.
患者の容体もどうやら～いている There is *a lull* in the condition of the patient. / The patient *is* barely *out of danger* now.
この1週間株式相場は～いている During the past week there has been *a lull* in the stock market.
3 〖ある場所に定着する〗 ¶ 郊外に一軒家を見つけて,やっと～きました We managed to rent a solitary house in the suburbs and *made it our home*.
家主に明け渡しを迫られたが～く先が見つからないので困っている We are asked to quit our house by the landlord, but we find it difficult to obtain another house to *live in*.
どうせその辺に結論は～くだろうと思った I expected their opinions would *settle down to* such a conclusion after all.
4 〖釣り合う〗 ¶ テーブルの大きさがどうもこの部屋には～かない It seems to me the size of the table *is ill proportioned to* this room.
そのソファは部屋のここに置くと～く気がする I think the sofa will *be* just *right* here for the room.
5 〖じみな〗 ¶ これは～いた柄ですね This is a *quiet* (≒ *sober*) pattern, isn't it?

おちつ·ける【落ち着ける】 ¶ 心を～ける calm *oneself* ; compose *oneself*.

おちど【落ち度】 〔a〕 fault ; blame. ¶ これはあなたの～ではない This is not your *fault*. / You *are* not *to blame for* this.

おちの·びる【落ち延びる】 ¶ もはやこれ以上～びることはできない We cannot *make good our escape* any longer. この村は昔平家の落武者が～びてきた所と言われている This village is said to have been the very place where some of the fugitive warriors of the Heike family *came to live*.

おちば【落ち葉】 fallen (≒ dead) leaves.

おちぶ·れる【落ちぶれる】 ¶ 彼は～れてだれも寄りつかなくなった Everybody keeps away from him now that he *has become poor*. 彼は仕事で失敗して～れた He *was brought low* because of his failure in business.

おちぼ【落ち穂】 gleanings. ¶ ～を拾う人 a gleaner.

おちめ【落ち目】 ¶ 彼も～になった His fortune *sank* (≒ *declined*).

おちゃ【お茶】 ¶ どうにか～を濁して切り抜けた Somehow I managed to *go through with* it. / I somehow *bluffed my way out of* the situation.

おちゃっぴい a saucy child (≒ girl).

おちゃのこ【お茶の子】 (お茶菓子) cake ; (たやすいこと) an easy task. ¶ そんなことは～さいさいだ That *is a cinch*. / That *is simple and easy*.

おちょぼぐち【おちょぼ口】 pursed-up lips.

お·ちる【落ちる】 **1** 〖落下する〗 fall. ¶ 階段から～ちて大けがをした I *fell* down the stairs and was badly hurt.
バスががけから谷へ～ちた The bus *fell* over the precipice into the ravine.
木の葉が水面に～ちた The leaves *fell* on the water.
2 〖崩れる〗 ¶ 地震で壁が～ちた The earthquake made the walls *crumble down*.
大水で橋が～ちた The flood made the bridge *give way*.
3 〖下落する〗 ¶ 今学期は成績が～ちた I have not done very well at school this term.
今月はストライキで生産が～ちた This month production *has decreased* on account of the strike.
こう暑くては能率が～ちる In this heat our efficiency *drops*.
そんなことをすると信用が～ちる If you do such

お

a thing, you will *lose* credit. / Such an act would *lower* (≒ *hurt*) your credit.
そんなことを言うときみの人格が～ちる Your words *are a disgrace to* yourself. / What you say *is beneath* your dignity.

4 〚その人のものになる〛 ¶ 競売の結果，その名画は彼の手に～ちた The famous picture was set up at auction and *was knocked down to* him.

5 〚悪くなる・衰える〛 ¶ 風が～ちた The wind *has died away*.
最近では彼女の人気は～ちている Recently her popularity *has been declining*.
この洗剤を使うと汚れがよく～ちる If you use this cleanser, the stains will *come out* very well.

6 〚落第・落選する〛 ¶ ぼくは大学の試験に～ちた I *failed* 〔*in*〕 the entrance examination for the university. (米では in をはぶく).
あの人はこの前の選挙では～ちた He *was defeated* (≒ *was unsuccessful*) *in* the last election.

7 〚漏れる〛 ¶ 名簿にきみの名が～ちている Your name *has been dropped from* the list. / Your name *is missing from* the roster.
上から２行めのところ，２字～ちている In the second line from the top of the page, two letters *have been left out*.

8 〚その他〛 ¶ きみの言うことはどうも腑(ふ)に～ちない I cannot *make out* exactly what you mean. / Your story doesn't *go down with* me.
彼はぼくらのしかけたわなにうまく～ちた He *fell* nicely *into* the trap we had laid for him.
彼は敵の術中に～ちた He *was caught in* the enemy's trap.
睡眠薬を飲まされて彼は深い眠りに～ちた He was given a sleeping drug and *fell into* a coma.

おつ【乙】(２番目) a second; (成績の) B; (後者) the latter. ¶ ～な味 *tasty* flavor. 彼はいつも～にすましている He always *puts on airs*.

おっかな・い ¶ そんなに～がるな Don't *fear* (≒ *be afraid*) so much. 彼は～そうにそっとそれをさわった He touched it *with fear*. そんな～いことはぼくにはとてもできない I cannot bring myself to such an *audacious* attempt.

おっかなびっくり ¶ 彼は～のぞきこんだ He peeped in *timidly* (≒ *with fear*). 彼は～部屋に入ってきた He came into the room *trembling with fear*.

おつき【お付き】an attendant; (侍女) a lady in waiting.

おっくう ¶ 手紙にいちいち返事するのはとても～だった It *was* very *troublesome* to answer each letter. 彼はそこまで行くのも～がった He *was* too *lazy* even *to* go there. 何事にも～がるな Don't *spare yourself* in anything.

おつげ【お告げ】an oracle; a divine message. ¶ ～を受ける receive *an oracle*.

おっちょこちょい a rash (≒ careless; thoughtless) fellow. ¶ 彼はまったく～だ He *is* quite *careless*. / He *is lacking in prudence*.

おっつかっつ ¶ ぼくの収入は彼と～のところだ My income *is about the same as* his.

おっつけ【追っ付け】soon; presently. ¶ 彼は～帰ってくるだろう He will be back *before long*.

おって【追っ手】a 〔party of〕 pursuer〔s〕.

おって【追って】later on; afterward.
¶ ～お話しします I'll tell you *later* 〔*on*〕. ～さたのあるまで until *further* notice.
—書き a postscript (手紙では P. S. と略す).

おっと【夫】a husband. ¶ ～のある女性 a *married* woman.

おっと ¶ ～危ない *Oh*, look out!

おっとせい【膃肭臍】〘動物〙 a fur seal.
¶ ～の毛皮 a sealskin.

おつとめ【お勤め】〔a〕 duty; (宗教の) 〔a〕 service.

おっとり ¶ 彼は～している He *doesn't trouble himself with small matters*.

おてあげ【お手上げ】¶ 万事～だ *It's all over with* me. / *I have given up all hope of* success. / Everything *has turned against me*.

おでこ the brow; the forehead. ¶ ～の人 a man with *a prominent forehead*.

おてのもの【お手のもの】*one's* strong point; *one's* speciality. ¶ スキーなら彼の～だ He *is expert in* skiing. (expert はこの場合ふつう [ikspə́ːrt] と読む). / He *is good at* skiing. / Skiing *is in his line*.

おてもり【お手盛り】a self-approved plan.

おてやわらかに【お手柔らかに】 ¶ ～願います Don't be too hard on me. / I hope you will not criticize me too severely.

おてん【汚点】a stain. ¶ この行為は彼の生涯に～を残した This behavior has left *a stain* on his career.

おでん Japanese hotchpotch.

おてんき【お天気】weather.
—屋 a fickle (≒ whimsical; moody) person.

おてんば【御転婆】a tomboy; a flapper.
¶ ～な saucy; forward; unladylike.

おと【音】**1** 〚音響・音階〛 〔a〕 sound. ¶ ～は空気の波といえる *Sound* is considered to be the waves of air.
なにか～が聞こえる Some *sound* can be heard.
それをたたくと妙な～がした When I tapped it, it made *a* strange *sound*.
太鼓の～が鳴り渡った The *rolls* of a drum resounded far and wide. / A drum *boomed* out.
波の～が聞こえてくる The *roar* (≒ *murmur*) of the waves is heard.
かすかに松風の～が伝わってくる The distant *sighing* (≒ *whisper*) of the wind is faintly heard among the pines.
時計の～が妙に気になって眠れなかった Strangely enough, the *ticking* of the clock kept me from falling asleep.
このレコードは低い部分の～がよく入っていない The

low *tones* are not good in this recording.

このピアノは～が狂っている This piano *is out of tune*.

塔は大きな～をたてて崩れ落ちた The tower collapsed with *a* tremendous *crash*.

ラジオの～を低くしてください *Turn down* the radio, please.

家人に気づかれないように，～をたてないで家を抜け出た I stole out of the house so as not to be noticed by my family.

表を通るトラックのうるさい～で勉強もできない Trucks passing our house *are* so *noisy* that I cannot settle down to my studies.

なんの～か．ガラスの壊れた～のようだ What is that *noise*? I think it's *a sound* of broken glass.

2 〖評判〗 ¶ 彼は～に聞こえた弓の名人だ He is a *well-known* master archer.

おとうさん【お父さん】 a father; (呼びかけ) papa; pa; dad; daddy; (米口語) pop.

おとうと【弟】a younger brother; *one's* little brother.

―分 a sworn brother; a favorite junior.

おどおど ¶ 彼は大聴衆の前で～した He *became timid* (≒ *became frightened*) before a large audience. / He *had a stage fright* before a large audience. 彼は～しながら私に質問した He asked me a question *timidly*.

おとがい【頤】⇒あご

おどか·す【脅かす】⇒おどす

おとぎばなし【御伽話】a fairy tale.

おどけ【戯け】fun; a joke.

おど·ける【戯ける】¶ 彼はばつの悪さを隠そうと～けてみせた He *played the fool* to hide his embarrassment. 彼は～けた格好をしてみせた He made a *comical* gesture.

おとこ【男】**1** 〖女性に対し〗 a man. ¶ ～のお子さんですか女のお子さんですか Is it a *boy*-baby or a girl-baby?

彼女には～友だちがたくさんいる She has numerous *boy* friends.

彼は～か女かわからない服装をしている He's dressed in such a way it's hard to tell whether he is *a man* or a woman.

彼女は～のようなことば遣いをする She speaks just like *a man*. / To hear her speak, one would think her to be *a man*.

～と女は平等の権利を持つ *Men* and women are endowed with equal rights.

～ばかりの生活で殺風景だ Mine is a *bachelor's* household and drab.

あんな～にかかってはかなわない I am no match for *him*.

だらしない～だ *He* is of a slovenly disposition.

息子もどうやら一人前の～になった My son seems to have become *a man*.

～ばかりの集まりだ It's a *stag* party.

2 〖りっぱな男の中の男〗 a man. ¶ ～ならやってみろ Have a try at it, if you consider yourself *a man*.

おまえも～じゃないか，そんなことができないとはだらしない Be *a man*! It is cowardly of you to back out of it.

それでもきみは～か．ひきょうなまねはするな Do you call yourself *a man* now? Don't act in a cowardly manner.

彼は～の中の～だ He is *a man among men*.

きみを～と思って頼む I ask you for help, for I believe you are *a man*.

それでは～がたたぬ By such an act, you will *lose your honor*.

その一件でぼくも～を下げた I *have lost my honor* in the recent affair.

3 〖情人・異性としての男〗 a lover. ¶ 彼女には～がいるんだ I know she has *a lover*.

おとこぎ【男気】chivalry. ¶ 彼は～がある He *is chivalrous*.

おとこざかり【男盛り】 the prime of manhood. ¶ 彼は～だ He is in *the prime of manhood*.

おとこずき【男好き】 ¶ この顔は確かに～のする顔だ This is certainly a face that *is attractive to men*.

おとこだて【男伊達】chivalry; a chivalrous person.

おとこで【男手】 ¶ ～が必要だ I want *a man* to help me.

おとこぶり【男振り】a man's appearance. ¶ なんと～のいい人だ What a *handsome-looking* man he is! あのひと言で彼は一躍～を上げた He had his *reputation* raised by that one remark of his.

おとこまさり【男勝り】¶ 彼女は～のところがある She has something *masculine* about her. / She is a *manly* (≒ *spirited*) woman.

おとこもち【男持ち】¶ この洋がさは～だ This is a *gentleman's* (≒ *man's*) umbrella.

おとこもの【男物】 men's things; (衣料品) men's wear.

おとこやもめ【男やもめ】a widower. ¶ ～にうじがわく It is proverbial that *widowers* are untidy.

おとこらし·い【男らしい】 manly; manful; strong; masculine. ¶ 彼は～いりっぱな態度だった He took up an attitude of *manliness*. きみは～く謝るべきだ You should make an apology *frankly*. 彼は～い顔つきだ He looks *strong* (≒ *brave*). その場の彼の態度はまことに～かった He really behaved *like a man* on that occasion. そんなことでぐずぐず言うのは～くない It is not *like a man* to complain of such a thing. / Aren't you *a man*? Don't be a coward!

おとさた【音沙汰】¶ 彼からその後～がない I haven't heard from him since then.

おどし【脅し】〔a〕 bluff. ¶ たぶんただの～だろう Maybe it is *a bluff*. そんな～文句を恐れるな Don't be afraid of such *threatening words*.

おとしあな【落とし穴】a trap; a pit; (わな) a snare. ¶ その動物は～に落ちた The animal fell into *a trap*. 私を仲間にさそいこむ～とは知らなかった I never suspected that it was *a trap* they set to make me an accomplice.

お

おとしい·れる【陥れる】¶ 彼はぼくを苦境に～れた He *landed* me *in* a difficult situation. 彼の術策に～れられた I *fell into* the traps he had set for me.

おとしだね【落とし種】an illegitimate child; a love child; a natural child.

おとしだま【お年玉】a New Year's gift (≒ present). ──つき年賀葉書 a New Year's lottery postal card.

おとしぬし【落とし主】¶ 時計の～が現われた The person who had lost the watch appeared.

おとしもの【落とし物】a lost article. ¶ ～をする *lose* a thing.

おと·す【落とす】1〖落下させる〗¶ 屋根の雪を～す *shovel away* the snow over a roof; *clear* a roof *of* snow.
敵機は多量の爆弾を～した The enemy planes *dropped* a large quantity of bombs.
月は湖面に影を～していた The image of the moon *was reflected* on the lake.
今彼は飛ぶ鳥を～す勢いだ He is now at the height of his prosperity.
戦いの幕は切って～された They *began* fighting. / They *opened* hostilities.
その話を聞いて思わず涙を～した Hearing the story, I *shed tears* in spite of myself.
父に雷を～された My father thundered at me.
2〖名声などを低下させる〗¶ そんなことをするときみの信用を～す By such conduct you will be sure to *lose* your credit.
彼はへたな演技で評判を～した His poor acting *detracted from* his popularity.
3〖スピード·音量などを〗¶ この先学校あり, スピードを～せ *Slow down* [your car]. [There is] a school ahead.
真夜中になるからテレビの音量を～しなさい *Turn down* the volume on the television set, as it is near midnight.
彼はいちだんと声を～してその秘密を語った *Dropping* his voice to a whisper, he confided his secret to me.
その選手は疲れていて, 調子を～している Being tired, the player *is in a bad condition* now. / Being tired, the player *is out of form* now.
その値段で売るのでは品質を～さないわけにはいかない In order to sell it at the price, the only thing we can do is to *lower* its quality.
難しすぎるから, もう少し問題の程度を～せ *Make* the problem a little *easier*. It is too difficult.
4〖失う〗¶ きのうバスの中で財布を～した Yesterday I *lost* (≒ *dropped*) my purse in the bus.
交通事故で危うく命を～すところだった I came near *losing my life* in the traffic accident. / I *was* nearly *killed* in the traffic accident.
5〖取り除く〗¶ 温泉につかって旅のあかを～した I bathed in the hot spring and *washed myself*. / I bathed in the hot spring and *washed off* the dirt.
鉄さくのさびを～してペンキを塗った I *removed* the rust from the iron railing and painted it.
私はひげを～したら若返った顔になった I *shaved off* my beard and looked much younger.
6〖漏らす〗¶ たいせつなことを言い～しましたからつけ加えます I *have missed* (≒ *have omitted*; *have skipped*) an important matter. Allow me to mention it now.
私はその文句を読み～していた I *have skipped over* the phrase. / I *have left out* the words in reading it.
答案に受験番号を書き～さないでください Take care that you don't *forget* to write your seat number in your examination paper.
7〖控除する〗¶ その費用は必要経費として～しなさい That is a legitimate *deductible* expense.
8〖競売で競り落とす〗¶ その名画は500万円で某画商の手で～された That famous painting *was knocked down* to a certain picture dealer for five million yen.
9〖その他〗¶ あの落語家はどこでこの話を～すのか I wonder to what ending the storyteller is going to bring his tale.

おど·す【脅す】¶ その男は私を殺すぞと言って～した The man *threatened* me *with* death. / The man *threatened to* kill me. 彼はピストルで人々を～した He *menaced* people with a revolver. 彼らは～されて服従した They *were frightened into* submission.

おとずれ【訪れ】1〖訪問·到来〗a call; a visit; coming. ¶ 春の～ the *coming* of spring.
2〖たより〗news; tidings.

おとず·れる【訪れる】¶ ローマを～れる *visit* Rome. われわれは先生を自宅に～れた We *called on* our teacher at his home. / We *went to see* our teacher at his home.

おととい【一昨日】the day before yesterday. ¶ ～の朝 the morning *before last*.

おととし【一昨年】the year before last. ¶ ～の春 the spring *before last*.

おとな【大人】an adult; a grown-up; a grown-up man; a man. ¶ ～になったら音楽家になりたい I want to be a musician when I *grow up*. この子どもは～のような口をきく This child talks like *a man* (≒ *a grown-up*).

おとなげな·い【大人げない】¶ きみのふるまいは～い Your behavior *is unworthy of a man* at your age. 彼は～い男だ He *is childish*. / He is not thoughtful enough for a man.

おとなし·い【大人しい】¶ ～い子ども (静かな子ども) a *gentle* (≒ *quiet*) child; (行儀のよい子ども) a *well-behaved* child; (すなおな子ども) an *obedient* child. ～そうな少年 a *quiet-looking* boy. ～くしなさい (静かに) *Be quiet*. / (行儀よく) *Behave yourself*. この犬は～い This dog *is tame*.

おとな·びる【大人びる】look like a grown-up. ¶ 彼女は年のわりに～びている She *looks old* for her age. 彼には変に～びたところがある There is something unpleasantly *precocious* about him.

おとめ【乙女】a maiden; a young girl; a

virgin; a damsel. ¶ ～の時代 *one's* girlhood; *one's* maidenhood.

おとも【お供】 a follower; an attendant. ¶ 彼は秘書を～にしていた He *was accompanied by* his secretary. 途中まで～しましょう I will *go* part of the way *with* you. 喜んで～いたしましょう I'm willing to *come with* you.

おとり【囮】 a decoy [bird]; a call bird; a lure. ¶ ～を使ってたかを呼び寄せた We used *a decoy bird* to lure hawks.

おどり【踊り】 dancing; a dance.
—子 a dancer; a dancing girl (dancing を強く言う. dancing と girl を同じ強さで言うと「踊っている少女」の意). **—場**(踊る所) a dancing hall; (特に米) a dance hall; (階段の) a landing.

おどりあが・る【踊り上がる】 ¶ ～って喜ぶ *leap* (≒ *dance*) for joy; *jump* with joy.

おどりかか・る【踊りかかる】 ¶ 彼は猛然と敵に～った He *sprang on* his enemy furiously.

おと・る【劣る】 be inferior (*to*); be second (*to*); below (≒ behind); be worse (*than*). ¶ 文学的才能では彼はだれにも～らない In literary gifts he *is second to none*. 女は男より社会的に～る Woman *is* socially *inferior to* man. この品物はあれより質が～る This article *is inferior* in quality *to* that. 英会話ではきみに～らない I *can* speak English *as well as* you. 彼女は姉に～らず美しい She *is no less* beautiful *than* her elder sister.

おど・る【踊る・躍る】 ¶ タンゴ(ワルツ)を～る *dance* the tango (waltz). 喜びで胸が～った My heart *leaped* (≒ *jumped*) with joy. 彼女は胸を～らせながら彼を待った She waited for him *with a leap of her heart*. / She waited for him *with a beating heart*.

おとろ・える【衰える】 become weak; lose vigor; decline; fall off; (しぼむ) wither; (力・名声などが) wane.
¶ 彼の健康は目だって～えてきた His health *has* notably *declined*. 彼も年のせいで視力が～えた His eyesight *got weaker* with age. 最近彼女の容色も～えた She *has* recently *lost her charms*. その国も既に～えかかっている The country *is* already *declining*.

おどろか・す【驚かす】 ¶ そのニュースは私を～せた The news *surprised* me. 彼の突然の死は一座を～せた His sudden death *astonished* all those present.

おどろき【驚き】 surprise. ¶ それを知ったときの彼の～はたいへんなものだった He *was* very much *surprised* to know it. そのときの彼の～は想像にあまりある I can hardly imagine how *astonished* he *was* then.

おどろ・く【驚く】 **1** 〖びっくりする〗 ¶ そんなことは～くにはあたらない You need not *be surprised at* such a thing. / That's nothing to *be wondered at*.
そいつは～いた Well, I never! / You don't say so!
隣が火事と言われて～いた I *was astonished* to hear that a fire had broken out next door.
彼がそんなことをしたとは～いた *It's surprising* that he should have done such a thing.
彼女の変わりはてた姿を見て～いた *Much to my amazement*, I found her dead and cold.
今から話すことに～かないでください *Prepare yourself for* what I am going to tell you. / I've got unpleasant news for you.
～たことに犯人は子どもだった We found *to our surprise* that the offender was a mere child.
～くべき速さでそのうわさは広まった The rumor spread *quite rapidly*. / The rumor spread *like wildfire*.
～くべき割合でその町の人口は増えた The population of the town increased at a *tremendous* rate.
2 〖恐怖する〗 ¶ いきなりピストルを突きつけられて～いた I *was frightened* (≒ *was scared*; *was terrified*) when without warning I had a revolver pointed at me.
家人に大声をあげられ,どろぼうは～いて逃げた When the family cried out, the robber *was frightened* and took to his heels. / The family's screams *frightened away* the thief.
3 〖感心する〗 ¶ きみの手際のよさには～いた I *wonder at* your skill. / I *really admire* your skill.
彼があんなに英語をうまくしゃべれるとは～いた I *admire* him *for* his fluency in speaking English. / I little thought he could speak English so well.

おないどし【同い年】 ¶ 彼は私と～だ He *is the same age as* I. / He *is* [*of*] *my age*. われわれは～だ We *are of an age*. / We *are* [*of*] *the same age*.

おなか【お腹】 stomach; belly. ¶ ～の子 the *coming* child. ～がすいた I *am hungry*. 今～がいっぱいだ My *stomach* is full now. 空腹で～が鳴る My *stomach* is rumbling from hunger. ～が痛い I have *a stomachache*. / I feel a pain in my *stomach*. 食べすぎて～をこわした I injured my *stomach* by eating too much. 彼女は～が大きい She *is pregnant*. / She *is with child*.

おながざる【尾長猿】 a long-tailed monkey.

おながどり【尾長鳥】 a blue magpie.

おながれ【お流れ】 ¶ 計画は～になった The plan *was given up*. / The plan *came to nothing*. 野球は雨で～になった The baseball game *was rained out*.

おなぐさみ【お慰み】 ¶ うまくいったら～ Give me a cheer if I do it successfully.

おなじ【同じ】 **1** 〖同一の〗 the same. ¶ 彼とぼくとは～学校を卒業した Both he and I graduated from *the same* school.
ぼくらはみな～町内に住んでいる All of us live in *the same* street.
これと～大きさの額をください Can you give me a picture-frame *as* big *as* this one?
これと～サイズで～型のくつをください Give me

shoes of *the same* size and style *as* these.
名は～だが違う人だ The name *is just the same*, but he is an entirely different person.
～労働には～賃銀を支払うべきだ *The same* amount of wages should be paid for *the same* labor.
それとこれとは～には論じられない These two matters are not to be mentioned *in the same breath*.
われわれはみな～道を歩いた仲だ We have all walked *the same* path together.
きみが同意しようとしまいと～ことだ *It does not make any difference* whether you agree or not. / *It does not matter* whether you agree or not.
結局～ことじゃないか *It comes to the same conclusion*, doesn't it?
右に～ *The same as* mentioned above.
彼らはみな～穴のむじなだ They are *birds of a feather*.
2 〖類似している〗¶ みな～ようなことを言った They expressed *similar* opinions about it.
ぼくもきみと～ような返事をもらった I've received an answer almost *the same as* yours.
どれもこれも～ようなくだらぬ作ばかりだ Any of these works is *as* poor *as* the other.
どれも～ように見えるが,違うのか They all look *alike*, but are they different?
これも～ように処理してください Handle this matter *in the same way*.
3 〖同然である〗¶ きみなんかいないも～だ You are *as good as* absent.
ここまでくれば仕事は終わったも～だ Well, the job is *practically* over.
4 〖どうせ〗 ¶ ～行くなら山がいい *If you are going anywhere*, you might as well go to the mountains.
～死ぬなら男らしく死ね *If I must die*, I will die like a man.
～買うなら品のよいのを買いなさい *As long as* you are going to buy some, buy quality.

おなじく【同じく】 in the same way; in the same manner; equally.

おなじみ【お馴染み】 familiarity; intimacy; (人) a friend; an old (≒ a familiar) acquaintance. ¶ 彼らと～になった I *became acquainted with* them. ～ですから安くいたしましょう As you are *an old customer*, you shall have it cheap.

おなら wind; (卑語) fart. ¶ ～をする break wind; fart.

おなんどいろ【お納戸色】 grayish blue.

おに【鬼】 a demon; (遊戯の) the tagger; it. ¶ ～のいぬ間に洗たく (諺) *When the cat is away, the mice will play.* 彼は仕事の～だ He is *a demon* for work. 彼は～の首でもとったように喜んだ He was overjoyed. 福は内,～は外 In with luck! Out with *the demon*! 今度はきみが～だ This time you're *it*. 来年のことを言うと～が笑う (諺) Next year is the devil's joke.

おにごっこ【鬼ごっこ】 tag; (目隠しの) blindman's buff. ¶ ～をする play *tag* (≒ *blindman's buff*).

おにば【鬼歯】 a projecting (≒ protruding) tooth.

おにばば【鬼婆】 a hag; a witch.

おにび【鬼火】 a will-o'-the-wisp; a jack-o'-lantern.

おにゆり【鬼百合】〖植物〗 a tiger lily.

おね【尾根】 a ridge. ¶ ～伝いに歩く walk along the *ridges*.

おねじ【雄ねじ】 a male screw; a bolt.

おの【斧】(まさかり) an ax; 英 an axe; (手おの) a hatchet.

おのおの【各】(めいめい) each; (みんな) all; (すべて) every (おもに単数名詞をとる). ¶ ～が意見を持っている *Each* has his own opinion.

おのずから【自ら】(自然に) naturally; (ひとりでに) of itself; of its own accord; (自発的に) spontaneously; of *one's* will.

おのの・く【戦く】 ¶ 恐れ～く tremble with (≒ for) fear.

おのぼりさん【お上りさん】 a country visitor; a sightseer from the country.

おのれ【己】 I; myself; oneself. ¶ ～をむなしくする be self-sacrificing; be modest. ～に打ち勝つ be master of *one*self; conquer *one*self.

おは【尾羽】 ¶ 彼はすっかり～うち枯らしていた He *was in bad, distressed circumstances.* / He *looked* very *down at heels*.

おば【伯母・叔母・小母】 ⇒おばさん

おばあさん【お祖母さん】 a grandmother; (小児語) a grandma.

おばあさん【お婆さん】 an old lady (≒ woman).

おばけ【お化け】 a ghost; a specter; a goblin; (怪物) a monster.
—屋敷 a haunted house.

おはこ【十八番】 *one's* forte; (演奏・演技など) *one's* favorite performance; (論題など) *one's* favorite topic. ¶ ～を出す ride *one's hobby*.

おばさん【伯母さん・叔母さん・小母さん】(叔母さん) an aunt; (小母さん) a lady. ¶ よその～ *a* strange *lady*.

おはじき【お弾き】 (玉) a marble; (遊戯) a game of marbles. ¶ ～をする play *marbles*.

おはち【お鉢】 (飯びつ) a rice tub; (順番) *one's* turn. ¶ ～が(順番が)私に回ってきた My *turn* has come 〔round〕.

おはつ【お初】 **1** 〖初物〗 the first product of the season. ¶ モモの～を食べる eat *early* peaches.
2 〖初対面〗 the first meeting. ¶ ～にお目にかかります I am glad to meet you.

おばな【雄花】 a male flower.

おはよう【お早う】 Good morning. (morning を強く言う. good を強く言うと「さようなら」の意). ¶ ～ございますと言う say *good morning* (*to a person*); bid (*a person*) *good morning*.

おはらい【お祓】 purification.

おはらいばこ【お払い箱】¶〜になった I *was dismissed.* / I *was discharged.* / I *lost my place.* / (口語) I *was fired.*

おはり【お針】¶〜のけいこを受ける take *sewing* lessons.

—子 a needlewoman.

おび【帯】an *obi* (英語で説明すれば a long, broad sash tied about the waist over a Japanese *kimono*). ¶〜を結ぶ tie (≒ do) up an *obi*. 〜を解く untie (≒ undo) an *obi*. 〜に短し,たすきに長し It is good for neither one thing nor the other.

おび·える【怯える】¶悪夢に〜える *suffer from* a nightmare. 彼女は気を失うほど〜えていた She *was frightened* out of her wits.

おびきだ·す【おびき出す】¶彼らはその少年を家から〜した They *lured* the boy *away from* his house.

おびきよ·せる【おびき寄せる】decoy; lure; entice.

おひざもと【お膝下】¶陛下の〜である東京 Tokyo where His Imperial Majesty lives; Tokyo, the Imperial capital.

おびただし·い【夥しい】¶通りは〜い人だかりだった There was a *great* crowd of people in the street. 彼は頼りないこと〜い He is *quite* unreliable.

おびどめ【帯止め】an *obi*-clasp.

おひとよし【お人好し】(気だてのよい) a good-natured person; (だまされやすい) a simple-minded person; a credulous person; (ばかな) a simpleton; a soft-headed person; a fall guy; a sucker.

おびふう【帯封】a wrapper. ¶新聞に〜をする *wrap* a newspaper.

おひや【お冷や】water; (ご飯) cold rice.

おびやか·す【脅かす】menace; threaten; intimidate. ¶それは世界の平和を〜すものだ It *is a menace to* world peace. 最近彼は脅迫状に〜されている Recently he *has been menaced* by threatening letters.

おひゃくど【お百度】¶彼の家に〜を踏んで,やっと彼をわが社に引き抜くことができた I *visited* him *again and again*, till I managed to buy him over to our company. 彼女は息子の全快を祈って神社で〜を踏んだ She *walked in the precincts of the shrine one hundred times praying* fervently for her son's recovery.

おひらき【お開き】¶パーティーは5時に〜になった The party *adjourned* (≒ *was closed*) at five o'clock. 会も〜にしよう Let's *adjourn* the meeting.

お·びる【帯びる】**1**〖身につける〗wear. ¶昔は武士は刀を〜びて町を歩いた In olden times the *samurai* walked along the street, *wearing* swords at their side.

2〖受け持つ〗¶彼がどのような任務を〜びて来日したのか明らかでない It is not known what kind of a mission he was sent to Japan *on*.

重要な使命を〜びて彼はワシントンに向かった He started for Washington *on* some important mission.

3〖含み持つ〗¶彼は酒気を〜びていた He *was tipsy* (≒ *was intoxicated; was under the influence of liquor*).

彼はふだんは赤みを〜びた顔色をしているが,きょうは顔色が悪い He usually *looks ruddy*, but today he is pale.

その運動はしだいに反戦的性格を〜びてきた The movement *has* gradually *assumed* (≒ *taken on*) an anti-war character.

しだいに話がすごみを〜びてきた The story *has become* more and more ghastly (≒ terrible).

その知らせでみなの顔は憂色を〜びてきた They *looked sad at* the news.

おひれ【尾鰭】¶事実に〜をつけて話すな Don't *exaggerate* the fact.

おひろめ【御披露目】announcement; introduction.

オフィス an office.

—ガール an office girl.

おふくろ【お袋】*one's* mother.

オブザーバー an observer.

おぶさ·る【負ぶさる】¶少年は父親の背に〜っていた The boy *was riding on* his father's *back*. 彼に〜るな(頼るな) Don't *rely on* him.

オフセット〖印刷〗an offset.

—印刷 offset printing.

おふだ【お札】a charm; a talisman; an amulet; a phylactery.

おぶつ【汚物】(不潔物) dirt; filth; (台所の) garbage.

オブラート a wafer (オブラートはドイツ語の Oblate から).

おべっか flattery. ¶彼はいつも社長に〜を使っている He *is* always *currying favor with* the president. / He *is* always *making up to* the president. 〜つかい a flatterer.

オペラ an opera.

—グラス〔a pair of〕opera glasses; an opera glass.

オペレッタ〖音楽〗an operetta.

おぼえ【覚え】**1**〖記憶·回想〗¶そんなことを言った〜はない I don't *remember* having said anything of that kind.

顔に〜のあるような気がする I *remember* seeing him before. / I think I saw him somewhere.

この筆跡に〜はないか Don't you *recognize* this handwriting?

1度彼女とそこへ行った〜がある I *remember* going there with her once.

まったく身に〜のない話だ I *am* entirely *innocent of* such a matter.

身に〜があるだろう Admit your guilt!

2〖理解力〗¶きみは仕事の〜が遅い You are slow at *learning* your job.

この子は〔物〕〜が悪くて困る I'm sorry this child is slow to *learn*.

3〖自信〗¶私もそのことなら多少腕に〜がある I *am* more or less *confident of* my ability in such matters.

4〖経験〗〔an〕experience. ¶ぼくも彼にはひどい目に会った〜がある I *have had a* similar

お

bitter *experience* of having a hard time with him.
そういう場面に出会った～のない人はまれだ There are few who *have* not *experienced* such a situation.
5〘信任・信用〙esteem. ¶ 彼は社長の～があまりめでたくない He *is* not *in the good books of* the president of his company.
このごろ彼は社長の～がめでたいようだ He seems to stand high in the president's *estimation* (≒ *esteem*) now. / He seems to *be* highly *thought of* by the president.

おぼ·える【覚える】**1**〘習得する〙learn. ¶ ぼくは自動車の運転を１か月で～えた I *learned* how to drive a car in a month.
ぼくは英語を～えるのには苦労した I worked very hard to *learn* English.
やっと少しは仕事を～えた I finally managed to *learn* how to do this work.
一度スキーの味を～えると，やめられなくなる Once you enjoy skiing, it is hard to quit.
フランス人の会社で働いているとき，いくらかフランス語を聞き～えた I *picked up* a little French while working in a French company.
2〘記憶する〙remember. ¶ その場でなにを言ったか少しも～えていない I don't *remember* what I said there at all.
私は昔のことはよく～えている I *remember* old days well.
あの晩のことはかすかに～えている I *have a dim recollection of* that evening. / My mind is vague about that evening.
あなたの母上の若いころのお姿をまだはっきり～えています I *remember* clearly how your mother looked in her younger days.
きみのところの電話番号は～えやすい Your phone number is easy to *remember*.
その辛らつさは身にしみて～えている The severe criticism *sank deeply into my mind*.
～えていろ，きっと仕返しをしてやるから *Remember!* You shall pay for this. / I shall make you pay for this.
あの先生のお説教はもうそらで～えている I *have learned by heart* the teacher's preaching.
コンピューターにどういう項目を～え込ませるのか What kind of things do you have the computer *memorize*?
3〘感じる〙feel. ¶ 急に胸に痛みを～えた Suddenly I *felt* a pain in my heart.
そろそろ冬の寒さを～えるころとなった The cold winter season is approaching.

おぼし·き【思しき】¶ アメリカ人と～き人に日本語で話しかけられた I was spoken to in Japanese by a man *looking like* an American.

おぼしめし【思し召し】¶ いかほどでも～でけっこうです Give me what[ever] *you think fit*. ～にかなうお部屋が見つからないかもしれません I am afraid you may not be able to find the room *you like*. せっかくの～ですがお受けすることはできません I am sorry, but I cannot accept *your kindness*.

おぼつかな·い【覚束ない】¶ 彼の成功は～い *I am doubtful as to* his success. 彼女の回復は～い *There is little hope of* her recovery.
彼は～い足取りで歩いていた He was walking with *unsteady* steps.

おぼ·れる【溺れる】¶ 彼は荒波にのまれて～れた He *was drowned* in a rough sea. 危なく～れるところだった I *was* nearly *drowned*. / I narrowly escaped *drowning*. ～れる者はわらをもつかむ(諺) *A drowning man will catch at a straw*. 酒に～れるな Don't *abandon yourself to* drinking. / Don't *give yourself over to* drinking.

おぼろ【朧】¶ 今では～げな記憶にすぎなくなってしまった I have only a *vague* memory of it now.

おぼろづき【朧月】a hazy moon.
―夜 a hazy moon-lit night.

おぼん【お盆】(器) a 〔serving〕 tray；(うら盆)〔宗教〕*Bon*；Feast of Lanterns.

おまいり【お参り】¶ 伊勢神宮に～する *worship at* the Grand Shrines at Ise. 人の墓に～する *visit a person's* grave.

おまえ【お前】you；(夫婦・親子・恋人間で)〔my〕 dear；darling；(子どもに) my boy (≒ child).

おまけ【お負け】(割引) a discount；(付録・景品) a gift. ¶ これは～です We'll give you this *for nothing*. あの店では100円～してくれた They *discounted* (≒ *made a discount of*) one hundred yen. ～に雪が降りだした *To make* 〔*the*〕 *matters worse*, it began to snow.

おませ ¶ ～な子 a *forward* (≒ *sophisticated*; *precocious*) child.

おまつりさわぎ【お祭り騒ぎ】merrymaking；merriment.

おまもり【お守り】a charm. ¶ 災難よけの～ *a charm* against evils.

おまる (寝床の中で用いる便器) a bedpan；(寝室で用いる便器) a closestool.

おみき【御神酒】*sake* offered before the altar；(酒) *sake*. ¶ 祭壇に～をささげる offer *sake* before the altar.

おみこし【お神輿】**1**〘神社の〙¶ ～を担ぐ carry about *a portable shrine*.
2〘比喩的に〙¶ ～を上げる(立ち上がる) rise from *one's* seat；(始める) set out.
～をすえる(動こうとしない) do not rise from *one's* seat at once.

おみそれ【お見それ】¶ ～してたいへん失礼いたしました I am very sorry I couldn't recognize you. / You have the advantage of me.

おむつ a diaper.

オムレツ an omelet〔te〕.

おめ【お目】¶ (A氏を紹介されて)初めて～にかかります How do you do, Mr. A? I'm very glad to meet you. (こう言われて答えるときは，How do you do? I'm very glad to meet you.). (受付などから) Aさんが～にかかりたいとおっしゃってお見えです Mr. A is here to *meet* you. いずれ近いうちにその絵を～にかけます I'll *show* you the picture one of these days. あの彫刻が～にとまりましたか Did that sculpture *attract* your attention?

おめい【汚名】〔a〕 disgrace；〔a〕 dishonor.

¶彼は汚職官吏の～を着せられた He *was branded as* a corrupt government official. ついに彼は詐欺師の～をそそいだ He could wipe off the *disgrace* (≒ *bad name*) of a swindler.

おめおめ〔と〕 shamelessly; ignominiously. ¶よくまあ〔平気で〕～帰れたものだ What a shameless man you are to come back *unconcernedly*!

おめかし dressing smartly; (化粧) making up. ¶彼女は鏡の前で～している She *is titivating* 〔*herself*〕 before the mirror.

おめがね【お眼鏡】 ¶彼は社長の～にかなった He *found favor with* the president. / He *found favor in* the president's *eyes*.

おめし【お召し】 ¶この服をちょっと～になってみますか Will you *try on* this dress?

—もの *one's* dress (≒ clothes). **—列車** the Imperial train.

おめずおくせず【怖めず臆せず】 boldly; fearlessly; without hesitation.

おめだま【お目玉】 a scolding; 〔a〕 reprimand; 〔a〕 censure; blame. ¶遅刻してうんと～を食った I *had a* good *scolding* for having been late. / I *was scolded* very sharply for having been late.

おめでた【お目出度】 ¶昨年はあの一家は～続きだった Last year one *happy event* followed another in the family. おたくの奥さん～だそうだね I hear your wife *is expecting a baby*.

おめでた・い【お目出度い】 ¶～い男 a *foolish* man.

おめでとう【お目出度う】 Congratulations! ¶合格～ I *congratulate* you *on* your success. ～, 男の子のパパになったんだってね *Congratulations*; you have just become the father of a son. 新年～ A Happy New Year. クリスマス～ A Merry Christmas 〔to you〕. 誕生日～ Happy birthday to you. / Many happy returns of your birthday.

おもい【思い】 **1** 〖気持ち・感じ〗 ¶まったく死ぬ～だった I *felt* as if I were going to die.

いやな～をさせてすみませんでした I'm sorry I have made you *feel* unhappy.

金がなくてずいぶんつらい～をしたこともある I *have experienced* a hard time over lack of money.

2 〖思索・配慮〗 ¶彼は長い間～にふけっていた He remained buried in *thought* for a long time.

彼女は遠く故郷に～をはせていた Her *thoughts* wandered back to her distant home.

事態をどう説明したらいいか彼は一生懸命に～を凝らした He *thought over and over* how to explain the situation.

それに～を致さなかったのは私の失敗だ It was my mistake not *thinking of* it.

それはきみの～すごしだ You *worry too much*.

3 〖予期・期待〗 ¶きみにそんなことを言われるとは～もよらなかった It is the last thing *I expected to* hear from you.

彼が不合格とは～もかけぬことだった *It is quite surprising that* he should have failed. / His failure was quite *a surprise*.

問題は～のほか難しい The question is more difficult than *I had expected*.

4 〖願望〗 ¶首尾よく合格し, 多年の～がやっとかなった I have realized my *long-cherished dream* of passing the examination.

きみの～をかなえてあげよう I'll satisfy your *desires*.

やっとのことで～を遂げた I managed to gain *my object* at long last.

彼女の～のままにさせなさい Let her *have her own way*.

なんでも自分の～のままになるとはかぎらない Things will not always turn out as you *wish*.

5 〖愛情〗 ¶彼は彼女に長いこと～を寄せていた He *was in love with* her for a long time. / He *was sweet on* her for a long time.

ほんとに彼女を愛しているなら, 率直に～を打ち明けなさい If you really love her, you should tell her frankly.

おも・い【重い】 (重さが) heavy; (重大な) grave; serious; (気分が) heavy; oppressive; depressed.

¶この荷物は～い This baggage *is heavy*. 彼は～い罰を受けた He was *severely* punished. 彼には～い責任がある He is burdened with a *heavy* responsibility. 頭が～い I *feel heavy* in the head. 彼女の病気は～い She is *seriously* sick. どう見ても彼の罪は～い His offense *is grave* in every respect. ～い気分をいかんともすることができなかった I could find no way of relieving my *heavy* heart. 彼は～い気分で職を辞さなければならなかった He could not but resign his post *with a heavy heart*.

おもいあが・る【思い上がる】 ¶彼の～った広言 his *vain* boasts. 彼は成功に～っている He *is vain of* his success. / He *conceits himself over* his success.

おもいあた・る【思い当たる】 ¶それを聞くと～る節がある That *reminds* me *of* a story I once heard. 彼女の名は～らない I cannot *think of* her name.

おもいあま・る【思い余る】 ¶まったく～って彼に相談した As I *was* quite *at a loss* what to do, I consulted with him.

おもいおもい【思い思い】 ¶～に as *one* pleases (≒ likes); each in *one's* own way; according to *one's* own fancy (≒ taste; wish).

おもいかえ・す【思い返す】 ¶もう一度よく～してごらん *Think* it well *over again*. ～してやめてほしい I hope you'll *think better of* it.

おもいがけな・い【思いがけない】 ¶～い客 an *unexpected* visitor. まったく～いときに彼が現われた He came up when *I least expected* him. 彼にまた会うなんてまったく～いことだった *Little did I expect* to meet him again.

おもいきって【思い切って】 (大胆に) boldly; daringly; resolutely; (非常に) desperately; extremely; exceedingly. ¶～彼の案に反対し

お

た I *dared* (≒ *ventured*) to oppose his plan. この際～たばこをやめることにした I *have resolved* to give up smoking.

おもいきり【思い切り】¶～やってみた I *did my best*. 彼を～なぐった I struck him *with all my might*. 彼は～がいい(過ぎたことにくよくよしない) He does not worry himself about what has been done. 彼は～が悪い(決断力に欠ける) He is lacking in *decision*.

おもいこ·む【思い込む】¶彼は自分で天才だと～んでいる He fully *believes* that he is a genius. 彼は～んだら徹底的にやりぬく Once he *has determined* to do a thing, he will do it thoroughly.

おもいし·る【思い知る】¶今度こそ彼も～ったにちがいない I'm sure he *has learned his lesson* this time. いまに～る(後悔する)ときが来るぞ The time will surely come when you'll *be sorry for* it. / The time will surely come when you'll *repent of* it.

おもいだ·す【思い出す】recollect; remember. ¶5年前の北海道の生活を～す I *recollect* my life in Hokkaido five years ago. その小説の題名が～せますか Can you *think of* the title of the novel? 彼はそのペンを見て学生時代を～した He looked at the pen and *was reminded of* his school days. その人の名前を～してください Please try to *remember* the name of the man. なにかを～したらしく, 彼女は泣いていた She was weeping, probably because she *thought of* something.

おもいた·つ【思い立つ】¶～ったが吉日(諺) *There is no time like the present.* / *Tomorrow never comes.*

おもいちがい【思い違い】〔a〕misunderstanding;〔a〕misapprehension;〔a〕misconception; a mistake.
¶きっとそれはきみの～だ You must *be mistaken*. / It must be some *misunderstanding* (≒ *misapprehension*) on your part. 彼をアメリカ人だと～をした I *have taken* (≒ *have mistaken*) him *for* an American.

おもいつき【思いつき】an idea. ¶それはいい～だ That's *a* good (≒ happy) *idea*. なにかいい～はないか Don't you have any good *suggestion* to make?

おもいつ·く【思いつく】¶適当なことばが～かない I can't *think of* the right word. / The right word doesn't *occur to* me.

おもいつ·める【思い詰める】¶彼女はまだ自分の不幸を～めている She *is* still *brooding over* her bad luck.

おもいで【思い出】a memory; a remembrance; a reminiscence. ¶～の記 a book of *reminiscences*. 京都の～ *reminiscences* of Kyoto. 彼女はいつも～にふけってばかりいる She is always indulging in *reminiscences*. 彼はぼくに大学時代の～を話してくれた He gave his *memories* of his college days to me. その旅行は～になってみると, 非常に楽しいものとなるだろう The trip will afford *a* most pleasing *reminiscence* in later years.

おもいでばなし【思い出話】reminiscences. ¶昔の～を語り合った We exchanged *reminiscences* of the good old days.

おもいどおり【思い通り】¶～に問題を解決することができた I could solve the problem *to my satisfaction*. / I could solve the problem *to my heart's content*. なんでも～になるというわけにはいかない You cannot *have everything your*〔*own*〕*way*. / You cannot *have your*〔*own*〕*way in everything*.

おもいとどま·る【思いとどまる】give up; abandon; desist (*from*). ¶頼むからひとりでそこに行くのは～ってくれ For God's sake, *give up going* there by yourself. なんとかして彼がその娘と結婚するのを～らせた I managed to *dissuade* him *from* marry*ing* the girl.

おもいなお·す【思い直す】⇒おもいかえす

おもいなしか ¶～物音が聞こえたような気がした *I fancied* that I heard a noise. / *It seemed to me* that I heard a noise.

おもいなや·む【思い悩む】¶彼は就職がうまくいかないのを～んでいた He *worried* much *about* his failure to find a job. その問題の解決法にはまったく～んでいる I *am* completely *at a loss* how to settle the matter.

おもいのこ·す【思い残す】¶～すことはない I have nothing to *regret*. もうこの世に～すことはなにもない I can die at peace at any moment.

おもいのほか【思いの外】unexpectedly; against (≒ contrary to) *one's* expectation. ¶試験は～やさしかった The examination was easier than *I had expected*.

おもいのまま【思いのまま】¶彼に～にさせなさい Let him *have his own way*. なんでも自分の～になるとは限らない Things will not always turn out *as you wish*.

おもいもよらな·い【思いも寄らない】¶きみにここで会おうとは～かった *I never dreamed of* meeting you here. / You are *the last* person *I expected to* see here.

おもいや·られる【思いやられる】¶きみの行く末が～られる *I feel very anxious about* your future.

おもいやり【思いやり】sympathy; compassion; consideration. ¶～のある人 a *sympathetic* person. ～のあることば *sympathetic* words. ～のない人 an *unsympathetic* person; a cold person. 彼女は老人に～がある She *is sympathetic to* the old. / She *is considerate of* the old.

おもいや·る【思いやる】¶彼の将来を～る *think of* his future. 彼の父親の嘆きを～ると when I *consider* his father's grief.

おもいわずら·う【思い煩う】⇒おもいなやむ

おも·う【思う・想う】**1**〖考える・信じる・感じる〗
¶ぼくもそう～う I *think* so, too.
きみにそれができると～うか *Are* you *sure* that you can do it?
それで十分だと～う I *suppose* it will be enough.
彼は既にロンドンに立ったと～っていた I *thought* that he had already left for London.

われわれのチームが勝つと〜った I *expected* that our team would win the game.
私が正しいと〜う I *believe* I am right.
彼はどうもどこかが変だとは〜わないか Don't you *think* there is something wrong with him?
もうだめだと〜った I *gave* it *up* as hopeless.
彼の言動を内心不愉快に〜った In my heart I *was displeased with* what he did.
悪く〜うな Don't *think ill of* me.
ひと眠りしたいと〜った I *wanted* to have a nap.
よい天気なので散歩に出てみたいと〜った As it was fine, I *intended* to go out for a walk. / As it was fine, I *thought of* going out for a walk.
2〖評価する〗 ¶ 彼は商才にたけていると〜う I *consider* him to have great business ability. / I look upon him as a man of great business ability.
彼らはぼくのことをよく〜ってくれなかった They did not *think well of* me.
彼はよい教師だと〜われている He *is regarded as* a good teacher.
きみは金がすべてだと〜っているのか Do you *regard* money *as* everything?
3〖不審に思う〗 ¶ 彼はぼくをだまそうとしているのではないかと〜った I *suspected* that he was going to cheat me.
その話を聞いておかしいなと〜った I *felt* strange when I heard it.
4〖懸念する〗 ¶ 試験に落ちるのではないかと〜った I *feared* (≒ *was afraid*) that I would fail in the examination.
あすは雪になるのではないかと〜う I *am afraid* that it will snow tomorrow.
きみの考え違いではないかと〜う I *am afraid* that you are mistaken.
5〖たいせつに思う・愛する・思い懐かしむ〗 ¶ 心ひそかに彼女のことを〜い続けた I have continued to *love* her in my heart.
お互いに〜い〜われる仲だった They *loved* each other.
きみのためを〜うからこそこう言うのだ I say this for your good.
子を〜わぬ親はいない Every parent *yearns after* his children. / There are no parents who do not *love* their children.
彼はぼくのことを〜ってくれているのだろうか I wonder if he *is interested in* me.
6〖希求・願望する〗 ¶ 英語を勉強しようと〜う I *intend* (≒ *am going*) *to* study English.
〜ったとおりにやりなさい Do as you *please*.
〜っていたことがかなえられた What I *dreamed of* came true.
物事はなかなか〜うとおりにはいかない Things do not turn out as one *wishes*.
〜う存分遊びなさい Play as much as you *like*.
これと〜う人物はなかなかいない There are very few worthy men to speak of.
7〖つもりだ〗 ¶ もうよそうと〜う I *am thinking of* giving it up.
あすは田舎に行こうと〜う I *am going* to my native village tomorrow.
やろうと〜えばやれないことはない There is nothing that cannot be done, if we *have a mind to* do it.
8〖想像する〗 ¶ ぼんやりしてなにを〜っているのか What *are* you *daydreaming* about?
それを〜うと涙が出る Tears come into my eyes when I *think of* it.
将来を〜うと希望がわく When I *picture* my future *to myself*, my mind is filled with hope. / When I *think of* my future, my mind is filled with hope.
9〖記憶する・追想する〗 ¶ 今〜えばぼくも当時は若かった When I *think of* it, I was young then. / When I *look back to* it, I was young then. / When I *come to recollect* now, I was young, then.
〜えばあのころは楽しかった I *remember* that I had a good time of it then.
あれはたしか去年の今ごろだったと〜う I *am sure* that it was about this time last year.
10〖予想する〗 ¶ 〜ったとおりの結果になった It ended as I *had expected*.
こんなことになろうとは〜ってもみなかった I did not *expect* at all that it would turn out like this. / I little *dreamed* that it would turn out like this.
試験は〜ったよりやさしかった The examination was easier than I *had expected* (≒ *had anticipated*).
ここできみに会えるとは〜わなかった I did not *expect* that I would meet you here.
どうせそうだろうと〜っていた I *thought* as much.

おもうぞんぶん【思う存分】 to *one's* heart's content; to the full; as much as *one* likes; (徹底的に) thoroughly; completely.

おもうつぼ【思う壺】 ¶ 彼は彼らの〜にはまった He *fell into the snare* spread by them. 事は彼の〜にはまった It worked satisfactory to him. / It went on as he wanted.

おもうまま【思う儘】 ¶ 〜にふるまう have *one's* own way. 〜にさせておく allow *a person* to do *as he pleases*; let *a person have his own way*.

おもおもし・い【重重しい】 grave; serious. ¶ 〜口調で in a *grave* (≒ *serious*) tone. 〜しく gravely; seriously; solemnly; with dignity. 〜さ gravity; seriousness; solemnity; dignity.

おもかげ【面影】 ¶ 彼女には美人だった若いころの〜がいくぶん残っている She retains *something of* her youthful beauty. 今の彼には往年のスタープレーヤーの〜はまったくない There is not the slightest *trace* in him of a star player of his young days. 城は今なお昔日の栄華の〜をとどめている The castle still retains some *traces* of its former grandeur.

おもかじ【面舵】〔航海術〕 the starboard; (号令) 困 Right!; 困 Starboard! ¶ 〜をとる turn 〔the helm〕 to starboard.

おもき【重き】 weight; emphasis; dignity; importance; value. ¶ 彼らは教育行政に〜を置く They *lay emphasis on* educational

お

administration. / They *attach importance to* educational administration. 閣僚の中でも彼は～をなす He *plays a leading role* among the Cabinet ministers. われわれは彼の意見に～を置かない We *make no account of* his opinion.

おもくるし・い【重苦しい】¶ ～い映画 a *dismal* motion picture. しばらくの間～い沈黙が続いた There was an *oppressive* silence for a while. ～い気分で床についた I went to bed with a *heavy* heart. 胃が～い I feel a *dull* pain in the stomach. 胸が[圧迫されて]～い I feel *oppressed* in the breast.

おもさ【重さ】weight. ¶ それは～はどのくらいあるか How much does it *weigh*? 彼はリンゴの～を測った He *weighed* the apple. ～が1キロある It *weighs* one kilogram. 彼は部長としての～が足りない Although he is head of the department, he doesn't have the proper *dignity*.

おもし【重石】a weight; a heavy stone. ¶ 漬け物に～をする put *a weight* on salted vegetables.

おもしろ・い【面白い】interesting. ¶ 彼の話はいつも～い His conversation *is* always *interesting*. テニスは～いですか *Is* it *fun* playing tennis? ゆうべは～かった I *had a good time* yesterday evening. たいへん～いひと晩だった I *enjoyed* the evening very much. 彼の話しぶりは～かった His way of talking *was amusing*. ～くない映画だった It was a *dull* movie. 形勢はだんだん～くなくなってきた The situation *became* more *unfavorable* to us. なんとも～い勝負だった It was quite an *exciting* game. どうも彼女の病状は～くないようだ It seems she really *is in a critical condition*. この品は～いように売れている This article is selling *exceedingly* well.

おもしろはんぶん【面白半分】¶ ～に in (≒ for) fun; in joke. 私は～に彼女をおどかした I frightened her *just for fun*.

おもしろみ【面白み】interest; enjoyment; fun. ¶ この岩石は～のある形をしている The shape of this rock *is interesting*. ここに花を置くと～が倍加する Put flowers here, and you will be able to add *interest*.

おもた・い【重たい】¶ この荷物は～い This baggage *is heavy*. 気分が～い I *feel depressed* (≒ *feel low-spirited*). まぶたが～くなった I *was sleepy*.

おもだった【重立った・主立った】chief; important; principal; leading; main.

おもちゃ【玩具】a toy; a plaything. ¶ ～の自動車 a *toy* car. ～で遊ぶ play with *a toy*. ナイフを～にしてはいけない Don't *toy with* a knife.

―屋(店) a toy store (≒ 囲 shop); (人) a toy dealer.

おもて【表】 **1** 〚家の外・玄関などがある前の方〛 ¶ ～でだれか人の声がする I hear somebody talking *outside*. ～から見るとりっぱな家だ From *outside* the house is impressive. 地震でびっくりして～に飛び出した The earthquake made us run out into *the street* (≒ *the outside*). ～の玄関の方にお回りください Come round to *the front door*.

2 〚顔・顔色〛 the face. ¶ 彼は怒りを～に現わした He *showed* his anger. 彼女は悲しみを～に出すまいとつとめた She tried to *hide* her grief.

3 〚裏面に対する表面〛 ¶ (貨幣の)～が出ればぼくの勝ち, 裏が出ればぼくの負け *Heads* I win, tails I lose. 裏か～か *Heads* or tails? (ふつう複数形). どちらがこの紙の～か裏かわかるか Can you tell which side is *the surface* of this piece of paper? 封筒の～にあて名を書く write an address on the *front* of an envelope (イギリスではふつう差出人の住所・氏名は封筒のすみに書く). 彼女はまちがって布地の裏～を逆にして裁断した She cut the cloth *the wrong side out* by mistake. / She cut the cloth *inside out* by mistake.

4 〚野球〛 ¶ 7回の～に 3点とられた We lost three runs in *the first half* of the seventh inning.

5 〚うわべ〛 ¶ ～ばかりとりつくろってもしかたない It will be no good to make up *appearance*.

おもてぐち【表口】the front door.

おもてげんかん【表玄関】the front door. ¶ 東京の～ *the front door of* Tokyo.

おもてざた【表沙汰】(公表) publication. ¶ ～にする(公表する) make (*a matter*) publicly known; (裁判に訴える) bring (*a matter*) before the court. ～になる(公表される) be made public; (訴えられる) be brought to the court.

おもてだ・つ【表だつ】¶ ～って彼の意見に反対できない I cannot oppose his opinion *openly* (≒ *in public*).

おもてどおり【表通り】the main street; 囲 the street.

おもてむき【表向き】¶ 会社ではそのような行為は～には禁じられている Such conduct is *officially* forbidden in the office. これが彼が欠席した～の理由だ This is the *ostensible* reason why he stayed away from the meeting. ～は出張ということで北海道に出かけたが, 実際はどうかわからない *Ostensibly* he went on an official trip to Hokkaido, but I don't know whether or not it was true.

おもな【重な・主な】chief. ¶ 使節の～目的 the *chief* aim of the mission. 今月の～スポーツ行事 the *main* sports events of this month. 関東地方の～河川 the *principal* rivers in the Kanto district. きょうの新聞の～記事 the *biggest* news in today's paper. この事件で～役割を演じた者はみな捕まった Those who took a *leading* part in the plot have all been arrested. 悪い道路は交通事故の～原因の一つだ Bad roads are one of the *primary* causes of traffic accidents.

おもなが【面長】¶ 彼の顔は～だ He has *an oval face*.

おもに【重荷】(重い荷物) a heavy load. ¶ 子どもはしばしば両親の～になる Children are often *a burden* to their parents. あなたのおかげで心の～がおりた You have taken *a load* off my mind. 心の～がおりた *A load* of anxiety is off my mind. / I feel relieved. この仕事は私には～だ This work is *too much for* me.

おもに【主に】chiefly; mainly; (大部分) for the most part. ¶ 日本人の食べ物は～米だ The food of the Japanese is *chiefly* rice. 夏休みは～海岸で過ごした I spent *most* of the summer vacation at the seaside. 聴衆は～女性だった The audience consisted *mainly* of women.

おもね·る【阿る】¶ 彼は権力者に～る He *fawns upon* the authority. 彼はけっして上役に～らない He never *flatters* his superiors.

おもはゆ·い【面はゆい】¶ ～いね I feel much *abashed* (≒ *embarrassed*).

おもみ【重み】(物の) weight; (人物としての) dignity. ¶ 本の～で戸が開かない The door will not open under the *weight* of the books. あの議長には～がない That chairman is wanting in *dignity*. / The chairman does not befit the chair. 彼のことばには千鈞(せんきん)の～がある His words carry great *weight* with us.

おもむき【趣】¶ お申し越しの～考慮いたします I will take note of what you wrote in your letter. いつものやり方とは全然～を変えてみよう Let's depart from the usual practice. 10年前とは辺りの～が全然変わっている The surroundings are not what they were ten years ago. 現在の建物には～がない The building which stands now has no *attractive features*. この庭には深山の～がある This garden has *an appearance* of mountain glens.

おもむ·く【赴く】¶ 彼は遭難者の救助に～いた He *went to* the rescue of the victims. 彼は敢然として死地に～いた Fearlessly he *rode into* the jaws of death.

おもむろに【徐ろに】¶ 彼は～話しはじめた He began to talk *after a little pause*. 彼は～意見を述べた He *calmly* expressed his opinion.

おももち【面持ち】a look; an expression. ¶ 彼は困惑した～であった He *looked* troubled. / He wore *a* troubled *look*. 彼女はけげんな～だった She *looked* puzzled.

おもや【母家·母屋】the main house (≒ building).

おもやつれ【面窶れ】¶ 彼は睡眠不足で～している He *looks haggard* from lack of sleep.

おもゆ【重湯】thin rice gruel.

おもり【錘】(釣り糸の) a sinker; (はかりの) a weight. ¶ 釣り糸に～をつける *weight* a fishing line; put *a sinker* to a line.

おもわく【思わく】expectation. ¶ なにか～があるにちがいない I'm sure he has some *plot* in his mind. / I'm sure he has some *secret intention*. ～どおりだ The whole thing has turned out just *as I calculated*. / The whole thing turned out just *as I wished*. 彼はここへは～があってやって来たのだ He has come here with *a purpose*.

おもわし·い【思わしい】¶ 結果は～くない The result *has* not *been satisfactory*. 彼の健康は～くない He is not in the best of health. 彼の病気は～くない His sickness has not taken a *favorable* turn.

おもわず【思わず】¶ ～知らずやったことだ I did it *unintentionally*. この妙技に観衆は～かっさいした There arose a *spontaneous* burst of applause at the fine play among the spectators. ～吹き出してしまった I burst out laughing *in spite of myself*. ～かっとなって彼をなぐった I hit him *on the spur of the moment*.

おもわせぶり【思わせぶり】¶ 彼は～な話し方をする His manner of talking *is suggestive* (≒ *is mystifying*). 彼はなにか～なまなざしを私に向けた He gave me a *significant* look. 彼女は～な女だ She *is* quite *coquettish*.

おもわぬ【思わぬ】¶ ～不覚をとった We suffered an *unexpected* defeat.

おも·われる【思われる】¶ 彼の報告は真実には～われない His report does not *sound* true. これまでだれもそれに気づいたようには～われない It *seems* that no one has noticed it. それは実行不可能のように～われます It *seems* impractical to me. そんなことはわけなく～われた It *looked* very easy. 彼は通俗作家と～われている He *is regarded as* a popular writer.

おもん·ずる【重んずる】¶ 生命をなによりも～ずる *value* life before everything else. 日本では家柄を～ずる傾きがある In Japan we have a custom of *making much of* our birth. われわれは彼の意見を～じなければならない We should *respect* his opinions.

おもんぱか·る【慮る】consider. ¶ あまり先のことを～っておくびょうになってはいけない Don't get nervous by *taking* too much *thought for* your future.

おや ¶ ～, なんだって? *What?* What did you say? ～, どうして? How's that, *eh*? ～まあ O dear me! ～, ああ, そうなの *Oh!* I see. / ～っ, みんななくなっちゃった *Why!* It's all gone.

おや【親】**1**〖肉親の〗a parent; (両親) parents; (父親) a father; (母親) a mother.
¶ この～にしてこの子あり (諺) *Like father, like son*.
彼はまだ～のすねかじりだ He is still dependent on his *father*.
2〖トランプなどの〗the dealer; (賭博の) the banker. ¶ だれが～ですか Whose *deal* is it?

おやおもい【親思い】filial affection. ¶ 彼は～だ He *is devoted to his parents*. / He *loves his parents very much*.

おやがいしゃ【親会社】a parent company; a holding company (子会社の株の大半を所有

お

しているだけで, 生産に関与しない).

おやがかり【親掛かり】¶ まだ～の身だ I *am* still *dependent on my father*. / I *am living at the expense of my parents*.

おやかた【親方】¶ 大工の～ a master carpenter.

おやがわり【親代わり】¶ おじが私の～だ My uncle is my *foster father*.

おやぎ【親木】(木の切り株の) a stool; a parent plant; (宿り木の) a host plant.

おやこ【親子】parent and child. ¶ その夫婦は～ほど年が違う The couple differ in age as *parent and child*. ～の縁を切る break the ties of *parent and son*. ～の情はいつの世も同じだ The mutual affection between *parent and child* has been the same since ancient times.

おやごころ【親心】¶ それが～というものだ Such is *the natural desire of parents*.

おやごろし【親殺し】a parricide; (父親殺し) a patricide; (母親殺し) a matricide.

おやじ【親父・親爺】**1**〖父親〗a father; a dad. ¶ ～は裏庭にいる *Dad* (≒ *Father*) is out in the backyard.
田舎の～は今はすっかり元気です *The old man* in the country is in good shape now.
2〖上長の者〗¶ うちの～きょうきげんが悪いぞ(部下の者同士で) Be careful. *The old man* looks sour today.

おやしお【親潮】the Kurile Current.

おやしらず【親知らず】a wisdom tooth.

おやす・い【お安い】¶ ～いご用だ Oh, that's nothing. / That's no bother at all. / That's pleasure. ～くないね Aren't you too sweet on each other?

おやすみ【お休み】¶ ～なさい Good night. ゆっくり～になってください Take *a* good *rest*, please. きょうは学校は～だ We have no school today. あすは～だ Tomorrow is *a holiday*. あすは～にしましょう Let's have *a holiday* tomorrow.

おやつ【お八つ】afternoon tea; tea break; (おもに米) coffee break. ¶ ～の時間だ It's time to have *afternoon refreshment(s)*. / It's tea time. ～にしよう Let's have *coffee break* now.

おやばか【親馬鹿】¶ 彼の～にも困ったものだ I'm disgusted with his *fond indulgence in his children*.

おやぶね【親船】¶ ～に乗ったつもりで私に任せなさい You can entrust me with the whole business and no worry.

おやぶん【親分】a chief; a boss.
—肌 ¶ 彼は～肌だ He *is magnanimous*.
—風 ¶ 彼は～風を吹かす He *is bossy*.

おやま【女形】(俳優) a female impersonator; a man-actress. ¶ この劇の～はだれがやるのですか Who *acts the part of a woman* in the drama?

おやもと【親元】¶ 彼は～を離れて東京へ出て来た He left *home* (≒ *his parent*) to live in Tokyo.

おやゆずり【親譲り】¶ 彼の短気は～だ His quick-temper *comes from his father*. / He *inherited* his father's quick-temper. 彼は～の財産で裕福に暮らしている He lives quite comfortably on his *family* property. / He lives quite comfortably on his *inherited* property from his father.

おやゆび【親指】(手の) a thumb; (足の) a big toe.

およぎ【泳ぎ】¶ ひと～しよう Let's have *a swim*. 彼は～がうまい He is *a good swimmer*.

およ・ぐ【泳ぐ】swim. ¶ この川を～いで渡れますか Can you *swim* across this river? 川に～ぎにいこう Let's go *swimming* in the river. / Let's go for *a swim* in the river. 彼は時流に乗って～げない人だ He doesn't know how to *swim* with the tide. 打つときからだが～いでいる(野球で) Your posture *is tottering* when you hit the ball.

およそ【凡そ】¶ ～20人の人が行方不明だ *About* (≒ *Some*) twenty persons are missing. 損害は～10億円に上った The damage was *roughly* estimated at a billion yen. 計画について～のところを教えてください Give me a *fair* idea of your project. そんなことは～考えられない That's *quite* unthinkable.

およばずながら【及ばずながら】¶ ～助力いたします I will do *what little I can* to help you. ～もやってみましょう I will try *to the best of my ability*.

およばれ【お呼ばれ】¶ 私も～にあずかりました I, too, had the honor of *being invited*.

および【及び】and.

およ・ぶ【及ぶ】**1**〖達する〗¶ 交渉は深更に～んだ The negotiations *extended* till late at night.
会議は延々3時間に～んだ The meeting *lasted* three hours.
自動車の列は1キロ以上に～んだ The motorcars *queued* for more than one kilometer.
風速毎秒25～30メートルに～んだ The wind blew at a speed of 25 to 30 kilometers a second.
霜害はその地方全体に～んだ The frost damage *extended to* the whole district.
あすの行楽の人出は数万に～ぶと予想される The weekenders are expected to *come up to* tens of thousands tomorrow.
被害総額10億円に～んだ The damage *amounted to* a billion yen.
話がそのことに～ぶとみな黙った All of them became silent when the talk *turned on* the subject.
彼の影響は現代の詩人にまで～んでいる His influence *has extended* even *to* contemporary poets.
両方とも酔ってけんか口論に～んだ Both got drunk and *started* quarreling.
この期に～んでなにを言うか *At this stage*, what have you to say? / It's too late to back out now.

そこまでは考えが〜ばなかった I ought to have known better.

2 〚できる・匹敵する〛 ¶ その仕事はとても私の力には〜びません The task *is beyond my power*. / I *am not equal to* the job.

彼は私など〜びもつかぬよい腕を持っている I *am not nearly so* skillful as he.

力の〜ぶかぎり助力しましょう I'll help you *with everything I have*.

〜ばずながら私もその仕事に協力させていただきましょう I'll gladly work together with you *though my share may be humble*.

想像も〜ばぬ美しい所だ The place is splendid *beyond imagination*. / It is a too beautiful place for words.

英作文にかけては組じゅう彼に〜ぶ者はない No one in our class can *match* him in English composition.

3 〚…するには及ばない〛 ¶ そんなことをするには〜びません You *need not* do such a thing.

わざわざ出迎えに来るには〜びません *Don't trouble yourself to* meet me.

ご返事には〜びません You *need not* send me an answer.

あわてるには〜ばぬ 〔*There is*〕 *no* hurry.

心配するには〜びません *There's nothing to* be worried about.

およぼ・す 【及ぼす】 ¶ 台風は関東一円に被害を〜した A typhoon *damaged* the Kanto area.

彼の演説は感化を〜した His speech *exercised* an influence over them.

オラトリオ 〔音楽〕 an oratorio.

オランウータン 〔動物〕 an orang-〔o〕utan.

オランダ (公式には) the Netherlands (単数および複数扱いされる); (一般には) Holland.

—人 a Hollander; a Dutchman. **—語** Dutch.

おり 【折り】 **—箱** a chip box. 二つ**—本** a folio. 四つ**—本** a quarto.

おり 【折】 **1** 〚機会〛 a chance; an opportunity. ¶ 〜があったら彼にそう伝えましょう I will tell him to that effect at the first *opportunity*.

〜があればとねらっていた I have been watching (≒ waiting) for *a chance*.

〜をみて彼に忠告します I'll wait for *a* suitable *chance* to warn him.

またとない〜だ It's now or never!

〜あるごとに彼は故郷の名物を送ってくれる *Now and then* he sends me special products from my hometown.

〜がありしだい, ご返送いただきたい Please send it back to me at your earliest *convenience*.

あの方にはまだお目にかかる〜を得ておりません I have had no *opportunity* of meeting him yet.

これは彼女の〜にふれて詠んだ歌です These are some of the poems that she wrote on certain *occasions*.

2 〚その時〛 ¶ 〜よく自動車工場で働いている人がいて車の故障を直してくれた *Luckily* (≒ *Fortunately*), I had my car repaired by a man working in a motor company.

〜も〜電燈が消えて会場の混乱に輪をかけた The hall was thrown into confusion all the more because the lights went out just at the very *moment*.

その〜にはまたよろしく願います I look forward to your continued help.

〜も〜とて, なんのおもてなしもできませんがひとつ召し上がってください *Unfortunately* I can't offer you much, but please help yourself to this.

ご上京の〜にはお立ち寄りください Please drop in *when* you come up to Tokyo.

〜もあろうに, こんなときに会社を休むとは困ったやつだ What a lazy fellow he is to be absent from office at such *a time*.

3 〚季節〛 ¶ 寒さ厳しい〜からお体おたいせつに Please take good care of yourself in this cold *season*.

おり 【澱】 (砂・どろなどの沈殿物) sediment; (酒などの) dregs; lees; (コーヒーの) grounds.

¶ 〜が沈んだ The *dregs* have settled.

おり 【檻】 (獣の) a cage; (家畜の) a pen; (牢獄の独房) a cell; (牢獄全体) a prison; a jail.

¶ 〜の中のライオン a *caged* lion; a lion in *a cage*.

おりあい 【折り合い】 ¶ 妻は両親と〜が悪い My wife finds it difficult to live *on* good *terms with* my parents. 彼は重役とは〜がよくない He often *has trouble with* the director.

おりあ・う 【折り合う】 ¶ 〜うには時間がかかった It took much time to *reach an agreement* (≒ *reach a compromise*). なんとか〜えないものかね Can't we *effect a compromise*?

おりあしく 【折り悪しく】 unfortunately; unluckily.

おりいって 【折り入って】 ¶ 〜頼みがある I have a special favor to ask of you.

オリーブ 〔植物〕 an olive.

おりえり 【折り襟】 a turn-down collar.

¶ 襟は〜にしてください I want to have the collar turned down.

オリエンテーション orientation. ¶ 1週間新1年生に〜を行なう We shall give a week of *orientation* to the freshmen.

おりおり 【折折】 ¶ 四季〜の花が花壇に咲く Flowers of *each season* bloom in our flower garden.

オリオン 〔天文〕 Orion. ¶ 〜の三つの星 Orion's Belt.

おりかえし 【折り返し】 (衣服の) a lapel; (本の) a flap. ¶ 〜ご返事を請う Please send your reply *by return*.

—運転 ¶ 2駅間の〜運転をしている Trains *are shuttling* between the two stations. **—地点**(マラソンの) the turn.

おりかえ・す 【折り返す】 ¶ ズボンのすそを〜した I *turned up* my trousers (≒ pants). 事故のため電車はその駅で〜している Owing to an accident, trains do not go farther than that station, and *turn back* from there.

おりかさな・る 【折り重なる】 ¶ 列車に急ブレーキをかけたので人々が〜って倒れた The motorman braked the train suddenly and many

お

passengers *fell one upon another*.

おりかさ·ねる【折り重ねる】¶ 毛布はきちんと～ねてあった Blankets *were folded* neatly.

おりかばん【折り鞄】a brief case; a portfolio (複 portfolios).

おりがみ【折り紙】¶ ～で折りづるを作った I folded *colored paper* into a paper crane. この品物の品質は～つきだ Good quality of this article *is guaranteed*. / It's a *guaranteed* article. 彼は～つきの秀才だ He is a student of *acknowledged* genius.

おりから【折から】¶ ～大粒の雨が降りだした *Just then* a heavy rain began to fall. 気候不順の～ご自愛ください Please take good care of your health *in this* unseasonable weather.

おりこみ【折り込み】―広告 an inserted bill.

おりこ·む【折り込む】¶ そで口を少し～む make a tuck in the sleeve a little. 端を内側に２インチ～む turn the end two inches inside.

おりこ·む【織り込む】¶ 原案にあなたの考えを～みましょう Your idea will *be incorporated in* the plan.

おりたたみ【折り畳み】―いす a folding chair. ―傘 a telescopic umbrella. ―ベッド a folding bed. ―ボート a folding boat.

おりたた·む【折り畳む】¶ ふろしきをふたつに～む *fold* a wrapping cloth double.

おりづめ【折り詰め·折詰】―弁当 a luncheon packed in a chip box.

おりづる【折り鶴】a folded paper crane.

おりま·げる【折り曲げる】¶ ページの角を～げる *fold* 〔*over*〕 the corner of a page. ワイシャツのそでを～げる *turn up one's* shirt sleeves.

おりめ【折り目】**1**〖折り目のしわ〗a crease; a fold. ¶ (プレスした)ズボンの～ the *crease*〔*s*〕 of *one's* trousers.
この布は～がつきやすい This cloth *creases* (≒ *makes creases*) easily.
2〖作法〗¶ 彼は～正しい人だ He is a *well-mannered* man. / He has *good manners*. 彼はぼくに～正しくあいさつした He greeted me *politely* (≒ *courteously*).

おりめ【織り目】¶ ～の粗い(細かい)布地 a cloth of a loose (fine) *texture*.

おりもと【織り元】a weaver; a textile manufacturer.

おりもの【織物】cloth; textile fabrics.
―業 the textile trade. ―工芸 textile art. ―工業 the textile industry.

おりもの【おり物】a discharge from the womb; (あとざん) the afterbirth; (月経) menstruation.

お·りる【下りる·降りる】¶ この道から～りて歩けばよい You can *get down* by this path. 丘を～りていくと小屋が見えてきた *Going down* the hill, I caught sight of a cottage. 次の駅で～りたほうがいい You had better *get off* at the next station. ヘリコプターはここに～りた The helicopter *landed* here.

オリンピック the Olympic Games. ¶ ～は参加することに意義がある *The Olympics* are significant as far as we participate.
―委員会 the Olympic Committee. ―組織委員会 the Olympic Organizing Committee. ―大会 the Olympic Games. ―村 the Olympic village. 国際―委員会 the International Olympic Committee.

お·る【折る】**1**〖ぽきりと折る〗break. ¶ スキーで足の骨を～った While skiing I *broke* my leg. 鉛筆の心を～ったからあなたのを貸してください Please lend me your pencil. I *have broken* the lead of mine.
公園の木の枝を～ってはいけません The public are requested not to *damage* the trees in the park.
2〖折り畳む〗fold. ¶ 紙を四つに～る *fold* a piece of paper in four.
子どもにツルを～ってやった I made paper cranes for the children by *folding* square pieces of paper.
そのことの書いてあるページを～っておいた I *turned down* the pages relating to the article.
3〖慣用的表現〗¶ とうとう彼も我を～って彼女の願いを聞いた At last he *gave in* to her wishes.
ぼくもいろいろとほねを～ったが，うまくいかなかった All my trouble was for nothing. / After all the trouble I have taken, things did not go well.
お正月の来るのを指～り数えて待った We counted the days left till the New Year's Day.

お·る【織る】¶ この布は羊毛とナイロンで～ってある This cloth *is woven* of wool and nylon.

オルガニズム〖生物〗an organism.

オルガン an organ (英語の organ はふつう教会などの pipe organ のこと. 日本の家庭用オルガンは harmonium, reed organ などという).
¶ ～をひく play 〔on〕 the *organ*.
―奏者 an organist.

オルグ an organizer (オルグは日本的省略).

オルゴール a music box (オルゴールはオランダ語から).

おれい【お礼】thanks; (謝礼) a reward; a fee. ¶ ご親切に対して厚く～を申し上げます *Thank you* very much *for* your kindness.
～に及びません 答 You are welcome. / Don't mention it. ～をもらうことはできない I can't accept *a reward* from you. 彼は先生に～をしない He doesn't pay *a fee* to his teacher.
―参り visiting a shrine for thanksgiving.

お·れる【折れる】**1**〖まがり折れる〗¶ この木はなかなか～れない This tree won't *break*.
彼は腕が～れた He *had* his arm *broken*.
2〖譲歩する〗yield. ¶ 彼らもついに～れた(譲った) They *gave way* at last. / They *gave in* at last.

オレンジ an orange.
―エード orange ade.

おろおろ ¶ ～した声で in a *broken* (≒ *faltering*) voice. 彼はその知らせを聞いてまったく～した He *was* so *bewildered* at the news.

おろか【愚か】¶ ～な foolish; stupid. ～にもあの男を信じてしまった I *was foolish enough to* believe in him.
―者 a fool; a foolish person.

おろか【疎か】¶ 彼は住む家は～, 食べる物もない He has nothing to eat, *to say nothing of* a house to live in.

おろし【卸】wholesale. ¶ 品物を～で買う We buy goods *wholesale*. このカメラは～で2万円です This camera is worth twenty thousand yen *at* (≒ 囲 *by*) *wholesale*.

―値 a wholesale price. ―売業者 a wholesaler ; a wholesale dealer.

おろし【颪】¶ 赤城～ *a wind blowing down* Mt. Akagi.

おろ·す【卸す】sell 〔at〕 wholesale. ¶ 定価の6掛けで～す They *sell wholesale* at sixty percent of the price. そうは問屋が～さない That's expecting too much.

おろ·す【下ろす·降ろす】 **1**〖上から下へ移す〗 bring down. ¶ 3階からどうやってその荷物を～そうか How shall we *bring* the things *down* from the third (≒ 囲 second) floor ?

その箱を本だなから～してください Please *bring down* the box from the shelf.

トラックからクレーンを使ってその機械を～した We *pulled down* the machine from the truck by a winch.

彼は路傍の石に腰を～した He *sat down* on a stone by the roadside.

この一件は彼の陳謝ということで幕を～した His apology *settled* the matter once and for all.

やっと肩の重荷を～した This *has relieved* me *of* my burden.

2〖乗り物から出す〗 ¶ 次の停留所で～してください Please *drop* me at the next stop.

電車の前のドアが開かないので後ろのドアから乗客を～した The passengers *were let off* the rear door as the front one did not open.

エンジンの故障で乗客は全部飛行機から～された All the passengers *were led out of* the airplane because it had engine trouble.

3〖堕胎する〗 ¶ おなかの子どもを～さなければ母親の体が危ない Without *abortion*, the mother's life is in danger.

彼女は胎児を～した She *had* (≒ *procured*) *an abortion*.

4〖貯金を引き出す〗 ¶ 銀行から10万円～してきてくれ Please *draw* a hundred thousand yen from my account for me.

もう～す貯金がない I have no balance to *be withdrawn*.

5〖錠·引き金などを〗 ¶ 金庫の錠を～しておいたか Did you *lock* the safe ?

6〖切って整える〗 ¶ 庭の木の枝を～したのでさっぱりした Now I feel refreshed because I'*ve pruned* the twigs in the garden.

7〖新品を出して使う〗 ¶ 彼女は～したばかりの着物にしみをつけた She stained the clothes she had worn for the first time.

きょうはお客さまが来られるからこのタオルを～しなさい *Use* this new towel as we have guests today.

おろそか【疎か】¶ 勉学を～にしない I'll never *neglect* my studies. 彼はけっしてあなたの忠告を～にしていない He never *forgets* (≒ *disregards*) your advice.

おわい【汚穢】muck ; dirt.

おわり【終わり】an end. ¶ これで仕事は～だ Now the work *is over*. 2時間めの～に先生の話があった The teacher gave us a talk *at the end of* the second period. 休暇も～だ The holidays *have come to an end*. 会の～近く彼が姿を見せた Toward *the close of* the meeting he made his appearance. 彼はもう世も～だと言っている He says that *the end of* the world will come before long. 夏も～になって涼しくなった Now we are about *the end of* summer, and it has become cool. 食事の～にアイスクリームを食べた I finished off my meal with ice cream.

おわ·る【終わる】end. ¶ 学校は4時に～る School *is over* at four. 会はようやく～った The meeting *has come to an end* at last. 仕事は遅くとも今晩じゅうに～る予定だ The work is to *be finished* in the course of tonight at the latest. 道路工事はまだ～らない The road-work *has* not *been completed* yet. 弁論大会は成功に～った The speech contest *ended in* success.

おん【音】a sound. ¶ ～の美しい語 a *melodious* word. その語の～は悪い The word *sounds* harsh.

おん【恩】(人に施す恩) kindness ; (人から受けた恩) an obligation. ¶ ご援助いただいたご～はけっして忘れません I will never forget your kind help. 彼には非常に～を受けている I *am under a* great *obligation to* him. / I *am* greatly *obliged to* him. 彼はいつも～に着せる He always reminds me of his *kindness*. 他人に～を売るな Never demand gratitude of (≒ from) others. 彼は～をあだで返すような男だ He is a man who returns evil for *good*.

おんいん【音韻】〖言語学〗a vocal sound ; a phoneme.

―学 phonology. ―変化 phonological transition. ―法則 phonological law.

おんかい【音階】〖音楽〗the 〔musical〕 scale.

おんがえし【恩返し】¶ 彼に～をする *repay* his *kindness* to me. いつか～をしたいと思っています Some day I will *repay your great kindness* to me.

おんがく【音楽】music. ¶ ～の先生 a *music* teacher. ～の好きな先生 a *musical* teacher. 彼女には～の天分がある She has a talent for *music*. 彼は～がわかる(わからない) He has an (no) ear for *music*.

―映画 a musical film. ―家 a musician. ―会 a concert. ―界 music circles. ―学 musicology. ―学校 a music school. ―コンクール a music contest. ―史 the history of music. ―堂 a concert hall. ―理論 musical theory.

おんかん【音感】a sense of sound.

―教育 acoustic training.

おんがん【温顔】a gentle look ; a kindly face.

お

おんぎ【恩義】⇒おん
おんきゅう【恩給】a pension. ¶ ～がつく be entitled to *a pension*. 彼は～をもらって退職した He retired on *a pension*. 彼は～で暮らしている He lives on *a pension*. / He is *a pensioner*.
おんきょう【音響】〔a〕sound.
—効果 sound effect. ¶ このホールの～効果はすばらしい The *acoustics* of this hall are excellent. / This hall is very good for sound.
オングストローム〘物理〙an angstrom.
おんけい【恩恵】a favor; a benefit. ¶ 彼に～を施した I did him *a favor*. 彼らは文明の～を受けていない They don't enjoy the *benefits* of civilization.
おんけつどうぶつ【温血動物】a warm-blooded animal.
おんけん【穏健】¶ ～な思想 a *moderate* view.
—派 the moderates.
おんこ【恩顧】a favor; patronage. ¶ 彼からいろいろと～を受けた I received *favors* from him.
おんこう【温厚】¶ 彼は～篤実の士である He is *gentle* and sincere.
おんさ【音叉】〘音楽・物理〙a tuning fork.
おんし【恩師】*one's* teacher. ¶ 小学校時代の～ my *teacher* in the primary school days.
おんし【恩賜】an Imperial gift. ¶ ～の時計 an *Imperial gift* watch.
おんしつ【温室】a greenhouse; a hothouse.
—栽培 a hothouse growth. —植物 a hothouse plant. —育ち a person brought up in prosperity.
おんしゃ【恩赦】an amnesty. ¶ 彼らは～を受けて帰宅した They returned home under *an amnesty*.
おんじゅん【温順】¶ ～な動物 a *docile* (≒ *tame*) animal.
おんしょう【温床】¶ 悪の～ *a hotbed* of vice.
おんしょう【恩賞】¶ 彼は～を賜わった He was granted *a reward*. / He *was rewarded*.
おんじょう【温情】〔a〕warm heart; 〔a〕warm feeling. ¶ ～ある処置 a *generous* dealing. ～あることば *warm-hearted* words.
おんしらず【恩知らず】ingratitude; (人) an ungrateful person. ¶ 彼は～な男だ He is *an ungrateful man*. / He *is ungrateful*.
おんしん【音信】correspondence; (消息) news; a letter. ¶ 先月来彼からなんの～もない I'*ve heard* nothing *from* him since last month.
おんじん【恩人】a benefactor. ¶ 彼は私の命の～だ I owe him my life. 彼はこのクラブの～だ He is *a benefactor* of this club.
オンス an ounce.
おんせい【音声】a voice.
—学 phonetics. —言語 spoken language.
—表記 speech notation.
おんせつ【音節】a syllable.
単— a monosyllable.
おんせん【温泉】a hot spring; a spa. ¶ 彼は～へ静養に行った He went to *a hot spring* for his health.
おんそ【音素】〘言語学〙a phoneme.
おんそく【音速】the velocity (≒ speed) of sound.
—ジェット機 a sonic jet plane.
おんぞん【温存】¶ 力を～する *keep one's* strength *in store* (≒ *in reserve*).
おんたい【温帯】〘地理〙the temperate zone.
—植物 the temperate zone flora.
おんたい【御大】a boss.
おんだん【温暖】warmth. ¶ 気候は～だ The climate *is mild*.
—前線 a warm front.
おんち【音痴】¶ 彼は～だ He *has no ear for* music. 彼女はまったくの方向～だ She *has no sense of direction*.
おんちゅう【御中】Messrs. (messieurs の略).
¶ 田中商会～ *Messrs*. Tanaka & Co.
おんちょう【音調】a tune; a tone; (快い) melody.
おんてい【音程】〘音楽〙a〔musical〕interval.
おんてん【恩典】favor; a generous treatment. ¶ 授業料免除の～がある Some students are exempt from school tuition by *a special privilege*.
おんと【音吐】¶ ～朗々として in *a* clear ringing *voice*.
おんど【温度】〔a〕temperature. ¶ ～をはかる take the *temperature*. ～が上がる(下がる) The *temperature* rises (falls). ～を調整する adjust the *temperature*. ～は零下５度である The *temperature* is five degrees below zero. / The thermometer stands at five degrees below zero.
—計 a thermometer.
おんど【音頭】¶ 歌の～をとる *lead* the song. 万歳の～をとる *lead* a cheer. 彼はその運動の～をとった He *took the initiative of* the movement.
おんとう【穏当】¶ 彼は～な処置をとった He took a *proper* measure. 彼女の考えは～でない Her view *is not reasonable*.
おんどく【音読】¶ 本を～する *read* a book *aloud*.
おんどり【雄鳥・雄鶏】a cock; a rooster.
おんな【女】a woman (複 women). ¶ ～の子 a girl. ～っぽい womanish. 彼女も～になった She *has reached* (≒ *grown to*) *womanhood*.
—あるじ a mistress; (宿屋の) a landlady.
—形 a female impersonator; an actor who plays a woman's part. —ぎらい a woman-hater. —坂 a gentle slope.
おんなごころ【女心】a woman's heart. ¶ ～と秋の空 Woman is as fickle as April weather. / Women and autumn skies are treacherous.
おんなざかり【女盛り】the prime of womanhood. ¶ 彼女は～だ She is in *the prime of womanhood*. 彼女は～を過ぎた She is past her *prime*.
おんなだてらに【女だてらに】unwomanly; woman as she is.

おんなで【女手】¶ 彼女は５人の子どもを～ひとつで育てた She brought up her five children entirely *by herself* (≒ *by her own efforts*). ～の手紙 a letter written *in a woman's hand*.

おんなもち【女持ち】¶ ～のかさ a *women's* umbrella.

おんならし・い【女らしい】¶ ～い (～くない)しぐさ a *womanly* (an *unwomanly*) manner.

おんぱ【音波】a sound wave.

おんぴょうもじ【音標文字】a phonetic sign (≒ alphabet).

おんびん【音便】〘言語学〙a euphonical change; euphony.

おんびん【穏便】¶ 彼はこの問題を～に済ましたがっている(内々に) He wants to settle this matter *privately*. / (穏やかに) He wants to settle this matter *peacefully*.

おんぶ【負んぶ】¶ 赤ん坊を～する *carry* a baby *on one's back*. 他人に～する (頼る) rely on (another).

おんぷ【音符】a musical note; a note.

おんぷ【音譜】a score.

おんぼろ ¶ ～な服 *worn-out* clothes. ～校舎 a *weather-beaten* school house.

おんりょう【音量】the volume. ¶ ～を上げる (下げる) turn the *volume* high (low).

おんりょう【怨霊】a revengeful ghost.

おんわ【温和】¶ ～な人 a *gentle* person. ～な気候 a *mild* climate.

か

か【可】(評点) passable; C (優, 良の次). ¶ ～もなく不可もない It is neither *good* nor bad.

か【科】(学科) a department; a course; 〘生物〙a family. ¶ 英語～ the *department* of English; the English *course*.

か【課】(学課) a lesson; (会社などの) a section. ¶ 第１～ *Lesson* One; the first *lesson*. 資料～ *a* data *section*.

か【蚊】a mosquito. ¶ ～に食われる be bitten (≒ be stung) by *a mosquito*. ～の鳴くような声で in a *very faint* (≒ *very thin*) voice.

か【香】smell; scent. ¶ 木の～ the *smell* of fresh wood. 花の～ the *fragrance* of flowers.

-か【-日】a day. ¶ 展覧会は８月２～から５～間開かれる The exhibition will be open for five *days* beginning on *the 2nd of August*.

-か **1**〘疑問〙¶ どうしたのです～ What is the matter with you? / What's wrong?

どうかしたのです～ Is there anything the matter with you? / Is anything wrong?

ご気分はいかがです～ How are you? / How are you feeling?

これはいかほどです～ How much 〔is this〕? / How much does this cost? (後者は形式ばった表現).

あの人はイギリス人～どうか知らない I don't know if he is English or American (≒ an Englishman or an American).

また映画に行くの～と父は私に言った My father asked me if I was going to the movies again.

なにか買いたいものがあります～ Is there anything you wish to buy?

きょうだれか来ました～ Did anybody come today?

2〘提案・依頼〙¶ お茶をいかがです～ Would you have some tea? (Would you like to have some tea? という必要はない. ただし How would you like some tea? はよい).

もう帰ってもいいです～ May I leave now? / Can I go back yet?

私たちといっしょにピクニックに行きません～ How about going on a picnic with us?

きみの履歴書を1通送ってくれません～ Please send me a copy of your personal history.

3〘選択〙¶ きみは行くの～行かないの～ Are you coming or not?

私と結婚するの～しないの～決めてください Tell me if you will marry me.

土曜日～日曜日に会合を開こう Let's have a gathering 〔*either*〕 on Saturday *or* on Sunday.

4〘不確実〙¶ この中古車は30万円～そこらだろう I think this used car costs *around* three hundred thousand yen.

あの婦人は40歳～そこらだろう She is *probably* forty or so.

彼は静岡～どこかに住んでいるらしい He seems to live 〔*somewhere*〕 *around* Shizuoka.

家を出る～出ないうちに雨が降りだした It began to rain *soon after* I left home. (No sooner had I left home than it began to rain. は今ではほとんど用いない).

できる～どうかやってみたまえ Have a try to see *if* you can do it.

試合を続行する～どうかまだ未定です It is not yet decided *if* (≒ *whether*) we will continue the game.

5〘意外・反語など〙¶ そんなばかな話があるもの～ Nobody would believe such a silly thing. / I won't believe a word of it.

もう食べてしまったの～ Have you eaten it up

already?
なんだ本は売り切れ～ Why, you mean the book has been sold out!
こんなセーターが5,000円もするの～ Is this sweater really worth five thousand yen?
なんだきょうは日曜～ Oh, is it Sunday today? / Oh, I've completely forgotten that it's Sunday today.
なんだそんなこと～ Oh, is that all?
6〖その他〗¶ あなたは試験に合格なさったと～ I hear you have passed your examination.
あ, そう～ Is that so?
そうだったの～ Oh, is that what really happened? / Oh, that's the whole truth, is it?

が【我】(自己) self; (自我) ego; (我意) self-will. ¶ ～の強い人(自己を主張する人) a *self-assertive* person; (がんこな人) an *obstinate* person. 彼はあくまで～を張って意見を変えようとしない He *sticks to* his own opinion. 彼は～を通した He *had his* 〔*own*〕 *way*. ついに彼も～を折って私の意見に従った He at last *gave in to* my opinion.

が【蛾】a moth.

-が **1**〖しかし〗but. ¶ 私は背が低い～, 弟は大男だ I am short, *but* my brother is very tall.
彼女は美しい～, とても傲慢(ごうまん)だ *Though* she is beautiful, she is very haughty.
朝はパン食だ～, 昼と夜は御飯を食べる I eat bread for breakfast, *but* rice for lunch and supper.
2〖しかして〗and. ¶ 彼の奥さんに紹介された～, とても美しい人だった I was introduced to his wife, *and* found her very beautiful.
箱根へ行った～, 雪で真っ白だった I went to Hakone, *and* found the place covered with white snow.
その映画を見た～, とても愉快だった I saw the movie, *which* was very pleasant.

があがあ ¶ ～鳴く(カエルなど) croak; (アヒルなど) quack; (ガチョウなど) cackle.

カーキいろ【カーキ色】khaki.

ガーゼ gauze.

ガーター a garter.

ガーターあみ【ガーター編み】garter stitch.

カーディガン a cardigan.

カーテン a curtain. ¶ ～を開け放った We drew back the *curtains*. 窓に～を引いた We drew the *curtain* across the window.

ガーデン a garden.
—パーティー a garden party.

カード a card. ¶ ～で整理する arrange on *a card* system.
—式簿記 bookkeeping on the card system. —索引 a card index.

ガード (陸橋) a girder bridge; (球技の) a guard.

ガードレール a guardrail.

カーニバル a carnival.

カーネーション a carnation.

カーバイド〖化学〗carbide.

カービンじゅう【カービン銃】a carbine.

カーブ a curve; (野球の) a curve ball.
¶ 彼のボールはバッターの手元で～する His ball *curves* just before it reaches the batter.
道路は～が多かったので自動車はスピードを落とさなければならなかった The automobile had to slow down for many *curves* in the road. 道があそこで～する The road *curves* there.

カーペット a carpet.

ガーベラ〖植物〗a gerbera.

カーボン a 〔piece of〕 carbon 〔paper〕.

カール a curl; a ringlet. ¶ 彼女は髪を～した She *curled* her hair. 生まれつき～している髪 naturally *curly* hair.

ガール a girl.
—スカウト the Girl Scout. —フレンド a girl friend.

かい【回】(度数) a time; (野球) an inning; 英 an innings. ¶ アメリカには2～行っている I have been to America *twice*. 彼はこれまで5～遅刻した He has been late five *times*. 九州には何～か行っている I have been to Kyushu several *times*. もう1～やってもいいですか May I try *once* again? (野球で)試合は延長10～にまで及んだ The game went to 10 *innings*.

かい【会】a meeting. ¶ ～が催された *A meeting* was held. その～には出たほうがいい You had better be present at the *meeting*. これはいったいなんの～だろう I wonder what this *gathering* is about. まもなく～は終わるだろう The *meeting* will break up before long. この～にはだれでもすぐ入れる Anyone can join the *society* any time. あす～が招集されている The *meeting* is to be called tomorrow.

かい【貝】a shellfish; (殻) a shell.

かい【下位】a low rank. ¶ 彼の～に甘んじることはできない I cannot accept a subordinate position to his.
—打線 (野球) low ranking batters.

かい【甲斐】(益) use; (効果) effect; result.
¶ 科学的研究の～あって彼は問題を解決できた *Thanks to* a scientific study, he succeeded in solving the problem. 彼女は努力の～があった Her efforts *have been rewarded*. あらゆる努力の～なく彼は失敗した He failed *in spite of* all his efforts. あんなやつに話したってなんの～があるんだ What is the *use* of talking to such a fellow? 彼女を待ったが～がなかった I waited for her *in vain*. 妻に死なれて, 生きる～がない Having lost my dear wife, I have nothing to live for.

かい【解】(解明・説明) explication; elucidation; (解法) a solution; a key.

かい【櫂】an oar; a paddle.

-かい【-界】a world; circles. ¶ 実業(文学)～ the business (literary) *world*. 動(植)物～ the animal (vegetable) *kingdom*.

-かい【-階】a floor; 米 a story; 英 a storey (floor は建物の階を示し story は「何階建て」の意味になる). ¶ 1～ 米 the first floor; 英 the ground floor. 2～ 米 the second floor; 英 the first floor. 2～建ての家 a house of two *stories* (≒ *storeys*); 米 a two-*storied* house; 英 a two-*storeyed* house. 彼らは3～に住んでいる They live on the 3rd *floor*. その建物は何～建てですか *How high* is the building? 6～建てです It is six *stories high.* / It is six-*storied.*

がい【害】harm. ¶ 酒は健康に～があるだろうか Does *sake injure* your health? たばこは～があるらしい Smoking seems to *be harmful.* ～のない虫もいる There are some insects that *are harmless* (≒ *do no harm*). この遊びは益どころかむしろ～がある This game does more *harm* than good.

がい【我意】¶ ～を通す have *one's* own way.

-がい【-外】¶ 市～に *outside* the city. 屋～で *out of* doors; outdoors. 専門～である be *not in* (≒ be *out of*) *one's* line.

-がい【-街】¶ 商店～ a shopping *street* (≒ *center*). 繁華～ busy *quarters.* 住宅～ a residential *quarter* (≒ *district*).

かいあお·る【買い煽る】〘株式〙bull the market.

かいあく【改悪】a change for the worse. ¶ それは～された It *changed for the worse.*

かいあげ【買い上げ】purchase; buying; (政府の) 米 procurement.
—値段 ¶ 政府の～値段 the government's *buying* (≒ *purchasing*) price.

かいあ·げる【買い上げる】purchase; buy.

かいあさ·る【買い漁る】¶ 彼女は最新流行のドレスを値段にかかわらず～った She *bought* the latest dresses, dear or cheap.

かいい【怪異】¶ ～な彫刻が飾られた部屋 a room decorated with *grotesque* sculptures.

かいい【魁偉】¶ 容貌(ようぼう)～な人 an *imposing* man.

かいいぬ【飼い犬】a house dog. ¶ ～に手をかまれた(恩をあだで返した) He *returned evil for good.*

かいいれ【買い入れ】buying; purchase.
—価格 the purchase price.

かいい·れる【買い入れる】buy; purchase.

かいいん【会員】a member (*of* a club); (総称) membership. ¶ ～になる become *a member*; join a society. この会は5,000人の～がいる This society has (≒ enrolls) *a membership* of 5,000 (≒ has 5,000 *members*).
—証 a membership card. **—**制 the membership system. **—**名簿 a membership list.
正(特別; 名誉)**—** a regular (a special; an honorary) member.

かいいん【改印】¶ ～する change *one's* seal.
—届 a notice of the change of *one's* seal.

かいいん【海員】a seaman (複 seamen); a sailor; (乗組員全員) a crew. ¶ ～になる *go to sea* (go to the sea は「海岸へ行く」こと).
—組合 a seamen's union. **—**宿泊所 a sailors' home. **—**保険 seamen's insurance.

かいいん【開院】¶ ～式 the opening ceremony of the Diet.

かいうけにん【買い受け人】a purchaser; a buyer.

かいう·ける【買い受ける】buy over; take over; acquire (*a thing*) by purchase.

かいうん【海運】shipping; marine transportation.
—界 shipping circles. **—**業 the shipping business. **—**業者 a shipping agent; (総称) shipping interests.

かいうん【開運】¶ ～のお守り a charm for *luck.*

かいえん【開演】¶ 午後6時～ *The curtain rises* at 6 p. m.

がいえん【外延】〘論理〙extension; denotation.

がいえん【外苑】¶ 神宮～ *the Outer Gardens* of the Meiji Shrine.

かいおうせい【海王星】〘天文学〙Neptune.

かいおき【買い置き】(予備品) a reserve stock; (貯蔵品) a stock. ¶ 安全かみそりの刃の～が少なくなった The razor blade *reserve stock* has dwindled. かん詰めの～はたくさんある We *have a good stock of* canned goods.

かいか【怪火】a mysterious fire; a fire of unknown origin.

かいか【階下】¶ ～に(で) downstairs. ～におりる go *downstairs.*

かいか【開化】¶ 文明～の時代 a *civilized* age.

かいか【開花】**—**期 the flowering time.

かいか【開架】**—**式図書館 an open access library. **—**図書室 an open-shelf room.

かいが【絵画】(一般に) a picture; (絵の具の) a painting; (ペン・クレヨン・鉛筆の) a drawing. ¶ 詩の～的な美 the *pictorial* beauty of a poem.
—館 a picture gallery.

がいか【外貨】(貨幣) foreign money (≒ currency); (貨物) foreign goods. ¶ 手持ちの～ (Japan's) *foreign exchange* holdings. ～を獲得する obtain *foreign money.*
—準備高 foreign currency reserves. **—**預金 foreign currency deposit. **—**予算 a foreign exchange budget.

がいか【凱歌】¶ 強敵と戦って運よく～を奏することができた We *gained a* lucky *victory* over the powerful enemy.

ガイガーけいすうかん【ガイガー計数管】a Geiger counter.

かいかい【開会】the opening of a meeting. ¶ 議会は明日～される The Diet *opens* tomorrow. ～の辞を述べる give *an opening address.* 議長が～を宣した The chairman *called* the meeting *to order.* 議会は～中だ The Diet *is now in session.*
—式 the opening ceremony.

かいがい【海外】foreign countries. ¶ ～に abroad. 彼は～に暮らしている He lives *abroad.* 彼は昨年特派員として～に派遣された He was sent *abroad* as a correspondent last year. 最近～に遊びに出かける若者が増えた The number of young people traveling *abroad* has recently increased. 彼はこの秋～から帰る He will return from *abroad* this fall. 彼は～の事情に非常に明るい He knows very well about *foreign* affairs.
—放送 overseas broadcasting. **—**旅行 a foreign tour; a travel abroad.

がいかい【外界】¶ 洪水のため～との交通はすべてとだえた All *external* communication was stopped by the flood.

がいかい【外海】the open sea ; the high seas.
かいがいし・い【甲斐甲斐しい】¶ 彼女は朝から晩まで～く働いた She worked *hard* from morning till night.
かいかく【改革】(革新) reform ; (改善) improvement. ¶ 教育制度の～に着手する start an education system *reform*.
—者 a reformer. 行政— administrative reform. 宗教—(イギリスの) the Reformation; (一般に) religious reformation.
がいかく【外角】〔数学〕an external angle.
—球〔野球〕an outside ball.
がいかく【外郭】—団体 (付属機関) an auxiliary organization ; (政府の) an extra-governmental organization.
かいかた【買い方】(買い手) a buyer ; (相場の) a bull.
かいかつ【快活】¶ ～な少年 a *cheerful* boy.
がいかつ【概括】a summary ; a summing-up. ¶ ～的な general ; summary. ～的に言えば *generally* speaking ; on the whole.
かいかぶ・る【買い被る】¶ きみは彼女の能力を～っている You *think too much of* her ability. / You *overestimate* her ability. 彼はぼくを～っている He *takes* me *for better than* I am.
かいがら【貝殻】a shell.
—細工 shellwork.
かいかん【会館】a hall; an assembly hall.
かいかん【快感】a pleasant feeling ; an agreeable sensation. ¶ ～を感ずる feel pleasant.
かいかん【快漢】a jolly (≒ nice) fellow (≒ guy).
かいかん【怪漢】a suspicious fellow.
かいかん【開巻】¶ ～第1ページに on the first page.
かいかん【開館】¶ 博物館は午前9時に～する The museum *opens* at 9 a. m. 図書館は毎日～している The library *is open* every day.
かいがん【海岸】the seaside ; the seashore ; (波打ち際) the beach. ¶ 夏休みには～へ行く We go to *the seaside* for our summer vacation. ～を散歩する walk along *the seashore*. 彼は～に別荘を持っている He has a villa *by the seaside*. ～の涼しい夏の夜 a cool summer evening *at the seaside*. ～で貝を拾う gather shells *on the beach*. 男の死体が～に打ち上げられた A man's body was washed *ashore*.
—線 a coastline. —地方 a seaside district.
—通り the sea front.
がいかん【外観】(an) appearance. ¶ ～は当てにならない *Appearances* are deceptive. その建物の～はりっぱだ The *exterior* (≒ *façade*) of the building is fine. / The building looks fine *externally*. それは～はまったく革のように見える It has all the *appearance* of leather.
がいかん【概観】a general view. ¶ 彼はその問題の～を述べた He gave *a general survey of* the matter. / He *surveyed* the matter.
かいき【買い気】〔株式〕a bull.
かいき【会期】(会議の) a session ; (期間) a term. ¶ 議会は今～中だ The Diet *is* now *in session*. ～は来月末まで延長された The *term* was extended till the end of next month.
かいき【怪奇】mystery. ¶ ～な扮装(ふんそう) a *grotesque* make-up.
—小説 a thriller.
かいき【皆既】〔天文学〕—日食 a total solar eclipse. —月食 a total lunar eclipse.
かいき【開基】〔仏教〕(寺院・宗派を開くこと) the foundation (≒ founding) (*of* a temple) ; (開いた人) the founder.
-かいき【-回忌】¶ 母の七～ the sixth *anniversary of* my mother's *death*.
かいぎ【会議】a conference ; a meeting.
¶ ～を開く hold *a conference* (≒ *a meeting*). ～を招集する call *a conference*. ～に出席する attend *a conference*. 彼らはその問題について今～中だ They are now sitting on the question. その件について何回も～を重ねてきた We have had many *conferences* in regard to the matter. その問題は近く～にかけられる The problem will soon be submitted to *a meeting*.
—室 a conference room. 講和— a peace conference. 国際— an international conference. 秘密— a secret conference.
かいぎ【懐疑】doubt ; 米 skepticism ; 英 scepticism. ¶ 彼は人生に対し～的になっている He has *doubts about* life. / He *is skeptical* (≒ 英 *is sceptical*) *about* life.
—主義 米 skepticism ; 英 scepticism. —論者 米 a skeptic ; 英 a sceptic.
がいき【外気】the air ; the open air. ¶ 窓を開けて新鮮な～を入れる open windows and let in *the* fresh *air*. 外に出て涼しい～に当たりなさい Go out and enjoy a cool *air*. それを～に当てたほうがいい You had better expose it to *the air*. / It should *be aired*.
かいきせん【回帰線】〔天文学〕〔地理〕the tropic.
南(北)— the Tropic of Capricorn (Cancer).
かいきねつ【回帰熱】recurrent fever.
かいぎゃく【諧謔】a joke ; humor. ¶ ～を解する have a sense of *humor*.
かいきゅう【階級】a class (「地位」は a rank で,「等級」は a grade). ¶ あらゆる地位, ～の人がそこに集まった People of all ranks and *classes* gathered there.
—意識 class consciousness. —制度 the class system. —闘争 class struggle (≒ conflict). 上流— the upper class(es). 中流— the middle class(es). 下層— the lower class(es). 知識— the educated class(es). 労働— the working class(es).
かいきゅうだん【懐旧談】reminiscence ; retrospection. ¶ ～をする talk about old times ; reminisce.
かいきょ【快挙】a brilliant achievement.
かいきょう【回教】Mohammedanism.
—寺院 a mosque. —徒 a Mohammedan.
かいきょう【海峡】a channel. ¶ イギリス～ *the* English *Channel*. ドーバー～ *the Straits* of

Dover (固有名詞につけるときは Straits として複数形で単数扱い).

かいきょう【懐郷】 ¶ ～の情に耐えない I *yearn for home*. / He *is homesick for his home*. 彼は～の情やみがたく故郷に帰った He returned to his home town *of homesickness*.

かいぎょう【改行】 ¶ ～する write on another line.

かいぎょう【開業】 ¶ 新しい医者がこの通りで～した A new doctor *established himself* on this street. 彼は弁護士を～した He *established himself* as a lawyer. 彼は内科医を～している He is *a physician in practice*. 銀行は明日から～する The bank *begins business* tomorrow. 彼は薬屋を～した He *opened* a drugstore.

―医 a medical practitioner ; (内科も外科もやる一般開業医) a general practitioner.

がいきょう【概況】 a general condition. 天気― a general weather condition.

かいき・る【買い切る】 ¶ だれがその品物を～ってしまったのか Who *bought up* all the articles?

かいきん【皆勤】 ¶ ことしは会社は～だ I *have never absented myself* from office this year.

―賞 a reward for regular attendance.

かいきん【解禁】 lifting of a ban. ¶ アユ漁は6月に～になる The *ayu* season *opens* in June. 政府はその品物の輸入を～した The Government *lifted* (≒ *removed*) *the ban on* the import of the goods. 誘拐(ゆうかい)事件の記事はまだ～になっていない The ban on the publication of the abduction case has not been *removed* (≒ *lifted*).

がいきん【外勤】 outside duty. ¶ 彼は今月は～だ He *is on outside duty* this month.

かいきんシャツ【開襟シャツ】 a sport shirt ; a shirt open at the neck.

かいぐい【買い食い】 ¶ ～をする spend *one's* pocket money on candies.

かいぐん【海軍】 the navy.

―軍人 a naval man ; a sailor. ―士官 a naval officer. ―兵学校 the naval academy.

かいけい【会計】 account(s) ; accounting ; (勘定書) 米 a check ; 英 a bill ; (支払い) payment. ¶ ～は私がします I will pay the *bill*. ～をお願いします 米 *Check*, please. / 英 *Bill*, please. ～は乱れている The *accounts* are in disorder.

―係 an accountant. ―士 an accountant. ―年度 a fiscal year. ―簿 an account book. 一般― general account. 公認―士 a certified public accountant. 特別― special account.

かいけい【塊茎】 〘植物〙 a tuber.

がいけい【外形】 an outward form ; appearance. ¶ それは～も実質もともによい It is good in essence as well as in *outward form* (≒ *appearance*).

かいけつ【怪傑】 a wonder man.

かいけつ【解決】 solution. ¶ 住宅不足問題を～することは非常に困難だ It is very difficult to *solve* (≒ *settle*) the housing shortage problem. その問題はいまだに満足な～をみるにいたっていない The problem does not come to *a* satisfactory *solution*. 依然未～な問題となっている It remains an *unsolved* problem.

かいけつびょう【壊血病】 〘医学〙 scurvy.

かいけん【会見】 an interview. ¶ 彼に～を求めた I asked for *an interview* with him. 彼と初めて～した I had the first *interview* with him. / I *interviewed* him for the first time. 彼は記者～で公式声明を発表した He issued an official statement at *the press interview*.

かいけん【懐剣】 a dagger.

がいけん【外見】 an appearance ; the outside. ¶ ～で人を判断するな Don't judge (of) a man by his *appearance* (≒ by *appearances*). 彼は～はいなか者のように見える He has the *appearance* of a rough fellow. 彼は～は粗野だが心はやさしい男だ He is a kind man with *a* rough *exterior*.

かいげんれい【戒厳令】 martial law. ¶ その市は目下～が敷かれている The city is now under *martial law*.

かいこ【蚕】 a silkworm. ¶ ～を飼う raise *silkworms*. ～から生糸をとる obtain raw silk from *silkworms*.

かいこ【回顧】 recollection. ¶ 私の少年時代を～する *look back on* my boyhood.

―録 *one's* reminiscences ; *one's* memoirs.

かいこ【懐古】 ¶ それは彼の～趣味を表わしている It shows his liking for the good old days.

かいこ【解雇】 dismissal ; discharge. ¶ 彼は仕事をさぼったため会社を～された He *was dismissed from* the company for neglect of his duty. 3ヵ月前に～予告をする give three months' notice to *a person*.

―手当 a dismissal allowance.

かいご【改悟・悔悟】 repentance ; remorse. ¶ 彼は早まった結婚を～した He *repented of* his hasty marriage. 彼は自分の愚行に～の涙を流した He shed tears of *remorse* for his folly.

かいこう【回航】 ¶ その船は長崎へ～された The ship *was brought to* Nagasaki.

かいこう【海港】 a seaport.

かいこう【開校】 ¶ その学校は10年前に～された The school *was founded* ten years ago. その学校は～20年になる The school *has been open* for twenty years.

―記念日 the anniversary of the foundation of a school.

かいこう【開港】 ¶ ～する *open* a port.

かいこう【海溝】 a deep.

かいこう【邂逅】 ¶ 汽車の中で彼に～した I *came across* him (≒ *met* him *by chance* ; *encountered* him) in the train.

かいごう【会合】 a meeting ; a gathering. ¶ われわれは数人の実業家と～した We had *a meeting* with several businessmen. 彼らは年に1度～する They *meet together* once a year.

がいこう【外交】 diplomacy. ¶ 彼の言うことは

か

〜上の問題だ What he says is a *diplomatic* problem. これらの両国は〜上の関係を続けている These two countries have *diplomatic* relations with each other. 彼女は生命保険の〜をやっている She is a life insurance saleswoman.
—員 a canvasser; a salesman; (女の) a saleswoman. —官 a diplomat; a diplomatist. —関係 diplomatic relation. —辞令 diplomatic language. —手腕 diplomacy. —団 the diplomatic corps.

がいこう【外港】an outport.

かいこういちばん【開口一番】¶ 彼は〜政府のインフレ対策を攻撃した He *opened his speech with* an attack against the Government policy against inflation.

がいこうせい【外向性】〚心理学〛 extroversion. ¶ 〜の人 an extrovert.

かいこく【戒告】a warning. ¶ 〜を与える give *a warning (to a person)*.

かいこく【海国】a maritime country; (島国) an island country.

かいこく【開国】(国交の開始) the opening of a country to foreign intercourse.

がいこく【外国】a foreign country. ¶ 〜から帰ったばかりだ I have just returned from *abroad*. 彼はしばしば〜を旅行する He often travels *abroad*. 〜へ行ったことがありますか Have you ever been *abroad*? この果物は〜産だ These fruits are *of foreign growth*.
—行き ¶ この船は〜行きだ This ship is bound for *abroad*. —行き郵便 outgoing mails. —為替 foreign exchange. —為替相場 foreign exchange rate. —語 a foreign language. —航路 a foreign [service] route. —人 a foreigner. —人登録法 the Alien Registration Law. —製 ¶ この万年筆は〜製だ This fountain pen is *of foreign make*. —船 a foreign ship. —貿易 foreign trade.

がいこつ【骸骨】a skeleton. ¶ 彼は〜のようにやせている He is *a* mere *skeleton*. / He is reduced to *a skeleton*.

かいこ・む【買い込む】¶ 金製品を〜む *lay in* gold goods.

かいこ・む【掻い込む】¶ 彼はかばんを小わきに〜んで走っていった He ran away *carrying* the bag *under his arm*.

かいごろし【飼い殺し】¶ 〜にする keep (an employee) for life.

かいこん【悔恨】remorse. ¶ 彼は〜の念にかられている He is smitten with *remorse*. 彼は〜の涙にくれていた He was in bitter tears of *remorse*.

かいこん【開墾】clearing; reclamation; cultivation. ¶ その荒れ地は〜された The wasteland *was brought under cultivation*. 彼らは森を〜している They *are clearing* the forest for *cultivation*.
—事業 reclamation work. —地 a reclaimed land.

かいさい【快哉】¶ 〜を叫ぶ yell for delight.

かいさい【皆済】full payment. ¶ 〜する pay in full; pay off; clear off (*one's* debts).

かいさい【開催】¶ 展覧会は来月〜される The exhibition will *be held* (≒ *be opened*) next month. 国際会議は目下ニューヨークで〜中である The international conference *is* now *meeting* (≒ *in* now *session*) in New York.

かいざい【介在】¶ あのふたりの間には複雑な事情が〜する There *lie* complicated circumstances between the two.

がいさい【外債】a foreign loan; (証券) a foreign bond. ¶ 5,000万ドルの〜を募る raise *a foreign loan* of fifty million dollars.

かいさく【改作】[an] adaptation. ¶ この劇は小説から〜したものだ This play *is adapted* from the novel. / This play is *an adaptation* from the novel.

かいさく【開削】excavation. ¶ 運河を〜する *cut* (≒ *make*) a canal.
—工事 excavation works.

かいさつ【改札】¶ 〜する examine tickets; (はさみを入れる) punch tickets. 〜はもう始まっている The wicket is already open.
—口 a wicket. —係 a ticket examiner.

かいさん【解散】(会合の) breakup; (議会・団体などの) dissolution. ¶ 会は混乱のうちに〜になった The meeting *broke up* in confusion. 駅で〜した We *broke up* at the station. 警察は群衆を〜させた The police *broke up* the crowd. 彼らは組合を〜した They *dissolved* the partnership. 国会は近く〜になるだろう The Diet will soon *be dissolved*.

かいざん【改竄】¶ 小切手を〜する *raise* a check. 公文書を〜する *alter* a public document.

がいさん【概算】a rough estimate. ¶ 〜する *estimate* roughly; make *a rough estimate* (*of*). 〜で at *a rough estimate*; roughly. 日本の人口は〜1億2000万である The population of Japan *is roughly estimated* at one hundred and twenty million.

かいさんぎょう【海産業】the marine products industry.

かいさんぶつ【海産物】marine products.

かいし【怪死】a mysterious death.

かいし【開始】beginning; commencement; opening. ¶ その会社と取引を〜した We *opened* (≒ *started*) an account with the company. 決勝戦は1時に〜された The finals *began* at 1 p.m.

かいじ【海事】maritime affairs.
—法〚法律〛the law of admiralty. —裁判所 the Admiralty Court.

がいし【外紙】a foreign newspaper; (総称) the foreign press.

がいし【外資】foreign capital. ¶ 〜導入 the induction (≒ introduction) of *foreign capital*.

がいし【碍子】〚電気〛an insulator.

がいじ【外耳】〚解剖学〛the auricle.
—炎〚医学〛otitis externa.

がいして【概して】generally; generally speaking; in general; as a rule; on the whole.

かいしめ【買い占め】〚商業〛a corner; cornering; coemption; 〔株式〕 a bull corner.

かいし·める【買い占める】 buy up; make a corner (*in*). ¶彼はその店の品物を～めた He *bought up* all the goods of the store. その会社は沿線の土地を～めた The company *bought up* all lands along the railroad line.

かいしゃ【会社】 a company; a firm. ¶～を設立する establish *a company*. 彼の～は倒産した His *company* went bankrupt.
—員 an office worker. 運送— a transfer company. 商事— a trading company. ¶彼は商事～に勤めている He is employed in *a trading company*. 保険— an insurance (≒ 英 assurance) company.

かいしゃ【膾炙】 ¶このことわざは人口に～されている This proverb *is well known to everyone*.

がいしゃ【外車】 an imported car; a foreign-made car.

かいしゃく【解釈】 〔an〕 interpretation. ¶私の話は誤って～された My talk *was* falsely *interpreted*. この文章はいろいろに～される This sentence can *be interpreted* in many ways. / This sentence admits of several *interpretations*. 彼の沈黙は譲歩と～された His silence *was interpreted* as a concession.

かいしゅう【回収】 withdrawal; retrieval. ¶くず物の～ *collection* of rubbish. 不良製品の～ *withdrawal* of bad goods. 売掛金を～する *collect* bills.

かいしゅう【改宗】 conversion. ¶彼は彼らをカトリック教から新教に～させた He *converted* them from Catholicism to Protestantism. 彼女はキリスト教に～した She *turned* Christian. / She *was converted to* Christianity.
—者 a convert.

かいしゅう【改修】 repair; improvement. ¶道路は～中だった The road was under *repair*〔s〕.
—工事 repair works.

かいじゅう【怪獣】 a monster.

かいじゅう【海獣】 a sea animal.

かいじゅう【懐柔】 ¶彼に贈り物をして～した I *conciliated* him with a present. 彼を～して味方にした We *won* him *over to* our side.
—策 a conciliatory measure.

かいじゅう【晦渋】 ¶～な文章 an *ambiguous* (≒ *abstruse*) passage.

がいじゅうないごう【外柔内剛】 ¶彼は～である He *is gentle in appearance, but sturdy in spirit*.

がいしゅつ【外出】 ¶彼は少し前に～した He *went out* a moment ago. 彼は今～中だ He *is out* now. 夜遅くまで～していてはいけない You must not *be out* till late at night. 一日じゅう～しなかった I *stayed at home* all day.
—着 outdoor clothes; street clothes.

かいしゅん【改悛】 repentance. ¶彼の～の情は明らかだ He shows sincere *repentance*.

かいしょ【楷書】 ¶～で書く write in *the square style* (≒ *the block letters*).

かいじょ【解除】 ¶彼らの武装を～した We *disarmed* them *of* their weapons. 責任を～された I *was absolved from* my obligation.

かいしょう【甲斐性】 ¶～のない人 a good-for-nothing. ～のある人 an *able* man.

かいしょう【快勝】 ¶日本はサッカーでインドに～した Japan *won an easy victory over* India in soccer.

かいしょう【解消】 dissolution. ¶彼女は彼との婚約を～した She *broke off* her engagement to him. 彼はその契約を～した He *canceled* the contract.

かいしょう【改称】 the change of a title (≒ name; designation).

かいじょう【回状】 a circular 〔letter〕. ¶～を回す send *a circular* 〔*letter*〕.

かいじょう【会場】 a meeting place.

かいじょう【海上】 the sea. ¶彼は～を5時間も漂っていた He was floating *on the sea* for five hours.
—自衛隊 the Marine Self-Defense Forces. —保安庁 the Marine Safety Agency. —保険 marine insurance.

かいじょう【階上】 ¶～の部屋 an *upstairs* room. 彼は～へ行った He went *upstairs*.

かいじょう【開場】 ¶～する open. 午後1時～ The doors *open* at 1 p. m.

がいしょう【外相】 the Foreign Minister.

がいしょう【外傷】 an injury. ¶彼は交通事故で頭に～を負った He suffered *injuries to* his head in the traffic accident.

がいしょう【街娼】 a streetwalker; a prostitute; a whore.

かいしょく【会食】 ¶彼と～の約束がある I have an appointment to *dine* with him. その夜われわれは～した We *dined together* that evening.

かいしょく【解職】 dismissal; discharge. ¶彼は不正直のかどで～された He *was fired* (≒ *was dismissed*) for dishonesty. 彼はその職から～された He *was relieved of* the post.

がいしょく【外食】 dining (≒ eating) out. ¶土曜日の夜は～する I *dine out* on Saturday evening.

かいしん【会心】 ¶勝者は～の微笑を浮かべた The winner smiled a *complacent* (≒ *self-satisfied*) smile. これは彼の～の作だ This is the work *after his own heart*.

かいしん【改心】 ¶彼は～の見込みはない He is beyond (≒ past) *reclaim*. / It is no use trying to *reform* him. 彼はすっかり～している He *has* completely *reformed himself*.

かいしん【改新】 renovation.

かいしん【回診】 ¶医者はまもなく～に来る The doctor will soon *come round to see* you.

かいじん【灰燼】 ¶その大邸宅は～に帰した The magnificent house *was reduced to ashes* (≒ *was burnt down*).

かいじん【海神】 the sea god; (ローマ神話) Neptune; (ギリシア神話) Poseidon.

がいしん【外心】 〔数学〕 a circumcenter.

がいじん【外人】 a foreigner; an alien.

か

—教師 a foreign teacher. —選手 a foreign player. —部隊 a foreign legion.

かいず【海図】a chart. ¶〜に載っていない島 a *chartless* (≒ an *uncharted*) island.

かいすい【海水】sea water. ¶〜が船に浸入してきた *Sea water* came into the boat.

—着 (女性の) 困 a bathing (≒ swimming) suit; 図 a bathing dress; (男性の) trunks. —帽 a bathing cap.

かいすいよく【海水浴】sea bathing. ¶江ノ島に〜に行く We go *sea bathing* at Enoshima. / We go to Enoshima for *sea bathing*.

—場 a bathing beach (≒ place); (海岸の町) a bathing resort; 図 a watering place. —客 a sea bather.

かいすう【回数】¶〜を重ねて練習すると上達する If you *repeat* your practice, you will improve yourself.

—券 a coupon ticket. ¶10回の〜券 a ticket of ten *coupons*.

がいすう【概数】an approximate number. ¶受験者の〜は6,000人だ The number of examinees *approximately amounts to* 6,000.

かい・する【解する】¶彼女は詩を〜さぬ She cannot *appreciate* poetry. 彼は音楽を〜さぬ He *has no ear for* music. 彼は私の皮肉を賛美と〜した He *took* my irony as a compliment.

かい・する【介する】¶彼女がなんと言おうと少しも意に〜さぬ I *don't care a bit* (≒ *don't mind at all*) what she says. そのうわさは友だちを〜して知った I knew the rumor *through* my friend.

がい・する【害する】¶彼女の感情を〜するつもりはなかった I meant no *hurt* to her feelings. 人の感情を〜するな Never *injure* the feelings of others. 彼は粗食で健康を〜した Poor food *impaired* his health. 彼は過労で健康を〜した He *injured* his health by overwork.

かいせい【改正】(改訂) [an] amendment; (改良) improvement; (変更) [an] alteration. ¶憲法の〜には反対だ We are against the *revision* of the Constitution. 規則は少し〜されている The regulation has several *amendments*. 交通規則がこの春〜された The traffic regulations *have been revised* this spring.

—案 a reform bill.

かいせい【改姓】a change of *one's* family name.

かいせい【快晴】fine weather. ¶休み中は〜に恵まれた We were lucky to have *fine weather* during the holidays.

かいせき【会席】a meeting place.

—料理 a simplified Japanese dinner; a set menu of select food served on an individual dinner-tray.

かいせき【解析】〘数学〙analysis.

—幾何学 analytical geometry.

がいせき【外戚】a maternal relation.

かいせつ【開設】establishment; opening. ¶児童相談所が〜された A child consultation center *was established*. 彼は新しく病院を〜した He *has set up* a new hospital.

かいせつ【解説】explanation; a commentary. ¶その規則を〜してくれませんか Will you *explain* the rule to us? 彼はその理論をわれわれに〜した He *expounded* the theory to us. 彼は時事問題を〜した He *commented on* current events.

—者 a commentator; (ラジオ・テレビのニュースの) a newscaster. —書 (手引き) a guide; (製法などの) a how-to book; (問答体の) a question-answer book; (参考書) a reference book; (評釈書) a commentary. —付き目録 a descriptive catalogue. ニュース— a news commentary.

がいせつ【概説】a general statement; an outline. ¶哲学〜 *an introduction to* philosophy.

がいせつ【外接】¶〜する be circumscribed. —円 a circumscribed circle.

かいせん【回旋】rotation; revolution; involution. ¶〜状の〘植物〙involute (内旋の); convolute (包旋形の); 〘動物〙involute (貝殻などがらせん状に巻いた).

—起重機 a rotary crane.

かいせん【回線】〘電気〙a circuit.

電話— a telephone circuit. —図 a circuit diagram.

かいせん【回船】—問屋 a shipping agent.

かいせん【海戦】a naval battle.

かいせん【開戦】the outbreak of war. ¶〜する open war (*against* a country); go to war (*with* a country).

かいせん【改選】reelection. ¶議長の〜を決議した We decided to *reelect* the chairman.

かいせん【疥癬】〘医学〙an (≒ the) itch; (犬・牛などの) mange.

かいぜん【改善】improvement. ¶設備はまだ〜の余地がある The accommodations leave much room for *improvement*. 労働組合は待遇の〜を要求した The labor (≒ trade) union demanded *betterment* of treatment.

がいせん【外線】(電話) the outside line. ¶〜をお願いします Can I call *outside*, please?

がいせん【凱旋】a triumphal return. ¶〜する return in triumph.

—門 a triumphal arch.

がいぜんせい【蓋然性】probability.

かいそ【改組】reorganization. ¶会社を〜する *reorganize* a company.

かいそ【開祖】the founder (*of* a temple); (元祖) an originator.

かいそう【回送】¶郵便は新住所に〜してください Please *forward* my mail to my new address.

—車 an out-of-service train.

かいそう【回漕】—業 shipping business (≒ trade). —店 a shipping agent.

かいそう【回想】recollection; reminiscence. ¶若い時代を〜する *look back upon* (≒ *recollect*) *one's* younger days.

—録 reminiscences; memoirs.

かいそう【会葬】¶彼の葬儀には多くの人が〜した Many people *were present at his funer-*

al. / Many people *attended his funeral.*

かいそう【快走】¶ ヨットが順風に乗って～している The yacht *is sailing fast* with the wind.

かいそう【改装】¶ 寝室を～して居間にした The bedroom *was converted into* a sitting room. 建物は～された The building *was redecorated* (≒ *was reconstructed*).

かいそう【改葬】reinterment ; reburial. ¶ ～する reinter ; rebury.

かいそう【海草】seaweeds.

かいそう【海藻】marine algae.

かいそう【階層】a social stratum (≒ level).

かいそう【壊走】¶ 敵は～した The enemy *ran away in disorder*. / The enemy *was put to flight*.

かいぞう【改造】reconstruction ; reorganization. ¶ 内閣を～する *reorganize* (≒ *reshuffle*) the Cabinet. 店舗はただいま～中だ The shop *is* now *under reconstruction*. 彼は家を店舗に～した He *remodeled* his house *into* a store.

かいぞえ【介添え】a helper ; an assistant ; (決闘などの) a second ; (花婿の) a best man ; (花嫁の) a bridemaid.

かいそく【会則】the regulations (≒ rules) (*of* a society).

かいそく【快速】a high speed. ¶ 車は時速70マイルの～で走った The car ran at *a high speed* of seventy miles an hour.
—船 a fast (≒ sailing) ship ; an ocean greyhound. —列車 a fast train.

かいぞく【海賊】a pirate ; a sea robber ; a sea rover. ¶ ～行為を働く commit (≒ practice) *piracy*.
—船 a pirate ship. —版 a pirate edition.

がいそふ【外祖父】a maternal grandfather ; a grandfather on *one's* mother's side.

がいそぼ【外祖母】a maternal grandmother ; a grandmother on *one's* mother's side.

かいそん【海損】sea damage ; 〘保険〙 an average. ¶ ～精算 an average adjustment.

がいそん【外孫】a child of *one's* daughter married into another family.

かいだ【快打】〘野球〙 a clean hit.

かいたい【解体】¶ 老朽船を～する *scrap* an old ship. 機械を～する *take* a machine *to pieces*. その構造物は巨大なので～して運んだ The structure was so huge that we *dismantled* it and carried it in pieces.

かいだい【改題】¶ ～する change the title.

かいだい【解題】a bibliographical introduction ; explanatory notes.

かいたく【開拓】development. ¶ 彼らは荒野を～した They *reclaimed* the waste land. 私どもは新市場を～した We *have opened* a new market. われわれはみずからの運命を～しなければならない We must *carve out* our career by ourselves. それはまだ未～の分野だ That belongs to an *unexplored* field.
—者 a pioneer ; a settler.

かいだく【快諾】¶ 彼の～を得た I have got his *ready* (≒ *willing*) consent.

かいだし【買い出し】(日用品の) shopping ; (買い込み) laying in ; (食料を探して買う) food-hunting.

かいだ·す【掻い出す】¶ ボートの水を～す *bail out* a boat.

かいたた·く【買い叩く】beat down the price.

かいだめ【買い溜め】(行為) hoarding ; (物品) hoardings. ¶ 彼は大量に米の～をしている He *has hoarded* a vast amount of rice.

かいだん【会談】a conference ; a talk. ¶ 彼らはその件に関して数回にわたって～した They held a series of *talks* about the matter. ～は2時間に及んだ The *conference* (≒ *talk*) continued for two hours·

かいだん【快談】a pleasant talk. ¶ ～する talk pleasantly ; enjoy a pleasant chat.

かいだん【怪談】a ghost story.

かいだん【階段】stairs ; (入り口の) doorsteps. ¶ ～の上(下)に at the head (foot) of the *stairs*. ～をのぼる(おりる) go up (down) the *stairs*.

がいたん【慨嘆】¶ 彼の行為は～に耐えない His behavior *is deplorable* (≒ *is disgusting*).

かいだんじ【快男子】a fine (≒ splendid) man ; (米口語) a nice guy.

ガイダンス guidance. ¶ 新入生に～を行なう give *guidance* to freshmen (*as to* the curriculums).

がいち【外地】an overseas land ; a foreign country.
—勤務 overseas service. —生活 overseas life.

かいちく【改築】rebuilding ; reconstruction. ¶ 納屋を住居に～した We *remodeled* our barn *into* a house. 橋は～中だ The bridge *is* now *under reconstruction*.

かいちゅう【回虫】a roundworm. ¶ ～がわく get *roundworms*.

かいちゅう【改鋳】(貨幣の) recoinage ; (鐘などの) recasting ; remolding. ¶ ～する recoin ; recast ; remold.

かいちゅう【海中】¶ ～に飛び込む jump into *the sea* ; (船上から) jump *overboard*.

かいちゅう【懐中】—電灯 ㊊ a flash 〔light〕; ㊖ an electric torch ; a torch. —時計 a watch.

がいちゅう【害虫】an injurious (≒ a harmful) insect ; (総称) vermin (ふつう複数扱い).

がいちゅう【外注】an outside order.

かいちょう【回腸】the ileum.

かいちょう【会長】the president (*of* a society) ; the chairman (*of* a committee). ¶ ～になる take the chair.

かいちょう【快調】¶ エンジンは～であった The engine was *in good condition*. 最初の1,000メートルは～に飛ばした I ran the first thousand meters *in my best condition* (≒ *on top condition*).

かいちょう【海鳥】〘鳥類〙 a seabird ; a seafowl.

かいちょう【諧調】melody ; harmony.

かいちょう【開帳】¶ ～する (仏像を) *unveil* (≒ *exhibit*) a Buddhist image ; (賭博を) *open* a game of gambling.

がいちょう【害鳥】an injurious (≒ a harmful; a noxious) bird; (総称) vermin.

かいちん【開陳】¶ いろいろの意見が～された Various opinions *were set forth*.

かいつう【開通】¶ 不通区間は6時に～する見込みだ The damaged section is expected to *be reopened* at 6. 両市間の新自動車道は10日に～する The new highway between the two cities will *be opened for traffic* on the tenth.

—式 an opening ceremony (*of* a railway).

かいづか【貝塚】a shellmound; a kitchen midden.

かいつけ【買いつけ】(商品の) buying; purchase. ¶ ～の店 *one's favorite* store.

かいつぶり〘鳥類〙a [little] grebe.

かいつま·む【掻い摘まむ】¶ ～んで言うと to be short; in short; to make a long story short; to put it briefly; briefly speaking.

かいて【買い手】a buyer. ¶ これはすぐに～がつく You will find *a* ready *buyer* for it. 彼はその家の～を求めている He is looking for the *buyer for* the house. その値段では～がつかない The price does not tempt *buyers*.

—市場 a (≒ the) buyer's market.

かいてい【改訂】revision. ¶ ～する revise.

—版 a revised edition.

かいてい【階梯】(階段) steps; stairs; (はしご) a ladder; (手段) a stepping stone; (手引き) a guide (*to*); a primer (*to*).

かいてい【海底】the bottom of the sea.

—火山 a submarine volcano. —電線 a submarine cable. —トンネル an underground tunnel.

かいてい【開廷】¶ ～する open (≒ hold) a court. ～中である The court *is sitting* (≒ *is in session*).

かいてき【快適】pleasant; comfortable.

¶ ～なドライブ a *pleasant* drive. 夏を～に過ごす pass summer *comfortably*; spend a *pleasant* summer.

がいてき【外敵】a foreign enemy (≒ invader).

がいてき【外的】outward; external; outside.

¶ ～証拠 *external* evidence.

かいてん【回転】[a] rotation; a revolution; a convolution. ¶ 地球は太陽のまわりを～する The earth *revolves* (≒ *rotates*) around the sun. プロペラは1秒間に5回～する The propeller makes 5 *revolutions* a second. 資金を～させる They *turn over* the fund. 彼女は頭の～が早い She has a nimble wit. / She has a quick mind.

—競技〘スキー〙slalom. —資金 a revolving fund. —軸 the axis of rotation; a shaft. —ドア a revolving door. —窓 a pivoted window. —率 a turnover rate.

かいてん【回天】¶ ～の偉業 a great work to save a nation on the verge of ruin.

かいてん【開店】¶ 電気器具店を～する *open* an electrical appliance store. その店は去年～した The store *was opened* last year. デパートは10時に～する The department store *opens* at 10 a.m. ～休業 No business is done.

—祝い ¶ ～祝いに in celebration of *the opening of a store*.

がいでん【外電】a foreign dispatch (≒ telegram); a cable[gram]; (外報) foreign news.

ガイド a guide.

—ブック a guidebook.

かいとう【会頭】¶ 商業会議所～ *the president* of the Chamber of Commerce.

かいとう【怪盗】a mysterious thief.

かいとう【回答】a reply; an answer. ¶ 口頭による～でけっこうです *An* oral *answer* will do.

かいとう【解答】an answer; a solution.

¶ 数学の問題の～を出す *clear up* mathematical questions. 生徒の質問に～する We *answer* the students' questions. 彼の～は正しい (間違っている) His *answer* is correct (wrong).

—者 a solver.

かいとう【快刀】¶ ～乱麻を断つ give clear-cut solutions to whatever difficult problems come *one's* way; *cut the Gordian knot*.

かいどう【会堂】(教会堂) a church; (校内などの) a chapel; (公会堂) a hall; an assembly hall.

かいどう【怪童】an extraordinary infant.

かいどう【街道】a highway; a highroad.

かいどう【海棠】〘植物〙an aronia.

がいとう【街燈】a street lamp.

がいとう【街頭】a street. ¶ ～で on (≒ 英 in) *the street*.

—演説 a stump (≒ wayside) speech; a soapbox oratory. —写真 a street snapshot. —募金 a street collection of subscription.

がいとう【該当】¶ その行為は商法第13条に～する The dealings *come under* article 13 of the Commercial Code. ～する項目を○で囲め Put a circle around each item when *applicable*. 人相書きに～するような人物は見つからなかった Nobody *answering to* the description could be found. その学校はわが国の中学校に～する The school *corresponds to* our junior high school.

がいとう【外套】米 an overcoat; 英 a greatcoat; (マント) a cloak.

かいどく【買い得】(買い得品) a bargain. ¶ その車はその値段なら～だ The car is *a bargain* at such a price.

かいどく【解読】¶ 暗号を～する *decode* a code. なぐり書きの手紙を～する *decipher* (≒ *make out*) a badly written letter.

—者 (暗号などの) a decoder.

かいどく【回読】¶ ～する read (a book) in turn.

がいどく【害毒】evil; harm; poison. ¶ 社会に～を流す exert *a harmful* (≒ *an evil*) *influence* on society; *poison* society.

かいと·る【買い取る】buy; purchase.

かいなら·す【飼い慣らす】tame. ¶ その動物は～

せない The animal cannot *be tamed*.

かいなん【海難】 a shipwreck; a sea disaster. ¶ ～にあう meet with *a sea disaster*.
—救助（船を）sea rescue; salvage;（人を）lifesaving. —信号 an SOS. —審判 inquiry of marine accidents.

かいにゅう【介入】 intervention. ¶ われわれは他国の戦争に～すべきでない We must not *intervene in* a war between other countries.

かいにん【解任】 dismissal. ¶ 私はその職を～された I *was dismissed from* (≒ *was relieved of*) the post. 素行不良の故に彼を～した I *discharged* him for his misconduct.

かいぬし【買い主】 a buyer; a purchaser.

かいぬし【飼い主】 the owner; the master (*of* a dog). ¶ ～のない犬 an *ownerless* (≒ a *homeless*) dog.

かいねこ【飼い猫】 a domestic cat.

がいねん【概念】 a general idea;〖哲学〗a concept; a notion. ¶ ～的な conceptional; notional; general. ～的に generally; conceptionally; notionally.

かいば【飼い葉】 feed; fodder. ¶ 馬に～を与える *feed* a horse.
—おけ a manger.

かいはい【改廃】 ¶ 省内部局の～が近く行なわれる *Reorganization* of the ministry will be made in near future.

がいはく【外泊】 ¶ ～する stay out for the night; sleep out.

がいはく【該博】 ¶ ～な知識〔a〕*profound* knowledge;〔an〕*exhaustive* knowledge.

かいばしら【貝柱】 an adductor〔of a shellfish〕.

かいはつ【開発】 development;（資源など）exploitation;（土地・才能など）cultivation. ¶ 天然資源を～する *develop* (≒ *exploit*) natural resources. 新しい宇宙ロケットを～する *develop* a new type of space rocket.
—計画 development project. —途上国 a developing country. 未—地域 undeveloped areas.

かいばつ【海抜】 ¶ 富士山は～12,385フィートある Mt. Fuji is 12,385 feet *above the sea*.

かいはん【改版】 ¶ ～する issue a revised edition.

かいひ【回避】 evasion; avoidance. ¶ 責任を～する *evade* (≒ *shirk*) *one's* responsibility.

かいひ【会費】 a〔membership〕fee; dues;（月月の）monthly dues. ¶ クラブの～は月額500円です The monthly club *dues* are 500 yen. / The monthly *fee* for the club is 500 yen. このパーティの～はひとり5,000円だ The *fee* for this party is 5,000 yen a head.

がいひ【外皮】 skin; husks (*of* grain); crust (*of* a pie).

かいびゃく【開闢】 ¶ ～以来 since the beginning of the world; since the world began. ～以来の出来事 an *unprecedented* event.

かいひょう【開票】 ¶ 午後4時に～は行なわれる The votes will *be counted* at 4 p. m.
—所 a ballot counting place. —立会人 a ballot-counting overseer (≒ witness);（主として英）a scrutineer.

かいひょう【海豹】〖動物〗a seal; a sea leopard.

がいひょう【概評】 a general view (≒ comment).

かいひん【海浜】 the seashore; the seaside; the beach.

かいふ【回付】 transmission. ¶ その手紙は彼の新住所に～された The letter *was forwarded to* his new address.

がいぶ【外部】 the outside. ¶ ～の人 an outsider. 秘密が～に漏れた The secret leaked (≒ slipped) *out*.

かいふう【海風】〖海事〗〖気象〗a sea breeze (≒ wind).

かいふう【開封】 ¶ 手紙を～する *open* a letter. 手紙を～で出す send a letter *unsealed*.

かいふく【回復】 **1**〖回復の〗recovery. ¶ 彼〔の病気〕はまったく～の見込みはない He is quite beyond *recovery*. / There is not a chance of his *recovery*. / He has no chance of *recovery*.
彼は～の見込みは十分ある There is a good chance of his *recovery*. / He has a good chance of *recovery*.
2〖回復する〗¶ 彼もまもなく健康を～するだろう I hope he will soon *recover* (≒ *get well*).
彼も徐々に健康を～しつつある He is *getting better* (≒ *is recovering*) slowly.
ぼくの健康も完全に（ほとんど）～した I *have* quite (almost) *recovered*.
彼は体力を～しつつある He *is recovering* his strength.
彼女は意識を～した She *recovered herself*. / She *recovered* her consciousness. / She *came to herself*.
ぼくらは友情を～することができるだろう We will be able to *recover* the friendship that formerly existed between us.
ついに彼は名誉を～することができた At last he could *retrieve* his honor.
天候はまもなく～するだろう I hope it will soon *clear up*.
治安が完全に～するまでには二, 三か月かかるだろう It will take two or three months till law and order *are* completely *restored*.

かいふくしゅじゅつ【開腹手術】 an abdominal operation; laparotomy.

かいぶつ【怪物】（化け物）a monster;（怪人物）a mystery man; a sphinx;（偉物）a prodigy. ¶ 政界の～ *a* political *sphinx*.

がいぶん【外聞】（評判）reputation;（体面）decency. ¶ それは彼の～にかかわることになる It will affect his *reputation*. 彼は非常に～を気にする男だ He thinks very much of his *reputation*. 彼女の素行は彼女の一家の～にかかわる Her conduct is a big scandal to her family. 恥も～もない We can't afford to care about *decency*.

がいぶん【外分】〖数学〗external division. ¶ ～する divide externally.

か

かいぶんしょ【怪文書】(けしからぬ) a reprehensible document; (不可解な) a mysterious document.
かいへい【海兵】a marine; a sailor.
—隊 困 the Marine Corps; 英 the Royal Marines.
かいへい【開平】〖数学〗evolution; the extraction of a square root. ¶ ～する extract the square root (*of*).
かいへい【開閉】¶ ～する open and shut (≒ close).
—器 a switch. 自動—器 an automatic switch. —橋 a drawbridge.
かいへい【皆兵】¶ 国民～制度 a universal conscription system.
かいへん【改変】change; reformation.
かいへん【改編】reorganization. ¶ 組織を～する *reorganize* a system. 本を～する *re-edit* a book.
かいへん【海辺】the seaside; the seashore.
かいほう【介抱】nursing; care. ¶ 彼女は徹夜で病人を～した She *sat up* all night *with* the sick person. / She *cared for* the sick person. / She *attended on* the sick person all night.
かいほう【会報】a bulletin; a report; (学術協会などの) the transactions; a journal.
¶ 同窓会～ *an* alumni *bulletin*.
かいほう【快方】¶ 彼は～に向かっている He *is getting better*. / His illness *is taking a favorable turn*.
かいほう【快報】good news; a joyful report.
かいほう【開放】opening. ¶ その図書館は一般に～されている The library *is open to* the public. ～禁止(掲示) Close the door after you. / Don't *leave* the door *open*. 彼は～的な性格の男だ He *is frank* by nature.
かいほう【解法】a solution; a key to solution.
かいほう【解放】emancipation. ¶ 貧困からの～ *freedom from* poverty. やっと～された I *am* quite *free* now. 7時になるまでは仕事から～されない I *am* not *released from* duty till seven.
奴隷— the emancipation of slaves. ¶ リンカーンは奴隷を～した Lincoln *emancipated* the slaves. 婦人—運動 a movement for the emancipation of women; Women's Lib; women's lib; Women's Liberation.
かいぼう【海防】coast (≒ coastal) defense; sea patrolling.
—艦 a coast defense ship.
かいぼう【解剖】(学術上の) anatomy; dissection; (検死の) autopsy; 困 a post-mortem 〔examination〕. ¶ 彼の死体は～に付された His body was submitted to *dissection*. 動物を～する *dissect* an animal.
—学(術) anatomy. —学者 an anatomist; a dissector. —室(台; 刀) a dissecting room (table; knife). —図 an anatomical chart. —模型 an anatomical specimen. 生体— vivisection.

がいほう【外報】foreign news; news from abroad; a foreign telegram.
がいぼう【外貌】an outward appearance.
がいまい【外米】foreign (≒ imported) rice.
かいまき【搔い巻き】a sleeved quilt.
かいまく【開幕】(始まり) the opening; the commencement. ¶ ～第1戦 the *opening* game. 国会の～ the *opening* of the Diet. ～は何時ですか When does the *curtain rise*?
かいまく・る【買い捲る】〖株式〗¶ 株を～る *bull* stocks.
かいま・みる【垣間見る】peep through (a hedge) at; catch a glimpse (*of*).
かいみょう【戒名】a posthumous Buddhist name.
かいみん【快眠】a sweet sleep.
かいむ【会務】affairs of a society.
かいむ【皆無】¶ 彼が治る見込みは～だ There is *no hope of* his recovery 〔*at all*〕. 私は英語の知識は～だ I know *no* English *at all*. / I know *not a word of* English.
がいむ【外務】foreign affairs.
—省 the Foreign Office; the Ministry of Foreign Affairs. —大臣 the Foreign Minister; the Minister of Foreign Affairs; 英 the Foreign Secretary.
かいめい【改名】¶ いつXからYに～なさったのですか When did you *change your name* from X to Y?
かいめい【解明】elucidation; (文学作品などの) explication. ¶ その秘密を～できない I cannot *explain* the mystery.
かいめつ【壊滅】destruction. ¶ その町は地震でまったく～した The town *was* totally *destroyed* by the earthquake. ～的打撃を与える inflict a *deadly* blow (*on*).
かいめん【海面】〔the surface of〕the sea; the sea surface. ¶ ～は鏡のように穏やかであった *The sea* was as smooth as glass.
かいめん【海綿】a sponge. ¶ ～状の spongy. ～でインクを吸い取る *sponge up* ink.
がいめん【外面】the outside; outward appearance. 彼は～は穏やかに見える He looks gentle *in appearance*.
—描写 an external description.
かいもく【皆目】at all; quite; utterly; entirely; completely; altogether.
かいもど・す【買い戻す】buy back.
かいもの【買い物】shopping; (品物) a purchase. ¶ 彼女は～に出かけるのが好きだ She likes to *go shopping*. きょうは少し～がある I have some *shopping* to do today. 銀座で少し～をした I *did* some *shopping* in Ginza. / I *made* some *purchases* in Ginza. それはよい～だった It was a 〔*good*〕 *bargain*.
—かご a shopping basket. —客 a shopper.
かいもん【開門】the opening of the gate.
¶ 午前9時～ The gate *opens* at 9 a. m.
がいや【外野】〖野球〗〖クリケット〗the outfield.
—手 an outfielder. —席 the outfield bleachers.

かいやく【解約】cancellation of a contract. ¶契約を～する *cancel* a contract. 彼はその機械の注文を～した He *cancelled* his order for the machine.

かいゆ【快癒】complete recovery. ¶彼は～した He completely *recovered*. / He *was restored to health*. / He *got well completely*.

かいゆう【回遊】―切符 an excursion (≒ a circular) ticket; 英 a round-trip ticket (米では往復切符の意味).

がいゆう【外遊】a foreign travel; a trip abroad. ¶～する go abroad. 彼は～中だ He *is now on a foreign tour*.

かいよう【海洋】the ocean; the sea(s).
―学 oceanography. ―科学 oceanics. ―気象台 a marine meteorological observatory. ―性気候 an oceanic climate.

かいよう【潰瘍】〖医学〗an ulcer (発音は[ʌ́lsə]). ¶～ができる *An ulcer* forms.

がいよう【外洋】the open sea; the ocean.

がいよう【概要】⇒がいりゃく

がいようやく【外用薬】an application; a medicine for external application.

かいらい【傀儡】a puppet; a tool. ¶人の～となって働く act as another's *tool*.
―政権 a puppet government.

がいらい【外来】―患者 an outpatient. ―語 a borrowed word; a word of foreign origin. ―思想 foreign (≒ alien) ideas. ―者 a stranger; (訪問者) a visitor.

かいらく【快楽】pleasure; enjoyment; ¶～にふける indulge in *pleasure*; give *oneself* to *pleasure*.

かいらん【回覧】circulation. ¶この手紙は～してください Please *read* this letter and *pass* it *on*.
―雑誌 a circulating magazine. ―板 a circular note (≒ notice).

かいらん【解纜】¶～する unmoor; weigh anchor.

かいらん【壊乱】¶この映画は風俗を～するおそれがある We fear this film might *be corruptive of* (≒ *be detrimental to*) public morals. / We fear this film might *be demoralizing*.

かいり【海里・浬】a nautical mile; a sea mile; a knot.

かいりき【怪力】Herculean strength; superhuman power.

かいりく【海陸】land and sea. ¶～両棲(りょうせい)の動物 an *amphibious* animal.

かいりつ【戒律】(Buddhist) precepts; commandments.

がいりゃく【概略】an outline. ¶その小説の～を述べよう I am going to give you *an outline* (≒ *a summary*) *of* the novel.

かいりゅう【海流】an ocean current; a current.
日本―(黒潮) the Japan Current.

かいりゅう【開立】〖数学〗the extraction of a cubic root.

かいりょう【改良】improvement. ¶～を施す bring about *improvement*. (牛馬などの)品種を～する *improve* the breed. この仕事は～の余地がある There is some room for further *improvement* of this work. / This work leaves something to be desired.
―種 a select breed.

がいりん【外輪】(船の) a paddle wheel.
―船 a paddle steamer.

かいれい【回礼】a round of complimentary visit. ¶年始の～をする *make* 〔*a round of*〕 New Year's *calls*.

かいれき【改暦】(暦法改正) a calendar reform; (新年) a new year.

かいろ【回路】〖電気〗a circuit. ¶～を閉じる(開く) break (open) the *circuit*.
―しゃ断器 a circuit breaker. ―制御器 a circuit controller. 集積― integrated circuit (I. C. と略記する).

かいろ【海路】a sea route. ¶～ハワイへ行く go to Hawaii *by sea* (≒ *by ship*; *by boat*; *by water*). 待てば～の日和あり (諺) *Everything comes to those who wait*.

かいろ【懐炉】a pocket body warmer.

がいろ【街路】a street.

かいろう【回廊】(寺院の) a cloister; a corridor; a passage; (画廊) a gallery.

がいろじゅ【街路樹】a street tree.

がいろん【概論】an introduction; an outline. ¶文学～ *an introduction to* literature.

かいわ【会話】〔a〕conversation; 〔a〕talk; (対話) a dialog.
英― English conversation. ―体 a conversational style.

かいわい【界隈】the neighborhood; the vicinity. ¶彼はこの～では顔がきく He is influential *in this district* (≒ *in this neighborhood*; *around here*).

かいわん【怪腕】¶～をふるう display *one's wonderful* (≒ *remarkable*) *ability* (*in doing*).

かいん【下院】the Lower House; 英 the House of Commons; 米 the House of Representatives.
―議員 a member of the Lower House; 米 a congressman.

か・う【支う】prop up; support (a thing) with a prop.

か・う【買う】**1** 〚購入する〛buy. ¶この家を安く～った I *bought* this house at a low price.
この本を安く～った I *bought* this book cheap.
この土地は高い値段で～った I *paid* an exorbitant amount *for* this land.
彼は5万円の旅行かばんを～った He *bought* a travel bag for fifty thousand yen. / He *bought* a fifty thousand yen travel bag.
友人からカメラを3万円で～った I *paid* thirty thousand yen *for* my friend's camera.
この家はいくらで～ったのですか About how much did you pay for this house?
この車をだれか20万円で～う人はいないか Is anyone interested in *buying* this car for two

hundred thousand yen?
別荘を～う金が少し足りない I don't have quite enough money to *buy* a villa.
彼女にイタリア製のハンドバッグを～ってやった I *bought* her a handbag made in Italy.
彼の親切は金では～えない You can't *buy* his kindness.
ごほうびになにを～ってあげようか What shall I *buy* for you (≒ *get* you) as a reward?
2 〖引き起こす〗 ¶ 人の恨みを～うようなことをした覚えがない I don't remember giving anyone cause to hate me.
社長の怒りを～った I angered my boss.
彼女の歓心を～うためにしたことだ It was done to *catch her attention*.
3 〖求める〗 ¶ 彼はけんかを～って出た He himself *took on the quarrel*. / He *took up the challenge*.
その事件に彼は一役～っているらしい He seems to *be involved* (≒ *be mixed up*) in that matter.
4 〖認める〗 ¶ 彼の才能を高く～う人は多い There are many who *respect* his talents.
彼は実直というところを～われた He *was chosen* for his sincerity.
彼の語学力を高く～いすぎるな Don't *overestimate* his grasp of language.
彼の誠意は～ってやるべきだ We should *recognize* his serious efforts.

か・う 【飼う】 (飼っておく) keep (a dog); (飼育する) raise (chickens; sheep; cattle).

カウボーイ a cowboy.

かうん 【家運】 the fortunes of a family.
¶ ～が傾いている My *fortunes* are on the wane (≒ decline).

ガウン a gown.

カウンセラー a counselor; 圏 a counsellor.

カウンター a counter. ¶ ～で支払ってください Please pay at the *counter*.

カウント a count. ¶ ～はワンストライク，ツーボールだ The *count* is two balls and one strike. (アメリカでは日本とは逆にボールを先に，ストライクをあとに言う).
—アウト ¶ 彼はレフリーに～アウトを宣せられた He *was counted out* by the referee.

かえうた 【替え歌】 a parody.

かえ・す 【返す】 (金を) pay back; repay; (物を) return; (もとへもどす) put (*a thing*) back (*to*).
¶ 1,000円はあすお～しします I will *pay back* 1,000 yen to you tomorrow. あした～すから3,000円貸してください Will you please lend me 3,000 yen on condition that I *repay* you tomorrow? 先日お貸しした本をお～しいただけませんか Won't you *give* me *back* the book I lent you the other day? この雑誌は今度の日曜日に～す I will *return* this magazine to you next Sunday. 彼には～すことばもない I don't know how to *answer* him. 彼は恩をあだで～した He returned evil for good.

かえ・す 【孵す】 hatch (an egg; a chicken).

かえすがえす 【返す返す】 (なんども) repeatedly; (かさねがさね) really; exceedingly.

かえだま 【替え玉】 a substitute; a dummy.
¶ ～を使う employ *a substitute*.

かえち 【替え地】 a substitute lot.

かえって 【却って】 (反対に) on the contrary; (むしろ) rather. ¶ 働いたのが～体によかった I *got the better for* the work. なまじ知っているということは～危険だ A little learning is *rather* dangerous. 少量の酒は～薬だ A little drink does you more good than harm. きみは悪くない，悪いのは～ぼくのほうだ You are not to blame; *on the contrary*, it is I who am to blame. / It's my fault, not yours.

かえで 【楓】 a maple; 圏 a sycamore.

かえり 【帰り】 return. ¶ ～は遅くなりそうだ I shall be late in *coming home*. 彼の～は何時ごろだろう What time will he *return*? ～を急いでいるようだ He seems to *be hurrying home*. ～の支度をしなさい Get ready to *depart* (≒ *leave*). ～は何時になるかわからない I cannot tell what time (≒ when) I shall *be back*. 学校からの～に彼に会った I happened to meet him *on my way home* from school.

かえりうち 【返り討ち】 ¶ 彼は～にあってしまった He was killed by the man on whom he had been seeking revenge.

かえりざき 【返り咲き】 (花木の) the second bloom; (復帰) a comeback.

かえりざ・く 【返り咲く】 ¶ 彼は10年ぶりに政界に～いた He *came back* to politics after his ten-year absence. 彼は大使として～いた He *was reinstated* as [an] ambassador. 彼女は映画界に～いた She *made her comeback* on the screen.

かえり・みる 【省みる】 ¶ まじめに自分を～みなさい *Reflect upon* yourself seriously.

かえり・みる 【顧みる】 ¶ 昔を～みるとすべてが懐かしい When I *look back upon* my past, everything is dear to me. 他人のことをまったく～みない人もいる There are some people who do not *take* others *into consideration*. 彼の意見は～みられなかった No one *paid regard to* his opinion. 一身を～みず現場へ急いだ *Sacrificing myself*, I hastened to the spot.

かえる 【蛙】 a frog; (食用の) a bullfrog.
¶ ～が鳴く The *frog* croaks. ～が跳ぶ The *frog* hops. ～の子は～ (諺) *Like father, like son*.

かえ・る 【帰る】 ¶ 彼はやがて～るだろう He will *come back* before long. 8時までには～りなさい *Come back home* by eight. すぐ～ってくるよ I'll *be back* in a moment. 人が変わって～ってきた He *came back* a changed man. お～りなさい Welcome home! 駅からは歩いて～れる I can *walk home* from the station. 早く～ったほうがいい You had better *come home* at once. もうそろそろ～らなければなりません I think I must be going now. 間もなくわれに～った I *came to myself* soon.

かえ・る 【孵る】 ¶ ひなが～った The brood *are out*. 卵は3週間で～る The eggs will *hatch* in three weeks.

か·える【変える】¶ 彼は一瞬顔色を～えた Suddenly he *changed* color. きょうは道を～えて行こう I will *take a different way* today. 先月名古屋に住所を～えた I *removed to* Nagoya last month. 水は熱によって蒸気に～えられる Water *is changed* into steam by heat. 日を～えて彼を訪ねてみましょう I will visit him again *some other time*.

か·える【替える·換える·代える】¶ そのころは衣類を米に～える人もいた In those days there were some people who *changed* clothes *for* rice. これとそれとを～えたい I should like to *replace* this *with* that. このカメラを別なカメラと～えられないかしら I wonder if I could *have* this camera *exchanged* for another.

かえん【火炎】 a flame ; a blaze.
—びん a fire-bottle ; a Molotov cocktail ; an oil bomb.

かお【顔】1〖身体の一部〗 a face (eyes, ears, nose, mouth, chin などはそれぞれ a feature という. これが集まって features (顔) となる. 日本語の顔は head (頭) の訳語を用いなければならぬこともある).
¶ 彼女の～は丸い She *is* moon-*faced*.
彼女の～は長い She has *a* longish *face*. (long face は「憂うつな顔」の意味がある).
彼女の～は美しい She has *a* beautiful *face*.
彼女の～は醜い She *is* quite *plain*.
彼女の～は白い She *is* pale-*complexioned*.
彼女の～は黒い She *is dark* (≒ *is tanned*).
彼女の～は荒れている Her *face* is rough.
互いに驚いて～を見合わせた They *looked at each other* in surprise.
犯人の～はよく覚えている I remember the criminal's *face* very clearly.
窓から～を出してはいけません Don't put your *head* out of the window. (この場合, 顔は face ではなく head を用いる).
化粧室に行って～を直していらっしゃい Go to the rest room and fix your *face* (≒ *make-up*).
彼女は～を伏せて黙っていた She hung her *head* in silence. (face でなく head を用いる).
二目と見られぬ〔醜い〕～だ It's *an* ugly *face*.
日本人ばなれの～をしている She *looks* quite exotic.
彼女は整った～をしている She has *a* well-shaped *face*.
2〖表情〗(an) expression. ¶ 彼は悲しそうな～をした He *looked* sad.
彼はうれしそうな～をした He *looked* overjoyed (≒ happy).
彼はいやな～をした He *grimaced*.
彼はつまらなそうな～をした He *looked* bored.
彼は不思議そうな～をした He *looked* puzzled.
彼はおかしそうな～をした He *seemed* tickled. / He *seemed* amused.
彼は驚いたような～をした He *looked* surprised. / He *looked* shocked.
彼はたいくつそうな～をした He *wore a* bored *expression*.
彼はうんざりしたような～をした He *seemed* disgusted. / He *seemed* fed up.
彼は怒ったような～をした He *looked* angry.
彼は寂しそうな～をした He *looked* lonely.
彼はがっかりしたような～をした He *seemed* discouraged.
彼はなに食わぬ～をした He *wore an* innocent *look*.
彼は恥ずかしそうな～をした He *seemed* embarrassed.
彼はそ知らぬ～をした He *pretended* not *to* notice anything.
彼は得意げな～をした He *seemed* proud. / He *wore a* proud *expression*.
彼は困ったような～をした He *wore a* troubled *expression*.
彼は渋い～をした He *showed* displeasure.
彼はほっとした～をした He *looked* relieved.
彼女は～を赤くした She *blushed*. / She *turned red*.
それを聞いて彼は～を曇らせた His *face* clouded over the news.
彼は～をひきつらせた He *looked* tense.
3〖態度など〗 ¶ 途中で会っても彼は知らん～をしている He *ignored* (≒ *cut*) me in the street.
ちゃんと～に書いてあるじゃないか It's written on your *face*.
私は～から火の出る思いだった I was never so embarrassed.
彼はそんなことは少しも～に出さない He didn't *show* it at all.
ひとりでいい～するな Don't take all the credit.
ここではそんな大きな～はするな Don't *act* so big here.
彼はなに食わぬ～で会社に出てきた He came to the company as if nothing had happened.
4〖慣用的表現〗 ¶ 彼はときどき研究室に～を出す He sometimes shows his *face* at the laboratory.
～がそろったら出かけよう Let's leave when everyone is here.
～を洗って出直してこい How can you say that? / Think it over and speak again.
きみには合わせる～がない. I can't *face* you.
彼とは毎日～を突き合わせている I *see* him every day.
この付近では彼の～は売れている He's *well known* around here.
彼は～でそれを手に入れた He used his *influence* to get it.
彼は業界に～のきく男だ He's quite a big man in the business circles.
今度だけはぼくの～を立ててほしい Please do this for me just this once.
ぼくの～をつぶさないでくれ Don't make me *lose face*.
私たちの～に泥を塗るようなことはしないでほしい Don't do things that will smear our reputation.
あの人は～を売るためにそんなことをしたのだ He did that *for face*.
私の～に免じて彼を許してやってください Please forgive him *for my sake*.

かおあわせ【顔合わせ】¶ きのうはほんの～をやった We just *met together* (≒ *introduced one* *another*) yesterday.

かおいろ【顔色】a complexion. ¶ 彼女は〜がよい She *looks* well. / She has *a* fine *complexion*. 子どもたちは怖くて〜を変えた Children *turned pale* (≒ *changed color*) with fear. 子どもは大人の〜をうかがう Children study the pleasure of adults. 彼は別に〜を変えなかった His face did not *show any emotion*. きみの〜ですぐそれとわかった I could see it easily in your *face*.

かおかたち【顔かたち】looks ; features. ¶ 〜のよい女の子 a *good-looking* girl.

かおく【家屋】a house ; a building.

かおだし【顔出し】¶ 忙しくて親戚(しんせき)に〜もできない I am too busy to *visit* my relatives.

かおだち【顔だち】looks ; features. ¶ きれいな〜の女の子だ She has good *features*. / She is good (≒ nice ; fine)-*looking*.

かおつき【顔つき】a countenance ; looks.

かおなじみ【顔馴染み】¶ あそこにはきみの〜が大ぜいいる You will find many *old familiar faces* there.

かおぶれ【顔触れ】personnel (ふつう複数扱い). ¶ 新内閣の〜に新鮮味がない The *personnel* of the new Cabinet lack freshness. / There are very few new *faces* in the new Cabinet.

かおまけ【顔負け】¶ 専門家が〜するような技術の持ち主だ He has such a wonderful technique that he *puts* experts *into the shades* (≒ *puts* experts *to blush*). 彼女はあまりずうずうしいのでこちらが〜だ I *am shocked at* her impudence.

かおみしり【顔見知り】¶ 彼とは10年余の〜だ I *have known* him for over ten years.

かおみせ【顔見せ・顔見世】*one's* debut ; *one's* first appearance on the stage.
—興行 a theatrical show of a newly organized company.

かおむけ【顔向け】¶ 世間に〜ができない I dare not *show myself in public*. 彼女に〜ができない I am ashamed to appear before her.

かおやく【顔役】a man of influence ;(俗語) a big shot.

かおり【薫り・香り】fragrance ; scent ; smell. ¶ コーヒーの〜 the *aroma* of coffee. これはよい〜がする This *smells* nice (≒ sweet ; good). この花は強い〜がする This flower has *a* strong *smell*.

かか【呵呵】¶ 〜大笑する laugh loudly ; roar with laughter.

がか【画架】an easel.

がか【画家】a painter ; an artist.

がか【雅歌】〔聖書〕the Song of Solomon.

がが【峨峨】¶ 〜たる山々 *rugged* mountains.

かかあ【嚊・嬶】a wife.
—天下 a petticoat government. ¶ 彼の家は〜天下だ He is *a henpecked husband*.

かがい【課外】¶ 〜の読み物 *outside* reading.
—活動 extra-curricular activities. —講義 an extra-curricular lecture ; a university extension.

がかい【瓦解】collapse ; downfall ; fall ; breakup. ¶ 〜する collapse ; fall ; break up.

かがいしゃ【加害者】an assailant.

かかえ【抱え】¶ 一〜の薪 an *armful* of firewood. いく〜もある大木 a big tree measuring several *arms'* stretches round. お〜の運転手 a chauffeur.

かか・える【抱える】¶ 病人を〜えている I have a sick person *on my hands* (≒ *to attend to*). 彼は運転手を〜えている He *keeps a* chauffeur.

カカオ a cacao (複 cacaos).

かかく【価格】(値段) a price ; (価値) value ; worth. ¶ 不作で野菜の〜が高くなる Vegetables will *be expensive* because of a bad harvest. 土地の〜に応じて課税する levy a tax according to the *value* of a land. そのダイヤの指輪を100万円の〜で売る sell the diamond ring at *a price* of one million yen.
—協定 an agreement on prices. —調整 price adjustment. —統制 price control. 最低(最高)— the minimum (maximum) price. 生産(消費)者— the producer (consumer) price.

かがく【化学】chemistry.
—記号 a chemical symbol. —工業 the chemical industry. —式 a chemical formula. —繊維 a synthetic fiber. —反応 a chemical reaction. —肥料 chemical fertilizer. —兵器 a chemical weapon. —変化 a chemical change. —療法〔医学〕chemotherapy. 応用— applied chemistry. 有機(無機)— organic (inorganic) chemistry.

かがく【科学】science. ¶ 〜的な scientific. 〜的に scientifically.
—技術 scientific technique. —研究 scientific research. —者 a scientist. —書 a scientific book. —小説 a science fiction. —知識 scientific knowledge. —博物館 the Science Museum. 応用— applied science. 自然— natural sciences. 社会— social science. 人文— the humanities.

ががく【雅楽】Japanese court music ; ceremonial music.

かか・げる【掲げる】¶ 日本の旗を〜げた船 a steamer *flying* the Japanese flag. その記事は第1面に〜げてある The article *is printed* on the front page.

かかし【案山子】a scarecrow.

かか・す【欠かす】¶ 彼は一度も〜さず会に出席した He *never missed* a single meeting. / He *regularly* attended the meeting.

かかと【踵】the heel. ¶ 彼女は〜の高い靴をはいている She wears high *heels*.

かがみ【鏡】a mirror. ¶ 〜を見る look at *oneself* in *a mirror*. 〜が曇っている The *mirror* is dim. 海面は〜のようだった The sea was as smooth as *glass*.

かがみ【鏡・鑑】a model ; a pattern. ¶ 婦人の〜 the *model* of womanhood.

かが・む【屈む】stoop down ; bend down. ¶ 彼女は部屋のすみに〜んでいた She *crouched* in a corner of the room.

かが·める【屈める】¶ 彼らは腰を～めてあいさつした They greeted *with a stoop*.

かがやかし·い【輝かしい】¶ ～い業績 a *brilliant* achievement. ～い未来 a *bright* future.

かがやか·す【輝かす】¶ 彼の業績は国威を～す His achievements will *exalt* (≒ *enhance*) our national prestige.

かがやき【輝き】brilliancy; brightness; splendor.

かがや·く【輝く】¶ 太陽は明るく～いている The sun *is shining* brightly. 月は夜～く The moon *shines* by night. 彼女の手にはダイヤモンドが～いていた The diamond *was sparkling* in her hand. 彼の目は喜びに～いていた His eyes *were sparkling* with joy. その知らせを聞くや彼の顔は喜びに～いた His face *brightened* with delight at the news.

かかり【係】(任務) charge; (費用) expenses. ¶ ～の人 a person *in charge*. ホテル住いは～がかかる It's *expensive* to live in a hotel.
—員 a clerk [in charge].

-がかり【-掛かり】¶ 5人～の仕事 a job *requiring* five persons to do. それは1日～の仕事だ That task *takes* a whole day. 10人～でそれを運んだ We carried it *with the combined labor* of ten.

かかりあい【掛かり合い】implication (*in*); involvement. ¶ そのことに～になった I *was mixed up in* (≒ *was involved in*) the matter. それになんの～もない I *have nothing to do with* it.

かかりきり【掛かりきり】¶ 彼はその仕事に～だ He *is tied down* to the work. 彼女は子どもに～だ The child *takes all her time*.

かかりつけ【掛かりつけ】¶ ～の医者 *one's* family doctor.

かがりび【篝火】a bonfire; a campfire; (合図の) a signal fire.

かか·る【掛かる·懸かる·架かる·係る·罹る】**1**〚物に接して〛¶ 壁に絵が～っている A picture *is hanging up* on the wall.
上着はハンガーに～っている Your coat *is on* the hanger.
2階の窓にはしごが～っている A ladder *is standing against* the second floor window.
ストーブになべが～っている *There is* a pot *on* the stove.
2〚設けられる〛¶ 戸にかぎが～っていた The door *was locked*.
この川には橋がたくさん～っている There are a lot of bridges over this river.
3〚要する〛¶ ここから大阪までは車で2時間～る It *takes* two hours by car from here to Osaka.
5分も～らないうちにそこに着いた I arrived there *in less than* five minutes.
彼が全快するまでにまだ3週間は～るだろう It will *be* three weeks more before he gets well.
この仕事には大いに金が～る It *costs* a lot to do this work.
宴会にはひとり5,000円の会費が～った It *cost* five thousand yen per man for the dinner party.
相続税はいくら～りましたか How much was your inheritance tax?
このカメラには税金は～らない This camera *is duty-free*.
屋根の修理には手数が～る It *takes* much trouble to repair the roof.
4〚始まる…しかかる·従事する〛¶ 月が出～っている The moon *is starting to* rise.
そろそろ日が暮れ～った Night *is coming on*.
彼は彼女の家の前に来～った He *was coming near* to her house.
子どもがおぼれ～っている There's a child *drowning*.
小鳥が死に～っている The bird *is dying*.
マラソンの先頭はもう箱根に～るころだ The leading runner in the marathon race must *be getting near* Hakone by now.
そのことばが口から出～った The word *was on the tip of my tongue*.
ぼつぼつ仕事に～るころだ Now is the time to *set about* the work.
彼女は子どもの世話に～りっきりだ She *is always busy* looking after her children.
きのうは採点に～りっきりだった I *spent all day* yesterday looking over the examination papers.
毎日こんな仕事に～ってはいられない I cannot *spend time* on this kind of work every day.
5〚依存する〛¶ 治療費は全部加害者に～ってきた The guilty party *had to pay* the whole of the doctor's fees.
この責任はすべて私に～っている The responsibility for this *lies* entirely *on* me.
この仕事はあなたの手腕に～っている This work *depends on* your ability.
事の成否は～ってきみの努力にある It *depends* entirely *upon* your effort whether it will succeed or not.
6〚対抗する〛¶ さあ, ～ってこい Come on!
きみに～ってはかなわない You are a rough customer to deal with. / I *am no match for* you.
ふたりいっしょに～ってくるとはひきょうだ It is not fair for two of you to *attack* me together.
猟犬は獲物に～っていった The hound *went after* the game.
7〚汚れ·水などが〛¶ 上着にほこりが～った The dust *fell* on my coat.
ズボンに泥水が～った My trousers *were splashed* with mud.
イチゴにクリームが～っている There's cream on the strawberries.
作物に火山灰が～った The crop *was covered* with volcanic ashes.
彼にその事件の嫌疑(けんぎ)が～った Suspicion of the affair *fell upon* him.
8〚上演する·上映する〛¶ その劇場では今なにが～っていますか What *is on* at the theater now?
その映画館では今どんな映画が～っていますか What

film *is on* at the movie theater now?

9 〖医者にかかる〗¶ 彼女は今風邪で医者に～っている She *is* now *under the care* of the doctor with a cold.

10 〖電話〗¶ きみに電話が～っていますよ There's a telephone call for you.
どこから電話が～ってきたのですか Who's calling?

11 〖その他〗 ¶ ネズミがネズミ取りに～った A rat *was caught* in the rattrap.
けさは車のエンジンがなかなか～らない This morning the motor won't *start*.
またお目に～りたいものです I'd like to *see* you again.
気に～ることがひとつある There is one thing which *weighs* on my mind.
彼の声は鼻に～っている He has a *nasal* voice.
彼女の髪にはパーマが～っていない She doesn't have her hair *permed*.

かか·る【罹る】¶ 病気に～った I *fell* (≒ *was taken*) ill. 私は神経痛に～っている I *am suffering from* neuralgia. 風邪に～った I *caught* 〔a〕 cold. 風邪に～っている I *have* a cold.

かかる【斯る】 such; like this ¶ ～人 *such* a person. ～次第で *such* being the case; as it is.

かが·る【縢る】 hemstitch; (つくろう) darn. ¶ くつ下を～る *darn* socks; *stop* socks from running. ボタンの穴を～る *work* button holes.

-がか·る ¶ 黄色～った緑 *yellowish* green. 芝居～った動作 a *dramatic* action.

かかわらず【拘らず】¶ 雨にも～彼は出かけていった He went out *in spite of* the rain. 風が強いにも～船は出帆した The boat set sail *despite* the strong wind. 会合は晴雨に～行なわれる The meeting will be held *rain or shine*. 好むと好まざるとに～それをやらなければならない You must do it *whether you like it or not*. 年齢のいかんに～だれでもその競技会に参加できる Everybody can take part in the meet, *regardless of* age. あれほど金持ちなのにも～彼女は満足していない She is still dissatisfied *in spite of* all her riches. / *With all* her riches she is not contented.

かかわり【係わり】 ¶ ぼくはそのことにはなんの～もない I *have nothing to do with* it.

かかわ·る【係わる】 ¶ それは私の名誉に～ることだ It *affects* (≒ *reflects upon*; *compromises*) my honor. / My honor *is at stake*. 生死に～る大問題だ It is a vital question. / It is a matter of life and death. 今そんなことに～っていられない This is no time to *concern ourselves in* (≒ *be mixed up in*) a matter like that.

かかん【果敢】¶ 彼は～にそれをやろうとしている He *is resolute in* his attempt.

かき【柿】〘植物〙(木·実) a persimmon.

かき【垣】 a fence. ¶ 庭の周囲に～を巡らした We put *a fence* around the garden.
石― a stone fence.

かき【牡蠣】〘貝類〙 an oyster.
―がら an oystershell. ―フライ a fried oyster. ―養殖 oyster farming (≒ culture). ―養殖場 an oyster farm. 生― a raw oyster.

かき【下記】¶ ～の条項 the *following* items. 出席者(列席者)は～のとおり The attendants are *as follows*.

かき【火気】 fire.
―厳禁(掲示) No Fire. / (燃焼しやすいものに書いて) Inflammable.

かき【夏期】 summer.
―休暇 a summer vacation; summer holidays. ―講習 a summer course (≒ session).

かぎ【鉤】 a hook. ¶ ～形の hooked; hook-shaped.

かぎ【鍵】 a key. ¶ 成功の～ the *key* to success. これが玄関の～です This is the *key* to the front door. この～で戸に錠をかけてください Lock the door with this *key*. この～では戸は開きません You cannot unlock the door with this *key*. トランクに～をかけることを忘れるな Don't forget to *lock up* your trunk. 宇宙の神秘を解く～ *a key* to the mysteries of the universe.
―穴 a keyhole. 合い― a fellow (≒ duplicate) key.

がき【餓鬼】(いたずらっ子) a naughty child; an urchin; an imp.
―大将 the boss of naughty children.

かきあ·げる【書き上げる】 ¶ 論文は～げましたか *Have* you *finished writing* the monograph?

かきあ·げる【掻き上げる】 ¶ 乱れた髪を～げる *comb up one's* stray locks.

かきあつ·める【掻き集める】¶ みんなの金を～めても2,000円しかなかった We had only two thousand yen among us all.

かきいれ【書き入れ】(記入) an entry; (書き込み) a note.

かきいれどき【書き入れ時】¶ 書店は4月と9月が～だ Books *sell best* in April and September. 雨の午後はタクシーの～だ A rainy afternoon is *the busiest time for* taxi drivers.

かきい·れる【書き入れる】(記入する) enter (the sum); make an entry (*of*); (用紙に書き込む) fill in a form. ¶ 余白に覚え書きを～れた I *scribbled* notes in the margins.

かきおき【書き置き】(置き手紙) a note (≒ letter) left; (別れの) a farewell message; (遺書) a 〔written〕 will.

かきおく·る【書き送る】 write to (*a person*); send a letter to (*a person*).

かきおとし【書き落とし】 an omission in writing.

かきおと·す【書き落とす】 leave out (a word); miss (a word).

かきおろし【書き下ろし】(小説) a newly written novel; (戯曲) a newly written play.

かきかえ【書き換え】(書き直し) rewriting; (更新) renewal; (名義変更) transfer.

かきか·える【書き換える】(書き直す) rewrite; (更新する) renew (a driver's license-card);

(名義を) transfer. ¶ 彼は別荘を息子の名まえに〜えた He *transferred* his villa *to* his son.

かきかた【書き方】(習字) penmanship; (書式) a form; (手紙などの) how to write (a letter).

かきくも·る【掻き曇る】¶ 一天にわかに〜って大粒の雨が降りはじめた Suddenly *it got quite dark* and began to rain heavily.

かきことば【書き言葉】written language.

かきこみ【書き込み】⇒ かきいれ

かぎざき【鉤裂き】¶ くぎに引っかけてズボンに〜をつくった I *tore* my trousers on a nail.

かきしる·す【書き記す】write (≒ put) down.

かきそ·える【書き添える】¶ 彼女の手紙には彼と結婚することに決めたと〜えてあった She *added* in her letter that she decided to marry him.

かきぞめ【書き初め】the first writing of the year; the New Year's writing.

かきだし【書き出し】(書きはじめ) the beginning; (抜き出し) the extracted paragraph.

かきだ·す【掻き出す】¶ 石炭がらを炉の外に〜す *rake out* the coal ashes.

かきた·てる【書き立てる】(盛んに書く) write up; (ほめて) write up; (けなして) write down.

かきた·てる【掻き立てる】¶ 好奇心を〜てる *stir up* curiosity. 火を〜てる *stir up* (≒ *poke*) the fire.

かぎたばこ【嗅ぎ煙草】snuff. ¶ 〜をかぐ take *snuff*.

かきちら·す【書き散らす】¶ 彼は数冊の月刊雑誌に連載小説を〜している He *is dashing off* serial novels for several monthly magazines.

かきつけ【書き付け·書付】(書類) a paper; a note; a document; (勘定書) a bill.

かぎつ·ける【嗅ぎつける】¶ スキャンダルを〜ける *smell out* a scandal. 犬はネコを〜けた The dog *scented* a cat.

かぎって【限って】¶ きみに〜 you, of all persons; you alone. その時に〜って at that particular time. 彼女に〜まさかそんなことはやりそうもない That's the last thing I should expect her to do.

かきつばた【燕子花】〖植物〗an iris; a flag.

かきとめ【書留】registration. ¶ 手紙を〜にする *register* a letter.

—小包 a registered parcel. —料金 the registration fee. —郵便 registered mail (≒ 圏 post); (1通の手紙) a registered letter.

かきと·める【書き留める】¶ 彼が私に言ったことはすべて〜めた I *wrote down* (≒ *made a note of*) all he said to me.

かきとり【書き取り】dictation. ¶ 〜をやらせる give *dictation* (to the class).

かきと·る【書き取る】write down. ¶ 秘書に手紙を〜らせた I *dictated* a letter *to* my secretary.

かきなお·す【書き直す】(書き改める) write over; (清書する) write out fair; make a fair copy.

かきなが·す【書き流す】¶ 手紙を〜す *write off* a letter; *write* a letter *with facility*.

かきなぐ·る【書きなぐる】¶ 報告書を一気呵成(かせい)に〜った I *dashed off* the report at a stretch.

かきぬき【書き抜き】(抄録) an extract; a selection.

かきぬ·く【書き抜く】¶ 本の一節を〜く *extract* a passage *from* a book.

かきね【垣根】(木のさん) a fence; (生けがき) a hedge.

かきの·ける【掻き退ける】¶ 彼は人を〜けて進んだ He *pushed his way* through a crowd.

かきのこ·す【書き残す】¶ 彼は伝言を〜した He *left* a message [behind].

かぎばな【鉤鼻】a hooknose.

かぎばり【鉤針】a hook; a crochet needle.

かきま·ぜる【掻き混ぜる】¶ 卵3個分の白身に茶さじ1杯分の砂糖を入れてよく〜ぜなさい *Mix* the white of three eggs *and* a spoonful of sugar.

かきまわ·す【掻き回す】(攪拌) stir (coffee); churn (milk); ransack (a drawer). ¶ 学校は彼らのためにまったく〜されてしまった Our school *was thrown into* hopeless *confusion* by them.

かきみだ·す【掻き乱す】¶ 彼の心はその知らせを聞いて〜された He *was disturbed to* hear the news.

かきむし·る【掻き毟る】¶ 彼は髪を〜った He *tore* his hair. それを聞いて胸を〜られる思いがした I *got my heart nearly broken* at the news. / It *went to my heart* to hear it.

かきもの【書き物】[a] writing; a document. ¶ 〜をする write.

かきゃくせん【貨客船】a cargo-passenger boat.

かきゅう【下級】a lower class.

—官吏 a minor official. —裁判所 a lower court. —生 a lower-class boy (girl).

かきゅう【火急】¶ 〜の場合には in case of *emergency*; in *an emergency*.

かきょう【佳境】¶ 物語が〜に入る We are now in *the most interesting part of* the story.

かきょう【華僑】overseas Chinese merchants.

かぎょう【家業】*one's* trade; *one's* business. ¶ 私は〜を継がなくてはならない I have to succeed to my *father's occupation*.

かきょく【歌曲】a song. ¶ ドイツ〜 *a* German song.

かきよ·せる【掻き寄せる】¶ 落ち葉を〜せる *rake up* fallen leaves.

かぎり【限り】**1**〖限界〗a limit. ¶ 命には〜がある There is *a limit* to *one's* life.

金銭には〜がある Money *is not boundless*.

欲望には〜がない There is no *limit* to one's desire.

2〖…限り〗¶ きょうに〜この席に座ってよろしい You may sit in this seat *just for today*.

その図書館は明日〜で閉鎖される The library is to be closed to the public after tomorrow.

できる〜お助けしましょう I'll help you *as much as I can* (≒ *as much as possible*).

できる〜のことはした I did *all* I could.

かぎりな·い【限りない】¶ 彼女は息子に〜い愛情

をそそいだ She devoted herself to her son. 〜く砂ばくは続いていた The desert reached to the horizon.

かぎ·る【限る】¶ 会員は40歳未満に〜る Membership *is limited to* those who are under forty. スピーチの時間はひとり10分に〜られている Speeches *are limited to* ten minutes, not more. 風邪をひいたら寝るに〜る When you catch a cold, *nothing is better than to* take to your bed.

かく【画】(字の) a stroke. ¶ 3〜の字 a three-*stroke* character.

かく【格】(地位) [a] rank; (等級) a class; 〘文法〙 a case. ¶ 彼は〜が上だ He is of a higher *rank*. 彼はわれわれとは〜が違う(上だ) He is far above us in *social ranking*. / He is not on the same *level* with us.

—変化〘文法〙 [a] declension.

かく【核】(果実の) a stone; a core; (細胞の) a nucleus (複 nuclei).

—エネルギー nuclear energy. **—基地** a nuclear station. **—実験** a nuclear test. **—戦争** a nuclear war. **—弾頭** a nuclear warhead. **—爆発** a nuclear explosion. **—反応** a nuclear reaction. **—武装** nuclear armament. **—物理学** nuclear physics. **—分裂** nuclear fission (≒ division). **—兵器** a nuclear weapon; nuclear arms. **—兵器所有国** a nuclear power. **—融合** nuclear fusion. **原子—** an atomic nucleus.

か·く【欠く】¶ きみは常識を〜いている You *are lacking in* common sense. 彼女は親切心を〜いている She *is wanting in* kindness. 義理を〜いてはならない Never *fail* in social obligations. 彼の行動は礼を〜いている He is impolite in his manners. 水はわれわれの生活に〜くべからざるものだ Water *is indispensable to* our life. 毎日の生活に事〜く人もある There are some people who *lack* (≒ *want for*) the necessaries of life (≒ for living).

か·く【書く】write. ¶ ここに名前を〜いてください Please *write* your name here. 鉛筆でなくペンで〜いてください Please *write* with a pen and not with a pencil. これはある小説家の〜いた随筆です This is an essay *written* by a novelist. 彼に手紙を〜こうと思っている I am going to *write* to him. だれか黒板に答えを〜く人はいないか Is there anyone who will *write* the answers on the blackboard? きのう大火があったときょうの新聞に〜いている Today's paper *says* that a great fire occurred yesterday. 掲示にはなんと〜いてありますか What does the notice *say*?

か·く【描く·画く】(絵の具で) paint; (鉛筆·クレヨンなどで) draw. ¶ 彼は油絵を〜いた He *painted* a picture in oils. その絵は鉛筆で〜かれている The picture *is drawn* in pencils. / The picture *is drawn* with a pencil. 風景画を〜くのが好きだ I am very fond of *drawing* (≒ *painting*) a landscape.

か·く【掻く】¶ 頭を〜く *scratch one's* head.

か·ぐ【嗅ぐ】¶ バラを〜ぐ *smell* (≒ *have a smell of*) a rose.

かぐ【家具】furniture (1個の家具は a piece (≒ an article) of furniture という. また furnitures とはいわない).

¶ 〜一式 a set of *furniture*. 部屋に〜を備えつける *furnish* a room. わが家には〜は少ない We have little *furniture*.

—店 a furniture store.

がく【学】(学問) learning; study; scholarship. ¶ 彼は〜がある He *is learned* (≒ *is erudite*). / He has (≒ shows) much *knowledge*.

がく【額】**1**〘絵の額〙 a picture frame; a tablet. ¶ 写真を〜に入れる *frame* a photograph.

2〘量·金額〙 an amount; a sum.

がく【萼】〘植物〙 a calyx (複 calyxes; calyces).

かくあげ【格上げ】¶ その学校は大学に〜された The school *was raised* (≒ *was upgraded*) to college *status*. 彼は支店長に〜された He *was promoted* to a branch manager.

かくい【各位】¶ 〜には後程お知らせがあります There will be an announcement to *the members* later.

かくい【隔意】¶ 〜なく frankly; without reserve. お互いに〜なく話し合った We had a *frank* exchange of views. / We had a *heart-to-heart* talk.

がくい【学位】a degree. ¶ 彼は東大で医学博士の〜を受けた He received the *degree* of Doctor of Medicine (≒ *an* M. D. *degree*) from Tokyo University. / He received *a* Tokyo University M. D. *degree*.

—論文 (修士) a master's thesis; (博士) a doctor's thesis.

かくいつ【画一】(画一化) standardization; (組織化) regimentation. ¶ 教育制度の〜化 the *regimentation* of educational system. 自動車部品を〜化する *standardize* the automobile parts. 〜的に uniformly.

かくいん【客員】an associate member; an honorary member.

—教授 a visiting professor.

がくいん【学院】a school; an academy; an institute.

かくう【架空】¶ 〜の人物 an *imaginary* (≒ a *fictitious*) character. 〜の話 a *made-up* story.

かくえきていしゃ【各駅停車】¶ 〜の青森行き *a local train* (≒ *a slow train*) for Aomori. この列車は〜だ This train *stops at every station*.

がくえん【学園】a campus; a school.

—生活 school (≒ college; campus) life.

かくかい【各界】¶ 〜の指導者 leaders of *various circles*. 〜を代表する名士たち notables representing *various departments* of society.

かくかく【斯く斯く】¶ 〜の場所で〜の時間に at *such and such* a time and at *such and such* a place.

かくがり【角刈り】a crew cut. ¶～にする cut *one's* hair square.
かくぎ【閣議】a cabinet council.
がくぎょう【学業】school work; studies. ¶～を続ける(終える；怠る) continue (complete; neglect) *one's studies*. 彼は～優秀だ He *has done well at school*.
がくげい【学芸】arts; art and science. ―会 literary exercises; a class day. ―大学 a college of liberal arts and education. ―欄 the fine arts and literature page (≒ columns).
がくげき【楽劇】a musical play; an opera.
かくげつ【隔月】¶～に every other month.
かくげん【格言】a maxim; a proverb; a saying.
かくげん【確言】¶彼は～を避けた He avoided to *make a definite statement*. 彼があのときその場にいたとは～できない I cannot *say for certain* that he was there at that time.
かくご【覚悟】(決心) resolution; (用意のあること) preparation. ¶そうする～をきめている I *am resolved to* do so. なにが起ころうとも～はできていた I *was prepared for* anything to happen.
かくさ【格差】a gap; [a] difference. ¶賃金～を是正する correct wage *disparity*. 学校間の～を取り除かねばならない We must get rid of the *difference in quality* of schools.
かくざい【角材】square lumber. ¶5インチの角材 a five inch *square timber* (≒ *stave*).
かくさく【画策】¶彼はその地位をねらって～した He *schemed for* the position. 彼はいろいろ裏で～している He *is working* behind the scene. 彼はなにかよからぬことを～している He *is up to* no good.
かくさげ【格下げ】¶彼は仕事を怠けて～された He *was moved down to a lower position* for neglecting his work.
かくざとう【角砂糖】lump (≒ cube) sugar; a lump [of sugar].
かくし【隠し】―カメラ a hidden camera; a candid camera. ―マイク a concealed microphone
かくじ【各自】⇒ めいめい
がくし【学士】(学位) a bachelor; (大学卒業生) a university (≒ college) graduate. ―院 the [Japan] Academy. ―会館 the University Alumni Association Hall. 文― Bachelor of Arts. 理― Bachelor of Science.
がくし【学資】school expenses. ¶彼が～を出してくれる He pays my *school expenses*.
がくし【楽士】a bandsman; a musician.
かくしき【格式】formality; (社会のしきたり) social rules. ¶～ばらずに without *formality*. 彼は～を重んじる He sticks to *formality*. / He is observant of *social rules*. ～ばったことは好きではない I don't like to *stand on formality*.
がくしき【学識】scholarship; learning. ¶彼は～がある He *is learned*. / He has much *knowledge*. この会は～経験者からなっている The society consists of men of *learning* and experience.
かくしげい【隠し芸】a parlor trick; a stunt.
かくしご【隠し子】a love-child; a bastard.
かくしだて【隠しだて】¶きみにはなんの～もしていない I have no *secret* from you. / I *keep* nothing *from* you. そんなに～しなくてもいいでしょう You need not *be* so *secretive*.
かくじつ【隔日】¶～に every other day.
かくじつ【確実】certainty; soundness. ¶～な情報 a *reliable* information. 彼が来ることは～だ He *is sure to* come. 彼が合格することは～だ *It is certain* that he will pass the examination. 成功する～な方法を知りたい I want to know the *sure* way to succeed. ～にはそれを知らない I do not know it *for certain*. ―性 reliability.
がくしゃ【学者】a scholar. ¶彼は～はだの男だ He is of a *scholarly* turn of mind. 彼は～ぶっている He assumes an air of *a scholar*. / He *is pedantic*.
かくしゃく【矍鑠】¶彼は80歳でまだ～としている He *is* still *spry* at eighty. / He *is* still *strong and healthy* at eighty.
かくしゅ【各種】every kind; all sorts (*of* cars).
かくしゅ【馘首】dismissal; discharge. ¶～する dismiss; discharge; (口語) fire.
かくしゅう【隔週】every other week. ¶～の水曜日に on *every other* Wednesday.
かくしゅう【各週】every week.
かくじゅう【拡充】expansion. ¶軍備を～する *expand* armaments. 組織を～する *enlarge* an organization.
がくしゅう【学習】learning; study. ¶英語を～する *learn* English. ―指導要領 a course of study.
がくじゅつ【学術】(学問) learning; (学識) scholarship; (科学). science. ¶～研究を振興する promote *scientific* researches. ～上の意義 a *scientific* significance. ―会議 the [Japan] Science Council. ―用語 a technical term. ―論文 a scientific essay; a treatise.
かくしょ【各所】¶～に everywhere; in various places.
かくしょう【確証】a positive proof. ¶彼が有罪であるという～はない There is no *positive proof* that he is guilty. / We have no *positive proof of* his being guilty.
がくしょう【楽章】〔音楽〕a movement.
がくしょく【学殖】⇒ がくしき
かくしん【革新】reform. ¶教育制度を～する *reform* the educational system. 会社は多くの技術～を行なった The company has put through many technical *improvements*. ―政党 a reformist political party. ―勢力 the progressive force.
かくしん【核心】the core; the heart. ¶事件の～に触れる get at *the heart* of a matter.

か

かくしん【確信】conviction. ¶ 彼は正しいと私は～する I *am sure* that he is right. 彼はすべてがうまくいくことを～している He *is confident* that everything will get on well. これだけは～をもって言える I can say this much with *confidence*. 彼らは無罪であると～している I *have a conviction* that they are innocent.

かくじん【各人】everyone; every one; everybody (everybody は everyone よりも口語的). ¶ ～各様の考えがある *Everyone* has his own idea.

かく·す【隠す】hide; (秘密にする) make (*something*) secret. ¶ 彼はすばやく財布をポケットに～した He quickly *hid* the purse in his pocket. やがて彼は姿を～した Soon he *disappeared*. 彼は木の陰に身を～した He *hid himself* behind the tree. 彼らは宝石類を床下に～しておいた They *hid* the jewels under the floor. 彼は部下にその計画を～した He *kept* the plan *from* his men. 彼らは彼の離婚をしばらく～していた They *kept* his divorce *secret* for a time. 事実はすべて～さずに言ってほしい I want you to tell me everything you know of the fact.

かくすい【角錐】〘数学〙a pyramid.

かく·する【画する】¶ AとBとの間に一線を～する *draw* a line between A and B. 新時代を～する発明 *an epoch-making* invention.

かくせい【隔世】¶ 当時を思うと～の感なきを得ない When I think of those days, I cannot but feel that I am now living in quite a different age.

—遺伝〘生物〙reversion; atavism.

がくせい【学生】a student. ¶ 全～ all *the students* (*of*).

—運動 a student movement. —会館 the Students' Hall. —時代 *one's* student (≒ school) days. —自治委員会 a student council. —自治会 a student government. —生活 college (≒ campus) life. —服 a school uniform.

がくせい【学制】the school system.

—改革 a reform of the school system.

がくせい【楽聖】¶ ～シューベルト Schubert, *the master of music* (≒ *the great musician*).

かくせいき【拡声器】a loud-speaker; a megaphone.

かくせいざい【覚醒剤】a stimulant.

がくせきぼ【学籍簿】a school (≒ college) register. ¶ ～に載っている学生総数は 1,000 人だ The total registration of students is one thousand.

かくぜつ【隔絶】isolation; separation. ¶ 外界から～される *be separated* (≒ *be isolated*) from the outer world.

がくせつ【学説】a theory. ¶ 新しい～を立てる set up *a* new *theory*.

かくぜん【画然】¶ ～と clearly; distinctly. ～と区別する make a *sharp* distinction (*between*).

がくぜん【愕然】¶ その知らせを聞いて～とした I *was very surprised* (≒ *amazed*; *startled*) *at* the news.

がくそく【学則】a school regulation.

かくだい【拡大】magnification; expansion. ¶ 対中貿易の～ trade *expansion* with China. 戦火の～ the *spread* of war. 反乱はその国の全土に～した The revolt *spread* through the whole of the country. 内乱はさらに～するおそれがある The rebellion is likely to *escalate* still further. 大統領は戦争～を避けると約束した The president promised to avoid a *wider* war. この顕微鏡は物を500倍に～する This microscope *magnifies* objects 500 times.

—鏡 a magnifier; a magnifying glass.

がくたい【楽隊】a brass band; a 〔musical〕 band.

かくだん【格段】¶ 彼は英語に～の進歩を示した He showed *great* (≒ *remarkable*) progress in English.

がくだん【楽団】a band; an orchestra.

がくだん【楽壇】the musical world; musical circles.

かくち【各地】every place; each place; various places. ¶ ～の天気 the weather of *various parts of the country*. 世界～から集められた珍品 rare articles collected from *many parts* of the world. 日本の～で *all over* Japan; in *all parts* of the country.

かくちょう【拡張】expansion; extension; enlargement. ¶ 軍備～ military *expansion*. 道路を～する *widen* the streets. 事業を～したい I want to *expand* my business. 店を～する計画をしている He is planning to *enlarge* the store. 販路の～に全力をつくそう Let's do our best to *enlarge* (≒ *extend*) the market for our goods.

かくちょう【格調】¶ ～の高い文章 writing in *noble* (≒ *dignified*) style.

がくちょう【学長】a president; a chancellor.

かくづけ【格付け】rating; grading. ¶ これらの品物を～することは困難だ It is difficult to *rate* these articles. その会社は日本の有名企業の中で第２位に～されている The company *ranks* second among the famous companies in Japan.

かくてい【確定】decision. ¶ 会の期日はまだ～していない The date of the meeting *is* not *decided* yet. その船の難破は～的になった We *are certain* the ship has been lost. 彼の死刑は～した His death sentence *has been finalized*. 彼がその仕事を引き受けることは～的だ It *is definite* that he will take the job.

所得税—申告 the final income-tax return.

カクテル cocktail.

—ドレス a cocktail dress. —パーティー a cocktail party.

かくど【角度】an angle. ¶ ～を測る take (≒ measure) the *angle* (*of*). この～から見ると viewed from this *angle*. これは地面と45度の～だ This forms *an angle* of 45 degrees *to* the earth. 船は30度の～で左舷(さげん)に傾斜していた The ship listed to port at the *angle* of 30 degrees. 人生はいろいろな～から見るべきだ

We must view life from various *angles*.
がくと【学徒】a student; a scholar.
かくとう【格闘】a fight; a grapple. ¶ ～する fight (≒ grapple) (*with a person*).
かくとう【確答】a definite answer; a decided answer. ¶ 私には～しかねる I am not in a position to *give a decided answer*.
がくどう【学童】a schoolboy; a schoolgirl; a pupil (pupil は小・中学生または家庭教師の生徒などに用いる).
かくとく【獲得】acquisition. ¶ 知識の～ the *acquirement* of knowledge. 権利を～する *acquire* a right.
かくにん【確認】certification. ¶ 部屋にはだれもいないことを～した I *made sure* that there was nobody in the room.
かくねん【隔年】every other (≒ second) year.
がくねん【学年】a school year; an academic year; 米 a grade; 英 a form. ¶ 彼は中学2～に在学中だ He is in the second *grade* of the junior high school. / He is a second *grade* junior high school boy.
—〔末〕試験 a final examination; a final.
かくのうこ【格納庫】a hangar.
がくは【学派】a school. ¶ フロイト～ the Freudian *school*.
がくばつ【学閥】an academic clique; school affiliations. ¶ ～を作る(打破する) form (break down) *an academic clique*.
かくはん【攪拌】¶ ～する stir〔up〕; whip; (卵・クリームなどを) beat; (バターをつくるためにミルクを) churn.
—器 an agitator; a stirrer.
がくひ【学費】school expenses; (大学の) a college fee. ¶ 彼は大学の卒業までの～を出してくれた He paid my *expenses* through the university.
かくぶ【各部】every part; every department. ¶ 機械の～を調べる look into *every part* of a machine. ～を統一する co-ordinate the *departments* (≒ *sections*).
がくふ【岳父】the father of *one's* wife; a father-in-law.
がくふ【楽譜】music; a score. ¶ ～なしでひく play without *music*. ～を見ずに歌う sing *by ear*. ～を読む read *music*.
がくぶ【学部】a faculty; a department.
法(医; 工)— Faculty of Law (Medicine; Engineering). —教授会 a faculty meeting. —長 a dean. 図書館— a school of library science.
がくふう【学風】academic traditions.
がくぶち【額縁】a〔picture〕frame. ¶ 絵を～に入れる put a picture into *a frame*; *frame* a picture.
かくへき【隔壁】a partition.
かくべつ【格別】¶ ～に重要な事柄 a matter of *special* importance. きょうのこの暑さは～だ This is a *very* hot day. 「何か変わったことがあるか」「～に変わったこともない」 "What news?" "Nothing *in particular*." / "Is there any news?" "No news *to speak of*."
かくほ【確保】¶ 永続的な世界平和の～ *maintenance* of durable world peace. 彼は生活の安定を～している He *is secure of* his livelihood.
かくほう【確報】reliable news; authentic reports.
かくぼう【角帽】a〔square〕college cap.
がくほう【学報】a school bulletin.
がくぼう【学帽】a school cap.
かくほうめん【各方面】¶ ～の援助を仰がねばならない We must ask help on *every side*. あの人は～に顔が広い He has acquaintances in *all classes* of people.
かくま・う【匿う】¶ 逃亡者を～う *shelter* a runaway.
かくまく【角膜】〖解剖学〗the cornea.
—移植〖医学〗cornea transplantation. —炎〖医学〗inflammation of the cornea.
かくめい【革命】a revolution. ¶ ～を起こす start *a revolution*. 彼らは～を断行するにちがいない It is certain that they will carry out *a revolution*. テレビは生活に～をもたらしたといえよう It may be said that television *has revolutionized* (≒ *has made a radical change in*; *has caused a revolution in* ways *of*) our life.
フランス— the French Revolution.
がくめい【学名】a technical term; a scientific name (≒ term).
がくめん【額面】(券面価格) face value; par. ¶ 証券の～ a denomination. ～価格で at *par*. ～で通用する pass at *par*. うわさは～どおりには受け取れない We cannot take a report at its *face value*. 彼はいつも相手のことばを～どおりに受け取る He always takes others at their words.
がくもん【学問】study; learning; (学識) scholarship; (勉強) studies. ¶ 彼は～好きだ He is fond of *learning*. あの人は～がある He is a *learned* man. あの人は～がない He *is uneducated*. ～はあっても賢明とはいえない人もある There are some people who, though *learned*, cannot be said to be wise. 天文学は私にとってやりがいのある～だ I believe that astronomy is *a subject* worth my studying.
がくや【楽屋】a dressing room; a greenroom. ¶ ～裏の工作 *backstage* maneuver.
かくやく【確約】¶ それを～します I *give you my word for* it. ～はいたしかねます I can hardly make *a definite promise*.
かくやす【格安】¶ ～に at a reasonable price. テレビは～で手に入る Televisions can be bought *at a very moderate price*. この品は～になっている This article is *a good buy*.
がくゆう【学友】a schoolmate.
—会 a students' association. —会会報 an alumni bulletin.
がくようひん【学用品】school things (≒ supplies).
かぐら【神楽】sacred music and dance.
かくらん【攪乱】disturbance. ¶ 平和を～する *disturb* (≒ *upset*) peace. 敵の後方を～する *harass* the enemy's rear positions.
かくり【隔離】isolation. ¶ この患者は～すべきだ

か

This patient must *be kept in isolation*.
—病院(病室) an isolation hospital (ward).

がくり【学理】 a theory. ¶ 社会の変化を～的に研究する study social changes *theoretically*.

かくりつ【確率】 probability. ¶ 私が成功する～は10分の1だ The *probability* of my success is one to ten. さいころの偶数の目が出る～は2分の1だ In tossing dice there is a fifty percent *probability* of an even number turning up.

かくりつ【確立】 establishment. ¶ 彼の地位は～された His position *was firmly established*.

かくりょう【閣僚】 a Cabinet Minister.

がくりょく【学力】 scholarship. ¶ 彼は～がある He *is a good scholar*. 彼女は～がない She *is poor scholastically*. ～ではとても彼にかなわない I am no match for him in point of *scholarship*.

がくれい【学齢】 school age. ¶ 彼はことし～に達した He reached *school age* this year. 彼は～に達していない He is under *school age*.

かくれが【隠れ家】 a hiding place. ¶ 犯人の～をつきとめる find out *a* criminal's *hideout*.

がくれき【学歴】 a school career; an academic career. ¶ 彼は～がない He has no *formal schooling*. 彼はほとんど～がない He has had little *schooling*. / He has no *college background*.

かくれもない【隠れもない】 ¶ それは～事実だ It is a *well-known* (≒ an *obvious*) fact.

かく·れる【隠れる】 ¶ 彼はどこかに～れている He *is hiding* 〔*himself*〕 somewhere. / He *lies concealed* somewhere. どうして～れていたのだ Why *have* you *been hiding yourself*? 彼は門の陰に～れた He *concealed himself* behind the gate. この少年はよく～れてたばこを吸っている This boy often smokes *on the sly* (≒ *secretly*). 彼は世に～れて暮らしている He is living *in seclusion*. ふたりはよく～れて会っていた The two met each other *in secret*. 彼は慈善事業という美名に～れて悪事を働いた He committed crimes *under the cloak of* charity. 彼は～れた天才といわれている He is said to be an *unknown* genius.

かくれんぼう【隠れん坊】 ¶ ～をする play hide-and-seek.

かくろん【各論】 a discussion of details. ¶ 詳細は～で述べる The details shall be dealt with in *a special treatise* (≒ *thesis*).

がくわり【学割】 a special discount for students.

かけ【掛け】 (掛け売り) credit; trust. ¶ ピアノを～で買う buy a piano *on credit*. これは～でも売っている These are also sold *on instalment*.

かけ【賭け】 betting. ¶ ～をする make *a bet*. ～に勝つ(負ける) win (lose) *a bet*. そのことで彼と～をした I *laid* him *a bet* on that matter.

-かけ【-掛け】 ¶ 帽子～ a hatrack. 食べ～のバナナ a half-eaten banana. 吸い～のたばこ a half-smoked cigarette. 彼はやり～の仕事をそのままにして外へ出た He went out, leaving the work half done. 彼は読み～の本を再び読みはじめた He resumed the book which had been left unfinished.

かげ【影·陰】 **1** 〚物の影〛 ¶ 木立の～がだんだんのびてきた The *shadow* of the trees grew longer and longer.
彼の家はビルの～になってしまった The building *has* completely *shaded* his house.
障子にツバキの木の～が映っていた The *shadow* of a camellia fell on the *shoji*.
山は湖水に美しい～を投げかけていた The lake reflected *a* beautiful *image* of the mountain.
彼は自分の～にもおびえた He was afraid of his own *shadow*.
彼女は～の形に添うように，いつも夫のそばを離れなかった She followed her husband *like a shadow*.
彼は～の薄い人だ He is an *unimpressive* man.
2 〚姿〛 ¶ 彼はもう～も形も見えなくなっていた He *is* entirely *out of sight* now.
彼は見る～もなくやつれはてた He was worn *to a shadow*.
犯人たちはまったく～を潜めてしまった The culprits have gone into hiding somewhere.
3 〚背後〛 ¶ ～であの人の悪口を言うな Don't speak ill of him *behind his back*.
事件の～には常に女がいる There is always a woman *behind* an affair.
彼はすばやく電柱の～に隠れた He hid 〔himself〕 quickly *behind* an electric-light pole.
彼は～になり日なたになって，彼女のために尽くしている He is doing all he can for her both openly and *secretly*.
どうもこの事件は彼が～で糸を引いているらしい He seems to *be behind* this affair pulling the strings.
飛行機は雲の～に隠れた The airplane has disappeared *behind* the clouds.
4 〚その他〛 ¶ あの人は～のある人だ He is a man of *doubtful* character.
その事件は私たちに暗い～を投げた The accident cast *a shadow* over us.

がけ【崖】 a precipice. ¶ 彼は～から下をのぞいた He looked over the *cliff*. 大きな石が～をころがり落ちた A big stone rolled down the *precipice*. ～をよじ登る climb up *a cliff*.
—くずれ a landslide.

-がけ【-掛け】 ¶ 命～で働く work *at the risk of one's life*. われわれは3人～で腰かけた We sat three in the seat. 彼は浴衣～で現われた He appeared (≒ made his appearance) informally dressed. 帰り～にちょっとお寄りします I will drop in on you *on my way home*. 起き～に近くを散歩した I took a walk in my neighborhood *as soon as I got up*. 本を定価の8～で売る sell books at eighty *percent* of the price.

かけあい【掛け合い】 negotiations. ¶ 隣家にへいのことで～に行った I visited my neighbor to *negotiate* about the matter of the fence.

かけあ·う【掛け合う】¶値段は会社と～いなさい *Negotiate with* the company about the price. 責任者に～おう Let's *talk over* the matter *with* the person responsible for it.

かけあし【駆け足】a run. ¶駅まで～で行った I *ran to* the station. ～で世界旅行をする make a *hurried* tour round the world.

かけい【家系】lineage.
—図 a family tree.

かけい【家計】household economy; family budget.
—簿 a domestic account book. ¶～簿をつける keep *a domestic account book*; keep *a family budget book*.

かけうり【掛け売り】a sale on credit. ¶～する sell *on credit*.

かげえ【影絵】a shadow picture (手や指で影を作る遊びは外国にはない).

かけおち【駆け落ち】elopement. ¶～する elope (*with a person*).

かけがえ【掛け替え】¶彼の～のない子が行方不明だ His *dearest* child is missing.

かけがね【掛けがね】a latch. ¶とびらに～をかける *latch* a door. とびらの～をはずす *unlatch* a door.

かげき【過激】¶～な運動をする take *excessive* exercise. 彼はしばしば～なことを言う He often makes *violent* remarks.

かげき【歌劇】an opera.

かけきん【掛け金】an instalment. ¶今月分の～ this month's *instalment*. 3,000円の保険の～を払う pay the insurance *premium* of three thousand yen.

かけきん【賭け金】a wager.

かげぐち【陰口】backbiting. ¶他人の～を言ってはならない Never *speak ill of* others *behind* their *backs*.

かけごえ【掛け声】a shout. ¶～をかけた We *shouted* our encouragement. ～ばかりで仕事は進まない There is much *shouting* but little progress.

かけごと【賭け事】⇒ かけ（賭け）

かけことば【掛けことば·懸け詞】a pivot-word.

かけこ·む【駆け込む】¶救いを求めて交番に～んだ I *ran* for refuge *to* the police box.

かけざん【掛け算】multiplication. ¶～をする do *multiplication*.

かけじく【掛け軸】a hanging picture.

かけず【掛け図】a wall map (⇔ chart).

かけだし【駆け出し】a greenhorn. ¶～の新聞記者 a *cub* reporter.

かけちが·う【掛け違う】¶～って彼に会えなかった I just *missed* him. 電話を～った I *had the wrong number*.

かけつ【可決】adoption; passage. ¶議案は～された The bill *was passed*. 動議は100票対7票で原案通り～された The motion *was carried* as drafted by 100 votes against 7.

かけつ·ける【駆けつける】run to (a place). ¶救急車はすぐ現場に～けた An ambulance soon *arrived at* the scene of the accident. 警察はすぐ現場に～けた The police *were soon on* the scene. 消防車は10分後に現場に～けた Fire engines *came rushing to* the scene after ten minutes.

かけっこ【駆けっこ】¶～をする run *a race*.

かけて ¶春から夏に～ from spring to summer. 週末に～ over the weekend. 英会話に～は彼にかなう者はいない He is second to none *in* English conversation. 私の名誉に～最善を尽くすことを誓います I swear *upon* my honor to do my best.

かけどけい【掛け時計】a wall clock; a grandfather['s] clock.

かけとり【掛け取り】(こと) bill-collecting; (人) a bill-collector.

かげながら【陰ながら】secretly. ¶彼は母親のことを～案じている He is *secretly* anxious about his mother.

かけぬ·ける【駆け抜ける】run through (the crowd).

かけね【掛け値】an overcharge; (誇張) exaggeration. ¶～のないところ彼の言うことは信用できる *Frankly speaking*, he can be trusted. ～なしに彼はすぐれた学者だ He is *undoubtedly* an excellent scholar.

かげのこえ【陰の声】(ラジオなどの) the mystery voice.

かけはし【掛け橋】a suspension bridge.
¶彼はふたりの間の～として働いた He acted as *a go-between* for them.

かけはな·れる【懸け離れる】¶ふたりの意見は～れている The opinions of the two *are far apart* from each other. この訳文は原文の意味と～れている This translation *is quite different* from the original in meaning. 彼の演説は現実から～れたものだった What he remarked in his speech *was far away* from the facts.

かけひ【筧】a water pipe.

かけひき【駆け引き】bargaining. ¶～する bargain. ～のある cunning. 彼は～がうまい He is a good hand at *bargaining*. 商売の～は難しい It is difficult to *deal with the tricks of* the trade. 彼は仕事の～を覚えるのが早い He is quick to learn the *ropes*.

かげひなた【陰日向】¶彼は～のある人間だ He is *a double-dealer*. / He is *two-faced*. あの人はまったく～なく働く人だ He works quite *conscientiously*.

かけぶとん【掛け布団】a coverlet; a quilt.

かげべんけい【陰弁慶】a braggart; a blustering coward.

かげぼうし【影法師】a shadow.

かげぼし【陰干し】¶～する dry in the shade.

かけまわ·る【駆け回る】run about. ¶彼は金策にあちこち～っている He *is busy* trying to raise money.

かげむしゃ【影武者】a general's double.

かけもち【掛け持ち】a part-time job. ¶彼はふたつの学校を～で教えている He is teaching at two different schools.

かけもの【掛け物】a hanging picture.

か

か

かけよ·る【駆け寄る】¶ 人に～る *run up* to *a person*.

かけら【欠片】a broken piece. ¶ 彼の行為には誠意の～もない There is not *a speck of* sincerity in his conduct.

か·ける【掛ける·懸ける·架ける】**1**〖つるす·下げる〗hang. ¶ 壁にはピカソのデッサンが～けてあった A rough sketch by Picasso *was hanging* on the wall.

上着はハンガーに～けなさい Please *put* your coat *on* the hanger.

2〖上に置く〗¶ テーブルには新しいテーブル掛けが～けてあった *There was* a new tablecloth *on* the table.

ストーブにやかんを～けてください Please *put* the kettle on the stove.

この川に橋を～けるのはそんなに難事業ではない It is not such a hard job to *build* (≒ *construct*) a bridge over the river.

3〖立て掛ける〗¶ 彼は屋根にはしごを～けた He *put up* (≒ *leaned*) a ladder *against* the roof.

4〖ふりかける〗¶ その料理はソースを～けて召し上がってください I think you need sauce on the dish.

彼女は庭で花に水を～けている She *is watering* the flowers in the garden.

水道のじゃ口が凍っていたので, 熱いお湯を～けた As the faucet (≒ tap) was frozen, I *poured* hot water *on* it.

5〖(時間や金を)使う〗¶ もうこれ以上このことに時間を～けている余裕はない We can't afford to *spend* any more time on this.

彼女は1年以上も～けてあの小説を書いた It *took* her more than a year to write the novel.

彼は事務所の落成式に大金を～けた He *spent* a lot of money on the inauguration ceremony of his office.

6〖心にかける〗¶ ご心配をお～けしてすみません I am sorry to *trouble* you. / I am sorry to *have caused* you *anxiety*. (文語).

彼にめんどうを～けないようにしなさい Try not to *give* him *trouble*.

彼のことはいつも心に～けている I always *keep* him *in mind*.

7〖腰をおろす〗¶ 彼らはベンチに並んで腰を～けた They *sat down* on the bench side by side.

どうぞお～けください Please *be seated*. / Please *sit down*. (be seated は sit down よりもていねいな表わし方).

8〖掛け算〗¶ 7に8を～けると56になる Seven 〔*multiplied*〕 by eight make〔s〕 fifty-six. (形式ばった言い方) / Eight *times* seven make〔s〕 fifty-six. (7×8=56 はふつう Seven times eight is fifty-six. と読む; 2×3=6 は Twice three is six. という).

9〖その他〗¶ 服にブラシを～けてください Please *give* my clothes *a brush*.

彼女は眼鏡を～けている She wears spectacles.

次はどのレコードを～けましょうか Which record shall I *play* next?

彼に電話を～けた I *rang* him *up*. / I *called* him 〔*up*〕. / I *phoned* him.

彼は広島から電話を～けてきた He *called* from Hiroshima.

用意ができたらぼくに声を～けてくれ Please *call out*, if you are ready.

戸にかぎを～けるのを忘れた I forgot to *lock* the door.

まだこの家には火災保険を～けてない This house *is* not *insured* against fire yet. / We *have* not *got* this house *insured* yet.

増築した部分にも税を～けてきた The new extension *was taxed* as well. / A tax *was put* on the new extension as well.

この問題は裁判に～けるつもりだ I will *bring* this case *to trial*.

この問題は次の会議に～けて決定されることになる This question is to be decided by the next conference.

か·ける【欠ける】¶ 彼は自制心に～けている He *lacks* self-restraint. / He *is lacking in* self-restraint. コーヒーカップの縁が～けている The edge of the coffee cup *is broken off*. その全集は第3巻が～けている The third volume *is missing* in the complete works. 月は～けかかっている The moon *is on the wane* (≒ *is in her wane*).

か·ける【翔ける】¶ 空を～けるカリの群れ a row of wild geese *flying* high in the sky.

か·ける【賭ける】¶ 彼はそのレースに有り金を全部～けた He *betted* (≒ *staked*) *on* the race all the money he had then. 彼はその実験に生命を～けた He *risked* his life for the experiment.

かげ·る【陰る·翳る】¶ 陽が～った The sun *is behind the clouds*. / Clouds *darkened* the sun.

かげろう【陽炎】heat wave.

かげん【下弦】¶ ～の月 a waning moon.

かげん【加減】**1**〖程度·調節〗¶ 息子の愚かさ～には母も手を焼いている His mother is quite at a loss for the way her son acts foolishly.

ちょっとした～で, 出来栄えがぐんと違う *A slight difference* in handling results in great success.

彼女はうつむき～にしていた She remained bending slightly forward.

「湯～はどうですか」「ちょうどいい～です」"How is the bath?" "It is just right." (湯加減を見るにはひじを使うことが多い).

ひょっとした～で足を捻挫(ねんざ)してしまった I *happened to* sprain my ankle.

子どもは力を～することを知らないものだ A child is apt to forget how to *allow for* its strength.

彼はいい～なことばかりしている He does everything in a *perfunctory* manner.

冗談もいい～にしろ Stop your joking!

私につきまとうのもいい～にしろ Do stop following me about!

2〖料理〗¶ 料理の味は調味料のさじ～で決まる The taste of food depends on the good use of seasonings.

シチューの味～はいかがですか How do you like the stew?

スープは塩～がたいせつだ With soup the amount

of salt you put in is important.

3 〖健康〗 ¶ お～はいかがですか How *are* you *feeling*?

ちょっと～が悪いので失礼します Well, I must be going now, because I *feel unwell*.

きょうはだいぶ～がいいので起きてみた I got out of bed, because I *am much better* today.

4 〖影響〗 ¶ 天候の～で古傷が痛む I feel a pain in my old injury *because of* the weather.

どうした～かおなかが痛む *I don't know why*, but I have a stomachache.

かげん【寡言】¶ ～の人 a *reticent* person; a man *of few words*.

かこ【過去】**1** the past; (人の) *one's* past days (≒ life). ¶ ～のある女 a woman with *a* 〔*shady*〕 *past*.

～は～として水に流そう Let *bygones* be *bygones*.

～数年間 for (≒ during) the *past* few years.

—帳 the death register 〔of a family〕.

2 〖文法〗 the past 〔tense〕.

—完了 the past perfect 〔tense〕. **—分詞** a past participle (分詞とは動詞と形容詞の役を分けもつ(participate) 詞の意味から).

かご【籠】a basket; (鳥の) a cage. ¶ ～の鳥 a bird in *a cage*; a *caged* bird. 一～のリンゴ *a basketful* (≒ *basket*) of apples.

—細工 basketwork. **買い物—** a shopping basket. **紙くず—** a waste-paper basket.

かご【駕籠】(インドや日本の) a palanquin; (西洋のいすかご) a sedan chair; (古代ローマの) a litter.

かご【加護】¶ 神の～を祈る pray to God for *help*. 神の～により thanks to God; under divine *protection*.

がご【雅語】an elegant word.

かこい【囲い】an enclosure; (垣の) a fence; (家畜などの) a corral; a pen. ¶ ～をする enclose; fence (≒ rail; rope) off.

かこう【下降】a fall; a descent; a drop.

—線 ¶ 物価は～線をたどっている Prices show *a downward curve*. / Prices *are declining* (≒ *are going down*).

かこう【火口】a crater.

—原 a crater-basin. **—〔原〕湖** a crater lake.

かこう【加工】¶ この工場では皮を～する This factory *processes* leather.

—業 processing industries. **—業者** a process manufacturer. **—食品** processed food. **—品** finished goods. **—貿易** processing trade.

かこう【河口】the mouth of a river; a river mouth; (潮が流れ込むような広い) an estuary.

かこう【河港】a river port; an inland port.

かこ・う【囲う】(囲む) enclose; surround; (貯蔵する) keep; store.

かごう【化合】chemical combination. ¶ 水素は酸素と～して水となる Hydrogen *combines* with oxygen to form water.

—物 a 〔chemical〕 compound.

がごう【雅号】a pen name; a pseudonym.

かこうがん【花崗岩】〖鉱物〗 granite.

かこく【過酷】¶ ～な労働条件 *severe* (≒ *hard*) working conditions. ～な批評 *severe* (≒ *bitter*) criticism.

かこ・つ【託つ・喞つ】¶ わが身の不運を～つ *deplore* (≒ *lament*) *one's* ill luck. 無聊(ぶりょう)を～つ *complain about* (≒ *of*) ennui (about のほうがふつう).

かこつ・ける【託ける】¶ なにかしらに～けて on some *pretext* (≒ *pretense*) or other. 病気に～けて *under the pretext of* illness.

かこみ【囲み】(囲い) an enclosure; (包囲) 〔a〕 siege. ¶ ～を解く raise *a siege*.

—記事 a boxed item.

かこ・む【囲む】surround; encircle. ¶ テーブルを～んで座る sit *around a* table.

かこん【禍根】¶ ～を絶つ eliminate *the root of evil*. それは将来に～を残すことになろう I am afraid 〔that〕 it will be *the cause of trouble* in the future.

かごん【過言】exaggeration. ¶ …と言っても～ではない It is not too much (≒ It is no exaggeration) to say that....

かさ【笠】(竹笠) a bamboo hat; (すげ笠) a sedge hat; (ランプなどの) a shade. ¶ 彼は親の威光を～に着ている He shelters himself under his father's influence.

かさ【傘】an umbrella; (日傘) a parasol; a sunshade. ¶ ～をさす put up (≒ hold) *an umbrella*. ～を広げる (つぼめる) open (close) *an umbrella*.

—立て an umbrella stand. **折り畳み—** a collapsible (≒ telescopic) umbrella.

かさ【暈】a halo (複 halo〔e〕s). ¶ 月が～をかぶっている The moon has *a halo* (≒ *a ring*) around it.

かさ【嵩】(容積) bulk; volume; size; (量) quantity. ¶ ～にかかって arrogantly. ～にかかった態度 an *overbearing* attitude.

かざあな【風穴】an air hole; a ventilator.

かさい【火災】a fire.

—保険 fire insurance. ¶ 家に～保険をかける *insure* a house *against fire*; *get one's* house *insured*. **—報知機** a fire alarm.

—予防週間 Fire Prevention Week.

かざい【家財】household belongings (≒ effects; goods); (家具) furniture (どんな場合にもこの語には不定冠詞はつかない).

かさかさ ¶ 北風で落ち葉が～と鳴っていた The fallen leaves *were rustling* in the north wind. 冷たい風で手が～になった My hands have got *dry and rough* with a chill wind.

がさがさ ¶ クマがやぶの中から～と出てきた A bear came *rustling* out of the bush.

かざかみ【風上】the windward. ¶ 彼の家は火の～にある His house *is on the windward side of* the fire. 彼は～にもおけない He's such *a dirty fellow*.

かさく【佳作】a fine 〔piece of〕 work.

かさく【家作】米 a house for rent; 英 a house to let (掲示には To let とするのがふつう).

かざぐるま【風車】a windmill; (おもちゃの) a paper windmill.

か

か

かささぎ【鵲】〘鳥類〙a magpie.
かざしも【風下】leeward. ¶ 彼の家は火元の～にあったから助からなかった His house was burnt down because it was *to the leeward of* the fire.
かざ・す【翳す】¶ 彼は額に手を～した He *shaded* his eyes with his hand.
がさつ ¶ ～な男 a *rude* fellow. 彼は態度が～だ He *is rough* in manner.
かさな・る【重なる】¶ あの一家は～る不幸に会った The family had *one* misfortune *after another*. 乗客は～って倒れた The passengers fell *one upon another*. ことしはクリスマスが日曜に～る Christmas *falls on* Sunday this year.
かさねがさね【重ね重ね】¶ ご親切, ～お礼申し上げます I'd like to express my *hearty* thanks for your kindness. ～ご迷惑をおかけして申しわけありません I'm sorry to give you *so much* trouble.
かさねて【重ねて】¶ …であることは～申すまでもないと思います I don't think it's necessary to *repeat* that....
かさ・ねる【重ねる】¶ 彼らは本を机の上に～ねた They *piled up* books on the desk. その小説は10版を～ねた The novel *went through* ten impressions. 彼は苦労に苦労を～ねてやっと成功した He *went through* many hardships and was able to succeed in the end. ～ねて質問します Let me ask *another* question. ～ねて言う必要はない You need not *repeat* it.
かさば・る【嵩張る】be bulky; grow voluminous. ¶ ～った bulky; voluminous.
かさぶた【瘡蓋】a scab; a slough. ¶ ～ができる *A scab* forms.
かざみ【風見】(鶏の形の) a weathercock; (矢形の) a 〔weather〕 vane.
かさ・む【嵩む】¶ 最近教育費が～む一方だ School expenses *have been piling up* recently.
かざむき【風向き】the wind; the direction of the wind. ¶ ～が南に変わった *The wind* has shifted to the south. ～(形勢)がだんだん悪くなる *Things* are getting hard with us. / *Things* are turning against us.
かざよけ【風除け】a windbreak.
かざり【飾り】an ornament; a decoration.
¶ 新年のお～ New Year's decoration. 身のまわりの～ personal *adornment*. ～のボタン an *ornamental* button. 着物にレースの～をつけた I *ornamented* a dress with lace. 彼の～のない態度には感心した I was deeply moved by his *artless* attitude.
―窓 a show window. ―物 an ornament; a decoration.
かざりけ【飾りけ】¶ 彼は少しも～のない人間だ He is quite a *modest, plain* man.
かざ・る【飾る】¶ 部屋を花で～る *decorate* a room with flowers. ショーウインドーはきれいに～られていた The show window *was* prettily *dressed*. 婦人は宝石で身を～っていた The woman *was decked up* with jewels. 子どもたちの作品を～ろう Let us *exhibit* the children's works.
かさん【加算】addition. ¶ ～する add.
―機 an adding machine.
かざん【火山】a volcano (複 volcanoes); (活火山) an active volcano; (休火山) a dormant volcano; (死火山) an extinct volcano.
―活動 volcanic activity. ―岩 a volcanic rock. ―帯 a volcanic zone. ―弾 a volcanic bomb. ―灰 volcanic ashes. ―脈 a volcanic range (≒ chain).
かさんかすいそ【過酸化水素】〘化学〙hydrogen peroxide.
かし【貸し】a loan; lending; (売掛金) a bill; a charge account. ¶ 彼には1万円の～がある He owes me ten thousand yen. 勘定がまだ～になっています Your account still remains unsettled.
―事務所 an office for (≒ 英 to) rent. ―ビル a building for (≒ 英 to) rent.
かし【樫】〘植物〙an oak. ¶ ～の実 an acorn.
かし【河岸】a riverside; a river bank; (魚市場) a fish market.
¶ きょうは～を変えよう(別の所へ行こう) Let's go over to another place.
かし【カ氏・華氏】¶ ～50度だ It's fifty degrees F. / It's 50° F. (英米ではふつう華氏を用いているからとくに断わって華氏 F. ということは少ない. またイギリスでは1978年からメートル法に変わる. アメリカもこれにならう. したがって摂氏 centigrade を使うことになる)
―寒暖計 a Fahrenheit thermometer.
かし【仮死】〘医学〙syncope. ¶ 彼女は今～状態に陥っている She is now in *a syncopic state*.
かし【菓子】(総称) confectionery; (カステラなどのケーキ類) cake; (砂糖菓子) 〔a〕 candy; 英 sweets; (ビスケット類) a cookie; 英 a biscuit; (パイ・タートなどの総称) pastry.
―屋 a confectionery; a candy store; 英 a sweet shop.
かし【歌詞】(歌曲の) the text; (オペラの) libretto.
かし【下肢】the legs.
かじ【舵】(舵機) a helm; (舵板) a rudder; (舵輪) a steering wheel. ¶ 彼はうまく～をとって岩の間をくぐり抜けた He *steered* the boat skillfully through the rocks. 彼がこの船の～をとっている He *is at the helm*. なんとか彼が～をとってくれるだろう I hope he will *manage* everything properly somehow.
―取り a helmsman; a steersman.
かじ【火事】a fire. ¶ ゆうべこの辺で～があった Last night there was *a fire* around here. 学校が～だ The school *is on fire*. きのうの～でふたりが焼け死んだ Two were burnt to death by the *fire* yesterday. ～はすぐ消し止められた The *fire* was immediately put under control. ～は郵便局から出た The *fire* started in the post office. ～の原因はたばこだ Tobacco was the cause of the *fire*. 彼は～で自宅を全焼した He had his house burnt down by the *fire*.
かじ【家事】household affairs; family chores. ¶ 私は母の～を手伝っている I help my mother with *housekeeping*. だれが～をやってくれるのですか Who takes care of your

household affairs? あすは～の都合で出席できません I will be unable to come tomorrow *for family reasons*. ～はいっさい娘に任せてある I depend on my daughter for all the *family matters*.

がし【餓死】starvation. ¶ ～する die of hunger. ～寸前 *be* nearly *dying from hunger*.

かじか【鰍】a bullhead; a miller's-thumb.

かじか【河鹿】a singing-frog (英米人には想像できぬ動物).

かしかた【貸し方・貸方】〔商業〕the credit side; the creditor. ¶ これは～につけるのですか借り方につけるのですか(帳簿で) Does this item go among *the credits* or the debits?

かじか・む ¶ 指が冷たくて～んでいる My fingers *are numb* (≒ *are benumbed*) with cold.

かしかり【貸し借り】¶ これで～はないね This settles the accounts between you and me, doesn't it? / This makes us even, doesn't it?

かしかん【下士官】(陸軍) a noncommissioned officer (NCO と略す); (海軍) a petty officer.

かじきまぐろ【かじき鮪】a swordfish.

かしきり【貸し切り】¶ 車は～だ The car *is reserved*.

―バス a chartered bus.

かしきん【貸し金】a loan. ¶ ～はいくらですか How much is the *loan*?

かしこ・い【賢い】¶ なんと～い子どもだ What a *bright* child! (bright はとくに子どもに対して用いる. また clever を用いると悪賢い意味を含むことがある). この少年は～そうに見える This boy looks *intelligent*. この少女は5歳にしてはたいへん～い This girl *is* very *intelligent* for a five-year-old child. 彼はいつも～く立ちまわる He always acts *with sagacity*.

かしこさ【賢さ】(賢明さ) wisdom; (如才なさ) tactfulness; (利口さ) cleverness; (抜けめなさ) shrewdness; smartness.

かしこま・る【畏まる】¶ ～りました All right, 〔sir〕. / Certainly, 〔ma'am〕. 彼はじっと～っていた He sat straight respectfully. そんなに～らないでください Take it easy. (とくに米語用法). / Get relaxed. / Make yourself at home (≒ comfortable).

かししつ【貸し室】㊇ a room for rent; ㊈ a room to let (≒ to be let).

かしず・く【傅く】wait upon (*a person*); attend on (*a person*); serve (*a person*).

かしだおれ【貸し倒れ】¶ 彼に100万円～になった We made a loan of one million yen to him, which we never got back.

かしだし【貸し出し】¶ 図書館の本の～は24時間以内に返却と定められている The book *loaned out from* (≒ *taken out of*) the library must be returned within 24 hours.

かしちん【貸し賃】(家・土地などの) rent; (乗り物の) hire.

かしつ【過失】a mistake. ¶ 大きな～をおかす make *a* big *mistake*. ～を見逃す overlook *an error*. だれの～でもない Nobody is *to blame*. / No one is responsible for the *error*.

―死 an accidental death. ―致死 an accidental homicide.

かじつ【果実】fruit (単数形で集合的意味を表わす. また複数形はめったに用いない).

―酒 fruit liqueur.

かじつ【過日】the other day (ふつう副詞的).

がしつ【画室】a studio; an atelier.

かしつけ【貸し付け・貸付】loaning.

―勘定 a loan account. ―金 a loan. ―残高 a debit loan. ―信託 a loan trust. 信用― an open credit. 長期― a long loan. 当座― a call loan; a day-to-day loan.

かしつ・ける【貸し付ける】lend.

かしほん【貸本】a book to loan out.

―屋 a circulating (≒ lending) library.

かしま【貸間】㊇ a room for rent; ㊈ a room to let (≒ to be let).

かしまし・い【姦しい】clamorous.

カシミア cashmere.

かしゃ【貨車】(貨物列車) ㊇ a freight train; ㊈ a goods train; (無蓋の1台) ㊇ a freight car; ㊈ a waggon; (有蓋の) ㊇ a boxcar; ㊈ a covered waggon.

かしや【貸家】㊇ a house for rent; ㊈ a house to let (≒ to be let).

かしゃく【仮借】¶ ～なく罰する punish *ruthlessly* (≒ *without mercy*).

かしゃく【呵責】¶ 良心の～を感ずる feel the *pricks* of conscience. 良心の～にたえかねて警察に自首した He gave himself up to the police, *conscience stricken*.

かしゅ【歌手】a singer.

流行― a pop (≒ popular) singer.

かじゅ【果樹】a fruit tree.

―園 a fruit garden; an orchard. ―栽培 fruit-growing.

かしゅう【歌集】a collection of poems; (選歌集) an anthology.

かじゅう【荷重】〔機械工学〕load.

かじゅう【果汁】fruit juice.

がしゅう【我執】tenacity; obstinacy.

かしょ【箇所・か所】¶ 数～誤りがある There are some mistakes in it. まだ数～回る所がある I have several calls to make yet. 1～気に入らないところがある There is one *point* that doesn't appeal to me. 東海道線は数～不通だ Railroad service is paralyzed at several *places* on the Tokaido Line. その～は訳しにくい That *passage* is difficult to translate.

かしょう【仮称】a tentative name.

かしょう【過小】¶ 彼は私の能力を～評価している He *underestimates* my abilities. 自分を～評価するな Don't *belittle* yourself.

かじょう【下情】¶ ～に通じている be well acquainted with *low life*; have a good knowledge of *the life of the lower classes*.

かじょう【過剰】―投資 investment to excess. 人口― overpopulation. 生産― overproduction.

かじょう【箇条】an item; an article. ¶ 要求

を～書きにする put down demands *in an itemized form.*

がじょう【画帖】a picture album; a sketchbook.

かしら【頭】the head; (リーダー) a leader. ¶～右!(号令) Eyes right! 彼は人の～となれる人物ではない I don't think he can *stand at the head of others.*

-かしら ¶彼は病気なの～ *I wonder* if he is sick. なぜ怒っているの～ *I wonder* why he is angry.

かしらもじ【頭文字】a capital letter; (姓名の) an initial. ¶～で書き始める begin with *a capital letter.* 語を～で書く *capitalize* a word.

かじりつ・く【齧り付く】¶大臣の地位に～く *cling to* a Cabinet position. 彼はその仕事に～いている He *sticks to* that job. 石に～いてもやる I will carry out the work *at any cost.*

かじ・る【齧る】¶ネズミが壁を～って穴をあけた The rats *gnawed* a hole through the wall. 親のすねを～る *be dependent on one's* parents. 彼はスポーツならなんでも多少は～っている He *knows a bit of* every sport.

かしわ【柏】〖植物〗an oak.

かしわ【黄鶏】(鳥) a brown-feathered domestic fowl; (肉) chicken.

かしわで【柏手】¶神前に～を打つ *clap one's hands* before a shrine.

かしん【過信】¶自己の能力を～する *overestimate one's* own ability.

かじん【家人】¶～の留守中に while none of *the family* is at home.

かじん【歌人】a poet; (女) a poetess.

かじん【佳人】a beauty; a beautiful woman. ¶～薄命 (諺) *Whom the gods love die young.*

かす【粕・滓】¶コーヒーの～ coffee *grounds.* 人間の～みたいなやつ *dregs* of society.

か・す【貸す】**1**〖金品などを〗¶あした返すから1,000円～してくれ *Lend* me one thousand yen; I'll return it to you tomorrow.
1週間の約束で彼女にレコードを～してある I *have lent* her a record just for one week.
たばこの火を～してください May I have a light, please?
2〖使用させる〗¶電話を～してください May I *use* your telephone? (May I borrow... または Lend me... とは言わない).
パーティーをしたいのでお宅の広間を～していただけませんか I'd like to give a party, so I hope I could *use* your hall.
鉛筆を削りたいのです. ナイフを～してください Could you *lend* me a knife to sharpen my pencil (with)? (口語では with ははぶく).
3〖賃貸する〗¶2階の部屋を月1万円で～している The room upstairs *rents for* ten thousand yen a month.
ルームクーラーを夏じゅう1万円で～す店がある Some shops *hire out* air-conditioning units at ten thousand yen for a whole summer.
別荘を月5万で～すがだれか借り手はいないか Is there anyone who wants to take my villa on a lease of fifty thousand yen a month?
あの店では自転車を1時間300円で～している They *hire out* bicycles for three hundred yen an hour at that shop.
4〖慣用的表現〗¶冷蔵庫を運ぶから手を～してください Could you *help* me carry the refrigerator?
きみの知恵を～してほしいのだが I'd like to have your advice.
彼にはないしょなんだ, ちょっと耳を～してくれ There's something I want to tell you. But you mustn't tell him.
彼はぼくの忠告には耳を～そうともしない He does not *listen to* my advice at all.
彼が成功したのは私が力を～してやったからなのだ He owes it to my aid that he has succeeded.

かず【数】a number. ¶箱の中の鉛筆の～を数える *count* the pencils in a case. この子は5以上の～は数えられない My child cannot *count* above five. テレビの～はどんどん増えて今ではほとんどの家庭が持っている The *number* of television sets has increased so remarkably that today most homes have got them. 日本では文字の読めない人の～は少ない Few people are illiterate in Japan. ～限りない動物がこの公園にいる There are *countless* animals in this park.

ガス gas; (濃霧) (a) dense fog. ¶～をつける(消す) turn on (off) the *gas.* ～を引いてもらう have *gas* laid on. どこか～漏れしている The *gas* leaks somewhere. ～の出が悪い The *gas* does not come out well. 腹に～がたまって困る I suffer from *gas* in the bowels.
—会社 a gas company. —管 a gas pipe. —工事人 a gasman; a gas fitter. —こんろ a gas range. —ストーブ a gas heater. —代 gas rates. —タンク a gas tank. —中毒 gas poisoning. —メーター a gas meter. 天然— natural gas. 毒— poison gas.

かすか【幽か・微か】¶～な望みさえない I have not *the faintest* hope. ～な声で in a *faint* voice. 富士山が～に見える Mt. Fuji is *dimly* seen.

かすがい【鎹】a cramp. ¶子は～ A child is *a pledge* of conjugal love.

かずかず【数数】¶～の楽しい思い出 *lots of* happy memories.

カスタード custard.

カスタネット castanets (ふつう複数形).

カステラ sponge cake.

かずのこ【数の子】herring roe.

かすみ【霞】a mist. ¶野に～がかかっている *A mist* hung all over the field.
—網 a fowling net.

かす・む【霞む】¶涙で目が～んだ My eyes *were blurred* with tears. 遠方に島が～んで見える An island is *dimly* seen in the distance, *wrapped in mist.* 彼女が来るとほかの者はみな～んでしまった All the people present *were outshone* by her appearance.

かす・める【掠める】¶彼は利益の大半を～め取った He *pocketed* most of the profits. 彼は人の目を～めてそれを持ち去った He took it away *stealthily*. 飛行機が屋根を～めて飛んでいった The airplane *skimmed* the roof of the house. 台風が半島の南端を～めた The typhoon just *touched* the southern end of the peninsula in its course.

かずら【葛】〘植物〙a vine; a creeper.

かすり【絣】a splashed pattern.

かすりきず【掠り傷】a scratch. ¶ 運よく～ひとつ受けなかった Luckily I didn't get even *a scratch*.

か·する【化する】¶ その町は焦土と～した The whole town was burnt to the ground.

か·する【課する】¶ 輸入飲料酒には関税が～せられている The customs duties *are imposed on* imported alcoholic drinks. あなたが～するどんな任務でもやりぬくつもりです I am ready to perform any task that you will *impose on* me. どんな刑罰を裁判官は彼に～したのか What penalty did the judge *inflict upon* him?

かす·れる【掠れる】¶ 彼はどなって声が～れた He shouted himself *hoarse*. きょうは声が～れているね You *sound husky* today. その先は字が～れていて読めない It is impossible to read the handwriting after that sentence, because the ink *becomes faded*. / The words thereafter are illegible because they *have faded away*. (後者は文語).

かせ【枷】(手かせ) handcuffs; (足かせ) shackles; fetters.

手—足— ¶ 手～足～をはめられた I *was handcuffed and fettered*. / I was put on *handcuffs* and in *fetters*.

かぜ【風】**1**〘そよ風・突風など〙a wind. ¶ 冷たい～が北から吹いている The chilly *wind* is blowing from the north.

～が東に変わった The *wind* has shifted to the east.

けさは少し～がある(あまり～がない) There is a little *wind* (little *wind*) this morning.

強い～が吹いている There is *a* strong *wind* blowing. / The *wind* is blowing strong. (後者は文語).

～が出てきた(ないだ) The *wind* has risen (has dropped).

少し酔ってしまった, ～に当たりに外に出てみよう I am a little tipsy; I think I'll go out *for a breath of air*.

冬服は～を当ててしまった I *aired* my winter clothes before putting them away.

～に乗ってバイオリンの音が聞こえてくる The sound of a violin was carried (≒ was borne) on the *wind*.

どこからともなく～が花の香りを運んできた The fragrance of flowers was borne on the spring *breeze*.

扇風機の～に長い間当たっていると体に毒だ It is bad for the health to sit in front of an electric fan for a long time.

～でテレビのアンテナが飛んでしまった The television antenna has been blown off by the *wind*.

～薫る季節ももうじきだ The warm season is just around the corner.

2〘慣用的表現〙¶ ～の便りによると彼は元気でいるようだ I heard from someone that he is in good health.

どうした～の吹き回しか, 突然彼が訪ねてきた He unexpectedly came to see me, though I don't know how it came to happen.

彼はいつも肩で～を切って歩く He always swaggers when he walks.

意見しても彼はどこ吹く～というような顔をしている When I talk to him, he has a nonchalant, I-don't-know-anything look on his face.

彼はすぐに役人～を吹かせる He always comes the government official over us. (come は「…ぶる」の意味の他動詞で米口語).

あすはあすの～が吹く Tomorrow brings its own fortune.

かぜ【風邪】a cold. ¶ ～をひいた I caught 〔a〕 *cold*. ひどい～をひいている I have *a* bad *cold*. ～がなかなか抜けない I cannot shake off my *cold*. また～をひきなおした I have caught *a* fresh *cold*. ～が治りかけている My *cold* is going now. 彼は～で休んでいる He is absent with *a cold*.

—ぎみ ¶ ～ぎみだ I have *a* slight *cold*. / I have a touch of *cold*. 鼻— ¶ 鼻～をひいている I have *a cold* in the head.

かぜあたり【風当たり】¶ この家は～が強い The wind blows hard against this house. ぼくに～が強かった Everybody was very critical against me.

かせい【火星】〘天文学〙Mars.

—人 a Martian.

かせい【加勢】help; assistance; support. ¶ どちらにも～するな Don't *commit yourself to* either side. ちょっと～してくれ *Help* me, please. いまに～にいく I will come to your *assistance*.

かせい【家政】housekeeping. ¶ ～を処理する manage *household affairs*; keep house. 彼女は～の切りまわしがうまい She is *a good housewife* (≒ *a good housekeeper*).

—科(学部) the department of domestic science (≒ home economics). —学 domestic science; home economics (ふつう単数扱い; 米大学生は俗に home ec [ek] とも言う).

かせい【苛性】〘化学〙—カリ caustic potash. —ソーダ caustic soda.

かぜい【課税】taxation; (税) a tax. ¶ 100万円以上の所得は～される *Tax* is payable on income over a hundred thousand yen. 去年はどれだけきみの所得に～されたか How much did they *tax* on your income last year?

—所得 the assessable (≒ taxable) income. —率 the tax rate. 累進— progressive taxation.

カゼイン casein.

かせき【化石】a fossil. ¶ 植物は白亜紀に～になった The plant *fossilized* in the cretaceous period.

—動物(植物) a fossil animal (plant).

かせぎ【稼ぎ】(収入) an income; earning. ¶ 私は～が少ない I have *a* poor *income*. きょ

うは～が少なかった I had small *earnings* today.

かせ·ぐ【稼ぐ】¶ 彼は1日に1万円～ぐ He *earns* ten thousand yen a day. 私は翻訳で小づかい銭を～いでいる I *earn* my pocket-money by translating foreign books. われわれはなんとかして時を～がねばならぬ We must *gain* time somehow.

かぜぐすり【風邪薬】a cold remedy; (錠剤) a cold tablet.

かせつ【仮設】¶ 橋を川に～した A temporary bridge was built across the river.

かせつ【仮説】a hypothesis (複 hypotheses). ¶ ひとつの～を立てる set forth *a hypothesis*.

かせつ【架設】construction; building. ¶ 橋を～した They *built* a bridge across the river. 電話を～した I *had* a telephone *installed* in my house.

カセット a cassette.
—テープ a cassette tape. —テープレコーダー a cassette tape recorder.

かぜとおし【風通し】¶ その部屋は～がいい(悪い) The room *is well* (≒ *not well*) *ventilated*.

かせん【下線】an underline. ¶ 語に～を引く *underline* a word.

かせん【化繊】synthetic fiber.

かせん【河川】a river.
—工事 river conservation works.

かせん【架線】¶ 電車の～ *a* trolley *wire*. ～工事中だ The *wiring works* are in progress.

がぜん【俄然】all of a sudden; suddenly.

かそう【下層】—階級 the lower classes. —社会 the lower strata of society. —雲 the lower layer of clouds.

かそう【火葬】cremation. ¶ 遺体は～に付された The body *was cremated*.

かそう【仮装】disguise. ¶ 彼女は若い男に～した She *disguised herself* (≒ *was disguised*) as a young man.
—行列 a fancy dress parade. —舞踏会 a fancy ball; a masked ball.

かそう【仮想】imagination; supposition.
—敵国 a potential (≒ hypothetical) enemy country.

がぞう【画像】a portrait; an image.

かぞえ【数え】¶ ～で10歳です I am in my tenth [calendar] year.

かぞえうた【数え歌】a counting song.

かぞえあ·げる【数え上げる】¶ それらをひとつひとつ～げるのはたいへんだ It takes a lot of trouble to *count* them one by one.

かぞえきれな·い【数え切れない】¶ そんな事件は～いほどある Such accidents *are numberless*. 空の星は～い There are *innumerable* stars in the sky.

かぞえた·てる【数え立てる】¶ 彼は彼女の欠点を～てた He *picked out* her faults one by one.

かぞ·える【数える】count. ¶ 怒りを鎮めるため20～えた I *counted* twenty to suppress my anger. 1から100まで～える *count* from one to one hundred. ～え違っているようだからもう一度～え直してくれ You seem to *have counted wrong* (≒ *have miscalculated*); please *count* once *again*. 彼は世界の大詩人の中に～えられる He *ranks* (≒ *is reckoned*) among the world's greatest poets.

かそく【加速】acceleration. ¶ ～する increase the speed. 自動車はふつう3段～になっている Cars usually have three *accelerations*.
—運動 an accelerated motion. —装置 an accelerater.

かぞく【家族】a family. ¶ ご～は何人ですか How large is your *family*? ～はみな元気です My *family* is (≒ are) in good health. (家族構成員のひとりひとりをさすときは family は複数, 家族をひとつの全体としてみなすときは単数; ただし会話ではふつう How *is* your family?—*They are* fine, thank you. という). ～を養う support *one's family*. 私の～は5人だ There are five members in our *family*.
—計画 family planning. —制度 the family system. —手当 family allowance.

かぞく【華族】(男) a peer; (女) a peeress; (総称) the nobility; the peerage.

かそくど【加速度】〖物理〗acceleration.

ガソリン gasoline; gas; 英 petrol.
—スタンド a gas (≒ gasoline; filling) station.

かた【形·型】**1**〖形状·様式〗a style; a model. ¶ これは1970年～のフォルクスワーゲンだ This is *a* 1970 *model* Volkswagen.

古い～のテレビはほとんど売れない Old-*fashioned* television sets hardly sell now.

いろいろな～の洗たく機が出回っている There are various *models* of automatic washers on the market.

こんな～の家を作りたい I want to build my house on this kind of *model*. (have a house built という必要はない).

彼女は流行の～をとり入れたスーツを作らせた She had her suit made according to the latest *fashion*.

このくつは, なかなか～がくずれない These shoes will not get out of *shape*.

私にはどんな髪の～が似合うでしょうか What kind of *hairstyle* suits me?

どんな～の顔だちですか, 丸～とか卵～とか What does he look like? Is his face round or oval for example?

2〖模様·鋳型〗a model. ¶ どろぼうの足跡が見つかったので, せっこうで足の～をとった We found tracks left by the robber and took plaster casts of his *footprints*.

なべは溶けた鉄を～に入れて作る Saucepans *are molded* out of melted iron.

3〖大きさ〗¶ 大～のハイヤーを頼んでくれ Please hire a large-*sized* taxi.

最近は小～のカメラが流行だ Small-*sized* cameras are now very popular.

4〖慣例〗¶ ～にはまった生活はとてもできない I can no longer endure such a *conventional* life.

最近の学校教育は～にはまった人間をつくってしまう The school education of today is apt to build up *stereotyped* students.

5 〖抵当〗 ¶ 土地, 家屋すべて～に入っている The land and the house *are* all *in mortgage*.

株券を～に100万円貸してくれ Lend me one million yen *on* the stock.

かた【方・片】 ¶ 仕事の～をつけよう Let's *finish* the work. やっとのことで借金の～をつけた I *have paid off* the debt at long last. 問題の～がついた The matter *has been settled*.

かた【肩】1 〖身体の〗 the shoulder. ¶ 彼は釣りざおを～にして出かけていった He went out with a fishing rod on his *shoulder*.

彼は～をすくめた He shrugged his *shoulders*.

だれかに～をたたかれた Someone tapped me on the *shoulder*.

よく～が凝る I often *have a stiff neck*.

彼は～越しに私を見た He looked at me over his *shoulder*.

2 〖慣用的表現〗 ¶ きみが彼の～を持つのはよくわかる It is understandable that you *are taking his side*.

弁舌にかけては彼と～を並べる者はいなかった He *had no equal in* eloquence.

かた【過多】 excess ; superabundance. ¶ 私は胃酸～だ I have *indigestion*. (胃酸過多の学名は acid dyspepsia). キャベツは市場に供給～になっている The market *is oversupplied* with cabbages.

-かた【-方】 ¶ 彼の歩き～はおかしい He is strange in his *manner of* walking. 彼は話し～がうまい He is good at speaking. 私は車の運転のし～を知らない I don't know *how to* drive a car. 彼は絵の見～を知らない He does not know *how to* appreciate pictures. さまざまのやり～を試みたが失敗した I tried various *methods* in vain. 彼は私の父～のおじだ He is my uncle on the paternal *side*.

がた ¶ この洗たく機に～がきた The washing machine *has got decrepit* (≒ *has broken down*). ぼくの体に～がきている I *feel rickety* all over these days. 家に～がきた The house *is in bad disrepair*.

-がた【-方】 ¶ 5割～増す increase by *some* fifty percent. 敵～ the enemy's *side*. 朝～ *toward* morning.

かたあし【片足】 one leg. ¶ ～で立つ stand *on one's leg*. ～の one-legged.

かた・い【堅い・固い・硬い】1 〖物について〗 ¶ それは石のように～い It *is hard* (≒ *is thick*) as a stone.

この肉は～い This meat *is tough*.

～い結び目がほどけない I cannot untie the *tight* knot.

くつが～くて痛い The shoes *are* so *tight* that my feet hurt.

2 〖その他〗 ¶ 彼は～い商売をしている He is engaged in a *solid* business.

彼は～い人だ He *is reliable* (≒ *is trustworthy*).

彼は～い信念を持っている He has a *firm* conviction.

～い約束をした I made a *solemn* promise.

文体が～い The style *is stiff*.

彼は口が～い He *is close-mouthed*.

彼は頭が～い His head *is thick*. / He *is stubborn*.

きみの成功は～い Your success *is assured*. / You can *be certain of* success.

～い話はこれくらいにしよう So much for such *serious* discussion.

そんなに～いことを言うな Don't *be* so *rigid*.

守りが～い The defense *is strong*.

～いところ100万はもうかる We can get a profit of one million yen *at the lowest estimate*.

かだい【課題】 a subject ; a theme. ¶ 作文の～は「友情について」だ The *theme* assigned for the composition is 'On Friendship.' 民主主義の育成こそ日本に負わされた～だ The *task* ahead of Japan is to foster democracy.

かだい【過大】 ¶ 人の能力を～評価する *overestimate* a person's ability. 事態の難しさを～評価する *exaggerate* the difficulties of the situation. ～な要求をする make an *excessive* demand (*for*).

がだい【画題】 (題名) the title of a painting ; (絵にかく事柄) the subject matter of a painting.

かたいじ【片意地】 ¶ ～を張るものではない Don't *be* so *stubborn* (≒ *obstinate*).

かたいなか【片田舎】 a remote village ; the back country.

かたうで【片腕】 ¶ 彼は私の～として働いてきた He has been my *right-hand man*.

がたおち【がた落ち】 ¶ 彼の人気は～だ His popularity suffered *a sharp decline*. 今月の収入は～だ This month's earnings *dropped sharply*.

かたおもい【片思い】 ¶ ～に悩む suffer from *one-sided love*.

かたおや【片親】 a parent. ¶ ～がない be fatherless (≒ motherless). ～のない子 a fatherless (≒ motherless) child.

かたがき【肩書き】 a title ; (学位) a degree. ¶ 私は博士の～がある I have *a* doctor's *degree*. 日本では～がものをいう *Titles* speak in Japan.

かたかけ【肩掛け】 a shawl ; a stole ; a shoulder scarf.

かたかた (音) a clatter ; a rattle. ¶ ～音をたてる make *a clatter*. 風で窓が～いう The windows *rattle* in the wind.

かたがた【旁】 ¶ 近況報告～ごあいさつまでに筆をとりました I am writing just to say hello to you as well as to let you know how I am getting along. (これは日本語の直訳で, 英語の手紙ではあまり用いない). 散歩～公園に出かけた *By way of* a stroll I went to the park. (形式ばった文体). 商用～観光にアメリカまで行く I am going to America on business *combined with* sightseeing.

がたがた (音) a clatter ; a rattle. ¶ 戸が～する The door *makes a clatter*. 寒くて歯が～鳴る My teeth *clatter* with cold. ひざが～震える My knees *shake* (≒ *tremble*). ぼろ車が田舎道を～と走っている A shabby car *is jolting* along the country road. 歯が～になる My teeth *are getting very bad*.

かたかな【片仮名】*katakana* (英語で説明すれば the Japanese syllabary).

かたがみ【型紙】¶ 洋服の～ *a paper pattern* for a dress ; *a dress pattern*.

かたがわ【片側】one side. ¶ ～に on *one side* (*of*).

—通行 one-way traffic. —通行止め(掲示) One side closed to traffic.

かたがわり【肩代わり】¶ 人の借金の～をする *assume* the payment of *a person's* debt; *shoulder a person's* debts.

かたき【敵】an enemy ; a foe. ¶ 彼は殺された父の～を討った He *revenged* his father's death. こんなひどいしうちをした彼に～を討ってやらねばならぬ I must *revenge myself upon* him *for* this ill-treatment.

—討ち [a] vengeance. —役 a villain's part. 恋— a rival in love. 商売— a competitor in business.

かたぎ【堅気】¶ ～な商売 a *clean, honest* business. ～になる start on an *honest* life ; begin to live a *decent* life.

かたぎ【気質】¶ ヤンキー～ Yankeeism. 当世学生～ *a characteristic feature* of today's students. 芸術家～の人 a man of artistic *temperament*.

かたく【家宅】a house.

—捜索 a search of the house. ¶ ～捜索される have *one's house* searched. —捜索令状 a search warrant. —侵入罪 trespass. ¶ ～侵入罪に問われる be charged with *trespass*.

かたく【堅く・固く】¶ 扉を～閉ざす shut the door *tight* (≒ *tightly*). ～信じる be *positive* (*about a matter*) ; believe *firmly*. 申し出を～断わる be insistent on declining the offer. ～その報道を否定する *persistently* deny the report. ～禁じられている be *strictly* forbidden.

かたくな【頑な】¶ ～な stubborn ; obstinate.

かたくな・る【堅くなる・固くなる】¶ パンが～った The bread *has gone stale*. そんなに～らないでください Please relax. / Don't *be so formal*. 彼は女性の中にいると～る He *doesn't feel at home* among ladies.

かたくり【片栗】〖植物〗a dog['s]-tooth violet.

—粉 [dog-tooth violet] starch.

かたくるし・い【堅苦しい】¶ ～いふんい気 a *restrained* atmosphere. ～い表現 a *stilted* expression. ～い人 a strait-laced man. ～いことは抜きにしよう Let's put aside *formalities*. あまり～く考えるな Don't take it too *seriously* (≒ *literally*).

かたぐるま【肩車】¶ ～に乗る sit on *a person's* shoulders. 子どもを～に乗せる carry a child on *one's* shoulders.

かたこと【片言】baby talk. ¶ ～を言う babble. ～の英語を話す speak *poor* English.

かたさ【堅さ・固さ】hardness ; firmness ; solidness ; (堅牢さ) solidity ; sturdiness ; (硬さ) stiffness ; (肉の) toughness.

かたじけな・い【忝い】¶ ～いおことば *gracious* words. まことに～く存じます I feel truly grateful.

かたじけのう・する【忝うする】¶ 皇太子殿下のご臨席を～した We *were* greatly *honored with* the Crown Prince's presence.

かたず【固唾】¶ ～をのむ hold *one's* breath. ～をのんでゲームを見守る watch the game *breathlessly*.

かたすかし【肩透かし】¶ ～をくわす dodge a blow ; (相手をそらす) put *a person* off.

かたすみ【片隅】a corner ; a nook.

かたち【形】(形状) [a] form ; [a] shape ; [a] figure ; (形式) [a] formality. ¶ ～がいい(悪い) well-(ill-)*shaped*. 変な～をしている have *a* peculiar *shape*. 内容より～にとらわれている be more concerned with *form* than substance. ～だけのために merely for *form's* sake. ～のうえでは友好関係を保っている assume *an outward appearance* of cordiality.

姿— ¶ 姿～が美しい have a graceful *figure*.

かたちづく・る【形作る】make ; form ; shape ; (構成する) make up ; constitute. ¶ …の中核を～る *constitute* the nucleus of....

かたちんば【片ちんば】¶ ～の手袋 an *odd* glove.

かたづ・く【片付く】¶ 部屋の中は～いている The room *is in good order*. がらくたは1日たてば～くだろう The odds and ends will *be cleared away* in a day. 問題は簡単には～くまい The matter will not *be disposed of* (≒ *be settled*) with ease. 事件はまだ～かない The matter *has* not *been settled* yet. 隣の娘さんは昨年～いた My neighbor's daughter *got married* last year.

がたつ・く (家具などが) be wobbly (≒ shaky ; rickety) ; (もめごとで) be in an upset (because of the trouble).

かたづ・ける【片付ける】¶ テーブルの上を～ける *clear* the table. ここに散らばっている本を～けてほしい I want you to *put away* these books scattered here. まずこの仕事を～けなければならない I must *finish* this work first of all. まずこの事件を～けることが第一だ You must *dispose of* this problem before everything else. このさらの残りものを～けてください *Eat up* what is left on the plate. 娘を医者に～けた I *married* my daughter *to* a doctor.

かたっぱしから【片っぱしから】¶ 本を～読む devour books *one after another*.

かたつむり【蝸牛】〖動物〗a snail.

かたて【片手】one hand. ¶ ～でボールを受けとめる catch a ball *with one hand* ; catch a ball *one-handed*.

かたておち【片手落ち】¶ ～の解決 an *unfair* solution. 一方の言い分だけを聞くのはまことに～な話だ It is obviously *unfair* to listen to just one side of the story.

かたてま【片手間】¶ あの人は主婦業の～にフランス語の勉強をしている She is a housewife and studies French *in her spare time*. それはほんの～仕事だ It's just a *trifle* job.

かたどおり【型通り】¶ ～の話 a *conventional* (≒ *standard*) speech. ～の文句 a *stock* expression ; a *hackneyed* phrase ; a cliché (フランス語から). 式は～に行なわれた The ceremony was held *formally*. 彼は～の文章で辞表を書いた He wrote his resignation *in due form*. ～のあいさつをしてすぐ帰った I returned immediately after a *formal* salutation.

かたとき【片時】¶あなたとは～も離れられない I cannot part from you even *for a moment*. (人と別れるとき part *with* とするのはまれ).

かたど・る【象る】 pattern (≒ model) after ; copy from ; reproduce. ¶富士山を～った記章 a badge *in the shape of* Mt. Fuji.

かたな【刀】 a sword (発音 [sɔːrd] に注意). ¶～を抜く draw *the sword*. ～をおさめる sheathe *the sword*. ～を差す wear *a sword*. ～のさびとなる *be put to the sword*.
—かじ a swordsmith.

かたならし【肩慣らし】〔競技〕a warm-up. ¶ピッチャーは今～の最中だ The pitcher *is* now *warming up*.

かたは【片刃】 a single-edged tool.

かたばかり【形ばかり】¶～の贈り物 (ささいな) a *very little* gift ; (古くさい) a *stereotyped* present.

かたはだ【片膚】¶彼のために～を脱いだ I *lent* (≒ *gave*) *a hand to* him. 彼のためなら～を脱ぐつもりだ I will *use all my influence* in his favor.

かたはば【肩幅】 the width across *one's* shoulders. ¶彼は～が広い He has broad *shoulders*. / He *is* broad-*shouldered*.

かたはらいた・い【片腹痛い】¶あんな弱いチームが優勝できると考えてるなんて～い話だ Isn't it *a scream* (≒ *a joke*) that such a poor team should expect to win the pennant?

かたパン【堅パン】 pilot (≒ ship) biscuit ; hardtack (主に船上または海軍用 ; 乾パンと同じ).

かたひざ【片膝】¶～をつく kneel on *one knee*. ～立てる raise (≒ lift) *one knee*.

かたひじ【片肘】¶～をつく lean on *one elbow*.

かたぶつ【堅物】(俗語) a square.

かたほう【片方】 one side ; (一方のがわ) the other side (≒ party). ¶～のくつがない *The mate* to the shoe is missing. ～の手で持ち上げる lift (*something*) with *one* of *one's* hands.

かたぼう【片棒】¶～をかつぐ take a hand (*in*).

かたぼうえき【片貿易】 a one-way trade.

かたまり【固まり・塊】(塊) a lump ; a mass ; (団) a group ; a cluster ; a crowd. ¶彼は土の～を投げた He threw *a clod*. 彼はけちの～だ He is *an incarnation* of stinginess.

かたま・る【固まる】¶この物質は乾くと～る This material *hardens* when it dries. まだセメントは～らない The cement *has* not *set* 〔*hard*〕 yet. 敷石の上に泥が～った Mud *has caked* on the paving stone. まだ決心が～らない I have not made up my mind yet. 雨降って地～る (諺) *After a storm comes a calm*. あそこに数人～っているのはなんですか What are those men standing in *group*? ふたり以上～って歩く walk in *groups* of two or more. その店に人が～っていた People *thronged* the store.

かたみ【片身】(魚の) a sliced side of a fish.

かたみ【形見】 a memento (複 -es, -s) ; a remembrance. ¶母の～分けをする distribute *one's* deceased mother's *mementos* (*to* ; *among*). 母の～としてとっておいてください Please keep this as *a remembrance* of my deceased mother.

かたみ【肩身】¶～が広い feel proud. あんな親を持ってあの子も～が狭かろう He must *be ashamed of* having such parents.

かたみち【片道】 one way.
—乗車券 米 a one-way ticket ; 英 a single 〔ticket〕.

かたむき【傾き】(傾斜) inclination ; slope ; slant ; (傾向) a tendency ; a trend ; a bent ; a disposition. ¶柱の～を直さなくてはならない We must have the *inclined* pillar mended. 彼には破壊的な～がある He *is disposed to* destroy a thing. (be disposed to の同意語句に be apt to, be liable to などがある).

かたむ・く【傾く】¶あの家は～いている That house *is leaning*. その塔はどちらへ～いているのですか Which way *is* this tower *leaning*? 柱は右の方に～いている The pillar *has a tilt to* the right. 彼は私の考えに～いた He *leaned toward* my view. 日は西に～いた The sun *has gone down* in the west. 家運は～き始めていた Their fortune was beginning to *decline*. このバスは～いて走っている This bus is running *in a leaning position*.

かたむ・ける【傾ける】¶体を～ける *lean one's* body. 人の話に耳を～ける listen to *a person's* speech. 杯を～ける drink *sake*. 彼女はひとり息子に愛情を～けた She *fixed* her affection *on* her only son.

かため【固め】¶国の～をおろそかにする neglect the national *defense* effort. 夫婦の～ marriage vows.

かため【堅め】¶卵ふたつを～にゆでてください Boil two eggs *fairly hard*, please.

かた・める【固める】¶まず仕事の土台を～めることだ You must *build up* the foundations of the work first of all. 粘土細工は日光に当てて～めるのがよい It is better to *dry* the clay work in the sun. 彼はもう身を～める年ごろだ He is now old enough to *get married*. 彼はこぶしを～めて私をにらんだ He stared at me with his fists *clenched*. 彼は地位を～めたといっていいだろう It may be said that he *has secured* his position.

かたやぶり【型破り】¶～のあいさつ an *unconventional* address. 彼は～のことを平気でする He doesn't care about social conventions. たまには～なことをやってみたくなる Sometimes I am tempted to do something quite *unusual*. あの男は～な人間だ He is a man of *extraordinary* character.

かたよ・る【片寄る・偏る】¶～った考え a *partial* (≒ *prejudiced*) idea. 彼の議論は～っている His argument *is one-sided*. ～った食事をとらないようにする take a well-balanced diet.

か

かたりあ·う【語り合う】¶ 日本の将来を～ *talk about* the future of Japan. 私たちは終夜～った We *talked together* all night. 私は彼とその計画について～った I *had a talk with* him *about* the plan.
かたりあか·す【語り明かす】¶ そのことについて彼と～す talk away the night with him about the matter.
かたりて【語り手】a narrator.
カタル〔医学〕catarrh.
大腸— colitis catarrh.
かた·る【語る】¶ 真実を～る *tell* the truth (真実はふつうひとつだから *the* truth, うそはたくさんあるから tell *a* lie と言う). ～るに足らぬ作だ The work is not worth *mentioning*.
かた·る【騙る】¶ 金を～られた I *was swindled* 〔*out of money*〕. 彼はぼくの名を～った He *used* my name.
カタログ a catalog ; a catalogue.
かたわら【傍ら】¶ 道の～に by the roadside. 彼は工員として働く～, 夜学に通った He attended a night school, *while* working as a mechanic in the daytime.
かたわれ【片割れ】(共謀者) an accomplice. ¶ 彼も～だ He, too, is *a party to* the plot.
かたん【加担】(加わること) participation ; (共謀すること) conspiracy. ¶ 彼は陰謀に～した He *was a party to* the conspiracy. / He *took part in* the conspiracy.
かだん【花壇】a flower bed ; a flower garden.
かだん【歌壇】the literary circles of *tanka* poets.
かだん【果断】¶ 彼は～にやってのけた He dispatched it *with resolution*. / He took a *quick* action on it.
がだん【画壇】painting circles ; the artists' world.
カタンいと【カタン糸】cotton 〔thread〕.
かち【勝ち】a victory. ¶ われわれが～をおさめた We *won* (≒ *gained*) *a victory*. きみの～だ The game is yours. ～に乗じて敵を急追した We pursued the enemy hot, following up the *victory*.
かち【価値】value. ¶ この本は読む～がある This book *is worth* reading. 外見だけで人間の～は判断できない We cannot judge a man's *worth* only by his appearance. この絵は彼にはたいへん～がある This picture *is of* great *value* to him. ～ある人間とはどんな人間ですか What is meant by a man *of value*? このさらには美術的～はない This dish *is of* no artistic *value*. この小説は三文の～もない This novel *is of* no *value*. 彼の誠実さは賞賛されるだけの～がある His faithfulness *is worthy of* praise. この宝石は10万円の～がある This jewel *is worth* a hundred thousand yen.
-がち【-勝ち】¶ あすは曇り～の天気だろう Tomorrow will be cloudy most of the time. 彼女は留守～だ She is away from home most of the time. だれでもあわてるとまちがいはし～なもの We *are* all *liable to* make mistakes, when we are in a hurry.
かちあ·う【かち合う】¶ 今度の祭日は日曜と～う Our next national holiday *falls on* Sunday. 両方の会が～わないとよいのだが I hope both meetings will not *be held at the same time*.
かちかち ¶ 道が～に凍っている The road is frozen *hard*. 時計の～いう音が気になって, すぐには眠れなかった I couldn't sleep at once, because the *ticktacks* of a clock got on my nerves.
かちき【勝ち気】¶ 彼女は～な娘だ She *is* quite *unyielding*. / She is a girl *of spirit*. ～にはやるな Don't be rash in winning a game.
かちく【家畜】(牛) cattle (形は単数だが複数に扱う) ; (牛·ブタ·羊等の総称) livestock (単·複同形).
かちこ·す【勝ち越す】¶ ぼくのほうが2回～している I *have* two *wins against* you.
かちどき【勝ち鬨】¶ われわれは～を上げた We *gave a shout of triumph*. / We *shouted triumphantly*.
かちと·る【克ち取る】¶ 権利は与えられるものでなく～られなければならぬ Rights are not given, but must *be acquired*.
かちぬ·く【勝ち抜く】¶ 彼は決勝戦まで～いてきた He *won through* up to the finals.
—き戦 a tournament.
かちほこ·る【勝ち誇る】¶ 彼らは敗れた敵に～っていた They *triumphed over* their beaten enemy. 彼らは～って帰国した They returned home *in triumph*.
かちめ【勝ち目】¶ ～がありそうだ *The odds* (≒ *chances*) are in my favor. ～がなさそうだ *The odds* (≒ *chances*) are against me. とても～はない The game *is hopeless*. / We *stand no chance against* them.
かちゅう【渦中】¶ 論争の～に巻き込まれた I was drawn into the *vortex* of the controversy. 彼は政争の～に身を投じた He threw himself into the *vortex* of political strife.
かちょう【課長】the chief of a section.
がちょう【鵞鳥】a goose (複 geese) ; (雄) a gander ; (雌) a goose (複 geese) ; (子ども) a gosling.
かつ【活】¶ 元気がないから彼に～を入れてやろう Let's *cheer* him *up*, he is so depressed. 死中に～を求めようと決めた We were determined to *risk losing ourselves*.
かつ【渇】thirst. ¶ ～をいやす relieve *one's thirst*.
かつ【且つ】and. ¶ 有効～適切 *both* effective *and* suitable. ～, それは高価すぎる *Besides*, it is too expensive.
か·つ【勝つ】win ; (打ち破る) defeat ; beat ; (征服する) conquer. ¶ 100メートル競走に～った I *won* the 100-meter dash. わがクルーは2艇身の差でYクルーに～った Our crew *defeated* the Y-crew by two lengths. きみにはどうしても～てない I *am no match for* you. 彼は私にチェスで～った He *was victorious over* me in chess. 彼のこの絵は青が～っている In this picture of his blue is the *predominant* color.
かつあい【割愛】¶ 時間の都合で～する *omit*

(*something*) for want of time.

かつお【鰹】a bonito.

—節 a dried bonito.

かっか【閣下】(呼びかけて) Your Excellency; (三人称) His (Her) Excellency. ¶ 大統領～(呼びかけ) Mr. President.

がっか【学科】a subject. ¶ きみの好きな～はなんですか What are your favorite *subjects*?

—試験 examinations in academic subjects.

がっか【学課】school work; a lesson.

¶ ～の下調べをする prepare *one's lessons*.

がっかい【学会】(団体) a scientific society; (会合) an academic meeting. ¶ ～で研究を発表する read a paper at *a meeting of the association* (≒ *society*).

言語— a linguistic society.

がっかい【学界】learned circles.

かっかく【赫赫】¶ 彼は～たる成功をおさめた He has achieved a *brilliant* success.

かっかざん【活火山】an active volcano.

がつがつ ¶ 彼は食事を～食べた He ate the meal *hungrily* (≒ *greedily*). / He *devoured* the meal. そんなに～するな Don't *be* so *covetous* (≒ *greedy*).

がっかり ¶ その報に接して～した I *was disappointed to* hear the news. 彼がいないからといって～するな Don't *be discouraged* because he is not here. まったく～させるやつだ What a *disappointing* man he is! 少なからず～したようすだった He seemed not a little *disappointed*. 会が延期になって～した *To* my *disappointment* the meeting was put off.

かっき【活気】spirit; energy; life. ¶ この町は～がある This town *is lively*. この辺りはそれほど～がない There does not seem to *be* much *life* in this neighborhood. 株式市場は再び～を帯びてきた The stock market has become *active* again. 彼はいつでも～にあふれている He is always full of *vigor*. 彼は～のない顔をしている He looks so *inactive*.

がっき【学期】a term; (2学期制度の) a semester; (4学期制の) a quarter.

—試験 米 finals; end-of-term examinations.

がっき【楽器】a musical instrument.

かっきてき【画期的】¶ ～な出来事 an *epoch-making* event.

かつぎや【担ぎ屋】(迷信家) a superstitious person; (やみ屋) a blackmarket peddler.

がっきゅう【学究】a scholar. ¶ ～生活に入る enter into a *scholarly* life.

がっきゅう【学級】a class. ¶ ～担任 a *homeroom* teacher; the teacher in charge of *a class*.

かっきょう【活況】activity. ¶ 相場は～を呈した The market *was bullish* (≒ *was rising*).

市場は～を呈している The market *is lively*.

取引は～を呈している Trade *is brisk*.

がっきょく【楽曲】a tune; a piece of music.

かっきり ¶ 正午～に *just* at noon. 時間～にまにあった I was *on time*. ～1,000円かかった It cost me *just* a thousand yen.

かつ･ぐ【担ぐ】¶ 肩に～いでそれを運んだ I *carried* it *on my shoulder*. 彼女はぼくを～いだ(だました) She *played a trick on* me. そんな役に～ぎ出されるのはごめんだ I refuse *being chosen* as the one fit for such a job. 彼女は縁起を～ぐ She *is* very *superstitious*. / She really *believes in omens*.

がっく【学区】a school district.

がっくり ¶ 彼女は～うなだれた She *dropped her head*. 彼は入試に落ちて～きている He failed in an entrance examination and *is broken down in disappointment*.

かっけ【脚気】〘医学〙beriberi.

かっけつ【喀血】hemoptysis. ¶ 彼は突然～した He *spat* (≒ *coughed*) *out blood* suddenly.

かっこ【各個】¶ ～撃破で彼らを説得してその計画を中止させよう We'll persuade them *one by one* to give up the plan.

かっこ【括弧】parentheses (単 parenthesis).

¶ 語を～で包む put a word in *parentheses*.

角— brackets. 大— braces. 二重— double parentheses.

かっこ【確固】¶ ～たる信念 a *firm* belief.

かっこう【郭公】〘鳥類〙a cuckoo.

かっこう【滑降】—競技 a downhill race.

かっこう【格好】**1**〖形体･体裁など〗shape.

¶ 彼は～のいい体つきをしている He is well-*proportioned*.

彼女はなんとなく～が悪い She is somehow ill-*proportioned*.

あの少女は～がいい That girl has *a* fine *figure*

この子は歩く～がおかしい This child has *a* strange *gait*.

この服を着ると～よく見える You *look* nice in this dress.

なんとおかしな～だ How strange you *look*!

彼は気どった～をして歩く He walks in *an* affected *way*.

みじめな～の男 a miserable-*looking* man.

この庭は～がついてきた This garden has begun to *take form*.

この部屋にこの家具では～がつかない This piece of furniture *looks out of place* in this room.

2〖手頃だ〗¶ この値段は～だ The price *is moderate* (≒ *is reasonable*).

このスーツケースは旅行に持っていくのに～だ This suitcase *is good for* carrying on a journey.

これは彼らが住むのに～な部屋だ This is a *suitable* room for them to live in.

～な家がなかなか見つからない It has never been easy for us to find a *suitable* house.

がっこう【学校】a school (はっきり授業を表わすときは冠詞をつけない); (総称) an educational institution.

¶ ～に入る enter *a school*. ～に通う go to (≒ attend) *school*. ～を休む be absent (≒ stay away) from *school*. ～を卒業する leave *school*; (特に大学) 米 graduate from (≒ 英 graduate at) *a college*. ～を中途退学する leave *school*; quit *school*. ～は8時に始まる *School* begins at 8 a. m. あさっては～は休みだ

There will be no *school* (≒ *lessons*) the day after tomorrow.
—教育 school education. —生活 school life. —友だち a schoolfellow; a schoolmate.

かっこく【各国】every country. ¶ヨーロッパ～ European *countries*.

か

かっさい【喝采】applause; cheers. ¶割れるような大～を博する win a storm (≒ thunder) of *applause*. 彼が通ると群衆は～した The crowds *cheered* as he went by.

がっさく【合作】collaboration; (作品) a joint work. ¶その戯曲はぼくと彼の～だ I *collaborated on* the drama *with* him.

がっさん【合算】¶雑費を～すると総支出は10万円以上になる The total expenditure will amount to over a hundred thousand yen when we *add up* sundries.

かつじ【活字】a printing type; (総称) type. ¶この本は～が大きいので読みやすい This book is printed in such large *type* that it is easy to read.
—体 ¶～体で書く write *in print*.

かっしゃ【滑車】a pulley.

がっしゅうこく【合衆国】the United States [of America]; the States; U. S. A.; U. S.

がっしゅく【合宿】¶毎年夏に～して野球の練習をする We *stay in the same dormitory* to practice baseball every summer.

がっしょう【合唱】〔音楽〕chorus. ¶～する sing in chorus; sing together.
—団 a chorus; a glee club; (教会の) a choir. 混声— a mixed chorus. 二部— a double chorus; a chorus of two parts.

がっしょう【合掌】¶～する press *one's* [open] hands together in prayer.

かっしょく【褐色】brown. ¶～の brown.

かっすい【渇水】(水不足) a water shortage.
—期 the dry season.

かっせいたん〔そ〕【活性炭〔素〕】〘化学〙activated (≒ active) carbon.

かっせん【割線】〘数学〙a secant.

かっせん【合戦】a battle; a fight.

かっそう【滑走】gliding; (氷上の) skating; (飛行機の) (地上) taxiing; (空中) volplaning.
¶彼を乗せた飛行機は～しはじめやがて飛び立っていった His plane began to *taxi* and took off [from the runway].
—路 a runway; (仮設の) an airstrip.

がっそう【合奏】〘音楽〙a concert; an ensemble. ¶～する play in concert.

カッター (裁断機) a cutter; (軍艦などに積み込むボート) a cutter.

かったつ【豁達】¶～な a generous; broad-minded.

かっちゅう【甲冑】armor.

がっちり ¶体格の～した男 a *strongly-built* man. 彼女はなかなか～屋だ (しまり屋だ) She *is* rather *tightfisted*.

かって【勝手】1〘台所〙a kitchen. ¶～道具は整頓(せいとん)しておきなさい You should see to it that *kitchen* utensils are always arranged properly.
八百屋の御用聞きが～口から入ってきた The grocer is at the *back door* to take orders.
2〘ようす・事情〙¶この会社へ入ったばかりなのでまだ～がよくわかりません I don't know much about my job yet, because I am new to the office.
初めての土地なので～がわからない I don't *know my way about* in this area because I am a stranger here.
この屋敷の～は私がよく承知しています I know *every nook and corner* of this house.
3〘わがまま・随意〙¶あまり～ほうだいなことをするな Don't try to *get* everything *your own way*.
そんな～なことを言ってはいけない Don't *be* so *selfish* (≒ *self-centered*).
自分～にやってはいけない You must not do *as you please*.
たいへん～で申しわけありませんが, 今度の会は失礼いたします *Please excuse me*, but I am afraid I cannot attend the party.
なにをしようと私の～じゃないか I can do anything I like. / I am my own master.
彼は～なまねばかりする He will *have* everything *his own way*.
人間は～なものだ Men *are selfish*.
彼は～気ままな生活を楽しんでいる He is enjoying life doing as *he pleases*.
これは危険だから～に使ってはいけない You must not use this *without permission*. It's dangerous.
どうぞこのウイスキーを～に飲んでください Please *help yourself to* this whisky.

かつて【嘗て・曾て】once; (疑問) ever; (否定) never. ¶～の首相 a *one-time* (≒ *former*) Prime Minister.

がってん【合点】¶～だ All right. / (米口語) O. K. どうも彼の話は～がいかない I can't *understand* him. 彼は～のいかないようすだ He looks *puzzled* (≒ *perplexed*).

かっと ¶～なって in a fit of anger (≒ passion; rage). 彼はほんのささいなことですぐ～なる He *flares up* at the least thing.

カット (さし絵) a cut; (映画で削除された部分) a cut. ¶(テニス・卓球で) 球を～する *cut* a ball.
「ハムレット」のせりふであまり長いのは上演の際にしばしば～されることがある Some of the speeches in "Hamlet" are so long that they *are* often *curtailed* in the theater.

ガット (楽器・ラケットなどの) gut.

かっとう【葛藤】trouble; conflict; complications; struggle; (反目) feud.

かつどう【活動】activity; action. ¶～的な生活 an *active* life. その火山は現在～中である The volcano *is* now *in activity*.
—家 an active (≒ energetic) person; a man of energy. —範囲 the scope of activity. —力 activity; vitality.

かっぱ【河童】a water imp; a *kappa*; (泳ぎの達人) a good swimmer.

かっぱ【喝破】¶～する declare; proclaim.

かっぱつ【活発】¶～な少年 a *brisk* boy. ～な議論 a *lively* discussion. 彼は動作が～である

He *is quick* in action. 女の子にしては〜すぎる She *is* too *active* for a girl. 日本の対米貿易は〜になってきた Japan's trade with America *has been brisk*.

かっぱらい【掻っ払い】(行為) stealing ; (人) a sneak thief.

かっぱら·う【掻っ払う】¶ だれかがぼくの時計を〜ったにちがいない Someone must *have stolen* my watch.

かっぱん【活版】type printing.

がっぴょう【合評】a joint review.

カップ(優勝杯) a cup ; a trophy (trophy は優勝旗·優勝盾などもいう).

かっぷく【恰幅】¶ 〜のいい人 a man *of stout build* ; a *portly* man.

カップル a couple. ¶ 似合いの〜 *a* well-matched *couple*.

がっぺい【合併】union ; combination ; (会社などの) merger ; (領土など) annexation. ¶ AとBを〜する *unite* (≒ *merge*) A with B. 合衆国はテキサスを1845年に〜した The United States *annexed* Texas in 1845. 1972年にA社はB社と〜した In 1972 A Company *was merged with* B Company. そのふたつの会社は〜してもっと大きな会社になった The two companies *were merged into* a larger company.

かっぽ【闊歩】¶ 街頭を〜する *stalk* (≒ *strut* ; *swagger*) along a street.

かつぼう【渇望】a longing ; a yearning. ¶ …を〜する *earnestly desire* to do ; *be anxious* to do ; *be longed* to do.

かっぽう【割烹】cooking.
—着 a cooking apron.

がっぽん【合本】the bound volume (*of* the magazines).

かつやく【活躍】activity. ¶ そのストでは彼が最も〜した He *played the most active part in* the strike. 彼は政界で大いに〜している He is one of the leading figures in politics.

かつやくきん【括約筋】〘解剖学〙a sphincter.

かつよう【活用】**1**〘応用〙practical use ; application. ¶知識を〜する *put one's* knowledge *to practical use*. 彼は金の〜の仕方を知っている He knows how to *make good use of* money.
2〘文法〙(動詞の) conjugation ; (語尾の) inflection ; (格の) declension.
¶ 〜する conjugate ; inflect.

かつようじゅ【闊葉樹】〘植物〙a broad-leaved tree.

かつら【桂】〘植物〙a Japanese Judas tree.

かつら【鬘】a wig ; false hair. ¶ 〜をつける wear *a wig*.

かつりょく【活力】vitality ; energy. ¶ 〜に満ちあふれた青年 a young man full of *vitality*.

カツレツ a cutlet. ¶ 牛肉の〜 *a* beef *cutlet*.

かつろ【活路】¶ 夜陰に乗じて，辛うじて〜を見いだすことができた Taking advantage of darkness, we were able to find out *a means of escape* with difficulty.

かて【糧】¶ その日その日の〜を得る earn *one's* daily *bread*. 読書は心の〜である Reading is our mental *food*.

かてい【仮定】assumption ; supposition ; (仮説) hypothesis (複 hypotheses). ¶ 彼らが来るだろうと〜して準備している I am preparing *on the assumption* that they will come. そのうわさがほんとうだと〜しよう *Let us suppose* that the rumor is true. きみが言ったことが正しいと〜すると… *Suppose* what you said is true, ...
—法〘文法〙the subjunctive mood.

かてい【家庭】a home ; a family. ¶ 彼の〜を訪ねてみたい I intend to visit his *home*. 彼が〜を持ってから10年になる It is ten years since he made *a home*. 彼は〜の事情で仕事をやめた He left his work for *family* reasons. 〜には〜のよさがある *Home* has a merit of its own.
—教師 a tutor. **—裁判所** a family court. **—生活** family life. **—争議** a family dispute. **—用品** household articles. **—欄** a domestic column. **—料理** home cooking.

かてい【過程】process ; course. ¶ 動物の進化の〜 the *process* of the evolution of animals.

かてい【課程】a course ; (教科課程) a curriculum. ¶ 高校の〜を終了する finish the whole *course* of a high school. 英語がその小学校の〔教科〕〜には含まれている English is included in the *curriculum* of the elementary school.

カテゴリー〘論理学〙a category.

-がてら ¶ 散歩〜本屋に行った I went to a bookstore *while* taking a walk.

かでん【家伝】¶ 〜の妙薬 a secret remedy *handed down from father to son*. 〜の秘法 a *hereditary* secret.

がでんいんすい【我田引水】¶ そんなことを言うのはきみの〜というものだ It *is self-centered* (≒ *is selfish*) of you to say so.

かど【角】a corner. ¶ 〜に薬屋がある There is a drugstore on the *corner*. 次の〜を右に曲がると郵便局がある Take the next *turning* to the right and you will find the post office. 〜から7軒めの家がおじの家だ The seventh house from the *corner* is my uncle's. そう言うと〜が立つ It will *sound harsh* for you to say so. 彼は目に〜を立てて怒った His eyes flashed in anger.

かど【廉】¶ 選挙違反の〜で *on the charge of* the Election Law violation.

かど【過度】¶ 〜の運動 *excessive* exercise. 〜の同情 *immoderate* sympathy.

かとう【下等】¶ 彼は〜な人間だ He is a man *of low character*.
—動物 a lower animal.

かとう【過当】¶ 〜な税金 *undue* taxes. 〜な報酬 an *extravagant* reward. 〜な賛辞 an *undeserved* praise.
—競争 an excessive competition.

かどう【花道·華道】〔the art of〕flower arrangement ; floral art.

かとき【過渡期】a transitional stage (≒ period). ¶ 日本の農業は今〜だ Agriculture in Japan is now in *a transitional stage*.

かとく【家督】¶ 彼が〜を継いだ He inherited his father's *house and estate*.

か

―相続権 the right of succession to a house. ―相続人 (男) an heir; (女) an heiress.

かどぐち【門口】the front door; the entrance. ¶ 彼を~まで見送った I saw him to *the front door*.

かどで【門出】departure. ¶ いよいよきみも社会に~することになる Now you *are going out in the world*. おふたりの新生活の~を祝して乾杯しよう Let's drink to good luck on the couple *starting* their new life.

カドミウム〔化学〕cadmium.

かとりせんこう【蚊取り線香】a mosquito-repellent incense.

カトリック (教) Catholicism; (教徒) a Catholic. ―教会 the Roman Catholic church.

かどわか·す【勾かす·拐す】¶ 子どもを~す *kidnap* a child.

かとんぼ【蚊蜻蛉】〔虫類〕a crane fly.

かな【仮名】*kana*; the Japanese syllabary. ¶ 電報は~で書く We write our telegram in *kana*. 名前には~をつけてください Please add *kana* to your name.

かなあみ【金網】a wire net; (総称) wire netting.

かない【家内】(家族) a family; (妻) a wife. ―工業 a domestic industry.

かな·う【叶う】¶ 私の長い間の望みが~った My long-cherished wishes *have been realized*. 彼は~わぬ恋とあきらめた He gave up his love for *hopeless*.

かな·う【適う·協う】¶ この作品は私の期待に~う This work *comes up to my expectation*. ご期待に~うよう努力します I will do my best to *meet your expectations*. これはぼくの目的に~う This *serves my purpose*.

かな·う【敵う】¶ 英語ではきみは彼に~わない You *are* no *match for* him *in* English. ゴルフではだれも彼に~わない No one can *match* him *in* golf. こんな高値では~わない Such an unreasonable price is more than we can *bear*. この暑さには~わない I *can't bear* the heat. / It's *unbearably* hot.

かなえ【鼎】a tripod. ¶ ~の軽重を問われる have *one's* ability questioned.

かなかな【蜩】〔虫類〕a cicada.

かなきりごえ【金切り声】a shrill voice; a raw shriek. ¶ 彼女は~を出して助けを求めた She *shrieked* (≒ *gave a shriek*) for help.

かなぐ【金具】¶ ドアーの~ *metal fixtures* (≒ *fittings*) of a door.

かなけ【金け·鉄気】¶ この水は~がある This water tastes *iron*.

かなし·い【悲しい】¶ ~い歌 a *sorrowful* song. それは~い出来事だった It was a *sad* incident. もうこの人がいないと思うと~い *It makes me sad* to think that he is gone forever. ~いことに彼女の息子は若死した *To her sorrow* her son died young.

かなしさ【悲しさ】grief. ¶ ~のあまり寝込んでしまった I was ill in bed in the excess of my *grief*. 教育のない~でこの本の意味がわからない For want of education I cannot understand this book.

かなしみ【悲しみ】sorrow; sadness. ¶ 彼女は~に沈んでいた She was in deep *grief*. 彼女は~に暮れていた She was overwhelmed by *sorrow*. / She *was heart-broken*. ~に耐えられなかった I was overcome with *sorrow*. 彼女は人知れぬ~を味わっていた She tasted the bitterness of hidden *sorrow*.

かなし·む【悲しむ】¶ 皆はその作家の死を~んだ Everybody *grieved over* the death of the writer. 彼までもが私の不成功を~んだ Even he *felt sad* that I had failed. 礼儀を知らない人が多いのは~むべきことだ It is a matter for *regret* that there are many people who have no manners at all.

かなた【彼方】¶ ~に見えるのが浅間山だ The mountain you see *over there* is Mt. Asama. はるか~に in the distance; far off. 海の~から from *beyond* the sea.

かなだらい【金盥】a metal 〔wash〕 basin.

かなづち【金槌】a hammer. ¶ ~で木にくぎを打ち込む drive a nail into the wood with *a hammer*; *hammer* a nail into the wood. 私は~だ (泳げない) I can't swim a stroke. / I can't swim at all.

かな·でる【奏でる】¶ 琴で美しい調べを~でる *play* a beautiful tune on the *koto*.

かなぼう【金棒】(鉄棒) an iron rod.

かなめ【要】¶ 扇の~ the *rivet* of a fan. 肝心~のところで失敗した I failed *at a critical moment*.

かなもの【金物】㊊ hardware; ㊇ ironmongery.

―屋 ㊊ (店) a hardware store; (人) a hardware dealer; ㊇ (店) an ironmongery; (人) an ironmonger.

かならず【必ず】certainly. ¶ ~お伺いします I will *never fail to* call on you. 彼は~会に出席するだろう He will be present at the meeting *without fail*. 彼は~時間までに来る He *is sure to* come by the fixed time.

かなり【可也·可成】¶ この川は~深い This river is *fairly* deep. きょうは~暖かい It is *pretty* warm today. ~待たされた I was kept waiting for *rather* a long time. 見通しは~暗い The anticipation is *rather* hopeless. ~の金額 a *considerable* sum of money. ~の収入 a *handsome* income. ~の成功 a *tolerable* success.

カナリア〔鳥類〕a canary.

―諸島 the Canary Islands. ローラー― a roller.

かに【蟹】a crab. ¶ ~の甲 a carapace. ~のはさみ claws. ~は横へはう The *crab* crawls side-ways.

―工船 a crab-packing vessel.

がにまた【蟹股】¶ ~の男 a man with *bandy-legs*. 彼は~で歩く He walks *bandy-legged*.

かにゅう【加入】(参加) joining; (加盟) affiliation; (電話の) subscription. ¶ 日本は国連に~している Japan *is affiliated with* the United

Nations. 会に〜する *join* an association.
—者 a member. 電話—者 a telehone subscriber.

カヌー a canoe.

かね【金】1〖金属〗〔a〕metal. ¶ このドアは〜でできている This door is made of *metal*.

2〖金銭・財産〗money. ¶ あの本を買いたいが，〜の持ち合わせがない I want to buy the book, but don't have any *money* with me. (困では I have no money. とはあまり言わない).

世界一周をしたいが〜がかかりすぎる I want to make a round-the-world trip, but I'm afraid it takes too much *money*.

こういう仕事はあまり〜にならない This kind of work doesn't *pay* very much.

彼は息子の教育には〜を惜しまない He is ready to *pay* for his son's education.

彼は株ですっかり〜をなくした He lost all his *money* on the stock market.

彼は〜に困って盗みをはたらいた *Financial difficulties* drove him to steal.

彼は土地を売って〜をこしらえた He sold his land to raise the necessary amount of *money*.

〜に糸目はつけないからぜひその土地を売ってくれ Please sell me that land. I'm ready to *pay* you as much as you want.

彼は母の形見の指輪まで〜に換えてしまった He *sold for money* (≒ *changed into money*) the ring his mother left him at her death.

子どもの命は〜には換えられない *Money* cannot pay for the life of a child.

世の中には〜で買えないものだってある Not everything can be bought with *money*.

計画はできた，あとは〜の問題だけだ We have already made a plan, but the matter of *money* still remains.

この庭はずいぶん〜がかかっている A lot of *money* was spent in laying out this garden. / It cost〔me〕a large amount of *money* to lay out this garden.

彼には〜の心配はさせたくない I don't want him to worry about *money*.

〜がものを言う世の中になってしまった In today's world *money* talks (≒ *money* is everything).

〜を寝かしておいてはもったいない．なにかに投資しよう What a terrible waste to let the *money* just lie idle! I'll invest it.

彼の家は〜にあかして建てた家だ He built his house regardless of *expenses*.

地獄の沙汰も〜次第 (諺) *Money makes the mare*〔*to*〕*go*.

〜の切れ目が縁の切れ目 The end of *money* is the end of love.

時は〜なり (諺) *Time is money*.

1ドルは日本の〜にすると，約300円だ A dollar is equivalent to 300 yen in Japanese *money*.

これは〜を山ほど積んでも手に入らぬ This is not to be had *for love or money*.

彼女は〜に目がくらんだ She was blinded by *money*.

先立つものは〜 *Money* is always the first consideration.

かね【鐘】 a bell; (組み合わされた鐘) chimes.
¶ 入り相の〜 *an* evening *bell*. 〜をつく sound *a bell*. 〜が鳴る *A bell* rings. 教会の〜は11時を告げた The church *bell* rang out eleven.
—つき堂 a belfry.

かねかし【金貸し】 a money lender. ¶ 彼は〜をしている He is running *a moneylending business*.

かねぐり【金繰り】 ¶ 不景気でわが社の〜は思わしくない *Financing* is not favorable to our company on account of bad business. 彼は〜で忙しい He is busy *raising funds*.

かねじゃく【曲尺・矩尺】 a carpenter's square; a metal measure.

かねずく【金ずく】 ¶ 彼は〜で選挙に勝った He has got a victory in the election *by force of money*. 〜では買えないものもある Money cannot buy everything.

かねつ【加熱】 ¶ 牛乳を〜殺菌する *heat-treat* milk. 食器を〜して消毒する give tableware *heat-treatment*.

かねつ【過熱】 ¶ エンジンが〜している The engine *is overheated*. 景気は〜している Business *is too much brisk*.

かねづかい【金使い】 ¶ 彼は〜が荒い He *spends money freely*. / He *is extravagant*.

かねづまり【金詰まり】 shortage of money. ¶ 年末になると〜になる At the end of the year *money is tight*.

かねづる【金蔓】 a source of revenue. ¶ 彼はいい〜をつかんだ He found *a* rich *financial supporter*.

かねて【予て】 ¶ 〜の打ち合わせどおり according to the *previous* arrangement. 〜の彼の望みはやっとかなった His *long-cherished* desire has at last been realized. パリには〜から行きたいと思っていた I have *often* wanted to visit Paris.

かねばなれ【金離れ】 ¶ 彼は〜がいい He *is generous with his money*. 彼は〜が悪い He *is stingy*.

かねまわり【金回り】 financial condition. ¶ 彼は今〜がよい He has plenty of money now. 彼は〜が悪い He is short of money. / He is hard up.

かねめ【金目】 ¶ 〜の物 a *valuable* article; valuables.

かねもうけ【金儲け】 moneymaking. ¶ 〜をする make (≒ earn) money. 彼は〜がうまい He is clever at *making money*. なにかうまい〜の話はないか Do you know any *moneymaking* scheme?

かねもち【金持ち】 a rich man; (大富豪) a millionaire. ¶ 〜たち the rich; rich people. 〜と貧乏人〔*the*〕*rich* and〔the〕poor (対照的にならべると the を省くことが多い). 彼は土地の売買で〜になった By dealings in estate he *made a fortune*.

か・ねる【兼ねる】1〖兼職・兼用〗¶ 彼は会社でふたつのポストを〜ねている He *holds* two positions in the firm.

この部屋は食堂も〜ねている This room *serves* as a dining room, too.

首相は今のところ外相をも～ねている The Prime Minister now *holds* the portfolio of the Foreign Minister *as well.*
大は小を～ねる(諺) The greater serves for the lesser.
彼は仕事と遊びを～ねて北海道へ旅行に出かけた He went on a trip to Hokkaido *both* on business *and* for pleasure.
2 〖…しかねる〗 ¶ 今すぐにはご返事いたし～ねます I am sorry I *could not* give my answer right now.
このことについてはちょっと申し上げ～ねます I *am in no position to* make any comments on this matter.
申し上げ～ねますが,隣の部屋にお移りいただけませんか *Excuse me*, but could you move to the neighboring room?
その案には承諾し～ねる I *am unable to* consent to the plan.
この問題はとても私にはわかり～ねます This problem *is far above* (≒ *is beyond*) my comprehension.
彼はどんなことでもし～ねない He will stop at nothing.

かねんせい【可燃性】 inflammability; combustibility.
—物 inflammables; combustibles (ふつう複数形).

かのう【可能】 a possibility. ¶ 不可能を～にする turn an impossibility into *a possibility*. われわれがその計画を達成するのは～である We *can* carry out the plan. / It *is possible* for us to carry out the plan. …の～性は十分ある There is *a* very strong *possibility* (≒ It is highly *possible*) that....

かのう【化膿】 suppuration. ¶ 傷口を不潔にしておくと～する If you leave a cut dirty, it will *fester*.
—菌 a suppurative germ. —性疾患 a suppurative disease.

かのじょ【彼女】 she (彼女の her; 彼女に(を) her); (愛人) *one's* sweetheart; a girl friend.

かば【樺】〘植物〙 a birch.

かば【河馬】〘動物〙 a riverhorse; a hippopotamus (複 hippopotamuses; hippopatami); (口語) a hippo.

カバー (覆い) a cover. ¶ 本の～ a [book] jacket; a wrapper. (野球で) セカンドが一塁を～した The second baseman *covered* first base. 赤字を～する収益 a profit enough to *cover* (≒ *make up*) the deficit.

かばいろ【樺色】 reddish yellow.

かば・う【庇う】 ¶ わが身を～う(体に気をつける) *take care of oneself*. 彼は私を～ってくれた He *stood up for* me. 親ガモは子ガモを～って犬と戦った A mother duck fought against a dog to *protect* her duckling *from* it.

がはく【画伯】 a [noted; famous] painter; an artist.

がばと ¶ ～床をけって起きた I sprang out of bed. 彼は～飛び起きた He jumped (≒ sprang) to his feet.

かばやき【蒲焼き】 (ウナギの) broiled eel.

かばり【蚊鉤】 a fly.

かはん【河畔】 ¶ ポトマック～の桜並木 a row of cherry blossoms *on the banks of* the Potomac River.

かばん【鞄】 a bag; (書類入れ) a brief case; (小型の旅行かばん) a suitcase; (大型の旅行かばん) a trunk.

がばん【画板】 a drawing board.

かはんしん【下半身】 the lower half (≒ part) of the body.

かはんすう【過半数】 the majority; the greater part (*of*). ¶ ～を占める have (≒ get; hold) *a majority*. 出席者の～の賛成を得て彼は会長に選ばれた He was elected chairman by *the majority* of those present.

かひ【可否】 right or wrong; (賛否) ayes and noes. ¶ 投票で法案の～を決める decide a bill by vote. 彼は全員にその計画の～を問うた He put the plan to the vote of all the members.

かび【黴】 mold; mildew. ¶ ～の生えたパン *moldy* bread. パンに～が生えた This bread *got* (≒ *grew*) *moldy*.

かび【華美】 gaiety; splendor. ¶ 近ごろ生活が～に流れている Recently people have become too *extravagant* in their way of living.

かびくさ・い【黴臭い】 ¶ ～い地下室 a *musty* basement. このパンは～い This bread *smells musty*.

かひつ【加筆】 ¶ ～する correct; improve. 彼の作文に～して直してやった I *made* some *improvements* on his composition.

がびょう【画鋲】 米 a thumbtack; 英 a drawing pin.

か・びる【黴びる】 get (≒ become) moldy.

かびん【花瓶】 a vase.

かびん【過敏】 ¶ 病人はどうしても神経が～になる A sick person is apt to become *oversensitive* (≒ *nervous*).

かふ【下付】 a grant. ¶ 免許状を～する *grant* (≒ *issue*) a license (*to a person*). 彼らは土地を政府から～された They received *grants* of land from the Government.
—金 a [government] grant.

かふ【寡婦】 a widow.

かぶ【株】 (切り株) a stump; (株式) stocks. ¶ そばの松の切り～に腰をおろして休んだ I took a rest, sitting on *a stump* of the pine near by. ～でしこたまもうけた I made a lot of money on the *stock* market. 彼はこのごろ～をやりだした He has begun to speculate in *stocks* of late. このところ～は上がっている *Stocks* have been rising these days. 彼はその会社の～を1,000～持っている He holds a thousand *stocks* in the company. 彼は彼女にお～を奪われた He has been outrivaled by her.
優良— gilt-edged stocks.

かぶ【蕪】〘植物〙 a turnip.

かぶ【下部】 the lower part.
—構造 a substructure. —組織 a substructure.

がふ【画布】 a piece of canvas.

かふう【家風】 a family tone (≒ tradition). ¶ うちの嫁はわが家の～に合わない My daughter-in-law is not in harmony with our *family tradition*.

がふう【画風】a style of painting (≒ drawing).

カフェイン〘薬学〙caffeine.

カフェテリア a cafeteria.

かぶか【株価】〘経済学〙a stock price. ¶ ～の値上がり(値下がり) a rise (fall) in *stocks*. ～が上がる(下がる) *Stock prices* go up (down).

がぶがぶ ¶ 水を～飲む drink water *freely* (≒ *heavily*).

かぶき【歌舞伎】the *kabuki*. ¶ ～十八番 eighteen popular *kabuki* dramas.

かふく【禍福】¶ 人生の～ *the ups and downs* of life.

かふくぶ【下腹部】the abdomen; (陰部) the private parts.

かぶけん【株券】米 a stock 〔certificate〕; 英 a share.

かぶしき【株式】**—**会社 a stock company (株式会社は 米 Co., Inc.; 英 Co., Ltd. と略す). **—**市場 a stock (≒ 英 share) market. **—**相場 stock prices (≒ quotations). **—**取引所 a stock exchange. **—**配当 a stock dividend. **—**仲買人 a stockbroker.

カフス cuffs (ふつう複数形). ¶ ～ボタン a *cuff* button; cuff links.

かぶ·せる【被せる】¶ その箱に土を～せる *cover* the box with earth. 歯に金を～せる *crown* a tooth with gold.

カプセル a capsule.

かふそく【過不足】¶ この菓子をみんなに～なく配りなさい Distribute these candies *equally* among all.

かぶと【冑·兜】a helmet. ¶ ついに彼も～を脱いだ He *owned* (≒ *admitted*) *himself beaten* at last. 勝って～の緒を締めよ Never be proud of your success.

かぶとがに【兜蟹】〘動物〙a horseshoe crab.

かぶとむし【兜虫】a beetle.

かぶぬし【株主】米 a stockholder; 英 a shareholder. ¶ 彼はあの会社の大～だ He is one of the heavy *stockholders* in (≒ of) that company.

—総会 a general meeting of stockholders.
—配当金 dividends to stockholders.

かぶや【株屋】a stockbroker.

かぶり【頭】¶ 彼は～を振った He *shook his head* in denial.

かぶりつき【噛り付き】the front row. ¶ ～で芝居を見る enjoy a play in *the front row of the main floor*.

かぶりつ·く【噛り付く】bite (*at something*).

かぶ·る【被る】¶ 帽子を～りなさい *Put on* your hat. (「帽子をかぶる」は put on *one's* hat, 「かぶっている」は wear *a* hat と言うのがふつう). 彼は帽子を～っていた He *had* his hat *on*. 本はほこりを～っていた The books *were covered with* dust. 子どもは布団を頭から～って眠っていた The child was lying asleep, with the coverlet over his head. 彼はひとりで罪を～った He *took the blame for* the crime alone. 暑ければ水を～ったらいい If you feel hot, *pour* water *upon yourself*. 船は大波を～った Huge waves washed over the boat.

かぶれ【気触れ】(皮膚の) a rash; an eruption. ¶ アメリカ～の男 an *Americanized* person.

かぶ·れる【気触れる】(ウルシに) be poisoned (*with* lacquer); (感化される) be influenced (*by* new ideas).

かふん【花粉】pollen.

かぶん【過分】¶ ～な報酬 a *generous* (≒ an *excessive*) fee. ～のおほめにあずかりまことに恐縮です I am afraid I am not worthy of such *high* praise. / I am afraid I don't deserve such *high* praise.

かぶん【寡聞】¶ ～にしてまだ知りません I'm afraid I haven't heard anything about it yet.

かぶんすう【仮分数】〘数学〙an improper fraction.

かべ【壁】a wall. ¶ ネズミが～に穴をあけた A mouse gnawed a hole in the *wall*. 会合は賃金問題で～に突き当たった The meeting *deadlocked* (≒ *reached a deadlock*) over the wage issue. ～に耳あり (諺) *Walls have ears*.

かへい【貨幣】money; (硬貨)〔a〕coin; (通貨) currency. ¶ ～を自動販売機に入れる drop *a coin* to a slot. ～を発行する issue *coins*. ～を鋳造する mint *coins*.

—価値 the value of money (≒ currency).
—制度 the monetary (≒ currency) system.
—単位 a monetary unit. 流通**—** coinage in circulation.

がべい【画餅】¶ 計画は～に帰した The plan *fell* (≒ *was dashed*) *to the ground*.

かべかけ【壁掛け】〔a〕tapestry.

かべがみ【壁紙】wallpaper. ¶ ～を壁にはる put *wallpaper* on the wall.

かべしんぶん【壁新聞】a wall newspaper.

かへん【可変】**—**資本 variable capital.

かべん【花弁】a petal.

がペン【鵞ペン】a quill〔pen〕.

かほう【加法】〘数学〙addition.

かほう【果報】a good fortune. ¶ ～は寝て待て (諺) *Everything comes to those who wait*.
—者 a lucky (≒ fortunate) person.

かほう【家宝】a family treasure; (先祖伝来の) an heirloom.

がほう【画法】〔a〕drawing technique.

がほう【画報】a pictorial; a graphic (≒ an illustrated) magazine.

かぼそ·い【か細い】¶ ～い神経質な少年 a *slender* nervous boy.

カボチャ【南瓜】a pumpkin; a squash.

かま【釜】an iron pot; (湯沸かし) a kettle.

かま【窯】an oven; a furnace.

かま【鎌】a sickle; (大がま) a scythe. ¶ 彼に～をかけた(誘導尋問をした) I *asked* him *leading questions*.

がま【蝦蟇】a toad.

かま·う【構う】**1**〖気にかける〗¶ 世間がどう言おうがいっこうに～わない I do not *mind* whatever the world may say.

彼は部屋が汚れていようがまったく～わない He does not *care* a bit even if his room is dirty.
彼女にはとても自分のことなど～っている暇はない She has no time to *look after herself* (≒ to *care about herself*). / (身のまわりを) She is too busy to *keep herself neat and tidy*.
彼女は着る物に～いすぎる She *is* too *particular about* what to wear. / She *cares* too much *about* dress.
彼は身なりなど～わない He *is careless about* dress.
あなたが死のうが生きようが私はいっこうに～わないんだ It doesn't *matter* to me at all (≒ It doesn't *make* any *difference* to me) whether you live or die.
かってにいただきますがいいでしょうか. ええ, 私にお～いなく May I help myself? Yes, that's all right with me (≒ Please go ahead).
小切手でも～いませんか. ええ, ～いませんとも Will a check do? Yes, it will certainly *do*.
たばこを吸っても～いませんか. はい, どうぞ Do you *mind* my smoking? Certainly not.
彼女はなりふり～わず勉強に専念している She is devoting herself to study without *caring about* her personal appearance.
仕事が第一, 家庭のことなど～っていられない Work is my prime concern, I cannot *trouble myself about* household affairs.
2 〖干渉する〗 ¶ 彼ももう大人だ, あまり～いすぎるのもよくない He is a grown-up man now. It is no good to *meddle* in his affairs too much. 私に～わないで好きにさせてくれ *Keep away from* me, and let me do as I like.

かまえ 【構え】 (構造) structure; (外観) appearance; (様式) style. ¶ 彼の新築の家はなかなかりっぱな～の家だ His new-built house has *a* fine *appearance*.

かま・える 【構える】 ¶ 彼もついに一戸を～えた He *has set up* his own home at last. 彼は失敗してものんきに～えている He is not disappointed at his failure. のんびり～えろよ Take it easy.

かまきり 【蟷螂】 a mantis.

がまぐち 【蝦蟇口】 a purse; (札入れ) a wallet.

かまくび 【鎌首】 ¶ ヘビが～をもたげた A snake raised its *head*.

かま・ける ¶ つい仕事に～けてごぶさたばかりして申しわけありません I must apologize to you for not writing to you so long, because *I've been absorbed in* my duties.

かます 【叺】 a straw bag.

かます 【魳】 〖魚類〗 〔a〕 barracuda.

かまたき 【罐焚き】 a fireman; a stoker.

かまち 【框】 a doorframe; a window frame.

かまど 【竈】 a cooking stove; an oven.

かまぼこ 【蒲鉾】 boiled fish-paste. ¶ ～形の建物 a *semicircular* building.

かまもと 【窯元】 (人) a potter; (所) a pottery.

がまん 【我慢】 (忍耐) patience; endurance; (自制) self-control. ¶ 彼の無礼には～できない I cannot *endure* his rudeness. この寒さにはとても～できない I cannot *stand* this cold at all. 私は～できないくらい虐待された I was ill-treated beyond all *bearing*. この騒々しさには～できない I *have lost patience with* this noisiness. なんて～強い人だ What a *patient* man he is! ここが～のしどころだ This is where our *patience* is required. とりあえずは手持ちのペンで～しよう I will *make the best of* the pen I have.

かみ 【上】 ¶ 滝はこの川の3マイル～にある The fall is three miles *above* this river.

かみ 【神】 a god; (キリスト教の) God. ¶ ～の恵み *divine* grace; the grace of *God*. ～かけて, そんなことはしなかった *By God*, I never did it. 私は～を信ずる I believe in *God*. 彼がどこにいるかは～のみぞ知る *God* (≒ *Heaven*) knows where he is.

かみ 【紙】 paper. ¶ ～3枚 three sheets of *paper* (まとまった紙形でなければ three pieces と言う). ～に書く write (*something*) on *paper*. ～で包む wrap (*something*) in *paper*.
—包み a paper parcel. **—**表紙 a paper cover. **—**袋 a paper bag.

かみ 【髪】 hair; (1本) a hair (頭髪全体は hair だが, 顔にかかった髪やみだれた数本の髪は hairs となる).
¶ 彼女は～をほどいた She let down her *hair*. 彼女は～を結っていた She was doing her *hair*. ～をとかす comb *one's hair*. ～を洗う shampoo *one's hair*. 彼は～をまん中(左側)で分けている He parts his *hair* in the middle (on the left hand side). 彼女は黒い～をしている She has dark *hair*. 彼は～をかきむしって泣いた He tore his *hair* and cried. 彼女は～を短く(長く)している She wears her *hair* short (long). 私はあの理髪店で～を刈った I had my *hair* cut at the barber's. 彼の～は最近めっきり白くなった Recently his *hair* has turned noticeably gray (≒ white).
—の毛 ¶ ～の毛を1本抜いた I plucked out *a hair*. ～の毛が抜ける I am losing my *hair*. 彼女はずいぶん～の毛が多い She has very heavy *hair*.

かみあ・う 【嚙み合う】 ¶ 歯車が互いにうまく～っている The teeth *gear into* each other.

かみいれ 【紙入れ】 a wallet; a pocketbook.

かみがかり 【神懸かり】 ¶ 彼女は～だ She is *a fanatic*.

かみかぜ 【神風】 a divine wind. ¶ ～タクシー a reckless *Kamikaze* taxi. ～特攻隊員 a *Kamikaze* pilot.

がみがみ ¶ 彼女はいつも彼に～言う She always *snaps at* him.

かみき 【上期】 the first half-year; the first half of the year.

かみきりむし 【髪切り虫】 〖虫類〗 a longicorn.

かみき・る 【嚙み切る】 ¶ 糸を～る *bite* a thread *in two*.

かみきれ 【紙切れ】 ¶ 1枚の～ a piece (≒ scrap) of paper.

かみくず 【紙屑】 wastepaper. ¶ そんなものは～同然だ Such a thing is *a mere scrap of paper* (≒ *as good as wastepaper*).

—かご a wastebasket; 英 a wastepaper basket.

かみくだ·く【噛み砕く】 ¶ 犬はその骨をこなごなに～いた The dog *crushed* (≒ *munched*) the bone to pieces with its teeth. 事の真相を彼に～いて話して聞かせた I explained the truth to him *in simple language*.

かみころ·す【噛み殺す】 ¶ 野犬が幼児を～した A stray dog *bit* an infant *to death*. あくびを～す *stifle* (≒ *suppress*) a yawn.

かみざ【上座】 ¶ ～に座る take *the head of the table*.

かみざいく【紙細工】 ¶ ～の人形 a *paper* doll.

かみしばい【紙芝居】 a picture-story show.

かみし·める【噛み締める】 ¶ よく～めなさい *Chew* it *strongly*. 心の底から自由の喜びを～めた We *tasted* the joy of freedom from 〔the bottom of〕 our heart.

かみそり【剃刀】 a razor. ¶～の刃 a razor's edge. ～をとぐ sharpen *a razor*. ～を当てる *shave one*self. 彼は～のように鋭い He is a man 〔as〕 sharp as *a razor*.

安全**—** a safety razor. 電気**—** an electric shaver.

かみだのみ【神頼み】 ¶ 苦しいときの～ Man turns to God only in his trouble. / (諺) *Danger past, God forgotten*.

かみつ【過密】 ¶ 人口～な都市 an *overpopulated* city. その市の人口～な地域 a *crowded* district of the city.

かみつ·く【噛み付く】 ¶ 犬は私の右手に～いた The dog *bit* me in the right hand. 突然彼は私に～いてきた(食ってかかった) Suddenly he *flew in my face*.

かみて【上手】 (川の) the upper course; (舞台の) the right of the stage (客席から見て, 舞台の右の方).

¶ 突然～から悪漢が現われた Suddenly a rascal appeared on *the right of the stage*.

かみなり【雷】 thunder (雷の音を言うときはふつう thunders となる). ¶ ～の音 a peal of *thunder*. ～が鳴っている It *is thundering*. / The *thunder* is rolling. 彼の家に～が落ちた His house was struck by *lightning*. 彼は～に打たれて死んだ He was struck dead by *lightning*.

かみはんき【上半期】 the first half-year; the first half of the year.

かみひとえ【紙一重】 ¶ その差は～だ There is only *a very slight difference* between the two.

かみまき〔たばこ〕【紙巻き〔たばこ〕】 a cigaret〔te〕.

かみやすり【紙鑢】 sandpaper.

かみよ【神代】 ¶ ～の昔から from *the age of gods* downward.

かみわ·ける【噛み分ける】 ¶ 彼は酸いも甘いも～けた人だ He *knows the sweets and bitters of life*.

かみわざ【神業】 the work of God; (奇跡) a miracle. ¶ これぞまさしく～だ This is *a miracle* itself.

か·む【噛む·咬む】 ¶ 子どもが野良犬に～まれた A child *was bitten* by a stray dog. つめを～むな Don't *bite* (≒ *gnaw*) your nails. 食事はよく～みなさい *Chew* your food well. 彼に～んで含めるように教えた I taught him *painstakingly*.

か·む【擤む】 ¶ 鼻を～む *blow one's* nose.

ガム chewing gum.

がむしゃら ¶ ～な男 a *reckless* fellow. 彼は～にその計画を実行に移した He put the plan into practice *recklessly*.

カムバック (口語) comeback. ¶ 彼女はテレビ女優としてみごとに～した She made *a* splendid *comeback* as a TV actress.

カムフラージュ camouflage. ¶ ～する camouflage; deceive; disguise.

かめ【瓶】 a jar; a jug.

かめ【亀】 a tortoise; a turtle. ¶ ～の甲 a tortoise shell. ～の甲より年の功 Sense comes with age. / Wisdom grows with age.

かめい【下命】 ¶ ぜひ当店にご～ください We hope to be favored with your *orders* (≒ *contract*).

かめい【加盟】 joining; affiliation; participation. ¶ 日本は1956年に国連に～した Japan *became a member of* the United Nations in 1956.

—者 a member; a participant.

かめい【仮名】 an assumed name; a nom de plume (フランス語から). ¶ ～で under an assumed name. 彼はジョンソンという～で通っていた He went by *the alias* of Johnson.

かめい【家名】 ¶ その事件で彼の～は上がった The incident raised *the reputation of his family*. 彼の行為は～を汚した His conduct brought disgrace on his *family name*.

カメオ a cameo.

がめつ·い ¶ 彼は～い男だ He *is avarice* itself. / He is an incarnation of *avarice*. 彼は金銭については～い He *is grasping* as regards money. / He *is* extremely *tightfisted* with money.

カメラ a camera. ¶ …に～を向けてパチリとやる snap the *camera* at…. 満開の桜を～に収める *take a photograph of* blooming cherry blossoms.

—アイ a camera eye. **—アングル** a camera angle. **—マン** a cameraman.

カメレオン 〘動物〙 a chameleon.

かめん【仮面】 ¶ ～をかぶる put on *a mask*. ～を脱ぐ drop (≒ put off; pull off; throw off) *a mask*. 悪人の～をはぐ *unmask* a villain.

がめん【画面】 (テレビ·映画の) a screen; a picture.

かも【鴨】 〘鳥類〙 a 〔wild〕 duck. ¶ いい～になる become *an easy victim of*; fall *an easy victim to* (*a person's* trick).

かもい【鴨居】 a door-head; a lintel.

かもく【科目·課目】 a course; a subject.

教養**—** (大学の) academic liberal arts subjects. 試験**—** an examination subject. 選択**—** an optional subject; 米 an elective 〔subject〕. 必修**—** a required subject.

かもじ【か文字·髢】 a false (≒ an artificial) lock of hair; a hair piece; a wig.

か

か

かもしか【羚羊】〖動物〗an antelope.

-かもしれない ¶そのうわさはほんとう〜 The rumor *may* be true. 彼は未婚〜 *Maybe* he is unmarried. ひょっとすると雨が降る〜 It *might* rain. そこには行かなかったほうがよかった〜 It *might* have been better for me not to visit the place.

かも・す【醸す】¶彼のその発言は物議を〜した His speech *caused* (≒ *gave rise to*) trouble. その音楽は楽しいふんい気を〜し出した The music *created* (≒ *produced*) a comfortable atmosphere.

かもつ【貨物】goods.
—自動車 a truck; 英 an autotruck; 英 a motor-lorry. —船 a freighter. —輸送 freight traffic. —列車 米 a freight train; 英 a goods train.

かもめ【鴎】〖鳥類〗a sea gull; a sea mew.

かや【榧】〖植物〗a torreya nuafera; a [nut-bearing] torreya.

かや【蚊帳】a mosquito net. ¶〜をつる put (≒ hang) up *a mosquito net*. 〜をはずす take down *a mosquito net*.

がやがや noisily; clamorously. ¶〜騒ぐな Don't make *a noise*.

かやく【火薬】[gun] powder.
—庫 a [powder] magazine. —製造所 a powder mill. 合成— compound powder. 黒色— black gunpowder. 綿— guncotton.

カヤック a kayak.
シングル— a single kayak. ペア— a pair kayak.

かやぶき【茅葺き・萱葺き】—屋根 a thatched roof.

かやり【蚊遣り】¶〜をたいて蚊を追い払う *smoke* (≒ *smudge*) mosquitoes *away*.
—火 a smudge.

かゆ【粥】rice porridge; rice gruel.

かゆ・い【痒い】¶〜い所をかく scratch where *one itches*; scratch an *itchy* spot. ああ〜い Oh, how it *itches*! 彼はぼくの〜い所に手が届くように親切だ He is very considerate to me. 彼に悪口を言われても痛くも〜くもない I *am* quite *indifferent* (≒*am callous*) *to* his abuse.

かよい【通い】¶〜のお手伝いさん a *living-out* maid. ヨーロッパ・南米〜の船 ships *plying* between Europe and South America.

かよ・う【通う】**1**〖往復する〗¶その村には1日に1本しかバスが〜っていない The bus *goes to and from* the village only once a day.
東海道新幹線は東京・博多間を〜うようになった The new Tokaido Line now *runs* between Tokyo and Hakata.
2〖通勤・通学する〗¶彼は歩いて学校へ〜っている He *walks to* school. (go on foot とは言わない).
彼は自家用車で会社に〜っている He *goes to* his office in his [own] car. (*one's* own car という言い方はアメリカ人はあまりしない).
ここから学校に〜うのに1時間かかる It takes an hour to *go* from here *to* the school.
彼は子どもたちを大学に〜わせるため借金までした He went so far as to borrow money in order to *send* his children to college.
彼は東京の大学に〜っている He *attends* a university in Tokyo.
3〖流通する・巡る〗¶母の気持ちがやっと息子に〜った The mother's mind *communicated with* her son's at last.
この絵には描いた人の心が〜っている This picture *communicates* the mind of the painter.
心の〜い合っている者どうし仲よくしよう Let's be good friends who are always open with one another.
4〖しばしば行く〗¶図書館に〜ってその作家について調べた He *paid* frequent *visits to* the library to study about a certain writer.
病院へまだ1か月も〜わなければならない I will still have to *go to* the hospital for as long as a month.

かようきょく【歌謡曲】a popular song.
—歌手 a popular singer.

がようし【画用紙】drawing paper.

かようせい【可溶性】solubility.

かようび【火曜日】Tuesday.

がよく【我欲】self-interest; selfishness.
¶彼は〜の強い男だ He is a very *selfish* man.

かよわ・い【か弱い】¶彼女は〜い寡婦の身で3人の子どもを育てた Though a *weak* widow, she has brought up three children entirely by her own hands.

から【空】¶〜の箱 an *empty* box. 頭が〜の人間 an *empty-headed* person. 財布を〜にした I *emptied* my wallet *to its last penny*. 財布が〜だった The wallet contained nothing. / I found the purse *empty*.

から【殻】a husk; a hull; (貝・果物・ピーナッツ) a shell; (卵) an eggshell; (豆腐の) bean-curd refuse. ¶自分の〜に閉じこもる withdraw into *oneself*.

-から **1**〖場所〗¶雨が急に降りだしたので駅〜うちまで走って帰った It began to rain suddenly, I ran *from* the station to my house.
太陽は東〜昇る The sun rises *in* the east.
海〜吹いてくる風が涼しい The wind *from* the sea is cool.
列車の窓〜顔を出すな Don't stick your head *out of* the train window. (face とは言わない).
彼は新潟〜東京へ働きに来ている He comes *from* Niigata to Tokyo to work.
カーテンを開けると窓〜部屋に日がさし込んできた When I drew the curtain aside, the sun streamed into the room *through* the window.
ふろ〜あがったら暖かくしていなさい Keep yourself warm after taking a bath.
30ページの5行目〜読みなさい Read *from* the fifth line on page thirty.
戸だな〜ウイスキーを出して飲みはじめた He took the whisky *out of* the cupboard and began to drink it.
彼は私の頭のてっぺん〜足のつま先までじろじろ見た He stared at me *from* head to foot.

2 〖時〗 ¶ 学校は8時半～始まる School begins *at* half past eight.
新学期は4月～始まる The new term begins *in* April.
きのう～なにも食べていない I have eaten nothing *since* yesterday.
思いたったが吉日, きょう～日記をつけよう There is no time like the present; I will begin to keep my diary *from* today *on*.
きのうは午前10時～午後5時まで仕事で外出した Yesterday I was out on business *from* ten in the morning to (≒ 米 through) five in the afternoon.
結婚して～もう5年になる It is five years (≒Five years have passed) *since* we got married. (米口語では It has been five years とも言う).
私は子どものころ～ミカンが大好きだった I have been very fond of tangerines *ever since* I was a child.
今～出かけても汽車にもう間にあわない Now it is too late to catch the train.
家族全員が帰宅して～夕食にしよう Let us have supper *after* all the family have returned home.
昼～首相の演説が始まる The prime minister's speech will begin *at* noon.
今度～は絶対遅刻しないように You must never come late *again*.
日本の大学を出て～アメリカの大学で2年ほど勉強した *After* graduating from a university in Japan, I studied in a university in America for two years or so.
3 〖原料・材料〗 ¶ 毛糸は羊の毛～できる Woolen yarn is made *from* wool.
日本の酒は米～つくる Japanese *sake* is made *from* rice.
4 〖原因・理由・出所〗 ¶ 親切心～したことがかえって裏目に出た What I did *in* (≒ *out of*) kindness brought about untoward results.
痛い～そっと包帯を巻いてくれ It hurts, *so* please be careful how you dress it.
たばこの火の不始末～火事を起こすことが多い Fires often break out *owing to* (≒ *in consequence of*) the careless handling of tobacco.
彼のちょっとしたいたずら～友だちに大けがをさせてしまった His friend was seriously injured *on account of* his petty mischief.
天気がいい～ピクニックに出かけよう It's a nice day, *so* let's go on a picnic.
危ない～火のそばに近寄ってはいけない Don't come near the fire, *as* it is dangerous.
だれ～こんな大金を借りたのだ Who on earth have you borrowed all this money *from*?
この文章は「ハムレット」～とってある This sentence is taken (≒ is quoted) *from* "Hamlet."
事業の元手は父親～出ている The enterprise is financed by my father. / The capital in the enterprise is invested by my father.
5 〖根拠〗 ¶ 彼の顔つき～判断すれば試験に受からなかったらしい Judging *from* his look, he seems not to have passed the examination.
わが家の経済状態～いって, そんな高価なものはとても買えない Judging *from* the economic condition of our family, we cannot possibly afford to buy such an expensive thing.
私の立場～するときみの考えには賛成しかねる *From* my standpoint I cannot agree to your opinion.
歩き方～みて, すぐ彼だとわかった I knew him *by* his walk at once.
若さ～そんな乱暴なことばが出たのだろう He used such violent language probably *because* he is young.
6 〖順序・その他〗 ¶ きょうはだれ～始めようか *With* whom shall I begin today?
1～100まで数えなさい Count *from* one to a hundred. (one hundred とすればいっそう意味が強くなる).
敵～身を守る術を覚えておきなさい You must learn the art of defending yourself *against* an enemy.
きみ, 田中さん～電話ですよ Mr. Tanaka wants you on the phone. / Mr. Tanaka is on the phone.

がら【柄】**1** 〖模様〗 a pattern. ¶ この～は私の好みに合わない This *pattern* (≒ *design*) is not to my taste.
彼はよく～もののワイシャツを着ている He is often seen wearing a *patterned* shirt.
2 〖体格・資格〗 ¶ あの子どもは～が大きい(小さい) That child *is of a* large (small) *build*.
この仕事は私の～に合わない This job is not in my *line*.
彼はスポーツマンといえる～ではない He *has* no *claim* to be called a sportsman.
私は人を指導する～ではない It is not for me to lead people.

カラー (襟) a collar.

カラー (色) color.
—写真 color photography. —テレビ color television (受像機の意味なら a をつける). —フィルム color film. スクール— school color. ローカル— local color.

がらあき【がら明き】 ¶ バスは～だった We had the bus almost to ourselves.

から・い【辛い】 (塩辛い) salty; (ひりひりと) hot. ¶ 彼は点が～い He *is severe* (≒ *is strict*) *in* marking.

からいばり【空威張り】 bluff; bluster. ¶ 彼はよく～する He often *bluffs*.

からか・う ¶ 子どもを～う *play a joke on* a child. 犬を～う *amuse oneself with* a dog.

からかみ【唐紙】 (紙) bamboo paper; (ふすま) a sliding screen; a sliding door; a *fusuma*.

からから【乾乾】 ¶ のどが～だ I *am parched* with thirst. 道路は日照りで～だった The road *was parched* up by the sun.

がらがら ¶ ～の電車 an *empty* train. 映画館は～に空いていた The movie theater *was quite empty*. 荷車が～と通る A cart *rattles* along the road. あの堂々たる建物すら～と崩壊した Even that imposing building *crumbled down* to dust (≒ pieces).

か

からくさもよう【唐草模様】an arabesque design (≒ pattern).
からくじ【空籤】a blank. ¶ ～を引く draw *a blank*.
がらくた rubbish; trash.
—市 a rummage sale. —道具 worn-out furniture.
からくち【辛口】¶ ～の酒 *dry sake*.
からくも【辛くも】¶ ～失明を免れた I *came very near* losing my sight. / I *barely* managed to keep my sight.
からくり【絡繰り】mechanism; a trick.
¶ それにはなにか～があるはずだ There must be some *trick* in that.
から·げる【絡げる】bind up; tuck up.
からげんき【空元気】a show of courage; mere bravado; sham courage.
からさわぎ【空騒ぎ】¶ つまらぬことに～するな Don't *make* much *fuss about* trifles. / Don't *fuss about* trifles.
からし【芥子】mustard. ¶ ～の種 *mustard* seed. ～はぴりっとする *Mustard* stings.
—菜 a mustard〔plant〕.
からす【烏】a crow; a raven.
から·す【枯らす】(草木を) kill; wither; blight; blast; (木材を) season.
から·す【涸らす】¶ 泉を～す *dry up* a fountain.
から·す【嗄らす】¶ 声を～す get husky (≒ hoarse). 声を～してしゃべる talk *oneself* hoarse. 彼女は帽子を振って声を～して叫んだ She *shouted herself hoarse* while waving her hat.
ガラス【硝子】glass.
—器 glassware. —工場 a glass industry. —細工 glass work. —戸 a glazed door. —びん a glass bottle. —窓 a glass window; a window pane. —屋 a glazier.
からすがい【烏貝】〘貝類〙a fresh-water mussel.
からすぐち【烏口】a drawing pen.
ガラスばり【ガラス張り】¶ わが国の政治は～の中で行なわれていない The state affairs of our country are not administered *before the public*. 帳簿は～だ(ごまかしはない) We have never cooked up the books.
からすむぎ【燕麦】〘植物〙oats.
からぜき【空咳】¶ ～をする make *a dry cough*.
からせじ【空世辞】¶ ～を言う pay *empty compliments* (*to a person*); pay *lip service* (*to a person*).
からだ【体】**1**〘肉体·体格〙a body. ¶ 彼はいい～をしている He *is well-built* (≒ *is of strong build*). / He has *a* strong *build*.
彼女はきゃしゃな～をしている She *is of* slender *build* (≒ *frame*).
最近太ってきて洋服が～に合わなくなった Recently I have put on so much weight that my clothes don't fit me any more.
子どもの～はすぐ服に合わなくなる Children soon outgrow their clothes.
彼は年をとるとともに～つきが父親に似てきた As he has grown older, he has come to resemble his father in *build*.
彼は～を張って私の子どもを救ってくれた He risked his own *life* to rescue my son from danger.
彼は～だけ大人だが, 考えはまだ子どもだ Although he has the *body* of an adult, he still is very childish in his thinking.
じんましんで～じゅうにぶつぶつがいっぱいできた I got little spots all over my *body* because I had hives.
夕立で～じゅうびしょぬれになった I was caught in a shower and got drenched *to the skin*.
～がふたつあっても足りないほど忙しい I'm so busy that even if there were two of me, I couldn't get everything done.
あまり～を使わないでいると～がなまってしまう If you don't use your *body*, it gets completely out of shape.
きょうの午後は～があいている I am free this afternoon. / I have nothing to do this afternoon.
2〘健康〙health. ¶ 運動不足は～に悪い Lack of exercise is bad for the *health*.
適度の運動は～によい Moderate exercise is good for the *health*.
最近～の調子がよくない Lately I haven't been feeling well.
彼は順調に～が回復してきている(医者が言う) His condition is improving satisfactorily. / He is getting better and better all the time.
毎晩夜更かしばかりしていると～をこわすよ You will ruin your *health* if you continue to sit up late every night.
1日も早くじょうぶな～になりたい I want to get better as soon as possible.
こんなに忙しくては～が続かない I don't think I can stand the strain of this hectic life.
どうぞお～をたいせつに(病人に) Please take care of yourself.
からたち【枳殻】〘植物〙a trifoliate orange.
からっかぜ【空っ風】a dry wind.
カラット ¶ 18～の金 18-*carat* gold.
からっぽ【空っぽ】¶ その箱は～だ The box *contains nothing*. / The box *is empty*. 彼の頭の中は～だ He is an *empty-headed* person.
からつゆ【空梅雨】a dry rainy season.
からてがた【空手形】a fictitious bill.
¶ ～を出す fly *a kite*. 彼の約束はいつも～で実行されたことがない His promise always proves to be *an empty one*.
からとう【辛党】a drinker; a tippler.
からに【空荷】¶ ～で行く *go* unloaded. リバプール港から～で出港した商船 a merchant ship bound *in ballast* from Liverpool.
からぶり【空振り】a miss; an empty swing.
¶ ～する swing wide; miss the ball; fan the air.
からまつ【落葉松】〘植物〙a larch〔tree〕.
からま·る【絡まる】¶ ツタの～った松の木 a pine tree *entwined* with ivy. その問題は複雑な事情が～っている Complex circumstances *are involved* in this problem.
からまわり【空回り】¶ ぬかるみで自動車のタイヤが～した The car *slipped* on the muddy road.

彼の努力も～に終わった All his efforts *were wasted*.

-がらみ 【-搦み】 ¶ 50～の年格好の男 a man *around* (≒ *about*) fifty.

からみあ·う【絡み合う】¶ その問題は多くの他の問題と～っている The question *is entangled* with many others. 2本のひもが～ってどうしてもほどけない The two strings *are entangled*, and won't come loose.

からみつ·く【絡み付く】¶ 朝顔がかきねに～いている A morning glory *entwines* the hedge.

から·む 【絡む】 ¶ つるが大木に～む A creeper *entwines* a big tree. 彼は酔うと人に～む When he gets drunk he always *picks a quarrel* with others. きみはいやに～んだものの言い方をするね You *are insinuating*, aren't you?

からめて【搦め手】(城の) the postern; the rear. ¶ ～から城を攻める attack a castle *from behind*; (比喩的に) approach *a person by the backdoor*.

からりと ¶ ～晴れた空 a *cloudless* sky. ～晴れ上がっている It *is clear as crystal*.

がらりと ¶ 戸を～開ける *throw open* the door. 彼は～態度を変えた He *suddenly* changed his attitude.

か·られる【駆られる】¶ 自責の念に～られる *be seized with* remorse. 好奇心に～られて *out of* curiosity. しっとに～られて *driven by* jealousy.

がらんと ¶ ～した広間 an *empty* hall. その屋敷は～していてだれもいなかった The house *was empty* and nobody was there.

かり【仮】¶ ここは～の事務所だ This is a *temporary* office.

—採用 ¶ 彼は～採用になった He was hired *on trial*.

かり【狩り】hunting. ¶ ～に行く hunt; go *hunting*.

ウサギ— ¶ ウサギ～に行く go hare *hunting*. ホタル— firefly hunting. 紅葉— maple viewing. キノコ— mushroom gathering.

かり【借り】a debt; a loan; (買い物での) a bill. ¶ 彼に1,000円の～がある I *owe* him a thousand yen. ～を払う clear off *a debt*; pay *one's debts*. 彼には古い～がある I *owe* him *a debt* of long standing. 彼にはいろいろ世話になって～がある I *owe* him *a* real *debt* of gratitude for his kindness.

かり 【雁】 a wild goose (複 wild geese).

カリ【加里】〘化学〙kalium.

かりあ·げる【刈り上げる】¶ 頭を～げる *trim one's* hair *up*; *cut one's* hair *short*.

かりあつ·める【駆り集める】¶ 学生たちを～めてチームの応援に行った We *rounded up* a gang of students and went to cheer for our team.

かりいれ【刈り入れ】a harvest; gathering.

—時 harvest time.

かりいれきん【借入金】a loan. ¶ 銀行からの～ *a loan* from a bank.

かりい·れる【刈り入れる】¶ 作物を～れる *harvest* a crop. 大麦を～れる *reap* a field of barley.

カリウム〘化学〙kalium; potassium.

ガリウム〘化学〙gallium.

カリエス caries.

脊椎(せきつい)— tuberculosis of the spine.

かりかし【借り貸し】¶ これでお互い～なしだ Let's call it quits, shall we?

かりかた 【借り方·借方】〘商業〙the debtor (Dr. と略す). ¶ ～と貸し方 *debtor* and creditor.

—勘定 debtor account.

カリカチュア caricature.

かりかり ¶ ～としたビスケット *crisp* biscuits. この菓子は食べると～する This cake *is crisp*.

がりがりもうじゃ【我利我利亡者】a grasping fellow; a selfish person. ¶ 彼はまったく～だ He is *avarice itself*.

かりぎ【借り着】borrowed clothes.

カリキュラム a curriculum.

かりき·る 【借り切る】 ¶ バスを～る *hire* (≒ *charter*) a bus. 旅館1軒を～る *reserve* a whole hotel.

かりこみ【狩り込み】a round-up. ¶ 不良のいっせい～をする *make a* sweeping *round-up* of a gang of street roughs.

かりこ·む 【刈り込む】 ¶ 頭の毛を短く～む *crop one's* hair *short*. 庭の芝生を～む *trim* the turf in the garden.

かりごや【仮小屋】a shack; a booth.

かりさしおさえ 【仮差し押さえ】 provisional seizure.

かりしゅっしょ【仮出所】provisional release.

かりしょぶん【仮処分】provisional disposition ¶ ～を申請する apply for *provisional disposition*.

かりずまい 【仮住まい】 a temporary residence. ¶ この家はほんの～です This is only my *temporary residence* (≒ *dwelling*).

かりそめ【仮初め】¶ ～にもそんなことを試みてはいけない You should not try it *for a moment*. ～にもそんなばかなことはするな *Never* do such a foolish thing *on any account*. 彼の恋は～の恋だった His was a *fleeting* love.

かりたお·す 【借り倒す】 fail to pay *one's* debt; bilk *a person*. ¶ 用心しなさい, 彼は～すかも知れないから Be careful; he *won't pay you back*. / Be careful; he might *cheat you out of your money*. / Be careful; you might *be bilked*.

かりだ·す【駆り出す】round up; chase. ¶ 昼休みに部屋の掃除に～された I *was urged to* sweep the room up during noon recess.

かりた·てる【駆り立てる】¶ 国民を戦争に～てる *spur* a nation to war.

かりちょういん 【仮調印】〘外交〙an initial signature.

かりちん【借り賃】(物) hire; (土地·家屋·ピアノなど) rent. ¶ この車の～は1日4,000円です The *rental* of this car is 4,000 yen a day.

かりて 【借り手】 a borrower; (家·土地) a tenant; a renter; a lessee.

か

か

かりとじ【仮綴じ】¶ ～の本 a *paper bound* book.

かりと·る【刈り取る】¶ 実った稲を～る *reap* (≒ *gather in*) ripened rice plants. 悪の芽を～る *nip* evil in the bud.

かりに【仮に】¶ ～気分がよくても働くのはまだ無理です *Even if* you feel better, you are not yet well enough to work. ～きみの言うことが正しいとしても，それは現実的でない *Granted that* your statement is correct, it is far from realistic. ～も法を犯すようなことはするな You must not *even for a moment* violate a law. ～この本を使おう I will use this book *for a time*.

かりぬい【仮縫い】a fitting. ¶ 背広の～をしてもらった I *had* a new suit *fitted* on me.

かりね【仮寝】a nap; a doze.

がりばん【ガリ版】a mimeograph. ¶ ～を切る(刷る) mimeograph.

カリフラワー〘植物〙a cauliflower.

かりもの【借り物】a borrowing. ¶ 彼の意見は～だ He *has borrowed* ideas. このモーニングは～だ I *borrowed* this morning coat.

かりゅう【下流】the lower part〔of a river〕. ¶ 淀川の～に on the *lower* Yodo River. ～へ流れる go *down* the river. 5キロ～に橋がある There is a bridge five kilometers *down* the river.

がりゅう【我流】¶ ピアノを～で弾きます I am a *self-taught* pianist. 彼は正規のレッスンも受けずに～でギターを弾いている He plays the guitar *in his own way* without taking regular lessons.

かりょう【加療】¶ 彼は入院～中だ He *is receiving medical treatment* in hospital.

かりょう【科料】〘法律〙a minor fine. ¶ 4,000円の～に処せられる *be fined* 4,000 yen.

がりょう【雅量】generosity. ¶ 彼は～がある He *is tolerant* (≒ *is broad-minded*). 彼は～がない He *is intolerant* (≒ *is narrow-minded*).

かりょく【火力】heat. ¶ コークスは～が強い Coke has strong *caloric force*.
　—発電 thermal (≒ steam) power generation. **—発電所** a steam-power plant.

か·りる【借りる】**1**〘借用する〙borrow. ¶ きのう彼にバス代を～りたがまだ返してない He paid the bus fare for me yesterday, but I haven't paid him back yet.
5万円足りない，彼に～りよう I need fifty thousand yen more. I'll *borrow* it *from* him.
この本を～りたいんですが(図書館で) May I *check* this book *out*, please?
先週図書館で～りた本をなくしてしまった I have lost the book I *borrowed from* the library last week.
電話をお～りできますか Can (≒ May) I *use* your phone?
おトイレをお～りできますか(個人宅で) Can (≒ May) I *use* your bathroom?
私は質屋に時計を持っていって5,000円～りた I *pawned* my watch for five thousand yen.
2〘賃借りする〙¶ 私は月2万円でこの部屋を～りている I *pay* twenty thousand yen *rent* for my room.
土地を～りて家を建てた I built a house on a *rented* plot.
家を～りるときはまわりの環境をよく調べてからにしなさい Before you *rent* a house, you should check up on the surroundings.
公園でボートを～りて乗った We enjoyed ourselves rowing a boat in the park.
3〘助けなど〙¶ 彼の助けは～りたくない I don't want to *lean on* him.
人の手を～りてまで実行したいとは思わない I don't want to ask anyone to help me do it.
この問題についてお知恵をお～りしたいのですが I'd like you to give me some advice about this problem.

か·る【刈る】(髪を) cut; clip; (羊毛を) shear (a sheep); (穀物を) reap; gather in; (草を) mow.
¶ 下葉を～る *trim off* the lower leaves.

か·る【駆る】¶ 車を～って野原を走った I *drove* across the field.

かる·い【軽い】¶ この荷物は私には～い This load *is light* for me. ～い食事をとった We had a *light* meal. ～い風邪をひいた I caught a *slight* cold. ～い頭痛のため学校を休んだ Because of a *slight* headache I absented myself from school. その子どもは～い日射病に襲われた The child suffered from *a touch of* the sun. 口の～い男だ What a gossipmonger he is! 彼はついていくだけだから責任が～い As he has only to follow the party, he has no responsibilities.

かるいし【軽石】a pumice stone.

かるがるし·い【軽軽しい】¶ ～い言動は慎め Be careful of your speech and behavior. ～く事を起こすな Don't *be rash in* starting anything. 彼の申し出を～く断るわけにいかぬ We can not refuse his offer *lightly*.

かるがる(と)【軽軽(と)】easily; lightly; without any difficulty.

かるく·する【軽くする】¶ 荷を～する *lighten* a burden (≒ load). 税を～する *reduce* taxes. 苦痛を～する *lull* (≒ *mitigate*; *mollify*; *relieve*) a pain. 刑を～する *reduce* a sentence (*to a person*).

かるくち【軽口】¶ ～をたたく crack *jokes* (*with a person*).

カルシウム〘化学〙calcium.

かるた【骨牌·歌留多】cards.

カルテット quartet.

カルデラ〘地質〙a caldera.

カルテル cartel.

かるはずみ【軽はずみ】¶ ～な行ない a *rash* act. ～なことをする act *hastily*.

かるわざ【軽業】acrobatic feats (≒ performance); acrobatics (職業または曲芸の意味ではふつう単数扱い).
　—師 an acrobat.

かれ【彼】he (彼の his; 彼に(を) him).

かれい【鰈】flat fish.

かれい【華麗】splendor; magnificence.

¶ ～な splendid ; magnificent ; gorgeous.
カレー curry.
—粉 curry powder. —ライス curry and rice.
ガレージ a garage.
かれえだ【枯れ枝】a dead branch.
かれき【枯れ木】a dead tree.
がれき【瓦礫】trash ; debris.
かれくさ【枯れ草】dry grass ; hay.
かれこれ【彼此】¶ 人のことを～言うな You must not talk about others. ～言わずに始めなさい Begin without *making a fuss* about it. ～するうちに時間が過ぎた We spent time *as we tried one thing and another.* / Time passed (≒ went by), *as we did this and that.* ～時間だ Time is *nearly* up. 彼は～60歳だ He *is hard upon* sixty.
かれつ【苛烈】¶ ～な戦い a hard-fought (≒ fierce) battle. 戦いはますます～になった The battle became *fiercer and fiercer.*
かれは【枯れ葉】a withered (≒ dead) leaf.
か·れる【枯れる】¶ 草は熱い太陽に照らされて～れた The grass *withered* in the hot sun. よく～れた木材 well *seasoned* wood.
か·れる【涸れる】¶ 井戸の水が～れた The well *ran dry.*
か·れる【嗄れる】¶ ～れた声 a *husky* voice. 声が～れてしまった My voice *grew* (≒ *became*) *hoarse.* 声が～れるまでしゃべった I *talked myself hoarse.*
かれん【可憐】¶ ～な乙女 a *pretty* (≒ *lovely*) girl.
カレンダー a calendar. ¶ ～をめくる tear a sheet of the *calendar.*
かろう【過労】overwork ; excessive work. ¶ 彼は～から倒れた He has broken down through *overwork.* 近ごろ～ぎみだ I am afraid I *have been overworking myself* of late. / I am afraid I *have been working too hard* of late.
がろう【画廊】an art (≒ a picture) gallery.
かろうじて【辛うじて】¶ 溺死(できし)するところを～助かった He *narrowly* (≒ *only just*) escaped drowning. ～終列車にまにあった We had *barely* enough time to catch the last train.
かろやか【軽やか】¶ ～な足どりで with *springy* (≒ *light*) steps.
カロリー a calorie. ¶ ～のある食事 food with high *calorific value.* この食事は1,000～ある This food has one thousand *calories.*
ガロン a gallon.
かろん·ずる【軽んずる】¶ 命を～ずる *make little of one's* life. 敵を～ずるな Don't *despise* your enemy.
かわ【川·河】a river ; a stream. ¶ 利根～を上る(下る) go up (down) the *River* Tone (≒ the Tone *River*) (川の名は必ず冠詞をつける). ～を渡る cross *a river.* 浅い所を歩いて～を渡る wade across *a stream.* ～の水が増えた The *river* has risen. ～の水が減った The *river* is low.
かわ【皮·革】(皮膚) the skin ; (皮革) a hide ; (くだものの) rind ; (樹皮) a bark. ¶ 背中の～がむけた The *skin* on my back has peeled. 桃の～をむく *peel* a peach (指で) ; カキの～をむく *pare* a persimmon (ナイフで). 彼はリンゴを～ごと食べる He eats an apple *skin and all.* (apple や persimmon のように薄い皮のものは skin で, orange のように厚い皮のものには rind 〔and all〕を用いる). 木の～をはぐ *flay* a tree. なんと面の～の厚い男だ What a *brazen-faced* fellow he is!
がわ【側】a side. ¶ 西(左)～に on the west (left) *side.* 反対～に on the opposite *side.* 両～に on either (≒ each) *side.* 大西洋の向こう～で on the other *side* of the Atlantic. 金～の時計 a gold watch. 学生～の考え the point of view on the *part* of students. 学生の～についた I *took sides* (≒ *took part*) *with* the students.
かわい·い【可愛い】¶ ～い子ネコ a *pretty* kitty. 赤ちゃんのあしはなんて～いんだ What *tiny* feet a baby has! ～い子には旅をさせよ (諺) *Spare the rod, and spoil the child.* だれでも自分の子どもは～いものだ Everybody *loves* his own children. / No other children *are sweeter* than *one's* own children. この子はまったく～げのない子だ This is a child with nothing *childlike* (≒ *sweet*) in him.
かわいが·る【可愛がる】¶ 彼女はあの犬を～っている She *takes good care* (≒ *takes loving care*) of that dog. / That is her *pet* dog. 彼は娘をとても～っている He *loves* his daughter dearly. / She is the apple of her father's eye.
かわいさ【可愛さ】¶ ～余って憎さ百倍(諺) Excessive *tenderness* switched to hundredfold hatred. / Who loves too much hates in like extreme.
かわいそう【可哀相】¶ 彼は～な男だ He is a *poor* creature. あの方があんな扱いをうけたなんて実に～だ Oh! What a *pity* 〔it was〕 that he should have been treated like that. それを見て～だと思わない者はいないだろう No one could look at it *without pity.*
かわいらし·い【可愛らしい】¶ ～い女の子 a *charming* girl. ～い手 a *tiny* hand. 子どものくせに～さがない He is a child with nothing *childlike* in him.
かわうお【川魚】a river fish.
かわうそ【獺】an otter.
かわか·す【乾かす】¶ 日光で洗たく物を～す *dry* the washing in the sun. ぬれたズボンを火で～す *dry* wet trousers over the fire.
かわかぜ【川風】a river breeze (≒ wind).
かわかみ【川上】the upper part of a river. ¶ 5キロ～に橋がある There is a bridge five kilometers *up the river.*
かわき【乾き】drying ; dryness. ¶ ナイロンのシャツは～が早い Nylon shirts *dry* well.
かわき【渇き】thirst. ¶ 泉の水でのどの～をいやす quench *one's thirst* at a fountain.
かわぎし【川岸】a riverside ; a river bank.
かわきり【皮切り】(初め) the beginning ; the start. ¶ 100メートル競走を～に運動会が始まった

The program of the athletic meeting *began with* a 100-meter dash.

かわぎり【川霧】a river fog (≒ mist).

かわ・く【乾く】¶ ～いた地面 *dry* ground. 冬の～いた風 a *dry* wind in winter. よい天気なので洗たく物がすぐ～く The washing *dries* well as it is fine.

か

かわ・く【渇く】¶ ひどくのどが～いている We *are parched* with a deadly thirst. 走ったのでのどが～いている We *are thirsty* with running.

かわぐち【川口】a river mouth ; an estuary.

かわざんよう【皮算用】¶ 取らぬたぬきの～ (諺) *Don't count your chickens before they are hatched.*

かわしも【川下】the lower part of a river. ¶ ～3マイルの所に滝がある There is a waterfall three miles *down the river*.

かわ・す【交わす】¶ あいさつを～す *exchange* greetings.「お休み」のあいさつを～したあとで after *an exchange* of good nights.

かわ・す【躱す】¶ 彼は危うく身を左に～して命びろいをした He barely saved himself by *dodging* to the left.

かわすじ【川筋】the course of a river.

かわせ【為替】exchange ; money order. ¶ ～で5,000円送った I sent five thousand yen by *money order*.
—相場 the exchange rate. —手形 a bill of exchange. 外国— foreign exchange. 郵便— a postal money order.

かわせみ【川蟬】〘動物〙a kingfisher.

かわぞい【川沿い】¶ ～の村 a village *along the river*. ～に歩く walk *along a river*.

かわぞこ【川底】a riverbed. ¶ ～に沈む sink to *the bottom of the river*.

かわった【変わった】¶ 彼の名前は～名前だ His name is an *uncommon* one. 彼には～ところがある He *is* a bit *of an eccentric*. ～ことを言う人だ What a *queer* thing he says! なにかもっと～本を見せてください Show me a *different* book.

かわって【代わって】¶ …に～ in place of ; in another's place ; instead of ; on behalf of ; in succession to. 私が彼に～出席した I attended *in his place*.

かわと【皮砥】a razor strop. ¶ ～でとぐ *strop* a razor.

かわどこ【川床】a riverbed.

かわはば【川幅】¶ ～は50メートルある The river is fifty meters *wide* (≒ *in width*).

かわひも【皮紐】a strap ; a 〔leather〕 thong.

かわびょうし【皮表紙】a leather cover. ¶ ～の本 a *leather-bound* book.

かわびらき【川開き】a river festival. ¶ 両国の～ the *river carnival* at Ryogoku.

かわぶくろ【皮袋】a leather-bag.

かわむこう【川向こう】the opposite side of a river. ¶ ～に *across* the river.

かわや【厠】a rest room ; a lavatory.

かわら【瓦】a tile. ¶ ～で屋根をふく roof (a house) with *tiles* ; *tile* a roof.
屋根— a roofing tile. 鬼— a tile with the figure of a devil. —ぶきの家 a house roofed with tiles.

かわり【代わり】**1**〚代用〛¶ 私の～にこの書類を彼に渡してください Hand this document to him *for* me.
木の葉がさらの～になった A leaf *served as* a plate.
子どもにとって母親の～になれる人はいない To a child nobody can *replace* his mother.
母の～に私が来た I have come *in place of* my mother.
秘書が辞めてしまった. ～の人が必要だ My secretary has now left me, so I need someone to *take her place*.
この料理は牛肉の～に豚肉を使ってもよろしい You can use pork *instead of* beef when you prepare this dish.
2〚代償〛¶ スカートを作ってもらう～に彼女にセーターを編んでやった I knitted a sweater for her *in exchange for* the skirt she made me.
この本を貸してやる～に別な本を貸してくれ If I lend this book to you, lend me another.
彼に数学の宿題をやってもらう～に英語の宿題をやってやった He did my mathematics homework for me, and I did his homework in English *in return*.
3〚食物の〛¶ シチューのお～をした I asked for *a second helping of* stew.
もう1杯お～はいかがですか How about *another helping*?
お～できますか May I have some more?
4〚けれども〛¶ 安い～にすぐいたみそうだ It is cheap, *but* it won't wear well.
彼は朝早く起きる～に寝るのも早い He gets up early in the morning *and so* he goes to bed early at night.
彼女は勉強はよくできる, その～運動はからっきしだめだ She is a good scholar, *but* a very poor athlete.

かわり【変わり】**1**〚変化〛a change. ¶ このふたつの部屋はまったく～はない There is no *difference* at all between these two rooms.
私の考えに～はありません I still have the same opinion as before.
この品とその品に～はありませんか Is there any *difference* between this article and that?
きのうは別に～はなかった Nothing *unusual* happened yesterday.
ここも大阪も品物に～はない The quality of the article is the same here as in Osaka.
どの道～はない It doesn't make much *difference*.
2〚健康などが〛¶ 彼の病状には～がない There is no *change* in the condition of his sickness.
お～ありませんか How are you getting on?
私は別に～ありません There is nothing the matter with me.

かわりあ・う【代わり合う】¶ ～って休憩をとった We had a rest *by turns*.

かわりだね【変わり種】(例外) an exception. ¶ 彼は政界の～だ He is *a peculiar figure* in political circles.

かわりばえ【代わり栄え】¶ いっこうに～がしない

It's none the better for it. 彼ではいっこう～がしない He is only *a poor substitute*.

かわりは·てる【変わり果てる】¶ その町のようすはまったく～てた The town *is quite changed*.

かわりめ【変わり目】 a change; a turning point. ¶ 陽気の～に左脚が痛む My left leg aches *with the change of* seasons.

かわりもの【変わり者】 a queer fellow; an eccentric [person].

かわ·る【代わる】¶ 水力が火力に～る Water power *replaces* heating power. 新しいものが古いものに～る The old *gives place to* the new. A先生がB先生と～った Mr. A *was succeeded by* Mr. B.

かわ·る【変わる·換わる】**1** 〖変化する〗¶ 風が北に～ったので急に寒くなった The wind *shifted to* the north and it suddenly became cold.

彼女は子どもに死なれて人が～ったように陰気になった After her child died she became so melancholy that she seemed to be quite another woman.

彼の気の～らないうちにその計画を決定した We decided on the plan before he would *change his mind*.

2 〖異なる·普通と違う〗¶ このいすの形は～っている This chair has *unusual* shape.

3 〖移る〗¶ 上記の所へ住所が～りました I *have moved to* the above address.

彼は東京の本社に～った He *was transferred to* the head office in Tokyo.

窓側の席に～りたい I would like to *move to* the window seat.

かわるがわる【代わる代わる】 by turns; in turn; alternately.

かん【寒】¶ ～の入り(明け) the beginning (end) of *the coldest part of winter*.

かん【感】 feeling; sensation. ¶ ～きわまって涙を流す be moved to tears. …の～がする impress *a person* as...; give *a person* an impression of....

かん【巻】 a volume; a book. ¶ 第1～ the first *volume*; vol. I; book I. 3～より成っている著作 a work in three *volumes*.

かん【勘】¶ ～が良い(悪い) be quick- (slow-) *witted*; have a quick (slow) *perception*; be sharp (dull). ～でやる depend on *intuition*.

かん【棺】 a coffin; (特に米) a casket.

かん【環】 a ring.

かん【簡】¶ 彼の説明は～にして要を得ている His explanation *is brief* and to the point.

かん【艦】 a warship; a man-of-war.

かん【癇】¶ ～の強い irritable; peevish; touchy; hot-tempered. その学生の長髪が彼の～にさわった He *was irritated by* the student's long hair.

かん【燗】¶ ～をする heat (≒ warm) *sake*. 酒の～がついた The *sake* is warm enough.

かん【罐·鑵】 a tin; 米 a can.

-かん【-間】¶ 10年～ *for* ten years. 過去10年～に *during* (≒ *for*; 特に米 *in*) the past ten years. 10分～の休憩 a ten minutes' recess. 友人～に *among a person's* friends.

がん【願】¶ ～をかける offer a prayer with a vow (*to* a god; *at* a shrine).

がん【癌】〔医学〕 cancer. ¶ ～ができる develop *a cancer*. それが政党政治の～だ It is *a cancer* to party politics.

がん【雁】 a wild goose (複 wild geese).

かんあん【勘案】¶ …という事実を～する *take into consideration* the fact that....

かんい【官位】 official rank.

かんい【簡易】 ―裁判所 a summary court; a police court. ―保険 postal life insurance.

かんいっぱつ【間一髪】¶ ～のところで死を逃れる escape death *by a hair's breadth*; have a *hair-breadth* escape from death.

かんえい【官営】 ―事業 a government enterprise.

がんえん【岩塩】 rock salt.

かんおけ【棺桶】 a coffin; 米 a casket. ¶ ～に片足を突っ込む have one foot in the grave; be near death.

かんか【感化】 influence. ¶ この子どもは彼に～された This child *was influenced by* him. テレビは子どもにはよい～のみならず悪い～も与える Television exerts *a* bad as well as *a* good *influence* upon children.

がんか【眼下】¶ ～に under *one's* eyes; just below *one's* eyes.

がんか【眼科】〔医学〕 ophthalmology. ―医 an ophthalmologist; an eye doctor.

がんか【眼窩】〔解剖学〕 an eye socket; an eyehole; an eyepit.

かんがい【干害】 a drought disaster. ―地 a drought-stricken area.

かんがい【感慨】¶ ～無量だった My heart was full [of deep emotion].

かんがい【灌漑】 watering; irrigation. ¶ 土地を～する *water* land.

がんかい【眼界】 the field of vision; sight; view. ¶ ～内に within *the field of vision*. ～に入る come in *sight*. ～を去る go out of *sight*.

かんがえ【考え】**1** 〖思考·思索〗[a] thought. ¶ きみの～を率直に述べなさい Frankly, what do you *think* about it? / Frankly, what's your *opinion*?

きみの～は保守的すぎる Your *ideas* are too conservative.

彼の～はかなり左翼的だ He has very leftist *thoughts*.

自分の～がまとまらないまま討論会に出た I joined the debate before my *ideas* had taken final shape.

私の～では彼は高血圧だ I *think* (≒ In my *opinion*,) he is suffering from hypertension.

彼の話を聞いたら私の～がぐらついてしまった What he said caused me to waver in my *conviction*.

最近の社会情勢についてあなたはどういうお～をお持ちですか What do you *think* of the present social conditions?

2 〖意向〗 an intention. ¶ 子どものころ大きくなっ

か

か

たら漫画家になる～を持っていた As a child I wanted to become a cartoonist when I grew up.

彼は日本美術を研究する～で日本に来た He came to Japan *to* study Japanese fine arts.

彼は私に会社を継がせる～だ He *wants* me to succeed him as president of his company.

3〖思いつき〗an idea. ¶ そいつはうまい～だ That's *a* good *idea*.

その金を慈善事業に寄付するとはよい～だ Contributing the money to charity is *a* good *idea*.

4〖期待・想像〗 ¶ 物事はそう～どおりには運ばないものだ Things don't always turn out as we *wish*.

計画は～どおりに進んでいる The plan is working as we *thought*.

5〖判断・分別〗¶ そんな～のないことをするな Don't *be* so *imprudent*.

彼も若いからどうも～が足りない He seems to lack *prudence* because he is still young.

きみの～はまだ甘い Your way of *thinking* is too optimistic.

彼は前後の～もなく家を飛び出した He ran away from home without stopping to *think*.

自分ひとりの～で決めないでだれかに相談してみなさい It's better to talk it over with someone than to try to decide all by yourself.

結果を～に入れてもう一度考えなおしなさい You must *think of* the consequences and think it over again.

かんがえこ・む【考え込む】¶ 何を～んでいるのだ What *are* you *thinking* so *deeply* (≒ *seriously*) *about*? 彼女は娘の話を聞いて～んでしまった She *fell into thought* when she heard her daughter's story.

かんがえつ・く【考えつく】¶ どうしたら彼を助け出せるか～かない I can't *think of* any way I can possibly help him.

かんがえなお・す【考え直す】¶ ～してみましょう I will *consider* it *once more*. ～してほしい I hope you'll *think better of* it.

かんがえよう【考えよう】¶ ものは～だ It all depends upon your way of *thinking*.

かんが・える【考える】**1**〖思考する〗think. ¶ この問題をきみはどう～えるか What do you *think of* this problem?

物事はもっと真剣に～えなければいけない You have to *take* things more seriously.

もっともっと～えるべきことはたくさんあるはずだ You ought to have many more important things to *think about*.

会社は社員の家庭の事情などあまり～えない Companies don't *give* much *thought to* the employees' situation at home.

彼は～えに～えたあげく旅行はやめることにした After *thinking* and *thinking* he finally decided to give up going on the trip.

しばらく～えさせてください Let me *think* it *over* for a few days.

その問題は～えれば～えるほどわからなくなった The more I *thought over* the problem, the more puzzling it became.

これからの社会をよく～えて自分の進むべき道を決めるべきだ You should *think over* what is going to happen in the world and try to decide what the best road is to take.

くだらないことを～えるな Don't bother your head over trivial things.

彼が言ったことについてよく～えてみた I *reflected upon* what he had said.

親はいつも子どものことを～えているものだ Parents *are* always *anxious about* their children.

万一のことを～えて，貯金をしておくほうがいい You should save money for a rainy day.

2〖想像する・予想する〗expect; imagine. ¶ ひとりでいると物事を悪い方にばかり～えてしまう When I am alone, I tend to *take* too pessimistic *a view of things*.

彼の絵が展覧会に入選したとは～えられない It *is* quite *unthinkable* that his picture should have been accepted by the exhibition.

彼があんなに喜んでくれるとは～えてもみなかった I little *thought* he would be so delighted.

私が～えていたより彼はずっと老けていた He was much older than I *had thought*.

とても～えられないことが彼女の身に起こった Something quite *unexpected* has happened to her.

みんなが～えていたほど事件は大きくならなかった The incident did not assume as serious proportions as *had been feared*.

試験は～えていたよりもやさしかった The examination was easier than I *had expected*.

3〖みなす・推定する〗regard. ¶ 彼は若いころは発明狂と～えられていた When he was young, he *was thought of* as an invention maniac.

ピカソは今世紀最大の画家だと～えられている Picasso *is regarded as* the greatest artist of this century.

4〖判断する〗judge. ¶ 彼女の態度から～えると彼女はそのことを前から承知していたようだ *Judging from* her attitude, she seems to have been aware of it for a long time.

私のやることは絶対に正しいと～える I *am positive* that what I do is absolutely right.

5〖…しようと思う〗¶ 私は学校の先生になろうと～えている I *am thinking of* becoming a schoolteacher.

この計画はどんなことがあろうと実行しようと～えている I *think* I will go ahead with this plan, no matter what happens.

6〖思い出す〗¶ 子ども時代のことをあれこれ～えていた I *was thinking about* my childhood.

死んだ母のことを～えていた I *was thinking of* my dead mother.

去年のヨーロッパ旅行のことを～えると楽しくなってくる *Thinking of* my European tour last year made me very happy.

かんかく【間隔】an interval; a space. ¶ 10メートルの～で at *intervals* of ten meters. 10分の～で at ten minutes' *intervals*. 一定の～を置いて at regular *intervals*. ～をあける leave *spaces*.

かんかく【感覚】sense; sensation; feeling. ¶ ～が鋭い(鈍い) have keen (dull) *senses.* 寒さで～がない be benumbed with (≒ by) cold. 脚の～がなくなった I have no *feeling* in the leg.

かんがく【官学】a government school.

かんがく【管楽】〘音楽〙the wind 〔music〕. —器 a wind instrument.

かんがく【漢学】Chinese literature (≒ learning; classics); Sinology.

かんかつ【管轄】control; jurisdiction. ¶ 文部省の～下にある be under *the jurisdiction* (≒ *control*) *of* the Education Ministry.
—官庁 the competent authorities.

かんが·みる【鑑みる】¶ …という事実に～みて *considering* the fact that....

カンガルー a kangaroo (複 kangaroos).

かんかん ¶ ～に怒る blaze with fury; be in a fume; 米 get mad with anger. 鐘が～鳴る The bells *clang.* ～日が照っている The sun *is blazing.*

かんがん【汗顔】¶ ～の至りである I am deeply ashamed of myself.

かんき【寒気】the cold. ¶ ～が緩んだ *The cold* has become a bit mild.

かんき【換気】ventilation. ¶ 部屋の～をする *air* (≒ *ventilate*) rooms. ～がよい(悪い) *be* well (badly) *ventilated.*
—口 a ventilator. —扇 a ventilation fan.

かんき【勘気】¶ 人の～を被る incur the *displeasure* of *a person*; fall into *disgrace* with *a person.*

かんき【喚起】¶ 世論を～する *rouse* (≒ *stir up*) public opinion. 世人の注意を～する *call* (≒ *arouse*) public attention (*to*).

かんき【歓喜】delight; great joy. ¶ 勝利に～する *rejoice over* a victory. ～して in great *delight.*

かんきつるい【柑橘類】citrus fruit; oranges.

かんきゃく【観客】(見物人) spectators; onlookers; the audience. ¶ そのだしものにはいつも～が多い The program always draws *a* large *audience.*

かんきゅう【感泣】¶ ～する be moved to tears.

かんきゅう【緩急】¶ いったん～あれば in case of *emergency.* ～よろしきを得る be discreet in dealing matters.

がんきゅう【眼球】〘解剖学〙an eyeball; the globe of an eye.

かんきょ【閑居】¶ 小人～して不善をなす (諺) *Idleness is the parent of all vice.*

かんきょう【環境】surroundings; circumstances (常に複数形); environment. ¶ ～に左右される be influenced by *one's surroundings.* ～に順応する adapt *one*self to *one's environment.*
—衛生 environment hygiene.

かんきょう【艦橋】the bridge (*of* a warship).

かんきょう【感興】interest. ¶ ～が湧く be inspired (*at*). ～をそそる(そぐ) excite (spoil) *interest.*

がんきょう【頑強】¶ ～な抵抗 a *stubborn* resistance. ～に否定する deny *persistently.*

かんきり【罐切り】a can (≒ 英 tin) opener.

かんきん【換金】¶ 証券を～する *realize one's* security.

かんきん【監禁】confinement; imprisonment; detention. ¶ ～する confine; imprison; detain; lock up.
不法— illegal detention.

がんきん【元金】the principal.

かんく【管区】the district under jurisdiction.

かんく【艱苦】hardships. ¶ ～をなめる go through *hardships.* ～に耐える endure *hardships.*

がんぐ【玩具】a toy; a plaything.
—店(商) a toy shop (dealer); 米 a toy store (dealer).

がんくつ【岩窟】a cave; a cavern.

がんくび【雁首】(きせるの) the bowl 〔of a pipe〕; (首) a head. ¶ ～をそろえる line up; gather.

かんぐ·る【勘繰る】guess at (the truth); conjecture; surmise; suspect.

かんぐん【官軍】the government troops (≒ forces); the loyal forces. ¶ 勝てば～ (諺) *Might is right.*

かんけい【関係】**1** 〘関連〙〔a〕relation. ¶ 両国間の～は非常に緊迫してきた *Relations* between the two nations have become extremely tense.
彼は漱石と英文学との～を研究している He is studying the *effect* of English literature on Soseki's work. / He is studying the *relationship* between English literature and Soseki.
中国と日本とは昔から～が深い China and Japan have long had deep *ties.*
政治は国民生活に深い～がある Politics *has* very *much to do with* the life of the nation.
スイカの出来と天気は～がある Weather *influences* the growth of watermelon.
あの人ときみとはどういうご～ですか In what way *are* you *connected with* him? / How did you come to know him?
私はあの男とはまったく～がない I *have nothing to do with* that man.
この文章は前後の～がはっきりしない There is no *connection* between the beginning and ending of this sentence.
あの会社と～をつけてくれる人はいないか Don't you happen to know someone who can *make contacts with* that firm for me?
彼らとは～なく，われわれだけでこの計画は実行する We intend to go ahead with the plan without them.
彼が今どこでなにをしていようと私にはまったく～がない Such things as where he is and what he is doing now *are no concern of mine* (≒ *are none of my business*).
—閣僚 the Cabinet ministers concerned.

か

—諸国 the countries concerned. —書類 all the documents related to (the matter). —者 the persons concerned. —代名詞〘文法〙a relative pronoun. —当局 the authorities concerned.

2 〚関与〛 ¶ その事件に～のあった者は彼だけだ He was the only man *involved in* the incident.

彼の問題にはもう～したくない I want to *stay out of* his problem.

その汚職事件にはある大臣が～していた A certain cabinet member *was involved in* the bribery case.

3 〚影響〛 ¶ だれが議長に選ばれても, 私にはあまり～がない It does not *matter* very much to me who is elected chairman.

気候の～でこの果物は日本ではできない This fruit cannot be produced in Japan *because of* the climate.

公共料金の値上げは国民生活に大いに～してくる A rise in public utility charges greatly *affects* the cost of living.

きみの無責任な発言が彼の死にまったく～がないとはいえない It cannot be said that your irresponsible remark *has nothing to do with* his death.

子どものころの育て方は性格に大いに～がある *One's* character is molded chiefly by his upbringing.

天気の～で頭痛がする I have a headache *because of* the weather.

4 〚男女の〛 ¶ 彼と彼女は清い～だ They are just friends.

私たちの～をもっと早く両親に話しておくべきだった I should have told my parents much earlier about our *relationship*.

あんな女なんかとは～をたて *Break off with* that girl.

かんけい【奸計】a trick. ¶ ～をめぐらす think out (≒ devise) *a nasty trick*.

かんげい【歓迎】welcome. ¶ みんなが彼を暖かく～した Everyone *received* him warmly. / Everyone *gave* him *a* warm *welcome*. 私が～のことばを述べた I gave an address of *welcome*. 女性ならだれでも～します Every woman will *be welcome*.

—会 a reception. ¶ メキシコ帰りの彼のために～会が催された They held *a reception* in honor of him who had just come back from Mexico.

かんげき【感激】inspiration; deep emotion. ¶ ～する be deeply moved (≒ be impressed; be inspired; be touched) (*by*; *with*). ～の涙を流す be moved to tears.

かんげき【観劇】theater going. ¶ ～に行く go to the theater.

かんげき【間隙】¶ ～を縫って進む creep along between (some obstacles); make *one's* way through.... 一瞬の～をうかがう watch for *an unguarded moment*.

かんげざい【緩下剤】a laxative; an aperient.

かんけつ【完結】conclusion; completion. ¶ ～する (終わる) be concluded; be completed; (終える) conclude; complete. 次号～ (雑誌の予告) To be concluded.

かんけつ【間欠】¶ ～的な intermittent. ～的に intermittently; by fits and starts.

—泉 a geyser. —熱 intermittent fever.

かんけつ【簡潔】¶ ～な concise; terse; brief. ～に答える answer *briefly*.

かんけん【官憲】officials; the authorities; (警察) the police.

かんげん【甘言】¶ ～に乗せられる be deceived with (≒ be taken in by) *honeyed words*. ～をもって誘い出す *coax* (*a person*) out. ～をもって物を奪う *coax* (*a thing*) out of (*a person*). ～をもって誘う *coax* (*a person*) *to* do (≒ *into* doing).

かんげん【換言】¶ ～すれば in other words.

かんげん【還元】〘化学〙reduction; (分解) resolution; (酸化物) deoxidization. ¶ ～する be reduced (*to*); resolve itself (*into*). その利益は社会に～されるべきだ The profit must *be returned to* the community.

—剤(作用) reducing agent (process).

かんげん【諫言】¶ ～する give (≒ make) *warning* (*of a thing to a person*).

がんけん【頑健】¶ ～な strong; strongly built; stout; robust.

かんげんがく【管弦楽】an orchestral music.

—団 an orchestra. —法 orchestration.

かんこ【歓呼】¶ ～の声をあげる give *cheers* (*to*). ～の声で迎えられる be greeted with *hearty cheers*.

かんご【看護】¶ ～する nurse; tend.

—婦 a 〔sick-〕nurse. —婦会 a nurses' agency. —婦長 a head nurse; a matron. —婦養成所 a nurses' training school.

かんご【漢語】a Chinese word.

がんこ【頑固】stubbornness; obstinacy.

¶ ～な obstinate; stubborn; stiff-necked; (片意地な) headstrong; bigoted; persistent. ～に obstinately; stubbornly; persistently.

かんこう【刊行】publication; issue. ¶ ～する publish; issue.

—物 a publication. 定期—物 a periodical.

かんこう【敢行】¶ ～する dare to *do*; carry out resolutely; take a decisive action.

かんこう【感光】〘写真〙exposure 〔to light〕; sensitization. ¶ このフィルムはまだ～していない This film *is* not yet *exposed*.

—紙 sensitized paper. —薬 sensitizer.

かんこう【慣行】〔a〕custom. ¶ ～に従って according to *custom*.

かんこう【観光】sightseeing. ¶ ～に行く do (≒ see) the sights (*of* London).

—客 a tourist; a sightseer. —事業 the tourist industry. —船 a sightseeing ship. —団 a sightseeing (≒ tourist) party. —地 a tourist resort. —バス a sightseeing bus. —旅行 a sightseeing tour.

がんこう【眼光】¶ ～が鋭い have piercing (≒ penetrating) *eyes*. ～紙背に徹する read between the lines.

かんこうちょう【官公庁】government and

public offices.

かんこうれい【箝口令】the gag law. ¶ ～をしく prohibit the mention (*of*).

かんこく【勧告】advice; counsel; recommendation; 困〔a piece of〕advice.

¶ 敵に降伏を～する *urge* the enemy *to* surrender. 人に辞任を～する *advise a person to* resign. 医師の～に従って on a doctor's *advice*. 彼は私の～に従った He followed my *recommendation*.

かんごく【監獄】a prison; 米 a jail; 英 a 「gaol.

かんこつ【顴骨】a cheekbone.

かんこつだったい【換骨奪胎】¶ これは中国の物語を～したものだ This is *an adaptation from* a Chinese story.

かんこどり【閑古鳥】〘鳥類〙a cuckoo. ¶ ～が鳴く(閑散としている) The place is deserted.

かんこんそうさい【冠婚葬祭】ceremonial occasions.

かんさ【監査】(検査) inspection; (会計の) audit. ¶ 会計を～する *audit* accounts.

—役 an auditor.

かんさい【完済】¶ ～する pay off a debt; complete a payment.

かんさい【関西】the Kansai districts.

かんさいき【艦載機】a deck plane; a ship plane.

かんざいにん【管財人】(遺産の) an administrator; (清算の) a receiver.

かんさく【間作】〘農業〙catch-cropping; (作物) a catch crop.

がんさく【贋作】a counterfeit.

かんざし【簪】an ornamental hairpin.

かんさつ【監察】inspection. ¶ ～する inspect; supervise.

—官 an inspector; a supervisor.

かんさつ【観察】an observation. ¶ ～する observe; survey; watch. ～を誤まる make *an* incorrect *observation*.

—力 ¶ ～力が鋭い have a keen power of *observation*.

かんさつ【鑑札】a license. ¶ 飲食店の営業の～ *a* trade *license* of a restaurant.

かんさん【換算】change; conversion. ¶ ドルを円に～する *change* dollars into yen. 邦貨に～して約100万円 about a million yen *in* Japanese money (≒ currency). 人間の労力に～して *in terms of* manpower.

—表 a conversion table. —率 exchange rates.

かんさん【閑散】leisureliness; (市場が) dullness. ¶ 市況は～だ The market *is bad* (≒ *is dull; is depressed*).

—期 a slack season.

かんし【冠詞】〘文法〙an article.

定— a definite article. 不定— an indefinite article.

かんし【監視】watch; observation; lookout; supervision. ¶ 厳重に～する *watch* closely; keep *a* close (≒ strict) *watch* (*on; over*). 行動を～する *keep an eye on* the movement (*of a person*).

—所 a watchhouse; an observatory. —船 a guard (≒ patrol) boat. —人 a guard; a watchman.

かんし【漢詩】a Chinese poem; (総称) Chinese poetry.

かんし【環視】¶ 衆人～の中で in public; *in full view* of the crowd.

かんし【鉗子】a forceps.

かんじ【感じ】**1** 〚感覚〛feeling; a sense.

¶ きみがそれをくれるなんて妙な～だ I *feel* it strange that you should give it to me.

さわるとざらざらした～でした It *felt* rough. / It was rough *to the touch*.

他人のじんましんを見ると自分までかゆいような～がしてくる When I see someone with a rash, I *feel* myself itching.

寒くて手足の～がまるでない My limbs *are numb* with cold.

急に頭の中がからっぽになったような～がした I suddenly *felt* as if my head were empty.

体が空中に浮き上がったような～がした I *felt* as if I were floating in the air.

2 〚印象〛an impression. ¶ 彼は明るい～の人だ There is something cheerful about him.

彼は～のいい人だ (～の悪い人だ) He is an *agreeable* (a *disagreeable*) man.

彼の話し方は～がいい He has an *agreeable* way of talking.

その本を読んでも別になんの～も受けなかった That book didn't impress me at all.

彼に会ってどんな～を受けましたか How did you *feel* when you saw him?

面接のときはよい～を与えるようきびきび答えなさい When you have an interview, be energetic in your answers so as to give *a* good *impression*.

たまに和服を着るとずいぶん～が変わるものだ You *look* quite *different* when you wear Japanese clothes.

一般的には赤い色は暖かい～がし，青は冷たい～がする In general red gives *a feeling* of warmth and blue of cold.

彼の後ろ姿はとてもさみしそうな～がした From the back, there was something very lonely about his form.

その絵は夕暮れの～がよく出ている The *atmosphere* of twilight is well brought out in that picture.

かんじ【漢字】a Chinese character (≒ ideograph).

—制限 limitation (≒ reduction) of Chinese characters. 当用— Chinese characters for daily use.

かんじ【幹事】a manager; a secretary; (旅行などの) a managing treasurer.

—長 the chief secretary.

がんじがらめ【雁字搦め】¶ 彼を～にした We *bound* him *firmly hand and foot*.

かんしき【鑑識】judgment; discernment.

—課 the identification section. —家 a connoisseur. —眼 connoisseurship. ¶ 彼は芸術品に対して～眼がある He has *a* good *discerning eye* for works of art. / He is *a* good *judge* of works of art.

かんじき【樏】〔a pair of〕snowshoes.

がんしき【眼識】¶ 彼は～ある人物だ He is a *discerning* person. 専門家の～でないとこの区別はつかない Nothing but an expert's *eye* can distinguish between the two.

か

がんじつ【元日】New Year's Day.

かんじつげつ【閑日月】¶ 退職して～の生活を田舎で送る lead *a quiet life* in the country after retirement. 英雄～あり A great man has a serene mind.

かんして【関して】¶ この点に～はなにも知らない I know nothing *in this respect*. この問題に～はこれだけしかわかっていない This is what we have learned *as regards* this matter. その件に～はなにも知りません I have nothing *about* it. 私に～はどちらでもかまわない Either will do *as far as I am concerned*.

かんしゃ【官舎】an official residence.

かんしゃ【感謝】thank; gratitude; appreciation. ¶ ～のしるしとして as a token of *one's gratitude*. 心より～します I express my heartfelt *thanks* to you. ～の申しようもありません I have no words to express my *thanks*./ I can never *thank* you enough. ～感激です I *am full of gratitude*.

—祭 Thanksgiving Day. —状 a letter of appreciation.

かんじゃ【患者】a patient; a case. ¶ ～を診察する examine (≒ see) *a patient*. ～に付き添う tend *a patient*. あの医者は～が多い The doctor *has a large practice*. その病院は～を50人収容できる The hospital can accommodate fifty *patients*. 赤痢～がたくさん出た Many *cases* of dysentery occurred.

外来— an outpatient. 新— a new case. 入院— an inpatient.

かんしゃく【癇癪】a temper; a rage. ¶ 彼はすぐ～を起こす He easily *gets out of temper*./ He easily *loses his temper*. 彼は～を起こしている He *is in a temper*.

—玉 ¶ 彼はついに～玉を破裂させた At last he *got into a temper*. —持ち ¶ 彼は～持ちだ He *is hot-tempered*.

かんしゅ【看守】㊊ a jailer; ㊈ a gaoler.

かんしゅ【看取】¶ 彼らの魂胆を～した I *saw through* their motives.

かんじゅ【甘受】¶ どんな非難も～する I *submit myself to* every sort of reproach.

かんしゅう【慣習】〔a〕custom. ¶ 彼らはまだその古い～を守っている They still keep up the old *custom*. 彼らはその古い～を破った They broke the old *custom*.

—法 the common law. 商— a commercial practice.

かんしゅう【監修】supervision. ¶ 百科辞典の～をする *supervise* the compilation of an encyclopedia. この辞典は３人の言語学者の～になる This dictionary was compiled *under the supervision of* three linguists.

—者 an editorial supervisor.

かんしゅう【観衆】spectators; an audience (単複両構文をとる). ¶ ～は興奮した The *audience* was (≒ were) excited. / The *spectators* got excited. ～の大部分はアメリカ人だった The *audience* were mostly Americans.

かんじゅせい【感受性】sensibility. ¶ 彼は～が強い男だ He *is sensitive*. / He has *a* fine *sensibility*. 彼女は色に対する～が鋭い She *is sensitive to* color. / She has *a* fine *sensibility for* color.

かんしょ【寒暑】¶ 日本は～の差がはなはだしい *The heat and cold* are extreme in Japan.

かんしょ【甘蔗】〔植物〕a sugar cane.

かんしょ【甘藷】〔植物〕a sweet potato (㊐ sweet potatoes).

かんじょ【寛恕】¶ ご～をお願いします I humbly ask for your *forgiveness*. / I humbly beg your *pardon*.

がんしょ【願書】an application. ¶ ～を提出する send in *an application*. ～を受けつける receive *applications* (*for* admission). ～に所用の書き入れをする fill in *an application*.

かんしょう【干渉】interference; intervention; interposition. ¶ 他国の内政に～した We *interfered in* the domestic policy of another country. 互いに～しないで生きよう Let's go on living without *meddling in* each other's affairs. 子どもにはあまり～しないほうがいい Children ought to be left alone sometimes.

かんしょう【環礁】an atoll.

かんしょう【完勝】¶ 相手チームに～した We gained *a complete victory over* the opposing team.

かんしょう【感傷】sentimentality. ¶ 幼時を思って～的になった I *became sentimental* remembering my childhood.

かんしょう【観照】contemplation; meditation. ¶ ～的な生活 a *contemplative* life. 人生を～する *meditate on* life.

かんしょう【観賞】¶ 草花を～する *admire* flowering plants.

—魚 an ornamental fish. —用植物 a decorative plant.

かんしょう【鑑賞】appreciation. ¶ 彼には英詩は～できない He cannot *appreciate* English poetry. 私の趣味は音楽を～することだ My hobby is to listen to music.

—力 ¶ クラシック音楽の～力を養わなければならない You must cultivate the *appreciation* of classical music.

かんしょう【緩衝】—器 a shock absorber; (車の) a bumper (≒ ㊈ a buffer); (汽車の) a fender. —地帯 a neutral zone. ¶ 休戦条約によって～地帯を設ける set up *a neutral* (≒ *buffer*) *zone* by a truce treaty.

かんじょう【勘定】**1**〖金銭的〗(計算) calculation; counting; (支払い) payment; settlement.

¶ 札入れの中の金を～する *count* the money in *one's* wallet.

彼は～がへただ He is poor at *figures* (≒ *calculation*).

～はだれが払うのだ Who will pay the *bill*? ～頼みます Check (≒ 英 Bill), please. きょうは～日だ This is a *setting* (≒ 英 *quarter*) day. あの店は毎月1回～を取りにくる The store sends a servant to collect the *bill* every month.
―高い ¶ あの人は～高い He is a *calculating* person. / He *is* quite *calculating*.
2 〖考慮〗 ¶ 彼の意見を～に入れなくてはいけない We must *take* his opinion *into account* (≒ *consideration*). この問題は～に入れないでおこう Let's *leave* this matter *out of account*.

かんじょう【感状】 a letter of appreciation; (軍隊の) a citation. ¶ 彼は勇敢な行為により～をもらった He *was cited for* his bravery.

かんじょう【感情】 feeling; emotion. ¶ 彼は～を込めて話した He spoke with *feeling*. 他人の～を害さないように気をつけなさい Be careful not to hurt the *feeling* of others. そのとき彼はだいぶ～が高ぶっていた He *was* quite *excited* at that time. 彼は少し～的になっている He *is being* a little *emotional*. 人間は～の動物だ Man is a creature of *feelings* (≒ *emotion*; *impulse*). / All men *are sensitive*. / All men have *feelings*. 個人的な～を抑えて事を処せ Deal with the matter, suppressing your personal *feelings*.

かんじょう【環状】 ¶ ～7号線 the seventh *circular* (≒ *loop*) road.
―線 a loop line. **―道路** a circular road.

がんしょう【岩礁】 a shore reef.

がんじょう【頑丈】 ¶ ～ないす a *strongly built* chair. ～な身体 a *stout* body. 彼の足は～だ He has *sturdy* legs. この家は～にできている The house is *strongly* built.

かんしょく【官職】 a government post; an official post. ¶ ～につく enter *the government service*. 彼は～についている He is *a civil servant*.

かんしょく【間食】 ¶ ～をする eat between meals.

かんしょく【閑職】 a sinecure; a leisurely post. ¶ 彼は～にまわされた He has been transferred to *an easy post*.

かんしょく【感触】 (the sense of) touch. ¶ この毛皮はざらざらした～だ This fur is rough *to the touch*. この服地は～が柔らかい This dress material is soft *to the touch*.

がんしょく【顔色】 ¶ すると彼は～を失った He *lost color* then. / He *turned pale* then. 彼女の歌は本職の歌手でも～をなからしめるうまさだ Her song *puts to shame* even a professional singer.

かん·じる【感じる】 **1** 〖知覚する〗 feel. ¶ おなかに痛みを～じる I *feel* (≒ *have*) a pain in the stomach. けさはいつもより寒さを強く～じる I *feel* much colder than usual this morning. 睡眠薬のおかげでまもなく眠けを～じた I *felt* sleepy soon after taking some sleeping tablets. 落葉を見るとなんとなく寂しさを～じる Falling leaves somehow make one *feel* lonely. スイッチにさわったら,ぴりっと電気を～じた When I touched the switch, I *got* an electric shock. 苦味は舌の先が一番よく～じる The tip of the tongue *is* most *sensitive to* a bitter taste. 水が冷たく～じられる季節がきた The season when water *feels* chilly has come. 必要を～じないから自分の家を持たないのだ I don't have my own house because I don't *feel* it is necessary. 自分の愚かさかげんを痛いほど～じた I *felt* very keenly how stupid I was. 体に～じない程度の地震はたびたび起こっている A barely *perceptible* earthquake sometimes occurred. 危険を～じて列車からすぐ降りた As soon as I *sensed* danger, I got off the train. 穏やかならぬ形勢を～じとった I *took in* the extraordinary situation.
2 〖感動する〗 be impressed (*by*). ¶ 彼には十分恩義を～じている I *feel* deeply indebted to him. 遠回しに言ったので彼はなにも～じなかったらしい He seems to *have been unaware of* what I was driving at because I was too indirect. ～じるところがあって酒をやめた *For certain reasons* (≒ *For reasons of my own*) I have given up drinking. 彼女の手紙には細やかな愛情が～じられる There was *a feeling* of warm affection in her letter. 彼のことばは誠意が～じられるので人を引きつける He attracts everybody because his words are full of sincerity. あなたのご注意には十分～じ入っています I *am* deeply *thankful to* you for your kind advice. 彼女はいくら親切にしてやってもなにも～じない She does not *appreciate* any kindness of others. 彼に対して友情を～じている I *have* friendly *feelings for* him. 常日ごろ迷惑に～じていることがあればこの場で話しなさい If there is anything that *troubles* you in your everyday life tell me about it.

かんしん【歓心】 ¶ 彼は私の～を買うためにそうした He did it to *win my favor*.

かんしん【寒心】 ¶ それは～にたえない It is *a matter for* deep *regret*. / It *is* very *regrettable*.

かんしん【感心】 wonder; admiration. ¶ ～に to *one's admiration*. ～な少年だ What a *laudable* boy! 彼の誠実さにはいつも～する I *am* always *impressed* with his faithfulness. 私たちはみな～してその子どもたちをながめた All of us watched the children with *admiration*. ～, ～! Well done! / Excellent! このケーキはあまり～しない I *don't care much for* this cake.

かんじんちょう【勧進帳】 a subscription list.

かんじんもと【勧進元】 a promoter. ¶ ～をす

か

る promote ; act as promoter.

かんすい【完遂】completion. ¶ 仕事は～された The work *has been completed* (≒ *has been accomplished*). / The work *has been brought to completion*.

かんすい【冠水】¶ ～する be flooded ; be submerged ; be under water.

か

かんすい【鹹水】salt water.
—魚 a saltwater fish. —湖 a salt lake.

がんすいたんそ【含水炭素】〘化学〙carbohydrate.

かんすう【関数】〘数学〙a function.
三角— a trigonometric function. 代数— an algebraical function.

かん・する【関する】¶ 文学に～する本はあまり読んでいない I have read few books *on* literature. 彼は法律問題に～する権威だ He is an authority *on* law. これは個人の名誉に～する問題だ This is a problem *concerning* personal honor. 私に～する限り so far as *I am concerned*, ...

かん・する【緘する】¶ そのことに関しては彼は口を～して語らなかった He *kept silent about* the matter.

かんせい【完成】completion ; accomplishment. ¶ そのビルはまもなく～する The building will soon *be completed* (≒ *be finished*). ついに彼は小説を～させた At last he *finished* writing his novel. (finish *to* write とは言わない). ついに彼の発明は～した At last he *perfected* (≒ *completed*) the invention.
—品 finished goods.

かんせい【官製】¶ ～の government-made.
—はがき 米 a postal card ; 英 a postcard.

かんせい【乾性】¶ ～の dry.
—油 dry oil.

かんせい【喚声】a shout. ¶ 観衆はファインプレーにどっと～をあげた The spectators gave *a shout* in admiration of the fine play.

かんせい【歓声】cheers ; a shout of joy.
¶ 彼らはその朗報を聞いて～をあげた They gave *a joyous shout* at the good news. / They *shouted with joy* at the good news.

かんせい【慣性】〘物理〙inertia. ¶ ～の法則 the law of *inertia*.

かんせい【管制】control. ¶ ～下におく bring (*something*) under *control*.
—官 an air traffic controller. —室 a control room. —装置 controlling gear. —塔 a control tower. 燈火— control of light ; light control. 報道— news censorship.

かんせい【閑静】¶ ここら辺りは～ですね This neighborhood is *quiet*, isn't it ?

かんぜい【関税】customs ; customs duties (customs はつねに複数). ¶ ～は支払った The *customs* were paid. その国は輸入品にはかなり高い～をかける The country imposes pretty stiff *duties* on imported goods. ～は1割引き上げられた The *customs duties* were raised by 10%. これには～がかからない The goods are *free of duty* (≒ *duty-free*).
—政策 a tariff policy. —法 the Customs Law. —率 a tariff rate.

かんせき【漢籍】a Chinese classic〔al〕book ; (総称) Chinese classics.

がんせき【岩石】a rock. ¶ この山は～が多い This mountain is *rocky*.

かんせつ【間接】¶ ～の原因 an *indirect* cause. きみも～にこの事件に関係がある You, too, are *indirectly* concerned with this affair. それは～に知った I heard the news *at second hand*.
—照明 indirect lighting. —税 an indirect tax. —話法 indirect narration.

かんせつ【関節】〘解剖学〙a joint. ¶ 腕の～がはずれた The *joint* of my arm became dislocated. 彼は肩の～がはずれた He had his shoulder put *out of joint*.
—炎 〘医学〙arthritis. —リューマチ 〘医学〙articular rheumatism.

がんぜな・い【頑是無い】(あどけない) innocent ; (頼りない) helpless.

かんせん【官選】¶ 日本では知事は～ではない The governor *is* not *appointed by the government* in Japan.
—弁護人 an official council ; a court-appointed lawyer.

かんせん【感染】(間接の) infection ; (接触の) contagion. ¶ 彼はインフルエンザに～した He *was infected with* influenza. / He *caught* the flu.
—経路 the infection route. —源 the source of infection.

かんせん【艦船】vessels ; (軍艦と船舶) warships and steamers.

かんせん【幹線】a trunk line ; a main line.
—道路 a trunk road ; a highway.

かんせん【観戦】¶ テレビで野球を～する *watch* a baseball game on TV.

かんせん【汗腺】〘解剖学〙a sweat gland.

かんぜん【完全】perfection. ¶ 実験は～な成功だった The experiment was a *complete* success. タイプライターを～にマスターした I mastered typewriting *thoroughly*. 大地震のため町は～に破壊された Because of the great earthquake the town was *completely* destroyed.
—無欠 ¶ この世の中で～無欠はありえない There cannot be *perfect* things in this world.
—犯罪 a perfect crime. ¶ 彼は～犯罪を計画した He planned *a perfect crime*. —試合 a perfect game. ¶ 彼は～試合をやりとげた He pitched *a perfect game*.

かんぜん【敢然】¶ ～と敵に向かう face the enemy *bravely* (≒ *boldly*).

かんぜん【間然】¶ この解説は～するところがない This explanation leaves nothing to be desired.

がんぜん【眼前】¶ ～の光景 a view *before us*. ～の利益 *immediate* profit.

かんぜんちょうあく【勧善懲悪】encouraging the good and punishing the evil.

かんそ【簡素】simplicity. ¶ ～な生活〔a〕*simple* (≒ *plain*) life. 手続きを～化する *make* the procedure *simple*.

がんそ【元祖】(一家の先祖) the first father of a family; (創始者) a founder; an originator; a father. ¶ 医学の～ *the father* of medical science.

かんそう【乾燥】¶～する dry up; (乾く) become (≒ get) dry. ～した空気 *dry* air.
—芋 dried sweet potatoes. —果実 desiccated fruit. —器 a drier; a desiccator. —季 the dry season. —剤 desiccant. —室 a drying room.

かんそう【感想】 impression[s]; feeling[s].
¶ パリのご～はいかがですか What is your *impression* of Paris? / How does Paris *impress* you? / How do you *find* Paris? ご～をどうぞ We wish to hear your *comments*. ～を述べる give *one's impressions* (*of*); describe *one's feelings* (*of*).

かんそう【歓送】 —会 a farewell party; a send-off.

かんぞう【肝臓】〔解剖学〕 the liver.

がんぞう【贋造】 counterfeiting. ¶～する counterfeit; forge; fabricate.
—紙幣 a counterfeit; a forged note; a false note.

かんそうきょく【間奏曲】〔音楽〕 an interlude; an intermezzo.

かんそく【観測】〔an〕 observation. ¶～する observe. 希望的～ *a* wishful *observation*; wishful *thinking*. 私の～では彼は絶対現われない In my *opinion* he will never appear.
—気球 an observation balloon. —者 an observer. —所(天体の) an observatory; (軍隊の監視所) an observation post. 天体— astronomical observation.

かんそん【寒村】 a poor village; a deserted village.

カンタータ〔音楽〕 a cantata (イタリア語から).

カンタービレ〔音楽〕 a cantabile (イタリア語から).

かんたい【寒帯】 the Frigid Zones.
—植物 an arctic plant. —動物 an arctic animal.

かんたい【歓待】 welcome; hospitality; a warm reception. ¶～する receive (*a person*) hospitably (≒ warmly). ～を受けて感激した I was deeply impressed by the *hearty welcome*.

かんたい【艦隊】(大きな規模の) a fleet; (小規模の) a squadron.
連合— a combined fleet.

かんだい【寛大】 generosity; magnanimity.
¶～な処置をとる deal with (*a person*) *leniently*. 彼は子どもには～なところを見せた He showed *generosity* in dealing with children. 彼は～にふるまった He *was generous in* behavior.

がんたい【眼帯】 an eye bandage.

かんだか・い【甲高い・疳高い】¶～い声 a *shrill* voice.

かんたく【干拓】 reclamation. ¶～する *reclaim* land *by drainage*.
—工事(事業) reclamation works. —地 dried land; reclaimed land.

かんたん【感嘆】 admiration. ¶～する admire; wonder (*at*). ～すべき admirable; wonderful.
—詞〔文法〕 an interjection. —文 an exclamatory sentence.

かんたん【肝胆】¶ ふたりは～相照らす仲だ The two *are on friendly terms* with each other. / They are *great* (≒ *close*) friends.

かんたん【簡単】 simplicity; brevity. ¶～な仕事 a *light* work; a *simple* work. ～な手続き a *simple* procedure. ～には説明できない *Brief* explanation is almost impossible. ～には解決しそうにない The problem is not likely to be solved *with ease*. ～に食事しましょう Let's have a *light* meal. ～に述べましょう I will state it *briefly*. ～に言えば in brief.

かんだん【間断】¶～なく incessantly; constantly; continuously.

かんだん【閑談】(静かな話) a quiet talk; (打ちとけた雑談) a chat; a casual talk. ¶～する have *a casual talk*.

かんだん【歓談】 a pleasant talk. ¶～する have *a pleasant talk* (≒ *chat*) (*with*).

がんたん【元旦】 New Year's Day.

かんだんけい【寒暖計】 a thermometer.
¶～は10度を示している The *thermometer* reads ten degrees.

かんち【感知】¶ ゆうべの地震は人体に～できない程度のものだった The earthquake last night was too slight to *be felt* bodily.

かんち【関知】¶ われわれの～するところではない We have nothing to do with it. / It is no concern (≒ business) of ours.

かんち【奸智】 guile; craft. ¶～にたけた人 a man full of *guile*.

かんちがい【勘違い】 misunderstanding.
¶ 彼は～している He *is mistaken*. ～はだれにでもあるものだ Everyone *misunderstands* (≒ *makes a mistake*) once in a while.

がんちく【含蓄】 an implication. ¶～のあることば *suggestive* (≒ *pregnant*) words. このことばはなかなか～がある This expression is full of *implicit meaning*.

かんちゅう【寒中】¶～に in the middle (≒ midst) of winter.
—水泳 midwinter swimming.

がんちゅう【眼中】¶～におかない take no notice of; ignore; disregard. あの連中のことは彼の～にない Such persons *are beyond his notice*. / Those people *are utterly disregarded* by him.

かんちょう【干潮】〔a〕 low ebb; 〔a〕 low tide.
¶～時に at *low tide*. 今は～だ Now the tide *is low* (≒ *is on the ebb*).

かんちょう【官庁】〔a〕 government office.
—街 a government office quarter.

かんちょう【館長】 a director.

かんちょう【浣腸】 an enema. ¶～する administer (≒ give) *an enema* (*to*).
—薬 an enema.

かんちょう【間諜】 a spy.

か

かんちょう【艦長】the captain; (旗艦の) the flag captain.
かんつう【貫通】¶ 弾丸が頭部を~した The bullet shot *through* his head. トンネルが~した The tunnel *has been dug through*.
かんつう【姦通】adultery; illicit intercourse. ¶ ~する commit *adultery* (*with*); have *illicit intercourse* (*with*).
かんづ・く【感づく】¶ 私の行動はだれかにあやしいと~かれているらしい It seems that someone *is getting suspicious of* my conduct. うすうす~いてはいた I'*ve been* dimly (≒ vaguely) *conscious of* it. / I *have* dimly *sensed* it. ~かれてはまずい Don't *incur suspicion*.
かんづめ【罐詰め】canned food; 英 tinned food. ¶ ~にする can; 英 tin. ~の豆 *canned* (≒ 英 *tinned*) beans. 彼はホテルに3日間~にされた(仕事のために) He *was confined* in a hotel for three days.
—業者 a canner; a packer. —工場 a cannery.
かんてい【官邸】an official residence.
かんてい【鑑定】(判定) judgment; (評価) estimation; (専門家の) an expert opinion. ¶ 美術品の~ *judgment* of art objects. 絵を~する *judge* a picture. 骨董(こっとう)品の~を専門家に依頼した I asked to *have* the curios *judged* by a connoisseur. この筆跡を~してくださいませんか Won't you give me *an expert opinion* on this handwritings? ⌈test.
—家 a connoisseur. 精神— a psychiatric
かんてつ【貫徹】¶ 初志を~する *accomplish* (≒ *carry out*) *one's* original intention. 目的を~する *achieve one's* end; *accomplish one's* purpose. 要求を~する *fulfill one's* demand.
カンテラ a [metal] handlamp.
かんてん【寒天】(食品) agar; agar-agar; a jelly; (寒空) freezing weather.
かんてん【観点】a point of view. ¶ この~から見ると judging from this *point of view*. あらゆる~に立って調査した We examined it from every possible *angle*.
かんでん【感電】¶ ~する receive an electric shock.
—死 ¶ ~死する be killed by an electric shock; be electrocuted.
かんでんち【乾電池】a dry cell; a dry battery.
かんど【感度】sensitiveness; sensitivity. ¶ ~がよい be very (≒ highly) sensitive. ラジオの~ the *sensitiveness* of a radio. マイクの~がよい The microphone picks up sound very well.
かんとう【完投】¶ (野球で) ~する throw throughout the game.
かんとう【官等】official rank (≒ grade).
かんとう【巻頭】¶ ~に at the beginning of a book. この雑誌の~に彼の文が載っている This magazine begins (≒ opens) with his essay.
かんとう【敢闘】¶ ~する fight courageously.
—精神 fighting spirit; combative spirit.
かんとう【関東】the Kanto districts. ¶ ~平野 the Kanto plain.
かんどう【勘当】disinheritance. ¶ 息子を~する *disinherit* (≒ *disown*) *one's* son.
かんどう【間道】a secret path; a bypath; a byroad.
かんどう【感動】excitement; impression. ¶ ~しやすい人 an *impressionable* person. 彼の成功を聞いて家族一同~した All the family *were moved* at the news of his success. 氏の受賞は人々に大いなる~を与えた His winning the prize has created *a* great *sensation* among the public.
かんとく【監督】superintendence; (人) a superintendent; (スポーツの) a manager; a coach; (映画の) a director.
¶ 工事の~は彼だ He *is overseeing* the construction work. 彼はその子どもたちの~を命じられた He was ordered to *take charge of* the children. 仕事は田中氏の~のもとにやりなさい Do your work under the *direction* of Mr. Tanaka. 彼が試験の~だった He *presided over* the examination. 彼は~不行き届きのかどで罰せられた He was punished *for falling down on his supervision* (≒ *for his mismanagement*).
かんどころ【勘所】the point. ¶ 彼は問題の~をおさえている He holds *the essentials* of the matter. ~を逃がさない He never misses *the point*.
がんとして【頑として】firmly; stubbornly. ¶ ~応じない He *turns a deaf ear to* it.
カントリークラブ a country club.
かんな【鉋】a plane. ¶ 板に~をかける *plane* a board. ~をとぐ whet *a plane*. ~の刃 *a plane* iron.
—くず shavings.
カンナ〔植物〕a canna.
かんない【管内】¶ ~に in (≒ within) *the jurisdiction*.
かんなん【艱難】hardships; adversity. ¶ ~に耐える bear (≒ go through) *hardships*. ~辛苦の末ようやくやり遂げた He accomplished his task after a lot of *difficulties*.
かんにん【堪忍】(忍耐) patience; (許すこと) forgiveness. ¶ その子どもを~してやろう I will *forgive* the child. ~袋の緒が切れた I can no longer *put up with* it. / This is the limit of my *forbearance*.
カンニング cheating (cunning とは言わない). ¶ 試験で~をする *cheat* in an examination.
かんぬき【閂】a bar; a bolt. ¶ 門に~をかける (はずす) *bolt* (*unbolt*) a gate.
かんぬし【神主】a Shinto priest.
かんねん【観念】(考え) an idea; a notion; a conception; (あきらめること) resignation.
¶ ~的な議論 an *ideal* argument. 義務~のない男 a man who has no *sense* of duty. 時間の~がない have no *sense* of time. これまでと~した I gave up. / I abandoned (≒ gave up) all my hope.

—論 idealism.

がんねん【元年】 ¶昭和～ *the first year* of Showa.

かんのう【完納】 full payment. ¶～する pay completely (≒ fully); pay the whole amount. 割り当てを～する *pay* the distribution *in full*.

かんのう【官能】 sense. ¶～的快楽 *sensual* pleasures.

かんのう【感応】 (電気の) induction; (心理的) sympathy.

—コイル an induction coil. —電気 induced current.

かんのん【観音】 〘仏教〙 *Kannon*; the goddess of mercy.

—開き a pair of folding doors.

かんぱ【看破】 ¶真の意図を～する *see through a person's* true aim.

かんぱ【寒波】 a cold wave. ¶ニューヨークはこの冬最大の～に見舞われた The biggest *cold wave* hit (≒ swept) New York this winter.

カンパ a campaign.

資金— a fund-raising campaign.

かんぱい【完敗】 ¶～する be completely defeated; suffer *a complete defeat*.

かんぱい【乾杯】 a toast. ¶～! Here's to you! / To your health! 太郎と花子のために～ *Here's a toast* for Taro and Hanako! ～の音頭をとる propose *a toast*. A氏の前途(健康)を祝して～する *drink* to the glorious future (health) of Mr. A.

かんばし·い【芳しい】 ¶～い香り〔a〕*sweet* (≒ *fragrant; agreeable*) smell. その人の評判は～くない He has a *bad* reputation. 結果は～くなかった The results *were unsatisfactory*.

カンバス 〔a piece of〕canvas.

かんばつ【旱魃】 a drought; a spell of dry weather.

がんばり【頑張り】 ¶～が足りないぞ Don't yield (≒ give in) easily. 彼は～が足りない He has no *guts*.

がんば·る【頑張る】 ¶～れ Hold out! / Stick to it! / Never say die! もっと～れ Work harder! 彼は自分は知らないと～った He *insisted* that he knew nothing about it. 彼は自分の意見を～り通した He *stuck to* his own opinion.

かんばん【看板】 a signboard. ¶～を出す put (≒ hang) up *a sign*. 社会保障を～にして *for* (≒ *in*) *the cause of* social security; (悪い意味) *under the cloak of* social security. もう～です(閉店) It's 〔the closing〕 time. / Time, gentlemen.

—娘 a draw. —屋 a sign painter. 一枚— a shining star.

かんぱん【甲板】 a deck.

上(中; 下)— the upper (middle; lower) deck. 前(後)— the forecastle (quarter) deck.

かんぱん【乾板】 〘写真〙 a dry plate.

かんパン【乾パン】 hardtack.

かんび【完備】 ¶その学校は体育館やプールが～している The school facilities are complete with its fine gymnasium and swimming pool. 電気·水道·ガス～の家 a house *supplied with* gas, electricity and water.

かんび【甘美】 ¶～なメロディー a *sweet* melody. ～な夢を追う pursuit *one's beautiful* dream.

かんぴ【官費】 ¶～で留学する study abroad *at government expense*.

かんびょう【看病】 ¶手厚い～ careful *nursing*. 病人を寝ずに～する sit up with a sick person; *nurse* all through the night.

かんぴょう【干瓢】 dried gourd shavings.

がんびょう【眼病】 an eye disease.

かんぶ【患部】 the affected part.

かんぶ【幹部】 the leaders; (会社の) the management.

かんぷ【還付】 ¶税金を～する *pay back* a tax.

かんぷ【完膚】 ¶～なきまでに completely; thoroughly; unsparingly.

かんぷう【完封】 〘野球〙 ¶相手チームを～する *shut out* the opponent team.

かんぷう【寒風】 a cold (≒ an icy) wind.

かんぷく【感服】 admiration; wonder. ¶～する admire; wonder at; be struck with admiration. 彼の親切さにはほとほと～する His kindness toward me commands (≒ claims) my heartfelt *admiration*.

かんぶつ【乾物】 dried goods; groceries.

—屋 a grocery; 英 a drysaltery; (人) a grocer; a drysalter.

カンフル 〘薬学〙 camphor.

—注射 a camphor injection.

かんぶん【漢文】 (文章) Chinese composition; (文学) Chinese classics.

かんぺいしき【観兵式】 a military review.

かんぺき【癇癖】 a short temper. ¶～が強い be short-tempered; be hot-tempered.

かんぺき【完璧】 perfection. ¶～な perfect; faultless; flawless; ideal. ～を期する aim at *perfection*. ～に近い出来だった The result *was* almost *ideal*.

がんぺき【岸壁】 a quay; a pier; a wharf. ¶船を～に横づけする bring a boat alongside *a pier*.

かんべつ【鑑別】 discrimination; judgment; discernment. ¶～する discriminate; judge; discern; distinguish; tell (*between* A *and* B).

かんべん【勘弁】 ¶～してください Please *pardon* me. もう～できない This is more than we can *forbear*. / This is past our *endurance*. 今度だけは～してください *Forgive* me for this once. それだけは～してください(やりたくない) I will do anything else 〔but that〕.

かんべん【簡便】 ¶～な simple; easy; handy.

かんぼう【官房】 —長官 the Chief Secretary of the Cabinet. 大臣— the Minister's Secretariat〔e〕.

かんぼう【感冒】 流行性— influenza; (口語) flu.

かんぼう【監房】 a cell; a ward.

かんぽう【官報】 the official gazette.

かんぽう【漢方】 Chinese medicine.

—医 a herb doctor. —薬 a herb medicine.

か

がんぼう【願望】¶長年の～が達せられる attain *one's* long-cherished *desire*.
かんぽうしゃげき【艦砲射撃】bombardment from a warship; a shelling.
かんぼく【灌木】a shrub; (群) a bush; a shrubbery.
かんぼつ【陥没】depression; subsidence. ¶～する sink; cave in.
かんぽん【完本】a complete book; an unabridged edition; (端本に対して) a complete set.
がんぽん【元本】〘商業〙the principal; the capital.
ガンマせん【ガンマ線】〘物理〙gamma rays.
かんまつ【巻末】¶～に付記する add at *the end of the book*.
かんまん【干満】ebb and flow; flux and reflux. ¶～の差が激しい There is a wide range between tidelines.
かんまん【緩慢】¶～な市況 a *dull* market. 疲れで彼らの動作が～になってきた They got too tired to be active.
かんみ【甘味】a sweet taste; sweetness. —料 sweetening materials.
がんみ【玩味】¶名作を～する *fully appreciate* a great work.
かんむり【冠】a crown; a coronet. ¶～を曲げる get angry (*with a person; at a thing*). 彼はたいへんなお～だ He *is filled with fury*. / He *is in a fury*.
かんめい【感銘】〔a deep〕impression. ¶深い～を覚える *be* deeply *impressed*. ～を与える *impress* (*a person*); make *a* great *impression on* (*a person*).
かんめい【簡明】¶～な simple and plain; concise. 彼は～に答えた He answered *briefly and to the point*.
がんめい【頑迷】stubbornness; obstinacy. —固陋 ¶～固陋な stubborn and obstinate.
がんめん【顔面】the face. —神経痛〘医学〙facial neuralgia.
かんもう【冠毛】〘動物〙a crest;〘植物〙a pappus (複 pappi); down.
がんもく【眼目】¶新企画の～ the *main object* of the new plan.
かんもん【喚問】summons. ¶～する summon (*a person for* examination).
かんもん【関門】a gateway. ¶入試の～を突破する get through *the barriers* of the entrance examination.
かんやく【完訳】¶～する make *a complete translation* (*of*).
かんやく【漢訳】a Chinese translation. ¶～する translate into Chinese.
がんやく【丸薬】a pill.
かんゆ【肝油】cod-liver oil.
かんゆう【官有】government ownership. —林 government (≒ state) forests.
かんゆう【勧誘】invitation. ¶保険の～をする *canvass for* the contraction of insurance. 入部を～する *solicit* for membership. —員 a solicitor; a canvasser.
がんゆう【含有】¶～する contain. —量 ¶鉱石の銀～量 the silver *content* of an ore.
かんよ【関与・干与】participation. ¶～する participate (*in*); take part (*in*).
かんよう【肝要】¶～な important; necessary.
かんよう【寛容】generosity; tolerance. ¶～の精神 the spirit of *tolerance*.
かんよう【慣用】usage. ¶～の common; customary; (語句の) idiomatic. —語(句) an idiom; an idiomatic expression.
がんらい【元来】¶これは～きみとは無関係だ This has nothing to do with you *in itself*. / *Essentially*, this is none of your business. この本は～子どものために書かれたものであった This book was *originally* intended for children.
かんらく【陥落】(城の) fall; surrender. ¶～する(城が) fall; surrender; (地盤が) sink; fall. その日はたいへん忙しかったが, 彼の誘いに～して彼といっしょに映画に行った I was very busy that day, but *was persuaded into going* to the movies with him.
かんらく【歓楽】pleasure; amusement. ¶人の世の～をきわめ尽くす drink the cup of *pleasure* to the dregs; *enjoy oneself* to the full in life. —街 an amusement center.
かんらん【観覧】inspection. —券 an admission ticket. —者 a spectator. —席 a seat; (野球の) a stand. —料 an admission fee.
かんらん【橄欖】〘植物〙an olive〔tree〕. —油 olive oil.
かんり【官吏】a government official. 高級— a high〔government〕official; a senior civil servant.
かんり【管理】management. ¶彼はその工場を～している He *manages* the plant. この寮は～が行き届いている This dormitory *is* well *managed*. この建築物は市の～下にある This building *is under the supervision of* the city.
がんり【元利】principal and interest. ¶～合計5万2,000円になる The amount with interest added is fifty-two thousand yen.
がんりき【眼力】〔an〕insight; observation. ¶彼の～には狂いがなかった His *observation* was not wrong. 彼の～には恐れ入った His *penetrating insight* is astonishing.
かんりつ【官立】—大学 a governmental university.
かんりゃく【簡略】brevity. ¶～な報告 a *brief* report. 手続きを～にする *simplify* the formalities.
かんりゅう【貫流】¶～する *flow* (≒ *run*) *through* (the plain).
かんりゅう【寒流】a cold current. ¶千島～ the *cold* Kurilian *currents*.
かんりょう【完了】completion. ¶旅行の準備を～した I *have finished* (≒ *have completed*) preparing for my trip. 出発の準備が

〜した We *are* now *ready* for starting.
—時制〘文法〙 the perfect tense.

かんりょう【官僚】(人) a bureaucrat.
—主義 bureaucratism; redtapism. **—**政治 bureaucracy; bureaucratic government.

がんりょう【顔料】cosmetics; (絵の具) paints; colors.

かんるい【感涙】¶ 〜にむせぶ be moved to tears.

かんれい【寒冷】**—**前線〘気象〙a cold front.
—地 a cold district. ¶ 〜地手当 a cold allowance.

かんれい【慣例】a custom; a convention.
¶ 〜に従う follow the *custom*. 〜により in accordance with *custom*. 国により社会の〜がいろいろ異なる Social *customs* vary in different countries.

かんれき【還暦】¶ 〜を祝う celebrate *one's* sixtieth birthday (英語になく日本だけ).

かんれん【関連】¶ その問題に〜して *in relation to* (≒ *in connection with*) the matter. きみの答えは質問には全然〜がない Your answer has no *relation* to the question. その事に〜して質問があります I want to ask a question *in connection with* the matter.
—事項 related matters.

かんわ【閑話】**—**休題 Now let's return to the main subject.

かんわ【緩和】alleviation; mitigation.
¶ 緊張を〜する *ease* the tense situation. 制限を〜する *lighten* the restrictions (*on*). 住宅難を〜する *relieve* the shortage of housing.

き

き【気】**1**〘心の傾向・性質〙¶ 〜の小さい人だ He *is faint-hearted* (≒ *is chicken-hearted*).
彼女は〜が強い She *is bold* (≒ *is daring*; *is unafraid*; *is unflinching*).
ぼくは〜が短い(早い) I *am quick-tempered.* / I easily *lose my temper*.
〜の弱いことを言うな Don't *be* so *weak-willed.* / Don't *be* so *feeble-willed*.
あの人とはどうも〜が合わぬ I can't *get along well with* him.
われわれは〜の合った仲だ We *are on congenial terms*.
まだまだ〜は若いつもりだ I still feel young *at heart*.
きみは〜がいいからすぐに他人の言うことを信じてしまう You *are good-natured* and too ready to believe others.
2〘心の働き・つもり・意欲〙¶ そんなことを言うとは彼は〜が狂っている He must *be crazy* (≒ *has lost his mind*) to say such a thing.
その事件以来彼は多少〜がふれている He *has been* a little *out of his mind* since the accident.
試験の前日に遊んでいる学生の〜が知れない *I'm* simply *amazed to* see the student playing around on the day before the test.
〜が向いたらやりましょう I'll do it when I *feel like* it.
それではぼくの〜がすまぬ I wouldn't *feel easy* then.
きみの〜のすむようにしたまえ Do it any way you *like* to.
〜の向くままに近所を散歩した I walked around the neighborhood *aimlessly*.
彼に試験不合格を知らせるのは〜が重かった I *felt heavy-hearted* to tell him of his failure in the examination.
なんの〜なしにそう言っただけで, 別に悪い〜があってのことではありません I just said so without thinking much about it. I didn't *mean* anything serious.
なんの〜なしに本をめくっていたら若いころの母の写真が出てきた I was just turning over the pages of a book, when I found a picture of my mother in her early days.
頭が痛くて勉強する〜がしなかった I didn't *feel like* studying because of the headache.
今更言いわけする〜にもなれなかった I *wasn't disposed* to make any excuse then.
それを聞いて〜が変わったらしい On hearing it, he seems to *have changed his mind*.
いったいやる〜はあるのかね Do you really *have a mind to* do it?
〜ばかり焦って体がいうことをきかぬ I'm only too much in a hurry to do it, but I'm helpless. / The *spirit* is willing, but the flesh is weak.
早く彼女に会いたいと〜がせいた I *was impatient to* see her.
怠けないでもっと〜を入れてやりなさい Don't be so lazy, *be* more *earnest*.
彼はあの女に〜があるらしい He seems to *be fond of* her.
ずいぶん〜の多い人だね Isn't he interested in all kinds of things?
彼はその試合で大敵を破り大いに〜をはいた He beat his great (≒ strong) rival at the match and achieved a tremendous success.
〜をとりなおして再び仕事に立ち向かった I *took heart* (≒ *pulled myself together*; *col-*

lected myself; *gathered myself up*) and set to work again.

～のはっているときは風邪はひかないものだ When you *are tense and determined* in something, you won't catch cold.

まだまだ～を緩めるな Don't *breathe easy* yet.

1セットとって思わず～が緩んだ I *felt relieved* after winning the first set.

彼はなぐられて～を失った He was knocked and *fainted* (≒ *became senseless*).

3〖心遣い·注意·配慮·心配〗¶ 彼に言われたことが妙に～になった Somehow I couldn't get over what he said to me.

人の言うことをあまり～にするな Don't *be* too *nervous about* what people say.

そんなことで～にやむことはない You don't have to *be worried about* such a thing.

試験の結果がどうなろうとあまり～にしてない I'*m* not so *anxious about* the results of the examination.

～は心だ This is just to show my thanks.

いつも私のことを～にかけていてくださってありがたく思っております I appreciate your kindly *looking after* me.

彼女は若いのによく～がつく Though young, she *is* quite *thoughtful*.

彼の入ってきたのに～がつかなかった I didn't *notice* him coming in.

～がついてみるともう夜は明けかかっていた The day was already breaking when I *was aware of* it. / I found it was almost light.

彼女がそれに～がつかぬはずはない I'm sure she *has noticed* it. / It can't be that she *has* not *noticed* it.

暗いから道に迷わぬように～をつけなさい *Be careful* not *to* lose your way in the dark.

彼を堅くならせまいと彼女はいろいろ～をつかった She *saw to it that* he would not feel too nervous.

あたりに～をくばり彼はこっそり私の部屋の戸をたたいた *Looking around carefully*, he knocked at my door quietly.

そんなに～をまわすな Don't *be* so *suspicious*.

どうもよけいなことを言ったので～がとがめる *I feel sorry* for having said something I shouldn't have.

こんな格好で彼女に会うのは～がひける *I am ashamed to* meet her looking like this.

そんなことがわからぬとは～がきかぬやつだ He must *be stupid* not *to* see such a thing.

なかなか～のきいた, しゃれた文句だね That's quite a *sensible* and witty expression.

～が散るといけないからテレビをつけるな Don't turn on the TV lest you should *disturb* him.

彼は妙に～を持たせる言い方をする He talks in a *suggestive* sort of way.

汽車が出るのに彼が姿を見せず～が～でなかった He didn't turn up when the train was about to start, so I *was* quite *worried*.

借金を返したので～が楽になった I paid back the debt and I *feel relieved* (≒ *feel easy*).

どんな結果になるか一同～をもんだ We *were* all *anxious* (≒ *uneasy*) *about* how it would turn out.

味方チームが優勝するかどうか, 見ていて～がもめた We *were excited to* see if our team would win or not.

彼とは～のおけぬ仲でなんでも言える I *am on friendly terms with* him, and can say anything to him.

そんな～のはる席には出たくない I don't *want* to attend such a *formal* gathering.

4〖心に与える感じ·気分〗¶ 彼にそう言われてみるとあまりいい～がしない It's rather *unpleasant* to hear him talk like that.

そんなこと言われりゃだれだって～を悪くする Anybody would *feel bad* (≒ *be hurt*) if he is told such a thing.

彼はみんなにおだてられていい～になっている He *is pleased with himself for* being flattered by all.

どうもうまくいかぬ～がした I *was afraid that* it would not work out well.

初めから相手に負ける～はしなかった I never *thought* I would be beaten from the beginning.

彼とは二度と会えぬ～がした I *felt that* it would be the last time to see him.

彼女の話を聞いているとあてにならぬ～がした Listening to her, I *thought* she was not reliable.

彼はゴルフをして～をまぎらわそうとした He tried to *forget* it by playing golf.

人を人とも思わぬ彼の態度が～にくわぬ His presumptuous behavior *gets on my nerves*.

30年も先にならなきゃ結果がわからないとは, ずいぶん～の長い話だ What a *slow* business, that it should take thirty years to know the results!

～の遠くなるようなばく大な金額だ That's a *tremendous* amount of money, indeed.

5〖空気·水蒸気などの気体〗¶ 久しぶりに山の～を十分に吸ってきた I have breathed in deeply the mountain *air* after a long time.

6〖香·味〗¶ ～の抜けたビールを飲まされた I was served *stale* (≒ *flat*) beer.

ふたをしないとコーヒーの～が抜ける If you don't keep the lid closed, the coffee will lose its *freshness*.

酒のびんはよく洗わないと酒の～が残る Unless you wash a *sake* bottle well, the *smell* will remain.

昨夜飲みすぎてまだ酒の～が体に残っている I overdrank last night, and have a hangover.

き【機】〔an〕opportunity; an occasion.

¶ 彼はすかさずその～に乗じた He took advantage of the *opportunity* at once. ～が熟するのを待とう Let's wait for *a* more favorable *opportunity*. 彼は～を見るに敏だ He is quick to seize *an opportunity*. 彼との再会の～を逸した I missed the *chance* to see him again.

き【木】1 a tree; (木材) wood; (材木) 米 lumber; 英 timber.

¶ ～で作った箱 a box made of *wood*; a *wooden* box.

2 〖慣用的表現〗 ¶ 彼は私の頼みに対して～で鼻をくくったような返事をした He treated my request snappishly.

それは～に竹を継ぐようなものだ It is just as if the fox's skin were sewn to the lion's.

～によって魚を求む go up a tree for fish.

き【生】 ¶ ウイスキーを～で飲む drink whisky *straight* (≒ *neat; short*).

き【奇】 (奇妙さ) strangeness; (新奇) novelty; (風変り) eccentricity. ¶ 彼は非常に～を好む He is very fond of *novelty*. 彼は～をてらってあんな格好をしている He wears such strange clothes in order to *make himself look eccentric*. 事実は小説よりも～なり (諺) *Fact is stranger than fiction*.

-き【-忌】 〔a period of〕 mourning. ¶ 一周～ the first anniversary (*of a person's* death).

ぎ【義】 (正義) righteousness; justice; (信義) honor. ¶ 彼は～を重んずる人だ He is a *righteous* man. / He values *honor*. ～を見てせざるは勇なきなり To see what *is right* and not to do it is a want of courage.

ぎ【儀】 ¶ 私～ I; as for me. この～はいかが取り計らいましょうか How shall I treat this *affair*? その～ばかりはお許しください I'm awfully sorry I cannot accept *that*.

ギア 〔a〕 gear. ¶ 4段～付きの車 a car with four *gears*. 車の～を入れる put the car *in gear*. ～を変える shift *gears*.

ロー― low gear. トップ― top gear.

きあい【気合い】 a cry. ¶ 彼は「えい」と～をかけた He shouted "Ei." どうも～が入らない Anyhow I'*m* not *in the mood*. 彼にもっとがんばるように～を入れた I *inspired* him *to* work much harder.

きあけ【忌明け】 expiration of the period of mourning.

きあつ【気圧】 atmospheric pressure. ¶ ～の谷 a trough of *atmospheric pressure*.

―計 a barometer. ―配置 the distribution of atmospheric pressure. 高(低)― high (low) 〔atmospheric〕 pressure.

きあわ・せる【来合わせる】 ¶ たまたま彼がそこに～せていた He *happened to be* there.

きあん【起案】 ¶ 請願書を～する *draw up* a petition.

ぎあん【議案】 (議会の) a bill; (会議の) a question. ¶ ～を可決(否決)する adopt (reject) *a bill*. ～を提出する introduce (≒ bring in) *a bill*.

きい【奇異】 ¶ それは彼に～な感じをいだかせるだろう It will strike him as *strange*. こういうと～な感じがするかもしれない This may *sound strange*.

キー a key.

―ホールダー a key ring (キーホールダーは和製英語). ―ボックス a keyboard. ―ステーション the key station. ―パンチャー a key puncher.

きいきい ¶ 階段が～鳴るのを耳にした We heard the stairs *squeak*.

―声 a squeaky (≒ piping) voice.

ぎいぎい ¶ ～音のする床 a *creaky* floor. その古い家は風で～ときしんだ The old house *creaked* with the wind.

きいちご【木苺】 〖植物〗 a raspberry.

きいっぽん【生一本】 ¶ 灘(なだ)の～ *genuine Nada sake*. ～な男 a *simple and honest* man.

きいと【生糸】 raw silk.

―検査所 a silk conditioning house. ―商 a raw silk merchant; (商業) raw silk trade.

きいろ【黄色】 yellow; yellow color.

きいろ・い【黄色い】 yellow. ¶ ～い声 a *shrill* (≒ *piping*) voice. ～い声を出す scream. 彼はまだくちばしが～い (未熟だ) He *is* still *green*. / He *is* just *a greenhorn*.

きいろがかった【黄色がかった】 yellowish.

きいん【起因】 ¶ …に～する be caused by; originate in; come from.

ぎいん【議員】 (一般の) a member (*of* an assembly); (日本の国会の) a Dietman; a Dietwoman; (アメリカの) a congressman; a congresswoman.

区(市; 県)会― a member of the ward (municipal; prefectural) assembly.

ぎいん【議院】 the House; the Diet (国によりその呼び名は異なり, 日本では衆議院は the House of Representatives, 参議院は the House of Councilors; アメリカの下院は the House of Representatives, 上院は the Senate; イギリスの下院は the House of Commons, 上院は the House of Lords).

―運営委員会 the House Operation (≒ Steering) Committee.

きう【気宇】 ¶ ～広大な人 a *broad-minded* man.

きうつり【気移り】 ¶ どのネクタイを買うかあれこれ～して決めかねる I am quite puzzled which tie to take.

きうり【胡瓜】 〖植物〗 a cucumber.

きうん【気運・機運】 (機会) the time; 〔an〕 opportunity; (傾向) a tendency. ¶ 社会主義化の～が高まっている There is *a* growing *tendency* toward socialism. 和平会談の～がいよいよ熟した At last *the time* is ripe for starting peace talks.

きえ【帰依】 conversion. ¶ 彼は仏教に～している He *is converted to* (≒ *believes in*) Buddhism.

きえい【気鋭】 ¶ 新進～の作家 a young and promising writer; an up-and-coming writer.

きえい・る【消え入る】 ¶ ～るような声で in a *faint* voice.

き・える【消える】 1 〖火・燈火がなくなる〗 go out. ¶ 急に電燈が～えた The light *went out* all of a sudden.

暖炉の薪が～えかかっていた The firewood in the fireplace *was* almost *dying*.

風でマッチの火が～えた The light of the match *was blown out* by the wind.

火事はなかなか～えなかった The fire *was* not easily *extinguished* (≒ *put out*).

みんなが立ち去ったあとは，火の〜えたようにひっそりしてしまった After they left, it *was all very quiet and still* (≒ *was all silent as a grave*).

2 〖見えなくなる〗 disappear. ¶ 彼の姿はやみに〜えた He *disappeared* into the dark.

飛行機はたちまちのうちに視界から〜えた The plane *went out of sight* in no time.

隊員の姿は吹雪の中に〜えていった The members of the party *vanished* in the snowstorm.

3 〖いなくなる〗 disappear. ¶ 彼は会議の途中いつの間にか〜えた He *disappeared* during the meeting without being noticed.

おまえどこへ〜えていたんだ Where in the world have you been?

恥ずかしくてどこかに〜えてしまいたかった I was so ashamed that I felt like *disappearing* (≒ *hiding myself*).

幽霊の姿は〜えて二度と現われなかった The ghost (≒ apparition) *vanished* never to reappear.

4 〖形や音などがなくなる〗 ¶ もう辺りの山々の雪もすっかり〜えた The snow on the surrounding mountains *has* all *melted away*.

庭にはところどころに雪が〜え残っていた The snow remained here and there in the garden.

この着物のしみはうまく〜えない I can't *get rid of* the stain on this dress.

ここのところは紙がこすれて字が〜えて読めない The paper *is rubbed out* here, and the letter is unreadable (≒ illegible).

このけしゴムはよく〜える This eraser *works well.* / This eraser *is quite good.*

このマジックで書けばなかなか〜えない If you use (≒ write with) this 'magic pen', it won't *come off* (≒ *fade out*).

きえん【気炎】 big talk. ¶ 彼らは〜をあげていた They *were talking big.* われわれは彼の怪〜にすっかり当てられた We were all victims to his *bombast*.

きえん【奇縁】 a strange chance (≒ fate). ¶ ここでお目にかかるなんてなんという〜でしょう What *a strange fate* 〔it is〕 to meet you here!

ぎえんきん【義援金】 contribution. ¶ 〜を募る raise *contribution*.

きえんさん【希塩酸】〘化学〙 dilute hydrochloric acid.

きおいた·つ【気負い立つ】 ¶ 彼はそのニュースを聞いて〜っていた He *was excited* to hear the news.

きおう【既往】 past. ¶ 〜は問わない We don't consider what has been done. / Let bygones be bygones.

—症 the past diseases of a patient; a case history.

きおく【記憶】 memory; recollection; remembrance.

1 〖記憶する〗 ¶ その当時のことを〜していますか Do you *remember* those days?

その学生の名前は〜している I *remember* the student's name.

あの人が2番めに演説したのをはっきり〜している I can *recall* clearly that he was the second to make a speech.

先生の言ったことを全部〜して，そのまま答案に書こうなんていうのはばかげている It's ridiculous to try to *memorize* everything the teacher says and to write it down at the examination.

2 〖記憶は〗 ¶ 彼女がはっきり申し出を断わったというきみの〜は確かか Are you sure you *remember* right that she flatly declined the offer?

3 〖記憶が〗 ¶ 確かにぼくはそう言った〜がある I *remember* distinctly having said so.

その場でなにをしたか〜がない I don't *remember* what I did there.

どうもこのごろ〜が衰えて(鈍って)きた My *memory* is rather shaky (≒ often fails me) recently. / My *memory* is starting to fail me recently.

4 〖記憶に〗 ¶ その熱戦のもようは今なお私の〜に残っている The scene of the exciting game is still vivid in my *mind*.

その飛行機事故はまだわれわれの〜に新しい The plane crash is still fresh in our *memory*.

ぼくの〜にまちがいなければ，確かに彼女はその場に居合わせた If *I remember right* (≒ If *I'm not mistaken*), I'm positive she was there.

そんなことは私の〜にない I can't *recollect* such a thing. / It has escaped my *memory*.

5 〖記憶を〗 ¶ 10年前の〜を頼りに彼の家を捜したが見つからなかった I looked for his house from what I *remembered* ten years before, but in vain.

おぼろげな〜をたどっているうちに，当時父は存命だったことに気づいた Tracing back my faint *memory* I found out that my father was still alive then.

自動車事故に会って以来あの人は〜を喪失している After the auto accident he lost his *memory*.

あの席でだれがなんと言ったか〜を呼び起こしてほしい I want you to *recall to your mind* what was said at the meeting and by whom.

6 〖合成語〗 ¶ このごろ〜力が悪くなった My *memory* has failed recently.

きみの〜力はすばらしい You have *a* splendid *memory*.

2,000の単語を1週間で覚える〜術を教えてやろうか Do you want me to tell you how to *memorize* 2,000 words in a week?

きおくれ【気後れ】 ¶ 彼の前にでるとぼくは〜する I *feel* (≒ *get*) *nervous* in his presence. その光景を見て彼女は〜してしまった She *lost her nerve* at the sight.

きおち【気落ち】 disappointment. ¶ 打ち続く不幸に彼はすっかり〜している He *is* completely *discouraged* by a series of misfortunes.

きおん【気温】 temperature. ¶ 急に〜が摂氏32度までも上がった The *temperature* suddenly rose as high as 32° C. 〜が摂氏零下5度まで下がった The *temperature* fell (≒ dropped) to 5° C. below zero.

きおん【基音】〘物理〙〘音楽〙 a fundamental note.

ぎおん【擬音】 sound effects (複数扱い).

きか【気化】 evaporation. ¶ 〜する evaporate.

—器 an evaporator ; (内燃機関の) a carburetter. **—熱** evaporation heat.

きか【奇禍】 an accident. ¶ ～に会う meet with *an accident*.

きか【帰化】 naturalization. ¶ 日本に～する *be naturalized* as a Japanese ; *be naturalized* in Japan.

—人 a naturalized person (≒ citizen).

きか【幾何】 geometry. ¶ ～学的な geometrical.

—級数 a geometrical series (≒ progression). **—学模様** a geometrical pattern. 平面(立体 ; 球面 ; 解析)**—学** plane (solid ; spherical ; analytical) geometry.

きが【飢餓】 starvation ; hunger. ¶ ～に瀕(ひん)する face *starvation* ; be on the verge of *starvation*.

ぎが【戯画】 a caricature ; a comic picture. ¶ 人の顔を～化する *caricature* a man's face.

きかい【奇怪】 ¶ ～な事件 a *strange* affair. ～な風説 a *wild* rumor.

きかい【機械・器械】 **1** a machine ; (機械類) machinery.

¶ 停電で～が止まった The *machine* stopped because the electricity was cut off.

～が故障して当分の間動かない The *machine* won't work for a while because it is out of order.

その～を取り扱える熟練工はあまりいなかった There weren't many skilled workers who could handle (≒ operate) the *machine*.

このセーターは ～ で 編んだものだ This sweater *is machine-knitted*.

このごろは～で作ったくつが多い Recently most shoes *are machine-made*.

人手を省くため事務の～化をはかろう To save the number of people, let's use *machines* for office work.

大農でなければ農業の～化は採算がとれない Unless you engage in large-scale farming, the *mechanization* of agriculture will not pay.

そういう～じかけになっているとは知らなかった I didn't know that the *machinery* made it work like that.

—工学 mechanical engineering. **—文明** mechanical civilization. 医療**—** medical appliances (≒ instruments). 工作**—** a machine tool. 精密**—** a precision instrument.

2〖習慣的に〗¶ 彼は毎日会社に行ってただ～的に仕事をしているだけだ He goes to his office just to do his daily routine.

この問題はそう～的に簡単に割り切れるものではない This problem isn't anything you can settle so easily in a businesslike manner.

彼女の指先は～的にタイプを打ちつづけた Her fingers kept on tapping the typewriter *mechanically*.

原料から製品になるまでの仕事は全部～的に行なわれる The process from raw material to the product is all done by *machine*.

きかい【機会】 a chance ; an opportunity.

1〖機会が〗¶ これからはわれわれも海外へ行く～が増えてくる In future there will be more *chances* for us to go abroad.

このことについて彼とゆっくり話す～がなかった I didn't have *a chance* to talk this matter over with him.

～がありしだい, きみを郷里から呼び寄せるつもりだ As soon as I get *a chance*, I mean to invite you from the hometown.

2〖機会に〗¶ こんな～になかなか巡り会えるものではない Such *an opportunity* will hardly ever come.

それを～に彼は酒を断った Seizing the *occasion*, he stopped drinking.

この～に私の考えを述べさせていただけたことを感謝いたします I thank you for the *opportunity* of expressing my opinion.

彼女とは偶然の～に知り合った I came to know her *unexpectedly* (≒ *by chance*).

その件についてはまた次の～にいたしましょう Let's leave that matter till the next *occasion*.

時間がありませんから, それの詳しい説明は別の～に譲ります As there is not enough time, I will leave the full explanation of it for another *occasion*.

3〖機会を〗¶ 彼はあらゆる～をとらえて公害の恐ろしさを説いた He took every *chance* to speak of the horror of pollution.

ぼくの立場を弁明する～を与えてください Let me have *a chance* to explain myself.

会議は混乱し, それを提案する～を失った The conference was in disorder and I lost the *chance* of suggesting the proposal.

まだあの方にお目にかかる～を得ておりません I haven't had the *chance* of meeting him yet.

4〖その他の助詞などとともに〗¶ きみの真価を発揮する千載一遇の～だ It's *a* rare *opportunity* to show your true ability.

事の真相をただす～は何度もあった There were *times* when we could have inquired into the truth.

きがい【危害】〔an〕injury ; harm. ¶ ～を加える do *(a person) harm* (≒ *an injury*); inflict *an injury*. ～を被る sustain *injuries (from)*. ～を免れる escape *unhurt*.

きがい【気概】 spirit ; backbone ; pluck ; mettle. ¶ ～のある男 a man *of pluck* (≒ *of mettle*). ～がない have no *spirit*. ～を示す show *one's mettle*.

ぎかい【議会】 (国会) a national assembly ; (日本) the Diet ; (アメリカ) Congress ; (イギリス) Parliament. ¶ 第50～ the fiftieth session of *the Diet*. ～を召集する call *the Diet* in session. ～を解散する dissolve *the Diet*.

—政治 parliamentary government. **—制度** the parliamentary system. **—主義** parliamentarism.

きがえ【着替え】 (衣服) extra clothes. ¶ ～をする *change* clothes. ～3枚 three *changes* 〔*of clothes*〕.

きか・える【着替える】 *change one's* clothes. ¶ 晩餐会のために～える *dress* for dinner.

きがかり【気掛かり】anxiety; worry; concern. ¶ 将来が～になる I *feel anxious* (≒ *feel uneasy*) *about* the future.

きかく【企画】a plan; planning. ¶ ～する plan; form (≒ lay) a plan.

—力 planning ability. ¶ ～力のある人 a man of *great enterprise*; an *enterprising* man.

きかく【規格】a standard; a norm. ¶ 自動車の部品を～化する *standardize* the parts of an automobile.

—判 a standard size. —品 standardized articles (≒ goods).

きがく【器楽】instrumental music.

きがけ【来がけ】¶ ～に彼に会った I saw him *on my way here* (≒ *while coming here*).

きかげき【喜歌劇】a comic opera; an operetta (複 operettas, operetti).

きかざ·る【着飾る】dress up. ¶ 彼女はきょう～っている She *is dressed up* today. / She *is gaily dressed* today. 彼女は豪華に～っている She *is dressed up to the nines*.

きか·せる【聞かせる】¶ 彼はその手紙を読んで～せてくれた He kindly *read* the letter for me. 頼むといつも彼は歌を～せてくれた He always *sang* for me if I asked him to. ひとつギターを～せてあげましょうか Shall I *play* the guitar for you? 新聞には子どもに～せたくない話がたくさんある In newspapers there appear many things which I don't want to *let* the children *know* (≒ *hear*).

きか·せる【利かせる】¶ 気を～せる *use one's* head. はばを～せる *exercise* influence *on* (≒ *over*). 塩を～せる *season* (food) with salt.

きがた【木型】wooden pattern. ¶ 帽子の～ *a* hat *block*. くつの～ *a* shoe *tree*.

きがね【気兼ね】constraint; hesitation. ¶ ～して with *reserve*. ～なく without *reserve*. 彼の前では～してしまう I cannot help *feeling constraint* in his presence.

きがまえ【気構え】preparedness; anticipation; expectation. ¶ 敵の攻撃に対する～ *preparedness* for the enemy attack. 彼らには弱い者を助けようとする～がない They *are* not *ready to* help the weak.

きがる【気軽】¶ 彼は～に何事も引き受けてくれる He *is* always *ready to* take anything upon himself.

きかん【気管】〖解剖学〗the trachea (複 tracheas, tracheae); the windpipe.

—支 a bronchus (複 bronchi). —支炎〖医学〗bronchitis.

きかん【器官】an organ.

生殖— the genital (≒ sexual) organs. 発声— vocal organs.

きかん【機関】**1**〖エンジン·機械〗an engine; a machine.

¶ 船は～の故障で漂流している The boat is drifting because of *engine* trouble.

—士 a locomotive driver; 米 an engineer. —長 a chief engineer. —区 an engineer's ward. —庫 a locomotive depot. —室 an engine room. 内燃— an internal combustion engine. 補助— an auxiliary engine.

2〖手段·設備·機構〗a means; an institution; a system.

交通— ¶ いっさいの交通～が途絶した All the *traffic* came to a standstill. 通信— ¶ 通信～がまひの状態になった Telephone and telegram *services* (≒ All the communications) were paralyzed. 教育— an educational institution. 行政— an administrative organ. 金融— a financial agency.

きかん【季刊】a quarterly [magazine].

きかん【奇観】a wonderful sight; a wonder. ¶ コロラドの～ the *wonderful spectacles* of Colorado.

きかん【既刊】¶ ～の already (≒ previously) published (≒ issued).

—図書目録 a list of books already published.

きかん【帰還】a return; (本国へ) a repatriation. ¶ ～する return; come home.

—者 a returnee; a repatriate. —兵 a returned soldier.

きかん【基幹】a mainstay.

—産業 basic (≒ key) industries.

きかん【期間】a term; a period. ¶ 一定の～内に within *a* definite (≒ certain) *period of time*. 有効～ the *term* of validity; the available *period*.

きかん【旗艦】a flagship.

きかん【汽罐】a [steam] boiler.

—室 a boiler room; (船の) a stokehold.

きかん【亀鑑】a paragon; a pattern; an excellent example.

きがん【祈願】[a] prayer; supplication.

¶ 平和への～ *a prayer* for peace.

ぎかん【技官】a technical officer.

ぎがん【義眼】a false (≒ an artificial; a glass) eye.

きかんき【利かん気】¶ ～の女の子 a girl *of spirit*. ～の人 (負け嫌いの) an *unyielding* man.

きかんし【機関誌】an organ. ¶ 各政党はそれぞれの～を通じ日本とその国との国交回復問題を論じた Political parties expressed their opinions on the restoration of diplomatic relations between the country and Japan through their respective *party publications*. 業界の～に各社の本年度新型車の紹介がある You will find all the new cars of this year represented in the *official bulletin* of the trade association.

きかんしゃ【機関車】a locomotive.

蒸気— a steam locomotive. ディーゼル— a Diesel locomotive. 電気— an electric locomotive.

きかんじゅう【機関銃】a machine gun.

軽— a sub machine gun.

きき【危機】a crisis (複 crises). ¶ 内閣の～ *a* cabinet *crisis*. ～に瀕(ひん)する be in *a critical condition*; be in *a critical situation*: come to *a crisis*.

—一髪 ¶ ～一髪というとき at the *critical*

moment; in *a pinch*. われわれはその事故から～一髪で助かった We escaped the accident *by a hair's breadth* (≒ *a hairbreadth*).

きき【鬼気】¶～迫る恐ろしい映画 *a bloodcurdling* horror movie.

きき【喜喜】¶～として merrily; joyfully; cheerfully.

ぎぎ【疑義】⇒ぎもん

ききあわ·す【聞き合わす】make inquiries (*about*); inquire (*about*).

ききい·る【聞き入る】¶彼らはその話に～ったThey *listened attentively to* the story.

ききい·れる【聞き入れる】¶要求を～れる *grant* a request. 人の希望を～れる *comply with* another's wish. 忠告を～れない *refuse* an advice.

ききうで【利き腕】the right arm (≒ hand); the more dexterous arm (≒ hand).

ききお·く【聞き置く】(覚えておく) hear (≒ keep) in mind; (聞くだけにする) hear and give no answer.

ききおと·す【聞き落とす】¶彼は一語も～さなかった He did not *fail to hear* a single word. / He did not *miss* a single word.

ききおぼえ【聞き覚え】¶～のある声 a *familiar* voice. その声には～がなかった The voice *was unfamiliar to* me.

ききかいかい【奇奇怪怪】¶～な事件 a *very strange* affair. ～な話 a *most monstrous* story.

ききかえ·す【聞き返す】ask again (≒ back).

ききかじ·る【聞き齧る】¶彼は子どものときに英語を～った He *picked up a smattering of* English when he was a child. 彼女はフランス語を～っている She *has a smattering of* French.

ききぐるし·い【聞き苦しい】disagreeable to hear; unpleasant to the ear; (声) harsh (voice).

ききごたえ【聞き応え】¶～のある講演 a lecture *worth listening to* (≒ *hearing*); an *impressive* talk.

ききこみ【聞き込み】dope; information; (うわさ) a hearsay.
—捜査 the search by questioning neighbors.

ききこ·む【聞き込む】¶彼らは彼についてなにか～んだようだ They seem to *have heard* something about him.

ききざけ【利き酒】¶彼は～がうまい He is an excellent wine taster.

ききじょうず【聞き上手】a good listener.

ききすて【聞き捨て】¶～ならぬことば an *unpardonable* (≒ an *inexcusable*) remark. それは～ならぬ I cannot *pass it over*. 彼はぼくの忠告を～にした He *ignored* my advice.

ききそこな·う【聞き損う】fail to hear.

ききだ·す【聞き出す】¶彼らからなにも～せなかった I could not *draw* any information from them.

ききただ·す【聞き糺す】¶事実を～す (確かめる) *ascertain* (≒ *make sure of*) the fact. その男の名前を彼女に～した (尋ねた) I *inquired of* her the man's name.

ききちがい【聞き違い】¶～をする mishear; (誤解する) misunderstand. ⇒ききちがえる

ききちが·える【聞き違える】¶きみは彼のことばを～えたに違いない You must *have misheard* his remark. / You must *have heard* his remark *incorrectly*.

ききつ·ける【聞きつける】¶その騒ぎを～けて現場へ人々は駆けつけた At the uproar people rushed to the place.

ききつたえ【聞き伝え】hearsay. ¶それを～で知った I have it from (≒ by) *hearsay*.

ききづら·い【聞き辛い】¶～い声 a *harsh* voice. ～い話 an *unpleasant* story.

ききて【聞き手】a hearer; a listener; (聴衆) an audience.

ききとが·める【聞き咎める】reprove; find fault with (what *one* says).

ききどころ【聞き所】¶この話の～ *the most interesting part* of this story. 彼の話の肝心な～ *the most important part* (≒ *point*) of his speech.

ききとど·ける【聞き届ける】¶われわれの願いは～けられた Our request *was granted*.

ききとり【聞き取り】hearing. ¶～の試験 a *hearing* test.

ききと·る【聞き取る】¶どうも彼の言うことがよく～れない I can hardly *catch* what he says. 彼はあまり早口で言うことがよく～れない He speaks so fast that I cannot *follow* him. 雑音でニュースはほとんど～れなかった The noise made the newscast almost *inaudible*.

ききなお·す【聞き直す】¶あやふやな箇所を彼に～しておこう Let's *ask* him *again* what we could not understand well.

ききなが·す【聞き流す】¶私の切なる願いを彼は～した He *was deaf to* my entreaties. どうせ実行できない案だと思ったので～しておいた As I thought it was impossible to carry out the plan, I *paid no attention to* (≒ *took no notice of*) it.

ききな·れる【聞き慣れる】¶～れた名 a *familiar* name. ～れると雑音もさして気にならないものだ Noises do not grate upon the ear after we *have got used to* them. ～れない専門語が次々と飛び出してくるのには参った A flood of *strange* technical terms upset me very much.

ききにく·い【聞き難い】¶彼の発音は不明瞭(ふめいりょう)で～い His pronunciation is so inarticulate that it *is hard to follow* (≒ *catch*) what he says. 彼にこんなことは～い It needs courage to ask him such an awkward question.

ききほ·れる【聞き惚れる】¶彼らはその音楽に～れた They *were charmed* (≒ *were enchanted*) *with* the music.

ききみみ【聞き耳】¶病人は彼女の来るのに～を立てた The sick man *listened for* her coming. 彼のことばを聞きとろうと～を立てていた I *was straining my ears* to catch his words.

ききめ【効き目】effect; virtue. ¶その薬はいくら

か～があるだろう The medicine will *have* some *effect* on you. / The medicine will *do* you some *good*.

ききもの【聞き物】¶今週のラジオの～ this week's radio *highlights*. それは～だ That's *worth listening to*.

ききもら·す【聞き漏らす】¶そのところは～した I *failed to catch* the point. 彼の住所は～した I *forgot to ask* his address.

ききゃく【棄却】〖法律〗rejection; dismissal. ¶抗告を～する *dismiss* (≒ *reject*) an appeal.

ききゅう【危急】an emergency; a crisis.
¶～を救う save (*a person*) from *imminent emergency*. ～存亡のときには in case of *emergency*.

ききゅう【気球】a balloon. ¶～を上げる fly *a balloon*.
観測― an observation balloon. 係留― a captive balloon.

ききゅう【帰休】¶彼は～中だ He *is* home *on leave*.
一時―制度(労務者の) a layoff system.

ききょ【起居】¶～をともにする live together (*with a person*).

ぎきょ【義挙】a worthy (≒ noble) undertaking; a heroic deed (≒ act).

ききょう【帰京】¶～する return to Tokyo.

ききょう【帰郷】homecoming. ¶墓参のために～する *return home* to visit the family grave.

ききょう【桔梗】〖植物〗a Chinese bellflower.

ききょう【奇矯】¶彼は時々～な言動でわれわれを驚かす He sometimes surprises us by his *eccentric* conduct.

きぎょう【企業】an enterprise. ¶～の合理化 rationalization of *enterprise*.
―家 an enterpriser. ―化 commercialization. ―整備 industrial adjustment. 公共―体 a public corporation. 大― a large-scale enterprise. 中小― medium and small-sized enterprises. 中小―者 medium and small-scale industrialists. 零細― a smallest scale enterprise.

きぎょう【機業】the textile industry.

ぎきょう【義侠】chivalry.
―心 ¶彼は～心に富んでいる He is full of *chivalry*.

ぎきょうだい【義兄弟】a brother-in-law.
¶～の契りを結ぶ make brothers (*with a person*); swear to be brothers (*with a person*).

ききょうりょうほう【気胸療法】〖医学〗a pneumothorax treatment.

ぎきょく【戯曲】a drama; a play. ¶～を書く write *a drama*. 小説を～化する *dramatize* a novel.
―作家 a dramatist; a playwright.

ききわけ【聞き分け】¶～のよい子ども a *docile* (≒ *easily taught*; *obedient*) child. ～の悪い子 a *naughty* (≒ an *obstinate*) child.

ききわ·ける【聞き分ける】¶10種類以上の鳥の声を～けられる I can *recognize* more than ten kinds of birds *by listening to* them. きみはものの道理が～けられないのか Can't you *hear* reason?

ききん【飢饉】〔a〕famine. ¶～に苦しむ suffer from *famine*. 大～がその国の東部を襲った *A* big (≒ severe) *famine* visited the eastern part of the country.
水― a water famine.

ききん【基金】a fund; a foundation. ¶～を集める raise *funds*. ～を設定する establish (≒ create) *a fund* (*for*).
国際通貨― the International Monetary Fund (I. M. F. または IMF と略す). 日本国際交流― the Japan Foundation.

ききんぞく【貴金属】precious metals.
―商(店) a jewelry store; (人) a jeweler.

きく【菊】〖植物〗a chrysanthemum. ¶～の節句 the *Chrysanthemum* Festival. ～の紋章 a *chrysanthemum* crest.
―人形 a chrysanthemum figure.

き·く【聞く·聴く】**1**〖聞こえる〗hear. ¶変な音を～いた I *heard* a strange sound.
時計が2時を打つのを～いた I *heard* a clock strike two.
そのニュースをラジオで～いた I *heard* the news over the radio.
2〖傾聴する〗listen to. ¶いいか,よく～け Now, *listen to* me.
ぼくの言うことを終わりまで～いてからにしてくれ Wait till you *hear* me *out*./ Wait till I finish my sentence[s].
そんなくだらぬことを～いている暇はない I have no time to *lend my ear to* such a trifle.
3〖聞き知る〗¶その話は～かなかったことにしておこう I am going to pretend that no words had passed between you and me about the matter.
どこからそんな話を～いたんだ Where did you *pick up* such a story?
～くところによると,彼はちかぢか辞めるそうだ From what I *have heard*, he is going to leave his office in the near future.
そういう先例は～いたことがない I *have* never *heard of* such a thing before.
4〖聞き入れる〗¶彼は医者の忠告も～かず不摂生の限りを尽くした *Disregarding* his doctor's advice, he indulged in excesses.
そんな忠告なんか～くものか I am not going to *follow* such advice.
ぼくの願いもたまには～いてくれ I hope you will *grant* my request once in a while.
この子は先生の言われることならよく～きます My son *listens* only *to* what teachers say.
おれの言うことを～かぬと承知しないぞ If you do not *listen to* what I am going to say, you will be sorry for it.
彼は同僚たちの意見を～かないで独断で事を処理した He decided for himself without *consulting* his colleagues' opinions.
5〖問う·尋ねる〗¶これがうそだと思うなら彼に～いてみたまえ Why don't you *ask* him if you don't believe it?

このことについては専門家の意見を～いてみる必要がある I think we must *refer* the matter *to* the experts.

近所に花屋があるかと～かれた I *was asked* if there was a flower shop near by.

き・く【利く・効く】**1**〖効き目がある〗¶この薬は風邪によく～く This medicine *is effective* against a cold.

薬が～いたらしく，熱が下がってきた The medicine must *have worked*. The fever is coming down.

あの子はしかられたのがだいぶ～いたらしい I think the boy has learned the lesson by getting a good scolding.

3回表のホームランが～いた The homer in the top of the third inning *was decisive*, I think.

2〖よく働く・できる〗¶彼は中風で左手が全然～かない He lost the freedom of his left arm after a stroke.

風邪で鼻が～かない I have lost my sense of smell on account of a cold.

ネコは暗やみでも目が～く A cat can see in the dark.

茶器についてはよく目が～いていられますね You have an expert eye for tea ceremony utensils.

あの子はなかなか気が～く She is a *clever* girl.

なかなか～いたようなことを言うね You are very *clever*, aren't you?

車が横にスリップしてブレーキが～かなかった The car skidded (≒ slipped sideways), and the brakes did not *work*.

この自動車はブレーキがよく～かない This car has faulty brakes.

年をとると無理が～かなくなる We cannot strain ourselves so much in our old age.

けがをしてから体の自由が～かない I have lost the freedom of movement since the accident.

どうもこの子はがんばりが～かぬ The boy seems to lack endurance.

この上着はまだまだ裏返しが～く This jacket (≒ coat) is still good for turning.

この生地は洗たくが～く This cloth is washable.

きぐ【器具】an appliance; (備えつけの) a fixture.

消防―― a fire-fighting appliance. 照明―― lighting fixtures. 電気―― an electrical appliance.

きぐ【危惧】a fear; misgivings. ¶大いなる～ *a* strong *fear*. 彼の計画を～する向きもある Some people *have misgivings about* his plan.

きぐう【奇遇】an unexpected meeting.

¶きみとここで会うなんてまったくの～だ What *a happy coincidence* to meet you here!

きぐう【寄寓】¶おじの家に～することになろう I will *lodge with* (≒ *live with*; *stay with*) my uncle.

きぐすり【生薬】a drug.

――屋 a druggist; a drugstore; 英 a chemist's shop.

きくずれ【着崩れ】¶この背広はまだ～がしない This suit keeps its original shape yet.

きぐち【木口】(材質) the quality of timber; (切り口) a cross-section of wood.

きくばん【菊判】a small octavo; a medium octavo.

きぐみ【木組み】a wooden frame. ¶この家の～はがっしりしている This house has *a* massive wooden *framework*.

きぐらい【気位】¶彼女は～が高い She is a *proud* (≒ an *arrogant*) woman. / She *holds* her *head high*.

きぐろう【気苦労】(心配) care; (心配ごと) cares; worries.

¶われわれのことで母は～が絶えない My mother *is* always *worrying* 〔*herself*〕 *about* us.

彼女は～のために病気になった It is *cares* that made her sick. / *Cares* marred her health.

彼女は～が多い She has a great many *cares*.

彼は全く～がない He is free from *cares* of every kind.

きけい【奇形】deformation; (人または物) a deformity.

――児 a deformed child. 先天的―― a congenital (≒ an inborn) deformity.

きけい【詭計】a trick. ¶～を用いて by *a trick*. 彼は野望達成のためあらゆる～を用いた He used every *cunning artifice to* accomplish his ambition.

ぎけい【義兄】a brother-in-law (複 brothers-in-law).

ぎげい【技芸】(特殊な技術) art; (美術と工芸) arts and crafts; (手芸) handicrafts; (芸事) accomplishments.

きげき【喜劇】a comedy.

――作家 a comedist; a comic dramatist. ――女優 a comedienne. ――俳優 a comedian. 軽―― a light comedy. どたばた―― a slapstick comedy; a noisy farce. どたばた――映画 a slapstick motion picture.

きけつ【帰結】end; result; conclusion.

¶それはその事件の当然の～として考えられることだ It is to be expected as *a* natural *consequence* of the incident.

きけつ【既決】――事項 a matter settled (≒ decided).

ぎけつ【議決】a resolution; a decision. ¶満場一致で戦争反対が～された The *decision* against war was made unanimously.

――権 the vote.

きけん【危険】danger; risk.

1〖危険だ〗¶飛行機の旅は～だと思いますか Do you think it *is dangerous* to travel by air? 「*risky*.

その事業は～すぎる The enterprise *is* too

夜更けにひとり歩きするのは～だ It *is dangerous* to walk alone late at night.

引火爆発の～がある There is some *fear* of the inflammables blowing up.

2〖危険が〗¶そんなに毎日その薬を飲むと中毒の～がある Daily use of the medicine may cause poisoning.

この種の手術には多少の～が伴う Operations of this kind involve some *risk*.

3 〖危険を〗 ¶ 彼は生命の～を感じた He felt *a danger* to his life.
～を顧みず猛火の中に飛び込んだ Braving the *danger*, he ran into the raging fire.
池のまわりにさくを立てて子どもが落ちる～を防いだ They built a fence around the pond to prevent children from falling into it.
彼の病状は～を脱した He has passed the *critical* condition.
原子力の発展は人類破滅の～をはらんでいる The increasing use of nuclear power can possibly lead to the total annihilation of mankind.
4 〖危険に〗 ¶ 火の手が強く一時は私の家も～になった The fire gathered so much strength that my house *was* also *in danger* for a while.
こう自動車が多くては,われわれの生命は絶えず～にさらされているといってよい With so many cars around us, our lives are always exposed to *danger*.
修復する費用がなく，その建造物は倒壊の～に瀕(ひん)している The building is on the verge of collapse, since there is no fund to meet the cost of repair.
5 〖合成語〗 ¶ 彼は～人物だ. 注意しろ Watch him. He is a *dangerous* character.
彼は当局から～人物としてにらまれている He is marked by the police as a public menace.
現体制を批判すると～思想だときめつけるのはおかしい I do not see why criticisms against the established order should be at once regarded as *dangerous* thoughts.
たばこは肺がんの～性を有する Smoking is a possible cause of lung cancer.
あの一帯は放射能汚染の～区域に指定されている That district as a whole is designated as a radiation-polluted *danger* area.

きけん【棄権】(投票の) abstention (*from* voting); (権利の) renunciation (*of one's* right); (競技の) withdrawal (*of one's* entry).
¶ 投票を～する *abstain from* voting. 権利を～する *give up* (≒ *abandon*) *one's* right. 競技の初めから～する *withdraw one's* entry. 競技の途中で～する *drop out of* a race.

きげん【起源・起原】 origin; rise. ¶ 文明の～ the *origin* of civilization. ある習慣の～を調べる trace the *origin* of a custom. その習慣は中国に～をもっている The practice owes its *origin* to the Chinese. 茶道の～は16世紀以前にまでさかのぼる The *origin* of the tea ceremony dates back before the 16th century.

きげん【紀元】 an era. ¶ ～1500年に in the year 1500 of the Christian *era*; in 1500 A. D. ～前50年 50 B. C.

きげん【期限】 a term. ¶ ～が切れる前に before the *term* expires. 締め切りの～を定める fix *a term* (≒ *a deadline*) (*for*). 支払いの～を延期する extend the *term* of payment. 手形は今月の10日に～が来る The bill falls (≒ becomes) *due* on the 10th of this month.
～が来たら本を図書館に返してください Please return the book to the library when it is *due*.
―切れ ¶ ～切れの際には at the expiration of the *term*. この手形は～切れだ This bill *is overdue*. 有効― the term of validity. ¶ この切符の有効～は3日間だ This ticket *is good* (≒ *is effective*) for three days.

きげん【機嫌】 **1** 〖安否〗 *one's* health. ¶ その後ご～はいかがですか How have you been?
ご～伺いにまいりました I am here to see *how you are doing* (≒ *how you are getting along*).
ご両親様のご～いかがですか How are your father and mother?
2 〖気分〗 temper; mood; humor. ¶ 赤ん坊は～が悪いと変な泣き方をする Babies cry fretfully when they do not *feel well*.
なんで彼はあんなに～が悪いんだ Why *is* he *in a bad temper*? / What made him *feel so depressed*?
そんなささいなことで～を悪くするな Don't *get sore* over such a trivial matter.
ぼくの試験の成績が悪いと母は～が悪い My mother *is displeased* when I did not do well in the exam.
彼は～よくぼくを迎えた He welcomed me *warmly*.
彼女は夫の～をとるのがうまい She has tact in *pleasing* her husband.
ちょっとほんとのことを言いすぎて,彼女の～を損じた I told her the truth too frankly, and that hurt her *feelings*.
3 〖あいさつ〗 ¶ ご～よう. さようなら Good-by! / So long! / Good luck!

ぎこ【擬古】 **―主義** pseudoclassicism. **―文** a pseudoclassical style.

きこう【気孔】 a pore; (植物の) a stoma (複 stomata).

きこう【気候】 climate; (天候) weather (climate はある地方の平均的気候; weather は特定の日の天候を指す).
¶ 暑い(乾燥した)～ *a* hot (dry) *climate*. 不順な～ unseasonable *weather*. ～の変わり目に at the change of *season*. 日本は～が温和だ Japan has *a* mild *climate*.

きこう【奇行】 an eccentricity. ¶ 彼は～でもって知られている He is well-known for his *eccentricities* (≒ *eccentric conduct*).

きこう【紀行】 〔a book of〕 travels; a travel sketch. ¶ ヨーロッパ～ 〔*a book of*〕 *travels* in Europe.

きこう【起工】 ¶ ～する (建築・鉄道・運河など) break ground; (船) lay down a keel. 来週新しい住宅計画を～する We will *break ground on* the new housing project next week. 大型タンカーが～された *The keel* of the supertanker *was laid down*.
―式(一般に) a commencement ceremony; (土木建築などの) a ground breaking ceremony.

きこう【起稿】 ¶ ～する start writing; begin to write.

きこう【寄稿】a contribution. ¶ 新聞に～する *write for* (≒ *contribute to*) the newspaper.
—家 a contributor.

きこう【帰航】¶ ～の途につく start on *a voyage home*.

きこう【寄港・寄航】¶ その船は神戸に12日に～する The boat will *call at* Kobe 〔Harbor〕 on the 12th.
—地 a port of call.

きこう【機構】machinery; organization; structure. ¶ 会社の～ the *organization* of a company. 社会の経済～ the economic *structure* of 〔a〕 society. コンピューターの～ the *mechanism* of a computer.
—改革 reorganization. 国際— an international organization.

きこうぼん【稀覯本】a rare book.

きごう【記号】a sign; a symbol. ¶ ト音～〘音楽〙G clef. 数学の～ *a* mathematical *symbol*.
発音— a phonetic symbol(≒ sign). 化学— ¶ 化学～Hは水素を表わす The chemical *symbol* H stands for hydrogen.

きごう【揮毫】¶ ～する (書を) write; (絵の具で絵を) paint; (ペン・えんぴつ・クレヨンなどで絵を) draw. 漢詩を～する *write* a Chinese poem.

ぎこう【技巧】art; technique. ¶ ～的に優れている excell in *craftsmanship*. ～を凝らした文章 a highly *polished* sentence. ～に走った作品 a too *elaborate* work. そのバイオリニストは～がすぐれている The violinist is *a* good *technician*.
—家 a technician.

きこうし【貴公子】a youth of noble birth; a noble-looking young man. ¶ ～然とした態度 *princely* manners.

きこえ【聞こえ】fame; reputation. ¶ 彼はやめたといえば～がいいが, 実は首になったのだ It *sounds* harmless enough to say he has resigned, but actually he was fired.

きこえよがし【聞こえよがし】¶ 彼は～に私の悪口を言った He spoke ill of me *intentionally in my hearing*.

きこ・える【聞こえる】**1**〘耳に入る〙hear. ¶ 耳を澄ましてもなにも～えなかった I strained my ears but I could not *hear* anything.
遠くかすかに汽車の音が～えた I *heard* a faint sound of a train passing a long distance away.
階下で赤ん坊の泣いているのが～える I *hear* the baby crying downstairs.
あの人の声はかん高くてよく～える His voice *sounds* shrill and clear.
このラジオは壊れていて～えない The radio is out of order and does not work.
彼女は右の耳が～えない She *is deaf in* her right ear.
年をとると耳がよく～えなくなる When you get old, you lose your sense of *hearing*.
2〘ある感じに響く〙sound. ¶ きみの話し方はもっともらしく～える Your version of the story *sounds* very reasonable.
そう言うと皮肉に～える That *sounds* sarcastic.
そんな表現はいまどきの若者たちには非常に妙に～える Such an expression *sounds* very odd *to* the youngsters nowadays.
3〘よく知られている〙be famous. ¶ 彼の名は社会教育家として～えている He *is famous* (≒ *is well-known*) as a social educationist.
ピアニストとして彼女の名声は海外にも～えている Her name *is known* as a pianist even abroad.
そんなことをすると世間の～えが悪いからよせ Don't do it, or it may cause a scandal.
～えた料理店だ It's a *name* restaurant.

きこく【帰国】¶ ～の途につく leave for home.
大使は本国政府と打ち合わせのため～中だ The ambassador *is back in his country* for consultation with the home government.
使節は～の途上にある The delegation *is* now *on its way home*. 彼は３年ぶりでロンドンから～した He *returned* (≒ *came*) *home* from London after three years' absence.

ぎごく【疑獄】a scandal; a graft scandal. ¶ 石油～事件 *an* oil *scandal*. ～事件に連座する be involved in *a graft scandal*.

きごこち【着心地】¶ ～のよい服 a *comfortable* dress 〔to wear〕.

きごころ【気心】¶ ～のよくわかっている友 a very *close* friend. ～の知れた友人 a *dependable* friend. 私どもはお互いに～の知れた間柄だ We know each other well. / We are on *familiar* terms.

きこしめ・す【聞こし召す】¶ 彼は一杯～している He's *a bit tight*. / He *is tipsy*.

ぎこちな・い ¶ ～い態度 an *awkward* manner. 彼は～い手つきで客に茶の接待をした He *clumsily* served tea to the guests.

きこつ【気骨】backbone. ¶ 彼は～のある男だ He is a man *of mettle*. / He has *backbone*.
彼は～がない He has no *backbone*. / He lacks *backbone*.

きこなし【着こなし】¶ 彼女は～がうまい She *dresses herself* right. / She is a good dresser.

きこり【樵】a woodcutter; a woodman (複 woodmen); a lumber man; a lumberjack; a logger.

きこん【気根】〘植物〙an aerial root.

きこんしゃ【既婚者】a married man; (女性) a married woman; (履歴書など) married.

きざ【気障】〔an〕 affectation. ¶ ～なネクタイ (けばけばしい) a *flashy* (≒ *showy*) tie. 彼の～な態度がいやだ I don't like his *affectations* (≒ *affected manners*). 彼は～な話し方をする He speaks in an *affected* manner.

きさい【奇才・鬼才】〔a〕 genius; exceptional talent; (人) a genius; a prodigy. ¶ 文壇の～ *a genius* in the literary field; *a* literary *giant*.

きさい【起債】¶ 道路建設のために～する *issue* bonds to finance the highway construction.

きさい【記載】mention; entry. ¶ 新聞に～されているとおり as *printed* in the newspaper. そ

の項目を帳簿に～する *make an entry of* the item in an account book. 「item.
—事項(帳簿などの) an entry; a mentioned

きざい【器材・機材】 machine parts.

きさく【気さく】 ¶ 彼は～にだれとも話をする He is always willing to have a *friendly* chat with anyone. 彼は～だ He *is unpretentious* (≒ *is frank*). / He is a *jolly* fellow.

ぎさく【偽作】 a fake; a spurious work. ¶ ピカソの絵の～ a *fake* picture of a Picaso.

きざし【兆し】 a symptom; a sign. ¶ 不景気の～が見える The *symptoms* of economic depression are apparent. 各所に春の～が感じられる There is *a sign* of spring everywhere.

きざ・す【兆す】 ¶ 邪念が彼の心に～した A wicked thought *grew up* in his mind.

きさま【貴様】 you.

きざみつ・ける【刻み付ける】 ¶ 彼は自分の名を木の幹に～けた He *carved* his name on the tree. そのことばを深く心に～けた I *kept* those words deep in my memory.

きざみめ【刻み目】 a notch; a nick. ¶ 1センチごとに棒に～を入れる *notch* a stick at intervals of one centimeter.

きざみたばこ【刻み煙草】 pipe tobacco.

きざ・む【刻む】 ¶ タマネギを〔細かに〕～む *mince* an onion. 仏像を～む *carve* a statue of Buddha. 墓石に銘を～む *engrave* inscriptions on the tomb stone. そのことばは深く心に～まれている These words *are engraved on* my mind. / These words *are kept* deep *in* my memory. 時計が時を～む The clock *ticks away*.

きさらぎ【如月】 February.

きさん【起算】 ¶ 着手してから～して100日めに on the 100th day *counting* from the start.

きさん【帰参】 ¶ 彼の～がかなった He *was reinstated in* his former office.

ぎさん【蟻酸】〔化学〕formic acid.

きし【岸】 the shore; (川の) a bank; (海の) the coast; the beach. ¶ ボートを～に上げる have a boat up *the beach*. 船が～に着く The ship reaches *shore*.
川— a river bank. 向こう— the other bank 〔of the river〕; the farther bank; the other side of the river.

きし【起死】 —回生 ¶ ～回生の思いがした I felt as if I had been delivered from the grip of death.

きし【騎士】 (馬に乗っている武士) a rider; a horseman; (ヨーロッパ中世の武士の称号) a knight.
—道 knighthood; chivalry.

きし【旗幟】 ¶ ～を鮮明にする clarify *one's* stand; take a stand; take *one's* stand.

きじ【雉・雉子】〔鳥類〕a pheasant.

きじ【生地】 cloth; texture; material. ¶ ワイシャツの～ broadcloth. ナイロンの～ nylon *cloth*. ～の細かい of fine *texture*. 男子服の～ suit *material*. 婦人服の～ dress *material*. 婦人服向けのウールの～ woolen *material* for ladies' dresses. 薄い服の～ thin silk *material*. これが彼の～のままの姿だ This is what he really is.

きじ【記事】 an article; an account; a story; news (news は形は複数であるがそれに続く動詞は news を単数として扱う).
¶ 選挙の～ election *news*. いい～になる make good *news*. ～を書く write *an article*. ～の掲載を差し止める ban the publication of *the news*.

ぎし【技師】 an engineer. 「neer.
建築— an architect. 土木— a civil engi-

ぎし【義士】 a loyal retainer.

ぎし【義姉】 a sister-in-law (複 sisters-in-law).

ぎし【義歯】 a false tooth (複 false teeth).
¶ ～を入れる have *a false tooth* put in.

ぎし【義肢】 an artificial leg; a wooden (≒ fixed) leg.

ぎじ【疑似】 —コレラ false cholera. —赤痢 quasi-dysentery.

ぎじ【議事】 proceedings. ¶ 彼が～を進行した(妨害した) He expedited (obstructed) the *proceedings*.
—堂 an assembly hall; (米州の) a capitol.
—日程 the order of the day; the agenda.
¶ その項目は～日程に入れられた(からのぞかれた) The item was included in (was excluded from) the *agenda*. —録 the record of the proceedings. 国会—堂 the Diet Building; 米 the Capitol.

ぎしき【儀式】 a ceremony; (宗教の) a service.
¶ ～は厳かに行なわれた The *ceremony* was performed with solemnity.

ぎしきば・る【儀式ばる】 ¶ 彼らは～ってあいさつを交わした They exchanged greetings *ceremoniously* (≒ *formally*). 彼はいつも～って堅くなっている He always *stands on ceremony*.

きしつ【気質】 nature; disposition; temperament. ¶ 激しい～ *a* fiery *temperament*. アメリカ～ *an* American *trait*.

きじつ【期日】 a date. ¶ 出発の～は近づいた The *date* for departure drew near. ～は12月8日ときまった The *date* was fixed for December 8. ～までに願書を出してください Please submit a written application by *a fixed date*. 借金返済の～が迫る *The date* to pay back my loan is coming up. 手形返済の～はいつですか When does the bill fall due?

きし・む【軋む】 ¶ 床が～む The floorboards *squeak*. 戸が～む The door *creaks*.

きしゃ【汽車】 a train. ¶ 名古屋へ行く～ *a train* for Nagoya. 彼はその～に乗っていた He was on (≒ 英 in) the *train*. どの～に乗ったらいいでしょう Which *train* shall I take? その町には～で行くといい The *train* might be most convenient for you to get to the town. 11時発の～を待ったほうがいい You had better wait for the 11:00 *train*.

きしゃ【記者】 a journalist; (新聞) a newspaperman; 英 a pressman; (地方駐在の) a correspondent; (外勤の新聞記者や雑誌の記者) a reporter. ¶ 彼はタイムズの～だ He is *a*

reporter for *the Times*.
—会見 a press conference. —クラブ a press club. —席 (競技場の) a press box; (議会の) a press gallery. —団 an editorial corps; a corps of reporters. 運動— a sports writer.

きしゅ【旗手】 a standard-bearer; an ensign (旧イギリス陸軍).

きしゅ【機首】 the nose [of an aircraft].
¶ 飛行機は〜を北方に向けた The plane *turned its course* northward. パイロットは〜を下げた(上げた) The pilot kept the *nose* down (up).

きじゅ【喜寿】 ¶ 〜の祝い *one's* 77th birthday celebration (英米には77歳の誕生を祝う習慣はない).

ぎしゅ【技手】 an assistant-engineer.

ぎしゅ【義手】 an artificial arm.

きしゅう【奇習】 a strange custom.

きしゅう【奇襲】 a surprise attack. ¶ 敵陣を〜した We *surprised* the enemy's camp./ We *took* the enemy camp *by surprise*. 要塞(ようさい)を〜して占領した We captured the fort *by surprise*.

きじゅう【機銃】 a machine gun.

きじゅうき【起重機】 a crane; a derrick.

きしゅく【寄宿】 (間借り) lodging; (食事つきの) boarding. ¶ 学生時代山田家に〜していた I *lodged at* Mr. Yamada's (≒ *with* Mr. Yamada) during my school days. 〜制の学校 a *boarding* school.
—舎 a dormitory. ¶ 学生の半数は〜舎に入っている Half of the students stay in the *dormitory*.

きじゅつ【奇術】 a conjuring trick; a legerdemain; magic. ¶ 彼は〜をやった He practised *a conjuring trick*. / He *conjured*. / He *did* (≒ *performed*) *magic tricks*. 彼は〜で帽子から鳩を三羽とりだした He produced three pigeons out of his hat by *magic*.
—師 a magician; a juggler; a conjurer; a conjuror.

きじゅつ【記述】 description. ¶ 〜する describe.

ぎじゅつ【技術】 art; skill. ¶ この仕事は熟練した〜を要する This work requires technical *skill*. すりも一種の〜だといえる Picking pockets may be said to be a kind of *art*. その案は〜的に実行不可能だ It is *technically* impossible to carry out the plan.

きじゅん【基準】 a standard; a criterion.
¶ 判断の〜をどこにおいたらよいか What should our *standard* for judgment be?
—価格 a standard price. —賃金 standard wages.

きじゅん【帰順】 submission. ¶ ゲリラは政府に〜した(〜を誓った) The guerrillas *submitted* (pledged *allegiance*) to the government.

きしょう【気性】 a temperament; a temper.
¶ 彼は〜が荒い He is of *a* violent *temperament*. 彼の〜はよくわかっている I know his *temper* well. 彼は怒りっぽい〜の男だ He has *a* hot *temper*.

きしょう【気象】 weather; atmospheric phenomena. ¶ 〜を観測する make *meteorological* observations.
—衛星 a meteorological satellite. —概況 general weather condition[s]. —学 weather survey; meteorological observation. —測候所 a weather station. —台 a meteorological observatory. —台員 a weather man. —庁 the Meteorological Agency. —通報 a weather report; (ラジオなどの) a weather forecast. —レーダー a weather radar.

きしょう【記章】 a medal; a badge.

きしょう【起床】 ¶ 6時が彼の〜時間だ Six o'clock is his *rising* hour. / He *gets up* at six in the morning.

きしょう【希少】 ¶ 〜価値 *scarcity* value.

きじょう【机上】 ¶ 〜の空論 a *desk* theory. 〜の計画 a *desk* (≒ *paper*) plan.

きじょう【気丈】 ¶ 〜な女 a *very firm* woman; a woman *of strong character*.

ぎしょう【偽証】 false evidence; 〚法律〛 [a] perjury. ¶ 〜する give *false evidence*; perjure *one*self.
—罪 perjury. ¶ 〜罪を犯す commit *perjury*.

ぎじょう【議場】 an assembly hall; a chamber; (議会) the House.
¶ 〜は大混乱だった *The House* was in an uproar.

きじょうぶ【気丈夫】 ¶ あなたさえいてくだされば大へん〜だ Your presence will make me feel very *secure*.

ぎじょうへい【儀仗兵】 a guard of honor; an honor guard.

きしょく【気色】 ¶ まったく〜の悪い話だ That's quite a *disgusting* story.

きしょく【喜色】 ¶ 彼は〜を満面に浮かべて賞品を受け取った *Smiling* broadly, he received the prize. / He *was all smiles* (≒ His face *beamed with pleasure*) when he received the prize.

きしょく【寄食】 ¶ 彼女はおじの家に〜している She *lives with* her uncle *at his expense*. / She *sponges on* her uncle. (後者は口語的).

きし・る【軋る】 grate; creak. ¶ ドアがギーと〜った The door *grated*. 車輪の〜る音 a *grating* noise of the wheels.

きしん【鬼神】 gods; deities; spirits; demons.

きしん【帰心】 ¶ 彼は〜矢のごとしであった He *was quite sick for home*.

きしん【寄進】 contribution.

きじん【奇人】 an eccentric person.

きじん【貴人】 a nobleman; a noble.

ぎしん【疑心】 suspicion; doubt. ¶ 彼は〜暗鬼でひと晩じゅう眠れなかった *Suspicion* kept him awake all night long. / *Doubt* troubled his sleep all night.

ぎじん【義人】 a righteous man; a public-spirited man.

ぎじん【擬人】 personification.
—化(法) personification. ¶ 動物を〜化する *personify* animals.

き

キス a kiss. ¶彼女の赤ちゃんのほおに～をした I *kissed* her baby on the cheek.

きず【傷・瑕】1〘身体のけが〙(傷口) a wound; (傷あと) a scar; (かすり傷) a scratch; (切り傷) a cut; an incision; (深い切り傷) a gash; (ひっかき傷) a scratch; (打撲傷) a bruise.
¶～は浅いから心配はいらない The *wound* is not so serious, so don't worry.
～は重く彼の生命にかかわるかもしれぬ The *injury* is serious enough to endanger his life.
まだあのとき受けた～がときどき痛む The *wound* I got then still hurts from time to time.
その戦闘で彼は右肩に～を負った In that battle he *was injured* on his right shoulder.
踏みはずして左足に軽い～をした I *had* my left leg slightly *injured* by missing my steps.
この～は治るまで1か月かかるだろう The *injury* will take one month to heal completely.
すぐ医者に行って～の手当をしてもらいなさい Go to the doctor right away and get your *injury* treated.
この顔の～は残るでしょうか Will the *scar* on the face remain?
2〘品物のきず〙a flaw. ¶このダイヤには～はない The diamond *is flawless* (≒ *is perfect*).
この茶器はよくできているが,惜しいことに小さな～がある This tea bowl is very well made, but it is a pity that it has *a* small *flaw*.
彼が送ってくれたナシの大部分は～がついていた I found that most of the pears that he sent to me *were bruised*.
柱に～をつけて彼の背の高さを測った I measured his height by *marking* the pillar.
たいせつな品物ですから,～をつけないように注意してください As this is a very precious article, please be careful not to *damage* it.
3〘欠点・汚名〙a failing; a defect.
¶あの人は約束をたがえるのが～だ He often breaks his promise, and that is his *failing*.
彼はまじめでよく働くが,人づきあいの悪いのが玉に～だ Though he is earnest and hardworking, unsociability is his *defect*.
そんなことをするときみの名に～がつく Doing such a thing will *disgrace* your name.

きずあと【傷あと】 a scar. ¶ほおに～のある男 a man with *a scar* across his cheek. 彼のひたいの～は消えた The *scar* on his forehead died away. ～がいまだにある The *scar* still remains. 彼は顔に犬にかまれた～がある He has on his face *a scar from* the bite of a dog.

きすう【奇数】 an odd number.

きすう【基数】 a cardinal number.

きすう【帰趨】 ¶自然の～として as *a* natural *consequence*. きょうの試合で優勝の～が決まるだろう Victory will be decided by today's game.

きすうし【基数詞】 the cardinal numerals.

ぎすぎす ¶彼女はどうも～している She has a very *stiff* (≒ *rigid*) manner. 彼女は～とやせこけている She is a mere [walking] skeleton.

きず・く【築く】 ¶城を～く *build* a castle. 巨万の富を～く *amass* (≒ *pile up*) great riches. 彼は下積みから今日の地位を～いた He *has risen up to* his present position from the bottom.

きずぐすり【傷薬】 [an] ointment. ¶私は彼の手に～を塗ってやった I rubbed his hand with *an ointment*.

きずぐち【傷口】 a wound; an opening wound.

きずつ・く【傷つく】 be (≒ get) injured (≒ hurt; wounded). ¶～いた人たち *wounded* persons.

きずつ・ける【傷つける】 ¶彼は右腕をひどく～けられた He *was* badly *injured* on the right arm. その事件で彼の名誉は著しく～けられた His reputation *was disgraced* by the scandal. そのひと言が彼女の自尊心を～けた That one word *hurt* her pride. 彼のおかげでぼくまで信用を～けられた Even my reputation *was spoiled* (≒ *suffered*) because of him.

きずな【絆】 bonds; fetters; ties. ¶因襲の～を断ち切る break the *bonds* of convention. 親子の～ the *bonds* between parents and children.

きずもの【傷物】 (品物) a flawed article; (娘) a ruined girl.

き・する【期する】 ¶彼らには～するところがある They *are expecting a great thing*. 彼には多くを～しえない We cannot *expect* much *from* him. 再会を～して別れた *Promising to* meet again we parted [from each other]. 次の日曜日を～して集まろう Let's meet next Sunday. ～せずしてふたりは出会った The two met [each other] *unexpectedly*.

き・する【帰する】 ¶どっちにしても～するところは同じだ Whichever alternative you may take, *the result* will be the same. その書類は彼の手に～した The documents *fell into* his hands. 彼の名案も水泡(すいほう)に～した His splendid plan *came to* nothing. 突然の出火のため彼の家は灰燼(かいじん)に～した His house *was reduced to* ashes in the sudden fire. 彼は成功を幸運に～した He *attributed* his success *to* luck.

ぎ・する【擬する】 ¶彼は次の市長に～せられている He *is recommended as* the next mayor.

ぎ・する【議する】 ¶国事を～する *deliberate on* the affairs of state.

きせい【気勢】 spirit; vigor. ¶彼らは～があがっている They are in high *spirits*. 彼は～があがらない He is out of *spirits*. / He is in low *spirits*. そのニュースはわれわれの～をそいだ The news *discouraged* us. そんな～をそぐようなことは言うな Don't say such a *discouraging* thing.

きせい【奇声】 a queer voice. ¶～を発する utter *a startling voice*.

きせい【既成】 ―観念 an accomplished idea (≒ notion). ―作家 a renowned writer; a writer of established fame. ―事実 an accomplished fact. ―秩序 an established order.

きせい【既製】**—**品 ready-made goods. **—**服 a ready-made suit; a ready-to-wear suit.

きせい【帰省】¶ 〜する go [back] home. 学生たちは夏休みで〜中だ The students *are home* for the summer holidays (≒ on summer vacation).

きせい【寄生】parasitism. ¶ 〜する be parasitic on; be a parasite on.
—植物(動物) a parasitic plant (animal). **—**虫 a parasite.

きせい【規正】correction. ¶ 〜する correct.

きせい【規制】regulation. ¶ ダンプカーの都心乗入れは〜されている Dump trucks *are restricted from* entering the heart of the city.
交通**—** traffic regulations.

きせい【期成】**—**同盟 a league for carrying out a plan; a union to carry out a design.

ぎせい【犠牲】a sacrifice; a victim. ¶ その大事業に多大の〜を払った We *paid* dearly to achieve the great work. 彼は余暇を〜にして患者のために働いた He worked for the patient *at the sacrifice of* his own leisure. 子どものために多大な〜を払う人もある Some people make great *sacrifices* for their children. 地震の〜になった人は数知れなかった Innumerable people were made *victims* of the earthquake.

ぎせいご【擬声語】〘言語学〙an onomatopoeia; an onomatopoetic word.

きせき【奇跡】a miracle; a wonder. ¶ 〜が起こった *A miracle* occurred. 〜を行なう work *a miracle*. 〜的成功 a *miraculous* success. 彼が助かったのは〜だ His escape was *a miracle*. 〜的に miraculously.

きせき【軌跡】〘数学〙a locus. ¶ 次の方程式の〜を求む Find the *locus* of the following equation.

ぎせき【議席】¶ 衆議院議員の〜を得る win *a seat* in the House of Representatives. 〜を失う lose the *seat*.

きせずして【期せずして】by accident; by chance; accidentally; unexpectedly.

きせつ【季節】a season. ¶ 一年のこの〜には at this *season* of the year. 〜の変わり目に at the change of *season*. リンゴは今が〜だ Apples *are* now *in season*. この果物は〜はずれだ This fruit *is out of season*. 今やまさに旅行の〜だ It is just the *season* for a trip now. この記事は〜おくれだ This article *is out of fashion*.
—風 a seasonal wind; the trade wind; (インド洋の) a monsoon. **—**労働者 a seasonal worker.

きぜつ【気絶】a swoon; a fainting fit.
¶ アッパーカットを食って彼は〜した The uppercut knocked him *senseless*. 知らせを聞いて彼女は〜するところだった She nearly *fainted* at the news.

きせる【煙管】a [tobacco-]pipe. ¶ 〜をやる(不正乗車) steal a ride on a train with no ticket for the middle part of the way.

き·せる【着せる】¶ 女の子が人形に服を〜せている A girl *is dressing* a doll. お客にオーバーを〜せてあげなさい *Help* the visitor *on* with his overcoat. 娘たちは母親に着物を〜せてもらう The daughters are helped into their *kimonos* by their mother.

きぜわし·い【気忙しい】¶ 年末はいつも〜い We *are* always *restless* at the end of the year. 〜い人 a *fussy* man.

きせん【汽船】a steamer; a steamship; (大洋航路などの定期船) a liner; an ocean liner. ¶ 〜で行く go by *steamer* (≒ *boat*; *ship*).

きせん【基線】the base[-]line.

きせん【機先】¶ 敵の〜を制する *forestall* the enemy.

きせん【貴賤】¶ 〜の別なく high and low alike.

きぜん【毅然】¶ 〜たる態度で with a *resolute* (≒ *firm*) attitude. 〜と resolutely; firmly.

ぎぜん【偽善】hypocrisy.
—者 a hypocrite.

きそ【起訴】prosecution; indictment; (民事) litigation; legal proceedings. ¶ 彼は殺人罪で〜された He *was indicted for* murder.
—状 an indictment; a bill of indictment.

きそ【基礎】the foundation. ¶ 〜的な fundamental. 〜的な勉強をしなさい Get *a foundation* of learning. 英語を〜から勉強したほうがいい You must study English from *ABC*. 彼の理論はS博士の研究が〜になっている His theory *is based on* the studies of Dr. S.

きそう【奇想】¶ まったく〜天外の思いつきだ That's quite a *fantastic* idea!

きそう【起草】¶ 憲法を〜する *draft* a constitution.
—者 a drafter.

きそう【寄贈】presentation. ¶ 彼は蔵書を図書館へ〜した He *presented* (≒ *donated*) his books to the library.
—者 a contributor; a donator. **—**書 a presentation copy.

きそ·う【競う】compete (≒ contend; vie; contest) (*with a person for* a prize).

ぎそう【擬装】camouflage. ¶ 〜する camouflage; disguise *oneself*.

ぎぞう【偽造】[a] forgery. ¶ 〜する forge. 小切手は〜だった The check was *a forgery*.
—小切手 a forged note. 文書**—** forgery of a document.

きそく【気息】¶ 彼の会社は〜えんえんたる状態だ His company is on the verge of bankruptcy. 彼は〜えんえんとしてたどりついた He arrived *breathlessly* (≒ *out of breath*).

きそく【規則】a rule; regulations. ¶ 〜に従いなさい Obey the *rules*. 〜を守るのは当然のことだ It is natural to observe *regulations*. 〜を破ると罰せられる If you break the *rules*, you will be punished. バスは交通〜に違反した The bus driver broke traffic *regulations*. 彼は〜正しい生活をしている He is leading a *regular* life. ここでは門限は10時という〜になっている It is the *rule* here that you should come back before ten.

きぞく【帰属】reversion. ¶ 小笠原諸島は再び日本に～した The Ogasawara Islands *reverted* to Japan again.

きぞく【貴族】(総称) the nobility; (個人) a noble; a peer. ¶ ～と平民 *peers* and commons. ～的顔だちの人 a man of *noble* features. 彼は～の生まれだ He is of *noble* birth. それは彼の～趣味に合わない It is against his *aristocratic* taste.
—社会 the aristocracy. —政治 aristocracy.

ぎそく【義足】an artificial leg; a false leg.

きそくずくめ【規則尽くめ】¶ ～のやり方ではだめだ Everything does not go by rule. 彼は～だ He is a stickler for regulations.

きそくただし・い【規則正しい】¶ ～い生活をする He has *regular* habits. ～く食事しなさい You must have meals *regularly*. 彼の～さに目を見張る I look at his *regularity* in astonishment.

きそん【既存】¶ ～の建物 the *existing* building.

きた【北】the north. ¶ ～へ(北方に) 〔to the〕 *north* (*of*); (北部に) in the *north* (*of*); (北端に) on the *north* (*of*). ～の風 a *north* wind. ～向きの家 a house facing *north*; a house with a *northern* aspect. ～へ向かって出発する leave *north*; leave *toward the north*. その村はこの町の～の方30マイルにある The village is 30 miles *north of* this city.

ギター a guitar. ¶ ～を弾く play the *guitar*.

きたい【気体】gas; vapor.
—燃料 gaseous fuel. —物理学 aerology.
—力学 aeromechanics; aerodynamics.

きたい【期待】anticipation; expectation.
¶ 彼の成功を～する I *expect* him to succeed. きみがコースを全部走り通すとはだれも～していなかった No one *expected* you to run the whole course. 仕事の出来栄えは～していたほどではなかった The result of the work was below our *expectations*. 彼はみんなの～を裏切った He *let* everyone *down*. 彼は～はずれの話をした He made a *disappointing* speech.

きたい【機体】(飛行機の) a body. ¶ ～はめちゃくちゃに壊れた The *airplane* cracked up.

ぎだい【議題】a topic (≒ subject) for discussion; an agenda. ¶ その問題は～に上らなかった The *topic* has not been taken up for discussion. 本日の～はその件です Today we are going to place the matter on the *agenda*.

きた・える【鍛える】¶ 鉄を～える *forge* iron (*into* steel). 身体を～える *build up one's* body (≒ *one*self). 精神を～える *train* the will. 若いときの苦労が彼をどんな困難にもくじけない男に～え上げた A lot of troubles in his youth made him as manly as not to be discouraged by any misfortune.

きたかいきせん【北回帰線】the Tropic of Cancer.

きたく【帰宅】¶ ～の途中で彼に会った I met him *on my way home*. 彼は～の途についた He started *on his way home*. / He *left for home*.

きたく【寄託】deposit; 〔法律〕bailment.
¶ 彼は書類を弁護士に～した He *deposited* the papers with his lawyer.

きた・す【来す】¶ 計画に混乱を～す *throw* the plan into confusion. 株式恐慌を～す *cause* a stock-exchange panic. 台風のため工事の完成に支障を～した The typhoon proved a hindrance to the completion of the construction.

きたての【来たての】¶ この市に～人 a *newcomer* to the city. ～の先生 a *new* teacher.

きだて【気だて】disposition; nature. ¶ ～のよい good-*natured*; kind-*hearted*. ～の悪い ill-*natured*; bad-*tempered*. ～のよい子 a good (≒ nice) boy. 思いやりのある～のよい人 a warm, good-*natured* man.

きたな・い【汚い】**1** 〚不潔な〛dirty. ¶ 手が～いから洗ってきなさい Go and wash your *dirty* hands.
工場を誘致したおかげで空気も海も～くなった Having allowed a plant to be built caused the air and the sea to *be polluted*.
白っぽいものはすぐ～くなる Whitish clothes easily *get soiled*. / Whitish clothes quickly *show soiling*.
子どもはきれいな服を着せても，すぐ～くする Even if you put fine clothes on a child, he will *soil* them in a little while.
そのごみ箱は～いからさわるのではありません Don't touch the garbage case, as it *is not clean*.
2 〚乱雑な〛untidy. ¶ きみの部屋は～い. 少しは整頓(せいとん)しなさい Your room *is untidy*. Why don't you put it in order?
きみの字は～くて読めない You write such *a poor hand* that I can hardly read it.
3 〚みすぼらしい〛shabby. ¶ そんな～い格好をしてみっともない Aren't you ashamed that you are *shabbily* clothed?
4 〚卑劣な・不正な〛dirty. ¶ そんな～い手を使うな Don't play such a *dirty* trick on me.
どうも彼のやり口は～い His way of doing it *is unfair*, I should say.
5 〚けちな〛mean. ¶ あの人は金に～い He is *a miser*. / He *is mean about* money. / He *is* quite *tight* (≒ *close-fisted*).

きたはんきゅう【北半球】the Northern hemisphere.

きたる【来る】¶ ～日曜日に *next* Sunday; on Sunday *next*.

きたん【忌憚】reserve. ¶ この問題について～なくご意見を述べてください Please give your opinion on this matter *frankly* (≒ *outspokenly*). ～なく言えば彼は芸術家ではない *Frankly speaking*, he is not an artist.

きだん【気団】〔気象〕an air mass. ¶ オホーツク～ the Okhotsk *air mass*.

きだん【奇談】(変わった実話) an exciting true story; (冒険談) an adventure story.

きち【吉】〔a〕good luck; 〔a〕good omen.

きち【危地】danger. ¶ ～に陥る get into *danger*. ～を脱する get out of *danger*. その計画

を実行すれば私は彼らを～に陥れることになるかもしれない I might *endanger* them to put the plan into practice.

きち【既知】 ¶ ～の事実 an *already-known* (≒ a *well-known*) fact.

—数〘数学〙 a known number (≒ quantity).

きち【機知】 wit. ¶ ～に富むことば a *witty* remark. 彼は～に富んでいる He is *a wit* (≒ *a witty man*).

きち【基地】 a base.

空軍— an air base. 作戦— a base of operation. 中継— a relay base.

きちがい【気違い】 (男) a madman; (女) a madwoman. ¶ ～になる go (≒ run) *mad*. ～じみた計画 a *mad* scheme. そんなことをするのはまったく～ざただ It would be sheer *madness* to do such a thing. 彼の行動は～じみている He is nearly *a madman*. 彼のジャズ好きは～じみている He *is mad about* jazz. / He *has a mania for* jazz. / He is *a* jazz *maniac*.

写真— an ardent photo fan; a photo maniac. 釣り— a fishing maniac.

きちく【鬼畜】 ¶ 彼は～のような人間だ He is *a brute*. / He is *a brute* of a man.

きちにち【吉日】 a lucky day.

きちゃく【帰着】 ¶ 種々の異論があるが～するところは同じだ In spite of different opinions, they have *arrived at* (≒ *reached*) the same conclusion.

きちゅう【忌中】 mourning.

きちょう【記帳】 ¶ 出納簿に支出額を～する *make an entry of* the expenditure in an account book.

きちょう【帰朝】 ¶ ～する return home; return from abroad.

きちょう【機長】 a captain.

きちょう【基調】 the keynote (*of*); the basis (*of*). ¶ 日本の憲法は平和と民主主義を～としている The constitution of Japan *is based on* peace and democracy.

きちょう【貴重】 ¶ ～なご意見 a *valuable* opinion. それは私にとって～な経験であった That was a very *valuable* experience for me. ～な時間を無駄にするな Don't waste your *precious* time.

—品 valuables.

ぎちょう【議長】 (委員長・座長) the chairman. ¶ 彼がその会の～をつとめた He *presided* (≒ *took the chair*) at the meeting.

—職権 the authority as chairman. 参議院— the President of the House of Councilors. 衆議院— the Speaker of the House of Representatives.

きちょうめん【几帳面】 ¶ 彼女は時間には～だ She *is punctual*. 彼は万事に～だ He *is precise in* doing everything. / He does everything *on the square*. 彼は勘定の支払いには非常に～だ He *is regular in* his payment.

きちんと ¶ 彼女の仕事ぶりはまったく～したものだ She *is* perfectly *accurate in* her work. 出たあとは～ドアを閉めなさい Close the door behind you. ドアには～錠をかけなさい Lock the door *securely*. 病人は寝床の上に～座った The patient *sat up* in bed. 身なりの～した人 a *neat* person. ～かたづいた部屋 a *neat* room. 部屋を～かたづける *put* a room *in order*. 部屋をいつも～しておく *keep* a room *neat* (≒ *tidy*). 机の上を～かたづけなさい *Clear up* your desk. 脱いだくつは～そろえよ *Arrange* your shoes you took off. 彼は～5時に来た He came *just* at five. 彼はいつでも時間を～守る He *is* always *punctual*. その上着は～合った The jacket *exactly* fitted me.

きちんやど【木賃宿】 a cheap rooming house; 俗 a flophouse.

きつ・い 1 〚性格・目つきなどが〛 brave; strong; manly. ¶ 彼女は～い女だ She is a *manly* (≒ *strong-minded*) woman.

この子は～くて(しっかりした子で)なかなか泣かない This child does not cry readily for very little reasons.

彼女は～い顔だちをしている She has *sharp* features.

彼は急に～い顔になった He looked *stern* suddenly.

2 〚仕事・ことばなどが〛 hard; stern. ¶ ～い仕事 *hard* work.

～いことば *biting* words.

～い返事 a *sharp* answer.

彼のことばは～かった His words *were sharp as a needle*.

3 〚窮屈な〛 tight. ¶ このくつは私には～すぎる These shoes *are* too *tight* for me.

きつえん【喫煙】 smoking.

—室 a smoking room. —車 a smoking car; a smoker; 英 a smoking carriage.

きづかい【気遣い】 ¶ 彼が遅れる～はない There is no *fear* of his coming late. どうぞお～なく Please don't *worry about* me. 財布がなくなる～はなかった There was little *likelihood* of the purse being lost.

きづか・う【気遣う】 ¶ 彼の健康が～われる We *are anxious about* his health. 彼の気持ちを害するのを～ってほんとうのことを言わなかった I did not tell him the truth *for fear* of offending him.

きっかけ【切っ掛け】 a chance; a clue. ¶ 玄関のベルを～にうまく部屋から出られた As the front door bell *happened to* ring, I succeeded in getting out of the room. その件について彼と相談するにはよい～だった It was *a* good *chance* to have a talk with him about the matter. 彼は問題解決の～をつかんだ He got *a clue* for solving the problem.

きっかり exactly; just. ¶ 1,000円～の買い物 a purchase of *just* a thousand yen. 6時～に *exactly* at six; at six *sharp*.

きづかれ【気疲れ】 mental fatigue. ¶ 子どもたちを連れて買い物に出かけると～してしまう We *are mentally fatigued* when we go shopping with children.

きづかわし・い【気遣わしい】 ¶ あすの天気が～い I *am anxious about* the weather tomorrow.

き

きっきょう【吉凶】¶ 自分の〜を占ってみる read *one's own fortune*.

キック kick.

—オフ〘フットボール〙a kickoff. —ボクシング Thai boxing.

きづ・く【気づく】¶ 彼は自分の欠点に〜いていた He *was conscious of* his own faults. 彼はその危険に〜いていた He *was aware of* the danger. きみに〜かなかった I didn't *notice* you. 家に帰るまで時計がなくなっているのに〜かなかった I didn't *notice* my watch missing till I got home. いつ財布がないのに〜きましたか When did you *miss* your purse? 彼らが〜かないうちに，彼女は立ち去ってしまっていた She had left before they *knew* it. 彼は〜かれずにこっそりその家に入り込んだ He stole softly into the house without *being noticed*.

ぎっくりごし【ぎっくり腰】¶ 彼は今〜だ He's suffering from *a slipped disk*. / He has *a slipped disk*.

きつけ【着付け】dressing. ¶ 彼女は着物の〜がうまい She *dresses herself* well in her *kimono*.

きつけ【気付け】¶ 〜にブランデーを飲む take a glass of brandy as *a restorative*.

—薬 a restorative; a stimulant.

きづけ【気付】¶ …〜A様 Mr.A, care of (≒ c/o).... …〜で人に手紙を出す write a letter to *a person* [in] *care of*....

きっさき【切っ先】the point of sword; the sword point. ¶ 〜をつきつけられて at the dagger point.

きっさてん【喫茶店】a coffee shop; a coffee house (アメリカには日本でいう喫茶店は皆無に等しい. drugstore とか café とか snack bar というところで，スタンドに腰掛けて，コーヒー・アイスクリーム・コーラ等を飲む. 看板などはすべて Teas and Coffees とだけある).

きっすい【喫水】draught; draft. ¶ 〜の浅い(深い)船 a ship of light (deep) *draft*; a shallow (deep) *draft* ship. 〜5メートルの船 a vessel of 5 meter *draft*. この船は〜が浅い(深い) This ship *draws* light (deep).

きっすい【生粋】¶ 〜の江戸っ子 a Tokyo man *to the backbone*.

きっ・する【喫する】¶ 敗北を〜する be defeated; (競技で) lose a game.

きづち【木槌】a mallet.

ぎっちょ a left-hander. ¶ 〜の left-handed.

きっちょう【吉兆】[a] good (≒ lucky) omen.

きっちり (正確に) accurately; (整然と) neatly; (ちょうど) just.

キッチン a kitchen.

きつつき【啄木鳥】〘鳥類〙a woodpecker.

きって【切手】a [postage] stamp. ¶ 封筒に50円〜をはる put *a* fifty-yen *stamp* on an envelope. 〜で200円送る send two hundred yen in *stamps*. 〜を収集する collect *stamps*.

—収集家 a stamp collector; a philatelist. —帳 a stamp album. 記念— a memorial stamp.

きっての【切っての】¶ 学校〜秀才 *the brightest* boy in the whole school.

きっと certainly; surely. ¶ 彼は〜成功する He will *surely* succeed. / *I'm sure* he will succeed. / He *is sure to* succeed. 今晩〜電話します I'll call you up this evening *without fail*. 明朝〜やってこい *Be sure and* (≒ *to*) come tomorrow morning. 彼女は〜音楽の天才なんだ She *must* be a musical genius.

キッド (子やぎの皮) kid. ¶ 〜のくつ(手袋) *kid* shoes (gloves).

きつね【狐】a fox; (雌狐) a vixen. ¶ 〜のえり巻き a *fox-fur* muffler. まったく〜につままれたようでなにがなんだかさっぱりわからなかった I was so bewildered that I did not know at all what was what.

—色 yellowish-brown. —狩り fox hunting. —つき a person possessed by a fox. —火 a will-o'-the-wisp.

きっぱり clearly; distinctly. ¶ 彼の申し出を〜断わった I *positively* (≒ *flatly*) refused his offer. なくした金のことは〜あきらめた I gave up the lost money *decisively*.

きっぷ【切符】a ticket. ¶ 彼は私に上野までの〜を買ってくれた He bought me *a ticket* to Ueno. この〜は新宿経由横浜行きと書いてある This *ticket* reads to Yokohama by way of (≒ via) Shinjuku. 〜をなんとかなりませんでしょうか Couldn't you provide me with facilities to get *a ticket* for it?

—売り場 a ticket office; 英 a booking office. 片道— a one-way ticket; 英 a single ticket. 往復— a round-trip ticket; 英 a return ticket.

きっぽう【吉報】good news. ¶ 〜を待つ look forward to *good news*.

きづまり【気詰まり】¶ 知らない人と食事をするのは〜だ I *feel embarrassed* (≒ *feel ill at ease*) when I dine with a stranger.

きつもん【詰問】intense questioning. ¶ 〜する question (*a person*) severely.

きづよ・い【気強い】¶ 彼といっしょに旅行できるなら，まったく〜い I will *feel* quite *secure* if I can travel in his company.

きて【来手】¶ 高給を出せば〜はいくらでもある If you pay a high salary, you could easily hire *employees*.

きてい【既定】¶ 〜の事実 an *established* fact. 〜の方針 a *pre-arranged* program.

きてい【規定】(条項) a provision; (規則) a regulation; a rule; (体操の) regulation problems.

¶ 〜どおりに according to the *regulations*. 〜の書式で in *due* (≒ *proper*) form. 学生自治会の〜 the *regulations* of the student council. その点に関し日本の法律にはなんら〜はない There is no *provision* in Japanese law on the point.

ぎてい【義弟】a brother-in-law (複 brothers-in-law).

ぎていしょ【議定書】a protocol.

きてき【汽笛】a whistle. ¶ 列車の〜 the

whistle of a train. 列車は～を鳴らした The train *whistled.*

きてん【起点】the starting point. 「point.

きてん【基点】the starting point; a cardinal

きてん【機転】tact; quick wit. ¶ 彼は～がきく He *is quick-witted.* 彼は～をきかせてひとりにしてくれた He *used his wit* (≒ *tact*) *to* leave me alone. とっさの～で難を逃れた I escaped danger *by my quick wit* (≒ *by my tact*).

ぎてん【疑点】a doubt; a question.

きと【帰途】*one's* way home. ¶ われわれは～についた We started *on our way home.*

きど【木戸】a wicket; a door; (劇場などの切符売り場) a box office; a ticket office.

—御免 free admission. —銭 an admission fee. —番 a doorkeeper.

きどあいらく【喜怒哀楽】¶ ～を顔に表わす show *one's feelings.*

きとう【気筒】〔機械〕a cylinder. ¶ 6～のエンジン a six-*cylindered* engine.

きとう【祈禱】a prayer. ¶ ～する pray. 食事前に～する say *grace* before meals.

—師 a conjurer; a conjuror.

きどう【軌道】(天体などの) an orbit; (電車の) a railway; a line. ¶ 人工衛星を～に乗せる put an artificial satellite into *orbit.* 彼の仕事は～に乗った His work *has got under way.* 仕事は～に乗っていますか *Are* you *getting along well* in your work?

きどう【機動】—作戦 mobile operations. —部隊 a task force. —力 mobile power. 警視庁—隊 the Metropolitan Police Riot Squad.

きどうしゃ【気動車】a Diesel train.

きどうらく【着道楽】love of finery. ¶ 彼女は～だ She *loves finery.* / She has a weakness for fine dress.

きどうりょく【起動力】motive power.

きとく【危篤】¶ 彼は～だ He *is in a critical condition.* / He *is seriously ill.* 彼は昨夜～に陥った He *fell into a critical condition* last night. 「チチキトク」の電報を受け取った I got a wire saying "Father *critical.*"

きとく【奇特】¶ ～な行ない a *praiseworthy* conduct.

きとくけん【既得権】vested rights (≒ interests).

きどり【気どり】affectation; pretension.

¶ 彼らは夫婦～で暮らしている They live together like man and wife.

—屋 (もったいぶった人) a pretentious person; (めかしや) a coxcomb.

きど・る【気どる】¶ いつも彼は変に～ってしゃべる He always has an *affected* way of speaking. 彼は学者を～っている He *poses as* a scholar.

きなが【気長】¶ ～に返事をお待ちしております I'm waiting for your answer *patiently.*

きなくさ・い【きな臭い】¶ ～いにおいがする I smell something *burning.*

きなこ【きな粉】ground soybean.

きなん【危難】a danger; a distress. ¶ ～を逃れる escape *danger.*

キニーネ quinine (発音は [kwini:n]).

きにいり【気に入り】a pet; a favorite. ¶ 彼は主人の～だ He *is in favor with* his master.

きにい・る【気に入る】¶ この部屋は～った I *am pleased with* this room. / I *like* this room. 私の運転が～らなければ，乗らないでください If you don't *like* my driving, please don't get in the car. ここの料理がたいへん～った I *have taken a liking to* (≒ *have become fond of*) the dishes here. (買いものなどで) ～りましたか Do you *like* it?

きに・する【気にする】¶ ～するな Never *mind.* (Don't mind. とは言わない). そんなことはちっとも～していない I don't *mind* it at all. 向こうに着いてからのことなど～しないでいい You need not *trouble yourself* about what you should do after you have reached the destination.

きにな・る【気になる】¶ 彼の結婚のことがなんとなく～る I *am* somewhat *concerned about* his marriage. きょうの会合のことがどうしても～る I cannot but *be worried about* today's meeting.

きにゅう【記入】entry. ¶ 空所に答えを～する *fill* an answer in the blank. 申込書に～する *fill* in an application form. 帳簿に金額を～する *enter* a sum in a book.

きにん【帰任】¶ ～する return to *one's* post.

きぬ【絹】silk. ¶ ～のドレス a *silk* dress. ～のような silky. ～を裂くような音がした I heard a *piercing* (≒ *shrill*) noise.

きぬいと【絹糸】〔a〕silk thread.

きぬおりもの【絹織物】silk fabrics; silk cloth.

きぬけ【気抜け】¶ 彼女は息子の死で～している She *is depressed* by the death of her son. 彼らは試験が済んでみな～したようだ As the examinations are over, they all look *absent-minded.*

きぬずれ【衣擦れ】the rustle of a dress.

きぬた【砧】a block for beating cloth.

きね【杵】a pestle; a pounder.

きねづか【杵柄】¶ 彼は昔取った～で，今でもテニスはうまい *A veteran in* tennis, he can still play it well.

きねん【祈念】¶ 彼の無事を～する I *pray for* his safety.

きねん【記念】commemoration. ¶ これを～するものを考えている I am thinking of something to *remember* this by. 4月23日はシェイクスピアを～する日である April 23 is the day we *commemorate* Shakespeare. この偉人を～して銅像が建てられた A bronze statue was erected *in commemoration of* the great man.

—切手 a commemorative stamp. —号 a commemoration number (≒ issue). —日 a memorial day; (年ごとの) an anniversary. —品 a souvenir; a memento; a keepsake. 卒業— ¶ 彼らは卒業～に松を植えた They planted a pine tree *in memory of* their graduation. 結婚—日 *one's* wedding anniversary.

ぎねん【疑念】〔a〕doubt; 〔a〕suspicion (「あや

き

しい点がありそうだ」という疑念には suspicion を用い,「真実性がなさそうだ」という疑惑には doubt を用いる).

¶ 彼の動機に～をいだいている (動機が不純ではないかなどと) I have *a suspicion about* his motives. 彼の正直に対してはなんの～もない There is no *doubt* (≒ *uncertainty*) *about* his honesty. 私に対する～を晴らしたい I want to clear away any *suspicion about* me.

きのう【昨日】yesterday. ¶ それはまるでつい～のように思われる It seems as if it were only *yesterday*. ～の新聞 *yesterday*'s paper. ～きょうの問題でない It is not a new matter. ～の敵はきょうの友 *Yesterday's* enemy, today's ally.

きのう【帰納】〘論理〙induction. ¶ ～する induce.

—法 induction; the inductive method.

きのう【帰農】¶ ～する return home to farm.

きのう【機能】function. ¶ 電気が止まれば社会の全～がまひするだろう If electricity stops, all the *functions* of society will be paralyzed. その器官は消化の～を果たしている The organ *functions* as a digestive one. / The organ *works* for digestion.

ぎのう【技能】skill. ¶ ～のある人 a *skilled* man. ～をみがく improve *one's skill*.

きのきいた【気の利いた】¶ 彼は～話をする He makes a *clever* speech. これは～贈り物だ This is a *thoughtful* present. 彼は～ことを言う What he says *is to the point*. / What he says *hits the right spot*. きみのそのネクタイは～ネクタイだ That tie of yours is *in good taste*.

きのこ【茸】a mushroom. ¶ ～狩りに行く go to gather *mushrooms*.

きのどく【気の毒】¶ ～にその老人は口がきけなかった The *poor* old man could not speak. それはお～に It *is too bad*./ *I am sorry* [to hear it]. 彼にはほんとに～した *I was* very *sorry for* him. 彼は～な境遇にいる He is in a *sad* (≒ *poor*) circumstance.

きのどくが・る【気の毒がる】¶ 彼女は～ってくれた She *felt sorry for* me. / She *felt sympathy with* me. / She *sympathized with* me.

きのない【気の無い】¶ 彼女は私に～返事をした She gave me a *cool* (≒ *half-hearted*) answer.

きのぬけた【気の抜けた】¶ ～ビール *vapid* beer. 彼は～顔をしている He has a *dull* (≒ *stupid*) look.

きのぼり【木登り】tree climbing. ¶ サルは～がじょうずだ A monkey is good at *climbing trees*.

きのみきのまま【着の身着のまま】¶ 火事だと聞いて～で家を飛び出した At the fire alarm, I rushed out of the house *with nothing but the clothes* I *wore*.

きのめ【木の芽】a bud. ¶ ～が出てきた *A bud* has sprouted (≒ has come out). / The trees *are in bud*.

きのり【気乗り】¶ その話にはどうも～がしない I have little *interest* in the proposal. それは～のする仕事でない It is not an *interesting* (≒ *attractive*) job.

きのりうす【気乗り薄】¶ 彼は～な顔をしている He looks *unwilling* (≒ *uninterested*).

きば【牙】(象などの) a tusk; (犬などの) a fang. ¶ ～をとぐ(比喩的に) prepare for hostilities; forge *one's* sword. ～をむく snarl; show the *fangs*.

きば【木場】a lumberyard; 英 a timber yard.

きば【騎馬】—警官 a mounted policeman. —戦 a cavalry battle game.

きはい【気配】〘株式〙the tone of the market.

きばえ【着栄え】¶ 彼女が着るとどんな着物でも～がする Any dress *looks fine* if she wears it.

きはく【気迫】spirit. ¶ ～に満ちた full of *vigor*; high-spirited.

きはく【希薄】¶ 上空に上るにつれて空気が～になる The higher one goes up in the sky, the *thinner* the air becomes.

きはずかし・い【気恥ずかしい】¶ 人前に出るのは～い I *feel shy* in the presence of others.

きはつ【揮発】¶ ～性の液体 *volatile* liquid. —油 volatile oil.

きばつ【奇抜】¶ 彼は～なことを考える His idea *is eccentric*. ～な格好をしている He is *strangely* dressed. なにか～な趣向はないだろうか Some *novel* idea is desirable.

きば・む【黄ばむ】turn yellow. ¶ ～んだ yellowish.

きばらし【気晴らし】amusement; diversion. ¶ ～に散歩に出かけた I went out for a walk to *refresh myself*.

きば・る【気張る】¶ 大いに～って外車を買った I *treated myself to* a foreign-made car. あと2,000円～ってほしい I ask you to *pay* two thousand yen *more*.

きはん【規範】a standard; a norm.

—英文法 a normative (≒ standard; prescriptive) grammar of the English language.

きばん【基盤】a base; a foundation.

きはんせん【機帆船】an engine-powered boat.

きひ【忌避】evasion. ¶ 兵役を～する *evade* military service. 裁判官を～する *object to* a judge. 良心的徴兵～ *a* conscientious draft *objection*.

きび【黍】〘植物〙millet.

きび【機微】inner workings; secrets; [a] subtlety. ¶ 人情の～にふれる encounter the *subtlety* of human nature. これは外交上の～に属する This is *a* diplomatic *secret*.

きびき【忌引き】an absence for mourning.

きびきび ¶ 彼は動作が～している He *is quick in* action. 彼は～した口調で命令を下した He gave a *crisp* order.

きびし・い【厳しい】¶ ～い暑さが何日も続く The heat wave continues for many days. 彼は子どもにとても～い He *is* very *strict with* his children. ～い顔つき a *severe* (≒ *stern*) look. ～い情勢 *grave* situations. ～い訓練

a *rigorous* discipline. ～い規則 *strict* (≒ *rigid*) rules. 先生は生徒を～くしかった The teacher scolded a pupil *sternly*.

ぎひつ【偽筆】forged handwriting; a forgery. ¶ ～の絵 a *forged* picture; a *counterfeit* drawing.

きびょう【奇病】a strange disease.

きひん【気品】dignity; nobility. ¶ あの婦人にはどこか～がある There is something *graceful* (≒ *noble*) about that lady.

きひん【貴賓】a distinguished (≒ an honored) guest; (皇族) an Imperial guest.
—室 a reception room for honored guests.
—席 a place for honored guests.

きびん【機敏】¶ 彼は動作が～だ He *is quick in* action (≒ movement). 彼は～に立ちまわる He acts *smartly* (≒ *cleverly*).

きふ【寄付】contribution; donation. ¶ 赤十字になにがしかの～をした I *contributed* some money *to* the Red Cross. 困った人への～を募っている We *are making a collection for* the needy.
—金 a contribution; a donation; a subscription. —者 a contributor.

ぎふ【義父】a father-in-law.

ギブアンドテーク give-and-take.

きふう【気風】(精神) spirit; (個人の) temper; character. ¶ この学校は質実な～で知られている This school is well known for the *spirit* of simplicity and sincerity.

きふく【起伏】undulations; ups and downs. ¶ ～のある地形 an *undulating* (≒ *rolling*) land. 彼の人生は～に富む His life is full of *ups and downs* (≒ *good and bad fortunes*; *rises and falls*; *vicissitudes*).

きぶく·れる【着膨れる】swell with clothes.

きふじん【貴婦人】a [noble] lady.

ギプス ¶ 腕に～をする apply *a plaster* to *one's* arm.

きぶつ【器物】a vessel; a utensil; (家具) furniture.

ギフト gift.
—チェック a gift check.

きぶとり【着太り】¶ ～する swell with clothes.

きふる·す【着古す】wear out. ¶ ～してぼろぼろのズボン *worn-out* trousers. 彼の上着は～されていた His jacket *was worn out*.

きぶん【気分】mood. ¶ ～がいい We are in a good *frame of mind* ～はいかがですか How do you *feel* now? ～がすぐれない I don't *feel* well. もうだいぶ～がよくなった I *feel* better now. 歌をうたう～にはならない I am in no *mood* to sing. 彼は彼女の～を害した He hurt her *feelings*. 絵をかく～にはなれない I do not *feel like* painting.
—転換 ¶ ～転換に散歩に出かけた I went out for a walk *for a change* (≒ *to change my mood*).

ぎふん【義憤】indignation.

きへい【騎兵】a cavalryman; a horseman. ¶ ～100人 a hundred horse. ～と歩兵 horse and foot.
—隊 cavalry; horse (集合的な意味で用いられふつう複数扱い).

きへき【奇癖】a queer (≒ an eccentric) habit.

きべん【詭弁】sophistry. ¶ 彼は～をろうする He is apt to *quibble*. / He has a way of *sophisticating*.
—家 a sophist.

きぼ【規模】a scale. ¶ 大～に on *a* large *scale*. 工場の～を拡大する enlarge the *scale* of the factory. 彼らは大～(小～)に土建業をやっている They do construction work *on a large scale* (*on a small scale*). その計画の～は大きい The *scale* of the plan is large. / The plan is laid *on a* large *scale*.

ぎぼ【義母】a mother-in-law.

きほう【既報】¶ ～のとおり会議を開催します We will hold the meeting *as previously reported* (≒ *as already announced*).

きほう【気泡】a bubble.

きほう【気胞】〘植物〙a bladder.

きぼう【希望】[a] hope.

1〘希望に〙¶ 若いうちはいろいろと～に燃えるものだ Young people are full of *hope*. / We are filled with *hope* while young.
大方のご～に応じ, 秘宝を公開します In order to meet your *wishes*, we would like to exhibit the treasures.
残念ながらご～にそいかねます I am sorry, but I cannot meet your *requirements*.
親の～に反して娘はその結婚を断わった The daughter refused the proposal against her parents' *expectations*.
ご～に反した結果を生み申しわけありません I am very sorry that the result was contrary to your *wishes*.

2〘希望を〙¶ きみの～をかなえてあげたい I would like to *meet your request* (≒ *satisfy your demands*).
なにが起ころうと～を失ってはいけない Whatever happens, do not lose your *hope*.
前途に～を持って毎日着実に働きなさい Work steadily every day with a *hopeful* prospect for the future.

3〘希望する〙¶ 両者ができるだけ早くなんらかの妥協に達することをわれわれは～する We *hope* that both parties will reach some agreement as soon as possible.
おふたりが幸福な家庭をつくられることを～します I *expect* both of you will establish a happy home.
そんなことを～したって, ～するほうが無理だ You can't reasonably *wish for* such a thing.

4〘その他の助詞などとともに〙¶ ぼくの将来の～は医者になることだ My *hope* for the future is to become a doctor. / I *wish* to be a doctor in the future.
この世から貧困をなくしたいというのが彼の～であった His *hope* was to rid the world of poverty.
きみの～どおりに事が運ぶかどうかわからない I am not sure whether everything will be carried out as you *wish*.
彼はこちらの～どおりの条件でその仕事を引き受けてく

れた He consented to take over the job on the condition we *requested*(≒ *laid down*).
そんなのは～的観測というものだ That might be called "*wishful* thinking."
—者 a person who desires to (do); (志願者) an applicant.

きぼね【気骨】¶～のおれる仕事 a *troublesome* job. その仕事は～がおれる The work means *a great strain on my nerves.*

きぼり【木彫り】wood carving. ¶～の人形 a *wooden* doll.

きほん【基本】a basis (複 bases); a foundation. ¶代数の～ the *elements* of algebra.
—給 a basic wage (≒ salary). —原理 a fundamental principle. —語彙(ごい) a basic vocabulary.

きほんてき【基本的】¶きみの考えは～にまちがっている Your idea is *fundamentally* wrong.
—人権 fundamental human rights.

ぎまい【義妹】a sister-in-law (複 sisters-in-law).

きまえ【気前】generosity. ¶～のよい男 a *generous* (≒ *open-handed*) man. 彼は～よく金をだす He *is generous* (≒ *liberal*) *with* his money. 彼の～よさには驚いた I was amazed at his *generosity*.

きまぐれ【気紛れ】a caprice; a whim. ¶～な天気 a *changeable* weather. ～な男 a *whimsical* man. その計画は一時の～ではけっしてなかった The plan was no *whim* of the moment. ～に whimsically; waywardly.

きまじめ【生真面目】¶～な性質 a *serious* (≒ *sincere*) nature. ～な若者 a *sober* young man.

きまず・い【気まずい】¶～い思いをした I *felt embarrassed.* / I *felt awkward.* ふたりの仲はいまは～くなっている They *aren't on good terms* as before.

きまつ【期末】the end of a term.
—決算 terminal accounts. —テスト a terminal examination. —手当 a terminal allowance.

きまって【決まって】¶彼はいつも～遅刻する He *always* comes late. 彼は～日曜日にやってくる He *regularly* shows up on Sundays.

きまま【気儘】¶それはあまりにも～すぎる That's too *selfish*. 彼は～な行動をした He *had his own way.* / He acted *as he liked*. 今度だけは～にさせてください Please let me *do what I like* (≒ Please let me *have my own way*), just for this once.

きまよい【気迷い】hesitation.

きまり【決まり】**1**〖規則〗a rule. ¶それが社の～だ That is one of our office *rules*.
～を無視するわけにはゆきません We cannot disregard the *rules*.
～は守ってほしい I want you to obey the *rules*
このことについては別にはっきりした～があるわけではない There is no set *rule* about this. / There is no fixed *rule* as to this.
～は～として,この場合例外を認めるわけにはいきませんか I admit that there is *a rule*, but can't you close your eyes just this once?
社の～として,こうしています We do it this way according to the *rules* of the company.
2〖習慣〗¶酒を飲むと息子の自慢をしはじめるのがあの人のお～だ He *never* drinks *without* boast*ing* of his son.
きみのお～の言いわけは,もう聞き飽きた I am fed up with your *same* old excuse.
—文句 ¶また～文句の彼のお説教が始まった He has started on his *usual* lecture again.
3〖決着〗¶できるだけ早くこの仕事の～をつけてほしい I want this work to *be brought to a close* (≒ *be finished*) as soon as possible.
この問題はそう簡単に～のつく問題ではない This problem cannot *be solved* so easily.
月末までには借金の～をつけなくてはならぬ I must *pay* (≒ *repay*; *discharge*) my debts by the end of the month.
こんなことではいつまでたっても～がつかぬ If we go at this rate, things will never *be settled*.
4〖秩序〗¶いろいろ仕事が山積し,どれから手をつけていいかまだひとつも～がついていない As I have a lot of work to do, I am at a loss what to begin with, leaving everything *unsettled*.
財産を処分し,ひととおり～をつけるのに1か月かかった It took 〔me〕 one month to dispose of the estate and *settle* things in the main.
5〖ぐあい〗¶借金しているので彼女に会うのは～が悪かった I *felt abashed* (≒ *felt embarrassed*; *felt awkward*) to see her as I owed her money.
子どもは～悪そうにぼくにあいさつした The child greeted me *shyly* (≒ *bashfully*).
こんなみすぼらしい格好であの人に会うのは～が悪い I *feel ashamed* to meet him in such shabby clothes.

きまりきった【決まり切った】¶～声明書ではおもしろくない A *stereotyped* statement is not interesting. 彼は～ことばかり言う He always speaks of what *is hackneyed*.

きま・る【決まる】**1**〖決定〗¶話がなかなか～らなかった We could not *settle* the matter easily.
一度～ったことを蒸し返すな Don't rehash what *was* once *decided*.
皆でお祝いすることに～った(贈り物をする) All of us *decided* to send a gift. / (めでたい日を祝う) All of us *decided* to celebrate the occasion.
開会式は今月の10日に～った The date of the opening ceremony *was fixed* (≒ *was arranged*) for the 10th of this month.
結論は既に～っている The conclusion *is* already *formed*.
勝敗は最後の5分で～るものだ The last five minutes *determines* the issue.
きみの腹は～っているのか Have you *made up your mind*?
2〖当然・確実〗¶そんなことをすれば損するに～っている If you do such a thing, you *are bound to* lose.
われわれはいつかは死ぬに～っている It is in the course of nature that we should die. / All men must die sooner or later.

夏は暑いに〜っている Summer is naturally hot.

そんなことは〜っているじゃないか That's a matter of course.

3 〖決まった〗 ¶ 〜った手続きを踏む go through *due* formalities.

なにか〜った書式でもあるのですか Is there any *prescribed* (≒ *due*) form?

別にこれと〜った習慣はありません We have no particular *established* usage.

ぎまん 【欺瞞】 deception; 〔a〕 deceit.

きみ 【君】 (親しい相手に) you; (国王) an emperor; a sovereign; (主人) a lord; a master.

きみ 【黄身】 〔a〕 yolk; a yellow.

きみ 【気味】 a feeling; a touch; a shade.

¶ うす〜の悪い笑い a *sinister* smile. その足音は〜が悪かった The footsteps made me *uneasy* (≒ *nervous*). 階下に〜の悪い音がした I heard *uncanny* sounds downstairs. いい〜だ Serves you right!

-ぎみ 【-気味】 ¶ 少し疲れ〜だ I am *a little* tired. ぼくは風邪〜だ I have *a touch of* cold./I have a slight cold. 物価は少し上がり〜だ The prices are *a bit* higher. 食事は控え〜にしたほうがいい You should be moderate in eating. 彼は多少遠慮〜に発言した He spoke *rather* reservedly. 彼は近ごろ慢心〜だ He shows *a dash of* conceit these days.

きみじか 【気短】 ¶ 彼は〜だ He *is quick-tempered* (≒ *is hot-tempered; is short-tempered*).

きみつ 【気密】 ━構造 an air-tight structure. ━室 an air-tight chamber.

きみつ 【機密】 a secret. ¶ 〜を守る(漏らす) keep (let out) *a secret*. 外交上の〜 diplomatic *secrets*. 〜が漏れた The *secret* leaked out (≒ is out).

━費 secret service money. ━文書 confidential (≒ classified) documents.

きみゃく 【気脈】 ¶ 彼は敵と〜を通じている He *has a secret understanding with* the enemy./He *is in collusion with* the enemy.

きみょう 【奇妙】 ¶ 彼はそれを〜に思った He thought it *strange*. 彼は〜な高い声で話す He speaks with *queer* shouts. 彼は〜な歩き方をする He has a *queer* way of walking. 彼女が来ないなんて〜だ *It is strange* (≒ *funny*) that she should not come. 〜なことにぼくはそれを聞いていなかった *Strange to say*, I have not heard it.

きみわる・い 【気味悪い】 ¶ 〜い顔つき *sinister* countenance.

ぎむ 【義務】 **1** (本分) duty; (責務) 〔an〕 obligation; (責任) responsibility.

¶ 権利を主張する以上〜も果たさねばならぬ So long as you insist upon your rights, you must perform (≒ do; fulfill) your *duty*.

都民である以上都民税を納める〜を負っている As a resident of Tokyo, you have the *duty* to pay the residence tax.

その工場は大気汚染防止装置をつける〜を怠っていた They neglected their *duty* to equip the factory with anti-air-pollution apparatus.

親は子を扶養する〜がある Parents are under *an obligation* to support their children.

それをやるのがきみの〜だ It's your *duty* to do it./You *are bound to* do it.

そのような際には違約金を払うように法律で〜づけられている You have the legal *obligation* to pay a penalty in such a case.

彼は上役に言われて〜的にその仕事をかたづけた He finished the work from a mere sense of *duty*, as he was ordered by his superior.

あの人は〜的な仕事はいやがってなかなかやろうとしない He is very reluctant to do an *obligatory* work.

2 〖合成語〗 ¶ 日本の〜教育は9年制である There is a nine-year *compulsory education* system in Japan.

その奨学金を受けた者が，その会社で働く〜年限は3年である Those who are supported by the scholarship are under *an obligation* to serve for three years in the company.

あの人は〜観念に乏しい He is wanting in *a sense of duty*.

きむずかし・い 【気難しい】 fastidious; (怒りっぽい) irritable; testy. ¶ 彼は食事に〜い He *is fussy* (≒ *is particular*) *about* his food. そう〜いことを言うな Don't *be* so *particular about* that. 彼は〜い顔をして私を見た He looked *frowningly* at me. 彼は非常に〜い男だ He *is* very *hard to please*.

きむすめ 【生娘】 a virgin; a maid; a maiden.

きめ 【木目】 (木の) grain; (膚の) texture.

¶ 〜の細かい膚 a *fine-grained* skin. 〜の粗い肌 a *coarse* skin. 〜の細かい報告書 a *minute* report.

きめい 【記名】 register; signature. ¶ 芳名録にご〜ください Please *sign your name* in the visitors' list.

━投票 an open vote (≒ ballot); a signed vote.

ぎめい 【偽名】 an assumed (≒ a false) name; an alias. ¶ 〜を使う assume *a false name*; take *a fictious name* (≒ *an alias*). 〜で under *a false name*; under *another name*.

きめこ・む 【決め込む】 ¶ たぬき寝入りを〜む *pretend* to sleep. 彼は発表の前から合格だと〜んでいる He *takes it for granted* that he will pass the entrance examination before the results are announced.

きめだま 【決め球】 〖野球〗 a winning shot.

きめつ・ける 【極め付ける】 ¶ 本人の弁解も聞かずになんでも彼が悪いと〜けるのはよくない It is not good to put everything down to him and give him a scolding without giving him a chance to defend himself.

きめて 【決め手】 a trump card. ¶ ぼくにはまだ〜がある I hold *trumps*. 彼にはまだ〜があった He had still *trump card to play*.

き・める 【決める】 **1** 〖決定する〗 decide. ¶ そんな子どもに将来の職業を〜めろというのは無理だ It is too much to ask such a little child to *decide on* his future occupation.

き

まず予算を～めてください Please *make* an estimate first.
やるかやらぬかどちらかに話を～めてほしい *Decide* 〔as to〕 whether you will do it or not.
私は一度～めたことは変えるわけにはゆかぬ I cannot change what *has* already *been decided* once.
結婚式の日どりは～めてあるのか *Have* you *fixed* the date of the wedding ceremony?
全会一致でこの作を1位と～めた The committee *decided* unanimously *to* give first place to this work.
どういう段取りでやるのか細かに～めましょう Let's *map* (≒ *work*) *out* a detailed plan.
みんなで～めた約束は守っていただきたい I want you to keep the promise which we *have made* together.
2 〖決心する〗 ¶ ぼくは行かないことに～めた I *made up my mind* not *to* go.
ぼくはそれに賛成することに～めた I *decided to* approve it.
3 〖常例としている〗 ¶ 日曜には人に会わぬことに～めている I *make it a rule to* be not at home to anyone on Sundays.
毎朝私は散歩することに～めている Every morning I go out for a stroll.
朝食は卵2個, パン1切れ, 果汁と～めている My morning meal *regularly* consists of two eggs, a slice of bread and fruit juice.
4 〖思い込む〗 ¶ そんなことは簡単だと～めてかかったのが失敗だった I failed because I *assumed* that it was easy.
あの人は必ずこの試合に勝つと～めている He *takes it for granted that* he'll win this game without fail.

きも【肝】(肝臓) the liver; (度胸) courage; nerve; spirit. ¶ 彼は～がすわっている He has iron *nerves*. 彼は～が太い He *is bold*. / He *is daring*. 彼は～が小さい He *is timid*. / He *is lily-livered*. その事実をあなたは～に銘じておくべきだ You must have the fact impressed on your *mind*. その大地震に～をつぶした I *was terribly frightened* by the big earthquake. 自動車にひかれそうになって～を冷やした I *was* greatly *shocked at* being nearly run over by a car.

きもいり【肝入り】 ¶ …の～で(主催で) under the auspices (≒ sponsorship) of…; (世話で) through the good offices of….

きもち【気持ち】 **1** 〖頭・胃など体の容体〗 ¶ ～が悪くなって吐いた I *felt* sick and vomited.
この薬を飲めば～がよくなる If you take this medicine, you will *feel* well.
2 〖気分・心境〗 ¶ つい～よくなって居眠りをした I *felt* so comfortable that I dozed off.
赤ん坊は～よさそうに眠っていた The baby was sleeping *comfortably*.
久しぶりに勝利を味わい一同いい～だった All of us *were happy*, as we gained a victory after a long interval.
あの人は～のいい人だ He is an *agreeable* person.
これは日当たりのいい～のいい部屋だ This is a *comfortable* sunny room.
その化けねこの話は～が悪い That tale of a goblin cat *gives me the creeps* (≒ *makes me creepy*).
彼はなんとなく～の悪い人相をしている There is a certain *sinister* look about him.
喜んでいいかどうか妙な～だ I *feel* strange as I don't know whether I should be glad or not.
まったく泣きたい～だ I *feel like* crying, indeed.
まだ船に乗っているような～がする I *feel* as if I were still on board a ship.
子どもにかえったみたいな～がする I *feel* as if I were a child once again.
彼の言いわけを聞いているといやな～になった I *was disgusted by* his excuse.
相手の～にもなってみろ Enter into another's *feelings*.
ぼくの～もくんでくれ Please enter into my *feelings*. / Please *sympathize with* me. / Please grasp (≒ catch) my *idea*.
きみのほんとの～はどうなんだ What are your real *intentions*?
そう率直に言ってくれれば, ぼくの～もすっきりする Now that you have told me so plainly, I *feel* refreshed.
相手の～を悪くさせるようなことは言うな Don't tell others what hurts their *feelings*.
なんとか彼の～を和らげてほしい Please try to calm down his *anger*.
あわてるな. もっと～を落ち着けろ Don't be in a hurry. Keep cool.
いつまでもその～を変えないで, まじめに働いてくれ I want you to work earnestly with determination.
3 〖快く〗 ¶ 彼女は～よく承諾してくれた She gave a *willing* consent. / She *willingly* consented.
あの人はなにを言いつけられても～よくやってくれる He *is willing to* do whatever he is told to do.
彼は～よく私を迎え入れた He received me *with a good grace* (≒ *with warm hands*).

きもの【着物】 clothes; dress; clothing; (和服) a *kimono*. ¶ ～を着る dress *oneself*; put on *one's clothes*. ～を脱ぐ undress *oneself*; take off *one's clothes*. ～を着替える change *clothes*.

きもん【鬼門】(方角) the "demon's gate"; the northeastern quarter; (比喩) an unlucky quarter; (弱点) a weak point.

ぎもん【疑問】(質問) a question; (疑念) a doubt; a question. ¶ 私は彼のことばには～をいだいている I have some *doubt about* his words. / I *doubt* his words. それには～の余地がない There is no *question about* it. そんなことが起こるかどうか～だ It *is questionable* if such a thing would happen. 彼が正直だということについて私には～の余地はない I believe *beyond all doubt* that he is honest. 彼に宿題の～をただした I checked the *doubtful points* of the homework with him.
―詞 an interrogative. **―符** a question

mark. —文 an interrogative sentence.

ギヤ gear. ¶ ～を入れる thrust the *gear lever*. 車の～をセカンドに入れる throw a car in *second gear*. 車は低速(高速; トップ)～で走っていた The car was going in low *gear* (high *gear*; top *gear*). 彼はすばやく～をいれかえた He *shifted gears* quickly.

ぎゃあぎゃあ ¶ ～泣く (子供が) squall; (鳥が) squawk; (猫が) caterwaul.

きゃく【客】1 〖訪問者〗 a visitor; a guest.
¶ お～さまです Somebody is at the door. / There's a knock (≒ ring) at the door.
主人は～を玄関まで出迎えた The master of the house came out to greet *visitors* at the door.
お～さまを応接室にお通ししなさい Show the *guest* into the drawing room.
きょうはお～をしなければならない I must give (≒ have) a party today.
お～を夕飯に招待した I invited (≒ asked) *guests* to dinner.
2 〖顧客〗 a customer. ¶ ふいの～ *a* chance (≒ casual) *customer*.
婦人～ *a* woman *customer*.
お～さまはご予約をなさっていますか Have you booked, sir?

きやく【規約】(協定) an agreement; a contract; (規則) a rule. ¶ ～を守る(破る) keep (break) the *rules*.

ぎゃく【逆】 the opposite; the contrary.
¶ ～に contrariwise. ～の順序で in the *reverse* order. 彼のことばは事実と～だ What he says *is contrary to* the truth. われわれは～の方向に行った We went in the *opposite* direction. ～は必ずしも真ならず *Converses* are not always true. それは私の考えとちょうど～だ That *is* the very *opposite of* what I meant. 彼の言うこととすることはまったく～だ He says one thing and does another. / His deeds *do not agree with* his words. 彼をやっつけようと思ったら～にやっつけられた I was going to knock him down, but *instead* I was knocked down by him. 彼はいつも～にとる He always takes me *by contraries*.

ギャグ a gag. ¶ 彼はよく～を飛ばす He often pulls *gags*. ～がうまい He is good at telling *gags*.

きゃくあし【客足】 customers. ¶ ～が落ちた *Customers* have fallen off.

きゃくあつかい【客扱い】 ¶ あの店員は～がうまい(悪い) That shop assistant gives good (bad) *service*.

きゃくいん【客員】 a guest member; an honorary member.
—教授 a visiting professor.

きゃくいん【脚韻】 a rhyme. ¶ この4行は1行おきに～を踏んでいる These four lines *rhyme* alternately.

ぎゃくこうか【逆効果】 a contrary (≒ reverse) effect. ¶ 彼の演説は～だった His speech *worked negatively*. 彼の抗議は～をきたした His protest had *a contrary effect*.

ぎゃくこうせん【逆光線】 backlight; counterlight. ¶ ～で写真を撮る take a picture *against the light*.

ぎゃくコース【逆コース】 the reverse course.

ぎゃくさつ【虐殺】 slaughter; massacre.
¶ ～する slaughter; massacre.
—者 a slaughterer. 集団— mass slaughter; genocide.

ぎゃくさん【逆算】 ¶ ～する count (≒ calculate) backward.

きゃくしつ【客室】(ホテルの) a guest room; (飛行機・船の) a cabin.
—係 (ホテルの) a room clerk.

きゃくしゃ【客車】 米 a coach; a passenger car; 英 a railway carriage.

ぎゃくじょう【逆上】 ¶ 激怒のあまり～した I *felt quite beside myself with* rage. 彼はその知らせを聞いて～した He *was beside himself at* hearing the news. / The news *turned his head*.

きゃくしょく【脚色】 dramatization. ¶「アンネの日記」を～する *dramatize* "the Diary of Anne Frank."

ぎゃくすう【逆数】〖数学〗 a reciprocal [number].

ぎゃくせつ【逆説】 a paradox. ¶ それは～的だ That sounds *paradoxical*. ～的に言えば *paradoxically* speaking.

きゃくせん【客船】 a passenger [boat]; a steamer; (定期の) a liner.

ぎゃくせんでん【逆宣伝】 ¶ 彼らは盛んに～をやっている They are carrying on an active *counterpropaganda*.

きゃくせんび【脚線美】 the beauty of leg lines. ¶ 彼女はみごとな～だ She has *shapely legs*.

ぎゃくたい【虐待】 ill-treatment. ¶ 動物を～するな You must not *be hard upon* (≒ *be cruel to*) animals. / Don't *treat* animals *cruelly*.

きゃくだね【客種】 ¶ デパートと専門店では～が違う Department stores and speciality stores have different *customers* respectively.

ぎゃくたんち【逆探知】 ¶ 彼らの秘密を～した We *spied out* their secret *conversely*.

きゃくちゅう【脚注】 footnotes.

ぎゃくて【逆手】 ¶ 彼は相手の発言を～にとってやりこめた He *took advantage of* his opponent's statement.

ぎゃくてん【逆転】 ¶ 彼のヒットで試合の形勢は～した His hit *turned the tables in our favor*.

きゃくどめ【客止め】 ¶ その劇場は連日満員～の盛況だ The theater *is drawing more than a full house* every day.

きゃくひき【客引き】 a tout; a runner.

ぎゃくひれい【逆比例】〖数学〗 an inverse proportion. ¶ ～する be in inverse proportion (*to*).

ぎゃくふう【逆風】 ¶ ヨットは～をついて走った The sail-boat sailed against *an unfavorable* (≒ *a contrary*) *wind*.

きゃくほん【脚本】 a play; a drama; (映画などの) a scenario. ¶ ～を上演する stage *a play*.

き

—家 a playwright; a playwriter; (映画の) a scenario writer.

きゃくま【客間】(大邸宅では) a drawing room; (普通の家では) a sitting room; a lounge.

ぎゃくもどり【逆戻り】¶ 通行止めだったので～した Because the street was blocked, we *turned back*.

ぎゃくゆしゅつ【逆輸出】 re-exportation. ¶ ～する re-export.

ぎゃくゆにゅう【逆輸入】 re-importation. ¶ ～する re-import.

ぎゃくよう【逆用】¶ 原子力エネルギーを～してはならない We should not *make a reverse use of* atomic energy. きみは彼の親切を～してはならない You must not *take advantage of* his kindness.

ぎゃくりゅう【逆流】 a back current. ¶ 川が～しはじめた The river began to *flow backward*.

きゃしゃ【花車・華奢】 delicate; slim. ¶ ～な体つきの人 a man of *delicate* constitution. ～な子ども a *frail* (≒ *slightly-built*) child. この机は～にできている This table *is breakable* (≒ *is fragile*).

きやす・い【気安い】¶ 私たちはお互いに～く話し合える仲だ We *are frank with* each other. / We *are on speaking terms with* one another.

キャスチングボート ¶ 彼はその問題に関する～を握っている He holds *the casting vote* about the issue.

キャスト the cast [of a play].
オールスター— an all-star cast.

きやすめ【気休め】 mere consolation. ¶ そう思うと少し～になる It gives me some *consolation* to think so. これ以上～を言わないでください Don't speak *soothing words* to me any more.

きゃたつ【脚立】 a footstool; a stepladder.

キャタピラ a caterpillar.

きゃっ ¶ 彼女は毛虫を見て～と叫んだ She *screamed* (≒ *gave a shriek*) at the hairy caterpillar.

きゃっか【却下】 dismissal; rejection. ¶ 彼の願書は～された His application *was turned down* (≒ *was rejected*).

きゃっかん【客観】¶ その問題を～的に考察した We viewed the matter *objectively*.
—性 objectivity. ¶ 彼が言っていることはほとんど～性がない His statement has little *objectivity*. —情勢 ¶ ～情勢は依然重大だ Our *objective* situation is still grave. —主義 objectivism. —テスト an objective test.

きゃっきゃっ ¶ 子どもたちが外で～言って遊んでいる The children *are frolicking about* outdoors.

ぎゃっきょう【逆境】 adversity. ¶ 彼は今～にある He *is* now *in adversity*. 彼は勇敢に～と闘った He struggled bravely *against adverse fate* (≒ *with adversity*).

きゃっこう【脚光】 the footlights. ¶ 彼はマスコミの～を浴びている He *is in the spotlight* (≒ *limelight*) *of* mass communication.

ぎゃっこう【逆行】¶ そんな政策は時勢に～する Such a policy *goes against* the times.

キャッチ ¶ よその船からの無線を～した I *caught* a wireless message from another ship. なにか情報を～しましたか *Have* you *obtained* any information?
—フレーズ a catchphrase; a catchword. —ボール catch.

キャッチャー〔野球〕 a catcher.
—ボート〔捕鯨〕 a catcher.

キャップ ¶ 万年筆の～ the *cap* of a pen (万年筆は fountain pen と言わないでもよい). びんの～ the *cap* of a bottle.

ギャップ a gap. ¶ ふたりの間には非常に大きな性格上の～がある There is *a* large *difference* between their characters.

キャデー〔ゴルフ〕 a caddie.

ギャバジン〔織物〕 gabardine.

キャバレー a cabaret.

きゃはん【脚絆】 leggings; gaiters.

キャビア〔料理〕 caviar[e].

キャビネ〔写真〕 a cabinet-size photograph.

キャプテン a captain.

キャベツ a cabbage.
—巻き a rolled cabbage. 花— (カリフラワー) a cauliflower.

ギャラ [a] guarantee. ¶ 彼の～は安い His *guarantee* is small.

キャラコ〔織物〕 calico.

キャラバン (隊商) a caravan.

キャラメル a caramel.

ギャラリー a gallery.

キャリア a career. ¶ 彼はオリンピック選手としての～がある He has *a career* as an Olympic athlete.

きゃんきゃん ¶ 子犬が～鳴いている A puppy *is yapping* (≒ *is yelping*).

ギャング (ひとり) a gangster; (一団) a gang.

キャンセル cancellation. ¶ 注文を～する *cancel* an order. 旅館の予約を～した We *canceled* the hotel reservation.

キャンデー a candy.
アイス— a popsicle.

キャンパス campus. ¶ ～で on the *campus*.

キャンプ a camp; camping. ¶ ～に行く go *camping*. 森で～する *camp out* in the woods.
—場 a camping ground. —ファイア a campfire. —村 a camping village. —用品 a camping outfit.

ギャンブル a gamble; (行為) gambling.

キャンペーン a campaign. ¶ その新聞は暴力追放の～を開始した The newspaper launched *an* anti-gangster *campaign*.

きゅう【旧】¶ 学園を～に復す restore the campus *as it was*.
—正月 New Year's Day according to the lunar calendar. —知事 an ex-governor.

きゅう【急】 1〖即刻〗¶ 事態の解決は～を要する The solution of the situation admits of *no delay*. インフレ対策は～を要する問題だ The anti-inflation policy needs *immediate* attention.

〜な用事ができて, 会に欠席した Some *pressing* business turned up, so that I could not attend the gathering. / Some *urgent* business prevented me from attending the meeting.

2 〖突然〗 ¶ 彼は〜に態度を変えた He changed his attitude *suddenly*.

〜にそう言われてまごついた I was embarrassed by the *sudden* request.

〜にロンドンに出張を命ぜられた I was *suddenly* ordered to leave for London.

運転手は〜に右にカーブを切った The driver turned *sharply* to the right.

彼女の死はあまりにも〜だったので, 皆茫然(ぼうぜん)とした Everyone was stunned by her *sudden* death.

温度が〜に変化した The temperature changed *all at once*.

3 〖危急〗 ¶ 風雲〜をつげた The situation became *critical* (≒ *threatening*).

火災や洪水の〜に備えて, 重要書類をまとめておいた I collected important documents to provide against *emergencies*, such as fires and floods.

国家の〜に当たっては, そんなぜいたくは許されぬ You must not indulge in such luxury at a time of national *emergency*.

4 〖鋭い角度・傾斜〗 ¶ この先〜カーブ多し There are many *sharp* turns beyond this point./ (掲示) *Sharp* Turns Ahead.

〜に曲がる道は危険だ The road which turns *sharply* is dangerous.

〜な坂道をのぼりきった所に彼の家があった His house stood at the head of a *steep* slope.

〜な階段ですから気をつけてください Please watch your step as the stairs *are steep*.

5 〖急速〗 ¶ この川は流れが〜だ This river has a *swift* current. / There is a *swift* current in this river.

きゅう 【級】 a class. ¶ 彼は〜では1番だ He is at the top of the *class*. われわれは同じ〜だ We are in the same *class*.

きゅう 【灸】 moxa cautery. ¶ 背中に〜をすえる *cauterize* the back *with moxa*. 彼の怠け癖に〜をすえてやろう I will *punish* him *for* his laziness.

-きゅう 【-級】 ¶ 1万トン〜のタンカー a tanker in the ten thousand ton *class*. 大臣〜の人物 a man of the minister *class*. 柔道で1〜昇進した I have been moved up to the next *grade* in *judo*. 一線〜の投手 a *topflight* pitcher. この酒は一〜品だ This *sake* is of first-*rate* quality.

きゆう 【杞憂】 ¶ あなたの思っていらっしゃるのは〜にすぎません You *are troubling yourself unnecessarily*. / Your fears *are* utterly *groundless*.

ぎゅう 【牛】 (牛肉) beef.

—かん canned beef. —舎 a cowshed.

ぎゆう 【義勇】 —軍 a volunteer army. —兵 a volunteer.

きゅうあい 【求愛】 courtship. ¶ 彼はその女性に〜して成功した He *wooed* (≒ *made love to*) the girl and won her hand.

きゅうあく 【旧悪】 ¶ 彼の〜がばれた His 〔*past*〕 *crime* came to light. 彼の〜をあばいてやれ Let's expose his *past misdeeds*.

きゅういん 【吸引】 ¶ この電気掃除機は〜力が強い This vacuum cleaner has strong *sucking force*.

ぎゅういんばしょく 【牛飲馬食】 ¶ 〜する eat and drink heavily (≒ greedily).

きゅうえん 【休演】 ¶ 彼は病気のため1週間〜している On account of illness he *has been absent from the stage* for a week. 改装のため〜中だ There is *no performance* because of repairs.

きゅうえん 【救援】 relief ; rescue. ¶ 〜する relieve ; rescue. すぐ彼らの〜に赴いた We went to their *rescue* at once. (rescue の前の所有格は目的関係を表わすことが多い).

—資金 a relief fund. —隊 a relief (≒ rescue) party. —物資 relief goods.

きゅうか 【旧家】 an old family. ¶ 彼は土地の〜の出だ He is (≒ comes) of an *old* local *family*.

きゅうか 【休暇】 a vacation (㊥では holiday は holy (聖なる)と関係があるという連想から単なる休暇は vacation のほうを好んで用いる).

¶ 暑中〜に during summer *vacation* (慣用として定冠詞を省く). 来週から〜だ Our *vacation* begins next week. 2日間の〜をとった I took *a* two-day *holiday*. 〜は3週間だ The *holidays* are three weeks long. 〜で故郷に帰っている He is at home *on vacation*. 1週間の〜をヨーロッパで過ごした I spent a week's *vacation* in Europe.

きゅうかい 【休会】 recess. ¶ 国会は目下〜中だ The Diet *is in recess* (≒ *is not in session*) now. 〜を宣言する call (≒ declare) *a recess*.

きゅうかく 【嗅覚】 the sense of smell. ¶ 犬は〜が発達している Dogs have *a* keen *nose* (≒ *a sense of smell*).

きゅうがく 【休学】 temporary absence from school. ¶ 彼は病気で1年間〜した He *absented himself from school* for a year because of sickness.

きゅうかくど 【急角度】 ¶ 〜の方向転換をする make a *sharp* change in direction ; take a *sudden* turn.

きゅうかざん 【休火山】 a dormant (≒ an inactive) volcano ; a sleeping volcano.

きゅうかん 【休刊】 ¶ きょうは新聞〜日だ There is no newspaper 〔issued〕 today.

きゅうかん 【急患】 an emergency (≒ urgent) case ; a sudden illness.

きゅうかんち 【休閑地】 idle land ; 〔a〕 fallow land.

きゅうかんちょう 【九官鳥】 a mina bird ; myna〔h〕 bird.

きゅうぎ 【球技】 a game in which a ball is used.

きゅうきゅう 【救急】 first aid.

き

—車 an ambulance. —箱 a first-aid box. —病院 an emergency hospital.

きゅうきゅう【汲汲】¶彼は金もうけに～としている He *is bent on* making money.

ぎゅうぎゅう ¶箱にがらくたを～詰め込んだ We *squeezed* rubbish *into* the box. ～いう目に会わせてやろう I will let them have it./ I'll teach them a lesson they'll never forget. 彼は～いう目に会わせられた He recieved *a severe drubbing*. このくつは歩くと～鳴る These shoes *squeak* when we walk with them on.

きゅうきょ【旧居】*one's* old house; *one's* former residence.

きゅうきょ【急遽】¶～対策を立てる make a counterplan *in a hurry*. 彼は～上京してきた He *hurried* up to Tokyo.

きゅうきょう【旧教】the Catholic Church; the Roman Catholic Church.
—徒 a〔Roman〕Catholic.

きゅうぎょう【休業】closure; suspension of business. ¶当日は銀行は～だ Banks *are closed* for the day.
臨時— temporarily closed. 本日—(掲示) Closed today.

きゅうきょく【究極】¶～の目的 an *ultimate* object.

きゅうきん【給金】pay; wages.

きゅうくつ【窮屈】¶～なズボン *tight* trousers. おじの家で～な思いをした It *was not comfortable*, staying at my uncle's. 規則にしばられる～な仕事はいやだ A *strictly* (≒ *rigidly*) regulated work isn't in my line

きゅうけい【休憩】a rest; a recess; a respite; (幕あい) an interval; an intermission.
¶授業の合間に10分～する We take *a* ten-minute *recess* between classes.
—時間 a recess; an interval; a rest period. —室(所) a rest room (米 劇場などで手洗所の意); (ホテルなどの) a lobby; a lounge; a foyer.

きゅうけい【求刑】¶～する demand a penalty. 検事は被告に終身刑を～した The prosecutor *demanded* life imprisonment for the accused.

きゅうけい【球茎】〘植物〙a bulb; a corm.

きゅうけい【球形】a globular form. ¶～の ball-shaped.

きゅうげき【急激】¶大都市の～な人口増加 the *rapid* increase in population of large cities. ～に温度が下がった The temperature has dropped *suddenly*.

きゅうけつ【吸血】—鬼 a vampire; a blood sucker. —こうもり a vampire〔bat〕. —動物 a blood sucker.

きゅうご【救護】relief. ¶～する relieve. 彼は被災者の～に当たっていた He was engaged in *relief* work of the sufferers.

きゅうこう【旧交】¶～を温める renew *one's old friendship* (*with a person*).

きゅうこう【休校】¶流感のため2週間～になった School *was closed* for two weeks because of the flu.

きゅうこう【休航】¶この航路は冬季～する This〔steamship〕service *is suspended* during the winter.

きゅうこう【休講】¶本日(3時限の授業は)～ *No* (third period) *lecture* today. A教授本日～(掲示) *No lecture* will be given today by Prof. A.

きゅうこう【急行】an express〔train〕. ¶10時20分発の～ the 10:20 *express*. ～で行けばまにあうだろう If you go by *express*, you will be in time. ～は30分ごとに出ている *Express trains* run every thirty minutes. 彼は現場に～した He *hurried to* the spot.

きゅうごう【糾合】¶彼は同志を～して旗揚げをした He *rallied* kindred spirits and rose in arms.

きゅうこうか【急降下】a sudden drop; a〔nose〕dive; a swoop. ¶～する(飛行機が) dive; swoop; make a nose dive.
—爆撃機 a dive bomber.

きゅうこうばい【急勾配】a steep slope.
¶～の階段 a *steep* flight of stairs.

きゅうこく【急告】an urgent notice. ¶～! 明朝9時から10時まで停電になります *Urgent!* The electric current will be off from 9:00 to 10:00 a.m. tomorrow.

きゅうこく【救国】¶～の英雄 the hero of *national salvation*.

きゅうこん【求婚】a proposal (≒ an offer) of marriage. ¶彼は彼女に～した He *asked for* her *hand*. / He *made a proposal to* her.
—者 a suitor.

きゅうこん【球根】a bulb; a tuber (ユリ, チューリップ, タマネギ, スイセンなどは bulb; tuber はジャガイモなど).

きゅうさい【休載】¶作者病気につき漫画「…」を一時～します Because of the author's sickness the comic strip "..." will *not appear* for a while.

きゅうさい【救済】aid; help. ¶公害被害者の～ *relief* to the sufferers from public nuisance. ～する *help* (*a person*) out of.
—策 a relief measure. —事業 relief works. 難民— the relief of the destitute.

きゅうさく【旧作】*one's* old work. ¶～を書き改めることにした I have decided to rewrite my *old work*.

きゅうし【九死】¶～に一生を得る have a narrow (≒ hairbreadth) escape; escape by a hair's breadth (≒ the skin of *one's* teeth).

きゅうし【旧師】*one's* old (≒ former) teacher.

きゅうし【急死】a sudden death. ¶～する die suddenly; die a sudden death.

きゅうし【急使】an express messenger; a courier.

きゅうし【臼歯】a molar〔tooth〕.
小— a premolar〔tooth〕; a false molar.

きゅうじ【給仕】a waiter; (事務所の) an office boy. ¶お客さんの食事のお～をしなさい *Serve* the guests at dinner. / *Wait on* the guests at table. だれか～がご用を承りましたか *Are* you *waited upon*?

ぎゅうし【牛脂】beef fat ; 〔beef〕 tallow.
きゅうしき【旧式】¶ ～な old-fashioned ; out-of-date. ～な人は革新に反対する A person *following old lines* is against innovation.
きゅうじつ【休日】a holiday. ¶ 学校の創立記念日は～だ We have *a holiday* on the anniversary of the foundation of our school.
きゅうしふ【休止符】〘音楽〙a rest ; a pause.
ぎゅうしゃ【牛舎】a cowshed.
きゅうしゅ【鳩首】¶ ～協議する put (≒ lay) heads together ; counsel together.
きゅうしゅう【旧習】old customs.
きゅうしゅう【吸収】absorption. ¶ 砂地は水をよく～する The sandy soil *absorbs* water well. 知識を～する *gain* knowledge. 大企業が同系の小企業を～する A large enterprise *absorbs* lesser ones of the same kind.
きゅうしゅう【急襲】a sudden attack. ¶ ～する make *a sudden attack* (*on*).
きゅうしゅつ【救出】¶ ～する rescue ; save.
きゅうじゅつ【弓術】archery ; bowmanship.
きゅうしょ【急所】a vital part ; (要点) the vital point ; (痛い所) a sore (≒ tender) spot. ¶ ～を打つ hit (*a person*) in *a vulnerable spot*. 問題の～はここだ This is *the point* of the problem. 彼の批評は～をついている His criticism *hits home*.
きゅうじょ【救助】rescue. ¶ 彼はこれまでに何人かの人命を～した He *has saved* several lives until now. だれかが叫んで～を求めている Somebody is crying for *help*. 一行の～に赴かなければならない We have to go to the *rescue* of the party.
—信号 an SOS. —船 a rescue boat.
きゅうじょう【休場】(建物などの) closure ; (人の) an absence. ¶ 劇場は改装のため～中だった The theater *was closed* for renovation. 横綱は病気のため～している The *sumo* champion *is staying away from the ring* because of sickness.
きゅうじょう【球状】¶ ～の ball-shaped ; spherical ; globular.
きゅうじょう【球場】a baseball ground (≒ field) ; a ball park.
きゅうじょう【窮状】distress ; a sad plight. ¶ 彼らは～を訴えた They complained of their *distress*.
きゅうしょく【休職】suspension from duty (≒ office ; service). ¶ 彼は病気のため～中だ He *is under suspension* owing to his sickness.
きゅうしょく【求職】¶ 彼は～のため上京した He came up to Tokyo *seeking employment*.
—者 a job hunter (≒ seeker) ; an applicant.
きゅうしょく【給食】¶ ～する provide meals (*for a person*) ; furnish (*a person*) *with* food.
—費(学校の) the expense for school lunch 〔program〕.
ぎゅうじ・る【牛耳る】¶ 党を～る *be the leader of* a party. その討論では彼が～っている He *is taking the lead* in the discussion.

きゅうしん【休神・休心】¶ 無事当地に到着しました. 他事ながらご～ください I am happy to say that I have arrived here safe and sound. (「ご休心ください」は文字どおりには Please set your mind at ease. だが, このような文脈では, 英語では上記のようにいうのが普通. また I am happy to say that の部分はないほうが英語らしい)
きゅうしん【休診】¶ 本日～(掲示) No consultation (≒ examination) today.
きゅうしん【急進】¶ ～的 radical ; extreme.
—派 the radicals.
きゅうしん【球審】〘野球〙a ball umpire.
きゅうじん【求人】the offer of situation. ¶ 今は～難の時代だ This is a hard time to *get workers for a job*.
—広告 a want ad ; (新聞で) Classified Ads. (この英語は求人・求職・貸間・貸家などをふくむ).
きゅうしんりょく【求心力】the centripetal force.
きゅうす【急須】a teapot.
きゅうすい【吸水】suction.
—ポンプ a sucking (≒ suction) pump.
きゅうすい【給水】¶ ～する supply water (*for* a city) ; supply (a town) with water. その都市の～が止まった The *water supply* to the town failed.
—車 a water wagon. —所 a water station. —設備 water-supply facilities. —塔 a water tower. 時間— an hour-restricted supply of water.
きゅうすう【級数】〘数学〙progression.
等差— arithmetical progression.
きゅう・する【給する】¶ 日給2,000円を～する *pay* a daily wage of two thousand yen. 衣食を～する *provide* (*a person*) *with* food and clothing. 食費を～する *supply* (*a person*) *with* food expenses.
きゅう・する【窮する】¶ ～すれば通ず There is always a way out. 彼は問い詰められて返答に～した He was pressed for an answer, and *did not know* what to reply.
きゅうせい【旧姓】*one's* former name ; (女性の) *one's* maiden name. ¶ 安田朝子(～高村) Asako Yasuda, *formerly* (≒ *nee*) Takamura.
きゅうせい【急性】¶ ～の病気 an *acute* disease. ～リューマチ *acute* rheumatism.
きゅうせい【救世】—軍 the Salvation Army.
—主 the Savior.
きゅうせい【急逝】a sudden death. ¶ ～する die suddenly.
きゅうせかい【旧世界】the Old World (しばしばヨーロッパを指す).
きゅうせき【旧跡】a historic site (≒ scene) ; ruins.
きゅうせつ【急設】¶ ～する lay (≒ set up) (telephones) quickly ; build (classrooms) speedily.
きゅうせっきじだい【旧石器時代】the Old Stone Age.
きゅうせん【休戦】cease-fire. ¶ ～する stop fire.
—会談 a cease-fire conference. —記念日

き

(第1次大戦の) Armistice Day (アメリカでは1954年に Veterans' Day と改称). ―協定 a cease-fire agreement.

きゅうせんぽう【急先鋒】 a leader; a forerunner. ¶ 彼女はこの大運動の～に立っている She *leads the van of* this great campaign.

きゅうぞう【急造】 ¶～する build (≒construct) in haste.

きゅうぞう【急増】 a jump; a sudden increase. ¶ 交通事故が～した Traffic accidents *have increased rapidly* (≒ *suddenly*).

きゅうそく【休息】 rest; repose. ¶ 横になって～する lie at rest. ちょっと(じゅうぶんに)～する take a little (good) *rest*.

きゅうそく【急速】 ¶ 日本の産業は最近～の進歩を遂げた Japanese industry has recently made *rapid* progress. この町は～に発展した This town has become larger (≒ has grown) rather *rapidly*.

きゅうたい【旧態】 ¶ 彼の考えには～依然たるものがある His idea *is old-fashioned*.

きゅうだい【及第】 ¶ 試験に～する *pass* an examination.
―点 the passing mark.

きゅうたいりく【旧大陸】 the Old World.

きゅうだん【球団】 a baseball team.

きゅうだん【糾弾】 impeachment. ¶ 収賄の件で～する *impeach (a person) for* taking a bribe.

きゅうち【旧知】 ¶ 彼とは～の間柄だ I *have been good friends with* him for a long time.

きゅうち【窮地】 a difficult situation. ¶ ～に陥る be put in *a dilemma*; stand *at bay*. その事件で彼らは～に追い込まれた They *were brought* (≒ *were driven*) *to bay* by the accident.

きゅうちゅう【宮中】 the Imperial Court.

きゅうつい【急追】 ¶ 敵の～をかわす evade *a hot pursuit* of an enemy. 敵を～する *pursue* an enemy *hotly*.

きゅうてい【休廷】 ¶ ～する hold no court.

きゅうてい【宮廷】 the Court.

きゅうていしゃ【急停車】 ¶ 列車は～して危うく事故を起こさずにすんだ The train *stopped suddenly* and narrowly avoided the traffic accident.

きゅうてき【仇敵】 a sworn enemy.

きゅうてん【急転】 ¶ 情勢が～した The situation took a *sudden* turn (≒ change). ～直下その事件は解決した The incident has come to an *immediate* solution.

きゅうでん【宮殿】 a palace.

きゅうと【旧都】 an old (≒ a former) capital.

きゅうとう【急騰】 an upswing; a sudden rise. ¶ 物価が～した Prices have taken *a sudden jump*.

きゅうどう【弓道】 archery.

ぎゅうとう【牛痘】〘医学〙cowpox; vaccinia.

ぎゅうなべ【牛鍋】 *sukiyaki*; beef cooked in the Japanese style.

きゅうなん【救難】 ―訓練 relief training. ―作業 relief work. ―船 a rescue ship. ―隊 a wrecking crew. ―対策 a relief measure. ―トラック(列車) a wrecking lorry (train).

きゅうに【急に】 ⇒きゅう(急)

ぎゅうにく【牛肉】 beef.

きゅうにゅう【吸入】 inhalation.
酸素―器 an oxygen inspirator.

ぎゅうにゅう【牛乳】 〔cow's〕milk. ¶ グラス1杯の～ a glass of *milk* (英 では牛乳は暖めないから a cup of milk とは言わない). ～を搾る *milk* a cow. ～で育てる feed (≒ raise) (a baby) on *milk*; feed *milk* to a baby. ～を配達する deliver *milk*.
―びん a〔milk〕bottle. ―屋 a milkman.

きゅうねん【旧年】 the old year; last year.

きゅうは【急派】 ¶ 軍隊を前線へ～する *dispatch* troops to the front.

きゅうば【急場】 ¶ ～のまにあわせ a *temporary* measure; a stopgap. ～の処置 an *emergency* measure. 借金をして～を切り抜けた I tided over *the pinch* by borrowing money. この金があれば～を切り抜けられる This money will tide me over *the crisis*.

キューバ Cuba.
―人 a Cuban.

ぎゅうば【牛馬】 ¶ 人を～のようにこき使う work people *hard* (≒ *like a beast*).

きゅうはく【急迫】 ¶ ～した国際関係 a *tense* international relationship. 食糧事情の～ food *stringency*. 情勢は～した The situation *has become tense*.

きゅうはく【窮迫】 ¶ 政府は財政的に～している The government is in financial *difficulty*.

きゅうはん【旧版】 an old edition.

きゅうばん【吸盤】〘動物〙a sucker; a sucking desk.

きゅうひ【給費】 ¶ 彼らは奨学金を～されていた They *were supported* by scholarships.
―生 a scholarship student; a scholarship holder.

ぎゅうひ【牛皮】 cowhide.

キュービズム〘美学〙cubism.

きゅうびょう【急病】 a sudden illness.
¶ ～にかかる be suddenly taken ill (誤って have suddenly taken ill とすることがある. 必ず be 動詞を用いること); be seized with *a sudden illness*.
―人 an emergency case.

きゅうふ【給付】 donating; delivery. ¶ 人に物を～する *furnish a person with* goods.

きゅうぶん【旧聞】 ¶ それは～に属することだ That is *an old story*.

きゅうへい【旧弊】 ¶ 彼は～な考えを持っている He has *old-fashioned* ideas.

きゅうへん【急変】 ¶ 彼の病状は～した His condition *has taken a sudden turn*. 彼の態度はそれを聞いて～した His attitude *changed suddenly* upon hearing it.

きゅうほう【急報】 a hurried report. ¶ ～する report promptly; send an emergency call.

きゅうぼう【窮乏】 poverty. ¶ 彼らはひどい～に陥っていた They were reduced to *wretched* *poverty*.

きゅうむ【急務】urgent business. ¶ ～に応ずる meet *the most urgent need*. 被災地の再建に着手することが～だ *It is urgently needed to* start the reconstruction of the stricken area.

きゅうめい【究明】¶ 原因を～する *inquire into* the cause (*of*). 科学者はその問題を～するだろう The scientists will *look into* the matter. / The scientists will *clarify* the matter.

きゅうめい【糾明】¶ 汚職事件を～する *examine* the corruption case *closely*.

きゅうめい【救命】―具 life preserver. ―索 a life line. ―ボート a life boat.

きゅうめん【球面】〖数学〗a spherical surface.

きゅうやく【旧約】―聖書 the Old Testament.

きゅうゆ【給油】refueling; supply of oil. ¶ ～する refuel; feed (≒ supply) oil (*to*).
―所 an oil (≒ a gas) station. ―船 a tanker. 空中― air-to-air refueling.

きゅうゆう【旧友】an old friend.

きゅうゆう【級友】a classmate.

きゅうよ【給与】〔an〕allowance; supply; a salary. ¶ 制服を～する *supply* (*a person*) *with* uniform.
―所得 earned income. ―水準 a wage level. ―生活者 a wage earner. 現物― an allowance in kind. 最低― a minimum wage.

きゅうよ【窮余】¶ ～の一策 *the last* (≒ *the final*) resort. 食物がなくなったので～の一策として野草を食べた Because of the food shortage, we *had to resort to* eating wild grass.

きゅうよう【休養】〔a〕rest; (病後の) recuperation. ¶ ひと月ほどいなかで～する I'll go to the country to *repose* for a month. きみは～をとる必要がある You need some *rest*.

きゅうよう【急用】an urgent appointment. ¶ ～で on *urgent business*. ～で伺えません *Urgent business* prevents me from calling on you.

きゅうらい【旧来】¶ ～の悪習 *old* abuses.

きゅうらく【及落】¶ ～を決める decide the result of an examination.

きゅうらく【急落】〖経済学〗〖商業〗a slump; a sharp decline. ¶ 相場は～した The market suffered *a sharp* (≒ *severe*) *decline*. 物価が～した Prices *dropped suddenly*.

きゅうり【胡瓜】a cucumber.

きゅうりゅう【急流】a rapid stream. ¶ いかだで～を下る shoot *the rapids* on a raft. ～をさかのぼる follow up *a torrent*.

きゅうりょう【丘陵】a hill; heights; an eminence.
―地帯 hilly districts. 多摩― the Tama heights.

きゅうりょう【給料】pay; a salary; wages (payは一般的な語, salaryは精神的な仕事の給料, wagesは筋肉労働の賃金で通例複数).
¶ 彼は～が高い(安い) He *is* well (poorly) *paid*. ～を10万円もらう get *a salary* of a hundred thousand yen. ～が1万円上がった My *salary* has been raised by ten thousand yen.
―取り a salaried man; (総称) the salaried class; 米 a white collar worker. ―日 (おもに米) payday (文中ではふつう不定冠詞を省く. アメリカの payday は大てい金曜日. イギリスでは1年に4回払いのとき a quarter day という).

きゅうれき【旧暦】the old calendar. ¶ ～では according to *the old calendar*. ～で by *the old calendar*.

ぎゅっと ¶ ～人の手を握る *squeeze* (≒ *press*) *a person's* hand.

きょ【居】¶ ～を東京に定める make *one's home* in Tokyo. 昨年ここに～を構えた I *moved* here last year. / We *were settled* in this house last year.

きょ【虚】¶ 敵の～をつく *catch* the enemy *off guard*. ～をつかれた I *was taken by surprise*.

きよ【寄与】a contribution. ¶ 科学の進歩に重大な～をする make *an* important *contribution* to the progress of science.

きよ・い【清い】¶ ～い水 *clear* water. 心の～い人 a person with *pure* heart. ～き一票を投じる cast a *clean* vote.

きょう【京】(首都) a capital; (京都) the city of Kyoto.

きょう【経】a sutra; the Buddhist scriptures. ¶ ～を読む chant (≒ recite; read) *a sutra*.

きょう【興】interest; fun. ¶ ～にのって in *fun*. ～をそぐ spoil the *fun*. トランプに～ずる *play* cards; *have fun with* playing cards. ～にのって詩を作る write a poem *on a flight of imagination*; *be inspired to* write a poem. 小説に～がわく *get interested in* a novel. 虫の声が名月に～を添えた Chirps of the insects *added special interest* in the moon viewing〔party〕.

きょう【凶】misfortune; ill luck. ¶ 占いは～と出た My fortune bodes me no good.

-きょう【-強】¶ 50キロ～ *a little over* 50 kg. 10分～ *a little more* than ten minutes.

-きょう【-狂】an addict; a fan. ¶ カメラ～ *a* camera *fan* (≒ *enthusiast*). 競馬～ *a* horse race *fan*. 野球～ *a* baseball *fan*.

きょう【卿】Lord; Sir; (大臣) a minister; a secretary (Lord は姓につき, Sir は名につける. George Sansom なら Lord Sansom か Sir George となる).

きょう【今日】today. ¶ ～は何曜ですか What day of the week is it *today*? (day はふつう曜日, date は日付. したがって What day is it? と言えば曜日を聞くことになる). ～の午後はだれかが訪ねてくるだろう Someone will come and see me *this* afternoon. ～じゅうにこの本を読み終えたい I want to finish〔reading〕this book *today*. ～から日記をつけよう I will keep a diary from *today* on. ～は一日楽しかった We have spent a wonderful day *today*. / We had a nice time *today*. ～の新聞はどこにありますか Where is *today's* paper?

きよう【紀要】a bulletin; memoirs. ¶ 大学の

き

き

～ *a* university *bulletin*.

きよう【起用】¶そこには新人が～されるはずだ A new man is to *be appointed to* that post.

きよう【器用】¶～な人 a *handy* man. 彼は～に木彫細工をする He *skillfully* carves figures in wood. 彼は～に立ちまわる He makes his way *cleverly* in the world.（日本語でも英語でも軽蔑の気持ちがこもる）. ～貧乏.（諺）*Jack of all trades and master of none.*

ぎょう【行】a line. ¶～をかえる begin *a* new *line*. 1～おきに書く write on every other *line*. 3～目に in the third *line*. ～をする（宗教の）practice *austerities*.

ぎょう【業】¶医を～とする be a doctor by *profession*; work as a doctor. ～を終える complete *one's studies*; finish school.

きょうあく【凶悪】¶～な犯罪 a *brutal* crime. **―**犯 a brutish (≒ brutal) criminal.

きょうい【胸囲】chest measurement. ¶～が90センチある I measure 90 centimeters *round the chest*.

きょうい【脅威】a menace; a threat. ¶～を与える menace; threaten; be *a menace* to (the enemy).

きょうい【強意】emphasis.

きょうい【驚異】a wonder; a marvel.
¶自然の～ nature's *wonders*. ～的な大記録を作る establish (≒ make; complete) a *wonderful* record. 科学は～的な発達を遂げた Science has made *marvelous* progress.

きょういく【教育】education.
1〖教育を〗¶息子には最高の～を受けさせたい I want to give my son the highest *education*.
新入社員は半年の～を受けたのち各職場に配置される Incoming partners are attached to posts after a half year *training*.
私は戦時中の～を受けている I had (≒ got; received) *education* during the war.
個人個人の性格・能力に応じた～をしなければならない People must *be educated* according to their individual characters and abilities.
そういう～をするには優秀な教師と多大の費用がいる It takes superior teachers and great expense to conduct such *education*.
彼は正規の～を受けていない He has no school *education*.
私はそのような方面の～はあまり受けていない I *have* not *been educated* in such a field.
2〖教育は〗¶知育偏重の～は感心しない. もっと人格的な～を目指すべきだ Too much intellectual *training* is not good. It is the liberal *education* that counts.
～は学校ばかりに任せられるものではない We can't leave *education* to school only.
3〖教育する〗¶そういうがんこな人を～することはできぬ I cannot *educate* (≒ *instruct*; *train*) such a pigheaded person.
若い人には人との応対の仕方を～する必要がある We must *train* youth in the right manner of receiving people.
4〖その他の助詞とともに〗¶あの国は一般に～の水準が低い In that country people have a low standard of *education* generally.
家庭での～もたいせつだ *Training* at home is also important.
私は～がないから, そんな難しいことはわかりません I don't understand such a difficult thing, because I have had little *schooling*.
―学 pedagogy; pedagogics. **―**心理学 pedagogical psychology. **―**者 an educationist; an educator. **―**費 educational expenses.

きょういん【教員】a [school] teacher (米では初等教育の先生は女性が多いので teacher は女性名詞として用いられることが多い); (男) a schoolmaster; (女) a schoolmistress; (全体) the teaching staff.
―組合 a teacher's union. **―**免許状 a teacher's license (≒ certificate).

きょうえい【競泳】a swimming race (≒ match). ¶～大会 a *swimming* meet.

きょうえき【共益】¶～のために for the *public good*; in the interest of the public.
―事業 a public enterprise.

きょうえん【共演】¶3大スターの～ three great stars *coacting*. A氏とB氏が～する Mr. A and Mr. B are to *appear together*.

きょうえん【供宴・饗宴】a banquet (ふつうスピーチや乾杯があり, 大人数のものを言う). ¶ホテルでは大～が催されていた A big *banquet* was being held in the hotel.

きょうおう【供応】an entertainment. ¶～を受ける *be treated* to dinner. ～する *invite* (≒ *treat*) *a person* to dinner.

きょうか【狂歌】a comic poem; a satirical poem.

きょうか【教化】education; instruction; enlightenment; (福音による) evangelization.
¶～する educate; instruct; enlighten; evangelize.
―運動 an educational campaign (≒ movement). **―**事業 educational work.

きょうか【教科】a course of study; the curriculum; (科目) a subject.

きょうか【強化】reinforcement. ¶陣容を～する *reinforce* the staff.
―合宿 a training camp. **―**食品 enriched food.

きょうかい【協会】an association; a society.

きょうかい【教会】a church (イギリスでは国教以外の教会は chapel と言う. また大学や大病院などの付属礼拝堂はどんなに大きくても chapel である).
¶～へ行く go to *church* (礼拝に関係のあるときは church に the をつけない. 次例も同じ). ～でお祈りをする pray in *church*.
―員 a church member; (全体) a flock; a congregation. **―**堂 a church; a cathedral.
ローマカトリック**―** the Roman Catholic Church. 長老(監督; 組合)**―** Presbyterian (Episcopal; Congregational) Church. メソジスト(バプテスト)**―** the Methodist (Baptist) Church.

きょうかい【教戒】[an] admonition.

—師 a prison chaplain.

きょうかい【境界】 a border; a boundary; a frontier (border は境界線および付近の地域. boundary が地理的分類であるのに対して frontier は政治・軍事的な境界):
¶ ～線を引く fix *the boundaries*; draw *a line* between the two. ～線を越える cross *the border*. この川が隣の牧場との～だ This river forms *the boundary* between our pasture and the neighboring one.

きょうがい【境涯】 ¶ 彼は気の毒な～だ He is leading *a* miserable *life*.

ぎょうかい【業界】 the industry. ¶ ～の大立て者 the leading figure *in the business*.
—紙 a business paper. 出版— the publishing world.

きょうかく【胸郭】 the chest; the thorax (複 the thoraxes, the thoraces). ¶ ～成形術 thoracoplasty.

きょうかく【侠客】 a chivalrous person; a street knight. ¶ 彼は～はだの男だった He had a touch of *chivalry* in his character.

きょうがく【共学】 mixed education; 米 coeducation. ¶ たいていの公立学校は～だ Most public schools *are coeducational*.

きょうがく【驚愕】 amazement; astonishment. ¶ その知らせを聞いて～した I *was astonished at* (≒ *was astonished to* hear) the news. / The news *astonished* me greatly.

ぎょうかく【仰角】 the angle of elevation.

きょうかしょ【教科書】 a textbook. ¶ 英語の～ *an* English *textbook*. 数学の～ *a textbook on* mathematics. 検定済み～ *an* authorized *textbook*.

きょうかつ【恐喝・脅喝】 a threat; a menace. ¶ ～する threaten; menace.
—状 a threatening (≒ blackmailing) letter.

きょうかん【凶漢】 a villain; a ruffian; a rascal; (暗殺者) an assassin; a murderer.

きょうかん【共感】 sympathy. ¶ ～を覚える feel *sympathy* with. ～を得る win the *sympathy* of. 彼の意見に～する I *have* great *sympathy with* his opinion. / I *agree with* him. そのキャンペーンは大ぜいの人の～を呼んだ The campaign awoke *sympathy* in many people.

きょうかん【教官】 a teacher (日本語の「教官」は正しくは公務員にのみ用いる); an instructor; a professor; (全体) the teaching staff.

ぎょうかん【行間】 space between the lines. ¶ ～を読む read *between the lines*; peruse (文語).

きょうき【凶器】 arms; a [murderous] weapon.

きょうき【狂気】 madness. ¶ 台風が来ているのに漁に出るなんて～のさただ It is *madness* to go fishing when a typhoon is coming on.

きょうき【狂喜】 ¶ ～する go (≒ be) wild with joy; be beside *one*self with joy. ～して in *wild joy*; in *a rapture of delight*.

きょうき【狭軌】 a narrow gauge.

きょうき【驚喜】 [a] pleasant surprise. ¶ ～する be pleasantly surprised (*at*; *to* hear).

きょうぎ【協議】 conference. ¶ ～する talk over (a matter); confer with (*a person*). ～のうえ after *conference*; by *mutual agreement*. ～中 (人が) be in *conference*; (事柄が) be under *discussion*.
—会 a conference; a council. —事項 a subject (≒ an item) of discussion.

きょうぎ【狭義】 a narrow sense. ¶ ～に解釈する interpret *in a narrow sense*.

きょうぎ【教義】 a doctrine; a creed; a dogma (複 dogmas; dogmata). ¶ ～上 in *doctrine*; in accordance with *doctrine*.

きょうぎ【競技】 a game; a match; a meet; (baseball, football などは game. boxing, wrestling などは match. swimming は meet を用いる); a contest; a competition.
¶ ～に参加する take part in *a game*. ～に勝つ (負ける) win (lose) *a game*.
—会 an athletic meet; a competition. —種目 sporting events. —場 a ground; (陸上競技の) a field; a stadium.

ぎょうぎ【行儀】 manners; behavior. ¶ 彼は～がよい(悪い) He has good *manners* (bad *manners*). 彼はなんて～が悪いんだ How ill-*mannered* he is! 彼は～よくしてましたか Did he *behave himself*? お～はどうしたの(子どもに向かって) Where are your *manners*?
—作法 etiquette.

きょうきゅう【供給】 supply; (ガス・水道などの) service. ¶ あの会社がガスをわれわれの家庭に～する That company *supplies* gas *to* our houses. / That company *supplies* our houses *with* gas. 需要と～のバランスがとれている An adequate balance between demand and *supply* is maintained.
—過多 oversupply. —源 a source of supply. —者 a supplier. —不足 short supply; shortage.

ぎょうぎょうしい【仰仰しい】 (表現が) exaggerated; (態度が) ostentatious. ¶ 彼の言い方はいつも～い He always *exaggerates*. ～い歓迎がかえって客を不愉快にした The guest was displeased at the *ostentatious* reception.

きょうきん【胸襟】 ¶ そのことについて～を開いて語り合った We talked on the subject *without reserve*. / We had a *heart-to-heart* talk on the subject.

きょうく【教区】 a parish. ¶ ～内の信者 a parishioner.

きょうぐ【教具】 teaching tools.

きょうぐう【境遇】 circumstances (この意味では常に複数). ¶ 彼は恵まれた(恵まれない)～にある He is in prosperous (needy) *circumstances*. 人間は～に左右されやすい We are apt to be influenced by our *environment*. 彼は～に打ち勝って成功した He succeeded in life against unfavorable *circumstances*.

きょうくん【教訓】 a lesson; teachings (ふつう複数形). ¶ その事件は彼らによい～となることだろう The incident will give them *a* valuable *lesson*. 彼の失敗を～としよう Let his failure be *a lesson* to us.

きょうげき【挟撃】¶敵を～する *attack* the enemy *from both sides*.

ぎょうけつ【凝結】congelation; condensation. ¶水蒸気が～して水となる Steam *condenses into* water.
—点 the freezing point. —器 a freezer.

き

きょうけん【狂犬】a mad dog.
—病 rabies; hydrophobia.

きょうけん【強健】¶～な体 a *strong* (≒*stout*) body.

きょうけん【強権】¶政府は非常事態を宣して～を発動した The government, declaring a state of emergency, *took strong measures*.

きょうげん【狂言】(能) a *no* farce; (作りごと) a fake; a trick. ¶〔能〕～はお好きですか Do you like a *no* comedy? 歌舞伎座の～はなんですか What is the *program* of the Kabukiza Theater? 彼が強盗に襲われたと言っていたのは～だった He invented *a lie* that he had been robbed.
—自殺 a mock suicide.

きょうこ【強固】¶彼は意志～な人物だ He is a man of *strong* will. / He has a *strong* will. 団結を～にしよう Let's *strengthen* our unity.

ぎょうこ【凝固】(氷などの) congelation; (血液などの) coagulation. ¶水が～して氷になるWater *congeals into* ice.
—点 a freezing point.

きょうこう【凶行】(殺人) murder; (犯罪) a crime. ¶～の現場 the scene of *a crime*. ～を働く commit *a crime*.

きょうこう【恐慌】a panic. ¶～で銀行もつぶれた Even some of the banks smashed owing to the *panic*. 彼らは～状態に陥った They were seized with *a panic*.
株式— a stock-exchange panic. 金融— a financial panic.

きょうこう【強行】¶無理な計画の～が災難を招く The *enforcement* of an impractical plan causes a disaster.

きょうこう【強硬】¶～な反対意見 a *strong* opposite opinion. 彼は～に反対しつづけた He *firmly* kept saying "No." ～手段に訴える take *strong* measures. ～な態度をとる take a *stiff* attitude.

きょうごう【強豪】a veteran. ¶～ぞろいのチーム a team of *veteran players*.

ぎょうこう【僥倖】〔good〕luck. ¶～で彼は成功した *By good luck* he succeeded.

きょうこうぐん【強行軍】a forced march.

きょうこく【強国】a strong country; a power. ¶世界の～ the *powers* of the world.

きょうさ【教唆】instigation. ¶彼らは彼を～して犯罪を実行させた They *instigated* him *to* a crime.

きょうさい【共催】¶この展覧会は新聞社とデパートが～した This exhibition has been held under the *joint-sponsorship* of the newspaper office and the department store.

きょうさい【恐妻】—家 a henpecked husband. —病 wife-phobia.

きょうざい【教材】teaching materials.
—研究 a study of teaching materials. —費 expenses for teaching materials.

きょうさいくみあい【共済組合】a cooperative society; a co-op.

きょうさく【凶作】a poor crop. ¶～の年 a *lean* year. ことしは米が～だ We have *a poor crop* of rice this year.

きょうざつぶつ【夾雑物】an admixture.

きょうざ·める【興覚める】¶～めた顔つきで with a *bored* look. 彼の長々と語る自慢話にはみんな～めした His proud long talk of himself *spoiled the pleasure* of the company.

きょうさん【共産】—圏 the Communist bloc. —主義 communism. —主義者 a communist. —党 the Communist Party.
—党員 a communist. —化 ¶彼らはその国の～化を意図している They intend to *communize* the country.

きょうさん【協賛】support; approval. ¶これは新聞社の主催, 文部省～による展覧会だ This exhibition *is* sponsored by the newspaper office and *supported* by the Ministry of Education.

きょうし【教師】a teacher (軽べつ的には a pedagogue が用いられる).
—用参考書 a teacher's manual. 家庭— a tutor; (女性) a governess.

きょうじ【凶事】a misfortune; a disaster (被害者が多いときに用いる).

きょうじ【教示】instruction; teaching.
¶～する teach; instruct.

ぎょうし【凝視】¶彼女はその男の顔を～した She *stared* him *in* the face. / She *stared at* his face.

ぎょうじ【行司】a *sumo*〔-wrestling〕referee.

ぎょうじ【行事】an event. ¶それは年中～の一つだ It is one of *the chief events of the year*. きのうわが校の創立80周年記念の～が行なわれた The eightieth anniversary of the foundation of our school was celebrated yesterday.

きょうしつ【教室】a classroom; a schoolroom.
階段— a〔lecture〕theater.

ぎょうしゃ【業者】traders. ¶～間の競争が激しい There is keen competition among *the traders concerned*. ～を呼んで入札させた I let *the traders* make a bid.

きょうじゃく【強弱】strength; strength and weakness.

きょうしゅ【教主】the founder of a religion.

きょうじゅ【享受】¶文化生活を～する *enjoy* a cultural life.

きょうじゅ【教授】teaching; (人) a professor.
¶イギリス文学の～ *a professor* of English literature. 彼女は生け花の～をしている She *teaches* (≒*gives lessons in*) flower arrangement.
—会 a faculty meeting. —法 a teaching method. 助— an assistant professor. 個

人— ¶バイオリンの個人～を受ける take *private lessons* in violin. 名誉— an emeritus professor.

ぎょうしゅ【業種】a type of industry. ¶～別(の)電話帳 a telephone directory classified by industry.

きょうしゅう【強襲】an assault. ¶敵陣を～する *make an assault on* a fort. 彼の一打は三塁～のヒットとなった His hit was too much for the third-baseman to handle.

きょうしゅう【郷愁】homesickness. ¶～にかられる feel homesick. ～やみがたいものがある I long very much for my home.

きょうしゅうじょ【教習所】a training school. 自動車— a driver's school. ダンス— a dancing school.

きょうしゅく【恐縮】¶わざわざお知らせくださって～に存じます *It's very kind of you to* tell me the news. まことに～ですが, それを取っていただけますか *I'm sorry to trouble you, but* will you please pass it to me? (ふつうは Excuse me, but... でじゅうぶん). 勘違いを指摘されて～した I *was ashamed to* have my careless mistake pointed out.

ぎょうしゅく【凝縮】condensation.
—ウラン enriched uranium.

きょうしゅつ【供出】a delivery. ¶彼らは割り当てられたように米を～した They *offered* rice as officially allotted.
—価格 a delivery price. —米 delivered rice.

きょうじゅつ【供述】〖法律〗a deposition.
¶～する depose.
—者 a deponent. —書 an affidavit; a written statement.

きょうじゅん【恭順】¶彼は国王に～の意を表した He *swore allegiance to* the king.

きょうしょ【教書】a message. ¶アメリカ大統領の～ President's *message* to Congress. 大統領の年頭～ the President's annual State of the Union *message* to Congress.

ぎょうしょ【行書】a semi-cursive writing of Chinese penmanship.

きょうしょう【協商】an entente.

きょうじょう【教条】dogma; doctrine.
—主義 dogmatism; doctrinism.

ぎょうしょう【行商】(人) a peddler. ¶～する peddle.

ぎょうじょう【行状】conduct; behavior.
¶きみの～は悪い You *are behaving* badly.

きょうしょく【教職】the teaching profession.
¶卒業したら～に就きたい I'd like to *be a teacher* after graduation.
—員 the teaching staff. —員組合 a teachers' union. —課程 an education (≒ a teaching) course.

きょうしん【狂信】fanaticism. ¶彼は新興宗教を～している He *fanatically believes in* a newly-risen religion.
—者 a fanatic.

きょうしん【強震】a severe earthquake.
¶昨夜当地に～があった *A severe earthquake* was felt here last night.

きょうじん【凶刃】¶大統領は暗殺者の～に倒れた The president fell a victim to *an assassin's dagger*.

きょうじん【狂人】a madman.

きょうじん【強靭】¶～な体 a *strong* body.

きょうしんざい【強心剤】a heart medicine; a heart tonic.

きょうしんしょう【狭心症】〖医学〗angina pectoris.

ぎょうずい【行水】¶～する have a bath in a tub.

きょうすいびょう【恐水病】〖医学〗hydrophobia.

きょう·する【供する】¶諸氏のご高覧に～する We *submit* it *to* your inspection. それは一般の縦覧に～されている It *is open to* the public. 茶菓を～する *serve* refreshments (*to*).

きょう·ずる【興ずる】¶子どもたちがボール遊びに～じている There are children *playing with a ball* (≒ *having fun at a ball game*).

きょうせい【強勢】〖音声学〗stress; emphasis; accent. ¶第2音節に～をおく put *stress* on the second syllable.

きょうせい【強制】compulsion; enforcement. ¶～的に彼にやらせた I *forced* him *to* do it. そうするように～された I *was compelled to* do so.
—管理 compulsory administration. —執行(処分) compulsory execution. —調停 compulsory mediation.

きょうせい【矯正】correction; remedy.
¶どもりを～する *cure* (*a person*) *of* stammering.

ぎょうせい【行政】administration. ¶彼は～的手腕がある He has *administrative* ability.
—官 an administrator. —機関 an administrative organ. —整理 administrative reorganization.

ぎょうせき【業績】results; achievements.
¶彼はりっぱな～を発表した He showed excellent *results* to the world. 建築界における彼の偉大な～に対して賞が贈られた A prize was given to him for his great *achievements* in the world of architecture. あの会社は～不振に悩んでいる The company is suffering from *business depression*.

きょうそ【教祖】the founder of a religion.
¶彼は経営学界では～的存在である He is *a king* in the world of business management.

きょうそう【競争】competition. ¶今は～の時代といわれる It is said that this is an age of *competition*. あの男とではとても～にならない I *am no match for* him. ～に最後に勝つのは努力家だ It is the hard workers that *win* finally. 私は学問で他の人たちと～をすることもできる I can *compete with* others academically.
—相手 a rival. —意識 competitive consciousness. —試験 a competitive examination.

きょうそう【競走】a race. ¶彼と～してみよう Let's *race* him. ウサギとカメが～した A hare and a tortoise *had a race with* each other.

き

き

彼は自分の車をバスと～させた He *raced* his car *against* a bus.

—車 a racing car; a racer. —者 a racer; a runner; (短距離の) a sprinter. 障害物— an obstacle race; (ハードル) a hurdle race. 自転車— a cycle race. 100メートル— the 100-meter dash (≒ race).

きょうそう【競漕】a boat race; a regatta.

きょうぞう【胸像】a bust; a bronze (≒ stone) likeness.

ぎょうそう【形相】¶ 彼は必死の～であった He had *a* desperate *look* on his face. ものすごい～で with *a* furious *look*.

きょうそうきょく【狂想曲】〘音楽〙a rhapsody.

きょうそうきょく【協奏曲】〘音楽〙a concerto (複 concertos).

バイオリン— a violin concerto.

きょうそうざい【強壮剤】a tonic.

きょうそくぼん【教則本】a textbook; a manual.

きょうそん【共存】coexistence. ¶ 平和～していく *coexist* in peace.

きょうだ【強打】hard-hitting. ¶ ～する hit hard; give *a heavy blow*.

—者 a heavy (≒ hard) hitter; (野球の) (米口語) a slugger.

きょうたい【狂態】a crazy conduct. ¶ 彼は酒を飲んで～を演じた He *got wild* in drink.

きょうたい【嬌態】coquetry. ¶ 彼女は～を示して彼の気を引いてみた She tried to attract his attention by *acting coquettishly*.

きょうだい【兄弟】(男の) a brother; (女の) a sister; (ふたり以上) brother[s] and sister[s]. ¶ われわれは 3 人～だ There are three of us children. ～は他人の始まり *Brothers* mark the first step toward estrangement.

—愛 brotherly love; sisterly love. —げんか ¶ 彼は～げんかはめったにしない He rarely *quarrels with his brothers*. —分 a sworn brother.

きょうだい【強大】¶ ～な strong; powerful; mighty.

きょうだい【鏡台】a dresser; a dressing table.

きょうたく【供託】a deposit; (委託) a trust. ¶ お金を銀行に(人に)～する *deposit* money *in* a bank (*with a person*).

—金 a deposit. —物 a deposit.

きょうたん【驚嘆】wonder; admiration. ¶ 私は～のあまり声が出なかった I was so overcome with *wonder* that I could not speak. 彼の進境は～に値する His progress well deserves *admiration*. 私は大自然の神秘に～した I was lost in *wonder* at the mysteries of great nature.

きょうだん【凶弾】¶ 彼は～に倒れた He was shot to death by an assassin. / He was killed by an assassin's bullets.

きょうだん【教団】a religious body; an order.

日本基督— the United Church of Christ in Japan.

きょうだん【教壇】the platform. ¶ ～に立つことに決心をした I've made up my mind to *become a teacher*.

きょうち【境地】a stage; a state. ¶ 彼は画境に新～を開いた He cleared (≒ broke) *a* new *ground* for the world of art. 修行によって無我の～に達することができる One can reach (≒ attain) the *state* of selflessness by training.

きょうちくとう【夾竹桃】〘植物〙an oleander.

きょうちゅう【胸中】¶ 彼は親友に～を打ち明けた He opened his *breast* to his intimate friend. 彼の～を察するにあまりある I truly *sympathize with* him.

ぎょうちゅう【蟯虫】〘虫類〙a thread worm; a pinworm.

きょうちょ【共著】a joint work; a collaboration. ¶ これは彼と私との～だ This is *a joint product* of us two.

きょうちょう【凶兆】[a] bad omen; [an] evil omen.

きょうちょう【協調】cooperation; (調和) harmony. ¶ われわれは～して困難を乗り越えた We *cooperated* in overcoming the difficulty. ここでは労使～がうまくいっている Here capital and labor *cooperate* (≒ *are getting on*) well with each other.

きょうちょう【強調】emphasis. ¶ 女らしさを～したデザイン a design *stressing* womanliness. 地震研究の必要を～する *stress* (≒ *emphasize*) the need of earthquake research.

きょうつう【共通】community. ¶ この欠点はわれわれすべて～に持っている This defect *is common* in all of us. 両者に～点を見いだす find something *in common* between the two. 彼らは利害関係が～している They have *common* interests. 彼はわれわれの～の友人である He is our *mutual* friend.

きょうてい【協定】an agreement. ¶ 彼らは～して価格を上げた They raised the price *by agreement*. 貿易～を結ぶ conclude *a* trade *agreement* (*with* America).

—価格 an agreed price. —書 an agreement; a written agreement. 紳士— a gentleman's agreement.

きょうてい【教程】a lesson. ¶ 彼は45～で普通自動車免許を取った He got a driving license for an automobile after forty-five *lessons*.

きょうてき【強敵】a strong (≒ powerful) enemy; (競争相手) a powerful rival.

きょうてき【狂的】¶ ～な態度 an *insane* (≒ *crazy*) behavior.

ぎょうてん【仰天】¶ その知らせを聞いてびっくり～した I *was* greatly *astonished* (≒ *was astounded*) *at* the news.

きょうてんどうち【驚天動地】¶ ～の事件 a *most sensational* (≒ *most shocking*) event.

きょうと【凶徒】a villain; an outlaw.

きょうと【教徒】回— a Mohammedan. キリスト— a Christian. 仏— a Buddhist.

きょうど【強度】strength; intensity. ¶ 鋼の～ the *strength* of steel. 彼は～の近眼だ He is *very* near-sighted.

きょうど【郷土】*one's* home [town; village]; *one's* native place. ¶ 彼はわが～の町の誇りである He is the pride of our *home town*.

—誌 a local history; a chronicle of a province. —色 ¶ 〜色豊かな土産物 a souvenir rich in *the local color*.

きょうとう【共闘】 a joint struggle (≒ strike). ¶ 組合は賃上げの〜を組んだ The unions planned *a joint strike* for higher pay.

きょうとう【教頭】 an assistant principal; a vice-principal.

きょうどう【共同】 collaboration; cooperation. ¶ 皆の間には明確な〜の目的がなかった They didn't have any definite *common* aims. その部屋を3人〜で使っていた The three of them had the room for *common* use./ The room *was shared by* the three. これは8人の学者が〜で研究したものだ This is the product of *combined* efforts of eight scholars. 皆で〜一致して事に当たろう We should *be united* against the trouble. / Let's *be united* against the trouble. 皆の足並みがそろわず〜してやるのが困難になった On account of a lack of unity among us, it became difficult to work *together*.
—組合 a co-operative society. —経営 ¶ この店は彼女とぼくとの〜経営だ She and I *operate* (≒ *run*) this shop *in partnership*. / This store *is kept going jointly* by her and me. —声明 ¶ 両国は明日正午〜声明を発表する予定だ The two countries are going to issue *a joint statement* at noon tomorrow. —戦線 ¶ われわれは〜戦線を張った We *united ourselves to* do it. —体 a community. —謀議 conspiracy. —募金 the community chest.

きょうどう【教導】 teaching; instruction. ¶ 〜する teach; instruct.

きょうとうほ【橋頭堡】 ¶ 〜を築く secure *a bridgehead* (≒ *a beachhead*) (beachhead は海岸の場合).

きょうねん【凶年】 a bad year; (不作の年) a year of famine (≒ bad harvest).

きょうねん【享年】 ¶ 彼は〜65歳であった He *died at* 〔*the age of*〕 sixty-five.

きょうは【教派】 a sect; a denomination.

きょうばい【競売】 auction. ¶ 彼の家は〜に付された His house was put up to (≒ at) *auction*. / His house was sold by *auction*.
—価格 a price offered by a bidder; a bid.
—人 an auctioner.

きょうはく【強迫】 —観念 a fear complex; an obsession.

きょうはく【脅迫】 〔a〕 threat; 〔a〕 menace. ¶ 彼はその男を殺すと〜した He *threatened* the man *with* death. 彼は〜して彼女に承諾させた He *threatened* her *into* consent.
—状 a threatening letter.

きょうはん【共犯】 complicity; conspiracy. ¶ 彼はその犯罪の〜である He is *a partner to* the crime. 彼は〜のかどで逮捕された He was arrested on a charge of *complicity*.
—者 an accomplice.

きょうふ【恐怖】 fear; terror. ¶ 彼は〜に震えていた He was shivering with *fear* (≒ *terror*). 子どもたちはその光景を見て〜にかられた The children *were terrified at* the scene.
—症 phobia. —政治 terrorism. 高所—症 acrophobia.

きょうふ【教父】 (神父) Father; (洗礼のときの) a godfather.

きょうぶ【胸部】 the breast; the chest.
—疾患 a chest disease; a lung trouble; tuberculosis. —レントゲン検査 a chest X-ray examination.

きょうふう【強風】 a strong wind; a wind storm. ¶ 〜注意報が出ている We are warned against *a strong wind*.

きょうへき【胸壁】 〔軍事〕 a breastwork; a parapet.

きょうへん【凶変】 a calamity; a disaster. ¶ アメリカには暗殺, 暴動のような〜が続いている The U.S. is plagued by assassinations, riots, and such like *disorders*.

きょうへん【共編】 ¶ この本はふたりの学者の〜だ This book has been edited by two scholars. / This book has been brought out under the *co-editorship* of two scholars.

きょうべん【教鞭】 ¶ 彼は大学で〜をとっている He *is teaching at* a university.

きょうほ【競歩】 〔競技〕 a foot race.

きょうほう【凶報】 bad news. ¶ 彼が死んだという〜に接し驚いている I'm surprised at the news of his death.

きょうぼう【共謀】 conspiracy; a plot. ¶ 彼は彼女と〜して悪事を働いた He *plotted with* her in the crime. 彼らは〜して政府転覆を計った They *conspired* to overthrow the government.
—者 a plotter; a conspirator.

きょうぼう【凶暴】 ferocity; brutality. ¶ 〜な fierce; brutal; savage. 狂人が〜性を発揮した The lunatic showed his *ferocity*.

きょうぼく【喬木】 a tall (≒ large) tree.

きょうほん【狂奔】 ¶ 一日中金策に〜した I *was madly busy* making money all day.

きょうほん【教本】 a textbook.

きょうまん【驕慢】 ¶ 〜な態度 an *arrogant* air; arrogance; haughtiness.

きょうみ【興味】 interest. ¶ 私はヨーロッパの絵画にたいへん〜がある I *am* deeply *interested in* European pictures. 彼は映画には〜がない He has no *interest in* movies. テニスにはだんだん〜が出てきた I have found my *interest in* tennis rising gradually. 彼はたくさんのことに〜を持っている He has a variety of *interests*. 彼の演説は〜しんしんたるものがあった His speech was full of *interest* to me.

きょうむ【教務】 school affairs. ¶ 〜主任 the head of the *instruction* department.

ぎょうむ【業務】 business. ¶ 本日は平常どおり〜が行なわれる Today's *business* is to be done as usual. / *Business* as usual today. 彼は怠ることなく〜に励んでいる He attends to his *business* diligently. 〜は拡張されるだろう *Business* will be extended. このエレベーターは〜用だ This elevator is for *business* use.

きょうめい【共鳴】(音の) resonance ; (意見に) sympathy. ¶ 彼の主義主張に大いに～した I heartily *sympathized with* his cause.
—者 a sympathizer. —箱〘物理〙a resonance box (≒ chest).

きょうもん【経文】a sacred book (≒ scripture) of Buddhism.

きょうやく【共訳】joint translation. ¶ ～する translate jointly.

きょうやく【協約】an agreement. ¶ 組合は会社と労働～を結んだ The union concluded *a* labor *agreement* with the company.

きょうゆ【教諭】a teacher.

きょうゆう【共有】joint ownership. ¶ その土地はわれわれの村の～である The land belongs to our village. きみとはそれを～したくない I don't like to *share* it *with* you.
—物(財産) common property.

きょうよう【共用】common use. ¶ 隣の家と井戸を～している We *share* a well *with* the neighboring house.

きょうよう【強要】¶ 寄付は～してはならない We must not *exact* (≒ *demand*) a subscription〔from others〕. 彼は彼女にその支払いを～した He *demanded* that she should pay for it.

きょうよう【教養】culture ; refinement.
¶ ～のある cultured ; sophisticated ; refined. ～を身につけるよう努力する make efforts to be a *cultured* (≒ *well-educated*) man.

きょうらく【享楽】enjoyment. ¶ 人生を～する *enjoy* life ; lead a *gay* life. 彼は人生を～的に考えている He has an *epicurean* view of life.
—主義 epicureanism. —主義者 an epicurean.

きょうらん【狂乱】frenzy ; madness. ¶ 彼女は悲しみのあまり～せんばかりだ She *is beside herself with* grief. 彼女は子どもを失って以来半～の状態だ She *has been* almost *mad* since she lost her child.

きょうり【教理】a doctrine ; a tenet. ¶ キリスト教の～ Christian *doctrine*.

きょうり【郷里】*one's* home ; *one's* own town (≒ country) ; 米 *one's* home town.

きょうりゅう【恐竜】〘古生物〙a dinosaur.

きょうりょう【狭量】¶ ～な人物 a *narrow-minded* person. 彼は～だから他人が自由に行なうことを好まない He *is* so *intolerant* that he is unwilling to let others do as they choose.

きょうりょう【橋梁】a bridge.

きょうりょく【協力】cooperation. ¶ 全員～して校庭の掃除をした All of us *worked together* to sweep the schoolground.
—者 a cooperator ; a co-worker.

きょうりょく【強力】¶ 彼の選任には外部から～な推挙があった For his nomination, there was a *strong* push from outside.

きょうれつ【強烈】¶ この絵は～な印象を与える This picture leaves a *strong* impression.

ぎょうれつ【行列】a procession. ¶ ～の先頭 the head of *a procession*. ～に割り込んではいけません Don't break into *a line*. ～して切符を買う buy a ticket standing in *a line*.
大名— the procession of a feudal prince.
ちょうちん— a lantern procession (≒ parade).

きょうれん【教練】military exercise (≒ drill).

きょうわ【共和】—国 a republic ; a commonwealth. —制 republicanism. —政治 republican government. —党(アメリカ) the Republican Party.

きょうわ【協和】harmony ; concord. ¶ このふたつの音は～しない These two sounds do not *harmonize*〔*with each other*〕.
—音〘音楽〙a consonance.

きょえいしん【虚栄心】vanity. ¶ ～の強い女 a woman full of *vanity*. 彼女は～が強い She *is vain*. それは彼の～を満足させた It satisfied his *vanity*.

ぎょえん【御苑】an Imperial garden.

きょか【許可】permission. ¶ それには警察の～が必要だ *Permission* of the police is necessary. ～なしで写真を撮ってはならない You must not take photos without *leave*. 外出の～は得られなかった I could not get *permission* to go out. 彼が学校の～を得たというのはうそだった His statement that he had got *permission* of the school turned out to be false. この病院では午後5時以後外出は～されない In this hospital they *are* not *permitted* to go out after five in the afternoon. 入学を～されたのはたった15人だった Only fifteen students *were admitted* to this school.

きょかい【巨魁】¶ 密輸組織の～ *the ringleader* of a smuggling gang.

ぎょかい【魚介】marine animals ; fishes and shells (≒ shellfishes) ; (特に 米) sea food.

きょがく【巨額】an enormous amount.
¶ 賭博(とく)場で～な金をもうけた I won *a large sum* at the casino. そのビルの建築費は数億円という～に達した The building cost the *enormous sum* of several hundred million yen. / The building cost came to *an enormous total* of several hundred million yen.

ぎょかくだか【漁獲高】a haul (≒ catch)〔of fish〕; a fish catch.

きょかん【巨漢】a man of gigantic stature ; a giant.

ぎょがん【魚眼】—レンズ a fisheye lens.

きょぎ【虚偽】falsehood. ¶ 彼は法廷で～の申し立てをした He made a *false* statement in court.

ぎょぎょう【漁業】fishery.
—会社 a fishing establishment. —組合 a fishermen's union. —権 a fishing right. —条約 a fishery agreement. 遠洋(近海)— ocean (coast) fishery.

きょきょじつじつ【虚虚実実】¶ それは～の駆け引きだった It was a case of *diamond cut diamond*. / It was a case of *cunning outwitting cunning*. / It was a case of *shrewdness against shrewdness*.

きょきん【拠金】a contribution. ¶ …のために～

する *raise money* for....

きょく【曲】〘音楽〙music. ¶ ショパンの～を演奏する play *a* Chopin's *composition*. ～に合わせて踊る dance to the *music*. ～のない話 a *dull* (≒ *insipid*) story. いつも同じ趣向では～がない It *is not fun* to do it always in the same way.

きょく【局】 ¶ その～に当たる deal with the situation.
無線── a wireless〔telegram〕station. 郵便── a post office.

きょく【極】 a pole; (絶頂) the height; the climax. ¶ 地球の～ the terrestrial *poles*. 磁気の～ magnetic *poles*. 平家の一族はそのとき繁栄の～に達した The Heike clan were then at *the summit* (≒ *zenith*) of their prosperity. われわれは疲労の～に達していた We were *dead* tired.

きょく【巨軀】 a massive figure; a big frame.

ぎょく【漁区】 a fishing ground; a fishing area.

ぎょぐ【漁具】 fishing implements; fishing tackle.

きょくう【極右】 the extreme right.
──思想 an ultra-rightist ideology (≒ idea).
──団体 an ultra-rightist organization.

きょっかい【曲解】 ¶ 彼は私の考えを～している He *misunderstands* me. それは事実の～だ It is *a distortion* of facts.

きょくがい【局外】 ¶ 争いの～に立って冷静に判断する judge fairly by observing the struggle from *the outside*.
──中立 ¶ ～中立を守る observe (≒ maintain) *neutrality*. ～中立の態度をとる maintain an attitude of a bystander.

きょくがくあせい【曲学阿世】 ¶ ～の徒 an academic flatterer; an intellectual time server.

きょくげい【曲芸】 tricks;〔acrobatic〕feats. ¶ 綱渡りの～ *a* tightrope *feat*.
──師 an acrobat; a stunt performer.

きょくげん【極言】 ¶ ～すれば彼は天才でなく狂人だ *To put it strongly* (≒ *Perhaps I am going too far in saying this, but*), he is not a genius but a madman. 彼を不正直だと～する気はない I won't *go so far as to say* that he is dishonest.

きょくげん【極限】 bounds; an extremity; a limit. ¶ 彼は疲労が～に達している He has reached the *limit* of fatigue.

きょくさ【極左】 the extreme left.
──思想 an ultra-leftist ideology (≒ idea).
──分子 the extreme left; communistic elements.

ぎょくざ【玉座】 the Imperial throne; the Emperor's chair.

きょくじつ【旭日】 ¶ 彼は～昇天の勢いだ His star is rising.

きょくしょう【極小】 ¶ ～の infinitesimal; irreducible.
──値 the minimum value.

ぎょくせき【玉石】 ──混交 a jumble of wheat and tares; a medley of chaff and grain.

きょくせつ【曲折】 bends; windings. ¶ ～のある人生 *ups and downs* of life. 多くの～を経て結論に達した We came to a conclusion after much *parley*.

きょくせん【曲線】 a curved line; a curve.
──美 the beauty of curves; (脚の) shapely legs.

きょくだい【極大】 ¶ ～の greatest.
──値 the maximum value.

きょくたん【極端】 an extrerme; extremity. ¶ 彼は何事も～に走る He is a man who runs to *an extreme*. 彼女は彼を～にきらっている She hates him *to the utmost*. 彼は～に楽天家だ He is *extremely* optimistic.

きょくち【局地】 ¶ 梅雨前線は～的に大雨を降らせた We had *regionally* much rain because of the rainy season front.
──戦争 a local war.

きょくち【極地】 the pole; a polar region.
──探検 a polar expedition.

きょくち【極致】 the consummation; the perfection. ¶ 芸術の～ *the highest reach* of art. この絵は美の～に達している This picture is a work of *ideal* beauty.

きょくちょう【局長】 (郵便局の) a postmaster; the head of a post office; (官庁などの) the director; the chief of a bureau; (新聞社の) a managing editor.

きょくてん【極点】 the climax.

きょくど【極度】 ¶ ～の神経衰弱にかかる suffer from nervous prostration *very badly*. ～に緊張する be strained *to the limit*. 彼はその事件を～に楽観している He takes an *extremely* optimistic view of the case.

きょくとう【極東】 the Far East. ¶ ～の the Far Eastern.

きょくどめ【局留め】 general delivery; 医 poste restante; (書状の表記) "To be called for." ¶ 小包を～で出す send a package *to general delivery*; address a package *poste restante*.
──郵便 mail to general delivery.

きょくのり【曲乗り】 (馬の) circus riding; (自転車の) trick cycling; (自動車の) stunt driving; (飛行機の) stunt flying.
¶ ～をする do *stunt* (≒ *trick*) *riding*.

きょくぶ【局部】 a part; a section; (患部) the affected part. ¶ 台風の被害は～的なものですんだ The damage of the typhoon was limited to one particular locality.
──麻酔 local anesthesia.

きょくほく【極北】 the extreme north; the north pole.

きょくめん【曲面】 a curved surface.
──体 a solid body with a curved surface.

きょくめん【局面】 the situation. ¶ ～は一変してわれわれに有利になった *Affairs* took a turn favorable to us. その政策は混乱した～を打開した The policy broke the confused *situation*.

きょくもく【曲目】 a program.

き

きょくりょく【極力】¶ 彼の計画に～反対した I *stoutly* opposed his plan. 警察は～治安の回復に努めた The police *did their best* to maintain public peace./ The police tried to maintain public peace *as much as possible*.

ぎょくろ【玉露】refined green tea. ¶ ～を一ぷく入れる make a cup of *refined green tea*.

きょくろん【極論】¶ ～すればすべての責任は彼にある *To say more bluntly*, he is answerable for all.

ぎょぐん【魚群】a shoal of fish.
—探知機 a fish detector.

きょこう【挙行】¶ 結婚式を～する *solemnize* a wedding. 入学式を～する *perform* (≒ *celebrate*) an entrance ceremony. 卒業式は昨日～された The graduation ceremony *took place* (≒ *was held*) yesterday.

きょこう【虚構】〔a〕fiction ; a falsehood.
¶ まったくの～ *an* out-and-out *fabrication*.

ぎょこう【漁港】a fishing port.

きょこく【挙国】¶ ～一致してそれに対処せねばならぬ *The whole nation* must be solid for coping with it. / *The whole nation* must be united in facing the difficulty.

きょしき【挙式】a ceremony ; a celebration ; (特に 複) exercises. ¶ ～する hold a ceremony.

きょじつ【虚実】truth 〔or falsehood〕.

きょしてき【巨視的】macroscopic. ¶ (物事を)～に見る take a *broad* view of (*things*).

ぎょしゃ【御者】a driver ; a cabman ; a coachman.

きょじゃく【虚弱】¶ ～な人 a man *of delicate health* ; a man *in poor health*.
—児 feeble children ; children of weak constitution. —体質 constitutional tendencies to disease.

きょしゅ【挙手】¶ ～の礼 a *hand* salute ; a military salute. 採決は～により行なう decide (*on something*) by *show of hands*. 賛成の人は～を願います Those in favor, please indicate by *show of hands*.

きょしゅう【去就】¶ ～に迷う be at a loss as to *how to act*. きみが～を決すれば万事うまくいく It will go well if only you define your *attitude*.

きょじゅう【居住】—権 the right of living (≒ residence). —者 a resident. —地 a residential area (≒ quarter ; district).

きょしゅつ【拠出】donation ; contribution.
¶ 社会事業に資金を～する *offer* (≒ *raise*) funds for welfare service.

きょしょ【居所】¶ ～を定める make *one's* home ; settle down. (郵便物の)～不明 Wrong Address.

きょしょう【巨匠】¶ 文壇の～ a *celebrated* (≒ *distinguished*) writer.

ぎょじょう【漁場】fishing grounds (ふつう複数形).

きょしょく【虚飾】affectaion ; foppery.
¶ ～のない人〔柄〕an *unaffected and honest* man. ～を好む人だ He is fond of *display* (≒ *empty show*).

ぎょしょく【漁色】philandering.
—家 a philanderer ; a debauchee.

きょしん【虚心】impartiality. ¶ 私の忠告を～に聞きなさい Listen to my advice *frankly* (≒ *with an open mind ; with no prejudice*). ～坦懐(たんかい)に話し合おう Let's talk *frankly* (≒ *without reserve*) together. / Let's have a *heart-to-heart* talk.

きょじん【巨人】a giant ; (偉人) a great man.
¶ 政界の～ *a colossal figure* in the political world.

きょすう【虚数】〘数学〙an imaginary number.

ぎょ·する【御する】 ¶ 彼は～しがたい He is a difficult fellow to *manage*. 彼女は～しやすい She is easy to *please*. この子は～しがたくなった This boy has gone beyond *control*.

きょせい【去勢】castration. ¶ この牛は～してある This ox *is castrated*.
—牛 a bullock. —馬 a gelding. —雄鶏 a capon. —術 castration.

きょせい【巨星】a big (≒ giant) star. ¶ ～ついに落つ *The great star* has fallen in the end.

きょせい【虚勢】〔a〕bluff. ¶ ～を張る make *a bluff* ; make *a show of power*.

ぎょせい【御製】an Emperor's〔*tanka*〕poem; a poem by His Majesty.

きょぜつ【拒絶】refusal. ¶ それは断固として～しなければならない We must *refuse* it flatly. 彼はにべもなく～した He gave me *a* flat *refusal*. 会社は社員の賃上げ要求を～した The company *rejected* its employees' demands for high wages.
—反応 a rejection reaction.

ぎょせん【漁船】a fishing boat ; a fisher boat.

きょぞう【巨像】a colossal statue ; a colossus (複 colossi ; colossuses).

きょぞう【虚像】〘物理〙a virtual image.
¶ ～と実像 images real and *unreal*.

ぎょそん【漁村】a fishing village ; a sea village.

きょたい【巨体】a big body ; a gigantic figure. ¶ 彼は暑さで～を持て余している He is gasping in hot weather with his *massive, plump figure*.

きょだい【巨大】¶ ～な huge ; gigantic.
—科学 a big science.

きょだく【許諾】(許可) permission ; (承諾) consent ; approval.

きょだつ【虚脱】prostration. ¶ 彼女は夫を失ってからすっかり～状態に陥ってしまった She's *been* utterly *disheartened* (≒ She's *been* utterly *upset*) since her husband died.

きょっかい【曲解】misconstruction. ¶ 彼は私の言ったことを～している He *misconstrues* my words. それは事実を～するものだ It's *a distortion* of the fact.

きょっけい【極刑】capital punishment (capital は元来「頭」の意. 斬首に由来するから).
¶ 罪人を～に処す condemn a criminal to *capital punishment*.

きょっこう【極光】the aurora.
ぎょっと ¶その音で～した I *started at* the noise. いきなり犬にほえられて～した I *was frightened* as a dog suddenly barked at me.
きょてん【拠点】a base ; a foothold ; a lodgment. ¶ゲリラの～ *a base* of guerillas. 販売拡張のため各地に～を作った We established *footings* in various places in order to extend the market.
きょとう【巨頭】a leader ; a magnate. ¶政界の～ a *leading* statesman. 米ソ～会談 a U.S.-Russia *top* conference. 3～会談 a "*Big* three" talk.
きょどう【挙動】behavior ; doings. ¶～の怪しい男 a suspicious-*looking* man. 彼の～はどうもまともでない His *conduct* is out of the common.
—不審 ¶～不審の男を逮捕する arrest a man *acting strangely*.
きょときょと ¶～辺りを見まわす look around *one restlessly*.
きょとん ¶彼はびっくりして～とした顔をした He *looked stupefied* in amazement.
ぎょにく【魚肉】fish ; fish meat.
きょねん【去年】last year. ¶～の5月に in May *last year*.
きょひ【拒否】refusal. ¶社長は組合の要求を～した The president *rejected* the request of the union.
—権 a veto. ¶～権を行使する veto ; exercise *one's veto* (*on*).
ぎょふ【漁夫】a fisherman ; a fisher. ¶～の利を占める gain the third party's profit. 彼は会社と労働組合を対決させて～の利を占めた He *played* the company *off against* the labor union. / He *profited himself* by causing the company to fight the labor union. (He made a profit for himself... と言えば金銭的に己れを利したことになる).
きょほう【虚報】a false report ; false news.
きよほうへん【毀誉褒貶】praise and (≒ or) censure ; praise or blame. ¶彼は世間の～は気にしない He is quite indifferent to (≒ He cares nothing for) public *criticism*.
きょまん【巨万】¶～の富を築く make *a vast fortune* ; accumulate *immense* (≒ *vast*) *wealth* ; become a millionaire.
ぎょみん【漁民】fishermen.
きょむ【虚無】nihility ; nihil.
—主義 nihilism. —主義者 a nihilist.
きょめい【虚名】a false reputation ; an empty name. ¶～を博す win *a false reputation*.
きよ·める【清める】purify ; make clean.
¶心身を～めて初もうでをした I *purified myself* and made the first visit to the shrine.
ぎょゆ【魚油】fish oil.
きょよう【許容】¶その程度の誤差は～できる This much of an error can *be permitted* (≒ *be tolerated ; be allowed*).
—量 ¶放射能汚染は～量を超えている The radioactive contamination is beyond its *tolerance level*.
きょらい【去来】¶胸中に～する思い出 memories *recurring* to *one's* mind. 白雲の～する空 the sky with white clouds *floating* (≒ *flying*) in it.
ぎょらい【魚雷】a torpedo.
—艇 a torpedo boat. —発射管 a torpedo tube.
きよらか【清らか】¶～な心 a *pure* heart. 彼は～な生涯を送った He lived *honestly* all [through] his life. / He led an *honest* life.
きょり【巨利】¶～を博す profit *enormously* ; make *an enormous profit*.
きょり【距離】distance. ¶京都から東京までの～はどのくらいですか How *far* is it from Kyoto to Tokyo? 学校はここから歩いて15分の～だ The school is a fifteen minutes' walk from here. 地球と太陽の～を教えてください Please tell me the *distance* between the earth and the sun. 自転車で100キロはかなりの～だ One hundred kilometers is a good *distance* for a bicycle. 公園は家から歩いていける～にある The park is within walking *distance* from my house.
きょりゅう【居留】—地 a [foreign] settlement. —民 ¶アメリカの日本～民 the Japanese *residents* in America ; (総称) the Japanese *colony* in America.
ぎょりょう【漁猟】fishing and hunting ; (漁業) fishery.
ぎょるい【魚類】fishes.
きょれい【虚礼】formalities ; empty forms. ¶～を廃する dispense with *mere formalities*.
きょろきょろ ¶～辺りを見まわす look around *restlessly*.
ぎょろぎょろ ¶目を～させる *goggle* (≒ *roll*) *one's* eyes.
きよわ【気弱】¶そんな～なことでどうするのだ Such *a faint heart* won't do. / Have the nerve.
きらい【嫌い】¶犬は～だ I *dislike* dogs. / I *don't like* dogs. あれから野球が～になった I *have lost interest in* baseball since then. 彼は食べ物に好き～がある He has likes and *dislikes* in food.
きらい【機雷】a mine. ¶～を敷設する lay *a mine* ; place *mines* [in the sea].
—敷設艦 a mine layer [boat]. 敷設— a submarine mine.
きら·う【嫌う】dislike ; hate ; loathe. ¶彼女はタマネギを～う She *dislikes* onions. 彼は結婚を～う He *has antipathy to* marriage. 相手～わずけんかする He quarrels with whomever he intends to. 彼は時を～わず話し込む He constantly has a long talk.
きらきら ¶～とまたたく星 *twinkling* stars.
ぎらぎら ¶太陽が一日じゅう～と照りつけていた The sun *glared* down on us all day.
きらく【気楽】¶～にしたまえ Make yourself *at home* (≒ *comfortable*). ～にやりなさい *Take it easy*. やっと～になった I *got relaxed* at last.

き

きら·す【切らす】¶その品は今～している The article *is out of stock* now. / The article *is* all *sold out.* 今小づかい銭を～している I'*m out of* (≒I'*m short of*) my pocket money.

きらびやか ¶彼女は～に着飾ってパーティーに出かけた She went to the party *in gala dress.*

きらめ·く【煌く】¶空に星が～いていた There were stars *glittering* (≒*twinkling*) in the sky.

きらら【雲母】〘鉱物〙mica.

きらわれもの【嫌われ者】¶彼はクラスの～だ He *is disliked* by everybody in his class.

きり【切り】**1**〖際限〗bounds; limits. ¶彼の欲には～がない His greed knows no *limits* (≒*bounds*).

彼はこぼしはじめたら～がない *There is no end to* his grumbling.

2〖切れ目·決着〗a period. ¶～がよい be a good place to leave off.

…に～をつける put *a stop* (≒*an end*) to….

きり【霧】mist; fog (mist よりも地上に近く濃い). ¶深い～ *a* dense (≒thick) *fog.* 急に～が晴れた The *fog* suddenly cleared up. 山に～がかかっている The mountain is hidden in *mist.* 湖面に～が立ち込めている It *mists* over the lake. ～が深くなる The *fog* thickens. アイロンをかける前に着物に～を吹く *spray* the clothes before *one* irons them.

きり【桐】〘植物〙a paulownia. ¶総～のたんす an all-*paulownia* chest of drawers.

きり【錐】(もみ錐) a gimlet; (突き錐) an awl; (木工用の) an auger; (金·石用) a drill. ¶～をもむ drive *a gimlet* (*into something*).

-きり ¶失敗したのは1回～だ I failed *only* once. これっ～もう二度と許してやらないよ I'll forgive you *just for once.* / *Once for all* I forgive you. ケーキはこれ～ですか Is this all the cake [there is]? 彼とはあれっ～会っていない I haven't seen him ever since [that time].

ぎり【義理】duty. ¶彼は～堅い He has a sense of *duty.* 彼には～がある I have *an obligation* to him. 彼にそんなに～を立てることはない You do not have to take so much trouble for him. きみは彼女に～を欠いている You fail in your *duty* to her. ～を知らないやつだ How ungrateful he is! これも～と人情にはさまれた例だ This is another instance of a man torn between love and *duty.* 彼は～にも誠実とはいえない He is anything but a faithful man.

きりあげ【切り上げ】¶もうそろそろ～どきだ It is time to *wind* it *up.*

きりあ·げる【切り上げる】**1**〖やめる〗leave off; stop. ¶きょうはこれくらいで～げよう Well, it's time to *leave off work* today. / Let's call it a day.

2〖数·平価を〗小数点以下は～げる *raise* the decimals to a unit; count decimals as one.

平価を～げる *revalue* the currency *upward.* 円を～げる *revalue up* the yen.

きりいし【切り石】a hewn stone; (集合的に用いて) ashlar.

きりうり【切り売り】¶学問の～はしたくない I hate to *peddle out* my knowledge. / I hate to *sell* my knowledge for a living.

きりおと·す【切り落とす】¶枝を～す *cut off* twigs and branches.

きりかえ【切り替え】(更新) a renewal; a change; a switchover. ¶頭の～ *a* mental *switchover.* 鉄道のダイヤの～ *change* of a train schedule.

きりか·える【切り替える】change; convert; (更新) renew. ¶きみは頭を～える必要がある You have to *change* your way of thinking. 6月1日から新しい時間割りに～える We're going to *have a new timetable* on June 1. 工場の仕事は戦時産業から平和産業に～えられた The *switchover* from wartime to peacetime industry took place in our factory.

きりかか·る【切りかかる】¶刺客は大刀を振りかぶって～った The assassin *attacked* me with a sword raised over his head.

きりかぶ【切り株】a stump; (稲などの) a stubble.

きりきざ·む【切り刻む】mince. ¶タマネギを～む *chop up* onions [*into small pieces*].

きりきず【切り傷】a cut; a gash; an incision. ¶ほおに～のある男 a man with *a cut* (≒*a scar*) on his cheek.

きりきり ¶頭が～痛む I have a *splitting* headache. おなかが～痛む I have a *sharp shooting* pain in my stomach.

—舞い ¶忙しくて～舞いする move about busily with pressure of work.

ぎりぎり ¶～の値段 *the lowest* [*possible*] price. 彼は学校に時間～のところでまにあった He *was almost late* for school. これが私の譲歩できる～の線だ This is *the very limit* to which I can concede.

きりぎりす a grasshopper.

きりくず·す【切り崩す】¶山を～す *cut through* a mountain. 組合を～す *split* a labor union. ストライキを～す *break* a strike.

きりくち【切り口】(木口) a cut end; (傷口) an opening; (おのなどの) a kerf.

きりこ【切り子】a facet.

—ガラス cut glass.

きりこうじょう【切り口上】¶～であいさつする make an address *in set terms.* ～で返事をする make a *stiff* reply.

きりこみ【切り込み】a cut.

きりこ·む【切り込む】cut deep into; (敵陣に) fight *one's* way into.

きりさ·げる【切り下げる】¶ポンドの平価を～げる *devaluate* the pound.

きりさめ【霧雨】a drizzle. ¶～が降っている It *is drizzling.*

ギリシア Greece.

—語 Greek. —人(単数) a Greek; (複数) the Greeks.

キリシタン【吉利支丹·切支丹】early Christianity in Japan; (人) early Christians in Japan.

きりす·てる【切り捨てる】¶一刀のもとに～てる *cut down* with one stroke of the sword. 小

数点第3位以下を〜てる *omit* the figure below the third decimal place.

キリスト【基督】Christ; Jesus Christ.
—教 Christianity. —教徒 a Christian.
—降誕祭 Christmas.

きりたお·す【切り倒す】(木を) fell; (木·人などを) cut down.

きりだし【切り出し】(小刀) a pointed knife; (話の) an opening.

きりだ·す【切り出す】¶ 材木を山から〜す *get* (≒ *bring down*) timber out of a mountain. 彼はしばらくためらって用件を〜した He *broached* the matter after some hesitation. 彼はいつも黙っているから, 私のほうから話を〜さねばならない I have to *break the ice,* as he always keeps silence.

きりつ【起立】¶ 全員〜 Everybody *up*! 一同ご〜ください Will the audience please *rise*?
—投票 a rising vote.

きりつ【規律】order; regularity; discipline.
¶ 〜のある orderly; methodical; disciplined. 厳格な〜 rigorous *discipline*. 〜の厳重な strict in *discipline*. この学校は〜が正しい The school is under good *discipline*. 彼は学校の〜を破った He broke the school *regulations*.

きりつ·ける【切りつける】strike (≒ cut) at *a person*.

きりづま【切り妻】a gable.
—屋根 a gable roof.

きりつ·める【切り詰める】¶ 費用を〜める *cut down* (≒ *reduce*) expenses. 〜めた生活をする live on very little.

きりとりせん【切り取り線】a perforation line; a perforation. ¶ カレンダーを〜の所で切る tear off the calendar at the *perforation line*.

きりと·る【切り取る】cut off; cut out; clip.

きりぬき【切り抜き】a clipping; 英 a cutout.
¶ 雑誌の〜 *a* magazine *clipping* (≒ *cutting*).
—帳 a scrapbook.

きりぬ·く【切り抜く】¶ 新聞の記事を〜く *cut* articles *from* a newspaper. 絵を〜く *cut out* a picture.

きりぬ·ける【切り抜ける】¶ 財政的困難を〜ける *weather* [*through*] financial difficulties. 不況を〜ける *tide over* the bad times.

きりばな【切り花】a cut flower.

きりはな·す【切り放す·切り離す】¶ 魚の頭を〜す *cut* a fish's head *off*. 機関車と客車を〜す *detach* a locomotive *from* a train. 政治と経済は〜して論ずることはできない It is impossible to discuss politics *apart from* (≒ *without including*) economics.

きりはら·う【切り払う】¶ 枯れ枝を〜う *prune off* (≒ *prune down*) dead branches. われわれは木を〜った We *cleared away* the trees.

きりばり【切り張り】¶ 障子を〜する *patch* a paper screen.

きりひら·く【切り開く】¶ 決死隊が血路を〜いた The storming party *cut their way* through the enemy. 彼らは密林を〜いて道をつくった They *cut out* a path through a thick jungle. 彼は林を〜いた He *cleared* the land of trees.

きりふき【霧吹き】a sprayer.

きりふだ【切り札】a trump. ¶ 彼には〜があった He had still his *trump card to play.* 組合はストライキという最後の〜を出した The labor union is now put to its last *trump* (≒ *resort*) of going on a strike.

きりぼし【切り干し】dried strips of radish.

きりまく·る【切りまくる】¶ 彼は敵を〜った He *cut* the enemy *down right and left*.

きりまわ·す【切り回す】¶ 世帯を〜す *manage* household affairs. 彼は会社をひとりで〜している He *handles* the entire management of the company.

きりみ【切り身】a slice; a cut. ¶ マグロの〜 *a slice* of tuna.

きりむす·ぶ【切り結ぶ】¶ 両剣士は激しく〜んだ Both swordsmen crossed their swords hard with each other.

きりもみ【錐揉み】〘航空〙a tail spin. ¶ 飛行機は〜しながら落ちていった The plane went down *making a tail spin* (≒ *turning round and round*).

きりもり【切り盛り】¶ うまく一家を〜するのは主婦のつとめだ It is the duty of a housewife to *run* a household skillfully.

きりゃく【機略】¶ 〜に富んでいる男 a man [*full*] *of resources*. 〜縦横な resourceful; tactful.

きりゅう【気流】an air current.
下降— the descending air current. 上昇— the ascending air current.

きりゅう【寄留】¶ おばの家に〜して通学する go to school by *residing temporarily* at *one's* aunt's.
—地 *one's* temporary residence.

きりゅうさん【希硫酸】〘化学〙dilute sulfuric acid.

きりょう【器量】(顔だち) personal appearance; (才能など) ability; capacity; caliber; (面目など) dignity.
¶ 〜よしの女 a beautiful (≒ well-featured; good-looking) woman. 〜自慢の女 a woman who is vain of her good *looks*. 彼には首相の〜はない He *is* not *competent* enough *to* be a prime minister. 彼はばかなまねをして〜を下げた He lost his *dignity* on account of his foolish act.

ぎりょう【技量】ability. ¶ 〜のある able; talented. 〜を発揮する display *one's ability* (*in*). 仕事をする十分の〜がある *be competent to* do a task.

きりょく【気力】spirit; vigor; energy.
¶ 〜のある energetic; full of energy; vigorous. 〜がない lack *vigor*. 〜に乏しい人 a man lacking *vigor* (≒ *energy*). 〜が衰える lose *one's vigor* (≒ *energy*). 〜を回復する regain *one's vigor*.

きりり ¶ 〜と引き締まった顔つき a man with *clear-cut* features.

きりん【麒麟】〘動物〙a giraffe.

—児 an infant (≒ a youthful) prodigy.

き·る【切る】 1〖刃物で〗cut. ¶ のこぎりで寸法どおりに板を〜る *cut* a board with a saw to measure.
彼ははさみでその布地をずたずたに〜ってしまった He *cut* the cloth to pieces with scissors.
この紙を半分に〜ってください *Cut* this paper in half, please.
この包丁では肉が薄く〜れない I cannot *cut* meat thinly with this kitchen knife.
この切符は〜ってあるから使えません This ticket is not valid as it *has* already *been punched*.
2 〖縁を絶つ〗 ¶ あんな者とは手を〜ったほうがいい You had better *be done with* (≒ *break with*) such a fellow.
親子の縁は〜っても〜れぬ Parent and child are inseparably connected.
ふたりは〜っても〜れぬ仲になっている They *are hand in* (≒ *and*) *glove with* each other. / They *are inseparably bound up* with each other.
3 〖電流·電話を〗 ¶ スイッチを〜る switch off; shut off.
うるさいからテレビを〜ってくれ *Turn off* the television set as it is distracting.
だれかが電源を〜ったので，機械がみな止まってしまった Somebody *cut* the power supply, so that all the machines stopped.
そう言って彼女は電話を〜った So saying, she *rang off* (≒ *hung up*).
4 〖息をとぎらせる〗 ¶ そこで〜って読まないと意味が通じない If you don't read *with a pause* there, you can't make yourself understood.
5 〖下まわる〗 ¶ 恐らく10秒を〜る大記録が出たことと思われる A great record of *under* 10 seconds has probably been established.
貯水量は10万トンを〜っている The weight of the reservoir water *is less than* a hundred thousand ton.
原価を〜ってまで売る必要はない You need not sell *below* cost.
6 〖慣用的表現〗 ¶ 不要と思われる箇所は遠慮なく〜ってください *Strike out* (≒ *Delete*) freely the lines which you think unnecessary.
トランプをよく〜る *shuffle* the cards.
すぐ10万円の小切手を〜ってくれ *Make out* a check for a hundred thousand yen at once, please.
身を〜る寒さだ It is *piercing* (≒ *biting*) cold.
打球は風を〜って飛んだ The batted ball *hurtled through* the air.
ヨットが波を〜って走っていた The yacht *was ploughing through* the waves.

きる【着る】 wear. ¶ 彼は上着を着た He *put on* a suit. 彼は外套(がいとう)を着ている He *wears* a coat. 新しい服を着て出かける go out *in* a new dress. 赤い服を着ている She *has* a red dress *on*. 彼女は黒い服を着ていた She *was dressed in* black. 外套を着たままで入ってかまいません You may come in *with* your coat *on*. このオーバーを着てごらんなさい *Try* this overcoat *on*.

きれ【切れ】 a piece; a scrap; (布) cloth; (細片) a strip. ¶ 肉2〜 two *pieces* (≒ *slices*) of meat. パン1〜 *a slice* of bread. 木綿の〜 cotten *cloth*.

きれあじ【切れ味】 ¶ 〜のよいナイフ a knife which *cuts* well. かみそりの〜を試す test the *sharpness* of a razor. 包丁の〜が鈍った The kitchen knife *has become dull*.

きれい【奇麗·綺麗】 1〖美しい〗beautiful; pretty. ¶ 〜な花ですね What a *pretty* flower it is! お〜な方ですね She is *an attractive* girl (≒ *a charming* lady).
街は〜に着飾った娘でにぎわっていた The street was full of young girls all dressed up in their *gay* clothes.
あの人は〜な歯並びをしている He has a *beautiful* (≒ *regular*) set of teeth.
あなたは〜に写っていますね You look very *beautiful* (≒ *handsome*) in the picture.
彼女は〜な字を書く Her handwriting is very *neat*. / She writes in a *beautiful* (≒ *clear*) hand.
2 〖清潔〗 ¶ 手を〜にしなさい Wash your hands.
お客が来るから部屋を〜にしておいて *Tidy up* the room. I am expecting a visitor.
あなたのハンカチはいつも〜ですか *Is* your handkerchief always *clean*?
どうしたらいつまでも〜な水と〜な空気を確保できるか How can we *keep* our water *clear* and our air *clean* forever?
3 〖公正な·異状ない〗 ¶ これは〜な金だから遠慮なく納めてください Do not hesitate to take my *honest* money.
彼の履歴は〜だ(きずがない) He has an *excellent* (≒ a *clean*) record.
レントゲン写真の結果胸は〜だ The X-ray test has shown that there is nothing wrong with the lungs.
〜に勝負をしたまえ Play *fair* to win or to lose.
4 〖すっかり〗 ¶ 彼は一晩でその金を〜に使ってしまった He spent *all* his money in a single night.
彼は前に約束したことなど〜に忘れてる His earlier promise has *completely* slipped from his mind.
〜さっぱり手を切った We broke our relations *for good*.

きれいごと【綺麗事】 ¶ そのようなことを〜で済ますとは驚いた I am surprised that he should *whitewash* such a thing.

きれいずき【綺麗好き】 ¶ 彼女は〜だ She *is fond of cleanliness*.

ぎれい【儀礼】 courtesy; etiquette. ¶ 〜的に訪問する pay a *courtesy* visit.

きれぎれ【切れ切れ】 ¶ 電話が遠くて彼の言っていることは〜に聞こえる I can hear only *fragments* of what he says because the voice is not distinct over the telephone.

きれくち【切れ口】 (木口) a cut end; (傷口) an opening; (断面) a section.

きれじ【切れ地】cloth ; stuff.

きれつ【亀裂】a crack ; a fissure. ¶ 大きな～が地面にできた There was made *a* big *crack* (≒ *fissure*) in the ground. 地震で壁に～が生じた The wall *was cracked* in places because of the earthquake.

きれなが【切れ長】¶ ～な目 a *long and slim* eye.

きれはし【切れ端】scraps. ¶ 木の～ *a piece* of wood. 肉の～ *a scrap* of meat.

きれま【切れ間】¶ まもなく雲の～が見えてきた Soon there appeared some *breaks* in the clouds.

きれめ【切れ目】a break ; a pause ; an interval. ¶ 話の～に in the *pause* of a conversation. 雲の～から太陽の光がさした The sun broke through the clouds. 仕事の～に一服やる have (≒ take) a smoke in *one's spare moments* from *one's* work. 金の～が縁の～ (諺) *When poverty comes in at the door, love flies out at the window.*

きれもの【切れ者】an able man ; a man of ability ; a shrewd person. ¶ 彼はなかなかの～だ He is a *competent* (≒ *smart*) man.

き・れる【切れる】**1**〖切断される〗¶ 糸がぷっつり～れた The string *snapped.*

電球が～れた The electric bulb *has burned out.*

電気が～れた The electric current *failed.*

架線が～れて電車が不通になった The overhead contact wire *was down,* and the train service was suspended.

額が～れて血がにじんでいた There was *a cut* in the brow and blood was coming out of it.

2〖切れ味〗¶ このかみそりはよく～れる This razor *shaves* very well.

この包丁はあまり～れない This knife *is dull.* / This knife doesn't *cut* well.

はさみが～れなくなったから研いでください The scissors *have no edge* at all. Can you sharpen them for me ?

3〖堤防が〗¶ 堤防が～れて全村水びたしとなった The river bank *broke* (≒ *collapsed*) and the whole village was flooded.

4〖つながりがとだえる〗¶ 話し中に電話が～れた The telephone *was disconnected* while I was talking.

船との連絡が～れた Contact with the boat *was lost.*

5〖息が〗¶ 走ってきたので息が～れる I *am out of breath* as I ran all the way.

6〖尽きる〗¶ 彼は薬が～れると手が震える When the medicine *loses its hold* (≒ *loses its effectiveness*) his hands begin to shake.

貸し出しの期限が～れた The book *is overdue.*

きみの持ち時間はあと1分で～れる Your time will *be up* in a minute.

燃料が～れたので不時着するよりしかたがなかった We *ran out of* fuel, and had to make an emergency landing.

7〖擦り切れる〗¶ 彼は外套(がいとう)もズボンもすそが～れてみじめな格好だった He was in a miserable condition ; his overcoat and his trousers *were worn out* (≒ *were frayed*).

8〖鋭い〗¶ 彼女は頭のよく～れる人だ She has a very *sharp* mind. / She *is smart.*

あの投手のカーブはよく～れる The pitcher throws a good curve.

9〖慣用的表現〗¶ 彼は手の～れるような1万円札をぽくにくれた He handed me a *crisp* ten-thousand yen note.

きろ【岐路】crossroads. ¶ われわれは今や人生の～に立っている We are now at the *crossroads* of life.

きろ【帰路】¶ ～につく start on *one's way home.* 大阪からの～京都に立ち寄った *On my way back from* Osaka I stopped over at Kyoto.

キロ a kilo. ¶ 8～の道のり an eight *kilometers'* distance.

—メートル a kilometer.

—グラム a kilogram.

—リットル a kiloliter.

—サイクル a kilocycle.

—ワット a kilowatt.

—ワット時 a kilowatt-hour.

きろく【記録】**1**〖書きとめること・書きとめたもの〗a document. ¶ 会議のもようを～しておきなさい Keep *a written account* (≒ *the minutes*) of the meeting.

その発言は～にとめないでほしい What I have just said *is off-record.*

のちの証拠になるから, それを～にとっておいてください *Put* it *down on paper,* because it will serve as evidence.

議事の～をだれがとりますか Who is to keep the *records* (≒ *minutes*) of the meeting ?

彼がその事件に関係していたことは古い～に残っている *An old document* says that he had a hand in the affair.

そういう細かいことまでいちいち～する必要はない It is not necessary to *record* (≒ There is no need of *recording*) every minute detail.

これが開会式の～映画だ This is a *documentary* film of the opening ceremony.

会議の～係は私がやる I will be glad to be the *secretary* in the meeting.

2〖競技の〗a record. ¶ きみの走り高跳びの最高～はいくらだ What is your best *record* in the high jump ?

彼は100メートル自由型世界～保持者だ He is a world *record* holder in a hundred meter free-style swim.

彼は砲丸投げの日本新～をつくった He established *a* national *record* in shot put.

この競技の～係はだれですか Who is responsible for keeping the *records* in this athletic meeting ?

3〖慣用的表現〗¶ この夏は～破りの暑さだ We are having a *record*-breaking heat wave this summer.

本年の米作は～的な生産高を示した We had a *record* (≒ *bumper*) harvest of rice this year.

ギロチン a guillotine.

ぎろん【議論】argument ; discussion ; dispute. ¶ ～好きな性格 *argumentative* character. そのことについて彼と～する *argue* with

き

him *about* the matter. ～に勝つ win the *argument*. 激しく～する have *a* hot *discussion* (≒ *dispute*). 彼相手では～にならない There is no *arguing with* him. それは～の余地がない It admits of no *dispute*. / It is beyond *dispute*. その問題は盛んに～された The question *was* frequently *discussed*. その問題は～の価値がない The subject does not bear *discussion*.

きわ【際】a brink ; an edge ; a side. ¶ 橋の～ *near* a bridge ; *close by* a bridge. がけの～ the *edge* of a precipice. 海～の家 a house *by* the seaside. 窓～の席 a seat *near* the window. いまわの～に in the *moment* of death ; on (≒ at) *one's* deathbed.

ぎわく【疑惑】suspicion ; doubt ; misgivings. ¶ ～をいだく have (≒ entertain) *a doubt* (*on*). 彼の～を解こうと努めた I tried to clear myself of his *suspicion*. 彼の言ったことはわれわれの心に～を起こさせた What he said raised many *doubts* in our mind. それは彼の～を呼び起こした It awakened his *suspicions*.

きわだ·つ【際立つ】¶ ～って conspicuously ; remarkably ; prominently. ～った性格 *striking* character. ～った才能 *conspicuous* ability. 彼はだれよりも～って数学ができる He is *far* ahead of others in mathematics.

きわど·い【際疾い】¶ ～いところで助かった We had a *narrow* escape. ～いところで難を逃れた I escaped *by a hair's breadth*. ～いプレーだった It was a *close* play.

きわまりない【窮まりない】¶ 危険～ be *extremely* dangerous.

きわま·る【窮まる】¶ 彼の態度は失礼～る His manner is *extremely* impolite. 進退～っている I *am in a dilemma*. / I *am at my wit's end*. / I *am driven to the wall*. 私は感～ってことばも出なかった I was nearly choked *with emotion*.

きわみ【窮み】the height ; the extremity. ¶ 喜びの～ the *utmost* joy.

きわめて【極めて】very ; extremely ; exceedingly.

きわ·める【窮める·究める】¶ 事の真相を～める *reach* (≒*get at*) the truth of the matter. 人々は彼の勇敢さを口を～めてほめそやした People spoke of his bravery *in the highest terms*. 学問を～める make a profound study. ぜいたくを～める be most luxurious. 横暴を～める be extremely tyrannical.

きわもの【際物】seasonable (≒ seasonal) articles.

きん【金】gold. ¶ ～色の golden. ～の指輪 a *gold* ring. ～を捜す search for *gold*. ～をかぶせる overlay (*something*) with *gold*.

—メダル a gold medal.

きん【菌】a bacillus (複 bacilli) ; a germ ; (キノコ) a fungus (複 fungi ; funguses).

きん【禁】¶ 彼は知らず知らずに～を犯した He violated the *prohibition* without being aware of it.

ぎん【銀】silver. ¶ ～の食器 a *silver* plate.

—ぱく a silver leaf. —メダル a silver medal.

きんいつ【均一】¶ 100円～で at a *uniform* price (≒ rate) of a hundred yen each. 商品の品質を～にする *equalize* (≒ *make equal*) the quality of the goods.

きんいん【近因】the direct (≒ immediate) cause (*of*).

きんえん【禁煙】¶ 禁煙(掲示) No Smoking. / Smoking Prohibited. 車内では～だ *Smoking is prohibited* in the cars. 彼は～しようとしたが 1 週間ともたなかった He tried to *quit smoking*, but it lasted less than a week.

きんか【金貨】(個々の) a gold coin ; (総称) gold coin (≒ currency). ¶ ～で払う pay *in gold*. ～の準備 a *gold* reserve.

—本位 the gold 〔coin〕 standard.

ぎんか【銀貨】a silver 〔coin〕.

ぎんが【銀河】〖天文学〗the Milky Way ; the Galaxy.

—系 the galactic system.

きんかい【近海】the neighboring (≒ home) waters.

—漁業 inshore (≒ coastwise) fishery. —航路 a coastwise route. —物 ¶ この魚は～物だ This is an *inshore* fish.

きんかい【金塊】a gold bar ; a nugget.

きんがく【金額】an amount (≒ a sum) of money. ¶ これは～にして数百万円に相当する品物だ This article *is worth* several million yen.

きんがしんねん【謹賀新年】〔I wish you〕 a Happy New Year.

ぎんがみ【銀紙】silver paper.

きんがわ【金側】¶ ～の時計 a *gold* watch.

きんかん【近刊】a recent issue. ¶ ～の latest ; (近日出版の) forthcoming ; in preparation. その本の～予告を新聞で見た I saw in the newspaper advertisement that the book *is coming out shortly*.

きんかん【金冠】a 〔gold〕 crown. ¶ 歯に～をかぶせる *crown* a tooth.

きんかん【金環】a gold ring ; (太陽の) the corona.

—食 an annular eclipse of the sun.

きんがん【近眼】myopia ; near-sightedness ; short-sightedness. ¶ ～の人 a *near-sighted* person. ～になる become *short-sighted*.

きんかんがっき【金管楽器】〔a〕 brass.

きんきじゃくやく【欣喜雀躍】¶ 彼は採用通知をもらって～した He *leapt with joy* to receive the notification of employment.

きんきゅう【緊急】emergency ; urgency. ¶ 非常に～を要する事柄 a matter *of great urgency*.

—質問(議会での) an emergency interpellation. —集会 an emergency session. —対策 emergency measures. —動議 an urgent motion.

きんぎょ【金魚】a goldfish.

—ばち a goldfish basin (≒ bowl).

きんきょう【近況】the recent state. ¶ 市場の～ *the recent condition* of the market. ～をお知らせください Please let me know how you are getting on.

きんきょり【近距離】a short distance. ¶ ～にある be at (≒ within) *a short distance* (*from*).
—列車 a local train.
きんきん【近近】shortly; before long.
きんぎん【金銀】gold and silver.
きんく【禁句】a tabooed word. ¶ 病気の話は彼の前では～だ We *shouldn't talk* about sickness before him.
きんけん【近県】neighboring prefectures.
きんけん【金権】the power of money; financial influence.
—主義 plutocracy.
きんげん【金言】a wise saying (≒ saw).
きんげん【謹厳】¶ ～な態度 a *serious* (≒ *grave*) manner. 彼は～そのものだ He is as *grave* (≒ *solemn*) as a judge./ He is a picture of *sincerity*.
きんこ【金庫】a safe; a strong box. ¶ ～を破る break *a safe*. ～から金を盗む rob *a safe* of money. 金を～にしまう put money in *a safe*.
—破り safe-cracker; safe-breaker. 貸し— safe-deposit.
きんこ【禁固】imprisonment. ¶ 犯人は放火のかどで5年の～に処せられた The culprit got five years' *imprisonment* for arson. 彼は盗みのために10か月の～刑に処せられた He underwent ten months' *imprisonment* for theft.
終身— imprisonment for life.
きんこう【近郊】the suburbs; the outskirts. ¶ 東京の～に in *the suburbs* of Tokyo. 東京およびその～ Tokyo and *vicinity*.
きんこう【均衡】balance; equilibrium. ¶ 勢力の～ *balance* of power. ～を保つ(失う) keep (lose) the *balance*. ヨーロッパにおける勢力の～を回復する restore the *equilibrium* of power in Europe.
きんこう【金鉱】(鉱山) a gold mine; (鉱石) gold ore. ¶ ～を掘り当てる strike *a gold vein*.
きんごう【近郷】¶ 東京～の農家 farmers in *a village near* Tokyo.
ぎんこう【銀行】a bank. ¶ ～に金を預ける deposit money in *a bank*. ～に100万円の預金がある I have *a bank* account of a million yen at *a bank*. ～から金をおろす draw money from *a bank*.
—員 a bank clerk. —家 a banker. —預金 a bank deposit.
きんこつ【筋骨】¶ ～たくましい男 a man *of sturdy build* (≒ *strong muscle*).
きんこんしき【金婚式】a golden wedding.
ぎんこんしき【銀婚式】a silver wedding.
きんさく【近作】*one's* recent work. ¶ これは彼の～だ This is his *recent* (≒ *latest*) *work*.
きんさく【金策】¶ 彼は～で忙しい He is busy to *get a loan*. / He is busy [in] *raising money* (≒ *funds*).
きんし【近視】near-(≒ short-) sighted. ¶ ～になる become *near-*(≒ *short-*) *sighted*. ～的なものの見方 a *short-sighted* view; a *short range* view.
きんし【金糸】gold thread.
きんし【禁止】prohibition. ¶ 酒類の販売を～する *prohibit* the sale of liquor. ～を解く remove *prohibition*. 核実験の～ *a* nuclear test *ban; a ban on* nuclear testing. 車内喫煙は～されている Smoking in the car *is forbidden*. コーヒーを飲むのを～されている I *am forbidden to* drink coffee. この池で泳ぐことは～されている We *are prohibited to* bathe in this pond.
きんじさん【禁治産】〚法律〛incompetency. ¶ ～の宣告を受ける be declared *incompetent*.
—者 a person adjudged incompetent; an interdict. 準—者 a quasi-incompetent.
きんじち【近似値】an approximate value. ¶ 3.14は円周率の～である 3.14 is the *approximate value* of the circular constant.
きんじつ【近日】¶ ～中に soon; one of these days; in a couple of days; in a few days.
きんじつてん【近日点】〚天文学〛the perihelion.
きんじとう【金字塔】a pyramid. ¶ 彼は工学上の～を打ち立てた He accomplished *a monumental work* in engineering.
きんしゃ【金紗・錦紗】thin silk crêpe.
きんしゅ【金主】a financier. ¶ 事業の～ *a financier* (≒ *a sponsor*) for an enterprise.
きんしゅ【禁酒】abstinence from drink (≒ liquor); temperance; (法律上の) [liquor] prohibition.
¶ 胃を悪くしたので～した I *stopped drinking* because I suffered from stomach trouble.
—運動 a temperance movement; a dry campaign. —国 a prohibition country. —主義 teetotalism. —主義者 a teetotaler. —法 the prohibition (≒ dry) law.
きんしゅく【緊縮】¶ 財政を～する *retrench* in finance.
—財政 a reduced budget.
きんしょ【禁書】a banned book.
きんじょ【近所】the neighborhood. ¶ ～の人人 *one's* neighbors. この(その)～には in this (that) *neighborhood*; around here; near here. 彼は学校のすぐ～に住んでいる He lives *within a stone's throw of* the school. 昨夜の火事で～の人々は大騒ぎをした The fire last night alarmed the whole *neighborhood*.
—迷惑 ¶ ～迷惑になってはいけません You must not make yourself *a neighborhood nuisance*. —づきあい ¶ 彼らは～づきあいがよくない They do not get on well with their *neighbors*.
きんしょう【僅少】¶ ～な謝礼 a *trifling* fee. ジャイアンツは～の差で勝った The Giants won by a *narrow* margin.
きんじょう【金城】¶ 農村は保守党の～湯池だ The rural community is *a stronghold* of the conservative party.
きんじょう【錦上】¶ ご夫妻のパーティーへの出席は～さらに花を添えるものであった The party *was graced* (≒ *was honored*) by the attendance of the couple.
きんしん【近親】a close relative; a near relation.

き

—結婚 intermarriage. —者 a near (≒ close) relative.

きんしん【謹慎】 home confinement. ¶ 彼は校則を破ったため3日間～を命じられた He *was put on his good behavior* for three days because he broke school regulations.

きん・ずる【禁ずる】 ¶ 未成年者の喫煙は法律によって～じられている Smoking by a person under age *is prohibited* by law. 釣りはこの湖では～じられている Angling *is banned* in this lake. それを見て失望を～じえなかった I *could not help* being disappointed at the sight.

ぎん・ずる【吟ずる】 sing (a song); recite (a poem).

きんせい【均整】 symmetry. ¶ ～のとれた体 a *symmetrical* (≒ *well proportioned*) physique.

きんせい【近世】 modern age (英語では modern は文芸復興以後現代に及ぶ).

—語 a modern language. —史 modern history. —文学 modern literature.

きんせい【金星】〔天文学〕Venus.

きんせい【禁制】 prohibition; a ban. ¶ キリスト教～は明治維新後ようやく解かれた The *ban on* Christianity was removed only after the Imperial Restoration.

—品 contraband goods; prohibited goods. 女人— ¶ 女人～の山 a holy mountain *not open to* women.

ぎんせかい【銀世界】 ¶ 一夜明けると一面の～だった I woke to find the whole place *covered with* (≒ *mantled in*) *snow*.

きんせきぶん【金石文】 an inscription on a stone monument.

きんせつ【近接】 approach. ¶ 台風は日本本土に～中だ The typhoon *is approaching* the main island of Japan.

きんせん【金銭】 money. ¶ ～上の問題 *pecuniary* matters. 親切は～には換えられない Kindness cannot be measured in terms of *money*. 命は～には換えられない Life cannot be bartered for *gold*. 彼はすべてを～で見積もる He sees (≒ measures) everything in terms of *money*. ～ずくで for [love of] *money*.

—出納係 a cashier. —出納簿 an account book; a cashbook. —登録器 a cash register.

きんぜん【欣然】 gladly; readily.

きんせんか【金盞花】〔植物〕a common marigold; a yellow ox-eye.

きんそく【禁足】 confinement. ¶ 3日間の～を命ずる order (*a person*) to *stay indoors* for three days; place (*a person*) under three days' *confinement*.

きんぞく【金属】 metal[s].

—塩 metallic salts. —元素 metallic elements. —工 a metal worker. —工業 the metal industry. —性 metallic character. —製品 an article of metal; metal goods. 貴(軽; 重; 卑)— a precious (light; heavy; base) metal.

きんぞく【勤続】 continuous service. ¶ 50年～する serve in a firm for fifty years; be in the company's service for fifty years. 20年～のベテラン a veteran who has worked for twenty years.

—年数 ¶ ～年数に応じて according to *one's length of service*.

きんだい【近代】 modern times; the modern age. ¶ 工業の～化が進んでいる The industries have *become* more and more *modernized*. 彼の作品は～的センスにあふれている His works are full of *modern* sense.

—思想 modernism. —性 modernity. —文学 modern literature.

きんだか【金高】 an amount (≒ a sum) of money. ¶ かなりの～ *a* considerable *amount of money*.

きんだん【禁断】 prohibition. ¶ ～の木の実 the *forbidden* fruit. 麻薬の～症状 *forbidden* symptoms of drugs.

きんちてん【近地点】〔天文学〕perigee.

きんちゃく【近着】 ¶ ～の雑誌 magazines *of recent arrival*.

きんちょう【緊張】 tension; mental strain. ¶ 会議場には～した空気が流れていた The conference room was filled with a *tense* atmosphere. 笑いは精神の～を柔らげる Laughter relaxes mental *tension*. 両国間には依然として～状態が続いている The two countries are still in a *tense* relationship.

きんちょう【謹聴】 ¶ ～, ～ Hear! Hear! / Listen! Listen! 彼は一語も漏らすまいと～している He *is all attention*. / He *is all ears*. あの人の話は～に値する His speech is worth *hearing*.

きんてい【謹呈】 ¶「～」(著書などを贈るときに添えることば) with the author's compliments.

きんてい【欽定】 —憲法 a constitution granted by the Emperor. —訳聖書 the Authorized Version [of the Bible] (A.V. と略すこともある).

きんでい【金泥】 gold paint.

きんてき【金的】 the bull's-eye. ¶ 彼の作品は芸術院賞の～を射止めた His work was awarded the Prize of Art Academy.

きんてんさい【禁転載】 Reproduction forbidden (≒ prohibited). / No photographs allowed.

きんとう【近東】 the Near East.

中— the Middle and Near East.

きんとう【均等】 equality; uniformity. ¶ 分け前を～に分担する *equalize* the share. 教育の機会～ *equality* in opportunity in education.

ぎんなん【銀杏】 a gingko nut.

きんにく【筋肉】 muscle[s]; sinew[s]. ¶ ～たくましい若者 a powerfully *muscled* young man; a *well-muscled* young man. 彼は～が発達している His *muscles* are well developed. ～の発達には運動がよい Physical exercises develop *muscles*.

—組織 muscular tissue. —注射 an intramuscular injection. —労働 physical (≒ manual) labor. —労働者 a physical (≒ manual) worker.

きんのう【勤王・勤皇】loyalty to the Emperor; royalism. ¶ ～の士 a patriotic royalist.
きんば【金歯】a gold tooth. ¶ ～を入れる have *a gold tooth* put in.
きんぱい【金杯】a gold[en] cup.
きんぱい【金牌】a gold[en] medal.
ぎんぱい【銀杯】a silver cup.
ぎんぱい【銀牌】a silver medal.
きんぱく【金箔】gold foil; beaten gold; (比較的薄い) a gold leaf. ¶ ～をかぶせる plate (*a thing*) with *gold*; gild.
きんぱく【緊迫】tension; strain. ¶ ～した国際関係 a *tense* international relationship. ～した社会情勢 an *acute* social situation. ～を緩和する ease *tensions*.
きんぱつ【金髪】golden hair; blonde. ¶ ～の少女 a *golden-haired* girl; a *blonde* girl.
ぎんぱつ【銀髪】¶ ～の紳士 a *silver-haired* gentleman.
きんばり【金張り】¶ ～の腕時計 a *gold-plated* wrist[-]watch.
ぎんばん【銀盤】¶ ～の女王 a queen on the *ice*.
きんぴか【金ぴか】¶ ～のたばこケース a *glittering* cigarette case.
きんぴん【金品】money and other valuables.
きんぶち【金縁】¶ ～の額 a *gilt*-frame.
—眼鏡 gold-rimmed spectacles.
きんぷん【金粉】gold dust.
ぎんぷん【銀粉】silver dust.
きんべん【勤勉】diligence; industry. ¶ ～に働く work *hard* (≒ *diligently*). 日本人は～だと言われてきた The Japanese have been said to be a *diligent* people. / It has been said that the Japanese *are industrious*.
きんぽうげ【金鳳花】〖植物〗a buttercup.
きんボタン【金釦】¶ ～の制服 a uniform with *brass buttons*.
きんほんい【金本位】gold standard.
—制 gold standard system.
ぎんほんい【銀本位】silver standard.
—制 silver standard system.
きんまんか【金満家】a millionaire; a man of wealth.
ぎんみ【吟味】¶ ～した品 a *carefully selected* article. 資料を～する *investigate* the data. 料理の材料を～しよう Let's *be careful in selecting* the materials for cooking.
きんみつ【緊密】¶ 彼は私と～な連絡をとっている He is in *close* touch with me. 彼らは～に協力している They are in *close* co-operation. / They are co-operating *closely*.
きんむ【勤務】duty; service. ¶ 彼は～中だ(～が明けた) He *is on duty* (*off duty*). そこでは8時間～だ They have an eight-hour day. ニューヨーク支店～を命じられた I have been appointed to *work* in the New York branch office.
—条件 ¶ 彼らの～条件はよい Their *working* conditions are good.
きんむく【金無垢】¶ このカップは～だ This cup *is of solid gold*.
きんめっき【金鍍金】gold-plating. ¶ この時計は～だ This watch *is gold-plated*. これには～がしてある This *is gilded with gold*. ～がはげている The *gilt* has come off.
きんモール【金モール】gold braid; 米 gold lace.
きんもくせい【金木犀】〖植物〗a fragrant olive.
きんもつ【禁物】¶ 車内では喫煙は～だ Smoking *is forbidden* in the train. 食堂でそういう話は～だ That kind of talk is *a taboo* during meals. この患者に肉類は～だ This patient *must be kept off* meat. 「(*of*).
きんゆ【禁輸】an embargo on the export
—品 articles under an embargo; contraband [goods].
きんゆう【金融】the money market (≒ situation); finance. ¶ ～が緩慢である *The money situation* is easy. ～引き締め策をとるべきだ We should adopt a tight *money* policy. / *The money situation* should be tightened.
—界 financial circles. —機関 a banking organ. —業 financial business; money lending operations. —業者 a financier. 住宅—公庫 the Housing Loan Corporation.
ぎんゆうしじん【吟遊詩人】a minstrel.
きんようび【金曜日】Friday.
きんよく【禁欲】control of the passions; asceticism.
—主義 asceticism; stoicism. —生活 an ascetic life.
きんらい【近来】recently; these days. ¶ ～にない快挙 the most spectacular undertaking *in recent years*. それは～まれな出来事だ It is an incident we have seldom heard of.
きんらん【金襴】gold brocade.
きんり【金利】interest. ¶ ～を引き上げる(引き下げる) raise (lower) *the rate of interest*. ～が高い(安い) *Money* is dear (cheap). ～が緩む(引き締まる) *Money rates* are eased (stiffened). ～は日歩30銭だ *Money interest* is at the rate of thirty sen a day.
きんりょう【禁猟】prohibition of shooting.
—期 the closed (≒ 英 close) season. —区(地) a game preserve.
きんりょう【禁漁】prohibition of fishing.
—期 the closed (≒ 英 close) season. —区(場) a marine preserve.
きんりょく【金力】[the influence of] money; the power of wealth (≒ money). ¶ 今は～がものをいう世界ではない This is not the world where *money* is everything.
きんりょく【筋力】muscular *strength* (≒ *power*); physical strength.
きんりん【近隣】⇒きんじょ
きんるい【菌類】fungus (複 fungi).
きんれい【禁令】a prohibition; a ban.
きんろう【勤労】labor; exertion.
—意欲 a will to work. —階級(大衆) the working class (masses). —感謝の日 Labor Thanksgiving Day. —者 a worker; a laborer. —所得(税) an earned income (tax).

く

く【九】(九つ) nine ; (9番め)〔the〕ninth.

く【区】(区域) a district ; a section ; (都市の小区分) a ward. ¶ バスは1区70円です The bus fare is 70 yen *a section*.
選挙— an electoral district ; a constituency. 文京— Bunkyo Ward.

く【句】(文法上の) a phrase ; (一節) a passage ; a clause ; (詩の一節) a verse ; (俳句) *haiku*-poetry.

く【苦】 pain ; trouble. ¶ 物事を～にしない人 an *easy-going* person. 彼は～もなくその問題を解いた He solved the problem *without difficulty* (≒ *with ease*). 彼女は試験を～にしている She *worries about* (≒ *is anxious about*) examinations. 彼は物事を～にしない He *takes things easy*. そんなことを～にするな Take it easy. / Don't *worry about* it.

ぐ【具】 ¶ すし(みそ汁)の～ the *ingredients* of *sushi* (*miso* soup). 芸術は宣伝の～に供されることもある At times art is used as *a tool* of propaganda.

ぐ【愚】 folly ; foolishness. ¶ ～にもつかぬことを言う talk *nonsense*. それはまったく～の骨頂だ It is indeed the height of *folly*.

ぐあい【具合】 ¶ きょうは体の～はいかがですか *How are you feeling* today? けさはずっと～がいい I *feel much better* this morning. 彼はいつもどこか～が悪いと言っている He always says that *something is wrong with* him. 私はここ二, 三日体の～が悪い I *have been sick* these few days. この時計はどうも～が悪い *There is something wrong with* this watch. お仕事の～はいかがですか *How are you going on with* your work? こんな～にやってほしい I want you to do it 〔*in*〕 *this way*. 万事～よくいっている Everything *is all right*.

くい【悔い】 repentance ; regret. ¶ 百年の～を残す leave irretrievable *repentance* behind.

くい【杭】 a post ; a stake. ¶ ～を打ち込む drive in *a stake* (≒ *a post*). ～を立てる set up *a post*. 出る～は打たれる(諺) A tall tree catches much wind. / Envy will pursue merit as its shade.

くいあ・う【食い合う】 ¶ 候補者どうし互いに票を～っている The candidates *are ruining each other's number of votes*.

くいあら・す【食い荒らす】 eat away. ¶ 作物は野ネズミにすっかり～された The crops *have been eaten up and spoiled* (≒ *ruined*) by wood-mice.

くいあらた・める【悔い改める】 ¶ ～めれば罪は許される *Repentance* will wipe out sin. 彼は前非を～め真人間になった He *repented of* his past error and became a new man.

くいあわせ【食い合わせ】 ¶ ハッカとジャガイモは～が悪いということだ Peppermint and potatoes are said to *disagree with* each other.

くいいじ【食い意地】 gluttony. ¶ ～が張っている be greedy ; be gluttonous.

くいい・る【食い入る】 ¶ 彼はこちらを～るように見詰めている He *is staring hard at* me. / He *is staring into* my face.

くいき【区域】 region; sphere; district; zone; (巡回などの) *one's* rounds (≒ beats). ¶ 巡査が担当～を見まわっていた A policeman was on his *beats*. / A policeman was making his *rounds*.
危険— a danger zone. 住宅— a residential quarter (≒ district). 配達— a delivery zone.

ぐいぐい ¶ 綱を～引く pull a rope *with violent jerks*. ビールを～飲む *gulp down* a glass of beer.

くいけ【食い気】〔an〕appetite. ¶ ～ざかりの若者 a young man *with good* (≒ *healthy*) *appetite*. 私には色気より～だ *Food* is more enchanting to me than love.

くいこみ【食い込み】 a loss ; a deficit. ¶ 1万円の～だった It was *a loss* of ten thousand yen.

くいこ・む【食い込む】(侵入) encroach ; (損失) leave a deficit. ¶ 人の地盤に～む(選挙の) *encroach upon* (≒ *on*) another person's constituency. リュックサックが重くて肩に～んでいる The rucksack is so heavy that it *cuts into* the flesh of my shoulders. 会議が長引いて昼休みに～んでしまった The meeting took time and *encroached upon* the lunch break. 日本品はアメリカ市場に～んでいる Japanese goods *are making inroads into* the American market.

くいさが・る【食い下がる】 persist ; hold on.
¶ われわれは次々に質問して彼に～った We asked him questions one after another *ceaselessly* (≒ *harassingly*).

くいしば・る【食いしばる】(歯を) clench *one's* teeth. ¶ 彼は歯を～って痛みをこらえた He stood up the pain *with his teeth set*.

くいしんぼう【食いしん坊】 a glutton.

クイズ a quiz.
—番組 a quiz program. ¶ ～番組の司会者 a quizmaster.

くいだおれ【食い倒れ】 ¶ 京の着だおれ, 大阪の～ People in Kyoto are extravagant in dress and those of Osaka in food.

くいちがい【食い違い】a discrepancy. ¶ 彼らの間に意見の～が生じた *A difference* (≒ *A clash*) of opinion has arisen between them.

くいちが・う【食い違う】¶ 今までのところ事がすべて～ってきた Everything *has gone wrong* (≒ *has gone amiss*) *with* me so far. まるっきり彼の意見と～う His opinion *differs* entirely *from* mine. / I *differ* entirely *with* him〔in opinion〕.

くいちぎ・る【食いちぎる】tear off with *one's* teeth. ¶ 犬は綱を～ろうとしていた The dog was trying to *bite* (≒ *eat*) the rope *off*.

くいちら・す【食い散らす】eat away. ¶ 子どもたちがおやつを～した The children *ate away* their refreshments.

くいつ・く【食いつく】bite. ¶ 魚がえさに～きはじめた Fish began to *take the bait*. 犬が私に～いた A dog *bit* me.

くいつく・す【食い尽くす】eat up. ¶ 食糧を～す *eat up* all the provisions.

くいつな・ぐ【食い繋ぐ】¶ 彼は新しい職を見つけるまで退職金で～がなければならない He must *eke out* his livelihood on his discharge allowance till he finds a new job.

くいつぶ・す【食い潰す】¶ 自分の家督を～す *eat up one's* patrimony.

くいつ・める【食い詰める】¶ かつての金持ちも今は～めている Once a very rich man, he *is* now *down and out*. 彼は東京を～めて郷里へもどった *Down and out* in Tokyo, he went back to his native place.

ぐいと ¶ ～戸を引く pull a door *with a jerk*. ウイスキーを～一口で飲む empty a glass of whisky *in one gulp*.

くいどうらく【食い道楽】(人) a gourmet; (事) epicurism.

くいと・める【食い止める】check. ¶ 損害を最小限に～める *reduce* the damage to a minimum. われわれは敵の攻撃を３時間にわたって～めた We *held off* the enemy's attack for three hours.

くいな【水鶏】a water rail.

くいにげ【食い逃げ】bilking. ¶ ～する run away from the restaurant without paying *one's* bill.

くいのば・す【食い延ばす】¶ ２日分の食べ物を４日間～す *make one's* food for two days *last* for four days.

くいはぐ・れる【食いはぐれる】(食事を) miss; (仕事を) lose *one's* means of livelihood. ¶ 寝坊して朝食を～れた I overslept myself and *missed* my meal. 技術者は～れることはない Engineers are assured of a living.

くいぶち【食い扶持】¶ 月給から～を入れる pay for *one's board* out of *one's* salary.

くいもの【食い物】(たべもの) food; provision; (犠牲) a victim; a prey.
¶ 彼らは家出娘を～にしている They *prey upon* the runaway girls. 彼は詐欺師の～になった He *fell a prey to* the swindler. / He *became the prey of* the swindler. 彼は娘を～にしている He *lives on* his daughter.

く・いる【悔いる】¶ ～いることはなにもない I have nothing to *repent of*. 学校のころの不勉強を～いる I *repent of* having been idle in my school days. / I *regret* not having worked harder in my school days.

クインテット〘音楽〙a quintet〔te〕.

くう【空】the air; space; (虚空) the void; (空虚) emptiness. ¶ ～を打つ(つかむ) beat (grasp at) *the air*.

く・う【食う】**1**〘食物を〙eat. ¶ 日本人は魚を生で～う The Japanese *eat* fish raw.
2〘虫類が〙bite. ¶ 虫が～った本 a moth-*eaten* book.
蚊に～われた I *was bitten* by mosquitoes.
この着物は虫に～われている This dress *was eaten* by moths.
書物はところどころ虫が～っていた Moths *ate into* the book here and there. / The book *was damaged* here and there by moths.
3〘魚がえさを〙bite. ¶ きょうは魚が～ってこない I haven't had *a bite* today.
今の時期がこの辺では魚がよく～う This is a good season for fish to *be biting* around here.
4〘生計を立てる〙live. ¶ それだけの収入じゃとても～っていけない I cannot *live* on such a poor income.
別に～うに困ってるわけではないから心配しなくてもよい Don't worry. I *have enough to live on*.
5〘消費する〙¶ この車はガソリンを～う This car *consumes* a lot of gasoline.
この道楽は金を～う This hobby *costs* a lot of money.
その手続きを済ますのに予想外に時間を～った It *took* me longer than I had expected to go through due formalities.
6〘謀られる〙¶ 彼に一杯～わされた I *was* fairly *taken in* by him.
その手は～わぬ I know that trick of yours. / You shan't outsmart me.
7〘奪われる〙¶ 彼は同じ党の候補者にかなり票を～われて落選した He was defeated in the election, his votes *being encroached upon* by the candidate of the same political party. (文語体).
新しいスーパーマーケットができて，うちの店はかなり客を～われた Our store *has lost* many customers because the new supermarket opened.
8〘慣用的表現〙¶ ずいぶん人を～ったことを言うね Do you take me for a fool?
彼は人を～った顔つきをしている He has a *provoking* look.

くうい【空位】a vacant post; a vacant throne; vacancy.

ぐうい【寓意】an allegory; a moral. ¶ イソップ物語は～に富んだ物語だ Aesop's Fables *are* very *allegorical*.

くうかん【空間】space; (余地) room. ¶ 時間と～ time and *space*. トランク内の～ the *space* in the trunk. まだ～がある There is enough *room*.

く

くうき【空気】〔an〕air；(ふんい気) an atmosphere. ¶ 新鮮な〜を吸う draw fresh *air*. 新鮮な〜を入れる let in fresh *air*. 室内の〜を浄化する purify the *air* of the room. この部屋は〜の流通がよい The room *is* well *ventilated*. 不安な〜が町じゅうに漂っている An unsettled *air* hangs over the town. 彼は自由な〜の中で育った He was brought up in *an atmosphere* of freedom. 平和な〜が会議に漂っていた *An atmosphere* of peace pervaded the conference.
—汚染 air pollution. —銃 an air gun. —制動機 an air brake. —調節 air conditioning.

くうきょ【空虚】emptiness；vacancy. ¶〜な数年 *blank* years.

ぐうぐう ¶〜寝る be *fast* asleep. 〜いびきをかく snore *loudly*. 腹が〜鳴る My guts *are growling*. / My stomach *rumbles loudly*.

くうぐん【空軍】an air force〔service〕.
—基地 an air base.

くうげき【空隙】an opening；a gap；vacant space；a crevice.

くうこう【空港】an airport. ¶〜に着く land at *an airport*.

ぐうじ【宮司】the chief priest of a Shinto shrine.

くうしゅう【空襲】an air-raid. ¶その市は〜を受けた The city *was attacked from the air*. / The city *was air-raided*.

ぐうすう【偶数】an even number. ¶〜日に on *even-numbered* days.

ぐう・する【遇する】¶彼は人を〜する方法を知らない He does not know how to *treat* others.

くうせき【空席】a vacant seat；room. ¶バスの〜 *a vacant seat* in the bus. (2階つきバスの) 上の方に〜がある There is *room* at the top. 彼らの辞任によって生ずる〜 the *vacancies* that will be made by their resignation.

くうぜん【空前】¶彼は〜の大成功を収めた He gained an *unparalleled* (≒ *unprecedented*) success. 会は〜の大盛会だった The meeting was a *record-breaking* success. それは〜絶後の壮挙だ It is *the first and the last* splendid undertaking.

ぐうぜん【偶然】an accident；a chance.
¶〜の出来事 an accident. 〜の出会い a *chance* (≒ an *accidental*) meeting. 彼の成功はまったく〜だった His success was *a* mere *chance*. それはまったく〜の一致だ It's quite *a coincidence*. 〜彼に会った I *happened to* meet him. / I met him *by chance*. 私がその場所を知っていたのはまったく〜だった *It chanced that* I knew the place. 私が勝ったのは〜だった I won the game *by a fluke*.

くうそ【空疎】¶〜な話 an *unsubstantial* talk.

くうそう【空想】a fancy；a vision. ¶それは単に〜にすぎない It is *a* mere *fancy*. 〜にふける indulge in *fancies*. 〜をたくましくする give full (≒ free) play to *one's fancy*.
—家 a dreamer. —科学小説 a science fiction (S.F. と略記する).

ぐうぞう【偶像】idol. ¶民衆の〜 the *idol* of the people. 富を〜化する *idolize* wealth；*make an idol* of wealth.
—崇拝 idol worship.

ぐうたら ¶〜な人間 a *good-for-nothing* fellow.

くうちゅう【空中】¶たくさんの風船が〜に流れていった Many balloons were floating *in the air*. ヒバリは〜高く舞い上がった A skylark flew up *into the air*. ジェット機は〜に文字を描いた The jet wrote the letters *in the sky*.
—写真 an air photo. —戦 an air battle. —分解 ¶飛行機は〜分解してしまった The plane *broke up to pieces in the air*. —輸送 air transportation. —楼閣 ¶彼らはただ〜楼閣を描いているだけだ They *are building castles in the air*.

クーデター coup d'état. ¶彼らは〜で政権を取った They rose to power by carrying out *a coup d'état*.

くうどう【空洞】a cave；a cavern；〖医学〗a vomica (複 vomicae).

ぐうのね【ぐうの音】¶彼はまったく〜も出なかった He *was completely defeated*.

くうはく【空白】a blank. ¶〜に書き入れなさい Please fill out *blanks*. 彼の記憶には〜の時期がある There is *a blank* in his memory. 政治の〜 *a* political *vacuum*.

くうばく【空漠】¶〜たる平原 a field *vast in extent*.

ぐうはつ【偶発】¶〜の accidental. 一連の〜的事件 a series of *accidents* (≒ *unexpected happenings*).

くうひ【空費】waste. ¶時間と金を〜する *waste one's* time and money (*upon*).

くうふく【空腹】hunger. ¶〜だ I *am hungry*. 〜を訴える complain of *hunger*. 彼はジャガイモを食べて〜をいやした He *satisfied his hunger on* potatoes. 〜にまずいものなし (諺) *Hunger is the best sauce*. / *Nothing comes wrong to a hungry man*.

くうぶん【空文】a dead letter；a scrap of paper. ¶その条約は〜となった The treaty has become *a dead letter*.

くうぼ【空母】an aircraft carrier.

くうほう【空砲】¶〜を撃つ fire *a blank shot*.

クーポン a coupon.
—券 a coupon ticket.

くうゆ【空輸】¶救援物資を〜する *carry* relief goods *by air*.

くうらん【空欄】a blank.

くうり【空理】¶〜空論 an empty, abstract theory.

くうれい【空冷】¶〜式エンジン an *air-cooled* engine.

くうろ【空路】an air route. ¶〜ホンコンに飛ぶ *fly* for Hongkong. 彼は〜帰国した He returned home *by air*.

ぐうわ【寓話】an allegory；(動物寓話) a fable.

クエーカー (教徒) a Quaker.
—教派 Quakerism.

くえき【苦役】hard toil (≒ work)；(懲役) penal servitude.

くえない【食えない】(食用にならない) not good to eat ; (生活できない) be unable to get along ; (こうかつな) sly.
¶ このカキは～ This persimmon *is not good to eat.* / This persimmon *is not edible.* 10万円の月給では～ I *cannot live* on my salary of a hundred thousand yen. あいつは～男だ He is a *crafty* (≒ *foxy*) fellow.

くえんさん【枸櫞酸】〘化学〙 citric acid.

くかく【区画】division.
―整理 (土地) land readjustment ; (都市) town planning. ¶ ～整理する readjust *town lots.* 行政― an administrative division (≒ district).

くがく【苦学】¶ ～して大学を出る work *one's* way through college. 彼は～した He supported himself while studying.

くがつ【九月】September.

くかん【区間】the section (*between* A *and* B). ¶ 不通～ a damaged section.

ぐがん【具眼】¶ ～の士 a *discerning* person ; a man *of judgment.*

くき【茎】a stalk ; a stem.

くぎ【釘】a nail. ¶ ～を抜く(打つ) pull out (drive) *a nail.* ～がゆるんだ The *nail* has started. 人に言わぬように彼に～を刺しておいた I *warned* him not *to* tell it to others. それはぬかに～だ It has no effect. / It is sowing the sand.
犬― a spike. 金― an iron nail. 木― a peg.

くぎかい【区議会】the ward assembly.
―議員 a member of the ward assembly.

くぎづけ【釘付け】¶ 壁にたなを～にする *nail* a shelf *to* the wall. 絵が壁に～になっている The picture *is nailed* on the wall. 驚きのあまり彼はその場に～になった Surprise *nailed* him to the spot.

くぎぬき【釘抜き】pincers.

くきょう【苦境】a difficult situation ; adverse circumstances. ¶ 彼は～に陥った He got into *a difficult situation.* 彼はまもなく～を脱するだろう He will soon get out of *a difficult situation.* 今～にある I am now in *difficulties.* 彼らがぼくの～を救ってくれた They helped me out of the *difficulties.*

くぎょう【苦行】asceticism ; mortification.
¶〔難行〕～する practice *asceticism* (≒ *mortification*).

くぎり【区切り・句切り】an end ; a stop ; a pause ; a period. ¶ ここで行をかえると話の～がつく When you begin a new line here you can *punctuate* a story. ～のよいところで休もう Let's have a rest when we *come to a period.*

くぎ・る【区切る・句切る】space ; (文章を) punctuate ; (仕切る) mark off. ¶ 彼は一語一語を～って言った He *punctuated* each word. 部屋はカーテンでふたつに～ってあった The room *was separated* (≒ *was partitioned*) into two by a curtain.

くく【九九】a multiplication table.

くく【区区】¶ この問題については意見が～まちまちだ Opinions *are divided* (≒ *are various*) on this point. ～たる問題にこだわる be particular about the *trifles.*

くぐりど【潜り戸】a side door.

くく・る【括る】tie ; bind ; fasten. ¶ 本をひもで～る *bind* books with a piece of string. 文をかっこで～る *put* a sentence *in brackets.* 彼は絶望のあまり首を～った He *hanged himself* out of despair.

くぐ・る【潜る】get through ; pass through.
¶ 門を～る *pass through* a gate. 彼は巧みに法の網の目を～った He cunningly *evaded* the law. 敵の猛射を～って川を渡った We got across a river *under* the enemy's fierce fire.

くげ【公家】a courtier ; a nobleman.

くけい【矩形】a rectangle.

くげん【苦言】¶ そのことに関して～を呈したい Let me give you *candid advice* on the matter.

ぐげん【具現】embodiment. ¶ その時代精神は完全に彼の作品の中に～されていた The spirit of the age *was* perfectly *embodied* (≒ *was* perfectly *realized*) in his writings.

くさ【草】grass ; (雑草) a weed ; (薬草) a herb.
¶ ～の葉 blades (≒ leaves) of *grass.* ～の根 *grass* roots. ありふれた～ common *grass.* ～でおおわれた庭 a *grass*-grown garden ; a garden covered with *grass.* 彼は庭の～を取っている He *is weeding* the garden.
―競馬 a local horse race. ―相撲 a local *sumo* tournament. ―野球 sand-lot baseball. ―枕 a travel ; a journey.

くさ・い【臭い】¶ このナイフはタマネギ～い This knife *smells of* onion. この肉は変に～い This meat *smells bad.* / This meat *has a bad smell.* 彼の息は～い His breath *smells* (≒ *stinks*). 彼はいつもビール～い His breath always *smells of* beer. この計画は～い (いんちき臭い) The plan *smells fishy.* 彼が～い(怪しい) *I am suspicious of* him.

くさいきれ【草いきれ】fume[s] of grass.

くさかり【草刈り】mowing. ¶ 庭の～をする *mow* the garden.
―機 a mower.

くさき【草木】plants [and trees]. ¶ ～も眠る丑三つどきに(真夜中に) at dead of night ; when even the river goes to sleep. (後者はしゃれた言い方). 最近の彼は～もなびく勢いだ He *is* now *carrying everything before* him.

くさくさ・する ¶ きょうは～してしようがない I *feel blue* today.

くさ・す【腐す】¶ 彼は人のことを～してばかりいる He *is* always *speaking ill of* others.

くさとり【草取り】¶ 庭の～をする *weed* a garden.

くさのね【草の根】¶ ～を分けても彼を捜し出せ You must find him *whatever happens.*

くさば【草葉】¶ ～の陰で under the sod ; in *one's* graves.

くさばな【草花】a flower ; a flowering plant.

くさび【楔】a wedge. ¶ ～を打ち込む drive in *a wedge.* 両国を結ぶ～となる be *a tie* that binds two countries.

くさぶえ【草笛】a reed pipe.

くさぶかい【草深い】¶ ～田舎 an *out-of-the-way* village; a *backwood* (≒ *remote*) village.

くさぶき【草葺き】¶ ～屋根 a *thatched* roof. ～の小屋 a *thatched* hut.

くさみ【臭み】a bad smell (≒ odor). ¶ この魚は～がない This fish is free from *smell*. 彼の話し方には～があっていやだ I don't like his *affected* way of speaking.

くさむら【草むら】a bush.

くさら·す【腐らす】rot; spoil; corrode. ¶ 暑さが卵を～す Heat *spoils* eggs. わらや草を～して堆肥(たいひ)にする Straw and weeds *are allowed to rot* and used as manure. 湿気は鉄の道具を～す Moisture *corrodes* iron tools. つまらぬことで気を～すな Don't *be discouraged* by trifles.

くさり【鎖】a chain. ¶ 犬を～でつなぐ *chain up* a dog. 犬は～でつないである The dog is kept on *a chain*.

ぐさり ¶ 彼は短刀で背中を～とやられた He *was stabbed* in the back with a dagger.

くさ·る【腐る】1〖腐敗する〗¶ ～った卵 a *bad* (≒ *rotten*) egg.

～った果物 *spoiled* fruit.

～りかけの肉 meat that *is going bad*.

魚は暑いとすぐ～りやすい Fish is easy to *go bad* in hot weather.

この魚は明朝まで～りません This fish is sure to *keep good* overnight.

～ってもタイ An old eagle is better than a young crow.

2〖気持ちが〗¶ 宿題が多くて～っている He *is blue* because he has a lot of homework to do. ～ってしまう I *am disgusted*. 彼は思うようにいかなくて～った He *was embittered with* frustrations.

3〖堕落する〗¶ 彼は心まで～っている He *is rotten* to the heart.

くされえん【腐れ縁】an inseparable relation; a fatal connection. ¶ 彼らの～はどうにもならない They cannot cut *the troublesome connections* with each other.

くさわけ【草分け】an early settler; a pioneer. ¶ 彼は日本の歌劇界の～だ He is *a pioneer* in Japanese opera.

くし【串】a spit; a skewer. ¶ 魚を～に刺す *skewer* a fish. 魚を～に刺して焼いた We broiled a fish on *skewers*.

―カツ a spitted cutlet. ―だんご a spitted dumpling.

くし【櫛】a comb. ¶ ～の歯 the teeth of a *comb*. ～で髪を解かす *comb* [down] *one's* hair.

くし【駆使】¶ 彼には部下が～できない He cannot *have* his subordinates *at his beck* [and *call*]. 彼は得意の英語を～して商談をまとめた He succeeded in making a good bargain *with his excellent command of* English.

くじ【籤】a lot; lottery. ¶ ～に当たった The *lot* fell on me. / I drew *a* winning *number*. ～で順番を決めよう Let's decide turns by *lot*.

―運 ¶ 彼は～運が強い He is lucky in *lottery*. 当たり― ¶ 当たり～を引く draw a prize in the *lottery*. 貧乏― ¶ 貧乏～を引く draw *a bad lot*.

くじ·く【挫く】(手足を) sprain; (気を) discourage; dispirit. ¶ 転んで足首を～いた I had a fall and *sprained* the ankle. あいつの鼻柱を～いてやれ I'll *humble* his pride. 弱きを助け強きを～くはわれらのつとめ It is our duty to help the weak and *fight* the strong. 敵の戦意を～く *break* the enemy's fighting spirit. 雨で出足を～かれた The rain *discouraged* me *from* going out.

くしくも miraculously; strangely enough.

くじ·ける【挫ける】¶ 彼は1度ぐらいの失敗で～けるような男ではない He is not a man to *be discouraged* by a single failure. 彼は手首が～けた He *had* his wrist *sprained*. / He *got* his wrist *broken*.

くじびき【籤引き】¶ だれがお使いに行くか～で決めよう Let us decide by *lot* who shall go on an errand.

くじゃく【孔雀】(雄) a peacock; (雌) a peahen; (ひな) a peachick. ¶ 尾をひろげた～ a peacock in his pride.

―石〖鉱物〗malachite.

くしゃくしゃ ¶ ～のハンカチ a *crumpled* handkerchief. ～の髪 *tangled* hair. この生地はすぐ～になる This kind of cloth is easy to *get crumpled*. 最近気が～して困る I *feel blue* these days.

くしゃみ【嚔】a sneeze. ¶ 風邪をひくと～が出る We *sneeze* when we have a cold.

ぐしゃり ¶ 卵が床に落ちて，～とつぶれた The egg fell to the floor and *was crushed*.

くじょ【駆除】¶ 害虫を～する *get rid of* (≒ *exterminate*) noxious insects.

くしょう【苦笑】a bitter smile. ¶ 彼のぶしつけな質問に思わず～した I *smiled bitterly* (≒ I *smiled a bitter smile*) at his rude question in spite of myself.

くじょう【苦情】a complaint. ¶ 工場は近所の～を無視した The factory ignored neighborhood *complaints*. きみが～を言う理由はない You have no cause to *complain*. 彼はいつも～ばかり言っている He *is* always *complaining about* something or other. いつも～が絶えない There are constant *troubles*.

ぐしょう【具象】concreteness. ¶ この詩ではなにが～されていると思いますか What do you think *is embodied* in this poem?

―芸術 the figurative arts. ―詩 concrete poetry.

くじら【鯨】a whale.

ざとう― a humpback whale. しろながす― a sulphur-bottom. まっこう― a sperm whale.

くしん【苦心】trouble; hard toil; hard effort. ¶ せっかくの～が水泡(すいほう)に帰すだろう All your *pains* will go for nothing. 彼の論文には～の跡が見える His paper bears traces of great *efforts*. 彼らは数年間～惨憺(さんたん)の末ついにその橋を完成した They completed the bridge after several years of *much labor*. われわれは～惨

憺したのだがその割りには得るものが少なかった We *worked very hard* and got little for all our pains.

—談 an account of *one's* hard (≒ bitter) experiences.

ぐしん【具申】 ¶ 彼は上司に意見を～した He *gave* his opinion *to* his superior.

くす【樟】〖植物〗(クスの木) a camphor tree.

くず【屑】 waste; rubbish; 米 trash. ¶ パンの～ crumbs. ぼろ～ rags. 鉄の～ scraps. のこぎりの～ scobs. 彼らは社会の～だ They are the *dregs* (≒ *scum*) of society. 彼は人間の～だ He is just *a good-for-nothing*.

—入れ a trash can; a dust bin.

くず【葛】〖植物〗 an arrowroot; (でんぷん) arrowroot starch.

ぐず【愚図】 ¶ 彼は～な男だ He is *a laggard*. あいつはなにをするにも～だ He *is slow in* doing anything.

くすくす ¶ 少女たちはひそひそ話をしては～笑った The girls whispered and *chuckled* (≒ *giggled*) together.

ぐずぐず【愚図愚図】 ¶ ～言うな Don't *grumble*. なにを～しているんだ What *are* you so *long about*? ～している(はっきりしない)人はきらいだ I can't bear an *irresolute* man. 彼は～してなかなか仕事にとりかからない He *is* very *slow to* do his work. ～しないですぐやりなさい Don't *be long about* it./Do it at once. ～してはいられない There is not a moment to be lost. ～言わないで言われたとおりにやりなさい Don't *complain* and do as you are told.

くすぐった·い【擽ったい】 ticklish. ¶ 足が～い My foot *tickles*. 彼は～がり屋だ He is *a ticklish person*. 小さなことを大げさにほめられて，ちょっと～かった I *felt* rather *flattered*, overpraised for a trifle.

くすぐ·る【擽る】 ¶ ～るな Don't *tickle*! 人のわきの下を～る *tickle a person* under the arm.

くず·す【崩す】 pull down; break; destroy; (金を) change. ¶ 古い家屋を取り～す *demolish* (≒ *pull down*) an old house. 1,000円札を100円玉に～す *change* (≒ *break*) a one-thousand-yen note into ten one-hundred-yen coins. どうぞおひざをお～しください Please *make yourself at ease*. 字を～して書く write *in running style*.

ぐずつ·く【愚図つく】 ¶ 天気が～くもようだ It seems that the weather will remain unsettled.

くずてつ【屑鉄】 scrap iron.

くす·ねる pilfer; pinch. ¶ 会計係が売上金の一部を長年～ねていた The accountant *has been pocketing* part of the sales for many years.

くすぶ·る【燻る】 smoke. ¶ 焼け跡はまだ～っている *Smoke is* still *hovering* over the scene of the fire. いろりが～っている The fireplace *is smoking*. 木が～っている Logs *are smoldering*. 家にばっかり～っているな Don't *stay indoors* all day long. 田舎に～っているのはいやだ I don't want to *vegetate* (≒ *lie buried*) in the country. 彼はまだあの会社に～っている He still *leads a humdrum life* in that firm.

くずや【屑屋】 a ragman; 米 a junkman; a junk dealer; (店) a junk shop.

くすり【薬】 **1**〖薬剤·薬品〗 medicine (調合しないものは drug). ¶ 3日分の～をあげます I will give you *medicine* for three days.

この～を1服飲めばすぐよくなります A dose of this *medicine* will soon cure your sickness.

この～は頭痛によく効く This *medicine* is effective for headache.

この～はちっとも効かない This *medicine* does not work at all.

この～は苦くて飲めない This *medicine* is too bitter for me to take.

この～(塗り薬)をつけると膚の荒れが治ります This *liniment* will cure your rough skin.

—代 charge for medicine. —箱 a medicine chest. —びん a medicine bottle. 胃— a stomachache remedy. 風邪— a cold cure (≒ tablet). 傷— an ointment. 粉— a powder. 眠り— a sleeping drug (≒ pill). 飲み— an internal medicine. 目— eyewash; eye-lotion.

2〖役に立つもの〗 ¶ こんなものは毒にも～にもならぬ It will *do* neither *good* nor harm.

彼は毒にも～にもならぬ男だ He is just *a nobody*./He is a *good-for-nothing* fellow.

きみがそんな目に会うのもいい～だ Those experiences of yours will be *a good lesson* to you.

あんなことを言って，少し～が効きすぎたかな *Have* I *been too harsh on* him to say that much?/I'm afraid I *was too blunt with* him.

3〖少量〗 ¶ 彼にはそんな殊勝な心掛けなど～にしたくもない He *has not an ounce of* such a laudable aim.

この小説にはユーモアなど～にしたくもない *There is not a spice of* humor in this novel.

くすりや【薬屋】 (店) 米 a drugstore; 英 a chemist's shop; (人) 米 a druggist; 英 a chemist.

くすりゆ【薬湯】 a medicated bath.

くすりゆび【薬指】 the third finger; (特に左手の) the ring finger.

くず·れる【崩れる】 crumble down [to pieces]. ¶ ～れかかったあばら屋 a *tumble-down* shack. ～れかかった城壁 *moldering* walls. 地震のためにその家はガラガラと音をたてて～れ落ちた Owing to the earthquake, the house *crashed* to the ground (≒ *fell down* with a crash). この服は型が～れない This dress *keeps its shape*. この帽子は型が～れない This hat *retains its shape*. その帽子は型が～れている The hat *is out of shape*. 天気が～れてきた The weather *is getting worse*. 壁が～れた The wall *gave way*.

くすんだ ¶ ～色合い a *dark* (≒ *dull*) color; a *subdued* color.

くせ【癖】 **1**〖習慣〗 a habit. ¶ 食前に手を洗う～をつけなさい Form *a habit* of washing your hands before each meal.

この子はつめをかむ～がなかなかなおらない This child

cannot possibly get rid of the bad *habit* of biting his nails.
一度ついた～はなかなか抜けないものです Once you get *a habit,* it will stay with you.
甘やかすと～になる Indulgence will *spoil* him.
なくて七～ Every man has his *faults.*
2〘片寄った性癖〙 ¶ どうもあの人には～がある I'm afraid he has his peculiar ways.
彼女の髪の毛は～がある She has *kinky* (≒ *curly*) hair.
これは～のある文章で読みづらい I find it difficult to read such *affected* sentences.
きみの文体には～がある There is *a mannerism* about your style.
もっと～のない英語をまねたまえ Try and learn *plain* English.
ひと～ありげな人物だ He is apparently a *cross-grained* man. / He is a *sinister-looking* man.
彼は人の言うことにいちいち反対する～がある He *has a way of* taking exception to whatever others say.

くせに【癖に】 ¶ 彼は子どもの～大人みたいな口をきく He is a mere child, *and yet* he talks as if he were a grown-up. 彼女は彼の住所を知っている～, 教えてくれない *Though* she must know his address, she won't tell it to me. 男の～泣くな You are a man. Don't cry like a girl.

くせもの【曲者】(怪しい者) a suspicious fellow; (老かいな人) an old fox.

くせん【苦戦】a desperate battle. ¶ 彼は今回の選挙では～の末やっと勝った It was after *a close contest* that he won in the last election. わがチームは目下～中だ Our team is now having *a close game.*

くそ【糞】 excrement; (家畜などの) dung; droppings. ¶ ええ～! Damn! / Heck! ～食らえ I'll see you hanged first. 文法など～食らえだ Grammar *be hanged!*

くそどきょう【糞度胸】¶ 彼の～にはだれもかなわない Nobody can be equal to him in *dauntless courage* 〔*in the face of danger*〕.

くそまじめ【糞真面目】¶ 彼はなんて～な男なんだ How *serious and rigid* he *is!*

くそみそ【糞味噌】¶ ～に言われてすっかり悲観してしまった I *was called all names* and quite discouraged.

くだ【管】a pipe; a tube. ¶ 彼は飲むといつも～を巻く He always *grumbles* (≒ *babbles*) over his glass.

ぐたい【具体】 concreteness. ¶ ～的に concretely; definitely. もっと～的に言えば to be more *concrete.* もっと～的に説明してくれ Give us a more *concrete* explanation. 計画を～化する *give shape to* a plan. 案は～化し始めた The plan began to *take shape.* 近く～策がとられる *Concrete* steps will be taken in near future.

くだ·く【砕く】break; crush; shatter. ¶ さらをこなごなに～く *break* a dish into pieces. 彼の希望は打ち～かれてしまった His hopes *were broken* (≒ *were shattered*). 娘を慰めようと心を～いた He *took great pains to* cheer up his daughter. ～いて(やさしく)話してくれ Explain *plainly* (≒ *in plain words*).

くたくた ¶ 疲れて～だ I *am tired out.* / I *am exhausted.*

くだけた【砕けた】¶ ～文体 *easy* style. ～解説 a *plain* explanation. ～人だ He is a *jolly* fellow. / He has good sense. ～態度で in a *free* (≒ an *easy*) manner.

くだ·ける【砕ける】break; go to pieces. ¶ 窓ガラスが～けた The windowpane *broke* (≒ *was broken*). 波が岩に当たって～ける The waves *break* on the rock. ガラスの～ける音がした I heard the smash of *broken* glass.

ください【下さい】¶ 本を買うから500円～ *Let me have* five hundred yen to buy books. この絵をよくごらん～ *Please* look at this picture carefully. 停車場へ行く道を教えて～ませんか *Would you be so kind as to* tell me the way to the station?

くだ·す【下す】¶ 彼はその仕事をただちに行なうようにとの命令を～した He *ordered* (≒ *gave orders*) that the work 〔should〕 be done at once. (should がないのはアメリカ用法). 裁判官は死刑の判決を～した The judge *pronounced* a sentence of death. 腹を～している My bowels *are loose.*

くたば·る ¶ ～ってしまえ Go to hell! / Go to the devil! / Be hanged to you!

くたびれもうけ【草臥れ儲け】¶ 骨折り損の～だった It was *a mere waste of labor.* / I *had all my trouble for nothing.*

くたび·れる【草臥れる】 get tired; get exhausted. ¶ 待ち～れた I *got tired from waiting* for him. この外とうはすっかり～れてしまった This overcoat *is* utterly *worn out.*

くだもの【果物】(個々の) a fruit; (総称) fruit. **—**ナイフ a fruit knife. **—**屋 a fruit store; (人) a fruit dealer.

くだらな·い【下らない】¶ ～いことをそう心配するな Don't get worried about *trifles.* ～い小説を読む暇があったらもっと勉強しなさい You ought to work harder instead of wasting time over *cheap* (≒ *trashy*) novels. ～いことを言うな Don't talk *nonsense.* なんだ～い How *absurd!* / Nonsense!

くだり【下り】decline; (列車の) a down train. ¶ われわれは保津川～を楽しんだ We enjoyed *a trip down* the Hozu rapids. ここから～になる Here the road *slopes down.* ～は今出たところだ The *down train* has just left.
—坂 a downward slope. ¶ 彼の運命は～坂だった His fortune *was on the decline.*

くだり【件】(箇条) an article; a provision; (節) a passage; a paragraph.

くだ·る【下る】go down; fall; descend. ¶ 山を～る *descend* (≒ *go down*) a mountain. 川を～る *descend* (≒ *go down*) a river. 舟は日本ラインを矢のように～った The boat *shot down* the Japan Rhine Rapids. 戦闘中止命令が～った A cease-fire order *was issued.*

全被告に無罪の判決が～った All the accused *were found* not guilty. 被告には死刑の判決が～った The accused *was sentenced* to death. 腹が～っている My bowels *are loose.* その事故での死者は50人を～らない *No less than* fifty persons were killed in the accident.

くだんの【件の】 ¶ ～男 the man *in question.* ～問題 the *above-mentioned* problem.

くち【口】1 〖身体の一部〗 a mouth. ¶ 赤ん坊の～にまだなにか入っている There is something left in the baby's *mouth.*
～をあーんとあけてごらん Open your *mouth* wide.
そんなに～をとがらせるな Don't pout like that. / Don't purse up your lips.
～にものをほおばってものを言うものでない Don't speak with your *mouth* full.
彼は～をへの字に曲げて困った顔をした He looked troubled and pursed his *mouth.*
～をきりりと結ぶ keep *one's lips* tight shut.
あなたの～は臭い You have *a* foul *breath.*
2 〖ことばをしゃべること・ことば〗 ¶ なかなかお～がおじょうずで You *are a flatterer.*
彼は～の悪い人だ What *a sharp tongue* he *has*! / He *is* very *sarcastic.*
世間の～がうるさい *Tongues* are wagging. / People *will talk.*
あいた～がふさがらない That *beats me* hollow. / I'*m* absolutely *floored.*
あの人は～が重い He *is taciturn.* / He *is discreet.*
あの人は～が軽い He *is talkative.* / He *is unreserved.* / He *is* too *outspoken.*
あの人は～が堅い He is a *close-mouthed* (≒ *tight-lipped*) man.
つい～が滑ってひと言多かった I *made a slip of the tongue.*
～が酸っぱくなるほど言っても彼にはわからない I *told* him *over and over again,* but in vain.
～のきき方に注意しなさい You ought to be cautious of your *tongue.*
彼とは～をきくものか I will never *talk* with him.
彼は私のために～をきいてくれた(口添えをした) He *put in a good word* for me.
犯人はなかなか～を割らなかった The criminal refused to *open up.*
よくもぼくにそんな～をきけるね How dare you *talk* to me like that?
だれがこの件について～を切ることになっているのか Who is to *be the first to speak* about this matter? / Who is going to *break the ice* on this matter?
一同～をきわめて彼女のことをほめた They all *spoke* in the highest praise of her. / They all *spoke* of her in the highest terms.
みなは～をそろえて彼の悪口を言った All of them unanimously *spoke ill of* him.
みんなで～を合わせて真相をかくしている They *are acting in concert* to hide the truth.
もっと～を慎みなさい Be more careful of your *tongue*!
ふたりの間が世間の人の～に乗るようになった People are beginning to *talk about* the relation between the two.
そんなことは～にするな Don't *talk about* it.
～には出さなかったが不満の色はありありと見てとれた He did not *say* it, but apparently he was dissatisfied. / Though not *mentioned,* dissatisfaction was quite clear in his face.
～は災いのもと Out of the *mouth* comes evil.
～はちょうほう, なんとでも言える Thanks to your *mouth,* you can say what you please.
彼は～では偉そうなことを言うが実際はなにもできやしない He *talks* big, but it is all *talk.* / He is all *talk* and no deed.
つい～から出任せのうそを言った I told a lie on the spur of the moment.
あの人は～も八丁手も八丁だ He is as ready in *talk* as in deed. / (話すことと書くことが) He *speaks* and writes with equal facility.
～で言うより手のほうが早い He strikes before he *speaks.*
3 〖味覚・味わうこと〗 ¶ お～にめしませんかもしれませんがおひとつどうぞ You may not like it, but please try it. (アメリカ人はこういうけんそんはあまりしない. 'Go ahead. I hope you like it.' と言う).
きみの～に合うかどうか知らないがぼくは好きだ I do not know whether it *suits your taste,* but I like it.
彼は～が肥えている(おごっている) He *has a delicate palate.*
4 〖生計〗 ¶ そんなにたくさん居候されたら～が干上がっちまう I myself will *starve* if I have to feed so many hangers-on.
5 〖就職口〗 ¶ なにかぼくに適当な～があったら知らせてください Please 〔write and〕 let me know when there is *a* suitable *job* for me.
うまい～がかかってきた I was lucky enough to find *employment.*
6 〖種類・割り前の数〗 ¶ 1～申し込みます I am ready to subscribe for *a share.*
お申し込みは1～でも幾百～でもけっこうです We welcome subscriptions of one *share* to hundreds.
ぼくにもひと～その仕事に乗せてくれ Let me in on the deal, will you?
7 〖種類〗 ¶ この～の品は今ではつくっていません We are not producing this *line* of goods now.
この～の品は今在庫していません This *brand* is now out of stock.
8 〖始まり〗 ¶ まだ宵の～だ It is still early in the evening.
9 〖出入り口・穴〗 ¶ このせんはこのびんの～に合わない This stopper is not good for the *mouth* of this bottle.
たるの～をあける *tap* a cask of *sake.*
びんの～にふたをする *cork* a bottle.
家屋は荒れて壁に大きな～がぽっかりあいていた There was *a gaping hole* in the wall of the ruined house.

ぐち【愚痴】 an idle complaint. ¶ 彼はいつも～ばかり言っている He *is* always *grumbling* about something. 彼は～っぽい男だ He is ready to *grumble.* / He is a *querulous* fellow.

くく

くちあたり【口あたり】¶この酒は～がよい This *sake tastes* nice. / This *sake is mellow*.

くちうつし【口移し】¶～に気つけ薬を彼に飲ませた I made him swallow a restorative *from my mouth*.

くちえ【口絵】a frontispiece.

くちかず【口数】¶あの人は～が多い He *is talkative*. 彼は～が少ない He *is quiet* (≒ *is taciturn*).

くちがね【口金】(びんの) a 〔metal〕 cap; a crown cap; a capsule; (財布などの) a frame.

くちきき【口利き】¶友だちの～でこの会社に就職できた I obtained a position in this company by (≒ through) *the good offices* of a friend.

くちぎたな·い【口汚い】foulmouthed; abusive. ¶人を～くののしる *abuse a person*; *call a person names*.

くちく【駆逐】¶敵を～する *drive away* the enemy. 害虫を～する *wipe out* harmful insects.

—艦 a destroyer.

くちぐせ【口癖】*one's* burden; *one's* favorite phrase. ¶彼は～のように…と言う He always says that....

くちぐちに【口口に】¶みな～不平をとなえた Everybody complained *in his own way*. みな～賛成と言った *There was a chorus of* "Ayes."

くちぐるま【口車】¶あの人の～に乗るな Don't let yourself be taken in by his *smooth talk* (≒ *fair speech*). セールスマンの～に乗ってこんな高い品物を買わされた A salesman *talked* me *into* buying such an expensive thing.

くちげんか【口喧嘩】dispute; quarrel. ¶～する quarrel; have words (*with a person*).

くちごたえ【口答え】a back talk; a retort. ¶親に～するな Don't *talk back* to your parent〔s〕.

くちごも·る【口籠る】¶～って返事する reply *hesitatingly*; *falter out* a reply.

くちさがな·い【口さがない】gossipy; scandal-loving.

くちさき【口先】¶彼は～ばかりでなかなか実行しない He *is all talk* and no deed. 彼は～がうまい He is *a glib* (≒ *smooth*) *talker*.

くちずさ·む【口ずさむ】(歌を) hum (a tune); sing to *one*self.

くちぞえ【口添え】good offices. ¶よろしくお～お願いします I would appreciate it if you would *put in a good word in my behalf*. あなたの～がなければとても就職できなかっただろう But for your *recommendation* I would not have got this job.

くちだし【口出し】¶彼は人の話にすぐ～する He always *meddles in* other people's business. ～しないでくれ Don't *butt in*. / Don't *chip in*. / Mind your own business.

くちづけ【口づけ】a kiss.

くちづたえ【口伝え】an oral tradition. ¶その事件は～に知れわたった The news of that incident traveled far by *word of mouth*.

くちどめ【口止め】¶彼からその事件に関して～された I *was told* by him *not to mention* the matter to anybody.

—料 hush money.

くちなおし【口直し】¶薬を飲んだあと～にあめを食べた After taking the medicine I ate some candy to *kill the bitter taste*.

くちなし【山梔子】〘植物〙a Cape jasmine; a gardenia.

—色 gamboge.

くちば【朽ち葉】dead (≒ rotted) leaves.

—色 yellowish brown; russet.

くちばし【嘴】a beak; a bill. ¶よけいな～を入れるな Don't *poke your nose into* another's business. / *Keep* 〔*your nose*〕 *out of* this.

くちばし·る【口走る】let out; blurt out. ¶彼女は気が違ったようにあらぬことを～った She *uttered* something incoherently as if she had gone mad.

くちは·てる【朽ち果てる】rot away; fall into decay; fall to ruins.

くちはばった·い【口幅ったい】¶～いことを言うな Don't talk *impudently*. ～い言い方をして恐縮ですが Please excuse me if I *sound presumptuous*, but....

くちび【口火】¶彼が政府反撃の～を切った He *was the first to* open an attack against the Government. 新聞のキャンペーンが～となって全国で交通安全運動が盛んになった *Stimulated by* the press campaign, the traffic safety movement has become brisk throughout the country.

くちひげ【口髭】a mustache. ¶～を生やす grow *a mustache*.

くちびる【唇】a lip (ふつう lips). ¶～をかむ bite *one's lip*.

くちぶえ【口笛】a whistle. ¶～を吹く whistle.

くちぶり【口振り】the way of *one's* talking. ¶彼は会社で最も重要な人物であるかのような～だ He *talks as if* he is the most influential person in his company.

くちべた【口下手】¶私はどうも～で, 考えていることの半分も言えない I *am* so *poor in expressing myself* 〔that〕 I cannot say half of what I want to.

くちべに【口紅】rouge; (棒状の) a lipstick. ¶～をぬる put *lipstick* on *one's* lips.

くちまね【口真似】mimicry. ¶赤ん坊は～でことばを覚える A baby learns to talk through *imitation*. オウムは人の～をじょうずにする A parrot is good at *mimicking* human speech.

くちもと【口元·口許】¶あの少女は～がおかあさんにそっくりだ The girl resembles her mother very much *around the mouth*. ～に微笑を浮かべながら with a smile playing *about one's lips*.

くちやかまし·い【口喧しい】particular; snippy; censorious. ¶彼は食べ物については～い He *is particular about* food. あまり子どもに～くしないほうがいい Don't *be* too *nagging* at your children.

くちやくそく【口約束】a verbal promise.

¶ 彼の～はあてにならない You cannot depend too much on his *word*. ～では契約したことにはならない *A verbal agreement* does not constitute a formal contract.

くちゃくちゃ ¶ チューインガムを～かむ chew gum *noisily*.

くちゅう【苦衷】¶ 彼は私の～を少しもわかってくれない He has no sympathy for my *predicament*.

くちゅうざい【駆虫剤】an insecticide; (虫下し) a vermicide.

くちょう【口調】a tone. ¶ 興奮した～で in *an* excited *tone*. 彼は偉そうな～で話をする He talks *smugly*. 私は激しい～で生徒をしかった I scolded the student *sharply*. 彼は演説～でいつも話をする He always talks as if he were making a speech.

くちょう【区長】a chief of the ward. ¶ 千代田～ the *director* of Chiyoda Ward.

ぐちょく【愚直】simplicity and honesty. ¶ ～な too honest.

くちよごし【口汚し】¶ お～ですが, どうぞ召し上がってください This is nothing special, but please help yourself.

く・ちる【朽ちる】¶ ～ちかかった橋 a *crumbling* bridge. 彼の名声は永久に～ちないだろう His fame will never *die*.

くちわ【口輪】a muzzle. ¶ 犬に～をはめておく *keep* a dog *muzzled*.

くつ【靴】shoes (米 では「短ぐつ」「編み上げぐつ」をいい, 英 では「短ぐつ」で,「編み上げぐつ」は boots). ¶ 彼は～をはいた He put on his *shoes*. ～を脱ぐ take off *one's shoes*. ～を1足(2足)買った I bought *a pair of* (*two pairs of*) shoes. ～をみがく *polish* (≒ *shine*) *one's* shoes. この～は私にはちょうどいい *These shoes* are big enough for me. この～は私には窮屈だ *These shoes* are too tight for me. (this shoe とすると「片方のくつ」).

—底 the sole of a shoe. **—**ぬぐい a door mat. **—**ひも 米 a shoestring; 英 a shoelace. **—**ブラシ a shoebrush. **—**べら a shoehorn. **—**みがき(人) 米 a bootblack; 英 a shoeblack. **—**屋(人) a shoemaker; (店) 米 a shoe store; a shoemaker's [shop]. 雨**—** rain shoes. 運動**—** gymnasium (≒ gym) shoes; sports shoes; (ゴム底) sneakers. 子ども(紳士; 婦人)**—** child's (man's; woman's) shoes.

くつう【苦痛】pain; suffering. ¶ ～にうめき声をあげる groan with *pain*. じっと～に耐える endure the *pain* stoically.

くつがえ・す【覆す】¶ 一審の有罪判決が再審で～された The initial verdict of "guilty" *was reversed* at a new trial. コペルニクス説は当時の人々の世界観を一挙に～した The theory of Copernicus *turned* the world's thought of itself *upside down*.

くつがえ・る【覆る】overturn; tip over; be overthrown; (船が) capsize.

クッキー a cookie.

くっきょう【屈強】¶ ～な若者 a *powerfully-built* young man.

くっきょく【屈曲】winding; bending. ¶ ～の多い海岸線 a *rugged* (≒ *much indented*) shoreline.

くっきり[と] clearly; distinctly.

クッキング cooking.

—スクール a cooking school.

ぐつぐつ ¶ 2時間ほどシチューを～煮込む *simmer* the stew for about two hours.

くっし【屈指】¶ 日本～の大金持ち one of the richest men in Japan. ～の人物 a *leading* (≒ *distinguished*) man.

くつした【靴下】(長い) stockings; (婦人用) hose (単複同形); (短い) socks. ¶ ～をはく(脱ぐ) put on (take off) *stockings*.

—止め garters; 英 suspenders.

くつじゅう【屈従】submission; servitude. ¶ 涙をのんで敵に～する swallow *one's* pride and decide to *surrender* to the enemy.

くつじょく【屈辱】a disgrace; a humiliation. ¶ ～を感ずる feel humiliated. ～を受ける be humiliated (*by*). ～感を与える give *a person* a sense of *humiliation*. ～に耐える swallow *an insult*.

ぐっしょり ¶ ～濡れる be soaked to the skin; be drenched to the bone. 男の子は汗で～だった The boy *was dripping with sweat*.

クッション a cushion. ¶ ～のきいたソファー a deep-*cushioned* sofa; a sofa with good *springs*.

くっしん【屈伸】elasticity. ¶ ～運動をする do bending and stretching exercises.

くつずみ【靴墨】shoe polish. ¶ ～をくつに塗る *black* shoes.

ぐっすり ¶ ～眠る sleep *well* (≒ *soundly*; *fast*).

くっ・する【屈する】yield; bow. ¶ ひざを～する *bend* the knee. 指を～する *count* on the fingers. 権力に～する *yield* to authority. 度重なる失敗にも～せず, 彼は仕事を続けた Never *discouraged* by repeated failures, he persevered in his work.

くつずれ【靴擦れ】a shoe sore. ¶ 左のかかとに～ができた I've got *a blister* on my left heel.

くっせつ【屈折】refraction. ¶ 光の～ *refraction* of light. 光線が45度に～する A light beam *is refracted* at a forty-five degree angle.

—角 the angle of refraction. **—**語 an inflected word. **—**光線 a refracted ray. **—**望遠鏡 a refractor; a refracting telescope. **—**率 refraction index.

くったく【屈託】¶ 彼女はなんの～もない寝顔をしている She *looks so free from worry* in her sleep. ～のない生活を送る lead a *carefree* life.

ぐったり ¶ ～疲れる be *completely* worn out; be *dead* tired. ～といすに腰をおろす sit down *wearily* in a chair; *slump* into a chair.

くっつ・く stick to; adhere to. ¶ キャラメルが歯に～いてしまった Some caramel *stuck to* my teeth. 彼は先頭の走者にぴったり～いて走っている He is running at the heels of the front runner. あのふたりはいつも～いて歩いている(比喩的に) Those two *are inseparable*.

くっつ·ける glue; stick; (結合) join. ¶ にかわで2枚の板を～ける *glue* two boards together. 書くとき，行間をあまり～けすぎないように When you write, *leave enough space* between your lines.

くってかか·る【食って掛かる】turn upon. ¶ 彼は約束が違ったと私に～った He *flew at* me for breaking my promise.

ぐっと ¶ 言い返したいところを彼は～こらえた He wanted to talk back, but bit his lip. あわれな物語は私の胸に～こたえた The sad story brought a lump to my throat. ビールを一息に～飲み干した He took a long draft of beer. きのうから～寒くなった The temperature has dropped *sharply* since yesterday. 去年に比べるとことしの冬は～暖かい This winter is *markedly* milder than last year's.

くっぷく【屈服】surrender; submission. ¶ 敵に～する *surrender* to the enemy.

くつろ·ぐ【寛ぐ】¶ どうぞお～ぎください Please *make yourself at home.*

くつわ【轡】a bit. ¶ 試験が難しくて仲間は～を並べて落第した The examination was so hard that all of us flunked *without exception.*

くでん【口伝】¶ この漢方薬の作り方はわが家の～だ The way to mix this herb medicine *has been handed down by word of mouth* from generation to generation in our family.

ぐでんぐでん ¶ ～に酔う get *dead* (≒ *blind*) drunk.

くど·い【諄い】lengthy; tedious; (味が) thick. ¶ ～い説明 a *lengthy* (≒ *wordy*) explanation. 彼の話は～くていやだ His *long-winded* talk is really annoying. このスープは味が～い This soup *is* too *rich* [for me]. 彼は～いお説教をするので生徒にきらわれている His pupils loathe him because he gives them *irksome* lectures all the time.

くとう【苦闘】¶ 長年の～が今日の彼の成功をもたらした A long series of *hard struggles* have brought great success to him.

くとうてん【句読点】a punctuation mark; a full stop; 米 a period. ¶ 文に～をつける *punctuate* a sentence.

くどく【功徳】virtuous deeds. ¶ 彼は正直の～で商売に成功した He succeeded in his business because of his honesty. 彼は生前貧しい人に～を施したのできっと極楽往生できるだろう Since he *was charitable to* the poor, he is sure to go to Paradise.

くど·く【口説く】¶ 父を～いて自動車を買ってもらった I *persuaded* my father to buy a car. 彼は彼女に結婚してくれと～いた He *courted* her.

くどくど〔と〕【諄諄〔と〕】¶ ～同じことを言う dwell (*on*); harp on the same string.

ぐどん【愚鈍】stupidity; silliness.

くないちょう【宮内庁】the Imperial Household Agency.
—御用達 Purveyors to the Imperial Household. —長官 the Director of the Imperial Household Agency.

くなん【苦難】hardship. ¶ 人生の～に耐える stand any kind of *trial* (≒ *hardship*). 彼は長い間～の道を歩んだ He struggled through *the thorny path of life* for a long time. / He *was in great distress* over a long period.

くに【国】a country; (国家) a state. ¶ ～をあげて彼の訪問を歓迎した *All the country* welcomed his visit. 彼はいつも自分の～の自慢ばかりしている He is always boasting of his own *country*. 私の～は鹿児島だ I *come* (≒ *am*) *from* Kagoshima. あなたのお～はどちらですか *Where* do you *come from*? / *Where are* you *from*? ～の両親へ手紙を書いた I wrote a letter to my parents *at home*.

くにく【苦肉】¶ ～の策をとる take *desperate measures*.

くにざかい【国境】the frontier; the border; the boundaries.

ぐにゃぐにゃ ¶ それは日光ですぐ～になる It *is* easily *melted into a shapeless mass* by the sunshine.

くぬぎ【椚】〔植物〕a kind of oak.

くね·る【曲る】¶ まがり～った道 a *winding* path. ヘビは身を～らせて進む A snake goes *wiggling* on.

くのう【苦悩】distress; agony. ¶ ～の色が彼の顔に現われた A look of *distress* came over his face.

くはい【苦杯】¶ 昨年われわれはさんざん～をなめた We *were miserably defeated* last year. / We suffered *a miserable defeat* last year.

くば·る【配る】¶ 先生は試験問題を生徒に～った The teacher *distributed* examination papers to the students. 彼がトランプのカードを～った He *dealt* the cards. 郵便配達人は1日2回郵便物を～って歩く The mailman *delivers* the mail twice a day. 道を横断するときは車に気を～りなさい You must *be watchful for* cars when you cross the street.

くび【首】**1**〖身体の〗a neck; (顔を含めて首から上) a head. ¶ 窓から～を出すと危険だ It is dangerous to put your *head* out [of] the window.
彼は～を縦に振って同意した He *nodded* in agreement.
彼女が～を横に振った(同意しなかった)のには驚いた I was surprised at her shaking her *head*.
その返答に彼は～をかしげた He inclined his *head* to one side at the answer.
2〖慣用的表現〗¶ 彼は息子の帰りを～を長くして待っている He *is looking forward to* his son's return.
彼は借金のため～が回らない He is deeply in debt.
そんなことを言うと彼は～になるだろう If he says such a thing, he will *be dismissed.*

くびかざり【首飾り】a necklace; a rivière. ¶ 真珠の～ *a* pearl *necklace*.

くびかせ【首枷】(刑具) a cangue.

くびき【頸木·軛】a yoke.

くびきり【首切り】(解雇) dismissal. ¶ 会社は

経営不振のため 50 人の～をした The company *dismissed* (≒ *discharged*; (米口語) *fired*) fifty workers owing to its financial difficulty.

くびじっけん【首実検】an identification. ¶ 犯人の～をした We *examined* the criminal.

ぐびじんそう【虞美人草】〔植物〕a field poppy; a red poppy.

くびす【踵】a heel. ¶ ～を返す(引き返す) turn back. 弔問客が～を接して訪れた Mourners came *one after another*.

くびすじ【首筋】the nape; the scruff [of the neck]. ¶ ～が寒い My *neck* feels cold. ～をつかんでネコをつかまえた I took a cat by *the scruff of its neck*.

くびったけ【首っ丈】¶ 彼は彼女に～だ He is off his head about her. / He's deeply in love with her.

くびっぴき【首っ引き】¶ 辞典と～で英字新聞を読む read an English newspaper *frequently referring to* a dictionary.

くびつり【首吊り】hanging *one*self; (人) a person who hanged himself. ¶ ～する hang *one*self.

くびれ【括れ】a compression; a constricted part. ¶ 胴の～ a waist. びんの口の～ a bottleneck; a neck. ひょうたんの～ *the narrow part* of a gourd.

くび·れる【括れる】be constricted. ¶ この池は中央が～れている This pond *is narrow* in the middle.

くびわ【首輪】a necklace; (犬の) a collar.

くぶ【九分】¶ ～どおり nine-tenths; almost; all but. ～九厘 ten to one; in nine cases out of ten; in all probability. もう～どおりできた It has been *practically* complete.

くふう【工夫】an invention; a device; (手段) a means; (計画) a plan. ¶ 新しいやり方を～した We *thought of* a new plan. / We *contrived* a new way. ～をこらして新製品を作った We *managed to* make new products. 彼の～に任せよう Let us leave it to his own *devices*.

くぶん【区分】(分割) division; section; subdivision; (区画) a compartment; a partition; (分類) classification.

くべつ【区別】a difference; a distinction. ¶ はっきりした～ *a* sharp *distinction*. 男女の～なしに without *distinction* of sex. 人間と動物を～する *distinguish* man *from* animals. 彼には善悪の～もわからぬ He does not *know* right *from* wrong. きみは公私をはっきり～しなければならぬ You must *draw a sharp line* between public and private affairs. 天然真珠と人工真珠を～する *discriminate* (≒ *tell*) natural pearls *from* artificial ones.

く·べる【焼べる】put (paper) into the fire; burn. ¶ 古い手紙を火に～べた I *put* old letters *into the fire*. ふろにまきを～べる *lay wood on the fire* in the bath furnace.

くぼち【窪地】low ground; a basin; a sunken place; a hollow.

くぼみ【窪み】a depression; a hollow. ¶ 土地の～ a depression. 目の～ the *hollow* about the eyes. ほおの～ *a pit* in the cheeks; *sunken* cheeks.

くぼ·む【窪む】cave in; sink; become hollow. ¶ 目の～んだ人 a person with *sunken* eyes. 大型トラックが通ったので道が～んだ A big truck *has caused a depression*. 夜おそくまで勉強したので彼の目が～んだ As he worked late at night, he *had hollows* about his eyes.

くま【隈】¶ 目の縁に～ができる have *shadows* under (≒ round) the eyes. ～なく捜す look *in every nook and cranny*; search *every corner* (≒ *everywhere*). 月は～なく辺りを照らした The moon cast its bright light *all around* (≒ *all over the ground*).

くま【熊】a bear. ¶ ～の皮 bearskin.

ぐまい【愚昧】¶ ～な stupid; 米 dumb.

くまで【熊手】a rake; a fork; a bamboo rake; (酉の市の) a lucky rake.

くまどり【隈取り】(顔の) make-up; shading.

くまばち【熊蜂】〔虫類〕a hornet.

くみ【組】a class; (競技の) a team; a party. ¶ この～には生徒が何人いますか How many pupils are there in this *class*? ふたりずつ～になって出た We went out *in pairs*. 8 人で～をつくった We made *a party* of eight. 3 人～の強盗が捕まった *A threesome* of robbers were caught.

くみあい【組合】an association; (労働者の) a union; (同業組合) a guild. ¶ 私はその～に加入した I joined the *association*. われわれは新しい消費者～をつくった We organized the new consumers' cooperative *association*.
—員 a member of the association (≒ union). —運動 union activities. —幹部 a union leader. —専従者 a paid union official. —組織 union organization. —費 union dues. 生活協同— a co-op; a coop; a cooperative. 労働— 米 a [labor] union; 英 a trade union.

くみあ·げる【汲み上げる】pump up; draw up. ¶ ポンプで地下水を～げる *pump up* underground water.

くみあわせ【組み合わせ】assortment; (競技の) matching. ¶ トーナメントの～が決まった The tournament *matching* has been fixed.

くみあわ·せる【組み合わせる】combine; assort; join together; pair (*a person*) with; (ゲームで) match (*a person*) against.

くみいと【組み糸】a braid; a plaited thread.

くみい·れる【組み入れる】weave into. ¶ 旅行の計画に工場見学を～れた We *included* the visiting of a factory in the trip plan.

くみうち【組み討ち】a grapple; a close struggle; 米 (乱闘) a free-for-all.

くみか·える【組み替える】rearrange; recompose. ¶ 日程を～える *rearrange* the schedule.

くみかわ·す【酌み交わす】drink (*sake*) together. ¶ 友人と酒を～した I *drank together* with my friends.

くみきょく【組曲】〔音楽〕a suite; a selection.

く

くみこ·む【汲み込む】¶ふろおけに水を～む *fill* a bathtub with water.

くみしやす·い【与し易い】¶彼は～い相手だ He *is easy to deal with.*

くみ·する【与する】join; support; side with. ¶どちらにも～しません I maintain neutrality. 彼は私を裏切って敵方に～した He betrayed me and *joined* the enemy.

くみだ·す【汲み出す】ladle out; (ポンプで) pump out. ¶バケツで池の水を～した We *bailed out* water from the pond with buckets.

くみたて【汲みたて】¶～の井戸水 *freshly drawn* water from a well.

くみたて【組み立て】construction; constitution; (機械の) assembling. ¶～方がわからない I don't know how to *assemble* (≒*fit together*) these parts. ～式本だな a *fabricated* bookshelf.

くみた·てる【組み立てる】put together; assemble; construct. ¶私はテレビを～てた I *put together* a television set.

くみちょう【組長】(組の頭) a leader; a head; (級長) a class monitor.

くみつ·く【組みつく】¶どろぼうに～いた I *grappled with* a robber.

くみと·る【汲み取る】(液体を) draw up; drain; bail out. ¶人の心を～る *guess* another's idea. 彼の気持ちを～ってやりなさい You should *enter into* his feelings. / You should *sympathize with* him. ┌tion.

くみはん【組み版】(印刷) a forme; composi-

くみひも【組み紐】a braid; a plaited cord.

くみふ·せる【組み伏せる】¶格闘の末犯人を～せた I grappled with a criminal and *pinned* him *down.*

く·む【組む】**1**〖組み合わせる·交差させる〗cross. ¶彼は腕を～んで考え込んだ He *folded* his arms and was lost in thought.
彼は腕を～んで傍観している He just looks on with *folded* arms.
ふたりは腕を～んで歩いていた The two were walking *arm in arm.*
組合員たちは腕を～んで部外者を通さなかった The union members put out a picket to exclude the outsiders.
彼は脚を～んでソファーに腰かけていた He sat down in the sofa *crossing* his legs.
このひもは３種類の糸で～んである This cord *is braided* with three kinds of string.
2〖構成する·組み立てる〗¶家の工事のため足場が～まれた Scaffolding *was set up* to build a house. / They *put up* a scaffolding for building a house.
彼は木材をいかだに～んで運んだ He *made a raft* of timber and transported it.
隊を～んで街中を歩いた We walked about the streets *in groups.*
3〖活字を並べる〗set 〔up〕. ¶この箇所はすこし小さな活字で～んでください *Put* this part *in* smaller *type.* / I want this line *set up in* smaller *type.*
この記事を版に～むのにどのくらい(費用が)かかりますか How much does it cost to *set up* printing blocks for this article?
4〖仲間になる·組になる〗unite. ¶みだりに徒党を～むな Don't *form* a clique without thought.
ぼくと～んで仕事をしませんか How about going into business *with* me?
私たちが～んだらあの敵は倒せる If we *unite,* we can defy the enemy.
彼は政敵と～んでいたそうだ He is said to *be in league with* his political rival.
5〖取り組む〗meet. ¶両力士は～み合ったまま動かなかった Both *sumo* wrestlers *grappled* with each other and would not move an inch. / Two *sumo* wrestlers didn't move a bit, *locking themselves* in each other's arms.
ふたりはむんずと～んでしばしもみ合った They *grappled* and struggled back and forth.
両チームは四つに～んで渡り合った Both teams *played an evenly-matched game.*
6〖為替を〗¶１万円の為替を～む *draw* a bill for ten thousand yen.
彼あてに為替を～んだ I *drew* a bill in favor of him.

く·む【汲む】draw; ladle; (酒を) drink. ¶バケツで水を～む *draw* water with a bucket.

くめん【工面】¶旅費の～がつかない I cannot *raise money* for the trip. なんとか～して授業料を払った I *managed* somehow *to pay* the tuition.

くも【雲】**1** a cloud. ¶白い～ *a* white *cloud.*
～の峰 a *cloud* bank.
～の切れ目 a break in the *clouds.*
太陽は～におおわれた The sun was covered with *clouds.* ┌sky.
空には～ひとつない There is not *a cloud* in the
山々は～にそびえていた The mountains rose above the *clouds.*
月が～間に現われた The moon appeared among the *clouds.*
月が～間に隠れた The moon disappeared behind the *cloud.*
～足が速い The *clouds* are moving fast.
2〖慣用的表現〗¶彼は～をつくばかりの大男だ He is a *towering* man.
それはまったく～をつかむような話だ It is quite an *ambiguous* story.
彼はどこかに～隠れした He *hid himself* in some secret place.

くも【蜘蛛】a spider. ¶～の巣 a *spider's* web; a cobweb. ～の糸 a *spider's* thread. 彼らは～の子を散らしたように逃げまどった They dispersed in all directions.

くもがたじょうぎ【雲形定規】a French curve.

くもつ【供物】an offering.

くもゆき【雲行き】¶この～では雨が降りそうだ The *appearance of the clouds* forebodes rain. 政界の～では近く総選挙が行なわれそうだ Judging from the political *trend,* a general election will be held soon. 国際収支の～が怪しくなって

きた *Things* are taking an ugly turn in the international market.

くもら·す【曇らす】(顔を) frown ; cloud. ¶ それを聞いて彼は顔を～せた He *frowned* at the news. / He *wore a gloomy look* at the news. 涙に声を～せながら彼はそれを読んだ He read the message *losing his voice in tears*.

くもり【曇り】cloudiness. ¶ ～後晴れ *cloudy* (≒ *overcast*), fine later. このところ～がちだ The weather *has been cloudy* these days. あすは～らしい It will probably be *cloudy* tomorrow. この鏡には～がある There is *a blur* in this mirror. ～のない心 a *serene* mind ; a mind without *a blot*. 彼の心には一点の～もない There is not *a blur* in his mind.

くも·る【曇る】(天候が) be (≒ become) cloudy ; (ガラスなどが) be (≒ become) dim ; (心が) be gloomy.
¶ 涙で～った目 eyes *dim* (≒ *misted*) with tears. 湯げで部屋一面が～った Steam *clouded* the room. ふろ場の蒸気で眼鏡が～った The steam in the bathroom *misted* my glasses. 雨の前で空が～った The sky *was overcast* before the rain.

くもん【苦悶】agony ; anguish. ¶ ～する be in agony ; be in anguish ; suffer with *agony*. 彼は～の末息を引き取った He breathed his last *in agony*.

ぐもん【愚問】a silly (≒ foolish) question.

くやくしょ【区役所】a ward office.

くやし·い【悔しい】regrettable ; mortifying. ¶ 優勝のチャンスを逃がして，ほんとうに～い I truly *regret* (≒ I *feel sorry about*) having missed the chance of gaining the victory ! 彼は失敗して～がっている His failure *has made* him *vexed* (≒ *chagrined* ; *sorry*).

くやしなみだ【悔し涙】¶ ～にくれる be vexed (≒ be chagrined) to tears.

くやしまぎれ【悔し紛れ】¶ ～にとんだことを口走った I uttered extraordinary words *out of vexation* (≒ *out of spite*).

くやみ【悔やみ】condolence[s]. ¶ お～のことば words of *condolence*. 父を亡くした彼にお～を言う express my *condolence to* him on the death of his father ; *condole with* him whose father died. お～を申し上げます Please accept my *condolences*.
—状 a letter of condolence.

くや·む【悔やむ】(後悔する) regret ; (悲しむ) mourn. ¶ 今さら～んでもしかたがない It is no use *repenting* now. 友の死を～む *condole* a friend upon his death.

くゆら·す【燻らす】¶ 葉巻を～す *smoke* (≒ *puff at*) a cigar.

くよう【供養】masses for the dead. ¶ ～する hold a [memorial] service (*for*). これが彼にはなによりの～になります Nothing is *a* greater *consolation* to his soul than this. 死者の成仏を祈って～した *Masses were said for* the peace of the dead souls.

くよくよ·する worry (*about*). ¶ ～することはない You needn't *worry* [*about it*]. / Take it easy. いったいなにを～しているのだ What *are* you *brooding* (≒ *fretting*) over ?

くら【倉·蔵】a warehouse ; a storehouse ; (穀物倉) a granary. ¶ ～に入れる put in storage.

くら【鞍】a saddle. ¶ 馬に～を置く *saddle* a horse. ～をはずす *unsaddle* a horse.

くらい【位】(帝位) throne ; (官職) rank ; (数字の位) order ; (品位) dignity ; (階級) grade. ¶ ～が上がる be advanced in *rank*.
—負け ¶ 彼は～負けしている He is unworthy of his *rank*. 彼女と比べると彼は～負けしている He *is outranked* by her.

くら·い【暗い】**1**〖明暗〗dark ; (薄暗い) dim ; (陰気な) gloomy. ¶ ～い部屋 a *dark* room. 薄～い電燈がついている部屋 a *dimly* lighted room.
～い夜だった It was a *dark* night.
～い所でなにをしているのか What are you doing *in the dark* ?
彼は～くなってから外出した He went out *after dark*.
～くならぬうちに帰ってきなさい Come back *before dark*.
～くなるまで待とう Let's wait *till dark*.
空がだんだん～くなってきた It is getting *darker*.
2〖前歴·情感など〗¶ 彼には～い過去がある He is a man with a *shadowy* past.
彼女の顔には～い影がさした *A cloud* (≒ *A shadow*) passed over her face.
私の前途は～い My prospects *are gloomy*. / I have a *dark* future before me.
3〖うとい〗¶ 彼女は世事に～い She *knows little of* the world. / She *is ignorant of* the world.
私はこの辺りの地理に～い I'*m a stranger* here.

-くらい ; -ぐらい **1**〖およそ·だいたい〗some ; about. ¶ 彼女は30歳～だ She is *about* thirty years old.
10分～で駅に行けます You can get to the station in *about* ten minutes.
5分～したら彼が来た *About* five minutes later he appeared.
それ～のところ(価格)で手を打とう Let's conclude the bargain *at this price*.
この辺の地価は5年前の倍～だ The price of land near here is *about* twice as much as it was five years ago.
どの～金がかかりますか *How much* does it cost ?
距離（長さ；高さ；深さ；幅；厚さ）はどの～ですか How far (long ; high ; deep ; broad ; thick) is it ?
2〖程度·比較〗so... ; that... ; like... ; as... as.... ¶ その～のことはぼくにだってできる I myself can do *that much*.
それ～のことはだれだってできる Anybody can do a thing *like that*.
1杯～はつきあえよ Why not have *a glass or two* with us ?
はがき～は出しておきなさい You might write *at least* a letter.

く

それがまちがってる～はきみにだってわかるはずだ You *are expected to* know that it is wrong. / You *ought to* know that it is wrong.
ハムレット～は読めるだろう You must be able to read "Hamlet" *at least*.
受取りを書かせる～のことはしておきなさい You may *at any rate* ask him to write a receipt.
それができるのはあの人～のものだ Nobody but he can do it. / He is perhaps the only man that can do it.
彼～人をばかにした者はない No one has ever despised others so much as he.
あのとき～恥ずかしい思いをしたことはない I have never had more disgrace than I had at that time.
いやになる～宿題を出された I am simply buried under my homework. / I am almost disgusted with so much homework.
ものも言えない～疲れた I was *too* tired *to* say anything.
一寸先も見えない～霧が濃かった It was *so* foggy *that* we could not see an inch ahead.
騒音がひどくて耳がつんぼになる～だ The noise is deafening.
私にだって彼～の英語はしゃべれます I can speak English *as well as* he. (well に強勢を置く).
これ～の大きな家に住みたいものだ I want to live in *such* a big house〔*as* this〕.
あの人が怒る～だからよくよくのことだった He got angry, I'm sure it was something terrible.
きみ～の年なら,そのネクタイはそんなにはでではない The tie is not so showy for *such* a young fellow *as* you.
3〖どうせ…なら〗rather...than.... ¶ 中途でやめる～なら初めからやるな Leave it undone, rather than leave it halfdone.
どうせ行く～なら今すぐ行きなさい *If* you go *at all*, go right away.

グライダー a glider.

くらいどり【位取り】¶ ～をまちがえた I got〔the〕digits wrong. / I calculated on a wrong unit.

クライマックス〔a〕climax ;〔a〕culmination. ¶ ～に達する reach the *climax*. この小説の～はふたりの再会場面だ The *climax* (≒ *culmination*) in the novel is the scene in which the two meet again.

グラウンド (野球の) a baseball ground ; (フットボールの) a football ground.
—マナー ground manners ; playing manners.

くらがえ【鞍替え】¶ 最近彼はテニスからゴルフに～した He *has* recently *shifted* his allegiance from tennis to golf.

くらがり【暗がり】darkness ; the dark. ¶ ～で in *the dark* (≒ *the darkness*).

くらく【苦楽】pleasure and pain. ¶ 彼らは3年間共同生活をして～をともにした They lived together for three years and shared their *joys and sorrows*.

クラクション a horn ; a klaxon. ¶ ～を鳴らす blow *a klaxon* (≒ *a horn*).

くらくら ¶ 頭が～する My head *swims*. 見下ろした瞬間～した I *felt dizzy* when I looked down.

ぐらぐら ¶ いすの脚がどうも～する The legs of the chair *are* rather *unstable*. 突然～ときてたなの上の物がみんな落ちた Suddenly *there was an earthquake* and everything fell from the shelves. やかんの湯が～煮え立っている The water in the kettle *is boiling*. 彼の心はまだ～している He *is* still *wavering* (≒ *is* still *undecided*) in his mind.

くらげ【水母・海月】〘動物〙a jellyfish.

くらさ【暗さ】darkness. ¶ ～は暗し, 腹はへり, 私はまったく泣きたい気持ちだった What with the *darkness* and hunger, I felt like crying.

くらし【暮らし】living ; livelihood. ¶ 彼は英語を教えて～を立てている He is earning his *livelihood* by teaching English. 彼女は～に困っている She is hard up for money. 収入以上の～をするな Don't *live* beyond your income. 身分相応の～をしなさい You must *live* within your income. 近ごろの物価高で～が楽でない We are rather badly off owing to the recent high living costs.
—向き ¶ 彼は～向きがよい(悪い) He is well (badly) off.

グラジオラス〘植物〙a gladiolus (複 gladioli ; gladioluses).

くらしきりょう【倉敷料】warehouse charge ; storage.

クラシック (古典) a classic ; (音楽) classical music.

クラス a class.
—会 a class meeting. **—**メート a classmate.

くら・す【暮らす】live. ¶ 彼らは幸福に～している They *live* happily. いかがお～しですか How *are* you *getting along*? 月10万円で～している I *live* on a hundred thousand yen a month. 遊んで日を～す idle *one's* time away.

グラス a glass.

クラッカー a cracker.

ぐらつ・く totter. ¶ テーブルが～いている The table *is wobbling*. 彼の決心は～いた He *wavered* in his resolution. / His resolution *was unsteady*.

クラッチ (自動車の) a clutch ; (ボートの) a crutch. ¶ ～を踏む step on the *clutch-pedal* ; let in the *clutch* ; put the *clutch* in.

くらばらい【蔵払い】a clearance sale ; a rummage sale.

グラビア gravure ; photogravure.

クラブ (会) a club ; (トランプの) a club. ¶ ～に加入する join the *club*. (トランプ) ～の1 the ace of *clubs*.
—員 a member of the club ; a club member. **—**活動 club activities ; extra-curricular activities.

グラフ a graph. ¶ ～を作る make *a graph* (*of*).
棒**—** a bar graph.

グラブ〘野球〙a glove.

グラフィックデザイナー a graphic designer.

グラフィックデザイン graphic design.

クラフトし【クラフト紙】kraft paper.

-くらべ【-比べ】¶ 力～ *a contest* of physical

strength. 腕～ *a contest* of skill. がまん～ *a contest* of endurance (≒ perseverance).

くらべもの【比べ物】¶ それはこれとは～にならない It can't *stand comparison with* this. 彼はあなたとはとても～にならない He *is no match for* you.

くら·べる【比べる】compare (*with*; *to*). ¶ ふたりの背の高さを～べる *compare* the two in stature. 富士山と～べたら高尾山なんか問題にならない Mt. Takao is no comparison for Mt. Fuji.

グラマー〔ガール〕 a glamor girl.

くらま·す【眩ます】¶ 彼は借金も返さず行方を～した He *disappeared* before he had paid his debt. 人の目を～そうたってそうはさせない I won't *be deceived* by you.

くら·む【眩む】¶ 光の強さに目が～んだ I *was dazzled* by the strong beams. 目も～むばかりの閃光(せんこう) a *dazzling* flash of light. 目も～むばかりの高層建築 a lofty building which almost *dazzles one's* eyes. 彼は金に目が～んだ He *was blinded* by money.

グラム【瓦】a gram (≒ 英 a gramme)(記号「は g).

くらやみ【暗闇】darkness; the dark. ¶ ～で in *the dark*; in *the darkness*. ～になる grow dark. 真っ～ utter darkness; pitch-dark. ～に乗じて under the cover of night.

ぐらり ¶ ～と大きくゆれて車はひっくりかえった There was *a* great *jolting*, and the car toppled over.

クラリネット a clarinet.
—奏者 a clarinetist; a clarinet player.

くらわ·す【食らわす】¶ 一発～したら黙ってしまった I *struck* him with my fist, and then he fell silent.

グランドピアノ〔音楽〕a grand piano.

グランプリ a great prize; a grand prix.

くり【栗】(木) a 〔sweet〕 chestnut tree; (実) a 〔sweet〕 chestnut. ¶ ～のいが a *chestnut* bur. ～色の *chestnut*-colored; nut brown.

くり【庫裏】the living quarters of a temple.

くりあ·げる【繰り上げる】move up; advance. ¶ 予定を～げて帰国した I returned earlier than scheduled. 5時限が4時限に～げになった The fifth period *was moved up to* the fourth. 次点を～げて当選にした The runner-up was declared the victor in the polls.

くりあわせ【繰り合わせ】¶ 時間の～がつかず失礼いたしました I am very sorry I could not *find time* to come. 万障お～のうえご出席ください Please *arrange* to come by all means.

クリーク a creek.

グリークラブ a glee club.

クリーナー a cleaner; a vacuum cleaner.

クリーニング cleaning; laundry. ¶ スーツを～に出す send *one's* suit to the cleaner's. 上着をすぐ～してもらいたい I'd like to *have* my coat *cleaned* at once.

クリーム cream; (アイスクリーム) ice 〔cream〕; (コールド) cold cream; (バニシング) vanishing cream. ¶ ～色の壁 a *cream*-colored wall. 生— fresh cream.

くりい·れる【繰り入れる】put in. ¶ 残金は来年度の予算に～れる The balance is to *be transferred to* next year's budget. 収益は建築資金に～れられる予定だ The profit is expected to *go to* the building fund. 利子は自動的に元金に～れられる The interest *is* automatically *added to* the principal.
—れ金 money transferred.

グリーン green.
—ピース green peas. **—ベルト** a greenbelt.

クリーンヒット〔野球〕a clean hit. ¶ ～を飛ばす smash out *a clean hit*.

くりかえし【繰り返し】a repeat; a repetition; (歌の) a refrain. ¶ 同じことの～だ This is mere *repetition* of the same thing. みんなでいっしょに～のところを歌おう Let's join in singing the *refrain*.

くりかえ·す【繰り返す】repeat; reiterate. ¶ ～してください Please *repeat* it. / (目上に対して,またはていねいに言うとき) I beg your pardon. (この場合文尾を上がり調子に言う). 何回でも～して試みた He tried it *repeatedly* (≒ *again and again*).

くりくり ¶ ～した目 *big round* eyes. 目玉を～させる *roll one's* eyes.
—坊主(頭) a clean-shaven head; (人) a boy with a clean-shaven head.

ぐりぐり ¶ 目を～させる *roll* (≒ *goggle*) *one's* eyes. わきの下に～ができた *A hard lump* has formed under my armpit.

くりげ【栗毛】¶ ～の馬 a chestnut 〔horse〕; a bay 〔horse〕.

クリケット cricket.

くりこし【繰り越し】transfer; a carry-over. ¶ 前期～ *a transfer* (≒ *balance*) *carried forward from* the last account. 5万円の～がある There is *a balance* of fifty thousand carried forward.

くりこ·す【繰り越す】transfer; carry forward. ¶ 次期へ～す *carry the balance to* the next account. 次年度へ～す *carry* (a sum) *to* the following year.

くりごと【繰り言】tedious talk. ¶ ～を言う grumble; complain; harp on the same string. 老人(老い)の～ the *tedious talk* (≒ *garrulity*) of the aged.

くりこ·む【繰り込む】¶ 利益の一部を運動資金に～む *transfer* part of the profit *to* the campaign fund. 彼らは会場に～んできた They *streamed into* the site.

くりさ·げる【繰り下げる】move down. ¶ 締切日を1日～げる *defer* the closing date by a day. 会を次の水曜日まで～げる *put off* (≒ *postpone*) the party till next Wednesday. 1時間めの講義を3時間めに～げる *move* the first period lecture to the third.

クリスタル crystal.
—グラス crystal glass.

クリスチャニア〔スキー〕Christiania 〔turn〕.

クリスマス Christmas (Xmas ともつづる).
—イーブ Christmas Eve. **—カード** a Christmas card. **—ツリー** a Christmas tree. **—プレゼント** a Christmas present.

く

グリセリン〘化学〙glycerin.

くりだ·す【繰り出す】¶ 糸を～す *let* (≒ *draw*) *out* (a) thread. 大ぜいの人がデモに～した A large number of people *sallied forth* to join a demonstration. 続々と新手を～して戦った *Sending out* fresh troops, we continued the battle.

クリップ a (paper-)clip ; (髪のカール用の) a curling pin ; a curler.

グリップ a grip ; a handle.

グリニッジ ―標準時 Greenwich (Mean) Time (GMT). ¶ 今～標準時でちょうど12時です It is exactly twelve o'clock *by GMT*.

くりぬ·く【刳り貫く】hollow out. ¶ 子どもたちはカボチャを～いて，ハローウィーンの仮面を作った The children *scooped out* a pumpkin and made a Halloween mask.

くりの·べる【繰り延べる】¶ 会の会期が２日～べられた The term of the meeting *was extended* two days.

くりひろ·げる【繰り広げる】unfold ; open. ¶ 若人の祭典が～げられた The festival of youth *was presented*.

くりょ【苦慮】¶ 政府はその対策に～している The government *is having much trouble in* dealing with the matter.

グリル a grill ; a grillroom.

くる【来る】**1**〘来着する〙¶ 10時に事務所に来てください Please *come* to my office at ten (o'clock).

忙しければ強いて来るには及びません You don't have to *come* if you are busy.

さあ東京に来たぞ Here we are in Tokyo.

今ごろなにしに来たんだ *What has brought* you *here* at this time?

バスは５分ごとに来る The bus *comes* every five minutes.

それを彼に言いだすチャンスが来ない I can't find any opportunity to break the subject to him.

郷里からしばらく便りが来ない I haven't heard from home for a long time.

大きな危険が迫って来た Pressing danger was approaching.

2〘来訪する〙¶ たまには遊びに来てください Please *come and see* me once in a while. (come to see me より米口語的).

留守にだれか来ましたか Did anyone *come* (to see me) during my absence?

3〘期日が〙¶ 誕生日が来れば19になる I'll be nineteen years old at my next birthday.

ことしは春が来るのが遅い Spring is late in *coming* this year.

あと１週間で夏休みが来る We'll *have* summer vacation in a week.

約束の日がとうとうやって来た At last the appointed day *came*.

4〘風雨が〙¶ ひと雨来そうだ It threatens to rain. 雨が降って来た It *has begun to* rain. / It *started* raining.

ひどいあらしが来るぞ We shall *have* a heavy storm.

5〘由来する〙¶ この語はラテン語から来ている This word *is derived from* Latin.

その様式は中国から来た The ceremony *originated in* China.

外国から来た思想はなかなか消化しにくい The ideas *brought from* abroad cannot be easily digested.

6〘起因する〙¶ 彼の病気は過労から来ている He has become ill through overwork. / His illness *comes of* overwork.

この熱は単なる風邪から来ている This fever *has come of* a mere cold.

スピードの出しすぎから来る事故が多い Many car accidents *come from* the violation of the speed limits.

この争いは労使の相互不信から来ている This struggle *results from* distrust between capital and labor.

7〘なってくる〙¶ しだいに春めいて来た It *has* gradually *become* spring-like.

寒くなって来た It *is getting* cold.

疲れて来るといらいらする I become irritated when I *get* tired.

数学がおもしろくなって来た I *am getting* interested in mathematics.

夜が更けて来た The night *is getting* late.

8〘…してくる〙¶ 彼はこれまでいろいろな経験を経て来た He has had many experiences till now.

今千葉へ行って来たところだ I *have* just *been to* Chiba.

今旅行から帰って来たばかりだ I *have* just *come back* from my trip.

9〘慣用的表現〙¶ さあ，来い Come on!

どうも彼の言うことはピンと来ない His explanation *is* not *to the point*.

そう言われて頭に来た I *was stung to the quick* by what he said.

相手がそう来るならこっちはこうする If he *assumes such an attitude*, I will cope with it in my own way.

く·る【繰る】turn over. ¶ 子どもたちは暦を～ってクリスマスを待ちわびた The children *looked up* the calendar and counted the days till Christmas.

ぐる ¶ ～になる plot together ; conspire (*with*). あのふたりは～だ Those two *are plotting* (≒ *are working*) *together*.

くるい【狂い】(手順の) confusion ; disorder ; (ひずみ) a warp. ¶ 機械に～が生じた The machine *got out of order*. われわれの目に～はなかった Our observation *proved exact*.

くるいざき【狂い咲き】blooming out of season.

くるいじに【狂い死に】¶ 彼は～した He *died crazy*.

クルー a crew.

くる·う【狂う】**1**〘気が〙¶ とうとう彼女は気が～った At last she *went mad* (≒ *crazy*).

不幸にも彼は気が～った Unfortunately he *became insane*.

彼女は痛みで気も～わんばかりだった She *was*

mad with pain.
彼女はその知らせを聞いて悲しみのあまり気も～わんばかりであった She *was beside herself with* grief at the news.
2 〖機械・計画などが〗 ¶ぼくの時計は～っている My watch *is out of order*.
計画が～った The plan *has gone wrong*. / *There was a hitch* in my plan.
順序が～っている The order *is wrong*.
このテレビはどこかが～っている Something *is wrong with* this television set.
大雪のため列車のダイヤはすっかり～ってしまった The train schedules *were* greatly *disrupted* owing to the heavy snow.
ねらいが～って当たらなかった I *missed* the mark./ I *failed to hit* the target.
彼の判断は～っている His judgment *is erroneous.*

グループ a group.
くるくる ¶～回る spin ; whirl. ～働く work *like a beaver* (≒ *bee*).
ぐるぐる ¶木のまわりを～走りまわる run *round and round* a tree. 綱を棒に～巻きつける wind a rope *against* a pole.
くるし・い【苦しい】painful ; (無理な) strained ; far-fetched ; (困難な) difficult ; hard ; (困窮) needy.
¶急に駆けたので息が～くなった I ran so suddenly that I *was* quite *out of breath*. ～い立場にある He is in a *painful* (≒ an *awkward*) position. 彼はよく～い言い逃れを言う He often makes a *lame* excuse. 彼は5人家族で生活が～い He *is in needy* (≒ *narrow*) *circumstances*, supporting a family of five. ～いときの神頼み (諺) *Danger's past, God's forgotten.* 彼も心の中は～いのだ He *is suffering* under a mental burden.
くるしまぎれ【苦し紛れ】¶問いつめられて～にまたうそをついた Questioned, he told another lie *in distress* (≒ *in desperation*).
くるしみ【苦しみ】pain ; suffering ; agony.
くるし・む【苦しむ】suffer (*from*) ; (困る) be troubled (*by*) ; (悩む) be worried. ¶彼は～まずに大往生をとげた He died *in peace* (≒ *without suffering*). 高熱で一晩じゅう～んだ I *suffered from* a high fever all the night. 彼は父親の残した借金に～んでいる He *is troubled with* his father's debts. 彼の言動には理解に～むものがある We *are puzzled by* his behavior.
くるし・める【苦しめる】¶自白しなかったので, さんざん～められた As I did not confess, I *was* badly *tormented.* ユダヤ人は世界の方々で～められた The Jewish people *were persecuted* in many parts of the world. そんなことをすれば自分で自分を～めるようなものだ If you do so, you will only make matters worse for yourself.
くるぶし【踝】the ankle ; the anklebone.
くるま【車】(一般の車) a vehicle ; (自動車) a 〔motor〕 car ; an automobile. ¶～で駅まで行こう Let's go to the station by *car* (≒ (タクシーで) *taxi*). / Let's *drive* to the station. ～を呼んでください Call (≒ Get) me *a taxi*, please. 流しの～ *a* cruising *taxi*. 日比谷公園で～を(タクシーを)降りた We got out of the *taxi* at Hibiya Park. (「バスから降りる」はふつう get off a bus と言う). 彼の～に乗った I got into his *car*. (「バスに乗る」はふつう get on a bus と言う).
くるまいす【車椅子】a wheelchair.
くるまえび【車蝦】a prawn.
くるまざ【車座】¶～になって座る sit *in a circle*.
くるまよせ【車寄せ】a porch ; an entrance.
くるま・る【包まる】¶その晩は毛布に～って眠った That night I slept, *wrapped up* in a blanket.
くるみ【胡桃】a walnut ; (木) a walnut-tree.
—割り nut-crackers.
-ぐるみ【-包み】¶町～の交通安全運動をやっている They are having a traffic safety campaign *throughout the city.*
くる・む【包む】wrap up. ¶荷物はむしろに～んであった The package *was wrapped up* (≒ *was done up*) in a mat.
ぐるり【周囲】¶あの家は～に高い木がある That house has tall trees *around.*
くるりと ¶台風は～向きを変えた The typhoon turned its course suddenly *round.*
くるわ・す【狂わす】¶この事件が彼の人生を～せた This accident *miscarried* his course of life. 物価の急上昇が計画を大幅に～せた The rapid rise of commodity prices greatly *upset* the plan.
くれ【暮れ】(夕方) evening ; nightfall ; sunset ; dusk ; (年末) the end of the year. ¶秋の～ in *late* autumn. 日の～がたに toward *evening.* 年の～にはみな忙しい Everybody is busy toward *the end of the year.*
クレープシャツ a crepe shirt.
グレープ grape. ¶～ジュース *grape* juice.
クレーム 〖商業〗 a claim. ¶その輸入品には～がついた There was *a claim* lodged against the imported product.
クレーン a crane ; a derrick.
クレオソート 〖化学〗 creosote.
くれぐれも【呉れ呉れも】¶～お体をおたいせつに Take good care of yourself. (健康な人には用いない). ～息子をよろしくお願いいたします I would appreciate your keeping an eye on my son. / I leave my son in your hands.
クレジット 〔a〕 credit. ¶～を設定する create (≒ set up) *a credit.*
—カード a credit card.
クレゾール 〖化学〗 cresol.
ぐれつ【愚劣】¶よくもそんな～なことができたものだ How could you dare to do such a *mean and stupid* thing ?
くれない【紅】crimson ; deep red.
クレバス a crevasse.
クレムリン the Kremlin.
クレヨン 〔a〕 crayon. ¶12色の～ twelve colored *crayons.* ～で絵をかく draw a picture *in crayon.*
—画 a picture in crayon.

く

く·れる【暮れる】¶ 日が～れる Night *falls.* 日が～れかかっている Night *is falling.* / The day *is drawing to a close.* / Evening dusk is gathering. やがて春も～れる Spring *is drawing to an end.* 彼に急に死なれて途方に～れている I *am* entirely *at a loss* what to do after his sudden death. 彼は息子を亡くして悲嘆に～れている By the death of his son, he *is overwhelmed with* sorrow. これからどうしてよいか思案に～れている I *am wondering* what to do after now.

く·れる【呉れる】¶ わざわざ自分で持ってきて～れた He *was kind enough to* bring it to me by himself. 彼は本を～れた He *gave* me a book.

ぐ·れる go wrong (≒ astray).

クレンザー cleanser ; 〔a〕 cleansing powder.

クレンジングクリーム cleansing cream.

ぐれんたい【愚連隊】〔street〕 gangsters ; 〔a gang of〕 hooligans.

くろ【黒】black 〔color〕; blackness. ¶ 彼はどうも～らしい (疑わしい) He *is suspicious.* それで彼が白か～かはっきりする It will clarify whether he *is guilty* or not (≒ innocent).

くろ·い【黒い】black. ¶ 色が～い He *is dark.* / He *is dark-complexioned.* だいぶ～く日焼けしましたね You'*ve got* quite *tanned.* / You've *got* quite *a sunburn.* (tan は好い感じを与える日焼けであるが, sunburn はひりひり痛むときに多く用いる). あの男は腹が～い He *is evil-hearted.* / He *is black-hearted.*

くろう【苦労】**1**〘ほねおり·心配〙〔a〕 trouble ; 〔a〕 worry. ¶ 金のことではまったく～する I *am* always *hard up.*

彼は金の～なんてしたことがない He has never had financial *worries.*

あの子のことじゃ～のしどおしだ My son is *a* constant *nuisance.*

家を建てるのにはずいぶん～した I've had to *go through* a lot of *hardship* to build my house.

言いわけをするのに～した I *racked my brains* to make an excuse.

英語にはずいぶん～させられた I had to *work very hard* to learn English.

若いうちに～をさせたほうがいい The young should *struggle with adversity.* (形式ばった形).

きみはまだ～が足りない You have not seen enough of life.

～してやっとこれまでになれた I have seen many *hardships* to raise myself to the present station.

彼のことで人に言えぬ～がある I have plenty of unexpressed *worries* about him.

女手ひとつで母はいろいろ～が多かったに相違ない My mother, a widow, must have undergone various *hardships* through her life.

子どものことでは～が絶えぬ We *have no end of anxiety* over our children.

いろいろ～をかけてすみません I am sorry to *have troubled* you so much.

やっときみの～も報われそうだ Your *efforts* seem to bear fruit at last.

彼は～に～を重ねてやっと赤字経営を脱した He *suffered hardship upon hardship,* until at last he came out of the red.

優勝できてこれまでの～も忘れた We have won the victory, and have forgotten all the *hardships* that we have gone through.

これだけ資料を集めるのはたいへんな～だったろう You must *have taken great pains* to collect such data as these.

入試のことが今から～の種だ Entrance examinations are a source of *cares* from now on.

彼女は生活の～ですっかりやつれていた She was haggard through her worldly *cares.*

2〘その他〙¶ ご～さま Thanks for your *trouble.*

遠路ご～さま Thank you for coming all the way. (having come としないでよい).

ご～千万なことだ (よせばいいのに) He might have spared himself the *trouble.*

彼は～性だ He always takes things too seriously. / He is a man of nervous temperament.

彼は酸いも甘いもかみわけたなかなかの～人だ He is a sensible man, because he has tasted the sweets and bitters of life.

ぐろう【愚弄】mockery ; derision. ¶ 人をそんなに～するものではない Don't *make fun of* others like that.

くろうと【玄人】(専門家) a professional ; (熟練者) an expert ; a specialist. ¶ ～の女 a woman *of the gay world.* 彼は～はだしの腕前だった His skill *put a professional to shame.*

クローク a cloakroom.

クロース (本の表紙) book cloth. ¶ ～製の本 a *clothbound* book ; a book with a *cloth* binding.

クローズアップ a close-up. ¶ 問題が再び～されてきた The problem *has been highlighted* again.

クローバー〘植物〙a clover.

グローブ a glove.

クローム〘化学〙chrome ; chromium (Cr).
—メッキ chromiun plating. —鋼 chrome steel.

クロール crawl strokes ; the crawl. ¶ ～で泳ぐ swim *the crawl.*

くろかみ【黒髪】dark hair.

くろこ【黒子】〘演劇〙a prompter.

くろこげ【黒焦げ】¶ ～になる burn black ; be burnt black ; be charred.

くろざとう【黒砂糖】brown sugar.

くろじ【黒字】¶ 収支は～だ The balance *is in the black.*

くろしお【黒潮】the Black (≒ Japan) Current ; the Black Stream.

くろしょうぞく【黒装束】〔a suit of〕 black clothes. ¶ ～の男 a man *dressed in black.*

くろしろ【黒白】¶ ～のフィルム *monochrome* film. ～をはっきりさせる必要がある We must clarify which is *right* and which is *wrong.*

クロスカントリーレース a cross-country race.

クロスゲーム a close game.
クロスワードパズル a crossword puzzle.
グロス a gross.
くろず・む【黒ずむ】become darkish. ¶ ～んだ darkish; blackish; swarthy.
くろダイヤ【黒ダイヤ】a black diamond; (石炭) coal.
グロッキー ¶ 昨夜遅くまで勉強したので, けさは少し～だ As I studied till late last night, I *am* a bit *groggy* this morning.
くろつち【黒土】black soil; fertile land.
くろっぽ・い【黒っぽい】darkish; blackish; (皮膚・顔色が) swarthy.
グロテスク ¶ ～な grotesque; bizarre.
クロノメーター a chronometer.
くろパン【黒パン】black (≒ brown) bread.
くろビール【黒ビール】porter; ㊥ black beer.
くろびかり【黒光り】¶ 旧家の柱や床が～している The wooden pillars and flooring of the old house give out *a black luster*.
くろぼし【黒星】a black dot; (負け星) a defeat mark. ¶ 政府の物価対策は～続きだ The Government has made a series of *failures* in its price policy.
くろまく【黒幕】¶ 彼は政界の～だ He *controls* politics *from behind* (≒ *behind the scenes*). 彼が陰謀の～だ He is the *wirepuller* of the plot.
くろまめ【黒豆】a black soybean.
くろみ【黒味】¶ 建物は煤煙(ばいえん)で～を帯びている The building *is darkish* (≒ *is slightly dark*) with soot.
くろめ【黒目】the iris of the eye. ¶ ～がちの少女 a *dark-eyed* girl.
くろやき【黒焼き】¶ イモリの～ a *charred* newt.
くろやま【黒山】¶ 海岸は～のような人だかりだった There were *a large crowd of people* at the seashore.
くろゆり【黒百合】〘植物〙a Japanese black fritillary.
クロレラ〘植物〙chlorella.
クロロホルム〘薬学〙chloroform. ¶ 彼は患者に～で麻酔をかけた He applied *chloroform* to the patient.
クロロマイセチン〘薬学〙chloromycetin.
―軟膏(なんこう) a chloromycetin salve.
くろわく【黒枠】a black frame. ¶ ～付きの写真(はがき) an *obituary* photo (card).
ぐろん【愚論】a foolish argument; an absurd view.
くろんぼう【黒ん坊】a Negro; a colored man; (女) a colored woman (最近は black people も用いるようになった).
くわ【桑】〘植物〙a mulberry. ¶ ～の実 a mulberry. ～を摘む pick *mulberry leaves*. 蚕に～をやる feed *mulberry leaves* to silkworms.
くわ【鍬】a hoe. ¶ ～で土地を耕す till the soil with *a hoe*.
くわい【慈姑】〘植物〙an arrowhead.
くわ・える【加える】add. ¶ 2に3を～えると5 Two and three is (≒ are) five. 10に5を～えるといくつになるか If you *add* five to ten, what number do you get? 彼の頭に一撃を～えた I *struck* him on the head. 彼は罰を～えられるべきだ He should *be punished*.
くわ・える【銜える・啣える】¶ 彼は口にたばこを～えている He *is holding* a cigarette *in his mouth*. ネコがなにか～えて逃げた A cat ran away *with something in its mouth*. この子どもは指を～える癖がある This child has a habit of *putting* his finger *in his mouth*.
くわし・い【詳しい】¶ 彼はその理由の～い説明をした He gave *a full and detailed* account of the reason. / He explained the reason *in full*. 彼女はロンドンに～い She *knows* London *well*. 彼は日本のことに～い He *is familiar with* things Japanese. 彼は法律に～い He *has a good knowledge of* law. これ以上～くは述べられない I can't *go into details* about this matter any more. ～くは説明書をごらんください For further *details* (≒ *particulars*), please refer to the explanatory note.
くわずぎらい【食わず嫌い】¶ 彼のジャズぎらいは～だ He *has prejudice against* jazz.
くわせもの【食わせ者】¶ 彼は見かけによらぬ～だ He is *an impostor* (≒ *a sham*) at heart.
くわ・せる【食わせる】¶ このレストランではおいしい魚を～せる You *are* nicely *served with* good fish at this restaurant. 妻子を～せるのは容易ではない It is no easy thing to *support* a wife and chidren. 彼の態度にまんまといっぱい～された I *was* nicely *taken in* by his manners.
くわだて【企て】an attempt. ¶ われわれの～は彼の病気で実現できなかった Our *plan* was upset by his illness. 彼らの反乱の～は失敗に終わった They failed in the *attempt* to rebel against the Government.
くわだ・てる【企てる】¶ 彼らは世界一周旅行を～てている They *are planning for* a trip around the world. 彼らは大統領の暗殺を～てた They *made an attempt on* the life of the President. 彼らは会社の設立を～てたが失敗した They *attempted to* establish a firm, but failed. 彼は新しい企業を～てている He *has been undertaking* a new enterprise.
くわばら ¶ ～, ～ Heaven help me!
くわ・れる【食われる】¶ 食うか～れるかの争い a *life and death* struggle.
くわわ・る【加わる】¶ 車は坂を下っていくにつれて速度が～った The car *gained* speed as it went down the slope. 日ごとに寒さが～っている It is getting colder day by day. 彼はその一行に～った He *joined* the party. ぼくは競技に～るつもりだ I am going to *join* (≒ *take part*) *in* the game. 彼は会議に～らなかった He did not *take part in* the conference.
くん【訓】¶「犬」という字の～は「いぬ」だ The Japanese pronunciation of a letter "犬" is "inu."
くん-【勲-】¶ ～1等 the First Order of Merit.
-くん【-君】¶ 吉田～ *Mr.* Yoshida.
ぐん【軍】¶ 将軍は数万の～を率いている The general commands ten thousands of *troops*.

く

ぐん【郡】a district.
ぐん【群】a group(*of* people). ¶彼の英会話は～を抜いている He *is well above the average in* English conversation.
ぐんい【軍医】an army surgeon; a medical officer.
くんいく【訓育】education; discipline.
ぐんか【軍歌】a war song; a martial song.
くんかい【訓戒】¶先生はその少年に二度とカンニングしないように～した The teacher *admonished* the boy never to cheat in an examination again. 警察は彼を～して釈放した The police dismissed him with *a caution* (≒ *a warning*).
ぐんがくたい【軍楽隊】a military band.
ぐんかん【軍艦】a warship; a man-of-war. —旗 a naval ensign; 英 the white ensign.
ぐんき【軍紀】¶～の維持 the maintenance of *military discipline*. ～を乱す violate *military discipline*. ～が乱れている The *soldiers' morals* have been corrupted.
ぐんき【軍機】¶彼は敵に～を漏らした He let out *military secrets* to the enemy.
ぐんき【軍旗】the colors; a standard.
ぐんきょ【群居】¶この池には水鳥が～している Water birds *live in flocks* in this pond.
—動物 a gregarious animal.
くんくん ¶子犬は部屋の外で～鳴いている The puppy *is whining* outside the door.
ぐんぐん ¶列車は～スピードを上げた The train speeded up *steadily*. 彼の病気は～よくなった He is getting *steadily* better.
くんこう【勲功】¶彼はこの戦争で～を立てた He rendered *distinguished services* to the country in this war.
ぐんこう【軍港】a naval port.
ぐんこく【軍国】—主義 militarism. —主義者 a militarist.
くんし【君子】a man of honor; a virtuous man. ¶～は危きに近寄らず(諺) *The wise man* does not court danger. ～は豹変(ひょうへん)す *The wise man* can adapt himself to any surroundings.
くんじ【訓示】instructions. ¶指揮官は部下に～をした The captain gave *instructions* to his men.
ぐんし【軍使】the bearer of a flag of truce (truce は「一時休戦」の意味).
ぐんじ【軍事】¶この運河はわが国にとって～的に重要である This canal is of *strategic* importance for our national defense.
—基地 a military base. —機密 military secrets. —教練 military training.
くんしゅ【君主】a sovereign; a monarch; a ruler.
—国 a monarchy. —制 monarchism. —独裁 autocracy.
ぐんじゅ【軍需】—工場 a munition plant. —産業 munition industries. —品 munitions. —補給基地 a railhead.
ぐんしゅう【群集】a crowd (集合体を指すときは単数扱いで, 個々を指すときは複数扱い).
—心理 mob (≒ mass) psychology.
ぐんしゅく【軍縮】disarmament.
くんしょう【勲章】a decoration; an order; a medal. ¶彼は軍功により～を授かった He *was decorated* for his brilliant services in the war. 彼はその功績により女王より～を授かった He was awarded *an order* for his merits by the Queen.
ぐんしょう【群小】¶～国 the *lesser* nations.
ぐんじん【軍人】(一般に) a soldier (高級将校をふくむ); (将校) an officer; (陸軍) a soldier; (陸軍将校) a military officer; (海軍) a sailor; (海軍将校) a naval officer; (空軍) an airman; (空軍将校) an air force officer.
¶彼は陸軍(海軍; 空軍)～になった He joined the *army* (*navy*; *air force*). 彼は～かたぎが抜けきれない He cannot rid himself of *the military spirit*.
—あがり(の人) an ex-soldier. —恩給 a military pension. —生活 a military life.
くんせい【薫製】¶魚を保存するために～にする *smoke* fish to preserve them.
—サケ〔a〕smoked salmon. —ニシン〔a〕smoked herring.
ぐんせい【軍政】¶占領地に～を敷く establish *a military government* at the occupied territory.
ぐんせい【群生】¶この山には高山植物が～している Many alpine plants *grow in crowds* in this mountain.
ぐんせい【群棲】¶この島には野猿(やえん)が～している Wild monkeys *live in flocks* on this island.
ぐんぜい【軍勢】¶わが～は10万 Our *forces* amount to 100,000.
ぐんそう【軍装】¶～の将兵 soldiers and officers *in uniform*; (戦闘の) soldiers and officers *in combat uniform*.
ぐんそう【軍曹】a sergeant.
ぐんぞう【群像】a group. ¶ラオコーン～ the Laocoön *group*.
ぐんぞく【軍属】a civilian.
ぐんたい【軍隊】an army. ¶彼は(陸軍の)～に入っている He *is in the army*. (海軍は the navy, 空軍は the air force となる). 彼らは～に入った They joined the *army*.
—教育 military training. —行進曲 a military march. —生活 (陸軍の) army life; (海軍の) navy life.
くんだり ¶どうしてきみは九州～まで行くのか Why do you go *all the way down to* Kyushu?
ぐんだん【軍団】〘軍事〙a corps (複 corps).
くんでん【訓電】a telegraphic instruction. ¶大使は政府に～を要請した The envoy asked the Government for *telegraphic instructions*. 大統領は特使に～を送った The President gave *instructions* to the special envoy *by wires*.
くんとう【薫陶】instruction. ¶彼は母親からよい～を受けた He received good *instruction* from his mother. 私は田中先生の～を受けた I *studied under* Mr. Tanaka.
ぐんとう【軍刀】a saber.

ぐんとう【群島】a group of islands; an archipelago. ¶フィリピン～ the Philippines; the Philippine *Islands.*

くんどく【訓読】the Japanese reading of Chinese characters.

ぐんばい【軍配】(相撲の) an umpire's fan. ¶行司は横綱に～を上げた The *sumo* umpire declared the *yokozuna* wrestler the victor.

ぐんばつ【軍閥】the military clique.

ぐんび【軍備】armaments. ¶～を縮小する reduce *armaments.*

ぐんぶ【軍部】¶～が政治権力を握っている *The military authorities* seize the political power.

くんぷう【薫風】a gentle breeze in early summer.

ぐんぷく【軍服】a military uniform; (海軍の) a naval uniform.

ぐんぽうかいぎ【軍法会議】a court-martial. ¶スパイは捕らえられ,～にかけられた The spy *was* arrested and *court-martialed* (≒ *tried by court-martial*).

ぐんむ【軍務】military (≒ naval) service. ¶3年～に服した He *served* three years *in the army* (≒ (海軍) *navy*).

ぐんもん【軍門】¶彼らは力尽きて敵の～に下った They *surrendered* when they could no longer fight.

ぐんゆう【群雄】¶当時は～割拠の世の中であった In those days *local leaders competed with* (≒ *rivaled*) one another for power. 現在の政界は～割拠の時代だ The political circles have entered a period of *rival leaders.*

ぐんよう【軍用】―機 a war-plane; a military plane. ―金 war funds. ―犬 an army dog. ―列車 a troop train.

ぐんらく【群落】¶その辺では高山植物が～をなして生えている Over there, alpine plants are growing *in groups* (≒ *in colonies*).

くんりん【君臨】domination. ¶イギリス国王は～するも統治せず The English sovereign *reigns,* but does not rule. 彼は今や産業界に～する大資本家だ He is now a great businessman *dominating* the industrial world. / He *is* now *a czar* (≒ *baron*) *of* the industrial world.

くんれい【訓令】an instruction. ¶政府はただちに交渉を再会せよという～を発した The Government gave *instructions* to reopen the negotiations without delay.

くんれん【訓練】training; drill; (練習) practice. ¶これらの人たちは看護婦としての(十分な)～を受けてきた These girls have been (well-) trained as nurse. 彼らは目下～中です They *are undergoing training* (≒ *are being trained*). 英語を十分に使いこなせるには何年もの～が必要です It takes years of *practice* to have a good command of English. 火事の避難～が近いうちにある We are going to have *a* fire *drill* very soon.

くんわ【訓話】a lesson. ¶けさ校長先生の～があった The principal spoke to us this morning.

け

け【気】(気味) a touch; a shade; (気配) a sign; (疑い) a supicion. ¶この部屋はまったく火の～がない This room is quite unheated. その家にはまったく人～がなかった There was no *sign* of life in the house. / The house was utterly deserted. 彼には糖尿病の～がある He has *symptoms* of diabetes.

け【毛】(総称) hair; (1本の) a hair. ¶柔らかい(堅い)～ soft (coarse) *hair.* 縮れた～ curly (≒ crisp) *hair.* ～が濃い(薄い) thickly-(thinly-) *haired.* ～が生える(抜ける) *Hair* grows (falls out). ～が薄くなっている I'm losing my *hair.* ～のシャツ a *woolen* shirt. その話を聞いて私は身の～もよだつ思いだった The story made my *hair* stand on end. / The tale *gave me the creeps.* 当時彼の英語の知識は中学生に～の生えた程度であった At that time, his knowledge of English *was just a little* (≒ *no*) *better than* a junior high school pupil's.

-け【-家】¶徳川～ the Tokugawa *family;* the Tokugawas. 常陸の宮～ the royal *family* of Hitachi.

げ【下】the low class; the low grade; (下巻) the last (≒ second) volume. ¶彼の成績はクラスの～の～だ He is in the very bottom of his class.

けあな【毛穴】pores 〔of the skin〕.

けい【兄】¶～たりがたく弟たりがたし There is little to choose between them. / They are on a par with each other. AとBとはテニスでは～たりがたく弟たりがたしだ A is B's *match for* tennis playing.

けい【系】(系統) a system; (血統) descent. ¶太陽～ the solar *system.* アイルランド～アメリカ人 an Irish-American; an American of Irish *descent.* 日～二世 a nisei; an American-born Japanese. 保守～の議員 a Conservative.

けい【計】¶一年の～は元旦にあり New Year's Day is the key of the year. 三十六～逃げるにしかず(諺) The best policy is to run away (≒ retreat). / Discretion is the better part of valor. 収入は～100万円になります The income *comes to a total of* a million yen.

けい【刑】 punishment; penalty. ¶ ～に服する serve *one's* sentence. ～に処する condemn (*a person*) to a penalty. 罪人に重い～を科する inflict severe *punishments* on criminals. 彼は窃盗罪で罰金～を宣告された He was fined for theft. 彼は禁固３年の～に処せられた He was sentenced to three years' imprisonment. / He got three years in jail. ～を減じて釈放せよ Reduce his *sentence* (≒ *penalty*) and set him free.

けい【罫】 a 〔ruled〕 line. ¶ ～のないノート an *unruled* notebook. ～を引く rule *lines*.

-けい【-景】 ¶ 近江八～ the eight most beautiful places of Omi; the eight famous sights of Omi. 第２幕第１～ Act II, *Scene* I.

げい【芸】 (技芸) an art; (たしなみ) an accomplishment; (演芸) a performance; (曲芸) a trick. ¶ 彼は～が細かい He is mindful of details (≒ particulars). / He is meticulous in performance. 一～に達した人 an *accomplished* man. 彼は～で身を立てている人だ He earns his living as an artist. ～は身を助ける *Accomplishments* are a friend in need. 犬に～を仕込んでいる I am teaching my dog *tricks*.

けいあい【敬愛】 ¶ ～するＡ君 My *dear* Mr. A. (あいさつなどで) ～する諸先生 our *respected* professors. 彼はその人を～していた He *loved and respected* the man.

けいい【経緯】 details; circumstances. ¶ 彼はその事件の～を説明してくれた He told us *the whole story* (≒ *all details*) of the affair.

けいい【敬意】 respect. ¶ 老人には～を払うべきだ We should *have respect for* old people. / We should *show* (≒ *pay*) *respect to* old people. 田中氏に～を表して晩餐(ばん)会が催された A dinner party was given *in honor of* Mr. Tanaka.

けいえい【経営】 management. ¶ 事業を～する *run* (≒ *manage*; *operate*; *carry*) an enterprise. 喫茶店を～する *keep* (≒ *run*) a coffee shop. 彼の～のもとに事業は大いに発展した The enterprise has achieved a great expansion under his 〔good〕 *management*. それはアメリカ人～の会社だ It is an American-*run* (≒ *-operated*) company. なかなか～の才のある男だ He has much *business ability* (≒ 米 *executive ability*).

—学 business management. **—コンサルタント** a management consultant. **—者** a manager; 米 an executive; (所有主) a proprietor; (総称) the management. ¶ ～者側と労働者側 *management* and labor; *capital* and labor. **—費** 米 operating costs; 英 running expenses. **個人—** a private enterprise.

けいえん【敬遠】 ¶ 彼は口やかましいのでみなから～されている He is so sharp-tongued that everyone *keeps a respectful distance from* him. ～の四球を与える give a batter *a walk* (≒ *a base on balls*) intentionally.

けいおんがく【軽音楽】 light music.

けいか【経過】 (時の) passage; expiration; (事の) progress. ¶ 出発してから５時間～した Five hours *have passed* since we started. 会議の～を報告する report the *progress* of a conference. 彼は今までの事件の～を詳しく話してくれた He gave us a full account of *how the affair had developed*. 手術の～はよい The operation was successful. / The *result* of the operation is satisfactory.

けいかい【警戒】 (警備) guard; (用心) caution; precaution. ¶ 彼は脱走するおそれがあるので十分～するように言われた I was told to *keep close* (≒ *strict*) *watch over* (≒ *on*) him, since he might run away. 彼に金をだまし取られないよう～せよ You must *be careful* not to be cheated out of your money by him. 彼の表情が変わったので～した The change of his look *put me on guard*. 火災の～を特に厳重にしなければならない We should *take* special *precautions against* fire. 彼は病気が再発しないよう～している He *is on guard against* a relapse.

—色 warning coloration. **—線** a police cordon.

けいかい【軽快】 ¶ ～なメロディー a *rhythmical* melody. ～な服装で in *light* dress; in *casual* wear; *lightly* dressed. ～な足どりで with *light* steps.

けいかく【計画】 a plan; a project; a scheme; a program. ¶ 綿密な(行き当たりばったりの)～ *a* careful (happy-go-lucky) *plan*. ～的な犯行 a *premeditated* crime. ～的な詐欺 a *well-organized* fraud.

¶ 彼は３か年～で世界一周旅行の金をためた On *a* three-year *plan* he saved enough money to make a trip around the world. 彼らは夏休みの～を立てている They are making *plans* for the summer vacation. 有給休暇にはなにか～があるか Do you have any *plans* for your paid vacation? 彼は勉強の～を立てて実行中である He drew up *a plan* of study and is carrying it out. きみは将来の～を立てなければならない You must make *plans* for the future. ～がうまくいった(失敗に終わった) The *plan* worked well (has failed). ～が狂ってしまった My *plan* went wrong. 万事～どおりにいった Everything went according to *plan*. その～は進行中だ The *plan* is under way. 彼らは新しいダムを～した They *projected* a new dam.

—委員会 a project team. **—経済** planned economy; economic planning. **—者** a planner; a projector; a designer. **長期—** a long-term plan. **都市—** city planning. **政府—案** a government program.

けいかん【景観】 a sight; a view. ¶ 雄大な～ *a* grand *view*.

けいかん【警官】 a policeman; 英 a constable; 米 (巡回の) a patrolman; (米俗語) a cop; (英俗語) a bobby; (総称) the police.
婦人— a policewoman (複 -women).

けいがん【慧眼】 insight; perspicacity; observant eye; sagacious eye. ¶ 彼は非常な～

の持ち主だ He is a man of great *insight.* / He has *penetrating* eyes.

けいき【刑期】 the term of imprisonment. ¶ 彼は５年の～を終えてきのう出所した He *completed* (≒ *served out*) his sentence of five years and was set free yesterday.

けいき【計器】 a meter. ―飛行 instrumental navigation. ¶ ～飛行をする fly on *instruments.*

けいき【契機】 a chance; an opportunity; a turning point. ¶ アメリカの参戦を～にして with America's entry into war. 原子爆弾の投下が終戦の～となった The use of atomic bombs ended the war.

けいき【景気】 business condition; (活気) liveliness. ¶ ご商売の～はどうですか How is your *business* doing? わが社は～がいい Our company *is doing a flourishing business.* ～がいい (活況を呈している) *Business* is brisk. ～が悪い(不～だ) *Business* is dull. ～は上向いている *Business* is looking up. / Business is improving. ～は下向いている *Business* is declining. ～の回復 a revival of *business.* ～の後退 *business* recession. ～の変動 industrial fluctuation. 彼はいつも～よく金を使う He always spends his money *freely.* 彼は一杯飲んで～をつけた He *enlivened* himself with a drink.

好― prosperity. 不― depression.

けいきかんじゅう【軽機関銃】 a light machine gun.

けいきょ【軽挙】 ¶ ～妄動は慎まねばならない No rashness! / Don't act *rashly* (≒ *on impulse*). ～妄動を戒めておいた I warned him against *rashness.*

けいきんぞく【軽金属】 light metals.

けいく【警句】 a witty remark; an epigram. ¶ ～を吐く make *a witty remark* (≒ *an epigram*).

けいぐ【敬具】 Sincerely (≒ Truly) yours (イギリス系では Yours sincerely がふつう. Yours truly はより正式なとき); Yours respectfully (官庁・会社に対する formal な手紙などに用いる場合が多い).

けいけい【炯炯】 ¶ 眼光～として人を射る感じだ He has such *sharp* (≒ *penetrating*) eyes as would see you through.

けいけん【経験】 experience.

1〘経験が〙 ¶ 私はアメリカ人に日本語を教えた～がある I *have experience in* teaching Japanese to Ame ricans.

そのことについては苦い～がある I *have had* bitter *experience in* that matter.

外国生活の～がありますか Have you *ever* stayed abroad?

この社会では知識よりも～がものをいう As far as this society is concerned, *experience* counts for more than knowledge.

やはり～がものをいう *Experience* will win in the long run.

～がないとやれない Without *experience,* it is difficult to do.

2〘経験の〙 ¶ この仕事は～のない人には無理だろう This is probably difficult work for an *inexperienced* man to do.

３年以上～のある人が欲しい We want a person with more than three years' *experience* behind him. / We need men with *experience* more than three years.

3〘経験に〙 ¶ 今度のことはとてもいい～になった This was *a* good *lesson* for me.

彼は人生～に富んでいる He has wide *experience* in life.

4〘経験を〙 ¶ ～を積んだ保母さんなら安心だ An *experienced* nursery teacher can be relied upon.

5〘その他の助詞などとともに〙 ¶ そのつらさは～した者でないとわからない Only the person who *has gone through* it himself knows that bitterness.

初めての～なのでうまくいくかどうか不安だ This is my first *experience* in my life and I wonder if I can do it well.

何事も～だ *Experience* is a good teacher.

彼は～は浅いが腕はしっかりしている He is wanting in *experience,* but skillful (≒ skilled) in his work.

私の～では, 運転免許をとって２年めぐらいに事故を起こしやすい *In my experience* we are apt to have a traffic accident the second year after we have got a driving license.

6〘合成語〙 ―者 ¶ ～者は知る Only the person who has gone through it himself knows that much. / *An experienced person* (≒ *An expert*) knows. ―年数 ¶ 給料は学歴と～年数とで決められている A salary is to be decided according to one's school career and the years of *experience.* ―談 the narrative of *one's* personal experience (*about*). ―論 empiricism.

けいけん【敬虔】 ¶ ～なクリスチャン a *devout* Christian.

けいげん【軽減】 decrease; reduction. ¶ 負担を～する *lighten* the burden. 税を～してほしい We would like to *have* the tax *reduced* (≒ *lightened*).

けいこ【稽古】 exercise; practice; training. ¶ ピアノの～をする(自分で) *practice* the piano; (先生について) *take lessons in* the piano. だれについて生け花を～しているのですか Who is your teacher of flower arrangement? / Who *are* you *taking lessons in* flower arrangement from?

舞台― ¶ 演劇クラブの部員は舞台～をしている The members of the Dramatic Club are having *a stage rehearsal.*

けいご【敬語】 a term of respect; an honorific. ¶ 目上の人と話をするときは～を使いなさい You should *be polite* (≒ *use respectful terms*) in speaking to your seniors.

けいご【警護】 ¶ 警察の～のもとに under police *escort.*

けいこう【傾向】 tendency; trend; inclination. ¶ 世論の一般的～ the general *trend* of

け

け

public opinion. ヨーロッパにおける言語学の最近の～ the recent *trend* of linguistics in Europe. 毎年物価は上がる～にある Prices *tend upward* (≒ *tend to rise*) every year. / Prices have (≒ show) *a* rising *tendency* every year. 彼は飲みすぎる～がある He *is inclined* (≒ *is apt*) *to* drink too much. アメリカには巨大主義の～がしだいに高まりつつある In America there is *a* growing *tendency toward* jumboism. そんな方策をとると排日運動という望ましからぬ～を助長するだろう Such measures will develop an undesirable *tendency* of anti-Japanese movement.

けいこう【携行】 ¶ 午後は雨の見込み.雨具～のこと It will rain in the afternoon. *Take* your umbrella *with* you.

けいこう【螢光】〖物理〗fluorescence.
—体 a fluorescent substance. —燈 a fluorescent lamp (≒ light).

けいこう【経口】 —避妊薬 a contraceptive; a birth-control pill; the pill.

げいごう【迎合】 ¶ 時代の流れに～する *go with* the current of the times. 他人の説に～する *echo* another's opinion. 権力に～する *follow* (≒ *wait on*) the wishes of the powers.

けいこうぎょう【軽工業】 light industry.

けいこく【警告】 caution; warning. ¶ その晩は外へ出ないように～しておいた I *gave* him *warning* not *to* go out that evening. 彼はわれわれの～を聞き入れなかった He would not listen to our *advice* (≒ *warning*). 災害は～なしにやってくる Accidents will come *unawares* (≒ *without warning*).

けいこく【渓谷】 a ravine; (深い谷) a glen; a gorge.

げいごと【芸事】 accomplishments; an art.

けいこつ【頸骨】〖解剖学〗a neck-bone.

けいさい【掲載】 ¶ 彼の記事があすの新聞に～されることになっている His article is to *appear* (≒ *come out*) in tomorrow's paper. ～禁止 a press ban; prohibition of printing.

けいざい【経済】 **1**〖国・社会の経済〗economy; (財政) finance. ¶ 日本はいまや～大国といわれている Japan is now called one of the great *economic* nations.
彼はその国の～事情に詳しい He is well acquainted with the *economic* conditions in that country.
その国は輸出不振で～的に窮迫している The country is in *financial* difficulty because of export depression.
その国はわが国に～援助を仰いできた The country has asked for our *financial* support.
—界 the economic world. —学 economics. —学者 an economist. —企画 an economic planning. —活動 an economic activity. —記事 financial news. —原論 the principles of economics. —記者 a reporter of financial news. —政策 an economic policy. —使節 the economic mission. —闘争 a wage dispute. —白書 an econoimc white paper. —欄(面) the financial section (≒ column; page). —力 financial power. 自由— free economy. 統制— controlled economy.
2〖一家の経済〗¶ わが家の～は危機に瀕(ひん)している Our [household] *budget* is at its worst.
そうしたいが家の～が許さない I should like to do so, but I *cannot afford* it.
そんなぜいたくをするとうちの～が成り立たなくなる If we live so high, we cannot control our *domestic expenses*.
わが家の～は苦しくなる一方だ Our *domestic economy* is becoming worse and worse.
3〖節約〗¶ ～の点から言えば石油ストーブがいちばんです From the *economical* point of view, the kerosene stove is the best.
その案は～的にみて採算がとれない The plan does not pay from the *economical* point of view.
地下鉄で行ったほうがずっと時間の～になる You can *save* more time by subway.
高くても品質のよい物が結局～的になる An article of high price but of good quality *pays* in the long run.
いらない物を買うのは不～だ It *is* not *economical* to buy unnecessary things.
この製品は電力をあまり食わず～的にできている This instrument *is economical* and does not consume much electric power.
この品のほうが～的にみてお得です This *is* more *economical*.
もう少し時間を～的に使いたまえ Try and *make economical* (≒ *better*) *use of* your time.
私の女房は～観念がない My wife lacks *common sense in housekeeping*. / My wife is not *an economical housekeeper*.
きみはなかなか～観念が発達しているね You *are* very *economy-minded*, aren't you?
時速20ノットがこの船の～運転速度だ Twenty knots per hour is the *economic speed* for this ship.

けいさつ【警察】 the police (常に複数扱い).
¶ 盗難を～に届け出た I informed *the police* of the theft. ～に訴える complain to *the police*. すりは～に突き出された The pickpocket was handed over to *the police*. 犯人は～に自首した The criminal gave himself up to *the police*. 被害者たちは～に保護を求めた The sufferers asked for *police* protection.
—官 a policeman; (婦人) a policewoman. —犬 a police dog. —権 police power. —署 a police station. —署長 the chief of a police station. —庁 the National Police Agency.

けいさん【珪酸】〖化学〗silicic acid.
—塩 silicate.

けいさん【計算】 accounts; calculation; reckoning. ¶ 彼は～が速い (遅い; うまい; へただ) He is quick (slow; good; poor) at *figures* (≒ *accounts*). 彼は～をまちがえた He *calculated* wrongly. / He *miscalculated*. この～はまちがっている These *figures* are wrong. 借金はいくらになるか～してください Please *figure up* how much I owe you. 料金は距離で～するCharges *are calculated* by distance. 予定外の費用も～に入れて，旅費は十分用意した We provided ourselves with enough money for traveling, *taking* unexpected expenditures *into account.* ぼくはきみが助けてくれるものと～していたのだ I *figured* (≒ *counted*) *on* your helping me.

—係 an accountant. —器 a calculating machine; a calculator. —尺 a slide rule. —書 a statement of accounts. —簿 an account book.

けいし【罫紙】ruled (≒ lined) paper.

けいし【軽視】¶ その事件は～すべきでない You should not *treat* the case *so lightly.* 彼を～して会議に呼ばなかった We *ignored* him and did not ask him to attend the conference.

けいし【警視】a police superintendent.

—総監 the Superintendent-General of the Metropolitan Police. —庁 the Metropolitan Police Office (≒ Board).

けいじ【刑事】(刑事巡査) a〔police〕detective.

—局 the Bureau of Criminal Affairs. —事件 a criminal case. —訴訟 a criminal action (≒ suit). —訴訟法 the Criminal Procedure Code. —犯 a criminal offense.

けいじ【啓示】revelation.

けいじ【掲示】a notice. ¶ ～を出す put up *a notice.*

—板 a bulletin board; 英 a notice board.

けいじ【慶事】a happy event.

けいじか【形而下】¶ ～の問題 a *physical* (≒ *material*) matter.

けいしき【形式】a form. ¶ あまり～にこだわらぬように Don't stick too much to *forms* (≒ *formalities*). ～を踏むことは必要である It is necessary to go through *formalities.* それは単に～上の問題だ It's only *a matter of form.* ただ～的にその問題を処理しただけだ I treated the matter only *perfunctorily.*

—主義 (特に文学上の) formalism. —主義者 a formalist.

けいじじょう【形而上】¶ それは～の問題である It is a *metaphysical* (≒ an *abstract*) matter.

—学 metaphysics. —詩 (詩人) a metaphysical poetry (poet).

けいしゃ【傾斜】an inclination; a slant; (坂などの) a slope; (上り) an acclivity; (下り) a declivity; (船の) a list; an incline.

¶ あの塔は少し東へ～している That tower *leans* slightly to the east. たいていの人の筆跡は右に～している Most handwritings *slant* to the right. その土地は海の方に～している The land *slopes* toward the sea.

—角 an angle of inclination. —度 gradient. —面 a slope; an inclined plane; an incline.

げいしゃ【芸者】a *geisha*〔-girl〕; a singing girl; an entertainer. ¶ ～をあげて騒いだ We made merry *calling in* (≒ *hiring*) *geishas.*

けいしゅ【警手】a guard.

けいしゅう【閨秀】—画家 a woman painter. —作家 a woman writer. —詩人 a poetess (a lady painter (writer) は言外に冷やかし・軽べつの響きを含む).

げいじゅつ【芸術】art (芸術一般の場合は無冠詞. ただし「建築は芸術である」というように，芸術の一分野を意味する場合，Architecture is *an art.* と冠詞をとる).

¶ 彼は～に幅広い関心を持っている He has wide-ranging artistic interests.

—愛好家 an art lover. —院 the Art Academy. —家 an artist. —祭 an art festival. —作品 a work of art. —至上主義 art for art's sake; aestheticism.

けいしょう【景勝】¶ ～の地 a *scenic* area (≒ spot).

けいしょう【敬称】a term of respect. ¶ あの人たちの名は～をつけて呼びなさい Call them by their appropriate *titles*〔*of respect*〕. ～は略します We omit *honorifics.* / *Honorifics* are omitted.

けいしょう【軽症】a mild case. ¶ ～の小児まひにかかる suffer a *mild* attack of polio. 幸いに彼の小児まひは～ですんだ Luckily his attack of polio *was not so serious.*

けいしょう【軽傷】a slight injury. ¶ 事故で～を負った He *suffered a minor injury* (≒ *was slightly injured*) in the accident.

けいしょう【軽少】¶ ～ですが，お納めください This *is not much,* but I hope you'll accept it.

けいしょう【継承】inheritance; succession. ¶ ジョージ 6 世のあとエリザベス 2 世が王位を～した After George VI Elizabeth II *succeeded to* the throne.

けいしょう【警鐘】an alarm bell. ¶ この事件は世人に～となるだろう This incident should be *a lesson* for us all.

けいじょう【刑場】an execution ground.

けいじょう【形状】form; shape.

けいじょう【計上】¶ 諸経費を～する *add up* all the expenses. その費用を来年度の予算に～する *make an appropriation* for that item in the next〔fiscal〕year's budget.

けいじょう【経常】—歳入 current (≒ ordinary) revenue. —費 current (≒ ordinary) expenditures; (運営費) working expenses; operating costs. —予算 the ordinary (≒ regular) budget.

けいじょうみゃく【頸静脈】〘解剖学〙the jugular〔vein〕.

けいしょく【軽食】a light meal; a snack; (口語) a bite.

けいしん【軽震】a small earthquake.

けいず【系図】genealogy; lineage; pedigree; (表) a family (≒ genealogical) tree. ¶ 山田家の～をさかのぼって調べる trace back Mr. Yamada's *family line*; trace back the pedigree of the Yamadas.

けいすう【計数】¶ 彼は～に明るい He is good at *figures.* 彼の理論は～的にも証明される His theory can also be proved *mathematically.*

けいすう【係数】〔数学〕a coefficient.

け

膨張― a coefficient of expansion.

けいせい【形成】 formation. ¶人格の～ the *formation* of character. 子供の性格の～期 the *formative* years of a child's character. 地殻が～されはじめたのはいつごろか When did the earth's crust begin to *form*? 今こそ人間～に最もたいせつな時期である This is the most crucial period for the *development* of man's personality.

けいせい【形勢】 the situation; the outlook; the prospects. ¶～がよい(悪い) *The situation* is favorable (unfavorable). 天下の～はいかが How are *things* in the world? ～は好転しつつある *Things* are getting better. ～はますます悪化した *Things* went from bad to worse. ～は彼に有利に(不利に)なった The *tide* turned to (against) him.

けいせき【形跡】 (証跡) signs; (痕跡) marks; traces. ¶この近くに犯人が隠れている～がある There is some *evidence* that leads us to suspect that the criminal is in hiding nearby. 原始人の～ *traces* of primitive men.

けいせき【珪石】〘化学〙〘鉱物〙 silica; silex.

けいせき【螢石】〘鉱物〙 fluorite.

けいせん【経線】〘地理〙 meridian; longitude.

けいそ【珪素】〘化学〙 silicon (記号 Si).

けいそう【係争】 dispute; (訴訟) a law suit. ¶その事件はまだ～中だ The [law] suit *is* still *in dispute* (≒ *is* still *disputed*).

けいそう【軽装】 light dress. ¶～で登山へ出かけた I went mountain climbing *casually dressed* (≒ *in a casual dress*).

けいそう【珪藻】〘植物〙 diatom.

―土 diatomaceous soil.

けいぞく【継続】 continuation; continuance. ¶交渉を～する *continue* negotiations. 契約を～する *renew* the contract. 借款の～を依頼した I requested *an extension of* the loan.

けいそつ【軽率】 carelessness; thoughtlessness; rashness. ¶～な行ない a *rash* act. ～なことば an *indiscreet* (≒ *ill-advised*) remark. すぐに結論づけるのは～だ It *is unwise* to jump to conclusions. 彼の～さには驚いた I was surprised at his *indiscretion* (≒ *rashness*).

けいたい【形態】 form; shape; figure.

―学〘生物〙 morphology. ―論〘言語学〙 morphology.

けいたい【携帯】 ¶～する carry; take (≒ bring) (*a thing*) with (*one*). ～用の portable. ～に便利な handy; easy to carry.

―ラジオ a portable radio; a transistor. ―品 *one's* personal effects (≒ belongings). ¶この写真が彼の～品のなかに見つかった This picture was found among *his personal effects*. ―品預かり所 ㊍ a checkroom; ㊏ a cloakroom.

けいだい【境内】 the sacred enclosure (≒ precincts); the grounds.

けいちゅう【傾注】 ¶彼は資力と能力のすべてをこの事業に～した He *devoted* all his money and ability *to* this undertaking.

けいちょう【軽重】 ¶よく事の～を判断してからにしなさい Do it after weighing *the importance of the matter* carefully.

けいちょう【傾聴】 ¶～する listen attentively (*to*); pay attention (*to*). ～に値する意見だ The opinion is worthy of *attention*.

けいちょう【慶弔】 ¶～電報は8番窓口で受け付けている Telegrams of *condolences and congratulations* are accepted at Window 8.

けいちょう【軽佻】 ¶～浮薄なふるまい *frivolous* conducts.

けいてき【警笛】 (汽車などの) a whistle; (自動車などの) a horn; a honk. ¶～鳴らせ(掲示) Sound the *horn*.

けいと【毛糸】 woolen [worsted] yarn. ¶～の手袋 *woolen* gloves.

けいど【経度】 longitude.

けいど【軽度】 ¶～の火傷 *first-degree* burns. ～の神経衰弱 a *slight* nervous breakdown.

けいとう【系統】 a system. ¶～的に配列されている be arranged *systematically*. ことばの～的な研究 a *systematic* study of language. ～立てて物事を考える structure *one's* thinking. ～立てて述べる give a *systematic* account (*of*). 命令～がはっきりしていない The *chain* of command is not clearly defined. この犬は秋田犬の～に属している The dog belongs to the Akita *pedigree*.

けいとう【傾倒】 ¶彼はシェイクスピアに～していた He *was a great admirer* (≒ *adorer*) of Shakespeare.

けいとう【鶏頭】〘植物〙 a cockscomb.

げいとう【芸当】 a performance; a stunt; a feat. ¶綱渡りの～ *a* tight rope *act*. そんな～は彼にはできない That's something he can never do. そんな危ない～はしないほうがいい You shouldn't try anything so risky.

けいどうみゃく【頸動脈】〘解剖学〙 the carotid [artery].

けいにく【鶏肉】 chicken.

げいにく【鯨肉】 whale meat.

げいにん【芸人】 an entertainer; a performer. ¶彼はあれでなかなかの～だ He doesn't seem much, but he is quite *talented*.

げいのう【芸能】 public entertainment.

―界 the entertainment world. ―人 a performer; an entertainer.

けいば【競馬】 horse racing; a horse race. ¶～にかける gamble on (≒ bet on) the horses. ～で金をする lose money at the *races*.

―狂 a horse racing mania. ―場 a race track; the turf.

けいはいしょう【珪肺症】〘医学〙 silicosis.

けいはく【軽薄】 ¶～な態度 *frivolous* manners. 彼は～な人間と思われたくなかった He did not want to be considered *frivolous*.

けいはつ【啓発】 enlightenment. ¶彼と接して～されるところが多かった I *have learned* a great deal by associating with him. その書で大いに～された I *was much enlightened* by the book.

けいばつ【閨閥】 *one's* wife's family's influential groups.

けいばつ【刑罰】a punishment; a penalty.

けいはんざい【軽犯罪】a minor offense (≒ 英 offence); misdemeanor.
—法 the Minor Offense Law.

けいひ【経費】expenditure[s]; expense[s]; a cost; an outlay. ¶ ～を削減する cut down *expenditures*; economize *expenditures*. その企画はばく大な～がかかった The project involved large *expenditures* (≒ *outlays*). それは～がかかりすぎるおそれがある I fear it will *cost too much*.

けいび【軽微】¶ わが方の損害は～である The damage to us *is minor*.

けいび【警備】guard. ¶ 首相官邸の～を強化する tighten the *security guard* at the premier's official residence. 警官がデモの～にあたっている The police *are on the alert for* a possible demonstration.
—員 a guard.

けいひん【景品】a bonus; a free gift. ¶ ～つき売り出し中 a bargain sale with *a premium* (≒ *a prize*).

げいひんかん【迎賓館】a [Government] guest house.

けいふ【系譜】genealogy; *one's* pedigree; a line; a family (≒ genealogical) tree.

けいぶ【頸部】the neck; 〖解剖学〗 cervical region.

けいぶ【警部】a police inspector.
—補 an assistant police inspector.

げいふう【芸風】¶ 彼の芸に独自の～が見られるようになった His acting is beginning to show a personal style.

けいふく【敬服】¶ 彼の冷静な判断力にはみな～した We all *bowed* (≒ *took off our hats*) *to* his cool judgment. / We *thought highly of* his impartial judgment.

けいぶつ【景物】¶ 竹の雪も冬の～のひとつだ The snow on the bamboo is one of the *attractive features* of winter scenery.

けいべつ【軽蔑】contempt. ¶ 彼は大学出でないと～する He *looks down on* anyone who hasn't had a college education. 彼は私を～したような目つきで見る He always gives me a *disdainful* (≒ *contemptuous*; *scornful*) look.

けいべん【軽便】¶ ～さがこの考案品の特徴のひとつだ One of the special features of this device is its *ease in handling*.
—鉄道 a light railway; a narrow-gauged single track railroad.

けいぼ【敬慕】¶ 小学校の恩師を今も～しています I greatly *adore* my grade school teacher even today. / My *respect* for my primary school teacher continues to this day.

けいほう【刑法】criminal law; a penal code. ¶ それは～に問われるだろう It will be charged with *a criminal offense*. ～上の問題点 a controversial issue in *criminal law*.
—学者 a criminologist.

けいほう【警報】an alarm; a warning.
津波— a *tsunami* (≒ tidal wave) warning.
暴風— a storm (≒ gale) warning.

けいぼう【警棒】a [policeman's] club; a billy [club]; 英 a truncheon.

けいみょう【軽妙】¶ ～な文体 a *light and witty* (≒ *easy*) style. ～なしゃれを言う make *wisecracks*; tell *witty* jokes.

けいむしょ【刑務所】a prison; a jail; 英 a gaol; 米 a penitentiary. ¶ ～に入れられる be sent to *prison*. ～から出てくる be released from *prison*.

げいめい【芸名】a professional name; (映画俳優の) a screen name; (舞台俳優の) a stage name.

けいもう【啓蒙】enlightenment. ¶ この本には大いに～された I *was* much *enlightened* by this book. / I *learned* a great deal *from* this book.
—運動 the Enlightenment; a campaign for enlightenment. —思潮 philosophy of enlightenment.

けいやく【契約】a contract. ¶ その家を買う～に署名した I signed *a contract* to buy the house. 土地の代金を現金で支払う～をした I *contracted* to pay cash for the land. 彼はその～を破棄した(解除した) He broke the *contract*. きみはその～を履行しなければならぬ You must fulfill the *contract*. その会社と大豆を1トン買う～を結んだ I *contracted* (≒ *made a contract*) with the company to buy a ton of soybeans. 彼は～の履行を主張している He insists upon the fulfillment of the *contract*. 彼は～の更新を望んでいる He wants to have his *contract* renewed. 彼は3年～で月約10万円で雇われた He was engaged at a monthly salary of a hundred thousand yen on *a* three-year *contract*. 彼はある放送会社とテレビ出演～を結んだ He signed *a* TV *contract* with a broadcasting company. 彼女はある映画会社と～している She *is under contract to* some motion picture company.
—違反 [a] breach of contract. —者 a contractor. —書 a written contract. ¶ 彼らは互いに～書を取り交わした They exchanged *written contracts* with each other. 個人— ¶ 個人～で by private *contract*. 長期— ¶ 長期～で by a long-term *contract*. 社会— a soical contract.

けいゆ【経由】¶ シベリア～でヨーロッパに行ったものだ We used to go to Europe *via* Siberia. 新宿～で東京駅に行くのが便利でしょう It will be convenient for you to go to Tokyo Station *by way of* Shinjuku.

けいゆ【軽油】light oil; gasoline; gas.

げいゆ【鯨油】whale oil.

けいよう【形容】description; metaphor.
¶ この美しい山の景色を～することばがない I can find no word to *describe* the beauty of this mountain.
—詞 an adjective; a modifier.

けいよう【掲揚】¶ 国旗を～する *hoist* a nation-

al flag. 「patrol.
けいら【警邏】¶～中の巡査 a policeman *on*
けいらん【鶏卵】an egg; a hen's egg.
けいり【経理】management; administration.
けいりし【計理士】a public accountant.
けいりゃく【計略】a trick. ¶～にかかって破滅する *be entrapped to* destruction. 彼を～にかけてうんと言わせる *entrap* him *into* consenting. 彼は自分の目的を達するために～を用いた He resorted to *tricks* to gain his end. ～に富む男 a man full of *craft*. 「(*at*).
けいりゅう【係留】mooring. ¶～する moor
—所 moorings (複数形). —気球 a captive balloon.
けいりゅう【渓流】a mountain stream (≒ torrent).
けいりょう【計量】¶～する measure; weigh.
—器 a meter.
けいりょう【軽量】lightweight.
—級 the lightweight class. —級選手 a lightweight.
けいりん【競輪】a bicycle (≒ cycle) race.
—場 a bicycle race track. —選手 a cycle racer; a professional bicycle racer.
けいるい【係累】encumbrances; dependents. ¶～のある(ない)人 a man with (without) *dependents*. 彼は～が多い He has *a* large *family*. / He has many *dependents* on him.
けいれい【敬礼】salutation. ¶～! Salute! 将校に(国旗に)～をする *salute* an officer (a national flag).
けいれき【経歴】a career; *one's* background. ¶～がよい(悪い) have *a* good (bad) *career* (≒ *record*). 彼は外交官としてりっぱな～を持っている He has *a* good *career* as a diplomat. 彼は手短に自分の～を話した He briefly outlined his *career*. 彼の～はどんなものか What is his *background*?
けいれつ【系列】a series. ¶～化する serialize. この会社はわが社の～だ This company is a subsidiary of our company.
—会社(子会社) a subsidiary [company].
—店 a chain store.
けいれん【痙攣】convulsions; a spasm; cramp. ¶～を起こす fall into *a fit of convulsion*. 足が～する *be convulsed* in the leg. ～がおさまった The *spasm* passed off. 彼は水泳中足の筋肉が～を起こした He was seized with *a cramp* in the leg while swimming.
けいろ【毛色】¶彼は～の変わった人間だ He is a *queer* (≒ an *eccentric*) person.
けいろ【径路・経路】a course; a route. ¶同じ～をたどる follow the same *course*. この旅行でたどった～ the *route* followed in the present journey. 別な～で送る send (*a thing*) via different *route*. ヨーロッパへ最も早く行ける～ the quickest *route* to Europe. 帰りの～ *a* homeward *route*.
感染— the route of infection. 入手— means of acquisition. 「aged.
けいろう【敬老】¶～の日 a day to respect the
—会 a respect-for-the aged meeting.
ケーキ a cake (一般にケーキというときには不可算名詞として扱い, 具体的に1個, 2個と数える場合には可算名詞).
ゲージ a gauge.
ケース a case. ¶こういう～は今までなかった We haven't had such *a case*. ひとつの具体的な～を考えてみよう Let us take *a* definite *example*.
シガレット— a cigarette case.
ゲートル gaiters. ¶～をつけて歩く walk with *gaitered* legs. ～をつける put *gaiters* on; wear *gaiters*.
ケープ a cape.
ケーブル a cable.
—カー a cable car. —鉄道 a cable railway.
海底— a submarine cable.
ゲーム a game. ¶～をしよう Let's play *a game*. ジャイアンツは3～差で首位に立った The Giants led the other teams by three *games*.
けおと・す【蹴落とす】¶彼を川に～す *kick* him into a river. 人を～して自分の立身出世をはかる try to win success *at the sacrifice* (≒ *at the expense*) *of* others.
けおり【毛織り・毛織】woolen (≒ 英 woollen).
—物 woolen fabrics. —物商人 a woolen draper. —物工場 a wool mill.
けが【怪我】a hurt; an injury; (ナイフ・弾丸などによるけが) a wound. ¶頭部の～ *an injury to* the head. 彼は頭にひどい～をした He *was* seriously *wounded in* the head. 交通事故で～をした I *got hurt* (≒ *was hurt*) in a traffic accident. ～をしないよう注意しなさい Be careful not to *hurt yourself*. 彼は～はなにもしなかった He received no *hurt* whatever.
—人 an injured person; (総称) the injured.
げか【外科】surgery. 「tion.
—医 a surgeon. —手術 a surgical opera-
げかい【下界】this world; the lower world. ¶われわれは山頂から～をながめた We looked down upon the *lowlands* from the mountain top.
けが・す【汚す】¶家の名を～す *bring disgrace on one's* family. 末席を～す have the honor of being present (*at*).
けがらわし・い【汚らわしい】¶～い話 a *filthy* (≒ *dirty*) talk. 見るも～い The very sight *makes me sick*.
けがれ【汚れ】(不浄) pollution; stain; uncleanliness; (汚点) a stain; a blot. ¶～ない stainless; clear. 家門の～ *a stain upon one's* family. ～ない身体 a *pure* (≒ *unsoiled*) body.
けが・れる【汚れる】get dirty; be stained; be polluted. ¶～れた金 *ill-gotten* money. ～れた心 an *impure* (≒ *degraded*) heart.
けがわ【毛皮】fur. ¶～のついたコート a *fur* lined coat.
げき【劇】a drama; a play. ¶～を書く write *a play*. ～を上演する stage *a drama*.
—中— a play within a play.

げき【檄】a declaration ; a manifesto. ¶ われわれは～を飛ばして彼のための後援会を作った We issued *a written appeal* and formed a society for the support of him.

げきえいが【劇映画】a film drama ; a movie.

げきえつ【激越】¶ ～な口調で in a *fiery* (≒ *vehement*) tone.

げきか【劇化】dramatization. ¶ 小説を～する *dramatize* a novel.

げきか【激化】¶ 戦闘はなお～しつつあり The battle *is becoming* still *fiercer*.

げきげん【激減】¶ 農村の人口が～している The population of rural districts *is decreasing sharply*.

げきさく【劇作】¶ ～する write a play.
—家 a playwright ; a dramatist.

げきしょう【激賞】eulogy ; a high praise.
¶ ～する praise highly. その小説は発表されるやいなや多くの批評家から～された As soon as the novel was made public, it won many critics' *high praises*.

げきじょう【劇場】a theater ; a playhouse.

げきじょう【激情】passion ; a violent emotion. ¶ ～にかられるままに彼は大罪を犯してしまった Carried away by *a fit of passion* he committed a great crime.

げきしょく【激職】a busy office. ¶ ～につく undertake *an arduous task*.

げきしん【激震】a severe earthquake (≒ shock).

げき・する【激する】¶ 販売競争はますます～しつつある The sales war *is getting fiercer* these days. 彼は～しやすい性質だ He has a very *excitable* character. / He easily *gets excited* by nature.

げきせん【激戦】a fierce battle ; a severe fight. ¶ 東京１区は有力候補が多くかなりの～だった Because there were many strong candidates in the first Tokyo constituency, they had *a close race*.
—地 a hard-fought field ; (選挙) a closely contested constituency.

げきぞう【激増】a sudden increase. ¶ 日本は人口が～した Japan *has* suddenly *shown a marked increase in* her population. 注文が～しててんてこ舞いをした *A sudden rush of* orders kept us working hard.

げきたい【撃退】¶ 敵を～する *drive away* an enemy. 彼らは大損害を受けて～された They *were driven back* with great losses.

げきだん【劇団】a troupe ; a dramatic company. ¶ 市川団十郎～ Ichikawa Danjuro and his *troupe*.
—員 a member of a dramatic company.

げきだん【劇壇】¶ ～に出る go (≒ come) on *the stage*. ～を去る go off *the stage*. フランス～を飾る名優のひとり one of the stars of the French *stage*.

げきちん【撃沈】¶ ～する sink (a ship).

げきつい【撃墜】¶ ～する shoot down (a plane).

げきつう【激痛】an acute pain. ¶ 頭に～を感ずる feel *a violent pain* in the head. ～をじっと忍ぶ endure *one's severe pain* stoically.

げきてき【劇的】¶ ～な効果 a *dramatic* effect. ふたりは～な再会をした The two met again *in a most pathetic way*. / The two met again *most dramatically*.

げきど【激怒】〔wild〕rage ; violent anger. ¶ 彼は放蕩(ほうとう)息子に～した He *raged against* (≒ *at*) his prodigal son.

げきどう【激動】excitement. ¶ 全世界に～が広がった *Immense excitement* prevailed throughout the world.

げきどく【劇毒】a deadly poison.

げきとつ【激突】¶ 学生と警察との間に～が起こった *A violent clash* took place between the students and the police. 車は列車に～した The car *crashed* into the train.

げきは【撃破】¶ 敵を～する *put* the enemy *to rout* ; *destroy* the enemy.

げきひょう【劇評】dramatic criticism.
—家 a dramatic critic.

げきへん【激変】¶ 気候の～ *a sudden change* of weather. ～する change suddenly (≒ violently).

げきむ【激務】press of business. ¶ ～につく undertake *a difficult task*. ～で倒れる break down through *overwork*.

げきめつ【撃滅】destruction ; annihilation. ¶ 敵を～する *destroy* (≒ *annihilate*) the enemy.

げきやく【劇薬】a powerful drug ; a deadly poison.

けぎらい【毛嫌い】¶ ～する hate ; be prejudiced against ; have a prejudice against.

げきりゅう【激流】a torrent ; a swift current. ¶ ～にのまれる be swept away by *a rapid stream* (≒ *a torrent*).

げきりん【逆鱗】¶ 彼の不用意な一言が社長の～に触れた His careless word incurred the manager's *displeasure*.

げきれい【激励】encouragement. ¶ ～する encourage ; cheer up ; stimulate.

げきれつ【激烈】¶ ～な競争 *fierce* competition. ～なことば *violent* language.

げきろう【激浪】¶ 船は～に翻弄(ほんろう)された The ship was tossed about by *the huge waves*.

げきろん【激論】a heated argument. ¶ その問題についてわれわれは～をした We *had a hot discussion over* the matter. ～が行なわれていた There was *a heated discussion* going on.

けげん【怪訝】¶ ～そうな顔で with a *suspicious* look. その知らせを聞くと彼は～そうな顔をした He *looked dubious* (≒ *looked doubtful*) at hearing the news.

げこ【下戸】a poor drinker ; a nondrinker. ¶ 彼は～だ He *does not drink*. / He *is temperate* (≒ *is abstemious*).

げこう【下校】¶ ～する come home from school.

げこくじょう【下克上】¶ それが～というものだ That's an instance of the juniors dominating the seniors.

けさ【今朝】this morning.

けさ【袈裟】a surplice.

け

げざい【下剤】a laxative.
げざん【下山】¶～する descend (≒ go down) a mountain.
けし【芥子】〘植物〙a poppy.
げし【夏至】the summer solstice; the midsummer.
けしいん【消印】a postmark. ¶ニューヨークの～のある手紙 a letter *postmarked from* New York.
けしか･ける【嗾ける】¶犬を～けて彼を追わせた I *set* the dog *at* him. 彼は労働者を～けてストライキをさせた He *instigated* the workers *to* go out on strike. 彼は彼らを～けて暴動を起こさせた He *incited* them *to* a riot.
けしからぬ【怪しからぬ】¶～やつ a *shameless* fellow. ～ふるまいをする behave *improperly* toward (*a person*). 彼の態度は～ His attitude *is unpardonable*.
けしき【気色】¶～ばむ grow excited; be stirred. 彼は怒る～も見せなかった He showed no *sign* of anger.
けしき【景色】a scene; a view; (一地方全体の風景) scenery. ¶海辺の～ coast *scenery*. ～のよい場所 a *scenic* spot. 丘の上からの～は私の記憶に鮮やかに焼きついている The *view* from the hilltop is strongly impressed on my memory.
げじげじ【蚰蜒】〘虫類〙a flat millipede; a centipede; (きらわれ者) a skunk. ¶彼は～のようにきらわれている He is hated *like a viper*.
けしゴム【消しゴム】an eraser; a 〔pencil〕rubber. ¶～で文字を消す rub out a letter with *an eraser*. エンピツ書きを～で消す erase pencil marks with *a pencil rubber*.
けしずみ【消し炭】cinders.
けしつぶ【芥子粒】a poppy seed. ¶～くらいの大きさのダイヤモンド a diamond *as small as a pin's head*.
けしと･ぶ【消し飛ぶ】¶爆発で工場は跡形もなく～んだ The factory *was* completely *blown off* by the explosion. 彼の元気な顔を見て心配は～んだ My anxiety suddenly *disappeared* (≒ *scattered*) on seeing his cheerful face. 汚職事件であの会社の信用は～んでしまった The corruption case *ruined* the credit of that company.
けしと･める【消し止める】¶火事は消防隊によって～められた The fire *was put out* by the fire brigade.
けじめ difference; distinction. ¶AとBの間になんらかの～をつけなければならない Some *line* must *be drawn between* A *and* B. 彼は公私の～がつかない男だ He does not know how to *draw the line between* public *and* private life.
げしゃ【下車】¶終点で～する *get off the train* at the terminal.
げしゅく【下宿】¶彼は私の家に～している He *is boarding at* my house. 私はおじのところに～している I *am boarding with* my uncle.
—代 the lodging fee. —人(食事つきの) a boarder; (食事なしの) 米 a roomer; 英 a lodger. —屋(食事つきの) a boarding house; (食事なしの) 米 a rooming house; 英 a lodging house. 素人— a private boarding house.
げしゅにん【下手人】a murderer. ¶少女殺しの～はだれか Who *murdered* (≒ *killed*) the girl?
げじゅん【下旬】the latter part of the month. ¶9月～に toward *the end of* September.
けしょう【化粧】toilet; dressing; make-up. ¶～する make up; put *make-up* on. 念入りな～をする make *an* elaborate *toilet*. 彼女は～をしすぎる She uses too much *make-up*. 彼女は～をすると見違えるようにきれいになる When she *puts make-up on*, she becomes so beautiful that one may not recognize her.
—台 a toilet table. —代 beauty expenses. —道具 a toilet set. 厚(薄)— heavy (light) make-up.
けしん【化身】an incarnation. ¶彼は悪の～だ He is the *incarnation* of a devil. / He is an *incarnate* devil.
け･す【消す】**1**〘燈火を〙¶明かりを～す *put out* the light.
寝る前に電気を～しなさい *Switch off* the light before going to bed.
2〘火を〙¶彼はたばこの火を踏み～して立ち上がった He rose to his feet, *stamping* a cigarette *out*.
その火事を～すのに化学消防車が出動した The chemical fire engine was sent to *put out* (≒ *extinguish*) the fire.
出かける前にガスの火を～し忘れた I forgot to *turn off* the gas before leaving home.
3〘字・痕跡(こんせき)・汚点などを〙¶黒板の字を～す *wipe out* (≒ *erase*) the words on a blackboard.
消しゴムでインクのしみを～そうとしたが～せなかった I tried to *erase* an ink spot, but in vain.
まちがった字は線を2本引いて～しなさい *Cross out* the wrong word with two lines.
彼の政策はその国の歴史に～すことのできない汚点を残した His policy left an *unremovable* stain on the nation's history.
4〘姿を〙¶彼女はやみの中に姿を～した She *disappeared* in the darkness.
それ以来彼は町から姿を～した He *disappeared* from the town since then.
5〘音・におい・毒などを〙¶この血清はマムシの毒を～す This serum *neutralizes* the poison of an adder.
口臭を～すいい薬がある There is a good medicine to *remove* foul breath.
これは冷蔵庫のいやなにおいを～す This is effective to *take away* the nasty smell in the icebox.
自動車のマフラーは音を～す装置だ The muffler of the car is a device for *deadening* sound.
げすい【下水】sewage; a drain. ¶～を作る(詰まらせる; 掃除する) layout (block; clean) *a drain*. ～がつかえた The *drain* is stopped up.

—管 a sewer pipe. —工事 drainage works. —設備 sewage system. ¶この町の～設備はよい The city has good *sewers.* —道 a drain.

ゲスト a guest.

けず·る【削る】¶鉛筆を～る *sharpen* a pencil. 費用を～らなければなるまい We will have to *cut down* our expenses. そのページに収まるように記事を～った I *cut down* the article to make it fit the page. われわれは彼の名前をリストから～った We *have crossed* (≒ *struck*) *off* his name *from* the list.

げせん【下船】¶～する get off (≒ leave) a ship.

げそく【下足】(集合的にくつ·サンダルなど) footgear.

—札 a check for footgear. —番 ¶～番に～を預けた We left our *footgear* with the *caretaker* 〔*of footgear*〕.

けた【桁】figure. ¶2～の数字 double (≒ two) *figures.* 4～の数字(金額) a number (sum) of four *figures.*

げた【下駄】〔wooden〕clogs. ¶～をはく(脱ぐ) put on (take off) *clogs.* 彼に～を預けた(すべてをまかせた) I *left everything to* him. / I *put myself in* his *hands.*

けだか·い【気高い】¶彼にはどことなく～いところがある There is something *noble* about him.

けだし【蓋し】(おそらく) maybe ; probably ; (結局) after all ; in the long run.

けたたまし·い ¶～い女の悲鳴が聞こえた I heard the *piercing* cry of a woman. ～く消防車のサイレンが鳴った The siren of the fire engine went off *noisily.*

けたちがい【桁違い】¶この割り算の答えは～だ There is *a mistake of units* in the answer of this division. 彼の家はうちとは～に大きい His house is *much* bigger than mine.

けた·てる【蹴立てる】¶船は波を～てて進んだ The ship tore ahead through the waves.

げたばこ【下駄箱】a clog cabinet ; a boot cupboard.

けたはずれ【桁外れ】¶～の秀才 an *extraordinarily* bright person.

けだもの【獣】a beast ; a brute. ¶～のような男だ He is *a beast* of a man. / He is *a brute.*

けだる·い【気怠い】¶日光浴の快い～さ the delicious *languor* of a sun bath. 睡眠不足でなんとなく～い Somehow I *feel listless* from lack of sleep.

げだん【下段】(寝台の) the lower berth. ¶刀を～に構える hold *one's* sword low.

けち stinginess ; niggardliness. ¶～な人 a *stingy* (≒ *mean*) fellow. ～な家(そまつな) a *humble* (≒ *shabby*) house. ～な根性(いやしい) a *mean* spirit. ～な考え a *narrow-minded* idea. 彼はよく人に～をつける人だ He *is* always *finding fault with* another. 手始めから彼には～がついた He had a *bad* beginning. その計画にはやがて～がついた The plan met with *an unlucky accident* soon.

けちくさ·い【けち臭い】¶～いひと a *stingy* (≒ *mean*) fellow. ～い考え a *narrow-minded* idea. ～い手当て a *niggardly* allowance. 金には～くないつもりだ I *am* not *mean with* money.

けちけち ¶～した stingy ; niggardly.

ケチャップ ketchup ; catchup ; catsup.

けちら·す【蹴散らす】¶敵を～す *rout* the enemy ; *put* the enemy *to rout.*

けちんぼう【吝嗇坊】a miser ; a niggard ; a tightfisted fellow.

けつ【決】a decision. ¶全員で賛否の～をとった We *put* the matter *to the vote* of all present. 審査員はその問題について～をとった The judges *took a vote on* the question.

けつあつ【血圧】blood pressure. ¶～が高い(低い) I have high (low) *blood pressure.* ～を計ってもらった I had my *blood pressure* measured. ～は120です My *blood pressure* is 120.

—計 a tonometer. 高— high blood pressure ; hypertension. 低— low blood pressure ; hypotension.

けつい【決意】determination. ¶彼は～を固めた He strengthened his *determination.* / He *was determined.* / He *decided.* ～を新たにする make *a* fresh *resolve.*

けついん【欠員】a vacancy ; a vacant position. ¶～を補う fill 〔up〕 *a vacancy.*

けつえき【血液】blood. ¶私の～はO型だ I have Type O *blood.*

—型 a blood type. —銀行 a blood bank.

けつえん【血縁】blood relation ; the ties of blood.

—関係 blood relationship.

けっか【結果】〔a〕result ; 〔an〕effect. ¶原因と～ cause and *effect.* ことしはよい～を期待できない We can't expect *a* good *result* this year. 彼の努力はまずい～になった His efforts *resulted* badly. 試験の～はあす発表される The examination *results* will be published tomorrow. 実験の～は満足すべきものだった The *results* of the experiment were satisfactory. その～彼女は病気になった The *result* was that she got ill. 彼の成功は努力の～だ His success is the *product* of hard work.

けっかい【決壊】¶大雨で堤防が数か所～した The bank *broke down* in several places owing to the heavy rain.

けっかく【結核】consumption ; tuberculosis. ¶彼は～にかかった He developed *consumption.* 彼は～だ He has *consumption.* / He suffers from *consumption.* 彼は過労で～になった He overworked himself into *consumption.*

—患者 a consumptive (≒ tuberculosis) patient. —療養所 a sanatorium for tuberculous people.

げつがく【月額】the monthly sum. ¶この仕事に～4万円の手当は悪くない *A monthly allowance* (≒ *pay*) of forty thousand yen for this job is not bad.

けっかん【欠陥】a defect ; a fault. ¶～のある defective. 人格上の～ *a defect* in character. 推論上の～ *a flaw* in *one's* reasoning. 精神

的に～のある人 a person mentally *deficient*. 彼はこの計画の～を指摘した He pointed out the *defects* of this plan.

―車 a defective car.

けっかん【血管】a blood vessel; (俗語) a vein. 毛細― a capillary vessel.

げっかん【月間】¶ 交通安全～ Traffic Safety *Month*. ～50万部の売り上げがある We sell five hundred thousand copies *a month*.

げっかん【月刊】monthly publication.

―誌 a monthly 〔magazine〕.

けっき【血気】¶ ～盛んな若者 a young man *in full vigor*; a *hot blooded* youth.

けっき【決起】¶ 労働者は～してゼネストを行なった The laborers *roused themselves* up to a general strike.

―大会 a rally.

けつぎ【決議】a resolution; a decision. ¶ 議会の～によりその法案は可決された Through the *decision* of the Diet, the bill was passed. 組合大会でストライキの決行を～した We *decided* to go on strike at the general meeting of the Union.

―案 a resolution. ¶ ～案を採択する (提出する; 否決する) adopt (introduce; vote down) *a resolution*.

けっきゅう【血球】blood corpuscles. 赤― red blood corpuscles. 白― white blood corpuscles.

げっきゅう【月給】a monthly salary (≒ pay); (聖職者などの) a monthly stipend. ¶ かなりの～をとる get (≒ draw) *a* good *salary*.

―日 the payday. ―取り a salaried man.

けっきょ【穴居】cave dwelling.

―時代 the cave age. ―人 a cave dweller.

けっきょく【結局】finally; after all; eventually. ¶ ～彼は当代一番の大詩人だ *In conclusion*, he is the greatest poet of the age. 彼は一晩じゅうやってみたが～失敗した He tried all night but failed *after all*. ～損にはならないと思う I trust that, *in the long run*, I shall not be a loser. ～次のような結果になった *In the last analysis* it gave the following result. ～彼らは安全な場所に着いた *In the end* they reached a safe place.

けっきん【欠勤】absence 〔from *one's* duties; from *one's* office〕. ¶ 彼はやむをえず～した He was obliged to *be absent from his office*. 彼は～がちだ He is not regular in his attendance.

―者 an absentee. ―届 a notice of absence. ¶ ～届を出す report *one's absence*. 無断― absence without leave.

げっけい【月経】menstruation; menses (ふつう複数形をとる); periods. ¶ ～不順 *menstrual* irregularity.

げっけいかん【月桂冠】laurels; a laurel crown. ¶ ～を得る win *laurels*.

げっけいじゅ【月桂樹】〔植物〕a laurel.

けっけいもじ【楔形文字】a cuneiform character.

けっこう【欠航】¶ 台風のため次の函館行き連絡船は～する The next ferryboat for Hakodate will *be cancelled* because of the storm.

けっこう【血行】blood circulation. ¶ ふろに入ると～がよくなる Taking a bath will improve our *blood circulation*.

けっこう【決行】¶ ゼネストを～する *call* a general strike. 雨天でも明日のマラソン大会は～する We will *hold* a marathon race tomorrow even if it rains. スト～中である be on strike.

けっこう【結構】**1** 〘りっぱ〙 very well. ¶ ～なお品を頂きありがとうございます Many thanks for your *nice* present.

～なお召しものですね What a *wonderful* suit.

～なご身分だね Yours is really an *enviable* position.

スポーツも～だが勉強もたいせつだ Having an interest in sports is *all right*, but you must not neglect your studies.

日光を見ないで～というな (諺) *See Naples and then die.*

2 〘十分に〙 well enough; quite. ¶ これで～りっぱに見える This looks *fairly* imposing.

この酒～いける This *sake* tastes *fairly* good.

へただなんて言ったくせに～やるじゃないか Though you say you are unskillful, I'm surprised how good you are at it.

今から行っても～まにあう There is still time *enough*.

彼の英会話は～うまい He is a *pretty good* speaker of English.

もう1杯いかが．いや，もう～です How about another glass? *No, thank you.*

鉛筆で～です．ちょっと貸してください A pencil *will do*. Lend me one, please.

じょうぶならどこの製品でも～ Any company's product *will do*, if it is durable.

いくら差し上げましょうか．1,000円で～です How much do you want? A thousand yen *will do*.

そんなにご心配していただかなくて～です．ひとりで帰れます You *need not* be worried so much. I can go home by myself.

けつごう【結合】〔a〕union; 〔a〕combination. ¶ AとBを～させる combine A with B.

げっこう【月光】moonlight. ¶ ～を浴びて in the *moonlight*.

げっこう【激高・激昂】(憤激) rage; fury; (興奮) excitement. ¶ ～して with *agitation*. ～した群衆は自動車に火をつけた The *agitated* mob set fire to the cars.

けっこん【結婚】**1** marriage. ¶ ～する marry (*someone*); get married to (*someone*).

～おめでとう,お幸せで Congratulations on your *wedding*! I wish you happiness.

娘の～の話がやっとまとまった My daughter's *marriage* has just been arranged.

彼女の～のお祝いになにを贈ろうか What shall I present her as *a wedding gift*?

彼は彼女に～の約束をした覚えはないと言い張った He denied having promised to *marry* her.

彼は彼女に～を申し込んだが断わられた He *proposed to* her, but she refused him.

～の日どりはもう決めましたか Have you fixed the date for your *wedding ceremony*?
彼女は２度めの～でやっと幸せをつかんだ She secured true happiness in life by her second *marriage*.
彼は彼女と来月～するそうだ He will *be married to* her next month, I hear.
姉は22で～した My sister *was married* at the age of twenty-two.
私どもは～して10年になります We *have been married* for ten years.
彼女は～してふたり子どもがいる She *got married* and is a mother of two.
父は娘を知人の息子と～させたく思った Her father wanted her to *marry* his friend's son.
彼はまだ～していない He *is* still *single*.
2 〖合成語〗 ¶ ふたりの～ひろう宴はホテルたちばなで盛大に行なわれた They held *a* gorgeous *wedding reception* at Hotel Tachibana.
ふたりは幸福な～生活を送っている They are leading *a* happy *married life*.
きょうは私たちの～記念日です Today is our *wedding anniversary*.
～式当日に区役所に～届をしなさい You must have your *marriage* registered at the ward office on the very day of your *wedding*.
ふたりは教会できのう～式を挙げた They held their *wedding ceremony* at church yesterday.
もうきみもそろそろ～適齢期だ You have already reached the *marriageable age*.
ぼくの息子はアメリカ人と国際～をした My son took an American girl in *an* international *marriage*.

けっこん【血痕】 a bloodstain. ¶ ～のついた bloodstained ; bloody. ～をたどる trace *blood drops*.

けっさい【決済】 settlement. ¶ 貿易収支はドルで～している We *settle* the payments of trade in dollars.

けっさい【決裁】 approval ; decision. ¶ ～する approve ; decide (*on*). ¶ この計画についてあなたの～を仰ぎます I submit this plan for your *approval*.

けっさく【傑作】 a masterpiece. ¶ これは安井画伯一代の～だ This is the artist Yasui's *best work* in his life. 彼の旅行談はまったく～だ The story of his trip *is* quite *interesting*.

けっさん【決算】 settlement 〔of accounts〕. ¶ ～する settle an account. 昨年度収支の～報告をした I rendered *an account* of the last year's balance.
—期 a term for settlements of accounts.

げっさん【月産】 a monthly production. ¶ この工場では自動車を～１万台造っている The factory has *a monthly output* of ten thousand cars.

けっし【決死】 ¶ ～の覚悟で at the risk of *one's* life. ～の覚悟でわが身を守る defend *oneself desperately*; defend *oneself regardless of danger* (≒ *with the courage of despair*).

けっしきそ【血色素】 hemoglobin.

けつじつ【結実】 fruition. ¶ 多年の研究の～ the *fruit* (≒ *result*) of *one's* years of study. 彼の長年の研究がついに～した His lifelong study finally *bore fruit*.
—期 the fruiting season.

けっして【決して】 ¶ 彼は～早起きしない He *never* gets up early. 初任給９万なら～悪くない A starting salary of ninety thousand yen is *by no means* bad.

けっしゃ【結社】 an association ; a society. ¶ ～の自由 freedom of association.
秘密— a secret society.

げっしゃ【月謝】 a monthly fee ; (学校の) a monthly school fee. ¶ この学校の～は10,000円だ The *school fee* is ten thousand yen a month.

けっしゅう【結集】 concentration. ¶ 全国の労働者の力が～された They *concentrated* the force of all the laborers in the country.

げっしゅう【月収】 a monthly income.

けっしゅつ【傑出】 ¶ ～した人物 a *prominent* figure. 彼は実業家では～している He *is outstanding* (≒ *is prominent*) among businessmen.

けつじょ【欠如】 lack. ¶ 彼は常識がひどく～している He *is* badly *wanting in* common sense. 彼の失敗の原因は経験の～であった His failure was due to *lack* of experience.

けっしょう【決勝】 **—戦** the final match (≒ game ; contest). **—点** the goal.

けっしょう【結晶】 (作用) crystallization ; (結晶体) a crystal. ¶ 努力の～ *the fruit* of *one's* industry.

けっしょう【血漿】 〔blood〕 plasma.

けつじょう【欠場】 ¶ 彼はけがのため10日間～した He *was absent* for ten days *from* the match because of his injury.

けっしょうばん【血小板】 a blood platelet.

けっしょく【欠食】 **—児童** an undernourished schoolchild.

けっしょく【血色】 complexion ; color of the face. ¶ 子どもたちは全員～がよい All the children *look well*.

げっしょく【月食】 a lunar eclipse ; an eclipse of the moon.
皆既— a total eclipse. 部分— a partial eclipse.

けっしん【決心】 resolution ; determination. ¶ 堅い～を示す show *a fixed determination* (*to*). 堅く～する take *a* firm *resolution*. ～を新たにする make *a fresh determination*. 彼は外国へ行く～をした He *made up his mind* to go abroad. 彼は～を変えなかった He did not change his *resolve*. 家族のことを考えると～が鈍った The thought of my family shook my *resolution*.

けっしん【結審】 the conclusion of an examination.

けっ·する【決する】 ¶ 態度を～する *define one's* attitude. 勝負を～する *decide* a contest. 意を～する make up *one's* mind.

けっせい【血清】 〔blood〕 serum. ¶ 毒ヘビにか

け

まれた人には一刻も早く～を注射しなければいけない You must give a *serum* injection to a person bitten by a poisonous snake.

けっせい【結成】formation; organization. ¶南極探検隊を～する *organize* an expedition to the South Pole.

けつぜい【血税】tax paid by the sweat of *one's* brow.

けっせき【欠席】absence. ¶私はこの学校に入学してから1日も～していない I *have* not *missed* a day since I entered this school. 彼はよく学校を～する He *is* often *absent from* school. ―裁判 judgment by default. ―届 a report of absence. 無断― absence without notice (≒ leave). 無断―者 an absentee without leave.

けっせき【結石】〖医学〗a stone; a calculus. じん臓― a kidney stone.

けっせん【決戦】¶天下分け目の～ a decisive battle. 敵に～をいどむ wage *a decisive battle* with the enemy.

けつぜん【決然】¶～と resolutely; firmly.

けっせんとうひょう【決選投票】a final vote (≒ election).

けっそう【血相】¶彼は～を変えて私の部屋に飛び込んできた He rushed into my room *with a desperate look* (≒ *with a desperate countenance*).

けっそく【結束】¶われわれは～して難局に当たらねばならない We must *bind ourselves together* (≒ *be united*) *closely to* deal with the difficult situation.

けつぞく【血族】blood relationship; blood ties. ―結婚 a consanguineous marriage.

げっそり ¶彼女はほおが～こけた Her cheeks *have sunk remarkably.* 彼は病気のため～やせた He *grew very thin* because of illness.

けっそん【欠損】a loss; a deficit. ¶その会社と取引をして10万円の～となった Our transaction with the company resulted in *a loss* of 100,000 yen. われわれはどうにかして～を補う必要がある We must make up for the *deficit* in some way or other. 会社は～続きだ The company suffered a succession of *losses.*

けったく【結託】conspiracy. ¶その商人はどろぼうと～して盗品故売を行なった The merchant dealt in stolen goods *in conspiracy with* a robber.

けったん【血痰】blood phlegm (発音は [flem]).

けつだん【決断】determination; [a] resolution. ¶今こそこの件について～を下すべきときだ Now is the time to reach *a definite decision* about this matter. 彼には～力がある He is quick in *decision.*

けっちゃく【決着】¶われわれはその問題の～をつけなければならない We have to *get* the dispute *settled up.* 係争中のその問題は～をつけるのが難しい The case is hard to *settle.*

けっちん【血沈】precipitation of blood. ¶～を調べる examine the *precipitation of one's blood.*

ゲッツー a double play. ¶ふたりの走者が～を食らった Two runners *were put out at a time* (≒ *were victims of a double play*).

けってい【決定】determination; conclusion; decision. ¶行動方針を～するべき時期だ It is already time we *determined* our course of action. きみももう今後の方針を～する年になった You are old enough to *decide on* your future course. 彼は何事によらず独断的な～をする He always makes *an* arbitrary *decision* in everything. この事件は彼の運命を～した The incident *decided* his fate. ～はきみしだいだ The *decision* is up to you. きみの～は賢明だ You have made *a* wise *decision.* 彼の失敗は～的となった His failure has become *decisive.* 彼は～的な誤りをおかした He has made a *fatal* mistake.
―版 a definitive edition.

けってん【欠点】a fault; a defect. ¶～のない人は少ない Few people are free from *faults.* 彼は人の～ばかり捜している He *is* always *finding fault with* others. ～を直す correct *one's fault.* ～のない作品 a *flawless* work. 彼女の～にもかかわらず彼は彼女が好きだった He loved her with all her *faults.* 自分の～を認めます I acknowledge my *fault.*

けっとう【血統】lineage; stock. ¶～がよい come of *a* good *stock.* 悪い遺伝のある～ *a* tainted *stock.* 彼は外国人の～をひいている He is of alien *blood.* 彼の～は家康までさかのぼることができる We can trace his *descent* (≒ *line*) back to Ieyasu. ～は争えないものだ (諺) *Blood will tell.*
―書 (純血家畜の) a pedigree. ¶～書付きのコリー a *pedigreed* collie.

けっとう【決闘】a duel. ¶～を人に申し込む challenge *a person* to *a duel.* ～をいどまれる be challenged to *fight.* 拳銃(けんじゅう)の～ *a* gun *duel.*

けっとう【結党】¶人民党は～後まもなくたくさんの小さなグループに分裂した The People's Party was split into many small groups soon after it *was established.*

けつにく【血肉】¶～を分けた兄弟 a brother *by blood.* 母は～の情にほだされてわが子の罪をかばった The mother protected her son from natural affection for him.

けつにょう【血尿】hematuria.

けっぱい【欠配】〔株式〕non-dividend. ¶その株は前期は～であった The shares brought *no dividend* last term.

けっぱく【潔白】purity; innocence. ¶身の～を証明するためにはできることはなんでもやらなければならない You must do all you can to prove your *innocence.* その男は～であることがわかった The man proved to *be clear.* 彼は～だ He *has clear hands.* / He *is clean-handed.*

けつばん【欠番】a missing number. ¶不吉な数字なので4と13はよく～にする Because 4 and 13 are considered unlucky numbers, they *are* often *omitted.*

げっぴょう【月評】a monthly review.

げっぷ [a] belch. ¶～が出た I *belched.*

げっぷ【月賦】困 the monthly installment plan; 英 the monthly hire-purchase (system). ¶ ～でその車を買う契約をした I contracted to buy the car *on the monthly installment plan* (≒ *by monthly installments*). 車の～を毎月50,000円払う I pay *an installment* of 50,000 yen on the car every month. 電気掃除器の次回の～金がない I don't have the next *installment* on the vacuum cleaner.
けつぶつ【傑物】a great man; a giant.
けっぺき【潔癖】fastidiousness; love of cleanliness. ¶ ～な男 a *fastidious* man. 彼は～すぎてつきあいにくい He *is* so *fastidious* that he is difficult to get along with.
けつべつ【決別】a farewell. ¶ ～の辞 a *farewell* address (≒ word).
けつべん【血便】bloody excrement.
けつぼう【欠乏】want; lack. ¶ 当時は世界的に食糧が～した There was a world-wide food *shortage then.* 彼らは資金に～している They *lack* (≒ *are lacking in*) funds.
げっぽう【月報】a monthly bulletin (≒ report).
けっぽん【欠本】a missing volume. ¶ この全集は第1巻が～になっている The first volume *is missing* from this set.
けつまくえん【結膜炎】〘医学〙conjunctivitis.
けつまず·く【蹴躓く】¶ 彼は石に～いてころんだ He *stumbled over* a stone and fell.
けつまつ【結末】(結果) the result; (終わり) a conclusion; a close. ¶ できるだけ早くこの問題の～をつけたい I want to *bring* this problem *to a close* as soon as possible. 両者の論争はちょうど予想どおりの～になった The controversy between the two *came out* just as I had expected. その映画の～はどうなるのですか How does that movie finally *come out*? 問題は最終的に～がついた The question *has* finally *been settled.*
げつまつ【月末】the end of the month.
けづめ【蹴爪】a spur.
げつようび【月曜日】Monday.
けつれい【欠礼】¶ 喪中につき年賀を～します Being in the mourning, I shall refrain from offering you the New Year's greetings.
げつれい【月例】¶ ～の研究発表会 a *monthly* meeting for reading papers.
げつれい【月齢】the moon's age; the age of the moon.
けつれつ【決裂】a breakdown; a rupture. ¶ 労資の交渉は～した The negotiations between capital and labor *came to a rupture.*
けつろ【血路】¶ われわれは～をひらいて脱出した We *cut a way through* the enemy's ranks and fled. / We *found a way of escape cut through* the enemy's ranks.
けつろん【結論】a conclusion. ¶ 早急な～を出すな Don't form *a* hasty *conclusion.* 異なった～に達したがやむをえないことだ We have arrived at *a* different *conclusion*, but it cannot be helped. ～として今回のご提案にはまったく反対であると申し上げざるをえません *In conclusion* I have to say that I am deadly against this proposal.
げてもの【下手物】a grotesquerie; a piece of folkcraft.
げどくざい【解毒剤】a detoxication; an antidote. ¶ ミルクはある種の毒に対し～の役をするといわれている Milk is said to be *an antidote* for some poisons.
けとば·す【蹴飛ばす】¶ 小石を～す *kick away* a small stone.
けなげ【健気】¶ ～な少年 a *brave* (≒ *a gallant; an admirable*) boy.
けな·す【貶す】speak ill of; disparage; abuse. ¶ 友人を～すものではない Don't *speak ill of* your friends. あれは人のことを～す以外に能がない男だ All he can do is to *abuse* others.
けなみ【毛並み】¶ 彼は～がよい He is of good stock. / He is a person of upper class ancestry.
けぬき【毛抜き】(a pair of) tweezers.
げねつざい【解熱剤】an antifebrile.
けねん【懸念】anxiety; (a) fear; (a) worry. ¶ 彼は事業に失敗する～が大いにある There is *a* strong *fear* that he may fail in the enterprise. ～が現実となった My *anxiety* was justified later. / My *fear* (≒ *apprehension*) proved to be true.
けば【毛羽】nap; fluff; pile. ¶ 布に～を立てる raise *nap* on cloth. ～の粗いラシャ woolen cloth with *a* rough *nap.*
けはい【気配】an indication; a sign. ¶ 人の来る～がする I *feel* someone coming. あの家には人の住んでいる～がない We see no *sign* of life about the house.
けはえぐすり【毛生え薬】a hair-grower.
けばけばし·い【毳毳しい】¶ あの女はいつも～い身なりをしている That woman is always dressed *gaudily.*
けばり【毛鉤】a feather jig.
げびた【下卑た】vulgar; indecent. ¶ 彼はとても～人だ He is a very *mean* fellow. あの子どもたちは～ことば遣いをする Those children have a *vulgar* manner in speech.
けびょう【仮病】a feigned illness. ¶ ～を使う feign illness; play sick; pretend to be ill.
げひん【下品】¶ ～な vulgar; mean; low.
けぶか·い【毛深い】¶ ～い男 a *hairy* man.
けむ【煙】smoke. ¶ 彼は～に巻かれて死んだ He was suffocated to death by *smoke.* 彼の手品はわれわれを～に巻いた His tricks *mystified* us.
けむ·い【煙い】¶ この部屋はたばこの煙で～い This room *is full of* cigarette *smoke.* / The air of the room *is thick with the fumes* of cigarettes. 暖炉のまきがいぶって～い With the firewood in the fireplace smoldering, the room *is smoky.*
けむくじゃら ¶ ～な大男 a *hairy* tall man.
けむし【毛虫】a hairy caterpillar.

け

¶ 彼は友だちから〜のようにきらわれている He is hated like *a viper* (≒ *a serpent* ; *a poison*) by his friends.

けむた·い【煙たい】 ¶ 部屋の中が〜い The room *is full of smoke*. 部下は彼を〜がっている His subordinates *keep* him *at a respectful distance*. あの人といっしょにいるととても〜い I *feel* rather *awkward* in his presence.

けむり【煙】 smoke ; (臭気の強い煙) fumes.
¶ その部屋は〜が立ち込めていた The room was full of *smoke*. 火山は〜を吐いている The volcano *is emitting smoke* (≒ *is smoking*). 〜がもうもうとあがっている Volumes of *smoke* are rising up. 彼は〜に巻かれて死んだ He was suffocated to death by *smoke*. 部屋にたばこの〜が立ち込めている The room is thick with *tobacco fumes* (≒ *cigarette smoke*). (tobacco fumes は「パイプたばこの煙」で, cigarette smoke は「両切りたばこの煙」をいう). 火のない所に〜はたたぬ (諺) *There is no smoke without fire*.

けむ·る【煙る】 ¶ このストーブはいやに〜る The stove *smokes* badly. 湿った薪が〜っている The damp wood *is smoldering*. 山々が霧に〜っている The mountains *are dimmed* (≒ *are obscured*) by fogs. 町が小雨に〜っている The town *is veiled* (≒ *looks dim*) by a drizzling rain.

けもの【獣】 a beast ; a brute.

げや【下野】 ¶ 彼は〜を決意した He made up his mind to *leave* (≒ *resign*) *office*.

けやき【欅】 a zelkova [tree].

けやぶ·る【蹴破る】 ¶ 彼らはドアを〜った They *broke open* the door *by kicking*.

けらい【家来】 a retainer ; a follower ; (封建時代の) a vassal.

げらく【下落】 ¶ 物価の〜 *a fall in* prices. 小豆の相場が急に〜した The red bean market *fell* suddenly. 物価は〜しつつある Prices *are going down* (≒ *are declining*; *are becoming lower*). 家庭で夫の地位が〜した A husband *has dropped in* his position at home.

げらげら ¶ 彼は〜笑った He laughed *boisterously*.

ゲラずり【ゲラ刷り】 a galley proof.

けり ¶ 仕事の〜はつきましたか *Have* you *finished* your work? レポートの〜はついた I *am through with* the report. 2社間のいざこざは無事に〜がついた The trouble between the two companies *was settled in peace* (≒ *came to a peaceful settlement*).

げり【下痢】 loose bowels ; diarrhoea. ¶ ぼくはよく〜をする I often *have loose bowels*.
—止め a binding medicine ; an astringent.

ゲリラ a guerrilla. ¶ ピストルを振りまわして〜は銀行に入ってきた Brandishing automatic pistols, the *guerrillas* burst into the bank.
—戦 a guerrilla war. **—**部隊 a guerrilla gang.

け·る【蹴る】 kick. ¶ ボールを〜る *give a kick at* a ball ; *kick at* a ball. 彼は憤然と席を〜って退場した He *stamped out of the room* indignantly. われわれの要求はきっぱり〜られた Our claim *was rejected* (≒ *was turned down*) flatly.

ゲルマニウム〘化学〙germanium (記号は Ge).

ゲルマン (民族) the Germanic race ; (語) Germanic.

ケルン〘登山〙a cairn.

げれつ【下劣】 meanness ; baseness. ¶ 非常に〜な男 a very *mean* (≒ *depraved*) fellow. そんな〜なことばを使ってはいけません Don't use such *vulgar* (≒ *coarse*) words.

けれど〔も〕 ¶ 失敗した〜もう一度やり直すつもりだ *Though* I failed, I will try again. / I failed, *but* I will try again. 雨が降ってはいる〜, たいへん暖かい It is raining, *and yet* very warm. いろいろ困難はあった〜, 彼は成功した He succeeded *in spite of* all the difficulties. / He succeeded *for all* the difficulties.

けれん ¶ 彼はほんとうに〜のない人だ He is not *a show-off* indeed. 彼は〜味がある He is full of *showmanship*. / He knows a lot of *showmanship*.

ゲレンデ〘スキー〙a slope.

ケロイド〘医学〙keloid ; cheloid.

けろり〔と〕 ¶ 歯の痛みが〜とよくなった I was *suddenly* relieved of my toothache. 約束を〜と忘れてしまった I have *entirely* forgotten the promise. 赤ん坊は少し前に泣いていたのに〜としている The baby screamed a moment ago, but now he *remains quiet*. 彼は財布をなくしたのに〜としている Though he lost his purse, he *remains cool*.

けわし·い【険しい】 ¶ 〜い山道 a *steep* mountain path. われわれの前途はますます〜くなってきた Our future is becoming still more *serious*. / Our future is turning down to a more *critical* stage. 〜い顔つき a *grim* look.

けん【件】 an affair ; a case. ¶ 例の〜はどうなりましたか What has become of *the matter*? お申し越しの〜につき近日中にお答えいたします We will respond to the *matter* mentioned in your letter pretty soon. きょうの交通事故はたった2〜だた Today's traffic accidents are only two *cases*.

けん【券】 (切符) a ticket ; (切り取り券) a coupon ; (債券) a bond.
回遊**—** a circular ticket. 食**—** a food coupon. 入場**—** an admission ticket.

けん【県】 a prefecture.
—人会 an association of people from a prefecture. **—**知事 a prefectural governor. **—**庁 a prefectural office. **—**民 the people of a prefecture.

けん【兼】 and ; at the same time. ¶ (下宿などの) 居間〜寝室 a bed-sitting room ; a bed-sitter. 居間〜食堂 a living *and* dining room. 台所〜食堂 a kitchen-dining room. 総理大臣〜外務大臣 the Prime Minister *and concurrently* the Foreign Minister (concurrently を省けば口語的. 文にしなければ省かないほうがよい).

けん【険】 ¶ 〜のある顔 a *sharp* look. 箱根は天下の〜として知られていた Hakone was known as *an impregnable pass*.

けん【剣】a sword ; (短剣) a dagger. ¶ 彼と～を交える cross *swords* with him. ～を抜く draw *one's sword*. 彼は～をとっては日本一だ He is the best swordsman in Japan.

けん【腱】〔解剖学〕a tendon.
アキレス— Achilles' tendon.

けん【鍵】〔音楽〕a key. ¶ 88～のピアノ a piano with 88 *keys*.

-けん【-軒】 ¶ 彼は角から２～めに住んでいる He lives in the second *house* from the corner. 昨晩私の家の３～先で火事があった Fire broke out three *doors* off from my house last night. 角を曲がって一～め the first *house* round the corner.

げん【言】 ¶ 彼は～を左右にして損害の責任をとろうとしなかった He used unclear expressions to avoid the responsibility for the loss. 正直は最上の政策であることは～をまたない *It is needless to say* (≒ *It goes without saying*) that honesty is the best policy.

げん【弦】 ¶ バイオリンの～ *a* violin *string*.

げん-【現-】 ¶ ～会員 the *present* members. ～内閣 the *present* Cabinet.

-げん【-減】 ¶ 彼は毎月3,000円の収入～となる His income will *be reduced by* 3,000 yen every month. 米の生産量はことしは15パーセント～であった Rice *fell* (≒ *decreased*) in its production by 15 percent this year.

けんあく【険悪】 ¶ 空模様が～になった The sky *is threatening*. / The weather is *stormy*. 国際情勢は～化している The international situation *is taking on an ugly look* (≒ *is taking a serious turn ; is deteriorating*). 彼は～な顔つきをしている He wears a *grim* expression. / He looks *dangerous* (≒ *menacing*).

けんあん【懸案】 an outstanding problem. ¶ 長年の～ a *long standing* question. 日中間の～ a question *pending* between Japan and Red China.

げんあん【原案】 the original plan ; (議会の) the original bill. ¶ 彼らが事業計画の～を作成した They made *the original plan for* the business project. 予算案は～どおり可決された The budget passed *in its original form* (≒ *as drafted*).

けんい【権威】〔an〕authority ; power. ¶ 彼は子どもたちに～がない He has no *authority over* his children. 彼は部下に対する～を失墜した He lost his *power* (≒ *influence*) *over* his men. 彼は天体物理学の世界的～だ He is *a* worldwide *authority on* astrophysics. 裁判官はその～を保持しなければならない The judge should maintain the *dignity* of his position.

—筋 ¶ そのニュースを～筋から聞いた I got the news from some *authoritative* source.

けんいん【検印】 a seal〔of approval〕. ¶ ～のない製品は保証されない Articles with no *seal* are not secured.

けんいん【牽引】 traction. ¶ 機関車が貨車を～している A locomotive *is pulling* freight cars.

—車 a tractor. —力 pulling capacity.

げんいん【原因】 a cause ; the origin. ¶ ～と結果 *cause* and effect. 出火の～ the *origin* of the fire. 事故の～を明らかにしなければならぬ We must clear up the *cause* of the accident. その交通事故は彼の不注意な運転が～だった The traffic accident *was caused by* his careless driving. いかなる～でこの戦争は起こったのか What *has caused* this war? / What was the *cause* of this war? 彼の病気は不節制が～だ His sickness *results* from intemperance. ～不明の火事 a fire of unknown *origin*. ～不明の病気 an *ill-defined* disease.

けんうん【絹雲】〔気象〕a cirrus (複 cirri).

けんえい【県営】 ¶ この競馬場は～だ This turf *is under prefectural management*. ～住宅に住んでいる I live in a *prefecture-managed* residence.

げんえい【幻影】 an illusion ; a vision. ¶ 彼は常に失敗の～におびえている He always labors under *a delusion* of his failure.

けんえき【権益】 rights and interests.
既得— vested interests. 特殊— special interests.

けんえき【検疫】 quarantine ; medical inspections. ¶ その家に赤痢が出て～中だ Dysentery is out at the house and the house *is in quarantine*.

—官 a quarantine officer. —所 a quarantine station. —船 a quarantine ship.

げんえき【現役】 active duty. ¶ 彼はまだ～でやれる選手だ He can still play as an *active* member. 彼は昨年～を退いた He retired from *active service* last year. ～の (新卒業生の) 入試合格率が年年高くなっている The percentage of the students who pass the entrance examination for colleges upon graduation from high schools becomes higher every year.

—将校 an officer on the active list. —兵 a soldier in active service.

けんえつ【検閲】 inspection ; (出版物・映画などの) censorship. ¶ その本は首尾よく～をパスした The book passed *censorship* successfully. 彼らは映画の～に抗議している They are protesting the film *censorship* system. 所持品は厳重な～を受けた Our belongings *were examined* rigidly.

—官 a censor ; an inspector.

けんえん【犬猿】 ¶ 彼らは～の仲だ They *are on extremely bad terms*. / They *lead a cat-and-dog life*.

けんお【嫌悪】 disgust ; hatred. ¶ 彼はそれに対して～の念をいだいている He *hates* it. / He has *a hatred* (≒ *dislike*) for it. (文語体).

けんか【喧嘩】 (口論) a quarrel ; (殴り合い) a fight. ¶ 彼らの間に～が始まった *A quarrel* arose among them. ぼくはささいなことで彼女と～した I *quarreled* (≒ *had a quarrel*) with her about a trifle. ぼくは～は苦手だ I'm no good at *fighting*. 彼はぼくに～を吹きかけた

け

He *fastened a quarrel on* me. 彼は非常に～早い He *is* very *quarrelsome*.
―腰 ¶ 彼は～腰で話している He is talking *in a defiant attitude*. ―両成敗 In *a quarrel* both sides are to blame.

げんか【言下】 ¶ 彼の提案は～に退けられた His proposal was rejected *flatly* (≒ *decidedly*).

げんか【原価】 the cost. ¶ この時計の～はいくらですか What is *the cost* [*price*] of this watch? きみにはこのカメラを～で(～を割って)差し上げましょう You may take this camera *at cost* (*below cost*).
―計算 cost accounting. 生産― the prime cost.

げんか【現下】 ¶ ～の住宅事情 the *present* housing condition. その国の～の情勢は重大な局面に至っている The *existing* state of affairs in the country has come to a crisis.

げんか【減価】 ―償却 depreciation.

げんが【原画】 the original picture. ¶ ゴッホの～ *the original picture* by Gogh.

けんかい【県会】 a prefectural assembly.
―議員 a member of a prefectural assembly.

けんかい【見解】 an opinion; a view. ¶ それは～の相違だ It is *a matter of opinion*. 宗教については, きみとぼくは～を異にする You and I have different *opinions* (≒ *views*) on religion. ぼくは彼らとは～を異にする I do not share their *opinions*. その点に関してはあなたと同一～だ I hold the same *view* with you on that point.

けんがい【圏外】 out of sphere. ¶ その候補者は当選～だ The candidate *is out of the running*. / *There is no possibility of* his being elected. 彼は政治の～にある He *keeps away from* (≒ *stands aloof from*) politics. 彼は優勝～へ脱落した He has fallen *out of the sphere of* a victory.

げんかい【限界】 a limit; a bound. ¶ ものには～というものがある Everything has its *limit*. / There is *a limit* to everything. 彼は自分の能力の～を心得ている He knows his *limitations*. 体力の～を知らねばならない We must recognize our physical *limitation*.
―効果〔経済学〕marginal utility.

げんかい【厳戒】 ¶ 警官が官邸を～している The policemen *are keeping a strict watch* around the official residence.

げんがい【言外】 ¶ 彼は～に不満をほのめかした He *hinted at* (≒ *alluded to*) his dissatisfaction.

けんかく【剣客】 a fencer; a swordsman.

けんがく【見学】 ¶ 放送局を～する *visit* a broadcasting station. 印刷所を～する *visit* a printshop *for information*.

げんかく【幻覚】 [a] hallucination. ¶ 彼女は～に襲われやすい She is subject to *hallucinations*. / She is apt to *be hallucinated*.

げんかく【厳格】 ¶ ～な先生 a *severe* (≒ *stern*) teacher; a taskmaster; (女性) taskmistress. ～なしつけ *rigorous* (≒ *rigid*) discipline. 彼は子どもには～だ He *is severe* (≒ *is strict*) *with* his children. 彼は～に育てられた He was brought up *rigorously*.

げんがく【弦楽】 ―器 a stringed instrument.
―四重奏 a string quartet.

げんがく【減額】 a reduction. ¶ 経費を30パーセント～した We *have reduced* (≒ *have cut down*) our expenditure by 30 percent.

けんかしょくぶつ【顕花植物】〔植物〕a phanerogam.

けんがん【検眼】 an eye examination. ¶ ～してもらった I *had my eyesight tested*.
―鏡 an ophthalmoscope.

げんかん【玄関】 the front door; the entrance; the hall; the porch. ¶ ～から入る enter at *the front door*. だれか～にいる There is someone at *the front door*. 彼は彼女を～まで見送った He *saw* her *to the door*.
―払い ¶ 彼に～払いを食わされた He *turned* me *away at his door*. 彼女は彼らに～払いを食わした She *denied herself to* them.

げんかん【厳寒】 intense cold. ¶ ～の候となりました *The coldest season* has come.

けんぎ【建議】 a proposal; a motion. ¶ 委員会は理事会に合理化政策を～した The committee *proposed* a rationalization policy *to* the board of directors. 彼らは政府にインフレ阻止政策を～した They *memorialized* an anti-inflation policy to the Government.

けんぎ【嫌疑】 suspicion. ¶ 彼に殺人の～がかかった *Suspicion* of the murder fell upon him. / He *was suspected of* the murder. なんで～がかかったのか What caused the *suspicion*? 彼はスパイの～を晴らした He cleared the *suspicion* of being a spy. 彼は詐欺の～で逮捕された He was arrested on [the] *suspicion* of fraud.
―者 a suspect.

げんき【元気】 spirits. **1**〖勢いのいいこと〗¶ もっと～を出せ Cheer up!
一同彼の無事の知らせを聞いて～を取り戻した All of us recovered our *spirits* upon hearing the news of his safety.
そんなことで～をなくすなんてだらしない How silly you are to *lose heart* over such a trifle!
なんとかして彼に～をつけてやらねば I must try and *cheer* him *up* by some means.
どうかしたのか. ばかに～がないね Is there anything the matter with you? You *look* rather *depressed* (≒ *look down in the mouth*).
なかなか～がいいな You are full of *vitality*, aren't you?
なかなか～のいい子どもだ The boy *is brimful with vigor*.
いくら年をとっても, まだそれぐらいのことをする～はある Though old, I *am* still *vigorous* enough for such a thing.
弁当を食べたらまた～が出てきた The lunch improved my *spirits*.
もうものを言う～もなかった He *was* too *depressed* to utter a word.
そのひと言が私を～づけてくれた The very word

encouraged me.
みんなで〜よくこの歌をうたおう Let's put some life in this song.
きょうも一日〜よく働きましょう Let's get the job done well today. / Let's do a good job of work today. / Let's work *hard* today.
子どもたちは〜いっぱい砂浜を駆けまわった The children ran about the sandy beach *in high spirits.*
2 〖健康なこと〗 ¶ みなさまお〜ですか How *is* your family 〔*getting along*〕?
おかげさまで〜にしております Thank you, *we are keeping well.*
みなさんお〜でなによりです I am glad 〔to see〕 *you are keeping well.*
どうだ, 〜でやっているかね Well, *are* you *strong and healthy*?
家族一同〜に暮らしております All 〔of〕 my family *are very well.*
彼も今はすっかり〜になった He *is* now *up and about* again.
彼は医者にかかったことがないほど〜だ He *is* so *healthy* that he has never consulted a doctor.
では, お〜で Good luck to you!

げんきづ·ける【元気づける】¶ 彼が来てくれたので私たちはたいへん〜けられた We *were* much *encouraged by* his arrival.

けんきゃく【健脚】strong in walking. ¶ きみはなかなか〜〔家〕だ You are *a* very *good walker.*

けんきゅう【研究】〔a〕 study. ¶ 彼は〜に専念している He is devoted to his *studies.* 彼は原子力の〜を始めた He began his *studies* of atomic energy. (ふつう *one's* studies となる). 彼女はフランス文学を〜した She *studied* French literature. あなたの専門の〜はなんですか What *are* you *majoring* (≒ *specializing*) *in*? この問題はとくと〜する必要がある It is necessary to *take* this matter *into* serious *consideration.* この案は目下5人のグループで〜中だ This plan *is under study* by a group of five persons. 彼は「シェイクスピア〜」を書いた He wrote "*A study* of Shakespeare."
—員 a research worker (≒ scholar). —活動 research activities. —室 (大学の) an office. —所 a research institute. —資料 research materials. —費 research funds. —論文 a treatise (*on*); a paper (*on*). —心 ¶ 彼は〜心旺盛(おうせい)だ He is full of *the research spirit.* —家 ¶ 彼はこん虫の〜家だ He *studies* insects. / He is *a student* of entomology.

けんぎゅう【牽牛】〖天文〗〔the〕 Altair.

げんきゅう【言及】reference. ¶ 彼はそのことについてはごく簡単にしか〜しなかった He only *referred* briefly *to* the matter.

げんきゅう【原級】the original class. ¶ 彼は成績不良のため〜留め置きになった They didn't move him up to the senior class because of this poor grades.

げんきゅう【減給】¶ 彼らは1割〜されることになった Their *wages were reduced* by ten percent.

けんきょ【検挙】an arrest. ¶ 彼は汚職で〜された He *was arrested for* corruption.

けんきょ【謙虚】modesty; humbleness.
¶ 〜に自分の行動を反省すべきだ You should *be modest enough to* reflect on your conduct.

けんぎょう【兼業】a side business. ¶ あの店では荒物屋とたばこ屋を〜している They *have* a general store which sells tobacco. / The kitchenware dealer serves also as a cigarette store.
—農家 a farmer who has a second job.

げんきょう【元凶】a ringleader. ¶ 暴動の〜たちはまもなくみんな捕らえられた All the *ringleaders* of the riot were arrested before long.

げんきょう【現況】¶ 気象〜 *the present state of* the weather.

げんぎょう【現業】non-clerical work (≒ business); field work. ¶ 大蔵省印刷局は〜の官庁のひとつだ The Finance Ministry Printing Office is one branch of the government's *non-clerical* business. 人員を事務から〜に振り向けた Some clerks were transferred to *non-clerical jobs.*
—員 a non-clerical worker.

けんきん【献金】a donation; a contribution; (教会での) offering; offertory (とくに礼拝のとき集められるもの).
政治— political donations.

げんきん【現金】**1** 〖金〗 cash; ready money. ¶ 私はなんでも〜で買う I buy everything *for cash.* / I pay *cash* for everything.
支払いは〜でも月賦でもけっこうです Payment may be made either *by cash* or in monthly instalments.
彼は〜をあまり持っていない He is short of *cash.* / He doesn't have much *money* with him.
〜で買うから値段を負けたまえ As I am paying *in cash,* will you reduce the price (≒ will you give me a discount)?
〜なら当店では5分引きにします We shall take off five percent *for cash.*
銀行へ行ってこの小切手を〜に換えてきてくれ Go to the bank and *cash* this check.
—書留〔郵便〕 a cash registered mail. —支払い a cash payment. —正価 a cash price. —出納簿 a cash book. —取引 cash transaction (≒ market).
2 〖打算的な〗 ¶ 彼は〜な人間だ He is a *calculating* (≒ *mercenary*) man.

げんきん【厳禁】strict prohibition. ¶ 場内ではたばこは〜されております We are very sorry to say that smoking *is strictly prohibited* in the hall. 酔っぱらい運転は法律により〜されている Drunken driving *is strictly prohibited* by law.

げんけい【原形】the original form. ¶ 〜を失う (保つ) lose (keep) its *original form.* 法隆寺の壁画は〜に復された The mural paintings of the Horyuji Temple were restored to

け

their *original forms.* その遺跡は～をとどめぬまでに破壊されてしまった The remains were destroyed beyond recognition.

げんけい【原型】 a prototype ; a model. ¶ ロダンの彫刻は～から同一の作品がいくつか作られている Some pieces of Rodin's sculptures are moulded on the same *prototype.* 裁断のための型紙は～をもとにして製図される A dress pattern for cutting is drawn on the *prototype.*

け

げんけい【減刑】 reduction (≒ mitigation ; abatement) of penalty. ¶ 裁判官は情状を酌量して彼を～した The judge *reduced his penalty* in consideration of extenuating circumstances.

けんけつ【献血】 blood donation. ¶ ～する give (≒ donate) blood.

—者 a blood donor.

けんげん【権限】 a function ; (代理人の) competence. ¶ 私には許可を与える～はない I have no *competence* to give leave to do so. 法律で～を与えられていないことをやってはいけない You should not do what you *are* not *authorized to* by law.

けんけんごうごう【喧喧囂囂】 ¶ 会は終始～たるものだった The meeting *was in an uproar* (≒ *was uproarious*) from beginning to end.

けんご【堅固】 firmness ; steadiness. ¶ 彼は志操～な人だ He has a *firm* purpose. 敵は～な陣地によっている The enemy has held a *strong* fortress. その城はなかなか～にできていた That castle was very *strongly* (≒ *solidly*) built.

げんご【言語】 language. ¶ アフリカではどんな～が話されていますか What sort of *languages* do they speak in Africa? この湖の美しさは～に絶する The beauty of the lake *is beyond words.*

—学 linguistics. —学者 a linguist. —失調 aphasia. —障害 speech defect.

げんご【原語】 the original word (≒ language). ¶ オペラのアリアを～で歌う sing an operatic aria *in its original tongue.*

けんこう【健康】 health. **1**〖健康を〗 ¶ ～を害した I injured my *health.*

彼はまもなく～を回復するだろう He will *recover his health* (≒ *get well*) soon.

彼女は～を保つために適度の運動をやっている She takes moderate exercise to keep her *health.*

～を増進したい I want to promote my *health.*

2〖健康に〗 ¶ ～に注意しなさい You must take good care of yourself.

彼は～に恵まれている He is blessed with *good health.* / He enjoys *good health.*

早寝早起きは～によい It is good for *health* to keep early hours.

～によいスポーツ a *healthy* sport.

3〖その他の助詞などとともに〗 ¶ ～な子ども a *healthy* child.

彼は～である He *is well.* / He *is in good health.*

彼女は～がすぐれない She *is in poor* (≒ *bad*) *health.*

4〖合成語〗 —診断 ¶ ～診断を受ける undergo *a health examination.* —美 ¶ ～美に輝く少女 a girl of *healthy* (≒ *physical*) *beauty.* —保険 ¶ ～保険に入っている be on the *health insurance* list. —保険医(証) a health insurance doctor (card).

けんごう【剣豪】 a great swordsman.

げんこう【言行】 words and deeds (≒ action); speech and behavior. ¶ 彼は～一致の人だ He is *a man of his word.* / He is a man who will *act up to what he says.*

げんこう【原稿】 a manuscript ; a copy ; a draft.

—用紙 a copy paper. —料 payment for a manuscript ; manuscript fee.

げんこう【現行】 ¶ ～制度のもとでは under *the present* system. ～の英語教科書は何冊ありますか How many English textbooks *are now in use*?

—犯 ¶ あの男は盗みの～犯で捕まった He was caught *in the act of* stealing. —法 ¶ ～法のもとでは警察は彼を処罰するわけにはいかない The police cannot punish him under *the existing law.*

けんこうこつ【肩胛骨】 a shoulder blade ; 〖解剖学〗 a scapula (複 scapulae).

けんこく【建国】 the founding of a state (≒ nation).

—記念日 the state foundation anniversary.

げんこく【原告】 〖法律〗 a plaintiff ; an accuser.

げんこつ【拳骨】 a [clenched] fist. ¶ 彼は～で私を殴った He struck me with his *fist.*

げんこん【現今】 ¶ ～の若い者 *present-day* young men ; young people *of today.*

けんさ【検査】 an inspection ; an examination. ¶ ～を受ける take (≒ go through) *an examination.* 会計を～する *audit* accounts. プールの水を厳密に～する *make a* strict *examination* of the water of the pools.

—官 an inspector ; an examiner ; (会計の) an auditor. —済み(はり紙など) Examined. —役 an inspector ; (相撲の) a referee. 身体— a physical (≒ medical) examination ; a medical check.

けんざい【健在】 ¶ 彼はまだ～だ He *is* still *well.* / He *is in good health.*

げんざい【原罪】 the original sin.

げんざい【現在】 the present. ¶ ～[で]は now ; at present. ～の状態で[は] in the *present* state of things ; under *existing* circumstances. ～まで up to *the present.* ～までに up to date ; down to date. それらは～の状態のままにしておきなさい Leave them *as they are.* ～の心境はただもう夢のようです I feel *now* as if I were dreaming. 当市の3月1日～の人口は6万です The population of this city *as of* March 1 is sixty thousand.

—完了〖文法〗 the present perfect. —時制〖文法〗 the present [tense]. —高 the stock (≒ amount) in hand. —分詞〖文法〗 present participle.

げんさく【原作】the original work.
—者 the [original] author (≒ writer).

けんさつ【検察】—官 ㊊ a prosecuting attorney; a public prosecutor; ㊋ a public procurator. —庁 the Public Prosecutor's Office. —当局 the prosecutory authorities.

けんさつ【検札】ticket check.
—係 a ticket examiner.

けんさつ【賢察】¶ それはまったくご〜どおりです It is quite as *you have conjectured*. どうかご〜願います I beg you will *sympathize with* me.

けんざん【検算】verification of accounts; checking. ¶ この1列の答えの〜をしてみなさい *Prove* (≒ *Check*; *Go over*) this row of answers.

げんさん【減産】curtailment of production. ¶ 鉄鋼生産を20パーセント〜する *curtail* (≒ *reduce*) steel production by 20 percent.

げんさんち【原産地】the country (≒ place) of origin; (動植物の) the habitat; the original (≒ natural) home.

けんし【犬歯】an eye-tooth; a canine tooth; 〚解剖学〛(特に人間の) a cuspid.

けんし【検死・検視】an inquest; a coroner's inquest; an autopsy (解剖して死因を調べる); a post-mortem [examination].
¶ 〜の結果, 毒殺ということが判明した The *autopsy* revealed that the man had been poisoned. 彼の遺体は係官が〜に来るまで路上に放置されていた His body was left on the street until a coroner came to *examine* it.
—官 a coroner.

けんじ【堅持】holding fast (*to*). ¶ 世界情勢がどのように変化しようとも,日本は世界平和の原則を〜していかねばならない No matter how the world situation may change, Japan must *stick to* the principle of world peace.

けんじ【検事】a public prosecutor; a prosecuting attorney; (検事側) the prosecution.

げんし【原子】an atom.
—エネルギー atomic energy. —核 an atomic nucleus. —時計 an atomic clock. —爆弾 an A-bomb. —爆発 an atomic explosion. —番号 atomic number. —病 an atomic disease. —物理学 atomic (≒ nuclear) physics. —物理学者 an atomic physicist. —兵器 an atomic weapon; atomic arms. —量 atomic weight. —力 atomic energy. —力空母(潜水艦) an atomic aircraft carrier (submarine). —力時代 the atomic age. —力発電 atomic power generation. —炉 an atomic reactor (≒ furnace).

げんし【原始】the beginning; genesis. ¶ 〜的な方法で in a *primitive* way.
—時代 the primitive times (≒ ages). —人 a primitive [man]. —林 a primeval forest.

げんし【原紙】(謄写版用) a stencil paper; (蚕卵紙用) an eggsheet.

けんしき【見識】[high] views. ¶ 〜のある人 a man *of insight*; a man of *discrimination*. 彼は高い〜を持っている He has *high views*. 彼のそういう考えも一つの〜だと思う Such an idea of his is *a fine view*. 彼らは〜ばっていてつきあいにくい As they *stand on dignity* (≒ *have an air of importance*), it is hard for us to get along with them.

けんじつ【堅実】steadiness. ¶ 彼は〜な意見を持っている He has *sound* views. あの人はなかなか〜な人だ He is a very *steady* man.

げんじつ【現実】reality; actuality. ¶ 〜を直視する face *realities*. きみは〜に即した解決策を考えるべきだ You should try to find a solution that is adapted to the *realities*.
—化 realization. —主義 realism. —主義者 a realist.

けんじゃ【賢者】a wise man; a sage.

げんしゅ【元首】the sovereign; the chief of a nation.

げんしゅ【厳守】¶ 時間を〜する be punctual [to the minute]. 秘密を〜する *keep* a secret *strictly*. 1時開会,時間〜のこと The meeting opens at one o'clock. Please *be punctual*./The gathering is to be opened at one o'clock. Please be sure not to be late.

けんしゅう【研修】a training. ¶ 月に1回社員のためにセールスの〜が行なわれる A *training* in salesmanship is given to the company staff once a month.
—所 a training institute. —生 a trainee.

けんじゅう【拳銃】a pistol; a revolver; ㊊ a gun. ¶ 人に〜を向ける point *a gun* at a person. 〜を突きつけられて脅迫された I was threatened at the *gun* point.

げんしゅう【減収】(収穫) a decrease in production; (歳入) a revenue decrease; (収入) an income decrease.
¶ ことしの米作は例年に比べると5パーセント〜の見込み This year's rice crop is likely to be five percent down under the average year's crop.

げんじゅう【厳重】strictness; severity. ¶ 市民たちは役人の不親切に対して市当局へ〜な抗議を行なった The citizens raised (≒ made) a *strong* protest against the unkind municipal officers. 国会周辺の警戒は〜をきわめている The neighborhood of the Diet building is very *closely* guarded.

げんじゅうしょ【現住所】the present address.

げんじゅうみん【原住民】natives; aborigines; primitive inhabitants.

げんしゅく【厳粛】solemnity; seriousness.
¶ 式は〜に執り行なわれた The ceremony was performed *solemnly* (≒ *with solemnity*). 国歌の吹奏が始まると〜な気持ちになったものであった As soon as the national anthem began, we used to be inspired with awe. 〜な口調で in *solemn* tones.

けんしゅつ【検出】detection. ¶ 牛乳びんからは毒物が〜された Poison *was detected* from the milk bottle.

けんじゅつ【剣術】fencing; swordsmanship.

げんしょ【原書】the original. ¶ シェイクスピアを

け

け

～で読む read Shakespeare *in the original*.

けんしょう【肩章】 shoulder straps.

けんしょう【検証】 an inspection.

現場— ¶犯行の現場～が行なわれた *An inspection* of the scene of the crime was performed.

けんしょう【憲章】 a charter.

国際連合— the United Nations Charter; the Charter of the United Nations. 児童— the Children's Charter. 大西洋— the Atlantic Charter.

けんしょう【懸賞】 a prize. ¶～に当選する win *a prize* 〔in a contest〕. その家の人は～を出して行方不明になった犬を捜した The family offered *a reward* for the lost dog. その犯人の首には1,000ドルの～がかかっていた *A prize* of 1,000 dollars was set on the criminal's head.

—金(品) a prize; a reward; an award. —〔当選〕小説 a prize 〔winning〕 novel. —当選者 a prize winner. —論文 a prize essay. —募集 ¶～募集に応ずる enter *a prize contest*.

けんじょう【謙譲】 modesty; humility. ¶金もうけをしようとしている場合に～の美徳を発揮していてはだめだ It does not do to behave *modestly* (≒ *with modesty*) when you are bent on making money.

げんしょう【現象】 a phenomenon (複 phenomena). ¶自然界の～ the *phenomena* of nature; *a* natural *phenomenon*. 一時的～ *a* passing *phenomenon*. 戦後の～ *a* postwar *phenomenon*.

—界 the phenomenal world. —論 phenomenalism. —学 phenomenology.

げんしょう【減少】 〔a〕 decrease. ¶米の需要は年々～してきている The demand for rice *has been decreasing* (≒ *has been on the decrease*) year by year. 学生数がこれ以上～するのを食い止めなければならない We have to check *a* further *decrease* in the number of students.

げんじょう【現状】 the present condition (≒ situation; state of things). ¶日本の～では裁判に年月がかかりすぎる *Under the present condition* (≒ *Under the existing circumstances*) of Japan lawsuits take too many years to be settled. 原因調査のため焼け跡は当分～のままにしておく In order to find out the cause of the fire we are going to leave for the time being the ruins *as they are* 〔*now*〕. われわれは～に不満である We are not content with *things as they are*. ～を変革する必要がある We must reform *the present condition*.

げんしょく【原色】 primary colors. ¶～のはでなシャツ a showy shirt of *primary colors*.

—版 a heliotype. 三— three primary colors.

げんしょく【現職】 the present post. ¶～の官吏 a government official *in active service*; a public servant *on the active list*.

げんしょく【減食】 reduction of diet (≒ food). ¶彼は中年太り解消のため～をしている He *is on a diet* (≒ *is dieting*) because of his middle age spread.

げん･ずる【減ずる】 lessen; decrease. ¶20から6を～ずると14になる Twenty *minus* six is fourteen. / Six from twenty leaves fourteen. / *Subtract* six from twenty. This leaves fourteen. 輸出が2割～じた Exports *fell off* (≒ *decreased*) by 20 percent.

けんしん【検針】 the inspection of a meter. ¶水道(ガス)の検針をする *inspect* the water (gas) meter.

けんしん【検診】 a medical examination; a physical checkup. ¶彼は癌(がん)予防のため定期的に～を受けている He gets *a checkup* for cancer at regular intervals. 学校はその医者に生徒の～を頼んだ The school authorities asked the doctor to *examine* the students' *health*.

—日 a medical examination day. 集団— collective medical examination. 定期— regular health checkup.

けんしん【献身】 devotion. ¶彼は世界平和の達成に～した He *devoted himself to* the establishment of world peace. 彼は民族の自主･独立に～的な努力をした He *was devoted to* the cause of national freedom and independence. 彼女は重傷者の看病に～的につとめた She *devotedly* cared for the seriously injured persons.

けんじん【堅陣】 ¶敵の～を抜く take the enemy's *stronghold*. わがチームのバックスは～を誇っている The backs of our team are proud of their *strong defense*.

げんしん【原審】 ¶～を破棄する Overrule the *original judgment*.

げんじん【原人】 a primitive (≒ primeval) man; a pithecanthrope.

ペキン—(学名) *Sinanthropus pekinensis*.

けんすい【懸垂】 chinning. ¶ぼくは～が10回できる I can *chin the bar* ten times.

げんすい【元帥】 (陸軍) a general 〔of the army〕; 英 a 〔field〕 marshal; (海軍) a fleet admiral; 英 an admiral of the fleet.

げんすい【減水】 ¶日でりで貯水池の水が半分に～した The water〔s〕 of the reservoir has fallen by half because of dry weather.

げんすいばく【原水爆】 〔an〕 atomic and 〔a〕 hydrogen bombs; A and H bombs.

けんすう【件数】 ¶交通事故の～ *the number* of traffic accidents. 火災～ *the number* of fires.

げんせ【現世】 (この世) this world (≒ life); (現代の世の中) the present (≒ modern) world. ¶～のつらさ hardship of life. ～の煩悩 *mundane* desires; worldly ambitions.

けんせい【県政】 a prefectural administration.

けんせい【権勢】 ¶ヒトラーは独裁者としてほしいままの～をふるった Hitler wielded his *power* over everything as a dictator.

けんせい【憲政】 constitutionalism. ¶～を敷

く adopt *constitutional government.* ～擁護運動 the movement (≒ cause) of defending *constitutionalism.*

けんせい【牽制】 check. ¶ そんなことをしてぼくを～したってだめだ You can't *check* my desires in such a way. ピッチャーは一塁に～球を投じた The pitcher *pegged* the runner on the first base. ～攻撃 a *containing* attack.

げんせい【厳正】 ¶ ～な判断をしていただきたい I hope you will pass a *fair and impartial* judgment. 国民は～な裁判を望んだ The people wanted *strict* justice [to be done by the court].

—中立 ¶ われわれは～中立を守っている We are keeping a *strict* neutrality.

げんぜい【減税】 tax reduction. ¶ 大幅な～をしなければならない We need *a* big *tax reduction.* / *A* big *tax reduction* is necessary.

げんせいだい【原生代】〔地質学〕the Proterozoic era.

げんせいどうぶつ【原生動物】 a protozoan.

げんせいりん【原生林】 a virgin (≒ primeval) forest.

けんせき【譴責】 reproof. ¶ 彼は公務怠慢のかどで～〔処分〕を受けた He *was reprimanded* (≒ *was reproved*) *for* his neglect of the public duty.

げんせき【原石】 a raw ore ; an ore. ¶ ダイヤモンドの～ a rough diamond ; an uncut diamond.

けんせきうん【巻積雲】〔気象〕a cirro-cumulus (複 cirro-cumuli).

けんせつ【建設】 construction. ¶ 彼らはここに36階建ての高層ビルを～した They *built* a 36 storied skyscraper here. 目下国内各地で高速道路を～中だ Superhighways *are* now *under construction* everywhere in the country. 平和国家の～に努めなければならない We must devote ourselves to the *establishment* of a peaceful country. ～的に物事を考えよう Let's take everything into consideration *constructively.* 彼の意見には～的な要素が少しもない There is nothing *constructive* in his opinion.

—会社 a construction firm. —省 the Ministry of Construction. —大臣 the Minister of Construction.

けんぜん【健全】 ¶ ～な思想 *healthy* (≒ *wholesome*) ideas. ～な精神は～な肉体に宿る (諺) *A sound mind in a sound body.* 子どもを～に育てるための環境作りが望まれる Providing good surroundings to raise children *soundly* is desirable.

—娯楽 healthy amusement. —財政 a sound financial (≒ fiscal) policy ; a sound finance.

げんせん【源泉】 ¶ 知識の～ *a source* of information.

—課税 taxation at the source [of income] ; a source tax.

げんせん【厳選】 ¶ ～された優良品 choice goods ; superior goods *rigidly selected.* ～して入選作品を決めた We *carefully selected* the winning pieces of work. ～の結果懸賞当選者が決まった As a result of *careful selection* the prize winners have been chosen.

げんぜん【厳然】 ¶ ～たる事実 a *solid* fact ; a *hard* fact ; a *grim* reality. 彼は～として節をまげなかった He *resolutely* did not change his principle.

けんそ【険阻】 ¶ ～な山道 a *steep* (≒ *rugged*) mountain path.

げんそ【元素】 an element ; a chemical element.

—記号 the symbol of an element. —分析 ultimate (≒ elementary) analysis.

けんそう【喧噪】 noise ; tumult. ¶ ～のちまた a *noisy* street. 市場は～をきわめていた The market *was very noisy* (≒ *was in tumult ; was in an uproar*).

けんぞう【建造】 construction ; building. ¶ 造船工たちは大型タンカーを～中だ The shipbuilding workers *are* now *building* a mammoth tanker.

—計画 a construction (≒ building) program. —物 a building ; a construction.

—能力 ¶ このドックは20万トンの～能力がある This dockyard is capable of *building* a two hundred thousand ton ship.

げんそう【幻想】 a fantasy ; a fancy. ¶ ～的な音楽 *dreamy* music.

—曲 a fantasia ; a fantasy.

げんそう【舷窓】〔航海〕a porthole ; a port.

げんぞう【現像】〔写真〕development. ¶ フィルムを～する *develop* film.

—液 a developer ; a developing solution.

けんそううん【巻層雲】〔気象〕a cirro-stratus (複 a cirro-strata) ; a sheep cloud.

けんそく【検束】 [an] arrest. ¶ ふたりの学生がデモ行進中～された Two students *were arrested* during the demonstration march.

げんそく【原則】 a principle ; a general rule. ¶ 憲法は国の～を定めたものだ The Constitution is the provision of the national basic *principles.* フェアプレーがすべての運動競技の～だ Fair play is the essential *principle* for all the games and sports. ～として生徒間の金銭の貸借は禁じられている *As a* [*general*] *rule,* borrowing or lending money among students is forbidden. ～的にきみの考え方は正しい Your idea is right *in principle.* ～的な問題から討議しよう Let's talk about the *basic* problems first. ～に立ち返って考え直そう Let's reconsider it from the *fundamental* viewpoint.

げんそく【減速】 speed reduction. ¶ 時速30マイル以下に～せよ *Reduce speed* (≒ *Slow down*) to less than 30 miles per hour.

—装置 reduction gear.

げんそく【舷側】〔航海〕the [ship's] side ; (水面上の) the broadside.

けんそん【謙遜】 modesty. ¶ 彼は態度の～な人だ He *is modest* in his behavior. そんなことおっしゃってずいぶんとご～ですね You *are* very *modest,* aren't you ?

げんそん【現存】 ¶ 日本に～する最古の建物 the

oldest building *existing* in Japan. ～の人々 people *alive*.

けんたい【倦怠】ennui; fatigue; weariness. ¶ときどき生活に～を感じる I sometimes *feel weary* (≒ *tired*) *of* life.

—感 ¶～感に悩まされた I *was in great boredom*. —期 the stage of ennui 〔in married life〕.

げんたい【減退】decline; decrease. ¶暑さのため食欲が～する My appetite *falls off* because of the heat. 年をとると視力が～する As we grow older our sight *fails* (≒ *falls off*; *declines*). 食欲～ *a loss* of appetite.

げんだい【現代】the present age (≒ day); modern times; this age; our time; today. ¶～の科学 *modern* science. 彼は～的センスの持ち主だ He *is modern in* his feelings.

—思想 modern thought; modernism. —文学 contemporary literature.

けんたん【健啖】¶きみの～なのには驚く What an appetite you have! / What a heavy eater you are!

—家 a heavy eater; a glutton.

けんち【見地】a point of view; a standpoint; a viewpoint. ¶科学的～から from *a* scientific *standpoint* (≒ *viewpoint*; *point of view*). 専門家の～から from the *viewpoint* of a specialist.

げんち【現地】the spot. ¶記者は事件の発生した～に飛んだ Reporters flew to *the* 〔*very*〕 *place* where the accident happened.

—報告 a report from the spot; reportage.

げんち【言質】a pledge; a promise; a commitment. ¶団交で使用者側の～を取った In the course of collective bargaining we obtained the employer's *pledge*. 彼はなんの～も与えなかった He did not make any *promise*. / He did not commit himself to any sort of *promise*.

けんちく【建築】building. ¶彼の家は今～中だ His house *is* now *being built* (≒ *is* now *building*; *is* now *under construction*).

—家 an architect. —業者 a builder. —許可 a building permit. —材料 building materials. —費 building expenses; the cost of construction. 木造(コンクリート)— a wooden (concrete) building.

けんちじ【県知事】a 〔prefectural〕 governor.

けんちょ【顕著】¶～な発展 a *remarkable* (≒ *marked*) advance. 物価の値上がりがますます～になった A price rise has become more and more *conspicuous*. この点に改善への努力のあとが～に見られる *Striking* evidences of your efforts at improvement are seen in this point.

げんちょ【原著】the original 〔work〕.

—者 the author.

けんちょう【県庁】a prefectural office (≒ government); (県当局) the prefectural authorities. ¶～所在地 the seat of *prefectural government*.

けんちょうぎ【検潮儀】a tide gauge; a tide register.

けんつく【剣突く】¶～を食わせる give a rebuff (*to*); rebuke; scold. ～を食う get a rebuff; get scolded.

けんてい【検定】(認可) authorization; official approval; (検査) examination; inspection. ¶この教科書は文部省～済みだ The textbook *is approved* by the Ministry of Education.

—試験 an examination for a certificate. —制度 an authorization system; an official examination system. 教科書—制度 the textbook authorization system. 資格—制度 the qualification system.

けんてい【献呈】dedication; (進呈) presentation.

げんてい【限定】¶受験資格を～する *determine* the qualifications for examination.

—版 a limited edition.

げんてん【原典】the original; a text. ¶この文は～から引用した I quoted this passage from *the original*. ～に当たってみた I consulted *the original text* (≒ *the first-hand source*).

げんてん【減点】a demerit mark. ¶彼の素行記録には既に3点～が記録されている He already has three *demerits* on his behavior record. 彼は綴りをまちがえて2点～された He lost two marks because he made a mistake in spelling. 反則者は～する An offender will receive *a more reduced number of* 〔*merit*〕 *marks*.

けんでんき【検電器】(検流計) a galvanometer; (験流器) a galvanoscope; (漏電の) a detector.

げんど【限度】a limit; bounds. ¶～を定める set (≒ fix) *a limit* (*to*). 月5万円の～内で within the *limit* of fifty thousand yen a month. 物には～がある There is *a limit to* (≒ *in*) everything.

けんとう【見当】(推測) a guess; a conjecture; (ねらい) an aim; (方向) a direction. ¶まあそんな～だ You *are about right*. 彼がなにを考えているのかだいたい～がつく I can *imagine* what he has in mind. / I'*ve got a rough idea of* what he is thinking. 警察は彼の身元の～が全然つかない The police have no *clue to* his identity. その住所はだいたいこの～だ The address is roughly in this *direction*. 彼は40歳～にちがいない He must be *about* forty. 旅費は5万円～かかるだろう The traveling expenses will be *about* fifty thousand yen. 修繕費のおおよその～を教えてくれませんか Could you tell me the *probable* cost of repairs?

けんとう【健闘】¶ご～を祈る Good luck 〔to you〕! 彼は困難をものともせず～した He *fought bravely* against difficulties.

けんとう【検討】examination; investigation. ¶～する examine; check up. もう一度それを～してください Won't you *think* it *over* again?

けんとう【拳闘】boxing.

けんどう【県道】a prefectural highway.

けんどう【剣道】*kendo*; 〔the art of Japanese〕 fencing; sword〔s〕manship.

げんとう【幻燈】(幻燈のスライド) a lantern slide;

(幻燈機) a magic lantern. ¶ ～を映す project pictures with *a magic lantern.*

げんとう【舷燈】〔航海〕a side light.

げんとう【厳冬】a severe (≒ hard) winter.

げんどう【言動】*one's* speech and action. ¶ ～を慎みなさい Be careful in your *speech and action.* / Be careful about *what you say or do.* / Mind *your P's and Q's.* 彼の～はりっぱだ His *speech and conduct* are fine.

けんとうちがい【見当違い】¶ ～な発言 an *irrelevant* speech. 彼は～の方へ行ってしまった He has gone in the *wrong* direction. きみの推測は全然～だ Your guess *is* quite *wide of the mark.* / You are guessing pretty *wrongly.* それはまったくの～だ You are quite *mistaken.* ～の所を捜してもむだだ It is no use looking for it at the *wrong* place. 私の言うことに～な解釈をしてもらっちゃ困る I don't want you to *take* my words *amiss.*

げんどうりょく【原動力】(推進力) driving force; (動機) a motive; (動力) motive power.

げんとして【厳として】¶ それは～存在する事実だ It is a *solid* fact. 富士の高根は～そびえ立っている The lofty peak of Mt. Fuji rises *impressively* high 〔above the clouds〕.

けんどじゅうらい【捲土重来】¶ 今度は勝つぞと～を期する be resolved to make another attempt for victory with redoubled efforts.

けんない【圏内】¶ 射程～に *within* range. 共産～の国 a country *within the sphere of* Communist influence. 勢力～にある be *within the sphere of* influence. 台風～に入る be *within* the typhoon area. 彼は当選～にのし上がってきた He has got into *the bounds* of possibility of winning the election. / He is beginning to have a fair chance of winning the election.

げんなり ¶ 彼のお説教には～した I *got tired of* his usual lecture. テスト, テストで思っただけでも～だ Test after test all the time! The mere thought of it *makes* us *sick.* 甘い物は～するぐらい食べた I've had sweets enough. I'*m getting sick at* the sight now.

げんに【現に】actually; really; (たとえば) for instance. ¶ そのことは～この耳で聞いた I heard it with my own ears. / I heard it at first hand.

けんにょう【検尿】〔医学〕examination of urine; a urine test.

けんにん【兼任】¶ 彼はふたつの会社の役員を～している He holds an executive position in two companies. 首相が外相を～する The Prime Minister *serves concurrently* as Foreign Minister.

けんにん【堅忍】¶ 彼は～不抜の精神で勉強し, 優等で卒業した He studied *perseveringly* and graduated with honors.

けんのう【献納】¶ これはみな神社への～品だ These are all *offerings* to the shrine.

けんのう【権能】¶ これは彼の～を超えた問題である This is a matter beyond his *authority* (≒ *power*).

げんのしょうこ〔植物〕a cranesbill; a crane's-bill.

けんば【犬馬】¶ 彼のために～の労をとろう I am prepared to serve him. / I will render to him what little service I possibly can.

けんぱ【検波】〔電気〕detection.
—器 a detector.

げんば【現場】the scene; the spot. ¶ 警官が事故の～に急行した The police hurried to *the scene* of the accident. スリは～でつかまった The pickpocket was caught *in the very act of* stealing. 今～には5人のセールスマンがいる We now have five salesmen *in the field.* 彼はそのとき～にいた He was *on the spot* at the time.
—監督 a field overseer. —検証 an investigation of the scene of crime.

げんぱい【減配】a dividend cut. ¶ 会社は今期配当を2分～した The company *reduced its dividends* by 2 percent this term.

げんばく【原爆】an atom〔ic〕bomb; an A-bomb.
—実験 an A-bomb test. —症 an A-bomb disease. —戦争 an atomic war; (核戦争) a nuclear war.

げんばつ【厳罰】severe punishment. ¶ 彼は～に処せられた He *was severely punished.* 違反者には～をもって臨むつもりである We'll *deal severely with* offenders.

けんばん【鍵盤】the keyboard (*of* a piano).

げんばん【原板】〔写真〕a film negative.

けんび【兼備】¶ 才色～の女性 a woman *with both* beauty *and* intelligence; a beautiful *and* intelligent woman.

けんびきょう【顕微鏡】a microscope. ¶ ～で細菌を調べる examine the germ through *a microscope.* 200倍の～ *a microscope* of two hundred magnifications.
—写真 a micrograph; a photomicrograph. 電子— an electron microscope.

けんぴつ【健筆】¶ 彼は相変わらず～をふるっている He still *wields a productive pen.*

げんぴん【現品】—在庫 the goods in stock. —引き換え払い cash on delivery (C.O.D.).

けんぶ【剣舞】a sword dance. ¶ 彼は美しい～を舞った He performed *a* beautiful *sword dance.*

げんぶがん【玄武岩】〔鉱物〕basalt.

けんぶつ【見物】sightseeing. ¶ ～する go sightseeing (*in, at, around*). 東京～を楽しみにしている I look forward to *seeing the sights of* Tokyo (≒ *visiting* Tokyo). ロンドンの名所～は楽しかった I enjoyed *sightseeing* in London. 彼らはみな高見の～をしていた They all *remained mere spectators.*
—席 a seat; a stand. —人(観光の) a sightseer; (見る人) an onlooker; a spectator.

げんぶつ【現物】the actual (≒ real) thing. ¶ 代金は～と引き換えでけっこうです You can pay for it on delivery. ～を見なければなんとも言えない I can't say either way without seeing *the*

け

goods. 彼女は金でなく～(品物)で借金を支払った She paid the debt *in kind* rather than with money.

けんぶん【見聞】(知識) information;(経験) experience;(観察) observation. ¶ 彼は～が広い He *has had wide experience.* / He *is well-informed.* / He *has seen much of life.* われわれは旅行をして～を広めた We increased our *knowledge* by traveling.
—記 a record of *one's* experiences.

けんぶん【検分】inspection.
下— a preliminary examination. 実地— ¶ そこを実地～した I *inspected* the place *in person.* / I *made a personal inspection* of the place.

げんぶん【原文】the 〔original〕 text;(原書) the original. ¶ シェイクスピアを～で読んだ I read Shakespeare's works *in the original.* これは～に忠実に訳してある This is a faithful translation of *the original.*

げんぶんいっち【言文一致】¶ ～で書く write in a colloquial style.

けんぺい【権柄】¶ 彼は私に対して～ずくな態度をとった He *domineered over* me.

けんぺい【憲兵】a military policeman (an MP; an M.P.).
—隊 the military police.

けんべん【検便】a stool test (stool は腰掛け式の便器の意味から). ¶ 学校では年1回～を行なう The school makes *a stool test* for the students once a year. ～用の便を医者に届けた I sent a specimen (≒ sample) of my *stools* to the doctor.

げんぼ【原簿】〘簿記〙a ledger.

けんぼう【権謀】¶ 彼は～術数にたけている He is clever at *tricks.* / He is a *crafty* person.

けんぽう【憲法】a constitution. ¶ これは～に違反している This is against *the Constitution.* / This *is unconstitutional.* ～改正の動きがある There is a movement to revise *the Constitution.* 戦後新しい～が公布された *A* new *Constitution* was proclaimed after the war.
—記念日 Constitution Memorial Day.

げんぽう【減法】〘数学〙subtraction.

げんぽう【減俸】a salary reduction. ¶ 彼は10パーセント～された His salary *was cut down* (≒ *was reduced*) by ten percent.

けんぼうしょう【健忘症】〘医学〙amnesia; (忘れっぽいこと) forgetfulness. ¶ 彼は～にかかっている He *is very forgetful.* / He *is forgetting things.*

げんぼく【原木】lumber.

けんぽん【献本】(著者からの) a complimentary copy;(本屋からの) an inspection copy.
¶ ～する *present* a copy.

げんぽん【原本】the original 〔book〕; the text.

けんま【研摩】¶ レンズを～する *grind* a lens.

げんまい【玄米】hulled (≒ unpolished) rice.

けんまく【剣幕・見幕】a fierce look; a threatening attitude. ¶ 彼はものすごい～で私に食ってかかった He turned upon me *with a terrifying look* (≒ *with a threatening attitude*).

げんみつ【厳密】¶ ～に言えば *strictly* speaking. ～に調べる examine *closely.* それは～な調査を要した It required a *close* investigation. ～な意味ではそれとこれとは違う They are different in a *strict* sense 〔of the word〕.

けんみん【県民】the people of a prefecture.

けんむ【兼務】¶ 彼は会計課長と庶務課長を～している He *is concurrently* chief of both the accounting *and* the general affairs sections.

けんめい【賢明】wisdom; good sense. ¶ それは～な判断だった It was a *wise* judgment.

けんめい【懸命】eagerness; earnestness.
¶ それは彼の～な努力のたまものだ It is the fruit of his *earnest* work. 彼は毎日～に努力した He worked *very hard* every day.

げんめい【言明】a statement; a declaration.
¶ それについてはっきりした～を避けた I avoided making any definite *statement* about it.

げんめい【原名】the original name.

げんめい【厳命】a strict (≒ rigid) order.
¶ ただちに出発せよと～を受けた I *was strictly ordered* to start at once.

げんめつ【幻滅】disillusionment. ¶ 彼女の不実に～の悲哀を感じた I *was disillusioned by* her dishonesty.

げんめん【原綿】raw cotton.

けんもほろろ ¶ ～のあいさつ a *curt* answer. 彼女の訴えに彼は～だった He *was very cold* to her appeal. ～に追い払われた I was *flatly* (≒ *curtly*) told to leave.

けんもん【検問】inspection; examination.
¶ 警官は彼女を～した The police *checked up on* her.
—所 a checking point.

げんや【原野】a wild plain; a wilderness.

けんやく【倹約】economy; thrift. ¶ 今月はできるだけ～しなければならない This month I have to *economize* as much as I can. 自分でやれば500円の～になる It will *save* you 500 yen if you do it by yourself. 子どもたちはクリスマスのためにお金を～している The children *are saving money* for Christmas. 彼女は時間を～して使っている She *is economical* of her time.

げんゆ【原油】crude oil.

げんゆう【現有】¶ ～勢力 the *existing* strength.

けんよう【兼用】combined use. ¶ ここは居間と食堂の～だ This is used (≒ This serves) both as a living room and a dining room. この机は彼と～だ I *share* this desk *with* him.

けんらん【絢爛】gorgeousness; brilliancy.
¶ 歌手は～たる衣装で現われた The singer appeared *dazzlingly* dressed. ～たる文体 an *ornate* (≒ a *high-flown*) style.

けんり【権利】a right;(請求権) a claim;(権限) authority. ¶ ～と義務 *rights* and duties. 法律上の～ legal *rights.* 条約上の～ treaty *rights.* ～を行使する exercise *one's right.* われわれはその部屋に入る～がある We have *a* (≒ *the*) *right* to enter the room. われわれには彼を止める～はない We have no *right* to stop him.

彼は〜を失った(放棄した) He lost (abandoned) his *rights.* きみの〜を主張しなさい Stand on your *rights.* 彼は土地の使用の〜を主張した He claimed *a right* to the use of the land. その家は当然の〜で彼女のものだ The house belongs to her by *rights.*

げんり【原理】a principle; a theory.

けんりつ【県立】¶〜高等学校 a *prefectural* high school.

げんりょう【原料】raw (≒ crude) material. ¶日本は多くの〜を輸入している Japan imports a lot of *raw materials.*

げんりょう【減量】a loss in weight (≒ quantity). ¶彼女は最近〜に努めている She *is reducing* these days.

けんりょく【権力】power; authority. ¶彼は総理大臣としてほしいままの〜をふるった He wielded (≒ exercised) the *power* of the Prime Minister at will.

—争い a struggle for power. 国家— state authority. —主義 authoritarianism. —政治 power politics.

けんろう【堅牢】solidity; durability. ¶この箱は〜にできている This box is *strongly* (≒ *solidly*) made.

げんろう【元老】¶政界の〜 an *elder* statesman. 医学界の〜 an *influential senior member* of the medical world.

げんろん【言論】speech; discussion. ¶〜の自由 freedom of *speech* (冠詞つけない); (新聞・雑誌の) the freedom of *the press* (the をつける). 〜の圧迫 pressure (≒ oppression) on *public opinion.*

—界 the press. —機関 an organ of public opinion.

げんろん【原論】a theory; a principle. ¶経済学〜 the *principles* of economics.

げんわく【眩惑】dazzlement. ¶彼の話じょうずに〜されだまされた We *were dazzled* and deceived by his clever speech.

こ

こ【子】a child (複 children); (男の子) a boy; (女の子) a girl; (犬の) a puppy; (ネコの) a kitten; (牛の) a calf (複 calves).

¶この〜はとても利口な〜だ This is *a* very bright *boy.* かわいい〜には旅をさせよ(諺) *Spare the rod and spoil the child.* 〜を持って知る親の恩 He knows not what parental love is who has no *children.* 〜を知ること親に如(し)かず The parents are the best judges of their *children.* かけごとで元も〜もなくした He lost everything by gambling.

こ【弧】an arc. ¶〜を描く draw *an arc.* 〜を描いて飛ぶ fly *in an arc.*

こ【故】¶〜山田氏 the *late* Mr. Yamada.

こ【個】¶リンゴ5〜 five apples. 3〜のせっけん three *pieces* (≒ *cakes*) of soap.

こ-【小-】¶〜1時間 about an hour; nearly an hour (about は1時間以上のこともあるが, nearly はつねに1時間以内の意になる).

ご【五】five.

ご【後】¶その〜 afterward[s]; after that. その〜彼には会っていない I have not seen him *since.* 3日〜に three days *later* (≒ *after*) (主として過去のことに用いる). 1週間〜に *in* a week (主として現在以後に用いる).

ご【語】a word.

ご【碁】*go.* ¶〜を打つ play *go.*

—石 a *go* piece. —盤 a *go* board.

ごあいさつ【御挨拶】¶これは〜だね Well! This is a surprise!

コアカリキュラム a core curriculum.

こあたり【小当たり】¶われわれはまず彼に〜してみた We first *sounded* his opinion *in a roundabout way.*

こい【恋】love. ¶〜する love; have a tender feeling (*toward*); fall in *love* (*with*). 〜に破れる be disappointed in *love.* 〜に悩む be lovesick.

こい【鯉】a carp (複 carp).

こい【故意】¶彼が〜にやったのなら許せない If he did it *intentionally* (≒ *on purpose*), he is inexcusable.

こ・い【濃い】(色が) deep; dark; (液体が) heavy; thick; (霧が) dense; thick; (コーヒーなどが) strong.

¶〜いスープ *thick* soup. 〜いまつげ *thick* eyelashes. 敗色が〜い There are growing signs of defeat. 彼女の化粧は〜い She makes up *heavily.* 血は水よりも〜い Blood *is thicker* than water. 彼女は私の〜い血縁だ She is a *close* relative of mine. 私にお茶を〜く入れてください Would you please make tea *strong* for me?

ごい【語彙】a vocabulary. ¶彼女は〜が豊かだ She has *a* rich *vocabulary.* / Her *vocabulary* is rich. 貧弱な〜を豊かにする enrich *one's* poor *vocabulary.* 基本〜 *a* basic *vocabulary.*

こいがたき【恋敵】a rival in love; a rival suitor.

こいき【小意気】¶〜な smart; stylish. 〜に smartly; stylishly.

こいこが・れる【恋い焦がれる】burn with passion (*for*); be consumed with love (*for*).

ごいさぎ【五位鷺】〘鳥類〙a night heron.

こいし【小石】a small stone; a pebble.
こいじ【恋路】¶ 人の～のじゃまをする thwart *a person's loves.*
こいし・い【恋しい】¶ ふるさとが～い I *am sick for* home. / I *miss* home. 母が～い I *long for* my mother.
こい・する【恋する】⇒こい
こいつ【此奴】¶ ～め! You *villain* (≒ *scoundrel*)!
こいなか【恋仲】¶ 彼らは～だ They *are in love with* each other.
こいにょうぼう【恋女房】*one's* beloved wife. ¶ 彼女は彼の～だ He married her for love.
こいぬ【子犬・小犬】a puppy; a little dog.
こいのぼり【鯉幟】¶ ～を立てる put up *a carp streamer.*
こいびと【恋人】(男) a lover; (女) a love (男女1組なら lovers でよい).
こいぶみ【恋文】a love letter.
コイル a coil.
こいわずらい【恋煩い】love sickness. ¶ ～をする be lovesick.
こう【功】credit; honor; merits. ¶ ～なり名とげる be distinguished forever after meritorious work; win fame and name. ～を立てる distinguish *oneself*; render distinguished services. 彼は～を急ぎすぎる He is too eager for *success.* ～により in recognition of *one's services*; for *one's services rendered.* 年の～ the *merit* of age.
こう【行】¶ どこまでもきみと～をともにするつもりだ I will go with you wherever you go.
こう【孝】¶ 父母に～を尽くす *be dutiful to one's* parents.
こう【効】efficacy; virture. ¶ この薬は胃病に～あり This medicine *is good for* stomach trouble.
こう【幸】¶ ～か不幸か予想は的中した *Happily* or unhappily it was just as we expected.
こう【稿】¶ その点については～を新たにする I am going to write on it in another *article.*
こう【項】〖数学〗a term; (条項) a clause; an item; (文章の) a paragraph. ¶ 第2条第2～ Article II, Clause 2. 内～ internal *terms.*
こう【甲】(足) the instep; (手) the back; (カメなど) a shell; a tortoise shell; (甲乙の) grade A. ¶ かめの～より年の功 (諺) Experience counts. / Sense comes with age.
こう【香】incense. ¶ ～をたく burn *incense.* ～をかぐ smell *incense.*
-こう【-公】¶ 近衛～ *Prince* Konoe. 熊～八～ Jack and Joe.
-こう【-港】a port; a harbor (port は港のある都市を重視して, harbor は港そのものを主としていう. harbor は防波堤などで風・波を防いでいる港. port は貨物船・客船などが荷役をする港. 一般には両方の要素を備えているものが多い). ¶ 東京～ Tokyo *Harbor.* 神戸～ the *Port* of Kobe; Kobe *Port.*
こ・う【請う】¶ 一夜の宿を～う *ask* for a night's lodging. 人に助けを～う *appeal* to *a person* for help. 慈悲を～う *beg for* mercy. 人の許しを～う *beg a person's* pardon. 彼は私に許しを～うた He *begged* me to forgive him. これのご一覧を～う I *beg* to submit this to your inspection.
こう【斯う】¶ ～言って彼は立ち去った *So* saying, he left. ～しなさい Do it *this way.* 実は～だ The fact is *this.* / It is like *this.* / This is what happened. / I tell you what. ～なっては, もうおしまいだ Now that things have come to *this,* there is no way out. 長いこと～はしていられない I cannot go on *like this* for a long time.
ごう【合】(容量の単位) a *gō* (=0.18 liter). ¶ 富士山の八～目 *the* eighth *stage* (≒ *station*) of Mt. Fuji.
ごう【号】a number; an issue; (雅号) a pen name. ¶ ～は大観 an artist with *a pen name* of Taikan. 彼はみずから大拙と～した He called himself Daisetsu.
ごう【業】¶ 彼の不勉強には～を煮やしている I *am impatient with* his laziness.
ごう【郷】¶ ～に入っては～に従え (諺) *When in Rome, do as the Romans do.* / *Do in Rome as the Romans do.*
こうあつ【高圧】¶ ～的手段 a *coercive* measure. 役所の言い分は非常に～的だった The office showed us a very *oppressive* attitude.
—がま a high-pressure pan. **—線** a high-tension line (≒ wire).
こうあん【公安】**—委員** a public safety commissioner. **—条例** the Public Safety Regulations.
こうあん【考案】¶ ～する design; devise. **—者** an originator.
こうい【行為】an action; an act. ¶ 親切な～ *an act* of kindness. 残忍な～ *a* cruel *act.*
こうい【好意】a favor; a kindness. ¶ 彼に対して～を持っている I have *a friendship* for him. ご～を感謝いたします I wish to offer my gratitude for your *kindness.* 彼はその考えに～的だ He *is friendly to* that idea. 彼に～を寄せている人もある There are some who look on him with *favor.* 人の～を無にするな You should accept the *favor* of another with thanks. / You should prove worthy of the *favor* shown. (このように2様に解される). …の～により through the *good offices* (≒ *courtesy; kindness*) of....
こうい【皇位】the Imperial Throne. ¶ ～につく succeed to (≒ ascend) *the Imperial Throne.*
こうい【高位】¶ ～高官の人 a man *of high rank* and office; a man *of distinction.*
こうい【校医】a school physician.
ごうい【合意】〔an〕agreement; consent. ¶ ～する agree; consent. ～のうえで by *mutual* (≒ *common*) *agreement.* ～が成立する reach *an agreement*; be in agreement. ～に基づく based on *an agreement.*
—書 a statement of mutual agreement. **—離婚** a divorce by mutual agreement.
こういう【斯ういう】¶ ～ふうにする I will do it

this way. 〜まちがいはよくある *This kind of* mistake is quite frequent. 〜色が欲しかった I wanted a color *of this kind.* 実は〜次第です This is exactly how it happened. 〜ことは二度としてはいけない You should never do *such a thing* 〔as this〕 again.

こういしつ【更衣室】a locker (≒ dressing) room.

こういしょう【後遺症】〘医学〙 a sequela (複 sequelae); an after-effect 〔of a disease〕. ¶ 〜が残るかもしれません I am afraid there may be *an after-effect.*

こういっつい【好一対】a good pair (≒ match). ¶ ふたりはまことに〜のご夫婦です They are *a* very *well-matched couple.*

こういってん【紅一点】the only female (in the company).

こういん【行員】a bank clerk.

こういん【工員】a factory worker (≒ hand); a workman; an operative.

こういん【光陰】¶ 〜矢のごとし(諺) *Time flies like an arrow.* (like an arrow は実際にはあまりつけ加えない).

こういん【拘引】arrest; custody. ¶ 〜する take *a person* into custody; put *a person* under arrest. 彼女は〜されている She *is under arrest.* / She *is held in custody.*

ごういん【強引】¶ 〜にその案を彼に納得させた We *forced* him *to* consent to the proposal. 彼の交渉は〜だった He negotiated most *forcibly.*

ごうう【豪雨】¶ 〜になるだろう We shall have *a heavy rain.*

こううりょう【降雨量】the amount of rainfall.

こううん【幸運】good luck (≒ fortune). ¶ 彼女は〜にも自動車事故で生き残った She *was lucky* (≒ *was fortunate*) enough to survive the car accident. / *Fortunately* she survived the car accident. ご〜を祈ります I wish you *the best of luck.* / I wish you *good luck*! / *Good luck*!

—児 a fortune's favorite; a lucky person.

こううんき【耕運機】a cultivator.

こうえい【公営】¶ 競馬は〜になった Horse racing was placed under *municipal management.*

—企業(官・国営) a government enterprise; (地方都市営) a municipal enterprise. **—**住宅 municipal housing.

こうえい【光栄】glory; honor. ¶ 彼は文化勲章授与の〜に浴した He had the *honor of* receiving the Order for Cultural Merits. お招きにあずかり〜です It is *a* great *honor* for me to be invited. 今夕みなさまにお話する機会を得たことは私の大きな〜と存じます I *feel highly honored* (≒ I consider it *a great honor*) to have the opportunity of speaking to you this evening.

こうえい【後衛】(軍事) the rear guard; (テニス) the back player.

こうえい【後裔】a descendant; an offspring; (集合的に) progeny.

こうえいへい【紅衛兵】the Red Guard.

こうえき【公益】¶ 〜のために in *the interest of the public.* 〜をはかる promote *the public interest.*

—委員 the public utilities commission. **—**事業 a public utility. **—**質屋 a public pawnshop. **—**法人 a public-service corporation.

こうえき【交易】trade; commerce; barter. ¶ 〜する *trade* (*with*); engage in *foreign trade* (*with*). 日本は中国との〜をもっと盛んにすべきだ Japan should increase the *trade* with China.

こうえつ【校閲】revision. ¶ 〜する revise; look over. K博士〜の本 a book *revised* by Dr. K.

—者 a reviser.

こうえん【公演】a public performance. ¶ 〜する play; perform 〔before an audience〕; present.

こうえん【好演】a good performance; good acting.

こうえん【公園】a park. ¶ 国立〜 *a* national *park.* 自然〜 *a* natural *park.* 日比谷〜 Hibiya *Park* (ふつう無冠詞).

こうえん【後援】support; backing. ¶ 政府の〜を得る have government *support.* 経済的に〜する *support* (*a person*) financially; give financial *support* (*to a person*). 彼女を〜してあげなさい Give her *support.* ある会社の〜で with the *support* of a certain company; under the *sponsorship* of a certain company; *sponsored* by a certain company.

—会 a sponsors' association. ¶ A氏の〜会を作る organize a society for the support of Mr. A. **—**者 a sponsor; a supporter.

こうえん【講演】a lecture; a speech. ¶ 〜する give *a* lecture (*on*); make a speech; lecture (*on*); address a meeting (*on*).

—会 a lecture meeting. **—**者 a lecturer. 公開**—** a public (≒ open) lecture.

こうえん【高遠】¶ 〜な理想 a lofty ideal.

こうお【好悪】¶ 彼は人の〜が激しい He *is* very *partial to* his friends.

こうおつ【甲乙】¶ 両者は〜をつけがたい There is little difference between the two. / They are peas from the same pod.

こうおん【高音】¶ このステレオは〜が特にきれいだ You can get a clear sound with this stereo-set, especially with *higher tones.*

こうおん【高温】high temperature. ¶ 摂氏100度の〜ならばたいていの細菌は死ぬ Most bacteria will die at the temperature of one hundred degrees C.

ごうおん【轟音】¶ 〜とともにジェット機は飛び立った The jet took off with *a deafening roar.*

こうか【工科】an engineering department.

—大学 an engineering college; a school of engineering.

こうか【効果】effect. ¶ 展示会の色彩〜が人々を感心させた People were impressed by the color *effect* of the exhibition. 鼻薬をきかした〜はてきめんだった The tip *worked* at once. 大

売り出しの宣伝をしただけの～があった The advertisement of our grand sale *was* quite *effective* as we had expected. あれだけやってみたが～はなかった With all our efforts, it *was of* no *effect*. 大いに～的にやりなさい Do it *in a* most *effective way*. / Do it most *effectively*.

こ

こうか【降下】¶ 彼らは落下傘(らっかさん)で地上に～した They *landed* by parachutes.

こうか【高価】¶ そんな～な品は不要だ I don't want such *expensive* articles.

こうか【高架】──鉄道 an elevated railroad; the L (≒ the El) (米, とくに New York で); 英 an overhead railway.

こうか【校歌】a school (≒ college) song.

こうか【硬化】¶ 相手は急に態度を～させてきた They suddenly *stiffened* (≒ *hardened*) their attitude.

動脈── hardening of the arteries; 〖医学〗 arterial sclerosis.

こうか【硬貨】a coin; hard money (≒ cash).

こうが【高雅】¶ あの人の～な文に打たれた I was impressed by his *refined* style of writing.

こうが【黄河】the Yellow River.

ごうか【豪華】¶ きょうの夕食は～だ What a *wonderful* feast we are having this evening! 彼女は～な衣装をたくさん持っている She has lots of *gorgeous* dresses.

こうかい【公海】the high seas. ¶ ～の自由 freedom of *the seas*.

こうかい【公開】¶ ～する *make* (*a thing*) *open* 〔*to the public*〕. それは寺の秘仏として～はされていない It *is* not *open to the public* since it is treasured by the temple as a sacred image.

──講座 extension lectures. ──状 an open letter.

こうかい【後悔】repentance. ¶ ～する repent (*of one's* folly); be sorry (*for* a remark). ～先に立たず (諺) *Repentance* comes too late. / *It is no use crying over spilt milk.*

こうかい【航海】a voyage. ¶ 彼らは世界一周の～に出た They went on *a voyage* around the world. その船は横浜からハワイへの～中に行方不明になった The boat was lost *on the voyage* from Yokohama to Hawaii. 楽しい～をなさいますように I *wish* you *a* happy *voyage*. / Bon voyage! (フランス語から. 船旅でなくても用いる). ～中海は荒れた (静かだった) We've had *a* rough (quiet) *voyage*.

──権 the right of navigation. ──士 a mate; a navigation officer. ¶ 一(二; 三)等～士 the chief (second; third) mate. ──術 〔the art of〕 navigation. ──図 a chart. ──長 the chief navigator. ──日誌 a ship's log; a voyage log; a ship's journal; a logbook. 遠洋── ocean navigation. 処女── a maiden voyage. 練習── a training voyage.

こうがい【口外】¶ この話は～無用に願います Let's keep the news to ourselves. / Remember this is just between you and me.

こうがい【口蓋】〖解剖学〗the palate.

こうがい【公害】environmental pollution (public hazards はさける). ¶ 市当局は～防止のためになんの策も講じていない The city has taken no measures for preventing *environmental pollution*.

──対策 pollution countermeasures. 産業── industrial pollution. 騒音── noise pollution.

こうがい【郊外】the suburbs; the outskirts (郊外の1箇所は a suburb of Tokyo のようにする). ¶ 彼の家は～にある He lives in *the suburbs*.

──電車 a suburban train.

こうがい【構外】¶ ～の(～に) outside the *grounds* (≒ *compound*).

こうがい【梗概】an outline. ¶ 小説の～を説明する give (≒ tell) the *outline* of a novel.

こうがい【港外】¶ 漁船がいっせいに～へ出ていく The fishing boats are leaving the port all together. 貨物船が～に停泊しているA freighter lies at anchor *off the harbor*.

ごうかい【豪快】¶ ～に笑う give a *hearty* laugh.

ごうがい【号外】an extra.

こうかいどう【公会堂】a public hall.

こうかく【口角】¶ 彼らは～あわを飛ばして論じ合っている They are having a heated discussion.

こうかく【広角】──レンズ a wide-angle lens.

こうがく【工学】engineering.

──博士 a doctor of engineering. ──部 the department of engineering.

こうがく【光学】optics.

──機械 an optical instrument.

こうがく【後学】¶ ～のために聞いておいた I asked *for my own information*. / I asked *for future reference*. 彼は熱心に～の指導に当たった He put his heart into the guidance of his *juniors*.

こうがく【高額】a large sum 〔of money〕.

──所得者 a person with a large income.

──紙幣 a bill of a high denomination.

ごうかく【合格】passing; success (*in*). ¶ 検査に～する *pass* inspection. 試験に～する *pass* (≒ *succeed in*) an examination.

──通知 a notice of success. ──者 a passer; a successful candidate. ──点 a passing mark. ¶ ～点に達する get the *passing mark*.

こうがくしん【向学心】love of learning. ¶ 新入生はみな～に燃えている The freshmen *are* all *eager to learn*.

こうがくねん【高学年】higher classes 〔of a school〕.

こうかくるい【甲殻類】〖動物〗the Crustacea.

こうかつ【狡猾】¶ ～な cunning; sly. ～に craftily; cunningly. ～さ cunning; craft.

こうかっしょく【黄褐色】yellowish brown.

こうかん【公刊】publication. ¶ ～する *publish* (a book).

こうかん【公館】a Government building. 在外── diplomatic offices abroad.

こうかん【好感】goodwill; (好印象) a favorable impression. ¶ 彼の話は聴衆に～を与えた His talk *impressed* the audience *favorably*. / His talk gave the audience *a*

favorable impression. 彼は〜の持てる人だ He is a *likable* person. 私は彼に〜を持っている I have *friendly feeling toward* him.
こうかん【好漢】 a nice fellow.
こうかん【交換】 exchange; (物々交換) barter. ¶ その問題について互いに意見を〜した We *exchanged* views on the problem. 私と席を〜してくれませんか Will you *exchange* (≒ *change*) seats with me? 彼と贈り物を〜した I *exchanged* gifts with him. 日本語と〜で彼に英語を教えた I taught him English *in exchange for* Japanese. 米と砂糖を物々〜した We *bartered* rice *for* sugar.
—教授(学生) an exchange professor (student). —局(電話の) 米 a central office; 英 a telephone exchange. —手 a 〔telephone〕 operator. —所(手形の) a cleaning house. —条件 the terms of exchange. —台 a switchboard.
こうかん【交歓】 exchange of goodwill.
—会 a get-together 〔meeting〕; a reception. —競技 a friendly game.
こうかん【高官】 a high official.
こうかん【鋼管】 a steel pipe.
こうかん【巷間】 ¶ 〜伝えるところによれば彼は父の死でばく大な財産を相続したそうだ *It is said* (≒ *People say*) that he inherited a huge fortune on his father's death.
こうがん【紅顔】 ¶ 〜の美少年 a *handsome* young boy.
こうがん【厚顔】 ¶ 〜無恥な shameless. 彼の〜には驚いた How *impudent* (≒ *shameless; brazen-faced*) he *is*! / His *impudence*!
こうがん【睾丸】〘解剖学〙 testicles.
こうかんしんけい【交感神経】〘生理学〙 the sympathetic nerve.
こうかんぱん【後甲板】 the afterdeck; the quarterdeck.
こうき【公器】 ¶ 新聞は社会の〜だ The newspaper is *a public organ* of society.
こうき【広軌】 a broad gauge. ¶ 〜鉄道 a *broad-gauge* railroad (≒ 英 railway). 東海道新幹線は〜だ The Tokaido New Line *is broad gauged.*
こうき【光輝】 glory; splendor. ¶ 〜ある伝統 the *glorious* tradition (*of* our school).
こうき【好機】 a good opportunity (≒ chance). ¶ 〜到来 Now is the time. この〜を逃がしてはならない You must not miss this *chance.*
こうき【好奇】 ¶ いまでは外国人を〜の目で見る人は少ない Now few people look up on foreigners with *curiosity* (≒ *a curious eye*).
こうき【後期】 the latter period; (2学期制の学校の) the second semester. ¶ 〜の試験 *final* examinations; finals.
こうき【香気】 sweet smell; fragrance; aroma.
こうき【高貴】 ¶ 〜な noble. ここへは〜の方がたもよくお忍びでいらっしゃる Even *dignitaries* often pay private visits to this place.
こうき【校旗】 a school banner.
こうき【校規】 a school regulation.
こうき【綱紀】 〔official〕 discipline. ¶ 役所の〜の緩んでいる証拠に汚職が盛んに起こっている The frequent corruption cases reflect the loose *discipline of the office.* 〜粛正 enforcement of *official discipline.*
こうき【後記】 a postscript (P. S. と略記す). ¶ 編集〜 *a postscript* by the editor.
こうぎ【広義】 a wide sense. ¶ そのことばを〜に解すればなにも問題はない If we take the word *in a broad sense,* there is no problem in the matter.
こうぎ【抗議】 protest. ¶ 市民は新しい計画に〜した The citizens *made a protest against* the new project. 彼の軽率な発言に〜した I *objected to* his careless remarks.
—集会 a protest rally. —デモ a protest demonstration. —文 a note of protest; a written protest.
こうぎ【講義】 a lecture. ¶ 〜に出る attend *a lecture.* 〜をする *lecture* (≒ *give lectures*) (*on* Modern Japan).
こうぎ【交誼】 friendship. ¶ 〜を結ぶ cultivate (≒ form) *friendship* (*with* many people).
ごうき【剛毅】 ¶ 〜な sturdy. 〜に with fortitude. 〜さ fortitude.
ごうき【豪気】 ¶ 〜な plucky; brave; stout-hearted. 〜さ a stout heart. 彼は〜に見える He looks quite *bold.*
ごうぎ【合議】 ¶ 会の運営は会員の〜によってなされる The management of the society is carried out by the *mutual consent* of the members.
—制 a council system.
こうきあつ【高気圧】 ¶ 北日本は〜におおわれている *High atmospheric pressure is* over northern Japan.
こうきしん【好奇心】 curiosity; an inquisitive mind. ¶ 〜が強い be curious (*about*). 〜を満足させる satisfy *one's curiosity.* 〜にかられてやった I did it out of *curiosity.* その話に〜をそそられた The story aroused my *curiosity.*
こうきゅう【好球】〘野球〙 a nice ball. ¶ 〜を見逃す miss *a fair ball.*
こうきゅう【恒久】 ¶ 〜の(的) eternal; everlasting (文語的). 〜性 permanency. 〜平和 *permanent* peace.
こうきゅう【高級】 ¶ 〜な high-class; high-grade.
—官僚 a higher official. —品 an article of superior (≒ high) quality; a first-class article.
こうきゅう【高給】 a high salary. ¶ 彼は〜を取っている He *is highly paid.* / He is earning *a high salary.*
こうきゅう【硬球】 (テニス・野球などの) a *hard* (≒ *regulation*) ball.
ごうきゅう【号泣】 ¶ 彼女はその知らせを聞いて〜した She *cried bitterly* to hear the news.
ごうきゅう【豪球・剛球】〘野球〙 a fast ball.
こうきゅうび【公休日】 a 〔legal〕 holiday; a day off.

こ

こうきょ【皇居】the Imperial Palace. ¶～前広場 the Imperial Palace Plaza.

こうきょう【公共】¶～の物をたいせつにしよう Take good care of *public* properties.
—企業体 a public corporation. —事業 a public enterprise. —施設 a public establishment. —職業安定所 the Public Employment Security Office. —心 a sense of public morality. —団体 a public body (≒ organization).

こうきょう【好況】¶～の prosperous; (市場) brisk.

こうぎょう【工業】industry; the manufacturing industry. ¶～化 industrialization. ～化する industrialize (a country).
—高校 a technical high school. —地帯 an industrial (≒ a manufacturing) area. —都市 an industrial (≒ a manufacturing) city. 家内— home (≒ domestic) industry. 軽— light industry. 手— handicraft. 重— heavy industry.

こうぎょう【鉱業】mining [industry].

こうぎょう【興行】a show; a performance. ¶夜の～ a night performance. 昼の～ a matinee. その一座は1日3回～する The troupe gives three *performances* a day.
—界 the entertainment world. —権 producing rights. —主 a promoter.

こうぎょう【興業】an industrial enterprise.
—銀行 an industrial bank.

こうきょうがく【交響楽】a symphony.
—団 a symphony orchestra.

こうきょうきょく【交響曲】a symphony.

こうきょうし【交響詩】a symphonic poem.

こうぎょく【紅玉】(リンゴ) a Jonathan; 〖鉱物〗 a ruby.

こうぎょく【黄玉】〖宝石〗a topaz.

こうきん【公金】public money (≒ funds). ¶～を横領する embezzle *public funds*.

こうきん【拘禁】confinement; detention. ¶彼は警察に～されている He *is confined* (≒ *is detained*) at the police station.

ごうきん【合金】an alloy. ¶銅と亜鉛の～ *an alloy* of copper and zinc.

こうく【鉱区】a mine lot; a mining area; a mining district.

こうぐ【工具】a tool; an implement. ¶～一式 a set of *tools*.

こうくう【航空】aviation.
—会社 air lines; (主に英) airways (複数形). —管制官 an air-traffic controller. —管制塔 a control tower. —基地 an air base. —自衛隊 the Air Self-Defense Force. —写真 an aerophotography; an aerial photograph. —術(学) aeronautics. —書簡 an aerogram; an air[-mail] letter. —測量 an aerial survey. —大学 an aviation college. —地図 an aerial map. —標識 an air beacon. —便 airmail. —物理学 aerophysics. —母艦 an aircraft carrier; a carrier. —路 an air line; an airline; an airway.

こうぐう【皇宮】—警察 the Imperial Guards.

こうぐう【厚遇】a warm reception; kind (≒ good) treatment; hospitality. ¶その会社は技術者を～する The technicians *are well paid* at the company.

こうぐん【行軍】a march; marching. ¶われわれは1日に60キロを～した We *marched* 60 kilometers a day.

こうけい【口径】a caliber. ¶32～のピストル a 32-*caliber* revolver. 大～レンズ a *wide-angle* lens.

こうけい【光景】a sight; a scene; a spectacle; a view. ¶空から眺めるローマの～は美しい The air *view* of Rome is very beautiful.

こうけい【後継】succession.
—者 a successor. ¶彼は父の財産の～者である He is *heir* to his father's estate. / He is his father's *successor* to his estate. A氏の～者として彼は大統領に選ばれた He has been elected president, *succeeding* Mr. A. —内閣 a succeeding (≒ an incoming) Cabinet.

こうげい【工芸】industrial arts.
—家 a technologist. —品 industrial products.

ごうけい【合計】a total; the sum total (total は形容詞). ¶われわれの出費は～10万円に達した Our expenses *reached a total* of (≒ *totaled to*; *amounted to*; *made*) 100,000 yen. リンゴは～50個ある There are fifty apples *in all* (≒ *altogether*; *all told*). 彼女は費用を～した She *added up* the expenses.

こうけいき【好景気】prosperity; a boom; good times. ¶この国のどの市場も～だ Every market *is booming* (≒ *is brisk*) in this country.

こうげき【攻撃】an attack; an assault.
¶～を始める open *an attack* against. 人の意見を～する *attack a person's* opinions. 要塞(ようさい)を～する make *an assault* on the fortress. ～は最上の防御だ The *offensive* is the best defense. 野党は政府の物価政策を～した The opposition parties *criticized* (≒ *made an attack against*) the government's policy on prices [of commodities].
いっせい— a joint attack. 人身— a personal attack. 総— a general attack. 側面— a flank attack.

こうけつ【高潔】¶～な人柄 a man of *noble* (≒ *upright*) character. 彼の～さには感心する I am impressed with his *noble-mindedness* (≒ *loftiness*).

ごうけつ【豪傑】a hero; a great man. ¶彼は～を気どっている He wears a *heroic* air. / He poses as *a hero*.
—笑い ¶彼はいつも～笑いをする He always laughs a hearty laugh. —はだ ¶彼は～はだだ He *is gallant* (≒ *is heroic*). / He has something of the *hero* in his composition.

こうけつあつ【高血圧】high blood pressure. ¶彼は～だ He suffers from *high blood pressure*.

こうけっか【好結果】a good result. ¶～を生

む produce (≒ bring about) *a good result*; prove *successful*; be *a success*.

こうけん【公権】 civil rights. ¶ 〜剝奪(はくだつ)(停止) deprivation (≒ suspension) of *civil rights*.

こうけん【後見】 guardianship; wardship. ¶ 彼は弟の〜人になった He became *a guardian* for his brother.

こうけん【貢献】 (a) contribution; service. ¶ 彼は科学の進歩に重要な〜をした He made *an* important *contribution* to the development of science. / He greatly *contributed* to the development of science. 社会になんらかの〜をするよう努力すべきだ We should try to *do something for* society. 彼は大学に大いに〜した He rendered great *service* to the university.

こうげん【公言】 ¶ 自分は政府の支持者だと彼は〜した He *professed himself* to be a supporter of the government.

こうげん【巧言】 flattery; flattering speech; fair words. ¶ 彼の〜に惑わされるな Don't be carried away by his *honeyed speech*.

こうげん【光源】〘物理〙 a source of light.

こうげん【抗原】〘生理〙 an antigen.

こうげん【高原】 a plateau; a tableland. ¶ われわれは夏を志賀〜で過ごした We spent the summer at Shiga *Heights*.

ごうけん【合憲】 ¶ 〜性 constitutionality.

ごうけん【剛健】 strong and sturdy; manly. ¶ 〜な精神 a *virile* spirit.

こうげんがく【考現学】 a study of modern phenomena.

こうこ【公庫】 the municipal treasury. 金融— a finance corporation. 国民金融— the People's Finance Corporation.

こうこ【後顧】 ¶ こうして彼は〜の憂いなく出発できた Thus he was able to go free from *anxiety about his home*.

こうご【口語】 colloquial (≒ spoken) language; spoken words. —英語 spoken English. —体 a colloquial style; colloquialism. —文 spoken language.

こうご【交互】 ¶ 彼らは苦しみと楽しみを〜に味わった They had trouble and pleasure *alternately*. 満潮と干潮は〜に起こる The ebb and flood *alternate*. 彼らは野獣から身を守るために〜にしか眠らなかった They slept only *by turns* in order to guard against wild beasts.

ごうご【豪語】 ¶ 彼は必ず優勝すると〜している He *boasts* that he is sure to win.

こうこう【口腔】 the mouth; the oral cavity. —衛生 the hygiene of the mouth; oral hygiene.

こうこう【孝行】 filial duty. ¶ 彼は〜息子だ He is a *dutiful* son. 彼は両親に〜している He *is devoted to* (≒ *is dutiful to*; *is thoughtful for*) his parents.

こうこう【高校】 (日本での正式の呼び方は) an upper secondary school (アメリカでは a senior high school). —生 a high school student.

こうこう【航行】 sailing; navigation. ¶ 太平洋を〜する *sail* across the Pacific Ocean. 海岸にそって〜する *sail* along the coast. 東に向けて〜する *sail* east. 風に逆らって〜する *sail* against the wind. 船は〜中です The boat is *at sea* (≒ *on a voyage*; *undersail*).

こうこう【膏肓】 ¶ 彼の病〜に入る He *is incorrigible*. / He is past praying for. / His malady is too far advanced for remedy. / There's no hope for him.

こうこう【皓皓・煌煌】 ¶ 〜たる月の光 the *bright* moonlight. 月は〜と照っていた The moon was shining *brightly* (≒ *bright*).

こうごう【皇后】 an empress; a queen. ¶ 〜陛下 Her Majesty the Empress.

ごうごう【囂囂】 ¶ 彼は〜たる非難を浴びた He was *loudly* denounced.

ごうごう【轟轟】 ¶ 列車は〜と音を立てて鉄橋を渡った The train *rumbled* across the iron bridge. / The train crossed the iron bridge with a *roaring* (≒ *thundering*) noise.

こうこうがい【硬口蓋】 the hard palate.

こうごうし・い【神神しい】 divine; heavenly; holy; solemn; awe-inspiring; awesome.

こうごうせい【光合成】〘化学〙 photosynthesis.

こうこうや【好好爺】 a good-natured old man.

こうこがく【考古学】 archaeology. —者 archaeologist.

こうこく【公告】 a public (≒ an official) notice; an announcement. ¶ 国立大学の入学試験要項が〜された They made *a public announcement* of the entrance examination requirements for the national universities.

こうこく【広告】 an advertisement. ¶ 新聞や雑誌にその商品を〜した We *advertised* the goods (≒ put *an advertisement* for the goods) in newspapers and magazines. 新聞の〜に応じた I answered the *advertisement* in a newspaper. ビラで店員を求める〜をした I *advertised for* a clerk by handbills. —業 advertising business. —代理店 an advertising agent. —塔 an advertising tower. —放送 a commercial broadcast. —欄 an advertising column. —料 advertising rates. 三行— classified ads. 死亡— an obituary (notice). 新聞— a newspaper advertisement. テレビ— a TV commercial.

こうこく【公国】 a dukedom.

こうこく【抗告】〘法律〙 a complaint. ¶ 判決に〜する *appeal against* a sentence.

こうこつ【恍惚】 rapture; ecstasy. ¶ 〜となる be *in raptures*. 〜と聞きほれる listen *in rapture*. 〜の人 a *senile* person.

こうこつかん【硬骨漢】 a man of firm character.

こうこつぎょ【硬骨魚】 a teleost.

こうさ【交差】 intersection; crossing. ¶ そこで2本の道が〜している Two roads *cross* (*each other*). 鉄道はこの地点で〜している The railroad lines *intersect* at this place. —点 a crossing; an intersection; a junction. 平面― a level crossing. 立体― a grade crossing.

こうさ【考査】a test ; an examination.

こうさ【公差】〖数学〗a common difference.

こうざ【口座】an account. ¶ 銀行に～を開く open *an account at* (≒ *with*) a bank.
振替貯金― a postal transfer account.

こうざ【講座】a chair ; a lectureship ; (講義) a lecture ; a course. ¶ フランス文学の～を担当する hold (≒ fill) the *chair* of French Literature. 哲学の～が欠員になっている The philosophy *chair* is vacant. ラジオの英語～ a radio *lecture* (≒ *course*) in English.
公開― an extension course ; an open lecture.

こうさい【公債】a public loan ; a government bond. ¶ ～を発行する issue *bonds*.

こうさい【交際】an association. ¶ 彼に彼らと～しないように忠告した I advised him not to *associate with* them. 彼は有名な政治家との～を求めている He seeks the *company* of famous statesmen. 外国人と～がない I have no *association with* foreigners. 私は彼と親密な～を続けている I *am on* friendly *terms with* him. 彼とただちに～を絶った I *broke off with* him at once. 彼は～好きである He is a *sociable* man. 彼は～が広い (狭い) He has wide (narrow) *acquaintances*.
―費 social expenses.

こうさい【光彩】brilliancy ; luster. ¶ 彼女の出席は今夜の会合に～を添えた Her presence added *luster* to the meeting tonight. 彼は政界で～を放つ He *makes* (≒ *cuts*) *a brilliant figure* in the political world.

こうさい【虹彩】〖解剖学〗the iris.
―炎 iritis.

こうざい【功罪】¶ 彼の～相半ばしている His *merits and demerits* are balanced.

こうざい【鋼材】steel.

こうざいりょう【好材料】an excellent material ; a favorable factor.

こうさく【工作】construction ; building.
¶ ～の時間 the *handicraft* hour. ふたりは裏で～していた They *were maneuvering* behind the scenes. 平和～をする make a peace move.
―品 handicrafts. ―機械 a machine tool. 政治― political maneuvering. 宣伝― propaganda maneuvers. 補強― reinforcement work.

こうさく【交錯】mixing. ¶ 利害が～して意見がまとまらなかった Their interests *were* so *complex* that they could not come to an agreement.

こうさく【耕作】farming ; cultivation ; tillage. ¶ 彼らはその土地をくまなく～した They *cultivated* every bit of available land. この畑は～しやすい The field *plows* well.
―者 a farmer. ―地 cultivated land. ―地域 the area under tillage. ―物 farm produce.

こうさく【鋼索】a steel wire rope ; a cable.

こうさつ【考察】consideration ; study. ¶ その問題を注意深く～した We *gave* careful *consideration to* the question.

こうさつ【絞殺】strangulation. ¶ ～する strangulate.

こうさん【公算】¶ 彼が成功する～は大きい(ない) There is strong (little) *probability* that he will succeed. 彼がわれわれの味方になってくれる～が大いにある There is every *probability* that he will support us.

こうさん【降参】surrender. ¶ 敵はわが軍に～した The enemy *has surrendered to* us. この暑さには～だ I *can't stand* the heat. / The heat *is unbearable*.

こうざん【高山】a high mountain.
―植物 an alpine plant ; (総称) an alpine flora. ―病 mountain sickness.

こうざん【鉱山】a mine.
―業 the mining industry. ―労働者 a mine worker ; a miner.

こうさんぶつ【鉱産物】mineral products.

こうし【小牛・子牛】a calf (複 calves). ¶ ～の皮 calf 〔skin〕. ～の肉 veal.

こうし【公私】¶ あの方には～ともとてもお世話になっている We are deeply indebted to him *both in public and private* (≒ *both officially and privately*). ～の別をはっきりさせる draw a line between *official and personal matters*. ～を混同する mix up *public and private matters*.

こうし【公使】a minister. ¶ 特命全権～ an envoy extraordinary and minister plenipotentiary.
―館 a legation. ―館員 〔a member of〕 the legation staff.

こうし【光子】〖物理〗a photon.

こうし【行使】¶ 黙否権を～する *exercise* the rights to remain silent. 要求がけられたので, 組合幹部は実力を～することに決定した Since their demand was turned down, the union leaders decided to *use* (≒ *appeal to*) force.

こうし【講師】a lecturer ; an instructor.
¶ ～になる be appointed 〔*a*〕 *lecturer*.
専任― a full-time lecturer. 非常勤― a part-time lecturer.

こうし【格子】(戸の) a lattice ; (窓の) a lattice work ; a bar ; (天井の) a coffer.
―じま cross stripes ; tartan checks ; square patterns. ―戸 a lattice door. 鉄― an iron bar ; grille.

こうし【嚆矢】¶ A氏をもって～とする Mr. A was the *first to* do.... / The *first attempt* (to do...) was made by Mr. A.

こうじ【麹】malt ; (酵母) yeast ; leaven.

こうじ【小路】an alley ; a narrow street ; a lane.
袋― a blind alley.

こうじ【工事】works ; construction 〔work〕.
¶ ～中である be under construction. ～中 (立て札) Men at work. この先道路～中(立て札) Road Work Ahead.

こうじ【公示】a public announcement. ¶ 選挙の投票日が～された The voting day *was announced publicly*.

こうじ【公事】public (≒ official) affairs; public business.
こうじ【好事】¶ ～魔多し(諺) *There's many a slip between the cup and the lip.*
こうじ【後事】¶ 友人に～を託してあります I have already asked a friend to look after my *affairs* while I am away.
ごうし【合資】¶ ～会社 a limited partnership. ～会社木下商店 Kinoshita & Co., Ltd.
こうしき【公式】〘数学〙a formula (複 formulas; formulae); (儀式) formality. ¶ その計画は～の席で発表された The project was announced at a *formal* occasion. 両国首脳の～会談は来月初めに東京で行なわれる A *formal* conference between the heads of the two countries will be held in Tokyo early next month. ～の発表 an *official* statement. 彼は近くアメリカを～訪問する予定だ He will shortly pay a *formal* visit to the United States.
—戦〘野球〙a pennant race.
こうしき【硬式】—野球 hard-ball baseball. —テニス tennis (軟式テニスは日本以外にない).
こうしせい【高姿勢】an aggressive (≒ a high-handed) attitude. ¶ 彼は近ごろいやに～だ He has been taking up *a high-handed attitude* lately.
こうしつ【皇室】the Imperial Household (≒ Family).
こうしつ【硬質】—ガラス hard glass. —陶器 hard earthenware (≒ china; porcelain).
こうじつ【口実】an excuse. ¶ 彼はやることになにかいつも～を作るたちだ He always *finds* (≒ *makes*) some *excuse* for everything he does. 病気を～にして申し出を断わった I declined the offer *on* (≒ *under*) *the pretext of* illness. 会合に欠席する～がない I can't find *an excuse* for staying away from the meeting.
こうじつせい【向日性】〘植物〙(positive) heliotropism. ¶ ～の植物 a *heliotropic* plant.
こうしゃ【公社】a public corporation.
日本専売— the Japan Monopoly Corporation. 日本電信電話— the Nippon Telegraph and Telephone Public Corporation.
こうしゃ【巧者】¶ 彼は交渉にかけては～な男だ He is *an expert* in negotiations.
こうしゃ【公舎】an official residence.
こうしゃ【後者】the latter. ¶ ～の場合には事態はわれわれにとってかなり不利となるであろう *In the latter case,* things will become pretty unfavorable for us.
こうしゃ【校舎】a schoolhouse; college; a school (≒ college) building.
こうしゃく【公爵】男 a duke; a prince (prince はイギリス以外の国の公爵). ¶ サウサンプトン～ the Duke of Southampton. ～夫人 女 a duchess; a princess.
こうしゃく【侯爵】a marquis. ¶ ～夫人 a marchioness.
こうしゃく【講釈】(講義) a lecture; (講談) storytelling.
こうしゃぐち【降車口】an exit; (掲示) Way Out.
こうしゃほう【高射砲】an anti-aircraft gun; a flak.
こうしゅ【攻守】offense and defense. ¶ ～所をかえる turn the tide of the war. 彼はきょうの試合で～に活躍した He showed *active plays in* today's game.
こうしゅ【絞首】—刑 ¶ ～刑に処せられる be put to death by *hanging*. —台 the gallows (単数扱い).
こうしゅう【口臭】bad (≒ foul) breath.
こうしゅう【公衆】the public. ¶ ～の面前で in public. ～のために働く work for the benefit of *the public*; work *for the general good*.
—衛生 public health (≒ hygiene). —電話 a public telephone. —道徳 public morality. —便所 a public lavatory; a rest room; (男子用の掲示) Men; (女子用の掲示) Women. —浴場 a public bath.
こうしゅう【講習】a course. ¶ 交通法規の～を受ける take *a short course in* traffic regulations. 水泳の～をする give *a course in* swimming.
こうしゅうは【高周波】〘電気〙high frequency.
こうじゅつ【口述】¶ ～する state orally; dictate.
—試験 an oral examination. —筆記 notes. —人〘法律〙a public speaker.
こうじゅつ【後述】¶ 詳細は～する Full particulars will *be mentioned later*.
こうじゅほうしょう【紅綬褒章】a Red Ribbon Badge.
こうじょ【皇女】a princess; an Imperial (≒ Royal) Princess.
こうじょ【控除】subtraction; deduction.
¶ 生命保険料は課税所得金額から～される The premium on life insurance *is deducted* from taxed income.
—額 the amount deducted. 基礎— basic deduction. 勤労— earned income exemption.
こうしょう【公称】—資本 authorized capital. —馬力 nominal horsepower.
こうしょう【公傷】an injury incurred while on duty.
こうしょう【交渉】**1**〚話し合い〛negotiation.
¶ ～はまとまった We *have come to terms*.
～を開始した We opened *negotiations*.
～は失敗に終わった The *negotiations* ended in failure.
～は不調に終わった The *negotiations* have been broken off.
ボーナスについて会社と～した We *negotiated* with the company about the bonus.
その件は目下彼と～中だ *Negotiations* are under way for the matter with him.
土地の買収について銀行と～中だ We *are treating with* the bank about the purchase of land.
われわれはついにその～を打ち切った The *negotiations* have not come to a conclusion.
—委員 a delegate; a negotiating committee. 団体— collective bargaining (特に労

資間の交渉を言う). 直接— direct negotiations. 予備— preliminary negotiations. 和平— peace negotiations.

2 〚交際など〛 ¶卒業以来彼とは～がない I haven't got *in touch with* him since my graduation.

こうしょう【考証】〔an〕investigation. ¶江戸時代の風俗を～する *make investigations on* the manners and customs in the Edo Era; *make researches after* (≒ *for*) the manners and customs in the Edo Era.
時代— historic investigation.

こうしょう【鉱床】〚鉱物〛〔mineral〕deposits. ¶銅の～ *a deposit* of copper.

こうしょう【哄笑】 a loud laugh; loud laughter. ¶～する laugh loudly; roar with laughter; burst out laughing.

こうしょう【高尚】 ¶～な趣味 *refined* taste; ～な思想 a *lofty* (≒ *noble*) idea. ～ぶる be priggish; be prudish; be snobbish.

こうじょう【口上】(伝言) a verbal message; (陳述) a statement.
—書き a verbal note. 前— an introduction; a prologue.

こうじょう【工場】 a factory; a mill; works; a plant.
—地帯 a factory district. —長 a factory superintendent. 自動車修理— an automobile repair shop. 製紙— a paper mill.

こうじょう【交情】 friendship; intimacy (intimacy は男女間の情交を意味することがある).

こうじょう【向上】 advancement; improvement; elevation. ¶彼の英語の学力は目覚ましく～した He *has* remarkably *improved in* his ability of English. 戦後の青少年の体位の～は目覚ましいものがある The *improvement* of the physique of the rising generation since the war has been quite remarkable. 黒人の社会的地位を～させる *elevate* (≒ *raise*) the social status of the colored people. 彼には～心がない He has no *desire to improve himself*.

こうじょう【厚情】 ¶ご～に感謝します Thank you for your *kindness*. / I appreciate your *kindness*.(アメリカに多い)./(やや形式ばって) I am much obliged to you for your *kindness*.

ごうしょう【豪商】 a wealthy (≒ rich) merchant.

ごうじょう【強情】 obstinacy. ¶そんなに～を張るものではない Don't *be* so *obstinate*. 彼は～っぱりだ He is an *obstinate* person.

こうじょうせん【甲状腺】〚解剖学〛 the thyroid gland.
—ホルモン thyroxin〔e〕.

こうしょうにん【公証人】 a notary.

こうしょく【公職】〔a〕public office. ¶～につく take up *a public office*. ～にある人は清廉潔白でなければならぬ Those who hold *a public office* must be honest and upright. 彼は汚職事件に関係したために～から追放された He was purged from *a public office* because he was involved in the bribery case.

こうしょく【好色】 ¶～な男 a lewd man; a lecher.
—文学 erotic (≒ pornographic; obscene) literature; pornography.

こうしょく【黄色】 —人種 the yellow race.

こうしん【行進】 a march; a parade. ¶通りを～する *parade* the street.
—曲 a march. 結婚—曲 a wedding march.

こうしん【交信】 telegraph communication. ¶無線で基地と～する *communicate* with the base by wire.

こうしん【更新】 renewal. ¶だれが400メートル自由型の世界記録を～するのだろうか Who will *make a new* world *record* for the four hundred meter free style event? 近いうちに借地契約を～しなければならない I must *renew* my lease before long.

こうしん【後進】 a younger man; a junior. ¶～に道を譲る make way for the promotion of *younger men*.

こうじん【公人】 a public man (≒ person); (公務員) a public servant; a government official; 〔米〕 an office-holder.

こうじん【後塵】 ¶彼の～を拝するなんてごめんだ I can't stand being second to him.

こうじん【幸甚】 ¶この物をご笑納くだされば～の至りです I shall *be* very *happy* if you accept this present. 折り返しご返事くだされば～に存じます We shall *appreciate* your immediate reply to this letter.

こうしんじょ【興信所】 〔米〕 a detective agency; an inquiry office (≒ agency).
—員 a private detective (≒ investigator).

こうじんぶつ【好人物】 a good-natured man; a good (≒ nice) fellow.

こうしんりょう【香辛料】 spice; condiments.

こうず【構図】 composition. ¶その絵は～がよい(悪い) The picture *is* well (ill) *composed* (≒ *planned; designed*).

こうすい【香水】〔a〕perfume;〔a〕scent; (総称) perfumery (〔米〕では a perfumery として perfume の意味に用いることもある).
¶～入りのせっけん *perfumed* (≒ *scented*) soap. ～をつける use *perfume*. 彼女は～をつけていた She *was perfumed*.

こうすい【硬水】 hard water.

こうすい【鉱水】 mineral water.

こうずい【洪水】 a flood; a deluge; an inundation (flood は一般的な語, deluge は大雨による洪水, inundation は川・湖などのあふれた洪水を言う).
¶ノアの～ the Deluge; the Flood. この村は毎年～にあう This village suffers from *a flood* every year. 田畑は一面の～だった All the fields *were flooded*. どこへ行っても車の～だ You will see *a flood of* cars wherever you go.

こうすいりょう【降水量】 precipitation.
¶年間～ the annual *precipitation*.

こうずか【好事家】 a dilettante (〔複〕 dilettantes; dilettanti).

こう·する【抗する】 ¶時流に～するのは損だ It

does not pay to *go against* the stream. / It is not wise to *be against* public opinion.

こう·ずる【高ずる·亢ずる·嵩ずる】¶ 彼は胃潰瘍(かいよう)が～じて胃がんになった His stomach ulcer *developed* into stomach cancer. 彼女のわがままは～ずるばかりであった She became *more and more* selfish.

こう·ずる【講ずる】¶ 彼は論語を～じている He *gives lectures on* the *Analects of Confucius.* そのことに関して前後策を～じなければなるまい We have to *take* (≒ *devise*) remedial measures for the matter. ～ずべき策がない We cannot find out any proper measures to *take* (≒ *adopt*).

こうせい【公正】(正義) justice ; (公平) fairness ; impartiality. ¶ ～な判決(判断) a *fair* judgment. 彼の意見はいつも～だ He *is* always *impartial* in his opinion. / His opinions *are* always *impartial.* われわれは何事にも～な態度で臨まなくてはならない We must *be fair* to everything. / We must assume an *impartial* attitude toward everything.

こうせい【攻勢】the offensive. ¶ 平和～ a peace *offensive.* 敵軍は突如～に出た The enemy suddenly *took the offensive.* わがチームは終始～をとった Our team *were on the offensive* throughout the game.

こうせい【更正】¶ 税金の額を～してもらった I *had* the assessment of my tax *revised.*
—決定 reassessment of a tax.

こうせい【更生】¶ 犯罪者の～は大きな問題だ The *rehabilitation* of released prisoners is a big problem. 非行少年を～させる *regenerate* a juvenile delinquent.

こうせい【厚生】public welfare.
—施設 welfare facilities. —省 the Ministry of Public Welfare ; the Welfare Ministry (米 では the Department of Health, Education and Welfare). —大臣 the Minister of Public Welfare (米では the Secretary of Health, Education and Welfare). —年金 a welfare pension (≒ annuity). —年金保険 the welfare pension insurance.

こうせい【後世】after ages ; (人) futurity ; future generation. ¶ 彼は～に名を残すだろう His name will become historic. ～恐るべき青年だ(有望な) He is a young man of great promise. / (危険人物) He will be a dangerous person to society *in the future.*

こうせい【恒星】a fixed star.
—時(日 ; 年) sidereal time (day ; year).

こうせい【校正】proofreading. ¶ ゲラ刷りを～する *read* proofs.

こうせい【構成】organization ; composition. ¶ 文章の～を考える consider how to *organize* a passage. 委員会は5人の委員によって～されている The committee *consists* (≒ *is made up*) *of* five members. ふたつの異なった人種がひとつの社会を～している Two different races *form* a single community. 空気を汚染させることは犯罪を～する Polluting the air *constitutes* a crime.
—要素 a constituent ; a component.「sis.

ごうせい【合成】composition ; 〖化学〗synthesis.
—語 a compound word. —ゴム synthetic rubber. —樹脂 synthetic resin. —繊維 synthetic (≒ chemical) fiber. —洗剤 synthetic detergent. —染料 synthetic dyestuff.

ごうせい【豪勢】¶ ～な家(料理) a *gorgeous* house (dinner). ～な生活をする live *in* 〔*grand*〕 *style* ; live *in luxury.*

こうせいせき【好成績】¶ 彼らの実験は～をあげた They *did well in* their experiments. / They got *good results in* their experiments. リーグ戦で～を収めた We *did well in* the league tournament.

こうせいのう【高性能】high performance.
¶ ～の機械 a *highly efficient* machine. ～の受信機 a *high-fidelity* receiver.

こうせいぶっしつ【抗生物質】〖生物〗antibiotic 〔substance〕.

こうせき【功績】¶ 彼は国家に～があった He *rendered distinguished services* (≒ *performed great services*) *to* his country. 彼は会の発展に～があった He *contributed a great deal to* the growth of this society. / We owe the growth of this society to him. 長年の研究の～が認められた Many years of his *study* (≒ *research*) was recognized. この物質を発見したのは彼の～だ We must give him all the credit for discovering the substance.

こうせき【鉱石】a mineral ; an ore ; (ラジオの) a crystal. ¶ ～受信機 a *crystal* 〔radio〕 set.

こうせき【洪積】—世(期) 〖地質〗the diluvial epoch. —層 a diluvial formation. —台地 a diluvial terrace.

こうせきうん【高積雲】〖気象〗an alto-cumulus (複 alto-cumuli).

こうせつ【公設】¶ ～の病院 a hospital *supported by public funds.* ～市場 a *public* market.

こうせつ【交接】sexual intercourse ; coitus ; (交尾) copulation. ¶ ～する have sexual intercourse (*with*) ; copulate (*with*).
—不能 impotence ; impotency.

こうせつ【降雪】a snowfall. ¶ 20センチの～を見た *Snow fell* twenty centimeters deep.
—量 〔the amount of〕 snowfall.

こうぜつ【口舌】¶ ～の徒 a man *of many words* ; a man who is all talk and no action.

ごうせつ【豪雪】heavy snowfall.

こうせん【口銭】commission ; brokerage.
¶ 小売店は売り上げに対して2割の～をとる The retail stores take *commissions* of twenty percent (≒ twenty percent *commissions*) *on* the sales made.

こうせん【公選】public election. ¶ 国会議員は～される the Dietmen *are elected by popular vote.* 知事は～制だ The prefectural governorship is *an elective office.*

こうせん【交戦】a war ; a battle ; an engagement. ¶ 両国は～中である The two countries

are at war with each other. わが軍は敵と～中である Our troops *are fighting with* (≒ *against*) the enemy. / Our forces *are engaging* the enemy.
—区域 a war zone; a combat area. —権 the belligerent rights. —国 belligerents. —状態 a state of war (*with*).

こ

こうせん【光線】light; (ランプなどの) a ray; (太陽などの) a beam. ¶ ～が悪くて本が読めない I can't read in the poor *light*.
—分析 spectrum analysis. —療法 phototherapy; actinotherapy. X— X-rays. 殺人— a death ray.

こうせん【抗戦】¶ 彼らは徹底的に～した They *fought* to the last. (実際の戦闘の場合). / They *made* do-or-die *resistance*. / They *resisted* with an indomitable will.

こうせん【鉱泉】a mineral spring; (温泉場) a spa; (鉱水) mineral water.

こうぜん【公然】¶ ～の秘密 an *open* secret. 彼はその提案に対して～と反対意見を述べた He *openly* opposed the proposal.

こうぜん【昂然】¶ ～として triumphantly; in high spirits.

こうぜん【浩然】¶ ビールを飲んで～の気を養った I *refreshed myself* (≒ *felt buoyant*; *felt free*) with a glass of beer.

ごうぜん【傲然】¶ 彼はいつも～と構えている He always *assumes a haughty attitude*. / He always *holds his head high*. 彼は～たる態度のためになかなか好かれない He is not popular because of his *arrogance*. ～と arrogantly; haughtily.

ごうぜん【轟然】thunderously. ¶ ジェット機が～たる爆音を残して飛び立った The jet plane took off *with a thunderous noise* (≒ *a deafening roar*). ピストルが～となった The gun went off *with a loud report*.

こうせんてき【好戦的】bellicose; warlike.
¶ ～な国民 a *warlike* (≒*bellicose*) nation.

こうそ【控訴】an appeal (*to* a higher court).
¶ 彼は最高裁判所へ～した He *appealed to* the Supreme (≒ High) Court. 彼の～は却下された His *appeal* was quashed.

こうそ【酵素】〘化学〙enzyme; ferment.

こうぞ【楮】〘植物〙a paper mulberry.

こうそう【抗争】〔a〕contention. ¶ 激しい内部の～があった There was *a* serious internal *struggle* (≒ *strife*). 彼らは主導権をめぐっての～を繰り返した They *were* always *contending for* the leadership.

こうそう【後送】¶ 負傷した兵士は～された The wounded soldiers *were sent back to the rear*. お荷物は～いたします I'll *send* your baggage to you *later*.

こうそう【高僧】a high (≒ high-ranking) priest; (キリスト教の) a prelate.

こうそう【高層】—雲〘気象〙an alto-stratus (複 alto-strati). —気流 the upper air current. —建築 a tall (≒ lofty) building; a skyscraper.

こうそう【構想】a design; a plan. ¶ まず～を練らなくてはならない First, we must make *a* detailed *plan*. / First of all I must sort out my *ideas*. 彼の論文は～が雄大だ His thesis is grand in *conception*. その小説の～はすばらしい The novel has *a* wonderful *plot*. ～力に富んだ心 an *inventive* (≒ *imaginative*) mind.

こうそう【広壮】¶ ～な邸宅 a *stately* mansion; a *magnificent* residence.

こうぞう【構造】structure; a construction; frame. ¶ アメリカ社会の～ the *structure* of American society. 文の～ the *structure* (≒ *construction*) of a sentence; sentence *structure*. 日本経済の二重～ the dual *structure* of Japanese economy. この橋は～上欠陥があるにちがいない This bridge must be *structurally* defective. / There must be a *structural* defect in this bridge.
—言語学 structural linguistics (単数扱い). —主義 (社会学・言語学などの) structuralism.

ごうそう【豪壮】¶ ～な住まい a *gorgeous* (≒ *splendid*) house.

こうそく【拘束】〔a〕restriction; 〔a〕restraint; binding; (監禁) confinement; custody.
¶ 彼は一晩身柄を～された He *was kept in custody* overnight. その契約に私は～されない The contract does not *bind* me.
—時間 actual (≒ compulsory) working hours.

こうそく【校則】school regulations; the rules of school; campus regulation.

こうそく【高速】¶ ～で at *a high speed*.
—道路 a superhighway; an express highway; a freeway; 英 a motor way.

こうぞく【皇族】the Imperial (≒ Royal) Family; (個人) an Imperial (≒ a Royal) prince (≒ princess); (総称) royalty.

こうぞく【後続】following; succeeding.
¶ ～の車はなかった There were no cars behind us.
—部隊 reinforcements.

こうぞく【航続】¶ この飛行機は～距離が長い This plane has *a* long *range*.

ごうぞく【豪族】a powerful clan.

こうそくど【高速度】—映画(写真) a fast motion picture. —鋼 high-speed steel. —撮影 high-speed photography.

こうた【小歌・小唄】a ballad; a ditty; a *kouta* song; a short simple song.

こうたい【交替】change; relief; a shift. ¶ 彼らは順番に～で車を運転した They drove the car *by turns* (≒ *in turn*). 彼らは8時間～で働く They work eight-hour *shifts*. 投手は～になった The pitcher *was relieved by* another pitcher.
—時間 the changing time. —制 ¶ 彼らは昼夜2～制で働く They work *a two-shift system*.

こうたい【抗体】〘生理〙an antibody.

こうたい【後退】〔a〕retreat. ¶ 彼は1歩～した He *took a step backward*. 彼は車をゆっくり～させた He *backed* his car *up* slowly. 景気の～がありそうだ There will be *a recession* in our economy.

こうだい【広大】¶～な屋敷 a *magnificent* (≒ *huge*) mansion. ～な原野 *vast* plains.

こうたいこう【皇太后】the Empress Dowager; the Queen Mother.

こうたいし【皇太子】the Crown Prince. ¶～殿下 His Highness the Crown Prince. イギリス～ the Prince of Wales. ～妃 the Crown Princess.

こうだか【甲高】¶私の足は～だ I have *high insteps*.

こうたく【光沢】gloss; luster; sheen. ¶～のある lustrous; glossy; brilliant. 宝石の～を出した（磨いて） I *gave a polish to* the jewel. / I *polished* the jewel. この絹は～がある This silk *is glossy*. その金の指輪は～を失った The gold ring lost its *luster*. この真珠の～をごらんなさい Look at the *shine* of this pearl.

ごうだつ【強奪】robbery. ¶～する rob with violence; seize. 強盗は銀行から数百万ドルを～した Bandits *robbed* the bank *of* millions of dollars.

こうたん【降誕】birth; (キリストの) the Nativity. ¶キリストの～ the *Nativity* of Jesus Christ. キリスト～祭 Christmas.

こうだん【公団】a public corporation. ―住宅（１戸の家） a housing corporation apartment 〔house〕; (団地) a housing complex (≒ project) of the housing corporation. 道路（住宅）― a 〔public〕 highway (housing) corporation.

こうだん【講談】storytelling; (話そのもの) a story; historical incidents and anecdotes. ―師 a storyteller. ―本 a storybook.

こうだん【講壇】a 〔lecture-〕platform; a rostrum.

こうだん【後段】the latter part.

ごうたん【豪胆】¶～な人 a *bold* (≒ *fearless; courageous*) man; a man *of nerve*.

こうだんし【好男子】a handsome man; a good-looking man.

こうち【高地】a plateau; a high land.

こうち【拘置】confinement. ―所 a detention room; a lockup.

こうち【耕地】arable land. ―面積 cultivated acreage.

こうち【巧緻】exquisiteness. ¶～をきわめた文体 an *elaborate* style.

こうち【狡智】¶～にたけた人 a *crafty* (≒ *tricky; cunning*) person.

こうちく【構築】construction. ¶～する construct.

こうちゃ【紅茶】black tea. ¶～を入れる make tea. ―こし a tea strainer. ―茶わん a tea cup.

こうちゃく【膠着】adhesion; agglutination. ¶雨季の到来とともに戦線は～状態になった With the advent of the rainy season, the battle *was brought to a standstill*. ―語 agglutinative language.

こうちゅう【甲虫】〘昆虫〙a beetle. ―類 Coleoptera; beetles.

こうちょう【好調】¶このような景気の～は一時的な現象にすぎない The present wave of *prosperity* is merely a temporary phenomenon. 彼の好意で万事～に進んだ Thanks to his goodwill, everything progressed *favorably* (≒ *smoothly*).

こうちょう【紅潮】¶彼は興奮するといつも顔面が～する His face *becomes flushed* whenever he gets excited.

こうちょう【高潮】climax; high tide. ―点 high water mark.

こうちょう【校長】a principal; a headmaster.

こうちょうかい【公聴会】a public hearing. ¶～はあす開かれる The *public hearing* will be held tomorrow.

こうちょく【硬直】stiffening. 死後― rigor mortis.

こうちん【工賃】a wage; wages; pay.

こうつう【交通】(車などの往来) traffic; (交通の手段) communication; (輸送・輸送手段) 米 transportation; 英 transport. ¶この道路は～が激しい（ほとんどない） There is heavy (little) *traffic* on this road. きのうはその道路は～止めになった The road *was closed to traffic* yesterday. 故障車が～の妨害になった A car that had broken down obstructed the *traffic*. 吹雪で～が途絶(まひ)した *Traffic* was held up (was paralyzed) by the snowstorm. ―安全週間 Traffic Safety Week. ―違反 violation of traffic rules. ―機関 means of transportation. ―規則 traffic regulations (≒ rules). ―事故 a traffic accident. ―渋滞 traffic jams. ―巡査 a traffic policeman. ―信号 a traffic signal (≒ light). ―整理 traffic control (≒ regulation). ―道徳 traffic morality (≒ morals). ―費 traffic expenses. ―網 a traffic network.

こうつごう【好都合】¶電話をかけようかと思っていたら～なことに本人が現われた I was thinking of phoning to him, when *to my great convenience* he made his appearance.

こうてい【公定】―価格 official price. ―歩合 an official rate.

こうてい【工程】¶～は順調に進んでいる *The progress of work* is satisfactory.

こうてい【行程】¶500キロの～は昔はたいへんなものだった Covering the *distance* of 500 kilometers was no easy matter in former days.

こうてい【肯定】affirmation; acknowledgment. ¶黙っているということはその案を～したことになる To say nothing is to *acknowledge* the plan.

こうてい【皇帝】an emperor.

こうてい【校訂】revision. ¶本を～する *revise* a book.

こうてい【校庭】school grounds; a campus.

こうてい【高低】¶～のある土地 an *uneven* land; undulating ground. 値段の～ *ups and downs* (≒ *fluctuations*) of price.

こうてい【高弟】*one's* leading (≒ best) disciple.

こうでい【拘泥】adhesion. ¶そんなことにいつまでも～しないことだ You must not *adhere to* (≒ *cling to*) such a thing so indefinitely.

こ

こうてき【公的】public ; official.
こうてきしゅ【好敵手】a good match. ¶ついに彼は～に出会った He found his *mate* (≒ *match*) at last.
こうてつ【更迭】a change ; a reshuffle. ¶大臣の～ a *reshuffle* of a minister. 大臣を～する *change* a minister.
こうてつ【鋼鉄】steel.
こうてん【公転】〘天文学〙revolution.
こうてん【好天】fine weather.
こうてん【好転】¶景気はいっこうに～しない Business does not *turn for the better* at all. いまは八方ふさがりだがそのうち～しよう Everything goes against us now, but things will *take a favorable turn* before long.
こうてん【交点】〘天文学〙a node.
こうてん【荒天】stormy weather. ¶一行は～をついて出発した The party left facing the *stormy weather*.
こうてん【光点】a luminous point.
こうでん【公電】an official telegram.
こうでん【香典】a present made in condolence. ¶御仏前に～をあげて合掌した Giving *a monetary offering* to the spirit of the deceased, I prayed.
こうでんかん【光電管】〘電気〙a phototube ; a photoelectric cell ; 〘テレビ〙a cathode-ray tube.
こうでんち【光電池】〘物理〙a photovoltaic cell.
こうてんてき【後天的】¶～に(な) *a posteriori* (ラテン語). 病気は先天的なものと～なものとに分けられる Diseases are divided into those of inheritance and those acquired *in the course of one's life*.
こうど【高度】height ; high degree. ¶～の先進国 a *highly* developed country. ～3,000メートルの上空はかなりの寒さだ It is pretty cold in *an altitude* of three thousand meters. 今度の問題はあまりに～すぎた The present problem *was* too *advanced*.
—計 an altimeter ; a height indicator.
こうど【硬度】solidity ; hardness. ¶岩石の～ the *hardness* (≒ *solidity*) of a rock.
こうど【光度】luminosity.
—計 a photometer.
こうとう【口頭】¶申し込みは～でもよい You may make your application *by word of mouth*.
—試問 an oral examination.
こうとう【高等】advanced ; higher.
—学校 ⇒こうこう(高校) —技術 high technique. —教育 higher education (大学教育のこと). —裁判所 a high court. —動物 the higher animal.
こうとう【高踏】¶～的な文学 *high-browed* literary work.
こうとう【高騰】¶物価の～ *sudden rising* of the prices ; price *hike*.
こうとう【喉頭】〘解剖学〙the larynx.
—科学 laryngology. —がん larynx cancer. —結核 larynx tuberculosis.

こうとう【好投】〘野球〙clean pitching. ¶～する pitch cleanly.
こうどう【行動】an action ; a movement. ¶若いときは衝動に駆られて過激な～をすることがあるものだ Pressed by impulse, young people often *act* excessively. 他人といっしょにいるときは自分かってな～は慎まねばならぬ You must not *go* (≒ *have*) *your own way* when you are with others. 選手は監督の指示に従って～するべきだ Players should *act* according to their manager's direction. ～的な男 a man of *act*.
—主義 behaviorism. —派 activism. —半径 a cruising radius.
こうどう【坑道】(横坑道) a level ; a drift ; (立て坑道) a shaft ; a pit ; (地下道) an underground 〔passage〕.
こうどう【黄道】〘天文学〙the ecliptic.
—吉日 a lucky day. —光 the zodiacal light.
こうどう【講堂】a hall ; a lecture hall ; an auditorium.
ごうとう【強盗】a burglar.
ごうどう【合同】¶ふたつの会社は～して新しい会社ができた The two companies *were amalgamated* (≒ *were merged*) to form a new company.
—委員会 a joint committee. —協議会 a joint council. —葬 a joint funeral. —庁舎 a common building for government offices.
こうとうぶ【後頭部】the back of *one's* head.
こうとうむけい【荒唐無稽】an absurdity. ¶その話はまったく～だ The story *is* quite *absurd*.
こうどく【鉱毒】mine pollution ; copper poisoning.
こうどく【購読】subscription. ¶雑誌を～する *subscribe to* a magazine.
—者 ¶この週刊誌は～者が多い This weekly *has a large circulation*.
こうどく【講読】reading ; translation. ¶～する read (works of Shakespeare).
こうとくしん【公徳心】public morality.
こうどくそ【抗毒素】〘医学〙an antitoxin.
こうない【坑内】a pit.
—夫 a pit worker ; an underground miner.
こうない【校内】¶～対抗体育競技会 an *inter-class* athletic meet.
こうない【港内】¶～におけるそのような事故は珍しい Such an accident *in* (≒ *within*) *the harbor* is rather rare.
こうない【構内】premises. ¶学校の～ school *grounds* ; (特に米) a campus. 駅の～ the station *precinct*.
こうないえん【口内炎】〘医学〙stomatitis.
こうなん【後難】future troubles. ¶～を恐れて黙っていては暴力団の思うつぼになる If you remain silent for fear of *future troubles*, you will fall into a snare just as the terrorist group wishes.
こうにゅう【購入】¶～する buy ; purchase.

こうにん【公認】official recognition. ¶ ～する recognize officially; authorize.
—会計士 a certified public accountant. —記録 an official record. —候補 a nominated candidate.

こうにん【後任】succession; (人) a successor. ¶ 彼が私の～として来る He will *succeed* me. / He will be my *successor*. 彼の～はだれでしょうか Who will *take* his *place*? / Who will *succeed* him?

こうねつ【高熱】a high fever (≒ temperature).

こうねつひ【光熱費】fuel and light expenses.

こうねつびょう【黄熱病】〖医学〗yellow fever.

こうねん【光年】〖天文学〗a light year.

こうねん【後年】afterward.

こうねん【高年】old age.
—者 the aged.

こうねんき【更年期】the menopause.
—障害 climacteric suffering.

こうのう【効能】effect; virtue. ¶ 薬草の～ the *virtue* of herbs. ～のある efficacious; effective.

ごうのう【豪農】a wealthy farmer.

こうのとり【鸛】a [Japanese] stork.

こうのもの【香の物】pickles; pickled vegetables.

ごうのもの【剛の者】¶ 彼こそ日本一の～だ He is *the bravest person* in Japan.

こうは【光波】light waves.

こうは【硬派】the stalwart party. ¶ 彼は～だ He is on *the solid* (≒ *stalwart*) *side*.

こうば【工場】a factory; a mill.

こうはい【交配】crossing; cross-breeding. ¶ 品種改良のためにいろいろな～が行なわれる Various *cross-breeding* is done for improvement of breed.

こうはい【後輩】*one's* junior[s]; an underclassman. ¶ 私は彼より３年(だいぶ)～だ I am three years (many years) his *junior*.

こうはい【荒廃】ruin. ¶ この建物は～している This building *lies in ruins*.

こうはい【興廃】¶ 皇国の～この一戦にあり *The fate* (≒ *rise or fall*) of our Empire depends upon this engagement.

こうはい【光背】a halo.

こうばい【勾配】a slope; an incline. ¶ ～がゆるい(急だ) The *slope* is gentle (steep). 道路は20度の～で上がっている The road rises at a twenty degree *slope*.

こうばい【紅梅】〖植物〗red (≒ pink) plum blossoms.

こうばい【公売】a public sale. ¶ 彼の不動産は～に付せられた His real property *was put up for public sale*. / His property *was offered at public auction*.

こうばい【購買】purchase.
—組合 a cooperative society. —者 a purchaser; a buyer. —力 purchasing (≒ buying) power.

こうばいすう【公倍数】〖数学〗a common multiple.
最小— the least common multiple (L. C. M.).

こうはく【紅白】¶ ～の幕 a *red and white* curtain; a curtain *in red and white stripes*.
—試合 a match (≒ game) between the red and white camps.

こうばく【広漠】¶ ～たる原野 *a vast expanse of* plains.

こうばし·い【香ばしい】aromatic; fragrant. ¶ なにか～いにおいがする There is some *fragrant* smell.

ごうはら【業腹】¶ まったく～なことだ I *am* quite *angry at* that.

こうはん【公判】a public trial. ¶ ～に付する put (a case) on *trial*; bring (a case) to *trial*. 彼は～中である He *is on trial*.

こうはん【後半】the latter half. ¶ 18世紀の～ *the latter* (≒ *second*) *half of* the eighteenth century; *the later* eighteenth century.

こうはん【広範】¶ ～な権限 a *wide* power. ～な知識 an *extensive* knowledge.

こうばん【交番】a police box.

こうはんい【広範囲】¶ この本の内容は～に及んでいる The contents of this book cover *a wide range*.

こうはんせい【後半生】¶ あの人の～は実に悲惨なものだった *The latter half of his life* was a miserable one indeed.

こうひ【工費】the cost of construction; labor cost. ¶ 総～ the total *cost of construction*.

こうひ【公費】public expenditure. ¶ その事業は～で行なわれることになっている The work is to be carried on *at public expense*.

こうび【交尾】copulation; pairing. ¶ ～する copulate; pair.
—期 the pairing (≒ mating) season.

こうび【後尾】the rear. ¶ 遅れてきた人たちは行列の～に並んだ Those who came late stood *in the rear* (≒ *at the back*) of the queue.

ごうひ【合否】¶ ～はまだわからない *Success or failure* has not been announced yet.

こうヒスタミンざい【抗ヒスタミン剤】〖薬品〗an antihistamine.

こうひょう【公表】a public announcement; publication. ¶ ～する announce officially. 氏名を～する *make* the name (*of* a criminal) *public*. 事の性質上～をはばかる問題だ The nature of the matter being what it is, we hesitate to *announce* it *officially*.

こうひょう【好評】favorable criticism. ¶ その本は大学生の間で～を得ている The book *is enjoying great popularity* among college students. その小説は～だ The novel *was well received*.

こうひょう【高評】¶ ご～を賜わりたく存じます I am anxious for *your comment* on this work.

こうひょう【講評】[a] comment; [a] criticism. ¶ 展示品に対する～が審査員によって行なわれた Some *comments* on the exhibits were given by the judges. 私の作文に対する先生の～はかなり厳しいものであった The teacher passed pretty severe *criticism* upon my composition.

こうびん【後便】¶ その詳細は～で知らせます I will inform you of its details *by next mail* (≒ *in my next letter*).

こうふ【工夫】a navvy; a workman. ¶ 鉄道(線路)～ *a* railway *workman*; a linesman.

こうふ【公布】(一般の) publication; (法令などの) promulgation. ¶ 新しい法律を～する *promulgate* a new law.

こうふ【交付】¶ 地方都市に補助金を～する *grant* a subsidy *to* provincial cities.

—金 a grant; a subsidy.

こうふ【坑夫・鉱夫】a miner.

こうぶ【後部】the rear; (船の) the stern.

こうふう【校風】school tradition (≒ customs; spirit); the discipline of a school.

こうふく【幸福】happiness; (幸運)〔good〕luck; (福祉) welfare. ¶ ～とはなんぞや In what does *happiness* consist? 一生～に暮らしたいものだ I want to live *happily* all my life. / I want to lead a *happy* life all my life. / I would like to *be happy* ever after. 彼らは～な家庭生活を営んでいる They are leading a *happy* family life.

こうふく【降伏】surrender.

無条件— an unconditional surrender. ¶ 敵は無条件～をするようにわれわれに要求してきた The enemy demanded that we should *surrender unconditionally* to them.

こうふく【校服】a school uniform.

こうぶつ【好物】¶ 私の～は甘い物だ My *favorite food* is sweet stuffs.

こうぶつ【鉱物】mineral.

—学 mineralogy. —学者 a mineralogist. —質 mineral matter. —油 mineral oil.

こうふん【公憤】¶ ～にかられる be carried away by *public indignation*.

こうふん【興奮】excitement; stimulation; agitation. ¶ きみは～しやすい You *are* easily *excited*. 彼は～のあまり大声で叫んだ In his *excitement* he shouted at the top of his voice. この冒険物語は少年少女を～させずにはおかないであろう This adventure story will never fail to *excite* young boys and girls. そう～するな Don't *be* so *emotional*. / Don't *excite yourself* so much. / Don't *get excited*. 会場は～のるつぼと化した The hall was turned into a scene of wild *excitement*.

こうふん【口吻】¶ 彼は会社をやめたいという～を漏らした He *hinted* (≒ *suggested*) that he wanted to quit the company.

こうぶん【構文】the construction of a sentence.

こうぶんしょ【公文書】an official document. ¶ 彼女は～偽造のかどで告訴された She was indicted for forgery of *official documents*.

こうべ【頭・首】¶ ～を垂れる hang down *one's head*. ～を巡らす(後ろを見る) look back (≒ backward).

こうへい【工兵】a military engineer.

こうへい【公平】impartiality; disinterestedness. ¶ あの人は～無私なので私は尊敬している I respect him for his perfect *impartiality*. あの先生はあらゆる生徒に～だ That teacher *is impartial to* all his students. 彼のそのやり方は～を失している That method of his is far from *fair*. ～に言えば彼の言うことは当を得ている *To do him justice*, what he says is to the point. ～な取り扱いを受けた I was *impartially* treated. 彼は財産を子どもたちに～に分けてやった He divided his property *equally* among his children.

こうへん【後編】(後半) the latter part (*of* a book); (続編) the concluding part; a sequel.

ごうべん【合弁】—会社 a joint concern (≒ company; complex). 日比—事業 a Filipino-Japanese joint undertaking.

こうほ【候補】¶ 彼は学生自治会の次期会長の～に立った He *became a candidate* (≒ *ran*; *stood*) for the next presidency of the student council. わが党は前回の市長選挙でふたりの～を立てた Our party *ran* (≒ *put up*) two *candidates* in the last mayoralty election.

—者 a candidate. ¶ われわれは公認～者の数を四, 五名にしぼる必要があろう We must get the list of recognized (≒ official) *candidates* down to four or five. 社会党の公認～者は全部当選した The whole Social Democratic *ticket* was returned. 非公認—者 an unofficial candidate.

こうぼ【公募】¶ うちの会社では株式を～することはやっていない We do not *offer shares for public subscription*. その会社では社員を～中である The firm *is inviting applications for admission* from job-applicants.

こうぼ【酵母】yeast; brewers' yeast.

—菌 yeast fungus (複 funguses; fungi).

こうほう【公法】〘法律〙public law.

—学者 a publicist. 国際— international law.

こうほう【公報】an official report (≒ bulletin).

こうほう【広報】public relations (P. R. と略す); public information.

—課 a public relation's section. —活動 public relations.

こうほう【後方】the rear. ¶ ～の rear; back. ～に(方向) backward; (位置) behind; in the rear.

こうほう【高峰】a high (≒ lofty) peak.

こうぼう【興亡】rise and fall. ¶ わが国の～は若者の双肩にかかっている *The rise or fall of* this country rests on the shoulders of young people.

こうぼう【弘法】¶ ～も筆の誤り(諺) *Even Homer sometimes nods*. ～筆を選ばず(諺) *A bad workman complains of his tools*.

ごうほう【号砲】a signal gun. ¶ ～一発, マラソンのスタートは切られた With *the report of a gun*, the marathon was started.

ごうほう【合法】¶ ～的な手段に訴える appeal to *lawful* means.

ごうほう【豪放】¶ ～な open-hearted; lion-hearted; (おおざっぱな) large-minded; broad-minded. ～磊落(らいらく)な open-hearted; broad-minded.

こうぼく【公僕】a public servant.

こうほん【校本】a text.

こうほん【稿本】a manuscript; a MS (複 MSS); (下書き) draft.

こうま【小馬・子馬】(小形の) a pony; (子馬) a colt.

こうまい【高邁】¶ ～な理想 a *lofty* (≒ *high-flown*) ideal.

こうまん【高慢】self-conceit; pride. ¶ あの人は～そうな顔つきをしている He *looks proud* (≒ *looks self-conceited; looks haughty*). ～の鼻をくじく humble *a person in his pride*.

ごうまん【傲慢】arrogance; haughtiness.
¶ ～無礼な男 an *insolent* fellow. 彼はだれにも～だ He *is haughty* to everybody. ～さ arrogance.

こうみえても【こう見えても】¶ ～ぼくは大学生だ I'm a college student, you know. *You perhaps wouldn't guess it* 〔*from*〕 *looking at me*. ～私は外交官だ *I don't know what you take me for*, but I am a diplomat.

こうみゃく【鉱脈】a vein of ore. ¶ 金の～を掘り当てる strike *a* gold *vein*.

こうみょう【功名】a great exploit. ¶ ～を立てる achieve *a meritorious* (≒ *glorious*) *deed*; distinguish *one*self. ほんとにけがの～だ It was indeed *mere luck*.
―心 aspiration.

こうみょう【光明】a light; glory; (希望) hope. ¶ ようやく前途に一縷(いちる)の～が認められた A ray of *hope* was at last seen before us.

こうみょう【巧妙】¶ 彼の仕事の～さはあらゆる人の賞賛するところとなっている The *dexterity* with which he has done his job is highly spoken of by everybody. 彼の～な話しぶりには感心する I heartily admire his *clever* manner of speech.

こうみん【公民】a citizen.
―館 a public hall. ―権 civil rights; citizenship. ―教育 civic education.

こうむ【公務】(公用) public service; (公職) official business.
―員 a civil servant; a public official; a government official.

こうむ【校務】school affairs (≒ duties).

こうむてん【工務店】a building constructor's office.

こうむ・る【被る】¶ あの方にはひとかたならぬ恩義を～っている I *am* deeply *indebted to* him. 住民は台風のために大きな被害を～った The inhabitants *suffered* heavy damage because of the typhoon. 主人の不興を～ったので彼はしょげている He is disheartened because he *has incurred* his master's displeasure.

こうめい【高名】fame; renown. ¶ ～な学者 a *famous* (≒ *noted; famed*) scholar; a scholar *of high renown* (≒ *repute*). ご～はかねがね伺っております I have heard a great deal about *your fame*.

こうめい【公明】¶ ～正大な fair; fair and square. ～正大にふるまう behave *fairly and squarely*.
―選挙 a clean election.

ごうめい【合名】―会社 an unlimited partnership. ¶ ～会社渡辺商会 Watanabe & Co.

ごうも【毫も】¶ そんなつもりは～ない I *hardly* intend to do so. 私は死を～恐れない I have *not the slightest* fear of death.

こうもく【項目】an item. ¶ 私は報告書を５～に分けた I divided my report into five *heads*. それはこの～に含まれている It is included under this *head*.

ごうもくてき【合目的】¶ まずわれわれの手段の～性を検討しなければなるまい The first thing that we must do is to consider whether 〔or not〕 our measure *suits the purpose*.

こうもり【蝙蝠】a bat. ¶ 鳥なき里の～ In the kingdom of the blind the one-eyed man is king.
―がさ an umbrella.

こうもん【校門】the gate of a school.

こうもん【肛門】〔解剖学〕the anus.
―科 proctology.

ごうもん【拷問】torture. ¶ 彼らは囚人を白状するまで～した They *tortured* the prisoner until he made a confession.

こうや【荒野】a wilderness; a waste; a desert land.

こうや【紺屋】a dyer; (店) a dyer's. ¶ ～のあさって(諺) *Jam tomorrow and never jam today*.

こうやく【公約】a public promise (≒ pledge). ¶ 選挙の～を果たす carry out (≒ fulfill) campaign *pledges*.

こうやく【膏薬】a plaster; (軟膏) a salve; unguent; vintment. ¶ ～を張る plaster (*one's* foot); apply *a plaster* (*to* a sore place).

こうやくすう【公約数】〔数学〕a common measure (≒ divisor).
最大― the greatest common measure (G.C.M.).

こうゆ【香油】perfumed 〔hair〕 oil balm.

こうゆう【公有】public ownership.
―財産 public property.

こうゆう【交友】¶ 彼は～が多い He has a lot of *friends*. 彼の～関係などを調べる必要がある It's necessary to check up his *associates*.

こうゆう【校友】a schoolmate; a schoolfellow; (同窓) 米 (男) an alumnus (複 alumni); (女) an alumuna (複 alumunae); 英 an old boy; (女) an old girl.
―会 (在学生の) a students' association; (卒業生の) an alumni association; (会合) an alumni (≒ old boys') meeting.

ごうゆう【剛勇・豪勇】valor; bravery; daring.

ごうゆう【豪遊】¶ ～する have a spree; spend much money in pleasures.

こうよう【公用】¶ ～で on *official business*.
―語 the official language.

こうよう【孝養】filial duties. ¶ 彼は両親に対し

てできるかぎりの～を尽くした He *was* as *dutiful to* his parents as he could.

こうよう【効用】 an effect; utility. ¶温泉はある種の病気に対して～があるThe hot-spring cure *has a good effect on* some kinds of diseases.

こうよう【紅葉】 red leaves. ¶うちの庭のカエデの葉もすっかり～した The leaves of the maple in my garden *have turned* completely *red*.

こうよう【高揚】 ¶国民の愛国心を～する *exalt* patriotism among the people.

こうようじゅ【広葉樹】 a broad-leaved tree.

ごうよく【強欲】 greed; avarice. ¶～な greedy; avaricious; covetous. ～に greedily; avariciously.

こうら【甲羅】 a shell. ¶カメの～ the *shell* of a turtle. 砂浜で～を干す bask (≒ bathe) in the sun on the sands. ～を経た相手だからだまされないよう用心せねばならない We must be careful not to be taken in because he is such *an old fox* (≒ *an old timer*).

こうらく【行楽】 ¶～シーズン the season of *holidaymaking*. 絶好の～日和 an ideal day for *a picnic*.

—客 a holidaymaker; 米 a vacationist.
—地 a holiday (≒ pleasure) resort.

こうらん【高覧】 ¶ご～に供したく存じます I beg to submit it to *your inspection*.

こうり【小売り】 retail sale. ¶～をする sell at retail.

—商 a retail merchant (≒ dealer). —値 a retail price.

こうり【公吏】 a public official (≒ servant; employee); a civil servant.

こうり【公理】〔論理〕〔数学〕an axiom; a maxim.

こうり【功利】 utility. ¶～的に物事を考える form the *utilitarian* point of view.

—主義 utilitarianism. —主義者 a utilitarian.

こうり【高利】 ¶～で金を貸す lend money *at high interest*.

—貸し usury; (人) a usurer.

こうり【行李】 a basket (≒ wicker) trunk (≒ suitcase); a plaited wickerwork basket.

ごうり【合理】 ¶彼の議論は～的だ His argument *is rational* (≒ *is reasonable*). 彼は～的にその問題を解決した He solved the problem *rationally* (≒ *reasonably*). 経営の～化 the *rationalization* of management. 産業を～化する *rationalize* industry.

—主義 rationalism. —主義者 a rationalist.

ごうりき【強力】(山案内人) a mountain guide.

こうりつ【公立】 ¶～の public: (市立の) municipal; (県立の) prefectural; (都立の) metropolitan.

—学校 英 a public school (イギリスで public school と言うと上流子弟などの学ぶ寄宿制の大学進学または公務員養成の私立中等学校を意味するので注意する必要がある. イギリスで一般に公立学校は county school と言う).

こうりつ【効率】 efficiency. ¶機械の～ mechanical *efficiency*. 生産の～を高める raise the *efficiency* of production.

こうりつ【高率】 ¶～有利な郵便貯金 *high-interest* postal savings.

こうりゃく【攻略】 ¶敵陣を～する *capture* an enemy position.

こうりゅう【交流】〔電気〕an alternating current. ¶両国間の文化の～は今後ますます活発になることであろう Cultural *exchanges* between the two nations will become more and more brisk from now on.

国際—基金 the Japan Foundation.

こうりゅう【拘留】 custody; detention. ¶彼は1週間の～に処せられた He was sentenced to a week's *detention*. 警察はさらに尋問を続けるために容疑者を～することにした The police decided to *detain* the suspect to make further inquiries.

こうりゅう【興隆】 rise; prosperity.

ごうりゅう【合流】 ¶渡良瀬川は栗橋で利根川に～する The River Watarase *joins* the River Tone at Kurihashi. われわれは先発隊と現地で～した We *joined* (≒ *met*) the advance party at our destination.

—点(川の) the confluence (≒ junction) 〔of two rivers〕.

こうりょ【考慮】 consideration. ¶彼の提案は～の価値がある His proposal is worth *consideration*. うちでは人を雇うに当たって学歴は～に入れない When we employ people, we *leave* their academic background *out of consideration*. この度の決定についてはまだまだ～の余地がありそうだ This decision seems to leave some room for *consideration*. なにを買うにつけても価値と品質の2点は～に入れなければならない Price and quality are two *considerations* in buying anything. 登山計画を立てるに当たっては, そのころの天候も～に入れねばならない We must also *take into consideration* how the weather will be at that time of the year in making a climbing plan.

こうりょう【香料】(薬味) spices; (化粧品の) perfume. ¶～を加える spice; season with *spice*.

こうりょう【稿料】 fee for a manuscript.

こうりょう【荒涼】 ¶見渡すかぎり～たる原野が広がっていた As far as the eye could reach, there spread a vast expanse of *desolate* (≒ *wild*) plains. 寺は～とした風景の中に立っていた The temple stood in the midst of very *bleak* scenery.

こうりょう【校了】 finishing (≒ final) proofreading; (符号) O. K.; Corrected. ¶～にする finish correcting the proof.

こうりょう【綱領】(基本方針) a general plan; general principles. ¶政党の～ *a* party *platform*.

こうりょく【効力】 an effect. ¶新薬も彼にはなんの～も発揮しなかった The new drug *did* him no *good* at all. 月日がたつと薬の～は薄れていく The medicine will lose its *effect* with the passage of time. この条約は向こう5年間～を有

することになる This treaty shall hold *good* for the period of five years from now on. われわれの契約はあと二, 三週間で～がなくなる Our contract will be *null and void* in another couple of weeks.

こうりん【降臨】the advent ; 〔a〕 descent.
—節〘キリスト教〙Advent.

こうれい【恒例】an established custom.
¶ ～により as usual ; according to the 〔time-honored〕 custom. ～の usual ; traditional.

こうれい【高齢】an advanced age. ¶ 彼女は100歳の～で亡くなった She died *at the* 〔*advanced*〕 *age* of hundred.
—者 the aged ; a person advanced in age.

こうれい【好例】a good example.

ごうれい【号令】an order ; a command.
¶ 天下に～する *rule over* (≒ *hold sway over*) the whole country. 先生が「集まれ」と～をかけた The teacher *ordered*, "Fall in !"

こうれつ【後列】the back (≒ rear) row.

こうろ【行路】journey. ¶ 長い人生～のうちにはいろいろなことがあるものだ You will see many things in your long *journey* of life.

こうろ【香炉】an incense-burner ; (つり香炉) a censer.

こうろ【航路】a course ; a route. ¶ 横浜シアトル～ the Yokohama-Seattle *run* (≒ *line*).
～を開く launch (≒ inaugurate) a regular *service* (between the two ports). 欧州～に船を就航させる put a ship on the European *service*.
—標識 a beacon ; a nautical mark. 定期— a regular line. 不定期— an occasional line.

こうろう【功労】distinguished service.
—者 a person of distinguished service ; a person who has done good service.

こうろうい【公労委】the Public Corporation Labor Commission.

こうろん【口論】a dispute. ¶ 彼と～した I *had a quarrel with* him. ふたりはつまらぬことから～になった A mere trifle led to *a quarrel* between the two.

こうろんおつばく【甲論乙駁】the pros and cons. ¶ ～した We debated for and against the matter. / We *argued* the matter *pro and con*.

こうわ【講和】peace.
全面— an overall peace. 単独— a separate peace. —条約 a peace treaty. ¶ 両国間に～条約が調印された *Peace* was signed between the two countries. —会議 a peace conference.

こうわ【講話】a lecture ; a talk.

こうわん【港湾】harbors.
—施設 harbor facilities. —労働者 a longshoreman ; a stevedore.

こえ【声】a voice. **1**〘声が〙¶ 彼は～が大きい(小さい) He speaks *loudly* (*low*).
彼女は～がよい She has *a* sweet *voice*.
彼は～がよく通る He has *a* good *voice*.
秋だ, 虫の～が聞こえだした Autumn has come! Insects have begun singing.
あの歌手は高い(低い)～がよく出る The singer has *a* very high-pitched (low-pitched) *tone*.
政府を非難する～が高い The government is *loudly* attacked.
彼はぼくの～が届く(届かない)所にいた He was within (out of) hearing me.
2〘声を〙¶ 静かにしてください. ～をたててはいけません Be quiet, and don't *talk*.
～を出して読みなさい Read 〔it〕 *aloud*.
彼は～を張り上げてそのことを強調した He stressed it *at the top of his voice*.
お出かけのときは私にちょっと～をかけてください When you go out, *let me know of* it.
彼は～をからして叫んだ He shouted himself *hoarse*. / He shouted in *a* hoarse *voice*.
彼女は急に～を潜めた She suddenly lowered her *voice*.
悲惨な事故の知らせに皆～をのんだ They cried in silence at the disaster.
彼女は～をはずませて「はい」と言った She said yes in *a* cheering *voice*.
突然後ろから～をかけられた Suddenly someone *called to* me from behind.
その知らせを聞くと, 彼は～をあげて泣いた He *cried* at the news.
彼らは～をそろえてその歌をうたった (合唱で) They sang the song *in chorus*. / (斉唱で) They sang the song *in unison*.
3〘声に・声も, など〙¶「火事だ!」という～に, あわてて外へ飛び出した On hearing somebody shout "Fire !", I dashed out of the house in a flurry.
彼は感激して～も出なかった He was too deeply moved to say even a word.
大きな～では言えないが, 彼は偽善者だ *Between ourselves*, he is a hypocrite.
4〘合成語・その他〙¶ 彼は突然涙～になった His *voice* suddenly sounded tearful.
大～で in *a* loud *voice* ; loudly.
小～で in *a* low (≒ small) *voice*.
泣き～で in *a* tearful *voice*.
ねこなで～で in *a* coaxing *voice*.
蚊の鳴くような～で in *a* weakly *voice*.
笑い～ laughter.
叫び～ a cry.
掛け～ a shout.
鼻～で in *a* nasal *voice* ; through the (≒ *one's*) nose.
つくり～ *a* feigned *voice*.
うめき～ a moan.
かすれた～ *a* husky (≒ hoarse) *voice*.
うなり～ a groan.
きんきん～ *a* squeaky *voice*.
すねた～ *a* sulky *voice*.
太い～ *a* deep *voice*.
細い～ *a* thin *voice*.
明るい～ *a* cheering *voice*.
良心の～ *a voice* of conscience.
民衆の～ the *voice* of the people (文語体ではまれにラテン語 vox populi を用いる) ; a grass roots *voice*.
～なき～ the hope of the people.

こ

こえ【肥】 manure ; a fertilizer ; (下肥) night soil. ¶ ～をやる manure (a garden) ; put manure (*on*).
—おけ a night soil bucket.

ごえい【護衛】 guard ; escort ; (軍艦などの) convoy ; (米大統領などの) secret service men (≒ agents).
¶ 屈強な若者が数人～として大臣のあとについていった Several hefty young men followed the minister as *bodyguards.* 首相は警官に～されて会に出席した The prime minister attended the meeting *under* police *escort.*
—艦 a convoy ; an escort. **—**兵 a guard ; a military escort.

ごえいか【御詠歌】 a pilgrim's hymn.

こえがかり【声掛かり】 ¶ 人のお～で on the *recommendation* of *a person* ; at the *suggestion* of *a person.*

こえがわり【声変わり】 ¶ その少年はまだ～していない The boy's voice *has* not *cracked* (≒ *broken*) yet.

こえた【肥えた】 fat ; stout ; plump ; (肥りすぎの場合) obese ; (地味の) rich ; fertile. ¶ ブタのように～女 a woman *fat* as a pig. ～土地 *rich* soil.

こえだ【小枝】 a twig ; a sprig ; (花などをつけた) a spray.

ごえつどうしゅう【呉越同舟】 ¶ ～だ Hostile parties go together.

こ・える【肥える】 (地味が) grow rich (≒ fertile). ¶ あの人は音楽を聞く耳が～えている He *has a trained ear for* music. 彼は口が～えている He *is fastidious about* his food. 目の～えた人 a connoisseur.

こ・える【越える・超える】 ¶ 碓氷峠を～えて長野県側に入った We *crossed* 〔*over*〕 the Usui Pass into Nagano Prefecture. 彼の危険状態も峠を～えた He *is out of danger* now. 彼の生まれた村はその川(山)を～えた所にある His native village lies *across* the river (≒ *beyond* the hills). 彼は60の坂を～えている He *is over* sixty./ He *is on the wrong side* of sixty. その事故による死傷者の数は100名を～えた *More than* a hundred persons were killed or injured in the accident. / There were *over* a hundred casualties in the accident.

こおう【呼応】 ¶ …と～して in concert (≒ cooperation) with… ; in response to…. AとBとは～している A *forms connection with* B. / A *is a counterpart of* B.

ゴーカート a go-cart.

コークス coke.

コース a course. ¶ 日帰り～ *a* one-day *course* of a trip. 人気のあるハイキング～ *a* popular hiking *course* (≒ *route*). 彼は最終～で抜かれた He was outstripped *on the last lap.* 今晩はフル～の食事をおごろう I will stand you *a full course* dinner this evening. 台風の～が東にそれた The typhoon *veered round to* the east. 彼は芸術の～を選んだ He opted for *a course* of art.

ゴーストップ a traffic signal (≒ light) (ゴーストップは go と stop からできた和製英語).

コーチ coaching ; (人) a coach ; a coacher. ¶ ～する coach. 水泳の～ *a* swimming *coach.*

コーチャー a coach ; a coacher. ¶ ～ズボックス a *coach's* (≒ *coaching*) box (特に三塁の).

コーチン【交趾】 a cochin. ¶ 名古屋～ *a cochin* of Nagoya breed.

コート (上着) a coat ; (外とう) a coat ; (テニスなどの) a (tennis) court.

コード (電線) a cord ; (法典・符号) a code.

こおとこ【小男】 a little (≒ small) man ; (小人) a dwarf ; a pigmy.

こおどり【小躍り】 ¶ ～して喜ぶ dance (≒ leap) for joy (*at*).

コーナー a corner. ¶ 手芸品の～ *a* handicraft *corner* (≒ *section*).

コーヒー coffee. ¶ ～を入れる make *coffee.* ～を1杯いかがですか Would you like a cup of *coffee?*

コーラス a chorus. ¶ ～をする sing *in chorus.*

コーラン〔宗教〕 the Koran.

こおり【氷】 ice. ¶ 池の～が解けだした The *ice* on the pond began to melt. ～の上で滑って転んだ I slipped on the *ice.* 湖の～はスケートができるほど厚かった The *ice* on the lake was thick enough for skating. ～が割れる The *ice* cracks. 池に～が張り詰めていた The pond *was iced over.* 水は～のように冷たかった The water was *icy* cold.
—砂糖 crystal sugar. **—**水 iced water ; (飲み物) shaved ice. **—**漬け icing. **—**詰め packing in ice. **—**まくら an ice pillow. **—**屋 an ice shop ; (人) an ice man. ぶっかき**—** chipped ice.

こおりつ・く【凍りつく】 ¶ 洗たく物がロープに～いてしまった The wash *froze to* the rope.

こお・る【凍る】 ¶ 昨夜はひどく～った It *froze* hard last night. 水は華氏32度で～る Water *freezes* at 32°F. 水道管が～ってしまった The water pipes *froze.* バケツの水がかちかちに～っている The bucket water *is frozen* hard. その光景を見て恐怖で血が～る思いがした The sight *made* my blood *freeze.* / The sight *froze* my blood.

コール call.
—サイン a call sign. **—**ナンバー a call number. **—**マネー call money.

ゴール a goal. ¶ ついに走者は～に入った At last the runner reached the *goal.* (サッカーで) 球を～に入れた I *kicked* (≒ *scored*) *a goal.* 彼らはめでたく結婚に～インした They got married happily. 「line.
—キーパー a goalkeeper. **—**ライン a goal

コールタール coal tar. ¶ 彼はその板に～を塗った He *tarred* the board.

コールテン corduroy. ¶ ～のズボン corduroys.

ゴールデンアワー prime time. ¶ この映画は～に放映される This picture will be shown *in prime time.* 「days.

ゴールデンウイーク "Golden Week" holi-

コールドゲーム a called game. ¶ 試合はにわか雨のため～になった The game *was called off*

owing to a shower.
ゴールドラッシュ gold rush.
こおろぎ【蟋蟀】 a cricket. ¶～が鳴いている *Crickets* are chirping.
コーンビーフ corned beef.
こがい【子飼い】 ¶～の社員 a empolyee brought up in the master's house; a member [of a company] trained from apprenticeship.
こがい【戸外】 ¶われわれは田舎で～の生活を楽しんだ We enjoyed an *outdoor* life in the country. 暇なときは～で過ごした I spent my spare time *in the open* [*air*].
ごかい【誤解】 a misunderstanding; misapprehension. ¶彼は私が言ったことを～した He *misunderstood* what I said. 彼はきみを～している He *misunderstands* you. きみは彼の～を解くために, もう一度彼と話し合ったほうがいい You had better talk to him once more to clear up his *misunderstanding*. 彼女はその問題について, なにか～している She has *a misunderstanding* about the matter. きみはこのところの意味を～している You *have misunderstood* this passage. それは彼のほうの～だ That's *a misunderstanding* on his part. これは～を招きやすい This *is misleading*.
こがいしゃ【子会社】 a subsidiary company.
コカイン〘化学〙 cocain[e].
こかく【顧客】 a customer; (集合) clients.
ごかく【互角】 ¶その両チームは実力は～だ The two teams *are well matched*. 両チームは～の勝負をした The two teams *played an even game*. きみと彼は技術的には～だ You and he *are equal in* skill. きみは彼とはとても～には戦えない You *are no match for* him.
ごがく【語学】 linguistics. ¶彼には～の才がある He has a *linguistic* talent.
—教師 a language teacher; a language instructor. —者 a linguist.
こかげ【木陰】 ¶われわれはしばらく～で休んだ We rested for a while *under a tree* (≒ *in the shade of a tree*).
こが・す【焦がす】 ¶敷物を～す *burn* the rug. 机にたばこで～した跡がいくつかある There are several cigarette *burns* on the desk. アイロンが熱すぎたのでシャツを～してしまった The iron was so hot that I *singed* the shirt.
こがた【小形・小型】 small size.
—自動車 a midget car; a mini-car. —トラック a light truck.
こがたな【小刀】 a knife (複 knives).
こかつ【枯渇】 ¶エネルギーの源泉を～させる *dry up* the springs of energy. 天然資源を～させる *exhaust* the natural resources.
ごがつ【五月】 May. ¶～の節句 the Boys' Festival.
—人形 dolls for the Boys' Festival.
こがね【小金】 a small sum of money.
¶世間のうわさではあの老人は～をため込んでいるそうだ It is generally reported that the old man has *a considerable sum of money*.
こがね【黄金】 —色 gold (≒ golden) color.
—虫 a May beetle; a gold bug.
こがら【小柄】 ¶～な女 a *small* woman; a woman *of small stature*. 彼はアメリカ人にしては～だ He *is of small build* for an American.
こがらし【木枯らし】 late autumn and winter wind. ¶～が静まった *The chilly wind* has dropped. ～が樹間を吹き荒れた *The chilly wind* raved through the trees.
こがれじに【焦がれ死に】 ¶彼女は彼に～した She *died of love* for him.
こがわせ【小為替】 ¶1,000円の～ *a money order* (≒ 英 *a postal order*) *for* 1,000 yen.
ごかん【五官】 the five organs of sense.
ごかん【語感】 ¶彼は～が鋭い He has *a* keen *sense of language*.
ごかん【語幹】〘言語学〙 a stem.
ごがん【護岸】 —工事(川の) bank protecting works; embankment; (海の) shore protecting works.
こき【古希】 ¶彼は～に達した He has reached *the age of three score and ten*. われわれは彼の～を祝った We celebrated *his 70th birthday*.
こき【呼気】 expiration; exhalation.
ごき【語気】 ¶彼は～荒く(～鋭く)私の不注意を責めた He reproached me *in an angry tone* (*in a sharp tone*) for being careless.
ごき【誤記】 an error in writing. ¶この帳簿には～がたくさんある There are a lot of *clerical errors* in this account book.
ごぎ【語義】 the meaning of a word.
こきおろ・す【扱き下ろす】 ¶彼はわれわれの計画をばかげていると～した He *denounced* our plan *as* absurd. 彼は彼女の小説を新聞の書評で～した He *wrote down* her novel in a newspaper book review.
ごきげん【御機嫌】 ¶～よう Good-bye. / Good luck to you! ～はいかがですか How are you?/ How do you do? 彼は社長の～をとるのがうまい He is very good at *pleasing* (≒ *courting*) his boss.
こきざみ【小刻み】 ¶～に歩く walk *with quick steps* (≒ *with shortsteps*). 彼は恐れで～に震えていた He *was all of a tremble* for fear.
こぎだ・す【漕ぎ出す】 begin to row; row out. ¶釣り舟を湖の中心に～す *row out* a fishing boat to the center of a lake.
こきつか・う【扱き使う】 ¶彼は部下を～う He *works* his men *very hard*.
こぎつ・ける【漕ぎ着ける】 ¶われわれはなんとかボートを岸まで～けた We *managed to row* to the shore. 交渉は両者の非常な努力で, この段階まで～けられた The negotiation *came to* this stage with great efforts on both sides.
こぎって【小切手】 米 a check; 英 a cheque. ¶～を現金に替える cash *a check*. ～に横線を引く cross *a check*. 彼に10万円の～を書いた I drew *a check* for 100,000 yen on him. ホテル代を～で払った I paid my hotel bill *in check*.
—帳 a check book. 銀行— a bank check. 不渡り— a dishonored check.
こぎて【漕ぎ手】 a rower; an oarsman.

ごきぶり〘虫類〙a cockroach.
こきみ【小気味】¶きみが彼の高慢の鼻をへし折ったなんてまったく～よい話だ It *is* very *pleasant* that you have humbled his pride. / You *have been smart* enough to humble his pride.
こきゅう【呼吸】breathing; respiration. ¶不規則な～ irregular *breathing*. 彼は～が困難になった He fell into labored (≒ difficult) *breathing*. 彼は～が早い He *breathes* fast. 彼は～が止まった He ceased *breathing*. ～は普通だ The *respiration* is normal. 彼は人を扱う～を知っている He *has tact* (≒ *has knack*; *has secret*) *in* dealing with others.
—運動 breathing exercise. —器 respiratory organs. —器病 a respiratory disease. 深— deep breathing. 人工— artificial respiration.
こきょう【故郷】*one's* home; *one's* home town (都会や村にも用いる). ¶～からの手紙 a letter from *home*. 彼は16のとき～を出た He left *home* when he was sixteen. 彼は～ににしきを飾った He returned to his *old home* full of honors. 彼は～を恋しがっている He *is homesick*. 仙台は私の第二の～だ Sendai is my *second home*.
こぎれ【小切れ】a small piece of cloth.
こぎれい【小綺麗】¶彼女はいつも～ななりをしていた She *was* always *neatly dressed*. へやは～だ The room *is tidy*.
こく【酷】¶いま彼のあら捜しをするのは～だ It *is hard* on him to find fault with him now.
こく【酷】body. ¶～のある酒 *sake* of *good* (≒ *full*) *body*. ～のある料理 a *substantial* dish.
こ・ぐ【漕ぐ】row. ¶ボートを～ぐ *row* a boat.
ごく【獄】a prison; a jail. ¶彼は～に投じられた He was put in *prison*.
ごく【極】extremely; very. ¶彼女は～少ししか食物が食べられなかった She was able to eat *only a little* food. 彼がこんなに早く起きるのは～まれだ It *is very rare* for him to get up so early.
ごく【語句】words and phrases.
ごくあく【極悪】¶～〔非道〕な男 a *most wicked* man; a devil. ～非道な行為 a *monstrous* (≒ *devilish*) deed.
こくい【国威】national power; influence of a nation. ¶それはわが国の～を宣揚することになろう It will enhance our *national prestige*. その事件は日本の～を傷つけた The event injured (≒ impaired) Japanese *prestige*.
こくい【黒衣】black clothes. ¶～を着た女 a woman *in black*.
ごくい【極意】the essential principle; the chief point. ¶～をきわめる master the *secret* of (*kendo*).
こくいっこく【刻一刻】¶形勢は～と変化している The situation is changing *every moment*.
こくいん【刻印】a stamp. ¶王冠の～のある貨幣 a coin *stamped with* a crown.
ごくいん【極印】a hallmark. ¶彼は裏切り者という～を押されて死んだ He died *branded* (≒ *stamped*) as a traitor.
こくう【虚空】¶～をつかんで彼は倒れた He fell down *grasping at the air*.
こくうん【国運】¶これはわが国の～を左右する重大問題だ This is the most important problem to influence *the destiny of our country*.
こくえい【国営】nationalization; state ownership. ¶～の事業 a *government* enterprise. 彼は鉄鋼業の～化を強く主張している He insists on *nationalizing* the iron and steel industry.
こくえん【黒煙】black smoke.
こくえん【黒鉛】〘鉱物〙black lead.
こくおう【国王】(a queen に対し) a king; (世襲の立憲君主) a monarch; (小さい国の王様) a prince.
¶スエーデン～ the *King* of Sweden. モナコ～ the *Prince* of Monaco.
こくがい【国外】outside the country.
¶彼はスパイ行為のかどで～に追放された He *was expelled* on a charge of espionage. ～追放 expulsion.
こくがく【国学】Japanese classical studies.
—者 a Japanese classical scholar.
こくぎ【国技】a national game. ¶相撲は日本の～といわれる *Sumo* is said to be *the national sport* of Japan.
こくご【国語】(ある一国の国語) a language; (自国語) the national language; (日本語) the Japanese language.
—改良 the Japanese language reform. —教師 a teacher of Japanese. —読本 a Japanese reader. —問題 the language problem.
こくこく【刻刻】every moment; momentarily.
ごくごく〔と〕¶～と彼はコップの水を飲んだ He *gulped down* a glass of water.
こくさい【国債】(公債) a government loan; (公債証書) a government loan bond.
こくさい【国際】¶それは～的行事だ It is an *international* event. 彼は～的に有名だ He is *internationally* famous. 彼の訪問は～的友好関係をもたらすだろう His visit will improve *international* relations.
—会議 an international conference. —関係 international relations. —管理 international control. —機構 an international organization. —語 a world (≒ an international) language. —司法裁判所 the International Court of Justice. —情勢 the international situation. —人 a cosmopolitan. —親善 international friendship. —通貨基金 the International Monetary Fund (IMF). —法 international law. —見本市 an international trade fair. —問題 an international problem. —連合 the United Nations (UN). —連盟 the League of Nations. —労働機構 the International Labor Organization (ILO).
ごくさいしき【極彩色】¶～のカレンダー a *richly* (≒ *gorgeously*) *colored* calendar.
こくさく【国策】a national policy. ¶～の線に沿って経済の発展に努力すべきだ We should try

to develop our economy in line with the *national policy.*

こくさん【国産】home production. ¶ ～の自動車 a *homemade* car.

—品 a home product. ¶ ～品の愛用を奨励する encourage the use of *home* (≒ *domestic*) *products.* 彼は長年～品愛用運動に携わっている He has been engaged in the "Buy Japanese" campaign for many years.

こくし【国史】the national history; the Japanese history.

こくし【酷使】¶ わずかばかりの金でこんなに～されてはたまらない I can't stand *being worked* so *hard* on such a small allowance. 頭を～する *overtax one's* brain.

こくじ【告示】a notice; an announcement. ¶ 彼の任官は9月1日づけ官報に～された His appointment *was announced* in the Official Gazette dated September 1.

—板 a bulletin (≒ notice) board. 内閣**—** the Cabinet Notification.

こくじ【国字】characters coined in Japan; the Japanese script.

こくじ【国事】national affairs. ¶ 彼は～に携わっている He participates in the *affairs of state.* 彼は～に奔走した He took an active part in the *affairs of state.*

こくじ【国璽】the Seal of State; the Great Seal.

—尚書 Lord Privy Seal.

こくじ【酷似】a close resemblance. ¶ 彼らふたりはお互いに～している They *bear a close resemblance to* each other. 彼は父親に～している He *has a strong resemblance to* his father. この詩はワーズワースの詩に～している This poem *closely resembles* Wordsworth's.

ごくし【獄死】¶ ～する die in prison.

こくしょ【国書】(信書) the sovereign message; (信任状) credentials.

こくしょ【酷暑】severe summer. ¶ ～の候 the *hottest* season. 東京のこの～にはまったく閉口だ Really I can't stand such *an intense heat* as this in Tokyo.

こくじょう【国情・国状】the condition of a country. ¶ 現下の悲しむべき～ the present deplorable *conditions of the country.* 日本の～に通じているアメリカ人は意外に少ない Only few Americans are versed in Japanese *affairs* (≒ *things* Japanese).

ごくじょう【極上】the highest quality.

—品 an article of the best (≒ finest; highest) quality.

こくしょく【黒色】black; black color.

—火薬 black [gun] powder.

こくじょく【国辱】a national disgrace (≒ dishonor). ¶ その事件は日本の～問題だ The affair is *a disgrace to* Japan.

こくじん【黒人】(男) a Negro (複 Negroes); a colored man; (女) a Negro woman; a colored woman (黒人の女性は a Negro woman よりも a colored woman を好む); a black; (一般的に) colored people.

—種 the Negro race; the colored race. **—**選手 a Negro player. **—**暴動 a Negro riot. **—**問題 the Negro question. **—**霊歌 a Negro spiritual.

こくすい【国粋】national characteristics.

—主義 ultranationalism. **—**主義者 an ultranationalist.

こくぜ【国是】a national (≒ state) policy.

こくせい【国政】the national administration; the government of a country. ¶ 彼は～にあたろうと決心した He determined to administer *the affairs of state.*

こくせい【国勢】**—**調査 ¶ 来年～調査が行なわれる The *census* will be taken next year.

こくぜい【国税】a national tax.

こくせき【国籍】nationality. ¶ ～を失う (回復する) lose (regain) *one's nationality.* あなたの～はどこですか What is your *nationality*? / May I ask your *nationality*? 彼は～はフランス人だが血統は日本人だ He is a Frenchman in *nationality,* but a Japanese in blood.

—不明機 a plane of unknown nationality. 二重**—** dual (≒ double) nationality. 無**—**者 a person of no nationality; a denationalized person; an expatriate.

こくそ【告訴】accusation; complaint. ¶ 彼は収賄で～された He *was accused of* taking bribes. その件は示談が成立したので彼は～を取り下げた As the case was settled out of court, he withdrew the *complaint.*

—状 a letter of complaint. **—**人 an accuser; a complainant.

こくそう【国葬】a national (≒ state) funeral.

こくそうちたい【穀倉地帯】¶ 新潟県は日本の～だ Niigata Prefecture is one of the *granaries* (≒ *great rice crop regions*) in Japan.

こくぞく【国賊】a traitor [*to one's* country]. ¶ 人を～呼ばわりする denounce *a person* as *a traitor to his country.*

こくたい【国体】the fundamental character of a country; (国民体育大会) the National Athletic Meeting.

こくたん【黒檀】〘植物〙an ebony.

こくち【告知】a notice; a notification.

—板 a notice (≒ bulletin) board.

こぐち【小口】small amounts. ¶ ～の金 *a small sum of* money. (営業に必要な)～の現金 *petty* cash. ～の当座預金 *petty* current deposit.

こぐち【木口】¶ このヒノキ材は～10センチだ This Japanese cypress wood is ten centimeters across at *the cut end.*

ごくちゅう【獄中】¶ ～で in prison.

—記 a diary written in prison.

こくちょう【黒鳥】a black swan.

ごくつぶし【穀潰し】a good-for-nothing. ¶ あいつはとんでもない～だ He *is not worth his salt* at all. / He is *a good-for-nothing.*

こくてい【国定】**—**教科書 a national authorized textbook. **—**公園 a quasi-national park.

こくてつ【国鉄】(日本国有鉄道) the Japanese National Railways.

こくてん【黒点】a black spot. ¶ 太陽の～ a sun *spot*.

こくでん【国電】a National Railways electric train.

こ

こくど【国土】a country ; a territory.
—開発 national land development. —計画 national land planning ; a program for national land development. —防衛計画 a national defense program.

こくどう【国道】a national road.

ごくどう【極道】¶ 彼は若いころ～の限りを尽くした While young he *led a* very *dissipated life*.
—者(放蕩の) a prodigal ; (邪悪な) a scoundrel.

こくない【国内】the interior. ¶ ～事情がよくなった The *domestic* conditions have improved. 今夏1か月間の～旅行をした This summer I *traveled in Japan* for a month.

こくないしょう【黒内障】〘医学〙black cataract.

こくなん【国難】a national crisis.

こくねつ【酷熱】intense heat. ¶ そこは～の地だ It *is scorchingly hot* there.

こくはく【告白】a confession. ¶ 信仰の～ *a confession* (≒ *profession*) of *one's* faith. 彼の愛の～に彼女はびっくりした His *declaration* (≒ *profession*) of love astonished her. 彼はキリスト教の信仰を～した He made *profession* of faith in Christianity. / He *confessed* Christianity. 彼女は牧師に罪を～した She *confessed* her sin to a priest.

こくはつ【告発】〘法律〙(検事の) prosecution ; indictment ; (民間の) complaint. ¶ 彼は殺人の罪で～された He *was indicted for* murder. / He *was accused of* murder. われわれは彼を～した We *made a complaint against* him.

こくばん【黒板】a blackboard ; a greenboard.
—ふき an eraser.

こくひ【国費】national expenditure. ¶ 彼は～で旅行した He traveled *at government expense*.

こくび【小首】¶ 彼は不思議そうに～をかしげた He *inclined his head slightly to one side* doubtfully.

ごくひ【極秘】strictly confidential. ¶ 彼らはその事件を～にした They *kept* the affair *in absolute secrecy*. 議事は～のうちに行なわれた The proceedings were conducted *in profound secrecy*.
—文書 a classified document. —事項 ¶ これは～事項だ This *must be kept absolutely secret*.

こくびゃく【黒白】black and white ; (正邪) right and wrong. ¶ 人と～を争う contend with *a person* as to which is right.

こくひょう【酷評】severe criticism. ¶ 彼の新著は新聞でさんざんの～を浴びた His new work *has been severely criticized* in the newspapers. それは～だ That *is hard on* me.

こくひん【国賓】a national guest. ¶ われわれは彼を～として遇した We treated him as *a national guest*.

こくふ【国富】national wealth ; the wealth of a nation.

こくふく【克服】conquest. ¶ 厳しい寒さや幾多の困難を～した We *overcame* severe cold and many other difficulties.

こくふく【克復】restoration ; return.

こくぶん【国文】(日本の文学) Japanese literature ; (日本の言語) the Japanese language ; (一般的な意味では, それぞれ) a national literature ; a national language.
—科 the department of Japanese literature ; the Japanese literature course. —学 Japanese literature. —学者 a scholar of Japanese literature. —法 Japanese grammar.

こくべつ【告別】leave-taking. ¶ ～の辞 a *farewell* speech ; (弔辞) a *funeral* oration.
—式 a funeral service.

こくほう【国宝】a national treasure.

こくほう【国法】the national law ; the law of the land.

こくぼう【国防】national defense. ¶ ～を強化する strengthen *the national defense*.
—軍 the national defense army (≒ forces). —計画 a national defense plan (≒ program). —省 ㊍ the Department of Defense ; the Defense Department. —費 national defense expenditure.

こぐまざ【小熊座】〘天文学〙the Little Bear ; Ursa Minor.

こくみん【国民】a nation ; a people. ¶ ～の祝日 a national holiday. 日本～ the Japanese 〔people〕.
—運動 a national movement. —感情 a national sentiment. —性 national character. —所得 the national income ; the annual income of the whole nation. —総生産 gross national product (GNP). —投票 a plebiscite ; a popular vote. —年金 a national pension.

こくむ【国務】state affairs ; the affairs of state. ¶ 総理大臣は～をつかさどる大臣の最高責任者である The prime minister is the most responsible of the ministers who administer the *affairs of state*.
—省 ㊍ the Department of State. —大臣 a minister of state. —長官 ㊍ the Secretary of State.

こくめい【国名】the name of a country.

こくめい【克明】¶ ～に faithfully ; scrupulously. 彼は日記に毎日の仕事を～に書き留めている He keeps a *scrupulous* (≒ *meticulous*) diary of his daily work.

こくもつ【穀物】㊍ grain ; ㊧ corn ; cereals.
—倉 a granary.

こくゆ【告諭】an official notice ; a proclamation.

こくゆう【国有】state ownership. ¶ 鉄道を～化する *nationalize* railroads.

—財産 national property. —地 national land. —林 a national forest.

こくようせき【黒曜石】〘鉱物〙obsidian.

ごくらく【極楽】 the paradise of the Buddhists; heaven; paradise. ¶ 彼は～往生した He *died in peace*. これはまったく～のようだ This is quite *a paradise* on earth.
—鳥 a bird of paradise.

こくりつ【国立】 ¶ あの劇場は～だ That theater *is supported by the State*.
—銀行(劇場；公園；大学；博物館；病院) a national bank (theater; park; university; museum; hospital).

ごくりと ¶ 彼は薬1服を～飲んだ He took the dose *at a gulp*. / He *gulped down* the dose.

こくりょく【国力】 (力) national power; (資源) national resources.

こくるい【穀類】 grain; corn.

こくれん【国連】 the United Nations; the UN; the U.N. (単数扱い).
—安全保障理事会 the United Nations Security Council. —憲章 the United Nations Charter. —総会 the United Nations General Assembly. —大使 the Ambassador to the United Nations. —本部 the United Nations Headquarters.

ごくろう【御苦労】 ¶ ～さま(さん) Thanks for your trouble! たいへん～をかけました I'm very sorry to have given you such trouble.

こくろん【国論】 public opinion. ¶ ～を統一する unify *public opinion*. 再軍備反対へと～を盛り上げる arouse *public sentiment* against rearmament.

こぐん【孤軍】 ¶ 彼の～奮闘のおかげで多くの生命が救われた It was due to his *unaided effort* that so many lives were saved.

こけ【苔】 moss. ¶ ～むした庭 a *moss*-covered garden. 岩に～が生える *Moss* grows on a rock.

ごけ【後家】 a widow.

こけい【固形】 —食 solid food. —燃料 solid fuel. —物 a solid; a solid substance.

ごけい【互恵】 reciprocity; mutual benefits.
—条約 a reciprocal treaty.

ごけい【語形】 a word form.
—変化 inflection. —論 morphology.

こけおどし a bluff; a false front. ¶ この計画の後援者に偉そうな名前をのせているのはただの～にすぎぬ Lining up all these high-sounding names as sponsors of the project is just *a window-dressing*.

こげくさ・い【焦げ臭い】 ¶ 台所で～いにおいがする I *smell something burning* in the kitchen. 御飯が～い This rice *tastes burned*. (have a smoky smell は燻製のような場合の味に用いる).

こけこっこう ¶ 雄鶏は～と鳴いた The rooster cried "*Cook-a-doodle-doo*!"

こけし a 'kokeshi' doll (英語で説明すれば a Japanese painted wood〔en〕doll).

こげちゃ【焦げ茶】 umber; dark brown.
¶ ～色 dark brown.

こけつ【虎穴】 ¶ ～に入らずんば虎児を得ず(諺) *Nothing venture, nothing have.*

こげつ・く【焦げ付く】 ¶ ～き貸し金 *frozen* credit (≒ loans). 銀行が会社に融資した貸付金が～いた The bank *is unable to collect its loan to* a company. 目玉焼きがフライパンに～いた I burned fried eggs and they *stuck to* the pan.

こけらおとし【こけら落とし】 opening of a new theater. ¶ 国立劇場の～に「勧進帳」が上演された The National Theater *was formally opened* with the showing of "Kanjincho."

こ・ける【痩ける】 ¶ ～けたほお *hollow* cheeks.

こ・ける ¶ 彼は何時間も眠り～けていた He *was sleeping on* for hours. 彼らは笑い～けた They *bent over with laughter*.

こ・げる【焦げる】 ¶ おもちが真っ黒に～げてしまった Rice cake *burned* black.

こけん【沽券】 dignity; prestige. ¶ そんなことをしてはきみの～にかかわる It would discredit your reputation to do such a thing. / It would be to your discredit to do such a thing. 大統領の～にかかわるような発言をした The President made a statement which was beneath the *dignity* of his office.

ごけん【護憲】 safeguarding the constitution.
—運動 a movement for safeguarding the constitution.

ごげん【語源】 the origin (≒ derivation) of a word; an etymology.

ここ【個個】 ¶ ～の問題 *individual* questions. われわれはこれらの問題を～に解決しなければならない We should settle these problems *one by one*. 彼らは～に意見を発表した They expressed their opinions *individually*.

ここ【呱呱】 a cry of a baby at its birth.
¶ ～の声をあげる be born; come into the world; see the light of day.

ここ【此処・此所】 this place; here. ¶ 正午まで～で待ちなさい Wait *here* till noon. ～へ来てください Please come *here*. 彼の家は～から遠い His house is a long way from *here*. ～から駅まで歩きましょうか Shall we walk from *here* to the station? ～しばらくはこの金でまにあう This money will do *for the time being*. ～二,三日彼に会っていない I have not seen him *for the last few days*. 彼は～二,三日はまだ休むだろう He will be absent *for the next few days*. ～だけの話だが,彼女は胃がんにかかっている *Between ourselves* (≒ *Between you and me*), she gets stomach cancer. きょうは～まで(授業が終わったとき先生が) So much for today.

ここ【古語】 an archaic word.

ごご【午後】 afternoon. ¶ ～3時に at three〔o'clock〕*in the afternoon*; at 3:00 *p.m.* きょうの～ this *afternoon*. 木曜の～に on Thursday *afternoon*. 仕事を終えるのに～じゅうかかってしまった It took me *the whole afternoon* to finish the work.

ココア cocoa.

ここう【虎口】 jaws of death. ¶ 彼は～を脱した

こ

He *had a narrow escape*.

ここう【糊口】living. ¶ 彼女のかせぎで一家は～をしのいでいる Her earnings *barely keep* the family *going*. / The family *lives on her earnings*.

ここう【古豪】a veteran.

ごこう【後光】a halo (複 halos; haloes); nimbus (複 nimbuses; nimbi).

こごえ【小声】a whisper; a murmur. ¶ ～で話す whisper; speak *in a low voice* (≒ *in a whisper*).

こごえじに【凍え死に】¶ ～する freeze to death; die of cold.

こご·える【凍える】¶ 今夜は～えるように寒い It *is freezing* tonight. 手がすっかり～えてしまった My hands *become numb with cold*. 彼は～えた手に息をかけて暖めていた He was blowing upon his *frozen* hands to warm them up.

ここかしこ【此処彼処】¶ ～をさまよい歩く wander *from place to place*. 小鳥が～に飛んでいる Some birds are flying *here and there*.

ここく【故国】*one's* homeland; *one's* native land (≒ country).

ごこく【護国】¶ 死して～の鬼とならん I will die so that my spirit may become *a guardian god* (≒ *genius*) *of the state*.

ごこく【後刻】¶ ～参上します I will make a call on you *later*.

ここぞ ¶ 彼らは～とばかりに敵を攻めたてた They took full advantage of the opportunity to stage a concentrated attack on the enemy.

ここち【心地】feeling; sensation. ¶ 天にも昇る～がした I *felt* as if I had soared up to heaven.

ここちよ·い【心地よい】¶ ～い春の日ざしを浴びる enjoy the *pleasant* spring sunshine. 昨夜は～く眠れた I had a *good* night's sleep last night.

こごと【小言】a scolding; a rebuke. ¶ 彼は遅くまで出歩いたといって息子に～を言った He *scolded* (≒ *rebuked*) his son *for* being out late. 母はなにやかやと一日じゅう～を言っている(ぶつぶつ言っている) My mother *grumbles about* one thing or another all day long.

ここと【戸毎】¶ 正月には～に門松が立てられる Pine-tree decorations appear *at every gate* at the New Year.

ここに【此処に·是に】here. ¶ ～おいて at this point; hereupon.

ここのか【九日】¶ 9月～ September *the 9th*. ～間の休暇 a *nine-day* vacation.

ここのところ【此処の所】lately; these days.

ここら ¶ ～でちょっと休もう Let's stop and have a rest *around here*. 彼は～あたりに住んでいる He lives *around here* (≒ *in this neighborhood*). ～で仕事を切り上げよう Isn't it *about time* to call it a day?

こころ【心】(心情) heart; (意志) will; mind; (感情) feeling.

1〖心の〗¶ ～の優しい女性 a *gentle-hearted* woman.

～の狭い男 a *narrow-minded* man.

かたくなな～の人 a *stubborn-minded* man.

～の平和 *one's* peace of *mind*.

～のこもった贈り物 a *heartfelt* present.

2〖心を〗¶ 彼は留学をとりやめることに～を決めた He *decided to* give up going abroad for study.

彼の純情さには,ぼくもまったく～を打たれた His simple-heartness deeply *moved* me.

その計画には大いに～を引かれている I *am* very *interested in* the plan.

彼は娘の不幸な結婚に～を痛めている He *is worried about* his daughter's unhappy marriage.

そんなつまらないことに～を悩ますな Don't *worry yourself about* such a trifle thing.

～を鬼にして彼の頼みを断わった I felt very sorry for him, but refused his request coldly.

彼もやっと～を打ち明けてくれた At last he *opened up to* me.

ぼくもこれからは～をいれかえる I will *reform myself* from now on.

彼の～を和らげることはできない You cannot soften his *heart*.

みんなで～を合わせてその仕事をやりとげた We finished the work *with one accord*.

3〖心が〗¶ 彼らは互いに～が通い合っていない They don't *understand* one another.

ぼくには彼の～が見抜けない I cannot *see through* him.

4〖心から〗¶ 彼らはみんな～から楽しそうに笑った They laughed *heartily*.

すばらしい贈り物を頂いて,～からお礼を申し上げます Thank you [*from the bottom of my heart*] for your beautiful present.

彼女はきみに～から感謝している She thanks you *heartily*.

彼らは～からの歓迎を受けた They received a *warm* welcome.

5〖心に·心にも〗¶ 彼は～にもないことを言う男だ He expresses a sentiment foreign to his *heart*.

いい考えが私の～に浮かんだ I hit upon a good idea. / A cute idea came across my mind.

こころあたり【心当たり】¶ だれがこんなことをしたか～がおありですか Do you *have any idea* who might have done a thing like this? 彼は不在ですが～を捜してみます He is not home now but I can check *where he might be*.

こころある【心ある】¶ ～人々 *thinking* (≒ *concerned*) people. ～人々は風紀の乱れを嘆いている All *concerned* citizens are deploring the corruption of public morals.

こころいき【心意気】¶ 彼の～に感じて協力することにした Impressed by his *fine spirit*, I have decided to cooperate with him.

こころえ【心得】(知識) knowledge; (概念) a notion; (経験) experience. ¶ 彼女は多少琴の～がある She *knows* a little bit *about* playing the *koto*. / She *knows how to* play the *koto*. 学生寮の～を守りなさい You should observe the dormitory *rules*. この本には初心者の～が記されている The book lists the *cautions* for beginners. 課長～ an *acting* chief of the section.

こころえがお【心得顔】 a knowing look. ¶ 彼は～でうなずいた He nodded *knowingly*.

こころえちがい【心得違い】 misbehavior. ¶ 変な～を起こさぬよう気をつけてくれ Be careful not to *fall into bad ways*. もしきみがそんなふうに考えてるのだったら, それはとんだ～だ If that is what you think, you *are* entirely *wrong*.

こころ·える【心得る】 ¶ 彼女は家事についてはひととおり～えている She *knows* a bit about running a house. / She *knows* how to do the routine housework. ～えました O. K. / I understand all right.

こころおきなく【心置きなく】 ¶ あとは引き受けました. ～アメリカにご出発ください You just go to the States, and *don't worry about anything*. I will look after everything. あの人と～話し合った I talked with him freely *without any reserve*.

こころおぼえ【心覚え】 ¶ そんなことを言った～もある I *vaguely remember* saying something like that. ～にメモをとっておいた I made some notes *so as not to forget*.

こころがかり【心掛かり】 ¶ 国に残した妻子のことが～だ I *am concerned about* my wife and children I left behind in my country.

こころがけ【心掛け】 ¶ ～の良い人 a *right-minded* person. ～の悪い人 a *wrong-headed* person; a *misguided* person. 彼がそうするのは良い～だ It *is right of* him *to* do that. ちゃんとかさを持ってくるとは～がいい It *is prudent of* you *to* remember to bring an umbrella.

こころが·ける【心掛ける】 ¶ 毎日つとめて運動するよう～けている I *make it a point to* do as much exercise as possible every day. 月々少なくとも3,000円は貯金するよう～けている I *try to* save (≒I *aim at* saving) at least three thousand yen a month.

こころがまえ【心構え】 preparedness; readiness. ¶ まさかのときの～はできている I *am prepared for* the worst. 彼はふだんからどんなことにもびくともしない～ができている His *inner resources* are such that he can meet any emergency.

こころがわり【心変わり】 a change of mind. ¶ いったんそうと決めたら～は許されない Once you made up your mind, you cannot *change* (≒*retract*) *it*.

こころぐるし·い【心苦しい】 ¶ 私のためにいろいろお骨折りいただき～く存じます *I feel guilty* (≒*I am sorry*) *about* letting you do so much for me. あんなことをしたあとであの人に会うのは～い I *have qualms about* meeting her after what I did to her. 借金も返せず～く思っています I *feel bad about* having been unable to pay you back the money. 父が経済的に苦労しているのに大学に行くのは～い I *don't feel right about* going to college when my father struggles to make ends meet.

こころざし【志】 (希望) a desire; a wish; (決心) a resolution; (目的) an object; (大望) an ambition.
¶ ～を立てる make *a resolution* (*to* do *something*); have *an ambition* (*to* do *something*). ～を遂げる attain *one's aim*. せっかくのお～ですからありがたく頂きます I am glad to accept your *nice present*. 人の～を無にするものではない You should not let their *kindness* be of no avail. / You should not treat people's *favor* so lightly. 事～と違った Things did not turn out as I *had intended*.

こころざ·す【志す】 ¶ 科学者を～す *aspire to be* a scientist. 文学に～す *intend* (≒*aspire after*) a literary career.

こころじょうぶ【心丈夫】 ¶ もう～だ Now I *feel secure*. / Now I *feel at ease*.

こころづかい【心遣い】 thoughtfulness; consideration; (心配) concern; care. ¶ 私へのお～, まことにありがとうございます I greatly appreciate your 〔*kind*〕 *interest in* me.

こころづくし【心尽くし】 (配慮) thoughtfulness; care; (親切) attentions. ¶ お～の品々をお送りいただきありがとうございます Thank you for your *thoughtfulness* in sending me those gifts.

こころづけ【心付け】 a tip. ¶ ボーイに～を500円やる give a waiter five hundred yen as *a tip*; *tip* a waiter five hundred yen.

こころづよ·い【心強い】 encouraging. ¶ あなたがそばにいてくれるので～い I *feel reassured* by your presence. / I *feel comforted* (≒*feel encouraged*) when you are with me.

こころな·い【心ない】 ¶ ～いことばを浴びせる speak *heartless* (≒*cruel*) words (*to a person*). ～い人々の手によって公園の花が手折られる Flowers in the park are plucked by *inconsiderate* people.

こころならず〔も〕【心ならず〔も〕】 unwittingly; unwillingly; (本心に反して) reluctantly.
¶ ぼくは～その案に同意した I agreed to the plan *against my will*.

こころにく·い【心憎い】 (うまい) superb; remarkable. ¶ ～い腕前 a *superb* technique.

こころのこり【心残り】 regret. ¶ 今死んでも～はない I would *have no regrets* even if I die now. あなたにお目にかかれずここを立ち去るのはほんとうに～だ I *feel* most *reluctant to* leave here without seeing you. あの子のことが～で死んでも死にきれない That child is *a source of great concern to* me, and I simply cannot die, leaving him behind.

こころばかり【心ばかり】 ¶ これは～の感謝のしるしです This is just a *small* token of my gratitude.

こころひそかに【心密かに】 ¶ 彼は怠けたことを～悔いている He repents *inwardly* of having been idle.

こころぼそ·い【心細い】 helpless; discouraging; lonely. ¶ 夜道をひとりで歩くのは～い I *do not feel secure*, walking alone at night. ことばのわからぬ国では～い We *feel lost* (≒*feel helpless*) in a country where we do not know the language. 年をとるとだんだん～くなる

You *feel* more *alone* as you grow older. 懐が～くなってきた My pocketbook *is getting alarmingly empty.*

こころまち【心待ち】¶よい返事を～にしている I *am looking forward to* a favorable reply.

こころみ【試み】(ためし) a trial; a test; an experiment; (企て) an attempt; a venture. ¶～に彼にやらせてみてはどうだろう How about giving him a chance 〔to prove himself〕? ～にそれをやってみよう I'll give it *a try.*

こころ·みる【試みる】¶新しい方法を～みる *try* a new method. アルプス登山を～みる *attempt* to climb the Alps.

こころもち【心持ち】¶湯上がりでいい～だ I *feel refreshed* after the bath. ～涼しくなった It has become *a bit* cooler.

こころもとな·い【心もとない】uncertain; unreliable. ¶日本の将来がどうなるか～いかぎりだ We *cannot but feel apprehensive* about the future of Japan. きみの運転では～い I *don't feel quite safe* when I am in the car that you drive.

こころやす·い【心安い】familiar; intimate. ¶私たちはごく～い間がらです We *feel at home with each other.* 彼女はだれとでもすぐ～くなる She *makes friends with* anybody. 身知らぬ人と～く話す talk with a stranger *in a friendly manner.*

こころやすだて【心安立て】¶～についよけいなことを申し上げてしまいすみません I beg your pardon for having made an uncalled-for remark *out of familiarity.*

こころゆくまで【心行くまで】¶彼は～歌った He sang *to his heart's content.*

こころよ·い【快い】comfortable; pleasant. ¶海辺から～い風が吹いてきた We had a *refreshing* (≒ *comfortable*) breeze blowing from the beach. 散歩のあとの入浴は実に～いものだ How *pleasant* it is to have a bath after a walk!

こころよく【快く】¶～眠る sleep *well* (≒ *soundly*). 彼は～承諾してくれた He consented *readily* (≒ *willingly*). 彼のでしゃばりを～思わない人が少なくない Not a few people *feel hurt* (≒ *feel offended*) *at* his interference.

ここん【古今】¶源氏物語はまさに～を通じての名作だ *The Tale of Genji* is really one of the greatest masterpieces *through all ages.* 子を思う親の愛は～東西を問わず永遠の真理である Love of *one's* children is the eternal truth *for all ages and in all places.*

ごこん【語根】the root of a word.

こさ【濃さ】(色の) depth; (液体の) thickness; density.

ごさ【誤差】an error.

ござ【茣蓙】a mat.

ごさい【後妻】a second wife. ¶彼は50代で～を迎えた He *remarried* (≒ *married a second wife*) in his fifties.

こざいく【小細工】petty tricks. ¶あまり～をするのはぼくの性に合わない Resorting to *petty tricks* is alien to my nature.

コサイン〔数学〕cosine.

こざかし·い【小賢しい】shrewd; smartish. ¶～いことを言う say something *smartish.* ～く立ちまわる behave *shrewdly.*

こざかな【小魚】small fish.

こさく【小作】tenancy.
—人 a tenant; a tenant farmer.

こざっぱり ¶彼女はいつも服装が～している She *is* always *neat* in her dress.

こさめ【小雨】a light rain; a drizzle; a fine rain. ¶～が降る It *rains lightly.*

こざら【小皿】a small plate.

こさん【古参】a senior. ¶彼のほうが私よりずっと～だ He is much *senior to* me.
—兵 a senior comrade.

ごさん【誤算】miscalculation. ¶コンピューターでもときには～がある Even a computer sometimes *makes miscalculation.* 当局は情勢分析において重大な～を犯した The authorities *made a* gross *error* in analyzing the situation.

ごさんかい【午餐会】a luncheon party (luncheon は公式のもので lunch は一般的).

こし【腰】**1**〖腰部〗the waist; the hips. ¶祖母はだいぶ～が曲がっている My grandmother *is* pretty *bent* with age.
きょうは～が痛い I have a pain in my *hips* today.
凍った道で滑って～を強く打った I slipped and fell on the frozen road, and hit my *waist.*
彼は～を伸ばして深呼吸した He *stretched himself* and breathed deeply.
老人は～を曲げてとぼとぼと歩いた The old man trudged *bending forward.*
水が～まで来た The water rose up to my *hips.* / The water has got *waist-deep.*
2〖すわる·立つ〗¶歩き疲れて公園のベンチに～をおろした I was tired from walking, and *sat down* on a bench in the park.
彼はやっと～を上げて歩きだした He *stood up* finally, and began walking.
3〖慣用的表現〗¶彼は相手に強く出られると, すぐ～砕けになる When someone shows a firm front, he *is* soon *daunted.*
彼女は驚いて～を抜かした She *was paralyzed* with fright.
人の話の～を折るな Don't *cut in* while I'm talking. / Don't *interrupt* me in my talk.
ひとつ～をすえてこの仕事をやってみたまえ *Settle down* to this job.
彼はだれにでも～が低い男だ He *is very polite to* anybody.

こじ【固持】persistence. ¶彼はがんとして自説を～した He resolutely *held fast to* his own opinion.

こじ【固辞】refusal. ¶～する refuse positively.

こじ【孤児】an orphan. ¶彼は7歳で～になった He *was orphaned* at seven.
—院 an orphanage. 戦災— a war orphan.

こじ【故事】a historical allusion. ¶彼は～来歴に詳しい He is well versed in *the anecdotes and history.*

こじ【誇示】display. ¶ 大国はとかく国力を〜するきらいがある Major powers are liable to *make an ostentatious display* of their own national strength.

-ごし【-越し】¶ 彼らは5年〜の交際が実ってめでたく結婚にゴールインした Their intercourse of *five years' standing* bore fruit in a happy marriage. 私は毎朝かきね〜にお隣にあいさつする I greet my neighbor *over* the fence every morning. 背の高い彼は電車の中で人の肩〜に新聞を読むことがよくある Being a tall man, he often reads newspapers in a train *over* others' shoulders.

ごじ【誤字】a wrong word; (印刷) a misprint.

こじあ·ける【抉じ開ける】wrench open; break (≒ force) open. ¶ 錠前を〜ける *force* a lock *open*.

こしあん【漉し餡】strained bean jam.

こしいた【腰板】〖建築〗panels.

こしかけ【腰掛け】(台) a seat; a bench; (一時の職) a temporary post.
¶ ほんの〜のつもりでこの会社に入った I entered this company with the intention of working only for a time.

こしか·ける【腰掛ける】take a seat; seat *oneself*.

こしかた【来し方】¶ 〜行く末 *the past* and the future.

こしき【古式】¶ 〜にのっとる in accordance with *an ancient ceremony*. 〜ゆかしい祭り a festival *suggestive of the good old times*.

こじき【乞食】a beggar. ¶ 〜をするほどに落ちぶれる be reduced to *beggary*.
—根性 a mean spirit.

こしぎんちゃく【腰巾着】*a person's* shadow. ¶ 彼は社長の〜にすぎない He is just *a minion* of the president of his company.

こしけ【白帯下】〖医学〗leucorrhea.

ごしごし ¶ このような汚れは〜洗えばすぐ落ちる You can wash off such a stain by rubbing *briskly*.

こしたんたん【虎視眈眈】¶ 敵は常に〜と攻撃のチャンスをねらっている The enemy is *continuously* watching for an opportunity to attack us.

こしつ【固執】insistence. ¶ そんなに自説を〜するとは彼も我が強い How obstinate he is to *stick to* his views so much! 敵は無条件停戦に〜した The enemy *insisted upon* the unconditional cessation of arms.

こしつ【個室】a private room.

こしつ【痼疾】a chronic disease.

こじつ【故実】¶ 彼は〜に明るい He is quite familiar with *old customs and manners*.

ごじつ【後日】in the future. ¶ これは〜の証拠にとっておきましょう Let's keep this for the *future* evidence. この件につきましては〜あらためてご返事申し上げます About this affair, I will reply *some day*.
—談 recollections.

こしつき【腰つき】¶ 病み上がりだからどうもふらふらした〜だ Being a convalescent, I *am not steady on my legs*.

ゴシック Gothic.
—活字 Gothic type. **—**建築 Gothic architecture. **—**様式 Gothic style.

こじつけ distortion. ¶ 彼の理屈はたいてい〜だ His talk *is* usually *far-fetched*. あの人は〜がうまい He is good at *sophistry*.

こじつ·ける ¶ ひねくれ者だから何事によらず〜ける Perverse as he is, he *distorts* almost anything. 〜けて by a stretch of language.

ゴシップ gossip. ¶ 〜に花を咲かせる engage in *gossiping*.

ごじっぽひゃっぽ【五十歩百歩】¶ どちらをとっても〜だ Whichever you may choose, there will *not be much difference* [*between the two*].

こしぬけ【腰抜け】cowardice; (人) a coward; a weak-kneed.

こしぼね【腰骨】the hucklebone.

こしゃく【小癪】¶ そんなことをするとは〜なやつだ How *impudent* (≒ *saucy*) he is to do such a thing!

こしゅ【固守】adherence. ¶ 伝統を〜する *stick to* traditions.

こしゅ【戸主】the head of a family.

ごじゅう【五十】fifty.

ごじゅうおん【五十音】the Japanese syllabary. ¶ 名簿は〜順だ The list is arranged *in Japanese alphabetical order*.
—図 the systematic table of the Japanese syllabary.

ごじゅうしょう【五重唱】〖音楽〗quintet[te].

ごじゅうそう【五重奏】〖音楽〗quintet[te].

こじゅうと【小姑·小舅】a sister-in-law; a brother-in-law (*one's* husband's brother とは言わないが, 意味はわかるので付加的解説ならよい).

ごじゅうのとう【五重の塔】a five-storied pagoda.

ごしゅきょうぎ【五種競技】the pentathlon.

ごじゅん【語順】word order.

こしょ【古書】an old book.
—店(古本屋) a used bookstore.

ごしょ【御所】an Imperial Palace.

ごじょ【互助】mutual aid.
—会 a friendly society.

こしょう【小姓】a page.

こしょう【湖沼】lakes and marshes.

こしょう【故障】[a] trouble. ¶ この時計はときどき〜する This watch sometimes *doesn't work well*. そのテレビは〜している The TV set *is out of order* (≒ *is broken*). バスが〜したので約束の時間に遅れてしまった I was late for the appointed time through the *breakdown* of the bus. 飛行機の墜落の原因はエンジンの〜によるものだった It was because of the *breakdown* of the engine that the plane crashed. エンジンに〜を起こして, ぼくの車は動かなくなってしまった *An* engine *trouble* caused my car to stop working. 体になにか〜のある人は申し出なさい Those who *have something wrong with* them, please report to me. 新幹線の工事計画には〜が生じた A project to build the New Main Line *was frustrated*. 新工場の

建設は〜なく進んでいる The building of a new factory is going *all right* (≒ *with no hitch*).

こしょう【胡椒】pepper. ¶ 〜の風味がよくきいている This is really well flavored with *pepper*.

ごしょう【後生】¶ 〜だから今度だけは見のがしてください *For God's sake*, please let the matter pass for this once. 彼は母からもらったお守りをいつも〜大事に持っている He always *treasures* the charm which his mother gave him.

ごじょう【互譲】mutual concession. ¶ 〜の精神 the spirit of *compromise* (≒ *concession*).

こしょく【古色】an antique look. ¶ この寺はすべてが〜蒼然(ぜん)としている This temple *looks time-honored* (≒ *looks hoary*) in everything.

ごしょく【誤植】a misprint; a printer's error.

こしらえごと【拵え事】a fake; a fiction. ¶ それは〜だから説得力を欠いている As it is *a fake*, it is lacking in persuasive power.

こしら・える【拵える】⇒つくる

こじら・す ¶ 先月は風邪を〜せて長く寝込んだ Last month I was tied to bed for a long time by *making* a cold *worse*. 彼の突然の辞任が問題をさらに〜せた His sudden resignation *complicated* the matter more seriously.

こじ・れる ¶ 風邪が〜れて肺炎になった His cold *grew into* pneumonia. ふたりの間はますます〜れていった The relations between the two men *became* more and more *strained*.

こじわ【小皺】little wrinkles. ¶ 目じりの〜 *wrinkles* (≒ *crow's-feet*) at the outer corners of the eyes. 彼の顔には〜がよっている His face is seamed with *wrinkles*.

こじん【故人】the departed; the deceased. ¶ この本の著者は既に〜となっている The author of this book *is* already *dead*. 〜のA氏 the *late* Mr. A.

こじん【個人】an individual. ¶ 〜の権利 the rights of the *individual*. 私の〜的な問題 my *private* affair; my *personal* matter. 私〜の意見ではその提案に賛成だ *Personally* I (≒ I *for one*) agree to the proposal. 私は〜の資格でその会合に出席した I attended the meeting in my *private* capacity. 彼とは〜的にはなんの関係もない I have no *personal* contact with him. 彼女を〜的に知っているわけではない I have no *personal* acquaintance with her. 彼は〜的感情に支配されやすい He is apt to be affected by *personal* prejudice.
—教授 private lessons. ¶ 彼女からピアノの〜教授を受けた I took *private* piano *lessons* from her. 彼に英会話の〜教授をした I gave him *private lessons* in English conversation. —差 ¶ 〜差を認める recognize *differences among individuals*. —主義 individualism. —主義者 an individualist. —タクシー an owner-driver taxi.

ごしん【誤診】a wrong diagnosis. ¶ どんな名医でも時には〜する The most experienced doctor sometimes makes *a wrong* (≒ *mistaken*) *diagnosis of* a person's illness. 医者は私の症状を結核と〜した That doctor *diagnosed* my case *wrongly* as tuberculosis.

ごしん【誤審】misjudgment.

ごしん【護身】¶ 〜用のつえ a stick for *self-protection*.
—術 the art of self-defense.

こ・す【越す】(越える) go over; (年月を過ごす) pass; (超過する) be over; (引っ越しする) move. ¶ 彼はボートで川を〜した He *crossed* the river by boat. 彼らは丘を〜していった They *went over* the hill. 彼の人気も峠を〜した His popularity *passed* its peak. 彼女は重病であったが, 今は峠を〜した She has been seriously ill, but *has got over the crisis* (≒ *has turned the corner*) now. 彼はもう60歳を〜した He *is over* sixty. それに〜したことはない Nothing can be better than that. 郊外へ〜す *remove to* the suburbs.

こ・す【漉す・濾す】¶ 茶を〜す *strain* tea. コーヒーのかすを〜して取る *strain out* coffee grounds. 水を使う前に汚れを〜して取り除く *filter out* all dirt before using water.

こすい【湖水】a lake.

こすい【鼓吹】¶ 向学心を若者に〜すべきだ A love for learning must *be inspired* in youth. 国民に愛国心を〜する *inspire* the nation *with* patriotism.

こす・い【狡い】cunning; sly; underhand. ¶ 〜いことをするな Don't do a *tricky* thing. あの〜い男のほうがわれわれより役者が一枚上だ That *sly* fellow is a cut above us.

こすう【個数】¶ これらの品物は〜に制限なくお買い上げいただけます You can buy as many of these articles as you like.

こすう【戸数】the number of houses. ¶ 〜30ばかりの村 a hamlet of about thirty *families*.

ごすう【語数】the number of words.

こずえ【梢】a twig; a treetop.

コスチューム costume.

コスト〔a〕cost. ¶ 〜を割って売る sell *below cost*. この品物を1個につき100円で売れば〜を割らなくてもすむ If we sell this article at one hundred yen a piece, we can cover the *cost*. 生産〜の切り下げを図る try to reduce the *cost* of production.
—高 the high cost (*of* an article).

コスモス〘植物〙a cosmos.

こす・る【擦る】¶ 毎朝体を粗いタオルで〜ることにしている I usually *rub* myself *down* with a coarse towel every morning. 戸が床に〜れる The door *rubs* on the floor. それはすぐ〜れて取れるだろう It will *rub out off* easily.

ご・する【伍する】¶ 日本は著しい経済成長を遂げ今や世界の経済大国に〜する段階にまでなった Japan has shown such remarkable growth in her economy that she now *ranks among* the economic powers of the world. 彼は先輩連に〜して大いに活躍している He is leading a very active life, *taking rank with* his seniors. 彼はベテランジャーナリストに～して仕事をすることができるだけの才能を持っている He is talented enough to work *side by side with* veteran journalists.

こせい【個性】individuality ; 〔a〕 personality. ¶ はっきりした～を持った人 a man of marked *individuality*. この競争の激しい世界では～に欠けていては成功はおぼつかない Those who are lacking in *personality* cannot hope to succeed in this competitive world. 自分の～を発揮できる会社に勤めたい I want to work for a company in which I can work out my *individuality*. 彼女には～がある She has *personality*. 彼女は非常に強い～を持っている She has *a* very forceful *personality*.

こぜい【小勢】a small number of men. ¶ ～ながら, われわれは敵に対してがん強に戦った Although greatly *outnumbered*, we put up a stubborn fight against the enemy.

こせいだい【古生代】〖地質学〗the Paleozoic era.

こせいぶつ【古生物】extinct plants and animals. ―学 paleontology. ―学者 a paleontologist.

こせき【戸籍】*one's* family register. ¶ 彼女はまだ夫の～に入っていない She has not yet had her name entered in her husband's *family register*. 彼の～を調べる inquire into his *family register*.
―抄本 an abstract of *one's* family register. ―謄本 a copy of *one's* family register.

こせこせ ¶ つまらないことに～するような人間は大成しない A man who *fusses* (≒ *makes a fuss*) about trifles will not be a somebody. つまらないことに～するな Don't *be fussy* (≒ *make a fuss*) about nothing.

こぜに【小銭】small money ; 〔small〕 change. ¶ ～で払う pay *in small change*. ～の持ち合わせがない I have no *change* with me.

こぜりあい【小競り合い】a skirmish.

こせん【古銭】old coin.

ごせん【互選】¶ 会長は会員の～によって決められる The president will be elected *by mutual vote* from among the members of the society.

ごぜん【午前】the morning ; a. m. ¶ ～に *in* the *morning*. ～中 all 〔the〕 *morning*. 10日の～に *on* the *morning* of the 10th.

こせんきょう【跨線橋】an overbridge.

ごせんし【五線紙】〖音楽〗music paper.

こせんじょう【古戦場】an old (≒ ancient) battlefield (≒ battleground). ¶ 関が原の～ the *battlefield* of Sekigahara.

-こそ ¶ それで～きみだ That's *what I expected of* you. それで～男だ That *is worthy of a* man. 見つかったらそれ～たいへんだ If this is found out, there will be all hell to pay. 彼のフランス語はそれ～フランス人のようだ He speaks French *just like* a Frenchman. こちら～おわびしなければなりません *It is I who* must apologize.

こぞう【小僧】(奉公人) an apprentice ; a shop-boy ; (少年) a boy ; a kid ; (お寺の) a novice. ¶ はなたれ～ *a* snotty *urchin*. 彼は大工のところへ～に入った He *was bound apprentice* (≒ *was apprenticed*) *to* a carpenter.

ごそう【護送】escort. ¶ 犯人は警官に～されて東京へ連行された The criminal was brought to Tokyo *under* police *escort*. 囚人を～する *carry* (≒ *transport*) a prisoner.
―車 [米] a patrol wagon ; [英] a prison van.
―船隊 a convoy.

ごぞうろっぷ【五臓六腑】entrails ; bowels. ¶ 酒が～にしみわたる *Sake* is intoxicating.

こそく【姑息】a makeshift. ¶ ～な手段をとって急場をしのごうとしてもむだだ It is no use trying to tide over the crisis by resorting to *makeshifts*.

ごそくろう【御足労】¶ このような遠い所まで～をおかけして申しわけありません I'm sorry *to have made you come such a distance*. It must have been a great deal of trouble.

こそこそ ¶ ～話す talk *in whispers*. ～立ち去る sneak away (*from*).

ごそごそ ¶ 押し入れのすみでなにか～音がした I heard something *rustling* in a corner of the closet.

こぞって【挙って】¶ 彼らは～そうだと言った They all answered "yes" *to a man*. 彼らは～辞職した They resigned *in a body*. 家族～ピクニックに行った The *whole* family went on a picnic.

こそどろ【こそ泥】a sneak (≒ petty) thief.

ごぞんじ【御存じ】¶ そんなことは～のはずです You ought to *know* such a thing. ロンドンには～の方がいらっしゃいますか Do you have any *acquaintances* in London ?

こたい【固体】a solid 〔body〕. ¶ ～燃料 a *solid* fuel.

こたい【個体】an individual.

こだい【古代】ancient times ; antiquity.
―史 ancient history. ―人 the ancients (英語では主としてギリシア・ローマ人). ―文学 ancient literature. ―文明 ancient civilization.

こだい【誇大】exaggeration.
―広告 a sensational advertisement. ―妄想(もうそう)狂 megalomania.

ごたい【五体】¶ 生まれた子どもは～満足だ The new-born baby *is without any physical defect*. その事故で命の助かった人で～満足な者はひとりもいなかった Those who survived the accident suffered some injury or other.

こたえ【答え】an answer. ¶ この問題に～を出すのに相当な時日がかかると思う I am afraid that it will be long before I can work out *a solution* for this problem.

こた・える【答える】answer ; reply. ¶ この質問に～えなさい *Answer* me this question. そのことについてはなにも知らないと彼は～えた He *answered* that he knew nothing about it. 彼女はなにも～えてもらえなかった She got no *answer* from him. 彼からの批評に～えてその論

文を書いた I wrote the article *in reply to* a remark from him.

こた・える【応える・対える】¶ 両親のことばは彼らの胸に強く～えた The parents' words *came* (≒ *went* ; *struck*) *home* to them. 友人の尽力に～えなければならない We must *reward* our friend *for* his services. この種の重労働は私のような老人には～える This sort of hard work *tells on* an old man like me.

こた・える【堪える】¶ この菓子はおいしくて～えられない This cake is *irresistibly* tasty. / I *cannot resist* the cake.

こだか・い【小高い】¶ ～い丘 a *small* hill.

こだから【子宝】¶ ～に恵まれている be blessed with many *children*.

ごたごた〔a〕trouble. ¶ 家庭内の～については口外無用 Keep domestic *trouble* to yourself. あの家庭は～が絶えない The family *is* always *in trouble*. だれだって友人と～を起こしたくはない Nobody wants to *get into trouble with* his friends. 引っ越してきたばかりだから, 部屋が～している The room *is in a mess* (≒ *is in sad disorder* ; *is untidy*), I've just moved in here.

こだし【小出し】¶ 食糧が不足してきたので船長は食糧を～に出した Since the food supply was running low, the ship's captain *doled out* the rations. 委員会は慈善事業の資金を～に出した The committee *doled out* the funds of the charity.

こだち【木立】a grove ; a cluster of trees.

こたつ【火燵・炬燵】a charcoal footwarmer ; a Japanese fireplace with a coverlet ; a Japanese covered heating system.

こだね【子種】¶ 夫婦は～に恵まれなかった The couple were not blessed with *children*.

ごたぶん【御多分】¶ ハイカーの～にもれず, 彼らはあとにがらくたをたくさん残していった *As is usual with* hikers, they left a lot of litter behind them. 一年のこの時期には, 同業者の～にもれずうちの会社も火の車だ At this time of year we are hard up for money just *like* everybody else of the same trade.

こだま【木霊・谺】an echo. ¶ 山は爆発の音で～した The hills *echoed* (≒ *resounded*) with the explosion.

こだわり ¶ きみたちも～を捨てて仲直りをしてはどうだね How about forgetting all that has passed (≒ How about letting bygones be bygones) and being friends again?

こだわ・る【拘る】¶ 彼は形式に～る He *sticks to* (≒ *is a stickler for*) formality. あまり細かいことに～っていてはいけない You should not *be* too *particular about* trifles.

こたん【枯淡】¶ この小説家の文体に最近独特な～の味が出てきた This novelist has recently begun to develop a *simple but elegant* (≒ *easy and sober*) style of his own.

こち【鯒】〔魚類〕a flathead.

こち【故知】¶ ～に倣う follow *another's example*.

こちこち ¶ 冷凍室の野菜はみんな～に凍っていた All the vegetables in the freezing compartment *were frozen stiff*. 粘土をひなたに出したままにしておくと～になってしまう If you leave the clay in the sun, it will *be dried and hardened*. 彼は緊張のあまり～になってろくに口もきけないほどであった He *was* so tense and *stiff* that he could not talk properly. 彼はあがって～になっていた He *was* too nervous and *stiff*.

ごちそう【御馳走】entertainment. ¶ 今度の日曜に友人を招いてお茶を～しようと思う I think I'll invite my friends and *entertain* them at tea next Sunday. 6品つきの～が出た *A dinner* of six courses was served. 私は昨晩アメリカの友人にすき焼きを～してあげた I *treated* my American friends to *sukiyaki* last evening. このビールはぼくが～する This glass of ale *is on me*. われわれは彼に～になった We *were treated to* a good dinner by him. ～さまでした Thank you〔for your *entertainment*〕./ Thank you for the hospitality. 私のような老人にとっては冬には火がなによりの～だ In winter fire is *a great treat* to old people like me.

ゴチック Gothic. ⇒ゴシック

ごちゃごちゃ a mess. ¶ 書類を机の上に～にしておくな Don't *leave* your papers *in confusion* on the desk. 自由と放縦を～にしている若い人が多すぎる There are too many young people who *confuse* liberty *with* license. 引き出しの中はなにもかも～になっていた Everything *was jumbled up* in the drawer.

こちょう【誇張】exaggeration. ¶ 会社の規模についての彼の話はひどい～だ His story about the size of his company is *a* gross *exaggeration*. あの人は物を～して言う He has a habit of *making a mountain out of a molehill*. その物語は信じがたいほどに～されている The story *is* incredibly *exaggerated*. 彼は現代のニュートンであると言っても～ではない It is no *exaggeration* to say that he is a Newton of today.

ごちょう【伍長】〔軍〕a corporal.

ごちょう【語調】a tone. ¶ 辛らつな～で話す speak *in* acid *tones*.

こちら ¶ ～へどうぞ *This way*, please.（電話で）～は山本です Hello, *this* is Yamamoto speaking. ～のおちどです It is a fault *on our part*. ～へおいでの節にはお立ち寄りください Drop in if you come *my way*. ～がさっきお話した田中さんです *This* is Mr. Tanaka we've been talking about. 道路の～側で遊ばなくてはいけません You have to play *this side*〔*of*〕the road. ～へ来て何年になりますか How long have you lived *here*?

こぢんまり ¶ ～した家 a *little snug* house.

こつ a knack. ¶ 小さい子どもを扱う～を覚えるのにかなりかかった It took me long to acquire the *knack* of dealing with little children. 彼はわずかな時間でも利用する～を知っている He has *a knack* for employing to advantage all odd moments. その～をのみこめばすぐやれる It's quite easy when you have the *knack* of it. 欠かさず練習をやってようやく～をつかんだ I have at

〔long〕last learned the *ropes* after putting in regular practice.

こつ【骨】 a bone ; (遺骨) ashes. ¶ 〜を拾う(骨上げをする) gather *a person's ashes*.

こっか【国花】 the national flower. ¶ 日本の〜は桜である *The national flower* of Japan is a cherry blossom. (アメリカの州花は a state flower).

こっか【国歌】 the national anthem.

こっか【国家】 a state ; a nation ; a country. ¶ 彼らは新しい〜を建設するために努力している They are endeavoring to build up *a new nation*. 彼は外交官として〜に尽くした He served his *country* as a diplomat. 彼は〜のために命を投げ出した He laid down his life for the sake of his *country*. 〜的見地からその問題をよく考えるべきだ We should think over the matter *from a national point of view*.

—管理 state (≒ government) control. **—経済** national economy. **—公務員(個人)** a national public official ; a civil servant ; (総称) national public service personnel. **—試験** a state examination. **—主義** nationalism. 共産(社会 ; 資本)主義**—** a communist (socialist ; capitalist) country. 警察**—** a police state. 福祉**—** a welfare state.

こっかい【国会】 (日本の) the Diet ; (アメリカの) Congress ; (イギリスの) Parliament.

—議員 a member of the Diet ; a Dietman ; (アメリカの) a Congressman ; (イギリスの) a member of Parliament (an M. P.). **—議事堂** the Diet Building ; (アメリカの) the Capitol ; (イギリスの) the Houses of Parliament. **—図書館** the Diet (≒ 米 Congress) Library.

こづかい【小使】 a servant ; (女) a maid servant.

こづかい【小遣い】 pocket money. ¶ 月に3,000円の〜をもらっている I receive *a monthly allowance* of three thousand yen. / I get three thousand yen a month for *pocket money*.

こっかく【骨格】 the build ; the frame of the body. ¶ 彼の〜はたくましい He is a man *of* sturdy *build*.

こっき【克己】 self-restraint. ¶ 〜に富む人 a *self-denying* person ; a man *of self-restraint*. 〜のない人 a person who lacks *self-control*.

こっき【国旗】 a national flag. ¶ 日本の〜 *the national flag* of Japan ; the Japanese flag ; the sun-flag. アメリカの〜 the American flag ; the Stars and Stripes ; the star-spangled banner. イギリスの〜 the British flag ; the Union Jack. フランスの〜 the French flag ; the Tricolor. ソ連の〜 the Soviet (≒ Russian) flag ; the Hammer and Sickle. 〜を掲げる hoist (≒ fly) *a national flag*.

こっきょう【国教】 a state religion. ¶ イギリス〜 the Church of England ; the Anglican Church.

こっきょう【国境】 a frontier ; a boundary. ¶ 〜の町 a *border* town. 〜を守る guard *the frontier*. 〜問題を解決する settle *the boundary problems*. 〜を固める fortify *the frontier*.

—線 a border line.

こっきん【国禁】 ¶ 彼らは〜を犯して起訴された They were prosecuted for violating *the legal prohibition* (≒ *the prohibition by law*).

こっく【刻苦】 toil ; labor. ¶ 彼は〜勉励の末大学者となった He *worked hard* and became a great scholar. / He made a great scholar through his *untiring industry*.

コック (水道などの) a cock ; a tap ; 米 a faucet ; (料理) a cook. ¶ 〜を開ける (閉める) turn the *tap* on (off).

こづ・く【小突く】 ¶ しかられて頭を〜かれた I was scolded and *had* my head *thrust* a little backward. 私はひじで隣に座っている彼を〜いた I *poked* him sitting next to me with my elbow.

こっくり ¶ 子どもは〜うなずいた The child *nodded in assent*. 彼は〜居眠りをしていた He *was nodding* (≒ *was rocking*) in a doze.

こづくり【小作り】 ¶ 〜の男 a *little* man ; a man *of small build* (≒ *of small stature*).

こっけい【滑稽】 ¶ 彼は〜なことを言って人を笑わせる He makes everyone laugh by saying *funny* things. あれで大成功のつもりだから〜だ What *nonsense* it is (≒ How *ridiculous* it is) that he does believe it a great success ! あれで学生だというのだから〜だ It is indeed *absurd* that he should pass for a student.

こっけん【国権】 national rights (≒ power).

こっこ【国庫】 the National Treasury.

¶ 費用は〜負担となる The expenses is paid out of *the National Treasury*.

—補助 a state (≒ government) subsidy.

こっこう【国交】 diplomatic relations. ¶ その国は隣国と〜を断絶した (結んだ) The country broke off (entered into) *diplomatic relations* with its neighboring countries. 日本は中国と〜を回復した Japan has restored her *diplomatic relationship* with China.

ごつごうしゅぎ【御都合主義】 opportunism.

こっこく【刻刻】 ¶ 〜と新しいニュースが入っている We are receiving news after news *every moment* (≒ *moment by moment*).

こつこつ ¶ 彼は〜努力する型だ He is a *hard and tireless* (≒ *assiduous*) worker. だれかが戸を〜たたいている Somebody *is tapping at* the door.

ごつごつ ¶ 〜した文体 a *stiff* style. 〜した岩 a *rugged* (≒ *ragged*) rock. 〜した手 a *bony* hand.

こっし【骨子】 the gist (*of*). ¶ 彼の演説の〜 the *sum and substance* of his speech.

こつずい【骨髄】〘生物〙the marrow. ¶ あの男には恨み〜に徹する I *bear* him *a bitter grudge*. / I *have a deep grudge against him*.

—炎〘医学〙osteomyelitis.

こっせつ【骨折】 fracture〔of a bone〕. ¶ スキーで足を〜した I *had* my leg *broken* (≒ *fractured*) while skiing.

こつぜん【忽然】¶ 彼は～として姿を消した He disappeared *suddenly* (≒ *as if by magic*).

こっそう【骨相】physiognomy.
—学 phrenology ; (人相学) physiognomy.

こっそり[と] ¶ 彼に～そのことを話しなさい Tell him *secretly* about the matter. 私は彼から前もって～それを聞いておいた I had learned it from him *on the quiet* beforehand. 私は～透き間からのぞいてみた I *stole a glance* from the opening.

ごっそり[と] ¶ どろぼうに新調のスーツを～やられた I had *all* my new suits stolen by the thief.

こった【凝った】¶ ～クリスマスの飾りつけ(手のこんだ) *elaborate* Christmas decorations. ～服装の女性(ぜいたくな) a lady in an *extravagant* dress.

ごったがえ・す【ごった返す】¶ 部屋は～している The room *is in a mess*(≒ *is in confusion; is topsy-turvy*). 駅は行楽客で～している The station *is overcrowded with* holiday-makers.

こっち ¶ ～のほうがいい *This* [*one*] is better. / I like *this* better. ～へ来なさい Come *here* (≒ *this way*).

こづち【小槌】a mallet. ¶ 打ち出の～ *a* magic *mallet* [with the same power as a magic wand].

ごっちゃ ¶ このふたつの問題を～に考えてはならない Never *confuse* the two problems. 分類したカードが～になってしまった The classified cards *got mixed.*

こっちょう【骨頂】¶ この暑いのに帽子もかぶらずに歩いていくなんて愚の～だ It *is very stupid of you* (≒ *is absolute folly*) to walk on such a hot day without a hat.

こつつぼ【骨壺】a cinerary urn.

こづつみ【小包】a parcel ; (小包郵便) parcel post. ¶ その本は～[郵便]にして送った I sent the book by *parcel post.* 田舎から～が届いた *A parcel* arrived from my home. ～を書留で送る mail *a package* registered.

こってり[と] ¶ 中華料理は～したものが多い Many Chinese dishes *are rich in taste.* ～しかられた I had a *good* scolding.

こっとう【骨董】a curio.
—品 a curio ; an antique. —屋(人) a curio (≒ curiosity) dealer ; (店) a curio (≒ curiosity) shop.

コットン cotton fabric ; cotton clothes.
—紙 cotton paper.

こつにく【骨肉】¶ ～の愛 love for *one's flesh and blood.* ～の間がら *family* relationship ; kinship ; brotherhood. ～相食む *The relations* are at feud with each other.

こっぱ【木っ端】¶ びんが落ちて～みじんに割れた The bottle fell down and was broken *to pieces.*

こつばん【骨盤】〘医学〙the pelvis (複 pelves).
¶ ～部 the pelvic wall.

こっぴどく ¶ 彼に～しかられた I was *severely* scolded by him. / I was given a *good* scolding by him. 彼に～どなられた I *was stormed* (≒ *was thundered*) *at* by him.

こつぶ【小粒】a grain. ¶ 彼は政治家としては～だ As a statesman he is *a man of small caliber.* さんしょは～でもぴりりと辛い *Small* man as he is, he is smart enough.

コップ a glass ; (大型の) a tumbler. ¶ ～1杯の水 *a glass* of water. ビールを～に半分 half *a glass* of beer. ～の中のあらし a storm in *a teacup* ; an *internal* trouble.

こっぷん【骨粉】powdered bones ; bone dust (≒ meal).

コッペパン a roll.

こつまく【骨膜】〘医学〙the periosteum (複 periostea).
—炎 periostitis.

こつん[と] ¶ 頭を～たたかれた I *was rapped* on the head.

ごつん[と] ¶ 彼と頭と頭を～ぶつけた I *bumped* my head *against* his.

こて【鏝】(洋裁の) an iron ; (理髪の) a curling iron ; (左官用の) a trowel.

こて【小手】a forearm ; fencing-gloves ; (剣道の) a gauntlet.

ごて【後手】〘将棋・囲碁〙the defensive hand. ¶ 災害対策は～に回らぬことが肝心だ Countermeasures against calamities must not *be too late.*

こてい【固定】¶ ～の fixed ; stationary ; permanent. ～する fix ; settle. ひもの一端を～して円を描く draw a circle by *fixing* an end of a string.
—概念 a fixed idea. —客 a regular customer. ¶ あの店は～客が多い That store has many *regular customers.* —給 a fixed salary ; fixed wages ; a regular pay. —資本 fixed capital. —資産 fixed assets. —資産税 the fixed property tax.

こてきたい【鼓笛隊】a drum and fife band.
—長 a drum major ; (女性) a drum majorette.

こてこて ¶ 彼女は～おしろいを塗っている She is [too] *thickly* powdered.

ごてごて ¶ その絵の色は～しすぎる The colors of the picture *are too gaudy.*

こてさき【小手先】¶ ～の策を弄(ろう)するな Don't try any *low tricks* on me.

こてしらべ【小手調べ】¶ 彼と試合をする前に～にちょっと彼の実力を試してみた I *tested* his real ability before I played a match against him.

こてん【古典】a classic ; (古典文学) the classics. ¶ 源氏物語は日本の代表的～文学だ *The Tale of Genji* is *a* representative Japanese *classic.* これは～的名著だ This is a fine book worthy of the name of *classic.*
—音楽 classical music. —学者 a classical scholar ; a classicist. —学派 a classical school. —主義 classicism. —文学 classical literature.

こてん【個展】a private show. ¶ 彼は銀座で自分の絵の～を開いた He gave *a private exhibition* (≒ *show*) of his own paintings at the Ginza.

こ

ごてん【御殿】a palace.
こと【琴】a *koto.* ¶ ～をひく play the *koto.*
こと【事】**1** 〖事柄〗a matter ; an affair.
¶ そんな～をしてはいけない You mustn't do such *a thing.*
彼の言う～がぼくにはわかる I understand him.
きょうはやる～がなにもない I am free today. / I have nothing to do today.
自分の～は自分でしなさい Look after yourself.
どうしてそんな～をしたのか What made you do it ?
この本にはおもしろい～がたくさん書いてある There are a lot of interesting *things* in this book.
われわれは～の真相を確かめなければならない We must disclose the real facts of *the case.*
たいへんな～をしてしまった I've got into a mess./ (人のものを壊したときなど) I was very awkward.
きみにちょっと話したい～がある I have something to talk to you.
～の起こりは彼の不注意からだ It happened through his carelessness.
彼の言う～は正論だ He is right. / *What* he says is right.
正直も～によりけりだ Honesty does not always do you good.
その～なら彼も承知だ He knows about the *matter,* too.
その～ならどうかご心配なく Please don't trouble yourself about it.
大事な～を忘れていた I have forgotten *an* important *thing.*
それはきみの知った～ではない It has nothing to do with you.
2 〖事情〗circumstances. ¶ ～ここに至っては, 彼も親に話さざるをえまい Now 〔that〕 *things* have come to such a pass, he has to tell it to his parents.
～によると彼はきょうは来ないかもしれない He may not come today.
そんな～では, きみはとても志望校に入れない *As things go,* you will not be able to enter your desired school.
きみたちの間にそんな～があったとは少しも知らなかった I did not know such *a thing* had happened to you all.
驚いた～には, 彼はまた試験に落ちた I am very surprised to learn that he failed the examination again.
3 〖出来事・やっかい事〗an event ; troubles.
¶ いかなる～が起ころうとも, ぼくはそこへ行くつもりだ Whatever happens, I will go there.
そいつは～だ Good heavens !
強いて彼と～を構える必要はない I don't have to make *troubles* with him on purpose.
4 〖必要〗¶ 今更彼にそんなことを言う～はない You don't have to tell him such a thing any longer. / There is no more *need* for you to tell it to him.
こちらからわざわざ彼を訪ねる～もない We *needn't* go all the way to see him on our part.
急ぐ～はない There is no *occasion* for haste./ We don't have to hurry.
なにも怒る～はない There is no *occasion* to be angry.
5 〖習慣〗¶ 毎朝野菜ジュースを1杯飲む～にしている I drink a glass of vegetable juice every morning. (「…ことにしている」は every morning があれば make it a rule to... という必要はない).
6 〖予定〗¶ 彼は明朝9時に羽田に着く～になっている He *is due at* Haneda at nine tomorrow morning.
私がその会議に出席する～になった It *was decided* that I attend the conference.
7 〖経験〗¶ きみはハワイへ行った～がありますか *Have* you ever *been to* Hawaii ?
私はまだ富士山へ登った～がありません I have not climbed Mt. Fuji yet.
そんなばかげた話はまだ聞いた～がない I never heard such an absurd story.
8 〖決心〗¶ いろいろ比べてみて, 結局この本を買う～にした I *decided* to buy this book, after comparing it with others.
熱があるので残念ながら学校を休む～にした I was sorry to be absent from school, because I had fever.
あすからたばこをやめる～にした I *have made up my mind to* give up smoking from tomorrow.
9 〖噂〗¶ 来年からそれは廃止になるとの～だ *I hear that* (≒ *It is said that ; They say that*) it will be abolished next year.
こと【古都】(古い都) an old (≒ ancient) capital ; (昔の都) a former capital.
こと【糊塗】¶ その場を～してのがれた I *shuffled through* the difficulty. / I *talked myself out of* the trouble.
-ごと【-共】¶ 箱～ください Give it to me, box *and all.* 家を地所～買った I bought the house *together with* the land. リンゴを皮～食べる eat an apple, peel *and all.*
-ごと【-毎】¶ 4時間～にその薬を飲む take the medicine *every* four hours. あのチームは一試合～に強くなる *Every* match makes that team stronger. ひと雨～に暖かくなる It is growing warmer *with every* rainfall. 彼は会う人～にお辞儀をした He bowed to *whomever* he met.
ことあたらし・い【事新しい】¶ ～く述べるまでもない It is needless to say anything *more* about it.
ことう【孤島】a lonely island ; a solitary island.
こどう【鼓動】¶ 心臓の～が止まった His heart stopped *beating.* 心配のあまり心臓の～が激しくなった Overcome with anxiety my heart started to *throb* violently.
こどうぐ【小道具】〔stage〕 properties.
—方 a property man (≒ master).
ことか・く【事欠く】¶ 水には～かない We have enough supply of water. 当時彼らは食べるのに～くような生活を送った In those days they lived such a hard life that they often lacked food. あの会社は資金には～かない That firm *has* never *suffered lack of* funds. /

That company *has been free from want* of funds so far.

ことき・れる【事切れる】¶ 駆けつけたときには，彼はもう〜れていた When I hastened to the spot, he *had* already *died* (≒ *was* already *dead*).

こどく【孤独】solitude; loneliness. ¶ 〜な生活を送る live *alone*; live *in solitude*; live a *solitary* life.

ことこと〔と〕¶ なにか〜音がしている I hear something *pattering*. 〜戸をたたく音がする There is *a tap* at the door. 彼女は〜かゆを煮ている She is taking much time to make gruel.

ことごと【事毎】¶ 彼は私に〜に反対する He opposes me *in every way*. 〜に失敗するのでくさっている As I fail *in everything*, I feel gloomy. / Failure in *every* attempt has made me depressed.

ことごとく【悉く・尽く】¶ 所持金を〜使いはたした I spent *all* the money I had with me. 彼らの計画は〜失敗に終わった Their plans have failed *one and all*.

ことこまかに【事細かに】minutely. ¶ 今それを〜述べる暇がない I have no time to *go into its details*. 事情を〜説明する give a *detailed* account of the situation.

ことさら【殊更】¶ 〜にやったわけではない I did not do it *intentionally* (≒ *on purpose*). 反感を買ってまでも〜彼に反対しようとは思わない I won't *dare* to disagree with him if it incurs his ill feeling.

ことし【今年】this year. ¶ 建築完成には〜いっぱいかかる It will take the rest of *this year* to complete the building. 〜じゅうにはこの問題の解決の手がかりを得たい We hope to find a key to this problem before the end of *this year*.

ことた・りる【事足りる】¶ 彼がいなくても十分〜りる We can *do well* without him. 生活には〜りている I can *get enough* to live on. さしあたり 50,000 円あれば〜りる Fifty thousand yen will *do* for the present.

ことづか・る【託る】¶ 彼から返事を〜ってきた Here is the answer he *asked* me *to hand* [*to*] you.

ことづけ【託け】a message. ¶ 彼女へ〜をお頼みしたいのだが May I ask you to give my *message* to her? 彼から会には少し遅れると〜がありました He sent me *word* he would be a little late for the meeting. なにか彼にお〜がありましたら伺っておきますが Would you leave *a message* for him?

ことづ・ける【託ける】¶ 今夜来てくれるようにと〜けてきました I *have left a message* for him that we want him to come to see us this evening.

ことなかれしゅぎ【事なかれ主義】a peace-at-any-price principle. ¶ 官僚の〜の態度 the bureaucrats' attitude of "never do anything liable to criticism."

ことなった【異なった】different; unlike; dissimilar; (別の) other; another; (種々の) varied. ¶ 〜趣味の人々 people with *dissimilar* tastes.

ことな・る【異なる】¶ 失礼だがその点では私の意見は〜る I beg to *differ* (≒ *disagree*) *with* you on that point. 国によって習慣は〜る Customs *differ* in different countries. 流行は時と場所で〜る Fashion *varies* with time and place. 人によって意見は〜る Each has his own opinion.

ことに【殊に】¶ ことしの冬は〜寒い It is *exceptionally* (≒ *unusually*) cold this winter.

ことに・する【異にする】¶ 彼と私は見解を〜する He and I *differ in* opinion. / I *differ from* him *in* opinion. / My opinion *is different from* his.

ことのほか【殊の外】unusually; extremely; exceedingly. ¶ 彼らは準備に〜手間どった They took much more time and trouble in preparation *than expected*.

ことば【言葉】(言語) language; (国語) a language; (語) a word; (表現) an expression; (方言) a dialect.

1〖言葉を〗¶ そのパーティーの席で彼は初めて私に〜をかけてきた He *spoke to* me for the first time at the party.

彼の家で初めて彼女と〜を交わした I *talked with* her at his house for the first time.

彼は私の〜をさえぎった He *cut* me *short*.

彼は急に私たちの話に〜をさしはさんだ Suddenly he *interrupted* us.

軽々しく彼の〜を信じてはいけない Don't believe *him* thoughtlessly.

きみはもっと〜を慎んだほうがいい You must be more careful in your *speech*.

彼は〜を濁して，はっきり諾否を言わなかった He did not answer yes or no, saying ambiguous things.

あまり突然の知らせで，〜を返すことができなかった The news was broken so suddenly that I could not *speak* anything.

彼女の〜をかりれば，彼は「おとなの赤ちゃん」だ To express (≒ put) it in her *terms*, he is 'a baby man.'

お〜を返すようですが，事態はもっと重大です You may be right, but the situation is more critical than you think. (端的には I disagree with you だが，訳例のほうが穏やかである).

2〖言葉では・言葉も〗¶ その夜景のすばらしさはとても〜では言えないくらいだ The beauty of the night view *is beyond description*.

彼女はあきれて，しばらくは〜も出なかった She *was struck dumb* for a while with amazement.

3〖言葉に〗¶ あの人の〜には少しなまりがある He *speaks* with a slight accent.

彼はそんな〜にだまされるような男ではない He is never deceived into believing such *words*.

ではお〜に甘えて，お先に失礼いたします Excuse me for going first. (会話では，through your kindness などと言う必要はない).

4〖言葉が〗¶ どうもうまい〜が浮かばない *A good expression* does not come across me by any means.

外国で〜が通じないときほど困ることはない We will be in the most awkward position when we cannot *make ourselves understood* in a foreign country.

5 〖合成語・その他〗 ¶ 上品な(下品な)〜 refined (vulgar) *words*.

秋田の〜 Akita *accent*.

〜数の多い人 a *talkative* man.

〜数の少ない人 a man *of few words*.

彼は〜巧みに彼女を説得した He *persuaded* her in honeyed *words*. (persuade の中に「ことば巧みに」の意味も入る).

あまり人の〜じりをとらえるようなことを言うな Don't catch me in my own *words*.

彼はとても乱暴な〜遣いをする He speaks in vulgar *language*.

先輩の前ではもっと〜遣いに注意したほうがいい You must be more careful about your *speech* before your senior.

ことぶき【寿】(祝い) congratulations ; *one's* best wishes ; (長命) a long life.

こども【子供】a child (複 children). ¶ 〜らしい無邪気さ *childlike* innocence. 〜っぽい計画 a *childish* attempt. 〜の日 *Children's* Day. (テレビ・ラジオの)〜の時間 the *Children's* hour. 〜の本 books for *children*. 彼は〜が多い He has many *children*. 〜のときから彼女を知っている I have known her from her *childhood*. 〜のころ私は体が弱かった In my *childhood*, I was delicate. 結婚して〜を生むのは女のつとめだ It is the duty of a woman to marry and bear *children*. そんなことでは〜の使いだ That's *a fool's errand*.

―銀行 a children's bank. ―心 a childish mind. ―服 children's wear (≒ clothes). ―部屋 a nursery〔room〕. ―だまし ¶ それでは〜だましだ That's a *childish trick*. そんな〜だましの手に乗るもんか I know much better! ―扱い ¶ 私は彼に〜扱いされるのがいやだ I hate to be treated as (≒ like) *a child* by him.

こともなげ【事もなげ】¶ 〜な態度をとる assume a *nonchalant* air. 〜に in a *nonchalant* manner. 彼はそれを〜にやってのけた He dispatched it quite *casually*.

ことり【小鳥】a small bird ; (愛称) a birdie ; (鳴鳥) a singing bird.

ことわざ【諺】a proverb ; a saying. ¶ 〜にいわく The *proverb* says.... 〜にもあるとおり as the *proverb* says (≒ goes ; puts it).

ことわり【断わり】(わび) an apology ; (拒絶) a refusal ; (辞退) declining ; (招待などに対する) regrets ; (許可) leave ; (予告) a notice. ¶ 彼に〜の手紙を出した I wrote him my *regrets*. そんな会はお〜だ I *refuse* to attend such a gathering. 〜なしに彼は欠席した He was absent *without notice*. 〜なしに外出するな Don't go out *without leave* (≒ *without permission*). 駐車お〜(掲示) *No* Parking. 立ち入りお〜(掲示) Off limits. / *No* trespassing. はり紙お〜(掲示) Post *no* bill. (「…お断わり」の掲示は No… で表わすことが多い. また, 自転車お〜 Cycling Prohibited のように Prohibited を用いることもある).

ことわ·る【断わる】**1** 〖こばむ・拒絶する〗 refuse ; decline.

¶ その件は君が彼に頼んでも〜られるだけだ He must *decline* the offer, though you ask him to accept it.

勉強が忙しくなりそうなので, 家庭教師の口を〜った It seemed I would become busy studying, so I *threw up* my tutoring job.

一も二もなく〜られた I *was met by a* flat *refusal*.

その申し出はていよく〜った I *declined* the offer with thanks.

お昼の弁当は〜ってください Please *cancel* the order for my lunch.

風邪をひいたので, 会議の出席を〜った I caught cold, so I *declined* to attend the conference.

2 〖前もって言う・許可を得る〗 ¶ 彼は病気で来られぬと〜ってきた He *excuses himself* because of illness.

だれに〜って外出したのだ By whose *permission* did you go out?

ひどく頭痛がしたので, 先生に〜って早退した Because I had a bad headache, I left school earlier by my teacher's *permission*.

当社を辞めるときは１か月前にその旨〜ってください Please *give* me a month's *notice* when you leave this company.

3 〖解雇する〗 ¶ 雇用者を〜るときは１か月の猶予を与える When we *dismiss* our employees, we give them a month's warning.

彼はあまり遅刻や欠勤が多いので〜った We *dismissed* him because he was too often late or absent from the office.

こな【粉】(粉末) powder ; dust ; (穀粉) flour.

こなぐすり【粉薬】a powder.

こなごな【粉粉】¶ コップが落ちて〜に砕けた The glass fell and broke *in* (≒ *to* ; *into*) *pieces* (≒ *fragments*).

こなし【熟】¶ 彼女は身の〜が上品だ She has *a* graceful *carriage*. / She *carries herself* gracefully.

こな·す【熟す】¶ 胃は食べた物を〜す A stomach *digests* what one has eaten. あの役者はりっぱに役を〜している That actor *is performing* his part very well.

こなみじん【粉微塵】⇒こなごな

こなゆき【粉雪】fine (≒ powdery) snow.

こな·れる【熟れる】¶ 〜れやすい食物 *digestible* food. 彼の文章は〜れていて自然だ His style *is natural* and idiomatic.

こにもつ【小荷物】a package ; a parcel. ¶ 着替えなどは〜で送る I will send changes of clothes as *a package* (≒ *a parcel*).

コニャック cognac.

ごにん【誤認】a misconception. ¶ 信号の〜で大事故となった The *mistake in perceiving* a signal caused the disastrous accident.

こにんずう【小人数】a small number of people ; a few persons. ¶ 〜の家族 a *small* family. 〜のグループに分かれて in *small* groups.

こぬかあめ【小糠雨】 a drizzling (≒ misty; fine) rain; a drizzle.

コネ〔クション〕 a connection. ¶ 彼にはよい～(親類などの)がある He *is* well-*connected*. 知事に～がある I *have a pull with* the governor.

こねこ【子猫】 a kitten; a kitty.

こ·ねる【捏ねる】 ¶ 子どもが泥を～ねている Children *are fingering with* mud. 粘土を～ねる *knead* clay. へ理屈を～ねるな Don't *quibble*. / Stop *talking nonsense*. その子はだだを～ねて言うことを聞かなかった The child *fretted* and wouldn't listen.

ご·ねる ¶ 土地立ち退き問題で～ねる人が多い There are a lot of people *making dogged complaints* about their eviction problem. 彼は～ね得をした He had his way by *making garrulous complaints*.

この【此の】 this (複 these). ¶ ～3月に卒業した生徒 *this* year's March graduates. それは～夏には完成する It is to be completed in the *coming* summer. ～二, 三日 *these* few days.

このあいだ【此の間】 ¶ つい～から練習を始めたところです We began our practicing *only a few days ago*. ～の例の件はどうなりましたか What has become of the matter you talked about *the other day*?

このあたり【此の辺り】 ¶ ～にガソリンスタンドはありませんか Is there any gas station *around here*? きょうは～でやめておこう So much for today.

このうえ【此の上】 ¶ ～は当たって砕けろだ Now let's make an attempt *anyhow*. ～がまんできない I cannot bear it *any longer*. ～もない品 *the choicest* stuff; *the first-rate* article. この席でお話できるのは私にとって～もない名誉です It is *the greatest* honor for me to talk on this occasion. 彼はまじめ～もない He is a man *as* serious *as* 〔serious〕 *can be*.

このかた【此の方】 (この人) this gentleman (≒ lady); this person; (以来) since. ¶ 学校創立～ *since* the foundation of this school. 3年～ *these* three years.

このくらい【此の位】 ¶ その箱は～の大きさだ The box is *about* this size. ～やっておけばいいだろう *This much* will be enough. ～のことにへこたれるものか It's tough, but I'll get it done. 2階にまだ～本がある I have *as many* more books upstairs.

このごろ【此の頃】 ¶ いつも～は天気がくずれやすい The weather is likely to break *at this time of year*. ～の若い者 young men of *today*.

このさい【此の際】 now; on this occasion; (今の事情では) under these circumstances.

このさき【此の先】 (今後) hereafter; in future; (ここより先) farther 〔on〕; beyond this. ¶ ～の十字路 the *next* intersection. ～は行き止まりだ The street *ahead* is a dead end.

このつぎ【此の次】 ¶ この問題を～までにやってきなさい This exercise is to be done by *next* lesson. 残りは～にしよう Let us do the rest *next time*. もっとお話したいのですがまたいつか～にしましょう I will tell you more about it *another time*.

このとおり【此の通り】 ¶ すぐ～やりなさい Do it *in this manner* (≒ *like this*) at once. バスは～満員だ The bus is full of passengers *as you see*.

このとき【此の時】 ¶ ～には既に手おくれだった It was already too late *by that time*. 皆～とばかり日ごろの恨みを晴らした They all *took this opportunity to* pay off old scores. ～になってあわててもだめだ It is no use getting flurried *now*. ちょうど～彼がはいってきた He came in *at this* very *moment*.

このは【木の葉】 a leaf (複 leaves). ¶ ～が散る The *leaves* fall. 舟は～のように揺れていた The boat 〔was〕 tossed about like *a leaf*.

このぶん【此の分】 ¶ ～なら2週間もあれば仕上がるだろう It will be completed in two weeks if things go on *like this*. ～ではあすは雨かもしれない *From* the look of the sky, it will rain tomorrow, I fear.

このへん【此の辺】 ⇒このあたり

このほか【此の外】 besides this; in addition to this. ¶ ～の物も見せてください Show me *another* (≒ *some others*). これほどの物は～にはない There is nothing like this. ～に盗まれた物はない Nothing *else* was stolen.

このま【木の間】 ¶ 月が～からもれていた The moon was shining *through the trees*.

このまえ【此の前】 ¶ ～お貸しした本を返してください Please return the book I lent you *before* (≒ *the other day*). ～の日曜日に映画を見た I saw a movie *last* Sunday (≒ on Sunday *last*).

このまし·い【好ましい】 ¶ ～い青年 a *nice* young man; a *likable* young person. きみの成績はどうも～くない Your school record *is* not quite *up to the standard*. ～からざる傾向 an *undesirable* tendency.

このまま【此の儘】 ¶ ～にほうっておけない We cannot leave the matter *as it stands* now. ～にしておきなさい Leave it *as it is*.

このみ【好み】 〔a〕 liking; 〔a〕 fancy. ¶ 人によって～が違う Every man has his 〔own〕 *taste*. どれにしようとお～しだいです(より取り自由) You can take your *choice*. / You can take whichever you like. / You can select according to your *preference*. 私には格別～はない I have no particular *choice*. それは私の～に合っている It suits my *taste*. / It is very much *to* my *taste*. 青が私の～の色だ Blue is my *favorite* color. 彼は～が難しい人だ He is fastidious in his *taste*. 彼女の着物の～は下品だ Her *taste in* dress is vulgar. / She has no *taste in* dress.

このみ【木の実】 (堅果) a nut; (漿果) a berry; (果実) a fruit.

この·む【好む】 ¶ 読書を～む I *like* (≒ *am fond of*) reading. 冬よりも夏を～む I *prefer* summer *to* winter. それは彼の～むところだ It is just what he *likes*. ネコは～まぬ I don't *like* (≒ *care for*) a cat. (care for はおもに否定文・疑問文に用いる). きみはなにを～んで立候補などしたのだ

Why did you *choose to* be a candidate?
〜むと〜まざるとにかかわらず, それをなさねばならぬ We have to do it whether we *like* it or not.

このよ【此の世】this world. ¶ 〜の苦労も少しは知った I have learned something of *life*. 彼はもう〜に思い残すことはなかった He has done everything he wanted to do *in this world*. 彼はもう〜の人ではない He *is no more*. 〜がいやになった I am sick of *life*. 〜のものとも思われぬ美しい景色だ The scenery is of *heavenly* beauty.

ごば【後場】〘株式〙 the afternoon session (≒ market). ¶ 〜の寄り付きは安値だった *The afternoon market* opened low.

こはく【琥珀】amber.
—色 amber〔-colored〕. —酸 succinic acid.

ごはさん【御破算】¶ 〜で願いましては Count up again, please. これまでの話はみな〜にしてください Let me *withdraw* my offer (≒ what I have said) up to now. すべては〜だ All *comes to nothing*. / We must *make a fresh start*.

こばしり【小走り】¶ 彼女は〜にロビーを通り抜けた She passed through the lobby *with hurried steps* (≒ *at a quick pace*).

ごはっと【御法度】¶ それは〜だ It *is prohibited*. / It *is forbidden*.

こばなし【小話・小咄】a short story; a storiette; a short comic story; a joke.

こはば【小幅】(布地)〔cloth of〕single breadth; (相場) a narrow range.

こば·む【拒む】refuse; decline; reject (refuse は最も普通の語, decline は辞退・謝絶の意, reject は激しく拒絶する意味で用いる).
¶ 依頼を〜む *refuse* a request. 要求を〜む *reject* a demand. 支払いを〜む *refuse* payment; *decline to* pay.

こはる【小春】—日和 an Indian summer; 英 St. Martin's summer.

コバルト〘化学〙cobalt.
—色 cobaltic color. —爆弾 a cobalt bomb. —ブルー cobalt blue; azure blue.

こはん【湖畔】the shores of a lake; a lakeside. ¶ 〜のホテル a *lakeside* hotel; a hotel *by the lake*.

こばん【小判】a *koban* (英語で説明すれば a gold coin of old Japan). ¶ ねこに〜(諺) *Casting pearls before swine*.
—形の oval〔-shaped〕. —ざめ a suck〔ing〕 fish; a remora.

ごはん【御飯】〔boiled〕rice; (食事) a meal.
¶ 〜を食べる have (≒ take) *a meal*. 〜をたく boil (≒ cook) *rice*. 〜どきに人を訪ねないほうがいい You must not call on a person at *meal* time.

ごばん【碁盤】a *go-ban*; a *go* board. ¶ 〜の目 the squares of a *go* board.
—じま check; checkers.

こび【媚】flattery.

ごび【語尾】the end of a word.
—変化〘文法〙inflection; (名詞の) declension; (動詞の) conjugation.

コピー a copy. ¶ 〜をとる copy; take *a copy* 〔*(of)*〕.
—ライター a copywriter.

こびと【小人】a dwarf; a pigmy.

ごびゅう【誤謬】a mistake; an error.

こびりつ·く ¶ その事件はしばらく私の頭に〜いて離れなかった The event *stuck in* my mind for a while. なにかねばねばした物が指に〜いてしまった Something sticky *has adhered to* my fingers.

こ·びる【媚びる】flatter. ¶ 権勢に〜びる *fawn upon* the powerful.

こぶ【瘤】(皮膚の) a wen; (打ぼくなどによる) a lump; (はれもの) a bump; (らくだの) a hump; (木の) a knot; a gnarl.
¶ 頭をドアにぶつけて〜をこしらえた I bumped my head against the door and had *a lump* on it.

こぶ【昆布】a sea tangle; kelp.

こぶ【鼓舞】¶ 隊員の士気を〜する *stimulate* (≒ *stir up*) the morale of the troops.

ごふ【護符】a charm; a talisman.

ごぶ【五分】five percent. ¶ 年利〜で金を貸す lend money at an annual interest of *five percent*. 現金払いなら〜引きします We make *five percent* discount for cash. 両者の力は〜と〜だ The two *are equal in ability*. / The two *are equally matched*.

こふう【古風】¶ 〜な文体 an *archaic* style. 彼女は今どきには珍しいくらい〜な人だ She *sticks to* (≒ *keeps to*) *the old customs*, quite rare in the present age.

ごふく【呉服】米 dry goods; clothes; 英 drapery.
—屋 米 a dry goods store; 英 a draper's shop; (人) 米 a dealer in dry goods; 英 a draper.

こふくしゃ【子福者】¶ 彼は〜だ He *is blessed with many children*.

ごぶごぶ【五分五分】¶ チャンスは〜だ The chances *are even*. 〜の条件においてのみ提案に応じる We are ready to accept your proposal only on *even* (≒ *equal*) terms. その患者の助かる見込みは〜だ The patient has a *fifty-fifty* chance to live. 勝負は〜だろう The game will end in *a draw*.

ごぶさた【御無沙汰】¶ 長らく〜して申しわけありません I'm very sorry I *haven't written you for quite a long time*.

こぶし【拳】a fist. ¶ 〜を固める clench *one's fist*. 〜を振り上げる shake *one's fist* (*at*).

こぶつ【古物】antiques; curios.
—商 an antique shop; a curiosity shop; a secondhand shop; (人) an antique dealer.

こぶとり【小肥り】¶ 〜の女 a *plump* woman.

こぶね【小舟】a boat.

コブラ〘動物〙a cobra.

ゴブランおり【ゴブラン織り】¶ 〜の壁掛け a *Gobelin* tapestry.

こぶり【小降り】¶ 間もなく〜になるだろう Before long *it* will *be raining less hard*.

こふん【古墳】an old mound; an ancient tomb.

こぶん【子分】a follower; (総称) a following.

¶さすがに大物政治家だけに～も多い Great statesman as he is, he has *a* large *following*. 彼らはいわば親分～の関係だ Their relation is, so to speak, that of a boss and *a henchman*.

こぶん【古文】ancient (≒ archaic) writing.

ごへい【語弊】¶こう言うと～があるかもしれないが, The word may *be misleading*, but.... / I may *be wrong in saying* that....

ごへい【御幣】¶～かつぎもほどほどにしなさい Do stop being too *superstitious*!

こべつ【戸別】¶～訪問する make a *house-to-house* visit; visit *from door to door*.

こべつ【個別】¶～に individually.
—折衝 separate negotiations.

コペルニクス ¶～の地動説 the *Copernican* theory. ～的転回 *Copernican* change.

ごへんけい【五辺形】a pentagon.

ごほう【語法】(慣用法) usage; (言葉使い) expression; diction. ¶～上の誤り *a* wrong *expression*.

ごほう【誤報】a fake report. ¶結局それは～だった After all the report proved to *be incorrect*. / After all it turned out to be *a false report*.

ごぼう【牛蒡】〔植物〕a burdock.
—抜き ¶警官隊は座り込みをしている学生デモ隊を～抜きにして進んだ The police broke through the party of students on a sit-down strike by *pulling them out one by one*.

こぼ·す【零す】¶水を～す *spill* water. 涙をぽろぽろ～す *shed* drops of tears. 不運を～す *make complaints against one's* hard lot; *complain of* (≒ *about*) *one's* misfortune.

こぼね【小骨】small bones. ¶～のある魚 a *bony* fish.

こぼ·れる【零れる】(水などが) spill; (あふれる) overflow. ¶彼女は～れんばかりのあいきょうがある She has *overflowing* smiles.

こぼ·れる【毀れる】¶こんなに刃が～れているのだから,よほど堅い物を切ったにちがいない He must have cut something tremendously hard, since the edge *has got* so *blunt* as this.

こぼんのう【子煩悩】¶～な父親 a *fond* father.

こま【駒】a horse; a pony; (将棋の) a chessman. ¶～を動かす (将棋) move *a chessman*; make a move.

こま【齣】(映画の) a frame. ¶歴史のひと～ *a scene* of history.

こま【独楽】a top. ¶～を回す spin *a top*.

ごま【胡麻】〔植物〕a sesame. ¶今更ぼくに～をすってもだめだ Now it's no use *flattering* me.
—油 sesame oil.

コマーシャル a commercial.

こまいぬ【狛犬】a lion dog; (神社などの) a guarding lion (≒ dog).

こまか·い【細かい】¶今～いお金の持ち合わせがない I don't have any *change* about me now. 彼は～い点にはふれなかった He didn't go into *details*. 彼の～い心遣いには感謝している I very much appreciate his careful regard for *detail*. この1,000円札を～くしてくれませんか Will you please *break* (≒ *change*) this one thousand yen note? あまりにも～い字で, ほとんど読めない She writes so *fine* that I can hardly read it. この土の塊を～く砕いてくれ *Pound* this clod. 彼女は神経が～い She *is sensitive*. そんな～いことを気にするな Don't be nervous about such *trifles*. 彼は～いことに気のつく男だ He has careful regard for *details*. 彼女は金銭には～い She *is strict in* money. このくしは歯が～い This comb has *fine* teeth. あの俳優は実に芸が～い His acting *is* very *elaborate*.

ごまかし【誤魔化し】a deception; eyewash. ¶彼の親切は～にすぎない His kindness is nothing but *a sham*. 彼くらい～のじょうずな人もいない He is second to none in *inventing a good excuse*.

ごまか·す【誤魔化す】¶彼は甘言で～された He *was deceived with* fair words. 彼は大金を～した He *pocketed* a large sum of money. 彼は金銭出納簿を～した He *falsified* the account book. 彼は私に量目を～した He *gave* me *short measure*. 年齢を～す *misrepresent one's* age. 彼は事故を～して説明した He *gave a false account of* the accident.

こまぎれ【小間切れ】hashed meat. ¶肉を～にしてもらう *have* meat *chopped* (≒ *hashed*).
—肉 chopped meat; mincemeat.

こまく【鼓膜】the eardrum; the tympanum (複 -s; tympana). ¶～を破る rupture *the tympanum*.

こまごま【細細】¶～した small; petty. ～と minutely; in detail.

ごましお【胡麻塩】salt with parched sesame.
—頭 gray hair.

こましゃく·れる ¶あの子は最近急に～れてきた Recently he *has* suddenly *become* very *cheeky* (≒ *saucy*). この子はなんと～れたことを言うのだろう How *precociously* (≒ *pertly*) she talks!

こまた【小股】¶～の切れ上がったいい女 a *slim and stylish* woman. ～に歩く walk *with short steps*.

こまづかい【小間使い】a lady's maid; a chambermaid; 米 a parlormaid.

こまった【困った】¶これはまことに～問題だ This is really a *difficult* problem. ～ことにその事件の目撃者がまったくいない *The trouble is* that there is no eyewitness at all.

こまどり【駒鳥】〔鳥類〕a robin.

こまね·く【拱く】¶腕を～く *fold one's* arms. 手を～いていることは許されない We should not *remain idle* without doing anything.

こまねずみ【高麗鼠·独楽鼠】〔動物〕a Japanese dancing mouse. ¶～のように働く work *as hard as a bee*; be *as brisk as a bee*.

こまめ ¶彼は～に便りをくれる He writes to me *very often*. 彼は～に働く He *is very diligent*. / He *is as brisk as a bee*.

こまもの【小間物】米 fancy goods; 英 haberdashery; 米 (紳士用装身具類) haberdashery.
—屋 米 a fancy〔goods〕shop; 英 a haber-

dashery.

こまやか【細やか・濃やか】 ¶ ～な親子の愛情 *warm* parental love. ～な神経と～な友情 *delicate* sensibility and *close* friendship.

こまら・せる【困らせる】 ¶ 彼はわざと突拍子もない質問をして先生を～せる He *perplexes* (≒ *embarrasses*) his teachers by asking them quite unexpected questions. あいつは生意気だから，ちょっと～せてやろう As he is so impudent, we will just *put* him *in trouble*.

こまりもの【困り者】 a good-for-nothing.

こま・る【困る】 **1**〖難儀する〗 ¶ 彼は動脈硬化で～っている He *is suffering from* hardening of the arteries.

彼は少し耳が遠くて～るが体はまだまだじょうぶだ Though he *has* some *difficulty in* hearing, he still enjoys good health.

軽はずみについたうそで非常に～った経験がある *I've been involved in a great deal of trouble* due to a lie which I told thoughtlessly.

2〖困窮する〗 ¶ 彼は金に～っていた He *was hard up* (≒ *was pressed*) *for* money.

年をとって金に～らない人は幸福者だ Those who *are well off* in their old age are happy.

生活に～っている人々を救済する relieve *the needy* (≒ *the destitute people*).

私の目の黒いうちは金に～るようなことはさせない You shall never *want for* money as long as I live.

3〖当惑する〗 ¶ 彼女におせっかいをやかれて私はたいへん～った I *was* greatly *annoyed at* her interference.

なぜ結婚しないのかと聞かれ彼は～った顔をしたBeing asked why he did not marry, he *looked embarrassed*.

あの人の物すごいいびきにはだれでも～る Nobody can *stand* his terrible snoring.

彼は返事に～った He *was at a loss for* an answer.

こみ【込み】 ¶ 私の月給は税～で月10万円だ My salary is one hundred thousand yen a month, *taxes included* (≒ *before tax*). 夕食と朝食の２食～で１泊3,000円だ The charge is three thousand yen for one night stay with two meals, breakfast and dinner.

ごみ【塵・芥】 (ちり) dust; (くず・廃物) rubbish; trash.

こみあ・う【込み合う】 ¶ いまごろは幹線道路はほとんどどこも～っている About this time almost all the trunk roads *are crowded*. けさの電車はいつもほどは～っていない This morning the tramcar *is* not so *jammed* (≒ *packed*) as usual.

こみあ・げる【込み上げる】 ¶ 故郷の山々を見た瞬間懐かしさが～げてきた The moment I saw the mountains of my home town, my heart *was filled with* a sense of nostalgia. そのニュースを聞くだけで涙が～げてきた I *was moved to tears* only by hearing the news.

こみい・った【込み入った】 ¶ ～った事件 a *complicated* case. ～った細工 *elaborate* workmanship. これには～った事情があるに違いない There must be some *complicated* circumstances behind that.

ごみごみ ¶ ～したスラム街 *squalid* slums.

こみだし【小見出し】 a subtitle.

こみち【小道】 a lane; (路地) an alley; (山などの) a path.

コミッショナー a commissioner.

コミッション commission. ¶ 売り上げに対して５パーセントの～をとる We receive *a commission* of five percent on the sales made.

ごみとり【ごみ取り】 a dustpan.

ごみばこ【ごみ箱】 an ash can (≒ box); (食べ物の残り物を捨てる) a garbage can; 英 a dust bin.

こみみ【小耳】 ¶ ちょっと～にはさんだのだが，彼女はその事件に関係があったらしい I just *happened to overhear* that she seemed to be involved in the case.

コミュニケーション communication.

マス― mass communication.

コミュニスト a communist.

コミュニズム communism.

こ・む【込む・混む】 be crowded; be packed. ¶ ～んだ電車 a *crowded* train. 手の～んだ仕掛け an *elaborate* contrivance.

ゴム【護謨】 gum; (弾性の) 〔India〕 rubber. ¶ ～の木 a *rubber* tree; a *gum* tree. ～底のくつ *rubber-soled* shoes.

―消し an eraser. ―長ぐつ rubber boots. ―ひも an elastic band. ―まり an India rubber ball.

こむぎ【小麦】 wheat; 英 corn.

―粉 wheat flour. ―畑 corn fields.

こむずかし・い【小難しい】 ¶ ～い理屈は抜きにして，はっきりした返事をください Don't go into details; just give me your definite answer. 彼はさっきから～い顔をして黙っている *Looking sullen*, he hasn't spoken a word for some time.

こむすめ【小娘】 a young girl.

こむら【腓】 the calf (複 calves) 〔of the leg〕.

―返り a cramp in the calf.

ごむりごもっとも【御無理御尤も】 ¶ 彼は～と頭ばかり下げている He never opposes, no matter how unreasonable others may be.

こめ【米】 rice. ¶ ～をとぐ wash *rice*. ～をたく boil *rice*. 三度三度～の飯が頂けるとは幸せなことだ What a blessing it is that we can have *rice* three times a day.

―俵 a sack of rice. ―粒 a grain of rice. ―所 a rice producing area. ―櫃 a rice box. ―屋(人) a rice-dealer; (店) a rice-shop.

こめかみ【顳顬】〖解剖学〗 the temple.

コメット〔天文学〕 a comet.

コメディアン a comedian.

コメディー a comedy.

こ・める【込める】 ¶ 弾丸を～める *load* a gun. 心を～めた贈り物 a gift *with one's best wishes*. 力を～めて打つ strike *with all one's might*. 諸手当～めて彼の月収は約10万円だ All allowances *included*, he makes about one hundred thousand yen a month.

ごめん【御免】¶ ～ください（詫び）Excuse me. / I beg your pardon. /（部屋へ入るとき）May I come in? /（人の足などを踏んだとき）I'm sorry. / Sorry. お先へ～ Excuse my going ahead of you. 冗談は～だ *No* joking, please. そればかりは～こうむる I would do anything but that. やっとお役～になった I am finally relieved of my office.

こも【菰】strawmatting; a rush mat.

こもかぶり【薦被り】a *sake* cask wrapped in a rush mat.

ごもく【五目】¶ ～並べをする play *gomoku.*

こもごも【交交】¶ 悲喜～至った I was filled with a *mixed* feeling of joy and sorrow. ～立って歓迎の辞を述べた We *took turns in* stand*ing* up to say a word of welcome.

こもじ【小文字】a small letter.

こもち【子持ち】¶ 彼は3人の～だ He *has* three *children.* ～のサケ a *seed* salmon. 彼はいい～だ He *has a large family.*

ごもっとも【御尤も】¶ ～なお考えです You *are quite right.* / That *is only reasonable.* あなたがお怒りなるのも～です You *have every reason to* get angry.

こもり【子守】nursing; tending a baby;（人）a〔dry〕nurse; a baby sitter. ¶ ～をする tend a baby; baby-sit.

―歌 a nursery song.

こも・る【籠もる】¶ 彼は家にばかり～っている He *seldom goes out.* / He *keeps to his house.* 彼は寺に～って修行している He is leading an austere life at a temple. 煙が部屋に～っている The room *is filled with* smoke. 彼の心の～った贈り物には感謝している I am grateful for his *thoughtful* gift.

こもん【顧問】a counselor; an adviser.

―弁護士 a legal adviser.

こもんじょ【古文書】ancient manuscripts; archives.

こや【小屋】a cottage; a hut. ¶ ～を掛ける put up *a shed*;（サーカスが）pitch *a circus.*

こやぎ【子山羊】a kid.

こやく【子役】a child-actor.

ごやく【誤訳】mistranslation. ¶ この本には～が多い There are many errors in this translation.

こやし【肥やし】manure;（人造の）fertilizer. ¶ この畑はよく～がきいている This field *is* well *manured.*

こや・す【肥やす】¶ 彼は役目を利して私腹を～した The post gave him a good chance to *fill* (≒ *live*) *his pocket.* ほんものを見て目を～す *cultivate* an〔appreciative〕eye by studying genuine works of art.

こやすがい【子安貝】〖貝類〗a cowrie.

こやま【小山】（丘）a hill;（塚）a mound.

こやみ【小止み】a lull. ¶ 雨が一日じゅう～なく降った It rained all day *without a break.* 雨が～になった The rain *is breaking.*

こゆう【固有】¶ 日本人～の礼儀正しさ politeness *characteristic* of the Japanese. 人にはそれぞれ～の才能がある Everyone has some abilities *of his own.* われわれは日本～の文化を守らねばならぬ We must keep the *traditional* culture of Japan.

―名詞〖文法〗a proper noun.

こゆき【小雪】a light snow.

こゆび【小指】（手の）a little finger;（足の）a little toe.

こよい【今宵】this evening.

こよう【雇用】employment. ¶ 全住民を～するのは不可能だ It is impossible to *employ* the whole population.

―者 an employer. 被―者 an employee.

ごよう【御用】**1**〖用事〗business. ¶ なんの～でしょうか What can I do for you? /（商店で）Can I help you?

なにか～はありませんか Is there anything that I can do for you?

お安い～です With pleasure. / Certainly.

～のときはベルを鳴らしてください When you *want me,* please ring the bell.

お安い～だ It is no trouble at all.

田中さん，部長が～です Mr. Tanaka! The director *wants you.*

当地にお出かけの～はなんですか What made you come here?

～の方は受付まで Please inquire at the receptionist.

2〖注文〗an order. ¶ きょうはなにか～はありませんか Do you have any *order* today?

―聞き 困 a roundsman; an order taker. ―組合 a company union. ―商人 a merchant under government patronage. ―新聞 a government organ. ―邸 an Imperial villa. ―始め the opening of official business in the New Year. ―納め the closing of official business for the year. 宮内庁― under the patronage of the Imperial Household.

ごよう【誤用】a misuse.

こよみ【暦】a calendar;（年鑑）an almanac. ¶ ～のうえでは春だがまだずいぶん寒い It is already spring in the *calendar,* but it is still quite cold.

こより【紙縒・紙撚】a paper-string.

こら hey; there. ¶ ～待て *Hey,* wait! / Halt there!

コラール〖音楽〗choral.

こらい【古来】¶ ～の風習 an *old* custom.

こら・える【堪える・怺える】¶ もう～えられない I can't *stand* that any longer. 吹き出したいのをやっと～えた I barely managed to *keep myself from* bursting into laughter. じっと～えて時節を待て *Have patience* and wait for your chance. ご立腹でしょうがどうぞ～えてください Please *forgive* me if I have offended you.

ごらく【娯楽】amusement; recreation; entertainment.

―施設 recreation facilities. ―場 a place of entertainment.

こらしめ【懲らしめ】a lesson; punishment. ¶ その失敗は彼にはいい～になった The failure was *a* good *lesson* to him.

こらし·める【懲らしめる】chastise. ¶ 彼を～めてやろう He must *be taught a lesson*.

こら·す【凝らす】¶ 工夫を～した装置 a device of great ingenuity. 工夫を～す *exert one's* ingenuity. 彼はひとみを～して暗やみを見詰めていた He was staring into the darkness. 息を～して様子をうかがった *Catching* my breath, I tried to see.

コラム a column.

ごらん【御覧】¶ ～! Look! / Have a look at it! もう～になりましたか *Have* you *seen* it yet? ちょっと右手を～ください Just *look* to your right. ～なさい. だから私が注意したでしょう *There*, didn't I tell you so? とにかく読んで～なさい Just read it anyway.

こり【凝り】¶ 肩の～がひどい I am suffering badly from *stiff* shoulders.

こり【梱】a bale; a pack.

コリー〘動物〙a collie.

こりかたま·る【凝り固まる】¶ 空気に触れると血はじきに～る When exposed to air, blood soon *becomes clotted*. 彼は新興宗教に～っている He is a *fanatical* believer in the new religion.

こりくつ【小理屈】a quibble. ¶ 彼は～をこねるのが好きだ He is fond of arguing for argument's sake.

こりこう【小利口】¶ 彼は～な口をきく He talks as if he knew everything.

こりごり【懲り懲り】¶ 株に手を出すのはもう～だ I *have learned to my cost what it is to* dabble in stocks. 彼の手伝いをするのはもう～だ I will *never* help him again. / I *have had enough of* helping him.

ごりごり ¶ のこぎりで～木を切る音がする I hear the *grating* sounds of a saw cutting wood.

こりしょう【凝り性】enthusiasm; fastidiousness. ¶ ～な人 a *fastidious* person; a devotee.

こりつ【孤立】isolation. ¶ 本隊から～してついに降伏せざるをえなくなった *Cut off from* the main force, they were finally forced to surrender. 彼はクラスで～している He *has no friends* in his class. / He *is isolated* (≒ *is lonely*) in the class.

ごりむちゅう【五里霧中】¶ 新しい環境に飛び込んで今は～の状態だ I *am all at sea* (≒ *am in a fog*) in my new surroundings.

こりゃ ¶ ～たいへんだ Good heavens! / My goodness! ～, おもしろい How interesting! ～いかん God forbid!

ごりやく【御利益】divine favor. ¶ 神に祈れば～があるでしょう God will answer your prayers. 観音様の～で商売が繁盛している Under *the divine protection* (≒ *the divine patronage*) of Kannon, the shop enjoys a flourishing business.

こりょ【顧慮】consideration. ¶ 彼女は他人の迷惑など～しない She doesn't *mind* what trouble she may cause other people. / She *has* no *consideration for* other people's feelings.

ごりょう【御陵】an imperial mausoleum.

こりょうり【小料理】a light meal; a snack. —屋 an eating house.

ゴリラ〘動物〙a gorilla.

こ·りる【懲りる】¶ これに～りてもう二度と株には手を出すまい Hereafter he will know better than to dabble in stocks. 彼は痛い目に会っても～りるということを知らない He has not a knack of learning from experience.

コル〘登山〙a col.

こ·る【凝る】**1**〘肩などが〙¶ 肩(首筋)が～っている I *have a stiff shoulder* (*a stiff neck*). 肩の～らない本 a book for light reading. **2**〘熱中する〙¶ 彼女は音楽に～っている She *is mad about* music. / She *is keen on* music. / She *devotes herself to* music. 彼はテニスに～っている He *is a devotee of* tennis. 彼は平和運動に～っている He *is a votary of* peace movement.

コルク a cork. ¶ ～のせんをする(抜く) cork (uncork) (a bottle).

コルセット a corset; 園 stays.

コルト a Colt〔revolver〕.

ゴルフ golf. ¶ ～をする play *golf*. ～をする人 a *golf* player; a golfer. —クラブ a golf club. —バッグ a golf bag. —リンク golf links; a golf course.

これ【此れ】this. ¶ ～はきみのですか Is *this* yours? ～とあれとどちらが好きですか Which do you like better, *this* or that? ～こそ長い間捜し求めていた本だ *This* is the very book I have been looking for for a long time. 今のところ～といって言うことはない There is nothing *in particular* to say right now. ～が世の中というものだ *That*'s what the world is like. / *Such* is life.

これから【此れから】(今) now; (今後) hereafter. ¶ ～出かけるところです We are just going out. ～はもっと気をつけます I will be more careful *in future*. ～がたいへんだ The worst is yet to come. きみたちはまだ～の人間なのだ You have a promising future ahead of you. ～の青年に社会の期待するところは大きい Society expects much of the *coming* generation.

これぎり【此れぎり】once for all; all; (否定) never again. ¶ 持っているのは～だ This is *all* I have. 彼の顔を見るのは～だ I shall *never* see him *again*. ～だから助けてくれ Help me *just for this once*.

コレクション a collection. ¶ 切手の～ *a collection* of postage stamps. 切手の～をする *collect* stamps.

これくらい【此れ位】¶ その魚は～の大きさだった The fish was as big as *this*. ～でもうよかろう *That* will be enough. ～のことでへこたれるな Don't let *such a trifle* discourage you.

これこれ【此れ此れ】¶ ～のときには～せよと教えてある I have advised him to do *such and such* a thing on *such and such* an occasion.

これしき ¶ ～の金ではなにも買えない We can buy

nothing with *such a little* money. ～のことでへこたれてはいけない Don't give in for *such a trifle*.

コレステロール〔生化学〕cholesterol.

コレスポンデンス correspondence.

これだけ ¶ きょうは～ *So much for* today. / (会などおしまいにしようというとき) Let's call it a day. ～は忘れないでください Remember *this very thing*. / Don't forget *this much*. 彼についてわかっていることは～だ *This much* is known of him. ～勉強すれば試験に合格するだろう I hope I will pass the examination after *so much* effort. 人数が～では野球のチームはできない We cannot make up a baseball team with *such a small* number of people.

こればかり ¶ ～はだれにもあげられない I can't give this to anyone *for all the world*. ～の給料では一家５人の生活はまかなえない I cannot support a family of five on *such a small* salary.

これはこれは Well, ... ¶ ～ようこそおいでくださいました *Bless me*, how nice of you to come!

これほど【これ程】¶ ～頼んでも彼は首を横に振るだけだった He only shook his head, *for all* my asking. ～ありがたいことはない Nothing is *more* welcome to me *than this*. ～おもしろい本は読んだことがない I have never read *such* an interesting book *as this*.

これまで【此れ迄】 **1**〚今まで〛¶ きみは～なにをしていましたか What have you been doing *all this while*?

～のところ事態は好転してきた *So far* the state of affairs has been turning for the better.

～にも何回かその町を訪れたことがある I have visited the town a few times *before*.

2〚現状〛 ¶ 彼が～になったのは彼の母親のおかげだ He owes what he is to his mother.

3〚最後〛 ¶ もはや～だ It's *all up* (≒ *over*) *with* me.

勝負～ Time is up.

これみよがし【これ見よがし】¶ 彼女は新車を～に乗りまわしている There she goes *showing off* her new car. 彼女は～にダイヤの指輪をはめている She wears a diamond ring *for show*.

コレラ〔医学〕cholera.

━患者 a cholera patient; a case of cholera. **━菌** a cholera germ. 疑似━ false cholera.

ころ【頃】¶ その～ in those days; at that time. 子供の～ in *one's* childhood; when *one* was a child. 来週の半ば～ *about* the middle of next week.

ごろ【語呂】 ¶ そのことばは～がいい The word *sounds well*. / The word *is euphonious*. そのことばは～が悪い The word *sounds stiff*. / The word *lacks euphony*.

━合わせ a game of rhyming; a pun.

ゴロ〔野球〕 a grounder. ¶ ～を打つ hit *a grounder*.

ころあい【頃合い】¶ ～の値段 a *moderate* (≒ *reasonable*) price. ～の大きさ *handy* size. よい～に彼は姿を現わした He showed himself *at the right moment* (≒ *in good time*). ～を見はからって彼に失敗を打ち明けた I confided the failure to him by *taking advantage of the right time*.

コロイド〔化学〕colloid.

━溶液 colloidal solution.

ころう【故老・古老】¶ この町の～ *the aged* (≒ *elders*) of this town.

ころが・す【転がす】¶ ドラムかんを納屋まで～して運んだ I *rolled* a drum can *along* to the barn.

ころがりこ・む【転がり込む】¶ ボールが川の中に～んだ The ball *rolled into* the stream. おじの遺産が～んだ I *came into* a fortune on my uncle's death. やっかい者が～んできた An unwelcome guest *has come to live at my expense*. 幸運が～んだ It was a windfall.

ころが・る【転がる】¶ ボールが～ってみぞに落ちた The ball *rolled along* into the ditch. 足もとにきみの探しているお金が～っている The coin you are looking for *lies* at your feet. 芝生に～って日光浴をした I *lay down* on the lawn basking in the sun.

ごろく【語録】sayings. ¶ 毛沢東～ Mao Tsuo Tung's *Sayings*.

ころげお・ちる ¶ 彼はいすから～ちた He *fell off* his chair. 彼は酔っ払って階段を～ちた He *fell* (≒ *tumbled*) *down* the staircase dead drunk.

ころころ ¶ 卵がかごの中から～と転げ出した Some eggs came *rolling* out of the basket.

ごろごろ **1**〚音が〛¶ ～と雷が鳴る It *thunders*. / The thunder *rolls*.

ネコがのどを～鳴らしている The cat *is purring*.

2〚物がころがる〛 ¶ たるを～転がした I *rolled* a barrel *over and over*.

あたりには大きな石が～している Big stones *lie scattered* all around.

3〚無為に〛¶ お天気がよいのに家で～しているのはもったいない It's sheer nonsense to *idle away your time* at home on such a fine day.

彼は失業して家で～している He *remains idle* at home unemployed.

ころし【殺し】a murder. ¶ 昨夜近所で～があった *A murder* was committed in my neighborhood last night.

━文句 insinuating (≒ endearing) words; a killing expression. **━屋** a killer; a murderer; an assassin.

ころ・す【殺す】kill. ¶ ネコはネズミを～した The cat *killed* a mouse. 彼を生かすも～すも私の自由だった His life was in my hands. 彼は虫も～さぬような無邪気な顔をしている He looks as innocent as a new-born baby. 彼らは息を～して演説に聞き入っていた They were listening to his speech *breathlessly* (≒ *with breathless attention*).

コロタイプ〔印刷〕a collotype.

ごろつき（暴漢）a ruffian; a bully; a rough.

コロッケ〔料理〕croquette.

コロナ〔天文学〕a corona.

ごろね【ごろ寝】¶ 昨夜はみんな～した Last night we all *slept with our clothes on*.

ころ·ぶ【転ぶ】¶ 石につまずいて～ぶ *stumble* (≒ *trip*) *over* a stone. ～んでもただは起きない男だ He *turns everything to account* (≒ *to profit*). どちらへ～んでも損はない I'll have nothing to lose *either way*. ～ばぬ先のつえ (諺) *Look before you leap.*

ころもがえ【衣替え】change of dress. ¶ ～する change *one's* dress (≒ clothes).

ころりと ¶ 彼は試合で～負けてしまった He was *easily* beaten in the match. 彼はきのう～死んでしまった He died *suddenly* yesterday. 彼は口がうまいのでだれでも～だまされる Everyone is *easily* deceived by his glib, smooth talk.

ごろりと ¶ 彼はソファーの上に～横になった He threw himself down on the sofa.

コロン a colon (:).

こわ·い【恐い】¶ 子供はほえる犬が～い Children *are afraid of* (≒ *are scared by*) barking dogs. 私は地震が～い I *dread* earthquakes. ～くてそれが見られなかった I *was afraid to* see it. そんなことをしたらあとが～いぞ If you do such a thing, you *will be sorry for* it. そんなに～い顔をするな Don't *look* so *fierce*. 彼は～いもの知らずだ He does not know what *fear* is.

こわ·い【強い·剛い】hard; stiff. ¶ (毛の)～いはけ a *stiff* brush. ～い髪の毛 *wiry* hair. ～い飯 *hard-boiled* rice.

こわいろ【声色】¶ 彼は～がうまい He is good at *speaking in an assumed voice*. 彼はあの俳優の～を使った He *imitated the voice* of the actor.

こわが·る【恐がる】¶ やけどした子は火を～る A burnt child *dreads* the fire. 彼はいつも死を～っている He *is in* constant *fear of* death. その惨状を見て彼女は～った She *was frightened* (≒ *was scared*) *at* the terrible sight.

こわき【小脇】¶ 彼はかばんを～にかかえていった He carried a bag *under his arm*.

こわけ【小分け】a subdivision. ¶ これは数項目に～できる This can *be subdivided into* several items.

こわごわ【怖怖】timidly; hesitatingly. ¶ ～洞窟(どうくつ)の中をのぞき込んだ We looked into the cave *with fear*.

ごわごわした ¶ のりがきいて～シーツ a very *starchy* sheet.

こわ·す【壊す·毀す】**1**〖物を〗destroy; break. ¶ だれがこのさらを～したのか Who *broke* this dish?

彼らはその門を～した They *destroyed* the gate. 彼らはその古い建物が～されるのを見ていた They watched the *destruction* of the old building.

2〖健康·美観を〗¶ 彼女は体を～している She *is in bad health*.

彼は胃を～している He *has* stomach *trouble*. その建物はその地のひなびた美しさを～した The building *destroyed* the rural beauty of the place.

こわだか【声高】¶ ～な話し声 a *loud* voice. ～に loudly; in a loud voice.

こわば·る【強張る·硬ばる】stiffen; become stiff. ¶ ～った顔つき a *stiffened* look. あまりの恐ろしさに体じゅうが～って身動きできなかった *Stiffened with* fear, all my limbs failed me.

こわれもの【壊れ物】a fragile article. ¶ ～注意(包装の表記) Fragile—Handle with Care.

こわ·れる【壊れる·毀れる】¶ ～れたいす a *broken* chair. ～れた置き時計 a *broken-down* clock. この茶わんは～れやすい This cup *is fragile*. コップはこなごなに～れた The glass *was smashed* to pieces. この機械はすぐにまた～れた This machine *got out of order* again very soon. この衝突で彼の車はすっかり～れてしまった His car *was* completely *wrecked* by the crash.

こん【根】〖数学〗a root; (根気) patience. ¶ 彼は～が続く He *is patient*. / He is a man *of patience*. ～を詰めて勉強する work *with perseverance*.

—仕事 a painstaking work. 平方(立方)**—** a square (cubic) root.

こん【紺】dark blue; navy blue. ¶ ～の背広 a *dark blue* (≒ *navy blue*) suit.

こんい【懇意】¶ 彼は私の～な友人だ He is a *good* (≒ an *intimate*) friend of mine. 私と彼はごく～な間がらだ I am *on friendly terms with* him.

こんいん【婚姻】〔a〕marriage.

—届 registration of *one's* marriage.

こんかい【今回】⇒こんど

こんかぎり【根限り】¶ この1年間～勉強した I have studied *as hard as I can* (≒ *with untiring energy; with tenacity*) for the last one year.

こんがらか·る ¶ 糸が～った The thread *has got entangled*. 話が～ってきた The story *is becoming complicated* (≒ *is becoming confused*).

こんがり〔と〕¶ トーストが～焼けた The toast is done *brown*.

こんかん【根幹】the basis (*of*). ¶ 日本の産業の～ *the basis* of Japanese industry.

こんがん【懇願】entreaty. ¶ 彼に承諾してくれるように～した I *begged*〔*of*〕him *earnestly* (≒ I *entreated* him) to consent.

こんき【今期】this session; this term. ¶ 当社の～の配当は1割2分です *This term* our company is to distribute a dividend at the rate of 12 percent. その議案は～の国会に提出されるはずだ The bill is expected to be presented at *this session* of the Diet.

こんき【根気】patience; perseverance. ¶ ぼくは～が続かない I lack *patience* (≒ *perseverance*). 彼は～よく勉強を続けた He studied *patiently* (≒ *with perseverance*). 彼は何事にも～がいい He *is patient in* anything.

こんき【婚期】marriageable age. ¶ ～の娘 a *marriageable* daughter. 彼女は～を逸してしまった She has lost *a chance of marriage*.

こんきゃく【困却】¶ すっかり～している I *am* quite *at a loss*. / I *am* greatly *embarrassed* (≒ *perplexed*).

こんきゅう【困窮】poverty; penury. ¶ 彼の生活は～している He *is badly* (≒ *miserably*)

こ

こ

off. / He is living in *poverty.*

—者 ¶ ～者に救いの手を差し伸べる extend a helping hand to *the poor and needy.*

こんきょ【根拠】 the basis; a foundation. ¶ ～のある報道 a *well-grounded* (≒ *an authentic*) report; news from *informed sources.* ～のない話 a *groundless*(≒ *baseless*) rumor. 彼は科学的～に立ってその現象を説明した He explained the phenomenon *on a* scientific *basis.* なにを～に彼が犯人だというのか *On* what *authority* do you say he is the criminal?

—地 a base (*of* operations).

こんぎょう【今暁】 early this morning.

ごんぎょう【勤行】〘仏教〙a religious service.

こんく【困苦】 hardships; privations. ¶ ～に耐える endure *hardships.*

ゴング a gong.

コンクール a contest; a *concours* (コンクールはフランス語から. 英語ではあまり用いられない).

こんくらべ【根比べ】 ¶ どちらがが まん強いか彼と～をした I *competed with* him *in perseverance.*

コンクリート concrete. ¶ ～の建物 a *concrete* building.

—ブロック a concrete block. **—ミキサー** a concrete mixer. **鉄筋—** ferroconcrete; reinforced concrete.

ごんげ【権化】 an incarnation. ¶ 悪の～ *a* devil *incarnate*; an *incarnate* devil; the *personification* of evil.

こんけつ【混血】 ¶ 彼女は白人と黒人の～だ She is *a mulatto.*

—児 a half-blood (≒ breed). ¶ 彼は日印の～児だ He is a man *of Japanese and Indian extraction* (≒ *of mixed Japanese and Indian parentage*).

こんげつ【今月】 this month. ¶ ～中に in the course of *this month*; during *this month.* ～10日 the tenth of *this month*; (商業文の書き方) (*on*) the 10th *inst.*

こんげん【根元】 the origin; the root. ¶ 悪の～ *the root* of evil. 国際間の協調が世界平和の～をなす International cooperation *lies at the root of* world peace.

こんご【今後】 in future; after this; hereafter. ¶ ～二度と同じ過ちを繰り返してはいけない Don't repeat the same mistake *in future.* ～は酒を飲みすぎないように注意しなさい Be careful not to overdrink yourself *from now on.* ～ともよろしく Happy to have seen you.

こんこう【混交】 mixture; intermixture.

こんごう【混合】 mixture.

—肥料 compound fertilizer. **—物** a mixture; a compound; (酒・薬など) a blend.

こんごうりき【金剛力】 ¶ 彼は～を振り絞ってバーベルを差し上げた He lifted the barbell *with all his might* (≒ *with all his strength*).

ごんごどうだん【言語道断】 ¶ 彼のふるまいはまったく～だ His conduct *is indescribably outrageous.*

こんこん ¶ キツネが～と鳴く A fox *yelps.* 彼は～とせきをしている He is suffering from a dry cough.

こんこんと【懇懇と】 (繰り返して) repeatedly; (親身になって) earnestly.

こんこんと【滾滾と】 ¶ ～わき出る泉 a *gushing* fountain; a fountain *gushing forth* (≒ *gushing out*).

こんこんと【昏昏と】 ¶ 彼は～眠っている He is *fast* (≒ *sound*) asleep. / He is sleeping *like a log* (≒ *like a top*).

コンサート〘音楽〙a concert.

—ホール a concert hall. **—マスター** a concertmaster.

こんざつ【混雑】 congestion. ¶ ～した通り a *congested* (≒ *crowded*) street. 交通の～を緩和する relieve the traffic *congestion* (≒ *jam*). クリスマスイブの銀座は人出でたいへんな～だ On Christmas Eve, Ginza street is *crowded with* a great number of people. その駅は朝夕の通勤客で非常に～する The station *is jammed with* a great rush of commuters every morning and evening. 彼は～にまぎれて行方をくらましてしまった He disappeared *in the confusion.*

コンサルタント a consultant. ¶ 経営～ *a* management *consultant*; *a consultant* on business methods.

こんじ【今次】 ¶ ～の大戦 the *recent* (≒ *last*) world war.

こんじ【根治】 ¶ その病気を～する方法はない There is no *complete cure* (≒ *complete remedy*) for the disease.

こんじき【金色】 a golden color. ¶ ～に輝く屋根 a roof bright with *gold.*

こんじゃく【今昔】 ¶ ～の感に耐えない We are surprised that things have changed too much. / We are impressed with the change of times. / The rapid change of times is impressive.

こんしゅう【今秋】 this autumn (≒ 米 fall).

こんしゅう【今週】 this week. ¶ ～中に during (≒ within) *this week.*

こんじょう【今生】 ¶ 私は彼に～の別れを告げた I bade him a *last* farewell. 彼は～の名残にもう一度京都見物をしたがっていた He wished to visit Kyoto *once again before he died* (≒ *for the last time in his life*).

こんじょう【根性】 ¶ ～のある男 an *untiring* (≒ *tenacious*) man; a man *with guts.* ～の腐った人 a *mean* person.

こんしん【混信】 interference; jamming. ¶ 両者の周波数が近似しているのでラジオの～が避けられない *Interference* is hardly avoided, because these two radio signals are of approximately the same frequency.

こんしん【渾身】 ¶ ～の力を振り絞って with all *one's* might (≒ energy); with might and main.

こんしんかい【懇親会】 a friendly reunion; 米(口語) a get-together〔meeting〕.

こんすい【昏睡】 a coma; a trance. ¶ 彼はしばらく～状態だった He was for some time in

〔a state of〕*a coma.*

こんせい【混成】 —チーム a mixed (≒ combined) team. —旅団 a mixed brigade. —物 a mixture; a medley. —語〘言語〙a hybrid.

こんせい【混声】〘音楽〙a mixed voice.
—合唱 a mixed chorus.

こんせい【懇請】 an earnest request. ¶ 会社は銀行に融資を〜した The company *made an earnest request for* a loan from the bank.

こんせき【痕跡】 marks; traces; tracks. ¶ まったくその〜をとどめていない There is no *trace* 〔of it〕 left behind. 彼女には絞殺された〜がある There are *evidences* of her having been strangled.

こんせつ【懇切】 ¶ 〜な指導 *kind* instruction.

こんぜつ【根絶】 extermination. ¶ 悪習を〜する *get completely rid of* bad habits. ネズミを〜する方法はない There is no way to *exterminate* the rats.

こんせん【混戦】 a confused fight; a melee. ¶ 今年のペナントレースは〜もようだ This season's pennant race seems to *be in confusion.*

こんせん【混線】 confusion. ¶ 電話が〜している The lines *are crossed.*

こんぜん【渾然】 ¶ 彼らは〜一体となってその仕事を完成した They performed the task *in perfect cooperation.* 弦とピアノとが〜一体となった演奏であった The violinist and the pianist played *in perfect harmony.*

コンセント〘電気〙a 〔plug〕 receptacle; an outlet.

コンソメ *consommé* (フランス語).

こんだく【混濁】 ¶ 彼の意識は〜したままだった He remained in a state of *dimmed* consciousness.

コンダクター〘音楽〙a conductor.

コンタクトレンズ a contact lens. ¶ 〜をはめる wear *a contact lens.*

こんだて【献立】 a menu; (特別な) a diet.

こんたん【魂胆】 an intention; a secret design. ¶ 彼にはなにか〜がありそうだ He seems to have some *secret plan.* 彼は彼女をだます〜だ He *intends to* deceive her.

こんだん【懇談】 ¶ 折り入ってご〜したいことがあります I have something in particular to *talk over with* you.
—会 a gathering for informal exchange of ideas.

コンチェルト〘音楽〙a concerto.
ピアノ— a piano concerto.

こんちゅう【昆虫】 an insect. ¶ 〜採集する *collect* insects.
—学 entomology. —学者 an entomologist. —採集 insect collecting. —採集網 an insect net. —標本箱 an insect cabinet.

コンツェルン〘経済〙a concern.

コンテ〘映画〙continuity.

こんてい【根底】 the foundation. ¶ この実験は彼の説を〜から覆した This experiment overthrew his theory *from its bottom.* 学生の騒動は大学を〜まで動揺させた The students' violent disturbances have shaken the university *to its* 〔*very*〕 *foundation.* これらすべての〜に横たわっている思想はなにか What concept lies behind all these?

コンディション a condition. ¶ 体の〜がよい I *am in good condition* (≒ *am in good shape; am in good form*). 試合に備えて〜を調えた I *got myself conditioned for* the game.

コンテスト a contest. ¶ 彼女は美人〜で1位になった She won the first prize in the beauty *contest.*

コンテナ a container.

コンデンサー〘電気〙a condenser.

コンデンスミルク condensed milk.

コント *conte* (フランス語); a tale; a short story.

こんど【今度】 **1**〘次回〙next time. ¶ 〜はきみの番だ *This* is your turn.
〜いらっしゃるときは, 奥さんもお連れください Bring your wife with you *next time.*
〜の日曜日に映画に行きませんか Let's go to the movies *next* Sunday.
〜だけは許してやる I'll let you off for *this once.*
どうもすみません. 〜からは気をつけます I'm very sorry. I'll be more careful *from now on.*
失敗したのは〜が初めてではない *This* is not the first time that I have failed.
外国へ行くのも〜が最後だ *This* is the last time that I will go abroad.
〜という〜は, もう許さない I'll never pardon you *for this time.*
この件は〜にしましょう Let's discuss this matter *later* (≒ *next time*).
〜出る下田行きは, 2番線から出る The *next* train for Shimoda starts (≒ leaves) from the second track.
2〘最近〙soon; shortly. ¶ 〜のヨーロッパ旅行では, ずいぶん彼の世話になった He helped me a great deal during my *last* tour of Europe.
〜の試験では, きみは英語がひどく悪かった You did very badly in English during *the late* examinations.
〜隣に越してきた田中です. どうぞよろしく My name is Tanaka. I moved into the house next quite *recently.* 〔I'm glad to meet you.〕
〜彼が建てた家を見た I saw the house he built *lately.*
〜の英語の先生は, 私は大好きだ I like *this* new English teacher very much.
〜彼は大使としてフランスへ行くことになった He is going to France as an ambassador *very soon* (≒ *in very near future*).

こんとう【昏倒】 ¶ 彼女は息子の血まみれな顔を見て〜した She *swooned* (≒ *fainted*) at the sight of her son's bloody face. 彼は疲労で〜した He *fell in a faint* from fatigue.

こんどう【混同】 confusion. ¶ われわれは自由と放縦を〜しがちだ We are apt to *confuse* liberty *with* license. 私はこれまであなたを妹さんと〜していた I *have mistaken* you *for* your sister up to now.

ゴンドラ (ベニス・飛行船) a gondola. ¶ ～の船頭 a gondolier.

コントラスト contrast. ¶ ～が強い The *contrast* [between them] is striking.

コントラバス 〔音楽〕 a contrabass.

コントラルト 〔音楽〕 contralto (複 contraltos).

コントロール control. ¶ その投手は～がない(ある) The pitcher has no (good) *control*.
　―タワー a control tower [of an airport].

こんとん【混沌】chaos. ¶ 政治情勢は～としている The political situation *is chaotic* (≒ *is in a state of chaos*). 形勢は～として予断を許さない The situation *is* so *chaotic* that we cannot predict anything definite.

こんな ¶ ～人は初めてだ I have never seen *such* a man. ～天気のよい日に家にいるのは惜しい It is a pity to stay [at] home on *such* a fine day [as this]. 彼は～ふうにそれをした *This is the way* he did it. / He did it *this* way. ～事情だから, 大学には行けない *Such being the case*, I can't go to college.

こんなん【困難】difficulty. ¶ 多くの～を乗り越える overcome many *difficulties* (≒ *hardships*). 解決～な問題 a problem *difficult* to solve. 彼はあらゆる～に耐えた He endured every possible *hardship*. 彼の申し出を断わるのに～した I *had difficulty* [*in*] declining his offer. / I *found it difficult to* decline his offer.

こんにち【今日】today. ¶ ～の世界 the world [*of*] *today*. ～の日本は昔の日本でない Japan is not what she used to be. 私の～あるのはあなたのおかげです I owe you what I am *today*. ～は(午前なら) Good morning. / (午後なら) Good afternoon.

こんにゅう【混入】¶ そのウイスキーには多量のメチルアルコールが～されていた A lot of methyl alcohol *was added to* the whisky. 不純物が～されている There *is* something impure *mixed* in it.

コンパ ¶ きょうはクラスの～がある We have *a* class *party* today.

コンバイン 〔機械〕 a combine.

コンパクト (化粧品入れ) a compact.
　―カー a compact [car].

コンパス compasses (ふつう複数形). ¶ ～1個 a pair of *compasses*. ～で円をかく make circles with *a compass*. ～の大きい人 a *long-legged* man.

こんばん【今晩】¶ ～は Good evening. ～は非常に涼しい It is very cool *this evening*.

コンビ a combination. ¶ 彼と～になろう I'll *form a pair with* him.

コンビーフ corned beef.

コンビナート industrial complex (コンビナートはロシア語の *kombinat* から).

コンビネーション a combination.

コンピューター a computer. ¶ ～にかける computerize. ～にデーターを入れる feed data to *a computer*. ～で計算する run up figures on *a computer*.
　数字式― a digital computer.

こんぶ【昆布】〔植物〕 a sea tangle; kelp.

コンプレックス 〔心理〕 complex. ¶ きみには～を感じている I *feel inferior to* you.
　インフェリオリティー― inferiority complex.

コンベア a conveyer.
　ベルト― a belt conveyor; 英 a conveyer belt.

こんぺき【紺碧】dark blue. ¶ ～の空 a *deep blue* sky.

こんぼう【棍棒】a club.

こんぼう【混紡】mixed spinning. ¶ このズボンは毛とナイロンの～だ This pair of trousers is of [*mixed*] wool and nylon.

こんぽう【梱包】packing. ¶ ～する pack (*a thing*).

こんぽん【根本】the basis; the foundation; (本質) the essence. ¶ 教育の～問題 the *fundamental* problem of education. 民主主義の～原理 the *basic* (≒ *radical*) principles of democracy. わが国の外交政策の～的な変更 a *fundamental* change in our diplomatic policy. その両者は～的に異なっている The two are *fundamentally* different.

コンマ a comma. ¶ ～以下は切り捨て omit the figure after *the decimal* [*point*]. 彼は～以下の人物だ He is *a nobody*.

こんまけ【根負け】¶ 彼の粘り強さには～した I *was not equal to* his patience. / He *outdid* me *in* patience. 彼の熱意に～して承諾した I was compelled to accept it by his earnestness.

こんみょうにち【今明日】¶ ～中にご返事します I'll give you an answer *in a day or two* (≒ *sometime today or tomorrow*).

こんめい【混迷】confusion; bewilderment. ¶ ～する政界 *confused* political circles.

こんもう【懇望】an earnest desire. ¶ 彼は社長就任を～された He *was earnestly requested to* become the president.

こんもり ¶ ～と茂った森 a *thick* (≒ *shady*) wood.

こんや【今夜】this evening; tonight.

こんやく【婚約】an engagement. ¶ 彼は彼女と～した He *got engaged to* her. 彼は彼女と～している He *is engaged to* her.
　―指輪 an engagement ring. **―者** (男) a fiancé; (女) a fiancée.

こんよく【混浴】mixed bathing.

こんらん【混乱】confusion; disorder. ¶ 国内は～状態である The country *is in confusion* (≒ *is in disorder*). 頭が～している I *am confused*.

こんりんざい【金輪際】¶ ～こんなことをするな *Never* do such a thing again.

こんれい【婚礼】a wedding.

こんろ【焜炉】a small kitchen range.

こんわく【困惑】embarrassment. ¶ 失業してどう暮らしていこうかと～している Being out of a job, I *am at a loss* how to make my living.

さ

さ【差】〔a〕difference. ¶ ふたつの間には大きな～がある There is *a* great *difference* between the two. きみの言うことと彼の言うことの間にはさほどの～はない There is not much *difference* between what both of you say. Aクルーは半艇身の～でBクルーに勝った The A crew defeated the B crew by half a boat's *length*.

ざ【座】 ¶ 妻の～ the *position* of a housewife. 彼の失言で～が白けた His careless remark cast a chill over *the party*. 彼は～を取り持つことがうまい He is good at *keeping the table amused*.

さあ ¶ ～すっかり話してくれ *Come*, tell me all about it. ～出かけよう *Now* let's go. ～始めるぞ *Here goes!* ～バスが来た *Here* comes the bus. ～たいへんなことをやっちゃった *Oh*, what have I done! ～駅に着いた *Here* we are at the station. ～どうかな *Well*, I can't tell.

サーカス a circus.

サークル a circle. ¶ 読書～に入る join *a* reading *circle* (≒ *group*).

—活動 circle acticism. 演劇— a dramatic circle (≒ club).

ざあざあ ¶ 雨が～降っている It is raining *heavily* (≒ *hard*). / It *is pouring*.

サージ (服地) serge.

サーチライト a searchlight. ¶ その建物に～を向けた We turned the *searchlight* upon the building.

サード〔野球〕(塁)〔the〕third base; (人) a third baseman.

サーバー〔球技〕a server.

サービス service. ¶ あの店は～がよい(悪い) That store gives good (poor) *service*. このホテルは料理はうまいが～は悪い The food is good at this hotel, but the *service* is poor.

—ステーション a service station. —料 ¶ ～料をふくむ(メニューなどで) Service complis (フランス語). ～料として15パーセントを勘定書におつけしてあります We added 15 percent to the bill for *service* (≒ *cover charge*). ～料は頂いておりません No charge is made for the *service*. このホテルでは～料はとっていますか Do you make *a service charge* at this hotel?

サーブ ¶ きみが～する番だ It is your *service*. / It is your turn to *serve*. 彼女の～は強い(弱い) Her *service* is strong (weak). 彼の～はうまい(まずい) He *serves* well (badly).

サーベル a sabre.

さあらぬ【然有らぬ】 ¶ ～体(てい)で with an innocent-looking air; as if nothing had happened; nonchalantly.

サーモスタット a thermostat.

さい【才】 ¶ 彼女は文筆の～がある She has *a talent* (≒ *a gift*; *a genius*) *for* writing. / She is a *born* (≒ *gifted*) writer. 彼は一度にふたつのことができる～がある He has *a faculty for* doing two things at once.

さい【際】 ¶ 非常の～は(に) *in case of* emergency; *in* an emergency. この～彼に忠告する必要がある It is necessary to give him advice *at this time*. ご上京の～はぜひお訪ねください Don't fail to come and see me *when* you come up to Tokyo.

さい【犀】〔動物〕a rhinoceros.

さい【賽・采・骰子】 a die (複 dice). ¶ ～の目 the spots on *a die*. ～の目に切る cut into *small cubes*. ～は投げられたり The *die* is cast.

さい【差異】〔a〕difference; 〔a〕distinction. ¶ このふたつの品物には～はない There is no *difference* between these two articles.

さい【歳】 ¶ 12～の少年 a boy *of* twelve; a twelve-*year-old* boy. 彼は何～ですか. 20～です How *old* is he? He is twenty〔*years old*〕. 彼は80～で死んだ He died at〔the *age* of〕eighty. / He lived to be eighty.

ざい【在】 ¶ ～米邦人 the Japanese *in* the United States. 彼は奈良の～に住んでいる He lives in *a village near* Nara.

ざい【材】(材木) wood; 英 timber; 米 lumber; (材料) material; stuff; (人材) a man of ability; a competent person.

ざい【財】〔a〕fortune; wealth; riches; property. ¶ 彼は土地ブローカーをして～をなした He *made a fortune* out of land-jobbing.

さいあい【最愛】 ¶ ～の妻 *one's*〔*be*〕*loved* (≒ *dearest*) wife.

さいあく【最悪】 ¶ ～の場合にはぼくはきみを助ける *If the worst comes to the worst*, I will help you. ～の事態を覚悟していなければならぬ We must be prepared for *the worst*. 事態は～になった Things *have come to the worst*.

ざいあく【罪悪】(宗教上・道徳上の) a sin (*against*); (法律上の) a crime (*against*). ¶ ～を犯す commit *a sin* (≒ *a crime*).

—感 a sense of guilt.

ざいい【在位】 ¶ 現エリザベス女王の～中に in the *reign* of Queen Elizabeth II. 彼は10年間～した He *reigned over* the country for ten years.

さいうよく【最右翼】 the extreme right wing.

さいえん【再演】 a second performance. ¶ その劇団はハムレットを～した The theatrical company *performed* "Hamlet" *again*. / The theatrical company *gave a second performance* of "Hamlet." その芝居は評判がよかったので～された The play *was presented again* because it was well received.

さいえん【菜園】 a kitchen garden; (市場向けの) a market garden; 米 a truck garden.

さいえん【才媛】 a talented girl; an accomplished lady. ¶ 彼女はまれにみる～だ She is *a lady of* rare *talents*. 彼女は女子大でいちばんの～だ She is at the top of the women's college.

さ

サイエンス science.
—フィクション science fiction (sf と略す).

さいか【西下】 ¶ ～する go (≒ proceed) west; start for the Kansai district.

さいか【災禍】 a disaster; 〔a〕 calamity.

さいか【裁可】 ¶ 国王のご～を得た We secured *the Royal* (≒ *Imperial*) *sanction*. それは天皇のご～を仰いだ It was submitted for *the approval of His Majesty the Emperor*.

ざいか【財貨】 property; wealth.

ざいか【罪科】 an offense.

さいかい【再会】 ¶ われわれは～を約した We promised to *meet again*. きのう 10 年ぶりでたまたま彼と～した Yesterday I happened to meet him after ten years' interval.

さいかい【斎戒】 purification.
—沐浴 purification of mind and body.

さいかい【際会】 ¶ 非常事態に～する *be confronted* (≒ *be faced*) *with* emergency.

さいかい【再開】 reopening; 〔a〕 resumption. ¶ 国会は～された The Diet session *was resumed*. 労使間の交渉はまもなく～される Negotiations between labor and management will soon *be reopened*. 家族の～ *a* family *reunion*.

さいかい【最下位】 the lowest rank; the bottom; the cellar. ¶ チームは～だ The team *is in the cellar*. / The team *ranks lowest*. / The team *is lowest in rank*. 彼はクラスの～だ He *is at the bottom* of the class.

さいがい【災害】 a calamity; a disaster. ¶ 関東各地は台風のため多大の～を生じた The Kanto district have suffered *a* great *disaster* from the typhoon.
—対策 countermeasures against calamities. —地 the stricken district. —防止 prevention of disasters. —保険 accidental insurance. —補償 accident compensation.

ざいかい【財界】 (金融界) the financial world; financial circles; (実業界) the business world; business circles. ¶ ～の巨頭 a leading financier.
—人 a financier; a businessman.

ざいがい【在外】 —研究員 a research student abroad. —資産 overseas assets. —代理店 a foreign agency. —邦人 Japanese residents abroad.

さいかく【才覚】 (才知) a ready wit; (工面) management. ¶ 彼の～で会が成功した The meeting was a success thanks to his *good* (≒ *excellent*) *management*. 彼はなかなか～のある男だ He is an *able* man. / He is a man *of ability*.

さいがく【才学】 ability and learning.

ざいがく【在学】 ¶ ～中に while in (≒ at) school; during *one's* school (≒ college) days. 彼は大学に～中だ He is an undergraduate. / He is a college student.

さいかくにん【再確認】 reconfirmation. ¶ 電話でホテルの予約を～してください Please *confirm* my hotel reservations *once more* by telephone.

さいかふ【再下付】 a reissue; a regrant. ¶ 運転免許状の～を申請する apply for the *reissue* of a driver's license. ～する reissue; renew.

さいかん【再刊】 republication; reissue. ¶ その新聞は 3 年後に～された The newspaper *was republished* three years later.

さいき【才気】 ¶ ～のある人 a *clever* (≒ *witty*) man. ～煥発(かんぱつ)な人 a *brilliant* (≒ *very clever*) man.

さいき【猜忌】 jealousy. ¶ ～の目 jealous eyes; yellow looks.

さいき【再起】 recovery. ¶ ついに彼は長い病気から～した He *recovered* (≒ *got well*) *from* his long illness. その国は戦争の痛手から～した The country *recovered from* the effects of the war. 彼女は夫を励まして激しいショックから～させた She encouraged her husband to *recover from* the violent shock. 彼女はオフェリアの役で舞台に～した She *made a comeback* on the stage in the part of Ophelia. 彼は重傷で～不能だ He has been too severely wounded to *recover*.

さいきねつ【再帰熱】〘医学〙recurrent fever.

さいぎ【再議】 reconsideration. ¶ ～に付する refer (*a matter*) to a committee for *reconsideration*.

さいぎ【猜疑】 suspicion. ¶ 彼は～心が強い He is of a *suspicious* nature.

さいきだいめいし【再帰代名詞】〘文法〙a reflexive pronoun.

さいきょ【再挙】 a second attempt. ¶ 彼は国へ帰って～をはかった He went home to *make another attempt*.

さいきょう【最強】 ¶ 日本～のチーム *the strongest* team of Japan.

ざいきょう【在京】 ¶ ～中はお世話になりました Thank you for your kindness *during my stay in Tokyo*. 彼は今～している He *is staying in Tokyo* now.

さいきょういく【再教育】 re-education. ¶ ～する re-educate.

さいきん【最近】 ¶ ～は京都に行っていない I have not visited Kyoto *lately*. ～いつ映画を見たか覚えていない I do not remember when I saw a movie *last*. 彼は～海外から帰国したばかりだ He has just *recently* returned from abroad. ～までその事実を知らなかった I have been ignorant of the fact till quite *recently*. ～数年間に彼の英語は著しく進歩した He has made remarkable progress in English *in the past* (≒ *in the last*) several years.

さいきん【細菌】a germ; a virus; a bacterium (複 bacteria).

—学 bacteriology. —学者 a bacteriologist. —性疾病 germ diseases. —戦術 bacteriological (≒ germ) warfare. —培養 germiculture.

ざいきん【在勤】¶ 彼の船舶会社に～中に during his *service with* the shipping company. 彼は神戸税関に～している He *holds a post at* the Kobe Customs. / He *works for* the Kobe Customs.

さいく【細工】workmanship. ¶ すばらしい～だ What *a* splendid *piece of work*! この～はみごとなものだ How fine this *piece of work* is! ～は流々,仕上げをごろうじろ (諺) Wait and see how this *work* will turn out. この貝がらに～ができますか Can you *work on* this shell? きわめて精巧な～を施した壁だった The wall *was* most cunningly *wrought*. この人形は～がすばらしい This doll is of exquisite *workmanship* (≒ *craftsmanship*).

—場 a workshop. —人 an artisan; a craftsman. 貝— shellwork. 金物— metalwork. しんちゅう— brasswork. トウ— rattan work.

さいくつ【採掘】mining. ¶ 石炭を～する *mine* (≒ *dig*) coal.

—権 mining rights.

サイクリング cycling. ¶ ～に行く go *cycling*.

サイクル〔電気〕a cycle.

サイクロトロン〔物理〕a cyclotron.

さいくん【細君】a wife.

さいぐんび【再軍備】rearmament. ¶ ～する rearm. ～には反対だ I am opposed to *rearmament*.

サイケ ¶ ～調 psychedelic.

さいげい【才芸】talent and accomplishments.

さいけいこく【最恵国】¶ ～待遇(条項) *the most-favored-nation* treatment (clause).

さいけいれい【最敬礼】¶ ～する bow deeply (≒ politely) to (*a person*); make a deep bow to (*a person*).

さいけつ【採血】¶ 彼らは多くの人から～している They *are collecting* (≒ *are gathering*; *are receiving*) *blood* from a lot of people. (draw blood というと比喩的になり,けんかをしたり,人の血を絞りとる冷血漢のような印象を与える).

さいけつ【採決】a vote; (イギリス議会の) a division. ¶ その問題は～に付された The question *went* (≒ *came*) *to the vote*. / The question *was put to the vote*. 彼らはその問題について～をとった They *took a vote on* the question.

さいけつ【裁決】〔a〕 judgment; 〔a〕 decision; (陪審員の) a verdict. ¶ ～する judge; decide; give *one's* decision; bring in a verdict. われわれは彼の～を仰いだ We asked him for *a decision*.

さいげつ【歳月】¶ ～人を待たず (諺) *Time and tide wait for no man*. ～がたった *Years* went by.

さいけん【再建】rebuilding; reconstruction; rehabilitation. ¶ その寺院は～された The temple *was rebuilt*. 彼らは荒廃した神社の～にとりかかった They began to *reconstruct* the ruined shrine.

さいけん【債券】a 〔loan〕 bond; (社債) a debenture. ¶ ～を発行する issue *bonds*.

記名— a registered bond. 国庫— 米 a treasury bond; 英 an exchequer bond. 貯蓄— a savings debenture.

さいけん【債権】credit. ¶ あの人に対して私は～がある I have *a claim against* (≒ *on*) him.

—者 a creditor.

さいげん【再現】(再び現われること) reappearance; (再び現わすこと) reproduction. ¶ 警官たちは事故現場を～した The policemen *reproduced* the accident scene.

さいげん【際限】a limit. ¶ この問題はいくら議論しても～がない *There is no end to* the argument on this matter.

ざいげん【財源】a source of revenue; (資金) funds. ¶ なんとか別に～を求めることができた We managed to obtain *a* new *source of revenue*. 目下～に窮している We are now at a loss for *a source of revenue*. 新しい家を建てるだけの～がない I do not have enough *funds* to build a new house.

さいけんさ【再検査】re-examination.

さいけんとう【再検討】re-examination.

¶ その問題は～されねばならぬ The problem must *be re-examined*.

さいこ【最古】¶ 世界～の木造建築 *the oldest* wooden building in the world.

さいご【最後】the last. **1**〖最後の〗¶ これがきみに与えられた～のチャンスだ This is *the last* chance given to you.

彼の～のもようをお聞かせください Would you please describe his *last* moments?

～の手段として法廷で争う We will take (≒ bring) the matter into court as *the last* resort. / We will go to law as *the last* measure.

～の手はずもととのった *The final* arrangements have been made.

2〖最後に〗¶ きのう～にこの部屋を出た人はだれですか Who was *the last* to leave this room yesterday?

彼女と～に会ったのは5月の10日だった It was on the tenth of May that I saw her *last*.

～にひと言お礼のことばを申し上げたい I would like to add a few words of gratitude (≒ appreciation) *in conclusion*.

～に皆で校歌をうたった *At the end* we all sang our school song together.

～に笑うものは誰か Who has *the last* laugh?

3〖最後は・最後を・最後だ〗¶ この話の～はどうなるのですか? How will the story come out *in the end*?

きみに会うのもこれが～だろう This is perhaps *the last* time that I may see you. / This might be *the last* chance for me to see you.

あれが母の声を聞いた～だった That was *the last*

さ

time I heard my mother's voice.
帝劇の舞台が彼の～となった The stage at the Imperial Theater was his *last* public appearance. / We saw *the last* of him on the stage at the Imperial Theater.
今シーズンの～を飾るにふさわしい熱戦だった It was such a close game that it perfectly rounded off this season.
彼は悲惨な～を遂げた He met *a tragic end*. / He *died a sad death*.
4 〖最後まで〗 ¶ 私の言い分を～まで聞いていただきたい I would like you to *hear* me *out*.
～まで彼はなにを聞かれても黙りとおした Whatever questions he was asked, he kept his mouth shut *to the last*.
～の～までどちらが勝つかわからなかった Nobody was able to tell which side would win *until the very last*.
どんなことがあっても～までがんばれ Whatever happens, hold on *to the last*.
この本はおもしろくて～まで一気に読んだ This book was so interesting [that] I *read* it *through* at a sitting (≒ at a stretch).
5 〖最後には〗 ¶ ～には彼も譲歩した He, too, gave in *finally*.
～にはぼくの真意もわかってくれるだろう He will understand what I really mean *eventually*.
6 〖…したら最後〗 ¶ 彼は言いだしたら～あとに引かない *Once* he has said something, he will never withdraw it.
彼に飲ましたら～きりがない *Once* you offer him a drink there will be no end of it.
ばれたら～首だよ You will be fired at *once* if it is found out.
彼ににらまれたら～だ We *are lost* if he is out to get us.
7 〖合成語〗 ¶ 組合はストライキ決行の～通牒(つうちょう)を会社に突きつけた The labor union presented *an ultimatum* for the strike to the company executives.
わが国は～通牒を相手国に送り国交断絶を辞さぬ姿勢を示した Our government sent *an ultimatum* and showed a strong attitude that we were ready to break off diplomatic relations.

さいご【最期】 ¶ 彼は～まで意識があった He was conscious *to the last*. 彼は父の～にまにあった He was present at his father's *deathbed*.

ざいこ【在庫】 ¶ ご注文の本は～しております(～しておりません) The book you have ordered *is in stock* (*is out of stock*). その店にはたくさんのおもちゃの～がある That store has *a* large *stock* of toys.
—品 goods in a storehouse; stored goods.

さいこう【再考】 ¶ ～の余地が十分ある There is plenty of room for *reconsideration*. きみはそのことを～してくれませんか Won't you *reconsider* the matter? ～した結果，それはあきらめることにした *On second thoughts*, I decided to give it up.

さいこう【再興】 ¶ 頼朝は源家を～した Yoritomo *restored* the Minamoto family. 彼はすたれた芸道の～につとめた He tried hard to *revive* the extinct art.

さいこう【採光】 lighting. ¶ その部屋は六つの窓から～している The room *is lighted* by six windows. ～のよい(悪い)部屋 a *well-lighted* (an *ill-lighted*) room.

さいこう【採鉱】 mining.
—学 mining engineering. —権 mining rights.

さいこう【最高】 ¶ ボストンで～温度75度に達した In Boston the temperature reached *a maximum* of 75°. 世界で～の山 *the highest* mountain in the world. 彼が～投票を得た He polled *the largest number of* votes.
—点(試験) the highest point (≒ mark); (投票) the largest vote. —学府 the seat of the highest learning. —記録 the best record. —検察庁 the Supreme Public Procurator's Office. —裁判所 the Supreme Court. —値段 the ceiling price.

さいこうき【砕鉱機】 a crushing machine; a crusher.

ざいこう【在校】 ¶ この学校には1,000人の生徒が～している In this school a thousand students *are enrolled*. 彼は中学校に～している He *is in junior high school*. / He *is a junior high student*.

ざいごう【在郷】 —軍人 an ex-soldier; an ex-service-man; 〔米〕 a veteran.

ざいごう【罪業】 ¶ 彼はかずかずの～を重ねた He committed many *sins*. / He *lived in sin*.

さいこうちょう【最高潮】 the climax; the peak. ¶ 試合が～に達する The game reaches *the climax*. 旅行ブームは今が～だ Enthusiasm of traveling has got to *the peak*.

さいこうふ【再交付】 ¶ 証明書は～できない The certificate is not to *be issued for the second time*. 彼に旅券を～した We *issued* him a *new* passport.

さいこうほう【最高峰】 ¶ エベレストは世界の～だ Mt. Everest is *the highest mountain* in the world. 彼は日本医学の～といわれる He is said to be *the high-water mark* (≒ *the highest authority*) of Japanese medical science.

さいこく【催告】 [a] notification; demand; (株式払込) a call.
—書 a call notice.

さいころ【賽子・骰子】 a die (〔複〕 dice); a bone. ¶ ～を振る cast (≒ throw) *a die*.

サイコロジー psychology.

さいこん【再婚】 ¶ 彼女は2年後に～した She *remarried* (≒ *got married again*) two years later.
—者 a digamist; a deuterogamist.

さいさい【再再】 ¶ ～注意したがききめがない I *often* (≒ *repeatedly*) advised him in vain.

さいさき【幸先】 ¶ 彼は～よく人生を乗り出した He *got a good start in* life. 彼の事業は～がよかった His work has begun *under fair* *auspices*.

さいさよく【最左翼】the extreme left wing.

さいさん【採算】¶この仕事は～がとれる(とれない) This work *is profitable* (*is unprofitable*).

独立—制 the self-supporting accounting system.

さいさん【再三】over and over again; very often; repeatedly.

ざいさん【財産】property. ¶～をつくる make *a fortune*. 彼は5億円の～を残して死んだ He died, leaving *a fortune* of five hundred million yen behind. ～を差し押さえられた I had my *property* seized. 人々の生命～を保護するのが彼らの役目だ It is their duty to protect the life and *property* of people. ～を目あてに結婚する男もいる There are some men who marry for *money*.

—家 a man of property. —税 a property tax.

さいし【才子】¶彼はなかなかの～だ He is really *a clever man*. (日英両語とも軽べつ的なひびきがある)

さいし【妻子】*one's* wife and children.

¶～ある人 a married man with children.

さいし【祭司】a priest; an officiating priest.

さいじ【細事】a trifle; a trivial matter.

¶われわれは～にむとんじゃくになりがちだ We are apt to be indifferent to *trifles* (≒ *trivial matters*). ～にこだわるな Don't worry about *trifles*.

さいしあい【再試合】a return game (≒ match); a rematch.

さいしき【彩色】coloring; painting.

—画 a colored picture. —版 chromatic printing; a colored print.

さいじき【歳時記】a literary calendar (外国にはこの種のものがない).

さいしけん【再試験】a re-examination. ¶私は～を受けた I *took a test again*. 先生はテストに合格しなかった人々を～した The teacher *re-examined* those who had failed the test.

さいじつ【祭日】a national holiday; a red-letter day. ¶敬老の日を～とする We make the Respect-for-Age day *a national holiday*.

ざいしつ【材質】the quality of the material.

さいして【際して】¶東京出発に～彼は別れを告げに来た *When* he left Tokyo, he came to see me to say good-bye. 危機に～は冷静であれ Be calm *in case of* emergency.

さいしゅ【採取】¶石油からアルコールを～する extract alcohol from petroleum.

—高 output.

さいしゅ【祭主】(喪主) the chief mourner; (司会者) the master of ceremonies.

さいしゅう【採集】collection. ¶こん虫を～する *collect* insects.

—家 a collector.

さいしゅう【最終】¶～的な打ち合わせ a *final* preliminary arrangement.

—電車 the last train. —回 the last inning.

ざいじゅう【在住】¶東京～の同窓生 a schoolmate *resident* in Tokyo. ニューヨークにはたくさんの日本人～者がいる There are a lot of Japanese *residents* in New York. / Many Japanese *are living* in New York.

さいしゅつ【歳出】¶～は歳入を超過した The *expenditure* was in excess of the revenue. ～が毎年増える *Annual expenditure* increases every year.

歳入— revenue and expenditure.

さいしゅっぱつ【再出発】¶～する start afresh. ～を期してがんばることだ I expect you to *make a fresh start*.

さいしょ【最初】¶～の the first; initial. ～に first. ～から from the first; from the outset. ～は at first; at the outset. 彼が～にやった He was *the first to* do it. 私の名が名簿の～にある My name *is at the head of* the roster.

さいじょ【才女】a talented woman; a woman of ability; an intelligent woman. ¶～の輩出する時代 the time when *women of ability* come forward in succession. 天下の～を集める call together *intelligent women* all over the country.

ざいしょ【在所】(いなか) the country; (故郷) *one's* native place.

さいしょう【最小】¶世界で～の国 *the smallest* country in the world. われわれは被害を～に食い止めた We checked the damage *to a minimum*.

—限 the minimum. —公倍数 the lowest common multiple (略語 L.C.M. または l.c.m.). —公分母 the lowest common denominator (略語 L.C.D. または l.c.d.).

さいしょう【宰相】the premier; the prime minister.

さいじょう【最上】the best. ¶料理は～のものだった The cooking was *of the best*. ～の品 *the best* thing.

さいじょう【斎場】a funeral hall.

ざいじょう【罪状】—認否〔an〕arraignment.

さいじょうきゅう【最上級】the highest class; 〘文法〙the superlative degree.

¶形容詞の～ *the superlative degree* of adjective.

—生 a senior student.

さいしょく【才色】¶花嫁は～兼備だ The bride *is both beautiful and talented*.

さいしょく【菜食】a vegetable diet. ¶私たちは～をしている We *live on vegetables*.

—主義 vegetarianism. —主義者 a vegetarian.

ざいしょく【在職】¶～10年以上の人が5人いる There are five people who *have served* (≒ *have been in service*) for over ten years. 彼はまだ～している He *is* still *in office*. それは私の～中に起きた It happened during my *tenure of office*.

さいしん【再審】re-examination; retrial.

¶この件の～を要求する We apply for *a new trial* to this case. / We demand *a retrial* to this case. 殺人事件は上級裁判所で～された

The murder case *was retried* (≒ *was re-examined*) in a higher court.

さいしん【細心】¶通りを横切るときは～の注意を払え *Take every caution* (≒ *Be most careful*) when you cross the streets. 彼は自分の仕事に～の注意を払った He gave *the most scrupulous* (≒ *the closest*) *attention* to his business. 彼は～の注意を払ってそれを研究した He studied it *with the greatest care* (≒ *very prudently*; *very scrupulously*).

さいしん【最新】¶これは～流行の帽子だ This is *the newest style* in hats. ～の資料 an *up-to-date* material.

—型 the newly-made type. ¶この機械は～型だ This machine is *of the latest* (≒ *of the most up-to-date*) model. —式 the newest one.

さいじん【才人】¶彼はなかなかの～だ He is *a man of* much *ability*. / He is *a* very *clever man*.

サイズ size. ¶～が合う(合わない) be (be out of) *one's size*. ワイシャツの～はいくつですか What *size* shirt do you take (≒ need)?

さいせい【再生】¶トカゲは失った尾を～する Lizards *reproduce* their lost tails. 録音テープを～する *transcribe* the recorded tape.

—ゴム rejuvenated rubber. —紙 reclaimed paper. —品 a reproduced article.

ざいせい【財政】finance. ¶～上の financial. この会社は～が豊かだ The *finance* of this firm is very good. 彼は会社の～に通じている He is well versed in the *finances* of the firm. この都市は目下～が困難な状態にある This city is now in *financial* trouble. この学校の～は改善されなければならない The *finances* of this school should be improved.

—援助 financial assistance. —家 a financier. —学 public finance. —投資 financial investments.

ざいせい【在世】¶この彼の著作は彼の～中に不朽の名著となった This book of his has become a classic *in his lifetime*.

さいせいき【最盛期】(出盛り) the season; the best time; (全盛) the golden age; the height of prosperity.

¶今はブドウの～だ It is *the season* (≒ *the best time*) *for* grapes. イギリスの～はエリザベス1世の治世であった *The golden age* of England was the reign of Elizabeth I.

さいせいさん【再生産】reproduction.

ざいせき【在籍】〔a〕enrol〔l〕ment. ¶彼はまだ～している He *is* still *on the roll* (≒ *on the register*). その大学には日本人学生が多数～している The university has *a* large *enrolment* of Japanese students.

さいせつ【細説】¶～する explain minutely; explain in detail.

さいせん【賽銭】a money offering.

—箱 an offertory box.

さいせん【再選】¶彼は会長に～された He *was re-elected* president. ～を妨げない Nobody is precluded from *being re-elected*.

さいぜん【最前】¶彼から～電話があった I got a call from him *a little while ago* (≒ *a short time ago*).

さいぜん【最善】¶われわれは～を尽くした We did *our best*. / We did *everything in our power*. / We did *what we could*. ～の方法を考える I'll think of *the best* way.

さいぜんせん【最前線】the front; the spearhead.

さいぜんれつ【最前列】¶彼は～にすわっていた He sat in *the firsh row*.

さいそく【細則】detailed rules.

さいそく【催促】〔a〕demand; an urgent request; a call; a claim.

¶図書館員はその本の返済を～した The librarian *pressed* me to return the book. あつかましくも彼は私に謝礼を～した He had the face to *remind* me *of* the payment of the reward. 彼は借金の支払いを～しかねていた He hesitated to *demand* payment of a debt. 子どもにおやつを～された My children *called for* refreshments. 私は返事をしろと矢の～を受けた I *was* hourly *pressed for* an answer. ～がましいことを言うな Don't say what sounds like *demand*.

サイダー soda pop (英米でいうサイダー(cider)はリンゴから作った飲み物(発酵している一種の酒)).

さいたい【妻帯】¶彼は～していてふたりの子どもがある He is a *married* man with two children.

—者 a married man.

さいだい【最大】¶世界～のタンカー *the biggest* tanker in the world. ～瞬間風速30メートルで吹いた The wind blew at *the maximum* velocity of 30 meters a moment.

—限 the maximum. —公約数 the greatest common measure (G. C. M. と略す).

さいだい【細大】¶私は～漏らさず報告した I explained *everything in detail* (≒ *to the minute detail*). 私は～もらさず観察した I observed *both the general effect and the minute details*.

さいたく【採択】¶教科書の～ the *choice* of a textbook. 議案を～する *adopt* a bill.

ざいたく【在宅】¶あすはご～ですか Will you *be* 〔*at*〕 *home* tomorrow?

さいたん【採炭】coal mining. ¶1880年にはアメリカ合衆国で約7千万トンの石炭が～された In 1880 they mined about 70,000,000 tons of coal in the United States of America.

—機 a coal cutter. —夫 a pitman. —量 an output of coal.

さいたん【載炭】coaling. ¶～する coal; take in (≒ on) coal.

さいたん【最短】¶～コースを行く take *the shortest* course.

—距離 the shortest distance.

さいだん【祭壇】an altar. ¶～を設ける prepare *an altar*. ～に花を供える decorate *an altar* with flowers.

さいだん【裁断】decision; judgment. ¶われわれはこの事件についてはまったく彼の～を信頼した We entirely relied upon his *judgment* in this matter. 彼の～は敏速だ He is prompt in *decision*. 洋服屋はきのう私の上着を～した The tailor *cut* a coat for me yesterday.

―機 a cutter.

ざいだん【財団】a foundation. ¶ ロックフェラー～ the Rockefeller *Foundation*.

さいち【才知】intelligence. ¶ ～のある人 a man *of wit*. ～にすぐれた人 a man *of* excellent *intelligence*.

さいちゅう【最中】¶ それは会議の～に起きた It happened *in the midst* (≒ *middle*) *of* the conference. その家は建築の～だ The house *is in course of* construction. 私は夏の～にかぜをひいた I caught cold *at the height of* the summer. 今相談の～です The consultation *is in progress*./The talk *is in full swing*./We are talking now.

ざいちゅう【在中】¶ 5,000円～の財布 a wallet *containing* five thousand yen. 写真～(封筒に) "Photo(s)." 印刷物～(封筒に) "Printed Matter."

さいちゅうもん【再注文】a repeated order.

さいちょうさ【再調査】re-examination; re-investigation.

さいてい【最低】¶ 試験で～の成績をとった I got *the lowest* mark in the examination. あんなことをするとは彼は～だ *How stupid* he is to do such a thing!

―賃銀 the lowest wages. ―限 ¶ ～限100人は確保したい I would like to secure 100 people *at the lowest*.

さいてい【裁定】decision. ¶ われわれは委員会の～に従った We obeyed the *decision* of the committee. ～する decide; adjudge.

仲裁― an award; a peacemaking ruling.

さいてき【最適】¶ 英作文に～な本 *the best* book for writing English. 植物の生長に～な条件 *the optimum* (≒ the *fittest*) conditions for the growth of plants. この仕事には彼が～だ He is *most suited* for this work.

さいてん【祭典】a festival. ¶ スポーツの～ *a festival* of sports; *a* sports *festival*.

さいてん【採点】marking; grading. ¶ 答案を～する *mark* (≒ *look over*) papers. 彼は～が甘い(辛い) He is generous (severe) in *marking* (≒ *grading*). 答案は100点満点で～する Your papers will *be marked* (≒ *be graded*) on the basis of 100.

―表 a list of marks; (競技の) a scorebook.

―簿 a mark (≒ grade) book.

さいど【済度】salvation. ¶ 衆生(しゅじょう)を～する *save* the world; *deliver* mankind. 彼は～しがたい男だ He *is beyond* (≒ *past*) *salvation*.

サイド a side. ¶ ～からゴールをねらう try to shoot a goal from the *side*.

―カー a sidecar. ―スロー〘野球〙a side throw. ―ボード a sideboard. ―ポケット a side pocket. ―ライト a sidelight. ―ライン a sideline. ―リーダー a supplementary reader (サイドリーダーは和製英語). ―ワーク a job; a sideline; an extra work (サイドワークは和製英語).

さいど【再度】again; twice; for the second time. ¶ ～の遠征 a *second* (≒ *another*) expedition. ～試みる try *again*; make *another* attempt.

さいどく【再読】¶ ～する read again; reread. この本は～に値する This book is worth *reading again*.

さいな・む【苛む】¶ それ以来彼は良心に～まれている He *has been* ever since *pricked* by his conscience. / He *has been conscience-smitten* ever since.

さいなん【災難】(不幸) a misfortune; bad luck; (災禍) [a] disaster; a calamity; (不慮の出来事) a mishap; an accident.

¶ ～に会う(を免れる) suffer (escape) *a misfortune*. 彼は細君に死なれてからはまったく～続きだ He has had a series of *misfortunes* ever since he lost his wife. とんだ～でしたね That's *too bad*. ～と思ってあきらめるのですね Get over it; you're in *bad luck* (≒ *hard luck*).

―よけ a charm against misfortunes.

さいにゅう【歳入】(国家の) [annual] revenue. ¶ ～が増える The [annual] revenue increases.

―歳出 revenue and expenditure.

さいにゅうがく【再入学】re-entrance.

¶ 大学に～を許可される *be readmitted* to a college.

さいにん【再任】reappointment. ¶ 彼は議長に～された He *was reappointed* chairman.

ざいにん【罪人】a criminal; an offender.

ざいにん【在任】¶ ～する hold (≒ fill) office; be in office. イギリス～のA氏 Mr. A who *is in office* in England. ～中に彼と知り合った I came to know him *while in office* (≒ *during my term of office*).

さいにんしき【再認識】¶ ～する have a new understanding (*of*).

さいねん【再燃】recrudescence; revival.

¶ 学制問題が～してきた The problem of educational system *has come to the fore again*.

さいのう【才能】[a] talent; ability. ¶ ～教育 *genius* education. ～のある人 a *talented* (≒ *gifted*) man; an *able* man. 彼は音楽の～がある He *has* [a] *talent* (≒ *gift*) *for* music. この分野における彼の持って生まれた～を伸ばしたい I want to cultivate his natural *ability* in this line (≒ field). 彼はすばらしい劇作の～を発揮した He displayed his unusual dramatic *talents*.

さいはい【采配】a baton of command.

¶ ～を振る command; direct; hold the leadership; take the management (*of*).

さいばい【栽培】growing; cultivation. ¶ 庭で菊の～をする *grow* (≒ *cultivate*) chrysanthemums in the garden. イチゴを温室で～する *grow* strawberries under glass.

促成― intensive culture; forcing. 水― water culture.

さいばし・る【才走る】be smart (≒ clever; witty; forward); (早熟である) be precocious.

さ

¶ ～った人 a *clever* man; a wit.

さいはつ【再発】 return; relapse; recurrence; recrudescence. ¶ 彼の胃がんが～しまいかと心配だ I'm very much afraid he may *relapse into* stomach cancer. ～の恐れはまったくない There is no fear at all that he will *have a relapse*. ごたごたがまた～した Another trouble has broken out.

ざいばつ【財閥】 the plutocrats; a financial clique; the *zaibatsu*. ¶ 三菱～ the Mitsubishi *zaibatsu* (≒ *financial group*).

サイバネティックス cybernetics.

さいはん【再犯】 (罪) a second offense.
—者 a second offender.

さいはん【再版】 reprinting; (第2版) a second edition (≒ impression). ¶ ～する reprint. 近くその本の～が出るだろう *A second edition* of the book will soon be issued. その本は～中である The book *is reprinting*.

さいばん【裁判】 (裁くこと) justice; (公判) a trial; (判決) judgment. ¶ ～にかける try (*a person*; a case); put (*a person*; a case) on trial. ～を受ける be tried; stand *one's* trial; be on trial. ～で勝つ(負ける) win (lose) *a* 〔*law*〕*suit*. ～ざたにする bring in *a lawsuit* (*against a person for a matter*); bring (*a matter*) before *the court*. 彼は窃盗罪で～を受けている He *is on trial for* theft.
—官 a judge; (総称) the bench; the court. —権 jurisdiction. —長 the chief judge; (最高裁の) the chief justice. 確定— (最高裁判所の場合) a final judgment (≒ decision); (最高裁以下の場合) a finalized judgment (≒ decision). 欠席— judgment by default. 正式— a formal trial. 略式— a summary trial.

さいばんしょ【裁判所】 a court 〔of justice〕; a law court; (建物) a courthouse. ¶ ～に出頭する appear in *court*.
家庭— a family 〔affairs〕 court. 簡易— a summary court. 管轄— a competent court. 刑事— a criminal court. 高等— a high court. 最高— the Supreme Court. 初審— a court of first instance. 巡回— a circuit court. 地方— a district court. 民事— a civil court.

さいひ【採否】 (議案などの) adoption or rejection; (雇用関係の) employment or rejection. ¶ 彼の提案について投票によって～を決めよう We move that his proposal *be voted on*.

さいひ【歳費】 (費用) annual expenditure; (手当) an annual allowance. ¶ ～の値上げを要求する demand an increase of *annual allowances*.

さいひょうか【再評価】 revaluation. ¶ ～する revalue.

さいひょうせん【砕氷船】 an icebreaker.

さいふ【財布】 a purse; a wallet; (女物の) 米 a pocketbook. ¶ ～のひもを締める(緩める) tighten (loosen) the purse strings. 彼は～の底をはたいてシェイクスピア全集を買った He emptied his *purse* to the last penny to buy the complete works of Shakespeare.

さいぶ【細部】 ¶ ～にわたって検討する go into *details*.

さいぶつ【才物】 a clever person; a man of talent; a man of parts.

ざいぶつ【財物】 property; 〘経済学〙 goods.

さいぶん【細分】 subdivision. ¶ ～する subdivide (*into* parts).

ざいべい【在米】 ¶ ～5年 five years' stay in America. ～中 during *one's* stay in America.

さいべつ【細別】 subdivision. ¶ ～する subdivide.

さいへん【砕片】 ¶ ガラスの～ *splinters* of glass.

さいへんせい【再編成】 reorganization.
¶ クラスを～する必要がある This class needs to *be reorganized*.

さいほう【裁縫】 sewing; needlework.
¶ ～する sew; do needlework. ～を習う(教える) take (give) lessons in *needlework*. 彼女は～がじょうずだ She is good at *sewing*.
—台 a sewing table. —道具 a sewing set. —箱 a sewing box; 米 a housewife [hʌzif].

さいぼう【細胞】 〘生物〙 a cell. ¶ 共産党の～ *a* communist *cell*. ～をつくる organize *a cell*. ～を破壊する destroy *a cell*. ～の cellular.
—学 cytology. —組織 cellular tissue. —分裂 cell division; segmentation. —膜 the cell wall.

ざいほう【財宝】 treasures; riches.

さいほうそう【再放送】 rebroadcast〔ing〕.
¶ 入選作品を～する *rebroadcast* a winning 〔piece of〕 work.

さいほく【最北】 ¶ ～の northernmost. 青森市は本州の～端にある The city of Aomori lies in *the northernmost* part of the Main Island.

サイホン a siphon; 英 a syphon. ¶ ～の原理 siphonage.

さいまつ【歳末】 the end of the year; the year-end. ¶ ～大売り出し a special *year-end* sale.

さいみつ【細密】 ¶ ～な minute; close; detailed.
—画 an elaborately painted picture.

さいみん【催眠】 —剤 a sleeping pill. —術 hypnotism; mesmerism. ¶ ～術をかける *hypnotize* (*a person*); *mesmerize* (*a person*). そのときはまるで～術にかけられたような感じだった At that time I felt as if I *were hypnotized*.

さいみん【細民】 the indigent; the poor; paupers.

さいむ【債務】 debts; obligations; liabilities.
¶ ～を履行する pay *one's debts*; meet *one's liabilities*. 私は彼に～がある I'*m indebted to* him. / I'*m in his debt*. / I *owe* him some money.
—国 a debtor nation. —者 a debtor. —証書 a bond. —不履行 default of obligations.

ざいむ【財務】 financial affairs. ¶ 私は～担当

だ I'm one of the staff of the *financial affairs* section.
—局 the Regional Financial Bureau; the Finance Bureau. —顧問 a financial adviser. —長官 米 the Secretary of Treasury.

ざいめい【罪名】charge. ¶彼は強盗の～で起訴された He was charged with robbery. / He was indicted *on the* (≒ *a*) *charge* of robbery.

さいもく【細目】details. ¶勘定の～を書き出す *itemize* (≒ *specify*) the account. ～はあとで通知します I'll notify you of its *details* later.

ざいもく【材木】米 lumber; 英 timber. ¶～を切り出す lumber. ～で家を建てる build a house of *wood*. この～は充分乾燥している This *wood* has been well seasoned.
—置き場 米 a lumberyard; 英 a timberyard. —屋 米 a lumberman; 英 a timber dealer.

ざいや【在野】¶～の政治家 a politician *of the opposition*. 彼の～時代に while he *was out of power* (≒ *was out of office*).

さいゆ【採油】¶菜種から～する *extract oil* from rapeseed.

さいゆうしゅう【最優秀】¶本年度の～映画 *the best* film of the year.
—賞 the first prize. —選手 the most valuable player 〔of the year〕.

さいゆしゅつ【再輸出】re-exportation. ¶～する re-export.

さいゆにゅう【再輸入】reimportation. ¶～する reimport.

さいよう【採用】(採択) adoption; (雇用) employment. ¶きみのアイディアが気に入ったので～しようと思う I like your idea and I think I will *adopt* it. この教科書は多くの学校で～されている This textbook *is used* in a great number of schools. 彼は若い婦人を秘書として～した He *engaged* a young woman as a secretary.
—試験 an examination for service. —条件 hiring qualifications. —申し込み an application for employment.

さいらい【再来】¶彼はジンギスカンの～といわれた He was said to be "*a second* Genghis Khan" (≒ "*the reincarnation* of Genghis Khan"). 黄金時代が近い将来～するだろう The golden age will *come again* in the near future.
—患者 a person on the sick list.

ざいらい【在来】¶～のやり方を改める change the *conventional* (≒ *traditional*) method.
—品種 a native kind.

さいり【犀利】¶～な観察 a *keen* observation. ～な眼力 a *penetrating* glance.

ざいりゅう【在留】¶～する reside; stay; live. ワシントン～の日本人 the Japanese *residents* in Washington, D.C. ～の resident; living (*at*; *in*).
—民 residents. —邦人 Japanese residents abroad; overseas Japanese.

さいりょう【最良】¶わが生涯の～の年 *the best* (≒ *happiest*) year〔s〕 of my life.

さいりょう【裁量】decision; discretion. ¶自分自身の～で at *one's* 〔own〕 *discretion*. すべて会長の～にゆだねられている Everything is left to the president's *discretion*. どちらの道を行くかはきみの～に任せる It is *within your discretion* (≒ *up to you*) to decide which way to take (≒ go).

ざいりょう【材料】materials; stuff; (資料) data (単 datum); (成分) ingredients; (題材) subject matter; 〘株式〙 a factor; news. ¶彼の伝記の～を集める collect *materials* for his biography.
—費 the material cost. 建築— building materials. 好— good materials (≒ data; news). 実験— materials for experiments.

ざいりょく【財力】financial power (≒ ability); (財産) wealth; means. ¶～のある人 a man *of wealth*. 彼は自分の～に頼りすぎる He trusts his *financial power* too much.

ザイル a rope (ザイルはドイツ語の Seil から由来した語). ¶登山家たちは体を～で結び合っていた The climbers were on the *rope*. / The climbers *were roped* together.

さいるい【催涙】—ガス tear〔-〕gas. —弾 a tear〔-gas〕 bomb.

さいれい【祭礼】a festival.

サイレン a siren. ¶～を鳴らす sound *a siren*. 試合開始の～が鳴った The *siren* signaled the beginning of the game.

サイレント —映画 a silent picture.

サイロ a silo.

さいろく【採録】(抄出) extraction; (記録) recording (*in* a book). ¶彼の詩集からいくつか詩を～した We *extracted* (≒ *selected*) several poems from his book 〔of poems〕. 民話を～する *record* (≒ *transcribe*) old folk tales.

さいろく【載録】record; transcription. ¶雑誌に～された論文 an essay which *appeared* in a magazine; a magazine article.

さいわい【幸い】happiness. ¶あすお会いできれば～です I should *be happy* if I could meet you tomorrow. 彼も合格して～でした *I'm glad* that he too passed the examination. ～彼は現われなかった *Fortunately*, he did not appear. 彼は自動車にぶつけられたが, ～けがはしなかった He was hit by a car, but *luckily* he was not injured. 彼が来たのでこれ～といっさいを彼に任せた I *took advantage of* his coming and left everything up to him.

サイン (合図) a sign; a signal; (署名) a signature; (芸能人などがファンに贈るサイン) an autograph. ¶〘野球〙二塁手に～を送る *signal* the second baseman. バッテリー間の～ *a signal* between the battery mates. 書類に～する *sign* the papers. 小切手に～する *sign one's name* to a check. 彼の～をもらった I got his *autograph*.
—ブック an autograph album. —ボール an autographed ball.

サイン〘数学〙sine (記号 sin).

さ

ざいん【座員】a member of the troupe (≒ company); (総称) the troupe (≒ company). ¶ ～一同に成り代わりまして厚く御礼申し上げます I should like to express our hearty thanks for your coming on behalf of *the troupe*.

サウスポー a southpaw. ¶ ～の投手 a southpaw.

サウナ the sauna. ¶ ～にはいる take *a sauna bath*.

サウンドトラック a sound track.

サウンドボックス a sound box.

さえ【冴え】¶ 今が腕の～の見せどきです Now is the time to show your *skill*. 頭の～にかけては彼にかなう者はいない As far as *intelligence* is concerned, he is second to none.

-さえ ¶ そんなことは子ども～知っている *Even* a child knows it. その作家は名前～聞いたことがない I have not *even* heard the name of the novelist. 自分の名前～書けない人もいる Some people can*not so much as* write their own names. 雨はやまず風～出てきた The rain did not stop and the wind rose *besides*. 音～出さなければなにをやってもいい You may do anything, *so long as* you don't make a noise. 雨～降らなければなあ If *only* it were not rainy! もう少し早く来て～いれば，彼に会えたのだが If *only* I had come a little earlier, I could have met him. とにかくきみは話を聞き～すればそれでいいのだ You have *only* to listen to what he says.

さえぎ・る【遮る】interrupt; obstruct; bar; hinder; cut off; shut out. ¶ 人の話を途中で～るのは失礼である It is rude to *interrupt a person* (≒ *cut a person short*). 木に～られて海が見えなかった Trees *obstructed* our view of the sea. 倒木が道を～っている Fallen trees *obstruct* (≒ *block up*) the road. 厚いカーテンによって光が～られていた The thick curtains *shut out* the light. 月は雲に～られて見えなかった The moon *was screened* by the clouds.

さえずり【囀り】chirping.

さえず・る【囀る】sing; twitter; chirp; (ウグイス・ヒバリなどが) warble; trill.

さえつ【査閲】[an] inspection; [an] examination; check. ¶ 年1回～を受ける *be inspected* once a year.

さ・える【冴える】¶ 月の光が～えている The moon shines *brightly* (≒ *bright*). ～えた夜空に無数の星が美しい Numerous stars twinkle brightly in the *keenly cold* night sky. ～えない顔色だね You look *glum*, don't you? 夜が更けるにつれて目がますます～えた As the night went on, my *wakefulness increased*. 昨夜彼は頭が～えていた He had a *clear* head last night. 腕の～えた職人を見つけることは難しい It is hard to find a *skilled* artisan. 回を追うごとに彼の投球は～えていった As the game advanced he *got skilled* in pitching. 自分の仕事に腕の～えた老年 "old hands" *skilled* at their jobs.

さお【竿・棹】a pole; a rod. ¶ 三味線の～ the neck. 釣りの～と糸 *rod* and line. たんす1～ a cabinet.

さおさ・す【竿さす・棹さす】¶ 流れに～して進んだ We *punted* up a stream. 彼は巧みに時流に～す He *swims with the tide* cleverly. 情に～せば流される Pole along in the stream of emotion; and you will be swept away by the current.

さおだけ【竿竹】a bamboo pole.

さか【坂】a slope. ¶ 上り～ *an* upward *slope*. 下り～ *a* downward *slope*. ～を上った(下った)所に at the head (foot) of the *slope*. 急な(なだらかな)～ *a* steep (gentle) *slope*. 記録的売り上げののち，商売は下り～になった After the record sales, business *declined*. 彼女は40の～を越している(越していない) She *is on the wrong side of* (*is on this side of*) forty.

さか【茶菓】refreshments (通例，複数形で用いる); tea and cakes. ¶ その会では～も出なかった No *refreshments* were served at the party.

さかい【境】a border; (国と国との) a boundary. ¶ それが恋愛と友情との～だ It is the *border line* between love and friendship. 彼は交通事故に会って生死の～をさまよった He *hung between life and death* because of a traffic accident. その山は山形県と宮城県の～にある The mountain rises *on the borders of* Yamagata and Miyagi Prefectures.

さかえ【栄え】prosperity. ¶ 御代に永久の～あれ A *brilliant* era last for ever!

さか・える【栄える】¶ その国は～えた The country *prospered well*.

さかき【榊】a *sakaki*; a sacred tree.

さがく【差額】¶ 収入と支出の～ the *difference* between the totals of the balances of an account. 貿易の～ the *balance* of the trade.

さかぐら【酒蔵】a room for storing *sake*; (酒場) a pub.

さかさ【逆さ】inversion. ¶ アルファベットを～に言ってごらん Try to say the alphabet *backward*. うっかり切手を～にはった I glued a stamp *upside down* by mistake. だれかがほうきを～に立てた Someone put a broom *the wrong end up*. きみの言うことは順序が～だ What you say is *putting the cart before the horse*. ネコの毛を～になでる rub a cat *the wrong way*.

さかさま【逆様】inversion. ¶ 湖面に富士山が～に映っている Mt. Fuji is reflected *head foremost* on the surface of the lake. 頭から～に水の中に飛び込む plunge *head first* into the water. ～に木から落ちた I fell from a tree *head over heels*.

さがしあ・てる【捜し当てる】¶ とうとう彼の居どころを～てた At last I *found out* (≒ *located*) his whereabouts. 字引でそのことばを～てた I *found out* (≒ *looked up*) the word in a dictionary.

さかし・い【賢しい】clever; bright; quick-witted.

さがしだ・す【捜し出す】¶ 旧友を～した He

searched out an old friend. その本を～した I *dug up* the book. 彼は他人の粗を～すのが好きだ He likes to *point out* others' faults.

さがしまわ·る【捜し回る】 ¶ 彼は仕事を～っている He *is looking about for* a job.

さがしもの【捜し物】 ¶ 彼はなにか～をしている He *is looking for* something.

さが·す【捜す·探す】 search; look for; seek. ¶ 彼は途中で落とした本を～しにいった He went to *find* the book he had lost on the way. 彼らは盗まれたピストルはないかと，彼の家の中を～した They *searched* his house for the stolen revolver. 私たちは彼の家を～しているところです We *are searching for* his house. (search a house (家の中を捜す), search a pocket (ポケットの中を捜す), search for a house (家を捜す) の違いに注意). 職を～している I *hunt for* a job. 貸間を～しているところだ I *am looking for* a room for rent. 地図でバス停を～した I *looked up* a bus stop on the map. だれを～しているんだ Who *are* you *looking for*? 会社でタイピストを～している A typist *is wanted* in the company.

さかずき【杯】 a *sake*-cup; a *sake*-glass. ¶ 別れの～ *a* parting *cup*. ～をあける empty *one's cup*.

さか·せる【咲かせる】 ¶ 四，五人が集まって話に花を～せた Several of us got together to *converse livelily*. この仕事でひと花～せるつもりだ I am going to *create a great sensation* by this work.

さかだい【酒代】 drink money; pourboire; (心づけ) a tip; a gratuity.

さかだち【逆立ち】 ¶ きみは～ができますか Can you *stand on your head*? 英語では～しても彼にはかなわない I could be no match for him in English, *however hard I might try*.

さかだ·つ【逆立つ】 stand on end. ⇒よだつ

さかだ·てる【逆立てる】 set on end; bristle up; erect. ¶ 犬は髪を～ててうなった The dog growled *with his hair standing on end*.

さかだる【酒樽】 a *sake* barrel; a *sake* cask.

さかて【酒手】 (酒代) drink money (≒ penny); pourboire; (心づけ) a tip; (余分の賃銀) an extra. ¶ これは～だ Here is something for you.

さかて【逆手】 ¶ 彼は刀を～に持って現われた He appeared *grasping a sword with the point downward*. 打ちかかってくる相手の腕を～に取った I grasped the thrusting arm of the opponent who were striking at me.

さかな【魚·肴】 ［a］fish (fish は単数·複数ともに fish; 種類をいうときはまれに複数に fishes を用いる). ¶ 彼は～を3匹捕らえた He caught three *fish*. この池にはたくさんの～がいる There are many kinds of *fish*［*es*］in this pond. (この場合でも fish がふつう). これは酒の～に向いていない This is not a fit food to be eaten with *sake*.

さかなで【逆撫で】 ¶ ～しながら顔をそった I shaved *against the grain*.

さかなみ【逆波】 a head-sea.

さかねじ【逆捩じ】 ¶ 彼にみごとに～を食わせてやった I *turned the tables on* him very well.

さかのぼ·る【遡る·溯る】 (上流へ) go up; go upstream; (過去へ) go back; retroact to. ¶ サケがこの川を～る Salmons will *go up* this river. 6月に～ってベースアップする Our salary increase *retroacts to* June. この法規は4月1日に～って有効だ This law is effective *retroactive to* April 1. 話は1940年代に～る The story *goes back to* the 1940's.

さかば【酒場】 a bar; 困 a saloon; (英口語) a pub.

さかま·く【逆巻く】 rise and fall; toss about; roll and move like waves; surge. ¶ ～く大波 *surging* billows. ボートは～怒濤(どとう)に翻弄(ほんろう)された The boat was tossed about by the *rolling* waves.

さかもり【酒盛り】 ¶ 彼らは盛大な～を開いた They held *a grand drinking bout*.

さかや【酒屋】 (人) a liquor merchant; (店) a liquor store; (醸造会社) a *sake* brewing company.
¶ 彼の家は造り～だ He runs a *sake* brewing company.

さかゆめ【逆夢】 ¶ その夢は～だった The dream was just contrary to the truth.

さから·う【逆らう】 ¶ 彼はよく両親に～う He often *disobeys* (≒ *contradicts*) his parents. 彼らはよく教師に～う They often *oppose* their teacher. 彼女は父の意に～って，アメリカへ行った She went to America *against* her father's will (≒ *contrary to* her father's wishes). 流れに～ってボートをこいだ We *rowed* the boat *against* the stream. 世の風潮に～わないほうがいい You had better not *swim against* the current. 時代に～う *go against* the stream of the times.

さかり【盛り】 **1**〖絶頂〗¶ イチゴは今が～だ Strawberries *are* now *in season*.
桜も～を過ぎた Cherry blossoms are past their *peak*.
ツツジが今を～と咲き誇っていた The azaleas were blooming *in all their glory*.
花の～は短いもの (人について) The *prime* of youth is but short. / One's *best days* pass swiftly.
夏の暑い～に汗水たらして働いた I worked hard *in the height* (≒ *heat*) *of* the summer.
今が東京では暑い～だ The heat in Tokyo *is at its height* now.
もうぼくも人生の～を過ぎた My *best days* are gone now. / I am past my *prime*.
小学6年生といえば遊びたい～だ Sixth-graders like playing.
彼女は若い～だ She *is in the prime* of youth.
2〖…ざかり〗¶ 食べ～の子にはそれだけではとても足りません That can hardly be enough for *growing* children.
40といえば男～だ A man in the forties *is in the heyday* (≒ *prime*) *of his life*.
きみは今が働き～だ You *are in the prime of your life*.

さ

この子は今が伸び～だ This child is growing fast.

3 〖交尾欲〗 ¶ うちの犬は～がついて近所の犬が押し寄せ困っている My dog *is in heat* now, and I am bothered by the dogs in the neighborhood hanging around her.

さがり【下がり】(下落) fall; decline; depreciation.

さがりめ【下がりめ】¶ 物価は～だ Prices show *a downward* (≒ *falling*) *tendency*.

さが・る【下がる】**1** 〖垂れ下がる〗 hang. ¶ 軒につららが～っていた Icicles *were hanging* from the eaves.

デパートの屋上から垂れ幕が～っている The signs *are hanging* from the roof of the department store.

店先に休業の札が～っていた There was a notice *hanging* on the door saying the store was closed.

物干竿にはたくさん洗濯物が～っていた There was a lot of washing *hanging out* on a clothesline (≒ clothes rod).

風のため電線が切れて垂れ～っていた The electric wires *were blown down* by the wind.

小枝に実がたくさんなり～っていた The branches *were heavy with* fruit.

2 〖低くなる〗 ¶ 彼の目じりは～っている He has *down-slanting* eyes.

その額は右が少し～っているから1センチばかり上げてください The frame is a little *low* at the right side, so would you raise it by one centimeter?

地下水をくみ上げたので地盤が～った Since the subterranean water was overused, the land began to *sink*.

着付けがへたで着物のすそが～っていた She was not so good at dressing up, so the hems of her *kimono* did not match.

彼の努力には頭が～る I *take off my hat to* his efforts.

3 〖温度が〗 fall. ¶ やっと熱が～った My fever *abated* at last.

夜になって急に温度が～った The temperature *fell* suddenly when night came.

当地では真冬でも温度が0度以下に～ることはない The temperature here never *falls* below zero even in the middle of winter.

4 〖価値が〗 ¶ 米ドルの価値が大いに～った The U. S. dollar *was devaluated* sharply.

ミカンの値段はひどく～った The price of tangerines *has* terribly *come down*.

物価が～る見込みはない There is no prospect for prices to *go down*.

午前中の株式相場は～りぎみであった Stock prices in the morning *were* more or less *declining*.

サービスが悪いと店の評判が～るよ If you don't serve the customers well, the store will *lose* its good reputation.

そんなことをするときみの男が～る Such conduct will *aishonor* you.

大臣の値うちも～ったものだ The prestige of a minister *has dropped* these days.

5 〖地位・成績が〗 ¶ 敗戦後日本の国際的地位は～った The position which Japan had occupied in international society *was lowered* after the end of the war.

今回の異動で会社での彼の地位は～った He *was demoted* after reshuffling of personnel.

今度の試験で成績が10番も～った I was ten places *down* after the last exam.

久しく練習していないので剣道の腕が～った Since I have neglected practicing [Japanese] fencing for some time, I seem to *have lost* my skill.

営業成績は～る一方であった The results of the business *were getting worse and worse* (≒ *kept falling*).

6 〖退く〗 ¶ (駅のアナウンス)白線の内側にお～りください Please *step back* and keep behind the white line.

後ろに1歩～ってください Take a step backward.

～れ Keep back!

次の間に～っていなさい You may *retire* to the next room.

一歩～って,もう一度(謙虚に)考えなおしてみよう Let us *step back* and give it one more thought (≒ think it over more throughly; consider it other ways).

7 〖時があとになる〗 ¶ 時代はずっと～って,鎖国のおきては解かれた Many years *later*, the nation gave up its isolationism.

8 〖下付する〗 ¶ 退職一時金が～った The lump-sum severance pay *was given*.

9 〖下手に行く〗 ¶ その店はこの通りを100メートルばかり～った所にあります The store is one hundred meters *down* the street.

さかん【左官】a plasterer.

さかん【盛ん】**1** 〖盛んだ〗 ¶ この町では野球が～だ Baseball *is* very *popular* in this town.

若者たちの間ではスキーが～だ Skiing *is in fashion* among youngsters.

ひところはわれわれの学園も学生運動がとても～だった The students *were* very *active* in political movements on our campus at one time.

ここはお茶の栽培が～だ A lot of tea is grown around here.

昨夜のパーティーはなかなか～だった The party last night was *a great success*.

彼は老いてますます～だ He *is vigorous* in his old age.

なかなかお～ですな (成功している) You *are doing very well*, aren't you? / (広く人と交際する) You *are getting around* a lot, I hear. / (楽しく過ごしている) You *are having a nice time*, aren't you?

2 〖盛んな〗 ¶ ～な拍手を浴びて彼女は舞台に立った Amidst *a storm of* applause she appeared on the stage.

～な声援に送られて彼は打席に立った While the crowd cheered *wildly*, he stood at the batter's box.

ブラジルはサッカーの～な国だ Brazilians are *ar-*

dent fans of soccer. / Brazilians are noted for their *enthusiasm* for soccer.

その町は昔から綿織物の～な町だ The town *has flourished with* the production of cotton fabrics from old days.

3 〖盛んに〗 ¶ ストーブのまきは～に燃えていた The wood in the fireplace was burning *briskly*.

彼らはそのことについて～に議論していた They were engaged in a *hot* (≒ *heated*) argument over the matter.

彼は～に彼女の悪口を言った He *was loud in* denouncing her.

若いころはマージャンを～にやった I used to play mah-jong *quite a lot* when I was young.

これは今～にテレビで宣伝している品物だ Here is the article which is being *extensively* advertised on TV.

4 〖盛んにする・盛んになる〗 ¶ 国際交流をもっと～にしなければならない International exchange programs should *be* more and more *expanded* (≒ *be promoted; be encouraged*). / We must *further* international exchange programs.

適当の運動は頭脳の働きを～にする A proper amount of physical exercise *stimulates* the workings of the brain.

海外旅行熱は若い女性の間に～になってきている Young women *are getting* more and more *interested in* traveling abroad. / Traveling abroad *is getting* very *popular among* young women.

さがん【砂岩】〖地質〗 sandstone.

さがん【左岸】 the left bank 〔of a river〕(左岸・右岸は川下に向かっていう).

さき【先】 **1** 〖先端〗 a point. ¶ 鉛筆の～が丸くなった The pencil *point* is not sharp.

この棒の～はとがっていて危ない It is sharp and dangerous at *the end* of this stick.

針の～でつついてみなさい Prick it with *a* needle *point*.

指の～をけがした I hurt the *tip* of my finger.

半島の～は深く切り立った断崖(だんがい)になっていた There was a cliff rising steeply at the *tip* of the peninsula.

彼女の家はぼくのところから目と鼻の～にある She lives *a stone's throw from* my house.

つま— the tip of the toe ; a tiptoe ; (くつの) the toe 〔of shoes〕. ペン— 米 a pen point ; 英 a nib.

2 〖前方〗 ahead. ¶ この～は行き止まりだ This is a blind alley.

信号の少し～で車を止めてください Stop the car a little *beyond* the traffic signal.

角から3軒～に彼女の家がある Her house is *three doors from* the corner.

それから少し～に行くと右側にホテルが見えます You'll see the hotel on the right, if you go a little further *ahead*. / Go straight *ahead*, and soon you'll find a hotel on your right.

立川から～は不通だ Traffic is tied up *beyond* Tachikawa.

(道路の)～がつかえている The road is blocked *ahead*.

～がつかえているのでぼくの番はなかなかきそうもない There are some people waiting *before* me, and I will have to have a long wait.

一寸～も見えぬ真っ暗やみだった It was pitch-dark and we could not see an inch *ahead*.

彼はぼくの10メートルばかり～を走っていた He was running about ten meters *before* me.

3 〖前もって・より早く〗 beforehand. ¶ ～に手を打っておきなさい Take all possible steps *beforehand*.

代金は～に払っていただけませんか Would you please pay *in advance*?

きみよりぼくのほうが～に着くだろう I'll get there *earlier* than you.

お～に帰らせていただきます Excuse me, but I must be leaving now.

4 〖順位・地位がより前〗 ¶ 経済の発展より福祉をより～に考えるべきだ We should place priority on public welfare *before* economic development.

この仕事を～にしてください Do this work *first thing* (≒*first of all*).

お～に失礼 Excuse me, but I must be going now.

どうぞお～に Please go *first* (≒ *ahead*). / After you, please.

～を急いでおりますので失礼します Please excuse me, I must be getting on.

～を争って逃げだした They all struggled to get out.

～の方から順に中へお入りください Step inside in order, please.

5 〖将来〗 the future. ¶ ～のことは考えないこと Don't think of *the future*.

あんな調子では～が思いやられる The way he is, I feel uneasy about *how he will end up*.

～の見通しは明るい We have a pleasure in *prospect*. / We have *a* good *prospect*.

お～真っ暗だ We have no prospect for *the future* at all. / *The future* is dark.

3年～はどうなるだろう How will it turn out three years *later*?

娘が結婚するのもそう遠い～のことではない My daughter will be married *in the near future*.

きみたちはまだまだ～が長い You have the whole *future* before you.

もうぼくもあまり～が長くない I have but a short time to live. / Death is just around the corner for me.

それから～のことは任せる I'll leave *the rest* to you.

彼のやることは～が知れてる I can easily imagine what he will do.

それから～ふたりは幸せだった They lived happily here *after*.

老い— the remainder of *one's* life; the rest of *one's* life.

6 〖続き〗 ¶ それから～はどうなったのですか Go on

with *the rest* of your story.
その～のことが聞きたい I would like to know *what follows*.
さて, これから～がどうやってよいか難しい Well, it is difficult to see *what to do next* (⇆ *to see the next step*).
7 〖以前に・かつて〗 ¶ ～にお願いした件につきご返事下さい Please let me hear from you concerning the matter I asked you *the other day*.
そのことは～に申し述べたとおりです It is just as I stated *previously*.
8 〖目的の所・着く場所〗 ¶ 彼女の立ち寄った～をあたってみなさい I suggest that you inquire at *every place she visited*.
行く～をはっきりしておいてください Let me know clearly *where you are going*.
東京に出てきたけれど落ち着く～がない I have come up to Tokyo, but can't find *any place* where I *stay*.
9 〖先方の相手〗 ¶ ～さまの気持ちも考えてみなさい Try and think of *the other party's* feeling.
～でいやと言うならこの話はよそう If *the other party* refuses, we'll stop this negotiation.

さき【左記】 the undermentioned; the following. ¶ 彼のことばは～のとおりである His words are *as follows*. ～の本が入要だ I need *the following* books. ～の学生が試験に合格した *The following* students have passed the examination.

さぎ【鷺】 a heron; (白サギ) a white heron.
¶ それではまるで～をカラスと言いくるめるようなものだ It seems as though you talked black into white.

さぎ【詐欺】 swindling. ¶ 彼はしばしば～を働く He often *swindles*. 彼女はたやすく～にかかる She *is* easily *swindled*. 彼は彼女を～にかけて金を巻き上げた He *swindled* (⇆ *cheated*) her *out of* her money.
―師 a swindler.

さきおととい【一昨昨日】 three days ago.

さきおととし【一昨昨年】 three years ago.

さきがけ【先駆け】 ¶ 水仙は春の～だ Daffodils *herald* the coming of spring. / We know the coming of spring by daffodils. 婦人服ではパリが流行の～だ Paris *leads* the fashion in a lady's dress.

さきごろ【先頃】 (先日) the other day; some time ago; (近ごろ) recently; lately.

さきざき【先先】 (行く所) places *one* goes to; (未来) the future. ¶ 行く～でいやな顔をされた I was given the cold shoulder *wherever I went*. ～のことまで心配していたらなにもできない If we thought of *the distant future*, we couldn't do anything at all. 彼は～のことは心配しないたちだ He is never anxious about *the future*.

サキソホン〖音楽〗 a saxophone.

さきだ・つ【先立つ】 ¶ 出発に～って彼を訪ねた I called on him *prior to* my departure. それは最初の事件に～つこと5年だった It was five years *preceding* the first incident. 彼はひとり息子に～たれた His only son *died before him*. / He *survives* his only son. その本は欲しいが今は～つものがない I want the book, but I don't *have enough money to buy* it. なにをするにも～つものは金だ We can't do anything if we don't have money.

さきどり【先取り】 taking before others; taking in advance. ¶ 貸し金の利子を～する *take in advance* the interest of a loan. 時勢を～した経済政策だ It is a kind of economic policy *anticipating* the trend of the times.

さきばし・る【先走る】 ¶ ～ったことをするな Don't *be too hasty in* doing so.

さきばらい【先払い】 ¶ 郵便料金～で彼に小包を送った I sent him the parcel C. O. D. (⇆ cash on delivery). 家賃を3か月～した I *prepaid* three months' house rent. 利息を～しなければならない We must *prepay* the interest.

さきぶれ【先触れ】 an advance (⇆ previous) notice.

さきぼう【先棒】 ¶ 私は彼らのお～を担がされた I was used by them to serve their purpose./ They *made* me *a cat's-paw*.

さきぼそり【先細り】 tapering; taper. ¶ ～する taper〔off〕; grow gradually lean. この商売も時代の波で～の運命にある This business is destined to *decline* with the change of the times.

さきほど【先程】 ¶ ～彼から電話がありました He rang me up *a little while ago*.

さきまわり【先回り】 ¶ 彼の～をして駅に着いた I arrived at the station *before* him. 彼は話の～をする悪い癖がある He has a bad habit of *anticipating* another's story.

さきみだ・れる【咲き乱れる】 bloom all over; bloom in profusion. ¶ 庭には花が～れていた Flowers *bloomed beautifully* all over the garden.

さきもの【先物】〖商業〗 futures.
―買い forward buying. ¶ ～買いには多少の危険が伴う *Forward buying* involves some risk. ―取引 futures deals. ―予約 forward contract.

さきゅう【砂丘】 a sand hill; (海辺の) a dune.

さきゆき【先行き】 the future; 〖商業〗 market prospects. ¶ その商売の～は明るい The business *prospects* are bright.

さぎょう【作業】 work; operations. ¶ すぐ～を始めなければいけない You must start *work* at once. 大規模な難破船の引き上げ～が始まった Large-scale salvage *operations* were started. 爆破～中に彼はけがをした He was injured during blasting *operations*. ～中止もやむをえなかった We could not help suspending *operations*.
―時間 working hours. ―場 a workshop. ―条件 job requirements. ―能率 work (⇆ operation) efficiency. ―服 working clothes.

ざきょう【座興】 fun; amusement; playfulness. ¶ ～にトランプの手品をやってみせた I juggled with cards *to amuse the company*. ほ

んの～のつもりでそう言っただけだ I said it just *for fun*.

ざぎょう【座業】a sedentary occupation (≒ work).

さきわけ【咲き分け】¶ ～の朝顔 multi-colored morning-glories.

さきわたし【先渡し】future (≒ forward) delivery. ¶ ～で買う(売る) buy (sell) for future delivery.

さきん【砂金】gold dust; alluvial gold.
—鉱業 alluvial mining.

さきん·ずる【先んずる】¶ 彼の思想は時代に～じていた His ideas *were ahead of* (≒ *were in advance of*) the age. 彼は何事も人に～じてやる He *takes the initiative in* doing anything. 社会の要求は個人の要求よりも～ずるべきだ Social claims should *take* 〔*the*〕 *precedence of* personal ones. ～ずれば人を制す(諺) *First come, first served*.

さく【作】(作品) a work; a piece; (収穫) a harvest; a crop. ¶ 彼女の初期の～ her early period *work*. 彼の最も評判のよい～ his most popular *work*. 高村光雲の～ *a sculpture* by Koun Takamura. 東山魁夷の～ *a picture* by Kaii Higashiyama (作品が彫刻·絵画などと, はっきりしているときは a sculpture, a picture, a painting (油彩) などとする). この探偵小説(漢詩)はだれの～ですか Who wrote this detective story (Chinese poem)?

さく【策】¶ 私は確たる～はない I don't have *a* definite *plan*. ～を実行に移す carry *a plan* into execution. 彼を救うためあらゆる～が講ぜられた All possible *steps* were taken to save him. もうこうなっては～の施しようがない There's nothing to be done about it now.

さく【柵】a fence. ¶ 鉄の～ *an* iron *fence*; 英 *an* iron *railing*. 芝生を～で囲む enclose the lawn with *a fence*.

さ·く【咲く】bloom; come out; blossom; come into flower. ¶ チューリップの花が～いている The tulips *are in bloom*. リンゴの木に花が～いている The apple trees *are in blossom*. (観賞用の花には bloom を用い, 実のなる木の花には blossom を用いる). バラが～きそろっている The roses *are in full bloom*. 話に花が～いた The chat *became animated*.

さ·く【裂く·割く】¶ 彼はその紙をふたつに引き～いた He *tore* the paper *in* two. 彼女はかっとなって, その手紙をずたずたに～いた She got mad and *tore* the letter *into* little *pieces*. その知らせを聞くと私は胸が～かれる思いがした The news *broke my heart*. 戦争がふたりを引き～いた The war *separated* the two. 中傷が彼と彼女の仲を引き～いた Spiteful gossip *severed* him from her. ちょっと時間を～いてくれませんか Can you *spare* me a few minutes? 今時間を～くことはできません I have no time to *spare*.

さく-【昨-】¶ ～年 *last* year. ～晩 *last* evening. ～夜 *last* night. ～4月15日は私の誕生日だった Yesterday, April 15, was my birthday. (last morning, last afternoon, last day とはいわない. それぞれ yesterday morning, yesterday afternoon, yesterday という).

さくい【作為】artificiality. ¶ ～的行為 an *intentional* doing. 彼がそうしたのは～か偶然かわからない I don't know whether he did it *on purpose* or by accident.

さくい【作意】an idea; a design; a conception; a motif.

さくいん【索引】an index (複 indexes, indices). ¶ 書物の～ *an index to* a book. この本の～はよい This book *is* well *indexed*. ～をつける *index* a books; provide a book with *an index*. 専門用語はみんな～に出ている All the technical terms *are indexed*.

さくがら【作柄】(一地方または一季節の全農作物) the crops; (一農地または一種類の作物) a crop. ¶ ことしの小麦の～は良かった (悪かった) The wheat *crop* has been good (poor) this year.

さくがんき【削岩機】a rock drill.

さくぐ【索具】rigging.

さくげん【削減】a cut; 〔a〕 reduction; curtailment; 〔a〕 retrenchment. ¶ 予算の～ *a reduction* (≒ *a cut*) in the budget. 経費を1割～しなければならぬ We must *cut down* (≒ *reduce*) the expenses by ten percent.

さくご【錯誤】a mistake; an error.
試行— trial and error. 時代— 〔an〕 anachronism.

さくさく ¶ 彼らは～と雪を踏んで歩いていた They *were crunching* through the snow. そのミュージカルは批評家のあいだで好評～である The musical *is very highly esteemed by* critics. / The musical *is very popular among* critics.

ざくざく ¶ 堅い雪はわれわれの足の下で, ～と砕けた The hard snow *crunched* under our feet. 彼らは砂利を～踏んで進んだ They *crunched* on gravel. 彼女は玉ネギを～切った She *chopped* an onion *up noisily*.

さくさん【酢酸】〘化学〙acetic acid.
—塩 acetate. —銅 copper acetate.

さくし【作詞】¶ ～する make a song. A氏～の歌 a song with words by Mr. A.
—家 a poet; a versemonger.

さくし【策士】(悪い意味の) a schemer; (良い意味の) a tactician. ¶ ～策におぼれる (諺) Good swimmers are most often drowned.

さくじつ【昨日】yesterday.

さくしゃ【作者】an author; (女) an authoress; a writer; (演劇の) a dramatist; a playwright.

さくしゅ【搾取】exploitation; squeezing.
¶ 資本家の～ capitalist *exploitation*. 中間～ intermediary *exploitation*. 彼は貧民階級から～した He *squeezed* (≒ *exploited*) the poor.

さくじょ【削除】elimination; cancellation.
¶ 最後の語は～したほうがいい You had better *strike off* (≒ *cross out*) the last word. 彼の名前を名簿から～した We *struck* his name *off* the roster.

さくず【作図】drawing; 〘数学〙construction. ¶ ～する draw a figure ; 〔数学〕 construct.

さく·する【策する】¶ 野党はひそかに法案阻止を～している The Opposition Party *is* secretly *planning to* reject the bill.

さくせい【作成】¶ 報告書を～する *draw up* (≒ *make out*) a report.

さくせん【作戦】(全体的な作戦計画) strategy ; (軍事行動) operations ; (戦術) tactics. ¶ ～を練る consider *a plan of operations*. ～を開始する begin *operations*. ～を誤る commit a *tactical* error. ～を変えたほうがよい We must change our *tactics*.

—会議 a council of war. —基地 a base of operations.

さくぜん【索然】¶ 興味～としている be devoid of interest ; be dry.

さくそう【錯綜】¶ 問題は非常に～している The matter *is* very *complicated*.

さくづけ【作付け·作付】planting.

—面積 the planted acreage ; the area under cultivation.

さくどう【策動】maneuvering ; 英 manoeuvring. ¶ 彼が陰で～しているのだ He *is maneuvering* behind the scenes.

さくにゅう【搾乳】milking.

—場 a dairy ; a dairy farm.

さくねん【昨年】last year.

さくばん【昨晩】米 last evening ; 英 yesterday evening.

さくひん【作品】a 〔piece of〕 work ; a product ; a production. ¶ バイロンの～集 Byron's *works*. 学生の～の展示 an exhibit of students' *works*. 彼の初期(後期)の～ his *early* (*late*) *work*. シェイクスピアの～をなにか読んだことがありますか Have you ever read *any of Shakespeare's works*?

さくふう【作風】a〔literary〕style. ¶ 彼はA氏の～をまねている He models his *style on* (≒ *after*) Mr. A's. / He imitates (≒ emulates) Mr. A's *style*.

さくぶん【作文】〔a〕 composition ; a short essay. ¶ 彼女の～はよく書けている Her *composition* is well written. この斬新(ざん)な案を単なる～に終わらせてはならない We should not let this original plan end in *a* mere *blueprint*.

英— English composition. 自由— free composition.

さくほう【作法】technique. ¶ 小説～ *how to* write novels.

さくぼう【策謀】¶ 彼は～にたけている He is adept at (≒ in) *intrigue*.

—家 a schemer.

さくもつ【作物】(一農地または一種類の作物) a crop ; (一地方または一季節の全農作物) the crops. ¶ この土地は～がよくできる This land *yields* good *crops*. 農夫は～をつくる Farmers *raise crops*. 今がその～を植えつける(取り入れる)のにいちばんよい時だ Now it is the best time to plant (gather) the *crop*. 日照りで～がだめになった Because of the drought, the *crops* have failed.

さくや【昨夜】last night.

さくら (大道商人の) a decoy ; a bonnet ; (劇場などの) a claquer (集合的には claque). ¶ 客の中には～もまじっている There are some *decoys* among the customers.

さくら【桜】〔植物〕(木) a cherry tree ; (花) cherry blossoms. ¶ ～は今満開だ The *cherry trees* are in full blossom. ～はもう散った The *cherry blossoms* are over. ぶどう酒で彼女のほおは,ほんのり～色だ Her cheeks *are* slightly *flushed* with wine.

—草 〔植物〕 a primrose. —肉 horseflesh. —紙 a paper handkerchief ; toilet paper. —もち sweet bean paste in flour wrapped in a cherry leaf.

さくらん【錯乱】distraction ; derangement. ¶ 彼の自殺の原因は精神～だ His suicide is due to *mental derangement*. 彼らは恐怖で精神～をきたしている They *are driven to distraction* (≒ *are distracted*) by fear.

さくらんぼ【桜桃】a cherry. ¶ ～の種 a *cherry* stone.

さぐり【探り】¶ 彼に～を入れてみよう I'll *feel* him *out*. 手で～って進んだ I felt my way. 彼はこちらの意向に～を入れてきた He *is sounding* us *on* the matter.

さくりゃく【策略】a stratagem ; a trick ; an artifice ; a scheme. ¶ ～を用いて彼から金をせしめた I got money from him *by a trick*.

さぐ·る【探る】¶ ポケットを～る *search one's* pockets. ポケットの財布を～る *feel one's* pockets for *one's* wallet. 人の意向を～る *sound a person's* mind. 敵情を～る *spy on* the enemy.

さくれい【作例】an example 〔of writing〕; a model sentence ; a model for composition. ¶ 彼はわれわれに～を示した He gave *a model example* to us.

さくれつ【炸裂】explosion. ¶ ～する explode; blow. 爆弾が～して多くの人々が死んだ A bomb *exploded* and killed many people.

ざくろ【柘榴·石榴】〔植物〕 a pomegranate.

—石 〔鉱物〕 garnet.

さけ【酒】*sake* ; (酒類) alcoholic drinks. ¶ どんなお～がお好きですか. 甘口ですか辛口ですか Which *sake* do you like better, medium-sweet or dry? この～はこくがある This *sake* is of good body. この～は強い This is *a* strong *sake*. この～は弱いから女性にも向く This *liquor* is suitable for women, because it is light. 私は～は一滴も飲めない I *do not touch a drop*. / I'*m a total abstainer*. 彼女は～が強い She *is a heavy* (≒ *good*) *drinker*. 彼は～が好きだ He likes *drinking*. / He is fond of *drink*. 彼は～を断った He quit (≒ gave up) *drinking*. 私の家は田舎で～をつくっている My family own a *sake* brewery in the country. 彼は1杯の～でもすぐ赤くなる He is easily flushed with a single cup of *sake*. 彼は～臭いにおいをぷんぷんさせていた I could *smell liquor* on his breath. 一杯～はどうです? What about *a drink*?

さけ【鮭】〘魚類〙a salmon (単複同形).
—かん 米 canned salmon; 英 tinned salmon. 塩— salted salmon. くん製の— smoked salmon.

さけい【左傾】¶ 彼の思想は〜している His ideas *are toward the left*.

さけぐせ【酒癖】¶ 彼は〜が悪い He *is a vicious* (≒ *quarrelsome*) *drinker*.

さげすみ【蔑み】contempt; scorn; disdain.

さげす·む【蔑む·貶む】despise.

さけのみ【酒飲み】a drinker. ¶ 大〜 *a* heavy (≒ hard; good) *drinker*. 彼は大〜だ He *drinks like a fish*.

さけび〔ごえ〕【叫び〔声〕】a shout; a cry; (悲鳴) a scream; (ほえる声) a howl. ¶ 彼は助けてくれと〜声をあげた He raised *a shout* for help. 助けを求める〜声が部屋の中から聞こえた *A scream* for help came from inside the room. 遠くにオオカミの〜声を聞いた I heard the *howl* (≒ *roar*) of a wolf in the distance. 戦争反対の〜は人々の心の底からの願いである *An outcry* against war is a hearty wish of all people.

さけ·ぶ【叫ぶ】¶「止まれ」と彼は〜んだ "Stop!" he *shouted*.「助けて」と彼女は〜んだ "Help!" she *cried*. 彼女はびっくりしてキャーと〜んだ She *screamed* (≒ *gave a scream*) in fright. 勝利の知らせに思わず万歳を〜んだ They *gave* involuntary *cheers* of *Banzai* at the news of victory. 戦争反対を〜ぶ *raise an outcry against* war. 待遇改善を〜ぶ *clamor* for higher wages.

さげまく【下げ幕】a drop curtain.

さけめ【裂け目】a rent; (割れ目) a fissure; (深いもの) a chasm; (浅いもの) a chink. ¶ 壁の〜 *a crack* in the wall. 堤防の〜 *a crevasse* in the levee. ワイシャツの〜 *a tear* in the shirt.

さ·ける【裂ける】tear ([tɛə] と発音する); break; give away; bust; rend. ¶ この布はすぐ〜ける This cloth *tears* easily. ぼくの上着はくぎにひっかかって〜けた My jacket *tore* on a nail. 板はふたつに〜けた The board *was split* in two. 船の帆はぼろぼろに〜けた The sails of the ship *were torn* to ribbons.

さ·ける【避ける】avoid; evade; avert; shirk; elude; keep away (*from*); get out of *a person's* way.
¶ 彼女は私を〜けているらしい She seems to *be avoiding* me. 悪友とのつきあいは〜けるべきだ You must *avoid* bad company. ふたりの意見の衝突は〜けられない The conflict of opinion between the two *is inevitable*. 難しい問題を〜けてやさしい問題を先にやりなさい *Put off* the difficult questions and try to answer the easy ones first.

さ·げる【下げる·提げる】¶ 知らない人が私に頭を〜げた(おじぎをした) A stranger *bowed* to me. 彼は給料を〜げられるかもしれない He might *have* his salary *decreased*. このぜんを〜げて下さい Please *clear* the table. 半音〜げる(音楽で) flatten. 包みを〜げる *bring* (≒ *carry*) a bundle〔in *one's* hand〕.

さげわた·す【下げ渡す】(釈放する) release; (許可する) grant.

さげん【左舷】port. ¶ 〜に船が見える There is a ship in sight to *port*. 船は〜に傾いた The ship listed to *port*.

ざこ【雑魚】small fish; small fry.

ざこう【座高】the sitting height.

さこく【鎖国】〔national〕isolation; seclusion. ¶ 徳川幕府は〜を行なった The Tokugawa Shogunate *closed the country to foreigners*.
—主義 a national isolation policy.

さこつ【鎖骨】〘解剖学〙the collarbone.

ざこつ【座骨】〘解剖学〙the hipbone; the hucklebone.
—神経 the sciatic nerve〔s〕. —神経痛 hip gout; sciatica.

ざこね【雑魚寝】¶ 〜する sleep together in a huddle.

ささ【笹】〘植物〙(竹類) bamboo grass; (竹の葉) a bamboo leaf.
—ぶね a bamboo-leaf boat. —やぶ bamboo bush.

ささい【些細】¶ 〜なことを気にする worry about *trifles*. 〜なことでけんかする quarrel over *trifles*.

ささえ【支え】(支持)〔a〕support; (支柱) a stay. ¶ このたなは〜がいる This shelf must have *a support*. 精神的〜 *a* mental *support*; *a* moral *support*.

さざえ【栄螺】〘貝類〙a turbo (複 tarbos).
¶ 〜の壺焼き *a turbo* cooked in its own shell.

ささ·える【支える】¶ 屋根は4本の柱で〜えられている The roof *is supported* with four posts. 彼はステッキで体を〜えた He *supported himself* with a stick. 彼女は女の細腕で一家を〜えている She *supports* the family on her limited means. 敵を〜えられない We cannot *keep* the enemy *in check*.

ささくれ (つめの) an agnail; a hangnail. ¶ 〜ができた I had *a hangnail* (≒ *an agnail*).

ささく·れる ¶ 竹の棒が〜れる The bamboo stick *gets splintery*. 彼女の気持ちは今〜れたようになっている She is now ready to *get irritated* at everything.

ささげ【大角豆】〘植物〙a cowpea.

ささげもの【献げ物】an offering. ¶ 神に〜をした I made *an offering* to God.

ささ·げる【捧げる】**1**〚献呈する〛¶ 彼は身命を国に〜げた He *sacrificed himself* for his country.
彼は研究に一生を〜げた He *devoted* his whole life *to* his researches.
その本は彼に〜げられた The book *was dedicated to* him.
彼は神に祈りを〜げた He *prayed* (≒ *offered* prayers) *to* God.
2〚持ち上げる〛hold up; lift up; (銃を) present. ¶ 〜げ銃(つつ) (号令) Present arms.

ささつ【査察】〔an〕inspection; investigation. ¶ 〜する inspect; investigate.

空中── 〔an〕 aerial inspection. ──官 a inspector.

さざなみ【小波・細波・漣】a ripple; a wavelets. ¶湖には～が立っていた There were *ripples* on the lake. そよ風で湖面に～が立ちはじめた The breeze began to *ripple* the surface of the lake.

ささみ【笹身】(鶏肉の) the breast flesh of a chicken.

さざめき (騒ぎ) a noise; an uproar; a hubbub.

ささやか【細やか】small; little; tiny. ¶彼に～な贈り物をした I gave a *little* present to him. 田中氏のために～な祝宴を催した We held a *small* feast in honor of Mr. Tanaka. 彼は～な資本で商売を始めた He started a business with a *small* capital. 彼は～に暮らしている He lives *in a small way*. / He is making a *scanty* life.

ささやき【囁き】a whisper; a murmur; whispering. ¶風の～ the *whisper* of the wind. 小川の～ the *murmur* of a stream. 隣の部屋から彼らの～が聞こえた I heard them *whispering* in the next room.

ささや・く【囁く】whisper; murmur; talk (≒ speak) in whispers. ¶彼は彼女にひと言, ふた言～いた He *whispered* a word or two *to* her. 私は彼にすぐ出発するように～いた I *whispered* him *to* start at once. 彼女はいつも～くように話す She always talks *in whispers* (≒ *in a whisper*). 彼は彼女に愛のことばを～いた He *murmured* words of love in her ear. / He *whispered to* her that he loved her. 物価が上がりそうだといううわさがどこへ行っても～かれている Everywhere you hear dark *whispers* of rising prices.

ささ・る【刺さる】¶指にとげが～った A thorn *has stuck* in my finger.

さざんか【山茶花】〘植物〙a sasanqua.

さじ【匙】a spoon. ¶このカップに砂糖を2～入れてください Put two *spoonfuls* of sugar in this cup. ～に山盛り一杯の砂糖 a heaping *spoonful* of sugar. 医者たちも彼には～を投げた The doctors *have given* him *up*. 私はこの事件には～を投げた This case is beyond my power.

大── a tablespoon. 茶── a teaspoon.

ざし【座視】¶友人の窮状を～するに忍びない I can't *stand by watching* my friend in need of help.

さしあ・げる【差し上げる】(持ち上げる) hold up; lift up; (進呈する) give; offer.

¶なにを～げましょうか(商店で) What can I do for you? / May I help you? 飲み物でも～げましょうか May I *offer* you a drink? お茶をもう1杯～げましょうか Would you like another cup of tea?

さしあたり【差し当たり】(当分) for the present; for the time being; (只今のところ) now; at present. ¶～2万円もあれば足りるだろう Twenty thousand yen will do (≒ be enough) *for the present*. ～いらない物はしまっておきなさい Put aside the things that you don't need *now*.

さしいれ【差し入れ】¶これが彼への～です This is *a present to* him in prison. 私は彼に本を1冊～した I *presented* a book *to* him in prison.

──口(郵便) a letter drop.

さしえ【挿し絵】an illustration. ¶～入りの本 an *illustrated* book.

──画家 an illustrator.

さしお・く【差し置く】¶なにを～いても first of all. 費用の問題は～いて，私にはそれをやる時間がない *Leaving aside* the question of expenses, I have no time to do it. 先輩を～いて彼は昇進した He was promoted *over* his seniors' *heads*.

さしおさえ【差し押さえ】attachment; 〔a〕 seizure; distraint.

──物件 seized (≒ attached) goods. ──令状 a warrant of seizure (≒ attachment).

さしおさ・える【差し押さえる】¶彼の財産を～えた I *attached* his property. 彼は俸給を～えられた He *had* his salary *attached*.

さしか・える【差し替える】¶番組は一部～えることがあります Part of the program is subject to *change*.

さしかか・る【差し掛かる】¶駅に～った所で列車は止まった The train stopped just when it *was getting to* the station. 峠に～ると急に雨が降りだした It began to rain just as we *came to* the pass.

さしかけ【指し掛け】¶彼は将棋を～にして座をはずした He rose from his seat, leaving the chess game *unfinished* (≒ *halfway*).

さしか・ける【差し掛ける】¶彼は私にかさを～けてきた He *held* an umbrella *over* me.

さじかげん【匙加減】(手加減) allowance; consideration; (薬の調合) prescription. ¶塩の～が難しい It is difficult to decide how much salt to use. 彼の～でどうにでもなる Everything is left to his *discretion*. / Everything is decided at his *discretion*.

さしがね【差し金】(そそのかすこと) incitement; instigation; (入れぢえ) suggestion. ¶この子がそうするのは彼の～だろう He may *have stirred* this boy *up to* do so. きみのすることはみんな彼の～だと思う I think you do everything *on his suggestion*.

さしき【挿し木】a cutting. ¶～をする plant *a cutting* (*from* a gum). ～がついた The *cutting* has taken root.

さじき【桟敷】a stand; (劇場の) a box.

天井── a gallery. 正面── the grand tier. 2階── the dress circle.

ざしき【座敷】(部屋) a room; (客間) a drawing room. ¶お客様を～へお通ししなさい Show the guest to the *room*. お～がかかっているよ You are called. / You are wanted. (芸者に) ～がかかる have an engagement; be hired (≒ called) by a client.

さしこ【刺し子】quilted clothes.

さしこみ【差し込み】(電気の) an outlet; a

socket ; (病気の) acute pain ; 〘医学〙 a spasm ; gripes. ¶ トースターのコードを～に入れる *plug in* a toaster. 急に～が起きたのでしばらくいすに座りこんでいた I had *a spasm* and was kept sitting in the chair.

さしこ･む【射し込む】¶ 日光が部屋に～んでいる The room *is sunny*. / The sunlight *is streaming in* the room.

さしこ･む【差し込む】¶ プラグを～む *put in* a plug. 急に腹が～んできた I *had a* sudden *stomachache*. / I *had acute pain in the stomach*.

さしころ･す【刺し殺す】¶ 彼は彼女を～した He *stabbed* her *to death*.

さしさわり【差し障り】an obstacle ; an hindrance. ¶ 彼は～があって欠席した He was absent because of some *trouble*. その話は彼には～がある The story *is offensive to* him.

さししめ･す【指し示す】¶ 地図を～して説明した I explained it by a map. / I *pointed to* the map to explain it.

さしず【指図】orders ; directions. ¶ きみの～は受けない I don't take my *orders from* you. 先生の～で作業をする We work *under* our teacher. きみが～する必要はない There is no need for you to give *directions*.

さしずめ【差し詰め】(今のところは) for the present ; for the time being ; (今) at present ; (けっきょく) in the end.
¶ このようすでは～きみがリーダーだ Then you are expected to be the leader *in the end*.

さしせま･る【差し迫る】¶ 期日が～っている The time *is pressing* (≒ *is close at hand*). ～った用事があるので帰ります I must be going because I have something to do now. 現在のところ～った問題はない I don't have any *pressing* matter at present.

さしだしにん【差出人】a sender. ¶ ～不明の手紙 an *anonymous* letter.

さしだ･す【差し出す】¶ 呼び出しが来たので代人を～した I was called and *sent* someone in place of me. 受付に名刺を～した I *presented* my visiting card *to* the receptionist.

さしたる【然したる】¶ ～損失でもない It is *not* a *heavy* loss. 彼の反対など～ことではない His objection *doesn't matter a great deal*. 今は～仕事もない I have nothing *particular* to do now.

さしつかえ【差し支え】(さしさわり) a hindrance; an interference ; (不便) an inconvenience ; (先約) a previous engagement.
¶ 今度の日曜なら～ない I shall *be free* next Sunday. 彼は大きな赤ん坊だといっても～ないだろう He *may* be called a grown-up baby. この本がなくても～ない I *can well get on without* this book. ひざが痛むが歩くのには～ない I have a pain about my knee, but I *can* still walk all right. ～なければこれをお持ちください Please take this with you, if you *don't mind*. この箱を開けても～ありませんか Do you *mind* my opening this box? ～があってあすはお目にかかれません I cannot see you tomorrow, as I have *a previous engagement*.

さしつか･える【差し支える】(さしさわりがある) be interrupted ; (先約などで) be engaged ; (必要なものがなくて) be short of ; be pressed for (money). ¶ あすは～えるから明後日おいでください I shall *be busy* tomorrow, so please call on me the day after. 彼は毎日の暮らしに～えている He is living a hand-to-mouth life.

さして【差し手】〘将棋〙 a move ; 〘碁〙 a hand.

さして【然して】¶ 失業しても彼は～生活に困らないだろう Though he loses his job, he won't find it difficult to make a living.

さしで【差しで】¶ ～飲もう Let's drink tête-à-tête.

さしでがまし･い【差し出がましい】¶ 彼の～い助言 his *uncalled-for* advice. ～くあれこれ言うな Don't *put yourself forward*. ～いようだがひと言注意しておく *This is none of my business*, but let me give you a piece of advice.

さしでぐち【差し出口】¶ よけいな～はしないほうがいい You had better *mind your own business*. (had better を用いるとおどし文句に近いきびしい表現になる). ～をたたくな Don't make *uncalled-for remarks*.

さし･でる【差し出る】¶ 私は～出たことをして恥をかいた I was put to shame because I *was too forward*.

さしとお･す【刺し通す】¶ 千枚通しを紙の束に～す *pierce* an eyeleteer *through* a sheaf of papers.

さしと･める【差し止める】¶ 内容の公表を～められた The publication of the details *was banned*.

さしの･べる【差し伸べる】¶ 彼に救援の手が～べられた A helping hand *was extended to* him. 幼児が手を～べた The little child *held out* its hand.

さしはさ･む【挟む･挿む】¶ 彼は本にメモを～んだ He *put* a note *between* the pages of a book. 突然彼は口を～んだ Suddenly he *cut in*. (in は副詞). 口を～んですみません I'm sorry to *interrupt* you. だれも疑いを～む者はいない Nobody is doubtful of it.

さしばな【挿し花】flower arrangement.

さしひか･える【差し控える】¶ はっきり言うことは～える I *don't want to say* positively. 私の意見は～えておく I *reserve* my opinion. (反対意見ないしは酷評したいときのおだやかな決まり文句).

さしひき【差し引き･差引】deduction. ¶ 貸借を～する *strike* a balance. ～あと100円払ってください Pay a balance of a hundred yen. ～勘定は私の貸し(借り)になります The balance of the account is for (against) me.

さしひ･く【差し引く】¶ かかった費用は～いてください *Take* the cost 〔*away*〕 from my pay. 会費を給料から～いてください *Take* (≒ *Deduct*) the fee from my pay. 税金を～くと収入はゼロだ We get no income *after* tax 〔*reduction*〕.

さしまね･く【差し招く】¶ 彼は私にいっしょに来るように～いた He *beckoned* me to come along.

さしまわし【差し回し】sending a car round to. ¶ 政府～の自動車 the car sent round

さ

from the government.

さしみ【刺身】 sliced raw fish. ¶ カツオの～ sliced bonito ; slices of raw bonito. ～のつま garnishings served with raw fish.

さしむかい【差し向かい】 ¶ ～で食事した We had dinner *face to face*. 彼女と～でテーブルについた I *sat down across the table from* her.

さしむ·ける【差し向ける】 ¶ 先方へ使いを～ける *send* a messenger to the house. 彼を迎えに車を～けた We *sent* a car for him.

さしも ¶ ～じょうぶな彼もついに寝込んだ *Strong as he was*, he fell ill at last. (形式ばった文体). ～の大火もやっと下火になった *Such* a big fire burnt low at length.

さしもど·す【差し戻す】 ¶ この書類は不備のため～す We *send* this paper *back* because it is not properly filled in. 彼は判決を～した He *referred* the decision *back*.

さしゅ【詐取】 fraud ; swindle. ¶ 彼は偽領収書で私から金を～した He *swindled* money *out of* me by a false receipt. / He *swindled* me *out of* my money by a false receipt. 彼は主婦たちから金を～した He *cheated* housewives *out of* their money.

さしょう【査証】 a visa ; a visé. ¶ 旅券に～がおりた I *had* my passport *visaed*. (visa'd ともつづる).

さしょう【詐称】 ¶ 氏名を～する *assume* another name. 彼は大学出と～した He *represented* himself *falsely as* (≒ *to be*) a college graduate. / He *pretended to* have a college background.

さじょう【砂上】 ¶ ～の楼閣 a castle in the air ; a castle in Spain.

ざしょう【座礁】 ¶ ～する run ground. 船は港の外で～した The ship 〔*was*〕 *stranded* outside the port.

ざじょう【座乗】 ¶ 指揮官の～する軍艦 a warship *with* the commander *on board* ; a warship *manned* by the commander.

さしわたし【差し渡し】 a diameter. ¶ ～1メートルの円 a circle one meter *across* (≒ *in diameter*) ; a circle with *a diameter* of one meter.

さじん【砂塵·沙塵】 dust. ¶ 強風が～を巻き上げる A strong wind raises *dust*.

さす【砂州】 a sandbar.

さ·す【刺す】 pierce. ¶ 彼は彼女の横腹を短刀で～した He *stabbed* her side with a knife. ハチに～された I *was stung* by a bee. かわいそうに赤ん坊は足を蚊に～された The poor baby *was bit* by mosquitoes in the leg. 彼は足にくぎを～したので歩くことができなかった A nail *had stuck in* his foot and now he could not walk. 走者は二塁寸前で～された (野球で) The runner *was put out* just in front of the second base. ～すような寒さ biting (≒ sharp) cold.

さ·す【指す】 ¶ コンパスは常に北を～す The compass always *points to* the north. 人を指で～すのは失礼だ It is rude to *point at* others. きみのことを～しているのではない I don't *mean* you. / I don't *hint at* you. 先生は生徒を順番に～した The teacher *called on* his students in turn. 京都を～して出発した We left *for* Kyoto. 将棋を～そうか Shall we *play* Japanese chess ? だれの～す番だ Whose *turn* is it ? もう～す手がない I have no chance to *move* my piece.

さ·す【射す】 ¶ この部屋は一日じゅう日が～している The sunlight *shines into* this room in all the daytime. 雲間からときどき日が～す The sunlight *breaks* now and then *through* the clouds.

さ·す【挿す】 ¶ 花びんに花を～す *put* flowers in the vase. 上着のえりに赤い羽根を～している wear a red feather on *one's* lapel.

さ·す【差す】 ¶ 機械に油を～す *oil* a machine. 目薬を～す *put* a drop of medicine (≒ eye lotion) into *one's* eyes. 彼女の顔に赤みが～した Her face *was tinged with* red. / (はにかむ) She *turned* a little scarlet. 潮が～す The tide *rises*.

さすが【遉·流石】 ¶ ～名人だけあってみごとだ He is so good as to *deserve to* be called a master. ～は大選手だ He is *truly* a great player. ～の大広場も人であふれた The square, *though* large, was crowded with people. それだけは～に言い出せなかった I couldn't speak of it, *though*.

さずかりもの【授かり物】 ¶ これは天からの～だ This is *a* heavenly *gift*. 子どもは神からの～だ The child is *a blessing*.

さずか·る【授かる】 ¶ 私は3人の子どもを～っている I'*m blessed with* three children. 彼は功績に対し勲章を～った He *was awarded* a medal for his merit.

さず·ける【授ける】 ¶ 女王は士官に勲章を～けた The Queen *awarded* the officer a medal. 彼は弟子に秘伝を～けた He *taught* the secret to his disciple.

ザスペンス suspense. ¶ ～に満ちた物語 a very *thrilling* story ; a story full of *suspense*. その物語は私には最後の最後まで～に満ちていた The story kept me in *suspense* till the very end.

さすらい【流離·漂泊】 ¶ ～の旅 a *wandering* journey. 彼は～の旅から帰ってきた He returned from his *wanderings*.

—人 a wanderer.

さすら·う【流離う·漂泊う】 wander ; roam. ¶ 彼は田舎をあてもなく～った He *wandered over* the country. (wander に「あてもなく」の意味が入っているので wander のあとに aimlessly はなくてもよい).

さす·る【摩る·擦る】 (こする) rub ; (なでる) pat ; stroke. ¶ ほっとして胸を～った I gave a sigh of relief. 背中を～ってもらった I *had* my back *rubbed*. (英米人はあまりしない行為). 犬の頭を～ってやった I *patted* a dog on the head.

ざせき【座席】 a seat. ¶ ～におつきください Take *a seat, please*. / Please be seated. 彼は老人に～を譲った He gave *a seat* 〔up〕 to an old man. ～を予約しましたか Have you reserved *a seat*? まだ100人分の〜がある There are a hundred *seats* more. 彼は〜についたままだった He *kept seated*. / He *sat* on a chair. (sit は「座席についている」(状態)の意味が普通.「座席につく」(行為)は sit down という).

させつ【左折】¶ 十字路を〜する *turn* 〔*to the*〕 *left* at the crossing (to the はほとんど用いない).

ざせつ【挫折】failure; collapse. ¶ 計画は途中で〜した The plan *has broken down* halfway.

-さ·せる (許可) let (*a person*) do; (強制) make (*a person*) do. ¶ 彼は息子を外出〜せた He *let* his son go out. 彼は娘に勉強〜せた He *made* his daughter study. 彼には好きなように〜せるがいい You may *let* him have his own way. 時計を修理〜せよう I will *have* my watch repaired. 彼にこの一節を訳〜せよう I will *have* him translate this passage. 子どもたちに部屋の掃除を〜せた He *made* his children sweep the room. 彼にいっさいを説明〜せなさい Try to *make* him explain the whole incident.

させん【左遷】relegation; degradation; demotion. ¶ 彼はあまり仕事をしないので〜された He *was demoted* as he did not do much work.

ざぜん【座禅】¶ 寺にこもって〜を組む *sit in meditation* in a temple.

さぞ【嘸】¶ 雨に降られて〜困ったでしょう Caught in the rain, you must have been troubled. 〜かし彼は喜んだでしょう *How* glad he must have been!

さそい【誘い】(招き) an invitation; (誘惑) temptation; enticement. ¶ 彼は〜に乗ってそうした He was tempted to do so. 〜のすき *faked* unguardedness.

さそいあ·う【誘い合う】¶ 仲間を〜って出席する *ask each other* to be present.

さそいだ·す【誘い出す】¶ 友だちを映画に〜した I *asked* a friend *to* go to the movies. ひとりの女がその子を外に〜した A woman *lured* the child *away* from home.

さそいみず【誘い水】pump priming. ¶ 彼の発言が〜となって(きっかけとなって)議論となった His utterance *led to* a discussion.

さそ·う【誘う】¶ いっしょに行こうと友を〜った I *asked* a friend *to* go with me. 彼の〜いでパーティーに出た I attended the party because he *asked* me *to*. 途中〜ってあげよう I'll *call for* you on the way. / (車で) Let me *pick* you *up* on the way. 6時ごろ〜うよ I'll *stop by for* you about six. 彼は少年を悪事に〜った He *tempted* a boy *to* do evil. その話は聞く人の涙を〜った The story *brought* tears to the listeners. / The story *moved* the listeners to tears. 彼の話しぶりは聴衆の眠りを〜った His speech *induced* the audience to sleep (文語体).

ざぞう【座像】a sitting statue.

さそく【左側】the left 〔-hand〕 side.

—通行(掲示) Keep left (米では右側通行, 英・ヨーロッパでは左側通行).

さそり【蠍】〔動物〕a scorpion.

—座 the Scorpion.

さそん【差損】a loss from the difference of quotations.

さた【沙汰】(命令) an order; directions; (通知・たより) 〔a〕 notice; information; news; (うわさ) a rumor; (事柄) an affair.

¶ 〜のあるまで待ったほうが賢明だ It would be wise of you to wait for *instructions*. 彼がそんなことを言うとは正気の〜ではない He cannot be *sane* (≒ *in the right mind*) to say so. 映画どころの〜ではない Movies are *out of the question*. 彼からはこの1週間なんの〜もない I *have heard nothing from* him for a week. 地獄の〜も金しだい(諺) *Money makes the mare* 〔*to*〕 *go*.

さだまった【定まった】¶ 〜書式 a *given* (≒ *regular*) form.

さだま·る【定まる】¶ 天候もこのごろ〜った The weather *is settled* these days.

さだめ【定め】(規定) a law; a rule; (運命) a fate; a destiny. ¶ この世の〜 the *fate* of this world. 法の〜に従う observe law.

さだめし【定めし】(きっと) surely; certainly; (たぶん) probably. ¶ ご両親も〜お喜びのことでしょう *I'm sure* your parents are very glad of it.

さだ·める【定める】¶ 目標を〜める *set up* a goal. 法の〜めるところにより *as provided* by law. そこにねらいを〜めてピストルを発射した I *aimed* and fired a pistol at it.

ざだん【座談】a conversation; a talk; a discussion (discussion は軽い談話の意味にも用いる). ¶ 彼は〜がうまい He *is a good talker*.

—会 a discussion meeting; (シンポジウム) a symposium.

さち【幸】¶ 海の〜, 山の〜 delicious food; marine and farm products. 〜多かれと祈ります I wish you *good luck*. / *Good luck!*

ざちょう【座長】the chairman; (女) the chairwoman (ただし呼びかけには男の場合は Mr. Chairman, 女には Madam Chairman という); 米 the moderator; (興行の) the proprietor. ¶ 彼は〜をつとめた He *was in the chair*. / He *took the chair*. 彼はシンポジウムの〜をつとめた He *presided at* the symposium. 彼を〜にして会議が開かれた A conference was held with him *in the chair*. / A conference was held under his *chairmanship*.

さつ【札】a bank note; 米 a bill; paper money. ¶ 1,000円〜 *a* thousand-yen *note*. 5ドルの〜 *a* five-dollar *bill*.

—束 a roll of notes. —入れ a pocketbook; a wallet.

-さつ【-冊】¶ 3〜の本(同じ本の) three copies; (異なる本の) three books. この百科事典はあと2〜で完結します This encyclopedia will be complete in two more *volumes*.

ざつ【雑】a miscellany. ¶ 〜な rough; rude; gross; (雑多な) miscellaneous. 彼は仕事が〜だ He *is careless with* his work. 彼は〜な文章を書く He writes in a *slipshod* style. このペンは出来が実に〜だ This pen is of quite a *cheap* make. 〜の部 miscellanies.

さ

さつい【殺意】¶彼は彼女にたいして～をいだいている He *intends to murder* her.

さつえい【撮影】photographing. ¶彼らを～した I *took a picture* (≒ *photograph*) of them. 別れのシーンを～した We *filmed* (≒ *shot*) the parting scene.

—技師 a cameraman. —所 a film (≒ movie) studio. 室内— indoor photographing. 夜間— night photographing.

ざつえき【雑役】odd jobs.

—夫 an odd〔-job〕man; a handy man. —婦 a maid of all work; [英](日雇いの) a charwoman.

ざつおん【雑音】〔a〕noise; (ラジオの) jarring and grating. ¶ラジオに～が入る The radio program is disturbed by *noises*.

さっか【作家】a writer; an author; (小説家) a novelist.

新進— a rising writer. 女流— a woman writer (≒ novelist).

ざっか【雑貨】general merchandise; (食料も含めて) groceries.

—商 grocery business; (人) a grocer. —店 [米] a general store (ふつうは drugstore で雑貨を売っている); [英] a general shop.

サッカー soccer; association football.

さつがい【殺害】killing; murder. ¶彼らは大統領の～を企てた They plotted the *murder* (≒ *assassination*) of the president.

さっかく【錯角】〔数学〕alternate angles.

さっかく【錯覚】an illusion; a hallucination. ¶ふるさとに帰ったような～に陥った I *felt as if* I was back again in my home town. 人人はこれが世界平和のかぎになると信じているが、それはたいへんな～だ People believe this will be the key to world peace, but that is *a* great *illusion*. 縦の線のほうが長く見えるのは目の～だ It is *an* optical *illusion* that the vertical line is seen to be longer.

ざつがく【雑学】¶彼は～の大家だ He is a *well-informed* man. / He *knows something of* (≒ *about*) *everything*.

さっかしょう【擦過傷】a scratch; an abrasion.

サッカリン saccharin〔e〕.

ざっかん【雑感】casual thoughts; miscellaneous impressions.

さっき【殺気】bloodthirstiness. ¶彼らは～だって彼に詰め寄った They drew closer to him *with blood in their eyes*. 会場には～がみなぎっていた There was great *excitement* prevailing all over the hall. 彼らは～だった群衆を静めることができなかった They could not calm down the *excited* crowd.

さっき【先】(すこし前) some time ago; a little (≒ short) while ago; (ちょうどいま) just now. ¶彼は～までこの部屋にいた He was in this room *a little time ago*. そのことについて～言ったばかりだ I mentioned the matter only *a little while ago* (≒ *a moment since*). ～うちに帰ってきたばかりだ I returned home *just now*.

さつき【皐月】〔植物〕an azalea.

ざっき【雑記】miscellaneous notes; miscellanies; (メモ) memo〔randum〕s.

—帳 a notebook. 身辺— a memoir; miscellaneous personal notes.

さっきゅう【早急】¶その問題の～な解決が望まれる The *immediate* solution of the problem is needed. / It's necessary to solve the problem *without delay* (≒ *as soon as possible*).

ざっきょ【雑居】¶一家に3世帯が～している There are three families *living together* in the same house.

さっきょく【作曲】〔musical〕composition. ¶これは彼の作詩～だ This is a song with both words and *music* by him. 彼はオペラを～している He *is writing* an opera. 彼は音楽を教えるし～もする He teaches music and also *composes*.

—家 a composer.

さっきん【殺菌】sterilization; disinfection; (低温殺菌) pasteurization.

—牛乳 sterilized (≒ pasteurized) milk.

サック (指の) a finger stall. ¶眼鏡の～ *a case* for spectacles (英語の sack は粉, 石炭などの袋で, 固いのは case).

ざっくばらん ¶～な批評を歓迎する *Outspoken* comments are welcome. ～に言えば to be *frank* 〔with you〕; *frankly* speaking. 彼は～な人柄だ He is an *outspoken* man. 彼女はなんでも～に言う女だ She *is outspoken* in her remarks. そのことについて～に話し合おう Let's talk about it *frankly*.

ざつけん【雑件】sundries; miscellaneous matters.

ざっこく【雑穀】〔minor〕cereals; [米]〔minor〕grain; [英]〔minor〕corn.

—商 a corn dealer.

さっこん【昨今】¶～はどうも生活しにくい *Nowadays* it is rather difficult to make a living. ～はそういう学者にめったにお目にかかれない Such scholars are rarely to be met with 〔in〕*these days*. (*in* をつけるのは古風な言い方).

ざっこん【雑婚】a mixed marriage; an intermarriage.

さっさと ¶～歩きなさい Walk *briskly* (≒ *quickly*). ～しろ *Be quick! / Hurry up!* 彼は～宿題をかたづけた He *made short work of* his homework. 退社時間が来ると彼はいつも～帰ってしまう When the closing hour comes round, he always *hurries to* leave his office.

サッシ a sash〔window〕.

アルミ— an aluminum sash.

さっし【察し】(推測) guess; (理解) understanding; (思いやり) consideration; 〔a〕sympathy.

¶彼は～がいい He *is understanding* (≒ *is sensible*; *is quick to see*). なんて～が悪い人間か How *insensible* (≒ *slow of understanding*) he *is*! ぼくが言わんとすることがなんだか～がつかないのか Can't you *make out* what I am going to say? お～のとおりです You are right〔in your *judgment*〕./You'*ve guessed* right.

さっし【冊子】 a pamphlet; a booklet.

ざっし【雑誌】(一般の) a magazine;(専門の) a journal;(定期刊行物) a periodical;(定期報告) a bulletin.

¶～を取る take〔in〕*a magazine*(困はほとんど in を用いない); subscribe to(≒ for) *a magazine*. ～に寄稿する write for *a magazine*.

―記者 a magazine editor; a journalist. 月刊(週刊)**―** a monthly (weekly) magazine (しばしば magazine を省く). 総合**―** a general magazine.

ざつじ【雑事】(日常の) routine; (家庭の) chores. ¶数か月前から日常の～に追われて忙しい I've been busy with *chores*(≒ *routine work*) for the past several months. ～はまず第一にかたづけるべきだ You must get through your *trifles* first. / The *miscellaneous affairs* should be disposed of before anything else. 彼女は家庭の～に追われて本を読む暇もない She is too busy with *domestic chores* to have time to read.

ざっしゅ【雑種】〔生物〕a cross; a hybrid; (特に犬) a mongrel. ¶～を作る cross (one breed) with (another); hybridize. ラバはロバと馬の～である A mule is *a hybrid* animal which is half donkey and half horse.

ざっしゅうにゅう【雑収入】 miscellaneous incomes; sundry receipts.

さっしょう【殺傷】 bloodshed. ¶強盗が3人を～した The burglar *killed and wounded* three persons.

ざっしょく【雑食】 **―**動物 an omnivorous animal.

さっしん【刷新】〔a〕reform;〔a〕renovation. ¶新政府は数々の根本的～を行なった The new government made radical *reforms*(≒ *innovations*).

さつじん【殺人】 murder. ¶～を犯す commit *murder*. 列車は～的混雑だ The train is *deadly*(≒ *terribly*) crowded. (terribly は女性が好んで用いる強意の副詞).

―罪 murder. **―事件** a murder case. **―犯** a murderer (女性形は a murderess); a killer; a homicide. **―未遂** an attempted murder. **―光線** deathray.

さっ·する【察する】 ¶～するところ彼は入学試験に落ちたらしい I *think* he has failed〔in〕the entrance examination. 彼のなまりから～すると九州出身にちがいない *Judging from*(≒ *by*) his accent, he must be from Kyushu. 彼の悲しみは～するにあまりある You can't *imagine* how grieved he is. / His grief *is beyond imagination*. 彼女の顔つきで彼はいっさいのようすを～した He *read* the whole story in her face(≒ look). お～しいたします *I* quite *sympathize with* you. / *I am sorry*. きみは彼の努力を～してやるべきだ You should *appreciate* his efforts.

ざつぜん【雑然】 ¶～とした部屋 a room *in disorder*; an *untidy* room. たくさんの参考書が机の上に～と積んである A lot of reference books are heaped *in a disorderly fashion* on the desk. ～と集めた資料はほとんど役に立たない The materials which are collected *indiscriminately* are of little use.

さっそう【颯爽】 ¶～たる姿で現われる appear in a *dashing* get up. 彼女はスキーを担いで～と出かけた She started out with skis on her shoulder *dashingly*(≒ *in high spirits*).

ざっそう【雑草】 weeds. ¶庭の～を取る *weed* a garden.

さっそく【早速】 at once; immediately; promptly; without delay.

¶～適当な対策を講じよう I'll take some proper measure〔to meet this situation〕*right away*. ～ですが, どんなご用件ですか Well, what do you want with me? I'd like you to come to the point at once. 彼が帰りしだい～お電話します I'll phone(≒ call) you *as soon as* he comes back. ～お聞き入れくださいまして恐縮です We're very much obliged to you for your kindness to grant our request *promptly*.

ざった【雑多】 ¶～な人々 *various kinds of* people.

さつたば【札束】 a stack of notes; a roll of bills.

ざつだん【雑談】 a gossip; a chat; an idle talk. ¶昔のことを～しながら楽しいひとときを過ごした We had *a* nice time *talking about* our old times. / We had *a* pleasant *chat* about old times for a little while.

さっち【察知】〔an〕inference. ¶事の真相を～する *perceive* the truth of a case.

さっちゅうざい【殺虫剤】 an insecticide; an insect powder.

¶～をまく sprinkle *an insect powder*(液体ならば *spray* a DDT solution のように spray を用いる).

さっと【颯と】 suddenly; (すばやく) quickly.

¶～水洗いする wash (*something*) *quickly*; give (*something*) a *quick* washing in water. 彼女は～顔を赤らめてうつむいてしまった She blushed and dropped her head. / She looked down with a blush. 彼は～ドアを開けると部屋に飛び込んできた *Flinging* the door *open*, he dashed into the room. ～風が吹いてきた There was *a gust of wind*. 彼は～軍を引き揚げた *All of a sudden* he withdrew his army.

ざっと【雑と】(大体) about; roughly; (概数) in round numbers; (あっさりと) lightly.

¶～20万円が必要だ *About* two hundred thousand yen is needed. 作家としての彼の月収は～50万円といわれる His income as a writer is *roughly* estimated at five hundred thousand yen a month. この絵は～見積もって30万円だ This painting is worth three hundred thousand yen by *rough* estimate. ビルの完成まで～3年かかった It took three years *or so* to complete the construction of the building. 私の野球は～こんなぐあいだ This is

さ

how I play baseball. 彼のエッセーに～目を通した I *glanced over* his essay.

さっとう【殺到】a rush; a flood. ¶ 出願者が事務所に～した Applicants *flooded* the office. 注文が～した There was *a flood* (≒ *a rush*) of orders. 方々から抗議の手紙が～した Letters of protest *poured in* from everywhere (≒ all quarters). 出口に人が～してけが人がいくらか出た People *rushed to* the exit, and some of them got hurt.

ざっとう【雑踏】a crowd. ¶ 休日の街はひどい～になる The streets *are* terribly *crowded* on holidays. / There are large *crowds* of people on the streets on a holiday. この時間, 駅はいつも～する The railroad stations *are* always *congested* with passengers at this time of the day.

さ

ざつねん【雑念】¶ ～を去る free *one's* mind from *worldly thoughts*.

ざっぱく【雑駁】¶ ～な議論 an *incoherent* argument. 彼は～な知識しか持ち合わせていない He is only a man of *patchy* (≒ *unsystematic*) knowledge.

さつばつ【殺伐】¶ ～とした事件 a *bloody* case. ～な気風 a *warlike* spirit. 世相が～になる There is a public tendency for people to *grow wild*. / People *are getting wild*.

さっぱり 1〚身なりが〛¶ きょうは～した身なりをしているね You are *neatly* dressed today, aren't you?

いつも身なりを～していなさい You should *be neat and tidy* at all times.

床屋に行って～していらっしゃい You must *have* your hair *trimmed* at the barber's.

2〚気分が〛¶ 言うだけ言ったら～した Now I have had my say, I *feel the easier* for it. よく寝たのでけさは気分が～している I slept soundly and *feel refreshed* this morning.

3〚性格が〛¶ 男は女と違って～しているからいい Men have the advantage of being more *open-hearted* than women.

あの人は性格が実に～している He is indeed a man of *frank* disposition.

いつまでもくよくよしないで～しろよ Don't worry so! *Cheer up!*

4〚あとになにも残らないようす〛¶ そう釈明されてもなんとなく～しない I *am not altogether satisfied with* your explanation.

彼女のことはきれい～あきらめろ Get her out of your thoughts. / Forget her.

5〚味が〛¶ あまり肉ばかり食べているので, なにか～したものが欲しい I've had too much meat, and want something *plain and simple*.

これは味が～していてうまい This food *is* very *light* and tastes good.

6〚全然〛¶ きみの言うことは～わからない I cannot understand you *at all*. / I cannot *make head or tail of* what you say.

ぼくの英語は～通用しなかった I could not make my English understood *at all*.

景気はどうだ. ～です How are you getting along in your business? Not too good.

このごろは～ですね Things *do not look promising*, do they?

ざっぴ【雑費】sundries; sundry (≒ miscellaneous) expenses.

さつびら【札びら】¶ ～を切る spend money freely; make money fly.

さっぷうけい【殺風景】¶ ～な生活 a *dull* (≒ *prosaic*) life. ～ななかめ a *dreary* sight; a *bleak* landscape.

ざつぶん【雑文】a literary miscellany; (複数形として) miscellanea.

—家 a miscellanist; a miscellaneous (≒ hack) writer. —集 miscellanea; miscellanies.

ざっぽう【雑報】miscellaneous news (≒ paragraphs); general news.

さつまいも【薩摩芋】a sweet potato.

ざつむ【雑務】routine work; miscellaneous business (≒ duties). ¶ このごろは～に追われて忙しい I am very busy with *one thing and another* these days. 先に～を処理しなさい Dispose of *routine business* first. (やや文語) / Get through your *odd jobs* first.

ざつよう【雑用】¶ ～で使い走りする go on errands to do *odd jobs*.

さつりく【殺戮】massacre ([mǽsəkər] と発音); slaughter; butchery. ¶ 原爆によって大量～を企てる attempt mass *slaughter* by atomic bombs. 戦闘のたびごとに大～が行なわれた Every battle resulted in *a* frightful *slaughter* (≒ *massacre*). 原住者は多くの移民を～した The natives *massacred* many of the settlers.

さて well; now; (話かわって一方) in the meantime; in the meanwhile.

¶ ～, それでは次の問題に移ろう *Well then*, let's discuss the next problem (≒ subject). ～, これには困った *Well*, that's the trouble. ～, 相談したいことがあるのだ *Now*, I have something to talk over with you.

さてい【査定】assessment. ¶ 財産を～する *assess one's* property. 税金を～する *assess* a tax. 土地は500万円と～された The estate *was assessed* at five million yen.

—価格 assessed value. —額 an assessment. —者 an assessor.

サディスト a sadist.

サディズム sadism.

さてお・く【さて置く】¶ なには～きこの仕事を仕上げてもらいたい I want you to finish this work *before everything else*. 冗談は～き, 事態の進展はどうですか *Joking aside*, how are the things going on? 向こうに着いたらなにを～きお手紙を差し上げます I'll write to you *before everything else* as soon as I get there.

さてさて well, well ...; (実に) how ...!; what ...!; Oh, dear!; indeed; truly.

¶ ～月日のたつのは早いものだ *Indeed* time flies like an arrow.

さてつ【砂鉄】〚鉱物〛iron sand.

さてつ【蹉跌】a setback. ¶ 彼は事業に～をきたした He *had a setback in* his business. これ

で学生運動は大きな～をきたすであろう This will *be a* serious *setback to* the student movement.

さては ¶ ～一杯食わされたか *Oh, dear!* I have been fooled! (Oh のあとにはコンマをつけるのがふつう. O はやや古い). ～あのとき助けてくれたのは彼だったのか *Oh,* it was he that helped me then. 彼はなだめたり, 哀願したり, ～おどしたりした He coaxed, implored *and finally* threatened me.

サテライト a satellite.

—スタジオ a satellite studio.

サテン satin.

さと【里】(村里) a village; (生地) *one's* home town; (田舎) the country.

¶ ～に帰る go into *the country* (必ず into を用いる. to は別の意味になる). 妻は今～に帰っている My wife is staying now with her parents. そんなことをするとお～が知れる That will betray your *origin* (≒ *character*).

さと·い【聡い】¶ 彼は目が～い He has *sharp* (≒ *keen*) vision. 彼は耳が～い He has a *sharp* ear. あの子はなかなか～い He is a very *clever* boy. (clever には「悪がしこい」の意味も加わることがある) / The child *is* very *bright*. (bright は子供に用いるのがふつう). 彼は利に～い He *is* very *keen on* the dollars. / He *is* very *alive to* his interests.

さといも【里芋】〔植物〕a taro.

さとう【砂糖】sugar. ¶ ～づけの果物 *candied* (≒ *sugared*) fruits. コーヒーに～をお入れしましょうか Would you like to have *sugar* in your coffee? 紅茶にいくつ～を入れますか How many *sugars* in your tea?

—きび sugar cane. —カエデ sugar maple. —大根 sugar beet. —ばさみ(食卓用) sugar tongs. 角— cube (≒ lump) sugar. ¶ 角～ひとつ a lump of sugar.

さどう【作動】¶ エンジンを～させる *start* an engine (start a car としても同じで, 車を走らせることにはならない). 機械を～させる *set* a machine *going*.

さどう【茶道】tea ceremony.

さとおや【里親】a foster parent; (父) a foster father; (母) a foster mother.

さとがえり【里帰り】¶ ～する make *one's* first call at *one's* old home after *one's* marriage.

さとご【里子】(受け入れたほうからいえば) a foster-child; (送り出したほうからいえば) a child put out to nurse. ¶ 彼は幼いとき母方の祖父母のところへ～に出された When he was very young, he *was put out to nurse* with his grandparents on the mother's side.

さとごころ【里心】homesickness. ¶ 外国に長くいるとだれでも～がつくものだ Everybody will *get homesick* when he stays long in a foreign country.

さと·す【諭す】¶ 彼が二度とそんなことをしないようにこんこんと～した I seriously *advised* him not *to* do such a thing again. もっと勉強するように彼に～した I earnestly *told* him *to* study harder.

さとり【悟り】spiritual awakening; understanding; comprehension. ¶ あの子は～のよい(悪い)子だ The child is quick (slow) of *comprehension*. その禅僧は若いときに～をひらいた The Zen priest *had spiritual awakening* (≒ *was spiritually enlightened*) when he was young.

さと·る【悟る】realize; understand; (察知する) read; (感づく) sense; (自分の悪いことに気づく) come to *one's* senses.

¶ 人は自分の義務を～るべきだ One should *be conscious of* one's duty. 彼は自分の過ちを～った He *found out* his own error. 真理を～るのは簡単ではない It is no easy matter to *perceive* the truth. ～ったようなことを言う人だ How wisely he talks! 人に～られぬように歩く walk so as not to *be noticed* by others. なんとか～られずに家を抜け出た I managed to escape from the house *unnoticed*.

サドル a saddle.

さなえ【早苗】rice sprouts; early sprouts of rice.

さながら【然乍ら·宛ら】¶ 彼はこじき～の姿をしていた He looked *just like* a beggar. 彼は～母国語のごとく英語を話す He speaks English *as if* it were his mother tongue.

さなぎ【蛹】(特にチョウの) a chrysalis (複 chrysalises, chrysalideslides); (一般的) a pupa (複 pupas, pupae).

さなだ【真田】—ひも a braid; a plait. —虫 a tapeworm.

サナトリウム a sanatorium (複 sanatoriums, sanatoria); (おもに 米) a sanitarium.

さのう【砂嚢】a sandbag; (鳥などの) a gizzard; a ventriculus (複 ventriculi).

さは【左派】the left wing (≒ faction) [of a political party]; (人) a leftist. ¶ 社会党～ *the leftwing* of the Socialist Party.

さば【鯖】〔魚類〕a mackerel (ふつう単複同形). ¶ 彼は～を読んだ He *counted less than* the actual number. / He *cheated* me *in counting*.

さはい【差配】(管理) agency; management; superintendence; (家屋などの) a house agent. ¶ ～する act as agent; manage; superintend.

—人 an agent.

さばき【裁き】judgment; decision. ¶ ～を下す decide; judge.

さばく【砂漠】a desert. ¶ サハラ～ the Sahara *Desert*; the *Desert* of Sahara.

さば·く【捌く】¶ この在庫品を～くのは容易ではない It's no easy matter to *sell* these goods in stock. 仕事が多すぎて～ききれない I have too many things to *do*.

さば·く【裁く】¶ 紛争(事件)を～く *pass judgment on* a strife (a case). 棺を覆うまで人を～くな Don't *pass judgment on* a man until he has died.

さばけた【捌けた】¶ 彼は～人だ He is *a man of the world*. 彼らはなかなか～人たちだ They are *sociable* people. きみはなかなか～ことを言う

You *talk sense*, don't you?

さば·ける【捌ける】sell; be sold. ¶この品はよく〜ける This article *sells* well. 彼の能弁のおかげで在庫品はたちまち〜けた Thanks to his eloquence, the goods in stock *were sold* at once.

さばさば ¶部屋の中がすっかりかたづいて〜した気持ちだ The room is set in perfect order and I*'ve felt refreshed in mind and body*.

さはんじ【茶飯事】¶そんなことは日常〜だ That's *a daily happening*. / That's *a matter of no importance*.

さ

さび【寂】sobriety. ¶〜のある声 a *trained* (≒ *seasoned*) voice. この庭にはだいぶ〜が感じられる This garden has quite *an antique* (≒ *sober*) *look*.

さび【錆·銹】rust. ¶〜がつく gather *rust*. ナイフの〜を落とす rub the *rust* off a knife. その刀は〜だらけだった The sword was eaten up with *rust*. 身から出た〜 You've made your bed, now lie in it.

さびし·い【寂しい】lonely; lonesome; deserted; dreary; (笑い顔などが) mirthless. ¶この辺はあまりにも〜い This neighborhood *is* too *lonely*. 彼は〜い顔をしている He looks *depressed* (≒ *lonely*). 彼女がいなくてたいへん〜い I *miss* her very much. この部屋には花がないのが〜い I *miss* the flowers in this room. その〜い公園を歩いている人がいた Someone was walking in the *deserted* park.

さびしさ【寂しさ】loneliness; lonesomeness; solitude.

さびどめ【錆止め】¶〜のため屋根にはペンキが塗られた The roof was painted to *prevent rust*〔*ing*〕.

ざひょう【座標】〘数学〙co-ordinates.
—軸 the co-ordinate axis.

さ·びる【錆びる】rust; become rusty. ¶このナイフはすぐ〜びる This knife *gathers rust* easily. 機械は長い間使わないと〜びつく A machine *becomes rusty* when it is not used long.

さび·れる【寂れる】decline; become desolate. ¶〜れた村 a *deserted* village. あの町は最近すっかり〜れてしまった The town *has fallen into decay* of late.

サファイア〘鉱物〙a sapphire.

ざぶざぶと with splashes. ¶〜冷水を体にかけた I *dashed* cold water *on* myself. 彼らは〜川を渡った They *paddled* in the water. 彼女は〜着物を洗濯した She washed her clothes in plenty of water.

サブタイトル a subtitle. ¶書物に〜をつける put *a subtitle* to a book. その映画の〜は「…」である The film bears the *subtitle* "…".

ざぶとん【座布団】a cushion. ¶〜を敷く(〜に座る) sit down on *a cushion*.

サフラン〘植物〙a saffron.

ざぶんと ¶〜水に飛び込んだ I *splashed into* the water.

さべつ【差別】〔a〕distinction; discrimination. ¶老若男女の〜なく without *distinction* of age and sex. あの店では常連とそうでない人を〜する At that store they *discriminate* between regular customers and strangers.
—待遇 discriminative treatment. —関税 differential duties. 人種— segregation; (黒人に対するもの) Jim Crow.

さほう【作法】〔rules of good〕manners; etiquette. ¶近ごろの若い人は〜を知らない Young people today *are ill-mannered*. / Young people today have no *manners*. 〜を習う learn good *manners*. お茶の〜 good *manners* in tea ceremony. そんなことをするのは〜に反することだ It's against *etiquette* to do such a thing. 彼女は厳格な〜をしつけられた She has been brought up in strict *etiquette*.
行儀— good manners. 不— a breach of etiquette.

さぼう【砂防】sand erosion control; sandbank fixing.
—工事 sand guard work; anti-sand erosion work. —ダム sand guard dam. —林 afforestation for sand erosion control.

サボテン〘植物〙a cactus (複 cactuses; cacti); a prickly pear. ¶〜のとげ a *cactus* needle (≒ prickle; spine).

さほど【然程·左程】¶それは〜だいじなことではない That's not *very* important. 彼の病気は〜ひどくはない He is not *so very* ill.

サボ·る ¶仕事を〜る *neglect one's* work. 学校を〜る *play truant from* school (英語の sabotage は, 労働争議で労働者が機械類を壊したりして, 生産妨害をすることをいう).

ザボン〘植物〙a shaddock; (小形のもの) a grapefruit.

さま【様】(人名につける敬語) (男性には) Mr. (複 Messrs.); (既婚女性には) Mrs. (複 Mmes.); (未婚女性には) Miss (複 Misses).
¶中村〜 Mr. Nakamura (太郎様, 花子様のような個人名には Mr., Miss などはつけない). おとう〜 Father.

さま【様】a state; condition; appearance. ¶彼女は子どもたちの喜ぶ〜を見て涙を流した She shed tears to see her children pleased. 彼とは〜を異にしているのだ My *condition* is quite different from his.

ざま【様·態】¶〜見ろ *Serve you right!* その〜はなんだ *Shame on you!* ふりかえり〜なぐられた *As soon as* I looked back I was struck.

サマー summer.
—スクール a summer school. —スーツ a summer suit. —タイム 英 summer time; 米 daylight-saving time.

さまざま【様様】¶〜の理由 *various* reasons. 〜の物 *all sorts of* things. 人の心は〜だ So many people, so *many* minds.

さま·す【冷ます】¶湯を〜す *cool* hot water. この薬は熱を〜す This medicine *reduces* fever. 熱意を〜す *cool a person's* enthusiasm (*for*).

さま·す【覚ます·醒ます】¶昨夜夜中に変な物音で目を〜した In the middle of last night I *was waked*〔*up*〕by a strange sound. ゆうべは何

度も目を～した Last night I *had a broken sleep*. 一晩じゅう目を～したまま床の中で横になっていた I lay *awake* in bed all night. その失敗は彼の夢を～した The failure *disillusioned* him *from* his dreams. / The failure *awakened* him *from* his illusions. 彼は今風に吹かれて酔いを～している He is now standing in the breeze to *make himself sober*.

さまたげ【妨げ】〔a〕hindrance ;〔an〕obstruction ;〔an〕interference. ¶ 迷信は進歩への～となる Superstition is *a hindrance* (≒ *a bar*) *to* progress. 病気は働きの～になる Sickness *prevents* one *from* working. テレビは勉強の～になる Watching television *disturbs* us *in* our studies.

さまた·げる【妨げる】 ¶ 彼の勉強を～げないように注意しなさい You must take care not to *disturb* him *in* his studies. きみの成功を～げるものはなにもない There is no *obstacle* in the way of your success. / Nothing *stands in the way of* your success. 大雪が汽車の運行を～げた The heavy snowfall *checked* the progress of the train. 会長の再任は～げない The president *may* be reappointed.

さまよ·う【彷徨う】 ¶ 道に迷って山中を～った I lost my way and *wandered* in the mountains. 彼はときどき当てもなく町を～い歩くことがあった He would often *wander* about the streets aimlessly. ～えるオランダ人 Flying Dutchman.

さみだれ【五月雨】 early summer rain. ¶ ～のころ in *the rainy season*. ～がしとしとと降っている *Early summer rain* is falling gently.

さむ·い【寒い】 cold ; chilly. ¶ きょうはかなり～い It's very *cold* today. ことしの冬は～い We have a *severe* winter this year. / It's *been* very *cold* this winter. たいへんお～くなりました It's *getting colder*. / The *cold* days have come. 夜が～くて寝られない The nights *are* so *cold* that I can't get to sleep easily. ～いね How *cold* it *is* ! / Bitterly *cold*, isn't it ? お～い社会福祉政策 a *poor* policy for the welfare of society.

さむがり【寒がり】 ¶ 私はすごい～だ I *am* exceedingly *sensitive to the cold*.

さむが·る【寒がる】 ¶ ここでは夏でも～る人が多い Many people here *are sensitive to the cold* even in summer.

さむけ【寒け】 a chill. ¶ 夜中に急に～がした I had sudden *rigor* in the night. 少し～がする I have *a* slight *chill*.

さむさ【寒さ】〔the〕cold ; (冬) winter. ¶ 厳しい～ *the* intense *cold*. ～に耐える stand *the cold*. ～を防ぐ protect *one*self from *the cold*. ここは冬でも～知らずだ The winter *is mild* here. (冬に温かいのは warm とは言わない). ことしは30年来の～だそうだ It is said that this is *the severest* winter we have had for thirty years. ぼくは～に弱い I *am* very *sensitive to the cold*. 子供たちは～にふるえていた The children were shivering with *cold*.

さむざむ【寒寒】 ¶ ～とした desolate ; bleak.

さむぞら【寒空】 ¶ ～の下で under *the wintry sky*. 彼はこの～に着る物もない He has no clothes in *cold weather*.

さむらい【侍】 a *samurai* ; a warrior.

さめ【鮫】〔魚類〕a shark.
—皮 sharkskin. **—膚** goose skin.

さめざめ ¶ ～と泣く cry *bitterly*.

さ·める【冷める】 cool. ¶ コーヒーが～めた The coffee *has got cold*. ～めないうちにあがってください Eat it before it *cools off*, please. 彼の野球も熱が～めた He *has lost interest in* baseball. 試合の興奮はまだ～めていない The excitement of the match *has* not *abated*. 日本人は熱しやすく～めやすいといわれる The Japanese are reputed to be *fickle* people.

さ·める【褪める】（色が主語で）go off ; fade away ;（物が主語で）lose color. ¶ この表紙の色はすぐ～める The color of this cover will easily *go off* (≒ *fade away*). この着物は色が～めない This dress will not *lose color*. この色は洗っても～めない This color will *stand washing*. この生地は洗っても～めない This fabric will *wash*.

さ·める【覚める·醒める】（目が）wake up ;（酔いが）become sober ;（迷夢から）be disillusioned ; be awakened.
¶ 目が～める wake up ; awake. 眠りから～める *awake from one's* sleep. 目の～めるような美人 a woman of *dazzling* beauty. すっかり酔いが～めた I'*m* quite *sober* now. 失敗してやっと彼も目が～めた Failure *disillusioned* him *from* his dreams. / Failure *awakened* him *from* his illusions.

さも【然も】 ¶ ～ありなん Quite possible ! / It ought to be *so*. / It's quite natural that it should be *so*. 彼女は～うれしそうに笑った She smiled with *evident* satisfaction. 彼は～なんでも知っているようなことを言う He talks *as if* he knew everything.

さもし·い ¶ ～い根性 a *mean* mind. いくら貧乏してもそんな～いことはできない However poor I may be, I am above such *meanness*.

ざもと【座元】 the proprietor of a theater.

さもないと【然も無いと】 or ; otherwise ; if not. ¶ タクシーで行きなさい，～まにあわないから Take a taxi, *or* (≒ *otherwise*) you will not be in time. (or の代わりに otherwise を用いると少し形式ばった形になる).

サモワール a samovar.

さもん【査問】 inquiry ; inquisition. ¶ 関係者を呼んで～する collect all the parties concerned and *inquire into* the matter.
—委員会 an inquiry commission.

さや【莢】 a pod ; a shell ; a husk. ¶ 豆の～をむく *shell* peas.

さや【鞘】（刀の）a sheath. ¶ 刀を～に収める put a sword back in the *sheath* ; *sheathe* a sword. 夫婦げんかを元の～に収める make up a quarrel between man and wife. (夫婦げんかが)元の～に収まる be reconciled. ～を取ってかせぐ get a margin.

さやえんどう【英豌豆】〔植物〕peas.
さゆ【白湯】hot water.
さゆう【左右】right and left. ¶ ～をよく見て渡れ Look *right and left* carefully and cross the street. 船が～にゆれた A ship rolled *right and left*. 世論を～することはできない It is impossible to *sway* the tide of public opinion. 人の言に～されるな Don't let others *influence* you. 人は境遇に～される Man *is influenced* by circumstances. / Man is a creature of circumstances.
ざゆう【座右】¶ ～の銘 a motto. ～の書 *one's deskside* (≒ *favorite*) book. 彼は聖書を～に備えている He has the Bible *at his elbow*.
さよう【然様】(その通り) so; yes; indeed; (間投詞) well; let me see. ¶ 彼に～お伝えください Please tell him *so*. ～なことは聞いたこともございません I haven't heard *such a thing*.
さよう【作用】action; operation; 〔a〕 function; process. ¶ この機械は電気の～によって動く This machine is operated by the *action* of electricity. 放射能の人体に及ぼす～ the *action* of radioactivity on the human body.
相互── 〔an〕 interaction. 同化── assimilation. 反── 〔a〕 reaction. 副── a subsidiary ill effect.
さようなら【然様なら・左様なら】good-by〔e〕. (adieu, farewell などは古い用法. 親しい間では See you. とだけ言うことが多い). ¶ みなさん, ～ *Good-by*〔*e*〕, everybody! 彼に～を言おう Let's say *good-by*〔*e*〕 to him. ～も言わずに行ってしまった He left without even saying *good-by*〔*e*〕 to us. ではあすまで～ See you tomorrow. (Good morning., Good evening., Good afternoon. なども, 語尾を下げて言うとイギリスでは「さようなら」の意味を表わす).
さよく【左翼】(隊形の) a left wing; (政治・思想の) the left wing; (人) a left winger; (野球) the left field.
──作家 a leftist writer. ──思想 leftism. ──手(野球) the left fielder. ──運動 the leftist movement. ──団体 a leftist organigation.
さより【細魚】〔魚類〕a halfbeak.
さら【皿】(深皿) a dish; (平皿) a plate; (大皿) a platter; (はかりの) a scale. (紅茶などの受け皿) a saucer.
¶ 野菜ひと～ *a dish* of vegetables. 5～の料理 a five-*course* dinner. 食後の～洗いは私の仕事だ It's my job to wash the *dishes* after a meal. 目を～のようにしてそれを捜しまわった We looked about for it *with our eyes wide open*.
さら new. ¶ ～の new.
さらいげつ【再来月】the month after next.
さらいしゅう【再来週】the week after next.
さらいねん【再来年】the year after next.
さら・う【浚う・渫う】¶ 家の前のみぞを～わねばならない We have to *clear out* the open ditch in front of our house. その川は～う必要がある The river wants *dredging*. 川を～って犯人の捨てたレーンコートを捜した We *dragged* the river for the raincoat which the criminal had thrown away into it.
さら・う【攫う】(持ち去る) carry off; (誘かいする) kidnap. ¶ 犯人は子どもを～ったもよう The criminal seems to *have kidnapped* the child. 彼はひとりで学芸会の人気を～った He *monopolized* popularity on that day of school theatricals. 彼は賞品を全部～っていった He *carried off* all the prizes. / All the prizes fell to him. 彼は大波に足を～われた He *was carried off* his feet by a large wave.
ざらがみ【粗紙】rough paper.
さらけだ・す【曝け出す】¶ 彼は私の秘密を皆の前に～そうとした He tried to *disclose* (≒ *lay bare*) my secret in company. 自己の無知を～すのはなかなかつらいことだ It is quite hard for us to *have* our ignorance *exposed* (≒ *revealed*). なにもかも～してしまったほうがいい You had better *confess* everything.
さらさ【更紗】〔cotton〕 print; chintz.
インド── India print.
さらさら【更更】not at all; in the least.
¶ そんな下心は～ない I have *no* such secret desires *whatever* (≒ *at all*). いやだなどとは～思っていない I have *not the least* intention to refuse it.
さらさら〔と〕 (風の音が) sough; (木の葉の音が) rustling; (水の音が) murmuring; (すらすらと書く) fluently; readily. ¶ きのうの雪は～とした軽い雪だった The snowflakes which fell yesterday were as *fine* and light as dry sand. (fine は「細かい」の意味). 昔この辺に小川が～と流れていた Many years ago there used to be a brook *murmuring* down around here. 木の葉が～と音をたてた The leaves of trees *rustled*. その外国人は筆をとって～と日本字を書いた The foreigner took up a pen, and wrote down some Japanese characters *with great* (≒ *amazing*) *ease*. / The foreigner wrote down some Japanese characters *with a facile pen*.
ざらざら ¶ 表が～した板 a board with a *rough* surface. 砂ぼこりで机の上が～だ The surface of the desk *feels rough* with dust. 彼女は袋の豆を～とあけた She emptied a bag of beans *with a rattling sound*.
さらし【晒し・曝し】(漂白) bleaching; (さらした布) bleached cotton (≒ cloth). ¶ ～のじゅばん an undershirt of *bleached cotton*.
──首 a gibbeted (≒ an exposed) head. ¶ ～首にする gibbet a head. ──粉 bleaching powder. ──者 a pilloried criminal; a criminal exposed to public view. ──木綿 bleached cotton.
さら・す【晒す・曝す】(漂白する) bleach; (風雨に) expose; (暴露する) expose. ¶ 布を薬品で～す *bleach* cloth in chemicals. 現場では多くの危険に身を～して作業をしていた They were at work on the spot, *exposed to* many dangers. 風雨に～されて壁の色があせた Wind and rain have faded the color of the wall.
サラダ 〔a〕 salad.
──オイル salad oil. 野菜── a vegetable salad.

ざらつ·く ¶このキャンデーは舌に～く This candy *feels rough to* the tongue. 砂ぼこりで家中～いている Every nook and corner of the house *is dusty* (≒ *is covered with dirt and dust*).

さらに【更に】 ¶～精進してください I expect you to make *further* efforts. それについて思い当たることは～ない I have *not the slightest* idea of it. / It reminds me of nothing *at all*.

ざらに ¶それくらいの誤りは～ある Such mistakes *are very common* (≒ *are by no means rare*). そんな花は～はない That kind of flower *is very rare* (≒ *is rarely to be found*).

さらばかり【皿秤】 a balance.

サラブレッド a thoroughbred (馬の場合は語頭を大文字ではじめるのが普通). ¶彼は実業界の～といわれている He is said to be *a thoroughbred* in the business circles.

ざらめ【粗目】 〔unrefined〕 granulated (≒ crystallized) sugar (granulated sugar はざらめといっても日本のもののような大きな結晶でないが, さらりとしている).

サラリー a salary. ¶彼は月8万円の～をもらっている He gets *a salary* of eighty thousand yen a month. / He *is paid* eighty thousand yen a month.

—マン a salaried man; a white-collar worker.

さらりと (すんなりと) smoothly; easily; (まったく) entirely; altogether. ¶この生地は～した膚触りだ This cloth feels *smooth*. 彼女は～した性格の持ち主だ She is a woman of 〔a〕 *frank* disposition. そんな記事は～読んで済ましておいたほうがいい You had better *glance down* (≒ *skim over*) such an article. けんかのことなど～忘れてしまっている I have forgotten *all* about the quarrel. 彼は相手の抗議を～受け流すのが得意だった He was dexterous in *evading* (≒ *parryring*) the protest of his opponent. たばこは～やめられるものではない We cannot *entirely* quit smoking.

サリー (インドの女性の着る) a sari.

さりがた·い【去り難い】 ¶その場を～い気持ちだった I *felt it hard to leave* the spot.

ざりがに【蝲蛄】〘動物〙 a crawfish; a crayfish.

さりげな·い【然り気ない】 ¶彼女は～くふるまった She behaved *indifferently* (≒ *as if she cared nothing about it*). 彼らは～いようすでその家に出入りした They frequented the house *as if they had nothing to do with the matter*.

サリチルさん【サリチル酸】 salicylic acid.

サリドマイド〘薬学〙 thalidomide.

—児 a thalidomide baby.

さる【猿】 a monkey; (類人猿) an ape.

¶～のような monkey-like; monkeyish. ～の人まね *A monkey* will mimic a man. ～も木から落ちる(諺) *Even Homer sometimes nods*.

さ·る【去る】 **1** 〘ある場所から行ってしまう〙 leave. ¶彼はこの世を～った He *departed from* this life. / He *passed away*. (上品な言い方).
彼女はそう言ってその場を～った So saying, she *left* the place.
職場を～らねばならぬ日がきた The day has come for me to *quit my job*. / The day has come for me to *resign from my office*. (ていねいな言い方).
多くの借財を残して彼は大阪を～った He *left* Osaka, leaving a huge debt behind him.

2 〘行ってしまう〙 ¶～る者は追わず If they want to *go*, let them go. (諺ではない. cf. Welcome the coming, speed the parting guest. (ホーマーのことばの英訳)).
～る者は日々に疎し(諺) *Out of sight, out of mind*.
あらしは～った The storm *has passed*. / The storm *is over*.
冬～り春きたる Winter *is over*; spring is here. (cf. For, lo, the winter is past, ...the time of the singing of birds is come. (聖書のことば).
ひとりふたりと～ってゆき, 最後に彼女と私だけになってしまった One by one the people *left* and soon I was alone with her.
10年の月日があっという間に～っていった Ten years *passed* in a twinkling.

3 〘消滅する〙 ¶危険は～った Now the danger *has passed* (≒ *is gone*).
一難～ってまた一難 (諺) *Out of the frying pan into the fire*. / Hills peep o'er hills and Alps on Alps arise. (Pope のことば).
その疑いがなかなか念頭から～らなかった The doubt *haunted* (≒ *lingered in*) my mind.
ひどい痛みは～りましたが, まだ起きられない The sharp (≒ severe) pain *is gone*, but I still can't leave my bed.

4 〘隔たる〙 ¶この案は理想を～ることはなはだしい This plan *is far from* ideal. / The plan *leaves a lot to be desired*.
サンフランシスコを～ること西へ30マイルの地点を飛行中です We are flying over a point thirty miles west of San Francisco.

5 〘過ぎた·前の〙 ¶会は～る10日に行なわれた The assembly was held on the tenth *of this month*.
今を～る10年前のきょう, ぼくは初めて東京に来た Ten years *ago* today, I came to Tokyo for the first time.
彼は～5月に死んだ He died *last* May.

さる【然る】 (ある) a certain. ¶～人の話ではこうだった According to *a certain* person, it was so. それは～所での出来事であった It happened at *a certain* place.

ざる【笊】 a bamboo basket.

—そば *soba* served on a wickerwork bamboo plate. **—碁** an unskillful *go*-playing.

さるぐつわ【猿轡】 a gag. ¶強盗に～をかまされた The burglar put *a gag* in my mouth. / I *was gagged* by the burglar.

さるしばい【猿芝居】 a monkey show.
¶ばかな～はよせ Don't resort to such *a shal-*

low trick. / Don't make such a *transparent* (≒ *thin*) excuse.

さるすべり【猿滑り・百日紅】〔植物〕a crape myrtle.

さるぢえ【猿知恵】¶それは～というものだ It might be called *shallow cunning* (≒ *shallow craftiness*).

サルチルさん【サルチル酸】〔薬品〕salicylic acid.

さるのこしかけ【猿の腰掛け】〔植物〕a shelf fungus.

サルバルサン〔薬品〕salvarsan.

サルビア〔植物〕a salvia ; a sage.

サルファざい【サルファ剤】〔薬品〕sulfa.

サルベージ salvage.

―船 a salvage boat.

さるほどに【然るほどに】(やがて) by and by ; (その間) meanwhile ; in the meantime.

さるまた【猿股】shorts ; underpants ; briefs. ⇒パンツ

さるまね【猿真似】an awkward imitation ; an act of apish mimicry.

さるまわし【猿回し】a monkey leader (≒ showman).

さるもの【然るもの】¶彼も～だ He is *somebody*. 敵も～だった The enemy was *no mean* adversary.

ざれうた【戯れ歌】a comic song.

されき【砂礫】pebbles.

サロン(客間) a *salon* ; 米 (酒場の意味で) a saloon ; (マレー人などの腰巻き) a sarong.

さわ【沢】(沼地) a swamp ; a marsh ; (谷間) a valley.

さわかい【茶話会】a tea party (ふつう午後に催されるもの. tea を強く読む).

さわがし・い【騒がしい】¶休み時間の教室は～い The classroom *is* very *noisy* at recess. / The children *make a noise* in the classroom during a break. 世間がだんだん～くなってきた More and more *unrest* is prevailing in the world.

さわが・せる【騒がせる】disturb; make a stir ; create a sensation. ¶世間を～せた事件だった It was a *sensational* affair. / The incident *caused* (≒ *created*) *a great sensation* (≒ *stir*) in the world. 子どもたちをあんなに～せておくなんて彼女もずいぶん無神経だ How careless she is to leave her children *making such a noise*! 敵軍はその国の北辺を～せた The enemy *disquieted* (≒ *molested*) the northern frontier of the coutnry.

さわぎ【騒ぎ】an uproar ; a sensation. ¶～が起こった There occurred *an uproar*. グラウンドは大～だった The whole ground was in *an uproar*. この～はなんですか What is this *noise* (≒ *row*) about? その知らせで社内は大～になった The news created *a sensation* in the office. ～は静まりそうにない It seems difficult to restore quietness. 笑うどころの～ではない It is no laughing matter.

さわぎた・てる【騒ぎ立てる】¶～てたら, どろぼうは逃げた When we *made an outcry* the thief ran away. / Because we *raised an alarm*, the thief vanished. つまらぬことで世間は～てている The world *is making a great fuss* about a trifle. ヘビが出たと言って～てた They *cried* snake. / They *gave* (≒ *raised* ; *uttered*) *a cry* of "Snake!"

さわ・ぐ【騒ぐ】¶～ぐな Don't *be noisy*. / Keep quiet. 彼はよくつまらぬことに～ぐ He often *makes a fuss* about trifling things. 学生たちは教室で～いだ The students *made a noise* in the classroom. 酒を飲んで～ぐのは感心しない I don't think it praiseworthy to *have a drinking spree*. 賃銀の値上げを要求して～いでいる They *are clamoring* for a raise in pay. ふたりの結婚は大いに新聞で～がれた Their marriage *was writtten up* in the newspapers. 彼は～がずじっとしていた He remained silent with composure.

ざわざわ rustling. ¶会場が～した There was *a general stir* (≒ *restlessness*) in the audience of the hall. 木の葉が風で～していた The leaves 〔of trees〕 *were rustling* in the breeze.

ざわつ・く be noisy ; (木の葉が) rustle. ¶教室内が～いていた There was *a commotion* in the classroom. 彼が現われたので, ～いた気分が一掃された His appearance made them quiet. / His appearance calmed them down.

ざわめき a stir ; 〔a〕 commotion ; noises. ¶あちこちから～が起こった There arose *a stir* here and there. 木の葉の～が聞こえる The leaves are heard *rustling*.

ざわめ・く ¶彼の発言に一瞬会場は～いた His utterance caused *a* momentary *stir* among the audience.

さわやか【爽やか】¶～な初秋の朝であった It was a *refreshing* morning in early autumn. 心身ともに～な気分になった I *felt refreshed* in mind and body. / It *refreshed* me in body and mind. 彼は弁舌～に演説した He made an *eloquent* speech.

さわら【椹】〔植物〕a Japan cypress.

さわら【鰆】〔魚類〕a *sawara* ; a Spanish mackerel.

さわり【触り】(義太夫の高潮場面) an emotional passage ; (話のポイント) the point of a story. ¶その歌の～のところだけ聞かせてください Please sing me only *the most moving* (≒ *impressive*) *passages* of the song.

さわり【障り】(悪い影響) a bad effect ; (害) harm ; (故障) 〔a〕 hindrance. ¶小説を読むのもいいが, 勉強の～にならない程度にしなさい You may read novels, but not to the extent that it *interferes with* your studies.

さわ・る【触る】touch ; feel. ¶指で～って調べてみた I *felt* it with my fingers to examine it. だれかが肩に～るのを感じた I felt someone *touch* me on the shoulder. 足になにか～った I *felt a touch* on my foot. ～らぬこと(掲示) Hands off. / Don't *touch*. ～らぬ神にたたりなし(諺) *Let sleeping dogs lie*.

さわ・る【障る】¶夜ふかしは体に～る It *is bad*

for your health to sit up late at night. 人の気に～るようなことは言うな Don't say anything that will *offend* (≒ *hurt*) others. どうもあのことがしゃくに～ってしかたがない That is the cause of my *offense*. / I cannot but *feel offended* (≒ *vexed*) *at* it. (文語体). この種の仕事はひどく神経に～る This kind of work *gets on* (≒ *is trying to*) my nerves.

さわん【左腕】 ━投手 a southpaw; a left-handed pitcher.

さん【三】 three; (第3) the third. ¶ ～度 three times; thrice (thrice は古語またはインドで用るいのみ). 第～に thirdly; in the third place. 第～者 a third person. ～分の1 a (≒ one) third. 5分の～ three-fifths.

さん【産】 1 〖出産〗〔a〕 childbirth. ¶ 初めてのお～なので妻は実家に帰っている My wife has gone home to her parents for her first *childbirth*.

お～は女の大役だ *Childbearing* is an important role for women.

お～は軽かった(重かった) She had *an* easy (*a* difficult) *delivery*.

彼女はこの6月にお～だ She *is expecting* in June.

彼女はアメリカから帰る途中船の中でお～をした She *gave birth* on board while coming back from America.

彼女はお～で死んだ She died in *childbed*.

2 〖出身〗 ¶ 彼は熊本の～だ He *is* (≒ (口語) *hails*) *from* Kumamoto. / He *was born in* Kumamoto.

3 〖産出〗 ¶ 日本～の米 Japanese-*grown* rice.

静岡～のミカンはおいしい Oranges *from* Shizuoka taste good.

このテレビは国～だ This is a home-*manufactured* TV set.

外国～の米は内地～のに比べ品質が劣る Imported rice is not so good as home-*grown* rice. / Imported rice is inferior in quality to home-*grown* rice.

これは青森～のリンゴだ These apples *came* (≒ *come*) *from* Aomori.

これはアフリカ～のライオンだ This is an African lion.

4 〖財産〗 a fortune. ¶ 彼は医薬品で～をなした He made *a fortune* by selling medical supplies.

彼は土地ブームで一躍～をなした He amassed *a great fortune* during the land boom.

彼はその事業に～を傾けた He exhausted his *fortune* in that enterprise.

さん【算】 ¶ 敵は～を乱して逃げまどった The enemy fled *in disorder* (≒ *in confusion*).

さん【酸】 an acid. ¶ ～性の acid. ～味 acidity. この金属は～に弱い This metal is easily affected by *acids*.

さん【桟】 (戸の) a bolt; (障子の) a frame. ¶ ～をおろす *bolt* the door. ～をはずす *unbolt* the door.

さん【惨】 ¶ ～たる(場面が) disastrous; frightful.

さん【賛】 praise; eulogy; a legend. ¶ 絵に～をする write *a legend* on the picture.

-さん【-山】 ¶ 富士～ *Mt.* Fuji.

-さん【-様】 (男性に対して) Mr.; (既婚の女性に対して) Mrs.; (未婚の女性に対して) Miss ¶ 加藤～ *Mr.* (≒ *Mrs.*; *Miss*) Kato (原則として家族名にのみ用いる).

さんい【賛意】 ¶ 出席者の大半がその案に～を表した The greater part of those present expressed (≒ gave) *assent* (≒ *approval*) *to* the plan. / Most of those present supported (≒ assented to) the plan.

さんいつ【散逸】 ¶ 文化財の～を防ぐ努力をすべきだ Efforts should be made to prevent cultural properties from *being scattered and lost*. 戦災で貴重な資料が～した The war damage *made* the precious data *gone to be lost*.

さんいん【参院】 (参議院) the House of Councillors.

さんいん【産院】 a maternity hospital.

さんか【参加】 participation. ¶ サマーセミナーに～する *participate in* (≒ *take part in*) a summer seminar. オリンピックは～することに意義がある The significance of the Olympiad is to *participate in* the Games. / It is more important to *participate* than to win *in* the Olympic Games. その会合に有志として～した I *joined* the party as a volunteer. ハイキングにはクラス全員が～した All the class *took part in* the hiking.

━者 a participant. ¶ 100メートル競走の～者は9人いた The one hundred meter race had nine *entries*.

さんか【産科】 obstetrics.

━医 an obstetrician. ━婦人科 obstetrics and gyn〔a〕ecology.

さんか【惨禍】 calamity; a disaster; ravage. ¶ 原爆の～は目を覆うばかりだ The *great damage* (≒ *ravage*) by the atomic bomb is too horrible to be seen.

さんか【酸化】 oxidation. ¶ この金属は～しやすい This metal *is oxidizable*. / This metal easily *oxidizes*.

━アルミニウム an oxide of aluminium. ━カルシウム an oxide of calcium. ━剤 an oxidizer. ━物 an oxide. 一━炭素 carbon monoxide. 二━炭素 carbon dioxide. ━鉄 oxidized steel; oxide of iron.

さんか【賛歌】 ¶ 愛の～ *a song in praise* of love. クリスマス～ *a* Christmas *carol*.

さんか【傘下】 ¶ ～の労組 *affiliated* (≒ *subsidiary*) labor unions. その社はその～に50以上の子会社を持つ大会社である The company is very big with more than fifty small ones *under its control* (≒ *influence*).

さんが【参賀】 ¶ 通りは～の人波でごったがえした The street was overcrowded with quite a lot of people going to *offer congratulations* at the Imperial Palace.

さんかい【山海】 ¶ 彼らは～の珍味でもてなしてくれ

た They entertained me with *foods of all lands and seas.* / They entertained me with *all sorts of dainties.*

さんかい【参会】 attendance.
—者 ¶～者は少数だった There was *a* small *attendance.*

さんかい【散会】 ¶会は午後5時に～した The meeting *adjourned* (≒ *broke up*) at 5 p. m. これで～といたします Now let's *close* (≒*adjourn*) *the meeting.*

さんかい【散開】〘軍隊〙deployment. ¶～する deploy (troops); spread out.

さ

さんがい【惨害】 a disaster; 〔a〕 calamity; severe(≒ heavy) damage. ¶戦争の～は忘れられない The *ravages* of war are not to be forgotten. 台風で大～を被った The typhoon brought *a* great *disaster* to us.

さんがい【三階】 the third floor (≒ story); 英 the second floor (≒ storey). ¶～に住む live *on the third floor* (≒ *in the third story*). ～建ての家 a three-storied (≒ three-story) house.

ざんがい【残骸】 remains; ruins; a wreck. ¶衝突して大破した自動車の～ the *wreckage* of crashed cars. ヨットの～が岸に打ち寄せられた The *wreck* of a sail-boat was cast upon the shore by the waves.

さんかく【三角】 a triangle. ¶この窓は～だ This window is *triangular* shaped.
—関係 a love triangle. —関数 trigonometrical function. —筋 a deltoid 〔muscle〕. —巾(きん) a triangle bandage. —定規 a set square. —州 a delta. —測量 triangular surveying. —法 trigonometry. 正(直角)—形 an equilateral (right-angled) triangle.

さんかく【参画】 participation in planning. ¶彼はその計画に～している He *is participating in* the project.

さんがく【山岳】 mountains.
—地帯 a mountainous region. —部 a mountaineering club.

さんがく【産学】 industrial circles and university.
—協同 collaboration between industrial circles and university. ¶～協同路線を助長する promote collaboration between *industry and university.*

さんがく【産額】 the 〔amount of〕 production; the output. ¶米の～ the *production* of rice. この島での石油の～はたいへんなものだ An enormous *quantity* (≒ *amount*) of petroleum is produced in this island. この国の鉄の～は年々増えている The *production* of iron in this country is increasing year by year.

ざんがく【残額】 the remainder; the balance. ¶預金の～は1万円だ The *balance* of the deposit money is ten thousand yen. / I have *a balance* of ten thousand yen in our bank. ～は月末までにお払いください You are requested to pay *the remainder* by the end of this month. (balance は銀行などの預金の残高で，支払いの残りにはふつう使わない).

さんがつ【三月】 March.

さんがにち【三が日】 three New Year days. ¶～は会社は休みだ We are free from work during *the first three days of the year.*

さんかん【山間】 ¶～の町 a *hill* town. ～の小村 a small village *among the mountains.*

さんかん【参観】 a visit; (視察)〔an〕 inspection. ¶学校を～する *visit* a school. 工場を～する *pay a visit of inspection* to a factory.
—者 a visitor.

さんかんおう【三冠王】〘野球〙 the triple crown.

ざんき【慚愧】 shame; humiliation; (後悔) remorsefulness. ¶いざというときになんの助けにもなれませんでまったく～に耐えません *I'm very sorry* (≒ *I'm quite ashamed of myself* when I think) I couldn't be of any help to you at the most critical time.

さんぎいん【参議院】 the House of Councillors.
—議員 a member of the House of Councillors.

さんきゃく【三脚】 a tripod.
—いす a three-legged stool. 二人— a three-legged race.

ざんぎゃく【残虐】 cruelty; brutality.
—行為 a cruel (≒ brutal) act.

さんぎょう【産業】 industry. ¶自動車～はわが国の主要～のひとつである The automobile *industry* is one of the chief *industries* of our country. ～化を近代化と混同してはならない We must not confuse *industrialization* with modernization.
映画— the cinema industry. —界 the industrial world; the industrial circles. —革命 the Industrial Revolution. —組合 an industrial association. —国 an industrial country. —資本 industrial capital. —組織 industrial organization. —道路 an industrial road. —復興 industry reconstruction. —別単一組合 an industrial union. —予備軍 an industrial reserve army.

さんぎょう【三行】 —広告 three-line advertisements. —広告欄 classified ad columns.

ざんぎょう【残業】 overtime work. ¶きょうは8時まで～だ We *work overtime* till eight.

ざんぎり【散切り】 ¶頭を～にしている He has his hair *cropped.*
—頭 a cropped head.

ざんきん【残金】 the balance; the money left 〔over〕; the arrears. ¶月賦の～を支払った I paid the *remainder* of the monthly instalment. ～はほとんどない We have little money left.

サングラス 〔a pair of〕 sunglasses; dark glasses.

さんけ【産気】 ¶彼女は～づいた Her labor has started. / She has begun to feel labor pains.

ざんげ【懺悔】 (告白) a confession; (後悔)

repentance. ¶罪を神に～する *confess one's* sins to God. どうか私の～をお聞きください Please listen to my *confessions*.

さんけい【三景】 ¶日本～とは松島・天の橋立・厳島の三つである Matsushima, Ama-no-Hashidate, and Itsukushima are *the best three of beauty spots* (≒ *the three views*) in Japan.

さんけい【山系】 a mountain chain (≒ range; system). ¶ヒマラヤ～ the Himalaya *Mountains*; the Himalayas.

さんけい【参詣】 ¶神社に～する go to a shrine to worship a god. 寺に～する make a pilgrimage to a temple.
—人 a worshipper; a visitor to a temple (≒ a shrine).

さんげき【惨劇】 [a] tragedy; a tragic event. ¶～の現場 the scene of the *murderous tragedy*. この家で一家皆殺しの～が行なわれた *A tragedy* of the massacre of all the family took place in this house.

ざんげつ【残月】 the moon at dawn; a morning moon.

ざんげん【讒言】 a false charge; [a] slander. ¶彼は～で陥れられた He was trapped by *a false charge*.

さんげんしょく【三原色】 three primary colors.

さんけんぶんりつ【三権分立】 respective independence of the three powers of administration, legislation, and judicature; separation of the administrative, legislative, and judicial powers.

さんご【産後】 ¶彼女は～の肥立ちがよい She is doing well *after childbirth*.

さんご【珊瑚】 coral. ¶～のブローチ a *coral* brooch.
—海 the Coral Sea. —礁 a coral reef. —虫 a coral insect.

さんこう【参考】 [a] reference; (助け) help. ¶きみの助言はたいへん～になった Your advice *was of much help* (≒ *service*) *to* me. / Your advice was *a* good *guide* (≒ *reference*). ご～までに私の意見をお聞かせしよう I have some suggestions *for your reference*. のちのちの～のためとっておこう I will keep it *for* future *reference*.
—書 a reference book. —書目(しばしば巻末の) a bibliography. —資料 reference materials (≒ data); data (複数扱い; 米 では単数扱いも; 単数形 datum はほとんど用いない). —人 a witness.

ざんごう【塹壕】 (防ぎょ用の) a trench; (からぼり) a moat. ¶～を掘る dig *a trench*. 兵隊は～から撃った The soldier shot from *trenches*.

さんごく【三国】 ¶～一の花婿(花嫁) an ideal husband (wife).
—干渉 the Triple Intervention. —協定 the Tripartite Agreement. —同盟 the Triple Alliance. —人 a third national. 第— a third power.

ざんこく【残酷】 cruelty. ¶子どもにそんなことをするのは～だ It *is cruel* to do such a thing to children. 失敗をすべて彼の責任にするのは～だ It *is heartless* of you to ascribe your failure solely to him. 彼は～にもその犬を打ちのめした He *was cruel enough* (≒ *had the cruelty*) to beat the dog.

さんこのれい【三顧の礼】 courteous invitation to take office. ¶社長は～をとってその学者を社に迎えた The president *most earnestly asked* the scholar *to* work for his company.

さんさい【山菜】 wild plants [for eating].
—料理 a dish of edible wild plants.

さんざい【散在】 lie scattered; be strewn; (場所を主語にして) be dotted; be strewn.
¶その村には人家が～している The village *is dotted with* houses. ゴルフ場はこの辺り一帯に～している Golf links *are scattered* all over the district.

さんざい【散財】 (浪費) squandering; (豪遊) a spree. ¶とんだ～だった It was really *waste of money*. きのうはとんだご～をかけました I am sorry to *have put* you *to so much expense*.

ざんざい【斬罪】 execution; beheading. ¶その殺人者は～に処せられた The murderer *was beheaded*.

さんさく【散策】 a walk; a ramble. ¶この庭は～するのにちょうどいい This garden is suitable for *walking* in.

さんざし【山査子】〘植物〙a hawthorn.

ざんさつ【惨殺】 ¶一家が～された The whole family *was cruelly murdered*. / The whole family *was butchered*.
—死体 a mangled body; a butchered corpse. —者 a murderer; a slayer.

さんざっぱら terribly. ¶～しかられた I was *severely* scolded. ～待たされた I was kept waiting *for a long time*. 彼は～悪口を言った He called me *all kinds of* [bad] names.

さんさん【燦燦】 ¶～たる陽光 *brilliant* rays of the sun. ～と太陽が輝く The sun shines *bright* (≒ *brightly*).

さんざん【散散】 thoroughly; completely; (ひどく) terribly; awfully; mercilessly. ¶まったく～な目に会った I *had a hard time of it*. ～待たされた I was kept waiting for a long time. 彼らには～迷惑をかけた I gave them *not a little* trouble. ～怒られた I was scolded *severely*. あらしで花が～になった The storm has ruined all the flowers.

さんさんくど【三三九度】 ¶～の杯をする exchange nuptial cups.

さんさんごご【三三五五】 by twos and threes; in group of twos and threes.
¶～散歩を楽しんだ We enjoyed a walk *by twos and threes*. 子どもたちは～連れだって学校へ行く Children go to school *in groups of twos and threes*.

さんし【蚕糸】 silk yarn.
—業 sericultural industry. —試験場 a sericultural laboratory.

さ

さんじ【三次】 the third time. ¶ ～にわたる南極探検 the Antarctic expedition of *three times*; a *third time* Antarctic expedition. 第～伊藤内閣 *the third* Ito Cabinet.
―方程式 a cubic equation.

さんじ【三時】 ¶ お～ですよ Come on, children. Let's have *afternoon tea*. / It's *afternoon tea* (≒ *coffee*) *break*.

さんじ【参事】 (会社の相談役) a councillor; (参与) a secretary.

さんじ【産児】 a new 〔born〕 baby.
―制限 birth control; family planning. ¶ ～制限をする practice *birth control*.

さんじ【惨事】 a terrible accident; a disaster (disaster は大ぜいの事故のとき. ひとりやふたりの事故では accident を用いる).
¶ 交通の～ *a* traffic *disaster*.

さんじ【賛辞】 a praise; words of praise.
¶ あなたに心からの～を呈したい I would like to pay you *a* sincere *compliment* (≒ *a* hearty *tribute*). / I sincerely *admire* you.

ざんし【残滓】 residue; residuum (燃焼・蒸発などの化学的変化の残留物には residuum を用いる); (かす) remnants; (液体のかす) dregs.

ざんし【惨死】 a tragic death. ¶ 彼はテロリストのひどい仕打ちに会って～した He *was murdered in a cruel way* by terrorists. / He was assaulted by terrorists and *was killed in a cruel way*.

さんしきすみれ【三色菫】〔植物〕 a pansy; a heartsease; a heart's-ease (昔失恋の悲しみをいやす花と信じられていたことからこの名がある); a viola tricolor.

さんじげん【三次元】 three dimensions.
¶ ～の three dimensional. ～の世界 a world of *three dimensions*.

さんしつ【蚕室】 a silkworm raising (≒ rearing) room.

さんしつ【産室】 a lying-in room; (病院の) a maternity ward; a delivery room.

さんしゅ【三種】 ¶ ～の神器 the Three Sacred Treasures passed down to the successive emperors of Japan.
第**―**郵便物 third-class mail.

さんじゅう【三重】 ¶ それは～の目的を持っている It has a *triple* purpose. それは～の安全装置がついている It has a *triple* safety device. 彼女は盲目, 聾唖(ろうあ)の～苦を背負っていた She was *triply* (≒ *trebly*) handicapped — blind, deaf and mute.
―唱(奏) a trio. **―**の塔 a three-storied pagoda.

さんじゅう【三十】 thirty; (第30) the thirtieth. ¶ 彼は～代のはじめに有名になった He became famous in his early *thirties*.

さんしゅつ【産出】 production. ¶ 日本は生糸の～国として知られていた Japan was well-known for its (≒ her) raw-silk *products*. / Japan was well-known as *a* raw-silk *producing country*. 肥沃(ひよく)な土地は豊かな作物を～する Fertile land *yields* (≒ *produces*; *gives*) good crops.

さんしゅつ【算出】 calculation; computation. ¶ 経費は複雑な式で～される The cost *is calculated* by a complicated formula. 私の～では, あなたの分は 1,000 円です *I've worked out* your share of the expenses at one thousand yen.

さんじゅつ【算術】 arithmetic. ¶ 子どものころは～が得意だった I was good at *sums* (≒ *figures*) when I was a child. ～の問題 an *arithmetical* problem.
―級数 arithmetic progression. **―平均** arithmetic〔al〕 mean.

さんじょ【賛助】 support. ¶ ～出演する act (play) as a guest star.
―会員 a supporting member.

ざんしょ【残暑】 lingering summer heat; the second summer. ¶ ことしの～はなかなか厳しい *The heat of late summer* is severe this year.

さんしょう【参照】 reference. ¶ 10ページ～ See page 10; *Cf*. p. 10. (*cf*. は compare または confer と読む. 文頭では *C* はふつう大文字). ～する refer (*to*); compare (*with*).

さんしょう【山椒】〔植物〕 a Japanese pepper; a prickly ash. ¶ 彼の言うことはいつも「～は小粒でもぴりりとからい」というところがある He is not considered to be a very important person, but his comments *are* always *piquant* (≒ *challenging*; *pungent*).

さんじょう【山上】 the top of a mountain.
¶ ～の垂訓〔聖書〕 the Sermon on the Mount.

さんじょう【三乗】〔数学〕 cube. ¶ 2 の～は 8 The *cube* of 2 is 8. / 2 multiplied by its square is 8.
―根 a cubic root. **―べき** the third power.

さんじょう【惨状】 a disastrous scene.
¶ 事故現場は～を呈していた The scene of the accident presented *a terrible sight* (≒ *spectacle*).

さんしょううお【山椒魚】〔動物〕 a 〔giant〕 salamander.

さんしょく【三食】 three meals. ¶ 1 日～は普通だ We usually have *three meals* a day. 彼は～ともパン食だ He has bread with each meal.

さんしょく【三色】 ¶ 原色には赤, 黄, 青の～がある There are *three* primary *colors*, *i. e.* red, yellow and blue.
―旗 a tricolor 〔flag〕 (これは特にフランス国旗を意味する).

さんしょく【蚕食】 invasion; encroachment; an inroad. ¶ ～する encroach 〔up〕on; invade (徐々に知らないうちに侵入する意味では encroach 〔up〕on を, 明らかな敵対行為で侵入する意味では invade).

さんじょく【産褥】 childbed; confinement.
¶ 彼女はいま～についている She is now in childbed. / She is now confined.
―期 a lying-in period. **―熱** childbed (≒ puerperal) fever.

さんしん【三振】〔野球〕 three strikes; a

strike-out; a fan. ¶ 次の打者は～した The next batter *was struck out.* 彼は相手チームから15～を奪った He *struck out* (≒ *fanned*) 15 batters of the opposite team.

ざんしん【斬新】 novelity; originality.

¶ ～な企画 a *new and original* (≒ *novel*) plan.

さんすい【山水】 hills and rivers; (風景) landscape; scenery.

—画 a landscape 〔painting〕.

さんすい【散水】 watering. ¶ 庭に～する sprinkle a garden with water. 街路に～する water the streets.

—機 a 〔water〕 sprinkler. —車 a motor sprinkler; a water cart.

さんすう【算数】 (算術) arithmetic; (数学) mathematics.

サンスクリット Sanskrit (Skr., Skt.).

—学者 a Sanskritist; a Sanscrit scholar.

さんすけ【三助】 a bathhouse attendant.

さんずのかわ【三途の川】 the Styx.

さん·する【産する】 produce. ¶ 米は多く平野部に～する Rice *is* mostly *produced* (≒ *is yielded*) in the plains. ニシンは北海道近海に～する Herrings *are caught* off the coast of Hokkaido.

さんせい【三世】 (日系米人の) a *sansei* (複 *sansei, sanseis*); a third-generation Japanese-American.

さんせい【酸性】 〖化学〗 acidity. ¶ ～の土壌 *acid* soil. この物質は土壌を～化する This substance *acidifies* soil.

—酸化物 an acid oxide. —反応 〔an〕 acid reaction.

さんせい【賛成】 agreement; approval; support; (動議に対しその) supporting.

¶ ～! 異議なし *Yes!* (≒ *Agreed!*) No objection. きみはこのことに～か反対か *Are* you *for* or against this? / *Are* you *in favor of* this or not? 採決の結果は法案に対して～10票, 反対8票だった The result of the voting was 10 *for* and 8 against the bill. ～多数と認めます I see that *the ayes* have it. もっと詳しく説明してくれなければ～も反対も言えぬ Unless you explain it in more detail, I can't say *yes* or no. ぼくもきみの意見に～だ I *agree with* you. / My opinion *is the same as* yours. / I *am in agreement with* your opinion. ～の方はご起立を願います All *in favor,* please stand up. 市長はその計画に～の意を表明した The mayor expressed his *approval of* the project. この案は住民の～を得ることは難しい It is difficult for this plan to obtain the *support* of the people. 3分の2以上の～を得なければ, この案は撤回する I will withdraw my proposal, if it doesn't receive a two-thirds majority. この結論には～しかねる点が多い In many respects I *disagree on* (≒ *about*) this conclusion. 委員の大多数はその計画に～した Most of the committee members *supported* the plan. 残念ながらこの予算案には～いたしかねる I am sorry but I can't *approve of the* budget. その提案に～します I *second* the proposal.

さんせいけん【参政権】 the right to vote; suffrage; franchise.

婦人— woman (≒ female) suffrage.

さんせき【山積】 ¶ 仕事が～している I have *too much* (≒ *a lot of*) work to do.

ざんせつ【残雪】 the remaining snow.

さんせん【三選】 election for the third term.

¶ 彼は首相に～された He was elected prime minister for the third term. 現知事の～は絶対に阻止する We will take every possible measure to prevent the reelection of the present governor for the third consecutive term.

さんせん【参戦】 entry into a war. ¶ アメリカの～が第2次大戦の勝敗を決した The *entry* (≒ *participation*) of the United States played a decisive role in World War II.

さんぜん【参禅】 ¶ 彼は円覚寺で～した He practiced *Zen* meditation in Enkakuji temple. / He joined the *Zen* cult held at Enkakuji temple.

—者 a *Zen* votary.

さんぜん【燦然】 ¶ ～たる宝石 *brilliant* (≒ *glittering*) jewels. ～と輝く shine *bright* (≒ *brightly*).

さんぜん【産前】 before childbirth. ¶ 彼女は～産後の休暇をとっている She is taking *maternity* leave.

さんそ【酸素】 〖化学〗 oxygen. ¶ 患者に～吸入をする give a patient *oxygen* inhalations; make a patient inhale *oxygen*. ～を除去する deoxygenate. ～で処置する oxygenate.

—吸入器 an oxygen inhaler. —テント an oxygen tent. —溶接 oxygen welding.

さんそう【山荘】 a mountain villa (≒ 米 cottage).

ざんぞう【残像】 〖心理学〗 an afterimage.

さんぞく【山賊】 a bandit; a brigand; a highwayman; a mountain robber (bandit はイタリア語の bandito から出た語で, 特に山中の追いはぎを意味するが, また一般に盗賊・人殺しなどの無法者をも意味する. brigand は群れをなす盗賊の一味, highwayman は馬に乗って旅人を襲う盗賊).

さんそん【山村】 a mountain village.

ざんそん【残存】 ¶ ～している史料 *surviving* (≒ *remaining*) historical records.

さんだい【参内】 ¶ ～する visit (≒ go to) the Imperial Palace.

ざんだか【残高】 a balance. ¶ ～はいくらでしょうか What is the *balance*?

繰越— the balance carried over; the balance brought forward.

サンタ=クロース Santa Claus (Saint Nicholas, Father Christmas ともいう).

サンダル a pair of sandals; sandal shoes.

さんたん【賛嘆】 admiration; praise. ¶ 彼の行為は～に値する His conduct deserves (≒ is worthy of) *the highest admiration*.

さんたん【惨憺】 ¶「試験の結果はどうだった」「～たるものだ」"How did the test turn out?"

さ

"*Miserable.*" ～たる光景 a *frightful* (≒ *horrible ; tragic*) sight. 昨日の試合は～たる負け方をした We *suffered a crushing* (≒ *serious; terrible*) *defeat* in the game Yesterday. 苦心～してその仕事を完成した I *took great pains to* accomplish my task. / I finished my work *with great* (≒ *infinite*) *pains*.

さんだん【三段】 —式ロケット a three-stage rocket. —跳び hop, step, and jump; triple jump. —論法〘論理〙a syllogism. —構え three-way. ¶～構えの防禦 a three-way (≒ three) fold defense.

さんだん【散弾】 a shot; a slug.
—銃 a shotgun.

さんだん【算段】 ¶やりくり～して10万円の金を用意した I *have* somehow *managed to* raise a hundred thousand yen.

さんち【山地】 a mountainous district (≒ region); a hilly country.

さんち【産地】 a producing (≒ growing) district; (動物・植物の) the home; the habitat. ¶青森はリンゴの～として知られている Aomori is well-known as *an* apple-*producing district*. / Aomori is a famous apple country. 秋田は美人の～だ Akita *is productive of* beautiful women. / Akita is *the home* of beautiful women.

さんちょう【山頂】 the top of a mountain. ¶ついに～をきわめた At last we reached *the summit* (≒ *top*) *of the mountain*. ここが～だ This is *the highest point of this mountain*.

さんてい【算定】 calculation; computation. ¶被害は総額2億円と～された The total amount of the damage *was estimated at* two hundred million yen. / The damage *amounted to* two hundred million yen. ～を誤らぬように Be careful not to make a mistake in *calculation*.

ざんてい【暫定】 ¶これは～的な見積もりだ This is a *provisional* estimate. この件は～的にそのように考えておきたい We would like to consider the matter that way *for the time being*. / We would like to take this point of view *tentatively*. (恒久的なものができたときにそれと「置きかえられるもの」という意味では provisional を用い，また「しばらくの間」の仮のものという意味で，temporarily または for the time being が用いられる．これに対して「実験的に試みるもの」という意味では tentative を用いる)．
—予算 a provisional budget.

さんど【三度】 three times; thrice. ¶～に1度くらいは返事をください I'm looking forward to hearing from you *once in* three times. 当地へ来たのは～めだ This is *the third time* I have been here. 彼は～の飯よりテニスが好きなほどだ He *is crazy* (≒ *mad*) *about* tennis. 彼は～めの正直で試験に合格した As the proverb goes, *third time* was really lucky, he passed the examination in his third attempt.

サンドイッチ sandwiches.
—マン a sandwich man; walking billboards. 野菜(ハム)— vegetable (ham) sandwiches.

さんとう【三等】 the third class; the third rate. ¶彼は競争で～になった(3等賞) He won *the third prize* in the race. / (3番だった) He was *the third* 〔to reach the goal〕 in the race.
—国 a third-rate power; a minor country. —親〘法律〙a relation of the third degree.

さんどう【山道】 a mountain road.

さんどう【参道】 the approach to a shrine.

さんどう【賛同】 support; approval. ¶われわれの計画にご～いただけますか Will you *support* (≒ *approve* 〔*of*〕) our plan? その決議は全員の～を得て採択された The resolution was adopted by unanimous *consent*.

ざんとう【残党】 the remnants of a defeated party.

さんとうきん【三頭筋】〘解剖学〙the triceps.

さんとうせいじ【三頭政治】 triarch; triumvirate.

さんとうぶん【三等分】 ¶リンゴを～する *divide* an apple *equally in three parts*.

サントニン〘薬品〙santonin.

サンドバッグ〘ボクシング〙a sandbag.

サンドペーパー sandpaper.

さんにん【三人】 three persons; three men. ¶～組の強盗 *a trio of* robbers. ～寄れば文殊の知恵(諺) Two heads are better than one.

ざんにん【残忍】 cruelty; brutality. ¶～な行ない a *brutal* act. 彼のやり方は～きわまりないものだった He did it in a most *atrocious* (≒ a very *cruel*) way. 彼は～な人間だった He was *a brute* 〔*of a man*〕. / (冷酷な人間) He was *cold-blooded*.

さんにんしょう【三人称】〘文法〙the third person.
—単数 the third person singular.

さんねん【三年】 three years. ¶～めごとに every third year. ～ごとの triennial. 高校～生になった I am *a 3rd-year student* at a high school. 彼女は大学の～生だ She is a junior in her college. (junior は高校・大学においてあと1年残したときの学年をいうから，3年制の高校なら2年生，4年制の大学なら3年生となる．したがって3年制高校の3年生なら I am in my senior year となる)．私の息子は小学校～生だ My son is in the third grade. / My son is *a third grader*.

ざんねん【残念】 regret; (失望) disappointment. ¶～な regrettable; disappointing. もっと早く出発しなかったのが～だ I *regret* not starting earlier. / I *regret* not having started earlier. 彼の急死が～でならない I deeply *regret* his sudden death. もう二度と彼に会えないというのは～なことだ It is *a matter of regret* that I can't see him any more. ～ながら，彼の招待を断わった I declined his invitation *with regret.* / I *regretfully* declined his invitation. 〜ながら, お手伝いできない *To my regret* (≒ *I'm sorry, but*) I can't help you. (to *one's* regret という言い方はやや文語的. 次例の to *one's* disappointment も同様). 〜ながら, 実験はまた失敗した *I regret to say that* the experiment failed again. 〜ながら, 彼は来なかった *To my disappointment* he did not come. 〜無念 What a pity! / What a shame!

さんば【産婆】a midwife. ¶ クラブの結成にあたって彼が〜役をつとめた He *assisted* in the establishment of our club.

さんばい【三倍】three times. ¶ 2を〜すると6になる *Three times* two makes six. あと10年もすると自動車の数は〜ぐらいになろう In ten years' time the number of cars will *be three times as* great *as* it is today.

さんぱい【参拝】worship; a visit. ¶ 〜する worship (*at*). (日本でいう参拝に相当する英米語はない. 普通なら visit くらいでよい).

—者 a worshipper. ¶ 神社は〜者でにぎわった The shrine was very crowded with *worshippers*.

さんぱい【惨敗】a crushing (≒ overwhelming; serious) defeat. ¶ 対校試合で〜を喫した We *were beaten utterly* at the interschool match.

さんぱいきゅうはい【三拝九拝】¶ 〜してやっと承知させた After *entreating* him *very earnestly*, I succeeded in persuading him to do it.

さんばがらす【三羽烏】a trio. ¶ 彼の馬術は日本で〜のひとりといわれるほどの腕前だ He has so excellent horsemanship that he can be said to be one of the *trio* in Japan.

さんばし【桟橋】a [landing] pier; a [landing] stage. ¶ 船が〜に横づけになる The ship comes alongside the *pier*.

さんぱつ【散発】¶ 相手のチームはヒットを〜するだけだった The opposing team did nothing but *scatter* hits.

さんぱつ【散髪】hairdressing. ¶ 〜する have *one's* hair *cut*. (アメリカでは, いわゆる散髪を haircut というと頭髪を切り, 簡単にえりにかみそりを当てる程度のことをいう).

さんばん【三番】¶ マラソンで〜になった I ran *third* in a marathon race. 彼が〜めの兄だ He is *the third* older brother. 〜勝負で2番勝った I won twice in *a three-game match*.

ざんぱん【残飯】left-over rice; the leftover; leavings.

さんはんきかん【三半規管】〘解剖学〙semicircular canals.

さんび【賛美】praise; glorification; admiration. ¶ その詩で詩人は人生を〜している The poet *sings the praises of* life in that poem. 彼は旧師の徳を〜する文を書いた He has written an article in which he *has glorified* his old teacher's virtue.

さんぴ【賛否】approval or disapproval; yes or no; for and against. ¶ その案には〜両論があった There were arguments *pros and cons* about the plan. 議長が議案について〜を問う The chairman takes the *ayes and noes* as to the bill. 〜は同数である The *ayes and noes* are equally divided.

さんびか【賛美歌】a hymn; a psalm. ¶ 〜を歌う sing *a hymn*.

—集 a hymnbook.

さんぴょう【散票】scattered votes. ¶ 彼の得票は〜が多かった His poll was full of *scattered votes*.

さんびょうし【三拍子】〘音楽〙triple time. ¶ ワルツは〜だ Waltz is *triple time*. 〜がそろっている選手は少ない Only a few players *are all-round*.

ざんぴん【残品】the remaining stock; unsold goods. ¶ 特価品の〜が少ない The *stock* of the bargain items is running short.

さんぶ【三部】three parts; three volumes.

—合奏 (合唱) a trio.

さんぷ【産婦】a woman in childbed; a woman in her confinement.

さんぷ【散布】scattering; dispersing; sprinkling. ¶ 農薬を〜する *scatter* agricultural medicines.

ざんぶ【残部】the remainder; the remnant; the remains; the rest.

さんぶさく【三部作】a trilogy. ¶ この絵は彼の〜のひとつだ This picture is one of his *trilogy*.

ざんぶと ¶ 私は洋服を着たまま〜水に飛び込んだ I *plunged* (≒ *jumped; plumped*) into the water with my clothes on.

さんぷく【山腹】a hillside; a mountainside. ¶ 〜にある家 a house *on a hillside*. 私の別荘は〜にある My cottage is *halfway up the hill*.

さんふじんか【産婦人科】obstetrics and gynecology.

—医 a gynecologist.

さんぶつ【産物】a product; a production; produce. ¶ 青森の重要な〜はリンゴだ Apples are *a* staple *product* in Aomori. この植物標本は彼の夏休み中の努力の〜だ These botanical specimens are the *fruit* of sheer labor during his summer vacation.

サンプル a sample. ¶ 〜を取り寄せる order *a sample*. セールスマンは〜を見せてくれた The salesman showed *samples*.

さんぶん【散文】prose; prose writing. ¶ 〜的な人物だ He is a *prosaic* (≒ *matter-of-fact*) man.

—詩 a prose poem. ¶ 彼のその景色の描写は〜詩といってもいいくらいだ His description of the scenery may be called *a prose poem* (≒ *a poem in prose*).

さんぶん【三分】trisection. ¶ 〜の1 one third; a third. 〜の2 two thirds. 生徒の〜の1はきょう欠席した *One third* of the pupils stayed away from school today. その国は敗戦で国土を〜された As a result of the defeat in the war the country was divided into *three* *parts.*

さんぽ【散歩】a walk; a stroll. ¶～する take *a walk*; go 〔out〕 for *a walk*. 犬を～させる *walk a* dog.

さんぽう【三方】**1**〖3方面〗¶その町は～山に囲まれている That town is surrounded by hills *on all sides but one* (≒ on *three sides*).

2〖神前などに物を供するための道具〗 a small wooden stand (≒ table).

さんぼう【参謀】〔軍事〕the staff; (ひとり) a staff officer; (相談役) an adviser; a counselor.

¶彼は社長の～だ He is a member of the president's *brain trust*. / He is *a brain truster to* the president.

—長 the chief of staff. **—**本部 the General Staff Office.

さんぽう【山砲】a mountain gun; (総称的に) mountain artillery.

さんま【秋刀魚】〔魚類〕a mackerel pike.

さんまい【三昧】(夢中になること) absorption; devotion. ¶読書～にふける *be absorbed* (≒ *be immersed*) *in* reading. 彼らはぜいたく～に暮らしている They are living *high* (≒ *in luxury*).

さんまいめ【三枚目】a comedian. ¶彼は～の役が得意だ He is good at playing a part of *a comic actor*.

さんまん【散漫】diffuseness; vagueness; looseness; desultoriness. ¶頭脳の～な人 a *loose* thinker. 彼は学習態度が～である He bears himself *vaguely* toward learning.

さんみ【酸味】acidity; sourness. ¶～のある sour; acid. レモンは～が強い A lemon has *a* strong *acid taste*.

さんみいったい【三位一体】trinity. ¶陸海空～の作戦が行なわれる The Army, Navy and Air Forces, forming *a trinity*, will undertake an action.

—論 trinitarianism; the doctrine of trinity. **—**論者 a trinitarian.

さんみゃく【山脈】a mountain range; a range of mountains. ¶アルプス～ the Alps. 日本アルプス～ the Japan Alps.

ざんむ【残務】remaining (≒ unsettled) affairs. ¶会社の～を整理する I'll arrange the affairs for the company. / I'll wind up the company.

—整理 settlement of the unfinished business; liquidation.

さんめんきじ【三面記事】city (≒ local) news. ¶きのうの事故が～に出ている Yesterday's accident is reported in *the police news page*.

さんめんきょう【三面鏡】a three-side mirror.

さんもん【三文】a farthing; cheap. ¶早起きは～の得(諺) *The early bird catches the worm*. 二束～の値うちもない It is not worth *a farthing* (≒ *a penny; a button*).

—オペラ the beggar's opera. **—**小説 a cheap novel. **—**文士 a literary hack; a hack writer; a penny-a-liner; (特に㊥) a word monger.

さんもん【山門】the main gate of a Buddhist temple; a temple gate.

さんや【山野】fields and mountains. ¶～を駆けめぐる run and roam over *fields and hills* (≒ *hill and dale*).

さんやく【三役】(政党の) the three top-ranking (≒ leading) officials 〔of a political party〕; (組合などの) the three top-ranking union officers; (相撲の) the *sumo* wrestlers of the three highest ranks under *Yokozuna*.

¶ひとりで～を演じる play *three parts*.

さんやく【散薬】powder medicine.

さんよ【参与】(関係) participation; (役名) a counselor. ¶政治に～する *have a voice in* politics. 彼を会社の～として迎えた We engaged him as *a company consultant*.

ざんよ【残余】the residue; the rest; the remainder; remains; leavings.

—額 the balance.

さんようすうじ【算用数字】Arabic figures (≒ numerals).

さんらん【産卵】egg-laying. ¶～する lay eggs; spawn.

—期 the breeding season. ¶サケの～期を迎えた The *breeding season* of the salmon has come.

さんらん【散乱】scattering; dispersing.

¶紙が部屋じゅうに～していた The room *was littered* all over *with* scraps of paper.

さんりゅう【三流】the third rate. ¶彼女は歌手としては～にすぎない She is only a *third-rate* singer.

ざんりゅう【残留】¶私はこの土地に～する I'll *remain* here.

—部隊 remaining forces.

さんりん【山林】mountains and forests; a forest on a mountain. ¶～を作る *afforest* mountains. ～を伐採する *deforest* mountains.

—業 a forestry industry. **—**保護 forest conservancy. **—**学 forestry.

さんりんしゃ【三輪車】a tricycle.

さんるい【三塁】〔野球〕〔the〕 third base.

—手 a third baseman. **—**打 a three-base hit; a three-bagger.

ざんるい【残塁】¶ランナーは二塁に～になった The runner *was left on* the second *base*.

サンルーム a sunroom.

さんれつ【参列】attendance; presence; participation.

¶彼の送別会に～した I *attended* the farewell party held in honor of him.

—者 an attendant; those present. ¶～者の中には政界の名士が多かった Among *those present* were many prominent figures in politics.

さんろく【山麓】the foot of a mountain.

¶富士～を行く go along the base of Mt. Fuji.

し

し

し【氏】(敬称) Mr. (複 Messrs.) ; (氏族) family. ¶ 田中～ *Mr.* Tanaka. 田中～夫妻 *Mr.* and Mrs. Tanaka. ～は有名だ *He* is well-known.

し【史】 history ; annals.
日本― Japanese history. 現代― contemporary history.

し【四】 four.

し【市】 a city ; a town. (行政区画) a municipality.
―町村 cities, towns and villages. ―当局 the municipal authorities. 京都― Kyoto city ; the city of Kyoto.

し【死】 death. ¶ 父の突然の～がぼくの一生を変えた My father's sudden *death* has changed the course of my life. なにが彼女を～に追いやったのだろうか What drove her to *die*? ドライバーはいつでも～に直面しているようなものだ We may fairly say that drivers always face *death*. 彼の～は近い He is on the verge of *death*. あのときさみは生と～の境をさまよっていた At that time you were wandering between life and *death*. ～はやすく生はかたい It is not hard to *die*, but hard to know how to live well. 若くしていった彼の～を悼まずにはいられない We cannot help mourning him who *died* young. あのときにはぼくも～を覚悟した At that moment I prepared myself for *death*. 過労が彼の～を招いた Overwork caused his *death*. 1台あとのバスに乗ったので危うく～を免れた I narrowly escaped *death*, by taking the next bus. 降伏するよりは～を選んだほうがいい I would rather choose *death* than surrender. 彼は～を決してことにあたった He took up the work *at the risk of his life*. 彼らは～を賭(と)して戦った They fought *to the death*.
―の商人 a merchant of death. ―の灰 lethal ash ; fallout. 自然― a natural death. 事故― an accidental death. ショック― death from the shock (*of*).

し【師】 a teacher ; a master ; an instructor. ¶ われわれはA博士を～と仰いでいる We look up to Dr. A as our *teacher*.

し【詩】(概念的) poetry ; (具体的) a poem. ¶ ～を作る(味わう) compose (appreciate) *a poem*. ～にうたう sing (*a thing*) in *a poem*.

し【資】(資本) funds ; capital ; (素質) qualities. ¶ 米塩の～ a means of living.

じ【字】 a letter ; a character ; a word ; (筆跡) a hand ; handwriting. ¶ うちの息子は～を覚えはじめた My son has begun to learn how to *write*. きれいな(きたない)～を書く He writes *a good* (*an awful*) *hand*.

じ【地】 ¶ ～が出る act in a natural way. ～をならす level *the ground*. 彼の生涯は小説を～で行ったようなものだ His life is just like a novel. この酒は～のものです This is the *sake* of *the place* (≒ *the local sake*). 白の～を赤に染める dye red on *a* white *ground*. ～の文がよい The *descriptive* (≒ *narrative*) *part* is good.
―酒 *sake* of local production. ―卵 home-produced eggs.

じ【辞】 ¶ 閉会の～を述べるように頼まれた I was asked to give *a* closing *address*. ～を低くして彼に助力をお願いした I *politely* (≒ *humbly*) asked him to help me with my work.

じ【痔】〘医学〙 piles ; h(a)emorrhoids. ¶ ～が悪い I have *piles*.

-じ【-時】 ¶ 今1～3分過ぎだ It's now three past one. 毎～60キロの速さで走った We drove at a speed of 60 kilometers *per hour*. ⇒なんじ

しあい【試合】 a game. ¶ 雨で～はなかった The *game* was cancelled because of the rain. あすは野球の～がある There will be *a* baseball *game* tomorrow. 卓球の～を見たいと思う I am going to see *a game* of ping-pong. テニスの～を申し込まれた I was challenged to *a game* of tennis.
最終― the last game. 第1― the first game (≒ round). 夜間― a night game. 練習― a practice game.

じあい【自愛】 self-regard ; self-love ; self-indulgence. ¶ ご～を祈ります I hope (≒ pray) that you will *take good care of yourself*.

じあい【慈愛】 affection ; kindness ; love ; benevolence ; tenderness. ¶ ～深い affectionate ; benevolent ; kindhearted ; amiable. ～に満ちた彼女のまなざしに私は元気づけられた Her *warm-hearted* look encouraged me.

しあがり【仕上がり】 completion ; accomplishment. ¶ この作品は～がよい This work has *a* good *finish*. ～に気をつけなさい Be careful during the *final touches*.

しあが・る【仕上がる】 ¶ この工事はもうすぐ～る予定です This construction work will *be completed* before long.

しあげ【仕上げ】 ¶ ～をよくしなさい Try to have *a* good *finish*. 彫刻の最後の～をしている He *is putting the finishing touches to* the sculpture. このガラス細工は～がきれいだ This glass work *is* prettily *finished*.

しあ·げる【仕上げる】 ¶二,三日で～げてください Please *get* it *finished* within a few days. 土曜日までにこの仕事を～げることは難しい It is difficult to *finish* this work before Saturday. ズボンを日曜日までに～げていただけますか Won't you *have* my trousers *finished* by next Sunday? 彼は独学で～げた人だ He is a self-taught man.

しあさって【明明後日】 two days after tomorrow; three days hence.

ジアスターゼ〘生化学〙 diastase.

しあつりょうほう【指圧療法】 finger-pressure therapy; *shiatsu* 〔therapy〕.
 —師 a *shiatsu* therapist.

しあわせ【幸せ】 happiness. ¶彼らは田舎で～に暮らしている They live *happily* in the country. / They lead a *happy* life in the country. ～なことに私たちには若さと活力がある *Fortunately* we are young and energetic. / We *are fortunate* enough to be young and energetic. 仲間と苦楽をともにできることほど～なことはない Nothing is *happier* than to be able to share joys and sorrows with our companions.

しあん【私案】 *one's* 〔private〕 plan. ¶ホテル経営の～を出そうと思います I think I will suggest (≒ propose) *my* 〔*private*〕 *plan* for hotel management.

しあん【思案】 ¶彼は～にくれていた He *was lost in thought*. / He *was absorbed in meditation*. 私はそのことについてあれこれと～をめぐらした I *thought hard about* it. ～に余ってきみに相談にきた As I *didn't know* (≒ *was at a loss*) *what to do*, I have come for your advice. / As I *was at my wits'* (≒ *wit's*) end, I have come to you for advice. 卒業後どうするかは目下～中です I *am* now *thinking about* what to do after graduation. 恋は～のほか Love is blind.

しあん【試案】 a tentative plan. ¶これはほんの～に過ぎない This is only *a tentative plan* just for your consideration.

シアン〘化学〙 cyanogen.

しい ¶～っ, 黙って *Hush* (≒ *Sh*; *Hist*; *Mum*; *Whist*)! Be silent. / Be quiet! ネコを～っと言って追い払った I *shooed away* a cat.

しい【椎】〘植物〙 a pasania. ¶～の実 an acorn 〔of the *pasania*〕.

しい【恣意】 ¶～的な決定をするな Don't make an *arbitrary* decision.

じい【自慰】 self-consolation; masturbation.

じい【侍医】 a court physician.

じい【辞意】 *one's* intention to resign.
 ¶～を表明する announce *one's resignation*. ～を漏らす hint at *resignation*. ～を撤回する withdraw *one's resignation*. 彼の～は堅い He is firm in his resolution to *resign*.

じいうんどう【示威運動】 demonstration.
 ¶彼らは政府の外交政策に反対する～をした They held *a demonstration against* the government's diplomatic policy.

しいか【詩歌】 poetry; (漢詩と和歌) Chinese and Japanese poetry. ¶～管弦の遊びにふけった貴族たち the nobles who were indulged in the pleasure of *poetry* and music.

しいく【飼育】 ¶家禽(かきん)を～する *breed* poultry. 熱帯魚を～する *keep* tropical fish.
 —係(家畜の) a breeder; (鳥などの) a fancier.

じいしき【自意識】 self-consciousness. ¶彼女は～が強い She *is* very *self-conscious*.
 —過剰 excessive self-consciousness.

シーズン the season. ¶スキーの～が待ち遠しい I am waiting impatiently for *the* skiing *season* to come. 行楽地は～中は人々でにぎわう Places of tourist resort are crowded with people during *the season*.
 —オフ an off-season.

シーソー a seesaw. ¶～で遊ぶ play at *seesaw*.
 —ゲーム a seesaw game.

しいたけ【椎茸】 a *shiitake* 〔mushroom〕.

しいた·げる【虐げる】 oppress; tyrannize; (迫害する) persecute. ¶弱い者を～げる *oppress* (≒ *tyrannize over*) the weak. ～げられた人々 the oppressed.

シーツ a 〔bed〕 sheet.

しいて【強いて】 ¶～言えばこの本のほうが少しよい This book is, *if anything*, a little better. ～そうするには及ばない You don't have to do so *against your will*. ～ごいっしょにとおっしゃるなら お止めしません If you *insist on* accompanying me, I won't stop you.

シート (席) a seat; (雨おおい) waterproof canvas.
 —ノック seat knocking. **—**ベルト a seat belt. 切手**—** a sheet of postage stamps; 〔postage〕 stamps in a sheet.

シード〘競技〙 ¶その学校は～校だ The school team *is seeded*.
 —選手 a seeded player.

ジープ a jeep.

シームレスストッキング 〔a pair of〕 seamless stockings.

シーラカンス〘魚類〙 a coelacanth.

シール a seal.

し·いる【強いる】 force (≒ press) (*upon a person*); compel (≒ force; impel) (*a person*) to do. ¶人に酒を～いる *force sake upon a person*. ここの従業員は過重な労働を～いられる The employees here *are compelled* (≒ *are forced*) to work too hard. 子どもに～いられてピクニックに出かけた We *were pressed* by our children to go on a picnic with them.

しいれ【仕入れ·仕入】 buying 〔in〕; laying in 〔a〕 stock.
 —先 a supplier; a vendor. **—**高 the amount of goods laid in. **—**値 the cost (≒ buying) price. **—**品 stocks (≒ goods) on hand.

しい·れる【仕入れる】 lay (≒ get) in a stock; stock (goods). ¶冬物を～れる *stock* (≒ *buy in*) winter goods. 私どもはもう十分品物を～れてある We *have* (≒ *keep*) a large stock of goods now. 情報を～れる *get in* information.

じいろ【地色】 the ground color.

しいん【子音】 a consonant.

有声(無声)― a voiced (voiceless) consonant.

しいん【死因】the cause of *a person's* death. ¶彼の～を究明しなければならぬ We must investigate *the cause of* his *death*. 彼の～ははっきりしない He *died from* some unknown *cause*. 彼女の～は過労だった *Her death was due to* overwork. / Overworking is *the cause of her death*.

しいん【試飲】¶このスープを～してみてください Won't you *sample* this soup?

シーン a scene.
ラスト― the last scene. ラブ― a love scene.

じいん【寺院】a Buddhist temple.

しいんと ¶その町は～静まりかえっていた *A profound silence* prevailed all over the town. 彼のひと言で場内は～なった A single word of his reduced the assembly to *deep silence*.

じいんと ¶その映画を見て目頭が～熱くなった I *was moved to tears* at the movie. / *Tears were ready to come to my eyes* when I saw the movie.

じう【慈雨】a welcome (≒ beneficial) rain. ¶干天の～ *a beneficial* (≒ *a welcome*) *rain* during the dry season.

しうち【仕打ち】a treatment. ¶私はひどい～を受けた I received *a* bad *treatment*. / I *was treated* badly. 私はこんなひどい～にはがまんできない I cannot put up with such *a* harsh *treatment*.

しうんてん【試運転】a trial. ¶新車の～ the *trial* of a new car. 彼はその機械を～してみた He *gave* the machine *a trial*. その船は～中だ The ship *is on her trial trip* (≒ *voyage*). 列車は～では時速200キロ出た The train ran at a speed of 200 kilometers per hour *on trial*.

しえい【市営】municipal management. ¶その保育所を～にすべきだ The nursery school should *be municipalized* (≒ *be placed under municipal management*). ～の municipal.
―アパート a municipal apartment house. ―事業 a municipal undertaking. ―バス a city bus.

しえい【私営】¶～の施設 an institution *under private management*.
―鉄道 a privately owned railway; a private line. ―バス a private bus.

じえい【自営】¶彼は～で商売している He is doing business *on his own* [*account*]. ～の independent; self-supporting.
―事業 an independent enterprise; an owner management.

じえい【自衛】self-defense. ¶～する defend (≒ protect) *oneself*. ～の策を講ずる devise a means of *self-defense*. ～上そうせざるをえなかった I could not help doing so *in self-defense*.
―権 the right of self-defense. ―隊員 Self-Defense Force soldier (≒ member). 陸上(海上; 航空)―隊 the Ground (Maritime; Air) Self-Defense Force.

シェーカー a [cocktail] shaker.

シェード shade; a [lamp] shade.

シェービングクリーム shaving cream.

しえき【使役】employment; service. ¶かつては領主が土木工事に農民を～した Formerly [feudal] lords *set* (≒ *put*) peasants *to* public *works*.
―動詞〘文法〙a causative verb.

ジェスイット a Jesuit.
―会 the Society of Jesus (日本ではヤソ(耶蘇)会ともいう. S.J. と略す).

ジェスチュア [a] gesture. ¶彼は～たっぷりの話し方をする He speaks with [*an*] exaggerated *gesture*. それは単なる～にすぎない It is *a* mere *gesture*.
―遊び 米 charades (単数扱い); a charade (発音は [ʃərɑ́:d]).

ジェット jet.
―機 a jet; a jet plane; a jet airplane. ―機関 a jet engine. ―気流 a jet stream. ―コースター a roller coaster; 英 a switchback (ジェットコースターは和製英語). ―旅客機 a jetliner; a jet liner.

ジェネレーション a generation. ¶～の違い a difference in *generation*.

シェパード a shepherd dog.

シェリー (スペイン産白ぶどう酒) sherry.

シェルパ a Sherpa (複 -s, または単複同形).

しえん【支援】support. ¶革新候補を～する *support* (≒ *back up*) a reformist candidate.
―者 a supporter.

しえん【紫煙】tobacco smoke; blue smoke [of tobacco]. ¶彼はゆうゆうと～をくゆらしていた He *was smoking* placidly. / He *was puffing* slowly at his cigar.

しえん【試演】a trial performance; demonstration.

しお【塩】salt. ¶(食卓で)～をとってください Pass me the *salt*, please. このスープは～が少しききすぎている This soup *is* a bit too *salt*[*y*] (≒ *oversalted*). これは甘～だ This *is* not well *salted*. / This *is* lightly *salted*.
―入れ (食卓用の) a saltcellar; (台所用の) a salt box.

しお【潮】a tide. ¶～が差している The *tide* is rising. ～が満ちている(状態) The *tide* is at the full. ～が引いている The *tide* is ebbing. / (状態) The *tide* is down. 鯨が～を吹く A whale *spouts* (≒ *blows*). それをよい～に, 皆帰りだした They *took occasion to* leave there.

しおあじ【塩味】¶この魚は～にしたほうがいい You had better *season* this fish *with salt*.

しおかげん【塩加減】¶～がよい(悪い) It *is well* (*badly*) *seasoned*. この焼き肉の～をみましょう I'll taste this roast meat to see how it *is seasoned*.

しおかぜ【潮風】a sea breeze. ¶～に吹かれて海岸を散歩した I enjoyed walking in the *sea breeze* along the beach.

しおから【塩辛】¶イカの～ *soused* cuttlefish (soused の発音は [saust]). カツオの～ *salted guts* of bonito.
しおから·い【塩辛い】salt; salty; briny; (少し) saltish. ¶海水は～い The sea water *is salty*. これは少し～い This *is saltish*.
しおくり【仕送り】an allowance. ¶彼は実家から月々3万円の～を受けている He is given *a* monthly *allowance* of thirty thousand yen by his parents at home. 月々母に生活費の足しにいくらか～している I *send* some money *to* my mother every month as part of her living expenses. 1週間すれば国もとから1万円の～があるはずだ I expect *a remittance* of ten thousand yen from home in a week.
しおけ【塩気】saltiness; saltishness; salty taste; a touch (≒ flavor) of salt. ¶～を含んだ風 a *salt-bearing* wind. ～が足りない want *a touch of salt*.
しおさい【潮騒】the sea roar.
しおざけ【塩鮭】a salted salmon.
しおさめ【仕納め】the last work to be done.
しおしお[と]【悄悄[と]】¶彼は～帰ってきた He came back *downhearted* (≒ *crestfallen*).
しおだし【塩出し】¶魚の～をする *desalt* fish; *remove the salt from* salted fish.
しおづけ【塩漬け】salted food. ¶野菜の～ *pickled* vegetables. 魚の～ *salted* fish. 魚を～にする *preserve* fish *in salt*; *salt* fish.
しおどき【潮時】(よい機会) an opportunity; a good chance; (潮流) the tidal hour. ¶ものには～というものがある There is *a time* for everything. ちょうどよい～に彼は辞意を表明した Just *at the right moment* he announced his resignation. ～を見て席を立った I *seized an opportunity to* rise up from my seat. / I *took occasion to* leave my seat.
シオニズム Zionism.
しおひがり【潮干狩り】¶～に行く go *gathering sea shells* [at low tide].
しおみず【塩水】salt water; brine. ¶それらを～につけなさい Steep them in *salt water* (≒ *brine*).
しおもの【塩物】salted fish.
しおやき【塩焼き】¶魚の～ fish *broiled with salt*.
しおらし·い ¶彼らは～い態度で私の話を聞いていた They were listening to me in a *modest* attitude. 彼はなかなか～いことを言う He says quite *pretty* things.
ジオラマ a diorama.
しおり【枝折り·栞】a bookmark[er]; (案内) a guide; a guidebook. ¶修学旅行の～ *a guide to* the school excursion. 読みかけの本に～をはさんだ I put *a bookmark[er]* between the leavesof the book I had not yet done with.
—戸 a wicket made of branches and twigs.
しお·れる【萎れる】¶～れた花 *drooping* flowers. 朝顔は昼までには～れてしまう Morning glories *wither* by noon. 彼は～れていた He *was out of spirits*.
しおん【紫苑】〔植物〕an aster.
しおん【子音】a consonant. ⇒ しいん
しおん【歯音】〔音声学〕a sibilant.
しか【鹿】a deer (単複同形); (雄) a stag; (雌) a hind; (子) a fawn. ¶～の皮 deerskin. ～の肉 venison. ～を追う者は山を見ず(諺) Scenery is lost on the keen sportsman.
しか【市価】the market price. ¶あのスーパーではなんでも～の半値だ They sell everything at half *the market price* in that supermarket. これは～2万円以上もする万年筆だそうだ They say this fountain pen has *the market value* of more than twenty thousand yen. ～の2割引きで求められます You can get it at a discount of twenty percent of *the market price*. 材木の～が下がっている The lumber market is declining.
しか【史家】a historian.
しか【歯科】dental surgery.
—医 a dentist; a dental surgeon. —医院 a dentist's [office]. —大学 a dental college.
しか【賜暇】leave of absence.
-しか ¶これ～ない This is *all* I have. これ～方法はない *No other way* is to be found. 1度～行ったことがない I have been there *only* once. 会社に入って1年に～ならない It's *only* a year since I entered this company. あの人の言うことはうそと～思えない I cannot help thinking what he says is a lie.
しが【歯牙】¶彼はぼくの忠告など～にもかけない He *pays no heed to* my advice. / He *simply ignores* my advice. / He does*n't care a bit about* my advice. ～にかけるに足らない It *is beneath one's notice*.
じか【自家】¶この工場は～発電装置がある This factory has *its own* power plant. 彼は～用の飛行機を持っている He has a plane *for his personal use*. ～製のクッキー *home-made* cookies.
—中毒 auto-intoxication.
じか【耳科】〔医学〕otology.
じか【時価】the current price. ¶この宝石類は全部で～5,000万円と見積もられている These jewels, in all, are estimated at fifty million yen today. ～で買いとろう I will buy it at its *current price*. ～100万円のダイヤモンド a diamond worth a million yen *in current prices* (≒ *in today's money*).
じか【磁化】〔物理〕magnetization.
じか【時下】at this time of year; at present; now.
じが【自我】self; ego. ¶～が強い selfish; egoistic. ～の解放 the emancipation of *ego*. ～を没却する efface *oneself*. 彼もそろそろ～を主張する年ごろだ He is old enough to *assert himself*.
しかい【市会】a city (≒ municipal) assembly.
—議員 a member of the city (≒ municipal) assembly. —議長 [the] chairman of

the city (≒ municipal) assembly.

しかい【司会】chairmanship. ¶今度の会の～をするのはだれですか Who will be the *chairman* at the next meeting? / Who will *preside over* (≒ *at*) the next meeting? A氏の～で開会した The meeting was opened *under the chairmanship of* Mr. A. 彼は～がうまい He is a good hand at *presiding over* a meeting.

—者 a chairman; a chairwoman; (テレビ番組などの) the master of ceremonies (MC, M.C. と略すことがある).

しかい【視界】sight; view; the field of vision. ¶～が広い(狭い) *The range of vision* is wide (narrow). ～がきく(きかない) *Visibility* is good (poor). やがて陸地が～に入ってきた We soon *came in sight of* land. / Soon land *came in sight*. 飛行機が飛び立ちやがて～から消えた An airplane took off and soon *went out of sight*. 濃霧のため～が 20 メートルになった The dense fog decreased *visibility* to 20 meters.

しかい【斯界】this circle; the line; the subject. ¶彼は～の権威だ He is an authority *on the subject* (≒ *in the line*). ～の功労者 a man of merit *in this circle*.

しかい【死海】the Dead Sea.

しがい【市外】the suburbs. ¶大阪の～に住む live *on the outskirts* (≒ *in the suburbs*) of [the city of] Osaka.

しがい【市街】(市) a city; a town; (街路) [the] streets.

—戦 street fighting. —電車 米 a streetcar; 英 a tramcar. 新(旧)— the new (old) town.

しがい【死骸・屍骸】a dead body; a corpse.

じかい【次回】next time; the next occasion. ¶～の会 the *next* meeting. ～完結(雑誌など) To be concluded.

じかい【自戒】self-discipline; self-admonition. ¶心から～を望みます I do hope you will exercise *self-discipline*.

じかい【自壊】—作用 disintegration.

じかい【磁界】〔物理〕〔電気〕the magnetic field.

じがい【自害】suicide. ¶ピストルで～する *commit suicide* (≒ *kill oneself*) with a pistol.

しがいせん【紫外線】ultraviolet rays.

しかえし【仕返し】revenge; retaliation. ¶いつか彼に～してやる I will *revenge myself on* him some day. 彼は～がこわいから黙っていた The fear that he might *be revenged* made him silent.

しかく【四角】a square. ¶～な文字 *angular* characters. 真～ *a* regular (≒ true) *square*. ～ばった顔 a *stiff* face. ～しめんな性格 [a man of] *square* character.

しかく【死角】the dead angle. ¶少女は～に入っていたので運転手には見えなかったらしい The girl seems to have been in the driver's *blind spot* (≒ *dead angle*).

しかく【刺客】an assassin. ¶～におそわれる be attacked by *an assassin*. 大統領は～の手にたおれた The president *was assassinated*.

しかく【視角】〔物理〕the angle of vision; the optic angle; the visual angle.

しかく【視覚】sight. ¶年をとるにつれ～が衰える Our [*sense of*] *sight* weakens as we grow old. このポスターは大いに～に訴えるところがある This poster has much to appeal *visually* to passers-by. 小鳥は犬よりも～がよいそうだ I hear birds have better *sight* than dogs.

—教育 visual education. —教具 visual aids.

しかく【資格】**1**〖身分・地位〗a capacity. ¶私は業界代表の～でその会議に出た I attended the conference *in the capacity of* a trade delegate.

私は今一父兄としての～で発言しています I am now speaking *in my private capacity* as one of the parents.

この地区に住む一住民としての～で質問いたします I would like to ask a question *in the capacity of* an inhabitant of this district.

今のところ彼は学長代行の～だ For the time being he *is entitled to* be the acting president of the university.

2〖身分・地位を得るのに必要な条件〗qualifications. ¶教員の～をとる obtain *qualifications* as a teacher.

そんな人に教員の～はない Such a man *is* not *eligible for* a teacher at all.

彼は弁護士の～を持っている He has a lawyer's *license*.

大学卒の～がないので，彼はいつまでも課長になれない He will never be promoted to a section chief, for (≒ because) he is not a university graduate.

彼は～のないものの悲哀をつくづくと感じた He felt such a deep sorrow as an *unqualified* person usually experiences.

入会の～は厳しいのでしょうか Are the *requirements* for membership severe?

彼なら～充分その仕事をりっぱにやってのけられる I believe he *is* quite *equal to* the task.

きみにはそんなことを要求する～はない You have no *right* to ask for such a thing.

熱戦の末辛勝，準決勝進出の～を得た Winning after a close game, we obtained *the right* to go into the semifinals.

彼ならその時代の劇文学を批評する～がある He *is* fully *qualified to* review the drama of that period.

そのようなおほめのことばを受ける～はございません I don't *deserve* such words of praise.

—審査 screening. 選挙— the elective franchise. 入学— requirements for admission. 応募— requirements for application. 無—者 an unqualified person. 有—者 a qualified person.

しがく【史学】historical science; historical studies.

—科 the history course.

しがく【私学】a private school; (大学) a private college (≒ university). ¶彼は～に学ん

でいる He is studying at *a private college* (≒ *a private university*).

しがく【詩学】poetics; (韻律学) prosody.

しがく【視学】(学校の視察) school inspection. (視察する人) a school inspector.

—官 a government school inspector.

じかく【自覚】consciousness. ¶責任を～すべきだ You should *be aware* (≒ *be conscious*) *of* your responsibility. 彼は自分の短所を～していない He *is* not *aware of* his own defects. 私は事態の認識について国民の～を促した I urged the nation to *wake up to* the realization of the situation.

—症状 a subjective symptom.

じかく【字画】strokes in a Chinese character.

じかく【耳殻】〘解剖〙 the concha (複 conchae); a pinna (複 pinnae).

しかけ【仕掛け・仕掛】(装置) a device; (わな) a trick. ¶このおもちゃは電気で動く～になっている This toy is electrically driven. われわれは相手の～を待った We waited for the opponent to *attack*. 大～の演出 production *on a large scale*.

—花火 set fireworks. 電気— an electric device.

しか・ける【仕掛ける】¶クマにわなを～けた I *set* a trap *for* bears. ～けた仕事をやめる羽目になった I was forced to stop the work before it was completed. けんかを～けたのは彼のほうで私ではない It was he, not I, that *picked* (≒ *provoked*) the quarrel.

しかざん【死火山】an extinct volcano. ¶この火山は～だ This volcano *is extinct*.

しかし【然し】but; however; though; although; nevertheless.

しかじか【然然・云云】such and such; so and so. ¶これこれ～の本 *such and such* books. ～のことを説明する explain *so and so*. あちらのようすはこれこれ～です *Such* 〔*and such*〕 is his state of affairs.

じがじさん【自画自賛】self-praise. ¶彼はいつも～ばかりしている He always *blows his own trumpet*.

じかしんけい【耳下神経】〘解剖学〙the parotid.

じかせん【耳下腺】〘解剖学〙the parotid gland.

—炎 parotitis.

じがぞう【自画像】a self-portrait.

しかた【仕方】**1**〘方法・やり方〙a way; a method; a means. ¶はじめは英語の勉強の～がわからなかった At first I did not know *how to* learn English.

出納簿の記入の～が正常でない The account book is not filled in in the proper *way*.

配列の～が悪い It is arranged in the wrong *way*.

このごろの若者はあいさつの～もろくに知らぬ The young men of today do not know *how to* make a proper greeting.

練習の～が根本からまちがってる Your *method* of practicing is fundamentally wrong.

フグ料理の～を知っていますか Do you know *how to* cook a globefish?

なんだ，この掃除の～は What! The *way* you have swept the room!

2〘どうにもならぬ・やむをえぬ〙¶これはまったく～のないことであった It was quite an *unavoidable* thing.

～がないのでこれを使っている I *am obliged to* make use of it.

ああ言われちゃ，なんとも～がない What can I do if he says that sort of thing?

～がない，きみの言うとおりになる *It can't be helped*. I'll do just as you say.

謝るよりほかに～がなかった *There was nothing for it but to* apologize.

ストのため歩いてゆくよりほかに～なかった I *had no choice but to* walk because of the traffic strike.

相手がうんと言わぬことには～がない *There is no help for it*, unless the other party says "yes."

こちらが悪いんだからいくら非難されても～がない We *deserve* their reproaches, as we are in the wrong.

だれもやろうと言わない．～ないからぼくがやることにした There was nobody ready to do it, so I *was obliged to*.

何度も頼まれたので～なしに承知した I agreed *unwillingly* as I was asked again and again.

社長の命令なら～ない *There is no contending against* the president's order.

もうやってしまったことは～ない What's done can not be undone.

これも運命だから～ない After all we *must accept* our fate.

若いんだから～がない We must *make allowance for* his youth.

金を取り立てようたって相手が一文なしじゃ～がない However hard we may try, we cannot get money back from someone who is penniless.

3〘無益だ・役にたたぬ〙¶陰で悪口を言ったって～ない *There is no use in* speak*ing* ill of others behind their backs.

今更じたばた騒いでも～ない *It is no use* strug*gling* now.

泣いたって～ない *It is no use* cry*ing*.

まったく～のないやつだ，へまばかりやって What a stupid fellow you are! Can't you do anything right?

あんなまぬけじゃ～ない I don't know what to do with such a fool.

それっぽっちの金じゃ～がない Such a small amount of money *is far from sufficient* for the purpose.

4〘がまんできない〙 ¶虫に刺されてかゆくて～ない This insect bite itches *like mad*

昨夜あまり寝てないので眠くて～ない I am *terribly* sleepy, because I could not sleep well last night.

子どものことが気になって～なかった I *could not help* feel*ing* uneasy about my child.

東京は暑くて～ありません It is *unbearably* hot

in Tokyo.

たくさんの人が泳いでいるのを見ると自分も泳ぎたくて〜なかった I *wanted very much to* swim myself when I saw a lot of people swimming there.

赤ん坊が一晩じゅう泣いてうるさくて〜なかった I *could not put up with* the baby's crying all night.

じかたび【地下足袋】rubber-soled socks. ¶〜で作業する work in *rubber-soled socks.*

じがため【地固め】¶敷地を〜する *solidify* (≒ *level*) the building site.

じかだんぱん【直談判】direct negotiation. ¶〜する negotiate with (*a person*) personally. 〜で支払いを納得させた I persuaded him to pay the money *by direct negotiation* (≒ *by negotiating with him personally*).

しかつ【死活】life and death; life or death. ¶この計画が成功するかどうかがこの会社の〜にかかわる問題だ Whether this project will be successful or not affects *the very fate* of our company.

—問題 a matter of life and (≒ or) death.

しがつ【四月】April.

じかつ【自活】¶〜している学生 a *self-supporting* student. 彼は16歳で〜しはじめた He began to *support himself* at sixteen. / He began to *earn his living* at sixteen. 〜の道を考えたまえ You must think of [some means of] *earning your own livelihood.*

しかつめらし·い【鹿爪らしい】¶〜い顔つき a *grave* (≒ *solemn*) look. 〜くあいさつを述べる salute *formally* (≒ *ceremoniously*). 〜くお辞儀をする make a *formal* bow.

しかと【確と】exactly; for certain; positively; (明白に) clearly; (かたく) firmly; tightly. ¶〜頼んだ I ask you *from the bottom of my heart.* 準備が整っているか〜見届けたい I *will see* [*to it*] that everything is ready.

しがな·い ¶〜い商売 *humble* (≒ *petty*) business. 〜い恋 *hopeless* love. 〜い暮らしをする live a *miserable* life.

じかに【直に】¶それについて彼の気持ちを〜聞いてみましょう I'll go and sound him about that *myself.* 〜頼んでみなさい Go and ask him *directly* (≒ *in person*). 壁に〜はってはいけません Never paste it *right* on the wall. ぼくはその話を彼から〜聞いた I heard the story *directly* from him.

じがね【地金】(金属) ground metal; (本性) *one's* true character. ¶〜は鉄だ The *ground metal* is iron. とうとう〜が出た He has revealed *his true character* at last. それで彼はうっかり〜を出した That made him *betray himself* unintentionally.

しかねない【為兼ねない】¶彼は脱獄も〜 He *is capable of* breaking out of prison. 彼は遅刻も〜 He *is liable to* be late. 彼女はあまりにも意気消沈しているので自殺も〜 She is so dejected that *there is a possibility* that she will commit suicide. あの調子ではとんだ乱暴も〜 If matters go on at this rate, he would be outrageous beyond imagination.

しかばね【屍】a dead body; a corpse. ¶生ける〜 *a* living *corpse.*

しがみつ·く ¶つり皮に〜く *hang on to* a strap. 彼は一度〜いたら放さない Once he *clings to* it, he never takes his hands off. 子どもが母に〜いた The child *held on to* his mother.

しかめつら【顰め面】a wry face; a frown. ¶〜をする make *a wry face* (≒ *a grimace*). 彼はいつも〜をしている He always *looks sullen* (≒ *looks sulky*).

しか·める【顰める】¶顔を〜める make *a grimace* (≒ *a wry face*); *frown* (*at*; *on*). 彼は顔を〜めて座っていた He sat there *frowning* (≒ *with a frown*).

しかも【然も·而も】besides; moreover; and yet; for all that. ¶雨の中を出かけた. 〜かさも持たずに I started in the rain, *and that* without an umbrella. 疲れきっていた. 〜空腹だった I was tired out, and, *what was worse*, I was hungry. しかられて〜改めない Although he was scolded, he has not repented yet. 全力で走って〜敗れたのならしかたがない If you ran with all your speed *and yet* you lost the race, it couldn't be helped. 彼女は美人で〜気だてがいい She is beautiful, *and* kindhearted *too.*

しかりつ·ける【叱り付ける】¶呼び出して〜けた I called him and *gave a good scolding to* him. 頭から〜けられた I *was called down* severely. (アメリカの口語用法).

しか·る【叱る】scold; give (*a person*) a scolding. ¶彼を〜ってやった I *have given* him *a scolding.* / I *have scolded* him. うるさいからといって子どもを〜るな Don't *be cross with* the child for being noisy.

しかるべき【然るべき】(適当な) proper; due; right; (かなりの) respectable; considerable. ¶それについては彼が謝って〜だ It is *proper* (≒ *natural*) that he should apologize for it. その役にはだれか〜人を捜そう Let's find somebody *suitable* for the position. よい教育を受ければ〜生活が約束される Good education will promise a *decent* (≒ *respectable*) life.

しかるべく【然るべく】¶〜取りはからってください Please see to it *as you think best.* 〜処置してほしい I want you to deal with it *in a proper way.*

シガレット a cigaret[te].

—ケース a cigarette case. —ホルダー a cigarette holder.

しかん【士官】an officer.

海軍— a naval officer. —学校 a military academy. —候補生 a cadet. 陸軍— a military officer.

しかん【弛緩】relaxation.

しかん【史観】a historical view.

唯物— historical materialism.

しかん【子癇】〔医学〕eclampsia.

しかん【歯冠】the crown (of a tooth).

しがん【志願】(申請) application; (進んでやること) volunteering. ¶A大学の入学を〜した He *applied for* admission to A University. 戦争が始まるや彼は～して従軍した He *volunteered* for military service as soon as war was declared. 彼女は～して辺地へ赴いた She *volunteered* to be sent to a remote place (*as* a teacher).

—者 an applicant. **—書** a written application; an application form. **—兵** a volunteer.

じかん【次官】 a vice-minister; an undersecretary.

大蔵**—** a Vice-Minister of Finance. 事務**—** a permanent secretary. 政務**—** a parliamentary vice-minister.

じかん【時間】1〚時刻〛time. ¶ 予定の～になっても彼女は来なかった She did not turn up at the appointed *time*.

～は何時ですか What *time* is it now?

東京駅に8時集合. ～厳守のこと Gather at Tokyo Station at 8 o'clock *sharp*.

もう寝る～だ It is about *time* to go to bed.

もうそろそろ彼が帰ってきてもいい～だ He should be coming home soon. / It is about *time* he came home.

もう～です. 答案を出してください *Time* is up. Hand in your papers.

彼は～をよく守る He *is very punctual*.

彼は～きっちりに現われた He turned up *on time*.

彼女はいつも約束の～に遅れる She *is* always *behind time for* appointments.

～をまちがえないでください Be sure to remember the *correct time*.

きょうは帰りの～が遅くなる I'll *be late* coming back today.

いつもの～においでください Please come and see me at *the usual time*.

約束の～にやっとまにあった I was barely *in time* for the appointed hour.

言われたとおりの～に行ったが彼は不在だった He was absent, though I called on him at his *appointed time*.

～を西部標準時に合わせる *set a watch to* Western standard time.

毎日毎日～に縛られて生活するのがいやになった I am tired of living every day with so little *time* to call my own.

殺人の行なわれた～は1時と2時の間と思われる We guess the murder was committed between one and two.

運命を決する～が刻一刻と迫ってきた The fatal *hour* is pressing every moment.

バスは～どおりに運行されている The bus is running *on time* (≒ *on schedule*).

飛行機は30分ほど～より遅れて空港に着いた The plane arrived at the airport half an hour *behind schedule*.

駅の時計で～を合わせてきた I have *set my watch* by the station clock.

～がなくなりかけた *Time* is running out.

その発表は～的にみてまずかった The announcement *was* not *timely*.

～的要素も十分考慮に入れて計画を立てなさい Make careful plans with due regard to *time*.

2〚時刻と時刻との間〛¶ ここから何～かかりますか. バスで2～かかります *How long* does it take from here? It takes two *hours* by bus.

この仕事は～がかかる It takes a lot of *time* to do the work.

いくら～をかけてもいいから正確に調べてください Check up exactly on the matter. You may spend as much *time* as you like.

そんなことをするのは～のむだだ It only wastes *time*. / It's a mere waste of *time*.

話に夢中になって～のたつのも忘れた I was so deep in conversation that I was unaware of *the* passage of *time*.

～がたつにつれ皆焦燥の色を濃くした *As time* passed, we came to feel more and more impatient.

～はどんどんたっていくし, 彼女は来ないし, 気が気でなかった I felt nervous that she did not turn up though *time* went by quickly.

出発までもう～がなかった I had already no *time* before I started.

もう少し～がたてば真相も判明しよう The truth will be revealed with the lapse of *time*.

ぼくにはそんなことにかまっている～はない I have no *time* to waste on such a matter.

そのことについて前もってきみと相談する～がなかった I had no *time* to consult with you about it beforehand.

まだまだ～はたっぷりあるから落ち着いてやりなさい Relax before you do it. You have plenty of *time*.

彼はわざわざ～をさいてぼくのところを訪ねてくれた He *took time off* his busy work to call on me.

私どものために貴重な～をさいてくださってありがとうございます Thank you for having spared your valuable *time* for us.

なんとか～のつごうをつけていただけませんか Couldn't you *make time* to be present?

自分の～がなくてよわっている The trouble is that I have no *time* to call my own.

機内に閉じ込められている間どうして～を過ごしましたか How did you spend *your time* while you were shut up in the plane?

彼はひまで～を持て余している He does not know how to use *time*.

汽車の出るまでパチンコをして～を過ごした I spent *the time* playing a game of pinball before the train started.

どうして～をつぶそうか困っていたところだ I am just at a loss how to *kill time*.

コンピューターは～と労力を節約する The computer *saves time* and labor.

彼女は～の使い方がへただ She does not *make good use of her time*.

あれこれ言いわけを言って彼が来るまで～をかせいだ I *gained time* until he came, making variousexcuses.

これはとても一, 二～ではできません. もう少し～を延ばしてください I cannot finish this in *an hour* or two. Please give me a little more *time*. 大事なことですから，考える～をください As it is important, I would like to ask for some *time* to think it over.

もはや彼の辞任は～の問題だ His resignation is now *a question of time*.

～を制限されると，落ち着いてものが考えられない When *time* is limited thus, I cannot think it over in a settled frame of mind.

食後1～，2錠服用のこと Take two tablets *an hour* after each meal.

3 〚授業時間〛 ¶ 2～めはなんの授業ですか What lesson do you have for the second *period*?

英語の～に当てられた I was asked to answer a question in the English *class*.

月曜日には6～授業があります We have six *lessons* on Monday.

ぼくの学校は1～，45分の授業です Our school period is 45 minutes for each *lesson*.

—外手当 an overtime allowance. —外労働 overtime work. —給 payment by the hour. —給水 a time-restricted water supply. —帯 a time period. —表 a timetable. 営業— business hours. 勤務— work hours. 現地— local time. 授業— school hours. 夏— daylight saving time; 英 summer time.

じかんぎめ【時間ぎめ】 ¶ タイピストを～で雇った We engaged a typist *by the hour*.

じかんぎれ【時間切れ】 ¶ 試合は～で引き分けになった The game ended in a tie, as *time ran out*.

しき【式】(儀式) a ceremony; a rite; (方法・型) a method; a style; (数式) a formula (複 formulas; formulae).

¶ ～を挙行する hold *a ceremony*. 山田～方法 Yamada's *way* (≒ *method*) of doing things. アメリカ～ホテル an American-*style* hotel. ゴシック～建築 Gothic architecture. 彼は～の計算がうまい He is good at *figures*. 理論を～で表わす *formularize* a theory.

しき【士気】 morale; fighting spirit. ¶ 戦いに勝って軍隊の～があがっていた The *morale* of the army was high after its victory in battle. ～が衰えている The *morale* is low. これは大いにチームの～に影響する This has much effect on the whole team's *morale*.

しき【四季】 the four seasons. ¶ このあたり一帯は～の変化にとんでいる The whole district is rich in changes of *the* 〔*four*〕 *seasons*. この公園は～を通じて美しい This park is good to look at *all through the year* (≒ *all year round*). この庭園は～折々の花で彩られる This garden is beautifully colored with flowers of *each season*.

しき【死期】 the time of death; the last hour. ¶ 彼の～が近づいている He is lying on his deathbed. / He is on the brink of death. 余病が～を早めた Complications hurried his death.

しき【私記】 a private record.

しき【指揮】 command; (監督) superintendence. ¶ 課長の～を受けて働く work under the *command* (≒ *direction*) of the chief. オーケストラを～する *conduct* an orchestra. 首相の～を仰ぐ ask *orders* from the Prime Minister. 部隊を～する *command* a troop. 社長みずから陣頭～をとった The president himself *took* personal *charge of* the staff.

—官 a commander; a commanding officer. —者 (オーケストラの) a conductor; (合唱団・社会運動などの) a leader; (探検隊などの) a commander. —台〔音楽〕 a podium. —棒 a baton.

しき【紙器】 (紙製品) a paper-made article; (紙容器) a paper container.

しぎ【鴫】〔鳥類〕 a snipe.

じき【直】 at once; soon; (直接) directly.

¶ ～お正月だ The New Year is coming *soon* (≒ *at hand*). 彼は～帰ります He will be back *very soon* (≒ *in a few minutes*). 彼の家は～隣だ His house is *just* next to mine.

—弟子 *one's* direct pupil. —取引 (直接取引) direct transaction; (現金取引) cash transaction.

じき【次期】 next time; next term. ¶ ～国会 the *next* session of the Diet. ～首相 the *next* Prime Minister. ～大統領 the President *for the next term*. ～大統領に立候補する run for the *next* presidency.

じき【時期】 (時) the time; (期間) the period; (季節) the season. ¶ 今はそれをする～ではない This is not *a* good *time* to do it. 今こそ登山にもってこいの～だ This is *a* good *season* for climbing.

じき【時機】 a chance; an opportunity.

¶ ～を待つ wait for *an opportunity* (≒ *a chance*). ～をとらえる(逃がす) seize (miss) *an opportunity*. まだ～を得ない The *time* is not ripe yet. ～を見て話そう I will *bide my time* before telling it to him. 何事も～を逃がしてはだめだ Everything is fruitless if it is *behind time*.

じき【磁気】 magnetism.

—あらし a magnetic storm. —鉱 magnetite. —録音器 a magnetic recorder; (テープによる) a magnetic tape recorder.

じき【磁器】 porcelain; china〔ware〕.

じぎ【字義】 the meaning (≒ signification; sense) of a word. ¶ この語は～どおりに使われている This word is used *in a literal sense* (≒ *literally*).

じぎ【時宜】 circumstances; the occasion.

¶ ～を得た処置をとる take *timely* (≒ *suitable*) action. 彼は～にかなったあいさつをした He offered (≒ extended) *appropriate* greetings.

じぎ【児戯】 child's play; (子どもらしさ) childishness. ¶ このような企ては～に等しい Such an attempt *is quite childish* (≒ *is mere child's play*).

しきい【敷居】 the threshold; (戸口の) a doorsill; (窓の) a window sill. ¶ ～が高くなりました

I feel awkward in calling on you. / I feel it awkward to come here. 二度と私の家の～をまたぐな Never cross the *threshold* of my house again. / Never *darken my door* again. / Never come to my house again.

しきいし【敷石】a flagstone ; a flag. ¶～を敷いた道 a road *paved* (≒ *flagged*) *with stone*.

しきいた【敷き板】decking ; planking ; (ボートの) a bottom board.

しきうつし【敷き写し】a tracing. ¶その模様の～をしてみよう I will try to *make a tracing* of the patterns.

しぎかい【市議会】a city council.
—議員 米 a city (≒ town) councilman ; an alderman ; 英 a city (≒ town) councilor.

しきがわ【敷き皮】(敷物) a fur cushion ; (くつの) an inner sole.

しきかん【色感】the color sense. ¶優れた～の持ち主 a man of excellent *sense of color*.

しききん【敷金】a deposit. ¶あの借家の～は家賃の１か月分だ The house is to let on *a deposit* corresponding to a month's rent.

しきけん【識見】discernment ; insight ; judgment. ¶～が高い人 a man of broad and intelligent *views* ; a man of *discernment* (≒ *wisdom*).

しきこう【色光】〘写真〙colored light.

しきさい【色彩】color ; 英 colour. ¶美しい～の本 a *colorful* book ; a book *full of colors*. この小説は文学的～に乏しい This novel lacks *a* literary *tinge*. その行事は宗教的～が強い The event has *a* strong *tinge* of religion. 私は～感覚が鋭い I have a keen *color* sense. / My sense of *color* is keen. 彼は～感覚が優れている He has a remarkable sense of *color*.

しきし【色紙】a square piece of fancy paper.

しきじ【式辞】a ceremonial address ; a congratulatory address. ¶彼は卒業式の～を述べた He gave *an address* at the commencement. / He made *a ceremonial* (≒ *a congratulatory*) *address* at the graduation exercises.

しきじ【式次】the program of a ceremony.

じきじき【直直】¶彼は社長～の命令で大阪支店に転勤した He was transferred to the Osaka branch by the president's *direct* orders. ご主人に～にお目にかかりたい I'd like to see your husband *personally* (≒ *in person*).

しきしゃ【識者】intelligent people. ¶その問題について～の意見を聞きたい I should like to invite the opinions of *the intelligent* (≒ *the informed*) on the subject.

しきじゃく【色弱】〔slight〕color-blindness.

しきじょう【式場】a ceremonial hall.

しきじょう【色情】sexual desire ; sexual appetite ; lust. ¶～を挑発する excite *sexual desire*.
—狂(病名) sexual insanity ; erotomania ; (人) a sexual maniac ; an erotomaniac.

しきせ【仕着せ】clothes provided by the employer ; livery. ¶店員はそろいの～を着て仕事をしている The clerks are working in *livery*.

しきそ【色素】coloring matter ; 〘生物〙pigment.
—欠乏症〘医学〙albinism. —細胞 a pigment cell.

じきそ【直訴】a direct appeal. ¶～する make *a direct appeal* (*to*).

しきそう【色相】〘物理〙a hue.

しきだい【式台】a stoop.

しきたり【仕来たり】¶～にとらわれるな Be free from *convention*. / Don't be a slave to *old customs*.

ジギタリス〘薬品〙digitalis ; 〘植物〙〔a〕digitalis ; 〔a〕foxglove.

ジギタリン〘薬品〙digitalin.

じきだん【直談】a personal interview.
¶彼と～した I had *a personal interview* with him. / I *negotiated directy* with him.

しきち【敷地】a site ; ground. ¶この付近は住宅用の～に造成されつつある The place around here is being turned into *a* building *lot*. その工場の～はまだ決まっていない The *site* for the factory is not yet fixed.

しきちょう【色調】color tone. ¶柔らかい～の風景画 a landscape of mild *color tone*.

しきつ·める【敷き詰める】¶砂利を～めた道 a road *covered all over with* gravel ; a gravel road ; a *gravelled* path. 床にじゅうたんを～めた I *spread* a carpet *all over* the floor. 部屋にじゅうたんを～める *cover* the room with a carpet. じゅうたんの～めた部屋 a *carpeted* room.

しきてん【式典】a ceremony ; rites.

じきに【直に】¶彼は～ここへ来る He will *soon* be here. / He will be here *in a minute*. ～よくなります You will be well again *before long* (≒ *in a few days*). もう～春になる Spring *is near at hand*. / Spring *is drawing near*. 彼は～かっとなる He *easily* gets excited.

じきひつ【直筆】an autograph ; *a person's* own writing. ¶漱石の～の手紙 an *autograph* letter of Soseki. これは彼の～の手紙だ This letter was written by himself.

しきふ【敷布】a〔bed〕sheet.

しきふく【式服】a ceremonial dress ; ceremonial clothes.

しきぶとん【敷き布団】a mattress ; a sleeping mat.

しきべつ【識別】discrimination. ¶彼は～力のある人だ He is a man of *discrimination*. この両者は容易に～できる These two can *be* readily *distinguished*〔*from* each other〕. / These two *are* readily *distinguishable*〔*from* each other〕. きみくらいの年齢なら善悪の～はつきそうなものだ You are old enough to *tell* (≒ *know*)〔what is〕right *from*〔what is〕wrong. / You ought to know better.

じきまき【直播き】sowing the field with rice seed.

しきみ【樒】〘植物〙a Chinese anise.

しきもう【色盲】color blindness. ¶彼は～だ He is *color blind* (≒ *a color blind person*). 赤緑— red-green blindness.

しきもく【式目】a code.

しきもの【敷物】a carpet ; a rug. ¶床に～を敷く spread *a carpet* (≒ *a rug*) on a floor ; *carpet* a floor.

じぎゃく【自虐】self-torturing. ¶彼は～性が強い He shows a strong tendency to *self-torture*.
—症 masochism. —症患者 a masochist.

しきゅう【子宮】the womb ; 〖解剖学〗〖医学〗 the uterus.
—外妊娠 extrauterine pregnancy. —がん uterine cancer. —内膜炎 endometritis.

しきゅう【支給】supply ; (支払い) payment. ¶被災者に食糧が～された Food *was supplied* (≒ *was furnished*) to the sufferers. 彼らの月給は毎月25日に～される They *are paid* on 25th every month. 彼は世間並みの俸給を～されている He *has* (≒ *is given*) an average pay. 昼食代として1,000円～された I *was allowed* a thousand yen for lunch. / An allowance of a thousand yen *was given* me for lunch money.

しきゅう【四球】〖野球〗¶ピッチャーは彼に～を出した The pitcher gave him *four balls*. / The pitcher walked him *on four balls*. 彼は～で一塁に出た He *walked* to first base 〔*on four balls*〕.

しきゅう【死球】〖野球〗¶彼は～を受けて倒れた He was hit by *a pitched ball* and fell on the ground. (a dead ball はピッチャーの投球が打者にあたったあとで試合が中断される球などをいうことに注意).

しきゅう【至急】¶～にご返事をください I'm expecting your *immediate* (≒ *prompt*) answer. / Please give me your answer *as soon as you can* (≒ *as soon as possible*). この問題は～解決されなければならない This problem must be solved *without delay*. 彼は～アメリカから帰国した He *hurried* back from America. ぼくは大～その仕事をかたづけた I finished the work *with all* 〔*possible*〕 *dispatch*.
—電報 an urgent telegram.

じきゅう【自給】¶あの国は食糧を～自足している That country *is self-sufficient* in food.

じきゅう【持久】—戦 a protracted war. —力 endurance ; sustaining (≒ staying) power ; stamina.

じきゅう【時給】payment by the hour.

しきゅうしき【始球式】〖野球〗¶知事が～を行なった The governor *threw the first ball*.

しきょ【死去】death.

じきょ【辞去】¶夕方彼の宅を～した I *left* his house toward evening. / I *took* 〔*my*〕 *leave of* him in the evening.

しきょう【市況】the market. ¶活発な～ *a* brisk *market*. 閑散な～ *a* dull *market*. ～が回復する *The market* recovers. ～が崩れる *The market* collapses. ～は活発である *The market* is active. ～は相変わらず堅調だ *Market conditions* remain firm.
株式— the stock market.

しきょう【司教】〖宗教〗(カトリック) a bishop.

しきょう【詩興】poetical inspiration.

しぎょう【始業】commencement of work. ¶この店は10時から～する This store *opens* at ten. ～のベルが鳴っている There goes the *beginning bell* (≒ *work-bell*)!
—式 the opening ceremony. —時刻 the opening time.

じきょう【自供】confession ; acknowledgement. ¶彼は罪を～した He *confessed* his guilt. 彼女は罪を犯したと～した She *confessed herself* 〔*to* be〕 guilty. 彼はその金を盗んだと～した He *confessed* that he had stolen the money. / He *confessed to having stolen* the money.

じぎょう【事業】(仕事) work ; (企業) an enterprise ; an undertaking ; (実業) business. ¶新たに～を起こす start *a* new *enterprise*. ～を縮小する reduce *business*.
—家(企業家) an enterprising man ; (実業家) an industrialist ; a businessman. —資金 business funds. —所得 an income from *one's* enterprise. —税 an enterprise tax. 教育(社会 ; 慈善)— an educational (a social ; a charitable) work. 公共— a public utility enterprise ; public service. 国営(民営 ; 国家)— a government (private ; state) enterprise.

しきょうひん【試供品】a sample.

しきょく【支局】a branch office.

しきよく【色欲】lust.

じきょく【時局】the situation ; (非常の) a crisis ; an emergency. ¶われわれは今重大な～に直面している We are confronted with *a grave situation* (≒ *an emergency*). ～を収拾する save (≒ improve) *the situation*. 時としてわれわれは困難な～に対処しなければならないことがある Sometimes we must meet (≒ deal with) *the* difficult *situation* (≒ *crisis*). ～を改善するには忍耐強い努力が必要だ It takes patient efforts to improve *the situation*.

じきょく【磁極】〖物理〗a magnetic pole.

しきり【仕切り】¶2室間の～ *a partition* between two rooms. ～の二つあるかばん a bag with two *compartments*.
—書(送り状) an invoice ; (計算書) a statement of accounts. —壁 a partition 〔wall〕.

しきりに【頻りに】(しばしば) very often ; frequently ; (絶えず) continually ; (盛んに) very hard ; (熱心に) eagerly ; intently.
¶惨事が～起こる Disastrous affairs take place *frequently* (≒ *very often* ; *one after another*). 雨が～降っている It is raining *very hard*. 彼は～きみに会いたがっていた He was *very* eager to see you. 亡き母のことが～思い起こされる I am *continually* reminded of my dead mother. そんなことをしないようにと彼は～私に警告してくれた He warned me *repeatedly* against doing such a thing. 彼は～政

界で名をあげたがっている He *eagerly* (≒ *earnestly*) desires to cut a brilliant figure in the political world.

しき·る【仕切る】¶部屋を二つに~る *divide* (≒ *partition*) a room *into* two compartments. 3月末で帳簿を~る We *settle accounts* at the end of March. 両大関とも十分に~って立ち上がった Both *sumo* champion wrestlers took a long time to *get off the mark to fight*.

しきん【至近】—距離 the shortest range; point-blank range. —弾 a near hit.

しきん【資金】capital; funds; (基金) a fund. ¶~を調達する raise the *capital* (≒ *funds*). ~を出す furnish *funds*. 彼らは貧困者の救済~の募集を始めた They started collecting (≒ raising) *a fund* for the relief of the poor and needy. 工場をつくる~が足りない We are short of *funds* for building a new factory. 彼女は結婚~をかせいでいる She is working for *money* to marry on. わが社は~難に陥っている Our company is in *financial difficulty*.

運転(運動; 回転; 救済; 奨学; 準備)— a working (campaign; revolving; relief; scholarship; reserve) fund.

しきん【賜金】a grant of money.

しぎん【詩吟】recitation of Chinese poems.

しきんせき【試金石】a touchstone. ¶この作品は彼の将来の~となるだろう This work will be *a touchstone* (≒ *a test*) of his ability.

しく【市区】streets; a municipal district.

しく【詩句】a line; a verse.

し·く【敷く】¶砂利を~いた道 a *graveled* (≒ *gravel*) road. 運動場に砂を~いてもらった We *had* our school yard *sanded*. どうぞ座布団をお~きください Please *sit* (≒ *be seated*) *on* the cushion. 自分で布団を~きなさい *Make* your own bed. あの当時は軍政を~いていた We had a military government at that time. 彼らは城の前に陣を~いた They *made* a camp in front of the castle of their enemy. 2都市間に鉄道が~かれることになっている A railroad is to *be made* (≒ *be laid*) between the two cities.

し·く【如く·若く·及く】¶子を見ること親に~かず The parent is *the best* judge of the child. 用心に~くはない *There is nothing like* caution. / *Nothing is better than* caution.

じく【軸】(中心) a pivot; (心棒) an axis (複 axes); (車の) an axle; (機械の) a shaft; (茎) a stem; a stalk; (巻き物) a scroll; a roll; 〔数学〕axis.
¶マッチの~ matchwood; (1本) a matchstick. ~を床の間にかける hang *a scroll* 〔*-picture*〕 in the alcove.
—受け a bearing. ペン— a penholder.

じく【磁区】〔物理〕a magnetic domain.

じく【字句】¶~にこだわる adhere too closely to *the wording*. 協約の~を修正する make some change in *the wording* (≒ *the phraseology*) of an agreemant.

じくう【時空】〔物理〕space time.

しぐさ【仕草】manners; behavior; gestures.

¶耳の聞こえない人は~で話す The deaf talk (≒ communicate) by *gestures*.

ジグザグ ¶~に進む go *in zigzag*; zigzag.
—行進 a zigzag parade; a snake march.

しくしく ¶~泣く sob; mourn. おなかが~痛む I *have a griping pain* in my bowels.

じくじく ¶汗が~出る The sweat *oozes* out. 雨で~した山道を登った We went up the mountain path *wet* with rain.

しくじり a mistake. ¶なんという~をしでかしたんだ What *a blunder* you made! 彼はよく~をする He often makes *mistakes* (≒ *errors*). 何度も~を重ねてやっと彼はその仕事を終了した After repeated *failures*, he has finished the task at last.

しくじ·る make a mistake; commit an error. ¶入学試験に~る *fail in* the entrance examination. 彼は会社を~った He *has got fired*. / He *has been discharged*.

しくつ【試掘】prospecting. ¶彼らは石油の~をした They *prospected for* oil.
—権 prospecting rights.

シグナル the signal. ¶~が青に変わった *The* 〔*traffic*〕 *signal* (≒ *sign*) turned green.

しくはっく【四苦八苦】¶借金で~している I *am greatly distressed with* debts. 彼は家族を養うのに~している He *is hard put to it to* support his family. 英語で意志を伝えようと~した I *struggled hard to* make myself understood in English.

しくみ【仕組み】(構造) construction; structure.

しく·む【仕組む】¶彼らは政府に対して陰謀を~んだ They *plotted* against the government. この小説はその事件をみごとに~んでいる This novel *is* skillfully *constructed* from the incident. / The plot of this novel *is* skillfully *taken from* the actual incident.

シクラメン〔植物〕a cyclamen.

しぐれ【時雨】a drizzling rain; drizzle.

しぐ·れる【時雨れる】¶夕方所により~れるかもしれない It may *drizzle* toward evening in some places.

しけ【時化】(海の荒れ) stormy (≒ rough) weather; (不漁) a poor catch of fish.

しけい【死刑】death penalty; capital punishment. ¶人を~に処する *put a person* to *execution*; *execute* him. 彼に~を宣告する *sentence* him *to death*. ~の廃止を唱える advocate abolition of *capital punishment*.
—囚 a criminal under sentence of death; a condemned criminal.

しけい【私刑】lynch; lynching.

しけい【紙型】a mold; a paper mold.
¶~をとる make *a paper mold* (*of*)

しけい【詩型·詩形】verse form.
—論 prosody.

じけい【自警】self-warning; vigilance.
—団 a vigilance organization; a watch committee. —団員 a vigilance man.

じけい【次兄】*one's* second brother.

しげき【史劇】a historical play (≒ drama).

しげき【刺激】stimulation; a stimulus. ¶このにおいは目を～する This smell *is irritating to* the eyes. 酸は鼻を～する Acid *is stimulating to* the nose. からしは舌を～する Mustard *bites* the tongue. この騒音は神経を～するからやめてほしい I want this noise stopped, because it *irritates* the nerves. 彼はのんびり屋だから，なにか～を与えたほうがいい Since he is too quiet and easy, he had better be given some *incitement*. ほめることはよい～を与える Praise is *a* good *stimulant*. 彼はよい本を読んでもなんの～も受けない Even when he reads a good book he *is* not *stimulated* at all. あまりにも～のない毎日だった Our everyday life *was* too *dull*. このごろは～の強い映画が多すぎる There are too many movies that *are* too *exciting*. その番組は私にはあまりにも～が強すぎた That program *was* too *exciting* for me. 彼らは～のない生活をきらう They dislike a *monotonous* life. 彼は～を求めて都会にやってきた He came to the city for *excitement*. 通貨膨張による産業への～は大きかった The *stimulation* of industry by inflation was considerable.

しげき【詩劇】a poetic drama; a verse drama.

しげしげと【繁繁と】¶彼は～喫茶店に足を運ぶ He *frequents* a tea room. / He is a *frequent* caller at a tea room. 彼女は子どもの寝顔を～見た She gazed *hard* (≒ *fondly*) at the face of her sleeping child.

しけつ【止血】¶タオルで～した I *stopped the bleeding* with a towel.

—剤 a hemostatic.

じけつ【自決】¶乃木将軍は～した General Nogi *committed suicide*.

民族— racial self-determination.

しげみ【茂み】a thicket; a bush. ¶庭の～ *a thicket* of a garden. ～を分けて山頂に出た Making our way through the *bushes*, we reached the top of the mountain.

しけ·る【湿気る】¶せんべいが～てまずい This *senbei* doesn't taste good as it *is damp*. 日本では6月がいちばんものの～る月です In Japan June is *the wettest* month of the year.

しけ·る【時化る】¶沖合いは～ている It *is stormy* out at sea. 彼は試験に失敗して～た顔をしている He *looks gloomy* (≒ *looks downcast*) as he has failed in the examination. 彼は～たやつだ He is a *stingy* (≒ *miserly*) fellow.

しげ·る【茂る】grow thick; be luxuriant; be overgrown (≒ covered) (*with*). ¶雑草の～った庭 a garden *overgrown* with weeds. 木の～った小高い山 a *thickly wooded* hill. 庭の杉の木がよく～っている The Japan cedars in the garden *have grown leafy*.

しけん【私権】〔法律〕a private right.

しけん【私見】¶～では in *my opinion*. これは私の～にすぎない This is only *my personal* (≒ *private*; *individual*) *opinion*.

しけん【試験】**1**〖人の知識・能力等を問題を出して試す〗examination. ¶あすは英語の～がある We have *an* English *examination* tomorrow. 来週数学の～をします Next week I will give you *a test* in mathematics.

当日簡単な～を行ないます *A* simple *examination* will be held on the day.

来年は大学の入学～を受けなければならない I have to take the entrance *examination* of the university next year.

彼は～に合格した He has passed the *examination*.

彼は1番の成績で～に通った He passed the *examination* with top marks.

彼女は～に落ちた She failed in the *examination*.

～に合格するしないは運と能力が半々だ It depends upon fortune and ability whether one will pass the *examination* or not.

～で山をかけた I outguessed the *examination* questions.

これは～に出そうな問題だ This question seems likely to be asked in the *examination*.

～，～というから勉強がいやになるのだ Referring to the *examination* too often disinclines us for work.

～の採点で忙しい I am busy looking over *the examination papers*.

～の日時はおって知らせる The date and time of the *examination* will be given later on.

ちょっと彼の人物を～してくれませんか Will you give him *a* short character *test*?

ぼくの英語の力が～されているようでこわかった I felt uneasy that I might *be* being *tested* on my ability in English.

2〖物の性質・性能等を試す〗¶新車の性能の～をした The performance *test* of new cars was held.

厳密な～の結果，このエンジンは公害防止基準に合格した This engine satisfied the pollution prevention standard by *a* strict *test*.

～をしてみると，試作品には二，三の欠陥があることがわかった A few defects were found in the experimental articles by that *test*.

～の方法により結果が違ってくる The results differ according to the *testing methods*.

今そのクーラーを～的に使っている We are making *experimental* use of the air-conditioner.

もうそのことは～済みだ It *has* already *been proved*.

3〖合成語〗—科目 examination subjects. —官 an examiner. —管 a test tube. —地獄 the ordeal of entrance examinations. —準備 preparation for the examination. —場 an examination room. —飛行 a test flight. —飛行士 a test pilot. —問題 an examination problem. —用紙 examination papers. 学力— an achievement test. 学年— an annual examination. 学期〔末〕— a term examination. 検定— a certificate examination. 口述— an oral test. 公務員— an examination for public officials. 採用— an examination for employment. 資格— a qualifying examination. 進級— an examination for promotion. 人物— a personality test. 卒業— a graduation examination. 中間— a midterm examination. 追— another examination. 入社— a test for employment in a business company. 筆記— a written examination. 模擬— a sham examination. 水産—場 a fisheries experiment station. 農事—場 an agricultural experiment station. リトマス—紙 litmus paper.

しげん【至言】a wise saying ; a maxim. ¶…とは～だ *It is well* (≒ *truly*) *said* that.... / *There is much truth in the saying* that.... 彼の言はまさに～だ What he said is really *a wise saying*.

しげん【資源】resources. ¶海の～を開発する exploit (≒ develop) the *resources* in the sea. 米国は天然～が豊富だ The United States of America is rich in natural *resources*.
—開発 exploitation of resources. 人的— man-power ; human resources. 天然— natural resources.

じけん【事件】(出来事) an incident ; (法律的な) a case ; (事柄) a matter. ¶それは大～だった It was *a* serious *affair*. 最近数年間においての最も恐ろしい～ the most horrible *incident* in the last few years. あの弁護士に～を依頼しよう Let's entrust that lawyer with the *case*. 彼は～をもみ消そうとした He tried to hush up the *matter*. 目撃者は～の詳細を警察に報告した The witness reported in detail to the police about the *incident*.
殺人— a murder case. 恋愛— a love affair.

じげん【次元】a dimension. ¶3～の空間 three-*dimensional* space. 4～の世界 the four-*dimensional* world. これとそれとは～を異にする This is quite different from that.

じげん【時限】¶きょうの3～めに英語の授業がある We have an English lesson at the third *period* (≒ *hour*) today.
—爆弾 a time (≒ delayed-action) bomb.

しご【死後】¶～の世界 the world *after death*. これはその作家の～発表された This is a *posthumous* work of the writer. 死体は～30時間を経過した The body *has been dead* for 30 hours.
—硬直〘医学〙*rigor mortis* ; post-mortem stiffness.

しご【死語】〘言語学〙a dead language ; (廃語) an obsolete word.

しご【私語】a whisper. ¶授業中～はやめなさい Don't *whisper* in class.

しご【詩語】a poetic word (≒ diction).

じこ【自己】self ; *one*self ; ego. ¶～を知る know *one*self. ～紹介する introduce *one*self. ～流で in *one's* own way (≒ style).
—嫌悪(けんお) self-disgust. —批判 self-criticism.

じこ【事故】(できごと) an accident ; an incident ; (故障) a trouble ; a hitch. ¶途中～もなく着きました I arrived here safe without any *trouble* on the way. ～もなく目的を達成した I achieved my purpose without *hindrance* (≒ *a hitch*). 不注意が～を引き起こす Carelessness causes *accidents*.
交通— a traffic accident. ¶毎日この国では平均3人の交通～死がある Every day, on an average, three persons are killed in traffic *accidents* in this country. 自動車— a car accident. 鉄道— a railroad accident.

じご【事後】¶彼から～承諾を得た I obtained his approval *after the fact*. / I obtained his *ex post facto* consent. 彼から～報告をうけた I received an *ex post facto* report from him.

じご【持碁】a game of *go* that ends in a tie.

じこあんじ【自己暗示】〘心理学〙autosuggestion. ¶彼は～にかかりやすい He is subject to *autosuggestion*.

しこう【至高】supremacy ; sublimity. ¶神は～の存在だ God is the *supreme* being.

しこう【志向】¶われわれが～するのは世界平和である What we *aim at* is world peace.

しこう【指向】—性アンテナ a directional antenna.

しこう【私行】*a person's* private affairs. ¶彼の～は目にあまる His *private doings* are intolerable. / His *private conduct* is unbearable. 彼の～を暴いてやろう I am going to expose his *private affairs*.

しこう【施行】¶この法律は公布の日に～される This law shall *take effect* (≒ *be in force*, *go into operation*) as from the day of its promulgation.
—期日 the date of enforcement. —期間 a period of effectiveness.

しこう【思考】thinking ; thought.
—力 thinking power ; contemplative faculty. ¶～を高める develop my *thinking power*.

しこう【嗜好】〔a〕taste. ¶それは私の～にかなっている It suits my *taste* (≒ *fancy*).
—品 a luxury ; an article of luxury ; (食品) a favorite food.

しこう【歯腔】〘解剖〙a dental cavity.

じこう【耳孔】〘解剖〙the auditory canal ; an ear hole.

じこう【事項】a matter ; an item.
調査— matters for investigation. 関連— relevant matters.

じこう【時好】¶彼のデザインは～に投じた His design has caught the *public fancy*.

じこう【時効】〘法律〙prescription ; a statutory limit ; limitation. ¶～が取得された The *prescription* has been acquired. 選挙違反は3か月で～になる Violations of Election Laws shall *be extinguished by prescription* after three months.

じこう【時候】¶～のあいさつ *seasonal* greetings (クリスマスその他の). ～はずれの暖かさ (寒さ) the *unseasonable* warm (cold) weather. ～の変わり目には健康に気をつけなければならない We should take care of ourselves at the change of *seasons*.

じごう【次号】¶この物語は～で終わる This story is to be concluded in our *next*. ～完結 To be concluded. 以下～ To be continued.

しこうさくご【試行錯誤】trial and error. ¶われわれは～を重ねたあとでそれに成功した We succeeded in it through *trial and error*.

じごうじとく【自業自得】¶私の～だ I have no one to blame for it but myself./I alone am to blame. 彼が落ちぶれたのも～だ His ruin is of his own making.

じごえ【地声】*a person's* natural voice. ¶声の大きいのは～だから致し方ない I cannot help my *natural* loud *voice*.

しごく【至極】¶～もっともな意見です Yours is *quite* a reasonable opinion. / You are *quite* right. 夫婦の仲は～円満だ The couple are getting on *very* well with each other. 獲物を逃がして残念～ I'm *most* regretful that I missed the game.

しご・く【扱く】¶彼は稲の穂を～いてもみを落とした He *drew* the ears of rice *through his hand* to take the unhulled rice off them. 彼らは新人部員を～いた They *put* the new members of their club *through a hard course of training*. 彼はあごひげを～いていた He *was stroking* his beard. 彼は槍を～いて敵に向かった He *worked* (≒ *plied*) a spear through his hand to fight with his enemy.

じこく【自国】*one's* 〔own〕 country. —語 *one's* mother tongue.

じこく【時刻】time. ¶出発の～ the starting *time*. 約束の～ the appointed *time* (≒ *hour*). ～は3時30分です The *hour* is 3 : 30. もう昼食の～だ It is *time* for lunch. 彼が在宅する～をねらって彼を訪問した I *timed* my visit *to* find him at home.

—表(列車の) a railway timetable; 米 a railroad schedule.

じごく【地獄】hell; Hell; Hades; the inferno. ¶この世の生き～ *a hell* on earth; *an* earthly *hell*; an inferno. ～で仏に会ったようだ I feel as if I had found "a friend in need." ～のさたも金しだい(諺) *Money makes the mare to go*. / Money is the key to all doors.

—耳 sharp (≒ keen) ears. 交通— a terrific traffic jam. 試験— the examination evil.

しごせん【子午線】〘天文学〙the meridian. 本初— the prime (≒ standard) meridian.

しこたま ¶彼は株で～金をもうけた He made *a lot of* money on the stock market.

しごと【仕事】**1**〘職業・任務〙¶今どんな～をしていますか. 建築関係の～をしています What kind of *work* are you doing now? I am doing construction *work*.

彼は輸出の～をしている He is in the export *business*.

彼はいろいろの～に手を出したが, どれも成功しなかった He tried his hand at various kinds of *businesses*, but was not successful in any of them.

彼は～をさがしている He is looking for *a job*.

なかなか～が見つからないで困っている I am at my wit's end to find *a job*.

彼は～がなくてぶらぶらしている He is hanging around with nothing to do.

やっと彼のおかげで～にありつけた Through him I landed (≒ got; secured) *a job* at last.

こんな割りの悪い～はごめんだ I don't want to have anything to do with such *an* unprofitable *business*.

牧野博士は植物分類を一生の～とされた Dr. Makino made the classification of plants his *lifework*.

これは一生の大～として行なう価値が十分にあるThis is really worth doing as my *lifework*.

彼は～でロンドンへ行った He went to London *on business*.

2〘心・身を動かして働くこと, 労働・作業〙¶さあ, ～にかかろう Well, let's get started.

お～中を失礼します I am sorry to interrupt you while *you are working*.

彼の～のじゃまをしてはいけませんよ Don't disturb him while *he is working*.

彼は今ホテルの一室を借りて～をしている He is doing his *work* in a room at a hotel.

彼は～をしている最中に突然倒れた He suddenly passed out while *at his work*.

ちょうど～を終えたところです I have just finished my *work*.

もうじゅうぶん一日分の～をした I've done *a* good day's *work*.

きょうはこれぐらいで～をよそう So much for today. / Let's *call it a day*.

あすは何時から～を始めますか When will you begin *work* tomorrow?

あすは午前中だけで～を打ち切ろう I'll *work* only in the morning tomorrow.

～が山ほどあるんで, ゴルフなんかしていられない I have heaps of *work* to do, so I have no time to think of playing golf.

1日休んだらこんなに～がたまってしまった I have such a lot of *work* on my hands because I took a day off.

このところ～に追われどおしだ I have lately been very pressed with *business*. / These days *business* has kept me on the go.

ちょっとは～がはかどったかね Have you made any progress in your *work*?

彼女はとても熱心に～をする She *works* very hard.

あの人は～はていねいだが遅い He is thorough but slow in his *work*.

あの職人は～が雑だ That artisan is very sloppy in his *work*.

彼は～が早くしかも正確だ He *works* quickly yet accurately.

あの人は～がよくできる He is good at his *job*.

彼女の～ぶりには感心した I was impressed by how eagerly (≒ earnestly; well) she *worked*.

し

きょうは〜でとても疲れた I am very tired from *working* today. (tired with はさける).
こう暑くては〜にならない It is so hot [that] I can't *work*.
そのことが心配で〜が手につかない I am so anxious about it that I cannot concentrate on my *work*.
〜の合間にでもちょっと行って彼のようすをみてきてください Please go and see how he is when you have some spare time.
いいかげんな〜はしないでほしい Don't give up halfway through your *work*. / Don't fudge your *work*.
彼は〜の虫だ He is *a* hard *worker*.
彼は〜の鬼だ He is a demon for *work*.
彼は〜をしないでむだ口ばかりきいている Instead of *working*, he just talks away the time.
こんな〜は朝飯前だ This *job* is as easy as pie.
これは大〜だ, とてもぼくひとりではできない This is such *a* big *job* that I cannot possibly do it by myself.
この〜はあと1時間もすればできる This *work* will be finished in an hour or so.
〜が半端になるから, 夜業をしてでもきょうじゅうにやり終える The *work* is not over yet, and I'll work on it at night so it will be ready for tomorrow.
3 〖労作・作品・業績〗¶ 彼はその方面の研究に関してりっぱな〜をした He has done *a* marvelous *job* in the field of research.
あの学者はりっぱな〜をした That scholar has done remarkable *work*.
この作品は彼が生涯の〜として取り組んだものだ This is the work he has concentrated on as his *lifework*.
—着 work clothes; a smock; overalls. **—**師 a workman; (事業家) a businessman. **—**台 a workbench. **—**賃 pay. **—**場 a workshop. **—**箱 a workbox; a toolbox. **—**部屋 a workroom. 賃**—** a job; piecework. 手**—** hand[i]craft; hand[i]work. 野良**—** farm work. 針**—** sewing; needlework.

じこひはん【自己批判】self-criticism.

しこみ【仕込み】(教育・訓練) training; education; (仕入れ) stocking. ¶ 彼はイギリス〜の紳士だ He is a gentleman *educated* in England. 彼はイギリス〜の標準英語を話す He speaks the Queen's English *mastered* in England.
—づえ a sword cane.

しこ・む【仕込む】¶ 彼は犬に芸を〜んだ He *trained* his dog *to* do some tricks. 彼はよく〜んだ犬を1匹飼っている He keeps a *well-trained* dog. 彼女は娘に作法を〜んだ She *taught* good manners *to* her daughter. 彼は子どもに英会話を〜んだ He *got* his child *to learn* English conversation. 彼らはたくさんの冬物を〜んだ They *stocked up* a lot of winter goods.

しこり【凝り】¶ 肩に〜ができた (肩がこる) I *feel stiff* in the shoulder. / (腫れもの) I've got *a tumor* in the shoulder. われわれふたりの仲の〜が解けた There is no more *ill feeling* between us. その事件はふたりの間に感情的〜をのこした The case left *an antagonistic feeling* between the two.

しこん【歯根】the root of a tooth; (歯ぐき) gums.

しこん【紫紺】bluish purple.

しさ【示唆】suggestion. ¶ その問題の解決法を〜してくれたのは彼女だ It was she who *suggested* the solution of the problem. 彼女の〜を受けて問題を解いた I solved the problem on her *hint*. これは非常に〜に富んだ文章だ This is a very *suggestive* sentence.

しさ【視差】〖天文・写真〗the parallax. ¶ 太陽の〜 the solar *parallax*.

じさ【時差】difference in time. ¶ 東京とサンフランシスコでは8時間の〜がある There is eight hours' *difference* between San Francisco and Tokyo time.
—出勤 differentiation of the office attendance hours.

しさい【子細】(理由) [a] reason; (詳細) details; (意味) meaning. ¶ 〜あって彼は姿を見せなかった He was absent *for a* certain *reason*. 〜はあとで説明する予定です As regards the *details*, I am going to explain it later on. なにか〜ありげな話しぶりだった He spoke somehow *significantly*. 事の次第を〜に述べた He made a *detailed* explanation of the whole affair. われわれは彼の申し出を〜に検討した We examined his offer *carefully* (≒ *minutely*).

しさい【司祭】(旧教の) a priest.

しざい【資材】material.
建築**—** construction materials.

しざい【私財】*one's* private funds. ¶ 彼は慈善事業に〜を投じた He spent his *private funds* on charity work. 彼女は〜を投じて病院を設立した She founded a hospital *at her own expense*.

じざい【自在】¶ このアンテナは伸縮〜だ This antenna *is capable of* expansion and contraction. 彼は左手で自由〜に絵が描ける He can draw a picture *quite easily* with his left hand. 彼女はフランス語が自由〜だ She *has a good command of* French.
—画 freehand drawing. 自由**—** freely; at will; at *one's* pleasure.

しさく【思索】meditation; speculation. ¶ 彼は〜にふけっていた He was lost in *contemplation*.
—家 a thinker.

しさく【詩作】¶ 〜する make (≒ compose) poems.

しさく【試作】(製作) trial manufacture; (栽培) trial growing. ¶ それを〜するのに3年かかった It took me three years to make it *as an experiment*. 彼は新種の稲を〜した He raised a new kind of rice plant *by way of experiment*.
—品 a trial product.

じさく【自作】¶ これらは私の〜の詩だ These are

the poems *of my own making*. 彼は～自演した(戯曲を) He acted [himself] in a play of his own writing. / (音楽を) He performed a piece of music of his own composing.

―農 a landed farmer.

しさつ【視察】 inspection; observation.

¶ 大臣が現地を～した The minister *made an* on-the-spot *inspection*. 彼らはイギリスの教育制度を～するためにイギリスへ行った They went to England to *inspect* the English educational system. 彼は毎週1回, 工場を～する He *inspects* the factory once a week.

―団 an observation group. ―旅行 an inspection tour.

じさつ【自殺】 suicide. ¶ ～する kill *oneself*; commit suicide. 彼はピストル～した He *shot himself to death*. 彼は首つり～した He *hanged himself*. 彼は服毒～をはかった He attempted *suicide* by taking poison. 彼の行為は～的だ His act *is suicidal*.

―未遂(者) an attempted suicide.

しさん【資産】 (一般の) property; a fortune; means; (会社・法人などの) assets.

¶ ～と負債 *assets* and liabilities. ～の凍結 freezing of *assets* (≒ *credits*). 彼は一代で～を作った He made *a fortune* in his lifetime. 彼女の両親は彼女に1億円の～を残した Her parents left her *a* large *property* (≒ *legacy*) worth one hundred million yen.

―家 a rich (≒ wealthy) man. ―株 income stock.

しさん【四散】 ¶ 暴徒たちは警官を見ると雲を霞と～した The rioters *dispersed* at the sight of the police.

しざん【死産】 a stillbirth. ¶ 彼女は女の子を～した She gave birth to a *dead* (≒ *stillborn*) baby girl. 彼女は子どもが～だったので嘆き悲しんだ She was grief-stricken over the birth of her *stillborn* child.

じさん【持参】 ¶ あすの遠足には必ず弁当と飲み物を～しなさい For our excursion tomorrow, be sure to *bring* (≒ *take*) your lunch and something to drink *with you*. 雨が降りそうだから, かさを～したほうがいい You must *carry* an umbrella *with you*, because it is likely to rain.

―人払い小切手 a bearer check. ―金 a dowry. ¶ 彼は娘に～金を持たせた He *endowed* his daughter at marriage. 彼は～金欲しさに金持ちの娘と結婚した He married a rich man's daughter for her *dowry*. 彼は～金つきの娘と結婚した He married a girl with *a dowry*. 彼は娘にたくさんの～金を用意した He provided *a* large *dowry* for his daughter.

しし【猪】 (いのしし) a wild boar.

しし【獅子】 (雄) a lion; (雌) a lioness. ¶ ～身中の虫 a thorn in *one's* side. 彼は敵と～奮迅の勢いで戦った He fought with the enemy like *a lion* (≒ *a devil*).

―鼻 a pug nose. ―舞い a lion dance; a dance with a lion's mask. ―使い a lion tamer.

しし【嗣子】 (男) an heir; (女) an heiress.

しし【志士】 a patriot. ¶ 勤王の～ a loyalist; a loyal spirit.

しし【四肢】 the limbs; the legs and arms; the members.

¶ ～を十分に伸ばして体操をした I practiced gymnastics by stretching my *limbs* fully.

しし【孜孜】 ¶ 彼は毎日～として働いた He worked *diligently* (≒ *assiduously*; *very hard*) every day.

しじ【支持】 support. ¶ その政策は全国民の～を受けた The policy had the *support* of the whole nation. / The policy *was supported* by the whole nation. きみの～する政党はなんですか What party do you *support*? われわれは平和主義を～する We *support* pacifism.

―者 a supporter.

しじ【私事】 private matters; personal affairs. ¶ 話は～にわたりますがお聞きください Excuse me for being *personal*, but please listen. あまり他人の～にわたらないようにしてください Please don't go into others' *private affairs*.

しじ【死児】 a dead child. ¶ ～の歳を数えてもしかたがない *It is no use crying over spilt milk*. (「こぼれたミルクのことで泣いてもしかたがない」という英語の諺が, この意味に近い).

しじ【指示】 instructions. ¶ 彼は彼女になんの～も与えなかった He gave no *instructions* to her. ～どおりにやりなさい Do it *as indicated*. 彼の～を受けるべきだ You must receive *instruction* from him.

しじ【師事】 ¶ 彼女は有名なバイオリニストのメニューヒンに～した She *was a pupil of* Menuhin, a famous violinist. 彼は佐藤教授に～して2年間経済学を勉強した He studied economics, *under* professor Sato's *instruction* for two years.

しじ【四時】 ¶ その山の頂は～雪におおわれている The top of the mountain is covered with snow *all the year round*.

じじ【時事】 current events. ¶ ～を論ずる discuss *current events*. 彼は～に明るい He is well-informed of *current affairs*.

―英語 current English. ―問題 current topics. ―解説 comment on current topics; news commentary. ―解説者(ラジオやテレビの) a news commentator.

じじい【爺】 (老人) an old man; an old thing (人に thing を用いると, 軽べつまたは親しみを表わす); (祖父) a grandfather. ¶ 欲ばり～ *a* greedy *old man*. くそ～ Stupid *old thing*!

じじこっこく【時時刻刻】 from hour to hour; hour by hour. ¶ 山の天候は～と変わる The weather in the mountains changes *from hour to hour*. 新しい情報が～と入ってくる New reports are coming (≒ are pouring) in *one after another*.

ししそんそん【子子孫孫】 ¶ これは～に至るまでの名誉です This will be a great honor even *to my remotest descendants*. ～に至るまでこの宝を伝えよ Hand down this treasure to *posterity*.

ししつ【私室】a private room. ¶やたらに～をのぞいてはいけません You must not look into *a private room* without permission.

ししつ【紙質】¶この本は～がよい(悪い) This book is made of *paper of good* (*poor*) *quality*.

ししつ【資質】nature. ¶すぐれた～を持った人 a *highly talented* person.

じしつ【自室】*one's* own room.

しじつ【史実】a historical fact.

じじつ【事実】a fact. ¶それは～だった That was *a fact*. それは動かし難い～だ It is *an* established *fact*. ～この子はりこうだ *In fact* this boy is bright. ～彼は信頼できる人物だ He is *really* a trustworthy man. ～その案は実現不可能だ *Actually* the plan is impracticable. 彼が正直なのは～だ *It is true* that he is honest. 彼のことばは～となった What he said *came true*. きみの言うことは～に立脚していない What you say is not based on *facts*. ～を否定することはできない It is impossible to deny *the fact*. 彼が不正を働いたという～がわかった That he did wrong proved to *be true*. ～は小説より奇なり *Fact* is stranger than fiction. そのうわさは～無根だった The rumor turned out to *be groundless* (≒ *be false*). 彼はその運動の～上の指導者だった He was the *virtual* leader of the movement.

じじつ【時日】time. ¶～がたつにつれて彼もその悲しみを忘れるだろう *As time passes* (≒ *As the days go by*) he will forget the grief. ～が切迫している *Time* presses. / There is no *time* to lose. 次の会合の～を定めよう Let's fix the *date* (≒ Let's choose the *day*) for the next meeting. 完成までにはかなりの～を要する It takes considerable *time* to complete it. 首相の訪米の～は未定だ The *date* of the premier's departure for America is not decided yet.

しじみ【蜆】〘貝類〙a corbicula (複 corbicu-lae).

ししゃ【支社】a branch office.

ししゃ【死者】a dead person; (総称的に) the dead; the deceased; (事故などの) the killed; a casualty (「死んだ人」という最も無色の表現が a dead person. the dead は常に複数扱いだが, the deceased は単・複両方の場合があり,「亡くなられた方」というように敬意をこめた場合に用いる. 事故の報告などで「死傷者…名」という場合のことばが casualty であり, これは死者のみならず負傷者も含まれる).
¶～3名 Three people [were] killed. 幸いその事故では乗客から～はでなかった Fortunately none of the passengers were killed in the accident. その鉄道事故で10人の～をだした Ten lives were lost in the railroad accident.

ししゃ【使者】a messenger. ¶彼らはフランスに～をやった They sent *a messenger* to France. 彼は停戦交渉の～として敵陣に乗り込んだ He went to the enemy's camp *on a mission of* negotiating the cease-fire.

ししゃ【試写】a preview; a private showing. ¶その映画の～会は明日午後催される The *preview* [of the film] will be given tomorrow afternoon.

ししゃ【試射】test firing.
—場 a firing range.

ししゃく【子爵】a viscount.
—夫人 a viscountess.

じしゃく【磁石】(マグネット) a magnet; (羅針盤) a compass. ¶～の針(羅針盤の) the needle of *a compass*. ～は鉄を引きつける *A magnet* attracts iron.
棒— a bar magnet. 馬蹄— a horseshoe magnet.

じじゃく【自若】self-possession; calmness. ¶彼はいかなることが起こっても～としている He will not lose his *self-possession* come what may. (文語体). / Nothing will make him lose his *self-possession*.

ししゃごにゅう【四捨五入】¶小数点3位以下～する *round off* the fractions *to* three decimal places.

ししゅ【死守】¶彼らは陣地を～した They *defended* their position *to the last*. / (必死になって) They *defended* their position *desperately*.

ししゅ【詩趣】¶彼の書くものは～に乏しい His writings are lacking in *poetry* (≒ *poetic feeling*). / His works are *prosaic*.

じしゅ【自主】¶～の精神 the spirit of *independence* (≒ *self-reliance*). 彼は～的に考える男だ He is an *independent* thinker. 彼には何事によらず～性がない He is lacking in *independence* in everything he does. 多くの植民地が～的な政府を作ろうと努力していた Many colonies were struggling to establish *autonomous* governments. われわれはもっと～的に考え行動すべきではないだろうか Shouldn't we think and act more *independently*? われわれは～的に話を決めるべきだ We should make an agreement *of our own free will*.
—権 autonomy. 関税—権 tariff autonomy.

じしゅ【自首】¶彼は警察に～した He *surrendered himself to* the police. / He *gave himself up to* the police. 彼に警察に～するようにすすめた I advised him to *deliver himself to* the police.

ししゅう【詩集】a collection of poems; (諸家の作品集) an anthology. ¶テニソン～ Tennyson's *Poetical Works*; *Collected Poems* of Tennyson.

ししゅう【刺繍】embroidery. ¶彼女はハンカチに～をした She made (≒ did) some *embroidery* on a handkerchief. 彼女はハンカチに模様を～した She *embroidered* some figures *on* a handkerchief. / She *embroidered* a handkerchief *with* some figures.
—台 an embroidery frame. —糸 embroidery thread.

しじゅう【四十】forty. ¶～代の男 a man in his *forties*. 彼は～過ぎ(前)だ He is over (under) *forty*. / He is on the wrong (right) side of *forty*. 彼女は～前後だろう I should say she is around *forty*.

しじゅう【四重】―唱(奏) a quartet(te). 弦楽―奏団(曲) a string quartet.

しじゅう【始終】(いつも) always ; all the time ; (やすみなく) continually ; (たびたび) very often. ¶ 彼は～不平ばかり言っている He is *always* complaining. 彼は～仕事のことばかり考えている He is thinking of his business *all the time*. 彼は～たばこを吸っている He is *continually* (≒ *incessantly*) smoking. 私は～その市を訪れる I visit the city *very often* (≒ *frequently*). そのできごとの一部～を話してみませんか Will you give *a full detail of* the incident?

じしゅう【自習】¶ 私は数学を～した(ひとりで勉強した) I *studied* mathematics *for myself*. / (独学で習得した) I *taught myself* mathematics. ―時間 study hours.

じしゅう【次週】〔the〕next week ; the following week.

じじゅう【自重】dead load ; dead weight.

じじゅう【侍従】a chamberlain.
―長 the Grand Chamberlain. ―武官 a military (naval) aide-de-camp to His Majesty.

しじゅうから【四十雀】〔鳥類〕a tit ; a titmouse.

しじゅうくにち【四十九日】¶ 明日は彼の～だ Tomorrow is *the forty-ninth day after his death*.

しじゅうはって【四十八手】¶ 相撲には～ある There are *forty-eight different ways of attacking* in *sumo* wrestling. / There are *forty-eight different forms of attack* in *sumo* wrestling. 彼は金もうけの～を心得ている He knows *all the tricks of* moneymaking. / He knows *the secret of* how to make money.

ししゅく【私淑】¶ 氏は私の～している人のひとりだ He is one of those I *admire* through his works.

しじゅく【私塾】a private school.

じしゅく【自粛】self-discipline. ¶ 政治家の～を望む We want the people who are engaged in government to practice stricter *self-discipline*.

ししゅつ【支出】expenses ; expenditure (文語的な語). ¶ 今月は～が多い Heavy *expenses* have to be paid this month. 収入と～とのバランスを保つことは難しい It is difficult to keep revenue and *expenditure* in balance. 資金の中から５万円～した I *paid* fifty thousand yen out of the fund. 不必要な～を避けなければならぬ We must avoid unnecessary *expenditure of money*.

ししゅんき【思春期】adolescence ; 〔the age of〕puberty (「少年少女時代から成人へ移行する期間」という比較的幅のある意味(主として10代の年代を指す)では adolescence を用い,「性行為が可能になる時期」というある一時期を指すには puberty を用いる. ふつう男子14歳から, 女子12歳からとされる). ¶ あの子ももう二, 三年で～に達する The boy will reach *puberty* in a few years. ～の少女の心は傷つきやすい The mind of a girl *at puberty* is extremely delicate. / The mind of an *adolescent* girl is extremely delicate.

ししょ【支署】a branch office ; (警察などの) a branch station ; a local branch.

ししょ【支所】a branch office.

ししょ【司書】a librarian.

ししょ【死所】¶ 遂に彼は～を見出した At last he found out the place where he could die peacefully.

しじょ【子女】¶ 良家の～ *the sons and daughters* of good families. ～の教育 the education of *children*.

じしょ【辞書】a dictionary ; a wordbook ; (古典語の) a lexicon ; (特定用語の) a glossary. ¶ ～を引く consult (≒ look up in) *a dictionary*. ～でその語を調べなさい Look up the word in the *dictionary*. / Study the word in the *dictionary*.

じしょ【自署】¶ 彼女は契約書に～しなかった She did not *sign* the contract. / She did not *sign* her *name* in the contract.

じしょ【地所】land ; (宅地・敷地) a plot ; a lot ; (所有地) an estate (「宅地用または墓地用などの小区画の土地」は a plot または a lot という. また「…用地」の意味では a parking lot (駐車場)のように lot を用いる.「広い屋敷のある所有地」の意味では estate を用いる).
¶ 私は小さな～を持っている I have *a* small *piece* (≒ *tract*) *of land*. 彼はいなかに広い～を持っている He has *a* large *estate* in the country. 家を建てるために100平方メートルの～を買った I purchased 100 square meters of *land* to build a house〔on〕.
―周旋人 an estate agent.

じじょ【次女】*one's* second daughter. ¶ これが～の花子です This is my *second daughter* Hanako.

じじょ【侍女】a waiting maid (≒ woman) ; a lady's maid ; (王公の) a lady-in-waiting ; a lady attendant.

ししょう【支障】a interference ; hindrance ; a hitch. ¶ それは仕事の進行上～をきたす It will *interfere with* (≒ *hinder* ; *retard* ; *impede*) the progress of the work. なんの～もなく without *a hitch*.

ししょう【師匠】a master ; a teacher. ¶ 生け花を～について習う study flower arrangement under *a teacher*.

しじょう【史上】¶ ～空前の大事件だった It was one of the greatest incidents that the world had ever seen.

しじょう【市場】a market. ¶ 新製品を来月には～に出す予定である We will put the new products on the *market* next month. 安い米がまもなく～に出まわるだろう Low-priced rice will be on the *market* shortly. 新製品の～を開拓しなくてはならない We have to open up *a market* for our new products. ～を拡張するにはどうしたらよいか How can we extend our *market*? ～性がある(ない)品物 (un-)marketable goods. 彼らは外国に新しい～を求めている

They are trying to find (≒ They are seeking) *a* new foreign *market*. 彼らは～を独占するであろう They will engross the *market*. 彼らは世界のダイヤモンド～を牛耳っている They control the diamond *market* of the world.

—価格 a market price. —性 marketability. —操作 market operations. —調査 market research (≒ survey). 売り手(買い手)— a seller's (buyer's) market. 卸売り— the wholesale market. 外国(国内)— a foreign (home ; domestic) market. 株式— a stock exchange (≒ market). 金融— a money market.

し

しじょう【至上】 —善 the supreme good. —命令 a supreme order. 芸術—主義 [the doctrine of] art for art's sake.

しじょう【私情】 personal feelings. ¶ 政治に～をさしはさむのはよくない It is wrong to admit *personal feelings* into politics. いま, われわれは～をすてなければならぬ Now we must set aside our *personal feelings*.

しじょう【紙上】 ¶ ～の計画 a *paper* plan. 乱闘事件が～をにぎわした The news of the riotous fight flooded *the paper*.

しじょう【試乗】 a trial ride. ¶ 新型車に～する *have a trial ride in* a car of the latest model.

しじょう【詩情】 poetic sentiment. ¶ この辺りの風景は～をかきたてる The scenery around here arouses our *poetic sentiment*.

しじょう【誌上】 ¶ その記事を週刊誌の～で読んだ I read the article in a weekly magazine.

じしょう【自称】 ¶ ～民主主義の守護者 a *self-styled* guardian of democracy. ～作家 a *would-be* author (would-be は「…志望の」「既に…気どりの」のようにまだ達せられない望みを詐称する意味があるのに対して, self-styled は現在の事実に反して自分でかってに詐称する場合に用いる). 大山太郎と～する男が訪ねてきた A man who *calls himself* Taro Oyama came to see me.

じしょう【事象】 (現象) a phenomenon (複 phenomena) ; (出来事) a happening ; an occurrence ; (傾向) tendency ; trend.

じじょう【自乗】〘数学〙 a square. ¶ 3を～せよ *Square* 3. / *Multiply* 3 *by itself*. 3の～は9だ The *square* of 3 is 9. / Three *squared* makes (≒ is) nine.

じじょう【事情】 circumstances. ¶ ～を聞きたい I want to hear about the *circumstances*. ～によっては許してもいい I may forgive you according to *circumstances*. いかなる～があっても最後までやる I will do it to the last under any *circumstances*. ヨーロッパでは～が違っている In Europe *matters* are different. 彼は欧米の～に詳しい He is well versed in European and American *affairs*. ～をはっきりさせてほしい I want *matters* to be cleared up. どんな～があってもパーティーには出席する I will attend the party no *matter* what happens. ～が許すかぎりルーマニアへ行きたい As far as *circumstances* will permit, I will visit Rumania. 家庭の～で学校をやめる人もある Some students leave school for family *reasons*. このような～だから, 出発を延期します *Such being the case*, I will put off my departure. こういう～で行けない I can't go because of these *circumstances*.

じじょう【磁場】〘物理〙 the magnetic field.

ししょうじ【指小辞】〘文法〙 a diminutive.

じじょうじばく【自縄自縛】 ¶ そんなことを言い張るときみは～に陥る If you persist in your opinion, you will be caught in your own trap.

ししょうしゃ【死傷者】 ¶ 幸い交通事故に～はなかった Fortunately there were no *casualties* in the traffic accident. その地震による～数は1万人に及んだ The *toll* of the earthquake reached ten thousand people.

ししょうせつ【私小説】 a novel depicting the author's real experiences in his private life ; a private life novel.

ししょく【試食】 ¶ われわれはその新食品を～してみた We *sampled* the new food product. / We *tested* the new food product by *sampling* it. これおいしいよ. ～してごらん This is real good. *Have a try!*

—会 a sampling party.

じしょく【辞職】 resignation. ¶ 彼は責任をとって～した He *resigned* his office from a sense of responsibility. 彼は～させられた He was forced to *resign*. (定年などで退職するのは retire を用いる).

—願い ¶ 彼は～願いを出すつもりだ He is going to tender (≒ hand in ; turn in) his *resignation*. 彼の～願いは受理された His *resignation* was accepted. 総— ¶ 内閣の総～ the general *resignation* of the cabinet. 内閣は総～した The cabinet *resigned en bloc*.

じじょでん【自叙伝】 an autobiography. ¶ ～ふうの小説 an *autobiographical* novel. —作者 an autobiographer.

ししょばこ【私書箱】 a post-office box ; P. O. box ; P. O. B. ¶ 東京中央郵便局～381号 P. O. B. No. 381 Tokyo Central Post Office.

ししん【私心】 ¶ 彼は～のない男だ He is an *unselfish* man. この事業には～を離れて当たる I will do this work without *a selfish motive*.

ししん【私信】 a private (≒ personal) letter (≒ message) ; (総称) private (≒ personal) correspondence.

ししん【指針】 ¶ 人生の～ *a guiding principle* of *one's* life. 速度計の～ *a needle* (≒ *an indicator* ; *a pointer*) of a speedometer.

しじん【詩人】 a poet ; (女) a poetess (今では男女とも poet というのが普通). ¶ 彼は～はだの男だ He *is poetic*. / He is something of *a poet*. 桂冠(けいかん)— a poet laureate.

じしん【自身】 ¶ 宿題はきみたち～の力でやること You are supposed to do your homework *by yourselves*. 母が留守のときは私～で食事の支度をする When my mother is away, I prepare meals *for myself*. (「自身で」に当たる by *oneself* は「単独で」「人の助けを借りずに」の意味であるが, *for oneself* は「独力で」の意味のほかに, 「自身の〔利益の〕ために」という意味を含む). きみ～の考えはどうなのか What is *your own* opinion? その物質はそれ〜では毒ではない The substance is not poisonous *in itself*. 私〜にもよくわかりません I'm not quite sure of it *myself*. 私〜は反対ではない *Personally* (≒ *For myself*) I'm not against it. これは自分〜で書いた英語の手紙だ This is an English letter *of my own writing* (≒ *that I wrote myself*).

じしん【自信】 self-confidence. ¶ 私は自分に〜がある I have *confidence* in myself. 私は自分に〜がついた(失った) I gained (lost) *confidence* in myself. 彼女はたいへん〜が強い She has great *confidence* in herself. 彼は自分の力量に対する〜を欠いている He lacks *confidence* in his own strength. 〜を持って行動しなさい Act *with confidence*. 試験に合格する〜がある I *am confident* (≒ *sure*) *of* pass*ing* the examination. 彼は〜に満ちた態度で話した He spoke *with confidence* (≒ *in a confident manner*).

─過剰 overconfidence. ¶ 自信〜の人 an *overconfident* person.

じしん【地震】 an earthquake. ¶ 今朝, 弱い〜を感じた I felt *a* slight *earthquake* this morning. 昨夜の〜は長かった The *earthquake* last night was long. 彼の家は〜でこわれた His house was destroyed by *an earthquake*. 日本は〜が多い *Earthquakes* are frequent in Japan. / We have frequent *earthquakes* in Japan. 強い〜がその市を襲った *A* strong *earthquake* shook the city. 〜の予知は可能か Is it possible to predict *earth quake*?

─学 seismology. **─学者** a seismologist. **─観測** seismometry. **─観測所** a seismological observatory. **─計** a seismograph; a seismometer. **─帯(国)** an earthquake zone (country).

じしん【磁針】 a magnetic needle.

じじん【自刃】 ¶ 彼は〜した He *killed himself* (≒ *committed suicide*) *with a sword*.

ししんけい【視神経】〘解剖学〙 optic nerves; ophthalmic nerves.

ジス JIS (the Japanese Industrial Standard しから).

─マーク a JIS mark.

しずい【雌蕊】 ⇒めしべ

じすい【自炊】 ¶ 私は〜している I *cook for myself*. / I *do my own cooking*.

しすう【指数】〘数学〙 an index 〔number〕.

知能─ intelligence quotient (I.Q. と略す).

物価─ a price index.

しすう【紙数】 ¶ 私の〜は尽きた My *space* is exhausted. 〜に制限がある *Space* is limited.

しずか【静か】 ¶ 〜に! Be *quiet*! / Hush! / (だまれ) Shut up! / (騒ぐな) Don't make such a noise! 5分間〜にしていてください Please *keep quiet* for five minutes. 彼は〜に酒を飲んでいた He was having a *peaceful* drink. 海上は〜だ The sea *is calm*. 彼女は〜に歩いた She walked *quietly*. 弟がいなくて家の中は〜だ It *is quiet* in the house now that my brother is away. 湖の水は鏡のように〜だ The water of the lake *is* as *calm* as the surface of a mirror. 会場は水を打ったように〜だ The hall *is hushed*.

しずく【雫】 a drop. ¶ 〜が落ちる *Water* drops. かさから〜が落ちている The umbrella *is dripping*.

しずけさ【静けさ】 ¶ あらしの前の〜のようだ It is like *silence* before a storm. 夜の〜中でフクロウがほーほーと鳴いた The owl hooted in the *stillness* of night.

しずしずと【静静と】 ¶ 葬列が〜通りを進んでいく The funeral procession is proceeding *slowly* along the street. 〜茶が運ばれてきた Tea was served *with composure*.

シスター (カトリック教の修道女) a sister.

システム a system.

─工学 system engineering.

ジステンパー〘獣医〙 distemper.

ジストマ〘医学〙 肝臓─ distoma hepaticum. 肺臓─ pulmonary distomiasis.

じすべり【地滑り】 a landslide; 㐧 a landslip.

しずま·る【静まる】 ¶ 風は〜った The wind *has gone down*. 間もなくあらしは〜った The storm *has calmed down* soon. 反乱は〜りそうもない The revolt is unlikely to *be suppressed*. ついに暴動は〜った At last the revolt *was put down*. 一帯は〜りかえった The whole place *has become* as *quiet as death*. しばらくの間, その部屋は〜りかえっていた The room *was silent* for a while. 会場はじっと〜りかえって彼のピアノの演奏に耳を傾けた The hall *was hushed* and all the audience listened to his piano.

しず·む【沈む】 1〖船や太陽が〗 ¶ ボートは〜んだ The boat *sank* into the water.

暴風のため船は〜んだ The ship *sank* by the violent wind.

ボールは水の底に〜んだ The ball *sank down* to the bottom of the water.

日が地平線に〜むのを見た I saw the sun *sink* below the horizon.

太陽は東から昇り西に〜む The sun rises in the east and *sets* in the west.

2〖人の気分が〗 ¶ そんなに〜んでないで, 元気をだせ Don't be so *out of spirits*. Cheer up!

彼は(気分が)〜んでいる He *looks blue*.

彼女はいつも〜みがちだ She *is* always *in low spirits*.

しず·める【沈める】 ¶ 船を〜める *sink* a ship.

しず·める【静める】 ¶ この騒ぎを〜めてほしい I want to *have* this uproar *suppressed*. 彼の怒りはなかなか〜められそうもない It seems difficult to *calm* his anger. そのくすりは彼女の神経を〜めた The medicine *quieted* her nerves.

し·する【資する】 ¶ 団体生活は人格形成に〜するところがある A group life *is helpful to* build*ing* up our character. その発明は科学の進歩に〜するところ大であろう The invention will *contribute* greatly *to* the progress of science.

じ·する【辞する】 ¶ 午後3時に彼の家を〜した I *left* his house at three in the afternoon. われらは国のためには死をも〜さず We *are ready to* die for our country.

しせい【市政】 municipal administration (≒

government).

しせい【市制】¶この町に～が敷かれて10年になる It is ten years since this town *was incorporated as a city*.

しせい【至誠】sincerity. ¶～天に通ず *Sincerity* moves heaven.

しせい【私製】―はがき a private post card.

しせい【市井】¶～の人 a man on (≒ in) the street.

しせい【姿勢】a figure; a posture. ¶彼は～がよい(悪い) He has *a* good (poor) *figure*. 無理な～をとるな Don't assume *an* unnatural *posture*. 彼は～を正した(身体をまっすぐにする) He erected his *figure*. ～を正して(気持ちを引きしめて)その仕事に当たりなさい *Brace yourself up for* the task. 前向きの～でその問題に当たろうと決心した We determined to deal with the matter *rapidly and wisely*. 近ごろ彼は高(低)～だ Recently he *has borne himself* haughtily (modestly).

しせい【施政】administration.
―方針 an administrative policy; 米 a party line. ―方針演説 a speech of administration policies.

しぜい【市税】a city tax; a municipal duty.

じせい【自生】¶野山に～する植物 *native* (≒ *wild*) plants in mountains and fields.

じせい【自制】self-control; self-restraint.
―心 ¶私は～心を失った I lost my *self-control* (≒ *temper*). 彼は～心に欠けている He has no *control over himself*. / He is *incontinent*.

じせい【時世】the age. ¶こんな不景気のご～では廃業もやむをえない We cannot help closing down our store *in these times of* business depression.

じせい【時勢】the times. ¶～におくれている be behind *the times*. ～におくれるな Keep up with *the world*. ～におくれる fall behind *the times*. ～に逆らう swim against *the stream* (≒ *the current*). 彼は～に先んじている He is ahead of *the times*. 彼は～おくれの人間だ He is an *old-fashioned* man.

じせい【時制】〘文法〙the tense.
未来(現在; 過去)― the future (present; past) tense.

じせい【辞世】¶～の歌(句) *one's* dying poem (words); *one's* swan song.

じせい【磁性】〘物理〙magnetism. ¶～を帯びた鉄 *magnetic* iron.

しせいかつ【私生活】*one's* private life. ¶～に干渉しないでくれ Hands off my *private life*.

しせいじ【私生児】an illegitimate child; a natural child; a love child. ¶彼は～だ He *was born out of wedlock*.
―認知 bastardization.

しせき【史跡】a historic spot. ¶古代ローマの～ *historic relics* of ancient Rome. ～を保存する preserve *historic remains*.

しせき【史籍】a history; a historical book.

しせき【歯石】tartar. ¶～を取ってもらおう I'll have the *tartar* removed from the teeth.

じせき【次席】(地位が次席の人) an official next in rank; (受賞者などの) the second winner.
―検事 an associate public procurator.

じせき【自責】¶～の念にかられた I *felt guilty*. / I *felt a guilty conscience*.
―点〘野球〙an earned run.

しせつ【私設】―ポスト(特に 米) a mailbox.
―秘書 a private secretary. ―鉄道 a private railroad.

しせつ【使節】(一行) a mission; (ひとり) an envoy.
親善― a goodwill envoy. 文化―団 a cultural mission. 貿易―団 a trade mission.

しせつ【施設】(建物) an establishment; an institution; (設備) equipments; facilities.
公共― public facilities. 厚生― welfare facilities. 娯楽― recreation facilities. 教育― educational facilities. 軍事― military establishments.

じせつ【自説】*one's* [own] opinion. ¶彼は～を曲げない He sticks to his *opinion*. ついに彼は～を捨てた At last he changed his *opinion*.

じせつ【時節】the season. ¶桜の～だ It's *the* cherry blossom *season*. ～を待とう I will wait for *a* better *chance*. ～到来だ *My time* has come. / My clock has struck. ～がくれば彼も有名になるでしょう *In due time* he will be famous. ～がら口を慎め Be careful in speaking in view of *the times*.

しせん【支線】¶鉄道の～ a branch line.

しせん【視線】*one's* eyes. ¶彼に～を注いだ I fixed my *eyes* on him. 彼から～をそらした I turned away my *eyes* from him. ～が合った Our *eyes* met. 彼女の冷たい～に耐えられない I cannot bear her unfriendly *look*. 世界じゅうの～が日本に集まっている The *eyes* of the world are focused upon Japan.

しせん【詩選】an anthology (*of* Japanese poetry).

しせん【死線】¶彼はいくたびか～を越えてきた He has passed through many *crises*. 彼女は～をさまよっていた She was hovering between life and death.

しぜん【自然】**1** nature. ¶詩人は～を愛した The poet loved *nature*.
この国の～の美しさは格別だ *Nature* in this country is unspeakably beautiful.
彼は～に帰れと主張した He insisted that every man should return to *nature*.
この町の～は日ごとに失われていく *Nature* in this town is being destroyed day by day.
2 〖おのずと〗¶親が子を愛するのは～である It *is natural* for parents to love their children.
彼のこの人のよさは～に備わったものだ This good nature of his has been *naturally* formed.
車が～に動きだした The car began to move *of itself*.
この辺ではこの種の植物は～に伸びる This sort of plant grows *naturally* in this neighborhood.
～のなりゆきに任せるほかはない There is no other way to be found than to let *nature* go on

her course.
—科学 natural science. —現象 a natural phenomenon. —主義 naturalism. —増 a natural increase. —淘汰(とうた) natural selection. —発火 spontaneous combustion. —発生 spontaneous generation. —保護 the conservation of nature. —描写 a description of nature. —界 the natural world. —死 a natural death. —崇拝 nature worship. 不— ¶彼の態度は不〜だった His manner *was artificial*.

じせん【自選】 ¶〜の歌集 a collection of poems *selected by the author*.

じせん【自薦】 ¶〜他薦合わせて10名いる There are ten candidates including those who *recommend themselves*.

じぜん【次善】 ¶〜の策 *the second-best* policy.

じぜん【事前】¶そのことについて〜に彼らと相談した I consulted with them about the matter *beforehand* (≒ *in advance*). その計画は〜に漏れてしまった The plan had leaked out before it was put into practice.
—運動(選挙の) pre-election campaigning. —協議 a prior consultation. —運動 advance preparations.

じぜん【慈善】charity.
—市 a charity bazaar. —音楽会 a charity concert. —事業 charities ; charitable work. —団体 a charity ; a charitable organization. —家 a charitable person. —興業 a charity performance. —病院 a charity hospital.

しそ【紫蘇】〖植物〗a beefsteak plant.

しそ【始祖】the founder.

しそう【死相】 ¶彼の顔には〜が現われていた *The shadow of death* was on his face.

しそう【志操】¶彼は〜堅固だ He is *a man of principle*.

しそう【思想】thought ; an idea. ¶過激〜の持ち主 a radical ; a Radical ; a thinker of radical *sentiments*. 〜調査は違憲だ *Thought control* is against the Constitution. 彼の〜はマルクス主義の影響を受けている His *thought* (≒ *idea*) is tinged with Marxism. 彼の〜は穏健(過激)だ He has *a* sober (radical) *thought*. 彼女の小説は〜に乏しい Her novel is poor in *thought*.
—家 a thinker. —劇 a problem play. —問題 a thought problem. —運動 a thought movement. —犯 an offense involving dangerous thoughts. 西洋— Western thought (≒ ideas). 東洋— Eastern thought (≒ ideas). 現代— modern thought. 科学— scientific thought.

しぞう【死蔵】¶長年〜されていた古文書 ancient manuscripts which *have been hoarded* many years.

じぞう【地蔵】¶路傍の石〜 a stone image of *Jizo* by the roadside.

しそうのうろう【歯槽膿漏】〖医学〗pyorrh(o)ea ; Riggs' disease.

しそく【子息】a son.

じそく【時速】¶車は〜60マイルで走った The car ran at 60 *miles per hour*. (60 m.p.h. と略して書ける). その列車の最高〜は200キロだ The train has a maximum speed of 200 *kilometers per hour*. (200 k.p.h. と略して書ける).

じぞく【持続】¶その薬の効果は長時間〜する The medicine takes *durable* effect. 市場の好調は当分〜しよう The favorable trade condition will *last* for a while.

しそこな・う【為損う】 ¶二度と〜うな Don't *make* another *blunder*.

しそん【子孫】a descendant ; an offspring (複数の意味にも用いる) ; (集合的) posterity. ¶彼は〜にばく大な財産を残した He left a big fortune to his *descendants*. 彼らは有名な小説家の〜たちだ They are the *descendants* of a famous novelist.

じそんしん【自尊心】pride ; self-respect.
¶彼女の〜は傷つけられた Her *pride* was hurt. 彼は〜が強い He is a man of great *self-respect*. そんなことはぼくの〜が許さない I have too much *pride* to do such a thing.

した【下】**1**〖場所・位置〗¶ベッドの〜にだれか隠れている Somebody is hiding *under* the bed.
ネコが縁の〜に入っていった A cat went *under* the veranda.
橋の〜にボートがつながれている A boat is moored *under* the bridge.
電話は階段の〜にある The telephone is *at the foot* (≒ *bottom*) of the stairs.
ホースの先をもっと〜に向けなさい Turn the nozzle of the hose further *down*.
海峡の〜をトンネルが通っている There is a tunnel *under* the channel.
彼はじっと〜を向いたままだった He kept looking *downward*.
がけのふちから〜を見ると目まいがしそうだった I felt dizzy when I looked *down* from the edge of the precipice.
ひざの〜まで水につかった The water reached *below* the knees.
ずっと〜の方に人家らしいものが見える I can see something like a house *down below*.
絵の右〜の方に画家の署名がある I can see the signature of the painter *down* at the right hand side (≒ *at* the *bottom* right).
ネコがベッドの〜から出てきた The cat appeared from *under* the bed.
子どもたちが山の〜から登ってくるのが見えた I saw children coming up the slope from the *foot* of the mountain.
掘ってみたら〜から昔の土器が出てきた When I dug into the ground, I found a piece of ancient earthenware.
なくしたかぎは布団の〜から出てきた The lost key was found *under* the mattress.
照明は〜から当てるほうが効果的だ The lighting is more effective when it is from *below*.
〜から3行めを見てください Please look at the last line but two. / Please look at the third line from *the bottom*.

2 〖階下〗 ¶すぐ行くから～で待っていてくれ I am coming in a moment, so wait *downstairs*.
このエレベーターは～に参ります This elevator is going *down*.
～に行くとき, ついでにこれを持っていってくれないか When you go *downstairs*, would you take this?

3 〖年齢〗 ¶～の子ももう小学校２年です The *younger* child is already in the second grade (≒ a second grader).
これがぼくのすぐ～の弟です This is my immediate *younger* brother.
妹はぼくより二つ～です My sister is two years *younger* than I. / My sister is two years my *junior*.
彼女は二つ年～の男と結婚した She got married to a man who was two years her *junior*.

4 〖地位・身分・力量・価値〗 ¶あの人の～で働くのはごめんだ I won't work *under* him.
～からの突き上げでストは回避できなかった Pressured by *the lower ranks*, the organization was not able to avoid the strike.
～から出るとすぐつけあがる He always presumes upon my *condescension*.
今度のベースアップは～に厚く上に薄くなっている The new raise in wages is more favorable to *the younger ranks* than the older.
地位はあの人のほうが～です He *is below* me in rank.
株価はそれより～にはならないだろう The price of the stock will not fall *lower* than that.
英語の成績はぼくより～なのに, 英語をしゃべるのはぼくよりうまい His marks in English *are below* mine, but he can speak better than I.
彼はぼくより中学で１級～の生徒だった He *was* a grade *below* me in the junior high school.
～にもおかぬもてなしを受けた They accorded me the utmost courtesy. / They gave me a warm welcome. / They treated me very courteously.

した【舌】 **1** a tongue. ¶～を出す put out *one's tongue*.
熱いスープで～をやけどした The hot soup burned my *tongue*.
きみの～は荒れている Your *tongue* is rough.
彼は非常に興奮して, 乾いたくちびるを何度も～でなめた He was so excited that he passed his *tongue* repeatedly over his dry lips.
～が真っ白だ My *tongue* is coated.
彼は～がもつれる He *has difficulty in articulation*.

2 〖比喩的・慣用的表現〗 ¶彼は陰で～を出しているにちがいない He must *be laughing in his sleeve*.
彼の雄弁には～を巻いた I *was astounded at* his eloquent speech.
その～の根も乾かぬうち彼はまた犯罪を犯した He committed a crime again while *the words were fresh from his mouth*.
二枚～を使うな Don't *be double-tongued*.

しだ【歯朶・羊歯】〔植物〕 a fern ; (総称) fernery.

じた【自他】 ¶彼は～ともに許すその道の権威だ He is a *commonly* acknowledged authority on the field.

したあご【下顎】 the lower jaw.

したい【死体】 a dead body ; a corpse. ¶彼は～となって発見された He was found *dead*. ～の引取人が現われなかった No one claimed *the body*. 昨夜身元不明の～が近所で発見された Last night *an* unidentified *body* was found in my neighborhood. 彼らは～の身元をはっきりさせることができなかった They could not identify the 〔*dead*〕 *body*.
—遺棄 abandonment of a corpse (≒ dead body). **—解剖** dissection of a dead body ; (検死のための) an autopsy. **—仮置き場** a deadhouse.

したい【姿態】 a figure. ¶彼女の～はすばらしい She has *a* wonderful *figure*.

したい【肢体】 the limbs ; the body and limbs. ¶均整のとれた～ a well-proportioned *figure*.
—不自由児 a crippled (≒ handicapped) child.

したい ¶あすは天気にしたいものだ *I hope* it'll be fine tomorrow. なにもしたくない I don't *feel like* doing anything. ああもしたいこうもしたいと思いながらなにもできなかった I *want to* do this and that, but so far have done nothing. 彼はいつもしたいほうだいのことをする He *gets his own way* in everything he does. / He *has everything his own way*. / He *has his fling*.

しだい【次第】 **1** 〖事情〗 circumstances. ¶事の～を説明してください Will you please explain *how it came to happen*?
このような～で結果はまだわからない *Such being the case*, the result is unknown yet.
このような～で私は行かれない These *circumstances* have made it impossible for me to go.

2 〖するやいなや〗 ¶天候がよくなり～運動会は行なわれる The athletic meet is to be held *as soon as* it clears up.
わかり～結果をご連絡します The result shall be known to you *the instant* I know it.
先方にご到着になり～お電話をください Please phone me *the moment* (≒ *the instant*) you arrive at your destination.
チャンスがあり～北海道に行きたい I am inclined to go over to Hokkaido *immediately* the chance is offered to me.
つごうがつき～ご返事します I will answer you *immediately after* the first opportunity is offered.
手当たり～に本を読んでいる I am reading books *at random*.

3 〖によって決まる〗 ¶成功も失敗も運～だ Success or failure *depends on* fortune.
すべてはきみの決意～だ All *is dependent on* your decision.
それは事と～による *That depends*.

じたい【自体】 ¶その計画～おかしい The plan *itself* is absurd. 現代では広告することはそれ～—

つの事業となっている In our times advertising has become a business *in itself*.

じたい【字体】¶どんな～にしますか In what *type* do you want it to be printed? あなたの名前をわかりやすい～で書いてください Please write your name *in an easily legible hand.* / (英語ではふつう活字体で書くから) Print your name.

じたい【事態】the situation. ¶彼は～を収拾するために最善をつくした He did his best to settle (≒ save; solve) *the situation*. 彼はその～に対処することができなかった He could not meet (≒ manage) *the situation*. ～を改善しなければならぬ We must improve (≒ better) *the situation*. ～は楽観を許さない *The situation* is still grave. / *The situation* doesn't warrant optimism. これによって緊急～が生ずるのは必定だ This will inevitably bring about a *tense* (≒ *threatening*) situation. ～は悪化の一途をたどるばかりだ *Things* are getting worse and worse. ～が好転した *The situation* has had a favorable turn. その国はいまや非常～にある The country is now in *a state* of emergency.

じたい【辞退】¶彼の援助の申し出を～した I *declined* his offer of help. 彼に～の手紙を出した I sent him my *regrets*. 彼は私にも行ってくれと言ったが,私はうまく彼の依頼を～した He wanted me to go too, but I managed to *excuse myself from* his request.

じだい【次代】¶～の青少年 *the younger* (≒ *the rising*) generation. ～を担う人々 those who are to lead *the next generation*.

じだい【地代】land rent. ¶月5,000円の～でけっこうです You may pay five thousand yen per month for *land rent*.

じだい【時代】**1** (時期) an age; an era; a time; (1代) a generation. ¶戦争は～の流れを大きく変えた The war greatly changed the trend of *the times*.

それを見てつくづくと～の流れを感じた When I saw it, I keenly felt the change of *the times*.

彼は～の波に乗っている He is riding on (≒ moving with) the wave of *the times*.

～の要求に応じる人材を育てなければならぬ We must bring up men of talent who meet the needs of *the times*.

今は～の変わっていることを悟らねばだめだ We must understand things are not what they used to be.

～とともに人間の趣味・嗜好(しこう)は変わる Human interest and taste change with *the times*.

彼は～に取り残されるのを恐れた He feared that he would be behind *the times*.

彼の作品は～を超越して今なおわれわれに強く訴える His works transcend *time*, strongly appealing to us even today.

若者の行動は～を反映している The conduct of young people reflects *the times*.

次の～を背負うのはきみたちだ It is you who will be the support and driving force of the next *age*.

それは～に逆行する考え方だ Such a point of view does not fit *the times*.

彼は～に背をむけたまま一生を終えた He lived out his life with his back turned on the world.

～に逆らって生きようとしたとて無理だ It is impossible to swim against the current of *the times*.

彼は～の反逆児であった He rebelled against *the times*.

利にさとい者は競って～を先取りしようとする Those people who have a quick eye for gain prepare in advance to meet the demands of the future.

そんな考えではこれからの～は生き抜けない In this *day and age* you can't get anywhere with that kind of thinking.

祖父の～にはテレビはなかった In my grandfather's *day* television was unknown.

昨今は情報過多の～といってよい You can say that we live in *an era* of excessive information.

20世紀は原子力の～だ The 20th century is *an* atomic *age*.

私どもの古きよき～が懐かしい I long for the good old *days*.

この川に再び魚が住める～が来るであろうか Will *the time* come when fish can live in this river again?

ぼくにもそのような夢を描いた～があった I also had such a dream at *a certain stage of my life*.

京都に都のあった～を平安～という The *days* when Kyoto was the capital of Japan is called the Heian *Era*.

この刀はかなり～を経たものだ This sword *is time-worn*.

今は原子力が日常生活に利用される～だ This is *a time* in which atomic power is used in daily life. (In this age ...ではじめてもよい).

2〖合成語〗¶その模様は～おくれだ That pattern *is old-fashioned* (≒ *is out of date*).

その時代にテレビがあったと思うのは～錯誤だ It *is anachronistic* to think that television was known at that time.

新婚～にはアパート1間で生活した We lived in a one-room apartment when we were newly married.

あの老人の言うことは～ばなれがしている That old man's words *are out of keeping with the times*.

～色豊かな祭りの行事が繰り広げられた The festival abounded in events full of *period color*.

学生～にはあまりアルバイトなどしないがいい You had better not do so much part-time work in your *school days*. (in *one's* school days, in *one's* boyhood などはやや改まった表現).

シェイクスピアとベーコンとは同～の人だ Shakespeare and Bacon were *contemporaries*. / Shakespeare was *a contemporary* of Bacon.

—劇 a historical play. **—思潮** the trend (≒ current) of the times. **—小説** a period novel. —物 an antique [article]. 宇宙— the cosmic age. 新— a new age (≒ epoch; era). 神話— the mythological (≒ legendary) age; the age of fables. 青春— *one's* youthful days; *one's* youth; when *one* was young. 石器— the stone age. 徳川— the time of the Tokugawa Shogunate. 明治— the Meiji Era (≒ Period). 封建— the feudal age (≒ days; times).

じだいしゅぎ 【事大主義】 flunk[e]yism; toadyism; worship of the powerful.
—者 a flunk[e]y; a toady.

し

しだいに 【次第に】 gradually. ¶ 彼は～有名になった *Gradually* he became famous. 彼女は～快方に向かっている She is *gradually* getting better. ～寒くなってきている It is getting *colder and colder*. きみの給料は～上がるだろう Your salary will rise *by degrees*.

した･う 【慕う】 ¶ この子は母親を～って泣いている This child is crying *for* her absent mother. 彼女は彼を～ってローマまで行った She *followed* him to Rome. その教授は学生たちから非常に～われている The professor *is the idol of* his students. われわれは彼を～っている We *have a regard for* him. 彼女は亡き夫を～っている She *cherishes her* late *husband's memory*. われわれはその偉人の人格を～っている We *admire* the personality of the great man. 彼女は彼をとても～っている She *loves* him very much. / She *is* deeply *attached to* him.

したうけ 【下請け】 a subcontract. ¶ 彼はその仕事を私に～させた He *subcontracted* (≒ *sublet*) the work *to* me. 私は～仕事の条件についてはなにも話されていない I am told nothing of the conditions under which the *subcontracted work* is carried out.
—業者 a subcontractor. —工場 a subcontract factory (≒ plant).

したうち 【舌打ち】 ¶ 彼はその考えを聞くと軽べつして～した He *tutted* the idea.

したえ 【下絵】 a rough sketch; (縫いとりなどの) a design. ¶ その景色の～を描いた I made *a rough sketch* of the view. 彼女はししゅうの～を描いた She made *a design for* embroidery.

したが･う 【従う】 ¶ 法律に～わなければならない We must *obey* the law. 彼の命令には絶対～いなさい *Obey* his orders by all means. 少年は母に～って門をくぐった The boy *followed* his mother through the gate. 外国人は日本に来ると日本人の習慣に～うようになる After coming to Japan, foreigners come to *follow* the customs of the Japanese. ご忠告には必ず～います I will *take* your advice without fail. 学校の決定に～うほかはない There is no other way than to *abide by* the decision of the school. 彼は私の忠告に～った He *yielded to* my advice. 目上の者に～うべきです You should *bow to* your elders.

したが･える 【従える】 ¶ 子どもを～えてやってくるのはだれですか Who is coming toward us, *followed by* children? 彼は付け人を～えて入ってきた He came in *with* his attendants.

したがき 【下書き】 ¶ 彼は論文を仕上げるのに3通りも～をした He made three different *drafts* of his essay before he had it in final form.

したがって 【従って】 **1** 〖…のとおりに〗 according to; in accordance with; in obedience to. ¶ 本は著者別に～本棚にならんでいる The books are placed on the shelves *according to* authors.
彼らは上官の命令に～行動した They acted *in obedience to* their superior officers.
きみの御要望に～彼女に手紙を書いた *In accordance with* your wishes, I have written to him.
2 〖つれて〗 as; in proportion as; in proportion to. ¶ 南へ行くに～だんだん暑くなる It becomes warmer and warmer *as* you go south.
英語を学ぶに～興味が増してきた *In proportion as* I learn English, I became more interested in it.
われわれは年をとるに～, 思慮分別が増してくる We are prudent *in proportion to* our age.

したがって therefore; consequently.

したが･る ¶ 彼らはすぐに議論を～る They *are* always *ready to* dispute. 彼はしきりに洋行～っている He *is anxious* (≒ *is eager*; *is impatient*) *to* go abroad.

したぎ 【下着】 (集合的に) underwear; underclothing (単数扱い); underclothes (複数扱い); an undergarment.

したく 【支度･仕度】 (用意･準備) preparations; arrangements; (装備) equipment; outfit; (服装) dressing.
¶ 彼は旅行の～をしている He *is preparing for* a trip. 食事の～をしなければならない I have to *get* a meal *ready*. 夕食の～をしましたか Did you *prepare* supper? 彼女は外出の～をしている She *is dressing* [*herself*] *up for* going out. 息子の旅行に十分な～をしてやる *equip one's* son fully *for* his trip. ぼくのほうは出発の～ができているがきみはどうですか *I'm* quite *ready* to go, but how about you? 旅行の～はすべて完了した All *arrangements* have been made for our trip. お食事の～ができました(召使のことば) Dinner *is served*. 彼はりっぱな～をして娘を嫁がせた He married his daughter *in grand style*. 女の外出の～は長いものだ Women take so much time in *dressing* when going out.
—金(嫁入りの) a wedding allowance. —部屋 a dressing room.

じたく 【自宅】 *one's* [own] home. ¶ ～にいる be *at home*; (米口語) be *home*. ～にいない be out; be not at home. 彼を～に訪ねる visit him at his *house* (≒ *home*).
—療養 home treatment. —診療 consultation at the doctor's office.

したくちびる 【下唇】 the lower (≒ under) lip. ¶ ～をかむ(感情を殺すため) bite *one's* lip.

したげいこ 【下稽古】 (練習) practice; (劇･音

楽などの) a rehearsal. ¶ 彼らは講堂で今度の劇の～をしている They *are rehearsing* (≒ *are having a rehearsal*) for a new play at the auditorium. 彼は昨夜演説の～をした He *practiced* his speech last night.

したけんぶん【下検分】 a preliminary inspection. ¶ 旅行のコースを～する make *a preliminary inspection* of the course of our trip.

したごころ【下心】 a secret end. ¶ 彼はなにか～あって私のために働いているのだろう Probably he works for me *with some secret end* (≒ *object*) *in view*. 私はそうしようと思う～は全然ありません I have the least *intention* of doing so.

したごしらえ【下拵え】 preliminary arrangements; preparations; prearrangement. ¶ 彼女は料理の～をしておいた She made *preliminary arrangements* for the dishes.

したさき【舌先】 ¶ 彼はだれでも～三寸で言いくるめる He persuades everybody *with a glib tongue*. 彼はなんでも～でごまかす He *talks* anything *away*. 彼女は～三寸でうまいこと言って彼をだました She cheated him by *flattery*

したじ【下地】 foundation; (ペンキの下塗り) the first coat. ¶ 彼女は語学の～があった She had *an aptitude* for languages. 彼女は音楽の～が十分できている She has *a good grounding* in music. / She is *well grounded* in music.

しだし【仕出し】 outgoing order. ¶ 当店はパーティーの料理の～をいたします We *cater* for parties. / We *supply dishes to order* for parties. / We accept *outgoing order* for parties. ～を10人前注文した I ordered food for ten persons.

—屋(人) a caterer; (店) a caterer's shop. **—料理** dishes suppplied to order.

したし・い【親しい】 good; close; intimate. ¶ 彼は私の～い友人だ He is a *good* (≒ *close*) friend of mine. 私たちはお互いに～い間柄だ We are on *good* terms with each other. / We are on *intimate* terms with each other. (intimate を用いると男女関係を連想させることがあるので異性間では避けられる). ～き仲にも礼儀あり (諺) A hedge between keeps good manners.

したじき【下敷き】 ¶ 文房具店で～を1枚買った I bought *a celluloid board laid under writing paper* at a stationer's. 家族の者がみな倒れた家の～になって死んだ All the members of the family were crushed to death *under their fallen house*.

したしく【親しく】 ¶ ふたりは～なった The two persons became *intimate*. 彼と私は～している He and I are on *friendly* terms. / I am on *good* terms with him. ヨーロッパ各国を～見聞した I made a *personal* observation of European countries. ⇒したしい(親しい)

したしさ【親しさ】 intimacy; familiarity. ¶ ふたりの～はみんなの語り草であった Everybody talked about the *intimacy* (≒ *familiarity*) between the two.

したしみ【親しみ】 intimacy; familiarity. ¶ ～のある声だった It was an *intimate* voice. 彼はいつも～やすい態度で話す He always speaks in a *friendly* way.

したし・む【親しむ】 ¶ あの家の人はみな～みやすい His family *are* all *friendly*. 彼はだれからも～まれていた He *was familiar with* everybody. 本に～めるのは学生の特権だ It is the privilege of students to be able to *take to* books. われわれは自然に～むべきだ We should *commune with* nature.

したしらべ【下調べ】 preparation. ¶ 私はまだあすの授業の～がしてない I *have* not *prepared* tomorrow's lessons yet. ～を十分にして教室に出る I go to the class *well-prepared*.

したたか【強か】 ¶ ～に飲む drink *heavily*. ～に酔う be *dead* (≒ *blind*) drunk; be drunk *like a fish*. 私は～打たれた I got a *sound* beating.

—者 ¶ 彼はなかなかの～者だ He is just *a scoundrel*.

したた・める【認める】 ¶ 手紙を～める *write* a letter. 軽い食事を～める *take* (≒ *have*) a light meal.

したたらず【舌足らず】 ¶ 彼の発音は～だ He speaks *with a lisp*. / He *lisps*. 私の説明に～の点があって誤解された My explanation, which turned out to *be dissatisfactory*, caused a misunderstanding.

したたり【滴り】 a drop. ¶ 軒先の雨の～ the *raindrops* from the eaves.

したた・る【滴る】 ¶ 彼の額から汗が～り落ちている His forehead *is dripping* 〔with sweat〕. / The sweat *is dripping* from his forehead. 彼の上着からしずくが～っていた His coat *was dripping*. 彼は水も～るいい男だ He is *extremely* handsome. 緑～る青葉のころが好きだ I love the season of *fresh* green foliage.

したつづみ【舌鼓】 ¶ 彼はスープに～を打った He *smacked his lips over* the soup. 彼はビフテキに～を打って食べた He ate the beefsteak *with great relish*. 彼はごちそうに～を打って食べた He ate the fine dish *with much gusto*.

したっぱ【下っ端】 a subordinate; an underling. ¶ ～役人 a *petty* (≒ *minor*) official.

したづみ【下積み】 ¶ ～の荷物 goods in the *lower layer*. 彼は一生～の生活をした He *lived in obscurity* all through his life.

したて【下手】 ¶ こちらが～に出れば彼は必ずつけあがる The more I *stoop* (≒ *humble myself*), the haughtier he is sure to become.

したて【仕立て・仕立】 tailoring. ¶ ～の申し分のない洋服 a perfectly *tailored* suit. きみの服は～がよい Your clothes *are* well *made* (≒ *tailored*). 彼らは特別～の列車で京都へ行った They went to Kyoto by a special train.

—物(縫うこと) tailoring; sewing; (仕立てた物) newly-made clothes. **—屋(男子用)** a tailor; (女子用) a dressmaker. **—おろし** ¶ 彼は～おろしの服を着ていた He wore a brand-new suit. **—代** ¶ ～代はいくらですか What is the charge for the *tailoring* 〔of it〕?

した·てる【仕立てる】¶どこでお～てですか Where did you *have* your suit *made*? / (女性服) Who is your dressmaker? / (男子服) Who is your tailor? 馬車を～てる *prepare* a carriage. 彼は息子を医者に～てるつもりだ He wants to *make* a doctor *of* his son.

したなめずり【舌なめずり】lick *one's* lips (≒ fingers). ¶彼はおいしいケーキが食べたくて～している He *is licking his lips* (≒ *fingers*) in the hope of eating sweet cakes.

したぬり【下塗り】¶彼は盆に漆の～をした He gave the tray *the first coat* of lacquer.

し

したば【下歯】the lower teeth.

したばえ【下生え】undergrowth; 米 underbrush.

じたばた ¶今更～してもだめだ It's no use for you to *struggle* now. / Don't *make a scene*. It's too late.

したばたらき【下働き】¶～のお手伝いさん a *kitchen* maid. 彼は私の～をしている He *works under* me.

したはら【下腹】the abdomen. ¶～に力を入れる strain *one's abdomen*. ～が激しく痛む I have a sharp pain in *the abdomen*. (abdomen は belly の婉曲語).

したび【下火】¶火事も～になってきた The fire *is burning down*. 野球熱も冬が近づいて～になった The rage for baseball games *has declined* because winter is coming. 彼の人気は～になっている His popularity *is on the wane*. 騒動が～になった The trouble *has quieted down*.

したまち【下町】a downtown. ¶私は東京の～に住んでいる I live *in downtown* Tokyo. 彼女は母親と～へ買い物に行った She went *downtown* with her mother to do some shopping. あの娘は～ふうのつくりだ She is dressed *in downtown* fashion.

したまわ·る【下回る】¶ことしの米作は平年作を～った The rice crop of this year *is below* the average one. 売り上げが予想を大幅に～った The sales *are* much *lower* (≒ *less*) *than* expected.

したみ【下見】(下見板) a weatherboard; (下検分) a preliminary inspection.

したむき【下向き】¶ライトを～にする *lower* a light. 景気が～になってきた Business *is going down*. / The market *is declining*. / The market *shows a downward tendency*.

したやく【下役】(地位) (a) subordinate position; (人) a subordinate [official].

したよみ【下読み】(準備) preparation; (脚本などの) a rehearsal. ¶あすの授業の～をした I *have prepared* (≒ *have made preparations for*) tomorrow's lessons.

じだらく【自堕落】¶～な男 a sloven. ～な女 a slut; a slattern; a loose woman. 彼女はニューヨークで～な生活を送っている She is leading a *loose* life in New York.

したりがお【したり顔】¶～をして話す speak *triumphantly*; speak *with a triumphant* (≒ *an elated*) *look*.

しだれざくら【垂れ桜】a drooping cherry tree.

しだれやなぎ【垂れ柳】a weeping willow.

しだ·れる【垂れる】droop; hang down.

したわし·い【慕わしい】beloved; dear.

したん【紫檀】〖植物〗a red sandalwood. ¶～の机 a table of *red sandalwood*.

しだん【師団】a division.
—長 a divisional commander.

しだん【詩壇】the poetical circles; the world of poetry.

じだん【示談】a private settlement. ¶～にする *settle* a matter *privately*. ～で解決するため努力がなされた Efforts have been made to effect *a private settlement* (≒ *a settlement out of court*). 弁護士の勧めにより訴訟を～にした On the advice of the counsel, the case *was settled out of court*. 私は～に応じなかった I did not agree to *an out-of-court settlement*. 私は債権者と～して借金を半分に負けてもらった I *have made a composition with* my creditors for one-half.
—金 money paid by way of compromise; composition.

じだんだ【地団駄】¶彼は～を踏んでくやしがった He *stamped his foot* in frustration.

しち【七】seven. ¶第～ the seventh.
—回忌 the sixth anniversary of *a person's* death. —五調 the seven-and-five syllable meter. お—夜 a feast in celebration of the seventh day of a child's birth.

しち【質】pawn. ¶時計を～に入れて2,000円借りた I *pawned* my watch *for* 2,000 yen. 彼は時計を～に入れた He *put* his watch *in pawn*. 私の時計は～に入れてある My watch is *in pawn* (≒ *in pledge*). ～が流れないように質屋に利子を入れた I paid the interest so that I might not *forfeit the pawn*. 時計を～から出した I took my watch out of *pawn*.
—ぐさ a pawn; an article for pawning. —流れ a forfeited pawn. —札 a pawn ticket.

しち【死地】¶やっとのことで～を脱した We had a narrow escape from *death*. 兵士は敢然として国のために～に赴いた The soldiers *went into the jaws of death* bravely for the sake of their country.

じち【自治】self-government. ¶～の精神 the spirit of *self-government*. 学園の～を守る defend the right of *self-government* of a college.
—会(学生の) a student council; a students' union. —権 the right of self-government. —省 the Autonomy Ministry. —制 the system of self-government. —体 a self-governing body; an autonomy. —領 英 a self-governing dominion (もとのカナダ·オーストラリアなどを指す); a self-governing colony.

しちがつ【七月】July.

しちごさん【七五三】¶～のお祝い the celebration of a child's *third, fifth and seventh years*.

しちじゅう【七十】seventy. ¶第～ the seventieth.

―年祭 the seventieth anniversary.

しちてんばっとう【七転八倒】¶～の苦しみで in the death agony. 彼は苦痛で～した He *writhed in agony with* pain.

しちふくじん【七福神】the Seven Gods of Good Fortune (⇆ Luck).

しちめんちょう【七面鳥】〔動物〕a turkey; (雄) a turkey cock; (雌) a turkey hen.

しちや【質屋】a pawnshop. ¶～の主人 a pawnbroker. ～に通う frequent *a pawnshop*. 彼は～をやっている He keeps *a pawnshop*. / He is *a pawnbroker*.

公設― a public pawnshop.

しちゅう【支柱】a pillar; a support. ¶テントの中に～を立てる set up *a pillar* to support a tent. 彼は一家の～となって働いた He *supported* his family.

しちゅう【市中】¶川が～を流れている A river runs *through the city*. この品は～どこでも出回っている You can get this in any store *in the city*. ～は火の消えたようだ *The town* looks deserted.

―銀行 a city bank.

シチュー stew.

しちょう【支庁】a branch office.

しちょう【市庁】a municipal office; a city hall.

しちょう【市長】a mayor. ¶横浜～ *the Mayor* of Yokohama.

―選挙 a mayoral election.

しちょう【思潮】the current (⇆ trend) of thought.

文芸― the trend of literature. 時代― the spirit of the age.

しちょう【視聴】¶世界の～を集めた出来事 an incident which attracted universal *attention*.

―者 an audience. ¶テレビの～者 *a* TV *audience*; (ひとり) *a* TV *viewer*. ―率 audience rating. ¶その歌謡番組は20%以上の～率を占めている The popular song program has *a rating* of more than twenty percent.

しちょう【試聴】an audition.

―室 an audition room.

じちょう【次長】a vice-chief; a vice-director.

―検事 the assistant procurator general.

じちょう【自重】¶今後はもっと～してもらいたい I want you to *be* more *prudent* from now on. くれぐれもご～ください Please *take* the best *care of* yourself.

じちょう【自嘲】self-scorn.

しちょうかく【視聴覚】auditory senses.

―教育 audio-visual education. ―教材 audio-visual aids.

しちょうそん【市町村】cities, towns and villages.

しちょく【司直】the judicial authorities; (法官) a judge.

じちんさい【地鎮祭】a ground-breaking ceremony.

しっ Sh! / Hush! / Hist! ¶ネコを～と言って追い払う *shoo* a cat away.

しつ【室】a room. ¶～外で outdoors. ～内で indoors.

しつ【質】quality. ¶これは～がよい(悪い) This is of good (poor) *quality*. 製品の～を高める improve the *quality* of the goods. 量より～がたいせつだ *Quality* is more important than quantity. ことしの入学者の中には～の悪い者が多い Among those who entered this year, there are many who are poor in *scholastic ability*.

じつ【実】¶～のところフランス語はひと言もしゃべれないんです *To tell the truth*, I can't speak a word of French. ～に偉い人だ He is a *really* great man. ～に美しい絵だ *How* beautiful the picture is!

しつい【失意】disappointment. ¶～の人 a *disappointed* man. 彼女は今～のどん底にある She *is* now *at the nadir of her fortune*.

じついん【実印】a registered seal. ¶証書に～を押した I put my *registered seal* to the instrument.

しつう【歯痛】¶～がする I have *a toothache*.

じつえき【実益】profit. ¶～がある be actually profitable. この仕事は趣味と～を兼ねている This work combines *profit* with a hobby. / This work *is* not only interesting but *profitable*.

じつえん【実演】a demonstration. ¶～をして料理を教える teach *a person* how to cook by *a demonstration*.

しっか【失火】an accidental fire. ¶その建物は～で焼けた The building was destroyed by *an accidental fire*. (a fire だけでもよい).

じっか【実科】a practical course.

じっか【実家】*one's* parents' home (⇆ house). ¶妻の～ the house of *one's* wife's parents.

じっかい【十誡・十戒】the Ten Commandments.

じつがい【実害】harm; damage. ¶この計画は～がある This plan *is damaging*. ～のあることはやめるべきだ You must stop doing what *is harmful*.

しっかく【失格】disqualification. ¶彼は予選で～となった He *failed to qualify* for the semifinals.

―者 a disqualified person.

じつかぶ【実株】〔株式〕a real stock; a spot share.

しっかり【確り】¶～ロープにつかまりなさい Hold on *fast* to the rope. このかばんを～持っていてください Please hold this briefcase *tightly*. 窓を～閉めておきなさい Keep the window shut *tight*. 彼は～した体格だ He has a *well-built* physique. あの老人は足もとが～している That old man *is firm* on his legs. 年はとっても足どりは～している In spite of his old age his step *is steady*. あの人は～した人物だ He is a *trustworthy* man. この家は土台が～している This house is built on *steady* foundations. 彼は

し

〜した考えを持っている He *is sound in* thought. 〜勉強せよ Study *hard*. 〜しろ Pull yourself together. / (がっかりするな) Cheer up! / (あわてるな) Take it easy! / (病気・大けがに負けるな) Don't give way!

しっかん【疾患】a trouble; a disease.
¶ 目の(肺の)〜 *an* eye (*a* lung) *trouble*.

じっかん【実感】¶ 当時われわれは戦争に負けたのだということを〜としてはよくわからなかった In those days we did not *realize fully* that we had lost the war. この絵は正に〜がよくでている This picture *is true to nature*.

し

しっき【湿気】moisture; damp. ¶ これを〜をうけないようにしておかなければいけない You must keep this free from *moisture*. 〜が多いので物にかびが生える Everything becomes moldy because the air *is humid* (≒ *is damp*). 〜の多い外に出ているな Don't stay outside in the *damp*. 〜のない所に置きなさい Keep it in a *dry* place.

しっき【漆器】lacquered 〔japan〕ware; lacquer.

しつぎ【質疑】a question; an interrogation; (国会での) an interpellation. ¶ 講師は聴衆の〜に答えた The lecturer answered *questions* put by the audience.
—応答 questions and answers.

じつぎ【実技】an exercise. ¶ 体操の〜 gymnastic *exercises*. (略して gym). 私は法規は合格したが, 運転の〜で落第した I passed the test of traffic laws, but failed in the *driving test*.

しっきゃく【失脚】a downfall; loss of position. ¶ 外交政策を誤ったため大統領は〜した The recent blunder in the foreign policy brought about the *downfall* of the President.

しつぎょう【失業】unemployment. ¶ 私は〜中だ I *am out of work*. / I *am out of a job*. 〜している人は案外多い There are more *unemployed* people than are expected. 彼は〜した He *has lost his work*.
—者 an unemployed person; (複数) the unemployed (複数扱い). **—対策** an unemployment policy. **—手当** an unemployment allowance. **—保険** unemployment insurance. **—問題** the unemployment problem.

じっきょう【実況】the scene; the actual state of things. ¶ 野球の試合の〜放送をする keep up *a running commentary* (≒ *a live coverage*) on a baseball game. われわれはその試合の〜放送を聞いていた We were listening to *the play-by-play broadcast* of the game.

じつぎょう【実業】industry; business.
—家 a businessman; (女性) a businesswoman. **—界** business circles. ¶ 彼は〜界にいる He *is* now *in business*. 彼は学校を出たら〜界に入る He will *go into business* when he leaves school. **—学校** a vocational school; 米 a business college.

しっきん【失禁】〖医学〗incontinence.

シック ¶ 〜な洋服 a *chic* suit.

しっくい【漆喰】mortar; plaster. ¶ 壁に〜を塗る *plaster* a wall.

しつく・す【為尽くす】¶ あの男は悪事の限りを〜した He *committed all sorts of* wicked deeds. 彼は若いころ, 道楽を〜した He *indulged in all kinds of* dissipation when he was young.

しっくり ¶ 彼とどうも〜いかない I do not get on with him *very well*.

じっくり〔と〕¶ そのことについて〜考える時間がほしい I want ample time to *think over* the matter. 〜勉強にとりかかろうではないか Let's *settle down* to our studies. ぼくの言うことを〜聞いてくれ Please listen to me *carefully*.

しっけ【湿気】⇒しっき

しつけ【仕付け・躾】discipline; training. ¶ 彼女は家庭の〜が非常にやかましい She is very strict in home *discipline*. あの子は〜のよい子どもだ He is a good-behaviored boy. / That boy *is well-bred*. あの娘は〜が悪い That girl *is ill-bred*.

しつけ【仕付け】tacking.
—糸 tacking thread.

しっけい【失敬】¶ 彼はぼくに向かっていつも〜なことを言う He always says *rude* things to me. 一足先に〜するけれどいいでしょうか Do you mind if I *leave* before you? じゃあ〜 So long. / Well, good-bye. 〜なことを言うな None of your *cheek*! これは〜した I beg your pardon.

じっけい【実兄】*one's* own elder (≒ older) brother.

じっけい【実景】the actual view; the actual scene.

じっけい【実刑】a prison sentence. ¶ 彼は5年の〜を宣告された He was given *a* five year *prison sentence*.

しつ・ける【仕付ける】¶ 子どもたちはよく〜けてある The children are under proper *discipline*. 子どもたちがりっぱな市民になるよう〜けることはたいせつなことだ It is important to *train* 〔*up*〕 children to be good citizens. 〜けない仕事で非常に疲れた I am very tired from the work that *I am not used to*.

しっけん【識見】insight; judgment. ¶ 〜の高い人 a man *of* great *insight*.

しつげん【失言】a slip of the tongue; a misstatement. ¶ われわれは彼に〜を取り消すように求めた We told him to retract his *misstatement* (≒ *word*). 大臣は〜をわびた The Minister apologized for his *slip of the tongue*.

じっけん【実見】¶ 〜する witness; observe; see with *one's* own eyes.

じっけん【実験】an experiment; a test.
¶ 化学の〜 *a* chemical *experiment*; *an experiment* in chemistry. 〜は大成功だった The *experiment* was a great success. 彼は核〜の禁止を提案した He proposed a ban on nuclear *tests*. その計画はまだ〜の段階にある The plan is still in an *experimental* stage. 〜によって知識を得る人もある Some people learn by *experiment*. 彼らは電気の〜をし

ている They are making *an experiment* in electricity. 動物～は成功だった The *experiment* on animals was successful.

―室 a laboratory. **―台**(実験材料) a guinea pig. **―物理学** experimental physics.

じっけん【実権】 real power. ¶ 彼が国政の～を握っている He *holds the real power* (≒ *the reins*) *of* government. 会社の～を握っているのは彼だ He *exercises controlling influences on* the company. / It is he who *has a great influence over* the company.

じつげん【実現】 realization; actualization. ¶ 父の遺産のおかげで彼は大学へ行くという夢を～できるようになった His father's legacy made it possible for him to *realize* his dream of going to college. 彼の理想は～されるに至った His ideal has been brought to *realization*. 人類の夢が～した The dream of mankind *has come true*. きみの計画は～性がない Your plan is impossible of *realization*. / Your plan *is infeasible*.

しつこ・い ¶ ～いこじき a *persistent* beggar. ～い攻撃 *persistent* attack. ～い食事 *heavy* food. 彼はいっしょに映画に行くように～くぼくをさそった He *persistently* invited me to go to the movies with him. この子はほんとに～い This child *is* much too *affectionate*.

しっこう【失効】 invalidation. ¶ その契約は～した The contract became *null and void*.

しっこう【執行】 execution; performance. ¶ 彼は公務の～にあたって非常に厳格であった He was very strict in the *execution* of official duties. 国会は法を制定し，大統領はそれを～する Congress makes laws; the President *executes* them.

―委員 an executive committee. **―官** an executive officer. **―者** an executor. **―手続き** proceedings. **―部** an executive. **―命令** an order of execution. **―令状** execution. **仮―** provisional execution. **死刑―人** an executioner.

じっこう【実行】 practice; action. ¶ 計画を立てるほうがそれを～するより難しいことがよくある It is often more difficult to make plans than it is to *carry* them *out*. 彼はその計画を～に移した He *put* the plan *into practice*. その考えを～しようとしたがだめだった The idea did not work *in practice*.

―委員会 an execution committee.

じっこう【実効】 ¶ ～のある措置 *effective* measures. 予防策はまったく～がなかった The precaution *was* quite *inefficacious*.

しっこうゆうよ【執行猶予】 a stay of execution; probation. ¶ 彼は懲役1年，～3年の刑に処せられた He was sentenced to one year in prison with *a* three-year *stay of execution*.

しっこく【漆黒】 ¶ 外は～のやみだ It *is pitch dark* (≒ *as dark as pitch*) outside.

しつこさ persistence. ¶ あの男の～はがまんがならない I can't bear his *persistence*.

じっこん【昵懇・入魂】 intimacy; familiarity. ¶ われわれは彼とだんだん～になった We have gradually formed *an intimacy* with him. 彼とは～な間柄だ I am *on* friendly *terms* with him.

じっさい【実際】 (理論に対しての) practice; (実状) an actual state; (事実) a fact. ¶ 理論と～は一致しない Theory does not coincide with *practice*. これが交通戦争の～だ This is *the actual state* of the 'traffic war.' ～は，ぼくはあの夜家にいた The *fact* is, I was home that night. 彼女はだまっていたが，～は彼女はフランス語がしゃべれるのだ She was silent. But, *as a matter of fact*, she can speak French. ～のところ私の家にはそんな便利なものはない *To tell the truth*, we do not have such a convenient thing in our house. 私は～にこわかったんです I was *really* afraid. ～にはこううまくはいかないだろう I am afraid things will not turn out so well. ～にやってみればわかる You will see what it is once you have done it *in practice*. ～彼には失望した I was *in fact* disappointed in him. 彼には～腹が立つ I feel angry with him *indeed*. 彼は～より若く見える He looks younger than *he really is*. 彼は～的な人物だ He is a *practical* man. ～問題として彼には政治家としての能力がない *As a matter of fact*, he is not capable as a statesman.

―家 a practical man. **―所得** a real income.

じつざい【実在】 existence; reality. ¶ ～しない unreal. この小説中の人物は～の人のように書かれている The characters in this novel seem quite *real*. ハムレットは歴史上～の人物だったか Was Hamlet a *real* person in history? そういうことは～する Such a thing *is* truly *existent*.

―論〔哲学〕realism. **―論者** a realist.

しっさく【失策】 an error; a mistake. ¶ 彼はまた大～をやった He made *a* terrible *mistake* again. / He *blundered* again.

しつじ【執事】 a steward; a butler.

じっし【十指】 ¶ 彼は～に余る論文を書いた He wrote more than *ten* papers.

じっし【実子】 *one's* own child; *one's* true child. ¶ われわれには～がないので養子をもらった Because we have no *children of our own*, we have adopted a child.

じっし【実施】 operation; execution; enforcement. ¶ これらの規則は6年も前から～されている These rules *have been in operation* for six years. 法律は厳正に～されねばならない The law must *be* rigorously *enforced*. 新規則は来週火曜日に～される The new regulations will *come into operation* next Tuesday.

―計画 an enforcement plan.

しつじつ【質実】 ¶ 彼は～な生活を送っている He lives a *sober and simple* life.

じっしつ【実質】 essence; substance. ¶ これら二つの物は～においてはほとんど同じだ These two things are almost the same *in essence*. この

文は美文にはちがいないが～がまったくない This essay is written in an elegant style, to be sure, but it is totally lacking *in substance*. 外見を～と見誤ることのないよう注意すべきだ You should take care not to mistake the appearance for *the substance*. 彼女の説明は～的には正しい Her explanation is correct *in substance*. われわれはお互いに～的には一致している We are in *substantial* agreement with each other.

—賃金 take-home pay; real wages.

じっしゃかい【実社会】¶ この3月，彼は大学を卒業して～に出た He graduated from college and *went into the world* this March.

じっしゅう【実収】 a net income; a real income; take-home pay. ¶ いろいろ差し引きして～5万円ほどだ I have *a net income* of 50,000 yen after various deductions.

じっしゅう【実習】 practice; exercise; actual training. ¶ ～する have *practical training*.

—生 apprentice. 教育**—生**(教生) a student teacher.

じっしゅきょうぎ【十種競技】 the decathlon.

しつじゅん【湿潤】¶ ～の地 *moist* places.

しっしょう【失笑】¶ その返事に一同～した There was *a* general *laugh* at that answer. / Everybody *burst out laughing* at the answer.

じっしょう【実証】 an actual proof; substantiation. ¶ これを～してくれるものはなにもない There is no *proof* of this. / Nothing can *prove* this. そうとも思われるがまだ～を握っていない I consider it a possibility but I *have* not yet *come to proof*. 詐欺を～するものはなにもなかった There was no *actual evidence* of fraud. 彼のアリバイは～された His alibi *was corroborated* (≒ *was confirmed*). それは彼の行動に関する陳述を～した It *bore out* (≒ *substantiated; verified*) the statement of his movements. 彼の陳述には十分な～があった There was ample *corroboration* of his statement.

—主義 positivism.

じつじょう【実状・実情】 the actual circumstances; the true state of affairs. ¶ ～が彼にわかりかけてきた *The real state of the case* dawned upon him. われわれは～を知らされる必要がある We must be informed of *the true state of affairs*. 彼には～がさっぱりわからなかった He did not know at all *how things stood* (≒ *the actual circumstances*).

しっしん【失神・失心】 a faint; a swoon. ¶ 彼女は突然～しそうになった Suddenly she *felt faint*. 彼女は～した She *fainted*. / She *passed out*. / She *lost consciousness*. 彼女は驚きのあまり～した She *fainted* [*away*] from fright. 彼女は血を見て～した She *fainted* (≒ *swooned*) at the sight of the blood. 彼女は～状態から覚めた She recovered consciousness. / She came to herself.

しっしん【湿疹】〘医学〙 eczema; moist [humid] tetter.

じっしんぶんるいほう【十進分類法】 the decimal classification.

じっしんほう【十進法】 the decimal system.

じっすう【実数】 the actual number; 〘数学〙 a real number.

しっ·する【失する】¶ 救援は遅きに～した They *lost* (≒ *missed*) a chance to extend a helping hand. 彼は彼女についてずいぶん礼を～したことを言った He made a very *rude* remark about her.

しっせい【失政】 misgovernment.

じっせいかつ【実生活】 real life. ¶ ～ではそんなことはありえない I don't believe in it in *real life*.

しっせき【叱責】 a rebuke. ¶ 私は彼の怠惰を～した I *scolded* him for his laziness.

じっせき【実績】 actual results; achievements. ¶ すばらしい～が認められた His distinguished *services* were appreciated. その弁護士はあの事件で～をあげた The lawyer *made a name for himself* in that case.

じっせけん【実世間】 the everyday (≒ actual) world.

じっせん【実践】 practice. ¶ それはただちに～された It *was* at once *put in* (≒ *into*) *practice* (≒ *action*). 彼は自己の理念を～躬行(きゅうこう)した He put his personal theory into *actual practice*.

—道徳〘哲学〙 practical morality.

じっせん【実戦】 actual fighting; a battle; an action. ¶ ～では彼は冷静で機略縦横の指揮官だった *In action* he was a cool and resourceful leader. 彼は～に参加中負傷した He was wounded *in an action*. 彼は陸軍中佐として～に参加した He *saw active service* as lieutenant colonel.

じっせん【実線】 a solid line.

しっそ【質素】 simplicity; plainness. ¶ 彼女の服装はたいへん～だ Her dress *is* very *plain*. 彼女は～な暮らしをしている She lives *simply*. / She lives a *simple* life. 彼女は～だが小ざっぱりした服装をしていた She was *poorly* (≒ *simply*) but neatly dressed. 昼食はパンとサラダの～な食事だった Lunch was a *simple* meal of bread and salad. それは～な調度の小さな部屋だった It was a small *poorly* (≒ *plainly*) furnished room. 彼らはどちらかというと～な感じの家に住んでいる They live in a somewhat *modest* house.

しっそう【疾走】¶ 車が私のかたわらを～していった The car *shot* (≒ *swept*) past me. 車は通りを～した The car *tore* down the street.

しっそう【失踪】 disappearance. ¶ 彼は突然～した He *disappeared* suddenly. / He made *a* sudden *disappearance*. ～した人を捜している We are tracing the *missing* man. 彼は～してしまっている He *is missing*.

じっそう【実相】 the true aspect; the real aspect. ¶ これらの写真は彼らの生活の～をとらえている These pictures show their *real aspects*.

じつぞう【実像】〘物理〙 a real image.

しっそく【失速】〘航空術〙 stall. ¶ 飛行機は～し

た The airplane *stalled*. 旅客機は～して墜落した The airliner crashed by *stall*.

じっそく【実測】〔actual〕survey. ¶土地を～する *survey* (≒ *make a survey of*) the land.
—図 an ordnance〔survey〕map.

じつぞん【実存】 existence.
—主義 existentialism. ¶～主義の作家 an *existentialist* writer. —主義者 an existentialist. —哲学 existentialist philosophy.

しった【叱咤】¶～する scold ; give (*a person*) a scolding ; rate.

しったい【失態】 a blunder ; a fault. ¶彼はときどき大～を演じる He *blunders* at times. / He committs *a blunder* sometimes. / He *makes a fool of himself* at times.

じったい【実体】〖哲学〗substance. ¶～を伴った議論 a *solid* argument. ～のない理論 an *unsubstantial* theory.
—論〖哲学〗substantialism. —論者 a substantialist.

じったい【実態】 the actual condition.

しったかぶり【知ったかぶり】¶彼はそれについて～をした He *pretended to know* all about it.

しったつり【執達吏】 a bailiff ; a process server.

じつだん【実弾】(弾丸・小銃弾) a bullet ; (砲弾) a shell. ¶ピストルには～がこめてある The revolver *is loaded*. / There are some *bullets* in the revolver.
—射撃(大砲の) target practice with loaded shells.

しっち【失地】 a lost territory. ¶選挙で～回復をしてみごとカムバックした He had a nice comeback in the election with his *lost territory* recovered.

しっち【湿地】 damp ground ; marsh ; morass.

じっち【実地】¶私はその考えを～に試したいと思う I want to test the idea *in practice*. ～に役だつことを二，三言わせていただきます I'll make some *practical* suggestions. それについては～に役だつ知識を持っている I have a good *working* knowledge of it.
—検証 an on-the-spot inspection. ¶警官が～検証に訪れた Policemen came to *inspect the scene*. —指導 practical guidance. —調査 an on-the-spot survey. —体験 actual experience.

じっちゅうはっく【十中八九】 in nine cases out of ten ; probably.

じっちょく【実直】¶～な働き手 an *honest* (≒ a *conscientious*) worker. 彼は～さを買われて会長に選ばれた As we duly appreciate his *sincerity* (≒ *integrity*), we elected him president.

しっつい【失墜】¶彼の信用は～した He *lost* his *credit*. 彼の勢力は～しはじめたもようだ His ascendency over them seems to *grow weaker*.

じつづき【地続き】¶～の土地 an *adjoining* land. 距離をおいてながめるとその島は本土と～のように見える Seen from a distance, the island seems to *be contiguous to* the mainland.

じってい【実弟】 *one's* real (≒ younger) brother (real brother は half-brother (父または母を異にする兄弟)と対比してまれに用いる).

しっと【嫉妬】 jealousy. ¶彼は私に～している He *is jealous of* me. 彼は～した He *grew jealous*. その場面を見たとき，彼女の心にむらむらと～心が起こった *Green envy* overspread her at the scene. ～深い女にはうんざりだ I am sick of a *jealous* woman.

しつど【湿度】 humidity. ¶空気中の～を測定する determine the *humidity* of the atmosphere. ～が高い We have high *humidity*. ～は60パーセントだ The *humidity* is 60 percent.
—計 a hygrometer.

じっと ¶私は彼女の目を～見詰めた I looked her *full* in the eyes. 彼女は彼を～見た She looked *hard* (≒ *steadily*) at him. それを聞いて～していられなかった The news made me uneasy. 動いてはいけない。～していなさい Don't move. Keep *quiet*. 彼は～横になっていた He lay *still*. 子どもはかたときも～していられないものだ Children cannot keep *still* even a moment. 彼女は悲しみを～こらえることができた She could control her grief *patiently*. 彼はその損害を～こらえた He suffered the loss *in silence*. 彼は～考えこんでいた He was thinking *deeply*. 彼は彼女を～観察した He studied her *very carefully*. ひとことも聞きもらさないように～彼の話に耳をすましていた I listened *attentively* to what he says not to miss a single word.

しっとう【執刀】¶A博士の～で手術が行なわれた The operation *was performed by* Dr. A.

じつどう【実働】 —時間 actual working hour.

しっとり ¶草の葉が朝露に～とぬれている The leaves of grass are *heavily* moist with morning dew.

じっとり ¶シャツは汗で～とぬれていた My shirt *was soaked through* with sweat.

しつない【室内】¶この植物は～においたほうがよい You had better put this plant *indoors*. (indoors は副詞). 子どもたちは～で遊んでいる Children are playing *in the room*.
—装飾 interior decoration. —楽 chamber music. —プール an indoor swimming pool. —遊戯 indoor games.

じつに【実に】¶～すばらしい It's *really* wonderful. ～簡単だ It's *quite* simple. / It's simple *enough*. ～失礼な男だ *How* impudent he is! ～いやなやつだ *What* a nasty fellow he is! ～熱心だ He is zealous *beyond words*. / He is very *keen on* it.

しつねん【失念】¶そのことについてはすっかり～しておりました I *have* quite *forgotten* all about it.

じつの【実の】 true ; real. ¶血を分けた～子 *one's* flesh and blood (ひとりにもふたり以上にも用いられる).

じつは【実は】 in truth ; really. ¶～私はあの人を高く評価していない *In truth* I don't make much of him. ～その件についてきのう彼と相談した *As a matter of fact*, I consulted with him about the matter. 〜彼がきらいだ *To be frank with you*, I don't like him. 彼がなぜ怒ったか〜私にもよくわからない I don't *really* know why he got angry.

ジッパー a zipper; a zip fastener.

しっぱい【失敗】 failure. ¶ 彼は試験に〜するだろう He will *fail in* an examination. 手術は〜に終わった The operation *was unsuccessful*. 実験は〜だった The experiment *failed*. 〜をおそれてはいけない You should not be afraid of *failure*. 一生懸命やったが〜した He tried hard *in vain*. その小説は完全な〜作だ The novel is *an* absolute *failure*. 計画は〜に終わった The plan *went wrong*. 〜は成功の母(諺) *Failure* is the mother of success.

じっぱひとからげに【十把一絡げに】 all together; sweepingly; in a wholesale manner; indiscriminately.

しっぴ【失費】 expenses; expenditure.

じっぴ【実費】 actual expenses; (原価) cost. ¶ 生産〜を下げる reduce the *cost* of the product. あとで〜精算します I'll settle accounts paying *actual expenses* later. 〜だけ頂きます Pay me only *the cost price*. これらの品物を〜で売った(原価で) I sold these goods *at cost*.

しっぴつ【執筆】 ¶ 彼は哲学に関する論文を〜中だ He *is writing* a treatise on philosophy. 彼は科学書を〜中である He *is at work upon* a scientific book. その本の〜は順調に進んでいる I am getting on well with the book. その本の〜が完了した I've got the book off.
—者 the writer; the author.

しっぷ【湿布】 a compress. ¶ 患部を〜する apply *a compress* to the affected part.
温— a hot compress. 冷— a cold compress. ¶ のどに冷〜をした I applied *a cold compress* to my throat.

じっぷ【実父】 *one's* [real] father.

しっぷう【疾風】 a gale. ¶ 〜のように like *a whirlwind*.

じつぶつ【実物】 a real thing. ¶ 〜そっくりの模型 a model like *a real thing*. それはまるで〜のようだ It looks like *a real thing*. これは〜ではなく写しだ This is not *an original* but a copy.
—大 ¶ 〜大の像 a *life-size* statue. …の〜大のモデルを作る make a *full-size* model of.

しっぺいがえし【竹篦返し】 retaliation. ¶ 〜する retaliate; give tit for tat.

しっぽ【尻尾】 a tail. ¶ 犬の〜 *a* dog's *tail*. 犬は〜をふっていた The dog was wagging its *tail*. 〜をつかまれては相手の言うなりになるほかない I cannot help obeying him as he *found my fault*. そしらぬ顔をしているがじきに〜を出すだろう Though he affects ignorance, I'm sure he will soon *show his true colors*.

じつぼ【実母】 *one's* [real] mother.

しつぼう【失望】 a disappointment. ¶ その小説には〜した The novel *disappointed* me. / The novel was *a disappointment*. 彼には〜した I *was disappointed in* him. 彼らはすごく〜した They *were* terribly *disappointed*. 〜してはいけない Don't *be discouraged*. 彼は容易に〜する男ではない He would not *despair* so easily. 彼が試験に落ちたので父は大いに〜した He failed in the examination *to the great disappointment* of his father.

しっぽうやき【七宝焼】 *cloisonné* ware.

しつぼく【質朴】 simplicity. ¶ 彼は〜な性格の人だ He has a *simple and honest* disposition.

しっぽり thoroughly; (しんみり) quietly. ¶ 〜ぬれる(文字どおりぬれる) be wet through; be thoroughly soaked. 〜語る(しんみり話す) have a quiet talk.

しつむ【執務】 office work; official duties. ¶ 〜中にすごく気分が悪くなった I got very sick while I *was at work*. 彼は午前9時から午後5時まで〜する He *works* in the office from nine in the morning to five in the afternoon.
—時間 office hours.

じつむ【実務】 (事業) business; (実務) practical affairs. ¶ 法律の〜は彼が担当している He transacts the legal *business*. 彼は〜のことはなにも知らない He knows nothing of *business*. 彼は学校を出たら〜につくことになるだろう He will *go into business* when he leaves school.
—家 ¶ 彼はなかなかの〜家だ He is a good man of *business*. / He has *business* ability.

しつめい【失明】 loss of eyesight. ¶ 彼は事故で〜した He *lost his eyesight* (≒ *went blind*) as a result of an accident.

しつもん【質問】 a question. ¶ 〜に答えてください Please answer my *question*. もうひとつ〜してもいいですか May I ask another *question*? もう〜はありませんか Do you have any more *question*? 先生はわれわれにたくさん〜をした The teacher asked us many *questions*. / The teacher put many *questions* to us. 〜は認めない No *questions* are allowed. 市長は〜攻めにあった The mayor faced (≒ met with) a barrage of *questions*. 委員はみんなで彼に〜を浴びせた All the committee members rained *questions* on him.
—者 a questioner. —書 a written inquiry. —戦 interpellations.

しつよう【執拗】 obstinacy; persistence. ¶ 彼は〜に実験を行ないつづけた He *persevered with* his experiments.

じつよう【実用】 practical use; utility. ¶ 〜向きのハンドバッグ a *utility* handbag. それは〜価値がない It is *of* no *practical use*. このかばんは重くて〜向きではない This bag is too heavy to *be practical*. それは〜に供しうるかどうか疑問だ It is doubtful *whether it can be put into practical use*.
—英語 practical English. —新案 a utility model. —品 a utility article.

しつら·える provide; set; place; establish.

じつり【実利】 actual profit.
—主義 utilitarianism.

しつりょう【質量】 〔物理〕 mass; (品質と量) quality and quantity. ¶ 〜不変の法則 the principle of the conservation of *mass*. これは～ともにそれより優れている This is better both in *quality and quantity* than that.

じつりょく【実力】*one's* real ability. ¶ ～を判定するのは難しい It is difficult to judge *a person's real ability*. 彼は～ある才人というべきだ He may well be called a *capable* man. 各自～に応じてやればよい Everyone is expected to do his best according to his *ability*. このごろは～がものをいう世界だ Nowadays *real ability* talks (≒ tells; counts) in the long run. 彼は～のある先生だ He is an *able* teacher. 彼の数学の～はたいしたものだ He has indeed *a good command* of mathematics. きみは英語の～をつけなければいけない You must *improve yourself* in English. 試験で～を十分発揮できなかった I could not *do myself justice* in the examination.

—行使 use of force. **—**者 a competent man; (政界の) an influential man.

しつれい【失礼】rudeness. ¶ 彼は～なことを言った He said something *rude* [to me]. ～ですがどなた様ですか Might I ask your name? ～ですが郵便局へ行く道を教えてくださいませんか *Excuse me*, but won't you tell me how to get to the post office? 彼は～にも私と話しながらあくびをした He *was rude* enough to yawn while talking with me. 留守をして～いたしました *I am sorry* I was away. たいへんお待たせして～しました *I am sorry* to have kept you waiting so long. ご返事もせず～いたしました *I am very sorry* I have not answered you. ちょっと～してもよろしいですか May I *interrupt* you? お先に～します *Excuse me*, [but] I must be going now.

じつれい【実例】an example; (例証) an illustration. ¶ ～をひとつ挙げて見ます Let me give *an example*. それは今述べたことのこの上もなくよい～だ It is *a* perfect *illustration* of what I have said.

しつれん【失恋】a broken heart; disappointment in love; lost love. ¶ 彼は～した He *was disappointed in love*.

じつろく【実録】an authentic record.

じつわ【実話】a true story.

して【仕手】(能) a protagonist; (相場) a rigger.

-して ¶ 若く～既に実力を認められた Even when he was young, he was looked upon as an able man. 3人～出かけた We three went out.

してい【私邸】*one's* private residence.

してい【子弟】young people; children.

してい【師弟】master and pupil; teacher and student. ¶ 彼らは～の関係を結んだ They became *master and pupil*.

してい【指定】appointment. ¶ 彼は～の時間に姿を現わした He showed himself at the *appointed* time. 彼は集合時間と場所を～した He *appointed* the time and place of meeting.

—券 a ticket for a reserved seat. **—**席 a reserved seat.

しでか·す【仕出かす】¶ 彼はなにを～すかわからない There is no knowing what he will *do*. / I can't tell what he will *do*.

してき【指摘】¶ 彼は私の誤りを～した He *pointed out* my mistakes. 彼は理論上の私の弱点を～した He *put his finger on* my logical weakness. ご～の箇所既に改良を加えました I have already improved on what you *told* me to.

してき【史的】**—**現在 〔文法〕 the historical present. **—**事実 a historical fact.

してき【私的】personal; private. ¶ ～な問題に口出ししてもらいたくない I don't want you to interfere in my *private* affair. これは私の～見解だ This is *my* point of view. ～な感情は抜きにして考えるべきだ This is to be considered without any *personal* feeling on your part.

してき【詩的】poetic; poetical. ¶ それは～だ That sounds *poetic*. 彼女の文章は～な表現にあふれている Her sentences are full of *poetic* expressions. この描写には～なところがある There is something *poetic* in this description.

—正義 poetic justice.

してつ【私鉄】a private railroad; a privately-owned railroad.

じてつ【磁鉄】magnetic iron.

じてっこう【磁鉄鉱】magnetite.

-しては ¶ 彼は年に～ふけて見える He looks old *for* his age. 春に～寒すぎる It is too cold *for* spring. 私と～最善を尽くしたつもりだ *As for* me, I think I have done my best. 彼は教育者と～落第だ He is a failure *as* a teacher. 彼は今日の学生と～勤勉だ He is a diligent student *as* students *go* nowadays.

-しても ¶ それに～, ずいぶん高いなあ *Even so*, how expensive it is! 彼が来ると～, かなり遅れるだろう *Even if* he should come, he will be pretty late. 水はたとえあるに～, ごくわずかだ There is little water, *if any*. かりに彼が不注意だったと～, あの過失は見逃すわけにはいかない *Granting* (≒ *Granted*) that he was careless, I cannot overlook that fault of his. 彼と～, それ相応の犠牲を払ったつもりでいるらしい He seems to think that he has made reasonable sacrifices *on his part*.

してや·る【為て遣る】¶ 彼の計画はみごとに図に当たり, ～ったりとほくそえんだ His plan worked so well that he smiled, saying to himself, "*Success is mine now.*" まんまと彼に～られた I *was* nicely *taken in* by him.

してん【支点】〔物理〕a fulcrum (複 fulcrums, fulcra).

してん【支店】a branch [shop]. ¶ その会社はローマに～をだした The company opened *a branch office* in Rome.

してん【視点】a viewpoint; a point of view. ¶ ～を変えて考える think from *a* different *point of view*.

しでん【市電】a [city] streetcar.

じてん【次点】¶ 彼は～で当選した He obtained *the second largest number of votes*. / He was *the second* successful candidate. 彼は～で落選した He headed the list of unsuccessful candidates.

じてん【自転】 rotation. ¶ 地球の～で昼夜ができる The *rotation* of the earth *on its axis* makes day and night. 地球は～している The earth *revolves* (≒ *rotates*) *on its axis*.

じてん【事典】 a cyclop(a)edia.
百科—— an encyclop(a)edia.

じてん【辞典】 a dictionary. ⇒じしょ

じてん【時点】 ¶ これが現在の～において考えられる最善の方法だ This is the best way I can think of *at the moment* (≒ *at this present moment*).

じでん【自伝】 an autobiography.

じてんしゃ【自転車】 a bicycle. ¶ 彼は～で学校へ行く He goes to school *by bicycle* (≒ *on a bicycle*). きみは～に乗れますか Can you ride *a bicycle*? 彼は～でぼくを訪ねてきた He called on me *by bicycle*.

しと【使途】 ¶ 使った金の～を明らかにすべきだ You should *account for* the money spent. ～不明の金が多額にのぼった There was a large expenditure of money *unaccounted for*. その金の～は何ですか What did you spend the money for?

しと【使徒】 an apostle.
十二—— the 〔Twelve〕 Apostles (≒ Disciples).

しど【示度】 a reading. ¶ 気圧の中心～は1,000ミリバール The central pressure *shows* 1,000 millibars. 温度計の～は摂氏36度となっている The thermometer *reading* is 36°C. (英・米では日常生活では華氏を用いる).

しど【視度】 ¶ ～良好である The *visibility* is good.

しとう【死闘】 a death (≒ desperate) struggle.

しとう【至当】 ¶ 彼のとった処置は～と考えられる The measure he has taken is considered 〔to be〕 *reasonable*.

しどう【私道】 a private road (≒ path).

しどう【始動】 ¶ エンジンを～させる *start* an engine.

しどう【指導】 guidance. ¶ 彼に息子の水泳の～を頼んだ I asked him to *teach* my son how to swim. 彼らは有名な柔道家の～を受けている They are under the *guidance* of a famous *judo*-man. 彼の～で実験を行なった We made an experiment under his *guidance*. 彼はその運動で～的役割を演じた He played the *leading* part in the movement. 彼に演劇の～を仰ぎたい We want to look to him for *guidance* in acting. 彼女はわれわれに歌の～をしてくれた She *taught* us singing. チームの～をしてくれた He *coached* the team for the game.
—者 a leader. —力 leadership. —員 an instructor. —教師 a guidance teacher. —主事 a teacher's consultant; a supervisor. —案 a teaching plan. —法 a method of guidance. —原理 a guiding principle.

しどう【斯道】 ¶ 彼は～の大家だ He is an authority *on the subject*. / He is an expert *in the art*.

じどう【自動】 ¶ この機械は～的にスイッチが切れる This machine is switched off *automatically*.
—エレベーター an automatic elevator. —火災報知機 an automatic fire alarm. —計算器(タクシーの) a taximeter. —操縦装置 an autopilot. —調整装置 a self-adjustment apparatus. —とびら an automatic door. —販売器 a slot machine; an automatic vending machine. —ピアノ a pianola; an autopiano. —巻き ¶ この時計は～巻きだ This watch is a *self-winding* one.

じどう【児童】 a child (圏 children). ¶ 小学校の～ school *children*. 学齢期前の～ preschool *children*. ～向きの本 books for *children*; *children's* books.
—学 p(a)edology. —劇 a juvenile drama. —憲章 the Children's Charter. —心理学 child psychology. —心理学者 a child psychologist. —相談所 a children's welfare clinic; a child consultation center. —福祉法 the Juvenile Welfare Law. —文学 juvenile literature. —文学者 a writer of juvenile stories.

じどうし【自動詞】 〘文法〙 an intransitive verb.

じどうしゃ【自動車】 a car; 困 an automobile; 圏 a motorcar; a motor. ¶ ～を運転する drive *a car*. 彼は～で通勤する He goes to office *by car*. 私は彼の～に乗った I got into his *car*. (get on a car とは言わない). 私は～で行った I rode *in a car*. 彼の家の前で彼の～からおりた I got out of his *car* in front of his house. (get off a car とは言わない). 彼はぼくを～に乗せてくれた He *gave* me *a ride in his car*. / He *gave* me *a lift in his car*.
—運転手 an automobile driver; a driver; (雇いの) a chauffeur. —事故 an automobile accident. —免許証 a driver's license. —レース a motor race; an auto race. —学校 a driving school. —旅行 a motor trip. —損害保険 automobile insurance. 貸し— a rental car. 貨物— 困 a truck; 圏 a lorry.

しどけな・い ¶ 彼女は～い格好をしている She is *disorderly* in her dress.

しと・げる【為遂げる】 ¶ 彼はとうとうその仕事を～げた At last he *accomplished* the work.

しとしと ¶ 雨が～降っている It is raining *softly* (≒ *gently*). / It *is drizzling*.
—雨 a drizzling rain.

じとじと ¶ ～する天気 *damp* (≒ *moist*; *sticking*) weather.

しと・める【為留める】 ¶ 彼は1発でクマを～めた He *killed* a bear at a shot.

しとやか【淑やか】 ¶ ～な娘 a *graceful* (≒ *gentle*) girl. 彼女は物腰が～だ She is *graceful* in manner. / She bears 〔herself〕 *gracefully*.

しどろもどろ ¶ 彼は～な答弁をした He made an *incoherent* explanation. 彼は～で答えた

He answered *falteringly*.

シトロン〔植物〕a citron; (飲料) citron water.

しな【品】(品質) quality; (品物) an article; goods (goods は複数扱いで, many や数詞などをつけない).

¶これは〜がよい (悪い) This is of good (poor) *quality*. / This is superior (inferior) in *quality*. この〜はよく売れる This *article* sells well. てまえどもは〜を落とすようなことはいたしません We don't lower the *quality*. ほかにご入用の〜はございませんか, 奥様 (店員のことば) What is the next *article*, madam? これらの〜をみんな同じ店で買った I bought all these *articles* at the same store. あの店は〜が豊富である They have lots of *goods* on hand at that shop. / The store *is* well *stocked*. 所変われば〜変わる (諺) Each country has its own customs. 彼女は〜をつくる She *is coquettish*.

シナ China. ⇒ちゅうごく(中国)

しない【市内】¶私の家は〜にある My house is *in the city*. 彼は〜の中心に店をもっている He has a store in the center of *the city*.

—電車 a streetcar. —配達無料 free delivery within the city. —版 the city edition.

しない【竹刀】a bamboo sword.

しな·う【撓う】¶竹はよく〜う The bamboo *is pliant* (≒ *is easy to bend*). きみの指はよく〜うね How *supple* your fingers *are*!

しなうす【品薄】¶その商品は〜だ The *stock is short* (≒ *is small*).

しなかず【品数】¶あの店は〜が少ない(多い) *The number of articles* in that store is small (large).

しなぎれ【品切れ】¶今卵は〜だ Eggs *are* now *out of stock*. / Eggs *are* now *all sold out*. / The stock of eggs *has run out*.

しなさだめ【品定め】¶彼は新入社員の〜をしている He *is estimating* (≒ *is weighing*) the abilities of the new staff members.

しなじな【品品】various articles (≒ goods); (各種) various kinds.

しなだ·れる【撓垂れる】¶彼女は酔ってぼくに〜れかかってきた She was so drunk as to *lean against* me coquettishly.

しな·びる【萎びる】wither; shrivel. ¶老人の〜びた手 an old man's *withered* hand. 〜びたトマト a *shriveled* tomato.

しなぶそく【品不足】¶これは〜になっている These articles *have run short*. 〜がはなはだしい There is *a* great *shortage of goods*. 〜になりつつある We are running *short of goods*. 木材が〜になっている There is *a shortage* of lumber.

しなもの【品物】an article; goods (複数扱いで, many や数詞などつけない). ¶この店の〜はまちがいがない *Things* (≒ *Goods*) sold at this store *are very good*. ⇒しな(品)

しなやか【嫋か】¶〜な手 *delicate* (≒ *supple*) hands; *slender* hands. 〜な体 a *lithe* body. 〜な指 *flexible* fingers. 柳が〜に風になびいている The willows are bending (≒ bowing) *gently* to the wind.

じならし【地均し】ground-leveling. ¶〜する level the ground.

じなり【地鳴り】¶〜がしている The earth *is rumbling*. ゴーッと〜がして山崩れが起こった There occurred a landslide the moment I heard the *ground rumble*.

シナリオ a scenario (複 scenarios).

—ライター a scenario writer; a scenarist.

しな·れる【死なれる】¶彼は両親に〜れた He *was bereft of* his parents.

しなん【至難】¶それは〜の業だ It is a *most difficult* task. きょうじゅうにこの仕事を終わらせるのは〜の業だ It seems *next to impossible* for me to finish this work today.

しなん【指南】¶彼は剣術の〜をしている He gives fencing *lessons*. / He is a fencing *master*.

—役(番) an instructor; a master.

じなん【次男】*one's* (≒ a) second son.

しにおく·れる【死に後れる】survive (≒ outlive) (*a person*).

しにがお【死に顔】*a person's* face after death. ¶彼の〜は美しかった He *looked* peaceful *in death*.

しにかか·る【死にかかる】¶彼は〜っている He *is dying*. / He *is at death's door*. / He *is at the point of death*.

しにかた【死に方】¶彼は幸福な〜をした He *died a happy death*. / He *died happily*. 彼は悲惨な〜をした He *died a miserable death*. / He *died miserably*.

しにがね【死に金】¶彼に金をやっても〜だ To give him money is to *throw away money*.

しにがみ【死に神】Death. ¶彼は〜にとりつかれている He is possessed by *Death*. / He is in the grip of *Death*.

シニカル cynical.

しにぎわ【死に際】¶彼の〜のことばに深く心をうたれた I was deeply moved by his *last* (≒ *dying*) words. 〜に重大な告白をした He made a serious confession *at* his *deathbed*.

しにく·い【為悪い】¶その善悪は判断〜い *It is difficult* to tell whether it is right or wrong. そこが説明〜い点なのだ That is the point where I *feel* much *difficulty in* explaining.

シニシズム cynicism.

しにせ【老舗】an old shop (≒ store); a shop of long standing. ¶あの店は明治初年にできた〜だ That store was established at the beginning of the Meiji era.

しにぞこない【死に損い】¶この〜め! (老人について) You *good-for-nothing old man!* / (男に対する悪口として) You *bastard!*

しにそこな·う【死に損う】¶彼は交通事故で〜った He *was almost killed* in a traffic accident.

しにた·える【死に絶える】¶オオカミは日本では〜えてしまった Wolves *have died out* in Japan. あの旧家は〜えた That old family *is extinct*.

しにはじ【死に恥】¶ ～をさらす die a shameful death.

しにばしょ【死に場所】¶ 彼は～を得た He got *a place to die in*.

しにばな【死に花】¶ 彼は～を咲かせた He *died a glorious death*.

しにみず【死に水】¶ 彼には～を取ってくれる息子がいる He has a son to *attend his deathbed*.

しにめ【死に目】¶ 彼の～に会えなかった I could not *be present at his death*. / I could not *have the last look at him* before his death.

しにものぐるい【死にもの狂い】¶ 彼は大家族を養うために～になって働いた He worked *madly* (≒ *very hard*) to support his big family.
彼は金を手に入れようと～の努力をした He *made desperate efforts* to gain money.

しにわか・れる【死に別れる】¶ 彼は早く両親に～れた He *lost his parents* when [he was] quite young. / He *was left an orphan* in his early childhood. 彼は妻に～れた He *was bereaved of* his wife.

しにん【死人】a dead person; (死者たち) the dead. ¶ その事故で多くの～が出た A lot of *people were killed* in the accident. / There were many *deaths* in the accident. ～に口なし(諺) *Dead men tell no tales*.

じにん【自任】¶ 彼は日本一の画家だと～している He *flatters himself* that he is the best painter in Japan. 彼は釣りの名人をもって～している He *considers himself to be* an expert angler. / He *looks upon himself as* an expert angler.

じにん【自認】¶ 彼は自分のまちがいを～した He *admitted* that he was wrong. / He *acknowledged* his mistake.

じにん【辞任】resignation. ¶ 彼は～を申し出た He *tendered* (≒ *offered; handed in*) his *resignation*.

し・ぬ【死ぬ】**1** die. ¶ 彼が～んだのは5年前だ It was five years ago that he *died*.
彼はひとり寂しく～んだ He *died* lonely.
彼は若くして～んだ He *died* young.
チャイコフスキーはコレラで～んだ Tchaikovsky *died of* cholera.
彼の兄はけががもとで～んだ His brother *died from* wounds.
彼は交通事故のため～んだ He *was killed in* a traffic accident.
彼は酒を飲みすぎて～んだ He *drank himself to death*.
彼は雪のなかで凍え～んだ He *was frozen to death* in the snow.
彼が～んで50年になる He *has been dead* these fifty years.
～ぬまであの日の出来事は忘れないだろう I shall never forget the events of that day *as long as I live*.
彼はぽっくり～んだ He *died* a sudden death. / He *died* suddenly.
彼らは病気になり, つぎつぎに～んだ They sickened and *died off* (≒ *died one by one*).
2〖慣用的表現〗¶ 彼は彼女を～ぬほど愛した He loved her *madly*.
私は～ぬほど退屈だ I am bored *to death*.
彼は～ぬほど母親に会いたがっている He *is dying to see* his mother.
疲れて～にそうだ I *am dying from* fatigue.
病人は～んだように眠っていた The patient *was in a dead sleep*.

じぬし【地主】a landowner; (土地・家屋を所有して貸す)(男) a landlord; (女) a landlady.

シネスコ〔映画〕CinemaScope (商標名).

じねつ【地熱】terrestrial heat. ¶ ～を発電に利用する utilize *terrestrial heat* to generate electricity.

シネラマ〔映画〕a Cinerama (商標名).

シネラリア〔植物〕a cineraria.

じねんじょ【自然薯】a Japanese yam.

しの【篠】¶ ～突く雨 a downpour; a *torrential* (≒ *pouring*) rain.

しのうこうしょう【士農工商】the military, agricultural, industrial, and mercantile classes.

しのぎ【鎬】¶ 両軍～を削って戦った The two armies *fought desperately with* each other.

-しのぎ【-凌ぎ】¶ これは一時～にすぎない This is *a* mere *temporary makeshift*. 彼は退屈～にときどき歌をうたう He sings songs *by way of recreation* from time to time. 私は退屈～に漫画を読む I read cartoons to *kill time*.

しの・ぐ【凌ぐ】**1**〖耐える〗¶ ～ぎがたい暑さ *unbearable* (≒ *intolerable*) heat.
～ぎやすい気候 a *mild* climate.
ぼくにはこの冬の寒さはとても～げない I can't possibly *bear* (≒ *stand*) the cold of this winter.
2〖防ぐ〗¶ 雨を～ぐためにレインコートを着た He put on the raincoat to *keep off* the rain.
どこかその辺の小屋であらしを～ごう Let's *find shelter* (≒ *take shelter*) from this storm in a cottage near here.
3〖切り抜ける〗¶ これだけあれば当分は～げる This will *last me* (≒ *tide me over*) for the present.
彼は独力でその難局を～いだ He *pulled through* the difficulty for himself.
ひと切れのパンとコップ1杯の水で飢えを～いだ I *satisfied* my appetite on a slice of bread and a glass of water.
4〖まさる〗¶ 老人の元気には壮者を～ぐものがあった The old man *outdid the young* (≒ *put the young to shame*) *in* energy.
彼は国王を～ぐ勢力を持っていた He *surpassed* the king in power.
東京は人口においてはロンドンを～いでいる Tokyo *exceeds* London *in* population.

しのごの【四の五の】¶ ～言わずに一生懸命仕事をしなさい Work hard *without grumbling*.

シノニム a synonym.

しのはい【死の灰】radioactive dust; fallout.

しのば・せる【忍ばせる】¶ 彼は短刀を懐に～せた He had a dagger *concealed* in his bosom.

足音を～せて階段を上った I went up the stairs *with stealthy steps* (≒ *on tiptoe*; *stealthily*).

しのびあい【忍び会い】a secret meeting.

しのびあし【忍び足】¶ 彼は～でぼくに近寄ってきた He came up to me *stealthily* (≒ *with stealthy steps*).

しのびこ·む【忍び込む】¶ どろぼうは勝手口から～んだ The thief *sneaked* (≒ *stole*) *in* by the back door.

しのび·でる【忍び出る】¶ 彼はだれにも見られず家から～出た He *slipped* (≒ *stole*) *out of* the house without being seen.

しのびなき【忍び泣き】¶ 彼女は～した She *sobbed* (≒ *wept*) *silently*.

しのびよ·る【忍び寄る】¶ 秋がいつしか～る Autumn *draws near unnoticed*. 谷間に夜が～る The night *creeps* (≒ *steals*) across the valley. 斥候は敵陣近く～った The scout *advanced stealthily to* the enemy camp. ネコはネズミに～った The cat *stole up on* the mouse.

しのびわらい【忍び笑い】a giggle; a chuckle. ¶ 彼女はときどき～した She *giggled* (≒ *chuckled*) now and then. / She sometimes *laughed in her sleeve*.

しの·ぶ【忍ぶ】¶ 彼らは非常な辛苦を耐え～ばなければならなかった They had to *endure* great hardships. 不便はできるだけ～んでほしい I want you to *put up with* the inconveniences as much as possible. 人目を～んで彼女に会った I met her *secretly*. 人目を～んでだれと会ったのですか Who did you meet *in secret*? この無礼は～びがたい Such rudeness *is intolerable* to me. この光景は見るに～びない I cannot *endure* seeing this.

しの·ぶ【偲ぶ】¶ 過ぎし日々を～ばせる品々 things *reminiscent of* the old days; *reminders of* the past. 亡き母を～ぶ *think of one's* dead mother. この写真は小学校時代を～ばせる This photograph *reminds* me *of* my elementary school days. われわれは同窓会を開いて，なつかしい大学生活を～んだ We held our alumni meeting and *talked about* the good old college life.

しば【芝】turf. ¶ 彼女は～を刈っている She is mowing the *lawn* (≒ *grass*). 彼は庭を芝生にするため～を置いている He is laying *turf* in the garden to make a lawn. (lawn は「芝生」で，turf (芝)を置いてつくる).

—刈り機 a lawn mower.

しば【柴】brushwood; (薪) firewood. ¶ 森に～刈りに行く go to the woods to gather *firewood*.

じは【自派】*one's* own party.

じば【地場】〘株式〙the local market.

じば【磁場】〘物理〙the magnetic field.

しはい【支配】rule; control; domination. ¶ この考え方が世論を～している This thought *sways* public opinion. 人間は環境に～される Man is a creature of circumstances. 王は二十数年も国を～した The king *ruled* his country as long as twenty odd years. この辺りはフランスの～下にあった This district was once under French *rule*. 彼は感情にすぐ～される He is ready to *be influenced* by personal feelings. なにが運命を～するかわからない We don't see beforehand what *controls* our destiny. 地球上の生物は自然の法則に～される All creatures on the earth *are subject to* nature's laws.

—階級 the ruling class. —者 a ruler. —人 a manager.

しはい【紙背】¶ 眼光～に徹する read between the lines.

しはい【賜杯】天皇— a trophy given by the Emperor.

しばい【芝居】**1**〘演劇〙a play. ¶ ゆうべ～を見にいった I went to see *a play* yesterday evening.

その～は2か月上演された The *play* ran for two months.

～はそんなに好きでもない I don't like the *theater* so much.

意外にもその～はさほど当たらなかった Unexpectedly the *play* was not a great success.

2〘比喩的に〙¶ 彼の話しぶりは～がかっている His manner of speaking *is dramatic*.

彼は～をやっているのだから，気をつけたほうがいい Since he *is* merely *playing a trick on* you, you had better be on the alert.

あの政治家はたいへん～っ気がある That statesman is *a real showman*.

彼の話し方は～っ気たっぷりだった His speech was full of *showmanship*.

彼の微笑はことによると～かもしれない Maybe his smile is *a fake*.

彼が泣いているのは実は～だった He seemed to be weeping, but he *was* really *acting*.

素人(しろうと)— theatricals; [米] dramatics. —愛好家 a playgoer; a theatergoer. —見物 playgoing; theatergoing. —小屋 a playhouse.

しばい【試売】a trial sale.

—品 goods on trial sale.

しばえび【芝蝦】〔動物〕a prawn.

じはく【自白】confession. ¶ 彼らは彼の～を強要した They forced *a confession* from him. 彼は絶対に～しなかった He did not *confess* by any means. 彼は金を盗んだことを～した He *confessed* that he had stolen the money. 殺人容疑者は犯行をすっかり～した The suspected murderer (≒ The murder suspect) *made a* full *confession of* his crime. / The suspected murderer fully *confessed himself* to be guilty.

じばく【自爆】suicidal (≒ self-blasting; suicide) explosion. ¶ ～する (船) scuttle *oneself*; be scuttled; selfblast; (飛行機が敵に体当たりする) dash *one's* plane (into an enemy position).

しばし【暫し】¶ 待て～ Wait *a minute* (≒ *a moment*), please. ～の別れだ Good-by *for the present*.

し

しばしば【数・屢】often; frequently.
¶彼は夜～外出する He *often* goes out in the evening. このような事故は～起こる Such accidents *are frequent*. / Such accidents take place *frequently*.

じはだ【地膚】(皮膚) skin; (地表) the surface of the ground. ¶白い(黒い)～ a fair (dark) *skin*. 彼女は～がきれいだ She has *a* clear *skin*.

しばたた・く【瞬く】¶彼女は急に光を当てられて, 目を～かせた She *blinked* 〔*her eyes*〕 at the sudden light.

じばち【地蜂】〘昆虫〙a mud-wasp.

しはつ【始発】(電車・列車) the first train.
¶私は上りの～で学校へ行く I go to school by *the first* up *train*.
—駅 the starting station; a terminal; 図 the terminus.

じはつてき【自発的】¶～な申し出 a *voluntary* (≒ *spontaneous*) offer. 彼はその仕事をしようと～に申し出た He *volunteered* to do the job. 彼は～に援助を買って出た He offered his help *of his own accord* (≒ *willingly*). 彼は～に多額のお金を孤児院に寄付した He made a *voluntary* contribution of much money to the orphanage. 彼は～にその情報を提供した He *volunteered* 〔to give〕 the information.

しばふ【芝生】a lawn. ¶彼は～をかっている He is mowing the *lawn*. ～に横たわった I lay on the *lawn*. ～に入るべからず(掲示) Keep off the *grass*.

じばら【自腹】¶その分はわたしが～を切ろう Let me *pay for that* (≒ *pay the expenses*) *out of my own pocket*.

しはらい【支払い】payment. ¶彼は私に～を請求した He asked me to *pay*. 彼は即時～を求めた He demanded prompt *payment* of the bills. ～は延期してもらおう I will ask to have my *payment* postponed. すべて～済みだ I *have* already *paid* for everything.
—期限 the date of payment. **—条件** the terms of payment. **—停止** the suspension of payment. **—手形** a bill payable. **—人** a payer.

しはら・う【支払う】pay; discharge; repay.
¶手形を～う *honor* a bill; *meet* a note. スーパーマーケットでは現金で～わなければならない We must *pay* cash at the supermarket. いつも彼が勘定を～う He always *pays* the bills. 早速借金を～った Soon after that I *cleared* (≒ *discharged*) my debt.

しばらく【暫く】¶～すると彼はここに現われるだろう He will turn up here *in a short time* (≒ *in a little while*). ～したら, もう一度彼に電話してみよう I will phone him again *in a while*. ～すればその仕事は完成するだろう It will *not* be *long before* the work is completed. ～して, ドアをノックする音が聞こえた *After a while* there was a knock at the door. ～お待ちください Wait *a minute* (≒ *a bit*), please. ～待とう Let's wait *for a while*. ～休みましょう Let's take a rest *for some time*. ～でした It's *a long time* since I saw you last. / I haven't seen you *for an age*. ～はこれで十分だろう That will be enough *for the present* (≒ *for the time being*). ～ぶりで避暑に海岸へ行った I went to the seaside to avoid the heat *after a long absence*.

しば・る【縛る】bind (≒ tie) up. ¶彼はひもでぼくの両手を～った He *tied* my hands 〔*up*〕 with a cord. どろぼうは手足を～られた The thief *was bound* hand and foot. 新聞紙を～って束ねた I *bound* the papers *into* a bundle. 彼は仕事に～られている He *is tied* (≒ *chained*) *to* his business. 時間に～られるのはいやだ I hate to *be restricted* by time. とかく因襲に～られやすい人がいる Some people are apt to *be fettered* by convention.

しはん【市販】¶この品は既に～されている This article *is* already *on the market* (≒ *on sale*). 新製品が～されるのも間近いことだろう It will not be long before the new article *is put on the market* (≒ *appears on the market*).
—品 an article on the market.

しはん【師範】a teacher; a master; (女) a mistress. ¶剣道の～ *a* fencing *master*.
—学校 a normal school. 高等**—学校** a higher normal school. **—代** an assistant master; an acting master.

しはん【紫斑】**—病**〘医学〙purpura.

じばん【地盤】**1**〚土地〛the ground. ¶この家の～は固い This house stands on firm *ground*.
彼の家の～は軟らかい. いつなんどき地震で倒れるかもしれない His house stands on soft *ground*. It might be destroyed by an earthquake at any moment.
この辺の～は年々沈下する *The ground* around here sinks year after year.
—沈下 ground subsidence.
2〚地歩〛footing; foothold. ¶民主主義はこの国では確固たる～を築いた Democracy has established *a secure footing* (≒ *foothold*) in this country.
彼の政界での～は揺るぎないものになったようだ It seems that his *footing* in the political world has become secure.
3〚勢力範囲〛a sphere of influence; (選挙の) a constituency. ¶当市は彼の～だ This city is his *sphere of influence*.
都会が彼の選挙～だ He has established his *constituency* in urban districts.

しはんき【四半期】¶第1～ the first *quarter* 〔of the year〕.

しはんぶん【四半分】a quarter; a fourth part.

しひ【私費】*one's* own expense. ¶私は～でアメリカに留学した I went to America to study *at my own expense* (≒ *on my own* 〔*account*〕).

じひ【自費】¶彼は詩集を～出版した He published a book of poems *on his own* 〔*account*〕 (≒ *at his own expense*).

じひ【慈悲】mercy. ¶あの人は～深い方だ He *is merciful* (≒ *is kind-hearted*). ～を垂れたまえ Please have *mercy* (≒ *pity*) on me. / Show *mercy* to me. ご～ですからお話しください Tell me *for mercy's sake* (≒ *for God's sake*). 神の～にすがりたい気持ちだった I felt like throwing myself on the *mercy* of God. / I felt like imploring the *mercy* of God upon me.

じび【耳鼻】the nose and ears.
—科 otorhinology. —咽喉(いんこう)科 otorhinolaryngology. —咽喉科病院 a nose, ear, and throat hospital.

じびき【字引】a dictionary. ¶その単語を～で引いてみなさい Look up the word in your *dictionary*. 彼はその会社の生き～だ He is *a* walking *dictionary* of the company.

じびきあみ【地引き網】a dragnet.

じひつ【自筆】*one's* own handwriting.
¶～の手紙 an *autograph* letter; a letter *in one's own handwriting*. これは彼の～の手紙だ This letter *was* really *written by himself*.

じひびき【地響き】a thud; a roar. ¶木が～をたてて倒れた The tree fell *with a thud*. ～をたてて列車が通り過ぎた The train *roared past*.

しひょう【指標】an index (複 indexes, indices).

しびょう【死病】a fatal (≒ mortal) disease.
¶癌は～のひとつだ Cancer is one of the *fatal diseases*.

じひょう【辞表】a resignation. ¶彼は～を提出したが却下された He sent in his *resignation*, but it was rejected. 彼に～を取り下げるようにすすめた I advised him to withdraw his *resignation*.

じひょう【時評】comments on current events. ¶新聞の～は芳しくなかった Press *comments* were not favorable.
文芸— a literary review.

じびょう【持病】a chronic disease; an old complaint. ¶また神経痛の～が起こった I have had a return of my *old complaint* of neuralgia. / I have had attack of my *chronic disease* of neuralgia again. 頭痛が私の～だ Headache is *a chronic disease* with me.

しびれ【痺れ】¶足に～がきて立てない I can't stand up; my legs *have gone to sleep* (≒ my feet *are asleep*). 彼は～をきらして返事を催促した He *impatiently* asked for an answer.
—エイ〘魚類〙an electric ray. —薬 an anesthetic.

しび·れる【痺れる】¶～れた足 *benumbed* feet. 寒さで指が～れた My fingers *are numbed* (≒ *have got benumbed*) with cold.

しびん【溲瓶】a chamber pot.

じびん【次便】米 the next mail; 英 the next post. ¶～で by next post (≒ mail).

しぶ【渋】astringent juice. ¶カキの～を抜く remove the *astringency* of persimmons.

しぶ【支部】a branch office.

しぶ【市部】urban districts (≒ areas).

じふ【自負】¶彼はフランス語にかけてはだれにも負けないと～している He *flatters himself* that he is second to none in French.
—心 ¶彼は～心が強い He *is self-conceited*. / He *thinks highly of himself*. 彼は～心を傷つけられた His *pride* was hurt.

じふ【慈父】a loving father.

しぶ·い【渋い】(味が) astringent; rough; (地味な) sober; quiet; (あかぬけた) refined; (気むずかしい) sullen; sour.
¶～いカキ an *astringent* persimmon. ～いぶどう酒 *rough* wine. ～い色 *sober* (≒ *quiet*) color. ～い声 a *trained* voice. ～いドレス a *tasteful* dress. 彼は好みが～い He has a *refined* (≒ *quiet*) taste. 彼は洋服の趣味が～い He has *good* taste in clothes. あの人は～い顔をしている He *looks sullen*.

しぶがき【渋柿】an astringent persimmon.

しぶがっしょう【四部合唱】〘音楽〙a vocal quartet(te); a chorus in four parts.

しぶがっそう【四部合奏】〘音楽〙a quartet(te).

しぶき【飛沫】spray. ¶われわれは滝の～をあびてぬれた We were wet from the *spray* of a waterfall. ～を立てて舟が走っている The boat is sailing in a cloud of *spray*. 波が岩に当たって～があがった The waves dashed against the rocks sending up much *spray*.

しふく【私腹】*one's* own pocket. ¶彼は大衆をだまして～を肥やしている He fools the public and *fills* (≒ *lines*) *his own pocket*.

しふく【私服】plain clothes; civilian attire.
¶～の刑事 a *plain-clothes* policeman; a plainclothesman.

しふく【雌伏】¶～して機の至るのを待った I *lay low* waiting for a chance.

ジプシー a gipsy; a gypsy (a Gypsy と G を大文字でも書く). ¶～の娘 a *gypsy* girl. ～の占い師 a *gypsy* fortuneteller. ～のほろ馬車 a *Gypsy* van. 放浪の～ *a* vagabond *Gypsy*.

しぶしぶ【渋渋】unwillingly; reluctantly.
¶～彼の招待に応じた I *unwillingly* accepted his invitation. その子は～お使いに行った The boy went on an errand *reluctantly*.

しぶつ【死物】a dead thing. ¶その法律も～化した(名目だけになった死法) The law has now become *a dead letter*.

しぶつ【私物】¶きみは公共物を～化してはならない You must not *convert* the public property *to your own use*. これは私の～です This is my *personal belongings* (≒ *private property*; *personal effects*).

じぶつ【事物】things; affairs.

ジフテリア〘医学〙diphtheria.
—血清 antidiphtheria serum.

しぶと·い ¶彼はすごく～かった He *was as obstinate* (≒ *stubborn*) *as a mule*. 彼は交渉の際なかなか～い He *is stiff* in his negotiations. あいつは全く～いやつだ What nerve he's got!

しぶみ【渋味】astringency; (ぶどう酒などの) a rough taste; (趣味) a refined taste.

しぶ·る【渋る】¶ 彼は私に金を出すのを～った He *grudged* (≒ *was unwilling to give*) me money. 返事を～った I *hesitated* to answer./ I tried to *evade* an answer. 彼女はかなり～った後, 私の提案に賛成した She agreed to my proposal after much *hesitation*.

しぶろく【四分六】¶ もうけを～に分けた We divided the profit at *the ratio of 6 to 4*.

しぶん【四分】¶ ～の1 a quarter ; onefourth. ～の3 three quarters ; threefourths.
—円(儀) a quadrant.

しぶん【死文】a dead letter. ¶ この法律は～と化している This law has *proved* (≒ *turned out*) *a dead letter*.

じぶん【自分】¶ その本はあなたご～のものですか Is that *your own* book? みんな～の家を持っている Everybody has *his own* house. ～の家がない人もいる There are some people who have no house *of their own*. 彼は～の用事で北海道に行った He went to Hokkaido on *private* business. だれでも～の子どもはかわいい Everybody loves *his own* child. ～のことは～でやれ Do *your own* business *for yourself*. ～のものは～で責任をもつこと Be responsible for *your own* things. こんなやさしいことは～でやりなさい You should do this kind of easy thing *for yourself*. ～で彼のところに行きなさい You should visit him *personally*. どうして失敗したのか～でもわからない I *myself* don't understand why I failed. きみは～を知らなすぎる You are too ignorant of *yourself*. なんでも～の思うようにやりなさい Do everything *your own way*.

じぶん【時分】¶ 今～は家に着いているにちがいない He must have got home *by this time*. 去年の今～はアメリカにいた I was in America [about] *this time* last year. あすの今～に来る I shall come *about this time* tomorrow. 毎年今～は雨が多い We have a lot of rain *about this time* of the year. 子どもの～は物語を聞くのが好きだった I loved to listen to stories in my childhood. 若い～にはよく本を読んだ I read a great deal in my young *days* (≒ *when* [I was] young). もう寝る～だ It's *time* for you to go to bed. もう出かける～だ It is *about time* I went away.

じぶんかって【自分勝手】selfishness. ¶ ～な人だね You are a *selfish* fellow! 彼は何事にも～な行動をとる He will *have his own way* in everything. そんなに～なことを言うな Don't *be* so *selfish*. 彼は聖書を～に解釈する He interprets the Bible *in his favor* (≒ *as he likes*). それでは～すぎる That's too *selfish*./ It's too *selfish* of you. 人間なんて～なものだ Men *are selfish* beings.

しぶんごれつ【四分五裂】¶ 党内は～の状態だ The party *is divided against itself*. 大会は～の状態に陥った The general meeting has fallen into *great disorder* (≒ *utter confusion*).

しぶんしょ【私文書】a private document.

しへい【紙幣】paper money ; 米 a bill ; 英 a [bank] note. ¶ ～を発行(回収)する issue (recall) *paper money*. 金額の一部を～で支払う I pay part of the sum in *bills*.

じへいしょう【自閉症】〘心理学〙autism.

じべた【地べた】the ground. ¶ ～に座る sit on *the ground*.

しべつ【死別】¶ 彼女は2年前に交通事故で夫に～した She *lost* (≒ *was bereaved of*) her husband in a traffic accident two years ago.

シベリア Siberia. ¶ ～の Siberian.
—人 a Siberian.

しへん【紙片】a piece (≒ slip) of paper.

しへん【詩篇】〘聖書〙the Book of Psalms.

じへん【事変】an accident.
満州— the Manchurian incident.

じべん【自弁】¶ 交通費は～である The traveling expenses must *be paid out of our own pocket*.

しへんけい【四辺形】〘数学〙a quadrilateral.
平行— a parallelogram.

しぼ【思慕】¶ ～する have *a yearning* (*toward*).

じぼ【字母】(音標文字) a letter ; an alphabet ; (活字) a matrix ; a [printing] type.

じぼ【慈母】a loving (≒ an affectionate) mother.

しほう【四方】¶ 10キロ～に within *a radius of* 10 kilometers *round*.
—八方 ¶ ～八方に in *all directions*. ～八方捜しまわる search (≒ seek) *high and low* for (*something*). 人々は彼の演説を聞くために～八方から集まってきた People gathered *from all quarters* (≒ *from every quarter*; *from every direction*) to hear his speech. ～八方に気を配った I kept an eye *on all quarters*.

しほう【司法】(the administration of) justice.
—解剖 judicial autopsy. —官 a judicial officer. —行政 judicial administration. —権 jurisdiction ; judicial power. —試験 a judicial examination. —修習生 a judicial apprentice. —書士 a judicial scrivener. (国際)—裁判所 the (International) Court of Justice.

しほう【至宝】¶ 国の～ the *most valuable asset* of the country. アメリカ文学界の～ the *pride* of literary America. 彼はわが社の～だ He is *a* great *asset* to our company.

しほう【私法】〘法律〙private law.

しぼう【子房】〘植物〙an ovary.

しぼう【死亡】death.
—者 the dead ; the deceased ; (事故の) deaths. —者数 the number of deaths. ¶ 事故でたくさん～者が出た The accident caused many deaths. —証明書 a death certificate. —届け a notice of *one's* death. —率 the death rate. ¶ 幼児の～率 infant *mortality*. 肺がんによる～率 the *death rate* from lung cancer. —記事 an obituary.

しぼう【志望】[a] desire ; [an] ambition.
¶ 彼女は歌手になりたいという～をいだいている She conceives (≒ harbors) *a desire* to be a

singer. 彼は女優になりたいという私の～を笑った He laughed at my *ambition* to be an actress. 私は進学を～する I *wish* to enter a school of higher grade. 教員を～する人は少ない Few people *wish* to be a teacher. ～どおり外交官になった I have become a diplomat as I *wished*. ～学科はなんですか What is your *desired* course? 第1～学科が法科だ The course of my first *choice* is the law. ～校はA高校だ The school of my *choice* is the A Senior High School. 彼は第一～の大学入試に失敗した He failed in the entrance examination for the university of his first *choice*.

—者 an applicant. ¶ あの大学には～者が多い There are many *applicants* for entrance to the university.

しぼう【脂肪】(動物性) fat (ヘット); lard (ラード); grease. ¶ ～分の多い食物 *fatty* foods. ～の多い肉は好きでない I don't like *fatty* (≒ *fat*) meat. この肉は～が多すぎる This meat is too *fatty*. 彼女は前よりもだいぶ～がついた She has got much *fatter*. / She has put on weight. 運動して～を取る wear off the *fat*. あの人は～過多だ He *is too fat*.

じほう【時報】 time-signal. ¶ けさのラジオの～で時計を合わせた I set my watch by the radio 〔*time-signal*〕 this morning.

じぼうじき【自暴自棄】 desperation; despair. ¶ 彼は落第したために～に陥った He *grew* (≒ *became*) *desperate* at the failure. その失敗のために彼は～になった The failure drove him to *desperation* (≒ *despair*). とうとう～になって自殺した At last, *in desperation*, he killed himself.

しほうだい【仕放題】 ¶ なんでも～にするわけにはいかない You cannot *have your own way* in everything. / You cannot do everything *as you please* (≒ *as you wish*).

しぼ・む【凋む・萎む】 ¶ この花は間もなく～むだろう This flower will soon *fade*. 花がすっかり～んでしまった All the flowers *have withered away* (≒ *up*). 風船が～んだ The balloon *became deflated*.

しぼり【絞り】 1〖模様の〗¶ ～の浴衣 a *white-patterned* bathrobe.

豆～の手ぬぐい a towel with *a spotted pattern*.

2〖写真機の〗 a stop. ¶ ～を開ける(閉じる) open (close) the stop.

しぼりたて【絞りたて】 ¶ これは～の牛乳だ This milk *is straight from the cow*.

しぼ・る【絞る・搾る】 1〖液体を〗¶ タオルを固く～る *wring* a towel dry.

レモンを～る *squeeze* a lemon.

トマトを～ったほんものの天然ジュース a genuine, natural juice *squeezed* from tomatoes.

オリーブから油を～った They *extracted* oil from olives.

牛乳を～る *milk* a cow.

2〖知恵・涙・金などを〗¶ その問題解決に知恵を～った I *racked my brains* to solve the problem.

その場面は観客の涙を～った The scene *moved* the audience *to tears*.

彼は金を貧乏人から～り取った He *squeezed* money *out of* the poor.

金持ちの地主は小作人から高い地代を～り取った The rich landowner *racked* heavy rents *from* sharecroppers.

3〖とっちめる〗¶ 先生に～られた(きびしくしかられた) I *was severely scolded* (≒ *was called to task*) by my teacher. / (勉強で) I *was put to a hard drill* from my teacher.

警官に～られた(厳しく尋問された) He *was grilled* by a policeman.

4〖幕・レンズを〗¶ 幕を～って光を入れた I *gathered* 〔*up*〕 (≒ *drew aside*) the curtain to let in the light.

レンズを～れば写真は非常に鮮明になる The sharpness of the picture can be greatly improved by *stopping down*.

しほん【資本】 capital. ¶ 外国～の導入(流入) the introduction (inflow) of foreign *capital*. 計画を実施するに必要な～ the necessary *capital* to carry out a project. 事業に巨額の～を投ずる invest enormous *capital* in an enterprise. 1,000万円の～で商売を始める start business with *a capital* of ten million yen.

運転— a working capital. 金融— financial capital. 固定— fixed capital. —主義 capitalism. —主義経済 capitalistic economy. 修正—主義 modified (≒ revised) capitalism. 独占—主義 monopoly capitalism.

しほんか【資本家】 a capitalist. ¶ ～と労働者 *capital* and labor.

—階級 the capitalist classes.

しほんきん【資本金】 a 〔share〕 capital; 米 capital stock. ¶ ～10億円の会社 a company *capitalized* at one billion yen. その会社の～は5億円である The company has five hundred million yen as *capital*.

しま【島】 an island. ¶ (ああ出られては)とりつく～もない He made me feel utterly helpless. / He threw me upon my own resources.

しま【縞】 ¶ ～のズボン *striped* trousers. 彼は赤い～のはいった青いネクタイをしている He wears a blue tie with red *stripes*.

しまい【仕舞い・終い】 ¶ 夏休みもそろそろお～だ Our summer vacation *is coming to an end*. 私の話を～まで聞きなさい Hear me *out*. 音楽会のお～までいた I stayed *to the last* of the concert. 彼は～には酒を飲みすぎて死ぬことになるだろう He will drink himself to death *in the end*. ～には怒るよ *Finally* I'll be impatient of you. 彼ももうお～だ *It's all over* (≒ *up*) *with* him. 彼らの話は～はけんかになった Their conversation *ended in* a quarrel. 彼は～は刑務所行きだ He will *end up* in prison. きょう(の授業)はこれでお～ *So much for today*. お～ということにしよう *Let's call it a day*.

しまい【仕舞】(能の) a *no* dance in plain clothes.

しまい【姉妹】 sisters.

し

―校 a sister school. ―都市 a sister city (*to* New York).

しまいこ·む【仕舞い込む】¶ ポケットにハンカチを～む *tuck* (≒ *put*) a handkerchief [*away*] *into* a pocket. 彼はなんでも引き出しの中に～んだ He *put* everything *away* in the drawer.

しま·う【仕舞う·終う】1〖終わる〗¶ 早くやって～いなさい Do it quickly. もう手紙は書いて～った I have written a letter. もう仕事は終わって～った I *am through with* my work.

2〖かたづける〗¶ この時計を箱の中に～っておきなさい *Put* this watch *in* the box.

かぎは引き出しに～ったほうがいい You must *keep* the key in the drawer.

ボールはもとのところへ～っておきなさい *Put* the ball back where it was.

テーブルの上の物は全部～った All the things and wares on the table *have been put away*.

このことは自分の胸に～っておいた I *kept* this to myself.

3〖廃業する〗¶ 今店を～うのは非常に残念だ I am very sorry to *close up* the store now.

しまうま【縞馬】〖動物〗a zebra.

じまえ【自前】¶ 彼は～でその印刷機を買った He bought the printing machine *at his own expense*. 費用は～だ You must pay your expenses yourself.

じまく【字幕】〖映画〗(題) a title; (説明字幕) a subtitle; superimposition. ¶ 英語の～のフランス映画を見た I saw a French film with English *subtitles*.

しまぐに【島国】an island country.

―根性 insularism.

しまつ【始末】¶ この子は～に負えない This child *is hard to deal with*. この書類は～に困る This document *is unmanageable*. 事の～を聞きたい Let me hear *how it happened*. この問題は早く～をつけたい I'd like to *settle* this matter as soon as possible. 自分のことは自分で～しなさい Your own affairs must *be settled* by yourself.

―書 a written apology. ―屋 a thrifty person.

しまった Dear me! / My goodness!

しまながし【島流し】banishment; exile. ¶ 彼は捕らえられ～になった He was arrested and *was banished* (≒ *was exiled*) *to an island*.

しまへび【縞蛇】〖動物〗a striped snake.

しまり【締まり】¶ ～のある人(まじめな人) a *steady* person. 彼は～のない顔つきをしている He has a *loose-looking* face. 彼女の口もとはいつも～がない She has always *loosely-closed* lips.

―屋 a close-fisted person; (倹約家) a thrifty person; (けちん坊) a miser.

しま·る【締まる·閉まる】¶ この窓はうまく～らない This window will not *close* properly. もっと～ったほうがいい(まじめな) You had better *be* more *sober*. 彼は～った筋肉をしている He has *strong* muscles.

じまわり【地回り】¶ ～の(地方の) local; (沿岸の) coasting [ship].

じまん【自慢】(誇り) pride; a boast; (うぬぼれ) vanity. ¶ 彼の両親は彼の成功をたいへん～している His parents *take* much *pride in* (≒ *are very proud of*) his success. 彼は自分がやったことを～した He *boasted* what he had done. / He *spoke boastingly* about what he had done. 彼女はひとり息子を～している She *prides herself on* her only son. / She *makes a boast of* her only son. 彼が子どもの～をするのももっともだ He may well *be proud of* his children. 成功したことを～たらたら話した He talked very *boastfully* about his success. きみの言うことは～たらしい What you say smacks of *pride*. その公園はわが町の～の種だ The park is the *boast* of our town. その記録は彼にとって～するほどのものではない The record is not a *proud* one for him. ～じゃないが,ぼくはひとりでそれをしたんだ It may be said, *without exaggeration*, that I did it by myself.

しみ【染み】a stain; a spot. ¶ インクの～ an ink *stain*. インクの～のついたテーブルクロス a tablecloth *stained* with ink; a tablecloth with ink *spots*. 着物の～を抜く remove *stains* from a dress. 上着にインクの～をつける *stain* a coat with ink. その床にはインクの～がたくさんついている The floor has many ink *spots* (≒ *stains*). ブラウスについたこの～はなかなか抜けない This *stain* on my blouse will not come out.

―抜き ¶ 上着の～抜きに洗たく屋に出す send a coat out to the laundry for *stain removing*.

しみ【紙魚·衣魚】〖虫類〗(本を食う) a bookworm; (衣類を食う) a clothes moth.

じみ【滋味】¶ ～に富む食物 *delicious* (≒ *nourishing*) food.

じみ【地味】1〖色などが〗¶ 彼は～な色が好きだ He likes a *quiet* (≒ *sober*) color.

彼女はいつも～な着物を着ている She always wears a *quiet* dress.

彼女は～な身なりをしている She is *soberly* dressed.

このネクタイはきみには～すぎる This tie *is* too *plain* for your own use.

2〖性格などが〗¶ 彼は～な人だ He is a man *of quiet taste*.

彼は金持ちなのに～に暮らしている He is rich, but he leads a *plain* (≒ *simple*) life.

シミーズ a chemise.

しみこ·む【染み込む】¶ 水がみな地中に～んだ All the water *sank into* the ground. 彼らには軍国主義が深く～んでいる They *are* deeply *imbued with* a military spirit.

しみじみ【染染·沁沁】¶ 世の中が～いやになった I have become *quite* sick of life. ～友人と話をした I had a *quiet* talk with a friend of mine. 彼女は～赤ちゃんの寝顔を見た She had a *good* look at her baby's sleeping face. ～受験勉強がいやになった I have got *heartily* tired of studying for examinations. 彼は息子に～と言い聞かせた He talked *seriously* to his son. 彼の忠告が～胸にこたえた His advice *came home to* me. 彼は科学の重要性を～私にわからせてくれた He *brought home to* me the importance of science. 英語研究の必要を～と感ずる I *keenly* feel the necessity of English studies. 私は～しあわせ者だと思う I *fully* realize how happy I am.

しみず【清水】(わき水) spring water; (清い水) clear water.

じみち【地道】¶ 彼は～に暮らしている He lives *honestly*. / He makes an *honest* living. きみは～に努力しなければならぬ You must *persevere* in your efforts.

しみったれ a stingy person; a miser; a niggard.

しみで・る【染み出る】ooze out; exude.

し・みる【染みる】**1**〚浸透する〛¶ 汗がシャツに～みた The sweat *soaked* through my undershirt.

この紙にはインクが～みない Ink does not *blot* on this paper.

2〚痛む〛 ¶ ヨードチンキは傷口に～みる Iodine tincture makes the wound *smart*.

煙が目に～みる The eyes *smart* with smoke.

タマネギをきざむと目に～みる Mincing onions makes one *cry*.

冷水が虫歯に～みた The cold water caused a pang of pain to my decayed tooth.

冷たい北風が身に～みる The cold north wind *cuts the skin* (≒ *chills me to the bone*).

きょうの寒さは身に～みる The weather (≒ It) *is biting* cold today.

3〚感銘する〛 ¶ ご親切身に～みてうれしく思います I *am deeply thankful for* your kindness. / I *fully appreciate* your kindness.

彼は身に～みて仕事をするようになった He has come to *put his heart into* his work.

彼の忠告を身に～みて感じた His advice *came home to my heart*.

-じ・みる ¶ 子ども(気違い)～みたことをする He behaves himself *like* a child (a mad man). 彼の話は年寄り～みている His talk *smacks of* an old man. 彼の言動には気違い～みたところがあった He showed *a touch of* insanity in his speech and behavior.

しみん【市民】a citizen. ¶ 名古屋～(ひとりならば) *a citizen* of Nagoya. アメリカ～ *an* American *citizen*.

—権 citizenship. ¶ 彼はオーストラリアの～権を失った He lost the Australian *citizenship*. 彼はアメリカの～権を得た He acquired the United States *citizenship*. 名誉— an honorary citizen.

じむ【事務】business; office work. ¶ ～手続き *business* (≒ *office*) routine. 彼はその事柄を～的に処理した He handled the affair in a *businesslike* manner. 私は彼が～をとっているのを見た I saw him doing *office work*. 彼から～を引き継いだ I took over *business from* him. 彼に～を引き渡した I handed over *business to* him. だいぶ～がはかどった *Business* has made good progress. 土曜日の午後は～を行ないません On Saturday afternoons no *business* is transacted. 彼は～に明るい He is familiar with the *routine of the office*.

—員 a clerk; an office worker; (女) an office girl. **—官** a secretary; an administrative official. **—局** a bureau; an executive office. **—系統**(仕事) office work; non-productive work; (職員) office workers; non-productive workers. **—室** an office 〔room〕. **—所** an office. **—総長** a secretary general. **—長** a head clerk. **—当局** authorities directly in charge. **—取扱**(学長) an acting president. **—服** a working suit (≒ dress); 困 a duster. **—用品** office supplies.

ジム a gymnasium; (口語) a gym.

しむ・ける【仕向ける】¶ 辞職するように～けられた I *was forced to* resign. 彼はその提案を承諾するように～けられた He *was induced to* accept the proposal.

じむし【地虫】〘虫類〙 a grub; an earthworm.

しめい【死命】fate. ¶ それは敵の～を制する戦いだった It was the battle to seal (≒ decide) the *fate* of the enemy. われわれは敵に～を制せられている We are *at the mercy of* the enemy.

しめい【氏名】a name. ¶ ～を明かす disclose *one's name* (≒ *identification*). ～不詳の男 an *unidentified* man.

しめい【使命】a mission. ¶ 極東における日本の～ Japan's *mission* in the Far East. 重要な～を帯びて訪米した I visited the United States on *an* important *mission*. 彼はりっぱに～を果たすだろう He will fulfill (≒ carry out) his *mission* successfully. ～を果たせなかった I failed in my *mission*. 孤児を教育するのが彼女の～だった It was her *mission* to teach orphans.

しめい【指名】nomination; designation. ¶ 彼は議長に～された He *was named* (≒ *was nominated*) as chairman. 先生は彼を～したが彼は正しく答えられなかった The teacher *called on* him, but he could not answer correctly. 警察は犯人の～手配をした The police have made arrangements for the search of the identified criminal.

—解雇 a dismissal of workers by designation. **—手配人** a most wanted criminal. **—者** a nominator.

じめい【自明】¶ 彼の判断が誤りだったことは～の理だ *It is self-evident* that his judgment was erroneous. そんなことはだれでも～の理だと考えている Everybody *takes* such a thing *for granted*.

しめがね【締め金】a buckle; a clasp. ¶ ～をかける(はずす) buckle (unbuckle).

しめきり【締め切り・締切】closing. ¶ 申し込みの～はいつですか When does the time for application *end*?

—期日 the closing day (≒ date); the deadline.

しめき・る【締め切る】¶ 窓を一日じゅう～っておいては毒だ It is not good for the health to *keep* the windows *closed* all day long. 原稿はあす～る予定だ We are to *go* (≒ *send*) *to press* tomorrow. / Tomorrow is *the deadline*.

しめくくり【締め括り】 ¶最後の～はやはり彼が適任だ Nobody is better than he for its *final management*.

しめくく・る【締め括る】 ¶きのうは例によって彼のあいさつで～った Yesterday we *finished* the meeting with his address as usual.

しめこ・む【閉め込む】 ¶彼はその部屋に～まれた He *was shut up* in the room.

しめころ・す【締め殺す】 ¶彼女は彼に～された She *was strangled* by him.

しめし【示し】 ¶重役連がそんな破廉恥ぞろいでは社員に～がつかない Such shamefulness of the board of directors really sets a bad example to the workers.

しめしあわ・せる【示し合わせる】 ¶～せたとおり彼は彼女と駅前で落ち合った As *previously arranged*, he met her in front of the station. 彼らは～せたにちがいない They must *have conspired with* one another.

じめじめ (しめっぽい) damp; (憂うつな) melancholy. ¶～した部屋 a *damp* room. ここ当分～した天気が続くだろう *Damp* weather will continue for some time to come. 雨の日は～している It *is damp* in rainy weather. 彼女はいつも～とふさぎこんでいる She *is* always *in a melancholy mood*.

しめ・す【示す】 ¶訪問先の都市を地図で～してください Please *show* (≒ *point out*) on the map where the cities are which we are going to visit. なるべく早くきみの計画を～しなさい You should *tell* us your plan as soon as possible. 冬の東京で温度計が氷点下を～す日は少ししかない In Tokyo, the thermometer seldom *stands* below the freezing point in winter. 彼はすばらしい外交的手腕を～した He *showed* great diplomatic ability. 先生は生徒によい手本を～すべきだ The teacher should *set* a good example for his pupils.

しめ・す【湿す】 ¶タオルを～す *wet* a towel.

しめた ¶～,くじが当たった *How lucky!* The lot fell upon me. そこまでできれば～ものだ *Success is almost yours* since you have got that much.

しめだ・す【締め出す】 ¶門限に遅れると～される You will *be shut out of doors* if you are late for the closing time.

しめつ【死滅】 ¶人類の～する日がそう遠くないと予言する者もいる Some people predict that the time will not be far away when mankind will *perish* (≒ *die out*).

じめつ【自滅】 self-destruction; (自殺) suicide. ¶急激な環境の変化によって～する植物もある Some plants *bring about their own destruction* owing to a sudden change of their environment. 彼らは遅かれ早かれ～するだろう Sooner or later they will *ruin themselves*.

しめっぽ・い【湿っぽい】 wet; damp; (憂うつな) gloomy; melancholy. ¶～い布団 a *wet* (≒ *moistened*) bed. ～い天気には飽き飽きした We are all tired of the *damp* weather. 彼の話はいつのまにか～くなる His story is apt to become *gloomy* (≒ *dismal*) while he is not aware of it.

しめて【締めて】 in all; altogether. ¶～いくらになりますか How much does it amount (≒ come) to? ～6,000円です It *amounts to* (≒ *sums up to*) six thousand yen.

しめなわ【注連縄】 ¶～を張る stretch *sacred straw festoons*.

しめやか ¶～な雨 a *gentle* (≒ *soft*) rain. 雪が～に降っている Snow is falling *softly*.

しめり【湿り】 moisture; dampness; (雨) rain. ¶昨夜はいいお～だった Last night we had *a* welcome *rain*.

しめ・る【湿る】 be (≒ become; get) wet (≒ damp). ¶～った夜具 *damp* bedclothing.

し・める【占める】 ¶きのうのスピーチコンテストでだれが1位を～めましたか Who *took* the first place (≒ Who *stood* first) in yesterday's speech contest? 氏は日本の保守党の中できわめて重要な位置を～めている He *occupies* (≒ *holds*) a very important position in the Conservative Party of Japan. 日本の対外貿易ではアメリカとの貿易が5割を～めている Trade with America *accounts for* (≒ *forms*) 50 percent of all the foreign trade of Japan. 日本へ観光に来る外国人ではアメリカ人が7割を～めている Of the foreigners coming to Japan for sightseeing, 70 percent *are* Americans. 彼はその取引で巨利を～めた He *made* a big profit on the transaction.

し・める【締める・閉める】 (閉じる) shut; close; (きつくする) tighten; (しっかり留める) fasten; (合計する) sum up; (首をしめる) strangle; (節約する) economize.
¶戸を～めてください Please *shut* (≒ *close*) the door. ねじを～めてほしい I want the screw *tightened*. きみはベルトをきつく～めたほうがよい You had better *tighten your belt*. (「支出を切り詰める」の意味もある). 座席のベルトを～めるように言われた We were told to *secure* (≒ *fasten*) our seat belts. ネクタイを～める *wear* a tie. 彼はタクシーの代わりにバスに乗って経費を～めた He *economized* by using buses instead of taking taxis.

しめん【四面】 all sides. ¶日本は～を海に囲まれている Japan is surrounded *on all sides* by the seas. / Japan is a *seagirt* country. (seagirt は文語). 当時の彼は文字どおり～楚歌(そか)だった At that time he *was* literally *surrounded by foes*.

しめん【紙面】 space. ¶私に割り当てられた限られた～では,その問題を詳しく論じることはできません In the limited *space* allotted to me, I cannot discuss the problem in detail. ～が十分ないのでこの問題を詳しく述べることができない *Space* does not allow me to dwell on this problem.

じめん【地面】 the ground; (土地) land. ¶100平方メートルの～ *a land* of 100 square meters.

しも【霜】〔white〕frost; hoarfrost. ¶～がおりる It *frosts.*
しもがれ【霜枯れ】¶庭は～だ The garden *is frostbitten* (≒ *is frostnipped*).
じもく【耳目】¶世間の～を集める draw public attention.
しもざ【下座】¶～に座る take *a lower seat.*
しもじも【下下】the lower classes; the common people; (大衆) the masses.
しもたや【しもた屋】¶商店街にある～ *a home* in the shopping quarters.
しもて【下手】(下方) the lower part; (舞台) downstage. ¶私たちの母校はこの川の～にある Our school is situated *down this stream.*
じもと【地元】¶彼の現在の隆盛も～の応援があればこそだ He owes his present prosperity entirely to the support by *local people.* 計画は～の熱狂的な歓迎を受けた The plan met with enthusiastic favor by *the people of the district.* ～チームが優勝した *The home team* won the championship.
しもどけ【霜解け】thawing; a thaw.
—道 a thawing road.
しもばしら【霜柱】ice needles; frost columns; frostwork. ¶明朝はぐっと冷えて～が立つでしょう Tomorrow morning it will be much colder and *frost columns* will be formed in the ground.
しもはんき【下半期】the latter (≒ second) half of the year.
しもぶくれ【下ぶくれ】¶～の顔の娘 a girl *with plump cheeks.*
しもふり【霜降り】¶～の服 a *pepper-and-salt* suit.
しもべ【下部・僕】a servant.
しもやけ【霜焼け】a frostbite; chilblains. (frostbite のほうが chilblains よりもおもい霜焼け). ¶～のできた足 the *chilblained* foot. 左手に～ができた I have had *chilblains* on my left hand.
しもよけ【霜除け】¶木に～をした I put *a frost protector* to the tree.
しもん【指紋】a fingerprint. ¶～を残す leave *one's fingerprints.* ～をとる (指から) take *a person's fingerprints*; (物から) *fingerprint* (a door).
しもん【諮問】¶彼はその問題に関して専門の経済学者たちに～した He *consulted* the experts economists about the problem.
—案 a subject submitted for deliberation.
—機関 an advisory organ; a consultative body.
じもん【自問】¶～自答する answer *one's* own question; talk to *one*self.
しゃ【社】(会社) a company; a firm.
しゃ【紗】silk gauze.
しや【視野】view; a visual field. ¶もう10分も歩けば～はぐっと広がる Another ten minutes' walk, and you will enjoy *a* much wider *view.* 彼は～を広くしなければならぬ He must widen his *view of life* (≒ *mental vision*). ～の狭いことが彼の致命的な欠点だ Being a man of narrow *outlook on life* is his fatal weak point. 彼は～が狭い He is narrow in his *observation.*
じゃ【邪】(不正) wrong; (悪) evil; vice.
じゃ【蛇】a snake; a serpent. ¶～の道はへび (諺) One devil knows another.
じゃあ ¶～, きょうはここまで *Well,* so much for today. ～, きみはそれをまったく知らないんだね *Then,* you are quite ignorant of that, aren't you? ～, 実行は不可能ですね *If that is the case,* there is no carrying it out. ～, 私は断然反対だ *In that case,* I am absolutely against it.
ジャー (魔法びん) a vacuum bottle; a thermos (英語の jar は「口の大きなびん」をいう).
じゃあく【邪悪】wickedness. ¶～な wicked; evil; vicious.
ジャージー〘織物〙jersey. ¶～の服 a suit of *jersey.*
しゃあしゃあ ¶彼はよくも～とあんなことが言えるね *How shameless* he is to talk like that! 彼女の～した態度を見ると胸くそが悪くなる Her *brazen-faced* manners disgusts me.
ジャーナリスト a journalist.
ジャーナリズム journalism.
シャープ sharp. ¶彼の頭はきわめて～だ He is a man of very *sharp* intelligence.
—ペンシル a propelling pencil (シャープペンシルは和製英語).
シャーベット sherbet.
しゃい【謝意】thanks; gratitude. ¶みなさんのご協力に対し心からの～を表します I would like to express heartfelt *thanks* (≒ *gratitude*) for your cooperation.
ジャイロ —コンパス a gyrocompass. —スコープ a gyroscope.
しゃいん【社員】(会社員) a〔staff〕member; a member of the staff; (総称) the staff. ¶彼はその会社の～になった He joined *the staff* of the company. 彼はわれわれの会社の～だ He *is on the staff of* our company.
正— a regular member. 新入— a new member of the staff. 赤十字— a member of the Red Cross Society.
しゃえい【射影】〘数学〙projection.
しゃおく【社屋】the building of a company.
しゃおん【謝恩】¶このデパートは来週月曜から～大売り出しです They begin their *thank-you* sales in the department store next Monday. 卒業生による～会は3時に始まる The *dinner party* given by the graduating students *in honor of* their professors is to be held at three.
しゃか【釈迦】Shakya Muni; Gautama; Buddha. ¶～に説法(諺) It is teaching your grandmother how to suck eggs.
しゃかい【社会】society. ¶彼はこの4月～に出た He *went into the world* this April. 彼は大いに～のために尽くした He worked very much for *the public good.* 彼は～の福祉に貢献した功を認められた He won public recogni-

し

tion for having contributed to *public welfare*. ～は彼のような有能の士を求めている *Society* requires such an able man as he. 彼は～的な地位を欲した He wanted to win *social* position. 彼は～を改善することに一生をささげた He devoted himself to the improvement of *society*. 彼は～に人望のある政治家です He is a statesman who is popular with *people in general*. アリの～はたいへん組織だったものだ The *society* of ants is a well organized one. 彼は～の敵だ He is *a public enemy*. **—意識** social consciousness. **—運動** a social movement. **—科** social studies. **—科学** social science. **—学** sociology. **—教育** social education. **—福祉事業** social work. **—福祉事業家** a social worker. **—主義** socialism. **—主義者** a socialist. **—人** a member of society. **—生活** social life. **—政策** a social policy. **—制度** the social system. **—秩序** social order. **—党** the Socialist Party. **—不安** social unrest. **—奉仕** social service. **—保険** social insurance. **—保障** social security. **—保障制度** the system of social security. **—問題** a social problem. **一般—** the public in general. **上流—** the upper classes. **中流—** the middle classes. **下層—** the lower classes.

じゃがいも【じゃが芋】〖植物〗 a potato (複 potatoes); an Irish (≒ a white) potato (サツマイモと区別するときの言い方).

しゃが·む ¶ 彼は突然～みこんだ He suddenly *crouched* (≒ *squatted down*).

しゃがれごえ【嗄れ声】 a hoarse (≒ husky; throaty) voice. ¶ 彼は～だ He has *a hoarse voice*. 彼は～でしゃべった He talked *in a husky voice*.

しゃが·れる【嗄れる】 ¶ 彼の声は～れた His voice *became hoarse* (≒ *became husky*).

しゃかん【舎監】 a dormitory inspector; (女) a dormitory matron.

しゃぎょう【社業】 the company's business. ¶ あすこでは～を拡張している They are expanding their *business*. ～の興廃は社員の努力いかんによる The prosperity of *a company* depends upon the efforts of every member of the staff.

じゃきょう【邪教】 a heresy; a heretical religion. **—徒** a heretic.

しゃく【尺】 *shaku*, a Japanese foot (1尺は 0.303 meter; 0.995 foot).

しゃく【酌】 ¶ 彼にお～をした I *helped* him *to sake*.

しゃく【癪】 ¶ ～の種 a cause of *offense* (≒ *vexation*). 彼の言いぐさが～にさわる I *am offended* (≒ *am vexed*) *at* (≒ *by*) his remarks. 彼に負けるのは～だ I just *can't stand* being beaten by him. 高い税金ほど～にさわるものはない Nothing *is* so *irritating* (≒ *vexatious*) as a high tax.

しやく【試薬】〖化学〗 a reagent. **—品** (製薬会社の) a sample; a sample medicine.

-じゃく【-弱】 ¶ 15メートル～ *a little less than* fifty meters. 20分～で in *less than* twenty minutes.

じやく【持薬】 *one's* usual medicine. ¶ その薬を～として飲んでいる I take the medicine habitually.

しゃくい【爵位】 a title of nobility; a peerage. ¶ ～ある人 a *titled* person.

しゃくざい【借財】 a debt.

しゃくし【杓子】 a ladle. ¶ ねこも～も everybody. 彼は～定規で融通がきかない He pays too much attention to rules and regulations. / He is a stickler for rules and regulations.

じゃくし【弱視】〖医学〗 weak sight. ¶ ～の人 a *weak-sighted* person.

じゃくしゃ【弱者】 the weak. ¶ それは～を圧迫することだ It is to oppress *the weak*.

しゃくしゃく【綽綽】 ¶ 彼の態度はいつも余裕～としている He is always *free and easy*.

しやくしょ【市役所】 a city hall; a municipal office.

じゃくしょう【弱小】 ¶ ～の small and weak. **—国** a small and weak nation.

じゃくしん【弱震】 a slight earthquake shock. ¶ 昨夜～があった *A slight earthquake shock* was felt last night.

しゃくぜん【釈然】 ¶ 彼の説明では,どうも～としない I *am* not quite *satisfied with* his explanation.

じゃくたい【弱体】 ¶ それはわれわれの労働組合を～化させようとする謀略だ It is a plot to *weaken* our labor union. ～内閣は倒れた The *weak* cabinet fell.

しゃくち【借地】 leased land. ¶ この土地は20年契約の～だ I took this land *on a lease of* twenty years. **—権** leasehold. **—人** a tenant; a leaseholder. **—料** a ground rent.

じゃぐち【蛇口】 a faucet; a tap. ¶ ～を開ける(締める) turn *a faucet* (≒ *a tap*) on (off).

じゃくてん【弱点】 a weak point; a weakness. ¶ 彼の～を知っている I know his *weak point*. 彼は彼女の～につけこんだ He took advantage of her *weak point*. 彼はついに～を暴露した He revealed his *weakness* at last.

じゃくでん【弱電】 a weak electric current.

しゃくど【尺度】 a measure. ¶ 文明の～ *a barometer* (≒ *an index*) of civilization.

しゃくどう【赤銅】 ¶ 彼は日に焼けて～色をしている He has a *tanned* skin. / He *is brown* with sunburn.

しゃくとりむし【尺取り虫】〖虫類〗 a looper; 米 an inchworm.

しゃくなげ【石南花】〖植物〗 a rhododendron.

じゃくにくきょうしょく【弱肉強食】 The strong prey upon the weak.

しゃくねつ【灼熱】 ¶ ～の恋 a *passionate* (≒ *burning*) love. 砂ばくの～の太陽 a *scorching* sun in a desert.

じゃくねん【若年】 youth. ¶ 彼は～のころ,寺で過ごした He lived in a temple *in his youth*.

じゃくはい【若輩】(若者) a young man ; (未熟者) a greenhorn. ¶ ～ですが，どうぞよろしくお願いします *Young and inexperienced* as I am, I will do my best. I hope you will [kindly] help me.

しゃくはち【尺八】a bamboo flute.

しゃくぶく【折伏】〘仏教〙¶ 彼らは彼を～した They *converted* him *to* the new religion.

しゃくほう【釈放】release ; liberation ; discharge. ¶ 彼は刑務所から～された He *was released* (⇆ *was set free*) from prison.

しゃくめい【釈明】[an] explanation. ¶ きみはきみの行為を～すべきだ You should *explain* (⇆ *give an explanation for*) your conduct.

しゃくや【借家】a rented house. ¶ ～住まいをしている人は多い Many people live in *a rented house*.

―人 a tenant.

しゃくやく【芍薬】〘植物〙a peony.

しゃくよう【借用】¶ 20万円まさに～いたしました I acknowledge that I *owe* you two hundred thousand yen. 彼からこの本を～した I *borrowed* this book from him. グラウンドを～したいのですが I'd like to *hire* your ground. (hire は使用料を払って借りる). 電話を～したいのですが Can I *use* the telephone?

―証書 a bond of debt (⇆ loan) ; an IOU (I owe you. からできた). ¶ ～証書を入れて彼から10万円借りた I borrowed a hundred thousand yen from him, giving *an IOU* to him.

しゃくりあ・げる【嚇りあげる】¶ 少女は～げていた The girl *was sobbing convulsively*.

しゃくりょう【酌量】consideration. ¶ われわれは彼の貧困を～しなければならぬ We should *take* his poverty *into consideration*. 彼が若いことを～して彼は放免された *In consideration of* his youth, he was set free. 彼の罪には情状～の余地がない Nothing can *extenuate* his crime.

しゃけ【鮭】〘魚類〙a salmon. ¶ 薫製の～smoked *salmon*.

しゃげき【射撃】a shot ; fire. ¶ 敵のいっせい～を浴びた We were under the enemy's *running fire*. 敵に～を加えた We *fired at* the enemy. 的をねらって～した I *shot at* the target. 彼は～がうまい(へただ) He is *a good* (*bad*) *shot*. / He *shoots well* (*ill*).

しゃけつ【瀉血】〘医学〙depletion.

ジャケツ a jacket.

スポーツ― a sports jacket.

しゃけん【車検】(車の車体検査) an automobile inspection.

しゃけん【車券】(競輪の) a bicycle-race ticket.

じゃけん【邪険】¶ 彼は～にも私を追い返した He *was unkind* enough to drive me back. そんなに～にしないでください Don't *be* so *hard* on me.

しゃこ【車庫】(電車の) a car barn ; (自動車の) a garage.

しゃこ【蝦蛄】〘動物〙a squilla.

しゃこう【社交】society. ¶ 彼はなかなか～的だ He is quite a *sociable* man. / He *is* very *sociable*. 彼は～ぎらいだ He does not like *society*. 彼は～性に欠ける He lacks *sociability*. / He is *unsociable*.

―ダンス a social dance.

じゃこう【麝香】musk.

―鹿 a musk deer. **―ばら** a musk rose.

しゃこうしん【射幸心】a speculative spirit ; a gambling spirit.

しゃこく【社告】an announcement of a company.

しゃさい【社債】a bond ; a debenture.

長期― a long-term debenture. 短期― a short-term debenture. 貯蓄― a savings debenture.

しゃざい【謝罪】an apology. ¶ 約束を破ったことを深く～いたします I deeply *apologize to* you *for* breaking the appointment. その会社に新聞広告による～を要求した We demanded *a* public *apology* from the company in a newspaper.

―状 a letter of apology.

しゃさつ【射殺】¶ 彼は～された He *was shot to death*. / He *was shot dead*.

しゃし【斜視】¶ 彼は～だ He *has a squint*. / He *is squint-eyed*.

しゃし【奢侈】luxury. ¶ 彼女は～にふけっている She indulges in *luxury*.

―税 a luxury tax.

しゃじ【社寺】shrines and temples.

しゃじ【謝辞】(感謝) thanks ; (おわび) an apology. ¶ 彼らに～を述べた(感謝のことば) I expressed my *thanks* to them. / (わびのことば) I made *an apology* to them.

しゃじく【車軸】an axle. ¶ ～を流すような雨が降った It rained *in torrents*.

しゃじつ【写実】realism. ¶ ～的な作風 a *realistic* style.

―主義 realism. **―主義者** a realist. **―小説** a realistic novel.

じゃじゃうま【じゃじゃ馬】(馬) a vicious horse ; (女) a shrew ([ʃruː] と発音する).

しゃしゅ【社主】the proprietor of a firm.

しゃしゅ【射手】a shooter ; (砲手) a gunner ; (弓の) an archer.

しゃしゅつ【射出】emission ; projection. ¶ ～する emit ; project.

しゃしょう【車掌】(バス・電車の) a conductor ; (女の) a conductress (バスガールは和製英語) ; (汽車の) 米 a conductor ; 英 a guard.

しゃしん【写真】a photograph ; a picture. ¶ この～はだれが撮ったのですか Who took this *picture*? だれかに1枚～を撮ってもらおう I want to have my *photograph* taken by somebody. 彼女はいつも～うつりがよい She always *comes out well*. その～は非常によくうつっている The picture *has come out very well*. 彼は～ぎらいだ He hates cameras. この～を現像してください Won't you please develop this *film*? この～を1枚焼いてください Please make a print of this *film*. この～は引き伸ばせない

We cannot enlarge this *film*.
—家 a photo artist. —顔 the photographed face. —機 a camera. —電送 phototelegraphy. —版 a photogravure. —判定 a photo decision. —屋(人) a photographer; (店) a photographer's. —館 a photo studio. 航空— an air photo. 白黒— a monochrome photograph. 電送— a telephotograph. 天然色— a color photograph.

じゃしん【邪心】malice; a wicked heart. ¶私はきみに~をいだくものではない I bear you no *malice*.

じゃしん【邪神】a malevolent god; a heathen god.

ジャス JAS (JAPAN AGR Japan Agricultural Standard から).
—マーク a JAS mark.

ジャズ〘音楽〙jazz. ¶彼はその曲を~風に演奏した He played the music in the manner of *jazz*. 彼は~に夢中だ He is crazy (≒ mad) about *jazz*.
—ファン a jazz fan. —バンド a jazz band.

じゃすい【邪推】a groundless suspicion. ¶~深い性質 a *suspicious* nature. 彼は私が不正をしているのではないかと~している He has *a suspicion* that I am dishonest.

ジャスミン〘植物〙jasmine.

しゃ·する【謝する】(感謝する) thank (*a person*); (わびる) apologize to (*a person*). ¶きみの厚意を~する I *thank* you *for* your kindness. / I *appreciate* your kindness. 彼らに私のまちがいを~した I *apologized to* them *for* my mistake.

しゃせい【写生】a sketch. ¶私はその橋を~した I *made a sketch of* the bridge. 彼は動物園で動物を~している He *is sketching* the animals in the zoo.
—帳 a sketch book.

しゃせい【射精】〘生理〙ejaculation. ¶~する emit (≒ discharge) semen.

しゃせつ【社説】㊎ an editorial; ㊫ a leader; a leading article. ¶新聞は~で物価高を論じている The paper comments *editorially* on the rise of prices.
—欄 the editorial columns.

しゃぜつ【謝絶】refusal; denial. ¶われわれの申し入れは~された Our offer *was declined* (≒ *was rejected*).
面会—(掲示) No visitors. ¶患者は重態で面会~だ The patient is so seriously ill that any visitor *is not allowed* to see him. 縦覧—(掲示) No admission except on business.

じゃせつ【邪説】a heresy.

しゃせん【車線】¶6~のハイウエー a six-*lane* highway.

しゃせん【社線】a private railway line.

しゃせん【斜線】an oblique line.

しゃそう【社葬】a company funeral. ¶亡くなった社長の~はあす行なわれる The *company funeral* of the late president is to be held tomorrow.

しゃそう【車窓】a car (≒ carriage) window. ¶~に映る景色はすばらしかった The scenery seen from the *car window* was wonderful.

しゃそく【社則】the company regulations.

しゃたい【車体】the body of a car; the chassis (発音は [ʃǽsi]); (自転車の) the frame.

しゃたく【社宅】a company's house [for its employees]; a company house. ¶彼は~に住んでいる He lives in the *company house*.

しゃだつ【洒脱】¶あの作家は軽妙~な文体で知られている That writer is well-known for his *unconventional* style. 彼にはどことなく~なところがある There is *something of the Bohemian* about him.

しゃだん【遮断】interception; isolation. ¶洪水に襲われたその地域は1週間外部との交通が~された The flooded region *was cut off* from communication with the outside world for a week. この壁は外部の音を~することができる This wall can *exclude* the outside sounds.
—機(踏切の) a crossing gate.

しゃだんほうじん【社団法人】a corporate juridical person; an incorporated company; an incorporation.

しゃち【鯱】〘動物〙an orc; a grampus.

しゃちほこ【鯱】—立ち ¶彼には~立ちしてもかなわない He is *more than a match for* me.
—ばる ¶そんなに~ばるにはおよばない Don't *be* so *stiff* (≒ *formal*).

しゃちゅう【車中】¶~では彼と楽しくおしゃべりをした I had a pleasant chat with him *in the car* (≒ *on the train*).
—談(政治家の) an informal talk [by a traveling politician]; a press interview in a train.

しゃちゅう【社中】the members of a company; (芸人の) a troupe; a company.

しゃちょう【社長】the president; the head; (俗語) the boss.
副— the vice-president.

シャツ a shirt (ワイシャツのこと); an undershirt; an underwear. ¶~のえり a shirt collar. ~1枚になって仕事にとりかかった Stripped to the *shirt*, I got down to business. 彼は冬でも~1枚になって働く He works *in his shirt sleeves* even in winter.

しゃっかん【借款】a loan. ¶同国はわが国に10億ドルの~を申し込んだ The country asked this (≒ our) country for *a loan* of a billion dollars. 両国の間で10億ドルの~協定が成立した *A loan* agreement of one billion dollars was concluded between the two countries.

じゃっかん【若干】¶~の(数·量) some; (数) a few; a number of; (量) a little. その事故で学生~名がけがをした *Some* (≒ *A few*; *A number of*) students were injured in the accident.

じゃっかん【弱冠】an early age. ¶彼は~18

歳で世界の音楽コンクールに入賞した He won a prize at the world music contest at *the early age* of 18.

じゃっき【惹起】 ¶ 彼の発言によって大論争が～された His words *gave rise to* a big controversy. 戦争が財政危機を～した The war *brought on* a financial crisis.

ジャッキ a jack. ¶ 彼は～で車を上げて後輪タイヤを取り替えた He *jacked up* his car and changed the rear tire.

しゃっきん【借金】 a debt. ¶ 彼に1,000円～がある I *owe* him a thousand yen. 私は～を返した I paid my *debt*. この～を返すのに一生かかるような気がする I think I'll have to work all my life to clear off my *debt*. 私は～がない I am out of *debt*. 私は長い間～なしに暮らしてきた I have kept out of *debt* for a long time. 私は銀行から～をした I *borrowed money* from the bank. ～で首がまわらないほどだ I *am* deep *in debt*. ～を催促されるのはいい気持ちはしないものだ Nobody feels comfortable when he is urged to pay his *debt* (≒ when he is dunned for his *debt*). 彼は～を取り立てに来た He came to collect *debts*.

―取り a debt collector.

ジャックナイフ a jackknife.

しゃっくり a hiccup; a hiccough. ¶ 彼女は話しはじめたとたんに～が出た She got the *hiccups* just as she began to speak. どうしても～が止まらなかった I could not get rid of my *hiccups* by any means.

ジャッグル ¶ ～する〘野球〙juggle (a ball).

ジャッジ a judge. ¶ スピーチコンテストの～を頼まれた I was asked to act as *a judge* for the speech contest. / I was asked to *judge* the speech contest.

シャッター a shutter. ¶ (カメラの)～を切ってくれませんか Will you *press the shutter*? ひろう宴の間じゅう彼はパチリパチリと～を切りつづけた Throughout the reception he kept the *shutter* clicking. 午後8時に入り口の～を下ろすことになっている The door *is shuttered* at 8 p. m. / The *shutter* of the door is closed at 8 p.m.

シャットアウト (締め出し) shutting out; 〘野球〙 a shutout. ¶ 彼は仲間から～されている He *is shut out* of his company. ジャイアンツはタイガースに完全に～を食った The Giants got *a* complete *shutout* over the Tigers. ジャイアンツはドラゴンズを3対0で～した The Giants won *a* 3—0 *shutout* victory over the Dragons.

シャッポ a hat; a cap (シャッポはフランス語の chapeau から). ¶ きみの当を得た処置には～をぬぐ I must *take off my hat to* you for the adequate measure.

しゃてい【射程】 a range. ¶ 敵陣は～内(外)にある The enemy is within (out of) *range*. この大砲の～距離は10マイルだ This gun has *a range* of ten miles.

有効― the effective range.

しゃてき【射的】 shooting; rifle practice.

―場 a rifle (≒ shooting) range. **―屋**(遊戯の) a shooting gallery.

しゃでん【社殿】 a shrine; a sanctuary.

しゃとう【斜塔】 a leaning tower. ¶ ピサの～ *the Leaning Tower* of Pisa.

しゃどう【車道】 a roadway. ¶ ～に出てはいけない Don't step on to the *roadway*.

シャドー shadow.

―ボクシング shadow-boxing.

じゃどう【邪道】 an evil way. ¶ きみの練習の方法は～のように思われる I think there is something *wrong* with your method of practice. それは～だ That's not a proper way of doing it. / That's not proper.

しゃない【社内】 ¶ ～ではそれは公然の秘密だった It was an open secret *in the office*.

―結婚 an office marriage. **―電話** an interoffice telephone.

しゃなりしゃなり ¶ 彼女は着飾って～と歩いた Decked out in her best clothes, she walked *affectedly* (≒ *with a mincing gait*).

しゃにくさい【謝肉祭】 the carnival.

しゃにむに【遮二無二】 ¶ 彼らは～敵陣に突っ込んだ They dashed *recklessly* (≒ *desperately*) into the enemy. 母親は休暇中も～息子を勉強させた The mother *forced* her son to learn his lessons during the vacation.

じゃねん【邪念】 a wicked thought. ¶ ～は捨てるべきだ You've got to get rid of *wicked thoughts*. それを聞いて彼の心に一つの～が起きた At this *an evil desire* occurred to him.

じゃのめ【蛇の目】 (形) a double ring; (かさ) an umbrella with a bull's-eye design.

しゃば【娑婆】 this world; (囚人から見て) the outside world. ¶ 彼は刑を終えて～に出たばかりだ He has recently left prison after doing his time. もう～には用がない I have no more use for *this world*.

―っけ ¶ ～っけを捨てなければこの種の仕事に没頭できない You cannot devote yourself to this sort of work unless you give up *worldly ambitions*.

じゃばら【蛇腹】 (写真機の) bellows; (建物の) a cornice.

しゃひ【社費】 the expense of the company. ¶ ～で世界旅行ができるのはありがたい How happy I am to be able to make a round-the-world trip *at the expense of the company*!

ジャブ 〘ボクシング〙 a jab. ¶ 右頬に～をうけた I had *a jab* on my right cheek.

じゃぶじゃぶ ¶ 川の中を～渡った I *splashed* my *way* in a river. 彼女は～洗たくしていた She was washing *with splash*.

しゃふつ【煮沸】 ¶ 患者の衣類は～して消毒する We sterilize the clothing of the patient by *boiling*.

シャフト a shaft.

しゃぶ・る【舐る】 suck; (あめを) chew (candy). ¶ あの子どもは指を～る癖がある That child has a habit of *sucking* its fingers. 当分彼にはあめを～らせておこう I'll *yield to him* on purpose for the time being. あんな人のところにいたら骨

の髄まで～られてしまう If you stay with him, you'll *be squeezed to death.*

しゃへい【遮蔽】 ¶ ブドウだながその部屋を西日から～している The grapevine trellis *shades* the room from the afternoon sun.

シャベル a shovel. ¶ ～で雪をかいて道をつけた I *shoveled* a path through the snow.

しゃべ·る【喋る】 talk; chat; chatter. ¶ 彼はよく～る人だ He is *a* great *talker.* / He is a *talkative* man. 彼女は30分～りつづけた She *talked* on for half an hour. 私はよく彼と～った I *have* often *talked* with him. お茶をのみながら彼と～ったものだ I used to *have a chat* with him over a cup of tea.

しゃへん【斜辺】〘数学〙 the hypotenuse.

しゃほん【写本】 a manuscript 〔copy〕 (MS, 複 MSS と略す). ¶ その本は～だ The book is in *manuscript.* / That's a book in *manuscript.*

シャボン soap.

—玉 a soap bubble. ¶ 数人の小さい子どもたちが～玉を飛ばして遊んでいた Several small children were enjoying themselves blowing *soap bubbles.*

じゃま【邪魔】 **1** 〘妨害·障害〙 interruption; an obstacle. ¶ 勉強の～をしないでください Please don't *disturb* me in my study. 彼は勉強の～をされたので怒った He was angry because his studying *was interrupted.* 自転車が通行の～になっている There's a bicycle *standing in our way.* 話の～をしないでほしい I'd like you not to *interrupt* me while I'm talking. われわれの話の～をしないでくれ Don't *interrupt* our talk. スモッグが～であの高い塔が見えない We can't see that tall tower *for* smog. お～しました I am sorry to *have interrupted* you. この箱を～にならない所にどけてください Won't you *put* this box *out of the way*? 彼の仕事の～をしてはいけない Never *hinder* him in his work. ラジオの音が～で本が読めなかった The sound of the radio *was* so *disturbing* to me that I could not read.

2 〘訪問〙 ¶ あすお～したいのですが, いかがですか May I *come to see* you tomorrow? 五, 六分お～してもいいですか Won't you *spare* me *a few minutes*?

ジャム jam. ¶ イチゴ(リンゴ; ブドウ)～ strawberry (apple; grape) *jam.* スライスパンに～をつける spread *jam* on slices of bread; spread slices of bread with *jam.*

しゃむしょ【社務所】 a shrine office.

しゃめい【社名】 the name of a company (≒ firm).

しゃめい【社命】 order of a company. ¶ 彼は～でロンドンへ行った He went to London *by order of the company.*

しゃめん【斜面】 a slope; an inclined plane. ¶ 急～ *a* steep *slope.* なだらかな～ *a* gentle *slope.* 山の～ the *slope* of a mountain.

しゃめん【赦免】 〔a〕 pardon; 〔a〕 remission. ¶ 囚人は2年の刑期を～された The prisoner *was pardoned* two years of his sentence.

シャモ【軍鶏】〘鳥類〙 a fighting cock; a gamecock.

しゃもじ【杓文字】 a 〔large〕 wooden spoon.

しゃゆう【社友】 a friend of a company.

しゃよう【社用】 〔company〕 business. ¶ 彼は～で名古屋へ出張中です He is in Nagoya *on a business trip* (≒ *on business*).

—族 ¶ 銀座のナイトクラブは～族でいつもいっぱいだ The nightclubs on the Ginza are always full of clerks enjoying luxuries on the expense of their companies.

しゃよう【斜陽】 the setting sun.

—産業 a declining industry. **—族** a declining upper-class family.

じゃよく【邪欲】 a wicked desire.

しゃらくさ·い【洒落臭い】 ¶ ～いことを言うな None *of your cheeks*!

じゃらじゃら ¶ 彼は硬貨をポケットで～させた He *jingled* coins in his pocket. あんな女と～するな Don't *flirt with* such a girl.

じゃら·す ¶ ネコを～す play with a cat.

じゃり【砂利】 gravel; small pebbles. ¶ 道路には～を敷いてある The road *is graveled.* / The road is covered with *gravel.*

—道 a gravel road.

しゃりょう【車両】 vehicles; (鉄道の) cars; (鉄道の車両全部) rolling stock. ¶ ～を整備しておくのに忙しい We are busy keeping the *cars* in thorough working order. 次の～にお乗り換えください Please transfer to the next *car.*

—故障 a car trouble. **—連結機** a car coupling.

しゃりん【車輪】 a wheel. ¶ ～の一つがはずれてしまった One of the *wheels* has come off.

しゃれ【洒落】 a joke; a jest; a pun. ¶ あの人はいつも～ばかり言っている He *is* always *joking.* まったくおもしろい. それはうまい～だ How funny! That's *a* very good *joke.* あの男は～がうまい He is good at *jokes.* ぼくにはその～がわからない I can't see the point of the *joke.* 私はただ～に言っただけだ I only said it *in joke.* / I only said it *for a joke.* 彼はやたらにだ～を言う He often makes *bad puns.* 彼は最後まで～のめしたHe continued *joking* to the last.

しゃれい【謝礼】 thanks; (報酬) a reward; (礼金) a fee. ¶ 彼は彼の奉仕に対してなんの～も期待していない He does not expect any *reward* for his services. 人のしてくれたことに対して～を出すのは当然だ It is quite natural to *reward* people for their services. ガイドは過分の～を要求した The guide asked an excessive *fee.* 講師にいくら～を差し上げたらいいでしょう How much shall we *pay* to the lecturer?

しゃれき【砂礫】 gravel.

しゃれこうべ【髑髏】 a skull.

しゃ·れた【洒落た】 stylish; smart. ¶ 彼女は～れた身なりの女だ She is *stylishly* (≒ *smartly*) dressed. きみの帽子はなかなか～れたもの

だ You are wearing a very *stylish* hat. ～れた帽子を手に入れた I got a *fanciful* hat. 彼はなかなか～れたことを言うね He says a very *smart* thing, doesn't he? そこにはなかなか～れた庭園がある There is a very *tasteful* garden there.

しゃ·れる【洒落る】(冗談を言う) joke; (服装が) dress up.

じゃ·れる【戯れる】¶子ネコが小さなまりに～れていた A kitten *was playing with* a small ball.

ジャワ Java.
—人 a Javanese. **—語** Javanese.

シャワー a shower; a shower bath. ¶～を浴びてから夕食にしよう Let's *take* (≒ *have*) *a shower* before we eat supper.

シャン (美人) a beauty. ¶彼女はなかなか～だ She is quite *a beauty*. / She is *a* very *nice-looking girl*.

ジャングル a jungle.
—ジム a jungle gym.

じゃんけん a toss (じゃんけんは英米の銭投げに相当する). ¶～で決めよう Let's *toss up for* it. ～に勝った(負けた) I won (lost) the *toss*.

しゃんしゃん ¶彼は70歳になるがまだ～している He is seventy years old, and yet still *hale and hearty*.

じゃんじゃん ¶電話が～かかってくる I am *continually* called up on the telephone. 彼は～金をもうけた He made money *very fast*. まきを～燃やした I burned *a great deal* of wood.

シャンソン *chanson* (フランス語).
—歌手 a *chanson* singer.

シャンツェ〘スキー〙a ski jump; *Schanze* (シャンツェはドイツ語). ¶70メートル～ *a* 70 meter *ski jump*.

シャンデリア a chandelier.

しゃんと ¶～しろ *Pull yourself together*. / *Brace yourself up*. ～背筋を伸ばしなさい *Make* your back *straight*. / *Straighten* your back. 彼は年をとっても～している He is *hale and hearty* in spite of his old age.

ジャンパー a jumper; (皮製·ウール製のスポーツ用の) a Windbreaker (商標名); a windbreaker.

シャンパン champagne.

ジャンプ a jump. ¶～する jump.

シャンプー 〔a〕shampoo. ¶週に2度～で髪を洗う I *have a shampoo* (≒ *shampoo my hair*) twice a week.

ジャンボ a jumbo.
—ジェット機 a jumbo jet.

ジャンボリー a jamboree.

ジャンル *genre* (フランス語). ¶～別に分類した本 books classified according to *genre*.

しゅ【主】**1**〘神〙the Lord. ¶～よ, 哀れみたまえ *Lord*, have mercy upon us.
2〘主要〙¶楽しみが～, 実益は従だ Pleasure is our *main thing*, and profit is subordinate to it.
商売は金もうけが～だ Money-making is *the first thing* (≒ *the chief consideration*) in business.
この本は政治問題が～になっている This book is *primarily* (≒ *chiefly*) concerned with political matters.
彼が～になって働いている He *takes the initiative* in working.
私たちは～として計画について話し合うことになっている We are to talk *chiefly* about the plan.

しゅ【種】(種類) a kind; a sort; a class; (型) a type; (生物の種属) a species. ¶この～の品 articles of this *kind* (≒ *sort*). 同～の本 books of the same *class*. この～の人間 this *type* of man. この～の本は好きでない I don't like *this kind of book* (≒ *a book of this kind*). (a book of this kind のほうが this kind of book よりも強意的用法).

しゅ【朱】vermilion. ¶～塗りの柱 a *vermilion-lacquered* pillar. 彼は満面に～をそそいで怒った He *was flushed* (≒ *was red*) with anger. ～に交われば赤くなる (諺) *He who touches pitch shall be defiled therewith*.

しゅい【首位】the first place; the top. ¶彼はクラスで～に立っている He *is at the head* (≒ *top*) *of* his class. この国は鉄の生産において～を占める This country *ranks first* (≒ *holds* 〔*the*〕*first place*) in iron production.
—打者〘野球〙the leading hitter.

しゅい【趣意】(意味) sense; effect; (目的) a purpose; (要旨) the point. ¶ご～はわかる I understand *what you mean*. 来日の～はなんですか What is your *purpose* of having come over to Japan?

しゅいん【主因】the primary cause. ¶第2次世界大戦の～は何であったか What was *the primary cause* of World War II?

しゅう ¶～という音 a hiss; a hissing sound; (むちを振るときの) a swish.

しゅう【州】(米では) a state; (英では) a county; (大陸をいうとき) a continent. ¶～議会 a *state* assembly. ～立大学 a *state* university. ニューヨーク～ the *State* of New York. ヨーク～ the *County* of York; Yorkshire (固有名詞に続くと -shire [-ʃə] という発音となる). アジア～ Asia; the Asiatic *Continent*. 五大～ the Five *Continents*.

しゅう【週】a week. ¶今(先; 来)～ this (last; next) *week*. 先～のきょう today 〔last〕 *week*. 来～のきょう today 〔next〕 *week*. ～5日制 *a* five-day *week*. 今～のなかば about the middle of this *week*. きみに～1万円払います I will pay you ten thousand yen *a week* (≒ *weekly*).

しゅう【衆】(多数) a great number; (民衆) the people. ¶彼らは～を頼んで攻撃をかけた They attacked us, *relying upon their great number*〔*s*〕. / They attacked us *on the strength of their numerical superiority*. 博愛～に及ぼす extend benevolence *to all* (≒ *the masses*; *the people*).

-しゅう【-周】¶世界一～をする go round the world. グランドを5～する run five laps.

しゆう【市有】¶～の建物 a *city-owned* building.
—地 municipal (≒ city) land.

しゆう【私有】private ownership.
—地 private land. ¶この土地は私の〜地だ This land is *my own property*. **—**財産 private property.

しゆう【雌雄】male and female (英語では雄雌となる). ¶ひよこの〜の見分け方 how to distinguish between the *male and female* of a chicken. この試合で〜を決しよう In this match we will *fight to the last* (≒ *fight it out*). 両チームは〜を争おうとしている Both [the] teams are going to *strive* (≒ *contend*) *for victory*.

じゅう【十・拾】ten. ¶〜分の1 one-*tenth*. 〜代の人 a *teen*-ager. 〜代の男子 a boy *in his teens*. 彼はきみの〜倍も本を持っている He has *ten times as* many books *as* you have.

じゅう【従】¶その旅行では歩くことが主で観光を〜とした In the tour I *subordinated* sightseeing *to* walking.

じゅう【銃】a gun; a rifle. ¶〜を向ける aim *a gun* at (a bear). 〜を担う shoulder *a gun*. 〜を構えて with *a rifle* at the ready.

-じゅう【-中】¶きょう〜に終わらせたい I want to finish it *in the course of* the day. 昨夜は一晩〜雪だった It kept snowing *throughout* last night. あすは一日〜家にいる予定です I'll stay at home *all day* (≒ *all day long*) tomorrow. 冬〜スキーを楽しんだ I enjoyed skiing *all through* the winter. この歌は世界〜で人気がある This song is popular *all over* the world (≒ *all* the world *over*). 妹は家〜でいちばんおしゃべりだ My younger sister is the most talkative *of all* our family. 村〜水浸しになった *All* the village was flooded.

-じゅう【-重】¶2〜の twofold; double. 3〜の threefold; triple.

じゆう【事由】a reason; a cause.

じゆう【自由】freedom; liberty.

1〖自由を〗¶われわれは言論の〜, 信仰の〜を保障されている *Freedom* of speech and religion is guaranteed to us.

学問の〜をぜひとも守らねばならぬ We must defend academic *freedom* at any cost.

個人の〜を侵害してはならぬ We must not infringe upon personal *freedom*.

私たちは行動の〜を束縛された Our *freedom* of action was restricted. / Our hands were tied.

個人の〜を尊重するのが民主主義の原則である It is the principle of democracy to prize personal *liberty*.

交通事故で彼は手足の〜を失った He was disabled in a traffic accident.

2〖自由な〗¶彼は公務を退いてやっと〜な身となった He *was free to* enjoy himself as he liked after he retired from office.

5年の刑期を終えて彼は〜な身となった The prisoner *was released* (≒ *was set free*) at the expiration of his five-year term.

どうぞ〜な立場から発言してください Express your opinion on anything you like.

自分の〜な時間がそれほどお持ちになれるとはうらやましい I envy you for having so much *free* time.

こういう問題になると〜なとらわれない気持ちにはなかなかなりにくい In such a matter it is difficult to be *free* and easy.

3〖自由に〗¶今どき子が親の〜になるとでも思っているのか Do you think that parents can do with their children as they please nowadays?

金の力で人を自分の〜にしようとはとんでもない男だ What a fellow he is to *lead* a person *by the nose* with money.

この金はぼくの〜にはならぬ I cannot *use* this money *as I like*.

遠慮なくご〜になさっていてください Please *make yourself at home*.

総会の議事が終わればあとはご〜になさってください After the proceedings of the general meeting are finished, you can do whatever you please.

ご〜にご歓談ください Please have a pleasant talk.

要覧はご〜にお持ち帰りください Please [*feel free to*] keep the handbook.

見本はご〜におとりになってお試しください *Help yourself to* (≒ *Have*) a sample and try it out, please.

クリームとお砂糖はご〜にお入れください Please *help yourself to* cream and sugar.

男女が〜に交際できるようになったのは戦後のことだ It was only after the war that men and women could *freely* meet.

どうぞご〜になんでも質問していただきたい Please *don't hesitate to* ask whatever question you like.

彼は5か国語を〜に話せる He *has a good command of* five foreign languages.

ぼくだってもう高校生だ. 少しは〜にさせてください Now that I am in senior high school, let me *have my own way*.

4〖自由だ〗¶人は生まれながらにして〜だ Man is born *free*.

どうしようときみの〜だ You can do just *as you please*. / You *are at liberty* to do anything you like.

きみの将来を決めるのはきみの〜だ You *are at liberty* to decide upon your profession.

5〖自由が〗¶全身がまひして体の〜がきかなかった I was paralyzed from head to toe and could not make my limbs move as I wanted.

6〖自由の〗¶彼らは民族の独立と〜のために戦った They fought for the independence and *liberty* of the people.

7〖自由と〗¶〜と放縦(ほうじゅう)とをはき違えるな Don't mistake license for *liberty*.

—意志 free will; spontaneity. **—**営業 nonrestricted trade. **—**化 liberalization. ¶国際貿易の〜化が要求されている The *liberalization* of international trade is demanded. **—**画 a free drawing. **—**形〖スポーツ〗freestyle. **—**〔職〕業 a liberal profession. **—**教育 liberal education. **—** 競争 free (≒

open) competition. —経済 free economy. —契約 free booking. —結婚 free marriage (≒ union); common-law marriage. —研究 independent investigation; free inquiry. —港 a free port. —行動 free action; independent action; a free hand. —作文 a free composition. —詩 free verse. —市場 a free market. —主義(者) liberalism (a liberalist). —主義国 a free nation. —種目 a free event. —人 a freeman. —陣営 the democratic camp. —世界 the free world. —選択 free choice. —党 the Liberal Party; the Liberals. —討議 free discussion. —投票 free voting. —貿易 free trade. —貿易港 a free port. —放任 noninterference; laissez-faire. —民権運動 democratic right movement. —労働者 an independent (≒ a casual) laborer.

しゅうあく【醜悪】 ¶ ～な人相 *ugly* features. 裏での～な争い an *abominable* (≒ a *detestable*) quarrel behind the scenes.

じゅうあつ【重圧】 great pressure. ¶ 精神的～ mental *great pressure*. 彼はその提案を否決するようにとわれわれに～を加えた He put *great pressure* on us to reject the proposal.
—感 an oppressive feeling; (受け身的なら) an oppressed feeling.

しゅうい【周囲】 (周囲) circumference; (環境) surroundings. ¶ ～の山々 the *surrounding* mountains. ～の景色 the scenery in the *neighborhood*. この島の～はどのくらいありますか What is the *circumference* of this island? この湖は～5マイルある This lake is five miles *around* (≒ *in circumference*). 彼女の～の人たちが好きでない I don't like those *around* her. 家の～に木が植えてある The house *is surrounded by* trees. 彼は～を見まわした He looked *around*. ～がうるさいとなかなか勉強ができない We cannot possibly work hard in noisy *surroundings*. 私たちはとかく～の影響を受けがちだ We are apt to be influenced by the *surroundings*. 子どもは～の事物から学ぶ A child learns from its *surroundings*.

じゅうい【重囲】 ¶ 彼らはついに敵の～に陥った They *were closely besieged* (≒ *surrounded*) *by* the enemy.

じゅうい【獣医】 a veterinary surgeon; a veterinarian; (口語で) a vet.
—学 veterinary medicine. —学校 a veterinary college.

じゅういち【十一】 eleven. ¶ ～番め the eleventh.

じゅういちがつ【十一月】 November.

しゅういつ【秀逸】 excellence. ¶ ～な作品 an *excellent* work; a masterpiece. ～なしゃれ a *capital* (≒ *first rate*) joke.

しゅうう【驟雨】 a shower.

しゅうえき【収益】 earnings; proceeds; a profit. ¶ ～のあがる商売 a *profitable* (≒ *lucrative*) business. 彼はその取引で大きな～をあげた He made *a* large *profit* on the transaction. / He made large *profits* out of the transaction. 音楽会は予想以上の～をあげた The *proceeds* of the concert were greater than had been expected.
—金 earnings; proceeds. —率 an earning rate. —力 earning power.

しゅうえき【就役】 ¶ 船はヨーロッパ航路に～した The ship *has been placed on* the European line.

しゅうえん【終演】 ¶ ～は午後5時です *The curtain falls* at five p.m.

しゅうえん【終焉】 ¶ 文豪～の地 the place of the *death* of the great man of letters.

じゅうおう【縦横】 ¶ ～の機知 a *wealthy* wit; *a wealth of* wit. ～に走る道路 *a network of* streets. 下水が市内を～に貫通している The sewer system runs *in all directions* through the city. この地方は鉄道が～に通じている This district *is crisscrossed with* railroads. 彼はその問題について～にしゃべった He talked *freely* on the subject. 彼は社会で～に活躍している He has been acting *vigorously* in the society.

じゅうおく【十億】 米a billion; 英 a thousand millions.

しゅうか【集荷】 collection of cargo. ¶ 果物の～ fruit *collection*.

しゅうか【衆寡】 ¶ ～敵せず敗れた We were *outnumbered* by the enemy and were defeated.

じゅうか【銃火】 rifle fire; gunfire. ¶ ～を冒して敵に近づいた We approached the enemy *under fire* (≒ *defying the enemy's musketfire*). わが軍は敵と～を交えた Our army exchanged *fire* with the enemy.

しゅうかい【集会】 a meeting. ¶ 私たちのクラブは毎週月曜日に～を開く Our club holds *a meeting* every Monday. ～の自由 freedom of *meeting* (≒ *assembly*).
—所 a meeting place; an assembly hall. 不法— an unlawful assembly.

しゅうかいどう【秋海棠】〔植物〕a begonia.

しゅうかく【収穫】 a harvest; a crop. ¶ 麦の～が多いだろう We'll have *a* rich wheat *harvest*. / There is every prospect of *a* rich wheat *harvest*. ことしは米の～が多かった The rice *crop* has been large this year. / We had *a* large rice *crop* (≒ *harvest*) this year. 肥沃(ひよく)な土地は～が多い Good soil produces *a* large *crop*. 今回の旅行は大きな～であった The tour we have made is *a* great *success*. 彼の研究は医学界にとって大きな～をもたらした His research has yielded *a* rich *harvest* to the medical circles.
—期 the harvest time. —高 the crop; the yield. 今年の(米の)—予想高 the estimated〔rice〕crop for this year.

しゅうがく【就学】 —児童 school children. —年齢 school age. —率 the percentage of school attendance. 未—児童 pre〔-〕school children.

し

しゅうがくりょこう【修学旅行】a school excursion. ¶彼らは～で日光へ行った They went on *a school excursion* (≒ *an educational trip*) to Nikko.

じゅうがつ【十月】October.

じゆうかって【自由勝手】¶それはきみの～な言い分だ It *is selfish* of you to say a thing like that. 彼の～なふるまいを許すわけにはいかぬ I cannot let him have his own way.

しゅうかん【週刊】¶この雑誌は～だ This magazine *is published every week*. / This magazine is *a weekly*.

—誌 a weekly〔magazine〕.

しゅうかん【週間】a week. ¶2～ two *weeks*; a fortnight. 一,二～ *a week* or two.

愛鳥— Bird Week. 交通安全— Traffic Safety Week. 防火— Fire Prevention Week (いずれも冠詞は不要).

しゅうかん【習慣】〔a〕habit; (慣習) a custom (habit は個人のくせ, 習慣をいい, custom は個人または社会の習慣的ならわしとなっているものをいう). ¶～は第二の天性である (諺) *Habit is a second nature*. ～になるとなんでもやさしくなる *Custom* makes all things easy. 早起きの～を身につけなさい Form the *habit* of getting up early. 彼はいつも食後に歯をみがくことを～にしている He is in the *habit* of brushing his teeth after each meal. / He has *a habit* of brushing his teeth after each meal. その悪い～はできるだけ早くやめたほうがいい You had better give up the bad *habit* as soon as possible. 国が違えば～も違ってくる Different countries have different *customs*. 非常に熱いお湯にはいるのが私の～だ It is my *custom* to take very hot baths. 日本人は鮮魚をなまで食べる～がある There is *a custom* in Japan to eat fresh fish raw.

じゅうかん【縦貫】¶その地方を山脈が～している A range of mountains *runs through* the district.

じゅうがん【銃眼】a loophole.

しゅうき【周期】a period; a cycle. ¶この現象は～的に起こる This phenomenon occurs *periodically* (≒ *in cycles*).

—運動 a periodic movement. —律 the periodic law; the law of periodicity.

しゅうき【秋季】autumn; 米 fall. ¶きのう～運動会が催された The *autumn* athletic meet was held yesterday.

しゅうき【臭気】a bad smell; an offensive odor. ¶腐った魚は～を発する Stale fish gives off *a bad smell*. / Stale fish emits *an offensive odor*. ガソリンは胸がむかつく～がする Gasoline has *a nasty smell*. その～が鼻をつく It *stinks*. / It *is stinking*. / It is *offensive* to the smell. その～の抜き方がわからない I don't know how to remove the *nasty smell*.

-しゅうき【-周忌】the anniversary of *a person's* death. ¶祖父の3～ the second anniversary of grandfather's death (3周忌は死後2年目だから second である).

しゅうぎ【祝儀】(祝いごと) a celebration; (心づけ) a tip; (祝い物) a gift; a present. ¶きょうあの家では～がある They are to have *a celebration* in their family today. 彼に～をやった I *tipped* him. / I gave him *a tip*.

しゅうぎ【衆議】¶～一決した It was decided *unanimously*. / We *were unanimous in* deciding it.

じゅうき【銃器】(総称的) small arms.

じゅうき【什器】(1個) an article of furniture; (総称) household furniture; (作りつけの備品) fixtures.

しゅうぎいん【衆議院】the House of Representatives.

—議員 a member of the House of Representatives. —議長 the Speaker of the House of Representatives.

じゅうきかんじゅう【重機関銃】a heavy machine gun.

しゅうきゅう【週休】a weekly holiday. ¶あの店では～2日制だ They are on *a five-day week* in that store.

しゅうきゅう【週給】weekly pay (≒ wages). ¶彼の～は2万円だ His *weekly pay is* (≒ His *weekly wages are*) 20,000 yen. (イギリス・アメリカは週給が多いから pay, salary は週給を指すことが多い).

しゅうきゅう【蹴球】football.

—選手 a football player; a footballer. —チーム a football team. —場 a football field; 米 a gridiron. ア式— association football; soccer.

じゅうきょ【住居】a residence; a dwelling. ¶彼は～を郊外へ移した He removed〔his *residence*〕to the suburbs. 彼はここに～を構えた He *has settled*〔*down*〕here./He *has taken up his residence* here.

—費 housing expenses.

しゅうきょう【宗教】religion. ¶彼は～に凝っている He is devoted to *religion*. 彼は～によって救われた He attained salvation by believing in *religion*. あなたの～はなんですか What *religion* do you believe in?

—家 a religionist. —画 a religious picture. —界 the religious world. —改革〖歴史〗the Reformation. —学 the science of religion; (神学) theology. —劇 a religious drama. —裁判〖歴史〗the Inquisition. —団体 a religious body. —心 ¶彼は～心が起こったらしい He seems to *have turned religious*. —哲学 philosophy of religion. —問題 a religious problem. —文学 religious literature. 新興— a newly-born religion. 無— ¶彼は無～だ He professes *no religion*. / He is *an atheist*.

しゅうぎょう【修業】(勉学) study; (鍛練) training. ¶彼は高校1年を～した He *finished* the first year *course of* a high school. ～年限は3年である The course of *study* covers three years.

—証書 a certificate.

しゅうぎょう【就業】¶～中は面会謝絶です We are not allowed to see a visitor *while at* *work*.

―規則 office regulations. ―時間 the working hours; the business hours. ¶ 本社の～時間は1日7時間だ *The working hours* of our company are seven hours a day.

しゅうぎょう【終業】(授業の) the end of school; (仕事の) the close of work. ¶ ～のベルが鳴った The bell went for *the end of school*. / The *closing* bell in our school rang. 本日は～しました *Business is over* today.

―時間 the closing hour. ―式 the closing ceremony.

じゅうぎょういん【従業員】an employee; a worker.

しゅうきょく【終曲】〘音楽〙〘演劇〙the finale. ([finɑ́:li] と発音する. イタリア語から).

しゅうきょく【終局】¶ ～の勝利 an *ultimate* (≒ a *final*) victory. 大事件もいよいよ～に達した The great event *came to an end* (≒ *was brought to a close*) at last. ドラマは～に近づいた The play *drew to a close* (≒ *drew near a close*).

しゅうぎょとう【集魚燈】lamps for gathering fishes; fishes gathering lamps.

しゅうきん【集金】collection. ¶ 電気代の～ *collection* of electric charges. 彼は請求書の～に回っている He goes round to *collect bills*. 彼は月に1回～に来る He visits us once a month for *collecting money*.

―人 a collector.

じゅうきんぞく【重金属】a heavy metal.

しゅうぐ【衆愚】the vulgar herd (≒ crowd).

―政治 mobocracy.

じゅうく【十九】nineteen. ¶ ～番め the nineteenth.

ジュークボックス a jukebox; a juke.

シュークリーム *chou à la crème* (フランス語); a cream cake; a cream puff.

じゅうぐん【従軍】¶ 彼はその戦争に4か月～した He *served* four months in the war. 彼は第2次大戦に～中亡くなった He died *as a soldier* in World War II.

―看護婦 a war nurse. ―記者 a war correspondent. ―記章 a war medal.

しゅうけい【集計】a total. ¶ 費用を～すると5,000円になる The expenses *amount to* five thousand yen. / The expenses reach *a total* of five thousand yen.

じゅうけい【重刑】a heavy penalty. ¶ その犯罪者に～が科された The criminal *was punished severely*. / *A heavy penalty* was laid *on* the criminal.

じゅうけいしょう【重軽傷】a serious or slight injury. ¶ その事故で30人以上の乗客が～を負った Over thirty passengers *were seriously or slightly injured* in the accident.

しゅうげき【襲撃】an attack; a raid. ¶ 彼らは敵の本拠を～した They *attacked* (≒ *raided*) the enemy's base. 彼らは敵に～された They *were raided* by their enemy.

―者 a raider. ―隊 an attacking party.

じゅうげき【銃撃】¶ ヘリコプターから～が加えられた *Shots were fired* from the helicopter.

しゅうけつ【終結】an end; a close. ¶ 争議の～に努力するつもりだ We will make efforts to *settle* the dispute. 戦争は～した The war *was brought to an end*. / The war *ended*. 彼らはできるだけ早く戦争を～させようとした They tried to *bring* the war *to an end* as soon as possible.

しゅうけつ【集結】concentration. ¶ 全部隊が～した All the units *have gathered*. 警官の一隊がここに～しつつある A police force *is collecting* here.

―地 an assembly place.

じゅうけつ【充血】〘医学〙congestion. ¶ 本を読みすぎて目が～した I read too much and *had* the eyes *bloodshot*.

しゅうけん【集権】¶ 中央～ centralized administration.

しゅうげん【祝言】a wedding. ¶ 彼らは来月～をあげる They will *get married* next month. / They will have their *wedding* next month.

じゅうけん【銃剣】a bayonet. ¶ ～を銃の先につける fix *a bayonet* to the muzzle of a musket. 敵陣に～で突撃した We charged at the enemy's base with *bayonets*.

―術 bayonet fencing.

じゅうご【十五】fifteen. ¶ 第～ the fifteenth.

じゅうご【銃後】the home front. ¶ ～の人々 people in *the home front*.

しゅうこう【周航】sailing round. ¶ その船は世界の海を～した The steamer *sailed round* through the seas of the world. / The steamer *circumnavigated* the world.

しゅうこう【就航】¶ 新鋭船が南米航路に～した A new and powerful ship *entered service* (≒ *was put*) on the South American line.

しゅうこう【修好・修交】friendship. ¶ アメリカと～条約を結ぶ conclude a treaty of *friendship* (≒ *amity*) with America.

しゅうごう【集合】a gathering; a meeting; 〘数学〙a set. ¶ 8時に公園に～することになっている We are to *meet* in the park at eight. 隊長は部下にまわりに～せよと命じた The captain ordered his men to *gather* around him. 彼らはその問題を討論するためホールに～した They 〔*were*〕 *assembled* in the hall to debate on the subject.

―場所 a meeting place (*for*). ¶ ここが指定された～場所だ This is the place appointed for our *meeting*. ―名詞〘文法〙a collective noun. ―論〘数学〙the theory of sets.

じゅうこう【重厚】gravity. ¶ ～な感じのマホガニー材のドア a *solid-looking* door of mahogany. あの人は～な人柄という感じであった I was impressed with the *gravity* of his demeanor.

じゅうこう【銃口】a muzzle. ¶ 彼は私に～を突きつけた He pointed the *muzzle* of the gun

し

toward me. / He pointed his *gun* at me.

じゅうこうぎょう【重工業】heavy industry.

じゅうごや【十五夜】a full-moon night.
¶～の月 a full moon.

じゅうこん【重婚】bigamy. ¶彼は～を犯した He committed *bigamy*.
—者 a bigamist.

しゅうさ【収差】〔物理〕aberration (*of* light). 色— chromatic aberration. 球面— spherical aberration.

ジューサー a juicer.
—ミキサー a juicer-mixer.

し

しゅうさい【秀才】a bright (≒ brilliant) man. ¶彼は～の誉れが高い He has a high reputation of *being very brilliant* (≒ *very bright*).

じゅうざい【重罪】〔法律〕a felony; a serious crime. ¶彼女は～を犯した She committed *a serious crime*.
—者 a felon.

しゅうさく【習作】a study; an *étude* (フランス語). ¶この絵はまだ～の域を出ない This picture is a kind of *study*.

じゅうさつ【重殺】〔野球〕a double play.

じゅうさつ【銃殺】shooting [to death]; (刑の執行) execution by shooting. ¶反逆者は～された The traitor *was executed by shooting*.

しゅうさん【集散】collection and distribution. ¶この町は野菜の～地だ This town is *a trading center* of vegetables.

じゅうさん【十三】thirteen. ¶第～ the thirteenth.

しゅうさんしゅぎ【集産主義】collectivism.

しゅうし【収支】the income and expenses. ¶彼らは～計算をしている They are striking *a balance*. この仕事は～が合わない (わりが合わない) This work does not *pay*. ～が合わない The accounts do not *balance*. 日本の国際～は黒字(赤字)だ Japan's international *balance of payments* is in the black (in the red).

しゅうし【宗旨】*one's* religion; a sect.
¶彼とぼくは～が違う(宗教) He and I are different in *religion*. / (好み) I am different from him in taste. 彼は～変えをしてクリスチャンになった He changed his *belief* (≒ *religion*) and became a Christian.

しゅうし【修士】Master. ¶～号を受ける take *a master's degree*.
文学— Master of Arts.

しゅうし【終始】throughout; from beginning to end. ¶彼はその混乱の中で～平静を失わなかった He remained calm *throughout* the turmoil. ～彼は同じ態度を持ちつづけた He kept the same attitude *from beginning to end*. 彼は～一貫して平和論者だった He was a *consistent* advocate of peace. / He *lived and died* an advocate of peace. ～一貫して彼は原案を推した He supported the original bill *from first to last*. 会議は予算問題に～した The conference *kept to* budget problem.

しゅうじ【修辞】¶この詩の～は巧みだ The *rhetoric* of this poem is very good.
—学 rhetoric. —学者 a rhetorician.

しゅうじ【習字】calligraphy; handwriting; penmanship. ¶～の手本 a copybook. ～を習う practice *penmanship*.
—帳 a copybook.

じゅうし【重視】¶われわれは外交問題を～しなければならない We must *lay a stress on* diplomacy. われわれは彼の証言を～する We *make much of* his testimony. 私は彼の意見を～する I *attach importance to* his opinion.

じゅうし【十四】fourteen. ¶第～ the fourteenth.

じゅうじ【十字】a cross. ¶彼女は災いをさけるために～を切った She *crossed herself* to keep off evil.
—花植物 a crucifer. —軍 a crusade. —砲火 a cross fire. —路 a crossroads (単・複両方にあつかわれる).

じゅうじ【従事】¶彼女は家事に～している She *engages* (≒ *is engaged*) *in* house work. 彼は建築の仕事に～している He *follows* the profession of an architect. / He is an architect by profession. 彼は科学の研究に～している He *pursues* the study of science. 彼らは主として農耕と狩猟に～した Their major occupations were farming and hunting. 彼はどんな職業に～していますか What is his line? / What business is he in?

じゅうじか【十字架】a cross; (キリストの) the Holy Cross. ¶彼は～を負うて生きている(苦難に耐えて生きている) He *bears his cross*.
—像 a crucifix.

じゆうじざい【自由自在】¶彼は英語が～だ He *is at home in* English. 彼は3か国語が～だ He *has a good* (≒ *fluent*) *command of* three foreign languages. 左手で～に字が書ける I can write letters *freely* with left hand. 曲芸師は何枚ものさらを～に操った The acrobat manipulated several dishes *with the greatest ease*.

じゅうしち【十七】seventeen. ¶第～ the seventeenth.

しゅうじつ【終日】all day; from morning till night. ¶私は～本を読んで過ごした I spent *the whole day* reading.

しゅうじつ【週日】a weekday. ¶私は～はとても忙しい I am very busy *on weekdays*.

じゅうじつ【充実】fullness. ¶彼は～した生活を送っている He lives a *fruitful* (≒ *full*) life. 彼は気力が～している He *is full of* vigor. ～した食事をとった We had a *substantial* dinner. この図書館は～している This library *has a good collection* of books.

しゅうしふ【終止符】a period; a full stop.
¶その議論に～を打った We *put an end* (≒ *a stop*) *to* the discussion. その調査に～が打たれることになった The investigation *was brought to a close*.

じゅうしまつ【十姉妹】〔鳥類〕a lovebird.

しゅうしゃ【終車】(電車・列車) the last train; (バス) the last bus.

しゅうじゃく【執着】(愛着) attachment; (固執) persistence. ¶ 私はどんなものにも～を感じない I never *feel attached to* anything./I never *stick to* anything. 彼はいつまでも勝負に～する He *clings to* the issue of the game.

しゅうしゅう【収拾】 ¶ 事態は～できない It can't *be controlled.* / It *is uncontrollable.* It *is out of control.* 事態を～するため彼が現地に赴く He goes there in the hope of *settling* the affair. 彼にはその難事を～する力はない He is not one who can *cope with* the difficulty. その場を～するために全力をつくした I did my best to *save the situation.*

しゅうしゅう【収集】〔a〕collection. ¶ 切手の～に興味をもっている I am interested in *collecting* stamps. 彼の絵の～はたいした数だ He has *a* large *collection* of paintings. ～した新しい情報はこれだけだ This is all the fresh information I could *obtain.* 十分なデータが容易に～可能だ Sufficient data are easily *obtainable.* 彼は情報を～するためにそこへ行った He went there to *glean* information.

切手―家 a stamp collector.

しゅうしゅう ¶ ～と水が吹き出ている Water is spouting out *with hisses.*

じゅうじゅう【重重】 ¶ 私の落ち度については～おわびします I'm *very* sorry for my fault. / I beg you *a thousand* pardons for my fault. 息子に代わって～おわびします I *do* apologize for my son. そのことは～承知しております I know it *very well.* / I am *fully* aware of it.

しゅうしゅく【収縮】 contraction. ¶ 金属は冷えると～する Metals *contract* when they are cold. 急に筋肉が～した The muscles *contracted* suddenly. この布はぬれると～する This cloth *shrinks* when it gets wet.

―筋 contractile muscles.

しゅうじゅく【習熟】 ¶ 彼はその機械の取り扱いに～した He *got skilled in* handl*ing* the machine. 一つの外国語に～することは容易ではない It is not easy to *master* a foreign language. 彼は英語に～している He *is proficient in* English. 彼は潜水技術に～している He is an *expert* diver.

じゅうじゅつ【柔術】 *judo.*

じゅうじゅん【従順・柔順】 ¶ 彼は親には～である He *is obedient to* his parents. あの子は～な性質だ The boy has a *gentle* nature. その犬はとても～だ The dog *is* very *docile.*

じゅうしょ【住所】(すみか) a dwelling; (所番地) an address. ¶ ご～はどちらですか Where do you live? / What is your *address*? / May I have your *address*? ～を書いてください Please write down your *address.* 落ち着いたら～を教えてください Let me know your *address* when you settle down. 彼に私の～を教えた I gave him my *address.* ～が変わった I removed to *a* new *address.* 封筒に～が書いてなかった The envelope bore no *address.*

―録 an address book; a directory. 現― the present address. ―不定 ¶ 彼は～不定だ He has no fixed *abode.*

しゅうしょう【周章】 ¶ 彼は～狼狽(ろうばい)して逃げた He ran away *in confusion.* / He ran away *helter-skelter.* その知らせを聞くと彼らは～狼狽した The news *threw* them *into consternation.*

しゅうしょう【愁傷】 grief; sorrow. ¶ どうもこの度はご～さまでございます I *heartily sympathize* (≒ *condole*) *with you* on this bereavement.

じゅうしょう【重症】 a serious illness. ¶ 彼は～で回復は望み薄だ He *is seriously ill* and his recovery is extremely doubtful. 彼は～のノイローゼだ He has fallen *seriously* neurotic.

―患者 a very serious case.

じゅうしょう【重唱】 ¶ ふたりの女性が二～をした The two women performed *a duet.* 三(四)～ a trio (quartette).

じゅうしょう【重傷】 a serious injury. ¶ 彼は～を負った He *was seriously injured* (≒ *wounded*). / He received *a serious* (≒ *severe*) *injury.*

じゅうしょうしゅぎ【重商主義】 mercantilism.

しゅうしょく【修飾】 ornamentation; 〘文法〙 modification. ¶ 彼はいつも話を誇張し～を加える He always exaggerates and *embroiders* (≒ *embellishes*) his story. 副詞は動詞, 形容詞, 他の副詞を～する An adverb is used to *modify* a verb, an adjective, or another adverb.

―語 a modifier.

しゅうしょく【就職】 ¶ 会社に～した I *got a position* in a company. 彼は商社に～している He *is employed* in a business firm. / He *has a position* in a business firm.

―運動 job (≒ place) hunting. ―口 ¶ 彼は東京に～口を見つけた He *got a job* in Tokyo. 彼は～口の世話をしてくれた He found me *a job.* ～口を捜している I'm looking for *a position* (≒ *a job*). 彼には～口がない He is out of *a job.* ―志願者 an applicant for a position. ―試験 an employment examination. ―難 ¶ ～難だ It's difficult to get *a job.* / It's difficult to find *employment.*

じゅうしょく【住職】 the chief priest〔of a temple〕.

じゅうしょく【重職】 ¶ 彼はその会社の～についている He occupies *a responsible* (≒ *an important*) *post* in the company.

しゅうしん【修身】(学科) morals; (修養) moral training.

しゅうしん【執心】 devotion; attachment. ¶ 彼の彼女への～ぶりはたいしたものだ How deeply he *is devoted to* her! / He *is infatuated with* her. / He *is head over heels in love with* her. 目下の彼は金もうけにご～だ To earn money is now his principal thought.

しゅうしん【終身】 all *one's* life; for life. ¶ 彼は～独身を続けた He remained unmarried *all his life.*

―会員 a life member. ―年金 a life annuity. —禁固刑 imprisonment for life. —刑 ¶その凶悪犯は～刑に処せられた The felon got a *life* sentence.

しゅうしん【終審】the final trial.
—判決 the final verdict.

しゅうしん【就寝】¶～する go to bed. 私の～中に while I *am in bed*.

しゅうじん【囚人】a prisoner.
—服 the prisoner's uniform.

しゅうじん【衆人】the people; the public. ¶～環視のなかでそんなふるまいをするなんて Shame on you to behave like that *in public*!

じゅうしん【重心】the center of gravity.
¶私は～をとろうとした I tried to keep my *balance*. ～を失た I lost my *balance*.

じゅうしん【銃身】a barrel.

ジュース 1 〖テニスなどの〗deuce. ¶私は彼と再三～の接戦を繰り返した I played a match with him, which went to *deuce* again and again. ～アゲン *Deuce* again.
2 〖飲み物〗juice; a soft drink.

じゅうすい【重水】〘化学〙heavy water.

じゅうすいそ【重水素】〘化学〙heavy hydrogen; deuterium.

しゅうせい【修正】〔an〕amendment; revision; 〔a〕correction; (写真の) a retouch; retouching.
¶字句を～した I *made* some *changes* in the wording. その議案は何回も～された The bill *has been amended* many times. 彼は自分の案に～を加えた He *revised* his plan. 彼はその法案の～を提案した He proposed *an amendment* to the bill. 彼はその写真を～した He *retouched* the photograph.
—案 an amendment. —予算 a revised budget.

しゅうせい【終世・終生】all *one's* life. ¶わが～の友 my *lifelong* friend. ご厚情は～忘れません I shall never forget your kindness *as long as I live*.

しゅうせい【習性】〔a〕habit. ¶魚は光に集まる～がある The fish have the *habit* of gathering around the light.

しゅうせい【集成】collection. ¶彼はその作家についての諸家のおもな注釈を～して1冊の本にした He *compiled* important notes and commentaries by many scholars on the writer into a volume.

じゅうせい【銃声】the report of a gun; a shot. ¶遠方に1発の大きな～を聞いた We heard a loud *report* in the distance.

じゅうせい【獣性】beastliness; brutality.

じゅうぜい【重税】(徴税) heavy taxation; (税金) a heavy tax. ¶～に苦しんでいる We are groaning under *heavy taxation*. 政府は勤労者に～を課してきた The government has imposed *a heavy tax* on wage earners.

じゆうせき【自由席】an unreserved seat.

しゅうせき【集積】accumulation; a pile. ¶ごみの～ *a pile* of dirt. 知識の～ the *accumulation* of knowledge.
—回路 an integrated circuit. —所(貨物などの) a depot ([dépou] と発音する).

じゅうせき【重責】an important duty; a heavy responsibility. ¶彼は大臣の～を果たした He fulfilled his *important duty* as a minister. ついに彼はその～を引き受けた At last he assumed *the heavy responsibility*. 私はこの～に耐えられるだろうか Am I equal to this *important mission*?

しゅうせん【周旋】(仲介) agency; (あっせん) good offices. ¶彼に職を～してやった I *found* him a job. 彼に～してもらってその職にありついた *By his good offices* I got the position. / He *exercised his influence* in getting me the position. 彼は土地売買の～をしている He is *a* land *agent* (≒ *broker*). 彼の～でその家を買った I bought the house by his *agency*. 彼はわざわざふたりの間にたって～の労をとってくれた He was kind enough to *act as an intermediary for* both of us.
—業 brokerage. —業者 a broker. —人 an agent; an intermediary. —屋 a broker; an agent; (雇人の) an employment agent; (土地・家屋の) a real estate agent. —料 brokerage; commission.

しゅうせん【終戦】the end of a war. ¶～後の教育 the *postwar* education. ～以来35年が過ぎた Thirty-five years have passed since *the end of the war*.

しゅうぜん【修繕】repair; mending (mend は「構造の簡単な小さなもの」の修繕に用い, repair は「家などの大きなものや, 自動車・テレビ・時計などの複雑なもの」の修繕に用いることが多い. またアメリカの口語では, repair, mend のかわりに, しばしば fix〔up〕が用いられる).
¶タイヤのパンクを～してもらった I *had* the flat tire *mended*. 家を～してもらった I *had* my house *repaired*. 時計を～してもらった I *had* my watch *repaired* (≒ *fixed*). 屋根は～の必要がある The roof is in need of *repair*. このくつは～が必要だ These shoes need *cobbling*. このテレビは～がきかない This television *is beyond repair*. 橋は～中です The bridge *is under repair*.
—工場 a repair shop. —道具 repair tools. —費 repairing expenses.

じゅうぜん【従前】¶仕事の方法は～どおりにする We'll do our work *as before*.

しゅうそ【宗祖】the founder of a sect.

しゅうそ【臭素】〘化学〙bromine.

じゅうそう【縦走】¶この夏われわれは日本アルプスを～する We will *traverse* the Japan Alps this summer. 奥羽山脈は東北地方を～する The Ou Mountain Range *runs through* the Tohoku district.

じゅうそう【重曹】〘化学〙sodium bicarbonate; (俗称) baking soda.

しゅうぞく【習俗】manners and customs.

じゅうそく【充足】¶欠員を～する *fill up* the vacancy.

じゅうぞく【従属】subordination; dependence. ¶大国に～するばかりでは独立国とはいえない The country which is always *dependent* upon a big power can't be called an independent country.

—国 a dependency; a subject country.
—節〘文法〙a subordinate (≒ dependent) clause.

じゅうそつ【従卒】an orderly.

しゅうたい【醜態】¶ 彼は人前で〜をさらした He *made a show of himself* in public. 〜を演じた I *behaved in a shameful manner*. / I *have made a mess*. / I *cut a sorry figure*.

じゅうたい【重体・重態】a critical condition. ¶ 彼は出血多量で〜だ He is *seriously ill* with excessive loss of blood. 彼女はきのう〜に陥った She fell into *a critical condition* yesterday.

じゅうたい【渋滞】delay; congestion. ¶ 交通の〜 traffic *congestion*. 生産の〜 *delay* in production. 道路は車で〜している The street *is congested with* cars. 工事が〜している The construction *is delayed*.

じゅうたい【縦隊】a file. ¶ 4列〜に並ぶ stand in fours. 1列〜で in single *file*; in Indian *file*. われわれは2列〜で行進した We marched *in file* (≒ *in double columns*).

じゅうだい【十代】*one's* teens (13歳から19歳まで). ¶ 〜の少年(少女) a teen-ager. 彼はまだ〜だ He is still in his *teens*.

じゅうだい【重大】importance. ¶ きみに〜な相談がある I have something very *important* to talk over with you. 彼は事の〜さに気がついていない He is not aware of the *importance* of the affair.

—視 ¶ 私はそれを非常に〜視する I *attach* great *importance to* it. / I take it very *seriously*. **—事** ¶ それは〜事だ It is *a matter of great importance*.

しゅうたいせい【集大成】compilation. ¶ それは万葉集を〜した研究である It is a work of scholarship in which the various texts of the *Manyoshu are compiled*.

じゅうたく【住宅】a house; a residence.

—金融公庫 the Housing Loan Corporation. **—公団** the Housing Corporation. **—地** a residential quarter (≒ area). **—難** housing shortage. **—問題** the housing problem.

しゅうだん【宗団】a denomination.

しゅうだん【集団】a group; a mass; a body. ¶ 暴徒が〜となって押し入った Rioters made a rush into the house *in a body*. 彼がその〜のリーダーだ He is the leader of the *group*.

—安全保障 collective security. **—結婚** group marriage. **—就職** mass employment. **—心理** group (≒ mob) psychology; group mind. **—生活** group life. **—中毒** mass poisoning. **—発生** a mass outbreak (of cholera).

じゅうたん【絨毯・絨氈】a carpet; a rug. ¶ 階段には〜が敷いてある The stairs *are carpeted*.

ペルシァ**—** a Persian carpet ([pə́ːʃən] または [pə́ːʒən] と発音する).

じゅうだん【銃弾】a bullet.

じゅうだん【縦断】¶ 台風が本土を〜した The typhoon *flew through* (≒ *cut across*) Japan proper from south to north.

—面 a vertical (≒ longitudinal) section.

じゅうたんさんソーダ【重炭酸ソーダ】〘化学〙bicarbonate of soda.

しゅうたんば【愁嘆場】a pathetic scene.

しゅうち【周知】¶ これは〜の事実だ It is a fact *known to all*. / It is a well-known fact. / This is a matter *of common knowledge*. 〜のごとく, 彼は非常な正直者だ *As everybody knows*, he is a very honest man.

しゅうち【衆知】¶ 〜を集める ask wise counsels from many people.

しゅうち【羞恥】shyness; (恥辱) shame. ¶ 彼女は〜のまなざしで彼を見た She cast a *shy* glance upon him. 彼女は〜で顔を赤らめた(恥辱で) She blushed for *shame*. / (恥ずかしさで) She blushed *shyly*.

—心 ¶ 彼は〜心で顔があげられない He can't look up with the sense of *shame*.

しゅうちく【修築】repair. ¶ こんなぼろ家は〜したとてむだだ It is no use trying to *repair* such a dilapidated house. その寺は〜中だ The temple is *under repair*(*s*).

しゅうちじ【州知事】the governor of a state.

しゅうちゃく【執着】(愛着) attachment; (固執) persistence; adherence. ¶ 彼女はなくした時計にいつまでも〜している She never loses her *attachment to* the lost watch. 彼女は住みなれた家に強い〜をもっている She has a strong *attachment to* her dear old house. そんなことにあまり〜するな Don't *stick to* that too much.

しゅうちゃく【終着】¶ 新宿〜は20時の予定です The train is to arrive at Shinjuku Terminal at 20.

—駅 the terminal station; the terminus.

しゅうちゅう【集中】concentration. ¶ 彼は何事にも注意を〜できない He can't *concentrate* his attention *on* anything. / He can't *concentrate upon* anything. 敵は北部国境に兵力を〜している The enemy *has massed* (≒ *has concentrated*) their troops on their northern borders.

—安打〘野球〙an avalanche of hits. **—豪雨** a heavy rain concentrated on a certain area. **—砲火** concentrated fire. **—講義** an intensive course. ¶ 英文学の〜講義 *an intensive course in* English literature.

しゅうちゅう【集注】(集注本) a variorum (edition). ¶ シェイクスピア〜(本) *a variorum edition* of Shakespeare.

しゅうちょう【酋長】a chieftain.

じゅうちん【重鎮】a leading man; a prominent man. ¶ 彼は政界の〜である He is *a prominent* (≒ *an influential*) *figure* in the political world.

しゅうてい【舟艇】¶ 上陸用〜 a landing craft (単複同形).

しゅうてん【終点】the terminal〔station〕; the terminus. ¶ 駅の～にはタクシーがたくさん待っている There are many taxis waiting at the *terminal*.

じゅうてん【重点】(強勢) emphasis; stress; (重要) importance; (優位) priority. ¶ この学校は外国語学習に～をおいている This school *puts* (≒ *lays*) *great emphasis on* the study of foreign languages. この地区を～的に調査しよう We will make a *priority* investigation of this district.
—主義 a priority system.

じゅうてん【充塡】filling. ¶ 虫歯にセメンを～してもらった I *had* my decayed teeth *plugged* (≒ *filled*) with cement.

じゅうでん【充電】¶ バッテリーは～する必要がある The battery must *be charged*.
—器 a charger.

しゅうでんしゃ【終電車】the last train (≒ car).

しゅうと【舅】a father-in-law.

しゅうと【宗徒】a follower; a believer.

シュート shot. ¶ 彼は～をした(バスケット) He *shot* a ball. / (フットボール) He *shot* a goal. 次のボールは内角に～した (野球) The next ball *shot* inside.

ジュート〘植物〙jute.

しゅうとう【周到】¶ 手術は～な注意のもとに行なわれた The operation was performed with *scrupulous* (≒ *careful*) attention. そのために前もって～な準備をした I made *thoroughgoing* preparations for it. 彼は用意～な男だ He is a *careful and prudent* man.

しゅうどう【修道】—院 (男の) a monastery; a cloister; (女の) a convent; a nunnery. —院長 (男) an abbot; a prior; (女) an abbess; a prioress. —女 a nun; a sister. —僧 a monk; (托鉢の) a friar.

じゅうとう【充当】appropriation. ¶ そんな企てにその金を～するのは当を得ていない The *appropriation* of the money *for* that undertaking is not right. 予備費を赤字の補塡に～せざるをえない We have to *appropriate* the reserve fund *for* the deficit.

じゅうどう【柔道】*judo*.
—家 a *judo* expert. —師範 an instructor of *judo*.

しゅうとく【拾得】¶ さいふを～する *find* (≒ *pick up*) a purse.
—者 a finder. —物 a found article.

しゅうとく【習得】¶ その技術を～するのに3年かかった It took me three years to *master* (≒ *acquire*; *learn*) the technique.

しゅうとめ【姑】a mother-in-law.

じゅうなん【柔軟】¶ 彼は～な体の持ち主だ He is a man of *flexible* build. / He has a *lithe* figure. 政府は野党に～な態度で臨んでいる The government shows a *flexible* stand to the opposition. もっと～な心を持ってほしい I want you to have a more *flexible* mind.
—性 flexibility; elasticity. —体操 cal〔l〕isthenics (複数扱いに注意).

じゅうに【十二】twelve. ¶ 第～ the twelfth.
—月 December (Dec.). —宮 the signs of the zodiac. —支 the twelve horary signs.

じゅうにく【獣肉】meat; flesh.

じゅうにしちょう【十二指腸】〘解剖学〙a duodenum.
—潰瘍 duodenal ulcer. —虫 hookworm.

じゅうにぶん【十二分】¶ もう～に頂きました I have had *more than enough*. 彼は実力を～に発揮しなかった He did not show his ability *to the full*. 彼はその事実を～に知っていた He was *fully* aware of the fact.

しゅうにゅう【収入】an income; earnings; (国家の) a revenue; (受入金) receipt; (収益金) proceeds.
¶ 彼は～が少ない(多い) He has a small (large) *income*. 月5万円の～がある I have (≒ earn) *an income* of fifty thousand yen a month. 彼は文筆で相当な～を得ている He *makes a* good *income* by his pen. 彼は月にどのくらい～があるのか How much does he *make* a month? 彼は～以上(以内)の生活をしている He lives beyond (within) his *income*.
—印紙 a revenue stamp. —役 a treasurer.

しゅうにん【就任】assumption of office.
¶ 彼の新しい地位の～ the *assumption* of his new post. 彼は会長に～した He *took office* as the president. ～して以来ちょうど1年たった It is just one year since I *took up* the present *post*. 彼は市長に正式に～した He *was inaugurated* as mayor.
—演説 an inaugural address. —式 an inaugural ceremony; an inauguration.

じゅうにん【住人】a dweller; an inhabitant.
¶ 千葉の～だ I'm *an inhabitant* in Chiba. / I *live* in Chiba.

じゅうにん【重任】(重い責任) a heavy (≒ grave) responsibility; an important duty; (再任) reappointment.
¶ 彼は委員長の～を果たした He fulfilled his *important duty* as the chairman of the committee. 彼は～をおびてワシントンへ行った He went to Washington on *an important mission*. 氏は総理大臣に～した He *was reappointed* to be prime minister.

じゅうにんといろ【十人十色】(諺) *So many men, so many minds.* / *Everyman has his humor.* ¶ 食べ物の好みは～だ Everyone has his own taste for food. 人の考えは～だ Each man has his own opinion.

じゅうにんなみ【十人並み】¶ 彼女は～の器量だ She is *average*-looking. 彼は～のことしかできない He is a man of *average* (≒ *ordinary*) ability. 彼の知能は～だ His intellectual faculties are *up to the average*. 彼女の仕事ぶりは～以上だ Her work *is above the average*. 絵は～とまではいかない I *am below the average* in painting.

-しゅうねん【-周年】an anniversary. ¶ 開校10～記念日 the tenth *anniversary* of the founding of our college.

しゅうねん【執念】(執着心) a deep attachment; (復しゅう心) vindictive feeling. ¶ 〜深く persistently; revengefully. 彼は科学の研究に〜をもやした He *devoted exclusively to* the study of science. 彼女は〜深い She *is revengeful* (≒ *is tenacious*; *is spiteful*). 彼の〜深さにはあきれた I am amazed at his *tenacity* (≒ *persistence*).

じゅうねん【十年】ten years; a decade. ¶ 彼は〜一日のごとく働いた He worked hard for years *without a break*. / He worked *tirelessly*. 初めて彼に会ったときに〜の知己のように感じた I felt at the first meeting as if he were an old friend of mine.

じゅうのうしゅぎ【重農主義】〘経済学〙physiocracy.

しゅうは【周波】〘電気〙a cycle; (周波数) frequency. ¶ NHKは〜数590キロサイクルで放送する The Japan Broadcasting Corporation broadcasts in the *frequency* of 590 kilocycles.
高(低)— high (low) frequency.

しゅうは【秋波】an amorous glance. ¶ 彼女は彼に〜を送った She cast *an amorous glance* at him.

しゅうは【宗派】a sect; a denomination.
—心 sectarianism. ¶ 彼は〜心の強い男だ He is a sectarian.

しゅうはい【集配】collection and delivery. ¶ 郵便を〜する *collect and deliver* mails.
—人(郵便の) 米 a mailman; 英 a postman.

じゅうばい【十倍】ten times. ¶ 彼はぼくの〜も本を持っている He has *ten times as many* books *as* I have.

じゅうばくげきき【重爆撃機】a heavy bomber.

じゅうばこ【重箱】a nest of lacquered boxes. ¶ そのようなことで〜のすみをつつくようなことを言うな You should not *be too particular about* such a thing.

じゅうはち【十八】eighteen. ¶ 第〜 the eighteenth. 鬼も〜番茶も出花(諺) *Everything is good in its season.*
—番 ¶ 化学は彼の〜番だ Chemistry is his *strong point*. / He *excels in* chemistry. あの歌が彼の〜番だ That is his *favorite* song.
—金 gold 18 carats fine.

しゅうばん【週番】weekly duty. ¶ 彼は今週〜だ He is on duty *this week*.

しゅうばん【終盤】the final stage. ¶ 選挙戦は〜に入った The election campaign has got into *the final stage*.

じゅうはん【重版】¶ その本はまもなく〜になるだろう The book will soon *go into its second edition*. その本は何回も〜になった The book *went through many editions*. (厳密には単に版を重ねる重版は a second impression で改訂または増補の重版は a second edition という).

じゅうはん【従犯】an accessory (*to* a crime).

しゅうび【愁眉】¶ その知らせを聞いて彼は〜を開いた He *felt relieved* to hear the news.

じゅうびょう【重病】a serious sickness. ¶ 彼女は〜だ She *is seriously* (≒ *dangerously*) *sick*.
—患者 a serious case.

しゅうふく【修復】restoration. ¶ 法隆寺の〜 the *restoration* of the Horyuji Temple. 寺の〜工事ができた The temple *has been repaired*.

しゅうぶん【秋分】the autumnal equinox. ¶ 〜の日 *the Autumnal Equinox* Day.
—点 the autumnal equinoctial point.

しゅうぶん【醜聞】a scandal. ¶ 〜が世間に広まった The *scandal* was noised abroad.

じゅうぶん【重文】〘文法〙a compound sentence.

じゅうぶん【十分・充分】**1**〘数量などがたっぷり〙¶ 時間はまだ〜ある There is still *plenty of* time left.
食糧は〜ある We have *sufficient* food.
20人分の食糧は〜ある There is *enough* food for twenty people.
あと1時間あれば〜だ One more hour will *be enough*.
千円で〜だ One thousand yen *is enough*.
ありがとうございます. もう〜頂きました I've had *enough*, thank you.
〜食べて〜眠りなさい *Eat your fill* and sleep *well*.
2〘完全に・申し分なく〙¶ 彼がその申し出を断わる理由は〜ある There is *good* reason why he should reject the offer.
歩いても〜時間にまにあう Even if you walk all the way, you will *surely* be in time.
それで〜だ That'*s enough*.
ゆうべは〜楽しんだ I enjoyed myself *to the full* last evening.
彼女には私の言う意味が〜わかっている She knows well *enough* what I mean.
彼は人生の苦しさを〜知っている He knows the bitterness of life *to the full*.
私は自分の思っていることを〜に言い表わせないのが残念だ I am sorry I cannot express myself *to my heart's content*.
〜な注意を望みます I want you to *be very careful*.
この本は〜読む価値がある This book is *well* worth reading.

しゅうへん【周辺】circumference; outskirts; environs. ¶ 彼らは国会の〜をデモ行進した They made a demonstration parade *around* the Diet Building. 彼は東京〜のどこかに住んでいる He lives somewhere *on the outskirts of* Tokyo.

しゅうほう【週報】a weekly bulletin.

しゅうぼう【衆望】popularity. ¶ 彼は市民の〜を一身に集めている He *wins great popularity* (≒ *is very popular*) among the citizens. 彼は〜を担って代議士に立候補した He ran for the Diet *with popular support*. 彼は〜にこたえることができなかった He failed to meet *public expectation*.

じゅうほう【重砲】a heavy gun; (総称) heavy artillery.

じゅうほう【銃砲】guns; firearms.
—店 a gun shop.
じゅうぼく【従僕】a servant.
しゅうまく【終幕】an end; a close. ¶ 事件もいよいよ～を迎えた The affair is coming to *an end*.
しゅうまつ【終末】an end.
しゅうまつ【週末】the weekend. ¶ この～には釣りに行くつもりだ I'm going to go fishing this *weekend*. 私は～を伊豆で過ごすことにしている I make it a rule to spend *the weekend* in Izu.
—旅行 a weekend trip. —旅行者 a weekender.

し

じゅうまん【十万】a hundred thousand.
—億土 Paradise; Elysium.
じゅうまん【充満】fullness; impregnation. ¶ 部屋にガスが～していた The room *was full of* gas. 国内に不平が～している Complaints are heard all over the land.
じゅうみん【住民】a dweller; an inhabitant; a resident. ¶ 東京には, 1,000万の～がいる Tokyo has ten million *inhabitants*.
—税 the inhabitants' tax. —登録 resident registration.
しゅうめい【襲名】succession to *a person's* name. ¶ 彼は団十郎を～した He *succeeded to* the name of *Danjuro*.
じゅうめん【渋面】a wry face; a sullen look. ¶ ～をつくるな Don't make *a wry face*. 彼は～をつくって出ていった He went out *with a sullen look*.
じゅうめんたい【十面体】a decahedron.
しゅうもく【衆目】all eyes; public attention. ¶ ～の見るところ彼は偉人だ *It is universally admitted* that he is a great man.
しゅうもん【宗門】a sect.
じゅうもんじ【十文字】a cross. ¶ ～の cross-shaped. ～に crosswise.
しゅうや【終夜】all night; the whole night.
—運転 ¶ 大みそかには国電は～運転をする On New Year's eve, there is *all-night* train service by JNR. —営業 ¶ 私の家の近くに～営業のスナックがある There is an *all-night* snack bar in my neighborhood.
しゅうやく【集約】¶ 彼は今までの討論を要領よく～した He *arranged* cleverly the arguments so far.
—農業 intensive agriculture.
じゅうやく【重役】a director.
—会 the board of directors. —会議 a directors' meeting.
じゅうゆ【重油】heavy oil; crude oil.
しゅうゆう【周遊】a 〔circular〕 tour; 圏 a round trip. ¶ 北海道を～する make *a tour* through Hokkaido.
—券 a circular tour ticket; 圏 a round-trip ticket. 世界—旅行 an around-the-world tour.
しゅうよう【収用】expropriation. ¶ 鉄道線路敷設のため土地を～する *expropriate* land for the purpose of building a railroad.
しゅうよう【収容】accommodation. ¶ 彼は病院に～された He *was admitted to* a hospital. 彼らは刑務所に～された They *were sent to jail*. 彼らは捕虜を収容所に～した They *sent* war captives *to* the concentration camp. その会場は2,000人を～することができる The hall *admits* (≒ *seats*) two thousand people. ホテルは3,000人を～する設備がある The hotel *has accommodations for* three thousand people. 駐車場には200台の車を～することができる There is enough space for two hundred cars in the parking lot.
—人員 the number of persons to be admitted. —力(劇場などの) a seating capacity (*of* 800); (ホテルなどの) accommodations (*for* 100 people).
しゅうよう【修養】culture; cultivation. ¶ ～を積んだ人 a *cultured* person. 彼は若いころ～に励んだ He made a great effort to *improve himself* in his youth. 彼は精神～が足りない He lacks moral *training*.
じゅうよう【重用】¶ 有能な人材を～する *give* an able man *a high position*.
じゅうよう【重要】importance. ¶ 彼はこの会社の～な地位にいる He is in an *important* position in this firm. 彼はこの地域の～な人物のひとりに数えられている He is counted among the most *important* characters in this district. 世界の平和を維持することはきわめて～である It is very *important* to maintain the peace of the world. なぜこの問題が～なのかわからない I cannot understand the *importance* of this problem. この問題はさほど～でない This problem is not so *important*. これはほとんど～でない This is of little *importance*. 彼のことばは私には～でない His words do not *weigh with* me at all. / I'm not concerned with what he said.
—書類 important papers. —人物 a very important person; (米・口語) a VIP; a V. I. P. —視 ¶ 物価問題はもっと～視すべきだ We should *take the matter of* commodity prices *more seriously*.
しゅうようじょ【収容所】(捕虜・政治犯の) a concentration camp; (難民の) the DP camp (DP は displaced persons の略).
しゅうらい【襲来】¶ ～する(台風などが) visit; strike; (敵が) attack; invade. 寒波の～が近い A cold wave *is coming*. 関西地方は台風の～を受けた The Kansai district *was visited by* a typhoon.
じゅうらい【従来】(今まで) until now; (以前は) formerly; in the past. ¶ ～の体育館 the *former* gymnasium. 彼は～どおり親切だった He was as kind *as before* (≒ *as in the past*).
しゅうらく【集落】a village.
しゅうらん【収攬】¶ 人心を～する *win* the hearts of the people.
じゅうらん【縦覧】¶ 選挙人名薄は今一般の～に供せられる The voters' list *is now open to the public*.
—室 a reading room. —謝絶 (掲示) No

visitors allowed. ―随意(掲示) Admission free.

しゅうり【修理】repair; mending (家などの大きなものや, 自動車・テレビ・時計など複雑なものは mend より repair を用いることが多い. また米・口語では mend, repair のかわりにしばしば fix〔up〕が用いられる).

¶彼はこわれたドアを~している He *is mending* a broken door. このくつは~が必要だ These shoes need *mending*. 時計を~してもらわなければならない I must *get* (≒ *have*) my watch *repaired*. その時計はとても~してもむだだ The watch *is beyond repair*. その車は~の必要がある The car is in need of *repair*. 橋は~中だ The bridge *is under repair*〔*s*〕. 彼はなんでも~するのが上手だ He is good at *fixing* everything.

―工場 a repair shop. ―所(電気器具などの) a service station.

しゅうりつ【州立】¶~の state.

―大学 a state university.

しゅうりょう【修了】completion. ¶彼は中学の全課程を~した He *completed* (≒ *finished*) the whole course of study at a junior high school.

―証書 a certificate.

しゅうりょう【終了】an end; a close. ¶第2次世界大戦は1945年に~した World War II *ended* in 1945. 戦争は国王の死によって~をみた The war *was brought to an end* by the king's death. 行事は成功裏に~した The event *came to a* successful *end*. 競技会は~した The athletic meet *has come to a close*.

じゅうりょう【重量】weight. ¶貨物の~をはかる *weigh* the freight. それは~が300キロある It *weighs* three hundred kilograms.

―感 ¶なんと~感のある船だ What a *massive* ship it is! ―不足 short weight. ―超過 overweight. ―トン dead-weight tonnage.

じゅうりょうあげ【重量挙げ】weight lifting. ¶~の選手 a weight lifter.

じゅうりょうきゅう【重量級】heavyweight. ¶ボクシングの~の試合は迫力がある The match by *heavyweight* boxers is impressive.

じゅうりょく【重力】〔物理〕gravity; gravitation. ¶~の法則 the law of *gravitation*.

無―状態 weightlessness.

じゅうりん【蹂躙】¶彼はわれわれの人権を~した He *infringed* our human rights. 都市は敵軍によって~された The city *was overrun* by the enemy army.

シュールリアリズム〔美学〕surrealism.

しゅうれい【秀麗】¶眉目(びもく)~な若者 a *handsome* young man. ~な富士の姿 the *graceful* figure of Mt. Fuji.

じゅうれつ【縦列】a column; a file. ¶~をつくる form *a file*.

しゅうれっしゃ【終列車】the last train.

しゅうれん【修練】training; practice.

¶彼は水泳の~を積んだ He *practiced* swimming hard.

しゅうれん【収斂】astringency. ¶光線は一点に~する Rays *meet in a focus*. この薬は血管を~させる This medicine causes the blood vessel *contract*.

―剤 an astringent.

じゅうろうどう【重労働】heavy labor; hard labor. ¶裁判官は彼に~2年の刑を宣告した The judge sentenced him to two years' *hard labor*.

しゅうろく【収録】recording. ¶野鳥の鳴き声をテープに~する *tape*〔*-record*〕the chirpings of wild birds.

じゅうろく【十六】sixteen. ¶第~ the sixteenth.

―分音符〔音楽〕a semiquaver. ―ミリカメラ a 16 mm movie camera. ―ミリフィルム a 16 mm movie film.

しゅうわい【収賄】bribery;〔a〕graft. ¶100万円を~する *accept* a million yen *bribe*. ~で起訴される be prosecuted for *taking bribes*.

―事件 a bribery case; a graft case. ―者 a bribee; a grafter.

しゅえい【守衛】a guard; a janitor; (議院などの守衛官) a sergeant-at-arms.

じゅえき【樹液】sap. ¶~の多い sapful; sappy. ~のない sapless.

じゅえきしゃ【受益者】a beneficiary. ¶費用は~負担にすべきだ The *beneficiaries* should bear (≒ share) the expenses.

しゅえん【主演】¶アラン=ドロン~の映画 a film *starring* Alain Delon. 彼女がその映画で~した She *starred* in the film. 彼女がその映画の~女優に選ばれた She was chosen as *a leading actress* of the film.

しゅえん【酒宴】a banquet; a feast; a revel. ¶彼を招いて~を催した We held *a banquet* (≒ *a feast*) in honor of him.

しゅかい【首魁】a ringleader.

しゅかく【主客】¶彼とは~転倒して私が優位に立った I *turned the tables on* him.

しゅかく【主格】〔文法〕the subjective case; the nominative case.

じゅがく【儒学】Confucianism.

―者 a Confucianist.

しゅかん【主幹】(主筆) the chief editor; the editor in chief; (編集長) the managing editor.

しゅかん【主観】subjectivity. ¶彼は自分の~を交えずに話すことができる He can speak without *subjectivity*. 彼の判断は~が強すぎる His judgment is too *subjective*.

しゅかん【主管】superintendence; management.

―事項 matters in *one's* charge.

しゅがん【主眼】the principal consideration. ¶われわれの教育の~とするところは, 学生の人格の向上である Our *principal consideration* in educating the students is to improve their character.

しゅき【手記】a note; a memo〔randum〕.

¶彼の~は死後出版された His *notes* (≒ *memoirs*) were published after his death.

しゅき【酒気】¶彼は~を帯びている His breath

し

smells of liquor. / He is under the influence of liquor.

しゅぎ【主義】a principle; a cause. ¶ 私は〜としてそれに反対した I was against it on *principle*. 自分ひとりでなんでもやるのが彼の〜だ It is his *principle* to do anything whatever for himself. 彼は〜のために死ぬと言っている He says he would die for his *cause*. 彼は自分の〜を曲げない He sticks to his *principle*. 〜に反することをやってはならぬ Never do what is against your *principle*. 〜のない人もいるものだ Some people have no *principle*. この店はもうけ〜ではない This store is not operated for profit alone.

し

じゅきゅう【需給】supply and demand.

しゅきょう【酒興】merriment; (余興) an entertainment. ¶ 彼のトランプの手品が〜を添えた His card tricks added to the *merriment*.

しゅぎょう【修行・修業】(訓練) training; (宗教的禁欲生活) austerities. ¶ 彼は講道館で柔道を〜した He *practiced judo* at the Kodokan. 彼は5年間寺にこもって〜を続けてきた He *has practiced austerities* in the temple for five years. 私はまだまだ〜が足りない I'*m* not sufficiently *trained* yet. 碁に熟達するには多年の〜が必要だ It requires many years of *training* to master *go*.

じゅきょう【儒教】Confucianism.

じゅぎょう【授業】school; a lesson; a class. ¶ きょうは〜はない We have no *school* today. きのうは〜は3時間だった We had three *lessons* yesterday. 〜は9時に始まる *School* begins at 9 a.m. きょうの〜はこれまで So much for *today* (≒ *today's lesson*). 音楽の〜は好きでない I don't like *a* music *lesson*. 当日雨天ならば平日どおり〜がある If it rains on that day, we will have *school* as usual.

—中 ¶ 彼女は歴史の〜中にいねむりをした She slept during the history *class*. 彼は〜中だ He *is teaching* his class. 〜中に教室を出てはいけない Never go out during the *lesson*.

—時間 ¶ 〜時間は9時から4時までだ *School* hours are from 9 a.m. to 4 p.m. —料 school fee.

しゅぎょく【珠玉】a gem; a jewel. ¶ 〜の文章 a *superb* style. 〜のような1編の詩 *a gem* of a poem.

じゅく【塾】a private school. ¶ 彼は英語の〜を開いている He keeps *a private English school*.

—生 a private school pupil. そろばん— a private abacus school.

しゅくあ【宿痾】a chronic disease; an old complaint.

しゅくい【祝意】(人に対して) congratulation. (行事など) celebration. ¶ 彼の成功に〜を表した I *congratulated* him *on* his success. われわれは彼らの成功に〜を表して目抜き通りを行進した We marched down the main street *in celebration of* their success. (入学・卒業・結婚などでその人を祝うときは congratulate を用い，行事・祝いの式などを行なって祝う意味では celebrate を用いる).

しゅくえん【祝宴】a banquet; a feast. ¶ 彼の成功を祝う〜を開いた We gave *a banquet* to celebrate his success.

しゅくが【祝賀】—会 a celebration. —パレード a celebration parade.

しゅくがん【宿願】*one's* long-cherished desire; *one's* heart's desire. ¶ 彼は〜を達した He attained his *long-cherished desire*.

じゅくぎ【熟議】deliberation; careful consultation. ¶ 〜したが結論に達しなかった We didn't come to a conclusion in spite of *careful consultation*.

じゅくご【熟語】an idiom; an idiomatic phrase.

しゅくさいじつ【祝祭日】a public holiday; a national holiday; a red-letter day.

しゅくさつばん【縮刷版】a smaller-sized edition.

しゅくじ【祝辞】a congratulatory address; congratulations. ¶ 彼の成功に〜を述べた I *congratulated* him *on* his success. / I *offered* him *congratulations on* his success.

じゅくし【熟視】stare; gaze. ¶ 彼は彼女の顔を〜した He *stared* her *in the face*. / He *stared* (≒ *gazed*) *at* her.

しゅくじつ【祝日】a fete day; a festival; a red-letter day; (宗教上の) a feast day.

しゅくしゃ【宿舎】a lodging; a hotel. ¶ われわれの〜は設備がすばらしい Our *lodgings* have excellent accommodations. 彼らの〜には市内のホテルが使われている They are staying at *hotels* in the city.

しゅくしゃ【縮写】¶ 1,000分の1に〜した地図 a map *on a scale of* one to a thousand. 〜する make a reduced copy (*of* a map).

—図 a reduced drawing; a miniature copy.

しゅくしゃく【縮尺】a reduced scale. ¶ 〜5万分の1の地図 a map *on a scale of* 1 : 50,000.

—図 a map on a reduced scale.

しゅくしゅく【粛粛】¶ 軍隊は〜と進軍した The army marched on *solemnly* (≒ *in solemn silence*).

しゅくじょ【淑女】a lady.

しゅくしょう【縮小】reduction. ¶ 軍備の〜 the *reduction* of armaments; disarmament. 人員の〜 *a* personnel *cut*. 不必要な人員を〜した We *cut down* unnecessary personnel. わが社は事業を〜した Our company *reduced* the business. 工場は生産を〜した The factory *cut down* production.

しゅくず【縮図】a reduced drawing; a miniature copy; an epitome. ¶ 実物の10分の1の〜 a drawing *on a scale of* one-tenth. 学校は社会の〜である School is a *miniature* society. / School is the society in *miniature*. 芝居は人生の〜である A play is *an epitome* of life.

じゅく・す【熟す】¶ 多くの果実は秋に〜す Many fruits *ripen* in autumn. このスイカは〜していな

い This watermelon *is green.* カキはもうすぐ～す Persimmons will soon *be ready for eating* ～したリンゴを木からとった I picked a *ripe* apple off the tree. 機運が～した The opportunity *has matured.*

じゅくすい【熟睡】 a sound sleep; a good sleep. ¶ 彼は～している He *is fast asleep.* 昨夜は～した I *slept well* last night. / I *had a good sleep* last night.

しゅく・する【祝する】 ¶ 彼の成功を～して晩餐(ばんさん)会を開いた We gave a dinner *in celebration of* his success. / We held a dinner to *celebrate* his success. / We held a dinner to *congratulate* him on his success. (事柄を祝うときは celebrate を用い, 人を祝うときは congratulate を用いる).

しゅくせい【粛正】 ¶ 官界の綱紀～が必要である Rigorous discipline must *be enforced* among the Government officials.

しゅくせい【粛清】 a purge; a cleanup. ¶ 政党は不穏分子を～した The political party *was purged of* its riotous members.

しゅくだい【宿題】 homework; 困 an assignment; (未解決の問題) a pending question. ¶ ふつう夕食後～をやる I usually do *my homework* after supper. 先生は難しい～を出した Our teacher set us *a* difficult *homework.* 次回の会合までその問題を～にした We *left* the question *in abeyance* until we met together next.

—帳 a homework notebook.

じゅくたつ【熟達】 ¶ 彼は水泳を教えることに～している He *is skilled in* teaching swimming.

じゅくち【熟知】 ¶ 彼はその事情を～している He *knows* the situation *well.* 彼は日本の事情を～している He *is familiar with* things Japanese.

しゅくちょく【宿直】 night duty. ¶ 今夜の～はきみの番だ It is your turn to *be on night duty* tonight.

—員 a person on night duty. —室 a night duty room.

しゅくてき【宿敵】 an old enemy. ¶ 彼は不倶戴天の～だ He is *a mortal enemy.*

しゅくてん【祝典】 a celebration. ¶ その学校は創立80周年の～をあげた They held the *celebration* of the 80th anniversary of the foundation of the school.

しゅくでん【祝電】 a congratulatory telegram. ¶ 人に～を打つ send *a person a congratulatory telegram (for).*

しゅくとう【粛党】 a purge of disloyal elements from a party. ¶ ～する purge disloyal elements from the party.

しゅくとく【淑徳】 feminine virtue; chastity.

じゅくどく【熟読】 careful reading. ¶ 本を～する *read* a book *carefully.* この本は～に値する This book is worth *careful reading.*

しゅくば【宿場】 a post town.

しゅくはい【祝杯】 a toast. ¶ 彼のために～をあげた(乾杯した) We *drank a toast to* him. / We *toasted* him. 彼の成功を祝って～をあげた We *drank in celebration of* his success.

しゅくはく【宿泊】 〔a〕 lodging. ¶ 民家に～する *stay* in a private lodging. 土曜日は伊東のホテルに～した I *put up at* (≒ *stayed at*) a hotel in Ito on Saturday. ホテルに～を申しこんだ I reserved a room at the hotel. 彼はおじの家に～している He *is staying with* his uncle. そのホテルには500人～できる The hotel has *sleeping accommodations* for five hundred guests.

—所 a lodging. —料 hotel charges. 簡易—所(イギリスの) a common lodging house.

しゅくふく【祝福】 a blessing. ¶ ふたりの結婚は両親や友人から～された Their marriage *was very warmly received* by their parents and friends. 彼に～あれ God *bless* him!

しゅくへい【宿弊】 long-standing evils. ¶ 多年の～を除去しなければならぬ We must eliminate *long-standing evils.*

しゅくほう【祝砲】 a salute of guns. ¶ 彼のために19発の～が撃たれた *A 19-gun salute* was fired in his honor.

しゅくぼう【宿望】 *one's* long-cherished desire. ¶ 彼は多年の～を達した He realized his *long-cherished desire.*

しゅくめい【宿命】 destiny; fate. ¶ こうなるのも～だったのだと思ってあきらめろ You should take your *destiny* as it is. / Resign yourself to your *fate.* 彼らは～的な対立関係にあった They were set up in *fatal* opposition.

—論 fatalism. —論者 a fatalist.

じゅくりょ【熟慮】 deliberation. ¶ ～する deliberate; think out. 彼は慎重～の後, その計画を実行に移した He carried out the plan after *due consideration.*

じゅくれん【熟練】 skill; dexterity. ¶ ～した電気技師 a *skilled* (≒ *skillful*) electrical engineer. 彼はピアノの調律に～している He *is skilled in* tuning a piano. それは大いに手の～を要する It needs much manual *skill.*

しゅくん【主君】 *one's* lord; *one's* master.

しゅくん【殊勲】 distinguished services. ¶ 彼は第2次大戦で～を立てた He rendered *distinguished services* in World War II.

—賞 a distinguished service medal. —打〖野球〗a winning hit. 最高—選手 the most valuable player.

しゅけい【主計】 an accountant; (軍隊) a paymaster.

しゅげい【手芸】 handicraft; manual arts.

—品 fancywork; a handicraft.

じゅけいしゃ【受刑者】 a convicted prisoner; a convict.

しゅけん【主権】 sovereignty; sovereign power. ¶ ～在民 The *sovereignty* rests with the people. その国の～を尊重しなければならぬ We must respect the *sovereignty* of the country. 日本の～が侵犯された Japanese *sovereignty* was violated.

—者 a sovereign; a ruler.

じゅけん【受験】 ¶ 彼は東大を～した He took (≒ sat for) the entrance *examination* to

Tokyo University.
—科目 subjects of examination. ¶ きみは指定した〜科目を〜すればよい You have only to *take examinations* in specified subjects. —資格 ¶ 彼には〜資格がない He is not qualified to *take an examination.* —準備 ¶ 彼は教員検定試験の〜準備をしている He is preparing for a teachers' certificate examination. —生 an examinee ; (受験準備中の学生) a student preparing for an entrance examination. —料 an examination fee. —番号 an examinee's number. —票 an admission ticket for examination.

し

しゅご【主語】〘文法〙 the subject.
しゅご【守護】 protection. ¶ 彼は神の〜を信じている He believes in divine *protection*.
—神 a guardian deity ; a genius. —聖人 a patron saint.
しゅこう【手工】 handiwork ; manual work.
—品 a handicraft.
しゅこう【手交】 ¶ 外務大臣は駐日英国大使に公文書を〜した The Foreign Minister *delivered* an official note *to* the British Ambassador to Japan.
しゅこう【趣向】 (計画) a plan ; (考え) an idea ; (くふう) a device ; (意匠) a design. ¶ まったく新しい〜 *an* entirely new *plan*. それはおもしろい〜だ That's *a* happy *idea*. そのパーティーを楽しくするためにできるだけの〜をこらした We invented all the possible *devices* to make the party merry. 〜をかえて, 釣りに行こうじゃないか Let's go fishing *for a change*.
しゅこう【酒肴】 food and drink.
—料 food and drink money.
しゅごう【酒豪】 a good (≒ heavy) drinker.
じゅこう【受講】 ¶ 夏季講習はだれでも〜が許される Anyone is allowed to *attend* the summer *course*.
—生(者) an attendant. ¶ 彼の講義は〜者が多い(少ない) There is *a* good (poor) *attendance* at his lecture. —料 tuition fee.
しゅこうぎょう【手工業】 handiwork.
しゅさ【主査】 (調査官) a chief investigator ; (試験官) a chief examiner.
しゅさい【主宰】 supervision ; superintendence. ¶ A博士が〜する科学研究所 the science laboratory *under the supervision* (≒ *superintendence*) *of* Dr. A. 彼がその雑誌を〜している He *is the chief editor of* the magazine.
—者 the chairman ; the leader.
しゅさい【主催】 sponsorship ; auspices.
¶ それは文部省〜で開催された It was held *under the sponsorship* (≒ *auspices*) *of* the Ministry of Education.
—者 the sponsor ; the promoter. —国 a sponsor nation.
しゅざい【取材】 ¶ 記者はその事故を〜するために名古屋へ行った The reporter went to Nagoya to *cover* the accident. 彼はその小説の〜のためにロンドンへ行った He went to London to *gather data for* his novel. この小説は事実に〜している This novel *is based on* facts.
しゅざん【珠算】 abacus calculation.
しゅさんち【主産地】 a chief producing district. ¶ 種なしブドウの〜 *the chief producing district* of seedless grapes. 青森は日本のリンゴの〜である Aomori prefecture is *the main producer* of apples in Japan.
しゅし【主旨】 the main point. ¶ 彼の演説の〜を説明してくれたまえ What is *the main point* of his speech? その計画は結局失敗に帰したという〜の手紙を彼から受け取った I received a letter from him *to the effect* that the plan turned out to be a failure. この文章の〜はなかなかつかみがたい I cannot quite grasp the *meaning* of this passage. 〜をはっきりさせなさい You must make your *point* clear.
しゅし【趣旨】 ¶ ご〜はわかりました I understand *what you mean*. 本会の〜をご説明申し上げます Let me explain the *object* of our society.
しゅじ【主事】 a director ; a manager ; (政府機関の) a secretary.
指導— a supervisor ; a teacher's consultant.
じゅし【樹脂】 resin.
合成— synthetic resin. 天然— natural resin.
しゅじい【主治医】 (主担当の) the attending physician ; (一家がかかりつけの) a family doctor (≒ physician).
しゅじく【主軸】〘数学〙 the principal axis.
しゅしゃ【取捨】 ¶ この場合〜選択が難しい It is difficult to *make a wise choice* in this case. 〜選択の余地はあまりない You haven't much *choice*.
しゅじゅ【種種】 ¶ ドラッグストアでは〜さまざまの物が売られている A wide (≒ great) *variety* of articles is sold at a drugstore. 万国博には〜の国々からたくさんの人が来ている Many people from *different* countries gather together at the International Exposition. 彼は〜の理由で, その会に欠席した He was absent from the meeting for *various* reasons.
じゅじゅ【授受】 ¶ 財産の〜は簡単なものではない *Transfer* of properties is no easy matter. 金銭の〜は慎重にすべきだ You should be careful in *giving or receiving* money.
しゅじゅう【主従】 master and servant ; employer and employee ; (主人と家来) lord and retainer.
しゅじゅつ【手術】 an operation. ¶ 彼は腕に〜を受けた He had *an operation* on his arm. 彼は盲腸炎の〜を受けることになっている He is to undergo *an operation* for appendicitis. その患者は〜中である The patient is *under the knife*. S博士の執刀で〜を受けた I *was operated on* by Dr. S. アデノイドを取るのはそう難しい〜ではない Removal of adenoids is *an* easy *operation*. 彼は〜しても手おくれだった It was too late to perform *an operation* on him.
—着 an operating gown. —室 an operating room. —台 an operating table. —料 charges for an operation.

しゅしょう【主将】(競技の) the captain; (軍の) the commander-in-chief.

しゅしょう【主唱】¶ 戦争中日本は「アジア人のアジア」を～した During the war Japan *took the lead in advocating* "Asia for the Asiatics." 彼は世界平和の～者である He *is an advocate* of world peace.

しゅしょう【首相】the premier; the prime minister. ¶ 佐藤～ *Premier* Sato.

しゅしょう【殊勝】¶ あの怠け者が朝早くから勉強とは～なことだ Just imagine the lazy boy studying so hard *like a good one* since early in the morning. 彼は～にも英会話を勉強する目的でロンドンへ行った He went to London *with a good intention* to learn English conversation. ～にも酒を慎んでるのか Have you abstained from drinking, *like a penitent sinner?*

しゅじょう【衆生】every living thing; all creatures; all life.

じゅしょう【受賞】¶ 彼はノーベル文学賞を～した He *was awarded* the Nobel prize for literature. 彼は最高点で～した He *won the prize* with the highest mark.

—者 ¶ 文化勲章の～者 *a* Cultural Medal *winner*. 彼はノーベル賞の～者だ He is a Nobelist. / He is *a* Nobel prize *winner*.

じゅしょう【授賞】¶ ～する award (≒ give) a prize. ノーベル賞～式 the Nobel-prize *awarding* ceremony.

しゅしょく【主食】the staple food. ¶ 日本人は米を～としている Rice is *the staple food* for Japanese people. / Japanese people *live* 〔*mainly*〕 *on* rice.

しゅしょく【酒色】¶ 彼は～にふけっている He gives himself up to *wine and women*. / He indulges in *sensual pleasures*.

しゅしょく【酒食】food and drink.

しゅしん【主審】the chief umpire; (ボクシングなどの) the chief referee.

しゅじん【主人】(戸主) the head of a family; (雇い主) a master; an employer; (旅館の)(男) a landlord; (女) a landlady; (夫) *one's* husband; (客に対して)(男) a host; (女) a hostess; (店の主人) a proprietor; an owner.

¶ ご～はご在宅ですか (斎藤さんの奥さんに対して) Is Mr. Saito 〔at〕 home today? ～は仕事で大阪へ行きました My *husband* went to Osaka on business. 彼はきびしい～の下で働いている He works under *a* strict *master*. 彼があの店の～だ He is the *proprietor* of the store. 彼女は園遊会の～役をつとめた She acted as *hostess* at the garden party.

—公 a hero. 女—公 a heroine.

じゅしん【受信】¶ 当地はテレビの～状態がよくない *Reception* of the television programs is unsatisfactory here. 宇宙船からの情報をここで～する Here we *receive* messages transmitted from spaceships. ロンドンからのテレックス通信を～した I *received* a telex message from London.

—機 a receiver; a receiving-set. —局 a receiving office (≒ station). —人 an addressee.

しゅす【繻子】satin. 「stitch.

—織 satin weave. —縫い〖手芸〗satin

じゅず【数珠】a rosary; a string of beads. ¶ 僧侶(そうりょ)は～をつまぐって念仏を唱えた The priest chanted a prayer to Buddha, *counting his beads*.

—玉 a bead. —つなぎ ¶ 暴徒たちは～つなぎにされた The rioters *were tied in a row*. 高速道路に自動車が数マイルにわたって～つなぎになって立ち往生していた A string of cars were held up for miles along the expressway.

しゅせい【守勢】¶ われわれは～に立たざるをえなかった We had to *be on the defensive*.

しゅせい【酒精】alcohol.

じゅせい【受精】〖生物〗fertilization; impregnation. ¶ ～する be fertilized (≒ impregnated).

—卵 a fertilized egg.

じゅせい【授精】fertilization.

人工— artificial impregnation (≒ insemination).

しゅせいぶん【主成分】the chief ingredient; the principal element. ¶ それはミルクが～になっている It has milk for its *main* (≒ *chief*) *ingredient*.

しゅせき【手跡】a hand; handwriting.

¶ 彼のみごとな～に感じ入った We were deeply impressed with his good *hand*.

しゅせき【主席】the head; the chief.

—検事 the chief public prosecutor. —全権 the chief delegate. —判事 the chief judge.

しゅせき【首席】¶ 彼はクラスの～だ He *is at the top* of the class. 彼は昨年大学を～で卒業した He graduated *first on the list* from college last year. あのふたりはクラスで～争いをしている The two are contending for *the top* in the class.

しゅせきさん【酒石酸】〖化学〗tartaric acid.

しゅせん【主戦】—投手 an ace pitcher; the top pitcher. —論 jingoism. —論者 a jingoist; a war advocate.

しゅせんど【守銭奴】a miser; a niggard; a skinflint.

じゅそ【呪詛・呪咀】a curse.

しゅぞう【酒造】*sake* brewing; (ジン・ウイスキーなど) distilling.

—家 a *sake* brewer; a distiller. —業 the *sake* brewing industry; the distilling industry. —場 a brewery; a distillery. .

じゅぞう【受像】a television image. ¶ ～はきわめて鮮明である The *image televised* is very clear. ブラウン管が古くて～がぼける The *image received* is not clear because of the old Brown tube.

—機 a TV set; a receiving set. —面 the television screen; the telescreen.

しゅぞく【種族】(人種) a race; (部族) a tribe; (動植物の) a family; a species. ¶ ～間の闘争 intertribal strife; conflicts between the *tribes*.

―保存本能 the instinct of tribe-preservation. ―本能 a racial instinct.

しゅたい【主体】 the subject; 〘法律〙 the main constituent. ¶ ～の 〘哲学〙 subjective. ～的(に) independent(ly). 生徒会が～となって学校祭の準備を進めた The student council *took the initiative in* preparing for the school festival.

―性(主観) subjectivity; (個性) individuality; (独立性) independence. ¶ 各人の～性を確立する establish *one's individuality*.

しゅだい【主題】 the subject [matter]; the [main] theme.

―歌 a theme song.

じゅたい【受胎】 conception. ¶ 結婚後半年以内に～するのが普通である Women usually *conceive* within half a year of marriage.

―告知(聖母マリアの) the Annunciation. ―調節 birth control.

じゅたく【受託】 ¶ その件に関する書類いっさいを～された I *was entrusted with* all the relevant documents to the matter.

じゅだく【受諾】 acceptance. ¶ あなたの申し入れを～します I will *accept* your offer. その地位につくことは～しかねます I cannot *accept* the position.

しゅだん【手段】 a method; a means. ¶ ～は目的を達成するためのものだ *A means* is for attaining a purpose. ことばは伝達の～だ Language is *a means* of communication. それは目的に対する～にすぎない That is *a* mere *means to* an end. 目的は～を選ばない The end justifies the *means*. きみは～を誤った You took *a* wrong *measure*. ほかに～は見当たらない That is the only *way* to do it. 政府はインフレ防止の～をとるだろう The government will take any *step to* prevent inflation. 彼は～を選ばずに金をもうけようとした He tried to make money *by fair means or foul*. 犯人を見出すべくあらゆる～を講じなければならない Every *measure* should be taken to find the criminal. 彼は事業を成功させるためあらゆる～を講じた He took every possible *means* to make his work successful.

しゅち【主知】 ―主義〘哲学〙〘文学〙 intellectualism. ―主義者 an intellectualist.

しゅちゅう【手中】 ¶ 総督は住民の生殺与奪の権を～に握っている All the lives of the inhabitants *are at the mercy of* the governor. その地方の大半を敵は～に収めた The greater part of the province *fell into the hands* of the enemy. 私の生命は彼の～にあった My life *was in his hand*.

じゅちゅう【受注】 ¶ きょうは大口の～があった We *received* a large *order* today.

―高 the amount of orders received.

しゅちょ【主著】 *one's* major writings; *one's* important books.

しゅちょう【主張】 insistence; assertion. ¶ 彼は自己の権利を～している He *claims* his own rights. 彼はあくまで～を通すだろう He will *stick to* his opinion to the last. 彼はその品を自分のものだと～してやまない He persistently *claims* that the article is his. 彼は自己の無罪を～する He *asserts* his innocence. / He *insists on* his innocence. もう支払は済んだと彼女は～している She *insists* on having already paid the money. 彼の～は正しいと私は信じている I believe his *assertion* to be right. その金は自分が盗んだのではないと彼は～している He *insists* that it is not he himself that stole the money. 彼がどうして～を曲げたのかわからない I don't see why he conceded *a point*. 彼はあくまでも～を曲げなかった He *sticked to* his opinion.

しゅちょう【主調】〘音楽〙 the keynote.

―音 the keynote.

しゅちょう【主潮】 the main current.

しゅちょう【首長】 a head; a chief.

―選挙 the election of local heads.

じゅつ【術】 art; means. ¶ 彼は保身の～にたけている He has mastered the *art* of protecting his status. なんの～も弄(ろう)しません I won't use any *trick* whatever.

しゅつえん【出演】 performance. ¶ 学校の劇に～する *perform* [*a part in*] *a play* at school. 彼の息子は先月テレビに～した His son *appeared* on television last month. 彼は国立劇場に～した He *appeared* on the stage of the National Theater. 初～するときにはだれでもあがる Everybody suffers from stage fright when he *makes his first appearance on the stage* (≒ *performs for the first time*). それはスター総～の映画だ It is a film with *an all-star cast*.

―者 the performers; the players; the cast. ―料 a performance fee. ―契約 booking.

しゅっか【出火】 a fire. ¶ ～の原因を究明しなければならない We must investigate the cause of the *fire*. 昨夜あのレストランから～した *A fire broke out* at the restaurant last night. 彼の家から～した火がたちまち近隣をなめ尽くした *The fire which started* in his house destroyed the neighboring houses in almost no time.

しゅっか【出荷】 (量・物) shipment; (行為) shipping. ¶ 野菜を東京に急行便で～する We *ship* vegetables to Tokyo by express. 品物は貨車で～された The goods *were shipped* by rail.

―先 a destination. ―者 a shipper. ―案内 a shipping advice. ―機関 a shipping agency. ―量 ¶ ～量が少ないので高値を保っている The scarcity of *shipment* keeps the prices high.

じゅっかい【述懐】 recollection[s]; reminiscence[s]. ¶ 彼は大学生活についておもしろい～をしてくれた He gave us interesting *reminiscences* of his college life.

しゅっかん【出棺】 ¶ 午後1時～ The funeral procession will leave the house at 1 p.m.

しゅつがん【出願】 application. ¶ 特許を～中

です *Application* for a patent is pending. (「特許出願中」(広告文) は "Patent applied for"). 彼はそのミシンの特許を～した He *applied for* a patent on the sewing machine.

―者 an applicant. **―期日** the time limit for application.

しゅっきん【出金】 ¶ くだらぬ義理合いで～が多くて困っている I am vexed with having to *spend money* often for respectability's sake.

しゅっきん【出勤】 attendance. ¶ 午前9時に～する I *come to office* at 9 a.m. 彼はきょうは～日だ He *is on duty* today. 彼はまだ～してきていない He *is* not *at office* yet. きょうは午後からの～だ I'*m on the afternoon turn* today. 彼女はいつも～が早い She *is* always early *at office*. 24時間交通ストのため～した者が非常に少なかった Very few people *came to work* because of a 24-hour traffic strike. 彼の～状態はよくない He is not regular in his *attendance* at his office.

―時間 the office-going hour; the hour reporting for duty. **―日数** the number of attendances. **―日** *one's* work[ing] day. **―簿** an attendance book.

しゅっけ【出家】 (僧侶) a priest; a monk; (日本・中国の僧) a bonze (日本語から). ¶ 彼は～して仏に仕えた He entered the priesthood. / He became *a bonze*.

しゅつげき【出撃】 a sally; a sortie (通例包囲された陣地からの出撃). ¶ 夜明けとともに～する *sally forth* at dawn.

しゅっけつ【出欠】 ¶ ～をとる call the roll. 彼は～常ならぬ He is irregular in *attendance*.

しゅっけつ【出血】 bleeding. ¶ 彼のけがをした足から～しはじめた His wounded leg began to *bleed*. ～を止めようとして固く包帯を指に巻いた I bandaged the cut finger tightly to stop *bleeding*. 医者は注射をして傷の～を止めた The doctor shot an injection to *stanch* the wound. 切り傷の～が止まらなかった The *bleeding* from the cut didn't stop. 多少の～(損失)は覚悟しなければなるまい We must be prepared for some *losses*.

―多量 ¶ 彼は～多量で死んだ He died from excessive *bleeding*. / He died from too much *loss of blood*. / He *bled* to death. **―販売** a sacrifice sale. **内―** internal haemorrhage.

しゅつげん【出現】 appearance. ¶ 怪物が～した A monster *appeared*. 不思議な彗星が昨夜～した A strange comet *made its appearance* last night. ジェット機の～以来,旅行はずいぶんスピードアップされた Since the *advent* of the jet aircraft, travel has been speeded up very much. 新政党の～は政界地図を塗りかえた The *appearance* of the new political party has changed the political climate.

じゅつご【述語】 〘文法〙 a predicate.

―動詞 a predicate verb.

じゅつご【術語】 a technical term.

しゅっこう【出向】 ¶ 大蔵省に～を命じられた I was ordered to *be transferred to* the Ministry of Finance.

しゅっこう【出校】 ¶ A教授はきょうは～されません Professor A is unable to *meet his classes* today. ご～になるのは何曜日ですか On what days of the week do you *teach at* (≒*come to*) *school*?

しゅっこう【出航】 ¶ 午後2時～の予定である The ship is to *depart* at 2 p.m. 日新丸はサンフランシスコに向けきのう～した The Nisshinmaru *set sail for* San Francisco yesterday. こんな悪天候のもとで～するのは危険だ(飛行機) It's dangerous to attempt *a flight* under such a threatening sky.

しゅっこう【出港】 departure. ¶ 横浜を～する *leave* Yokohama [port]. 税関はその船の～を許した The customhouse granted *clearance* to the ship. ～を停止する *lay* (≒ *put*) *an embargo on* a ship. ～停止を解く *lift* (≒ *remove*) *an embargo on* a ship.

―船 an out-going ship. **―手続き** clearance procedure. **―通知書** a clearance notice.

しゅっこう【出講】 ¶ 何曜日にご～願えますか On what days of the week will you *give* us *lectures* (≒ *teach* us)? 彼は非常勤講師として本学に～している He *lectures* at this college as a part-time teacher.

じゅっこう【熟考】 careful consideration. ¶ その問題を～してみたうえでご返事いたしましょう We will answer you after *considering* the matter *carefully*. これがわれわれの～の末の結論だ This is the conclusion we have reached after *careful consideration*. その問題は目下～中だ The matter *is under consideration*. 行動を起こす前によくその問題を～すべきだ We should *think* the problem *over* before acting. これは日本人が最も真剣に～すべき問題だ This problem demands the most *serious consideration* of the Japanese people.

しゅっこく【出国】 ¶ 彼がどういう経路で～したか不明だ It remains a mystery by what route he *got out of the country*. もう～手続きはすっかり済ませた I have taken all the necessary procedures for *leaving the country*.

しゅつごく【出獄】 ¶ 彼は～した He *was released from prison*. / He *came out of prison*.

じゅっさく【術策】 a trick; a trap. ¶ きみは～を弄(ろう)しすぎる You resort to *tricks* too often. われわれは敵の～にはまった We have fallen into our enemy's *trap*. / We *were entrapped* by our enemy.

しゅっさつ【出札】 **―係** 米 a ticket clerk (≒ agent); 英 a booking-clerk. **―所** 米 a ticket office; 英 a booking office.

しゅっさん【出産】 birth; delivery. ¶ いつご～の予定ですか When *is* your baby *expected*? 彼女の～はもうすぐだ She is going to *have a baby* pretty soon. / She *is expecting a baby* pretty soon. 彼女は男児を～した She *gave birth to* a baby boy. / She *was de-*

し

livered of a baby boy.

—届 the registration of a birth. —率 the birth rate. —休暇 a maternity leave.

しゅっし【出資】〔an〕investment. ¶ 彼はその事業に〜することを渋った He was reluctant to *make an investment in* the enterprise. 私は貯金をはたいてある事業に〜した I *invested* all of my savings *in* a business enterprise. 彼はこの事業に〜している This enterprise *is financed* by him.

—額 the amount of investment. —者 an investor; (後援者) a financial supporter.

しゅっしゃ【出社】 ¶ 以後〜に及ばず You needn't *come to office* any more. 彼女はまだ〜していません She *is* not *at office* yet.

しゅっしょ【出所】 (出どころ) the origin; the source; (出獄) release from prison.

¶ 〜の確かな情報か Is the information from *a* reliable *source*? この句の〜はキーツだ This phrase *is quoted from* Keats. 彼は〜(出獄)してから更生した He turned over a new leaf after he *was released from prison*. 彼は仮〜(出獄)を許された He *was released from prison* on parole. / He *was paroled*.

しゅっしょう【出生】 birth. ¶ 〜の秘密 the secret of *one's birth*.

—地 *one's* birthplace. —年月日 the date of *one's* birth. —率 the birth rate.

しゅつじょう【出場】 (参加) participation; (出演) appearance. ¶ テニスのトーナメントに〜する *take part in* a tennis tournament. 彼は国体の体操競技に〜した He *participated* (≒ *took part*) *in* the gymnastics competition in the National Athletic Meet. その競技への彼の〜は取り消された His *entry* for the game was canceled. 彼はそのレースに自分の馬を〜させた He *entered* his horse for the race. 今夜の演芸会にご〜なさりたい方はほかにおいでですか Is there anyone else who wants to *perform* at the entertainment this evening?

—者(参加者) a participant; (競技に出場する人) a player; (演芸会などに出場する人) a performer; (競技出場者総称) the entry.

しゅっしょく【出色】 ¶ 〜の作品 an *excellent* (≒ *outstanding*) work. 〜の出来栄えだ The workmanship *is superb*.

しゅっしょしんたい【出処進退】 a course of action. ¶ 彼は〜を誤った He took *a* wrong *course of action*.

しゅっしん【出身】 ¶ ご〜はどちらですか. 広島です Where *do you come* (≒ *are you*) *from*? I *come* (≒ *am*) *from* Hiroshima. 参加者の約 6 割は大学〜者であった About sixty percent of the participants were college graduates. 彼は社会党〜の知事だ He is a governor *from* the Socialist Party.

—校 *one's* Alma Mater (ラテン語の「慈母」の意味から). ¶ 〜校はどちらですか What school did you *graduate from*? ぼくたちは〜校が同じです We attended the same college. —地 *one's* native place; *one's* home town.

しゅつじん【出陣】 ¶ 〜する go to the front; take the field.

しゅっすい【出水】 a flood. ¶ 通りは 3 メートル〜した The streets *were flooded* to a depth of three meters.

しゅっせ【出世】 success in life; (昇進) promotion. ¶ 彼は〜すると思う I hope he will *succeed in life*. / I hope he will *get on* (≒ *be advanced*) *in the world*. その事件は彼の立身〜の妨げになるだろう The event will be an obstacle to his *advancement in life*. 〜するばかりが能じゃない *Success in life* is not everything. 校長になるなんて, 彼もたいした〜をしたものだ What *a* great *success* he has attained to have become a principal! 彼は会社で〜が早かった He has won quick (≒ rapid) *promotion* in the company.

—頭 ¶ 彼は大学の同級生のなかでは〜頭だ He is *the most successful* of our college classmates. —作 ¶ それが彼の〜作だ The work *made him famous*.

しゅっせい【出征】 ¶ 多くの若者が〜していった Many young men *have gone to the front*.

しゅっせき【出席】 presence; attendance.

¶ 彼女は〜している She *is present*. 私はそのパーティーに〜した I *attended* (≒ *was present at*) the party. 彼はその会合に〜しなかった He *was absent from* the meeting. 先生は時間の初めに〜をとる Our teacher *calls the roll* (≒ *makes a roll call*) at the beginning of the class. きみは私の講義に何回〜しましたか How many *attendances* have you made at my lecture? 彼女は〜がよくない She is irregular in her *attendance*.

—者 ¶ その会合には〜者が多かった(少なかった) There was *a large* (*small*) *attendance* at the meeting. —簿 a roll; an attendance book. —率 the attendance percentage.

しゅつだい【出題】 ¶ 期末試験の〜範囲 the range of possible *questions* in a term-end examination. 某大学入試の〜傾向 the tendency of entrance axamination *questions* of a certain university.

—者 ¶ その問題の〜者は彼だ It is he who *set the question*.

じゅっちゅう【術中】 ¶ われわれは敵の〜に陥った We fell into the enemy's *trap*. / We were caught in the enemy's *trap*.

じゅっちゅうはっく【十中八九】 ¶ 彼は〜成功するだろう He will succeed *in nine cases out of ten*. 〜彼はここに来るだろう *Most likely* he will come here.

しゅっちょう【出張】 (会社員の) a business trip; (公務員の) an official trip. ¶ 先月は福岡へ〜した I *made a business trip to* Fukuoka last month. 彼は〜中だ He *is away on official business*. 彼は今〜で大阪に来ている He is now in Osaka *on a business trip*. 海外へ〜を命じられた I received an order to go abroad *on official business*.

—員(役人) a dispatched official; (販売の) a traveling salesman; (代理人) an agent. —教授 ¶ 彼女はピアノの〜教授をしている She gives private lessons in piano at her pupil's home. —所 a branch office. —旅費 a traveling allowance.

しゅっちょう【出超】〔経済〕an excess of exports〔over imports〕. ¶ 3月の～は50億円にのぼった The *excess of exports* in March amounted to five hundred million yen.

しゅってい【出廷】¶ 彼は～しなかった He did not *appear in court*. 彼は～している He *is in court*.

しゅってん【出典】the source. ¶ この語句の～を教えてください Please give *the source of* this phrase. 引用にはいちいち～を明らかにした I indicated *the source* of each quotation.

しゅっとう【出頭】appearance. ¶ 裁判所に～を命じられた I was ordered to *appear* in court. 本人が～しなければいけない You must *appear* in person. 彼は警察に～した He *presented himself* at the police station.
—命令 a summons. 任意— voluntary appearance.

しゅつどう【出動】¶ 軍隊の～ the *mobilization* of troops. 機動隊が～した A riot squad *went into action*. 軍隊はそこへ～を命じられた The troops were ordered *to go* there. パトカーは～の準備を調えていた Squad cars were getting ready for *action*. 自衛隊が罹災(りさい)者の救助に～した The Self-Defense Forces *took action* to rescue the sufferers.

しゅつにゅう【出入】⇒でいり
—国管理庁 the Immigration Bureau.

しゅつば【出馬】¶ 彼は国会議員選挙に～するだろう He will *run for* (≒ *stand for*) Diet. 懸案解決に大臣の～を仰いだ We asked for the minister to *participate in* the solution of a pending problem.

しゅっぱつ【出発】departure; a start. ¶ ～の時間がきた The time for our *departure* has come. 私は～を延ばした I put off (≒ postponed) my *departure*. 彼らはパリからローマへ～した They *started from* (≒ *left*) Paris for Rome. 彼は新潟からナホトカへ船で～した He *embarked for* Nakhodka at Niigata. 彼は世界一周旅行に～した He *started on* an around-the-world trip. 飛行機は午前10時にパリからロンドンに向かって～する The plane *takes off* from Paris for London at 10 a.m. 彼の飛行機の～時刻を忘れた I forgot *the departure time* of his plane. 彼は人生の～点を誤った He *made a wrong start* in life.

しゅっぱん【出帆】¶ 彼はニューヨークへ向かって～した He *sailed for* New York. / He *set sail for* New York.
—日 the sailing day.

しゅっぱん【出版】publication. ¶ ～の自由 freedom of *the press*. その本の～年月日は不明だ The *publication* date of the book is unknown. その本はいつ～の予定ですか When is the book to *be published*? その本はまだ～されている The book *is* still *in print*. その本はもう～されていない The book *is* now *out of print*. その作品はイギリスで10種類以上の版が～されている There are more than ten editions of the work *in print* in Britain.
—界 the publishing world. —記念会 a party in honor of the publication of *a person's* book. —業 the publishing business. —権 the publication right. —社 a publishing company; a publisher. —物 a publication. —部数 the number of issues. 自費— ¶ 彼女はその本を自費～した She *published* the book at her own expense. 限定— limited publication. 予約— publication by subscription.

しゅっぴ【出費】expenses; expenditure (文語的な語). ¶ ～をきりつめなければならない I must cut down my *expenses*. ～を制限しなさい Limit your *expenditure*. ～がだいぶかさんだ My *expenses* have increased considerably. その計画の実行には多額の～を要する It will require very heavy *expenditure* to carry out the plan.

しゅっぴん【出品】exhibition; (出品物) an exhibit. ¶ バラをフラワーショーに～した I *exhibited* my roses at the flower show. 彼の絵はその画廊に～されている His paintings *are exhibited* (≒ *are on exhibition*) in the art gallery. ほかに数点おもしろい～があった There were several other *exhibits* of interest.
—点数 the number of exhibits. —目録 a catalog of exhibits. —者 an exhibitor. —物 an exhibit. ¶ ～物には手を触れないでください Please don't touch the *exhibits*.

じゅつぶ【述部】〔文法〕the predicate.

しゅっぺい【出兵】the dispatch of troops. ¶ 日本はシベリアに～した Japan *sent* (≒ *dispatched*) *troops to* Siberia.

しゅつぼつ【出没】¶ 人里近くにクマが～する Bears *appear frequently* in the neighborhood of the village. 海賊が島々に～した Pirates *infested* the islands.

しゅっぽん【出奔】¶ 彼は郷里を～した He *ran away* from home. 彼はその娘と～した(駆け落ちした) He *eloped with* the girl.

しゅつらん【出藍】¶ 彼は～の誉れが高い He *surpasses* (≒ *excels*) his *master* (≒ *teacher*).

しゅつりょう【出漁】¶ 捕鯨船団は南氷洋に～した A fleet of whalers *went out fishing* to the Antarctic.
—区域 a fishing area.

しゅつりょく【出力】output; generating power. ¶ ～2万キロワットの発電所 a power plant with the *capacity* of twenty thousand kilowatts of electricity. ～1,000馬力のモーター a motor that can develop a thousand h.p.
—計 an output meter.

しゅつるい【出塁】¶ ～者はない There is not any runner on base. 彼はフォアボールで～した He *took his base* on balls. 彼は～した He *got to first base*.

しゅと【首都】a capital; a metropolis.

―圏 the metropolitan circle.

しゅとう【種痘】vaccination. ¶～を受けた I *was vaccinated.* / I *took vaccination.* ～がついた The *vaccination* has taken.
―証明書 a vaccination certificate.

しゅどう【手動】¶機械は万一の場合には自動式から～式に切りかえられる In an emergency the machine is to be changed from self-operating to *hand-operated.*
―ブレーキ a hand brake.

じゅどう【受動】¶～的な passive.
―態〖文法〗the passive voice.

し

しゅどうけん【主導権】¶彼らが～を握っている They have *the initiative* (≒ *the leadership*). 激烈な～争いがあった There was a fierce contention for *the initiative.*

しゅとく【取得】acquisition. ¶彼は不動産を～した He *acquired* real estate.
―者 an acquisitor. ―税 an acquisition tax.

しゅとして【主として】chiefly; mainly.

じゅなん【受難】¶キリストの～ the *sufferings* of Christ〔on the cross〕; the Passion.
―劇(キリストの) a Passion play.

ジュニア a junior. ¶～サイズのブラウス a *junior-sized* blouse.

しゅにく【朱肉】vermilion inkpad.

じゅにゅう【授乳】¶赤ちゃんに～する *nurse* (≒ *suckle*) a baby.
―期 the lactation.

しゅにん【主任】the chief; the head. ¶彼が英語の～です He *is the head of* (≒ *is responsible for; chairman of*) the English department. 彼女が1年の～だ She *is in charge of* the lst year class.
会計― the chief treasurer. 教務― the chief of the instruction department. 捜査― the chief investigator. 編集― the chief editor; the editor in chief.

しゅぬり【朱塗り】¶～のお盆 a *vermilion-lacquered* tray.

しゅのう【首脳】the head; the leader.
¶社会党の～部 *the leading members* of the Socialist Party. 政府～ *the leaders* of the government. 米ソ～会議 a *top-level* conference between the United States and Soviet Russia. 5か国～会談 a five-power *summit* conference.

じゅのう【受納】acception. ¶つまらぬものですがご～ください Won't you please *accept* this gift of mine?

しゅはん【主犯】the principal offender.

しゅはん【首班】the head. ¶内閣の～ *the head* of a Cabinet. 共産党～内閣 a Communist-*headed* Cabinet. 議会は彼を～に指名した The Diet designated him to *the premiership.*

しゅび【守備】defense; (野球) fielding. ¶敵の攻撃にそなえて～陣地を強化する strengthen the *defenses* against the enemy's attack. 外野の～を固めた(野球) We strengthened the outfield. われわれは～についた(球技で) We *took to the field.* それは～ではうまいチームだった It was a strong team *on defense.* 彼は～がうまい(へただ) He is good (poor) at *fielding.*

しゅび【首尾】(結果) the result; (始めと終わり) beginning and end. ¶ヨットは～よく太平洋を横断した The yacht *succeeded in* sailing across the Pacific. その計画は最初から上～だった The plan *was successful* from the beginning. すべては～よくいった All *went well.* 商談の～はいかがでしたか *How* did the negotiation *come off*?
―一貫 ¶彼の言行は～一貫している There is *consistency* between his words and actions.

じゅひ【樹皮】the bark.

しゅひつ【主筆】¶新聞の～ *the chief editor* (≒ *the editor in chief*) of the newspaper.

しゅひつ【朱筆】¶誤りの箇所に～を加える correct errors.

じゅひょう【樹氷】trees covered with ice.

しゅひん【主賓】the guest of honor. ¶パーティーの～ *the guest of honor* at the party. 彼を～として晩餐(ばん)会が開かれた A dinner party was given *in honor of* him.

しゅふ【主婦】a housewife; a mistress. ¶一家の～ the *mistress* of a house.
―連〔合会〕the Housewives' Federation.

しゅふ【首府】a capital. ¶日本の～, 東京 Tokyo, the *capital* of Japan.

しゅぶ【主部】(主要部) the main part; 〖文法〗a subject.

しゅぶん【主文】the text; 〖文法〗the principal clause. ¶判決の～ *the text* of a decision.

じゅふん【受粉】〖植物〗pollination; fertilization.
人工― artificial fertilization.

しゅべつ【種別】classification.

しゅほ【酒保】a canteen; 米 a post exchange; P.X.; PX.

しゅほう【手法】a technique. ¶彼は日本画に西洋の～をとり入れた He introduced a Western *technique* into a Japanese drawing.

しゅほう【主峰】¶アルプスの～ *the highest peak* of the Alps.

しゅぼうしゃ【首謀者】a leader. ¶暴動の～ the *leader* (≒ *ringleader*) of the riot.

しゅみ【趣味】**1**〖楽しみ〗〔a〕taste. ¶彼は園芸に～がある He has *a taste* for gardening.
読書が彼の唯一の～だ Reading is his only *pastime.*
きみの～はなんですか What is your *hobby*?
私の～は旅行だ My *hobby* is traveling.
ゴルフには～がなくなった I have lost *interest* in golf.
それは～の問題と言える It may be a matter of *taste.*
彼は無～の人だ He is a man of no *taste.*
彼は多～の人だ He is a man of varied *tastes.*
2〖趣・気質〗¶彼は洗練された～の人だ He is a man of refined *taste.*
野球は私の～に合わない Baseball is not to my *taste.*

彼女は服装の～がすばらしい She has excellent *taste* in dress.
彼女の服装は～が悪い Her clothes are *in bad taste*.
彼のネクタイは～がいい He has good *taste* in ties.
このカーテンはあまり～がよくない This curtain is not in the best of *taste*.
シュミーズ a chemise.
じゅみょう【寿命】1〚生命〛a life; a life span. ¶息子の死が彼の～を縮めた His son's death shortened his *life*.
そのことが彼女の～を延ばした It prolonged her *life*.
日本人の～はどんどん伸びている The *life span* of the Japanese is rapidly growing longer.
彼の～も終わりだ His *life span* is nearly over.
医学の発展は人間の～を延ばした The development of medicine has lengthened a man's *life*.
ツルは～が長い Cranes *are long-lived*. / Cranes have *a* long *life*.
人間の平均～は延びた *The average life span* of a human being has been prolonged.
彼は～で死んだ He *died a natural death*.
2〚その他〛¶この電池は～がきたらしい The battery seems to have run down.
その流行は～が短かった The fashion had *a* short *life*.
しゅむ【主務】 —官庁 the competent authorities.
しゅもく【種目】 an item; (競技の) an event. ¶営業～ *items* of business. 彼は水泳競技の5～に優勝した He won the championship in five *events* of the swimming match.
しゅもく【撞木】 a wooden bell hammer.
じゅもく【樹木】 trees. ¶～のない山 *a treeless* mountain. ～の茂っている島 a *wooded* island.
じゅもん【呪文】 a spell; an incantation.
¶彼女は～を唱えはじめた She began to utter *an incantation* (≒ *a spell*).
しゅやく【主役】 the leading part; (男優) a leading actor; (女優) a leading actress. ¶その劇の～はだれですか Who is *a leading actor* in the play? 新人がその映画の～を演じた A new face played *the leading part* of the film. / A new face *starred* in the film.
彼はその運動の～だった He played *the leading part* of the movement.
じゅよ【授与】 conferment. ¶彼に文学士の称号が～された The degree of B. A. *was awarded to* (≒ *was conferred on*) him.
彼はノーベル文学賞を～された He *was awarded* the Nobel prize for literature. 校長から卒業証書が～された Diplomas *were granted* us by the director.
しゅよう【主要】 ¶～な chief; main; principal; essential; important.
—産業 key industries. —産物 leading (≒ staple) products; staples. —人物(劇などの) a central figure; the major characters. —都市 principal cities. —部 the main part.
しゅよう【腫瘍】〚医学〛a tumor (≒ 英 tumour).
悪性— a malignant tumor. 脳— a brain tumor.
じゅよう【受容】 acceptance.
じゅよう【需要】 〔the〕 demand. ¶～と供給 *demand* and supply. ～が供給を上回る The *demand* exceeds the supply. ～はかなり減じた The *demand* has considerably abated. 供給は～を満たせない The supply cannot meet the *demand*. たばこは大いに～がある There is *a* great *demand* for tobacco. / Tobacco *is in* great *demand*.
しゅよく【主翼】 the main planes.
しゅら【修羅】 ¶～のちまた a scene of bloodshed; a scene of carnage.
ジュラき【ジュラ紀】〚地質〛the Jurassic period.
ジュラルミン duralumin.
しゅらん【酒乱】 ¶彼は～だ He is *a vicious drunk*. / He loses his reason when he is drunk.
じゅり【受理】 acceptance. ¶彼の辞表は～された His resignation *was accepted*.
しゅりけん【手裏剣】 a dirk; a dart.
じゅりつ【樹立】 establishment. ¶彼らは新政府を～した They *established* (≒ *set up*) a new government. 彼は世界新記録を～するだろう He will *make* (≒ *establish*) a new world record.
しゅりゅう【主流】 the main current (≒ stream). ¶ドイツ哲学の～ *the main current of* German philosophy. 党の～派 the faction *in power*; *the leading faction* of a party.
しゅりゅうだん【手榴弾】 a 〔hand〕 grenade (grenade はスペイン語で「ざくろ」のこと. 形が似ていることから).
—兵 a grenadier.
しゅりょう【首領】 ¶山賊の～ *the chief* (≒ *the boss*) of bandits.
しゅりょう【狩猟】 hunting; shooting (hunting は広く狩猟に用いるが, イギリスではおもにキツネ狩り, ウサギ狩りなど銃を用いない狩猟に用いる. またかなりぜいたくなスポーツと考えられている).
¶彼らは～に出かけた They went *hunting* (≒ *shooting*).
—家 a hunter; a sportsman. —期 the hunting season. —禁止期 the close season. —場 a hunting ground. —法 the game law. —免許状 a shooting license.
しゅりょう【酒量】 ¶きみは～が多い You *drink heavily*. / You are *a heavy drinker*. きみは～を減らしなさい You must drink less.
じゅりょう【受領】 receipt. ¶金1万円まさに～いたしました *Received* with thanks the sum of ten thousand yen.
—証 a receipt. —者 a receiver.
しゅりょく【主力】 the main force. ¶主要教科に～を注いだ I *devoted myself to* the chief subjects. 彼は数学の勉強に～を注いだ He *concentrated all his energies on* the study of

し

mathematics.

—艦 a capital ship. —艦隊 the main fleet.

しゅるい【種類】a kind; a sort. ¶あらゆる〜のスポーツ all *kinds* (≒ *sorts*) of sports. 数〜のリンゴ several *kinds* (≒ *sorts*) of apples. この〜の花 this *kind* of flower; a flower of this *kind* (kind of につづく名詞にはふつう冠詞をつけない. kind of が形容詞のような役割をつとめるからである). どんな〜の小説が好きですか What *kind* (≒ *sort*) of novel do you like? 公園にはあらゆる〜の花々が咲きみだれている There are all *kinds* (≒ *sorts*) of flowers blooming in the park.

じゅれい【樹齢】¶〜300年の老木 an ancient tree of three hundred years old.

しゅれん【手練】skill. ¶〜の早業でその球を捕った He caught the ball *as quick as lightning*.

しゅろ【棕櫚】〖植物〗a hemp palm.

じゅわき【受話器】a receiver. ¶〜をとる(置く) take up (put down) *a receiver*. 彼は〜を耳に当てた He put the *receiver* to his ear. 彼は〜をとってダイヤルをまわした He picked up the *receiver* and dialed the number. 彼女は〜をはずしっぱなしにしておいた She left the *receiver* off the hook.

しゅわん【手腕】ability. ¶〜のある人(〜家) a man of *ability*; an *able* man. 〜に欠ける人 a man wanting in *ability*. 彼の経営の〜は抜群だ His administrative *ability* is splendid. 彼は〜を十分に発揮できなかった He could not show fully his own *ability* (≒ *skill*). 彼はこの方面ではすばらしい〜を発揮する He shows great *ability* in this direction.

しゅん【旬】¶イチゴの〜 the strawberry *season*. サンマは今が〜だ Mackerel pikes *are* now *in season*. / This is the mackerel pike *season*.

じゅん【純】¶〜日本的な婦人 a *purely* Japanese lady. 彼女はほんとに〜な子だ She is a very *innocent* (≒ *simple*) girl. 彼は〜日本式の家をつくった He built a house of a *purely* Japanese style.

—金 pure gold.

じゅん【順】(順序) order; (輪番) turn. ¶先頭からひとりずつ〜にお入りください Please enter *one by one* from the head. 〜不同 No special *order* is observed. それらはＡＢＣ〜に並べられてある They are arranged in alphabetical *order*. それらを大きさの〜に並べなさい Arrange them *in order of* size. 彼らは年齢〜に(身長の〜で)並んでいる They stand *in order of* age (height). 申し込み〜に受け付けます You will be accepted *in order of* application.

じゅん-【準-】—公式試合 a quasi-official match. —優勝者 the second winner. —急 a local express. —決勝 a semifinal. —会員 an associate member.

じゅんあい【純愛】pure love.

じゅんい【順位】order; ranking. ¶〜決定戦 a *ranking* deciding match; (同点者間の) a play-off.

しゅんえい【俊英】a genius.

じゅんえき【純益】a net profit. ¶今月は100万円の〜をあげた I *netted* (≒ *gained a net profit of*) a million yen this month.

じゅんえん【順延】¶雨天〜 In case of rain, it will *be put off* (≒ *be postponed*) *till the first fine day*.

じゅんか【純化】purification. ¶日本語を〜する運動 the movement to *purify* the Japanese language.

じゅんかい【巡回】a patrol; a round. ¶保健婦が受け持ちの家を10日に１度〜する The health nurse *makes the round* of the families under her charge every ten days. 〜中の巡査にであった I saw a policeman *on patrol* (≒ *on his beat*). 夜警が所定の場所を２時間おきに〜する A night watch *goes on a tour* of the appointed place every two hours. / Night watchmen *patrol* their beats every two hours.

—区域 *one's* beat; *one's* round. —講演 a lecture tour. —診療所 a traveling clinic.

じゅんかいいん【準会員】an associate member (「準…」は(アメリカの) 準教授 an *associate* professor のように associate... で表わす).

しゅんかしゅうとう【春夏秋冬】(四季) the four seasons; (一年じゅう) all the year round (英語でも四季はふつう春から数えはじめる).

じゅんかつゆ【潤滑油】lubrication oil.

しゅんかん【瞬間】a moment; an instant. ¶彼は私を見た〜, 戸の陰に隠れた *The moment* (≒ *As soon as*) he saw me, he hid himself behind the door. (The moment のほうが文語的). 次の〜, 彼は走って逃げた *The next moment* he ran away. ちょうどその〜ドアが突然開いた The door opened suddenly *at the very moment*. うっかりした〜に, さいふを落とした In *an* unguarded *moment*, I dropped my purse.

じゅんかん【旬刊】¶この雑誌は〜だ This magazine is *published* (≒ *issued*) every ten days.

じゅんかん【循環】circulation. ¶入浴は血液の〜によい Taking a bath is good for the *circulation* of blood. 血液は私たちのからだを〜する Blood *circulates* in our body. 彼女は血液の〜がいい She has *a good circulation*. 部屋を暖かくしておくために, 熱湯がパイプの中を〜している Hot water *circulates through* pipes to keep rooms warm.

—小数 a recurring decimal. —線 a loop line. 景気— a business cycle.

じゅんきゅう【準急】a local express.

じゅんきょ【準拠】¶この報告書は確たる事実に〜している This report *is based on* the established fact.

じゅんきょう【殉教】martyrdom. ¶自由のために〜する *die a martyr to* liberty.

—者 a martyr. キリスト教—者 a Christian martyr.

じゅんきょう【順境】prosperity. ¶彼は今〜にある He *is* now *in favorable* (≒ *pros-*

perous) circumstances. われわれの事業は～に向かいはじめた Our business bagan to take *a favorable turn.*

じゅんぎょう【巡業】 ¶ その劇団はここ２年間～を続けている The company *has been on the road* these two years. 彼女はその一座に加わって～中の役者だった She was an actress *on tour* in the company.

—劇団 a touring theater ; a traveling company. 地方**—** a provincial tour.

じゅんきん【純金】 pure gold.

じゅんぎん【純銀】 pure silver.

じゅんきんちさん【準禁治産】 quasi-incompetence.

—者 a quasi-incompetent.

じゅんぐり【順繰り】 ¶ 彼らは～に眠った They slept *by turns* (≒ *in turn*). (by turns は「次から次へと」または「交互に」, in turn は「一定の順をふんで次から次へと」の意味で, 両者は必ずしも同じではない).

じゅんけつ【純潔】 purity ; chastity. ¶ ～な心 a *pure* heart. ～な乙女 a *chaste* girl. 彼女は～を守っている She keeps her *chastity.*

—教育 education in sexual morality.

じゅんけつしゅ【純血種】 thoroughbred. ¶ ～の馬 a Thoroughbred. ～のコリー犬 a *thoroughbred* (≒ *pure-blooded*) collie.

じゅんけっしょう【準決勝】 a semifinal 〔game〕. ¶ わがチームは～に進んだ Our team won its way to the *semifinal* 〔*game*〕. わがチームは～で敗れた Our team was defeated in the *semifinal.*

—出場選手 a semifinalist.

しゅんけん【峻険・峻嶮】 ¶ ～な岩 a *rugged* rock.

しゅんげん【峻厳】 ¶ ～な先生 a *severe* teacher. 彼は教室ではいつも～な態度だ He always takes a *stern* attitude in the class. 彼は弟子たちに～すぎる He *is* too *severe with* his disciples.

しゅんこう【竣工・竣功】 completion. ¶ その建物はまもなく～を見るであろう The building will soon *be completed.* / The building will soon be brought to *completion.*

—式 the completion ceremony (*of* the building).

じゅんこう【巡航】 ¶ ～中の軍艦 the warship *on a cruise.* 主力艦隊は太平洋を～中である The main fleet *is cruising* on the Pacific.

—船 a cruiser.

じゅんさ【巡査】 a policeman ; 英 a constable (巡査に呼びかけるには Policeman ! と言わないで, Officer ! と言う).

—部長 a police sergeant. **—派出所** a police box. 交通**—** a traffic policeman.

しゅんさい【俊才】 a genius.

しゅんじ【瞬時】 a moment. ¶ 時の流れは～もとどまらず Time does not stop *a moment.* 光は～にして消えた The light vanished *in a moment* (≒ *in an instant*).

じゅんし【巡視】 an inspection. ¶ 工場を～した I *inspected* (≒ *went over*) the factory.

—人 a guard.

じゅんし【殉死】 ¶ 乃木将軍は明治天皇のあとを追って～した General Nogi *killed himself on the death of* Emperor Meiji.

じゅんじ【順次】 ¶ 製品はできしだい～お届けします We'll send products *in order* as soon as they are manufactured.

じゅんしゅ【遵守・順守】 observance. ¶ 規則の～ the *observance* of the rule. 法律を～しなければならぬ We must *observe* the law. 交通規則の～は厳重に励行されなければならない The *observance* of traffic laws must be strictly enforced.

しゅんじゅう【春秋】 spring and autumn. ¶ 彼らは～に富む青年たちだ They are young men *with a brilliant future before* them.

しゅんじゅん【逡巡】 hesitation. ¶ ～するな, すぐやれ Don't *hesitate.* Do it at once. いくぶん～していたが, 彼はついに話しだした After some *hesitation,* he at last began to talk. ～せずに彼はその計画を実行に移した He carried out the plan without *hesitation.*

じゅんじゅん【諄諄】 ¶ 彼に～と人の道を説いた I taught him humanity *earnestly.*

じゅんじゅんに【順順に】 ¶ ～部屋に入りなさい Enter the room *by turns* (≒ *in turn*). ⇒じゅんぐり

じゅんじょ【順序】 order. ¶ 正確な～を乱すな Don't disturb the exact *order.* 彼は～よく事を処理した He dealt with the problem *in good order.* 彼女は資料を～よくまとめた She arranged the data *systematically.* ～だてて話をしないとわからない If you don't talk *systematically* (≒ *in due order*), you cannot make yourself understood. この本の並べ方は～がでたらめだ These books are arranged *disorderly* (≒ *in bad order*). まず第一に, きみは彼の両親とそのことを話し合うのが～というものだ First of all, you should talk it over with his parents.

じゅんしょう【准将】 a brigadier 〔general〕.

じゅんじょう【純情】 ¶ ～な青年 a *pure-hearted* (≒ *simple-hearted*) young man.

じゅんしょく【殉職】 death on duty. ¶ 彼は～した He *died while he was engaged in his regular work.*

—者 ¶ 彼は～者として取り扱われた He was treated as *a victim to his post of duty.*

じゅんしょく【潤色】 embellishment. ¶ ～の跡 the marks of *embellishment.* 彼は話に事実と異なることをつけ加えて～した He *embellished* his story with untrue details.

じゅん·じる【殉じる】 ⇒じゅんずる

じゅんしん【純真】 ¶ ～な少年 an *innocent* boy. 彼女は～だ She *is pure in heart.* ～な子どもの心を踏みにじるな Don't trample on *pure and simple* hearts of the children.

じゅんすい【純粋】 purity. ¶ ～のコリー(犬) a *thoroughbred* (≒ *pure-blooded*) collie. 彼は～のイタリア人だ He is an Italian *born and bred* in Italy. 彼は～な生き方を求めている He looks for a *pure* way of life. 彼の～さには深く

心を打たれた I am deeply impressed with his purity.
—理性〘哲学〙 pure reason.
じゅん·ずる【殉ずる】 ¶ 彼は国に〜じた He *died for* his country.
じゅん·ずる【準ずる】 ¶ クラブでは正会員に〜ずる取り扱いを受けている At the club I am treated the same as a regular member.
じゅんせい【純正】 **—中立** perfect neutrality. **—科学** pure science.
しゅんせつ【浚渫】 ¶ 川を〜する *dredge* a river.
—機 a dredge. **—船** a dredger. **—作業** dredging work.
じゅんぜん【純然】 ¶ 〜たる国産品 a *purely* home product. その贈り物を〜たるわいろと断定することは難しい I find it difficult to judge the present to be a *downright* bribe (≒ a bribe *pure and simple*). 彼は〜たる共産主義者だ He is a communist *through and through*.
しゅんそく【俊足】 ¶ 〜の外野手 a *swift-footed* outfielder. かつては彼は門下生中の〜と言われた He was once called *the most talented* among the disciples.
じゅんたく【潤沢】 abundance. ¶ 資金は〜だ We have *a good supply of* funds. / We have *ample* funds.
じゅんちょう【順調】 ¶ 工事は〜に進んでいる The work is going *well*. ここ10日間天気は〜だ We have had *favorable* weather these ten days. 手術後の彼女の経過は〜だ She *is doing well* (≒ *is getting better favorably*) after the operation.
しゅんと ¶ しかられて子どもたちは〜なった The children were scolded and *got silent*. 彼の落選の報に一同〜なった All of them *became disappointed and silent* at the news of his failure in the election.
じゅんど【純度】 purity.
しゅんとう【春闘】 (春季闘争) a spring labor offensive.
じゅんとう【順当】 ¶ 有力チームが〜に勝ち進んだ Powerful teams went on winning *in due to course*. 〜にいけば総会は午後4時までには終わるはずだ *If nothing happens*, the general meeting will end by four in the afternoon.
じゅんに【順に】 in order; by turns; in turn; one after another; one by one. ¶ 彼らは〜歌った They sang *one after another* (≒ *in turn*). ⇒じゅんぐり
じゅんのう【順応】 adaptation. ¶ 〜性のある人 an *adaptable* person. 彼女は新しい環境に〜できなかった She was not able to *adapt* (≒ *adjust*) *herself to* the new environment. 彼は時勢に〜して生きている He *goes with the tide*. / He *swims with the stream*. 彼は〜性に欠けている He lacks *adaptability*.
じゅんぱく【純白】 ¶ 〜のドレス a *snow-white* dress (英米では white は幽霊のような無気味なものの代名詞でもある).
じゅんばん【順番】 (順序) order; (交代) turn. ¶ 〜がくるまで待ちなさい Wait till it is your *turn*. 彼は〜を待っていた He was waiting for his *turn*. とうとうぼくの〜になった At last my *turn* has come. その店の前に〜に並んだ We stood in front of the store *in a queue*. われわれは〜に眠った We slept *in turn* (≒ *by turns*). ⇒じゅんぐり
じゅんび【準備】 preparation. ¶ 昼食の〜ができました Lunch *is ready*. 会の〜をしなさい *Make preparations* for the party. 彼は試験の〜で忙しい He is busy *preparing for* an examination. 〜はもういいですか *Are* you *ready*? ピクニックの〜をしなければならない We must *get things ready for* the picnic. 出かける〜をしておきなさい *Get ready to* start. 〜はオーケーだ Everything is *ready*. 〜なしにそれをしようとしてはいけない Don't try to do it without any *preparation*.
—委員 a comittee of arrangements. **—金** a reserve fund.
しゅんびん【俊敏】 ¶ 〜をもって鳴る男だ He is famous for his *brilliance*. (bright は子どもが利口な場合に用いる).
しゅんぷう【春風】 a spring breeze. ¶ 彼は常に〜駘蕩(たいとう)としている He *is* always *mild and genial*.
じゅんぷう【順風】 a favorable wind. ¶ ヨットは〜に乗って走った The sailboat *sailed before the wind*.
しゅんぶん【春分】 the vernal (≒ spring) equinox. ¶ 〜の日 the *Vernal* (≒ *Spring*) *Equinox* Day.
—点 the vernal equinoctial point; the vernal point.
じゅんぶん【純分】 (金・銀の) fineness; (金の) carat.
じゅんぶんがく【純文学】 polite literature.
しゅん·べつ【峻別】 ¶ われわれは公私を〜しなければならない We must *draw the sharpline* between public life and private one.
じゅんぽう【遵法・順法】 **—精神** a law-abiding spirit. ¶ 彼らは〜精神に欠けている They are lacking in *a law-abiding spirit*. **—闘争** a law-abiding labor struggle. ¶ 労働組合は〜闘争に突入した The labor union got into *a law-abiding labor struggle*.
じゅんぼく【純朴】 ¶ 〜な田舎の老人 a *simple-hearted* country old man.
しゅんみん【春眠】 ¶ 〜暁を覚えず In spring one sleeps peacefully and soundly.
しゅんめ【駿馬】 a swift horse.
じゅんめん【純綿】 pure cotton; all cotton. ¶ 〜のワイシャツ an *all-cotton* shirt.
じゅんもう【純毛】 all wool; pure wool. ¶ 〜のセーター an *all-wool* sweater.
じゅんようかん【巡洋艦】 a cruiser.
じゅんら【巡邏】 a patrol; a round. ¶ 彼は〜中だ He *is making his round*. / He *is on his round*.
じゅんりょう【順良】 ¶ 〜な人 a *good and obedient* person.
じゅんりょう【純良】 ¶ 〜な pure; genuine. 〜な蜂蜜 *pure* honey.

じゅんれい【巡礼】a pilgrimage; (人) a pilgrim. ¶彼らは聖地へ～に出かけた They *went on a pilgrimage to* the sacred places.

じゅんれき【巡歴】¶彼らは聖跡を～するために出発した They started to *visit one* sacred place *after another*.

しゅんれつ【峻烈】¶～な批評 a *severe* (≒ *scathing*) criticism.

じゅんれつ【順列】〔数学〕permutation.

じゅんろ【順路】the route. ¶印刷した掲示があって参観者のとるべき～を示してある Printed signs point *the route* to be followed by visitors.

しょ【書】(筆跡) a hand; (書いたもの) a writing; (本) a book. ¶彼は～がへただ(りっぱだ) He *writes a poor* (*an excellent*) *hand*. これは空海の～だ This is *a writing* by Kukai. これはぼくの愛読の～だ This is my favorite *book*.

しょ-【諸-】¶～説 *various* opinions. ～君 you, my friends. ～国 *various* countries.

-しょ【-署】¶警察～ *a* police *station*. 消防～ *a* fire *station*. 税務～ *a* taxation *office*.

じょ【序】(序文) a preface; (初め) a beginning. ¶彼の本に～を書いた I wrote *a preface* to his book. 彼はその書に～を寄せた He contributed *a preface* to the volume. これはほんの～の口だ This is only *a beginning*. 長幼の～あり The younger should give precedence to the elder.

じょい【女医】a woman (≒ lady) doctor (複数形は women doctors となる).

しょいこ・む【背負い込む】¶彼のおかげでぼく大な借金を～んだ I *am saddled with* (≒ *am contracted*) a large debt by him.

しょいちねん【初一念】¶彼は～を貫いた He fulfilled his *ever-present* (≒ *original*) *intention*. / He realized his *long-cherished desire*.

しょいなげ【背負い投げ】¶彼を～で投げとばした I *threw him over my shoulder*.

しょいん【所員】a member of the staff; (総称的に) the staff.

しょいん【署員】¶税務～ *a* tax office *clerk*. 消防～ *a* fire *officer*.

しょう【小】smallness. ¶大は～を兼ねる The greater comprises *the less*. 大中～の三つのサイズがある There are three sizes, large, medium, and *small*.

しょう【性】nature; temperament. ¶～に合った仕事 a *congenial* work. 教師は彼の～に合った職業ではない Teaching *is* not *congenial to* him. / He *is* not *suited for* teaching. 彼とぼくは～が合う He *is congenial to* me. 当地の気候は彼の～に合わなかった The climate here did not *agree with* him. 中華料理はぼくの～に合わない Chinese dishes do not *agree with* me.

しょう【省】(イギリス・ヨーロッパ・日本では) a ministry; (アメリカでは) a department. ¶外務～ the *Ministry* of Foreign Affairs. 国務～ the *Department* of State.

しょう【章】¶第1～ the first *chapter*; *Chapter* 1.

しょう【勝】a victory; a win. ¶われわれは2～零敗だった We had two *wins* and no defeats.

しょう【賞】a prize; an award. ¶ノーベル文学～ the Nobel *Prize* for Literature. 彼女はその展覧会で～を得た She won (≒ gained) *a prize* at the exhibition. この～はその小説家を記念して設けられた This *prize* was instituted in memory of the novelist. その映画は1973年度のアカデミー～を得た The film won the Academy *Award* for 1973.

1等— the first prize. 残念— a consolation prize. 特— a special prize. 副— a supplementary prize.

しょう【抄】an extract; an excerpt; a selection. ¶源氏物語～ *extracts* from "The Tale of Genji."

しょう【将】a commander; (指導者) a leader. ¶一軍の～ the *commander* of the army.

しょう【衝】¶交渉の～に当たる *be in charge of* negotiations. 交通の～ *the forcus* of the trade route.

しょう-【正-】¶～1時に *just* at one o'clock.

しよう【子葉】〔植物〕a seed leaf.

しよう【私用】¶彼は～で外出した He went out *on personal* (≒ *private*) *business*. それを～に使ってはいけない Don't use it *for private purposes*.

しよう【使用】use. ¶このカメラは～に耐えない This camera cannot *be used*. このホールは一般に～されている This hall *is in* general *use*. この方法は現在～されていない This method *is* not *in use*. これらの語はシェイクスピアの作品にはひんぱんに～されている These words *are of* very frequent *use* in Shakespeare's works. この機械は7年間も～されている This machine *has been in use* these seven years. 鉛筆の～は許されない The *use* of a pencil is not allowed.

—権 the right of using (*a thing*). —者 a user. —法 how to use (*a thing*).

しよう【枝葉】¶～末節の問題 a *side* issue. それは～末節のことだ That is *a mere detail*.

しよう【試用】trial. ¶新薬を～する *try* (≒ *make a trial of*) new medicine.

しよう【仕様】¶彼はもうどう～もない *There's nothing to be done for* him. 降参するよりほかに～はなかった *There was nothing for it but* to surrender.

—書(書き) specifications.

しよう【止揚】〔哲学〕sublation. ¶～する sublate.

じょう【上】¶彼女は～の成績だった Her school record *is above the average*. これらの品物は品質によって, ～中下に分けられる These articles are classified by quality as *fine*, medium, and bad.

—巻 the first book.

じょう【条】(箇条) an article; an item. (すじ) a line; a streak; a stripe. ¶第8～によって under *Article* 8. 憲法第9～ the ninth *article* of the Constitution. 一～の光 *a streak of* light. 彼はその規則を～を追って説明した He

し

explained the rules *item by item*.

じょう【情】affection; heart; emotion; human nature. ¶～の深い人 an *affectionate* man. その人は～の薄い人だった He was a *hard-hearted* man. 彼女は～にもろい She is an *emotional* woman. これは子に対する母の～をあらわす話だ This is a story of *a* mother's *love* for her children. 彼を使いにやるのは～において忍びない We *are unwilling to* send him on an errand. この手紙には～がこもっている This is a very *affectionate* letter.

し

じょう【錠】a lock; (なんきん錠) a padlock; (薬) a tablet. ¶その部屋には～がかかっている(いない) The room *is on* (*off*) *the lock*. その部屋は中から～がかかっていた The room *was locked* from the inside. ドアに～をかけるのを忘れるな Don't forget to *lock* the door. ～をおろした(開けた) I fastened (opened) the *lock*. 彼はその～をこじ開けた He broke open the *lock*. 彼女はかぎで～を開けた She turned the key in the *lock*. このトランクにはじょうぶな～がついている The trunk has *a* good *lock*. このドアは～がかからない This door will not *lock*. この薬を毎食後30分に3～ずつ飲みなさい Take three *tablets* of this medicine thirty minutes after each meal.
アスピリン── an aspirin 〔tablet〕. 糖衣── a sugar-coated tablet.

じょう【嬢】¶花子～ *Miss* Hanako. お～さんはお元気ですか How is your *daughter*?

-じょう【-畳】¶6～敷きの部屋 a six-*mat* room.

-じょう【-帖】¶数～の紙 several *quires* (⇐ *pads*) of paper.

じよう【滋養】nourishment; nutrition.
¶～に富む食物 a *nutritious* (⇐ *nourishing*) food.
──物 nutriment; nourishment.

じょうあい【情愛】¶～がこまやかな女 a *warm-hearted* woman.

しょうあく【掌握】¶彼は民心を～している He *has a hold on* people. アメリカ軍は制空権を～した The United States army *obtained* the command of *the air*.

しょうい【少尉】(アメリカの陸軍・空軍) a second lieutenant; (アメリカの海軍) an ensign.

しょうい【傷痍】¶～軍人 a *wounded* soldier.

じょうい【上位】¶彼は勉強ではクラスの～にある He takes *a high rank* among his classmates in schoolwork. 陸軍少佐は大尉の～である A major *ranks above* a captain.

じょうい【譲位】abdication. ¶皇帝は皇太子に～した The emperor *abdicated* in favor of the crown prince.

しょういだん【焼夷弾】a fire (⇐ an incendiary) bomb.

しょういん【勝因】the cause of victory.

じょういん【上院】㊎ the senate; ㊊ the House of Lords.
──議員 ㊎ a senator; ㊊ a lord.

じょういん【冗員】superfluous members.

じょういん【乗員】(個人) a member of the crew; (集合的に) the crew.

しょううちゅう【小宇宙】microcosm.

しょううん【勝運】¶彼は～に恵まれた(見放された) *Luck* was with (against) him.

じょうえい【上映】screening. ¶その集まりではチャップリン映画を～するつもりだ We are going to *show* a Chaplin film at the gathering. とてもロマンチックな映画が～された A very romantic film *was put on the screen* (⇐ *was shown*; *was run off*). その映画はただいま有楽座で～中だ The film *is now on* at the Yurakuza.

しょうえん【荘園】〖歴史〗a manor.
──制度 manorialism.

じょうえん【上演】performance. ¶歌舞伎座では今,なにを～していますか What'*s on* at the Kabukiza? その劇はニューヨークで～された The play *was staged* (⇐ *was performed*) in New York. 彼らは来月ハムレットを～することになっている They are going to *stage* (⇐ *give a performance of*) Hamlet next month. 新作オペラが当地で～される A new opera will *be brought on the stage* here.

しょうおう【照応】correspondence; agreement; accordance. ¶…に～する correspond *to* ...; agree *with* ....

じょうおん【常温】〖物理〗〖化学〗normal temperature.

しょうおんき【消音器】(自動車の) a muffler.

しょうか【昇華】〖物理〗〖心理〗sublimation.
¶～する sublimate.

しょうか【消火】¶彼らは～につとめた They *fought the fire*. 彼らは～できた They *put out* (⇐ *extinguished*) *the fire*.
──器 a fire extinguisher. ──せん a fireplug; a hydrant. ──用ホース a fire hose.

しょうか【消化】digestion. ¶この薬は～を助ける This medicine helps *digestion*. この魚は～がいい This fish is easy to *digest*. この論文を～するのはたいへんなことだ It is no easy thing to *digest* this thesis.
──器 the digestive organs. ──剤 a digestive. ──不良 indigestion. ¶彼はすぐ～不良を起こす He is likely to suffer from *indigestion*.

しょうか【商科】a commercial course.
──大学 a commerce college.

しょうか【唱歌】a song; singing.
小学── a song for schoolchildren. ──集 a collection of songs.

しょうか【頌歌】〖キリスト教〗a hymn; (クリスマスの) a carol; anthem.

しょうが【生薑・生姜】ginger.

じょうか【浄化】purification; a cleanup.
¶彼らは政界の腐敗を～した They *cleaned up* corruption in the political world. この機械は部屋の空気を～する This machine *purifies* the air of a room.
──装置 a purifier. ──運動 a cleanup movement.

しょうかい【商会】a company; a firm; a concern. ¶林～ the Hayashi *Company*;

Hayashi & *Co*.

しょうかい【紹介】 introduction. ¶ 兄を～します Allow me to *introduce* my brother to you. 彼に～してほしい I want to *be introduced* to him. 彼に正式に～されたことがありますか Have you ever *met* him *formally*? ディケンズを最初に日本に～したのはだれですか Who first *introduced* Dickens to Japan? 彼の～で入会したいと思う I am going to join the society through his *introduction*.

—者 an introducer. —状 a letter of introduction. 自己— self-introduction. 職業—所 a public employment agency.

しょうかい【照会】 inquiry; reference. ¶ 彼について前の雇い主に～した I *inquired of* his last employer *about* him. / I *made reference to* his last employer. 在庫品について本社に～した I *made inquiries to* our main office *as to* the stocks. 彼の身元はだれに～すればわかりますか Who is his *reference*?

—先 a reference. —状 a letter of inquiry.

しょうかい【詳解】 ¶ 旧約聖書の～ *a detailed commentary on* the Old Testament. 彼がその本に～をつけた He gave *a full commentary on* the book.

しょうかい【哨戒】 ¶ たくさんの船が沿岸を～中だ Many boats *are on patrol* along the coast.

—艇 a patrol boat. —機 a patrol plane. —線 a patrol line.

しょうがい【渉外】 public relations. ¶ 彼は会社で～の仕事にまわった He engaged in *public relations* in the company.

—係 a public relations man. —事務 public relations business.

しょうがい【傷害】 injury. ¶ ぼくのは公務上の～だ My *injury* was one I suffered while on duty.

—罪 a charge of injuring another. —事件 an injury case. —保険 accident insurance.

しょうがい【障害】 an obstacle. ¶ この問題が～になっている This problem *gets in the way*. 思わぬ～に出くわした We met with unexpected *obstacles*. 彼は話しことばに～がある He has *a* speeh *defect*. ～を乗り越えて目的を達成すべくベストを尽くしなさい Do your best to *get over difficulties* in order to attain your purpose.

—物 an obstacle. —物競走 a hurdle race. 言語— an impediment in speech. 胃腸— gastro-enteric trouble. 身体—者 a physically handicapped person.

しょうがい【生涯】 a life; a career. ¶ 私の～の友 my *lifelong* friend. 彼の～の事業 his *lifework*. 彼女は～独身で過ごした She remained unmarried *for life*. 彼は～幸福な生活を送った He lived happily *throughout all his life*. そのあとずっと幸せな～であった He lived happily *ever after*. 彼はきのう70年の～を閉じた He ended his *life* of seventy years yesterday. 彼はその研究に～をささげた He devoted all his *life* to the study. 彼女は～ロンドンで過ごした She spent all her *life* in London. 彼の親切は～忘れません I will never forget his kindness *as long as I live*.

じょうがい【場外】 ¶ 観衆は球場の～にあふれた The spectators *overflowed* the stadium.

—ホームラン an out-of-the-park homer.

しょうかく【昇格】 promotion. ¶ その短大は大学に～した The junior college *was raised to* the status of university. 彼は課長に～した He *was elevated to* the post of a section chief.

しょうがく【小額】 ¶ ～の金を寄付する subscribe *a small sum* 〔*of money*〕 to (the school).

—貸し付け a small loan. —紙幣 a small note. —貨幣 a small coin.

しょうがく【商学】 commercial science.

—士 a bachelor of commercial science. —博士 a doctor of commercial science. —部 the school of commerce; the department of commercial science.

じょうかく【城郭】 (城) a castle; (城のとりで) a citadel; (城壁) castle walls.

じょうかく【城閣】 the watchtower of a castle.

しょうがくきん【奨学金】 a scholarship. ¶ 彼はその大学で～を得た He won *a scholarship* at the college. 私は～を受けている I hold *a scholarship*. 彼は～を受けている学生である He is a student *on scholarship*. / He is *a scholar*. 彼女は～をもらって留学した She went abroad *on a scholarship*. 2年間1か月1万円の～を与えられた I was awarded *a scholarship* of ten thousand yen a month for two years. われわれの大学でも～制度を設けた Our college founded *a scholarship*.

しょうがくせい【小学生】 a grade schoolboy (≒ schoolgirl); schoolchildren.

しょうがつ【正月】 the New Year; (元日) New Year's Day. ¶ ～の休み *the New Year* vacation. 旧の～ *the New Year* by the lunar calendar.

しょうがっこう【小学校】 米 a grade school; an elementary school; 英 a primary school. ¶ 弟は～の6年生だ My brother is in the sixth grade. / My brother is a sixth grader. 彼は～しか出ていない He had only *a grade school education*.

—教育 elementary education. —教員 米 a grade school teacher; 英 a primary school teacher.

じょうかまち【城下町】 a castle town.

しょうかん【召喚】 a summons. ¶ 彼は警察からの～に応じた He obeyed *a summons* from the police. 彼は裁判所から～された He *was summoned to* appear in the court. 裁判所は彼に～状を発した The court issued *a summons* on him.

しょうかん【召還】 a recall. ¶ 大使が本国に～された The ambassador *was recalled* (≒ *was summoned home*).

しょうかん【将官】 (陸軍) a general; (海軍)

し

an admiral; a flag officer.
しょうかん【商館】a trading house.
しょうかん【償還】repayment; redemption.
¶ 債券は～された The bonds *were redeemed*.
国債は来年～期限がくる The national bond will *be due for redemption* next year.
５年後に～の債券 a bond *redeemable* in five years.
—金 a redemption fund.
じょうかん【上官】a senior officer.
じょうかん【情感】emotion; sentiment.
しょうかんしゅう【商慣習】commercial customs.
じょうかんぱん【上甲板】the upper deck.
しょうき【正気】**1**〘本気・まとも〙 consciousness. ¶ 彼は～だ He *is in his right mind*.
きみは～でそう言うのか Do you *really mean* what you say?
彼が～でそんなことを言っているとは思われない He does not seem to be saying that sort of thing *in earnest*.
彼は～とは見えない He does not seem to *be* quite *right in his mind*. / He does not seem to *be in his right mind*. ⌈at last.
やっと～にもどった He *has come to himself*
とても～のさたではない It's *madness itself*.
～の人間ならそんなことはしない A man *in his senses* cannot do such a thing.
2〘意識〙 sense. ¶ 彼は～を失った He lost his *senses*.
２時間後に彼は～に返った He regained *consciousness* two hours later.
彼は～を失っていた He *was out of his senses*.
その子どもを～づかせるのにはかなりの時間がかかった It took me quite a long time to *bring* the child *to his senses*.
しょうき【商機】a business chance (≒ opportunity).
しょうぎ【将棋】Japanese chess. ¶ ～をさそう Let's play *Japanese chess*. ～のこまと盤 *chessmen* and *a chessboard*.
—倒し ¶ 彼らは～倒しに転んだ They *fell over like* 〔*a lot of*〕 *ninepins*.
じょうき【上気】¶ 彼の顔は興奮で～していた He *was flushed* with excitement.
じょうき【上記】¶ ～のとおり相違ありません I affirm *the above* to be true and correct in every particular.
じょうき【常軌】¶ 彼のふるまいはまったく～を逸している His conduct *is* quite *abnormal* (≒ *extraordinary*). 資材の高騰はまったく～を逸している The cost of materials has advanced *beyond all reason*.
じょうき【蒸気】steam; vapor. ¶ この機械は～で動く This machine goes (≒ is driven) by *steam*. この汽罐(かん)はよく～を発生する The boiler *steams* well.
—機関 a steam engine. —船 a steamer. —ボイラー a steam boiler. —暖房 steam heating.
じょうぎ【定規・定木】a ruler; a rule. ¶ ～で線を引く draw a straight line with *a rule*.
雲形— a curved rule. 三角— a set square. T— a T square.
じょうぎ【情義・情誼】friendly feelings. ¶ 彼は～に厚い人だ He is very *kind and warm-hearted*.
じょうきげん【上機嫌】¶ ～で歩いて家へ帰った I walked home *in great* (≒ *high*) *spirits*.
しょうきぼ【小規模】¶ ～の学校 a school *on a small scale*. 彼の商売は～で経営されている His business is operated *on a small scale*.
しょうきゃく【焼却】¶ 関係書類は～された The related papers *were burned up*.
—炉 a refuse-burner.
しょうきゃく【償却】¶ 設備(減価)の～ the *depreciation* of equipment. 減価～資金 a *depreciation* fund.
じょうきゃく【乗客】a passenger; a fare. ¶ その船は～定員3,000名だ The steamer can carry three thousand *passengers*.
—案内所 an information office for passengers (駅などではただ Information と指示してある). —専務車掌 a passenger conductor.
じょうきゃく【上客】a good customer.
しょうきゅう【昇級】promotion. ¶ 彼は～が早かった He won quick *promotion*. 彼は部長に～した He *was promoted to* the chief of a department.
しょうきゅう【昇給】a rise in salary. ¶ 年々の～ *a* yearly *pay increase*. 私は15パーセント～した I had *a* fifteen percent *rise in salary*.
１時間100円の～だった I got *a wage increase* of a hundred yen an hour. われわれは２割の～を要求した We demanded *a* twenty percent *rise* (≒ *hike*) *in salary*. ～は物価の値上がりで帳消しになるだろう *Wage increases* will soon be offset by price increases. われわれは彼女の月給を10万円に～させるつもりだ We will *increase* her monthly *salary* to a hundred thousand yen.
じょうきゅう【上級】a high rank. ¶ 彼は大学で私の２年～だった He was my *senior* at the university by two years.
—官吏 a senior official. —裁判所 a higher court. —生 a senior.
しょうきゅうし【小休止】a short rest.
しょうきょう【商況】¶ ～は活発(不振)である *Trade* (≒ *Business*) is active (dull). ～は上り坂だ(下り坂だ) *Business* is *improving* (*declining*).
しょうぎょう【商業】commerce. ¶ ～の中心 the center of *commerce*. 彼は～に従事している He is engaged in *trade*.
—英語 business English. —学校 a commercial school. —都市 a commercial city. —美術 commercial art.
じょうきょう【上京】¶ 彼は目下～中である He *is up in Tokyo*. 彼女はきのう～してきた She *came up to Tokyo* yesterday.
じょうきょう【状況】circumstances; a situation. ¶ 険悪な～ *a* threatening *situation*. 彼にその～を説明した I explained the *circumstances* to him. 目下の～では彼はその会に出席

できないだろう *Uuder the present circumstances*, he will not be able to attend the meeting. ～は深刻化しつつある The *situation* is becoming tense. ～が悪化した The *situation* deteriorated. ～がどうなっているか知らせてください Let me know how the *situation* stands.

—証拠〘法律〙circumstantial evidence.

しょうきょくてき【消極的】¶彼は何事にも～だ He *is passive* in everything. そんな～な態度ではだめだ You must not take such a *passive* attitude. 彼の性質は～だ He is of a *passive* disposition. 私はその計画を～に支持した I gave a *passive* support to the plan. 彼を～にほめた I gave him a *cold* praise.

しょうきん【賞金】¶彼は1等～10万円を獲得した He got (≒ was awarded) the first *prize* of a hundred thousand yen.

じょうきん【常勤】¶～の先生 a *full-time* teacher.

じょうくう【上空】¶飛行機が8機東京湾の～を飛んだ Eight airplanes *flew over* Tokyo Bay. 飛行機は1万メートルの～でエンジンが故障した The engine of the airplane was out of order *at a height of* ten thousand meters.

しょうぐん【将軍】a general; (幕府の) a *shogun*. ¶グラント～ *General* Grant.

じょうげ【上下】up and down. ¶身分の～ *the upper and lower classes*. ～2巻の本 a book *in two volumes*. そのおもちゃの馬は首を～に動かした The toy horse bobbed its head *up and down*. 身分の～にかかわらずみなそこに集まった *High and low* gathered there. 東海道新幹線は～線とも不通 Both *up and down* trains are stopped on the New Tokaido Line.

しょうけい【小計】¶～はいくらでしょう What does *the total* come to?

じょうけい【上掲】¶～の above-mentioned.

じょうけい【情景】a scene; a sight.

しょうけいもじ【象形文字】a hieroglyph; a hieroglyphic character.

しょうげき【衝撃】a shock. ¶爆発の～でたくさんの人が大けがをした A lot of people were badly wounded by the *shock* of the explosion. 大統領急死のニュースは世界に大きな～を与えた The news of the president's sudden death gave *a* great *shock* to the world.

—波〘物理〙a shock wave. —療法〘医学〙shock treatment (≒ therapy).

しょうけつ【猖獗】¶流感が～をきわめている The flu *is raging*.

しょうけん【証券】(一般に証券類) securities; (公社債) a bond; (株券) a stock certificate. ¶彼は～類を銀行に預けてある He keeps his *securities* at the bank.

—会社 a securities corporation. —取引所 a stock exchange. 預かり— warehouse receipts. 有価— securities.

しょうげん【証言】testimony; witness. ¶彼に会ったことがあると～した I *testified* that I had seen him. 彼の無罪を～できる I can *testify* to his innocence.

—台 ¶～台に立つ take *the witness stand*.

じょうけん【条件】a condition; a term. ¶勤勉が第一の～だ Diligence is the first *condition*. この～に応じてください Won't you accept the *terms*? 一つ～をつけてきみの要求を認めよう I will acknowledge your request *on* one *condition*. 公平な～で取引をしたい Let's carry on trade *on* fair *terms*. 彼の失敗を考えると, まさに失敗の～がそろっていた When we consider how he failed, he was indeed full of *the causes of* failure.

—反射 conditional reflex. —文 a conditional sentence. 労働— work conditions.

じょうげん【上弦】¶～の月 a young moon; a waxing crescent.

じょうげん【上限】the highest limit; the ceiling.

しょうこ【証拠】evidence; 〔a〕 proof; testimony. ¶なんの～もない No *evidence* is to be found. どんな～がありますか What *evidence* do you have? これが確実な～だ This is *a* positive *proof*. 彼が犯人だという～はない There is nothing to *prove* that he has committed a crime. そのとき彼が家に不在だったという十分な～がある There is sufficient *evidence* that he was away from home then. 有罪を証明するためには法廷は～を必要とする In order to prove that a man is guilty a court requires *evidence*. なにを～にきみはそう言うのか What *proof* do you have of what you say? 彼のこの著書は学識の高いことの～だ This work of his *testifies* to his high standard of scholarship. 彼のろうばいしたようすは, なにかやましいことをしている～だろう His dismayed look seems to be *testimony* of his consciousness of guilt. 論より～(諺) *The proof of the pudding is in the eating*. ～不十分のため彼は釈放された He was set free for lack of *evidence*.

—固め the gathering of evidence. —金 a deposit. —書類 documentary evidence. —調べ the taking of evidence. —物件 an evidential matter.

しょうご【正午】noon. ¶彼らは～に昼食をとる They have lunch *at noon*.

じょうご【上戸】笑い— a merry drinker. 泣き— a maudlin drinker. 怒り— a vicious drinker.

じょうご【漏斗】a funnel. ¶～形の funnel-shaped.

じょうご【冗語】a redundant word; wordiness.

しょうこう【小康】a lull. ¶彼の病気は～を保っている There has been *a slight improvement* in his condition. 国際収支は～状態にある There is *a lull* in the balance of international payments.

しょうこう【昇汞】〘化学〙corrosive sublimate.

—水 a solution of corrosive sublimate.

しょうこう【昇降】going up and down. ¶それは電気で～する It *goes up and down*

(≒ *rises and falls*) by electricity.
—口 an entrance; (船内の) a hatchway. **—舵** the elevator push-pull rod. **—機** an elevator; 英 a lift.

しょうこう【将校】 an officer. ¶ 陸(海; 空)軍～ *a* military (*a* naval; *an* air force) *officer*. 高級～ *a* high-ranking *officer*.

しょうこう【商工】 **—会議所** a chamber of commerce and industry. **—業** commerce and industry.

しょうこう【焼香】 ¶ 仏前で～する *burn incense* for the dead.

し

しょうごう【称号】 a title; a name; (学位) a degree. ¶ 博士の～ *a* doctor's *degree*; a doctorate. 彼に名誉市民の～が贈られた The *title* of an honorable citizen was conferred on him.

しょうごう【商号】 (店名) a firm name; (商品名) a trade name.

しょうごう【照合】 checking; collation. ¶ 計算書を原簿と～する *check* an account with a ledger.

じょうこう【条項】 provisions; articles; clauses. ¶ 法文の～を検討する investigate (≒ examine) each *article* of the law. ～に基づいて under the terms.

じょうこう【乗降】 **—客** passengers getting on and off (the train).

しょうこうい【商行為】 business.

しょうこうねつ【猩紅熱】〔医学〕 scarlet fever.

しょうこく【小国】 a small nation.

しょうごく【生国】 ¶ 彼の～は高知だ Kochi is *his native province*. / He comes from Kochi.

じょうこく【上告】 a final appeal. ¶ ～を棄却された The *appeal* was dismissed (≒ was rejected). 上級裁判所へ～するつもりだ I will *appeal to* a higher court.
—審 a hearing of final appeal.

しょうこり【性懲り】 ¶ 彼は何度も失敗したのに, ～もなくまたやると言っている In spite of his repeated failures, he *insists on* making another attempt.

しょうこん【商魂】 ¶ 彼は～がたくましい He *is shrewd in business*.

しょうさ【小差】 ¶ ～で勝った We won *by a narrow margin*.

しょうさ【少佐】 (陸軍) a major; (海軍) a lieutenant commander.

じょうざ【上座】 ¶ 主賓が～に座った The guest of honor sat at *the top of the table*. / The guest took *the honored seat*.

しょうさい【商才】 business ability (≒ capacity); a knack for business. ¶ 彼は～にたけている He *is a shrewd businessman*. / He *is shrewd in business*.

しょうさい【詳細】 ¶ 彼はその事故を～に語った He told the accident *in detail*. / He gave *a full detail of* the accident. その事件の～な報告を受けた I received a *full* (≒ *detailed*) report on the event. さらに～については手紙でお知らせします *For further details* I will write to you.

じょうさい【城塞】 a fortress; a citadel.

じょうざい【錠剤】 a tablet.

じょうざい【浄財】 ¶ ～を募る raise *a subscription*.

じょうさし【状差し】 a letter rack.

しょうさっし【小冊子】 a pamphlet; a booklet.

しょうさん【勝算】 ¶ あすの試合はわれわれに～がある(ない) Tomorrow *the odds are in our favor* (*are against us*).

しょうさん【硝酸】〔化学〕 nitric acid.
—塩 a nitrate. **—カリウム** potassium nitrate. **—銀** nitrate of silver.

しょうさん【賞賛・称賛】 praise; admiration. ¶ その行為は～に値する The deed is worthy of *praise*. / It is a *praiseworthy* deed. われわれは彼の勇敢な行為を～した We praised him for his brave deed. 彼は人々の～を博した He won the *admiration* of the public. 彼の勇気は全市民の～の的となった His courage was the *admiration* of all the citizens. 私も彼を～する者のひとりだ I am one of his *admirers*, too.

しょうし【笑止】 ¶ それはまったく～千万だ It is utterly *ridiculous*.

しょうし【証紙】 a certificate stamp.

しょうじ【商事】 **—会社** a commercial (≒ trading) firm.

しょうじ【小事】 a trifle; a trivial matter. ¶ ～にこだわる stick at *trifles*.

しょうじ【障子】 a *shoji*; a paper sliding screen.

じょうし【上司】 *one's* superior 〔officer〕.

じょうし【上肢】 the upper limbs; the arms.

じょうし【城址】 the ruins of a castle.

じょうじ【情事】 a love affair.

じょうじ【常時】 (常に) constantly.

しょうじき【正直】 honesty. ¶ ～な人は信用される Those who *are honest* are trusted. ～は最良の策である(諺) *Honesty is the best policy*. ～者がばかをみることもある *Honesty* does not always pay. ～なところその案には私は反対だ *Frankly speaking*, I am against the plan. ～に言って私は英作文は苦手だ *To confess the truth*, I am not good at English composition.

じょうしき【常識】 common sense. ¶ それは～だ That is *a matter of common knowledge*. 彼は～に欠けている He lacks *common sense*. そんなことはもう～になっている Everybody knows that. ～のある人 a man *of common sense*. ～を働かせなさい I want you to exercise your *common sense*.

しょうしつ【消失】 ¶ 権利が～する The right *vanishes*.

しょうしつ【焼失】 ¶ 市の大半が～した The better part of the city *was burnt down* (≒ *was destroyed by fire*). その家は～を免れた The house escaped *the fire*.

じょうしつ【上質】 **—紙** the best quality paper.

じょうじつ【情実】personal considerations. ¶～にとらわれるな Don't be influenced by *personal considerations*. 彼の昇級には～がからんでいる He owes his promotion to some *private considerations*. 彼は～をいっさい排した He set aside all *private considerations*.

しょうしみん【小市民】people of the lower middle class.

しょうしゃ【商社】a〔trading〕firm.

しょうしゃ【勝者】a winner ; a victor.

しょうしゃ【照射】irradiation. ¶患部に放射線を～する *apply* radioactive rays *to* the affected part.

しょうしゃ【瀟洒】¶～な服装の紳士 a gentleman in *stylish* clothes. 彼は～な服装をしている He is *smartly* dressed.

じょうしゃ【乗車】¶～する *get on* (a bus ; a car ; a train). タクシーの運転手は～拒否をした The taxi driver rejected me.

——口 an entrance ; a way-in. ——券 a (railroad; streetcar) ticket. ——賃 railroad fare ; car fare.

じょうしゅ【城主】the lord of a castle.

じょうしゅ【情趣】¶～に富む山村 a *charming* mountain village. ～に富んでいる詩 poems full of *sentiment*.

じょうじゅ【成就】accomplishment ; achievement. ¶彼は事業を～させた He *accomplished* (≒ *achieved*) the enterprise. ついに大願～せり My prayer *is heard* at last.

しょうしゅう【召集】a call ; a summons ; (動員) mobilization ; (議会の) convocation. ¶臨時国会が～された An extra session of the Diet *was convoked* (≒ *was convened*). 彼は～されて戦争に行った He *was summoned* to〔go to〕war.

——令状 a call-up paper.

しょうじゅう【小銃】a rifle.

——弾 a bullet.

じょうしゅう【常習】¶彼は麻薬の～患者だ He takes a narcotic drug *habitually*. / He is a drug addict.

——犯 a habitual crime ; (人) a habitual criminal ;〘法律〙a recidivist.

しょうじゅつ【詳述】¶事件の原因を～する *explain* the cause of an incident *in detail*.

じょうじゅつ【上述】¶～の本 *above-mentioned* books. ～したとおり as *stated* (≒ *mentioned*) *above*.

じょうしゅび【上首尾】¶それは～だった It was *a great success*. 彼との交渉は～にいった We negotiated with him *successfully*.

しょうじゅん【照準】¶その獲物に慎重に～を合わせた I *trained* (≒ *aimed* ; *sighted*) my gun carefully *upon* (≒ *at*) the game. / I took *a* careful *sight* at the game.

じょうじゅん【上旬】¶3月～に *early* in March ; in *early* March.

しょうしょ【詔書】an Imperial edict.

しょうしょ【証書】a bond ; a deed ; (証明書) a certificate.

——貸し付け a deed loan. 卒業——(大学の) a diploma ; (学位を伴わない) a certificate.

しょうじょ【少女】a〔little〕girl. ¶～らしい遊び a *girlish* game.

——時代 girlhood. ——趣味 girlishness. ——小説 a story for girls.

じょうしょ【浄書】¶この作文は～しなさい *Make a fair copy of* this composition.

しょうしょう【少将】(海軍の) a rear admiral ; (陸軍の) a major general.

しょうしょう【少少】(量) a little ; (数) a few ; (程度) a bit. ¶～お待ちください One moment, please. 彼は東洋美術について～勉強した He studied *a little* about Oriental art. 彼女はほんの～フランス語が話せる She can speak *only a little* French. ぼくは～疲れた I am *slightly* (≒ *a bit*) tired. 砂糖を～くれませんか May I have *a little* sugar? 彼は～のミスは許してくれた He pardoned me *a few* mistakes.

しょうじょう【症状】(病状) the condition of illness ; (兆候) symptoms. ¶肺炎の～が現われている You have *symptoms* of pneumonia.

自覚—— a subjective symptom. 中毒—— toxic symptoms.

しょうじょう【賞状】a certificate of commendation ; (主として軍事的) citation. ¶私はことし学業優良の～をもらうことになった I'm to be awarded *a certificate* of efficient study this year.

じょうしょう【上昇】¶物価の～ *a rise in* price. 温度の～ *a rise in* temperature. 気温が～する The temperature *rises*. 彼の人気は～中である His popularity *is going up*. 景気が～する Business *is looking up*. わが社の利益は毎年～している Our company is making a larger profit year by year.

じょうしょう【常勝】¶～軍(チーム) an *invincible* army (team).

じょうじょう【上上】¶きょうはピクニックに～の天候だ This is *the best* weather for a picnic. / We can hope no better weather than this for the picnic. コンディションは～だ I'm in *the best* condition.

じょうじょう【上場】〘株式〙¶その会社の株は市場に～された The company's stocks *are listed in* the market.

——株 listed stocks. ——基準 listing requirements. ——廃止 delisting.

じょうじょう【情状】circumstances. ¶裁判官は～を酌量した The judge took the *circumstances* into consideration. 彼の犯罪は～を酌量の余地がない Nothing can *extenuate* his crime.

しょうしょく【小食・少食】¶彼は～だ He is *a light* (≒ *small*) *eater*.

じょうしょく【常食】¶日本人は米を～としている The Japanese *live on* rice. 牛は草を～にしている Cows *feed on* grass.

しょう･じる【生じる】¶そのため一大変化が～じた A great change *was brought about* by it. 火災のため幾多の問題が～じた A lot of problems *arose* because of the fire. 圧制は反乱を～じた Tyranny *gave rise to* a rebellion.

地震により少なからぬ損害が～じた Not a little damage *was caused by* the earthquake.

じょう·じる【乗じる】 ¶ 2に3を～じると6になる Two *multiplied* by three makes six. / Three times two is six. 彼は私の無知に～じた He *took advantage of* my ignorance. 彼らは夜陰に～じて逃亡した They escaped *under cover of* (≒ *taking advantage of*) darkness.

しょうしん【小心】 ¶ ～な人 a *timid* person. ～翼々たる scrupulous.

しょうしん【昇進】 promotion. ¶ 彼は～が早い He is quick in *promotion*. 私には～の見込みがない I have no prospect of *promotion*. 彼は実力で～した He has got *promotion* by merits.

しょうしん【傷心·傷神】 ¶ ～の人 a *heart-broken* person. 彼女は～のあまり自殺した *Grief* drove her to suicide.

しょうじん【精進】 (努力) devotion; (肉食を避ける) abstinence from meat. ¶ 彼は日夜仏道に～する He *devotes himself to* Buddhism.
—揚げ fried vegetables. —潔斎 religious purification. —料理 a vegetable diet.

じょうしん【上申】 ¶ この事実を当局へ～しなければならない We must *report* this fact to the authorities.
—書 a report.

じょうじん【常人】 an ordinary man.

しょうしんしょうめい【正真正銘】 ¶ この刀は～の正宗だ This is a *genuine Masamune* sword. 彼は～の日本人だ He is a *true* (≒ *genuine*) Japanese.

じょうず【上手】 ¶ 彼はピアノが～だ He *is good at* playing the piano. 彼女は泳ぎが～だ She is a *good* swimmer. 英語が～になりたい I want to *improve* my English. 彼はこのクラスでいちばんテニスが～だ He is *the best* tennis player in this class. 彼は話し～, 彼女は聞き～だ He is a *good* talker, while she is a *good* listener. タイプが～になった I *have become expert in* typewriting.

しょうすい【憔悴】 ¶ ～した顔 a *haggard* face. 彼は過労で～しきっている He *is* utterly *exhausted* (≒ *worn-out*) *with* overwork.

じょうすい【上水】 water supply; service water. ¶ 玉川～ *service water* from the Tamagawa.
—道 waterworks.

じょうすい【浄水】 clean water.
—場 a cleaning bed.

しょうすう【小数】〔数学〕a decimal.
—点 a decimal point. ¶ ～点以下第2位まで計算する calculate down to the second *decimal* place. 有限(無限)— a finite (an infinite) decimal.

しょうすう【少数】 a few; a small number. ¶ ～の賛成者 *a small mumber* of supporters. 反対者は～だった Only *a few* were against it. パーティーの出席者は～だった *A small number* of people attended the party. われわれは～精鋭主義を採っている We make it a principal to have *a few* capable members.
—党 a minority party. —派 a minority. —民族 a minority race. —意見 a minority opinion.

じょうすう【乗数】〔数学〕a multiplier.
被— a multiplicand.

じょうすう【常数】〔数学〕a constant.

しょう·する【称する】 call; (偽って) pretend. ¶ 大森と～する男 A man *named* Omori. 彼はブリッジの名人と～されている He *is called* a master of bridge. 彼は刑事と～して私の金をだまし取った *Representing himself as* a detective, he cheated me out of the money. 多忙と～して彼はパーティーに来なかった He did not attend the party *on* (≒ *under*) *the pretext of* being too busy. 彼は病気と～して働かない He *pretends to be* ill and never works.

しょう·する【賞する】 ¶ 彼らの善行を～し, 表彰した I *recognized* their good act and honored them. 彼の勇気は～するに足る His courage is worthy of *praise*.

しょう·する【証する】 ¶ 本校の生徒であることを～する I do hereby *certify* that he is a student of our school.

しょうせい【小生】 I.

しょうせい【小成】 ¶ ～に甘んじるな Don't be content with *a small success*.

しょうせい【招請】 invitation. ¶ 会議に彼を～した We *asked* (≒ *invited*) him to the conference.

じょうせい【情勢·状勢】 a situation. ¶ 緊迫した世界～ the tense world *situation*. ～が怪しくなる The *situation* becomes unstable. 彼にはこの難しい～が切り抜けられない He cannot manage this difficult *situation*. 現在の～はわれわれには不利だ The present *situation* (≒ *state of affairs*) is unfavorable to us.

じょうせい【上製】 —本 a *de luxe* edition.

じょうせい【醸成】 ¶ 酒を～する *brew sake*. その運動に協力する機運を～しよう Let's *produce* the mood to cooperate in the campaign.

しょうせき【硝石】〔化学〕niter (≒ 英 nitre).
チリ— Chile saltpeter.

じょうせき【定石】 ¶ そうするのが～になっている It's *a rule* to do so. 碁の～を学んだ I learned the *formulas* in the game of *go*.

じょうせき【上席】 seniority; an upper seat. ¶ 彼はテーブルの～についた He took *the head* of the table.

しょうせつ【小説】 a novel. ¶ 事実は～より奇なり Fact is stranger than *fiction*.
—家 a novelist. 懸賞— a prize novel. 新聞— a newspaper novel. 短編— a short story. 長編— a novel. 通俗— a popular novel.

しょうせつ【小節】〔音楽〕a bar.

しょうせつ【詳説】 detailed explanation. ¶ このことについてはあとで～する I'm going to *explain* the matter *in detail* later.

じょうせつ【常設】 —委員会 a standing

committee.

じょうぜつ【饒舌】¶～な talkative; garrulous; voluble.

しょうせっかい【消石灰】〖化学〗slaked lime.

しょうせっこう【焼石膏】plaster of Paris.

しょうせん【商船】a merchant ship; a merchantman; (全体) the merchant marine.
—隊 a marine fleet. —大学 a marine college.

しょうぜん【悄然】¶～と dejectedly. 彼は失敗して～としていた He *was dejected* at his failure.

じょうせん【上船・乗船】embarkation.
¶彼は午後3時に～した He *went on board the ship* at three in the afternoon. 彼は神戸で～してホンコンへ向かった He *took a ship* at Kobe for Hong Kong.

しょうぜんてい【小前提】〖論理〗a minor premise.

しょうそ【勝訴】¶被告が～した The defendant *won the case*.

じょうそ【上訴】an appeal. ¶最高裁判所に～する *appeal to* the Supreme Court.

しょうそう【少壮】¶～有為の実業家 a promising *young* businessman.

しょうそう【焦燥】¶～の感にかられながら彼を待った I waited for him *with impatience*.
—感 ¶彼は～感にかられていた He *was in a fret*. / He *was irritated*.

しょうそう【尚早】¶それを実行するのは時期～だ *It is too early* (≒ *The time has not yet come*) to carry it out.

しょうぞう【肖像】a portrait. ¶～をかいてもらった I had my *portrait* painted.
—画 a portrait. —画家 a portrait painter.

じょうそう【上層】(地層) the upper stratum (複 strata); (階級の) the upper classes; (建物の) the upper stories. ¶社会の～部 *the upper classes* of society.
—雲 the upper clouds. —階級 the upper classes. —気流 the upper air-current. —大気 the upper atmosphere.

じょうそう【情操】aesthetic appreciation. ¶～教育をする cultivate *one's aesthetic appreciation* (≒ *sensibilities*).

じょうぞう【醸造】brewing; distilling. ¶酒は米で～する *Sake is brewed* from rice. このブランデーは1939年の～だ This brandy *was distilled* in 1939.
—家 a brewer. —元 a brewery.

しょうそく【消息】news. ¶彼から～がありましたか *Have* you *heard anything* from him? 彼からはなんの～もない I *have heard nothing from* him. 彼の～はない I *have heard nothing of* him. 彼はここ1か月～を絶っている He *has been missing* for a month.
—通 ¶彼は経済界の～通だ He *is well versed in* economic matters.

しょうぞく【装束】a dress; costume.
¶白～の花嫁 a bride *dressed in* white.

しょうたい【小隊】a platoon.
—長 a platoon leader.

しょうたい【正体】true character. ¶盗人は～を現わした The thief has shown his *true colors*. 大男が～なく眠っている A big man *is sleeping like a log*. ～なく酔っている He *is dead drunk*. 電話の声の～はまだつかめない The *identity* of the voice on the telephone is still not clear.

しょうたい【招待】〔an〕invitation. ¶私は彼を夕食に～した I *invited* him to dinner. 彼の誕生日のパーティーに～された I *was invited to* his birthday party. ご～いただきありがとうございます Thank you for your kind *invitation*. 彼はイギリス政府の～でロンドンへ行った He went over to London *at the invitation of* the British Government.
—客 a〔invited〕guest. —券 an invitation card. —状 a letter of invitation. —日(絵画展などの) a preview.

じょうたい【上体】the upper part of the body. ¶～を反らす bend *oneself* back.

じょうたい【状態】a condition. ¶彼の商売は絶望～だ His business is in *a* helpless *condition*. 患者はまだ危険な～にある The patient is still in *a* critical *condition*. 球場はプレーできる～にある The baseball ground is in *a* playable *condition*.

じょうたい【常態】a normal condition; a usual state. ¶事故現場は～に復した The spot where the accident happened was restored to *a normal condition*. 彼の言動は～ではない His speech and behavior are *abnormal* (≒ *not normal*).

じょうだい【上代】ancient times (英米の ancient は主としてギリシア・ローマを指す).
—史 the history of remote antiquity. —文学 ancient literature.

しょうたく【沼沢】a marsh; a swamp.
—地 a swamp area.

しょうだく【承諾】a consent. ¶彼はヨーロッパ行きを～した He *consented* to go over to Europe. 彼は二つ返事で娘の結婚を～した He gave *a* ready *consent* to his daughter's marriage. 彼の～を得たほうがいい You had better have his *assent*. 彼は私の要求を～してくれるだろう He will be willing to *comply with* my request. 彼を説得して～させることは難しい It is difficult for me to persuade him to *agree with* me.

じょうたつ【上達】progress; improvement. ¶英会話が～した I *have improved in* (≒ *have made progress in*) my English conversation. / My English speaking ability *has* much *improved*. 彼はフランス語の～が早い(遅い) He makes rapid (slow) *progress* in French.

しょうだん【商談】a business talk. ¶私はその土地のことで地主と～した I *negotiated* with the landlord about the land. 1平方メートル20万円で彼とその～を取り決めた I *struck the bargain with* him at two hundred thousand yen a square meter.

じょうたん【上端】the upper end; the top.

じょうだん【上段】(寝台車の) an upper berth. ¶それらの本を本だなの～に並べた I placed those books on *the upper row* of the bookshelf. 寝台車の～に席をとった I took *an upper berth* in the sleeping carriage. 彼は刀を～に構えた He held his sword *over his head*.

じょうだん【冗談】a joke. ¶彼はよく～を言う He often *jokes*. 彼は～がわからない He has no sense of *humor*. ～ばかり言っている人にも困る We feel puzzled to have someone who *is* always *joking*. ～はやめてほしい None of your *jokes*! ご～でしょう You *are* only *joking*, aren't you? (比較的やわらかい言い方) / You must *be joking*! (強い言い方). ～もほどほどにすべきだ He is carrying the *joke* too far. 彼は～半分に私のことを「小犬」などと言う He calls me "Puppy" *half in joke*. 彼はまじめな顔をしてよく～を言う He often *cracks jokes* with a straight face.

しょうち【招致】¶この町に観光客を～する努力をなすべきである We have to make efforts to *invite* sightseeing tourists to our town.

しょうち【承知】¶そんなことは～している I *am aware of* that. ご～のように私はこの辺は初めてです *As you know*, I am a stranger here. 難しい手術だとは十分～しています I *know* well that it is a difficult operation. 彼は私の案を～した He *consented to* my proposal. すぐ～してくれた He *said yes* immediately. うそをつくと～しないぞ Don't tell a lie, *or I will not forgive you*. すぐやらないと～しないぞ Do it at once, *or you will be sorry for it*. はい, ～しました All right! 彼女の母親はふたりの結婚を～しないだろう Her mother will not *permit* the couple to be married.

しょうちゅう【掌中】¶彼は敵の～に落ちた He *fell into the enemy's hands*.

じょうちゅう【条虫】〘虫類〙a tapeworm.

じょうちょ【情緒】sentiment; emotion. ¶江戸～ an Edo *atmosphere*. 京都は古都の～豊かな街だ Kyoto is a city rich in the *atmosphere* of the good old days.

しょうちょう【小腸】〘解剖〙the small intestines.

しょうちょう【消長】¶企業の～ the *prosperity and decay* of an enterprise. 一国の～ the *rise and fall* of the country.

しょうちょう【象徴】a symbol. ¶～的な詩 a *symbolic* poem. ユリは純潔の～である The lily is the *symbol* of purity. / The lily is *symbolic* of purity. / The lily *symbolizes* purity. **—主義** symbolism. **—派の詩人(画家)** a symbolist.

じょうちょう【冗長】¶～な演説 a *tedious* speech. ～な表現 a *diffuse* (≒ *verbose*) expression.

じょうちょう【情調】an atmosphere; a mood. ¶江戸下町の～を味わった I enjoyed *an* Edo downtown *atmosphere*. 長崎には異国～がある There is *an* exotic *atmosphere* in Nagasaki.

じょうてい【上程】¶その法案は議会に～された The bill *was placed* (≒ *was presented*) *before Parliament*. 三つの議案を一括～した The three bills *were brought up* en bloc for discussion.

じょうでき【上出来】¶～だぞ *Well done!* ことしはミカンが～だ We *have very good harvest of* oranges this year. 試験はみんな～だった I *got high marks in* all my examinations.

しょうてん【昇天】ascension. ¶彼は安らかに～した He *breathed his last* peacefully. / (宗教的に言えば) His soul ascended to Heaven in peace. キリストの～ the Ascension.

しょうてん【商店】a store; 英 a shop. **—街** a shopping center. **—主** a storekeeper; a shop proprietor.

しょうてん【焦点】a focus. ¶彼は彼女にカメラの～を合わせた He *focused* the camera on her. この塔に～が合っている This tower *is in focus*. 彼は今ニュースの～だ Public attention *is centered on* him. **—距離** the focal distance.

じょうてんき【上天気】¶～にはここから富士が見える In *clear weather* we can see Mt. Fuji from here.

しょうど【焦土】¶町は～と化した The town *was burnt to ashes*.

じょうと【譲渡】¶権利の～ the *transfer* of rights. 土地の所有権を彼に～した I *transferred* the ownership of the land *to* him. **—証書** a deed of transfer; a conveyance.

しょうとう【小刀】a short sword; a dagger.

しょうとう【消燈】¶9時に～する We *put out lights* at nine. **—時間** ¶～時間は10時だ *Lights out* is at ten.

しょうどう【唱道】advocacy. ¶彼らは生活改善を～する They *uphold* the improvement of their lives. 彼は禁酒を～する He *advocates* temperance. 彼は禁煙運動を～している He *advocates* no-smoking movement.

しょうどう【衝動】an impulse. ¶やみの中を走りたい～にかられた I was driven by *an impulse* to rush through the darkness. 彼はよく～にかられて行動する He often acts *on impulse*. / He is an *impulsive* man.

じょうとう【上等】¶～のウイスキー whisky *of fine quality*. 特別～のかばん a bag *of extra superior quality*. これはあれよりも～だ This *is of better quality* than that. もっと～のを見せてくれ Show me a *better* one.

じょうとう【常套】¶商売の～手段 *a common trick* of trade. 詐欺師の～手段 a swindler's *old trick*.

じょうどう【常道】¶民主主義の～ *the fundamental rule* of democracy. これは商売では～だ This is the *common way* of trade.

しょうどく【消毒】disinfection; sterilization. ¶～済みのメス a *sterilized* knife. 彼が腸チフスにかかった後, 家は～された The house *was disinfected* after he had had typhoid. 外科医は器具を念入りに～した The surgeon carefully *sterilized* his instruments.

—器 a sterilizer. —剤 an antiseptic. —薬 a disinfectant.

じょうとくい【上得意】a good customer.

しょうとつ【衝突】collision. ¶ 自動車がへいに～した A car *ran into* the wall. バスとトラックが～して 30 分交通がまひした On account of *a collision* between a bus and a truck, the traffic was paralyzed for half an hour. (a collision *between* A and B は両方とも動いている場合と考えられるが a collision of A *with* B は B が動いていない場合もありうる). 船は岩に～した The ship *crashed into* the rock. 彼は息子としょっちゅう意見が～する He quite frequently *conflicts with* his son. ふたりの間には感情の～があった There was *a collision* of sentiments between the two. 彼らは意見が～することがめったにない They seldom *clash with* each other.

三重— ¶ あの十字路できのう三重～があった There was *a three-way collision* at that crossroads. 正面— ¶ トラックがミキサー車に正面～した A truck *collided head on with* a concrete mixer truck.

しょうとりひき【商取引】a commercial transaction ; a business deal.

じょうない【場内】¶ 彼らは～整理をした They restored order *in the hall*. ～は禁煙です You are not allowed to smoke *in the hall*. / Please refrain from smoking *in the hall*.

しょうに【小児】a child ; an infant.

—科 pediatrics (単数扱い). —科医 a children's doctor. —病 children's diseases. —病的 childish ; infantile. —まひ infantile paralysis ; polio〔myelitis〕.

しょうにゅう【鍾乳】—石 a stalactite. —洞(どう) a stalactite grotto.

しょうにん【承認】(賛成) approval ; (同意) agreement ; (認可) recognition. ¶ 法案は原案どおり～された The bill *was approved* in its original form. その計画は職員会議の～を得た The plan had the *approval* of the faculty meeting. 彼らはそれが事実であることを～した They *admitted* it to be true. 日本はその国の独立を～した Japan *recognized* the independence of the new state.

しょうにん【証人】a witness. ¶ 信頼できる～ *a* credible *witness*. 偽証する～ *a* lying *witness*. 彼は私を～に立てた He called (≒ took) me to *witness*. 裁判に被告の～として召喚された I was called as *a* defense *witness* at the trial.

—調べ examination of witnesses. —席 the witness box (≒ stand). 生き— a living witness.

しょうにん【商人】a merchant ; (小売商人) a store keeper.

じょうにん【常任】—委員 a member of a standing committee. —委員会 a standing committee. 国際連合～理事国 permanent members of the U. N. Security Council.

しょうね【性根】nature. ¶ ～の曲がった人 an *ill-natured* fellow. 彼の腐った～をたたき直さなければならぬ I must reform his *corrupt* nature. 彼は～のすわった人だった He was a *calm and bold* man. この仕事は～をすえてかからなければならない This undertaking requires great resolution on our part.

しょうねつ【焦熱】¶ 原爆で広島は～地獄と化した Hiroshima was made *a burning hell* by the atomic bombs.

じょうねつ【情熱】passion. ¶ ～的な愛 a *passionate* love. 彼は音楽に～を燃やしている He has a *passion* for music.

しょうねん【少年】a boy.

—院 a reformatory. —雑誌 a children's magazine. —時代 *one's* boyhood. ¶ 彼は～時代を京都で過ごした He spent his *boyhood* in Kyoto. —団 the Boy Scouts. —犯罪 juvenile delinquency. —犯罪者 a juvenile delinquent.

しょうのう【小脳】〘解剖学〙the cerebellum.

しょうのう【小農】a small farmer.

しょうのう【樟脳】〘化学〙camphor.

じょうば【乗馬】¶ 彼女は～が好きだ She likes *riding*.

—学校 a riding school. —クラブ a riding club. —ズボン riding breeches. —用長ぐつ riding boots. —練習 riding exercises.

しょうはい【勝敗】victory or defeat ; the issue. ¶ ～にこだわらずフェアプレーでやりなさい *Win or lose*, you have to play fair. ～は時の運 Luck leads *the issue* of the battle to success or failure. 彼のホームランが～を決した His homerun decided *the issue* of the game.

しょうはい【賞杯】a prize cup ; a trophy.

しょうはい【賞牌】a medal.

しょうばい【商売】**1**〘営業〙business ; trade ; (職業) an occupation. ¶ 日曜は～はいたしません Our shop is closed on Sundays.

～はうまくいっているか How is *business*?

ご～は? What line of *business* are you in? / What do you do? / What's your *job* (≒ *occupation*)?

～は花屋です I sell flowers. / I am a florist.

なにかもうかる～はないかね Do you know of any lucrative (≒ profitable) *business*?

～のこつがなかなかわからない It is difficult for me to learn the tricks of the *trade*.

彼の～のやり方はなかなか手堅い He is conservative in his〔*business*〕*dealing*. / He has *a* sound *business* method.

なかなか彼は～がうまい He has a good sense for *business*.

彼は～が不振で多大の借財を負った He fell into heavy debt on accout of a *business* failure.

この程度の売り上げでは～にならない Our sales are too small to yield a profit.

これでもけっこう～になるから不思議だ It is amazing that this kind of *business* pays at all.

東京のような大都会ではこのようなことも～になる In a large city like Tokyo, even this kind of thing like this can be *a* paying *business*.

彼はこの地方で自動車の～を手広く行なっている He

し

is one of the largest automobile dealers in this area.
この〜を始めるにはどのくらいの資金が必要ですか What is the initial capital required for this *business*? / How much initial capital is required for this *business*?
野球も趣味としてでなく〜となると楽じゃない Baseball is not easy, if you play it for money and not just for fun.
2 〖合成語〗 ¶ 彼はなかなか〜熱心だ He is an *enterprising* merchant.
先生という〜がらあまりむちゃなこともできない As a teacher, I mustn't do anything undignified (≒ unbecoming).
〜がらそういうことはすぐぴんとくる My *business interests* keep me wide awake to anything like that.
彼はなかなか〜気たっぷりだ He has an *enterprising* spirit.
ふたりは〜がたきだ They are *business rivals*.
彼は品もよく教養があり, ただの〜人ではない He is refined and cultured. He is more than *a mere merchant*.
ああいう本職の〜人にあっちゃかなわない There is no competing with *an old pro* like him.
ぼくの〜道具はペンと原稿用紙だ My *business requirements* are a pen and some writing paper.
〜がえをしようかと思っている I am thinking of changing my *business*.

じょうはく【上膊】〖解剖〗 the upper arm.

しょうばつ【賞罰】 reward and punishment.

じょうはつ【蒸発】 evaporation. ¶ 水は〜する Water *evaporates*. 彼は水を〜させた He *vaporized* water. アルコールは〜しやすい Alcohol *is volatile*. 彼女は〜した(行方不明になった) She *vanished* no one knows where.
—器 an evaporator. —熱 evaporation heat.

しょうばん【相伴】 ¶ 彼からパーティーにお〜するように招かれた He invited me to *partake of* the party.

じょうはんしん【上半身】 the upper half of the body; (特に女性) the bust. ¶ 〜裸になった I stripped to the waist.

しょうひ【消費】 consumption. ¶ そんなことには金を〜できない I cannot *waste* money *on* such a thing. あなたの家では毎月どのくらい電気を〜されますか How much electricity does your family *use* (≒ *consume*) every month?
—者 a consumer. —者価格 consumer〔s'〕 price. —高〔the amount of〕consumption. —物資 consumer〔s'〕goods.

しょうび【焦眉】 ¶ 〜の急の問題 a problem *of great urgency*; an *urgent* problem.

じょうひ【冗費】 unnecessary expenses.
¶ 〜を省く cut down *unnecessary expenses*.

じょうび【常備】 —軍 a standing army. —薬 a household medicine.

しょうひょう【商標】 a trademark. ¶ 〜を登録する have *a trademark* registered.
登録— a registered trademark.

しょうびょうへい【傷病兵】 sick and wounded soldiers (the sick and wounded となる場合が多い).

しょうひん【小品】 ¶ 音楽の〜 *a short piece* of music; *a* musical *sketch*. 文学の〜 a short piece; a〔literary〕sketch; an essay.

しょうひん【商品】 goods; consumer goods. ¶ あの店ではいろいろ外国の〜を売っている They sell various kinds of foreign *merchandise* at that store. たばこも〜の一つだ Cigarettes are *a commercial item*.
—券 a gift certificate. —陳列室 a showroom. —取引所 a commodity exchange. —仲買人 a commodity broker. —見本 a commercial sample. —名 a trade name. —目録 a catalog〔ue〕.

しょうひん【賞品】 a prize. ¶ 彼は1等の〜をもらった He was awarded *the* first *prize*.

じょうひん【上品】 ¶ 〜な服 an *elegant* dress. 彼は趣味が〜だ He *is refined in* his taste. 〜な少女に会った I met a *refined* girl. 彼女は〜に話す She has a *refined* manner of speaking. 彼女は服装が〜だ She is dressed in *refined* taste. 彼女にはどことなく〜なところがある There is something *refined* about her. 彼女はばかに〜ぶっている She is an *over-sophisticated* woman.

しょうぶ【勝負】 a game. ¶ 〜に勝った We won〔the〕*game*. 〜に負けた We lost〔the〕*game*. きょう〜をつけよう Let's win today! 〜はついた *The game* is over. 彼と私はいい〜だ He and I *are evenly matched*. 5,000円かけて彼と〜をした I *played* him for five thousand yen.
—ごと a game. ¶ 彼は〜ごとが大好きだ He is very fond of *gambling*. —師 a gambler.

しょうぶ【菖蒲】〖植物〗 an iris.

じょうぶ【丈夫】 ¶ 体を〜にするために適度の運動をしなさい Take moderate exercise to *build up a healthy body*. 彼は運動をして〜になった *His health has been improved* by exercise. 体が〜である I *am in good health*. この箱は〜にできている This box is *strongly* built. この生地は〜である This cloth *wears well*.

じょうぶ【上部】 ¶ 顔の〜 *the upper part of one's* face. ページの〜に at *the top of* the page.
—構造 a superstructure.

しょうふく【承服】 consent; acceptance. ¶ その条件には〜できない I cannot *accept* (≒ *agree to*) the conditions.

しょうふだ【正札】 a price tag; a price label. ¶ 彼は店の全部の商品に〜をつけた He *marked the price* on every article in his store. その本は2,000円の〜がついていた The book *was marked at* two thousand yen.

じょうぶつ【成仏】 "attaining Buddhahood." ¶ 彼は安らかに〜した He *died* peacefully.

しょうぶん【性分】 nature. ¶ 彼はおくびょうな〜だ He is cowardly *by nature*. 彼は秘密を守れるような〜ではない He is not the kind of a man as can keep a secret to himself. 私の～としてそんなことはできない *It is not in my nature* (≒ *It goes against my grain*) to do such a thing.

じょうぶん【条文】¶ 条約の～ the *text* of a treaty. 法律の～ the *provisions* of a law.

しょうへい【将兵】¶ 前線の～ the *officers and men* at the front.

しょうへい【招聘】invitation; engagement. ¶ わが社は彼を顧問として～した Our company *engaged* him as one of advisers. 彼は大学に教授として～された He *was called* as a professor to the university. 彼はフランス政府の～でパリへ行った *At the invitation of* the French government, he went to Paris.

しょうへき【障壁】a barrier; a fence.

じょうへき【城壁】a castle wall; walls.

じょうべき【乗冪】〖数学〗a power.

しょうへん【小片】a small piece; a fragment. ¶ ガラスの～が散らばっている *Small pieces* of glass are scattered.

しょうべん【小便】urine; water. ¶ 夜～に起きた I got up at night to *pass water* (≒ *pass the urine*).

じょうほ【譲歩】a concession. ¶ 互いに～して話をまとめる settle the dispute by mutual *concessions*. 彼はがんこでわれわれの要求に少しも～しない He is so obstinate that he makes no *concession* to our demand at all.

しょうほう【商法】〖法律〗the commercial law.

しょうほう【詳報】a detailed report.

しょうぼう【消防】fire-fighting; fire service. ―士 a fireman. ―自動車 a fire engine. ―署 米 a fire house; 英 a fire station. ―ポンプ a fire pump. ―隊 a fire brigade.

じょうほう【乗法】〖数学〗multiplication.

じょうほう【情報】information; news. ¶ 役に立つ～ a useful piece of *information*. 目下～を集めている We are collecting *information*. その事件に関してなにか～を手に入れたか Did you get any *information* about the event? われわれは敵についての～を交換した We exchanged *intelligence* of the enemy. 彼はヨーロッパにいるとの～がある It *is reported* that he is in Europe. なにか～はないか Have you got any *news*? / Is there any *news*? まだ～が来ていない No *information* has been received.
―機関 secret (≒ intelligence) service. ―処理 management of information. ―部 the information (≒ intelligence) bureau (≒ section). ―網 an intelligence network. ―ルート 米 a pipeline.

しょうほん【抄本】an extract; an abstract. 戸籍― an abstract of *one's* census register.

しょうほん【正本】the original.

じょうまえ【錠前】a lock. ¶ ～をかける lock (a door).

しょうまっせつ【枝葉末節】¶ ～にこだわる stick at *trifles*.

じょうまん【冗漫】¶ ～な演説 a *long, tiresome* speech. ～な文章 a *diffuse* style.

しょうみ【正味】¶ ～の目方 the *net* weight. ～1時間かかる It takes a *full* hour.

しょうみ【賞味】¶ 菓子を～する *enjoy* cakes.

じょうみ【情味】¶ ～豊かな人 a *warm-hearted* person. 古都には特有の深い～がある An old city is full of peculiar *charms*.

じょうみゃく【静脈】〖解剖学〗a vein. ―硬化症 phlebosclerosis. ―注射 a venous injection. ―瘤(りゅう) a varix (複 varices).

じょうむ【常務】―取締役 a director. ―理事 a standing director.

じょうむいん【乗務員】(列車の) a trainman; (電車の) a carman; (飛行機の) a crewman; (総称) the crew.

しょうむしょう【商務省】米 the Department of Commerce; 英 the Board of Trade.

しょうめい【証明】proof. ¶ この陳述は彼の無実を～する This statement *is proof of* his innocence. 無罪を～するには証拠が必要だ Evidence is necessary to *prove* innocence. この文面は彼の誠実さを～している This letter *proves* his sincerity. 彼の発言は彼がスペイン人であることを～した His remark *gave proof* that he was Spanish. 本大学を卒業したことを～します This is to *certify* that you have graduated from this university. この研究で彼は自分の説の正しいことを～した With this research he *proved* that his theory was right. この長さとこの長さの等しいことを～できますか Can you *show* that these two lengths are equal?
―者 a witness. ―書 a certificate.

しょうめい【照明】illumination; (舞台の) lighting. ¶ ～のよい(悪い)部屋 a well-*lighted* (dimly-*lighted*) room. 通りは明るく～が施されていた The streets *were* brightly *lighted up*. 強い～がその女優に当てられた The *spotlight* was focused upon the actress.
―係 an illuminator. ―器具 a lighting fixture. ―効果 light effect. 舞台― stage lightng.

しょうめつ【消滅】¶ 権利の～ the *lapse* of *one's* rights. 手続きをしないと権利が～する The right will *lapse* if you don't follow the necessary procedure.

しょうめん【正面】the front. ¶ ～から見た建物のながめ a *front* view of the building. 駅の～の入り口 a *front* entrance to the station. ～に見える山が富士だ The mountain *in front* is Mt. Fuji. ケースの～はガラス張りだ The case *is fronted* with glass.
―衝突 ¶ 彼の車はトラックと～衝突した His car had a *head-on* collision against (≒ with) the truck.

しょうもう【消耗】consumption. ¶ マラソンでまったく体力を～した I *am exhausted* by the marathon race.
―品 articles for consumption; consumer goods.

しょうもん【証文】a bond; a deed; (借金の) an IOU. ¶ ～をとっておいてある I hold the *deed*. ～を作らなければならぬ We must draw up the *deed*. ～を入れて彼から金を借りた I borrowed money from him on *a bond*.

しょうやく【抄訳】translation of selected passages. ¶ 彼は源氏物語を～した He *translated selected passages* from *the Tale of Genji*.

じょうやく【条約】a treaty. ¶ 彼はその～に調印した He signed the *treaty*. 日本はその国と通商～を結んだ Japan concluded *a* commercial *treaty* with the country. 合衆国はその～を破棄した The United States annulled the *treaty*.
—案 a treaty draft. —改正 treaty revision. —加盟国 a treaty power.

じょうやど【定宿・常宿】*one's* regular hotel.

しょうゆ【醤油】soy; soy sauce.

しょうよ【賞与】(ボーナス) a bonus; (賞金) a reward.

じょうよ【剰余】a surplus.
—金 a surplus〔fund〕. —価値 surplus value.

じょうよ【譲与】¶ 権利の～ the *transfer* of rights. 土地使用権を彼に～した I *transferred* him the right to the use of land.

しょうよう【商用】business. ¶ 彼は～で名古屋へ行った He went to Nagoya *on business*. ～で訪問した I made *a business call* on him.
—語 a commercial term. —文 commercial correspondence.

しょうよう【逍遙】a stroll. ¶ 森の中を～する *stroll* in a wood.

しょうよう【従容】¶ ～として死につく meet *one's* death *calmly*.

しょうよう【賞揚】¶ ～する admire; praise.

じょうよう【常用】¶ 彼は睡眠薬を～している He *takes* a sleeping drug *habitually*.
—漢字 Chinese characters in common use. —者 a habitual user (≒ drinker).

じょうようしゃ【乗用車】an automobile; a car.

じょうよく【情欲】passions; sexual desire; lust. ¶ 彼は～におぼれている He indulged in his *sensual pleasures*.

しょうらい【招来】¶ それは戦争の危機を～する It *leads to* a crisis of war.

しょうらい【将来】the future. ¶ きみは自分の～について考えなければならぬ You must think of your *future*. きみは～のために貯金すべきだ You should save money for *the future*. 彼は～大人物になる He will become a great man *in future*. 近い～パリに行く I will go to Paris *in*〔*the*〕*near future*. あなたには輝かしい～が待ち受けている You have *a* bright *future* before you. だれも自分の～のことはわからない Nobody can tell about his *future*. ～なにが起こるかだれにもわからない No one can tell what will happen *in future*. これは私の～の計画だ This is my plan *for the future*. 彼女の最近の小説はかなり～の楽しめるものだ Her recent novel is of considerable *promise*.
—性 ¶ ～性のある青年 a young man of *prospects* (≒ *promise*); a *hopeful* (≒ *promising*) young man.

しょうり【勝利】a victory; a triumph. ¶ 彼が～をおさめるだろう He will *win*. 彼らは大～を博した They *won* (≒ *gained*) *a* great *victory*. われわれのチームは5回戦って3回～を得た Our team *won* three *victories* in five games.
—者 a victor; (競技の) a winner. —チーム a winning team. —投手 a winning pitcher.

じょうり【条理】reason. ¶ ～にかなった説 a *reasonable* theory. それは～にかなう It stands to *reason*.

じょうりく【上陸】landing. ¶ 乗客は神戸で～した The passengers *landed* at Kobe. 船員は横浜で～を許された The crew were allowed to *go on shore* at Yokohama. 台風が本土に～するかもしれない The typhoon may *hit* the mainland.
—作戦 landing operations. —地点 a landing place. —用舟艇 a landing boat; (米海軍) a landing craft.

しょうりゃく【省略】omission. ¶ 紙面のつごうで一部～した The part *was omitted* for want of space. 細かい点は～する The minute details will *be omitted*. ～せずに without abridgment; in full.
—符号 an apostrophe. —文 an elliptical (≒ abridged) sentence. —法 ellipsis.

じょうりゅう【上流】(川の) the upper stream; (社会の) the upper classes. ¶ 江戸川の～ *the upper course* (≒ *reaches*) of the Edo River. この橋の3マイル～にダムがある There is a dam three miles *above* this bridge.
—社会 ¶ ～社会での習慣 customs of the *fashionable* society. —階級 ¶ ～階級の婦人 a *fashionable* lady.

じょうりゅう【蒸留】distillation. ¶ ぶどう酒を～してブランデーを作る We *distil* brandy *from* wine.
—水 distilled water. —装置 a distillatory apparatus.

しょうりょ【焦慮】anxiety; impatience.
¶ 彼には～の色が濃くなった He was getting *impatient*.

しょうりょう【少量】a small amount; a small quantity. ¶ ～の砂糖 *a small amount of* (≒ *little*) sugar.

しょうりょう【渉猟】extensive reading. ¶ 内外の文献を～する *range over* home and foreign books.

じょうりょくじゅ【常緑樹】an evergreen.

しょうれい【省令】a departmental regulation.

しょうれい【奨励】encouragement. ¶ 学問の～ the *encouragement* of learning. 彼らは科学的研究を熱心に～した They warmly *encouraged* scientific researches.
—金 a bounty (*on*).

じょうれい【条例】a regulation; an ordinance. ¶ 市～ *a* municipal *ordinance*.

じょうれん【常連】¶ 彼らはこの店の～だ They are *regular visitors to* this store.

じょうろ【如雨露】¶ ～で植木に水をやる water

the garden plants with *a watering can*.
しょうろう【鐘楼】 a bell tower; a belfry.
しょうろく【抄録】 an extract; an abstract. ¶ 原典を～する *make an extract from* the original text.
しょうろん【詳論】 full discussion. ¶ ～する *discuss* (a problem) *at length* (≒ *in detail*).
しょうわ【笑話】 a funny story.
しょうわくせい【小惑星】〔天文学〕an asteroid.
しょうわる【性悪】 ¶ ～な女 an *ill-natured* woman. なんて～な人間だ What a *wicked* (≒ *vicious*) fellow!
しょえん【初演】 the first performance.
じょえん【助演】 ¶ ～する support the leading actors.
—者 a supporting player (≒ actor; actress).
ショー a show.
—ウインドー a show window. —マン a showman. —ルーム a showroom.
じょおう【女王】 a queen. ¶ エリザベス～2世 *Queen* Elizabeth II.
—バチ a queen bee.
ショート (野球で) a shortstop; (電気の) a short circuit. ¶ ～してヒューズが飛んだ The fuse got burnt (≒ blown) out because of *a short circuit*.
—ケーキ a shortcake. —パンツ shorts.
ショール a shawl.
しょか【初夏】 early summer.
しょか【書架】 a bookshelf; a bookcase; (図書館の) a 〔book〕stack.
しょか【書家】 a calligrapher.
じょがい【除外】 exception. ¶ ～する except; exclude.
—例 an exception.
しょがくしゃ【初学者】 a beginner.
じょがくせい【女学生】 a schoolgirl; a girl student; 米 (男女共学制の) a coed.
しょかつ【所轄】 jurisdiction. ¶ ～の税務署 the taxation office *concerned*.
じょがっこう【女学校】 a girls' high school.
しょかん【所感】 (感想) *one's* impression〔s〕; (意見) an opinion. ¶ 彼はその問題について～を述べた He expressed his *opinion* on the problem. このことで一言～を述べたいと思います Let me say a few *words* about this.
しょかん【所管】 jurisdiction. ¶ その問題は彼の～に属する The matter comes under his *jurisdiction*.
—官庁 the competent authorities; the authorities concerned. —大臣 the Minister concerned.
しょかん【書簡】 a letter; (総称) correspondence.
じょかん【女官】 a court lady.
しょき【初期】 ¶ ～の作品 *one's early* works. 明治の～に *in the early years of* the Meiji era. がんは～に治療することがたいせつだ It is essential to cure cancer *in its early stages*.
しょき【書記】 a secretary; (特に雑用をする人など) a clerk.
—官 a secretary. —長 a chief (≒ head) secretary; (政党の) a secretary-general.
しょき【所期】 ¶ ～の目的を果たす achieve *one's desired* end. ～に反して実験は失敗した The experiment failed contrary to our *expectations*.
しょき【暑気】 heat. ¶ ～あたりする suffer from *the heat*.
しょきゅう【初級】 the beginners' class. ¶ ～英語 English *for beginners*; *elementary* English.
じょきょ【除去】 ¶ 彼は多くの弊害を～した He *removed* (≒ *got rid of*) many evils.
じょきょうじゅ【助教授】 an assistant professor.
じょきょく【序曲】〔音楽〕an overture; a prelude. ¶ これはその恐ろしい事件の～にすぎない This is only *a prelude* to the awful incident.
しょく【食】 (食物) food; (食事) a meal; (食欲) appetite. ¶ 食パン1～分 bread for one *meal*. 私は～が進む(進まない) I have *a* good (poor) *appetite*. 泳ぐと～が進む Swimming gives us *a* good *appetite*. われわれは1日に3～とる We take three *meals* a day.
日本— Japanese food. 栄養— nutritious (≒ nourishing) meal. 美容— a fat-reducing diet. 菜— a vegetarian diet.
しょく【職】 a job; an employment. ¶ 彼は今～がない He has no *job* now. ～のない人は少なくない Quite a few people *are unemployed*. 彼は～を求めている He is looking for *a job* (≒ *an employment*). 毎月何千人もの人が～を失っている Thousands of people lose their *jobs* every month. 彼が～についたのはほんの1年前だ It was only a year ago that he *was employed* (≒ *got the job*). 彼はようやく～にありついた He managed to find *employment*. 彼は～をかえないだろう He will not switch *jobs*. 彼女になにか適当な～を見つけてやりたい I want to find *a* good *job* for her. 彼は突然～を免ぜられた He was suddenly relieved of his *office* (≒ *post*).
しよく【私欲】 a selfish desire. ¶ ～に目がくらんで不正を行なった Blinded by *self-interest*, he did a dishonest thing.
しょくいん【職員】 (集合的に) the staff; (学校の) the teaching staff; (個人) a member of the staff; an employee. ¶ 彼はわれわれの学校の～だ He is on *the teaching staff of* our school. その病院には20名の～がいる The hospital has *a staff* of twenty men.
—会議 a staff (≒ faculty) meeting. —組合 a faculty union. —室 a teachers' (≒ faculty) room. —録 a list of government officials; 米 a blue book.
しょぐう【処遇】 treatment. ¶ 彼を公平に～してください I hope you will *treat* him fairly.
しょくえん【食塩】〔common〕salt.
—水 a solution of salt. —注射 a saline

injection.

しょくぎょう【職業】 an occupation. ¶ あなたの～は何か What is your *occupation*? 彼女の職業はタイピストだ Her *trade* is typewriting. 彼はどんな～に従事しているのか What *occupation* does he follow? ～をかえるのは容易ならぬことだ It is no easy thing to change *one's occupation*. 彼は文筆を～としている His *occupation* is writing. / He is a writer by *occupation*. 趣味と～は両立しがたい It is hard to match one's *occupation* and hobbies.

—安定所 an employment security office. —案内欄 the want ads column. —意識 job sensitivity. —教育 vocational education. —軍人 a career officer. —紹介所 an employment office. —選手 a professional player. —病 an occupational disease. —婦人 a professional woman. —別電話帳 a classified telephone directory. —補導 vocational guidance. —野球 professional baseball.

しょくご【食後】 after meal. ¶ 1日3回, ～30分に服用 To be taken three times a day thirty minutes *after each meal*.

しょくさん【殖産】 increase of production.

しょくし【食指】 ¶ あの本には大いに～が動いた I *had an itch for* the book.

しょくじ【食事】 a meal; a dinner; (まかない) board. ¶ まもなく～の用意ができます *Dinner* is going to be ready soon. ～の時間です It's time for *dinner*. ホテルで軽い～をとった I had *a* light *meal* at the hotel. 彼らは1日に4回～をする They have (≒ take) four *meals* a day. 彼女は～の用意をしている She is preparing *the table*. ～の前には手を洗いなさい Wash your hands before *meals*. 私が～のあとかたづけをした I cleared *the table*. 今晩は家で～をする I *dine in* this evening. 昨夜は外で～をした Last night I *dined out*. 部屋代は～つきで3万円だ The room rent is thirty thousand yen *with board*. 彼らは～中だ They *are at table* (≒ *are at dinner*).

しょくじ【食餌】 —療法 ¶ 彼女は～療法をしている(おもにやせるための) She *is on a diet*. 医者は病人に特別な～療法をさせている The doctor puts the patient on *a* special *diet*. / The doctor *diets* the patient.

しょくじ【植字】 typesetting; composition.

—機 a composing (≒ typesetting) machine. —工 a type-setter; a compositor.

しょくじゅ【植樹】 ¶ ～する plant a tree.

—祭 米 Arbor Day (4月または5月に米国各州で植樹する日).

しょくしょう【食傷】 ¶ 毎日同じような料理に～してしまった I *was surfeited with* the same dishes every day. 彼の苦労話にも～した I *was fed up with* the story of his life full of cares.

しょくしょう【職掌】 ¶ 彼は～がらその問題には詳しい His *duties* have made him familiar with the subject.

しょくせい【職制】 office regulations.

しょくせいかつ【食生活】 ¶ ～を改善する improve *one's diet*. ～を楽しくする increase the pleasure of *the table*.

しょくせき【職責】 duty; responsibility. ¶ ～を果たす do *one's duty*.

しょくぜん【食膳】 ¶ それは～に供された It was served on *the table*. それらの料理は～をにぎわした Those dishes gave variety to *the table*.

しょくぜん【食前】 ¶ ～30分に服用のこと To be taken half an hour *before meals*.

—酒 aperitif.

しょくだい【燭台】 a candlestick.

しょくたく【食卓】 a [dining] table. ¶ 彼らは～についた They *sat at table*. 彼女は～を離れた She rose from *the table*. 彼女は～の用意をした She *set* (≒ *laid*; *spread*) *the table*. 彼女は～をかたづけている She is clearing *the table*.

—塩 table salt.

しょくたく【嘱託】 a part-timer; a nonregular employee.

しょくちゅうどく【食中毒】 food poisoning. ¶ 彼はふぐを食べて～をおこした He was a victim of globefish *poisoning*.

しょくつう【食通】 a gastronomer; an epicure.

しょくどう【食堂】 a dining room; (料理店) a restaurant; (駅などの) a refreshment room.

—車 a dining car; a diner.

しょくどう【食道】 〘解剖学〙 the esophagus (複 esophagi).

—がん cancer of the esophagus.

しょくにく【食肉】 [edible] meat.

—獣 a carnivore. —類 the Carnivora.

しょくにん【職人】 a workman; an artisan. ¶ ～かたぎ an *artisan* spirit.

しょくのう【職能】 function.

—給 wages on job evaluation. —別組合 a craft union.

しょくば【職場】 (仕事場) a workshop; (持ち場) *one's* post. ¶ ～を放棄する desert *one's post*.

—会 a [work]shop meeting. —大会 a work[shop] rally. —結婚 ¶ ～結婚をする marry a man (≒ a woman) working in the same company.

しょくばい【触媒】 〘化学〙 a catalyst.

しょくパン【食パン】 bread.

しょくひ【食費】 food expense; (まかない費) a boarding charge. ¶ 部屋代と～ rooming and *boarding charges*. 毎月1万円を～として払っている I pay ten thousand yen for my *boarding charge* every month.

しょくひん【食品】 foodstuffs (ふつう複数形で用いる); food.

—衛生 food sanitation. —化学 food chemistry. —[加]工業 food industry.

しょくぶつ【植物】 a plant; a vegetable; (総称) vegetation.

—園 a botanical garden. —学 botany. —学者 a botanist. —採集 plant collecting. —質 vegetable matter. —繊維 a vegetable fiber. —標本 botanical specimens. —油 vegetable oil. 高山— an alpine plant. 熱帯— a tropical plant.

しょくぶん【職分】*one's* duty. ¶～を全うする do (≒ discharge; perform) *one's duties*. ～を守る be faithful to *one's duties*.

しょくぼう【嘱望】¶将来を～された青年 a *promising* young man. 彼は大いに将来を～されている Much *is expected of* him.

しょくみん【植民・殖民】colonization.
—地 a colony. —地開拓者 a colonist. —地政策 a colonial policy.

しょくむ【職務】〔a〕duty; duties. ¶～を遂行しただけだ I only performed my *duties*. 彼女は～を怠った She neglected her *duties*. 彼は～に従って行動した He acted *in line of duty*. 彼は～上きみにそうするように言ったのだ *As a matter of duty*, he told you to do so.
—質問 ¶～質問を受けた I was checked on by a policeman.

しょくもく【嘱目】¶教師や同級生から～されている人物 a person *much expected of* by his teachers and classmates.

しょくもつ【食物】food; foodstuffs. ⇒しょくひん

しょくやすみ【食休み】a rest after a meal.

しょくよう【食用】¶～になるキノコとそうでないものとがある Some mushrooms *are eatable* (≒ *are edible*), and others are not.
—ガエル an edible frog. —油 cooking oil.

しょくようじょう【食養生】a diet.

しょくよく【食欲】〔an〕appetite. ¶～がある(ない) I have *a good* (poor) *appetite*. それは私の～をそそった It quickened my *appetite*. 病人は～が衰えた The patient has lost his *appetite*. 戸外で大いに運動すれば～が出るでしょう Much exercise in the open air will give you *a good appetite*.

しょくりょう【食料】food; provisions.
—品店 a grocery.

しょくりょう【食糧】provisions; food.
¶われわれは5日分の～を持っていった We carried five day's *provisions*. 彼らの～は6日しかもたない Their *provisions* last only six days.
—不足 a food shortage. —問題(事情) the food problem (situation).

しょくりん【植林】afforestation. ¶彼はその土地に～した He *afforested* the land. / He *planted* the land *with trees*.

しょくれき【職歴】*one's* professional (≒ occupational) career.

しょくん【諸君】(男性だけの聴衆に対して) Gentlemen (呼びかけのときは [dʒéntlmən] と発音する); (女性相手なら) Ladies.

じょくん【叙勲】conferment of a decoration.
¶彼に～のさたがあった He was informed that he would *be conferred a decoration* (≒ *be decorated*).

しょけい【処刑】(処罰) punishment; (死刑執行) capital punishment; execution.
¶彼は～された He *was executed*. / (電気で) He *was electrocuted*.

じょけい【叙景】a description of scenery.
—文 a scenery sketch.

じょけつ【女傑】a great woman.

しょ・げる【悄気る】¶彼は～げた顔をしていた He *looked dispirited* (≒ *looked blue*). 彼女は～げていた She *was in low spirits*.

しょけん【所見】*one's* views (≒ opinions).
¶～を述べる express *one's views*. 一言～を述べる say a word (*on* a matter).

じょげん【助言】〔a piece of〕advice. ¶彼の～を求めた I asked his *advice*. 彼に用心するように～した I *advised* him to be cautious. 彼は私の～を聞き入れた He took (≒ followed) my *advice*. 彼は私の～を聞き入れようとしなかった He would not listen to my *advice*.

しょこ【書庫】a library; (図書館の) stacks.

しょこう【曙光】¶紛争の解決の～が見られる We see *promise* of a settlement of the trouble.

じょこう【徐行】(掲示) "Go slow" ¶途中10分間ほど～した We *drove slow* (≒ *drove slowly*) for ten minutes on the way.

しょこく【諸国】(世界の) various countries; (国内の) various provinces.

しょこん【初婚】¶彼女は～だ This is her *first marriage*. 彼は40歳で～だった He *married for the first time* at forty.

しょさい【書斎】a study.

しょさい【所載】¶その雑誌～の彼の記事が問題になった His article *printed* in the magazine has caused a trouble.

しょざい【所在】(人の) *one's* whereabouts; (物の) the seat. ¶彼の～を発見した We discovered his *whereabouts*. 彼は～をくらました He concealed his *whereabouts*. 彼の～は不明である His *whereabouts* is (≒ are) unknown. 責任の～を明らかにしなければならぬ We must make clear *where* the responsibility lies.

しょざいな・い【所在ない】¶退職して～い(なにもすることがない) I retired and *have nothing to do* now. ～さにドライブに出かけた *In order to beguile the tedious hours*, I went for a drive.

じょさいな・い【如才ない】¶～い人(機転のきく人) a *tactful* (≒ *smart*) man; (抜け目のない人) a *shrewd* man; (愛想のよい人) a *sociable* man. 彼は～く立ちまわる He acts *tactfully*. 彼女はだれにでも～い She *is affable* (≒ *is sociable*) to everybody.

しょさん【所産】¶彼の努力の～ the *fruits* (≒ *product*) *of* his effort.

じょさんぷ【助産婦】a midwife.

しょし【初志】¶彼は～を貫いた He carried out his *original intention*.

しょし【庶子】an illegitimate child.

しょじ【所持】¶私は多額の現金を～している I *have* a large sum of cash with me.
—品 ¶～品を改められた I had my *things* 〔*at hand*〕 examined.

じょし【女子】(大人) a woman; (子ども) a girl.
—学生 a girl student. —高校 a girls' high school. —大学 a women's college.

じょし【助詞】〘文法〙a particle.

じょじ【助辞】〘文法〙an auxiliary word.

し

じょじ【叙事】―詩 an epic. ―体 a narrative style. ―文 a narrative; a description.

しょしがく【書誌学】bibliography.

しょしき【書式】a fixed form. ¶ ～に従って欠席届を書く write a report of absence *in due form*. これは～が違っている This is not *in due* (≒ *proper*) *form*.

じょしゅ【助手】an assistant; a helper. ¶ 彼女は女子大の～をしている She works as [an] *assistant* in the women's college.

しょしゅう【初秋】early autumn; 米 early fall.

じょじゅつ【叙述】description. ¶ 事件のありのままを～する *describe* an event exactly.

しょしゅん【初春】early spring.

しょじゅん【初旬】¶ 3月～に *early* in March; *at the beginning of* March.

しょじょ【処女】a virgin; a maiden. ―宮〖天文学〗the Virgo. ―航海(飛行) a maiden voyage (flight). ―作 a maiden work. ―地 a virgin soil. ―峰 an unclimbed peak. ―膜〖解剖学〗the hymen.

しょじょう【書状】a letter.

じょじょう【叙情】―詩(総称) lyrical poetry; (個々の) a lyrical poem. ―詩人 a lyric poet.

じょじょうふ【女丈夫】a great woman.

じょじょに【徐徐に】¶ 車は～動きはじめた The car began to move *slowly*. 彼の英語は～ではあるが確実に進歩していっている He is making *slow* but steady progress in English. ～温度が下がりはじめた The temperature began to go down *gradually* (≒ *by degrees*).

しょしん【初心】¶ ～忘るべからず Don't forget *your first resolution*.

しょしん【初診】¶ ～の患者 a *new* patient. ―料 the fee for the first medical examination.

しょしん【所信】*one's* belief; (意見) *one's* opinion. ¶ ～を表明する express *one's opinion*. ～を断行する act according to *one's belief*.

しょしんしゃ【初心者】a beginner.

じょすう【序数】〖数学〗an ordinal [number].

じょすう【除数】〖数学〗a divisor.

しょ·する【処する】¶ 彼は難局に巧みに身を～した He *dealt* tactfully *with* the difficulties. 彼は厳罰に～せられるべきだ He *deserves* a severe punishment.

しょせい【処世】¶ 彼は～の術にたけている He knows well *how to get on in the world*.

じょせい【女声】―合唱 a female chorus.

じょせい【女性】a woman (複 women); (総称) woman; 〖文法〗the feminine gender. ¶ 教養のある～ *a* cultured *woman*. 女らしい～ *a* womanly *woman*. ～的な男 *a* womanish man (-ish がつくと軽べつ的感情が加わる).

じょせい【女婿】a son-in-law.

じょせいきん【助成金】a subsidy; a bounty.

じょせいと【女生徒】a schoolgirl.

しょせき【書籍】books; (出版物) publications. ―愛好家 a bibliophile; a lover of books. ―業組合 a publishers' guild. ―商 (人) a bookseller; (店) a bookstore. ―目録 a book catalog[ue].

じょせき【除籍】¶ 彼を会員から～しなければならぬ We must *strike* his name *off* the membership list. その学生は～された The student *was expelled* from school.

しょせつ【諸説】¶ その件については～紛々としている *Opinions* are divided on the matter.

じょせつ【序説】an introduction.

じょせつ【除雪】¶ 彼らは通りの～をしていた They *were clearing* the road *of snow*. (*clear the snow of* the road としないように注意). ―機関車 a Russel plow. ―車 a snowplow.

しょせん【所詮】after all.

しょせん【緒戦·初戦】¶ ～を飾る win *the first match* (野球·蹴球などなら match を game にかえる).

しょそう【諸相】¶ 現代生活の～ *various aspects* of modern life.

しょぞう【所蔵】¶ 大倉氏～の貴重な写本 precious manuscripts *owned by* (≒ *in the possession of*) Mr. Okura.

じょそう【女装】¶ ～の男 a man *in a woman's dress*.

じょそう【序奏】〖音楽〗an introduction.

じょそう【助走】¶ ～する run. ―路 a runway; (スキーの) an approach.

じょそう【除草】―機 a weeder. ―剤 a weed killer.

しょぞく【所属】¶ 彼は社会党に～している He *belongs to* the Socialist Party.

しょぞん【所存】(考え) [an] intention; (動機) a motive; (意見) an opinion.

じょそんだんぴ【女尊男卑】¶ アメリカには～の風習がある America is a woman's paradise. / In America women are put above men.

しょたい【所帯】(家庭) a household (この語には使用人もふくまれている); (家政) housekeeping. ¶ 彼らは結婚して～を持った They got married and started *housekeeping*. 彼女も～じみてきた She *got domesticated*. 彼女は～の苦労を知らない She does not know *domestic cares*. ―主 a householder. ―数 the number of households. ―道具 household goods. ―持ち ¶ 彼女は～持ちのいい奥さんだ She is good at *housekeeping*. ―やつれ ¶ 彼女は～やつれしている She *is worn with domestic cares*.

しょたい【書体】a style of penmanship; handwriting.

しょだい【初代】the founder; (第1代) the first generation. ¶ ～の校長 *the first* principal.

じょたい【除隊】¶ 彼は～になった He *got a discharge from* (≒ *was discharged from*) military service.

しょたいめん【初対面】¶ ～のあいさつを交わした We exchanged formal greetings of *the first meeting*. 彼とはきょうが～だった I *met* him *for the first time* today. ～の印象はどう

でしたか How was his *first* impression [on you]?

しょだな【書棚】a bookshelf.

しょだん【初段】¶ 彼は柔道の～をとった He was granted *the first grade* in *judo*.

しょち【処置】(処理) disposal; (方策) measures. ¶ 事故を～する *deal with* an accident. その問題の～に窮している I do not know how to *dispose of* the problem. 断固たる～をとらねばならぬ We must take decisive *measures*. 彼は～よろしきをえた He took *a* proper *step*. 私は～を誤った I took wrong *measures*. 彼はもう～なしだ There's nothing to be done about him.

しょちゅう【暑中】―見舞 ¶ 彼に～見舞を出した I wrote to him inquiring after his health in the hot season. (英米にはあらためて暑中見舞の便りを出す習慣はない). ―休暇 a summer vacation (㊍では during をつけると冠詞をつけずに during summer vacation という); summer holidays.

じょちゅうぎく【除虫菊】a pyrethrum.

しょちょう【所長】a head; a superintendent.

しょちょう【初潮】〔医学〕*one's* first menstruation.

しょちょう【署長】¶ 警察～ *the chief* of police.

じょちょう【助長】promotion. ¶ 無知は迷信を～する Ignorance *fosters* superstition.

しょっかく【触角】a feeler; an antenna (㊜ antennae).

しょっかく【触覚】the sense of touch.

しょっかん【食間】¶ この薬は～に飲みなさい Take this medicine *between meals*.

しょっき【食器】tableware. ―だな a cupboard.

ジョッキ a jug; (ふた付き) a tankard. ¶ ～1杯のビール a *jug* of beer.

ショッキング ¶ ～な事件 a *shocking* event.

ショック a shock. ¶ 彼女の死はぼくには非常な～だった Her death was *a* great *shock* to me. そのニュースは彼らに～を与えた The news gave them *a shock*. / The news came upon them with *a shock*. 彼らはその～から立ち直っていない They have not recovered from the *shock*. 私は彼の死の知らせを聞いて～を受けた I *was shocked* at the news of his death. ―死 ¶ 彼は～死した He died of *shock*. ―療法 shock treatment.

しょっけん【食券】a meal ticket.

しょっけん【職権】authority; official power. ¶ ～を行使する exercise *one's authority*. ～を乱用する abuse *one's authority*.

しょっこう【燭光】candle power. ¶ 40～の電光 a forty *candle power* bulb.

ショット a shot. ¶ ゴールに向かってのみごとな～ *a* nice *shot* at the goal.

しょてい【所定】¶ ～の場所(時間) the *appointed* place (time). ～の用紙に書き込む fill up a *prescribed* form.

しょてん【書店】a bookstore; ㊖ a bookshop; a bookseller's.

じょてんいん【女店員】a saleswoman; ㊍ a salesgirl; ㊖ a shopgirl. ¶ 売り場の～ *a salesgirl* attending at the counter.

しょとう【初冬】early winter.

しょとう【初等】―科 an elementary course. ―教育 elementary education. ―数学 elementary mathematics.

しょとう【初頭】¶ 19世紀の～ *the beginning* of the 19th century.

しょとう【諸島】¶ 南太平洋～ the South Pacific *Islands*.

しょどう【書道】calligraphy. ―家 a calligrapher.

じょどうし【助動詞】〔文法〕an auxiliary verb.

しょとく【所得】income; gain. ¶ 彼は～が多い(少ない) He has *a* large (small) *income*. ～以上の(以内の)暮らしをしている I live beyond (within) my *income*. 彼には年に500万円の～がある He has *an income* of five million yen a year. / His *income* is five million yen a year. ―税 an income tax. 勤労― earned income. 高額―者 a large-income earner. 不労― unearned income.

しょなのか【初七日】the sixth day after *a person's* death.

じょなん【女難】¶ 彼には～の相がある Fate will get him into *trouble with women*.

しょにち【初日】the first day; the opening day.

しょにんきゅう【初任給】a starting salary; an entrance salary. ¶ 彼の～は6万円だ His *beginning salary* is sixty thousand yen.

しょねん【初年】¶ 明治の～に in *the early years* of Meiji.

じょのくち【序の口】the beginning; (相撲) the lowest *sumo*-wrestler.

しょは【諸派】(政治の) the minor parties.

しょばつ【処罰】punishment. ¶ 人を～する *punish a person*.

しょはん【初犯】the first offense; (人) a first offender.

しょはん【初版】the first edition.

しょはん【諸般】¶ ～の事情が許すかぎり so far as *circumstances* permit. ～の事情を考慮しなければならぬ We must take *every circumstance* into consideration.

じょばん【序盤】¶ 選挙戦の～ *the first stage* of an election campaign. ―戦 ¶ わがチームはトーナメントの～戦で負けた Our team lost *at the first stage* of the tournament.

しょひょう【書評】a book review. ―家 a book reviewer. ―欄 book-review columns.

しょぶん【処分】(処置) disposal; (処罰) punishment. ¶ 彼はその土地を～した He *disposed of* the land. 自由に～できる財産を持っている I have property *at my own disposition*. 彼はその罪で厳重に～されるだろう He will *be* severely *punished* for the crime.

じょぶん【序文】a preface (*to*); a foreword.

しょほ【初歩】elements; rudiments; the ABC. ¶ 経済学の～ *the rudiments* (≒ *the*

ABC) of economics. 彼は英語の～から始めた He began with *the ABC* of English. 私は算数を～から勉強したい I want to learn arithmetic from *the beginning*.
じょほう【除法】〘数学〙 division.
しょほうせん【処方箋】 a prescription. ¶ 医者は私の頭痛に～を書いた The doctor *prescribed medicine for* my headache. / The doctor *wrote out a prescription* of my headache. (欧米では医薬分業だから処方箋はくれるが薬はくれない). 彼は～どおりに調合した He made up *a prescription*.

し

しょぼしょぼ ¶ ～した目 *blear* eyes. 雨が～降っている It *drizzles*.
じょまく【序幕】 the first act; a prelude (*to*).
じょまく【除幕】 ¶ 像の～をする *unveil* a statue. ―式 the unveiling ceremony.
しょみん【庶民】 the [common] people; (大衆) the masses. ¶ ～的なゲーム a *popular* game. このような宝石類は～の手には届かぬ This jewelry is beyond *the masses'* reach.
しょむ【庶務】 general affairs.
―係(人) a general affairs clerk. ―課 a general affairs section.
しょめい【書名】 the title of a book.
しょめい【署名】 a signature; (有名人の署名など) an autograph. ¶ 著者の～入りの本 a book with the author's *autograph*. その俳優の～入りの写真 the actor's *autographed* photograph. この書類に～してください Please *sign* these papers. その手紙にはだれの～があるか Whose *signature* does the letter bear? その手紙には彼女の～がある The letter *is signed by* her.
―運動 a signature-collecting campaign.
じょめい【除名】 expulsion. ¶ 彼は会から～された He *was expelled from* the club. / His name *was struck off* the membership list.
じょめい【助命】 ¶ ～を請う ask for *a person's* life.
しょめん【書面】 (手紙) a letter; (文書) a document. ¶ ～による返事 an answer *by letter* (≒ *in writing*).
しょもう【所望】 a desire; a wish. ¶ ご～によりフランスの歌をうたいます *At your request* I'll sing a French song.
しょや【初夜】 the bridal night.
じょや【除夜】 New Year's Eve. ¶ ～の鐘 *the watch-night* bell.
じょやく【助役】 (市の) a deputy mayor; (区・町の) a headman's assistant; (駅の) an assistant stationmaster.
しょゆう【所有】 possession. ¶ この小屋は彼の～だ He *owns* this cottage. 彼は多くの店を～している He *owns* a large number of stores. この庭園は彼の～となった This garden *has come into* his *possession*. この図書館はL大学の～である This library *belongs to* L University. 田中～(書物の裏表紙などに書く) *Belongs to* Tanaka.
―権 ownership. ―者 an owner.
じょゆう【女優】 an actress. ¶ 映画(テレビ)～ *a* film (TV) *actress*.
しょよう【所用】 ¶ 彼は～で外出した He went out *on business*.
しょよう【所要】 ¶ 飛行機でそこまで行く～時間は2時間だ It takes two hours to fly there.
しょり【処理】 management; disposal.
¶ 問題の～ the *disposal* of the matter. 事務の～ the *transaction* of business. ～すべき問題がたくさんある I have a lot of problems to *deal with*. 地震の予知にはまだ～すべき問題がたくさんある There are a lot of problems to *solve* before an earthquake can be predicted. その仕事を手際よく～した I *managed* the business skillfully.
じょりゅう【女流】 ¶ ～作家 a *woman* (≒ *lady*) writer (最近は lady よりも woman のほうがていねいな感じを与える); an authoress (author を女流作家の意味で用いることが多い).
じょりょく【助力】 help. ¶ 相互の～ mutual *aid*. 彼に～を仰いだ I asked him for *help*. 彼女にはきみの～が必要だ She needs your *help*.
しょるい【書類】 papers; documents. ¶ ～を提出する send (≒ hand) in the *papers* (教師が採点ずみの試験答案を学校に提出するのは send in のほうがよい). ～を整理しておきなさい Keep *the papers* in order (≒ file). 彼らは～を押収した They captured the *documents*.
―選考 ¶ 志願者は～選考された The candidates were selected by examining their *career papers*. ―送検 ¶ 事件は～送検となった The *papers* of the case were sent to the prosecutor's office.
ショルダーバッグ a shoulder bag.
じょれつ【序列】 a grade; order.
しょろう【初老】 ¶ ～の男 an *elderly* man.
しょろん【緒論】 an introduction.
しょろん【所論】 *one's* view; a personal view. ¶ ～を述べる give *one's opinion* (*on* an incident).
じょろん【序論】 an introduction.
しょんぼり ¶ 彼女は～とした顔つきで立っていた She stood *with a dejected expression*. 彼は～と立ち去った He went away *dejectedly*.
しら ¶ 彼は～をきった He *pretended not to know*.
じらい【地雷】 a land mine. ¶ ～をしかける lay *a mine*. ～に触れる strike *a mine*.
しらうお【白魚】〘魚類〙 a whitebait. ¶ 彼女の～のような指 her *delicate* fingers.
しらが【白髪】 [a] gray hair. ¶ ～交じりの髪 *grizzled* hair. 彼は少し～交じりになった His hair is beginning to *turn gray*. 彼は～が1本もない There is not *a gray hair* on his head. 彼は～を黒く染めている He has his *white hair* dyed black. 若～の人 a youth with *hoary hair*. ～染め a hair-dye.
しらかば【白樺】〘植物〙 a white birch.
しらかべ【白壁】 a white-plastered wall.
しらき【白木】 ¶ ～造りの神殿 a shrine built of *plain wood*.
しらぎく【白菊】〘植物〙 a white chrysanthemum.

しらくも【白雲】(雲) a white cloud; (病気) a scald head.

しら・ける【白ける】¶ 座が〜けた *A chill came over* the company. 彼の冷たい態度で一座が〜けてしまった His cold attitude *cast a chill over* the gathering.

しらこ【白子】(人) an albino; (魚) milt.

しらさぎ【白鷺】〔鳥類〕a white heron.

しらじらし・い ¶ よくもあんな〜いうそが言えたものだ How dare he tell such a *transparent* lie? (transparent はうそなどが見え透いていること. lie はアメリカ人・イギリス人はめったに用いない厳しい語. 非難の気持ちを含む. ふつうは falsehood がよい).

しらじらと【白白と】¶ 〜夜が明けはじめた Day broke. (英語では「昼が明ける」という).

じら・す【焦らす】¶ あまり子どもを〜してはいけない Don't *tease* the child too much. 彼女は彼を何年も〜しつづけて, 結局ほかの人と結婚した She kept *tantalizing* him for years, and then married somebody else.

しらずしらず【知らず知らず】¶ 〜身を乗り出して彼の話を聞いていた I was *unconsciously* leaning forward to listen to his story. 彼女は〜のうちに涙を流しはじめた She began to shed tears *in spite of herself* (≒ *without knowing it*).

しらずに【知らずに】¶ 彼は危険とは〜向こう側へ渡った He passed over to the other side *without knowing* its danger. (文頭を Not knowing ...で始めれば文語体).

しらせ【知らせ】a report; news. ¶ その〜はほんとうだ The *report* is true. 彼が急病になったという〜を受けた I received the *report* that he had suddenly fallen ill. 会合の〜を出した I sent them *an announcement* of the meeting. 先方からなんの〜もない We *have* not *been informed* of it by them. 母親に会えるという虫の〜があった He had *a presentiment* that he might see his mother.

しら・せる【知らせる】¶ 沖縄へ着いたらすぐ〜せてください Please *let* me *know* as soon as you arrive in Okinawa. 病気のことはだれにも〜せなかった I *told* no one *of* my illness. 彼は事件のことを私に〜せてくれた He *informed* me *of* the incident. 子どもには父親の死を〜せないほうがいい It is better not to *tell* the child *of* his father's death. すぐ盗難を警察へ〜せなさい *Report* a burglary *to* the police at once. 彼は息子にその事実を暗に〜せた He *suggested* the fact *to* his son.

しらちゃけた【白茶けた】whitish (-ish (…じみた)は悪い意味に用いることが多い).

しらない【知らない】¶ 〜人 a stranger. 〜土地 a *strange* place; an *unknown* land.

しらなみ【白波】¶ 沖に〜が立っている There are *white waves* on the ocean. / *White-crested waves* are to be seen in the offing. (white-crested waves は詩的表現. ただ waves だけでもよい. また ocean より sea のほうが詩的に響く).

しらばく・れる ¶ きみはその件について〜れようとしてもだめだ It is no use your trying to *feign* (≒ *pretend*) *ignorance* of the matter.

しらはのや【白羽の矢】¶ 彼に〜が立った He was made a goat. / He was chosen as a sacrifice 〔out of many〕. (悪い場合). / He was chosen as the proper man.

しらふ【白面・素面】¶ 彼は〜のときは紳士だ He is a gentleman *when sober* (≒ *when not drunk*).

シラブル a syllable. ¶ 語を〜に切る divide a word into *syllables*.

しらべ【調べ】¶ あすやるところの〜をしておこう I will *prepare for* tomorrow's lesson. 〜が済まないうちは外へ出られません You are not allowed to go out-of-doors until the *investigation* is over. 税関の〜は時間がかかる Customs *inspection* takes time. たえなる〜 *a* sweet *tune*.

しら・べる【調べる】investigate. ¶ 事故の原因を〜べる必要がある It is necessary to *investigate* the cause of the accident. 失敗の原因を〜べてごらんなさい *Examine* the reason for your failure. 彼は古文書を〜べている He *is looking over* old documents. 電話帳で彼の住所を〜べてください *Look up* his address in the telephone directory. 警官がどろぼうを〜べている The policeman *is interrogating* the thief. 税関で荷物を〜べられた I *had* my baggage *examined* at the customhouse. ポケットを〜べられた I *had* my pockets *searched*. あすの英語を〜べておこう I will *prepare for* tomorrow's English lesson. もう一度人数を〜べたほうがいい We had better *count* (≒ *check on*) the number of people again.

しらみ【虱】a louse (複 lice); (総称) vermin.
—つぶし ¶ 一軒一軒〜つぶしに調べた They *made a thorough search* from door to door.

しら・む【白む】¶ だんだん東の空が〜んでくる The eastern sky *is* gradually *turning gray*.

しらゆき【白雪】¶ 峰の〜 *the* 〔*white*〕 *snow* on the summit.
—姫 the Snow White.

しらんかお【知らん顔】¶ あの男は道で会っても〜をする When we meet on the street he completely *ignores* me. / When we meet on the street, he *cuts* me *dead*. その事件に彼は〜をしている He is *indifferent to* the matter.

しり【尻】**1** 〖体の〗 the hip. ¶ 彼女はお〜が大きい She has big *hips*.
彼女は赤子の〜を日に何回打つかわからない We cannot tell how often she spanks her baby's *bottom* in a day.
彼は先生に〜を向けて座っている He is sitting with his *back* to the teacher.
2 〖慣用的表現〗 ¶ 〜に火がついた I *am pressed by urgent business*.
彼は〜をもっていくところがない He has no one *to* whom he can *complain*.
彼女はいつも〜が落ち着かない She *is* always *restless*.
彼は〜が重い He is a *lazy* fellow. (idle fellow はさける).

し

彼女は～が軽い She is a *loose* woman. 彼はクラスで～から3番めだ He is third from the *foot* of the class. 彼は妻の～に敷かれている He *is henpecked*.

しり【私利】¶ 彼は～のみを図ってきた He has been seeking nothing but *his own interests*. 彼は～私欲で凝り固まっている He is a dogged egoist. / He is indifferent to anything but *his personal profit*.

しりあい【知り合い】an acquaintance (いまではひとりの知人の意味にしか用いない). ¶ 彼は～が多い He has *a* wide *acquaintance*. (この acquaintance は「知人」ではなく「面識」の意味). 彼は私の～だ I *know* him. / I *am acquainted with* him. (やや形式ばった言い方). 私は京都に～がいない I have no *acquaintances* in Kyoto. (acquaintance のように単数形にするのはやや古めかしい用法). どうして～になったのですか How did you *get in touch with* him at first? / How did you *come to know* him? 彼とは長年の～だ I *have known* him for a long time. ぼくはひょんなことから彼と～になったんだ I *picked acquaintance with* him. そのことについては～のアメリカ人に聞いてみます I'll ask an American of my *acquaintance* about the matter.

しりあ・う【知り合う】¶ 彼女とは音楽会で～った I *got acquainted with* her at the concert. 彼と～ってから3年になる I *have known* him for three years.

しりあがり【しり上がり】¶ ことしの売り上げは～に伸びた The sales account this year has shown *a rising tendency*. 彼の話し方は～の癖がある He always speaks *with a rising intonation*.

しりあて【尻当て】a seat-lining (*of one's* trousers) (ズボンのひざの裏につける「ひざすべり」や「尻当て」などは欧米のズボンにはない).

シリーズ a series. ¶ 古典文学～ the classical literature *series*. これは推理小説～の一巻である This book is one of the crime story *series*. ワールド― 〔野球〕 a World Series.

しりうま【尻馬】¶ 彼はすぐ人の～に乗る He *easily* (≒ *blindly*) *follows* the lead of another.

しりおし【尻押し】¶ 大ぜいの人の～で彼は当選した He was elected *by the backing of* a lot of people.

じりき【自力】¶ 最後まで～でやりなさい Do it *for yourself* to the last. (by oneself とすれば「ひとりで」の意味). 彼は～で出世した人だ He is *a self-made man*.

じりき【地力】⇒じつりょく

しりきれ【尻切れ】¶ 彼はなんでも～とんぼだ He *leaves* everything *unfinished* (≒ *half-done*).

シリコーン 〔化学〕 silicone.

しりごみ【後込み】¶ めんどうな仕事にみんな～した Everybody *shrank from* the troublesome job. いざとなるとみな～してしまった At the last moment, all *held back*.

じりじり ¶ ～と焼けつくような暑い日中を under the *broiling* (≒ *scorching*) sun. 敵のチームが～とわれわれを押してきた Our opponent team had the edge on us *little by little*.

しりぞ・く【退く】¶ 彼は一歩～いた He *took* a step *backward*. (文字どおりにも比喩的にも用いる). われわれは一歩も～かない決心をしていた We all were determined to *contest every inch of the ground*. 彼はことしの3月職を～いた He *retired from his office* (≒ *resigned his post*) this March. 彼は最近政界を～いた He *has* recently *retired from politics*.

しりぞ・ける【退ける】¶ 彼はわれわれの要求を～けた He *refused* our demands. われわれの意見はみなすげなく～けられた All our opinions *were* bluntly *rejected*.

しりつ【市立】¶ その病院は～だ The hospital *is run* (≒ *is maintained*) *by the city*. ―学校(図書館; 病院) a municipal school (library; hospital).

しりつ【私立】¶ その学校は～だ The school is a *private* institution. ―学校(大学) a private school (college; university). ―探偵 a private detective.

じりつ【自立】independence. ¶ 彼は30歳のとき～して印刷業を始めた At thirty, he *set up* his own printing house. 新興国は経済的に～しえないものが多い Many of the developing countries can't *be* economically *independent*.

じりつ【自律】―神経〔系〕 autonomic nerves 〔system〕.

しりとり【尻取り】¶ 英語で～遊びをしようじゃないか Let's *cap verses* in English.

しりぬ・く【知り抜く】¶ 10年もいるからその土地のことはなにもかも～いている Because he has lived in the place for ten years, he *knows* it *thoroughly*.

しりぬぐい【尻拭い】¶ 他人の失敗の～はごめんだ I don't like to *pay for* (≒ *repair*) another's blunder. 彼の借金の～をした I *paid* his debt *for* him.

じりひん【じり貧】¶ このままでいけばわれわれは～の状態になる We will *be headed for a worse lot* if things go like this.

しりめ【後目・尻目】¶ 彼は友人たちの反対を～に初めの要求を主張してきかなかった He never receded from the original demand, though his friends were not in favor of it.

しりめつれつ【支離滅裂】¶ ～な議論 an *incoherent* argument. 彼の言っていることは～だ He talks *incoherently*. / His speech *lacks consistency*.

しりもち【尻餅】¶ ～をつく fall on *one's* bottom (≒ buttocks) (buttocks は複数形に注意. buttocks より bottom のほうが口語的でいつでも用いることができる); fall backward.

しりゅう【支流】a branch; a tributary. ¶ 多摩川の～ *a tributary* 〔*river*〕 *to* the Tama 〔River〕.

じりゅう【時流】the current of the times. ¶ ～に逆らってもむだだ It is no use trying to run counter to *the current of the times*. 彼はいつも～を追う He always swims with *the current of the times*.

しりょ【思慮】 consideration. ¶ ～深い(のない)人 a *thoughtful* (*thoughtless*) person. ～の足りない行動 an *imprudent* (≒ a *rash*) act. 彼は年の割りには～分別がある He *is thoughtful* (≒ *is prudent*) for his age.

しりょう【資料】 materials; data (datum の複数形であるがアメリカではしばしば these data を this data のように単数扱い). ¶ 彼の伝記の～を集めている I am collecting *materials* (≒ *data*) for his biography.

しりょう【史料】 historical materials.

しりょう【飼料】 forage. ¶ 馬の～ *feed* for horses. 牛の～に干し草をやる *feed* cows *on* hay.
配合— assorted feed.

しりょく【死力】 ¶ 彼らは～を尽くして戦った They fought *desperately*.

しりょく【視力】 eyesight; sight. ¶ 彼女は～が弱い She *is weak-sighted*. / She has bad *sight* (≒ poor *eyesight*). 彼は私の～を検査した He tested my *vision* (≒ *eyesight*). 彼女は～を失った(回復した) She lost (recovered) her *sight*. 最近～がめっきり衰えた My *eyesight* has been remarkably failing of late.
—検査 the eyesight test. —表 the eyesight test chart; optotypes.

しりょく【資力】 means; funds. ¶ ～のある(ない)人 a man *of means* (*of no means*). その事業の～は十分ある We have enough *funds* for the enterprise. 彼らは～の不足に苦しんでいる They are suffering from lack of *funds*. 車を持つだけの～がない I don't have *means* enough to have a car.

じりょく【磁力】〘物理〙 magnetism; magnetic force.
—計 a magnetometer. —線 the magnetic line of force.

シリンダー a cylinder.
高(低)圧— a high-(low-)pressure cylinder. 蒸気— a steam cylinder.

しる【汁】(果汁) juice; (樹液) sap; (吸い物) soup. ¶ ～の多い果物 a *juicy* fruit. オレンジの～をしぼる squeeze *juice* out of (≒ from) an orange. オレンジの～を吸う *suck* an orange. 彼はうまい～をひとり占めにした(比喩的に) He had all the profit to himself.

し・る【知る】 **1**〘知識として持つ・記憶する〙 know. ¶ 彼はヨーロッパの事情をよく～っている He *is* very *conversant with* European affairs. / He *has a* very good *knowledge of* things European. / He *is* well *versed in* European affairs.
きょうの新聞で彼の死を～った I *have learned of* his death in today's paper.
この件についてはなにも～らない I *know* nothing *about* this matter.
その事件については今～ったところだ I *have* only just *heard about* this incident.
その後彼がどうしているか～りませんか Don't you *know* what has become of him since? (Do you know …でもほぼ同じ意味. 否定疑問文はなるべくさける).
これはまだだれも～らないことだ Nobody *knows* this yet.
これは内部事情をよく～った者の仕業にちがいない This must have been done by someone who *has* good inside *knowledge*.
彼はなんでも～っているようなふりをする He pretends to *know* (anything and) everything.
酒を飲んで酔っていたので，昨晩のことはなにも～らない Because I had drunk too much, I do not *remember* what I did last night.
2〘理解する・推量する〙 ¶ 病気になって初めて健康のありがたさを～る We do not *appreciate* the blessing of health till we lose it.
子を持って初めて～る親の恩 It is not till we come to have children of our own that we *know* our debt to our parents.
私を～ってくれるのはきみだけだ It is only you who *understand* me.
彼は人情の機微を～っている He *has a keen insight into* human nature.
自分の欠点を～ることがたいせつだ It is important to *know* one's own defects.
彼の実力は～る人ぞ～るだ Those will *appreciate* his real ability who can.
3〘知り合いである〙 ¶ 同窓会には～らない顔が多かった At the alumni reunion many of those present *were strangers* to me.
幸い～った人には出会わなかった Fortunately I did not meet any *acquaintances*.
彼なら子どものころから～っている I *have known* him since he was a mere child.
あの人は顔を～っている程度だ I *know* him only by sight.
4〘認める〙 ¶ 彼は作曲家として世界に～られている He *is known to* the world as a composer.
町で出会ったが彼女は～らん顔をして行ってしまった When I met her on the street, she *cut* me *dead* and walked away.
産児制限の必要を世界の人々に～ってもらいたい I want the people of the world to *recognize* the need of birth control.
5〘感知する・気がつく〙 ¶ しまった，そういう手があるとは～らなかった(ゲームなどで) My goodness! I never *thought of* that sort of move.
～らない間にうとうとしたらしい It seems that I must have dozed off.
南伊豆なら冬も寒さ～らずで過ごせる At South Izu you can pass the days without *feeling* the winter cold.
～らぬが仏(諺) *Ignorance is bliss.*
よく眠っていたのでけさの地震は～らなかった I was so fast asleep that I did not *feel* the earthquake this morning.
動物は自然の異変を～るのが早い Animals are quick to *notice* unusual changes in nature.
6〘かかわる〙 ¶ きみの～ったことではない That is none of your business. (乱暴な言い方. You have nothing to do with it. ならよい意味でも悪い意味でもよい). / That's no concern of yours.
彼がどうなろうと私の～ったことではない What will become of him is no concern of mine.
言うことが聞けないんだったら，もう～りませんよ If

し

you are naughty, I won't love you any more.

7 〖経験する〗 ¶ 彼はまだ世間を～らない He *has* not *seen* the world yet. / He *is* still *inexperienced* in the ways of the world.

20代の若者はあの戦争を～らない Young people in their twenties *have had* no *experience of* that war.

シルエット a silhouette; (影) a shadow (silhouette は非常に上品な語).

シルク silk.

―ハット a silk hat; a top hat (silk hat は古めかしい形, 特にアメリカでは a top hat という).

しるこ【汁粉】sweet red-bean soup with rice-cake.

しるし【印・標・徴】a sign. ¶ 赤鉛筆で～をつける *mark* with a red pencil. ここにある包みには～をつけてください Please put *marks* on these packages. 「星」～のノートを買った I bought a star *brand* notebook. お礼の～にこの品をお受け取りいただきたいのですが Please accept this as *a token* of my gratitude. (大げさな言い方. ふつうは Here is a little present for you. でじゅうぶん). 朝焼けは雨の降る～だ The morning-glow is *a sign* of coming rain. そのことは人類の進歩の確実な～だ That's *a* solid *proof* of human progress. 赤は危険の～として用いられる Red is used as *a signal* of danger.

しる・す【記す・誌す・印す】¶ 彼は日本上陸の第一印象を日記に～した He *wrote* 〔*down*〕 the first impressions of his landing on Japan in the diary. 人々は碑を建てて彼の輝かしい業績について～した People *gave an account of* his glorious achievements on the monument.

しれい【司令】―官 a commander. ―長官 the commander-in-chief. ―塔 a conning tower. ―部 the headquarters.

しれい【指令】an order; instructions. ¶ 彼らにそこにとどまるようにとの～を出した I gave them *instructions* to stay there. われわれは本部からの～によって行動する We act upon *orders* of the headquarters.

じれい【辞令】(任命書) a written appointment; (役人の) a government order. ¶ 大阪支店へ転任の～をもらった I received *a written appointment* of my transference to the Osaka branch.

外交― diplomatic tongue.

しれた【知れた】¶ 彼が負けるのは～ことだ It is *a matter of course* that he 〔should〕 lose the game. その本の値段は～ものだった The book cost me *only a trifle*. 彼の音楽の才能なんて～ものだ He has *not much* talent for music.

しれつ【熾烈】¶ 商売がたきどうしの～な戦いがあった There was *keen* competition between the rival dealers. 戦いは～をきわめた The battle *was* very *fierce*. / They had a very *severe* fight.

じれった・い ¶ 彼女のぐずにはいささか～くなってきた I *got* a little *impatient at* her dullness. なにをしてもうまくいかない, ああ～い Everything I do goes wrong with me. How *vexing*!

じ・れる【焦れる】¶ 彼は一日じゅう～れていた He *has been fretful* all day. そんなつまらんことで～れるな Don't *fret about* such trifles.

しれわた・る【知れわたる】¶ 彼の名は全世界に～った His name *has been known* all over the world. ～った事実 a *well-known* fact.

しれん【試練・試錬】a trial; an ordeal. ¶ 人生は～に満ちている Life is full of *trials*. 彼は少年時代に多くの～を受けた He underwent many *trials* when he was a boy. 彼は多くの～を切り抜けた He went through many *ordeals*. 彼女はその～に耐えた She endured the *ordeal*.

ジレンマ a dilemma. ¶ 彼は理想と現実の～に陥った He fell into *a dilemma* between the ideal and the reality.

しろ【白】(色) white; (無罪) innocence. ¶ ～が勝った The *White* team won the race. 彼(容疑者)は～だった He proved to *be innocent*.

しろ【城】a castle. ¶ ～を築く(攻め落とす) build (take) *a castle*. ～を明け渡す surrender (≒ give up) *a castle* (*to* the enemy).

しろあと【城跡】¶ ～を訪れた I visited *the ruins of a castle*. ～は今は公園になっている *The site of the castle* is now changed into a park.

しろあり【白蟻】〖虫類〗a white ant; a termite.

しろ・い【白い】white. ¶ なにか～いものが見える We can see something *white*. 色の～い女性 a woman with the *fair* complexion. 汚れた壁を～くした I painted the dirty wall *white*. 彼らは彼を～い目で見る They look at him *with contempt*.

しろうと【素人】an amateur. ¶ 彼女は歌手としては～だ As a singer she is *an amateur*. ダンスはずぶの～だ I am quite *a green hand* at dancing.

―演芸 amateur entertainment. ―下宿 a private boarding-house. ―芝居 an amateur dramatic performance. ―役者 an amateur actor. ―療法 home treatment. ―ばなれ ¶ 彼の考え方は～ばなれしている He thinks like a professional.

しろうり【白瓜】〖植物〗a white muskmelon.

しろくじちゅう【四六時中】¶ 彼は～考えごとをしている He is *always* thinking about something. 彼は～商売のことばかり考えている He is a businessman *all the time*.

しろくばん【四六判】a duodecimo.

しろくま【白熊】〖動物〗a white bear; a polar bear.

しろくろ【白黒】¶ 容疑者の～をはっきりさせる decide whether the suspect *is guilty or innocent*. 彼はその知らせを聞くと驚いて目を～させた He *was staggered* to hear the news.

―写真 a picture in black and white. ―テレビ a black-and-white TV set (会話では簡単に a black and white ともいう. またこれは白黒写真の意味にも用いる).

しろざとう【白砂糖】white 〔refined〕 sugar.

しろじ【白地】¶ 〜に赤いバラの模様 a design of red roses on *a white ground*.

しろしょうぞく【白装束】a white attire.
¶ 〜で in *white* (白装束は外国では清浄を意味するほかに, 幽霊・無気味なものを連想させることが多い).

じろじろ ¶ 彼は私の顔を〜見た He *stared* me *in the face*. / He *stared at* me.

シロップ syrup. ¶ 咳止め〜 cough *syrup*.

しろっぽ・い【白っぽい】¶ 〜いコート a *whitish* coat. 東の空が〜くなってくる The eastern sky *is growing light*.

しろぬり【白塗り】¶ 〜のテーブル a *white-painted* table.

しろねずみ【白鼠】〘動物〙a white mouse (複 mice).

しろぼし【白星】¶ 〜をかせぐ win *a victory mark*.

シロホン a xylophone.

しろみ【白味】whiteness. ¶ 乾くと〜を帯びてくる It becomes *whitish* when dry.

しろみ【白身】¶ 〜の魚 fish of *white meat*. 卵の〜 *the white* of an egg.

しろめ【白目】the white of an eye.

しろもの【代物】¶ 500円くらいの〜 *an article* of about five hundred yen. たいへんな〜を買わされた I was forced to buy *a wretched stuff*. 彼はやっかいな〜だ He is *a disturbing fellow*.

じろり ¶ 彼は怒って〜と私の顔を見た He *cast an indignant glance* at me. (形式ばった形). / He got angry and *looked at* me.

しろん【詩論】(詩学) poetics; (論文) an essay on poetry.

しろん【史論】a (≒ an) historical essay.

しろん【試論】¶ 文学〔についての〕〜 *an essay on* literature.

じろん【持論】*one's* cherished view. ¶ 子どもは厳しく育てろというのが彼の〜だ His *theory* is that children need strict discipline.

しわ【皺】wrinkle. ¶ 彼の顔には〜がよっている His face *is wrinkled*. 彼の顔には〜がまったくない There is not *a wrinkle* in his face. スカートの〜をのばす press out the *wrinkles* of a skirt. アイロンでハンカチの〜をのばす iron the *wrinkles* out of a handkerchief.

しわが・れる【嗄れる】¶ 〜れた声で話す talk *in a husky* (≒ *hoarse*) *voice*; talk *hoarsely*.

しわくちゃ【皺苦茶】¶ 1枚の〜の紙 a *crumpled* piece of paper. 〜の顔 a *wrinkled* face. このズボンは〜だ These trousers *are full of wrinkles*.

しわけ【仕分け・仕訳】(分類) classification; (選別) assortment; (簿記で) journalizing.
—〔明細〕書 a specification. —帳 a journal.

しわざ【仕業】¶ これはいったいだれの〜だ Who on earth *has done* this? これはきっと彼の〜だ He must *have done* this.

じわじわ ¶ 継ぎ目から〜と水がしみ出している Water is oozing *little by little* through a joint. 〜敵を攻める make a *slow but steady* attack upon the enemy.

しわす【師走】December.

しわよせ【皺寄せ】¶ 休んだ人の仕事が他の人に〜される The task of the one who is absent *is shifted to* someone else.

じわれ【地割れ】a crack in the ground. ¶ 地震で道路が〜した The earthquake caused *cracks in the road*.

しん【信】confidence. ¶ その国は世界の〜を得た(失った) The country gained (lost) the *confidence* of the world. 彼は〜をおくに足りる(〜をおくに足りぬ)人物だ He is a *trustworthy* (an *unreliable*) man.

しん【真】¶ 〜の愛国心 *true* patriotism. 〜の芸術家 a *true* (≒ *genuine*) artist. 〜のやみ *utter* darkness. 彼の演技は〜に迫っている His performance *is true to life*.

しん【心・芯】the marrow; (鉛筆) lead; (ろうそくなど) a wick; (果物) a core; (帯) a padding.
¶ 鉛筆の〜 the *lead* of a pencil. 石油ストーブの〜 the *wick* of an oil heater. リンゴの〜 the *core* of an apple. 〜のしっかりした人 a *trustworthy* person. 〜のある飯 *half-cooked* rice. 体の〜まで冷えきった I *was chilled to* the bone.

しん-【新-】¶ 〜制度 a *new* system. 〜内閣 a *new* Cabinet. 〜流行 the *latest* fashion.

しん-【親-】¶ 〜日的 *pro*-Japanese. 〜ソ派 a *pro*-Soviet group.

じん【仁】benevolence; humanity.

じん【陣】(陣形) 〔a〕battle array. ¶ 教授〜 *a* teaching *staff* (アメリカでは the faculty といえば高校教員にも用いる). 編集〜 *an* editorial *staff*. 報道〜 *a group of* pressmen.

しんあい【親愛】¶ 〜なる諸君 *Dear* friends! (英語の dear friend〔s〕などの dear には「親愛なる」という意味はほとんど感じられない); (スピーチで) Ladies and gentlemen! 〜の情を表わす(いだく) show *a deep affection* (*for a person*).

じんあい【塵埃】(ほこり) dust; (ごみ) rubbish.
¶ 〜にまみれた都会 a *dusty* city.

しんあん【新案】a new design (≒ idea).
¶ 彼の〜によるおもちゃ a *new* toy *designed* by him.
—特許 a new design patent.

しんい【真意】(意味) the true meaning; (気持ち) *one's* real intention. ¶ 〜を明らかにする disclose *one's real intention*.

じんい【人為】¶ 〜的に artificially.
—淘汰〘生物〙artificial selection.

しんいり【新入り】¶ 〜の弟子 a *new* disciple. 〜がひとり増えた Here is another *newcomer*.

しんいん【真因】¶ 事故の〜を究明する investigate *the true cause of* the accident. 彼の自殺の〜はこれだ This is *the true motive of* his suicide.

じんいん【人員】(人数) the number of the persons; (集合的に職員) the staff; the personnel (personnel は複数扱い. ふつう官公庁や会社の職員について言う).
¶ 事務所の〜を増やした(減らした) We increased (reduced) *the personnel* of our office. 必要な〜をそろえる get *a* necessary *number of persons*. その役所は〜が過剰である(不足である)

The office *is overstaffed* (*is understaffed*).

―整理 〔a〕personnel cut ; the reduction of the personnel.

しんうち【真打ち】 a headliner.

しんえい【新鋭】 ¶～の機械 an *up-to-date* machine. ～の選手 a *fresh* player.

じんえい【陣営】 ¶共産～ the Communist *camp*. 政治家たちはふたつの～に分かれた The statesmen were divided into two *camps*.

しんえいたい【親衛隊】 ¶大統領の～ the *bodyguards* of the president.

し

しんえん【深遠】 ¶～な学説 a *profound* theory. この語には～な意味が含まれている This word bears a *deep* meaning.

しんえん【深淵】 an abyss ; a gulf.

しんか【臣下】 a subject ; a retainer (イギリスで subject を用いる場合, アメリカその他の国では citizen を用いる. British subject と American citizen とを比較).

しんか【真価】 true worth ; true value. ¶彼の～を知っている I know his *true worth*. 彼は腕のいい外科医として～を発揮した He proved his *real worth* as a skillful surgeon.

しんか【進化】〔生物〕 evolution ; (発達) development. ¶動物はすべて～する All animals *evolve*. 人間はなにから～したか What *has* man *evolved* from? 社会全体が～する The whole world *advances*.

―論 the theory of evolution ; Darwinism. **―論者** an evolutionist.

じんか【人家】 a house. ¶トラックが～に突っ込んだ A truck ran into *a dwelling house*. そのあたりは～が密集している The locality is crowded with *houses*.

しんかい【深海】 a deep sea ; deep waters. **―魚** a deep-sea fish.

しんがい【心外】 ¶～な出来事 a *regrettable* happening. そんなことを言われるとは～だ *I am very sorry to* hear such a remark. きみの言うことはまったく～だ *I deeply regret that* you say so. 彼の裏切り行為は～にたえない Nothing is more *regrettable* than his betrayal.

しんがい【侵害】 violation ; trespass (violation は女性に対する暴行を意味するので, 避ける人がいる).

¶きみは彼女のプライバシーを～した You *violated* her privacy. 彼はぼくの人権を～した He *trespassed on* my human rights. その船は日本の領海を～した The ship *encroached upon* Japanese territorial waters.

じんかいせんじゅつ【人海戦術】 ¶～をとる adopt *human wave tactics*.

しんかいち【新開地】 a newly-opened land. ¶郊外の～ *a newly-opened lot* in the suburbs.

しんがお【新顔】 a newcomer ; a new face.

しんがく【神学】 theology.

―校 a theological school. **―者** a theologian. **―生** a theological student.

しんがく【進学】 ¶本校の学生の大部分は大学へ～する The great majority of the students of this school *go on to college*. (college には school と同様に冠詞をつけないことが多い).

じんかく【人格】 character ; personality. ¶～を尊重(無視)する respect(disregard) *one's personality*. ～を傷つける injure *one's character*. 彼はすばらしい～の持ち主だ He is a man *of fine* (≒ *noble*) *character*.

―教育 character building. **―者** a man of character. 二重**―**(者) (a man of) double personality.

しんかくか【神格化】 deification. ¶彼らは彼を～した They *deified* him.

じんがさ【陣笠】 ¶国会の～連中 *the rank and file* of the House ; the backbenchers.

しんがた【新型・新形】 a new style. ¶くつの最～ *the latest style* in shoes. 最～のクーラー an air-conditioner of *the latest model*.

―車 a new style car.

しんかぶ【新株】〔株式〕 a new stock.

しんがら【新柄】 a new pattern. ¶毛織物の～ *new patterns* on woolen fabrics.

しんがり【殿】 ¶退却に際しわれわれが～をつとめた We *brought up the rear* in the retreat. 彼が～に現われた He came *last*.

しんかん【信管】 a fuse. ¶爆弾に～をつける set *a fuse* in a bomb.

しんかん【新刊】 ¶～の図書 a new book ; a new publication. 今月の～ *new publications* (≒ *books*) of this month.

―目録 a list of new publications. **―予告** a notice of forthcoming publications.

しんかん【新館】 a new building.

しんかん【震撼】 ¶世間を～させる大事件 a *world-shaking* event. この事件は世間を～させた This incident *shocked* the world.

しんかん【森閑】 ¶部屋の中は～と静まりかえっている There is silence in the room.

しんがん【心眼】 ¶その塔は彼の～に映じた He saw the tower *in his mind's eye*.

しんかんせん【新幹線】 ¶～が開通した *The new trunk line* has been opened to traffic. 東海道**―** the New Tokaido Line.

しんき【心悸】 **―**昂進(こうしん) palpitation of the heart.

しんき【新奇】 novelty. ¶彼女は～を好む She likes *novelty* (≒ *curious things*). 彼は～をてらっている He displays his *originality*.

しんき【新規】 ¶彼は～に商売を始めた He started a *new* business. その銀行に～に預金を始めた I became a *new* depositor in the bank.

―まき直し ¶～まき直しで出直すつもりだ I will *make a new start* (≒ *start afresh*).

しんき【心機】 **―一転** ¶～一転して勉学に励んだ I *changed my mind* and studied hard.

しんぎ【信義】 faith ; fidelity. ¶人との～を守る(踏みにじる) keep (break) *faith* with *a person*.

しんぎ【真偽】 truth ; genuiness. ¶～のほどはわからない No one knows whether it is *true or not*. その報告の～を確かめた I ascertained *the truth* of the report.

しんぎ【審議】 discussion ; deliberation.

¶～を重ねた末 after much *deliberation.* まず第一にその議題を～しなければならぬ First of all, we must *inquire into* (⇆ *deliberate on; discuss*) the matter. (discuss がいちばん口語的). その問題は～中である The problem *is under deliberation.* その問題は～未了になった The problem *was shelved* (⇆ *was tabled*). その法案は継続～にまわされた The *deliberation* on the bill was carried into the next session. その問題は委員会の～に付託された The matter *was referred* (⇆ *was submitted*) *to* the committee.

じんぎ【仁義】(人道) humanity; (義理) duty; (やくざの) moral code. ¶～にはずれた行ない an *inhumane* deed.

しんきげん【新紀元】¶～を画する出来事 an *epoch-making* event. 本書は言語学史上に一～を開くことになるだろう This book will make *a new epoch* in the history of linguistics.

しんきじく【新機軸】a new device. ¶宣伝になにか～を打ち出そう Let's make some *innovations* in advertising.

しんきゅう【進級】promotion; (学校の) remove. ¶彼女は4年生に～した She *was promoted to* the fourth grade. 彼はことし3年に～する He is going to *get his remove to* the third form. (3年制高校(4年制大学)の最高学年は senior class と言い, その1年下を junior class と言う. したがって「高校2年(大学3年)に進級した」は He became a junior. でよい).

しんきゅう【新旧】¶～思想が鋭く対立している There is a terrible collision between *old and new* ideas. (新と旧の語順が反対になる点に注意).

しんきょ【新居】a new house. ¶～に移る move to *a new house.* 郊外に～を構える make *a new home* in the suburbs.

しんきょう【心境】a mental state. ¶～に変化をきたす change *one's mind.*

しんきょう【信教】¶～の自由は憲法に保障されている The Constitution guarantees freedom of *religion.* (freedom の成句にはふつう冠詞をつけない).

しんきょう【進境】progress. ¶最近彼のゴルフの～は著しい He has made remarkable *progress* in golf recently.

しんきょう【新教】Protestantism.
—徒 a Protestant.

しんきょうち【新境地】¶彼の研究はまったくの～を開拓した His studies have broken entirely *new ground.*

しんきょく【新曲】a new musical composition.

しんきょくめん【新局面】¶事件は～を迎えた The case is beginning to assume *a new aspect.* / The case is beginning to enter upon *a new phase.*

しんきろう【蜃気楼】a mirage.

しんきろく【新記録】a new record. ¶～を作る make (⇆ establish) *a new record.* 日本～ *a new* Japanese *record.*

しんきん【心筋】**—梗塞**(こうそく) myocardial infarction.

しんぎん【呻吟】¶彼は病床に～している He *is confined to bed suffering severely.* 人々は暴君のもとで～していた People *groaned* under the tyrant.

しんきんかん【親近感】familiarity; intimacy (intimacy, intimate は男女間の情愛を表わすことが多い). ¶彼に～を覚える I *feel friendly toward* him.

しんく【辛苦】hardships; trials; (労苦) pains; labor. ¶彼は若いときから人生の～をなめてきた He has gone through a lot of *hardships* since he was young.

しんく【深紅】crimson. ¶～の優勝旗 a *crimson* champion flag.

しんぐ【寝具】bed and bedclothes; bedding (複数にならない).

しんくう【真空】(状態) vacuity; (空間) [a] vacuum.
—管 a vacuum tube; 英 a vacuum valve. **—制動機** a vacuum brake. **—掃除機** a vacuum [cleaner]. **—放電** vacuum discharge. **—ポンプ** a vacuum pump.

じんぐう【神宮】a *shinto* shrine. ¶明治～ the Meiji *Shrine.*
—外苑(がいえん) the Outer Garden of the Meiji Shrine. **—球場** the Meiji Jingu Stadium.

ジンクス a jinx. ¶～を破る(かつぐ) break (believe in) *a jinx.*

シングル (ゴルフのふたりでする試合) single; (ベッドの) a single bed; (上着の) a single-breasted coat.
—ヒット a single [hit]; a base hit.

シングルス〘テニス〙singles. ¶～をする play *singles.*

シンクロ synchronization.
—ナイズドスイミング synchronized swimming.
—フラッシュ〘写真〙a synchro-flash.

シンクロトロン〘物理〙a synchrotron.

しんぐん【進軍】march; advance. ¶一行は～中である The party *is on the march.* 隊長は部下に～を命じた The captain ordered his men to *advance.*

しんけい【神経】**1**〘神経繊維〙a nerve. ¶彼は歯医者で歯の～を抜かれた He had the *nerve* of his tooth extracted at the dentist's.
彼は歯の～がまひしている His teeth *are dead.*
2〘気質的・感情的なもの〙¶彼は～が太い He *is bold.* / He *is insensitive.* / He has a lot of *nerve.*
あなたは～がにぶい You *are insensitive.*
彼女は～が細かい She *is* extremely *sensitive.*
この仕事はたいへん～をすりへらす This work is an extraordinary strain on my *nerves.*
彼はいつも～が高ぶっている He always has a lot of *nerve.*
きのうは～が高ぶって一日じゅうなにもできなかった Yesterday I *was* so *excited* that I could do nothing all day.
あの騒音は～にこたえる That noise is a strain on my *nerves.*
なんでもない. それは～だ Your sickness is not so serious. It is merely your *imagination.*

3 〚合成語〛 ―質 ¶ 彼は～質に見える He looks *nervous*. 彼はたいへん～質だ He *is all nerves*. ―衰弱 ¶ 彼は～衰弱にかかっている He is suffering from *a nervous breakdown*. ―戦 a war of nerves. ―組織 nervous tissues. ―中枢 the nervous center. ―痛 neuralgia. 視― the optic nerve. 運動― a motor nerve. 中枢― the central nervous system.

しんげき【新劇】 a new school of acting. ¶ ～の女優 an actress of *the new school*.

しんげき【進撃】 an attack. ¶ ～する attack; advance (*on*; *against*).

しんけつ【心血】 ¶ 彼は研究に～を注いだ He *devoted himself to* his studies. / He *put his heart and soul into* his studies.

しんげつ【新月】 ¶ 今夜は～だ There is *a new moon* tonight.

しんけん【真剣】 seriousness; (刀) a sword. ¶ ～なまなざし an *eager* (≒ *earnest*) look. 彼は～になって勉強している He is studying *heart and soul*. 彼はほんとうに～だ He *is* quite *serious*.

―勝負(ほんものの刀での) a fight with swords; (本気の勝負) a hotly contested game. ―味 ¶ 彼は～味に乏しい He lacks *sincerity*.

しんげん【進言】 [an] advice; a suggestion. ¶ 彼はわれわれの～をいれなかった He did not take (≒ accept) our *advice*. 彼は学制改革を～した He *suggested* that the educational system be reformed.

じんけん【人絹】 artificial silk; rayon (rayon は光沢があるので ray (光)にちなんでつくられた語. いまでは artificial silk よりも rayon を用いる).

じんけん【人権】 human rights (civil liberty と言えば法律で保障されている個人の自由を指す). ¶ われわれの基本的～は守られなければならぬ Our fundamental *human rights* must be defended. それは～問題だ It is a question of *human rights*. 彼らはわれわれの～を蹂躙(じゅうりん)した They trampled down our *human rights*.

―侵害 an infringement (≒ outrage) on people's rights. ―擁護委員 a Civil Rights Commissioner (civil rights はアメリカでは憲法修正個条により保障された権利を指す. 常に複数形). ―擁護局 the Civil Liberties Bureau.

しんげんち【震源地】 the earthquake (≒ seismic) center; the center of the earthquake.

じんけんひ【人件費】 personnel expenses. ¶ ～がかさむ The *personnel expenses* run up.

しんご【新語】 a new[-coined] word. ¶ ～を作る coin *a new word*.

じんご【人後】 ¶ 彼は誠実さの点では～に落ちない He *is second to none* in sincerity. 彼は語学にかけては～に落ちない He *is behind no one* in linguistic attainments. / He *is as good* a linguist *as anyone*.

じんご【人語】 ¶ 動物は～を解さない Animals don't understand *human speech*.

しんこう【信仰】 [religious] faith; belief. ¶ 仏教を～している I *believe in* Buddha. / I am a Buddhist. 彼は～を捨てた He abandoned his *faith*. それが動機で彼はキリスト教への～をますます深めた That made him deepen his *faith in* Christianity.

―心 faith. ¶ 彼女は～心が厚い She *is pious* (≒ *devout*). 彼女はキリスト教への～心を失った She lost her *faith in* Christianity.

しんこう【振興】 ¶ 産業を～する promote the development of industry. 貿易～策をとる take measures for the *promotion* of foreign trade.

しんこう【進行】 progress. ¶ 仕事は着々と～している The work *is making* steady *progress*. 工事の～はなかなか思うようにいっていない Little *progress* has been made with the construction work. 仕事の～はおくれている The *progress* of my work has been delayed. ～は順調だ We *are progressing* well *with* the work. お仕事の～はいかがですか How *are* you *getting on with* your work (≒ activities)? 議事は彼が～している He *is presiding over* the proceedings. 交渉は目下～中だ The negotiations *are* now *going on*.

しんこう【親交】 close friendship. ¶ 彼と～を結ぶようになった I *came into friendly relations with* him. ぼくはその作家と～がある I *am on familiar terms with* the writer. (intimate terms を用いると今では男女間の愛情を連想するから「親交のある友人」は a good friend のほうがよい).

しんこう【深更】 midnight. ¶ 討論は～まで及んだ The discussion continued *until late at night*. ～まで起きていた I sat up *late*. (till late としないほうがよい).

しんこう【新興】 ―国 a rising (≒ developing) nation (今では a developing country (開発途上国) が最も普通). ―宗教 a newly-risen religion. ―都市 ㊥ a boom town.

しんごう【信号】 (交通·通信の) a signal. ¶ ～は赤だった The *signal* showed "Stop." / The [*traffic*] *light* was red.

危険― a danger signal; a red flag (≒ light). 遭難― an SOS; a distress signal. 注意(安全)― a caution (clear) signal. 徐行(停止)― a slowdown (stop) signal. 交通― a traffic signal. ¶ 交通～を守る observe *a traffic signal*.

じんこう【人工】 ¶ この景色は～の美だ This sight is an *artificial* beauty. この庭園は～が加えられたものだ This garden *is man-made*.

―衛星 a man-made satellite. ―栄養 artificial feeding. ―降雨 rain-making. ―呼吸 artificial respiration. ―授精 artificial insemination. ―授粉 artificial pollination. ―頭脳 an artificial brain. ―孵化(ふか) artificial incubation. ―惑星 an artificial planet.

じんこう【人口】 1 〚人数〛 population (形容詞は populous). ¶ ～1,000万の都市 a city of ten million *population*; a city with *a population* of ten million. 東京の～はロンドンより多い The *population* of

Tokyo is larger than that of London.

この都市の～はいくらか What is the *population* of this city? (How many と population は いっしょに用いない).

東京は夜間～が少ない Tokyo has *a* small night *population*.

その町の～は動かない *Population* remains stationary in the town.

—増加(減少) an increase (a decrease) in population. —密度 population density. ¶～密度の高い都市 a *densely populated* city. —問題 the population problem. 過剰— excess (≒ overflowing) population. 農業— the agricultural population.

2 〖人の口にのぼる〗 ¶この詩はよく～に膾炙(かいしゃ)している This poem *is wellknown to the public*.

しんこきゅう【深呼吸】 ¶～をする draw a deep breath; breathe deeply.

しんこく【申告】 a report; (税関での) declaration. ¶税務所へ所得の～をしなければならない I must *report* the amount of my income to the tax office. (税関で)なにか～すべき物がありますか 〔Do you have〕 Anything to *declare*?

青色— a blue-paper report. 確定— a final return. 予定— a provisional return.

しんこく【深刻】 ¶彼は～な顔をしている He looks *serious* (≒ *grave*). 彼らは～な食料不足に苦しんでいる They are suffering from an *acute* shortage of food. あまり～に考えるな Don't be so *serious*! / Don't take it so *serious*. 石炭産業の不振がますます～化している Coal industry is getting more and more *aggravated*.

しんこん【新婚】 ¶～の夫婦 *a newly-married couple*. 彼らは～ほやほやだ They are *a newly-married couple*.

—旅行 a honeymoon. ¶～旅行はパリにします We are to *honeymoon* (≒ *spend our honeymoon*) in Paris.

しんさ【審査】 an examination; (調査) inquiry. ¶応募作品を～する *judge* applied works 〔for the prize〕. 彼の絵が～に合格した His picture *was accepted* 〔for the exhibition〕.

—委員会 a judging committee; (絵画の) a hanging committee. —委員 a judge.

しんさい【震災】 〔an〕 earthquake disaster. ¶私は～で多大の損害を受けた I suffered a lot from the *earthquake*. 関東大～ the Kanto *Earthquakes*.

じんざい【人材】 a man of ability; a man of talent; (総称) talent. ¶彼は広く～を集めた He collected all *the talent* of the world. 会社は有為の～を登用した The company employed *men of talent*.

しんさく【新作】 a new 〔piece of〕 work. ¶～を発表する publish *a new work*.

しんさつ【診察】 〔medical〕 examination. ¶医者は患者を～した The doctor *examined* (≒ *saw*) patients. ～を受けた I *consulted* a doctor. / I went to *see* a doctor. (動詞 see は doctor を主語にすれば「診察する」となり，患者が主語になれば「(医者の)診察を受ける」となる). 私は胃を～してもらった I *had* my stomach *examined*.

—時間 㷌 office hours; consultation hours. —室 㷌 an office; a consultation room. —日 a consultation day. —料 a medical fee.

しんさん【辛酸】 ¶生活の～をなめる go through every *hardship* of life.

しんざん【深山】 ¶彼は～に分け入った He made his way into *the depths of mountains*.

—幽谷 steep mountains and deep valleys.

しんし【紳士】 a gentleman (覆 -men).

¶～らしい風采(ふうさい) a *gentlemanly* appearance. ～らしくふるまう behave like *a gentleman*. 彼のいかにも～ぶったところが気に入らない I don't like his *snobbery*.

—協定 a gentleman's agreement. —録 a Who's Who; a directory.

しんし【真摯】 ¶彼の～な態度に深く打たれた I was deeply moved by his *sincerity*.

じんじ【人事】 ¶～を尽くして天命を待つ do *one's* best and leave the rest to God.

—異動 personnel changes. —院 the National Personnel Authority. —課 a personnel section. —行政 personnel administration.

しんしき【神式】 ¶葬儀は～により挙行される The funeral service will be carried out according to *shinto rites*.

しんしき【新式】 a new type; (方法) a new method. ¶～の機械 a *new-type* machine.

シンジケート〖経済学〗 a syndicate.

しんしつ【心室】〖解剖学〗 the ventricle 〔of the heart〕.

右(左)— the right (left) ventricle.

しんしつ【寝室】 a bedroom (イギリスでは２階建ての家の場合，寝室はふつう２階にある. He's coming down. といえば「彼はおりて(つまり起きて寝室からおりて)くる」の意味になることが多い).

しんじつ【真実】 the truth (真実は常に一つしかないから the をつけて the truth と言う. うそはいろいろあるから不定冠詞をつけて a lie または many lies と言う); reality. ¶～を語る speak (≒ tell) the *truth*. ～のところは，彼は彼女が好きでたまらないのだ *To tell the truth*, he is crazy about her.

—味 ¶その話は～味に欠けている The story lacks *reality*.

じんじふせい【人事不省】 faint. ¶彼女は～になった She *swooned* (≒ *fainted away*). 彼はまったく～になって倒れた He fell *in a dead faint*.

しんじゃ【信者】 a believer. ¶彼女はキリスト教の～になった She became a Christian.

じんじゃ【神社】 a *shinto* shrine.

—仏閣 shrines and temples.

しんしゃく【斟酌】 consideration; allowance. ¶われわれは事情を～して判断を下さねばならぬ We must make a judgment *taking the circumstances into consideration*. 彼の年がいかないという点を～してほしい I want you to *make* *allowance for* his youth.

しんしゅ【進取】¶ ～の気性〔a spirit of〕*enterprise*; an *enterprising* spirit. 彼は非常に～の気性に富んだ人だ He is a man *of great enterprise*.

しんしゅ【新種】a new species.

しんじゅ【真珠】a pearl. ¶ ～を養殖する culture *pearls*.

—貝 a pearl oyster. —細工 pearl work. —取り(採取) pearl fishery; (人) a pearl diver. —養殖 pearl culture. —養殖場 a pearl farm. 人造— an artificial pearl. 天然— a〔natural〕pearl. 模造— an imitation pearl. 養殖— a culture〔d〕pearl.

し

じんしゅ【人種】a human race. ¶ 彼はわれわれとは～が違うのだ(住む世界が違う) He *lives in* (≒ *belongs to*) *a different world from* ours.

—学 ethnology. —差別 racial discrimination (アメリカでは人種差別を segregation という語でしばしば表わす. また特に黒人に対する差別を Jim Crow と言う). 白色(黄色; 黒色)— the white (yellow; black) people.

しんじゅう【心中】a double suicide (英語には double suicide という習慣はまれ. したがって成句になっていない). ¶ 恋人たちは～した The lovers committed *a double suicide*.

—未遂 an attempted double suicide. 一家— a〔whole〕family suicide. 無理— a forced double suicide.

しんしゅく【伸縮】elasticity; flexibility. ¶ それは簡単に～する It easily *expands and contracts*.

—性 ¶ ～性のある布 *elastic* cloth. ～性のない布 cloth lacking *elasticity*. —自在 ¶ ～自在の elastic; flexible.

しんしゅつ【進出】¶ 政界に～する *enter into* politics; *enter* the political world. 国産品が海外市場に～する Home goods *make inroads into* the overseas market. そのデパートが東京に～しようと計画している The department store is planning to *extend its business to* Tokyo. 外国資本の日本～が目だつ There is *a* remarkable *advance* of foreign capital *into* the Japanese business world.

しんしゅつきぼつ【神出鬼没】¶ ～の犯人 an *elusive* criminal.

しんしゅん【新春】(新年) the New Year; (春) early spring. ¶ ことしはロンドンで～を迎えた I welcomed *the New Year* in London.

しんしょ【信書】a letter; (総称) correspondence. ¶ ～の秘密は守られねばならぬ We should protect the privacy of personal *correspondence*.

しんしょ【親書】¶ 大統領からの～ *a letter* with the President's autograph; the President's *autograph letter*.

しんしょう【心証】an impression; conviction. ¶ 私は彼の～を害した I hurt his *feelings*. 被告の態度は裁判官の～をよくした(悪くした) The defendant's attitude gave the judge *a* favorable (*an* unfavorable) *impression*.

しんしょう【身上】fortune; property. ¶ 彼は株で～をつくった(つぶした) He made (ruined) *a fortune* by a stock speculation.

しんじょう【身上】¶ 正直が彼の～だ Honesty is his sole *merit*.

—書 *one's* qualification statement. —調査 *one's* character investigation.

しんじょう【真情】genuine sentiment; true heart. ¶ 自分の～を吐露した I expressed my *genuine feeling*.

しんじょう【信条】(信念) a principle; (教え) a creed. ¶ 努力は私の～である It is my *principle* to make every effort. 信者として～を守る I observe *a creed* as a devotee.

じんじょう【尋常】normality. ¶ ～に勝負する play *fair*. これは～なことではない This *is out of the common*. この問題は～な方法では解決できない We cannot solve the problem through *ordinary* means.

しんしょうしゃ【身障者】a physically handicapped person.

しんしょく【浸食】corrosion; erosion. ¶ 海が海岸線を少しずつ～した The sea *ate away* the coastline little by little.

しんしょく【寝食】¶ 彼は～を忘れて研究を行なった He *devoted himself exclusively to* his studies. われわれは5年間～をともにした We *lived under the same roof* for five years. / We *lived together* for five years.

しんしん【心身・身心】¶ 彼は～ともに健康だ He is sound in *mind and body*. / He is in *mental and bodily* health. 彼は～とも疲労困憊(こんぱい)している He is exhausted *physically and mentally*.

しんしん【新進】¶ ～の作曲家 a *new* composer. ～気鋭の学者 a *young* and vigorous scholar.

しんしん【深深】¶ ～と夜が更けてきた The night *has grown* (≒ *has advanced*) *late*. 寒さが～と身にしみた The cold *pierced me to the bone*.

しんじん【信心】faith. ¶ ～深い女性 a *pious* woman. 彼は仏教を～する He *has faith in* Buddhism.

しんじん【新人】(芸能界の) a new face; (新参者) a newcomer.

—歌手 a new singer. —選手(野球の) a rookie.

しんじん【深甚】¶ 彼の好意に対して～の謝意を表したい I want to express my *deepest* gratitude for his favor.

じんしん【人心】¶ ～を一新する必要がある It is necessary to lead *the thought of the people* to an entirely different channel. 彼のことばは～を不安に陥れた His words made *public feelings* uneasy.

じんしん【人身】—攻撃 a personal attack. —売買 flesh traffic.

しんすい【心酔】¶ 彼はベートーベンの音楽に～している He *adores* (≒ *is an adorer of*) Beethoven.

—者 ¶ 彼はアメリカ～者だ He is *a maniac*

for (≒ *an adorer of*) American ways.

しんすい【浸水】¶ 300戸が床まで～した Three hundred houses *were flooded* floor-deeps.
—家屋 flooded houses.

しんすい【進水】¶ この船はことし1月に～した This ship *was launched* last January.
—式 a launching ceremony. —台 the launching platform.

しんずい【神髄・真髄】¶ 宗教の～ the *essence* of religion. 武士道の～ the *soul* of *Bushido*.

じんずうりき【神通力】a supernatural power; a divine power.

しん・ずる【信ずる】**1**〖信用する・確信する〗believe. ¶ 彼はどんなことでも～ずる He *believes* any sort of thing.
彼はまじめな人間だと～ずる I *believe* that he is a decent man. / I *believe* him to be a decent man. (後者は文語的).
そんなことはとても～じられない I can hardly *believe* such a thing.
私を～じてくださいませんか Won't you *believe in* me? (上例2文の違い: believe something (somebody) は一時的にある事(人)を信ずること, believe in とすれば永続的に信ずること).
自己を～じなさい *Have faith in* yourself.
そのことばは私にはとても～じがたい I simply can't *believe* those words.
彼が死んだとは～じられない It *is unbelievable* that he is dead.
私は彼女の合格を～じている I *am sure* she will pass.
彼は自分の能力を～じている He *is confident of* his own ability.
その話はあまりよくできすぎていて～じられないほどだ The story is *too good to be true*.
2〖神仏を〗¶ 私は神を～じない I don't *believe in* God.
彼は仏教を～じている He *professes* Buddhism.

しんせい【申請】application. ¶ 都の建設局へ建築許可を～した I *applied for* the building permit *to* the City Building.
—書 an application form; a written application. —人 an applicant; a petitioner.

しんせい【神聖】sacredness; holiness.
¶ ～な職業 a *divine* occupation. 審判は～である Judgment *is sacred*. ～なふんい気に打たれた I was impressed by the *holy* (≒ *consecrated*) atmosphere.
—ローマ帝国 the Holy Roman Empire.

しんせい【真性】¶ ～の天然痘患者 a *genuine* smallpox case.

しんせい【新制】—大学 a new system university. —高校 a senior high school. —中学 a junior high school.

しんせい【新星】〘天文学〙a nova; (新人) a new face.

じんせい【人生】life. ¶ ～とはそんなものさ Such is *life*. / *Life* is like that. (失敗や不幸があると欧米人(特にフランス人)はよくこう言う). ～は大いに楽しむべきだ *Life* is much to be enjoyed. ～は40から *Life* begins at forty.
—観 *one's* view of life.

しんせいめん【新生面】¶ 彼は語学研究に～を開いた He opened up *a new field* for linguistic studies. / He brought *a new phase* in linguistic studies.

しんせかい【新世界】a new world; (アメリカ大陸) the New World.

しんせき【親戚】a relation; a relative (アメリカ人は relative のほうを好む). ¶ 彼とは長年～づきあいをしている I*'ve been on very good terms with* him for a long time.

じんせき【人跡】¶ ～まれな奥地 an *unfrequented* back country. ～未踏の森 *a virgin* (≒ *an untrodden*) forest.

しんせつ【新雪】fresh snow. ¶ ～が朝日に輝く The *fresh snow* is glittering in the rising sun.

しんせつ【新設】¶ ～の会社 a *newly-established* (≒ *new*) company. 大学を～した We *established* (≒ *started*) a new university.

しんせつ【新説】a new theory. ¶ ～を唱える advance *a new theory*.

しんせつ【親切】kindness. ¶ ～な人 a *kind* person (kindly とすれば様子から判断して「親切そうな」の気持ちをふくむ). 老人に～にするのは当然だ It is natural for us to *be kind* to old people. 彼が出迎えにきてくれたのは～からだった It was *out of* (≒ *through*) *kindness* that he came to meet me. 宿屋では～な扱いをしてくれた I was treated *kindly* at the inn. ～にも道を教えてくれた He *was so kind as* to show me the way. ～にもわざわざその本を自宅まで持ってきてくれた He *was kind enough to* take the trouble to bring the book to my house. せっかくの彼の～が無になった His *kindness* was wasted, to my regret. ご～にありがとう Thank you for your *kindness*. ご～にそう言ってくださってまことにありがとう *It is* very *kind* (≒ *nice*) *of* you *to* say so.

しんせん【新鮮】freshness. ¶ ～な野菜 *fresh* vegetables. ～な空気 *fresh* air. 首相の演説には～なものはなにもなかった We found nothing *novel* in the Prime Minister's speech.

しんぜん【神前】¶ 結婚式は～で執り行なわれた The wedding was performed *according to shinto rites*.

しんぜん【親善】friendship; friendly relations. ¶ 日米間の～関係を維持しなければならぬ We must maintain *friendly relations* between America and Japan. 彼は日中間のいっそうの～をはかるために全力を尽くした He did his best to promote *closer relations* between Japan and China.
—使節団 a goodwill mission.

じんせん【人選】¶ 目下探検隊員の～中だ We *are* now *selecting* explorers suitable *for* the expeditionary party. 残念だが彼は～に漏れた We are disappointed that he was left out of *the choice*.

しんソ【親ソ】¶ ～政策をとる adopt a *pro-Soviet* policy.

しんそう【真相】the truth; facts. ¶ その事件

の～を知ろうと努めた I tried to get at *the truth* about the affair. 彼は～を語った(明らかにした) He told (revealed) *the truth.* ～は明らかになった *The truth* has come out.

しんそう【新装】¶～なったビル a *newly constructed* building. ～をこらした社屋 a *beautifully remodeled* company building.

しんそう【深層】 ━構造(言語学で) deep structure. ━心理学 depth psychology.

しんぞう【心臓】 the heart. ¶～は絶えず鼓動する *The heart* is always beating. 彼はよく～の発作を起こす He often has *heart attacks.* 彼は～が弱い(肉体的に) He is suffering from *a weak heart.* / (気が弱い) He *is* so *meek.* 彼はまったく～が強い(ずうずうしい) He *is* very *cheeky.*

━病 a heart disease. ━まひ a heart failure.

しんぞう【新造】¶～の豪華船 a *newly-built* luxury liner.

じんぞう【人造】 ━湖 a man-made lake. ━繊維 a synthetic fiber. ━人間 a robot. ━肥料 an artificial fertilizer.

じんぞう【腎臓】〔解剖学〕the kidney.

しんぞく【親族】 a relative ; a relation.

直系━ a lineal relative. 傍系━ a collateral relative. ━会議 a family reunion.

じんそく【迅速】¶彼は仕事を～にやってのける He *promptly* (≒ *quickly*) carries out his business. / He dispatches business *with speed.*

しんそこ【心底】¶彼は～から過ちを後悔した He regretted the mistake *heartily* (≒ *from the bottom of his heart*).

しんたい【身体】 a body.

━検査 a physical examination ; a health check. ━障害者 a physically handicapped person.

しんたい【進退】¶彼は～きわまってなすすべを知らなかった He *was between the devil and the deep sea* (≒ *was driven to the wall*) and did not know what to do. 彼はわれわれと～をともにするつもりだ He is going to *cast in his lot with* us.

━伺い ¶彼は責任を感じて～伺いを出した He submitted *an informal resignation* from a sense of responsibility.

しんだい【身代】 a fortune. ¶彼は株の投機で～をつくった(つぶした) He made (ruined) *a fortune* by a stock speculation. 彼は裸一貫で～をこしらえた He built up *a fortune* out of nothing. 彼は子どもたちにばく大な～を残した He left *a large fortune* to his children.

しんだい【寝台】 a bed ; (列車・船の) a berth. ¶～を予約する reserve *a berth.*

━券 a berth ticket. ━車 a sleeping car; 英 a sleeper. ━料金 a berth charge.

じんたい【人体】 a human body. ¶それは～に害を及ぼす It does harm to *a person.* それは～に大いに影響がある It has great influence upon *the human body.*

じんたい【靭帯】〔解剖学〕a ligament.

じんだい【甚大】¶台風による作物の被害は～だ The crop was *badly* damaged by the typhoon.

しんたいし【新体詩】(総称) the new-style poetry ; (詩の1編) a new-style poem.

しんたいりく【新大陸】(アメリカ) the New Continent ; the New World.

しんたく【神託】 an oracle.

しんたく【信託】 trust. ¶彼に財産を～した I *left* my property *in trust with* him. / I *trusted* my property *to* him.

━会社 a trust company. ━銀行 a trust bank. ━統治 trusteeship. ━預金 a trust deposit. 投資━ investment trust.

しんたん【心胆】¶彼の～を寒からしめた I made his blood run cold.

しんだん【診断】 diagnosis. ¶肺炎と～された My illness *was diagnosed as* pneumonia. あの医者はよく～を誤る The doctor sometimes makes *a* wrong *diagnosis.*

━書 a medical certificate. 健康━ a medical examination.

じんち【人知】 human intellect ; human knowledge. ¶～の及ばない beyond *human knowledge.*

じんち【陣地】 a position. ¶～を固める hold *a position.*

しんちく【新築】¶～中の家 a house *under construction.* 自分の家を～する *build* a house of *one's* own.

じんちく【人畜】¶これは～無害だ This will do no harm to either *man or beast.*

しんちゃ【新茶】 the first tea of the season.

しんちゃく【新着】 new arrival (物なら a をつける). ¶～の図書 a *newly-arrived* book. ～の洋画 a *newly-imported* foreign film.

しんちゅう【心中】¶彼の～は察することができない I cannot enter into his *feelings.* ～を彼に打ち明けた I *took* him *into my confidence.*

しんちゅう【進駐】¶当時ドイツ軍がパリに～していた Then the German army *was occupying* (≒ *was staying in*) Paris.

━軍 the occupation forces.

しんちゅう【真鍮】 brass. ¶～製品 *brass* ware.

しんちょう【身長】 height. ¶彼の～をはかった I measured his *height.* 彼女は～が伸びた She grew *taller.* (higher はさける). 彼は～はどのくらいありますか How *tall* is he? 彼は～が6フィート以上ある He is more than six feet *tall* (≒ *in height*).

━順 ¶彼らは～順に並んだ They formed a line *in order of height.* 平均━ ¶このクラスの男子の平均～は158センチある *The average height of* the boys of this class is 158 centimeters.

しんちょう【伸長・伸張】 expansion. ¶輸出を～する *increase* exports.

しんちょう【慎重】 care ; caution. ¶～な回答 a *careful* answer. ～なドライバー a *cautious* driver. ～な態度 a *cautious* attitude. 彼は何事にも～さを欠く He lacks *prudence* in everything. 彼女は何事をするにも～だ She *is* *careful in* doing anything. その問題は～に考慮中である The matter is under *careful* consideration. その問題は～に審議する必要がある It is necessary to give *careful* consideration to the matter. ～にやらなければいけない You must do it very *carefully*.

しんちょう【新調】 ¶ ～の上着 a *newly-made* suit. ～したばかりの旅行かばん a *brand-new* traveling bag. 洋服を～しよう I will *buy* a *new* suit. / (仕立てさせるなら) I will *get* a *new* suit made.

じんちょうげ【沈丁花】〘植物〙a daphne.

しんちょく【進捗】 ¶ 工事は～中である The construction *is under way* (≒ *is in progress*). 交渉はいっこうに～していない The negotiation has made no *progress*.

しんちんたいしゃ【新陳代謝】 renewal; (生理) metabolism. ¶ 人間の体は常に～する The human body is always subject to *metabolism*. 流行語は～が激しい A vogue word *is* always *replaced one after another*.

しんつう【心痛】 a heartache. ¶ 彼は息子のことを～している He *is worried about* his son. ～のあまり床についた He *was* so much *worried* that he was confined to bed.

じんつう【陣痛】 labor 〔pains〕. ¶ 彼女は～が始まっている She *is in labor* 〔*pains*〕. ～の発作があった There was *an onset of labor* 〔*pains*〕. 新企画の実現には～の苦しみが伴う We have much *trouble* in realizing a new scheme.

じんつうりき【神通力】 a magical power.

しんてい【進呈】 presentation. ¶ きみに～するものがあります I have *a present* (≒ *a gift*) for you. きみにこの本を～しよう This book is for you. / I will *give* (≒ *present*) this book *to* you. / I will *present* you *with* this book. 見本は無料で～します Samples *are presented* free.

しんていばん【新訂版】 a revised (≒ newly-revised) edition.

しんてき【心的】 mental. ¶ ～現象 *mental* phenomenon.

しんてん【進展】 progress. ¶ 交渉が～した The negotiation *has progressed*. 事件は意外な方向に～した The affair *progressed* in an unexpected direction. 万事うまく～している Everything *is shaping up* (≒ *is going on*) well.

しんてん【親展】 (封筒の上書き) Confidential. ¶ ～と書かれた手紙を受け取った I received a letter marked 'Personal.'

しんでん【神殿】 a shrine; a sanctuary.

しんでんず【心電図】〘医学〙〔an〕electrocardiogram (ECG).

しんと ¶ あたりは～静まりかえっている All is dead*ly still* (≒ *quiet*). 会場がまったく～なった *A* dead *silence* fell upon the hall.

しんど【進度】 progress. ¶ このクラスは歴史の～が遅れている This class is backward in history.

しんど【深度】 ¶ 湖の～を測る measure the *depth* of a lake.

—計 a sea gauge.

しんど【震度】 a magnitude 〔of an earthquake〕. ¶ さっきの地震は東京で～5の強震であった The earthquake we had a little while ago was a strong one of *magnitude* 5 in Tokyo.

しんとう【浸透】 saturation; permeation. ¶ 薬が皮下に～した The medicine *penetrated through* the skin.

しんどう【神童】 an infant prodigy.

しんどう【振動】 vibration; (揺れ) a shock; (小刻みな) a tremor. ¶ モーターの～ the *vibration* of a motor. 毎秒50の～ fifty *vibrations* per second. この車は乗っていて～が感じられない I cannot feel the *vibration* when I am on the car.

—器 a vibrator. —数 the number of vibrations.

しんどう【震動】 a tremor; a vibration. ¶ 爆発で大地が～した The explosion *made* the earth *shake*. 突然大きな～を感じた Suddenly I felt *a* big (≒ heavy) *shock*. 貨車が通るたびに家が～する The house *trembles* (≒ *vibrates*) whenever freight cars pass.

じんとう【陣頭】 ¶ 市長が～に立って災害復旧にあたった The mayor *took the lead in* restor*ing* the disaster.

じんどう【人道】 (道路) 米 a sidewalk; 英 a pavement; (人の守る道) humanity. ¶ ～に反する罪 a crime against *humanity*. 彼は捕虜を～的に取り扱った He treated war prisoners *with humanity*. そのような行為は～にもとる Such conduct *is inhuman*. / It is an *inhuman* act.

—主義 humanitarianism. —主義者 a humanitarian. —問題 a question touching (≒ affecting) humanity.

じんとく【人徳】 *one's* natural virtue. ¶ それは彼の～のしからしむるところだ That depends on his *natural virtue*.

じんど・る【陣取る】 ¶ われわれは敵の正面に～った We *pitched a camp* in front of the enemy. 彼らは最前列に～って声援していた They were cheering up in a front-row seat.

シンナー〘薬品〙thinner.

しんにち【親日】 ¶ ドイツ人は概して～的だ Germans are generally *pro-Japanese*.

—家 a pro-Japanese; a Japanophile.

しんにゅう【侵入】 (敵国への) invasion; (他人の所へ) intrusion; trespass. ¶ 敵が不意に～してきた The enemy *invaded* our country all of a sudden.

しんにゅう【進入】 ¶ 飛行機が滑走路に～してくる A plane *is approaching* along the landing strip.

しんにゅうせい【新入生】 (小・中学校の) a new pupil; (高校以上) a new student; (特にアメリカの大学の) a freshman (freshman は女性にも用いる).

しんにん【信任】 trust; confidence. ¶ 彼は上司の～を得ている He enjoys the *confidence* of his superiors. / He *is trusted by* his

し

superiors.
—状 credentials ; letters of credence. —投票 a vote of confidence.

しんにん【新任】¶ ～の校長 a *new* principal. 大臣は～のあいさつを述べた The minister made an *inaugural* address.

しんねん【信念】faith ; confidence. ¶ ～が強い(弱い)人 a man of strong (weak) *faith*. 彼には確固たる～がない He is not a man of unshaken *faith*. 彼は～をまげない He sticks to his *conviction*.

しんねん【新年】the New Year. ¶ ～おめでとう〔A〕Happy New Year〔to you〕. ～をパリで迎えた I greeted *the New Year* in Paris. 故郷で～を祝った We celebrated *the New Year* at our home town.

しんぱい【心配】1〖気がかり〗anxiety. ¶ なんの～もない人なんていない There is nobody who is completely free from *anxiety*. / There is nobody who has nothing on his mind. うちの子どもは親に～ばかりかける Our child always causes us *anxiety*. / Our child is a constant source of *anxiety* to us. 私は子どものころ病弱で親にずいぶん～をかけた I was weak in my childhood and gave a lot of *trouble* to my parents. もう～ありません，病人は峠を越しました You need not *feel anxious* any more, because the patient has turned the corner. 早く帰りなさい，うちの人たちが～するから Go home at once, or your family will *wonder* what's happened. 試験の結果が～で眠れなかった I *was* so *uneasy* (≒ *anxious*) *about* the result of the examination that I could not sleep. ～するな，私がついているじゃないか Don't *feel uneasy*, I'm with you. 私の将来についてご～には及びません，必ず成功してみせます You need not *be concerned about* my future ; I will certainly succeed. 彼女には～の種が絶えない She always has something on her mind. 彼はいつも金の～に追われている He is always pressed with money *worries*. ご～ごとが多くてたいへんですね I am sorry that you have a lot of *troubles*. 彼女は～のあまり病気になった She *was* so *anxious* that she fell ill. あすは雨の～はなさそうだ I don't think it will rain tomorrow. / You need not *be afraid* that it will rain tomorrow. 彼は～そうに私を見た He looked at me with *an anxious look* (≒ *a troubled face*). もう老後の～をしているのか（気にかける）Have you begun to *take thought for* your old age yet ? /（そなえる）Have you begun to *provide against* (≒ *for*) your old age yet ? よけいな～をするな Take care not to *worry* too much. / Don't *worry yourself* unnecessarily.
—性 ¶ きみもずいぶん～性だ You *worry too much*. / You *are of* a *worrying temperament*.
2〖世話〗¶ いい勤め口を～してあげよう I will get you a good position. 彼は帰りの旅費まで～してくれた He *was kind enough to* give me even the expenses for my return trip. いろいろ～してくれる人がいて，きみも幸せだ You are fortunate to have a person who *looks after* you in many ways. あの方に～していただいて娘もようやくかたづきました He *helped* to find a husband for our daughter, who is married at last.

シンパ〔サイザー〕a sympathizer.

しんぱん【侵犯】violation. ¶ 国境～ *a* border *violation*. 領空～ *a violation* of another country's territorial air.

しんぱん【新版】a new edition ;（新刊）a new publication.

しんぱん【審判】judgment ;（競技の）refereeing ; umpireship ;（審判員）a referee ; an umpire ; a judge.
¶ 最後の～ the Last Judgment. 彼は公平な～員だ He is *an* impartial *umpire*. ぼくがその野球の試合の～をつとめた I acted as *umpire* in the baseball game. ～の判定には服従すべきだ We should obey the *judge's* (≒ *umpire's*) decision.

しんぴ【神秘】〔a〕mystery. ¶ ～的教義 a *mystical* doctrine. ～的伝説 a *mystic* tradition. 宇宙の～ the *mysteries* of the universe. 仏像の～的な微笑 a *mysterious* smile of a Buddhist image. ～に包まれた事件 incidents wrapped in *mystery*. 彼女にはなにか～的なところがあった There was something *mysterious* about her.

しんぴ【真皮】〖解剖〗the true skin ; the derm.

しんびがん【審美眼】¶ 彼は～がある He has *an eye for the beautiful*. / He has *a sense of beauty*.

しんぴつ【真筆】a genuine handwriting ; *one's* own handwriting.

しんぴょうせい【信憑性】reliability. ¶ そのニュースは～がある(ない) The news *is reliable* (*unreliable*).

しんぴん【新品】a new (≒ brand-new) article. ¶ ～同様です This *looks brand-new*. / This *is as good as new*.

じんぴん【人品】¶ ～卑しからぬ人 a *respectable-looking* person.

しんぷ【神父】a father. ¶ ブラウン～ *Father* Brown.

しんぷ【新婦】a bride.

シンフォニー〔a〕symphony.

しんぷく【心服】¶ 彼は仲間から～されている He *enjoys the esteem of* his comrades. / He *is highly respected* by his friends.

しんぷく【振幅】〖物理〗amplitude〔of vibration〕.

しんぷく【震幅】the amplitude of an earthquake.

じんぶつ【人物】〔a〕character ;〔a〕personality. ¶ 彼はどんな～ですか What sort of *man* is he ? 彼は頼もしい～だ He is *a* promising

person. 彼はなかなかの～だ He is quite *a character*. 彼女はひとかどの～だ She is *somebody*. 彼は～がしっかりしている He has *a* steady *personality*. 彼の～には多くの人が敬服している Many people admire his *personality*. この店は～本位で店員を採用している This store goes *by character* in engaging clerks. 人物の点ではAよりBのほうがいい B is superior to A in *character*. 歴史上の～ *a* historical *figure*. 小説の中の～ *characters* in a novel.
—画 a portrait. —評 a personal sketch. 好— a good-natured man. 注意— a man on the black list.

しんぶん【新聞】a newspaper. ¶ ～を読む read the *newspapers*. ふたつ～をとっている I take in two *papers*. ～に昨夜の火事のことが出ている The *paper* says (≒ has a report) about the fire that occurred last night. ～を配達する deliver *newspaper*. 彼は～でさんざんたたかれた He was severely attacked in *the press*.
—界 the newspaper world. —記事 a newspaper account. —記者 a newsman. —社 a newspaper office. —週間 Newspaper Week. —種 a news item. —屋(人) a newsdealer; 英 a news agent; (店) a newspaper agency.

じんぶん【人文】civilization; culture.
—科学 cultural sciences. —科目 humanities. —主義 humanism. —地理 human geography.

しんべい【親米】pro-Americanism.
—家 a pro-American.

しんぺい【新兵】a new conscript; a recruit.

しんぺん【身辺】¶ われわれは彼の～を気づかっている We are anxious about his *personal safety*. 容疑者の～を洗わなければならぬ We must rake up a suspect's *past*. 彼は～を(持ち物を)整理している He is arranging his *belongings*.

しんぽ【進歩】progress; advance. ¶ 科学の～ the *progress* of science. 日本は諸外国に比べて科学技術が～している Japan *is ahead of* other foreign countries in scientific technique. 私は英語がちっとも～しない I *have made* no *progress in* English. 彼女の英会話は大いに～している She *is making* good *progress in* speaking English. (progress には形容詞がついても不定冠詞はつけない).
—派 the progressive group. ¶ 保守党内の～派 the *progressive* group within the Conservative Party.

しんぼう【心棒】(車輪の) an axle.

しんぼう【信望】(人望) popularity; (信用) confidence. ¶ ～のある(ない)人 a man of *popularity* (*no popularity*). 彼は学生たちの～を得た He gained *a popularity* with the students. 彼は部下の～が厚い He enjoys the utmost *confidence* of his followers.

しんぼう【深謀】¶ ～遠慮の人 a *prudent*, *far-sighted* man.

しんぼう【辛抱】patience. ¶ 彼は～強い He *is persevering*. きみはもう少し～したほうがいい You must be a little more *patient*. 何事にも～が肝心だ *Perseverance* is essential in everything. もうとても～しきれない My *patience* is worn out. ～強くやることが結局は成功への近道だ It is a short cut to success after all to advance *with perseverance*.

しんぽう【信奉】¶ キリスト教を～する人たち those who *profess* Christianity.
—者 a believer. ¶ マルクス主義の～者 *a believer in* Marxism.

じんぼう【人望】popularity. ¶ 彼は生徒に～がある(ない) He *is popular* (*unpopular*) *among* the pupils.

しんぼく【親睦】friendship. ¶ われわれは毎年1度同窓会を開いて～をはかる By holding an alumni association once a year we promote *friendship* among our old classmates.
—会 a social gathering; 米 a get-together. —団体 a party for promoting mutual friendship.

シンポジウム a symposium (複 symposia).

しんまい【新米】new rice.

しんまえ【新前】¶ ～のくせに大きなことを言うな That's a big word for *an upstart* like you. ～のくせに出しゃばりすぎる He is too forward for *a green* (≒ *new*) *hand*.

じんましん【蕁麻疹】〖医学〗nettle rash.

しんみ【新味】novelty. ¶ 彼の話は～に乏しかった I found his speech lacking in *novelty*.

しんみ【親身】¶ Aさんから～も及ばぬ世話を受けた I was looked after with *more than parental care* of Mr. A. 彼はいつでも～になって相談に乗ってくれる He always takes a *parental* (≒ *fatherly*) interest in me to give advice.

しんみつ【親密】intimacy. ¶ 彼とは特別に～な間柄だ I am on a specially *friendly* terms with him. (intimate は男女関係を意味するのでさける).

しんみょう【神妙】¶ 彼は～な顔つきをして現われた He appeared with a *serious* look. 彼の～なふるまいは彼らの深い感動を呼び起こした As he *behaved himself* they were moved profoundly.

しんみり ¶ 彼女の～した話し方には思わず引き込まれてしまう Her *heart to heart* talk captivates me in spite of myself. 彼女の話が始まると一同はいつのまにか～してしまった When she began to talk, all became *sad* before they were aware of it. 彼の話はどうも～したところがない His talk somewhat lacks *seriousness*.

じんみん【人民】the people; the public; 米 citizens (英では subjects のほうがふつう).
¶ ～の権利 the *people's* (≒ *civil*) rights.
—公社 a people's commune. —裁判 a people's court. —戦線 the Popular (≒ People's) Front. —投票 a popular vote; a referendum (複 referendums, referenda). —民主主義 public democracy.

しんめ【新芽】a bud; a shoot; a sprout.
¶ ～をふく sprout; bud.

し

じんめい【人名】a person's name.
—辞典 a biographical dictionary. —簿 a list of names; a roll; 米 a roster; (住所録) a directory.

じんめい【人命】〔a〕life. ¶ ～にかかわるような暴挙 a reckless attempt that may endanger *life*. ～を軽視する make light of *human life*. 多数の～を奪う carry off the *lives* of many people. ～を救助する save *a life*.

しんめんもく【真面目】¶ ～を発揮する show *one s true character*.

し

しんもつ【進物】a present; a gift.

じんもん【尋問】¶ 警官は不審な者を～する A policeman *questions* (≒ *examines*) those who look suspicious.
反対— a cross-question.

しんや【深夜】¶ ～に late at night. ～まで起きている sit up *late*. 論議は～まで続いた The discussion continued till *far into the night*.
—営業 midnight work. ¶ ～営業の open *at late hours*. —放送 midnight broadcasting.

しんやく【新薬】a new medicine.

しんやくせいしょ【新約聖書】the New Testament.

しんゆう【親友】a good friend; a close friend; a bosom friend.

しんよう【信用】confidence; credit; faith.
¶ きみのことばを～しよう I will *believe* you.
私を～してそれを任せてくれませんか Can't you *trust* me *with* it?
あれは～できる男だ He is a *trustworthy* man./ He is a *reliable* man.
彼のことばはどこまで～していいかわからない I do not know how far I can *believe* what he says.
彼なら～がおける We can put *trust in* him.
今回の事件でわが社の～は世間にがた落ちだ The present case has discredited our firm hopelessly with the public.
これでもぼくは社長に～がある In spite of this I stand high in the *estimation* of the president.(「これでも」が得意の気持ちを表わすなら I flatter myself that ...とする).
メーカーを～してこのテレビを買った I have bought this TV set because I *have confidence in* the manufacturer.
宝石は～のある店で買う I buy jewels at a *reputable* shop.
商売は客の～を得ることが第一だ The first consideration in business is to gain the *confidence* (≒ *trust*) of the customers.
いったん～を失ったら回復するのは容易ではない It is by no means easy to regain *confidence* once lost.
そのニュースは～できるのか Can we *give credence to* the news?
社員は会社の～を傷つけないように注意すべきだ Company employees should be careful not to disgrace the *reputation* of their company.
—貸し credit loan; loan on credit. —借り a debt of honor. —組合 a credit union. —金庫 a credit depository. —状 a letter of credit. —照会 a credit (≒ confidential) inquiry. —状態 financial (≒ credit) standing. —調査 credit research. ¶ 新しい会社と取引するときは～調査が必要だ It is necessary to make *credit research* in dealing with a new company. —取引 credit transaction; sales on credit. —保険 fidelity insurance.

じんよう【陣容】a staff. ¶ 敵の～が整わぬうちに攻撃せよ Attack the enemy before they *array for battle* (≒ *are in a battle formation*). 試合に負けたからといって特に～を変える必要はない There is no need of changing our *line-up* simply because we have lost a game.

しんようじゅ【針葉樹】〔植物〕a needle-leaf tree.

しんらい【信頼】trust. ¶ 彼は～できる男だ He is a *reliable* fellow. あの政治家は～できない That statesman is not to *be relied upon*. 彼は私の～を裏切った He betrayed my *confidence in* him. 彼は自己をあまりに～しすぎている He *is* too *confident of* himself. あの人の話はすべての人に～感を与える His speech inspires everybody with *confidence*. 私の～にこたえてくれた He proved worthy of my *trust*. 彼は主人の～にそうだろう He will enjoy the *confidence* of his master.

しんらつ【辛辣】¶ その批評家は～な皮肉で有名だ That critic is infamous for his *cutting* sarcasm. 彼は涼しい顔で～なことを言うのだからよけいこたえる Because he makes a *harsh* remark with quite a nonchalant air, it hits me all the harder.

しんり【心理】psychology; a mental state; mentality. ¶ 事件以来彼女は～的にまいっている She is *mentally* disabled since that affair.
—現象 a psychological phenomenon. —作用 mental process. —小説 a psychological novel. —描写 psychological description.

しんり【真理】truth (特別の分野の真理なら不定冠詞をつけ，また複数形にもなる. 例えば「科学的真理」は scientific truths). ¶ ～を探究する seek 〔after〕*truth*. 彼のことばにも一面の～がある His words contain some *truth*.

しんり【審理】a trial. ¶ その事件は目下～中だ The case is *under* (≒ *on*) *trial*.

しんりがく【心理学】psychology.
—者 a psychologist. 群集— mass (≒ mob) psychology. 形態— gestalt psychology. 児童— child psychology. 社会— social psychology. 深層— depth psychology. 犯罪— criminal psychology.

しんりゃく【侵略】aggression; invasion.
¶ ～する invade; encroach upon.
—軍 an invading army. —者 an aggressor; an invader. —戦争 a war of aggression.

しんりょ【深慮】¶ ～遠謀の人 a *far-sighted* 「man.

しんりょう【診療】medical examination and

treatment. ¶ ～を受ける receive *treatment*.
—時間 consultation hours. —所 a clinic.

しんりょく【深緑】 deep (≒ dark) green.

しんりょく【新緑】 fresh verdure.

じんりょく【人力】 man's power.

じんりょく【尽力】 ¶ この記念碑は彼の～により建立された This monument was built through his *efforts* (≒ *good offices*). 円満解決のためにできるだけ～しよう We will *make every effort* (≒ *do our best*) for its peaceful settlement.

しんりん【森林】 a forest; a wood.
—地 a forest land. —地帯 a forest belt (≒ zone). —鉄道 a forest railway. —保護 forest conservation.

じんりん【人倫】 morality; morals. ¶ ～にもとる行為 an *immoral* deed.

しんるい【親類】 a relation; a relative; a kinsman. ¶ 彼は私の～だ He is one of my *relatives*. / He *is related to* me. 遠い(近い)～ *a* distant (near) *relative*.
—縁者 friends and relatives.

じんるい【人類】 man; mankind; 〔動物学〕 homo sapiens.
—愛 love for humanity (≒ mankind); philanthropy. —学 anthropology. —学者 an anthropologist.

しんれい【心霊】 —界 the spiritual world. —学 psychics. —現象 a spiritual (≒ psychic) phenomenon. —術 spiritualism.

しんれき【新暦】 a new (≒ solar) calendar.

しんろ【針路】 a course; a route. ¶ 北北西に～をとる take *a* NNW *course* (N は north と読むから an N...とならない).

しんろ【進路】 a course; a direction. ¶ 人の～を阻む block (≒ stand in) *a person's way*. この島は台風の～にある This island is in the *path* of a typhoon.

しんろう【心労】 anxiety; worry; care.

しんろう【新郎】 a bridegroom.
—新婦 the bride and bridegroom; a newly wedded couple; 米 the newly-weds.

しんわ【神話】 a myth; (総称) mythology.
—学者 mythologist. —時代 the mythological (≒ legendary) age. ギリシア— Greek myths.

しんわ【親和】 friendship; fellowship.
—力 〖化学〗 chemical affinity.

す

す【州】 a bar; a shoal; a sand bank.
三角— a delta.

す【巣】 (鳥の) nest; (クモの) a cobweb; a 〔spider's〕 web; (ハチの) a beehive; (動物の) a den. ¶ ～を作る build *a nest*. クモが～を張る A spider spins *a web*.

す【酢】 vinegar. ¶ これは～がききすぎている This *is* too *sour* to eat. 野菜に～をかける *vinegar* vegetable.

ず【図】 **1** (絵) a picture; (図解) a figure; (図表) a diagram. ¶ 壁の～をよく見てください Look at the *picture* on the wall carefully. 第1～は成人病についてだ The first *figure* shows about diseases of adults. ～で説明しましょう Let me illustrate by *a diagram*.
2 〖調子にのる・好調だ〗 ¶ 彼はすぐ～に乗る He *is puffed up* easily. 幸いにも商売が～に当たった Fortunately my job *worked well*. 企画はまんまと～に当たった The attempt *has proved a complete success*.

ず【頭】 ¶ 彼はだれに対しても～が高い He *holds his head too high* to anybody. / He *is too haughty* to anybody.

すあし【素足】 a bare (≒ naked) foot.
¶ ～で歩く walk *barefoot*; go *barefooted*.

ずあん【図案】 a design. ¶ ～化する make *a design* (*of*). ～を作る design.
—家 a designer.

すい【粋】 ¶ 日本文化の～ the *cream* of the Japanese culture. ～なはからい a *considerate* judgment.

す・い【酸い】 sour; acid. ¶ 世の中の～いも甘いもかみわけた人 a man who has tasted *the sweets and bitters* of the world.

ずい【蕊・蘂】 〖植物〗 (めしべ) a pistil; (おしべ) a stamen (複 stamens, stamina).

ずい【髄】 (動物の) the marrow; (植物の) the pith.

すいあ・げる【吸い上げる】 ¶ ポンプで井戸から水を～げる *pump up* water from a well.

すいあつ【水圧】 water pressure; hydraulic pressure. ¶ ～が異常に高い The *water* (≒ *hydraulic*) *pressure* is extraordinarily high.
—機 a hydraulic press. —計 a water-pressure gauge; a piezometer.

すいい【水位】 water level. ¶ この川の通常～は5メートルだ The *water level* of this river usually stands five meters high.
—標 a water mark.

すいい【推移】 change; movement; transition. ¶ 時代の～ the *change* of the times. 当分は事態の～を見守るだけだ For the time being, all we can do is to watch the *state* of things.

ずいい【随意】¶きょうの午後は特にやることがないから各自〜に過ごしてよろしい There being nothing particular to do this afternoon, you may spend your time *as you please*. 出席は〜です Attendance *is voluntary*. 〜に freely; voluntarily; at will.
—科(目) an optional course (≒ subject). —筋〖解剖学〗 a voluntary muscle.

すいいき【水域】 waters; a water area. ¶カムチャツカ〜 the Kamchatka *sea area*. 利根川〜 the Tone *water basin*. テムズ河上流〜 the upper *reaches* of the Thames.

ずいいち【随一】¶当代〜の随筆家 *the greatest* essayist of our time.

スイートピー〖植物〗 a sweet pea.

スイートホーム a sweet home.

スイートポテト a sweet potato.

ずいいん【随員】 an attendant; a follower; a member of *a person's* suite. ¶全権大使の〜として *in the suite of* the ambassador plenipotentiary.

すいうん【水運】 water transportation. ¶大阪は昔も今も〜の便がよい Osaka enjoys good *water transportation* facilities, as she did in olden times.

すいえい【水泳】 swimming. ¶彼は〜がうまい He is a good swimmer. / He swims well.
—大会 a swim meet. —パンツ swimming trunks. —帽 a swimming cap. —着 a swimming suit; a bathing suit.

すいおん【水温】 water temperature.

すいか【水火】 fire and water. ¶〜をも辞さない(危険を恐れない) go through *fire and water*. 〜もいとわずに through thick and thin.

すいか【西瓜・水瓜】 a water melon.

すいか【誰何】 challenge. ¶通行人を〜する *challenge* a passer-by.

すいがい【水害】(こう水) a flood; (こう水による被害) flood damage. ¶幸いにも本年は〜はわりあいに少なかった Fortunately we had comparatively few *floods* this year. 〜は予想をはるかに上回った The *flood damage* far exceeded our expectations.
—地 a flooded district (≒ area). —被災者 flood sufferers (≒ victims). —救済 flood relief.

すいかけ【吸いかけ】¶〜のたばこ a *half-smoked* cigarette.

すいかずら〖植物〗 a honeysuckle.

すいがら【吸い殻】(巻きたばこの) a cigarette end (≒ butt; stub) (葉巻ならば cigarette の代わりに cigar を用いる).

すいがん【酔眼】 ¶〜もうろうとしてあらわれた He appeared *with dull and drunken eyes*.

すいき【水気】(水分) moisture; (水腫) dropsy. ¶〜がくる become dropsical.

ずいき【随喜】¶吉報に接して彼は〜の涙を流した He *wept for joy at* the glad news. / He *shed tears of joy at* the glad news.

すいきゅう【水球】〖競技〗 water polo.

すいぎゅう【水牛】〖動物〗 a buffalo (圏 -es, 「-s).

すいきょ【推挙】 recommendation. ¶〜する recommend.

すいぎょ【水魚】¶ふたりは〜の交わりを結んだ The two formed *a lasting friendship*.

すいきょう【酔狂】¶〜なふるまい *eccentric* behavior. そんなことをするとは〜にも程がある How *fanciful* he is to do such a thing!

すいきん【水禽】 a water fowl.

すいぎん【水銀】 mercury.
—温度計 a mercury thermometer. —柱 ¶〜柱がぐんぐんのぼった The *mercury* has been rising to a great height. —中毒 mercury poisoning. —燈 a mercury lamp. —軟膏(なんこう) mercurial ointment.

すいくち【吸い口】¶〜つき葉巻 a cigar with *a mouthpiece*. フィルターの〜がついた巻きたばこ a cigarette with *a* filtered *tip*.

すいけい【水茎】〖植物〗 a water-stem.

すいけい【水系】¶利根川〜 the Tone river *water system*.

すいけい【推計】 estimation. ¶〜する estimate.
—学 the theory of statistical inference; stochastics.

すいげん【水源】 the source (*of* a river). ¶この川の〜は山間の湖である This river *takes its rise* in the lake among the mountains.

すいこう【推敲】 polishing; improvement. ¶この作文は〜が必要だ This composition needs *polishing*. 原稿には〜に〜を重ねた I worked very hard at *polishing up* my manuscript.

すいこう【遂行】 accomplishment; performance; execution. ¶その計画を〜するのはたいへんだった We had much difficulty in *carrying out* the plan. 首尾よく任務を〜した I succeeded in *performing* my duty.

すいこう【水耕】 —栽培 water culture; tank farming. —場 a hydroponic farm.

すいごう【水郷】 a riverside district.

ずいこう【随行】¶彼は首相に〜してペキンへ行った He visited Peking *in the suite of* the prime minister. 彼は一行に〜した He *accompanied* the party.
—員 ¶彼は〜員のなかに加わっていなかった *The suite* did not include him. / He was not *a member of the suite*.

すいこ·む【吸い込む】¶彼は深く息を〜んだ He *drew* a deep breath. たばこの煙を〜んだ He *inhaled* cigarette smoke. 新鮮な空気を胸いっぱいに〜んだ I *breathed* the fresh air to the full. 砂地が水を〜んだ The sandy soil *absorbed* (≒ *sucked in*) water.

すいさいが【水彩画】 a watercolor〔painting〕. a painting in watercolor. ¶〜をかく paint *with watercolors*.
—家 a watercolor painter. —絵の具 watercolors.

すいさし【吸いさし】¶〜のたばこ a *half-smoked* cigarette; a butt.

すいさつ【推察】(推測)〔a〕 guess; (同情) sympathy; consideration. ¶ご〜のとおりだ

You've *guessed* right.

すいさん【水産】—業 the marine products industry. —試験所 a marine laboratory. —庁 the Fisheries Bureau. —物 marine products. —学校 a fishing school. —大学 a fishing college.

すいさんか【水酸化】—鉄 hydrated iron. —物 a hydroxide.

すいし【水死】 ¶ 彼は海で～した He *was drowned* at sea.

—者 a drowned person.

すいじ【炊事】cooking. ¶ ～する cook.

—係 a cook. —道具 cooking utensils. —場 a kitchen.

ずいじ【随時】(いつでも) at any time; (必要に応じて) as occasion calls.

すいしつ【水質】the quality of water. ¶ この井戸は～がよい The *water* of this well is good to drink. この湖の～を調べてください Please examine *the quality of the water* of this lake.

すいしゃ【水車】a water mill.

—小屋 a mill.

すいじゃく【衰弱】weakness; a weakened condition. ¶ 長患いで彼はかなり～している The prolonged illness *has* considerably *weakened* him. 病人は～がはなはだしい The patient *has become* much *weaker*.

すいしゅ【水腫】〘医学〙dropsy; an oedema (複 oedemas, oedemata).

すいじゅん【水準】a standard. ¶ この商品は～に達している This article has reached the *standard*. このカメラは世界の～を抜いている(～には達していない) This camera is above (below) the *level* of the best in the world.

生活— ¶ 日本人の生活～は高いといえるだろうか Is the *living standard* of the Japanese high? 同一— ¶ この2種のぶどう酒は同一～にある These two sorts of wines are on the same *level*.

ずいしょ【随所】(いたるところで) everywhere; (あちこちに) here and there.

すいしょう【水晶】crystal. ¶ この水は～のように澄んでいる This water is as clear as *crystal*.

—体〘解剖学〙the crystalline lens. 紫— amethyst.

すいしょう【推奨】praise; recommendation. ¶ 彼の勇気はまったく～すべきだ His courage is worthy of great *praise*. 彼は熱心にその計画を～した He warmly *recommended* the plan.

すいじょう【水上】¶ ～に浮かぶ float *on the water*.

—競技 water sports. —競技会 *a* swim meet. —警察 the water police. —スキー water ski. ¶ ～スキーをする water-ski. —生活 life on the water.

すいじょうき【水蒸気】steam; vapor.

すいしん【水深】the depth of water. ¶ ～を測った We sounded *the depth of the water*. この湖は～15メートルだ This lake *is* fifteen meters *deep* (≒ *in depth*).

—計 a hydrobarometer.

すいしん【垂心】〘数学〙an orthocenter.

すいしん【推進】propulsion. ¶ 彼がこの運動を～した He was *the driving force* of this movement.

—者 ¶ 彼がその計画の～者だ He is *a leader* of the plan.

すいじん【粋人】(世慣れた人) a man about town; (いきな人) a man of refined taste.

スイス Switzerland.

—人 a Swiss; (国民) the Swiss.

すいすいと lightly.

すいせい【水生・水棲】—植物 a water plant. —動物 an aquatic animal.

すいせい【水星】〘天文学〙Mercury.

すいせい【彗星】〘天文学〙a comet. ¶ 彼は～のように文壇に登場した He suddenly became famous in literary circles.

すいせい【水勢】the force of water; the force of a current. ¶ 大雨で川の～が増した The heavy rain has quickened the *flowing* of the river.

すいせいがん【水成岩】〘地質〙an aqueous rock.

すいせん【水洗】washing; flushing.

—便所 a flush lavatory.

すいせん【垂線】〘数学〙a perpendicular [line]. ¶ 三角形の底辺に向かって～をおろす fall *a perpendicular line* toward the base of a triangle.

すいせん【推薦】recommendation. ¶ この書物を先生の～で買った I bought this book *on the recommendation of* our teacher. この本を役に立つ参考書として,確信をもってきみに～できる I can confidently *recommend* you this book as a useful book of reference. 彼を会員に～したい I want to *recommend* him *for* membership. 候補者をひとり～してください Won't you please *nominate* a candidate?

—者 a recommender. —状 a letter of recommendation.

すいせん【水仙】a narcissus; (ラッパズイセン) a daffodil.

すいそ【水素】〘化学〙hydrogen. ¶ ～の hydric; hydrogenous.

—ガス hydrogen gas. —爆弾 a hydrogen bomb.

すいそう【水草】a water plant; an aquatic plant.

すいそう【水葬】a burial at sea. ¶ 遺体は～された The body *was buried at sea*.

すいそう【水槽】a water tank.

すいそう【吹奏】flute-blowing. ¶ ～する play on the flute. 国歌が～された The national anthem *was played* by the band.

—楽 wind instrument music. —楽団 a brass band. —楽器 a wind instrument.

すいぞう【膵臓】〘解剖学〙the pancreas.

—炎 pancreatitis.

ずいそうろく【随想録】*one's* essays; *one's* memoir.

すいそく【推測】a guess; [a] conjecture. ¶ 私の～は当たった(はずれた) I *guessed right* (*wrong*). そんなことは～にすぎない It is *a* mere *guesswork*. 事は～どおりに進展した The matter went on *as conjectured*. ～だけでいろいろ言ってみてもしかたがない It is of little use to talk merely by *conjecture*.

すいぞくかん【水族館】 an aquarium (複 aquariums, aquaria).

すいたい【衰退】 decline; decay. ¶ その国々はたちまち～した Those countries *declined* (≒ *decayed*) all of a sudden.

すいたい【推戴】 ¶ クラブは皇太子を総裁に～している The club *has* the Crown Prince *as* president. 彼を議長に～することにきまった We have decided to *have* him *as* chairman.

す

すいだし【吸い出し】 (膏薬) a blister.

すいだ·す【吸い出す】 ¶ 患部からうみを～した I *drew* the pus *from* the affected part.

すいちゅう【水中】 ¶ 海女たちは～で作業中です Women divers are now working *under water*. 大水のためその村は～に没した The village *was submerged by* the flood.

—眼鏡(水泳用の) swimming goggles; (水中をのぞくための, 箱形の) a water glass. —翼船 a hydrofoil.

すいちょく【垂直】 ¶ ～の perpendicular; vertical. ～に perpendicularly; vertically. ¶ 二つの直線は～に交わっている The two lines cross *perpendicularly* (≒ *vertically*). ヒバリは～に空高く昇っていった The lark went *straight* high up in the sky. 棒は地面に～に立っている The pole is erected *at right angles* on the ground. 旗ざおは～に立っていない The flag pole is *out of* [*the*] *perpendicular*.

—降下〔航空術〕a vertical descent. —線 a perpendicular line. —離着陸機 a vertical take-off and landing craft.

すいつ·く【吸い付く】 ¶ この虫はヒルのように足に～いて離れない This worm *sticks to* my leg like a leech. この動物は～いたら離れない This animal sticks fast to anything that touches it.

すいつ·ける【吸い付ける】 ¶ 磁石は鉄を～ける A magnet *attracts* iron.

スイッチ a switch. ¶ 彼は拡声器の～を入れた(切った) He *switched on* (*off*) the loudspeaker. ラジオの～を入れてください Please *switch on* (≒ *turn on*) the radio. テレビの～を切った I *switched off* (≒ *turned off*) the TV.

—ヒッター a switch hitter.

すいてい【水底】 the bottom of the water. ¶ 村はダム建設で～に没してしまった The village went down to *the bottom* of the big dam.

すいてい【推定】 presumption; assumption. ¶ 私の～では彼はまだ50前だ I *suppose* he is still in his forties. / I *suppose* he is still on this side of fifty. 大火の損害は2,000万円と～された The loss of the great fire *was estimated at* twenty million yen.

—相続人 the heir presumption. —量 an estimated volume.

すいてき【水滴】 a drop of water.

すいでん【水田】 a rice field; a paddy field.

すいとう【水痘】〔医学〕chicken pox.

すいとう【水筒】 囲 a canteen; 関 a water bottle.

すいとう【水稲】 paddy.

すいとう【出納】 receipts and disbursement; revenue and expenditure; incomings and outgoings ¶ ～をつかさどる take charge of *accounts*.

—係 a cashier. —簿 a cashbook; an account book.

すいどう【水道】 water; (地域全体の水道設備) water supply. ¶ この家には～がない This house has no *water* laid on. その辺は～が引けてない They have no *water supply* there. ぼくの家にガスと～を引いてもらった We had gas and *water* installed in the house. ～を止めて(出して)ください Please turn off (turn on) the *faucet* (≒ *tap*). ～を出しっぱなしにするな Don't leave the *faucet* (≒ *tap*) running. 井戸水は夏は～よりも冷たい Well water is colder than *city water* in summer.

—管(本管) a water main; (引き込み管) a water pipe. —工事 water supply works. —屋 a plumber. —料 a water rate; (家庭などで支払う) a water bill. 豊後— (海峡) the Bungo channel.

すいとりがみ【吸取紙】 blotting paper; (木の台につけた) a blotter.

すいと·る【吸い取る】 ¶ この吸取紙はインクをよく～る This blotting paper *soaks up* ink well. その水は海綿で～ったほうがいい You had better *soak up* the water with a sponge. / You had better *sponge up* the water.

すいなん【水難】 (海難) a disaster by water; (水死) drowning; (水害) a flood disaster.

すいばく【水爆】 a hydrogen bomb; an H-bomb.

—実験 a thermonuclear test; an H-bomb test. —弾頭 a hydrogen warhead; an H-bomb warhead.

すいばん【水盤】 a basin.

ずいはん【随伴】 ¶ ～する accompany (*a person*).

—者 an attendant.

すいはんき【炊飯器】 a rice cooker.

すいび【衰微】 decline; decay. ¶ ～する decline.

ずいひつ【随筆】 an essay.

—家 an essayist. —集 the collected essays (*of* Mr. A).

すいふ【水夫】 a sailor. ¶ ～になる become *a sailor*; *go to sea* (この意味では sea は冠詞なし).

すいぶん【水分】 water; (液汁) juice. ¶ ～の多い果物 *juicy* fruits. ～を吸収する absorb *water*.

ずいぶん【随分】 ¶ ことしは～暑い It is *very* hot this year. ～久しぶりだね I haven't seen you *so long*. 彼女は～変わってしまった She has changed *very much*.

すいへい【水平】 the level; the horizon. ¶ ～に horizontally.

—線 ¶ 太陽は～線上に現われた The sun appeared above *the horizon*. 太陽は～線の

下に没した The sun sank below *the horizon*. ―動 a horizontal shock. ―面 a horizontal plane; a level surface.

すいへい【水兵】a sailor; a seaman; a blue jacket.

―服 a sailor uniform. ―帽 a sailor hat. 1等― a first class-seaman. 2等― a second-class seaman.

すいほう【水泡】(あわ) the foam; a bubble; 〘医学〙 a blister; a vesicle.

¶すべての努力は～に帰した All the efforts *have come to nothing*. / All the efforts *were in vain*.

すいぼう【水防】flood control; flood defense.

―工事 anti-flood construction. ―対策 an anti-flood measure.

すいぼう【衰亡】ruin; fall. ¶ローマ帝国の～ *the decline and fall* of the Roman Empire.

すいぼくが【水墨画】a drawing in Indian ink.

すいま【睡魔】drowsiness. ¶午後になると～に襲われる I *get sleepy* (≒ *get drowsy*) in the afternoon.

すいみつとう【水蜜桃】〘植物〙 a peach.

すいみゃく【水脈】a water vein. ¶～を掘り当てる strike *water*.

すいみん【睡眠】sleep. ¶十分に～をとった I had *a* good *sleep*. ～は毎日8時間必要です We need eight hours' *sleep* every day. ～中に財布を盗まれた I had a purse stolen *in my sleep*. / I had a purse stolen *while I was sleeping*.

―時間 hours of sleep. ―不足 want of sleep. ―薬 a sleeping drug; (錠剤) a sleeping tablet.

すいめん【水面】the surface of the water. ¶木の葉が～に浮かんでいる The leaves are floating *on the water*. 魚が～に浮かびあがる Fish come up to *the surface* 〔*of the water*〕.

すいもの【吸い物】soup.

すいもん【水門】a sluice 〔gate〕; a floodgate.

すいよう【水溶】―液 a water solution. ¶塩の～液 *a* saline *solution*. ―性 ¶砂糖は～性である Sugar *is soluble in water*.

すいようび【水曜日】Wednesday.

すいよく【水浴】a bath; bathing. ¶川で～した I *bathed* in a river. けさ, 冷～をした I *took a cold bath* this morning.

すいらい【水雷】(魚雷) a torpedo; (機雷) a mine. ¶～を発射する discharge *a torpedo*. ～を敷設する lay *a mine*.

―艇 a torpedo boat.

すいり【水利】(船の便) water transportation; (水の便) water supply; (かんがい) irrigation. ¶大阪は～の便がよい Osaka has many facilities for *water transport*. ～の便が悪く大火事になった The fire became big *for lack of water*.

―組合 an irrigation association. ―権 water rights.

すいり【推理】inference; deduction. ¶資料から～する *deduce* (≒ *infer*) from the data.

―作家 a detective story writer. ―小説 a detective story (≒ novel); a crime fiction (主に英); a mystery (主に米). ―力 reasoning power.

すいりく【水陸】land and water.

―両棲(りょうせい)動物 an amphibian. ―両用機 an amphibian plane.

すいりゅう【水流】a current. ¶この川は～が急だ This river is swift in *current*.

すいりょう【水量】water volume. ¶雨で川は～が増した The river *rose* owing to the rain.

―計 a water gauge.

すいりょう【推量】guess. ¶あなたの～は当たっていない Your *guess* is not right. / You'*ve* not *guessed* right. それはまったく～の域を出ない It is only *a guesswork*.

すいりょく【水力】water power. ¶～を利用する make use of *water power*. この機械は～で動く This machine is driven by *water power*.

―タービン a water-power (≒ hydraulic) turbine. ―発電 water-power generation. ―発電所 a water-power station (≒ plant); a hydroelectric power station (≒ plant).

すいりょく【推力】(ロケットの) driving force.

すいれい【水冷】―式エンジン a water-cooled engine.

すいれん【睡蓮】〘植物〙 a water lily.

すいろ【水路】a waterway; a watercourse.

¶水を引くために～を掘る dig *a channel* to draw water.

―測量 a hydrographical survey. ―標識 a beacon. ―学 hydrography. ―図 a hydrographic map. 長―(水泳の) the long-distance course. ¶彼は長～で新記録を出した He made a new record in *the long-distance course*.

すいろん【推論】inference; deduction.

¶資料から～を下す *infer* (≒ *draw inferences*) from the data.

スイング ¶そのバッターはすばらしい～だ The batter has *a* wonderful *swing*. (ジャズの)スイングは好きでない I don't like *swing music*.

すう【数】a number; (数字) a figure. ¶十～日 ten-odd days. ～をかぞえる count *the number*. 彼は～に明るい He is good at *figures*. 敵は～においてまさる The enemy is greater in *number* than we.

す・う【吸う】(空気を) breathe 〔in〕; inhale; (たばこを) smoke; (吸収する) absorb. ¶新鮮な空気を～う *breathe* fresh air. 汁を～う *sip* soup. 一服～う *have* a smoke. 血を～う *suck* blood. たばこを～ってもいいですか Would you mind my *smoking*? 海綿が水を～う Sponges *absorb* water.

すうかい【数回】¶彼は～失敗した He failed *several times*.

すうがく【数学】mathematics. ¶～の問題 a *mathematical* problem.

す

―者 a mathematician. 高等― higher mathematics.

すうかげつ【数か月】¶彼が当地を去ってから～が過ぎた *Several months* have passed since he left here.

すうき【枢機】 the most important affairs. ¶彼は国政の～をゆだねられている He assumes the helm of state affairs.
―卿(きょう) a cardinal.

すうき【数奇】¶彼女は～な一生を送った She led an *unlucky* life. / Her life was marked by *vicissitudes*. 彼女は～な運命にもてあそばれた She was *the sport of fortune*.

すうけい【崇敬】 reverence; veneration.
¶～する revere; honor.

すうこう【崇高】¶その光景を見てなにか～の感に打たれた I was struck with something *sublime* to see the scene. 彼は～な精神の持ち主だ He *is high-minded*. / He has a *high* mind.

すうし【数詞】〘文法〙a numeral.

すうじ【数字】 a figure; a numeral. ¶4けたの～ four *figures*. 天文学的～ astronomical *figures*. 彼は～に明るい He is good at *figures*. 失業者の数は記録的な～になった The number of jobless people has reached record *figures*. 確かな～は示されなかった No reliable *figures* were given. ～上のまちがい a *numerical* error.
漢― Chinese numerals. 算用― Arabic numerals. ローマ― Roman numerals.

すうじ【数次】¶～の実験を重ねた I made *several* experiments.

すうしき【数式】 an expression; a formula.

すうじくこく【枢軸国】¶第2次世界大戦の～ *the Axis* in World War II.

すうじつ【数日】 several days. ¶彼に～前会った I met him *several* (≒ *a few*) *days ago*. その～前に彼に会った I had met him *a few days before*. ～後再び彼女に会った *A few days later* I met her again. ～来雨が降りつづいている It has been raining *for the past few days*.

すうじゅう【数十】¶～人 *scores of* men; *several tens of* men. ～万円 *hundreds of thousands of* yen.

すうすう ¶彼は～寝息を立てて寝ている He is sleeping *with a quiet breath*. 透き間風が～入る The draught *comes whistling in*.

ずうずうし・い【図図しい】¶まったく～い男だ How *impudent* he *is*! 彼は～くもこんなことを言う He *is impudent* enough to say such a thing. / He has the *impudence* (≒ *audacity*) to say such a thing.

ずうずうべん【ずうずう弁】¶彼は東北の～で話す He speaks with *a Tohoku accent*.

すうせい【趨勢】 a trend. ¶世の～に従う follow the *trend* of the times. 世界は平和への～にある The world *is drifting toward* peace. 物価の～は上向きである The *trend* of prices is uprising.

すうせい【趨性】 a tendency. ¶光に向く～ *a tendency* to run toward the light.

すうせん【数千】¶～人の人 *thousands of* people; *several thousand* people.

ずうたい【図体】¶彼は～が大きい He is a *big hulking* fellow.

すうち【数値】〘数学〙numerical value.
¶その式の～を出す get (≒ decide) the *numerical value* of the formula.

スーツ a suit.
―ケース a suitcase.

すうど【数度】 several times.

すうとう【数等】¶彼の能力は私より～すぐれている His ability is *far* (≒ *much*) better than mine.

すうにん【数人】 several persons; a few persons.

すうねん【数年】 several years. ¶彼に会ってからもう～たった *Several years* have passed since I saw him last. ～もすれば町は変わるだろう The town will change *in a few years*. 物価は～間上がりつづけている Prices have been rising *for several years*. ～後彼女はパリへ行った *Several years later* she went to Paris. ～前に彼に会った I met him *a few years ago*.

スーパーインポーズ〘映画〙superimposition.

スーパータンカー a supertanker.

スーパーマーケット a supermarket.

スーパーマン a superman.

すうはい【崇拝】 worship; admiration.
¶リンカーンを～している I *admire* Lincoln. / I *am an admirer of* Lincoln. 彼らは彼を生き神様として～している They *adore* him as a living god.

すうばい【数倍】 several times. ¶このビルは学校の～の高さがある This building is *several times* as high as our school.

すうひゃく【数百】¶～人の人 *hundreds of* people; *several hundred* people.

スープ soup. ¶濃い(薄い)～ *a* thick (thin) *soup*. 昼食に野菜～を飲んだ I had (≒ ate) vegetable *soup* for lunch. (drink soup とは言わない).

すうまん【数万】 tens of thousands (*of* people).

ズームレンズ a zoom lens.

スウェーデン Sweden.
―語 Swedish. ―人 a Swede. ―体操 Swedish gymnastics.

すうり【数理】 mathematics. ¶彼は～に明るい He is good at *mathematics*.
―統計学 mathematical statistics.

すうりょう【数量】 quantity; volume. ¶かなりの～の金 a considerable *quantity* of gold.

すうれつ【数列】〘数学〙progression.
等差― arithmetical progression. 等比― geometrical progression.

すえ【末】(終わり) the end; (将来) the future.
¶月の～に at *the end* of the month. ～の子 *the youngest* child. 彼は～の見込みはない He is not promising. / He has no bright *future*. この子の行く～が心配だ I am anxious about this child's *future*. 彼らは～を楽しみに

働いた They worked for their *future* happiness. 彼らの～は幸福だった They were happy *ever after*. 慎重に考えた～それをした I did it *after* careful consideration. 私にとっては～の問題だ It is a *trifling* matter to me. / It *doesn't matter* to me.

スエード ¶～のくつ *suede* shoes.

すえおき【据え置き・据置】deferment. ¶預金を3年間～にする *have* the deposit *deferred* for three years.

—公債 deferred bonds. **—**期間 the period of deferment. **—**貯金 deferred savings.

すえお・く【据え置く】¶年金が～かれた The annuity *was deferred*. 借金はそのまま～いた We *left* the loan *unredeemed*.

スエズ Suez.

—運河 the Suez Canal.

すえたのもし・い【末頼もしい】¶～い青年だ He is a *promising* young man.

すえつけ【据え付け】installation; placement; setting up. ¶～の本だな a *stationary* bookcase. このたなは壁に～になっている This shelf *is fixed* to the wall.

すえつ・ける【据え付ける】¶部屋にストーブを～けた I *had* a stove *installed* (≒ *fixed*) in the room. 屋上に天体望遠鏡を～けた I *set up* an astronomical telescope on the roof.

すえっこ【末っ子】the youngest child.

すえながく【末長く】¶～おつきあいをお願いします I hope we can be friends *for a long time*.

すえひろがり【末広がり】¶富士のすそ野は～だ The foot of Mt. Fuji *spreads out like an unfolded fan*. / The foot of Mt. Fuji *fans out*.

す・える【据える】¶機械を～える *install* a machine. 彼は目を～えて私を見た He *stared at* me. 腰を～えて仕事ができない I can't *settle down to* my work. 彼らは私の後釜(ごがま)に彼を～えた They *placed* him in my position (≒ place).

す・える【饐える】go bad; turn sour (≒ stale; rancid).

ずが【図画】drawing; (絵) a picture.
¶～をかく draw *a picture*; (色のついた) paint *a picture*.

—用紙 drawing paper.

スカート a skirt.
ギャザー**—** a gathered (≒ shirred) skirt. タイト**—** a tight skirt. フレア**—** a flared skirt. ミニ**—** a miniskirt. ロング**—** a long skirt.

スカーフ a scarf (複 -s, 英 scarves).

ずかい【図解】an illustration. ¶～の豊富な教科書 a textbook full of *illustrations*. それを～して説明した I explained it by *pictures* (≒ *diagrams*).

—辞典 a picture dictionary.

ずがいこつ【頭蓋骨】〖解剖学〗the skull; the cranium (複 -s, crania).

—骨折 a skull fracture.

スカイライン ¶アルプスの～ the *skyline* of the Alps.

スカウト a scout. ¶新人を～する *scout* a new talent.

すがお【素顔】an unpainted face; a face not made up. ¶彼女の～は美しい She is beautiful in her *unpainted face*. 彼女は写真顔より～のほうがいい The picture does not do her justice. 日本の～を見てほしい I'd like you to see *Japan as it is*.

すかさず【透かさず】at once; promptly; immediately; instantly; without a moment's delay. ¶～彼に一撃を与えた I caught him a blow *instantly* (≒ *at once; with no hesitation*). / I *lost no time in* catching him a blow.

すかし【透かし】a watermark. ¶～の入った紙 *watermarked* paper.

—彫り openwork.

すか・す【空かす】¶彼は腹を～している He *is* (≒ *feels*) *hungry*. 腹を～すために散歩した I walked to *aid digestion*.

すか・す【透かす】¶ガラスを～して彼を見ていた I was peering at him *through* the glass. やみを～して見た I *peered into* the darkness. お札を～して見る *hold* a banknote *up against the light*.

すか・す【賺す】¶おどしたり～したりして彼に言うことを聞かせた *What by threats and what by entreaties*, they succeeded in coaxing him into compliance. 私はなだめ～してその子を寝かしつけた I *coaxed* the child to go to bed.

ずかずか directly; straight[ly]; (許可なく) without leave; without permission; (無作法に) rudely. ¶彼はあいさつもなく～と部屋に入ってきた He came *rudely* into the room without ceremony.

すがすがし・い【清清しい】¶～い朝の風 a *bracing* (≒ *refreshing*) morning wind. 仕事をやりとげて～い気分だ I *feel refreshed* after completing a task. ちょっとひと眠りして～くなった I *refreshed myself* with a nap.

すがた【姿】**1**〖姿形〗a figure. ¶この馬は～がいい This horse has *a fine appearance*.
なんとがっちりした～の男だろう What *a* steady *figure* he has!
彼女は鏡の中の自分の～をながめている She is looking at *herself* in the mirror.
富士山がその～を現わしてきた Mt. Fuji has made its *appearance*.
山の～は格別美しかった The mountain *looked* unutterably beautiful.
キツネは美しい少女に～をかえた The fox *disguised himself as* a beautiful girl.
歌舞伎では男が女の～になって演技をする In *Kabuki* a male actor acts the part of a woman.

2〖出現〗an appearance. ¶まもなく湖は～を現わした The lake *came in sight* before long.
まだ彼は～を見せない He has not *made* his *appearance* yet.
事件以来彼は～を見せていない We *have seen nothing of* him since the event.

3〖様子〗¶彼はその小説の中でその一家の～をありのままに描いた In that novel of his he drew *a*

す

true picture of the family.
あなたの生まれた国のありのままの～を話してください Please tell me *all* about the country where you were born.

スカッシュ squash.
レモン― lemon squash.

ずがら【図柄】a pattern; a design. ¶はでな～の着物 a *kimono* of *a* gay *pattern*.

すがりつ・く【縋り付く】cling to; hold on to; hang on; lean on. ¶子は母親に～いて泣いた The child cried *clinging to* his mother.

すが・る【縋る】¶母のそでに～る子 a child *clinging to* his mother's sleeve. 老人はつえに～って歩いていた The old man was walking *leaning on* a stick. 人々の同情に～るのはいやだ I don't like to *appeal to* others *for* mercy.

す

ずかん【図鑑】a picture book.
動物(植物)― an illustrated animal (plant) book. 理科(社会科)― a picture book of science (social studies).

スカンク〔動物〕a skunk.

スカンジウム〔化学〕scandium.

スカンジナビア Scandinavia. ¶～の Scandinavian.
―人 a Scandinavian. ―半島 the Scandinavian Peninsula.

すかんぴん【素寒貧】a penniless fellow.
¶彼はばくちで～になった He *became penniless* (≒ *lost all his money*) through gambling.

すき【好き】**1**〘好む〙 ¶きみの～な物をなんでも買ってあげよう I will buy you anything you *like*.
きみの～な歌手はだれか Who is your *favorite* singer?
うちの子はサッカーが～で一日じゅうボールけりをしている Our boy *likes* soccer and he is kicking a ball all day long.
このごろラテン音楽が～になった I have recently come to *like* Latin music.
彼は酒がなによりも～だ He *is fond of sake* above all things.
ああいうタイプの女は～ではない A woman of that type doesn't *appeal to* me. / I *am* not *fond of* women of that type.
リンゴとブドウとどっちが～ですか Which do you *like* better, apples or grapes? / Which do you *prefer*, apples or grapes?
彼の～な学科は歴史だ His *favorite* subject is history.
彼ほどたばこの～な人も珍しい There are very few who *are* as *fond of* smoking as he.
きみの～なように仕事を進めてよろしい You may go ahead with the work as you *please*.
いつでも～なときにいらっしゃい You may come whenever you *like*.
休日は～なことをして過ごす I spend the holiday doing what I *like*.
まだ～な人ができないのか Haven't you got *a sweetheart* (≒ *a lover*) yet?
彼はもう大人だから～なようにさせておけ Let him do as he *likes*. He is grown up now.
～でお手伝いしているんですから報酬はいりません I do not want any reward, as I am helping you *out of my own choice*.
～こそ物のじょうずなれ(諺) What one *likes* one will do well. / *Liking* shows where one's talent lies.
2〘自分かってな〙 ¶彼は～なことばかり言って話をぶちこわす He says only what he *likes* and upsets everything.

すき【透き】(透き間) an opening; (裂け目) a crack; a slit; (余地) room; space; (ひま) leisure (㊎では [líːʒəl], ㊇では [léʒəl]); spare time; free time.

すき【透き・隙】**1**〘隙〙an opening; (さけめ) a chink; a gap. ¶戸の～から風が入ってくる The wind comes in through the *chink* in the door.
かきねの～からネコが庭に入ってきた A cat has come into our garden through *an opening* in the fence.
2〘機会・つけ込まれる油断〙a chance; an opportunity; an unguarded moment.
¶彼はひそかに～をねらっている He is secretly watching for *a chance*.
相手に～を見せるな Don't *lay yourself open to* attack.
彼は～を見せまいと懸命だ He is trying very hard to *be on the alert*.
彼の言うことには一分の～もない What he says *is unassailable*.
きみは～だらけだから気をつけたほうがいい You are *wide open*, so be careful.
忙しい中を～を見て昼食をとった I had lunch *in an interval of* my work.

すき【鋤】a spade; a plow; ㊇a plough.
¶～の刃 a plowshare; ㊇a ploughshare. 彼は～で土を掘っている He is digging the earth with *a spade*. 彼らは畑を～で耕している They *are plowing* the field.

すき【数奇・数寄】¶～をこらした茶室 a tea ceremony arbor *tastefully laid out* (≒ *elaborately designed*).

すぎ【杉】〔植物〕a 〔Japanese〕 cedar; a cryptomeria. ¶～の木 a *cedar* tree. ～の板 a *cryptomeria* board. ～の林 a *cedar* forest.

-すぎ【-過ぎ】past; after; (度合い) over; too much. ¶30～の男 a man *over thirty* (≒ *in his thirties*; *the other side of thirty*). 今10時少し～です It is a little *past* ten. 6時～に来たまえ Come and see me *after* six. 予定より10分～に着く arrive ten minutes *late*. 列車は定刻より10分～に着いた The train arrived ten minutes *behind time*. 食べ～に注意しなさい Be careful not to eat *too much*. たばこの吸い～は健康によくない *Excessive* smoking is not good for the health.

-ずき【-好き】¶犬～ *a* dog *lover*. 山～ *a* mountain *lover*. 酒～ a drinker. たばこ～ a heavy smoker.

スキー skiing; (道具) 〔a pair of〕 skis.
¶冬は～のシーズンだ Winter is the season for *skiing*. ～をはく(脱ぐ) put on (take off) *one's*

skis. ～でスロープを滑りおりる slide down a slope *on skis*. 毎年冬は菅平高原へ～に行く I go to Sugadaira Heights to *ski* every winter./I *go skiing* at Sugadaira Heights every winter.
—ぐつ ski boots. **—**場 a skiing ground. **—**ズボン a pair of ski pants. **—**服 a ski suit. **—**ヤー a skier.

すきかえ·す【鋤き返す】¶田を～す *plow* (≒ 英 *plough*) *up* a field.

すきかって【好き勝手】¶彼はいつも～なふるまいをする He always *has his own way*. / He always *does what he wants*.

すききらい【好き嫌い】*one's* likes and dislikes. ¶彼は食べ物の～が激しい He has strong *likes and dislikes* in food.

すきぐし【梳き櫛】a fine-toothed comb.

すきこの·む【好き好む】¶こんな不便な所に～んで住んでいるのではない I *am* not quite *willing* (≒ *contented*) *to* live in such an inconvenient place. なにも～んでそんな仕事を引き受けなくてもいいのに You need not take the job on yourself *of your own accord*.

すぎさ·る【過ぎ去る】pass away; go on; go by; elapse. ¶～った出来事 a thing *of the past*. あっというまに10年が～った Ten years *passed away* rapidly.

すきずき【好き好き】¶人にはそれぞれ～がある(たで食う虫も～)(諺) *There is no accounting for tastes*. それは～だ It is *a matter of taste*.

ずきずき ¶傷口が～痛む The wound *smarts* (≒ *hurts*; *throbs*) *with pain*. / I *have a throbbing pain* in the wound.

スキップ skip. ¶～する skip.

すきとお·る【透き通る】be transparent; be seen through. ¶～った水 *clear* water. ～った声で歌う sing in a *clear* voice. 彼女は薄いドレスを着ていたので肌が～って見えた She wore such a thin dress that her skin could *be seen through* it.

すぎな【杉菜】〘植物〙a field horsetail.

すぎない【過ぎない】only; mere; nothing but; no more than. ¶これはほんの一例に～ This is a *mere* example. それは単なるうわさに～ It is a *mere* rumor. / It is *no more than* a rumor. ただの風邪に～ This is *only* (≒ *nothing but*) a slight cold.

すきはら【空き腹】¶～にまずいものなし (諺) *Hunger is the best sauce*. / Nothing comes wrong to a hungry man. ～では仕事ができない We cannot work *on an empty stomach*.

すきま【透き間·隙間】an opening; (裂け目) a crack; (空間) a space; a crevice; a chink. ¶戸の～から光が漏れる A streak of light comes out through *an opening* in a door.

スキムミルク skim milk.

すきや【数寄屋·数奇屋】(茶室) a tea ceremony arbor; (風雅に造った家) a tasteful cottage.
—造り rustic work.

すきやき【すき焼き】*sukiyaki*.

スキャンダル a scandal. ¶～をもみ消す keep quiet *a scandal*. ～をでっち上げる make up *a scandal*. ～を暴く disclose *a scandal*.

すぎゆ·く【過ぎ行く】pass away; pass by; go on; (形容詞として) passing; fleeting.
¶年月は夢のように～く Days *are fleeting by*.

す·ぎる【過ぎる】**1**〘場所·時間について〙pass.
¶もう横浜駅は～ぎた We *have* already *passed* Yokohama Station.
眠っていて降りる駅をうっかり～ぎてしまった I was sleeping so soundly that I *went past* the station where I was to get off.
冬が～ぎて春が来た Winter *is over* and spring has come.
時が～ぎるにつれて彼は落ち着いてきた As time *passed on*, he calmed down.
3年～ぎて平和がやってきた Peace came *after a lapse of* three years.
彼が村を離れてはや5年は～ぎた *It is already* five years since he left the village. / Five years *have passed* since he left the village.
2〘出来事が〙¶～ぎたことを後悔してもはじまらない It is no use repenting what *is* already *past*.
～ぎたことは～ぎたことだ *Let bygones be bygones.*
3〘過分な·必要以上な〙¶彼には～ぎた奥さんだ She is *too* good a wife for him.
～ぎたるはなお及ばざるがごとし(諺) *Too much water drowned the miller*.
彼は冗談が～ぎるので人にきらわれる Since his jokes *go too far*, he is disliked by others.

-す·ぎる【-過ぎる】¶この仕事は私には難し～ぎる This work is *too* difficult for me. 彼はこういう仕事をするには若～ぎる He is *too* young *for* this sort of work. 食べ～ぎないよう気をつけなさい Be careful not to eat *too much*. 彼は働き～ぎる He *overworks himself*. どうもひとつ多～ぎるThere seems one *too many*. 人がふたり多～ぎる There are two persons *too many*. それは重量が1キロ多～ぎる It is one kilogram overweight. 1,000円よけいにもらい～ぎた I have got a thousand yen *too much*. 健康にはいくら注意しても注意し～ぎることはない You *cannot* be *too* careful of your health. このふろはあつ～ぎて私には入れなかった The bath was *too* hot for me to get in.

ずきん【頭巾】a hood.

スキンパウダー skin powder.

スキンローション skin lotion.

す·く【好く】¶彼はだれにも～かれる He *is loved* by everybody. 彼らは～いたどうしだ They love each other.

す·く【空く】¶おなかが～いた I *am* (≒ *feel*) *hungry*. 座席が～いている There are some *empty* (≒ *vacant*) seats. 今手が～いていますか *Are you free* now? 図書館は～いていた The library *was not crowded*. / I found the library *not crowded*.

す·く【梳く】¶髪を～く *comb one's* hair.

す·く【漉く】¶紙を～く *make* (≒ *manufacture*) paper.

す·く【鋤く】plow; 英 plough; till; break up (≒ turn over) (soil). ¶田を～く *plow* (≒

圏 *plough*) a field.

すぐ【直ぐ】**1** 〖直ちに〗 ¶～戻りますから待っていてください Please wait a little, I will be back *in a moment*.

急用ですから～来てください There's some urgent business for you, so please come *as soon as possible*.

手紙をもらったら～返事を出すものだ You should answer *quickly* when you receive a letter.

食後～運動するのはよくない It is not good for the health to take exercise *soon* after meals.

向こうに着いたら～電話しなさい Phone me *as soon as* you arrive there. / Give me a ring *as soon as* you arrive there.

用が済んだら～帰りなさい Come away *at once*, when you've finished.

事故を見たので～警察へ通報した I *lost no time in* alerting the police when I saw the accident.

2 〖まもなく〗 ¶バスはもう～来るだろう The bus will be here *soon*.

ひな祭りがくるともう～春だ Spring will come *soon* (≒ *shortly*) after the Doll's Festival.

入学試験はもう～だ The entrance examination *is close at hand*.

彼女はもう～28歳になる She *is close upon* twenty-eight.

もう～駅に着く We will reach the station *in a short time*.

雨は～にあがるだろう It will clear up *in no time*.

3 〖容易に〗 ¶ちょっと練習すれば～要領が覚えられる If you take a little practice, you will get the knack *easily*.

あの人の家は～見つかった I found his house *easily*. / His house *was easy to* find.

彼は～人の誘いに乗る He *is* too *ready to* be tempted.

彼女はちょっと無理をすると～体をこわす If she overworks herself a little, she *is apt to* fall ill.

彼はつまらぬことに～腹を立てる He *is quick to* take offense at a trifle. / He is *easily* offended at trifling matters.

あの子は泣き虫で, ちょっとしたことでも～泣く He is a crybaby and cries at *the least* provocation.

4 〖距離など〗 ¶私の家は駅の～近くだ My house *is close by* the station.

～そこまで来たのでお寄りしようと思いました I was in the neighborhood, so I thought I'd drop in.

彼は私の～前の席に座っていた He took his seat *just* in front of me.

私はきみの～あとを走っていた I was running *close* behind you.

～目の前で人が車にはねられるのを見た I saw a man knocked down by a car *right* before my eyes.

これが～下の弟です This is my younger brother *just* below me. (英語では younger, older はめったに用いない. またこの文は次のようにするほうがよい This is my 〔younger〕 brother. He is next to me in age.).

-ずく【-尽く】 by ; by means of ; for ; for the sake of. ¶腕～ででも取ってみせる I will take it *by force*. 相談～で決めた We have decided it *after much consultation*. とかく金～の世の中だ Money makes the mare to go.

すくい【救い】 help ; (宗教的な) salvation.

¶われわれは被害者に～の手を差し伸べなければならない We should extend *a helping hand* to the sufferers. 彼は大声で～を求めた He called (≒ cried) for *help*. 彼の人生観には～がない He holds an entirely *pessimistic* view of life.

—主 ¶道元は私の魂の～い主だ *Dogen* is the *salvation* of my soul.

すくいあ·げる【掬い上げる】 ¶数匹の金魚を～げる *scoop up* several goldfish. 彼は砂をバケツで～げていた He *was dipping up* sand with a bucket.

スクイズ 〖野球〗 a squeeze play. ¶われわれは9回に～で1点を入れた Our team *squeezed in* a run in the ninth inning.

—バント ¶私は絶好の～バントで彼をホームインさせた I *squeezed* him *in* with a perfect bunt.

—プレー a squeeze play.

すくいだ·す【救い出す】 ¶彼は火中から老人を～した He *saved* an old man *from* (≒ *out of*) a house on fire. 彼は私を窮地から～してくれた He *helped* me *out of* the difficulty.

すく·う【救う】 (危険から) help (*a person*) out of a difficulty ; (死から) save (*a person*) from death ; (苦痛から) relieve (*a person*) from a pain.

¶おぼれる子を～う *rescue* (≒ *save*) a drowning child ; *save* a child *from* drowning. 貧しい人を～う *relieve* the poor. 人命を～う *save* a human life. 世を～う *save* (≒ *redeem*) the world. 彼は～いようのない悪人だ He is a villain past (≒ beyond) *redemption*. 彼は困っている多くの男女を～った He *helped* many men and women in trouble.

すく·う【掬う】 scoop up ; (ひしゃくで) ladle ; (足を) trip ; clip. ¶水を手で～って飲む drink water *out of one's hands*. 魚を網で～う *scoop up* fish with a net. 足を～って相手を倒す *trip a person up*. 商売とはいえ彼の足を～うようなことをしてはいけない Don't *take advantage of* his weakness even for the sake of business.

すく·う【巣食う】 (巣を造る) build a nest ; (住みつく) have *one's* den (*at*; *in*); inhabit; haunt (a place).

¶鳥がこの木に～っている Some birds *nest* (≒ *have their nests*) in this tree. このあたりには不良が～っている Some bad boys *have their den* around this place.

スクーター a scooter. ¶～に乗る ride on *a scooter*.

スクープ a scoop. ¶彼は盗難ダイヤモンドの件を～して他の日刊紙を出し抜いた He *scooped* all

the other dailies with the story of the stolen diamond.
—記事 a scoop.
スクーリング schooling. ¶～を行なう(受ける) give (have) *schooling*.
スクール a school.
—バス a school bus.
スクエアダンス a square dance. ¶～をする have *a square dance*.
すぐさま【直様】¶～返事を書いた I wrote an answer *at once* (≒ *immediately*).
すくすく〔と〕 ¶このあたりは木が～のびる Trees grow *rapidly* around here. 少女は～成長している The little girl is *rapidly* growing.
すくな·い【少ない】¶彼は友人が～い He has *few* friends. 彼女は収入が～い She has a *small* income. 家族が～い I have a *small* family. 彼は口数が～い He talks *little*. 私の家は客が～い We *seldom* have a guest. この辺は人通りが～い There is *little* traffic around here. 出席者は～かった There were *only a few* present. 真相を知っている人は～い *Few* people know the truth. 時間が～い I have *little* time. 機会が～い I have *little* chance.
すくなからず【少なからず】not a little; not a few; greatly; considerably. ¶その知らせにはだれしも～驚いた Everyone was *considerably* (≒ *greatly; not a little*) surprised at the news.
すくなく〔と〕も【少なく〔と〕も】at least; to say the least of it; not less than. ¶～100人は来るだろう There will come a hundred people *at least*. / A hundred people will be present *in the minimum*. 彼は～2,000冊の本を持っている He has *no less than* two thousand books. 東京で暮らすには1か月に～5万円はかかる It will cost you *at least* fifty thousand yen a month to live in Tokyo.
すくなくな·い【少なくない】¶訪問客は～かった There were *not a few* visitors.
すくなめ【少な目】¶彼に～にぶどう酒をついだ I helped him to wine *with reserve*. / I served him *less than enough* wine.
すく·む【竦む】¶そのとき足が～んでしまった My knees *gave way* then. ヘビを見ると～んでしまう I *cower before* a snake. その恐ろしい光景を見て～みあがった I *cowered at* the horrible sight.
-ずくめ【-尽くめ】¶彼女は白～の服装だ She is dressed *all* in white. けっこう～のもてなしを受けた I enjoyed *princely* hospitality. 宝石～の王冠 a crown decorated *all over* with jewels.
すく·める【竦める】 ¶首を～める *duck one's* head. 肩を～める *shrug one's* shoulders.
スクラップ scrap. ¶彼は古い車を～として売った He sold his old car as *scrap*. その古い車は～にされた The old car *was scrapped*.
—ブック a scrapbook.
スクラム〔運動〕a scrum〔mage〕; a scrimmage. ¶彼らはすぐ～を組んだ(ラグビーで) They *scrummaged* at once. 学生たちは～を組んで通りを行進していた The students were marching along the street *arm in arm*.
スクリーン the screen.
スクリプター〔映画〕a scripter.
スクリプト〔映画〕〔放送〕a script.
スクリュー a screw〔propeller〕.
すぐれた【優れた】great; good; excellent. ¶～学識の持ち主 a man of *eminent* scholarship. 聖書は世界で最も～文学作品の一つである The Bible is one of the *greatest* literary achievements in the world.
すぐれな·い【勝れない】¶彼は顔色が～い He *looks pale* (≒ *looks unwell*). 彼は健康が～い He *is in poor* (≒ *bad*) *health*. / He *is poor in health*. / He *is out of health*. 私は気分が～い I *feel unwell*. / I *am out of sorts*. / I *am not in my form*.
すぐ·れる【優れる·勝れる】¶彼は体力に～れている He *excels in*〔physical〕strength. 彼は勇気の点ではだれよりも～れている He *is superior in* courage *to* any other person. / He *excels* (≒ *surpasses*) any other person *in* courage.
ずけい【図形】a figure.
平面(立体; 幾何学的)— a plane (solid; geometrical) *figure*.
スケート skating. ¶池に～に行く go *skating* on a pond.
—ぐつ a pair of skates. —リンク a skating rink; an ice rink.
スケール (規模) a scale; (器量) a caliber.
¶～の大きい(小さい) large-(small-) scaled. ～の大きい人物 a man of large *caliber*. その事業は空前の～で運営されている The business is conducted *on an* unexampled *scale*.
すげか·える【すげ替える】 ¶係長の首を～える *replace* the chief clerk.
スケジュール a schedule (米では [skédʒu:l]; 英では [ʃédju:l] と発音する); a program.
¶～を立てる make (≒ map) out *a schedule* (*of*; *for*); draw up *a program* (*of*). ～どおり as *scheduled*; according to *schedule*; on *schedule*. 都知事としての彼の～はぎっしり詰まっている His *schedule* as the Metropolitan Governor is very tight.
ずけずけ ¶彼は思ったことを～と言う He speaks out his mind *bluntly*. / He *does not mince* matters.
すけだち【助太刀】(決闘などで) assistance; (人) a second. ¶～を買って出た I proposed to act as *a second*. (手が足りないので)人に～する give *a person* a helping hand.
スケッチ a sketch. ¶パンダを～した I *made a sketch of* a giant panda. きみはなにを～しているのか What *are* you *sketching*?
—ブック a sketchbook.
すげな·い ¶彼は～い返事をした He replied *curtly* (≒ *coldly*). 彼女は彼に～くした She treated him *coldly*. / She *turned the cold shoulder to* him.
スコア a score. ¶わがチームは13対2の～で勝った Our team won by *a score* of 13 to 2. 彼が

す

〜を記録した He kept (≒ marked) the *score*. 〜は9回に3対3のタイになった The *score* was tied at 3 to 3 in the ninth inning.

—ブック a scorebook. **—**ボード a scoreboard.

すご·い【凄い】(気味が悪い) ghastly; grim; (恐ろしい) dreadful; horrible; terrible; (すばらしい) wonderful; amazing; (非常な) awful; tremendous.

¶〜い美人 a *strikingly* beautiful woman. 彼は〜い目つきをしている He has a *fierce* (≒ *dreadful*) look. 町は〜い人出だ The streets are *so much* crowded with people. 〜い腕前だ He is a man of *wonderful* (≒ *amazing*) ability.

ずこう【図工】(教科) drawing and manual arts; (製図工) a draftsman (複 a draftsmen).

スコール a squall.

すごく【凄く】 exceedingly; extremely; awfully; remarkably. ¶雨が〜降った It rained *heavily* (≒ *in torrents*). 〜寒い It is *extremely* (≒ *bitterly*) cold.

すこし【少し】 **1**〚数·量〛¶私はハワイに友だちが〜いる I have *a few* friends in Hawaii.

この図書館には仏教に関する本が〜ある There are *some* books on Buddhism in this library.

びんにウイスキーが〜残っている There's *a small quantity* of whisky left in the bottle.

コーヒーに砂糖を〜入れてください Please put *some* sugar in the coffee.

〜お金を貸してくれませんか Will you please lend me *some* money?

ビスケットを〜いかがですか Won't you take *some* biscuits?

お茶をもう〜頂けますか May I have *some* more tea?

私は英語の本は〜しか持っていない I have only *a few* English books.

飲み水はもう〜しか残っていない There is only *a little* drinking water left.

今月は〜も雨が降らない It has*n't* rained *at all* this month.

2〚程度〛¶彼のテニスは〜上達した He has made *a little* progress in tennis.

私はドイツ語とフランス語が〜わかる I can understand German and French *a little*. / I have *a little* knowledge of German and French.

この部屋は〜狭すぎる This room is *a little* too small.

ふたりの意見は〜違っている The opinions of the two are different *to a slight degree*.

きょうは〜気分がいい I feel *a little* better today.

きょうは〜頭が痛い I have *a slight* headache today.

彼女はきょうは〜どうかしている Something is wrong with her today.

彼のことばに〜腹が立った I was *somewhat* offended at his words.

弟さんの病気は〜はよくなりましたか Is your brother *any* better?

この計画が実現する可能性は〜はある There is *a slight* possibility that the plan will be realized.

もう〜で遭難するところだった *It was very close to* a disaster.

もう〜で車にはねられるところだった I *came very near* being run over by a car.

〜でも気のついたことがあったら言いなさい Tell me if you notice *anything at all*.

〜でも疑問があったら私に聞きなさい Ask me if you have *any* question *at all*.

彼は〜のことでもすぐ怒る He takes offense at *trifles*.

私は新しい仕事に〜ずつ慣れてきた I have got used to the new job *gradually* (≒ *by degrees*).

毎日〜ずつ日が長くなる The days are getting longer *little by little*.

それを聞いて彼は〜も驚かなかった He was *not* surprised *at all* to hear it.

彼の言うことは〜もわからない I can*not* understand *at all* what he says.

こんな結果になろうとは〜も考えなかった I *little* dreamed that it would end in such a result.

この本は〜も難しくありません This book is not difficult *in the least*. / This book is by no means difficult.

3〚時間〛¶彼は〜前に出かけた He went out *a little* while ago.

もう〜お待ちください Please wait *a little* longer.

疲れたから〜休みましょう We are tired, so let us rest *a while*. / We are tired, so let us take a *short* rest.

〜したら伺います I will call on you *a little later on*.

もう〜で大阪に着く We will reach Osaka *in a short time*.

もう〜で船に乗り遅れるところだった I *came very near* missing the ship.

家の完成までにはもう〜かかる It will take *some* time before the house is completed.

4〚距離〛¶学校は家からは〜ある The school is at a *short* distance from our house.

この道を〜行くと公会堂がある If you go *a little* way along this road, you will find a public hall.

〜離れて彼のあとをつけていった I tagged along *a little* behind him.

駅はもう〜ですから歩きましょう Let us walk, it *isn't very far to* the station.

事務所は駅から〜の所にある The office is at a *short* distance from the station.

すご·す【過ごす】¶本を読んで時を〜す *spend one's* time 〔in〕 reading. 志賀高原で夏休みを〜す *spend* the summer vacation at Shiga Highlands. 時をむだに〜す *waste* (≒ *idle away*) *one's* time. 酒を〜す drink *too much* (≒ *to excess*); overdrink *one*self.

すごすご【悄悄】 downcast; dejectedly; in dejection; crest-fallen.

スコッチ〔ウイスキー〕 Scotch 〔whisky〕.

スコッチツイード Scotch tweed.

スコットランド Scotland.

—人(男) a Scotchman; (女) a Scotchwoman; (総称) the Scotch; (一般的に) a Scot.

スコップ a scoop; (シャベル) a shovel.

すこぶる【頗る】 very; very much; highly; exceedingly; extremely; remarkably.
¶～元気です I am in *best* spirits. / I am *very* well. 彼女は～つきの美人だ She is a *most* beautiful woman.

すごみ【凄味】 ¶彼は～のある顔つきだ He has a *grim* (≒ *ghastly*) look. 彼は仕返しをするぞと私に～をきかした He *threatened* me *with* revenge. 彼は～をならべたてた He made *threatening remarks*.

すご・む【凄む】 ¶彼は私に～んだ He *threatened* me with violence. 強盗は金を出せと～んだ The robber *threatened* us, asking for money.

すこやか【健やか】 ¶～な healthy; sound. ～に well; healthily.

すごろく【双六】 *sugoroku* (日本の遊び); backgammon.

すさまじ・い【凄まじい】 terrific; terrible; tremendous; fierce; dreadful; amazing.
¶彼は～い意気込みでその仕事に着手した He set about the work with *tremendous* enthusiasm. 自動車が～い速力で走ってきた The car came running at a *terrific* speed. 彼は～い形相で私をにらみつけた He glared at me with a *fierce* look.

すさ・む【荒む】 ¶彼は～んだ生活を送っている He is leading a *dissipated* (≒ *dissolute*) life.

ずさん【杜撰】 ¶～な本 a *carelessly compiled* book. 彼はすることが～だ He *is careless in* doing anything.

すし【寿司・鮨】 *sushi* (英語で説明すれば vinegared rice ball with raw fish, etc. on).

すじ【筋】 1 〖線〗 line, stripe. ¶赤地に黒い～のはいったネクタイ a tie with black *stripes* on a red background.
ぼくの水泳帽は白に黒い～が2本ついている My white swimming cap is banded with two black *stripes*.
2 〖繊維〗 ¶ずいぶん～の多いサツマイモだ The sweet potatoes *are* very *stringy*.
エンドウの～を取ってくれないか Please *string* the green peas.
この肉は～が多くて少しかたい This meat *is stringy* and a little tough.
3 〖筋肉〗 ¶水泳中に足の～がつった I *got cramp in* my leg while swimming.
腰の～を少しもんでくれないか Won't you massage me round the hips for a while?
変なかっこうで眠って首の～を寝違えた I *have got a crick in* the neck from sleeping in a funny position.
肩の～が凝っている My shoulders are stiff.
4 〖血管〗 a vein. ¶彼女の腕は青い～が浮いている Her arms are marked with blue *veins*.
彼は額に青～を立てて怒った He was blue in the face with anger. / His *veins* stood out like whipcords with anger. / He *turned pale* with rage.
5 〖道理・手続き〗 ¶彼のすることは～が通っている What he does *is reasonable*. / There is *reason* in what he does.
彼の話は～が通らない What he says *is without rhyme or reason*. / What he says *is unreasonable*.
ここで契約を破棄するのは～が立たない It *is unreasonable* to break the contract now.
～を通して先方へあいさつに行くべきだ You should approach them through the *proper* channels.
～の通った正しいことなら，遠慮なく要求すべきだ You should demand without reserve what *is reasonable* and right.
6 〖話の運び〗 a plot. ¶その劇はどんな～でしたか What is the *plot* of the play?
彼は小説を書くとき，まず始めにだいたいの～を考える In writing a novel, first he works out *a* rough *scheme* (≒ *plan*) for it.
7 〖当局・方面〗 a source. ¶この情報は確かな～から出たものだ The news is from *a* reliable *source*.
アメリカ政府～の見解はまだわかっていない The view of the American Government *circles* is not known yet.
これはパリの外交～から得たニュースだ This is a piece of news we have had from the diplomatic *sources* in Paris.
信ずべき～からの報告によれば，また公定歩合が引き上げられるそうだ According to the report from *a* reliable *quarter*, the official bank rate will be raised again.
商社～の見方は非常に楽観的だ The views of the commercial *circles* are very optimistic.
8 〖素質〗 〔an〕 aptitude. ¶彼の碁はなかなか～がいい He has *a* considerable *aptitude for* the game of *go*.
9 〖助数詞〗 ¶山あいにきれいな渓流がひと～流れていた A clear mountain stream ran among the mountains.
飛行機雲がひと～ふた～見えた One or two vapor trails could be seen.

ずし【図示】 〔an〕 illustration. ¶～する illustrate; show in a graphic form; show by a diagram (≒ graph; figure). 家の位置を～する *illustrate* location of a house.

ずし【厨子】 a miniature shrine.

すじあい【筋合い】 〔a〕 right; 〔a〕 reason.
¶彼はわれわれの戦争反対運動をとやかく言えた～ではない He *has no right to* criticize our movement against war.

すじがき【筋書き】 (芝居などの) a plot; an outline; a synopsis (複 synopses); (計画) a plan; a program; a schedule.
¶この芝居の～は荒唐無稽(こうとうむけい)だ The *plot* of this drama is absurd. 何事も～どおりに運ぶとはかぎらない Everything does not always go on *as arranged*.

すじがね【筋金】 ¶～入りの社会主義者 a *diehard* (≒ *dyed-in-the-wool*) socialist. ～入りの海の男 a *staunch* seaman.

ずしき【図式】 a diagram.

すじこ【筋子】salmon roe.

すじちがい【筋違い】(筋肉の) a crick; (背理) absurdity. ¶首を~させた I got *a crick* in the neck. それは~の要求だ It is an *unreasonable* (≒ *absurd*) request.

すしづめ【すし詰め】¶~〔の〕電車 a *jam-packed* train. バスは~だった The bus *was jammed* (≒ *was packed to capacity*) *with* passengers. 彼らはその狭い部屋に~にされた They *were packed* into the small room. ~教室の解消が叫ばれてから久しい The improvement of *overcrowded* schoolrooms has long been clamored for.

すじみち【筋道】(道理) reason; logic; (話の) the thread. ¶~の通らない話 an *illogical* (≒ *inconsistent*) story. ~の通った意見 a *reasonable* (≒ *logical*) opinion. もっと~をたてて話しなさい Talk more *coherently* (≒ *methodically*).

すじむかい【筋向かい】¶~の家 the house *just across the street*. 私の家と~の家 the house *opposite to* my house.

すじめ【筋目】(折り目) a fold; a crease; a pleat; (血統) lineage; pedigree. ¶~正しい家柄 a family *of good lineage*.

すじょう【素性・素姓】(生まれ) birth; origin; (経歴) *one's* career; (身元) identity.
¶~のいい(卑しい)人 a man of good (humble) *birth*. ~は争われないものだ *Blood* will tell. ~のよしあしで人の価値は決まらない We cannot value a man's worth by his *birth*. 彼は~の知れない無気味な印象を与える人だ His *past life* being unknown, he gives us an uncanny impression.

ずじょう【頭上】¶飛行機が~高く(はるかに)飛んでいる A plane is flying *high up in the sky*. ボールが彼の~に落ちた A ball fell *on his head*. 鳥が~を飛び過ぎた A bird flew *overhead*.

ずしりと with a thud (≒ thump).

ずしんと ¶~音がした Dull sound was heard. / There was a dull sound. ~音をたてて倒れた It fell *with a thud*.

すす【煤】soot. ¶煙突に~がたまった *Soot* has collected on the chimney. 彼は~だらけの顔をしている He has a *sooty* (≒ *sooted*) face.

すず【鈴】a bell. ¶~の音 the tinkle (≒ tinkling) of *a bell*.

すず【錫】〖鉱物〗〖化学〗tin.
—鉱石 tin ore〔s〕. —製品 tinware. —はく tin foil.

すずかけ【篠懸け】〖植物〗a plane〔tree〕; 米 a sycamore.

すずかぜ【涼風】¶~が立つ *A cool breeze* in autumn begins to blow. / *Autumn wind* begins to breeze.

すすき【薄・芒】〖植物〗〔Japanese〕pampas grass.

すすぎ【濯ぎ・滌ぎ】¶洗たく物の~をよくしなさい *Rinse out* washed clothes in water.

すずき【鱸】〖魚類〗a〔sea〕bass (複 basses, (集合的) bass).

すす・ぐ【濯ぐ・滌ぐ】wash; wash out; rinse. ¶着物をきれいな水で~ぐ *rinse* the clothes in clean water. 口を~ぐ *rinse*〔*out*〕the mouth. 汚名を~ぐ *wipe out* a disgrace.

すす・ける【煤ける】¶~けた天井 a *sooty* ceiling. 天井が~ける The ceiling *gets smoked*. / The ceiling *is stained with soot*.

すずし・い【涼しい】cool; refreshing. ¶けさは~くて気持ちがいい It is pleasantly *cool* this morning. 朝晩めっきり~くなった It has got (≒ become) much *cooler* mornings and evenings. そのケーキを~い所に置きなさい Put the cake in a *cool* place. 彼女はとても~い目をしている She has very *bright* (≒ *clear*) eyes. ~い顔をしている He *looks unconcerned*. / He *looks indifferent*.

すずしさ【涼しさ】cool; coolness.

すずなり【鈴生り】¶ブドウが~になった Grapes have grown *in bunches* (≒ *in clusters*). 電車には人が~になっていた The train *was packed with* people.

すすはらい【煤払い】¶暮れの~をする *clean a house* at the end of the year. 天井の~払いをする *sweep off* (≒ *away*) *the soot* from a ceiling.

すすみ【進み】progress; advance. ¶工事の~が速い(遅い) The work makes rapid (slow) *progress*.

すずみ【涼み】¶公園へ~に行こう Let's go〔out〕to *cool ourselves* in the park. 彼らは夕~に出かけた They went out to *enjoy the cool* of the evening.
—台 a bench. —客 people who are out to cool themselves.

すす・む【進む】**1**〖前進する〗¶名を呼ばれた者は前へ~みなさい *Step forward* when your name is called.
船は南へ南へと~んだ The ship *went* on and on toward the south.
ロケットは金星目指して~んだ The rocket *made its way* toward Venus.
彼は人込みを押し分けるようにして~んでいった He *pushed* (≒ *elbowed*) *his way* through the crowd.
音の~む速さを知っていますか Do you know the velocity of sound?
敵軍は1日に20キロ~んできた The enemy *advanced* twenty kilometers in a day.
わが国はこれからどう~んだらよいか How is our country to *advance* hereafter?
彼の思想は時代よりもはるかに~んでいる His idea *is* far *ahead of* the times.
資材不足で工事が~まない We cannot *hasten* (≒ *go far with*) the work on account of the shortage of building materials.
計画は着々と~んでいる The plan *is making* steady *progress*.
研究は実用化の段階に~んでいる The study *has made* such *progress* that it can be put to practical use.
2〖仕事などがはかどる〗¶一生懸命やっても1日20ページしか~まない I can *finish* (≒ *read*) only twenty pages in a day even if I work very

す

hard.

きょうは朝早くから仕事をしたので，ずいぶん～んだ I *have made* good *progress with* my work, since I began to work early this morning. この前の授業は何ページまで～みましたか What page (≒ Where) did we *get to* in the last class?

3〖進歩する〗¶ 文明が～むにつれて自然は破壊されていく With the *advance* of civilization nature is ruined. アメリカやソビエトはロケットの技術が日本より～んでいる America and Russia *are ahead of* (≒ *are in advance of*) Japan in rocketry. 文化の～んだ国はおくれている国を助けるべきだ *Advanced* nations should give assistance to backward nations. 日本の科学は世界的水準にまで～んだ Japanese science *has come up to* the international standard. / Japanese science *has reached* the international level. 彼は～んだ考えを持っている He has *advanced* (≒ *forward*) views.

4〖上へあがる〗¶ この高校では卒業生の大部分が大学へ～む Most graduates of this upper secondary school *enter* university. われわれのチームはついに決勝戦に～んだ Our team *won its way to* the finals. 彼は一工員から社長にまで～んだ From being a mere worker he *made his way to* the presidentship.

5〖気が〗¶ 彼は～んでその難しい仕事を引き受けた He *was willing* (≒ *was eager*) *to* take upon himself the difficult work. 気が～まないから私はストライキに参加しません I will not join the strike, as I *am disinclined to* do so. 気が～まないままにその人に会った Though *unwilling*, I met him. 彼女は～んで話そうとするから，英会話の上達が速い She makes rapid progress in English conversation, because she tries to speak *of her own accord*. 彼は人がいやがることでも，～んでやる He is a man who does *willingly* what others do not like.

6〖時計が〗¶ この時計は1日に3分～む This watch *gains* three minutes a day. 腕時計が5分～んでいた My wrist watch *was* five minutes *fast*.

7〖食欲が〗¶ 秋は最も食が～む季節だ Autumn is the season when we have the best appetite. 塩ザケがあると食が～む Salted salmon gives us a good appetite. 食が～まないのは熱のせいだろう It is probably because of fever that you have a poor appetite.

8〖病気が進行する〗¶ 彼の病気はそんなに～んでいたのか *Was* his illness so *advanced*? / Was he in such a bad condition? 手術をしたが，がんが～んでいて手がつけられなかった An operation was performed, but his cancer was in such an *advanced* state that they could not do anything about it.

すず·む【涼む】¶ 川べりに座って～もう Let's sit on the bank of the river and *enjoy the cool breeze*.

すずむし【鈴虫】〔虫類〕a 'bell-ring' insect.

すすめ【勧め】(推薦) recommendation; (助言) advice; counsel; suggestion; (奨励) encouragement.

¶ 先生の～でその学校を選んだ *On* my teacher's *advice* I selected the school. A氏の～で映画会社に採用された *On the recommendation of* Mr. A. I was employed in the film producing company.

すずめ【雀】〔鳥類〕a sparrow. ¶ ～が鳴く *A sparrow* chirps (≒ twitters). 彼は私に～の涙ほどのはした金をくれた He gave me *only a trifle of* money.

すす·める【進める】¶ この計画を～めてください Please *go on with* this plan. きみはこの研究をもっと～めるべきだ You must *proceed* further *with* this study of yours. この交渉は～めていいだろうか Shall I be allowed to *go ahead with* these negotiations? この時計を5分～めてくださいませんか Would you *set* this clock *forward* by five minutes? 彼は位を1級～められた He *was promoted* one grade in rank. 仕事は～めてけっこうです You may *go on with* your work.

すす·める【勧める】¶ 彼は私にその小説を～めた He *recommended* the novel *to* me. 医者は彼に入院を～めた The doctor *advised* him *to* go to hospital. 彼は私にたばこを～めた He *offered* me a cigarette. 彼は私に大学に行くように～めている He *encourages* me *to* go to college. 彼はその仕事を無理に～めた He *pressed* me *to* do the work. 夕食に来てくれるよう彼女に～めてください Please *invite* her *to* supper.

すずらん【鈴蘭】〔植物〕a lily of the valley.

すずり【硯】an inkstone; an ink-slab.
—箱 an inkstone case.

すすりなき【啜り泣き】a sob. ¶ ～の声が起こった There was a sound of *sobbing*.

すすりな·く【啜り泣く】sob; whimper.
¶ 彼女は～きながら話をした She told the story *with a sob*. / She *sobbed out* the story. 少女の～く声が聞こえた A girl's *sobbing* voice was heard.

すす·る【啜る】¶ コーヒーを飲むときは～らないで少しずつ飲みなさい When you have coffee, don't *suck* it, but just sip it. 鼻を～るな Stop *sniffing*. 茶を～りながら話した We talked *over a cup of tea*.

すすんで【進んで】willingly; voluntarily; of *one's* own accord. ¶ 彼は人のいやがることもみずから～やる人だ He *is ready* (≒ *willing*) *to* do what others don't want to. 彼女は～病人たちの世話を申し出た She offered to take care of the sick *of her own accord*.

ずせつ【図説】an illustration; an explanatory diagram. ¶ この本は～が豊富だ This

す

book is fully illustrated by diagrams and pictures.

すそ【裾】(衣服の) the skirt; (婦人礼服の長い裾) the train; (ズボンの) the bottom; (山の) the foot.

¶ズボンの～に折り返しをつける put cuffs on *the bottom* of trousers. ズボンの～をまくって海辺を散歩した I walked on the seashore *with* my trousers *rolled up*. 富士山は～が長い Mt. Fuji *sweeps* far and wide. 山の～の一軒家 a lonely house at *the foot* of the mountain.

す

すその【裾野】 the foot (≒ base; bottom; skirts) of a mountain. ¶富士の～ *the skirts* (≒ *the foot*) of Mt. Fuji.

スター a star. ¶プロ野球の～ *a* pro (≒ professional) baseball *star*. 国際的映画～ *an* international film *star*. 彼は今やマスコミの～だ He is now *a star* of mass communication.

スターター a starter.

スタート a start. ¶彼らはいっせいに～を切った They *started* all in one body. 「ドン」と～の合図が鳴った "Bang!" went *the starting signal*. 彼はデパートの店員として人生の～を切った He *got his start in life* as a clerk in a department store. 彼はさい先のよい～を切った He *made a good start*. 彼は～がまずかった He *made a bad start*.

—ライン a balk line. **—**台 (短距離の) a starting block.

スターリング sterling.

—地域 a sterling area (イギリスの為替管理上の正式呼称は scheduled territories だが, 通称 sterling area という monetary area である).

スタイリスト (おしゃれ) a dandy; a fop; (衣類・室内装飾・車などのデザイナー) a stylist.

スタイル a style. ¶彼女は～がいい(悪い) She has *a* good (poor) *figure*. 彼女はほっそりとしたいい～だ She has *a* slender and graceful *figure*. これがパリの最新流行の～だ This is the latest *style* in Paris. 彼の文章は独特の～がある His writing has *a style* of its own.

—ブック a stylebook.

すたこら hurriedly; helter-skelter; in head long haste. ¶～と逃げだした He ran away *hurriedly* (≒ *in a hurry*). / He *scurried away*.

スタジアム a stadium.

スタジオ a studio.

テレビ**—** a TV studio.

すたすた quickly; rapidly; briskly.

ずたずた ¶彼女は着物を～に裂いた She *tore* her *kimono to* (≒ *into*) *shreds*. 紙を～に切った I *cut* 〔a sheet of〕 paper *to pieces* (≒ *to shreds*). 洪水で東海道線は～になった The flood *tore* the Tokaido line *into strips*.

スタッカート〘音楽〙staccato. ¶～風の演奏 a *staccato* style of playing.

スタッフ the staff. ¶彼は編集～の一員だ He is on the editorial *staff*. その大学はりっぱな教員～を有している The college has *a* good teaching *staff*.

スタミナ stamina. ¶彼は～がある(ない) He has much (no) *stamina*. ～をつけるために毎朝テニスをやる I play tennis every morning *to strengthen myself*. おいしい～料理で元気をつけた I *refreshed myself with* delicious nourishing dishes.

すだれ【簾】 a rattan blind. ¶～をおろす(上げる) let down (roll up) *a rattan blind*.

すた・れる【廃れる】 ¶この種の帽子はもう～れた This sort of hat *is out of fashion*. ボーリングも～れかけている Bowling *is going out of vogue*. 火ばちはもう～れてしまった A brazier *is out of use*. そんなことをすればぼくの男が～れる It should *be unworthy of* me.

スタンス〘野球〙〘ゴルフ〙〔a〕stance. ¶彼は～が広い His *stance* is a little too wide.

クローズド**—** closed stance.

スタンダード standard.

—ナンバー〘音楽〙a standard number.

スタンド (観客席) a stand; (ランプ) (机上の) a desk lamp; (床に置く) a floor lamp; (売り場) a stand. ¶～は満員だった The *stands* were full.

—イン a stand-in. インク**—** an inkstand. ガソリン**—** a gas station; a service station. コーヒー**—** a coffee stand. **—**プレー a standing play.

スタンプ a stamp. ¶記念～を絵はがきに押す affix *a* commemorative *stamp* to a picture card.

—インキ stamp ink.

スチーム steam. ¶部屋には～が通っている The room *is steam-heated*. / The room *is heated by steam*.

—暖房 steam heat; central heating.

スチール **1**〘野球〙a steal.

2〘鉱物〙steel. ¶～製の机 a *steel*-made desk.

3〘映画〙a still.

—写真 a still picture.

スチュワーデス a stewardess.

-ずつ【-宛】 ¶1日に5ページ～読む I read *five papers a day*. 彼らはひとり～部屋から出た They went out of the room *one by one*. 応募者は二, 三人～やってきた The applicants came *by twos and threes*. 少し～食べる We eat *little by little*. 3人に1枚～配る We distribute a sheet of paper to *every three persons*.

ずつう【頭痛】 a headache. ¶頭が割れるような～ *a* splitting *headache*. ～がする I have *a headache*. ひどい(少し)～がする I have *a* bad (slight) *headache*. 彼女は～持ちだ She is subject to *headaches*. 息子の病弱が～の種だ My son's ill health is *a cause of anxiety* (≒ *a severe headache*) to me.

すっからかん ¶財布が～になった I *became* quite *penniless*.

すっかり ¶彼の家は～完成した His house is *completely* built. ～忘れていた I have *clean* forgotten it. 故郷の町は～変わってしまった My hometown has *completely* changed. 彼女は～大人になった She is *quite* grown up. 彼はもう～だめだ It's all over with him. ～夜が明けた

It is *broad* daylight now. 〜きみに任せます I'll leave it *all* to you.

すっきり ¶ぐっすり眠ったあとで，まったく〜した気持ちだ I *am* quite *refreshed* after a sound sleep. 彼女は〜した服装をしている She is dressed *neatly*. すっきりした気持ちだ I've a *refreshed* frame of mind.

ズック ¶〜のくつ *canvas* shoes.

すっくと ¶彼は〜立ち上がった He rose *abruptly* to his feet.

ずっしり ¶〜と重い財布 a *well-* (≒ *richly-*) *lined* purse.

すったもんだ【擦った揉んだ】¶〜のあげくやっと事件がおさまった After *much wrangling* (≒ *much fuss*) the trouble came to an end. そのことで〜の騒ぎをした We *made a fuss* over it.

すってんころり ¶〜と転ぶ fall plump.

すってんてん ¶かけ事で〜になった I *lost all my money* in gambling. / I *became quite penniless* because of gambling.

すっと (直立して) straight; (すばやく) quickly; abruptly. ¶彼は〜席を立った(すばやく) He *sprang up* from his seat. 1杯のコーヒーで頭が〜した I *felt refreshed* with a cup of coffee. 言いたいだけ言って気持ちが〜した After I had said what I wanted to, I *felt my mind unburdened*.

ずっと (はるかに) very much; considerably; (続けざまに) all the time; through; (まっすぐに) straight.
¶ゴルフよりボーリングのほうが〜おもしろい Bowling is *far* more interesting than golf. 彼は〜よくなっている He is getting *much* better. 〜向こうに明かりが見えた I saw a light *in the distance* (≒ *far away*). 〜前に見たことがある I remember seeing it *long ago*. いままで〜ここにいた I have been here *for a long time*. 彼は3週間前から〜病気で寝ている He has been ill in bed for three weeks. 名古屋まで〜立ちどおしだった I was kept standing *all the way* to Nagoya. バス停まで〜走った I ran *all the way* to the bus stop. 彼は一日じゅう〜眠りつづけた He slept the whole day *through*. (この through は副詞). 彼女は一生〜独身だった She remained unmarried *all through life*. (この through は前置詞).

すっぱ·い【酸っぱい】sour; acid. ¶レモンは〜い果物だ A lemon is an *acid* fruit. このミルクは〜くなった This milk has turned *sour*. この牛乳は〜い This milk *tastes sour*. 口を〜くして彼に小言をいった I scolded him *over and over again*.

すっぱだか【素っ裸】stark-nakedness. ¶〜になって海に飛び込んだ I jumped into the sea, *stark-naked*. 事業に失敗して〜になった Failure in the business made him *penniless*.

すっぱぬき【素破抜き】exposure; disclosure.

すっぱぬ·く【素破抜く】¶彼女の離婚は週刊誌に〜かれた Her divorce *was disclosed to the public* by the weekly.

すっぱり ¶旅行は〜とあきらめた I gave up traveling *without the least regret*. たばこを〜とやめた I quit smoking *completely*.

すっぽか·す ¶彼はけっして約束を〜すようなことはしない He never *breaks his word*. 彼はその仕事を〜して外出した He went out *leaving* the work *undone*. 彼を〜した I *gave* him *the slip*.

すっぽり ¶彼は布団を〜かぶっていた He covered his body *completely* with a quilt.

すっぽん【鼈】a snapping turtle. ¶両者は月と〜の違いがある The two *are poles asunder* (≒ *apart*). / The two *are as far apart as the poles*.

すで【素手】¶彼は〜で戦うつもりだ He is going to fight *unarmed* (≒ *with bare hands*). 彼は〜で帰った He returned *empty-handed*.

すていし【捨て石】¶彼の死は民族独立のりっぱな〜になった His death proved to be a valuable contribution to racial independence.

すてうり【捨て売り】¶〜する sell (goods) at a sacrifice.

ステーキ 〔a〕steak; 〔a〕beefsteak.

ステージ a stage.

ステートメント a statement. ¶大統領はけさ〜を発表した The President announced his *statement* this morning.

すてお·く【捨て置く】¶その件はそのままに〜きなさい *Leave* the matter *alone* (≒ *as it is*). 彼のことは〜きなさい *Leave* him *alone*. そんなささいな誤りは〜きなさい *Overlook* (≒ *Forget*) such a trivial mistake.

すてき【素敵·素的】¶〜な食事 a *wonderful* dinner. 〜ながめ a *fine* view. 〜な日没 a *splendid* sunset. 〜な乙女 a *wonderful* girl. 〜な歌手 a *fine* singer. 〜なひとときを過ごした We had a *wonderful* time.

すてご【捨て子】a deserted child; (拾った) a foundling.

すてぜりふ【捨て台詞】¶「覚えてろ」と彼は〜を言った "You shall suffer for this!" he *cried over his shoulder*.

ステッキ a stick; (籐など) a cane; a walking stick.

ステップ ¶ワルツの〜 the waltz *step*. 汽車の〜(乗降台) the *step* of a train.

すでに【既に】already; long ago. ¶日は〜暮れていた It had *already* got dark. 彼は衰弱しすぎて〜手術には手おくれだ He is *too* weak *for* an operation. 時〜遅し It's *too* late now. 最終バスが〜出てしまっていた The last bus had *already* left.

すてね【捨て値】a sacrifice. ¶それを〜で売った I sold it *at a large sacrifice*. それを〜で買った I bought it *dirt cheap*.

すてば【捨て場】a dumping place; a dump. ごみ—— a dumping ground. ¶ごみの〜がどこにも見当たらなかった I did not find any place to throw rubbish into.

すてばち【捨て鉢】¶彼は失敗して〜になっている He *is driven to despair* by the failure. / He *is desperate at* the failure. / He *is in despair at* the failure. 〜になるな Don't *abandon yourself to despair*.

すてみ【捨て身】¶〜で敵と戦った I fought

against the enemy *at the risk of my life.* ～の戦法で相手チームを破った We won over our opponent team *like mad.*

す・てる【捨てる】 ¶この紙くずを～ててください *Throw away* the wastepaper. ごみをあき地に～ててはいけない Never *dump* the rubbish in vacant areas. ごみ～てるな(掲示) Don't *throw* it. / Be tidy. / (たとえば京都なら) Keep Kyoto clean. このびんの水を～ててはいけない You mustn't *pour out* the water in this bottle. 彼は妻を～てた He *abandoned* his wife. 彼は試合を～てた He *threw away* the game.

す

ステレオ (電蓄) a stereo.
—放送 stereophonic broadcasting. —レコード a stereo〔phonic〕record.

ステンドグラス stained glass. ¶～の窓 a *stained-glass* window.

ステンレス stainless steel. ¶～のスプーン a *stainless steel* spoon.

スト (ストライキ) a strike. ¶無期限～ *an* indefinite period *strike.* 首切り反対～ *a* counter-discharge *strike.* ～中である The *strike* is on. 彼らは～中である They *are on strike.* 彼らは～を計画中である They are organizing *a strike.* ついに～は実行された At last *a strike* has broken out. ～を宣言した We declared *a strike.* ～を解決するためにベストを尽くした We did our best to settle the *strike.* 従業員は～突入を決定した The workers decided to *go on a strike.* ～は中止された The *strike* has been called off.
—破り(人) a strikebreaker; (行為) strike-breaking.

ストア a store (主として米).
チェーン— a chain store. ドラッグ— a drug-store.

すどおし【素通し】 ¶～のガラス *plain* glass. ～の眼鏡 *plain* glasses.

ストーブ a stove; a heater (stove は cooking stove の意に使うことが多い. 普通の暖房用は heater のほうがよい).
¶きのう～をたいた I made a fire in the *stove* yesterday. / I heated *a stove* yesterday. この～はよく燃えている The *stove* is well burning.
ガス— a gas heater (⇔ stove). 石炭— a coal stove. 石油— an oil stove; a kerosene lamp. だるま— a potbellied stove. 電気— an electric heater. —リーグ〖野球〗a stove league.

すどおり【素通り】 ¶彼はぼくの家を～していった He *passed* our door *without dropping in.* 彼女は図書館の前を～した She *passed* the library *with no stopping.*

ストッキング stockings. ¶～2足 two pairs of *stockings.*

ストック **1**〖スキー〗ski sticks (ストックはドイツ語から).
2〖在庫品〗stock. ¶このネクタイは～がある(ない) This tie *is in stock* (*is out of stock*).

ストップ stop.

ストップウオッチ a stopwatch.

すどまり【素泊まり】 ¶～で1泊1,000円だった It cost a thousand yen to *stay overnight without meals.*

ストライキ (罷業) a strike. ⇒スト

ストライク〖野球〗a strike. ¶どうやら～をとった I managed to score *a strike.* カウントはツー～, ワンボールだ The count is one ball and two *strikes.* / The count is one and two. (英語ではワンボール, ツーストライクの順に言う).
—ゾーン the strike zone.

ストライプ a stripe.

ストリート a street.
メーン— the main street.

ストリキニーネ〖薬品〗strychnine.

ストレート ¶ウイスキーを～で飲む drink whisky *straight* (⇔ *short*).
—勝ち ¶～勝ちをした I *won a straight victory*〔*over* my opponent〕. —負け ¶～負けをした I *suffered a straight defeat*〔*from* my opponent〕.

ストレス〖医学〗stress. ¶休暇をとって～を解消する take a vacation and *relax* (⇔ *be released from stress*).
—学説 the stress theory. —病 stress disease.

ストレプトマイシン〖薬品〗streptomycin.

ストロー a〔drinking〕straw; (紙の) a sipper. ¶～で飲む suck (milk) through *a straw.*
—ハット a straw hat.

ストローク (ゴルフ・水泳) a stroke; (ボート) the stroke; the stroke-oar. ¶ワン～の差で勝つ win by *a stroke.*

ストローベリー a strawberry (ふつう複数形で用いる).

ストロボ an electronic flash; (商品名) a Strobo.

ストロンチウム〖化学〗strontium.

すとんと ¶～落ちる fall *with a thump.*

ずどんと ¶銃声が～鳴った *Bang!* went the rifle. / *Bang!* The rifle report reverberated.

すな【砂】 sand. ¶ぬかるんだ所に乾いた～をまく sprinkle dry *sand* over the muddy place. 右の目に～が入った I have got some *sand* in my right eye.

すなあらし【砂嵐】 a sandstorm.

すなお【素直】 gentleness; meekness; obedience; docility. ¶～な性質の人 a man of *gentle* nature. ～な子ども a *good* (⇔ an *obedient*) child. ～に人の言うことを聞きなさい(従う) Obey others *meekly.* / *Be obedient* to others (⇔ what others say). / (耳をかす) *Be ready to* listen to the advice of others. 彼は～に罪を白状した He confessed the crime *frankly.* 彼は～な字を書く His handwriting is free from mannerism.

すなけむり【砂煙】 a cloud of dust. ¶～をあげる raise *a dust cloud.*

すなじ【砂地】 a sandy place; (土壌) sandy soil.

スナック snack.
—バー a snack bar.

スナップ (ホック) a snap; (写真) a snapshot; (野球など) a snap. ¶彼女の～(写真)をとった I *took a snapshot of* her.

すなつぶ【砂粒】grains of sand.

すなどけい【砂時計】a sandglass; an hourglass.

すなば【砂場】(採取場) a sand pit; (遊び場) a sandbox.

すなはま【砂浜】a sandy beach; the sands.

すなぶろ【砂風呂】a sand bath.

すなぼこり【砂塵】a cloud of dust. ¶～が立った *A dust cloud* went up.

すなやま【砂山】a sand hill; dune.

すなわち【即ち・則ち】¶アメリカの第16代大統領～エイブラハム＝リンカーン the sixteenth president of the United States, *that is*, Abraham Lincoln. アメリカの国会は二院，～上院と下院から成る Congress consists of two houses, *namely*, the Senate and the House of Representatives. カナダでは2か国語，～英語とフランス語が用いられている In Canada they use two languages, *that is to say*, English and French.

すね【臑・脛】the leg; the shin. ¶彼は～に傷持つ身だ He *has a bad conscience*. / He is a man *with a shady background*. 親の～をかじっている I *live on my parents*.

す・ねる【拗ねる】¶子どもはおもちゃを買ってもらえないので～ねている The child *is in the sulks* because he can't get the toy he wants. 彼は世を～ねている He *lives a cynic life*.

ずのう【頭脳】a head; brains. ¶緻密(ちみつ)な～ *a* close *head*. 散漫な～ *a* loose *head*. 彼は～明晰(めいせき)だ He *is* clear-*headed*. / He has *a* clear *head*. 彼は～的仕事には向かない He is not suited for *brain* work. 彼はわが社の～といわれる人だ He is regarded as *the wisest head* of the firm.

―流出 brain drain. ―労働者 a brain (≒ mental) worker.

すのこ【簀の子】a hurdle.

―縁 hurdle-floored verandah.

すのもの【酢の物】a vinegared dish. ¶カキの～ *vinegared* oysters.

スパーク a spark. ¶～する spark.

スパート〘競技〙a spurt. ¶ラスト～をかける put on *a* last *spurt*. ランナーは最後の1周でラスト～をかけた The runner *spurted* forward in the last lap of the race.

スパイ (人) a spy; (行為) espionage. ¶われわれの仲間に～がいる We have *an* office *spy* among us. 彼に～をつけた We set *a spy* on him. ～につけられている I am shadowed by *spies*.

―活動 espionage 〔action〕.

スパイク (金具) a spike; (スパイクシューズ) spiked shoes.

スパゲッティ spaghetti.

すばこ【巣箱】(鳥の) a nest box; (ミツバチの) a 〔bee-〕hive.

すばしっこ・い ¶～い男(抜け目のない男) a *smart* (≒ *shrewd*) man; (機転のきく男) a *quick-witted* man. 彼は動作が～い He *is quick* (≒ *agile*) *in* his movements. 彼は～く(抜け目なく)立ちまわった He acted *shrewdly*.

すぱすぱ ¶たばこを～と吸う *puff away at* a cigarette. パイプを(葉巻を)～ふかす *puff away at one's* pipe (*one's* cigar). ダイコンを～と切る cut a radish *with quick ease*.

ずばずば ¶彼は～物を言う He *is outspoken*.

すはだ【素膚】bare skin. ¶～の美しい女 a woman of *a* clear *skin*. ～にワイシャツを着る put on a shirt *with no underwear* (≒ *next to the skin*).

スパナ a spanner; 米 a wrench.

ずばぬ・ける【ずば抜ける】¶～けた才能 an *outstanding* talent. ～けてスキーがじょうずだ He *excels* others at skiing. / He is *by far the best* skier. / He enjoys *great excellence* in skiing. あの相撲取は～けて強い That *sumo* wrestler is *by far the strongest* of all.

すばや・い【素早い】quick; speedy; swift; prompt. ¶～い動作 *quick* movement. ～く逃げる run away *quickly*.

すばらし・い【素晴らしい】¶～い景色 a *grand* view (≒ scenery). ～い天気 *splendid* (≒ *glorious*) weather. ～い人気 *great* popularity. ～い景気 a *great* boom. ～い住宅 a *fine* (≒ *splendid*) house. ～い経験 a *wonderful* experience. ～く大きなビル a *magnificent* building. ～い美人 a *strikingly* beautiful woman. ～い考え a *capital* idea. きみの記憶力はまったく～い What a *wonderful* memory you have!

ずばり ¶～と言う speak *frankly*; speak out. ～と質問に答える answer a question *decidedly*.

すばる【昴】〘天文学〙the Pleiades ([pláiədi:z]と発音し，複数扱い).

スパルタ Sparta. ¶子どもを～式に鍛える give *Spartan training* to *one's* children.

ずはん【図版】a plate; a figure; an illustration.

スピーカー a speaker.

ラウド― a loudspeaker.

スピーチ a speech.

テーブル― an after-dinner speech (table speech は和製英語). ¶晩さん会でテーブル～をした I made *a speech* at the dinner party.

スピーディー speedy; swift; quick; rapid. ¶～に動く move *quickly*. ～な処置をとる take a *quick* (≒ *prompt*) action. ～に speedily; swiftly; rapidly.

スピード 〔a〕 speed. ¶フル～で at full *speed*. 普通の～で at *an* ordinary *speed*. 猛～で at a great *speed*. ～を出す gather (≒ put on) *speed*; speed up. ～を落とす slow down. 彼の車は時速120キロの～で走っていた His car was running at *a speed* of 120 kilometers an hour.

―違反 speeding.

スピッツ〘動物〙a spitz 〔dog〕.

ずひょう【図表】a chart; a diagram.

スピロヘータ〘医学〙a spiroch〔a〕eta.

スフィンクス a sphinx (複 sphinxes, sphinges); 〘ギリシア神話〙the Sphinx.

スプーン a spoon. ¶～1杯の砂糖 *a spoonful of* sugar. ～2杯の塩 *two spoonfuls of* salt.

ずぶと・い【図太い】¶～い男(大胆な) a *bold*

す

man；(ずうずうしい) an *audacious* man. ～く構える take an *audacious* attitude. 彼は～い神経の持ち主だ He has *iron* nerves.

ずぶの utter；entire. ¶ 彼は商売には～素人(しろうと)だ He is an *unexperienced* person in business work. 彼は外交には～素人だ He is an *absolute* beginner in diplomacy.

ずぶぬれ【ずぶ濡れ】¶ ～になった I *got wet through.* / I *got wet* (≒ *drenched*) *to the skin.* きみは～だ You *are wet all over.* 頭のてっぺんから足のつま先まで～だ I *am wet from top to toe.*

す

ずぶり ¶ 人を～と刺す stab *a person* through. 片足が沼に～とはまった My foot was stuck *thoroughly* (≒ *well*) in the swamp.

スプリンター〔競技〕a sprinter.

スプレー a spray.

すべ【術】¶ まったくなすすべを知らなかった I was quite at a loss what to do. / I was quite at my wits' end. 彼は金をもうける～にたけている He is good at making money. / He knows well *how to* make money. / He has the *art* of making money.

スペア a spare. ¶ ～のタイヤ a *spare* tire.

スペイン Spain.

—語 Spanish. **—人**(ひとり) a Spaniard；(総称) the Spanish.

スペース〔a〕space；room. ¶ ～が足りないので for want of *space*. 十分な～(余地)がない There is not enough *space* (≒ *room*).

スペード〘トランプ〙a spade (ふつう複数形).

すべからく【須らく】by all means；necessarily.

スペクトル〘物理〙the spectrum.

—分析 spectrum analysis.

すべすべ ¶ この生地は～している This cloth feels *smooth*.

すべっこ・い【滑っこい】slippery；sleek；velvety；smooth. ¶ ビロードのような～さ velvety *smoothness*.

すべて【総て・全て】all；whole；entire；total. ¶ 費用は～で１万円だ The *total* cost is ten thousand yen. / The cost is ten thousand yen *in all*. ～は神が知っている God knows *all*. 計画は～の点で完全だ The plan is perfect *in every respect*. ～はきみの決心しだいだ *Everything* depends upon your decision. 金が～ではない Money is not *everything*.

すべら・す【滑らす】¶ 足を～してころぶ *slip* and fall. 筆を～す make *a slip* of the pen. 口を～す make *a slip* of the tongue. うっかり口を～して彼の名を言ってしまった I let his name *slip* from my lips.

すべり【滑り】a slip；a slide；sliding. ¶ 戸の～がよい The door *slides* well. この窓は～がよくない This window does not *slide* well.

—台(子どもの) a chute；a slide；(進水式の) a sliding platform.

すべりこみ【滑り込み】〘野球〙sliding. ¶ 頭からの～ head-first *sliding*. ～をする slide to a base. ～で列車にまにあった I was barely in time for the train. / I nearly missed the train.

すべりこ・む【滑り込む】¶ 走者はホームに(二塁へ)～んだ The runner *slid* home (*slid into* second base). 一塁に～んでセーフだった I *slid* safely *into* first base.

すべりだし【滑り出し】¶ ～がよい make (≒ get) a good *start* (*in*).

スペリング spelling.

すべ・る【滑る】glide；slide；slip；(試験などに) fail；(スケートで) skate. ¶ 彼は氷の上を～るのがうまい He is good at *skating*. 彼はスキーで坂道を～っていった He went *skiing* off down the slope. スキーで～って転ぶ人は多い Many people *slip* and fall while enjoying skiing. スケートで～ってしりもちをついた I *slipped* while skating and fell on my backside. 雨のため道が～った The road *was slippery* because of the rain. 列車はプラットホームを～るように出ていった The train *glided* out of the station. 階段で～らないよう気をつけなさい Be careful not to *slip* and fall on the stairs. 彼は試験でまた～った He *failed* the examination again.

スポイト a fountain pen filler (スポイトはオランダ語の spuit から).

ずほう【図法】〔製図〕drawing；draftsmanship.

透視**—** perspective drawing. 平面(投影)**—** projection.

スポークスマン a spokesman.

スポーツ a sport. ¶ ～をする enjoy *sports*；engage in *sports*；practice *sports*；take part in *sports* (play sports はさける). 彼は～が好きだ He is a lover of *sports*. ぼくの好きな～は野球だ My favorite *sport* is baseball. (単数形に注意).

—ウェア sportswear. **—カー** a sports car. **—界** the sporting world；sportsdom. **—センター** a sports center. **—欄** a sports section.

スポーツマン a sportsman.

—シップ sportsmanship. ¶ ～シップにのっとって戦う play *sportsmanlike*.

スポーティー ¶ 彼はいつも～な服装をしている He always wears *sporty* clothes.

ずぼし【図星】the mark；the bull's eye. ¶ まさに～だ You*'ve hit it right*. 彼は～を指されて白状した He *had his design spotted*, and confessed. / He *was rightly guessed*, and confessed.

スポット spot. ¶ 問題の焦点に～を当ててみよう Let's *focus* our attention *on* the most important point of the subject.

—ニュース spot news. **—ライト** a spotlight.

すぼ・める【窄める】¶ かさを～める *close* (≒ *shut*) an umbrella. 彼女は口を～めた She *pursed up* her mouth (≒ lips). 彼は軽べつしたように笑って肩を～めた He *shrugged* his shoulders giving a scornful laugh.

ずぼら ¶ ～な男 a sloven. ～な仕事 *slovenly* work. 彼は～な生活を送っている He is leading a *slovenly* life. 彼は何事によらず～だ He *is slovenly* in everything.

ズボン〔a pair of〕trousers；㊇ pants (㊈では「ズボン下」を意味する. また日本語のパンツは㊇㊈とも

に briefs という).

¶～をプレスしてもらった I had my *pants* pressed. すそに折り返しのある(ない)～ a pair of *pants* with (without) cuffs.

—下 米 drawers; 英 pants. —つり 米 suspenders; 英 braces. 替え— spare trousers. 作業— work trousers; (胸当てまでついた) overalls. 乗馬— riding breeches [brítʃiz]. 半— breeches; (子ども用) short pants; shorts.

スポンサー a sponsor. ¶テレビの～ *a* TV *sponsor*. ラジオ番組の～ *a* radio program *sponsor*. わが社があの番組の～だ Our company *sponsors* (≒ *is a sponsor for*) that program.

スポンジ a sponge.

—ケーキ sponge cake. —ボール a sponge ball.

スマート stylish (smart は英語では「抜け目のない」「鋭い」の意が主で衣服その他で使うことは少ない). ¶彼女の制服姿はとても～だ She *looks* very *stylish* in her uniform. 彼女は前よりもやせて～になった She has lost weight, and has a *graceful* figure. (become thinner はさける).

すまい【住まい】 a home; a house; a residence; (住所) *one's* address.

¶さしあたりホテル～だ I *am staying* at a hotel for the present. お～はどちらですか Where do you *live*? 店は銀座で～は鎌倉です I keep a store at Ginza and have my *home* at Kamakura. りっぱなお～ですね What *a* fine *house* you live in!

すましじる【澄まし汁】 clear soup; consommé.

すましや【澄まし屋】 ¶彼は～だ He *is stuck-up*.

すま・す【済ます】 ¶もう夕食は～せた I *have* already *had* supper. 早く仕事を～せなさい *Get* your work *finished* quickly. 用事を～せるまで待っていてください Please wait till I *have finished* my business. われわれは水なしでは～されない We cannot *do without* water. 朝食ぬきで～す人もある Some people *do without* breakfast. この作品を読むのに辞書なしでは～されない In reading this work we cannot *dispense with* a dictionary.

すま・す【澄ます】 1〖水を〗clarify. ¶濁った水を～す *make* muddy water *clear*.

2〖耳・心を〗¶じっと座って心を～せなさい Sit silently and *keep* your mind *clear*.

耳を～してごらんなさい Try to *listen carefully*. 耳を～して彼のラジオ放送の声を聞いた I *was all attention* listening to what he said on the radio.

3〖気取る〗¶彼は～した顔で外を歩いている He is walking about outside *with an affected air*.

彼は～している He *puts on airs*.

彼はいつもつんと～している He always *looks prim*.

彼は知らぬ顔で～している He *is playing the innocent*.

スマッシュ (テニスなどの) a smash; smashing.

すまな・い【済まない】 ¶～いけれど1,000円貸してくれませんか *May I trouble you* to lend me a thousand yen? きみにはたいへん～いことをした I have done you very *wrong*.

すみ【炭】 charcoal. ¶～をおこす make fire with *charcoal*.

すみ【墨】 Chinese ink; Indian ink; (固形) an Indian ink stick; (イカの) sepia. ¶～をする rub down *an Indian ink stick*. この～は濃い(うすい) This *ink* is thick (thin). ～で書く write *in Indian ink*. イカは身の危険を感じると～を吐く A cuttlefish ejects *a black, inklike fluid* when in danger. この二つは～と雪ほども違う These two *are as different as light from darkness*.

すみ【済み】 ¶代金は～ Paid. これできょうの仕事は全部～だ I *have* completely *done* my day's work. 朝食はお～ですか *Have* you *finished* your breakfast? きょうはこれで～としよう Let's *call it a day*.

検査— Examined.

すみ【隅・角】 a corner; a nook. ¶～から～まで捜した I looked *in every nook and corner*. / I left no *corner* unsearched. 彼女は礼拝堂の人目につかない～に座った She took her seat in *an* unobserved *corner* of the chapel. 封筒の左上の～に切手をはる put stamps on the left-hand *corner* of an envelope. 彼はなかなか～におけない He *is* very *smart*.

すみえ【墨絵】 Indian ink drawing. ¶彼の～の傑作 his masterpiece drawn in Indian ink.

すみか【住み処・栖】 a dwelling; (盗賊の) a den [of robbers]; (鳥・獣などの) a lie.

すみごこち【住み心地】 ¶これは～のよい家だ This is a *comfortable* house to live in.

すみこみ【住み込み】 ¶～のお手伝い a maid *who lives in*.

すみこ・む【住み込む】 live with *one's* master.

すみずみ【隅隅】 all the corners; every nook and corner. ¶部屋の～までよく掃除した I've swept *all the corners* of a room.

すみぞめ【墨染め】 ¶～の衣をまとった尼 a nun *in a black robe*.

すみつ・く【住み着く】 ¶親の代から当地に～いている We *have settled in* this place for two generations.

すみて【住み手】 ¶この家は～がない This is an unoccupied house.

すみな・れる【住み慣れる】 ¶彼は～れた村を出ていった He left his village *where he had lived for a long time*. 彼は～れた家を出ていった He has left his *old* house.

すみにく・い【住みにくい】 ¶～い国 a country *unfit to live in*. とかくこの世は～い Anyway, this world of ours *is not a very agreeable place to live* [in]. (口語では live *in* としないのがふつう). / It *is no easy thing to live* in the world of men.

すみび【炭火】 charcoal fire.

すみません【済みません】 ¶どうも～ I beg your pardon. (下がり調子に言う). (こんなに頂いて)どうも～ *I'm sorry to* put you to such expense. ～が, 駅へ行く道を教えてください *Excuse me, but* will you please tell me the way to the station? ～が，この答えを教えてください *May I trouble you to* give me the answer to this? ～，いっしょにいらしていただけませんか *Would you mind* coming with me? 遅れてきて～ *Pardon* me *for* coming late. お待たせして～でした I'*m sorry to* have kept you waiting.

すみやか【速やか】 ¶～な動作 a *rapid* action. ～な返答が望ましい A *prompt* answer is desirable. ～な行動をとるよう望みたい I want you to take *immediate* action. ～に現場に行くのがいちばんだ The best thing would be to go to the spot *without delay*. ～な救援活動が始まった *Rapid* (≒ *Prompt*) relief activities started. 仕事は～に進んでいる The work is making *rapid* progress. ～に rapidly.

すみやき【炭焼き】 charcoal making; (人) a charcoal burner.

すみれ【菫】 a violet. ¶～の花盛りだ *Violets* are in bloom.
三色── a pansy.

す･む【住む】 live. ¶彼がどこに～んでいるか知っていますか Do you know where he *lives*? この家は人が～んでいない This house *is uninhabited*. その地方には今でもたくさんのアメリカインディアンが～んでいる Many American Indians still *inhabit* the district. ～む家もなかった I had no house to *live* 〔*in*〕. ～めば都(諺) *There is no place like home*.

す･む【済む】 1 〖終わる〗 ¶朝食はもう～みました I *have* already *had* breakfast.
試験が～んでほっとした The examination *is over*, so I feel relieved.
用事が～んだらすぐ行きます I will come as soon as I *have finished* (≒ I *am through with*) my business.
仕事が～んだら遊びにいってよい You can go and play when your work *is done*.
～んだら書類を私にください Please give me the papers when you *have read* them *through*. / Please give me the papers when you *have done with* them.
～んだことはしかたがない(諺) *What is done cannot be undone*.
彼にあんなことを言って無事に～むと思うのか Do you think you can *get away with* saying that sort of thing to him?
あの一件は無事に～んだ The affair *was settled* without mishap.
このまま～むことではない The matter must not *be left as it is*.
2 〖まにあう〗 ¶この冬はストーブなしに～んだ I *managed* without the heater this winter. / I passed this winter without the heater.
きみが出席しなくても～むようにしておく I will *manage* so that you need not attend.
私が出なくては～まなくなりそうだ It seems it won't *be settled* without me.
弁償すれば～むという問題ではない It is not a matter to *be put right* only by reparation.
買い物は１度で～むように欲しい物をメモした I have made a list of what I want to buy so that I *need not* go shopping again.
彼の本があったので，新しい本を買わないで～んだ He had the book, so I *did not need* buy a new one.
生活費は月10万円で～ませている As for the cost of living I *get along* on ten thousand yen a month.
ことしは借金せずに～みそうだ I will be able to *make shift* without borrowing money this year.
電話で話せばわざわざ先方まで行かずに～む If you phone him, you *don't have to* go there (≒ to him).
私は甘党で，甘い物がないと気が～まない I have a sweet tooth and I can't *do without* sweet stuff.
3 〖謝罪〗 ¶～みませんで～むと思うか Do you think it's enough just to say "*Excuse me*"? ⇒すみません

す･む【澄む】 ¶空は～んできた The sky *became clear*. 水は～んでいる The water *is clear and bright*. 山の空気は～んでいる The air of the mountain *is clear*. 彼は～んだ目をしている He has *clear* eyes.

スムーズ ¶事は～に収まった The matter *has been smoothed over*. 仕事は～に運んだ The matter went *smoothly*. 会の進行は～だった The meeting advanced *favorably*.

ずめん【図面】 a drawing; a plan; (青写真) a blueprint. ¶～をかく(引く) draw *a plan*. ～を読みとる read (≒ look at) *a sketch of the blueprint*.

すもう【相撲･角力】 *sumo* wrestling; (勝負) a *sumo* wrestling match (game とは言わない); (力士) a *sumo* wrestler.
¶～をとる engage in *sumo*; enjoy *sumo*; wrestle (*with a person*) (play *sumo*, do *sumo* とは言わない). AとBでは～にならない A *is no match for* B. / A *is not B's equal*. / A cannot *bear comparison with* B. 人のふんどしで～をとる be generous at *a person's* expense; (成句) rob Peter to pay Paul.

スモッグ smog (<smoke+fog).

すもも【李】 〖植物〗(木) a plum; (実) a plum.

すやき【素焼き】 unglazed pottery; biscuit; bisque. ¶～のさら an *unglazed* plate.

すやすや〔と〕 peacefully; quietly. ¶子どもが～眠っている The child is sleeping *peacefully* (≒ *quietly*).

スライダー 〖野球〗 a slider.

スライド slide. ¶～を写す project *a slide*. 物価に応じて賃銀が～する Wages *slide* as prices change.
──制 a sliding scale.

ずらか･る ¶当番を～る *escape one's* duty.

ずら･す ¶出発の日を１日～す *put off one's* departure by one day.

すらすら ¶問題が～と解決した The problem was solved *smoothly* (≒ *with ease*). 彼はフランス語が～と読める He can read French *easily*. 手紙を～と書き流した He *dashed off* a letter. 事は～運ぶだろう The matter will go over *smoothly*.

スラックス 〔a pair of〕 slacks.

スラブ a Slav.
—語 Slavic; Slavonic. —人 a Slavic; Slavonic. —民族 the Slavs.

スラム a slum.
—街 the slums; a slum district.

すらり〔と〕 smoothly; graceful. ¶ ～した体つき a *slender* figure.

ずらり〔と〕 ¶ 着飾った人たちが～並んでいる Fine-dressed people are standing *in a row* (≒ *in a line*). 街には高級店が～並んでいる The street *is lined with* high-class stores.

スラローム 〘スキー〙 (回転競技) slalom.

スラング slang.

スランプ a slump. ¶ このところ～だ These days I *am in a slump*. 彼は～に陥った He *got* (≒ *fell*) *into a slump*. ～から抜け出ようと努力している I am making efforts to *wriggle out of* (≒ *get through*) *a slump*.

すり【刷り】 ¶ これは～がきれいだ This *is* well *printed*.

すり【掏摸】 (行為) pocket-picking; (人) a pickpocket. ¶ ～にやられる have *one's* pocket picked.

すりあが・る【刷り上がる】 ¶ ～ったばかりの本 books *wet from the press*. 本が～った Books *were off the press*.

すりあ・げる【刷り上げる】 ¶ やっと 1,000部 ～げた One thousand copies *were* finally *printed* (≒ *worked*) *off*.

スリーブ a sleeve.
ノー— ¶ ノー～のドレス a *sleeveless* dress; a dress with no *sleeves*.

すりえ【擂り餌】 ground food for birds; paste feed.

ずりお・ちる【ずり落ちる】 ¶ ベッドから～ちる *slip down* from the bed. ズボンが～ちた The trousers *worked down* (≒ *slipped down*).

すりか・える【すり替える】 ¶ ほんものと偽物とを～える *substitute* a false thing *for* a real one. 問題を～えて追求を逃れた I *substituted* the question *for* another to escape (≒ evade) a pursuit.

すりガラス【磨り硝子】 frosted glass.

すりきず【擦り傷】 an abrasion; a graze; a scratch. ¶ ～を負う get *a scratch*. ～程度で済んだ I got off only with *a scratch*.

すりき・れる【擦り切れる】 wear out; become threadbare. ¶ ぼろぼろに～れる be worn to rags. ズボンのすそが～れている The cuffs of my trousers *are worn out*. ひもが～れた The strings *were worn through*.

すりこぎ【擂り粉木】 a wooden pestle.

すりこ・む【擦り込む】 ¶ クリームを顔に～む *rub* cream *into* (≒ *on*) the face.

スリッパ slippers (ふつう, くるぶしも包むもの); (日本風のつっかけ式の) mules.

スリップ (滑ること・下着) a slip. ¶ 雨で車が～する The car *slips* (横すべりなら *skids*) because of the rain.

すりつぶ・す【すり潰す】 ¶ 豆を～す *grind* down beans *into powder*. ねじ山を～す *rub* screw threads *out of shape*.

すりばち【擂り鉢・摺り鉢】 an earthenware mortar. ¶ ～型の cone-shaped; conic〔al〕.

すりへら・す【磨り減らす】 ¶ 彼女は1週間でくつを～してしまった She *had* her shoes *down* at the heels in a week. あれこれ気をつかって神経を～してしまった I *exhausted* my nerves by worrying about this and that matter.

すりむ・く【擦り剝く】 ¶ 彼は転んですねを～いた He fell down and *skinned* his skin. 綱引で手が～けた I had the skin *scraped* from my hand at a tug of war.

すりもの【刷り物】 printed matter (郵便物の上に「印刷物在中」とするときは Printed Matter と書く).

すりよ・せる【擦り寄せる】 ¶ 母親は子どもにほおを～せた The mother *pressed* her cheek *against* her child's.

すりよ・る【擦り寄る】 ¶ 彼は徐々に～ってきた He *edged* 〔*closer*〕 *up to* me.

スリラー a thriller.

スリル a thrill. ¶ 危険な山で～を味わう get *a thrill* on a dangerous mountain. サーフィンはすごく～がある Surfing has *a great thrill*.

す・る【刷る】 print. ¶ この名刺を100枚～ってもらいたい I want to *have* one hundred copies of this card *printed*.

す・る【掏る・掏摸る】 ¶ ひとりの男が乗客の財布を～るところを見た I saw a man *picking* a passenger's *pocket of* his wallet. 人ごみの中で時計を～られた I *had* my watch *stolen* (≒ *picked*) in the crowd.

す・る【摩る・磨る・擦る】 ¶ 墨を～る *rub down* an ink-stick. マッチを～る *strike* a match. 彼は競輪で有り金全部～ってしまった He *lost* all his money at the cycle races. 彼はすりばちでゴマを～った He *ground* sesame seeds in the mortar.

する【為る】 **1** 〚行なう・なす〛 ¶ きょうはすることがたくさんある I have a lot of things to *do* today.
好きなようにしなさい *Do* as you like.
きみのすることはいつもどじだ You make a mess of whatever you *do*.
危ないことはしないほうがいい You had better not *run a risk*.
よいことをしたあとは気持ちがいい We feel happy after *doing* good.
なにか私のすることはありませんか Is there anything for me to *do*?
この会社に入ったらここの社員らしくしなさい Now that you have entered this company, you should *act* as an employee is expected to.
なんてばかなことをしたんだ What a foolish thing he *did*!
たまには運動をしなさい *Take* exercise now and then.
そんなことができるものならしてみろ Just try *doing* that.
することなすことみんなお門違いだった Everything went wrong with me.
2 〚従事する・役をする〛 ¶ 彼は神田で古本屋をしている He *keeps* a secondhand (≒ used) bookstore in Kanda.

す

彼は谷川岳でガイドをしている He *acts as* 〔a〕 guide on Mt. Tanigawa.
あの人はアメリカ貿易をして財をなした He made a fortune in the American trade.
学校を出たら教師をするつもりだ I intend to *be* a teacher after I am graduated from the university.
若いころはいろいろな商売をしたものだ When I was young, I used to *engage in* various kinds of business (≒ *follow* various occupations).
私が通訳をしてあげよう I will *act as* interpreter for you.
あなたはなにをして暮らしていますか What *are* you *doing* for a living?

す

3〖…にする〗¶息子を弁護士(医者)にする考えだ I intend to *make* a lawyer (a doctor) of my son. / I intend my son for the bar (the medical profession).
彼らはぼくをキャプテンにした They *made* me 「captain.
あなたをきっと幸せにする I will never fail to *make* you happy.
この小切手を現金にしてください Please *get* this check cashed. / Please cash this check.
彼は土地を金にした He raised money on his land.
風で落ちた果物をジャムにしよう Let's *make* jam with these windfalls.
4〖感じがする〗 ¶今変な音がしなかったか Didn't you hear a strange sound just now?
だれもいない隣の部屋から人の声がした I heard a voice from the next room, which I thought was empty.
この部屋はいやなにおいがする This room smells unpleasant.
この辺は夜遅くまで車の音がする We hear the noises of the traffic till late hereabouts.
5〖値する〗 ¶彼女は100万円もする指輪をしている She wears a ring worth as much as a million yen.
この家は4,000万円もした This house cost me forty million yen.
失礼ですが, あなたのくつはいくらしましたか Excuse me, but what did you pay for your shoes (≒ what did your shoes cost you)?
6〖時がたつ〗¶もう10日もすると涼しくなるだろう *In* ten more days it will be cool.
彼は1時間もしないうちに戻ってきた He came back *in* less than an hour.
二, 三年もすればこの子も手がかからなくなる *In* a few years this child will be able to look after himself.
7〖仮定〗¶きみでないとすると, いったいだれがやったのだ Who on earth has done it, if it is not you?
会を開くとすれば会場が必要だ If we hold a meeting, we need a place.
あした雨だとしたら, 試合はどうなるのか What will become of the match, if it rains tomorrow?

ずる【狡】¶(競技などで)彼はまた〜をした He *played foul* again. 彼は〜をきめこんで知らん顔をしている He *shirked his duty* and pretends not to know.

ずる・い【狡い】¶〜い人 a *tricky* man. 〜そうな人 a *sly-looking* man. 不意打ちを食わすとは〜い It's *unfair* to take me by surprise. それは〜いやり方だ That's a *dishonest* way. 彼はいつも〜く立ちまわる He always acts *cunningly*.

ずる・ける ¶〜けて時間をむだにしてはいけない Never *idle away* your time. この休みも〜けてなにもしなかった I did nothing but *be idle* (≒ *be lazy*) these holidays, too.

するする〔と〕¶マストに〜と旗を上げた They ran up the flag on the mast. 彼は〜と木に登った He climbed the tree *with ease*.

ずるずる〔と〕¶彼は長い綱を〜と引きずっていた He *was dragging* (≒ *was pulling*) *along* a long rope. なにもしないで〜と今日に至った Nothing has been done up to now.

ずるずるべったり ¶その事件は〜になっている The affair *is left unsettled*.

ズルチン〖薬品〗〖化学〗 dulcin.

すると (それでは) then; (そのとき) just then; (そこで) thereupon (文語的). ¶〜, この計画は取りやめということですか Do you intend to give up this plan, *then*? 〜, そこへひょっこり彼が現われた *Just at that time*, he appeared there by chance.

するど・い【鋭い】sharp. ¶〜いナイフ a *sharp* knife. この動物は〜い目をしている This animal has *keen* eyes. この子どもは頭が〜い This child *is shrewd* (≒ *is bright*). 彼は〜いことばで私に迫った He closed in on me in a *cutting* tone. 彼の〜い観察には敬服した I was deeply impressed by his *shrewd* observation. 犬は臭覚が〜い Dogs have an *acute* sense of smell. 右肩に〜い痛みを感じた I had an *acute* (≒ a *cutting*; a *piercing*) pain in my right shoulder. その評論家は〜い批評で知られている The critic is known for his *biting* criticism. 彼らはたちまち〜い批判に直面した Soon they faced a *cutting* criticism.

するめ【鯣】dried cuttlefish.

ずるやすみ【ずる休み】〔a〕 truancy. ¶寒いので〜した I *played truant from school* as I felt cold.

するりと ¶指輪が〜抜けた The ring *slipped off* the finger.

ずれ ¶両者の間の感覚の〜 *a difference* of sensibility between the two. 時代(年齢)の〜 *a disparity in* the times (age). 時間の〜 *a* time *lag*. その問題についてきみとぼくの間には考えの〜がある I *differ with* (≒ *differ from*) you *on* the subject. / I'm afraid I *don't agree with* you *on* the problem.

すれあ・う【擦れ合う】¶肩と肩とが〜うような雑踏だ People are jostling one another.

スレート a slate. ¶〜で屋根をふく slate a roof.
—がわら(石綿セメント板) asbestos. **—**ぶき ¶〜ぶきの屋根 a slated roof.

すれすれ ¶屋根〜に飛行機が飛んでいった An

airplane passed *close to* the roofs. 彼は〜のところで及第した He just *scraped through* the examination. / He *barely* passed the examination. 約束の時刻〜に着いた We arrived *barely in time for* the appointed time.

すれちが・う【擦れ違う】¶ 道で〜っても,彼は気づかなかった He didn't recognize me when he *passed* me on the street.

すれっからし【擦れっ枯らし】(女の) a jade. ¶ 彼女は〜で手に負えない She *is so saucy* (≒ *impudent*) that she has got out of hand.

す・れる【磨れる・擦れる】(こすれる) rub; (すり減る) wear. ¶ 彼女は〜れてないので純情だ She is a *pure-hearted* girl.

ず・れる ¶ 彼の考えは少し〜れている His opinion *is* a little *off* (≒ *beside*) *the point*. 旅行の日どりが2日〜れるらしい Our trip seems to *be postponed* two days. その手紙の写しをとったら,少し〜れてしまった The letter is not closely copied.

スロー slow.

—モーション映画 a slow-motion film.

スローガン a slogan. ¶ 彼らは「平和」を〜に掲げた They published *a slogan* "peace."

ズロース drawers; bloomers.

スロープ a slope. ¶ 急な〜を滑降する slide down *a* steep *slope*.

スローモー slow motion; (人) a dull fellow; a slow coach. ¶ 彼はなにをやらせても〜だ He *is slow in* doing anything. / He *is dull in* everything.

すわ【素破】¶ 〜,一大事! Good Heavens! 〜,一大事と驚いた I *am quite* (≒ *terribly*) *alarmed*. 〜,というときの準備をしておきなさい Prepare for *the worst* (≒ *an emergency*).

すわり【座り】¶ この置物は〜が悪い This statuette is not balanced.

すわりごこち【座り心地】¶ 新車のシートは〜がよい The seat of a new car *is comfortable to sit* 〔*on*〕.

すわりこみ【座り込み】a sit-in (≒ sit-down) strike; 英 a stay-in strike. ¶ 彼らは要求が通るまで〜を続けることにした They determined to continue their *sit-in strike* till their demands were satisfied.

—戦術 sit-in (≒ sit-down) tactics.

すわりこ・む【座り込む】¶ 彼らは重役室に〜んだ They *sat down* in the director's room 〔to have a talk with him〕.

すわ・る【座る・据わる】**1**〖席などに着く〗sit down; be seated. ¶ ちょっとの間〜っていてください *Be seated* for a while.

このいすに〜ってください Will you please *sit down* on this chair?

正面に〜りなさい *Take your seat* in front.

みんなはテーブルに向かって〜っていた Everyone *sat* at the table.

ちゃんと〜れないのですか Can't you *sit* straight 〔*up*?

彼はベッドの上で〜っていた He *sat up* in bed.

そのイギリス人は日本人のように畳の上に〜った The Englishman *squatted* in the Japanese manner on *tatami*.

このソファーにはゆうに5人が〜れる This sofa is big enough to *seat* five persons.

2〖慣用的表現〗¶ 彼は目が〜っている His eyes *are set*.

彼は度胸が〜っている He *is emboldened*.

すんか【寸暇】¶ 彼は〜をさいて彼女に会いに出かけていったものだった Whenever he could spare time from business, he went out to see her. 彼は〜を惜しんでピアノの練習をした He gave *every spare moment* to the practice on the piano. 〜もない I have *no time to spare*.

ずんぐり ¶ 彼は〜した体つきをしている He is *fat and short*.

すんげき【寸劇】a skit.

すんし【寸志】¶ 〜ですがお納めください Please accept *my present of gratitude* (≒ *my token of thanks*). お礼の〜までに彼に本を1冊送った I sent him a book *in token of my gratitude*.

すんじ【寸時】¶ 私は彼のことを〜も忘れられない I cannot forget him even *a moment*. 彼は約束どおり〜もたがわずやってきた He came *punctually to the minute*.

ずんずん ¶ 仕事は予定どおり〜はかどった The work progressed *rapidly* as arranged before. 彼は〜歩きつづけた He walked *on and on*. ピアノの腕が〜上達した I *have made rapid progress in* playing the piano. ふたりの間隔は〜開いていった The distance between the two has become *greater and greater*.

すんぜん【寸前】¶ その会社は倒産〜だ That company *is on the verge of* bankruptcy. ゴール〜に抜かれた I was outstripped by the next runner *just in front of* (≒ *just before*) the goal. 私は発車〜に飛び乗った I jumped into the train *just before* it left the station.

すんたらず【寸足らず】¶ あの人は少し〜だ He *is* a little *too short*.

すんだん【寸断】¶ 水害で交通が〜された Because of a flood disaster, the traffic *was cut in pieces*. 秘密書類が〜された The classified documents *were torn in* (≒ *to*) *pieces*.

すんづまり【寸づまり】¶ この服はやや〜だ This dress *is* rather *shortish*.

すんてつ【寸鉄】¶ 彼は〜人を刺すような皮肉を言う There is *biting* (≒ *cutting*) *sarcasm* in his talk. 彼は身に〜も帯びていない He *is* quite *unarmed*.

すんでに ¶ 〜トラックにひかれるところだった I *came* (≒ *went*) *near* being run over by a truck. 〜ころぶところだった I *very nearly* fell to the ground.

すんなり ¶ 彼女の姿はたいへん〜している She *is* very *slim* and charming. 反対もなく〜と決まった It was passed *unanimously* without any objection.

すんぴょう【寸評】a short review.

すんぶん【寸分】¶ これはあれと〜違わない This is *not a bit* different from that. / This is *just the same* as that.

す

すんぽう【寸法】¶へやの～を計る *measure* a room. 洋服の～をとってもらった I had my *measurements* (≒ *measure*) taken for a new suit. 犬小屋は～どおりに作ってほしい I want a kennel to be made according to the *measurements*.

せ

せ【瀬】(浅瀬) shallows; a shoal; (早瀬) rapids; a torrent. ¶そう言われると私の立つ～がない Now that I have heard of such a thing, it's *all over with* me.

せ【背】the back; (身長) height; stature; (山の) the ridge. ¶～をまっすぐに伸ばす straighten *one's back*. 山を～にして写真を撮った We had a photograph taken with mountains in the *background*. 彼は俗事に～を向けて研究に没頭した He devoted himself to his study without hearing about worldly affairs. 親切にしてくれた人たちに～を向けるな(背くな) Don't *turn your back on* those who were kind to you.

ぜ【是】(正しいこと) right; justice; what is right. ¶あなたはどちらの意見を～としますか Which opinion do you *approve of*? ～を～とし非を非としなければならない We must *call a spade a spade*.

せい【生】(生きていること) living; (生活) life; (生命) life. ¶～あるもの all living things. この世に～をうけてこのかた since *I was born* [in this world].

せい【姓】a family name; a surname; the last name.

せい【正】justice; right; (副に対して) the original; 〘数学〙(負に対して) plus; positive. ¶～の数 a *plus* quantity.

せい【精】**1**〘精力・努力〙energy; industry. ¶よくお～が出ますね How *hard* you *work*! さらにいっそう～を出して働きたまえ I hope you will *work harder*.
～も根も尽きはてた I *was* completely *exhausted*.
ウナギを食べて～をつけなさい Eat eels and *invigorate yourself*.
2〘精霊〙¶水の～ *a* water *nymph*; an undine.
森の～ *a* forest *nymph*; a dryad.

せい【背】stature; height. ¶彼は～が高い(低い) He is *tall* (*short*). 彼は～が180センチある He is 180 centimeters *tall* (≒ 図 *high*). 彼女はぼくより5センチ～が低い(高い) She is 5 centimeters *shorter* (*taller*) than I. 彼はもっと～が伸びるだろう He will *grow taller*. ～の順に並びなさい Stand in a line *in order of height* (≒ *stature*). ～の立たない所へは行くな Never go *out of* (≒ *beyond*) *your depth*. 彼女は～の立つ所にいた She kept within *her depth*.

せい【性】(性質) nature; (男女の) sex; 〘文法〙gender. ¶人の～は善であると言われている It is said that men *are born* good. 幼児に～の知識を与えようとしてもむだだ It is no use trying to tell a small child *the facts of life*.
―教育 sex education. ―行為 the sexual act. ―衝動 the sex urge. ―生活 *one's* sex life. ―道徳 sexual morality. ―犯罪 a sex crime. ―ホルモン sex hormone.

せい【静】quiet; inactivity; peace. ¶～的 statical; static.

せい【所為】¶遅刻したのはきみの～だ It is *because of* you that I was late. 彼は失敗を人の～にしている He *is putting the blame* for his failure *on* others. 負けたことをグラウンドの～にするのは感心しない I disagree with those who *attribute* their defeat *to* the conditions of the playground. 彼が委員を辞職したのは病気の～だ It was *on account of* his sickness that he resigned from the committee. だれの～でもない. きみが悪いのだ No one else *is to blame*. It's entirely your fault.

せい-【正-】¶～会員 a *regular* member. ～教授 a *full* professor. ～教員 a *regular* teacher.

せい-【聖-】a saint; a sage. ¶～パウロ Saint (≒ St.) Paul.

-せい【-製】¶日本～の品物 goods *of* Japanese *make*; goods *made in* Japan. イギリス～の服地 cloth *of* British (≒ English) *make*. この時計はスイス～です This watch is *of* Swiss *make*. / This is a Swiss-*made* watch. 銀～の食器 *silver* tableware. 革～の本 a book bound *in* leather.

-せい【-制】a system; an institution.
¶新～大学 a new-*system* college. 許可～ permission *system*. 4年～大学 a four-year college. 2年～大学 a junior college. 1日8時間～ an eight-hour day. 週48時間～ a forty-eight-hour week. 週給～ a weekly-pay *system*.

-せい【-世】¶ルイ14～ Louis XIV.

ぜい【税】a tax; (物品税) a duty; (国税) a national tax; (地方税) a local tax. ¶～はもう納めましたか Have you paid your *tax*? ～はあまりにも重い *Taxation* is too heavy. こんなものにも～がかかるとは驚いた I am surprised that this is subject to *duty*. ～を申告しなければならない I must fill in my *tax* return form.

—込み before tax. 財産— a property tax. 所得— an income tax. 遊興— an entertainment tax. 累進— a progressive tax.

ぜい【贅】¶ 彼は～を尽くした生活を送っている He lives a most *luxurious* life. 彼は～を尽くした家に住んでいる He lives in a house furnished with every *luxury*.

せいあつ【静圧】〔物理〕static pressure.

せいあつ【制圧】suppression. ¶ 敵の艦隊を～する *gain mastery over* the fleet of *one's* enemy. 彼らはデモ隊を完全に～した They *brought* the demonstrators *under complete control*. 暴徒は彼らの力では～できない状態になった The mob *was beyond their control*.

せいあん【成案】a definite plan (≒ program).

せいい【誠意】sincerity. ¶ 彼は～のある人だ He *is sincere*. / He is a man *of sincerity*. 彼はやることに～がない He *is insincere* (≒ He lacks *sincerity*) in whatever he does. 彼の～を疑う I doubt his *sincerity*. 彼にきみの～を示しなさい Show him your *sincerity*. ～を尽くして彼を説得した I persuaded him *in all sincerity*.

せいいき【声域】the range of a voice; a register. ¶ ～の広い歌手 a singer of *a* wide *register*.

せいいき【聖域】the sacred (≒ holy) precincts. ¶ 明治神宮の～ *the sacred precincts* of the Meiji Shrine.

せいいく【成育】growth. ¶ 動物の～のようすを観察する observe how animals *grow* (≒ *are reared*).

せいいっぱい【精いっぱい】with might and main; with all *one's* might.
¶ ～働きなさい Work *as hard as possible*. / Work *with all your might*. ～やった I *did my best*. / I *did everything in my power*. ～叫んだがだめだった I cried out in *as* loud a voice *as possible*, to no purpose. これが私にとっては～のところだ This is *the utmost limit of* my power. 家族を養っていくのが～だ It is *all I can do* to support my family.

せいいん【成員】a member; (集合的に) membership.

せいいん【成因】the origin.

せいう【晴雨】¶ ～にかかわらず rain or shine.
—計 a barometer. ¶ ～計は雨(晴れ)を指している The *barometer* points rain (fair).

せいうち【海象】〔動物〕a walrus; a sea horse.

せいうん【青雲】¶ ～の志のある青年たち young aspirants after fame; ambitious young men. 彼は～の志をいだいて上京した He went up to the capital *with high ambitions* (≒ *aspiring after greatness*).

せいうん【星雲】〔天文学〕a nebula. ¶ ～状の nebulous.

せいえい【精鋭】seasoned (≒ picked) troops; picked men. ¶ ～をよりすぐって全日本チームを編成した The all Japan team was organized by *the best players* in Japan. 大将は～をひきいて敵を破った The general led his *picked troops* to victory.

せいえき【精液】〔生理〕semen; sperm.

せいえん【声援】cheering; a shout of encouragement. ¶ 彼らは自分たちのチームを～した They *cheered* their team.

せいえん【製塩】salt manufacture.
—業 a salt making industry. —所 a salt factory.

せいおう【西欧】(東欧に対して) Western Europe; (ヨーロッパ) Europe; (ヨーロッパ,アメリカ) the Occident.
—化 Westernization. —諸国 the Western countries. —文明(文化) the Western civilization (culture).

せいおん【清音】〔音声学〕a voiceless sound.

せいおん【静穏】tranquility; calmness.
¶ 総会は～のうちに終わった The general meeting came to an end *in peace and quiet*.

せいか【生花】a natural flower; (生け花) flower arrangement. ¶ 神だなに～を供えた We offered *flowers* on the altar.

せいか【生家】*one's* parents' home. ¶ エジソンの～ the Edison's *home*. 彼は18歳のとき～を出た He left *home* at the age of eighteen. なつかしい～を訪ねるつもりだ I am going to visit *the old home* again.

せいか【正価】the [net] price. ¶ ～で買う buy *at a net price*.

せいか【正貨】specie; gold.
在外— specie held abroad (≒ overseas).

せいか【正課】the regular curriculum.

せいか【成果】the result; the fruit. ¶ 注目に値する～ *a* noteworthy *result*. 期待した～ *an* expected *result*. 彼は新しい療法でりっぱな～を収めた He got good *results* from a new treatment. 会議は～なく終わった The meeting ended without *result*.

せいか【声価】fame; reputation; renown.
¶ その著作は批評家としての彼の～を高めた The work enhanced his *reputation* (≒ *fame*) as a critic.

せいか【青果】vegetables and fruits.
—市場 a vegetable and fruit wholesale market.

せいか【盛夏】midsummer. ¶ ～の間たいてい都市を離れて暮らす I usually live out of town for *the hot summer days*.

せいか【聖火】(オリンピックの) the Olympic Torch. ¶ ～リレー the *sacred torch* relay.

せいか【聖歌】〔キリスト教〕a sacred song; a hymn; (クリスマスの) a carol.
—集 a hymnal; a hymnbook. —隊 a choir.

せいか【精華】the essence; the flower.
¶ 実にわが国芸術の～と呼ぶべきもの what we may call *the very flower* of our art. 騎士道の～ *the flower* of chivalry.

せいか【製菓】confectionery.
—会社 a confectionery company.

せいか【製靴】shoe-making.
—業 the shoe industry. —工場 a shoe-

せ

making factory.

せいかい【正解】 a correct answer (*to* a problem).

せいかい【政界】 the political world; political circles. ¶ 彼は～の実力者のひとりだ He is one of the bosses in *political circles*. 彼は30歳で～に入った He entered *the political world* at thirty. 彼は70歳で～を退いた He retired from *political life* at seventy.

せいかい【盛会】 a success; a successful meeting. ¶ 会は非常に～だった The meeting was *highly successful*. / The meeting was (≒ had) *a great success*. 御～を祈る My best wishes for *a successful meeting*.

せいかいいん【正会員】 a regular member.

せいかいけん【制海権】 the command of the sea.

せいかがく【生化学】 biochemistry.
—者 a biochemist.

せいかがく【性科学】 sexology.

せいかく【正確】 accuracy; correctness; exactitude; exactness; precision.
¶ ～な時刻を教えてください Tell me the *exact* (≒ *precise*) time. その部屋の～な広さはどのくらいですか What is the *exact* size of the room? ぼくは事実を～に述べた I stated the fact *precisely*. ぼくの時計は～だ My watch *keeps good time*. 彼女は時間に～だ She *is punctual*. そのニュースは全く～だ The news *is* quite *correct*. 彼は～な英語を書く He writes *correct* English. 彼は彼らに英語の～な発音を教えた He taught them an *accurate* pronunciation of English. この記事は～さを欠く(～だ) This report *lacks precision* (*is accurate*).

せいかく【性格】 character; personality.
¶ 彼は～のりっぱな人だ He is a man of fine *personality*. 彼は兄とは～がまったく違う He has *a* quite different *character* from his elder brother's. / He has *a character* quite different from his elder brother's. 彼女の人のよさは～だ She is kind *by nature*. 日本人の～をどう思いますか What do you think of Japanese *character*? 人間の～はごく小さいころに形成されるものだ A person's *character* is formed when he is quite small. この絵は彼の内気な～をあらわしている One can see his shy *character* in this picture. ～的には彼らふたりは合わない They don't get on well together. ～だからどうにもしかたがない He cannot help his own *nature*. / It's due to his *nature*, which cannot be helped.

せいかく【政客】 a politician.

せいかく【製革】 tanning.
—業 the tanning industry. —業者 a tanner.

せいがく【声楽】 vocal music.
—家 a vocalist. —科 a vocal music course.

ぜいがく【税額】 the amount of a tax; (決定された税額) an assessment.

せいかつ【生活】 life; (生計) living; livelihood. ¶ 彼は幸福な～を送っている He lives *a* happy *life*. 彼らは都会で～している They *live* in a city. アメリカ的な～の方法に慣れていない I am not yet used to the American *way of life*. 彼は月給だけで～している He *lives on* nothing but his salary. 彼は文筆を～の糧にしている He *is making his living* by writing. 当時南米への植民者の～はどんなでしたか What was the *life* of the colonists in South America like then?
—水準 the standard of living. ¶ ～水準は5年前より上がってきている The standard of *living* is better than it was five years ago. —費 the cost of living. —必需品 the necessaries of life. —物資 subsistence commodities. 学校— school life. 家庭— home life.

せいかん【製罐】 can manufacturing.

せいかん【盛観】 a grand sight.

せいかん【生還】 ¶ ～する return alive. 彼の二塁打で2者～した(野球) Two runners *reached the home plate* by his two-base hit.
—者 a survivor.

せいかん【静観】 contemplation. ¶ 時局の進展を～する *watch calmly* the development of the situation. われわれは～的な態度をとろう We will take *a watch and wait attitude*.

せいかん【精悍】 ¶ ～な顔つき a *dauntless* face. ～な目つきの男 a man with *eagle eyes*. ～に intrepidly; fearlessly; dauntlessly. ～さ intrepidity; fearlessness; dauntlessness.

せいがん【請願】 a petition; an application.
¶ われわれの～は許可された(却下された) Our *petition* was granted (was rejected). 議会に減税を～した We *petitioned* the House of Representatives *for* a tax reduction.
—書 a petition. ¶ 政府に～書を提出した We presented *a petition* to the Government.
—者 a petitioner.

ぜいかん【税関】 a customhouse; the customs. ¶ ～で手荷物を調べられた I got my baggage inspected at *the customs*. ～を通るのに40分以上かかった It took more than forty minutes to get through (≒ pass) *the customs*.
—申告書 a customs declaration. —手続き the customs formalities. —吏 a customs officer.

せいき【生気】 life; vigor; vitality. ¶ ～にあふれた青年 a *vigorous* young man. ～にあふれた顔の少年 a boy with an *animated* face. 彼は～にあふれている He is full of *vigor*. ～のない顔つき a *spiritless* face. ～のない演技 a *lifeless* performance. その知らせで彼は～をとりもどした He *was aroused* by the news.

せいき【正規】 regulation. ¶ ～の看護婦 a *regular* nurse. きみは～の手続きをふまなければならない You must follow the *regular* procedure. 彼は大学で～の法律の課程を修めた He finished the *regular* law course at college.
—軍 a regular army. —兵 a regular soldier.

せいき【世紀】 a century. ¶ 今～の最もすぐれた芸術家たち the greatest artists in the present *century*. われわれは20～に生きている We live in the twentieth *century*. 彼女こそ～の美女だ She is the most beautiful woman in the world.

せいき【精気】spirit; energy.

せいき【性器】the genitals.

せいき【生起】occurrence.

せいき【制規】regulations; rules.

せいぎ【正義】justice; righteousness; right. ¶～の味方 a friend of *justice*. われわれは～のために戦った We fought in the cause of *justice*.

—感 a sense of justice. ¶彼は～感が強い He has *a strong sense of justice*.

せいきゅう【性急】impatience; quick-temper. ¶～な人 a *short-tempered* man. 彼が正しいと～に結論を下すべきではない You should not decide *hastily* that he is right.

せいきゅう【請求】request; demand; claim. ¶即刻支払いを～した They *demanded* immediate payment. 彼は切符代2,000円を私に～した He *charged* me two thousand yen for my ticket. ～ありしだいカタログをお送りします We shall mail a catalogue *on request*. 本代は～しだい支払います I will pay for the books *on demand*. 彼は損害の補償を～してきた He *claimed* payment from me for damages.

—書 a bill. —人 an applicant. —払い payable on demand. 損害— a claim for damage.

せいきゅうりょく【制球力】control. ¶あの投手は球に偉力はあるが, ～がない That pitcher has great power but no *control*.

せいきょ【逝去】death.

せいぎょ【制御】control. ¶馬を～する *get control over* a horse. 情熱を～する *have control over one's* passions.

せいぎょ【生魚】(鮮魚) fresh fish; (生きているさかな) alive fish.

せいきょう【清教】Puritanism.

せいきょう【正教】orthodoxy.

せいきょう【政教】religion and politics.

—分離 the separation of religion from politics.

せいきょう【盛況】prosperity; success; hit. ¶会は満員の～だった The meeting was *a great success* crowded to capacity.

せいぎょう【生業】a calling.

せいぎょう【正業】a respectable business. ¶彼は～についている He follows *a respectable calling*. 彼を～につかせることは難しい It is hard to settle him in *a legitimate calling*.

せいぎょう【盛業】the completion of *one's* work.

せいきょういん【正教員】a regular teacher.

せいきょうと【清教徒】〘キリスト教〙a Puritan.

せいきょく【政局】the political situation. ¶彼は～を担当するような政治家ではない He is not a statesman to take the helm of *state affairs*. ～は重大な危機に瀕(ひん)している *The political situation* is in a serious crisis. 彼と現在の～を論じた I discussed *the* present *political situation* with him. 彼は～を収拾するため全力を尽くした He did his best to save *the political situation*.

せいきん【精勤】diligence; industry; (無欠勤) regular attendance. ¶彼は仕事に～している He *is diligent in* his work.

—者 a regular attendant. —賞 a diligence award.

ぜいきん【税金】a tax.

せいく【成句】a set phrase; an idiomatic expression.

せいくうけん【制空権】¶イギリス軍が～を握っている The British army has *the command of the air*.

せいくらべ【背比べ】¶～をしよう Let's see which is the taller. 彼と～をした I *compared my height* with his. 私は彼らふたりの～をしてみた I saw which of them was the taller. 彼らはどんぐりの～だ(ふたりのとき) There is little to choose between the two. / (3人以上) They are all nearly alike.

せいくん【請訓】a request for instructions.

せいけい【生計】living; livelihood. ¶彼はなんで～を立てていますか How does he get his *living*? 彼は自動車のセールスで～を立てている He obtains (≒ earns) *a livelihood* as a motor-car salesman. 彼は文筆でようやく～を立てている He earns (≒ gets) *a* bare *livelihood* by his pen. 彼は両親の～を助けている He helps his parents with their *living expenses*. / He *supports* his parents.

せいけい【西経】the west longitude. ¶～25度 twenty-five degrees *west longitude*.

せいけい【整形】¶彼女は鼻を～した(～手術を受けた) She had *a plastic operation* on her nose.

—外科 plastic surgery. —外科医 a plastic surgeon. —手術 plastic surgery operation. ¶～手術を受ける undergo plastic surgery operation.

せいけつ【清潔】cleanliness; purity. ¶～な clean; neat; pure. ～に cleanly; neatly; purely. ～な台所 a *clean* kitchen. 部屋を～にしておきなさい *Keep* your room *clean*. 彼はいつも手を～にしている He always *keeps* his hands *clean*.

せいけん【政見】political opinion (≒ view). ¶彼は～を発表した He stated his *political views*. 候補者の～発表会に出席した I attended the meeting at which the candidate declared his *political views*.

せいけん【政権】political power. ¶その党は～から離れた The party went out of *power*. その党が現在～を握っている The party is at present in *power*. その党は1930年に～を握った The party came into *power* in 1930. 彼らは極東に共産～を立てた They established the Communist *regime* in the Far East.

せいげん【正弦】〘数学〙a sine.

せいげん【制限】limit; restriction. ¶会員の数には～がある The members *are limited* in number. 費用は絶対必要なものだけに～されている The expenses *are limited* to what is absolutely necessary. 小づかいは月3,000円に～されている My pocket money *is restricted* to three thousand yen a month. 入会するのに年齢の～はない There is no age *limit* for entering the society. 自由はある程度の～を必要とする Freedom needs certain *limitation*. 用紙は～なく配付される The forms are to be distributed without *restriction*. ～が緩和されることはないだろう *Restrictions* will not be relaxed. 海外移住に～が加えられることはないだろう It is not likely that *restrictions* will be placed on emigration. この道路では時速 40 キロに～されている Speed *is limited to* forty kilometers an hour on this road. この問題の～時間は 60 分だ The time *allowed* for this question is sixty minutes.

せ

ぜいげん【税源】a source of tax revenue.

せいご【生後】after *one's* birth. ¶～2か月の赤ん坊 a two-month-old baby; a baby two months old. 赤ちゃんは～2週間で死んだ The baby died two weeks *after his birth*.

せいご【正誤】correction.
—表〔a list〕errata (単数形は erratum).

せいこう【生硬】crudity; crudeness. ¶～な文章 a *crude* style.

せいこう【成功】〔a〕success; (繁栄) prosperity. ¶勤勉こそ～への道だ Diligence is the way to *success*. 失敗は～のもとといわれる It is said that failures lead to *success*. アメリカの月着陸は大～を収めた America was crowned with *success* in landing on the moon. 彼は十分～の見込みがある He has a good chance of *success*. この仕事は～の見込みがない There is no prospect of *success*. 会は大～だった The meeting was *a* great *success*. 彼は実験に～した He *was successful in* his experiment. 彼は全コースを走破することに～した He *succeeded in* running the whole course through. ご～を祈ります I wish you *success*! 彼のその事業は～だった That enterprise of his was *a success*. 一応試みてはみたが～はしなかった We tried at any rate, but it was in vain. その試みは～裏に終わった The attempt *was successful*. 彼は俳優という職業を選んで～した He chose acting as his occupation and *made a success of* it. 彼はなにをやっても～する He *is successful* in everything.

せいこう【性向】disposition; inclination.
¶好奇心の強い～の人 a man of curious *disposition*.

せいこう【性交】coitus; coition; sexual intercourse. ¶～する have sexual intercourse; have coitus.

せいこう【製鋼】steel manufacture.
—所 a steel works.

せいこう【精巧】exquisitness; elaborateness.
¶非常に～な細工の宝石 a jewel *of exquisite workmanship*. 細工はきわめて～だ It *is of exquisite workmanship*. ～なはかり a *delicate* balance. きわめて～な機械 a machine *of excellent mechanism*.

せいこううどく【晴耕雨読】¶以来彼は～の生活を送った Since then he led a life of〔plowing and〕working in the fields when fine and reading at home in wet weather.

せいこうかい【聖公会】the Episcopal Church; the Anglican Church.
—員 an Episcopalian.

せいこうほう【正攻法】a frontal attack; an orthodox approach.

ぜいこみ【税込み】¶初任給は～で月 10 万円だ You are paid a hundred thousand yen a month *before tax* at the start. それは～の値段だ It is the price *including* (≒ *plus*) *tax*.

せいこん【精魂】energy; vitality. ¶彼はその仕事に～をこめた He put *his whole heart and soul* into the work.

せいこん【精根】energy; vitality. ¶彼はその仕事に～を傾けた He devoted all his *energies* to the work. ～尽きはてた I *was exhausted*.

せいこん【成婚】〔a〕marriage.

せいざ【正座】¶30分も～できない I cannot *sit up straight* even for half an hour.

せいざ【星座】a constellation.
—早見図 a planisphere; a star chart.

せいさい【正妻】a lawful (≒ legal) wife.

せいさい【生彩】life; vividness; liveliness.
¶～を欠くプレー a *lifeless* (≒ *dull*) play. 今晩の彼女の演奏はまったく～がなかった Her performance was utterly lacking in *vigor* this evening.

せいさい【精彩】luster; color. ¶その絵はひときわ～を放っていた It was a particularly *brilliant* picture.

せいさい【制裁】restraint; sanction; punishment; discipline. ¶社会的に～を受ける suffer social *punishment*. あんな人は～を加える必要がある Such a fellow deserves *punishment*.

せいざい【製材】sawing; lumbering.
¶～する saw up (logs).
—機 a sawing machine. —業 the sawing (≒ lumbering) industry. —所 a sawmill; a lumber mill.

せいさく【製作】manufacture; production.
¶当社は主として工作機械を～している Mainly we *manufacture* machine tools. / Our main products are machine tools.
—所 a factory; a plant; a mill. —費 production costs. —品 manufactures; manufactured goods (≒ products).

せいさく【制作】¶これはA氏の～にかかる絵だ This picture is the *work* of Mr. A.
—者 an author; a maker; (絵の) a painter.

せいさく【政策】a policy. ¶～を立てる shape *a policy* (*about*). 日本の対中国～ Japan's *policy* toward China. ～を実行に移す carry out *a policy*.
—協定 a policy agreement. 社会— a social policy. ¶社会～を検討すべき時期に来ている It is the time to investigate the *social policy*.

せいさつ【省察】consideration; reflection.

せいさつよだつ【生殺与奪】¶彼らに～の権を握られていてはなんとも手の施しようがない Nothing can be done now that they *hold the power of life and death over* us.

せいさん【正餐】a dinner.

せいさん【生産】production. ¶この国では多量の鉄が～される A great deal of iron *is produced* in this country.
—意欲 a zeal for production. —過剰 overproduction. —管理 production control. —技術 manufacturing technique. —指数 an index of industrial production. —者 a producer. —者価格 producer〔s'〕 price. —性 productivity. —制限 curtailment of production. —設備 production facilities. —高 output. —費 cost of production. —物 products. 国民総— the gross national product (GNP).

せいさん【成算】hope of success. ¶～があるのか *Are* you *sure of success*? ～はない I *am doubtful of success*. ～がある事業だと思う I *am* quite *confident of* the *success* of the enterprise. ～の立たない仕事には手を出すな Never concern yourself with a touch that offers little *hope of success*.

せいさん【清算】liquidation; (貿易の) clearing. ¶負債を～したらあとにはなにも残らなかった Nothing was left when we had *cleared off* our debts. 過去を～して出直す *liquidate* (≒ *bury*) the past and start life again.
—会社 a company in liquidation. 強制— forced liquidation. —人 a liquidator.

せいさん【青酸】〘化学〙cyanic acid.
—カリ potassium cyanide.

せいさん【精算】(精確な計算) an accurate account; (決算) adjustment; settlements of account. ¶～する adjust (an account).
—額 an adjusted amount. —書 a settlement of accounts. —所 a fare adjustment office.

せいさん【凄惨】ghastliness; grimness.
¶～な事故現場に顔を背けないものはなかった There were none but turned their faces away from the *dreadful* scene of the accident.

せいさんかくけい【正三角形】〘数学〙a regular triangle.

せいさんしき【聖餐式】Holy Communion.

せいし【生死】life and death; (安否) safety.
¶それは～にかかわる問題だ It is a matter of *life and death*. 彼はいまだに～不明だ His *fate* is still unknown. 彼らと～をともにするつもりだった I intended to share *the fate* with them. 彼は重傷を負って～の境をさまよっている Seriously injured, he is hovering between *life and death*.

せいし【正史】authentic history.

せいし【正視】¶まず事態を～することだ First of all, you should *look at* the fact *squarely*. あわれでとても彼女を～するにしのびなかった She looked so miserable that I couldn't bear to *look at* her.

せいし【制止】control. ¶暴力を～できない状態となっている Violence has gone beyond our *control*. 彼らには暴徒の乱入を～しきれなかった They couldn't *keep* the mob *from* running into it.

せいし【精子】〘生物〙a spermatozoon (複 spermatozoa).

せいし【静止】stillness. ¶～する stand still; rest. それは～の状態にある It is at *standstill*. / It is in *a stationary state*.

せいし【製糸】—業 the silk-reeling industry. —業者 a silk manufacturer. —工場 a silk mill (以上の製糸は絹糸 (silk) の場合で,木綿糸ならば cotton が用いられる).

せいし【製紙】paper making.
—機械 a paper-making machine. —業 the paper industry. —業者 a paper manufacturer. —工場 a paper mill.

せいじ【青磁】celadon porcelain. ¶～の花びん a vase of *celadon porcelain*.

せいじ【政治】politics. ¶彼は～を論じるのが好きだ He is fond of talking *politics*. 正しい～が行なわれれば,国民は幸福になる If *government* is carried on properly, our nation will become happy. こういう人々が国の～を行なっているのだ Such people *are administering the affairs of state*. ～の貧困が話題になっている Lack of proper *government* is much talked about. ～を明るくするよう各人が努力しなければならない Everyone should make efforts to make *politics* clean. 強力な～が望ましい Strong *government* is desirable.
—運動 a political movement. —家 a statesman; (やや悪い意のとき) a politician. —学 politics. —活動 political activity. —献金 political donation. —問題 a political problem. —感覚 political sense. ¶彼は～感覚が鋭い There is something sharp in his *political sense*.

せいじ【政事】governmental affairs.

せいじ【盛事】a grand enterprise.

せいしき【正式】formality. ¶～の学校教育 *regular* schooling. ～の手続きを踏む go through the due *formalities*. 彼は～に校長に会見を申し込んだ He *formally* asked for an interview with the principal. われわれはまだ～には結婚していません We are not *legally* married yet.

せいしき【整式】〘数学〙an integral expression.

せいしつ【性質】nature; character; quality.
¶もって生まれた～はどうにもしようがない A man cannot help his own *nature*. 人間の～はいろいろだ People are of various *qualities*. 彼女は移り気な～だ She has *a* changeable *disposition*. 気だてのよい～の人はだれからも好かれる A man of good *nature* is loved by everybody. そういう～の仕事はお断わりしたい I want to decline work *of that sort*. 問題の～上,緊急に決定する必要がある It needs to be decided immediately from the very *nature* of the matter.

せいじつ【誠実】sincerity; integrity.
¶～な人 a man of *integrity*. ～に働く work *honestly*.

せいじほう【正字法】〘文法〙orthography.

せいじゃ【正邪】¶～をわきまえる know *right*

せ

from *wrong*.

せいじゃ【聖者】 a saint. ¶～のような生活 a *holy* (≒ *saintly*) life.

せいしゃいん【正社員】 a regular employee.

せいしゃえい【正射影】〘数学〙 an orthographic projection.

せいじゃく【静寂】 stillness; quietness.
¶夜の～を破る break the *still* (≒ *silence*) of the night.

ぜいじゃく【脆弱】 ¶彼は生まれつき～だ He is *weak* (≒ *frail*) by nature.

せいしゅ【清酒】 [refined] *sake*.

ぜいしゅう【税収】 tax yields.

せいしゅく【静粛】 ¶～にしてください Be quiet, please. / (会議で) Order! Order!

せいじゅく【成熟】 ripeness; maturity; mellowness; full growth. ¶オレンジは秋に～する Oranges *ripen* in autumn. 彼は心身ともに～した青年だ He is a young man who *has matured* mentally and physically.
—期 puberty; age of puberty; the mellow age.

せいしゅん【青春】 youth; the spring of life. ¶～を楽しむ enjoy *one's youth* (≒ *spring of life*). ～の悩み mental struggle of *youth*.
—期 adolescence.

せいじゅん【清純】 purity. ¶彼女は心が～だ She is *pure* in heart.

せいしょ【清書】 a fair copy. ¶ノートを～する *make a clean copy of one's* notes. 原稿を～する *make a fair copy of one's* draft.

せいしょ【青書】 a blue-book.

せいしょ【聖書】 the Bible; the [Holy] scriptures.
旧約— the Old Testament. 新約— the New Testament.

せいじょ【整除】〘数学〙 divisibility.

せいしょう【星章】 a star badge.

せいしょう【斉唱】 a unison. ¶～する sing *in unison*.

せいじょう【正常】 normality; normalcy.
¶日ソ間の国交は速やかに～に復されるべきだ The *normal* diplomatic relation between Soviet and Japan should be restored immediately. 彼は～な神経の持ち主だ He has *normal* mentality. 教育の～化が先決問題だ How to *normalize* school education is the first consideration.

せいじょう【政情】 a political situation.
¶不手際な政策で～が不安定になった The poor measures caused the *political* instability.

せいじょう【清浄】 cleanness.
—野菜 clean vegetables.

せいじょう【性状】 character; nature; (気質) temperament.

せいじょうき【星条旗】 the Stars and Stripes (単数扱い).

せいじょうこうさい【星状光彩】 asterism.

せいしょうねん【青少年】 the youth; the younger generation.
—犯罪 juvenile delinquency.

せいしょく【生色】 a lively look; an animated countenance. ¶彼はやっと～を取り戻した He *recovered himself* after all.

せいしょく【生殖】 reproduction; generation.
—器 the sexual organs; genitals. —機能 generative (≒ reproductive) function. —細胞 a generative (≒ sex) cell. —腺 the genital gland. —力 generative power.

せいしょく【聖職】 (牧師の職) holy orders.
¶～につく take *holy orders*. 彼は～についている He *is in orders*. 教師は～だ Teaching profession is *sacred occupation*.

せいしょくかんばん【整色乾板】〘写真〙 an orthochromatic plate.

せいしん【精神】 the spirit; (意志) will; (魂) soul; (意図) intention. ¶もっと～を鍛えるべきだ You should cultivate your *mind* more than ever. 彼は～が異常だ He *is out of his mind*. / He is not in his right *mind*. ～を打ち込んでやりなさい Do this *heart and soul*. 彼は～を入れかえた He *turned over a new leaf*. ～を集中してやればできないことはないはずだ There is nothing you cannot do if you *concentrate your attention on* it. ～一到何事か成らざらん(諺) *Where there is a will, there is a way*. 健全な～は健全な肉体に宿る(諺) *A sound mind in a sound body*. その法律の～を尊重すべきだ We should respect the *spirit* of the law.
—鑑定 a psychiatric test. —薄弱 a weak mind. —薄弱児 a weak-minded child. —病 a mental disease. ¶彼は～病をわずらっている He is suffering from *a mental disease*. —病院 a mental hospital. —病患者 a mental patient. —分析 psychoanalysis. —分裂症 schizophrenia. —分裂症患者 a schizophrenic. —年齢 mental age.

せいじん【成人】 an adult; a grownup.
¶～の日 *Adults* Day. ～した娘 a *grownup* daughter. 坊ちゃんもご～なさいましたね How your son *has grown*!
—教育 adult education. —病 adult diseases. —向き映画 a film for adults.

せいじん【聖人】 a saint. ¶(皮肉に)きみも～になったものだ Have you turned *saint*?

せいしんせいい【誠心誠意】 sincerely; faithfully. ¶彼の訪問を～歓迎した We welcomed his visit *from the bottom of our heart*. 彼は質問に～答えた He answered the questions *in all sincerity*.

せいしんな【清新な】 new; fresh.

せいず【星図】〘天文学〙 a celestial map; a star chart.

せいず【製図】 drawing; (地図の) cartography.
¶～する draw; draft.
—家 a draftsman. —器 a drawing instrument. —板 a drawing board.

せいすい【盛衰】 vicissitude. ¶国家の～はこの一戦にかかっている The *destiny* of the country depends upon this battle. 栄枯～は世の習い Our life has its *ups and downs* (≒ *vicis-*

situdes). / *The rise and fall* is the way of the world.

せいずい【精髄】 essence. ¶ 源氏物語は日本文学の～である "*The Tales of Genji*" is the *essence* of Japanese literature.

せいすい【静水】 still water.

せいすう【正数】〔数学〕a positive number.

せいすう【整数】〔数学〕an integral number; a whole number.

せい·する【制する】 ¶ 敵の機先を～せよ *Get the start of* the enemy. 情欲は～しがたい The passions are hard of *control*. 真の紳士とはみずからを～するものである A real gentleman should *control* himself. 先んずれば人を～す (諺) *First come, first served*.

せいせい【精製】 refinement. ¶ 塩を～する *refine* salt. ～した砂糖 *refined* sugar.
—所 a refinery. **—法** a refining process.

せいせい【清清】 refreshment. ¶ 試験が済んで～した As the examination was over, I *feel relieved*. 勉強したあとの散歩は～する Taking a walk after studying is *refreshing*.

せいせい【生成】 formation ; generation ; creation.

せいぜい【精精】 at best ; at most. ¶ ～お安くしておきます We can reduce the price. ～お体をたいせつに Please take good care of yourself. 遠いので電報を打つのが～だ I can just manage to send a telegram as it is a long way from here.

ぜいせい【税制】 the taxation system.
—改正(改革) a tax reform. **—調査会** the taxation system research committee.

ぜいぜいと ¶ 彼は苦しそうに～息をした He *wheezed* with difficulty.

せいせいどうどう【正正堂堂】 ¶ 彼の態度は～たるものだ His manner *is fair and square*. 彼らは～と戦った They fought *fairly*. どんな競技でも～とやることが好きだ I love *fair play* in any play. 彼らに対して～とやれ *Play fair* with them.

せいせき【成績】 a result ; a record ; (個人の) standing. ¶ 彼は学校の～がよい He *does well* at school. 試験の～は悪かった I got bad *marks* in the examination. 彼女は学校の～はまあまあだ She *does pretty well* at school. 英語の～はよかったが数学の～は悪かった I got *a good mark* in English, but *a bad one* in mathematics. A君とB君とはどちらが～がいいですか Which is getting better *marks*, A or B? ～はあす発表される The *results of the examination* will be announced tomorrow. 新しい仕事で彼は相当の～をあげている He *has been doing fairly well* in his new job.
—表 a report card.

せいせき【聖跡】 a holy place with historic associations.

せいせつ【正接】〔数学〕a tangent.

せいせっかい【生石灰】〔化学〕quicklime.

せいせん【生鮮】 ¶ ～な fresh.
—食料品 fresh food ; perishables.

せいぜつな【凄絶な】 extremely weird.

せいせん【清泉】 a clear spring.

せいせん【精選】 ¶ 材料を～する *pick* (≒ *select*) materials *carefully*. ～されたブドウ *select* (≒ *choice*) grapes.

せいぜん【生前】 in (≒ during) *one's* life. ¶ ～の愛用品 *one's* relic. 彼は～読書を愛した He loved reading *while alive* (≒ *during his lifetime*).

せいぜん【整然】 ¶ ～たる都市計画 an *orderly* city planning. 彼らは～と行進した They marched on *in good order*. 彼の理論はまったく理路～としている His theory is thoroughly *logical*. 万事が～としていた Everything was kept *in proper order*.

せいそ【清楚】 neatness ; tidiness. ¶ ～な花 a *graceful* flower. 彼女は～な服装をしていた She was *neatly* dressed.

せいそう【正装】 full dress. ¶ 彼は～していた He was in *full dress*. ディナーのために～した I *dressed up* for dinner.

せいそう【盛装】 full dress. ¶ 夜会にはみな～です They will *be dressed up* at an evening party. ～の婦人 a lady *in full feather*.

せいそう【成層】 stratification ;〔地質〕bedding.
—火山〔地質〕a cone ; a conical volcano. **—圏**〔天文学〕stratosphere. **—岩**〔地質〕sedimentary rock.

せいそう【政争】 a political strife. ¶ ～が絶えない There is *an* endless *political strife*. 人事を～の具としてはならない You should not make a political issue of personnel administration.

せいそう【清掃】 cleaning ; (洗うこと) washing. ¶ 道路を～する *scavenge* streets.
—員(道路の) a street sweeper ; a scavenger ; (ごみ集め) a garbage man. **—車** a garbage wagon.

せいぞう【製造】 manufacture ; making. ¶ あの工場は扇風機を～している They *are producing* fans in that factory. この町では大量に顕微鏡を～している They *are turning out* microscopes in great quantities in this town. この菓子箱には～の年月日が記されていない The date of *manufacture* hasn't been put on this box of confectioneries. この道具はイタリアで～したものだ This tool is *of* Italian *make*.
—工業 the manufacturing industry. **—者** a maker ; a manufacturer. **—所** a factory. **—高** 〔the〕 output. **—能力** manufacturing capacity. **—費** manufacturing cost. **—品** manufactured articles. **—法** a manufacturing process. **—元** a maker ; a manufacturer.

せいそく【生息・棲息】 habitation. ¶ 水中に～する *live* in the water.
—地 a habitat.

せいそく【正則】 a regular system.

せいぞろい【勢揃い】 a line-up ; an array ; muster. ¶ 全員が門の前に～した All members *made an array* (≒ *lined up*) in front of the gate.

せいぞん【生存】existence; life. ¶ 月にはなにも生物は～していない No life *exists* on the moon.

—競争 the struggle for existence. ¶ ～競争の激しい時代 the age of the severe struggle for *existence*. —権 the right to live. —者 a survivor. ¶ 彼がその惨事のただひとりの～者だった He was the only *survivor* of the accident. 適者— the survival of the fittest.

せいた【背板】a backboard.

せ

せいたい【成体】〔動物〕an imago.

せいたい【生体】a living body.

—解剖 a vivisection. —解剖者 a vivisector. —学 somatology. —実験 an experiment on a living body.

せいたい【生態】a mode of life. ¶ サルの～を調べる study (≒ investigate) the *ecology* of monkeys. —学 ecology.

せいたい【声帯】〔解剖〕the vocal chord〔s〕. ¶ ～を震わす vibrate *the vocal chords*.

—模写 ¶ ～模写をする imitate (≒ mimic) another's voice.

せいたい【聖体】〔キリスト教〕Eucharist; the Host. —拝受 Holy Communion.

せいたい【政体】the form of government; a regime.

共和— the republican form of government. 民主— democracy.

せいたい【静態】¶ ～の statical; stationary.

せいだい【盛大】(りっぱなこと) grandeur; (繁栄していること) prosperity. ¶ ～な歓迎会 an *enthusiastic* reception. 祝賀会が～に開かれた They gave a *grand* celebration. 園遊会は～だった The garden party *was largely attended*. 彼の商売は～になっている His business *is prospering*.

せいたかくけい【正多角形】〔数学〕an equilateral polygon.

せいだく【清濁】¶ 彼は～併せのむ人物だ He is broad-minded enough to tolerate people of all shades of opinion.

ぜいたく【贅沢】luxury; extravagance.

¶ あれこれと～を言う ask too much; be too particular. 食べることぐらいは～しよう Let's try to live on *luxurious* food. 彼は～に暮らしている He lives in *luxury*. きみは～をやめなければいけない You must abandon *luxury*. 私にはそんな～はできない I cannot afford such *luxury*. この万年筆は私には～すぎる This pen *is* too *expensive* for me. ～を言うな Don't ask too much. ～を言えばきりがない One can never be completely satisfied. 彼女は～に育った She was brought up *in luxury*. 彼女は着る物に～すぎる She *is too extravagant with* her clothes.

せいだ・す【精出す】work hard (≒ with diligence); be industrious; be diligent. ¶ 畑仕事に～す *work hard* in the field.

せいたん【生誕】birth. ¶ A氏～の地 Mr. A's *birthplace*. B氏～100年祭 the centenary of the *birth* of Mr. B.

せいだん【政談】political talk.

せいだん【星団】a star cluster.

せいち【聖地】a holy place; a sacred place; the Holy Land (パレスチナを指す).

—巡礼 a pilgrimage to sacred places.

せいち【生地】*one's* birthplace.

せいち【整地】¶ 山林を～する *clear* the woodland. 建築のために～する *readjust the land* for construction.

せいち【精緻】exquisitness; fineness; delicacy; minuteness. ¶ ～な機械 a *delicate* machine. ～な筆 *minute* painting. ～をきわめた設計図 a plan drawn with utmost *minuteness*.

せいちゃ【製茶】tea manufacture.

—業 tea manufacture. —業者 a tea manufacturer. —工場 a tea factory.

せいちゅう【成虫】〔動物〕an imago (複 imagos, imagines). ¶ 幼虫から～になる grow out of a larva into *an imago*.

せいちゅう【精虫】〔生物〕a spermatozoon (複 spermatozoa).

せいちゅう【掣肘】restriction; restraint. ¶ なんの～も受けていない I am free from all *restraint*.

せいちゅう【正中】the middle.

せいちょう【正調】the orthodox tune.

せいちょう【政庁】a government office.

せいちょう【生長】growth. ¶ この木は～が早い This tree *grows* quickly. その木は十分に～した The tree has reached its full *growth*. それは小麦の～を早めるだろう It will promote the *growth* of wheat. その植物は～が止まった The plant stopped *growing*.

せいちょう【成長】growth. ¶ 子どもは～が早い Children *grow up* quickly. 彼もりっぱな若者に～した He *grew up* into a fine young man. それはがん細胞の～を止めるだろう It will halt the *growth* of cancer cells.

—株 growth stock. ¶ 彼は～株だ He is *a promising youth*. —産業 a growth industry. 経済—(率) (the rate of) economic growth. 名目(実質)—率 the nominal (real) growth rate.

せいちょう【清聴】¶ ご～ありがとうございました I thank you for your kind *attention*.

せいちょう【整調】(音楽の) tuning; (ボートの) a stroke. ¶ ボートの～をつとめる pull *stroke*.

せいつう【精通】¶ 彼女はフランス語に～している She *knows* French *well*. / She *has a good knowledge of* French. 彼は国際法に～している He *is well versed in* international law. / He *is an expert in* international law. 彼はアメリカ事情に～している He *is well acquainted with* American affairs.

せいてい【制定】enactment; establishment. ¶ 法律を～する *make* (≒ *enact*; *establish*) a law. 国旗を～する *create* a national flag.

せいてき【政敵】a political opponent; a political enemy. ¶ 彼は多くの～がある He has a lot of *political opponents*.

せいてき【性的】¶～な犯罪 a *sex* crime. ～な衝動 a *sex* urge. 非常に～な魅力のある女性 a woman with a strong *sex* appeal ; (米俗語) a very *sexy* girl ; a *glamor* (≒ *pin-up*) girl. 彼女は～魅力がある She has *sex* appeal. ～な記事 an *inflammatory* article. 彼らは～に早熟である They are *sexually* precocious.
—倒錯症 sexual perversion.

せいてき【静的】static ; statical.

せいてつ【精鉄】refined iron.

せいてつ【製鉄】iron (≒ steel) manufacture.
—会社 an iron (≒ a steel) manufacturing company. —業 the iron (≒ steel) industry. —業者 an iron (≒ a steel) producer. —所 a steel mill ; an ironworks.

せいてん【青天】the blue [sky]. ¶その知らせは私には～の霹靂(へきれき)であった The news was *a bolt from the blue* to me.
—白日 ¶彼は無罪の判決を受けて～白日の身となった He was given a decision of "not guilty," and *completely cleared of the charge*.

せいてん【晴天】fine (≒ fair) weather ; a clear sky. ¶本日は～なり It is *fine* today. ～が続いた We have had a long spell of *fine weather*.

せいてん【聖典】the sacred book.

せいてん【正典】〘キリスト教〙the canon ; the canonized books.

せいでんき【静電気】〘物理〙static electricity.

せいと【聖徒】〘キリスト教〙a saint. ¶～に列する *canonize (a person)*.

せいと【生徒】(高校以上の) a student ; (小・中学校の) (男子) a schoolboy ; (女子) a schoolgirl.
—会 a students' congress. ¶文化祭は～会が主催する The cultural festival is sponsored by the *students' congress*. 全校— the whole school ; all the school.

せいど【制度】a system. ¶～化する systematize. ～を確立する(改める; 廃する) establish (renovate ; abolish) *a system*. 新～は来年度から施行される The new *system* will be put into practice from next year on.
貨幣— the monetary system. 教育— the educational system. 社会— the social system. 封建— the feudal system ; feudalism.

せいど【精度】¶～の高い機械 a machine with a high degree of *accuracy*. この機械の～はすばらしい The *precision* of this machine is wonderful.

せいとう【正当】justice ; propriety ; (適法なこと) legitimacy ; lawfulness. ¶私は～な報酬を要求する I only claim a *just* reward. 彼は～な理由なしに参加を拒絶した He refused to take part in it without *sufficient* reason. どんなことも～に評価すべきである We should set (≒ put) a *proper* (≒ *just*) value upon anything. 彼は部下を～に扱う He *does* his men *justice*. 目的が手段を～化することがある It sometimes happens that the end *justifies* the means. ～な手続きもとらずに彼はそれを決めた He determined the matter without *due* process of law. 人を～に扱わない人は結局は憎まれる Those who do not give others their *due* come to be hated in the long run.
—防衛 self-defence. ¶～防衛のため彼は言い分を主張した He had his own say *in self-defence*.

せいとう【正統】orthodoxy ; legitimacy. ¶～の君主 a *legitimate* monarch. 彼はその流儀の～を受け継いでいる He is the *lineal* successor of the school.
—派 the orthodox school.

せいとう【政党】a political party. ¶～を結成する form *a* new *political party*.
—員 a party member (≒ man). —政治 party government (≒ politics). —内閣 a party cabinet.

せいとう【精糖】sugar refining ; (製品) refined sugar.

せいとう【製糖】sugar production.
—会社 a sugar manufacturing company. —業 the sugar manufacturing industry.

せいとう【製陶】pottery.
—業 the pottery manufacturing industry.

せいどう【青銅】bronze. ¶～の胸像 a *bronze* bust.
—器 bronze ware. —器時代 the Bronze Age. —細工 bronze work.

せいどう【正道】the path of righteousness ; the right path ; justice.

せいどう【聖堂】a temple ; a church ; a sacred edifice.

せいどうき【制動機】a brake. ¶～をかける apply (≒ put on) the *brakes*.
自動(真空)— an automatic (a vacuum) brake. 手動(足踏み; 電気)— a hand (a foot ; an electric) brake. 非常— an emergency brake.

せいどく【精読】careful reading ; (速読などに対して) intensive reading. ¶～する read (a book) carefully ; peruse (a book). ～は多読にまさる *Careful reading* (≒ *Intensive reading*) is better than extensive reading.

せいどようび【聖土曜日】Holy Saturday (復活祭前の土曜日).

せいとん【整頓】order ; arrangement ; adjustment. ¶彼はいつも身のまわりの物をきちんと～しておく He always *keeps* his things *in order*. 彼女は急いで部屋を～した She quickly *put* her room *in good order*. 出かける前に机の上を～しなさい *Clear up* your desk before you go out. ぼくの部屋はいつもきちんと～してある My room is always *neat and clean*. 彼の部屋はいつも～してない His room is always *untidy* (≒ *in disorder*).

せいなん【西南】southwest. ¶～の風が吹きはじめた The *southwest* wind began to blow. / The wind began to blow from the *southwest*. そこは本土の～端にある The place is at the *southwest* end of the mainland.

せ

その寺は京都の～部にある The temple stands in the *southwest* of Kyoto. 博物館は学校の～方にある The museum is 〔*to the*〕 *southwest of* our school.

せいなん【正南】the due south.

せいにく【生肉】raw meat.

せいにく【精肉】dressed meat.

—商 (店) a butcher shop ; (人) a butcher.

ぜいにく【贅肉】¶ 彼は～がつきはじめた He began to put on *superfluous flesh*. きみは～をとらなければいけない You should get rid of *superfluous flesh*.

せ

せいねん【成年】¶ ～に達する come of age ; attain (≒ reach) *one's majority*. ～に達しない be under age ; be not of full age.

未— a minor.

せいねん【生年】¶ ～月日 the date of *one's* birth.

せいねん【青年】a young man ; a youth ; (総称) young people ; the younger generation. ¶ 前途有為な～ *a* promising *youth*. 農村出身の～たち *young people* from the country. 彼の息子もりっぱな～になった His son has grown into *a* fine *young man*.

—学級 a special class for young people.

—男女 young men and women.

せいのう【性能】(機能) capacity ; ability ; (特質) property. ¶ ～のよい機械 a highly *efficient* machine. 機械の～をよくする raise the *efficiency* of a machine ; give the machine *a* greater *efficiency*. この機械は～が鈍った This machine became less *efficient*. エンジンの～を調べる test the *capacity* of an engine.

せいは【制覇】conquest. ¶ 彼は商業の面で世界の～を目指している He aims to *dominate* the world commercially. わがチームは高校野球大会で全国～を成し遂げた Our team *gained* (≒ *won*) *the championship* in the national interhighschool baseball games.

空中(海上)— the mastery (≒ command) of the air (seas).

せいばい【成敗】(裁断すること) judgment ; (罰) punishment.

両— ¶ けんか両～ In a quarrel both parties are to blame.

せいはく【精白】¶ ～する(米を) polish rice ; (砂糖を) refine sugar.

—米 polished rice. —糖 refined sugar.

せいはくじ【精薄児】a retarded child.

せいばつ【征伐】subjugation. ¶ 敵を～する *subjugate* (≒ *subdue*) the enemy. 海賊を～する conquer the pirates.

せいはん【正犯】〔法律〕the principal offense.

—者 the principal offender.

せいはん【製版】(版を作ること) plate-making ; (活字組み) type-setting. ¶ ～する make a plate.

せいはん【整版】〔印刷〕makeup ; justification.

せいはんごう【正反合】〔哲学〕thesis-antithesis-synthesis.

せいはんたい【正反対】direct opposition ; the exact opposite (≒ reverse). ¶ 彼は～の方向を指示した He pointed *the utterly opposite* direction. きみの意見とぼくの意見とは～だ Your views *are directly opposite to* mine. 事実は～だ The fact *is just the opposite*. 彼女の性格は彼とは～だ Her character *is the very opposite* of his. 私は～のことを考えていた I thought *quite the opposite*.

せいひ【生皮】a hide.

せいひ【政費】administrative expenditure.

せいひ【正比】〔数学〕direct ratio.

せいひ【成否】success or failure ; the result. ¶ ～はきみの心がけしだいだ *Success* depends upon your efforts. ～のほどは保証できない I am not sure of *success*. ～のいかんにかかわらずやってみなさい Try it regardless of *the result*.

せいび【整備】(改善) improvement ; (完備) complete equipment. ¶ 車を～する *fix* a car. 会場を～する *arrange* a hall.

—員(航空機の) a ground man ; (機械の) a repairman. —工場 a repair shop.

せいび【精美】surpreme beauty. ¶ ～な exceedingly.

せいび【精微】minuteness. ¶ ～な minute ; detailed.

せいひょう【製氷】ice manufacture.

—機 an ice machine. —工場(会社) an ice plant (company).

せいびょう【性病】a venereal disease.

せいひれい【正比例】direct proportion. ¶ 重さは量に～する The weight *is directly proportional to* the volume. / The weight *is in direct proportion to* the volume.

せいひん【清貧】¶ 彼は～に甘んじている He is contented with *honest poverty*.

せいひん【製品】manufactured goods (≒ articles) ; a product. ¶ 石油からの新しい～ *a* new petroleum *product*. これはその新会社の～だ This is the *product* of the new company. このカメラは日本の～だ This camera is *of* Japanese *make*.

アメリカ— articles of American make ; American-made goods. 外国— foreign products ; imported goods. ガラス— glassware. 絹— silk manufacture. 国内— home products.

せいひん【正賓】a guest of honor.

せいふ【正負】〔数学〕positive and negative ; plus and minus.

せいふ【政府】the government. ¶ 彼は新しい～を樹立した He set up *a* new *government*. これは～の機関だ This is a *governmental* organ.

—当局 the government authorities. 日本— the Japanese government.

せいぶ【西部】(一般に) the west ; (アメリカ西部地方) the West. ¶ 彼の家はその市の～(～地域)にある His house is *in the west of* the city. (to the west of... は「…の西方に」の意となる).

—劇(映画・劇・小説の) a Western.

せいふう【西風】a west wind.

せいふう【清風】a cool (≒ refreshing) breeze.

せいふく【正副】(役職の) principal and vice.

(書類の) original and copy. ¶ ～２通の送り状を作った We made out the invoice *in duplicate*.

—議長 the speaker and vice-speaker; the president and vice-president.

せいふく【征服】 conquest; subjugation; mastery. ¶ エベレストの～ the *conquest* of Mt. Everest. 人類の自然～ man's *conquest* over nature. アレキサンダー大王はペルシアを～した Alexander the Great *conquered* (≒ *made a conquest of*) Persia. 不得意な科目を～する *master one's* unfavorite subject.

—者 a conqueror.

せいふく【制服】 a uniform; (お仕着せ) a livery. ¶ 学校の～ *a* school *uniform*. ～の警官 a *uniformed* policeman; a police officer *in uniform*. 彼女はスチュワーデスの～を着ていた She was in *a* stewardess *uniform*. / She was *in the uniform of* a stewardess. 彼女は～を着て学校へ通う She goes to school *in uniform*.

せいぶつ【生物】 a living thing; a living creature; (総称) life. ¶ 月には～はいないらしい There seems to be no *life* (≒ *living things*) on the moon.

—界 the biological world. —学 biology. —学者 a biologist. —岩〘鉱物〙biogenetic rock. —検定 a biological assay.

せいぶつ【静物】 still life. ¶ 油絵の～(画) *a still life* in oils. 彼は水彩で～を２枚描いた He painted two *still lifes* in water colors. (覆 still lifes に注意).

—画家 a still-life painter.

せいぶつぶつりがく【生物物理学】 biophysics.

—者 a biophysicist.

せいふん【製粉】 milling.

—機 a flour mill. —業 the milling industry. —業者 a miller. —所 a flour mill.

せいぶん【正文】 the〔official〕text (*of* a treaty).

せいぶん【成文】 ¶ 法律を～化する *codify* a law. 慣習を～化する reduce the custom to *statuary form*.

—法 a written law.

せいぶん【成分】 a component; an ingredient. ¶ 文を～に分ける divide a sentence into *the elements*.

せいへい【精兵】 a crack troop; picked man.

せいへき【性癖】 a mental habit; a propensity. ¶ 彼は大げさに言う～がある He has *a way* of exaggerating. / He has *a propensity* for exaggeration.

せいべつ【性別】 ¶ ～に関係なく regardless of *sex*. カードに～を記入する enter *one's sex* in a card.

せいへん【政変】 a political change; a change of government. ¶ ～が起こるだろう *A political change* will take place. / (内閣の更迭) *A Cabinet change* will take place.

せいへん【正編】 the principal part〔of a book〕.

せいぼ【生母】 *one's*〔real〕mother.

せいぼ【聖母】 the Virgin Mary. ¶ ～の像(彫刻) a Madonna.

せいぼ【歳暮】 the year end; the end of the year; (贈り物) a year-end present. ¶ ～大売り出し the great *year-end*〔bargain〕sale. 彼にお～を送った I sent him *a year-end present*.

せいほう【西方】 the west. ¶ 村の～に〔*to the*〕*west* of the village. 町は～に広がっていく The town is extending *to the west*.

せいほう【製法】 a method of manufacturing. ¶ 土器の～ *how to make* earthenware; the *method* of *manufacturing* earthenware.

せいぼう【声望】 popularity; reputation; fame. ¶ ～のある人 a man *of good* (≒ *high*) *reputation*. ～のない人 a man *of poor reputation*. 彼はなかなか～がある He has *an* excellent *reputation*. / He *is in high repute*. 彼は急に～が高まった He came to sudden *fame*.

せいぼう【制帽】 (一般的な) a regulation cap; (学校の) a school cap. ¶ ～を着用する wear *a regulation cap*.

ぜいほう【税法】 the tax law.

せいほうけい【正方形】 a square.

せいほく【西北】 northwest. ¶ ～の風 a *northwest* wind. その市はわれわれの市の～にある The city is〔*to the*〕*northwest of* our city. われわれの大学は東京の～〔部〕にある Our college is *in the northwest of* Tokyo.

せいぼつ【生没】 birth and death. ¶ ～年不詳 dates of *birth and death* unknown.

せいほん【製本】 bookbinding. ¶ ～する *bind* a book. じょうぶな～の本 a book in durable *binding*. この本は～がよくできている This book *is* well *bound*.

—所 a bookbindery. —屋(人) a bookbinder.

せいほん【正本】〘法律〙the original〔copy; text〕.

せいまい【精米】 —機 a rice-cleaning machine. —所 a rice-cleaning mill.

せいみつ【精密】 (細かいこと) minuteness; closeness; (精確なこと) accuracy; precision. ¶ ～な機械 a *precise* machine. ～な地図 a *detailed* map. その機械の寸法を～に測定しなさい Measure the machine *closely* (≒ *with minute accuracy*). 病院で～な健康診断を受けた I took a *close* medical examination at the hospital.

—科学 an exact science. —機械 a precision machine. —工業 the precision industry.

せいみょうな【精妙な】 subtle; delicate; exquisite.

せいむ【政務】 —次官 a parliamentary vice-minister (≒ secretary). —調査会 the Political Affairs Research committee.

ぜいむ【税務】 —署 a taxation office. —署員 a tax collector. —署長 the superintendent of a taxation office.

せいめい【生命】 life. ¶数百人の～が失われた Hundreds of *lives* were lost. 彼は～の危険を冒してその子を救った He saved the child at the risk of his own *life*. 彼の～に別状はない There is no fear of his death. 彼の随筆の～は叙情性だ The *life and soul* of his essays is their lyricism. スポーツマンの～はフェアプレーである Fair play is the *soul* of a sportsman.
—保険 life insurance.

せいめい【声明】 a declaration; an announcement; a statement. ¶政府はその問題について次のような～を出した The government issued (≒ gave out) the following *statement* on the problem. その国は中立を～した The country *declared* neutrality. その問題に関して公式～はまだ出ていない No official *statement* has been issued yet on the matter.

せいめい【姓名】 *one's* [full] name.
—判断 onomancy.

ぜいもく【税目】 tax items; items of taxation.

せいもん【正門】 the front gate; the main entrance.

せいもん【声門】〔解剖〕glottis (複 glottises, glottides).

せいもん【声紋】 a voiceprint.

せいやく【制約】 a restriction; a limitation; (条件) a condition. ¶まず時間の～がある First I *am restricted* by time. 規則によって～される *be controlled* (≒ *be restricted*) by the rule. 農作物は天候に～される The crops *depend on* the weather.

せいやく【誓約】 [an] oath; [a] pledge.
¶彼は～を破った He broke his *promise*. ぼくは～は守る I keep my *promise*. 彼は全力を尽くすと～した He *made a promise* (≒ *promised*) to do his best. 彼は～を取り消した He withdrew his *promise*.
—書 a written promise (≒ pledge).

せいやく【製薬】 medicine manufacture.
—会社 a pharmaceutical company. —業 a pharmaceutical industry. —工場 a pharmaceutical factory.

せいゆ【精油】 refined oil.

せいゆ【製油】 oil manufacture.
—所 an oil factory (≒ refinery).

せいゆう【声優】 (ラジオの) a radio actor (女性は a radio actress).

せいよう【西洋】 the West; the Western countries; the Occident. ¶～の Western; European; Occidental.
—史 European history. —風 a Western style. —文明 Western civilization. —料理 Western food. —人 a Westerner; an Occidental.

せいよう【静養】 rest; (病後の) convalescence.
¶彼は～のために田舎へ行った He went into the country *for his health*. 家で～したほうがいい You had better *take a rest* at your home. 彼女は病後の～のために海岸へ行った She went to the seaside to *recuperate*. 自宅～中です I *am recuperating* at my home. 3週間の～を要する You need three weeks' *rest*. ～先(療養所)に彼を訪ねた I visited him in *a rest home*.

せいようひいらぎ【西洋柊】〔植物〕an ilex; a holly.

せいようすぎ【西洋杉】〔植物〕a cedar.

せいようすもも【西洋李】〔植物〕a plum; a damson.

せいよく【性欲】 sexual desire; flesh. ¶～の満足 satisfaction of *flesh* (≒ *lust*). 卵やカキは～を刺激する Eggs and oysters stimulate (≒ excite) *sexual desire* (≒ *appetite*). ～を満足させる gratify *one's sexual desire*.
—倒錯 sexual perversion. 変態— abnormal sexuality.

せいらい【生来】 nature. ¶彼は～のお人よしだ He *was born* a good-natured man. 彼は～うそつきだ He is a *born* liar. 彼女は～詩的な女性だ She is poetic *by nature*.

せいり【生理】 physiology. ¶よだれが出るのも～的な現象のひとつだ Slavering is one of *physiological* phenomena. 彼女は彼を～的にきらっている She hates him *instinctively*.
—学 physiology; physiological science. —学者 a physiologist. —休暇 a [woman's] monthly holiday; a special monthly leave for women. —日 *one's* menstrual period.

せいり【整理】 1 arrangement; regulation; adjustment; readjustment. ¶部屋の中を～する *put* a room *in order*.
彼は身のまわりの～をしていた He *was arranging* his personal belongings.
帳簿はまだ～がついていない The accounts *have* not *been adjusted* yet.
本だなの本を～してほしい I want my books *arranged* on the shelf.
けさの話し合いの記録を～しておきなさい Be sure to *keep* the records of what we talked about this morning *straight*.
彼のノートはいつもきちんと～してある His notebooks *are* always *kept neat*.
区画— city planning. —だんす a commode. 交通— the traffic regulation. 行政— administrative adjustment.
2〖負債を〗¶負債を～する *clear off one's* debt.
3〖人員を〗¶人員を～する *cut down* the staff; *reduce* the staff.
人員— reduction of staff.

せいりきがく【静力学】〔物理〕statics.

ぜいりし【税理士】 a licensed tax accountant.

せいりつ【成立】 (完成) completion; (組織が) formation; (存在が) existence; (事が成る) success.
¶予算が～した The budget *was approved*. 動議は～するかどうか疑問だ I doubt if the motion will *be carried*. この委員会は15人の委員で～する This committee *consists of* fifteen members. 議会はまだ～しない The House *is* not yet *formed*. 昨夜新内閣が～した A new cabinet *was formed* last night. 条約が～したのは10年前だった It was ten years

ago that the treaty *was concluded*. 両者の間に商談が～した A bargain *was arranged* between the two. 両者の間に和解が～した A settlement *was reached* between the two. 彼の出した案が交渉の～に役立った The plan he submitted was helpful in promoting the *success* of the negotiation.

ぜいりつ【税率】the taxation rate; the tax rate; (関税の) a tariff. ¶石油の～は改められるだろう *The tariff on* petroleum will be revised. われわれの所得に対する～は下げられるだろう *The tax rate on* our incomes will be lowered.

せいりゃく【政略】politics; a political maneuver. ¶～的な発言 a *political* utterance.
—結婚 a marriage of convenience.

せいりゅう【整流】〖電気〗rectification; commutation.
—管 a rectification tube. —器 a rectifier. —作用 rectifying action. —子 a commutator.

せいりゅう【清流】a clear stream.

せいりょう【声量】volume of *one's* voice. ¶彼は～が豊かだ He has *a* rich *voice*.

せいりょう【清涼】refreshing; cool.
—飲料 a soft drink.

せいりょう【正量】〖数学〗a positive quantity.

せいりょうな【精良な】excellent; fine; choice; picked; superior.

せいりょく【勢力】power; influence; (力) strength; force; (引き立て) pull. ¶彼はこの地方に～がある He has *power* in this district. / He *is influential* in this area. 彼は党内では～を持っている He is *powerful* in the party. 氏は経済界に大きな～を持っている He has very powerful *influence* in economic circles. 台風の～はだいぶ弱まった The typhoon has much weakened in *force*. 彼は仲間に対し絶大な～をふるっている He is exercising great *influence* over all the members. 昔は王が絶対の～を持っていた The king had absolute *power* over his people.
—争い ¶彼らは～争いをしている They are struggling for *power*. —家 a man of power. —範囲 *one's* sphere of influence. —下 ¶彼は何人かの人を～下に置いている He has several men under his *power*.

せいりょく【精力】energy; vigor. ¶～旺盛(おうせい)な人 an *energetic* (≒ a *vigorous*) man. 彼はその仕事に全～を傾けた He concentrated *all his energies to* the work. 彼は長いドライブで～を使いはたした He *is tired out from* the long drive. 彼は～的に仕事をする He works *vigorously* (≒ *with energy*). ゆっくり休んで～を養う take a sufficient rest to restore *one's energy*. 彼は～絶倫だ His *energy* is unbounded.

せいりょくりつ【静力率】〖物理〗static moment.

せいるい【声涙】¶～ともに下る演説をした He made a speech with tears rolling down his cheeks.

せいれい【聖霊】〖キリスト教〗the Holy Ghost (≒ Spirit).
—降臨祭 the Pentecost; the Whitsunday.

せいれい【政令】a government ordinance.

せいれい【精励】diligence; industry. ¶彼は研究に～している He studies *hard*. / He *is diligent in* his study. 自分の職務に～せよ *Devote yourself to* your duties.

せいれき【西暦】the Christian Era; A. D. (ラテン語の Anno Domini から). ¶～1970年 in A. D. 1970 (アメリカでは in 1970 A. D. と書くこともある).

せいれつ【整列】standing in row; a parade. ¶学生たちは1列に～していた The students *were drawn up in line*. 教師は少年たちを1列に～させた The teacher *drew* the boys *up in a line*. 兵隊たちは兵営の前に～した The soldiers *lined up* in front of the barracks. 彼らは(横に)2列に～した They stood *in two rows*. 彼らは(縦に)2列に～した They stood *in file*.

せいれつな【清冽な】limpid; clear.

せいれん【清廉】¶～潔白な人 a man *of integrity*; a *clean-fingered* man.

せいれん【精錬・製錬】refining; smelting. ¶金を～する *refine* gold. ～された鉄 *refined* iron.
—所 a refinery. 銅—所 a copper refinery.

せいろう【蒸籠】a steaming basket.

せいろう【晴朗】¶天気～である The weather *is fine*. / It *is clear and blue*. ～な clear; fair; fine. ～に clearly; fairly; finely.

せいろくめんたい【正六面体】a cube; a regular hexahedron.

せいろん【正論】a just (≒ sound) argument. ¶きみのは～だ I admit the justice of your argument.

セイロン Ceylon.
—紅茶 Ceylon tea.

セーター a sweater.

セーフ〖野球〗safe. ¶彼は一塁で～になった He was *safe* on the first base.

セーブ ¶まだいろいろやることがあるから, 力を～しておきたまえ *Save* your strength *for* further attempts.

セーフティバント〖野球〗a safety bunt.

セーラー ¶～服の少女 a girl in *a sailor suit*.

セールスマン a salesman.

せおいかご【背負い籠】a pannier.

せおいなげ【背負い投げ】a shoulder throw. ¶彼を～で投げた I *threw* him *over my shoulder*. ～を食わせる(人を裏切る) go back on *a person*.

せお・う【背負う】¶彼はリュックサックを～っている He *has* a rucksack *on his back*. 彼はその責任を全部～いこんだ He *took* all the responsibility *on his shoulders*. 彼は負債をうんと～っている He *is burdened with* a heavy debt. 彼は一家を～っている He *is the sole support of* his family. / He has a family to *support*.

せおおい【背覆い】(いすの) an antimacassar.

せおよぎ【背泳ぎ】a backstroke.

せかい【世界】**1** the world; (地球) the earth;

(宇宙) the universe. ¶ 〜は一つだ *The world* is one.
彼は1年にわたって〜じゅうを旅行した He traveled *all over the world* for a year.
〜じゅうの人はそのニュースを知っている *The whole world* knows the news.
彼は〜的に有名な植物学者だ He is a *world-famous* botanist.
アメリカは〜第一の富国である America is the richest country *on earth*.
—観 a world view; an outlook on the world. **—記録** a world record. **—漫遊** a round-the-world trip. **別—** another world. **—主義** cosmopolitanism.
2 〖生活の場面〗 ¶ 彼ら一団は新しい〜を求めて移住した Their group emigrated in search of *a new world*.
男の〜と女の〜はあらゆる点で異なっている The *world* of men is, in every respect, different from that of women.
子どもの〜にはおとなでは理解できないことがある In the *world* of children there are things that are beyond the comprehension of grown-up people.

せかせか ¶ 〜した人 a *restless* man. だれもかれも〜と動きまわっていた Everybody *was bustling about*.

せか・せる【急かせる】 hurry up; stir up. ¶ 〜せないでくれ Don't *hurry* me *up* (≒ *rush me*). 〜されるのは大きらいだ I hate to *be rushed*.

せかっこう【背格好】 ¶ 彼は〜が彼の父親とそっくりだ He is very like his father *in appearance*.

ぜがひでも【是が非でも】 ¶ 彼らは〜金をもうけようと思ってそれをした They did it in the hope of making money *by fair means or foul*. 〜勝ちたい I hope to win *by all means*. 〜来いと彼は言う He asks me to go *without fail*.

せが・む ¶ 彼は私に金を〜んだ He *teased* (≒ *pressed*) me *for* money. 彼はしきりにキャンデーを〜んでいる He keeps *teasing for* candy.

せがれ【倅・伜】 a son.

せがわ【背皮・背革】 a leatherback. ¶ 〜とじの本 a *quarter-bound* (≒ *leatherback*) book.

セカンド 1 〖野球〗 [the] second base; (二塁手) a second baseman.
2 〖自動車〗 the second gear.
3 〖ボクシング〗 a second.

せき【石】 ¶ 23〜の腕時計 a watch of 23 *jewels*.

せき【席】 a seat; a place; (余地) room. ¶ これはだれの〜ですか Whose is this *seat*? すぐ〜につきなさい *Take* your *seat* at once. このホールには500の〜がある This hall contains five hundred *seats*. この劇場にはいくつ〜がありますか How many persons can this theater *seat*? 今行ってもいい〜はとれないだろう Even if you start right now, you will be unable to *get* good *seats*. 老人に〜を譲らない若者もいる Some young men do not offer their *seats* to old people. 〜を取り替えていただけませんか Will you please *change seats*? 彼が入ってくるまで〜を立たないでください *Keep* your *seat* until he comes in. この図に示されているように〜についてください Please *be seated* as indicated by the plan of seats. 彼は仕事の〜にまだついていない He *has* not *sat down* to work yet. 彼は〜をけって出ていった He *flung out of* the room. あの人は〜の暖まる暇もない He *is* always *busy* (≒ *is* always *on the move*).
指定— a reserved seat.

せき【積】 〖数学〗 the product. ¶ 5と4の〜は20である The *product* of 5 by 4 is 20.

せき【籍】 (法的な) the census register; a domicile; (ポスト) membership. ¶ 彼は確かにその大学に〜をおいている He *is* surely *enrolled* in the university. 彼女は〜を入れた(抜いた) She had her name *entered in* (*removed from*) *the register*. 彼は東京に〜がある He *is domiciled* in Tokyo.

せき【関】 a barrier; a check point.

せき【咳】 a coughing; a cough. ¶ 〜をしてたんを吐き出した I *coughed up* phlegm. 彼女はひどい〜をした She *coughed* very hard. 彼は少し〜が出る He has *a* slight *cough*.
—止め薬 a cough medicine. **—止めドロップ** a cough drop. **から—** a dry cough; a hacking cough.

せき【堰】 a dam; (水門がついた) a sluice. ¶ 川の〜 *a dam* across a river. 〜を切ったように話しだす *burst out* speaking.

-せき【-隻】 ¶ 3〜の船 three ships.

せきあく【積悪】 *one's* old crimes.

せきうん【積雲】 〖気象〗 a cumulus (複 cumuli).

せきえい【石英】 〖鉱物〗 quartz.
—ガラス quartz glass.

せきえんこう【赤鉛鉱】 〖鉱物〗 crocoisite; crocoite.

せきが【席画】 (画) an offhand drawing; an impromptu painting; (画法) impromptu drawing.

せきがいせん【赤外線】 〖物理〗 infrared rays.
—写真 infrared photography. **—療法** infrared ray therapy.

せきがいぶ【赤外部】 infrared.

せきがいほうしゃ【赤外放射】 〖物理〗 infrared radiation.

せきがく【碩学】 a man of profound learning; a great scholar; an erudite person.

せきかん【石棺】 a stone coffin.

せきぐん【赤軍】 the Red Army; the Reds.

せきこ・む【急き込む】 ¶ 〜んで話す speak *impatiently*.

せきこ・む【咳き込む】 ¶ 彼は突然〜んだ He *got* (≒ *had*) *a fit of coughing*.

せきさい【積載】 carrying; loading.
—トン数 capacity tonnage. **—能力** carrying (≒ loading) capacity. **—量** loadage. ¶ 列車は〜量いっぱいの荷を積んで出発した The train left *with capacity load*.

せきざい【石材】 building stone.
—商 a stone dealer.

せきさん【積算】addition integration.
せきじ【席次】the seating order ; (学校の) class standing. ¶卒業の～ graduation *standing*. 彼はクラスの～が下がった He *lost his standing in the class*. 彼女はクラスの～が6番上がった She *gained in class standing* by six places.
せきじつ【昔日】former days ; former times; old days. ¶そこには～の面影もなし The place retains nothing of its *former* magnificence. 彼にはもはや～の面影はない He is but *the mere shadow of his former self*.
せきじゅうじ【赤十字】the Red Cross〔Society〕.
—看護婦 a Red Cross nurse. —病院 the Red Cross Hospital. —旗 the Red Cross flag. —条約 the Red Cross Convention.
せきじゅん【石筍】〘鉱物〙stalagmite.
せきしょ【関所】a barrier. ¶～を通る pass through *a barrier*.
せきじょう【席上】¶～で at the meeting. 会議の～で at the conference.
せきしょうも【石菖藻】〘植物〙an eelgrass.
せきしょく【赤色】red〔color〕.
—革命 a Red revolution. —テロ a Red terrorism. —リトマス試験紙 red litmus paper.
せきしん【赤心】sincerity ; *one's* true heart. ¶～を披瀝(ひれき)する reveal *one's inmost heart*.
せきずい【脊髄】〘解剖〙the spinal cord.
—麻酔 spinal anesthesia.
せきせいいんこ【脊黄青鸚哥】〘鳥類〙a grass parakeet.
せきせつ【積雪】snowfall ; drifted snow. ¶～2メートルに達した The *snow* was two meters *thick* (≒ *deep*). / We had *snowfall* of two meters. 汽車は～で立ち往生した The train *was snowed up*. / Because of the *deep snow*, the train was stopped. ～で動けなくなった We *were snow-bound*.
—量 a snowfall.
せきぜん【積善】¶～の家に余慶あり(諺) He who gives to the poor lends to the Lord.
せきぞう【石像】a stone image.
せきた・てる【急き立てる】¶皆を～てて寝かせた I *hastened* everyone *off* to bed. 彼に返事を～ててもむだだ It is no good *pressing* him *for* an answer.
せきたん【石炭】〘鉱物〙coal. ¶～を掘る dig *coal*. ～をたく burn *coal*. ストーブに～を入れる put *coals* in a stove.
—入れ a coalbox. —液化 coal liquefaction. —液化装置 coal liquefaction equipment. —ガス coal gas. —がら cinder. —酸 carbolic acid. —層 a coal bed ; a coal seam. —バケツ(室内用) a coal scuttle.
せきちく【石竹】〘植物〙a pink.
せきちゅう【脊柱】〘解剖〙the spinal column; the spine.
せきちんけんさ【赤沈検査】a sedimentation test.
せきつい【脊椎】〘解剖〙the backbone ; the vertebral column.
—カリエス vertebra caries. —動物 a vertebrate; a vertebral animal.
せきてっこう【赤鉄鉱】〘鉱物〙h(a)ematite.
せきどう【赤道】the equator ; the line.
¶～の equatorial. その船の位置は～直下にあった The ship was just on *the equator*. その距離は～を4回以上回る The distance is more than four times around the earth at the *equator*. この船はあす～を越える This ship will cross *the line* tomorrow.
—祭 the ceremony of crossing the line (≒ equator).
せきどうこう【赤銅鉱】〘鉱物〙cuprite ; red copper.
せきと・める【塞き止める】¶川が～められた A stream was *dammed up*.
せきとり【関取】a〔*sumo*〕wrestler.
せきにん【責任】responsibility ; (義務) an obligation ; *one's* duty ; (支払いの) liability.
1〖責任だ〗¶この失敗は私の～だ I *am responsible for* this slip-up.
2〖責任が〗¶こういうことになったのはきみにも～がある You *are* partly *to blame for* this.
われわれのひとりひとりが町を住みよくする～がある It is the *duty* of each and every one of us to keep the city comfortable to live〔in〕.
3〖責任は〗¶きみがこの子のめんどうをみる～はない You *are* not *expected to* look after the child.
4〖責任を〗¶自分の言ったことに～を持ちなさい You must *be true to* your words.
彼のせいではなかったが彼はその事故の～をとった He *took the blame for* the accident although it wasn't his fault.
私が～をもって彼に伝えましょう I will *see*〔*to it*〕that he gets the message.
この件については私が全～を負います I shall *assume* total *responsibility* in this matter.
社長は経営不振の～をとって辞任した The president *held himself responsible for* the slump in business, and left his post.
彼はさいごまでキャプテンとしての～をりっぱに果たした He remained a true captain to the last moment of his life.
～を回避してはいけない You must not shirk your *responsibility*.
それで～を果たしたと思うのか Do you think you have done your duty?
会社は水質汚染の～を問われている The company *is blamed for* the water pollution.
彼はとかく～を回避したがる He is likely to shirk his *responsibilities*.
そのことについては私も～を感じている I also feel that I *am* partly *to blame for* it.
5〖責任に〗¶きみの～においてやるなら私はなにも言わない I have no objection, as long as you do it on your own *responsibility*.
6〖責任の〗¶あのふたりはこの事故の～のなすり合いをしている They both blame each other for the accident.
まず～の所在を明らかにしよう Let us, first of all,

せ

find out where the *responsibility* lies.

7〖責任ある〗¶貴社の～ある回答を頂きたい I am expecting a *responsible* answer from your company.

彼は今度～ある地位についた He has recently risen to a *responsible* post.

それは～ある人の言うことばではない *A man of honor* is not expected to say such a thing.

8〖合成語〗¶クラスの共同～で教室をきれいにしなさい All the members of the class must work together to clean the classroom.

この事については私も連帯～を負います I will *answer* jointly *for* this matter.

彼は～感が強い He has *a* keen *sense of responsibility*.

この工場の～者はだれか Who *is in charge of* this factory?

せきねん【積年】many years; a number of years. ¶～の弊を打破しなければならない We must crush *long standing* evils.

せきのやま【関の山】¶試験は60点が～だ It is *all I can do* to get sixty marks in the examination.

せきはい【惜敗】¶試合は延長戦になったが, 結局～した The game extended to extra innings, and we *were defeated by a narrow margin*.

せきばく【寂莫】desolation; loneliness.

せきばらい【咳払い】¶彼は話す前に～をした He *cleared his throat* before he spoke.

せきはん【赤飯】steamed rice with red beans.

せきばん【石版】lithography.

—印刷 lithography. —画 a lithograph.

せきひ【石碑】a〔stone〕monument. ¶彼らはA氏のために～を建てた They built *a stone monument* to the memory of Mr. A.

せきひつ【石筆】a slate pencil.

せきひん【赤貧】dire poverty. ¶～に苦しむ suffer *the bitterest poverty*. 彼は～洗うがごとき状態にある He is in *extreme poverty*. / He is *as poor as a church mouse*.

せきぶつ【石仏】a stone image of Buddha.

せきぶん【積分】〖数学〗integral calculus.

—法 integration.

せきべつ【惜別】¶～の情に耐えない I shall miss you very much.

せきぼく【石墨】〖鉱物〗black lead.

せきむ【責務】¶～を果たす discharge *one's obligation*; do *one's duty*.

せきめん【石綿】asbestos.

せきめん【赤面】a flush. ¶～させる put *one* to shame; put *a person* to the flush. それを聞いて～した I *blushed* to hear it. 彼はまごついて～した He *blushed* confusedly. 恥ずかしくて～した I *blushed for* shame. 彼はそれを考えて～した He *blushed at* the thought of it.

せきゆ【石油】〖鉱物〗petroleum; oil. ¶～を掘り当てる strike oil.

—化学 petrochemicals. —かん an oil can. —業 the oil industry. —工業 the petroleum industry. —資源 petroleum resources. —ストーブ a kerosene heater (≒ lamp). —製品 oil products.

せきらら【赤裸裸】¶～な(率直な) frank; plain; outspoken. 彼は事の真相を～に語った He *frankly* told the truth of the matter. / He gave *naked* facts of the case. 彼は～に罪を告白した He made a *frank* confession of his sins.

せきらんうん【積乱雲】〖気象〗a cumulonimbus (複 cumulonimbuses, cumulonimbi).

せきり【赤痢】〖医学〗dysentery.

アミーバー— amoebic dysentery.

せきりょう【席料】(レストランなどの) a cover charge; (室代) the charge for a room.

せきりょう【寂寥】loneliness.

せきりん【赤燐】〖化学〗red phosphorus.

せきれい【鶺鴒】〖鳥類〗a wagtail.

せきろう【石蠟】paraffin.

せ·く【急く】hurry; be in a hurry. ¶そんなに～いてもはじまらない(気短になるな) Take it easy. / Take your time. / Don't *be* so *impatient*. / (急ぐな) What's the use of your *being in* such *a hurry*? ～いては事を仕損じる (諺) *Haste makes waste*. 彼は息が～いている He *is breathing hard*.

セクシー sexy. ¶彼女の声は～だ Her voice *is sexy*.

セクショナリズム sectionalism.

セクト a sect.

—主義 sectionalism.

せけん【世間】the world; society; the public; (世間の人) the people. ¶きみはまだ～を知らないのだ You know little of *the world* yet. 彼は～を知っている He has seen a lot of *the world*. ～の口はさぞうるさいことだろう Certainly *people will talk*. 5年前には彼女はまだ～に知られていなかった She was not known to *the world* five years ago. 彼は～に知れ渡っている He is known all over *the world*. ～の人は彼をばかだというが, 私はそうは思わない *They* say he is foolish, but I don't think so. 彼は～に顔向けができないと言っている He says he cannot look *the world* in the face. あの強盗は10年にわたって～を騒がした The robber *caused a sensation* as long as ten years.

—体 ¶彼が息子を大学に入れたがっているのは～体のためだ It is for the sake of *appearances* that he wants to send his son to a university. —なみ ¶彼らは～なみの暮らしをしている They *are making a decent living*. —話 ¶彼は～話をするのが好きだ He likes *having a chat*. —知らず ¶彼は～知らずだからすべてのものが彼にはめずらしかった Since he *knows but little of the world*, everything was splendid to him.

せこ【世故】worldly affairs; the world.

¶彼は～にたけた男だ He is a *worldly-wise* fellow. / He is a man *of the world*. 彼女は～にうとい She knows little of *the world*.

せこ【勢子】(狩猟の) a beater.

せじ【世事】worldly matters; the way of men. ¶彼はよく～に通じている He knows *the world* well. / He has seen much of *the world*. / He is rich in *worldly* wisdom.

セシウム 〖化学〗 cesium.

せし・める get; (人からだまし取る) cheat *a person* out of (money). ¶ 彼は母親を言いくるめてまんまとその金を〜めた He succeeded in *cheating* his mother *out of* the money.

せしゅう【世襲】 hereditary; patrimonial. ¶ 〜の財産 *hereditary* property. イギリスの女王は〜の君主である The queen of England is a *hereditary* ruler.

せじん【世人】 people; the world. ¶ 彼の新しい小説は〜の関心を引くにちがいない His new novel is sure to arouse *public* interest.

ゼスイット (人) a Jesuit.
—派 the Jesuits.

せすじ【背筋】 ¶ やみで女の悲鳴が聞こえたとき〜が寒くなった A cold shiver ran down my *spine* when I heard a woman scream in the dark. 〜がひどく痛む I have a sharp pain in my *back*.

ゼスチャー (身ぶり) a gesture; (ゲーム) charades (単数扱い). ¶ 彼の拒絶は単なる〜だ His refusal is merely *a gesture*.

ぜせい【是正】 ¶ 彼は国の悪弊をすべて〜すると約束した He promised to *put right* all the abuses in the country. そのような誤りは〜されねばならぬ Such a mistake must *be corrected*.

せせこまし・い ¶ 〜い部屋 a *poky little* room. 彼は〜い男(こせこせした男)だ He is a *fussy* fellow.

ぜぜひひ【是是非非】 ¶ 〜の態度を貫くべきだ We ought to stick to *the principle of being fair and just*.

せせらぎ【細流】 the murmur (*of* a stream); (小川) a small stream; a brook.

せせらわらい【せせら笑い】 a mocking laughter; a scornful smile. ¶ 彼の〜がしゃくにさわる His *scornful smile* makes me irritable.

せせらわら・う【せせら笑う】 ¶ 他人のまちがいを〜ってはいけない Don't *laugh* (≒ *jeer*) *at* the mistakes of others.

せそう【世相】 the world; social condition; aspects of life; the state of the world.
¶ 乱れた〜 wild *times*; *the* degenerated *world*. 現代〜の一面 an aspect of modern *life*. この事件の中に現代の〜がよく現われている This case sharply reflects the present *state of things*.

せぞく【世俗】 (風俗) the ways of life; manners and customs; (世間) the world.
¶ 彼は〜にとらわれるような人ではない He stands aloof from *the world*. 真の芸術家は〜にこびるようなことはしない A true artist will never try to curry favor with *the masses*. 死が近づくと人はだれでも〜的な事柄に興味を失う When a man is near death, he loses interest in *worldy affairs*.

せたい【世帯】 a household.
—主 the head of a household.

せだい【世代】 a generation. ¶ 若い〜の人々 the younger (≒ rising) *generation*. それは〜が違うためだ That's because we belong to the different *generation*.

—交番 〖生物学〗 alternation of generations.

せたけ【背丈】 ¶ ずいぶん〜が伸びましたね My, you've grown *tall*! 服の〜を詰めなければならない I have got to get the length of my coat shortened.

セダン a sedan 〔car〕.

せちがら・い【世知辛い】 ¶ まったく〜い世の中だ What a *tough* world we are in! / It's really *hard* to live nowadays. そんなに〜いことを言うなよ Be more generous. / Don't be so *mean* 〔*over* money matters〕.

せつ【節】 **1** 〖季節・時〗 a season; time; an occasion. ¶ この〜は雨が多い We have a lot of rain *these days*.
この辺にお立ち寄りの〜はお訪ねください Please drop in 〔at my house〕 *if you happen to* come this way.
お暇の〜はお遊びにおいでください Please come and see me *when* you are free.
その〜はお世話になりました I am grateful to you for your kindness *on that occasion*.
2 〖文章〗 a passage; a paragraph; a clause. ¶ 第1章第1〜を読みなさい Read Chapter I; *Paragraph* I.
この詩は四つの〜から成っている This poem consists of four *stanzas*.
この〜はいくつの文から成っていますか How many sentences are there in this *paragraph*?
3 〖節義〗 honor; fidelity. ¶ あの人はあくまでも〜を曲げない He remains true to his *principles* to the last.
彼は〜を守る人間だ He is true to his principles.

せつ【説】 (学説) a theory; (意見) an opinion. ¶ この〜には賛成できない I cannot approve of this *theory*. まったくお〜のとおりだ I quite agree with you. その問題についてはさまざまな〜がある There are various *opinions* about the matter. 彼は自分の〜を固守している He holds fast to his *views*. その〜を立てたのは世界的科学者だ It was a scientist of world-wide repute that built up the *theory*. その政治家の自殺〜が伝わっている There is *a rumor* that the statesman killed himself. あなたと私は〜を異にする You disagree with me in *opinion*.

せつえい【設営】 construction; (準備) arrangement. ¶ 中継基地を〜する *build* (≒ *construct*) a relay base.
—隊 a construction party.

ぜつえん【絶縁】 isolation; insulation.
¶ 彼は親類全部と〜した He *broke with* all his relatives. / He *had done with* all his relations. 電線をゴムで〜した They *insulated* wires by a covering of rubber.
—線 insulated wire. —体 an insulator. —テープ insulating tape. —抵抗 insulation resistance.

せっか【赤化】 Bolshevization. ¶ 彼は〜した He *turned red* (≒ *Red*).
—運動 a Red movement.

ぜっか【舌禍】 an unfortunate slip of the tongue. ¶ 文部大臣が〜事件を起こした The

Education Minister is severely criticized for what he said.

せっかい【切開】(外科的に) incision ; (手術) operation. ¶ 患部を～する *cut out* an affected part.

—手術 a surgical operation. ¶ 彼は胃の～手術を受けた He underwent *an operation* on his stomach.

せっかい【石灰】 lime. ¶ 畑に～をまく *lime* the field.

—岩 limestone. **—水** limewater. **—洞** a lime grotto. **—乳** milk of lime. **—肥料** calcium fertilizer. 消**—** slaked lime. 生**—** quick (≒ caustic) lime.

せつがい【雪害】 snow damage. ¶ 農作物は大きな～を被った The crops suffered serious *damage from snow*.

ぜっかい【絶海】 ¶ ～の孤島 a lonely island in *the distant sea*.

せっかく【折角】(苦心して) with much trouble ; (わざわざ) on purpose ; (親切に) kindly. ¶ ～の彼の努力が水のあわになった *After all his efforts* he failed. ～の休日が雨でだめになった The rain spoiled *the long-waited* holiday. ～のご招待ですが, あいにく先約がありますので行けません *I'm sorry*, but I can't accept your kind invitation because I have another appointment. ～彼に会いに行ったのに残念なことに彼は不在だった Though I went to see him *all the way*, he happened to be out to my great disappointment. 彼が～貸してくれた雨がさを電車の中に置き忘れてしまった I left the umbrella on the train that he *kindly* lent to me. ～手に入れた絵を盗まれてしまった I had the picture stolen that I got *with much effort*.

せっかち ¶ 彼は生まれつき～なたちだ He *is hasty-tempered*. / He *is hasty* by nature. ～に口をきいてはなりません Don't speak *hastily*.

せっかっしょく【赤褐色】 reddish brown ; russet ; auburn. ¶ ～の brownish red.

せつがんきょう【接眼鏡】 an eyepiece.

せっき【石器】 a stone implement.

—時代 the Stone Age. 新(旧)**—時代** the Neolithic (Paleolithic) Age.

せっき【赤旗】 a red flag.

せっきゃく【接客】 receiving guests ; service.

—係 a receptionist. **—業** a service trade.

せっきょう【説教】 a sermon ; (その行為) preaching. ¶ 毎日曜日教会に行って～を聞く Every Sunday we go to church to hear *a sermon*. 私に怠けるなといったお～はやめてくれ Don't *preach* me *a sermon* about being lazy.

ぜっきょう【絶叫】 a scream ; an exclamation. ¶ 彼は助けを求めて～した He *cried* (≒ *shouted*) *at the top of his voice* for help.

せっきょく【積極】 ¶ ～的 positive ; active. 彼は～的な人だ He is a man of *progressive* character. ただ否定的な批判をするのではなく, ひとつ～的に力を貸してください Don't just make a negative criticism, give us some *positive* help. 彼はその問題に対して～的な態度に出た He took up a *positive* attitude to the problem.

—策 ¶ ～策を採ることに決めた We decided to adopt *a positive policy*. **—性** positiveness. ¶ ～性のある positive.

せっきん【接近】(近づくこと) approach ; (近接) proximity ; (密接な関係) intimate relations. ¶ 台風が本土に～している A typhoon *is approaching* the main island of Japan. 日米の～を図ることがたいせつだ What is important is to attempt to establish *better relations* between Japan and America. 会議の期日がいよいよ～した The day of the conference *is drawing near*. 彼らは実力が～している They *are almost equal* in ability.

—戦(拳闘) infighting.

せっく【節句・節供】 a festival. ¶ ひなの～ the Doll's (≒ Girls') *Festival*. 端午の～ the Boys' *Festival*.

ぜっく【絶句】 ¶ ～する(役者がせりふを忘れる) forget *one's* lines. 彼は感きわまって～した He was so deeply moved that he *found no word to say*. / He was so deeply moved that he *didn't know what to say*.

セックス sex.

—アピール sex appeal. ¶ ～アピールのある女 a *sexy* woman ; a woman with a lot of *sex appeal*.

せっけい【設計】 a plan ; a design. ¶ 彼は自分の事務所を～した He made *a plan* for his own office. 彼は塔の～をあるデザイナーに依頼した He asked a designer to draw *a plan* for the tower. このビルは～がよい This building *is* well *planned*. 目下～中の機械は来月完成の予定だ The machine now under *design* is to be completed next month. この庭は彼の～によってつくられたものだ This garden *has been laid out* by him. この住宅はあまり～がよくない This house *is* not so well *planned*.

—者 a designer. **—書** specification. **—図** a plan. 生活**—** life planning.

せっけい【雪渓】 a snowy valley.

ぜっけい【絶景】 a grand view. ¶ この辺りの景色はまさに天下の～だ The scenery about here is unparalleled in the world. ～かな, ～かな. What a superb view this is!

せっけっきゅう【赤血球】〘生理〙 a red〔blood〕corpuscle.

—沈降速度 blood sedimentation rate. **—沈降速度検査** a sedimentation test.

せっけん【接見】 an interview ; a reception. ¶ 天皇が外国大使を～された The Emperor *received* the foreign ambassadors.

—室 a reception room. **—日** a reception day.

せっけん【石鹸】 soap. ¶ ～1個 a cake of *soap*. この～はあわ立ちがよい This *soap* lathers well. その汚れたシャツはよく～をつけて洗いなさい *Soap* the dirty shirt well. 手を～で洗いなさい *Soap* your hands. / Wash your hands with *soap* and water. ひげをそる前に～をぬる I *lather* my face before shaving.

—水 soapsuds. 化粧— toilet soap. 粉— soap powder. 洗たく— laundry soap. 薬用— medicated soap.

せっけん【席巻】¶～する overwhelm; carry everything before *one*; make conquest of.

せつげん【雪原】a snowfield.

せつげん【節減】reduction. ¶経費を～しなければならない We have to *cut down* (≒ *reduce*) expenses.

ゼッケン a player's number (ドイツ語の Zeichen から). ¶～10番の選手 a runner with No. 10.

せっこう【斥候】(人) a scout; (行為) scouting. ¶敵状偵察のために～を出した *Scouts* were sent out to get information about the enemy. 彼は～に出ている He is out *scouting*.
—隊 a reconnoitering party.

せっこう【石工】a stone cutter; a stone mason.

せっこう【拙攻】〔野球〕poor batting.

せっこう【石膏】plaster; 〔鉱物〕gypsum.
—像 a plaster statue. —模型 a plaster cast. 焼き— plaster of Paris.

せつごう【接合】union. ¶板を～する *fasten* the boards *together*.

ぜっこう【絶好】the best; ideal; perfect.
¶留学する～の機会だ This is *the best* chance for you to go abroad to study. ～の遠足日和だ This is an *ideal* day for〔going on〕a picnic. 彼の調子は今～調だ He *is in the best* condition now. / He *is in the pink* now.

ぜっこう【絶交】¶彼と～した I'*ve done with* him. / I'*m through with* him. 彼とは～するつもりだ I will *have nothing to do with* him.

せっこつ【接骨】bonesetting. ¶折れた腕を～してもらった I *had* my broken arm *set*.
—医 a bonesetter.

せっさ【切磋】¶彼は～琢磨(たくま)して人格をみがいた He *made great efforts* to train his mind. 彼は～琢磨して学問に励んだ He applied himself wholly and indefatigably to his studies.

せっさく【拙作】(まずい作品) a poor work; (自作の卑称) my〔humble〕work.

ぜっさん【絶賛】great admiration; high praise. ¶この映画は人々の～を博した This film *has won the highest praise* from the public.

せっし【摂氏】Celsius (Cels., C.).
¶きょうの温度は～20度だ The thermometer stands 20°C today. (20°C は twenty degrees centigrade と読む).
—寒暖計 a centigrade (≒ Celsius) thermometer.

せつじつ【切実】¶～に keenly; appositely; (心の底から) heartily; sincerely. ～な願い an *earnest* desire. 金の威力を～に感じた I *keenly* felt the power of money.

せっしやくわん【切歯扼腕】¶彼は計画が失敗したことを聞いて～してくやしがった He *ground his teeth with vexation* to hear that the plan had failed after all.

せっしゅ【接種】〔医学〕inoculation. ¶ワクチンを～する vaccinate; *inoculate a person with* a vaccine.
ツベルクリン— tuberculin inoculation.

せっしゅ【摂取】adoptation; intake. ¶外国の文化を～する *adopt* foreign cultures.

せっしゅ【節酒】temperance; moderation in drinking. ¶～する drink moderately.

せつじゅ【接受】¶無線電信を～する *pick up* a wireless message.

せっしゅう【接収】requisition. ¶建物を～する *take over* (≒ *requisition*) a building.

せつじょ【切除】〔医学〕resection. ¶～する cut off; rest.
肺葉—手術 pneumonectomy operation.

せっしょう【折衝】negotiation; a parley.
¶会社側は組合と～を重ねた The management continued *negotiations* with the labor union.

せっしょう【摂政】(人) a regent; (職) regency. ¶～をおく set up *regency*; appoint *a regent*.
—殿下 the Prince Regent.

せっしょう【殺生】destruction of life. ¶むやみに～するな Don't *kill animals* without reason. ～なことを言うな Never say such a *cruel* thing. / Don't be so *cruel* to me.
—戒 the Buddhist precept prohibiting killing.

ぜっしょう【絶唱】an excellent piece of poetry.

ぜっしょう【絶勝】the most beautiful scenery.

せつじょうしゃ【雪上車】a snowmobile.

せっしょく【接触】contact; touch; (衝突) collision. ¶彼は店で多くの人と～する He comes in *contact with* a variety of people in the store. 電線が塔のてっぺんに～している The electric wire *is touching* the top of the tower. あの電線に～すると危険だ It is dangerous to *touch* that wire over there. バスが自動車と～した A bus *hit* a car. 私の車はあやうく～事故を起こすところだった My car nearly *hit* another and there was almost an accident.

せっしょく【節食】¶～する eat moderately. 彼女は今～している She *is now on a diet*.

せつじょく【雪辱】vindication of *one's* honor. ¶彼はみごとに～を遂げた He succeeded in *removing his disgrace*.
—戦 a return match; a return game.

ぜっしょく【絶食】fasting. ¶私はきのう一日～した *Not* a morsel of food did I *take* for the whole of yesterday. / I *went without food* all yesterday.
—療法 a fast cure.

せっすい【節水】water saving. ¶干魃(かんばつ)のため～してください Please *save water* together for want of rain.

せっ·する【接する】(接触する) come into contact with; (隣り合う) touch; border on; (人に応対する) see *a person*; visit; (知らせを受け取る) receive; get.
¶彼の家は道路に～している His house *adjoins*

the road. この町は港に～している This town *borders on* the harbor. この一帯の荒れ地は湖に～している This stretch of waste land *borders on* the lake. Aの家とBの家は軒を～している A's house stands *side by side with* B's. この二つの円は～している These two circles *are tangent to* each other. 彼は一日にたくさんの来客と～する He *has* a lot of visitors every day. 吉報に～して私は少なからず喜んだ I was not a little delighted *at* the good news.

ぜっ·する【絶する】 ¶ 言語に～する苦しみを味わった I went through *unspeakable* hardships. / I tasted the bitterness *beyond words* (≒ *beyond description*). その作品は古今に～する名作だ The work has *no equal* in any age. その美しさは想像を～している The beauty is *beyond* all imagination.

せっせい【摂生】 care of health. ¶ ～につとめなさい Be *careful about your health*.
—家 a person careful about *one's* health.

せっせい【節制】 moderation. ¶ ～が第一だ Above all things, you must *be temperate*. 欲望は～すべきだ You should *control* your passions.

ぜっせい【絶世】 ¶ ～の美女 a woman of *peerless* beauty.

せつせつ【切切】 ¶ ～たる願い *one's earnest* (≒ *eager*) desire. 彼のことばは～とわれわれの胸に迫った His words produced a *deep* impression on us. / His speech appealed *profoundly* to our heart.

せっせと ¶ 彼は毎日～働いている He works *hard* every day. 彼は自動車教習所に～通っている He attends the drivers' school *frequently* (≒ *regularly*).

せっせん【接線】〔数学〕a tangent [line].

せっせん【接戦】 a close game (≒ fight). ¶ ～の末,やっと勝った After *the close game*, we won a victory by a slim margin. / *The close game* resulted in a final victory for our team.

ぜっせん【舌戦】 a verbal warfare. ¶ 両候補はテレビで～を交えた Both the candidates engaged in *a verbal contest* through television.

せっそう【節操】 constancy. ¶ 人は～を守ることが大事だ It is very important for us to keep our *principles*. / (女性が) It is essential for women to keep their *chastity*. 彼は～のない人だ He is an *unprincipled* (≒ *unfaithful*) man. 彼女は～のない女だ She has no *constancy* in love.

せっそく【拙速】 ¶ 兵は巧遅より～を尊ぶ "*Rough and ready in action*" is valued above "being slow and prudent" among the soldiers.
—主義 a rough-and-ready method.

せつぞく【接続】 connection. ¶ 山陽線は神戸で東海道線に～する The Sanyo line *connects with* the Tokaido line at Kobe. この列車は新大阪駅で「ひかり２号」に～する This train *connects with* "Hikari No. 2" at Shin-Osaka Station. この島は長い橋で本土に～している This island *is joined to* the mainland *with* a long bridge.
—駅 a junction. —詞〔文法〕a conjunction.

せっそくどうぶつ【節足動物】〔動物〕an arthropod ; (総称) the *Arthropoda*.

せったい【接待】 reception. ¶ 彼は昨晩客を10人も～した He *received* ten guests last evening. あの店ではお茶を～してくれる They *serve* tea *free* at that shop.
—係 a reception committee.

ぜったい【絶体】 ¶ 彼は～絶命のピンチに追い込まれた He was driven *to the last extremity* (≒ *to his wit's end*).

ぜったい【絶対】 absolutely. ¶ ～そんなことはない Such a thing *never* occurs. ～まちがいない It is *decidedly* correct. 彼の案には～反対だ I am *positively* against his plan. そんなばかなことは～にしないつもりだ I *won't* do such a silly thing. 彼は～に盗みはしていないと言う He *swears by God* that he has never committed theft. 彼はやると言ったことは～やる人だ He *is sure to* do what he says he will do. 彼の言うことには～従うべきだ You *ought to* obey what he says before everything else. ～に酒はやめたと彼は言っている He says he *has sworn off* drinking. 彼は医者から～安静を要すると言われている His doctor says that he must be kept *absolutely* quiet.
—温度 absolute temperature. —多数 an absolute majority. —値 the absolute value. —量 the absolute quantity.

ぜつだい【絶大】 ¶ ～なご支援をお願いします Please give us your *generous* support. ～なるご声援を感謝します A thousand thanks for your *sincere* encouragement. / I have no words to thank for your *enthusiastic* cheers.

せつだん【切断】 amputation ; cutting. ¶ 彼は右足を～した He *had* his right leg *amputated*.

ぜったん【舌端】 ¶ その討論会では～火を吐く論戦が繰り広げられた Very heated arguments were made at the debate.

せっち【設置】 creation. ¶ 組織委員会が～された An organizing committee *was set up* (≒ *was formed*). 本校は1900年に～された Our school *was established* (≒ *was founded*) in 1900.

せっちゃく【接着】 ¶ にかわで板を～する *glue* boards ; *fasten* boards with glue.
—剤 an adhesive agent.

せっちゅう【折衷】 a compromise. ¶ そのふたつの案を～してはどうか How about *making a compromise between* those two plans? / What about *blending* both plans?
—主義 eclecticism. 和洋— ¶ 和洋～の家 a house *in semi-foreign style*.

ぜっちょう【絶頂】 (山頂) the top ; (頂点) the peak ; the height. ¶ ついに彼らはエベレスト山の～をきわめた At last they reached *the summit* of Mt. Everest. そのとき彼は喜びの～に達した At that time, he was thrown into *an ecstasy* of delight. / He was then at *the climax* of happiness. 彼女は今人気の～にある She is now at *the peak* of her popularity. / Her popularity now attains its *zenith*.

せっちん【雪隠】(便所) a lavatory.

―詰め〘将棋〙¶王将は～詰めになった The king *was cornered*. / The king *was driven into one of the corners*.

せってい【設定】establishment. ¶祝日をもうひとつ～することになった It was decided to *establish* (≒ *institute*) another public holiday.

せってん【接点】〘数学〙a point of contact.

せつでん【節電】power-saving. ¶～する save electricity; economize 〔in〕 electricity.

セット **1**〚ひと揃い〛a set. ¶コーヒーの～ *a* coffee *set*.

2〚毛髪の〛¶彼女はきれいに髪を～した She had *a* beautiful wave *set* on her hair. / She *had* her hair *set* beautifully.

3〚テニス・野球〛¶テニスを1～やる play *a set* of tennis.

―オール〘テニス〙set all. **―ポイント**〘球技〙set point. **―ポジション**〘野球〙set position.

4〚映画・演劇〛a set.

オープン― 〘映画〙an open set.

せつど【節度】moderation. ¶～を守ってほしい I want you to *be moderate*. / I hope you will *obey orders*. ～ある行ないが望まれる It is desirable to *act on the rule*.

せっとう【窃盗】theft.

―罪 〔a〕 larceny.

せっとうじ【接頭辞】〘文法〙a prefix.

ゼットき【Z旗】¶～を掲げる raise (≒ hoist) *the battle flag*.

せっとく【説得】persuasion. ¶両親を～して上京した I came 〔up〕 to Tokyo after having obtained my parents' consent by *persuasion*. 数度の～も功を奏さなかった My repeated *dissuasion* couldn't alter his resolution. ～力のない文章だ This sentence has no *persuasive* power. / This is no *convincing* sentence.

せつな【刹那】¶衝突した～気を失った *The instant* (≒ *The minute*) my car crashed into another, I fainted. (the instant (≒ the minute) は接続詞的用法). 彼らは～的享楽にふけっている They indulge in *momentary* pleasures.

―主義 impulsiveness.

せつな・い【切ない】¶こんなに～い思いをしたことはない I never felt *distressed* so much before. ～い胸のうちを打ち明けた(悲しみ) I confessed my *heart-rending* sorrow. / (恋心) I confessed my *ardent* love.

せつなる【切なる】¶～願い *one's earnest* (≒ *fervent*) desire.

せつに【切に】¶～皆さんのご協力をお願いします I *sincerely* (≒ *ardently*) hope for your help.

せっぱく【切迫】pressure; urgency. ¶時間が～している The time *presses*. 事態が～している The situation *is acute* (≒ *is urgent*). 会場は～した空気に包まれた There was a *tense* atmosphere in the hall.

せっぱつま・る【切羽詰まる】¶彼は～って盗みを働いた He stole *under the pressure of necessity*.

せっぱん【折半】¶利益を～する *halve* the profit. 費用を～する *share* expenses (*with a person*); *go halves* (≒ *go fifty-fifty*) on expenses.

ぜっぱん【絶版】¶この本は～だ This book *is out of print*.

せつび【設備】equipment. ¶まず～を整えねばならない First of all we must complete the *arrangements*. 医務室を～すべきだ We should *equip* (≒ *fit*) *with* the medical office. 寮には運動のための～がある There are athletic *facilities* in the dormitory.

―投資 equipment investment. **―費**(資金) the cost of equipment; equipment fund.

防火― fire-prevention devices.

せつびじ【接尾辞】〘文法〙a suffix.

ぜっぴつ【絶筆】*one's* last writing. ¶これが氏の～となった This was the last article before his death.

ぜっぴん【絶品】an unrivaled article; a rarity.

せっぷく【切腹】¶～する commit *hara-kiri*.

せつぶん【節分】the parting of the seasons; (特に) the day before the beginning of spring.

せっぷん【接吻】kiss.

ぜっぺき【絶壁】a precipice; a cliff.

せつぼう【切望】an earnest desire. ¶ファンは彼の出場を～している Fans *earnestly desire* (≒ *long for*) his playing in the game. 彼は上京を～している He *is anxious* (≒ *is eager*) *to* go to Tokyo.

せっぽう【説法】¶それは釈迦(しゃか)に～だ(諺) *It's to carry coals to Newcastle*. / *It's like teaching your grandmother how to suck eggs*.

ぜつぼう【絶望】despair. ¶～して in despair. 人生に～してしまった I *have given up* my life. 病人はもう～だ The patient is *hopeless* of recovery. 彼は今～のどん底にいる He is now in the depth of *despair*. / He is thrown into utter *despair*. 情勢は～的である The situation is *hopeless*.

ぜつみょう【絶妙】¶～のコントロール a *miraculously nice* control.

ぜつむ【絶無】¶誤りが～とはいえない We cannot be sure to say that it is *free from* errors.

せつめい【説明】explanation. ¶彼の～はわかりやすかった His *explanation* was easy to understand. この原理をもう一度～してください Please *explain* this principle once again. これは図で～したほうがわかりやすい It would be better to *explain* this with a picture. ～は簡単にしてほしい I want your *explanation* to be brief and simple. この事情は理屈では～できない It is impossible to *reason out* this state of affairs. これはとても～できません This is

せ

unaccountable. その原因は〜を要する The cause needs *explanation*.
—者 an explainer. —書 an explanatory note.

ぜつめつ【絶滅】 extermination. ¶ 交通事故を〜しよう Let's try to *root* (≒ *wipe*) *out* traffic accidents. 害虫は〜した Harmful insects *died out* (≒ *became extinct*).

せつもう【雪盲】〔医学〕snow blindness.

せつもん【設問】 a question.

せつやく【節約】 economy. ¶ 費用を〜する *cut down* expenses. 経費の〜が必要だ *Economy* in expenditure is necessary. / We need *save* expenses.

せつゆ【説諭】 admonition. ¶ 警官は少年を〜して帰した The policeman released the boy *on reprimand*.

せつり【摂理】 Providence. ¶ 神の〜 the divine Providence; the Providence of God.

せつりつ【設立】 establishment. ¶ 彼がその会社を〜した He *established* (≒ *founded*) the company.
—者 a founder. —手続き formalities of incorporation. —費 organization expenses.

ぜつりん【絶倫】 ¶ 精力〜の男 a man of *unequaled* (≒ *unbounded*) energy.

せつれつ【拙劣】 ¶ 〜な演技 a *poor* (≒ *clumsy*) performance.

せつわ【説話】 a tale.
—体 narrative form. ¶ 〜体の小説 a novel written in *narrative* form. —文学 narrative (≒ legendary) literature.

せと【瀬戸】 a channel.
—内海 the Inland Sea [of Japan]. —引き enameled ware. —物 china; earthenware; porcelain; pottery; crockery.

せとぎわ【瀬戸際】 a critical (≒ crucial) moment; a crisis.

せなか【背中】 the back. ¶ 彼はわれわれに〜を向けた He turned his *back* to (≒ on) us. 彼と〜合わせに座った I sat *back to back with* him.

ぜにがめ【銭亀】 a spotted turtle; a little Japanese terrapin.

ぜにん【是認】 approval; recognition.
¶ 当局は彼の申し立てを〜した They *approved of* his declaration. / The authorities *admitted* his statement to be true. それは〜すべき事柄だ It is an *admissible* (≒ *allowable*) matter.

せぬき【背抜き】 ¶ 〜の服 an *open-backed* suit. 〜の上着 a coat with *unlined back*.

ゼネスト（ゼネラル ストライキ）a general strike.

せのび【背伸び】 ¶ 〜してやっとたなの上の本がとれた I was barely able to take down a book from the shelf by *standing on tiptoe*. 彼は〜して人とつきあう He pretends to be better than he really is.

せばま・る【狭まる】 get narrow. ¶ 道は急に〜って自動車は通れなくなった Suddenly the road *became* too *narrow* for cars to pass. 男女の賃銀の開きは〜る傾向にある The disparity in the wage level between man and woman tends to *be small*.

せば・める【狭める】 limit; narrow. ¶ 活動範囲を〜める *make one's* sphere of activity *small*.

セパレーツ〔服飾〕separates.

せばんごう【背番号】〔野球〕a uniform number.

ぜひ【是非】 **1**〖よしあし〗¶ きみは物事の〜を知っていてよい年ごろだ You are old enough to be able to tell *right* from *wrong*.
この方法の〜は簡単には決められない We cannot tell at once whether this method is *right or wrong*.
男女共学の〜について話し合った We talked about the *propriety* of coeducation.
2〖かならず〗¶ ことしは〜北海道へ行きたい I will go to Hokkaido this year *by all means*.
彼は〜富士山に登りたいと言っている He says he *is eager to* climb Mt. Fuji.
〜一度お訪ねください *Do* come and see me some day.
〜と言うならやりましょう I will try if you *insist upon* my doing so.
この小説を〜読みたまえ *Be sure to* read this novel.
3〖しかたない〗¶ 残念ながら失敗したが，〜もないことだった I failed to my regret, but *there was no help for it*.

せひょう【世評】 reputation; rumor.
¶ 彼は〜ほど正直者ではない He is not so honest *as they say*. 〜など気にかけはしない I don't care *what people say of* me.

せび・る ¶ 人に小づかいを〜る *tease a person for* pocket money.

せびろ【背広】〔米〕a business suit; 〔英〕a lounge suit.

せぶみ【瀬踏み】 ¶ 相手の出方を〜する *fly a trial balloon* to see what the other party will make.

せぼね【背骨】〔解剖学〕the spinal column; the spine.

せま・い【狭い】 narrow; (限られた) limited.
¶ この道は〜くてタクシーは通れない This lane *is* too *narrow* for a taxi to pass. あのあき地は野球をするには〜すぎる The vacant lot *is* too *small* to play baseball. 彼は了見が〜い He is a *narrow-minded* person. 彼女は視野が〜い She *is narrow* in opinion. 彼の科学についての知識はわりあい〜い His knowledge about science *is* rather *limited*. 彼は交際が〜い He has a *small* (≒ *narrow*) circle of acquaintances. 世間は広いようで〜いもんだ It's a *small* world after all.

せまくるし・い【狭苦しい】 ¶ 〜い家 a *narrow and close* house.

せま・る【迫る】 **1**〖近づく〗approach. ¶ 時間が刻々〜っていた Time *was pressing* little by little.
日没が〜っていた Sunset *was drawing near*.
谷間には夕やみが〜っている The evening dusk *is gathering* upon the valley.

彼には死が〜っていた He *was on the verge of* death.

2 〚しいる〛 force ; push on. ¶ 彼は必要に〜られて盗みを働いた He committed a theft *under the pressure of necessity*.

彼は自白を〜られたが, 断じて自白しなかった He *was pressed for* a confession, but he never confessed.

首相は辞職を〜られた The prime minister *was urged to* resign.

彼はあくまで私に釈明を〜った He *pressed* me *for* vindication obstinately.

せみ【蟬】〔虫類〕 a cicada ; 困 a locust. ¶ 〜が盛んに鳴いている A lot of *cicadas* are chirping noisily.

セミ- **—**ドキュメンタリー〔映画〕 a semidocumentary. **—**ファイナル(準決勝) semifinals. **—**プロ〔の〕 semiprofessional ; (口語) semipro.

せみしぐれ【蟬時雨】 ¶ 〜を聞きながら歩いた I walked among *the noisy chirps of numerous cicadas*.

ゼミナール a seminar.

せめ【責め】 responsibility. ¶ その〜は私にある I *am responsible for* it. 私が彼の失敗の〜を負う I *am responisble for* his failure.

せめい・る【攻め入る】 ¶ ついに1941年ナチスはソ連に〜った At last in 1941 the Nazis forces *invaded* the Soviet Union.

せめおと・す【攻め落とす】 ¶ 要塞(ようさい)を〜す *take* a fortress.

せめく【責め苦】 ¶ 地獄の〜を受ける be greatly tortured.

せめさいな・む【責め苛む】 ¶ 罪の意識に〜まれている I *am tortured* by the consciousness of my guilt.

せめて at most ; at least. ¶ 〜自分の部屋のあとかたづけくらいしなければだめだ You ought to get your room straightened *at least*. 〜500円ならこの本ももっと売れ行きがよいだろうに This book would sell better if the price were (≒ was) five hundred yen *at most*.

せめどうぐ【責め道具】 an instrument of torture.

せ・める【責める】 blame ; reproach. ¶ 彼女は夫の失敗を〜めた She *blamed* her husband *for* his failure. 彼は借金取りに〜められている He *is harassed* by creditors.

せ・める【攻める】 attack ; assault. ¶ 外国を〜める *attack* a foreign country.

セメント cement. ¶ 床に〜を塗る *cement* a floor. 石を〜で固めて石垣を作る *cement* stones to form a wall.

ゼラチン gelatin〔e〕. ¶ 〜状の gelatinous.

せり【芹】〔植物〕 a *seri* (近似語は parsley).

せり【競り】 auction. ¶ その絵は〜に出された The picture was put up at *auction*. それは〜で売られた It was sold by *auction*.

せりあい【競り合い】 ¶ この選挙ではA, B 2氏の激しい〜となった In this election there was *a* hot (≒ keen) *competition* between Mr. A and Mr. B. ゴール寸前でふたりの〜となった The two *competed with* each other *for* the first prize just before the goal.

せりあ・げる【競り上げる】 bid up. ¶ 収集家たちはその絵の値段を300万円にまで〜げた The collectors *bade up* the price of the picture till it reached three million yen.

ゼリー jelly ; (菓子) a jelly. ¶ 〜状になる(する) jelly.

せりうり【競り売り】 ¶ 〜する sell at auction.

せりおと・す【競り落とす】 ¶ その絵は50万円なら〜せると思った I expected to be able to *get* the picture *at the auction* for five hundred thousand yen.

せりふ【台詞・科白】 lines ; words. ¶ 彼女は〜をとちった She bungled in her *lines*. あの女優は〜がうまい The actress speaks her *lines* well. きみの〜は聞き飽きた We are weary of listening to your *words*.

セル serge.

セルフサービス self-service. ¶ 〜の食堂 困 a cafeteria ; a *self-service* restaurant.

セルフタイマー〔写真〕 a self-timer.

セルロイド〔化学〕 celluloid.

セレナーデ〔音楽〕 a serenade.

セロ〔音楽〕 a cello.

ゼロ【零】〔a〕zero. ¶ 彼の答案には〜をつけた I put *a zero* on his paper. 彼はその試験でまた〜をもらった He was given *a zero* again in the exam. 3対〜で負けた We were defeated by 3 to 0. 彼は正義感が〜だ His sense of justice *is at zero*. 彼女は母親としては〜だ She is a complete failure as a mother.

—敗〔野球〕 a shutout. **—**メートル地帯 an area zero-meter above sea level.

セロハン cellophane.

セロリー〔植物〕 celery.

せろん【世論】 public opinion. ¶ 〜に訴える appeal to *public opinion*. マスコミがしばしば〜を形成したり左右したりする Mass communication often forms and influences *public opinion*. 〜を喚起する arouse *public opinion*. 〜に耳を傾ける listen to *public opinion*.

—調査 a public opinion poll (≒ survey).

せわ【世話】 **1** 〚手数・やっかい・めんどう〛 trouble ; help ; assistance.

¶ 彼は〜の焼けるやつだ What *a nuisance* he is! / What a *troublesome* man! (口語では「主語＋動詞」は省くのがふつう).

あの子はあまり〜が焼けない That boy is easy to *look after*. / The boy gives little *trouble*.

こんなことできみに〜をかけたくはない I don't want to *trouble* you about a thing like this.

ぼくが困っていたときあの人にはずいぶんとお〜になった He *helped* me a lot when I was in trouble.

いまおじの家に〜になっている I am now staying at my uncle's house (≒ with my uncle).

在京中はひとかたならぬお〜になり感謝しております I am deeply grateful to you for the kindness you showed me during my stay in Tokyo. (あらたまった言い方. 口語体なら Thank you for everything you did ...とする).

さんざっぱら人様の〜になっておきながら, なんていう言いぐさだ After all I've done for you, you

せ

have the cheek to say that!
病人の～をする人がだれも見つからない I can't find anybody to *look after* the patient.
うちの子どもたちは犬の～をするのが好きだ My children like *taking care of* dogs.
赤ん坊の～で忙しく，出席できません I can't attend because I am so busy *looking after* my baby.
大学まで出て，まだ親の～になっているのか You have graduated from college, so it is time you stood on your own feet.
2〖周旋〗kind offices. ¶お嫁さんの～をしようか Shall I find you a wife?
だれかいい人を～してくれないか Will you find me a suitable man?
だれの～でここに勤めるようになったのか Who recommended you to this firm? / Who helped you to find employment here?
3〖おせっかい〗¶大きなお～だ That's none of your business. / Mind your own business.
いらぬ～は焼かないでくれ Don't poke your nose into my affairs. / Don't meddle in my affairs.
4〖合成語〗 **―**好き an obliging person. **―**女房 a good wife; a devoted wife. **―**人 a sponsor. **―**焼き a busybody. **―**役 a sponsor.

せわし・い【忙しい】busy.

せわしな・い【忙しない】restless. ¶彼はなんとも～い人だ He is quite a *restless* person.

せん【千】a thousand. ¶2～ two *thousand*. ～分の1 a (≒ one) *thousandth*. 幾～という人々 *thousands of* people.

せん【先】¶こちらから切り出そうとしたのだが，相手に～を越されてしまった I was going to speak about the subject, but he *was beforehand with* me. (やや文語体なら but を when にする).

せん【線】**1**〖一筋のもの〗a line. ¶まっすぐな～を引く draw *a* straight *line*.
彼女の絵の～の美しさは定評がある The beauty of *lines* in her paintings is proverbial.
この～の電車はいつも込む The trains on this *line* are always crowded.
上り**―** the up line. 下り**―** the down line. 三番**―** the track three. 上越**―** the Joetsu Line. 国内**―** the internal line. ローカル**―** a local line.
2〖方針〗¶この計画の～にそって仕事を進めてください Please proceed with the work *in line with* this plan.
3〖神経〗¶太っ腹に見えてけっこう～の細いところもある Indeed he looks daring, but in reality he *is delicate*.

せん【選】selection. ¶彼の作品は～に漏れた His work was left out of *selection*.

せん【栓】a stopper. ¶びんにコルクの～をする *cork up* (≒ *put a cork in*) a bottle. ガスの～をしめる(あける) turn off (on) the gas.

せん【腺】a gland.

ぜん【善】goodness. ¶～をなす do *good*. ～と悪とを見分ける distinguish (≒ tell) *right* from wrong. ～は急げ Never hesitate in doing what is *good*.

ぜん【禅】〔宗教〕*Zen*. ¶～をする practice *Zen*. **―**宗 the *Zen* sect. **―**寺 a *Zen* temple.

ぜん【膳】a table; (食事) a meal. ¶はし1～ a pair of chopsticks. 御飯1～ a bowl of rice. ～につく sit at *table*. ～をそろえる lay (≒ set) the *table*.

ぜん-【前-】¶～代議士 an *ex*-member of the Diet. ～カント派 *Pre*-Kantian philosophers. ～近代的な not modern; old-fashioned; *pre*-modern.

-ぜん【-然】¶彼はいかにも学者～としている He is just *like* a scholar.

ぜんあく【善悪】good and bad; right and wrong. ¶～をわきまえるべきだ You should know *good* from *evil*.

せんい【船医】a ship doctor.

せんい【戦意】a fighting spirit. ¶彼らは依然として～を示した They still showed *fight*. ～を失った We lost our *fighting spirit*.
―高揚(喪失) elation (loss) of fight.

せんい【繊維】a fiber; 英 a fibre.
―産業 the textile (≒ fiber) industry. **―**素〖生理〗fibrin; 〖化学〗cellulose. 化学**―** chemical fiber. 合成**―** [an] artificial (≒ synthetic) fiber.

ぜんい【善意】good will. ¶～でやったのだ I did it *in good faith*. 彼のことばを～に解釈しよう Let's take his words *in a favorable sense*.

ぜんいき【全域】¶都内～にわたって台風の被害を受けた The *whole* city of Tokyo has suffered from the typhoon. ルネッサンスは文化～にわたる改革運動であった Renaissance was a reformation movement in *all the fields of* culture.

せんいつ【専一】¶どうぞご自愛～に Please take good care of yourself. (手紙文では病人あて以外には書かない).

せんいん【船員】(総称) the crew; (ひとり) a sailor. ¶その船は～わずか10名であった The ship had *a crew* of only ten men. 彼は捕鯨船の～だった He was one of the *crew* of a whaling ship.
高級**―**(総称) the quarterdeck; (ひとり) a ship's officer.

ぜんいん【全員】all the members. ¶クラス～でその問題を話し合った All the class discussed the problem. 彼らは～一致で提案に賛成した They *unanimously* approved [of] the proposal.

せんえい【先鋭・尖鋭】¶近年学生の思想は～化している Recently students have become *radical* in their ideas.
―分子 a radical. ¶これは～分子の仕業だ This is the doing of *radicals*.

ぜんえい【前衛】(軟式テニスなどの) a forward player; (サッカーなどの) a forward.
―芸術 avant-garde art. **―**派 the avant-garde.

せんえつ【僭越】audacity. ¶～ですが，私が提案します Allow me to make a proposal. ～ながら一言いわせてもらえば，あなたの計画は実際にはできない話です If I *may be so bold as* to make a comment upon your plan, it is not practicable. ～ながら皆のためを思うからこう言うのだ I *made bold to* say this in the interest of all of us. ～にも彼は主賓の席についた He *was audacious to* sit at the head of the table.

せんおう【専横】¶彼は部下にはしばしば～なふるまいをする He often *tyrannizes over* his subordinates. そんなことを独断で決めるとは～だ It *is despotic* of him to make such a decision without consulting us.

せんおん【顫音】〘音楽〙a trill.

ぜんおん【全音】〘音楽〙a whole note.
—音階 the whole-note scale; the whole gamut.

せんか【専科】a special course.
—生 a special course student.

せんか【戦火】¶～がヨーロッパじゅうに広がった *The war* has spread all over Europe.

せんか【戦果】war result. ¶この戦闘でわれわれは多大の～を収めた We have achieved great *results* in the battle. これがきょうの～だ(比喩的) This is *the result* gained today.

せんか【戦禍】war damage. ¶住民は多大の～を被った The inhabitants suffered a lot of *war-damage*.

せんか【選科】(選択科目) an elective course.
—生 an elective student.

せんが【線画】line drawing.

ぜんか【前科】a criminal record. ¶彼には～がある He has *a criminal record*. 彼は～数犯だ He has been convicted several times. ～5犯の人 a man with five *previous convictions*.
—者 an ex-convict.

せんかい【旋回】turning; revolution. ¶艦は急に右～をした The ship suddenly *made a* right *turn*. 飛行機が空港の上を～している An airplane *is circling* over the airport.
—軸 a pivot. —飛行 a circling flight.

せんがい【選外】¶彼の詩は～となった His poem *was not accepted* (≒ *was rejected*).
—佳作 a good work left out of selection. ¶彼女の応募作品は～佳作となった Her entry in the competition won her *an honorable mention*.

ぜんかい【全会】¶彼は～一致で選ばれた He was elected *by a unanimous vote*.

ぜんかい【全快】¶もう～した I*'ve got quite well* now. まだ～には至っていない I *haven't* yet *completely recovered* [from illness]. その病気は～することはありえない The disease cannot *be completely cured*. 一日も早く～されるよう祈っております I do hope you will soon *get well* (≒ *be restored to health*).

ぜんかい【全壊】¶地震で彼の家は～した His house *was completely destroyed* by the earthquake.

ぜんかい【前回】the last time. ¶～までの粗筋 an outline of the story *up to the last instalment*. ～と比べて参加者が多い The number of the participants is larger than that of *the last time*.

せんがく【浅学】shallow knowledge.
¶～非才をも顧みず大役を引き受けた I have accepted the important role in spite of my *lack of knowledge and ability*.

ぜんがく【全額】the total amount. ¶その費用～を会社が負担する *The whole expenses* will be charged to the company. 彼は私に～を払いもどした He refunded *the whole amount* back to me. 土地代金～の払い込み完了 The money for the purchase of the estate has been paid *in full*. この株は～払い込み済みだ The stocks are *fully* paid up.

せんかくしゃ【先覚者】a pioneer. ¶この道の～ *a pioneer* in this field.

ぜんかてい【全課程】the whole course.
¶高等学校の～を終える finish *the* high *school course*.

ぜんかもく【全科目】¶～合格した I passed in *all subjects*. ～を修める必要がある It is necessary to complete *the whole course*.

せんかん【戦艦】a battleship.

せんかん【潜函】caisson.
—工法 the caisson manufacturing. —式建築法 the caisson method. —病 the caisson disease.

ぜんかん【全巻】¶百科事典を～まとめて買った I bought *the whole volumes* of the encyclopedia at once. ～を通じて彼の主張がはっきり出ている His position is clearly stated *throughout the whole book*.

せんき【戦記】a record of war; a war chronicle.

せんき【戦機】the time for fighting. ¶～が熟した The time has matured (≒ Now is the time) for opening hostilities.

せんぎ【詮議】¶いらぬ～だてをするな Don't poke your nose into our business. 彼らはくだらぬ～に時間をつぶした They *deliberated over* the matter idly for hours.

ぜんき【前記】¶～の全額 the *said* sum; the sum *mentioned above*. ～の件 the *above-mentioned* matter. 私あての手紙は～の所にご回送ください Please forward my letters to the *above* address.

ぜんき【前期】(1年2期制の学校で) the first semester (イギリスの学校では3期制が多く term を用いる); (上半期) the first half year.
¶.～からどれだけ繰り越しがあるのか How much is the sum brought over from *the preceding term*?

せんぎけん【先議権】¶予算の～は衆議院にある The House of Commons has the right to *prior deliberation* on a budget bill.

せんきゃく【先客】¶～がいたのでしばらく待っていた I waited for some time, because there was already a visitor before me.

せんきゃく【船客】a passenger.
1等— a first-class passenger; a cabin passenger. 3等— a third-class passenger.
—名簿 a passenger list.

せんきゃくばんらい【千客万来】¶けさから～だ

There has been a constant flow of visitors to my house since this morning.

せんきゅうがん【選球眼】 ¶彼はよい～を持っている He has *a* sharp *batting eye*.

せんきょ【占拠】 occupation. ¶彼らは事務所を不法～した They *took possession of* the office illegally.

せんきょ【選挙】 election. ¶～は先月20日に行なわれた The *election* took place on the 20th of last month. 彼は～に勝った He won the *election*. 彼は～に負けた He was defeated in the *election*. 彼は議長に～された He *was elected* chairman. 彼が～に打って出た He has run for *an election*.

—違反 election irregularities. **—運動** an election campaign. **—運動員** an election campaigner. **—演説** a campaign speech. **—管理委員** election judges. **—区** an election district. **—権** suffrage. **—公報** an election bulletin. **—事務所** an election office. **—人** an elector. **—人名簿** a poll-book. **—法** election law. **—法違反** violation of the election laws. **総—** a general election. **補欠—** a by-election.

せんぎょ【鮮魚】 fresh fish.

せんきょう【宣教】 missionary work.
—師 a missionary.

せんきょう【船橋】 a bridge.

せんきょう【戦況】 the war situation. ¶～はどうか How is the battle going on? ～はわれわれに不利であった The battle was not going in our favor.

せんぎょう【専業】 the speciality. ¶あの家は養蚕を～にしている The family *is specializing in* sericulture. ～農家 a full-time farmer.

せんきょく【戦局】 the tide of war. ¶～が悪化した *The tide of war* has turned against us. ～は味方に有利に展開している *The war* is going in our favor.

せんぎり【千切り】 ¶ダイコンの～ radish *chips*. ダイコンを～にする *chip* a radish.

せんきん【千金】 ¶春宵一刻値～ Every hour of a spring evening is worth *a thousand pieces of gold*. 一刻～(諺) *Time is money*. これは～に値する This *is priceless*.

せんきん【千鈞】 ¶彼のそのことばは～の重みがある This remark of his has *great weight* with us.

せんく【先駆】 ¶近代詩の～ *a forerunner* of modern poetry. ～のパトカー a police *pilot* car. 彼は業界の～者だ He is *a pioneer* in this field of business.

せんぐ【船具】 ship fittings; (船索の総称) rigging.

ぜんく【前駆】 **—症状**〖医学〗a premonitory symptom; a prodrome.

せんくち【先口】 ¶あすは～の約束がある We have a *previous* engagement tomorrow.

ぜんぐん【全軍】 (軍隊) the whole army; (スポーツ) the whole team.

せんぐんばんば【千軍万馬】 ¶彼は～の古つわものだ He is *an old campaigner*. / He is *a real veteran*.

ぜんけい【全景】 the whole view. ¶機上から東京の～を見た We saw *the whole view* of Tokyo from a plane. そこから町の～が見られる The place commands *the whole view* of the town.

ぜんけい【前景】 the foreground.

ぜんけい【前掲】 ¶～の論文 the article *mentioned above*.

せんけつ【先決】 ¶こっちが～問題だ This must *be settled first*. / This must *be decided before anything else*. まずやるかやらぬかが～だ Whether we really want to do it or not is *the first consideration*.

せんけつ【鮮血】 fresh blood. ¶シャツは～に染まった The shirt was stained with *blood*. (鮮血は文字どおりに訳せば fresh blood であるが, 体質を変える新しい血の意味でなければわざわざ fresh をつけない).

せんげつ【先月】 last month. ¶その記事は～号に載った The report of the event appeared in *the last month's* issue. ～3日は彼の誕生日だった The third of *last month* was his birthday.

せんけん【先見】 foresight. ¶彼には～の明があった He was *far-sighted*. / He was a man of *foresight*. 彼には～の明がない He is lacking in *foresight*.

せんげん【宣言】 declaration. ¶議長は開会を～した The chairman *announced* the meeting open. 大統領は国の独立を～した The President *declared* independence of the country.

—書 a declaration; a statement. **共産党—** the Communist Manifesto. **独立—** the declaration of independence. **ポツダム—** the Potsdam Declaration. **爆弾—** ¶それは爆弾～だった The *announcement* was a bombshell.

ぜんけん【全県】 ¶台風の被害は～に及んだ The typhoon did considerable damage to *the whole prefecture*.

ぜんけん【全権】 ¶そのことについてわれわれは彼に～を委任します We will invest him with *full powers* to deal with this matter. きみに～を任す I will leave the *whole business* in your hands.

—大使 an ambassador plenipotentiary. **特命—大使** an ambassador extraordinary and plenipotentiary.

ぜんげん【前言】 *one's* previous remarks. ¶～を取り消すつもりですか Are you going to take back *your words* (≒ *what you have said*)? 私は～を翻すつもりはない I refuse to retract (≒ withdraw) *my words*. 彼女は～を翻した She went back on *her words*.

ぜんげん【漸減】 a gradual decrease. ¶定員を～する *decrease* the fixed number *gradually*. 交通事故は～している Traffic accidents *are diminishing gradually*.

せんけんたい【先遣隊】 (軍隊の) an advance guard; (探検隊の) an advance party.

せんけんてき【先験的】*a priori*; transcendental.
—論 transcendentalism.

せんこ【千古】¶ 彼は文学界に～不滅の金字塔を打ち立てた He has built a golden monument of *immortality* in literature.

せんご【戦後】¶ ～の日本の教育をどう思うか What do you think of the *postwar* education in Japan? ～数年間はみじめな生活だった We lived through terrible times for several years *after the war*.
—派 postwar generation.

ぜんご【前後】**1**〘前と後ろ〙¶ まず～を見なさい Look to *the front and the rear* first of all. ～左右を見まわしたが, だれひとりいなかった I looked *around* me but there was no one to be seen.
船は～に激しく揺れた The ship *pitched* violently.
2〘時間・年について〙¶ 彼は～10年アメリカにいた He has been in America *for ten years in all*.
2時～においでください Please call on me *around* two.
彼女は40歳～に見える She looks *around* forty years old.
ふたりは30分の間に～してやってきた The two made their appearances, *with half an hour between them*.
3〘ことの脈絡・前後関係〙¶ 事件の～のことをもう一度考えてごらんなさい Try to consider the *consequences* of the event.
話が～している The story *is lacking in sequence*.
彼は逆上して～を忘れていた He *was beside himself* with excitement.
—不覚 ¶ やがて彼は～不覚となった Presently he *lost consciousness*. 彼は～不覚に眠っていた He *was sleeping like a log*. —関係 ¶ このことばの意味は～関係から判断すべきだ You should determine the meaning of this word from the *context*.

せんこう【先行】¶ 彼は時代に～する識見を持っている He *is ahead of* his times.

せんこう【先攻】¶ 試合はAチームの～で始まった The game started with the A-team *batting first*.

せんこう【専攻】a special study. ¶ 日本文学を～する *specialize* (≒ 米 *major*) *in* Japanese literature. ご～はなんですか What are (≒ were) you *majoring in*? / What's your *major*?
—科 a postgraduate course. —科目 a special study; a specialty; 米 a major.

せんこう【線香】a joss (≒ an incense) stick.
¶ ～を上げる offer *incense sticks*.
—立て an incense holder (≒ burner). —花火 toy fireworks. 蚊取り— a mosquito (≒ an anti-mosquito) stick; an insectifuge stick.

せんこう【選考】selection; choice. ¶ ～する select; make a choice. 新入社員を～中である New employees are under *consideration*.
彼は～に漏れた He was left out of *election*.
—委員 a screening committee. —基準 a criterion for evaluation.

せんこう【潜行】¶ 地下に～する go underground.

せんこう【潜航】underwater navigation.
¶ ～する navigate (≒ move) under water.
—艇 a submarine 〔boat〕.

せんこう【閃光】a flash 〔of light〕. ¶ 目もくらむような～ *a* blinding *flash*. ～を放つ flash; emit *flash*.

せんこう【穿孔】—カード a punch card. —機 a boring machine; a drill. —器 a puncher; a perforator.

ぜんこう【全校】(学校全体) the whole school; (すべての学校) all the schools.

ぜんこう【前項】the preceding clause; the previous paragraph; 〘数学〙 the antecedent.

ぜんこう【善行】good conduct; a good deed.
—章 a good-conduct badge (≒ medal).

ぜんごう【前号】the preceding (≒ last) number (≒ issue). ¶ ～から続く Continued from the *last issue*. (雑誌などの記載にはただ Continued. とだけ書く).

せんこく【先刻】¶ ～お見えになりました He arrived *a short time ago*. ～ご承知のとおり as you know.

せんこく【宣告】condemnation. ¶ 死刑を～する *sentence a person to* death. 死刑の～を受ける *be condemned to* death. 有罪の～を受ける be found guilty; be convicted. 無罪を～する acquit *a person* of the charge. 彼は5年の刑を～された He received *a* five-year *sentence*.
—書 a written sentence.

ぜんこく【全国】the whole country (≒ land). ¶ ～的に all over (≒ throughout) the country. ～的運動を起こす start a *nationwide* movement (≒ campaign). 流感が日本～に広がる The flu spreads *all over Japan*.
—区(選挙の) the national constituency.
—大会 (競技) a national meet; (集会) a national conference.

せんごくじだい【戦国時代】the age of civil wars.

ぜんごさく【善後策】¶ 彼らは～を練った They tried to work out *remedial measures* for the situation. 彼らは急いで～を講じた They resorted to *an expedient* in haste.

ぜんざ【前座】(事柄) an opening performance; (人) a minor performer; a curtain raiser. ¶ ～をつとめる play *a minor part*.

せんさい【先妻】*one's* former (≒ first) wife; (亡妻) *one's* late (≒ deceased) wife.

せんさい【戦災】war damage. ¶ ～を受ける suffer *war damage*.
—孤児 a war orphan. —地 war-damaged area.

せんさい【繊細】delicacy; fineness. ¶ ～な模様 *exquisite* design. ～な体つき a *slender* figure. ～な感受性 *delicate* sensibility.

せんざい【千載】¶ ～一遇のチャンスを逃す miss

せ

a golden opportunity.

せんざい【洗剤】cleanser; cleaning material; a detergent.

中性— a synthetic detergent.

ぜんさい【前菜】《料理》an *hor d'œuvre* (フランス語から); an appetizer.

せんざい【潜在】latency. ¶ 封建主義は今でも彼らの伝統の中に～している Feudalism *is* still *latent* in their tradition.

—意識 subconsciousness. —失業 latent unemployment. —失業者 the potential unemployed.

せ

せんさく【詮索】inquiry. ¶ ～好きな人 an inquisitive person. ～する look (≒ inquire; pry) into; scrutinize.

せんさばんべつ【千差万別】¶ ～の various; of various kind; an infinite variety of.

せんし【先史】prehistory.

—時代 the prehistoric age.

せんし【戦士】soldier. ¶ 無名～の墓 the tomb of the Unknown *Soldier* (≒ 英 *Warrior*) (米では Arlington 墓地の, 英では Westminster Abbey にあるものをさす). 自由の～ *a champion* of liberty.

せんし【戦史】a military history. ¶ ～に残る be recorded in *war history*.

せんし【戦死】death in battle (≒ action). ¶ ～する die in action; fall (≒ be killed) in action; die on the battlefield.

—者 a fallen (≒ dead) soldier; (総称) the war dead.

せんじ【戦時】wartime; a war period. ¶ ～中 during the war; in *wartime*.

—景気 a war boom. —経済 wartime economy. —公債 a war loan. —国際法 international law in time of war. —産業 the wartime industry. —体制 war structure. —保険 war risk insurance. —補償 war compensation (≒ indemnity).

ぜんし【全市】the whole city.

ぜんし【全紙】(全紙面) the whole paper; (全新聞) all the newspapers.

ぜんじ【漸次】gradually; slowly; little by little.

せんじぐすり【煎じ薬】medical decoction.

せんしつ【船室】a cabin.

特等— a stateroom. 1等(2等)— a first-(second-)class cabin. 3等— the steerage.

せんじつ【先日】the other day; a few days ago. ¶ ～の recent; late; of the other (≒ previous) day. ～来そのことを考えていた I have been thinking of it *for several days* (≒ *all these days*).

ぜんじつ【前日】the day before; the previous (≒ preceding) day. ¶ 試験の～に風邪をひいた I caught [a] cold *the day before* the examination.

せんじつ・める【煎じ詰める】¶ ～めれば失敗の原因は彼の努力不足だ *After all,* his failure was due to the lack of effort. その話は～めればこういうことになる The talk *boils down* to this that....

せんしゃ【戦車】a [war] tank.

—兵 a tank man; (総称) crew. —砲 a tank gun; (ロケット砲) a bazooka. 重(軽)— a heavy (light) tank.

せんじゃ【選者・撰者】a selector; a judge; (編纂者) a compiler.

ぜんしゃ【前者】(the latter に対して) the former; (this に対して) that; (the other に対して) the one.

せんしゅ【先取】¶ 1点を～する *score the first point* of the game.

—特権 priority.

せんしゅ【船主】a shipowner; 米 a shipping operator.

せんしゅ【船首】the bow; the prow; the head. ¶ ～から沈む sink from the *prow* (≒ *bow*).

せんしゅ【選手】a player; an athlete.

¶ 彼は野球の～だ He *is in* (≒ *on*) *the* baseball *team*. オリンピックに～を派遣する send representative *athletes* to the Olympic Games.

—権 a championship; a title. —権試合 a title match. —権保持者 a champion. 補欠— a substitute; an alternate.

せんしゅう【千秋】¶ 一日～の思いで待つ wait impatiently for (*a person*); look forward to (*a thing*) with longing.

せんしゅう【先週】last week. ¶ ～のきょう this day [*last*] *week*; a week ago today. ～の土曜日に last Saturday; on Saturday last (月曜などの場合は last Monday が今週の月曜になることもあるので Monday last week のほうがよい).

せんしゅう【選集】a selection. ¶ ブラウニング～ *selected poems* of Browning.

ぜんしゅう【全集】¶ シェイクスピア～ *the complete works* of Shakespeare.

ぜんしゅう【前週】(先週) last week; (その前の週) the week before; the preceding week.

せんじゅうしゃ【専従者】(労働組合) a full time union officer.

せんじゅうみん【先住民】aborigines.

せんしゅうらく【千秋楽】(興行の) the last day of a public performance; (一般に) a close; an end.

せんしゅつ【選出】election. ¶ 東京から～される *be elected from* (≒ *be returned for*) Tokyo. 全国区から～された参議院議員 a Councilor *elected* from the national constituency.

せんじゅつ【戦術】tactics. ¶ ～上の tactical. ～的に tactically. 新しい～に出る adopt new *tactics*.

—家 a tactician.

ぜんじゅつ【前述】¶ ～の above; above-mentioned; foregoing. ～のとおり as mentioned (≒ stated) above.

ぜんしょ【全書】百科— an encyclopedic series of handbooks. 法律— a compendium of laws.

ぜんしょ【善処】¶ 政府に～するよう申し入れる urge the government to *handle* the problem *with care*.

せんしょう【戦勝】a triumph; a victory.
—記念日 the anniversary of the victory.
—国 a victorious country (≒ nation).
せんしょう【僭称】¶ 会長の職を～する *usurp* the presidency.
せんじょう【洗浄】washing. ¶ 目を～する *bathe one's* eyes. 胃を～する *wash out one's* stomach.
—器 a washer; a syringe. —薬 a wash; a lotion.
せんじょう【戦場】a battlefield.
古— an ancient battlefield.
ぜんしょう【全勝】¶ ～する win a complete victory; make straight wins.
ぜんしょう【全焼】¶ ～する be burnt down 〔to the ground〕.
ぜんしょう【前哨】—基地 an advanced base. —戦 a 〔preliminary〕 skirmish.
ぜんじょう【前条】the preceding (≒ foregoing) item.
せんじょうてき【扇情的】¶ ～な小説 a *sensational* (≒ *suggestive*) novel. ～的な記事 *inflammatory* articles.
せんしょく【染色】dyeing.
—工場 a dye works. —体〘生物〙a 〔sex〕 chromosome.
せん・じる【煎じる】¶ 茶を～じる *brew* tea.
せんしん【専心】¶ 仕事に～する *devote oneself to one's* task. 一意～勉学に励む *be absorbed in one's* studies.
せんしん【線審】〘球技〙a linesman.
せんじん【千尋】¶ ～の谷 a bottomless ravine.
せんじん【先人】predecessors.
せんじん【先陣】the advance guards. ¶ われわれは攻撃の～を承ることになった We have been ordered to *lead the van of the attack*.
せんじん【戦陣】the front.
ぜんしん【全心】*one's* whole heart.
ぜんしん【全身】the whole body; 〘写真〙the full length. ¶ 彼は～に打撲傷を負った He got bruises *all over the body*. 彼女の～は怒りに震えた She trembled *all over* with anger. / Anger made her tremble *from top to toe*. ～汗だくになった I *was all in a sweat*. 彼は芸術に～全霊を傾けた He *devoted himself to* art.
—像〘写真〙a full length portrait. —不随 total paralysis. —麻酔 general anesthesia.
ぜんしん【前身】*one's* antecedents. ¶ 彼の～を洗ってくれ Investigate (≒ Inquire into) his *past history*. 彼女の～はいかがわしい She is a woman of shady *antecedents*. その会社の～をご存じですか Do you know the *predecessor* of the firm?
ぜんしん【前進】an advance; 〘号令〙Forward! ¶ 軍勢はネバ川まで～した The troops *advanced* to the Neva. 新たに一歩～をはかれ Try *to take a new step forward*.
—基地 an advanced base.
ぜんしん【漸進】¶ 人口の～的増加 a *gradual* increase in population. その政党の政策は～的である The party *is moderate* in policy.
—主義 moderatism; slow and steady policies. —主義者 a moderatist.
ぜんじん【前人】¶ ～未踏のジャングル a *trackless* jungle. ～未踏の分野 an *unexplored* (≒ *untrodden*) field.
せんしんこく【先進国】advanced nations.
せんす【扇子】a 〔folding〕 fan. ¶ ～を使う *fan oneself*.
センス sense. ¶ 彼にはユーモアの～がない He has no *sense* of humor. 彼女の服装には～がある Her dress shows *good taste*.
ぜんず【全図】¶ ロンドン～ *a complete map* of London.
せんすい【泉水】a fountain; a spring.
せんすい【潜水】diving. ¶ 海女の～を見たことがありますか Have you ever seen a woman diver *dive*? 船は見るまに～しはじめた The boat began to *submerge* (≒ *go under water*) in an instant.
—艦 a submarine. —夫 a diver. —服 a diving suit.
せん・する【宣する】announce; declare.
¶ 開会を～する *announce* the opening of a meeting. 休憩を～する *call* a recess. 戦いを～する *declare* war (*upon*).
せんせい【先生】a teacher; a master; an instructor; (医者) a doctor. ¶ ～! Sir! (Teacher! と呼びかけることはしない); (女の教師に) Ma'am!; (医者に) Doctor! 鈴木～! *Mr.* (≒ *Miss*; *Mrs.*) Suzuki! 彼は数学の～だ He is *a* mathematics *teacher*. / He is *a teacher* of mathematics.
せんせい【専制】autocracy; tyranny.
—君主 an absolute monarch; an autocrat. —君主政体 an absolute monarchy. —国 an absolute monarchy. —主義 absolutism; despotism; autocracy. —政治 an absolute (≒ autocratic) government.
せんせい【宣誓】an oath. ¶ 彼女は聖書に接吻(せっぷん)して～した She *took an oath* by kissing the Bible. 真実を語ると～せよ *Swear* to speak the truth. 供述の前に～させなさい *Administer* him *an oath* before making a statement.
—口述書 an affidavit. —式 administering of an oath. —書 a written oath.
ぜんせい【全盛】¶ 保守党は今や～を誇っている The conservative party *is in all its glory*.
—時代 ¶ フィレンツェの～時代は終わった *The heyday* (≒ *golden age*) of Florence was over. ～時代彼は豪奢(ごうしゃ)をきわめた He lived like a prince *in his best days*.
ぜんせい【善政】good government. ¶ 歴代の領主が～を施した The successive lords *governed wisely*.
せんせいじゅつ【占星術】astrology.
—師 an astrologer.
せんせいりょく【潜勢力】potential (≒ latent) power.
センセーショナル sensational. ¶ ～な犯罪 a *sensational* crime.
センセーション sensation. ¶ 彼女の出現は劇

界に一大～を巻き起こした Her appearance caused *a* great *sensation* in the theatrical world.

ぜんせかい【全世界】 the whole world.
¶～の青年男女 young men and women *throughout the world*. ～から選ばれた選手たち athletes selected *from all the nations of the world*. ～から集まる平和主義者たち pacifists coming *from all parts of the world*.

せんせき【船籍】 the nationality of a ship.
¶その船はフランスの～を持っていた The ship had French *nationality*. / The ship was registered French.

せんせき【戦跡】 the old battlefield; the scene of the old battle.

ぜんせつ【前節】 the preceding (≒ foregoing) paragraph.

ぜんせつ【前説】 ¶委員会の席上で彼は～を翻した He changed *his former view* at the committee meeting.

せんせん【宣戦】 declaration of war. ¶日本はアメリカに～を布告した Japan *declared war upon* the U. S. A.
—布告 a declaration of war.

せんせん【戦線】 the front.
共同— a united front. ¶野党は政府に対して共同～を張る意向である The parties in opposition intend to present *a united front* against the government. 人民— the people's front. 労働— the labor front.

せんぜん【戦前】 ¶現在ではすべてのものが～のレベルを越している Everything is now above the *prewar* level.

ぜんせん【全線】 ¶～が開通した *The whole line* was opened for service. ～が不通になった Traffic was tied up *all along the line*.

ぜんせん【前線】 the front line. ¶～の将兵 officers and men at *the front*.
寒冷(温暖)— a cold (warm) front.

ぜんせん【善戦】 ¶きのうの試合でわがチームは～した Our team *fought a good fight* in the game yesterday.

ぜんぜん【全然】 ¶彼は私の～知らない人だ I do not know him *at all*. / He is a *total* stranger to me. 彼の場合は～話が違う The case is *altogether* (≒ *wholly*) different with him. 私には～見当がつかない I *haven't the slightest idea* against it.

せんせんきょうきょう【戦戦恐恐】 ¶秘密がばれはしないかと彼は～としていた He *was terribly afraid* that the secret might come out.

せんせんげつ【先先月】 the month before last.

ぜんぜんじつ【前前日】 two days before.

せんぞ【先祖】 an ancestor; a forefather.
—代々 ¶～代々の墓 a *family* tomb. その家は～代々医者である They have been medical doctors *from father to son* (≒ *from generation to generation*). —伝来 ¶～伝来の地所 an *ancestral* estate. このつぼは～伝来のものである This vase has been handed down from our *ancestors*.

せんそう【船窓】 a porthole.

せんそう【船倉】 a hatch; a hold.

せんそう【戦争】 a war; (戦闘) a battle.
¶今彼らと～すべきでない We should not *make war* (≒ *take up arms*) *against* them now. 子どもたちが～ごっこをして遊んでいる Boys *are playing at soldiers*. ～はいつ起こるかもしれない *War* may break out at any moment. ～に負ける(勝つ) lose (win) *a war*. 冷たい～もこれで終わった The cold *war* is now over. 彼らはあの国と～している They *are at war* with that country.
—映画 a war film. —犠牲者 war victims. —景気 a war boom. —好き ¶もともと～好きの国民なのだ They are a *warlike* nation by nature. —成金 a war profiteer. —犯罪人 a war criminal. —文学 war literature. —放棄 renunciation of war. ¶日本は～放棄を宣言した Japan declared to *renounce war*. —未亡人 a war widow.

ぜんそう【前奏】 an overture.
—曲 an overture; a prelude.

ぜんそう【禅僧】 a *Zen* priest.

ぜんぞう【漸増】 a gradual increase. ¶当市の人口は～している The population of this city *is increasing gradually* (≒ *by degrees*).

せんぞく【専属】 ¶彼女は当社～である She *belongs exclusively to* our company. / She *is attached to* our firm.

ぜんそく【喘息】〘医学〙asthma.
—患者 an asthmatic.

ぜんそくりょく【全速力】 ¶少年は～で走った The boy ran *at full speed* (≒ *as fast as he could*). 彼女は車を～で飛ばした She drove the car *at top speed*. 船は～を出した The boat *put on full steam*.

せんそくわたし【船側渡し】 free alongside 〔ship〕 (f.a.s. と略す). ¶輸出契約は～の条件で結ばれた The contract of the export was made on f.a.s. basis.

センター (中心地区) a center; 〘野球〙 the center field; (中堅手) a center fielder.
—フライ ¶彼は～フライに終わってツーダウン He flied to *center* for two outs.

せんたい【船体】 a hull.

せんたい【船隊】 a fleet of ships.
捕鯨— a fleet of whalers. 輸送— a fleet of troop ships.

せんたい【蘚苔】〘植物〙 a moss; a bryophyte.
—学 bryology.

せんだい【先代】 *one's* father; *one's* predecessor; (時代) the last generation.

せんだい【船台】 stocks.

ぜんたい【全体】 the whole. ¶選手は～で何人か How many players are there *in all* (≒ *all together*)? ～から見てよく設計されている It is designed well *on the whole*. 料理は～に行き渡りましたか Have the dishes been served *to all*? このクラスの生徒は～にたいへん出来がよい *In general* the boys of this class are very bright. 体～が痛む I feel painful *all over*.

—主義 totalitarianism. **—**主義国家 a totalitarian country.

ぜんたい【全隊】 the whole troop. ¶～止まれ! (号令) [The troop] *Halt!*

ぜんだいみもん【前代未聞】 ¶～の大惨事 an *unheard-of* disaster. ～の大冒険 an *unparalleled* (≒ *unprecedented*) adventure. ～の好景気 a *record-breaking* boom. それは～の不祥事だ We've never heard of such a disgraceful affair before.

せんたく【選択】 choice; selection. ¶彼は職業の～を誤った He made *a* bad (≒ wrong) *choice of* occupation. / He was wrong in *choosing* his profession. それについては～の余地はない You *have* no *choice* (≒ *alternative*) in it.

—科目 (米) an elective; an optional.

せんたく【洗濯】 wash; washing; laundry; cleaning. ¶自分の物を～しなさい *Wash* your own things. これは～がきく This *is washable*. 彼女に～してもらいなさい *Have* them *washed* by her. シーツは～にやった I'*ve sent* the sheets *to the laundry*. / The sheets *are at the wash*. 鬼のいぬ間に～(諺) *When the cat's away, the mice will play.*

—板 a washboard. **—**せっけん washing soap. **—**物 ¶～物を干す hang out *the washing* to dry (washing にはいつも the をつけ, 集合的に用いる). **—**屋(店) a laundry; (人) a launderer; a laundress; a washerman; a washerwoman. 電気**—**機 an electric washing machine.

せんだつ【先達】 a guide; a leader; (先駆者) a pioneer.

せんだって【先達て】 the other day; a few days ago; (このほど) recently; lately. ¶～から返金を催促されている I have been urged to pay the debt *for some time past*.

ぜんだて【膳立て】 ¶お～は整っている It *is all set*. 歓迎のお～は十分にやってください I hope you will make satisfactory *preparations* (≒ *arrangements*) *for* the reception.

ぜんだま【善玉】 a good man. ¶～悪玉 *good* and bad.

せんたん【先端】 the point; the tip. ¶彼女はいつも流行の～を行く She always *leads* (≒ *sets*) the fashion.

せんたん【戦端】 ¶あげくの果てにわが国はアメリカと～を開いた In the end our country *opened hostilities* (≒ *war*) *with* the U. S. A.

せんだん【船団】 a fleet of vessels.

捕鯨**—** a fleet of whalers. 輸送**—** a convoyed fleet.

せんだん【栴檀】〘植物〙 a bead tree; (木材) bastard cedar. ¶～は双葉より芳し Genius displays itself even in childhood.

せんち【戦地】 the front. ¶～に行く go to the front.

センチ ⇒センチメートル; センチメンタル

ぜんち【全治】 complete cure. ¶彼はまもなく～しよう(病気の場合) He will *be completely cured* (≒ *be completely recovered*) before long. / (傷の場合) He will soon *be completely healed of* his wound. 彼は～1か月の傷を負った He suffered an injury which would take a month to *heal completely*.

ぜんちし【前置詞】〘文法〙 a preposition.

—句 a prepositional phrase.

ぜんちぜんのう【全知全能】 ¶～の神 Almighty God (God をはぶけば the をつける); God Almighty.

センチメートル centimeter (cm.).

センチメンタル sentimental. ¶～な小説には興味がない I am not interested in *sentimental* novels.

せんちゃ【煎茶】 green tea.

せんちゃく【先着】 ¶～500名様に粗品を差し上げます We will give presents to *the first* five hundred persons.

—順 ¶～順に席は割り当てられます The seats will be allotted *in the order of arrival* (≒ *by the order of receipt*). 申し込みは～順で締め切ります Applications will be accepted *on a first-come, first-served basis*.

せんちゅう【船中】 ¶～で一夜を明かす pass a night *on the ship*.

せんちょう【船長】 a captain.

ぜんちょう【全長】 the total length. ¶その船は～30フィートである The ship is 30 feet *long*.

ぜんちょう【前兆】 an omen; (特に不吉な) a portent; a foreboding; (しるし) a sign; a precursor; (病気などの) a symptom.

¶よい(悪い)～ *a good* (*an ill*) *omen*. あの黒雲はあらしの～だ Those clouds are *a sign* of a storm. / Those clouds *forebode* a storm. 彼が黙りこむのは荒れる～だ Silence *is ominous* of his violence.

ぜんつう【全通】 the opening of the whole line. ¶新線は来月～の予定です The whole new line is to *be opened to traffic* next month.

せんて【先手】 forestalling. ¶～をとる(将棋・囲碁) take (≒ obtain) *the initiative*. 敵の～を打って, われわれはその町を爆撃した We *forestalled* (≒ *anticipated*) the enemy's move by bombing the town.

せんてい【選定】 selection. ¶教科書を～する *select* textbooks.

せんてい【剪定】 pruning. ¶果樹を～する *prune* fruit trees.

—ばさみ pruning shears.

ぜんてい【前庭】〘解剖学〙 the vestibule [of the ear].

ぜんてい【前提】 a premise. ¶彼の行動は合法的なものであるという～のもとにのみ容赦できるものであった His conduct was only pardonable *on the assumption that* it was lawful. 彼は自分は正しいということを～としている He *assumes* that he is right. 両国は平和を～として話し合うべきである The two countries should talk with each other, *presupposing* peace.

せ

—条件 a precondition.

せんてつ【銑鉄】pig iron.

せんてん【先天】¶ 彼は～的なうそつきだ He is a *born* liar. 彼女は～的に運動神経が発達している She is quick *by nature* in her movement. ～性の病気 a *congenital* disease. ～的に音楽の才能がある He is *naturally* endowed with a musical talent.

せんでん【宣伝】〔a〕propaganda (誇張の意味をふくむこともあるのは日本語と同じ. 誤解をさけるためには publicity を用いる).
¶ 広告だけが～ではない Advertisement is not the only form of *propaganda*. 彼は～を言っているような気がする It seems that he is talking *propaganda*. 新製品をテレビで～している Newly-made articles *are being advertised* on television. この店は鳴り物入りで盛んに～している This store is carrying〔on〕*an* active *propaganda* with tantara. これはバーゲンセールの～だ This is *an advertisement* for a bargain sale. その会社は新車の～に乗り出した The company launched into *an advertising campaign* for their automobiles.
—係 a publicity man. —機関 a propaganda machinery (≒ organization). —費 publicity expenses. —ビラ a propaganda bill. —部 a publicity department.

せんと【遷都】¶ 一時東京～論がにぎやかだった Once there was much talk about the removal of Tokyo as Capital.

セント a cent. ¶ 1～銅貨 a penny. 5～ニッケル貨 a nickel. 10～銀貨 a dime. 25～銀貨 (米俗) two bits; a quarter. 50～銀貨 a half dollar.

せんど【鮮度】degree of freshness. ¶ きょうの魚は～が高い Today's fishes *are* very *fresh*. この魚は～が落ちた This fish has become inferior in *freshness*.

ぜんと【前途】〔a〕future; prospects. ¶ 彼は～有望だ He has *a* bright (≒ rosy) *future ahead*. この学生は～有望な青年だ This student is a *promising* young man. / This is a student *of great promise*. 彼らの～は暗い Their *prospects* are black. / They have *a* dark *future* before them. われわれの～は遼遠(りょうえん)だ We have a long way to go. / Our goal is far off. 日本の～にはいろいろな困難がある Various difficulties are lying in Japan's *future*. / Japan's *future* is full of difficulties. 彼は～を悲観して自殺した He became pessimistic about his *future* and killed himself.

ぜんど【全土】¶ スペイン～は戦禍の中にあった *The whole land* of Spain was at war.

せんとう【先頭】the lead; the head. ¶ 行列の～に立っているのは彼だ He *is at the head of* the procession. ゴール近くで彼が～に出た He gained *the lead* a little before the goal.

せんとう【戦闘】a battle. ¶ ～を始める get into *action*. ～に参加する see *combat*.
—員 a combatant. —機 a fighting plane. —訓練 field training. —準備 ¶ ～準備を整える prepare for *action*. —力 fighting capacity.

せんとう【銭湯】a public bath; a bathhouse.

せんとう【尖塔】a spire.

せんどう【先導】guidance. ¶ 作業は彼の～で行なわれた The work was conducted under his *guidance*.
—者 a leader. —車 a leading car.

せんどう【扇動】agitation. ¶ 彼は部下を～して反乱を起こさせた He *incited* (≒ *agitated*) his men *to* revolt. 彼に～されて彼らは活動を開始した They began their activities *at his instigation*.
—者 an agitator; an instigator. —政治家 a political agitator.

せんどう【船頭】a boatman. ¶ ～多くして船山に上る(諺) *Too many cooks spoil the broth*.

ぜんどう【善導】¶ 罪人を～するのはたいへんなことだ It is no easy task to *lead* criminals *in the right direction*.

ぜんどう【蠕動】¶ ～する vermiculate.
—運動 vermiculation.

ぜんとうこつ【前頭骨】〘解剖学〙the frontal bone.

ぜんなんぜんにょ【善男善女】the pious.
¶ 多くの～が集まった Many *pious men and women* gathered.

せんにち【千日】—紅〘植物〙a globe amaranth. —手〘将棋〙an endless circle of repetitive moves.

ぜんにちせい【全日制】—高校 a full-time upper secondary school (≒ senior high school) (upper secondary school は日本の高校にのみ用いる).

ぜんにほん【全日本】¶ ～の代表のひとり one of the representatives of *all Japan*.
—選手権 an all-Japan championship.

せんにゅう【潜入】¶ 彼は単身敵陣に～していった He *smuggled himself* all alone *into* the barracks of the enemy.

ぜんにゅう【全乳】whole milk.

せんにゅうかん【先入観】preconception.
¶ 人はとかく～にとらわれやすい Men are likely to be possessed by *a preconceived idea*. そういう考え方が彼の～となっている Such an idea *preoccupies* his mind. 共産主義に対して誤った～を持つ人は多い Many people have *a prejudice* against communism.

せんにょ【仙女】a fairy.

せんにん【専任】¶ 彼は某大学の～講師だ He is a *full-time* instructor at a certain university.

せんにん【選任】election. ¶ 彼は議長に～された He *was elected* chairman.

せんにん【仙人】a fairy; a hermit.

ぜんにん【善人】a good man. ¶ ～栄えて悪人滅ぶ *Virtue* triumphs over vice.

せんにんしゃ【先任者】a senior member.

ぜんにんしゃ【前任者】*one's* predecessor.
¶ 彼は～から仕事を引き継いだ He took over his job from his *predecessor*.

せんにんりき【千人力】¶ 彼は～だ He *is as*

strong as a thousand men put together. / He has *a Herculean strength*. あなたが仲間に入ってくだされば～です I *feel reassured to* have you as one of our members.

せんぬき【栓抜き】(コルク抜き) a corkscrew; (びんのキャップ抜き) a cap opener.

せんねん【先年】some years ago. ¶ ～以上の大雪になった It was the greatest snowfall that we had ever experienced.

せんねん【専念】¶ 勉学に～しなさい Work *hard*. (give *oneself* to... は悪い意味で用いられる). 彼は家業に～することになった He has decided to *attend to* (≒ *see after*) his family business. 今育児に～している I am taking care of my children. 彼は生涯子弟の教育に～した He *devoted his whole life to* the education of young people.

ぜんねん【前年】the previous year. ¶ 本年は～に比べて米が不作だ We have had a poorer crop of rice this year than that of *last year*.

せんのう【洗脳】brainwashing. ¶ ～する brainwash.

ぜんのう【全能】¶ ～の神 Almighty God; the omnipotent God.

ぜんのう【前脳】〔解剖学〕the forebrain.

ぜんのう【前納】¶ 会費を～する *pay* the membership fee *in advance*; *repay* the membership fee.

ぜんば【前場】〔株式〕the morning session.

せんばい【専売】monopoly. ¶ たばこは政府の～だ Tabacco *is monopolized by* the Government. この薬は当社の～だ This medicine is our *speciality*.

—特許 a patent. 日本—公社 the Japan Monopoly Corporation.

せんぱい【先輩】a senior. ¶ 彼は私の～だ He is my *senior*. / He is *senior* to me. 彼は私のかなり～だ He is my *senior* by many years. 社員の中では彼がいちばん～だ He is *the oldest member* of the staff.

ぜんぱい【全敗】¶ わがチームは～に終わった Our team *lost all games*.

ぜんぱい【全廃】¶ 米の配給制度を～することが決定した It was decided to *abolish altogether* the rationing system of rice.

せんぱいこく【戦敗国】a vanquished nation.

せんぱく【浅薄】¶ ～な学問はかえって危険だ A *little* learning is a dangerous thing. 彼は～な知識を振りまわす He shows off his *superficial* knowledge.

せんぱく【船舶】shipping; a ship. ¶ この港は～の出入りが激しい There are a lot of *ships* entering and leaving this port.

—会社 a shipping company. —業 the shipping industry. —業者 a shipping man. —用品 a ship's stores.

せんばつ【選抜】choice; selection. ¶ 50人からふたりの選手が～された Two players *were selected* from among the fifty applicants. 彼は～に漏れた He was left out in the *selection*.

—チーム a selected team. —試験 a selective examination.

せんぱつ【先発】¶ ～する start in advance.

—隊 an advance party. —投手〔野球〕a starting pitcher.

せんぱつ【洗髪】a shampoo. ¶ ～する wash *one's* hair. 人を～してやる give *a person a shampoo*.

せんばん【先番】¶ 将棋は名人の～で開始された The Japanese chess was started, the champion *making the first move*.

せんばん【旋盤】a lathe.

—工 a latheman; a turner. —工場 a turnery.

せんばん【千万】¶ 迷惑～だ I am *very much* annoyed. ～かたじけなく存じます *Many* thanks for your kindness. 彼が来ないとは遺憾～だ It is *a thousand* pities that he should not come.

せんぱん【先般】¶ ～申し上げた件につきお話したく存じます I wish to speak to you of what I told you *the other day*.

せんぱん【戦犯】a war criminal.

ぜんぱん【前半】the first half (*of* the twentieth century).

—戦 the first half of the game.

ぜんぱん【全般】¶ 文学～にわたって講演をした I made a lecture on *the whole field* of literature. 子どもの体位が～的に向上している The physique of children has *generally* been improved. / The *general* physique of children has been improved. 社会～がおかしくなっている The society *at large* has become eccentric.

せんび【戦備】war preparations. ¶ ～を整える prepare for war.

せんび【船尾】the stern.

せんぴ【戦費】war expenditure; the cost of war. ¶ あまりにも巨額の～を費やした We spent too large an amount of *money on the war*.

ぜんぴ【前非】¶ ～を悔いる repent of *one's past conduct*.

せんぴょう【選評】¶ 私が応募作品を～した I *selected and commented on* the applied works.

せんびょうしつ【腺病質】¶ 小さいときは～だといわれていた I was thought to *be sickly* while a little boy.

せんびん【先便】*one's* last letter; a previous mail. ¶ ～で申し上げたとおりです It is what I wrote in my *last letter*.

せんぷ【先夫】*one's* former *husband*.

ぜんぶ【全部】all. ¶ その本は～持っています I have *all* those books. きょうの新聞は～読んだ I have read today's paper *from beginning to end*. この厚い本を～読んだとは驚いた I am surprised that he should have read this thick book *from cover to cover*. たばこはもう～なくなった The cigarettes are *all* gone. 一行は～健康だ The party are healthy, *all of* us.

ぜんぶ【前部】the front part. ¶ 自動車の～

せ

the front part of the car. 最〜に座っていた I was seated in *the forefront*.

せんぷう【旋風】 a wirlwind; a tornado. ¶ 彼の小説は一大〜を巻き起こした His novel created *a* great *sensation*.

せんぷうき【扇風機】 an electric fan. ¶ 〜をつける(止める) turn on (off) *an electric fan*.

せんぷく【潜伏】 concealment. ¶ 病気には〜性のものもある Some of the diseases *are latent*. 犯人が市内に〜している The criminal *is hiding* somewhere in the city.

せんぷく【船腹】 bottoms.

ぜんぷく【全幅】 ¶ 彼に〜の同情を注ぎたい I want to sympathize with him *wholeheartedly*. 〜の支持を得た I was given *full* support.

せんぶん【線分】〔数学〕 a definite straight line.

ぜんぶん【全文】 the whole passage (≒ sentence). ¶ 条約の〜 *the full text* of a treaty. 報告書の〜 *the whole statement* of a report. 彼は〜を引用してそれの説明をした He explained it by quoting *the whole passage*.

ぜんぶん【前文】 the preamble; the above sentence. ¶ 憲法の〜 *the preamble* of a constitution. 〜で述べたように as above-mentioned; as previously stated.

せんべい【煎餅】 *senbei* (英語で説明すれば Japanese cracker).
—ぶとん thinly stuffed bedding.

せんぺい【尖兵】 a spearhead.

ぜんべい【全米】 ¶ 彼の就任演説は〜に放送された His inaugural address was broadcast to *all over America*.

せんべつ【餞別】 a parting present; a farewell gift. ¶ 私は彼に〜をおくった I gave *a parting present* (≒ *gift*) to him.

せんべつ【選別】 selection. ¶ 業界の〜化が急速に進んでいる *Selection of the best* in the business world is being rapidly made.

せんべん【先鞭】 ¶ 彼はがんの研究の〜をつけた He *took the initiative in* the study of cancer.

ぜんぺん【前編】 the first part (*of* a novel).

せんぺんいちりつ【千編一律】 ¶ 〜の monotonous. 彼女はいつも〜の話ばかりしている She always harps on *one* (≒ *the same*) string.

せんぼう【羨望】 envy. ¶ 彼の成功を見て〜の念を禁じえなかった I was filled with *envy* at his success. 彼は社内の多くの人の〜の的であった He was the *envy* of many people in the office.

せんぽう【先方】 the other party (≒ side). ¶ 〜の言うことを聞かねばなりません We must listen to what *the other party* (≒ *side*) says. 〜とよく話し合ってみた I talked out with *him* (≒ *her*; *them*).

せんぽう【戦法】 tactics; strategy. ¶ 彼は〜を誤った He made a mistake in his *strategy* (≒ *tactics*).

せんぽう【先鋒】 the vanguard; the van. ¶ 彼は労働運動の急〜だった He was among *the most active leaders* of the labor movement.

ぜんぼう【全貌】 the whole aspect. ¶ 事件の〜が明るみに出た *The whole affair* has been brought to light.

ぜんぽう【前方】 the front. ¶ 〜を注視した I gazed at *the front*. 美しい景色が〜に広がった A beautiful scenery spread out *before* us.

せんぼうきょう【潜望鏡】 a periscope.

せんぼつ【戦没】 ¶ 〜の遺族 the war bereaved.
—者 the war dead.

せんまい【千枚】 —張り ¶ 彼は面の皮が〜張りだ He *is brazen-faced*. —通し an eyeleteer.

ぜんまい【薇】〔植物〕 a flowering fern; an osmund.

ぜんまい【発条・撥条】 a spring. ¶ それは〜で動く It moves by *clockwork*. / It works by moves of *a spring*. 時計の〜を巻く wind up a watch.
—じかけ clockwork.

せんみん【選民】 the chosen people; the elect.
—思想 the idea of God's elect.

せんむ【専務】 —車掌 a conductor; 英 a guard. —取締役 a managing director.

せんめい【鮮明】 ¶ 〜な色彩 a *vivid* color. この小説では人物が〜にうつし出されている This novel gives a *vivid* description of each character. 印刷は〜だ The print *is clear*.

せんめつ【殲滅】 annihilation. ¶ 当地区の敵を〜した We *have wiped out* the enemy in this area.

ぜんめつ【全滅】 annihilation. ¶ わが部隊は敵の攻撃によって〜した Our unit has suffered *a crushing defeat* under the attack of the enemy. 尾瀬の高山植物は〜に瀕(ひん)している The alpine plants of Oze are on the verge of *annihilation*. この毒薬を使えばネズミは〜する This poison will *exterminate* the rats.

せんめん【洗面】 —器 a washbowl; a washbasin. —所 a lavatory; 米 a washroom; a rest room.

ぜんめん【全面】 ¶ 条約は〜的に改正された They made a *sweeping* (≒ *complete*) revision of the treaty. 先方の条件を〜的に受け入れた We accepted *all* the terms they asked.

ぜんめん【前面】 the front.

せんもう【繊毛】〔動物〕〔植物〕 a cilium (複 cilia).

せんもん【専門】 1〔学問・研究の専攻〕 speciality. ¶ 私の〜は法律学だ My *speciality* is law. 社会学は私の〜ではない Sociology is not in my *line*.
フランス文学が彼の〜だ He *specializes in* French literature.
彼は社会言語学を〜に研究している He *is making a special study* of social linguistics.
彼は動物学が〜ではないが, 動物に関する〜的知識を持っている Zoology is not in his *field*, and yet he has *professional* knowledge of various animals.
彼の〜はアジア史ではなくヨーロッパ史だ He *makes*

せ

a speciality of European history, not of Asian.

大学では生物学を～に勉強した I *majored in* biology at college.

—医 a medical specialist. —家 a specialist. —化 ¶ 学問は高度に～化されつつある Studies *are being* highly *specialized*. —外 ¶ 彼は～外のことはよくわからない He is not versed in what is outside his *field*. —分野 ¶ 数学は科学の～分野のひとつだ Mathematics is a *special* branch of science. —学校 a professional school. —教育 professional education. —語 a technical term. —誌 a professional magazine.

2 〖職業〗 ¶ この店は舶来品を～に扱っている The *speciality* of this store is foreign goods.• あの店は衣類だけが～だ That store *deals in* dresses *only*.

—店 a speciality store.

ぜんもん【前門】 ¶ ～のとら, 後門のおおかみ We found ourselves between the devil and the deep sea. / We found ourselves between Scylla and Charybdis.

ぜんや【前夜】 the previous night. ¶ 事件の～のことを話してくれ Tell me what happened *on the night before* the incident.

—祭 ¶ クリスマス～祭 Christmas *Eve*.

せんやく【先約】 a previous engagement. ¶ 残念ですが～があるので会には出席できません I regret that *a previous engagement* prevents me from attending the party. (文語体. 仲間同士なら I'm sorry I can't come to the meeting because I am busy. などでよい).

ぜんやく【全訳】 a complete translation.

せんゆう【戦友】 a war-comrade; a fellow-soldier.

せんゆう【占有】 occupation. ¶ あの土地建物を不法に彼は～している He unlawfully *occupies* the premises.

—権 the right of possession. —者 an occupant; a possessor.

せんよう【専用】 exclusive use. ¶ この駐車場はわが社の～だ This parking lot *is used exclusively* for our company. / This parking lot is for *the exclusive use* of our company.

—機 a plane for *one's* personal use. —車 a private (⇆ an owner's) car; a car for *one's* personal use. 自動車—道路 a route for the exclusive use of motor vehicles.

ぜんよう【善用】 ¶ 余暇を～する *make good use of* leisure.

ぜんら【全裸】 total nudity. ¶ ～の絵 a *nude* picture.

せんらん【戦乱】 disturbances; wars. ¶ その都市は～のちまたと化した The city was turned into the scene of *war*. ～のヨーロッパ *war-torn* Europe.

せんりがん【千里眼】 (人) a clairvoyant; (女) clairvoyante.

せんりつ【旋律】 melody.

せんりつ【戦慄】 shiver; shudder. ¶ ニュースは世間の人々を～させた The news made people *shudder with horror*. ～すべき事件 a *shivery* incident.

せんりひん【戦利品】 a trophy; a booty; spoils (通例複数).

せんりゃく【戦略】 strategy. ¶ ～上の退却 a *strategic* retreat. ～を立てる map out *a strategy*.

—家 a strategist. —爆撃 strategic bombing. —物資 strategic materials.

せんりゅう【川柳】 a *senryu* verse (英語で説明すれば a Japanese humorous poem consisting of 17 syllables in 3 lines).

せ

せんりょ【千慮】 ¶ ～の一失 an unexpected failure.

せんりょう【占領】 occupation. ¶ ～下の都市 a city under *occupation*. あの敵陣を～しなければならぬ We must *occupy* that enemy fort. 席は全部先に来た人に～された All the seats *were taken* by early comers.

—軍 the occupation forces. —地 an occupied area.

せんりょう【染料】 〔a〕 dye.

ぜんりょう【善良】 ¶ ～な市民 a *good* citizen.

せんりょうやくしゃ【千両役者】 an accomplished actor (⇆ actress).

せんりょく【戦力】 war potential. ¶ ～の増強 increase in *war potential*. ～なき国家 a country without *war potential*.

ぜんりょく【全力】 all *one's* power. ¶ 彼は仕事に～を傾けた He *devoted his whole energies* to the work. / He did the work *with all his might*. ～をあげてその問題の解決に努力しなければならない We must *do our best* to solve the problem.

ぜんりん【善隣】 ¶ ～のよしみ *neighborly* relation.

せんれい【先例】 a precedent. ¶ ～を破る break *a precedent*. ～に従う follow *a precedent*. これにはひとつも～がない There is no *precedent* for this. これを～としてはならない Do not take this as *a precedent*. ～に従って according to *precedent*.

せんれい【洗礼】 baptism. ¶ 彼女は～を受けてキリスト教徒になった She *was baptized into* the Christian faith. 日本は世界じゅうで原爆の～を受けた唯一の国だ Japan is the only country in the world that has received her *baptism* of A-bomb.

ぜんれい【前例】 a precedent. ⇒せんれい(先例)

せんれき【戦歴】 a war experience.

ぜんれき【前歴】 ¶ 人の～を調べる trace *a person's previous history*. ～を隠す conceal *a past of one's career*.

せんれつ【戦列】 ¶ 彼らは進んで～に加わった They voluntarily *went into the battle line*. 数人の負傷者が～から離れた Several wounded soldiers *left the battle line*.

ぜんれつ【前列】 the front row. ¶ 私は小柄なのでいつも～に並ぶ As I am short I always stand in *the front row*. ～の左から２番めはだれか Who is the second from the left in *the* *front row?*

せんれん【洗練】¶彼女の～されたふるまいはすべての人を魅了した All people were charmed with her *refined* (≒ *elegant*) manners.

せんろ【線路】⊞ a track; ⊞ a line. ¶～を敷く lay *a track*.
—工事 line construction. —工夫 a track-layer.

そ

そ【祖】(先祖) an ancestor; (創始者) the founder.

そあく【粗悪】¶～な品 a *bad* (≒ *coarse*) article; an article *of bad quality*; an *inferior* thing.

そいそしょく【粗衣粗食】coarse clothing and food. ¶彼は～に甘んじている He is content with *plain living*.

そいね【添い寝】¶母親は赤ちゃんに～している The mother *is lying with* her baby at her side.

そいん【素因】a basic factor; a primary cause. ¶この事件の～はどこにあるのか What is *the basic factor* of the trouble?

そう【相】(人相) physiognomy. ¶彼には英雄の～がある He *looks like* a man destined for a hero.

そう【想】¶ぼくは卒業論文の～を練っている I *am thinking over* my graduation thesis. 彼は～を新たに小説を書きあげた He *thought* the plot *over* again and has finished writing his new novel.

そう【装】¶～を新たに改訂版が出版された A revised edition was published *in new binding* (≒ *in renewed style*).

そう【僧】a priest; a bonze. ¶彼は禅寺の～となった He became *a Zen* temple *priest*.

そう【層】a layer; a seam; a bed; class. ¶化石が～をなして発見された Fossils were found in *strata*.
勤労— the working class. 古生—〖地質〗the Paleozoic stratum. 読者— a class of readers.

そう-【総-】—所得 a gross income. —人口 the total population (*of*). —選挙 a general election. —動員 a general mobilization.

そ・う【沿う】¶海に～った家 a house *on* the coast. 道に～った店 stores (≒ shopfronts) *on* the street. 道に～った街路樹 trees *lining* the street. 川に～って歩く walk *along* a river. 鉄道が海岸に～って通っている The railroad *skirts* (≒ *runs along*) the coast.

そ・う【添う・副う】satisfy; suit. ¶ご希望に～うようにつとめます I'll do my best to *satisfy* your desire (≒ *meet* your expectations). 残念ですがご希望に～いかねます We are very sorry we can't *meet* (≒ *grant*; *gratify*) your wishes.

そう【然う】1〖そのよう・そのように〗¶～, それなんだ *Yes*, that's it.
～とはかぎらぬ That's not always the case.
～は問屋がおろさない You're expecting too much. / That's what you think.
～ではない. 違う That is not *so*. You are wrong.
～だ, そのとおりだ *Yes*, that's right.
～なら～とはっきり言ってくれ Tell me frankly. / Speak straight from the shoulder.
ぼくは～は思わぬ I don't think *so*. / I don't agree with you.
～はさせない I won't let that happen.
～してくれ Do *it* for me.
～伝えてください Please tell him about it.
～けちけちするな Don't be *so* stingy. / Be more generous.
～堅苦しいことを言うな Don't be *so* particular.
～怒るな Don't be *so* angry.
彼は～ばかでもないらしい I don't think he is *such* a blockhead as he is said to be.
みんなが言うほど～悪いやつとも思えない I don't think he is *such* a bad fellow as he's generally said to be.
～あわてて行くこともあるまい We can afford to wait.
2〖否定語を伴って, たいして〗¶～お手間はかけません I won't take too much of your time. / I won't keep you very long.
不景気も～ひどいことにはならないだろう I hope things are not going to be as bad as people think.
3〖慣用的表現〗¶～いえば, 彼はあのときここにいた That reminds me that he was here at that time.
～かといってほかに名案も浮かばない Not that I have thought of a good plan.

ぞう【象】〖動物〗an elephant; (雄) a bull elephant; (雌) a cow elephant; (子) a calf elephant. ¶～の鼻 the trunk of *an elephant*.
—使い an elephant trainer (≒ driver); (東インドの) a mahout.

ぞう【像】an image; a figure; a statue. ¶天女の～(彫像) *a statue* of an angel. 神々の～(絵) *figures* of gods. (光が)レンズを通して～を結ぶ focus into *image*.

ぞう【蔵】¶A氏～のセザンヌの名作 a masterpiece by Cézanne *in the possession of* (≒ *owned by*; *property of*) Mr. A.

そうあい【相愛】¶ ふたりは～の仲だ They *love each other*. / They *are in love with each other*. / They *are lovers*.

そうあたり〔せん〕【総当たり〔戦〕】a round robin.

そうあん【草案】a draft. ¶ 報告書の～を書く *draft* (≒ *draw up*) a report. 憲法の～を起草する make *a draft* of a constitution.

そうあん【創案】an original idea. ¶ これはだれの～か Whose *idea* (≒ *plan*) is this?

—者 an originator; an inventor.

そうい【相違】**1**〘違い〙〔a〕difference. ¶ 英語と米語の～を説明してください Please explain the *difference* between British English and American English.

ふたりの間には意見の～がある There is *a difference* of opinion between the two.

黒と白には著しい～がある There is *a* striking *contrast* between black and white.

AとBとはたいへんな～だ A is *a great contrast to* B.

ふたりの見解の～はいかんともしがたい There is no help for the *difference* between the two.

彼の申し立ては事実と～している What he states *is contrary to* the fact.

右のとおり～ありません I *affirm* the above statement to be true in every detail.

案に～して彼は約束の場所に現われなかった *Contrary to* my expectations he did not make his appearance at the appointed spot.

2〘たぶん〙¶ 彼はその事実を知らないに～ない He *must* be ignorant of the fact.

彼はもう出かけたに～ない *There is no doubt that* he has already gone out.

そうい【創意】originality invention. ¶ ～に富んだ人 a man *of ideas*; a *creative* mind; an *imaginative* person. ～に富んだ作品 a work full *of originality*.

そうい【総意】the general will. ¶ 国民の～に基づいて条約を結ぶ conclude a treaty with *the general will* of the people.

そういう ¶ ～問題は難しい *Such kind of* questions are difficult to answer. ～音楽は私の好みに合わない *That sort of* music is not to my taste. あなたが～ことを言うとは驚いた I am surprised that you should say *so*. ～事情で私は彼の申し出を断わった *Such being the case*, I declined his offer. ～わけで私はきのうの会に欠席したのだ *That is why* I absented myself from the meeting yesterday. ～ことになるのも当然だ It is natural that *such* a situation should follow.

そういん【僧院】a monastery; a cloister; (尼の) convent.

そういん【総員】the whole number. ¶ クラスの～は40名だ The class is made up of forty students. ～5時に起床 *All hands* are supposed to get up at five.

ぞういん【増員】¶ 警察官を2,000名～する *increase the number of* policemen by 2,000.

そううつびょう【躁鬱病】〔医学〕manic-depressive insanity.

—患者 a manic-depressive.

そううん【層雲】〔気象〕a stratus (複 strati).

ぞうえい【造営】¶ 皇居を～する *build* the Imperial Palace. ～中 be under *construction*.

ぞうえん【造園】〔landscape〕gardening.

—家 a landscape gardener (≒ architect).

—学 landscape architecture. —術 landscape gardening.

ぞうえん【増援】¶ ～する reinforce. ～部隊が最前線に送られた *Reinforcements* were sent to the〔battle〕front.

ぞうお【憎悪】detestation; hatred. ¶ 人に～の情を抱く harbor *hatred* toward *a person*. ～すべき行為 a highly *detestable* deed.

そうおう【相応】¶ 身分～の暮らしをする cut *one's* coat according to *one's* cloth. 能力に～した給料をもらう get a salary *proportionate to one's* ability. 委員長は彼に～な地位だ Chairman is a *fit* position for him.

不— ¶ 身分不～の暮らしをする live beyond *one's* means.

そうおん【騒音】a noise. ¶ 町の～に悩まされる be annoyed by street *noises*.

—防止 prevention of noises. —防止条例 the antinoise law.

ぞうか【造化】creation; nature. ¶ ～の神 the Creator. ～の妙に感嘆する admire the wonders of *nature*.

ぞうか【造花】an artificial (≒ imitation) flower. ¶ ～の桜 paper cherry blossoms.

ぞうか【増加】increase. ¶ この国の人口は～しつつある The population of this country *is on the increase*. この町は住民の数が急速に～した The population of this town *has* rapidly *increased* in size. 日本からの輸出品は著しく～している The number of Japan's exports *is growing* remarkably. 悪質犯罪の～は見逃すことができない重大問題だ The *increase* in vicious crimes is a serious problem not to be overlooked.

—率 the rate of increase. 自然— a natural increase.

そうかい【爽快】¶ 早朝の気分は～だ We *feel refreshed* in the early morning air. 暑い日にひと泳ぎするとまったく気分～になる A swim on a hot day *is really refreshing*.

そうかい【総会】a general meeting (≒ assembly).

株主— a general meeting of shareholders. 国連— the United Nations General Assembly. 臨時(通常)— an extraordinary (ordinary) general meeting.

そうがい【霜害】frost damage.

そうかいてい【掃海艇】a mine sweeper.

そうがかり【総掛かり】¶ ～で all together; with united (≒ combined) efforts.

そうがく【奏楽】a musical performance. ¶ 国歌の～のうちに式が始まった The ceremony began with the *playing* of the national anthem.

そ

そうがく【総額】the total. ¶～で100万円に上る損害だ The damage amounts to a million yen *in all* (≒ *in total*). A社からの請求書は～いくらになるのか What is the *amount* (≒ *total sum*) of the bill from A company?

ぞうがく【増額】¶予算の～を要求する ask for an *enlarged* budget. 彼らは賃銀の～を要求してストライキを行なっていた They were on strike demanding *higher* wages.

そうかつ【総括】generalization; a summary. ¶～的意見を述べる give an *all-inclusive* opinion. 討論を～する *summarize* a debate.

そうかつ【総轄】¶事務を～する *superintend* all the office works.

そうがわ【総皮・総革】¶～製の本 a *leather-bound* book.

そうかん【送還】¶捕虜を本国へ～する *repatriate* the captives to their own country. 強制～ compulsory *repatriation*; deportation.

そうかん【壮観】a grand sight. ¶海で見る日の出は～だ The sunrise on the sea is *a grand view*. 編隊飛行は実に～だった The formation flight was *a fine spectacle* (≒ *a grand sight*).

そうかん【相関】correlation; interrelation.
—関係〔a〕correlation; coefficient. ¶気候と作物との間には～関係がある There is *a correlation* between climate and crops. **—作用** correlation.

そうかん【創刊】¶新聞を～する *launch* a newspaper. 1800年～ *Started* in 1800.
—号 ¶～号を発行する issue *the first number*.

そうかん【総監】an inspector general. 警視— the Metropolitan Police Superintendent-General.

ぞうかん【増刊】**—号** an extra number (≒ issue; edition).

ぞうがん【象眼】¶金銀の～をした宝石箱 a jewel box *inlaid with* gold and silver. 金属に～する inlay (*something*) on metal.
—細工 an inlaid work; an inlay.

そうがんきょう【双眼鏡】〔a pair of〕binoculars; (陸上用)〔a pair of〕field glasses; (海上用)〔a pair of〕marine glasses.

そうき【早期】an early stage.
—診断 early check. **—治療** early treatment. **—発見** early detection.

そうぎ【争議】a strike. ¶～を解決(調停)する settle (adjust) *a strike*. ～に参加する join in *a strike*. 彼らは～中だ They *are on strike*. / The *strike* is on.
—権 the right of strike. **—行為** a strike action. **—団** the strikers. 労働— a labor dispute.

そうぎ【葬儀】a funeral service (*for* the late Mr. A.). ¶～に参列する attend *a person's funeral*.
—店 米 a funeral parlor. 英 an undertaker's〔shop〕. **—屋(人)** 米 a mortician; an undertaker.

ぞうき【臓器】(内臓器官) internal organs; (はらわた) the viscera (單 viscus); the intestines; the bowels.
—移植 an internal organ transplantation.

ぞうきばやし【雑木林】a copse; a coppice.

そうきゅう【早急】¶～に immediately; without delay. ～に処置しなければならない We need a *prompt* action.

そうきゅう【送球】〖野球〗passing. ¶外野から本塁へ～する *pass the ball* from the outfield to the home base.

そうきょ【壮挙】a heroic attempt; a grand project. ¶南極探検の～につく go on *a heroic* (≒ *great*) *expedition* to the South Pole.

そうぎょう【創業】the commencement of an enterprise. ¶明治10年～ *Founded* in the tenth year of Meiji. ～50年を祝う celebrate the fiftieth anniversary.

そうぎょう【早暁】dawn; daybreak.

そうぎょう【操業】operation; work. ¶～を開始(続行; 休止)する begin (keep on; cease) *operations*. ～を短縮する cut down (≒ reduce; curtail) *operations*.
—時間 operating hours. **—短縮** operation reduction; reduced operation. **—費** operating cost. 完全— full operation.

ぞうきょう【増強】reinforcement. ¶国防力を～する *strengthen* (≒ *reinforce*; *increase*) national defense.

そうきょく【箏曲】*koto* music.

そうきょくせん【双曲線】〖数学〗a hyperbola.

そうきん【送金】〔a〕remittance. ¶郵便為替で5,000円～する *remit* (≒ *make a remittance of*) five thousand yen by postal money order.
—為替 a remittance check. **—先(受取人)** a remittee. **—手数料** remittance charge. **—人** a remitter.

ぞうきん【雑巾】a floorcloth; a dust cloth; a house-cloth; a mop. ¶～をかける wipe with *a wet cloth*; (床に) mop the floor.

そうきんるい【走禽類】〖鳥類〗runners; cursorial birds.

そうく【痩軀】¶長身～の人 a *tall and slim man*.

そうぐ【葬具】a funeral outfit.

そうぐ【装具】an outfit; equipment〔s〕. ¶登山の～を身につける *be equipped* for mountain-climbing.

そうぐう【遭遇】an encounter. ¶沖で　に～する *be overtaken* (≒ *be caught*) *by* a storm at sea. 敵に～する *meet* (≒ *come across*) the enemy.
—戦 an encounter.

そうくずれ【総崩れ】¶敵は～になった The enemy *was put to rout*.

そうくつ【巣窟】a den; a haunt. ¶その場所はネズミの～になっている The place *is infested with* rats. 盗賊の～ *a den* of robbers.

そうけ【宗家】(本家) the hereditary master; (創始者) the inaugurator; the founder.

ぞうげ【象牙】ivory. ¶～の塔 an *ivory* tower.

—色〔の〕 ivory-color〔ed〕. —細工 ivory work. —質〘解剖〙(歯の) a dentine. —製品 ivory manufactures.

そうけい【早計】overhastiness. ¶ そんなことで計画を放棄するのは～にすぎる It would be *rash* to give up the plan for such a reason. 彼は～にもそう結論を下した He so concluded *hastily*.

そうけい【総計】a total〔amount〕; the sum total; the gross. ¶ 支出～は100万円だ The *total expenditure* amounts to a million yen.

そうげい【送迎】welcome and farewell. ¶ さかんな～を受ける *be received and sent off* with cheers.

ぞうけい【造形】—美術 plastic arts.

ぞうけい【造詣】¶ 彼は美術に～が深い He *is well-informed of* (≒ *is at home in*) fine arts.

そうけだ・つ【寒気立つ・総毛立つ】¶ 恐ろしさに～った My hair stood on end with horror.

ぞうけつ【増結】¶ 電車を3両～する *add* three coaches to the train.

ぞうけつざい【増血剤】a blood-making medicine.

そうけん【双肩】¶ 母校の名誉がわれわれの～にかかっている The honor of our school *falls upon* our success. この仕事の成否は諸君の～にかかっている The success of this enterprise *rests upon* you *wholly*.

そうけん【壮健】¶ ご～でなによりです I am very glad to find you *in good health*.

そうけん【送検】¶ 犯人(書類)を～する send the criminal (the police report relating the criminal) to the prosecutor.

そうけん【創見】an original view. ¶ 彼の論文は～に富んでいる His thesis *is* quite *original*.

そうげん【草原】a plain; a grassland; (北米の) a prairie; (南米の) pampas; (ロシアの) a steppe.

ぞうげん【増減】¶ 月によって収益は～する The profits *vary* (≒ *fluctuate*) with the month.

そうこ【倉庫】a storehouse; a warehouse. ¶ 品物を～に入れる *store* (≒ *warehouse*) goods.

—会社 a warehouse company. —係 a warehouse keeper; warehousing business. —業者 a warehouseman. —料 warehouse charges.

そうご【相互】¶ そうすれば会員～の利益になるだろう It would be the *mutual* benefit of the members to do so.

—援助条約 a mutual assistance pact. —関係 mutual (≒ reciprocal) relation. —銀行 a mutual financing bank. —作用 reciprocal action. —扶助 mutual aid. —保険 mutual insurance.

ぞうご【造語】a coined word. ¶ それは彼の～だ This word *was coined* by him.

そうこう【草稿】a draft; notes; (原稿) a manuscript.

そうこう【装甲】—甲板 plate armor. —車 an armored motorcar; a tank. —列車 an armed train.

そうこう【操行】conduct; behavior; deportment. ¶ 彼は～の点がよい(悪い) He gets a good (poor) mark in *deportment*.

そうこう【然う斯う】¶ ～するうちに彼はもどってくるだろう He will be back *in the meantime*.

そうごう【相好】¶ 朗報を聞いて彼は～をくずして喜んだ His face *was radiant with joy at* the good news. / He *was all smiles at* the good news.

そうこうかい【壮行会】a send-off party; a farewell party.

そうごう【総合】synthesis. ¶ 各種の問題を～して考える think of every sort of problem *collectively*. あれこれ～してみると，この方法が最善のようだ *Putting this and that together*, I think this method is the best of all.

—課税 consolidated taxation. —競技 an all-round game. —計画 an all-round plan. —雑誌 an all-round magazine. —大学 a university. —点 the total count.

そうこうげき【総攻撃】a general attack. ¶ 敵に～を行なう make *a general attack* on the enemy.

そうこく【相克】a conflict. ¶ 理性と感情の～ *a conflict* between reason and sentiment.

そうこん【早婚】an early marriage. ¶ 彼は～だ He *married early* (≒ *young*).

そうこん【草根】the root of a plant.

—木皮 roots of herbs and barks of trees (grass roots とすると農牧民・一般庶民・根底などの意味にもなる).

そうごん【荘厳】solemnity; sublimity. ¶ 儀式は～に行なわれた The ceremony was performed *solemnly*. その神社の～さに心打たれた I was deeply impressed with the *solemnity* (≒ *grandeur*) of the shrine. なんという～な音楽だろう What *solemn* music!

そうさ【走査】scanning.

—線 a scanning beam; a scanning line.

そうさ【操作】operation; management. ¶ 機械を～する *operate* a machine.

金融— monetary manipulation (≒ operation). 市場— market manipulation (≒ operation).

そうさ【捜査】search; investigation; inquiry. ¶ ～はあらゆる方面にわたった The *search* was made in every direction. 警察は犯人の徹底的～を開始した The police began to make *a* thorough *search* for the criminal. ついにその～は打ち切られた At last the *search* came to be concluded.

—員 an investigator; a detective. —網 a dragnet. ¶ 町中に～網が敷かれた The *dragnet* was spread throughout the town.

そうさい【相殺】a counterbalance; a counteraction. ¶ このもうけであの損の～はできない That loss cannot *be compensated* by these gains. それはその効果を～するのにじゅうぶんでない

そ

It is not enough to *counteract* (≒ *offset*) the effect.

そうさい【総裁】a president; a governor. ¶党の～になる assume *the presidency* of a party.

日本銀行── the Governor of the Bank of Japan. 副── a vice-president. 名誉── an honorary president.

そうさく【捜索】a search. ¶彼らは彼の～に出発した They started *in search of* him. 警察がその部屋のすみずみまで～した The police *looked* in every nook and corner of the room.

──願い ¶彼は警察に息子の～願いを出した He asked the police to *search for* his missing son. ──令状 a search warrant; an order for search.

そうさく【創作】creation; an original work. ¶彼は～に携わっている He is engaged in *creative writing*.

──家 a novelist. ──活動 ¶彼は精力的に～活動を続けている He is energetically engaged in *creative activity*. ──力 creative power.

ぞうさく【造作】**1**〘家の〙the furnishings. ¶この家の～は(構造は)手がこんでいる This house *is* elaborately *built* (≒ *fixed*).

この家には一部しか～がついていない This house *is* partly *furnished*.

2〘顔の〙¶彼女は顔の～がいい Her *features* are lovely.

ぞうさつ【増刷】¶2万部～する *print additional* twenty thousand *copies*.

ぞうさな・い【造作ない】easy. ¶そんなことは～い That *is* quite *easy*. / I could do it quite *easily*. / There *is no trouble* at all. 彼はその仕事を～くやってのけた He finished the task *without any difficulty* (≒ *with ease*; *without any trouble*).

そうざらい【総ざらい】a general review. ¶もうこのへんで～をする必要がある Now we should *review all the lessons*.

そうざん【早産】a premature birth. ¶この子は～だった This baby *was born prematurely*. 彼の妻は～した His wife *gave birth to a baby prematurely*.

ぞうさん【増産】increased production. ¶彼は小麦の～に励んだ He worked hard to *increase* the yield of wheat. 合衆国はウランの新しい～計画を始めた The United States started a new plan for *increasing* uranium output.

そうし【相思】¶ふたりは～相愛の仲だ They *are in love with each other*.

そうし【創始】origination; creation. ¶その理論はA博士の～したものだ The theory *originated with* Dr. A.

──者 the originator; the founder.

そうじ【相似】resemblance; similarity.

──形 similar figures.

そうじ【掃除】cleaning; sweeping. ¶部屋を～する *clean* (≒ *sweep*) a room. 彼の部屋はいつも～が行き届いている His room *is* always *kept clean*.

──道具 scrubbing things. ──人 a cleaner; a sweeper; (街路の) a scavenger. ──婦 a charwoman; 米 a scrubwoman. 街路── scavengery. 電気──機 a vacuum cleaner.

ぞうし【増資】¶その会社は1億円から2億円に～した The company *increased the capital stock* from one hundred million yen to two hundred million yen.

そうしき【葬式】a funeral. ¶～を出す hold *a funeral*; perform *a funeral service*. 人の～に参列する attend *a person's funeral*.

そうしき【総指揮】¶～をとる take *the supreme command* (*of*).

──者 a supreme commander.

そうししゅつ【総支出】¶～はいくらになるか How much is *the total expenditure*?

そうじしょく【総辞職】¶そのため内閣が～するかもしれない It might cause *the general resignation* of the Cabinet. 彼らは～した They *resigned in a body*.

そうしつ【喪失】loss. ¶権利を～する *lose one's* right. 記憶を～する *lose one's* memory. 市民権を～した His civil rights *were forfeited*.

記憶── loss of memory. 自信── loss of confidence.

そうじて【総じて】¶日本人は～勤勉である *Generally speaking*, Japanese are diligent. 文化祭は～よくできた *On the whole* (≒ *In general*), the Cultural Festival was successful.

そうしはいにん【総支配人】a general manager.

そうしゃ【走者】¶(リレーの)第1～ the first *runner*; 最終～ the last *runner*; an anchor 〔man〕; (野球の)一塁～ *a* first-base *runner*.

そうしゃ【操車】marshaling.

──係 a train dispatcher. ──場 a marshaling yard.

そうしゃ【掃射】machine-gunning. ¶敵機の機銃～を受けた We *were machine-gunned* by the enemy airplanes.

そうじゅう【操縦】**1**〘乗り物を〙handling. ¶彼は飛行機の～ができる He can *fly* an airplane.

ヘリコプターの～はさほど難しくない It is not so difficult to *pilot* a helicopter.

──桿(かん) a control stick (≒ column). ──士 a pilot.

2〘人を〙¶彼は息子を巧みに～して自分の思いどおりのことをさせた He *maneuvered* his son *into* doing as he himself wanted.

彼は妻を思いのままに～している He *is turning* his wife *around his finger*.

ぞうしゅう【増収】(収入の) increased income; (収穫の) an increased yield. ¶昨年に比して2割の～となる It shows *an increase* of twenty percent over last year.

そうしゅうにゅう【総収入】the total income. ¶～の2割が図書費にかかる Twenty percent of *the total income* (≒ *the gross income*) is paid for books.

そうじゅく【早熟】precocity. ¶～な子 a *precocious* (≒ *premature*) child.

そうじゅつ【槍術】spear exercise.

そうしゅん【早春】early spring.

そうしょ【叢書】a series; a library. ¶フランス文学の～ *a library* of French literature.

そうしょ【草書】a cursive style. ¶～で書く write *in a cursive hand* (≒ *in a running style*).

ぞうしょ【蔵書】a collection of books.
¶彼の～はたいへん多い He has *a* large *collection of books*. / He owns *a* large *library*. 彼は3,000冊の～がある He has *a collection* of three thousand volumes.
—家 a book collector. —目録 a library catalogue.

そうしょう【宗匠】a master. ¶茶の湯の～ *a master* of tea ceremony.

そうしょう【総称】a general term. ¶これらを～して両棲(りょうせい)類と呼ぶ "Amphibia" is *a general term for* these animals.

そうじょう【奏上】¶政治全般について～した He *reported* the general political affairs *to the Emperor*.

そうじょう【相乗】multiplication.
—積 the product of a mass. —平均 a geometrical average.

そうじょう【僧正】a bishop.
大— an archbishop.

そうじょう【層状】¶石炭が～をなしている Coal *is stratified*.
—岩 a stratified rock.

そうじょう【騒擾】〔a〕disturbance.
—罪 the crime of sedition.

そうしょく【草食】—動物 a grass-eating animal. —類 herbivora (単 -vore).

そうしょく【装飾】〔an〕ornament; 〔a〕decoration. ¶～する decorate; ornament.
—品 ornaments; decorations. 室内— interior (≒ inside) decoration. 舞台— stage decoration.

そうしょく【僧職】holy orders. ¶～につく enter the *priesthood*; take orders. ～にある be in the *priesthood* (≒ *orders*).

ぞうしょく【増殖】increase. ¶魚類を～する *multiply* fish〔es〕.
—炉(原子の) a breeder reactor.

そうしれいぶ【総司令部】General Headquarters (G.H.Q. と略す).

そうしん【送信】transmission. ¶～する transmit a message.
—機 a transmitter.

そうしん【喪心・喪神】absent-mindedness.
¶～状態で absent-mindedly; distractedly.

ぞうしん【増進】promotion. ¶適度の運動をして健康の～をはからなければならぬ You must *improve* your health by moderate exercise. 食前の一杯は食欲を～する To have a drink before meals *improves* our appetite. 音楽は作業能率を～する Music *improves* our work efficiency.

そうしんぐ【装身具】personal ornaments; accessories.

そうすい【送水】—管 a water pipe. —本管 a water main.

そうすい【総帥】the leader (*of*).

ぞうすい【増水】¶豪雨のため川は2メートル～した Owing to the heavy rain, the river *has risen* two meters. ～のため堤を警戒しなければならない The river *has swollen*, so we must watch the bank carefully.

ぞうすい【雑炊】medley soup. ¶～を一杯すする sip a bowl of *porridge of rice and vegetables* (≒ *medley soup*).

そうすう【総数】the total number. ¶参加者の～は1万人に達した *The total* of the participants amounted to ten thousand.

そう·する【奏する】play. ¶楽隊が国歌を～しはじめた The band began to *play* (≒ *strike up*) the national anthem. 彼の努力が功を～した His efforts were successful.

そうすると【然うすると】¶～彼の言ったことはまちがいだ *Then* (≒ *If so*), what he said is wrong. ～結局うまくいかなかったのだね That means that it did not come off after all.

そうすれば【然うすれば】¶～私も助かる That would be of great help to me. ～反対できない *In that case*, I cannot oppose it.

そうせい【早世】an untimely death. ¶彼は～した He *died young*. / He *died at an early age*.

そうぜい【総勢】the whole men. ¶～でたった9人だった There were only nine *in all* (≒ *all told*). 家族～で出かけた *All* the family went out *together*.

ぞうぜい【増税】a tax increase; increase of taxation. ¶所得税が5パーセント～になった The income tax was increased by 5 percent.

そうせいき【創世記】〔聖書〕the Genesis.

そうせいじ【双生児】twins (双生児のひとりひとりは one of the twins と言う).
一卵生— identical twins. 二卵生— fraternal twins.

そうせいじ【早生児】a prematurely-born baby.

そうせき【僧籍】priesthood. ¶彼は～に入った He *became a priest* (≒ *a monk*). / He *took holy orders*. / He *was ordained priest*. 彼は～を離れた He *renounced the cloth*.

そうせきうん【層積雲】〔気象〕a strato-cumulus (複 -cumuli); a roll-cumulus.

そうせつ【総説】general remarks; an introduction.

そうせつ【創設】establishment; foundation.
¶この大学は1900年に～された The college *was founded* (≒ *was established*) in 1900.
—者 the founder; the father.

そうぜつ【壮絶】¶彼は～な最期を遂げた He died a〔n〕*heroic* death. ～な死闘が繰り返された *Fierce* struggles for life and death continued.

ぞうせつ【増設】¶学校を～する *build more*

schools. 図書館を～する *establish* (≒ *set up*) *more* libraries.

そうぜん【騒然】 ¶ 物情～たるありさまであった There was *public unrest* everywhere. 会場が～となった The hall was thrown into *an uproar*. 市場は～としていた The market was in *a tumult*.

そうせん【造船】 shipbuilding.
—技師 a naval (≒ marine) engineer. —技術 shipbuilding engineering. —業 shipbuilding industry. —所 a shipyard; a dockyard. —能力 shipbuilding capacity.

そ

そうせんきょ【総選挙】 a general election.

そうそう【早早】 early; quickly. ¶ ～に退散した I beat a *hasty* retreat. 入社～に失敗した I blundered *soon* after I entered the company. 来月～に上京する I'll go up to Tokyo *early* next month. 帰る～また出かける用事ができた *As soon as* I came home, I had to go out again on business.

そうそう【錚錚】 ¶ ～たる学者たち *prominent* (≒ *distinguished*; *eminent*) scholars. 各界の～たる人物 *outstanding* men from various spheres of life.

そうそう【然う然う】 **1** 〖しばしば〗 ¶ ～借金を延ばすことはできない I cannot put off the payment of debt *so often*.
2 〖思い出して〗 ¶ ～すっかり忘れていた *Oh, Yes!* I have clean forgotten it.
～, まさにそのとおりだ *Yes, yes,* you are quite right.

そうぞう【創造】 creation. ¶ 天地～のとき the time of *the Creation*. 神は地上の万物を～した God *created* all things on earth. これは～的な作品とはいえない This is not worth the name of an *original* (≒ a *creative*) work.
—者 a creator. —物 a creature; (総称的に) creation. —力 originalities. ¶ ～力を伸ばさねばならぬ We must develop our *originalities* (≒ *creative faculties*).

そうぞう【想像】 **1** imagination. ¶ どんなことになるかちょっと～もつきません I can hardly *imagine* how things are going to develop.
そのあとどうなったかはご～にまかせます You may *imagine* the rest.
そんなに～をたくましくするな Don't give free play to your *imagination* like that.
そんなことをすれば, ～もつかぬ膨大な額になります That would entail an *incredible* sum of money.
～を絶する大氷原が私たちの進路をさえぎっていた An *unimaginably* vast ice field blocked our way.
結果はきみの～したとおりだった The result was as you *had expected*.
そういう事態も～できぬことではない Such a situation *is* not *unthinkable*.
2 〖合成語〗 ¶ きみはなかなか～力に富んでいる You have *a* lively (≒ vigorous) *imagination*. / You *are* very *imaginative*.
勘が悪いな. もっと～力を働かしてみろ You're dull. Use your *imagination*.

きりんは～上の動物だ The "Kirin" is an *imaginary* animal.
これは当時のある画家の描いた地獄の～画だ This is a picture of hell as *envisaged* by a painter of the day.

そうそうきょく【葬送曲・送葬曲】 a funeral march.

そうぞうし·い【騒騒しい】 ¶ 部屋の中が～い The room *is noisy*. そんなに～くするな Don't *make* such *a noise*. 世の中が～い There is *public unrest* everywhere.

そうぞうしさ【騒騒しさ】 ¶ 都会の～を離れて生活したい I want to live a long way from the city *noise*.

そうそく【総則】 general rules.

そうぞく【相続】 succession; inheritance.
¶ だれが彼の財産を～するのか Who will *inherit* (≒ *succeed to*) his estate? 私が父のあとを～する I'll *succeed* my father. (地位・職業などを相続する意味では succeed *a person* とし, succeed to *a person* とは言わない).
—争い a dispute about (≒ a quarrel over) the succession. —財産 an inheritance; inherited property. —税 an inheritance tax; death duties. —人(男) an heir; (女) an heiress; (後継者) an successor. 遺産— succession to property. ¶ この土地は遺産～でぼくのものとなった I own this land by *inheritance*.

そうそふ【曾祖父】 a great-grandfather.

そうそぼ【曾祖母】 a great-grandmother.

そうそん【曾孫】 a great-grandchild.

そうだ【操舵】 steerage; steering. ¶ 彼は岩間を巧みに～していった He *steered* the boat skillfully through the rocks.
—室 a steering house. —手 a steersman; a helmsman; a quartermaster. —術 steersmanship; steering.

-そうだ **1** 〖ということだ〗 ¶ 彼は泳ぎがうまい～ *They say* he is a good swimmer.
彼はやがて渡欧する～ *I hear* that he will go over to Europe before long.
彼は校長をやめる～ *It is said* that he will resign the post of principal.
彼は高校を卒業している～ *We are told* that he has finished the high school course.
彼女は当分結婚しない～ *It is rumored* that she will remain unmarried for the time being.
あなたが間崎さんだ～ね You are Mr. Masaki, *I understand* (≒ *I presume*)?
2 〖のように見える〗 ¶ たなから今にも本が落ち～ The book *may* fall down from the shelf *at any moment*.
雨が降り～ It *is likely to* rain. / It *looks like* rain.
彼は見るからに健康～ He *looks* every inch in good health.

そうたい【早退】 ¶ 彼は会社を午後～した In the afternoon he *left* his office *earlier than usual*. 頭が痛くて学校を～した I *left* school *before it was over*, because I had a headache.

そうたい【相対】 ¶西とか東とかいうのは～的な概念である What is called "West" or "East" is a *relative* concept.

―性原理 the theory of relativity.

そうたい【総体】 all ; the whole body. ¶今度のテストは～によくできた The result of the last examination is *generally* good.

そうだい【総代】 a representative. ¶卒業生～に選ばれた I was chosen valedictorian (≒ the *representative* of the graduates). 彼が皆の～として謝意を表した He made an address of thanks *on* (≒ *in*) *behalf of* us all.

そうだい【壮大】 grandeur ; magnificence. ¶われわれはその渓谷の～さに心を打たれた We were deeply impressed with the *grandeur* of the canyon. ～なながめ a *magnificent* (≒ *grand*) view. ～な寺院 an *imposing* temple.

ぞうだい【増大】 increase ; enlargement. ¶失業者が～する Unemployment *goes on increasing*. 都市人口は～の一途をたどっている The population in cities steadily *increases*.

そうたいきゃく【総退却】 a general retreat. ¶敵は～中である The enemy *are in full retreat*. / The enemy *are retreating in all the fronts*.

そうだち【総立ち】 ¶満場～になって騒いだ The whole audience (≒ house) stood up in an uproar.

そうだつ【争奪】 a contest ; a struggle. ¶両者の政権の～はみにくいものとなった The *struggle* for political power between them became quite dirty.

―戦 ¶選手権の～戦が始まる *A contest for* the championship is going to start. 近ごろは熟練工の～戦が激しい Recently there has been *a* fierce *scramble for* skilled workers.

そうたん【操短】 curtailment of operations. ¶工場では3割の～を始めた Operations at the factory began to *be restricted* by thirty percent. 不景気のため～せざるをえない We have to *work for short time* on account of business depression.

そうだん【相談】 **1**〖検討・打ち合わせ〗 conference ; consultation. ¶彼と～のうえで返事する I'll give you a definite reply after *talking* it *over with* him.

～もしないでかってに決めるとは何事だ How preposterous of you to have decided without letting me know anything about it!

彼女はその問題のことで～にきた She came to *ask for* my advice about the affair.

例の件で～したいことがある I'd like to *talk over* that problem with you.

どうだ, きみたち, ～がまとまったかね Well, have you come to an agreement?

身の上**―欄** an agony column. 天気**―所** a weather information bureau.

2〖取りきめ〗 ¶どうもふたりの間でそういう～ができていたらしい It seems to me that such arrangements were made beforehand between them.

3〖慣用的表現〗 ¶そんなことはできない～だ It's an impossible proposition.

そうち【装置】 a system ; contrivance ; mechanism.

舞台**―** a stage setting. 防火**―** anti-fire provisions. 安全**―** a safety device.

ぞうちく【増築】 (増築する行為) extension of a building ; (増築された建物) an annex (*to* a building).

¶あの百貨店は目下～中だ *An extension* is now under construction at that department store. / They *are* now *enlarging* its building at that department store.

そうちょう【早朝】 ¶～から人出が多かった There were crowds of people *early in the morning*. われわれは明～出発する We'll start *early* tomorrow *morning*.

そうちょう【荘重】 solemnity. ¶式は～にとり行なわれた The ceremony was performed *with solemnity*. ～な音楽が奏でられた *Solemn* music was played.

そうちょう【総長】 a president.

大学**―** the president of a university ; (イギリスの大学) the chancellor. 検事**―** 米 the Public Prosecutor General ; 英 the Attorney General ; the Director of Public Prosecution. 事務**―** a secretary-general.

そうちょう【曹長】〔軍事〕米 a master sergeant ; 英 a sergeant major.

ぞうちょう【増長】 ¶彼のわがままが～する He *grows more and more* wayward (≒ selfish). 彼は最近～している He *has been puffed up* recently. / He *has grown impudent* recently.

そうで【総出】 ¶一家～で彼を迎えた *All* the family welcomed him.

そうてい【送呈】 ¶その本を～しましょう I'll *offer* (≒ *send*) the book.

そうてい【装丁・装幀】 binding ; (表紙の) design. ¶豪華な～の本だ It is a book in gorgeous *bindings*. その本は総革で～してある The book *is bound* in full leather. この本の～はよい This book *is* well *bound*.

―家 a designer 〔of books〕.

そうてい【想定】 the assumption ; a hypothesis. ¶ここから火が出たと～して退避訓練をしよう Let's take a refuge drill *on the assumption that* a fire has started here.

そうてい【漕艇】 rowing.

―競技 a boat race ; a regatta.

ぞうてい【贈呈】 presentation. ¶銀製のカップを彼に皆で～した We *made a present of* a silver cup *to* him. / We *presented* a silver cup *to* him. クラスで学校に絵を～した Our class *presented* the school *with* a picture. (著者が自著に署名して)～ With the compliments (≒ *With the best wishes*) of the author.

―者 a giver ; a presenter. **―品** a present.

そ

—本 a presentation copy.

そうてん【争点】 an issue; the point at issue. ¶ ～のずれた論争だ It is a dispute off *the point*. ～は人員整理にしぼられた The *dispute* was narrowed down to the problem of personnel cut.

そうてん【装塡】 ¶ 銃に弾(たま)を～する *load* a gun with bullets.

そうでん【相伝】 ¶ 一子～の秘法 the family secrets.

そうでん【送電】 transmission of electricity. ¶ この発電所は東京に～している This power station *supplies electricity* to the city of Tokyo.

—設備 power transmission. **—線** a power cable; a power line.

そうと【壮図】 an ambitious course. ¶ 彼の～はむなしかった His *heroic attempt* ended in failure.

そうとう【相当】 **1** 〖かなりの〗 ¶ 彼ももう～の年だ He is *rather* advanced in age.

この職はあの国では～重要な職だ This post is a *very* important one in that country.

彼女は～よい家柄の出だ She comes of a *fairly* respectable family.

彼も～なもんだ He is a *smart* fellow. / He is certainly a man *to be reckoned with*.

2 〖ふさわしい〗 ¶ 私は自分の力量に～する給料をもらっている I am getting a salary *commensurate to* (≒ *with*) my ability.

この行為は死刑に～する This deed *deserves* the death penalty.

3 〖同等の〗 ¶ 1ドルは何円に～するか What *is* one dollar *equivalent to* in Japanese money?

プライバシーに～する日本語はあるか Is there a Japanese word (≒ *a* Japanese *counterpart*) *for* 'privacy'?

その職は日本の文部大臣に～する That position *corresponds to* that of Japan's Education Minister.

彼は金額にして100万円に～する品物をわいろとして受け取った He accepted as a bribe an article *worth* a million yen.

そうとう【総統】 the president; (中国の) the generalissimo.

そうとう【掃討】 ¶ 敵を～中だ We *are clearing* (≒ *are ridding*) the battlefield of the enemy.

そうどう【騒動】 a riot; a commotion; trouble. ¶ 彼らはまた～を起こした They stirred up *troubles* again. / They started *a riot* again. 上を下への大～だった There was *an* utter *confusion*.

お家**—** ¶ 彼はお家～に巻き込まれた He was involved in *the family strife*. 米**—** a rice riot. 学校**—** ¶ 学校～が各地に起こっている There have been *school disturbances* (≒ *campus riots*) all over the country.

ぞうとう【贈答】 gift-giving.

—品 a present; a gift.

そうどういん【総動員】 general mobilization. ¶ 一家～で大掃除をした *All* the family joined in cleaning the whole house. ～令が下された *General mobilization orders* were given.

そうとく【総督】 a governor-general (複 governors-general).

—府(イギリス植民地の) the Government House. インド**—** the Viceroy of India.

そうトン【総トン】 gross tonnage. ¶ 2万～の船 a ship of twenty thousand *tons gross*.

—数 gross tonnage.

そうなめ【総嘗め】 ¶ われわれはリーグ戦で敵を～にした We *won a sweeping victory* 〔*over* all the teams〕 in the league series.

そうなん【遭難】 an accident; a disaster; (船の) a shipwreck. ¶ 冬山の～が多い There are a lot of *accidents* in winter mountains. 彼らは山で～した They met with *a disaster* in mountaineering. あらしで多くの船が～した Many ships *were wrecked* by the storm.

—救助隊 a rescue party. **—現場** the scene of the disaster. **—者** a victim; (生存者) a survivor. **—船** a ship in distress; a wrecked ship. **—信号** an SOS. ¶ ～信号を受けた We picked up *an SOS*.

ぞうに【雑煮】 *zoni* (英語で説明すれば rice cakes and vegetables boiled in a soup).

そうにゅう【挿入】 insertion; 〔数学〕 interpolation. ¶ その契約に免責条項を～しておかなければならぬ We must *insert* an exemption clause in the contract.

—句 a parenthesis.

そうねん【壮年】 manhood. ¶ 彼は既に～に達している He has already reached *manhood*. 彼は～時代に財をつくった He made a large fortune *in the prime of his life*.

そうは【走破】 ¶ 私は2時間かかって山道を30キロ～した I *ran* (≒ *covered*) 30 kilometers along the mountain road in two hours.

そうば【相場】 **1** 〖株・市況〗 (市価) the price; (投機) speculation. ¶ 米の～は上がっている *The price* of rice has risen.

彼は～に手を出している He is engaged in *speculation*.

～でたいへんな損をした I lost a lot of money in *speculation*.

彼は～でもうけた He made a lot of money in *speculation*.

—師 a speculator. 株式**—** a stock market. 為替**—** the rate of exchange. 小売**—** the retail price.

2 〖一般の評価〗 ¶ 正直者は融通がきかないものと～がきまっている An honest man *is generally considered to be* lacking in adaptability. 夏は暑いものと～がきまっている Summer is *always* a hot season, *as everyone admits*. 昔は牛乳屋は早起きと～がきまっていた Formerly milkmen were, *without exception*, early risers.

ぞうはい【増配】 (配当の) an increased dividend. ¶ 会社は来期は～をする The corporation will *pay a larger dividend* on stocks next term.

そうはく【蒼白】¶ 顔面が～になった He turned *pale* (≒ *white*).
ぞうはつ【増発】¶ 臨時列車を～する run *extra* trains. 公債を～する issue *additional* bonds.
そうはつき【双発機】a twin-engine[d] airplane.
そうはつせいちほうしょう【早発性痴呆症】〖医学〗dementia praecox.
そうばな【総花】¶ これまでは～式にやってきた We have been doing to please everybody. / We have so far followed an *all-round* policy. 予算の配分が～的で重点がない The allotment of the budget *is all-round* and has no stressed points.
そうばん【早晩】¶ この事件も～解決するであろう This affair will be settled *sooner or later* (≒ *in due course of time*).
ぞうはん【造反】¶ その学校にも～する者がだいぶんいた There were many *rebels* (≒ *insurgent faculty members*) in that school too.
そうび【装備】equipment; outfit. ¶ われわれは核兵器を～しない We will not *equip ourselves with* nuclear weapons. 彼女はじゅうぶん～を整えて登山した She climbed the mountain *well equipped with* necessaries.
そうひょう【総評】a general comment (*on*); (日本労働組合総評議会) General Council of Trade Unions of Japan.
そうふ【送付】¶ 法案を参議院に～する *refer* a bill *to* the House of Councillors for consideration.
そうふ【総譜】〖音楽〗a full score.
そうふう【送風】ventilation.
—機 a blower; a ventilator.
ぞうふく【増幅】〖電気〗amplification.
¶ 電流が真空管で～される The electric current *is amplified* in a vacuum valve.
—器 an amplifier.
ぞうぶつしゅ【造物主】the Creator; the Maker; (神) God.
ぞうへいきょく【造幣局】the Mint Bureau.
そうへき【双璧】the two greatest authorities. ¶ 彼らは画壇の～だ They are *the two* (≒ *the twin*) *greatest* painters.
そうべつ【送別】farewell. ¶ ～の辞を述べる make a *farewell* speech.
—会 a farewell party. ¶ A氏の～会を催す give *a farewell party* to Mr. A.
ぞうほ【増補】¶ ～する enlarge.
—版 an enlarged edition. 改訂—版 a revised and enlarged edition.
そうほう【双方】both sides; both parties. ¶ 彼はわれわれ～の友人だ He is our *mutual* friend. 労使～の言い分を聞く listen to the claims of *both* labor *and* capital.
そうほう【走法】a way of running.
そうほん【造本】binding. ¶ この本は～がしっかりしている This book *is* solidly *bound*.
そうほんけ【総本家】the head family.
そうほんざん【総本山】the head temple [of the Buddhist Sect].
そうまとう【走馬燈】a revolving lantern.
そうむ【総務】—会長(政党の) the Chairman of the Executive Council. —部 the general affairs department. —部長 a general manager.
そうむけいやく【双務契約】〖法律〗a bilateral contract.
そうめい【聡明】¶ ～な人 an *intelligent* man. 彼は～そうだ He looks *bright and wise*.
そうめいきょく【奏鳴曲】〖音楽〗a sonata.
そうめん【素麺・索麺】Japanese vermicelli; fine noodles.
そうめんせき【総面積】¶ 日本の～ *the total area* of Japan.
そうもく【草木】plants and trees; vegetation.
そうもくろく【総目録】a catalog; a complete (≒ full) list.
ぞうもつ【臓物】the entrails; guts; (鳥の) giblets; (牛・羊の) pluck.
そうゆかん【送油管】an oil pipe line.
ぞうよ【贈与】donation; presentation.
¶ 彼は父の遺産の一部をある福祉施設に～した He *presented* part of the property left by his father *to* a certain welfare establishment.
—税 a gift (≒ donation) tax.
そうらん【争乱】¶ 中東では～が絶えなかった There was no end of *troubles* in the Middle East.
そうらん【騒乱】[a] disturbance; troubles.
¶ ～が起こりそうだ *Troubles* seem imminent. 国内では～が絶えなかった The country was subject to continual *disturbances*.
—罪〖法律〗the crime of riot act.
そうり【総理】the Prime Minister.
—官邸 the Prime Minister's official residence.
ぞうり【草履】Japanese sandals.
そうりつ【創立】establishment; founding; foundation. ¶ 彼がこの学校を～した He *founded* (≒ *established*) this school. わが社は～50年になる Our company has reached the 50th year of its existence.
—記念日 the anniversary of the founding [of a school]. ¶ きのうわが社の～20周年記念日祝賀パーティーが開かれた The party to celebrate the 20th anniversary of the *founding* of our company was given yesterday.
—者 the founder. —総会 the inaugural (≒ general) meeting.
ぞうりむし【ぞうり虫】〖動物〗a paramecium (複 paramecia).
そうりょ【僧侶】a priest.
そうりょう【送料】(郵便の) postage; (荷物の) carriage. ¶ 本の～が値上がりした The *postage on* books was raised (≒ was increased). この小荷物の～はいくらになりますか What is the *carriage* for this parcel?
—無料 postage free; carriage free.
そうりょう【総量】(総重量) the gross weight; (総額) the total amount.
そうりょう【総領】the oldest (≒ eldest) child.

そ

—娘 the oldest (≒ eldest) daughter.
そうりょうじ【総領事】a consul general.
そうりょく【総力】all *one's* energy. ¶～をあげて戦う fight *with all one's energies.*
—戦 a total (≒ an all-out) war.
ぞうりん【造林】afforestation. ¶水害を防ぐために～した We *planted trees* to prevent floods.
そうるい【藻類】〔植物〕the algae; seaweeds.
そうるい【走塁】running. ¶彼は～がうまい He is good at *base running.*
そうれい【壮麗】grandeur. ¶～なベルサイユ宮殿 the *magnificent* (≒ *imposing*) Versailles Palace. ～な建築 a *splendid* building. ～な儀式 a *grand* ceremony.
そうれつ【壮烈】¶～な最期を遂げる die a *heroic* death.
そうれつ【葬列】a funeral procession.
¶～に加わる be in *a funeral procession.*
そうろ【走路】a track; a course.
そうろう【早老】premature senility.
そうろん【総論】general remarks; an introduction.
そうわ【総和】the sum total. ¶～を出す sum (≒ add) up.
そうわ【挿話】an episode.
ぞうわい【贈賄】bribery. ¶彼は50万円を市長に～した He *gave a bribe* of five hundred thousand yen to the mayor. 彼は～で訴えられている He is charged with *bribery.*
—罪 bribery. —事件 a bribery case.
そうわき【送話器】a transmitter; (電話の) a mouthpiece.
そえがき【添え書き】a postscript (P.S. と略す).
¶～する add a postscript (*to* a letter).
そえぎ【添え木】a splice piece; (腕などの) a splint. ¶植木に～をする *apply* a splice piece to the tree. 腕に～を当てる *splint* an arm.
そえぢ【添え乳】¶母親が～していた The mother *was suckling her baby in bed.*
そえもの【添え物】(付加物) an addition (*to*); (景品) a premium (*for*); (料理の) a garnish (≒ garnishings) (*to*); (付録) a supplement (*to*).
そ·える【添える】¶贈り物に名刺を～えて送ってよこした He sent me a present along *with* his 〔calling〕card. 彼の余興が会に彩りを～えた His entertainment *added to* the enjoyment of the party. 願書には写真を～えてください Present the application form *with* your photograph.
そえん【疎遠】(仲たがい) estrangement; (ごぶさた) *one's* long silence. ¶彼との間が～になった I *became estranged from* him.
ソークワクチン〔医学〕the Salk vaccine.
ソース sauce; (日本で言うソース) Worcester〔shire〕sauce. ¶～をかける put (≒ pour) *sauce* (*on*; *over*).
ホワイト— white sauce.
ソーセージ a sausage.
ウインナ— wiener; Vienna sausage.
ソーダ soda.
—水 soda water. —灰 soda ash.
ゾーン a zone. ¶デビスカップの東洋～ the Eastern *zone* of the Davis cup tournament.
ラッキー— 〔野球〕a lucky zone.
そかい【租界】a settlement. ¶ホンコンのイギリス～ the British *concession* (≒ *settlement*) in Hong Kong.
そかい【疎開】evacuation. ¶私たちは田舎に～した We *were evacuated to* the country.
そがい【阻害】a check. ¶社会の発展を～してはならない We must not *check* (≒ *arrest*) the development of society.
そがい【疎外】alienation.
—感 ¶だれも声をかけてくれないので彼は～感を覚えた He keenly felt that he was left out of the party because no one spoke to him.
そかく【組閣】¶～する form (≒ make) a cabinet.
そがん【訴願】a petition; an appeal. ¶処分取り消しを当局に～した We *petitioned* (≒ *appealed to*) the authorities *for* the revocation of the punishment.
そきゅう【遡及】¶～する retroact. 法律は既往に～せず The law *is* not *retrospective.* この法律は昭和49年3月31日に～する This law *becomes effective retroactive to* March 31, 1974.
-そく【-足】¶くつ1～ a pair of shoes.
そ·ぐ【削ぐ·殺ぐ】¶端を～ぐ *slice off* an end. 板を～ぐ *shave off* wood. 竹を～ぐ *sharpen* bamboo. 髪の毛を～ぐ *thin* the hair. 彼らの失策がその試合の興味を～いでしまった Their errors *spoilt* (≒ *killed*) our interest in the game. そのことで彼は大いに気を～がれた He *was* deeply *discouraged* over the matter.
ぞく【俗】¶～にそう言う It is *commonly* (≒ *generally*) said so. ～に言う,君子危うきに近寄らずだ *As the saying goes* (≒ *To use a common phrase*), fools rush in where angels fear to tread. ～な絵だ It is a *vulgar* (≒ *low*) picture. 彼は～なやつだ He is quite *a snob* (≒ *a vulgar fellow*).
ぞく【属】〔生物〕a genus.
ぞく【賊】(どろぼう) a thief; a robber; (謀反人) a rebel.
ぞく【続】¶「～アメリカ旅行記」"A Trip through America, *continued.*" この小説は正と～の2編から成っている This is a novel in two volumes —the first and *second* volumes.
-ぞく【-族】(家族) a family; (種族) a tribe; a race. ¶彼はマイカー～だ He is one of the owner drivers. 彼らは斜陽～だ They belong to the declining upper-class families.
ネコ— the cat family. モンゴル— the Mongol tribe.
ぞくあく【俗悪】¶～な趣味 *vulgar* taste. ～な本 a *low-brow* book.
そくい【即位】accession to the throne.
¶～する accede to the throne; ascend (≒ come to) the throne.

ぞくうけ【俗受け】¶このドラマは～する This drama will *appeal to popular taste*. 彼は～をねらった映画ばかり作る He produces only the films which will *meet the low taste of the public*. 彼の小説は高尚すぎて～がしない His novels are too lofty to *be appreciated by the public*.

ぞくえい【続映】¶その映画は1年以上も～している The movie has been run for more than a year. / The film show has continued for more than a year.

ぞくえん【続演】¶さらに1か月～する The show will be run for another month.

そくおう【即応】¶情勢に～して事態を処理する必要がある It is necessary to handle the matter *in conformity* (≒ *accordance*) *with* the circumstances (≒ situation).

そくおん【促音】〔the first part of〕a double consonant.

ぞくぐん【賊軍】a rebel army; rebels.

ぞくご【俗語】(集合的) slang; (個々の) a slang word (≒ expression); a slangy word.

そくざ【即座】¶～に immediately; promptly; instantly; on the spot.

そくし【即死】an instant death. ¶彼は自動車事故で～した He *was killed on the spot* in an automobile accident.

ぞくじ【俗事】worldly affairs; a routine work; a chore.

そくじつ【即日】the same day; the very day.

そくしゃほう【速射砲】a quick-firing gun; a quick-firer.

ぞくしゅう【俗臭】vulgarity. ¶～ふんぷんたる vulgar; worldly.

ぞくしゅつ【続出】¶交通事故が～した Traffic accidents *occurred in succession* (≒ *one after another*).

ぞくしょう【俗称】a common (≒ popular) name. ¶AはBと言う A *is commonly called* B.

そくしん【促進】promotion. ¶日米友好を～する *promote* mutual good-will between America and Japan. その条約は2国間の貿易を～すると確信する We are sure that the treaty will *give an impetus to* trade between the two countries. その薬が彼女の回復を～した The medicine *hastened* her recovery.

そくしん【測深】sounding. ¶～する sound. **—器** a depth finder; a sounder.

ぞくじん【俗人】the laity (複数扱い). ¶～の考えることは似ている What *worldly persons* think of differs little. / What *worldly persons* think is more or less the same.

ぞくじん【俗塵】¶ときには～を避けることが必要だ We sometimes have to be free from *the hustle and bustle of ordinary life*.

ぞくじんしゅぎ【属人主義】〔法律〕the personal (≒ nationality) principle; jurisdiction based on the nationality of the persons who commit criminal offenses.

そく・する【即する】¶それは事情に～した方法だった It was the way *based on* the fact. 時代に～した見方 the view to *meet* the contemporary social requirements.

ぞく・する【属する】¶ライオンはネコ科に～する The lion *belongs to* the cat family. 彼は政党に～さない He *is affiliated with* no political party. そのテーマはこの部門に～する The theme *belongs in* this category. かつてその国はイギリスに～していた The country *was* once *subject to* the Great Britain. 主権は国民に～する The sovereignty *rests with* the people.

そくせい【即製】¶～の料理 instant food.

そくせい【促成】**—栽培** forcing culture; intensive cultivation. ¶～栽培の野菜 *forced* vegetables.

そくせい【速成】quick mastery. ¶3か月の英語～講習 a three-month *intensive* course in English.

ぞくせい【族生】¶ヨモギが一面に～している Mugworts *are growing in clusters*.

ぞくせい【属性】an attribute.

そくせき【足跡】a footprint. ¶彼は国じゅうに～を印した He left his *footmarks* all over the country. 彼は日本の近代化に偉大な～を残した He *made a* great *contribution to* the modernization of Japan.

そくせき【即席】¶私は～に詩を作るのが得意だ I am good at *improvising* poems.
—料理 a quick lunch.

ぞくせけん【俗世間】the world; a mundane life.

ぞくせつ【俗説】a popular saying. ¶～では…と言われている It is *traditionally* said that ….

そくせん【側線】(鉄道の) a sidetrack; (魚の) a lateral line.

ぞくぞく ¶背中が～する I *feel chilly* on the back. うれしくて～した I *was thrilled* with joy.

ぞくぞく【続続】¶落伍(らくご)者が～と出た Lots of people dropped out *one after another*. 信者が～とお参りに来る Devotees come *in succession* to pay their respects to the god. 注文が～来た Orders *poured in*.

そくだい【即題】¶～で作文を書く write an *impromptu* composition.

そくたつ【速達】¶～で送る send a letter *by express*.
—郵便 express delivery post. **—料** a special (≒ an express) delivery charge.

そくだん【即断】an immediate decision. ¶～する decide promptly.

そくだん【速断】a hasty conclusion. ¶～する decide hastily.

そくち【測地】land surveying. ¶鉄道建設の～をする *make a geodetic survey* for constructing a railway.

ぞくちしゅぎ【属地主義】〔法律〕the territorial principle; the principle of territorial privilege for jurisdiction.

ぞくっぽ・い【俗っぽい】¶近ごろ軽井沢も～くなっ

た Karuizawa *has* recently *become more popularized* than before.

そくてい【測定】 measurement. ¶ ～する measure ; (土地を) survey ; (水深を) sound.

そくど【速度】 speed. ¶ 光の～はどのくらいですか How *fast* does light travel? 今回の台風の～は毎時50キロだった The *speed* of the last typhoon was 50 kilometers per hour. この車は1時間80マイルの～で走れる This car can *do* 80 miles an hour. 列車は～を増した The train gathered *speed*. 車は急に～を上げた(落とした) The car suddenly increased (decreased) *speed*. 伝書バトは時速約60キロの～で空中を飛ぶ A carrier pigeon travels through the air at *a speed* of 60 kilometers per hour. その作家は書く～がはやい The novelist *is* very *fast* in writing novels.

—計 a speedometer. —制限 speed limits. 最高— the maximum speed.

そくとう【即答】 a prompt (≒ ready) answer. ¶ ～する answer promptly. ～を求める ask *a person* to *answer immediately*.

ぞくとう【続騰】 ¶ 株価が～する Stock prices *increase continuously and acceleratedly*.

そくどく【速読】 rapid reading. ¶ ～する read fast (≒ rapidly).

ぞくねん【俗念】 a worldly mind ; an earthly desire.

そくばい【即売】 a spot sale. ¶ ～する *sell* a thing *on the spot*. 新刊書～会 an exhibition of new books for *sale on the spot*.

そくばく【束縛】 restraint. ¶ このところ時間に～されている I *have* always *been restricted* by time. 彼らは言論の自由を～した They *restricted* people's freedom of speech.

ぞくはつ【続発】 ¶ 事件の～ *a series of* events. 難問が～する Troubles *occur in succession*.

ぞくぶつ【俗物】 a worldly (≒ vulgar) man; a man of vulgate taste.

そくぶつてき【即物的】 ¶ ～なものの考え方 a view based on the realities.

そくぶん【側聞・仄聞】 ¶ ～したところによれば彼は離婚したそうだ From what I *heard by chance*, he got divorced. / I *heard casually* that he had divorced.

ぞくへん【続編】 a continuation (*of*) ; a second volume.

そくほう【速報】 a prompt report. ¶ ～する report promptly ; announce quickly. ニュースはテレビによって～された The news *was televised rapidly*.

ぞくほう【続報】 ¶ 事件の～が現地から送られてきた We received *a continued* spot *report*.

ぞくみょう【俗名】 a secular name.

ぞくむ【俗務】 mundane affairs ; routine work.

ぞくめい【俗名】 (学名に対して) a common (≒ popular) name.

ぞくめい【属名】〘生物〙 a generic name.

ぞくめい【賊名】 ¶ 彼は～をこうむった He *was branded as a rebel*.

そくめん【側面】 the flank ; the side. ¶ ～から彼らを援助すべきだ We should give *indirect* aid to them.

—運動 a lateral movement. —図 a side view ; a lateral view.

ぞくよう【俗謡】 a folk song ; a ballad.

ぞくりゅうけっかく【粟粒結核】〘医学〙 miliary tuberculosis.

そくりょう【測量】 measurement ; (土地の) survey ; (水深の) sounding. ¶ 土地を～する *survey* the land. 山の高さを～する *measure* [the height of] a mountain.

—技師 a surveying engineer ; a surveyor. —図 a plan of survey. —船 a surveying ship.

ぞくりょう【属領】 a subject province ; a dependent domain (≒ territory). ¶ オーストラリアはイギリスの～であった Australia was *a dependency on* Great Britain.

そくりょく【速力】 speed ; velocity. ¶ ～毎時2,000マイルの宇宙船 a spacecraft of two thousand mph *speed*. ～を減ずる reduce (≒ lessen) the *speed*. この船は平均30ノットの～で走る The ship makes an average *speed* of thirty knots.

最大— the maximum speed. 制限— regulation speed.

ぞくろん【俗論】 ¶ 私は～には耳をかさない I'm against *people's opinions*. / I don't bow to *conventionalism*.

そぐわな・い ¶ きみは学生として～い服装をしている You wear clothes *unsuitable for* a student. それはきみの持論に～い発言だ What you are saying now doesn't *suit* your own opinion. / Your speech *is different from* what you always think of.

そけいぶ【鼠蹊部】〘解剖〙 the inguinal part.

そげき【狙撃】 shooting ; sniping. ¶ 大統領は暴漢に～された The President *was shot* by a ruffian.

—兵 a sniper ; a sharpshooter.

ソケット〘電気〙 a socket ; a lamp holder.

そ・げる【削げる・殺げる】 ¶ 彼女のほおは肉が～げている She *has sunken* cheeks. / Her cheeks *have sunk in*.

そこ【底】 **1**〖物の〗 the bottom. ¶ 船は海の～に沈んだ The ship sank down to *the bottom* of the sea.

くつの～ the sole.

このかごは～が抜けている *The bottom* of this basket has come out.

コップの～にまだ少し砂糖が残っている There is still a little sugar left in *the bottom* of the glass.

2〖慣用的表現〗 ¶ 財布の～をはたいてしまった I have spent my money to the last penny.

彼は心の～からあなたに感謝している He is grateful to you from *the bottom* of his heart.

値段はもう～をついた The price has reached *the bottom*.

相場は～知らずの状態だ *The bottom* seems to have fallen out of the market.

彼にはなにか〜知れないところがある There is something *mysterious* in him.

そこ【其処】 ¶ 〜にはなにもなかった There was nothing *there*. 〜へはいつ行ったのですか When did you go *there*? 〜が問題だ *That*'s an important matter. 〜まではわからない I don't understand *that much*. 〜が心配な点だ *That*'s what I am afraid of. 〜がきみのまちがっているところだ *That*'s where you are wrong.

そご【齟齬】 ¶ 両者の間にははなはだしい〜がある There is remarkable *inconsistency* between the two. 計画に〜をきたした Our plan *went wrong*.

そご【祖語】〘言語学〙a parent language.

そこい【底意】 a secret intention. ¶ 相手の〜を見抜いた I could see through his *secret intention*. 彼の賛成は〜があってしたことだ His agreement resulted from his *intention* to do harm.

そこいじ【底意地】 ¶ 彼女は〜の悪い人だ She *is malicious* (≒ *spiteful*) *at bottom*.

そこいれ【底入れ】〘株式〙 ¶ 相場は今が〜だ The prices *have* now *touched* 〔*the*〕 *bottom*.

そこう【素行】 conduct; behavior. ¶ 彼は〜が修まらない He is loose in his *morals*. / He cannot *conduct himself* properly. 〜を慎め Be prudent in your *conduct* (≒ *behavior*). 〜を改めよ Mend your *ways*. / Reform yourself.

そこく【祖国】 *one's* motherland; *one's* fatherland; *one's* own country.

そこここ【其処此処】 ¶ 会場の〜に和服姿も見られる People in *kimono* are seen *here and there* in the hall.

そこそこ ¶ 1時間〜だ It takes *about only* one hour. 1キロ〜だ It is *no more than* one kilogram. これは100円〜だ It costs a hundred yen *or so*.

そこそこに ¶ 彼はあいさつも〜帰っていった He left us saying good-bye *hurriedly*.

そこぢから【底力】 ¶ 彼には〜がある He has enough *strength in reserve*. 彼はマラソンで〜を発揮した He showed *potential power* (≒ *energy*) in a marathon race.

そこつ【粗忽】 carelessness; rashness. ¶ 彼は〜にもまちがいをした *Carelessly enough* he made a mistake.

—者 ¶ 彼女は〜者だ She is *a blunderer* (≒ *a rash woman*).

そこで【其処で】 (その場所で) there; (それ故) therefore. ¶ 〜(それ故)わざわざきみを訪ねてきたんだ *So* (≒ *Therefore* (強意的)) I have come all the way to see you. 〜(さて)きみに頼みがあるんだが *Well, now,* I wonder if you could do me a favor.

そこな·う【損う】 1〘傷つける〙 ¶ 健康を〜わないようにしなさい Be careful not to *injure* your health.

よけいなものを入れすぎると食物の味を〜う If you add anything too much, it will *spoil* the taste of food.

高速道路は都市の美観を〜う Highways *spoil* the beauty of the city.

文学作品は翻訳によって原文の味が〜われることがある Literary works may *suffer* in translation.

2〘機会をのがす〙 ¶ 評判の映画を見〜った I *failed to* see that popular film.

急がないと電車に乗り〜うよ Hurry up, or you'll *miss* the train. / Unless you make haste, you will *miss* the train.

ごちそうを食べ〜った I *missed out on* a splendid dish.

そこなし【底無し】 ¶ 〜の沼 a *bottomless* swamp. 〜の大酒飲み an *extremely heavy* drinker.

そこに【底荷】 ballast. ¶ 船は〜だけで出帆した The ship set sail *in ballast*.

そこぬけ【底抜け】 ¶ 彼は〜の善人だ He is good *to the core*. / He is a man of no guile. 〜のばか a *perfect* fool. 〜騒ぎをする go wild; go on a spree.

そこね【底値】 the bottom price. ¶ 相場はきょうが〜だろう Market prices seem to reach *bottom* today.

そこ·ねる【損ねる】 ¶ 彼の気分を〜ねてしまった I *hurt* his feelings. / I *offended* him. 酒を飲みすぎて健康を〜ねた I drank too much and *fell ill*. 箱根へ行き〜ねた I *missed* the chance of going to Hakone.

そこのけ【其処退け】 ¶ 彼の腕前は本職〜だ His ability would *put* a professional *to shame*.

そこはかとなく ¶ バラの香りが〜漂う The fragrance of roses hangs *faintly* in the air.

そこひ【底翳】〘医学〙 白— cataract. 黒— amaurosis.

そこびえ【底冷え】 deep cold. ¶ けさは〜がする It *is biting cold* (≒ *is quite chilly*) this morning.

そこびかり【底光り】 ¶ 彼の作品は〜がする There is some *inexpressible beauty* in his work.

そこびきあみ【底引き網】 a trawl net; a drag-net.

そこら ¶ 〜を捜してごらん Look for it *around there*. それは300円か〜で買える You can get it for three hundred yen *or so*.

そこらじゅう【其処ら中】 ¶ 〜あなたを捜しまわった I looked for you *all over the place*. / I looked *everywhere* for you.

そさい【蔬菜】 vegetables; greens.

そざい【素材】 a material; (小説など) a theme; a subject matter. ¶ 彼は新しい小説の〜を集めている He is collecting *material*〔*s*〕 (≒ *data*) for his new novel.

そざつ【粗雑】 ¶ 〜な考え a *crude* (≒ *rough*) idea.

そし【阻止】 ¶ われわれは規則の改訂を〜した We *blocked* the revision of the regulations. 寒さで彼らの前進は〜された Cold *hindered* 〔them〕 their advance. だれも彼らのデモを〜できなかった Nobody was able to *stop* their demonstration.

そじ【素地】 an inclination; qualities. ¶ 彼女

には踊りの～がある She has *an aptitude* (≒ *an inclination*) for dancing. / She has in her the *makings* of a good dancer.

そしき【組織】organization. ¶ 人間の身体は複雑な～を持っている The human body has *a* complex *organization*. 南極探検隊を～する *organize* an expedition to the South Pole region. 内閣を～する *make* (≒ *form*) a cabinet. 委員会は6人の委員で～されている The committee *is composed of* six members. この問題については～的な研究が望ましい A *systematic* study of this problem is desirable. このグループは～的に仕事をする This group works *systematically*. 生物の～の構成単位は細胞だ The unit of the *structure* of living creature is the cell.

—委員会 an organizing committee. —網 the network of a system. —力 organizing ability. —労働者 organized laborers. 神経— nervous tissue.

そしつ【素質】character ; qualities. ¶ 彼はすぐ友人をつくるという恵まれた～を持っている He has *a gift* of making friends quickly. 彼には音楽の～がある He has *a genius* for music. 政治家としての～がある He has in him the *makings* (≒ *qualities*) of a politician.

そして and ; then ; now ; so.

そしな【粗品】a small gift. ¶ ～ですがお納めください I hope you will like this. (英語では「粗品」という発想がない).

そしゃく【租借】¶ イギリスはかつてシャンハイを中国から～した England once *obtained a lease on* Shanghai from China. / England once *leased* Shanghai from China.

—権 lease. —地 a leased territory.

そしゃく【咀嚼】mastication ; chewing. ¶ 食物をよく～する *chew* (≒ *masticate*) food well. 現代哲学をよく～することが必要だ We need to *digest* (≒ *appreciate*) modern thoughts well.

そじゅつ【祖述】¶ 彼は師の学説を～した He *expounded* (≒ *commented upon*) his teacher's theory.

—者 an expounder.

そしょう【訴訟】a lawsuit. ¶ 彼は～に勝つだろう He will win *a suit*. 残念ながら～に敗れた I am sorry I lost *a suit*. 彼は市長を相手どって～を起こした He entered *a lawsuit* against the mayor. 彼は賠償をとるため～を起こした He started *a suit* to collect damages.

—事件 a lawsuit. 刑事— a criminal suit. 民事— a civil suit.

そじょう【俎上】¶ 問題を～にのせる *bring up* a matter *for discussion*.

そしょく【粗食】¶ ときには～も必要だ We need to live on *simple diet* (≒ *poor food*) at times.

そしらぬ【素知らぬ】¶ 彼女は～顔をしていた She pretended not to know me. / She *took no notice of* me. / She *paid no attention to* me.

そしり【謗り・誹り】blame ; 〔a〕 censure ; a slander. ¶ 約束を守らないのだから不正直の～は免れない He is open to the *charge* of being dishonest because he does not keep his word.

そすい【疏水】a drainage canal.

そすう【素数】〚数学〛a prime number.

そせい【組成】¶ 水の～要素は酸素と水素だ Oxygen and hydrogen are the *elements* (≒ *component parts ; constituents*) of water.

そせい【粗製】—品 a crude article. —濫造 overproduction of inferior articles.

そせい【蘇生】revival. ¶ それを聞いて～の思いがした Hearing it I *felt relieved*.

そぜい【租税】taxes. ¶ われわれは重い～を課せられている We *are* heavily *taxed*.

そせき【礎石】a cornerstone. ¶ この建物の～は200年前にすえられた The *cornerstone* of this building was laid two hundred years ago. 彼はわが国に理論物理学の～をすえた He laid the *foundations* of theoretical physics in our country.

そせん【祖先】an ancestor ; a forefather. ¶ 彼は私の～に当たる He is *ancestor* to me.

—崇拝 ancestor worship. —伝来 ¶ ～伝来の土地 the soil which has been handed down from *one's ancestors* (≒ *forefathers*).

そそ【楚楚】¶ ～たる graceful ; neat ; (ほっそりした) slim.

そそう【阻喪】¶ 会社の従業員の士気が～してしまった The company employees *were* (≒ *became*) *demoralized*. 彼は今意気～している He *is in low spirits* now. / He *is depressed* now. 彼女はただ1度の失敗で意気～してしまった She *was disheartened* by a single failure.

そそう【粗相】a blunder ; carelessness. ¶ これは～をいたしました It *was* very *careless of* me. / I *was awkward*. お客に～のないようにしなさい Be courteous to the guests.

そぞう【塑像】a plaster image ; a plastic image.

そそ・ぐ【注ぐ】**1**〚水など〛¶ 花に水を～ぐ *water* flowers.

数人の消防士がホースで火に水を～いでいる Several firemen *are hosing* the fire.

びんからコップに水を～いだ I *poured* water out of the bottle into a glass.

大井川は駿河湾に～ぐ The Oi River *empties* 〔*itself*〕 *into* Suruga Bay.

2〚力・視線など〛¶ 彼は彫刻の大作に心血を～いだ He *devoted himself to* the great work of sculpture.

全力を～いで仕事をやりぬけ Carry out your work *with all your might*.

彼に目を～いだ I *fixed my eyes upon* him.

そそ・ぐ【雪ぐ】¶ 彼はりっぱに恥を～いだ He admirably *wiped away* his disgrace. 彼は汚名を～ぐことができた He could *clear himself of* the false charge. / He could *cleanse* his dishonor.

そそくさと ¶ 彼は～出ていった He went out *in*

そ

a hurry (≒ *hurriedly*). / He *hurried* out.

そそっかし·い ¶なんて〜い人なんだろう How *careless* (≒ *hasty*) he *is*! 彼はよく〜いことをする He often acts *thoughtlessly* (≒ *carelessly*).

そそのか·す【唆す】¶彼女は彼を〜していたずらをさせた She *egged* him on to mischief. 一部の学生は彼の理論に〜されて反抗的になった His theory *incited* (≒ *instigated*) some of the students *to* rebellion.

そそりた·つ【そそり立つ】¶雪山が空高く〜っている Snow-covered mountains *are towering* high in the sky.

そそ·る ¶その新鮮さが食欲を〜る Its freshness *whets* our appetite. その話が彼の好奇心を〜った The story *excited* his curiosity. 彼女の手紙は私の涙を〜った Her letter *brought tears into my eyes*.

そぞろ【漫ろ】¶彼の話にみな〜涙ぐんだ *In spite of themselves* they were all moved to tears by his story. 浜伝いに〜歩きをした We *strolled* along the beach.

そだ【粗朶】brushwood; a fag〔g〕ot.

そだち【育ち】breeding; growth. ¶氏より〜 *Breeding* is better than birth. 彼は〜がよい(悪い) He *is* well-(ill-)*bred*. 彼女の作法を見ると〜のよさがわかる Her manners show good *breeding*. 〜ざかりの子どもたちはよく食べる *Growing* children eat much. 彼は都会(田舎)〜だ He is city-(country-)*bred*.

そだ·つ【育つ】¶彼は東京で生まれ東京で〜った He *was* born and *bred* in Tokyo. / He *was* born and *brought up* in Tokyo. 彼は母乳(人工乳)で〜った He is a breast (bottle) *fed* baby. 寝る子は〜つ Babies *grow up* in their sleep.

そだて【育て】¶生みの親より〜の親 One owes more to *the foster parent* than to the real parent.

そだ·てる【育てる】¶彼女は女手ひとつで3人の子を〜てた She *raised* (≒ *brought up*) three children by herself. 父親は彼女を先生に〜てた Her father *educated* her *to* be a school teacher. その農夫は作物を作り家畜を〜てている The farmer *raises* crops and cattle.

そち【措置】a measure. ¶臨機応変の〜をとる take such *a step* (≒ *a measure*) as the occasion demands. 飲酒運転に対して強硬な〜をとる take strong *measures* against drunken drivers.

そちこち【其方此方】here and there; in places.

そちゃ【粗茶】¶〜をどうぞ Let me offer you *a cup of tea*.

そちら【其方】¶あす〜へ伺います I will call on *you* tomorrow. 〜の方を紹介してください Will you introduce *that* gentleman to me? 〜の品を見せてください Show me *the other* one. 〜のようすはいかがですか How are things going on *in your place*?

そつ【卒】¶彼は1973年の高校〜だ He *graduated* from high school in 1973. 1945年〜(全員)はまだみな健在だ *The class of* 1945 are still all alive.

そつ ¶彼は何事も〜なくやる He does everything *perfectly* (≒ *faultlessly*; *carefully*).

そつい【訴追】prosecution. ¶彼女は彼を殺人罪で〜した She *prosecuted* him for a homicide. 運転手はスピード違反で〜された The driver *was charged with* (≒ *was accused of*) speeding.

そつう【疎通】¶両者間に意志の〜を欠く There is want of *understanding* (≒ *communication*) between the two. お互いに意志の〜をはかった We tried to *understand* each other better.

ぞっか【俗化】vulgarization. ¶観光客が多すぎて古都をすっかり〜してしまった Too many tourists *have vulgarized* (≒ *have secularized*) the ancient capital of Japan. / Too many visitors *have spoiled* the ancient capital of Japan with vulgarities.

ぞっかい【俗界】secular life; the secular society; the world. ¶彼は〜のことに心をわずらわさなかった He was free from the common cares of *the world*. 彼は〜に超然としている He stands (≒ keeps; holds) aloof from *the everyday life*.

そっき【速記】shorthand. ¶彼女は〜を習っている She is learning *shorthand*. / She is taking lessons in *stenography*. あなたは〜できますか Can you write (≒ take down) *in shorthand*?

—者 a stenographer. —術 shorthand; stenography. —文字 a stenographic character. —録 shorthand notes; stenographic records.

ぞっきぼん【殺本】remainders; dumped books.

そっきゅう【速球】〖野球〗a fast ball.

—投手 a fast pitcher.

そっきょう【即興】improvisation. ¶彼はこれらの詩を〜的に書き上げた He composed these poems *extempore* (≒ *impromptu*; *extemporarily*). / He *improvised* these poems.

—曲 an impromptu. —詩 an impromptu (≒ improvised) poem.

そつぎょう【卒業】graduation. ¶彼は中学を〜した He *completed* the junior high school *course*. 彼はこの春大学を〜した He *graduated from* a university this spring. 彼は大学の建築科を〜した He *graduated* 〔*from* a university〕 in architecture. この道はもう〜しているつもりだ I think I *know everything* along this line. これを知っていれば,これは〜だ If you know this, you *have no more to learn*.

—式 ㊇ the commencement; ㊈ a graduation ceremony. —試験 a graduation examination. —証書 a diploma. —論文 a graduation thesis.

そっきん【即金】cash payment. ¶〜で新車の代金を払った I paid 〔*in*〕 *cash* for the new car. 代金は〜のこと *Cash* only. / No credit. その方法ですとまず〜で10パーセント払っていただきます On this plan you *pay* ten percent *down*.

そっきん【側近】¶ 首相の〜 *those close* to the prime minister. 大統領は〜を信頼していた The president trusted his *aides*.

ソックス socks.

そっくり ¶ 彼は父親〜だ He *is a carbon copy of* his father. / He *has a strong resemblance to* his father. / (特に気性など) He *is a chip of the old block*. この絵は実物〜だ This portrait *is true to life*. 飛騨の民家を〜そのまま東京に移築した The original farmhouse in Hida has been *wholly* removed to Tokyo. 報告は〜委員会に承認された The report *in its entirety* was accepted by the committee. 私の部屋は〜そのままにしておいてください Leave my room *as it is*. 骨ごと〜食べられる You can eat it, bone *and all*. それで〜全部だ That's *the lot*.

そっくりかえ·る【反っくり返る】¶ 彼はいすに〜っている He is sitting *thrown back* in his chair. / He *lords it over* in his chair.

そっけ【素っ気】¶ 彼の話は味も〜もなかった His story *was dry and dull* (≒ *dry as dust*).

そっけつ【即決】a summary decision (≒ trial; judgment).

—裁判 ¶ 彼は〜裁判を受けた He *was tried summarily*.

そっけな·い【素っ気ない】¶ 〜い返事をする give a *cold* (≒ *curt*; *flat*; *blunt*) answer. 彼女は私の申し出を〜くはねつけた She *flatly* rejected my proposal. 彼は私に〜い態度をとった He gave me a cold shoulder.

そっこう【即効】an immediate effect. ¶ その薬は頭痛には〜がある The medicine has *an immediate effect* on headache.

—薬 a quick remedy.

ぞっこう【続行】continuation. ¶ 交渉を〜する continue negotiations (*with*). 審議はまだ〜中だ The matter *is still under discussion*. 雨がやんでからまた試合を〜した We *continued* the game after the rain had stopped.

そっこうじょ【測候所】a meteorological station (≒ observatory).

そっこく【即刻】immediately; (米口語) right away; at once.

ぞっこく【属国】a tributary.

ぞっこん ¶ 彼は彼女に〜ほれ込んでいる He is *deeply* (≒ *madly*) in love with her.

そっせん【率先】¶ 彼が〜して掃除を始めた He *took the lead in* sweeping. 彼は〜垂範した He *took the initiative in* setting an example on others.

そっち【其方】⇒そちら

そっちのけ【其方のけ】¶ 彼は勉強を〜にして遊んだ He idled his time away *neglecting* his studies. 仕事も〜で雑談にふけっている *Instead of* working diligently, they are wasting their time talking with each other.

そっちゅう【卒中】〖医学〗apoplexy; stroke. ¶ 〜を起こす have *a stroke* 〔*of apoplexy*〕.

そっちょく【率直】¶ 彼は〜な人間だ He is a *candid* person. 〜さだけが彼のとりえだ *Frankness* alone is his merit. 〜に意見を言う人だ He *is outspoken* in his assertion of opinions. 〜に言えば, あなたのやり方はまちがっている *To be frank with you*, your method is wrong. 〜に答えなさい Give a *candid* answer.

そって【沿って】¶ 川に〜歩いた I walked *along* the river. 道路に〜ホテルが並んでいる Hotels stand in a line *along* the road.

そっと (軽く) lightly; (静かに) softly; (こっそり) stealthily. ¶ 〜階段をおりた I *stole down* the stairs. 彼は〜家を出た He *stole out of* the house. その問題は〜しておいたほうがいい You had better *leave* the matter *as it is*. 彼女を〜ひとりにしておいてやれ *Leave* her *alone*. 彼は優しく〜声をかけてくれた He was kind enough to talk to me *tenderly*. 彼は私の肩を〜たたいた He *patted* me *on* the shoulder.

ぞっと ¶ その光景を見て彼は〜した He *shuddered at* the sight. / The sight *sent a shudder through* him. 幽霊の話を聞いて私たちは〜した We *were terrified by* the ghost story. その事故を見て〜した I *was horrified at* the accident. 競馬はあまり〜しない I *don't care* so much *for* horse races.

そっとう【卒倒】fainting. ¶ 彼は暑さのため〜した He *fainted from* the heat. 彼女は傷を見て〜した She *fainted away at* the wound. 貧血を起こして〜した I became anemic and *swooned*. / Anemia made me *fall into a swoon*.

そっぱ【反っ歯】¶ 彼女の〜がかえって愛らしい *A projecting tooth* makes her all the more lovely.

そっぽ【外方】¶ 彼は〜を向いて返事もしなかった He *turned away* and gave no answer.

そで【袖】a sleeve. ¶ 〜のないドレス a *sleeveless* dress. 〜の長い(短い)シャツ a long-(short-) *sleeved* shirt. シャツの〜をまくる roll up the *sleeves* of *one's* shirt. 〜をだれかに引かれた I was pulled *by the sleeve*. 私は彼の〜にすがった I clung to his *sleeve* for mercy. ない〜は振れぬ(諺) Nothing comes out of the sack but what was in it. 〜すり合うも他生の縁(諺) A chance acquaintance is a divine ordinance.

—の下 ¶ 彼が〜の下を使うとは驚いた It is surprising that he should *bribe*.

ソテー sauté.

ポーク— a pork sauté.

そでぐち【袖口】a cuff. ¶ 〜が擦り切れている The *cuff* is worn out.

そでたけ【袖丈】*one's* sleeve length.

そてつ【蘇鉄】〖植物〗a cycad.

そでつけ【袖付け】an armhole.

そと【外】the outside ¶ 〜はたいへんな暑さだ It is extremely hot *outdoors*. 〜は雨らしい It seems to be raining 〔*outside*〕. 〜へ出よう Let's go *out*. 〜でしばらく遊んだ We played *out of doors* for a while. 〜で遊ぶのは健康によい It is good for the health to play *in the* *open air*. ～からは中のようすはわからなかった What was going on inside was not seen from *the outside*. 昼食は～でとろう Let's have lunch *out*. このごろは～で食べることが多くなった Recently, I often *dine out* (≒ *eat my meals out*). 彼はどこか～に出ている He *is out* somewhere.

そとう【粗糖】unrefined sugar.

そとうみ【外海】¶～は波が荒い Waves run high in *the open sea*.

そとがまえ【外構え】¶あの家は～はりっぱだ The house looks fine *externally*. / The house has *a fine appearance*.

そとがわ【外側】¶箱の～は緑色に塗ってある *The outside* of the box is painted green. 彼はへいの～に立った He stood *outside* the wall.

そとづら【外面】¶彼は～のいい男だ He is kind to everyone except his own people.

そとのり【外法】the outside measurement.

そとば【卒塔婆・卒都婆】a stupa.

そとぼり【外堀】¶城の～を埋める fill up *the outer moat* of the castle.

そとまた【外股】¶彼女は～に歩く She walks *with the toes turned out*.

そとまわり【外回り】(周囲) circumference; (軌道) the outer track; (外交員) a solicitor. ¶山手線の～の電車 the train on *the outer track* of the Yamanote Line.

そなえ【備え】(準備) preparation; (防備) defenses. ¶～あれば憂いなし(諺) *Readiness* is all. / Be always prepared.

そなえつけ【備え付け】¶図書館に～の辞書 dictionaries *kept* in the library. その旅館の各室には～の冷蔵庫がある Each room of the inn has a refrigerator for the guest's convenience.

そなえつ・ける【備え付ける】¶室内にはテレビが～けてある The room *is provided* (≒ *is equipped*) *with* a television. 講堂にラウドスピーカーが～けてある There is a loud-speaker *available* in the auditorium.

そな・える【供える】¶仏前に花を～える *offer* a nosegay to the altar.

そな・える【備える】¶万一に～える *prepare for* the worst. 将来に～える *provide for* the future. 試験に～えて猛勉強した I studied hard *in preparation for* the examination. いざというときに～えてこれだけは手もとに置いておきなさい *Keep* at least this *in hand* against a rainy day. この部屋には机といすがひとつずつ～えられている This room *is furnished with* a desk and a chair. 彼は威厳を～えた人物だ He is a *dignified* man. 彼は作曲の才を～えている He *is endowed with* the talent of composing music.

ソナタ〔音楽〕a sonata. ¶月光～ the Moonlight *Sonata*.

—形式 ¶～形式でつくられている It is composed in *a sonata* form.

そなわ・る【備わる】¶彼女には生来気品が～っている She *is endowed with* dignity and grace.

ソネット〔詩学〕a sonnet.

そねみ【嫉み】jealousy. ¶～深い男 a *jealous* (≒ *envious*) man. 彼はとかく人の～を受けがちだ He is apt to incur the *jealousy* of others.

そね・む【嫉む】¶人の才能を～む *envy a person's* ability. 彼らが彼の人気を～むのも無理はない It is no wonder that they should *be jealous of* his popularity.

その【其の】that (複 those).

そのうえ【其の上】on top of that; over and above ...; in addition 〔to that〕; moreover. ¶～言うこともない I have nothing *more* to say. ～悪いことに, 雨が降りだした *What was worse* (≒ *To make* 〔*the*〕 *matters worse*), it began to rain.

そのうち【其の内】¶～伺います I will call on you *before long*. ～雨が降ると思う I think it will rain *sooner or later*. ～結婚する I will be married *one of these days*. 一行は10人で, ～死を免れたのはたったふたりだった The whole party was ten in all, only two of whom could escape death.

そのかわり【其の代わり】¶ぼくにそれをくれ, ～きみにこれをあげる If you give it to me, I will give you this *in return*. 彼はきのうは非番だった, ～きょうは出勤している As he was off duty yesterday, he is on duty today.

そのくせ【其の癖】and yet; for all that. ¶あの人はまじめだが, ～だれにも信用されない He is diligent, *and yet* he is not trusted by anyone.

そのくらい【其の位】¶～はすぐわかる I understand *such a thing* (≒ *that much*) with ease. ～のことで争うのはばかげている It is foolish to quarrel over *such a trifle*. ～は1時間で読める I can read *that much* in an hour. きみくらいの年なら～の分別があってもいいはずだ You should *know better* at your age.

そのご【其の後】¶～お変わりありませんか How are you getting on? ～彼とは会っていません I have not seen him *since*. ～あの人はどうしただろう I wonder what has become of him *since*. ～すぐに彼は出発した He started *soon after*. ～数日間彼女は病気だった She was ill for several days *after*. ～1週間して私は彼女にまた会った A week *later* I met her again.

そのころ【其の頃】¶～には帰ってきます I will be back *by that time*. ～はまだ若かった I was still young *then* (≒ *at that time*). ～は商売はうまくいっていた Business was good *in those days*.

そのすじ【其の筋】the authorities. ¶～の命により場内禁煙(掲示) No smoking. By order. それは～に届けたほうがいい You had better report it to *the authorities*. ～から情報が入った There was a piece of information from *an official source*.

そのせつ【其の節】¶～はお世話さまでした Thank you for your kindness you showed to me *at that time*.

そのた【其の他】¶時計～数点がなくなっていた The clock and some *other* things were gone. 彼は犬,ネコ〜の小動物を飼っている He keeps a dog, a cat, and many *other* small animals.

そのため【其の為】¶〜に(その理由で)健康を害した I injured my health *for that reason*. / *That is why* I injured my health. 〜に(その目的で)彼に会った I met him *for that purpose*. 〜に(その結果)彼は学校に遅刻した *Consequently* he was late for school.

そのつど【其の都度】¶彼は〜不平を言った He complained *each time*. そこへ3回行って私は〜がっかりした I visited the place three times, and *every time* I went there, I was disappointed.

そのて【其の手】¶〜は食わない No good trying to deceive me that way! / None of your tricks. / I know a trick worth two of that.

そのとおり【其の通り】¶〜にします I will do *just like that*. 〜です That's right. / You're right.

そのとき【其の時】¶〜私は18歳だった I was eighteen years old *then*. 〜の校長は山田先生だった The *then* principal was Mr. Yamada. 〜までには帰っているはずだ I ought to be back *by that time*.

そのば【其の場】¶ちょうど〜に居合わせた I happened to be *there* (≒ *on the spot*). 〜で代金を払ってくれた He paid me the money *on the spot*.

―かぎり ¶彼はいつも〜かぎりのことを言う He always says something suitable just *for the occasion*. **―逃れ** ¶彼は〜逃れの言いわけをした He made an apology just to suit the *occasion*.

そのひぐらし【その日暮らし】¶彼は〜の生活だ He *lives from hand to mouth*. / He *lives from day to day*.

そのひそのひ【その日その日】¶〜の生活に追われている I am pressed with *day-to-day* life. 彼は〜を幸せに送っている He lives a happy life *day by day*.

そのへん【其の辺】about there. ¶〜の人に道を聞けばいい You may ask someone *in the neighborhood* which way to take. 〜の値段なら彼の言い値で買う If the price *is somewhere about there*, I will buy at his own price. 〜のことは聞いていない I have not heard of *anything about that*.

そのまま【其の儘】as it is. ¶彼女は母親の若いころ〜だ She is *the very image of* her mother in her girlhood. この建物は昔の姿を〜残している This building has maintained its aspect of former days *as it was*. 言われたことを〜やりなさい Do as you are told. 本を机に置いて〜立ち去った *Leaving* the book on the desk, he went away.

そのみち【其の道】the line; the field. ¶〜の大家 an authority *on the subject* (≒ *in the line*).

そのむかし【其の昔】in olden times; (そのころ) in those days; (物語などで) once upon a time.

そのむき【其の向き】¶事故を〜に届け出なければならぬ You must report the accident to *the authorities concerned*.

そのもの【其の物】the very thing. ¶彼は正直〜だ He is honesty *itself*. 彼は健康〜だ He is *the* [*very*] *picture of* health. 彼女は幸福〜だ She is *as happy as a lark*. この液〜は毒ではない This liquid is not poisonous *in itself*.

そば【側・傍】neighborhood; side. ¶彼の家は学校の〜にある His house stands *by* the school. 郵便局は湖の〜にあった The post office was *close to* the lake. 〜の駅から電話しなさい Telephone from *the nearest* station. 〜を通りかかるだれにでもいいから道を尋ねなさい Ask where you are of anyone passing *by*. しばらく私の〜を離れないでください Please *keep close to* me for a while.

そば【蕎麦】buckwheat noodles.
―粉 buckwheat flour.

そばかす【雀斑】freckles. ¶〜のある顔 a *freckled* face.

そばだ・つ【峙つ】¶波打ち際から高く〜つ岩壁 a cliff *towering* high from the beach.

そばだ・てる【欹てる】¶耳を〜てる *strain* (≒ *prick up*) *one's* ears.

そばづえ【側杖・傍杖】¶けんかの〜を食った I *was involved in* the quarrel. 事故の〜を食ってけがをした I hurt myself in the accident that I happened to *be involved in*.

ソビエト [the] Soviet Russia; the Union of Soviet Socialist Republics (略して U.S.S.R. で表わすことがある).

そび・える【聳える】¶雲に〜える山々 mountains *rising high* above the clouds. そのビルは町の上空に高く〜えている The building *towers high* over the town.

そびやか・す【聳やかす】¶肩を〜す *raise one's* shoulders. 彼は肩を〜して歩く He walks *with a defiant manner*. / He *swaggers*.

そびょう【素描】a rough sketch.

-そび・れる ¶彼に苦情を言おうと思ったが言い〜れた I *missed a chance to* say that I had some complaints against him. 昨夜は本を読んでいて寝〜れた Reading a book last night, I *failed to* get to sleep. 気まずくて,とうとうその問題は言い〜れてしまった I felt so awkward that I *couldn't dare to* (≒ *dared not*) refer to that matter.

そふ【祖父】a grandfather.

ソファー a sofa.

ソフト (帽子) 米 a soft hat; 英 a felt hat.

ソフトクリーム [soft] ice cream.

ソフトボール (球技) softball; (球) a softball.

そふぼ【祖父母】grandparents.

ソプラノ〖音楽〗soprano. ¶〜の歌手 a soprano singer.
メゾ― mezzo-soprano.

そぶり【素振り】behavior; a manner; bearing; a look. ¶彼は彼女に対してよそよそしい〜

をした He *behaved himself like* a stranger *toward* her. 彼の～でそのことがわかった I noticed it by his *manner*. 彼は何をするにもいやな～を見せない Whatever he does, he *shows* no *signs of* discontentment. 怪しい～の男 a man *acting suspiciously*; a man of suspicious *behavior*. 彼はいかにも意味ありげな～をする He *bears himself* in a very significant manner.

そぼ【祖母】a grandmother.

そほう【粗放・疎放】¶ 彼は元来～な男だ He is *careless* by nature.

—農業 extensive agriculture.

そぼう【粗暴】¶ 彼は性質が～だ He is of a *wild* disposition. 彼はことば遣いが～だ He *is rough of* speech.

そほうか【素封家】a rich man. ¶ 彼はこの地方の～に生まれた He was born of *a rich family* here.

そぼく【素朴】simplicity. ¶ ～な人柄 a *naive* nature. ～な考え a *simple* thought. ～な民芸品 a *simple* folkcraft work.

そぼふ・る【そぼ降る】drizzle. ¶ ～る雨 a *drizzling* rain.

そまつ【粗末】**1**〚質素な・つまらない〛¶ ～な家 a *humble* cottage.

彼はいつも～な服装をしている He is always *plainly* dressed.

～な食べ物がまずいとは言えない *Plain* food does not always taste bad.

彼の話のお～さにはあきれた I was surprised that his speech was so *poor*.

2〚疎略〛¶ 親を～にするとはたいへんなやつだ What a good-for-nothing fellow he is to *neglect* his parents!

金を～にするな Don't *waste* money *on worthless things*.

簡単に手に入るものはとかく～にしがちだ We are liable to *make light of* things easily obtainable.

そま・る【染まる】¶ この生地ならよく～る This cloth *dyes* well. 彼は血に～って倒れていた He lay in a pool of blood. 都会の若者は悪に～りやすい Young men in a big city are apt to *sink in vice*.

そむ・く【背く】disobey; go against. ¶ 彼のそのことばは私たちの期待に～くものだった That remark of his *went against* our expectations. 命令に～いた兵士たちはみな罰せられた The soldiers who *disobeyed* the order were all punished. 親の希望に～いて彼は大学を中退した He left the university in the middle of his course *against* his parents' wishes. 人の信頼に～くようなことをしてはならない Never do what *betrays* others' trust.

そむ・ける【背ける】¶ あまりのむごたらしさに顔を～けた I *turned away* my face *from* too horrible a scene. 彼はその恐ろしい光景から目を～けた He *averted* his eyes *from* the terrible sight.

そめ【染め】dyeing. ¶ ～がきれいにあがった The cloth *was dyed* well. この～はさめない This *dyeing* will not fade out.

そめもの【染め物】(染めること) dyeing; (染めた物) dyed goods.

—屋(店) a dye house; (人) a dyer.

そ・める【染める】¶ きれを黒く～める *dye* cloth black. 彼女は髪を茶色に～めた She *had* her hair *dyed* brown. それを聞くと彼女はほおを～めた She *blushed* to hear it.

そもそも【抑抑】to begin with. ¶ ～彼の顔つきが気に入らない *First of all*, I dislike his looks. ～やり方がまちがっている *To begin with*, the method is wrong. それが～の事の起こりだ It is the very cause of the affair.

そや【粗野】¶ ～なふるまいや～なことば遣いにはがまんできない I can't bear *rude* manners and *coarse* speech. 彼は～だが人間味はある He *is unpolished* but quite warm-hearted.

そよう【素養】attainments; groundwork.

¶ 彼には音楽の～がある He *is well grounded in* music. 彼女はフランス語の～がない She does not *know* French./She has no *knowledge* of French. 彼女は生け花の～がある She has *training* for flower arrangement.

そよかぜ【微風】a gentle (≒ soft) breeze.

そよ・ぐ【戦ぐ】¶ 若葉が風に～いでいる The fresh leaves *are swaying* in the wind.

そよそよ ¶ 春風が～と吹いている The spring wind is blowing *gently* (≒ *softly*).

そら ¶ ～急げ *Now*, hurry up! ～ごらん I told you! ～A君が来た Here comes A!

そら【空】**1**〚天〛the sky. ¶ ～は晴れていた The *sky* was clear.

ツバメが1羽～を飛んでいる A swallow is flying in *the air*.

泣きだしそうな～だった The *sky* looked watery.

～の旅は快適だった Traveling by *air* was splendid.

2〚慣用的表現〛¶ 長い詩を彼は～で読んだ He recited *from memory* a long poem.

彼はベートーベンの曲を～でピアノでひいた He played *by ear* one of Beethoven's compositions.

そのことばを～で覚えているのは彼ひとりだった It was he alone who *remembered* the remark.

彼は私の言うことを～吹く風と聞き流した He *took no notice of* what I said.

彼はしばしうわの～でたたずんでいた He was standing *absent-mindedly* for a while.

彼は～を使っていた He *pretended* (≒ *feigned*) *ignorance*. / He *pretended* not to know it.

そらいろ【空色】sky blue. ¶ ～のハンカチーフ a *sky-blue* handkerchief.

そらおそろし・い【空恐ろしい】¶ ～い子だ *I feel a vague fear to* the child. そんなことは考えただけで～い気がする The bare thought of it is enough to *make* me *dreadful*.

そら・す【反らす】¶ 胸を～す straighten *oneself* up.

そら・す【逸らす】¶ 彼女は彼から顔を～した She *turned away* her face *from* him. / She *averted* her eyes *from* him. 彼は人を～さない He has tact in dealing with people.

そらぞらし・い【空空しい】¶ ときどき彼は～いうそ

そ

をつく Sometimes he tells a *thin* lie. 彼はいかにも～い態度であった He behaved as if he were a stranger to me. 彼は私にいろいろ～いお世辞を言った He made me many *hollow* compliments.

そらだのみ【空頼み】¶ 干天に雨を望んだが～だった We *vainly hoped for* a rainfall during the dry season.

そらとぼ・ける【空惚ける】¶ 彼は～けた顔をしている He *pretends not to know about it*. / He *looks as if he knew nothing about it*. ～けてもむだだ It is no use *wearing an air of innocence*.

そらなみだ【空涙】¶ ～を流す shed *sham* (≒ *crocodile*) *tears*.

そらに【空似】¶ それは他人の～だ It is *an accidental resemblance*.

そらまめ【蚕豆・空豆】〖植物〗a broad (≒ horse) bean.

そらみみ【空耳】¶ だれか来たように思ったが～だった I only fancied I heard someone coming.

そらもよう【空模様】the look of the sky. ¶ ～が怪しい *The weather* looks threatening. / *It* is threatening to rain. この～ではあすは晴れないと思う From (≒ Judging from) *the look of the sky*, I don't think it will be fine tomorrow.

そり【反り】a curve; (板の) a warp. ¶ 熱で板に～がきた Heat *warped* the board. 彼とは～が合わない I cannot *get along well with* him.

そり【橇】(小型のそり) 米 a sled; 英 a sledge; (馬が引く大型のそり) a sleigh. ¶ ～に乗る drive in *a sledge*. ～で行く go in *a sledge*. ～を引く steer *a sledge*; pull *a sledge*.

そりかえ・る【反り返る】¶ 板が～った The board *was warped*. 彼はいすに～った He *threw back his head* in the chair.

ソリスト a soloist (ソリストはフランス語の soliste から).

そりみ【反り身】¶ 彼は～になって話した He spoke *with his chest thrown out*.

そりゃく【疎略】¶ 客を～に扱う *neglect* a guest; treat a guest *roughly*.

そりゅうし【素粒子】〖物理〗an elemental particle.

―論 the theory of elemental particle.

そ・る【反る】⇒そりかえる

そ・る【剃る】¶ (理髪店で)顔は～りますか Do you want *a shave*? 顔を～ってもらった I *had* my face *shaved*. けさはひげを～らなかった I did not *shave* 〔*myself*〕 this morning. ひげを～ってもらった I *had a shave* (≒ I *got myself shaved*) at a barber's. 彼はあごひげを～り落とした He *shaved off* his beard. ひげを～れよ You need *a shave*. ひげを～ってくれ I want *a shave*. 彼のひげは～りたてだった His beard *was freshly shaven*.

ゾル〖化学〗sol; colloidal solution.

それ【其れ・夫れ】it; that. ¶ ～はそうと彼は病気か *By the way*, is he ill? ああ～～ That's it! ～行け *Now*, go! ～, 走れ Now, run for it!

それかぎり【それ限り】⇒それきり

それから ¶ ～(次に)どうなった What happened *next*? ～(その後)彼はどうしている How is he getting along *since then*? ～それへとひっきりなしに問題が持ち上がった There came successively *one* trouble *after another*.

それきり【其れ限り】¶ 彼は～顔を見せない He has never come *since then*. ～さ(それで全部) That's all. なにもかも～さ(万事終わり) All is over.

それくらい ¶ ～のことで夫に愚痴をこぼすな You shouldn't complain to your husband about *such* a trifle. ～勉強すればだいじょうぶだ You are sure to pass the exam if you go on working *so much*.

それそうおう【それ相応】¶ ～のお礼はする I will offer a *reasonable* reward. 彼は危険な仕事はしているが, ～に高給をもらっている He is engaged in a dangerous job, but paid *reasonably* well. こちらにも～の考えがある We have a plan to meet it.

それぞれ【夫れ夫れ・其れ其れ】each; respectively. ¶ 思い思いに～休日を楽しんでいる Everybody enjoys his holidays *in his own way*. 佐藤と吉田は～銀行と出版社に就職した Sato and Yoshida took positions in a bank and a publishing firm *respectively*. 人～に生き方がある Everyone has *his own way of* living.

それだから so; therefore. ¶ ～泣いているのか *Is that why* you are crying? ～言わないことではない I told you *so*!

それだけ that much. ¶ さしあたり～あれば今は十分だ *So much* is all I want for the moment. ～のことで泣いたりするな Don't cry over *such* a trifle. ～はまっぴらだ I will do anything but *that*.

それで ¶ ～どうしました What did you do *then*? ～しばらく彼の家にやっかいになることにした *Therefore*, I decided to stay with him for a while. ～わかった I see it *now*. ～こそ男だ That's worthy of a man.

それでは ¶ ～またお目にかかりましょう *Well*, see you again. ～あまりかわいそうだ *That* would be too pitiful. ～私も賛成する *If that is the case*, I agree with you, too.

それでも ¶ ～彼は私の上京を許してくれない *Still*, he doesn't allow me to go up to Tokyo. 変に聞こえるかもしれないが, ～ほんとうだ It may sound strange, but it is true *for all that*.

それどころか on the contrary; far from that.

それとなく indirectly. ¶ ～彼に注意した I warned him of it *indirectly*. / I advised him *in a casual manner*.

それとも or; otherwise.

それなり ¶ その計画は～になっている The plan has been left *as it is*. それは～に意味がある It has significance *of its own*.

それに moreover; besides. ¶ 疲れていたし, ～おなかもすいていた I was too tired, *besides* I was hungry. ～しても来るのがおそい How late he is in coming *for all that*.

それはさておき ¶～，まず腹ごしらえをしよう Let's eat *first anyway*.

それはそうと【其れは然うと】¶～約束の物を持ってきてくれましたか *By the way* (≒ 囲 *Incidentally*), have you brought what you promised me? ～今何時ごろだろう *Well, now*, what time is it? ～, だれが手伝ってくれるのですか Who is going to help me *after all*? ～, いつか食事に来ませんか *Meanwhile* why don't you come and dine with us?

それはそれは ¶～りっぱな人だ He is an *extremely* fine gentleman. ～お疲れでしょう I know you must be *very* tired. ～住みよい所だ It is an *extraordinarily* nice place to live. ～ご親切にありがとう It's *very* kind of you. / I *really* appreciate your kindness. ～美しい景色だった The beauty of the scenery was *utterly* beyond description.

それほど【其れ程】¶～山へ行きたいのか Do you want to go mountain-climbing *so much*? 忙しいですか. いや, ～でもありません Are you busy? No, not *very* (≒ 囲 *pretty*). ～の勉強家なら試験に受かるだろう If he is *such* a hard worker (≒ If he is working *so* hard), he will pass the examination.

それまで【其れ迄】¶～に帰ってきなさい Come home *by then* (≒ *by that time*). ～は東京にいる I'll be in Tokyo *till then*. 病人は～よりも少しよくなったようだった The patient seemed to be a little better than *before* (≒ *he had been*). ～黙っていた人が口を開いた A man who had kept silence *up to that time* opened his mouth. ～は待てない I can hardly wait so long. ～にしなくてもよかったのに You should not have gone *so far*.

それゆえ【其れ故】so; therefore.

そ·れる【外れる·逸れる】¶話が～れた The conversation *turned on other subjects*. / The conversation *strayed from the subject*. 弾丸が的から～れた The bullet *missed the mark*. / The bullet *went wild*. 車はここでわき道へ～れた The car *turned off* the road here.

ソロ〖音楽〗a solo (複 solos; soli).

そろい【揃い】a set; a suit. ¶家具ひと～ *a set of* furniture. 洋服ひと～ *a suit of* clothes. みなさんお～でどちらへ Where are you going *all together*?

そろう【疎漏】¶万事～のないようにしてください See to it that everything *goes well*.

そろ·う【揃う】¶この会社には有能な社員が～っている This firm *has a good staff of* workers. この家には電気製品が～っている This house *has every sort* (≒ *has all kinds*) *of* electrical goods. 漱石全集が全部～っている I *have the whole set of* Soseki's complete works at home. 全員～いましたか Is everyone here? 一家～ってピクニックに出かけた We went out on a picnic *all together*. 彼らは～いも～ってみな小柄だった They were *all* small boys *without a single exception*. 彼らは～いも～って頭がよかった They were bright *one and all*. この通りの街路樹は高さが～っている The trees along this street are of *uniform* height.

そろ·える【揃える】¶書類を～えておいてください Please *get* me the *complete set of* the documents. その店は冬物を豊富に～えている They *have an abundant assortment of* winter things at the store. シェイクスピアを研究するなら，シェイクスピアの全集を～えたほうがいい If you are to study Shakespeare, you had better *have a complete set of* Shakespeare at hand. この仕事をするには50人～えなければならない This job requires fifty workers. 色は～えたほうがいい Colors had better *be harmonized*. すぐ出かけられるようくつを～えておきなさい *Get* your shoes *ready for* putting on so that you can go out immediately. 脱いだスリッパは～えておきなさい *Put* your slippers you have taken off neatly *side by side*.

そろそろ (ゆっくり) slowly; (やがて) by and by; now; (しだいに) gradually. ¶～歩きなさい Walk *slowly*. ～寝る時刻だ It is time to go to bed *now*. ～始めよう Let's get started *now*. 彼女も～結婚してもいい年ごろだ She is about the age to get married.

ぞろぞろ ¶毛虫が～はっている Caterpillars are creeping along *in a swarm*. パレードのあとを子どもたちが～ついていく Children *go swarming* after the parade.

そろばん【算盤】an abacus (複 abaci). ¶～で計算する count on *an abacus*. それでは～がとれない That won't *pay*.

—玉 a counter; a bead. **—ずく** ¶彼は何事も～ずくで考える He is never free from selfish interest.

そわそわ ¶彼は～している He *looks nervous*. ～と辺りを見まわした I cast an *uneasy* glance around me. そんなに～するな Don't *be* so *nervous* (≒ *restless*).

そん【損】**1**〖金銭的に〗loss. ¶5,000円の～をした I *lost* five thousand yen.

この取引で100万円の～をした We *lost* a million yen by that transaction.

ずいぶん～をしたものだ What *a* great *loss* I have *suffered*!

今どきそんな買い物をするのは～だ It is *a bad bargain* to buy such a thing now.

この～を埋めるにはどうしたらいいだろう What am I to do to *cover up this loss*?

～までしてこんな仕事をやることはない You need not do such a work *at a loss*.

相手に～をかけないようにしなさい Take care not to inflict *a loss* upon the other party.

投機でとんだ～をした I *lost* not a little on speculation.

2〖その他の得失〗¶彼の言うことを聞いても～にはならない You *lose nothing* by listening to him.

うそをつけば結局は自分の～になる Telling a lie results in our own *loss*.

卒業前に学校をやめるのは～だ It is *to your dis-*

そ

advantage to leave school before completing the whole course.
せっかく勉強したのに問題がやさしすぎて～をした I did my best in my study, and yet the questions were too easy, *to my cost*.
字を書くのがへたで～をしている Being a poor hand at writing letters results in *my disadvantage*.

そんえき【損益】profit and loss. ¶ ～を計算する balance *profit and loss* (≒ *loss and gain*). ～なし Neither *lost* nor *gained*.
—計算 a profit and loss account. —計算書 a statement of profit and loss.

そんかい【村会】a village assembly. ¶ ～議員 a member of *a village assembly*.

そんがい【損害】damage; a loss; an injury. ¶ 会社は10万円の～を受けた The firm suffered *a loss* (≒ *damage*) of 100,000 yen. その火災の～は1,000万円に及んだ The total *damage* caused by the fire amounted to 10,000,000 yen. その条約は国家に大きな～を与えた The treaty caused *a* considerable *loss* to the nation. その～を埋め合わせることはできない It is impossible to cover up the *loss*. ～は最小限度に食い止めねばならぬ We have to reduce the *damage* to a minimum.
—高 the extent (≒ amount) of damage.
—保険 insurance against damage.

ぞんがい【存外】¶ 読んでみたら～おもしろい本だ I found the book *more* interesting *than I had expected*. / I found the book *unexpectedly* interesting. ～に利口な子だった He proved to be *unexpectedly* bright.

そんけい【尊敬】respect; esteem. ¶ 多くの人は神に～の念をいだく Many people *feel respect for* God. 彼を～していますか Do you *respect* him? 私は彼を～する(しない) I *pay* my *respect* (no *respect*) *to* him.

そんげん【尊厳】dignity; majesty. ¶ 法の～を保つ uphold the *dignity* (≒ *majesty*) of the law.

そんざい【存在】existence. ¶ 私は神の～を信じる I believe in〔the *existence* of〕God. そんなものはこの世に～しない Such a thing does not *exist* in this world. 彼は詩人としては～を認められなかった He *was taken no notice of* as a poet. 彼は実業界では異色の～だ He is *a* unique *figure* in the business world.
—理由 ¶ この委員会の～理由がわからない I cannot understand〔*the reason*〕*why* this committee *exists*.

ぞんざい ¶ ～に扱うな(人を) Don't treat him *uncourteously*. / (物を) Don't handle it *roughly*. 彼は口のきき方が～だ He has a *rough* way of speaking. / He *is rough of* speech. 彼は～な手紙を書く He writes a letter *carelessly*.

そんしつ【損失】a loss. ¶ 彼の死はわが社にとって大きな～だ His death is *a* great *loss* to our firm. 洪水で1,000万円の～をまねいた The flood caused *a loss* of 10,000,000 yen.

そんしょう【損傷】damage;〔an〕injury. ¶ 彼の車は少し～を受けた His car *was injured* a little. / His car suffered *a* slight *injury*.

そんしょく【遜色】¶ 最近国産の自動車は外車と比べて～がない The home-manufactured cars these days *are* by no means *inferior to* foreign cars. AはBに～がない A *is equal to* B.

そん·じる【損じる】¶ 上役のきげんを～じた I *offended* my superior. 用紙を書き～じた I *failed to* fill the form properly.

そんぞく【存続】continuation. ¶ 私は旧制度の～に反対だ I am opposed to the *retention* of the old system. / I am opposed to *keep* the old system. 会社を～させたい I want to *continue* the firm.
—期間 the term of existence.

そんぞく【尊属】〘法律〙an ascendant; an ancestor; (総称) lineal ascendants.

そんだい【尊大】haughtiness. ¶ 彼はだれに対しても～に構える He *is haughty to* everyone. そう～ぶるな Don't *look* so *proud*. / Don't *look* so *haughty*.

そんたく【忖度】¶ 私は彼の心中を～しかねる I can't *guess* (≒ *conjecture*) what is in his mind.

そんちょう【村長】the chief of a village; the village master.

そんちょう【尊重】¶ 少数意見でも～しなければいけない We should *esteem* (≒ *value*; *think highly of*) the opinion of the minority as well. 伝統の～は文化的に意義がある *Respect* of tradition has a cultural meaning.

そんどう【村道】a village road.

そんとく【損得】loss and gain; self-interest. ¶ ～をはなれて仕事をすることもある Sometimes we can be free from *selfish interest*.
—ずく ¶ 彼の考えはいつも～ずくだ He considers his *personal interest* first of all.

そんな ¶ ～ときにはすぐ呼んでください Call me at once in *such* a case. ～物をどうするつもりだ What will you do with *such* a thing? ～ばかなことがあるか That's impossible. ～話は聞いたことがない I have never heard *such* nonsense. まあ～ところだ That's about it. ～ことがあるものか It can't be true. ～ことではいい絵はかけない You can't paint a good picture *if you go on like that*. ～つもりではなかった I did not mean it.
—こんな ¶ ～こんなで,そのことを忘れてしまった I got involved and forgot it.

そんなに ¶ なぜ～怒るのですか What are you *so* angry for? / What makes you *so* angry? ～急ぐな Don't be in *such* a hurry. ～無理をするな Don't overwork yourself.

そんぴ【存否】¶ 生存者の～を知らせてください Let me know whether there are any survivors or not.

ぞんぶんに【存分に】¶ ～お休みください Take *as much* rest *as* you *like* (≒ *please*). ～食べた(飲んだ) I *ate* (*drank*) *my fill*. 好きな音楽を～聴いた I enjoyed the favorite music *to my heart's content*. お気のすむように～してくだ

さい Deal with me *as you please*.

そんぼう【存亡】existence; fate. ¶ 国家は今や危急～のときである The national *existence* is now at stake. / It is a question of *life and death* for the nation.

そんみん【村民】the villagers; the village people.

ぞんめい【存命】¶ 亡父の～中はお世話になりました Thank you [very much] for your kindness to my dead father while he *was alive*.

そんもう【損耗】a loss. ¶ 機械の～がはなはだしい The machine *has worn* rapidly.

そんゆうりん【村有林】a village-owned forest.

そんらく【村落】a village; (小さい) a hamlet.

そんりつ【村立】¶ ～小学校 a *village* primary school.

そんりつ【存立】¶ 会社の～が危ぶまれている The *existence* of the firm is being threatened.

そんりょう【損料】hire; [a] rent. ¶ ～をとって物を貸す let out things *on hire*. ～5,000円で車を借りた I paid 5,000 yen for the *hire* of the car.

た

た【他】another; other; others. ¶ ～のために尽くしなさい Do good to *others*. ～に欠席者はありませんか Is there anyone *else* absent? ～は推して知るべしだ *The rest* may be inferred.
—府県 other prefectures. **—**方面 other fields.

た【多】¶ 彼の労を～とする We *deeply appreciate* his great service to us.

た【田】a rice field; paddy[-field]. ¶ ～を耕す plough *a rice field*.

だ【打】hitting. ¶ 彼は～の第一人者だ He is the leading hitter.

だあ ¶ 彼の答えを聞いてなみいる人は～となった All the people present *were dumbfounded at* his answer (≒ *to* hear his answer).

たあいな·い【他愛ない】⇒ たわいない

ダーク dark.
—スーツ a dark suit. **—**ホース a dark horse.

ダース a dozen. ¶ 鉛筆1ダース *a dozen* of pencils. ビール半～ half *a dozen* of bottles of beer. ～で買えばやすくなります You can buy [at a] cheaper [price] *by the dozen*.

ダーツ〖洋裁〗darts; (遊戯) darts.

ターバン a turban.

ダービー [the] Derby. ¶ 毎年～へ行く I go to *the Derby* every year. ～で1万円もうけた I gained (≒ made) ten thousand yen *on the Derby*.
ホームラン**—**〖野球〗a homerun derby.

タービン a turbine [engine].
蒸気(ガス)**—** a steam (gas) turbine.

ターボジェット a turbojet engine.
—機 a turbojet plane.

ターボプロップ a turboprop engine; a turbo-propeller engine.
—機 a turboprop plane.

ターミナル 米 a terminal; a terminal station; 英 a terminus.
—デパート a department store at a railway terminal.

タール tar. ¶ このたばこは～分が少ない This cigarette contains little *tar*.

ターン a turn. ¶ (水泳などで) ～がうまい (まずい) He makes *a* beautiful (poor) *turn*.
ユー(U)**—** [a] U-turn. ¶ U～禁止 (掲示) No "U" *turns* allowed.

タイ (国名) Thai; Thailand.
—語 Thai. **—**人 a Thai; a Thailander.

タイ a tie. ¶ 試合は5対5の～に終わった The game ended in a 5-5 *tie*. (読むときは five to five). 両チームは～になった The two teams *tied*.
—記録 a tie record. ¶ 彼は100メートル競走で世界～記録を出した He *tied with* world *record* for the 100-meter dash.

たい【体】¶ ボールから～をかわした I *dodged* the ball. それでは～をなさない That is in bad *form* (≒ *style*).

たい【対】**1**〖二つのものの間の関係〗¶ オックスフォード～ケンブリッジのボートレース the boat race *between* Oxford *and* Cambridge; the Oxford *vs.* Cambridge boat race (vs. は versus [vəːsəs] の略. against の意で, [əgéinst] とも発音される).
5～3で勝った We won the game by [a score of] 5 *to* 3.
資本家～労働者の闘争は果てしがない There will be no end to the struggle of labor *against* capital.
空**—**空ミサイル an air-to-air missile (A. A. M.). 地**—**空ミサイル a ground-to-air missile (G.A.M.). 空**—**地ミサイル an air-to-surface missile (A.S.M.). **—**ミサイルミサイル an anti-missile missile.
2〖相手への関係に用いて〗¶ 政府は～インド接近をはかっている The government is trying to improve the relations *with* India.
わが国の～中国外交は転換期に達した Our foreign policy *toward* China has reached a turning point.

たい【隊】a party; a band. ¶ ～を組んで歩く march *in a body*. 一～の兵士が走ってきた *A band* of soldiers came running.
合唱── a chorus; (教会の) a choir. 探検── an expedition. 航空── a flying corps. 陸軍(海軍)軍楽── a military (marine; naval) band.

たい【鯛】a sea (≒ gold) bream. ¶ 腐っても～(諺) An old eagle is better than a young crow. / If a diamond is thrown into the mire, it is a diamond still. / A diamond is valuable though it lies on a dunghill.

たい【他意】(他の意図) another intention; (悪意) ill will; malice. ¶ ～はありません I bear you no *ill will*. / I mean no harm.

-たい【-度い】¶ 父に会いたい I *want to* see my father. イタリアで暮らしたい I *wish* I could live in Italy. コーヒーが飲みたい I *feel like* drink*ing* a cup of coffee. お茶を飲みたいですか Would you *care for* a cup of tea? その映画をごらんになりたいですか Would you *like to* see the movie? とても泳ぎたい I *am dying for* a swim. すぐこの仕事をやってもらいたい I *want* you *to* do this immediately. きみにそんなことを言ってもらいたくない I don't *like* your saying such a thing.

-たい【-帯】a zone; (ベルト) a belt.

だい【大】**1**〖大きいこと〗largeness; greatness; (大きさ) size. ¶ この品には～中小の３種がある This article comes in three sizes: *large*, medium and small.
～は小を兼ねる (諺) *The greater* serves for the lesser.
その石を庭に運ぶのに～の男が７人がかりだった The effort of seven men was necessary to carry the stone to the garden.
10円玉～の石 a stone about *the size of* ten-yen coin.
こぶし～の石 a stone *as large as* a fist.
五月は～の月だ May has thirty-one days.
彼は～の字になって寝ころんでいた He was lying *at full length*.
2〖偉大なこと〗¶ 彼が今日の～を成したのはひとえに努力のたまものだ It is entirely owing to his efforts that he has attained to his present *greatness*.

だい【代】**1** (世代) a generation; (治世) a reign. ¶ 徳川５～将軍はだれですか Who was *the fifth Shogun* of the Tokugawa clan?
ジョンソンはアメリカ合衆国第何～の大統領ですか How many presidents were there in the United States before Johnson?
このでき事はエリザベス女王の～のことだ This happened in the *reign* of Queen Elizabeth.
この家は父の～に2度洪水に見舞われた This house was flooded twice in my father's *time*.
2〖年齢・年代の一区切り〗¶ 彼女は10～で結婚した She got married in her *teen's*.
100歳～の人々 centenarians.
1960年～の後半には世界でどんな事がありましたか What happened in the world in the latter half of the *1960's*?
3〖代金〗¶ この本のお～はいくらですか *How much* is this book?
部屋～は払った We have paid the *rent*.
お～は立て替えましょう I will pay the *charge* for you.

だい【台】(物をのせるもの) a stand; (肉などをのせて切ったり工作物をのせてくぎを打ったりするもの) a stock; (像などの台座) a pedestal; (演台) a platform.
¶ ３～の自動車 three cars. ２万円～ 20,000 to 30,000 yen price range.

だい【題】a title; a subject; a theme; a heading. ¶ ～をつける *entitle* (a book). その本はなんという～ですか What *is* the book *entitled*? / What is the *title* of the book? 先生は作文の～を出した The teacher gave us the *subject* (≒ *theme*) for composition. 彼は「雨」という～の詩を書いた He composed a poem *entitled* "The Rain." テストに５～出た Five *problems* were given in the test. / The test was made up of five *questions*.

だい-【第-】¶ ～10条～４項 the fourth clause of Article ten. ～五交響曲 Symphony No. 5; The Fifth Symphony (序数の場合は名詞の前, No. ...のときは名詞のあとにつけるのが原則).

たいあたり【体当たり】¶ 私は～してその男をはねとばした I knocked the man down by *dashing myself against* him. / I *hurled myself at* the man and knocked him down. 彼は～の演技をした He did his best in acting his part. / He devoted his whole energy to the performance of his part.

タイアップ a tie-up. ¶ 外国商社と～する *tie up* (≒ *cooperate*) with a foreign firm. 今度わが社はアメリカの会社と技術的な～ができた Recently we obtained technical *cooperation* from an American firm.

ダイアモンド diamond.

たいあん【大安】a lucky day. ¶ ～吉日をえらんで挙式する celebrate (≒ hold) a wedding on *an auspicious* (≒ *a lucky*) *day*.

たいあん【対案】a counterproposal. ¶ 政府原案に対して野党は～を出した The Opposition parties brought in *a counterproposal* against the Government bill.

だいあん【代案】an alternative plan.

たいい【大尉】(陸軍の) a captain; (海軍の) a lieutenant; (空軍の) 米 a captain; 英 a flight lieutenant.

たいい【大意】(概要) the gist; the substance; (趣旨) the purport; (概略) the general idea; an outline; a summary; a synopsis (複 synopses); a résumé (内容の具体的な点をまとめたものは *gist*, 話の目的または内容の中心課題を述べるものは *purport*, 細かな点を省いた概要は *substance* という. 重要点をまとめたものは *outline* または *summary* である. 論文などの概要は *synopsis* あるいは *résumé* という).
¶ 物語の～を述べましょう I will give (≒ tell) you *the outline* of the story. 論文の最後に英語で～を添えてください Please put *an* English *résumé* (≒ *synopsis*) at the end of your

paper.

たいい【体位】(体格) physique; physical condition; (姿勢) a posture. ¶国民の～が向上(低下)した The national *physique* has been improved (deteriorated). / The *physical standard* of the nation has risen (fallen).

たいい【退位】abdication; resignation. ¶皇帝は皇太子に位を譲って～した The emperor *abdicated* 〔*from*〕(≒ *gave up*; *resigned from*) *the throne* in favor of the crown prince.

たいいく【体育】(教科) physical education; (訓練) physical training. ¶～の日 Health-Sports Day.

―館 a gymnasium (複 gymnasiums; gymnasia); a gym. **―会** an athletic association (≒ club).

だいいち【第一】¶～章(課) *the first* chapter (lesson); Chapter (Lesson) *One*. ～交響曲 Symphony *No. 1*; *The First* Symphony. ～次世界大戦 World War *I*. それは～に重要なことだ That is *the most* important thing. / It is of *primary* importance. 健康が～だ Health is above everything else. まず～に健康に注意しなさい *In the first place* (≒ *Firstly*; *First of all*), you must take care of yourself. ～, 金がないじゃないか *First*, we have no money.

―印象 the first impression (*of*). **―組合** the first union. **―次産業** the primary industry. 安全― Safety first.

だいいちぎ【第一義】¶この仕事の～的目的はなにか What is *the most important* object of this work? 言語は～的に話しことばである Language is *primarily* speech.

だいいちにんしゃ【第一人者】a leading expert. ¶彼はその道の～だ He is *a leading expert in* the field. 彼は実業界の～だ He is a *topflight* (≒ *topnotch*; *first-rate*) businessman.

だいいちにんしょう【第一人称】〔文法〕the first person.

だいいっせい【第一声】*one's* first speech. ¶彼の～は全聴衆の注目を引いた His *first speech* attracted the attention of all the audience. 彼の帰国～を聞いた I heard his *first public speech* after returning from abroad.

だいいっせん【第一線】the first line; a front; the forefront. ¶～で戦う兵士たち the soldiers fighting in *the* 〔*fore*〕*front*. 彼はまだ～で活躍している He is still active in *the first line*. ～から退いた I retired from *active life*.

だいいっとう【第一党】(与党) the leading party. ¶野党～ *the chief* (≒ *No. 1*) opposition 〔party〕.

だいいっぽ【第一歩】the first step. ¶～を踏み出す take (≒ make) *the first step*. 1969年地球人類は月に～を印した Men from the earth *first set foot on* the moon in 1969.

たいいほう【対位法】〔音楽〕the counterpoint.

たいいん【退院】¶彼は明日～の予定だ He is going to *leave* 〔*the*〕 *hospital* tomorrow. 病人はあと2, 3日で～の許可が出るだろう The patient will *be discharged from the hospital* in a few days.

たいいん【隊員】¶彼らは南極越冬～である They are *members* of the wintering party at the Antarctic.

だいいん【代印】¶あなたの～をしましょう I'll *sign for* you. (欧米では日本のように印を押す習慣はなく, 代わりに署名をする).

たいいんれき【太陰暦】the lunar calendar.

たいえい【退嬰】¶彼は～的だ He *is unenterprising*. / His attitude *is not progressive*. 会社は～的な空気がみなぎっている The atmosphere of this company *is sluggish and stagnant*.

たいえき【体液】〔医学〕body fluid (血漿 (blood plasma); リンパ液 (lymph) などの体内の液体); 〔古生理学〕humors.

四― the four cardinal humors (昔, 西欧中世の生理学で, その配合の仕方によって人間の性質を定めると考えられていた四つの体内の液体で, 血液 (blood), 粘液 (phlegm), 胆汁 (choler), 黒胆汁 (melancholy) の４種類をいう).

たいえき【退役】retirement. ¶彼は60歳で～した He *retired from service* at the age of sixty.

―軍人 a retired soldier; an ex-service man.

だいえん【大円】〔数学〕the great circle.

たいおう【対応】(匹敵) match; (相応) correspondence. ¶～する２辺 two *corresponding* (≒ *homologous*) sides. イギリスのパブリックスクールは日本の高等学校に～する The public schools in Britain *correspond to* the senior high schools in Japan. その日本語に～する英語はない The Japanese phrase has no close *equivalent* (≒ *counterpart*) in English. いかにしたら時局に～できるだろうか How can we *cope with* the situation?

たいおう【滞欧】¶彼は～中に絵の仕事をした He worked in painting *during his stay in Europe*. 彼は３年間～した He *stayed* (≒ *lived*) *in Europe* for three years.

だいおう【大王】a great king.

えんま― *Yama*, the King of Hell. アレキサンダー― Alexander the Great.

だいおう【大黄】〔植物〕a rhubarb; a wine plant.

だいおうじょう【大往生】¶～を遂げる die a peaceful death. 彼は90歳で～を遂げた He *died at the great age of* ninety.

ダイオード〔電気〕a diode.

たいおん【体温】temperature; bodily temperature. ¶看護婦が患者の～をはかった The nurse took the *temperature* of the patient. 夕方に～が上が(下が)った My *temperature* rose (fell) toward the evening. ～は96度だ My *temperature* is 96°. (アメリカ・イギリスではふつう, 華氏 (Fahrenheit) で体温をはかる. したがって36°5′ などと摂氏でいうときには36.5°

た

Centigrade (thirty-six point five degrees Centigrade) のように，あとに Centigrade をつけていうほうがよい).

だいおん【大恩】¶ 彼は私にとって～のある人だ I *am deeply indebted to* him. / I *owe* him *a debt of great gratitude*.

たいおんけい【体温計】a clinical thermometer.

だいおんじょう【大音声】¶ 騎士は～に名のった The knight announced his name *in a very loud* (≒ *stentorian*) *voice*.

たいか【大火】a big fire; a conflagration. ¶ロンドンは1666年に～に見舞われた London was destroyed by *a great* (≒ *big*) *fire* in 1666. / *A great fire* broke out in London in 1666.

たいか【大家】an authority. ¶ 文壇の～ *an authority* in the literary world; a *distinguished* writer. ドイツ文学の～ *an authority* on German literature. 音楽の～ a *leading* musician; a *maestro*. 絵の～ *a first-rate* (≒ *master*) painter.

たいか【大過】a serious (≒ grievous) error. ¶ 幸いにも～なく職務を遂行することができた Fortunately I could discharge my duties without making any *serious* (≒ *grievous*) *errors*.

たいか【耐火】fireproof.
—金庫 a fireproof safe. —建築 a fireproof building; (構造) fireproof construction. —建築材料 fire-resisting building materials. —れんが a firebrick.

たいか【退化】degeneration; retrogression. ¶ 鯨はあと足が～している The whale has its hind legs *degenerated*. / The whale *is degenerated in* the hind legs.

たいか【滞貨】¶ ～の山 a huge pile of *stocks*. 国鉄の～は二，三日うちに一掃される見通しである The *freight congestion* of the Japan National Railways will be cleared up in a few days. ストライキのため郵便の～がたまりはじめた Mail delivery has begun to slow down because of the strike.

たいが【大河】a large (≒ big) river.
—小説 a long novel; a saga〔novel〕; (フランス語で) *roman-fleuve*.

だいか【代価】(値段) a price; (費用) cost. ¶ いかなる～を払ってもその計画を実行する I am determined to carry out the plan *at any price* (≒ *at any cost; at all costs*). 彼らは尊い人命を～に独立をかちとった They won the independence *at the cost of* valuable lives.

たいかい【大会】a mass (≒ grand) meeting; (総会) a general meeting (≒ assembly); (会議) a conference; a convention; (競技の) a meet; a tournament.
¶ 自由民主党は6月に党～を招集する予定である The Liberal-Democratic Party is scheduled to hold the party *convention* in June.
マラソン— a grand marathon-race meeting. 〔労働〕組合— the general meeting (≒ assembly) of the〔labor〕union.

たいかい【大海】an ocean; the sea; (雅語) the main; the〔great〕deep. ¶ ～の1滴 a drop in the bucket (≒ ocean).

たいかい【退会】withdrawal from membership. ¶ 先月はふたりが～した Two members *left* (≒ *withdrew from*) the society last month. / Two persons *resigned their memberships* last month. 彼は～の届けを出した He notified the society of his *withdrawal*. / He sent a notice of *withdrawal* to the society. / He gave notice of *resignation* to the society.
—者 a seceder.

たいがい【大概】**1**〘大部分・おおよそ〙¶ ～の出席者はその案に賛成だった *Most of* the people present agreed to the plan.
少女たちは～はイギリス人だった The girls were *mostly* English.
私は～は朝食後散歩する I *usually* take a walk after breakfast.
彼は～来るだろう He will *probably* come.
若い人たちは～冬より夏のほうが好きだ *Most* young people like summer better than winter.
きみは～成功するだろう You *are likely to* succeed.
日曜日は～出かける I am *generally* away on Sundays.
2〘いい加減に〙¶ 遊ぶのは～にしておけ *You shouldn't* waste your time *so much*.
冗談も～にしろ *You shouldn't* carry a joke *too far*.

たいがい【体外】¶ 老廃物は～に排出される Waste matter is expelled from *the body*.

たいがい【対外】¶ ～的な仕事 *international* works.
—関係 foreign relations. —政策 a foreign policy. —貿易 overseas (≒ foreign) trade.

たいかく【体格】a physique; a constitution. ¶ このごろの子どもは～がよい Children of today have *a* fine *physique* (≒ *constitution*). 彼は～が悪い He has *a* weak *constitution*.
—検査 a physical examination. ¶ ～検査を受けた I took (≒ underwent) a *physical* examination (≒ check).

たいがく【退学】(生徒が自分から) withdrawal from school; (退学処分) expulsion from school.
¶ 家庭の都合で～した I *left* (≒ *quit*) *school* for family reasons. 彼は論旨～を命じられた He *was expelled* (≒ *was dismissed*) *from school* at the request of the school authority. / *Expulsion from school* was imposed on him as a penalty. 彼は息子を～させた He *withdrew* his son *from school*.
—届 a notice of withdrawal from school.

だいがく【大学】(総合大学) a university; (単科大学) a college. ¶ 彼は～に行っている(大学生だ) He goes to *college*. / He is a *college* student. / He is in *college*. 彼は～の構内のどこかにいる He is somewhere on the *campus*.

～の自治 university autonomy.
―院 ㊥ a graduate school; ㊫ a graduate course. ―院生 a postgraduate; a graduate student. ―教授 a university (≒ college) professor. ―出身者 a college graduate; a university graduate. ―生 a university (≒ college) student; an undergraduate. ―生活 a college (≒ university) life; a campus life. ―総長 a university (≒ college) president; a chancellor. ―紛争 a campus (≒ university) dispute (≒ disturbances; riot); student unrest. ―町 a university town. 紛争― a university in trouble.

たいかくせん【対角線】〔数学〕a diagonal; a diagonal line.

だいかこ【大過去】〔文法〕the past perfect tense; the pluperfect tense.

だいかつ【大喝】¶ 彼に～一声しかられた I was scolded by him *in a voice of thunder.* / He *thundered out* the words of scolding to me.

だいがわり【代替わり】¶ その商店は～になった The store *has changed hands.*

たいかん【大患】a serious illness. ¶ 彼は～にかかった He *was taken seriously ill.* / He *is seriously ill.* / He *is in critical condition.* (後者２例はかかっているの意).

たいかん【大観】a general view (≒ survey). ¶ 現在の時局を～してみよう Let's make *a general survey of* the present situation. 次に来年度の世界経済情勢を～してみよう Next, let us take *a general view* of the world economy for the coming year.

たいかん【体感】bodily sensation.
―温度 effective temperature.

たいかん【退官】¶ 彼は定年で～した He *retired* 〔*from office*〕 because of the age limit. (定年に達せず辞職するのは *resign* という).

たいかん【耐寒】―訓練 training in the cold season. ―植物 a hardy plant. ―設備 winterization (エンジンに不凍液を入れたり，機械に雪をさける覆いをつけたりすること．動詞で使えば「自動車に不凍液を入れて耐寒準備をする *winterize* an automobile with antifreeze」のように使う).

たいがん【対岸】the opposite bank; the other side (*of* a river). ¶ この川の～へはどうすれば行けるでしょうか How can I get to *the other side* of the river? ホテルは湖の～にある The hotel is on *the opposite shore* of the lake. ～の松が見えますか Do you see the pine-trees on *the opposite bank*? この事件を～の火災視してはいけない We must not look on the incident with indifference.

たいがん【大願】ambition; aspiration (*ambition* は富・権力・名声などに対する強い願望で，よい意味でも悪い意味でも用いられる. *aspiration* は期待するのが少し無理に思われるような高い願望をいう). ¶ 彼女は偉大な女優になりたいという～をいだいている She has *ambition* (≒ *aspiration*) to be a great actress. 彼の～は成就した His *dream* came true. / He realized his *dream* (≒ *ambition*). / His *ambition* was realized.

だいかん【大寒】the coldest season; midwinter.

たいかんしき【戴冠式】the coronation〔ceremony〕.

たいき【大気】the atmosphere; the air.
―汚染 air pollution. ―圏 the atmosphere. ¶ ～圏外の平和利用 peaceful use (≒ exploitation) of *outer space.* ～圏内の核実験 a nuclear test in *the atmosphere*; an *atmospheric* blast of a nuclear device.

たいき【大器】a great talent; a person of great caliber. ¶ ～晩成 *Great talents* mature late.

たいき【待機】¶ 警官が～している The police *are on the alert.* / The police *are alerted.* 全員～するように命じられた All the members were ordered to *stand by.*

たいぎ【大義】justice; righteousness; (目的) a great cause; (忠義) loyalty and patriotism. ¶ 彼の行ないは～名分が立たない His conduct cannot *be justified.* / He has no *cause* for such a conduct.

たいぎ【大儀】¶ 彼は仕事が～そうに見える He *looks tired* from the work. 彼は～そうに歩いていた He was walking *heavily* (≒ *with heavy steps*).

たいぎ【体技】physical exercise.

だいぎ【台木】a trunk; a stock; a block. ¶ 私は桜の～に梅の接ぎ木をした I inserted a shoot (≒ graft) of a plum tree into the *trunk* (≒ *stock*) of a cherry tree. / I grafted a twig of a plum tree in *a block* of a cherry tree.

だいぎ【代議】―員 a representative; a delegate. ―制 the representative system. ―政治 representative government.

だいきぎょう【大企業】(大会社) a big business (≒ company; firm; concern).

だいぎし【代議士】(日本の) a member of the Diet; a Dietman; (アメリカの) a Congressman; a representative; (イギリスの) a Member of Parliament (an M. P.).

だいきぼ【大規模】¶ ～な工事 a *large-scale* work. 方言の調査を～に行なった We made a survey of dialects *on a large scale.*

たいきゃく【退却】〔a〕 retreat; 〔a〕 withdrawal. ¶ フランス軍は総くずれになって～した The French army were put to rout and *made a retreat.* ～を命ずる give (≒ issue) an order to *retreat*; order *a retreat.*
総― a full retreat. ¶ 彼らは総～中だった They were *in full retreat.*

たいきゅう【耐久】―消費材 durable consumer goods. ―力 durability; endurance; (人や国の) staying power; stamina. ¶ ～力に富む鋼 *durable* steel. この時計は～力がある This watch *lasts long.* この背広は～力がある This suit *wears long* (≒ *wears well*). この靴下は～力がなかった These socks *have worn badly.*

た

だいきゅう【代休】a compensatory day off. ¶彼は先週日曜日に出社したので〜をとった He took *a compensatory day off* because he worked in the office last Sunday.

だいきゅうし【大休止】a long rest. ¶部隊はその村で〜をとった The troops took *a long rest* in the village.

だいきゅうし【大臼歯】〘解剖学〙a true molar 〔tooth〕.

たいきょ【大挙】¶われわれは〜して彼のところに押しかけた We called on him *in crowds* (≒ *in a crowd*). 彼らは〜してその工場を訪れた They visited the plant *in great numbers*.

たいきょ【退去】¶船長は乗り組み員全員に〜を命じた The captain ordered all the crew to *leave* (≒ *quit*) the ship. 彼らは大学構内から〜を命じられた They were ordered *out of* the campus. / They were ordered to *leave* (≒ *evacuate*) the campus. 不法入国者は国外に〜を命じられた The illegal alien *was expelled* (≒ *was deported*) *from* the country.

たいきょう【胎教】prenatal care (≒ training).

たいぎょう【大業】a great work; a great enterprise. ¶国連は恒久世界平和の〜に踏み出した The United Nations set to *the great work* of establishing permanent world peace.

だいきょう【大凶】¶おみくじで〜と出た A written oracle told *a singular ill fortune*.

たいきょく【大局】the general (≒ whole) situation. ¶〜的見地に立つべきだ You should *take a large* (≒ *wide*) *view of things*. 〜を見誤るな Don't *take a wrong view of things*. 〜をはっきりつかむ必要がある We must *take a right view of the whole situation*. 〜に変化はなかった There was no change in *the general situation*.

たいきょく【対局】¶名人戦の〜が始まった The Japanese chess players' championship *tournament* is now going on. 碁の有名な両者が〜する The two famous *go*-game players will *have a match*.

だいきらい【大嫌い】¶彼が〜だ I *cannot bear* (≒ *cannot stand*) him. / I *hate* him. ニンジンは〜だ I *don't like* carrots *at all*.

たいきん【大金】a large sum of money. ¶〜を投じて事業を起こした He started an enterprise *at great cost*. 彼は〜を持ち逃げした He ran away with *a large sum of money*.

だいきん【代金】a price. ¶その品物の〜を払ってください I want you to *pay for* the goods. 彼は私に〜を立て替えてくれた He paid the *price* for me. 品物は〜引き換えでなければお渡しできません The goods are not delivered except in exchange for the *money*.
—引換 C. O. D.; c. o. d. (㊖ collect on delivery; ㊛ cash on delivery).

だいく【大工】a carpenter.
—仕事 (職) carpentry. —道具 carpenter's tools; (一式) a carpenter's kit.

たいくう【対空】—砲火 anti-aircraft fire. —ミサイル an anti-aircraft missile.

たいくう【滞空】—記録 a flight record. —飛行 an endurance flight.

たいぐう【待遇】treatment; (給料) pay; (ホテルなどのサービス) service. ¶そこでは〜がよかった(悪かった) I *was* warmly (coldly) *treated*. あの家ではお客に対する〜がよい(悪い) They *are hospitable* (*inhospitable*) to visitors at that house. あの会社は〜がよい(悪い) The employees *are well* (*poorly*) *paid* at that company. このホテルなら〜はよい(悪い) This hotel will give you good (poor) *service*. 〜を改善すべきだ You should *improve labor conditions* (≒ *increase pay; raise salary*).
課長— a person receiving similar treatment as the chief of a section.

たいくつ【退屈】tedium. ¶実に〜な話だった It was quite a *tedious* (≒ *boring*) talk. この本はまったく〜だ This book *bores* me *to death*. 〜しのぎに昨年の日記を読んだ I read my diary of last year *to kill time*.

たいぐん【大軍】a big army. ¶〜が押し寄せてきた *A large force* came surging upon us.

たいぐん【大群】(人の) a large crowd of people. ¶羊の〜 *a large flock of* sheep. イナゴの〜が発生した *A large swarm* of locusts were generated there.

たいけい【大計】(大きな計画) a great plan; (遠大な計画) a long-range plan. ¶国家百年の〜を立てる make *a great* (≒ *long-term; long-range*) *plan* 〔for the future〕 of the nation; establish a *far-sighted* national policy.

たいけい【大系】an outline. ¶「日本文学〜」"*An Outline* of Japanese Literature."

たいけい【体系】a system. ¶理論〜のしっかりした学説だ It is a theory with *a* complete *system*. 学問にはあらゆる理論の〜化が必要だ In pursuit of learning, it's necessary to *systematize* all the theories.
—化 systematization. ¶〜化する systematize.

たいけい【体刑】(体罰) corporal punishment; (懲役) imprisonment with hard labor; penal servitude.
¶彼は〜を科された *A corporal punishment* was inflicted on him. 裁判長は彼を10年の〜に処した The chief judge sentenced him to ten years' *penal servitude*.

たいけい【隊形】formation. ¶〜を整えた We put the *formation* in good order. 〜が乱れた The *formation* was in disorder.

だいけい【台形】〘数学〙a trapezoid.

たいけつ【対決】confrontation. ¶彼と〜した I *stood face to face with* him. われわれは彼と彼女を〜させた We *confronted* him *with* her. いずれ2大政党の〜が見られるだろう Sooner or later there will be *a showdown* between the two political parties.

たいけん【大圏】a great circle.
—コース the great circle route.

たいけん【大権】the supreme power; (君主の) a prerogative. ¶彼は〜を発動した He exercised the *Imperial* (≒ *Royal*) *pre-*

rogative.

たいけん【体験】personal experience. ¶この貴重な～を生かしてください Make the best use of this valuable *experience*. 彼は幾多の困難を～してきた He *experienced* (≒ *went through*) many hardships. / He *has known* all sorts of difficulties.

—談 the story of *one's* experience. ¶彼は私に～談を聞かせてくれた He told me of his *personal experience.*

たいげん【大言】tall (≒ big) talk; a loud boast; exaggeration. ¶彼はよく～壮語する He often *talks big* (≒ *talks tall; talks large*). ～壮語する人 a braggart; a boaster.

たいげん【体言】〘文法〙the substantives; the indeclinable parts of speech in Japanese grammar.

たいげん【体現】embodiment. ¶建築は建築家の考えを～したものだ A building *embodies* the architect's idea.

だいけんしょう【大憲章】Magna C(h)arta; the Great Charter.

たいこ【太古】ancient times. ¶～の動物の化石を発見した We discovered fossil animals *in remote ages*.

たいこ【太鼓】a drum. ¶～をたたく beat (≒ play) *a drum*.

たいご【対語】an antonym.

たいご【隊伍】the ranks; a line. ¶～を組んで通りを行進した We marched *in rank and file* on the street. / We paraded *in line* on the street. ～を整えた(乱した) We dressed (broke) our *ranks*.

たいこう【大公】a grand duke. ¶モナコ～ *the Grand Duke* of Monaco.

たいこう【大功】¶彼は国のために～を立てた He rendered *eminent* (≒ *meritorious; distinguished*) *services* to his country.

たいこう【大綱】general (≒ fundamental) principles. ¶条約の～が決まった *Fundamental principles* of the treaty were laid down. 政策の～を示した We gave *an outline* of our policy.

たいこう【対抗】opposition. ¶体力では彼に～できるが頭のほうではかなわない I *equal* him *in* strength but not in intelligence. 英会話では彼にはとても～できない He *is more than my match in* English conversation. 日米～水上競技大会が東京で開始された A Japan-U. S. A. aquatics was held in Tokyo.

—策 a counterplot. —者 a rival; an opponent. —馬(競馬の) a rival horse; (選挙の) *a person's* rival candidate.

たいこう【対校】—試合 an interschool match (≒ game); (大学の) an intercollegiate tournament (≒ match).

たいこう【退校】(任意の) withdrawal from school; (退学処分) dismissal from school. ¶彼は～した He left school. 彼は～処分を受けた He *was expelled* (≒ *was dismissed*) *from school.*

だいこう【代行】¶彼は学長の職務を～した He *acted for* the president.

—機関 an agency; a substitute machinery. 学長— the acting president.

たいこうしゃ【対向車】an on-coming car.

だいこうぶつ【大好物】a great favorite. ¶ジャガイモは～だ Potatoes are my *favorite food*. サンマは私の～だ I *am very fond of* mackerel pike.

たいこうぼう【太公望】an angler. ¶終日～をきめこんだ I indulged in angling all day long.

たいこく【大国】a large country; (強力) a big power; (偉大な国) a great country. ¶日本は世界の～の一つとなった Japan ranks among *the great powers* of the world.

だいこくばしら【大黒柱】¶家の～(建物の) *the central pillar* of a house. 一家の～ *the support* (≒ *the breadwinner*) of a family. 父は一家の～だ Father is *the support* (≒ *supporter*) of our family.

たいこだい【太古代】the Archaean Era.

たいこばら【太鼓腹】a portly belly; a paunch; a pot-belly. ¶～の人 a *pot-bellied* man.

たいこばん【太鼓判】(大きな判) a large seal. ¶彼が正直であることには～を押す I *vouch for* his honesty. 彼の成功には～を押す I *guarantee* his success.

だいごみ【醍醐味】a great charm. ¶釣りの～をきのうは十分に味わった I could fully enjoy myself in fishing yesterday.

だいごれつ【第五列】the fifth column.

だいこん【大根】〘植物〙a radish.

—おろし(食物) grated radish; (道具) a radish grater. —役者 a poor actor; (女優) a poor actress.

たいさ【大佐】(陸軍·空軍) a colonel (発音は[kəːnəl]); (海軍) a captain.

たいさ【大差】a great difference. ¶両者の意見に～はない The two opinions are about the same. / There is little *difference* of opinion between the two. 彼は～でゴールインした He reached the goal *with a long lead* on other runners. われわれは10点の～で敗れた We lost the game by *a wide margin* of ten points.

だいざ【台座】a pedestal; a dais.

たいさい【大祭】a grand festival.

たいざい【滞在】a stay. ¶私のロンドン～中に during my *stay* in London. 彼は京都に～中だ He *is staying* in Kyoto. 彼女はおばの家に～している She *is staying with* her aunt. 1週間ホテルに～する予定だ I am going to *stop at* a hotel for a week. パリには長く～するつもりだ I will *make a* long *stay* in Paris.

—客 a guest; a visitor. —地 the place of stay. —日数 the length of *a person's* visit. —費 (ホテルの) a hotel bill; hotel expenses.

だいざい【大罪】a great crime. ¶彼は～を犯した He committed *a serious* (≒ *capital; terrible*) *crime*. 七つの～ seven deadly *sins* (地獄に落ちる罪悪で pride, covetousness, lust, anger, gluttony, envy, sloth の七つをいう).

だいざい【題材】a theme; a subject matter.

¶作家はよい～を選ばねばならない A writer should select good *materials* for his work.

たいさく【大作】(大部の) a voluminous work; (傑作) a great work; a masterpiece.
¶～(絵・彫刻の) a picture (sculpture) of *large size*. 200号の～ a picture of *large size*, No. 200.

たいさく【対策】a counterplan; a countermeasure. ¶なにか～を立てるべきだ We should make up some *counterplan* for it. 新しい～を講ずる必要がある It is necessary for us to work out *a* new *countermeasure*. / It is necessary for us to take *measures* to meet with a new situation.

だいさく【代作】ghostwriting. ¶彼は最近A氏の小説の～をしている Recently he *has been ghosting* (≒ *ghostwriting*) novels for Mr. A. 彼の論文の～を頼まれた I was asked to *write* (≒ *compose*) an article *for* him.
—者 a ghost-writer.

たいさつ【大冊】a big book. ¶1,000ページの～ *a great* (≒ *bulky*) *volume* of 1,000 pages.

たいさん【退散】dispersion. ¶彼らはあわてて～していった They *ran away* in a flurry. 彼らは～を命じられた They were ordered to *disperse*. 悪魔～! Confusion to the devil!

たいざん【大山】a tall (≒ big) mountain.
¶～鳴動して,ねずみ一匹(諺) *Much cry, little wool*.

たいざん【泰山】¶国家を～の安きに置く place the state in a position of perfect security.

だいさん【第三】the third; No. 3.
—階級 the bourgeoisie. —国 a third power. —次産業 tertiary industry. —者 a third person; an outsider. —勢力 the third partisan group.

だいさんにんしょう【第三人称】〔文法〕the third person.
—単数 the third person singular. —複数 the third person plural.

たいさんぼく【大山木・泰山木】〔植物〕an evergreen magnolia.

たいし【大志】an ambition. ¶少年よ, ～をいだけ Boys, *be ambitious*. 少年のころは大科学者になろうという～をいだいていた When a boy I had *a very high ambition* to become a great scientist.

たいし【大使】an ambassador. ¶日本はアメリカに～を派遣した Japan dispatched *an ambassador* to the United States.
—館 an embassy. —館員 a member of the embassy. —夫人 an ambassadress. 駐日(駐米・駐英)— an ambassador to Japan (at Washington; to Great Britain). 特命全権— an ambassador extraordinary and plenipotentiary.

たいじ【退治】(征服) conquest; (撲滅) extermination. ¶あの悪者たちを～してくれよう I will *root* (≒ *wipe*) *out* those bad people. 彼らは怪物～の旅に出かけた They went on an expedition to *kill* a monster. 害虫を～しよう Let's *exterminate* (≒ *get rid of*) harmful insects.

たいじ【胎児】an embryo (妊娠2か月まで); a fetus (妊娠3か月以上).

たいじ【対峙】¶両軍が～した The two armies *faced* (≒ *confronted*) *with each other*.

だいし【台紙】a mount. ¶写真を～にはる *mount* a photograph.

だいじ【大事】**1**〖注意・大切にすること〗¶では体をお～に Please *take good care of* your health. / Please *look after* yourself.
生命を～にしなければならない We must *make much of* (≒ *think highly of*) our life.
親を～にするのはあたりまえだ It is natural that we should *take care of* (≒ *be filial to*) our parents.
物を～にして使おう Let us use things *with care*.
この品は～に使ってください Please use this article *carefully*.
この記録は～にとっておいてください Please keep this record *with care*.
風邪ぎみなので～をとって学校を休んだ Since I had a touch of cold, I stayed away from school *as a precaution*.
あまり～をとりすぎるとかえって悪い結果を生む Too much *care* will produce bad results.
2〖重要・貴重・たいせつ〗¶～な息子 a *precious* son; a *beloved* child.
彼は私にとって～な人だ He is an *important* person to me. / I *set a high value on* him.
これは彼から預かった～な品だ This is a *valuable* thing which he entrusted to me.
～なことを言い忘れていた I forgot to mention an *important* thing.
～な用件があるからすぐ来てほしい Please come as soon as possible, because a *serious* matter has turned up.
そこが～なのだ That's an *important* point. / That's the point.
なにより今は勉強が～だ Nothing *is* more *important* now than studying. / Right now studying *is above everything else*.
3〖危機〗¶火事は危うく～になるところだった The fire was just about to become *serious*. / The fire very nearly became *serious*.
4〖大きな仕事・企て〗¶だれがそんな～を企てたのだ Who planned such *a great undertaking*?
それは一～だ Good Heavens! That's *serious*.

ダイジェスト a digest. ¶～する digest (a book).
—版 a digest (≒ concise) edition.

だいしきょう【大司教】〔キリスト教〕an archbishop.

だいしぜん【大自然】Mother Nature; nature.
¶私は北海道の～の雄大さに大いに打たれた I was much impressed with the grandeur of *Mother Nature* in Hokkaido.

たいした【大した】¶彼はほんとうに～人物だ He is indeed *a great man*. 彼は自分では～人物だと思っている He thinks himself to be *somebody*. 彼は～教育は受けていない He is not *so*

た

well educated. 彼女は～物知りではない She does *not* know *so much*. 彼は～学者ではない He is *not so much of* a scholar. 彼の病気は～ことはない He is *not seriously* sick. この二つに～違いはない There is *not much* difference between the two. 彼の貯金は～額になるだろう The money he is saving will amount to a *big* sum. あなたの言うことは～ことではない What you say *is not* particularly *serious*. きみは～ものだ. 5つの問題を全部解けたのだから *I must hand it to you*. You have solved all five problems.

たいしつ【体質】a constitution. ¶ 彼はひ弱な～だ He has *a* weak *constitution*. その子には気の毒にも～的な欠陥があった The poor child had a *constitutional* defect. 彼女は生まれつき病気にかかりやすい～だった She was *constitutionally* predisposed to diseases. そんなことは私の～に合わない Such a thing doesn't suit my *constitution*. / Such a thing doesn't *agree with* me.

―改善 the improvement of a constitution.

たいしつ【耐湿】¶ 浴室には～性の材料が使われている The bathroom is usually made of *wet-proof* materials.

たいして【大して】¶ ～寒くなかった It was *not very* (≒ *not so*) cold. ～気にしません I *don't* mind it *so much*. そんなことは私には～関係がない It matters *little* to me. ～好みません I *don't* like it *too* well.

たいして【対して】**1**〖関して・就いて〗¶ 彼は老人に～たいへん親切だ He is very kind *to* old people.

この問いに～あなたならどう答えますか What would be your answer *to* this question?

ご好意に～心から謝意を表したい I heartily express thanks *for* your goodwill.

彼の功績に～賞が贈られた A prize was awarded *for* his distinguished services.

この裁判に～のあなたの態度はどうなのか What is your attitude *toward* this trial?

2〖反対に・対抗して〗¶ 彼が物静かなのに～彼女は活発だ He is quiet, *while* she is active. / He is *as* quiet *as* she is active.

法案は20に～200の多数で否決された The bill was rejected by a majority of 200 *to* 20.

敵に～は勇気を持つことだ You must be courageous *against* your enemy.

3〖…につき〗¶ この村ではふたりに～1台の車がある In this village there is a car *to* every two persons.

1,000円に～10円の手数料を払うことになっている We are to pay a commission of ten yen *for* one thousand yen.

たいしゃ【大赦】an amnesty. ¶ ～を行なう grant *an amnesty* (*to* criminals).

たいしゃ【退社】¶ ～する (退出する) leave the office. 彼は一身上のつごうで～した (会社をよす) He *resigned* for personal reasons.

たいしゃ【代謝】¶ ～する be replaced.

新陳― renewal; 〖生物〗metabolism.

だいじゃ【大蛇】a big snake; a huge serpent.

たいしゃいろ【代赭色】burnt sienna; red ocher; reddish brown.

たいしゃく【貸借】a loan; (帳簿上の) debt and credit. ¶ 彼との間に～関係はない I have no *accounts* to settle with him.

―期限 the term of a loan. **―対照表** a balance sheet.

だいしゃりん【大車輪】(鉄棒の) a giant swing. ¶ ～の活躍をする play a most active part.

たいじゅ【大樹】a big tree. ¶ 寄らば～のかげ When you take shelter go under a big tree.

たいしゅう【大衆】the masses; the general public. ¶ この問題は～に呼びかけるべきだ We should appeal to *the masses* for this matter.

～を見くびってはいけない Don't despise *the general public*. テレビ番組は～向きにつくられている Television programs are made for *the general public*. 当時は野球はまだ～化されていなかった Baseball *was* not *popularized* then. 政治の～化をもっと考えるべきだ You should consider *popularization* of politics more. この価格は～的といえる This may be said to be a *popular* price.

―課税 taxation on the general public. **―作家** a popular writer. **―雑誌** a popular magazine. **―食堂** an eating place. **―心理** mass psychology. **―文学** popular literature.

たいしゅう【体臭】body odor. ¶ 特異な～の文章 a writing of some *peculiar characteristics*.

たいじゅう【体重】weight. ¶ ～が増えた(減った) I have gained (lost) *weight*. 彼は入浴後に～をはかる He *weighs himself* after the bath. きみの～はどのくらいありますか How much do you *weigh*? 私の～は120ポンドです I *weigh* 120 pounds.

だいしゅきょう【大主教】〖キリスト教〗an archbishop.

たいしゅつ【退出】¶ 彼は宮中を～した He *left* the Imperial Palace.

―時刻 the closing hour.

たいしょ【対処】¶ 国民は力を合わせて難局に～した The nation *dealt with* (≒ *coped with*) the situation with united efforts.

だいしょ【代書】¶ ～する write for (*a person*): draw up for (*a person*).

―所(屋) a scrivener's office. **―人** a scrivener.

たいしょう【大将】**1**〖軍人の〗(陸軍) a general; (海軍) an admiral; (首領) a chief; a head.

2〖俗に〗a boss; a big shot. ¶ やあ～, 元気かい How are you, *old man*?

いや～, そんなことはできませんよ No, *boss*, we couldn't do it.

～はそのことになんと言ってた What did *the boss* say to that?

たいしょう【大勝】a great victory. ¶ ～を博す achieve *a great victory*.

たいしょう【対称】〖数学〗symmetry; 〖文法〗the second person. ¶ 線分を中心に～の位置に

点を打て Put a *symmetrical* dot on the other side of the line section. / Put *symmetrical* dots on either side of the line section. これらの点はX軸に対して〜をなしている These points *are symmetrical* with respect to the X-axis.

―式 a symmetrical expression. ―関数 a symmetrical function. 平面(線)― plane (line) symmetry.

たいしょう【対象】an object. ¶年少者を〜とした雑誌 a magazine *intended for* juvenile readers. 批評は〜を正しく見ることによって成立する A just criticism consists in grasping the *object* properly.

課税― property liable for taxation. 研究― an object of study.

たいしょう【対照】contrast; antithesis; (比較) comparison. ¶翻訳と原文を比較〜する *compare* the translation *with* the original work. 雪山の白さと空の青さが美しい〜をなしていた The snow-covered mountains *were in* an exquisite *contrast to* the blue sky overhead. 桜の花は青葉と美しい〜をなす Cherry blossoms *make a* beautiful *contrast with* the green leaves around them.

たいしょう【隊商】a caravan.

たいじょう【退場】exit. ¶〜する leave. 選手団が〜した The delegations of athletes *left* the sports field. 審判は選手に〜を命じた The umpire ordered the player out of the ground. 日本の大使は議場から〜した The Japanese ambassador *walked out of* the chamber. 俳優が〜した The actor *made his exit*. 観客はいつでも自由に〜できる The audience has free *exit* at all times. マクベス〜(卜書き) *Exit* Macbeth. 国王は従者を従えて〜(卜書き)*Exeunt* the king and his attendants. (exit は「退場せよ」の意で,単数の名詞のまえにおく. 複数の名詞のまえには exeunt となる).

だいしょう【大小】(大と小) big (≒large) and small〔ones〕; (大きさ) size. ¶〜さまざまのサルがいた There were a lot of *big and small* monkeys. / There were monkeys *of various size*. 事の〜を問わず報告することになっている We are supposed to report everything whether it *is important or not*. 川は〜にかかわらず,われわれの生活にたいせつなものである Rivers are very precious regardless of its *size*. / Rivers, *big or small*, are very precious to our life.

だいしょう【代将】(陸軍) a brigadier general; (海軍) a commodore; (空軍) an air commodore.

だいしょう【代償】compensation. ¶〜を求める demand *compensation* (*for something*). 〜を与える pay *compensation* (*for something*). 彼は損害をかけた〜として100万円を払った He paid one million yen *in compensation for* the damage he had given.

だいじょう【大乗】¶〜的見地に立って問題を解決せねばならぬ We have to settle the matter *from a broader viewpoint*.

―仏教 Mahayanist Buddhism.

だいじょう【台状】―火山 a trapezoid volcano.

だいじょうだん【大上段】¶刀を〜に振りかぶった I held the sword *above my head*.

だいじょうぶ【大丈夫】¶この釣り橋は〜だ This suspension bridge *is safe*. 病人はもう〜だ The patient *is out of danger*. 彼は〜合格する He *is sure to* pass the examination. その建物は火事でも〜だ The building *is proof against* fire. 〜, 危険はない *All right!* It's not dangerous. 彼は〜来る He will *certainly* come.

だいじょうみゃく【大静脈】〔解剖学〕the vena cava (複 venae cavae).

だいしょうり【大勝利】a great victory; (選挙の) a landslide. ¶〜を得る win *a great victory over* the enemy. 試合はわが校の〜となった The game ended in *an overwhelming victory* for our school.

たいしょうりょうほう【対症療法】a symptomatic treatment.

たいしょく【大食】¶〜は健康によくない *Eating too much* is not good for the health. 〜する eat too much; eat gluttonously.

―漢 a big eater; a glutton. 無芸― ¶私は無芸〜だ I have no accomplishments but eating.

たいしょく【退色】fading; faded color. ¶生地が〜しつつある The cloth *is growing dull in color*. この色は洗っても〜しない The color *stands wash*.

たいしょく【退職】retirement〔from office〕. ¶教授は昨年定年で〜した The professor *retired* under the age limit last year. 彼は病気のため〜した He *retired* (≒*resigned*) *from* office because of illness. ⇒たいかん(退官)

―金 a retiring allowance; (解雇の場合) a dismissal allowance. ―者 a retired employee. ―積立金 reserve for retirement allowance. ―年金 a retirement pension (≒annuity). ―年限 the age limit〔of retirement〕.

たいしょく【耐蝕】¶〜の材料 *anti-corrosive* material.

たいしょこうしょ【大所高所】¶この問題はもっと〜から考えなければならない We must consider the matter *from a broader point of view*.

だいじり【台尻】(銃の) the butt end〔of a rifle〕.

たいしん【対審】〔法律〕a trial; (対決) confrontation.

たいしん【耐震】¶〜の proof against earthquake; earthquake-proof.

―家屋 an earthquake-proof building.

たいじん【大人】a man of virtue; a fine gentleman; a great man. ¶彼は〜の風格がある He looks *a fine gentleman*. / He has all the qualities we find in *a fine gentleman*.

―国 a land of giants; a Brobdingnag (ガリバー旅行記にもとづいて).

たいじん【対人】¶彼は〜関係に注意を払った He

was very careful about *personal relations*.
たいじん【対陣】¶両軍は川をはさんで～した Both armies *faced each other* across a river.
たいじん【退陣】 resignation. ¶内閣は～した The Cabinet *resigned en bloc*. 国民は内閣の～を要求した People claimed the general *resignation* of the Cabinet.
だいしん【代診】a doctor's assistant. ¶先生の留守にふたりの患者を～した I *examined* two patients *on behalf of the doctor* while he was absent.
だいじん【大尽】a rich man; a millionaire. ¶～風を吹かす play the millionaire. ～遊びをする spend money in a royal style.
だいじん【大臣】a〔Cabinet〕minister; 英 a secretary; a Secretary of State. ¶～のいす ministership; a Cabinet position; a portfolio. 彼は～になるだろう He will be appointed *a* 〔*state*〕 *minister*. / He will *enter the Cabinet*. 彼は～をやめた He left *ministership*. / He *resigned from the Cabinet*.
—席(国会の) the ministerial bench. 総理— the Prime Minister; the premier. 外務— the Minister for Foreign Affairs; 英 the Foreign Secretary (アメリカでは the Secretary of State (国務長官)が外務大臣の職務をつかさどる). 文部— the Minister of Education. 大蔵— the Minister of Finance; 英 the Chancellor of the Exchequer.
だいじんぐう【大神宮】伊勢— the Grand Shrine at Ise.
だいしんさい【大震災】a great earthquake disaster. ¶関東～ the Kanto Earthquake disaster in 1923.
だいじんぶつ【大人物】a great man; a great character; a man of great caliber.
ダイス (さいころ) dice (単 a die) (単数形を使うことはめったにない. ひとつは one of the dice という).
だいず【大豆】a soybean; a soya bean.
—かす a bean cake. —油〔soy〕bean oil.
たいすい【耐水】waterproof; watertight.
たいすう【対数】〘数学〙a logarithm.
¶～の logarithmic.
—級数 logarithmic series. —計算尺 a logarithmic scale. —表 a table of logarithms. 自然(普通)— natural (general) logarithms.
だいすう【代数】〘数学〙algebra. ¶問題を～で解く solve a problem *algebraically*.
—学 algebra. —関数 an algebraic function. —記号 an algebraic symbol(≒ sign). —方程式 an algebraical equation.
だいすう【台数】number. ¶自動車の～がぐんぐん増えている The *number* of cars is increasing rapidly. / Cars are rapidly increasing *in number*.
だいすき【大好き】¶この子犬は牛乳が～だ This puppy *likes* milk *very much*. これは私の～な音楽だ This is my *favorite* music. 彼は野球が～だ He *is crazy about* baseball. 彼は映画が～です He *is very fond of* movies. / He *is a lover of* movies.
たい・する【対する】¶これがきみの質問に～する答えだ This is my answer *to* your question. 彼らは平和に～する関心が強い They show special interest *in* peace. それは社会に～するわれわれの義務です It is our duty *toward* (≒ *to*) the world. 彼の先生に～する態度は礼を欠いている His attitude *toward* teachers is not polite.
たい・する【体する】¶彼らは政府の命を～してその計画を実行に移した They put the plan into action *in accordance with* the orders of the government. きみの意を～して彼と交渉してみる I will deal with him, *keeping* your wish *in mind*.
だい・する【題する】¶彼は「行人」と～する作品を発表した He made public a work *entitled* (≒ *under the title of*) "Kojin."
たいせい【大成】¶彼はその研究をやっと～した He *accomplished* his researches on it at last. 彼はきっと実業界で～すると思う I am sure he will *attain to greatness* in the industrial world. 彼は学者として～した He became a great scholar. 彼は～しそうもない I am afraid he will never *do well*.
源氏物語— the Variorum Edition of "The Tale of Genji."
たいせい【大政】¶～奉還 the restoration of the sovereign power to the throne.
たいせい【大勢】**1** the general trend (≒ tendency); the situation; the current.
¶～を観望する observe *the situation* (≒ *the trend of the affairs*).
～に従う adapt *oneself* to *the trend of the times*; follow *the general trend*.
～の赴くところいかんともしがたかった I found it impossible to *swim against the current*.
～に変化はない There is no change in *the general situation*.
彼は～を察するに敏である He is quick in grasping *the situation*.
2〘決着〙¶試合の～は決した The game is almost decided. / This is *the beginnig of the end*.
～は既に決した The end is now in sight.
たいせい【対生】〘植物〙opposition; symmetry. ¶この植物の葉は～である The leaves of the plant grow in *opposition*.
—葉 opposite leaves.
たいせい【体制】a structure; a system; an order; an establishment. ¶現～を打破(維持)する destroy (maintain) the existing *structure* (≒ *establishment*). 資本主義の～が確立した The capitalistic *structure* has been established.
新— a new order. 政治— a political system. 反— anti-establishment.
たいせい【態勢】¶新入社員の受け入れ～が整った *Preparations* to receive new employees have been made. それには万全の～ができている All the necessary *arrangements* have been made for it.
たいせい【胎生】〘生物〙viviparity.
—学 embryology. —動物 viviparous

animals ; vivipara (複数).

たいせい【退勢】the declining fortune ; decline. ¶ ～を挽回(ばんかい)しようと努めた We tried hard to restore *the declining fortune*.

たいせい【泰西】the West ; the Occident.

たいせいよう【大西洋】the Atlantic〔Ocean〕. ―横断飛行 a transatlantic flight. ―航路 an Atlantic line. 北―条約機構 the North Atlantic Treaty Organization (NATO).

たいせき【体積】〔cubic〕volume ; (容積) capacity. ¶ 50立方メートルの～ the *volume* of fifty cubic meters.

たいせき【退席】¶ 気分が悪くなったので～した I *left the place* because I felt sick. 会の終わらぬうちに～した I *left the meeting* before it was over.

たいせき【堆石】a pile of stones ;〖地質〗a moraine.

たいせき【堆積】〖地質〗accumulation ; a heap ; a pile. ¶ その部屋にはいろいろのがらくた道具が～していた Various pieces of old furniture *were piled up* in the room.

たいせつ【大切】**1**〖大事な〗(重要な) important; (貴重な) valuable ; (重大な) serious.

¶ 時間ほど～なものはない Nothing *is* so *valuable* as time.

～なものはしまっておきなさい Put away your *valuables*.

彼は命より金のほうが～だ Money *is* more *valuable* to him than his own life.

このような重大な時機には彼は～な人物だ He is an *indispensable* man in this kind of emergency.

外国語を学ぶことはもっとも～なことのひとつだ It is one of the most *important* things to study foreign languages.

～な用事を思い出した I have just remembered something I have to do.

人生でいちばん～なことは一体何だろう I wonder what *counts* most in life.

2〖大切にする〗¶ 体は～にしなさい *Be careful of* your own health. / *Take good care of* yourself.

金より時間を～にする人は多い There are many people who *make more of* time than of money.

私の～にしている本が見つからない The book I *treasure* is missing.

親が子どもを～にするのは当然だ It is natural for parents to *be attentive to* their children.

彼はあの頃の思い出を～にしている He *treasures* (≒ *cherishes*) the memory of those days.

これは私が～にしているものだ These are my *cherished* things.

たいせつ【体節】〖生物〗an arthromere.

たいせん【大戦】a great war ; (戦闘) a great battle. ¶ 第２次世界～ World War II (発音は [wə́ːrld wɔ́ːr túː]) ; the Second World War.

たいせん【対戦】¶ あすA校と～する We will *have a game with* A school tomorrow. われわれは容易ならぬ敵と～した We *were confronted by* a formidable enemy.

―成績 the result of a match (≒ a game).

たいぜん【大全】a complete (≒ collected) work ; a complete collection.

たいぜん【泰然】¶ 彼は～自若としていた He *was perfectly calm and self-possessed*. / He *was perfectly composed*. 彼は～たる態度を守っていた He maintained a *calm* attitude.

だいせんきょく【大選挙区】a major constituency ; a large electoral district.

―制 a major constituency system ; a large electoral system.

たいせんしゃ【対戦車】―壕 an anti-tank trench. ―砲 an anti-tank gun.

だいぜんてい【大前提】〖論理〗the major premise ; the sumption.

たいそう【体操】gymnastics (gym. と略す) ; exercises. ¶ 私は毎朝～をする I *take exercises* (≒ *practice gymnastics*) every morning. 毎週～の時間が２時間ある We have two periods of *physical training* (≒ *education*) every week.

―器具 a gymnastic apparatus. ―選手 a gymnast. 室内―場 a gymnasium ; (口語) a gym. 柔軟(美容)― calisthenics ; calisthenic exercises.

たいそう【大層】¶ ～強い人だった He was a *very* strong man. 彼は～犬が好きだ He likes dogs *very much*. / He is a *great* lover of dogs. ～な人出だ There is a *big* crowd.

たいぞう【退蔵】hoarding. ¶ 多量の金を～する *hoard* a great deal of gold.

―物資 hoarded goods.

だいそう【代走】〖野球〗(代走者) a pinch runner. ¶ ～する run for another.

だいそうげん【大草原】a great plain ; (特に北アメリカのミシシッピ川流域の) a prairie.

だいそうじょう【大僧正】〖キリスト教〗〖仏教〗an archbishop.

だいそれた【大逸れた】¶ どうしてそんな～罪を犯したのか Why have you committed such a *reckless* crime ? そんなことをしでかすとは彼も～人間だ How *impudent* (≒ *audacious*) of him to have done it !

たいだ【怠惰】idleness ; laziness. ¶ 彼は～な生活を送っている He is leading an *idle* life. 彼は～のため会社を首になった He was dismissed from the company for *laziness*.

だいだ【代打】〖野球〗¶ ～する pinch-hit (*for*). ―者 a pinch hitter.

だいたい【大体】the main point. ¶ ～の話を説明してください Will you please explain the *outline* of the story ? ふたりは～同じ年ごろだ The two are *about* the same age. ～において計画はうまくいった *On the whole* the plan went well. ～あなたの言うとおりです *On the whole* you are right. 私が言いたいのは～次のようなことです What I want to say is *something like* this. 損害は～50万円だった The damages were *roughly* estimated at five hundred thousand yen. 日曜日は～外出します I *mostly* go out on Sundays.

だいたい【大隊】a battalion.
—長 a battalion commander.
だいたい【代替】substitution.
—物 a substitute.
だいたい【大腿】〘解剖学〙the thigh.
—骨 the thighbone.
だいだい【橙】〘植物〙a bitter (≒ sour) orange.
—色 orange; reddish yellow.
だいだい【代代】from generation to generation; generation after generation. ¶ 彼の家は～医者だ His family have always been doctors. この刀はわが家に～伝えられてきた This sword has been handed down *from generation to generation* in my house. 先祖～の墓 a family tomb.
だいだいてき【大大的】¶ 新製品を～に宣伝する make a *huge* advertising campaign of new products; advertise new products *widely*. ～に店を拡張したい We want to extend the store *on a large scale*.
だいたすう【大多数】the majority. ¶ ～がその案に賛成だった *The majority* were (≒ was) for the proposal. クラスの～の生徒は泳ぎができる *Most* pupils of the class can swim.
たいだん【対談】a talk; a conversation; a dialogue. ¶ あなたが彼と～されているのをラジオで聞きました I heard you *talk with* him on the radio.
たいだん【退団】¶ 彼はジャイアンツを～した He *left* the Giants.
だいたん【大胆】boldness. ¶ 彼の～さには舌をまく I marvel at his *boldness*. 彼女は～なデザインの洋服が好きだ She likes dresses of a *bold* design. 彼の～な行為のために事故にならずにすんだ His *bold* act prevented an accident.
—不敵 boldness; daring.
だいだんえん【大団円】the end; (悲劇の) a catastrophe; (幸せな) a happy ending.
¶ 長い物語もついに～となった The long story *has ended* (≒ *has come to an end*) at last.
だいち【大地】the earth; the ground. ¶ ～を踏む tread on *the earth*. 飛行機が～をけって飛び立った An airplane smoothly took off *the ground*.
だいち【台地】(高台) a terrace; (高原) a plateau (㊥ plateaux); a tableland; (アメリカ合衆国南部) a mesa.
だいち【代地】a substitute land. ¶ ～を提供しますから立ち退いてください We will provide *a substitute plot of land*, so please move.
たいちょ【大著】(量的に) a voluminous work; (名著) a great work; a masterpiece.
たいちょう【退庁】¶ ～する leave the office. ～時間は5時です The office closes at five.
たいちょう【隊長】a commander; a commanding officer.
小 (中; 大)— a section (company; battalion) commander.
だいちょう【大腸】〘解剖学〙the large intestine.
—カタル colitis. —菌 colitis germs.
だいちょう【台帳】a ledger. ¶ ～につける put (≒ enter) in *a ledger*. 「register.
仕入— a stock ledger. 土地— a land
たいちょうかく【対頂角】〘数学〙vertically opposite angles.
タイツ tights (複数扱い).
たいてい【大帝】a great emperor.
イワン— Ivan the Great. 明治— the Great Emperor Meiji.
たいてい【退廷】¶ ～する leave the court.
たいてい【大抵】generally; usually. ¶ ぼくは～6時半に朝食をとる I *usually* (≒ *generally*) take breakfast at half past six. この辺りの子どもは～バスで学校へ行く *Most* children living around this place go to school by bus. 小学生なら～はこの問題は解ける *Most* elementary schoolboys and schoolgirls can solve this problem. この町の道路は～舗装されている *Most of* the streets in this town are paved. ～彼女は来ないよ She will *probably* not come here. 広島なら～のところは知っている I know *almost all* the places in Hiroshima. こんな大家族を養うのは～のことではない It *is no easy* task to support this large family.
たいてき【大敵】a great (≒ powerful) enemy. ¶ 今度の試合では～と争うことになっている We are to face *a powerful rival* in the next match. シロアリは家の～だ White ants are *a formidable* (≒ *deadly*) *foe* to houses. ～たりとも恐れず小敵たりとも侮らず Don't fear *a powerful enemy* and don't underrate a powerless enemy.
油断— Security is the greatest enemy.
たいてん【大典】a great (≒ state) ceremony; (即位の) a coronation.
たいと【泰斗】a great authority. ¶ 彼は理論物理学の～だ He is *a great authority on* theoretical physics. 彼は日本画の～だ He is *a great master of* Japanese painting.
タイト —スカート a tight skirt.
たいど【大度】generosity; broad-mindedness.
たいど【態度】(心構え) an attitude; (ふるまい) manner; behavior. ¶ 彼の～は感心しない His *attitude* is to be blamed. 彼女の～をどう思いますか What do you think of her *manner*? どうも彼の～は気にくわない I somehow don't like his *manner*. 彼の傲慢(ごうまん)な～にみな閉口した Everyone was annoyed at his haughty *attitude*. 彼はがらりと～を変えた He has changed his *attitude* suddenly. あの少年は頭はいいが～が気にくわない He is a bright boy but his *bearing* is disagreeable to me. 彼の～になにか変わったところがありますか Is there anything unusual in his *attitude*? こそこそした～をとったため彼はあやしまれた He aroused people's suspicion on account of his stealthy *attitude*. われわれは彼に対して強い～を取るべきだ We should take *a* strong *attitude* toward him. この問題に対する～を今晩までに決めてほしい I want you to determine your *attitude* toward this problem before this

た

evening.

たいとう【台頭】¶新しい政治家の〜を期待している We expect new politicians will *gain power* (≒ *come to the fore*). 新しい平和運動がわが国では〜してきている A new peace movement *is gaining ground* (≒ *is gathering force*) in our country.

たいとう【対等】equality. ¶われわれは〜の立場で話し合った We talked with each other *on terms of equality* (≒ *on equal terms*). 彼と〜につきあう I associate with him *as equals* (≒ *on equal terms*). きみは彼らとは〜の立場にない You *are* not *on an equal footing with* them. ふたりは能力の点では〜だ Both *are equal in* ability.

だいとう【大刀】a long sword.

だいどう【大同】¶どの案も〜小異だ All of these proposals *are much the same*. 諸派は〜団結して運動を起こした The factions united and began the movement.

だいどう【大道】(大通り) a highway ; a street ; (道義) a great principle.

—芸人 a street entertainer. —商人 a street-stall keeper ; a hawker.

だいどうみゃく【大動脈】〘解剖学〙the main artery ; the aorta. ¶交通の〜 *the main artery* for traffic (between A and B).

だいとうりょう【大統領】the President.
¶ルーズベルト〜 *President* Roosevelt. 米国〜夫人 the first lady. 彼は合衆国の〜に選ばれた He was elected *President* of the United States.

—官邸 (アメリカの) the White House ; (一般の) the Presidential Mansion. —選挙(候補) a presidential election (candidate). 副— the Vice-President.

たいとく【体得】¶岩登りのこつを〜した I*'ve got the knack of* rock-climbing. 彼はその手品のこつを〜した He *mastered* the art of the trick.

たいどく【胎毒】〘医学〙congenital syphilis.

だいどく【代読】¶大臣の祝辞は彼が〜した He *read* the Minister's congratulatory address.

だいどころ【台所】a kitchen. ¶彼女は一家の〜をあずかっている She is in charge of the *household economy*.

—用品 kitchen utensils ; kitchenware. —仕事 kitchen work.

タイトル a title ; a championship. ¶彼は試合で〜を獲得した(奪われた) He gained (lost) the *title* in the match. 彼は〜を防衛した He defended the *title*.

—マッチ a title match. ノン—マッチ a non-title match.

たいない【体内】¶外科医は彼の〜から弾丸を摘出した The surgeon took out the bullet from his *body*.

たいない【対内】¶政府の〜問題が対外方策に反映する The government's *domestic* policies are reflected on the foreign policies.

たいない【胎内】the womb. ¶〜の子 a child *in the womb*.

—感染 prenatal infection.

だいなし【台無し】¶その失敗は彼の一生を〜にした The failure *ruined* (≒ *destroyed*) his life. せっかくのピクニックも雨で〜になった The long-awaited picnic *was wrecked* by the rain.

ダイナマイト dynamite. ¶〜で岩を爆破する blow up a rock with *dynamite*. 〜2本 two sticks of *dynamite*. 橋げたに〜をしかけた We set *dynamite* at the bridge girders.

ダイナミック ¶〜な演奏 a *dynamic* performance.

ダイナモ〘電気〙a dynamo (複 dynamos).

だい·なり【大なり】¶AはBより〜なり A *is bigger* than B. 〜なり小なり似たようなものだ They are much the same.

だいに【第二】the second. ¶〜, 第三の手を考えておく必要がある We have to consider *a second* and a third step. 研究は〜段階に入った The research has entered *the second* stage. 彼は〜のエジソンになりたいと思っている He wishes to be *a second* (≒ *another*) Edison.

だいにぎ【第二義】¶そんなことは〜的な問題だ Such a thing is a matter *of secondary importance*.

たいにち【対日】¶彼らの〜感情は好転した Their feelings *toward Japan* have changed for the better.

—外交関係 diplomatic relations with Japan. —請求権 the claim to Japan. —貿易 trade with Japan.

たいにち【滞日】¶彼は〜中にほうぼうを見物した He visited many places *while in Japan*. 彼は商用で〜中だ He *is* 〔*staying*〕 *in Japan* on business.

だいにゅう【代入】〘数学〙¶Xのところに5を〜する put 5 in the place of X.

だいにゅうほう【代入法】〘数学〙substitution.

たいにん【大任】(仕事) a great (≒ an important) task ; (使命) an important mission. ¶私は十分〜を果たすつもりだ I intend to do my *important duty* well. 彼は〜を帯びてアメリカに向かった He left for America *on an important mission*. われわれは無事〜を果たすことができた We succeeded in accomplishing our *great task* (≒ *heavy responsibility*).

たいにん【退任】retirement. ¶彼は昨年〜した He *retired* 〔*from office*〕 last year.

ダイニングキッチン a dinette.

たいねつ【耐熱】—ガラス heat-resisting glass. —テスト a heat-resistance test.

だいの【大の】¶彼は〜野球ファンだ He is a *great* baseball fan. 彼らは〜仲よしだ They are *great* friends. 〜の男が泣くなんてみっともないぞ It's a shame for *a man* to shed tears.

たいのう【滞納】nonpayment. ¶税金を〜している I *am in arrears* (≒ *am behindhand*) *with* the tax. / I *haven't paid* the tax.

—金 arrears. —所得税 an income tax in arrears. —家賃 the arrears of rent.

だいのう【大脳】〖解剖学〗 cerebrum (複 cerebrums; cerebra).
—皮質 the cerebral membrane.

だいのう【大農】—経営 a large-scale farming.

たいは【大破】 ¶ 彼の車はトラックと衝突して～した His car *was greatly* (≒ *badly*) *damaged* by the collision with a truck.

たいはい【大敗】 a complete (≒ crushing) defeat. ¶ わがチームは～を喫した Our team *was completely defeated*.

たいはい【退廃・頽廃】 corruption; decadence. ¶ ～的な風俗 *corrupt* (≒ *decadent*) manners. ～な映画 a *decadent* film. 今の社会は道徳的に～している The present society *is* morally *corrupted*.

だいばかり【台秤】 a platform scale.

たいばつ【体罰】 physical (≒ corporal) punishment. ¶ 児童に～を加えてはならない We should not give *physical punishment* to schoolchildren. / We shouldn't inflict *corporal punishment* on schoolchildren.

たいはん【大半】 the greater part. ¶ 市の～は焼けてしまった *The greater part* of the city was burnt down. 彼はおこづかいの～を本に使う He spends *most* of his pocket money on books. 彼は生涯の～を外国で暮らした He lived abroad *for the greater part* of his life. 学生の～はその運動には無関心だった *The majority* of the students were indifferent to the movement.

たいばん【胎盤】〖解剖学〗 the placenta (複 placentas; placentae).

たいひ【対比】 contrast. ¶ きみの作品と彼のとを～してみる必要がある You should *contrast* (≒ *compare*) your work *with* his. 新旧の車を～して見せている They show new and old cars *in contrast*.

たいひ【待避】 ¶ 船は港に～した The ship *took shelter in* the harbor.
—線 (鉄道の) a sidetrack.

たいひ【退避】 escape; evacuation. ¶ 火災現場から～する *escape* from the blazing area. 危険な場所から～する *remove* (≒ *evacuate*) from a dangerous place.
—所 (道路上の車の) a turnout.

たいひ【堆肥】 compost; barnyard manure.

たいひ【貸費】 a loan; advanced expenses.
—生 a scholarship student. —制度 the scholarship system.

タイピスト a typist.
英文— a typist in English. —学校 a typewriting (≒ typing) school.

だいひつ【代筆】 ¶ 彼に手紙の～をしてやった I *wrote* a letter *for* him.

たいびょう【大病】 a serious illness. ¶ 去年の秋に～をした I had *a serious* (≒ *bad*) *illness* last autumn.

だいひょう【代表】 representation. ¶ 選手の～は彼だ He is the *representative* of all the athletes. 彼が日本を～して会議に出席する He will *represent* Japan at the conference. 各党の～はまだ姿を見せていない The *delegates* of every party have not made their appearance yet. われわれはその会議に～を送った We sent *a representative* to the conference. あらゆる点で彼は現代の若者の～だ He *typifies* modern young men and women in every respect. 彼は一家を～して歓迎のあいさつを述べた He made a speech of welcome *on behalf of* his family. 彼は日本の～として申し分がない Japan *is* well *represented* by him.
—者 a representative. —番号 (電話の) a key number. —作 the most important work (*of*). —取締役 a representative director.

ダイビング【水泳】 diving.
スカイ— sky-diving. スキン— skin diving.

たいぶ【大部】 ¶ ～の著作 a *voluminous* work.

タイプ **1** 〖型〗 type; pattern. ¶ 古い～の人 a person of old *pattern*; a man of old-fashioned *type*.
彼はだれにも好かれる～の人だ He is an attractive man.
彼女は私の好きな～ではない She is not my *type*.
私はあの～の男が好きではない I don't like men of that *type*. / I don't like that *type* of men.
2 〖タイプライター〗 a typewriter. ¶ 彼女は～の腕がいい She *types* well.
彼女は～が早い She *types* fast.
彼は手紙を～で打っている He *is typewriting* a letter. / He is writing a letter on *a typewriter*.
この書類を～してください Will you *type* these papers for me?

だいぶ【大分】 ¶ ～暖かくなった It is getting *very* (≒ *rather*; *fairly*) warm. 取り消しが～あった *Quite a few* people cancelled their orders. / There was *a considerable number of* cancellations. 今学期は成績が～あがった I have done *much* (≒ *considerably*) better this semester. ～疲れたようですね You look *pretty* tired. この前におめにかかってから～たちますね It is *quite* a long time since I saw you last. その映画なら～前に見た I saw the movie *quite* some time ago. 今日は～気分がいい I feel *much* better today. 患者は～悪い The patient is in *serious* condition. 昨夜は～雨が降った It rained *heavily* last night.

たいふう【台風】 a typhoon. ¶ ～の目 the eye (≒ center) of *a typhoon*. 大型～が日本に近づいている *A* big *typhoon* is approaching Japan. ～は九州に上陸するだろう The *typhoon* will strike (≒ hit) Kyushu.
—圏内 the typhoon area. ¶ 関西地方は～圏内にはいるだろう The Kansai districts will be within *the typhoon area*.

たいぶつ【対物】 —貸し付け a loan on security. —契約 a real contract. —信用 real credit. —レンズ an object lens.

だいぶつ【大仏】 a huge statue of Buddha. ¶ 奈良の～ *the great* 〔*image of*〕 *Buddha* at Nara.

た

だいぶぶん【大部分】(名詞) the most part; the greater part; the majority; (副詞) for the most part.
¶学生の～がストに参加した *The majority* of the students joined in the strike. 彼は一生の～を外国で暮らした He spent *the greater part* of his life in foreign countries. この箱のリンゴは～腐っている *Almost all* 〔*of*〕 the apples in this box are rotten.

タイプライター a typewriter.

たいぶんすう【帯分数】〘数学〙 a mixed number.

たいへい【太平】peace; tranquil〔l〕ity. ¶天下～だ All the world *is at peace.* / All is right with the world. 人は～ムードに酔っている People are enjoying *a peaceful mood* (≒ *the blessings of peace*).

たいべい【対米】**—**貿易 trade with America. **—**輸出 exportation toward America.

たいべい【滞米】¶～中に while *one* was staying in the United States; during *one's* stay in the United States. 彼らは～中だ They *are* 〔*staying*〕 *in America.*

たいへいよう【太平洋】the Pacific 〔Ocean〕. **—**安全保障条約 the Pacific Security Pact. **—**沿岸 the Pacific coast; (アメリカの) the West coast. **—**〔沿〕岸標準時 the Pacific standard time. **—**横断航路 a transpacific line. **—**戦争 the Pacific War. 南(北)**—** the south (north) Pacific. 汎(はん)**—**会議 the Pan-Pacific Conference.

たいへいらく【太平楽】¶～をならべる talk a volume of nonsense; indulge in a happy-go-lucky talk.

たいべつ【大別】¶それらは～すると3種類になる They can *be classified into* three *large* (≒ *great*) *groups* (≒ *divisions*). / *Roughly classified,* they are of three categories.

たいへん【大変】**1** 〖非常に〗 very; much.
¶列車は～込んでいた The train was *very* crowded.
～お世話になりました I am *much* obliged to you for your help.
～困ったことになった I am in *great* trouble. / Things have come to a pretty pass.
この絵は～よくできている This picture is *very* (≒ *awfully*; *remarkably*) well painted.
2 〖異常の; 重大な; 大量・多数の; 困った〗
¶～だ, 火事だ *Good Heavens*! Fire! ～だ, だれか来てくれ *Hey*! Come here, someone! そんなことをしたら～だ If you do that, it will bring *serious* consequences.
～なことになった, 書類がなくなった This *is terrible*! I have lost the papers.
これだけのことをするのはなかなか～だ It's *something* just to do this!
5人の家族を養うのは～だ It *is by no means easy* to support a family of five.
いちいち返事を出すのは～だ It's *a lot of trouble* to send a reply to every letter.
この仕事はなかなか～だ This work *is* very *hard.*
もう少しで～な事故を起こすところだった I came very close to causing a *terrible* accident.
金融引き締めで産業界は～な事態を迎えた The tight-money policy has given rise to a *serious* state of affairs in the industrial world.
これは～な問題だ This is a *serious* matter.
これは～なごちそうですね This is a *splendid* (≒ *sumptuous*) dinner, isn't it?
きょうは～な寒さだ It is *awfully* cold today.
それはきみの～な思い違いだ It is a *great* misunderstanding on your part.
きみは～な約束をしたものだ You have made an *embarrassing* promise.

だいべん【大便】excrement; f〔a〕eces. ¶今日は2回～が出た *My bowels were open* twice today.

だいべん【代弁】¶母親の意向を娘が～した The daughter *spoke for* (≒ *spoke on behalf of*) her mother.
—者 a spokesman; (女) a spokeswoman.

たいほ【退歩】retrogression; a setback.
¶それは文明の～になる It will be *a going backward* in the way of civilization.

たいほ【逮捕】arrest; capture. ¶100名以上が～された More than a hundred people *were arrested.* 彼は窃盗の容疑で～された He *was arrested* for (≒ on a charge of) theft. きみを～する You *are under arrest.*
—状 a warrant of arrest; an arrest warrant. ¶彼に～状が出ている There is *an arrest warrant* out for him.

たいほう【大砲】a gun; a cannon (昔の大砲をいう). ¶～を発射する fire *a gun.* ～の音が聞こえる We hear the boom of *guns.*

たいぼう【耐乏】austerity. ¶～生活を送る lead a life of *austerity.*

たいぼう【待望】¶～の夏休みがやってきた The *long-expected* (≒ *long-awaited*) summer vacation is here at last. 彼女は帝劇で～の初舞台を踏んだ She made her *hoped-for* debut at the Imperial Theatre.

たいぼうちょう【体膨張】〘物理〙 cubic〔al〕 expansion.

たいぼく【大木】a big tree.

だいほん【台本】(劇の) a playbook; (映画などの) a script; a scenario.
—作者 a scripter; a script writer; a scenarist.

だいほんざん【大本山】the headquarters (≒ cathedral) (*of* a sect).

たいま【大麻】〘植物〙 a jute; a hemp.

タイマー a timer.
セルフ**—** a self-timer. パート**—** a part-timer.

たいまい【大枚】a big (≒ large) sum.
¶このカメラには～5万円払った I paid *as much as* (≒ *a good sum of*) fifty thousand yen for this camera.

たいまつ【松明】a torch; a torchlight; a firebrand. ¶～をともす kindle *a torch.*

たいまん【怠慢】negligence; neglect.
¶きみは職務～だ You *neglect* your duties. 彼は職務～のかどで戒告を受けた He was warned for *negligence* (≒ *neglect*) of duty. (neglect はふつう1回の行為に, negligence は常習的

な行為に用いる).

だいみょう【大名】a *daimyo*; a feudal lord.
—行列 a〔long line of〕*daimyo* procession.
—旅行 ¶ ～旅行をする travel like a prince.

タイミング timing. ¶ 正にいい～だった You did it at the right time. / You couldn't have done it at a better time.

タイム time; (試合中の) time-out; (写真の露出時間) time; exposure. ¶ レースの～を計る *time* a race. 彼の最高の～は58分15秒だ His best *time* is 58 minutes 15 seconds.
—スイッチ a time switch. —レコーダー a time clock. ラップ— lap time.

タイムリー timely. ¶ 政府は～な処置をとった The Government took *timely* (≒ *well-timed*) measures. ～ヒットを放つ make a *timely* hit.

だいめい【題名】a title.

だいめいし【代名詞】〘文法〙a pronoun.
¶ 貧乏が彼の～だった His name was a synonym for 'poverty.' / He was poverty itself.

たいめん【対面】an interview; meeting.
¶ 彼とは10年ぶりの～だった I *met* him after ten years' separation.
—交通 on-coming traffic. 初— the first meeting.

たいめん【体面】(名誉) honor; (威信) dignity.
¶ 彼は～を重んずる He respects his own *honor*. 教師としての～を保ちたかった I intended to keep up my *dignity* as a teacher. 学校の～を汚すような行為は許されない No one is allowed to injure the *prestige* of our school. 彼は～上そう言わなければならないのだ He is bound to say so *to save his face*.

たいもう【大望】an ambition; an aspiration.
¶ ～を持つ have *an ambition*. ～を果たす realize *one's ambition*. 彼は若いころ～に燃えていた He was an *aspiring* youth. / He was full of *ambition* when he was young.

だいもく【題目】a subject; a theme; a title.
¶ 彼は朝夕お～を唱える(お経を) He offers *sutra* every morning and evening.

タイヤ a tire; 英 a tyre. ¶ ～がパンクした We had *a* flat *tire*. / The *tire* punctured. すりへった～を新しい～ととりかえる change *an* old *tire* for a new one. ～に空気を入れる pump up *a tire*.
スノー— a snow tire. スペア— a spare tire.

ダイヤ **1**〘宝石〙〔a〕diamond. ¶ ～の指輪 a *diamond* ring.
2〘列車の〙a timetable. ¶ 冬の～にかわった The *timetable* was revised for the winter. 豪雨のために～が乱れている The *train timetable* is confused on account of the heavy rain.

たいやく【大役】an important mission; a heavy role. ¶ 支店創設の～をおおせつかった I was charged with the *important mission* of establishing a new branch. 彼は～をすばらしく演じた He played his *important part* splendidly.

たいやく【対訳】a translation printed side by side with the original.
—版 a bilingual version.

だいやく【代役】(人) a substitute; (映画) a stand-in; a double. ¶ 私が彼の～をつとめた I *filled in for* him. 彼女が入院中のタイピストの～をした She *substituted for* the typist who was in hospital. 彼の～として議長をつとめた I *took his place* as chairman. 彼の～としてハムレットを演じた I played (≒ acted) the part of Hamlet as *a substitute* for him. / I *understudied* him in the play of Hamlet.

ダイヤモンド〔a〕diamond.

ダイヤル a dial〔plate〕. ¶ ～を回す turn *a dial*; *dial* a number. ラジオの～を回す *dial* (≒ *turn a dial of*) the radio.

たいよ【貸与】loan. ¶ 学生に奨学資金を～する *loan* scholarships to students.
—金 a loan.

たいよう【大洋】the ocean.
—学 oceanography. —航路客船 an ocean liner.

たいよう【大要】an outline; a summary; a gist; an epitome; a résumé. ¶ 彼は論文の～を述べた He *summarized* the essay. / He gave *a summary* of the essay.

たいよう【太陽】the sun. ¶ ～の黒点 a sunspot. ～は輝いていた *The sun* was shining. ～は東から上り, 西にしずむ *The sun* rises in the east and sets in the west. ～の光線は木の間をもれていた The *sunbeams* came through the branches.
—学 heliology. —系 the solar system. —神 the sun god; (ギリシア神話の) Helios. —電池 a solar battery. —燈 a sun (≒ mercury) lamp. —熱 solar heat; the heat of the sun. —暦 the solar calendar.

だいよう【代用】substitution. ¶ 牛肉の～に魚, ブタなどを使う *substitute* fish or pork *for* beef. それはベッドの～になる It *serves as* a bed./ You can *use* it *for* a bed.
—教員 a substitute teacher. —食 substitute food. —品 a substitute〔article〕.

たいようしゅう【大洋州】Oceania.

たいよく【大欲】avarice; greed. ¶ ～は無欲に似たり(諺) *Grasp all, lose all.*

たいら【平ら】smooth; level; flat; even.
¶ ～な道路 a *smooth* road. ～なほうが表だ The *smooth* side is the right side. この機械は道を～にする This machine *levels* roads. どうぞお～に *Make yourself at home.*

たいら・げる【平らげる】¶ 賊を～げる *suppress* (≒ *subjugate*; *put down*) rebels. ごちそうをぜんぶ～げた I *ate up* (≒ *dispatched*) all the dishes. 飯を三杯ぺろっと～げた He *ate up* three bowls of rice in no time.

だいり【代理】representation; a deputy.
¶ 彼が私の～をつとめてくれる He will *take my place*. X先生がY先生の～をした Mr. X *acted for* Mr. Y. ～で彼が出席してくれる He will *represent me* at the meeting. 彼は父の～として渡英した He went abroad to Britain *on behalf of* his father. ～で彼に投票してもらおう I will have him vote for me *by proxy*.
—大使 a chargé d'affaires (発音は [ʃáːʒei

dæfέə] で, フランス語から). —店 an agency. —人 a representative. 校長— the acting principal. 保険—店 an insurance agency.

だいりき【大力】 ¶ ～の男 a man *of great strength.*

たいりく【大陸】 a continent.
—間弾道弾 an intercontinental ballistic missile (ICBM). —性気候 a continental climate. —だな the continental shelf. —文化 continental culture. —文学 continental literature. 暗黒— the Dark Continent. 新— the New Continent (≒ World).

だいりせき【大理石】〔鉱物〕marble. ¶ ～の像 a *marble* statue.

たいりつ【対立】 opposition. ¶ 委員たちの意見はこの件に関してまっこうから～している The committee *differ* widely *on* this problem. 彼の意見は私と～している His opinion *is* quite *contrary to* mine. / He holds quite an *opposite* opinion *to* mine.
—候補 ¶ 反対党が～候補を立てた The opposition put up a *rival* candidate.

たいりゃく【大略】(概要) an outline ; (摘要) a summary ; (ほぼ) almost ; nearly ; roughly. ¶ 彼は計画の～を話した He gave *an outline* of the plan. / He *outlined* the plan. / He gave *a short sketch* of the plan. 私の意見は～次のとおりです This is my *general* idea.

たいりゅう【対流】〔物理〕convection.
—圏〔気象〕the troposphere.

たいりょう【大量】 a large quantity.
¶ 彼は私に～のぶどう酒をくれた He gave me *a large quantity* of wine. サラダオイルを～に買った I bought salad oil *in large quantities* (≒ *in quantity*).
—解雇 mass discharge (≒ dismissal). —虐殺 mass murder; massacre. —生産 mass production ; large-scale production. —生産方式 a mass-production method.

たいりょう【大漁】 a good catch. ¶ きょうはサバが～だった We made *a good catch* of mackerel today.

たいりょく【体力】 physical strength ; bodily powers. ¶ 近ごろ～の衰えを感じる Lately I feel my *power* declining (≒ failing). 栄養のある物を食べて～をつけるべきだ You should increase (≒ develop ; build up) your *physical strength* with nourishing food.
—テスト a physical strength examination ; an examination of physical strength.

たいりん【大輪】(車輪の) a large wheel ; (花の) a large flower. ¶ ～のバラの花 a *large* rose.

タイル a tile. ¶ ～張りの浴室 a *tiled* bathroom. 流しに～を張る *tile* a sink.

ダイレクトメール direct mail.

たいれつ【隊列】 file ; ranks. ¶ ～をつくって in *file*. ～をつくって出て行く *file* out.

たいろ【退路】 the (path of) retreat. ¶ 敵の～を断つ cut off the enemy's *retreat*.

だいろっかん【第六感】 the (≒ a) sixth sense.
¶ ～でそれがわかった I knew that *by instinct*. / My *sixth sense* told me that.

たいわ【対話】〔a〕conversation ; a talk ; (ふたりの) a dialog〔ue〕. ¶ ～する converse (≒ talk) with *a person*. ～体で in *dialog* style.

たいわん【台湾】 Taiwan ; Formosa.
—人 a Formosan.

ダイン〔物理〕dyne.

ダウ —式平均株価 Dow-Jones average ; Dow-Jones index.

たうえ【田植え】 ¶ ～をする plant rice.
—歌 a rice planters' song. —時 the rice planting season.

ダウン down. ¶ ボクサーは第1ラウンドで～した The boxer *was downed* in the first round. コスト— cost down. ノック— knockdown.

たえい・る【絶え入る】 ¶ 彼女は～るように泣いた She wept as if her heart would break.

たえがた・い【耐え難い】 ¶ ～い寒さだ It is *intolerably* cold. それはぼくには～いことだ It is more than I can bear. / It *is intolerable* (≒ *unbearable*) to me. / It *is too much for* me.

だえき【唾液】 saliva. ¶ ～を分泌する secrete *saliva*.

たえしの・ぶ【耐え忍ぶ】 bear ; put up with ; endure. ¶ 彼はその悲しみを～んだ He *endured* the sorrow.

たえず【絶えず】 always ; incessantly.
¶ 彼女は彼と～口論ばかりしている She is *always* quarreling with him. ～努力をしなければならぬ We must make a *constant* (≒ *perpetual ; sustained*) effort.

たえだえ【絶え絶え】 ¶ 彼は息も～だった He was breathing very *feebly*. / He *was gasping for breath*.

たえて【絶えて】 ¶ 都会ではホタルなど～見かけない Fireflies have *hardly* ever been seen in towns. あれから～久しくあの方にはお会いしてません Since then I have *never* seen him.

たえなる【妙なる】 sweet. ¶ ～楽の音 *sweet* music ; an *exquisite* piece of music.

たえは・てる【絶え果てる】 ¶ 彼はやがて息も～てた Then at last he *breathed his last*. その種の生物は～ててしまった That species of animal *has become extinct*.

たえま【絶え間】 a break ; an interval. ¶ 雲の～から陽がさしてきた The sun began to stream through *a break* (≒ *a rift*) in the clouds. この通りは車と騒音の～がない There is a *constant* stream of cars and noise in this street.

た・える【耐える・堪える】 1 〖こらえる〗 ¶ あらゆる困苦に～えて彼は今日の地位を築いた *Enduring* all hardships, he has secured his present position.
彼ならどんな苦労にも～えられる He can *stand* any hardships.
慣れた人でなければこの暑さにはとても～えられない With the exception of those who are accustomed to it, nobody can possibly *stand* the heat.
彼は彼女に聞くに～えない悪口を言った He called her *unbearably* ugly names.
彼はその悲しみにじっと～えた He stolidly *endured* his grief.

彼らは耐えがたきを～え忍びがたきを忍んだ They *endured* the unendurable and bore the unbearable.

その土地に来て彼は今昔の感に～えなかった When he came there, he was deeply moved by the changes.

みなさまのご協力をいただき感謝に～えない *Thank you very much for* your cooperation. / *I appreciate* your cooperation.

優勝おめでとう. われわれ一同喜びに～えません Congratulations on your victory! We are all very glad.

2 〖もちこたえる〗 ¶ このガラスは高熱に～える This glass can *stand* intense heat.

このビルは震度 7 の地震にも～えられる This building can *stand* even an earthquake of an intensity of 7.

この車はまだ二, 三年は使用に～える This car can still be used for two or three years.

まだきみの体はその労働に～えられない You *are* not yet *strong enough* for that hard labor.

私にはとてもその重責には～えられそうもない I am afraid I could not possibly *bear up under* (≒ *stand*; *be equal to*) the heavy responsibility.

た·える 【絶える】 ¶ 食糧の供給は～えた The supply of food *has been cut off*. この山の頂きには一年じゅう雪が～えない The summit of this mountain is covered with snow all the year round. 彼ら一家は生活の苦労が～えない Their family are *always* suffering from some kind of trouble. / Their family are never free from care. この家には争いが～えない There are *constant* troubles in this family. 厄介が～えない There is *no end* of troubles.

だえん 【楕円】 an ellipse; an oval.

—運動 an elliptical movement. **—軌道** an elliptical orbit.

たお·す 【倒す】 **1** 〖転倒さす〗 ¶ ものすごいあらしが電柱を～した A severe storm *blew down* the telegraph pole.

電気スタンドを～さないように気をつけなさい Be careful not to *tip over* the desk lamp.

2 〖負かす〗 ¶ このチームを～すのは容易ではない It is not easy to *beat* this team.

彼が横綱を～したのは大殊勲だった He distinguished himself by *defeating* the champion *sumo* wrestler.

たおやか ¶ ～な乙女 a *graceful* maiden.

タオル a towel. ¶ ～で顔をふいた I dried my face on *a towel*. バス～で身体をふきなさい Dry yourself on *a bath towel*. (前置詞の on に注意).

—掛け a towel rack. **—地** toweling.

たお·れる 【倒れる】 **1** 〖転倒する〗 fall. ¶ 彼は～れた子供を抱き起こした He picked up a child who *had fallen*.

彼はその場にばったり～れた He *fell* limp on the spot.

そのマラソン選手は～れて立ち上がれなかった The marathon runner *fell down* and couldn't get up.

彼は人波に押されて～れた He *was pushed down* by the crowd.

地震でへいが～れた The wall *was knocked down* by the earthquake.

台風でたくさんの木が～された The typhoon *blew down* many trees.

脱線して客車は横倒しに～れた The passenger train jumped the track and *fell* over on its side.

2 〖病む〗 fall ill. ¶ 彼は過労で～れた He *broke down* from overwork.

仕事の完成を前にして彼は病に～れた He *fell ill* just before the completion of the work.

3 〖死ぬ〗 die. ¶ ～れて後やまん I am determined to do or *die*. / I won't give up if it kills me.

大統領は凶弾に～れた The president *was* shot and *killed* by a ruffian.

4 〖没落する·滅びる〗 collapse. ¶ 独裁政権はついに～れた At last the dictatorship *collapsed*.

経済政策の失敗で現内閣はいまにも～れそうだ On account of the mistaken economic policy the present Cabinet seems about to *fall* (≒ *collapse*).

不景気で多くの中小企業が～れた Because of the depression many minor enterprises *failed*.

たか 【高】 ¶ どんなに節約しても～が知れている However strictly you may save, your saving *won't amount to much*. 彼の腕前など大したことはないと～をくくっていた We *made light* (≒ *nothing*) *of* his ability. 彼は選挙に負けることはあるまいと～をくくっていた He *was* quite *optimistic* as to the result of the election.

たか 【鷹】 〖鳥類〗 a hawk; a falcon. ¶ 能ある～はつめを隠す (諺) *Still* (≒ *Smooth*) *waters run deep*.

—狩り hawking; falconry. ¶ ～狩りをする hawk. **—派の人** a hawk.

たか 【多寡】 ¶ 金額の～にかかわらず, 贈収賄はとがめられるべきだ Bribery is to be blamed regardless of the *amount* involved.

たが 【箍】 a hoop. ¶ たるの～が緩んだ The *hoop* of the barrel has gotten loose. 年のせいで彼もだいぶ～が緩んできた He has been losing his strength of character because of his age.

だが but; and yet. ⇒ しかし

たかい 【他界】 ¶ ～する die; pass away.

たか·い 【高い】 **1** 〖高さが〗 high; tall.

¶ ～い建物 a *high* building.

～い山 a *high* (≒ *lofty*) mountain.

あの人は背が～い He *is tall*.

彼は急に背が～くなった He became *tall* suddenly.

彼女は鼻が～くて美人だ She is a beautiful woman with *a Grecian nose*.

もう少し～い所に行けば, 町全体が見渡せる If you go a little *higher* up, you can see (≒ command) the entire town.

山が～くなればなるほど涼しく感じた In the mountain, *the higher* I was, the cooler I felt.

トンビが空～く舞っている A kite is flying *high*

up in the sky.
波が～いから水泳はよしなさい You must not swim, because the waves *are high*.
山～きがゆえに尊からず，木あるをもって尊しとす（諺） A mountain is valued, not for its *height* but for its trees.
2 〖地位・身分が〗 high. ¶ 彼はあの国では身分の～いほうだ He has *high* social position in that country.
～い地位についている人にはいろいろの苦労がある People in *high* positions experience numerous difficulties.
その役職とこの役職とはどちらが地位が～いのか Which is of *higher* social standing, this position or that〔one〕?
3 〖基準・程度が〗 high. ¶ この問題は普通の中学生には程度が～すぎる This question *is* too *difficult* for the ordinary lower secondary school student.
あの大学は程度が～いから入学しても苦労する The academic level of that university *is high*. So, even if you are admitted, you will have to work hard.
国民の生活水準を～くする *raise* the national standard of living.
4 〖人格・識見が〗 high; lofty. ¶ なかなか見識の～い人だ He has very *high* (≒ *lofty*) views./ He is a man of insight. / He is an original thinker.
彼は徳が～く皆に尊敬されている He *is virtuous* and respected by everyone.
さすがはお目が～い You are indeed a good judge.
5 〖理想・望みが〗 high; lofty. ¶ きみは望みが～すぎる You aim too *high*.
理想は～く持ちなさい Have (≒ Entertain) a *lofty* ideal.
彼は理想が～い He has *high* ideals.
彼女はお～くとまっているのでつきあいにくい She *is* so *haughty* that it is hard to associate with her.
6 〖音声・格調が〗 loud. ¶ この文章は格調が～い This is a *dignified* (≒ *elevated*) style.
ラジオの音が～いから低くしなさい The radio *is* too *loud*; turn it down.
しっ，声が～い Hush!
7 〖温度が〗 high. ¶ この冬は平年に比べて気温が～い The temperature of this winter *is higher* than the average of past years.
彼は風邪をひいて～い熱を出している He has a cold and has *high* fever.
温度を～くすれば物体は膨張する If you *heat* an object it expands. / An object expands with heat.
8 〖圧力が〗 high. ¶ 年をとると血圧が～くなる When we grow old, our blood pressure *goes up*.
～い気圧では沸点が上がる The boiling point rises under *high* atmospheric pressure.
9 〖名声・評判が〗 ¶ これが今日本で評判の～い小説だ This is the novel *much talked of* in Japan now.
彼は変なことで名を～くしたものだ He *has become widely known for* something strange.
あれが例の事件で悪名～い政治家だ He is the *notorious* statesman involved in that affair.
10 〖価値・金額が〗 high; expensive. ¶ あの店は～い That store *is expensive*.
物価がこう～くてはやりきれない We are unable to make both ends meet, with such *high* prices of commodities.
この土地は物価が～い Commodities *are high* in this district.
値段が～すぎる，まけなさい It's too *expensive*; come down.
そんな～い給料をきみには出せない We cannot pay you such a *high* salary.
そんなに～い金を出すのはばかげている It is absurd to pay so *much* money.
飛行機で行くより船で行くほうが～くつく It *is* more *expensive* to go by ship than by airplane.
中古車を買ったばかりに修理に追われて結局～くついた I bought a used car which has to be repaired often, so it *has proved expensive* after all.
きみの努力は～く買う I *appreciate* your effort *very much*.
われわれは会議の成果を～く評価している We *value* the result of the conference *highly*.
11 〖比喩的に鼻が〗 ¶ きみのおかげでぼくは鼻が～い You *do* me *proud*. / I *am proud of* you.
ちょっとの成功でそんなに鼻を～くするな Don't *be* so *elated with* (≒ *be* so *proud of*) such a small accomplishment.

たがい【互い】 each other. ¶ ～の mutual. ～に mutually. ～に助け合うことがたいせつだ It is important for you to help *each other* (≒ *mutually*). ～に励まし合った We encouraged *each other*. 私たちは～の家庭を訪ね合った We visited *each other's* homes. 私たちはお～の立場を理解し合わなければならない We must understand *each other's* situation. お～さまです It's the same with me.

だかい【打開】 ¶ 行き詰まりを～する *solve* (≒ *break*) the deadlock; *save* the situation. 難局を～する *overcome* (≒ *get over*) difficulties.

たがいちがい【互い違い】 ¶ ～に alternately. 日照りの日と雨の日が～に続いた There was a spell of sunny days *alternating with* rainy days.

たかいびき【高鼾】 a loud snore. ¶ 彼は～をかく He *snores loudly*. 彼の～でねむれなかった His *loud snores* kept me awake.

たが・う【違う】 ¶ 1分も～わず彼はやってきた He came *exactly on time*. / He came *punctually to the minute*.

たが・える【違える】 ¶ あの人は約束など～えぬ人だ He never *breaks* his word. / He is the last man to *break* his promise. / He is a man of his word.

たかが【高が】 only; merely. ¶ 彼は～政治屋だ He is a *mere* politician. / He is *no more than* a politician. / He is *nothing but* a politician.

たかく【多角】¶物事を～的に考える consider a matter *from many different angles* (≒ *from many different points of view*).
―経営 diversified (≒ multiple) management.

たがく【多額】a large sum (≒ amount) (*of* money). ¶～の失費 *heavy* expenses.

たかさ【高さ】height; altitude. ¶そのビルの～はどのくらいか How *high* is the building? / What is the *height* of the building? ～2,000メートルの山 a mountain two thousand meters *high*. 彼の声の～が気になる The pitch in his voice irritates me.

だがし【駄菓子】cheap candy; 英 cheap sweets.

たかしお【高潮】the flood (≒ major; high) tide.

たかだい【高台】a hill; an eminence; an elevation; a height.

たかだか【高高】**1**〖せいぜい・多くとも〗¶～1,000円 a thousand yen *at most*; *no more than* one thousand yen.
もうけは～10,000円だった All we got from that was *only* (≒ *merely*) ten thousand yen.
2〖高さ・音など〗¶塔が～とそびえ立っている There is a tower rising *high* (≒ *aloft*).
声～と皆で合唱した We all sang *loudly* together in chorus.
優勝チームは鼻～だった The winning team *were very proud*. (team はその各メンバーを考えるときは複数扱い).

だかつ【蛇蠍】a viper. ¶人を～のようにきらう hate (≒ abhor; detest) *a person* like *poison* (≒ *a serpent*; *a viper*).

だがっき【打楽器】〔音楽〕a percussion instrument.

たかっけい【多角形】〔数学〕a polygon.

たかとび【高跳び】〔競技〕the high jump.
走り― the running high jump. 棒― the pole jump (≒ vault); 英 the pole jumping.

たかとび【高飛び】¶犯人は～寸前に捕らえられた The criminal was arrested just before his *bolt* (≒ *decampment*). 犯人はホンコンへ～した The criminal *flew* (≒ *fled*; *made off*) to Hongkong from justice.

たかな・る【高鳴る】¶胸が～る My heart *throbs* (≒ *beats fast*).

たかね【高根・高嶺】¶富士の～ *the lofty summit* of Mt. Fuji. ぼくにとって彼女は～の花だ She is *a prize beyond my reach*.

たかね【高値】a high price; 〔株式〕a high. ¶その絵はかなりの～を呼んだ That picture fetched *a* pretty *high price*.
新―(株式) a new high.

たがね【鏨・鑽】a graver; a burin; a 〔cold〕 chisel.

たかのぞみ【高望み】¶きみは～しすぎる You *set* your *hopes too high*. / You *have an excessive* (≒ *inordinate*) *ambition*. 自分の実力以上に～してもだめだ It is no use expecting more than you are entitled to.

たかひく【高低】¶～のある土地 an *undulating* (≒ *uneven*) land.

たかびしゃ【高飛車】¶～な態度で in a *high-handed* (≒ an *overbearing*) manner. ～に出る act *high-handedly* (≒ *overbearingly*).

たかぶ・る【高ぶる】¶感情が～る get excited. 彼は神経が～っている His nerves *are highly strung*. 彼はまったく～らない男だ He *is* very *modest*. 彼女は～らない天才だ She is a *humble* genius.

たかま・る【高まる】¶欺瞞(ぎまん)的政策に～る怒り *mounting* (≒ *rising*) anger toward the deceptive policy. その問題に国民の関心がますます～っている The people *are getting more and more concerned with* the problem. 戦後婦人の社会的地位が～った After the war the status of women in society *has risen* (≒ *has been elevated*). 国会解散の気運が～っている The time *is getting ripe* for the dissolution of the Diet. それに対する反対の声が～ってきた Opposition to it *has become* more *clamorous*. 彼の作品に対して世評が～った His works *got a reputation*. / The popularity of his works *increased*.

たかみ【高み】height; an elevated position.
¶彼はいつも～の見物をきめこんでいる He always remains an unconcerned spectator.

たか・める【高める】¶教養を～める *cultivate oneself*; *heighten* (≒ *enhance*) *one's* culture. 生活水準を～める *raise* (≒ *improve*) *one's* living standard. 効果を～める *heighten* an effect. 能率を～める *increase* (≒ *enhance*) efficiency. 人格を～める *ennoble a person*. 名声を～める *enhance* (≒ *increase*) *one's* reputation.

たがや・す【耕す】¶田を～す *plow* (≒ 英 *plough*) a rice field. 土地を～す *till* (≒ *cultivate*) land.

たから【宝】a treasure; riches (複数扱い).
¶～の持ち腐れ a miser's gold buried in the ground. 子どもは社会の～だ Children are social *treasures*.
―捜し treasure-hunting. ―島 a treasure island. ―船 a treasure ship.

だから so; therefore; because. ¶彼はたいへん疲れていた．～早めに寝た He was very tired, 〔*and*〕 *so* he went to bed earlier than usual. / He was *so* tired *that* he turned in earlier than usual. 彼は病気～来られません He cannot come *because* he is ill. ～言わんこっちゃない I warned you about it. ～うまくいかないんだ *That is why* you cannot do it well. ～といって行かぬわけにもいくまい *Yet* (≒ *For all that*), I must go, mustn't I?

たからか【高らか】¶彼は声～に歌っていた He was singing *aloud* (≒ *in a loud voice*).

たからくじ【宝籤】a public lottery; (券) a lottery ticket. ¶彼は～で一等が当った He won the first prize in *a public lottery*.

たかり【集り】(行為) blackmail; (人) a blackmailer. ¶彼は～に会った He *was blackmailed*.

た

たか·る【集る】¶ハエが食物に～った Flies *collected* on the food. アリが砂糖に～る Ants *swarm* upon the sugar. 彼はちょくちょくたばこを～る He *bums* a cigarette now and then. 不良に金を～られた I *was robbed of* money by a street rough.

-たがる ¶子どもはなんでも知り～ Children *are anxious* (≒ *eager*) *to* know everything. 自家用車を持ち～人が多い Many people *want to* have their own cars.

たかわらい【高笑い】a loud laugh. ¶彼は満足そうに～した He *had a loud laugh* contentedly. / He *laughed aloud* in contentment.

たかん【多感】¶～な青春時代に in *one's emotional* (≒ *sentimental* ; *impressionable*) youth. 彼にも多情～な青年期はあったのだ Once he *was*, too, *passionate and emotional* in his younger days.

だかん【兌換】conversion.
—券(紙幣) a convertible note (≒ paper money).

たき【滝】a waterfall ; falls ; (大きな) a cataract. ¶華厳の～ the Kegon *Falls*. 汗が～のように流れる sweat *freely* (≒ *violently* ; *profusely*).
—つぼ the basin (≒ bottom) of a waterfall.

たき【多岐】¶話が～にわたる talk on many topics ; take up many topics for discussion.

たぎ【多義】¶～にわたる語 a word with *many meanings* ; a *multivocal* (≒ an *ambiguous*) word.
—性 ambiguity.

だき【唾棄】¶～すべき人物 a *detestable* (≒ *disgusting* ; *despicable*) person ; a wretch.

だきあ·う【抱き合う】¶ふたりの少女は～った The two girls *embraced each other*. ふたりは喜んで～った The two were much delighted and *embraced*.

だきあ·げる【抱き上げる】¶子どもを～げる *lift* a child *in one's arms*.

だきあわせ【抱き合わせ】¶チューブ入り歯みがきと歯ブラシを～で売る sell a tube of toothpaste and a toothbrush *at a tie-in sale*.
—販売 a tie-in sale.

だきおこ·す【抱き起こす】raise (*a person*) in (≒ with) *one's* arms ; help (*a person*) up.

だきかか·える【抱き抱える】¶彼女は子を～えて病院へ急いだ She hurried to the hospital *carrying* her child *in her arms*.

たきぎ【薪】firewood. ¶～を拾う gather *firewood*.

だきこ·む【抱き込む】¶彼らは彼を～んで悪事を働くつもりだ They are going to *win* him *over to their side* for an evil plot.

タキシード 米 a tuxedo ; 英 a dinner jacket.

だきし·める【抱き締める】embrace ; hug.
¶彼女はわが子を～めて泣いた She cried *pressing* her child *to her bosom*. / She cried *hugging* her child *tightly*.

たきだし【炊き出し】¶焼け出された人々への～をする distribute boiled rice to the victims of the fire.

だきつ·く【抱き付く】¶彼はその男の首に～いた He *threw his arms around* the man's neck.

たつけ【焚き付け】kindling.

たきつ·ける【焚き付ける】¶ふろを～ける *start a fire* in the bath heater. 甘言をもって若者を～ける *stir up* (≒ *inflame*) young men by means of flattery.

だきね【抱き寝】¶彼女はわが子を～した She slept with her baby in her arms.

たきび【焚き火】a fire. ¶落ち葉を集めて～をする rake up the fallen leaves to *make a fire*.

だきゅう【打球】〘野球〙batting ; (打ったボール) a batted ball.

だきょう【妥協】〔a〕compromise. ¶適当な線で～すべきだ You should try to *come to an understanding* on fair terms. ～の余地なし There is no room for *a compromise*. われわれは彼らと～した We *compromised with* them. 彼は～的な態度をとった He took a *compromising* (≒ *conciliatory*) attitude.
—案 a compromise〔plan〕.

たぎ·る【滾る】¶ポットの湯が～っている The pot *is boiling*.

たく【宅】¶社長のお～にはときどき伺います I sometimes call at our president's〔*house*〕. ～は(夫は)留守でございます *My husband* is not at home. お～のお子さんは何年生まれですか When was *your* child born?

たく【卓】a table ; a desk. ¶～を囲んで飲みかつ語った Sitting around the *table*, we drank and talked. 私はその問題について彼らと～をたたいて論じあった I argued vehemently with them on the matter.

た·く【炊く】¶飯を～く *boil* (≒ *cook*) rice.

た·く【焼く·焚く】¶薪を～く *burn* wood. 火を～く *make* a fire. ふろを～く *make* a bath ; *heat* a bath. 香を～く *kindle* incense.

だ·く【抱く】hold (*a person*) in *one's* arms ; hug (*a person*) ; embrace (*a person*).
¶(鳥が)卵を～く *sit* (≒ *brood*) *on* eggs. 赤ちゃんをちょっと～かせてください May I *hold* your baby?

たくあん【沢庵】pickled Japanese radish.

たぐい【類·比】¶ああいう～の人は苦手だ That *sort* of man is hard for me to deal with. 彼は～まれな名優だ He is a *matchless* actor. 彼は～ない人物だ He is a *rare* (≒ *unique*) character.

たくえつ【卓越】excellence ; superiority.
¶～した技量 *excellent* (≒ *superior*) ability. 人物技量ともに～した男だ He *is distinguished* (≒ *is prominent*) *in* character and ability.

だくおん【濁音】〘言語学〙a sonant ; a voiced sound.

たくさん【沢山】**1** 〖数や量が〗(数) many ; (量) much. ¶なんて～な人なんだ What *a lot of* people!
彼は本を～持っている He has *a lot of* books.
この県ではトマトが～とれる Tomatoes are produced *in large quantities* in this district.
あの店にはよい品が～ある *A large number of*

good articles are to be found in the store. 若い時代には楽しみが～ある There *is plenty of* pleasure in *one's* youth.

この池には魚が～いる This pond *is full of* fishes.

どうぞ～おとりください Please take *as much as you like*.

2 〘じゅうぶんだ〙 ¶もう～です *No more,* thank you.

彼の話はもう～だ I *want no more of* his speech.

私は毎晩3時間眠れば～だ It *is quite sufficient for* me to sleep three hours every night.

たくしあ·げる【たくし上げる】 ¶ワイシャツのそでを～げる *roll up one's* shirt sleeves. スカートを～げる *tuck up one's* skirt.

タクシー a taxi; a cab; a taxicab. ¶～を拾う pick up (≒ hire) *a taxi*. 流しの～ *a* cruising *taxi*. 駅まで～で行った I took *a taxi* to the station. / I went to the station *by taxi*.

—料金 the taxi fare.

たくじしょ【託児所】 a day (≒ public) nursery.

たくじょう【卓上】 **—**カレンダー a desk calendar. **—**電話 a desk telephone.

たくしょく【拓殖】 colonization.

—会社 a colonization company. **—**銀行 a colonial bank.

たくしん【宅診】 office consultation. ¶午前～午後往診 "Hours of Consultation: before noon, at office; afternoon, for calls."

たく·す【託す】 ¶彼は後事を息子に～すつもりでいる He intends to *commit* his affairs *to the care of* his son. 彼は大事を～すに足る人物だ He *is worthy of* a great responsibility. 彼女は子供たちをうばに～した She *left* her children *in charge of* a nurse.

だくすい【濁水】 muddy water.

たくせつ【卓説】 an excellent opinion.

名論**—** sound arguments and excellent views.

たくち【宅地】 (すでに家のある) residential land; a residence lot; (まだあき地の) building land; a building site; a house lot.

だくてん【濁点】 a sonant mark.

タクト 〔音楽〕 a baton. ¶～を振る take the baton; conduct an orchestra.

たくはつ【托鉢】 religious mendicancy.

¶～に出る go about as a begging priest.

—僧 a begging (≒ mendicant) priest.

たくばつ【卓抜】 ⇒ たくえつ

だくひ【諾否】 yes or no; consent or refusal.

¶～の返事 an answer *in the affirmative or negative*. ～をご一報ください Please tell us whether you *accept* it *or not*.

たくほん【拓本】 a rubbed copy. ¶碑文の～をとる *make a rubbing of* a monumental inscription.

たくまざる【巧まざる】 ¶彼には～ユーモアのセンスがある He has a *natural* sense of humor.

たくまし·い【逞しい】 ¶筋骨～い男 a *robust* (≒ *sturdy*) man. ～い腕 *muscular* (≒ *sinewy; brawny*) arms. ～い想像力 *strong* (≒ *vigorous*) imagination. ～い開拓者 an *energetic* pioneer. 彼は精神的にも肉体的にも～く成長した He *has grown vigorous* both physically and spiritually. この絵は～い気迫を持っている This picture *is full of vitality*.

たくましく·する【逞しくする】 ¶想像を～する *give free play* to *one's* imagination. 台風が猛威を～している The typhoon *is* now *raging with all its force*.

たくみ【巧み】 ¶彼は右に左に～に身をかわした He *skillfully* dodged to the right or the left. ～な口実を作ってその会に出なかった I made a *clever* excuse and was absent from the meeting. この指輪は～な細工をしてある This ring is of *exquisite* workmanship. 彼は人扱いが～だ He *is dexterous* (≒ *is ingenious*) *in* handl*ing* men. / He *knows how to* handle men.

たくらみ【企み】 a plan; a design; (悪だくみ) a plot; a conspiracy. ¶いろいろと～をめぐらす consider various *plans*. 人の～を見抜く see through another's *plot*. 政府を倒す～がばれた *A conspiracy* against the government came out.

たくら·む【企む】 plan; design; plot; conspire. ¶政府打倒の謀反を～む *conspire* to overthrow the government. 彼はあなたを陥れようと～んだのだ He *plotted* to trap you. 彼らは何か悪事を～んでいる They *are plotting* some evil.

だくりゅう【濁流】 a muddy stream.

たぐ·る【手繰る】 ¶ひもを～る *pull in* a string. 釣り糸を～る *reel in* a fishing line. 綱を～り寄せる *haul in* a rope. 記憶を～ってその人の名を思い出した I recollected his name by *tracing back* my memory.

たくろん【卓論】 a clever view.

たくわえ【蓄え】 (貯金) savings; (貯蔵) a store; a stock; (供給) supplies. ¶食料の～ *a store* of food; *a stock* of provisions. 石炭の～ *supplies* of coal. 彼には老後の～がある He has *some money saved* for his old age.

たくわ·える【蓄える】 ¶金(かね)を～える *save* money; *put by* money. 精力を～える *conserve one's* energy. 彼は大学時代に知識を～えた He *stored* his mind with knowledge in his college days. 燃料を～えておかねばならぬ We must *have* fuel *in store*.

たけ【竹】 a bamboo. ¶～の皮 a *bamboo-*sheath. 彼は～を割ったような性格の男だ He is a *straightforward* man. / He is a man of *frank* disposition.

—細工 bamboo work. **—**竿 a bamboo pole. **—**ぼうき a bamboo broom. **—**やり a bamboo-spear. **—**やぶ a bamboo grove.

たけ【丈】 (身長) height; stature; (長さ) length; (寸法) measure. ¶彼は身の～が6尺ある He *is* six feet *tall* (≒ *in height*). この外とうは私には～が長すぎる(短すぎる) This overcoat is too long (short) for me. 着物の～を短くしてもらった I had the *length* of the *kimono* shortened. 彼に思いの～を述べたい I want to *unbosom* (≒ *open up*) *myself* to him.

だけ【丈】 1 〖ばかり〗 alone ; only. ¶ぼく～家にいた I was home *alone*.
それ～が彼のとりえだ That's his *only* merit.
ほんとのことを言った～だ I said *only* what was true.
2 〖数量・程度〗 (数について) as many as ; (量について) as much as. ¶ガソリンを1,000円分～ください Give me one thousand yen *worth of* gasoline.
欲しい～持っていきなさい Take *as many as* (≒ (量の場合) *as much as*) you want.
これ～あれば十分まにあう This will be enough (≒ sufficient). / This much will do.
これ～はきみに言っておこう I will tell you this, *at least*.
それは，これ～の価値はない It hasn't *this much* value.
この本は1度は読む～の価値がある This book *is worth* read*ing* once. / This book *is worthwhile to* read once.
3 〖だけのことはある〗 ¶努力した～のことはあった I did not labor in vain. / The effort I made was rewarded.
金をかけた～のことはきっとある Money is never spent for nothing.
さすが専門家～あってそのことについて彼はよく知っている *As may be expected from* a specialist, he is well versed in the matter.
彼は苦労した～あって人情がある Like the man of the world 〔that〕 he is, he is warm-hearted.

たげい【多芸】 versatility. ¶～な役者 a *versatile* actor. ～な男 a man *of varied accomplishments*.

たけうま【竹馬】 stilts. ¶彼は～〔に乗ること〕がうまい He is good at walking on *stilts*.

たけがき【竹垣】 a bamboo fence.

だげき【打撃】 a blow ; a hit ; (野球) batting ; (損害) damage. ¶～がふるわなかった (野球で) The batters played poorly. 株価の暴落で私は大～を受けた The heavy decline in stocks gave me *a* severe *blow*.

たけだけし・い【猛猛しい】 ¶～い男だ He is an *audacious* man. 盗人～いとは彼のことだ He is quite shameless.

だけつ【妥結】 an agreement. ¶賃上げ交渉は円満に～した The wage increase negotiations *came to a* satisfactory *settlement*.

たけなわ【闌・酣】 ¶春も～である The spring *is in all its glory*. 宴も～である The banquet *is at its height*. 論戦は今や～である The discussion *is* now *in full swing*.

だけに ¶彼は頭がいい～に理解が早い He is quick to understand *because* he is smart by nature.

たけのこ【竹の子・筍】 bamboo shoots (≒ sprouts). ¶最近雨後の～のようにゴルフの練習場ができた Recently a lot of golf ranges have appeared *like mushrooms*.

た・ける【長ける・闌ける】 ¶彼は弁舌に～けている He is a *fluent* (≒ *persuasive*) talker. / He talks fluently.

たけ・る【猛る】 ¶～り狂う波 the *violent* waves. 私は～る心を静めようとした I tried to calm my *anger*.

たげん【多元】 ―性 plurality. ―描写 descriptions from different viewpoints. ―放送 a broadcast from multiple origination. ―方程式 a plural equation. ―論 pluralism. ―論者 a pluralist.

だけん【駄犬】 a mongrel.

たこ【凧】 a kite. ¶少年たちは～あげをしている The boys are flying *kites*. 彼は～をおろし始めた He began to draw in the *kite*.

たこ【蛸】 an octopus.
―つぼ an octopus trap ; (待避壕) a foxhole.

たこ【胼胝】 a callus ; a callosity. ¶足に～ができた *A callus* has formed on my foot. その話は耳に～のできるほど聞かされた I have heard the story a thousand times.

たこう【多幸】 good luck. ¶ご～を祈ります I wish you *good luck*!

だこう【蛇行】 ¶一筋の川が谷間を～している A stream *winds* through the valley.

たこうしき【多項式】 〔数学〕 a polynominal expression.

タコメーター a tachometer.

たごん【他言】 ¶この件は～をはばかる This is a secret 〔matter〕. / This is confidential. / Don't tell it to others. ご～無用に願います Let no one know this. / Keep it secret. / Don't tell it to others.

たさい【多才】 versatility. ¶～な人 a man *of versatile talents*. 彼は多芸～で聞こえている He is well known for his *versatility*.

たさい【多彩】 ¶～な行事祝典 the *variegated* celebration program.

たさく【多作】 ¶彼は～で知られた作家だ He is a noted *prolific* writer.

ださく【駄作】 a poor work ; rubbish. ¶この映画は～だ This movie *is mere rubbish*.

たさつ【他殺】 murder. ¶この事件は～の疑いが濃い There are strong suspicions of *murder* in this matter.

たさん【多産】 fecundity. ¶～な動物 a *prolific* (≒ *fecund*) animal.

ださん【打算】 calculation ; self-interest.
¶彼は～的な男だ He is a *calculating* man. それは～的な考えだ It is a *selfish* (≒ *egocentric* ; *self-seeking*) idea.

たざんのいし【他山の石】 ¶われわれはこれをもって～とすべきである We may learn a good lesson from it. きみはもって～とすべきである Let this be a good lesson to you.

たし【足し】 ¶こうして研究費の～にしていた I *supplemented* my research fund by doing this. 1,000円ではたいして～にはならない A thousand yen won't *help* much. ビスケットではたいして腹の～にはならない Crackers (≒ 囲 Biscuits) are not enough to stay hunger.

たじ【他事】 other things ; (他人の事) other people's affairs. ¶～を顧みる暇がなかった I have had no time to think about *other*

た

things. 無事帰宅しましたから～ながらご安心ください I am happy to inform you that I have safely arrived home.

たじ【多事】¶ 1976年は日本にとって～多端な年であった The year 1976 was quite an *eventful* one for Japan.

だし【出し】(だし汁) broth; (口実) a pretext. ¶ こんぶで～をとる make *broth* from kelp. このスープは～がきいている This soup is richly flavored with *broth*. 母親の病気を～にして彼女は学校を休んでいる She is using her mother's illness as *a pretext* (≒ *an excuse*) for being absent from school.

だし【山車】a float; a festival car.

だしあ·う【出し合う】¶ 私と彼とで費用を～いましょう I will *share* the expenses *with* him. 費用はみんなで平等に～うことになっている The expenses are to be equally divided.

だしいれ【出し入れ】¶ 車をガレージから～する *get* a car *in and out of* a garage. 私はいつもこの銀行で金を～する I *deposit and draw* money in this bank.

だしおし·む【出し惜しむ】¶ 彼はいつも慈善事業への寄付金を～む He *is* always *unwilling to* donate money to charity.

たしか【確か】**1**〘たぶん〙¶ ～去年の末のことだった It was at the end of last year, *if I remember correctly*.
失礼ですが, ～田中さんでしたね Excuse me, but I think you are Mr. Tanaka.
金額は～ 5,000 円だった The sum of money was five thousand yen, *if I am correct*.
彼女は～大阪の生まれだった She is from Osaka, *I believe*.
2〘確かに〙certainly. ¶ きみはあのとき～にそう言った You *certainly* said so then. / *I am sure* you said so then.
きみは～にそれを見たのか *Are you sure* you saw it?
お送りくださった品物～に受け取りました I have certainly (≒とくに強調するときは *indeed*) received the goods which you sent to me.
そう言われれば～におかしい話だ Since you mention it, it is strange.
～に安いが品質が悪い It is *undoubtedly* cheap, but the quality is poor.
3〘正気の·元気の〙¶ そんなことを言うとは気は～か *Are you in your right mind* to say such a thing?
こんな軽いけがで死ぬものか, 気を～に持て How could you die from such a slight injury? *Buck up!* (≒ *Get hold of yourself!*)
4〘確実な·しっかりした〙¶ ～な数字はつかめていない We have not got at the *correct* figure.
なにひとつ～なことはわかっていない I don't know anything, *exactly*.
これは～な情報だ This is *reliable* information.
～な筋からの情報 information from a *reliable* source; information on *good* authority.
～な証拠はあるのか Do you have any *strong* (≒ *positive*) proof?
だれか留守中に来たことは～だ *It is clear* (≒ *It is evident*) that somebody came to see me in my absence.
不景気になるのは～だ Bad times will *surely* come.
彼の人物は～か Is he a *trustworthy* (≒ *reliable*) man?
身元の～な者でないと雇えない We can only employ those who *are identified*.
～な人をよこしてくれ Please send me a *reliable* man.
彼は腕は～だ He is an *able* man
彼女の歌は音程が～だ She sings on pitch.
彼は足腰はまだ～だ He *is* still *strong enough to* get around.
～な足どりで歩く walk with *steady* steps.

たしか·める【確かめる】¶ われわれは彼の意向を～めたい We want to *ascertain* his intentions. 汽車が定時に着くかどうか～めましょう I'll *see* if the train is coming on time. 彼の安否を～めてください Will you *make sure of* his safety?/ Please *check* (≒ *find out*) whether he is safe or not.

だしがら【出し殻】¶ コーヒーの～ coffee *grounds*. お茶の～ used tea leaves.

だしき·る【出し切る】¶ 実力を～る *show one's* ability *to the full*.

たしさいさい【多士済済】¶ わが校の卒業生は～だ Our school has produced *a number of distinguished people*.

たしざん【足し算】〘数学〙addition.

だししぶ·る【出し渋る】¶ 彼はいつも寄付を～る He *is* always *unwilling to* make contributions.

たじたじ ¶ 虚をつかれて～の体だった He *flinched* as he was taken by surprise.

たしつ【多湿】high humidity. ¶ 日本の夏は高温～だ In Japan, we have high temperature and *high humidity* in summer.

たじつ【他日】some day; one day. ¶ ～お伺いいたします I'll call on you *some day* ～を期して努力してください Make every effort in anticipation for *the future*.

たしなみ【嗜み】¶ 彼は～がよい He is a man of good *taste*. / He has〔a〕good *taste*. 彼は行ないに～を欠く He lacks *modesty*. 彼女は～のよい身なりをしている She is dressed *with elegance*. 彼女はお花の～がある She *is accomplished in* flower arranging.

たしな·む【嗜む】¶ 彼は和歌を～む He *has a liking for tanka*. / (作ることを) He *likes* to compose *tanka*. 以後は～むがよい *Be* more *careful* hereafter.

たしな·める【窘める】¶ 私は彼の無礼を～めてやった I *reproved* him *for* his bad manners.

だしぬ·く【出し抜く】¶ 彼はわれわれを～いた He *has got ahead of* us. タイムズはこの事件で他紙を～いた The Times *beat* (≒ *scooped*) its rivals on this matter.

だしぬけ【出し抜け】¶ ～の質問にまごついた I was puzzled by the *unexpected* question. / I was puzzled as I was questioned *without warning*. 彼は～に私に会いにきた He made a *surprise* visit on me. / He came to see me *without notice* (≒ *quite unexpectedly*).

だしもの【出し物】(番組) a program. ¶ 今月の帝劇の～は何ですか What *is on* at the Imperial Theater this month?

だしゃ【打者】〖野球〗a batter; a batsman.
1番— a leadoff man. 強— a slugger; a hard hitter.

だじゃれ【駄洒落】a cheap joke; a pun.
¶ ～を飛ばす crack *a cheap joke.*

たしゅ【多種】many kinds; a〔large〕variety.
¶ ～多様な(の) various; varied; a great variety of. アメリカには～多様な人種が住んでいる There are *various* races of people in America. / There is *a great variety of* races in America.

だしゅ【舵手】(船の) a steersman; (ボートの) a coxswain.

たしゅみ【多趣味】¶ 彼は～だ He *has versatile tastes.*

だじゅん【打順】〖野球〗batting order.

たしょう【多少】¶ ～空腹を感じている I feel *a little* hungry. 彼女は～は英語を話すことができる She can speak English *a little.* 彼の言うことは～事実と食い違っている What he says is *some way* from the truth. 経済界のことは～は知っているつもりだ I think I know *something* about the economic world. ～にかかわらず寄付を募ります *Any amount of* contribution is to be accepted. きみは～は運動したほうがいい You must take *a certain amount of* exercise.

たじょう【多情】¶ 若い人は～だ Young people *are passionate.* あれは～な女だ She is a *fickle* woman. / She is a woman of *loose morals.*

たじろ・ぐ ¶ 野党の弁舌は首相を～がせた The vehement eloquence of the opposition party made the premier *shrink back.*

だしん【打診】〖医学〗percussion. ¶ 医者は患者の胸を～した The doctor *sounded* his patient's chest. その問題について彼の意向を～する必要がある We have to *feel* him *out* on the matter.

たしんきょう【多神教】polytheism.

た・す【足す】¶ 3に2を～す add 2 to 3. 用を～す do *one's* business.

だ・す【出す】**1**〖内から外へ〗¶ 列車の窓から首を～すな Don't *stick* your head out of the train window.
彼は失敗すると舌を～す When he fails, he *sticks out* his tongue.
ポケットから手を～しなさい *Take* your hands out of your pockets.
彼は手を～してぼくに握手を求めた He *held out* his hand to shake hands with me.
彼は名刺を～して来訪の目的を述べた He *presented* his card and explained the purpose of his visit.
ごみをやたらに道路に～してはいけない You must not *dump* garbage in the street.
2〖提出する・発送する〗¶ 入学願書を～す *send in* an application for admission to a school.
必要な書類を～す *send in* (≒ *submit*) the necessary papers.
辞表を～す *hand in* (≒ *tender*) *one's* resignation.
手紙を～す *send* a letter (*to*); write (*to*).
3〖発進させる〗¶ 臨時列車を～す *run* (≒ *operate*) a special train.
東京駅まで彼を迎えに車を～してください Please *send* a car to meet him at Tokyo Station.
金曜日に神戸へむけて船を～す We will *set sail* for Kobe on Friday.
4〖選出する〗¶ 保守党は市長候補者に彼を～した The Conservative Party *put* him *up* as a candidate for the mayor.
運動会の準備委員を各組から～す Each class *appoints* a member of the preparatory committee for the athletic event.
彼をわれわれのクラスの代表として～した We *elected* him as the representative of our class.
5〖話題を〗¶ ここでその話を～してくれるな Don't *bring* that matter *up* here.
このほかにきょうの会議に～す議題はない There is nothing else to *be submitted* to the conference today. / There is nothing else to *be brought up* for today's conference.
6〖発表する・出版する〗¶ あなたの名を～してかまいませんか May I *mention* your name?
このことでぼくの名を～されては困る I will be troubled if my name *is made public* in connection with this affair. / I don't want my name *mentioned publicly* in connection with this matter.
こういう専門的な本を～しても売れないだろう Such a specialized book as this would not sell, even if it *were published.*
本を有力出版社から～す *publish* a book by a leading publishing firm.
新聞に求人広告を～す *advertize* for help in a newspaper; *place* a want ad in a newspaper.
掲示を～す *put up* a notice.
展覧会に作品を～す *show* a product in an exhibition.
7〖露出する・露呈する〗¶ ひざを～す *show* (≒ *expose*) *one's* knees.
彼は怒りをおもてに～さない He *restrains* (≒ *contains*) his anger. / He does not *betray* his anger.
問い詰められて彼はぼろを～した Questioned closely, he *exposed* (≒ *unmasked*) himself.
彼はまた例の癖を～した He *showed* his usual habit again. / Again he *exhibited* his habit.
8〖音・光・におい・熱などを〗¶ 彼女は大きな声を～して泣いた She cried in a loud voice.
もう少し大きな声を～してください Please speak in a louder voice. / Please speak a little more loudly.
この工場は有害な廃棄物を～している This factory *has been producing* poisonous refuse.
木材は青い炎を～して燃えた The wood burned with a blue flame.
もっとスピードを～せ Go faster. / Speed up!
彼は高熱を～した He had a high fever.
この品は製造過程で多量の熱を～す A lot of heat

た

is generated in the process of manufacture of this article.

9 〖涙・血などを〗 ¶ その話を聞くと彼は思わず涙を～した Hearing the story, he *shed* tears in spite of himself.

子どもが転んで鼻血を～した The child fell down and his nose *bled*.

宿直の不注意から学校は火事を～した Owing to the carelessness of the person on night duty, the school building *caught* fire.

10 〖発揮する〗 ¶ もっと元気を～せ Cheer up! 馬力を～してきょうじゅうに仕事をかたづけよう I'll work hard and get this job done today.

11 〖産み出す〗 ¶ この学校はたくさんの有名人を～している This school *has produced* a lot of celebrities.

その事故で100人以上の死者を～した More than one hundred people *were killed* in the accident.

この事件で処罰者を～した Some *were punished* as a result of this incident.

彼はたくさんの犠牲者を～したことに責任を感じた He felt responsible for *having victimized* many people.

12 〖金を〗 ¶ 彼に学資を～してやった I *paid* his school expenses./I *paid for* his education.

この事業に資金を～した I *provided* funds for this enterprise./I *financed* this enterprise.

いくら～せばいいのですか How much money do you want me to *pay*?

それにそれだけの金を～す必要はない You need not *pay* so much money for it.

彼の誕生日の祝いにお金を少し～してあげよう I will *give* him some money in honor of his birthday.

13 〖提供する・もてなす〗 ¶ お客様にお酒を～してください Please *serve sake* to the guest.

彼女はぼくにお茶の1杯も～さなかった She did not *offer* me even a cup of tea.

14 〖課する〗 ¶ あの先生はたくさん宿題を～す The teacher *gives* a lot of homework.

命令を～す *give* orders; *issue* an order.

15 〖慣用的表現〗 ¶ 会に顔を～す *present oneself* (≒ *be present*) at a meeting.

よけいなことに手を～すな Don't do unwanted things. / Don't *stick* your nose where it doesn't belong.

そうやたらに口を～すな Don't *speak* thoughtlessly.

彼におどかされて皆手も足も～なかった Threatened by him, we were all quite at a loss what to do (≒ we were all helpless).

店を～す *open* a shop.

使用人に暇を～す *dismiss* an employee.

あまり働きすぎてあごを～さないように Don't *tire yourself out* by working too hard.

部品は下請けに～す We *sub-contract* for the manufacture of parts.

16 〖…しだす〗 ¶ それを言い～すときりがない If you *bring* that *up*, there's no end to it.

そのゲームは一度やり～すとおもしろくてやめられなくなる Once you *begin to* play the game, you will never give it up, as it is so interesting.

夜になると雪が降り～した When night fell, it *began to* snow.

その話を聞くと皆笑い～した All *burst into* laughter when they heard the story.

たすう【多数】 a large (≒ great) number; a multitude; (人数の) a mass; (採決の) the majority; a great part.

¶ 駅前にはいつも～の人がいる We always find *a large number* of people in front of the station. 自由党が～を占めている The Liberal Party has *the majority*. 彼らは～をたのんでいる They trust to *numbers*. 国民の～がその法案に反対だった *The majority* of the nation were against the bill.

―決 ¶ ～決で決めよう Let's decide by *majority*. **―党** the majority party.

だすう【打数】 〖野球〗 ¶ 彼は5～2安打だった He made two hits in five *at bats*.

たすか・る【助かる】 **1** 〖生命が〗 ¶ 彼は～る見込みがあるだろうか I wonder if there is any hope of his *recovery*.

この赤ん坊は～るだろう This baby *is expected to live*.

彼は自分では～らぬものとあきらめている He *has given himself up for lost*.

彼はおぼれかけたが運よく～った He was on the brink of being drowned, and yet fortunately he *was saved*.

この病気で～る人は少ない There are few who *survive* this disease.

2 〖有難い・役立つ〗 ¶ きょうは涼しくて～る *Thank goodness* it's cool today.

この機械は費用が節約できて～る This machine *saves* expense.

あの日外出しないで～った *I am thankful* I did not go out that day.

この参考書でたいへん～っている This reference book *is of great help to* me.

その場に彼がいてくれて～った His being on the spot *was helpful to* me.

たすき【襷】 a *tasuki*; a cord used for tucking up the *kimono* sleeves. ¶ ～を掛ける tuck up the *kimono* sleeves with a cord.

―がけ ¶ ～がけで働く work with *one's* sleeves tucked up.

たすけ【助け】 help; assistance. ¶ だれかが～を求めて叫んでいる Someone is crying for *help*. すぐ彼を～に行こう Let's go to his *rescue*. 彼の忠告はあまり～にはならなかった His advice did not *help* much. 人の～を借りずにこの仕事をやることは難しい It is difficult to do this work without *help* from others.

たすけあ・う【助け合う】 help each other (≒ one another) (each other はふたりの場合, one another は3人以上の場合とされているが厳密には守られていない).

¶ ふたりは～って山に登った They *helped each other* 〔climbing〕 up the mountain.

たすけだ・す【助け出す】 save; rescue; deliver.

¶ 消防士は火の中から子どもを～した The fireman *saved* a child from the fire. 彼らは遭難者を～した They *rescued* the sufferers.

た

たすけぶね【助け船】a lifeboat; a rescue boat; (助力) a help. ¶ 困っている人に~を出す *help a person* in distress; *help a person out.*

たす・ける【助ける】help. ¶ だれか~けてください *Help* me, somebody. / (急な場合) *Help, help!* 彼は私の宿題を~けてくれた He *helped* me *in* my homework. 彼は私に~けてほしいと言っている He says he wants my *help.* どうか命だけは~けてください Will you *spare* my *life*? ~けると思って私の願いを聞いてください Please grant my request *for mercy's sake.* 彼の提案は会の進行を~けた His proposal *was helpful in* the progress of the meeting. この薬は消化を~ける This medicine will *help* the digestion. 天はみずから~くる者を~く (諺) *Heaven helps those who help themselves.*

た

たずさ・える【携える】¶ 彼は大金を~えていた He *was carrying* much money *with* him. 彼は紹介状を~えて私を訪ねてきた He called on me *with* a letter of introduction. 私は彼と手を~えてこの事業をおこした I started this business *in co-operation* (≒ *in partnership*) *with* him. 全国民は相~えてその難局を切り抜けた All the nation *united their efforts* and tided over the difficulty.

たずさわ・る【携わる】participate (≒ take part) in; be concerned in (≒ with). ¶ 母は家事に~っている My mother is busy with housework.

ダスター〔コート〕 米 a duster; 英 a dustcoat.

たずねびと【尋ね人】a missing person.

たず・ねる【訪ねる】call on; pay a visit to. ¶ 私は先年その古都を~ねた I *visited* the ancient capital a few years ago. 先日彼を~ねた I *called on* him the other day.

たず・ねる【尋ねる】ask; inquire. ¶ お~ねしたいことがあります May I *ask* you something? 彼は疑問点を先生に~ねた He *asked* a question *of* his teacher. 外人が私に駅に行く道を~ねた A foreigner *asked* me the way to the station. 彼は私の両親の安否を~ねた He *inquired after* my parents' health. 私はその習慣の由来を~ねている I *am tracing the origin of* the custom.

たぜい【多勢】¶ ~に無勢ではかなわない There is no use fighting against *great odds.*

だせい【惰性】inertia; momentum. ¶ ~で朝寝がなおらない I can't get over the habit of oversleeping. 彼は~的に怠惰な生活を送っている He is leading a lazy life *out of habit.* ボールは~で転がっていった The ball rolled on by the force of *inertia.*

だせき【打席】〔野球〕at bat. ¶ 彼は~についている He *is at bat.* 彼は5~2安打だった He made two hits in five *at bats.* (at bats は名詞用法で「打席数」の意).

たせん【他薦】recommendation. ¶ その地位を求めて自薦~の候補がひしめいている The candidates who recommend themselves and those who *are recommended by others* are jostling each other for the post.

だせん【打線】〔野球〕the batting lineup (≒ line-up).

だせん【唾腺】〔解剖学〕the salivary glands.

たそがれ【誰そ彼・黄昏】¶ ~時に at *dusk* (≒ *twilight*); in the *twilight.*

だそく【蛇足】superfluity. ¶ ~を加える make an *unnecessary addition* (*to*). それは~だ That *is superfluous* (≒ *is redundant*).

たそくるい【多足類】〔動物〕myriapods.

たた【多多】¶ ~ますます弁ず The more, the better.

ただ【只】¶ ~の入場券 a *free* admission ticket. 彼女は~でネックレスをもらった She got the necklace *for nothing.* 入場は~だ Admission *is free* (≒ *is gratis*). 彼は~同様でその時計を売った He sold the watch *for almost nothing.* 彼は転んでも~では起きない He is so greedy that he would even squeeze water from a stone.

ただ【唯】¶ ~の人 a *common* (≒ an *ordinary*) man. ~1度 *only* (≒ *but*) once. 私の持っているのは~これだけ They are *all* I have. 彼女は~うれし涙にくれるのみだった She *could only* cry for joy. 彼は私を~ぼんやり見ていた He *only* (≒ *simply*; *merely*) saw me absentmindedly. 彼女は~ひとりで外国へ行った She went abroad 〔*all*〕 *alone.* きみは~彼に会いさえすればいい You *have only to* see him. 私は~彼のためにしただけだ I did *only* for his sake. ~一心にその研究にうちこみなさい Devote yourself exclusively to the study. これが~ひとつの証拠品だ This is the *only* (≒ *single*) piece of evidence.

だだ【駄駄】¶ そう~をこねるな Don't *be* so *fretful.*

ただい【多大】¶ その取引きで~の利益を得た I gained a *large* profit in the business. その火事で~の損害をこうむった *Serious* damage was caused by the fire. 私は洪水で~の損害をうけた I suffered a *great* loss from the flood.

だたい【堕胎】an artificial abortion.
—薬 an abortive medicine.

ただいま【唯今・只今】now. ¶ ~帰りました I have *just* come back. ~伺います I am coming *now.* ~, おとうさん *Hi,* Dad! 彼は~出張中です He is *now* away on official business. ~のところ列車の開通の見込みはない There is no prospect of the railroad being reopened *for the present.* 彼は~すぐ来ます He will come *in a moment.*

たた・える【称える】¶ 努力を~える *praise* (≒ *speak highly of*) an effort.

たた・える【湛える】¶ 彼は目に涙を~えていた His eyes *were filled with* tears. 彼女は目に涙を~えて出て行った She went out with her eyes *full of* tears. 彼は満面に笑みを~えてあらわれた He appeared *with smiles all over* (≒ *beaming with smiles*).

たたかい【戦い・闘い】(戦争) a war; (戦闘) a fight; a battle; a combat; (組織的な戦闘) an engagement; (交戦) an encounter; (争闘)

a struggle; a strife; a conflict. ¶ ～を宣する declare *war* (*against*). ～に勝つ(負ける) win (lose) *a battle*. 労使の～ the *struggle* between capital and labor. 世界平和のための～ *a struggle* for world peace. 彼に～をいどんだ I challenged him to *a fight*.

たたかいぬ·く【戦い抜く】¶ 選挙戦を～く *fight through* an election campaign. 勇敢に～く *fight it out* bravely.

たたか·う【戦う·闘う】fight. ¶ 彼らは平和のために～っている They *are fighting* for peace. 彼らの軍は数時間敵と～った Their forces *fought against* the enemy for several hours. 病人たちは死と～っている The sick people *are fighting against* death. 多くの困難と～わねばならぬ We have to *struggle against* a lot of difficulties. 彼らは幾多の誘惑と～った They *resisted* a lot of temptations. ～わずして勝った We won a victory over the enemy *without bloodshed*.

たたき【叩き】(料理) mince-meat; minced meat. ¶ カツオの～ *minced* bonito.

たたき【三和土】(土間) a concrete floor; an earthen floor.

たたきあ·げる【叩き上げる】¶ この会社の社長は店員から～げてきた人だ The president of this company is a man who *worked his way up* from a shop clerk to the present position.

たたきうり【叩き売り】a bargain sale; a discount sale.

たたきおこ·す【叩き起こす】(戸をたたいて起こす) knock (*a person*) up; (無理に起こす) rout (*a person*) out of bed.
¶ いっせいに～された We *were roused out of bed* all at once. 彼は夜中に戸をたたいて家人を～した He *knocked up* his household at midnight.

たたきおと·す【叩き落とす】¶ クリを～す *knock* chestnuts *down*. 小枝を～す *chop off* twigs.

たたきき·る【叩き切る】¶ 木を～る *chop* wood.

たたきこわ·す【叩き壊す】¶ かきを～す *break* a fence *down*.

たたきつ·ける【叩き付ける】¶ コップを地面に～ける *throw* a glass *against* the ground. 彼はかんしゃくを起こして本を床に～けた He lost his temper and *dashed* his book *to* the floor. 彼は私に辞表を～けた He *thrust* his resignation *at* me.

たたきのめ·す【叩きのめす】¶ 大ぜい寄ってたかって彼を～した A large crowd joined in *knocking* him *down*.

たたきふ·せる【叩き伏せる】¶ 暴漢を～せた I *knocked* the ruffian *down*. 相手チームを～せた We totally *defeated* the opposite team.

たた·く【叩く】**1**〘打つ〙beat. ¶ 戸を～いているのはだれだ Who *is knocking at* the door?
子どもはフォークでテーブルを～いていた The child *was hitting* the table with a fork.
突然だれかが私の肩を～いた Suddenly someone *tapped* me *on* the shoulder.
彼ははげしく机を～きながら演説した He made a speech *pounding on* the desk.
彼女はほこりをとるためじゅうたんを～いていた She *was beating* the dust out of the carpet.
観客はいっせいに手を～いた The spectators *clapped* their hands unanimously.
父親はいきなりその子のほおを～いた The father *slapped* the child *on* the face all of a sudden.
太鼓を～く *beat* a drum.
あられが窓を～いている Hailstones *are lashing* the window.
2〘慣用的表現〙¶ 彼の意見を～いてみたほうがよい You had better *sound* his point of view.
新聞でその俳優はひどく～かれた The actor *was attacked* (≒ *was criticized*) severely in the newspapers.
これ以上値段を～くことはできない The price cannot *be beaten down* any more.

ただごと【徒事·只事】a trivial matter; a commonplace. ¶ ～ではない物音 an *alarming* sound; a *fearful* (≒ *terrible*) sound.

たださえ【唯さえ】¶ ～困っているのにこの大雨だ *To make matters worse* (≒ *To add to my misery*), a heavy rain is falling.

ただし【但し】but; however; only. ¶ あすは行く, ～雨が降ればやめ I will go tomorrow, *but* I won't if it rains. 動物をそれほど好きではないが, ～ネコは好きだ I don't like animals so much *except for* cats. あす手伝いに行くが, ～2時間しか手伝えない I will help you tomorrow *on condition that* I cannot do so for more than two hours.

ただし·い【正しい】right. ¶ ～いことをやりなさい Do what *is right*. 彼の言うことは～いとは言えない What he says cannot be said to *be right*. あなたの考えは～い Your way of thinking *is correct*. この言い方は文法的には～いが, 実際にはこの言い方はない This expression *is* grammatically *correct*, but really there is no such expression. これはその時の～い描写だ This is a *just* description of the state of affairs. 彼は証拠を見せて自分の～いことを証明した He *justified himself* by showing evidence. ～いことをやればきっといつかは報いられる If you *do right*, you are sure to be rewarded some day. 私が～いというのは法律的に～いということではない By what *is correct* to me I don't mean what *is* legally *correct*.

ただしがき【但し書】a proviso (複 provisos; provisoes). ¶ ～付きの記録 a *provisory* record. その案は～付きで同意された The plan was approved of with *a proviso*.

ただ·す【正す】(訂正する) correct; rectify; (きょう正する) reform; set (≒ put) right.
¶ 姿勢を～す *straighten oneself*. 誤りを～す *correct* an error. 人の誤りを～す *set a person right*. 行ないを～す *reform oneself*; *reform one's* wrong ways.

ただ·す【糾す·糺す】¶ 彼の罪を～す *inquire into* his crime. 元を～せば originally. 彼の身元を～す *look into* his record.

ただ·す【質す】*ask* (*a person about a matter*);

ask (a question *of a person*). ¶ この件については専門家に～した I *consulted* an expert on the matter. 彼は政府の方針を～した He *asked* the Government policy.

たたずまい【佇まい】¶ 雲の～にも秋が感じられる Even the *appearance* of a cloud makes us feel the presence of autumn.

たたず·む【佇む】¶ しばし～む *stand still* for a while.

たた·せる【立たせる】¶ 教室のうしろに～せる (～せておく) *make* a pupil *stand* at the rear of the classroom; *keep* a pupil *standing* at the rear of the classroom.

ただちに【直ちに】(すぐに) soon; at once; immediately; directly; instantly; without delay; (直接) directly; straight.
¶ 彼は思ったことを～実行する He *immediately* puts into practice what he has in mind.

だだっこ【駄駄っ子】(甘やかされた子) a spoiled (≒ spoilt) child; (気難しい子) a fretful (≒ cross) child.

ただでさえ【唯でさえ】¶ ～成績がよくないのに遊んでばかりいては落第するのはあたりまえだ In addition to your bad school record, you are always playing around, so it is quite natural that you should fail the exam.

ただなか【直中】¶ 論戦の～に突然笑いが起こった Laughter occurred suddenly *in the middle of* the argument. 大海の～に船が2隻ただよっている Two ships are drifting *in the middle of* the ocean.

ただならぬ【啻ならぬ】¶ 彼は～ようすだった There was something *unusual* about him. ～物音がした An *alarming* sound was heard. 両国間は～状態だ The situation between the two countries *is tense*. 彼と彼女は～仲にある He *is very intimate* with her.

ただのり【ただ乗り】¶ ～する steal a ride (*on* a train). ～の乗客(米俗) a deadhead.

ただばたらき【ただ働き】¶ 彼は～も同じ安月給だ He works for *next to nothing*. せっかくの努力も～だった Nothing has come of my great efforts.

たたみ【畳】a mat; (総称) matting. ¶ ～を敷く lay *tatami*; mat (a floor). ～の上で死にたい I want to die in my bed.
—替え renewing (≒ refacing) of *tatami*.
—いわし a piece of dried small sardines.

たたみか·ける【畳みかける】¶ ～けて聞く press (*a person*) for an answer; rain (≒ shower) questions on (*a person*).

たたみこ·む【畳み込む】¶ ちゃぶ台の脚を～む *fold* the legs of a table. その教訓を頭に～んで忘れてはならない *Keep* the lesson *in your mind*, and don't forget it.

たた·む【畳む】fold. ¶ 紙を四つに～む *fold* a sheet of paper in four. この毛布をきれいにふたつに～んでほしい I want you to *double up* this blanket neatly. テントを～むのは簡単だ It is easy to *strike* the tent. 彼は店を～んだ He *closed up* his store. このことはきみの胸に～んでおいてほしい I want you to bear (≒ *keep*) this *in mind*.

ただもの【徒物·只者】¶ 彼は～でない He is not *a common person*.

ただよ·う【漂う】float; drift. ¶ 空に雲が～う Clouds *float* in the sky. 不安の影がわれわれに～う A cloud of uneasiness *is* (≒ *hangs*) *upon* us. 大きな氷山が～っていた A big iceberg *was drifting*. バラの甘い香が空中に～っている A sweet smell of roses *is* in the air.

ただよわ·せる【漂わせる】¶ それはかぐわしい香りを～せている It *gives off* a pleasing perfume.

たたり【祟り】a curse; an evil consequence.
¶ ～を恐れる fear *the evil consequence*. あとの～がこわい Future *trouble* is horrible./There will be the devil to pay./You'll have to pay dearly for it. この家には～がある There is *a curse* on this family. 弱り目に～目(諺) *Misfortunes never come single*.

たた·る【祟る】¶ あの一家は何かに～られている Some evil spirit *curses* the family. 大食が～って胃をこわした I had stomach trouble *from* eating too much.

ただれ【爛れ】a sore; an inflammation.
—目 a bleary (≒ sore) eye.

ただ·れる【爛れる】¶ 傷が～れる The wound *festers* (≒ *is inflamed*). ～れた生活を送る lead a *dissipated* life.

たたん【多端】¶ ～な人生 a *very eventful* life. 多事～ eventfulness; press of business.

たち【質】(性質) nature; character; (品質) quality; (気質) a disposition; temper; a temperament; (傾向) aptitude; an inclination.
¶ ～のよい(気質が) good-natured; (品質が) of fine (≒ superior) quality. ～が悪い(気質·性質が) ill-natured; wicked; vicious; (品質が) of poor (≒ inferior) quality. ～の悪い風邪 a *bad* (≒ *nasty*) cold. 彼は気の弱い～だ He is a weak-*minded* man. 彼は疲れやすい～だ He tires easily.

たち【太刀】a long sword. ¶ ～をはく wear *a long sword*. ～を抜く draw *a sword*. ～筋がよい be a good swordsman.

たちあい【立ち会い·立会】(出席) presence; (株式取引所の) a session. ¶ ～を求める request (≒ ask for) (*a person's*) *presence*. ～の警官 a policeman *present* (≒ *in attendance*). (株式取引所の)～停止 suspension of a session. 「さあさあ, お～」 "Come now! Your attention, please!"
—演説会(選挙の) a competitive speech meeting. **—人** an observer; (証人) a witness; (開票の) a teller.

たちあ·う【立ち会う】(出席する) be present; attend; (参加する) take part (*in*); (証人として) witness; be 〔a〕 witness. ¶ 参考人として～った I *was present* as a witness.

たちあがり【裁ち上がり】cutting 〔up〕. ¶ ～がきれいだ The *cut* is fine.

たちあがり【立ち上がり】¶ ～から好調だ He has done well *from the start*. あの投手は～が悪い That pitcher is bad *at the start*.

たちあが·る【立ち上がる】¶いすから～る *stand up* from *one's* chair. 彼はびっくりして～った He *started to his feet*. 平和運動に～る *rise up for* the peace movement. 彼は大火事の打撃から～った He *recovered from* the blow of a big fire.

たちい【立ち居】movement. ¶彼は～が不自由である He has difficulty in *moving about*. 彼女は～ふるまいがしとやかだ She is graceful in *movement*.

たちいた【裁ち板】a cutting (≒ a tailor's) board.

たちいた·る【立ち至る】¶重大な段階に～る *reach* (≒ *come to*) an important stage.

たちいり【立ち入り】entrance ;〘法律〙entry. ¶～禁止(掲示) Keep out. / 囲 Keep off. / Off-limits. 無用の者～禁止(掲示) No admittance except on business.

たちい·る【立ち入る】¶芝生に～るべからず(掲示) *Keep off* the grass. ここでは～った話はよそう Let's stop being too personal here.

たちうお【太刀魚】〘魚類〙a hairtail ; a scabbard fish.

たちうち【太刀打ち】(対抗) opposition. ¶英語では彼にとても～できない I *am no match for* him *in* English. 値段の点で, これはあれに～できない This cannot *compete with* that *in* price.

たちうち【立ち撃ち·立ち射ち】firing in a standing position. ¶～する fire in a standing position.

たちうり【立ち売り】¶新聞の～ the *hawking* (≒ *peddling*) of newspapers.

たちおうじょう【立ち往生】a standstill. ¶事故で列車が～した A train *was brought to a standstill* owing to an accident. 彼は演壇で当惑して～してしまった He *stood speechless* with embarrassment on the platform.

たちおく·れる【立ち後れる】¶当社は貿易不況に対する用意の点で他社に～れた Our company *is behind* other companies *in* the preparation for trade depression.

たちおよぎ【立ち泳ぎ】treading water. ¶～する tread water.

たちかえ·る【立ち返る】¶本題に～る *return to* the subject. 彼は本心に～った He *came to* his senses. / He *was brought back to* his senses.

たちかた【裁ち方】a cut ; cutting. ¶ドレスの～が悪い The *cut* of the dress is bad.

たちがれ【立ち枯れ】blight. ¶～の菊 a *blighted* chrysanthemum. ～する stand *blighted*.

たちかわり【立ち替わり】¶昨日は入り替わり～来客があった Yesterday I had visitors *in succession*. / Yesterday I had *one* visitor *after another*.

たちき【立ち木】a standing (≒ living ; growing) tree. ¶～を切る cut down *a tree*. 松を～で売る sell pine trees *as they stand*.

たちぎえ【立ち消え】¶計画は～になるだろう The plan will *fall through* (≒ *fail* ; *come to nothing*).

たちぎき【立ち聞き】¶人の話を～する *eavesdrop on* others' talk. ぼくはたまたま彼らの話を～してしまった I accidentally *overheard* their conversation. (eavesdrop は「他人の話を盗み聞きする」ことで, overhear は「偶然聞いてしまう」こと).
—する人 an eavesdropper.

たちき·る【断ち切る】¶紙を～る *cut* paper *asunder*. 関係を～る *cut off* the relationship ; *sever* (≒ *break off*) *one's* connections (*with*). 敵の退路を～る *cut off* the enemy's retreat ; *intercept* the enemy's retreat.

たちき·る【裁ち切る】¶服地を～る *cut out* the cloth.

たちぐい【立ち食い】a stand-up meal. ¶～する take a stand-up meal ; eat standing. すしの～をした I ate *sushi* standing.

たちぐされ【立ち腐れ】¶住む人もなく～になった家 a house long deserted and *run-down*.

たちくず【裁ち屑】waste pieces of cut cloth.

たちげいこ【立ち稽古】a rehearsal. ¶彼らは「ベニスの商人」の～をしている They *are rehearsing* "The Merchant of Venice."

たちこ·める【立ち込める】¶谷間に霧が～めている Mist *is hanging* over the valley. / The valley lies hidden in mist.

たちさ·る【立ち去る】¶彼は人知れずこの地を～った He *left* this place unknown. 彼に～れと言った I ordered him to *get away*. ～れ Begone ! / Get away ! / Get out of here !

たちさわ·ぐ【立ち騒ぐ】¶アンパイアの判定に見物人がものすごく～いだ The spectators *made a great deal of fuss over* the judgment of the umpire. 波風が～いでいる The sea *is rough*.

たちすく·む【立ち竦む】¶子どもは犬にほえられてその場に～んだ The child was barked at by the dog and *was frozen with fear*. / The child was barked at by the dog and *stood paralyzed with fear*.

たちつく·す【立ち尽くす】¶観衆はこの光景に胸を打たれてその場に～した The spectators *stood motionless* deeply impressed with this sight.

たちづめ【立ち詰め】¶満員電車で終着駅まで～であった I was forced to *keep standing* in the crowded train all the way to the terminal station.

たちどおし【立ち通し】¶場内が込んでいたので～で映画を見た The movie theater was so crowded that I had to *stand all through* the movie. 列車が込んで大阪まで～だった As the train was crowded, I had to *stand all the way to* Osaka.

たちどころに【立ち所に】¶彼は問題を～解いた He *promptly* solved the problem. この薬で胃の痛みは～治る This medicine will cure your stomach pain *at once*.

たちどま·る【立ち止まる】¶私はぎょっとして～った I *stopped* with a start. 彼女はショーウインドーの前に～っていた She *stood still* in front of the show window.

たちなお·る【立ち直る】¶ピッチャーは3回から～

った The pitcher *recovered himself* in the third inning. 秋には市況が～るだろう The market will *rally* next autumn. 国際収支は完全に～った The balance of international payments *has recovered* completely.

たちなら・ぶ【立ち並ぶ】¶ 街路にはモダンな店が～んでいる There *stand* fashionable stores *along* the street. 都心には高層ビルが～んでいる There *are* skyscrapers standing *in a row* in the center of the city.

たちのき【立ち退き】(移転) removal; (撤退) evacuation; (追いたて) eviction; (明け渡し) vacation. ¶ わが家は～を命じられた We were ordered *out of the house*. / We were ordered to *remove*.

—先 the new address; (一時の) the temporary address. —料 compensation for removal. —命令 an eviction order.

た

たちの・く【立ち退く】¶ 故郷を～く leave *one's* home town. 区画整理のために土地を～かなければならない We have to *move from* this place on account of city planning. 近所の学校へ～いた(避難した) We *took refuge at* a nearby school. 彼は家賃延滞のかどで～かされた He *was evicted* for not paying the rent.

たちのぼ・る【立ち上る】go up; rise; ascend. ¶ 森の向こうから煙が～っている Smoke *is rising* (≒ *is ascending*) from behind the woods.

たちば【立場】a position. ¶ 自分の～を考えなさい Consider your own *position*. 私の～をわかってほしい I want you to appreciate my *position*. この私の～になって考えてほしい I want you to put yourself *in my place*. 私はこの問題に関してはなにも言えない～にある I am not in *a position* to say anything about this matter. 自分の～を明らかにした I made my own *standpoint* clear. ～をかえて考えることもたいせつだ It is important to consider it from *a* different *point of view*. 彼らはむずかしい～にあった They were in *a* difficult *situation*. 彼はもう他人の～がわかってもいい年ごろだ He is old enough to understand the *situations* of other people.

たちはだか・る【立ちはだかる】¶ 強敵A校がわれわれのチームの前に～っている "A" school, our powerful rival, *stands right in the way* of our team.

たちはたら・く【立ち働く】¶ 彼女はこまめに～く She *works* like a bee.

たちばな【橘】〖植物〗a wild orange.

たちばなし【立ち話】¶ 彼と～をした I *exchanged a few casual words with* him.

たちはばとび【立ち幅跳び】a standing broad jump.

たちばん【立ち番】watch; (人) a guard. ¶ 彼は入り口で～をした He *stood guard* (≒ *kept watch*) at the entrance.

たちふさが・る【立ち塞がる】¶ 船の前方に大きな氷山が～っていた There was a great iceberg *in the path of* the ship. 彼は私の前に～った He *stood in my way*.

たちまち【忽ち】at once; in a moment; in an instant; (突然) suddenly; all at once. ¶ 彼はその難問を～解いた He solved the difficult problem *at once*. この薬で胃の痛みは～治る This medicine will remove your stomachache *in a moment*. 彼の新しい戯曲は～大評判になった His new play was an *immediate* success.

たちまわり【立ち回り】(格闘) a scuffle; a fighting; (演劇) a fighting scene. ¶ 警官はそのすりと大～を演じた The policeman had *a scuffle* with the pickpocket. 歌舞伎の～ *a fighting scene* in a Kabuki play.

たちまわりさき【立ち回り先】¶ 彼の～は知らない We don't know where he has gone.

たちまわ・る【立ち回る】¶ 彼は如才なく～って早く出世した He *played his part* smartly and won early success. 犯人は実家に～ったところを逮捕された The criminal was caught when he *visited* his home.

たちみ【立ち見】¶ ～する see a play from the gallery.

—客 a standee; (総称) the gallery. —席 standing room; the gallery.

たちむか・う【立ち向かう】¶ 私は大胆に困難に～った I boldly *confronted* the difficulty. 彼はひとりで3人の敵に～っていった He *fought* alone *against* three opponents.

たちもど・る【立ち戻る】¶ 本題に～って議事を進めよう Let's *return to* the main subject and expedite the proceedings.

たちゆ・く【立ち行く】¶ この高物価では生活が～かない We cannot *get along* with prices this high. その小さな店は辛うじて～く程度だった The small store barely *paid its way*.

だちょう【駝鳥】〖鳥類〗an ostrich.

たちよみ【立ち読み】¶ 彼はよく本屋で～する He often *reads books* (≒ *browses*) *in bookstores*. 雑誌の～をしていたらどなられた When I *was reading* a magazine *in a store*, the bookseller told me off.

たちよ・る【立ち寄る】¶ 一行は当地へ～った The party *stopped* here. 大統領はアジア訪問の途上, ホノルルに～った The president *stopped off* (≒ *stopped over*) *at* Honolulu on his way to Asia. たまにはお～りください Please *drop in on* us sometimes.

たちわざ【立ち技】〖レスリング・柔道〗a standing throw.

だちん【駄賃】(報酬) reward; a tip. ¶ お使いに行ってくれればお～をあげるよ I'll give you *something* if you will go on an errand for me. ほねおりのお～にこれをあげよう I will give you this for your trouble. 行きがけの～にこいつを失敬してきた I got hold of this while I was at it.

たつ【竜】a dragon.

た・つ【立つ・起つ・建つ】**1**〖人・動物が〗stand. ¶ 彼はぼんやりそこに～っていた He *was standing* there absent-mindedly. (He stood でもよい). そんな所に～っていないで早く中に入りなさい Hurry up and come in instead of *standing* in such a place.

乾杯しますからお～ちください I'd like to propose the toast to him. Would you kindly *stand*?

彼は演壇に〜って一礼した He *stood* on the platform with a bow.

犬が後ろ足で〜った The dog *stood* on his hind legs.

彼は便所へ〜った He went to wash his hands.

2 〖物・事が〗 ¶ 頂上に展望台が〜っていた *There was* an observatory at the top of the hill.

たくさんの看板が駅前に〜っていた A lot of placards *were put up* in front of the station.

いまにこの辺もたくさん家が〜つだろう A lot of houses will probably *be built* in this neighborhood.

市長の銅像が〜った A bronze statue *was erected* to the memory of the mayor.

3 〖舞い上がる〗 ¶ あらしが近づいてきたので波が〜っている The waves *are high* because a storm is approaching.

ほこりが〜たないように道に水をまきなさい Sprinkle water on the road to keep the dust down.

山頂に一条の火柱が〜つのが見えた A pillar of flames was seen to *shoot up* from the top of the mountain.

火のない所に煙は〜たない (諺) *There is no smoke without fire.*

4 〖うわさ・評判が〗 ¶ きみについて変なうわさが〜っている *There is* a strange rumor *abroad* about you.

彼は渡米するといううわさが〜っている *Rumor has it* (≒ *It is rumored*) that he is going to America.

たちまち彼はよい先生だとの評判が〜った Very soon he *won the reputation of* being a good teacher.

5 〖立ち去る・出発する〗 ¶ いつお〜ちですか When *are* you *leaving*?

彼は昨夜東京を〜って青森に向かった Last night he *left* Tokyo for Aomori.

彼は憤然として席を〜った He *left* his seat in a rage.

〜つ鳥跡を濁さず (直訳なら) A bird taking flight does not foul the water. / (意訳なら) It is an ill bird that fouls its own nest.

6 〖ある情況・地位におかれる〗 ¶ 30(歳)にして〜つ establish *oneself* at thirty.

人の上に〜つ lead others; play first fiddle.

この地区からは彼が区会議員に〜つ He is a candidate in this district for the ward assembly. / He *is running for* the ward assembly in this district.

きみは教壇に〜ってから何年になるか How many years have you been teaching? / How long have you had experience in teaching?

今度の事件で彼はしばしば苦境に〜たされた He often *found himself in* a difficult position because of the recent event.

7 〖決起する〗 ¶ 今こそ一致団結して平和のために〜ち上がろう Let's *rise* as one man for the cause of peace.

若者よ, 〜て *Be up and doing,* young men!

武器を取って〜つ日がきた The time has come to *rise* in arms.

彼がその気ならこっちも受けて〜とう If that is what he wants, I can't help *standing against* him.

8 〖感情がたかぶる〗 ¶ そういう話を聞くと腹が〜つ I cannot help *getting angry* when I hear such things.

彼は気が〜っている He *is* now *irritated* (≒ *is* now *excited*).

損をしまいとする気持ちが先に〜ってわれわれはしばしば用心しすぎる In trying to avoid a loss, we are often too careful.

9 〖目だつ〗 ¶ そう言えば角が〜つ If you said that, he would *see red.*

ふたりは人目に〜たないようにして会っていたものだ Both of them used to meet *secretly.*

10 〖用をする・優れている〗 ¶ この接着剤はいろいろなことに役に〜つ This adhesive agent *is useful to* everything.

彼は腕が〜つ He is *an able man.*

彼は弁が〜つ He is *an eloquent speaker.*

彼は筆が〜つ He is *a good writer.*

11 〖理論・筋道が通る〗 ¶ そういうふうに言えば筋道が〜つ There is *logic* in what you say. / What you say *is logical.*

そういう言いわけは〜たない That is a *lame* (≒ *poor*) excuse for it.

私の欠席は言いわけが〜たない My absence *is* not *excusable.*

9を3で割れば3が〜つ Nine divided by three makes (≒ is) three.

12 〖顔・義理などが〗 ¶ そんなことをされてはぼくの顔が〜たない I *am embarrassed* by what you did. / I can't *save my face* if you do such a thing.

あちらを〜てればこちらが〜たない I *am on the horns of a dilemma.* / I *am in a fix.*

それでは義理が〜たない That would be against my sense of duty (≒ honor).

13 〖しっかりしたものになっている〗 ¶ 計画は〜ったのか *Have* you *made* (≒*laid down*) your plan?

その件についてはなんの方針も〜っていない No policy *has been established* yet concerning the matter.

それだけの収入では暮らしが〜たない I cannot *make a living* on such an income.

彼の説は相対性理論の上に〜っている His theory *is based on* that of relativity.

生計が〜つか Can you make both ends meet?

た・つ 【断つ】 ¶ いつたばこを〜ったのですか When did you *quit* (≒ *give up*) smoking? 彼は息子を真人間にするため茶を〜っている He *has given up* tea for the purpose of making his son turn over a new leaf.

た・つ 【絶つ】 ¶ 彼は交通事故で命を〜った He *was killed* in a traffic accident. 彼とのつき合いは〜ったほうがよい You must *break off relations with* him.

た・つ 【裁つ】 ¶ スカートを〜つ *cut out* a skirt. 余分の布を〜ち落とす *cut off* the margin of the cloth.

た·つ【経つ】¶もう1年〜ってしまった A year *has* already *passed.* ふたりが会わなくなってもう8年〜った The two haven't seen each other for eight years. 時が〜つにつれて彼の優しさがわかってきた I came to appreciate his gentleness as time *went by.* 読書に夢中になって時の〜つのを忘れた I was so much absorbed in reading that I was almost unconscious of *the lapse of time.* 1週間も〜たないうちに彼はよくなった He got well *in less than a week.* 帰京して5日も〜たないうちに彼は発病した He *had scarcely* been in Tokyo for five days *when* he fell ill. あとどのくらい〜つと旅行に出発されますか *How long is it before* you start on your journey? この大木はもう50年〜っている This tree *is* fifty years *old.*

だつい【脱衣】¶〜する undress *oneself*; take off *one's* clothes.
—場(化粧室) a dressing room; (海水浴場など) a bathhouse; a bathing house.

だっかい【脱会】withdrawal from membership.
—届 a report of secession. —者 a bolter; a seceder. ¶〜者が多数あった Many *have left the association.*

だっかい【奪回】recapture. ¶わが方は敵から陣地を〜した We *recaptured* the position from the enemy. われわれは優勝旗を〜した We *won back* the championship flag.

たっかん【達観】¶彼は人生を〜している He *takes a philosophic view of* life.

だっかん【奪還】recapture.

だっきゃく【脱却】¶彼らはまだ旧態を〜できずにいる They cannot *get rid of* (≒ *free themselves from*) the old custom yet.

たっきゅう【卓球】ping-pong; table tennis. ¶〜をする play *ping-pong.*

だっきゅう【脱臼】〘医学〙dislocation. ¶彼は片ひざを〜した One of his knees *was put out of joint.* / He *dislocated* his knee.

タック〘洋裁〙a tuck.

タッグ —チーム a tag team. —マッチ a tag match.

ダッグアウト〘野球〙a dugout.

タックル〘ラグビー〙tackle. ¶〜する tackle (*a person*).

-たっけ ¶あの時は雨が降ってい〜 *I remember* it was raining then. よくあの川へ泳ぎに行っ〜 *I used to* go swimming in that stream.

-だっけ ¶きょうの当番はだれ〜 Who is supposed to be on duty today, *may I ask?*

たっけん【卓見】(先見の明) foresight; (名案) an excellent suggestion. ¶〜を発表する offer *excellent suggestions.*

たっけん【達見】far-sightedness. ¶〜ある far-sighted; far-seeing.

だっこ【抱】¶若い母親は産まれたばかりの赤ん坊を〜していた The young mother *was holding* (≒ *was carrying*) her new-born baby *in her arms.*

だっこう【脱稿】¶彼はその小説を〜した He *completed* (≒ *finished writing*) the novel.

だっこう【脱肛】〘医学〙proctocele; prolapsed rectum (複 recta).

だっこく【脱穀】threshing. ¶〜する thresh; thrash.
—機 a threshing machine.

だつごく【脱獄】prison(≒ jail)-breaking. ¶〜する break prison; escape from prison.
—囚 a prison breaker.

たっし【達し】a public (≒ government) notice; official orders. ¶その筋のお〜により by *police orders.*

だつじ【脱字】an omitted word (≒ letter).

だっしにゅう【脱脂乳】skim milk.

だっしめん【脱脂綿】absorbent cotton.

たっしゃ【達者】**1**〘壮健な〙in good health; well. ¶お〜で I hope you will *stay in good health.*
有難う, ぼくも〜です I *am fine,* thank you.
彼は〜で暮らしている He *is getting on well.*
彼は85歳になるが〜なものだ He, now eighty-five years old, *is* still *going strong.*
このところ彼は〜になった He has recently become *strong and healthy.*
彼は驚くほど足が〜だ He is a surprisingly *good* walker.
2〘上手な〙good. ¶あの人は口は〜だが, 筆は〜ではない He is a *good* talker but not a *good* writer.
彼女は英語ばかりでなくフランス語も〜に話す She speaks French as well as English *fluently.*
その子どもは計算が〜だ The child *is good at* figures.
彼女は英会話が〜だ She *is strong in* (≒ *is good at*) English conversation.
彼は水泳が〜だ He is a *good* swimmer.

だっしゅ【奪取】¶わが軍は敵陣を〜した We *captured* (≒ *seized*) the enemy position.

ダッシュ (競技) a dash; (記号) a dash (—); (数学) a prime (A′ は A prime, A″ は A double prime と読む).
¶彼はすばらしい〜でとび出した He started with *a good dash.*

だっしゅう【脱臭】deodorization. ¶〜する deodorize.
—剤 a deodorizer; a deodorant.

だっしゅつ【脱出】escape. ¶彼は国外に〜した He *escaped* from the country. 彼は苦境から〜したいともがいている He is struggling to *get out of* the difficulty.

だっしょく【脱色】decoloration. ¶〜する decolorize.
—剤 a decolorer.

たつじん【達人】a master (*of*); an expert (*at; in*); (哲人) a great (≒ master) mind.
¶彼は剣道の〜だ He is *an expert in* (≒ *at*) Japanese fencing.

だっすい【脱水】dehydration. ¶〜する dehydrate.
—機(遠心力を利用した) a spin-drier.

たっ·する【達する】**1**〘着く〙reach. ¶やがて頂上に〜した We *got to* the top of the mountain before long.

2〖数量が〗amount to. ¶ 集まった金は10万円にも～している The money collected *amounts to* as much as a hundred thousand yen.

この書庫の本は10,000冊に達した The books in this library *amounted to* ten thousand in number.

3〖目的を〗attain. ¶ 目的を～するようできるだけ努力しなさい Try to do your best in *attaining* your object.

彼は本望を～していかにも満足そうだった *Having attained* his long-cherished object, he seemed much satisfied.

4〖力量が〗¶ 彼の弁舌ぶりは名人の域に～している He *has attained* super skill in eloquence.

5〖年齢が〗¶ 彼は成年に～した He *came of age.*

だっ·する【脱する】¶ 彼は窮地を～した He *escaped from* the difficulty. / He *got out of* the difficulty. インドは1950年にイギリスの支配を～した India *freed herself from* Britain in 1950.

たつせ【立つ瀬】¶ きみに反対されては, ぼくは～がない Your opposition *puts* me *in a tight spot.* / Your opposition will *leave* me *quite helpless.*

たっせい【達成】achievement; attainment. ¶ 彼は目的を～した He *attained* (≒ *accomplished; realized*) his purpose.

だつぜい【脱税】tax evasion. ¶ 彼は所得税を～した He *dodged* (≒ *evaded*) his income *tax.*

—者 an tax dodger; a tax evader. **—品** smuggled goods. **—額** the amount of the tax evasion.

だっせん【脱線】(列車の) derailment; (話の筋の) digression. ¶ 電車が～した The train *left* (≒ *ran off*) *the rails.* / The train *was derailed.* 話が～した The talk *digressed from the subject.* / The talk *got sidetracked.*

だっそ【脱疽】〖医学〗gangrene.

だっそう【脱走】escape; desertion. ¶ 彼は兵営を～した He *escaped* (≒ *ran away; deserted*) from the camp.

—者 a runaway; a deserter. **—兵** a deserter.

だつぞく【脱俗】¶ 彼の書には～的な気風がある His handwriting shows that there is something *unworldly* about him.

たった【唯】only; merely; but; just. ¶ 彼は～今帰って行ったところだ He has *just* gone home. / He went home *just now.* (just now は現在完了とともには使わない). 彼は～500円しかくれなかった He gave me *only* (≒ *merely; no more than*) five hundred yen. 彼は～ひとりで山へ出かけた He went up the mountain *all alone* (≒ *by himself*).

だったい【脱退】withdrawal; secession. ¶ 彼は組合を～した He *withdrew from* the union. 日本は国際連盟から～した Japan *left* (≒ *seceded from*) the League of Nations.

タッチ **1**〖野球·競技〗a touch. ¶ キャッチャーは走者に～した The catcher *touched* the runner.

ランナーは2塁寸前で～アウトになった The runner *was touched out* just before the second base.

彼は～の差で2位になった He missed being first *by a fraction.*

2〖趣き〗a touch. ¶ この絵は生き生きした～で描いてある This picture is painted with *a* vivid *touch.*

彼女はやわらかい～でピアノをひく She plays the piano with *a* delicate *touch.*

3〖関係する〗¶ 私はその問題に～していません I have nothing to do with the matter.

だっちょう【脱腸】〖医学〗rupture; hernia. ¶ ～になる be affected with *hernia.*

—帯 a truss.

たって【達て】¶ ～会いたいとおっしゃるのなら, お目にかかりましょう I will see you if you *insist.* ～の望みというのでその絵を彼に譲った I gave up the picture to him in answer to his *earnest* request.

-たって ¶ そんなこと言っ～ぼくは知らないよ Don't blame me. That isn't my fault. / Don't blame me. I have nothing to do with it.

だって **1**〖でさえ·でも〗¶ サル～木から落ちることもある *Even* a monkey may fall from a tree.

私～そのくらいは知っている *Even* I know that much.

彼～その点では私と同じだ He is not different from me in that respect.

いくら寝ぼう～明日の朝は早く起きてください *Though* you *may* be a late riser, be sure to get up early tomorrow morning.

雨～出かけると彼は言っている He says he would go *even if* it rained.

「私は英作文はきらいだ」「私～きらいだ」 "I dislike English composition." "*So* do I."

「ぼくは疲れてはいない」「私～疲れてはいない」 "I am not tired." "*Neither* am I."

2〖接続詞として〗¶「よく間に合ったね」「～走り通したんだ」 "You were in time, weren't you?" "*Certainly, but* I ran all the way."

「どうして起きないんだ」「～眠いんだもの」 "Why don't you get up?" "*Because* I am sleepy."

だっとう【脱党】withdrawal from a party; secession. ¶ ～する leave a party; break away from *one's* political party.

—者 a seceder. **—届** a written report of *one's* secession from the party.

たづな【手綱】a bridle; the reins. ¶ 私は馬の～を引いて歩調をゆるめさせていた I *was reining in* my horse. 彼女は～を引いて馬を止めた She *reined up* her horse. 彼は馬の～をとった He held his horse by *the bridle.* 彼は～をゆるめた He slackened *the reins.* / He *gave* the horse *the reins.*

たつのおとしご【竜の落とし子】〖動物〗a seahorse.

だっぴ【脱皮】(へび·昆虫などの) ecdysis. ¶ 蚕は

～するごとに大きくなる A silkworm grows every time it *casts off the skin.*

たっぴつ【達筆】a good hand. ¶ 彼は～だ He *writes a good hand.* その手紙は～な女文字で書かれていた The letter was written in *a delicate* female *hand.*

タップダンス a tap dance. ¶ ～を踊る tap-dance.

たっぷり fully. ¶ まだ時間は～ある We have *plenty of* time left. 彼は～食べてあとはぐっすり眠る He *eats his fill* and then sleeps soundly. 彼はこの小説を書くのに～2年かかった This novel took him a *full* two years. 歩いて～2時間かかった It was a *good* two hours' walk. そこまでバスで～5時間かかる It takes *fully* five hours to reach there by bus.

だっぷん【脱糞】evacuation ; (糞) excrement. ¶ ～する empty *one's* bowels.

だつぼう【脱帽】¶ ～する take off *one's* hat ; raise *one's* hat. 彼は～しておじぎをした He *took off his hat* and bowed. / He bowed *in bareheaded respect.* ～! (号令) Hats off !

たつまき【竜巻き】(陸上の) a sandpillar ; (海上の) a waterspout ; (一般) a windspout ; tornado ; a whirlwind ; a cyclone.

¶ 見る見る海面に～がおこって近づいてきた Soon *a cyclone* appeared on the sea, moving toward us.

だつもう【脱毛】¶ ～する Hair *falls out* (≒ *falls off*).

—症 alopecia. 円形**—症** alopecia areata.

だつらく【脱落】(離脱) defection ; (抜け落ちる) falling off ; (脱漏) an omission.

¶ 彼はマラソンで～した He *dropped away* (≒ *gave up*) in a marathon race. 文中に～がある There are *omissions* in the sentences.

たて【縦】length. ¶ この箱は～が1メートルある This box measures a meter in *length.* ～の線を3本引く draw three *vertical* lines. この絵は～が25センチ, 横が50センチある This picture is 25 centimeters *long* (≒ *in length*) and 50 centimeters wide (≒ in width). カードを～に並べる arrange cards *lengthwise.*

たて【盾・楯】a shield ; (小型で円形の) a buckler. ¶ 立ち木を～にとって防戦した We fought in defense, using trees as *shields.* 彼は病気を～によくさぼる He slacks off in his work *on the plea of* illness.

たて【殺陣】a sword battle.

—師 a man who teaches actors how to fight with swords.

-たて【-立て】¶ ペンキ塗り～(掲示) 米 Wet Paint; 英 Fresh Paint. 大学出～の青年 a young man *fresh from* college. 焼き～のパン bread *hot from the oven.* 生み～の卵 a *newly-laid* egg. 洗い～のワイシャツ a *freshly-washed* shirt. 買い～の万年筆 a *brand-new* pen.

たで【蓼】〔植物〕a smartweed ; a knotweed.

¶ ～食う虫も好き好き(諺) *There is no accounting for taste*[*s*]. / *Every man to his taste.* / *Tastes differ.*

だて【伊達】dandyism ; show. ¶ 彼女は～にめがねをかける She wears glasses *for show.* 私はこの仕事を～やすいきょうでしているのではない I am not doing this job *only for fun.*

—男 a dandy ; a gallant ; a fop.

-だて【-立て】¶ 要らざる忠義～ an uncalled-for show of loyalty. 4頭～の馬車 a carriage and four. きみに何もかくし～していない I keep nothing secret from you. ささいな誤りをとがめ～するな Don't carp at minor errors. 2本～の映画を見に行った I went to the *double bill* movies.

-だて【-建て】¶ 8階～のビル an *eight-storied* building.

たてあな【縦穴・竪穴】a pit.

たてあみ【立て網・建て網】a drag-net.

たていた【立て板】¶ 彼は～に水を流すように説明した He explained with great fluency.

たていと【縦糸】warp ; the threads which run lengthwise.

たてうり【建て売り】¶ ～する sell a ready-built house.

—住宅 a ready-built house.

たてかえ【立て替え】payment for another.

¶ きみに1,000円～になっている There is a thousand yen to your debit.

—金 an advance.

たてか・える【立て替える】¶ すみませんが1,000円～えてくださいませんか Excuse me, but won't you *pay* a thousand yen *for* me ? / Excuse me, but won't you *accommodate* me *with* [a loan of] a thousand yen ? 彼にタクシー代を～えた I *lent* him his taxi fee.

たてか・える【建て替える】¶ 家を～えた I *have rebuilt* a house.

たてがき【縦書き】vertical writing. ¶ 日本語はふつう～にする We, in general, *write* Japanese *in vertical columns.*

たてかけ【建てかけ】¶ ～の家 a *partially built* house.

たてか・ける【立て掛ける】¶ はしごをへいに～ける *place* (≒ *rest*) a ladder *against* the wall.

たてがみ【鬣】a mane.

たてかんばん【立て看板】a standing signboard ; a billboard.

たてぐ【建具】furnishings ; fittings. ¶ ～付きの家 a *furnished* house. 部屋に～を備える *furnish* a room.

—屋 a joiner.

たてぐみ【縦組み】vertical typesetting.

たてこう【立て坑・縦坑・竪坑】a shaft.

たてごと【竪琴】a harp.

たてこ・む【立て込む】(混雑する) be crowded ; (忙しい) be busy. ¶ 展覧会場は～んでいる The exhibition-hall *is quite crowded.* 仕事が～んでたいへん忙しい I *am very busy with* a lot of work to do.

たてこ・もる【立て籠もる】¶ 敵は城に～っている The enemy *are entrenched in* a castle.

たてじく【縦軸】(機械の) a spindle ; (グラフの) a column ; a vertical line.

たてじま【縦縞】vertical stripes. ¶ ～の服 *striped* clothes.

たてつ・く【盾突く】¶ 彼は私によく～く He often

rebels (≒ *sets himself*) *against* me.

たてつけ【立て付け】¶この戸は～が悪い This door doesn't work well.

たてつづけ【立て続け】¶彼女はさっきから～にしゃべっている She's been talking *at a stretch.* 水を3杯～に飲んだ I took three glasses of water *in quick succession.* ジャイアンツは～に3度勝った The Giants won three games *in succession.*

たてつぼ【建坪】floor space. ¶～100平方メートルの家を買った I bought a house with 100 square meters of *floor space.* この家は～30坪だ This house has a *floor space* of 30 *tsubo* in all.

たてとお·す【立て通す】¶彼はあくまで自説を～した He *stuck to* his own view *to the last.* 彼は主人に義理を～した He *remained loyal to* his master.

たてなお·す【立て直す·建て直す】¶計画を～した We made a plan anew. 家を～す I'll *have* the house *rebuilt.* 財政を～した We *rebuilt* the national economy.

たてね【建値】official quotations.

たてひざ【立て膝】¶～をする sit with *one's* knee drawn up.

たてふだ【立て札】a notice board. ¶「立ち入り禁止」の～を立てる put up *a notice board* of "Keep off."

たてまえ【建て前·立て前】(建築の) the completion of framework (*of* a house); (方針) a principle; a rule.

¶私は10時に寝るのを～にしている I *make it a rule to* go to bed at ten.

たてまし【建て増し】an extension〔of a building〕. ¶子ども部屋を～した We *had* the children's room *enlarged.* 現在私の家は～中です *An addition* is being made *to* my house.

たてまつ·る【奉る】¶彼を会長に～っておこう Let's *honor* him as the president.

たてもの【建物】a building; a structure; (広壮な) an edifice. ¶この教会はルネサンス式～のひとつだ This church is a specimen of the Renaissance *architecture.*

たてやくしゃ【立て役者】(役割) a leading man; (指導者) a leader; (舞台での) a leading actor; a star.

¶彼は菊五郎劇団の～だ He is the *leading actor* of the Kikugoro theatrical troupe. 彼はこの会の～だ He is playing *a leading part* in this meeting.

たてよこ【縦横】length and breadth. ¶～十文字に crosswise; lengthwise and breadthwise.

-だてら ¶彼女は女～に酒を飲み歩く *Unbecoming for* (≒ *to*) *a woman,* she has taken to drinking. / *Woman though* (≒ *as*) *she is,* she has taken to drinking.

た·てる【立てる·建てる】 **1**〖建てる·直立させる〗¶家を～てる *build* a house.

自分の家を～てる *have one's* house *built*; *build one's* house. (build *one's* house のほうが口語的).

銅像を～てる *erect* (≒ *place*) a statue.

門に旗を～てる *display* a flag at the gate.

見やすい所に道路標識を～てる *post* a road sign in a prominent place.

看板を～てる *put up* a signboard.

卵を～てる *put* an egg *on end.*

2〖会社·学校などを〗¶孤児院を～てる *establish* an orphanage.

貿易会社を～てる *organize* a trade company.

3〖計画を〗¶夏休みの計画を～てる *make* a plan for the summer vacation.

4〖作り上げる〗¶一派を～てる *found* a school.

ひげを～てる *grow* a mustache.

これを説明する理論を～てるのは難しい It is difficult to *set up* a theory explaining this.

彼は異説を～てた He *developed* a different view.

5〖誓い·志を〗¶彼は志を～てて上京した He went〔up〕to Tokyo *with* an ambition.

彼は一生を教育にささげようと誓いを～てた He *has made a vow to* devote his life to education.

6〖筋道を〗¶ちゃんと順序を～てて仕事をする do *one's* work *in a correct order.*

筋道を～てて話す speak *logically.*

7〖顔や義理を〗¶先輩を～ててやれ *Pay due respect* to your seniors.

彼の顔も～ててやれ *Save* his face.

親は親として～てなさい Your parents should be given due respect.

ぼくは彼には義理を～てているつもりだ I believe that I *have* always *been true to* him.

8〖ある地位につかせる〗¶候補者に彼を～てた We *nominated* him as a candidate.

そういうことはなかに人を～てて交渉するものだ Such a matter should be negotiated indirectly *through* a third person.

彼を使者に～てよう Let's *send* him as a messenger.

9〖上方へあがらせる〗¶材木は黒煙を～てて燃えた The heap of lumber burned, *sending up* black smoke in the air.

湯げを～てて部屋の乾燥を防ぐ check the dryness of a room *with steam.*

車はほこりを～てて走りすぎた The car *raised* dust when it passed.

モーターボートが波を～てて近づいてきた A motorboat was coming near, *raising* (≒ *making*) waves.

10〖広める〗¶変なうわさを～ててくれるな Stop such an indecent rumor.

11〖音を発する〗¶声を～てるな Don't *raise* your voice!

あまり大きな音を～てると赤ん坊が目を覚ます If you *make* too much *noise,* you will wake up the baby.

12〖その他〗¶腹を～てる get angry.

ふろを～てる *heat* the bath.

た·てる【点てる】¶(茶道で) 茶を～てる conduct tea ceremony.

た·てる【閉てる】¶雨戸を～てる *close* the sliding doors.

た

だてん【打点】〚野球〛run〔s〕batted in (略して r.b.i.; RBI); a run. ¶ 彼は1試合に3～をあげた He drove in three *runs* in a game.
—王 the RBI winner.

だでん【打電】¶ 彼に～した We *telegraphed* 〔*to*〕 him. アメリカの友人に誕生日の祝いを～した I *cabled* birthday greetings to my friend in the U. S. A.

だとう【打倒】overthrow. ¶ 現在の政府を～すべきだ We must *overthrow* the present government. 彼の権威主義を～すべきだ We should *put an end to* his authoritarianism.

だとう【妥当】¶ ～な意見 a *right* (≒ *valid*) opinion. ～な経営方針 *proper* management policy. それは～な方法ではない It's not an *appropriate* measure.
—性 propriety; soundness; pertinence; validity.

た

たどうし【他動詞】〚文法〛a transitive verb.

たとえ【譬・喩】(ことわざ) a proverb; (直ゆ) a simile; (暗ゆ) a metaphor. ¶「時は金」という～がある *A proverb* says that "Time is money." ～にもあるように,大は小を兼ねるものだ As the *proverb* says, the greater serves for the lesser. ～を引いてその理論を説明してください Please explain the theory by *example*.

たとえ【仮令・縦令】¶ ～雨が降っても私は出かける *Even if* it rains, I will go out. ～何事が起こっても,私の決心は変わらない *Whatever* may happen, I will not change my mind. ～やってくるにしても8時過ぎになるだろう He will come after eight, *if* he *ever* comes. ～どんなに頭がよくとも,この問題は解けまい *No matter how* clever he may be, he will not be able to solve this problem. 彼の言うことは～全部ではないにしても半分は本当だ Half, *if not all*, of what he says is true. ～半年なにも食べなくともこの動物は死なない *Even though* this animal eats nothing for half a year, it won't die.

たとえば【例えば】for instance; for example. ¶ 体に害のあるもの,～酒,たばこなどはやめなさい Stop doing what is not good for the health, *for instance*, drinking and smoking. 大工道具を持っていますか,～金づち,のこぎり,かんななど Do you have carpenter's tools, *such as* a hammer, a saw and a plane?

たと・える【例える・譬える・喩える】¶ ～えて言うと so to speak; metaphorically speaking. われわれはしばしば美人の美しさを花に～える We often *compare* the beauty of a charming lady *to* a flower. 人生は航海に～えられる Life is to *be compared to* a voyage. その美しさはなににも～えようがない The beauty *is beyond description*. / The beauty *beggars description*.

たどく【多読】extensive reading. ¶ ～する read extensively.

たとする【多とする】¶ 彼の援助を～ We *appreciate* (≒ *are grateful for*) his assistance.

たどたどし・い【辿辿しい】¶ きみのは～い読み方だ You read *with difficulty*. 彼は～く歩いている He is walking with an *unsteady* gait.

たどりつ・く【辿り着く】¶ やっと目的地に～いた At last I *found my way to* my destination. やっと駅に～いた We *arrived at* the station at last.

たどりよみ【辿り読み】¶ 私の5歳の子が本を～する My five-year-old child can *spell out* a book. / My five-year old child *reads* a book *letter by letter*.

たど・る【辿る】¶ 足跡を～る *trace* footsteps. 川を上流の方に～って歩く *follow* a river up to its source.

たどん【炭団】a charcoal-ball.

たな【棚】a shelf; (網状の) a rack; (ブドウなどの) a trellis; (暖炉の上の) a mantelpiece.
¶ ～をつる make *a shelf*; fix *a shelf* (*to* the wall). 彼は自分のことを～に上げる He is unmindful of his own shortcomings. / He is wilfully ignoring his own faults. ～からぼたもちだ It's a piece of good luck. / It's a windfall.
大陸— a continental shelf.

たなあげ【棚上げ】¶ 彼らはその議題をしばらく～にした They *shelved* the bill for the time being. 彼らは会長を～にした They *put* the president *into pigeonhole*.

たなおろし【棚卸・店卸】**1**〚在庫調べ〛stocktaking. ¶ 昨夜～をした We *took stock* last night. / We *made an inventory of the articles in stock* last night.
～のため本日休業 Closed for *stocktaking* today.
2〚あらさがし〛¶ 彼らはよってたかって彼女を～した They, together, *found fault with* her. / They all *picked holes in* her character.

たなこ【店子】a tenant.

たなご【鱮】〚魚類〛Acheilognathus morikoae.

たなごころ【掌】the palm. ¶ ～を指すように明白なことだ It is as clear as day. ～を返すように態度を変える assume a completely changed attitude.

たなざらえ【棚浚え】clearance. ¶ ～の大売り出しをする hold a *clearance* sale.

たなざらし【店晒し】¶ あの品は半年も～になっている The goods *have lain on the shelf unsold* for half a year. ～の本 *shop-worn* (≒ *shop-soiled*) books.

たなばた【七夕】(星) the Weaver; Vega; (7月7日) the seventh of July.
—祭り the Festival of the Weaver Star.

たなび・く【棚引く】¶ 春には山野にかすみが～く The mist *lies* (≒ *hangs*) *over* hills and fields in spring. 汽船の煙が～いた The smoke *trailed* from the ship. / The ship left a trail of smoke behind it.

たなぼた【棚牡丹】a windfall. ¶ ～を期待してもだめだ It is no use expecting *a windfall* (≒ *a godsend*). 宝くじが当たったとはまさに～だ It's quite *a piece of good luck* that you should have won a prize in the public lottery.

たなん【多難】¶ それは～な時代であった It was an

age *full of troubles.*

たに【谷】 a valley ; (峡谷) a ravine ; a glen ; (深い峡谷) a canyon ; (詩語) a vale ; a dale. ¶ 彼は山を越え～を越えて歩きつづけた He walked on, up hill and down *dale.* 諺で, 虎はその子を千仭(せんじん)の～に突き落とすと言われている It is proverbially said that the tiger throws its young down the bottomless *ravine.* 気圧の～が通り過ぎてしまったからあすは天気がいいだろう The *trough* has passed away, so it will be fine tomorrow.

だに【壁蝨】 a 〔dog〕 tick. ¶ この犬には～がたかっている This dog is infested with *ticks.* 彼は町の～だ He is *a street vermin.*

たにあい【谷間】 a valley ; a ravine. ¶ ～の涼しい所で休んだ We had a rest in the cool of the *valley.* 急流が～を流れている A rapid stream runs in the *ravine.*

たにかぜ【谷風】 ¶ ひやりとする～がとても快い感じだった *A* cool *valley wind* was very refreshing.

たにがわ【谷川】 a mountain stream. ¶ われわれは～に沿って登っていった We went up along the *mountain stream.* 雨が降って～の水がふえた The rainfall caused the *mountain stream* to rise. ～が岩の上を激しく流れていた The *mountain torrent* was dashing over the rocks.

たにし【田螺】〔貝類〕 a pond (≒ mud) snail.

たにそこ【谷底】 the bottom of a ravine. ¶ 彼は車ごと～へ転落した He fell into *the bottom of a ravine* car and all.

たにま【谷間】 a valley. ¶ それは私の暗い青春の～であった It was *a gloomy moment* of my youthful days. 社会の～に住む人々は年々減少している The inhabitants of *the slum quarters* are decreasing year by year.

たにん【他人】 others ; (未知の人) a stranger. ¶ ～をあてにしすぎるな Never rely too much upon *others.* 彼女は私を～扱いした She treated me as *a stranger.* 彼女はあかの～だ She is *an utter stranger* to me. 彼は絶対に～を信じない He does not trust *others* at all. ～が入ったため家庭はめちゃめちゃになった Home life was spoilt with *a stranger* sharing it. これは～の空似だ It is *an accidental resemblance.* この家はほどなく～の手に渡るだろう This house will soon *fall into a stranger's hands.*

—行儀 ¶ 彼は～行儀にふるまう He *stands on formality.*

たにんずう【多人数】 a great (≒ good) many people ; a great number of persons. ¶ ～で彼らは会場に繰り込んできた They rushed into the hall *in great numbers.* 私は～の家族を養わねばならない I have a *large* family to support.

たぬき【狸】〔動物〕 a racoon dog ; a badger. ¶ 取らぬ～の皮算用 (諺) *Don't count the chickens before they are hatched.*

—寝入り ¶ ～寝入りをする pretend to be asleep. **—じじい** ¶ 家康は～じじいと呼ばれた Ieyasu was called *a foxy* (≒ *cunning*) *old man.*

たね【種】 1 〘種子〙 a stone ; a seed. ¶ 桃の～ *a stone* (≒ *a pit*) of a peach.
ナシの～ *a seed* of a pear.
小麦の～ *a grain* (≒ *a kernel*) of wheat.
～なしスイカ a *seedless* watermelon.
ホウレン草の～をまく sow spinach *seeds.*
麦の～をまく *sow* 〔the field〕 with wheat.
この植物は～から育てた This plant was grown from *seed.*
このミカンは～が多い This orange *is seedy.*
2 〘原因・材料〙 〔a〕 cause ; a source. ¶ 不平の～ the *cause* of complaint.
話の～にパンダを見に行きます I am going to have a look at a panda *to have a topic of conversation.*
ふぐを食べてみるのも話の～だ To eat globefish will be an adventure for me.
久しぶりに会ったので話の～が尽きなかった We *had no end of talk,* because we met each other after a long separation. (やや形式ばった形).
子どものことが私の苦労の～だ My child is *a source* of anxiety with me.
なかなか悩みの～が尽きず困る I am troubled, because all kinds of things to make me worry keep coming up.
それはけんかの～になりかねない I'm afraid it leads to *a bone* of contention.
その醜聞を～に劇が書かれた The scandal was woven into the play.
思い出すのも涙の～ The thought brings the tears into my eyes.
夫の帰宅が遅いのが彼女の不平の～だ Her husband's coming home late at night is the *seed* of her discontent.
自分でまいた～は自分で刈り取らねばならぬ You must reap what you *have sown.*
まかぬ～は生えぬ (諺) One must *sow* before one can reap.
3 〘秘密〙 a secret ; a trick. ¶ 手品の～を明かす show how the *trick* is done.

たねあかし【種明かし】 ¶ 彼は手品の～をした He *revealed his magic tricks.* うまくいった～をしよう I will *tell* you *the secret* of the success. その秘密の～をしてください Please *disclose* (≒ *reveal ; tell*) the secret. (disclose は形式ばった語).

たねあぶら【種油】 seed oil ; vegetable oil.

たねいも【種芋】 seed potatoes ; taroes.

たねうし【種牛】 a bull.

たねうま【種馬】 a stud-horse ; a breeding horse ; a 〔breeding〕 stallion.

たねぎれ【種切れ】 ¶ これで話は～だ Now I *have run short of* topics of conversation. もう私のやることが～になった I *have nothing more* to do next. 彼はいろいろな雑誌に寄稿するのでやがて～になるだろう He writes for so many magazines that he will *have written himself out* before long.

たねつけ【種付け】 mating. ¶ 競走馬の～の季節である This is the time of the year when they *mate* race horses.

たねほん【種本】 ¶ 彼の話の～はこれだ This is

the secret source of his story. これが私の講義の～だ This is *the source book* of my lecture.

たねまき【種蒔き】 sowing; seeding. ¶ 人々は早春に～する People *sow seed* in the soil in early spring.

―時 the seed-time.

たねもの【種物】 ¶ そばの～ a buckwheat noodle dish with other ingredients. 氷の～ shaved ice with sugar and fruit juice.

たねもみ【種籾】 seed-rice.

たねん【多年】 ¶ 彼は英文学を～研究した He studied English literature *for many years* (≒ *for a number of years*). 彼は～の努力の後成功した He succeeded after *many years'* hard labor. 彼らは～の知己だ They are friends *of many years' standing.* 彼は～の希望を実現した He realized a *long-cherished* desire.

―生 ¶ ～生の植物 a *perennial* plant.

た

-だの ¶ 行く～行かない～と彼女はわからないことを言う It is unreasonable of her *now* to say to go *and now* not to go. 赤～白～, さまざまな花が咲いている Various flowers, red, white *and so forth,* are in bloom.

たのし·い【楽しい】 happy. ¶ テニスは～い It *is pleasant* to play tennis. なんと～い一日だったろう What a *happy* day it was! ～い時代もあった We had a *good* time. 軽井沢で1週間を～く過ごした I spent a week *happily* at Karuizawa. 子どもたちは～く遊んでいる The children *are enjoying themselves.* ～いときもあれば苦しいときもある We have bad times as well as *good* times.

たのしげ【楽しげ】 ¶ みんな～に歌っている They are all singing *merrily* (≒ *joyously*). 部屋から～な笑い声が聞こえてきた A *happy* laughter came out of the room.

たのしさ【楽しさ】 ¶ ～と苦しさは交互にやってくる *Happiness* and suffering come to us by turns. 読書の～は比較するものがない Nothing can be compared with the *pleasure* of reading. 彼は人生の～を知らずに死んだ He died without knowing the *charm* of life. 読書の～は彼にはわからない He cannot find the *comfort* in reading.

たのしま·せる【楽しませる】 ¶ 秋には紅葉が日光を訪れる人の目を～せる Scarlet-tinged leaves *delight* the eyes of those who come to Nikko in autumn. 彼の話は聴衆を大いに～せた His story *amused* the audience so much. 彼は音楽で私を～せてくれた He *entertained* me with music.

たのしみ【楽しみ】 (快楽) [a] pleasure; (娯楽) amusement; (趣味) a hobby. ¶ 読書は私にとって～の一つだ Reading is *a pleasure* for me. カメラが私の唯一の～だ Taking photos is my only *hobby.* この仕事は私には義務でなく～だ This work is *a pleasure,* not a duty for me. 彼は～に小説を書いている He is writing novels *for pleasure.* 私たちは夏休みを～にしている We *are looking forward to* the summer vacation. あの子の将来が～だ That child *is full of promise.*

たのし·む【楽しむ】 ¶ 子どもたちは生活を～んでいる The children *are enjoying themselves.* 彼らはさわやかな秋の一日を～んでいた They *were enjoying* a refreshing autumn day. 音楽はひとりで～むのがよい Music *is* best *enjoyed* by oneself. 日曜日の午後をフォークダンスで～んだ We *enjoyed* the Sunday afternoon folk-dancing. 少女は犬とたわむれて～んでいた The girl *was amusing herself* by playing with a dog.

たのし·める【楽しめる】 ¶ 週刊誌一冊でけっこう半日～める A copy of a weekly is enough to *amuse* (≒ *entertain*) me half a day. あの遊園地は大人でも～める Even grown-up people *amuse themselves* in that recreation ground. テニスは老いも若きも～める遊びだ Tennis is a game *enjoyed* by young and old alike.

だのに ¶ 力の限り走った. ～列車に間に合わなかった I ran as fast as possible, *but* couldn't catch the train. くどいほど言っておいた. ～彼は忘れてきた I told him over and over again, *and yet* he left it behind.

たのみ【頼み】 a request. ¶ 彼はどうしても私の～を聞いてくれない He won't grant my *request.* あなたに～があるのですが I *have a favor to ask of* you. ひとつ私の～を聞いてください Would you *do* me *a favor*? この男は私が困ったときの最大の～だ This man is my best friend when I am in trouble. 彼はあまりにも自分の能力を～にしすぎている He *relies* too much *on* his ability. あの時あのナイフが私の～の綱だった That knife was my *only hope* then. もはや～の綱は切れた Now my *only hope* is gone. なんという～になる男だ What a *dependable* fellow he is! いざという時に～になる友こそ真の友だ *A friend in need* is a friend indeed. 彼はとても～にならない He is not to *be trusted* at all. このごろの天気予報はちっとも～にならない The weather forecast these days is not to *be relied upon* at all. 彼には金だけが～だ To him money is *everything.*

―がい ¶ 彼は～がいがある He is *reliable.*

たの·む【頼む】 1 〖依頼する·注文する〗 ask.

¶ 彼にすぐ来てくれと～んだ I *asked* him to come over at once.

彼に彼女を経済的に助けてやってくれと～んだ I *asked* him to help her financially.

今度の選挙にはぜひ～むよ Please *support* me in the coming election.

彼に～む気はしない I don't feel like *asking* any *favors of* him.

彼に～まれて娘の就職口を捜してやった *At his request* I found a job for his daughter.

ぼくは彼に応援を～んだ I *asked* him to back me up. / (応援演説を) I *asked* him to speak for me.

そんなことを人に～むことはない That is something you can do on your own.

きみでなければだめだ. ぜひ～む Only you can do it. Please do it for me.

彼は〜まれればいやとは言えぬたちだ He is the kind of person who can never turn anyone down.
〜むから相談に乗ってくれ Please give me your advice [on this].
〜まないのにそれをかってに送ってきた They sent it to me without *being asked*.
2 〖委託する〗 leave. ¶ 彼からこの品を〜まれてきた *At his request* I've brought this to you. (文語体) / He *asked* me to give this to you.
彼からあなたに伝言を〜まれた I have brought a message from him for you.
この仕事はだれに〜もうか Who (≒ Whom) shall we *ask* to do this?
ぼくが死んだらこの事業はきみに〜む I will *leave* this business *with* you after I'm gone. / I will *charge* you *with* this business after my death.
あとのことは万事〜む I would like to *leave* everything *to* you.
娘の教育はきみに〜む I would like to *place* my daughter's education *in your hands*.
留守中赤ん坊をよろしくお〜みします Please take care of my baby while I'm away.
3 〖頼りにする〗 depend on. ¶ 彼女は一家の柱と〜む夫に死なれた She lost her husband who had supported the entire family. / She lost her husband on whom the family *had depended* for everything.
多勢の助けを〜むのはひきょうだ It is not fair to get so many people to help you.
彼は自分の力だけを〜んでいる He is full of confidence. / He *relies* entirely *on* his own ability. / He doesn't *ask* anyone else for help.
彼は〜むに足る人物だ He is a *reliable* person. / He is a man you can *rely on* (≒ *upon*).
4 〖雇う・予約〗 get; call. ¶ ハイヤーを〜んでください *Get* (≒ *Call*) me a taxi, please.
お子さんに家庭教師を〜んであげよう I will *get* a tutor for your child.
至急医者を〜んでください Please *call* a doctor at once.
弁護士を〜んだほうがいい It would be better for you to *see* a lawyer (≒ *seek* legal advice).
飛行機の席は〜んでおいた I'*ve made a reservation* [*for* a seat] on the plane for you. / I'*ve made a* plane *reservation for* you.

たのもし・い 【頼もしい】 (有望な) promising; (頼みになる) reliable. ¶ 彼はなんて〜い少年だろう What *a promising* (≒ *hopeful*) boy he is! 利口な男の子が3人いるなんて, 〜いですね You have three bright sons! You can *expect* (≒ *hope*) *much from* them, can't you? 彼は〜い青年だ (頼みになる) He is a *reliable* young man. 現代の青年は〜い The young people today are to *be depended upon*. 彼は末〜い投手だ He has a great future as a pitcher.

たば 【束】 ¶ わら1〜 *a bundle* of straw. 花1〜 *a bunch* (≒ *a bouquet*) of flowers. まき1〜 *a fagot* of firewood. 書類1〜 *a sheaf* of papers. 彼は掘ったニンジンをみな〜にした He *bundled* all the carrots he had dug out of the earth. 〜になってかかってこい Come on, all of you *in a bunch*. / Come on *all at a time*.

だは 【打破】 ¶ 旧習 (現状) を〜する *do away with* the old practices (the existing state of things); *break down* the old practices (the existing state of things).

だば 【駄馬】 a draught horse; a pack horse; (下等な馬) a jade; a hack.

たばか・る 【謀る】 cheat. ¶ 人を〜るようなことはするな Never try to *cheat* others. 彼にうまく〜られた I *was* fairly *taken in* by him. / I *fell an easy victim to his trick*.

たばこ 【煙草】 (紙巻き) a cigarette; (葉巻き) a cigar; (パイプ用の) tobacco (tobacco はたばこ各種を含むこともある).
¶ 〜1箱 a pack of *cigarettes*. 〜の灰を床に落とさないよう気をつけなさい Be careful not to drop *cigarette* ash onto the floor. 彼は〜が好きだ He is fond of *smoking*. 彼は日に20本〜を吸う He *smokes* twenty *cigarettes* a day. このライターで〜に火をつけなさい Please use this lighter. 〜の火を貸してくれませんか Won't you please give me *a light*? 〜をやめて5年になる It is five years since I quit (≒ gave up) *smoking*. 彼はうまそうに〜を吹かしていた He was enjoying *smoking*. 彼はいつ見ても〜を吹かしている He is always puffing at *a cigarette*. 〜をすすめられた I was offered *a cigarette*. この部屋では〜はご遠慮ください Please refrain from *smoking* in this room.
—盆 a tobacco tray. **—屋** (人) a tobacconist; (店) a tobacconist's [shop].

たはた 【田畑】 a farm; fields. ¶ 〜を耕す cultivate *the fields*.

たはつ 【多発】 ¶ ここは事故〜の場所だ This is a place where accidents *occur frequently*.

たばね 【束ね】 ¶ 彼が町の〜をしている He *governs* the town. 彼はうまく一家の〜をしている He *manages* (≒ *controls*; *directs*) his household successfully.

たば・ねる 【束ねる】 ¶ 刈りとった稲を〜ねる *bundle* the rice cut down. 古新聞を〜ねる *tie up* the old papers *in a bundle*. 彼女はじょうずに髪を〜ねた She *bundled* her hair well.

たび 【旅】 a trip; a journey; an excursion (travels はふつう遠い旅行で, 複数形が多い. excursion は遠足のような団体旅行. expedition は調査・探検などの旅行. tour は視察・観光などの旅行. trip は商用または遊びの旅行. journey は長い旅で文語的. voyage は海または空の長い旅).
¶ 彼は月に1回〜をする He goes on *a trip* once a month. 彼は長い〜に出た He started on *a* long *trip*. 彼はあす〜から帰ってくる He is back from his *travels* tomorrow. あなたは船の〜と汽車の〜とどちらが好きですか Which do you like better, *traveling* by sea or *traveling* by land? 彼は世界一周の〜に出た He set off on *a trip* round the world. 四国

への～は快適だった The *trip* to Shikoku was comfortable for me. 彼は南米の～を計画中だ He is planning *a trip* to South America. 仕事がかたづいたから二,三日～に出るつもりだ Since I have done with my work, I intend to go on a few days' *trip*. 運悪く彼は～の空で病気になった Unfortunately he fell sick *while he was away from home*. ～は道づれ(諺) Good company makes the road shorter. ～の恥はかきすて(諺) Once over the borders, one may do anything. かわいい子には～をさせよ(諺) *Spare the rod and spoil the child.*

—芸人 a strolling player. **—**商人 a pedlar.

たび【度】¶ この～はおめでとう Congratulations! ひと～始めたら最後まで続けなければならぬ *Once* you begin you must continue to the last. われわれは会う～にその問題について議論した We discussed it *every time* (≒ *whenever*) we met.

たび【足袋】 *tabi*〔-socks〕; Japanese style socks. ¶ ～をはく put on *one's tabi*〔-socks〕.

—屋 a tabi〔-socks〕 store.

だび【荼毗】 cremation. ¶ 彼らは彼の死体を～に付した They *cremated* his remains. / They *reduced* his body *to ashes*.

たびかさな·る【度重なる】 ¶ ～る事故のため警官が沿道に配置された The police were stationed along the road because of *repeated* accidents. ～る催促も彼にはむだであった I pressed him *again and again*, but to no purpose.

たびがらす【旅烏】¶ どうせわれわれは～だ We are *birds of passage* after all. 彼は生涯～の生活を送った He remained *a wanderer* all his life. / He *led a wandering life*.

たびこうぎょう【旅興行】 ¶ 彼らは世界じゅう～をした They *made a provincial tour* throughout the world.

たびごころ【旅心】¶ あれこれ話を聞いていると～にかられた I was moved with *a desire* (≒ *yearning*) *for travels* while listening to this or that.

たびさき【旅先】 *one's* destination. ¶ 彼は～からたびたび便りをくれる He often writes to me *on his trip*. / He often writes to me *while traveling*. ～から昨夜遅く帰った I returned home from my *trip* late last night. ～で思いがけず友人に会った I met one of my friends unexpectedly *on my trip*.

たびじ【旅路】 a journey; a travel. ¶ ～につく go (≒ start) on *a journey*. この世の～ *one's* pilgrimage〔in life〕; life's pilgrimage. ～の終り the *journey's* end. 死出の～ the *journey* to the next world.

たびじたく【旅支度】 preparations for a trip. ¶ ～をする prepare for a trip. これで～は全部ととのった This completed *the outfit for the trip*.

たびだ·つ【旅立つ】¶ 彼はフランスへ向け～った He *started on a tour* for France. 彼は昨年あの世に～った He *departed this life* last year. / He *passed away* last year. / He *went to his long home* last year.

たびたび【度度】 often; many times; over and over again; frequently. ¶ 日本には～地震がある Earthquakes *often* shake Japan.

たびはだし【足袋跣】 feet in *tabi*-socks. ¶ 突然の地震に～で外に出た At the earthquake we ran out of the house *without our shoes on*.

たびびと【旅人】 a traveler; a tourist; a wayfarer.

たびまわり【旅回り】 ¶ ～の役者 a *traveling* player (≒ actor).

たびやつれ【旅窶】 ¶ 彼女は～した顔をしていた She *looked travel-worn*.

たびょう【多病】 ¶ 彼は～だ He *is of delicate health*. / He *is* rather *sickly*.

タフ ¶ 徹夜しても平気だなんて彼は～な男だ What a *tough* man he is (≒ How *tough* he is) to make nothing of sitting up all night.

—ガイ a tough guy.

タブー 〔a〕 taboo; 〔a〕 tabu. ¶ この会社では交通事故の話は～になっている We *put it under a taboo to* talk of traffic accidents in the office.

だぶだぶ ¶ 彼の上着はぼくには～だ His coat *is too loose* for me. ジュースを飲みすぎたので腹が～だ The bowels *are moving*, because I have drunk too much juice.

だぶつ·く ¶ ミカンが大豊作で～いている Oranges *are over-supplied* as a result of the heavy crop.

ダフや【ダフ屋】 a scalper.

たぶらか·す【誑かす】 cheat; deceive; swindle. ¶ 彼は他人を～してぼろもうけしている He makes easy money by *cheating* others. すんでのところで～されるところだった I *was* nearly *taken in*.

ダブル ¶ 彼は～の背広がよくにあう A *double-breasted* coat fits him well.

—スチール a double steal. **—**幅 double width. **—**プレー a double play. **—**ヘッダー a double header. **—**ベッド a double bed.

ダブ·る ¶ 同じ本を彼も買ってきたので～ってしまった As he bought the same copy as mine, we *have two copies of the same book*. 彼は大学で1年～った He *remained in the original class* at the university *for a year* (≒ *another year*). / 困 He once *failed to go up to the next grade* at the university. 昨年は天皇誕生日と日曜が～った The Emperor's birthday *fell on* Sunday last year.

ダブルス doubles. ¶ 混合～の試合は日本が勝った The Japanese team won *the mixed doubles*.

タブロイド a tabloid. ¶ ～版の新聞 a *tabloid* newspaper. ～版の新聞を発行する publish newspaper *in tabloid*.

たぶん【他聞】 ¶ この話は～をはばかることなのでそのつもりでいてください I want you to know that this is *a confidential matter* (≒ *between you and me*).

たぶん【多分】 probably. ¶ ～彼は来るだろう He will *probably* come. あすは～晴れるだろう It *is* *likely to* clear up tomorrow. ～あの人は商人だろう *Maybe* he is a merchant. あすは～参加できないかと思います *I am afraid* I shall not be able to join the party tomorrow.

たぶんに 【多分に】 ¶ 私の成功は～彼のおかげだ I owe my success *very much* to him. 彼は責任を果たさないという傾向が～ある He is *very much* inclined to be irresponsible. 彼は早口の傾向が～ある He has a *strong* tendency to speak too fast.

たべかけ 【食べかけ】 ¶ ～で席を立つ leave the table *without finishing one's meal*; leave the table *half way.* 夕飯を～のところへ来訪があった I had a visitor *while I was taking* supper.

たべごろ 【食べ頃】 ¶ このメロンはあすあたりが～だ This melon will *be good to eat* tomorrow. もう桃が～だ The peaches *are* now *ripe enough to eat.*

たべすぎ 【食べ過ぎ】 overeating; excessive eating. ¶ ～は体によくない It is bad for the health to *eat too much.*

たべずぎらい 【食べず嫌い】 ¶ 彼は魚の～だ He *has a prejudice against* fish. / He *is prejudiced against* fish.

たべつ·ける 【食べつける】 ¶ 彼は～けない物を食べて腹をこわした His stomach is upset from eating *unaccustomed* food. / His stomach is upset from eating something *he was not used to having.* ふだん～けているものが結局一番うまい You will find *usual* diet most agreeable to your taste.

たべのこし 【食べ残し】 leftovers; leavings. ¶ 犬はわれわれが与えた～をむさぼり食べた The dog devoured the *leftover* 〔*food*〕 we gave him.

たべのこ·す 【食べ残す】 ¶ ～すのは不作法だ It is bad manners to *leave your dish unfinished* (≒ *half-eaten*).

たべもの 【食べ物】 food. ¶ なにか～をさがした I looked for *something to eat.* 夏はとくに～に注意しなければなりません You must be very careful about your *food* especially in summer. 動物に～を与えないでください Please don't give *food* to animals. ぼくはあっさりした～を食べたい I want to take *a* light *meal.* あんまり栄養のある～ばかりとると健康に悪い Too rich *a diet* is not good for the health. あのホテルは～がよい That hotel *serves* (≒ *sets*) *a good table.* 出された～はみなおいしかった I enjoyed *everything offered at table.*

た·べる 【食べる】 **1** 〚食事〛 eat. ¶ この肉は生で～べられる This meat can *be eaten* raw.
何時に昼食を～べますか What time do you *have* lunch?
腹いっぱい～べると体に毒だ It is bad for the health to *eat* too much.
なにも～べるものがなかった There wasn't anything to *eat.*
この中のものをなんでもとって～べてください Please *help yourself to* anything in this box.
彼はなんでも～べるがちっとも太らない He *eats* every sort of food, and yet he never puts on weight.
彼は野菜だけしか～べない He *lives on* vegetables.
2 〚生活する〛 ¶ 彼は当分～べるのに困らない He *is well provided for* for the present.
月5万円ではとても～べられない We cannot *live on* fifty thousand yen a month.
彼は家族5人を～べさせるのに苦労している He has a lot of difficulty 〔in〕 *supporting* his family of five.

たべん 【多弁】 talkativeness. ¶ 彼はまったく～な男だ He is quite a *talkative* fellow.

だべん 【駄弁】 idle talk. ¶ このように～を弄(ろう)しても時間の浪費になるだけだ This *idle talk* is simply a waste of time. / Talking like this is nothing but a waste of time.

だほ 【拿捕】 capture. ¶ 漁船を～する *capture* (≒ *seize*) a fishing boat.

たほう 【他方】 another side (≒ place); the other side. ¶ 彼は非常な才能の持ち主だが～では常識に欠けている He is a man of great talent but *on the other hand* lacks common sense.

たぼう 【多忙】 busyness. ¶ 彼は～な毎日を送っている He *is very busy* every day. / He is leading a *very busy* life every day. 彼は山のような事務をかたづけるのでおそろしく～だ He *is* now *terribly busy* handl*ing* piles of desk work. 彼らは今取り入れで～をきわめている They *are* now *extremely busy with* the harvest. / They *are very busy* harvest*ing* at present. ～なため,ご返事が遅れました I am sorry I couldn't write you earlier as I *was busy.*

たぼう 【多望】 ¶ 彼は才能があるから前途なかなか～な青年である That young man has a great deal of talent, and *is* very *promising.*

だぼう 【打棒】 〖野球〗 ¶ ジャイアンツの～おおいにふるい圧勝した The batters of the Giants played well, and they won a great victory.

たほうめん 【多方面】 many directions. ¶ 彼は～にわたって活躍している He is actively engaged *in various fields.* 彼の趣味は～に及んでいる He has *a great variety of* taste. それを～から念入りに検討した I examined it minutely *from various angles.*

だぼくしょう 【打撲傷】 a bruise. ¶ 転んで5日間の～を受けた I fell down, and got *a bruise* which would take five days to heal.

だぼら 【駄法螺】 a big talk; a tall story. ¶ 彼はよく～をふく He often *talks big.* / He often *blows his own trumpet.* / He *is a big talker.*

だほん 【駄本】 a useless book.

たま 【玉·球·弾】 **1** 〚ボール〛 a ball; a bullet. ¶ ～を投げる throw *a ball.*
～を捕る catch *a ball.*
速い～を打つ hit *a fast ball.*
2 〚弾丸〛 ¶ 彼は～に当たって大けがをした He was severely wounded by *a bullet.*

た

この銃には～が入っている This rifle *is loaded.*

3 〖慣用的表現〗 ¶ 彼女の額には～のような汗が浮かんでいた *Beads* of sweat stood on her forehead.

～のような女の子が生まれた A *darling* baby girl was born.

彼は短気なことが～にきずである A quick temper is the only defect in his otherwise perfect character.

4 〖電球〗 ¶ この電気の～をはずしてほしいのですが Will you please take out this electric *bulb*?

たま 【偶】 ¶ ～の外出なのだから十分楽しんでいらっしゃい Go and have a good time, because you don't have the chance to go out so often.

たまいし 【玉石】 a round stone ; (大型のものは) a boulder.

たまがき 【玉垣】 the fence of a shrine.

たまぐし 【玉串】 a sprig (≒ branch) of a sacred tree offered to a god.

たま·げる 【魂消る】 ¶ 足音も立てずに現われるんだもの～げた You *startled* me by coming in so quietly. 彼にお前などに会ったことがないと言われたときには～げた I *was astonished* when he said that he had never seen me before. 彼女はそのおそろしい光景に～げて気を失った She *was* so *frightened at* the horrible sight that she lost her senses.

たまご 【卵】 **1** an egg ; (魚介類の) spawn (集合名詞的に用いる). ¶ ～の黄身(白身) the yolk (white) of *an egg.*

～を焼く(割る) fry (break) *an egg.*

～を半熟にする boil *an egg* soft.

この鶏は1日おきに～を生む This hen lays *an egg* every other day.

この鶏が～を抱きはじめてから2週間たった This hen has been sitting on the *eggs* for two weeks.

3週間で鶏の～はかえる Hen's *eggs* hatch in three weeks.

ウナギは海で～を生む Eels shoot their *spawn* in the sea.

—あわだて器 an egg beater. **—酒** eggnog. **—とじ** egg soup. **—焼き** an eggroll. かき— scrambled eggs. 生— a raw egg. ¶ 私は生～が好きだ I like to eat *an egg uncooked.* ゆで— a hard-boiled egg (半熟は a soft-boiled egg).

2 〖比喩的に〗 ¶ 医者の～ a *prospective* doctor.

画家の～ an artist *in embryo.*

たましい 【魂】 (霊) the soul ; (精神) the spirit. ¶ 彼は仕事に～を打ち込んでいる He is doing his work *with all his heart.* その女の美しさに～を奪われる思いだった I *was fascinated* (≒ *was captivated*) by her beauty. 刀は武士の～だ The sword is the *soul* of a *samurai.* これからは～を入れかえて一生懸命勉強します I promise I'll mend my ways and work sincerely. 彼女はすっかり意気消沈している. ～が抜けたみたいだ She looks completely dejected ; she has no usual *spirit* at all. 三つ子の～百までも (諺) *The child is father of the man.* (Wordsworth の詩から). 一寸の虫にも五分の～ (諺) *Even a worm will turn.* (忍耐にも限度がある, ということ).

だましうち 【騙し討ち】 a surprise attack ; a foul play. ¶ 彼は～にあって殺された He was *foully* murdered. ～をするのはひきょうなことだ It is unfair to *make a surprise attack.*

だま·す 【騙す】 cheat ; coax. ¶ 彼は人を～して金を奪うことをなんとも思わない He is not ashamed of *cheating* others *out of* their money. 彼は私たちを～そうとしていた He was attempting to *deceive* us. 彼はお人よしだからよく人に～される He is such a good-natured man that he *is* easily *taken in.* 彼女は子どもを～して薬を飲ませた She *coaxed* her child *to* take the medicine. 彼女は泣く子を～して寝かせるのがうまい She is good at *soothing* a crying baby into sleep. きみは彼にすっかり～された I'm afraid you*'ve been done* by him. あの男にうまいことばで～されてくだらない品物を買わないよう注意しなさい Take care not to *be wheedled* by him *into* buy*ing* worthless things.

たまたま 【偶偶】 accidentally ; (まれに) merely. ¶ 私は～そこに居合わせただけだ I just *happened to* be there. / I was there just *by chance.* (やや文語).

たまつき 【玉突き】 billiards. ¶ ～をする have a game at billiards.

—場 a billiard room. **—台** a billiard table. **—棒** a cue.

たまてばこ 【玉手箱】 ¶ 開けてびっくり～ an apple of Sodom ; a Pandora's box.

たまに 【偶に】 (時々) occasionally ; (まれに) rarely ; seldom. ¶ 私は～図書館に行く I *occasionally* go to the library. / I go to the library *now and then.* 旅に出かけることは～しかない I *seldom* (≒ *rarely*) go on a trip. そこには～行ってみることがあるくらいだ I *rarely* go there. 彼は～はいいことを言う *Sometimes* he says smart things. ごく～訪問客がある We have visitors *once in a* [*long*] *while.*

たまねぎ 【玉葱】 an onion. ¶ ～をきざむと涙が出る *Onions* make your eyes water when you cut them.

たまのあせ 【玉の汗】 drops of sweat. ¶ 彼の額から～がしたたり落ちていた *Drops of sweat* were streaming down from his brow. 彼の額には～がにじんでいた The *sweat* stood *in beads* upon his forehead. 彼は～を流して木を切り倒した He *was sweated* all over as he cut the tree down.

たまのこし 【玉の輿】 ¶ 女は氏なくして～に乗る (諺) A woman of no birth may *marry into the purple.* 彼女は元来はまずしい出なのだが, いわゆる～に乗って金持ちの奥方になった To tell the truth, she was from a very poor family but lucky enough to *marry a rich man.*

たまのり 【玉乗り】 balancing (≒ walking) on a ball.

たまむし 【玉虫】 〖昆虫〗 Chrysochroa elegans. ¶ その絹の布は～色の光彩を放つ The silk cloth gives out *iridescent* light.

たまもの【賜物・賜】a gift ; (天の恵み) a blessing. ¶ 彼がここまでになったのは長年努力した～だ His many years of hard work made him what he is. / His present success is *the fruit* (≒ *result*) of his many years of hard work.

たまや【霊屋】a great tomb ; a mausoleum.

たまよけ【弾除け】¶ 警官たちは～の武装をして殺人者を追跡した The policemen *armed themselves against bullets* and pursued the murderer. / The cops pursued the murderous villain *with bulletproof jackets on*.

たまらな・い ¶ 寒くて～い It is *unbearably* cold. 野球がしたくて～い I *am dying to* play baseball. 空腹でとても～い I *cannot bear* hunger. ビールが飲みたくて～かった I *was dying for* a drink of beer. 冬になるとスキーをしたくて～くなる In winter I *feel impatient to* go skiing. 頭が痛くて～い I *have a splitting headache*. 彼は不安で～い He *is oppressed with anxiety*. そんなに遠くては～い It is such a long way off that I *cannot bear* it. こんなことで文句を言われては～い Being complained about for such a thing *is too much for* me. そんなことがあっては～い That *is more than I can bear*. 仕事のあとの1ぱいのビールは～い There's nothing like a glass of beer after work.

たまり【溜まり】a place of resort. ¶ あの店は学生たちの～になっている That shop is *a favorite haunt* of students.

―場 ¶ この近くにタクシーの～場がある There is *a taxi stand* about here.

たまりかねて【堪りかねて】¶ 彼は主人の虐待に～逃げた He *was unable to bear* his master's ill treatment and ran away. 彼のからかいに～彼女はついどなってしまった *Being unable to put up with* his biting sneer, she burst out in anger.

だまりこく・る【黙りこくる】keep silent. ¶ 彼女は両親が何を聞いても～っていた She would not answer any question her parents asked and *kept* (≒ *remained*) *silent*.

だまりこ・む【黙り込む】¶ 話がその事件に行くと彼はきまって～んだ Whenever the case happened to be talked about, it was found that he *fell dumb* suddenly. 彼は腕を組んで～んだ He folded his arms and *sank into silence*.

たま・る【溜まる】(集まる) collect ; (水などが) stand ; (貯金が) be saved. ¶ 穴に水が～っている There's some water in the hole. 家の前に一面に水が～っていた *There was a pool of* water in front of the house. ごみが～った *There's a lot of* rubbish. 仕事が～って旅行もできない *There is so much work left to do* that I cannot even take a trip. 1か月で仕事がずいぶん～った In just one month a lot of work *has piled up*. 彼はだいぶ金が～った He *has saved* a lot of money. もし100万円～ったらどうしようか If I *saved* a million yen, what shall I do?

だま・る【黙る】¶ ～れ Shut up! ～っていろ Keep silent (≒ quiet). 彼はずっと～っていた He *remained silent* all the time. 彼は1時間も口をきかずに～っていた He *held his tongue* as long as an hour. 彼はそれきり～ってしまった He *said no more* about it. このことはぜひ～っていてほしい Be sure to *keep quiet* about this. きみに話したことは～っていてほしい I want you to *keep* what I have said *to yourself*. ～って学校を休んではいけない You must not stay away from school *without notice*. ～って出ていったのはだれだ Who was it that (≒ who) left *without a word*? ～って部屋に入らないようにしてください Be careful not to enter the room *without permission*. 私に～っていたとはけしからん What do you mean by *keeping* it *from* me? 彼の暴言にはとても～っていられなかった I could not *put up with* his violent words. とにかく～って仕事すればいいのです Anyway, *stop complaining* and get on with your work. ～って私についてきなさい *Don't say anything*, just follow me.

たまわ・る【賜わる】¶ アメリカ大使は陛下より拝謁を～った The American ambassador *was granted* an audience by the Emperor.

たみ【民】the people ; (国民) a people ; (民族) a race ; (臣下) subjects. ¶ 流浪の～ *a* wandering *people*.

だみごえ【濁声】a gruff voice ; a thick voice. ¶ 酔っ払いは太い～でどなっていた The drunkard was bawling *in a* deep *gruff voice*.

だみん【惰眠】¶ ～をむさぼる live in idleness. 成功したいなら今のように～をむさぼっていてはだめだ If you are to succeed, stop *idling away your time*, and work hard.

ダム a dam. ¶ その川に～を建設中である *A dam* is being built across the river. その川は～でせき止められた The river *was dammed*.

―サイト a dam-site. **―式発電** generation of electricity by water power.

たむけ【手向け】(供物) an offering ; (餞別) a parting gift ; a farewell present. ¶ 花を供えて故人の霊への～とした We *made an offering of* flowers to the deceased soul.

たむ・ける【手向ける】present ; offer. ¶ 亡き人人に花を～ける *offer* flowers to dead spirits.

たむし【田虫】〖医学〗a ringworm.

たむろ【屯】¶ あちこちに人々が～している People *are grouping* here and there.

ため【為】**1**〖役にたつこと・利益〗¶ そうするのがきみの～だ That *is good for* you. / It will *do* you *good*. / It *is for* your *good*.

きみの～を思って言っているのだ I'm telling you this *for* your own *good*.

みんなぼくの～を思ってやってくれたことだ They did it all *for* me.

そんなことをするのは子どもの～にならぬ It will be harmful *to* children.

子どもの～に親は苦労する Parents have to go through a lot *for* their children.

世の～人の～に働きたい I want to work *for* the public interest.

た

彼は国の～に命を捨てた He gave his life *for* his country.

新婚夫婦の～に乾杯しよう Let us drink a toast *to* the newlyweds.

2〘…にとって〙¶この失敗は彼の～にはよい薬だ This failure 〔of his〕 will *do* him some *good.* / He will learn a lesson from (⇋ by) this failure 〔of his〕.

夜更かしするのは体の～によくない It is bad *for* the health to stay up 〔at night〕. / Late hours are bad *for* the health.

3〘目的〙for ; in order to ; to. ¶彼は金の～に働く He works *for* money 〔rather than *for* the pleasure of working〕.

なんの～にそんなことをしたのか What did you do that *for?*

仏文学研究の～彼はパリに行った He went to Paris *to* study (⇋ *in order to* study ; *for the purpose of* studying) French literature.

成功する～にはもっと努力しなければならぬ If you want to be successful, you have to work harder.

平和の～に戦争するのは矛盾だ It is inconsistent to fight *for the cause of* peace.

4〘原因・理由・結果〙¶彼は寒さの～凍死した He was frozen to death. / He died *of* cold.

雨の～試合は中止になった The game was rained out. / The game was called off (⇋ was canceled) *because of* the rain.

風邪の～学校を休んだ I was absent from school *because of* a cold. / I couldn't go to school *because* I had a cold.

洪水の～にふたつの町が全滅した The two towns were destroyed completely *in consequence of* the flood.

きみがあんなことをした～にぼくまでおこられた I too got hell *for* what you did.

インフレの～生活が苦しくなった It has become difficult to live *owing to* inflation.

事故を起こしたのは彼女の不注意な運転の～だ Her careless driving resulted in an accident.

だめ【駄目】**1**〘役にたたぬ・不十分・無益〙useless. ¶この時計はもう～だ This watch *doesn't run* any more.

そのくらいの金では～だ That *isn't enough* money.

そんな小さな字引では～だ A small dictionary like that *is no good.*

そんな英語の勉強の仕方では～だ That is no way to study English. / That is not the way you should study English.

泣いたって～だ *It is no use crying*

彼は～な男だ He is 〔*a*〕 *good-for-nothing.*

2〘不成功・不可能・望みがない〙hopeless. ¶彼女に行くことを思いとどまらせようとしたが～だった I tried *in vain* to persuade her not to go.

体重を減らそうとしたが～だった I tried to lose weight, but *it was no use.*

霜で作物が～になった The frost *has spoilt* (⇋ *has ruined*) the crops.

やるだけやってみるが～だろう I will do my best but I'm afraid I *won't be successful* (⇋ I'm afraid *it's no use*). / All 〔of〕 my efforts will *be in vain.*

～とわかっていながら万一をたのんだ I knew I would *be a failure* but I took a chance.

3〘拒否・禁止〙¶～だ, 断わる *No,* I won't. (Will you ... ? などの答えとして)

笑っては～だ *Don't* laugh. / *Stop* laughing.

怠けてばかりいては～だ *Don't* be so lazy all the time.

急がなくては～だ You *have to* (⇋ *have got to*) hurry.

きみが行かなくては～だ You *have to* go.

4〘人が悪い状態になる〙¶もう病人は～だ The case *is* now *hopeless.*

彼は年をとって視力が～になってきていた He was old and his eyesight *was going.*

遊んでばかりいると人間が～になる If you keep fooling around, you will end as *a good-for-nothing.*

5〘慣用的表現〙¶やってくれますかと彼に～を押した *To make sure,* I asked him again to do it for me.

ためいき【溜め息】a sigh. ¶～をつく sigh ; draw a sigh. 帰り道がわかったのでみんなほっと安堵の～をついた Everybody *gave a sigh of relief* when they found the way home. ～をついて with *a sigh.*

ためいけ【溜め池】an irrigation pond ; a reservoir.

だめおし【駄目押し】¶彼は～のホームランを打った He smacked a home run to *make* the victory *doubly sure.* 彼は約束を守ると思うが～したほうがよい I think he will keep his promise but you had better *make sure* that he will do so.

ためこ・む【溜め込む】¶彼女は働いて得たお金をせっせと～んだ She *saved up* (⇋ *hoarded*) every coin she earned.

ためし【試し】an experiment ; a try ; a trial. ¶～に on *trial ;* for *a test* (⇋*try*). ドレスを～に着てみる *try on* a new dress. ～に1度ご用命ください Please give us *a trial.* 新しい車を～に使ってみる give a new car *a try* (⇋ *a trial*). ～に人を半年使ってみる give a person six month's *trial* ; take a person *on trial* for six months.

ためし【例】¶彼は時間どおり来た～がない I have never known him to come on time. いまだかつてそうした～がない There is no *precedent* for it.

ため・す【試す】(試みる) try ; (験す) test. ¶生徒の学力を～す *test* the students' degree of achievement. このやり方で問題が解けなかったらまた別のやり方で～してごらん If you cannot work out the problem this way, *try* another way. 新製品を～してみてください Please *give* our new product *a trial.* 彼は今度買った車の乗り心地を～した He took his new car out to *see* how it would run. 新薬は動物で十分～さなければならない *An* extensive *experiment must be made* with a new drug on animals.

ためつすがめつ【矯めつ眇めつ】¶ 彼は新しい機械に～眺め入っていた He examined the new machine *very closely.* / He examined the new machine *with scrutinizing eyes.*

ために【為に】¶ 彼は急に父をなくし，～大学進学を断念せざるを得なくなった His father died *so* suddenly *that* he was obliged to give up going up to college. 彼はひどい風邪を引いた，～会議には出席できなかった He had a bad cold, and *therefore* (≒ *for that reason*) could not attend the meeting.

ためら·う【躊躇う】hesitate. ¶ ～わずに without *hesitation.* ～いがちに hesitatingly; waveringly. 彼は話す前に～った He *hesitated* before speaking. いきさつがすっかりわかるまでは彼の味方につくことを～った I *hesitated about* tak*ing* his side until I knew the whole story. きみはあまり忙しそうだったので頼むのが～われた I *hesitated to* ask you; you looked so busy.

た·める【貯める·溜める】(貯蓄する) save (money); (貯蔵する) store (food).
¶ 彼は珍しい貝がらをずいぶんと～めている He *has a* large *collection of* rare shells. 非常用に食べ物を～めておく *store up* some food for emergency use. 支払いを～めないように注意しなさい Be careful not to *leave* your bills *unpaid.* 彼はその仕立屋の支払いを～めたまま姿をくらました He gave the tailor a slip *without paying* (≒ *without settling*) *his bills.* 未解決の問題をずいぶん～めてしまった I have many problems left unsolved. 彼女は目に涙を～めてさよならと言った She said good-by *with* tears in her eyes.

た·める【矯める】¶ 松の枝を～める *train* twigs of a pine tree. 悪いくせは小さいときに～めておかねばならない You must *cure yourself of* a bad habit when young. / You must *get rid of* a bad habit when young.

ためん【他面】the other side. ¶ 物事を一面から見ないで～からも見る必要がある You have to look at things from *different angles,* instead of only one. ～において on the other hand.

ためん【多面】many sides. ¶ ～的な人 a *many-sided* (≒ *versatile*) man.
—体 a polyhedron.

たもあみ【たも網】(金魚などをすくう) a spoon-net; (つり上げた魚をすくう) a landing net.

たもうさく【多毛作】multiple cropping.
¶ この地方の気候は～に適している The climate here is favorable to *multiple cropping.*

たも·つ【保つ】¶ 平和を～つのがわれわれのつとめだ It is our duty to *maintain* peace. 健康を～つには節制が必要だ In order to *preserve* our health, we need temperance. 彼は体面を～つことができなくなった He has become unable to *keep up* appearances. 社会の秩序を～つ *maintain* the order of the society.

たもと【袂】**1**〖衣服の〗the sleeves.
2〖橋の〗¶ 橋の～ at the *foot* (≒ *edge*) of a bridge.
3〖慣用的表現〗¶ ～を分かつ (別れる) part from *a person*; (絶交する) part company with *a person*; break with *a person.*

だもの【駄物】trash; rubbish.

たや·す【絶やす】¶ トキを地上より～してはならない We must not *let* Japanese crested ibises *die out* on the earth. / Efforts must be made to keep Japanese crested ibises from *disappearing* from the earth. 火を～さないようにする *keep* the fire *alive.* 彼のところは酒を～したことがない He never *runs out of sake.* / He never *lets sake out of stock.*

たやす·い【容易い】easy. ¶ この問題は～い This is an *easy* question. それは私にとって～いご用です That *is no trouble* for me. そんな申し出は～く承知できるものではない I can't accept such an offer so *readily.* 彼の家は～く見つかった I found his house *with no difficulty.* / I found his house *with ease.*

たゆまぬ【弛まぬ】¶ 彼は研究に～努力を重ねている He devotes his *steady* efforts to his studies. / He is engaged in his studies with *untiring* zeal. 彼は～努力を続け今日の成功をみた His present success is the fruit of his *indefatigable* (≒ *untiring*) diligence.

たゆ·む【弛む】¶ 仕事が成るまでは～むことなく励めよ Don't *slacken your efforts* till the work is done. 彼女は～まず毎日ピアノの練習に励んでいる She practices on the piano *untiringly* every day. うまず～まず untiringly; indefatigably; steadily.

たよう【多用】¶ ご～中を恐縮ですが二，三分お時間を頂けないでしょうか I know you *are very busy,* but could you spare me a few minutes?

たよう【多様】diversity.
多種— ¶ 多種～な品物が並べてあった *A great variety of* articles were displayed.

たより【便り】(文通) correspondence; (手紙) a letter; (消息) news; (情報) information.
¶ お～ありがとう Thank you for your *letter.* / I appreciate your *letter.* じきお～します I'll *write* 〔*to*〕 you soon. 最近彼から～がありましたか *Have* you *heard from* him lately? / Have you received *a letter* from him lately? 風の～に彼がパリで貧しく死んだことを聞いた *I hear* he died poor in Paris. / *The rumor says that* he died poor in Paris.

たより【頼り】reliance; dependence; (信頼) trust. ¶ 彼は～になる You can *rely on* him. 辞書を～に英語の小説を読んだ I read an English novel *with the help of* a dictionary. 彼はつえを～に歩いた He walked *leaning on* his stick.

たよりない【頼りない】¶ そんな～返事はもうたくさんだ I've had enough of your *vague* answers.

たよ·る【頼る】rely (≒ depend) 〔up〕on.
¶ ぼくには～れる友人がひとりもいない I have no friends to *turn to.* 他人に～ってばかりいてはだめだ Don't *rely* (≒ *depend*) *on* others for help so much. 私は彼を～って上京した I came to Tokyo *counting* (≒ *relying*) *on* his

た

help. 雲の中を計器に～って飛んだ We flew through the clouds *with the help of* the instruments. 金の力に～って彼はかって気ままにふるまった He *resorted to* his money to get his own way.

たら【鱈】〖魚類〗cod; haddock (アメリカに多い).

-たら ¶この町へ来～寄ってくれ Please call on me *if* you *happen to* visit this town. あす雨が降っ～会は延期される *If* it rains tomorrow, the meeting will be postponed. もし万が一あの人が来なかっ～たいへんだ *If* he should not come, I will be at a loss what to do. 時間があっ～お宅へ寄りたいのだが *If* I have time enough, I would like to call at your house. 彼の援助があっ～ありがたかったのだが *If* he had helped me, I should have been much obliged. もうおやすみになっ～ Will you go to bed now? そうやってみ～どうだ Why not try it?

た

たらい【盥】a tub.
━回し ¶与党は政権をいつも～回しにしている The Government party always *monopolizes* political power within their own clique.

だらく【堕落】fall; corruption. ¶人間は～した Human beings *have degenerated.* このごろの政治は～している Politics these days *is corrupt.* ひとり住まいになってから彼は～した He *has gone wrong* since he began to live by himself. ギャンブルは人間を～させる Gambling *leads* man *to ruin.* この村の人たちはみんな～している People in this village *are* all *degraded.*

-だらけ ¶どろ～のくつ muddy shoes. 血～の死体 a *bloody* corpse. 血～の服 *blood-stained* clothes. この本は誤植～だ This book *is full of* misprints. 彼のすねは毛～だ His legs *are hairy.* 机はほこり～だった The desk was thick with dust.

だら・ける ¶～けた試合が続いている A *dull* (≒ *boring*) game is going on. きみは少し～けている You *are* a little *lazy* (≒*slow*). ～けないでよく働け Work hard *without slackening your efforts.* 暑いとからだが～ける The heat makes us *feel weak* (≒ *feel languid*).

たらこ【鱈子】 cod's-roe; (塩づけの) salted cod's-roe.

-たらし・い ¶彼はいつまでも長～い演説をつづけた He has kept on with a lengthy speech. 彼女はいやみ～い口調で話をする She speaks with an ironical tone.

だらしな・い slovenly. ¶なんと～い男だ What a *slovenly* man he is! この部屋は～い This room *is untidy.* 彼女は身なりが～い She is *untidily* dressed. 彼は金銭に～い He *is loose about* money matters. 彼の机の上はいつも～い He always *keeps* his desk *untidy.* あんな男にごまかされるとは～い How *silly* you *are* to be deceived by such a man! 彼は～く金を使う He wastes his money *foolishly.* やることなすこと～い He *is slovenly in* everything that he tries.

たら・す【垂らす】¶カーテンが～してある A curtain *is hanging down.* 部屋には黒いカーテンが～してあった The room *was hung with* a black curtain. この馬は汗を～している The horse *is dripping with* sweat. 床に水を～すな Don't *drop* (≒ *dribble*) water on the floor. 彼は二, 三滴の水薬を水に～した He *let fall* a few drops of liquid medicine into the water. 子供は鼻水を～していた The child *was snivelling.*

たら・す【誑す】¶あの女は彼を～して多額の金を巻き上げた She *wheedled* a lot of money out of him. あの男は女を～す He will *seduce* a girl.

-たらず【-足らず】¶歩いて1時間～の行程だ It is *less than* an hour's walk. クラス会に集まったのは10人～だった There were *less than* ten present at the class party. 私は1時間～待った I waited for *nearly* an hour. 貧乏は恥ずるに～ We *need not* be ashamed of poverty.

たらたら **1**〖汗や血が〗¶汗が額から～と流れ落ちている Sweat *is dripping* (≒ *is trickling*) *down* from his forehead.
頭から血が～流れていた Blood *was running* from his head.
2〖お世辞・不平が〗¶彼はお世辞～だ He pays *a lot of* compliments. / He is flattering *profusely.*
彼女は不平～だ She is all complaints. / She *is full of* complaints.

だらだら ¶彼は仕事を～と続けた He went on working *in a slovenly way.* 彼の額から汗が～流れていた The sweat *was dripping* from his forehead. / His forehead was *all in a sweat.* 血が手から～流れた The hand was bleeding *a lot.* ～の坂 a *gentle* slope. ～と長い話 a *lengthy monotonous* talk.

タラップ a gangway.

たらふく【鱈腹】¶彼は夕食を～食べた At supper he ate *to the full* (≒ *as much as he wanted*). / At supper he ate *his full.*

だらり ¶ひもが1本～と垂れている A piece of string *is dangling.*

タランテラ〖音楽〗[a] tarantella.

-たり ¶彼女は泣い～笑っ～した She laughed *and* cried *by turns.* 見～聞い～して確かめた I confirmed it by seeing *and* hearing. 雨が降っ～やんだりしている It is raining *on and off* (≒ *off and on*). 彼は立っ～すわっ～して私を待っていた He waited for me *impatiently, now* standing, *and then* sitting. 勉強し～山登りし～して彼はとても忙しかった *What with* studying *and* [*what with*] climbing, he was very busy.

ダリア〖植物〗a dahlia.

タリウム〖化学〗thallium.

たりき【他力】**━本願**(宗教上の) salvation by faith; (依頼心) a sheer dependence on some one other than *one*self. ¶彼は何事も～本願だ He always *turns to others for help* in everything. 何事も～本願では向上しない You cannot be improved in anything by simply *depending on others.*

だりつ【打率】〔野球〕the batting average. ¶彼の〜は３割２分１厘だ He is batting .321. (point three two one と読む).

たりとも ¶一刻〜なまけるな Don't be lazy *even* for a moment.

たりな·い【足りない】¶あの男は少々〜い That man *is* a little *dull* (≒ *stupid*; *slow-witted*). この問題は論ずるに〜い The problem *is not worth* discussing.

たりゅうじあい【他流試合】¶〜をすると腕が上がるものだ *Contests with other schools* will improve skill.

たりょう【多量】abundance. ¶この国では〜の鉄が産出される This country produces *a large quantity of* iron. この国は〜の石油を海外に輸出している This country exports oil *in great quantity.* 安い外国品が〜に日本に入ってきた Inexpensive goods were imported *in large quantities.* この山脈には金が〜にある Gold is found *in abundance* in this mountain range. 彼は毎日〜の水を飲む He drinks *a great deal of* (≒ *a lot of*) water every day.

だりょく【打力】〔野球〕batting; hitting. ¶彼の〜はなかなかみごとだ He *hits* very well.

だりょく【惰力】〔物理〕inertia.

た·りる【足りる】**1**〘充分だ〙be enough. ¶これで〜りる This *is enough.*

これで〜りると思いますか Do you think this *sufficient*?

この劇場は優に１万人を収容するに〜る This theater *is large enough to* accommodate ten thousand persons.

彼は信用するに〜りる人間だ He is a *trustworthy* man.

彼の話はまさに傾聴するに〜りる His speech *is* indeed *worth* listening to.

今は食べ物は少しで〜りる Only a small amount of food *is sufficient* for me now.

2〘否定形の場合〙¶人手が〜りない We *are short-handed.* / We *are short of hands.*

当時は食物が〜りなかった Then we *had not enough* food. / We *were suffering from the shortage of* food then.

いくらお金が〜りないのか How much 〔money〕 *is wanting?*

少し資金が〜りない We *are* a little *short of* funds.

これでは本を買う費用に〜りない This *is not enough* for buying books.

1,000円に10円〜りない It *is* ten yen *short of* one thousand yen.

100円〜りない. 貸してください We *are short of* a hundred yen. Would you lend it to me?

鉛筆があと５本〜りない We *need* five more pencils.

あなたはまじめさが〜りない You *are lacking in* diligence.

彼は才能はあるが経験が〜りない He is a man of ability but *lacks* experience.

この本は３ページと４ページが〜りない Pages 3 and 4 *are missing from* this book.

健康にはいくら注意してもなお〜りない We *cannot* be careful *enough* of our health.

たる【樽】a cask; a barrel. ¶ビール〜 *a* beer *barrel.* 〜詰めの酒 *casked sake.* 〜詰めのビール *barreled* beer.

た·る【足る】¶信用するに〜る人 a *reliable* man; a *trustworthy* man. 〜るを知れ Be content with what you have. 衣食〜って礼節を知る (諺) Well-fed, well-bred.

だる·い【懈い】¶午後になると〜くなる I *feel weak* (≒ *feel languid*) in the afternoon. 足が〜い My legs *feel tired.* 彼は〜そうに歩いていた He was walking *languidly* (≒ *wearily*). 〜そうな声が部屋の中に聞こえた A *wearisome* voice was heard in the room.

たるがき【樽柿】persimmons turned mellow in a *sake* cask.

たるき【垂木】a rafter.

だるま【達磨】a tumbler; (仏教) Dharma. **—**船 a barge; a lighter.

たるみ【弛み】slack; (気分の) relaxation. ¶綱の〜をなくす pull in the *slack* of the rope. 彼のほおは〜ができている His cheeks *are sagging.* 心の〜は研究を進歩させない *Relaxed mind* prevents us 〔from〕 making good progress in our study. だれにもときには心の〜は起こる Everybody sometimes *gets slack* (≒ *gets lazy*).

たる·む【弛む】(物が) loose; (気分が) relax. ¶綱が〜んでいる The rope *is slackening.* 試験のあとは気持ちが〜む We *feel relaxed* after the examination. きみはこのごろ〜んでいる You *have been lazy* (≒ *have been slackening your efforts*) these days.

たれ【垂れ】(ポケットの) a flap; (汁の) sauce; gravy. ¶かばやきの〜 *sauce* for broiled eels.

だれ【誰】**1**〘疑問〙¶〜がそんなことを言った *Who* told you such a thing? / *Who* said so?

〜かいないか Is *anybody* home?

〜に頼まれてそんなことをしたのか *Who* told you to do that?

〜を推薦しようか *Who* (≒ *Whom*) shall we recommend?

〜からその話を聞いたか *Who* did you hear that from? / *Who* told you that?

この金は〜のか *Whose* money is this? / *Whose* is this money?

〜か英語を話す人はいないか Isn't there *anyone* who speaks English?

〜が〜かさっぱりわからなかった I could never tell *who* was *who.*

2〘打ち消し·否定の語を伴って〙¶〜も答えなかった *Nobody* answered.

〜のせいでもない *Nobody* is to blame. / It is *nobody's* fault.

〜にもそのことは言うな Don't tell *anyone* about it. / Don't breathe a word of it.

〜がそんなことを信ずるものか *Nobody* will believe a thing like that. / *Who* believes such a thing?

3〘どんな人も〙¶〜にも欠点はある *Nobody* is

た

perfect. / *Everybody* has a weak point. / We all have our faults.

〜だってそんなことは断わる *Nobody* would want to do that. / *Everybody* refuses that.

〜でもかまわぬ, ここに来てくれ Let someone come here ; I don't care *who*.

〜でもそんなことはできる *Anybody* can do it.

その仕事は〜でもよいというわけではない This job is not for *everybody*. / Not *everybody* can do this job.

ぼくは〜よりも早くその知らせを知った I was the very first to learn the news.

〜もが結果を知りたがった *Everybody* was anxious to know the result.

4 〖不特定の人〗 ¶ 〜かがやってくれるさ *Someone* will do it 〔for you〕.

きみたちのうち〜かがしたに相違ない *One* of you must have done it.

〜かほかの人のまちがいだろう It must be *somebody* else's fault. / It must be *someone* else, not me.

〜か適当な人を捜している We are looking for *some* qualified person.

5 〖暗に特定の人〗 ¶ 〜かさんのやりそうなことだ *Someone we all know* is likely to do that.

だれかれ 【誰彼】 ¶ 彼女は〜の区別なく微笑する She smiles on *everybody*. 彼は〜の区別なく信用する He trusts *everybody* indiscriminately.

だれぎみ 【だれ気味】 ¶ 聴衆は彼の話に〜だった The audience *got a little bored with* his speech. 休みには〜になる We are apt to *be a little relaxed* on holidays.

たれこ·める 【垂れ込める】 ¶ 戦雲が近東に〜めている The war clouds *are hanging* over the Near East.

たれさが·る 【垂れ下がる】 ¶ 旗が〜っている A flag *is hanging down*.

だれしも 【誰しも】 ¶ 〜そう考えているわけではない *Everybody* doesn't think so.

だれそれ 【誰某】 Mr. (≒ Mrs., Miss) So-and-so ; a certain person (わざと名前を明示するのを避ける場合に用いる). ¶ それは〜さんの言った話だ It is what *Mr. So-and-so* said.

だれだれ 【誰誰】 ¶ 〜が来たか *Who* (≒ *What persons*) came?

たれながし 【垂れ流し】 ¶ 汚水の〜 the *discharge* of filthy water. シアンが〜のままであった Cyanogen *has been trickling out freely*. / Cyanogen *has been thrown out unchecked*.

だれひとり 【誰一人】 ¶ そこには〜現われなかった *No one* (≒ *Nobody*) appeared there.

たれまく 【垂れ幕】 a curtain ; a hanging screen.

た·れる 【垂れる】 **1** 〖垂れさがる〗 hang down. ¶ 彼女の髪はひざまで〜れている Her hair *hangs down* to her knees.

雲は低く〜れていた The clouds *were hanging low*.

天井からシャンデリアが〜れている A chandelier *is hanging down* from the ceiling.

彼は頭を〜れてじっと立っていた He was standing *with bent head*.

天井から雨水が〜れている Rain water *is dropping* from the ceiling.

傷口からたらたら血が〜れていた Blood *was trickling* from the wound.

2 〖あわれみ·恵みを〗 ¶ 彼は貧しい人々にあわれみを〜れた He *took pity on* poor people.

神はすべての人に恵みを〜れたまう God *bestows* a favor on everybody.

だ·れる 【堕れる】 ¶ 聴衆が彼の演説に〜れてきた The audience *grew bored with* his speech. 午後になると気分が〜れる We *feel relaxed* in the afternoon. ここのところ市場は〜れている The market *has been dull* these days. 彼は〜れずによく働く He works hard and steadily.

タレント a talent.

テレビ── a T. V. star.

-だろう ¶ 彼は病気〜 *I think* (≒ *I guess*) he is sick. / *Perhaps* he isn't well. 彼女は成功する〜 *I hope* she will succeed. 彼らは失敗する〜 *I am afraid* they will fail. きっと彼はやってくる〜 *I am sure* he will come. 一体これはなん〜 What in the world is this? 彼はいつ出発するん〜 *I wonder* when he will start. ひょっとしたら彼は留守〜 *Maybe* he is away. なんというばかなことをしたの〜 What a silly thing I have done! 多分彼はこの町にいる〜 He is *probably* in this town. それは思いちがい〜 It *must* be some mistake. もし彼がこの場にいなかったら, 私は途方にくれていた〜 If he had not been in this place, I *should have been* at a loss what to do.

たわいな·い 【他愛無い】 absurd ; foolish ; idle. ¶ 彼らは〜い話に花を咲かせていた They were talking *absurd* nonsense. 彼は〜く眠りこけている He is sleeping *innocently*. 彼女は〜くだまされる She is deceived *easily*. 彼は〜い男だ He is a *silly* (≒ *foolish*) man. 彼は〜く酔っ払ってた He was *dead* drunk.

たわけ 【戯け】 a fool ; an idiot. ¶ 〜者が! You *fool*! 〜たことをするな Don't *make a fool of yourself*. / Don't *act silly*. / Don't *behave foolishly*. 彼はいつも〜たことを言っている He is always talking *nonsense*.

たわごと 【戯言】 nonsense ; a silly talk. ¶ 〜を言うな Don't talk *nonsense*!

たわし 【束子】 a scrubbing brush.

たわ·む 【撓む】 bend. ¶ 実がなって柿の枝が〜んでいる The branches of a persimmon *are bending* with fruit.

たわむれ 【戯れ】 ¶ こどもたちは〜に石をその池に投げ込んだ The boys threw stones into the pond just *for fun* (≒ *out of fun*). 私が〜に言ったことが真に受けられた What I said *in jest* (≒ *in joke*) was taken seriously. ふたりの愛は一時の〜であった Their love was *a* passing *fancy*. 〜に恋はすまじ You shouldn't fall in love *frivolously*. / You shouldn't play with love.

たわむ·れる 【戯れる】 ¶ ネコがまりと〜れる A cat

plays with a ball. 彼らは芝生で〜れている They *are frolicking* on the grass. 彼は女と〜れる He *flirts* with women.

たわら【俵】a straw bag.
米― a straw rice-bag.

たわわ ¶枝も〜に柿がなった The branches *are heavily laden with* persimmons.

たん【反】**1**〖土地約9.92アール〗¶〜当たりの収穫量 production per *tan.*
2〖反物の約12ヤール〗¶この反物は1〜いくらですか What does *a roll* (英語で説明すれば about 12 yards in length) of this cloth cost?

たん【短】shortness; (欠点) a defect. ¶長をのばし〜をおぎなう make up for *one's defects* developing *one's* strong points. 国家の改革は〜日月にはできない A national reform cannot be effected in a day (≒ in a short time).

たん【胆】(胆のう) liver; (勇気) courage; guts. ¶彼は〜斗の如し He *is very brave.* / He *is as brave* (≒ *bold*) *as a lion.* / He is a man of iron nerves.

たん-【単-】single; singular.

たん【端】¶彼らのけんかは誤解に〜を発した Their quarrel *started from* (≒ *originated in*) a misunderstanding.

たん【痰】phlegm. ¶〜がのどにからまる *Phlegm* obstructs the throat. 道端に〜を吐く *spit* on the street. 彼はよく〜が出る He coughs up much *phlegm.*
―つぼ a spittoon.

タン a tongue.
―シチュー〔a〕stewed tongue.

だん【暖】¶彼らは火のまわりで〜をとった They *warmed themselves* around the fire.

だん【壇】a platform; (教会の) a pulpit; (祭壇) an altar.

だん【団】(団体) a body; a group; a party. ¶彼らは一〜となって走り去った They ran away *in a group.* 彼は山中で山賊の一〜に会った He came across *a band* of robbers in the mountain.
観光― a sightseeing party. 使節― a mission; a delegation. 調査― a survey group.

だん【男】(男爵) a baron.
公侯伯子― (貴族) the peerage; duke, marquis, earl, viscount, and baron.

だん【断】a decision; judgment. ¶彼は最後の〜を下した He made *a* final *decision.*

だん【談】a story; an account.
冒険― ¶冒険〜は子どもをよろこばせる *An adventure story* amuses children. 旅行― ¶彼は旅行〜をしてくれた He gave us *an account of his travels.*

だん【段】**1**〖階段・段層の〗a stair; a step. ¶彼は階段の上から3〜めから飛び降りた He jumped off the third *step* from the top.
3〜重ねのサンドイッチ a three-*decker* sandwich.
2〜ベッド a double-*decker* 〔bed〕; two beds one above the other.
ロケットの第3〜はうまく点火した The third-*stage* booster was ignited on schedule.
2〖活字の組み方〗a column. ¶3〜抜きの見出しで with a three-*column* heading.
2〜組みのページ a double-*column* page.
3〖階級・程度〗¶柔道三〜の人 a *judo*-player of the third *grade.*
ここの冬は寒いどころの〜ではない It is freezing cold in the winter here.
4〖場合〗¶英語を話す〜になるとなかなか難しい *When it comes to* speaking English, I have a lot of difficulty.
5〖芝居の〗¶忠臣蔵の五〜目 the Fifth *Act* of *Chushingura.*
6〖次第・件〗¶失礼の〜お許しください I beg your pardon.

だんあつ【弾圧】oppression; suppression. ¶自由はけっして〜されるべきでない Freedom should never *be suppressed.* 警察がデモを〜した The police *suppressed* (≒ *controlled*) the demonstration.

だんあん【断案】a decision; a conclusion.

たんい【単位】**1**〖計算の〗a unit. ¶〜をまちがえて計算する calculate on *a* wrong *unit.*
〜時間の生産高が伸びた The production in the *unit* hour increased.
2〖授業の〗a credit; a unit. ¶大学卒業のためには100〜とらなければならない To complete the college course, it is required to take a hundred *credits.*
彼は〜が足りなくて卒業できない He hasn't got enough *credits* for graduation.

だんい【段位】a grade. ¶柔道の最高〜 the highest *grade* of *judo.*

たんいつ【単一】unity; simplicity. ¶指揮系統の〜化をはかる *simplify* the supervising system.
―神教 monotheism. ―為替レート a single exchange rate. ―経済 economy in the individual family basis.

だんいん【団員】¶消防〜 *a member* of the fire brigade.

だんうん【断雲】scattered clouds.

たんえき【胆液】〘医学〙bile; gall.

たんおん【単音】a single sound; (単音節) a monosyllable.

たんおん【短音】a short sound.

たんおんかい【短音階】〘音楽〙the minor scale.

たんか【担架】a stretcher. ¶負傷者を〜で運んだ We carried the injured on *a stretcher.*

たんか【単価】a unit cost; a unit price. ¶その品は〜100円で売られている The articles are sold at a hundred yen *apiece.*
生産― the unit cost of production.

たんか【炭化】〘化学〙carbonization.
―水素 hydrocarbon. ―物 carbide.

たんか【短歌】a 31-syllable Japanese poem.

たんか【啖呵】¶彼は私に向かって〜をきった He *swore* (≒ *hurled defiance*) *at* me.

だんか【檀家】a parishioner.

タンカー a tanker.
マンモス― a supertanker.

た

だんかい【段階】a stage ; (順序) a step ; a degree. ¶政局は新しい～に入った The political situation has entered upon *a* new *phase*. 当時科学はまだ幼稚な～にあった In those days science was still in its early *stage*. 生徒たちは能力に応じて三つの～に分けられる The students are divided into three *grades* according to their ability.

だんがい【弾劾】impeachment. ¶判事はわいろをとって～された The judge *was impeached for* tak*ing* bribes. / The judge *was accused of* taking bribes.

—演説 an impeachment address. —裁判所 an impeachment court.

だんがい【断崖】a precipice ; a cliff.

—絶壁 an overhanging cliff.

たんかだいがく【単科大学】a college.

たんかっしょく【淡褐色】light-brown.

¶～の鳥 a *light-brown* bird.

たんがん【単眼】〔動物〕a stemma (複 stemmata) ; an ocellus (複 ocelli).

たんがん【嘆願】〔an〕 entreaty ; an appeal ; (当局への) a petition. ¶政府に救済を～する *make petition to* the government for relief ; *petition* the government for relief. 彼はわれわれの～をいれた He listened to our *entreaty*. 彼にとどまってくれと～した We *entreated* (≒ *implored*) him *to* stay.

—者 a petitioner. —書 a petition. ¶新しい橋を造ってくれという～書を提出した We presented *a petition* asking the authority for a new bridge.

だんがん【弾丸】(小銃弾) a bullet ; (砲弾) a shell. ¶小銃に～を込める load a rifle with *a bullet*.

—ライナー a bullet-like line drive. —列車 a bullet train ; a flier.

たんき【単記】single entry.

—投票 a single vote. —投票制 a single ballot system.

たんき【単騎】a lone horseman. ¶彼は～敵中を突破した The horseman broke through the enemy's rank *single-handed*.

たんき【短気】quick (≒ short ; hot) temper ; (おこりっぽい) irritability. ¶彼は～だ He *is quick-tempered* (≒ *is short-tempered*). 彼が～なのにはあきれた I was amazed at his *irritability*. ～を起こさないようにしなさい Try not to *lose your temper*. 彼はとかく～を起こしやすい He is apt to *lose his temper*. ～なのが彼の唯一の欠点だ *Short temper* is his only defect. ～は損気(諺) *Out of temper, out of money*.

—者 a quick-tempered person.

たんき【短期】a short term.

—貸し付け a short-term loan. —契約 a short-term contract. —講習 a short course. —国債 a short-term bond. —大学 a junior college. —手形 a short-dated bill. —取引 a short-term transaction.

たんきかん【短期間】¶こんな～にこの仕事はとてもできない I cannot do this work *in* such *a short time*. 彼は～にそれをやってのけた He managed to do it *within so short a time*.

たんきゅう【探究】search ; investigation ; (研究) research ; inquiry. ¶科学者は真理を～する Scientists *search for* (≒ *investigate*) truth. 彼はその事の真偽を～した He *made an inquiry into* the truth of the matter.

—者 an investigator ; an inquirer.

だんきゅう【段丘】〔地理〕a bench ; a terrace.

たんきょり【短距離】a short distance.

—競走 a short distance race ; a dash. —選手 a sprinter.

タンク (容器) a tank ; (戦車) a tank.

—ローリー a tank-lorry. ガス— a gas tank.

タングステン〔化学〕tungsten.

たんぐつ【短靴】〔a pair of〕 shoes.

たんけい【短径】〔幾何〕(楕円の) the minor axis.

たんげい【端倪】¶彼は～すべからざる人物だ He is a *mystery* man.

だんけい【男系】male issue ; the male line. ¶～が家産を相続する *The male line* succeeds to the family property.

だんけつ【団結】unity. ¶～は力なり *Union* is strength. ～すれば必ず成功する If you *unite yourselves*, you are sure to succeed. ～してその仕事に当たりなさい *Band together* to do the work. みんなが～すればよいのだ All of you should *unite in a body*. ～して彼らと闘おう Let's *unite ourselves* against them. ～してその案に反対した We opposed the plan *in a body*.

—権 the right of organization. —心 cooperative spirit. —力 power of unity.

たんけん【探検・探険】expedition ; exploration. ¶深海の～は興味深い The *exploration* of the ocean depth is very interesting. 彼は南米～に出かけた He went on *an expedition* to South America. 無人島を～する *explore* an uninhabited island.

—家 an explorer. —隊 an expeditionary party. 南極— an antarctic expedition.

たんけん【短剣】a dagger ; a dirk.

たんげん【単元】〔哲学〕the monad ; 〔教育〕a unit.

—制度 the unit system. —論 monadism.

だんげん【断言】declaration ; affirmation. ¶彼はその旨を～してはばからなかった He was positive in his *declaration* (≒ *affirmation*) to that effect. 私はそれが事実であると～する I *affirm* (≒ *assert*) it is true. / I can *say positively* that it is true. それが事実であると～するのをはばかります I hesitate to *say* (≒ I refrain from *asserting*) that it is true.

たんご【単語】a word. ¶彼は英語の～をたくさん知っている He has *a* large *vocabulary* of English. (word は普通名詞, vocabulary は集合名詞).

—集 a collection of words ; a wordbook. 基本— basic words ; a basic vocabulary.

たんご【端午】¶～の節句は5月5日だ *The Boys' Festival* falls on the fifth of May.

タンゴ〔音楽〕tango.

だんこ【断固】¶ ～たる処置をとった We took *decisive* measures. 彼は～たる態度で使用人を追い払った He drove away the employee *firmly*. 彼は～たる決意で会に臨んだ He attended the meeting with a *firm* resolution. ～たる態度が望ましい A *firm* attitude is desired. ～として私はその申し出を断わる I will refuse the offer *flatly*. 彼らは～としてその案に反対した They opposed the plan *positively*.

だんご【団子】a dumpling. ¶ 花より～ (諺) *Pudding rather than praise*.
—鼻 a snub nose.

たんこう【炭鉱・炭坑】a coal mine ; colliery (建物・設備をも含む).
—会社 a colliery company. —業 the coal mining industry. —主 a coal mine operator ; a coal owner. —地帯 a coal mining region. —夫 a coal miner ; a collier.

だんこう【団交】(団体交渉) a collective bargaining. ¶ ～は物別れになった The *collective bargaining* reached no agreement.
大衆— a collective bargaining session.

だんこう【断交】a rupture ; a severance.
¶ 両国は～状態にある The two nations *are on hostile relations*. / The two nations *have severed diplomatic relations*.
経済— a rupture of economic relations.

だんこう【断行】¶ ～の時がきた The time has come to *take a decisive action*. ひとたび計画が決定すれば彼は必ずそれを～する Once a plan is decided, he never fails to *carry* it *out* (≒ *carry* it *into effect*) resolutely. 彼は熟慮～した He was deliberate in council, *prompt in action*. 反対はあったが私は改革を～した I *effected* a reform in spite of opposition. / I carried a reform into execution in spite of opposition.

だんごう【談合】¶ 長時間～したが話は少しもまとまらなかった We *conferred* (≒ *got our heads together*) for a long time and to no end at all. 彼らはうらで何か～している They are making some secret *arrangement*.

たんこうしき【単項式】〔数学〕a monomial 〔expression〕.

たんこうしょく【淡紅色】pink ; rose pink.

たんこうしょく【淡黄色】lemon yellow ; light yellow.

たんこうほう【単行法】〔法律〕a special law.

たんこうぼん【単行本】a book. ¶ 彼は講義を～として出版した He published *in book form* a course of his lectures.

だんこく【暖国】a warm country (≒ province ; climate).

たんこぶ【たん瘤】a wen ; a lump. ¶ 彼は彼らの目の上の～だ He is *an eyesore* (≒ *a nuisance ; an obstacle*) for them.

だんこん【男根】a penis.

だんこん【弾痕】a bullet mark. ¶ 船にはたくさんの～があった The boat showed a lot of *bullet marks*. / The boat was riddled with *shot*.

たんさ【探査】inquiry ; investigation. ¶ 警察はその事件の真相の～に乗り出した The police began to *inquire* (≒ *probe*) *into* the truth of the matter.

たんざ【単座】—式飛行機 a single seater (≒ aircraft).

ダンサー (職業ダンサー) a 〔taxi〕 dancer.

たんさい【淡彩】light coloring.
—画 a light-colored picture.

だんさい【断裁】¶ 不ぞろいな本の縁を～する cut the irregular edges of a book.
—機 a cutter ; a cutting machine.

だんざい【断罪】(有罪の判決) conviction ; condemnation ; (斬罪) beheading ; decapitation. ¶ 彼はその罪により～された He *was found guilty of* the crime.

たんさいぼう【単細胞】〔生物〕a single cell.
¶ 彼は～だ(単純な人だ) He *is quite stupid* (≒ *dumb*).
—生物 monad. —動物 (植物) unicellular animals (plants).

たんさく【単作】a single crop.
—地帯 one-crop area.

たんさく【探索】¶ 警察は犯人を～中である The police *are searching for* (≒ *are looking for ; are making a search for*) the criminal.

たんざく【短冊】a paper strip to write Japanese poems 〔on〕.

たんさん【炭酸】〔化学〕carbonic acid.
—塩 carbonate. —ガス carbon dioxide ; carbonic acid gas. —カリ potassium carbonate. —カルシウム(石灰) carbonate of lime. —紙 carbon paper. —水 carbonated water. —ソーダ sodium carbonate.

たんし【短資】a short-term loan ; 米 a call loan.
—市場 the short loan market.

たんし【短詩】a short poem ; (14行詩 ソネット) a sonnet.

たんし【端子】〔電気〕a terminal.

だんし【男子】a boy ; a man (複 men). ¶ ぼくも一個の～だ I am *a man*. ～として恥ずかしくない行動をとれ Behave *like a man*. ～の一言だ. 信じてくれ Do believe the word of *a gentleman*.

だんじ【男児】日本— ¶ 彼は日本～だ He is *a true Japanese*.

タンジェント〔数学〕tangent.

たんじかん【短時間】¶ それは～に完成されるだろう It will be completed *in a short time*.

たんしき【単式】〔数学〕a simple expression ; 〔簿記〕single entry.
—火山 a simple volcano. —簿記 bookkeeping by single entry.

だんじき【断食】a fast ; fasting. ¶ 彼らは10日間の～を行なった They performed *a fast* of ten days' duration. 彼らは2日間～した They *fasted* for two days.
—療法 a fast cure.

たんじじつ【短時日】¶ ～に in a short time ; in a day ; in a short period of time.

だんじて【断じて】absolutely ; positively.

た

¶ ～私は考えを変えません I will *never* change my mind. / *Nothing* will change my mind. そんなことをするのを～許すな *Don't on any account* permit him to do it. ～それを否定する I *positively* deny it. それは～正しい It is *certainly* right. それは～まちがいだ It is *absolutely* wrong.

たんしゃ【単車】 a motorcycle.

だんしゃく【男爵】 a baron. ¶ A～ Baron A. A～夫人 (イギリスでは) Lady A; (イギリス以外では) Baroness A.

だんしゅ【断種】 sterilization. ¶ 外科医はその狂人の～を行なった The surgeon *sterilized* the mad man.

たんじゅう【短銃】 a pistol; (連発式短銃) a revolver.

たんじゅう【胆汁】 bile; gall. ¶ 彼は～質だ He is a man *of choleric temperament.*

た

たんしゅく【短縮】 reduction. ¶ 授業時間は10分間～された The school hour *was shortened* by ten minutes. 労働時間の～を要求する We demand the *shorter* working hours. ことしの夏休みは2週間に～された The summer vacation this year *has been shortened into* two weeks.

—授業 shortened school hours. 操業— reduction of operation. ¶ 操業～しなければならぬ We have to *curtail* (≒ *reduce*) operation.

たんじゅん【単純】 simplicity. ¶ 彼女は子どものように～だ She *is* as *simple* as a child. 彼は考えの～な人だ He *is simple-minded.* 彼らは官庁用語の～化を行ないはじめた They began *to simplify* the official language. 語いの～化はけっして容易でない The *simplification* of vocabulary *is* by no means *easy.* 物事を～に考えるな Don't take things *simple and easy.*

—概念 a simple concept.

たんしょ【短所】 a fault; a weak point. ¶ きみは怒りっぽいところが～だ Quick temper is your *weak point* (≒ *fault; defect*). だれもおのおの長所と～がある Everybody has his own merits and *demerits.* 私は～を矯正せねばならない I must correct my *defects.* / I must make up for my *shortcomings.*

たんしょ【端緒】 the origin; the beginning; the start; (初歩) the first step; (手がかり) a clue (*to*); a key (*to*).

だんじょ【男女】 man and woman; male and female; both sexes. ¶ ～7歳にして席を同じうせず *Boys and girls* should sit apart after they have reached the age of seven. 部屋は若い～でかなりいっぱいだった The room was fairly full of young *men and women.*

—共学 ¶ わが国で～共学が実施されてから20年以上たった More than twenty years have passed since *coeducation* (≒ *mixed education*) started in this country. —混浴 ¶ ～混浴はここでは許されていない *Mixed bathing* is not allowed here. —差別 ¶ ～差別待遇は廃止されるべきだ Discriminating treatment between *men and women* should be abolished. —関係 ¶ 彼は～関係で苦労したことはない He has never had *a trouble with women.* —同権 equality between both sexes; equal rights for man and woman. 老若— ¶ 老若～を問わず会員になれます Everybody can be a member regardless of age or *sex.*

たんしょう【嘆賞・嘆称】 admiration. ¶ 彼女の服は友だちの～の的であった Her dress was the *admiration* of all her friends. 彼の勇気には～すべきものがあった His courage *was admirable* (≒ *was praise-worthy*).

たんしょう【探勝】 a sight-seeing trip. ¶ 彼は九州へ～の旅に出かけた He went on *a sight-seeing trip* to Kyushu. 彼は層雲峡を～するため北海道へ行った He went to Hokkaido to *do* (≒ *see*) *the sights of* Sounkyo.

たんしよう【単子葉】 —植物 a monocotyledonous plant; the monocotyledons.

たんじょう【誕生】 birth. ¶ みんながこの会の～を祝った Everybody celebrated the *birth* of this society.

—日 *one's* birthday. ¶ 私の～日は5月2日です My *birthday* is (≒ falls on) May 2. ～日おめでとう Happy *birthday* to you! 家族は祖父の80歳の～日を祝った The family celebrated their grandfather's eightieth *birthday.* —祝い ¶ 彼の～祝いに時計をプレゼントした I gave him a watch as *a birthday present.*

だんしょう【談笑】 a friendly talk; a chat. ¶ 彼と～した I enjoyed *a friendly chat* with him.

たんしょうとう【探照燈】 a searchlight.

たんしょく【単色】 a single color; a simple color. ¶ それは～で描かれている It is painted in *a single* (≒ *one*) *color.*

—画 a monochrome.

だんしょく【男色】 sodomy (homosexuality も近ごろは主として男色で, イギリスでは今これだけしか使わない).

—家 a sodomite.

だんしょく【暖色】 ¶ ～系の上着 a jacket of *a warm color.*

たんしん【単身】 alone; by *one*self. ¶ 彼は～でニューヨークに赴任した He started *alone* for his new post in New York.

たんしん【短針】 (時計の) the short hand; the hour hand.

たんじん【炭塵】 coal dust.

—爆発 a coal dust explosion.

たんす【簞笥】 困 a bureau; 困 a chest of drawers.

重ね— a double chest of drawers. 茶— a cupboard; a sideboard. 洋服— a wardrobe; a dresser.

ダンス a dance; dancing. ¶ ～のお相手をお願いできましょうか May I have you the next *dance*? 彼と～をした I *danced with* him. / I *had a dance with* him.

—教師 (男) a dancing master; (女) a dancing mistress. —教習所 a dancing school. —パーティー a dance; a dancing party; a ball. ¶ あのホテルでは毎晩〜パーティーがある At the hotel *dances* are held nightly. ―ホール a dance hall. 社交― a social dance. スクエア― a square dance. タップ― tap dancing. トウ― toe dancing.

たんすい【淡水】 fresh water.
―魚 a fresh-water fish. ―湖 a fresh-water lake.

だんすい【断水】 suspension of water supply. ¶ 工事のため今夜は水道は〜だ The water supply will *be suspended* (≒ *cut off*) tonight for repairs.

たんすいかぶつ【炭水化物】〘化学〙 a carbohydrate.

たんすいしゃ【炭水車】 a tender.

たんすいろ【短水路】〘水泳〙 a short course; a 25 meter course.
―記録 a short-course record.

たんすう【単数】〘文法〙 the singular number. ¶ この名詞は〜だ This noun is *in the singular*.

たん・ずる【嘆ずる】 (なげく) lament; regret; deplore; sigh; (感心する) admire. ¶ 〜ずべき lamentable; regrettable; (あっぱれな) admirable.

だん・ずる【断ずる】 (断定する) conclude; decide; (さばく) judge.

だん・ずる【談ずる】 ¶ 彼は時局を〜ずるのが好きだ He likes to *talk* about the 〔political〕 situation. それは〜ずるに足りないことだ It is not worth *mentioning*. あんな男はともに〜ずるに足らずだ Such a man is not worth *talking to*.

たんせい【丹精】 (努力) efforts; (苦心) pains; assiduity; labor. ¶ この作品は彼の〜の作だ This work has cost him *a great deal of labor*. / This is his *painstaking* work. これは彼の〜の結果だ This is the fruit of his *assiduous labor*. 〜してこの木をそだてた I have raised the plant *with utmost care*. 〜の甲斐がなかった All my *labors* have come to nothing.

たんせい【単性】〘生物〙 unisexuality.
―花 a unisexual flower. ―生殖 monogenesis.

たんせい【嘆声】 a sigh; a groan. ¶ 彼のみごとな絵にみな〜を放った Everybody uttered *a cry of admiration* at his entrancing picture. 彼の死に〜をもらした I heaved *a sigh of grief* at his death.

たんせい【端正】 smartness. ¶ 彼は〜な顔だちをしている He has a *decent* appearance. / He has *handsome* features.

だんせい【男声】〘音楽〙 a male voice.
―合唱 a male chorus. ―四重唱 a male quartet.

だんせい【男性】 the male sex; 〔a〕 man; 〘文法〙 the masculine gender. ¶ 〜的スポーツ a *manly* sport. 彼女は〜的な人だ She behaves like *a man*. グランド・キャニオンは〜的な景観だ The Grand Canyon is rich in *masculine* beauty.

だんせい【弾性】〘物理〙 elasticity.
―ゴム elastic gum.

たんせき【胆石】〘医学〙 a gallstone.
―病 cholelithiasis.

だんぜつ【断絶】 ¶ 彼の家は跡継ぎがないので〜した His family *has died out*. 両国は国交を〜した The diplomatic relations between the two countries *were broken off*. 世代の〜は防ぎようがない *The lack of communication* between the younger and the older generations is inevitable.
国交― rupture of diplomatic relations.

たんせん【単線】 a single track; a single line. ¶ 事故のため〜運転をしている Only *one-way traffic* is maintained on account of the accident.

たんぜん【端然】 ¶ 彼は〜とすわっていた He was sitting *straight*.

だんせん【断線】〘電気〙 disconnection. ¶ 電線があちこちで〜した Telegraph wires *were broken down* in many places. 〜のためこの電話は不通になっている This telephone line is interrupted on account of *broken wires*.

だんぜん【断然】 ¶ こちらのほうが〜いい This is *much* better. 冬より夏のほうが〜いい I like summer *much better* than winter. 3人の中で彼が〜野球がうまい He is *by far* the best baseball player of the three. その申し出を〜断わることにした I have decided *flatly* to refuse the proposal. 〜たばこはやめる *I swear* I will quit smoking.

たんそ【炭素】〘化学〙 carbon (C). ¶ 〜を化合させる carbonize. 〜を除く decarbonize.
一酸化― carbon monoxide. 二酸化― carbon dioxide.

たんそう【炭層】 a coal bed.

たんぞう【鍛造】 forging. ¶ それは鋼鉄から〜される It *is forged from* steel.

だんそう【男装】 men's clothes; male attire. ¶ 彼女はよく〜する I often see her in *men's clothes*. / She often *wears men's clothes*. 〜の麗人 a fair woman in *male attire*.

だんそう【断層】〘地質〙 a dislocation.
―地震 a dislocation earthquake. ―写真 (レントゲンの) a tomogram.

だんそう【弾奏】 ¶ ピアノを〜する *play* the piano.

たんそく【嘆息】 lamentation; a sigh. ¶ 天を仰いで〜した He looked up at heaven *with a deep sigh*. 彼は不運を〜した He *sighed over* his misfortune.

だんぞく【断続】 intermission. ¶ 〜的な雨がきょうで3日続いている It has been raining *off and on* for three days. 〜的に砲声を耳にした We heard the roar of guns intermittently.

たんそびょう【炭疽病】〘医学〙 anthrax.

だんそんじょひ【男尊女卑】 predominance of man over woman. ¶ 日本の田舎では〜の風習が残っている The custom of *treating women as inferior to men* still exists in some of the rural districts in Japan.

たんだ【単打】〘野球〙 a single 〔hit〕; a one-

base hit. ¶ 彼は～とホームランを打った He hit *a single* and a home run.
たんたい【単体】〘化学〙 a simple substance.
たんだい【短大】(短期大学) a junior college.
女子— a women's junior college.
だんたい【団体】 a party ; a group ; (組織体) an organization. ¶ ～で行動しなさい Act *as a group*. 30名以上の～に割引はありますか Are special reduced fares allowed for *a party* of not less than thirty? 10名の～でピクニックに出かけた We made up *a party* of ten and went on a picnic. その～は解散を命ぜられた The *organization* was ordered to be dissoloved.
—競技 team sports. —協約 a collective agreement. —訓練 group training. —行動 a united action; a corporate action. —生活 group life. —保険 group insurance. —旅行 a group excursion. ¶ ～旅行をした We had *a group going*. —割引 reduced fares for a party ; a party-trip reduction. 経済— an economic organization. 政治— a political party ; a political organization.
だんたいこうしょう【団体交渉】 collective bargaining.
—権 the right of collective bargaining.
だんだら【段だら】¶ ～じまの布 *checkered* cloth. ～染めの布 cloth in *multi-colored* (≒ *parti-colored*) stripes.
たんたん【淡淡】 ¶ 彼は現在の心境を～と語った He *frankly* spoke of his mind at present. 日本人は～とした味を好む The Japanese prefer *plain* tastes in food.
たんたん【坦坦】 ¶ 車は～たる道路を走りつづけた The car moved on along the *smooth* road.
だんだん【段段】(階段) 〔a flight of〕 stairs ; a staircase.
—畑 terraced fields.
だんだん【段段】(徐々に) gradually. ¶ ～暖かくなっている It is *gradually* getting warmer and warmer. その幼児は～歩けるようになるだろう *Little by little* the baby will be able to walk. ～やる気がなくなってきた I became *less and less* inclined to do it. 彼の話は～興味がなくなった His speech became *less and less* interesting. ふたりの友情は～深まって愛情に変った Their friendship *by degrees* grew into love. ～暗くなってきた It is growing dark*er* and dark*er*.
たんち【探知】 detection. ¶ 警察は犯人の行動を～した The police *detected* the criminal's activities.
—器 a detector.
だんち【団地】 a housing development.
—族 people living in housing development apartments. 工場— a collective factory. 住宅— a collective housing area.
だんち【暖地】 a warm place ; a warm district ; a mild climate.
だんちがい【段違い】¶ 彼はクラスで～に優秀だ He is *by far* the best boy in the class. 日本はアジア諸国の間で～の経済力を持っている Japan is on a *far* higher level of economic power than any other nation in Asia.
—平行棒 leveled parallel bars.
だんちゃく【弾着】—点 the point of impact.
—距離 range ; gunshot.
たんちょう【単調】 monotony ; dullness.
¶ ～なメロディー a *monotonous* melody. この仕事の～さにはうんざりだ I am awfully tired of the *monotony* of the work. たいていの人は～な生活を送っているものだ Most people are leading a *monotonous* life.
たんちょう【短調】〘音楽〙 a minor 〔key〕.
だんちょう【団長】 the head. ¶ 観光団の～ the *head* (≒ *leader*) of a tourist party.
だんちょう【断腸】 ¶ ～の思いで故郷を捨てた I left my hometown *with bleeding heart*. 彼の死を聞いて～の思いだった I *was in heart-breaking grief* to hear of his death.
たんちょうづる【丹頂鶴】〘鳥類〙 a red crested 〔white〕 crane.
たんてい【探偵】 detective work ; (人) a detective ; a private eye. ¶ 私の行動を～がつけていた *A detective* was on my track.
—小説 a detective story ; a crime fiction.
私立— a private detective ; a private eye.
だんてい【断定】 conclusion ; decision.
¶ 警察はこの件を殺人事件と～した The police *decided* that it was a murder. 陪審員は被告を有罪と～した The jury *concluded* that the accused was guilty. 調査の結果非は運転者にあると～された Upon investigation they *came to the conclusion* that the driver was to blame.
ダンディー (人) a dandy. ¶ 彼は～な服装をしている He is in a *showy* attire. 彼は会社一番の～だ He is the *dandiest* boy in his firm.
たんてき【端的】 ¶ ～に言えば私はその法案に反対だ *Frankly speaking*, I am against the bill. / *To be frank with you*, I am against the bill.
たんでき【耽溺】 addiction ; indulgence.
¶ 酒色に～する *give* (≒ *addict*) *oneself to* sensual pleasures.
たんでん【炭田】 a coal field.
たんとう【担当】 charge. ¶ 彼は3年を～している He *is in charge of* the third-year class. 私は英語を～している I *teach* English. 彼がその事件の～だ He *takes charge of* the case. 彼がクラブの会計を～している He *takes care of* (≒ *is responsible for*) the club accounts.
—者 the person in charge (*of* an affair).
たんとう【短刀】 a dagger. ¶ 彼は～でその男を刺した He stabbed the man with *a dagger*.
だんとう【暖冬】 a mild winter.
—異変 ¶ ことしは～異変だ We are having an unusually *mild winter* this year.
だんとう【弾頭】 a warhead.
核— a nuclear warhead.
だんとうだい【断頭台】¶ ルイ14世は～のつゆと消えた Louis XIV died on the *scaffold* (≒ *guillotine*).

た

だんどうだん【弾道弾】a missile.
大陸間— an intercontinental ballistic missile (ICBM). 中距離— an intermediate range ballistic missile (IRBM).

たんとうちょくにゅう【単刀直入】¶ ～に言えば to be frank with you; frankly speaking. ～に彼の考えを聞いてみた I *frankly* asked him what he thought of it. 彼は～に本題に入った He came *straight* to the point.

たんどく【丹毒】〖医学〗the rose; erysipelas.

たんどく【単独】¶ 彼女は～でその仕事をやっている She is engaged in the work *by herself*. 彼は～でその案を思いついた He hit upon the idea *for himself*. 私が～でこの機械をつくった I made this machine *without any help from others*. 彼は～行動をとった He acted *independently*.
—犯 a single-handed offense. —飛行 a solo flight.

たんどく【耽読】¶ 私も若いころはミステリーを～したものだ I used to *be absorbed in reading* mysteries in my youth.

だんどり【段取り】(予定) a program; a plan; (手はず) arrangements. ¶ 仕事の～を決める make *arrangements* for the work. これから先のはっきりした～を決めよう Let's map out *a* definite *plan* for the future. あすの～はどうなっているんだ What is the *program* for tomorrow? すべてきみの希望どおり～はととのった Everything *has been arranged* as you wished.

だんな【旦那】(主人) a master; (夫) a husband; (芸人のひいき客) a patron; (呼びかけ) sir; gentleman.
—芸 amateurism. —衆 gentlemen; the betters. —寺 *one's* family temple; a parish temple. 大— the old master. 若— the young master.

たんなる【単なる】 simple; mere. ¶ 彼は～好奇心から尋ねてみた He asked out of *mere* curiosity. それは～冗談だ It is a *mere* joke. それは～ささいなことだ It is a *simple* trifle thing.

たんに【単に】simply; merely; only. ¶ ～そう言っただけだ I *merely* suggested it. それはただ～子どもたちだけでなく両親にとっても重要なことである It is important *not only* for children *but also* for their parents.

たんにん【担任】charge; duty. ¶ 彼がこのクラスの～だ He *is in charge of* this class. 私がこのクラスを～している I *take charge of* this class. 彼は英語を～している He *teaches* English.
—学級 a class under (≒ in) *one's* charge.
—教師 a teacher in charge.

タンニン〖化学〗tannin.
—酸 tannic acid.

たんねん【丹念】¶ 教科書を～に読みなさい Read your textbook *carefully*. 彼はその件に関して～な調査を行なった He made an *elaborate* investigation into the matter.

だんねん【断念】¶ アメリカへ行くのを～した I *gave up* the idea of going to America. 彼は大学進学を～した He *gave up* the hope of entering a college. 天気が悪いのでみんなに登頂を～させた I *dissuaded* them all *from* reaching the mountain summit because of bad weather.

たんのう【胆嚢】〖解剖学〗the gall bladder.
—炎 cholecystitis.

たんのう【堪能】proficiency. ¶ 彼女は英会話に～だ She *is proficient in* English conversation. / She *is good at* English conversation. たくさん食べて～した I *have had enough*. 十分～させていただきました I enjoyed myself *to my heart's content*. Thank you.

たんぱ【短波】a short wave.
—受信機 (送信機) a short wave receiver (transmitter). —放送 short wave broadcasting. —無線機 a short wave wireless apparatus.

たんぱく【淡白】¶ ～な味 *plain* taste. ～な気性の人 a man of *frank* disposition. 彼は金銭に～だ He *does not care much about* money. / He *is indifferent to* money.

たんぱく【蛋白】〖生化学〗protein. ¶ 尿に多量の～がある There is much *albumin* in the urine.
—質 protein.

たんぱつ【単発】¶ ～の飛行機 a *single-engined* plane. ～で終わらせるのは惜しい企画だ The attempt is too good to be given up without another trial.
—銃 a single-barreled gun.

だんぱつ【断髪】bobbed hair; a bob.
¶ ～の娘 a *bobbed* girl.

タンバリン〖音楽〗a tambourine.

だんぱん【談判】〔a〕negotiation. ¶ 彼とその件について～しよう I will *negotiate with* him *about* (≒ *for*) that matter. ～は決裂した The *negotiations* were broken off. ～は行きずまった The *conference* came to a deadlock.
膝詰め— a pressing demand.

たんび【耽美】—主義 aestheticism. —主義者 an aesthete.

たんび【嘆美】admiration; adoration. ¶絶景を～する *admire* the grand sight (*of*).

たんぴょう【短評】a short comment. ¶ 彼女は彼の演説に～を下した She made *a short comment on* his speech.

ダンピング〖経済学〗dumping. ¶ 品物をその国に送って～した They *dumped* the goods into the country.

ダンプカー a dump truck.

タンブラー a tumbler.

たんぶん【単文】〖文法〗a simple sentence.

たんぶん【短文】a short sentence; a short piece; a short composition. ¶ 百字以内の～で要約せよ Summarize it in less than 100 words.

たんぺいきゅう【短兵急】¶ ～に解決しようとしても無理だろう It will be almost impossible for us to settle the matter *hastily*. そんなに～になるな Don't *be* so *impetuous*.

たんぺん【短編】―映画 a short film. ―集 a collection of short stories; collected short stories. ―小説 a short story; a sketch; a novelette.

だんぺん【断片】a piece; a fragment. ¶ 手紙の～ *a fragment* of a letter. ～的な知識 *scraps* of information; *fragmentary* knowledge. ～的にしかニュースが入らない Only *fragments* of news come to us.

たんぼ【田圃】a rice field; a paddy (field).
―道 a path (≒ lane) through rice fields.

たんぽ【担保】security; a mortgage. ¶ なにを～に入れてくれますか What can you offer as *security* for it? なにか確実な～を入れてもらいたい I must have some approved *security*. 家を～に入れて金を借りた I borrowed money *on* (*the*) *security of* the house. 無～で金を借りた I borrowed money *without security*. 自動車を～に取って金を貸した I lent money *on* (*the*) *security of* a motorcar. 彼は確実な～で金を貸す He lends money *on good security*. あの家は～に入っている The house *is under a mortgage*.
―付き貸付け a secured loan; a loan on security. ―付き社債 secured bonds. ―物権 real rights granted by way of security. 二重― double securities.

たんぼう【探訪】inquiry. ¶ 夜の東京の～はいかがでしたか How did you enjoy Tokyo by night?
―記事 a report (of inquiries). ―記者 a reporter; an interviewer.

だんぼう【暖房】heating. ¶ きょうは寒いので～を入れた It was so cold today that we turned our *heaters* on. その部屋は～がききすぎていた The room *was over-heated*. その部屋の～は快適だった The room *was* comfortably *heated* (*up*).
―器 a heater. ―装置 a heating apparatus (≒ system). 集中― central heating. スチーム― steam heating.

だんボール【段ボール】corrugated cardboard.
¶ ～の箱 a *corrugated cardboard* box.

たんぽぽ〘植物〙a dandelion. ¶ ～の冠毛 a pappus of *a dandelion* (pappus の複数形は pappi).

タンポン〘医学〙a tampon.

たんほんい【単本位】〘経済学〙―制 a single standard; monometallism.

だんまつま【断末魔】¶ 彼は～の叫びをあげた He gave *a death cry*. ～の苦しみを味わった I experienced *the death agony*.

たんまり ¶ ～もうかった I gained a *large* profit on the transaction. ボーナスを～もらった I got a *large* bonus.

だんまり【黙り】(無言) silence; (劇) a dumb show; a pantomime.

たんめい【短命】a short life. ¶ ～な short-lived; ephemeral. かげろうは～だ A may fly *is short-lived* (≒ *is ephemeral*). 才子～(諺) *Whom the gods love die young*.

だんめん【断面】a cross section. ¶ それは工業化された社会の一～を表わしている It reveals *a cross section* of an industrialized society.
―図 a cross section (*of* a ship).

たんもの【反物】㊜ dry goods; ㊎ drapery; (織物) cloth; textile; textile fabrics.
―屋 ㊜ a dry goods store; ㊎ a draper's.

だんやく【弾薬】ammunition.
―庫 a (powder) magazine. ―帯 a cartridge belt.

だんゆう【男優】an actor.

たんよう【単葉】〘植物〙a simple leaf.
―植物 a unifoliate plant. ―飛行機 a monoplane; (水上機) a hydromonoplane.

たんらく【短絡】¶ ～した議論に耳をかすな Don't listen to such an absurd "*short-circuit*" argument.

だんらく【段落】(終り・区切り) an end; a conclusion; (文章の) a paragraph. ¶ ちょうど仕事が一～ついた I have just finished part of the work. / The work has been brought to a period. この社説は五つの～に分けられる This editorial article can be divided into five *paragraphs*.

だんらん【団欒】¶ 一家～の楽しみは一日の苦労を忘れさせる *The pleasure of a happy home* makes us forget the day's cares.

たんり【単利】〘経済学〙simple interest.
¶ ～で計算する calculate *at simple interest*.

だんりゅう【暖流】a warm current.

たんりょ【短慮】(軽率) rashness; (短気) a quick temper.
¶ 彼に～をいましめられた He admonished me for my *quick temper*.

たんりょく【胆力】courage. ¶ 彼は～がある He *is courageous*. 彼は～を練る必要がある He has to develop *courage*.

だんりょく【弾力】elasticity. ¶ ～のあるゴムひも an *elastic* rubber band. ～のないゴムひも an *inelastic* rubber band. ～性のある交渉 a *flexible* negotiation.

たんりょくしょく【淡緑色】light green.

たんれい【端麗】gracefulnesss; elegance.
¶ 彼女は容姿～だ She has a *graceful* figure. 彼は～な顔だちをしている He *is handsome*.

たんれん【鍛練・鍛錬】(心身の) training; discipline. ¶ 心身を～しなさい *Train* your mind and body. 座禅を組んで心を～する I *discipline* my mind sitting in *zen*-meditation. 彼は～をつんで名選手になった He *was trained* to become a skillful player.

だんろ【暖炉】a stove; a fireplace; a hearth.
¶ ～にあたる warm *oneself* at *a fireplace*.

だんろん【談論】discussion; argument.
¶ その件については～風発だった The matter *was* warmly *discussed*. / The matter *was discussed* with great animation.

だんわ【談話】a talk; a conversation.
¶ 彼は来客と～中です He *is in conversation with* a visitor. 彼の意見は～の形式で発表された His opinion was published in the form of *an informal talk*.
―室 a parlor; a lobby; a lounge.

た

ち

ち【地】1〘土地・地方〙the earth. ¶ 〜の果て the end of *the earth*.

彼が初めてヨーロッパの〜を踏んだのは一昨年だ He *set foot* in Europe for the first time the year before last.

この〜ははるかに海をながめる景勝の〜だ This *place*, commanding a long view of the sea, is *a place* of scenic beauty.

この〜の産物を三つあげなさい Name three *local* products.

スイスはイタリアと〜を接している Switzerland *adjoins* (≒ *lies next to*) Italy.

2〘比喩的に〙¶ 彼の名声は〜に落ちた His reputation *was ruined*.

一敗〜にまみれた We were entirely defeated.

ち【知・智】(知恵) wisdom ; (知力) intellect. ¶ 彼は才と〜ともにすぐれている He excels others both in talent and *intellect*.

ち【治】¶ 〜にいて乱を忘れず We must always be prepared for emergency.

ち【血】1〘血液〙blood. ¶ ナイフで指を切って〜を出した I cut my finger with a knife and it began to *bleed*. (I had my finger cut としないでよい).

きみの歯ぐきから〜が出ている Your gums *are bleeding*.

事故現場には大量の〜が流れていた A lot of (≒ A huge amount of) *blood* covered the scene of the accident.

彼は足からぽたぽたと〜を垂らしていた *Blood* was dripping from his foot (≒ feet).

献血のため〜を 200cc 採ってもらった I had 200 cc of my *blood* taken for blood donation.

傷口に当てたハンカチに〜がにじんでいた The handkerchief on the wound was stained with *blood*.

早く包帯をして傷口の〜を止めなさい Bandage the wound quickly and stop the *bleeding*.

彼のシャツにべっとりと〜がついていた His shirt was thickly covered with *blood*.

彼の手は〜だらけだった His hands were stained with *blood*. / He had *blood*-stained hands.

戦場はやがて〜の海となった The battlefield soon turned into a pool of *blood*.

〜のしたたるようなステーキをごちそうになった They served me a beefsteak *cooked rare*. (圏では an *underdone* steak という).

その光景に彼女の顔から〜の気が引いた Her face turned pale at the sight.

また〜の雨が降りそうだ We may see *bloodshed* again. / There may be another *bloodshed*.

両家の間には〜で〜を洗う争いが繰り返されてきた *Bloody* quarrels have been going on between the two families.

2〘血縁〙¶ 私たちは〜を分けた兄弟だ We are brothers of the same *blood*.

彼は祖父の〜を引いて酒癖が悪い He *takes after* his grandfather and is a terrible drunk.

私はあのおばとは〜がつながっていない I'*m* not *related to* that aunt.

〜は争えないものだ *Blood* will out.

〜は水よりも濃い〘諺〙*Blood is thicker than water*.

3〘慣用的表現〙¶ その鳥は〜を吐くような悲しい声を出すといわれている The bird is said to sing in an extremely sad voice, as if its heart *were bleeding*.

これは〜のにじむような苦労をしてためた金だ I have saved this money through *strenuous* efforts. / I have saved this money *by burning the candle at both ends*. / This is the money I saved *by working myself to the bone*.

この田畑の開拓は彼の〜と汗の結晶といってよい The cultivation of this field may be said to be the fruit of his *struggle*.

彼はいささか〜の気が多すぎる He is rather hot-*blooded*.

きみも〜の巡りの悪い男だね You certainly *are stupid*! / How *dull-witted* you *are*!

きみには〜も涙もないのか How *cold-blooded* you *are*! / How can you *be* so *cruel*!

彼の青春の〜は燃えた The *blood* of youth kindled in him. / It stirred his *blood* of youth.

それは〜わき肉おどる冒険談だった The story of the adventure was simply *thrilling*.

ちあい【血合い】(魚の) blood-colored flesh.

ちあん【治安】public peace ; tranquility (ふつうは law and order「法と秩序」という).

¶ 警察は町の〜を保った The police kept (≒ maintained) *the peace* of the town. 〜を乱した者は検挙された Those who disturbed the *public peace* were arrested.

—警察 the peace police. —条令 the Public Peace Regulation.

ちい【地衣】〘植物〙a lichen.

ちい【地位】position. ¶ 彼女は〜が高い She has *an* important *post*. 彼らは〜が低い They are of low *standing*. 彼は〜も金もある He has both *position* and money. 彼は婦人の〜向上のため大いに力を尽くした He did a great deal to elevate the *status* of women in society. 〜のある人すべて偉人とはかぎらない Not all men *of position* are great. 彼はキャプテンの〜にふさわし

ち

い働きをした His performance was worthy of his *position* as the leader. 人間の価値は～とは無関係だ A man's worth has nothing to do with his *position*.

ちいき【地域】an area; a region. ¶ 疫病はあっという間にその～一帯に蔓延(まんえん)した The epidemic spread very quickly over *an* extensive *area*.

―給 a regional allowance. ―差 regional differences. ―社会 a local society; a community. ―代表 the delegation of a local union; local union delegates.

ちいく【知育】intellectual training (⇆ discipline). ¶ ～に偏する overemphasize *intellectual training*.

チークざい【チーク材】teak. ¶ ～の家具 *teak* furniture.

ちいさ·い【小さい】small. ¶ あの～い家が私の家だ That *small* house over there is mine. ～いネコが庭を歩いている A *little* kitten is walking in the garden. この帽子は私には少し～い This hat *is* a bit too *small* for me. ～い声で歌いなさい Sing in a *low* voice. ～い字で名前を書きなさい Write your name in letters of *small* size. (small letters とすると capital letters に対する小文字の意味になる)．彼女は気が～いのでひと言もいわなかった She *was* so *shy* that she did not speak a word. けんかは～いことから始まることが多い Quarrels often begin over *trivial* things.

ちいさく【小さく】¶ 肉を～切ってください Will you please cut the meat into *small* pieces? 彼はそう小さな人間ではないが，まわりが大きいので～見える He is not so small but those around him make him look *smaller*. もっとテレビの音を～してほしい I want you to *turn down* the television. どうしてそんなに～なっているのですか Why *are* you so *quiet*?

チーズ cheese.

―フォンデュ cheese fondue. 粉― powdered cheese.

チーター〖動物〗a cheetah.

チーフ a chief.

チーム a team. ¶ どの～にもチームカラーはある Every *team* has the characteristic of its own.

―ワーク teamwork.

ちうみ【血膿】bloody pus.

ちえ【知恵】wisdom. ¶ ～のある子ども a *bright* (⇆ *clever*) child. 彼女はあまり～がない She has little *intelligence*. その方法は～がない That is not a *wise* method. 彼は息子に～をつけている He is giving his boy *a hint*. お～を拝借したいのですが Won't you give me *a piece of advice*?

―比べ a contest of wits. ―者 a wise man. ―歯 a wisdom tooth. ―おくれ ¶ ～の子ども a *retarded* child.

チェア a chair.

アーム― an armchair. デッキ― a deck chair.

チェーン a chain.

―ストア 米 a chain store; 英 a multiple shop. ―ブロック a chain block.

チェコ（人）a Czech.

―語 Czech. ―スロバキア人 a Czechoslovak.

チェス chess. ¶ ～をやる play *chess*.

―盤 a chessboard.

ちえっ Phew! / Tut!

チェック **1**〖模様〗¶ ～のスカート a *checked* skirt.

～の服地 *tartan* cloth.

2〖照会〗¶ 在庫品を帳簿と～する *check* goods in stock with the book.

―イン check in. ―アウト check out. ¶ ～アウトのお時間は12時です *Check* out is at twelve. (check in はふつう動詞として用いる)．

チェロ〖音楽〗a cello (複 cellos).

―奏者 a cellist.

ちえん【遅延】delay; retardation. ¶ 事故で列車は２時間～した The train *was delayed* two hours by an accident.

チェンジ a change.

―アップ〖野球〗change-up. ―オブペース〖野球〗a change of pace.

チェンバロ〖音楽〗a cembalo.

ちか【地下】underground. ¶ 彼らは～で仕事をしている They are working *underground*. ～100メートルの深さになにかがある Something is hidden 100 meters *below the ground*. そこは～に豊富な資源がある It has rich natural resources hidden *underground*.

―運動 underground activities. ―茎 a subterranean stem. ―資源 underground resources. ―室 a basement; 米 a cellar. ―水 underground water. ―鉄 米 a subway; 英 an underground [railway]. ―道 an underground passage; 英 a subway; an underpass.

ちか【地価】land value; the price (⇆ value) of land.

ちか【治下】¶ インドは長年の間イギリスの～におかれていた India *was under the rule of* Britain for a long time. / India had fallen *under* the British *rule* for long.

ちかい【誓い】an oath. ¶ 禁煙の～を立てている I *have vowed* not to smoke. 二度とそんなことはするまいと～を立てた I *made a vow* not to do such a thing again. 彼は禁酒の～を守っている He *is under a vow* not to drink any alcoholics.

ちかい【地階】a basement; a cellar.

ちか·い【近い】**1**〖距離〗¶ 学校は私の家から～い The school *is near* my house. / The school *is close to* my house.

駅はこの道を行くのがいちばん～い This is *the nearest* way to the railroad station.

もっと～くに来なさい Come *nearer* (⇆ *closer*). 私たちの席は舞台から～すぎた Our seats *were* too *close to* the stage.

山頂は～い We have *almost* reached the summit. / The summit *is near at hand*.

2〖時間〗¶ もう12時～いから寝たほうがいい *It's nearly* twelve now. It's time you went

to bed.(過去形 went に注意).
また～いうちにお伺いします I'll come again *soon*./ I'll come and see you again *shortly*.
～いうちに彼は辞職するだろう He will probably resign *in the near future*.(in future「これからは」と区別すること).
もう夏休みも終わりに～い The summer vacation *is almost over* now. / We *are already at the end of* the summer holidays. / The summer vacation *is drawing to an end*.
ヒグラシが鳴くと秋も～い When the clear-toned cicadas begin to chirp, autumn *is near at hand* (≒ *is just around the corner*).
ぼくはいずれ～いうちに彼に忠告するつもりだ I will give advice to him *one of these days*.
3 〚ほとんど…; もう少しで…〛 ¶ 彼女は40に～い She *is nearly* forty. / She *is going on for* forty.
クラス会には30人～い人が集まった *Almost* thirty persons attended the class meeting.
彼の研究の完成も～い He will complete his research *before long*. / His study *is nearing* completion. / *It won't be long before* he accomplishes his research.
私の会社は最近の為替レートの変更で1,000万円～い損失を被った Our company suffered a loss of *almost* ten million yen on account of the recent change in the exchange rate.
そういうことは不可能に～い That's *almost* impossible. / Such a thing is *hardly* possible./ It *is next to* impossible.
4 〚近眼〛 ¶ ぼくは子どものときから目が～い I *have been short-sighted* since my childhood.

ちがい【違い】 difference. ¶ ふたりは身分の～があった There was *a disparity* (≒ *a difference*) in social positions between the two. このことばとあのことばの間に意味上の～はほとんどない There is little *difference* in meaning between this word and that. この方法でもその方法でもたいした～はない It *makes* little *difference* whether you take this way or that. ふたりの姉妹の年齢の～はどのくらいですか What is the age *difference* between the two sisters? 兄は私とふたつ～です My brother is two years older than I.

ちがいない【違いない】¶ 彼はこのことを知っているに～ He *must know* this. / *I'm sure* he knows this. きっと彼女がそれをやってくれたに～ She *must have done* it for me. きみはきっと成功するに～ *I'm sure* that you will succeed. / *You are sure to* be successful. それに～(そのとおりだ) That's quite true. / You're quite right.

ちがいほうけん【治外法権】 extraterritorial (≒ exterritorial) rights; extraterritoriality.

ちか·う【誓う】¶ 私は真実を話すことを天地神明に～う I solemnly *swear by* (≒ *to*) God [that] I will speak the truth. (儀式ばった固い言い方). ～ってうそは申しません I *promise* [that] I'll tell you the truth.
それは～ってうそはない I'll *give* you *my word* (≒ I'll *pledge my honor*) *for* that. / You can take word for that.
彼は自分の言にまちがいないと～った He *pledged* his word.
秘密にすることを～った We *were pledged to* secrecy.
彼は禁煙を～った He *swore off* smoking.
彼は禁酒を～った He *resolved* to give up drinking. / He *made an oath* to give up drinking. / He *swore off* drinking.
私は同じ誤りを繰り返すまいと心に～った I firmly *resolved* (≒ *determined*) not to make the same mistake again.
彼らは将来を～いあった They *promised* to each other to be man and wife. / They *promised* to get married.
彼らは国家に忠誠を～った They *pledged* to their country.

ちが·う【違う】**1** 〚異なる〛 differ (*from*).
¶「これがあなたのお宅ですか」「いや～います」 "Is this your house?" "No, it *isn't*."
この花とあの花は大きさが～う This flower *is different in* size *from* that.
彼の机と私の机はずいぶん～う His desk *differs* very much *from* mine.
馬とロバはどんな風に～いますか In what way *is* a horse *different from* a donkey?
彼は言うこととすることが～う What he says *does not agree with* what he does.
これは私がなくした本とは～う This is *not* the book I have lost.
ふたりの兄弟は性格がまるっきり～う The two brothers *are* entirely *different in* character *from* each other.
彼はそう言うが，私は考えが～う He says so, but I think *otherwise*.(彼が間違っているとはなるべく言わないでこのように言う).
これは私の注文したものとは～う This is *not* what I ordered.
値だんは大きさで～う The prices *vary* according to size.
これではない．～うのを見せてください This is not what I want. Please show me *another*.
今はあの時代とは全然～っている Things *have* entirely *changed* since that.
弟は兄と～って背が高い *Unlike* the older brother, the younger is tall.
2 〚間違う〛 ¶ この答えは～っている This answer is *wrong*.
計算を～った I *made a mistake* in calculation.

ちが·える【違える】 change. ¶ 今度は道を～えて行こう Now let's take a *different* way. 約束を～えないようにしなさい Never *break* your promise. バスを乗り～えた I took the *wrong* bus. あわてたため読み～えた In my hurry I *misread* it.

ちかく【近く】**1** 〚時間〛 ¶ ～お伺いします I'd like to come and see you *shortly* (≒ *before long*).
彼は～アメリカから帰る He'll *soon* be back from the United States.

子どもたちは夕方～家に帰っていった The children went home *toward evening*.

2 〖距離〗 ¶ 私の家は学校のすぐ～だ Our house *is* quite *close to* the school.

駅のすぐ～にホテルがある There is a hotel *close by* the railroad station.

この～に銀行はありませんか Is there a bank *around* here?

それを～から見てみよう Let's take a *close* look at it. / Let's look at it from *close at hand*.

私は遠くを見てまた～に目を向けた I looked at a distant view and turned my eyes to the *near* view.

もう少し～にお寄りなさい Please come a little 〔bit〕 *closer*.

3 〖およそ〗 nearly ; about ; almost (nearly は「もう少しで…近く」という意味で, ある数未満を意味する. これに対して about は「およそ…」という意味で, ある数以上でも未満でもよい. また almost も nearly と同じく, ある数未満を意味するが, nearly のほうが, 驚き・安心などの感じを強く表わす).

¶ その事故で50人～の人がけがをした *Nearly* fifty persons were injured in the accident.

もう真夜中～だった It was *nearly* midnight.

100人～の人が出席した *About* a hundred people were there.

ちかく【地核】〖地学〗 the earth's nucleus.

ちかく【知覚】(認識) perception ; (意識) consciousness ; (感覚) sensation.

━神経 sensory nerves. **━表象** perceived symbols ; percept.

ちかく【地殻】〖地学〗 the crust 〔of the earth〕.

ちがく【地学】 physical geography ; geology.

ちかごろ【近頃】 recently ; lately ; (このごろ) these days (recently, lately は現在完了形または過去形とともに用いられる. these days には口語では in をつけないのがふつう).

¶ ～の若い者はエチケットを知らない *Today's* youngsters (≒ Young people 〔*of*〕 *today*) do not know how to behave. 彼は～までここにいた He 〔has〕 lived here until *recently*.

ちかし・い【近しい・親しい】 ¶ 彼とは～い仲です He and I are good friends. / I'm *close* friends with him. 彼は彼女とは～い関係のようだ He seems to *be on intimate terms with* her. (intimate はかなり懇ろな関係を意味する. be on intimate terms with は一般には "Mr. Brown" というような呼び方でなく, 互いに "John" "Bill" というような first name で呼び合うような関係をいう).

ちかちか ¶ 明るすぎて, 目が～する Too much light *dazzles* my eyes. 星が～光っている The stars *are twinkling*.

ちかぢか【近近】 shortly ; before long ; in very near future.

ちかづき【近付き】 ¶ お～になれてうれしい I'm glad to *have met* you. (初対面の人への別れぎわのあいさつ). / I am very happy to *have made your acquaintance*.

ちかづ・く【近付く】 approach. ¶ 駅に～いた We *are approaching* (≒ *are coming near*) the railroad station. 休暇も終わりに～いている The vacation *is nearing* its end. 2学期が～いた The second term *is near at hand*. 春が～いてあたたかくなった Spring *drew near*, and it became warmer. 彼は～きにくい It is difficult to *talk to* him. ああいうグループには～かないほうがいい You must *keep away from* such a group.

ちかづ・ける【近付ける】 ¶ 関係者以外は～けない None but the persons concerned *are admitted*. (none but～ の none はふつう複数扱い). カメラをそれに～けた I *put* a camera *close to* the object. 彼は人を～けない He *keeps others away from him*. / He *is hard to approach*. / He *is unapproachable*. 彼は犬をこわがって～けない He is afraid of dogs and never *let* them *come near*.

ちかって【誓って】 ¶ ～うそは申しません *I swear* I will never tell a lie. / *I promise* 〔that〕 I'll tell the truth. / *On my honor* (≒ *word*) I'll never tell a lie.

ちかまわり【近回り】 a short cut. ¶ ～する take *a short cut*.

ちかみち【近道】 a short cut. ¶ ～をして帰った I came home by *a short cut*. 森を抜けて～をした I took *a short cut* through the woods. それがいちばんの～だ That's *the shortest way*. 努力以外成功の～はない Effort is the only *short cut* to success.

ちかめ【近め】 ¶ ～の球 a ball *on the inside*.

ちかよ・る【近寄る】 ¶ 彼には～りがたいところがある There is something unapproachable about him. / He is rather hard to approach. 彼には～らないほうがいい You'd better keep away from him. / You'd better leave him alone.

ちから【力】 **1** 〖物理的な力〗 power. ¶ この機械は～が強い This machine *is* very *powerful*. この車のエンジンは 90 度 C で最大の～が出る This car exerts its strongest *power* at 90 degrees centigrade.

風の～でこの風車は回っている The wind *powers* the mill. / The wind keeps the mill going.

蒸気機関は熱を～に換える The steam engine turns heat into *power*.

2 〖体力〗 strength. ¶ 女の～ではこの荷物は運べまい This baggage is too heavy to be carried by a woman. / I don't think any woman is strong enough to carry this baggage.

最後の～をふりしぼって頂上にたどりついた We reached the summit exerting what little *strength* we had left.

この知らせを聞いて体じゅうの～が抜けてしまった When I heard the news, all my *strength* was gone.

ふたりで～を合わせればこの石は動かせよう I think we can move this stone if we do it together.

もっと～を出して網を引け Pull the net much *harder*.

3 〖能力・力量〗 ability. ¶ 私にはこの問題を処理する～はありません It is not within my *power* to handle such a problem.

私は自分の～の限界を心得ている I know the

limitations of my *ability.*

天候を左右することは人間の～ではどうにもならぬ Controlling the weather is beyond man's *power.*

彼の数学の～はクラス一だ He is at the top of his class in mathematics.

あの先生はとても英語の～をつけてくれる The teacher is helpful in improving our English *ability.*

きみはだいぶ英語の～がついた You *have improved* much *in* your English. / You *have made progress in* your English. (progress は形容詞がついても冠詞は用いない). / You *have become proficient in* English.

この敗戦でわがチームは自分たちの～不足を痛感した When we lost the game, we fully realized the *weakness* of our team.

この社会では～のない者は脱落していくよりほかない In this society there is nothing that *the weak* can do but be left behind. / Those with no *ability* must simply be left behind in this world.

～のかぎりつとめた I tried *to the best of my power.*

4 〖頼り・助力〗 ¶ この計画を立てるにあたり彼はいろいろ～になってくれた He *was of* great *help to* us in planning this. / He *helped* us a lot *in* this plan.

人の～を借りることを考えてはいけない You should not expect the *help* of others. / Don't expect others to *help* you.

ぼくはきみだけを～と頼んでいるのだ You are the only person that I can *depend on.* / It is you that I *am counting on.*

5 〖効力・影響力〗 influence. ¶ 子どもの訓育に及ぼす教師の～は大きい The teacher's *influence* on his pupils' education is very great.

彼の発言は議論の趨勢(すうせい)を決めるに大きな～となった His statement had greatly determined the trend of the discussion.

彼は政府部内で相当な～を持っている He *is* quite *influential* in the government.

6 〖権力〗 ¶ お上の～でぜひこの問題を解決していただきたい We earnestly request the government to settle this problem.

警察の～も地に落ちたものだ The *authority* of the police is less far-reaching than it was.

7 〖気力〗 ¶ ～を落とさないことだ You should not *be discouraged.*

ちからいっぱい 【力一杯】 ¶ ～バットを振った I swung the bat *with all my force* (≒ *with all my might; with all my strength*). 彼らはその綱を～引っ張った They pulled the rope *with might and main.* この問題の解決に～がんばってみます I'll *do* (≒ *try*) *my best* to solve the problem. 私は～戸をたたいた I knocked at the door *as hard as I could.*

ちからおとし 【力落とし】 ¶ ご主人を亡くされさぞお～のことでしょう I can imagine how *grieved you are at* the loss of your husband.

ちからくらべ 【力比べ】 ¶ ～をしよう Let's see who is the strongest. / Let's see who is the stronger, you or I. (後者はふたりの場合).

ちからこぶ 【力瘤】 ¶ 腕を曲げると～ができる When you bend your arms, the muscles of your upper arms will *stand out* (≒ *swell up*) *in knots.* PTAがこの行事に～を入れている The P.T.A. *backs up* this program.

ちからしごと 【力仕事】 ぼくは～には向かない I'm not fit for heavy labor.

ちからずく 【力尽く】 ¶ 彼は～で自分の主張を通そうとする He tries to carry his point *forcibly* (≒ *by force*). / He always tries to make people agree to his opinion *by coercion.* 彼のやり方はいつも～だ He always carries matters *high-handedly.*

ちからぞえ 【力添え】 help; aid; assistance (この3語はほぼ同意に用いられるが, help は一般的な語で, aid は助けられる方が非力で助ける方が強大である意味が含まれ, assist はわき役としての助力を意味することがある).

¶ なにとぞお～を! Please *help* me. / I need your *help* badly. (口語的) / Will you please give us some *aid*? / May I ask for your *assistance*? ひとつお～を頂けないでしょうか Could I ask for your *assistance*?

ちからだめし 【力試し】 ¶ ～にやってみよう Let's *try our strength.* ～にテストを受けた I took the examination to *test my real ability.*

ちからつ・きる 【力尽きる】 ¶ 彼は～きてゴール寸前で倒れた He *was exhausted* and fell down right near the goal. 彼はついに～きてそこに倒れた Finally he fell down *exhausted.*

ちからづ・く 【力付く】 ¶ 少年は先生のことばで～いた The boy *was cheered up* (≒ *was encouraged*) by his teacher's words. 彼らは一休みするといくらか～いた They *were* a little *refreshed* after taking a rest.

ちからづ・ける 【力付ける】 ¶ 私は彼の成功に～けられた I *was encouraged at* his success.

ちからづよ・い 【力強い】 ¶ きみがそばにいてくれて～い I *feel* quite *at ease* with you. / Your presence *is* very *encouraging.* その小説は～い文体で書かれている The novel is written in *vigorous* style.

ちからぬけ 【力抜け】 disappointment; discouragement. ¶ すっかり～がした I *was* much *discouraged.*

ちからまかせ 【力任せ】 ¶ その綱を～に引っ張った I pulled the rope *with all my strength.* 彼はその男の頭を～になぐった He gave the man a *violent* blow on the head.

ちからまけ 【力負け】 ¶ 相手にわがチームは～している (緊張しすぎて負けている) Our team *is losing the game* because of the strain caused by nervousness. / (体力が劣っている) Our team *is inferior to* the opponent in strength.

ちからもち 【力持ち】 a strong man. ¶ 彼は縁の下の～だ He does a toilsome yet thankless task. 彼は気はやさしくて～だ He *is* kind [-hearted] and *strong.*

ちからわざ 【力業】 heavy work (≒ labor); manual work (≒ labor). ¶ ～では彼にかなわない I am not his equal in *physical work.*/

I cannot beat him at *physical strength.*

ちかん【置換】〘化学〙substitution ; replacement. ¶ 分子中の酸素をイオウと～する *substitute* sulfur *for* oxygen in a molecule.

ちかん【痴漢】a molester ; a sex maniac.

ちかん【弛緩】relaxation ; laxity ; slackness. ¶ 近ごろの道徳の～は実に嘆かわしい I cannot help deploring today's moral *corruption.* / The recent moral *laxity* is really deplorable. 彼はこのごろ精神が～している He *is lacking* in application these days.

ちき【知己】an acquaintance ; a friend. ¶彼には～が多い He has many *friends* (≒ *acquaintances*). / He is rich in *friends.* 彼と会って, 百年の～を得た思いだ I'm happy to say that I've found *a true friend* in him.

ちき【稚気】childishness. ¶ 彼には愛すべき～がある There is something amiably *childish* about him.

ちきゅう【地球】the earth ; the globe. ¶ ～の表面 the surface of *the earth.* ～の引力 terrestrial gravitation.

—儀 a 〔terrestrial〕 globe. **—物理学** geophysics.

ちぎょ【稚魚】fry ; young of fishes.

ちきょう【地峡】an isthmus. ¶ スエズ～ the *Isthmus* of Suez.

ちきょうだい【乳兄弟】(男) a foster brother ; (女) a foster sister.

ちぎり【契り】¶ 彼らは夫婦の～を結んだ They *became man and wife.* / They *got married.*

ちぎ·る【契る】¶ ふたりは二世を～った間柄だ They *are engaged.* / They *pledged themselves* to love each other eternally.

ちぎ·る【千切る】¶ 花びらを1枚～った I *plucked* a petal *off* the flower. メモ用紙を1枚～りとった I *tore* a leaf *out of* (≒ *from ; off*) a scratch pad.

ちぎれぐも【千切れ雲】scattered clouds.

ちぎれちぎれ ¶ 彼らは～になった断片を集めて原型を再現した They put the *broken* pieces together and restored the original form.

ちぎ·れる【千切れる】¶ 綱が～れた The rope *broke.* 本の表紙が～れた The front cover *came off* the book. 寒さで耳が～れそうだ A cold wind is biting my ears.

チキン chicken.

—ライス chicken and rice. ロースト**—** roast chicken.

ちく【地区】an area ; a district ; a zone ; a region (area は「ある特定の区域」, district は「行政上の区画」, zone は「境界線に囲まれた地区」, region は「他と異なった特徴のある地区」(たとえば a mountain (forest) region) を意味する).

¶ 彼らのチームが関東～の代表になった Their team represented the Kanto *area* (≒ *district*).

商業**—** the business zones (≒ section) ; the commercial area ; the business district ; the downtown area.

ちくいち【逐一】in detail ; (ひとつずつ) one by one. ¶ 彼は状況を～報告した He *made a detailed report of* the situation. われわれは問題を～審議した We discussed the problems *one by one.*

ちぐう【知遇】favor. ¶ 彼は師の～を得た He *won* his teacher's *favor.* / He *found favor with* his teacher.

ちくこう【築港】construction of a harbor.

ちくごやく【逐語訳】word-for-word (≒ literal) translation.

ちくざい【蓄財】¶ 彼は～に専念している He is only interested in *saving* 〔*up*〕 *money.*

ちくさん【畜産】livestock industry ; stock raising (≒ breeding ; farming).

—業者 a livestock raiser (≒ breeder).

ちくじ【逐次】successively. ¶ その新しいシリーズは～刊行される予定です The new series of books will be published *one after another* (≒ *at frequent intervals ; at short intervals*).

ちくしょう【畜生】**1** 〘動物〙a beast ; a brute. **2** 〘ののしりのことば〙 ¶ ～! (いまいましいことだ) Hang (≒ Confound) it! / (いまいましいやつだ) Hang (≒ Confound) you! / (しまった) Great Scott! / Oh, dear! / Dear me! / Dear God! / My Goodness! (多少女性的). / (なんてこった) Gosh! / God damn it! / Jesus Christ! / Doggone it. (最後の三つはかなり下品).

ちくじょう【築城】fortification. ¶ 太田道灌は江戸に～した Ota Dokan *built* (≒ *constructed*) *a castle* in Edo.

—術 〔the science of〕 fortification.

ちくじょう【逐条】¶ その法案は～審議された The bill was discussed *article by article* (≒ *clause by clause*).

ちくせき【蓄積】accumulation. ¶ 富 (知識 ; 疲労) の～ the *accumulation of* wealth (knowledge ; fatigue) ; the *accumulated* wealth (knowledge ; fatigue). 富を～する *accumulate* (≒ *store up*) wealth.

ちくぞう【築造】construction. ¶ ～する build ; construct.

ちくちく ¶ 針で～つつく *prick* with a needle. 歯が～痛む My tooth *is pricking* (≒ *is prickling*). 彼は話の間に～皮肉を言った There was a touch of irony in his talk. / He used *stinging* sarcasm in his speech.

ちくでん【逐電】escape ; flight. ¶ 事務員が会社の金を盗んで～した A clerk *ran away* (≒ *absconded*) with some amount of money belonging to the company.

ちくでんき【蓄電器】〘電気〙a condenser.

ちくでんち【蓄電池】〘電気〙a storage battery (≒ cell).

ちくのうしょう【蓄膿症】〘医学〙empyema.

ちぐはぐ ¶ このくつは～だ These shoes are *an odd pair.* 彼らは気持ちが～なまま別れた They parted *before they came to an understanding of each other.* / They parted *without understanding each other.* 彼の話は～になった His argument *was inconsistent* (≒ *was incoherent ; was illogical*).

ちくば【竹馬】¶ 彼とは～の友だ He and I *have*

been good friends since our childhood. / We *are friends from childhood.*

ちくび【乳首】a nipple ; a teat.

ちくり ¶ 針で～と刺す *prick* with a needle. 彼のことばに～としたものが感じられる There is something *stinging* in his words. / His remarks are a little *sarcastic*(≒ *ironical*). (sarcastic はしばしば相手を中傷する皮肉に, irony は事実と反対のことを言う皮肉に用いられる).

ちくわ【竹輪】fish paste shaped like a section of bamboo 〔trunk〕.

ちけい【地形】topography ; geographical features.

—図 a topographical map.

チケット a ticket.

ちけむり【血煙】a spray of blood.

ちけん【知見】knowledge. ⇒ けんぶん

ちご【稚児】an infant ; a child.

—行列 a *kimono*-clad children's procession in a Buddhist festival.

ちこう【地溝】a trough.

ちこく【遅刻】¶ 学校に～するな Don't *be late for* school. ぼくは～してしかられた I was scolded for *being late.* (late に強勢をおかないと意味が変わる).

—届 a report for being late ; a late 〔-〕report. —者 a late-comer.

ちこつ【恥骨】〔解剖学〕the pubis ; the pubic bone.

ちさ【萵苣】〔植物〕lettuce.

ちさい【地裁】(地方裁判所) a district court.

ちさん【遅参】¶ ～して申し訳ありません I'm very sorry I'*ve come late.*

ちし【地史】the terrestrial history.

ちし【知歯】a wisdom tooth. ¶ この子は～が生えかけている This boy is cutting (≒ is developing) his *wisdom tooth.*

ちし【地誌】a topography.

ちし【致死】—量 a fatal dose (*of*). ¶ この薬の～量はどのくらいですか What's the *fatal dose* of this medicine? / How much *is fatal* when you take this medicine? 過失—罪 accidental homicide. ¶ 彼は過失～罪に問われた He was accused of *accidental homicide.*

ちじ【知事】a 〔prefectural〕 governor. ¶ 千葉県～ the *Governor* of Chiba Prefecture.

ちしお【血潮】blood. ¶ ～に染まった遺品 *blood-stained* articles left behind.

ちしき【知識】knowledge ; information.

¶ この本はパズルに関する～を与えてくれた This book has given me *information* about puzzles. 彼は経済の～が多少ある He has some *knowledge* of economics. (some に強勢を入れて [sʌ́m] と読むと「かなりの」の意味になる). 私は数学の～がほとんどない I have little *knowledge* about mathematics. この本は～を広めるのにたいへん役立つ This book is useful in adding to our stock of *knowledge.* 日本についての～のない人は少なくない There are not a few persons who have little *knowledge of* (≒ *information on*) Japan. 彼は～のある人だ He is a *well-informed* man.

—階級 the intellectual〔s〕; the intelligentsia (この語はあまり用いない). —人 an intellectual. —欲 a thirst for knowledge.

ちじき【地磁気】〔地学〕terrestrial magnetism.

ちじく【地軸】the earth's axis. ¶ ～をゆるがす大音響が聞こえた There was a *terrific* (≒ *deafening*) noise 〔in my ears〕.

ちしつ【地質】geological features ; (土質) the nature of the soil. ¶ その地域に関しては非常に広範な～調査がまもなく行なわれることになろう A very extensive *geological* survey of that area will be carried out before long.

—学 geology. —学者 a geologist. —時代 the geological age.

ちしつ【知悉】¶ 彼はアメリカ文学を～している He *is well versed in* American literature. / He *has a complete knowledge of* American literature.

ちしま【千島】—列島 the Kurile Islands ; the Kuriles. —海流 the Kurilian Current.

ちしゃ【知者】a wise man ; a man of wisdom ; (総称) the wise.

ちしょう【知将】a resourceful (≒ well-advised) general.

ちじょう【地上】¶ ～の楽園 a paradise *on earth* ; an *earthly* paradise. 塔の高さは～50メートルある The tower rises 50 meters *above the ground.*

—権〔法律〕surface rights. —権所有者 a surface right owner. —権設定 settlement of surface rights.

ちじょう【痴情】〔a〕 blind passion ; lust ; (しっと) jealousy. ¶ ～のからんだ犯行 a crime of *a blind passion.*

ちじょうい【知情意】intellect, emotion, and volition.

ちじょく【恥辱】disgrace ; (侮辱) insult.

¶ この事件は学校にとって～だ This occurrence is *a disgrace* (≒ *shame* ; *dishonor*) *to* our school. 彼は甘んじて～を受ける決心をした He decided to submit to *disgrace.* 彼は満座の中で～を受けた He *was insulted* (≒ *was disgraced* ; *was humiliated*) before the whole company. 今こそ～をすすぐ時 Now is the time to wipe *disgrace*!

ちじん【知人】a friend ; an acquaintance.

¶ 彼は各界に～を多く持っている He has *a* wide *acquaintance* (≒ many *acquaintances*) in various circles.

ちじん【痴人】a fool ; an idiot ; a simpleton.

¶ そんなことは～のたわごとにすぎない That's nonsense!

ちず【地図】a map ; (地図書) an atlas ; (都市などの) a plan ; (産業などを主にするもの) a chart.

¶ 5万分の1の～ *a map* on a scale of 1 to 50,000. ～を調べる consult (≒ read) *a map.* ～で場所を探す look up a place on *a map.* ～に出ていなかった It was not on *a map.* ～を頼りに彼を訪ねた I visited him with the help (≒ aid) of *a map.*

掛け— a wall map. 白— a blank map. 歴史— a historical map (≒ atlas).

ち

ちすい【治水】river improvement; flood control. ¶ その川の～は成功した The *flood control* of the river turned out to be a great success.
——工事 embankment work; 米 levee works.

ちすじ【血筋】(血族) blood; (家系) lineage; [family] parentage. ¶ 彼は～がよい He is a man of good *origin*. 彼は狂人の～を引いている Madness runs in his *blood*. ～は争えないものだ *Heredity* will out.

ちせい【地勢】topography.
——図 topography.

ちせい【知性】intellect. ¶ ～的な顔 an *intellectual* face. ～のすぐれた人 a man *of intellect*. 彼にはほとんど～が見られない He shows little *intelligence*. 彼の話しぶりは感情に訴えるよりは～に訴える His speech appeals to the *intellect* rather than to the emotions.

ちせい【治世】a reign; a rule. ¶ 明治天皇の～に during the *reign* of the Emperor Meiji.

ちせき【地籍】a land register.

ちせき【治績】good administration. ¶ 彼は知事として大いに～をあげた His governorship resulted in a great success. 彼の～は大いに上がった His *administration* proved to be successful.

ちせつ【稚拙】¶ 埴輪(はにわ)はその～さ故にかえって愛される Clay images are loved the more because of their *naive* beauty. / Clay images are loved because of their beauty of *artless simplicity*.

ちそ【地租】a land tax.

ちそう【地層】〘地質〙a stratum (複 strata); a layer.

ちそう【馳走】a feast; a treat; a dinner.
¶ その晩は彼のところでご～になった That evening he *feasted* us. 感謝祭に彼らはご～を食べる On Thanksgiving Day they have *a feast*. 彼は一流のレストランで私たちに夕食をご～してくれた He *treated* us *to* dinner at a first-rate restaurant. 何をご～しようか What shall I *treat* you *to*? こんどは私がご～する番です It is my turn to *treat*. / You are my guest this time. ご～さまになりました Everything was delicious. / That was a wonderful dinner. いなかに居ることが私にはなによりのご～だ Staying in the country is the greatest *feast* to me now.

ちそく【遅速】(速力) speed; (進度) progress.

ちぞめ【血染め】¶ ～のハンカチ a *blood-stained* handkerchief; a handkerchief *stained with blood*.

ちたい【地帯】a zone; a region.
安全—— a safety zone; (市街電車などのとき) a traffic island. 工業—— an industrial area. 危険—— a danger zone. 中立—— a neutral zone. 森林—— forest zone. 綿花—— the cotton belt. 緑—— a greenbelt; a green belt.

ちたい【遅滞】delay. ¶ その計画を～なく実施してほしい It is desirable that the plan should be carried out *without delay* (≒ *immediately*).

チタニウム〘化学〙titanium.

ちだらけ【血だらけ】¶ 彼らは～になって戦った They fought with each other *covered with blood all over*.

ちだるま【血達磨】¶ 彼は～で倒れていた He was found lying *in a pool of blood*. / We found him lying *covered with blood all over*.

チタン〘化学〙titanium.

ちち【父】a father. ¶ 義理の～ a father-in-law; a foster father. ～のない子 a *fatherless* child. 天にましますわれらの～ our Heavenly *Father*; Our *Lord* in Heaven. この～にしてこの子あり (諺) *Like father, like son*. ～の日 Father's Day. チョーサーは英文学の～といわれる Chaucer is called the *father* of English literature.

ちち【乳】milk. ¶ この牛は～がよく出る This cow *milks* well. / This cow produces a lot of *milk*. 彼は毎朝牛の～を搾る He *milks* cows every morning. 彼女は～の出がとまった Her breasts have run dry. 赤ん坊に(自分の)～を飲ませていた She *was suckling* her baby.

ちち【遅遅】slow. ¶ 工事は～として進まない The works make *slow* progress. (progress に冠詞なし). / The works progress *at a snail's pace*.

ちちかた【父方】¶ 彼は～の親類だ He is related *on my father's side*. / He is a *paternal* relative.

ちちくさ・い【乳臭い】¶ 赤ん坊は～い Babies *smell of milk*. 彼はまだまだ～い(未熟だ) He is still a *green* boy. / He *is* quite *green as grass*. / He *is half-fledged*.

ちちくび【乳首】a nipple.

ちぢこま・る【縮こまる】¶ 寒さが厳しいので～って寝た I *was huddled* (≒ *huddled myself*) *up* in bed with the severe cold.

ちちばなれ【乳離れ】⇒ ちばなれ

ちぢま・る【縮まる】⇒ ちぢむ

ちぢみ【縮み】(織り) shrunken cloth; crepe; crape; watered silk.

ちぢ・む【縮む】shrink; (短くなる) be shortened; (小さくなる) contract. ¶ この布地は洗っても～まない This cloth won't *shrink* in the wash. ウール地のものは熱湯で洗うと～む Woolen cloth *shrinks* (≒ *contracts*) when washed in hot water. 隣の真っ暗な部屋でどさりと物の落ちる音がしたとき恐ろしくて～み上がった We *shrank* with fear (≒ We *were terrified*) when there was a thumping noise in the next dark room. 私は寿命の～む思いがした I felt as if my life were coming to an end.

ちぢ・める【縮める】(省略する) abridge; (短くする) cut down; shorten. ¶ 寿命を～める *shorten one's* life. 首を～める *duck one's* head. 文章を～める *abridge* a composition. 修業年限を～める *shorten* (≒ *reduce*) the term of study. 休暇を～める *cut down* the holidays. 上着のわきの下を少し～めてもらった I *had* my coat lightly *drawn in* under the arms.

ちちゅう【地中】¶ その宝は～に埋めてあった The treasure was found buried *in the earth*.

彼らはその爆弾を～から掘り出している最中であった They were digging the bomb *out of the ground.* その木は～深く根を張っていた The tree struck root deep *into the ground.*

ちちゅうかい【地中海】the Mediterranean 〔Sea〕.

ちぢら·す【縮らす】(髪を) curl (*one's* hair) ; (しわにする) shrink. ¶ 彼女は髪を～している She keeps her hair *in curl.*

ちぢ·れる【縮れる】(髪が) become curly ; be frizzled ; (しわになる) shrink ; be wrinkled.
¶ ～れ毛 a curl ; *curly* hair. 彼女は髪が～れている She has *curly* hair. / Her hair *is kinky.*

ちつ【膣】〖解剖学〗the vagina.

ちつ【帙】a folding case for a book or books.

ちっかぶつ【窒化物】〖化学〗a nitride.

チッキ a check. ¶ 荷物を～にする 米 *check* a baggage. 荷物を～にする (してもらう) 米 *have one's* baggage *checked* ; 英 *have one's* luggage *registered.* シカゴまでかばんを～で送ろう I will *check* my bag through to Chicago.

チック (整髪用品) a cosmetic.

ちつじょ【秩序】order ; method. ¶ ～を確立する establish *order.* その国の～は保たれている *Law and order* is maintained in that country. このごろの社会は～が乱れている Society these days *is out of order.* この人たちの議論にはほとんど～がない There is hardly any *order* in their discussion. 彼は～だって仕事をする He works *systematically* (≒ *methodically*). 彼の仕事ぶりには～がある There is *system* in his way of working. 彼は～だててものを考えない He has no *system* in his thinking.

ちっそ【窒素】〖化学〗nitrogen. ¶ ～と化合させる nitrogenize. 空気中から～をとる extract *nitrogen* from air.
—肥料 nitrogenous fertilizer (≒ manure). 空中—固定〔法〕atmospheric nitrogen fixation.

ちっそく【窒息】suffocation. ¶ この部屋は暑くて～しそうだ We *are smothering* (≒ *are suffocating*) in this sultrily stuffy room. こんな厳しい規則に縛られては～してしまう These strict rules *choke* (≒ *suffocate*) me.
—死 death from (≒ by) suffocation. ¶ その火事では多くの人が煙に巻かれて～死した Many people *were choked to death* with smoke in the fire.

ちつづき【血続き】blood relationship ; (人) a blood relative.

ちっと ¶ もう～時間が欲しい I want to have *a little more* time. ～は英語を話しもする I speak English *a little.* ～はわかったか Did you understand *even a bit?*

ちっとも ¶ ～疲れていない I am *not* tired *at all.* ～かまわない I *don't* mind *at all.* ～時間が残っていない We have *no* time left.

チップ 1〖心づけ〗a tip ; a gratuity. ¶ ～を出す tip ; give (≒ offer) *a tip.*
給仕に～を奮発した I generously *tipped* a waiter. ウエイトレスに～を25セントやった I *tipped* a waitress a quarter.
当館では～は絶対に頂きません *Tips* are most emphatically not accepted in our hotel.
2〖野球〗a tip.

ちっぽけ ¶ ～な tiny ; very small (≒ little).

ちてい【地底】the bowels of the earth.

ちてき【知的】¶ ～な顔 an *intellectual* face.
—生活 an intellectual life. —能力 intellectual faculties ; intellectual powers.

ちてん【地点】a spot ; a point. ¶ 便利な (危険な) ～ *a* convenient (dangerous) *spot.* たまたまその交通事故の起こった～に居合わせた I happened to be at the *spot* where the traffic accident took place.

ちどうせつ【地動説】the Copernican theory ; the heliocentric theory.

ちどめ【血止め】(薬) a styptic. ¶ とにかくその傷の～をするのが先決だ At any rate the first thing to do is to *stop the bleeding* of that cut.

ちどり【千鳥】〖鳥類〗a plover. ¶ 彼がひどく酔って～足で歩いているのを見た I saw him *reeling along* (≒ *tottering ; walking along unsteadily ; walking zigzag*) deadly drunk.

ちどん【遅鈍】stupidity ; dullness. ¶ ～な stupid ; dull.

ちなまぐさ·い【血なまぐさい】¶ ～い戦場 the *bloody* (≒ *sanguinary*) field.

ちなみに【因に】¶ ～彼は昨年暮れに死んでおります It may be said *in this connection* (≒ *in passing ; incidentally*) that he passed away toward the end of last year.

ちな·む【因む】¶ そのことに～んであなたのご存じのことをみんな話してください Please tell me all you know *in connection with* that matter. 彼はおじいさんに～んで William と名づけられた He was named William *after* (≒ 米 *for*) his grandfather.

ちにちか【知日家】a pro-Japanese.

ちぬ·る【血塗る】¶ 王家の～られた歴史 the *bloody* (≒ *blood-stained*) history of the royal family. 刃に～らずして平和は達成されなかった Peace was not achieved without *bloodshed.*

ちねつ【地熱】the subterranean heat.

ちのあめ【血の雨】¶ 彼らはその騒動で～を降らした They *shed blood* in the riot.

ちのう【知能】intelligence. ¶ ～の高い子 a child of high *intelligence.* ～を啓発する develop *one's intellectual faculties* (≒ *mental powers*).
—検査 an intelligence test ; an I. Q. 〔test〕. —指数 intelligence quotient. —程度 intellectual level. —年齢 the I. Q. age. —犯 an intellectual offense ; an intellectual crime ; a fraud. —率 intelligence quotient (I.Q. と略す).

ちのけ【血の気】¶ 彼は～の多い若者だ He is a *full-blooded* (≒ *hot-headed ; vigorous*) young man.

ちのみご【乳飲み子】a suckling 〔child〕.

ち

ちのめぐり【血の巡り】¶こんな簡単なことがわからないなんてなんと～の悪いやつだ How *slow-witted* (≒ *fat-headed*) you *are* not to understand such a simple thing!

ちのり【血糊】a clot of blood.

ちのり【地の利】¶あのデパートは～を占めている That department store gains *advantages of position.* / The department store *is well situated.*

ちはい【遅配】a delay. ¶彼らは給料の～で困っている They are suffering from *a delay* in the payment of wages. 郵便が数日～になっている The deliveries of letters *have been delayed* for a few days.

ちばし・る【血走る】¶受験生の目はみな～っていた The eyes of all the candidates for the examination *were bloodshot.*

ちばなれ【乳離れ】¶この子ももうすぐ～するだろう This baby will soon *be weaned* [from his mother].

ちばん【地番】a lot (≒ house) number (英語では日本の番地と違って1軒ごとに違う番号がついているものをいう).

ちび（背の小さな人）a very small man; (小さな子ども) a kid; a tiny tot.

ちびちび ¶彼は金を～と使う He uses his money *sparingly.* / He spends his money *in dribs and drabs.* 彼は酒を～と飲む He *sips* [*at*] *sake.* / He drinks *sake by sips.* / He drinks *in small sips.*

ちひょう【地表】the surface of the earth.

ちぶさ【乳房】the breast[s].

チフス〖医学〗—菌 a typhoid bacillus(複 bacilli). 腸— typhoid fever. 発疹(はっしん)— typhus. パラ— paratyphoid.

ちへいせん【地平線】the horizon; the horizontal; the skyline. ¶～上に above *the horizon* ～下に below *the horizon.*

チベット〖地名〗Tibet.
—語 Tibetan. —人 a Tibetan.

ちほ【地歩】a position; a ground; a standing. ¶彼は社内に有力な～を築いた He has obtained *an* influential *position* in his firm. 彼は文壇に確固とした～を占めている He has established *a* firm *footing* in the literary world.

ちほう【地方】**1**〚ひとつの地域〛a locality; a region; a district.
¶この～は雨が少ない We have only a little rain in this *district.*
この～はジャガイモの産地だ Potatoes are produced in *this part of the country.*
これはこの～では有名な建物です This building is famous in this *area.*
～によっては6月でも寒い It is cold even in June in some *parts* of the country.
この～の人々と仲よくしようとしている I try to be on friendly terms with the *local* people.
2〚首都以外・いなか〛¶彼は～に住んでいる He lives in *the country.*
あなたは～の出ですか Do you come from *the country*?
彼は～の大学を出ている He has graduated from a *local* university.
—官庁 a local office. —行政 local administration. —銀行 a local bank. —区 provincial constituencies. —警察 a provincial police. —公務員 a local public service employee. —裁判所 a district court. —紙 a local paper. —自治体 a local self-governing body. —巡業 a provincial tour. —税 local taxes. —都市 a provincial city. —版 a provincial edition. —団体 a regional body. —分離 decentralization of power. —分離主義 the decentralization system.

ちほう【痴呆】imbecility.
—症 dementia. 早発性—症〖医学〗dementia praecox.

ちぼう【知謀】resourcefulness. ¶～に富んだ人 a man of *resources.* 彼は要塞(ようさい)を攻略するために～をめぐらしていた He was employing all the *resources* at his disposal to take the fortress.

ちまき【粽】a bamboo leaves wrapped rice-dumpling.

ちまた【巷】(街) a street; (場所) a place.
¶その都市は戦火の～と化した The city became *a field of battle.* ～にいろいろの噂がとんでいる All sorts of rumors *are going round* (≒ *are rife*).

ちまつり【血祭り】blood-offering. ¶敵の先陣を～にあげた We *made a victim of* (≒ *victimized; annihilated*) the van of our enemy.

ちまなこ【血眼】bloodshot eyes. ¶みんなは～になって迷子を捜した They made *every possible* effort to find the lost child.

ちまみれ【血まみれ】¶ひとりの男が～になって死んでいた A man lay dead *covered* (≒ *smeared*) *with blood.* / A man lay *in the blood.*

ちまめ【血豆】a blood blister.

ちまよ・う【血迷う】¶彼は怒りに～った He *was mad* (≒ *was beside himself*) *with* rage. ～ってはいけない Don't *lose your mind.* 彼は～った He *ran amuck* (≒ *ran amok*).

ちみ【地味】the soil. ¶この地方は～が肥えている(やせている) The *soil* in this region is fertile (barren).

ちみち【血道】¶彼はその女優に～をあげている He *is crazy about* (≒ *is dead gone on*) the actress. 彼は競馬に～をあげている He *is utterly given up to* horse racing.

ちみつ【緻密】accuracy; minuteness; precision. ¶この研究には～さが欠けている This research work lacks *accuracy.* 彼は～な頭脳の持ち主だ He has a *fine* brain. / He has a head *for detail.* 登山には～な計画が必要だ Mountain climbing requires *careful* planning.

ちみどろ【血みどろ】¶彼は生活のために～の苦闘をした He had *the severest* (≒ *the hardest*) struggle for livelihood.

ちみもうりょう【魑魅魍魎】evil spirits (of

mountains and rivers); elves; sprites.

ちめい【地名】a place name.
—辞典 a geographical dictionary.

ちめい【知名】¶～の士 a *well-known* (≒ *noted*) person; a man *of note* (≒ *of distinction*).

ちめい【致命】¶彼の会社は～的な打撃をこうむった His firm suffered a *fatal* (≒ *mortal*) blow.
—傷 ¶頭の傷が彼の～傷だった His wound in the head proved *fatal*. / He died from the wound in the head. 首相の失言が内閣の～傷になった The premier's slip of the tongue proved *a deathblow* (≒ *a fatal blow*) to the cabinet.

ちゃ【茶】tea. ¶お～を1杯いかがですか Won't you have a cup of *tea*? / What about a cup of *tea*? 私は食後に必ず～を飲む I never fail to drink *tea* after meals. お～を入れてくれませんか Will you make *tea* for me? お～を入れかえてほしい I want *tea* made fresh. 彼女がお～をついでくれた She poured out *tea*. 会が終わると～が出た After the meeting *tea* was served. (「お茶とお菓子」ならば refreshments という). お～を飲みながらもう少し話し合いましょう Let's talk a little more *over tea*. このお～は出すぎている This *tea* is stewed. あすお～の会にお招きしたいのですが I want to invite you to a *tea* party tomorrow. 彼女は～を摘む仕事をしている She is engaged in picking *tea*. おへそが～を沸かすようなことをいうな Don't talk such nonsense!

チャージ〔サッカー・ラグビー〕charge.

チャーター ¶外国船を～する *charter* a foreign ship.
—機 a chartered plane.

チャーハン【炒飯】fried (≒ frizzled) rice.

チャーミング ¶～な目 *charming* eyes.

チャイム a chime.

ちゃいろ【茶色】〔light〕brown.

ちゃうけ【茶請け】teacake; tea biscuits; cookies; 〔between-meals〕refreshments.

ちゃうす【茶臼】a tea grinding handmill.

ちゃえん【茶園】a tea-garden; a tea-plantation.

ちゃか【茶菓】tea and cake; 〔light〕refreshments. ¶～を出す serve *a person* with *light refreshments*.

ちゃかい【茶会】a tea party; (日本のお茶会) the 〔Japanese〕tea ceremony.

ちゃがし【茶菓子】teacake; light refreshments; cookies.

ちゃか・す【茶化す】¶彼はなんでも～してしまう He *makes fun of* everything. / He *turns* everything *into jest*. 人の話を～さないでまじめに聞け Don't *make fun of* me, and listen to me in earnest.

ちゃかっしょく【茶褐色】¶～の brown〔ish〕.

ちゃがま【茶釜】a tea kettle.

ちゃがら【茶殻】tea grounds; used tea-leaves.

ちゃき【茶器】tea-things. ¶彼は～にこっている He is particular about *tea-things*.

ちゃきちゃき ¶彼は～の江戸っ子だ He is a *true-bred* (≒ *true-born*) Edokko. / He is an Edokko *to the backbone*. 彼は～の実業家だ He is a *leading* (≒ *competent*) businessman.

-ちゃく【-着】¶洋服3～ three suits 〔of clothes〕. 9時～の列車 the train *due at* nine; *the* nine *o'clock* train. マラソンで1～になった I *was the first to arrive* in the marathon race. / I *came in first* in the marathon race.

ちゃくい【着衣】(総称的に) clothing; wear.

ちゃくえき【着駅】the destination depot (≒ station).

ちゃくがん【着眼】¶彼は～がいい His *aim* is right. / His *viewpoint* is good.
—点 a point of view; *one's* viewpoint.
¶彼の研究は～点がいい His study *is to the point*. ここがその問題の～点だ This is *the very point* of the question you must pay attention to.

ちゃくざ【着座】¶～する take a seat; be seated.

ちゃくし【嫡子】(嫡男) the oldest son; the heir; (嫡出子) a legitimate child.

ちゃくじつ【着実】steadiness; soundness.
¶～な考えの人 a man of a *solid* (≒ *sober*) view. 彼は～な人だ He is a *trustworthy* (≒ *reliable*) man. / He is a man of *steady* character. 彼の店は～な営業をしている His store is run on a *sound* business basis.

ちゃくしゅ【着手】¶新しい事業にいつ～するつもりですか When will you *start* a new enterprise? 彼は新種を作る仕事に～した He *set about* originating a breed. / He *set himself to* originate a breed.

ちゃくしゅつ【嫡出】legitimacy.
—子 a legitimate child.

ちゃくじゅん【着順】¶彼らは～に列をつくった They stood in line *in the order of arrival*. ～が発表された *The result of the race* was announced.

ちゃくしょく【着色】coloring; coloration.
¶人工～した食品 artificially *colored* food. ～する color; paint.
—ガラス stained glass. —写真 a colored photograph. —剤 a coloring agent. —法 coloring.

ちゃくしん【着信】arrival of the post (≒ mail).

ちゃくすい【着水】(宇宙船の) splashdown.
¶宇宙船はみごとに～した The spaceship *alighted* (≒ *landed*) *on the water* successfully.

ちゃくせき【着席】¶～する take a (≒ *one's*) seat; sit down. ～してください Please *be seated*. / Please *take a chair*.

ちゃくそう【着想】an idea; a conception.
¶この小説は～がいい This novel *is* well *conceived*. / This novel is written on *a* clever *idea*.

ちゃくそん【嫡孫】the oldest grandson and heir.

ち

ちゃくだん【着弾】 **—**距離 ¶ 敵は〜距離外だ The enemy is out of *range*. 戦車が〜距離に入ってきた The tank came within *range*.

ちゃくち【着地】 landing. ¶ その選手の〜は完璧(かんぺき)だった(体操で) The athlete finished his performance with *a* perfect *landing*. 〜で体勢がくずれた His posture went out of balance when he finished his performance.

ちゃくちゃく〔と〕【着着〔と〕】 steadily. ¶ 準備は〜進められている The preparations are *steadily* progressing.

ちゃくでん【着電】 the arrival of a telegram.

ちゃくなん【嫡男】 the oldest son and heir apparent.

ちゃくに【着荷】 the arrival of goods.
—払い payment on arrival.

ちゃくにん【着任】 arrival at *one's* post.
¶ 本日〜しました I *have arrived at my post* today. 〜した大使を空港に迎えた We met the *newly-appointed* ambassador at the airport.

ちゃくふく【着服】 peculation; embezzlement. ¶ 彼は公金を〜した He *embezzled* (≒ *peculated*) public money.

ちゃくもく【着目】 ⇒ ちゅうもく

ちゃくよう【着用】 ¶ 本校の生徒は全員制服を〜のこと Every student of this school is supposed to *wear* uniform. 彼は制服を〜している He *is in* uniform.

ちゃくりく【着陸】 landing; alighting.
¶ 飛行機は定時に空港に〜した The airplane *landed* on time at the airport. / The airplane *made a landing* on schedule at the airport.
軟**—** a soft landing. 不時**—** a forced landing. 無**—**飛行 a non-stop flight.

ちゃくりゅう【嫡流】 the direct line of descent.

チャコ French chalk.

チャコールグレー charcoal gray.

ちゃこし【茶こし】 a tea strainer.

ちゃさじ【茶匙】 a teaspoon. ¶ 砂糖を〜に1杯入れる put *a teaspoonful of* sugar in (coffee).

ちゃしつ【茶室】 a Japanese tea-ceremony room (≒ house).

ちゃじん【茶人】 a master of the tea ceremony; (風流人) a man of refined taste.

ちゃせん【茶筅】 a tea whisk; a tea stirrer.

ちゃだい【茶代】 a tip; a gratuity. ¶ 彼は〜をはずんでくれた He *tipped* me generously.

ちゃたく【茶托】 a saucer.

ちゃだんす【茶簞笥】 a cupboard for tea-things; a tea-cabinet.

ちゃちな mean. ¶ 〜家だ It's a *jerry-built* house. / It's a *flimsy* (≒ *flimsily built*) house. それは〜時計だ That's a *cheap* watch.

ちゃちゃ【茶茶】 ¶ 人の話に〜を入れるな Don't *disrupt* our conversation.

ちゃっか【着火】 ignition; combustion.
—点 the ignition (≒ combustion) point.

ちゃっか【着荷】 the arrival of goods. ¶ 野菜の〜がおくれる The *arrival* of vegetables is late. / The vegetables are delayed in *arriving* here.

ちゃっかり ¶ 彼女はずいぶん〜している She is quite an *exacting* (≒ a *demanding*) girl. / She *is* very *self-assertive*.
—屋 a hardhead.

ちゃっきょう【着京】 ¶ 彼は午後1時飛行機で〜する He'll *reach Tokyo* by air at one p.m.

チャック a zipper; a fastener; a slide (≒ zip) fastener. ¶ 〜をかける *zip* 〔*up*〕(a jacket).

ちゃっけん【着剣】(命令) Fix bayonets!

ちゃっこう【着工】 ¶ その工事は6月に〜し, 12月に落成した The work *was started* (≒ *was begun*) in June and completed in December.

ちゃづつ【茶筒】 a tea caddy; a tea canister.

ちゃつぼ【茶壷】 a tea canister.

ちゃつみ【茶摘み】 tea-picking.

ちゃどうぐ【茶道具】 tea-things; a tea set.

ちゃどころ【茶所】(茶の産地) a tea-growing district; a tea-producing center. ¶ 宇治は〜だ Uji is famous for its tea.

ちゃのま【茶の間】 a living room; (茶室) a 〔Japanese〕 tea-ceremony room (≒ house).

ちゃのみ【茶飲み】 **—**茶わん a teacup. **—**友だち a crony; (老夫妻) an elderly couple; elderly friends.

ちゃのゆ【茶の湯】 tea ceremony; the art of ceremonial tea-making.

ちゃばしら【茶柱】 ¶ 〜が立つ have a tea stalk floating erect in *one's* tea〔, which is a sign of good luck〕.

ちゃばなし【茶話】 a chat; a gossip; a small talk.

ちゃばら【茶腹】 ¶ 〜も一時(いっとき) A cup of tea may stay hunger for a while. / Anything is better than nothing.

ちゃばん【茶番】 a farce. ¶ とんだ〜でお恥ずかしい I am ashamed of playing such *a farce*.
—狂言 a burlesque; a farce; a low comedy.

ちゃびん【茶瓶】 a teapot; a tea urn.

ちゃぶだい【ちゃぶ台】 a tea table; a dining (≒ an eating) table.

チャペル a chapel.

チャボ【矮鶏】〘鳥類〙 a bantam.

ちやほや ¶ 彼は〜されていい気になっている He *is puffed up* (≒ *is flattered*) by other persons' attentions. 彼は今あちこちで〜されている He *is being much waited upon* wherever he goes.

ちゃみせ【茶店】 a teahouse; a tea stall; a tea booth.

ちゃめ【茶目】 ¶ お〜な人 an urchin; a *playful* fellow.
—気 ¶ 彼は〜気がある He *is full of fun*. / He is quite a *playful* fellow.

ちゃや【茶屋】(茶商) a tea shop; (人) a tea merchant; (掛け茶屋) a tea stall (≒ booth); (料理屋) a restaurant.

ちゃらんぽらん ¶ 彼は〜なことを言う He says *nonsense* (≒ *irresponsible things*). / He does not mean what he says. 彼の仕事は～だ He does his work *by halves.*

チャリティー charity.

—ショー a charity show.

チャルメラ a reed pipe.

チャレンジ a challenge.

—ラウンド a challenger round.

ちゃわかい【茶話会】a tea party.

ちゃわん【茶碗】(食事用の) a rice bowl; (湯飲み) a teacup. ¶ ～1杯の飯 *a bowl* of rice. ～に飯を盛る serve boiled rice in *a bowl.*

—蒸し a thick custardy soup; a pot-steamed hotchpotch.

ちゃんこりょうり【ちゃんこ料理】a *sumo* wrestler's meal.

チャンス a chance. ¶ またとない～だ This is *a* capital *chance.* 彼を訪問する～がなかった I have had no *chance* to call on him. ～があったらパリにもう一度行きたい I want to visit Paris once more if *opportunity* offers. 彼は～は必ずものにする He never misses *an opportunity.* ～があったらすぐにでもそうしたい I will do so *at the earliest possible occasion.* ～はつくろうと思えばできるものだ We can make *an opportunity* if we are inclined to do so. カメラはシャッター～が重要だ In taking a photo it is important to release the shutter *at the right moment.*

ちゃんちゃらおかし・い How absurd (≒ ludicrous)!; Fiddlesticks! ¶ あんな男が国会議員に立候補するなんて～い *What a farce* (≒ *What a joke*) it is for a man like him to run for the Diet!

ちゃんちゃんこ a padded sleeveless coat.

ちゃんと **1** 〚もう・すでに〛 already. ¶ そのくらいのことは～知っているべきだ You ought to know that much *well.*

食事の用意は～できています Your meal is *quite* ready.

話のテーマは～決まっている The theme of my speech is *already* fixed.

2 〚きちんと〛 neatly. ¶ 彼は見かけは～している He looks *neat and tidy.*

いつ会っても彼女は～した身なりをしている Whenever I see her she is *neatly* dressed.

もう5歳なのだから, ～していなければだめだ Since you are five years old, you ought to behave *properly.*

彼は～仕事をする人だ He is a *neat* worker.

彼は～した仕事についている He is engaged in a *decent* job.

約束の時間までに～来てください Please come *punctually* before the appointed time.

家賃は月々～払っている I *never fail to* pay my rent every month.

部屋を～かたづけなさい *Tidy up* your room.

この部屋はいつも～かたづいている This room *is* always *in perfect order.*

チャンネル (テレビの) a channel. ¶ 12～ではなにをやってますか What is on *Channel* 12?

ちゃんばら a sword battle; (遊び) a sword play.

—映画 a sword picture; a sword film.

チャンピオン a champion.

—ベルト a champion belt.

ちゃんぽん ¶ 和洋～の料理が出た Japanese and Western dishes were served at the same time. 彼らはウイスキーと酒を～に飲んだ They took (≒ drank) whisky and *sake alternately* (≒ *by turns*). それは肉・野菜などを～にした料理だ It is a dish of meat, vegetables, etc. *mixed together.*

ちゆ【治癒】healing; cure. ¶ 傷は1週間で～した The wound *was healed* in a week.

ちゅう【中】(平均) average. ¶ 彼の学力は～くらいだ His scholarship *is average.* 彼女の学力は～よりは上(下)だ Her scholarship is above (below) the *average.*

ちゅう【忠】(忠義) loyalty; devotion; allegiance; (忠実) fidelity; faithfulness. ¶ 君に～, 親に孝 loyal to *one's* sovereign and dutiful to *one's* parents.

ちゅう【注】an annotation; a note. ¶ ～つきの版 an *annotated* edition. この本にはA博士の～がついている This book *is annotated* by Dr. A.

ちゅう【宙】**1** 〚空〛 the air; the sky. ¶ ～にぶらさがる hang *in the air*; hang *in mid air.* 風船が～に浮いた A balloon floated *in the air.*

2 〚その他〛 ¶長い詩を～でいう recite a long poem *offhand* (≒ *from memory*).

議論が～に浮いた The argument was up *in the air.*

-ちゅう【-中】¶ 3階建てのビルが建築～だ A three-storied building *is under construction.* 彼は目下勤務～だ He *is on duty.* 彼はアメリカを旅行～だ He *is on a trip* in America. 彼は電話～だ He *is on the phone* now. 打ち合わせの会は目下進行～だ The consultation *is under way.* 法案は審議～だ The bill *is under discussion.* その案は検討～だ The plan *is under examination.* 彼は今授業～だ He *is* now *in class.* 休み～にこの本を読み終えたい I want to read through this book *during* the holidays. (電話) お話し～です The line *is busy* (≒ *is engaged*).

ちゆう【知友】an intimate friend; a bosom friend.

ちゆう【知勇】wisdom and courage. ¶ 彼は～とも優れた武将だ He is a great general who is excellent in *wisdom and valor.*

ちゅうい【中尉】(陸軍) 米 a first lieutenant; 英 a lieutenant; (海軍) 米 a lieutenant junior grade; 英 a sublieutenant.

ちゅうい【注意】**1** 〚留意・注目・関心〛 attention. ¶ 今や人口問題に先進国の～が向けられている Now the advanced nations *are* greatly *concerned about* the population problem.

あの子はときどき他人の～を引きたいばかりにわざとおどけてみせる The boy sometimes behaves in a funny way to attract *attention.*

だれも彼の言うことに～を払う者はいなかった No one *paid attention to* him. / Nobody *paid* any

ち

attention to what he was saying.
へやを借りるときは部屋の採光に十分～しなさい When you rent a room you should *pay* enough *attention to* sunshine.
彼は別のことを言ってわれわれの～をそらそうとした He tried to divert our *attention* by talking about another subject.
下線の部分に～しながら次の文を訳しなさい Translate the following sentence *paying attention to* the underlined part.
私の言うことを～して聞きなさい Listen *carefully* to what I say.
よく～して見ていれば，やり方がわかります If you watch *carefully*, you can understand how to do it.
こういうミスがおきたのは私の～が足りなかったからだ It was through want of *care* on my side that the mistake occurred.
彼は私の言うことを～深くノートに書きとめていた He was *carefully* writing down what I was saying.
2 〖用心・警戒〗 care. ¶ お体にはくれぐれもご～ください Please *take great care of* yourself. / I hope you will *be* very *careful about* your health.
夏は特に食べ物に～する必要がある In summer we should *take* special *care about* (≒ *of*) our food.
道路の横断には左右をよく～しなさい When you cross a street, *be* very *careful to* look both ways.
懐中物にご～ください *Beware of* pickpockets.
子どもが危険な場所に近寄らないよう～していなさい Please *see to it that* the children don't go near dangerous places. / Please *be careful* not to let the children go to dangerous spots.
試験前には風邪をひかないよう～が必要です You should *take care* not *to* catch cold before the examination.
悪い友だちの仲間に入らないよう～しなさい *Try* not to get into bad company. / Avoid bad company.
ドライバーの～不足による交通事故が多い There are many traffic accidents due to lack of *care* on the driver's part.
3 〖警告・忠告〗 warning. ¶ 私はたばこをやめるよう医者に～された The doctor *advised* me *to* stop smoking.
あまり飲まないように彼に～してやった I *advised* him not *to* drink too much.
悪天候だから見合わせなさいと～したのに，彼は山へ出かけた Though I *warned* him (≒ In spite of my *warning*) *to* give up going because of the bad weather, he went to the mountains anyway.
あれほど～しておいたのにまたかさを忘れてきた Though I strongly *reminded* him *to* bring back the umbrella, he has forgotten it again.
ほかにご～いただくことはございませんでしょうか Is there any more *advice* you can give me?

遊泳禁止の～を無視して数人の若者が海に入った Some young men went into the water disregarding the *warning* prohibiting swimming.
―事項 hints; suggestions. ―信号 a warning signal. ―人物 a man on the black list. ―力 attentiveness. ¶ どうもうちの子どもたちは～力が散漫で困る The trouble with my children is that they *are* not *attentive*. 強風―報 a strongwind warning.

チューインガム a chewing gum ; a gum ; (棒状の) a stick of gum. ¶ ～をかむ chew *gum*.

ちゅうおう【中央】the center. ¶ 公園は市の～にある The park is in *the center* of the city. 机はへやの～にあった The desk was in *the middle* of the room.
―アジア Central Asia. ―官庁 the Central Office. ―気象台 the Central Meteorological Observatory. ―銀行 the central bank. ―市場 the central market. ―執行委員会 a central executive committee. ―集権 centralization. ―政府 the central government. ―線 (国電の) the Chuo [Electric] Line. ―標準時 central standard time. ―放送局 a key radio station. ―郵便局 the Central Post Office. ―労働委員会 the Central Labor Relations Committee.

ちゅうおう【中欧】Central Europe.

ちゅうおん 【中音】〖音楽〗 (男声) baritone (barytone とも書く) ; (女声) mezzo-soprano ; (音域) mediant.

ちゅうか【中華】(中国のこと) China.
―人民共和国 the People's Republic of China. ―そば lao-mien. ―ナベ a Chinese pan. ―民国 the Republic of China. ―料理 Chinese dishes (≒ food). ―料理店 a Chinese restaurant.

ちゅうかい【仲介】 mediation. ¶ ～の労をとる act as *a go-between* ; act as *an intermediary*. あの人に家の売買の～を頼んだ I asked him to act as *a* house *agent* for me.
―者 an intermediary ; a go-between ; an agent ; a mediator.

ちゅうかい 【注解】 a note ; an explanatory note ; an annotation ; a commentary ; a comment.
¶ いま～つきで「源氏物語」を読んでいる I am reading *The Tale of Genji* with *notes*. / I am reading *an annoted edition* of *The Tale of Genji*.
―者 an annotator ; a commentator.

ちゅうがい 【虫害】 insect (≒ vermin) damage. ¶ 稲作は～にみまわれた The rice crop suffered *insect damage*. / The rice crop *was damaged by insects*.

ちゅうがえり【宙返り】a somersault ; a somerset ; (飛行機の) a loop. ¶ 彼はすばらしい～をした He turned *a* beautiful *somersault*.
―飛行 a loop-the-loop flight.

ちゅうかく【中核】the kernel ; the core.
¶ 40代は社会の～だ The forties are *the core* (≒ *the center*) of the society.

ちゅうがく〔こう〕【中学〔校〕】(日本での正式の英語の呼び方は) a lower secondary school ; 米 a junior high school.
¶ ～時代にはよく遊んだものだ I used to play *in my junior high school days.*

ちゅうがくせい【中学生】a junior high school student (≒ boy ; girl).

ちゅうがた【中形・中型】a medium (≒ middle) size. ¶ ～の本 a *medium-sized* book.

ちゅうかん【中間】midway. ¶ この町は東京と名古屋の～にある This town is situated *halfway* between Tokyo and Nagoya. このふたつの駅の～に新しい駅がほしい A new station is needed *midway* between these two 〔stations〕. ここは桃色と赤の～の色で塗るとよい Here it is better to cover it with some color between pink and red.
―階級 the middle class. ―子〘物理〙a meson. ―試験 the midterm examination. ―小説 a quasi-novel. ―色 neutral tints. ―選挙 an interim election. ―報告 an interim report.

ちゅうかん【昼間】daytime ; day.
―人口 the daytime population.

ちゅうき【中気】〘医学〙palsy ; paralysis.
¶ 彼は～で寝たきりだ He has been laid up with *paralysis.*

ちゅうき【中期】¶ 江戸～の文学 literature about the *middle* of the Edo Era.

ちゅうき【注記】a note. ¶ 教科書に～する give *notes* on a textbook. これには何も～してない No *notes* are given on this point.

ちゅうぎ【忠義】loyalty ; fidelity ; devotion ; faithfulness. ¶ 国に～を尽くす *be faithful* (≒ *be devoted*) to *one's* country. ～な家来 a *loyal* retainer.
―者 a loyal person. ―立て ¶ 彼にそこまで～立てするには及ばない There's no need for you to be that *loyal to* him.

ちゅうきゅう【中級】the medium grade.
¶ ～英語講座 the *intermediate* English course.

ちゅうきょう【中共】the Chinese Communists ; Communist China ; (俗) Red China.

ちゅうきょり【中距離】―競走 a middle-distance race. ―選手 a middle-distance runner. ―弾道弾 an intermediate range ballistic missile (IRBM).

ちゅうきん【忠勤】faithfulness ; devotion ; loyalty. ¶ 秀吉は信長に～を励んだ Hideyoshi was a *faithful* servant to Nobunaga. / Hideyoshi *served* Nobunaga *faithfully* (≒ *devotedly*).

ちゅうきん【鋳金】casting.
―家 a metal worker.

ちゅうきんとう【中近東】the Middle and Near East.

ちゅうくう【中空】(中天) midair ; (うつろ) hollowness. ¶ グライダーが～に舞い上がった A glider flew up *in the air* (≒ *in the sky*). ～になった古木 an old *hollow* tree.

ちゅうぐらい【中ぐらい】¶ ～の大きさ *medium size.* ～の大きさの石 a *medium-sized* stone. 彼女の成績は～だ Her school record *is mediocre.* / Her school record *is neither very good nor very poor.*

ちゅうくん【忠君】loyalty ; devotion to *one's* master.
―愛国 loyalty and patriotism.

ちゅうけい【中継】relay ; rebroadcast.
―局 a relay station. ―放送 ¶ 全国に～放送する *broadcast* over a nation-wide network. 月着陸のようすは世界に～放送された The actual scene of landing on the moon *was broadcast* over a world-wide network.
実況(現場)― relay from the spot.

ちゅうけん【中堅】the backbone. ¶ 彼はわが社の～となった He proved himself *the backbone* of our company.
―作家 a writer of medium standing. ―人物 a leading figure.

ちゅうげん【中元】(贈り物) a *Bon* present ; a midyear gift. ¶ ～大売り出し a *midyear* sale.

ちゅうげん【忠言】good advice. ¶ ～耳に逆らう Good medicine is bitter to the mouth.

ちゅうこ【中古】―車 a used car. ―品 secondhand goods ; used articles.

ちゅうこう【中興】¶ 蕪村は俳諧(はいかい)～の祖である Buson is *the restorer* of *haiku* poetry. / Buson brought *haiku* to its present glory.

ちゅうこう【忠孝】loyalty and filial piety.
¶ 彼は～を全うした He did his duty both to his lord and to his parents.

ちゅうこく【忠告】advice. ¶ 彼に～したい I want to *advise* him. 医者は彼に泳ぐのをやめるよう～した The doctor *advised* him *to* stop swimming. 彼女に～してもむだだろう It will be 〔of〕 no use to give her *advice.* 彼はわれわれにいくつかの～を与えた He gave us some *advice.* 私の～に従ったほうがいい You had better follow my *advice.* 彼らは私の～を聞くべきだ They should take my *advice.*

ちゅうごく【中国】(日本の中国地方) the Chugoku Districts ; (中華人民共和国) 〔the People's Republic of〕 China.
―語 Chinese ; the Chinese language. ―人 a Chinese (複 Chinese) ; (総称) the Chinese. ―通 ¶ 彼は～通を自任している He professes to be *an authority on Chinese affairs.*

ちゅうごし【中腰】¶ ～で in a half-rising posture. ～で働く work with the body half bent.

ちゅうさ【中佐】(陸軍) a lieutenant colonel ; (海軍) a commander ; (空軍) 米 a lieutenant colonel ; 英 a wing commander.

ちゅうざ【中座】¶ 急用ができたので会議の途中で～した Because of urgent business, I *left the room before the conference was over.* 彼はよく無断で～する He often *leaves during the session* (≒ *leaves in the middle of the meeting*) without permission.

ちゅうさい【仲裁】mediation. ¶ ふたりの～に入った I *mediated for* the two. だれかけんかを～す

る人はいないか Is there anyone who can *arbitrate* the quarrel? 争議は〜に付せられた The dispute was referred to *arbitration*. この問題は〜裁判に付せられるべきだ This matter should be submitted to *arbitration*.

ちゅうざい【駐在】¶ その外交官は現在ワシントン〜である The diplomat *is* now *stationed in* Washington D.C.
—員 a resident officer; an official resident (*in* a country). —所 (巡査派出所) a police box; a police substation.

ちゅうさんかいきゅう【中産階級】the middle class[es]; the bourgeoisie; (人) the middle classes; middle-class people.

ちゅうし【中止】stoppage. ¶ ピクニックは〜となった The picnic *was called off*. 工事は一時〜になった The construction work *was suspended* temporarily. 病気のため彼は仕事を〜せざるをえない He has to *stop* work temporarily on account of sickness. 彼は計画を〜した He *gave up* the plan.

ちゅうし【注視】¶ 彼のスポーツカーは世間の人の〜を浴びた *The eyes* of the whole community *were fixed upon* his sports car. / His sports car *attracted a great deal of attention*.

ちゅうじ【中耳】〘解剖学〙the middle ear; the tympanum.
—炎〘医学〙tympanitis; otitis media.

ちゅうじく【中軸】the pivot; the axis (複 axes); (中心人物) a central figure.

ちゅうじつ【忠実】faithfulness. ¶ 犬は〜な動物だ Dogs are *faithful* animals. 彼は主義に〜だ He *is true to* his principle. 職務に〜でない人もいる Some persons *are* not *faithful to* their duties. この翻訳の文章には原文に〜でないところが多い In this translation there are a lot of passages that *are* not *faithful to* the original.

ちゅうしゃ【注射】an injection; a shot.
¶ 医者にビタミン剤を〜してもらった The doctor gave me *a* vitamin *injection* (≒ *shot*). / I had the doctor *inject* a vitamin preparation. 左の臀部にペニシリンの〜をしてもらった I got *a* penicillin *injection in* the left buttock.
—液 an injection; (ワクチン) a vaccine. —器 an injector; a syringe. —針 a needle. 予防— inoculation. ¶ コレラの予防〜を受けた I *was* (≒ *got*) *inoculated against* cholera.

ちゅうしゃ【駐車】parking. ¶ 道路の片側に〜する park [a car] along the side of the street.
—違反 a parking violation. —禁止 (掲示) No Parking. —場 米 a parking lot; 英 a car park.

ちゅうしゃく【注釈】a commentary; an annotation; explanatory notes. ¶ その本には詳しい〜がついている The book *is* fully *annotated*.
—者 an annotator; an commentator. —書 (版) an annotated edition; a book with annotations.

ちゅうしゅう【中秋・仲秋】midautumn.
¶ 〜の名月 the harvest moon.

ちゅうしゅつ【抽出】〘化学〙abstraction; extraction; 〘統計〙sampling. ¶ キノコから毒物を〜する *extract* poisons from mushrooms.
—検査 a sampling inspection. —物 an extract. 任意—法 a random sampling [method].

ちゅうじゅん【中旬】the middle of a month. ¶ 6月〜に in *the middle* of June; in mid-June.

ちゅうしょう【中小】—企業 medium and small-sized enterprises.

ちゅうしょう【中傷】slander. ¶ それは〜的報道にすぎない This is nothing but a *slanderous* report. そんなことを言うとは〜もはなはだしい To say such a thing is *a* gross *slander*. 他人を〜する *slander* others; *malign* others.

ちゅうしょう【抽象】abstraction. ¶ 彼の説明はあまりにも〜的だった His explanation *was* too *abstract*. こどもに〜的なことを言ってもわからない Children cannot grasp *abstract* ideas. 〜的でなくもっと具体的に説明してほしい I want you to explain more concretely instead of *abstractly*.
—画 an abstract painting. —芸術 abstract art. —名詞〘文法〙an abstract noun.

ちゅうじょう【中将】(陸軍) a lieutenant general; (海軍) a vice admiral; (空軍) 英 an air marshal.

ちゅうしょく【昼食】lunch; (社交上の昼食会などでの) luncheon; a midday meal.
¶ 軽い〜でもとりましょう Let's take (≒ have) *a* light *lunch*.
—会 a luncheon [party]. ¶ 来客のため〜会が開かれた *A luncheon* [*party*] was given in honor of the guests.

ちゅうしん【中心】the center. ¶ 大学は町の〜にある The university is in *the center* of the town. 江戸城を〜に発展したのが江戸だ The city that developed around Edo Castle was Edo. この都市は産業の〜だ This city is *the center* of industry. この小説はフランス革命のことが〜になっている This novel *centers on* the French Revolution. 彼が一行の〜だ He is *the leader* of the party.

ちゅうしん【中震】〘地学〙a medium shock (≒ earthquake).

ちゅうしん【忠臣】a loyal subject (≒ retainer).

ちゅうしん【衷心】¶ お父上の急死に際し〜よりお悔やみ申し上げます I wish to express my *deep* regret at the sudden death of your father.

ちゅうすい【虫垂】〘解剖学〙[vermiform] appendix.
—炎〘医学〙appendicitis.

ちゅうすい【注水】¶ 燃えている家に〜する *flood* a burning house *with water*.

ちゅうすう【中枢】the center; the pivot; the brain.
—神経 central nerves. —神経系統 the central nervous system. 神経— a nerve center.

ちゅうせい【中正】¶ 彼は常に～な意見をはく He *is* always *impartial* (≒ *unbias(s)ed*) in his opinions.

ちゅうせい【中世】the Middle Ages; the medi(a)eval times.
—史 medieval history. —文学 medieval literature.

ちゅうせい【中性】〘文法〙the neuter gender; 〘化学〙neutrality.
—子 〘物理〙 neutron. —洗剤 neutral cleanser. —反応 neutral reaction.

ちゅうせい【忠誠】loyalty; devotion. ¶ …に～を誓う pledge (≒ swear) *one's loyalty to (a person)*. ～を尽くす practice *loyalty to (a person)*; *be loyal* (≒ *devoted*) *to (a person)*.

ちゅうぜい【中背】¶ ～の人 a man of middle height.

ちゅうせいだい【中生代】〘地質〙 Mesozoic; the Mesozoic era.

ちゅうせき【柱石】a pillar and a foundation stone; a mainstay; a pillar. ¶ 彼は国家の～だ He is the *pillar* of the State.

ちゅうせき【沖積】〘地質〙 —世(期) the alluvial epoch. —層 alluvium. —土 alluvial soil; alluvium. —平野 an alluvium plain.

ちゅうせつ【忠節】loyalty; devotion.

ちゅうぜつ【中絶】an interruption; (妊娠の) an abortion. ¶ 戦争のため両国間の通商は急に～した The war suddenly *interrupted* the flow of commerce between the two countries. 彼女は何度も〔妊娠〕～をした She had a number of *abortions*.

ちゅうせん【抽選】a lottery; drawing.
¶ ～で by *lot*; by 〔the〕 *drawing* 〔*of*〕 *lots*. ～で順番を決める *draw lots for* turns. ～で当たった The *lot* fell on me. 1等は～で決めます The first prize will be decided by *lot*.
—券(番号) a lottery ticket (number).

ちゅうソ【中ソ】China and 〔Soviet〕 Russia.

ちゅうソ【駐ソ】¶ ～日本大使 the Japanese Ambassador to the Soviet Union.

ちゅうぞう【鋳造】casting; founding; (貨幣の) coinage. ¶ 活字を～する *cast* (≒ *found*) a type.
—所 a foundry.

ちゅうそううん【中層雲】〘気象〙 middle clouds.

ちゅうそつ【中卒】(中学卒業者) a junior high school graduate. ¶ このごろ～は求人難だ Recently, *junior high school graduates* are much sought after by employers.

ちゅうたい【中退】¶ 父が亡くなったのでやむなく大学を～した My father died, so I had to *leave* (≒ *quit*) the university.

ちゅうたい【中隊】a company; (歩兵の) an infantry company; (砲兵の) an artillery battery.
—長 a company commander.

ちゅうだん【中段】(剣道の構え) 〔be at〕 middle guard; (汽車の寝台の) a middle berth (≒ bunk).

ちゅうだん【中断】interruption; stoppage. ¶ 仕事を～して電話に出る *stop in the middle of one's* work to answer a telephone. 彼の演説は聴衆にやじられ何度も～した His speech *was* often jeered at and *interrupted* by the audience.

ちゅうちゅう ¶ 小鳥が～鳴いていた The birds *were chirping* (≒ *were twittering*). ネズミが～鳴く Mice *squeak*.

ちゅうちょ【躊躇】hesitation. ¶ ～するな Don't *hesitate*. ～せず承諾したほうがいい You should accept it without *hesitation*. そこを訪れるべきかどうか～している He feels some *hesitation* as to whether or not to visit the place. 何も～することはない There is no room for *hesitation*. 彼は～してすぐには答えられなかった He *hesitated* and did not answer immediately.

ちゅうてつ【鋳鉄】cast iron.

ちゅうてん【中天】the middle of the sky. ¶ 月が～にかかっている The moon hangs *high up in the sky* (≒ *in mid-air*).

ちゅうてん【中点】〘数学〙 the middle point (of a line).

ちゅうと【中途】¶ ～で退学する *give up* (≒ *quit*) school. 食事(仕事)の～で *in the middle* of a meal (*one's* work). 雨が降ってきたので～で引き返した As it began to rain we turned back *halfway*. その仕事を～でやめてはいけない You must not leave the work *unfinished*.

ちゅうとう【中東】the Middle East.

ちゅうとう【中等】the middle class.
—学校 a lower secondary school. —教育 lower secondary education. —教員 a lower secondary school teacher.

ちゅうどう【中道】the middle road. ¶ ～を歩む take the golden mean; choose a moderate course.
—政治 the middle-of-the-road politics.

ちゅうどく【中毒】poisoning. ¶ フグを食べて～を起した I *was poisoned from* eating swell-fish. ガス～で死んだ He *was poisoned* to death by gas.
—症状 toxic symptoms.

ちゅうとん【駐屯】¶ 橋を守るために10人の兵が常にそこに～している Ten soldiers *are* always *stationed* there to guard the bridge.
—軍 stationary troops; (守備の) a garrison; (占領地の) an occupation army.

チュートン —語 Teutonic. —族 the Teutons; the Teutonic race. —人 a Teutonic.

チューナー〘電気〙a tuner.

ちゅうなんべい【中南米】Latin America.
—音楽 Latin-American music.

ちゅうにかい【中二階】〘建築〙a mezzanine.

ちゅうにく【中肉】(中等の食肉) meat of medium quality. ¶ ～中背の人 a man of *medium build*.

ちゅうにち【中日】(なかび) the middle day; (彼岸の) an equinox (秋なら the autumnal equinox, 春なら the vernal equinox という).

ちゅうにち【駐日】¶ ～アメリカ外交団 the U.S. diplomats *in Japan*. ～アメリカ大使 the U.S.

ち

Ambassador *to Japan*.

ちゅうにゅう【注入】¶水をタンクに〜する *pour* (≒ *put*) water *into* a tank.

ちゅうねん【中年】middle age. ¶〜の人 a *middle-aged* person.

—太り ¶〜太りする develop a *middle-age*[*d*] *spread*.

ちゅうのう【中脳】〘解剖学〙the midbrain.

ちゅうのう【中農】a middle-class farmer.

ちゅうは【中波】〘電気〙medium wave.

チューバ〘音楽〙a tuba.

ちゅうばいか【虫媒花】〘植物〙an entomophilous flower.

ちゅうはば【中幅】(布の) medium width.

ちゅうばんせん【中盤戦】¶大統領選挙も〜に入った The presidential election has entered *the middle stage*.

ちゅうぶ【中部】¶千葉県の〜では in *the central parts* of Chiba Prefecture.

—地方 the Central Districts.

チューブ a tube. ¶自動車の〜 the inner *tube* of a car. 〜入り絵の具 *tube* colors.

ちゅうぶう【中風】〘医学〙palsy ; paralysis.

ちゅうふく【中腹】¶山の〜に小屋がある There is a hut *halfway up* (≒ *halfway down*) the mountain. (山を登ってゆくと「中腹に」は halfway up で, 山を下ってゆくと「中腹に」は halfway down).

ちゅうぶらりん【宙ぶらりん】¶その問題はまだ〜になっている(未決定の状態にある) The problem *hangs* still *in the balance*.

ちゅうぶる【中古】¶彼が買った車は〜だ He bought a *secondhand* car. / He bought the car *secondhand*. (この secondhand は副詞).

ちゅうべい【中米】Central America.

ちゅうへん【中編】the second part (前・後編に対して).

—小説 a medium-length story.

ちゅうぼそ【中細】¶〜の毛糸 knitting wool *of medium thickness*. 〜のペン a *medium-fine* pen.

ちゅうみつ【稠密】thickness. ¶東京は人口〜である Tokyo *is densely* (≒ *thickly*) *populated*. 人口〜地帯 a *densely populated* district.

ちゅうもく【注目】notice. ¶〜すべき発言だ It is a *noteworthy* comment. 彼の万能ぶりは〜に値する His all-round performance *is worthy of notice* (≒ *remarkable*). 彼女は観客の〜を引いた She attracted the *attention* of the spectators. 黒板に〜しなさい *Watch* the blackboard. あの人はすばらしい才能の割合に世間から〜されない In spite of his great talent, he *is taken* no *notice of*.

ちゅうもん【注文】**1** 〚発注・あつらえ〛an order. ¶食事はまだ〜していない We *have* not *ordered* our meals yet.

この本はアメリカに〜しなければならない This book has to *be ordered from* America.

アメリカに〜した本はまだ来ない The books I *ordered from* America have not been delivered yet.

外国に〜した本は届くのに3か月はかかる If you *order* books *from* abroad, it will take them at least three months to reach you.

ウエートレスは〜したものをやっと持ってきた The waitress has brought in my *orders* at last.

(食堂で)ボーイが〜をききにきた The waiter came to take our *orders*.

その品は既に〜済みだ The article *is* already *on order*.

この服は〜だ This suit is *made to order*.

2 〚要求〛 ¶すべてが〜どおりにいくとはかぎらない Everything does not go *as we expected*.

それは難しい〜だがやってみよう That's *a tall order*, but I'll try.

ちゅうや【昼夜】day and night. ¶1〜かかって仕事をやり上げた We completed the job in *twenty-four hours*.

—交替 ¶彼らは〜交替で働いている They work *in a double shift* (≒ *in shifts day and night*). **—**兼行 ¶〜兼行で働いた I worked *night and day* (≒ *day and night*).

ちゅうゆ【注油】oiling ; lubrication. ¶エンジンに〜する *oil* an engine.

ちゅうよう【中庸】moderation. ¶彼は〜を得た意見の持ち主だ He is a man of *moderate opinions*. 何事にも〜を守るというのが彼の人生哲学であった His philosophy of life was to *be moderate* in everything.

ちゅうりつ【中立】neutrality. ¶彼らはその問題に関して〜的態度をとっている They are taking a *neutral* attitude toward the problem. 彼は〜の立場をとっている He stands *neutral*. 新聞は〜を守るべきだ Newspapers should observe *neutrality*.

—国 a neutral country. **—**主義 neutralism. **—**地帯 a neutral zone. 厳正**—** strict neutrality. ¶その国は厳正〜を守っている The country observes *strict neutrality*.

チューリップ〘植物〙a tulip.

ちゅうりゃく【中略】an omission ; an ellipsis.

ちゅうりゅう【中流】(上流・下流に対して) the middle reaches.

—階級 (中産階級) the middle class[es] ; (人人) the middle class[es]. **—**家庭 a middle-class family.

ちゅうりゅう【駐留】¶その国に〜する *stay* in the country.

ちゅうるい【虫類】(昆虫) insects.

ちゅうわ【中和】〘化学〙neutralization ; (毒などの) counteraction. ¶アルカリは酸を〜する Alkalis *neutralize* acids.

ちょ【著】a book. ¶A氏の〜 *a book* [written] by Mr. A.

ちよ【千代】¶〜に八千代に forever and ever ; through all ages.

ちょいちょい (おりおり) [every] now and then ; (しばしば) often ; frequently.

ちょう【丁】¶〜か半か, どっちだ *Odd or even*, which do you choose? はさみ1〜 *a pair of* scissors.

ちょう【町】a *cho* (距離の a *cho* は約 109 me-

ち

ters; 面積の a *cho* は約 2.45 acres).

ちょう【蝶】 a butterfly. ¶ 彼女は～よ花よと育てられた She was brought up *with utmost care and affection*.

ちょう【長】 ¶ 一家の～ *the head* of a family. その分野では彼はきみより一日の～がある He *is* a little *ahead of* you in that line.

ちょう【腸】〘解剖学〙 the intestines; the bowels (複数形に注意). ¶ ～のぐあいが悪い I have *bowel* trouble. / I have some trouble in *the intestines*.

―捻転(ねんてん) a twist in the intestines. ―閉塞(へいそく) ileus. 大― the large intestine. 小― the small intestine.

ちょう【兆】 1〚前兆〛 a sign. ¶ 不景気の～ *a sign* of depression.

2〚数の単位〛 米 a trillion; 英 a billion.

-ちょう【-朝】 (歴代の王朝) a dynasty; (時代) an age; a period. ¶ 唐～ the Tang *Dynasty*. 平安～の女流作家たち women novelists in the Heian *period*. ビクトリア～ the Victorian *age*; *the reign* of Victoria.

-ちょう【-調】 ¶ ニ長～ D *major*; ニ短～ D *minor*. 七五～の in the 7-5 syllable *meter*. ぎこちない翻訳～の文体の小説 a novel written in a stiff translation *style*.

ちょう-【超-】 ¶ ～現実的な *super*natural. ～現実主義 *sur*realism. ～自然的 *super*natural. 公会堂は～満員で息苦しいほどだった The public hall was *quite* full to suffocation.

ちょうあい【寵愛】 ¶ 彼女は両親の～を一身に集めた She *was loved* most tenderly by her parents.

ちょうい【弔意】 condolence; sympathy. ¶ 衷心から～を表します (お悔やみを述べる) I express my sincere *condolences* to you. / Please accept my sincere *sympathy*. (口語的)

―金 condolence money.

ちょういん【調印】 signature. ¶ 両国代表が条約に～した The delegates of both countries *signed* the treaty.

―者 a signatory; a signer. ―国 a signatory 〔power〕. ¶ フランスとイタリアも～国だった France and Italy were among the *signatories* of the treaty.

ちょうえき【懲役】 imprisonment. ¶ 彼には～5年の判決が下された He was sentenced to five year's *imprisonment*.

終身― imprisonment for life.

ちょうえつ【超越】 ¶ 彼は世俗を～している He *is above* the world. 彼は自己の利害を～してその仕事をした He did the work *disregarding* his own benefit.

ちょうえんけい【長円形】 an oblong. ¶ ～のテーブル an *oblong* table.

ちょうおん【長音】〘音声学〙 a long vowel.

―符 (記号)〘音声学〙 a macron.

ちょうおん【調音】 (音声の) modulation; (楽器の) tuning.

ちょうおんかい【長音階】〘音楽〙 the major scale.

ちょうおんき【聴音機】 a sound locator.

水中― a hydrophone. 空中― an aerophone.

ちょうおんそく【超音速】 supersonic speed. ¶ ～で飛ぶ fly *at supersonic speed*.

―ジェット機 a supersonic jet plane. ―輸送機 a supersonic transport (SST).

ちょうおんぱ【超音波】〘物理〙 supersonic waves.

ちょうか【超過】 the excess. ¶ あなたの手荷物は規定の重量を～している Your baggage *is overweight*. その車は制限速度を～している The car *exceeds* the speed limit. 費用はぼくの最初の見積もりを大幅に～した The expense *exceeded* my original estimate by a great deal. 輸入の～は800万ドルになる Import *exceeds* export by eight million dollars. / The *excess* of imports over exports is eight million dollars.

―額 a surplus. ―勤務 overtime work; extra duties. ―勤務手当 overtime pay.

ちょうかい【町会】 a town assembly. ¶ 明日～が開かれる The *town assembly* will be held tomorrow.

―議員 a member of a town assembly.

ちょうかい【潮解】〘化学〙 deliquescence.

ちょうかい【懲戒】 disciplinary punishment. ¶ 彼は～処分を受けた He was submitted to *disciplinary action*.

―委員会 a disciplinary committee. ―免職 disciplinary dismissal. ¶ 彼は～免職になった He *was dismissed by way of disciplinary punishment*. / He *got disciplinary dismissal*.

ちょうかく【頂角】〘数学〙 a vertical angle.

ちょうかく【聴覚】 〔the sense of〕 hearing.

―神経 an auditory nerve. 視―教育 audio-visual education.

ちょうかん【長官】 a chief; a governor. 国務― 米 the Secretary of State. 防衛庁― the Director of the Defense Agency.

ちょうかん【朝刊】 a morning paper. ¶ タイムズの～ the *morning edition* of the Times.

ちょうかんず【鳥瞰図】 a bird's-eye view (*of* the district).

ちょうき【弔旗】 a flag at half-mast. ¶ 彼らは～を掲げた They *hung the flag at half-mast*. / They *half-masted the flag*.

ちょうき【長期】 a long time. ¶ 彼は～にわたる闘病生活を送った He struggled against the disease *for a long time*.

―貸し付け a long-term loan. ―計画 a longrange plan. ―興行 a long run. ―戦 a prolonged war. ―滞在 a long stay. ―予報 a long-range forecast.

ちょうきょう【調教】 (馬の) training; breaking. ¶ 馬を～する *train* (≒ *break in*) a horse.

―師 a horse trainer; a horse breaker.

ちょうきょり【長距離】 a long distance.

―競走 a long-distance race; a marathon 〔race〕. ―電話 a long-distance call. ―飛行 a long-distance flight. ―砲 a long-range gun.

ち

ちょうく【長駆】¶～して敵陣を突いた We *made a long march* to attack the enemy's position.

ちょうく【長軀】a high stature. ¶彼は～, 端麗な若者だ He is a *tall* and handsome youth.

ちょうけい【長兄】the eldest brother (囲では oldest も用いられる).

ちょうけい【長径】〖数学〗the major axis. ¶楕円(だん)体の～ *the major axis* of an ellipsoid.

ちょうけし【帳消し】¶借りを～にする *cancel* a debt; *wipe* (⇔ *write*) *off* a debt. やりあいはこれで～にして握手しよう Let's *call it quits*, and shake hands. この勘定を僕が持てばこないだの借りは～した If I pay this bill, it will *wipe off* the debt I owed you the other day〔, *and we are quits*〕.

ちょうこう【兆候・徴候】(病気の) a symptom; (一般に) a sign. ¶寒けがするのは風邪の～だ If you feel chilly, it is *a symptom* of a cold. 暴風雨の～が見えてきた There is *an indication* of an approaching storm. / There is *a sign* of a storm coming.

ちょうこう【聴講】attendance at a lecture. ¶講義を～する *attend* a lecture.
—者 (生) an auditor; (全体) an attendance. ¶その講義は～者が少なかった There was *a* poor *attendance* at the lecture. 彼はA大学に～生として籍をおいている He is enrolled as *an auditor* at A University. —料 an admission fee. —無料 (掲示) Admission free.

ちょうこう【長考】¶～する meditate for a long time. ～の末 after *a long meditation*.

ちょうごう【調号】〖音楽〗a key signature (♯ sharp; ♭ flat).

ちょうごう【調合】mixture; compounding. ¶この処方箋(せん)どおり～した I *made up* the prescription. その処方を病院の薬局で～してもらった I *had* the prescription *filled* at the pharmacist's office.

ちょうこうぜつ【長広舌】a long〔-winded〕speech. ¶彼の～にはうんざりした I had enough of his *long speech*.

ちょうこうそう【超高層】¶東京にも～のビルがあちらこちらに立ち並んでいる In Tokyo also we see *skyscrapers* towering here and there.

ちょうこく【彫刻】sculpture. ¶彼は木で仏像を～した He *carved* an image of Buddha in wood. 石に文字が～されているのがかすかに読める The letters *engraved* upon the stone can be dimly seen. (carve は木・石などをある形に刻んで造る; engrave は金属・石などの表面にある形を刻み込むの意).
—家 (彫りものの) an engraver; a carver; (塑像などの) a sculptor. —刀 a carving knife.

ちょうこっかしゅぎ【超国家主義】ultra-nationalism.
—者 an ultra-nationalist.

ちょうさ【調査】examination; investigation. ¶事の真偽を～してほしい I want you to *investigate* whether it is true or not. 事故の原因を～する *investigate* the cause of the accident. 彼の発言はほんとうなのかどうか～してください Please *check up* his remark. その問題は目下～中だ The matter *is under investigation*. この池の水質を～したい We want to *examine* the water of this pond. ～するとその書類はいいかげんであることがわかった *On examination* the documents were found to be random. 厳密な～が必要だ *A* close *examination* is required.

ちょうざい【調剤】preparation. ¶～する prepare a medicine. ⇒ ちょうごう (調合)

ちょうざめ【蝶鮫】〖魚類〗a sturgeon.

ちょうし【長子】the eldest child (囲では oldest も用いられる).

ちょうし【調子】**1**〖音調〗¶この楽器は～の高い部分がよくない The high-pitched *notes* of this musical instrument are not so good.
彼女は低い～でその歌をうたった She sang the song *in a low tone*.
～が高すぎて歌えないから1オクターブ下げてください The *pitch* is too high for me to sing. Could you lower it by one octave?
このピアノの～を合わせてください Please *tune* the piano.
彼女のバイオリンは～が狂っている Her violin *is out of tune*.
ピアノの伴奏に～を合わせて歌いなさい You must sing *in tune to* the piano accompaniment.
—はずれ ¶彼は～はずれの歌をうたった He sang *out of tune*.
2〖拍子・リズム〗¶彼女は足で～をとりながら歌った She sang *keeping time* with her feet.
私がうたいますから手拍子で～をとってください I will sing, so will you *keep time* by clapping?
みんなで～を合わせて踊りましょう Let's dance together *in tune*.
なかなか～のいい曲ですね It's quite *a* rhythmical *tune*, isn't it?
3〖語調・口調〗¶監督は強い～で審判員に抗議した The manager protested to the umpire *in a* severe *tone*.
彼の話し方はいつも～がなめらかだ His conversation is always smooth and flowing.
そこで講演者は突然声の～を変えた There the speaker suddenly changed the *tone* of his voice.
新聞は激しい～で政府を非難した The newspaper criticized the government *very strongly*.
見知らぬ男がなれなれしい～で話しかけてきた A stranger talked to me *in* too friendly *a manner*.
4〖ぐあい〗¶私は寒くなると体の～が思わしくない I don't *feel* well when it gets cold.
どうも腹の～がおかしい *Something is wrong with* my stomach.
このごろ体の～がとてもいい Recently I *feel* very fine. / I am in very good health now.
彼は頭の～がおかしいんじゃないか He is a little crazy (⇔ mad), isn't he? (crazy はとくに囲では異性に夢中であるという意味にとることが多い).
どうもエンジンの～が悪い Somehow the engine

doesn't *work well.* / There seems to be something *wrong with* the engine.

この時計は～が狂っている This watch doesn't *keep good time* at all. / This clock does not run properly.

きょうはあのピッチャーは～がいい Today that pitcher *is in good condition.*

彼のバッティングの～は落ちている His batting *is* not *up to the mark.*

あの棋士はこのところ少し～を乱している The chess player *is* not *in top form* recently.

この～だと向こうへ着くのはだいぶ遅くなりそうだ We will arrive there quite late if we travel *at this rate.*

今からその～では先が思いやられる If he *is like that* now, I can't help worrying about his future.

仕事の～はどうですか *How* is your business 「going?

万事～よくいっています Everything is going *splendidly.*

5 〖勢い・気分・態度〗 ¶ 彼はどんな人とでも～を合わせていく He can *get along with* anybody.

彼女は～に乗って言わなくてもいいことまでしゃべってしまった She said *without reserve* things she should not have said. / She *let her tongue slip.*

あまり～に乗っていい気になるな Don't *get carried* 「*away.*

彼は～に乗りすぎて事業に失敗した He *relied too much on luck,* and failed in his business.

彼は人にほめられるとすぐに～づく When anyone praises him, he *forgets himself.*

～のいい男だから，だまされないように用心しなさい He will say anything to flatter you, so take care not to be deceived.

—者 ¶ 彼は～者で軽はずみなところがある He is easily elated and behaves imprudently.

ちょうし【銚子】a *sake* bottle.

ちょうじ【弔辞】a memorial address. ¶ 彼は友人代表として～を述べた He *expressed his condolences* (≒ *made a memorial address*) as the representative of the friends of the deceased.

ちょうじ【丁子】〔植物〕a clove.

ちょうじ【寵児】¶ 運命の～ *the favorite* of fortune. 文壇の～ a *very popular* writer. 彼は今や時代の～だ He is now *the lion of the day.*

ちょうじかん【長時間】〔for〕many hours. ¶ ～その問題で論議を重ねた We discussed the matter *for a long time.* (long を副詞に用いるのはやや形式ばった語法).

ちょうしぜん【超自然】¶ ～的 supernatural; preternatural.

—主義 supernaturalism.

ちょうしゃ【庁舎】a government office building.

ちょうじゃ【長者】a rich (≒ wealthy) man.

—番付 a list of millionaires. 百万**—** a millionaire. 億万**—** a billionaire.

ちょうしゅ【聴取】¶ 判事は目撃者の証言を～した The judge *heard* the evidence of the eye-witness. 双方の代表委員の意見は当局より公平に～された The deputation of either party received *a fair hearing* from the authority.

—者(ラジオ) a wireless (≒ broadcast) listener. **—料**(ラジオ) a radio license fee. **—装置** a receiving apparatus (≒ set).

ちょうじゅ【長寿】long life; longevity.

¶ ～を保つ live long; enjoy *longevity.*

—法 the secret of longevity.

ちょうしゅう【徴収】levy; collection.

¶ 会員1名につき1か月500円～する *make a levy of* five hundred yen per member every month. 政府は税金を～する The government *levies* (≒ *collects*) taxes.

ちょうしゅう【徴集】levy; recruitment.

¶ 戦時には軍隊が～される Troops *are levied* in time of war. 大戦には数百万の青年が～された Several million young men *were called out* (≒ *were recruited*) in the war.

ちょうしゅう【聴衆】an audience; an attendance; hearers. ¶ 多数(少数)の～ *a* large (small) *audience* (≒ *attendance*). ～から割れるような拍手が起こった Thunderous applause arose among the *audience.*

ちょうじゅう【鳥獣】birds and beasts.

ちょうしょ【長所】a strong (≒ good) point.

¶ けんそんするところが彼の～であり短所でもある His modesty is at once his *strength* and weakness. マスコミ機関を通じて新製品の～を宣伝する advertise the *advantages* of newly produced articles through mass media. だれでも～もあれば短所もある Everybody has his *merits* and demerits.

ちょうしょ【調書】a written evidence (≒ record). ¶ 警察はその事件の～を作成した The police drew up *a written evidence* (≒ *record*).

ちょうじょ【長女】the eldest daughter (㊊では oldest も用いられる).

ちょうしょう【嘲笑】ridicule. ¶ 人々は彼を～した People *laughed at* him. 彼の行動は世間の～を招いた His behavior excited the *sneer* of the public. 彼は町じゅうの～の的となった He made himself the *laughingstock* of the whole town.

ちょうじょう【長上】*one's* superior. ¶ ～を敬う respect *one's elders* (≒ *seniors*).

ちょうじょう【頂上】the top; the summit.

¶ われわれはその山の～をきわめた We gained *the summit* of the mountain. 彼は今幸福の～にある He is now at *the peak* (≒ *the top*) of happiness. 今が寒さの～だ It is the coldest time of the year.

—会談 a summit meeting. ¶ 両国首脳が～会談を行なった The leaders of the both countries had *a summit meeting.*

ちょうしょく【朝食】breakfast. ¶ 私は～には卵を食べる I have eggs *for breakfast.*

ちょうじり【帳尻】the balance of accounts.

¶ 帳簿係は自分の盗みを隠すために～をごまかした The bookkeeper manipulated *the balance of accounts* (≒ *books*) to conceal his theft.

私には～を合わせることは苦手だ It is difficult for me to *make my accounts balance*.

ちょうしん【長針】(時計の) the minute hand ; the long hand.

ちょうしん【長身】tall stature. ¶ ～の男 a *tall* man.

ちょうしん【聴診】auscultation. ¶ ～する stethoscope.

—器 a stethoscope.

ちょうじん【超人】a superman. ¶ ～的努力 a *superhuman* effort.

ちょうしんけい【聴神経】〖解剖学〗the *auditory* (≒ *acoustic*) nerve.

ちょうすいろ【長水路】〖水泳〗a long course ; a 50-meter course.

ちょう·する【弔する】¶ 心から偉大な指導者の死を～する We heartily *mourn for* the great leader. / We heartily *lament* the death of the great leader.

ちょう·する【徴する】¶ 当局は種々の社会問題について学者の意見を～した The authorities *gathered* (≒ *invited*) the opinions of the scholars on the various kinds of social problems.

ちょう·ずる【長ずる】¶ 彼は～じて医師となった He *grew up to* be a doctor. 彼らは自然科学に～じていた They *were expert* (≒ *were adept*) *in* natural science.

ちょうせい【町政】town administration.

ちょうせい【調製】¶ 本剤は精選された原料から～されている This medicine *is prepared* (≒ *is compounded ; is made*) from the choicest materials.

ちょうせい【調整】regulation. ¶ この器械は部屋の湿度を～する This instrument *regulates* the humidity of the room. この机と腰掛けはどの子どもの身長にも合うように～できる The desk and the seat can *be adjusted to* the height of any child. 部屋の大きさによって音声を～しなければならぬ The voice must *be modulated* (≒ *be adjusted ; be controlled*) according to the size of the room. 私は彼らの意見の～ができなかった I was not able to *make* them *come to an understanding*.

ちょうぜい【町税】a town tax.

ちょうぜい【徴税】tax collection ; the levy of taxes. ¶ ～する collect taxes ; levy (≒ impose) taxes (*upon*).

—令書 a tax bill.

ちょうせき【潮汐】ebb and flow ; a tide.

—学 tidology. —点 a tidemark.

ちょうせつ【調節】regulation ; adjustment ; control ; (音量の) modulation. ¶ われわれはこの器械で室内の温度を～する We *regulate* the temperature of the room with this instrument. ラジオの～をして局番に合わせる *tune in to* the radio station. ラジオの音量を～する *modulate* the volume on a radio.

ちょうぜつ【超絶】transcendence ; excellence.

ちょうせん【朝鮮】Korea.

—語 Korean. —人 a Korean. —ニンジン a ginseng.

ちょうせん【挑戦】challenge. ¶ 彼にひと試合～しよう I'll *challenge* him *to* a game. 彼は～に応じるだろう He will accept the *challenge*. 彼はすぐに～的態度に出る He is quick to take a *defiant* attitude.

—者 a challenger. —状 a 〔written〕 challenge.

ちょうぜん【超然】¶ 彼はいつもクラスの者から～としている He always *stands* (≒ *keeps*) *aloof from* the class. 彼は何事にも～としている Nothing can influence him. / He cannot be influenced by anything. 彼はそんな卑しいことから～としている He *is above* such meanness.

ちょうそ【彫塑】plastic arts.

ちょうぞう【彫像】a 〔carved〕 statue.

ちょうそく【長足】¶ 現代の科学は～の進歩を遂げた Modern science has made *rapid* (≒ *great ; remarkable*) progress. 日本は外国貿易において～の進歩を遂げた Japan has made *rapid strides* in its foreign trade.

ちょうぞく【超俗】¶ 彼は～的だ He *keeps aloof from the world*.

ちょうだ【長打】〖野球〗a long hit. ¶ ～を打つ make *a long hit*.

—者 a long-ball hitter. —力 the long-ball power.

ちょうだ【長蛇】¶ 多くの人々が切符を買おうと～の列をなして立っていた A lot of people were standing *in a long line* (≒ *in a long queue*) to buy the tickets. ～を逸した I missed *a big chance*.

ちょうだい【頂戴】¶ お菓子を～ *Please give me* some candies. けっこうな贈り物を～してどうもありがとうございます Many thanks for your nice gifts. 十分～しました I *have had enough*. / I *have had plenty*. (人にすすめられて) 自由に～いたします I will *help myself to* it. 先生からお小言を～した I *got* a scolding from the teacher.

ちょうたいそく【長大息】¶ 彼は空を見上げて～した He *sighed deeply* looking up the sky.

ちょうたつ【調達】supply. ¶ 食料を～する *provide* food. 金を～する *raise* money. 政府は住民に物資を～した The government *furnished* the population *with* goods.

ちょうたん【長短】length. ¶ 2本の棒の～をはかる measure the *relative length* of the two sticks. 人はだれでも～それぞれある Every man has his *merits and demerits*.

ちょうたん【長嘆】⇒ ちょうたいそく

ちょうたんぱ【超短波】〖電気〗ultrashort waves.

—受信器 an ultrashort wave receiver.

ちょうチフス【腸チフス】〖医学〗typhoid fever.

ちょうちょう【町長】a town headman.

ちょうちょう【長調】〖音楽〗a major key. ¶ ハ～奏鳴曲 a sonata in C *major*.

ちょうちょう【蝶蝶】⇒ ちょう (蝶)

ちょうちょう【丁丁·打打】¶ 弁護士と証人の～はっしのやりとりが続いた *The thrust and parry* of barrister and witness continued. ふたりの侍は～はっしと切り結んだ The two *samurai* clashed swords *hotly.*

ちょうちん【提燈】a paper lantern. ¶ ～をともす light *a lantern.* ～に釣り鐘 It's a misalliance. / They are an ill-assorted couple.

—持ち a lantern-carrier; (比喩的に) a puffer. ¶ 彼は上役の～持ちをする He *holds a candle to* his superior. **—行列** a lantern procession (≒ parade).

ちょうつがい【蝶番】a hinge. ¶ 戸に～をつける *hinge* a door. 戸の～がはずれている The door *is off its hinges.*

ちょうつけ【帳付け】¶ 彼は宿屋の～をしている He is *a bookkeeper* of a hotel. / He *keeps accounts* in a hotel.

ちょうづめ【腸詰め】a sausage.

ちょうてい【朝廷】the 〔Imperial〕 Court.

ちょうてい【調停】mediation; intervention. ¶ だれか争議を～する人が要る Someone must *mediate* the dispute. 彼が二者の間を～した He *intervened* between the two. 労働者たちは～を求めることに同意した The workers agreed to ask for *arbitration.*

—案 a mediation plan. **—裁判** 〔a〕 court; 〔a〕 court arbitration. **—者** an arbitrator; an arbiter.

ちょうてん【頂点】the top; the zenith. ¶ 三角形の～ *the apex* of a triangle. 彼の一家は今や栄華の～にある His family is now at *the height* (≒ *the zenith*) of its prosperity. その作品は完成の～に達している The work attained *the acme* of perfection. ゲームのおもしろさは～に達した The game reached *its climax.*

ちょうでん【弔電】¶ ～を打つ send *a telegram of condolence.*

ちょうと【長途】a long distance. ¶ 彼は～の旅に出発した He started on *a long journey.*

ちょうど【調度】(必要品) supplies; (家具) furniture. ¶ 客間の～ drawing-room *furniture.*

ちょうど【丁度】just. ¶ ～昼食を終わったところだ I have *just* finished lunch. ～1時間待った I waited *just* 〔for〕 an hour. 彼は～30歳だ He is *just* thirty. ～1,000円しか持っていない I have *exactly* one thousand yen. ～2時に来てほしい I want you to come at two *sharp.* 講義は～始まったところだった The lecture had *just* begun. それは～私が話そうと思っていたことです That is *just* what I wanted to talk about.

ちょうとうは【超党派】¶ この件は～で解決すべきだ All parties should unite in settling this matter.

—外交 米 a bipartisan diplomacy; nonpartisan diplomacy.

ちょうどきゅうかん【超弩級艦】a super-dreadnought.

ちょうとっきゅう【超特急】a superexpress 〔train〕. ¶ ～で仕上げよう I'll finish it *in a great hurry.* / I'll *hurry through* the work.

ちょうトン【長トン】a long ton.

ちょうない【町内】¶ ～の人たち people living *in the same street.* われわれは同じ～に住んでいる We live *in the neighborhood.* ～の顔役 a man of influence *in the neighborhood.*

ちょうなん【長男】the eldest son (米では oldest も用いる).

ちょうにん【町人】a tradesman (複 -men).

ちょうネクタイ【蝶ネクタイ】a bow tie.

ちょうねんげつ【長年月】¶ 10年という～をかけて彼は自分の作品を完成した In *a long period of* ten years he completed his work.

ちょうねんてん【腸捻転】a twist in the intestines; volvulus.

ちょうは【長波】〔電気〕 a long wave.

ちょうば【跳馬】〔体操〕 long horse; (女子種目) vaulting horse.

ちょうば【帳場】(店の) a counter; (ホテルのフロント) the front desk; the office.

ちょうば【調馬】horse breaking; horse training.

ちょうはつ【長髪】¶ ～の青年 a *long-haired* young man.

ちょうはつ【徴発】requisition. ¶ 彼らは軍用としてトラックを～した They *put* the motor-trucks *in requisition for* war purposes. / They *requisitioned* the motor-trucks *for* war purposes.

—権 the right of requisition. **—令** a requisition order.

ちょうはつ【挑発】provocation; excitement. ¶ 彼の～的なことばに乗って腹を立てるな Don't lose your temper by his *provocative* words. ～的な服装が流行している *Provocative* dresses are much in fashion.

ちょうはつ【調髪】⇒ さんぱつ

ちょうばつ【懲罰】punishment; discipline. ¶ 規則に違反した者は～にかけられることになろう Those who are against the rules will *be disciplined* (≒ *be punished*).

—委員会 a disciplinary committee ¶ この問題は～委員会にかけられるべきだ This case should be referred to *a disciplinary committee.*

ちょうはん【丁半】(とばく) gambling. ⇒ばくち

ちょうふく【重複】duplication; overlap; (繰返し) repetition. ¶ ～は避けたほうがいい You must avoid *overlapping* (≒ *duplication*). きみの話は～している Your speech *is overlapping.*

ちょうぶつ【長物】¶ 無用の～ a useless thing; a superfluity; a good-for-nothing.

ちょうぶん【弔文】¶ 故A氏に対する～ *a funeral address* to the late Mr. A.

ちょうぶん【長文】¶ ～の手紙 a *long* letter.

ちょうへい【徴兵】¶ 彼は～にとられた He *was drafted* (≒ *was enlisted*). / He *was called up for military service.* 彼は～を逃れるために,あらゆる手を尽くした He made every effort to evade *military service.*

—忌避 evasion from conscription; 米 evasion of the draft. **—検査** a physical examination for conscription. **—制度** conscription. ¶ その国では間もなく～制度がしかれるだろう *Conscription* will soon be enforced in the country.

ち

ちょうへいそく【腸閉塞】〔医学〕ileus; intestinal obstruction.

ちょうへん【長編】—小説 a long novel. —漫画映画 a long cartoon picture.

ちょうぼ【帳簿】〔簿記〕a book. ¶～を調べた I checked the *books*. ～はつけていますか Do you keep *books*? その勘定を～に記入しましたか Did you enter the account in the *book*? 彼らは～の整理中だ They are adjusting *accounts*.
—係 a book-keeper; an accountant. —監査 an audit. —価格 book value.

ちょうぼ【徴募】enlistment. ¶義勇兵を～している We *are enlisting* volunteer soldiers.

ちょうほう【弔砲】¶故A氏の葬儀の～が放たれた The *funeral salute* was fired in honor of the late Mr. A.

ちょうほう【重宝・調法】¶～な人 a *useful* person. ～な物 a *convenient* thing. いい物を頂いて～しています I find your present very *handy*. 彼は会社で～がられている He *proves* (≒ *makes*) *himself useful to* his company. テレビは～なものだ A television is *a convenience*.

ちょうほう【諜報】—員 an intelligencer; a spy. —機関 an intelligence service. —部 an intelligence department (≒ bureau). —網 an intelligence network.

ちょうぼう【眺望】a view. ¶この山は～がいい This mountain commands *a* fine *view*. この部屋は暑いが～はいい It is hot in this room, but the *view* from here is splendid.

ちょうほうけい【長方形】a rectangle. ¶～の箱 a *rectangular* box.

ちょうほんにん【張本人】¶彼が事件の～だ He is *the ringleader* of the affair.

ちょうまん【腸満・脹満】〔医学〕abdominal dropsy.

ちょうまんいん【超満員】¶朝のラッシュ時には電車は勤め人や学生で～だ During the morning rush hours trains *are overcrowded* (≒ *are congested*) *with* office-workers and students. 公会堂は～で息苦しいほどだった The public hall *was quite full* to suffocation. ホテルは～だ The hotel *is full to the roof*.

ちょうみりょう【調味料】〔a〕condiment; a seasoning.
化学— a chemical condiment.

ちょうみん【町民】a townsman; townsfolk (複数扱い); the inhabitants of a town.

ちょうむすび【蝶結び】a bowknot. ¶彼女は髪に～のリボンをつけていた She had *a bow* of ribbon in her hair.

-ちょうめ【-丁目】¶柳町1～1番地2号 1-2 Yanagicho 1-chome (この方式が日本の表記法として決められている. 番地には外国でもふつう No. はつけない).

ちょうめい【長命】a long life; longevity. ¶彼は～の血統だ He belongs to a *long-lived* family. 現内閣は～だ The present Cabinet has long been in power.

ちょうめん【帳面】(ノート) a notebook.
¶～に書きこむ write down in *a notebook*.
—づら ¶～づらはきちんと合っている The *books* balance exactly. 彼は～づらをごまかした He falsified *accounts*.

ちょうもん【弔問】¶彼の遺族を～した I made *a call of condolence* on his bereaved family.
—客 a caller for condolence.

ちょうもんかい【聴聞会】a hearing.

ちょうや【朝野】¶～の名士がその葬儀に参列した Men of distinction *both in and out of office* attended the funeral.

ちょうやく【跳躍】a jump; jumping.
¶～する jump; spring; leap; skip.
—運動 a jumping exercise. —選手 a jumper. —板 a leaping board.

ちょうやく【調薬】⇒ ちょうごう

ちょうゆう【町有】¶あの土地は～だ The land *is under town ownership*.
—林 a town forest; a city forest.

ちょうよう【長幼】young and old. ¶～序ありという意見には賛成だ I support the idea that the young should give precedence to their elders.

ちょうよう【徴用】requisition. ¶彼は～された He *was put in requisition*.

ちょうらく【凋落】¶彼の会社は～の一途をたどっている His company *is in reduced circumstances*. 草木が～した Flowers and trees *withered*.

ちょうり【調理】cooking. ¶肉を～する *cook* meat (cook は「煮る, 焼く, 揚げる」などのように熱を用いて料理するときに限る. dress は cook の前の下ごしらえするの意).
—師 a cook. —台 a dresser.

ちょうりつ【町立】—幼稚園 a town kindergarten. —図書館 a town library.

ちょうりつ【調律】tuning. ¶ピアノを～してもらった I *had* my piano *tuned*.
—師 a tuner.

ちょうりゅう【潮流】(海) a tide; (風潮) a current; a tendency. ¶時代の～に逆らう swim against the *current* of the times. 時の～に従う swim with the *current* of the times.

ちょうりょう【跳梁】¶ならず者たちの～を許すわけにはいかぬ We cannot let scoundrels *have their own way*.

ちょうりょく【張力】〔物理〕tension.
—計 a tensimeter. 表面— surface tension.

ちょうりょく【聴力】〔the power of〕hearing.
¶年のせいで～が衰えた I lost my *hearing* with age. / My *hearing* got weaker with age.
—計 an audiometer.

ちょうるい【鳥類】birds; fowls; (雅語) the feathered tribe.
—学 ornithology. —学者 an ornithologist.

ちょうるい【蝶類】butterflies.

ちょうれい【朝礼】¶毎日～を行なう Every day we have the *morning assembly*.

ちょうれいぼかい【朝令暮改】an inconsistent policy.

ちょうれん【調練】drill; training; exercise.
¶～する drill; train. 新兵が～を受ける New

conscripts are put through *a drill.*

ちょうろう【長老】an elder; a senior. ¶ 政界の～ an *elder* statesman. 政党の～ *a senior member* of a political party. 村の～たち the village *seniors.*

ちょうろう【嘲弄】ridicule; mockery. ¶ 彼は町じゅうの人から～された He *was ridiculed* by the whole town.

ちょうわ【調和】harmony. ¶ この家具は部屋と～している The furniture *is in harmony with* the room. このふたつの音は～しない These two sounds do not *harmonize with* each other. カーテンとじゅうたんは～している The curtains *match* the carpet. これは～のとれた配列だ This is a *harmonious* arrangement. これらの品は～を欠いている These articles are lacking in *harmony.* 空の色と水の色が～している The color of the sky *is in agreement with* that of the water.

チョーク chalk. ¶ ～1本 a piece of *chalk* (普通名詞扱いで a chalk ともいう). ～で黒板に字を書く write letters *with chalk* on the blackboard.

ちよがみ【千代紙】paper with gay-colored figures.

—細工 gay-colored paper work.

ちょきちょき ¶ はさみで紙を～切る *snip* paper.

ちょきん ¶ 彼は糸の両端を～と切り落とした He *snipped off* the ends of the thread.

ちょきん【貯金】savings. ¶ 郵便局にいくらか～がある I have some *money deposited* in a post office. なるべく～しなさい *Save up* as much as possible. ～を少し引き出した I drew some of my *savings.* 月給の中から～しようと思う I want to *save* some amount out of my salary.

—箱 a piggy bank (ブタの格好をしているから). —通帳 a savings passbook. 郵便— postal savings. 積立— instalment savings. 月掛— monthly savings.

ちょくえい【直営】direct management.

¶ この食堂はAデパートの～だ This restaurant *is under the direct management* of A Department store.

ちょくげき【直撃】a direct hit. ¶ 教会は～を受けて破壊された The church *was hit directly* and destroyed by bombs.

—弾 a direct hit.

ちょくげん【直言】plain speaking. ¶ 上役に～する I'll *speak frankly to* my senior. あえて～すればもっとまじめにやらなければいけない *Frankly speaking,* you must work harder.

ちょくご【直後】¶ 皆の出発～彼は駆けつけた *Immediately after* they departed, he came in running. (この after は接続詞で Immediately after their departure, ... とすれば after は前置詞).

ちょくご【勅語】the Imperial Message.

教育— the Imperial Message on Education.

ちょくさい【直截】¶ ～な表現 a *plain* expression. ～に言えば in plain words.

ちょくし【勅使】an Imperial messenger.

ちょくし【直視】¶ 事態を～しなさい You must *look* the fact *in the face.*

ちょくしゃ【直射】¶ それには日光の～を受けないように注意しなさい Take care not to *expose* it *directly to* the sun. 彼は放射線の～を受けた He *was exposed direct to* the radiant rays.

ちょくじょうけいこう【直情径行】¶ ～の人 a man *of lively and impulsive disposition.*

ちょくしるい【直翅類】〖虫類〗orthoptera.

ちょくしん【直進】¶ この通りを突き当たるまで～してそれから左折しなさい *Go straight ahead* to the end of this street and turn left.

ちょくせつ【直接】¶ これが失敗の～の原因だった This was the *immediate* cause of our failure. 彼と～の知り合いではない I am not *personally* acquainted with him. これは～彼から聞いた情報だ This is the information I *personally* got from him. / This is the *first-hand* information I got from him. 私が～彼に会うつもりです I will see him *in person.*

—税 a direct tax. —目的語〖文法〗a direct object. —話法〖文法〗direct narration.

ちょくせん【直線】a straight line. ¶ ～を引く draw *a straight line.*

—距離 ¶ ここから海岸までは～距離で10キロある It is ten kilometers from here to the seaside, *as the crow flies.* —コース a straight course.

ちょくせん【勅撰】—和歌集 an anthology of Japanese poems collected by the Imperial command.

ちょくぜん【直前】¶ 発車～に駅に着いた *Just before* the train left, I arrived at the station.

ちょくそう【直送】¶ これは産地～のカキだ These are oysters *sent directly* from the oyster-producing center.

ちょくぞく【直属】¶ ～する be under immediate control (*of*). 彼には有能な～の部下が7人いる He has seven able men *under* his *direct control.*

ちょくだい【勅題】¶ 本年の～は「川」だ This year's *theme of the New Year's Imperial poem competition* is 'River.'

ちょくちょう【直腸】〖解剖学〗the rectum.

ちょくちょく now and then; at times.

¶ 最近彼には～会っている I have *often* seen him recently.

ちょくつう【直通】direct communication; a direct service. ¶ この列車は名古屋まで～だ This train *goes through* to Nagoya. A市とB市間には～バスがある There is a *through* bus service between A and B. 東京ベルリン間に～の航空路が新設された A *through* air service was started between Tokyo and Berlin.

—電話 a direct telephone.

ちょくどく【直読】¶ ～直解を練習しなさい Practice *rapid reading.*

ちょくばい【直売】direct sales. ¶ ～でそれを買った I bought it *at direct sales.* 信州リンゴの～だ The growers themselves *are selling* those Shinshu apples *direct to* us.

ちょくほうたい【直方体】a rectangular solid.

ちょくめい【勅命】¶ ～を奉じて in obedience to *the Imperial command.*

ちょくめん【直面】¶ 彼は難問に～している He *is faced with* a difficult problem. / He *is confronted with* a difficult problem.

ちょくやく【直訳】literal translation. ¶ ～する translate literally. 英語論文の～ *a literal translation* of an English article; *a word-for-word translation* of an English article. 締まりのない～的な文体 a loose, *metaphrastic* style. その文章を一字一句～する必要はない You need not *translate* those sentences *word for word.*

ちょくゆ【直喩】〘修辞〙a simile.

ちょくゆしゅつ【直輸出】direct export. ¶ 外国に原毛を～する *export* raw wool *direct to* a foreign country.
—品 direct exports.

ちょくゆにゅう【直輸入】direct import. ¶ 外国から原綿を～する *import* raw cotton *direct from* a foreign country.
—品 direct imports.

ちょくりつ【直立】¶ 旗ざおが～している A flagpole *stands erect.* / A flagpole *is straight up.*
—不動 ¶ 兵士は～不動の姿勢をとった The soldier *stood at attention.* / The soldier *stood erect and stiff.*

ちょくりつえんじん【直立猿人】a pithecanthrope; a Pithecanthropus erectus.

ちょくりゅう【直流】〘電気〙direct current (D.C. と略す).
—電動機 a direct current motor.

ちょくれい【勅令】an Imperial ordinance (≒ order); a Royal decree. ¶ ～が発せられた *An Imperial order* has been issued.

ちょくれつ【直列】〘電気〙series. ¶ 電池を～につなぐ connect cells *in series.*
—回路 a series circuit.

ちょげん【緒言】an introduction; introductory remarks.

ちょこ【猪口】a *sake*-cup.

ちょこざい【猪口才】¶ ～なことを言うな None of your impudence! / Don't be so impudent!

ちょこちょこ ¶ 彼は朝から晩まで～動きまわる He *bustles about* all day. 子どもは部屋の中を～歩いていた The baby *was toddling about* in the room.

ちょこなんと ¶ 子どもが座ぶとんの上に～座っていた A little child sat on the cushion *all alone.*

ちょこまか ¶ 彼はいつも～してうるさい He *is always on the move* and bothers me.

チョコレート chocolate. ¶ 1 枚の～ a bar (≒ stick) of *chocolate.* ～色の chocolate〔-colored〕.
板— a chocolate bar.

ちょさく【著作】writing; a book. ¶ 彼には経済に関する～が多い He has written a lot of *books* on economics.
—権 copyright. ¶ ～権のある作品 a *copyrighted* work. —権侵害〔literary〕piracy.
—者 a writer; an author.

ちょしゃ【著者】(男) an author; a writer; (女) an authoress (女流作家もいまでは author ということが多い); a woman (≒ lady) writer (woman を用いる方がふつう).

ちょじゅつ【著述】¶ 彼は～で生活している He lives *by writing.* / He got his livelihood *by his pen.*
—家 a writer; an author; a literary man.
—業 the literary profession; authorship.

ちょしょ【著書】a book; a work. ¶ 彼には科学に関する～がたくさんある He has written a lot of *books* on science.

ちょすい【貯水】—池 a reservoir. ¶ この～池は全市に給水する This *reservoir* supplies the entire city. —量 the volume of water kept in store. —槽(そう) a water tank.

ちょぞう【貯蔵】¶ 野菜は塩づけにして～される Vegetables *are preserved* in salt. 米を倉庫に～する *store* a warehouse with rice. リスはクルミを～する The squirrel *stores away* nuts. わが国には米を多量に～してある We *keep* ample *stocks of* rice in our country.
—庫 a storehouse. —物 stock; a supply. —米 stored rice. 冷凍— cold storage; refrigeration.

ちょたん【貯炭】a stock of coal.
—所 a coal yard. —量 the volume of coal in store.

ちょちく【貯蓄】saving; (金) savings. ¶ 月収の 1 割を～すべきだ You should *save* (≒ *lay by; put by*) 10 percent out of your monthly income. 老後に備えて～する人は多い Many people are cautious enough to *save* against old age. ～は常に奨励される *Savings* are always encouraged.
—運動 a savings campaign. —銀行 a savings bank. —債券 a savings bond. —性向 propensity to save.

ちょっか【直下】¶ われわれの船は赤道～を進んでいるところだった Our ship was sailing *directly* under the equator. / Our ship was sailing on the equator.
急転— ¶ 事件は急転～解決した The affair *took a sudden turn* toward solution.

ちょっかい ¶ 彼は他人のことに～を出すのが好きだ He likes to *meddle in* (≒ *poke his nose into*) other's affairs. ～を出すな Mind your own business.

ちょっかく【直角】a right angle. ¶ この線はあの線と～をなす This line *makes a right angle with* that. ひとつの線が他の線と～に交わる One line meets another *at a right angle.* 道路がそこで～に曲がっている The road *makes a right angle turn* there.
—三角形 a right-angled triangle.

ちょっかく【直覚】intuition. ¶ 私には～的にそれがわかった I knew it *intuitively* (≒ *by intuition; by instinct*).

ちょっかつ【直轄】¶ 文部省がその学校を～している The Education Ministry *controls* the school *directly*. それは大蔵省～の土地だ It is a lot *under the direct control of* the Finance Ministry.

ちょっかっこう【直滑降】〔スキー〕 a straight descent. ¶ ～する make *a straight descent*.

ちょっかん【直感】¶ 私は彼の気持ちを変えることができないと～した I *perceived immediately* that I could not change his mind.

ちょっかん【直観】intuition. ¶ 必ずしも～にのみ頼れない We cannot always rely on *intuition* alone. 彼はその場の状況を～的に総合する能力がある He is capable of comprehending the situation by *intuition*.

ちょっかん【直諫】remonstration. ¶ 私は彼の怠惰を～した I *remonstrated* (≒ *expostulated*) *with* him *against* his idleness.

チョッキ 米 a vest; 英 a waistcoat (頭からかぶる毛糸のチョッキは pullover と言うことが多い).

ちょっきゅう【直球】〔野球〕 a straight ball.

ちょっけい【直系】direct descent; direct line. ¶ ～の子孫 a *direct* descendant.
—会社 a controlled company; a direct affiliate. **—尊属** a lineal ascendant. **—卑属** a lineal descendant.

ちょっけい【直径】the diameter. ¶ ～3メートルの円をえがく draw a circle three meters *across* (≒ *in diameter*). この円の～はいくらか What is *the diameter* of this circle?

ちょっけつ【直結】direct connection. ¶ これはわれわれの生活に～する問題だ This is a problem *directly connected with* our daily life.

ちょっこう【直交】¶ AとBは～する A *falls at right angles with* B.

ちょっこう【直行】¶ 目的地へ～する予定だ We *are going direct* (≒ *straight*) *to* the destination. この汽車は大阪まで～します This train *runs through to* Osaka.

ちょっこう【直航】¶ この船はサンフランシスコに～している This ship *is sailing direct to* San Francisco.

ちょっと【一寸】**1**〘少しの間〙¶ 5時～前に家に帰った I returned home *a little* before five.
～の間にビルの建築がだいぶ進んだ The construction of the building has proceeded a good deal *in a short time*.
～お待ちください Please wait *a moment* (≒ *a minute*; *a second*). / *Just a moment*, please. / Could you wait *a moment*?
～考えさせてください Let me think *a while*. / I will think about it *a bit*.
～出かけてくる I'm just going out *for a while*.
～静かに Be (≒ Keep) quiet *for a while*.
～でもいいから，顔を出してくれませんか Will you please come *just for a short time*?
～お父さまにお目にかかりたいのですが I would like to see your father *just for a while*.
きみのノートを～見せてくれませんか Will you please let me have a look at your notebook?
あらしは～治まりそうにない I don't think the storm will *soon* abate.
学校の帰りに～友人の家に寄ってきた I dropped in at my friend's house on my way home from school.
2〘少し・わずか〙¶ ～お願いしたいことがあるのですが May I ask a favor of you? / I have something I would like to request you.
～困ったことになった We have a problem.
もう～砂糖を入れてください Please put in *a little* (≒ *some*) more sugar.
もう～で車にはねられるところだった I *narrowly* escaped being run over by a car. / I *almost* got run over by a car.
もう～というところで優勝を逸した We lost the game *by a hair's breadth*.
～は親のことも考えなさい You should think *a little* of your parents. / You should have consideration about your parents.
～でも良心があるなら，そんなことはできないはずだ If you had *any* conscience *at all*, you wouldn't do such a thing.
彼は～したことにすぐ腹を立てる He gets angry at *the merest* trifle.
彼は～したことにまで口を出す He interferes even in *little* things.
見知らぬ所では～した親切がとてもうれしいものだ When you are a stranger, *a little* kindness makes you happy.
彼の言ったことが～気になった What he told me worries me *a bit*. / I'm *a little* worried about what he said.
それは～言いにくい I hesitate to say it.
～ばかり心細くなってきた I feel *a little* lonesome.
～見ただけで偽札だとわかった At one glance I saw that it was a counterfeit bill.
3〘かなり・相当な〙¶ 彼は～した絵かきだ He is a *rather* (≒ *pretty*) famous painter. / He is *well* known as an artist. / He is *something* as an artist.
彼女は～したグラマーだ She is *something of* a glamour girl.
～まとまったお金が欲しい I need *quite a bit* of money.
彼は政界では～した顔だ He is *quite* well-known in the political circles. / He is *quite* considerably influencial in the political circles.
彼は～した邸宅に住んでいる He lives in *quite* a big mansion.
4〘否定を伴って，簡単に・容易に・なかなか〙¶ それは～できない相談です That's〔*quite*〕an impracticable thing to ask.
彼がどこにいるかは～わからない It's〔*rather*〕hard to know his whereabouts.
彼女が離婚するなんて，～考えられない It's *quite* unbelievable that she will divorce her husband.
5〘呼びかけ〙¶ ～，失礼ですが，山田さんですか Excuse me, but are you Mr. Yamada?
ねえ～，どうしてそんなに急ぐの *Hey* (≒ *I say*), why are you in such a hurry?

ちょっぴり ¶ これは～塩がからい This tastes *a*

little too salty. / This tastes *a bit* salty.

チョップ (あばらつきの肉) a chop ; (テニス・プロレスなど) a chop. ¶ ポーク～ *a* pork *chop.*

ちょとつ【猪突】¶ ～猛進する make a reckless (≒ wild ; headlong) rush.

ちょびひげ【ちょび髭】a moustache. ¶ 彼は～を生やしている He wears *a tooth-brush moustache.*

ちょぼく【貯木】a stock of lumber.
—場 a lumberyard.

ちょめい【著名】¶ ～の士 a *well-known* (≒ *celebrated*) person. 彼は豪力で～だ He *is noted for* his strength.

ちょめい【著明】¶ ～な(の) remarkable ; marked.

ちょろちょろ ¶ 小川が谷間を～流れていた The brook *trickled* through the valley. トカゲが～していた I saw a lizard *sneaking about.*

ちょろまか・す pilfer ; cheat. ¶ 彼は友人から金を～した He *pilfered* some money from his fellows. 彼らは売上金の大部分を～した They *pocketed* (≒ *peculated*) a large part of proceeds. 彼は会社から50万円～した He *embezzled* half a million yen from the company.

ちょろん【緒論】an introduction ; introductory remarks.

ちょん ¶ こんなことはばかでも～でもできることだ Nothing is easier than this. この事件はこれで～となった This *brought* the affair *to an end.*

ちょんぎ・る ¶ 茎からつぼみを～った I *snipped* a bud *off* the stem. 松の木から数本の枝を～った I *lopped* a few branches *off* the pine-tree.

ちょんまげ【丁髷】a topknot. ¶ 彼は～を結っている He wears *a topknot.*

ちらか・す【散らかす】scatter. ¶ 部屋を～す *put* a room *in disorder.* 子どもたちが部屋じゅうに紙くずを～した The children *littered* the room with bits of paper. おもちゃを～しっぱなしにしておいてはいけません Don't *leave* your toys *lying about.*

ちらか・る【散らかる】¶ 部屋が～っている The room *is in disorder* (≒ *is in a litter*). 道に枯れ葉が～っている Dead leaves *lie scattered* on the road.

ちらし【散らし】(広告) a handbill ; a leaflet. ¶ ～を配る distribute *handbills* (≒ *leaflets*).
—書き scattered writing. —薬(でき物の) a resolvent. —ずし *sushi* served in a bowl.

ちら・す【散らす】scatter ; (はれものなどを) resolve. ¶ われわれは自分の職務以外に気を～してはならない We should not *have* our minds *distracted* from our duty. その薬ははれものを～す The medicine *resolves* the tumor. ふたつの剣が火花を～した The two swords *made sparks fly.*

ちらちら ¶ 花びらが～風に散る Flower-petals *flit* (≒ *flitter*) in the wind. 雪が～している It *is snowing lightly.* 黒板に日が当たると～する The sunlight *glances* on the blackboard. 彼のうわさを～聞く We *occasionally* hear of him. 酔っぱらうと目が～する When you are drunk, *things will swim before your eyes.*

ちらつ・く ¶ 雪が～いている It *is snowing lightly.* 彼の面影が目の前に～く His image *haunts* me. 明かりが遠方に～いた A light *glimmered* in the distance. 木の間に湖が～いて見えた We *caught glimpses of* the lake through the trees.

ちらば・る【散らばる】¶ その部屋は～っていた The room *was in disorder.* 風で紙が部屋じゅうに～ったSheets of paper *were scattered about* in the room by the wind. その海にはたくさんの島が～っている The sea *is dotted with* a lot of islands. 彼の作品の大半は～ってしまって残っていない Most of his works *got scattered* and lost. 私の同級生はあちらこちらに～っている My classmates *are scattered* far and wide.

ちらほら ¶ 梅が～咲きはじめた Plum blossoms are coming out *here and there* (≒ *in twos and threes*). お客さんたちは～帰りはじめた The guests began to return *by twos and threes.* 聴衆の中にはアメリカ人が～いた The audience *was sprinkled with* Americans. 妙なうわさが～聞こえてくる A strange rumor *is circulating.*

ちらり ¶ その絵を～と見た I *cast a glance at* the picture. / I *caught a glimpse of* the picture. うわさを～と耳にした I *happened to* hear the rumor. / I heard the rumor *by chance.*

チリ Chile.
—硝石 Chile saltpeter. —人 a Chilean.

ちり【塵】dust. ¶ 部屋のすみに～がたまっている There is some *dust* accumulating in the corner of the room. テーブルには～がいっぱい積もっていた The table was thickly covered with *dust.* 部屋から～を掃き出した I swept the *dirt* out of the room. 部屋には～ひとつなかった The room *was spotless.* ～も積もれば山となる (諺) *Many a little makes a mickle.*

ちり【地理】(地理学) geography ; (地勢) geographical features ; topography. ¶ この町は～的条件に恵まれている This town enjoys a *geographical* advantage. 彼はこの町の～に明るい He is quite familiar with this town. / He knows his way about here. 私はこの土地の～に暗い I am a stranger here.
—学者 a geographer. 自然—学 physical geography. 商業—学 commercial geography. 人文—学 human (≒ descriptive) geography. 政治—学 political geography.

ちりがみ【塵紙】toilet (≒ privy) paper ; tissue〔paper〕.

ちりちり ¶ 彼女の髪は生まれつき～に縮れている Her hair *is* naturally *over-frizzled.*

ちりぢり【散り散り】¶ 一行はパリで～になった The party *broke up* in Paris. 驚いた子どもたちは～になって逃げた The frightened children ran away *in all directions.* 旅行者たちはいっしょにヨーロッパに行ったが, ～に帰宅した The travelers went to Europe together, but returned home *separately.*

ちりとり【塵取り】a dustpan.

ちりなべ【ちり鍋】a pot of fish and vegetables cooked before the diners; a pot of fish boiled with vegetables and other food and seasoned with vinegared soy.

ちりば・める【鏤める】inlay; set. ¶ その象牙(ぞうげ)は金銀が～められている The ivory *is inlaid with* silver and gold. (宝石などのときは studded with jewels). たくさんの宝石を～めた指輪 a ring *set with* many gems.

ちりめん【縮緬】〔silk〕crape; *crêpe* (フランス語).
──じわ fine crinkles.

ちりゃく【知略】resources. ¶ ～にたけた将軍 a *resourceful* general. 彼は～にたけている He is full of *resources*. / He *is quite resourceful*.

ちりょう【治療】treatment. ¶ A博士に足を～してもらった I *had* my leg *treated* (≒ *taken care of*) by Dr. A. 彼はだれの～を受けているのですか Who *is looking after* him? 歯の～にどのくらい日数がかかりましたか How long did it take you to *have* your tooth *treated*? 彼はまだ～を受けている He is still under *treatment*. この病気は～のしようがない This disease is beyond *medical treatment*. こういうおできの確実な～法を教えてください Won't you tell me *a* sure *cure for* a boil of this sort?

ちりょく【知力】intellect; mental power. ¶ 彼女は～において彼に劣る She is inferior in *mental faculties* to him.

ちりれんげ【散り蓮華】a petal-shaped porcelain spoon.

ちりんちりん tinkle-tinkle. ¶ 風鈴が風で～と鳴っている The wind bell is *tinkling* in the wind. そりを走らせるとそりの鈴が～鳴った The sleigh bell *jingled* as we rode.

ち・る【散る】scatter. ¶ 花はすっかり～った The blossoms *are* all *gone*. 風のため桜はみんな～ってしまった The wind has made all the cherry blossoms *fall*. 風で雲は～った The clouds *have been scattered* by the wind. テレビで気が～った The TV program *distracted* my attention. このインクは～りやすい This ink is apt to *spread*.

ちろちろ ¶ 炉でたき火が～燃えている The fire is burning *quietly* in the furnace. 小川が谷間を～流れていた The brook *trickled* through the valley.

ちわ【痴話】love-talk; lovers' talk.
──喧嘩 ¶ それは～喧嘩にすぎなかった The affair was only *a lovers' quarrel*.

ちん【狆】〘動物〙a lap dog; a Japanese spaniel.

ちんあげ【賃上げ】a wage increase. ¶ 労働者たちは～を要求した The workers demanded *higher wages* (≒ *a wage increase*). / The workers demanded to *raise wages*.
──闘争 a struggle for higher wages.

ちんあつ【鎮圧】suppression; repression. ¶ 謀反の～に軍隊が出動した Troops were used in the *suppression* (≒ *repression*) of the revolt. 政府は断固として暴徒を～した The Government *suppressed* (≒ *repressed*; *put down*) the mob firmly.

ちんうつ【沈鬱】melancholy; gloom. ¶ 彼女は～な顔をしていた She had a *gloomy* (≒ *dismal*; *melancholy*) face. / She looked *gloomy*. この重苦しい空気の中で彼の～はしだいにつのっていった In this heavy atmosphere his *depression* grew gradually.

ちんか【沈下】¶ 地盤～は重大な問題だ Ground *subsidence* (≒ *sinking*) is a matter of consequence. 地盤が～する The ground *subsides* (≒ *sinks*).

ちんか【鎮火】¶ 火事はすぐ～した The fire *was* soon *put out*. / The fire *was* soon *extinguished*. / The fire *was* soon *brought under control*.

ちんがし【賃貸し】¶ これらのボートは～する These boats *are on hire*. この車は1日2,000円で～する They *hire out* this car for two thousand yen a day.

ちんがり【賃借り】hire; (土地・家屋の) lease. ¶ 月5万円でアパートを～した I *leased* an apartment for fifty thousand yen a month.
──人 a hirer. ──料 rent.

ちんき【珍奇】novelty; rarity. ¶ ～な風習 *curious* manners. ～な動物 *strange* animals.

チンキ tincture.
ヨード── iodine tincture.

ちんきゃく【珍客】a welcome visitor. ¶ ゆうべ～があった I had *an unexpected visitor* yesterday evening. / Last night I had a visitor whose coming I had not expected.

ちんぎん【賃銀・賃金】wages. ¶ 彼はどのくらい～をもらっているのですか What are his *wages*? / How much does he *earn*? 彼らは～の値上げを要求した They demanded higher *wages*. 彼は1日2,000円の～で働いている He is working at the *wage* of 2,000 yen a day. / He is working at 2,000 yen a day. / He is being paid 〔*a wage* of〕 2,000 yen a day. あなたの会社は～がいいですか Does your office pay good *wages*?
──格差 the differentiation in wages. ──カット the reduction of wages. ──水準 a wage level. ──生活者 a wage earner. ──統制 wage control. ──ベース a wage base. ──労働者 a wage earner. 基本── the standard wages. 名目── nominal wages. 割り増し── extra wages.

ちんこう【沈降】sedimentation.
──速度 (赤血球の) 〔blood〕 sedimentation rate.

ちんこん【鎮魂】the repose of souls.
──曲 〔a〕 requiem. ──祭 a service for the repose of the deceased.

ちんざ【鎮座】¶ この社には大国主命が～まします The shrine *is dedicated to* Okuni-nushi-no-mikoto. 彼の顔にはまん中に大きな鼻が～ましましている A big nose is conspicuous in the middle of his face.

ちんし【沈思】¶ 彼は～黙考していた He *was lost in thought*. / He *was absorbed in meditation*.

ちんじ【珍事・椿事】an accident; a disaster. ¶ ～が起こった *An accident* happened.

ちんしごと【賃仕事】job〔work〕. ¶ ～をする do odd jobs; do piece work. 彼女は内職に洋裁の～をしている She takes in dressmaking to supplement a living.

ちんしゃ【陳謝】an apology. ¶ 彼は約束を破ったことをぼくに～した He *apologized to* me *for* breaking his promise. 失礼なことを申しまして深く～いたします I sincerely *apologize to* you *for* having said rude things.

ちんじゅ【鎮守】¶ ～の森 the grove of a tutelary shrine. ～の祭り the festival of a village shrine.

ちんじゅつ【陳述】a statement. ¶ 弁護人の～が行なわれた The lawyer *made* his *statement.*
—書 a written statement.

ちんじょう【陳情】a petition; an appeal. ¶ 農民は大臣に米価値上げを～した The farmers *made an appeal to* the minister to raise the price of rice.
—者 a petitioner. —書 a petition.

ちんせい【鎮静】quiet; calmness. ¶ ～する become calm; become quiet.
—剤 a sedative; a tranquilizer.

ちんせつ【珍説】a novel opinion. ¶ 彼についてはたくさん～がある There are many *amusing* (≒ *interesting; funny*) *stories* about him.

ちんたい【沈滞】dullness. ¶ ～した空気がみなぎっている A *dull* (≒ *stagnant*) atmosphere prevails. 商況は～している Business *is depressed.*

ちんたい【賃貸】lease. ¶ ～する rent; lease.
—価格 a rental value. —契約 a lease. —人 a lessor. —料 rent.

ちんたいしゃく【賃貸借】letting and hiring.

ちんだん【珍談】a funny story. ¶ 彼には～がたくさんある Many *funny stories* are told about him.

ちんちくりん ¶ ～な人 a dwarf; a midget; a runt; an *undersized* man.

ちんちゃく【沈着】coolness; composure; self-possession. ¶ ～な態度 a *calm* attitude; a *cool* manner. 彼は～に判断してそこに集った人人を安全なところへ誘導した He led the people gathering there into a safe place by his *self-possessed* (≒ *calm*) judgment.

ちんちょう【珍重】¶ その秘宝を～している I *prize* the cherished treasure. この名刀は～するに足る This noted sword is worth *valuing highly.*

ちんちょうげ【沈丁花】〖植物〗a sweet-smelling daphne.

ちんちろりん ¶ 鈴虫が～と鳴いている The bell-ring insect *is tinkling.*

ちんちん 1〘鈴の音など〙chink; tinkle.
¶ ～鳴る tinkle.
やかんが～沸いている The kettle *is singing.*
2〘犬の〙¶ 犬が～している A dog *is standing on his hind legs.*
(犬に向かって)～! Beg!

ちんつう【沈痛】¶ ～なおももちで with a *sad* look. ～な口調で in a *sad* tone.

ちんつうざい【鎮痛剤】an anodyne; a lenitive.

ちんてい【鎮定】suppression. ¶ 反乱は～された The rebellion *was put down.* / The rebellion *was suppressed.*

ちんでん【沈殿】precipitation; sedimentation; deposition. ¶ ～する settle; be deposited.
—物 a deposit; a sediment; (おり) dregs.

ちんどんや【ちんどん屋】a musical sandwichman; a ding-dong band for publicity; a publicity agent〔with drums and bugles〕(外国にこの種のものはない).

ちんにゅう【闖入】intrusion; trespass.
¶ デモ隊が首相官邸に～した The demonstrators *forced their way into* the premier's official residence.
—者 an intruder; a trespasser.

ちんば【跛】¶ 彼は交通事故で～になった A traffic accident *made* him *lame.* / A traffic accident *crippled* him. 彼はげたを～にはいている He is wearing *an odd pair* of clogs.

チンパンジー〖動物〗a chimpanzee.

ちんぴら an urchin; a kid; (不良少年) a punk.

ちんぴん【珍品】a rarity; (こっとう品) a curio. ¶ これはまさに～だ This is indeed *a rarity.* / This is indeed *a rare article.*

ちんぶ【鎮撫】¶ 自警団が暴徒を～した The vigilance committee *quieted* a mob.

ちんぷ【陳腐】¶ ～なことば a *hackneyed* remark. ～な冗談 a *stale* joke. あの人にしては～なことばだ What a *trite* remark for him to make!

ちんぶん【珍聞】(耳新しいこと) startling news; (珍談) a strange story. ¶ それは～だ It's *startling news* to me.

ちんぷんかんぷん ¶ ～でちっともわからない It *is all Greek to* me. 彼は～のことばかり言っている He *is* always *talking nonsense.* ～の返事をした He made an *incoherent* reply.

ちんべん【陳弁】¶ ～する plead; explain; expound. もっぱら～につとめた He did his utmost to *plead.*

ちんぼつ【沈没】¶ 船は乗組員もろとも～した The ship *sank* with all her crew. 船はどうにか～を免れた The ship managed to escape *being submerged.*
—船 a sunken ship.

ちんぽん【珍本】a rare book.

ちんまり ¶ ～した部屋 a *cozy* room. ～した庭 a *prettily arranged* garden.

ちんみ【珍味】a dainty; a delicacy. ¶ 彼のところで山海の～をごちそうになった We've enjoyed *every sort of delicacies* at his home.

ちんみょう【珍妙】¶ 彼は～な顔をしている He has a *queer* look. それは～な考えだ That's a *fantastic* (≒ *odd*) idea. / It's a fancy.

ちんむるい【珍無類】¶ 彼の話し方はまさに～だ His manner of speaking is *extraordi-*

nary. それは〜な出来事だった It was *the oddest* (≒ *queerest*) event we have experienced.

ちんもく【沈黙】 silence ; (無口) reticence. ¶ 〜を守る keep *silent*. 〜を破る break *silence*. 〜は金なり (諺) *Silence is golden*. 彼の一言で相手は〜した One word he uttered *silenced* his opponent. 重苦しい〜が続いた There continued weighted *silence*. 彼は長年の〜を破って新作を発表した He made a new work public after a long years' *silence*.

ちんゆう【沈勇】 cool courage. ¶ 〜な男 a *coolly courageous* man.

ちんれつ【陳列】 exhibition. ¶ 〜する exhibit ; display ; put on show. 店先に品物を〜する *display* goods in a show window. 種々の人形が目下〜中だ Various sorts of dolls *are on display*.

—館 a museum. —室 a show room. —だな a showcase. —品 an exhibit ; an article on display. —窓 a show window.

ちんろうどう【賃労働】 wage labor.

つ

つ【津】 a port ; (渡し) a ferry.

-つ ¶ 彼は行き〜もどり〜した He walked to and fro. 1枚の木の葉が浮き〜沈み〜流れていった A leaf drifted down the stream, *now* sinking *and now* rising. 世の中は持ち〜持たれ〜だ In this world we must *give and take*.

ツァー Tzar ; Czar.

つい【対】 a pair ; a couple ; a set. ¶ 〜にする pair ; make a pair. 1〜の椅子 *a couple of* chairs. このふたつは〜になっている These two *make a pair*. 1〜の茶わんが食卓の上にある There is (≒ are) *a pair of* cups on the table.

好一— ¶ ふたりは好一〜だ The two persons *are well-matched*.

つい ¶ それは〜きのうのことだった That happened *only* yesterday. 彼は〜今しがた出たところだ He left here *just now*. 〜笑ってしまった I laughed *in spite of myself*. 彼の言うことを〜承諾してしまった I consented to what he said *in spite of myself*. 〜そう言ってしまった I said it *without due consideration*.

ツイード〔織物〕 tweed. ¶ 〜の服を着た人 a man in *tweeds*. 〜の上着 a *tweed* jacket.

つい·える【潰える】 ¶ 敵軍の猛攻にあってわが軍は〜えた Our army *collapsed* by the fierce attack of the enemy.

ついおく【追憶】 recollection ; remembrance. ¶ 彼は〜にふけっている He is absorbed in *reminiscence*.

ついか【追加】 〔an〕 addition ; (補充) a supplement. ¶ 前に出した注文にもう3冊〜注文をした I ordered three books *in addition to* the order previously sent. もう2人前食事を〜しよう Let us order two *more* meals.

—予算 a supplementary budget.

ついき【追記】 a postscript (省略形としてP.S. を用いることがある). ¶ 〜する add *a postscript*.

ついきゅう【追及】 overtake. ¶ その時の彼の行動を〜する必要がある It is necessary to *catch* (≒ *get*) him as to what he was doing then. 彼は矢継早に質問されて〜された One question after another was put on him in attempting to prove his guilt or innocence.

ついきゅう【追求】 pursuit ; chase. ¶ 彼の〜しつつある問題は重大だ The problem he *is getting after* is very important. / The problem he *is pursuing* is very important. 利益を〜する *seek after* profits. 人生の目的を〜する *pursue* the purpose of *one's* life.

ついきゅう【追究】 investigation ; close inquiry. ¶ それ以上は〜できなかった The matter *was* not *pressed* any further. 真理を〜する *seek* truth.

ついく【対句】 a couplet ; an antithesis. ¶ 〜をなす make *an antithesis*.

—法 antithesis.

ついげき【追撃】 〔a〕 pursuit ; 〔a〕 chase. ¶ 逃げる敵を〜中である We are *giving chase to* the retreating enemy. 敵は〜をやめた The enemy gave up the *chase*.

—戦 a running fight.

ついご【対語】 a pair of words. ¶ この2語は〜になっている These two words *make a pair*.

ついこつ【椎骨】〔解剖学〕 a vertebra (複 vertebrae).

ついし【墜死】 death from a fall. ¶ 彼はロッククライミングをしていて〜した While he was climbing the mountain rocks, he *fell down to death*.

ついしけん【追試験】 a supplementary examination. ¶ 英語の〜を受ける take *a supplementary examination in* English. 〜を受けさせる give (*a person*) *a supplementary examination*.

ついじゅう【追従】 ¶ 権力家に〜する *follow* a man of power.

ついしょう【追従】 flattery. ¶ お〜を言うのはやめなさい Never say *flattering things*. 彼は上役に〜するのがうまい He is good at *flattering* his superiors. 彼の言動には〜的なところがある He has something *oily* in his speech and action.

—笑い ¶ 彼は〜笑いを浮かべた He had *a servile smile* on his face.

ついしん【追伸】a postscript (省略形として P.S. を用いる).

ついずい【追随】¶ 彼は他の〜を許さない He *is without a peer.* / He *is unrivaled.* 英会話にかけては彼は他の〜を許さない He *is second to none* in English conversation. 彼の大工仕事の技術は他の〜を許さない He has a *peerless* technique in carpentering.

ついせき【追跡】pursuit. ¶ 犯人を〜している警官 a policeman *in pursuit of* the criminal. パトカーは1台の車を激しく〜中だ A patrol car *is chasing* a car *in* hot *pursuit.* 30分〜してようやく彼を捕らえた I caught him after half an hour's *chase.*

—基地 (人工衛星などの) a tracking station.
—者 a pursuer.

ついぜん【追善】a memorial service for the dead; a mass [for the dead]. ¶ 彼の〜を営む予定だ I am to give *a memorial service for* him. あの名優の〜興行が行なわれた There was a performance given *in memory of* that great actor.

ついそ【追訴】¶ 〜する bring a supplementary suit (*against*).

ついぞ【終ぞ】¶ こんなものは〜見たことがない I have *never* seen such a thing.

ついそう【追想】remembrance; recollection. ¶ 幼時の〜にふけった I enjoyed *recalling memories* of my childhood. この絵を見ると幼いころのことが〜される This picture *reminds* me *of* my childhood. 小学校時代の〜にしばし時のたつのを忘れた *Reminiscing on* my elementary school days, I forgot the passing of time.

ついたち【一日】the first day of a month. ¶ 5月〜 *the first* of May; 1st of May; May 1 ([mei fə:st] と読む). 毎月〜に *on the first day of* every month.

ついたて【衝立て】a screen. ¶ この部屋は〜でふたつに仕切られている This room is partitioned with *a screen* into two.

ついちょう【追徴】additional collection. ¶ 彼は5万円の金を〜された(罰として) He was ordered to *forfeit* fifty thousand yen.

—金 money collected in addition; (罰金) a forfeit. —税 a tax collected in addition.

ついて【就いて・付いて】**1**〖に関して〗about. ¶ この問題に〜あなたはどう思いますか What do you think *of* this problem? 彼は日本文学に〜講演した He lectured *on* Japanese literature. 私に〜なら, それはたいした問題ではない *As for* me, that is of little importance.

2〖に沿って〗along. ¶ 川に〜約3キロ歩いた I walked about three kilometers *along* the river.

3〖のもとで〗under. ¶ 数学の大家に〜数学を勉強した I studied mathematics *under* a great mathematician.

ついで【序】a chance; an opportunity. ¶ この仕事の〜に彼を訪問したい *In the course of doing* this job, I'd like to call on him. お〜の節にお立ち寄りください Please call on me *when you happen to* come this way. 旅行の話の〜だがあなたは欧州に行ったことがありますか *Speaking of* traveling, have you ever been to Europe? 〜のありしだいかの地をひと目見たい I want to have a look at the place *at the first opportunity.* 〜にちょっとお話したいことがあります *Incidentally* (≒ *While we're at it*), there's something I'd like to talk to you about.

ついで【次いで】¶ 講演が終わり, 〜余興に移った The lecture came to an end, *and then* an entertainment followed (≒ was given). 琵琶湖に〜日本で大きな湖は何ですか What is the largest lake *after* (≒ *next to*) Lake Biwa in Japan? それに〜需要があるのは鉄だ Iron *comes second* in demand.

ついていく【付いて行く】(すぐあとから) follow; (おくれないで) keep up with. ¶ 彼に〜った I *went with* him. きみのあとに〜きます I'll *come after* you. きみの車が先に行ってくれ, ぼくはあとから〜く Drive ahead, and I'll *follow* you. ぼくはきみにおくれずに〜けない I cannot *keep up with* you. 彼は時勢に〜けなかった He could not *keep up with* the times.

ついてくる【付いて来る】¶ 犬は駅まで私のあとに付いて来た The dog *followed* me *to* the station.

ついてる ¶ きのうは万事〜てた Yesterday *everything was lucky to* me. これで勝てるなんて全く〜てる *Everything is to my advantage* to be able to win such an unfavorable game. きょうは全く〜てない *Everything goes wrong with* me today indeed. ここできみに会えるなんて〜てる *How lucky I am to* see you here. ぼくは〜てるときは大きな勝負をする I have a big game when *fortune is on my side.* 〜てて勝った I won *by a fluke.*

ついとう【追悼】mourning. ¶ 故人への〜の辞を述べた I gave *a memorial address* in honor of [*the soul* of] the deceased.

—会 a memorial service. ¶ 〜会を催す hold *a memorial service for* (*a person*); hold *a meeting in memory of* (*a person*). —演説 a funeral oration. —文 a memorial writing.

ついとつ【追突】a rear-end collision. ¶ 〜しないように注意してください Drive [your car] carefully so as not to *collide with* another car *from behind.* 〜されてむち打ち症になった Whiplash resulted when my car *was struck from behind.*

ついに【遂に・終に】at last. ¶ 戦いは〜彼の勝利に帰した The fight *ended in* his victory. 待ちに待ったが〜彼は姿を現わさなかった We waited and waited but he never came. 暴飲暴食のため〜彼は病の床についた He ate and drank immoderately *until at last* he was confined to bed. 〜彼は健康を回復した He recovered his health *at length.* 〜は彼もわかってくれるだろう He will understand me *in time.*

ついにん【追認】confirmation. ¶事実を〜する *confirm* (≒ *ratify*) a fact.

ついば·む【啄む】peck (*at*); pick (*at*). ¶小鳥が木の実を〜んでいる Birds *are picking* nuts. めん鳥はトウモロコシを〜んだ The hen *pecked* the corn.

ついひ【追肥】additional fertilizer.

ついぼ【追慕】¶懐かしい昔を〜した I *was nostalgic of* the good old days. 亡き母を〜して彼は涙にくれた He was choked with tears *remembering* his deceased mother.

ついほう【追放】banishment; expulsion. ¶彼らは王を〜した They *banished* the king. 彼は国外に〜された He *was expelled from* the country. 彼は公職を〜された He *was removed from* public office.

ついや·す【費やす】¶彼は書物に多額の金を〜す He *spends* a lot of money *on* books. あなたは週にどのくらいの時間をレジャーに〜しますか How much time do you *spend in* amusement? この駅は5億円を〜して出来上がった This station was completed *at the cost of* five hundred million yen. 一日の大部分を読書に〜す人もある Some people *spend* most of their time 〔*in*〕 reading. ただむだに時間を〜すことのないようにしなさい Try not to *waste* your time. このひとつの問題に5ページを〜した I *devoted* five pages *to* this single problem.

ついらく【墜落】a fall; a crash. ¶飛行機が〜した An airplane *crashed.* 彼はビルの屋上からまっさかさまに〜した He *fell* head over heels from the top of the building. ひとりの男が船から海中に〜した A man *fell* overboard.

つう【通】(物事に通じている人) an authority; an expert; (鑑定家) a connoisseur. ¶彼はなかなかの〜だ He is *a well-informed person.* 彼女は西洋〜だ She is *an authority on* (≒ *is well versed in*) things European. あの人は宝石〜だ He is *a connoisseur in* (≒ *of*) jewelery. 彼はどんなことでも〜を気どる He pretends to *be well-informed* (≒ *be well versed*) *in* everything.
情報— a man of full information; a well-informed man. 野球— an authority on baseball.

-つう【-通】¶手紙の写し1〜 *a copy* of a letter. 書類2〜 two *copies* of a document. 契約書を3〜作った We made three *copies* of the contract. ことしはクリスマスカードを10〜もらった I received ten Christmas cards this year.

つういん【痛飲】carousal. ¶きのう旧友に会って〜した Yesterday I met an old friend of mine and *drank deeply* (≒ *drank heavily; caroused*) with him.

つううん【通運】transportation.
—会社 a transportation company; 米 an express company.

つうか【通貨】currency. ¶〜の切り下げ devaluation. 〜の切り上げ revaluation. 〜の流通額 total amount of *money in circulation.* 日本では〜として円が使われている Yen is used as *currency* (≒ *current money*) in Japan. 勘定をその国の〜で支払った I paid the bill in *the current coin* of the country.
—膨張 inflation. —縮小 deflation.

つうか【通過】passage. ¶バスが1台目の前を〜した A bus *passed* in front of me. 列車はトンネルを〜した The train *passed* through the tunnel. この駅は〜することになっている The train *passes* this station *without stopping.* ジェット機が上空を〜した A jet *passed* over us. この議案は議会を〜した This bill *passed* the Diet. 議案の〜 the *passage* of a bill.

つうかい【痛快】a great pleasure. ¶きみと昔話をするのは実に〜だ *It is awfully pleasant* (≒ *It is extremely pleasant*) for me to talk about our early days with you. / *It gives* me *a great pleasure* to talk about our younger days with you. 会議で彼は〜な発言をした He made an *incisive* observation at the conference. この映画は実に〜だった I found this film *thrillingly pleasant.* 彼は〜な男だ He is a *jolly* fellow.

つうかく【痛覚】〘医学〙sense of pain.

つうがく【通学】¶毎日電車で〜している I *go to school* by train every day. / I *attend school* by train every day.
—生 a day scholar (≒ student).

つうかん【通関】entry; customs clearance. ¶〜する pass the customs.
—許可証 a goods clearance permit. —手数料 a clearance fee. —手続き customs formality. ¶〜手続きを済ます go through *customs formalities.*

つうかん【痛感】¶語学力の不足を〜している I *keenly feel* (≒ *fully realize*) that I am deficient in linguistic ability. / I *know very well* my poor language ability.

つうかん【通観】a general survey. ¶国内情勢を〜する *take a general veiw* (≒ *survey*) *of* the domestic affairs.

つうぎょう【通暁】¶彼は近代文学に〜している He *is well acquainted with* (≒ *is well versed in; is at home in*) modern literature. / He *is widely read in* modern literature.

つうきん【通勤】¶ずいぶん遠くから〜している者もいる Some of them *come to work* from very far. / Some of them *come to the office* from very far. 毎日の〜にかなりの時間をとられる *Commutation* takes me a great deal of time every day.
—者 a commuter. —手当 a commutation allowance. —定期 a commuter ticket. —電車 a commuter train.

つうげき【痛撃】a severe attack. ¶わが軍は敵に〜を与えた Our army *made a severe* (≒ *made a shattering*) *attack on* the enemy.

つうこう【通行】passage. ¶この道路は〜できない No one can *pass* along this road. この道は〜できる This road *is passable.* 自動車の〜は禁じられている Automobile *traffic* is closed.

―権 the right of way. ―税 a transit tax. ―止め the suspension of traffic. ¶ この通りは～止めだ This road *is blocked.* ―人 a passer; a passer-by (複 passers-by). ―料金 a toll. 一方―(掲示) One way only. 右側―(掲示) Keep to the right.

つうこく【通告】 notice; [a] notification. ¶ 一方的な～ one-sided *notice.* 組合は会社側にストライキを～した The labor union gave *notice* of a strike to the management. 転勤の～は1週間前に出される *A notification* of transference is issued a week in advance. / We are transferred at a week's *notice.* アメリカはわが国に条約の正式批准を～してきた The United States *communicated to* our country formal ratification of the treaty.

つうこん【痛恨】 mortification; deep regret. ¶ 一世一代の～事 [a matter of] *the greatest regret* of *one's* life. ～の涙 tears of *bitterness* (≒ *great sorrow*). 彼の事故死は～の至りだ It is a matter for *deep regret* that he was killed in an accident. / *To our great regret,* he was killed in an accident.

つうさん【通産】 ―省 the Ministry of International Trade and Industry. ―大臣 the Minister of International Trade and Industry.

つうさん【通算】 the total. ¶ わがチームは～7回めの優勝をした Our team has won seven victories *in all.* 1月から6月までの交通事故件数を～すると1万件になる The traffic accidents which have occurred from January to June *total* [*up to*] ten thousand.

つうし【通史】 ¶ 日本文学～ *the general history* of Japanese literature; *the outline* of Japanese literature.

つうじ【通じ】 passage; action of bowels. ¶ ～があった I had *an action of the bowels.* / My *bowels moved* well. 2日間～が止まっている I have had *no motion* for two days. ～をつけるにはどうしたらいいでしょうか What shall I do to *loosen the bowels*? / What shall I do to *move the bowels*? ～をよくするようにつとめる keep *one's bowels open.*
―薬 a laxative.

つうじあ・う【通じ合う】 ¶ 私たちは心が互いによく～う We *agree* very well *with each other.* 彼とはいくら話しても意志が～わない However often I talk to him, I cannot *make myself understood.*

つうじて【通じて】 ¶ この辺りは一年を～暑い It is hot *all the year round* in this neighborhood. 料金は全国を～同一である The fare is the same *all over* the country. 一年を～私がいちばん好きなのは夏だ I like summer best *of all the seasons of the year.* 本を～知識を得る We acquire knowledge *through* books. テレビを～外国のようすを知ることもできる We can learn something about foreign countries *through* television.

つうしょう【通称】 a popular name; an alias. ¶ 坂東妻三郎～坂妻 Bando Tsumasaburo, *alias* Bantsuma. 彼はタヌキという～で呼ばれている He *is commonly called* "Tanuki". / He *passes by the name of* "Tanuki".

つうしょう【通商】 commerce; trade. ¶ あの国との～には障害が多い There are plenty of troubles in *trading* (≒ *commercial relations*) with that country. わが国がアメリカと～を始めてから何年もたつ It is many years since we opened *trade relations* with America.
―航海条約 a treaty of commerce and navigation. ―産業省 the Ministry of International Trade and Industry. ―産業大臣 the Minister of International Trade and Industry. ―条約 a commercial treaty.

つうじょう【通常】 usually; in general. ¶ 家では～みな朝7時に起きる All my family *generally* get up at seven in the morning. 父は～6時に帰宅する *In general* (≒ *Usually*) my father comes home at six. あすは～どおり営業します Our store is open *as usual* tomorrow. / Business *as usual* tomorrow.
―会員 an ordinary member. ―国会 a regular session [of the Diet]. ―服 a business suit; everyday clothes; casual wear. ―郵便物 ordinary mail.

つう・じる【通じる】 **1** 〖至る・達する〗 ¶ この道は駅に～じています This road *leads* to the station. この村から仙台までバスが～じている There is a bus service between this village and Sendai. 銀座かいわいでは地下鉄が四方に～じている In the Ginza district subway lines *run* in all directions. 来年4月までにはこの町まで鉄道が～じる By next April a railway is going to *be laid* to this town. / This town will be brought into railway communication by next April. / Railway service will *be available* as far as this town next April. この渡り廊下は各病棟(びょうとう)に～じている This roofed passage *leads* to each ward.

2 〖了解される〗 ¶ ロンドンでは私の英語は～じなかった In London I could not *make myself understood* in English. この赤ちゃんのことばは母親にしか～じない Nobody but its mother can *understand* what the baby says. ここのところの意味がよく～じない I can't *catch* the meaning of this passage. / This passage *is unintelligible.* 彼には冗談はいっさい～じない Every joke *is lost upon* him. / He can't *see* a joke. / He *has* no *sense of* humor. ふたりはなにも言わなくても気持ちは～じていた Although the two didn't say anything, they could *sympathize with* each other.

3 〖通暁する〗 ¶ 彼はヨーロッパの経済事情に～じている He *is well informed about* European economic affairs. 彼は東西の文学に～じている He *is well read in* Eastern and Western literature. 彼は4か国語に～じている He *has a good command of* four languages.

彼は英文学に～じている He *is at home* (≒ *is well versed*) *in* English literature.
4 〖電流・電話などが〗 ¶ この電線には電流が～じている This wire *is charged with* electricity. / This wire *is alive*.
彼の家へ電話をかけたが～じなかった I could not *get through to* him by phone. / I could not *get* him on the telephone.
5 〖通知する・取り次ぐ〗 ¶ 先方には前もって話を～じておきました I *informed* him *of* the matter beforehand.
彼は玄関で来意を～じた He *stated* the objects of his call at the front door. / He *mentioned* the objects of his visit at the front door.
6 〖内通する〗 ¶ 味方の中にだれか敵軍に～じている者がある There is someone in our troops who *is connected* (≒ *is in touch*) *with* the enemy.
あのふたりは気脈を～じている There exists a secret understanding between them.
7 〖範囲・期間にわたる〗 ¶ これは従業員全体に～じる問題だ This problem *is common to* all workers.

つうしん【通信】 correspondence ; communication. ¶ ワシントンからの～は暴動を報じた *A dispatch* from Washington told us about the revolt. 本国との間の～は絶えた *Communication* between our country and this place has been interrupted. パリの友人とときどき～を交わしている I *correspond with* a friend of mine in Paris once in a while. 台風のため～はすべて絶えた All *communication* has been suspended by the typhoon. 無電でその島と～することもできる We can *communicate with* the island by wireless.
—員 a correspondent. —機関 an organ of communication. —教育 the correspondence course of education. —社 a news agency. —販売 mail-order business. —簿 a report card. —網 news gathering facilities.

つうじん【通人】 a man of the world ; a man of fashion. ¶ 彼は着ることにかけては～だ He *has a good knowledge of* clothing. 彼はやたらに～ぶる He very often pretends to be *a man of the world* (≒ *a man about town*).

つうせい【通性】 ¶ それは綿製品の～だ That is *a common quality* of (≒ *a property common* to) all cotton goods. 勤勉なことはドイツ人の～だ Diligence is *a habit common* to the Germans.

つうせつ【通説】 a common view ; a popular opinion. ¶ ～によると日本は昔大陸と陸続きであった *It is commonly accepted* that the lands of Japan were adjacent to the Continent.

つうせつ【痛切】 ¶ ～な批評 *severe* (≒ *sharp*) criticism. 住宅不足は～な問題だ Housing shortage is a *serious* problem. 健康のありがたさをそのとき～に感じた At that time I *keenly* felt what a blessing it is to be healthy. / The blessing of health *was brought home to* me at that time.

つうそく【通則】 general (≒ common) rules.

つうぞく【通俗】 ¶ ～的な読みもの a *popular* book. ～的な考え方 a *common* way of thinking. その本は～的に書いてある The book is written in *popular* style.
—小説 a popular novel. —性 popularity.

つうたつ【通達】 notice ; (a) notification.
¶ まだそのような～は来ていない We have not received such *notification* yet. / We *have* not *been notified of* it yet.

つうたん【痛嘆】 deep lamentation ; bitter grief. ¶ 彼がそんなことをしたなんて～にたえない *It is deplorable* (≒ *lamentable*) that he should have done such a thing.

つうち【通知】 notice ; (a) notification ; information. ¶ 彼からはなんの～もない I have heard nothing from him. 先方に着いたら～してください Please *tell* me (≒ *Let* me *know*) when you have arrived at your destination. 私の出発を～した I *informed* him *of* my departure.
—状 a notice ; (転居などの) an announcement. —預金 a deposit at notice.

つうちょう【通帳】 a passbook.
貯金— a savings passbook. 預金— a bankbook.

つうちょう【通牒】 a notice ; a notification.
¶ ドイツはイギリスに最後～を発した Germany issued *an ultimatum* to England.

つうてん【痛点】 a pain-spot.

つうどく【通読】 ¶ 私はその本を1週間で～した I *read through* the book in a week. / I *read* the book *from cover to cover* in a week.

ツートンカラー ¶ ～の自動車 a *two-tone* (≒ *two-toned*) automobile.

つうねん【通念】 a common idea ; a generally accepted idea. ¶ 10年もたつと社会～も変わってくるだろう *A commonly accepted idea* will change in ten years.

つうば【痛罵】 condemnation. ¶ 彼は私のことを～した He *criticized* (≒ *condemned*) me *severely*. / He *railed at* (≒ *against*) me *furiously*.

ツーピース a two-piece suit.

つうふう【通風】 ventilation. ¶ この部屋は～がよい(悪い) This room *is* well (badly) *ventilated*. 窓を開けて部屋の～をよくする *ventilate* a room by opening the windows.
—管 an air pipe. —機 a ventilator. —筒 an airduct.

つうふう【痛風】 〘医学〙 gout. ¶ ～にかかっている I am a martyr to *gout*. / I am afflicted with *gout*.

つうぶん【通分】 〘数学〙 ¶ 1/3と1/2を～して加えなさい Add one-third to a half by *reducing* them *to a common denominator*.

つうへい【通弊】 a common evil. ¶ ねばり強さのないのは都会人の～だ Lack of tenacity is *a weakness common to* city-dwellers. / People living in town *are apt to* lack tenacity. 時代の～を改めるよう最善を尽くすべきだ

つ

We should do our best to reform *evils prevailing* (≒ *abuses common*) in our own time.

つうほう【通報】 a report ; a bulletin. ¶ なにか異常があればすぐ警察へ～したほうがいい On finding something wrong, you had better *report to* the police (≒ *inform* the police *of* it) at once.
気象── a weather report.

つうやく【通訳】(人) an interpreter ; (事) interpretation. ¶ 彼は～なしで講演した He delivered a speech without *an interpreter*. 私の～をやってくれませんか Will you please *interpret* (≒ *act as interpreter*) *for* me? 私はS氏の～でT氏と会談した I talked with Mr. T through the *interpreter*, Mr. S.
同時── simultaneous interpretation ; (人の場合) a simultaneous interpreter.

つうよう【通用】 currency ; common use. ¶ ドルはこの国でも～する Dollars *are used* in this country, too. 英語は世界各国で～する国際語だ English is an international language *spoken* all over the world. 日本語は日本でのみ～する Japanese *is spoken* only in Japan. 彼のおうへいさはこの家では～するはずがない His impudence cannot *be tolerated* in this house. この理論は今日でも～する This theory *holds good* even today. この切符はもう～しない This ticket *is* not *good* (≒ *available*) any more. そのことばは今でも～する The word *is* yet *in common use*.
──期間 the term for which a thing is usable. ──門 the side gate.

つうよう【痛痒】 ¶ 結果がどうなろうと私は～を感じない I *have no concern with* the result. / What will become of it *does not make any difference* to me.

つうらん【通覧】 survey ; glance. ¶ 報告の書類を～した I *looked over* the report. / I *ran over* (≒ *glanced over*) the report.

ツーリスト a tourist.
──ビューロー a tourist bureau ; a travel bureau.

つうれい【通例】 usually ; commonly. ¶ 月曜に会議を開くことが～になっている We *make it a rule* to hold a conference on Monday. / Our *rule* is (≒ It is our *custom*) to hold a meeting on Monday.

つうれつ【痛烈】 ¶ ～な非難 *severe* reproval. ～な反対 *strong* (≒ *fierce*) opposition. 彼の行動は～に批判された His conduct was *bitterly* (≒ *severely*) criticized. 彼女はよく～なことを言う She often makes a *cutting* remark. / She has a *biting* tongue.

つうろ【通路】 a passage ; (劇場などの) an aisle. ¶ ～側の席 an *aisle* seat. ～に立ち止まってはいけない Don't keep standing *in the way*. / Don't keep standing *in the path*. ここはわれわれ社員の～だ This is the *passage* available for us members alone. ～をあけてください Please clear *a passage* for me.

つうろん【通論】 an outline ; an introduction.
数学── an outline of mathematics. 文学── an introduction to literature.

つうわ【通話】 a 〔telephone〕 call. ¶ 列車の中からでも～ができる We can *talk over the telephone* even in the train. 1～3分間の料金は60円だ The telephone rate is sixty yen for *a* three minutes' *conversation*. 今～中だ They *are speaking through the telephone*. / They *are speaking by telephone*. / *The telephone is* now *busy* (≒ *engaged*).
──料 the charge for a telephone call.

つえ【杖】(籐などの) a cane ; a walking stick. ¶ ～をついて歩く walk with *a cane*. 家族は彼を～とも柱とも頼りにしている He is *the sole support* of his family. / His family *relies on* him *as the sole support*. 転ばぬ先の～ **(諺)** *Look before you leap*.

つか【塚】 a mound.
一里── a milestone. 貝── a shell mound.

つか【柄】 a hilt. ¶ 彼は～も通れと突き刺した He thrust his dagger *home*. / He plunged his dagger *hilt-deep*. 彼は刀の～に手をかけた He put his hand on the *hilt* of his sword.

つが【栂】〘植物〙 a hemlockspruce.

つかい【使い】 an errand ; (人) a messenger. ¶ ～に行ってくださいませんか Will you please *run errands* for me? 彼を～にやった I sent him *on an errand*. ～の者に返事を欲しい I would like your answer through the *bearer* 〔of this note〕. ～をやって私のことばを伝えたい I'd like to send *a messenger* to deliver my message. ～に手紙を持たしてもいい You may send a letter by *a messenger*. 自分で行かずに～をやってもいい Instead of going yourself, you may send *a messenger*.

つがい【番】 a pair. ¶ 文鳥の～ *a pair* (≒ *a brace*) of paddybirds.

つかいかた【使い方】 way of using. ¶ この機械の～を教えてください Please teach me *how to operate* this machine. ～が乱暴なためこの道具はだめになった This tool wore out under rough *usage*. 彼は部下の～が荒っぽい He *handles* his men hard.

つかいこな・す【使いこなす】 ¶ この機械を～せる人は少ない Few can *handle* (≒ *manage*) this machine. 彼は人を～すのがうまい He is good at *managing* people. 彼はどんな楽器でも～す He *knows how to* play on musical instruments of any sort.

つかいこみ【使い込み】 peculation ; embezzlement.

つかいこ・む【使い込む】 ¶ 彼は会社の金を500万円も～んだ He *appropriated* five million yen from his company *for his own use*. 彼は公金を20万円も～んだ He *embezzled* as much as two hundred thousand yen of public money. 鉄びんは～むほどにつやが出る The longer we *use* an ironkettle, the more lustrous it becomes.

つかいす・ぎる【使い過ぎる】 ¶ 彼は金を～ぎる He *spends too much* money. あの人は部下を～ぎる He *overworks* his men. / He *works* his men *too hard*.

つかいて【使い手】a user; one who uses. ¶この機械には～がひとり足りない We lack one *person to operate* this machine.

つかいで【使いで】durability. ¶500万円あれば～がある Five million yen will *last you a long time.* 1万円では今は～がない Ten thousand yen does not *go far* these days.

つかいなら・す【使い馴らす】¶その機械を～すべきだ You should *accustom yourself to using* the machine. 馬を～す *break in* a horse.

つかいな・れる【使い慣れる】¶この機械も～れた I *am accustomed to using* this machine. ～れたペンで書こう I'll write with my *old* pen (I'll write with a pen I *am accustomed to use*). (be accustomed to の次には動名詞・動詞の原形のいずれも使用可).

つかいのこ・す【使い残す】¶材料をいくらか～した I *left* some of the material *unused.* 帰りの旅費は～しておいた I *left unspent* the traveling expenses for my return journey.

つかいはた・す【使い果たす】¶彼は旅先で金を～した He *spent all* the money on his trip. 私は今月の小づかいを全部～してしまった I *used up* all my pocket money for this month. 彼は死ぬ前に財産を～していた He *had gone through* his fortune before he died. 私は力をすっかり～してしまった I *have consumed* (≒ *have exhausted*) all my energies. / I *have put out all* my strength.

つかいふる・す【使い古す】¶～した食器 a *worn-out* dinner set. ～したじゅうたん a *threadbare* carpet.

つかいみち【使い道】〔a〕use. ¶この箱は～が全然ない This box *is* not *useful* at all. この紙は～が広い This paper can *be used* extensively. この壊れたいすは～がない This broken chair *is good for nothing.*

つかいもの【使い物】¶この机はまったく～にならない This desk *is of no use.* この機械はけっこう～になる This machine can *be* very *useful.*

つかいわけ【使い分け】proper use. ¶彼はことばの～を心得ている He knows how to *use the right word in the right place.*

つかいわ・ける【使い分ける】¶道具を～ける *use* tools *properly.* 彼女は5か国語を～ける She *can speak* five different languages. / She *has a good command of* five languages.

つか・う【使う】**1**〖物・器具を〗¶彼はナイフとフォークをじょうずに～う He *uses* a knife and fork skillfully.
てこを～ってこの石を運ぼう Let's move this stone *with* a lever.
うちのテレビには真空管が1本も～ってない No vacuum tubes *are used* in our television. / Our TV set does not *use* any vacuum tubes.
この防火建築にはどんな材料が～われているのか What kind of materials *are used* in this fire-proof building?
この車はまだ二,三年は～えるでしょう This car should *last* (≒ *go*) another two or three years.
この会議では英語とフランス語が～われる In this conference English and French are to *be used.*
もっと頭を～って仕事をしなさい *Make* better *use of* your brains in the work.
2〖人を使う・雇用する〗¶私の店では店員を8人～っている I *am employing* eight people in the shop. / I *have* eight *employees* in the shop.
きみは人を～うのがへただ You are not good in *handling* (≒ *managing*) people.
彼は人を～うのが実にうまい He is very clever (≒ tactful) in *handling* (≒ *using*) his men.
3〖消費する〗¶彼女は化粧品に相当のお金を～う She *spends* a considerable amount on cosmetics.
時間をもっと有効に～って勉強の能率を上げなさい Increase efficiency in your work by *making* better *use of* your time.
彼女は読書に多くの時間を～う She *spends* much time in reading.
暖房に灯油を～いすぎる. 節約しなさい You *use* too much oil for heating. Practice economy.
4〖操る〗¶文楽は人形を～う芝居だ *Bunraku* is the theatrical performance in which puppets *are manipulated.*
あの奇術師はトランプを～った手品がうまい That magician is skillful at *doing* conjuring with cards.
5〖ふろ・食事など〗¶赤ん坊にお湯を～わせるところだ I am going to *bathe* my baby now.
ここで弁当を～わせてください Let me *take* my lunch here.

つが・う【番う】pair; (鳥が) mate; (獣が) copulate.

つか・える【仕える】¶親のあるうちに親に～えるようにつとめなさい Try to *be filial* to your parents while they are alive. 彼女はその家に10年間～えた She *served* the family for ten years. 娘は病気の母親に～えた The daughter *attended on* her sick mother.

つか・える【使える】¶彼はなんにでも～える男だ He is a quite *useful* (≒ *serviceable*) man every way. この機械はだれでも～える This machine *can be handled* by anybody. これはなんにでも～える表現だ This is an *all-purpose* expression.

つか・える【支える】¶車が～えている Traffic *is held up.* 前に数台の車が～えている Several cars *are held up* in front. 骨がのどに～えた I *choked on* a bone. ～えながら彼は謝罪した He made an apology, *stammering.* ことばが～えてよく言えない My words *stick in the throat.* ～え～えしゃべった He spoke *haltingly.* キセルが～えている The pipe *is stopped* (≒ *is choked*) *up.* 仕事が～えている I *am very, very busy.* / I *am busy over* a lot of work.

つか・える【痞える】¶胸が～える I *feel heavy* in the stomach. / I *feel a pressure on* my chest.

つ

つが･える【番える】¶ 彼は弓に矢を～えた He *fitted* an arrow *to* the bow.

つかさど･る【司どる･掌る】¶ 彼が議事進行を～った He *took charge of* the proceedings. / He *was chairman of* the meeting. 首相が国務を～る The prime minister *administers* the affairs of the country.

つか･す【尽かす】¶ 家族のものは彼にあいそを～した All his family *were disgusted with* him. / He *was given up* by all his family.

つかずはなれず【つかず離れず】¶ 彼は上役とは～やっている He *keeps a relation neither too close nor too remote with* his superiors. 彼はわれわれに～の態度をとった He took a *non-committal* attitude toward us.

つかつかと ¶ 彼女は私に～歩み寄った She walked *directly* up to me. 彼女は～部屋に入った She entered the room *unannounced.* / She walked *straight* into the room. 名前を呼ばれると彼は～進み出た As soon as he was called by name, he *strode forward.*

つかぬこと【付かぬ事】¶ ～をお尋ねしますが, お国はどちらですか *Excuse my abrupt* (≒ *awkward*) *question,* but where do you come from?

つか･ねる【束ねる】¶ そのときは手を～ねて見ているよりしかたなかった I could not help looking on *with folded arms* at that time. / I could not help *being a* mere *looker-on* at that time.

つかのま【束の間】¶ ～の人生 a *brief* life. 彼女のことは～も忘れない I do not forget her even *for a moment* (≒ *for a minute*). ほっと一息つけたのも～, また忙しくなった I managed to take a rest, but it lasted *only a short while,* again I was busy. 一筋の希望の光も～に消え去った A ray of hope went out *in a moment* (≒ *in a minute*).

つかま･える【捕まえる･摑まえる】¶ 手すりをしっかりと～えた I *took* (≒ *caught*) tight *hold of* the handrail. 犯人を～えた We *arrested* the culprit. 相手の胸ぐらを～えた I *seized* (≒ *grasped*) him by the breast of his coat.

つかま･せる【摑ませる】**1**〖つかまえさせる〗¶ 自分の腕を～せた I *let* him *grasp* me by arms.
2〖金を〗¶ 彼に金を～せて言うことを聞かせた I *bribed* him *into doing* as he was told.
3〖にせ物を〗¶ 彼は物を知らぬ人に偽物を～せた He *passed off* an imitation *upon* an ignorant person. / He *palmed off* a fake *on* an ignorant person.

つかま･る【捕まる･摑まる】¶ ネズミが～った A rat *was caught.* スピード違反で～った I *was arrested* for violation of the speed limit. 柱にしっかり～りなさい *Hold on* tight *to* the pillar. つり革に～らないと倒れる Unless you *hold on to* a strap you will fall. 彼に2時間以上も～ってしまった I *was detained* by him for more than two hours.

つかみ【摑み】a grip; a hold. ¶ ひと～の砂 *a handful* of sand. 彼はそれをひと～にした He made one *grip* (≒ *grasp*) of it.

つかみあい【摑み合い】¶ 彼らは～のけんかをした They *grappled with each other.* 彼らは口論の末～になった Their quarrel ended in *scuffling.* / They proceeded from words to *grips* (≒ *grapples*).

つかみあ･う【摑み合う】¶ 互いに髪を～った They *dragged each other* by the hair.

つかみかか･る【摑みかかる】¶ 彼はいきなり私に～った He suddenly *grasped at* me.

つかみだ･す【摑み出す】¶ 無礼な者は～す I'll *turn* (≒ *throw*) a rude fellow *out* 〔*of doors*〕.

つかみどころ【摑み所】¶ ～のない話 an *evasive* (≒ *vague; pointless*) story. 彼は～のない人間だ He is a *sly* (≒ *tricky*) man. / He *is as slippery as an eel.* 彼の話は全然～がない One cannot get hold of *the point* of his story. なんという～のない話だろう What a *pointless* story! ～のない答え an *evasive* answer.

つか･む【摑む】grasp. ¶ ロープの端を～んだ I *grasped* the end of the rope. だれかが私の右腕を～んだ Someone *caught* me by the right arm. 両肩を急に～まれた Someone suddenly *caught* me by the shoulders. 彼はボールを～むと捕手めがけて投げた He *caught* the ball and threw it to the catcher. 新しい手掛かりが～めない No new clue can *be found.* ようやく真相を～んだ Finally we *arrived at* the truth. 要点を～むように努めなさい Do your best to *grasp* the point. おぼれる者はわらをも～む (諺) *A drowning man will catch at a straw.*

つか･る【浸かる】¶ 町じゅうが水に～った The whole street *was flooded* (≒ *was under water*). 大水でわが家は床上まで水に～った My house *was flooded* floordeep. / The flood came up above the floor of my house. 温泉に～る *take a bath* in a hot spring.

つか･る【漬かる】¶ つけ物が～った Pickles *are well-seasoned.*

つかれ【疲れ】fatigue; exhaustion. ¶ 長い旅行の～もだんだん抜けてきている I am gradually recovering from the *fatigue* of a long trip. ベンチに座って～を休めた I *rested myself* (≒ *had a rest*) on a bench. 眠って長時間のドライブの～をおとりください Please sleep off the *fatigue* of driving for many hours. まだ～が抜けない I can't get over my *fatigue* yet.

つかれき･る【疲れ切る】¶ 彼はもうまったく～っている He *is* quite *worn out.* / He *is exhausted.* ～ってもう一足も歩けなかった *Tired out,* I could not take another step. / I *was* too *tired* to walk any further. 彼は激務のために身も心も～っていた He *was* mentally and physically *exhausted with* hard work.

つかれは･てる【疲れ果てる】⇒つかれきる

つか･れる【疲れる】¶ 私は5分歩いても～れる I *get tired* even if I walk five minutes. 私は走るとすぐ～れる Running soon *makes* me *tired.* 長旅で彼は～れている I *am tired from* the long travel. この仕事はばかに～れる This work *is* very *tiring*. 畑仕事でくたくたに～れた Farm work *has worn* me *out*. 講演旅行は～れる Lecturing trips *are exhausting*. 電車の中で読書すると目が～れる Reading on the train *taxes* our eyes. あまり～れて話もできなかった I *was* too *tired* to speak.

つか·れる【憑かれる】 ¶ 彼はなにかに～れたようにしゃべりまくった He talked and talked as if *possessed*. / He talked away *like mad*.

つかわ·す【遣わす】 ¶ 外国へ特使を～す *dispatch* an envoy *to* another country.

つき luck; fortune. ¶ 彼は～に見はなされた He *is out of luck*. / His *luck* is out.

つき【月】1 〖天体の〗 the moon. ¶ ～がのぼっている *The moon* is rising.
やがて～が出るだろう *The moon* will appear soon.
～が満ちている *The moon* is full.
～が欠けた *The moon* is no longer full.
～の裏側 the other side of *the moon*.
～のない晩 a *moonless* night.
～とすっぽんの違いがある The two are as different as *chalk from cheese*.
2 〖暦の〗 a month. ¶ 彼は～に 1 回は旅行する He makes a trip at least once *a month*.
～に 2 万円は消費する I spend twenty thousand yen *a month*.
～が変わったらご返事します I will answer you next *month*.

つき【付き】 ¶ この家はガス～だ This house *is supplied with* gas. この紙はインクの～がいい This paper *takes* ink well. この材木は火の～が悪い This wood does not *catch* fire well. この雑誌は付録～だ There is an appendix *attached to* this magazine.

つき【突き】 a stab; a thrust. ¶ 彼は背後から短刀でひと～された He was given *a thrust* with a dagger from behind.

つき【尽き】 the end. ¶ ここで見つかったのが彼の運の～だ *His fate was sealed* at last when he was found out there.

-つき【-就き】1 〖ために〗 ¶ 雨天に～旅行はとりやめます We give up our trip *on account of* the rain.
病気に～きょうは欠席いたします Please allow me to absent myself today *because of* sickness.
入試に～授業は行なわれません There will be no class *because of* the entrance examination.
2 〖ごとに〗 ¶ 1 週に～ *per* week.
1 ドルに～ 3 個 three *for* a dollar.

つぎ【次】1 〖そのあと〗 next. ¶ ～の月曜日は休日です *Next* Monday is a holiday.
～の駅が名古屋です The *next* station is Nagoya.
彼の～の会長はだれでしたか What president came *after* him? / Who *succeeded* him as a president?
～はいつ来たらいいですか When shall I come *next*?
～はいったい何が起こるだろうか What on earth will happen *next*?
私の～に彼が話した He spoke *after* me.
きのうは～から～へと私のところに人が訪ねてきた Yesterday I *had a constant stream of* callers.
～から～へと物がなくなっている Various things have been lost *one after another*.
2 〖…に次いで〗 ¶ グループの中で私の～に背の高いのは彼だ *Next to* me he is the tallest in the group.
数学の～に私の好きな科目は物理だ The subject I like best *next to* mathematics is physics.
3 〖以下の〗 ¶ ～の注意をごらんなさい Look at the *following* notice.
～の文の誤りを正しなさい Correct the *following* sentences.

つぎ【継ぎ】 a patch.. ¶ ～の当たったシャツ a *patched* undershirt. ズボンの破れに～を当てた I put *a patch* on the hole of my trousers.

つきあい【付き合い】 association. ¶ あの人は～が多い He has *a* large *acquaintance*. 彼女は～が狭い She has few *acquaintances*. 彼はだれにも～がいい He *is friendly* to everyone. 彼は多くの作家と～がある He *associates with* a lot of writers. あの人との～はやめた I *broke with* him. お～で会に出席した I was present at the meeting *for companionship*.

つきあ·う【付き合う】 ¶ よい友人と～いなさい *Keep* good *company*. 夕食を～っていただけませんか Won't you have dinner with me? そういう人とは～わない I avoid *keeping company* with such people. 私の～っている仲間にそういう人はいない You won't find such people *in the company I keep* (≒ *among my associates*).

つきあかり【月明かり】 moonlight; moonshine. ¶ ～で手紙を読む read a letter in the *moonlight*; read a letter by *moonlight*. ～で外は明るい It is bright outside in *the moonlight*.

つきあ·げる【突き上げる】 ¶ 市民に～げられて当局はその方針を変更せざるをえなかった The authorities had to change the policy *at the loud demand of* (≒ *under pressure from*) the citizens.

つきあたり【突き当たり】 (路地などの) the end. ¶ ～に交番がある There is a police box *at the end* of the lane. 彼の家はこの道の～から 2 軒めだ He lives in the second but one house *at the bottom* of this lane. 廊下の～にドアがある There is a door *at the end* of the passage. この先は～になっている This is no through passage.

つきあた·る【突き当たる】 ¶ バスはへいに～った The bus *ran into* a wall. この先を～って左へ曲がってください(そこまで行く) Please turn to the left *at the bottom of* the road.

つきあ·てる【突き当てる】 ¶ うっかり運転を誤って車を電柱に～てた Driving absent-mindedly, I *ran* my car *into* an electric light pole.

つきあわ·せる【突き合わせる】 ¶ 原文と～せた I *checked* it up *with* the original. 月末には帳簿を～せる The books *are looked over* at the end of the month. わが社の製品を他社の製品と～せた We *compared* our products *with* those of other companies. あんな男と顔を～せているのはいやだ I don't like *being* 〔*face to face*〕 *with* such a man. / I don't like working *in the company of* such a man. ひざを～せてじっくり相談しよう Let's *sit knee to knee* and talk over the matter.

つぎあわ·せる【継ぎ合わせる】¶ ふたつの部分品を～せる *join* two pieces *together*.

つきおくれ【月後れ·月遅れ】¶ ～の雑誌 *a back number* of a magazine.

つきおと·す【突き落とす】¶ 彼らは彼を汽車から～した They *pushed* him *off* the train. 彼は彼女を断崖(だんがい)から～した He *thrusted* her *over* the cliff.

つきかえ·す【突き返す】¶ 抗議文を断固として～した I *rejected* positively the note of protest.

つきかげ【月影】(月光) moonlight. ¶ ～がさわやかだ The *moonlight* is bright.

つきがけ【月掛け】monthly installments. ━貯金 monthly installment deposit. ━保険 monthly installment insurance.

つぎき【接ぎ木·継ぎ木】grafting; (接いだ木) a grafted tree. ¶ 西洋スモモにナシを～した I *grafted* the pear *on* the plum.

つききず【突き傷】a stab.

つきぎめ【月決め】¶ ～の読者 a *monthly* subscriber. その楽団に～で契約した I made a contract with the band *by the month*.

つききり【付ききり】¶ 医者は彼に～だ The doctor *is in constant attendance upon* him. 彼女は彼のまくらもとに～だ She *is at his bedside all the time*.

つぎきれ【継ぎ切れ】a patch.

つきくず·す【突き崩す】¶ 敵陣の一角を～した We succeeded in *breaking* through the enemy line.

つきごと【月毎】¶ ～に every month; monthly.

つぎこ·む【注ぎ込む】¶ 水を手おけに～んだ I *poured* the water *into* the pail. 彼は全力を仕事に～んだ He *did his best in* his work. 金は全部土地に～んだ I *invested* all my money *in* land. 彼は有り金すべてをその株に～んだ He *put* all his money *into* the stock.

つきころ·す【突き殺す】¶ ナイフで～す *stab* (*a person*) *to death* with a knife.

つきころば·す【突きころばす】¶ 彼を～した I *knocked* him *down*.

つぎざお【継ぎ竿】a jointed fishing rod.

つきさ·す【突き刺す】¶ 膚を～すような冷たい風 a *biting* (≒ *cutting*) cold wind. 針が指に～さった A needle *stuck into* my finger. くぎが車のタイヤに～さった A nail *pierced* the tire of my car. 彼はその紳士を短刀で～した He *stabbed* the gentleman *with* a dagger.

つきずえ【月末】(*at*; *toward*) the end of the month.

つきすす·む【突き進む】go ahead; head. ¶ ボールを持ってゴールにまっしぐらに～んだ I *made a wild rush* to the goal with the ball. 南へ～んだ They *headed* south.

つきせぬ【尽きせぬ】infinite; boundless; endless. ¶ ～嘆き *infinite* sorrow. ～感謝 *boundless* gratitude. くめど～泉 a spring *never running dry*.

つきそい【付き添い】attendance; (人) an attendant. ¶ 病人に～をつける get *a helper* who will take care of a patient. ～の看護婦 a nurse *in attendance*.

つきそ·う【付き添う】¶ あす子どもの遠足に～っていかなければならない Tomorrow I must *accompany* my child on a school excursion. 彼は弁護士に～われて出廷した He appeared in court, *accompanied* by his lawyer. あの病院では病人の家族が～うことになっている A patient must *be cared for* by a member of his family in that hospital. 彼女には看護婦がふたり～っていた She had two nurses *attending on* her.

つきたお·す【突き倒す】knock down (*a person*).

つきだ·す【突き出す】¶ 窓から顔を～さないようにしなさい Never *stick* your head out of the window. 犯人は警察に～された The criminal *was handed over* to the police.

つぎた·す【継ぎ足す】¶ ここの廊下を～してもらった We *had* the hallway *enlarged*. (この文を *have* a hallway *added* とすると, 今まで廊下のなかった所に廊下をつくることになるから注意).

つきた·てる【突き立てる】¶ 岩壁の割れ目にピッケルを～てた I *drove* the pickel *straight* into the crack in the rock. ピンを指に～てた I *pricked* my finger with a needle.

つきたらず【月足らず】¶ ～の赤ん坊 a *premature* baby. この子は～で生まれた The baby was born *prematurely*.

つきづき【月月】every month. ¶ ～利子を支払う pay interest *every month*. ～の会費 *monthly* membership fee.

つぎつぎに【次次に】one after another. ¶ 家の人々は～風邪をひいた The family caught a cold, *one after another*. 客が～到着しはじめた Guests began to arrive *in a steady stream*. ～事故が起こった Accidents happened *in succession*.

つきつ·ける【突きつける】¶ 検事は被告に証拠を～けた The prosecutor *thrusted* (≒ *poked*) the evidence *at* the accused. 組合は会社に厳しすぎる要求を～けた The labor union *forced* an impossible demand *on* the management. 彼は私に短銃を～けた He *leveled* a gun *at* me.

つきつ·める【突きつめる】¶ 事故の原因を～める *probe into* the cause of an accident. そのことをそんなに～めて考えないほうがいい You shouldn't *brood over* it so much. 問題をとことんまで～めてみよう Let's *dig down into* the core of the problem.

つき·でる【突き出る】¶ がけが海中に～出ている A cliff *is jutting out* into the sea. 彼の肩甲骨は～出ている His shoulder-bone *sticks out*.

つきとお·す【突き通す】¶ 彼はやりを相手の胸にぐ

さりと〜した He *thrust* his lance *through* the opponent's chest.

つきとお·る【突き通る】¶ 弾丸が厚い壁の裏まで〜った A bullet *pierced through* the thick wall.

つきとば·す【突き飛ばす】¶ 彼を部屋の向こうに〜してやった I *knocked* him *across* the room. けんかして相手を〜した In a fist fight I *sent* the man *flying*.

つきと·める【突き止める】¶ 彼の動機を〜めた I *found out* what his motives were. 彼の居所を〜めた I *located* him. / I *found out* where he was. 失敗の原因を〜めた I *traced* (≒ *ascertaind* ; *pinpointed*) the cause of the failure.

つきなかば【月半ば】¶ 〜にして金がなくなった We ran out of money *in the middle of the month*.

つきなみ【月並】commonplace. ¶ この絵は〜だ This is just an *ordinary* (≒ *mediocre*) painting. 彼は〜なお世辞を言った He paid just a *routine* compliment.

つきぬ·ける【突き抜ける】¶ 弾丸は車の屋根を〜けた A bullet *went* (≒ *pierced*) *through* the top of the car.

つきの·ける【突き除ける】¶ 彼は人を〜けて前に出た He *shoved* (≒ *thrusted*) people *aside* to come forward.

つぎのま【次の間】the next (≒ adjoining) room ; (控え室) an antechamber.

つきのわ【月の輪】a halo around the moon ; (クマの) a white collar.

つぎはぎ【継ぎはぎ】patching. ¶ 〜だらけのズボン a *much patched* pair of pants ; pants *with patches all over*.

つきはじめ【月始め】the beginning of the month. ¶ 〜に計画を立てる make plans *at the beginning of the month*.

つきは·てる【尽き果てる】¶ 彼には愛想も〜てた I *am utterly disgusted with* him. 精も根も〜てた I *haven't an ounce of* energy left.

つきはな·す【突き放す】¶ 彼は親から〜された He *was rejected by* his parents. そんな〜した言い方はよしてくれ Don't talk as if you *couldn't care any more about* it.

つきばらい【月払い】monthly installments. ¶ 〜でテレビを買った I am paying for a television set *by monthly installments*.

つきひ【月日】(時) time ; days and months ; lapse of time. ¶ 〜のたつのは早いものだ How fast *time* flies! 〜がたつにつれて彼の悲しみも薄らぐだろう As *time* goes on, his grief will gradually lessen.

つきびと【付き人】(俳優の) a dresser ; (お付きの人) an attendant.

つきべつ【月別】¶ 売上高を〜に示してある We have our sales figures listed *each month*. 〜に使用料を払う pay a rent *by the month*.

つぎほ【接ぎ穂·継ぎ穂】¶ 話の〜がなくて困った I felt awkward, unable to *keep up the conversation*. 話の〜がなくなってしまった We *ran out of things to talk about*.

つきまと·う【付き纏う】¶ ごろつきに〜われて困った I was annoyed by a hoodlum who *persistently followed* me *around*. 子どもが母親に〜って離れない The child *tags along after* her mother wherever she goes.

つきみ【月見】¶ 〜の宴 a *moon viewing* party. 〜をしよう Let's *enjoy the moon*. / Let's *look at the moon*.

—草〘植物〙an evening primrose.

つぎめ【継ぎ目】a joint ; a connection. ¶ 管の〜から水がもる Water leaks from *where the two pipes are joined* (≒ *are connected*). 鉄管の〜が緩んできた The *joints* of the iron pipes have become loose. 〜なしの板 *a single piece* of wood.

つきもの【付き物】¶ 政治にスキャンダルは〜のようだ Scandal and politics seem to *go together*. / Scandal seems to *be mixed with* politics. 登山に危険は〜だ Danger *is a part of* mountain climbing. 詩人に貧乏は〜だ A poet's life *is accompanied with* poverty. 金もうけに冒険は〜だ We can*not* make money *without* risks.

つきもの【憑き物】¶ 彼は〜が落ちたような顔をしている He looks like a new man, freed from *the grip of the devil*.

つきやぶ·る【突き破る】¶ 車はへいを〜って止まった A car *crashed through* the fence and came to a stop.

つきやま【築山】a small hill (≒ mound).

つきゆび【突き指】¶ バレーボールをやって〜をした While playing volleyball, I *sprained one of my fingers*.

つきよ【月夜】a moonlit night. ¶ なんてきれいな〜だ What *a* charming *moonlight* (≒ *moonlit*) *night*! 今夜は〜だ *The moon is out* tonight.

つ·きる【尽きる】¶ あの絵は美しいという一言に〜きる That painting is *simply* beautiful. 彼には愛想が〜きた *I haven't any more* patience with him. 万策〜きた Every means *is exhausted*. いつまでたっても名残は〜きない It is getting more and more difficult to say goodbye. ふたりの話は〜きそうにない There seems to *be no end to* their talk. ついに彼の力は〜きた At last his strength *gave out*.

つきロケット【月ロケット】a moon rocket. ¶ アメリカは1969年に〜を打ち上げた America launched *a moon rocket* in 1969.

つきわり【月割り】¶ 私はこのテレビを〜で買った I bought this television set *on a monthly installment plan* (≒ *on monthly hire purchase system*).

つ·く【着く·付く·就く·点く】**1**〖到着する〗¶ 船は無事港に〜いた The ship *reached* (≒ *arrived in*) the port safely.

駅に〜いたときは列車が出たあとだった The train had already started when I *reached* the station.

ひかり３号は定刻に〜きますか Will the Hikari No. 3 *arrive* on schedule?

彼はきょうのＰＡＡ機で羽田に〜く予定だ He *is*

due at Haneda by PAA plane today.
私たちは暗くなってから家に～いた We *got* home after dark.
2 〖達する・届く〗 ¶ 彼は頭が天井に～くほど背が高い He is so tall that his head *touches* (≒ *reaches*) the ceiling.
洪水で水がとうとう床に～いた The flood water finally *reached* the floor.
3 〖身を置く〗 ¶ 私が部屋に入ったときには，みな席に～いていた When I entered the room, everybody *was seated*.
4 〖付着する〗 ¶ 彼の手には血がべっとりと～いていた His hands *were covered with* blood.
彼の上着の肩にはいつもふけが～いている The shoulders of his jacket *are* always *covered with* dandruff.
そのモモには虫が～いているから，食べてはいけない Don't eat that peach, as it *is worm-eaten*.
冷蔵庫に入れておいたらパンに変なにおいが～いた Some strange smell *has adhered to* the bread, which had been kept in the refrigerator.
5 〖付属する〗 ¶ この机には引き出しが左右に～いている This desk *has* drawers on the right and left side.
彼はガレージの～いた家を探している He is looking for a house *with* a garage.
この雑誌にはたくさん付録が～いている A lot of appendixes *are added to* this magazine.
その話にはまだもうひとつおまけが～いている The story *has* a supplementary episode.
6 〖身のまわりの世話をする・そばにいる〗 ¶ 彼には秘書がふたり～いている He *has* two secretaries.
しばらく病人に～いていてください *Tend* the patient for a while, will you?
なにが起こるかわからないからぼくのそばに～いていてくれないか *Stay with* me, as I don't know what will happen.
7 〖生じる・加わる〗 ¶ 彼は最近肉が～いてたくましくなった Recently he *has put on* weight and become stronger.
この社債には6分の利子が～く This bond *bears* 6 percent interest.
ことしは柿の木にひとつも実が～かない This year the persimmon tree *is fruitless*.
移植したトマトの苗はようやく根が～いた The tomato seedlings which I transplanted *have taken root* at last.
きみはだいぶ英語の力が～いた You *have become* very *proficient in* English.
最近夜更かしの悪い癖が～いた Recently I *have formed* a bad habit of sitting up late.
コーヒーを1杯飲んだらやっと人心地が～いた I *felt* quite *myself* after drinking a cup of coffee. / The cup of coffee greatly *refreshed* me.
柿の実に赤みが～いてきた Persimmons *have become* red.
ゆうべは犬の声が耳に～いて寝つかれなかった I couldn't get to sleep for a long while last night, as the dog was barking noisily.
8 〖残る〗 ¶ どろぼうの大きな足跡が庭にはっきり～いていた There were big and distinct footmarks *left* by the robber in the garden.
彼は顔にけがをして傷あとが～いた Wounded (≒ Injured) in the face, he *had* a scar.
9 〖味方になる〗 ¶ 子どもたちは母親に～いて，私の意見に反対する The children are against my opinion, *taking sides with* their mother.
けんかになると，彼はいつも強そうなほうに～く When a quarrel takes place, he never fails to *take part on* the stronger side.
10 〖あとを追って離れない〗 ¶ 案内しますから～いてきてください I'll show you the way. *Follow* me, please.
彼はどんなに努力しても級友たちの学力に～いていけない No matter how hard he tries, he cannot *keep up with* his classmates in the studies.
11 〖完成する〗 ¶ 電話がやっとうちにも～いた We *had* a telephone *installed* at last.
12 〖価が〗 ¶ この菓子は1個100円に～く This cake *costs* one hundred yen a piece.
たくさんお買いになれば安く～きます If you buy many of them, they *become cheaper*.
その肖像に300万円という値が～いた The portrait *was priced at* three million yen. / They *set* the value of the portrait *at* three million yen.
この家は高い値が～いている This house *is high* in price. / This house *is dear* (≒ *is expensive*).
安物買いは結局高く～く Bargain hunters are after all money losers. / (諺) *Penny-wise and pound-foolish*.
彼の怠慢は高いものに～いた He *paid dear* for his negligence. / His negligence *proved to be expensive*.
13 〖巣・餌(え)に〗 ¶ 鳥は夕方になると巣に～く Birds *fly home to roost* toward evening.
14 〖師事する〗 ¶ 彼女は彼に～いてバイオリンを習った She *took* violin *lessons from* him.
私は山田教授に～いて経済学史を研究している I am studying economic history *with* (≒ *under*) Professor Yamada.
15 〖職業に従事する・地位を占める〗 ¶ 彼は教職に～いている He *is engaged in* teaching. / He is a teacher. / He teaches [at a] school.
彼は今度会社の枢要な地位に～くことになった He is going to *occupy* an important position in the company.
彼は将棋で日本一の座に～いた He has become the champion player of the Japanese chess in Japan.
16 〖赴く〗 ¶ 夕方3人そろって家路に～いた We three *turned homeward* together toward evening.
彼らは南極探検の壮途に～いた They *went on* an Antarctic expedition.
17 〖点燈・点火される〗 ¶ この電燈はぐあいが悪くてなかなか～かない There is something wrong with this electric light. It fails to *come on*.
彼の部屋は一晩じゅう明かりが～いていた The light of his room *was on* throughout the night.
マッチが湿っていてなかなか火が～かない The match-

es won't *strike* as they are damp.

日本の家は木と紙だから火が～きやすい Japanese houses are easy to *catch* fire, because they are made of wood and paper.

18 〖慣用表現〗 ¶ 彼の自慢話は鼻に～く I *am sick* (≒ *am tired*) *of* his boasting. / His boasting has begun to *irritate* me.

あの娘に虫が～いてはいないだろうな She doesn't keep bad company, does she? / I hope she does not have a lover.

それが心配で彼女は仕事が手に～かなかった She couldn't *settle to work* because she was very anxious about it.

思わぬところから足が～いて犯人がつかまった An unexpected matter *supplied a clue* and the criminal was arrested.

つ・く 【突く・衝く・撞く】 **1** 〖突き刺す〗 ¶ 彼は敵の剣にのどを～かれて倒れた He *was stabbed* by the enemy in the throat and collapsed.

彼女は過って針で指先を～いた She *pricked* (≒ *prickled*) her finger with a needle by mistake.

2 〖押す〗 ¶ 満員電車の中でひじで胸を～かれた Someone *elbowed* me *on* the chest in the crowded car.

3 〖攻める〗 ¶ 相手はわれわれのチームの弱点を巧みに～いてきた They *took* full *advantage of* the weak point of our team.

彼に痛いところを～かれて困った I was embarrassed, as he *touched* me *on a sore spot.*

彼は虚を～かれてろうばいした He *was caught off* his *guard* and upset.

彼の質問は問題の核心を～いていない His question doesn't *get at the heart* (≒ *touch the core*) of the problem.

部屋に入ると異臭が鼻を～いた When I entered the room, an offensive smell *assailed my nostrils.* / When I entered the room, I *noticed an offensive odor.*

4 〖鐘・球などを〗 ¶ 5 時きっかりに鐘楼の鐘を～く We *strike* the bell of the belfry at five sharp.

四つ玉を～かせては彼の右に出る者はいない He is second to none in billiards.

5 〖冒す・ものともしない〗 ¶ ラグビーの試合は折からの風雨を～いて行なわれた The rugby game was played *in spite of* the wind and rain.

探検隊はあらしを～いて進んだ The expeditionary party advanced *through* the storm.

6 〖きれる〗 ¶ 干魃(かんばつ)のため都民の飲料水が底を～いた On account of a long spell of dry weather there is a serious shortage in the supply of drinking water for the Metropolitan citizens. / Tokyo is faced with a serious water shortage due to a draught.

長年の失業生活で彼の蓄えも底を～いてしまった On account of many years of unemployment his savings *touched bottom.*

つ・く 【吐く】 **1** 〖息をする〗 ¶ 一息～いてから次の仕事にかかろう Let us *have a short break* before we set about our next job (≒ task).

午前中は忙しくて息～く暇もなかった We were so busy in the morning that *we could not take a moment's rest* (≒ *there was no breathing spell*).

息も～かずにこの小説を読んでしまった I read the novel *at one go* (≒ *at a sitting*).

その知らせを聞いて彼女はほっとため息を～いた She *heaved a sigh* of relief at the news.

2 〖言う〗 ¶ 彼女はよくうそを～くので信用できない She *lies* so often (≒ She *is* such *a* congenital *liar*) that she cannot be trusted.

つ・く 【憑く】 ¶ 彼は悪霊にとり～かれている He *is possessed* (≒ *is haunted*) by an evil spirit.

私はきょうは～いている I *am lucky* today.

つ・く 【搗く・舂く】 ¶ もちを～く *pound* boiled rice; *make* rice-cake.

つ・ぐ 【次ぐ】 rank (≒ be) next (*to*). ¶ 大阪は東京に～ぐ大都会だ Osaka *is* the greatest city *next to* (≒ *only second to*) Tokyo.

これに～いでもうひとつの事件が起こった Another event *followed* this. 彼は会社で社長に～ぐ地位にいる He *is next in line to* the president of the firm.

つ・ぐ 【継ぐ】 inherit; succeed. ¶ 彼は父の財産を～いだ He *inherited* (≒ *succeeded to*) his father's property. 彼は父の志を～ぐことに決めた He has decided to continue working as his father wished. 彼らは夜を日に～いで働いている They are working *night and day.*

つ・ぐ 【接ぐ】 ¶ 台木に若木を～ぐ *graft* a shoot *on* a stock. 骨を～ぐ *set* a broken bone. それは木に竹を～いだような話だ That is an *inconsistent* (≒ *incongruous*) story.

つ・ぐ 【注ぐ】 pour. ¶ 彼は酒をグラスに～いだ He *filled* the glass *with sake.* 少し冷たい水を～いでください (鉄びんなどに) Please *pour in* some fresh water. 彼はお茶を～いでくれた (ついで出してくれた) He *poured out* a cup of tea.

つくえ 【机】 a desk. ¶ いつ行ってみても彼は～に向かっている I never call on him without finding him sitting at his *desk* (≒ *writing table*). / He is always at his *desk* (≒ *writing table*) every time I visit him.

つくし 【土筆】 〖植物〗 a horsetail.

つく・す 【尽くす】 ¶ 学校のためにできるかぎりのことを～した I *did all* I *could* for the school. 彼女は私にたいへん～してくれます She *does a great deal* for me. 彼は国のために～した He *served* his country. 全力を～してがんばりなさい Stick to it *with all your might.* 彼を見つけるためあらゆる手段を～した We *tried* every means to find him out.

つくだに 【佃煮】 food boiled in soy. ¶ 貝の～ shellfish *boiled down in soy.*

つくづく 【熟】 entirely; quite; keenly. ¶ 人生が～いやになった I am *quite* weary of life. われわれはときどき自分の欠点を～感じる We sometimes feel our shortcomings *keenly* (≒ *severely*). 私は～仕事がいやになった I have become *utterly* (≒ *completely*) disgusted with the work. 私は彼の親切を～感謝した I thanked for his kindness *heartily.* / I *greatly* appreciated his kindness. 彼の絵を～ながめた I watched his picture *earnestly* (≒ *keenly*; *attentively*).

つぐない【償い】 compensation; reparation. ¶ 彼は私のナイフをなくした～に新しいのをくれた He gave me a new knife as *compensation* (≒ *reparation*) for the one of mine he lost.

つぐな·う【償う】 ¶ 彼は死をもって過ちを～おうとした He tried to *atone* with life *for* the wrong he had done. 彼は私の損失を～ってくれると約束した He promised to *indemnify* me *for* my losses.

つくねんと ¶ 彼女は～廊下に座っていた She was sitting alone in the corridor *absent-mindedly* (≒ *absently*; *vacantly*).

つくばい【蹲】 a wash basin in the garden.

つぐみ【鶫】〘鳥類〙a thrush; a dusky ouzel.

つぐ·む【噤む】 ¶ 彼は口を～んでひと言も話さなかった He *remained silent*. / He *held his tongue*. / He *held his peace*. / He *shut his mouth*. 彼は口を～んだ He *pursed* 〔*up*〕 his lips.

つくり【作り·造り】 **1**〘構造〙structure; make. ¶ 彼はれんがの～の家に住んでいる He lives in a house *built of* brick.
この家具は材料はいいが～が悪い This furniture is good in material, but bad in *make*.
2〘体格〙build; stature. ¶ 彼女は小～の女だ She is a woman *of* small *stature*. / She is *of* slight *build*.
3〘化粧〙toilet; make-up. ¶ あの女は～が若すぎる She *dresses herself up* too young.

つくりあ·げる【作りあげる】 ¶ 彼は話を～げるのがうまい He *makes up* a fine story. / He is *a fine story-teller*. / (悪い意味) He skillfully *fabricates* a false story.

つくりか·える【作り替える】 ¶ 講堂は体育館に～えられた The auditorium *was converted* (≒ *was transformed*; *was changed*) into a gymnasium. 彼は物語を劇に～えた He *dramatized* the story.

つくりかた【作り方】 the way of making. ¶ トマトの～を教えてください Please tell me *how to grow* tomatoes. プリンの～を知りたい I want to learn *how to make* pudding.

つくりごえ【作り声】 a feigned voice. ¶ あの声は～だ That is *a feigned voice*. 彼は～で返事をした He answered *with* (≒ *in*) *a feigned voice*.

つくりごと【作り事】 a fabrication. ¶ きみの話はまったくの～だ Your story is *an* utter *fabrication*. これはとても～には思えない This does not seem to be *fiction*.

つくりざかや【造り酒屋】 (人) a *sake* brewer; (醸造所) a *sake* brewery.

つくりだ·す【作り出す】 ¶ 日本は年間数百万台の自動車を～している Japan produces (≒ *manufactures*; *turns out*) millions of cars in 〔the course of〕 a year. 彼は数々の名作を～した He *wrote* a lot of great works.

つくりつけ【作り付け】 ¶ ～の鏡 a *built-in* mirror. 本だなは～にした I *had* my bookshelf *built in*.

つくりなお·す【作り直す】 make (*a thing*) over; remake. ¶ 模型を～す *remake* a model. 私はくつを～させた I *had* my shoes *remade*.

つくりばなし【作り話】 a fable; a fiction. ¶ これは～であって実話ではない This is not a real story but *a made-up one* (≒ *a piece of fiction*). 彼はよく～をする He often *makes up stories*.

つくりもの【作り物】 an artificial product. ¶ ショーウインドーには～のケーキが並んでいた *Artificial* cakes were displayed in the show window.

つくりわらい【作り笑い】 a feigned laugh. ¶ ～をする force a smile; affect a laugh.

つく·る【作る·造る·創る】 **1**〘製造する·製作する·建造する·創造する·醸造する〙 ¶ うちの会社では5種類のトラックを～っている Our company *produces* five different models of trucks.
今われわれは大型タンカーを～っているところだ We *are building* a supertanker right now.
大都市ではどんどん地下鉄が～られている Many new subway lines *are under construction* in large cities.
雪国では家は雪の重みに耐えられるように～られる In snowy districts, houses *are* so *built* as to withstand the weight of snow.
女の子は人形を～るのが好きだ Young girls are fond of *making* dolls.
彼女がこの暖かいセーターを～ってくれた She *knitted* this warm sweater for me.
この木を使って本箱を～ろう Let's *make* a bookcase *out of* this piece of wood.
ウイスキーはなにから～られるか知っていますか Do you know what whisky *is made from*?
パンは小麦粉から～られる Bread *is made from flour*.
2〘文·作品などを〙 ¶ 彼は美しい詩を～る He *writes* beautiful poems.
彼は講演の草稿を自分で～った He *wrote* the draft of his speech for himself.
これは日本の民話から～られた劇だ The narrative of the play *was taken from* a Japanese folk tale.
シェイクスピアは多くの新語を～った Shakespeare *coined* many words.
3〘作成する〙 ¶ 新しい道路交通法が～られた New traffic regulations *have been made*.
早速この取引の契約書を～りましょう Let me *draw up* a contract for this bargain right away.
そのことについて細案を～ってくれませんか Will you *draw up* a detailed plan for it?
彼は学芸会のプログラムを～るのに忙しい He is busy *preparing* a program for our cultural festival.
4〘構成する·組織する〙 ¶ 彼は独立して新しい会社を～った He became independent, and *established* a new company.
彼らは組合を～った They *organized* a union of their own.

どうぞ明るい新家庭をお～りください I sincerely hope that you will *have* (≒ *make and keep*) a happy home.
公害のない住みよい町を～ろう Let us *create* a comfortable, pollution free environment for our town.
私たちは会社に写真クラブを～った We *made* a camera club in our company.
列を～ってお待ちください Please *form* a queue and wait.
選手たちは監督のまわりに円陣を～って座った The players sat *in a circle* around the general manager.
5 〖耕す・栽培する〗 ¶ 彼は家の近くに小さな畑を～っている He *keeps* a small vegetable garden near his house.
近ごろ稲の裏作に麦を～る農家が少なくなった Nowadays, instead of *planting* wheat, most farmers prefer to fallow their fields after rice harvest.
これは彼が丹精して～った菊だ These are the chrysanthemums he *raised* with love and care.
6 〖人を生む・養成(育成)する〗 ¶ あの夫婦は子どもを～らないつもりらしい It seems that the couple have no intention of *having* a child.
あの学校はりっぱな人間を～る The school *trains* men of fine character.
よい後継者を～るのは難しい It is not easy to *train* a good successor.
わが社は新しい会社だから, みなでよい社風を～っていきたい Our company is still young and we must work together to *establish* good precedents.
7 〖捏造(ねつぞう)する・わざとする〗 ¶ それは彼が～った話ではないのか Isn't that a story *invented* by him?
どうもその話は～りすぎている The story sounds too good to be true.
彼女は口実を～ってデートの申し込みを断わった She *cooked up* an excuse and declined the date.
彼女は無理して笑顔を～ってみせた She forced a smile on her face.
8 〖調理する〗 ¶ 彼女はケーキを～るのが得意だ She is very good at *making* (≒ *baking*) cakes.
すぐお昼を～りますからお待ちください I hope you will stay for lunch. I will *prepare* it in a few moments.
9 〖敵・味方を〗 ¶ 真の友を～るのは難しいことだ It is not so easy to *cultivate* true friendship.
敵を～ってはいけない Don't *make* enemies.
10 〖化粧する〗 ¶ 役者は顔を～るのに長い時間をかける Actors and actresses spend a long time in *make-up*.
私は母にまゆを～ってもらった I *had* my eyebrows *penciled* by my mother.

つくろい【繕い】(修繕) mending; repair; (ほころびなどの) darning. ¶ 家の～をするにはなかなか金がかかる It costs a lot of money to *repair* a house. 少女たちは自分のコートの～をした The girls *patched up* their own coats.

つくろ・う【繕う】¶ 服を～う *mend* a dress. くつ下を～う *darn* stockings. かぎ裂きを～う *patch* a tear. 世間体を～う *keep up* appearances. 人前では身なりを～わねばならない We must try to *look neat* in company.

つけ【付け】(勘定書) a bill; an account. ¶～で買う *buy* things *on credit*. ～にしておいてくれ *Charge* it *to my account* (≒ *credit*). / *Put* it *on my bill*. この店は～がきかない No *credit is given* at this shop.

つけ【就け・付け】¶ 雨に～風に～故郷を思い出す Everything I see and hear reminds me of my home. なんに～かに～金が必要だ We need money *on every occasion*.

つげ【告げ】an oracle; a revelation. ¶ 神のお～があった The 〔*divine*〕 *oracle* was delivered.

つげ【黄楊・柘植】〖植物〗a box tree; (材) boxwood.

-づけ【-付け】¶ 4月1日～のお手紙を受け取りました I received your letter *dated* (≒ *under date of*) April 1.

つけあが・る【付け上がる】¶ 子どもはおだてるとすぐ～る Children *are* easily *puffed up* by praises. 優しくしてやれば彼はすぐ～る He is apt to *take advantage of* my kindness.

つけあわせ【付け合わせ】vegetable taken with meat or fish; garnish.

つけあわ・せる【付け合わせる】¶ 肉料理に野菜を～せる *add* vegetable *to* meat.

つけい・る【付け入る】¶ 彼女は彼の人のよさに～った She *has presumed on* (≒ *has taken unfair advantage of*) his good nature.

つけおとし【付け落とし】(帳簿の) an omission in a bill.

つけおと・す【付け落とす】¶ 帳面に日時を～した I *forgot to put* the date in the book.

つけか・える【付け替える・付け換える】¶ 電球を新しいのに～えた I *changed* the electric bulb *for* a new one. 私はノートの表紙を～えた I *renewed* the cover of the notebook.

つけぐすり【付け薬】a medicine for external application.

つげぐち【告げ口】talebearing. ¶ 彼はいつもぼくのことを彼らに～する He always *tells* them *on* me. ～をする人 a talebearer; a telltale.

つけくわ・える【付け加える】¶ 彼の説明に私が～えることはなにもない I have nothing to *add to* his explanation. 彼を探険隊に～えることになった We decided to *let* him *join* the expedition.

つけこ・む【付け込む】¶ 私が知らないと思って～まないでください Don't *take advantage of* my ignorance.

つけたし【付け足し】an addition; (建物などの) an annex. ¶ ～にひと言述べさせてください Let me make an *extra* (≒ *additional*) remark.

つけた・す【付け足す】¶ それに説明を～す必要がある I have to *add* a supplementary explanation *to* it.

つけたり【付け足り】an accessory; an addition. ¶ それはほんの～にすぎない That is *a* mere *complement*. 視察は～で観光が彼らの目的だ

They are traveling for the *ostensible* purpose of inspection, but their true aim is sightseeing. / Inspection *is* just *nominal*; sightseeing is their true aim.

つけどころ【付け所】¶ そこが目の〜だ That's *the point to consider*. / That's *the point to aim at*. 目の〜がいい(悪い) You *aim* right (wrong). きみは私とは目の〜が違う You take *a* different *view of things* from mine.

つけとどけ【付け届け】bribes; an occasional present. ¶ 彼は盆暮れの〜を必ずする He never fails to make summer and year-end *presents*.

つけね【付け値】a bid; a price offered. ¶ 最初の〜は5,000円だった The first *bid* (≒ *offer*; *price offered*) was five thousand yen.

つけね【付け根】the base; the root. ¶ 足の〜 the groin. 首の〜 *the base* of the neck. 葉の〜 a leafstem.

つけねら・う【付け狙う】¶ 私は駅ですりに〜われた I *was followed* by a pickpocket at the station. 犯人は大統領の命を〜っていた The criminal *had designs upon* (≒ *had sought*) the life of the president.

つけひげ【付け髭】a false m[o]ustache. ¶ 〜をつける wear *a false m[o]ustache*.

つけびと【付け人】an attendant; an assistant.

つけまわ・す【付け回す】¶ 女の子を〜す *chase* (≒ *run after*) girls.

つけめ【付け目】an aim; an object. ¶ 彼の結婚は金が〜だった The true *object* of his marriage was her fortune. 彼女の親切さがこっちの〜だ Why don't you *take advantage of* her kindness?

つけもの【漬け物】pickles; pickled (≒ salted; preserved) vegetables.

—屋 a pickle shop.

つけやき【付け焼き】¶ 魚を〜にする *broil* fish *with soy*. 魚の〜 a *broiled* fish.

つけやきば【付け焼き刃】(にわか仕込み) a makeshift; borrowed wisdom.

つ・ける【着ける・付ける・就ける・点ける】**1**〖身にまとう〗 ¶ 彼はいつも警官の制服を〜けている He always *wears* his police uniform.

この犬は首輪を〜けていない The dog *has* no collar around its neck.

2〖着くようにする〗 ¶ 早くボートを岸に〜けてください Hurry up and *bring* the boat *ashore*.

彼は車を玄関にぴたりと〜けた He *drove up* his car *to* the entrance.

3〖位置にすえる〗 ¶ 子どもたちを各自の席に〜けてください Let every child *be seated*.

4〖付着させる・付属させる・接触させる〗 ¶ 用心のため戸に2種類のかぎを〜けた I *had* two different kinds of locks *fitted* (≒ *fixed*) in the door for safety.

車にスノータイヤを〜けた I *equipped* my car *with* snow tires.

花束には彼の名刺が〜けてあった His name card *was attached to* the bouquet.

彼は壁に耳を〜けて隣室の話を聞いた He *pressed* his ear *against* the wall and listened to the conversation in the next room.

5〖塗る〗 ¶ パンにジャムを〜けて食べよう I will *spread* jam *on* my bread.

彼女はいつもより濃くおしろいを〜けている She *is wearing* (≒ *has put*) more powder on her face than usual.

彼は髪にいっさい油を〜けない He *has* absolutely no hair oil.

私は足の傷を洗って赤チンを〜けた I washed my feet, and *applied* some mercurochrome *on* the cut.

ばかに〜ける薬はない No remedy for a fool. / He is a hopeless idiot.

6〖記入する〗 ¶ 来年は英語で日記を〜けることにしよう I have decided to *keep* an English diary next year.

きょうの売り上げを計算して帳簿に〜けてください Will you add up today's sale and *enter* the total *in* our account book?

この代金を私の勘定に〜けておいてくれ *Charge* it *to* my account.

7〖付き添わせる・雇う〗 ¶ 病人に看護婦を〜けてもらった I *had* the patient *attended* by a nurse.

被告には必ず弁護士を〜けることになっている As a rule, the defendant *is provided with* a lawyer.

8〖通じるようにする〗 ¶ 彼らはその村まで広い道を〜けた They *built* a wide road *to* the village.

私が先方に連絡を〜けましょう I will *contact* (≒ *get in touch*) *with* the other party.

9〖加える・つくり上げる〗 ¶ 弱い相手と戦わせて彼に自信を〜けさせた We let him fight with a weak opponent to *inspire* confidence in him.

峠で一休みして元気を〜けよう Let's have a short rest at the summit to *regain* our strength.

このまずい料理はだれが味を〜けたのか This food is terrible! Who *cooked* it?

該当する項目に○印を〜けてください *Put* a circle *on* the applicable item.

これからこの絵に絵の具で色を〜けるところだ I am going to *color* this drawing.

庭に足跡を〜けないように注意しなさい Be careful not to *leave* your footprints in the garden.

次の漢字にふりがなを〜けなさい *Affix* phonetic transcriptions in *kana to* the following ideographs.

早寝早起きの習慣を〜けなさい I advise you to *cultivate* the habit of keeping early hours.

彼は人のすることにいちいちけちを〜けたがる He is too ready to *find fault with* others.

10〖加担させる〗 ¶ 彼を味方に〜ければもうだいじょうぶだ Now that we *have won* him *to our side*, we have nothing to worry about.

11〖始める〗 ¶ どの仕事から手を〜けようか I do not know where to *begin*. / I do not know what I should *take up first*.

病気があまり進行しすぎていて，医師も手を〜けかねた The disease was too far gone that the doctor could do nothing about it.

12〖決定・終結する〗 ¶ 早く仕事のかたを〜けて帰る

としよう Let's *finish* our work quickly and go home.
慰謝料として10万円払うことに話を～けた We *settled the matter* with a solatium of a hundred thousand yen.
13 〖値を決める〗 ¶ 彼はその絵に100万円の値を～けて売りに出した He offered the painting for sale *at the price of* a million yen.
あの店の商品は値引きを見越して高い値段を～けてある Everything in that shop *is overpriced*, for discounts are expected.
14 〖注意〗 ¶ 暗いから気を～けて歩きなさい *Watch your steps*. It is dark.
私はあの学生の文才に目を～けている *I've been watching* the literary talent of that student.
15 〖尾行する〗 ¶ あの男を～けてくれ *Follow* the man.
犯人は刑事に～けられていることに気がつかなかった The criminal was not aware of the detective *shadowing* (≒ *dogging*) him.
この野ウサギの足跡を～けてみよう Let's *trace* these hare tracks.
16 〖従事・就職させる〗 ¶ うちでは子どもは早く職に～ける方針だ Both my wife and myself believe that our children should *get jobs* early.
見張りを部署に～ける *send* a watchman *to* his post.
17 〖点火する〗 ¶ たばこに火をお～けしましょう Let me *give* you *a light*.
その男は保険金欲しさに自分の家に火を～けた He *set fire to* his house, hoping to receive a large insurance.
スタンドの明かりを～けて勉強しないと目を悪くする Study with your desk lamp *on*, or you will hurt your eyes.
テレビを～けてくれませんか *Turn on* the television set, please.

つ·ける【浸ける】¶ 洗たくをする前に衣類を水に～けておきなさい *Soak* your clothes in the water before you wash them. 彼は頭をプールの中に～けた He *dipped* his head in the pool.

つ·ける【漬ける】¶ 彼は菜を塩で～けた He *pickled* greens in salt. 彼はカエルをアルコールに～けた He *preserved* a frog in alcohol.

-つ·ける ¶ ここは歩き～けた通りだ This is a *familiar* street *to* me. 彼は質素な生活をし～けている He *is accustomed to* a simple life. / He *is in the habit of* leading a simple life. 私はここで買い～けている I *am an old customer* here.

つ·げる【告げる】¶ 彼は真実を～げた He *told* us the truth. 彼は友人たちに最後の別れを～げた He *bade* a last farewell *to* his friends. 彼は名前を～げずに立ち去った He went away without *giving* his name.

つごう【都合】**1** 〖便宜・事情〗 circumstances; convenience. ¶ きょうは～が悪くてお伺いできません It *is* not *convenient* for me to come and see you today.
ご～のよい日を知らせてください Please let me know the date when you will *be free*. / Please let me know the day that *suits* you best.
いつでもあなたの～のよいときに来てください Come and see me whenever you *are free*. / Come and see me whenever it *suits* you. / Come and see me whenever it *is convenient* for you.
もしきょうご～が悪ければ, あすお会いしましょう If it *is* not *convenient* for you today, let us meet tomorrow.
他の人の～も聞かなくてはなりません We have to check others' *convenience*.
家の～であすは欠勤します I will take a day off tomorrow *for family reasons* (≒ *on account of family affairs*).
～によっては貸付金の返済期日を延ばしてもよい We might as well postpone the due date for the return of the loan, depending on the *circumstances*.
～の悪いことに列車が1時間も延着した *Unfortunately*, the train was delayed by one hour.
幸い万事～よく運びました Fortunately everything *has gone well*. / Fortunately everything *went smoothly*.
彼は自分の～だけで何事も決めてしまう He always makes an arrangement *at his own convenience*.
2 〖繰り合わせ・融通〗 ¶ なんとか時間の～がつきませんか Can't you *make time* somehow?
～がつきしだいお宅へ伺います I will call on you *at my earliest convenience*. / I will call on you as soon as I can *make it*.
明後日ならご～がつきますか Could you *be free* the day after tomorrow?
3 〖金の調達・融通〗 ¶ 家を買いたいのだが, 金の～がつかなくて困っている I am thinking of getting a house, but I am having a hard time *raising* the money.
やっと10万円～してきた I barely managed to *raise* a hundred thousand yen from various sources.
5,000円ばかり～してもらえませんか Could you *lend* (≒ 米 *loan*) me five thousand yen?
4 〖合計・全部で〗 ¶ 屋根の修繕に～30万円かかった It cost me the *total* of three hundred thousand yen to repair the roof.
受賞者は～8人になった The number of the prize winners came to eight *in all* (≒ *in total*).

つじ【辻】(町かど) a street corner; (十字路) a crossing; (街路) a street.
—強盗 a highwayman; a highway robber. **—**説法 street preaching.

つじつま【辻褄】¶ きみの話は～が合わない Your story *is not consistent* (≒ *is inconsistent*). 彼は～の合わないことを言う He talks *inconsistently*. / He *contradicts himself*. それは～の合わない言いわけだ It is a *lame* excuse.

つた【蔦】〘植物〙 an ivy.

-づたい【-伝い】¶ 私はいそ～に歩いた I walked *along* the shore. どろぼうは屋根～に逃げた The thief fled *from roof to roof*.

つた·う【伝う】¶ 枝を～って木にのぼる climb up a tree *by the help of* branches. 綱を～っておりる climb down *along* a rope. 川岸を～っていく go *along* the river.

つたえ【伝説】(伝説) a tradition ; (伝達) transmission ; report.

つたえき·く【伝え聞く】¶ ～くところによると富士山は一夜にしてできたものだ *The legends say that* (≒ *There is a tradition that ; According to the tradition*) Mt. Fuji rose in a night.

つた·える【伝える】**1**〖知らせる〗tell. ¶ このように～えてください *Tell* him so.
電話をくれるよう～えてほしい Please *tell* him *to* phone me.
彼はみんなにそのニュースを～えた He *told* the news *to* everyone.
その情報を彼に～える I will *convey* the information *to* him.
～えられるところによると，彼は殺されたそうだ *There is a rumor that* he was killed.
お母さんによろしくお～えください Please *remember me to* your mother. / *Give my best regards to* your mother.
2〖もたらす〗introduce. ¶ タバコは400年前にイギリスに初めて～えられた Tobacco *was introduced into* England 400 years ago.
3〖伝授する〗initiate. ¶ 彼は製作の秘けつを息子に～えた He *initiated* his son *into* the secret of the production.
4〖伝えのこす〗hand down. ¶ その話は子孫に～えられた The story *was handed down to* posterity.
この絵は代々～えられてきた家宝です This picture is our family treasure which *has been handed down* from generation to generation.
5〖伝導する〗transmit. ¶ 鉄は熱を～える Iron *transmits* heat.

つたな·い【拙い】(へたな) poor ; unskillful. ¶ 王は武運～く戦死した The king died an *unlucky* death in the war.

つたわ·る【伝わる】**1**〖昔から伝わる〗come down. ¶ この習慣は祖先からわれわれに～ったものだ This custom *has come down to* us from our ancestors.
この刀は代々わが家に～ったものだ This sword *has been handed down* from generation to generation in my family.
2〖広まる·進む〗spread. ¶ そのうわさは口から口へとたちまち～った The rumor *spread* rapidly from mouth to mouth.
彼の死は全世界に～った His death *was reported* all over the world.
光は音より速く～る Light *travels* faster than sound.
3〖沿って進む〗¶ 彼は木を～っておりた He *climbed down* the tree.
彼はへいを～ってのぼった He *climbed up* the wall.
涙が彼女のほおを～って流れた Tears *ran down* her cheeks.
4〖伝来する〗be introduced. ¶ 仏教は6世紀に日本に～った Buddhism *was introduced* (≒ *was brought*) into Japan in the sixth century.

つち【土】**1**〖土地〗earth ; soil. ¶ ここの～はよい *Soil* here is good.
～一升金一升の土地だ This *land* (≒ *soil ; earth ; dirt*) is worth its weight in gold.
～を深く掘る dig deep in *dirt*.
2〖慣用的表現〗¶ 顔色が～のようになった He *turned pale as ashes.*
彼は異国の～となった He died in *a* strange *land*.
あなたは外国の～を踏んだことがありますか Have you ever been abroad ?
横綱は今のところ～つかずだ This grand *sumo* champion *has a clean record* so far.
大関にきょう～がついた A champion *sumo* wrestler *was defeated* today.

つち【槌·鎚】a hammer ; (木製の) a mallet. ¶～で釘を打つ drive in a nail with *a hammer*. ～で金を薄くのばす *hammer* gold into thin leave.

つちいじり【土いじり】¶ 子どもたちは庭で～をしている The children are out in the garden *playing with mud.*

つちいろ【土色】¶ そのニュースを聞いたとたんに彼女の顔は～になった The moment she heard the news, she *turned ghastly* (≒ *deadly*) *pale.*

つちか·う【培う】foster ; cultivate. ¶ 愛国心を～う *foster* a patriotic spirit.

つちぐも【土蜘蛛】a ground spider.

つちくれ【土塊】a clod.

つちけむり【土煙】a cloud of dust. ¶ 荷車が田舎道をゴロゴロいって通ったときにものすごい～があがった When the wagon rumbled along the country road, it raised *a* tremendous *cloud of dust.*

つちふまず【土踏まず】the arch of the foot.

つちまみれ【土まみれ】¶ 彼は～になって働いた He worked *covered with mud.*

つちろう【土牢】a dungeon.

つつ【筒】a pipe ; a tube ; (鉄砲の) a gun barrel.

-つつ ¶ 悪いと知り～彼の日記を読んでしまった I read his diary *though* I knew it was wrong. 彼の成績は向上し～ある He is improving in his studies.

つつうらうら【津津浦浦】everywhere ; in every nook and corner of the country ; throughout the length and breadth of the country. ¶ 彼の名は全国～まで知れ渡っている His name is known *far and wide all over the country.*

つっかいぼう【突っ支い棒】a prop ; a support. ¶ へいに～をする *support* a wall *with a prop.*

つっかえ·す【突っ返す】¶ 彼はぼくの書類を不備だと言って～した He *thrust back* (≒ *refused to accept*) my papers, saying they were not in order.

つっかか·る【突っかかる】¶ 彼はだれにでも～る男だ He *turns on* any person. 彼は私目がけていきなり～ってきた He *knocked against* me all of a sudden.

つっか·ける【突っかける】¶ サンダルを～けて飛び出

した I dashed out *slipping* my feet *into* sandals.

つつがなく【恙無く】safe and sound ; safely ; (健康で) in good health. ¶ 任務を終えて〜彼は帰国した Having fulfilled his mission, he came home *safe and sound.* 母も〜暮らしております My mother *is* also *in good health.*

つづき【続き】continuance ; (続編) a sequel. ¶ この話の〜を知りたい I want to hear the *sequel* to this story. この話の〜はあしたのお楽しみ Tomorrow look for the *continuation* of this story.

-つづき【-続き】¶ 雨天〜で閉口した After *a long spell* of rainy weather I was depressed. 彼は不幸〜で気が狂った He went insane from *a series of* misfortunes.

つづきがら【続き柄】*one's* relation (*to*). ¶ 彼とあなたはどういう〜ですか How *are* you *connected with* him? 世帯主との〜をここに書いてください Please give your *relationship* to the head of your household.

つづきもの【続き物】a serial story ; a serial. ¶ この作家はいま新聞に〜を書いている This writer is writing *a* newspaper *serial.*

つっき・る【突っ切る】¶ 彼女は線路を〜って彼のあとを追った *Crossing* the track, she ran after him.

つつ・く【突く】**1**〖突く〗¶ 鳥がえさを〜いている The bird *is pecking at* the food. 彼にいきなりひじで〜かれた He *nudged* me with his elbow all of a sudden.
2〖なべを〗¶ なべをみんなで〜いた We *ate from the pan* together.
3〖あらをさがす〗¶ どこからも〜かれないようにしなさい Be careful that no one will *find fault with* you.

つづ・く【続く】**1**〖継続〗continue. ¶ 雨が〜いている It has been raining continuously. 雨の日が〜いた We *had a spell of* rainy days. このかんばつは当分〜くだろう We shall *continue to have* this drought for the time being. 戦争はまる4年〜いた The war *continued* a full four years. 今月は幸運が〜いている There has been *a run of* good luck this month. その事業は長く〜くだろう I think the business will *last* long. 会議は一日じゅう〜いた The conference *continued* all day. 同じような事故がこのところ〜いている Recently there have been the same sort of accidents *one after another.*
2〖通じる〗¶ この道は港に〜いている This road *leads to* the harbor. この廊下は隣の建物に〜いている This corridor *adjoins* the neighboring building.
3〖後続〗¶ 彼のあとに〜きなさい *Follow* him. 彼に〜く人がない There is no one to *succeed* him. 前ページから〜く *Continued* from the preceding page.

つづけざま【続けざま】¶ くしゃみが〜に出た I had *a fit of* sneeze. 彼は〜にビールを3杯飲んだ He drank three glasses of beer *in rapid succession.*

つづけて【続けて】¶ きのう4時間〜話をした Yesterday I lectured for four hours *at one stretch.* 彼は1週間も〜欠席することはなかった He hasn't been absent for a week *running.* 彼らのチームは3回〜敗れた They lost three *successive* games. 2度〜地震を感じた I felt earthquakes twice *in succession.* この映画はどのくらい〜上映されるだろうか I wonder *how long* this film will be shown.

つづ・ける【続ける】go on ; continue ; proceed ; keep up. ¶ 仕事を〜けてください Please *go on with* your work. 彼は話を〜けた He *went on* talk*ing*. 3時間以上講義を〜けた I *continued* to lecture for more than three hours. 彼は自転車の旅を〜けた He *continued* his trip on a bicycle. もうこれ以上商売を〜けることはできない Now I cannot *continue* my business any longer. 彼は30分以上歩き〜けた He *continued* to walk for more than half an hour. もうすこしこの問題を考え〜けよう We shall *continue* to consider this problem a little longer.

つっけんどん【突慳貪】¶ 彼はいつも〜な言い方をする He always speaks *sharply* (≒ *harshly*). 人をそんなに〜にあしらうものではない You must not treat others *in* such *a cold way.*

つっこみ【突っ込み】¶ これは〜の足りない研究だ This study lacks *exact research.*

つっこ・む【突っ込む】¶ 彼はポケットに手を〜んだまま私のところにやってきた He came up to me *with his hands in* his pockets. 3人の勇士は敵陣に〜んで壮烈な死を遂げた The three brave soldiers *plunged into* the enemy's line and died a heroic death. 彼女はなかなか〜んだ質問をする She makes rather *searching* inquiries. 学生にあいまいな点を〜まれることがある My students sometimes *question* me *closely* on my indefinite ideas.

つっころばす【突っ転ばす】¶ 相撲で相手を〜した I *pushed down* my opponent *with a thrust* in *sumo* wrestling.

つつさき【筒先】(銃の) the muzzle ; (ホースの) the nozzle.

つつじ【躑躅】〔植物〕an azalea.

つつしみ【慎み】discretion ; prudence. ¶ 〜のない人 an *indiscreet* person ; an *imprudent* person. 彼女の〜深い物腰は居合わせた人すべてに好感を与えた Her *gentle manners* (≒ *graceful bearing*) made a good impression on all those who were present there. あらゆることにもっと〜深くあるべきだ You should *be discreet* (≒ *be prudent ; be modest*) *in* everything.

つつし・む【慎む】¶ ことばを〜みなさい *Be careful in* what you say. もっと言動を〜むべきだ You must *be* more *discreet in* word and deed. 酒を〜んでいる He *abstains from* liquor. たばこを〜んだほうがいい You should *be moderate in* smoking. 今後こんなことのないよう

つ

〜みなさい *Be cautious* not *to* do such a thing again. 暴食を〜まないときみは病気になる You are sure to get sick unless you *keep from* overeating.

つつしんで【謹んで】¶〜お礼を申し上げます I offer you my *heartfelt* thanks. / I thank you *cordially*. この度のご不幸〜お悔やみ申し上げます I *respectfully* express my condolence on your sad bereavement. ご迷惑をおかけしたことを〜おわび申し上げます I *humbly* ask your pardon for my having caused you a lot of trouble.

つつそで【筒袖】 a tight sleeve; a tight sleeve *kimono*.

つった·つ【突っ立つ】¶なにをぼんやり〜っているのだ Why *are* you *standing* like a fool?

つっと suddenly; abruptly. ¶彼女は〜立ちあがってへやを出ていった She stood up *abruptly* and left the room. / She *sprang up to her feet* and went out of the room. 私のそばを何かが〜通り過ぎるのに気づいた I found something *suddenly* pass away beside me.

つつぬけ【筒抜け】 ¶秘密が先方へ〜だ Every secret *leaks out to* them. 隣の話が〜に聞こえる The neighbors' talks *come directly to my ears*.

つっぱ·ねる【突っ撥ねる】 ¶経営者は組合の要求を〜ねた The management *turned down* (≒ *rejected; refused*) the demands of the trade union.

つっぱり【突っ張り】 a prop; a support; (相撲の) a thrust.

つっぱ·る【突っ張る】 ¶泳いでいる間に足が〜った While swimming, I *had cramp in* my leg. 家を丸太ん棒で〜るようにしないと危ない It may be dangerous unless you *support* the house with a log.

つつまし·い【慎ましい】(節約した) frugal; (謙遜な) humble; modest; (うやうやしい) respectful. ¶彼は金持ちだが生活は〜い Rich as he is, he lives a *frugal* life. / Rich as he is, he is living *in a small way*. 彼女は〜い身なりをしている She is *humbly* (≒ *poorly*) dressed. / (おとなしい感じ) She is *quietly* dressed. / (飾りけのない) She is *plainly* dressed. われわれが話をしている間, 彼女は〜く後ろに控えていた While we were talking, she was sitting behind us *modestly*.

つつましやか【慎ましやか】¶あの店員はいつも〜な態度で客に接する That shop assistant always waits upon her customers *modestly*. 彼は私に〜に頭をさげた He bowed to me *respectfully*.

つつみ【包み】 a package; a parcel. ¶〜を解く open *a package*; unpack *a parcel*.
—紙 wrapping paper.

つつみ【堤】 a bank. ¶川の〜が切れた The *embankment* of the river gave away.

つづみ【鼓】 a hand drum; a *tsuzumi*. ¶〜を打つ tap *a drum* with *one's* finger tips.

つつみかく·す【包み隠す】 ¶なにもそう〜さなくてもいいだろう Why should you *keep* it *from* me? 〜さず言いなさい Tell the plain truth. / Confess everything. 彼はなに一つ〜しはしない He *conceals* (≒ *hides*) nothing *from* me. / He tells me everything *frankly* (≒ *openly*). 彼はなんでもかんでも〜そうとしている He *keeps* everything *secret* (≒ *to himself*).

つつ·む【包む】 **1** 〖くるむ〗 wrap. ¶本を紙に〜む *wrap* a book *in* paper.
彼は体を毛布に〜んで横になっていた He was lying, *wrapped in* a blanket.
付近一帯は霧に〜まれていた The entire district *was veiled in* a mist.
ビルは炎に〜まれた The building *was enveloped in* flames.
その話は神秘に〜まれている The story *is veiled in* mystery.
2 〖隠す〗 ¶〜まず白状しなさい Make a clean breast of what you have done.
3 〖着る〗 ¶彼女は白い衣服に身を〜んでいた She *was in* the white dress.

つづ·める【約める】 ¶〜めて言えばこうだ *In short* it is like this. この文章を2行に〜めて書きなさい *Condense* this sentence *into* two lines.

つづら【葛·葛籠】 a box of basketwork; a clothes box.

つづらおり【九十九折り】 ¶〜の山道 a *winding* mountain path.

つづり【綴り】(文字の) spelling; (書類の) file; (音節の) a syllable. ¶会議録の〜 *files* of the minutes. きみの作文には〜の誤りが多い There are lots of *misspellings* in your composition. あなたの〜はめちゃめちゃだ Your *orthography* is shocking.

つづりかた【綴り方】(単語の) spelling; (作文) [a] composition.

つづりじ【綴り字】 spelling.

つづ·る【綴る】(字を) spell; (文を) write; (とじる) bind. ¶思い出を文章に〜る *write down* something on *one's* recollections. ローマ字で名前を〜ってごらん Try and *spell* your name in Roman letters.

つづれ【綴れ】 —織り hand-woven brocade.
—にしき a gobelin tapestry.

つて【伝】(仲介者) an intermediary; (縁故) a connection; (引き) influence; (世話) good offices; (手だて) means.
¶彼は友人の〜でやっと職にありついた He managed to obtain a position through *the good offices* of a friend. あの会社にだれか〜でもおありですか Do you have *someone* in that company *who will use his influence for* you?

つと suddenly; abruptly. ⇒つっと

つど【都度】 every time; whenever. ¶彼は訪問の〜なにかお土産を持ってくる He gives me some presents *whenever* he calls on me. 彼らは検査の〜ひっかかる They fail to stand a test *each time* they are examined.

つどい【集い】 a gathering; a meeting.

つとに【夙に】(朝早く) early in the morning; (年少時に) early in life; (以前に) long ago.

つとま·る【勤まる】¶彼にはこの仕事は〜らない He

is unequal to (≒ *is unfit for*) this task. こうひどく使われてはとても〜らない I can never *stand* such hard work. 彼くらいの実力がある者ならどんな役も〜る A man of his ability *is equal to* any job (≒ *can fill* any office).

つとめ【勤め・務め】duty. ¶ お〜はどちらですか Where are you working? 〜としてやったまでだ I did it only *out of duty*. 勉学するのが学生の〜だ It is the *duty* of students to study. 彼は政治家としての〜を全うして死んだ He died after having fulfilled his *duty* as a statesman.

つとめあ·げる【勤め上げる】¶ 彼は定年までこの会社で〜げた He *worked* for this company till he retired under the age limit. 彼女は年期を〜げて帰ってきた She came home after she *had served out* her time.

つとめぐち【勤め口】a situation; a position; a job. ¶ 彼は〜をさがしている He is looking for *a position*. ようやく〜が見つかった Finally I found *employment*.

つとめさき【勤め先】*one's* place of employment. ¶ 彼は最近〜を変えた He has changed his *job* recently.

つとめて【努めて】¶ あの人たちには〜親切にしてあげなさい Be *as* kind *as possible* to them. 〜英語を読むようにしなさい Try to read English *as much as you can*.

つとめにん【勤め人】a salaried man.

つとめぶり【勤め振り】*one's* assiduity; *one's* service. ¶ 彼の〜はまじめそのものだ His *manner in his job* is diligence itself. 彼は私の〜が気に入らないようだ He seems dissatisfied with *my work* (≒ *the way I do my job*).

つと·める【努める・勉める・力める】¶ 義務を果たすべく〜めるのは当然だ It is natural to *exert yourself* to fulfill your duty. この語を正確に発音するよう〜めなさい *Try* to pronounce this word correctly.

つと·める【勤める・務める】**1**〖勤務する〗¶ 彼は商事会社に〜めている He *works* in a trading company.

2〖役を〗¶ みんな主役を〜めたがる Everyone is anxious to *play* a leading part.

3〖遂行する〗¶ 彼は2期議長を〜めた He *served* two terms as chairman.

つな【綱】a line; (太い) a rope; (細い) a cord; a string; (鉄条の) a cable. ¶ これで頼みの〜も切れた This put an end to *my last hope*. 2台の自動車を〜でつないだ We fastened the two cars with *a rope*. この木の間に〜を張る stretch *a rope* between these trees.

つながり【繋がり】connection; relationship. ¶ 彼とはなんの〜もない I *have* no *connection with* him. / I *have nothing to do with* him. 彼とぼくとは血の〜がある He *is related by* blood with me. / He and I *are of the same blood*. / He is my blood *relation* (≒ *relative*).

つなが·る【繋がる】¶ 家が五, 六軒〜っている There are five or six houses *linked together*. / Several houses come *in a line*. 彼はその事件に〜っている He *is involved in* the affair. 彼とぼくとは血が〜っている He *is related by* blood with me. どうやら首が〜ったので安心だ I feel relieved that I narrowly *escaped being fired*.

つなぎ【繋ぎ】a connection; a link. ¶ ひもの〜目が解けた The *knot* in the string came untied (≒ undone). 次の出演者の〜に手品をやってもらいたい I want you to do conjuring tricks *to fill up the gap* before the next entertainer comes. 鉛管の〜目が離れた The *joint* in the lead pipe has parted.

つなぎあわ·せる【繋ぎ合わせる】¶ 彼は短いひもを2本〜せて長いひもを1本作った He *tied* two short strings *together* to make a long one. このさおにきみのさおを〜せたらどうだろう How about *joining* this pole *to* yours?

つな·ぐ【繋ぐ】tie. ¶ 手を〜いで歩く walk *hand in hand*. 馬を木に〜ぐ *tie* a horse *to* a tree. 犬を鎖で〜ぐ *chain* a dog. 電話をパリに〜いでください Please *connect me with* Paris. 彼は水だけで命を〜いだ He *has sustained himself on* nothing but water.

つなひき【綱引き】¶ 〜をやる play at *a tug of war*. プログラムの次は〜です Next on our program is *a rope-pulling contest*.

つなみ【津波】a tidal wave. ¶ ものすごい〜が日本海沿岸各地を襲った A tremendous *tidal wave* struck various districts along the coast of the Japan Sea.

つなわたり【綱渡り】(事) ropewalking; (人) a tightrope walker. ¶ そんな危ない〜はやめなさい (比喩的に) Stop *leading such a precarious life*. / You shouldn't *take such a great risk*.

つね【常】¶ 彼は朝食後散歩するのが〜だ He *usually* takes a walk after breakfast. (He makes it a rule to...と言う必要はない). 日曜日にはピクニックに出かけるのが〜だった I *used to* go on picnics on Sundays. 彼はようすが〜でない He does not *look quite himself*. これがこの世の〜だ Such is life. ぶつぶつ不平をこぼすのが彼の〜だ He is *always* grumbling.

つねづね【常常】¶ 〜その件につき彼に注意しておいた I have *always* warned him about it. あの人は〜そのことについて不平をもらしている He is *always* complaining about it.

つねに【常に】always; usually. ¶ 〜健康に注意を怠るな You should be *always* careful of your health. / You must pay *continual* attention to your health.

つね·る【抓る】pinch. ¶ 彼女はいたずらっ子の手を〜った She *gave* the urchin *a nip on* his hand. わが身を〜って人の痛さをを知れ (諺) *He who lives in a glasshouse should not throw stones*.

つの【角】a horn; (シカの) an antler. ¶ これを知ったらきっと彼の細君が〜を出すぞ If his wife happens to know of this, she will surely *have a fit of jealousy*. 〜をためて牛を殺す The remedy is worse than the evil. 彼らはいつも〜を突き合わせている They *are* always

つ

at odds with one another.
—細工 a hornwork.
つのかくし【角隠し】a bride's hood (at a wedding).
つのぶえ【角笛】a bugle; a horn.
つの·る【募る】**1**〘募集する〙¶来月新会員を～る We'll *raise* new members next month. 電車に志願者を～るポスターがかかっている There hangs a poster to *invite* applicants in the train. 講堂建設の基金を～った We *raised* (≒ *collected*) funds to construct an auditorium.
2〘激化する〙¶この暑さで急に彼の病勢が～った His sickness suddenly *became serious* (≒ *became critical*) because of this heat. 暑さが～ってきた The heat *has become oppressive.*
つば【唾】spittle; spit; saliva.
つば【鍔·鐔】(刀の) a sword guard; (帽子の) a brim. ¶～の広い帽子 a broad-*brimmed* hat.
つばき【唾】spittle; saliva. ¶彼は床に～を吐いた He *spat* on the floor. 彼は手に～をしてからハンマーを振るいはじめた He *spat* on his hands before using the hammer. 天に～すれば報いはおのれにかえる Don't *spit* up into the air: it may fall back on you.
つばき【椿】〘植物〙a camellia.
—油 camellia oil.
つばさ【翼】the wings. ¶その鳥は～を広げると3フィートある The bird has a three-foot *wingspread.*
つばぜりあい【鍔迫り合い】¶零対零の～が続いた *A close game* continued, with no score on either side.
つばめ【燕】〘鳥類〙a swallow. ¶彼は～のような早業で敵を倒した He fell the enemy *as quick[ly] as lightning.* 若い～ (年下の恋人) a young lover.
つぶ【粒】(穀物の) a grain; (水滴などの) a drop. ¶～の小さい豆 small-(≒ fine-)*grained* beans. 大きい～の雨 large drops of rain. ～のそろった卵 eggs *of even size.* ～のそろった作品 *the best* (≒ *choice*) works. あの学校の選手は～がそろっている The players of the school *are all very good.*
つぶさに【具に·備に】¶その事故の原因を～調べた We investigated the causes of the accident *in detail.* ～辛酸をなめた I went through *many* hardships.
つぶし【潰し】¶彼は～がきく男だ He *is useful in any other work.* 時間～に映画を見にいった I went to the movies to *kill time.*
つぶ·す【潰す】crush. ¶転んで卵を～した I stumbled and *smashed* the eggs. 彼の顔を～した I *put* him *out of countenance.* 彼は身代を～した He *wasted* (≒ *dissipated*) his fortune. 暇を～す *kill* time.
つぶぞろい【粒揃い】¶～の選手たち *uniformly good* players.
つぶつぶ【粒粒】¶顔に～ができた *Pimples* broke out on the face. / I had *pimples* on the face.
つぶて【飛礫·礫】a stone; throwing a stone. ¶彼からはなしの～だ *I've heard nothing from* him.
つぶやき【呟き】muttering; (不平の) grumbling.
つぶや·く【呟く】mutter; (ぶつぶつ言う) grumble. ¶彼はひとり～いていた He *was muttering* to himself.
つぶより【粒選り】¶～の選手たち *select* (≒ *picked*) players.
つぶら【円】¶～なひとみ *round* eyes.
つぶ·る【瞑る】¶目を～る *close* (≒ *shut*) *one's* eyes. 彼は悪いことはどんなことにも目を～らない He never *shuts his eyes to* anything wrong. / He never *connives at* anything wrong.
つぶ·れる【潰れる】¶卵はすぐ～れる An egg *breaks* easily. 卵が1個～れた An egg *was broken.* シュークリームが～れた The cream puffs *are smashed.* 地震で私の家が～れた My house *collapsed* in an earthquake. あの店は～れかかっている The store is about to *fail.* あの会社は～れた The company *has gone under.*
つべこべ ¶～言うな Shut up. ～口出しするな Mind your own business. 彼はすぐ～言う He is apt to *answer back.*
ツベルクリン〘医学〙tuberculin. ¶～の検査を受ける take a *tuberculin* test.
—反応 tuberculin reaction.
つぼ【坪】¶12～の家 a house with a floor space of 12 *tsubo.* この土地は100～ある This land covers (≒ has) an area of 100 *tsubo.*
つぼ【壺】a pot; a jar. ¶それこそまさにこちらの思う～だ The very thing is *what we aim at.* われわれは敵の思う～にはまった We *have played into the hands* of the enemy. なにもかも思う～だ Everything turned out *as we wished.*
つぼま·る【窄まる】¶先の～ったズボン trousers *narrow* at the bottoms of the legs.
つぼみ【蕾·莟】a bud. ¶庭の木の～が出はじめた The trees in my garden began to *bud.* 桜の～がふくらんでいる The cherry trees *are in full bud.* 彼女は惜しくも～のうちに死んだ It is a pity that she passed away *before her bloom.*
つぼ·む【窄む】¶朝顔が～んでしまった The morning glories *have shut* (≒ *have closed*).
つぼ·める【窄める】¶かさを～める *close* (≒ *fold up*) an umbrella. 口を～める *pucker* (≒ *purse*) *up one's* lips.
つぼやき【壺焼き】¶さざえの～ a top shell cooked in its own shell.
つま【妻】a wife. ¶～をめとる marry; take a wife. 彼女は私のよい～になってくれるものと確信している I am sure that she will make me *a* good *wife.*
つま【妻】(さしみの) garnishings; a relish.
つまぐ·る【爪繰る】¶数珠を～る *tell* (≒ *count*) *one's* beads.
つまさき【爪先】the tips of toes. ¶足音をたてないように～で歩いた We walked *on tiptoe* so as not to make any noise. ～で立ってへいの中

をのぞいた We peeped over the fence *on tiptoe*. 彼は頭のてっぺんから～まで一分のすきもない身なりをしている He is *perfectly* dressed.

つまさ·れる ¶ 彼の身の上話を聞いてまったく身に～れた I *was deeply touched* when I heard him tell all about himself. 彼女は人の情けに～れた She *was moved* by the kindness of others.

つまし·い【倹しい】¶ ～い主婦 a *frugal* (≒ *thrifty*) housewife. 彼らは～く暮らした They led a *frugal* life. 彼は～い男だ He *is frugal of* his expenses. / He *is economical of* his money.

つまずき【躓き】stumbling; (失敗) a failure. ¶ 彼はちょっとした～で一生を棒に振った *A slight failure* brought about his ruin.

つまず·く【躓く】¶ 石に～いて倒れた I *stumbled* (≒ *tripped*) *over* a stone and fell. あの敷居に数回も～いた I *tripped on* that threshold several times. 彼は仕事に～いて自殺した He killed himself because he *failed in* his work.

つまだ·つ【爪立つ】stand on tiptoe.

つまはじき【爪弾き】a fillip. ¶ 彼は友人みんなから～にされた He *was shunned* (≒ *was disdained*) by all his friends.

—者 ¶ 彼は近所の～者だ He is *a regular pest* of the neighborhood.

つまび·く【爪弾く】¶ ギターを～く *play* the guitar with *one's fingers*.

つまびらか【詳らか·審らか】¶ 事故の原因を～にする必要がある We must *make* the cause of the accident *clear*. 彼の生死は～でない *It is little known* whether he is alive 〔or not〕. このことについて～にお話したい I want to talk about this *in detail*.

つまみ【摘まみ·撮み·抓み】(取っ手) a knob; (ひとつまみ) a pinch. ¶ ～を右に回す turn *a knob* to the right. ～が取れてしまった The *knob* has come off. 塩をひと～加えて料理に味をつけた I seasoned the dish with *a pinch of* salt.

つまみあらい【摘まみ洗い】¶ 衣服のすそについたどろのはねを落とそうとして～をしてみたがだめだった I tried *washing* the skirt of my dress to remove splashes of mud, but I couldn't.

つまみぐい【摘まみ食い】¶ 子どもはだれもいないのを見はからってお菓子を少し～した The child *ate* some candy when nobody was about. 彼は会社の金を～したために首になった He was fired because he *appropriated* some of the money of his company *for his private use*.

つまみだ·す【摘まみ出す】¶ 店から酔っ払いを～した We *threw* the drunkard *out of* the store. ネコが～された A cat *was dragged out*.

つまみもの【つまみ物】(ビールなどの) a relish.

つま·む【摘まむ·撮む·抓む】¶ 指で～んで食べる eat with *one's* fingers. 臭くて鼻を～んだ It was so stinking that I had to *hold my nose*. 要点を～んで話してください Please *give a summary of* it. どうぞお菓子をお～みください Please *help yourself to* cakes. きつねに～まれたような話だ *I'm quite puzzled* by it.

つまようじ【爪楊枝】a toothpick.

つまらな·い【詰まらない】¶ ～いことを言うのはやめたまえ Don't say *foolish* things. 彼は～いことに怒る He is offended by *trifling* things. そんな～いことを心配するな Don't worry over such *trifles*. 彼は～い人間だ He is a *worthless* man. まったく～い話だった The speech *was* very *boring*. / His speech *was* utterly *dull*. 彼はひとりぼっちで～いと言っている He says it *is boring* to be alone.

つまり【詰まり】¶ ～失敗だった (結局) *After all* it was a failure. とどの～は破産になった *The final result* was my bankruptcy. きみの言っていることは～こうだ (要するに) What you say comes to this, *in short*. 安物は～損だ (すなわち) Cheap things don't pay *in the long run*.

つま·る【詰まる】**1**〚ふさがる〛¶ このパイプは～っている This pipe *is stopped up*.
煙突にすすが～った The chimney *is choked up with* soot.
下水が～っている The drain *is choked up*.
鼻が～っていて, においがわからない My nose *is stuffed up* and I cannot smell a thing.
2〚窮する〛¶ 彼は金に～っている He *is hard up*.
一瞬彼女は返答に～った She *was* momentarily *at a loss for* an answer.
3〚いっぱい〛¶ その箱には本がぎっしり～っていた The box *was stuffed with* books.
彼は忙しくてスケジュールが～っている He is so busy 〔that〕 his schedule *is jampacked*.
いっぱいの人でホールは息が～りそうだった The hall *was* almost *stifling* because of the large crowd.
4〚短くなる〛¶ 日がいちばん～るのはいつだろう When *are* days *the shortest*?

つまるところ【詰まる所】¶ ～きみは勉強が足りないのだ *In short*, you haven't studied hard enough.

つみ【罪】(法律上の) a crime; (宗教·精神上の) a sin. ¶ 彼のほうに～があった He *was guilty*. 彼は～のないことがわかった He turned out to *be innocent*. 彼が～を犯したと聞いて驚いた I am surprised to hear that he committed *a crime*. 彼に～があるとは信じられない I cannot believe that he *is guilty*. 彼はみずからその～を負うと言っている He says he *holds himself to blame*. 彼が～を逃れたのは喜ぶべきことだ It is a matter for rejoicing that he escaped *punishment*. まったく～のない人はその中にひとりもいなかった There was no one among them who *was* completely *innocent* 他人のものをとったら, それはとりもなおさず～を犯したことになる If you have taken someone else's property, you are certainly to *be blamed*. 彼が～を隠しつづけるのは感心しない He is indeed blameworthy for concealing his *guilt*. 彼は殺人の～に問われた He *was accused of* murder. 赤ん坊はなんと～のない顔をしていることだろう What an *innocent* look the baby has!

つみ【詰み】¶ あと1手で～だ You *lose* by another move 〔of *koma*〕. / You *are check-*

つ

mated by another move.

-づみ【-積み】¶ 4トン〜のトラック a four-ton truck.

船— shipment.

つみあ·げる【積み上げる】¶ れんがを一つ一つ〜げる *lay* one brick upon another. ごみが山のように〜げられた Rubbish *was piled up* in a heap.

つみおくり【積み送り】shipment.

—人 a shipper; consignor. —品 a shipment; a consignment.

つみおく·る【積み送る】send 〔off〕; ship.

つみおろし【積み降ろし】¶ 荷の〜に忙しい We are busy *loading and unloading* goods.

つみか·える【積み替える】¶ 船から貨車に荷物を〜えた We *transferred* the goods from the ship to the train.

つみかさな·る【積み重なる】¶ 落ち葉が庭一面に〜っていた Fallen leaves *lay deep* all over the garden.

つみかさね【積み重ね】a heap; a pile. ¶ 成功は彼の努力の〜によるものだ Success was due to his *unbroken* (≒ *continuous*) efforts.

つみかさ·ねる【積み重ねる】¶ れんがを〜ねる *pile* bricks *up*. 机の上に本がうず高く〜ねられていた Books *were piled* high *up* on the desk. 実験を〜ねた後, ついに成功した We have succeeded after *a series of* experiments.

つみき【積み木】building blocks.

つみくさ【摘み草】¶ きのう川の土手に〜に行った We went *herb-gathering* on the bank of the river yesterday.

つみこみ【積み込み】loading; (船に) shipment.

—値段 free on board price (F.O.B. price と略す).

つみこ·む【積み込む】¶ 貨物を汽車に〜む *load* a train *with* goods (≒ freight). 船はその港で鉱石を〜んだ The ship *took on* 〔a cargo of〕 ore at the port.

つみすぎ【積み過ぎ】¶ この車は〜だ This car *is overloaded.*

つみす·ぎる【積み過ぎる】¶ 車に荷物を〜ぎてはいけない Don't *overload* the car.

つみだし【積み出し】shipment.

—人 a shipper. —港 a port of shipment.

つみだ·す【積み出す】¶ 石炭を貨車で〜す *send off* coal by rail.

つみたて【積み立て·積立】¶ 毎月1,000円を〜する *save* (≒ *lay aside*) a thousand yen every month.

—金 a reserve 〔money〕.

つみた·てる【積み立てる】¶ 彼女は給料の3分の1を結婚の用意に〜てる She *saves* (≒ *lay aside*) a third of her salary for marriage.

つみつくり【罪作り】¶ 子どもをだますなんて彼は〜な男だ It *is cruel* of him to cheat children. きみは時折〜なことをする You sometimes do a *cruel* (≒ *heartless*) thing.

つみとが【罪科】¶ 彼のようになんの〜のない男を逮捕するとは言語道断だ It is preposterous that the police should have arrested an *innocent* man like him.

つみと·る【摘み取る】¶ 子どもが芽を全部〜ってしまった Some children *nipped off* all the buds.

つみなお·す【積み直す】¶ トラックに材木を〜す *load* a truck *again with* timber.

つみに【積み荷】a load; (船の) 〔a〕 cargo.

¶ 〜を満載した船 a ship with *a* heavy *cargo*. 船に石炭を〜する *load* a ship *with* coal. この船の〜は石炭です This ship *has a cargo* (≒ *is loaded*) *with* coal.

—港 a port of shipment. —料 stowage. —目録 a manifest.

つみのこ·す【積み残す】¶ 荷物を〜す *leave* cargo *off*.

つみぶか·い【罪深い】¶ 〜い女 a *sinful* woman.

つみほろぼし【罪滅ぼし】¶ 〜のためにその仕事に一心を尽くした I devoted myself to the job *for my atonement*. 彼の業績が失敗の〜になった His achievements *atoned for* his fault.

つむ【錘·紡錘】a spindle.

つ·む【積む】**1** 〚積載する〛 ¶ 本を高く〜む *pile* books high.

本が山と〜んであった A great many books *were piled up*.

トラックは建築資材をたくさん〜んでいた The truck *was loaded with* building materials.

石炭を船に〜む *load* a ship *with* coal.

彼らは馬に荷を〜んでいた They *were packing* the horse.

2 〚蓄積する〛 ¶ 彼ほど経験を〜んだ人はいない No one *is* as *experienced* as he.

彼は巨万の富を〜んでいるという評判だ It is rumored that he *has accumulated* a big fortune.

もっと練習を〜みなさい You must practice harder.

3 〚提供する〛 ¶ どんなに巨額の金を〜まれても私はその仕事は引き受けられない No amount of money will make me accept the task.

つ·む【詰む】¶ あと1手で〜む *be checkmated* by another move. 目の〜んだ生地 *fine* cloth. この本は字がぎっしり〜んでいる The book *is closely printed*.

つ·む【摘む】¶ 若芽を〜む *nip* new shoots. 花(茶)を〜む *pick* flowers (tea). 悪の芽を〜む *nip* an evil in the bud.

つむぎ【紬】pongee.

つむぎいと【紬糸】spun thread.

つむ·ぐ【紡ぐ】¶ 糸を〜ぐ *spin* thread.

つむじ【旋毛】the whirl of hair on the head.

¶ 彼はすぐに〜を曲げる He easily *gets cross* (≒ *gets perverse*).

—曲がり ¶ きみみたいな〜曲がりは見たことがない I have never met such *a crank* (≒ *a perverse man*) like you.

つむじかぜ【旋風】a whirlwind.

つめ【爪】**1** (人の) a nail; (鳥·ネコなどの) a claw.

¶ 〜を切る cut *one's nail*.

〜を伸ばす grow *one's fingernails* long.

〜の手入れをする do *one's nail*.

〜の手入れをしてもらう get a manicure.

つ

〜を染める paint *one's nails.*
この子どもは〜でひっかく This child has a habit of *scratching.*
〜にあかをためないようにしなさい Be careful that your *nails* are not dirty.
きみの〜には泥が入っている There is dirt under your *nails.*
2 〖慣用的表現〗 ¶ 彼は〜に火をともすようなけちんぼうだ He is *a skinflint.*
能あるたかは〜を隠す (諺) *Still waters run deep.*

つめ【詰め】(将棋の) checkmating.

-づめ【-詰め】¶ 箱〜のリンゴ apples *packed in a case.* びん〜のマヨネーズ *bottled* mayonnaise. 1ダース〜のビール a case of a dozen bottles of beer. 文部省〜の記者 a reporter *assigned to* the Education Ministry. 終着駅まで立ち〜だった I *was kept* stand*ing* to the terminal station. (I *kept* stand*ing* とすれば自分の意志で立っていたことになる).

つめあと【爪痕】(ひっかきの) a scratch. ¶ 村にはまだ洪水の〜が残っている There are still left some *places destroyed* by the flood in the village.

つめあわせ【詰め合わせ】an assortment. ¶ チョコレートの〜1箱 a box of *assorted* chocolates. かん詰めの〜 *an assortment* of canned (≒ 英 tinned) food.

つめあわ・せる【詰め合わせる】¶ 果物を箱に〜せる *assort* fruits in a box.

つめえり【詰め襟】¶ 〜の学生服 a 〔boy's〕 uniform with a stand-up (≒ closed) collar.

つめか・える【詰め替える】 ¶ スーツケースを〜える *repack* a suitcase *with* (*something*). 彼はパイプにたばこを〜えた He *refilled* his pipe *with* tobacco.

つめか・ける【詰めかける】¶ 多数の買い物客がデパートに〜けた A large number of shoppers *crowded into* the department store. 火事場にやじうまが〜けた A crowd of people *thronged to* (≒ *besieged*) the scene of the fire.

つめきり【爪切り】nail scissors; a nail clipper.

つめき・る【詰め切る】¶ 病室に〜って父の看病をした I kept attending on my father 〔in hospital〕 without leaving his sickroom. 記者団が首相官邸に〜りだ A group of newspaper reporters *stick to* the premier's official residence.

つめこみ【詰め込み】¶ 〜主義の教育 *cramming* education. 入試準備のために先生は生徒に〜勉強をさせた The teacher *crammed* his pupils for the entrance examinations.

つめこ・む【詰め込む】¶ 箱に本を〜んだ I *packed* books *into* the box. かばんにいろいろの物を〜む *pack* a bag *with* all sorts of things. 小さな部屋にたくさんの人を〜んだ They *crowded* many people *into* a small room. この通勤電車にはぎっしり人が〜まれている This commuter train *is overcrowded.* 彼は知識を頭にいっぱい〜んでいる He *has stuffed* his head *with* knowledge.

つめしょ【詰め所】¶ (番兵の) a guardhouse; a guardroom; (守衛の) a guardsmen's office.

つめた・い【冷たい】**1** 〖水・風などが〗 cold. ¶ 〜い風が吹いている A *cold* wind is blowing.
〜い水を飲みたい I want to have a *cold* drink of water.
2 〖態度・関係が〗 cold. ¶ なんと〜い人だろう What a *cold-hearted* man 〔he is〕!
彼は私に〜い態度をとる He assumes an *indifferent* attitude toward me.
彼は〜い目つきで私をにらんだ He stared at me with a *glacial* look.
両国の間には長い間〜い戦争が続いていた There was a *cold* war between the two countries for a long time.

つめばら【詰め腹】¶ 彼は事故の責任を問われて〜を切らされた He *was forced to resign* because of his fault in the accident.

つめもの【詰め物】¶ クッションの〜 *stuffing* (≒ *padding*) in a cushion. 虫歯に〜をする *fill* a decayed tooth. にわとりの腹に野菜を〜にして丸焼きにした We roasted the chicken whole with vegetables *stuffed.* 虫歯に〜をしてもらった I *had* my decayed tooth *filled* (≒ *plugged; stopped*).

つめやすり【爪やすり】(マニキュア用) an emery board.

つめよ・る【詰め寄る】¶ 彼らは早く返事をしろと私に〜ってきた They *drew closer* (≒ *drew nearer*) *to* me, demanding my immediate answer.

つ・める【詰める】**1** 〖入れる・満たす〗 ¶ 衣類をスーツケースに〜める *pack* clothes in a suitcase.
布団に綿を〜める *stuff* a quilt *with* cotton wool.
彼は水をいっぱい〜めた水筒を持って出かけた He went out with a water-bottle *filled up* with water.
きのう歯にアマルガムを〜めてもらった I *had* my cavity *filled* with amalgam yesterday.
2 〖間隔を縮める〗 ¶ 席を〜めて座ってください Would you *sit closer together*? / Please *squeeze* a little *closer.*
バスが込んできたから奥の方に〜めましょう The bus is getting crowded, so let's *move on to* the back.
もっと行間を〜めて書かないと1枚に書ききれません *Crowd* it *in,* or you'll run over.
3 〖短縮する・切りつめる〗 ¶ スカートのたけを3センチ〜める *shorten* a skirt by three centimeters.
今月は食費を〜めないと家計が赤字になりそうだ We have to *cut down* 〔*on*〕 food expenses this month, otherwise the family budget would go into the red.
会社は今後経費を〜めることに決めた The company has decided to *cut down* 〔*on*〕 expenses hereafter.
4 〖勤務する〗 ¶ 万一に備えてぼくはきょうは朝から事務所に〜めている I have been at my post

since this morning preparing for an emergency.

この交番には必ず警察官が～めている Policemen *are* always *stationed* at this police box.

5 〖息・根気を〗 ¶ その光景を見て思わず息を～めた I *held my breath* at the scene in spite of myself.

そんなに根(こん)を～めて仕事をすると体に毒だ Working so *hard continuously* cannot be good to your health. / The strain of overwork could harm your health.

そう一日中～めて勉強しても能率が上がるまい Studying so *hard* all day long would not be efficient.

6 〖動けなくする〗 ¶ 将棋では相手の王を～めたほうが勝ちになる In the game of Japanese chess the one who *checkmates* the opponent's king wins.

つ

-つ・める 【-詰める】 ¶ 彼はそのバーに通い～めたものだ He used to frequent the bar. これ以上問い～めるのはよしてくれ Don't press me any more to answer the question.

つもり 【積もり・心算】 **1** 〖意向〗 intention. ¶ あしたスキーに出かける～だ I *am going to* go skiing tomorrow. / I *am planning to* go skiing tomorrow.

いつアメリカへ行く～ですか When do you *plan* (≒ *expect*) *to* leave for America?

実はきのうお訪ねする～だった Actually, I *meant to* visit you yesterday.

彼はどういう～であんなことを言ったのだろう What did he really *mean* by that? / With what *intention* did he say that?

冗談の～で言ったことが, たいへんな問題になってしまった I *meant* it as a joke but it caused a lot of trouble.

私はあなたを非難する～はまったくない I don't have the least (≒ the slightest) *intention* of blaming you.

そういう～ではなかった I didn't *mean* it.

それはきみのことを言っている～だった That *meant* you.

近く上京する～だ I *am thinking of going* (≒ *have a mind to* go; *have an intention of going*) to Tokyo before long.

何をする～だ What do you *intend to* do?

2 〖自負〗 ¶ 彼は自分では有能な～でいるのだから始末が悪い It is hard to deal with him, because he believes himself very competent.

出来栄えは自分ではそう悪くない～だった *In my estimation*, the result was not so bad.

3 〖仮定〗 ¶ ごちそうを食べた～で貯金しよう Let's save the money *instead of* spending it on a feast.

死んだ～でやればできないことはない Nothing is impossible to one who does not fear death.

4 〖予定〗 ¶ いまにめんどくさいことを頼むからその～でいてくれ I want you to *be ready for* a difficult job which I'll have to ask you to do before long.

つも・る 【積もる】 **1** 〖雪・ほこりなどが〗 ¶ 雪が5センチ～った The snow *lay* five centimeters deep.

この雪はあまり～るまい This snow won't *lie deep* (≒ *lie thick*).

その書類はたなざらしになってほこりが～っていた The papers lay upon the shelf, *covered with* dust.

2 〖感情について〗 ¶ 彼らは～る話に花を咲かせた They had an endless talk with each other about one subject after another.

あの人には～る恨みがある I have a *deep-rooted* hatred toward him.

つや 【艶】 ¶ 絹地の～ the *gloss* (≒ *luster*; *sheen*) of silk cloth. ～のある真珠 *glossy* (≒ *lustrous*) pearls. ～のない真珠 *lusterless* pearls. ～のある (つやつやした) 顔色 a *beautiful* (≒ *bright*) complexion. ～のない顔色 a *sallow* complexion. ～のある声 a *sweet* voice. ～のある髪 *glossy* hair. 床をみがいて～を出す *polish up* (≒ *bring out the luster of*) a floor. 革の～を消す take off the *shine* (≒ *luster*; *gloss*) of leather.

つや 【通夜】 ¶ 遺族と親戚(しんせき)の何人かが～をした The family of the deceased and some of their relations *kept* [*a*] *vigil* (≒ *held* [*a*] *wake*) during the night. (wake はおもにアイルランドで用いる語).

つやけし 【艶消し】 ¶ それで話も～だ It *spoils* the interest of the story.

—ガラス frosted (≒ matted; mat) glass.

—写真 a matted (≒mat) photograph.

—電球 a frosted electric bulb.

つやだし 【艶出し】 (皮革・金属など) polishing; (金属など) burnishing; (陶器など) glazing; (紙や布など) calendering; (木綿) mercerizing.

—機械 (紙や布の) a calender.

つやつや 【艶艶】 ⇒つや

つゆ 【露】 **1** 〖水滴〗 dew; (しずく) a dewdrop. ¶ ～にぬれた花 flowers wet with *dew*; *dewy* flowers.

～が下りる The *dew* falls.

2 〖慣用的表現〗 ¶ ～の命 an *ephemeral* life; a life *as ephemeral as dew*.

王女は20歳で断頭台の～と消えた The princess died on the scaffold at so early an age of twenty.

そんなこととは～知らず彼は旅行に出かけた *Entirely* unaware of it, he went on a trip.

私は彼の正直さを～ほども疑ったことはない I have not *in the least* doubted his honesty.

つゆ 【汁・液】 (スープ) soup; (肉汁) broth.

つゆ 【梅雨】 the rainy (≒ wet) season. ¶ ～の入り (明け) the setting-in (end) of *the rainy season*. ～に入った *The rainy season* has set in. ～が明けた *The rainy season* is over (≒ has ended).

つゆくさ 【露草】 〖植物〗 a dayflower; a spiderwort.

つよ・い 【強い】 **1** 〖体力・意志などが〗 strong. ¶ ～い動物 *strong* animals.

最後には～いものが勝つのは当然だ It is natural that *the strong* should win in the long run.

意志の～い人は簡単にはくじけない A man of *strong* will is not easily discouraged. 息子を体の～い子に育てた I trained my son to *be strong*. 鉄は熱に～い Iron *is strong to* heat.
2 〖得意・得手〗 ¶ 彼は船に～い He is *a good sailor*. 彼は酒が～い He is *a heavy drinker*. 彼は英語には～い He *is strong in* English.
3 〖風・光・においなどについて〗 ¶ ～い風 a *strong* wind. 光線が～いので外を歩けない The sunlight *is* too *intense* for me to walk outside. なにか薬のような～いにおいがする There is a *sharp* odor like medicine.
4 〖激しい・威勢のよい〗 ¶ 政府は民衆の～い抵抗を受けた The government was *strongly* resisted. 彼は口で～いことを言っているだけだ He only sounds fierce.

つよがり【強がり】¶ ～を言うのはやめなさい Stop *bluffing*. / No use of your *bluff*.

つよが・る【強がる】¶ 弱い者に限って～るものだ None but the weak will *bluff*. (形式ばった言い方). / *Bluffing* is the proof of being weak. 彼は人々の前で～ってみせた He *showed off his strength* before the people.

つよき【強気】〖株式〗 a bullish (≒ strong) feeling; firmness. ¶ 彼はいつも～に出る He always takes *an aggressive attitude*. 彼は～に試合を進めた He played the game *aggressively*. 市況は午後から～に転じた The market turned *bullish* in the afternoon.

つよく【強く】strongly. ¶ ひもを～引っぱる pull a cord *strongly*. もっと～生きることだ I want you to live a more *vigorous* life. この子は病弱なのでもっと～したい Since this child is weak, I want him to *become stronger*. この語は第2音節を～発音しなさい Pronounce this word *with emphasis* (≒ *with the accent*) *on* the second syllable. 太陽の光はたいへん～芝生に当たっていた The sun's rays shone *intensely* on the lawn. この点は～言うべきだ You must *emphasize* this point. その案には～抗議すべきだ The plan should be *firmly* resisted.

つよごし【強腰】¶ 政府は～だ The Government is taking *a firm attitude* (≒ *a firm stand*).

つよさ【強さ】strength; powerfulness. ¶ 光の～ the *intensity* of light. そのにおいの～ the *keenness* of the smell. チャンピオンはすばらしい～を示した The champion showed his splendid *strength* (≒ *power*).

つよび【強火】¶ ～で野菜をいためる fizzle vegetables over *a hot* (≒ *blazing*) *fire*.

つよふくみ【強含み】〖株式〗¶ 相場は～だ The market *is advancing* (≒ *is strong*).

つよま・る【強まる】¶ 火勢が～った The fire burnt *higher*. 風は夕方から～った The wind began to blow *harder* (≒ *stronger*) toward evening. 人々の間に不安が～った There was a *growing* anxiety among the people. あらしが～ってきた The storm has begun to *rage*.

つよみ【強味】a strong point; strength; an advantage. ¶ 彼の～は記憶力がよいことだ His *strength* (≒ *merit*; *strong point*) lies in his marvelous memory. 彼はチャンピオンらしい～をみせた He showed his splendid *strength* worthy of the name of champion.

つよめ【強目】¶ ひもを～に締める tie a cord *rather harder*.

つよ・める【強める】¶ 彼は語気を～めてそう言った He said so *emphatically* (≒ *with emphasis*). ガスの火力を～める *make* the heat of the gas *more intense*. 時として逆境が人の精神力を～める In some cases adversity *develops one's* will power.

つら【面】¶ どの～さげてそんな要求をするのか *How dare you have the face to* make such a request to me?

つらあて【面当て】¶ 彼の妻は彼への～に自殺をはかった His wife attempted suicide *to vent her spite* (≒ *spleen*) *upon* him. / *Having a spite at* (≒ *against*) him, his wife attempted suicide. 彼がそんな質問をしたのは私に対する～だ He asked me such a question *out of spite*.

つら・い【辛い】¶ きのうは～い目に会った I *had a hard time of it* yesterday. 早起きは～い *It is hard to* get up early. 彼らと別れるのは～かった *It was painful to* part from them. 私は今や～い立場にある I am now in a *difficult* position. 金のないのは～いことだ *It is tough* not *to* have any money. なんとも～い経験だった What a *bitter* experience I had! 旅行は～いものだった The trip *was full of hardships*. 商売は～いものだとつくづく感じた I felt keenly that trade is a *hard* thing.

つらがまえ【面構え】¶ ふてぶてしい～の男だ He is an audacious-*looking* man. 一癖ありげな～だ He is an evil-*looking* man. / The man has a sly *look*.

つらさ【辛さ】¶ 別れの～ the *pain* (≒ *sorrow*; *bitterness*) of parting. その労働の～ the *painfulness* of the labor.

つらだましい【面魂】¶ 大胆不敵な～の男 a man with (≒ of) *an* audacious *countenance*; an audacious-*looking* man.

つらつら【熟】¶ ～考えてみるに若いころなんと時間を浪費したことか *Upon reflection*, what a lot of time I wasted in my youth! (形式ばった文体).

つらな・る【連なる】¶ この国では東から西に～るアルプスをどこからでも見ることができる From anywhere in this country we can enjoy a fine view of the Alps *stretching* from east to west. 見渡すかぎり松原が～っている *There is a long stretch of* pine groves as far as the eye can reach.

つらにく・い【面憎い】¶ まったく～いやつだ He is quite an *offensive* fellow. / He is a *detestable* (≒ *hateful*) person. 彼は～いほど落ち着

いて答えた He replied with *provoking* calmness.

つらぬ·く【貫く】¶川は町を～いて流れている The river *runs through* the city. 弾は彼の腹部を～いた The bullet *shot through* his belly. 彼は初志を～いた He *carried out* his original intention.

つら·ねる【連ねる】¶彼は発起人として名を～ねた He *entered* his name *in* the list of the promoters.

つらのかわ【面の皮】¶彼は～が厚い He is a *brazen-faced* (≒ *impudent*; *shameless*; *cheeky*) fellow. いい～だ It serves him right.

つらよごし【面汚し】¶彼はとんだ一家の～だ He is indeed *a disgrace to* our family. 学校の～になるようなことはするな Never do anything which will be *a discredit to* our school.

つらら【氷柱】an icicle.

つら·れる【釣られる】¶彼は金に～れて悪い仲間に入った Money *allured* him *into* bad company. その広告に～れて多くの人々がその品物を買った Many people *were allured* (≒ *were enticed*) by the advertisement to buy the goods.

つり【釣り】**1**〖魚釣り〗fishing. ¶きのう～に出かけた Yesterday I went out *fishing*.
彼は～がうまい He is *a good angler*.
—糸 a fishing line. **—**ざお a fishing rod.
—仲間 a fellow angler.
2〖釣り銭〗¶～がありますか Do you have *change* for this?
お～はとっておきたまえ(タクシーの運転手などに) You may keep *the change*.
1万円でお～がありますか Can you give me *change* for ten thousand yen?
お～です Here is your *change*.

つりあい【釣り合い】¶よく～のとれた体 a well-*proportioned* physique. ～のとれた体をしている He *is* well-*proportioned*. 彼は体の～を失ってその場に倒れた He lost his *balance* and fell down on the spot. 両国の力の～が失われた The two nations have lost the *balance* of power.

つりあ·う【釣り合う】¶よく～った(～わない)夫婦 a well-*matched* (an ill-*matched*) couple. 古い家具は新しい部屋に～わない Old furniture does not *match* (≒ *harmonize with*) the new room. 彼女の帽子の色は服の色と～っている The color of her hat *harmonizes* (≒ *is in harmony*) *with* that of her suit. 仕事と～った報酬が欲しい I want to be paid *enough for* my labor. / I want to get a *reasonable* compensation *for* the work.

つりあが·る【釣り上がる】¶目の～った女 a *slant-eyed* woman.

つりあ·げる【釣り上げる】¶大きな魚を～げた I *landed* a big fish. 井戸から古バケツを～げた I *hooked up* an old bucket out of the well. 彼は目を～げて怒った He got angry with his eyes *upturned*.

つりおと·す【釣り落とす】¶～した魚は大きい The fish that *has escaped* looks always bigger than it really is.

つりかご【釣り籠·吊り籠】a hanging basket; (気球の) a gondola.

つりがね【釣り鐘】a temple bell. ¶～をつく strike *a temple bell*.
—堂 a belfry; a bell tower; a bell house.

つりがねそう【釣り鐘草】〘植物〙a 〔dotted〕 bellflower.

つりがねむし【釣り鐘虫】〘虫類〙a bell animalcule.

つりかわ【釣り皮】a strap. ¶～につかまる hang on to *a strap*.

つりこま·れる【釣り込まれる】¶彼の話に多くの人が～れた A lot of people *were attracted* by his story. 宣伝に～れてついそれを買ってしまった I *was allured* (≒ *was enticed*) by the advertisement to buy it.

つりさ·げる【釣り下げる】¶夏になるとわが家では軒に風鈴を～げる In summer we *hang* (≒ *suspend*) a wind-bell *from* the eaves of our house.

つりせん【釣り銭】¶1,000円札を出して300円の～をもらった I gave a thousand-yen bill and got three hundred yen in *change*. ～はいらないよ Keep the *change*. 彼は～をまちがえてよこした He gave me the wrong *change*.

つりだし【釣り出し】(すもうで) carrying the opponent out. ¶～で勝つ win by *carrying* the opponent *out*.

つりだな【釣り棚】a hanging shelf.

つりて【釣り手】(人) an angler; (かや·ハンモックなどの) a hanger.

つりてんぐ【釣り天狗】a self-styled angling master.

つりどうぐ【釣り道具】fishing tackle; a rod and line.

つりどうろう【釣り燈籠】a hanging lantern.

つりばし【釣り橋】a suspension bridge.

つりばり【釣り針】a fishhook. ¶～にえさをつける bait *a fishhook* (≒ *a hook*).

つりぶね【釣り船】a fishing boat.

つりぼり【釣り堀】a fishing pond.

つりわ【釣り輪·吊り環】(体操) the rings.

つる【弦】(弓の) a bowstring; (楽器の) a string; (なべの) a handle. ¶弓に～を張る *string* a bow. 矢は既に～を離れた The die is cast.

つる【蔓】(眼鏡の) bows; (植物の) a vine.
¶ブドウの～が松の木に巻きついていた Grape *vines* twined about the pine tree. キュウリの～が地をはう Cucumber *vines* run along the ground.

つる【鶴】〘鳥類〙a crane. ¶社長の～の一声で彼の案が採用された A word from the president made them decide to adopt his plans.

つ·る【吊る】¶壁に絵を～る *hang* a picture on the wall. かやを～る *put up* a mosquito net. 首を～る hang *one*self. 彼はズボンつりでズボンを～っている He is wearing trousers with suspenders.

つ·る【釣る】angle. ¶海で～る *fish* in the

ocean. 彼は魚を～っている He *is fishing*. この辺は～れる There is good *fishing* here. この湖はよく～れる This lake *offers good fishing*. この川では大きなサケが～れる Excellent salmon *fishing may be obtained* at this river.

つ·る【攣る】¶プールで泳いでいる間に右脚が～ってしまった While swimming in the pool, I *had a cramp in* the right leg.

つるぎ【剣】a sword.

つるくさ【蔓草】a vine ; (よじ登るもの) a climber ; (地をはうもの) a creeper.

つるし【吊し】¶ぼくは～の洋服は買わないことにしている I usually do not buy *ready-made* chothes.

つるしあ·げる【吊し上げる】¶学生たちは学長を～げた The students *put* the president *on trial*. / The students *cross-examined* the president. 乗客たちは駅長をなぜ電車が遅れているのかと～げた The passengers *subjected* the station master *to a kangaroo court* demanding why the train was delayed.

つるしがき【吊し柿】a dried persimmon.

つる·す【吊す】hang. ¶風鈴が軒先に～してある There is a wind-bell *hanging* from the eaves.

つるつる ¶彼女の膚は～している Her skin *is velvety*. 道が凍って～滑る The road *is* frozen and *slippery*. 彼は頭が～にはげている He *is as bald as marble* (⇆ *an egg*). / He has a *marble* head. 彼女は乾いたぞうきんで床を～にみがいた She *scoured out* the floor with a dry cloth.

つるはし【鶴嘴】a pickax〔e〕; a pick.

つるべ【釣瓶】a well bucket.

—打ち ¶彼らは銃を～打ちに撃った They fired many shots *in rapid succession*. **—落とし** ¶秋の日は～落としに沈む The autumn sun sinks *fast*. / Evening dusk gathers *very fast* in the fall.

つれ【連れ】a companion ; (総称) company. ¶旅行中に3人の人と～になった While on a trip, we picked up three *companions* (⇆ *fellow-travelers*). ～の人はいないのですか. いたのですがみんなホテルへ帰ってしまいました Are you with someone? I was. But everybody else has gone back to the hotel.

-づれ【-連れ】¶彼は5人～で旅行に出かけた He went on a trip *with* five companions. ゴールデンウイークには子ども～でハイキングに出かける人が多い During the "Golden week," many people go on a hike *with* their children.

つれあい【連れ合い】*one's* husband ; *one's* wife ; *one's* spouse.

つれこ【連れ子】a child by *one's* former (⇆ previous) marriage.

つれこ·む【連れ込む】¶われわれは容疑者を最寄りの交番に～んだ We *walked* the suspect to the nearest police box.

つれそ·う【連れ添う】¶～って10年になる We *have been married* for ten years. 彼は30年間～った妻に先立たれた He lost his wife who *had been married to* (⇆ *had lived with*) him for thirty years.

つれだ·す【連れ出す】¶きょうの午後彼を散歩に～そう I will *take* him for a walk this afternoon.

つれだ·つ【連れ立つ】¶みんな～って今度の日曜に彼のところへ遊びに行こうじゃないか Let's go and see him *in a body* (⇆ *all together*) next Sunday.

つれづれ【徒然】¶私は読書して旅の～を慰めた I *beguiled the tedium* of the trip by reading. (形式ばった文体). 入院中の～に彼女は編物を始めた While in hospital she took up her knitting to *kill time*.

つれて【連れて】¶年をとるに～忘れっぽくなる人が多い There are many people who become forgetful *as* they grow older. 日がたつに～彼の容体はよくなった *As* days went by (⇆ Day by day) his condition became better. 時がたつに～状態が複雑になっていった *As* time passed (⇆ *As* the day wore on), the situation became more and more complicated.

つれな·い【情無い】¶金がなくなったとたんにあの女は～くなった As soon as I became penniless, that woman *grew very cold to* me. あのかわいそうな人たちにそんなに～く当たるのはやめたほうがいい Don't *be* so *hard on* those poor people. / Don't treat those poor persons so *cruelly*.

つ·れる【連れる】¶子どもを動物園に～れていった I *took* my child to the zoo. 彼女は犬を～れて散歩する She takes a walk *with* her dog. ここへ息子さんを～れてきなさい *Bring* your son here. 男は警官に～れていかれた The man *was taken away* by the policeman.

つわぶき【槖吾·石蕗】〖植物〗a Japanese silver leaf.

つわもの【兵】a soldier ; a warrior.

つわり【悪阻】morning sickness.

つんざ·く【突ん裂く】¶耳を～くような爆発音が聞こえた I heard a *deafening* (⇆ an *ear-splitting*) explosion. 膚を～くような寒風が吹いていた A *piercing* (⇆ *cutting*) wind was blowing.

つんつるてん ¶こんな～のズボンをはいていたのではみっともない I feel quite ashamed of wearing such *short* trousers.

つんつん ¶きみのように～した娘は嫁にもらい手がないよ Nobody is willing to get married to an *unkind* girl like you.

つんと ¶あの娘はいつも～すましている That girl always *assumes a prim attitude*. いやなにおいが～鼻をついた An unpleasant smell *assailed* my nostrils. アンモニアは～したにおいがする Ammonia has a *pungent* smell.

ツンドラ the tundra.

—帯 the tundra area.

つんぼ【聾】deafness ; (人) a deaf person ; (総称) the deaf. ¶あの人は～だ He *is deaf*. / He *is hard of hearing*. 彼は右の耳が～だ He *is deaf in* the right ear. こういうことについてはわれわれはいつも～さじきに置かれている We *are* always *kept utterly uninformed* about these matters.

つ

て

て【手】1〘人の手・腕〙 a hand ; an arm. ¶ ～の甲 the back of the *hand*.
～のひら the palm of the *hand*.
～になにを持っているのですか What do you have in your *hand*?
彼女は老人の～をとって部屋に案内した She took the old man's *hand* and led him to the room. / By taking the old man's *hand*, she led him into the room.
品物を自由に～にとってごらんください Please feel free to take the articles in your *hand*.
展示品に～を触れないでください You are requested not to *touch* the articles exhibited. / Please keep your *hands* off the exhibits.
母子は～を取り合って再会を喜んだ The mother and the child rejoiced over their reunion, clasping each other's *hands*. / The mother and the child clasped each other's *hands* and rejoiced over their reunion.
彼はにっこり笑いながら私の～を握った He took my *hand* with a smile.
彼らは～を打って喜んだ They clapped their *hands* with (≒ for) joy.
さあみんな～をつないで円をつくりましょう Now let's all join our *hands* in a circle.
彼は墓の前にしゃがんで～を合わせた He squatted down before the grave and prayed with his *palms* held together.
私はポケットに～を入れて立っていた I was standing with my *hands* in my pockets.
彼は耳に～を当ててかすかな人声を聞こうとした He cupped his *hand* on the ear, trying to listen to the faint voice.
子どもはお菓子をくれと～を差し出した The boy put out his *hand* asking for some candy.
彼は出された食べ物にはいっさい～をつけなかった He didn't *touch* anything that was served.
～を放さないようにしっかり鉄棒につかまれ Don't let go your *hands*, but hold on fast to the 〔horizontal〕 bar.
彼女はさようならと言って～を振った She said good-bye and *waved*. / She *waved* a farewell. / She *waved* good-bye.
この案に賛成のかたは～をあげてください Those of you who approve of the plan, please raise your *hands*.
2〘所有〙 ¶ この本はどこで～に入れたか Where did you *get* (≒ *buy*) this book?
こんな大金をどうやって～に入れたか How did you come to *get* such a lot of money?
この情報は確かな筋から～に入れた I *got* this news from a reliable source.
この家がそんなに安く～に入るなんて信じられない I can't believe that you could *get* this house so cheaply.
この古文書は偶然私の～に入った These old documents *came into my hands* by chance. / I *got* these old documents quite unexpectedly.
先祖代々の家もとうとう人の～に渡ってしまった Even our hereditary property had to *be sold*.
さしもの要塞(ようさい)もついに敵の～に落ちた Though it was a strong fortress, the enemy *captured* it at last (≒ it *was* finally *captured* by the enemy).
この宝石は多くの人の～を経て私のものとなった This jewel came into my possession after going through the *hands* of many people.
ダイヤの指輪なんて私にはとても～が届かない A diamond ring is beyond my dreams.
そんな高い車にはとても～が出ない I couldn't possibly *buy* such an expensive (≒ a high-priced) car.
3〘人手〙 ¶ ～が足りなくて困っている The trouble with us is that we *are short-handed*. / We are troubled with lack of *manpower*.
あの家は～がそろっているから農作業がはかどる They have enough *people*, so the farming is well under way.
その手紙は何人かの～を経て彼のもとに届いた The letter reached him after going through many people's *hands*.
～を分けて事務所の大掃除をした We cleaned up the whole office, dividing the work among us.
忙しそうですね，～を貸しましょうか You seem to be very busy. Shall I lend you *a hand*?
忙しくてねこの～も借りたいくらいだ We are so busy that we would appreciate any help available.
4〘仕事・手数〙 ¶ ～があいたらちょっと来てください Please drop in when you *are free*.
今～がふさがっていますから，あとで行きます As I *am busy* now, I'll come later. / As I can't *leave* right now, I'll be coming a little later.
急ぎの仕事で～がはなせません I cannot *leave* this urgent business. / I *am busy with* something urgent just now.
いくら彼が働き者でもそこまでは～がまわらない He may be a hard worker, but he won't be able to do that much.
子どもたちも～がはなれて彼女にも暇ができた The

children have grown and need less *care*, so she has some free time to spare.

簡単な仕事にも～を抜いてはいけません You must *be careful in* your work, even if it is a simple one.

これは～のこんだ仕事なのでなかなかはかどらない As this is a *complicated* job (⇆ it takes time), I can't get it done so quickly.

5 〖手段・方法・方策〗 way; means; measure; method. ¶ その～はぼくには通用しないよ You can't trick me *that way*. / You are not going to deceive (⇆ trap) me *that way*. / I know a trick worth two of that.

次は別の～でいってみよう Let's take *a* different *approach*. / Let's change our *methods*.

彼はきたない～を使うから気をつけろ He uses dirty *tricks*, so you had better be careful.

彼は～を変え品を変えて彼女の関心を引こうとした He tried to attract her attention by every *means*.

八方～を尽くして捜したが彼は見つからなかった We searched for him in every way possible, but we could not find him.

敵はうまうまとわが方の～に乗った The enemy *was* easily *deceived* by our plan. / The enemy easily fell into our *trap*.

大事にならないうちに早く～を打ったほうがいい You must do something before it becomes serious.

なかなか～のこんだことをやるね What an *elaborate* work you are doing! / This must be a *painstaking* work you are doing.

どこからかたづけるか～のつけようがない Everything is in such a mess that I don't know how to put it in order.

火勢が強くて～の施しようがなかった The force of the fire was so strong that it was simply impossible to do anything. / The blaze was so fierce that we *were* simply *helpless*.

6 〖トランプ・将棋などで〗 ¶ きょうはつきがないのか，ちっともいい～がこない I have been out of luck today, and I never have *a* good *hand*.

彼は将棋で実にうまい～を打つ He makes very clever *moves* in [playing] Japanese chess.

7 〖技能・制御〗 ¶ 彼はだいぶ酒の～が上がった He can consume large quantities of drink now.

子どもも大きくなると親の～に負えなくなる When children grow up, parents can no longer *control* them. / When children grow up, they are beyond parents' *control*.

8 〖関係〗 ¶ 彼はいろいろな商売に～を出している He is doing all kinds of business. / He has many irons in the fire.

彼は商売の～を広げすぎ失敗した He over-extended his business and failed.

相場に～を出すのはよしなさい Don't engage in speculation. / I advise you not to go in for speculation.

彼はすぐ女に～を出したがる He likes to flirt with girls.

ぼくのことに～を出さないでくれ Please *leave* my affairs *alone*.

実業家として成功してから政治に～を出す人が多い There are many who *dabble in* politics after they have succeeded in business.

彼はようやくその女と～を切った At last he *broke away from* her.

私の意見がいれてもらえなければ，あなたと～を切ります If you will not consider my opinion, I will *have nothing to do with* you.

とうとう彼は悪事に～を染めるようになった Finally he *was reduced to* wrong-doing.

本人にやる気がないのなら，私も～を引きます If he is not willing to do it, I will withdraw my *hands* [from it], too.

9 〖種類〗 kind. ¶ この～の品をもっと見せてください Please show me some more of this *kind*.

この～で色の違う品はありませんか Do you have this in different colors?

その～の人間が多くて困る We are troubled by many people *like that* (⇆ *of that type*).

10 〖慣用的表現〗 ¶ 彼は～が早いからこの仕事は1日でかたづけるだろう As he is quick with his work he can probably finish it in a day.

彼女は心配ごとがあって仕事が～につかない She is worried about something, and can't concentrate on her work. / She is too worried to work.

この手紙は男名前になっているが女の～だ Though the sender's name is a man's, this letter is written by a woman.

～をこまぬいてふたりの争いを見ていた I watched them quarreling without attempting to help.

彼は～の切れるような1万円札を取り出した He took out a *brand-new* 10,000 yen note.

その問題に～をつけた生徒はひとりもいなかった None of the students *had tried to solve* the problem.

チャンピオンの技巧の前に挑戦者は～も足も出なかった Those who challenged the champion *were* completely *helpless* (⇆ *powerless*) before his skill.

先生はその生徒の扱いに～をやいている The teacher is having problems with that pupil.

私には～に余る仕事だ The work *is beyond my power*. / I *am not equal to* the task. / I'm afraid the work *is too much for* me.

彼女はかゆいところに～が届くように夫の世話をする She looks after her husband *with utmost care*.

政府は貧しい人たちに救いの～を差しのべるべきだ The government should *offer aid to* the poor.

ふたりは～に～をとって駆け落ちした The lovers eloped *together*.

悪かったと思うなら～をついて謝りなさい If you really feel sorry, you should apologize *from the bottom of your heart* (⇆ *on your knees*).

あの習字の先生は～をとって教えてくれる The penmanship teacher actually takes us by our *hand* and shows us how to write.

このけんかは最初に～を出した者が悪い The one who *struck* first is to be blamed in this quarrel.

彼は父の～となり足となって家業を助けている He is helping his father's business *in every way he can.*

～に汗を握る好試合だった The match was a *breath-taking* one.

彼の話を聞いているとそのときの状況が～にとるようにわかる When I listen to him, I almost feel as if I were at the actual scene. / When I listen to him, I have the feeling that I am at the scene.

そんなことをすると～が後ろにまわるよ If you do such a thing, the police will be after you.

両者はその条件で～を打った Both companies *agreed* on that condition.

どうです，5万円で～を打ちませんか Well, how about *settling on* fifty thousand yen?

て

で【出】 ¶ 彼は貴族の～だ He *is of a noble family.* 彼は九州の～だ He *comes from* Kyushu. あの花屋の娘は大学～だ The florist's daughter is *a* university *graduate.* 今晩の月の～は何時ごろですか What time will the moon *rise* this evening? このところこの品は～がよい This article *sells well* these days. ことしはブドウの～が早い Grapes have *come in* (≒ *ripened*) *earlier* this year. この神社は日曜日には人の～が多い There is *a* large *turnout* at this shrine on Sundays. この万年筆はインクの～が悪い This fountain pen does not write well. どうも水の～が悪い The water does not seem to *flow* smoothly. お茶の～がよい This tea *draws* well. Nさん，～ですよ Mr. N! It's time for you to *appear on the stage.*

-で 1〘場所・範囲〙 at; in. ¶ この電車に乗って渋谷～降りなさい Take this train and get off *at* Shibuya.

きのう上野駅～彼に会った Yesterday I met him *at* Ueno Station.

神田の本屋～この本を買ってきた I bought this book *at* a bookstore in Kanda.

こんな所～きみに会うなんて I've never dreamed of meeting you *here.* / I would never have thought of seeing you *at* a place like this.

この部屋～すこし待ちなさい Wait *in* this room for a while.

公園～日曜の午後をのんびり過ごした I spent a quiet afternoon *in* the park on Sunday.

大都会～暮らすのはもうあきあきした I am bored with life *in* a big city.

ラグビーはイギリス～始まったスポーツだ Rugby is a sport which began *in* England.

子どもは外～遊びなさい Children should go *outside* and play. / You children go out and play.

彼女は2階～勉強している She is studying upstairs.

2〘所用時間など〙 at; in. ¶ この仕事は1日～かたづくだろう This can be done *in* (≒ *within*) a day. / I can probably finish this work *in* one day.

あと1週間～ことしも終わりだ There is only a week left this year. / Only one week will bring us to the end of the year.

本日は正午まで～閉店させていただきます Today we shall close *at* noon.

3〘年齢〙 ¶ 彼は70歳～死んだ He died *at* [*the age of*] seventy.

母は18歳～お嫁にきたそうだ I understand that my mother got married *at* eighteen.

ぼくの友人で20代～大会社の重役になった人がいる There is a friend of mine who became the director of a big company *in* his twenties.

4〘手段・道具〙 ¶ バス～学校へ来る We come to school *by* bus.

アメリカへは飛行機～行きますか，船～行きますか Will you go to America *by* plane or *by* ship? / Are you going to fly or sail to America?

彼は午後の列車～東京に着く He will reach Tokyo *on* the afternoon train.

昔はそこまで馬～半日かかった In olden days it used to take half a day *on* horseback to get there.

入試の結果を電話（電報）～知らせなさい Phone (Wire) the result of the entrance examination to me. / Tell me *by* phone (*by* telegram) the result of the entrance examination.

この手紙を書留～出してください Please send this letter registered.

答案はインク～書いても鉛筆～書いてもよい The paper may be written *in* ink or *with* a pencil.

住所氏名は活字体～書いてください Please write your name and address *in* block letters.

ふつう作品名はイタリック体～印刷される We usually print the name of the work *in* italics./ The name of the work *is* usually *italicized.*

きみはそれをフランス語～言えますか Can you say it *in* French?

彼は双眼鏡～敵の動きを見ていた He was watching the enemy's movements *through* his binoculars.

私は新聞～そのニュースを知った I read the news *in* the newspaper.

ゆうべ野球の実況をテレビ～見た I watched the baseball game *on* television last night.

グリーン車～旅をするなんてぜいたくだ You are too extravagant to travel *in* a 'green car.'

金づち～くぎをまっすぐに打つのは難しい It is hard to drive in nails straight *with* a hammer.

犬を鎖～木につないでおきなさい *Chain* the dog to the tree.

彼はコップ～酒を飲みはじめた He began to drink *sake from* a glass.

人の親切は金～買えるものではない No amount of money can buy other people's kindness. / You cannot buy people's kindness *with* money.

彼はその問題を金～解決するつもりだ He intends to settle the matter *with* money.

彼は昼食代を1万円札〜払った He paid for the lunch *with* a ten thousand yen note.
支払いは小切手〜お願いします Please pay *with* a check.
ぼくは彼にいきなりげんこつ〜殴られた All of a sudden he struck me *with* his fist.
そんなこと〜話がつけられると思っているのか You don't think you can settle the matter *in* that way, do you?
駅は勤め帰りの人〜混雑していた The station was crowded *with* people returning from work.
5 〖材料〗 ¶ この家は木〜できている This house is made *of* wood. / This is a wooden house.
ビールは麦〜つくられる Beer is made *from* wheat.
紙〜人形をつくって遊びましょう Let's make a paper doll and play. / Let's play making paper dolls.
6 〖価格・費用〗 ¶ 彼はスポーツカーを200万円〜買った He got a sports car *for* two million yen. / He paid two million yen for a sports car.
この本を2,000円〜私に譲ってくれませんか Won't you sell the book to me *for* two thousand yen?
あなたの家はいくら〜売れましたか *At* what price could you sell your house?
私の給料だけ〜生活するのは苦しい It is rather hard to live *on* only my salary.
あの店では電化製品を卸値〜売っている They sell electric appliances *at* wholesale prices.
7 〖基準〗 a standard; a basis. ¶ この鉛筆はダース〜売っている This pencil is sold *by* the dozen.
このミカンはキロ〜300円もした These tangerines cost as much as three hundred yen *a* kilogram.
私はこの家を2年契約〜借りた I rented this house *on* a two years' lease. / I leased this house for two years.
車は時速80キロ〜走った The car ran *at* the speed (≒ rate) of eighty kilometers an hour.
あなたということは歩き方〜わかった I recognized you *by the way* you were walking.
この学校では生徒の性別〜クラスを分ける In this school we divide the pupils into different classes *by* their sex.
外見〜人を評価してはいけません You should not judge a person *by* his appearance.
彼女は日給〜会社に雇われている The company hired her *by* the day.
家に着いたのは私の時計〜9時だった When we reached home, it was nine *by* my watch.
8 〖原因〗 a cause. ¶ 雨〜遠足が延期になった The excursion was postponed *on account of* (≒ *because of*) the rain.
きのうも全国で3人の人が交通事故〜死んだ Yesterday, for instance, three persons died *in* nationwide traffic accidents.
彼は脳出血〜亡くなった He died *of* cerebral hemorrhage.
きのうは風邪〜欠勤した Yesterday I was absent from the office *because* I had a cold.
彼は私の忠告〜まじめになった He became very diligent *following* my advice.
彼は商用〜大阪へ出張中だ He is now *on* a business trip to Osaka.
奈良は法隆寺〜有名だ Nara is famous *for* the temple Horyuji.
子どもたちは夏休み〜山へ行っている The children have gone to the mountains *for* the summer vacation.
昨夜の火事〜彼は家を焼かれてしまった His house was burnt down last night. / His house was destroyed *by* fire last night.
9 〖様態〗 ¶ 彼は悲しそうな顔〜部屋に入ってきた He came into the room looking *depressed* (≒ *sad; unhappy*).
彼は喜色満面〜私にそのニュースを知らせに来た He came to tell me the news with his face beaming *with* smiles (≒ *with* all smiles; *with* a big smile).
野党議員は激しい口調〜首相を攻撃した The opposition member attacked the prime minister *in* a fierce tone.
彼女はだれに対しても誠実な態度〜接する She is sincere with everyone she comes into contact with. / She treats everyone *with* sincerity.
彼は首席〜大学を卒業した He graduated from college first on the list. / He was at the head of the class when he graduated from college.
10 〖人数〗 ¶ 彼らは3人〜私の家を訪ねてきた Those three came to see me.
この菓子をふたり〜分けなさい You can divide this cake *between* the two of you.
この仕事は私ひとり〜やったのではない I didn't do it all *by myself*.
11 〖そのうえに・そして・それで〗 ¶ 彼は勤勉〜心の優しい男だ He is *not only* diligent *but* kind-hearted.
彼は美人〜働き者の女性と結婚した He married a pretty *and* hard-working girl.
〜, 先方の返事はどうでしたか *And*, what was their answer?
〜, 結局うまくいかなかったのか *And*, you say it didn't go well after all?
12 〖たとえ…でも〗 ¶ どんなにがんばったところ〜, 仕事はきょうじゅうには終わらない *No matter how* hard you *may* try, it is impossible to finish it today.

てあい 【手合い】 ¶ あんな〜とはかかわらぬほうがいい You had better keep away from *that sort of people*.

であい 【出会い・出合い】 encounter. ¶ 彼との〜が私の一生の方向を決定した The *encounter* with him decided the course of my life.
—がしら ¶ ふたりは〜がしらに突き当たった They knocked against each other as they *passed*.

であ・う【出会う・出合う】 come across; meet; run into. ¶ 旅先で昔の友人に～った While traveling, I *came across* an old friend of mine. 旅行中に台風に～った I *was caught* in a typhoon during my journey.

てあか【手垢】 finger marks; dirty marks. ¶ ～のついた本 a *finger-marked* book; a book *soiled by the hand*.

てあき【手空き】 ¶ ～の人を集めてくれ Gather some *free* people. ～のときにこの仕事をやってくれないか Please do this work when you *are free* (≒ *are disengaged; are not busy*).

てあし【手足】 hands and feet; hand and foot; the limb[s]. ¶ 彼は私の～となって働いている He *renders helpful* (≒ *active*) *service* to me. / He waits on me *hand and foot*. 彼の～はしびれてきかない His *limbs* are benumbed into uselessness. 私は～を縛られた I was bound *hand and foot*.

であし【出足】 start. ¶ ～がよくないと成功はおぼつかない Unless you *make a good start* in life, you can't succeed. 投票の～がよい There is a fairly good *turnout* at the polls.

てあたりしだい【手当たり次第】 ¶ 彼はかんしゃくを起こして～に物をほうり投げた He lost his temper and threw *anything he could lay his hands on*. 彼は読書家で～に本を読む A great reader, he reads *anything that comes his way*.

てあつ・い【手厚い】 ¶ 負傷者は～い看護を受けた The injured people were treated *with tender care*. われわれはどこへ行っても～いもてなしを受けた We were received *cordially* (≒ We were given a *warm* reception) wherever we went. その住所不定の男は～く葬られた The man of no fixed address was buried *respectfully*.

てあて【手当】 **1**〘治療〙[a] treatment. ¶ この歯は早く～をしたほうがいい It would be better to *have* this tooth *looked after* soon. / You had better *have* this tooth *treated* soon.
転んでけがをしたので医務室で～してもらった I fell down and hurt myself, so I *had* the injury *dressed* in the infirmary.
負傷者たちはその場で医師の応急～を受けた The injured received [a] first-aid *treatment* by the doctors on the spot.
私の～をしてくれた医者はたいへん親切だった The doctor who *treated* me was very kind.
その傷は～を怠ったために大ごとになった The injury turned into a serious one because no proper *treatment* was given.
2〘給与・報酬〙 an allowance. ¶ 組合は家族～の5割アップを要求している The labor union is demanding a 50% raise in the family *allowance*.
先月は忙しかったので超過勤務～をたくさんもらった Last month I was so busy that I got quite a lot of overtime *pay*.
いろいろな～まで含めて月に手取り10万円です Including various *allowances* my net income is a hundred thousand yen a month.
3〘準備・予約〙 ¶ 彼は支店を開店するための商品の～を任されている He is to *provide* the commodities *for* opening a new branch.
私は引っ越しのトラックをまだ～していない I *haven't arranged for* a moving van (≒ truck) yet.

てあぶり【手焙り】 a small brazier.

てあみ【手編み】 ¶ ～のくつ下 a pair of *hand-knit* socks.

てあらい【手洗い】(便所) a lavatory. ¶ お～はどこですか Where can I *wash my hands*? / Where is the *washroom* (≒ *rest room*)?

てあら・い【手荒い】 ¶ あまり～いことをするな Don't use force. あの医者は患者を～く扱う That doctor treats his patient *roughly*. ～い連中 a *rough* crew.

である・く【出歩く】 ¶ 彼は夜よく～く He often *gads about* after dark.

てあわせ【手合わせ】(勝負) a game; a contest; a match. ¶ 将棋の～をする have *a game of* Japanese chess (*with*).

てい【体】 an attitude; an appearance. ¶ 彼はそしらぬ～でわれわれの方を見ていた He was watching us *unconcernedly*. ～よく断わられた I was refused *politely*. 彼は満足の～で部屋を出ていった He left the room *with an air of* satisfaction. 彼らはほうほうの～で逃げ出した They ran away *with bare life*.

てい【弟】 ¶ ふたりは兄たりがたく～たりがたし There is little to choose between the two.

てい【邸】 a residence; a mansion. ¶ 山田氏～ Mr. Yamada's *residence*.

てい【艇】 a boat.

てい【亭】(料亭) a restaurant; (あずま屋) an arbor.

ていあつ【低圧】 low pressure; 〔電気〕 low tension (≒ voltage).

ていあつ【定圧】 constant pressure.

ていあん【提案】 a proposal; a proposition; a suggestion. ¶ 労働組合員はその～を可決した The trade unionists adopted the *proposal*. …という～があった It *was proposed* that.... 会長の選出方法について～します Let me *make a proposal* on the way of electing the president.
—者 a proposer; a mover.

ていい【帝位】 the throne; the crown. ¶ ～につく accede to (≒ ascend; mount; come to) *the throne*. ～をつぐ(うばう) succeed to (seize) *the throne*. ～をゆずる abdicate *the throne* (≒ *crown*).

ティー(お茶) tea.
—カップ a teacup. **—スプーン** a teaspoon. **—タイム** teatime. **—パーティー** a tea party. **—ルーム** a tearoom.

ティーじょうぎ【T定規】 a T square.

ディーゼル Diesel.
—エンジン a Diesel engine.

ティーチングマシン a teaching machine.

ていいん【定員】[a] capacity. ¶ ～は守るべきだ We must be careful not to exceed the *capacity*. この劇場の～は500人だ This theater has *a capacity* of 500 seats. このバスの～は何人ですか What is the *seating capacity* of this bus? この会社の従業員の～は30名だ This firm has thirty employees. まだ～には及ばない The passengers have not reached *the fixed number* yet. この車は～以上乗せている This car *is overloaded*. この船は～以上の客を乗せては危ない This ship is dangerous if it carries more passengers than the *capacity*. この観光船は～を無視しているようだ This sightseeing ship seems to be ignoring *passenger capacity* on purpose. 委員会は～に達している The committee members have reached 〔the〕 *full quota*.

—増 the increase of the regular number.
—法 the personnel strength law.

ティーンエージャー a teen-ager ; a teener (13歳から19歳までをいう). ¶ ～の少女 a *teen-age* girl.

ていえん【庭園】 a garden. ¶ 日本式～を造る build *a* Japanese-style *garden*.
—術 landscape gardening.

ていおう【帝王】 an emperor ; a monarch ; a sovereign.
—切開 ¶ ～切開をする perform *a Caesarean operation*.

ていおん【低音】 a low tone ; 〘音楽〙 bass.
—歌手 a bass. —部 〘音楽〙 bass.

ていおん【低温】 a low temperature.
—殺菌 low-temperature pasteurization.

ていか【低下】 a fall ; a drop ; a decline. ¶ 最近学生の学力がとみに～している There has been *a* considerable *decline* (≒ *downslide*) *in* the students' scholastic attainments lately. 温度は氷点下５度まで～した The temperature *dropped* (≒ *declined* ; *fell*) to five degrees below zero. 品質が～した The quality of goods *deteriorated* (≒ *grew worse*). (人は) 貧しくなるとよく道徳も～する Poverty often causes (≒ leads to) the moral *degeneracy* of the people.

ていか【定価】 a fixed (≒ regular ; list) price. ¶ この本の～は1,000円だ This book *is priced at* 1,000 yen. ～を１割引き下げた We made a discount of ten percent on the *regular prices*. あの店では品物を～どおりに売る They sell their articles at the *fixed price* at that store.
—表 a price list.

ていかい【低回・低徊】 loitering in meditation; lingering. ¶ 故人となった恩師の旧宅を訪れたとき, 私は～去るあたわざるものがあった When I visited the old home of my deceased teacher, I could hardly tear myself away from it.
—趣味 dilettantism.

ていかい【停会】 suspension ; prorogation ; 〔an〕 adjournment.

ていかく【底角】 〘数学〙 a base angle.

ていがく【低額】 a small amount.
—所得者 people in the lower-income brackets ; underpaid people.

ていがく【定額】 a fixed amount. ¶ 積立貯金が～に達した The installment savings have come up to the *specified amount*.
—所得 a fixed income. —貯金 a fixed deposit.

ていがく【停学】 suspension from school. ¶ 彼は無期～に処せられた He *was suspended from school* for an indefinite period.

ていがくねん【低学年】 the lower classes (≒ grades). ¶ ～の生徒 children *in the lower grades*.

ていかん【定款】 the articles of association (≒ incorporation).

ていかん【諦観】 resignation. ¶ 世の中のことを～できるほど年はとっていない I am not old enough to *be philosophical about* the world (≒ *look upon* the world *with philosophy*).

ていかんし【定冠詞】 〘文法〙 the definite article.

ていき【定期】 a fixed term (≒ period). ¶ この湖には～の遊覧船がある There is a *regular* sightseeing vessel available on this lake. 委員会は～に開かれる The committee meeting is held *at regular intervals*. 機械は～に運転されている The machine is operated *regularly*. 会議は～的に催されることになっている The conference is to be held *periodically*.
—刊行物 a periodical. —券 米 a commuter's ticket ; 英 a season-ticket. —券購入証明書 a commuter's certificate. —試験 a regular examination. —船 a 〔regular〕 liner. —預金 a fixed deposit. ¶ 私は銀行に100万円の～預金がある I have *a fixed deposit* of a million yen in a bank.

ていき【提起】 ¶ 問題を～する *pose* (≒ *bring forward*) a problem. 妻のほうが離婚訴訟を～した The wife *started* divorce proceedings. / The wife *instituted* a divorce suit.

ていぎ【定義】 a definition. ¶ 三角形の～ the *definition* of a triangle. その本は「民主主義」ということばにどういう～を与えていますか What *definition* does that book give of the word 'democracy'?

ていぎ【提議】 a proposal. ¶ きょうの教授会で私は学生の定員を増やそうと～した At today's faculty meeting I made *a proposal* for increasing the number of students. 労働組合は社員の保養施設をもっと改善すべきだと会社に～した The labor union *suggested* to the company that recreational facilities for the workers should be improved more greatly.

ていきあつ【低気圧】 a low 〔atmospheric〕 pressure. ¶ ～の中心が海上にある The center of *a depression* is on the sea. 彼はきょう～だ (気げんが悪い) He *is in a bad temper* today.

ていきゅう【低級】 a low grade. ¶ ～な趣味 a *low* taste. ～な雑誌 a *cheap* magazine. ～なテレビ番組 *vulgar* TV programs.

ていきゅう【庭球】 〔lawn〕 tennis.

ていきゅうび【定休日】 a regular holiday. ¶ うちでは月曜日が～です We *are closed* on Mondays.

ていきょう【提供】 an offer. ¶ おもしろい情報を～する I will *give* you an interesting information. 私の家を会場に～しよう I will *offer* my house as the meeting place. 彼はこの問題について信頼すべき資料を～してくれた He *furnished* (≒ *produced*) reliable data on this subject. これはM社～の番組です This is a program *sponsored by* M company.

ていぎょう【定業】¶ きみは早く～につくべきだ You should get *a regular employment* (≒ *a regular job*) as soon as possible.

ていくう【低空】a low altitude (≒ sky).
—飛行 a low altitude flight. ¶ ～飛行をする fly *low* (≒ *at a low altitude*).

ていけい【定型】a fixed form ; a type.
—詩 rhymed verse ; a fixed form of verse.

ていけい【提携】co-operation. ¶ A社とB社は～して新しい事業を始めた A and B Cos. *joined hands* (≒ *tied up*) *with each other* to start a new enterprise. わが社の財政を建て直すにはあの会社と～しなければならない We must *be tied up with* that company in order to improve our financial condition.
技術— a technical tie up.

ていけい【梯形】a trapezoid.

ていけつ【締結】conclusion. ¶ 日本は1951年にアメリカと講和条約を～した Japan *concluded* a peace treaty with the United States in 1951.

ていけん【定見】a definite (≒ fixed) view (≒ opinion). ¶ 彼の無～さには驚かざるをえない I can't help being surprised at his lack of *fixed principle*.

ていげん【低減】decrease. ¶ 投票率の～を防ぐ prevent the *decrease* of the voting rate.

ていげん【提言】⇒ていあん

ていげん【逓減】successive diminution. ¶ 価値～の法則 the law of *diminishing* value.

ていこ【艇庫】a boathouse.

ていこう【抵抗】resistance. ¶ 彼はわれわれに～した He *resisted* us. 彼らは警官に頑強(がんきょう)に～している They are offering stubborn *resistance* to the policemen. 少なからぬ～が予想される Not a little *resistance* is to be expected. 彼ひとりで敵に最後の～をした He *made a last effort against* the enemy [all] by himself. きみのそういう考え方に私は～がある I cannot but feel *resistance* to your way of thinking. ～せず私に従いなさい Follow me *without complaining*. 彼の誘惑には～しがたい His temptation *is irresistible*. 負傷者は相当～したらしい We can see signs of strong struggle made by those who were injured. 空気の～ air *resistance*. 電気の～ electric *resistance*.
—力 ¶ 彼は病気に～力が弱い He has little *resistance* to disease. この子どもは～力をもっと大きくする必要がある We must increase this child's *resistance* to disease.

ていこく【定刻】a fixed time. ¶ ～までにおいでください Please come over by *the appointed time*. ～に開会した The meeting opened *punctually* (≒ *on time*). 列車は～より30分遅れて到着した The train arrived half an hour behind *time* (≒ *schedule*).

ていこく【帝国】an empire.
—議会 Imperial Diet. —主義 imperialism. —主義者 an imperialist. 大英— the British Empire.

ていさい【体裁】appearance. ¶ この箱は～がいい This box *looks smart*. 彼は～などかまわない He does not mind *how he looks*. これよりあれのほうが～がいい That one *looks better* than this. 上着を着ていないのは私ひとりだけだったので, ～が悪かった I was the only person without a suit, so I *felt awkward*. 彼は～のいいことばかり言っている He is always saying *pleasant things*. 彼女はとかく～ぶる She is likely to *put on airs*.

ていさつ【偵察】scouting ; reconnaissance. ¶ 彼は～に行ったが, 無事に帰ってきた He went *scouting* and returned safe. 彼は今敵の動きを～中だ He *is now on the scout* for the enemy's movements.
—機 a reconnaissance plane. —隊 a reconnoitering party.

ていし【停止】stop. ¶ 会社は支払を～した The firm *suspended* payment. その雑誌は発行を～された The magazine *was suspended*. 警官はバスに～を命じた The policeman ordered the bus to *stop*. エンジンは～している The engine *is turned off*. 仕事は一時～している The work *has come to a standstill* temporarily. 選手は1週間の出場～となった The player *was suspended* for a week.
—信号 a stop signal. —線 the stop line. 出場— suspension.

ていじ【丁字】¶ ～形の T-shaped.
—路 a three-forked road.

ていじ【定時】a fixed time. ¶ 列車は～に発車した The train started *on schedule*. / The train started *at the scheduled time*. 彼はいつも～に退社した He always observed *regular* [*office*] *hours*.
—制高校 a part-time high school. —総会 a regular general meeting.

ていじ【提示】presentation. ¶ 身分証明書を～してください *Show* us (≒ *Produce*) your identification card.

ていしせい【低姿勢】¶ 首相は野党に対して～をとった The prime minister adopted *a low* (≒ *modest*) *attitude* toward the Opposition party. 彼もこのごろはいやに～になってきた He has recently come to *act very courteously to* us.

ていしゃ【停車】a stop. ¶ 列車はこの駅で5分間～する The train *makes a* five minutes *stop* at this station.
一時— ¶ 踏切で一時～した I *brought* my car *to a momentary stop* at the railway crossing.

ていしゅ【亭主】(主人) the master ; (夫) *one's* husband. ¶ 彼女は～をしりに敷いている She *henpecks her husband*.
—関白 ¶ 彼は～関白だ He is the boss in his home. —持ち ¶ 彼女は～持ちの女には見えない She doesn't look *a married woman*.

ていじゅう【定住】settlement. ¶ 私は郷里に

〜することにした I made up my mind to *settle down* in my home town.

—者 a permanent resident. —地 a permanent abode (≒ home ; residence).

ていしゅうにゅう【定収入】a fixed (≒ regular) income.

ていしゅうは【低周波】〘電気〙low frequency.

ていしゅく【貞淑】virtue. ¶〜な妻 a *virtuous* (≒ *chaste* ; *modest*) wife.

ていしゅつ【提出】presentation. ¶答案を〜する *hand in* (≒ *turn in*) an examination paper. 弁護士は被告に有利な証拠を〜した The lawyer *produced* evidence in favor of the accused. 必要書類の〜を求められた I was asked to *submit* the necessary documents. 昨日辞表を〜した I *tendered* my resignation yesterday. 願書の〜は2月10日まで You are requested to *file* (≒ *send in*) your application not later than February 10.

ていじょ【貞女】a virtuous woman.

ていしょう【提唱】advocacy ; proposal. ¶彼は世界平和を熱心に〜した He earnestly *advocated* (≒ *proposed*) world peace. / He *was an* ardent *advocate of* world peace.

—者 an advocate. ¶彼女は産児制限の〜者として知られている She is known as *an advocate* of birth control.

ていしょく【定食】(料理店の) *table d'hôte* (フランス語) ; a regular meal. ¶そのレストランで〜をとった We had *a set supper* at the restaurant.

ていしょく【定職】a regular occupation (≒ job). ¶彼には〜がない He has no *fixed employment*. / He hasn't got any *steady job*.

ていしょく【抵触】collision ; confliction. ¶きみの行為は法律に〜している Your deeds *are against* the law. / Your deeds *are contrary to* the law. 彼は前日の言と〜する発言をした He made a remark *contradictory to* the one which he made the day before.

ていしょく【停職】suspension from duty. ¶彼は3か月の〜を命じられた He *was suspended from office* for three months.

ていしん【逓信】communication.

—事務 post and telegraphic service.

ていしん【艇身】a boat's length. ¶2〜の差で勝った We won the race *by two lengths*.

ていしん【挺身】¶彼は平和運動に〜した He *volunteered* (≒ *offered himself*) *to* conduct a pacifist movement.

でいすい【泥酔】drunkenness ; intoxication. ¶〜する get dead drunk. 昨夜は〜して家に帰った I returned home *dead drunk* last night.

—者 a drunk ; a drunken person ; a drunkard (泥酔癖のある人の意にも用いる).

ていすう【定数】a fixed number ; a quorum ; 〘数学〙a constant. ¶この会の委員の〜は7人だ Seven members shall form *a quorum* at this committee. 総会は〜に足りず流会となった The general meeting was called off for want of *a quorum*.

ディスカウント〔**セール**〕〔a〕discount〔sale〕.

ディスカッション〔a〕discussion. ¶平和について〜をした We *had a discussion about* peace. / We *discussed* peace.

ディスク a disk ; a disc.

—ジョッキー a disk jockey.

てい・する【呈する】¶彼に二, 三質問を〜した I *asked* him a few questions. 彼の偉業には賛辞を〜したい I want to *pay* a compliment to his great achievement. 市場は活気を〜した The market *became* active (≒ *displayed* activity). 水害現場は惨状を〜していた The floodstricken place *presented* a tragic sight. それは既にかっ色を〜していた It *has* already *turned* brown.

てい・する【挺する】¶彼は身を〜しておぼれかかっている幼児を救った He bravely *volunteered* to save the drowning child. / He saved the drowning child *at the risk of his own life*.

ていせい【訂正】correction. ¶誤りを〜する *correct* errors.

—版 a revised edition.

ていせい【帝政】imperial government (≒ rule).

—時代 the monarchical days. —ロシア Czarist Russia.

ていせいぶんせき【定性分析】〘化学〙qualitative analysis.

ていせつ【定説】an established theory. ¶彼の研究は学界の〜を覆した His study overthrew the *established theory* in academic circles. だれがこの絵を描いたかということについては〜がない There is no *accepted opinion* as to who painted this picture.

ていせつ【貞節】faithfulness. ¶〜な妻 a *faithful* (≒ *devoted* ; *virtuous*) wife. 彼女は〜を守った She *has led a chaste life*.

ていせん【底線】〘数学〙the base.

ていせん【停船】stoppage of a ship. ¶われわれの乗った船は濃霧のため一時〜した Our ship *was* temporarily *held up* in a thick fog. われわれは近づいてきた船に〜を命じた We ordered an approaching ship to *stop*.

ていせん【停戦】a cease-fire. ¶司令部は3日間の〜を命じた The headquarters ordered them to *suspend hostilities* for three days (≒ *make a* three-day *truce*).

—協定 a cease-fire agreement. ¶〜協定は忠実に守られた The *cease-fire agreement* was observed faithfully.

ていそ【提訴】¶労働委員会に不当首切りを〜した We *appealed* (≒ *presented a case*) to the labor relations board against the unfair dismissal of us workers.

ていそう【貞操】chastity. ¶〜のかたい婦人 a woman *of chaste reputation*. 最近の若い女には〜の観念がない人が多い Many young women today have little sense of *chastity*.

ていそく【定則】an established rule ; a law.

ていぞく【低俗】¶〜な趣味(映画) a *vulgar*

taste (movie). ～なテレビ番組 *lowbrow* TV programs.

ていそくすう【定足数】a quorum. ¶ 出席者は～に満たなかった The number of those who attended the meeting did not come up to *a quorum*.

ていたい【停滞】(貨物の) accumulation ; (資金の) a tip-up ; (支払いの) falling into arrears. ¶ 彼のところでは事業がひどく～している His enterprise *is* extremely *stagnant*. 大雪のため郵便物が～している Mail *has piled up* owing to the heavy snow. / The heavy snowfall caused postal *delays*.

ていた・い【手痛い】hard ; severe. ¶ 彼は～い批判を浴びた *Severe* (≒ *Incisive* ; *Sharp*) criticisms were leveled at him. 彼はきのうの試合で～い失策を演じた He made a *serious* (≒ *fatal*) error in the game yesterday.

ていたく【邸宅】a residence.

ていたらく【為体】a 〔despicable〕 state of things. ¶ まわりの人すべてから非難されて，彼はさんざんの～だった Bitterly criticized by everybody around him, he was in *a wretched plight*.

ていだん【鼎談】a three-man talk.

でいたん【泥炭】〘地質〙 peat ; turf.
──地 a peat bog ; a turbary.

ていち【低地】low ground ; low land. ¶ 雨で市内の～は浸水した所が多かった Many of the *low-lying sections* of the city were flooded as a result of the rainfall.

ていちゃく【定着】¶ この習慣がわが国に～するまでにまだかなり年月がかかるだろう It will be long before this custom *is fully established* in this country.
──液(剤)〘写真〙 a fixing solution (agent).
──氷 fast ice.

ていちょう【丁重】courtesy ; politeness.
¶ ご～なおもてなしまことにありがとうございました Thank you very much for your *respectful* (≒ *courteous*) treatment. あの人は～に取り扱ってください I hope you will treat him *courteously*.

ていちょう【低調】dullness. ¶ わが校のクラブ活動は概して～だ The club activities in our school *are* generally *inactive*. (経済で) 市場はきわめて～だ The market *is* deplorably *slow*. ～きわまる音楽会だった The concert *was* very *tedious*.

ていちょう【艇長】a coxswain ; a cox. ¶ 汽艇の～を勤める *coxswain* a boat.

ティッシュペーパー tissue paper.

ていっぱい【手一杯】¶ ～に商売を広げるのは考えものだ It is not wise of you to extend business *to the very limit of your means*. 子どもの世話だけで～だ I'*m too busy* just taking care of my children.

ていてい【亭亭】¶ ～たる松 *towering* pines.

ていてつ【蹄鉄】a horseshoe. ¶ 馬に～を打つ *shoe* a horse.
──工 a farrier ; a shoer ; a horseshoer.
──所(業) 〔a〕 farriery.

ていてん【定点】〘数学〙 (不動点) a fixed point.
──観測 fixed point observation. ──観測船 a ship weather station.

ていでん【停電】an electricity failure ; 〔a〕 power failure. ¶ ヒューズが飛んで～した The fuse has blown and the light *went out.* / The light *has fused*. ～のためエレベーターが止まった *The electric current was off* and the elevator stopped.

ていど【程度】**1** 〘範囲・限界〙 〔a〕 degree ; a limit. ¶ すべてものには～がある There is *a limit* to everything.
この案にはある～まで賛成だ I agree to this plan *to a certain extent*.
きみの言うことはある～まではわかる I understand what you say *to some extent*.
彼の言うことにはある～の真理がある There is *some* truth in what he says.
どの～彼の言うことを信じていいか疑わしい It is doubtful *to what extent* we can trust his words.
私にはこのような本は～が高すぎる This sort of book *is too difficult* for me.
これは高校～の問題だ This is a high school *level* problem.
この地方の被害の～は大きかった This district has suffered great damage.
この～なら試験はだいじょうぶだ If you get this mark in the examination, you will pass.
2 〘水準〙 ¶ 日本は文化の～が高い Japan is in *a* high *state* of culture.
生活の～をもっと上げる raise the *standard* of living.

でいど【泥土】mud ; mire.

ていとう【抵当】〔a〕 mortgage. ¶ 彼はなにを～にとったのですか What did he accept as *security*? 彼は自分の家を～に入れた He *mortgaged* his own house. この家は500万円の～に入っている This house *is mortgaged for* five million yen. この土地は100万円の～に入っている There is *a mortgage* of a million yen on the land. この家を～にして200万円を借りた I borrowed two million yen *on* this house. この建物はぎりぎりいっぱいの～に入っている This building *is mortgaged* to the limit.
──権 〔a〕 mortgage. ──物 a security. ──流れ 〔a〕 foreclosure. 1番── a first mortgage. 2番── a second mortgage. 二重── double mortgage.

ていとく【提督】an admiral. ¶ 艦隊の～ the *admiral* of a fleet. ペリー～ *Commodore* Perry.

ていとん【停頓】a deadlock ; a standstill.
¶ 戦局は依然として～したままだ The war situation *is* still *at a deadlock*. その事故によって道路工事が～した The accident brought the construction of the road to *a standstill*.

ていねい【丁寧・叮嚀】**1** 〘丁重〙 politeness.
¶ ～に politely.
～な手紙をもらった I received a *polite* letter.
ご～なお手紙ありがとう Thank you for your *polite* letter.

他人には～にしなさい *Be polite to* others.
あの店の主人はどんな客にでも～にする That storekeeper *is civil with* every visitor to his store.
彼女はこの家の人に対しては～にする She *is polite to* people in this family.
ばか― ¶彼があまりばか～なので人々は彼を奇異に感じている Since he *is excessively polite*, people think him an eccentric.
2 〖慎重〗 ¶この品は～に扱ってほしい I want you to handle (⇆ treat) this article *carefully*.
彼は仕事が～だ He *is careful in* his work.
この事件はもっと～に調査する必要がある It is necessary to make a more *thorough* investigation of this incident.
3〖わざわざ〗¶彼はご～に自分でその店を訪ねた He *took the trouble to* make a personal visit to the store.

でいねい【泥濘】mud; mire.

ていねん【定年】the age limit. ¶彼は来年3月で会社を～で退職する He is going to retire from the office *under the age limit* next March. 私のところは60歳で～だ We are to *retire* at sixty.
―制 age limit system.

ていのう【低能】feeble-mindedness. ¶～な男 a *weak-headed* (⇆ *weak-minded*; *feeble-minded*) fellow; an *imbecile* [fellow].
―児 a weak-minded child; an imbecile child.

ていはく【停泊】mooring; anchorage.
¶港に～中の船 a ship *at anchor* in the harbor. 船は2日その港に～した The ship *was* (⇆ *lay*; *rode*) *at anchor* for two days in the harbor. 船は東京湾に～した The ship *anchored* (⇆ *came to anchor*; *dropped anchor*) in the Bay of Tokyo.

でいばんがん【泥板岩】〖鉱物〗shale.

ていひょう【定評】[a] reputation. ¶この本は～がある Everybody says this is a good book.
彼は科学者として既に～がある His *reputation* is established as a scientist. / As a scientist, his *reputation* stands very high. 彼は公正な取引をすることで～がある He has *an excellent reputation for* fair dealing. あの男はペテン師だというのが～だ He is a *notorious* cheat. (notorious は感心しないことの場合に使われる).

ていへん【底辺】the base. ¶三角形の～ *the base* of a triangle. 社会の～に住む人々がそのスラム街にひしめいている The slum is crowded with the people of *the lowest class*. 彼らは社会の～に住んでいる They live *at the bottom* of the social ladder.

ていぼう【堤防】a bank; an embankment.
¶～が切れた The *bank* gave away.

ていほん【底本】the original text.

ていほん【定本】an authentic book.

ていめい【低迷】¶最下位に～するチーム a cellar-dwelling team. 市場は～状態だ The market *is dull* (⇆ *is weak*). 暗雲～する Dark clouds *are hanging low*.

ていめん【底面】〖数学〗the base. ¶円すいの～ *the base* of a cone.

ていやく【締約】the conclusion of a treaty.
¶日本はアメリカと平和条約を～した Japan *concluded* a peace treaty with the United States.

ていよく【体よく】¶われわれは～断わられた We were *politely* refused.

ていらく【低落】a fall; a decline. ¶相場は～の一途をたどっていた The market *was* steadily *falling* (⇆ *declining*).

ていり【低利】low interest. ¶～で at *low interest*. 銀行から～で資金を借りた I got a *low-interest* loan [of money] at a bank.

ていり【定理】〖数学〗a theorem. ¶ピタゴラスの～ Pythagorean *proposition* (⇆ *theorem*).

でいり【出入り】**1** 〖出入・訪問〗coming and going.
¶～する go in and out.
彼の家は人の～が多い There are a large number of *visitors to* his house.
この会社は人の～が絶えない They constantly have *visitors* in this firm.
私はM先生のところに月に2回～している I *call on* Mr. M. twice a month.
彼はPさんのところにしばしば～している He *frequents* Mr. P's house.
彼はこの部屋に～を許されている He *is allowed free access to* this room.
その少年は学校へ～を差し止められた School *was forbidden to* him.
―口 a doorway.
2 〖取引き〗¶あなたのところには～の肉屋がありますか Do you have a *favorite* butcher?
～の大工は親切だった Our *regular* carpenter was kind.

ていりつ【定率】a fixed rate.

ていりつ【低率】a low rate. ¶(手形などの)～の割引率 a *low* discount rate.

ていりつ【鼎立】¶現在三つの勢力が～している状態である At present the three powers *are opposed to* (⇆ *are fighting with*; *are struggling against*) one another.

ていりゅう【底流】an undercurrent.

ていりゅうじょ【停留所】a station; a stop.
¶バスの～ a bus stop; 米 a bus depot.

ていりょう【定量】a fixed quantity. ¶彼は自分の～以上に酒を飲んだ He *overdrank himself*.
―分析〖化学〗quantitative analysis.

ていれ【手入れ】**1** 〖世話・つくろい〗repair.
¶公園はよく～がしてあった The park *was well taken care of*. / The park *was well kept*.
この庭は～が行き届いている This garden *is in good repair*.
芝生は～中です The lawn *is* now *under repair*.
私は毎朝バラの～をする I *trim* the rose bushes every morning.
この裏庭はずっと～していない This back yard has been neglected.
この植木の～の方法がわからないで困っている I am

て

at a loss how to *take care of* this plant. 彼は毎朝自動車の～をしている He *takes care of* his car every morning. 彼は毎朝ひげの～をする He *trims* his beard every morning.
2 〘警察の〙 ¶ きょう早朝賭博(とばく)場に～があった There was *a raid* on the gambling place early this morning.

ていれい【定例】 a custom ; usage. ¶ その法案は～閣議で可決された The bill passed at the *regular* Cabinet meeting. ～によると総会は5月に行なわれる According to *practice* a general meeting is held in May.

ディレクター a director.

ディレッタンティズム dilettantism.

ディレッタント a dilettante (複 -s ; dilettanti).

てうす【手薄】 ¶ 防備の～な所を捜して突破しよう Let's find out *the weakest* point of defense and break through it.

てうち【手打ち】 ¶ 毎月100トンの石炭を買うことで～にした We made *a bargain* (≒*a contract*) 〔with the merchant〕 to buy 100 tons of coal every month.

デージー 〘植物〙 a daisy.

データ data (単 datum). ¶ その問題に関して満足すべき～が集まった Satisfactory *data* came to hand on the subject.
—バンク a data bank.

デート a date. ¶ 彼は彼女と～した He *dated* with her. / He made *a date* with her. 彼は彼女の～の相手だ He is her *date*.

テープ a tape. ¶ (船などの歓送迎用の) ～を投げる fling *a* 〔*paper*〕 *streamer*. 彼は100メートルレースで1着で～を切った He breasted *the tape* in the 100-meter dash. 彼の演説を～に取った I *recorded* his speech *on tape*. / I *taped* his speech.
—レコーダー a tape recorder.

テーブル a table. ¶ ～の上をかたづける clear the *table*.
—スピーチ an after-dinner speech ; a speech at a dinner party. (「テーブルスピーチ」は和製英語. a table talk は食卓を囲んでする談論のこと).
—クロース a tablecloth. **—**マナー table manners.

テーマ a theme. ¶ 戦争を～にした映画 a film with war *theme*. 研究論文の～は決まりましたか Have you decided the *theme* (≒*subject*) of your thesis? 人間愛はその作家が好んで用いる～である Humanism has been *a* favorite *theme* (≒*subject*) with the writer.
—ソング a theme song.

テール tail.
—エンド the tail end. **—**ライト a taillight.

ておい【手負い】 ¶ ～のトラ a *wounded* tiger.

ておくれ【手後れ】 ¶ 今から出発するのではもう～だ *It's too late to* start now. 彼はもう～だ (回復の見込みがない) I'm afraid he *is quite beyond recovery*. / I'm afraid he *has no chance to recover*.

ておけ【手桶】 a pail (発音は [peil]).

ておしぐるま【手押し車】 a handcart ; a push-cart ; a wheelbarrow.

ておち【手落ち】 a fault. ¶ それはぼくの～であってきみの～ではない It's my *fault*, not yours. / It is not you but I who *am to blame for* it. 私にはなんの～もないと思います I don't see that I *am to blame* in any way. ちょっとした～があって, ご返事が届かなかったのです Through *an oversight*, your letter was left unanswered.

ておの【手斧】 a hachet.

ており【手織り】 ¶ ～のじゅうたん a *hand-made* carpet. ～の木綿 *homespun* cotton cloth.

てかがみ【手鏡】 a handmirror.

てがかり【手掛かり・手懸かり】 (糸口) a clue ; (痕跡) a trace. ¶ 唯一の～は犯人が残していった眼鏡だけだった The only *clue* was a pair of glasses lost by the robber. 彼の行方を捜す～がまったくつかめなかった We failed to find any *trace* of him. 殺人者はなんの～も残さず消えてしまった The murderer disappeared without leaving any *trace* behind. 問題解決の～が見つからなかった We could find no solution to the problem. いろいろと調査したが～はつかめなかった All inquiries have drawn blank.

てがき【手書き】 handwriting. ¶ 書類の～のコピーをとる copy a document *by hand*.

でがけ【出掛け】 ¶ ～に雨が降りだした Just as I was going out, it began to rain.

てが・ける【手懸ける】 ¶ あれは私が最初に～けた仕事だ That was my first business. 私は小学生を～けたことがない I *have* no *experience with* primary school boys and girls. / I *have* no *experience in* teaching primary school boys and girls.

でか・ける【出掛ける】 ¶ これから～けるところだ I'm just *going out*. あす旅行に～ける I'm *starting* on a trip tomorrow. そろそろ～ける時間だ It's time to *start*. / It's time we *started*. 彼は今～けている He *is out* now. 彼女は買い物に～けている She *has gone* shopping.

てかげん【手加減】 consideration. ¶ 彼は若いのだから～してやらねばならない We should *make allowances for* his youth. / We should *take* his youth *into consideration*. / We should *consider* his youth.

てかご【手籠】 a 〔hand〕 basket.

でかした【出来した】 Well done! / Excellent! / Bravo!

てかせ【手枷・手械】 handcuffs.

でかせぎ【出稼ぎ】 ¶ 彼は冬は都会に～に行く He *works away from home* in a big city during the winter.

てがた【手形】 a draft ; a bill. ¶ 彼に5万円の～を振り出した I drew *a bill on* him *for* 50,000 yen. この～の割引をしてもらいたい I want to have this *bill* discounted. その～を現金に替えた I got the *draft* cashed. ～で支払っていいですか Can I pay *by draft*? その～はまもなく期限が来る The *bill* will soon fall due. この～は期日が過ぎている This *bill* is overdue.
—振出人 the drawer of a bill. **—**割引 dis-

counting of a bill. 受取── a bill receivable. 空── a windbill. 支払── a bill payable. 不渡── a dishonored bill (≒ draft). ¶ 彼は50万円の不渡～を振り出した He passed *a bad draft for* 500,000 yen. 約束── a promissory note.

でかた【出方】¶ あのときの彼の～には驚いた I was surprised at his *attitude* then. 先方の～しだいだ It all depends upon *how* he will *act*.

てがた·い【手堅い】steady; reliable; sound. ¶ ～い方針 a *steady* (≒ *sound*) plan. ～い商人 a *reliable* merchant. ～い投資 a *safe* investment. 彼は～い商売をしている He does a *conservative* business.

デカダン decadence. ¶ 彼は～な生活を送っている He leads a *decadent* life.

てかてか ¶ ～のはげ頭 a *shining* bald head. 彼はポマードで頭を～にした He *plastered* his hair with brilliantine pomade.

てがみ【手紙】a letter. ¶ 今～を書いている I am writing *a letter*. お～拝見しました I have received your *letter*. 6月1日づけのお～拝受しました I have received your *letter* dated [of] June 1. 彼に～を出そう I will *write* [*to*] him. お～ありがとう Thank you for your kind *letter*. 彼は週に1度父親に～を出す He *writes to* his father once a week. 彼に～の返事をまだしていない I have not answered his *letter*. 東京の娘から毎週～がくる I *hear from* my daughter in Tokyo every week. アメリカにいる友人と～のやりとりをしている I *correspond with* a friend of mine in America. この～の料金はいくらですか How much is the postage on this *letter*? 彼は退院したと～で知らせてきた He informed me *by letter* that he had left the hospital. 10時に駅に迎えにきてくれと彼は～でいってきた He sent me *a letter* asking me to meet him at the station at ten. その～は配達違いになった The *letter* has been misplaced.

てがら【手柄】a merit; an exploit. ¶ 彼はその戦闘で～を立てた He *distinguished himself* in the battle. それは彼の～だ The *credit* goes to (≒ belongs to) him. 彼は人の～を横取りした He took *credit* for the work done by another. そんなことをしても～にはならない You can't get any *credit* for that.
──話 ¶ 彼の～話を喜んで聞いた We listened with amusement to his *exploits*.

でがらし【出がらし】¶ ～のお茶 *thin* tea.

てがる【手軽】¶ ～な食事をとった I had a *light* meal. 紅茶とトーストで～な朝食をとった I took a *light* breakfast of tea and toast. この問題は～に考えるべきではない This problem must not be regarded *lightly*. 彼は暇があればだれとでも～に会ってくれる He *readily* gives anyone an interview if he has time to spare.

てき【敵】**1**〖争いの相手·害となるもの〗an enemy. ¶ ふたりはあらゆる点で～味方の関係にある The two *are opposed to* each other in every respect.
彼は味方は少なく～が多い He has few friends and many *enemies*.
彼は味方も多いが～も多い He has as many *enemies* as friends.
彼はすぐ～をつくる He makes *enemies* easily.
彼のような人間は人類の～だ Such a man as he is *an enemy* to the human race.
彼はその男を不倶戴天(ふぐたいてん)の～としている He looks upon the man as his sworn *enemy*.
彼は私を商売上の～としている He regards me as his business *rival*.
──艦 an enemy warship. ──機 an enemy plane. ──軍 an enemy troop.
2〖対抗者〗¶ 彼は私の～ではないといえる He may *be no match for* me.

でき【出来】¶ あの子は～がよい He is a *smart* boy. 彼は数学の～がよい He *does well in* mathematics. / He *is good at* mathematics. ことしの麦の～はどうですか How is the wheat *crop* this year? 去年は米の～がよかった We had *a* good (≒ rich) *harvest* of rice last year. この品物は～がよい(悪い) This article is of good (bad) *workmanship*. 安物は～がよくない The cheap one does not have good enough *quality or workmanship*.

できあい【出来合い】¶ ぼくは～の服でまにあう *Ready-made* clothes fit me. これは～で買った I bought it *ready-made*.

できあい【溺愛】¶ 彼は末っ子を～した He *doted upon* his youngest child. / He *loved* his youngest child *blindly*.

できあがり【出来上がり】¶ この品物の～はよいとはいえない This article cannot be said to *be* well *made*. ～はいつごろですか When will it *be completed*?

できあが·る【出来上がる】¶ ぼくの家ももうじき～る My house will soon *be completed*. 来週までに～らせてほしい I want to *have* it *ready* (≒ *finished*) by next week.

てきい【敵意】hostility. ¶ 彼は私に対して～を持っている He has (≒ feels) *hostility toward* me. 彼らは彼にあからさまに～を示した They showed *an* open *hostility to* him.

てきおう【適応】fitness; suitability; adaptation. ¶ 彼は環境によく～する He *adapts himself* well *to* his environment. 彼は今の仕事に非常に～している He *is* well (≒ best) *suited for* his present job.

てきがいしん【敵愾心】a hostile feeling. ¶ 彼らの～をあおるな Don't excite their *hostility*.

てきかく【的確】¶ 私は自分の考えを～に表現できない I cannot *adequately* (≒ *exactly*) express my opinion. 彼はわれわれの質問に～に答えた He made a *relevant* answer to our question. ～な判断が必要とされる *Impeccable* judgment is needed.

てきかく【適格】¶ 彼が～かどうか判定することは困難だ It is difficult to decide whether he *is competent* (≒ *is qualified*; *is adequate*) or not.
──者 a competent (≒ qualified) person; a person qualified (*for* a position).

てきぎ【適宜】¶ この本を～に分類してください Classify these books *as you think right*

て

(≒ *proper*). みんな各自の～な判断で行動した Everyone acted *on his own judgment* (≒ *on his own discretion*).

てきごう【適合】(一致) conformity; (適応) adaptation. ¶ 彼には新しい環境に～した生き方が望ましい It is desirable for him to *adapt himself to* the new environment. 彼は自分の習慣を彼らの習慣に～させようとした He tried to *conform* his habits *to* their habits.

てきこく【敵国】an enemy country; a hostile country.
仮想── a supposed enemy country.

できごころ【出来心】〔an〕impulse. ¶ 彼もほんの～からあんなことをしたのだ He has committed such a folly *upon a sudden impulse* (≒ *on the impulse of the moment*).

できごと【出来事】an event; (事故) an accident. ¶ 世界の～ world *events*. 日々の～ daily *events* (≒ *happenings*). そのとき恐ろしい～が起こった Then *a* dreadful *accident* happened. 彼らは会合での～を話し合った They talked over *what happened* at the meeting.

てきざい【適材】¶ 彼は委員長として～だ He is *the best* (≒ *the right*) *man* for the chairman.
──適所 the right man in the right place.

てきし【敵視】¶ 彼を～するのはよくない It is wrong to *regard* him *with hostility*. / It is wrong to *have hostility toward* him.

できし【溺死】death by drowning. ¶ 彼は波にのまれて～した He *was drowned* at sea. 彼は危うく～するところだった He narrowly escaped *drowning*.
──者 a drowned person. ──体 the body of a drowned person.

てきしゃ【適者】a fit person.
──生存 the survival of the fittest.

てきしゅ【敵手】(相手) an opponent; a match; (敵の手) enemy hands. ¶ その城は～に落ちた The castle fell into *enemy hands*.
好── a good match; a good rival.

てきしゅつ【摘出】extraction. ¶ 傷口からガラスの破片を～する *extract* (≒ *remove*) a small piece of glass from the wound.

てきしょう【敵将】an enemy commander.

てきじょう【敵状・敵情】¶ ～を探る reconnoiter *the enemy's movements*.

てきじん【敵陣】the enemy's line. ¶ ～を攻撃する make an attack upon *the enemy*〔*'s*〕*position*.

てきず【手傷】a wound; an injury. ¶ ～を負った I *was wounded*. / I received *a wound*.

テキスト a text; a textbook. ¶ 英語の～ *an* English *textbook*.
──ブック a textbook.

てき･する【適する】fit. ¶ この水は飲み水に～する This water *is good to* drink. 彼はその仕事に～している He *is suitable for* the work. この地方は野菜の栽培に～している This district *is suitable for* growing vegetables. この魚は食用には～さない This fish *is* not *good to* eat. この場所は確かに健康に～しているといえる This place can be said to *be good for* health. この国の気候は農業には～さない The climate of this country does not *suit* agriculture. 彼は学者に～している He *is suited for* scholar. このはさみは使用に～さない This pair of scissors *is* not *fit for* use. この種の食べ物は日本人には～していない This sort of food *is disagreeable to* the Japanese. この雑誌は５歳の子どもが読むには～さない This magazine *is* not *suitable for* a five-year-old child to read.

てき･する【敵する】¶ 議論では彼に～する人はいない No one can *match* (≒ *stand against*) him *in* argument.

てきせい【適正】¶ ～な価格 a *reasonable* price. ～な処置 a *suitable* measure.

てきせい【適性】fitness; aptitude. ¶ 飲料水としての～を調べる examine the *fitness* of the water for drinking.
──検査 an aptitude test. ¶ ～検査を受ける undergo *an aptitude test*.

てきせつ【適切】appropriateness. ¶ ～な行動 *apt* conduct. これは～な批評だ This is an *apt* criticism. まさに～な比喩(ゆ)だ This is indeed an *appropriate* simile. ～な処置が望ましい A *proper* measure is desirable. 彼は私に～な注意を与えてくれた He gave me an *appropriate* warning. 確かにきみの言うことは～だ What you say *is* certainly *to the point*. そのとき彼の言ったことばは確かに～だった His remark made on that occasion *was to the point*. どうも～な表現がない I cannot somehow find a *suitable* expression. この小説にこの題名は～ではない This title does not *fit* this novel. 彼は～に答えた He answered *properly*. まさにこの際～なことばといえる This is just the *right* word (≒ expression) in this case.

てきぜん【敵前】──上陸 landing on a hostile coast. ──逃亡 escape in the face of the enemy.

できそこない【出来損い】¶ ～の焼きリンゴ a *badly* baked apple. 彼はまったく～だ (ろくでなしだ) He is *a good-for-nothing*.

てきたい【敵対】hostility.
──行為 hostile actions; hostilities.

できだか【出来高】(産出高) production; 〘株式〙dealings. ¶ 米の～を調節する adjust the *production* of rice.
──払い ¶ ～払いの仕事 piecework. ～払いの職人 a pieceworker.

できたて【出来立て】¶ ～の new; brand-new; fresh; newly-made. このケーキは～だ This cake *is hot* (≒ *fresh*) *from the oven*.

てきだん【敵弾】¶ 彼は～に倒れた He was killed by *a bullet from the enemy*. / He was shot dead by the enemy.

てきだんとう【擲弾筒】a grenade discharger.

てきち【敵地】the enemy's land. ¶ ～に潜入する steal into *the enemy's territory*; steal into *the enemy's land*.

てきちゅう【的中・適中】¶ われわれの予想は～した Our expectations *came true*. 彼の矢は的に～

した He *hit* the mark.

てきど【適度】moderation. ¶ ～の睡眠は体によい *A proper amount* of sleep is good for the health. ～に飲食する eat and drink *in moderation* (≒ *moderately*).

てきとう【適当】**1**〖適当な〗moderate. ¶ ～な運動は体のためによい *Moderate* exercise is good for the health.
彼は息子に～な仕事を捜している He *is* looking for a *suitable* job for his son.
～なときに伺います I will call on you on a *proper* occasion.
彼こそこの地位にいちばん～な人物だ He *is* most *suitable* for this position.
～なことばが思いあたらなかった I could not think of a *suitable* word for it.
この随筆に～な題名を考えてほしい I want you to think of a *suitable* title for this essay.
～な条件があればお引き受けしましょう I will accept your offer on *fair* terms.
2〖適当でない〗 ¶ こんなときに笑うのは～でない Laughing *is improper* in such a case.
厚い羊毛の服は夏には～でない Thick woollen dresses *are* not *appropriate for* wearing in summer.
3〖適当に〗 ¶ ～にやってけっこうです You may do *as you think* (≒ *see*) *fit*.
～にはからっていただきたいのですが Won't you manage it *properly*?
4〖適当だ〗 ¶ この役には彼がいちばん～だ He is *the best person for* this office.

てきにん【適任】¶ 彼はその仕事に～だ He *is fit for* the work. 彼はその地位には最も～だと思う I think he is *the best man for* the post.

できね【出来値】〖商業〗a sale price.

できばえ【出来栄え】¶ 彼女の演奏はすばらしい～だった Her performance was wonderful. 彼の演説はみごとな～だった He made a very fine speech.

てきぱき ¶ 彼女は～と仕事をかたづける She does her work *in a brisk way*. / She *is quick in* her work. 彼は非常に～と話した He talked much *to the purpose*. ～とやれ Be quick [about it]! / Look sharp!

てきはつ【摘発】[a] prosecution; disclosure; [an] exposure. ¶ その汚職事件は～された The scandal *was laid bare*. 彼らは違反者を～した They *prosecuted* offenders. / They *brought* offenders *to justice*.

てきひ【適否】fitness; suitability; propriety. ¶ 彼のとった処置の～を論議した We disputed whether the measure he had taken was suitable to the occasion or not.

てきびし・い【手厳しい】rigorous; bitter; severe. ¶ このために彼は～い批判を浴びせられた This made him face *sharp* (≒ *harsh*) criticism. 彼はその政策を～く批判した He criticized the policy *bitterly*.

てきひょう【適評】a just criticism; an appropriate comment. ¶ 彼はこの問題について～を下した He made (≒ gave) *a just criticism on* this matter.

てきふてき【適不適】fitness; suitability. ¶ 自分の職業の～をよく知っている人は少ない Few people know for certain their own *fitness for* their occupation.

できふでき【出来不出来】¶ 彼の作品には～がある Some of his works are successful, others are not. 学校の科目に～があるのはやむをえない No one can do well every subject at school.

てきへい【敵兵】(集合的に) the enemy [troops]; (ひとり) an enemy [soldier].

てきほう【適法】legality. ¶ この処置は～だ These measures *are lawful*.
—行為 a legal (≒ lawful) act.

てきみかた【敵味方】opposite sides; both sides. ¶ その内戦では親子が～になって戦った Fathers and sons fought *on opposite sides* in the civil war. ～の死傷者は数知れぬほどだった There were countless casualties *on both sides*.

てきめん【覿面】¶ その子をほめてやったら効果は～だった My words of praise *took an instant* (≒ *immediate*) *effect upon* the child. 勉強で徹夜をするとその疲れが～に出る All-night hard work wears me down with fatigue.

できもの【出来物】a boil; a tumo[u]r; (はれもの) a swell.

てきや【てき屋】a [street-]booth keeper.

てきやく【適役】¶ 道化師を彼がやるとはまさに～だ He is *the best man* (≒ *best fitted*) *for* the role of a clown.

てきやく【適訳】a proper translation. ¶ この熟語の～がちょっと思いつかない I can't think of *a proper* (≒ *good*) *translation* of this phrase. / I can't *translate* this phrase *properly*.

てきよう【適用】[an] application. ¶ 彼は法律の～を誤った He made a mistake in the *application* of the law. この規則は一般に～される This rule *is* generally *applicable*. 彼の言うことはすべての場合に～される What he says *holds* in every case. この理論はこの場合には～できない This theory does not *apply to* this case. この方法は～の範囲が広い This method *is of wide application*.

てきよう【摘要】a summary. ¶ 講演の～ *a summary* (≒ *an outline*) of the lecture.

てきりょう【適量】a proper quantity. ¶ 酒の～を過ごす take (≒ drink) too much. 砂糖を～加える add *a proper quantity* of sugar to (*something*).

で・きる【出来る】**1**〖可能である〗can; be able to. ¶ 私は泳ぐことが～きるが, 彼は～きない I *can* swim, but he *cannot*.
私にはそんな残酷なことは～きません I *cannot* do such a cruel thing.
何事も努力すれば～きる If you make efforts, you *can* do anything. / With effort, one *can* do anything.
～きれば会合に出席したいと思います I'd like to attend the meeting if *possible*.
あすは～きるだけ早く出かけましょう Let's start *as* early *as possible* tomorrow.

〜きるだけの援助はさせてもらう I will help you *as much as* I *can.* / Let me give you *the greatest possible* assistance.

〜きるかぎりの努力はしたつもりです I feel that I have made my *best* effort. / I think I exerted all *possible* efforts.

それは〜きない相談だ That's *impossible.* / You ask for *an impossibility.* / It's a very *tall* order.

鳥のように飛ぶことが〜きたらなあ I wish I *could* fly like a bird.

もうひと月もおそばにいて看病〜きたらと思います I wish I *could* stay a month longer to nurse you.

2 〖完成する・完了する〗 ¶ 食堂に夕食の用意が〜きています Dinner *is ready* in the dining room.

遠足の用意が〜きたら早く寝なさい If you *have made* all preparations for the excursion, go to bed early.

3 〖つくられる〗 ¶ この畑はいろいろな野菜がよく〜きる This field *yields* a large variety of vegetables. / Various vegetables *grow* well in this field.

このスイカは九州で〜きたものだ This watermelon *was produced* in Kyushu.

ことしはミカンが〜きすぎて, 産地では困っている This year's *bumper crop* of mandarin oranges has brought about problems to the producers.

新宿には新しいビルが続々と〜きている New buildings *are being built* one after another in Shinjuku.

私たちの学校は25年前に〜きた Our school *was founded* twenty-five years ago.

この眼鏡のレンズは合成樹脂で〜きている The lenses of this pair of spectacles *are made of* synthetic resin.

地球はどのようにして〜きたのだろうか I wonder how the earth *was made.* / How did the earth *form,* I wonder.

この本はとても親切に〜きている A lot of consideration went into *the making* of this book.

4 〖発生する・生じる〗 ¶ 彼は顔ににきびがたくさん〜きた Lots of pimples *broke* (≒ *came*) *out* on his face.

足にまめが〜きて歩くのに苦労した I had difficulty in walking because of blisters on my feet.

台風はどうして〜きるのか Do you know how a typhoon *is spawned*?

急用が〜きましたのでお先に失礼します I'm afraid I'll have to leave early *due to* an urgent matter.

5 〖技能がすぐれる〗 ¶ 彼は数学がとても〜きる He *is* very *good at* mathematics.

彼女はどの教科も平均してよく〜きる She *does well in* every course of study.

勉強は〜きないけれど, 憎めない生徒だ He *is bad at* his studies, but good-natured.

試験はよく〜きましたか *Were* you *successful in* the examination? / Did you *obtain good results in* the examination?

6 〖人格がすぐれた〗 ¶ 彼はほんとによく〜きた人だ He is truly a *mature* man.

てきれい【適例】a good example. ¶ 〜をあげる give *good examples.*

てきれいき【適齢期】¶ 〜の娘 a young woman *of marriageable age.*

てぎれきん【手切れ金】consolation money. ¶ 〜を出す pay *consolation money.*

てぎわ【手際】efficiency; performance. ¶ 彼なら〜よくその仕事を処理できるだろう He could manage the work *efficiently.* 彼は〜よく交通整理をした He controlled the traffic *skillfully* (≒ *with skill*). 彼の〜はなかなかよい(悪い) He does it *cleverly* (*poorly*).

てきん【手金】earnest money; a deposit. ¶ 土地を買う契約をしたので〜を打った I *made a deposit on* the land I had made a contract to buy. いかなる事情があっても〜はお返しいたしません Under no circumstances shall the *earnest money* be refunded.

てぐす【天蚕糸】silkworm gut; catgut.

てぐすね ¶ 猟師は獲物が現われるのを〜ひいて待っていた The hunter *was on the lookout* (≒ *was eagerly watching*) *for* the game.

てくせ【手癖】¶ 彼は〜が悪い He *is light-fingered.* / He *has light fingers.*

てくだ【手管】an artifice; a trick. ¶ 女の〜にかからないように気をつけよ Take care not to be caught in a woman's *toils.*

てぐち【手口】a trick; a way of doing. ¶ これが彼の例の〜だ This is his same old *game* (≒ *trick*). この事件の犯行の〜は容疑者のと似ている The *style of work* in this crime is similar to that of the suspected man.

でぐち【出口】the way out; an exit. ¶ 彼と会場の〜で待ち合わせた I waited for him at the *exit* of the hall. 〜はこちらです This is *the way out.*

てくてく ¶ 駅まで〜(と)歩いた I *trudged* along the street to the station.

テクニカル technical.

—ターム a technical term. **—**ノックアウト a technical knockout (T.K.O. と略記する).

テクニック 〔a〕 technique; 〔a〕 technic. ¶ 確かにこのピアニストの〜は一流であるが, ぼくは彼の音楽性を高く評価する気にはなれない To be sure, his *pianism* is first-rate (≒ This pianist has first-rate *technique*), but I cannot bring myself to think highly of his musicality.

でくのぼう【木偶の坊】¶ 彼は〜のようにそこに立ったままであった He kept standing there *like a wooden figure.*

てくび【手首】a wrist.

てくらがり【手暗がり】¶ 右光線で字を書くと〜になる When we write lighted from the right, we *are troubled by the shadow of our own hand.*

でくわ·す【出くわす】¶ 街角で友人とばったり〜した I *came across* a friend of mine on the street. 知らないことばに〜すたびに辞書をひいていたのでは1日に何ページも読めない If you consult a dictionary every time you *come across* a word you don't know, you can read only a few pages a day.

てこ【梃子・梃】a lever. ¶ ～を使って路上の岩を取り除いた We removed the rock from the road with *a lever*. 彼は強情だから一度言いだすと～でも動かない He is so obstinate that he *never changes his opinion*.

てこいれ【梃子入れ】promotion. ¶ 政府はその企業に～をした The government *bolstered up* the enterprise.

てごころ【手心】(自由裁量) discretion ; (しんしゃく) allowance. ¶ 教師は採点に～を加えてはならない Teachers must not *use their discretion in* marking examination papers. きみが若いからといって警察は～を加えてはくれない You must remember that the police will *make* no *allowance for* your youth.

てこず・る【手古摺る】¶ 難事件に当局は～っている The authorities *are utterly puzzled* what to do with the difficult incident. まったくこの子のいたずらには～らされる This mischievous child always *gives* me *much trouble*. 彼らを説得して気を変えさせるのにはとても～った We *had a lot of trouble* trying to persuade them to change their minds.

てごたえ【手応え】(効果) an effect ; (抵抗) resistance ; (反応) a response. ¶ 打った瞬間ホームランの～があった I *knew* it would be a homer the instant I hit the ball. 彼はいくら注意しても～のない相手だ My warning *had little or no effect* (≒ *was lost*) *upon* him.

でこぼこ【凸凹】unevenness ; (不均衡) unbalance. ¶ バスは～道を進んでいった Our bus jolted along the *rough* (≒ *bumpy*) road. 従業員が給与の～を直してほしいと会社に要求した The employees asked the company to smooth out *their inequalities* in the pay scale.

デコレーション〔a〕decoration.
—ケーキ a fancy cake ; a party cake. クリスマス— Christmas decorations.

てごろ【手頃】¶ ～な moderate. この道具は私が使うのに～だ This is a *handy* tool for me. 値段の～なカメラが欲しい I want a *moderately* priced camera. ～な値段ならその本だなを買いたい I want to buy the bookshelf if the price *is moderate*. これは誕生日の贈り物に～の品だ This is a *proper* article for a birthday present. この箱は大きさが～だ This box is a *handy* size. ～な広さの家が見つからない A house of *convenient* size has not been found. 初心者に～な英和辞書をしりませんか Do you know any English-Japanese dictionary *fit for* beginners? 彼は夫婦で住むのに～な家を捜している He is looking for a house *suitable for* him and his wife to live in. このかばんは旅行家には～でしょう This briefcase seems *within the price range of* a tourist. これは休暇中に読むのに～な小説だ This is a *suitable* novel for you to read during the vacation.

てごわ・い【手強い】¶ ～い相手だった He was a *strong* (≒ *tough* ; *formidable*) opponent.

デザート dessert. ¶ ～にでたアイスクリームは実においしかった The ice cream served at *dessert* was delicious.

デザイナー a designer.
服飾 (工業) — a dress (an industrial) designer.

デザイン a design. ¶ 彼は新しい～を次々に考案した He devised new *designs* one after another.
商業 (工業)— a commercial (an industrial) design.

でさかり【出盛り】the season. ¶ 今はミカンの～だ Mandarin oranges *are* now *in season*. 今はちょうどカキの～だ This is *the season* (≒ *the best time*) for oysters.

てさき【手先】(指先) the fingers ; (手下) a tool. ¶ ～の仕事には慣れている I am used to *hand*[*i*]*work*. ～の器用な人だ He is clever with his *fingers*. あの娘はひどく～が不器用だ Her *fingers* are all thumbs. 彼は敵の～にされた He was used as *a tool* (≒ *an agent*) of the enemy. 彼はそのボスの～になった He made himself *a minion* (≒ *a cat's paw*) of the boss.

でさき【出先】¶ 彼の～はわかりません I don't know *where he has gone*. ～で彼になにか起こったのかしら I wonder what has happened to him *on the way*. ～から便りをくれた He wrote to me from *the place where he was staying*.
—機関 a branch office (*of*).

てさぐり【手探り】groping. ¶ ～で暗がりを進んだ He *groped his way* in the dark. かぎはないかとポケットの中を～した I *felt* in my pocket *for* the key. 彼は～でマッチ箱をさがした He *felt after* the matchbox. 私は～の状態で問題の解決方法を捜しているところだ I *am* now *groping for* a solution of the problem.

てさげ【手提げ】a handbag.
—かばん a satchel ; a brief case. —金庫 a portable safe ; a cashbox.

てざわり【手触り】〔the〕touch ; the feel. ¶ この布は柔らかい～だ This cloth is soft to *the touch* (≒ *feel*). ～のよい布地だ This cloth *feels* smooth. / This cloth has *a* soft *feel*. この～は絹ではない I know this isn't silk *by the feel*.

でし【弟子】a pupil ; a disciple ; (徒弟) an apprentice. ¶ 彼に～入りした I became his *pupil*. 彼は～をとる He takes *pupils*.
内— an apprentice. 兄弟— a fellow pupil.

てしお【手塩】¶ あの子は私が～にかけて育てた子だ He is a child I have brought up *with tender care*.

てしごと【手仕事】handiwork. ¶ 彼女は～をしない日はない She does *manual work* every day.

てした【手下】a follower ; a man (複 men). ¶ 彼には～が大ぜいある He has many *followers*. ～を使って悪事を働いた He ordered *his men* to commit a crime.

てじな【手品】jugglery ; magic ; conjuring ;

conjury. ¶ ～をやる do (≒ perform) *a conjuring* (≒ *magic*) *trick.* 彼は～がうまい He is good at *jugglery.* 彼は～の種明かしをしてくれた He showed us how the *trick* was done. 彼は～でポケットからハトをだした He produced a pigeon out of his pocket by *magic.*
—師 a juggler; a conjurer; a magician.

てじゃく【手酌】 ¶ 相手がいないので～で飲んだ As I was alone, I *helped myself to sake.*

でしゃばり【出しゃばり】 [an] intrusion; (人) an intruder. ¶ きみみたいな～は人から好かれない *Obtrusive* people like you are not liked by others.

でしゃば・る【出しゃばる】 ¶ 彼はいつも～る He always *thrusts* (≒ *pokes*) *his nose into* everything. ～るな Mind your own business! ～りすぎてはいけない You must be careful not to *be* too *forward* (≒ *pushing*).

て

てじゅん【手順】 (段取り) an arrangement; a plan; (順序) an order; (手続き) procedure. ¶ 仕事の～を決めよう Let's make *arrangements* for our work. 材料がなくなったので仕事の～が狂ってしまった Lack of materials upset our *plan.*

てじょう【手錠】 handcuffs (通例複数). ¶ ～をかける handcuff (*a person*).

-でしょう ¶ 午後から雨が降る～ *I think* it will rain in the afternoon./ (米口語) *I guess* it's going to rain in the afternoon. 急げばまにあう～ You *will* (≒ *may*) be in time if you hurry. この服があなたに合う～ This dress *will* suit you. 彼はきっと合格する～ *I hope* he will pass the entrance examination. 長い旅行でさぞお疲れのこと～ You *must* be very tired after a long trip. だれもこの私の案に賛成してくれない～ *I am afraid* nobody will support this proposal of mine. 彼はきょうは来ない～ *I don't think* he will come today.

てすう【手数】 trouble. ¶ これは～のかかる仕事だ This is *troublesome* work. このほうが～がかからないですむ This will be a less *troublesome* way. きみにそんなに～をかけたくない I don't like to give you so much *trouble.* この機械は大いに～を省く This machine will save you much *trouble.* お～をかけてすみません I am sorry to *have troubled you.* お～をかけてすみませんが，その本を彼に送ってくれませんか I'm sorry to *trouble you,* but will you send the book to him? お～ですがテーブルの上をかたづけていただけませんか *May I trouble you to* clear the table?

てすうりょう【手数料】 (口銭) a commission; (料金) a fee. ¶ 彼はいくら～を請求しましたか How much did he *charge for trouble*? 彼は私に売上げに対して10%の～を請求した He charged me ten percent *commission on* sales. 私は彼に5%の～を支払った I payed him five percent *commission.*

てずから【手ずから】 ¶ 式が終わったあとで天皇～苗を植えられた After the ceremony the Emperor planted young trees *himself* (≒ *in person; personally*).

てすき【手透き】 leisure. ¶ お～のときおいでください Call on me when you *have nothing particular to do* (≒ *have time to spare*).

てすき【手漉き】 ¶ ～の和紙 Japanese *handmade* paper.

でずき【出好き】 a gadabout. ¶ ～な女だ She is *a gadabout.* / She *is fond of gadding about.*

です・ぎる【出過ぎる】 ¶ 前へ～ぎるな Never *go* (≒ *step*) *too forward*! お茶が～ぎた The tea *is too strong* (≒ *is too stewed*). ～ぎたまねをするな Mind your own business. / Never *put yourself forward*!

デスク (机) a desk; (新聞の編集部) the desk. ¶ 社会部の～ *a deskman* in the local news section.
—プラン a desk plan.

てすじ【手筋】 ¶ 彼の字は～がよい(悪い) He *writes a good* (*bad*) *hand.* / He *has* (*doesn't have*) *an aptitude for handwriting.* 彼はなかなか碁の～がいい He has *a gift for* the game of *go.*

テスト a test. ¶ 英語の～を受けた We took (≒ had) *a test* in English. 自動車の性能を～した I had *a* performance *test* of the car. 先生は数学の～をした The teacher gave us *a* math *test.*
—ケース a test case. —パイロット a test pilot. 学力(知能)— an achievement (an intelligence) test.

デスマスク a deathmask.

てすり【手摺り】 a handrail; a railing.

てずり【手刷り】 hand-printing. ¶ ～の年賀状 a New Year's card *printed by hand.*

てせい【手製】 ¶ ～の家具 *homemade* furniture. このケーキは～だ These are *homemade* cakes. / These are cakes *of my own making.* 彼女のお～の料理をごちそうになった We were treated to some dishes she *cooked herself.*

てぜい【手勢】 ¶ ～を引き連れて敵陣に乗り込んだ I rushed into the enemy's camp *with my men.*

てぜま【手狭】 ¶ ～な仕事場でお気の毒です I am sorry this workshop *is too small for* you. この事務室は～で身動きもできないくらいだ We *have not room enough to swing a cat* in this office.

てそう【手相】 the lines of the palm. ¶ 彼は～を見る He can read *a person's palm* (≒ *hand*). 易者に～を見てもらった I had my *palm* read by a fortuneteller. あなたの～はよい You have *lucky lines in your palm.*
—見 a palmist. —学 palmistry.

でぞめ【出初め】 ¶ 新年の～式 the New Year's parade of fire brigades.

でそろ・う【出揃う】 ¶ 季節の花が一時に～った The flowers of the season *were all out* (≒ *came out fully*) at a time. みんな～ったから出発しよう Let's start as all of us *are here.*

てだし【手出し】 interference. ¶ ～する meddle (*in*). 他人のことに～をするな Never *interfere with* others. 先に～をするな Don't be the first to *pick up the quarrel.* 彼は女に～する機会をねらっている He is always looking for a chance to *make advances.* 彼は株に～して失敗した He *dabbled in* stocks, and ended in a failure. その問題には～したくない I don't want to *have anything to do with* the matter. 彼がこの問題に～したはずがない He cannot *have been mixed up in* this matter. 彼には～をするるな *Keep away from* him.

でだし【出だし】¶すべて～が大事だ It is very important how to *start* in everything. なかなかよい～だ We made *a* very good *start.*

てだすけ【手助け】〔an〕help. ¶目下母の家事の～をしている I *am* now *helping* my mother 〔to〕 keep house at home. 娘がひじょうに私の～になっている My daughter *is* very *helpful* (≒ *is a* great *help*) *to* me. 私には～をしてくれる人がひとりもいない I have no one to *help* me.

てだて【手だて】a means (means は単複同形). ¶経営を立て直すよい～はないか Don't you have *a* good *means* of rebuilding our business?

でたて【出たて】¶彼は大学～のうちの社員だ He is a fresh member of our company who *has just graduated from* a university. お茶の～をいれてあげましょう I will make you *fresh tea.* 彼は田舎から～で東京の生活のめまぐるしさにまごまごするばかりであった He, *fresh from* the country, was simply bewildered by the hectic life in Tokyo.

でたとこしょうぶ【出たとこ勝負】¶～で試験に臨んだ I went to take the exam *without making any preparations.*

てだま【手玉】¶相手を～にとった I *made sport of* my opponent.

でたらめ【出鱈目】nonsense. ¶～を言う talk *nonsense*; talk *at random.* 彼は～な男だ He is such an *unreliable* man. まったく～な話だ It's all *nonsense.* / It's quite a *tall* (≒ *made-up*) story. ぼくは～に本を読む I read books *at random.* / I am a *desultory* reader.

てぢか【手近】¶～にあるものからかたづける put in order anything *near at hand.* ～な例をあげて説明してあげよう I will explain it to you by giving a *familiar* example.

てちがい【手違い】(失敗) a mistake; a blunder; (事故) an accident. ¶私どもの～でご迷惑をかけて申しわけありません I am very sorry to have put you to much trouble by some *mistake* of ours. 計画がずさんで～が生じた As it was a careless plan, it *went wrong* with us.

てちょう【手帳】a notebook. ¶～に書く write down in *one's notebook.*

てつ【鉄】iron; (鋼鉄) steel. ¶～のカーテン the *iron* curtain. ～の意志 an *iron* will. ～を鍛えて刀をつくる The blade is forged from *steel.* ～は熱いうちに打て (諺) *Strike while the iron is hot.*

てつ【轍】¶前車の～を踏むなかれ Don't repeat the mistake of others. / Take a lesson from another's failure.

てついろ【鉄色】iron-blue; reddish-black.

てっかい【撤回】withdrawal; repeal. ¶前言を～すべきだ You have to *withdraw* your former statement. / You should *get* the proposal *abandoned.* 辞表を～した I *withdrew* my resignation.

てつがく【哲学】philosophy. ¶彼はすべて～的に考える He thinks of everything *philosophically.* これが私の～です This is my *way of thinking.*

—史 a history of philosophy. —者 a philosopher. —博士 Doctor of Philosophy.

てつかぶと【鉄兜】a steelhelmet; a trench helmet.

てづかみ【手掴み】¶彼はケーキを～で食べた He ate cake *with his fingers.* 彼は水にもぐってコイを～にした Diving in water, he *seized* a carp *by hand.*

てっかん【鉄管】an iron tube; an iron pipe.

てっき【鉄器】ironware; 米 hardware.

—時代 the Iron Age. ほうろう— enamelware.

てつき【手つき】¶不器用な～でカードを配る deal 〔the〕 cards with clumsy *hands.* 変な～をする *make* awkward *gestures* with hands.

デッキ (船) the deck; (列車の中の出入口など) the platform.

—チェア a deck chair.

てっきょ【撤去】〔a〕withdrawal; 〔a〕removal. ¶障害物を～する *remove* an obstacle. 工場を～する *take away* a factory. 軍隊を～する *withdraw* troops (*from*).

てっきょう【鉄橋】an iron bridge; (鉄道の) a railway bridge.

てっきり certainly. ¶このいたずらは～彼の仕業だと思った I concluded that he did the naughty thing.

てっきん【鉄琴】an iron xylophone (発音は [záiləfoun]).

てっきんコンクリート【鉄筋コンクリート】ferro-concrete. ¶～コンクリートの建物 a *ferro-concrete* building.

てつくず【鉄屑】scrap iron.

でつく・す【出尽くす】¶ご意見は～したようなので採決します As it seems that the last opinion has been said, let's come to a vote.

てづくり【手作り】¶～の梅酒 *home-made* plum-brandy. ～の人形 a *hand-made* doll.

てつけ【手付け】earnest money; a deposit. ¶1万円の～を払った I *made a deposit of* ten thousand yen. / I *placed* ten thousand yen *on deposit.*

てっけん【鉄拳】a fist. ¶～制裁を加える administer *fist law.*

てっこう【鉄鋼】iron and steel.

—業 the steel industry.

てっこう【鉄鉱】iron ore.

てっこうじょ【鉄工所】an ironworks.

てっこつ【鉄骨】a steel frame; an iron frame. ¶～の建造物 an *iron frame* building.

てつざい【鉄材】iron 〔material〕; steel.

て

てつざい【鉄剤】an iron preparation; a ferrous medicine.

てっさく【鉄柵】an iron railing; an iron fence.

てっさく【鉄索】a cable.

デッサン a sketch; a drawing; a design.

てっしゅう【撤収】〔a〕withdrawal. ¶ 軍隊を〜する *withdraw* troops (*from*).

てつじょうもう【鉄条網】barbed wire entanglements. ¶ 牧場のまわりに〜を張る put *barbed wire* around the meadow. 彼らは〜を突破して突き進んだ They broke through *barbed entanglements.*

てつじん【哲人】a philosopher; a sage; a man of wisdom.

てつじん【鉄人】an iron〔-bound〕man; an unyielding man.

てっ·する【徹する】¶ 彼は夜を〜して働く He keeps working *all night.* 彼女は夜を〜して病気の子供の看護をした She sat up *all night* with her sick child. 平和主義に〜する He *believes heart and soul in* pacifism. 骨身に〜して忘れない It *has sunk deep into* my mind never to be forgotten. 彼には恨み骨髄に〜する I *have bitter rancor against* him. 学問に〜しなさい You should *devote yourself to* the pursuit of learning.

てっせい【鉄製】¶ 〜の made of iron; iron made; steel.
—品 ironwork; hardware.

てっせん【鉄線】iron wire; steel wire;〘植物〙a clematis.

てっそく【鉄則】an iron rule. ¶ 民主主義の〜 *an iron rule* of democracy.

てったい【撤退】〔a〕withdrawal;〔an〕evacuation. ¶ 占領軍が〜した The occupation forces *withdrew* (≒ *pulled out*). デモ隊は飛行場を〜した A demonstration group *left* the airport.

てつだい【手伝い】(手助け) help; assistance; aid; (人) a helper; an assistant; a maid. ¶ お〜さん a helper; a maid. なにかお〜することがありますか Can I *be of help to* you? 彼はあまり私の〜をしない He does not *help* me very much. 至急〜が必要だ We want urgent *help.*

てつだ·う【手伝う】help. ¶ 彼の仕事を〜った I *helped* him *with* his work. 〜って彼に上着を着せてあげた I *helped* him *on with* his suit. 荷物を2階に運ぶのを〜ってください Please *help* me *carry* the baggage upstairs. ちょっと〜ってくれませんか Won't you *lend me a hand?* 彼はときどき仕事を〜ってくれる He sometimes *helps* me *with* my work.

でっち【丁稚】an apprentice; a shopboy. ¶ 私は呉服屋に〜奉公をした I *served my apprenticeship with* a draper. この店の主人は〜上がりだ The master of this shop has once been *an apprentice.*

でっちあ·げる【でっち上げる】¶ 彼は報告書を現地に行かずに〜げた He *made up* a report without visiting the spot.

てっちゅう【鉄柱】an iron pole.

てっつい【鉄槌】an iron hammer. ¶ 悪人に〜を下した They gave *a hard blow* to the villain. 当局は俗悪映画に〜を下した Indecent films *were banned by* the authorities. / The authorities *cracked down on* vulgar movies.

てつづき【手続き】〔a〕procedure; (正式の手続き) formalities; (訴訟手続き) proceedings. ¶ 法律上の正式〜 legal *formalities.* すぐ〜をとりなさい Go through the *formalities* at once. もう入社〜は済ませた I have gone through the entrance *formalities* to the firm. 入会の〜がわからない I don't understand *how to* join the association. 〜を怠ってはならない Never neglect the *procedure.* 〜は簡単だった The *formality* was simple. ふたりは離婚の〜をとった The couple took *proceedings for* divorce. アメリカの大学に入るにはどんな〜がいりますか What *procedure* should we follow in entering an American university? 彼は輸出の〜に明かるい He is familiar with export *procedure.*

てってい【徹底】thoroughness. ¶ その問題を〜的に調査すべきだ We should make a *thorough* investigation of the matter. 〜的改革が望まれる A *thorough* reform is needed. 医者はその患者を〜的に診察した The doctor *was thorough in* his examination of the patient. 彼を〜的にやっつけよう We will defeat him *soundly.* なにをやるにしても〜的にやりなさい Do whatever you undertake *thoroughly and completely.* 彼は女性の心理を〜的に研究した He made a *complete* study of the mentality of women. あの人の言い方はどうも〜しない Somehow he does not speak *to the point.* 自分の気持ちを人に〜させるのは難しいことだ It is difficult to *make ourselves understood perfectly.* 彼は〜した菜食主義者だ He is a *thoroughgoing* vegetarian.

てっとう【鉄塔】a steel tower; (高圧線用の) a pylon. ¶ 送電線の〜 *a* power transmission *pylon.*

てつどう【鉄道】a railroad; 英 a railway. ¶ この島には〜がない There is no *railroad service* on this island. このふたつの町の間には〜が通じている *A railroad* runs between the two cities. ここから仙台市まで〜が通じたのはいつですか When was the *railroad* laid from here to Sendai? 豪雪のため〜は一部不通になった On account of the heavy snowfall part of *the railroad service* was crippled.
—案内所 a railroad information bureau. —員 a railroad man; a railroader. —運賃 a railroad fare. —公安官 a railroad security officer. —工事 railroad construction. —工夫 (線路工夫) a tracklayer; (保線工夫) a trackman; a lineman. —事故 a railroad accident. —自殺 ¶ 彼はゆうべ〜自殺をした He *killed himself by throwing himself in front of a train* last night.

てっとうてつび【徹頭徹尾】thoroughly; in

every way; from beginning to end. ¶ 相手チームを～押しまくった We pressed the opposite team *from beginning to end.*

デッドエンド a dead end.

デッドヒート a dead heat. ¶ ～を演ずる run *a dead heat* (*with*).

デッドボール (野球で) a hit by pitch; (バスケット・サッカーなどで) a dead ball. ¶～を食う be hit by a pitched ball.

てっとりばや·い 【手っとり早い】 prompt; quick. ¶ ～く仕事をかたづけた I finished working *promptly.* / I did the work *with dispatch.* ～く言えばこうだ *In short* (≒ *To be short*; *In a word*), it is as follows.

デッドライン a deadline.

デッドロック a deadlock. ¶ ～に乗り上げる come to *a deadlock*; be deadlocked.

てつのはい 【鉄の肺】〔医学〕 an iron lung.

でっぱ 【出っ歯】 projecting teeth; protruding teeth. ¶ 彼はひどい～だ He has such *protruding teeth.*

てっぱい 【撤廃】 abolition; removal. ¶ 米の統制を～する *abolish* (≒ *lift*) the rice control. アメリカは黒人白人の差別待遇の～に熱を入れている American people are doing their best to *do away with* the discrimination between black and white.

でっぱ·る 【出っ張る】 ¶ ～った窓 a *projecting* window. あの広告板は道路に～っている The signboard *projects* into the street.

てっぱん 【鉄板】 an iron plate; a sheet of iron. ¶ ～で肉を焼く do meat on *an iron plate.*
—焼き cooking on an iron plate.

てっぴつ 【鉄筆】 a stylus.

てつびん 【鉄瓶】 an iron kettle.

でっぷり〔と〕 ¶ ～太った男 a *fat* man. ～太った重役 a *portly* director.

てつぶん 【鉄分】 iron. ¶ ～のある温泉 a hot spring containing *iron.* ホウレンソウには～が含まれている Spinage contains *iron.*

てっぺい 【撤兵】 the withdrawal of troops; evacuation; removal. ¶ ～する withdraw troops (*from*); evacuate (a place).

てっぺき 【鉄壁】 ¶ ～の守備 an *impregnable* defence. ～の陣 an *impregnable* (≒ *unassailable*) position. 金城～ an *impregnable* fortress.

てっぺん 【鉄片】 a piece of iron; a scrap of iron.

てっぺん 【天辺】 the top; the summit. ¶ 山の～に登った I reached the mountain *summit.* 彼は私を頭の～からつま先までじろじろ見た He stared at me *from top to toe* (≒ *from top to bottom*). 彼は頭の～がはげている He has a bald *pate.*

てつぼう 【鉄棒】 (鉄の棒) an iron bar; an iron club; (体操用具) a horizontal bar; (競技種目) the horizontal bar. ¶ ～で優勝した I was placed first in *horizontal bar exercise.*

てっぽう 【鉄砲】 a gun; a rifle. ¶ ～を撃つ shoot (≒ fire; discharge) *a gun.* 彼は私に～を向けた He leveled *a gun* at me. 家の近くで～の音を聞いた I heard *a gun* report near my house.
—傷 a bullet wound. —弾 a bullet.

てづまり 【手詰まり】 a standstill; a stalemate. ¶ 両者の交渉は～状態になった The two parties have come to *a standstill* (≒ *a deadlock*). ～状態である be at *a standstill* (≒ *a deadlock*). ～状態を打開する break *a deadlock.* (将棋で) ～だ I have no good move to make. / I *am stalemated.*

てつめんぴ 【鉄面皮】 impudence; shamelessness. ¶ ～な行為 *shameless* conduct. 彼は～な男だ He is an *impudent* (≒ a *cheeky*; a *brazenfaced*) fellow. 彼は～にも助けを求めてきた He *had the impudence* (≒ *cheek*) to ask for help.

てつや 【徹夜】 all night; throughout the night. ¶ ゆうべは～で勉強した I sat up *all night* studying last night. 彼女は病気の夫を～で看病した She sat up *all night* with her sick husband. ～の会議を開いた We had an *all-night* conference.

てつり 【哲理】 philosophy; philosophical principles.

てづり 【手釣り】 ¶ タイの～ the *hand-line fishing* of sea breams.

てづる 【手蔓】 (縁故) 〔a〕 connection; (仲介) 〔a〕 medium; (勢力) influence. ¶ 彼の～で就職した I got employment through his *influence.* 事件の～をつかんだ We found out the *connection* of the case. 彼は～をたどって金策に走りまわっている He is busy going for a loan of money, seeking *connections.*

てつわん 【鉄腕】 an iron arm.
—投手 an iron arm pitcher.

ててなしご 【父無し子】 (父のない子) a fatherless child; (私生児) an illegitimate child; a bastard.

でどころ 【出所】 the source; the origin. ¶ 麻薬の～を調べている We are looking for the *source* of the drug. うわさの～はどうも彼らしい The rumor seems to *have originated with* (≒ *from*) him.

テトラポッド a tetrapod.

てどり 【手取り】 (純益) a net profit; a net income. ¶ 私の給料は～で5万円だ My *take-home pay* (≒ My *salary after tax*) comes to 50,000 yen. 売り上げの～は15万円になる The *net proceeds* of the sale will come to 150,000 yen.

てとりあしとり 【手取り足取り】 ¶ 彼に～やっとそれをやらせた I *forced* him *to* do it. / I made him do it *with great patience.*

てなおし 【手直し】 ¶ 賃銀体系は～の要がある The wage structure needs to *be corrected* (≒ *be rectified*).

でなお·す 【出直す】 ¶ ～してまた参ります I will *call again.* 商売に失敗したのでまたゼロから～す I failed in business. I will *make a fresh start.*

てながざる 【手長猿】 a long-armed monkey.

てなぐさみ 【手慰み】 (遊び) amusement; (ばくち) gambling. ¶ ～に絵をかく I *amuse myself* *in* drawing

てなず·ける【手なずける】¶ 彼はライオンを～けるのが得意だ He is good at *taming* lions. 彼は部下を～けるのがへただ He is weak in *winning* his men's *heart*.

てなべ【手鍋】a pan.

てなみ【手並み】dexterity; skill. ¶ お～拝見(一戦を交える) I challenge you to a game.

てならい【手習い】(習字) penmanship. ¶ 六十の～ It is never too late to learn.

てな·れる【手慣れる】¶ 彼の機械の操作は～れたものだ He *is* quite *practiced in* operating a machine.

テニス〔lawn〕tennis. ¶ ～をする play *tennis*. ～の試合 a *tennis* match (≒ tournament). ～の選手 a *tennis* player. ～のラケット a *tennis* racket.

―コート a tennis court. 硬式(軟式)― hardball (softball) tennis.

デニム denim. ¶ 彼はよく～のズボンをはいている He often wears *denim* pants.

てにもつ【手荷物】(集合的) 米〔hand〕baggage; 英〔hand〕luggage. ¶ ～1個 a piece of *baggage*. たくさんの～ much baggage. 私はスーツケースを鹿児島まで～で送った I checked my *suitcase* through to Kagoshima.

―一時預かり所 a cloakroom; 米 a checkroom. **―**取扱所 米 a baggage office; 英 a luggage office. **―**車 a baggage car.

てぬい【手縫い】¶ ～のくつ *hand-made* shoes.

てぬかり【手抜かり】an omission; an oversight. ¶ ～のないようよく注意してください Be very careful not to *omit* (≒ *miss*) *anything*. / Be very careful that *nothing is neglected*.

てぬき【手抜き】¶ 彼は仕事を～する He *skimps* (≒ *scamps*) his work.

てぬぐい【手拭い】a towel. ¶ ～で手をふく wipe *one's* hand with *a towel*; dry *one's* hand on *a towel*. ～を絞る wring *a towel* dry.

―掛け a towel rack.

てぬる·い【手緩い】¶ それは運転者に～い罰則だ Those are *lenient* (≒ *mild*; *lax*) penal regulations for drivers. 彼は生徒に～い He *is easy with* his students. そんな～いしかり方では彼にはだめだ Such a *slack* way of scolding has no effect on him. 彼の仕事ぶりは～い He is a *sluggish* worker. / He *is* very *slow in* working.

てのうち【手の内】¶ 私は～を見透かされた(弱みを) I had my *weak points* detected. 彼は決して人に～を見せない(何を考えてるかわからない) He never *puts his cards on the table*. 彼の～がわかった(意図がわかった) I knew his *intentions*.

てのうら【手の裏】⇒てのひら

テノール〔音楽〕tenor.

―歌手 a tenor〔singer〕.

てのこう【手の甲】the back of the hand.

てのひら【手のひら】the palm (≒ flat) of the hand. ¶ 彼の意見は～を突然返すように変わる He makes a complete change in his opinion suddenly.

デノミ〔ネーション〕〔経済学〕redenomination.

では ¶ ～すぐ伺います *Then* I will call on you at once. ～田中さんに会ったのですか *So* you saw Mr. Tanaka? ～またあした *Well*, see you again tomorrow. ～あなたは将来なにになりたいですか *Now then*, what do you want to be in the future?

-では **1**〖場所〗¶ イギリス～今どんなスポーツが行なわれていますか What sports do they enjoy *in* England?

北海道～もう雪だろう It is probably snowing *in* Hokkaido.

ここから～そのビルは見えないだろう The building will not be seen from here.

2〖時〗¶ 今から～会にまにあわない Even if I start now, I shall not be in time for the meeting.

あす～遅すぎる. きょう仕上げたい Tomorrow is too late. I am going to finish it today by all means.

3〖判断すると〗¶ この空もよう～あすは雨かもしれない *Judging from* the look of the sky, it may rain tomorrow.

この分～きょうは終わりそうにない *If things go at this rate*, this will not be completed today.

彼はこんな勉強ぶり～とても合格の見込みはない He has no chance of passing the examination *if* he continues to study this way.

私の知るかぎり～そういう英語はない *As far as* I know, there is no such English expression.

4〖に関して·について〗¶ 日本語～これをなんといいますか How do you say this *in* Japanese?

彼は競走～だれにも負けない He has no equal *in* running a race.

これ～彼は喜ぶまい He will never be delighted *with* this.

漱石のもの～「三四郎」がいちばん好きだ *Of* all the works by Soseki I like 'Sanshiro' best.

私のほう～なにも文句はない *As for* me, I have no objection.

この方面～なんといっても彼が権威だ He is every inch an authority *in* this line.

彼～きみの代理はつとまらない He cannot take your place.

5〖程度〗¶ この部屋～会場には狭すぎる This room is too small for a meeting place.

彼への贈り物にこんな品～もったいない This sort of article is too good for him as a present.

このじゅうたん～どう見てもこの部屋には不釣り合いだ No matter how you look at it, this carpet is unsuitable for this room.

この弁当～とても足りない This lunch is far from sufficient to me.

6〖用具に関して〗¶ 眼鏡なし～新聞も読めない I cannot even read a newspaper *without* my glasses.

この鉛筆～字がよく書けない This pencil does not write well.

普通のはさみ～針金は切れない You cannot cut a wire *with* ordinary scissors.

このくつ～山には登れない I cannot climb a

mountain *in* these shoes.
7 〖では…ない〗 ¶ 彼はまじめそうに見えて実はまじめ〜ない He looks like a serious man, but he actually is not.
彼は1日1回どならない〜いられない He *has to* shout loudly at least once a day.
私は人と会うと話しかけない〜いられない I *cannot help* talking with everyone I meet.
厚めのくつ下をはかない〜この寒さにとても外には出られない We cannot go out in this cold weather *without* heavy stockings on.
この子は近くの公園に行くだけ〜満足しそうもない This child is not likely to be contented merely *with going* to a neighboring park.

デパート 困 a department store; 園 the stores.

てはい【手配】 arrangements; preparations. ¶ 品物をすぐ問屋に〜します I'll *arrange for* ordering goods from a wholesale store immediately. 彼の旅行の〜をした I *made arrangements for* his journey. 八方に〜して犯人を捜している The police are searching for a criminal by *sending policemen* in every direction. 外国の大統領がこの国を訪問するので警備の〜を依頼した Anticipating the visit of a foreign president to this country, we asked to *make arrangements* (≒ *make dispositions*) *for* his guard.

てばこ【手箱】 a hand-box; a casket.

てはじめ【手始め】 ¶ 〜に to begin with; at the outset.

てはず【手筈】 (準備) arrangements; (約束) an appointment. ¶ 彼がそのパーティーの〜をととのえた He *made arrangements for* the party. 彼と会合の〜をとりきめた I *made an appointment with* him.

てばた【手旗】 a flag.
—信号 flag signaling.

でばな【出端】 ¶ 仕事の〜をくじかれてがっかりした I was unhappy because I was baffled in the work *at the outset.* 彼女は〜をくじかれたがけっして勇気を失わなかった Though discouraged *at the start,* she never lost courage.

てばなし【手放し】 ¶ 彼はわが子の成績を〜でほめたたえる He admires the school records of his son *freely* (≒ *without reserve*). 彼は恋人を〜でのろける He talks *freely* about his sweetheart.

てばな・す【手放す】 ¶ 私はたいせつな家宝を〜した I *parted with* my valuable family treasure. 私は娘を〜したくない I hate *parting with* my daughter.

でばぼうちょう【出刃包丁】 a kitchen knife.

てばや・く【手早く】 quickly; smartly. ¶ 彼は仕事を〜くかたづける He finishes his work *quick and smart.* 彼女は食後のさら洗いを〜く済ませる She finishes washing-up *quickly.*

ではら・う【出払う】 ¶ 家族は全部〜ってしまった The family *are all out.*

でばん【出番】 *one's* turn. ¶ 〜を待っている I am waiting *my turn.*

てびき【手引き】 (案内・指導) guidance; (指導者) a guide; (入門) introduction. ¶ 今度の盗難事件は, 内部の者が〜をした An insider acted as *guide* in this theft.

デビスカップ 〖テニス〗 the Davis Cup.

てひど・い【手酷い】 harsh; (無情な) merciless; (残酷な) cruel. ¶ 〜い扱いを受けた I was given a *harsh* treatment. 〜い批判 a *harsh* (≒ an *unsparing*; a *scathing*) criticism. 彼は〜く罰せられた He was *severely* punished.

デビュー a debut. ¶ 彼女は14歳で〜した She *made her debut* at fourteen.

てびょうし【手拍子】 ¶ 〜を合わせて歌った We sang *beating time with the hands.*

てびろく【手広く】 ¶ 彼は園芸の商売を〜やっている He has a *large* trade in floriculture. 彼は牧畜業を〜やっている He has an *extensive* cattle-breeding business.

でぶ ¶ 〜の女 a *fat* woman.

てふき【手拭き】 a towel.

てぶくろ【手袋】 [a pair of] gloves; (二また手袋) [a pair of] mittens.

でぶしょう【出無精】 (人) a stay-at-home.
¶ 〜な stay-at-home.

てぶそく【手不足】 a shortage of hands.
¶ 〜だ be short of hands; be difficult in finding hands. われわれは〜で困っている We are suffering from *a shortage of hands.*

てふだ【手札】 (トランプ) a hand. ¶ 〜型の写真 a card-size photograph.

でぶでぶ ¶ 〜の男 a *very fat* man.

でふね【出船】 an outgoing ship.
—入船 ¶ 〜入船でにぎわう港 a port alive with incoming and *outgoing ships.*

てぶら【手ぶら】 ¶ 彼は魚釣りに出かけたが〜で帰ってきた He went fishing but came back *empty-handed.*

てぶり【手振り】 ¶ 〜で知らせた I let him know it by *gestures.*
身振り— ¶ 彼は身振り〜もおもしろく話す He speaks with attractive *gestures.*

デフレ[ーション] 〖経済学〗 deflation.
—政策 a deflationary policy.

でべそ【出臍】 a protruding navel.

てべんとう【手弁当】 ¶ 〜で働く work *without pay.*

でほうだい【出放題】 ¶ 彼は〜にほらを吹く He talks *at random.* 取り調べに対して彼は〜のことを言った When examined, he gave *haphazard* answers.

てほどき【手解き】 initiation. ¶ 私は彼から習字の〜を受けた I received *first lessons in* handwriting from him. 彼は電子計算機の使い方を〜してもらった He *was taught how to* use an electric computer.

てほん【手本】 (模範) an example; (習字の) a copybook. ¶ 習字の〜を見て書く write from *a copybook.* 彼女の人形をお〜にしてその人形を作った I made the doll on the *model* of hers. 彼の勤務ぶりは後輩のよい〜だ His diligence is *a* good *example to* young men.

てま【手間】 (時) time; (労力) labor; (手数) trouble. ¶ 機械のおかげで〜が省ける(時間) Ma-

て

chines save much *time* for us. 彼のおかげでずいぶん～が省けた(手数) He saved me a lot of *trouble*. このごろはインスタント食品のおかげで料理する～が省ける We can now save the *trouble* of cooking by the help of the 'instant' foods.

―仕事 an odd job; piecework. **―賃** pay; wages. **―ひま** ¶ それは～ひまのかかる仕事だ It will take (≒ require) much *time and labor*.

デマ a false rumor. ¶ ～を飛ばす start *a false rumor*. 近く大地震があるという～が飛んでいる *Rumor has it that* there will be a big earthquake in the near future.

てまえ【手前】 **1** 〚こちら〛 ¶ 郵便局は川の～にある The post office is on *this side* of the river. 彼の家の～にあき地がある There is a vacant area on *this side* of his house. 公園のすぐ～の小屋のところで待とう I will wait in front of the cottage just *this side* of the park. 渋谷のひとつ～の駅で降りると便利です It may be convenient for you to get off one station *this side* of Shibuya.
2 〚体面〛 ¶ 先生の～そんなことはとてもできない I cannot do such a thing *when I think of* my teacher. 世間の～彼は恥ずかしくていられないはずだ He shouldn't be able to show his face in public. 子どもたちの～こんなところは見せられない I cannot let the children see me in such a disgraceful situation. 誓った～もう酒は飲めなくなった I cannot drink *sake* any longer *in view of* my pledge. 人様の～ということを考えなさい Be careful to behave yourself *in others' company*.

でまえ【出前】 outside catering. ¶ 昼食はそばの～を頼んだ For lunch, we ordered bowls of buckwheat noodles to be delivered from the near shop. この店は～をやる This shop does *outside catering*.
―持ち a delivery boy.

てまえがって【手前がって】 selfishness. ¶ ～な男 a *selfish* man. 彼は～な人で困る I am suffering from his *selfishness*.

てまえみそ【手前味噌】 self-praise. ¶ 彼は～ばかり言っている He *is always praising himself*. ～を並べるのはやめなさい Stop *singing your own praises*.

でまかせ【出任せ】 ¶ 彼は口から～を言う He talks *at random*. / He says *at a venture*. 彼は口から～にうそを言う He tells *irresponsible* lies.

てまくら【手枕】 ¶ ～でうたた寝した I took a nap, *resting my head on my arm*.

でまど【出窓】 a bay (≒ bow) window.

てまど·る【手間取る】 ¶ 仕事に～って約束の時間に遅れた As my business *kept me long* (≒ *took time*), I was late for my engagement.

てまね【手真似】 a gesture. ¶ 彼は～で私を呼んだ He *gestured* me *to* come.

てまねき【手招き】 beckoning. ¶ 彼にこちらへ来るよう～した I *beckoned* 〔*to*〕 him *to* come here.

てまり【手鞠】 a handball.

てまわし【手回し】 (準備) preparation; (手はず) arrangements. ¶ 彼はいつでも～のよい人だ He *is* always *ready* (≒ *prepared*).

てまわりひん【手回り品】 personal effects (≒ belongings).

でまわ·る【出回る】 ¶ 店頭にミカンが～ってきた Oranges began to *come into the market*.

てみじか【手短】 ¶ ～に説明する make a *brief* (≒ *short*) explanation; explain *briefly* (≒ *in short*). ～に言えば in short; in brief; to be brief.

でみせ【出店】 a branch store (≒ shop).

てむかい【手向かい】 〔a〕 resistance. ¶ ～するな Don't *resist*.

でむかえ【出迎え】 ¶ 彼は空港で友人の～を受けた He *was met* (≒ *was received; was greeted*) at the airport by his friends. 彼を東京駅まで～に行くところだ I am going to *meet* him at Tokyo Station.

でむ·く【出向く】 ¶ 指定の場所に～く *go* to the appointed place.

でめきん【出目金】 a pop-eyed goldfish.

-ても ¶ どんなにつらく～やり通しなさい *However* (≒ *No matter how*) hard it *may* be, you should go through with it. 暇があっ～なく～, やる気があればやれる *Whether* you have time *or* not, you can do it, if you have a mind to do. 雨が降っ～来ます I'll come *even if* it rains.

デモ a demonstration. ¶ ～に参加する join a *demonstration* parade.

でも ¶ ～, 私は反対だ *But* I object to it. どうして来なかったのですか. ～忙しかったのです Why didn't you come? *Because* I was too busy.

-でも **1** 〚…であっても〛 ¶ いつ～電話をください Phone me *any time* that suits you. どれ～好きなカードをとりなさい Take *whichever* card you like. なん～いいから飲むものをください Won't you give me something to drink? *Anything* will do. 今すぐやらなくてもいい. あす～いい You do not have to do it at once. Tomorrow will do. この鉛筆～まにあう This pencil will do. 雨～出発することに決めた We have decided to start *even if* it rains. だれ～年をとっても学べるものだ *Nobody* is too old to learn.
2 〚なりと〛 ¶ 紅茶～おあがりになりますか Won't you have something to drink, *say*, a cup of tea? 新聞～読もうと思っている I am going to read a newspaper *or something*.
3 〚でさえ〛 ¶ この小説は子ども～読める *Even* a child can read this novel. こんなことはばか～知っている *Even* a fool knows that.

デモクラシー democracy.

てもち【手持ち】 ¶ ～の金 money *on hand*.

～の商品がある I have goods *in stock.* 日本の～外貨 Japan's foreign currency *holdings.*

てもちぶさた【手持ちぶさた】¶たばこがないとどうも～だ Having no cigarettes to smoke I somehow *feel ill at ease.*

てもと【手元】¶～にある資料 the data *in* (≒ *on*) *hand.* ～に置く keep (*something*) *at hand.* 夫婦は息子を～に引きとめたがった The couple wanted to keep their son *at home.* ～が狂って親指を金づちで打ってしまった I *missed the mark* and hit myself on the thumb with a hammer.

でもどり【出戻り】a divorced woman.

てもなく【手も無く】easily. ¶～彼にやりこめられた I was *easily* talked down by him.

でもの【出物】an article for sale. ¶ちょうどよい～があります We have just *a* good *article for sale.*

てもり【手盛り】¶お～案 a proposal *made to suit oneself.* お～予算には賛成できない We cannot support the *self-approved* budget.

デモンストレーション a demonstration.

デュエット〘音楽〙〘ダンス〙a duet.

でよう【出様】⇒でかた

てら【寺】a temple.
—男 a sexton; a temple servant. —銭 the proceeds of gambling tables.

てらい【衒い】〔an〕affectation. ¶彼女の～は鼻もちならぬ Her *affectations* are insufferable.

てら・う【衒う】¶才知を～う *show off one's* talents. 学問を～う make *a display* (≒ *a parade; a show*) of *one's* learning. 彼は学問を～いすぎる He *is* too *pedantic.*

テラコッタ terra-cotta.

てらしあわ・せる【照らし合わせる】¶AとBとを～せる *check* A *with* B. ⇒しょうごう

テラス a terrace.

てら・す【照らす】**1**〘光線〙shine. ¶太陽は地球を～す The sun *shines* on the earth.
月は砂ばくを～していた The moon *was shining* on the desert.
だれかが懐中電燈で夜道を～している Someone *is lighting* the way with a flash-light.
ろうそくで～して本を読む read a book *in candlelight.*
ネオンの光が通りを～している Neon lights *are lighting up* the street.
2〘参照する〙¶歴史に～してみると彼の言ったことは正しいことがわかる What he says turns out to be right *in the light of* history.
法律に～して彼の処分を決めたい We shall deal with him *according to* the law.
3〘その他〙¶ふたりは肝胆相～す仲だ The two *are on friendly terms with each other.*

デラックス de luxe; deluxe (フランス語から).
—本 a de luxe edition.

てらてら bright〔ly〕; shiny. ¶彼の作業ズボンは～と脂ぎっている His overalls *are glossy* with grease.

テラマイシン〘薬品〙terramycin.

てらまいり【寺参り】¶～を欠かさぬ I regularly *visit the temple.*

てり【照り】sunshine; (日照り) dry weather; a drought; (光沢) luster; gloss. ¶～が強い The sun is strong. ～が続く There has been *a* long *drought.*

テリア (犬) a terrier.

てりかえし【照り返し】reflection; (反射光) the reflected light. ¶夏の日ざしの～で暑い The *reflection* of the summer heat tells on us.

てりかえ・す【照り返す】reflect.

デリカシー delicacy.

デリケート delicate. ¶～な感覚 *subtle* (≒ *delicate*) senses. ～な問題 a *delicate* question. 両国の国際関係は～だ There is something *delicate* in the diplomatic relations between the two countries.

てりこ・む【照り込む】¶この部屋は日が～むのでとても暑い As the sunlight *shines into* this room, it is very hot here. こう～むと作物の出来が心配だ Such *a long spell of dry weather,* I am afraid, will not be good for the crops.

てりつ・ける【照りつける】¶太陽が砂浜に～けていた The sun *was beating down on* the sandy beach. ～ける太陽を木陰に避けた We sheltered ourselves under the trees from the *scorching* sun.

てりは・える【照り映える】¶紅葉の～える山道を登った I went up the mountain path with the scarlet maple leaves *shining beautifully in the sun.*

てりやき【照り焼き】¶マグロの～ tunny (≒ tuna) *broiled with soy.*

てりょうり【手料理】a home-made (≒ home-cooked) dish. ¶これはみんな妻の～です My wife cooked all these.

デリンジャーげんしょう【デリンジャー現象】〘物理〙Dellinger phenomenon.

て・る【照る】¶月が雲間から～っている The moon *is shining* brightly through the clouds. 降っても～っても rain or *shine.*

でる【出る】**1**〘内から外へ行く・出発する〙go out.
¶外へ出て運動しよう Let's *go out of* doors and take exercise.
あすは6時に家を出る予定だ I *am leaving* home at six tomorrow.
彼女は買い物に出ている She *has gone out* shopping.
こんな映画はつまらないから出よう This movie is boring. Let's *leave.*
彼女は黙って部屋を出ていった She *went out of* the room without a word.
バスは1時間に何本出ますか How many buses arrive and *depart* every hour?
その特急はどの駅から出ますか From what station does the limited express *start*?
田舎から出てきたばかりでまだ落ち着きません Since I *have* just *come up* from the country, I still feel nervous.
2〘現われる〙appear. ¶山の上に月が出た A moon *has risen* over the mountain.
うちの台所にはゴキブリが出て困る We are troubled by the *appearance* of cockroaches in

our kitchen.

あの家には幽霊が出る That house *is haunted* by ghosts.

きみのなくした時計はまだ出ませんか *Haven't* you *found* the watch you lost yet?

あの古墳から貴重な土器が出た Valuable earthen vessels *have been dug up* (≒ *have been unearthed*) from the ancient tomb.

もうイチゴが果物屋の店頭に出ている Strawberries *have* already *appeared* in the fruit stores.

あの辺りは痴漢がよく出る That area *is* often *troubled* by sexual deviants.

また彼の癖が出た He's at it again.

3 〖芽が〗 come out. ¶ 朝顔の芽がようやく出た The buds of a morning glory *have come out* at last.

彼はいつまでたっても芽が出ない Luck won't turn in his favor./ He has had constant ill luck.

4 〖出場する・参加する〗 appear; participate. ¶ 彼女は5歳のとき初めて舞台に出た She *made her debut* (≒ *made* her first *appearance* on the stage) when she was five.

彼女はどこの劇場に出ていますか At what theater *is* she *appearing* now?

彼はあすの弁論大会に学校の代表として出る He will *participate in* the speech contest on behalf of the school tomorrow.

おまえの出る幕じゃない This is no business of yours. / Mind your own business. / It doesn't concern you.

今度の総会には出ますか Will you *attend* the next general meeting?

きのうの民法の講義に出ましたか *Were* you *present at* (≒ Did you *attend*) the lecture of the Civil Law yesterday?

彼は今度の知事選挙に出る He is going to *run for* (≒ *stand for*) governor.

5 〖卒業する〗 graduate; work. ¶ 彼はこの4月に大学を出た He *graduated from* the university last April. (英では graduate at とも言う).

6 〖勤務する〗 ¶ 彼は区役所へ出ている He *works in* (≒ *at*) the ward office.

7 〖発生する〗 ¶ 朝になって強い風が出た A strong wind *rose* (≒ *blew*) toward morning.

ゆうべは高い熱が出て苦しかった Last night I suffered from a high fever.

8 〖流出する・放出する〗 ¶ 止めどもなく涙が出た I couldn't control the tears that *came to* my eyes.

汗が出て手が滑って力が入らない Since the hands are slippery with perspiration, I cannot get a firm grip.

煙突から真っ黒い煙が出ている The chimney *is giving off* deep black smoke.

大雨で水が出て村は水びたしになった The village *was flooded* by the heavy downpour.

会議中あくびが出そうになって困った I had a hard time suppressing my yawns during the conference.

9 〖由来する〗 ¶ 英語にはラテン語から出た語がたくさんある There are many words *of* Latin *origin* in English. / There are many words which *are derived* from Latin in English.

この村の名はその故事から出た The name of this village *owes its origin to* the historical incident.

それは彼女の親切から出たことばだ She said so *from* (≒ *out of*) kindness.

10 〖出版される・掲載される〗 come out; be in. ¶ その本はいつごろ出ますか When will the book *come* (≒ *be*) *out*?

5月号はきのう出たばかりだ The May number *appeared* (≒ *came out*) only yesterday.

週刊誌にきみの写真が出ている Your photograph *is* in the weekly magazine.

その記事はどの新聞にも出ている The news *is* in every newspaper.

11 〖産出される〗 produce. ¶ この鉱山からはスズが出る This mine *produces* tin.

私の県からは教育者がたくさん出ている Our prefecture *has produced* many teachers.

12 〖売れる〗 sell. ¶ このレコードはとてもよく出る This record *sells* very well. / This record *is in* very great *demand*.

今いちばんよく出ている小説はなんですか What novel is the best seller now?

13 〖通じる・達する〗 ¶ 駅へ出る道を教えていただけませんか Won't you tell me the way *to* the station?

14 〖議題・話題にのぼる〗 ¶ その問題は確かにきのうの会議に出た I'm sure the problem *came up* for discussion at yesterday's meeting.

きみのことが話題に出た You *became a topic* of conversation.

歴史の問題は何題出ましたか How many questions on history *appeared* (≒ *were there*)?

ついに結論は出なかった We didn't *come to* any conclusion after all.

15 〖供される・与えられる〗 be served. ¶ お昼にはサンドイッチが出た Sandwiches *were served* at lunch.

デザートにメロンが出た Melon *was served* for dessert.

優勝者にはトロフィーが出る A trophy will *be given* to the winner.

ボーナスはいつ出ますか When do we *get* our bonus?

16 〖態度をとる・行動する〗 ¶ 先方がどう出るかようすをみよう Let's wait and see what *move* he will *make*.

彼は強気に出てきた He *has taken an aggressive attitude*. / He's *on the offense*.

相手チームがどう出るかをみて作戦を立てよう Let's form a plan after we see what the other team *does*.

17 〖突き出る〗 ¶ 彼女はほお骨が出ている She has *high* (≒ *prominent*) cheekbones.

彼は近ごろおなかが出てきた He's been developing a potbelly recently.

枝がへいの外に出すぎている The branch *is reaching out* far beyond the fence.

18 〖超過する〗 ¶ 彼女は40歳を出ているにしては若く見える She looks young for a woman of

over forty.
着物を買ったら予算を1万円も出てしまった I *went* ten thousand yen *beyond* the budget when I bought the *kimono*.
きのうの会は会費では足が出た The fees *did not cover* the expenses of yesterday's meeting.
19 〖お茶が〗 ¶ このお茶はすぐ出なくなる This tea soon becomes watery.
20 〖力・スピードなどが〗 ¶ この車は何馬力出ますか What horsepower does this car *develop*?
この道路ならこの車でも時速100キロは出る Even this car *could run at the speed of* 100 kph along this road.

デルタ a delta.
—地帯 a delta region. —翼機 a delta-winged plane.

てるてるぼうず【照る照る坊主】a paper charm doll made by Japanese children looking forward to fine weather.

でるところ【出る所】¶ ～へ出てこの争いにけりをつけたい I want to settle up the dispute *before proper authorities*.

てれかくし【照れ隠し】 ¶ ～に話題を変えた *To hide my embarrassment* (≒ *awkwardness*) I changed the subject.

てれくさ・い【照れ臭い】¶ 知らない人たちの前でしゃべるのは～かった I *was embarrassed* to speak in the presence of strangers. 彼はほめられて～そうな顔をしていた Being praised he looked *awkward* (≒ *embarrassed*).

テレタイプ a teletype; a teletypewriter.
¶ ～で通信を送る *teletype* a message; send a message *by teletype*.

テレックス telex (telegraph-exchange の略).

テレビ television; (テレビ受像機) a television; TV. ¶ ～をつける turn on *a television*. ～はすぐ消してほしい I want the *television* turned off at once. ～で野球の試合を見た I watched a baseball game *on television*. あの人が～で坊っちゃんを演じた He played Botchan *on television*. 彼は今晩～に出る He will appear *on television* this evening. 今～でなにを放送していますか What *is being telecast* now? その野球試合は～で放送された The baseball game *was telecast* (≒ *was televised*).
—映画 a telefilm; a telepicture. —カメラ a television camera. —視聴者 a televiewer. —受像機 a television set. —電話 a television telephone. —ドラマ a teleplay. —塔 a television tower. —ニュース telenews. —番組 a TV program. —放送 a telecast. —放送局 a television station. カラー—受像機 a color TV set. カラー—放送 colorcast.

テレビンゆ【テレビン油】〖薬品〗turpentine oil.

て・れる【照れる】¶ 知らない人ばかりだったので彼はちょっと～れた He *felt* a little *awkward* because he knew nobody there. 彼は～れ屋だ He is a *bashful* (≒ *shy*) person.

てれん【手練】wiles ¶ まんまとそのうわき女の～手管にのせられた He fell an easy prey to the *wiles* of the coquette.

テロ terrorism. ¶ 大統領は～に倒れた The president fell a victim to *terrorism*.
—行為 terrorism. —戦術 terroristic tactics.

テロリスト a terrorist.

てわけ【手分け】¶ みんなで～して迷子を捜しに行った We went out *in parties* to search for a lost child. 全員で～して部屋の掃除をしよう Let's *divide the work* of cleaning the room *among* all of us.

てわた・す【手渡す】¶ この手紙を彼に～して下さい Please *hand* this letter *to* him.

てん【天】**1** (空) the sky; the heavens; (天意) Providence; Heaven. ¶ ～高く馬肥ゆる秋になった Now it is autumn, *the sky* is high and clear, and horses are growing fat.
～を摩する高層ビルがずらっと建ち並んでいた High buildings scraping *the sky* stood in a row.
それは～に向かってつばきするに等しい It is like spitting at *the sky*.
運を～に任せるつもりだ I will trust it to *Providence*.
～知る, 地知る *Heaven* knows and earth knows.
事をはかるのは人にある, 事をなすのは～にある Man proposes; *God* disposes.
～の助けを請うほかはない We cannot but call upon *Heaven* for help.
～はみずから助くる者を助く (諺) *Heaven helps those who help themselves*.
2 〖その他〗 ¶ 彼は入賞して～にも上る心地だった Having won a prize, he *was in the seventh heaven*.
彼は～地人の～の部に入賞した He won *the highest prize*.
～から降ったか地からわいたか, サルが1匹現われた There suddenly appeared a monkey as if it had fallen from *the sky*.
～にも地にもこれひとつだ This is the only thing *in the world*.

てん【点】**1** 〖小さいしるし〗 a dot; a spot. ¶ i や j の～を打つのを忘れてはいけません Don't forget to *dot* the i's and j's.
沖の船は～のように小さく見えた The boat in the offing looked like *a* small *dot* (≒ *spot*).
きょうは一～の雲もない日本晴れだ Today we have a clear, blue sky without *a speck* of cloud in it.
2 〖評点〗 a mark; a point. ¶ きのうの数学の試験で彼はいい～をとった He got very good *marks* in the math exam yesterday.
ぼくは100～満点の85～だった I obtained 85 *marks* (≒ *points*) out of 100.
つづりをまちがえただけで5～も引かれた I lost 5 *marks* (≒ *points*) just for a careless error in spelling.
歴史の成績は60～でかろうじて及第した I barely passed the history exam with 60 *marks*.
勤務評定を～であらわすことは難しい It is difficult to evaluate *one's* service in terms of *points*.
英語の先生は～が辛い(甘い) Our English teacher is strict (lenient) with *grades*.
文を途中で省略するときは～を三つつけなさい Use three *periods* (≒ *dots*) to indicate the

omission of words from a sentence.
小数〜以下3位まで求めなさい Calculate down to 3 decimal places.

3 〖競技の得点〗 a point. ¶ きのうの野球は最終回に3〜入れてぼくたちが勝った We scored 3 *points* in the last inning, and won the baseball game yesterday.

4 〖問題点・論点・観点〗 a point. ¶ 品質の〜は保証します *As far as* quality *is concerned,* we will guarantee it.
その〜はきみの言うことを信じよう I believe you *on that point.*
いろいろな〜できみと彼は異っている You are different from him *in many ways.*
性格の〜からみれば彼がもっとも適している *Viewed from the standpoint of* character, he is better qualified than anyone else.
どの〜からみてもきみのほうが彼よりまさっている *In all respects,* you are superior to him.

5 〖品物の数〗 ¶ 彼女は4〜セットの家具を買った She bought a set of furniture consisting of four *articles.*
盗まれたのは現金と衣類数〜だった Cash and several *items* of clothing were stolen.

てん【貂】〘動物〙 a marten.
黒— a sable. 白— an ermine.

でん【伝】a life; a biography. ¶ リンカーン〜 *a life* of Lincoln. いつもの〜でやればよい You may do it *in the usual way.*

でんあつ【電圧】〔a〕voltage. ¶ 高い(低い)〜 *a* high (low) *voltage.* 〜を上げる(下げる) increase (drop) *voltage.*
—計 a voltmeter.

てんい【天意】Providence; God's will. ¶ 彼は〜によって救われたように思われた He seemed to have been saved by *the Providence of God.*

てんい【転位】(位置)〔a〕transposition; (原子の)〔a〕dislocation; (染色体の) translocation.

てんい【転移】〘医学〙 metastasis. ¶ 胃がんが肝臓に〜した The stomach cancer *has spread to* the liver.

でんい【電位】electric potential.
—計 an electrometer. —差 potential difference.

てんいむほう【天衣無縫】¶ 彼の小説は〜だ His novel *is natural and flawless.* / His novel is a work of *artless art.*

てんいん【店員】㊍ a〔store〕clerk; a salesman; ㊇ a shopassistant; (おもに㊇) a shopman; (女) a shopgirl; (販売員) a salesclerk; (女) a saleswoman; a salesgirl.

てんうん【天運】fate; destiny. ¶ 彼は〜に身をゆだねた He resigned himself to his *fate.*

でんえん【田園】farms; fields; (いなか) the countryside.
—詩 a pastoral; an idyl. —詩人 a pastoral poet. —生活〔a〕country (≒ rural) life. —都市 a garden (≒ rural) city. —交響曲 Beethoven's symphony No. 6 "Pastoral."

てんか【天下】**1** 〖世間〗 the world. ¶ この著書で彼は〜に名をあげた By writing this book he made a name for himself *in the whole country.*
彼は〜に敵なしというふうに見える He looks as if he had no rival *in the world.*
この山は姿の美しいことで〜に知られている This mountain *is world-famous* for its beauty.
ふたりは〜晴れて夫婦になった The two became a *happy legitimate* couple.

2 〖政権〗 ¶ 彼が〜をとったのは300年も前のことだ It was as long as three hundred years ago that he conquered (≒ subdued) *the whole country.*
足利幕府は何年間日本の〜をとったのですか How long did the Ashikaga Shogunate *rule over the whole* of Japan?
社会党が〜をとる日はいつ来るだろうか When will the Social Democratic Party *come into power,* I wonder.
彼らは〜分け目の戦いに敗れた They lost *the most decisive* battle.

てんか【点火】ignition. ¶ ストーブに〜する *light* a stove. 木に〜する *ignite* wood.
—器 a lighter. —装置 an igniter. —プラグ a spark (≒ ㊇ sparking) plug.

てんか【添加】addition; annexing. ¶ 甘味を〜する *add* a sweet flavor (*to*).
—物 an addition.

てんか【転化】change; transformation.

てんか【転嫁】imputation. ¶ 責任を他人に〜する *shift* responsibility *to* someone else. 当局は事故の責任を被害者に〜した The authorities *laid* (≒ *threw*) the blame for the accident *on* the injured party.

てんが【典雅】¶ 彼女には〜な趣がある She looks *graceful.* 〜に装いをこらしていた She was *elegantly* dressed up. / Her dress *was of refined taste.*

でんか【伝家】¶ やむなく〜の宝刀を抜いた I was forced to resort to my last measure.

でんか【電化】electrification. ¶ 東北線は全線〜された The Tohoku line *was* entirely *electrified.* わが家はかなり〜している We *have* many *electrical appliances installed* in our house.
—計画 an electrification scheme. —事業 an electrification work. —住宅 an electrified home.

でんか【電荷】〘物理〙 an electric charge.

でんか【殿下】(3人称, 男性では) His Imperial Highness; (3人称, 女性では) Her Imperial Highness; (2人称では) Your Imperial Highness (動詞は3人称扱い).
¶ 〜は女王を訪問された *His Imperial Highness* paid a visit to the Queen.
皇太子— His Imperial Highness (H.I.H.) the Crown Prince. 皇太子妃— Her Imperial Highness the Crown Princess. 高松宮同妃両— Their Imperial Highnesses Prince and Princess Takamatsu. 英国皇太子— His Royal Highness the Prince of Wales.

てんかい【展開】(進展)〔a〕development; (拡

大)〔an〕expansion. ¶ 彼は新しい言語理論を～した He *developed* a new linguistic theory. 広々とした平野が眼前に～する A broad plain *spreads out* before us. すばらしい演技が～されてゆく A splendid performance *is* now *going on* on the stage.

てんかい【転回】a revolution. ¶ 船長は進路を90度～させた The captain made the boat take *a* 90 degree *turn*.

てんがい【天蓋】a canopy.

てんがい【天涯】¶ 彼は～孤独の身の上だ He is a person without a single relative.

でんかい【電解】〘化学〙electrolysis. ¶ 水は酸素と水素に～される Water *is electrolyzed into* oxygen and hydrogen.

—質 an electrolyte.

てんかぶつ【添加物】an additive.

食品— (色など) food additives.

てんかん【転換】conversion. ¶ あの国の政治は～期に来ている *A turning point* in politics has come in that country. 気分～に休憩しよう Let's take a rest *for a change*.

てんかん【癲癇】〘医学〙epilepsy. ¶ ～持ち an epileptic. 彼は～の発作を起こした He had an *epileptic* fit.

てんがん【点眼】¶ 1日3回この目薬を～してください *Drop* the eye lotion *in your eyes* three times a day.

—器 an eyedropper.

てんがんきょう【天眼鏡】a magnifying glass.

てんき【天気】**1** 〘天候〙weather. ¶ 今晩の～はどうだろう I wonder how the *weather* will be this evening.

この～は続くだろう I hope this *weather* will last long.

いやな～が続いている We have had nasty *weather*.

～は突然くずれた The *weather* broke suddenly.

～はよくなりそうだ The *weather* is likely to clear up.

～はなかなか定まらない The *weather* remains unsettled.

～がよくなりしだい出発しよう We will start as soon as it *clears up*.

山の～は変わりやすい The *weather* in the mountain is changeable.

～がよくても悪くても遠足に出かけよう Let's go on a picnic whether the *weather* is fair or foul.

～がよければ明日出発します We will start tomorrow, *weather permitting*.

—概況 a general weather condition. —図 a weather chart. —相談所 the Weather Information Bureau. —もよう the weather. —予報 the weather forecast. ¶ 案の定～予報は当たらなかった The *weather forecast* did not prove accurate, as I had feared. お—屋 a whimsical person.

2 〘晴天〙fine weather. ¶ なんといい～だろう How *fine* it is!

このところ～に恵まれている We have been blessed with *fine weather* these days.

てんき【転記】¶ 伝票から原簿に～する *post* an item from a slip to a ledger.

てんき【転機】a turning point. ¶ 70年代には産業界にひとつの～が来る *A turning point* will come in the industrial world in the nineteen-seventies. あの会社は今～に立っている The company is now on *the turning point*.

てんぎ【転義】a figurative meaning.

でんき【伝奇】—小説(物語) a romance.

でんき【伝記】a life; a biography. ¶ キュリー夫人の～ *a life* of Madame Curie.

—作者 a biographer. —物語 a biographical story.

でんき【電気】electricity; (電灯) an electric light. ¶ このエンジンは～で動く This engine is driven by *electricity*. ～を起こすものにはどんなものがありますか What sort of matter or phenomenon generates *electricity*? この針金には～が通じていない This wire is not charged with *electricity*. ～をつける turn on the *light*. ～を消す turn off the *light*. 突然～が消えた The *light* went out suddenly. 部屋に～を引く install *an electric light* in a room.

—アイロン an electric iron. —あんか an electric foot warmer. —医療機械 an electromedical apparatus. —ウナギ〘魚類〙an electric eel. —オルガン an electric organ. —会社 an electric company. —がま an electric oven. —かみそり an electric shaver. —機関車 an electric locomotive. —器具 an electric appliance. —器具店 an electric goods store. —技師 an electric engineer. —ギター an electric guitar. —計算器 an electric calculator. —工学 electrical engineering. —コンロ an electric cooker. —自動車 an electric automobile. —炊飯器 an electric rice cooker. —スタンド a desk lamp; (床の) a floor lamp. —ストーブ an electric heater. —洗たく機 an electric washing machine. —掃除機 a vacuum cleaner. —抵抗 electric resistance. —時計 an electric clock. —めっき electrogilding. —毛布 an electric blanket. —溶接 electric welding. —量 amount of electricity. —料金 electric charges. —療法 electric treatment. —冷蔵庫 an electric refrigerator. —炉 an electric furnace.

てんきゅう【天球】the heavens; (文語) the vault〔of Heaven〕.

でんきゅう【電球】an electric bulb. ¶ 100ワットの～ *a* 100 watt *bulb*. ～が切れた The filament has broken (≒ burnt out).

豆— a miniature bulb.

てんきょ【典拠】authority. ¶ これについてははっきりした～がある This is an *authentic* statement. この記事の～を示してください Cite the *authority* for this statement.

てんきょ【転居】〔a〕removal. ¶ この度下記の住

所に～しました We *have removed* (⇔ *have moved*) *to* the following address. 彼は京都から名古屋へ～した He *moved* from Kyoto to Nagoya.

—先 *one's* new address. —通知 ¶友人に～通知を出した I gave *notice of my removal* to my friends.

てんぎょう【転業】a change of occupation. ¶彼は～を決意した He decided to *change his business*.

—資金 funds for occupational change.

でんきょく【電極】an electrode; a pole.

てんきん【天金】a gilt top. ¶～の本 a *gilt-topped* book.

てんきん【転勤】transference. ¶彼は4月にニューヨーク支社に～を命じられた He *was transferred to* the New York branch in April.

て

てんぐ【天狗】(怪物) a long-nosed goblin; (自慢家) a boaster. ¶彼はほめられるとすぐ～になる He easily *becomes proud* (⇔ *becomes conceited*) when he is well spoken of.

てんくう【天空】the sky; the air.

てんぐさ【天草】〘植物〙an agar-agar.

てんぐだけ【天狗茸】〘植物〙a death cup.

デングねつ【デング熱】〘医学〙dengue〔fever〕.

でんぐりがえし【でんぐり返し】a somersault. ¶マットの上で～をする turn *a somersault* on a mat.

でんぐりがえ・る【でんぐり返る】turn heels over head. ¶軽自動車はトラックと衝突して～った The minicar collided with a truck and *turned upside down*.

てんけい【天恵】a blessing. ¶～豊かな国 a country blessed with (⇔ rich in) *natural resources*.

てんけい【天啓】a sign from heaven; revelation.

てんけい【典型】(模範) a model; (代表的なもの) a type; a paragon.

¶男らしさの～ *a model* of manhood. 近代文学の～ *representative* modern literature. ～的官僚 a *typical* bureaucrat.

でんげき【電撃】¶敵機はわれわれの町を～爆撃した The enemy planes *blitzed* our city. ～作戦を展開した We employed *lightning* (⇔ *blitz*) tactics. 彼は～的に仕事を処理した He finished his work *with lightning speed*.

てんけん【天険】a natural stronghold.

てんけん【点検】inspection. ¶前もって道具を～しておくべきだ You should *examine* your instruments beforehand. 彼が人員の～をした He *called the roll*.

でんげん【電源】sources of electricity; (コンセント) an outlet. ¶この部屋の～はどこですか Where is the *electric outlet* in this room? このラジオの～は交流・直流どちらでもよい This radio can play on alternating current as well as direct current.

—開発 development of power resources.

てんこ【点呼】〔a〕roll call. ¶先生は毎朝生徒の～をする The teacher *takes a roll call of* his students every morning. 彼は～に遅れた He was late for the *roll call*.

でんこ【電弧】〘電気〙an electric arc.

てんこう【天候】weather. ¶収穫は～に左右される The crop depends upon the *weather*. 山小屋で～の回復を待った We waited for the *weather* to improve in the mountain hut. ～が崩れる The *weather* breaks (⇔ deteriorates). 悪～をついて巡視船は出港した The patrol boat left port in spite of bad *weather*. (「形容詞+weather」には a も the もつけない).

全—機 an all-weather plane.

てんこう【転向】〔a〕conversion. ¶近ごろ釣りから～してゴルフに凝っている I stopped going fishing and I have been absorbed in golf recently. 彼は会社員から～して作家になった Leaving the company, he became an author.

—者 a convert.

てんこう【転校】¶彼は父の転勤のため大阪の学校へ～した He *changed* (⇔ *transferred*) *to a school* in Osaka, as his father was transferred to the Osaka office.

—生 a student transferred from another school.

でんこう【電光】lightning.

—石火 ¶彼は～石火のごとく仕事をかたづけた He finished his work *at a lightning speed* (⇔ *as quickly as lightning*). —ニュース an electric news tape.

てんごく【天国】heaven. ¶彼は～へ行った He went to *heaven*. 今の職場は私にとっては～だ I am very much satisfied with the present post.

歩行者— a pedestrians' paradise; a no-car area.

でんごん【伝言】a message. ¶あなたに～がある I have *a message* for you. 彼女への～を彼に言い残した I left *a message* for her with him. 彼への～を頼まれた I was asked to give him *a message*. 彼によろしくご～を頼みます Please *give my kind regards to* him.

—板 a message board.

てんさい【天才】(才能) genius; (人) a genius. ¶大～ *a* transcendent *genius*. 彼女は化学の～だ She is *a genius* in chemistry. 彼は～的なピアニストだ He is an *exceptionally talented* pianist.

—児 an infant genius; a gifted child.

てんさい【天災】a natural calamity; 〘法律〙an act of God. ¶昨年はたびたび～に見舞われた We were often visited by *natural calamities* last year. その事故は～と思ってあきらめた We accepted the accident as our fate (⇔ destiny).

てんさい【転載】reprinting. ¶この記事はニューヨークタイムズから～した The article *was reprinted from* the New York Times.

禁— Copyright reserved; Reproduction forbidden.

てんさい【甜菜】〘植物〙a〔sugar〕beet.

—糖 beet sugar.

てんざい【点在】¶たんぼの中に農家が～している The paddy fields *are studded* (⇔ *are* *dotted*) *with* farm houses.

てんさく【添削】correction. ¶ 答案を～してもらった I *had* my paper *corrected*.
通信— a correspondence course.

てんし【天使】an angel. ¶ ～のような少女 *an angel of* a girl; an *angelic* girl.

てんじ【点字】Braille (≒ braille) points; braille (Braill の発音 [breil]); raised type (≒ letters). ¶ ～を打つ *brialle* (a short story). ～の新聞(本) a newspaper (a book) in *raised type* (≒ *braille*).
—図書館 a braille library.

てんじ【展示】exhibition; display. ¶ 作品を～する *display* (≒ *exhibit*) works. 新しい自動車がショーウインドーに～してある New automobiles *are displayed* (≒ *are on display*) in the shopwindows.
—会 an exhibition; a show. ¶ 写真の～会 *a* photo *exhibition*. カメラの～会 *a* camera *show*. —会場 an exhibition hall. —館(博覧会などの) a pavilion. —物 an exhibit; (総称) exhibition.

でんし【電子】〘物理〙an electron.
—オルガン an electronic organ. —音楽 electronic music. —計算機 an electronic computer (≒ calculator). —顕微鏡 an electron microscope. —工学 electronics. —光学 electron optics. —レンジ an electronic oven.

でんじ【電磁】—気 electromagnetism. —波 electromagnetic waves.

てんじくあおい【天竺葵】〘植物〙a geranium.

でんじしゃく【電磁石】an electromagnet.

てんしゃ【転写】transcription. ¶ 原本から一部～した I *copied* some parts *from* the original. 発音記号で文章を～する *transcribe* a sentence *in* phonetic signs.

でんしゃ【電車】(市街電車) 米 a streetcar; 英 a tram; a tramcar (「列車」の場合は an electric train または単に a train).
¶ ～に乗る get on *a streetcar*. ～から降りる get off *a streetcar*. 東京ではバスや地下鉄が～にとってかわった In Tokyo buses and subways have replaced *streetcars*. ここから港までは～がある There is *an electric train service* from here to the harbor. 学校までは～で行く I go to school *by tram* (≒ *by streetcar*). ～に乗っていけばすぐだ Take *a train* and you will soon get there. ～の故障で会合に遅れた I was late for the meeting on account of the *train* breakdown. この～は東京駅に行きますか Is this *train* for Tokyo Station? ～は混んでいた The *train* was crowded.
—賃 a carfare.

てんしゃく【転借】(家屋・土地の) a sublease; subtenancy. ¶ 家を～する *sublease* a house.

てんしゅ【天主】God; the Lord of Heaven.
—教 Roman Catholicism.

てんしゅ【店主】米 a storekeeper; 英 a shopkeeper; the proprietor; (女) the proprietress.

てんじゅ【天寿】the natural span of life. ¶ 彼は～を全うして94歳で没した He *died a natural death* at ninety-four.

でんじゅ【伝授】instruction. ¶ 彼にバラ作りの秘法を～してもらった He *instructed* (≒ *taught*) me how to grow roses well. / He *initiated* me *into the secrets of* rose-gardening.

てんしゅかく【天守閣】a castle tower; a donjon.

てんしゅつ【転出】¶ 4月に大阪の支社に～した(転勤) I *was transferred to* the branch office in Osaka in April. 昨年神奈川県に～した(転居) We *moved out to* Kanagawa Prefecture last year.

てんしょ【添書】(紹介状) a letter of introduction; (推薦状) a letter of recommendation.

てんじょう【天上】heaven. ¶ ～(界)の幸福 *celestial* bliss. ～天下唯我独尊 Holy am I alone throughout heaven and earth.

てんじょう【天井】the ceiling. ¶ ～にハエが止まっている There is a fly on *the ceiling*. ぼくのへやの～はとても高い *The ceiling* of my room is very high.
—裏 ¶ ～裏でネズミがチューチュー鳴くのが聞こえた I heard mice squeaking in *the ceiling*.
—値 the ceiling price.

でんしょう【伝承】〔a〕tradition.
—文学 oral literature. 民間— folklore.

てんしょく【天職】a mission; a vocation. ¶ 彼は教師を～と考えて励んだ He did his best in teaching, believing that it was his *vocation*.

てんしょく【転職】a change of occupation. ¶ 若い人たちで～する人が多い There are not a few young people who *change their occupation* (≒ *job*).

でんしょばと【伝書鳩】a carrier pigeon; a homing pigeon.

てんしん【転進】¶ ～せざるをえなかった There was no way but to *change the course* (≒ *retreat* (退却の場合)).

てんしん【転針】¶ その船は航海の途中で～した The ship *changed its course* on the way.

でんしん【電信】telegraph; wire; (海底の) a cable. ¶ ～で知らせる inform by *telegraph*. 東京・鹿児島間の～は不通となった *Telegraphic communication* has been cut (≒ has been interrupted) between Tokyo and Kagoshima. 東京・小笠原間に～が開通した *Telegraphic service* has been established from Tokyo to Ogasawara.
—為替 a telegraphic money order; a telegraphic remittance. —機 a telegraph; telegraphic instruments. —技師 a telegrapher; a telegraph operator. —柱 a telegraph pole. —符号 a telegraphic code. 無線— 〔a〕wireless.

てんしんらんまん【天真爛漫】¶ ～な子ども a *simple and innocent* child. あの人は子どものように～だ He *is* as *naive* as a child.

テンス〘文法〙tense.

てんすい【天水】rain water.
—桶 a rain-water tank.

てんすう【点数】(評点) a mark ; (競技の) a score ; (品数) pieces. ⇒てん
—表 a list of marks ; a scorebook.

てん・ずる【転ずる】¶ 彼は学校時代の生活に話題を〜じた He *changed* the topic *to* the life in his school days. 彼は他に責任を〜じる癖がある He is apt to *shift* the responsibility *on to* others.

てん・ずる【点ずる】¶ ランプに火を〜ずる *light* a lamp.

てんせい【天成・天性】(a) nature ; (気質) temperament. ¶ 〜の詩人 a *born* poet. 彼は〜の政治家だ He *is born to be* a statesman. 彼女には〜の美しさがある She is beautiful *by nature.*

てんせい【展性】malleability. ¶ 〜に富んだ金属 a *malleable* metal.

でんせいかん【伝声管】a voice pipe (≒ tube) ; 米 a speaking tube.

てんせき【転籍】¶ 現住所に〜した I *had my registered domicile transferred* to my present address.

でんせつ【伝説】(a) tradition ; (a) legend. ¶ 〜によると富士山は一晩のうちにできたのだそうだ *The legend says that* (≒ *According to the legend*) Mt. Fuji arose in a night.

てんせん【点線】a dotted line ; (ミシン目の入った切り取り線) a perforated line. ¶ 〜で示された部分を和訳しなさい Put into Japanese the part shown in *dotted lines.* 〜(切り取り線)のところを切り取りなさい Tear the paper on the *perforated line.*

てんせん【転戦】¶ 彼は戦争中各地を〜した He *fought in one place after another* during the war.

でんせん【伝染】(間接の) infection ; (接触による) contagion. ¶ 〜は病菌によるものだ *Infection* is caused by germs. 天然痘は接触〜で広がる Smallpox spreads by *contagion.* この病気はけっして〜しない This disease *is* never *infectious.* その病気は非常に〜しやすい The disease *is* highly *contagious.* 笑いは〜する Laughter *is contagious.*
—病 (間接の) an infection ; an infectious disease ; (接触による) a contagion ; a contagious disease. —病患者 a case of infectious disease. —病病院 an infectious hospital. 法定—病 a legal epidemic.

でんせん【電線】(an) electric wire ; a telegraph wire (≒ line). ¶ 〜をひく lay on *an electric wire.*
—網 wire-webs. 海底— a (submarine) cable.

でんせん【伝線】(くつ下の) 米 a run ; 英 a ladder. ¶ くつ下が〜した There is *a run* in this stocking. 彼女の片方のくつ下は〜していた She had *a run* in her stocking.

てんそう【転送】¶ 手紙を下記の住所へ〜してください Please *forward* this letter *to* the following address. ご〜願います(手紙の表書きに書く場合) Please forward.

でんそう【電送】¶ これらの写真は現地から〜された(電信で) These photographs *were sent over the wires* from the scene. / (無線で) These photographs *were sent by wireless* from the scene.
—写真 a telephoto(graph).

てんたい【天体】a heavenly body. ¶ 〜の運動 the movements of *heavenly bodies.*
—観測 astronomical observation. —望遠鏡 an astronomical telescope. —力学 celestial mechanics.

てんたい【転貸】sublease. ¶ 彼はその家を私に〜した He *subletted* (≒ *subleased*) the house to me.

てんたく【転宅】⇒てんきょ

でんたつ【伝達】transmission. ¶ そのニュースは口から口へと〜された The news *was transmitted* from mouth to mouth. その伝言は正しく〜されなかった The message *was* incorrectly *transmitted.*

てんたん【恬淡・恬澹】¶ 彼は毀誉褒貶(きょほうへん)に対して〜としている He *is indifferent to* praise or blame.

てんち【天地】 1 〖天と地・世界〗 heaven and earth. ¶ こんなことは〜開闢(かいびゃく)以来初めてのことだ We have never had such an experience *since the beginning of the world.*
彼らは自由の〜を求めて国を離れていった They left their own country in search of *a land* of freedom.
神は〜の創造主だ God is the creator of *the universe.*
新— a new world. ¶ 彼らは新〜を求めて出発した They left for *a new world.* 別— a different world. ¶ ここはまったくの別〜だ This is indeed *a world of its own.*
2 〖その他〗 ¶ 政府のいうことと警察のいうことの間には〜の開きがある *There is all the difference in the world* between what the government said and what the police said.
〜神明に誓って二度とああいうことはしません *Upon my word* I will never do such a thing again.
このページは〜をあけてほしい I want to have spaces left *both at top and at bottom.*
—無用 (掲示) This side up.

てんち【転地】a change ; (転地療養) a change of air. ¶ 彼は軽井沢へ〜した He went to Karuizawa *for a change of air.*

でんち【電池】a battery. ¶ 〜を充電する charge *a battery.* 〜がなくなった The *battery* is run down. / The *battery* is dead.
—時計 a battery clock. 乾— a dry battery. 蓄— a storage battery.

でんちく【電蓄】an electric gramophone ; (ラジオ兼用の) 米 a radiophonograph ; 英 a radio gramophone.

てんちゅう【天誅】¶ 遂に彼にも〜がくだった At last he *was punished by Heaven.*

でんちゅう【電柱】(電信の) a telegraph pole ; (電話の) a telephone pole ; (電燈の) an electric light pole.

てんちょう【天頂】the zenith.
—儀 a zenith telescope. —距離 the

zenith distance.

てんで ¶ 彼は～ひとことも言わなかった He said nothing *at all*. 彼は私の言うことを～聞こうとしなかった He *would* pay *no* attention to my words. それは～問題にならない It is *altogether* out of the question. きみなんか～彼の相手にならないよ You are no match for him.

てんてい【天帝】God ; Providence.

てんてき【点滴】¶ 彼には～で輸血した We gave him *a drip transfusion*.
━注射 an intravenous drip injection.

てんてこまい【てんてこ舞い】¶ 彼は出発の準備で～だ He *is tremendously busy* preparing for his departure.

てんてつ【転轍】¶ 列車を～する *switch* a train (*into* a siding).
━機 米 a switch ; 英 points. 自動━機 an automatic switch.

てんてつ【点綴】¶ 海には小島が～している The sea *is dotted* with small islands.

てんてん【点点】¶ 血が～と落ちる Blood falls *in drops*. 海にはいさり火が～と見える The sea *is dotted* (≒ *is scattered*) with fishing flares.

てんてん【転転】¶ 各地を～とする *wander* from place to place. ～と住所を変える *often change one's* address. 陶器は持ち主の間を～とした The pottery *passed from hand to hand*. / The pottery *passed through many hands*. 彼は～と会社をかわった He *went from one* company *to another*.

てんでんばらばら ¶ 子どもたちは～に帰った Children went home *in all directions*. 彼らはやることが～だ Each of them is *doing only what he likes*.

でんでんむし【でんでん虫】a snail.

てんと【奠都】the transfer of the capital (*to* Kyoto).

テント a tent. ¶ ～を張る(畳む) pitch (strike) *a tent*. 彼らは森の中で～生活をした They *camped out* in the wood.

てんとう【店頭】the front of the shop.
¶ 彼は～に立っている(店員として) He *is behind the counter*. 品物を～に出した(売りに出した) We *put* goods *on sale*. この雑誌は～には出ない This magazine is not offered *on sale* to the public. ～はすごい人だかりだった *The store* was crowded with customers.
━広告 a window advertisement. ━装飾 window dressing. ━販売 over-the-counter sales.

てんとう【点燈】lighting. ¶ ～する *turn* (≒ *switch*) *on* a light.

てんとう【転倒】a fall. ¶ 彼はつまずいて～した He stumbled and *fell*. 彼女は滑ってすごい勢いで～した She slipped and *fell down* violently. 彼女はステージで気も～していた She *lost her presence of mind* on the stage. 彼の急死の知らせを聞いてまったく気が～してしまった I *was beside myself* to know his sudden death.
本末━ ¶ それは本末～というものだ That is the case of *putting the cart before the horse*.

てんどう【天道】(神) Heaven ; Providence ; (太陽) the sun.

でんとう【伝統】〔a〕tradition. ¶ これは～ある大学だ This is a university with *a* long *tradition*.
その大学は70年の～がある The university has seventy years' *tradition*.
この村の人たちは～を重んじている People in this village value *tradition*.
彼らは古来の～を守りつづけている They stick to time-honored *traditions*.
この集会には20年の～がある This meeting has *a history* of twenty years.
当地の祭りには 2000 年以上の～があるということだ I hear the festival of this place *goes back* more than two thousand years.
われわれは～に縛られたくない We are not inclined to be bound by *traditions*.
このしきたりはこの国の国民的～だ This custom is *a* national *tradition* of this country.
～を維持することがはたしていいことかどうか疑わしい I doubt if it is good to keep up *traditions*.
これはこの地方の～的な芸術だ This is a *traditional* art in this district.

でんとう【電燈】an electric light. ¶ ～をつける turn on the *light*. ～を消す turn off the *light*. この部屋には～が引いてある This room has *electric lights* installed. だれかが～をつけっぱなしておいた Somebody has left the *light* on.
━会社 an electric light company. ━料 electric light charges. 懐中━ a flashlight ; 英 an electric torch.

でんどう【伝動】〔機械〕transmission.
━装置 (特に自動車の) a transmission.

でんどう【伝道】mission〔s〕. ¶ キリスト教の～をする *preach* Christianity. 彼は一生を～に尽くした He devoted his life to *mission work*.

でんどう【伝導】transmission ; conduction.
¶ 金属は熱や電気を～する Metals *transmit* (≒ *conduct*) heat or electricity.
━性 conductibility ; conductivity. ━体 a conductor. ━率 conductivity.

でんどう【電動】━機 a motor ; an electric motor ; an electromotor. ━発電機 a motor dynamo (≒ generator).

でんどう【殿堂】a palace ; (神殿) a temple ; a sanctuary. ¶ 学術の～ the *sanctuary* of learning.

てんどうせつ【天動説】the Ptolemaic theory.

てんとうむし【天道虫・瓢虫】〔虫類〕a ladybird ; 米 a ladybug.

てんとして【恬として】¶ 彼は～恥じない He shows no sign of shame./ He does not feel any shame. 彼は世俗的成功など～顧みない He is *quite* indifferent to worldly success.

てんとりひょう【点取り表】a scorebook.

てんとりむし【点取り虫】米 a plugger ; 英 a grinder.

てんどん【天丼】a bowl of fried fish and rice.

てんにゅう【転入】¶ 彼は仙台から東京へ～した He *moved into* Tokyo *from* Sendai.

て

てんにょ【天女】a celestial maid; an angel.

てんにん【天人】a heavenly being; a fairy. ¶～の羽衣 a gossamer robe of *a celestial maiden.*

てんにん【転任】transference. ¶彼は本社から大阪へ～した He *was transferred from* the head office *to* the Osaka branch. 彼の～先を知っているか Do you know *his new post?*

でんねつ【電熱】electric heat.
—器(暖房用) an electric heater; (料理用) an electric [cooking] range; a hot plate.

てんねん【天然】nature.
—ガス natural gas. —記念物 a natural monument. —現象 a natural phenomenon. —資源 natural resources. —色 a natural color. —色映画 a color film. —色写真 a color photograph. —繊維 natural fiber.

てんねんとう【天然痘】〖医学〗smallpox.

てんのう【天皇】an emperor. ¶明治～ *the Emperor* Meiji.
—機関説 the Emperor-organ theory. —制 the Emperor system of Japan. —誕生日 the Emperor's Birthday. —杯 the Emperor's Trophy. —陛下 His Majesty the Emperor.

てんのうざん【天王山】(勝敗の定まる大事な機会) a crucial (≒ decisive) point.

てんのうせい【天王星】〖天文学〗Uranus.

てんば【天馬】(飛ぶ馬) a flying horse; 〖ギリシア神話〗Pegasus. ¶～空を行く push forward with irresistible force.

でんば【電場】〖物理〗an electric field.

でんぱ【電波】an electric wave; a radio wave. ¶彼は～を通じて親善のメッセージを送った He sent a goodwill message *through* (≒ *over*) *the radio.*
—探知機 a radar. —妨害 jamming.

でんぱ【伝播】spread. ¶文化の～を促進する promote the *spread* of civilization. 病気の～を防ぐ prevent the *spread* of the disease; prevent the disease from *spreading.*

てんばい【転売】[a] resale. ¶その品物の～は厳禁されている It is rigidly forbidden to *resell* the goods.

てんばつ【天罰】Heaven's judgement (≒ justice). ¶そんなことをすれば～を招くだろう It will incur *the wrath of Heaven.* そりゃ～だ It's *Heaven's justice.* / *Heaven's judgment* has overtaken him. ～てきめん(諺) *Swift is Heaven's vengeance.*

てんぴ【天火】an oven (発音は [ʌvn]). ¶～でケーキを焼く bake a cake in the *oven.*

てんぴ【天日】the sun[light]. ¶～で干す dry in *the sun.* ～にさらす expose to *the sun.*

てんびき【天引き】deduction. ¶われわれの所得税は給料から～される Our income tax *is deducted* from our salary. 利子を～して金を貸す loan money with interest *reduced in advance.* 給料の5パーセントを～貯金する deposit 5 percent of *one's* salary on *one's* payday.

てんびょう【点描】a sketch. ¶街頭風景の～ *a sketch* of the street scene.
—法〖絵画〗pointillism. 人物— personal sketches; the profile of a person.

でんぴょう【伝票】a slip; a chit; a tab. ¶～を切る give *a chit.* ～で品物を買う buy articles by signing *chits.* ～と引き換えに金を払う pay money in exchange for *a slip.* 売り上げ— a sales slip. 支払— a payment slip. 入金— a receiving slip. 振替— a transfer slip.

てんびん【天秤】(はかり) a balance; (てんびん棒) a pole. ¶物を～にかける weigh (*something*) in *a balance.* 彼は自分の損と得を～にかけてみた(よく比べて考えた) He *weighed* his losses *against* (≒ *with*) his profits.

てんぷ【天賦】a gift. ¶彼は早くから絵に対して～の才を発揮した He early showed his *natural talent* (≒ *gift*) for painting.

てんぷ【添付】¶～の書類 *appended* papers; *accompanying* documents. 写真を～して願書を提出する submit an application *with one's* photograph.

てんぷ【貼付】¶手紙に50円切手を～する *affix* a fifty yen stamp *to* a letter; *stick* a fifty yen stamp *on* a letter.

でんぶ【臀部】the bottom[s]; the hip[s]; (口語) the buttock[s].

でんぶ【田麩】fish mashed and seasoned.

てんぷく【転覆】¶船が大波を受けて～した Great waves *capsized* the ship. 車が列車に衝突して～した The car *was overturned* when it collided with the train. 彼らは政府を～させることをねらっている They are plotting to *overthrow* the cabinet.

てんぷら【天麩羅】*tempura*; Japanese fried food. ¶エビの～を揚げる *fry* lobster. エビの～ a *fried* lobster.

てんぶん【天分】(天性) [a] nature; (才能) [a] talent; a gift. ¶彼は音楽家としての～を備えている He is highly endowed with musical *talent.* / He has *a* great *gift* (≒ *talent*) *for* music. 子どもたちの～を生かすような教育をするべきだ We must teach the children so as to make the most of their *talents.*

でんぶん【伝聞】a rumor; hearsay. ¶～するところによれば国家の秘密はその新聞記者によってもらされたということである *It is said that* the state secret was leaked out by the newspaperman.

でんぶん【電文】a telegram; a telegraphic message; (海外からの) a cablegram. ¶結婚ひろう宴で友人から寄せられた多数のお祝いの～が読み上げられた A number of congratulatory *telegrams* from their friends were read aloud at the wedding reception.

でんぷん【澱粉】〖化学〗starch. ¶～質の食べ物 *starchy* food.

テンペラが【テンペラ画】a tempera.

てんぺん【天変】¶この国には～地異がとても多い This country is exceedingly subject to *natural disasters.*

てんぺん【転変】mutation. ¶ 彼は幾多の〜を経てきた He has experienced many *vicissitudes of fortune*.

てんぽ【店舗】㊮ a store ; ㊫ a shop. ¶ 〜改造中は休業します We will be closed until repairs on the *premises* have been finished. この通りを少し行った所に新〜を建築中です We are building new *premises* a few blocks from here along this street.

テンポ〘音楽〙tempo. ¶ われわれは急〜の時代の進歩についていけない We cannot keep up with the swift *tempo* of the day. / We cannot keep up with today's quick *tempo*.

てんぼう【展望】a view ; a prospect. ¶ 窓から〜がひらけている *A fine view* can be obtained from the window. / The window affords *a fine view*. ここが峡谷の〜がいちばんすばらしい所だ We can obtain the most picturesque *view* of the gorge here. この論文で彼はことしの政界を〜している In this article he *reviews* the political world of this year.
—車 an observation car. —台 an observatory.

でんぽう【電報】a telegram. ¶ その結果を彼に〜で知らせた I *telegraphed* the result *to* him. / I sent him *a telegraph* of the result. 〜でお知らせ下さい Please let me know *by telegram*. 手紙が着きしだい〜をください *Wire* me as soon as this letter reaches you. 今晩の会には出席できない旨の〜を彼から受け取った I received *a telegram* from him saying that he would be unable to attend the meeting tonight.
—為替 a telegraphic money order. —取扱局 a telegraph office. —料 a telegram fee. —局 a telegraph station. —頼信紙 a telegram form ; a telegraph slip.

でんぽう【伝法】¶ 彼は〜な口調で私にたんかをきった He swore at me in a *wild* tone.

てんまく【天幕】a tent. ¶ 〜を張る pitch *a tent*.

てんません【伝馬船】a junk ; a jolly boat ; a lighter.

てんまつ【顛末】(詳しい説明) a full account ; (事情) the circumstances. ¶ これまでの〜を話してください Please tell me the *whole* story. / Please give me *the full account* (≒ *detail*) of the matter. 彼女は息子がそのような罪を犯すに至った〜を話した She told us about *the circumstances* under which her son came to commit such a crime.

てんまど【天窓】a skylight.

てんめい【天命】destiny ; Providence. ¶ これも〜とあきらめよう Let's resign ourselves to *fate*. 人事を尽くして〜を待とう Let's do our best and leave the rest to *Providence*.

てんめつ【点滅】¶ 懐中電燈を〜させて仲間に合図をした We sent the signal to our friends by *turning* the flashlight *on and off*.

てんめん【纏綿】¶ 彼女の話しぶりには情緒〜たるものがあった She talked in very *sentimental* tones.

てんもう【天網】¶ 〜恢々疎にして漏らさず(諺) Heaven's vengeance is slow but sure. / God stays long but strikes at last. / God permits the wicked but not forever.

てんもん【天文】astronomy. ¶ 〜学的数字に達する reach *astronomical* figures.
—学 astronomy. —学者 an astronomer.
—台 an astronomical observatory.

てんやく【点薬】¶ 〜する drop lotion in the eyes.

てんやく【点訳】braille writing.

てんやもの【店屋物】a dish from a caterer.

てんやわんや ¶ 聴衆のだれかが「火事だ」と叫んだので, 場内は〜の大騒ぎとなった When someone in the audience cried, "Fire!" the whole house *was thrown into an utter confusion*.

てんゆう【天佑】the grace of God. ¶ 命をとりとめたことはまさに〜だ I escaped death *by the grace of Heaven* (≒ *miraculously* ; *by a miracle*).
—神助 the grace of Heaven (≒ God).

てんよ【天与】¶ 〜の才能 a *natural* gift ; a *native* talent.

てんよう【転用】diversion. ¶ 農地を宅地に〜することを禁止された We were prohibited from *using* arable land *for* building purposes.

でんらい【伝来】transmission ; introduction. ¶ 父祖〜の名刀 a celebrated sword *handed down* from *one's* ancestors. 祖先〜の家宝 *one's* family treasure. 茶は中国から日本へ〜した Tea *was introduced* (≒ *was brought over*) into Japan from China.

てんらく【転落】〔a〕fall ; 〔a〕downfall. ¶ 車はがけから〜した The car *fell* off the precipice. 彼はクラスのトップから最下位に〜した He *dropped* from the top to the bottom of the class. 彼は社長の地位から〜するに至った He came to *be degraded* from the presidency.
—死 death by a fall.

てんらん【天覧】His Majesty the Emperor's inspection ; (演芸などの) an Imperial Command ; ㊫ a Royal Command.
¶ この作品は〜の栄に浴した This work of art was honored with *His Majesty's inspection*. 〜に供する submit (*a thing*) to His *Majesty's inspection*.
—試合 an Imperial Command match.

てんらんかい【展覧会】an exhibition ; a show. ¶ 博物館で切手の〜が開かれている *An exhibition* of postage stamps is now on at the museum. 生徒の作品の〜を来る6日に開く We are going to hold *an exhibition* of the pupils' works on the 6th. 〜にきみの絵を出品したらどうだ How about showing (≒ displaying) your paintings in the *exhibition*?
—場 an exhibition gallery. 美術— an art exhibition ; an exhibition of works of art.

でんり【電離】〘電気〙〘物理〙electrolytic dissociation. ¶ 〜する dissociate ; ionize.
—層 the ionosphere.

でんりゅう【電流】an electric current. ¶ 〜を流したり切ったりするのにこの器具を使う This ap-

て

pliance is used to switch on or off *an electric current.* 〜が来ている(いない) The *current* is on (off). 〜の通じている電線 a *live* wire.

—計 a galvanometer. **—**遮断(しゃだん)器 a contact breaker. **—**量 amperage.

でんりょく【電力】 electric power (略して power ということが多い); electricity. ¶〜で動く機械 a machine run by *electricity*; a *power-driven* machine. この発電所はこの辺一帯に〜を供給している This power plant (≒ station) supplies this district with *electric power.* 市民の〜消費量はぐんぐん増加している The citizens' *power* consumption is going up by leaps and bounds.

—会社 an electric power company. **—**開発 power development. **—**計 a wattmeter. **—**資源 power resources. **—**制限 power restriction. **—**不足 ¶20数年前市民は〜不足に悩まされた About twenty odd years ago, the citizens suffered from *an electric power shortage.* **—**料金 power rates; electric charges.

でんれい【伝令】〘軍事〙 an orderly. ¶指揮官のところに〜を出した We sent (≒ dispatched) *an orderly* to the commander.

でんわ【電話】 a telephone; a phone. ¶彼に〜をかけなさい *Call* him *up.* / *Telephone* him. / 英 *Ring* him *up.* すぐ〜で彼に知らせた I told him *by telephone* (≒ *over the telephone*) at once. 彼のところには〜がない He has no *telephone.* きみに〜がかかっている You are called up on the *phone.* / You are wanted on the *phone.* だれか〜に出てほしい I want someone to answer the *phone.* 〜が遠い，もう少し大きな声で話してくれませんか I can't hear you. Would you please speak louder? 〜を切らないで待ってください Please wait *without ringing off* (≒ *without hanging up*). / *Hold the line,* please. 彼が〜に出ている He is speaking on the *telephone.* 〜が切れた The connection is broken off. 〜ではきみの声ははっきり聞きとれなかった The connection was too bad for me to hear you. こちらからまたお〜します I will *phone* (≒ *call*) you *back.* 〜をお借りしたいのですが May I use your *phone*? おるすに〜がありました Someone *called* you in your absence.

—加入者 a telephone subscriber. **—**機 a telephone. **—**局 a telephone office. **—**口 ¶彼女を〜口へ呼んでください Call her on the *telephone.* **—**交換手 a telephone operator. **—**交換台 a telephone switchboard. **—**室 (公衆電話の) 米 a telephone booth; 英 a telephone box. **—**帳 a telephone directory. **—**番号 a telephone number. **—**料 telephone charges. 共同**—** a party line. 切り替え**—** an extension. 公衆**—** a public telephone. 構内**—** a house phone. 国際**—** international telephone service. 市内**—** a local call. 卓上**—** a desk telephone. 長距離**—** a long-distance (≒ trunk) call.

と

と【徒】 fellow (おもに軽べつ的に). ¶無頼の〜 *a gang of* rogues; (ひとり) a gangster. 忘恩の〜 an ingrate.

と【都】 metropolis.

—議会(議員) (a member of) the Metropolitan Assembly. **—**知事 the Metropolitan Governor; the Governor of Tokyo. **—**庁 the Metropolitan Government Office. **—**電(バス) a [metropolitan] streetcar (bus). **—**民 a metropolitan; a citizen of Tokyo. **—**民税 the citizenship tax.

と【途】 way. ¶使節団は渡米の〜についた The mission *left for* America. アメリカから日本へ帰国の〜にある He *is on his way home* from America to Japan.

と【戸】 a door. ¶〜を開けて(閉めて)ください Please open (shut) the *door.* 〜が開いている The *door* is open. 〜が少し開いていた The *door* stood ajar. だれかが〜をたたいている Someone is knocking at the *door.* その〜を開けると台所へ出る The *door* opens into the kitchen. 指を〜にはさまれそうになった I nearly got my finger caught in the *door.* 彼は〜をバタンと閉めた He banged the *door.* 彼が入れないように〜をしめろ Close the *door* on to him. 人の口に〜は立てられぬ (**諺**) People will talk.

と **1** 〖…にかてて加えて〗 and. ¶ノート〜鉛筆を用意しなさい Bring with you a notebook *and* a pencil.

私には兄〜妹がいます I have an elder brother *and* a younger sister.

お茶〜ケーキを出してくれた He served cake *as well as* tea.

2 〖…とともに〗 ¶彼は彼女〜(いっしょに)出かけた He went out *with* (≒ *accompanied by*) her.

3 〖対象・相手〗 ¶そんな人〜はけんかをするな Don't quarrel *with* such a man.

彼〜はつきあうな Don't associate *with* him.

彼〜相談してからご返事する I will let you know

after a talk *with* him.
彼女～結婚することにした I decided to marry her.
4 〖発言・思考の内容を示す〗 ¶ 彼は来る～言ったのにまだ現われない He said [*that*] he would come, but he has not turned up yet.
彼女は近く結婚する～いううわさだ Rumor says *that* she is going to get married soon.
最初はいやなやつだ～思った At first, I thought *that* he was a disagreeable fellow (≒ person).
5 〖比較〗 ¶ お茶～コーヒー～どちらにいたしますか Which would you like, tea *or* coffee?
きみの時計はぼくの～同じだ Your watch is the same as mine.
私の成績を彼の～比べてみた I compared my school record *with* his.
6 〖…するとき〗 ¶ 彼は羽田に着く～すぐ家に電話をかけた He telephoned his family *on* his arrival at Haneda Airport.
よく見る～それはカタツムリだった *Upon* a closer look, I discovered it was a snail.
仕事を終わる～もう10時だった It was already ten *when* I finished my work.
ふたりは会う～けんかをする They never meet without quarreling.
春になる～花が咲く Flowers bloom *in* spring.
彼女は私の顔を見る～夫のぐちをこぼす She complains about her husband *every time* she meets me.
7 〖もし…ならば〗 ¶ 忘れ物をする～家へとりに帰らせますよ *If* you forget anything, I will send you home to get it.
雨が降る～試合は順延になる The game will be postponed *if* it rains.
そうだ～いいが I hope it is true.
8 〖…であろうと〗 ¶ どんな相手だろう～, 絶対に負けない *No matter* who plays against me, I am confident that I will win the game.
行こう～行くまい～, きみの自由だ *Whether* you go *or* not is really up to you.
好む～好まざる～にかかわらず, われわれはそれをしなければならぬ We must do it *whether* we like it *or* not.
家の者がなんと言おう～, 私の決心は変わらない *Regardless of* what my family might say, I am determined.
どんなに彼が急ごう～, その列車にはまにあうまい *No matter how* much he hurries, he won't be able to catch the train.
どうなろう～ぼくの知ったことではない I don't care a bit how it may turn out. / I don't care a bit what may happen.

ト 〔音楽〕 G. ¶ ～調 [the key of] G. ～長(短)調 G major (minor). 嬰(変)～調 G sharp (flat).

ど 【度】 **1** 〖回数〗 a time.
¶ 1～ once.
2～ twice.
2, 3～ two or three *times*; a few *times*.
何～その話を聞いたのですか *How often* have you heard the story?
5～やって5～とも失敗した I tried five *times*, and failed *each time*.
彼のチームは3～続けて負けた His team lost three games in a row.
2 〖温度計・角度・緯度などの〗 a degree. ¶ けさ6時の温度は5～だった The thermometer stood at five *degrees* at six this morning.
熱は37～だった My temperature was thirty-seven *degrees*.
熱は38～5分ある My temperature is thirty-eight point five.
東京は北緯何～ですか What *latitude* is Tokyo [*on*]?
ニューヨークは北緯41～にある New York is on *latitude* 41° N. / The *latitude* of New York is 41° N.
3 〖程度〗 ¶ 何事にも～を過ごさないよう注意しなさい Be careful not to *go too far* in anything.
きみはあまりにも酒の～を過ごしすぎる You drink *far too much*.
4 〖心の平静〗 ¶ どんなことがあっても彼は～を失うことがない Whatever may happen, he never *loses his presence of mind*.

ド 〔音楽〕 do. ¶ ハ調の～ fixed do.

ドア a door. ¶ ～をノックする knock at (≒ on) *a door*. ～を開ける(閉める) open (shut) *a door*. ～がすこし開いていた The *door* stood ajar.

どあい 【度合い】 a degree; an extent; a rate.

とあみ 【投網】 a cast net; a fishing net.
¶ ～を打つ cast *a fishing net*.

とある ¶ 途中, ～木の下でひと休みした On the way we took a rest under *a* tree. ～人物 *a certain* personage.

とい 【問い】 a question; an inquiry. ¶ 次の～に答えよ Answer the following *question*[*s*].
彼は先生によく奇妙な～を発する He often asks his teachers odd *questions*. / He often puts funny *questions* to his teachers.

とい 【樋】 a water pipe; a conduit. ¶ 落ち葉で～が詰まった The *water pipe* has been stopped up with fallen leaves. ～で水を引く draw water by means of *a pipe*.

といあわせ 【問い合わせ】 an inquiry. ¶ その新聞記事についての～が殺到している There has been a lot of *inquiries on* the article in the paper.
—先 a reference. **—状** a letter of inquiry.

といあわ・せる 【問い合わせる】 inquire. ¶ 本社に詳しく～せてみた I *inquired* (≒ *made inquiries*) at the head office for all particulars. 品物があるかどうか発売元に～せてみよう I think I will *address inquiries* to the general agency for the goods. 駅に電話して列車の着く時刻を～せてはどうですか Why don't you call [up] the station and *find out* what time the train comes in? ～せてみたらその報道は誤りだとわかった We found *upon inquiry* that the news was a mistake.

-という ¶ 田村～男がきのう私を訪ねてきた A man *named* Tamura called on me yesterday. むかしむかしある村に権兵衛～男が住んでいた Once upon a time there lived in a village a man, Gonbei *by name*. 彼が病気だ～知らせを受け取

った I heard the news *that* he was sick. 彼がその店で働いた〜事実はない It is not a fact *that* he has worked in that store. 「はい」と言うことは引き受けた〜ことだ The answer 'yes' means *that* he has accepted it.

といえど〔も〕【と雖〔も〕】¶ 聖人〜人間であるからには欠点がある *Even* a saint cannot be free from human weakness. 当たらず〜遠からず It is not far from the mark. 先生〜人間だ Teachers are common people, *too*. 老いたり〜記憶力は確かだ *Although* I am old, I still retain a good memory.

といかえ·す【問い返す】¶ 私は思わず相手に〜した I *asked back* involuntarily. 確認するために彼に何度も〜してみた I *asked* him *again and again* to confirm it.

といか·ける【問いかける】¶ 彼女は急に私にこう〜けてきた She suddenly *flung this question at* me.

といき【吐息】⇒ ためいき
青息— gasps and sighs.

といし【砥石】a whetstone. ¶ 〜でナイフをとぐ sharpen a knife on *a whetstone*.

といただ·す【問いただす】ask ; cross-examine. ¶ われわれは彼にことの真相を〜した We tried to get at the truth by *asking* him questions. わかるまで〜すことをお許しください Allow me to *question* you persistently until I can understand it fully. 嫌疑者を〜した We *cross-examined* the suspect.

ドイツ【独逸】Germany.
—語 German ; the German language. —人 a German ; (総称) the Germans ; the German people. —連邦共和国 the Republic of Germany. 西— West Germany ; the Federal Republic of Germany. 東— East Germany ; the German Democratic Republic.

どいつ ¶ きみは一体どこの〜だ *Who* the hell are you? どこの〜がやったんだ *Who* the devil has done this? 〜もこいつも意気地なしばかりだ You are indeed *all* a pack of cowards.

といつ·める【問い詰める】cross-examine. ¶ 検事は容疑者を〜めた The public prosecutor *cross-examined* the suspect (≒ *questioned* the suspect *closely*).

トイレ〔ット〕 a toilet room ; a lavatory ; a water-closet (W.C.) ; 米 a washroom ; (劇場などの) a rest room. ¶ 〜はどこですか Where can I wash my hands?
—ペーパー toilet (≒ lavatory) paper.

とう【当】¶ 〜を得た処置をする take a *proper* (≒ *suitable*) measure. 〜を得た助言を頂き感謝しております I am greatly indebted to you for your *judicious* (≒ *sensible*) advice. きみのは〜を得た考えだ Yours is a *good* idea. 彼の意見は〜を得ていない His opinion *is* not quite *correct*. / *His opinion is wide of the mark*.

とう【党】a party ; (仲間) a set. ¶ 4, 5人の人が集まって〜を組織した Four or five people formed *a party* (≒ *a clique*). 多くの人が〜に加入(を脱退)した Many people joined (left) the *party*. 〜の方針に従うべきだ We must follow the lines of the *party*.
—員 a member of a party. —首 the party leader ; the chief of a party. —大会 a party convention.

とう【等】**1** 〖等級〗a class. ¶ 競走で1〜になった He won *the first prize* in the race. 2〜で旅行した We traveled second *class*. 2〜片道切符を1枚ください Please give me a second-*class* single ticket.
2 〖など〗and so on ; etc. ¶ 鉛筆, ペン, 消しゴム〜を私に持ってきてください Please bring me pencils, pens, erasers, *and so on*. Xさん, Yさん, Zさん〜多くの作家が集まった There gathered a lot of writers such as Mr. X, Mr. Y, Mr. Z *and so forth*.

とう【塔】a tower ; (尖塔) a steeple ; a spire ; (東洋の寺院の) a pagoda. ¶ 五重の〜 *a* five-storied *pagoda*. 象牙(ぞうげ)の〜 an ivory *tower*. 教会の〜 *a* church *tower*. パリのエッフェル〜は高さはどのくらいありますか How high is the Eiffel *Tower* in Paris?

とう【籐】〖植物〗a cane ; a rattan.
—細工 rattan work.

とう【糖】⇒ とうぶん

とう【薹】a flowering stalk. ¶ フキの〜 a butterbur flower. 〜が立つ go (≒ run) to seed ; (盛りを過ぎる) be past *one's* prime.

-とう【-頭】a head. ¶ 牛3〜 three *head* of cattle (head は単複同形).

と·う【問う】¶ 彼の安否を〜うてみよう I will *inquire after* his safety. 彼は責任を〜われた He *was called to account*. 年齢を〜わず会に参加してよい Anyone can participate in the party *irrespective of* age. 値のいかんを〜わずぜひともその本は買いたい I want to buy the book by all means, *whatever* the price *may be*. 晴雨を〜わずピクニックを行なうとのことだ I hear that they will go on a picnic *rain or shine*. 彼は殺人罪に〜われるだろう He will *be charged with* murder.

と·う【訪う】¶ 〜う人もまれな目立たぬ場所 an inconspicuous place which attracts few *visitors*.

どう【堂】a temple ; (小さなもの) a shrine. ¶ 彼の話しぶりは〜に入ったものだ He makes an *excellent* (≒ *admirable*) speech.

どう【銅】copper.
—管 a copper tube. —線 copper wire. —像 a 〔bronze〕 statue.

どう【胴】(身体の) the trunk ; (衣服の) the body ; (楽器の) the frame ; (馬の) the barrel ; (船の) the hull.
¶ 彼は〜が長い He has *a* long *trunk*.

どう (馬に対するかけ声) soho!

どう【如何】**1** 〖疑問〗¶ 駅へは〜行ったらいいですか *How* can I get to the station? 「do? 〜するおつもりですか *What* do you intend to 〜彼に返事していいかわからない I don't know *how* to answer him.
景気は〜だね *How*'s your business? / *How*'s

everything going on?
日本の第一印象は～ですか *What* are your first impressions of Japan?
彼にあたってみたら～ですか *Why* don't you try to talk with him? / *Why* not try him? / *What about* seeing him?
その後病気は～ですか *How* have you been feeling?
結局話は～なりましたか *What* happened after all? / *What*'s the result of the story?
彼はその後～なったか *What* has become of him since then?
あの娘さんを～思いますか *What* do you think of that girl? / *How* do you like that girl?
2 〖その他〗 ¶ もう1杯コーヒーは～ですか *Won't you have* (≒ *Do you care for*) another cup of coffee?
病人は今急に～ということはない The patient will not suddenly change for the worse.
内容は～というわけではないが, 文章がわかりにくい The contents are not bad, but the style is hard to understand.
彼のことばは～ともとれる His words are rather ambiguous. / His words can be taken *in either way*.
～みても彼女は独身と思えぬ You would never think she was single.
そんな気の弱いことで～する You shouldn't be so weak-hearted. / *What*'s going to become of you if you're so faint-hearted?
～なりと好きなようにしたまえ Do as you please. / Go your own way.

とうあ 【東亜】 East Asia ; (東洋) the East ; (極東) the Far East.
—諸国 the East-Asiatic countries.

どうあげ 【胴上げ】 ¶ 勝ったチームの主将を～する *toss* the captain of the victorious team *shoulder-high*.

とうあさ 【遠浅】 a shoaling. ¶ この辺りの海は～になっている The sea about here *is shallow for a good distance from the shore*.

とうあつせん 【等圧線】 〖気象〗 an isobaric line.

とうあん 【答案】 (解答) an answer. ¶ 数学の～ *a paper in* mathematics. もう～を出してしまった I have already handed in my *paper*. ～を調べる look over (≒ grade) *examination papers*.
—用紙 an examination paper.

とうい 【当意】 **—即妙** ¶ 彼は～即妙に答えた His answer *was witty*. / He gave *a repartee*. 彼は～即妙の才がある He *is quick-witted*.

とうい 【等位】 **—節** 〖文法〗 a co-ordinate clause. **—接続詞** 〖文法〗 a co-ordinate conjunction.

とうい 【糖衣】 **—錠** a sugar-coated pill (≒ tablet).

どうい 【同位】 **—角** 〖数学〗 the corresponding angles. **—元素** 〖物理〗 an isotope.

どうい 【同意】 agreement ; consent. ¶ 彼は私に～した He *agreed with* me. 彼女は彼の提案に～した She *consented* (≒ *agreed*) *to* his proposal. 彼の～を得るのは難しかった It was difficult for me to obtain his *consent*.

どういう ¶ ～ことなのですか What's the matter? / Is anything the matter with you? / (相手の言ったことについて) What do you mean 〔by that〕? ～ものが欲しいのですか What do you want? ～わけで来なかったのか *Why* didn't you come? 彼らに～ふうに連絡したらいいでしょう *How* shall I contact them? ～ことになるかわからない I don't know *what* will become of it. ～ことになろうとも私はかまわない *Whatever* may happen I don't care.

どういご 【同意語】 a synonym.

とういす 【籐椅子】 a rattan (≒ cane) chair.

どういたしまして 【如何致しまして】 ¶ (礼を言われたときなど) (特に 米) You are welcome. / Not at all. / That's quite all right. / It's my pleasure. / Don't mention it.

とういつ 【統一】 unity ; unification. ¶ 目下国家を～することが必要だ What is necessary at present is to *unify* the nation. 彼がその国を～した He *brought* the country *into unity*. 多くの党派をひとつに～することは不可能だ It is impossible to *unify* a lot of parties. このチームは～を欠いている This team lacks *unity*. このクラスのほうがあのクラスより～がある This class has more *unity* than that. この集団には～がない This group of men *is divided*. その国は～ある国家といえない The nation cannot be said to be a *united* one.
—意見 a unified opinion. **—行動** united action. **—国家** a united nation. **—戦線** a united front. **—体** a united whole.

どういつ 【同一】 identity. ¶ ～の identical ; the same. 私はきみと～意見だ I *am of the same* opinion *as* you 〔are〕. これとそれは～のものだ This *is identical with* that. このふたつの犯罪は～犯人の仕業だ *The same* person committed these two crimes. ジキル博士とハイド氏は～人物だ Dr. Jekyll and Mr. Hyde are *one and the same* person.

どういつし 【同一視】 ¶ ふたりを～してはならない These two persons should not *be viewed* (≒ *be looked at*) *in the same light*. これらの問題は～してもよいものだ These problems could *be put in the same category*.

とういん 【党員】 a party member. ¶ 彼は共産党の～になった He joined the Communist Party. 彼は～として5年間も活動している He has been working in the party as long as five years.

とういん 【登院】 ¶ (議会へ) ～する attend (the House of Representatives).

とういん 【頭韻】 alliteration. ¶ パイプとペットは～を踏んでいる 'Pipe' *alliterates* with 'pet'.

どういん 【動因】 a motive ; motivation.
¶ その事件が～となって彼は会社を辞めた That incident *caused* (≒ *motivated*) him *to* resign the company.

どういん 【動員】 mobilization. ¶ 軍隊が～された An army *was mobilized*. 全署員を～して

と

警戒した All the police *were sent out* on the alert. その芝居は10万人の観客を～した The play *drew* a hundred thousand audience.
—令 mobilization orders.

とうえい【投影】(画法) projection.
—器 a projector. —図 a projection chart.
—図法 the method of projections. 頭上—器 Overhead Project (O.H.P と略す).

とうおう【東欧】 ¶～諸国 *East European* countries.

どうおん【同音】 —異義語 a homonym.

とうおんせん【等温線】 an isothermal line.

とうか【投下】 ¶爆弾を～する drop bombs (*on*). 私はばく大な資本を～した I *invested* a large amount of capital.
—資本 invested capital.

とうか【等価】 equivalence. ¶これらは～である These *are equivalent.*
—量〘化学〙an equivalent.

とうか【燈下・灯下】 ¶～に書をしたためる write a letter *by lamplight.*

とうか【燈火】 [lamp] light. ¶～親しむべき候となる The good season for reading is come.

とうか【糖化】 ¶でんぷんを～する *saccharize* starch.
—酵素 diastatic enzyme.

とうが【陶画】 a porcelain picture.

どうか【同化】 assimilation. ¶原住民は植民者と～しなかった The natives did not *adapt* (≒*adjust*) *themselves with* the settlers. 食物は～されて栄養となる Food *is assimilated into* nourishment.

どうか【銅貨】 a copper [coin]. ¶10円～ *a* ten yen *copper.*

どうか 1〘どうぞ〙 ¶～許してください Pardon me, *please.* / *Won't you* forgive me?
～食べる物を少しください *Please* give me something to eat.
～私の言うことを聞いてほしい *Will you please* listen to what I say?
～これをもう一回説明してくださいませんか *Would you mind* explaining it to me once more?
～これを受けとってください *Please* take this, *will you?*
2〘疑問〙 ¶来られるか～聞いてごらん Ask him *if* he can come.
うわさがほんとうか～疑わしい It is doubtful *whether* the rumor is true *or* not.
彼女が作家であるか～私は知らない I do not know *if* she is a writer.
あなたの申し出を受けるべきか～まだ決めていない We have not decided yet *whether* to accept your offer.

どうが【童画】 a nursery picture.

どうが【動画】 an animation; animated cartoon.

とうかい【倒壊】 collapse. ¶多数の家屋が地震で～した Many houses *fell down* because of the earthquake.
—家屋 ¶～家屋は200戸に達した The *collapsed* houses amounted to two hundred [in number].

とうがい【等外】(競技の) an also-ran. ¶彼は～だった He *failed to win the prize.* それは～に落ちることまちがいない It is sure to *fall under the regular grades.*

とうがい【当該】 ¶～校の説明を聞きたい I want to hear the explanation of the school *concerned.* ～官庁 the authorities *concerned.*

とうかいどう【東海道】 *Tokaido.*
—五十三次 The Fifty-Three Post-Stations of the *Tokaido.* —新幹線 The new *Tokaido* [trunk] line. —本線 The main *Tokaido* line.

とうかく【倒閣】 overthrowing the cabinet. ¶彼らは～を目指している They are aiming at *the downfall of the Cabinet.*
—運動 a movement to unseat (≒overthrow) the Cabinet.

とうかく【頭角】 ¶彼は幼いころから～をあらわしていた He *distinguished himself* as a child.

どうかく【同格】〘文法〙apposition. ¶ふたりは～である These two *are of the same rank.* 彼と私は資格のうえで～だ He *is equal in* the rank with me.

どうがく【同学】 ¶ふたりは～の友だ The two persons are *schoolmates.* われわれ3人は～の士だ We three are *companions in our studies.* / We three *study together in the same line.*

どうがく【同額】 the same amount (*of* salary).

どうかこうか ¶～毎日を暮らしている I am getting along *somehow.* 彼は2日かかって～村にたどりついた It was two days before he arrived at the village *somehow or other.* ～約束の時間までに仕事を終えることができた I *managed to* finish the work before the appointed time.

どうかして ¶～最後までやり通そう I will carry it out to the last *somehow or other.* ～彼の家族に知らせなければならない We must tell it to his family *by any means.*

どうか・する ¶彼は～している *There is something the matter with* him. この時計は～している *Something is the matter* (≒*is wrong*) *with* this watch. ～しましたか *Is anything the matter with* you? 彼は～するとおかしなことを言う He *sometimes* says strange things. 人は～するとまちがいをおかすことがある We *are apt to* make a mistake.

どうかせん【導火線】 a fuse. ¶その争いが戦争の～となった The trouble *gave rise to* war. 彼はダイナマイトの～に点火した He fired the *fuse* of dynamite.

とうかつ【統轄】 supervision; control. ¶部内を～する人 a person to *control* the department; a person who *is responsible for* the department.

どうかつ【恫喝】 ¶彼は殺すと言って私を～した He *threatened* to kill me.
—外交 bluff diplomacy.

とうから【疾うから】 ¶～わかっていたのだ I have *long since* been aware of it. 彼は～仕事にとりかかっていたのだ It was *a long time ago* that he began his task.

とうがらし【唐辛子】red pepper. ¶ この～はよくきかない This *red pepper* does not bite much.

とうかん【等閑】negligence.
—視 ¶ それは～視すべき問題ではない It is not a thing to *be ignored* (≒ *be neglected*).

とうかん【投函】¶ 手紙を～する *mail* (≒ 英 *post*) a letter.

とうかん【統監】supervision. ¶ 全軍を～する *supervise* the whole army.

とうがん【冬瓜】〔植物〕a wax gourd.

どうかん【同感】¶ 私も～です I *agree with* you. 私もあなたと～です I *am of the same opinion as* you.

どうかん【道管・導管】a conduit ; a pipe.

どうがん【童顔】a boyish face. ¶ 彼は～だ He is *juvenile-looking*. / He has *a child-like face*.

とうき【冬季・冬期】the winter season.
—オリンピック競技 the winter Olympic games. **—休暇** the winter vacation.

とうき【投機】speculation. ¶ 株の～をする *speculate in* stocks. ～に手を出す go in for *speculation*. ～として土地を買った I *ventured* to buy a tract of land.
—心 ¶ ～心をあおられた My *speculative spirit* was inflamed.

とうき【党紀】party discipline. ¶ ～を粛正する enforce *party discipline*.

とうき【党規】party rules.

とうき【陶器】earthenware (通例は集合的に扱う). ¶ ～の花びん a *china* vase.
—商 (店) a china shop ; (人) a crockery dealer. **—製造所** a pottery.

とうき【登記】registration. ¶ 新築した家を～した I *had* my newly-built house *registered*. この家はもう～済みだ This house *is registered*.
—係 a registrar. **—所** a registry office.
—簿 a register. **—料** a registration fee.

とうき【当期】the present term. ¶ ～利益金 the profits for this term.

とうき【騰貴】a rise ; a price hike. ¶ 物価は～するだろう Prices will *go up* (≒ *hike up*). ドル価が～した The dollar *appreciated*. 地価の～で土地の購入が困難になった The *rise* of the land value has made it difficult for us to buy land. 物価の～で生活も苦しくなった Owing to the *rise* of prices, we find it difficult now to make a living. 原料の～ぶりはたいへんなものだ The raw material *has gone up* a great deal〔in price〕.

とうぎ【党議】(会議) a party council ; (決議) a party decision. ¶ ～にはかりたい The question should be referred to the *party council*.

とうぎ【討議】discussion. ¶ 今講堂で～が行なわれている *Discussions* are now going on in the auditorium. 彼らは 1 週間にわたって教育問題を～した They *discussed* the educational problem for a week. 活発な～が望ましい *A hot discussion* is desirable. なんの問題を～中なのか知りたい I want to know what problem *is under discussion*. そろそろ～を始めよう Now let's begin the *debate*. 大いに～した結果, 提案は退けられた After much *debate*, the proposal was rejected. 明日何をするか～しよう Let's *discuss* what we shall do tomorrow.

とうぎ【闘技】a contest ; a competition ; a match.
—者 a contestant ; a competitor. **—場** an arena ; a ring.

どうき【同期】the same period. ¶ 彼とぼくは～だ He and I are *graduates in the same class*. 昨年の～に比べると寒い Compared with *the corresponding period* of last year, it is colder.
—会 a class reunion. **—生** a classmate ; a graduate in the same class.

どうき【動機】a motive. ¶ これを書いた～はなんですか What *caused* you to write this? こんなことをやった～は自分でもわからない I myself cannot see why I did such a thing. ぼくは純粋な～からそう言っているのだ I am speaking from *a* disinterested *motive*.

どうき【銅器】copperware.
—時代 the Bronze Age.

どうき【動悸】〔a〕palpitation ;〔a〕pulsation. ¶ ～が激しく打ちはじめた My heart began to *beat* fast.

どうぎ【同義】¶ このことばと～のことばをあげなさい Give a word *synonymous* with this word.
—語 a synonym.

どうぎ【胴着】underwear ; an undergarment ; a vest.

どうぎ【動議】a motion. ¶ ～を提出する make *a motion*. ～に賛成する second *a motion*. ～が可決(否決)された The *motion* was adopted (was rejected). 彼の～によりその議案は可決された The bill was passed on his *motion*.
緊急— an urgent motion.

どうぎ【道義】morality. ¶ それは～に反する That is against *morality*. 彼のあの行為は～上許せない That conduct of his is not to be permitted from the *moral* point of view. このごろの～の退廃ぶりはひどい The *demoralization* in recent years is too much.
—心 morality. ¶ 彼の～心に訴えたい I think I will appeal to his sense of *morality*.

とうきび【唐黍】〔植物〕Indian millet.

とうきゅう【投球】¶ ～する throw a ball. 彼の～は直球ばかりだ His *pitching* is full of straight balls.

とうきゅう【等級】a class ; a grade ; an order. ¶ この種の商品に～をつけるのは難しい It is not easy to *grade* these sort of articles. ～によって値段も違っている The prices differ according to the *class*.

とうぎゅう【闘牛】a bullfight ; (牛) a fighting bull.
—士 a bullfighter ; (スペインの) a matador ; (馬上の) a toreador. **—場** a bull ring.

どうきゅう【同級】the same class. ¶ 私は彼とは～だ He and I are in *the same class*. / He

と

is my classmate.
—生 a classmate.
とうぎょ【統御】rule; (統制) control. ¶ 部下を～する *control one's* followers. 国王は人民を～する The king *rules* (≒ *reigns*) *over* his people.
どうきょ【同居】¶ 私の家にふたりの人が～している Two persons are living with my family. 山田君のところに外人がひとり～中だ A foreigner is lodging at Yamada's (≒ with Yamada).
—人 an inmate; (下宿人) a lodger.
どうきょう【同郷】the same province.
¶ あの人は私と～だ He *comes from the same province as* I. 彼とは～のよしみで親しくなった I became familiar with him because of *the identity of the native place.*
—人 a person from the same province.
どうぎょう【同業】the same business.
—組合 a trade association; a guild. —者 a man of the same business (≒ trade); a fellow trader; (集合的に) the trade; the profession (知的職業には business や trade の代わりに profession を用いる).
とうきょく【当局】the authorities.
学校— the school authorities. 警察— the police authorities. 関係— (その筋) the authorities concerned; the proper authorities. —者 (単数) a (≒ the) person in authority.
どうぐ【道具】a tool.
—箱 a tool box. —屋 (家具や) a furniture dealer; (骨とう品や) a curio dealer. 家財— household goods. 商売— the tools of *one's* trade. 台所— kitchen utensils.
とうぐう【東宮】the Crown Prince (イギリス以外の皇太子をいう英語).
—御所 the Crown Prince's Palace. —職 the Board of the Crown Prince's Affairs.
どうくつ【洞窟】a cave; a cavern; a grotto.
とうけ【当家】this family. ¶ ～にはそういう名前の人はいません We have nobody of that name *in our family.*
とうげ【峠】a [mountain] pass; (頂上) the height. ¶ 寒さも今が～だ It's the coldest time in winter. 暑さも～を越した The hottest time of the year *is over.* 彼の病気は～を越した His illness *has passed the crisis* (≒ *has turned the corner*). 病人はきょうが～だ The invalid *is passing the crisis* today. われわれの仕事も～を越した Our work *is over the hump.*
どうけ【道化】drollery. ¶ ～じみたまねをするな Don't *make a fool of yourself.* / Don't *be funny.* 彼が～を演じた He played *the clown.*
—師 a buffoon. —芝居 a farce. —もの a jester. —役 a comic actor; a clown; a fool.
とうけい【東経】the east longitude. ¶ ～45度15分に at 45 degrees 15 minutes of *east longitude* (略して at Long. 45° 15′ E と記す).
とうけい【統計】statistics (複数扱い). ¶ 政府発表の～ *statistics* issued by the government. 彼が～をとった He *took statistics.* ～によれば, 死因のうち第1位はがんだそうだ According to *statistics,* the first cause of death is cancer. その問題について正確な～はまだ発表されていない Exact *statistics* on the subject are not yet published.
—学 statistics. —学者 a statistician. —表 a statistical table. 人口— statistics of population.
とうけい【闘鶏】a cockfight.
とうげい【陶芸】ceramic art; ceramics.
—家 a ceramist. —品 works of ceramic art.
どうけい【同系】¶ ～の会社 an *affiliated* (≒ *allied*) company.
—色 ¶ ～色のきれ *similar-colored* cloth.
どうけい【同型】the same type. ¶ 最近は～の犯罪が多い Recently crimes of *a similar type* (≒ *a similar pattern*) have occurred very often. ～の靴 shoes *of the same style.*
どうけい【同慶】¶ 入試合格とのことご～の至りです I *offer my hearty congratulations on* your success in the entrance examination.
どうけい【憧憬】[a] yearning. ¶ 外国に～をいだいている若者が多い Many young people have *a yearning for* foreign countries.
とうけつ【凍結】freezing. ¶ 日本の在外資産が一時～された The Japanese assets abroad *were frozen* for a time.
とうけん【刀剣】a sword.
—商 a sword dealer.
とうけん【闘犬】(戦い) a dogfight; (犬) a fighting dog.
どうけん【同権】equality.
男女— the equality of the sexes; equal rights for men and women.
とうこう【投降】surrender. ¶ ～する者が続出した One after another they appeared and *gave up* (≒ *laid down*) *their arms.*
—者 a surrenderer.
とうこう【投稿】a contribution. ¶ ～大歓迎 *Contributions* [are] cordially welcomed. (広告などでは are を省く). 彼は毎月雑誌に小説を～している He *contributes* a novel *to* a magazine every month. 彼はこの雑誌にしばしば～する He *is a* frequent *contributor* to this magazine.
—者 a contributor. —欄 the reader's columns.
とうこう【登校】¶ 毎日バスで～する I *go to* (≒ *attend*) school by bus every day. 受験者は9時までに～されたい The examinees are expected to *present themselves* by nine.
とうごう【投合】¶ われわれは意気～した仲だ We are *congenial* friends. 彼とは初対面で意気～した I *fell in with his views* when we met first.
とうごう【等号】〔数学〕the sign of equality.
とうごう【統合】synthesis. ¶ 学校をひとつに～する We *synthesize* schools. 天皇は国民～の象徴である The Emperor is the symbol of *the unity* of the people. 大学の～移転問題 the

と

problem of *integrating* and removing the college campus.

—参謀本部 米 the Joint Chiefs of Staff.

どうこう【同好】 the same taste. ¶～の士 persons *of the same tastes.*

—会 ¶テニス～会 an amateur tennis club.

どうこう【同行】 ¶途中まで～します I will *go* part of the way *with* you. 警察へ～していただきたい Please come *with* me to the police station. ～できなくて申しわけありませんでした I am sorry not to *have traveled with* you. ～5人 *a party of* five.

—者 fellow traveler.

どうこう【動向】 a trend. ¶世論の～ the *trend* of public opinion. 彼は経済界の～にたいへん敏感だ He is very responsive to economic *trends.* 時勢の～におくれてはいけない We must follow the *movement* of the times. / We should keep up with the world.

どうこう【銅鉱】 copper ore.

どうこう【瞳孔】〘解剖学〙 the pupil; the apple of the eye.

—拡大 the dilatation of the pupil. —縮小 the contraction of the pupil.

どうこう ¶～言ってもしかたがない What's done cannot be undone. / It's no use saying *this or that* now. ～せよと言われる覚えはない You cannot order me to do this or that. ～言うところはあるまい You can't have nothing to *complain of* (≒ *grumble at*).

どうこういきょく【同工異曲】 ¶これらの小説はいずれも～だ These novels *are more or less alike* (≒ *similar*).

とうこうせん【等高線】 a contour.

—地図 a contour-line map.

とうごく【投獄】 imprisonment. ¶彼は～された He *was imprisoned.* 無実の罪で～された He *was* falsely *put into prison.*

どうこく【慟哭】 lamentation. ¶国王の死に全国民が～した All the nation *wailed* (≒ *lamented*) the death of the king.

どうこくじん【同国人】 a fellow countryman.

とうごせん【等語線】〘言語学〙 an isogloss.

とうこん【当今】 these days; nowadays.

¶～の学生 students *of today.*

とうこん【闘魂】 a fighting spirit.

とうさ【等差】 equal difference.

—級数（数列）〘数学〙 arithmetical progression (series).

とうさ【踏査】 a survey. ¶そこをくまなく～しよう Let's *tread* the place from end to end. 史跡の実地～をした We made *a survey* (≒ *a field investigation*) *of* a historic scene.

とうざ【当座】 1〘一時〙 the time being. ¶1万円あれば～のまにあう Ten thousand yen will do *for the moment* (≒ *for the present*). これを～の費用にしてください Please use this for *immediate* expenses. ～の必要品だけ持っていったほうがいい You should take your *immediate* needs. ～しのぎにいくらか融通してほしい Won't you spare me some money as a *temporary* expedient?

2〘当座預金〙 a current account (≒ deposit). ¶その金は～〔預金〕へ預け入れることにした I have decided to deposit the money in my *current account.*

—貸し越し an overdraft.

どうさ【動作】 action; behavior. ¶～がにぶい（敏捷だ）He is slow (quick) in *action.* 彼女は～がしとやかだ She has graceful *manners.* 彼はどうぞと～で示した He *motioned* me *to* enter.

とうさい【搭載】 ¶船に武器を～した We *loaded* the ship *with* arms. / We *had* arms *on board.* 船に軍隊を～した We *embarked* troops *on board.* この船は12インチ砲6門を～している This ship *carries* six 12-inch guns.

とうざい【東西】 the east and the west.

¶～に大きな道路が走っている There is a wide road running *from east to west.* この村は～約20マイルだ This village is about twenty miles *from east to west.* このおきては古今～に通じる This rule is applicable to *all times and places.*

どうざい【同罪】 ¶きみも～だ You *are also to blame.* きみたちはふたりとも～だ Both of you *are equally guilty.*

とうさく【盗作】 plagiarism. ¶この詩は彼の作の～ではないか Isn't this the *plagiarism* from his poem? 他人の論文を～するなんてもってのほかだ You must not think of *plagiarizing* another person's essay.

とうさく【倒錯】 perversion. ¶～した精神の持ち主 a man of a *perverse* mind.

性的—者 a sexual pervert.

どうさつ【洞察】〔an〕insight. ¶彼は人間性をみごとに～していた He had *an* admirable *insight* into human nature. 彼は未来を～する目を持っている He is wise enough to *see into* the future. 彼には～力がある He is a man *of insight.*

とうさん【倒産】〔a〕bankruptcy. ¶当市では昨年だけで～が10を下らなかった In this city there were more than ten *bankruptcies* last year. 不景気で各地に～が続出した Owing to the depression, many companies *went bankrupt* (≒ *went into bankruptcy*) one after another in various places. あの会社の～はおもに運転資金の不足が原因である The *failure* of that company is chiefly attributed to the want of working capital.

どうさん【動産】 movable (≒ personal) property; movables.

どうざん【銅山】 a copper mine.

とうし【凍死】 death from cold. ¶山で10人が～した Ten persons *died of cold* (≒ *were frozen to death*) among the mountains.

—者 a person frozen to death.

とうし【投資】 investment. ¶新しい企業に多額の～をした I *invested* heavily *in* a new enterprise. ～して利益があった It proved *a* good *investment.* この事業には大金を～するつもりだ I

と

will *put* a large sum of money *in* this business. 今は土地を買うのが最も安全な～法とはいえない To buy land cannot be said to be the safest way of *investment* now.
―信託 investment trust. 一般―家 the investing public; general investors. 設備― investment in plant and equipment.

とうし【透視】 clairvoyance. ¶ レントゲンで胸部を～してもらった I *had* my chest *looked at through* the fluoroscope. 彼には未来が～できるとか He is said to be *a clairvoyant.*
―画法 perspective. ―検査 fluoroscopy.

とうし【闘士】 a fighter. ¶ 彼は組合活動の～だ He is *a fighter* in union activities. 彼女は女権運動の～だった She was *a champion* of woman's rights.

とうし【闘志】 fight; a fighting spirit. ¶ ～がない I have no *fighting spirit.* ～を示してほしい I wish you to show *fight.* ～を失ってはならぬ You must never lose *fight.*
―満々 ¶ 彼は～満々だ He is full of *fight.* 度重なる敗戦にもめげず, 彼らは～満々だ In spite of repeated defeats, they still have plenty of *fight* in them.

と

とうじ【冬至】 the winter solstice.
―線 the Tropic of Capricorn.

とうじ【当時】 in those days; then. ¶ ～私はロンドンに滞在中だった I stayed in London *at the time.* ～はまだ子どもだった *In those days* I was still a child. この町も～はにぎやかだった This town was crowded *at that time.* ～の思い出がよみがえってきた Memories *of those days* returned to me. 彼が～の市長だった He was the *then* mayor.

とうじ【湯治】 hotspring cure. ¶ 彼は草津に～に行った He went to *take the baths* at Kusatsu. 彼は～療養中だ He is now recruiting himself *at the spa.* ～がよく効いた The waters did me a great deal of good. (欧米では温泉につかる風習はない. 温泉療法では鉱泉を飲むのがふつう).
―客 a spa visitor.

とうじ【答辞】 a response. ¶ 卒業式では彼が～を読むことになっている He is due to make *an address in response* at the graduation.

どうし【同士】 a fellow. ¶ みんな日本人～だ We are all Japanese. 彼らはかたき～だ They are rivals (≒ enemies).
学生― fellow students. 恋人― lovers. 隣― next-door neighbors. うちわ― ¶ うちわ～だ We are members of the same family.

どうし【同志】 a comrade. ¶ 彼はわれわれの～だ He is *a kindred spirit* with us. ～を糾合した We gathered people who agree [with us].
―愛 comradeship.

どうし【動詞】〘文法〙a verb.
―変化 (の活用) conjugation. 規則(不規則)― a regular (an irregular) verb. 自(他)― an intransitive (a transitive) verb.

どうじ【同時】 ¶ 彼らは～に出発した They started *at the same time.* 彼が寝ると～に私は起きた I got up *the moment* he went to bed. 彼は勤勉であると～に頭もいい He is *both* (≒ *at once*) diligent *and* clever. この仕事は楽しいが, ～に多少危険でもある This work is pleasant, but *on the other hand* it is somewhat dangerous. 目的地に着くと～に彼はその場にぶっ倒れた *On* arriv*ing* at his destination, he fell down on the spot.
―通訳 a simultaneous interpretation; (人) a simultaneous interpreter. ―放送 (ラジオ・テレビの) a simulcast.

とうしき【等式】〘数学〙an equality.

とうじき【陶磁器】 pottery; chinaware.

とうじしゃ【当事者】 the person concerned. ¶ 争いの～に事情を聞いた We heard the contending *parties.* その件は～に一任すべきだ We should leave the matter entirely to *the parties concerned.* 本契約は各～においていつでも解約することをえる The contract may be canceled at any time by the other party.

どうした ¶ ～の? *What is the matter with* you? / *Is anything the matter with* you? ～らよいのだろう *What* shall I do? / I wonder *what* I should do. それが～ And *what* of that? / So *what?* これは～金だ *How* did you come by this money? 彼は～はずみか失敗した He somehow failed.

とうじつ【当日】 the day; (定められた日) the appointed day. ¶ 試験～に病気になってしまった Unluckily I got ill *on the very day of* the examination. 発行～のみ有効です This is valid *for the day of* issue only. ～限り通用の切符です It's a *day* ticket. ～雨天の際は順延 If it rains on *the appointed day,* it will be postponed till the first fine day.

どうしつ【同室】 ¶ 彼とぼくは寮では～だった He and I lived in *the same room* of the dormitory. / He and I were roommates in the dormitory.
―者 a roommate.

どうしつ【同質】 the same quality. ¶ ～の事件が続々と起きた Accidents *of the same sort* happened one after another.

どうじつ【同日】 the same day. ¶ 彼とぼくとは～の談ではない *There is no comparison between* him *and* me.

どうして【如何して】 (なぜ) why; (どのようにして) how. ¶ ～彼は怒っているのか *Why* is he angry? 彼女は～出かけたのですか *What made* her go out? ～勉強ができなかったのですか *What* prevented you from studying? 「きみがそれをやりなさい」「～?」 "You do it." "*Why?*" 「この本は読んではいけない」「～いけないの?」 "You mustn't read this book." "*Why not?*" その事故は～起こったのかだれも知らない No one knows *how* the accident happened.

どうしても 1〚ぜひとも〛by all means; at any cost. ¶ ～行かなければならない I must go *by all means.*
彼は～その仕事を引き受けると言ってきかない He *insists on* accepting the work.
彼は～自分の息子をヨーロッパに行かせたがっている He *insists* that his son [should] visit

Europe.
～彼に会いたい I *would give anything to* meet him.
～この仕事は完成させなければならぬ We must accomplish this work *at all costs* (≒ *at any cost*).
2〖否定的な意味で〗 ¶ この窓は～開かない This window *will not* open.
どこに置いたのか～思い出せない I cannot, *for the life of me*, remember where I put it.
～この問題が解けない I cannot solve this problem *however hard I try*.
彼は～それをするのをいやがった He flatly *refused to* do it.
私にはこの歌のよさが～わからない I cannot see the merit of this song *on any account*.
3〖その他〗 ¶ あの子は～女の子に見える That child is a girl *to all appearances*.
努力する者が～最後には成功する Those who work hard succeed *after all*.

とうしゃ【投射】 projection.
—角〘物理〙 an angle of incidence.

とうしゃ【透写】 tracing. ¶ 図面を～する trace a drawing.
—紙 tracing paper. —用具 a tracer.

とうしゃ【謄写】 copy ; transcription. ¶ 原稿を50部～印刷する *get* 50 *mimeograph copies* of a manuscript.
—版 a mimeograph. —版原紙 stencil paper.

とうしゅ【当主】 the 〔present〕 head (*of* a family).

とうしゅ【投手】〘野球〙 a pitcher. ¶ その試合では彼が～をつとめた He *pitched* (≒ *took the mound*) in the game.
—戦 a pitcher's battle. 勝利— a winning pitcher. 敗戦— a losing pitcher. 左— a southpaw ; a left-hand pitcher. 速球— a speedball pitcher. 完投— a go-through pitcher. 先発— a starting pitcher. 救援— a relief pitcher. —陣 the pitching staff.
—力 pitching power.

とうしゅ【党首】 the party leader.
—会談 a party leaders' talk.

どうしゅ【同種】 the same kind. ¶ 私たちは～の過ちをしがちである We are apt to make *the same kind of* mistakes.

とうしゅう【踏襲】 ¶ 彼は従来の政策を～する予定である He is to *follow* the former policy.

とうしゅく【投宿】 ¶ 駅前の旅館に～した We *stayed* (≒ *put up*) *at* an inn in front of the station.

とうしょ【当初】 ¶ ～の計画は実行できなかった We couldn't carry out the *original* plan.

とうしょ【当所】 ¶ ～には有名な寺がある There is a famous temple *here* (≒ *in this place*).
～ではタイピストを求めている *Our office* wants a typist.

とうしょ【投書】 ¶ 彼はよく新聞に～する He often *writes a letter to* the paper.
—家 a contributor ; a correspondent. —箱 a suggestion box. —欄 the readers' column.

どうしょ【同所】 the same place. ¶ ～にご郵送ください Please mail letters to *the above-mentioned address*.

どうしょ【同書】 the same book.

とうしょう【凍傷】 frostbite. ¶ 彼は足が～にかかった He *had* his feet *frostbitten*. / His feet *were frostbitten*.

とうしょう【闘将】 a brave leader.

とうじょう【東上】 ¶ 彼は来月～する He will *go up to Tokyo* next month.

とうじょう【登場】 appearance. ¶ 彼が～する機会がついに来た The opportunity of his *appearance* has come at last. 彼は政界にさっそうと～した He *made an* impressive *appearance* in politics. 多くの政治家がこの事件に～する(関係している) Many politicians *are involved in* this affair. 弁慶～(脚本で) *Enter* Benkei.
—人物(文学作品の) characters.

とうじょう【搭乗】 ¶ 飛行機に～する *board* (≒ *get on*) an airplane.
—員 a crew.

どうじょう【同上】 the same as above ; ditto (略語は do.).

どうじょう【同乗】 ¶ そのトラックに～した We *rode* on the truck *together*.
—者 a fellow passenger.

どうじょう【同情】 sympathy. ¶ 彼は私に～してくれた He *sympathized with* me. 彼に～する人は少なくない Not a few people *have sympathy for* him. 私は彼に心から～する I *have* (≒ *feel*) hearty *sympathy for* him. 彼は人々の～を得ようとした He tried to excite other people's *sympathy*. 彼に対する～の気持ちから私は彼を訪ねたのだ It was *out of sympathy with* him that I called on him. 世間の～が彼に集まった Public *sympathies* were centered on him. 彼に対して人々の～はしだいに高まった People's *sympathy for* him mounted gradually. 彼のリーダーとしての立場は確かに～すべきだ It is certain that his standpoint as a leader deserves our *sympathy*.
—者 a sympathizer. —スト a sympathy strike.

どうじょう【道場】 ¶ 剣道の～ *a* fencing *hall*. 柔道の～ *a judo hall*. 座禅の～ *a training hall* for the *Zen* sect.

とうじょうか【頭状花】〘植物〙 capitate flowers.

どうしょく【同色】 ¶ 彼の上着とネクタイは～だった His suit and tie *were* 〔*of*〕 *the same color*.

どうしょくぶつ【動植物】 animals and plants.
—界 the animal and vegetable kingdoms.

とうしん【刀身】 the blade of a sword.

とうしん【投身】 ¶ 彼女は海に～自殺した She *drowned herself* in the sea.

とうしん【東進】 ¶ 艦隊は～中 The fleet *is moving east*.

とうしん【答申】 a report. ¶ 委員会は文部大臣に～をした The committee *submitted a report to* the Education Minister.
—案 a draft report. —書 a report.

とうしん【等身】 ¶ ～大の人形 a *life-size* doll.

とうしん【等親】the degree of kinship.
¶三～ a relation in the third *degree* [of consanguinity].
とうしん【燈心】a wick.
とうじん【党人】a party man.
とうじん【蕩尽】¶彼は全財産を～した He *wasted* (≒ *squandered*) all his fortune.
どうしん【童心】the child's mind. ¶～にかえる recover the *innocence of a child*. ～を傷つける hurt the *feelings of children*.
どうしん【道心】—堅固 ¶～堅固な僧 a priest *of firm faith*. ～堅固な人 a man *of strict morals*.
どうじん【同人】a literary coterie; (同人のひとりは) a member (*of* a literary coterie).
—雑誌 a literary coterie magazine.
どうしんえん【同心円】〔数学〕concentric circles.
とうすい【陶酔】intoxication; [an] ecstasy. ¶彼らは美しい音楽に～した They *were intoxicated* (≒ *were fascinated*) *with* (≒ *by*) the beautiful music.
自己— self-intoxication.
とうすい【統帥】the supreme command.
¶三軍を～する *command* all the armed forces.
—権 the prerogative of supreme command. —者 ¶大統領は陸海空三軍の～者である The president is *the supreme commander* of the army, navy and air forces.
とうすう【頭数】the number of heads.
とう·ずる【投ずる】**1**〖投げる〗throw (*a thing*) into.
¶彼は次から次へと書類を火の中に～じた He *threw* the documents *into* the fire one after another.
彼はがけの上から水中に身を～じた He *threw himself into* the water from the top of the cliff.
2〖参加する〗join. ¶彼らはみな敵がたに～じた All of them *went over to* the enemy.
彼は暴漢の群れに～じた He *has joined* the band of rogues.
3〖資金を〗invest. ¶彼はその会社の株に持ち金全部を～じた He *invested* all his money *in* the company's stock.
私財を～じて図書館を建てた He built a library *at his own expense*.
100万円を～じて書庫をつくった I built my library *at a cost of* one million yen.
彼は巨額の金を～じて邸宅を買った He *paid a large amount of money* for his mansion.
4〖票を〗cast (a vote). ¶彼に一票を～じた I *voted for* him.
どう·ずる【動ずる】¶最悪の事態にも～じない覚悟ができている I *am prepared for* the worst. 彼はそのニュースに～じなかった He *was* not *agitated* (≒ *moved*) *at* the news. 女の子はものに～じやすい Girls *get excited* easily.
どうせ ¶人間は～死ぬのだ Man will die *after all*. ～勝つにきまっている We *are sure to* win. ～私はばかですよ I'm silly, *as you know*. ～やるなら，しっかりやれ If you do it *at all*, do it well. ～いつかはそれをやらなければならない I must do it *sooner or later*.
とうせい【当世】nowadays. ¶～そんな歌ははやらない *Nowadays* such a song doesn't get popular.
—風 ¶これが～風のやり方だ This is *an up-to-date way* of doing.
とうせい【統制】control. ¶政府の～は厳しすぎる The government *control* is too tight. 米が政府の～下にあったこともあった Rice was once under the government *control*. 式典は～がとれていた The ceremony *was well-organized*.
—経済 controlled economy. —品 controlled articles. 物価— price control.
とうせい【陶製】¶～の花瓶 an *earthen* vase.
どうせい【同性】¶彼女は～の間に人気がある She is popular with her *own sex*.
—愛 homosexuality; (女性間の) Lesbianism; (人) a homosexual; (俗語) a homo; (女性の) a lesbian.
どうせい【同姓】the same name. ¶この村には～の人が多い There are a lot of persons *of the same name*. 彼は私と～同名だ He has *the same name as* myself. / He is my *namesake*. 彼らは～異人だ They are different persons *of the same name*.
どうせい【動静】movements. ¶敵の～を探る spy on the *movements* of the enemy. 彼は政界の～に詳しい He knows well about the *situation* of political circles.
どうせい【同棲】cohabitation. ¶彼らは～している They are living together like husband and wife. 彼女はボーイフレンドと～している She *is cohabiting with* her boyfriend.
—者 a cohabitant.
どうぜい【同勢】¶～わずかに10人だった The *company* consisted of ten members only.
とうせき【投石】¶群衆が警官に～した The crowd *threw stones* at the policemen.
とうせき【党籍】the party register. ¶～を離れる leave the *party*. 彼は～を剝脱(はくだつ)された He was expelled from the *party*.
どうせき【同席】company. ¶パーティーでは彼と～だった I *sat at the same table with* him at the party. 彼が～しているとけっして退屈しない *In his company* we are never bored. 私たちは～する機会が多い We *are* often *in each other's company*. 彼女とは～したくない I don't like her *company*.
とうせつ【当節】¶～の青年は何事によらず自分勝手な行ないをする Young men *of today* have their own way in everything. ～そんな物ははやらない *Nowadays* (≒ *Today*) such a thing is out of fashion.
とうせん【当選】election. ¶彼は代議士に～した He *was elected to* the Diet. 彼は再度議長に～するだろう He is likely to *be elected* chairman again. この候補者は～の見込みがない（ある） This candidate *is out of the running* (*is in the running*). 彼は懸賞小説の1等に～した

He *won the first prize* in a novel contest.

—者 a successful candidate. —小説 a prize-winning novel. —無効 annulment of *a person's* election.

とうせん【当籤】prize winning. ¶ 宝くじの1等1千万円に～した I *won* the first prize of ten million yen in the public lottery. 彼は住宅の抽選に～した He *drew a lucky number* in the lottery for housing.

—者 a prize-winner. —番号 a lucky (≒ winning) number.

とうぜん【当然】naturally. ¶ それは～のことだ It is *a matter of course*. 彼の罰は～の結果だ His punishment is a *natural* result. 彼が罰せられるのは～のことだ He *deserves* punishment. / He *deserves* to be punished. ～の報復というべきだ It may well be said to be his just *deserts*. きみは～すぐ出発すべきだ You *ought to* start at once. きみが彼の忠告を聞くのは～だ It *is natural* that you [should] listen to his advice. 彼は～出発を延期すべきだった He *should* (≒ *ought to*) have postponed his departure.

とうぜん【陶然】¶ 彼は酔って～としていた He was *pleasantly* drunk with *sake*. 名曲に～と聞きほれた I *was fascinated with* the beautiful music.

どうせん【同船】¶ 彼と～だった I *was on board the same ship with* him. / I *took the same ship with* him.

—者 a fellow passenger.

どうせん【銅線】[a] copper wire.

どうせん【銅銭】a copper coin.

どうせん【導線】a leading wire.

どうぜん【同然】¶ 彼は死んだも～だ He is *as good as* dead. こんな本は紙くず～だ Such a book is *little* (≒ *no*) *better than* waste paper. この試合は勝ったも～だ We *practically* won the game.

どうぞ【何卒】please. ¶ ～お入りください *Please* come in. ～ケーキを自由につまんでください *Please* help yourself to [the] cakes. ～こちらへ This way, *please*. ～お許しください I beg your pardon.

とうそう【逃走】an escape; a flight; a getaway. ¶ 犯人が刑務所から～した A criminal *escaped* (≒ *ran away*; *got away*) from the prison. 強盗はまだ～中だ The robber *is* still *at large*.

—者 a runaway; a fugitive.

とうそう【闘争】a struggle; a strife.

—資金 struggle funds. —本能 ¶ どんな動物も～本能を持っている Any animal has *a fighting* (≒ *combative*) *instinct*. 賃上げ— a wage boost struggle; a struggle for higher wages. 年末— ¶ 組合が会社と年末～をした The union *struggled for the year-end bonus* with the company.

どうそう【同窓】¶ 彼と私は～だ He and I studied at the same school. 彼とは大学は～だ He and I are graduates of the same university.

—会（組織） an alumni association; a graduates' association; (会合) an alumni meeting. —生 a classmate; a graduate; 困 (男) an alumnus (覆 alumni); 困 (女) an alumna (覆 alumnae).

どうぞう【銅像】a bronze statue. ¶ ネルソンを偲(しの)んで～が建てられた *A bronze statue* was erected in memory of Nelson.

とうそく【党則】party rules.

とうそく【等速】〘物理〙uniform velocity.

とうぞく【盗賊】a thief; (強盗) a robber.

どうぞく【同族】(種族) the same race; (家) the same family.

—会社 a family partnership. —結婚 endogamy. —体〘化学〙a homologue.

どうそたい【同素体】〘化学〙an allotrope.

とうそつ【統率】leadership. ¶ 彼は全軍を～した He *commanded* all the armed forces. 彼はその政党をうまく～している He *leads* the party well. 彼は～力がある He has good *leadership*.

—者 a leader.

とうた【淘汰】dismissal; (生物) selection. ¶ 無能職員を～する *dismiss* incapable officials. 生存に適さないものは～される Those unfit for survival will *be weeded out* (≒ *be got rid of*).

自然— natural selection.

とうだい【燈台】a lighthouse. ¶ ～もと暗し (諺) *At the foot of the candle it is dark*.

—守 a lighthouse keeper.

とうだい【当代】the present age. ¶ 彼は～まれに見る才人だ He is a man of ability rarely to be met with *in the present age*. 彼は～随一の画家だ He is the greatest painter *of the day*.

どうたい【同体】¶ 両力士は～となって倒れた Both the *sumo*-wrestlers fell down *in a pile*.

どうたい【胴体】a body. ¶ 飛行機の～はまっ二つに折れた The *body* of the airplane was severed in two.

—着陸 a belly landing. ¶ 飛行機はやむなく～着陸した The plane was forced to make *a belly landing*.

どうたい【動態】¶ 人口の～を調査する examine *the movement* of population.

どうたい【導体】〘物理〙(電気の) a conductor.

不良— a bad conductor.

とうたつ【到達】arrival. ¶ 時間どおりに目的地に～した I *arrived at* my destination on time. 名人の域に～することは困難だ It is difficult to *be a master* (≒ *be an expert*). ついにわれわれは結論に～した At last we *have come to* the conclusion.

とうたん【東端】¶ 市の～にある公園 the park *at the east*[*ern*] *end* of the city.

とうだん【登壇】¶ ～する *mount* (≒ *step on*) a platform.

とうち【当地】this place; [down] here. ¶ ～にお越しのときはご一報ください Please let me know when you come *here*. ～は冬でも暖かい It is mild *here* even in winter.

と

とうち【統治】rule ; reign ; government. ¶天皇は日本を〜しない The Emperor doesn't *rule* (≒ *govern*) Japan. その国はフランスの〜下にある The country is under the *rule* of France.
—権 the supreme power ; sovereignty.

とうちほう【倒置法】〔文法〕〔修辞〕inversion.

とうちゃく【到着】arrival. ¶東京〜は午後5時の予定だ We are to *arrive in* Tokyo at 5 p.m. 自動車はまだ〜しない The car *has* not *come* yet. バスは5分後に〜するだろう The bus will *appear* in five minutes. さきほどお手紙〜しました Your letter *reached* me a while ago.
—順 ¶〜順にこちらに並んでください Stand in line *in order of arrival*. **—しだい** ¶あちらに〜しだいお知らせします I will tell you as I *have reached* there.

と

どうちゃく【同着】¶彼らは〜だった They *arrived at the same time.*

どうちゃく【撞着】conflict ; contradiction. 前後— ¶彼の話は前後〜している His story *is inconsistent.* 自家— ¶彼は自家〜した He *contradicted himself.*

とうちゅう【頭注】a headnote.

どうちゅう【道中】¶〜ご無事で I wish you a good journey ! / Bon voyage !

とうちょう【盗聴】(電話などの) wiretap. ¶電話の〜をする *tap* the telephone wires ; *wiretap* the telephone. ラジオの〜をする *listen to* the radio *without a license.*
—器 a wiretap.

とうちょう【登庁】¶大臣は朝11時に〜する The minister *goes to the office* at eleven in the morning.

とうちょう【登頂】¶一行はエベレスト〜に成功した The party succeeded in *reaching the top of* Mt. Everest.

どうちょう【同調】¶私はこの方針に〜していない I do not *sympathize with* this policy. 彼の意見に〜する者は少ない Few *agree with* him. 波長をVOAに〜させる *tune* the radio *in to* V.O.A.
—者 a sympathizer.

とうちょく【当直】duty ; watch. ¶今夜は〜だ I *am on duty* (≒ *am on watch*) this night.
—員 a man on duty (≒ watch) (watch は艦船の場合によく使う).

とうつう【疼痛】a pain. ¶背中に激しい〜を覚えた I had a sharp *pain* in the back.

とうてい【到底】not ... possibly ; after all. ¶私には〜そんなことはできません I *cannot possibly* do such a thing. その電車には〜まにあわない You *can* hardly reach the train in time. それでは〜無理だ It is *absolutely* impossible. 彼の提案は〜われわれには満足できない His proposal *is far from* being satisfactory to us.

どうてい【童貞】chasitity ; virginity.

どうてい【道程】¶東京から大阪までの〜 the *distance* between Tokyo and Osaka. 学問研究の〜は長い The *path* of learning is long. / Art is long.

とうてき【投擲】throw.
—競技 throwing events.

どうてき【動的】¶〜な表現 *dynamic* expressions. 彼は人間の心理を〜にとらえている He understands human psychology *in motion.*

とうてつ【透徹】penetration. ¶〜した理論 a *clear*[*-cut*] theory.

どうでも ¶それは〜いいことだ That *does not matter.* 〜きみのいいようにしなさい Do *as you please.* 成績など〜いい I *don't care at all* what my results are like. テレビなんか〜いいだろう *Never mind* television. きみの言うことは〜いいことではないか What you say *is a matter of no importance*, isn't it ? 彼の気に入るかどうかはぼくには〜いいことだ It *makes little difference to* me whether he likes it or not.

とうてん【東天】the eastern sky.
—紅〔鳥類〕a brown domestic fowl.

とうてん【読点】a comma. ¶〜を打つ use *a comma* (*between* clauses).

どうてん【同点】a tie. ¶試合は2対2の〜で引き分けになった The game ended in *a tie*, 2 to 2. 彼とテストが〜だった I had the *same marks as* he in the test. われわれは彼らと〜になった We *tied with* them. 試合は9回裏で〜になった The teams *tied* (≒ *drew*) at the second half of the ninth inning in the game. 彼は〜ホーマーをかっとばした He swatted the *tying* homer.

どうてん【動転】¶その光景にまったく心が〜した I *was* utterly *confounded* at the sight.

どうでんたい【導電体】〔物理〕an electric conductor.

とうど【凍土】frozen land.

とうと・い【尊い・貴い】(貴重な) precious ; (高貴な) noble. ¶〜い宝 a *precious* treasure. 〜いお方 a *noble* (≒ *high*) person. きみは健康の〜いことを知らない You don't know the *value* of health.

とうとう【到頭】at last ; at length ; after all. (at last, at length (ようやく)は否定文に用いない. after all は「いろいろあったがやはり結局は」の意味で否定文にも肯定文にも用いる).
¶彼は〜現われなかった He didn't show up *after all.* 彼は〜実験に成功した *At last* he succeeded in the experiment. 彼はしゃべりすぎて〜声がかれてしまった He talked *till* he became hoarse.

とうとう【等等】¶肉, 魚, 野菜〜 meat, fish, vegetables *and so on.*

どうとう【同等】¶あの会社は男女を〜に待遇する The company treats men and women *equally.* あのふたりの腕前は〜だ The two *are equal in* ability. 彼はわれわれと〜の立場でつきあう He associates with us *on equal terms.* 応募者は高校卒またはそれと〜の学力を有する者でなければならない The applicants must be high school graduates and *the equivalent.*

どうどう【同道】¶駅までご〜します I'll *accompany* you to the station. ご〜してもよろしいですか Could I *go with* you ?

どうどう【堂堂】¶〜たる大邸宅 a *magnificent*

(≒ *grand*) mansion. ～たる大男 a big *dignified-looking* man. 彼は～たる態度で答えた He answered in an impressive manner. ～とした試合ぶりだった He played in the match quite *fairly*. 彼らは～と戦った They fought *fair*. 大臣は自動車で～とやってきた The minister came *in style* in an automobile. 彼らは～たる議論を展開した They argued with each other *fairly and squarely*.

とうとうと【滔滔と】¶ 彼は～弁じた He spoke *eloquently*. 川は～流れていた The river was flowing *in torrents*.

どうどうめぐり【堂堂巡り】¶ われわれの議論は～するだけだった We were arguing *in a circle*.

どうとく【道徳】morality. ¶ ～は慣習から起こる *Morality* comes from customs. 彼は～を教えている He is teaching *morality*.
—家 a moralist. —観念 a moral sense. —教育 moral education. —心 a moral sense. —性 morality. —問題 a moral question.

とうとつ【唐突】¶ 彼はいつも～な発言をする He always speaks *abruptly*. 今それを言うのは～すぎる It *is* too *sudden* to say it now.

とうと・ぶ【尊ぶ・貴ぶ】value ; make much of ; (尊敬) respect.

とうどり【頭取】¶ 銀行の～ *the president* of a bank.

とうなす【唐茄子】〔植物〕a pumpkin.

とうなん【東南】southeast. ¶ 船は横浜の～30マイルの所にある The boat is located 30 miles *southeast* of Yokohama.
—アジア Southeast Asia.

とうなん【盗難】robbery ; (事件) a robbery. ¶ ～を警察に届けなければならない We must report the *robbery* (≒ *burglary*) to the police. 留守中に～に会った I *was robbed* in my absence. 昨夜その事務所に～事件が発生した *A robbery* took place at the office yesterday. ～防止につとめなさい Attend to the prevention of *robbery*.
—警報器 a burglar alarm. —品 stolen articles. —保険 burglary insurance.

とうに【疾うに】¶ それは～知っていた I knew it *long ago*.

どうにか ¶ ～こうにかして暖をとることができた I could keep warm *somehow* [*or other*]. ～試験に受かった I *barely* passed the examination. ～家族を養うことができた I *managed to* support my family.

どうにも ¶ ～彼の助けようがなかった I couldn't help him *anyhow* (≒ *in any way*). この暑さじゃ～やりきれない I *really* can't stand this heat. ～ならない It can't be helped.

とうにゅう【投入】¶ その事業に多額の資金を～した They *invested* a lot of money in the enterprise.

どうにゅう【導入】introduction. ¶ 外資を～する *introduce* foreign capital. 西洋文化の～ the *introduction* of Western culture. 生徒を新しい課に～する *introduce* pupils to a new lesson.

どうにょうかん【導尿管】〔解剖学〕the ureter.

とうにょうびょう【糖尿病】〔医学〕diabetes.
—患者 a diabetic.

とうにん【当人】the said person. ¶ ～を調べよう Let's examine *the person in question* (≒ *the person concerned*). その件については～は全然われ関せずだ *The man himself* is quite indifferent to the matter.

どうにん【同人】(同じ人) the same person.

とうねん【当年】(今年) this year ; (その年) that year. ¶ 彼女は～とって18歳だ She is eighteen years old *this year*.

どうねん【同年】¶ きみとは～生まれだ I was born *in the same year as* you. / I *am* [*of*] *your own age*. / I *am as old as* you.

とうの【当の】¶ ～本人にそれをやる気がない *The man himself* is not willing to do it.

どうのこうの ¶ 今更～言っても始まらない It is too late to *complain*. 彼のことを～言ってはいけない Don't try to *find fault with* him.

とうは【党派】a party ; (政党内の派閥) a faction. ¶ どの～にも属していない I don't belong to any *party*. その党にはいくつかの有力な～がある There are some powerful *factions* in the party. 彼らはその目的実現のために～を組んだ They formed *a party* to realize their object.
—心 party-spirit ; partisanship. 超—外交 supra-party diplomacy.

とうは【踏破】¶ 彼は全国を～した He *traveled through* the country *on foot*.

どうはい【同輩】*one's* equals. ¶ 彼は～の受けがいい He gets on well with his *colleagues*. ～のよしみで飲みにいこう Let's go and have a drink together.

とうはつ【頭髪】the hair [of the head]. ¶ ～が薄くなったね Your *hair* has become thin. 彼は～を長くしている He wears his *hair* long.

とうばつ【討伐】suppression ; subjugation. ¶ ゲリラを～する *subdue* guerrillas.
—軍 a punitive expedition.

とうばつ【盗伐】¶ ～する cut down trees without a license ; cut down another man's trees.

とうはん【登攀】¶ ヒマラヤを～する *climb* the Himalayas.
—隊 a climbing party. —者 a climber.

とうばん【当番】duty ; (順番) turn. ¶ きょうは私の～だ I'*m on duty* today. 今度はきみが～だ This is your *turn for duty*. きょうはきみが掃除～だ It is your *turn* to sweep the room today.

とうばん【登板】¶ (野球で) きのうの試合では彼が～した He *was a pitcher* in yesterday's game. / He *took the plate* (≒ *took the mound*) in yesterday's game.

どうはん【同伴】¶ 彼は家族～で箱根へ行った He went to Hakone *with* his family. あなたに～して行きたい I'd like to *accompany* you.
—者 a companion. —席 family seats. 夫人— ¶ 彼らは夫人～が普通だ They are gen-

と

erally *accompanied* by their wives.
どうばん【銅板】sheet copper.
どうばん【銅版】a copperplate.
—刷り a copperplate print; etching printing.
とうひ【当否】propriety; right or wrong. ¶ その理論の～を論じよう Let's discuss whether the theory *is right or wrong.* 手段の～は問題でない It matters little whether the measure *is proper or not.*
とうひ【逃避】escape. ¶ 彼は世間から～したい気持ちになっている He is disposed to *escape* from the world. 彼は～的な人生を送っている He *lives as a recluse.*
—行 an escape journey. —文学 escapist literature.
とうひ【党費】party expenses.
とうひ【等比】〔数学〕equal ratio.
—級数(数列) geometric progression.

と

とうひょう【投票】voting. ¶ 彼らは国民の～によって選ばれる They are elected by the *vote* of the people. これは～で決めるべきだ It must be decided by *vote.* ぜひ彼に～してください Do *vote for* him. 彼は大多数の～を得て当選した He won the election by a large majority. この法案に賛成の～をしよう Let's *vote for* this bill. その法案に反対の～をした We *voted against* the bill. 彼らはみな社会党に～した They all *voted* Socialist. ～の結果は賛成25, 反対8だった The *vote* was twenty-five ayes and eight noes. もう～は済みましたか Have you been to *vote* yet? この政党は～数の5分の1も得られなかった The party polled less than a fifth of the *votes* cast.
—者 a voter. —所 a polling place (≒ 英 station). —日 a voting day. —用紙 a voting paper. —率 a poll. ¶ 高い～率 *a* heavy *poll.* 低い～率 *a* light *poll.* 記名— an open vote. 無記名— a secret vote. 決選— final ballot. 信任— a vote of confidence. 不信任— a vote of non-confidence. 無効— a spoiled vote.
とうびょう【闘病】the fight against disease. ¶ 10年間～生活を送った I*'ve struggled against the disease* for ten years.
どうひょう【道標】a guidepost; a signpost.
どうびょう【同病】¶ ～相哀れむ（諺）Misery loves company. / Fellow sufferers pity each other.
とうひん【盗品】stolen articles.
とうふ【豆腐】¶ ～1丁 a cake of *tofu* (≒ bean curd).
とうぶ【頭部】the head. ¶ 自動車事故で～に負傷した I was injured in *the head* in the motorcar accident.
とうぶ【東部】the eastern part; (アメリカの) the East Coast. ¶ 東京の～地区では in *the eastern part* of Tokyo. あのアメリカ人は～の出身だ The American comes from *the East.*
どうふう【同封】¶ 切手を～しました I *enclosed* a postage stamp *with* this letter. 彼女の手紙には小切手が～してあった Her letter *enclosed* a check. 写真を1枚～します I send you a picture *under the same cover.* 3,000円の小切手を～しましたからお受け取りください *Enclosed* please find a check for 3,000 yen. (手紙のきまり文句).
どうふく【同腹】¶ ～の兄弟 brothers of the same mother.
どうぶつ【動物】an animal.
—園 a zoo; a zoological garden. —界 the animal kingdom. —学 zoology. —学者 a zoologist. —実験 a biological test. —性たんぱく animal protein. 高等(下等)— the higher (lower) animal.
とうぶん【等分】¶ 彼の財産は3～された His property *was divided into* three *equal parts.* 費用を～しよう Let's *share* the expenses *equally.* われわれ5人で利益を～する We *share* the profit among the five.
とうぶん【糖分】sugar. ¶ それは多量の～を含む It contains a lot of *sugar.* 尿の～の検査を受けた My urine was examined for *sugar.*
とうぶん【当分】for the time. ¶ ～この暑さは続く(しばらくの間) This heat will last *for some time.* ～来なくてよろしい(さしあたり) You don't have to come *for the present.*
どうぶん【同文】the same script. ¶ 以下～です The following sentences are *the same* as the previous.
とうへき【盗癖】kleptomania; a thievish habit. ¶ 彼には～がある He is *a kleptomania.* / He has *a thievish habit.*
とうへん【等辺】¶ 二～三角形 an *isosceles* (≒ *equilateral*) triangle.
とうべん【答弁】an answer; a reply. ¶ 彼に～を求めた We demanded *an answer* of him. 私には～しかねる I am not in a position to *answer* for it. その質問に対して担当者が～に立った The person in charge stood up to *answer* the question. 私には～のしようがなかった I didn't know how to *explain* it.
とうへんぼく【唐変木】a blockhead. ¶ この～め What *a fool*! / You *blockhead*!
とうほう【当方】¶ ～にもおいでください(私の家にも) Please call on *us,* too. それは～の過失です(私の方の) It's *my* fault. / It's a fault *on my part.* / I'm in the wrong.
とうほう【東方】the east. ¶ 市の～6キロの所に小高い丘がある There is a hill six kilometers *east of* the city.
とうぼう【逃亡】escape; getaway. ¶ 彼は国外に～した He *fled* the country. 犯人は西方へ～中 The criminal is now making his *escape* toward the west. 捕虜が～を企てた The prisoners attempted to *escape* from jail.
—者 a fugitive; a runaway.
どうほう【同胞】a compatriot; a fellow countryman. ¶ 海外の～ *compatriots* abroad.
—愛 brotherly love.
とうほく【東北】the northeast.
—地方 the northeastern districts.
とうほくとう【東北東】east-northeast (E.N.E.).
とうほん【謄本】a copy.
戸籍— a certified copy of the domiciliary

register. ¶ 戸籍～を取り寄せた I got *a certified copy of the domiciliary register* by mail.

とうほんせいそう【東奔西走】 ¶ 彼らは～して資金を集めた They *busied themselves to* raise funds. 彼はいつも～している He *is* always *on the move.*

どうまき【胴巻き】 a bellyband.

どうまごえ【胴間声】 a deep bass voice.

どうまわり【胴回り】 *one's* girth ; *one's* waist. ¶ 私は～が90センチある I measure 90 centimeters *in girth* (≒ *around the waist*).

とうみつ【糖蜜】 molasses ; syrup ; 英 treacle.

どうみゃく【動脈】〘解剖学〙an artery. ¶ 地下鉄は今や東京の～となっている The subway is now *one of the most important means of transportation* in Tokyo.

—硬化〔症〕〘医学〙arteriosclerosis ; sclerosis of the artery. ¶ わが社は今や～硬化の状態だ Our company *has come to a deadlock.* 大— the main artery.

とうみょう【燈明】 a sacred light. ¶ 神前に～を上げる offer *a light* (≒ *a taper*) before god.

とうみん【冬眠】 hibernation ; winter sleep. ¶ リスは目下～中だ Squirrels *are* now *hibernating* (≒ *are* now *in hibernation*).

とうみん【島民】 an islander.

とうむ【党務】 party affairs.

とうめい【透明】 transparency. ¶ ～な水 *clear* water. 無色～の液体 a colorless, *transparent* liquid.

—体 a transparent body. —度 transparency.

どうめい【同名】 the same name. ¶ 彼は～異人だった He was a different person with *the same name.* あの人と私は～なだけだ We have just *the same surname,* but are unrelated.

どうめい【同盟】 an alliance. ¶ 日本はイギリスと～を結んだ Japan made (≒ formed ; concluded) *an alliance* with England. わが国はかつてイタリア・ドイツと～を結んでいた Our country *was* once *allied with* Italy and Germany.

—休校 a school strike. —国 an ally ; an allied power. —条約 a treaty of alliance. —罷業 a strike ; 米 a walkout. 三国— a triple alliance. 日英— the Anglo-Japanese Alliance.

とうめん【当面】 ¶ これが～の仕事です This is the *immediate* work for you. ～の問題はなんでしょうか What's the *urgent* problem? / What's the question *of the day*? 始めから難問題に～した From the beginning difficult problems *faced* us. / We *were confronted with* great difficulties from the very start.

どうも ¶ ～ありがとう Thank you *very much.* ～すみません I am *very* sorry for you. ～わからない I cannot *somehow* understand this. ～あすは雨らしい *It is likely to* rain tomorrow. ～きょうはおかしい I don't feel well today. ～寒いね It's *quite* cold, isn't it? ～どこかで見た写真だ *I am sure* I have seen this photo somewhere before.

どうもう【獰猛】 ferocity. ¶ トラは～な動物だ Tigers are *fierce* (≒ *savage*) animals. 彼は～な顔つきの男だ He looks *fierce.* / He is a *ferocious*-looking man.

どうもく【瞠目】 opening *one's* eyes wide. ¶ 彼は近年～すべき業績をあげている He has produced *surprising* achievements in recent years. 彼の技量の進歩には～させられた I *was* quite *astonished at* the progress of his skill.

どうもと【胴元】 the banker.

どうもり【堂守り】 a temple keeper.

とうもろこし【玉蜀黍】〘植物〙maize ; Indian corn ; 米 corn.

どうもん【同門】 ¶ 彼とは～で学んだ間柄だ He and I were *fellow pupils.*

どうもん【洞門】 a tunnel.

とうや【陶冶】 cultivation ; training. ¶ 人格を～する *cultivate* (≒ *train ; build up*) *one's* character.

とうやく【投薬】 prescription ; medication. ¶ 患者に～する *prescribe* (≒ *give ; administer*) medicine to patients (prescribe のときは for も用いる).

どうやく【同役】 a colleague ; an associate.

どうやら ¶ ～歩き通した We walked all the way *somehow.* ～会にまにあった I *managed to* be in time for the meeting. ～彼の言うことはほんとうらしい What he says seems to be true *somehow.* ～雨らしい *It looks like* rain. ～彼は不在らしい *I am afraid* he is away from home. ～仕事を終えた I have *barely* finished my work. ～彼が犯人のようだ *It is likely that* he himself is the criminal.

とうゆ【燈油】 lamp oil ; kerosene.

とうゆ【桐油】 tung oil.

—紙 oil-paper.

とうゆうし【投融資】 investment and accommodation.

財政— investment and accommodation of financial funds.

とうよ【投与】 ¶ 患者には薬を～する *give* (≒ *administer*) medicine to a patient.

とうよう【当用】 present use.

—漢字 Chinese characters for everyday use. —日記 a diary.

とうよう【東洋】 the East ; the Orient.

—学 Oriental studies. —学者 an Orientalist. —諸国 the Eastern countries. —人 an Oriental ; the Orientals. —風 Orientalism ;〘建築〙Oriental style. —文明 Oriental civilization.

とうよう【盗用】 appropriation. ¶ 公金を～する *appropriate* (≒ *embezzle*) public money. あそこでは他社のデザインを～している They *are stealing* (≒ *are appropriating*) the designs of other companies.

とうよう【登用・登庸】 promotion ; appointment. ¶ 大いに人材を～すべきだ You should positively *promote* people on the merit of their talent.

どうよう【同様】 1〘似た〙¶ これは前のと～の例で

す This is *the same* example as we had before.
これと～の事件を手がけたことがある I have handled a case *similar to* this before. / I have handled a case *like* this before.
私にもそれと～の経験がある I have had a *similar* experience to that.
この車は新品～だ This car is *practically* (≒ *as good as*) new.
彼に金を貸すのはどぶに捨てるも～だ You *might as well* throw your money down the drain *as* lend it to him.
2 〖同じように〗 ¶ いとこと私とは兄弟～に育てられた My cousin and I were raised *like* real brothers.
きみが日本語が話せないと～ぼくも英語が話せない I can *no more* speak English *than* you speak Japanese.

と

どうよう【動揺】 (車) jolting ; (不安) unrest ; (騒ぎ) disturbance. ¶ この車は少しも～しない This car runs *smoothly*. 私の心は～していた My mind *was wavering*. 人心は～している People *are agitated*. 彼は民衆の～を抑えることに一生懸命だった He was working hard at repressing the people's *agitation*. 彼の発言は実業界に～をきたした His remark has brought about *disturbances* in the business world.

どうよう【童謡】 songs for children ; nursery rhymes.

どうよく【胴欲・胴慾】 avarice. ¶ ～な金貸し a *heartless* (≒ *cruel*) money-lender.

とうらい【到来】 arrival. ¶ そのうちチャンスが～する A chance will *come* (≒ *present itself*) soon.
—物 a present ; a gift.

とうらく【当落】 the result of an election. ¶ 彼の～は明朝判明する His *success or defeat in the election* will be known tomorrow morning. ～線上の人 candidates *whose chances go fifty-fifty*.

とうらく【騰落】 a rise and fall. ¶ 株価の～ the *fluctuations* of stock prices.

どうらく【道楽】 (遊興) dissipation ; (娯楽) a hobby. ¶ 若いころ～をした When young I led a *dissipated* (≒ *decadent*) life. / He *sowed wild oats* when young. ～もほどほどにしなさい You must not go so far as to *take pleasure for pleasure's sake*. 切手収集が唯一の～だ Stamps collection is my sole *hobby*. ～で絵をかいている I paint pictures *for pleasure*.
—息子 a prodigal son. **—者** a libertine. **食い—** an epicurean ; a gourmet.

どうらん【動乱】 disturbance. ¶ 社会的～ *a* social *upheaval*. アフリカに～が起こった *A riot* broke out in Africa.

どうらん【胴乱】 a satchel ; (植物採集用の) a collecting case ; a vasculum(複 vasculums ; vascula).

とうり【党利】 party interests. ¶ 彼らは～のみ求めた They pursued nothing but their own *party interests*.
—党略 ¶ ～党略に走りすぎたきらいがある They were too much swayed by *party policy and interests*.

どうり【道理】 (条理) reason ; (正当) right ; (妥当) propriety. ¶ 彼の言うことには～がある There is *reason* in what he says. 彼がそう言うのも～だ It *is natural* for him to say so. 彼は～を聞き分けない He won't listen to *reason*. なんと～のわからないことを言う人だ What *unreasonable* things he says! 彼の言うことは～にはずれている What he says *is against reason*. 彼がこの仕事を引き受ける～はない There is no *reason why* he should accept this work. 彼が黙っているのも～がある It *is* quite *reasonable* for him to remain silent. ～で彼は会に来なかった *It is no wonder that* he did not come to the meeting.

とうりつ【倒立】 standing on *one's* hands.

どうりつ【同率】 the same rate. ¶ 両チームが～で首位に立った Both led the other teams with *the same percentage of victories*.

とうりゃく【党略】 a party policy.

とうりゅう【逗留】 a stay. ¶ ～する stay.
—客 a guest ; a sojourner. **長—** ¶ 長～する make *a long stay*.

とうりゅうもん【登竜門】 the gateway to success. ¶ 芥川賞は文壇への～だ The Akutagawa Prize is *the gate* to the literary world in Japan. / 〔Receiving〕 The Akutagawa Prize means (≒ promises (若い人の場合)) success in the literary world in Japan.

とうりょう【投了】 〖囲碁・将棋〗 ¶ ～する give up the game for lost ; admit *one's* defeat.

とうりょう【頭領】 the chief ; the boss ; a leader.

とうりょう【棟梁】 a leader ; (大工の) the head carpenter.

どうりょう【同僚】 a colleague ; an associate ; a fellow worker.

どうりょく【動力】 〔motive〕 power.
—計 a dynamometer. **—炉** (発電用原子炉) an atomic 〔power〕 pile.

どうりん【動輪】 a driving wheel.

とうるい【盗塁】 〖野球〗 base stealing. ¶ 二塁～に成功する succeed in *stealing* second.

とうるい【糖類】 〖化学〗 saccharide ; saccharoid.

どうるい【同類】 (同種類) the same kind ; (共謀者) an accomplice.
—項 〖数学〗 a similar term.

とうれい【答礼】 a return salute. ¶ ～した I *answered* (≒ *returned*) *the salute*. / I *saluted in return*. 彼を～訪問した I *made a return call on* him. / I *paid a visit of courtesy to* him.

どうれつ【同列】 the same rank. ¶ われわれは〔彼等と〕～に扱われた We were treated as *the same in rank*.

どうろ【道路】 a road ; (街路) a street. ¶ この～はどこまで続いているのですか How far does this *road* go? ～の両側に杉の木が並んでいた Cedars lined the *road* on both sides.

—工事 road-mending. ¶ ～工事のため今はこの道は通れない Owing to *road-mending*, you cannot go along this road now. **—地図** a road map (*of*). **—標識** a road sign.

とうろう【燈籠】 a garden (≒ hanging) lantern.
—流し floating lanterns; a lantern display on the water. **石—** a stone lantern. **回り—** a revolving lantern.

とうろう【蟷螂】〘昆虫〙 a〔praying〕mantis. ¶ ～の斧 It's like throwing straws against the wind. ⇒ かまきり

とうろく【登録】 registration. ¶ 車の～は済ませてある I *have* already *registered* my car. 彼は歯医者として～した He *registered himself* as a dentist. 私はAという名で～されている I *am registered* as A. 彼は卒業生名簿に～されていない He *is* not *listed* among the graduates.
—商標 a registered trademark. **—済み**(掲示) Registered. **—番号** a register number. **—料** a registration fee. **金銭—器** a cash register.

とうろん【討論】 a debate; a discussion. ¶ その問題はまだ～中だ The question is still under *discussion*. その件については～する必要がある It's necessary for us to *discuss* (≒ *debate on*) the problem.
—会 a debate; a panel discussion. **公開—会** an open forum. **テレビ—会** a TV debate. **ラジオ—会** a debate on the air.

どうわ【童話】 a fairy tale.
—劇 a juvenile play. **—作家** a fairy-tale writer.

とうわく【当惑】 perplexity; embarrassment. ¶ 彼の訪問を受けて私は～した I *was perplexed at* his visit. 話をしてほしいと頼まれて私は～した I *was embarrassed* when I was asked to make a speech. なんと言ったらいいか彼は～した He *was at a loss* what to say. 彼は～して辺りを見まわした He looked around *in perplexity*.

とえい【都営】 **—バス** metropolitan (≒ city) buses. **—住宅** a municipally owned dwelling house.

とえはたえ【十重二十重】 ¶ ～の人がきを押しのけて前に出た I pushed my way to the front through a *big and thick* crowd of people.

どえら・い【ど偉い】 enormous. ¶ ～い事件が起きた A *shocking* (≒ *terrible*) accident occurred. ～い音がした There was a *prodigious* (≒ *tremendous*) noise. ～いことをしでかしたな What a *terrible* thing you have done! 町じゅう～い騒ぎだった The whole town was in a *great* uproar.

とお【十】 ten.

とおあさ【遠浅】 a shoal. ¶ この海岸は～だ This shore *is shallow to a considerable distance.*

とお・い【遠い】 1〘場所〙 distant; far. ¶ 学校は駅から～い The school *is distant* (≒ *is far*) from the station.
～い国に旅をしたい I want to make a journey to a *distant* country.
～い所へ引っ越した He moved *a long way off*.
彼ははるばる～い国から私を訪ねてやってきた He came all the way from a *distant* country to see me.
彼の家はここから～い所にある His house stands *a long way* from here.
～い眺めは見事だった The *distant* view was fine.
2〘時間〙 ¶ ～い昔から人間は火を使うことを知っていた From *remote* antiquity man has known how to use fire.
～い昔のことだった It was quite *a long time ago*.
3〘人間の関係が〙 ¶ 彼は私の～い親戚(しんせき)だ He is a *distant* relative of mine.

とおう【渡欧】 a visit to Europe. ¶ 彼は～の旅についた He started on *a journey to Europe*.

とおえん【遠縁】 a distant relation. ¶ 彼は私の～に当たる He is one of my *distant relatives*. / He *is distantly related to* me. 彼女は私の～の者と結ばれた She got married to one of my *remote relatives*.

とおか【十日】 ten days. ¶ 学校を～休んだ He absented himself from school *for ten days*. 彼が行方不明になって～だ This is *the tenth day* since he became missing.

とおからず【遠からず】 before long; in the near future; soon. ¶ ～連中はここに来る They will come here *before long*. ～平和がよみがえるだろう The day will come *soon* when we can enjoy peace again. ～その問題は解決すると思う I think the problem will be solved *in the near future* (≒ *before long*).

トーキー a talkie.
ハンディー— handie-talkie.

とおく【遠く】 1〘場所〙 far; far away; in the distance. ¶ どこか～へ行きたい I want to go to a *distant* place.
ここから～伊豆の山々が見える We can get a *distant* view of the Izu mountains.
～で鐘が鳴っている A bell is〔heard〕ringing *in the distance*.
ここは本土を～離れた島だ This is an island *remote from* the mainland.
この高いビルは～から見える This high building can be seen *from afar* (≒ *from a distance*).
2〘比較〙 ¶ 彼は兄に～及ばない He is *far* inferior to his elder brother.
3〘気が〙 ¶ 私は急に気が～なった I *fainted* all of a sudden.

とおざか・る【遠ざかる】 ¶ 船は岸から～っていった The ship *went away* from the shore. 飛行機は見る見る視界の外に～っていった The plane *flew out of sight* rapidly. 彼は世間から～っている He *holds aloof from* the world. 彼は文壇から～ってしまった He *has been out of* the literary circle.

とおざ・ける【遠ざける】 ¶ 悪友を～ける *avoid* (≒ *keep away from*) bad company. 余人

を～けて話した We *had a private talk.* / We *talked behind the closed door.*

とおし【通し】¶この汽車はシカゴまで～で行く This train goes *straight* (≒ *direct*) to Chicago. ―切符 a through ticket (*to* Rome). ―狂言 presentation of the whole play. ―矢 long distance archery.

-どおし【-通し】¶夜～起きている sit up *all* 〔*through the*〕 *night.* 赤ん坊が朝から泣き～だ The baby *keeps* crying since morning. 彼は勉強のし～だ He is *always* working at his desk. 彼は一日中働き～だった He was working all day.

トーシューズ 〔a pair of〕 toeshoes.

とお·す【通す】**1**〖通過させる·貫く〗¶ちょっと～してください Would you let me *pass,* please?/ Excuse me.

道をあけて彼を～してあげてください *Make way for* him, please.

守衛は私を～してくれなかった The doorkeeper wouldn't *let* me *in.* / The guard wouldn't *admit* me through the gate.

朝日が窓を～して部屋にさし込んでいた The morning sun streamed into the room *through* the windows.

部屋の空気がこもっているから窓を開けて風を～しなさい The room is stuffy. Why don't you open the window to *ventilate* it?

この布地は加工してあるから水を～さない This cloth *has been waterproofed.*

この物質は電気を～さない This material does not *conduct* electricity.

この合板は熱を～さない This board *is impervious to* heat (≒ *is heatproof*).

赤いガラスは赤の光線だけを～す Red glass *is pervious to* (≒ *transmits*) red light only.

この成績では～すわけにはいかない We can hardly *pass* you with such a poor record.

針に糸を～す *thread* a needle.

2〖案内する〗¶お～ししなさい *Show* him *in.*

ぼくは彼の書斎に～された I *was shown into* his study.

3〖続ける〗¶彼は夏冬～してシャツを1枚しか着ない He wears only one shirt *all* the year *round.*

外套(がいとう)なしで一冬～した I *did without* a coat *all through* the winter.

私は学生時代4年間皆勤で～した I *kept* attend*ing* school regularly without missing a single day *all through* the four years of college.

3日3晩雨が降り～した It *kept* raining for three days *on end.*

彼女は一生独身で～した She never married. / She *remained* unmarried all her life.

4〖意志などを貫く〗¶彼は一生自分の主義を～した He *maintained* his principle *all through* his life.

自分の意見を～そうとするのは彼の悪い癖だ The trouble with him is that he *sticks to* his own opinion.

そんなわがままを～そうとしてもだめです You can't *have your own way.*

彼はなにを聞かれても最後まで知らぬ存ぜぬで～した He *maintained* his innocence *throughout* the questioning.

5〖議案などを〗¶政府は予算案を3月中に～そうと懸命である The Government is making every effort to *push* the budget bill *through* by the end of March.

6〖目を〗¶会議の議題に目を～しておかなければならない I have to *look over* the agenda of the meeting.

この原稿にざっと目を～していただけませんか Would you briefly *look through* this manuscript?

7〖経由する〗¶ぼくは友人を～して彼女と知り合った I came to know her *through* a friend of mine.

先方は弁護士を～して和解を申し入れてきた The other party proposed a reconciliation *through the good offices of* a lawyer.

これは人を～して聞いた話です This is what I heard *through* others.

トースター a toaster.

トースト toast. ¶～1枚 a slice of *toast.* バターをぬらない～ dry *toast.*

とおせんぼう【通せん坊】¶男の子が～した A little boy *stopped* (≒ *barred*) *the way.* 木が倒れて～した A fallen tree *stopped* (≒ *barred*) *the way.*

トータル total. ¶来訪者の～は1000人に達した The visitors *totaled* 〔*up to*〕 a thousand.

トーダンス toedance.

トーチ a torch.

とおで【遠出】¶彼は～して留守だ He *is away* from home *on a trip.* 休日に車で～をする人が多くなった The number of people who *go out* in their cars on holidays has increased.

トーテム totem.
―ポール a totem pole. ―崇拝 totemism.

ドーナツ a doughnut.
―盤 an extended play; an EP record.

トーナメント a tournament. ¶われわれは大学対抗テニス～で優勝した We won the intercollegiate tennis *tournament.*

とおなり【遠鳴り】a distant roar. ¶潮の～が聞こえる *The distant roar* of the sea is heard.

とおの·く【遠退く】¶雷の音が～いていった The roll of thunder *faded away.* 卒業すると学校から足が～くものだ People *visit* their school *less often* after their graduation. 彼の友人たちも彼から～きはじめた His friends began to *keep away from* him.

とおのり【遠乗り】(馬) a long ride; (車) a long-distance drive. ¶～する(馬で) have a long ride; (車で) have a long drive.

とおび【遠火】¶～でもちを焼く toast a rice-cake over *a slow fire.*

とおぼえ【遠吠え】a distant bay (*of* a dog). ¶犬の～が聞こえる I hear a dog *howling.*

とおまき【遠巻き】¶彼らは男を～にした They *surrounded* the man *at a distance.*

とおまわし【遠回し】¶ ～の言い方はよせ Don't speak *in a roundabout way.* / Speak to the purpose. ～に注意した I advised him *vaguely.* 私は外出したいということを～に言った I *hinted* that I wanted to go out.

とおまわり【遠回り】a detour. ¶ ～する take a roundabout way ; make a detour.

とおみ【遠見】a distant view. ¶ ～がきく高台に登った I climbed up a hill which *gave a commanding prospect.* ～にはよく見えるものだ Things look better *at a distance.* / Distance lends enchantment to the view.

とおみみ【遠耳】¶ ～がきく have a sharp (≒ keen) ear.

ドーム a dome.

とおめ【遠め】¶ 今度の旅行は少し～にしよう Let's go on a trip *a little farther than usual* this time.

とおめ【遠目】¶ 彼は～がきく He can *see a long distance.* 彼女は～には美人に見える She looks beautiful *at a distance.*

とおめがね【遠眼鏡】a telescope.

ドーラン grease paint (Dohran はドイツの会社名). ¶ 彼女は～を顔にぬっている She *is very much made up.*

とおり【通り】**1**〖道路〗a street ; a road ; an avenue ; a passage. ¶ にぎやかな(寂しい)～ a busy (lonely) *street.*

彼の家はこの～に面している He lives on this *street.*

2〖交通・空気・水などの〗¶ この街道は～が激しい(少ない) There is a great deal of (little) *traffic* on this road.

下水の～が悪い The drain does not *run* well.

この部屋は風の～がいい This room *is airy.* / This room *admits air.* / This room *has fine ventilation.*

3〖種類〗¶ この問題の解き方は2～ある There are two *ways* of solving the problem.

4〖のように〗¶ ご承知(ごらん)の～ *as* you know (see).

いつもの～ *as* usual.

両親の言う～にしなさい You had better do *as* your parents advise you.

実験の結果は予期した～だった The result of the experiment *was what I had expected.*

おっしゃる～です You are right. / That's right.

ぼくが言った～でしょう Didn't I tell you ?

5〖声・文が〗¶ きみの声は～がいい Your voice *carries far* (≒ *carries very well*).

彼の文は～がいい His writing *is clear and legible.*

6〖通用〗¶ あの人は世間の～がよくない He has *an* unpleasant *reputation.*

彼女はここでは旧姓のほうが～がいい Here she *passes* better under her maiden name.

-どおり【-通り】¶ 彼は規則～行動した He acted *according to* the rule. 万事は計画～に進んだ Everything went *according to* arrangement. / Everything went *as planned.* 汽車は時刻～に着く Trains arrive *on time.* バスはなかなか時間～に来ない Buses seldom arrive *on schedule.* 彼の演奏は評判～の出来だった His performance *did credit to* (≒ *confirmed*) *the reputation* he had won. 家族の期待～彼は試験に合格した He passed the examination and *answered the expectation* of his family. 建築は九分～できあがった The building is *almost* (≒ *nearly*) completed. 彼は約束～3時に来た He came just at three *as he had promised.*

とおりあめ【通り雨】a [sudden] shower.

とおりいっぺん【通り一ぺん】¶ ふたりは～のあいさつをした They exchanged *perfunctory* greetings. ～の観察 *superficial* observation.

とおりがかり【通りがかり】¶ ～の人に道を尋ねた I asked the way of *a passer-by.* ～にお寄りしました I just dropped in *on the way.* ～の車 a *passing* car.

とおりかか・る【通りかかる】¶ 教会の前を～ったとき，時計が7時を打つのが聞こえた I heard the clock strike seven when I *was* just *passing by* the church. そのとき，たまたま学校のそばを～った I happened to *pass by* the school then.

とおりがけ【通りがけ】¶ 私は～に彼を訪ねた I dropped into his house *on the way.*

とおりこ・す【通り越す】¶ 橋を～して行った I *went past* the bridge. 風は冷たさを～して痛かった The wind *was more* cutting *than* cold. その案は実験の段階を～して実行の段階に達している The idea *has gone beyond* the experimental stage and reached the working stage.

とおりすがり【通りすがり】¶ ～に声をかけて行った He said "Hello" when *passing by.*

とおりす・ぎる【通り過ぎる】¶ あまり小さな家なので～ぎてしまうところだった The house was so small that I almost *passed* it *without noticing* it.

とおりそうば【通り相場】the current price. ¶ 彼はばかだというのが～だ He *passes as* a fool.

とおりぬ・ける【通り抜ける】¶ トンネルを～ける *pass through* a tunnel.

とおりま【通り魔】a phantom killer.

とおりみち【通り道】a passage ; a path ; a way. ¶ ～をあける(ふさぐ) clear (block up) the *passage.* 学校への～に *on the way to* the school.

とお・る【通る】**1**〖行き来する〗¶ この道路は車がたくさん～る There is heavy motor traffic on this road.

温泉と駅の間に電車が～っている Streetcars *run* between the station and the spa. / Streetcars *ply* from the station to the spa.

2〖通過する・経由する・合格する〗pass. ¶ パレードは銀座通りを～る The parade will *pass* along the Ginza.

いまここを～ったのが私たちの先生だ The man who *has walked past* here is our teacher.

時間がないから近道を～りましょう As we are pressed for time, let's *take a short cut.*

トンネルを～りぬけると視界が開けた *Coming out of* the tunnel, we found the view spread out before our eyes.

ヨーロッパへはシベリアを～って行くのが最も近い Going *via* Siberia would be the shortest way to Europe. / The shortest way to Europe is *by way of* Siberia.

この部屋は風がよく～る The room *is* well *ventilated.*

彼は国立大学の入学試験に～った He *passed* the entrance examination to one of the national universities.

憲法改正案が議会を～った The bill amending the National Constitution *passed* the House.

そのことが心配で飯ものどを～らないほどだった I was too anxious about it to have any appetite.

3 〖部屋などに入る〗 ¶ どうぞ中へお～りください Please come in. (普通の言い方). / Come on in. (くだけた, ときにぞんざいに聞こえる言い方).

私たちは客間に～ってしばらく待った We *were shown* (≒ *were ushered*) *into* the parlor and waited for a while.

4 〖通用する〗 ¶ この化粧品は世界の一級品で～っている These cosmetics *pass as* the best class in the world.

彼は学校では「ネコ」というあだ名で～っていた He *passed* under the nickname of "Cat" in school. / He *was known as* "Cat" in his school days.

彼はこの地方ではちょっと名の～った医者だ He is a considerably *well-known* doctor in this part of the country.

5 〖意味・論理が一貫する〗 ¶ 彼はなにやら意味の～らないことをぶつぶつ言っていた He was mumbling something *incoherent.*

彼の言うことは筋が～っている What he says *is consistent.* / He *sounds reasonable.*

6 〖許容される・認められる〗 ¶ その意見はおそらく～らないだろう That opinion may not *go down* with them.

そんな言いわけは～らない Such excuses *won't do.*

無理が～れば道理がひっこむ Where might is master, justice is servant.

7 〖届く・貫く〗 ¶ 彼女の声はよく～る Her voice *carries very well* (≒ *carries far*). / She has a *clear* voice.

この魚は火がよく～っていない This fish *is underdone* (≒ *is* still *raw*).

トーン a tone.

とか 【都下】 ¶ ～の学校 schools *in the capital* (≒ *the metropolis*).

とか 【渡河】 ¶ ～する cross a river. 歩いて～する wade across a river.

-とか ¶ 山田さん～いう人 *a certain* Mr. Yamada. 彼はアメリカへ行く～いう話だ *The rumor runs* (≒ *I hear*) *that* he will go to America. 机～いす～全部用意ができている Everything is ready—chairs, desks, and all others. 子供たちは動物園でライオン～クマ～オウム～ペンギン～珍しい動物や鳥をたくさん見た The children saw in the zoo a lot of strange animals and birds *such as* lions, bears, parrots, and penguins.

とが 【科】 (あやまち) fault ; blame ; (罪) a crime.

とかい 【都会】 a city ; a town. ¶ ～にあこがれる have a wish to live in *a city.* 私は～よりも田舎に住みたい I would rather live in the country than in *a town.*

—化 urbanization. ¶ ～化する urbanize. **—生活** city (≒ urban) life. **—人** a city-dweller. **大—** a great (≒ big) city.

どがいし 【度外視】 ¶ 費用は～した We *left* the expense *out of consideration.* 損得を～して事業を起こす undertake an enterprise *irrespective* (≒ *regardless*) *of one's* interest.

とがき 【ト書き】 stage directions.

とかく 【兎角・左右】 ¶ 冬は～風邪をひきやすい In winter we *are apt to* catch cold. こんな不注意は～事故を起こしがちだ Such carelessness *is liable to* cause an accident. ～するうちにその年も暮れた *Meanwhile* (≒ *In the meantime*) the year came to a close. ～事故は起こるものだ Accidents *will* happen. 彼については～のうわさがある He is a man of an *unfavorable* reputation.

とかげ 【蜥蜴】 〔動物〕 a lizard.

とか・す 【溶かす】 ¶ コップ 1 杯の水に砂糖をすこし～す *dissolve* some sugar in a glass of water.

とか・す 【解かす】 ¶ 太陽が雪を～す The sun *melts* snow. 髪を～す *comb one's* hair.

どか・す 【退かす】 ¶ 彼は人を～して前へ出た He forced his way through the crowd.

どかどか ¶ 彼らが～とへやへ入って来た They burst *boisterously* (≒ trooped *noisily*) into the room.

どがま 【土窯】 an earthen furnace.

とがめ 【咎め】 fault ; blame ; rebuke. ¶ 彼は良心の～に耐えかねた He could not endure the *pangs* (≒ *pricks*) of conscience. ～を受けてもしかたがない It deserves the *blame.*

とがめだて 【咎め立て】 faultfinding. ¶ 彼はなんでもぼくのやることには～する He *finds fault with* everything I do.

とが・める 【咎める】 ¶ 人の不注意を～めるものではない Don't *reproach* others *for* their carelessness. 暗がりで警官に～められた I *was challenged by* a policeman in the dark. 私は気が～める I *feel guilty.* / My conscience *pricks* (≒ *stings*) me. 彼の遅刻を～めた I *blamed* him *for* coming late. 彼は無届けで欠勤したために～められた He *got blamed for having* absented himself from office without notice. 彼は～めるように私を見た He looked at me *reproachfully.* 傷を～める *aggravate* (≒ *mortify*) a wound.

とがら・せる 【尖らせる】 ¶ 鉛筆を～せる *sharpen* a pencil. 彼は神経を～せている He *is all nerves.* 彼の言うことにそう神経を～せるな Don't *be* so *nervous* about his words.

とが・る 【尖る】 ¶ ～った屋根 a *pointed* roof. ～った鼻 a *sharp* nose. 先の～った棒 a *sharp-pointed* stick. ～った声 an *angry* voice.

どかん 【土管】 an earthen pipe.

どかん ¶ 爆弾が～と爆発した The bomb burst

with a noise like thunder. 大砲が～と鳴った The gun *blasted*. / *Bang!* went the gun. 花火を～と上げる We let off fireworks *with a great bang*.

とき【時】 **1** 〖時間・時刻〗 time. ¶ ～は金なり *Time* is money.
～のたつのは早いもので，お別れしてからもう３年になります *Time* really flies; it's already three years since I saw you last.
トランプ遊びに夢中になって，～のたつのも忘れていた We were so absorbed in playing cards that we had forgotten all about *the time*.
～がたつにつれてその記憶も薄らいだ As *time* passed, the memory of it became dim.
～がたてばぼくの真意もわかってもらえるだろう As *time* passes on, he will understand what I really meant.
ふたりの感情のもつれは～が解決してくれるでしょう *Time* will (≒ It will take *time* to) ease their misunderstanding.
災害は～を選ばずやってくる Disasters will come *at all hours*.
野党は動議を連発して～をかせごうとした The opposition party tried to *gain time* by making one motion after another.
はっきりした返事をしますからもうすこし～を与えてください I will give you my definite answer, so I wish you would give me a little more *time*.
火災発生の報を受けて，～を移さず消防車が出動した Being notified that a fire broke out, they *immediately* dispatched a fire engine.
この時計は正確に～をきざむ This clock keeps (≒ marks) accurate *time*. 「well.
このおんどりはよく～をつくる This cock *crows*
2 〖機会・時期〗 a chance; an opportunity; time. ¶ その会合の～と場所を知っていますか Do you know the *time* and place of the meeting?
今こそはっきり断を下すべき～だ *Now is the time to* give a definite decision.
ここは無理をせずに～を待つべきだ We should leave things as they are and wait for *an opportunity*.
その件は～をみて彼に話してみましょう As for this matter, I will talk it over with him when *a good chance* arises. 「*ly*.
彼の発言は～を得ていた His remark *was time*-
ちょうどよい～に来てくれた You have come just *at the right moment*.
服装は～と場所に適したものを着なさい You should dress according to *time* and place.
～と場合によってはそうしたとてかまわない You can do that *at certain times*.
それは～と場合による That depends.
～が～だから彼の言動も慎重だ As the *situation* is delicate, he is very careful of his speech and conduct.
若い～は二度とないのだからなんでも経験してみることだ Youth will never come again, so I would advise you to gain as much experience as you can.
私は子どもの～はたいへん弱かった I was extremely weak *when* I was a child.
3 〖折・場合〗 ¶ 本を読む～は姿勢を正しなさい Straighten yourself *when* you are reading.
私が帰途についた～はもう薄暗かった It was already dark *when* I started for home.
彼がたずねてきた～は，私は昼寝をしていた I was taking a nap *when* he came to see me.
私がいない～は秘書に聞いてください *If* I'm out please ask my secretary.
ご用の～はこのベルを押してください *If* you need any help, please ring this bell.
いざという～には私が力になってあげます *When* you really need help, you can depend on me.
4 〖その当時・時代〗 ¶ ～の将軍は吉宗であった The shogun of *the time* (≒ *the day*) was Yoshimune.
彼は～の風潮に迎合しなかった He did not compromise with *the public trend*.

とき【鴇】〖鳥類〗 a Japanese crested ibis.
━色 pale pink.

どき【土器】（総称） earthenware; (１箇) an earthen vessel.

どき【怒気】 anger. ¶ 彼は～を含んでその計画に抗議した He protested against the plan *in an angry tone*. 彼は～を満面にたたえている He *is black* (≒ *red*) *with anger*.

ときあか・す【解き明かす】 ¶ 人の急死に関する疑問を～す *dispel* (≒ *clear up*) the doubts concerning *a person's* sudden death (dispel は噂などによる疑問をはらすときなど).

ときおこ・す【説き起こす】 ¶ 彼は第一次大戦から～した He *started writing* (≒ *started talking*) *with* World War I.

ときおよ・ぶ【説き及ぶ】 ¶ 彼は人間の起源にまで～んだ He *referred to* (≒ *touched upon*) the origin of mankind.

ときおり【時折】 ¶ ～夕立が降るでしょう There will be showers *from time to time*.

ときかた【解き方】 ¶ この問題の～がわからない I don't know *how to solve* this problem.

ときかた【説き方】 ¶ 彼は～のこつを心得ている He knows *how to persuade*.

とぎしる【磨ぎ汁】 ¶ 米の～ water in which rice has been washed.

ときすす・める【説き勧める】 ¶ もっと勉強するように彼に～めた I *persuaded* him *to* study harder. 彼は私にタバコをやめるように～めた He *coaxed* me *to* give up smoking.

とぎすま・す【研ぎ澄ます】 ¶ ～した刀 a *keen-edged* (≒ *well-whetted*) sword.

ときたま【時たま】 once in a while; sometimes; occasionally; from time to time.
¶ ～機会があればコンサートに行く I go to the concert *from time to time* when an occasion presents itself.

どぎつ・い ¶ ～い色 a *loud* (≒ *flashy*) color. ～い化粧 *heavy* make-up. ～い表現 *strong* words.

ときつ・ける【説きつける】 ¶ 彼に仲間に加わるように～けた I *persuaded* him *to* join us (≒

と

into joining us).

どきっと ¶それを聞いたときはまったく〜した I *was startled* (≒*felt a shock*) to hear it. / It *startled* me. / It *gave* me *a shock*. / My heart missed a beat when I heard it.

ときどき【時時】sometimes; occasionally; now and then. ¶その〜で受け取る感じが違ってくる It gives varied impressions on different *occasions*.

どきどき ¶走ってきたので心臓が〜する My heart *is throbbing* violently as I came running all the way. 胸を〜させながら舞台のそでに立っていた I was waiting in the wing of the stage with *my heart beating fast with excitement*.

ときとして【時として】sometimes; occasionally; at times.

と

ときならぬ【時ならぬ】unexpected; untimely. ¶〜雪に驚いた I was surprised at an *unseasonable* snowfall. 彼の〜帰郷に家族の人々は心配した His *sudden* (≒ *unexpected*) return troubled his family.

ときに【時に】¶〜, 今何時でしょう *By the way*, what time is it? 〜ご用は何でしょう *Well* (≒ *Now*), shall we get to the point?

ときには【時には】¶〜寝坊することもある I oversleep myself *once in a while* (≒ *at times*).

ときのうん【時の運】¶勝敗は〜 Victory or defeat is *a matter of fortune*. / *Chance* plays a major part in deciding the issue of the battle. / The race is not always to the swift, nor the battle to the strong.

ときのこえ【関の声】¶〜をあげる raise *a war cry*; give *a battle cry*.

ときのひと【時の人】the man of the day. ¶彼も〜になった(話題にのぼる人になった) He has become *the topic of a talk*.

ときはな·す【解き放す·解き離す】¶犬を木から〜してやりなさい *Untie* the dog from the tree. 彼は犬を〜った He *set* the dog *free*. / He *let* the dog *loose*.

ときふ·せる【説き伏せる】¶彼を〜せて新車を買ってもらった I *talked* him *into* buying me a brand-new car. 彼女を〜せるのにはほねがおれた I had great difficulty [in] *talking* her *down*. 彼はアフリカに行きたがったが, 私は〜せてやめさせた He wanted to go to Africa, but I *argued* (≒ *persuaded*) him *out of* it. 〜せて彼の外国旅行をやめさせた We *talked* him *out of* his journey abroad.

どぎまぎ ¶外国人に駅に行く道を聞かれて〜した I *was embarrassed* (≒ *was confused*) when asked the way to the station by a foreigner. 彼は知らない人と会うといつも〜する Meeting strangers always *embarrasses* him. (やや文語的). 試験問題を見て〜した I *was perplexed* (≒ *was bewildered*) when I saw the test questions.

ときめか·す ¶彼女は恋人が来るのを胸を〜して待っていた She was waiting for her lover to come *with tremulous excitement* (≒ *with her heart fluttering in excitement*).

ときめ·く flutter; beat fast. ¶入試合格の喜びに胸が〜いた My heart *throbbed* with joy of success in the entrance examination.

ときめ·く【時めく】¶彼は今を〜く実業家のひとりだ He is one of the most *influential* (≒ *prosperous*) businessmen. 彼はかつては世に〜いたこともあった He *has had his day*. / He *has seen better days*.

どぎも【度肝·度胆】¶彼の無鉄砲さにはまったく〜を抜かれた I *was* really *astonished* (≒ *astounded*) *by* his recklessness. われわれの質問は彼らの〜を抜くものであった Our questions *frightened* them *out of their wits*.

ドキュメンタリー a documentary.
—フィルム a documentary film.

ドキュメント a document.

どきょう【度胸】courage; nerve. ¶彼はなかなか〜のある男だ He has plenty of *guts*. / He is a *courageous* man. 彼は〜のない男だ He is *a coward*. / He has no *guts*. 〜のある人でなければこんなめまいのするような高い所では働けない Only men of *steady nerve* can work at such dizzy heights. 彼のまちがいを指摘してやるだけの〜がなかった I had no *nerve* (≒ *courage*) to point out his mistakes to him. 彼は〜をすえて逆巻く海に飛び込んだ He *mustered up all his courage* to dive into the raging waves. 彼の〜を試してやろう Let's *put his courage to the test*. / Let's try to see how *courageous* he *is*.

どきょう【読経】sutra-chanting. ¶僧侶(そうりょ)の〜の声が流れてきた I heard the priests *reading* (≒ *reciting*) *the sutras*.

ときょうそう【徒競走】a footrace.

どきり ¶路上に急に子どもが飛び出したので〜とした I *was frightened* when I saw a little boy run into the street so suddenly.

とぎれとぎれ【跡切れ跡切れ】¶彼は〜に次のような話をした He *brokenly* told us the following story. 〜に聞こえてくる電車の音に夜通し眠れなかった The *intermittent* noise of the railway trains kept me awake all through the night.

とぎ·れる【跡切れる】¶彼の演説はしばしばかっさいで〜れた His speech *was* often *interrupted* by applause. 話がちょっと〜れた *There was a* momentary *pause* in the conversation. 敵の攻撃は〜れることなく一日じゅう続いた The enemy's attack continued all day *without intermission* (≒ *without interruption*). 彼の脈は〜れがちだった *There were intermissions* in his pulse.

ときわぎ【常磐木】an evergreen.

ときん【鍍金】gilding. ⇒めっき
—工 a plater. —術 the art of gilding.

どきん ¶その知らせに〜とした My heart *beat fast* at the news. / The news made my heart *throb* (≒ *thump*).

とく【得】profit. ¶投資で〜をした I *have profited* by investment. なんと〜な商売だろう What a *profitable* business! その取引で10万

円～をした We made *a profit* of 100,000 yen on the deal. 外国語を勉強しておいたほうが～だ It will *be to your advantage to* study a foreign language. そんなことを言っていったいどんな～があるのか *What is the use of* saying such a thing? うそをついて～になることもある You will sometimes *gain* by telling a lie. この方法のほうが～だ This method *is* more *advantageous.*

とく【徳】 virtue; moral excellence. ¶ ～の高い人 a man *of virtue*; a *virtuous* man. 隣人愛はキリスト教のひとつの～である Loving one's neighbors is *a* Christian *virtue.* あなたのこのような軽率な行為がお父さんの～を傷つけるのです Your careless conduct like this injures *the good reputation* of your father. 彼の好意を～としたい I should like to *appreciate* his kindness.

と・く【説く】（説明する）explain;（詳しく述べる）dwell on;（説得する）persuade;（説教する）preach.
¶ 彼はその原理を～いた He *explained* the principle. 彼は医学の将来について～いた He *dwelled upon* the future of medicine. 彼にはこの問題をどう～いていいかわからない I do not know how to *explain* the problem to him. 彼は学問の必要性を～いた He *preached* the need of learning. 彼は孔子の道を～いている He *is preaching* the morals of Confucius. 彼にその薬の効用を～いてもむだだ It is no use *explaining* the use of the medicine to him. 首相は減税の必要をこんこんと～いた The prime minister *dilated upon* the necessity of reducing taxes. 彼を～いてその企てをやめさせた I *persuaded* him *to* give up the attempt. / I *persuaded* him *out of* the attempt.

と・く【解く・融く】 **1**〖ほどく〗untie. ¶ 包みを～く *unpack* a parcel.
この結び目がどうしても～けない I can't *untie* this knot.
くつひもを～く *unlace one's* boots.
なわを～く *unfasten* a rope.
彼はやがて職を～かれた He *was relieved of* his post before long.
2〖解決する〗solve. ¶ 問題を～く *solve* a problem.
この誤解はなかなか～けそうもない It will be quite long before this misunderstanding *is removed.*

と・く【溶く】 dissolve. ¶ ペンキを油で～く *dissolve* paint in oil.

どく【毒】 **1**〖毒薬・害〗poison. ¶ そんなに食べては体に～だ If you eat so much, you will *injure* your health.
彼は～を飲んで死んだ He killed himself by taking *poison.*
この虫には恐ろしい～がある This worm has *a* deadly *poison* in it.
こんな暗い所での読書は目に～だ Reading in such a dark place *is bad for* the eyes.
～が彼の体じゅうに回った The *poison* spread throughout his system.
～をもって～を制す（諺）*Poison* quells *poison.*
2〖慣用的表現〗¶ ～を食わばさらまで（諺）*One may as well be hanged for a sheep as a lamb.*
彼の言うことは～にも薬にもならない What he says *is* neither *harmful* nor constructive. / What he says does neither good nor *bad* to you.

ど・く【退く】 ¶ さっさと～け *Get out of the way!*
彼は～いて彼女を通してやった He *stepped back* for her to go. / He *made way for* her.

とくい【得意】 **1**〖自慢・自負・満足・高ぶること〗¶ 彼女はちょっと先生にほめられるとすぐ～になる She *is delighted and proud* whenever her teacher praises her.
つまらないことで彼はすぐ～になる He *gets elated over* trifling matters.
社長に就任して彼は今～の絶頂にある Now president of the firm, he *is at the height of his glory.*
そのころが彼の最も～の時代であった Those were the days when he *felt* extremely *proud of himself.*
―顔 ¶ 彼は大きな魚を釣って～顔で家に帰った He caught a big fish and went home *triumphantly.* ―満面 ¶ 彼女は～満面でパリの話をした She spoke *with pride* about Paris.
2〖得手・じょうず〗¶ あなたの～の学科はなんですか What is your *favorite* subject?
私は音楽が～だ I *am good at* music. / My *favorite* subject is music.
彼女はカレーライスをつくるのが～だ She *is good at* making curry and rice.
彼は～の早業で相手を倒した He knocked his opponent down with his *favorite* trick.
彼女はお～の歌をうたった She sang her *favorite* song.
3〖顧客〗customer. ¶ あの方は当店の長年のお～さんです He has been our *client* for many years.
どの店も～を増やそうと懸命である Every shop is bent on increasing the number of *customers.*
常― ¶ 彼は愛想がないのでだいぶ店の常～をなくした He was not so friendly, so he lost many of *the regular clients.* 上― ¶ あの会社はうちの上～のひとつです That company is one of our *best customers* (≒ *best clients*).
―回り ¶ 彼は今～回りに出ている He *is* now *visiting his clients.*

とくい【特異】 peculiarity.
―体質〖医学〗idiosyncrasy.

どぐう【土偶】 an earthen figure.

どくえん【独演】 a solo. ¶ 今夜は彼が～した This evening he *performed alone* from beginning to end.
―会（音楽会の）a〔solo〕recital;（演芸などの）a one-man show. ―者 a soloist; a solo performer.

どくが【毒牙】（ヘビの）a〔poison〕fang. ¶ 詐欺

師は銀行家を～にかけた The swindler *preyed upon* the banker.
どくが【毒蛾】a poisonous moth.
とくがく【篤学】¶～の士 a *devoted* (≒ *diligent*) scholar.
どくがく【独学】self-education. ¶～の人 a *self-educated* (≒ *self-taught*) man. 彼は～で英語を学んだ He *learned* English *by himself* (≒ *without a teacher*).
どくガス【毒ガス】poison gas. ¶多くの兵士が～でやられた A lot of soldiers *were gassed*.
—弾 a poison-gas shell. —マスク a gas mask.
とくぎ【特技】special ability; speciality. ¶りっぱな英語が話せるのが彼の～だ His *strong point* is to speak good English. / He has *special ability* to speak good English. / His *speciality* is English speaking.

と

とくぎ【徳義】morality; honor. ¶彼は～を非常に重んじている He sets a high value upon *morality*. 彼の行為は～上許せない What he did was *morally* unpardonable.
—心 a moral sense; morality.
どくけ【毒気】¶彼の～を含んだ批評には全く腹が立った His *spiteful* (≒ *noxious*) criticism made me mad.
どくけし【毒消し】an antidote (*for* poison).
どくご【独語】〔a〕soliloquy. ¶「彼女の言うとおりかもしれぬ」と彼は～した He *said to himself*, "She may be right."
どくごかん【読後感】*one's* impression of a book.
とくさ【木賊】〘植物〙a scouring rush.
どくさい【独裁】dictatorship. ¶ソ連はかつてスターリンの～下にあった Soviet Russia was once under *the complete* (≒ *absolute*) *control* of Stalin. 彼は何事によらず～的だ He *is dictatorial* (≒ *despotic*) in everything.
—者 a dictator. —政治 autocracy.
とくさく【得策】¶黙っていたほうが～だ It *is wise* (≒ *is better*) to keep silent.
どくさつ【毒殺】¶～する poison (*a person*); kill (*a person*) by poison.
とくさんぶつ【特産物】a speciality.
とくし【特使】a special envoy; (大使) an ambassador extraordinary. ¶その問題を討議するためにアメリカに～が派遣された *A special envoy* was dispatched to America to discuss the problem.
どくじ【独自】¶彼は～の見解を発表した He expressed *his own* views. 彼は現在彼の先生とは違う～の研究をしている He is now engaged in research *independent of* his teacher. 彼はなにをするにも～の行動をとる He goes *his own way* in doing anything.
—性 individuality.
とくしか【篤志家】a charitable man; a philanthropist.
とくしつ【特質】a characteristic.
とくしつ【得失】merits and demerits. ¶彼はその政策の～を論じた He discussed *the merits and demerits of* the policy.
とくじつ【篤実】¶～な sincere. 温厚～な人 a *gentle and sincere* person; a true gentleman.
とくしゃ【特車】a tank.
とくしゃ【特赦】(政治犯などに対する) an amnesty; (個人に対する) a special pardon. ¶政治犯に対して～が行なわれた *A general amnesty* was granted to the political transgressors. 彼は～にあって出獄した He was let out of prison *under an amnesty*.
—令 an act of amnesty.
どくしゃ【読者】a reader; (定期購読者) a subscriber; (一般に) the reading public. ¶この新聞はたくさんの～を持っている This paper has *a* large *circulation*. この雑誌の～は少ない This magazine has *a* small *circulation*.
—欄 the reader's column. —層 the reading public.
どくじゃ【毒蛇】a venomous (≒ poisonous) snake.
どくしゃく【独酌】¶～で飲む drink *without company* (≒ *by oneself*).
とくしゅ【特殊】¶わが社はその会社と～な関係はない Our company has no *special* relations with the company. 同時通訳には～な才能が必要だ Simultaneous interpretation requires a *special* ability. 彼は彼女と～な関係にある He is on *intimate* terms with her.
—化 specialization. —学校 a special school. —鋼 special steel. —撮影 special photographing. —事情 special situations (≒ circumstances). —性 peculiarity.
とくじゅ【特需】¶～景気 a special procurement boom.
どくしゅ【毒酒】poisoned *sake*. ¶彼は～を盛られた He *had* his *sake poisoned*.
とくしゅう【特集】¶日曜の～記事 Sunday features.
—号 a special number.
どくしゅう【独習】self-study. ¶彼はギターを～した He *learned* to play the guitar *by himself*.
—書 (とらの巻) (米俗語) a horse; a pony; 英 a crib. フランス語—書 (書名) *French Self-Taught*.
どくしょ【読書】reading. ¶たいへんな～家 a great reader; (読書狂) a bookworm. ～百遍(ひゃっぺん)意おのずから通ず (諺) Repeated *reading* makes the meaning clear.
—週間 Reading Week. —三昧(ざんまい) ¶彼は毎日～三昧にふけっている He *is buried in books* every day. / He *is absorbed in reading* every day. —力 ¶この本は～力を養うのによい This book helps you cultivate your *reading ability*.
とくしょう【特賞】a special prize. ¶～は彼に行った The *special prize* went to him.
どくしょう【独唱】a vocal solo. ¶～する sing a solo.
—会 a recital. ¶～会を開く give a 〔song〕 recital.
とくしょく【特色】a characteristic. ¶この絵

はその時代の～をよく表わしている This picture *is* specially *characteristic of* the age. 進歩の精神が19世紀の～だ The nineteenth century *was characterized* (≒ *was marked*) by the spirit of progress. この精神が同校の～だ This spirit is (≒ constitutes) *a characteristic feature* of the school. 彼には他の作家にはない～がある He has something which distinguishes him from other writers. 彼の考えは～のないものだ His idea *is featureless* (≒ *is common*).

とくしん【得心】(承諾) consent; agreement; (満足) satisfaction. ¶ 説明に～がいく(満足する) *be convinced of* (≒ *be satisfied with*) an explanation. 彼に本気なのだということを～させた I *convinced* him *of* my seriousness. きみも彼のアメリカ行きに～した(同意した)わけではなかったのか You too *consented to* his leaving for America, didn't you?

どくしん【独身】 ¶ 彼は～だ He *is unmarried*. / He *is single*. 彼女はいまだに～だ She still remains *single*. 彼は一生～で通した He remained *single* all his life.

—者 a single (≒ an unmarried) person; (男) a bachelor; (女) a spinster; (独身の職業婦人) a bachelor girl. —生活 celibacy; (男) bachelorhood; (女) spinsterhood.

どくしんじゅつ【読唇術】 lip reading.

どくしんじゅつ【読心術】 mind-reading.

とく·する【得する】 ¶ それで～しようが損しようが大した問題ではない It doesn't matter whether I shall *gain* or not by that. 彼の援助の申し入れを受けたほうが～する It *is to your interest* to accept his offer of help.

どく·する【毒する】 ¶ このような小説は青少年を～するものだ Such novels will *poison* (≒ *do harm to*) young minds.

とくせい【特性】 a characteristic. ¶ ラクダの～は何日も水なしで持ちこたえられるところにある The camel *is characterized* by an ability to go for many days without water. せっけんには汚れを除く～がある Soap has the *property* (≒ *quality*) of removing dirt. 金銭に対する執着心はエジプト人の～であった The love of money has been *a* marked *characteristic* of the Egyptian.

とくせい【特製】 ¶ これはその会社～のくつです This is a pair of shoes *specially made by* the company.

—品 a specially-made article. —本 a specially bound book.

とくせい【徳性】 virtue. ¶ ～をみがく cultivate (≒ develop) *one's virtue*.

どくせい【毒性】 ¶ キノコには～のあるものが多い Many toadstools *are poisonous*.

とくせつ【特設】 ¶ ～する set up (≒ establish) specially.

—電話 a specially installed telephone.

どくぜつ【毒舌】 a spiteful tongue. ¶ 彼は政府の政策の失敗を～をふるって攻撃した He *bitterly* (≒ *scathingly*) *denounced* the wrong step the Government had taken.

—家 ¶ きみはなんという～家なのだ What *a spiteful* (≒ *bitter*) *tongue* you have!

とくせん【特選】 ¶ 彼の絵が展覧会で～になった His picture *won the highest honors* (≒ *was specially selected*) at the exhibition. ～の着物 a *kimono of special make*.

—品 deluxe articles. —品売場 the deluxe article saleroom.

とくせん【督戦】 —隊 a supervising army.

どくせん【独占】 〔a〕monopoly; monopolization. ¶ この会社が塩の製造を～している This firm *monopolizes* (≒ *has a monopoly of*) the production of salt. 彼がこの大きな部屋を～している He *has* this big room *to himself*.

—禁止法 the Anti-monopoly Law. —権 a monopoly. —事業 a monopoly; a monopolistic enterprise. —資本 monopolistic capital. —主義者 a monopolist.

どくぜん【独善】 self-righteousness. ¶ 彼の～的な態度が彼らの反感を買った His *self-righteous* (≒ *self-justified*) behavior aroused their antipathy.

—主義 ¶ 官僚の～主義 bureaucratic self-righteousness.

どくそ【毒素】 a toxin.

抗— an antitoxin.

どくそう【毒草】 a poisonous plant.

どくそう【独走】 a runaway victory. ¶ ことしのペナントレースは巨人が～するだろう The Giants will get *a runaway victory* in the pennant race this year.

どくそう【独奏】 a solo. ¶ バイオリン～ *a* violin *solo*.

—会 a recital. —者 a soloist.

どくそう【独創】 originality. ¶ ヘミングウエイに関する非常に～的な論文 a very *original* (≒ *unique*) essay *on* Hemingway. 彼には～的なところがある He has an *original* (≒ *inventive*) mind.

—力 originality. ¶ 彼は建物の設計において大いに～力を示した He showed much *originality* in the design of the building.

とくそく【督促】 ¶ 税金の支払を～された I *was pressed for* payment of taxes. / I *was urged to* pay taxes.

—状 a demand letter (≒ note); a letter of reminder.

ドクター a doctor.

—コース the doctor's course. —ストップ the doctor's order.

とくだい【特大】 ¶ ～のシャツ a *king-size*〔*d*〕(≒ *oversize*〔*d*〕) shirt.

—号 ¶ 新年～号 an *enlarged* New Year special edition.

とくたいけん【特待券】 a complimentary ticket.

とくたいせい【特待生】 a scholarship (≒ an honor) student. ¶ ～になる get *a scholarship*. あの大学には～制度がある The college has *a scholarship* system.

どくたけ【毒茸】 a toadstool.

とくだね【特種】 a scoop; an exclusive news

と

story. ¶〜で競争紙を抜く *scoop* the rival paper.

どくだん【独断】¶〜で予定を変更する change the plan *on one's own judgment* (≒ *on one's own responsibility*). 〜で事を行なう act *on one's own authority*. 〜的すぎる意見を主張する maintain (≒ insist) too *dogmatic* an opinion.

—専行 ¶〜専行する act *on one's own authority*.

どくだん【独弾】a solo. ¶ピアノの〜をする play *a piano solo* (≒ *alone*).

どくだんじょう【独壇場】¶ショパンの演奏にかけては彼女の〜だった *No one could be* her *equal at* playing Chopin. / She *was unrivaled* (≒ *matchless*) *as* a Chopin player.

とぐち【戸口】the door ; the doorway. ¶〜で待つ wait *at the door* (≒ *in the doorway*). 〜まで彼を送った I saw him to *the door*. 〜から〜へ from *door* to *door*.

とくちょう【特長】a strong point ; a merit. ¶時間のきちょうめんなのが彼の〜だ Punctuality is his *strong point*. そこがこの小説の著しい〜だ That's the outstanding *merit* of the novel. 人それぞれの〜を生かすべきだ One should make the most of his *characteristics*.

とくちょう【特徴】a characteristic. ¶この病気の〜は高熱が出ることだ A high fever *is characteristic of* this disease. 彼の話し方には〜がある There is *something striking* about his manner of speaking. / He has *a peculiar way* of speaking. エスキモー人の〜はいろいろある There are several different things that *mark* the Eskimos. 彼の顔は〜のある顔だ His face is a *peculiar* one. 彼の顔は〜のない顔だ His face is lacking in *character*. これがメキシコの天候の最も著しい〜のひとつだ This is one of the most remarkable *features* of the weather in Mexico. その国の地理的〜を述べなさい Describe the geographical *features* of the country. 象の〜は長い鼻である It is the long trunk that *characterizes* the elephant. この民族の〜は背の低いことだ This race *is distinguished by* shortness of stature.

どくづ·く【毒づく】¶彼は私に〜いた He *cursed* me. / He *called* me *names*.

とくてい【特定】¶〜の品 a *specific* article. ある〜の目的のためにそれをとっておく set it aside for a *specific* purpose.

とくてん【得点】(学校の成績の) a mark ; (競技の) a score. ¶彼は3科目に最高〜を取った He gained the highest *marks* in the three subjects. 100点満点でぼくの〜は97点だった I gained 97 *marks* out of a possible 100. ジャイアンツの〜は3点だった The Giants *scored* 3 points.

とくてん【特典】a privilege. ¶徴兵免除の〜 the *privilege* of exemption from military service. 授業料全額免除の〜を受ける enjoy *the privilege* of total exemption from school fees. 本会会員の〜は次のとおりです The *advantages* of membership in this society (≒ club) are as follows. 本校卒業者にはその大学へ無試験入学の〜がある The graduate of this school can enjoy the *privilege* of being admitted into the college without examination.

とくでん【特電】a special ; a special telegram. ¶UPI〜によれば according to the UPI's *special*. タイムズ宛ワシントン特電によれば *A* Washington *special* to the Times says that....

とくと【篤と】¶〜考える consider (the matter) *thoroughly*. 〜考えたうえで決定する decide it after *due* consideration. 〜調べる look *carefully* into (the matter). そのことは〜考えてから御返事致します I must consider the matter *thoroughly* before giving my answer to it. / I'll give my answer to it after *due* consideration.

とくど【得度】¶彼は50歳で〜した He *entered the Buddhist priesthood* at the age of fifty.

とくとう【特等】the highest prize. ¶福引きで〜が当たった I drew *the highest prize* in the lottery.

—席 a special seat ; (劇場の) a box. **—品** an extra fine article ; (口語) an A 1 article.

とくとうびょう【禿頭病】〔医学〕alopecia.

とくとく【得得】¶〜として語る speak *proudly* (≒ *triumphantly* ; *with a triumphant look*).

どくとく【独特】¶彼〜のやり方で in his *own* way. このお菓子はあの店〜のものだ This cake *is unique to* that store. / The cake is *a speciality* of that store. 彼の作品には〜な味がある His works have something *peculiar to* him. 彼女の歩き方は〜だ She has a *unique* way of walking.

どくどく ¶傷口から血が〜出た Thick blood flowed *profusely* out from the wound. / Thick blood *gushed out* rom the wound.

どくどくし·い【毒毒しい】¶〜い色 a *gaudy* color. 〜いキノコ an *unwholesome-looking* mushroom. 口紅を〜くぬる *thickly* rouge *one's* lips. 〜い物の言い方をする use *spiteful language* (≒ *bitter words*).

とくに【特に】specially ; especially ; particularly (especially と particularly はともに「とりわけ」の意で交換可能であるが，前者には「特によく，激しく」，後者には「いろいろあるなかで特に指摘すれば」という語感がある．specially は「特別に，わざわざ，もっぱら」という意が強い).

¶〜注意を払う pay *special* attention (*to*). 〜注意を促す call *particular* attention (*to*). ある政治家(〜名を秘す) a statesman (his name is *intentionally* withheld). この夏は〜暑い It is *especially* hot this summer. きょうは〜暑いね It's *especially* hot today, isn't it? きょうは〜やらねばならぬ仕事はない I have nothing *particular* to do today. このエッセーは〜日本の若い人々のために書かれたものである This essay

と

is written *specially* (≒ *expressly*) for the Japanese young people. ～言うべきほどのことはない There is nothing worthy of *special* mention.

どくにんじん【毒人参】〘植物〙園 a hemlock (米 アメリカツガ); a conium.

とくのうか【篤農家】 a hard-working farmer.

とくは【特派】 ¶ 人をフランスへ～する *dispatch a person* to France *for special purposes*.
—員 (新聞等の) a [special] correspondent. ¶ ニューヨークタイムズ東京～員 *a [special] correspondent* of the New York Times at Tokyo. —使節 a special envoy (≒ mission). —大使 an ambassador extraordinary.

どくは【読破】 ¶ ～する *finish* (a book); *read* (≒ *go*) *through* (a book).

とくばい【特売】 a [bargain] sale. ¶ ～する *sell* (something) *at a special price*.
—日 a special bargain day. —場 a bargain counter; (デパートなどの) a bargain sale floor. —品 a bargain. ¶ ～品をあさる hunt for good *bargains*.

どくはく【独白】 a monolog[ue]; a soliloquy. ¶ ハムレットの～ Hamlet's *monologue*. 舞台の上で～する *monologize* on the stage.

とくひつ【特筆】 ¶ なにも～すべきことはない There is nothing *worthy of special mention*. このことはわが家にとっては～すべき大事件であった This was a *big* event to our family. これはことしの～すべき出来事のひとつだ This is one of the *memorable* events of this year.

とくひょう【得票】 the number of votes polled. ¶ 彼の～はたったの200票だった He *polled* (≒ *got*) only two hundred *votes*.

どくふ【毒婦】 a vampire; a wicked woman.

どくぶつ【毒物】 [a] poison. ¶ ～を検出する detect *a poisonous substance*.

どくぶん【独文】 —科(科目) the German literature course; (学部) the department of German literature. —学 German literature. —学者 a scholar (≒ an authority) of German literature.

とくべつ【特別】 **1** 〚特に・たいへん〛 ¶ 彼は～背が高い He is *exceptionally* tall.
彼の書く小説は～難しい His novels are *extraordinarily* difficult.
ことしはツバメが来るのが～遅い Swallows are *unusually* late in coming this year.
彼女はドレスには～やかましい She is particular *especially* about her dress.
今は私には～必要なものはない I don't need anything *in particular* now.
この夏は～雨が多かった We have had an *unusual* amount of rain this summer.
きょうは～暑い It is *especially* hot today.
クラスの中で彼は～頭がいい He is one of the *most* intelligent students in the class.
この衣装は～の際に着るものです This dress is worn on *special* occasion.
2 〚別に・別な〛 ¶ これは～に犬のためにつくられた食べ物だ This is food *specially* prepared for dogs.
これらの患者は～な食事を与えられている These patients are given *special* meals.
～に親しい友人だけを招くつもりだ I intend to invite *especially* intimate friends of mine.
彼だけは～になっている He is given *special* treatment.
—扱い ¶ 私を～扱いしないでほしい Never give me *special* treatment. 彼だけを～扱いはできない I cannot *make* him *an exception*.
—委員 an extraordinary member of a committee. —会員 a special member. —国会 a special session of the Diet. —号(雑誌などの) a special number. —席 a reserved seat. —手当 a special allowance. —列車 a special train. —予算 a special budget. —弁護人 a special pleader.

どくへび【毒蛇】 a poisonous (≒ venomous) snake.

とくほう【特報】〘ジャーナリズム〙 a flash. ニュース— a news flash.

とくぼうか【徳望家】 a man of [established] virtue.

どくぼう【独房】 a cell.

とくほん【読本】 a reader. ¶ 英語の～ *an* English *reader*.
小学— a primary-school reader.

ドグマ a dogma; dogmatism.

どくみ【毒味・毒見】 ¶ ～する *taste* food *previously*.
—役 a taster.

とくむ【特務】 ¶ ～を帯びて on *special duty*.
—機関 the secret military agency.

どくむし【毒虫】 a venomous (≒ poisonous) insect. ¶ ～に刺される be stung by *a venomous* (≒ *poisonous*) *insect*.

とくめい【匿名】 anonymity. ¶ ～の手紙(投書)を出す send an *anonymous* letter (contribution). ～で小説を批評する criticize novels *anonymously*.
—社員 a silent partner. —投票 a secret ballot. —批評 anonymous criticism.

とくめい【特命】 ¶ ～を帯びて on *special mission*.
—全権大使 an ambassador extraordinary and plenipotentiary.

どくや【毒矢】 a poisoned arrow.

とくやく【特約】 a special contract. ¶ わが社はその会社と～を結んだ Our company made *a special contract* with the company.
—店 an agency; a chain store. ¶ ある会社の～店をする *hold the agency of* a company.

どくやく【毒薬】 a poison. ¶ 彼に～を盛る give him *a poison*.

とくゆう【特有】 peculiarity. ¶ 日本人～の風俗習慣 customs and manners *peculiar* to the Japanese. あらゆる動物にはそれぞれ～の本能がある Every animal has its *proper* instinct. その種族には～の言語がある The tribes have a language *of their own*. この文体は彼～のものだ This style *is peculiarly his own*. 金を愛することは昔からユダヤ人～の性質であった The love of money has always been *a marked characteristic* of the Jews.

とくよう 【徳用】 ¶それを買うほうが〜だ It's *economy* to buy it. 〜のストーブ(経済的な) an *economical* stove.

—品 an economical article.

どくりつ 【独立】 independence. ¶彼は〜して出版の仕事を始めた He started the publishing business *on his own account*. 彼は〜して生活している He *is earning his own living*. 彼はまだ〜できる年ごろではない He is not old enough to *stand alone*. 彼はグループから歌手として〜した He *became independent of* the group as a solo singer. アメリカは1776年に〜を宣言した The United States of America *declare independence* in 1776.

—記念日(アメリカの) Independence Day. —国家 an independent country. —採算制 the independent profit system. —心 ¶彼は〜心に富んでいる He is full of *the spirit of independence*. —戦争(アメリカの) the War of Independence. —宣言(アメリカの) the Declaration of Independence.

どくりょう 【読了】 ¶小説を一気に〜する *finish reading* a novel at a stretch; *read* a novel *through* without rest.

どくりょく 【独力】 ¶人には〜ではできかねることがなにかあるものだ There are some things one can't do *for oneself*. 彼は〜でその事業を起こした He built the enterprise *for himself*.

とくれい 【特例】(例外) an exception; (特別の例) a special case. ¶戦時の〜 *a* wartime *exception*. 〜を認める grant *exceptions*. 〜を設ける make *an exception* (*to* a rule). これは〜だ This is *a special case*.

—法 the Exception Law.

とくれい 【督励】 encouragement; stimulation. ¶もっと勉強するように子どもを〜する *urge* a child to study harder. 部下を〜して仕事をせかす *urge one's* men to push the work. ほうびを出すといって人を〜する *encourage a person* with prizes.

とぐろ ¶〜を巻いたヘビ a *coiled* serpent. ヘビが〜を巻いていた I found a snake *coiling itself up*.

どくろ 【髑髏】 a skull.

どくわ 【独和】 —辞典 a German-Japanese dictionary.

とげ 【刺・棘】(ばらの) a thorn; (草葉の) a prickle; (さかなの) a spine. ¶〜を指に立てる run *a thorn* into *one's* finger. 〜を抜く pull (≒ draw) out *a thorn*. 〜のあることば *stinging* (≒ *bitter*) words. 彼の言うことには〜がある He has a *sharp* tongue. ばらにとげあり (諺) *No rose without a thorn*.

とけあ・う 【溶け合う】 ¶そのふたつの金属は〜って新しい合金をつくる The two metals *melt into* a new alloy.

とけい 【徒刑】 penal servitude.

無期(有期)— penal servitude for life (a limited term). —囚 a convict.

とけい 【時計】(掛け時計・置き時計) a clock; (腕時計など) a watch.

1 〖時計は〗 ¶この〜は合っている This *watch* is correct.

この〜は正確だから信用できる As this *watch* keeps good time, you can trust it.

きみの〜は進んでいる Your *watch* is fast.

ぼくの〜は遅れている My *watch* is slow.

きみの〜はどのくらい進んでいますか How fast is your *watch*?

私の〜は5分進んでいる(遅れている) My *watch* is five minutes fast (slow).

私の〜は1時間に1分遅れる(進む) My *watch* loses (gains) a minute in an hour.

〜をラジオの時報に合わせる set *a watch* by the radio time signal.

〜を巻く wind up *a watch*.

〜は11時を打った The *clock* struck eleven.

〜を掃除して修繕してもらった I had my *watch* cleaned and mended.

2 〖時計の・時計を・その他〗 ¶〜のかちかちいう音だけが聞こえる Nothing but the ticking of *a clock* is to be heard.

あの〜を10分進めてほしい Please advance the *clock* ten minutes.

この〜では今5時だ It's five by this *watch*.

—仕掛け clockwork. —仕掛けの爆弾 a time bomb. —台 a clock tower. —屋(人) a watchmaker; (店) a watchmaker's. 置き— a table clock. 目ざまし— an alarm clock. 電気— an electric clock. ハト— a cuckoo clock.

とけこ・む 【溶け込む】 ¶環境に〜む *adapt oneself to* the surroundings. チームに〜む *become familiar with* each member of the team. 色がしだいに別の色に〜んでいく One color *is melting into* another. 海と空が水平線上で一つに〜んでいる The sea *melts into* the sky at the horizon.

どげざ 【土下座】 〔a〕 prostration. ¶人々は王の前に〜した People *prostrated themselves* before the king. 〜して頼む ask *with many prostrations*.

とけつ 【吐血】 ¶大量に〜する *eject* (≒ *spit*; *vomit*) a great deal of *blood*.

とげとげし・い 【刺刺しい】 ¶〜いことばを言う use *stinging* (≒ *harsh*; *bitter*) words; speak *harshly*. 〜い態度で with a *virulent* attitude.

と・ける 【解ける】 **1** 〖ほどける〗 become loose (≒ untied). ¶帯の結び目が〜けた The sash *came untied*.

〜けた帯のはし a *loose* end of a sash.

2 〖解決される〗 be solved. ¶彼の疑念はどうしても〜けない His doubt *has* not *been cleared* (≒ *dispelled*) by any means.

彼の怒りもようやく〜けた At last his anger *melted away* (≒ *was appeased*).

根本問題がまだ〜けてない The basic question *has* not *been solved* yet.

そんな問題は簡単に〜ける Such a question can easily *be solved*.

やっとそのなぞが〜けた At last I *have solved* the puzzle.

彼らの葛藤はまだ〜けない Their trouble *is* not *over*. / Their trouble *still continues*.

彼の心はなかなか〜けなかった He would not *relent* toward me.

3 〚雪などが〛 melt ; thaw. ¶ 雪は朝日を受けてたちまち〜けてしまった The snow *melted* rapidly in the morning sun.

池の氷は〜けた The ice in the pond *has melted* off.

池の氷は3月に〜ける The pond *thaws* in March.

去年の春は早く雪(氷)が〜けた It *thawed* early last spring.

と･ける 【溶ける】 ¶ 〜けやすい(にくい)金属 a *fusible* (an *infusible*) metal. 〜けやすい(にくい)粉末 *soluble* (*insoluble*) powder. 紅茶に入れた砂糖が〜ける Sugar *melts* in 〔black〕 tea. 多くの金属は熱で〜ける Most metals *melt* with heat. 塩は水によく〜ける Salt *is* easily *soluble* in water. / Salt easily *dissolves* in water.

と･げる 【遂げる】 achieve ; accomplish. ¶ 目的を〜げる *achieve one's* purpose. 年来の望みを〜げる *accomplish* (≒ *attain*) *one's* long-cherished desire. 最期を〜げる *meet one's* death. 非業の死を〜げる *die* an untimely death. 名誉の戦死を〜げる *die* a glorious death in war. (功成り)名を〜げる *win* fame ; *make one's* name. どんなに犠牲を払っても目的を〜げるつもりだ I will *accomplish* my purpose at any cost.

ど･ける 【退ける】 ¶ じゃま物を〜ける *get* an obstacle *out of the way*; *remove* an obstacle.

どけん 【土建】 ―業 civil engineering and construction enterprise. ―業者(会社) a civil engineering and building constructor (≒ construction company).

とこ 【床】 a bed. ¶ 〜につく go to *bed* ; (病気で) be ill in *bed*. 〜をとる make *a bed*. きれいなシーツを〜に敷く put clean sheets on *a bed*. 子どもを〜の上に寝かす lay a child down on the *bed*. 〜を離れる(起きる) get up ; (病床) leave *one's bed* ; recover from sickness. 〜の中で本を読む read 〔a book〕 in *bed*. 彼は風邪をひいて〜についている He is sick in *bed* with a cold.

―の間 an alcove. 河― a river bed. 苗― a seed bed ; a seed plot.

どこ 【何処】 **1** 〚疑問文〛 ¶ ここは〜ですか *What place* is this?

私を〜へ連れていくのですか *Where* are you going to take me?

銀行は〜ですか *Where* can I find the bank?

それは部屋の〜にありますか *In which part* of the room is it?

このバスは〜まで行きますか *How far* does this bus go?

あなたは〜のご出身ですか *Where* are you from?/ *Where* do you come from? / *What* is your home town?

けさきみは〜から来たのですか *Where* did you come from this morning?

その事故は〜で起こったか *Where* (≒ *In what place*) did the accident happen?

遠足の行き先は〜に決まりましたか Have you decided *where* to hold the picnic?

彼女は〜の大学へ通っているのですか *What* university does she attend?

この前はテキストの〜まで進みましたか *How far* did we go in this textbook last time?

〜の馬の骨ともわからない男の言うことを信じるのですか Do you mean to say that you believe what a complete stranger said?

はっきり〜そこで買ったと証明できますか Can you prove clearly that you have bought it at such and such a place?

2 〚疑問文以外〛 ¶ 〜ででもご都合のよい所でお会いします I'll meet you *anywhere* it suits you. / I'll see you *wherever* it is convenient for you.

彼女は〜にも見当たりません I can't see her *anywhere*.

〜へでも好きな所へ行ってよろしい You may go *wherever* you like. / You can go *anywhere* you choose (≒ wish).

私はきょうは〜へも行きたくない I don't feel like going *anywhere* today.

〜か行きたい所があったら言いなさい Tell me if there is *any place* you would like to visit.

日曜は〜へ行っても行楽客でいっぱいだ On Sundays, *no matter where* you may go, it is crowded with holidaymakers.

彼は〜か国立大学を出ている He is a graduate of *some* national university.

彼は〜へともなく消えてしまった He has disappeared *somewhere*.

さあ〜からでも向かってきなさい You can attack me *from anywhere* you like.

〜から手をつけていいかわからない I don't know *where* to begin.

神田のことなら〜から〜まで知っている I know *every inch of* Kanda. / I know Kanda very well, even to the back streets.

彼が女装すると〜から見ても男とは思えない When he dresses as a woman, you will never think that he is a man.

彼の言うことは〜まで本気なのか判断に苦しむ I can't make out how serious he really is.

会議は〜までいっても結論が出なかった The conference dragged on without any conclusion.

白い砂浜は〜までも続いていた The white sandy beach extended as far as the eye could reach.

いったんやろうと思ったことは〜までもやりとげるようにしなさい Once you have decided to do a thing, carry it out *to the end*.

彼は〜までもお人よしだ Isn't he *too* good-natured!

彼はなにを言われても〜吹く風と聞き流してしまう No matter what people may say to him, he doesn't care a bit.

どご 【土語】 a vernacular ; (方言) a dialect. ¶ 〜で話す speak in *a native language* (≒

a native tongue).

とこあげ【床上げ】recovery from sickness. ¶ ～をする leave *one's* bed; recover from sickness. ～の祝いをする celebrate *one's recovery from sickness.*

とこう【渡航】a voyage; a passage. ¶ 朝鮮へ～する *go over* to Korea; *take passage* for Korea.

━者 a passenger. **━手続き** ¶ ～手続きをする go through the due formalities for *going abroad.*

どこう【土工】a navvy.

どごう【怒号】a roar; a howl. ¶ 市場は売買のすさまじい～でいっぱいだった There was *a* loud *roar* of buying and selling in the market.

どこか【何処か】¶ ～にかさを置き忘れてきた I have left my umbrella [behind] *somewhere.* 彼は～この付近に住んでいる He lives *somewhere* in this neighborhood. 彼の話し方には～魅惑的なところがある There is *something* fascinating about his manner of speech. それには～不確かなところがある There is *something* uncertain about it. 彼女の顔つきは～寂しげなところがある She looks *somewhat* sad.

どこからともなく【何処からともなく】out of nowhere; from some unknown place; from nowhere; from where we know not (文語).

¶ 彼は～現われて, どこへともなく姿を消した He suddenly showed up and just as suddenly disappeared. ～彼女についての変なうわさが流れてきた Strange rumors about her reached us *from nobody knows where.*

とこしえ【常】¶ ～の愛 *everlasting* love. ～にきみを愛す I love you *forever.* この物語は～に語りつがれるであろう This story will be handed down *forever* from generation to generation. ～にきみがみ魂安かれ *Requiescat in pace!* (ラテン語のきまり文句). / *Long* may you rejoice in peace. (文語).

とこずれ【床擦れ】bedsores. ¶ 入院中に～ができた I had *bedsores* while I was in hospital.

どことなく【何処となく】¶ 彼には～こっけいなところがある There is *something* humorous about him. あの人は～威厳がある He has *certain* dignity about him. あのふたりは～似ている The two resemble each other *in some way or other.* ～体のぐあいが悪い I feel *vaguely* ill. 彼女は～育ちがよさそうに見える *Somehow* one gets the impression that she's from a good family.

とことん ¶ ～までやれ Do it *thoroughly.* / Go *the whole way.* ～まで戦おう Let us fight it *out.* ～まで彼に反対してやる I will stand against him *to the bitter end.* ～まで調べあげてやる I'll make a *thorough* investigation of the matter.

とこなつ【常夏】¶ ～の国 a land of everlasting (⇆ unending) summer; a land where summer never dies.

とこのま【床の間】an alcove.

とこばしら【床柱】a *tokonoma* post.

とこや【床屋】(店) 米 a barber shop; 英 a barber's [shop]; (人) a barber. ¶ ～の看板 a barber's pole.

とこやま【床山】(役者の) a wig-maker; (すもうの) a hairdresser for *sumo* wrestlers.

どこやら【何処やら】⇒どことなく

とこよ【常世】¶ ～の国 (不老不死の国) Heaven; a land of eternity (⇆ immortality); (黄泉) the under world.

ところ【所】**1**〖場所〗[a] place. ¶ どこか公害のない～に住みたいものだ I would like to live in some pollution-free *place.*

彼の家は交通の便利な～にある He lives in *a place* convenient for transport.

ここは私が生まれ育った～だ This is the *place* where I was born and grew up.

彼のいる～でその話をしてはいけません You must not mention that *in his presence.*

人のいない～で悪口を言うのはやめなさい Don't speak ill of others *behind their backs.*

彼は～かまわず大声を出す He speaks too loudly *no matter where he is.*

～もあろうにこんな～できみに会うとは Fancy meeting you here, *of all places!*

私が事故に会った～はもう少し先だ The *scene* where my traffic accident occurred is a little farther from here.

学校は家から歩いて15分の～にある It is [a] fifteen minutes' walk from my home to school.

どこへでもきみの好きな～へ連れていってあげる I'll take you along *wherever* you'd like to go.

この犬はぼくの体を～かまわずなめる This dog licks me *all over.*

～変われば品変わる So many countries, so many customs.

午後は～によって雷雨があるという予報だ The weather forecast says that in the afternoon there will be a thunderstorm *in some places.*

彼が庶務課長とはまさに～を得た人事だ It is a very *wise* personnel change that he was appointed chief of the general affairs section.

あらゆるものが～をえている Everything is *in its place.*

彼は～をえない He is *a misfit.*

2〖家・住所〗¶ この用紙にお～を記入してください Please write down your *address* on this form.

弟は大阪のおじの～に世話になっている My brother lives *with* our uncle in Osaka.

友だちの～に遊びに行ってきます I am going to call at my *friend's.*

━番地 an address. ¶ 彼の家の～番地をご存じですか Do you know *where* he lives?

3〖場合・時〗¶ ちょうど今起きた～だ I have *just* got up.

きみのうわさをしていた～だ We were *just* talking about you.

朝出かけようとしている～へ彼が訪ねてきた He came to see me in the morning *just* I was

going out.
ちょうどいい～へ来てくれた. ひとりでたいくつしていた～だ You've come at the right *moment.* I've been bored all by myself.
この～ずっと忙しくて，バテぎみです I have been so busy *lately* that I have nearly collapsed.
お忙しい～をおじゃまいたしました Excuse me for having interrupted you on such a busy day.
犯人は逃げだそうとした～を取り押さえられた The criminal was arrested *just when* he was going to run away.
もうすこしで車にはねられる～だった I was *almost* being knocked down by a car.
ほんのちょっとの～で，いつもの電車に乗り遅れた I missed the usual train *by a minute.*
お訪ねした～，先方は留守でした He was absent *when* I called on him.
きょうの～は大目に見ておいてやろう I will overlook it *just this once.*
4〘点・部分・事柄・関係〙¶ わからない～があったら質問してください Please ask me any question when you have anything you don't understand.
彼女のいちばんいい～は，すなおなことだ Obedience is her best quality.
この本には難しい～が多い There are a lot of difficult *passages* in this book.
きみの話には納得できない～がひとつある There is one *point* I am not convinced of in what you say.
彼女の顔にはどこか寂しそうな～がある Somehow she looks lonely.
彼の伝記を読むと教えられる～が多い（自分の経験として）I have learned much from his biography. /（人に対して）You will learn a lot if you read his biography.
彼には偏屈な～がある There is *something* eccentric in him. / He is *something* of an eccentric.
がんこな～など彼は父親にそっくりだ He resembles his father closely *in* his obstinacy.
彼女の言う～によると，彼は病気ではない *According to* her, he is not sick.
ああ言う～をみると，彼には自信があるのだろう *Judging from* what he says, he will probably be confident in it.
いまだに現われない～をみると，彼は欠席だろう *As* he has not come by this time, I think he is going to be absent.
5〘範囲〙¶ 私の知る～では計画に変更はない *So far as* I know, there is no change at all in the plan.
今の～騒ぎが起こるようすはない *Up to the present* there is no sign of commotion.
私の見た～，とても感じのいい娘だ *The way* I see her, she is a very attractive girl.
どのくらいボーナスが出ますか. 20万ぐらいの～ですかね How much do you expect as a bonus? Well, *maybe* two hundred thousand yen.

-どころ【-所】¶ 暑い～じゃない "Hot" is no name for it. お花見～ではない This is no time for going to see the cherry blossoms. / How could I think of cherry-viewing! それ～ではない That is out of the question. それができるかって？ できる～じゃない（大できだ）Could I do it, you say? Why, yes, rather. 忙しくてそれ～の話じゃない I am too busy to care about that.

ところが【所が】 but; however; while; on the contrary. ¶ 彼はいないと思った. ～そこにいた I did not expect him to be there, *but* he was there. 私は疲れている. ～彼は全然疲れていない I am tired, *while* he is not tired at all. 問題はやさしかった. ～解けなかった The problem was easy, *but* I could not solve it.

-どころか【-所か】¶ 貯金～今はやっとやっとの生活です *Far from* saving money, now I make a bare living. おもしろい～えらい目に会った *Far from* being amused, I had a terrible experience. 手助け～，この子はかえって仕事のじゃまだ *So far from* being a help to me, this boy disturbs me in my work. 彼は日本～世界じゅうに知れた学者だ He is a great scholar well-known *not only* in Japan *but also* all over the world. 彼はフランス語～英語も話せない He cannot speak Englih, *to say nothing of* French.

ところがき【所書き】 an address.

ところで【所で】¶ ～，どうしよう *Now,* what shall we do? ～，そろそろ出かけようか *Well,* shall we start? ～，あの男をどう思う *By the way,* what do you think of him? ～，1万円貸してくれないか *Incidentally,* could you lend me ten thousand yen? ぐずぐず言った～しかたがないじゃないか It is no use complaining, isn't it? 彼に話してみた～なんにもなりはしない It is quite useless *to* tell him. 今から出発した～まにあわない *Even if* we were to start now, we would not be in time. だれがやった～失敗するにきまっている *No matter who* tries, he is sure to fail.

ところてん【心太・心天】 gelidium jelly. ¶ 彼は～式に学校を出た He was allowed to leave his school as the graduation year came.

ところどころ【所所】 here and there. ¶ 雪が～に残っている The snow remains *here and there.* ペンキが～はげている The paint is off *in places.* ～に村や森が見える I can see a village *here* and a thicket *there.*

とざい【吐剤】〘医学〙 an emetic.

どざえもん【土左衛門】 a drowned body. ⇒できしたい

とさか【鶏冠】 a crest; a comb; a cockscomb.

どさくさ hubbub. ¶ ～に紛れて彼は姿を消した He disappeared *in the confusion.* 彼は火事の～に紛れて逃げた He escaped *in the bustle* of the fire. 彼は～に紛れて大もうけをした He took advantage of the *confusion* to make a great fortune.

とざ・す【閉ざす】 shut. ¶ 戸を～して部屋にこもっ

と

た I *shut* the door and kept indoors. この港は冬じゅう氷に～されている This harbor *is icebound* throughout the winter. 船はまる1日氷に～されていた The ship *was frozen in* for a whole day. 口を～す *keep one's* mouth *shut*.

とさつ【屠殺】slaughter. ¶～する *slaughter* ⌊(a pig). —場 a slaughter house.

どさどさ ¶書棚から本が～と落ちてきた Books fell down *with a thud* from the bookshelf. 数名の警官が～と彼の部屋に乱入した Several policemen rushed into his room *one after another*.

とざま【外様】being outside. ¶われわれは～だから仕方ない It cannot be helped, as we *are not in the favored group*.
—大名 an outside *daimyo*; a *daimyo* who was not a hereditary.

と

どさまわり【どさ回り】(劇団) a troupe of strolling actors and actresses. ¶彼は人気が落ちたので～をしている He is no longer popular and *is* now *on the road*. ～の一座 a theatrical company *on the road to tour a play*.

どさり ¶彼は～と本を机の上に置いた He *flopped* his books on the table. 彼はかばんを～と地面に置いた He put down his bag *with a heavy thud*.

とざん【登山】mountain climbing; mountaineering (mountaineering はやや改まった言い方). ¶～する go up a hill (≒ mountain); go mountain climbing; climb a mountain.
—家 a mountaineer; an alpinist. —づえ an alpen-stock. —鉄道 a mountain railroad. —熱 a craze for mountaineering.

とし【年・歳】**1** 〖暦年・年月〗 a year. ¶私の生まれた～に祖父が亡くなった My grandfather died *in the year* I was born.
～の始めにはいつも日記をつけようと決心する At the beginning of every *year* I make a resolution to keep a diary.
行く～を送り新しい～を迎えると気持ちが引き締まる Seeing the old *year* out and the new *year* in makes me feel sober and serious.
～が明けたらおじゃまにあがります I will visit you early *in the New Year*.
がんばって～のうちにこの仕事をかたづける I'll do my best to finish this job within *the year*.
どうぞよいお～を Have *a* happy new *year*!
～がたつにつれてこの事件も忘れられていく In the course of *years*, the affair will fade out of everybody's memory.
物価が～を追って上昇する Prices advance *year after year*.
2 〖年齢〗 ¶坊や, お～はいくつですか *How old* are you, sonny?
ぼくと彼は同じ～だ He and I *are the same age*. / I *am the same age as* he.
女の～はまったくわからない I can never tell a woman's *age*. / I can never tell *how old* a woman is.
彼女は～のわりに若く見える She looks young *for her age*. / She doesn't look her *age*.
彼は～に似合わず物知りだ He is knowledgeable *beyond his age*.
きみたちの～のころは私は苦労したものだ I was struggling for a living when I was your *age*.
私の言うことがわかってもいい～だ You *are old enough* to understand what I am telling you.
もうきみも結婚していい～だ It is *high time* you married.
名簿は～の順に並んでいる The names are listed according to *age*.
あなたも～をとりましたね You *have aged*, too, haven't you? / You*'ve grown old*, haven't you?
彼は今度の病気で10も～をとってしまったようだ He seems to *have put on* ten *years* after the last illness.
～はとりたくないものだ I don't want to *get old*./ I want to stay young.
ぼくももう～だなあ I *have put on years*. / I *am feeling my age*.
お互い～には勝てませんね We can't hold back the clock, can we?
彼はだいぶ～がいっている He *is* well *up in years*. / He *is of a good age*.
～のせいで細かい字が見えなくなってきた My *age* prevents me from reading the fine print.
彼は～に不足なく長生きして, 昨年亡くなった He had a full life and died last year.
～が違いすぎているので結婚はあきらめた On account of *age disparity* (≒ *age difference*) I gave up marrying her.
～相応のふるまいをしなさい Be your *age*. / Act your *age*.
死んだ子どもの～を数えてもしかたがない There is no point in dwelling upon might-have-beens.

とし【都市】cities.
—計画 图 city planning; 囷 town planning. —生活 city life; urban life. —生活者 a city dweller. —対抗野球 an Intercity Baseball Championship Series. 学園— a college city; a university city. 工業— an industrial city; a manufacturing city. 田園— a garden city; a rural city.

とじ【綴じ】binding. ¶この本は～がよくない This book *is* badly (≒ poorly) *bound*. これは～がしっかりしている This *is* well *bound*.
—糸 (本の) a binding thread; (着物の) a tacking thread. —方 binding.

どじ ¶まったく～なやつだ He is quite a *stupid* fellow. きょうは～ばかり踏んでいる Everything *goes wrong* with me today.

とじあわ·せる【綴じ合わせる】¶書類を～せる *file* (≒ *bind*) papers.

としうえ【年上】¶彼は私より四つ～だ He *is* four years *older* than I. きみは私よりふたつ～だ You are my *senior* by two years.

としおとこ【年男】a lucky-bean scatterer at the *Setsubun* ritual.

としがい【年甲斐】¶ 彼もなんという～もないことだ What a silly thing it is *for a man of his age!* 彼は～もない男だ He *must know better at his age.* / He *has put on years in vain.* ～もないまねはやめなさい Try and stop such a thing as you are old enough. あんな子どもとけんかするとは～もない It *is beneath your years* to make a quarrel with such a child. 彼は～もなく女に手を出した *Forgetting his age,* he made advances to a young woman.

としかさ【年嵩】¶ ～の人が彼らの代表としてやってきた An *aged* (≒ *elderly*) man came to see me as their representative. ～の人からどうぞ *Seniors* first!

どしがた・い【度し難い】be incorrigible. ¶ こんな失敗をするなんて, 彼もまったく～い It *is* quite *helpless* of him to make such a mistake like this.

としかっこう【年格好】¶ それは～50 くらいの人だった He was a man of about fifty〔*years of age*〕. きみぐらいの～の男を見かけなかったか Didn't you happen to see a man *about your age?* みんな同じ～だ They seem to *be* all *of an age.* / They seem to *be the same age.*

としご【年子】¶ あの姉妹は～だ They are *sisters born in two successive years.* / The sisters *were born within a year of each other.*

としごと【年毎】¶ 流行は～に変わっていく Fashions change *every year.* ～に女性の服装が華やかになる Women's dresses become more colorful *year by year.*

とじこみ【綴じ込み】a file. ¶ 書類の～ *a file* of papers. 週刊誌の～を作る *keep* weekly magazines *on file.*

とじこ・む【綴じ込む】¶ 書類を～む *keep* papers *on file.*

とじこ・める【閉じ込める】¶ きのうはかぜを引いて家に～められていた Yesterday I *was confined to* my house with a cold. 吹雪で一日家に～められた I *was kept indoors* by the heavy snow all day〔long〕. 一晩中故障した電車の中に～められた I *was kept in* the disabled car all through the night.

とじこも・る【閉じ籠もる】¶ この3日間かぜで～っている I *have been confined to* my house (≒ *have been kept indoors*) with a cold these three days. 彼は寺に～って修行している He is training himself *shutting himself up in* a temple. あの人はいつも家にばかり～っている He always *shuts himself up in* his house.

としごろ【年頃】**1**〚年配〛age. ¶ 彼はもう60歳に近い～だ He *is* now *about* sixty *years old.* ふたりは同じ～だ The two *are about the same age.* 彼女は私の妹の～だ She *is about* my sister's *age.* 彼ももうひとりで旅行できる～だ He *is old enough to* travel by himself.
2〚青春期〛¶ 彼女も～になった She has become of *marriageable age.*

としごろ *(cont.)*

彼には～の息子がふたりいる He has two *adolescent* sons.

としした【年下】¶ 彼は私より三つ～だ He *is* three years *younger* than I. / He is my *junior* by three years.

どしつ【土質】the nature of soil. ¶ ～がやわらかいので崩れやすい The earth is easy to break, as it is soft.

としつき【年月】years; time. ¶ これを仕上げるまでに多くの～を重ねた It took me *years and years* (≒ *a long time*) to finish this. / I have finished this after *many years'* work.

-として as; by way of. ¶ 私は友人～きみに言いたい I want to speak to you *as* a friend. 彼は警察官～尋問した He asked *in the capacity of* a police officer. 冗談は別～彼はどこから見てもそつがない *Joking apart,* he is faultless in every way. 言いわけ～彼はそれを言った He said that *by way of* excuse.

-としては ¶ 彼は学者～常識に欠ける *For* a scholar he lacks common sense. 18歳～彼は若く見える *Considering* that he is eighteen years old, he looks young. / He looks younger than eighteen years old. 彼はフランス人～日本語がじょうずだ He is good at speaking Japanese *for* a Frenchman. 私～その案は考えものだ *As for* me, I doubt if the plan is right.

-としても ¶ それが事実～私は驚かない I should not be surprised *even if* it were true.

どしどし ¶ ～質問しなさい Ask *as many* questions *as you like.*

としなみ【年波】*one's* increasing age. ¶ 彼も寄る～に腰が曲がっている He is bent in the back *under the weight of years.* だれも寄る～には勝てない Nobody can struggle against *advancing age.*

としのくれ【年の暮れ】the last days of the year. ¶ ～はだれも忙しい Everybody is busy *toward the end of the year.* ～が押し迫っている *The year end* is near at hand.

としのこう【年の功】¶ かめの甲より～ We learn by experience. / Experience teaches. あれだけのことができるのは～だ He *has not put on years in vain,* now that he can do so much.

としのせ【年の瀬】the last days of the year. ¶ ～は何かとあわただしい We pass *the end of the year* restlessly. / We are busy in some way or other *toward the end of the year.*

としは【年端】¶ ～もいかぬ子ども a *young* child.

としま【年増】a middle-aged woman. ¶ 彼女は～盛りだ She *is in full womanhood.* あの女はもういい～だ She *is rather advanced in age.* / She is a *middle-aged* woman.

とじまり【戸締まり】¶ 彼女は～をしないで出かけた She went out *leaving the doors unfastened.* ～を厳重にせよ *Fasten the doors* securely.

としまわり【年回り】¶ ことしは～が悪い I *am* not *lucky this year.* / This is *an unlucky*

と

year for me. / I *am in my unlucky year*.

とじめ【綴じ目】¶ ～が切れる *A seam* breaks.

としゃ【吐瀉】vomiting and diarrhoea. ¶ 患者が急に～した The patient had a sudden attack of *vomiting and diarrhoea*.

どしゃ【土砂】earth and sand.

どしゃくずれ【土砂崩れ】a landslide; a wash-out.

どしゃぶり【どしゃ降り】a heavy rain; a downpour. ¶ ～の雨だった It rained heavily./ It poured down. / It rained in torrents. 降れば～(諺) *It never rains but it pours*.

としゅ【斗酒】¶ 彼は～なお辞せずだ He *drinks like a whale* (≒ *a fish*). / He *is ready to down kegs of sake*.

としゅ【徒手】¶ 私は～で仕事を始めた I had nothing to start with. 彼は～空拳(くうけん)で北海道へ渡った He went over to Hokkaido *penniless*.

—体操 free gymnastics.

としょ【図書】books.

—閲覧室 a reading room. **—閲覧者** a reader; a visitor to library. **—閲覧料** a library admission fee. **—解題** a bibliography. **—室** a library. **—目録** a catalog[ue] of books.

とじょう【途上】¶ 新校舎は建築～にある The new school house *is* now *under construction*. 彼は成功の～にあった He *was in a fair way to* great success. この店は発展～にある This store is getting more and more prosperous. 帰宅の～, 彼に会った *On my way* home, I met him.

発展**—国** a developing country.

どじょう【泥鰌・鰌】〔魚類〕a loach. ¶ 柳の下にいつも～はいない You cannot always succeed twice running.

—汁 loach soup. **—ひげ** a poor mustache.

どじょう【土壌】soil. ¶ 肥沃(ひよく)な(やせた)～ fertile (poor) *soil*.

どしょうぼね【土性骨】¶ 彼は～のある男だ He has *a strong will* (≒ plenty *of guts*).

としょかん【図書館】a library. ¶ ～から本を借り出す take a book from *a library*.

—館員 a librarian. **—学** library science. **—長** the chief librarian. 学校**—** a school library. 国会**—** the Diet Library; 米 The Library of Congress. 巡回**—** a traveling library.

としょく【徒食】¶ 無為～で日を送る live an idle life; idle away *one's* time; live in idleness.

としより【年寄り】(老人) an old person. ¶ それは～の冷や水というものだ That is *an old man's* indiscretion. ～の言うことは聞くものだ You should listen to *an old man*. 彼女は～じみた顔をしている She looks much *older* for her age.

と・じる【閉じる】¶ 窓を～じる *shut* (≒ *close*) the window. 会を～じる *close* (≒ *adjourn*) the meeting; *break up* the party; *bring* the meeting *to a close*. 本を～じる *shut* (≒ *close*) a book.

と・じる【綴じる】¶ 本を～じる *bind* a book. 書類を～じておく *keep* papers *on file*.

としわすれ【年忘れ】¶ ～の会を開く hold *a year-end drinking party* (≒ *a year-end social gathering*).

としん【都心】the heart (≒ hub) of the city. ¶ ～に買物に行く go shopping *downtown*. 東京の～ *downtown* Tokyo.

どしん ¶ なにかが～と落ちた Something fell *with a thud*. たなから荷物が～と落ちた The bundles fell *plump* from the shelf. 車が～と音をたててへいにぶつかった A car *bumped against* the fence.

トス a toss. ¶ ショートはゴロをとって二塁手に～した The shortstop fielded the grounder and *tossed* the ball to the second baseman. ～できめよう Let's *toss*. / Let's decide by the *toss* (≒ *tossing*).

どす a dagger. ¶ ～のきいた声 a *threatening* voice. 彼は～のきいた声をしている His voice has *a touch of danger* (≒ *a threatening tone*).

どすう【度数】frequency.

—制 (電話の) the message (≒ call) rate system. **—料金** message (≒ call) rates.

どすぐろ・い【どす黒い】dark; dusky. ¶ ～い顔 a *swarthy* face. ～い血 *dark red* blood.

と・する【賭する】risk. ¶ 彼は命を～して戦った He fought *at the risk of* his life. 国を～して戦った We engaged in an *all-out* war. 会社は社運を～して新商品を発売した The company *staked* its future *on* the promotion of the new merchandise.

とすれば ¶ ～, 彼がおこるのも当たりまえだ *If that is the case*, it is no wonder that he should get angry.

どせい【土星】〔天文学〕Saturn.

どせい【怒声】an angry voice. ¶ 彼の～が聞こえた I heard his *angry voice*.

とぜつ【途絶】(中止) suspension; stoppage. ¶ 悪天候のため交通が～した All the transportation service *were blocked* (≒ *were suspended*) because of bad weather. その地方との通信が～した The communication with that area *has been cut off*. / The communication lines to that area *have been broken off* (≒ *have been interrupted*).

とそ【屠蘇】spiced *sake*. ¶ 彼は～気分が抜けていない He has not been sobered up from the merriment of the New Year's *spiced sake*.

とそう【塗装】¶ そのおもちゃはエナメルで～されている Those toys *are coated* with enamel. 壁の～が必要だ The walls need *a coat of paint*.

どそう【土葬】burial; interment; inhumation. ¶ 彼は死後3日目に～に付された He *was buried* (≒ *was interred*) three days after his death.

どぞう【土蔵】a stone treasure-house.

どそく【土足】¶ ～お断わり Please remove your shoes before entering. 彼らはずかずかと家に～であがりこんできた They walked into the house without removing their shoes.

どぞく【土俗】local custom.

—学 folklore.

どだい【土台】a foundation. ¶ この家は～がしっかりしている This house stands on *a* firm *foundation.* 勤勉こそ成功の～だ Diligence is the very *foundation* of success. 彼のその小説は戦争体験を～にしている That novel of his *is founded* (≒ *is based*) *on* his experience in war.

どだい ¶ それは～無理な注文だ *Altogether* it is a tall order to fill. ～なってない *To begin with,* the whole thing is preposterous. 彼の言うことは～おかしい What he says is *utterly* unreasonable.

とだ·える【跡絶える】¶ 通信がしばらく～えた The radio communication *was interrupted* for a while. 彼からの音信が近ごろ～えがちだ I *seldom hear from* him now. もうすぐ通りは人通りが～える The street will *be deserted* here soon.

どたぐつ【どた靴】shabby ill-fitting shoes; big clumsy shoes.

とだな【戸棚】a cabinet; (台所の) a cupboard; (食器の) a sideboard; (押し入れ) a closet.

どたばた ¶ 2階で～騒ぐな Don't *make too much noise* upstairs. 今更～しても始まらない It is [of] no use to *fuss about* now.

—喜劇 a slapstick.

とたん【塗炭】¶ 彼は～の苦しみをなめた He underwent *unspeakable* sufferings./ He went through an *agonizing* experience.

とたん【途端】¶ 家を出た～にだれかにつけられていると感じた I *no sooner* stepped out of the house *than* I became aware that someone was following me. 家に着いた～, 雨がざあっときた There came a heavy downpour *as soon as* (≒ *the moment*) I reached home.

トタン zinc.

—板 corrugated iron; tin[plate]; galvanized iron. —屋根 a zinc roof; a tin[plate] roof.

どたんば【土壇場】the last moment; (危機) a crisis. ¶ 彼は～に追いこまれた He was driven *to the wall* (≒ *into a corner*). 敵は～になって反撃に出てきた The enemy waited until *the last moment* to counterattack. 彼は最後の～になって計画を変えた He changed the plan *at the eleventh hour.*

とち【土地】**1**〖土地·土〗 land; (地所) an estate. ¶ この～は高価だ This *land* is expensive.

この～は広さどのくらいだろうか I wonder how large this *land* is.

この～はトマトの栽培に適している This *soil* is fit for the cultivation of tomatoes.

彼は軽井沢に～を買った He bought *a piece of land* in Karuizawa.

私は～に投資した I invested in *real estate.*

—家屋 land (≒ estate) and buildings. —家屋周旋業所 an estate agent. —価格 the value of the land. —所有権 land ownership. —台帳 a land ledger.

2〖所·地方〗¶ あの辺りの～にはまったく不案内だ I am an utter stranger to *the place.*

彼はこの村のことはよく知っている. ～の者だから He knows a lot about this village. He is a native of *the place.*

この辺りの～の名産物はなんですか What is the product of this *place*?

とちじ【都知事】¶ 東京～ the Governor of Tokyo Metropolis. 東京～選挙 the Tokyo gubernatorial election.

とちのき【栃·橡】〘植物〙 a horse chestnut.

どちゃく【土着】¶ ～の native; native-born.

—民 a native; (総称) the natives.

とちゅう【途中】**1**〖道の〗 on the way; (中途で) halfway; midway.

¶ ～で私は買い物をした I did my shopping *on the way.*

家へ帰る～で荷物を置き忘れた I left my baggage somewhere *on my way* home.

ここへ来る～彼を見た I saw him *on my way* here.

駅へ行く～でにわか雨に会った I was caught in a shower *on my way to* the station.

彼は学校へ往復の～この店に立ち寄る He drops in at this store *on his way to and from* school.

～までは走った I ran *part of the way.*

～までごいっしょしましょう I will go *part of the way* with you.

—下車 ¶ この切符では～下車ができない This ticket does not allow you to make *stopovers.* ～下車前途無効 No *stopover* is allowed by this ticket.

2〖事のなかば〗¶ ～で仕事をやめるな Don't give up your work *halfway.*

話の～で電話に呼び出された I was wanted at the phone *in the middle of* my talk.

お話の～ですが, あすご在宅ですか *Excuse me for interrupting you,* but will you be at home tomorrow?

とちょう【都庁】¶ 東京～ the Tokyo Metropolitan Government.

どちら【何方】**1**〖どこ〗¶ ～へいらっしゃるところですか *Where* are you going?

2〖どっち〗¶ 春と夏とでは～が好きですか *Which* do you like better, spring or summer?

～があなたの本ですか *Which* is your book?

～の道を行ったら駅に出られますか *Which* road leads to the station?

～の道を行っても駅に出られます *Whichever* road you take, you will be able to get to the station.

～も私の好きな本です *Both* [of the] books are my favorite ones.

彼らは～も英語を話さない *Neither of* them speaks English.

～の話もほんとうでない *Neither* story is true.

私は～もきらいだ I like *neither of* them.

～かが私のです *One or the other* is mine.

彼か私か～かが行きます *Either* he *or* I will go.

どれかひとつください. ～でもいいですから Please give

me one. *Either* will do.
〜でも好きなほうを持っていってください You may take *whichever* you like.
彼女は〜かといえば神経質だ She is, *if anything*, nervous.
彼は〜かといえば背が高い He is *rather* tall.

とち・る ¶あの俳優は舞台でせりふを〜った That actor *faltered* in his speech on the stage.

とっか【特価】 a reduced (≒ special) price. ¶この品を〜でお分けします We offer these articles at *special* (≒ *reduced*) *prices*.
—売り出し a sale. —品 a bargain item.

どっかい【読会】 a reading. ¶法案は第3〜を通過した The bill passed its third *reading*.

どっかいりょく【読解力】 reading comprehension.

どっかと ¶彼はいすに〜座った He *settled himself down comfortably* in the chair.

とっかん【突貫】(突撃) a charge; a rush.
—工事 rush work. ¶その道路は〜工事で完成された The road was completed *with great speed* (≒ *at a rush*).

とっき【突起】 a projection; 〔解剖〕 a process. 虫様— the vermiform appendix. 虫様—炎 appendicitis.

とっき【特記】 special mention. ¶これは〜に値する作品だ The work deserves *special mention*.

どっき【毒気】 ¶彼のことばに〜を抜かれた I *was* quite *taken aback* at his words. 彼女の〜を含んだ話し方におそれをなした I was terrified at her *malicious* (≒ *venomous*; *spiteful*) tongue.

とっきゅう【特急】 a limited express; a special express (途中停車駅が全然ない場合のみ a special express を使う). ¶〜ひかりで大阪に行った I went to Osaka on the Hikari *Limited* 〔*bullet train*〕.
「*sake*.

とっきゅう【特級】 —酒 the highest quality

とっきょ【特許】(専売の) a patent. ¶われわれは〜を出願中だ We are now applying for *a patent*. この新装置に対して〜を取った We obtained *a patent* for this new device. この製造過程はアメリカの〜を取ってある The manufacturing process holds *a patent* in the United States.
—権 a patent right. —庁 the Patent Agency. —品 a patent. —料 a patent fee.

とっく【疾っく】 ¶彼は〜の昔に亡くなった He died *long ago*. 8時の汽車は〜に出てしまった The eight o'clock train was gone *quite a while ago* (≒ *a long while ago*). 彼は〜に40を過ぎている He is *well* over forty.

とつ・ぐ【嫁ぐ】 marry (a man). ¶彼女はA家に〜いだ She *married into* A family.

ドック a dock. ¶船を〜に入れる *dock* a ship; put a ship into *dock*. 〜に入る go into *dock*. 〜から出る come out of *dock*.
浮き— a floating dock. 乾— a dry dock. 人間— ¶彼は人間〜に入った He entered the hospital for a thorough physical check.

とっくみあい【取っ組み合い】 ¶ふたりで激しい〜のけんかを始めた The two began to have a *hand-to-hand* fight.

とっくみあ・う【取っ組み合う】 grapple (*with a person*). ¶兄弟は〜った The brothers *grappled with each other*.

とっくり【徳利】 a bottle. ¶〜首のセーター a turtleneck; a 〔pullover〕 sweater.

とっくり ¶あすまで〜とこの問題を考えさせてください Let me *sleep on* (≒ *over*) this problem. きみの報告書を〜読ませてもらった I went over your report *very thoroughly*.

とっけい【特恵】 —関税 preferential tariff.

とつげき【突撃】 a charge; a dash; a rush.
¶騎兵隊は敵陣に〜した The cavalry *rushed to* the enemy's position./ The cavalry *charged* the enemy.

とっけん【特権】 a privilege. ¶大学教育はもはや少数者だけの〜ではなくなっている College education is no longer *a privilege* enjoyed by only a few. それらの〜は会員にだけ与えられる Those *privileges* are allowed to members only.
—階級 the privileged classes.

どっこい ¶〜そうはいかない No, no, that won't do; that can't. 彼らの実力は〜〜だ Their abilities *are just about the same* (≒ *go fifty-fifty*).

とっこう【特効】 special efficacy; special virtue.
—薬 a special remedy (*for* colds).

とっこう【徳行】 a virtuous act. ¶彼のかくれた〜が世に知られた His secret *virtuous act* became known to the public.

とっこう【篤行】 good deed.

とっこうたい【特攻隊】 a suicide squad; a forlorn hope.

とっさ【咄嗟】 off hand; impromptu. ¶〜には答えられない I cannot reply *off hand*. 彼の名前を〜に思い出せなかった I could not recall his name *on the spot*. 彼は〜に車のハンドルを右に切った He turned the wheel to the right *on the spur of the moment*. 彼は〜に答えた He answered *impromptu*.

どっさり ¶彼からお土産を〜もらった I got *a lot of* presents from him.

ドッジボール dodge ball.

とっしゅつ【突出】 ¶半島が海に〜している The peninsula *juts out* into the sea.

とつじょ【突如】 suddenly; all of a sudden.

どっしり ¶〜した態度 a *dignified* manner.

とっしん【突進】 a rush; a dash. ¶彼はゴール目がけて〜した He made *a wild rush* (≒ *dash*) *to* the goal. 彼は〜してくる列車に身を投げ出した He threw himself in front of the *on-coming* train.

とつぜん【突然】 suddenly; all of a sudden.
¶彼は〜逃げだした He ran away *suddenly*. 私は〜の彼の訪問にめんくらった I was embarrassed at his *sudden* visit. 事故は〜起こった The accident occurred *suddenly* (≒ *all of a sudden*). 彼は〜帰ってきた He came back home *unexpectedly*. 彼は〜姿を見せた He

made a *sudden* appearance. 夜中に～サイレンが鳴り響いた The siren rang out *without notice* in the middle of the night.
—変異〘生物〙 mutation; (もの) a sport.

とったん【突端】 the point; the tip. ¶ みさきの～ *the tip of* a cape.

どっちつかず ¶ 彼は～の返事をした He gave a *non-committal* (≒ an *evasive*) answer.

どっちみち ¶ ～まにあわない We won't be in time *anyway*.

とっち·める【取っ締める】 ¶ また窓ガラスを割ったので彼に～められた He *gave it to* me for breaking another windowpane. 彼を～めよう Let's *give* him *a rough time*.

とっつき【取っ付き】 (初め) the beginning. ¶ ～のいい (悪い) 人 an easy (a hard) person to get to know.

とって【取っ手】 a handle; a grip; (引き出しなど) a knob; (引き手) a pull. ¶ なべの～ the *handle* of a pan. ドアの～ *a* door *knob*. 引き出しの～がはずれた *A* drawer *handle* came off.

-とって ¶ 人口過剰はわが国に～大きな問題だ Overpopulation is of great concern *to* our country. 中国と国交回復することはわが国に～有益なことだ It is advantageous *for* our country to establish diplomatic relations with Red China.

とってい【突堤】 a breakwater; a quay.

とっておき【取って置き】 ¶ 彼は～のぶどう酒をふるまってくれた He served us the wine *stored* (≒ *kept*) *for very special occasion*.

とってお·く【取って置く】 keep; hold; reserve. ¶ 金を～く *save* money. 席を～く *reserve* a seat.

とってかえ·す【取って返す】 ¶ 電車にかさを忘れたのを思い出し, 駅に～した I remembered I left my umbrella on the train, so I *hurried back to* the station.

とって·くる【取って来る】 ¶ 新聞を～きてくれませんか Will you please *go and get* me the newspaper? (犬などに) ボールを～こい *Go and fetch* the ball!

とってつけた ¶ 彼は～ようなお世辞を言った He gave me an *awkward and insincere* compliment.

どっと all at once; suddenly. ¶ 水が～流れ込んできた The water *rushed in*. 聴衆は～笑った The audience *burst out* laughing (≒ *burst into* laughter). 涙が～あふれた Tears *welled up* into my eyes. 彼は～病の床についた He was *suddenly* taken ill. 日曜のハイカーたちが郊外に～繰り出した A crowd of Sunday hikers *swarmed* all over the countryside.

とつとつ【訥訥·吶吶】 ¶ 彼はその話を～として語った He told us the story *falteringly*.

とっとと ¶ ～出ていけ Clear out *right now*. 彼女は小またながら～歩く She takes small but *fast* steps. 彼は～歩き去った He walked away *hurriedly* (≒ *quickly*).

とつにゅう【突入】 ¶ 労組はストに～した The labor union *went* (≒ *rushed*) *headlong into* a strike. 敵陣に～した We *broke into* the enemy line.

とっぱ【突破】 ¶ 日本の人口は1億を～した The Japanese population *passed* the one-hundred million mark. 彼らは警察の非常線を～した They *broke through* the police cordon. 彼は入学試験の難関を～した He *passed* the entrance examination. / He *survived* the keen competition in the entrance examination.
—口 ¶ 彼がその～口を開いた He took the initial step in breaking the barrier.

とっぱつ【突発】 an outbreak. ¶ 大事件が～した A great incident *occurred*.
—事故 ¶ そんな～事故は防ぎようがない There is no way of preventing such *a totally unforeseen accident*. ～事件があいついで起こった *Unexpected events* occurred one after another.

とっぱん【凸版】 —印刷 letterpress; relief printing.

とっぴ【突飛】 ¶ 彼はいつも～なことをする He is always doing *wild* things. そんな～な要求は受け入れられない We cannot accept such a *preposterous* demand. 彼の～な発言にまごついた We were puzzled at his *absurd* suggestion. 宝石は～な値段で売れている Jewels are selling at *exorbitant* prices. ～な流行 *fantastic* fashions.

とっぴょうし【突拍子】 ¶ ～もない想像 an *extravagant* flight of fancy. ～もない行動 an *escapade*. 彼はときどき～もないことを言い出す He sometimes talks *recklessly*. ～もない夢 *fantastic* (≒ *extravagant*) dreams.

トップ top. ¶ 彼はクラスで～だ He *is at the top* (≒ *head*) *of* the class. / He *tops* his class. ことしはP大学が入試の～を切った P University *was the first to* give entrance examinations.
—会談 a summit conference. —クラス ¶ ～クラスの人々 *top* people.

とっぷう【突風】 a gust of wind; a gale.

とっぷり entirely; completely. ¶ 日は～暮れた It became *quite* dark. / The night *completely* closed in.

どっぽ【独歩】 ¶ 当代～の詩人 the *unique* poet of the age; the poet *unequalled* at present. 彼は独立～で頑張った He held on, *relying on himself* (≒ *standing on his own legs*). この業績は古今～のものだ This achievement *stands unique*. / This achievement *has no rival*.

とつめんきょう【凸面鏡】 a convex mirror.

とつレンズ【凸レンズ】 a convex lens.

-とて ¶ 彼～わかっていたであろう *Even* he may have known it. 知らぬこと～失礼しました I beg your pardon, but I didn't know it. 勝った～別に偉いことはない You are not necessarily a great man *even if* you won. いかにベテランだから～, 油断してはならぬ You should not be inattentive *because* you are an old timer in your line. 彼がここにいた～, しようがない *Even if* he were here, it would be no use.

と

どて【土手】a bank ; an embankment. ¶ ～を築く build *a bank* (≒ *an embankment*); *embank* (a river).

とてい【徒弟】an apprentice.

どてっぱら【土手腹】¶ ～を蹴られた I was kicked *on the side.*

とてつもない【途轍もない】¶ ～こと an *absurd* thing. ～要求を突きつけられた A *preposterous* demand was thrust before me.

とても【迚も】**1**〖非常に〗very ; so. ¶ 山頂は～寒い It is *very* cold at the top of a mountain.
私はそれが～おもしろかった I have enjoyed it *immensely.*
2〖どうしても〗by no means. ¶ この調子では～まにあわない If I go on (in) this way, I am afraid I can*not* make it *anyway.*
彼は～三十代の人とは見えない He *hardly* looks like a man in his thirties (as he really is).
～望みがない There is *no* hope *at all.*
～やりきれない I *couldn't* stand it *for all the world.*

どてら【縕袍】a padded dressing gown.

ととう【徒党】conspirators ; a faction. ¶ ～を組む band together ; form *a faction.*

どとう【怒濤】raging billows ; roaring waves. ¶ ～逆巻く絶海 the farthest seas with *angry waves.*

とど・く【届く】**1**〖着く〗¶ 手紙は～きましたか *Has* my letter *reached* you?/ *Have* you *received* my letter?
包みはまだ～かない The parcel *has* not *arrived* yet.
2〖達する〗¶ 彼は天井に手が～くくらい背が高い He is tall enough to *reach* the ceiling.
彼の息子は30に手が～く年ごろとなった His son is *almost* 30 years old.
本はすぐ手の～く所に置いてください Please put the book *within easy reach.*
目の～くかぎり空と海だった As far as the eye could *reach,* nothing was to be seen but the sky and sea.
この値段ではとても手が～かない The price *is* too *prohibitive* for me.
矢は的には～かなかった The arrow *fell short of* the mark.
ひもは短くて半分しか～かなかった The string was so short that it *reached* only halfway.

とどけ【届け・届】a report.
――先 a receiver's address. ――済み filed. 移転―― a removal notice. 欠席―― a report of absence. ¶ 欠席～は至急提出しなければならない The *notification of absence* must be submitted as soon as possible. 死亡―― ¶ 彼の死亡～を出した I *reported* his death.

とど・ける【届ける】send ; report. ¶ この書類を社長に～けてくれ Will you *send* this paper *to* the president? 落とし物を拾った人は～けてください It will be appreciated if anyone *hands over* a find to us. 盗難を警察に～けたか Have you *reported* the burglary *to* the police yet? 市に長男の出生を～けた I *registered* the birth of our first son *with* the city authorities.

とどこおり【滞り】stagnation. ¶ 家賃の～ *arrears* of rent. 郵便の～が増える More mails *are being delayed.* 税金は～なく支払うほうがいい You should pay your tax *promptly* (≒ *regularly*). ふたりの結婚式は～なく済んだ Their wedding ceremony went off *smoothly* (≒ *without a hitch*).

とどこお・る【滞る】¶ お勘定が２か月～っています Your account *has been standing unsettled* for two months. / Your account *has been left unpaid* for two months. 仕事が～っている I *am behind with* my work. 交通が～る The traffic *is jammed* (≒ *is congested*). 彼の家賃が～っている He *is behindhand* (≒ *is in arrears*) *with* the rent.

ととの・う【整う】¶ 昼食の準備が～った Lunch *is ready.* 用意が～いしだい会は開かれる The meeting is to be held as soon as the preparations *are completed.* 彼女は～った服装をしている She is *neatly* dressed. 彼女は～った顔だちをしている She has *regular* features.

ととの・える【整える】¶ 服装を～えなさい *Make* yourself *neat.* 彼女は毎朝髪を～える She *does* her hair every morning. 食事は11時までに～えてください *Get* our meal *ready* by eleven. お客のためにその部屋を～えた We *prepared* the room for visitors.

とどのつまり ¶ ～, その会は中止ということになった *In the end* (≒ *Finally; After all*) the meeting was broken off. ⇒けっきょく

とどま・る【止まる・留まる・停まる】¶ しばらくここに～っていなさい *Stay* here for a while. 雨のため外出せず家に～った The rain *kept* me *indoors.* 彼はなおも現職に～った He *remained* in his present position. 失望したのは彼ひとりに～らなかった He was not *the only* person that was disappointed. 彼女の才能は文学の世界のみに～らなかった Her talents *were* not *limited to* the literary world. 涙が～ることなく彼女のほおを流れた Tears trickled down her cheeks *incessantly.* 彼の横暴ぶりは～るところを知らなかった His ferocity *was boundless.* 彼の影響力は経済界のみに～らなかった His influence *was* not *confined to* the economic world. 物価は～るところなく上昇を続けた The prices *kept on* rising.

とどめ【止め】a finishing stroke. ¶ ～を刺す give (*a person*) a finishing blow ; put an end to (*a person*). わがチームはホームランで～を刺された A homerun gave *a coup de grâce* to us.

とど・める【止める・留める】¶ 反対意見を言うに～めた I *only* made an opposite remark. 他人がやろうとすることを無理に～める He *forces* others *not to do* what they want to do.

とどろか・す【轟かす】¶ 飛行機は爆音を～せて飛んでいった The airplane flew off *with a whirr.* 彼は全世界に名を～した He was known far and wide all over the world./ He enjoyed a world-wide reputation.

とどろき【轟き】a roar ; thumping. ¶ 雷の～

と

a peal. 大砲の～ the *roar* of a gun.

とどろ·く【轟く】roar. ¶ ～く波の音 the sounds of *roaring* waves. 砲声が～いた The *boom* of guns was heard. 私の胸が～いた My heart *was beating.* / My heart *was throbbing.* 彼の芸名は天下に～いている He has won worldwide fame as an actor. / He is much talked of as an actor.

とな·える【唱える】¶ 異議を～える take objection to; object to; be opposed to. 自然主義を～える *advance* naturalism. 万歳を～える give cheers. 禁酒を～える *advocate* temperance.

トナカイ【馴鹿】〘動物〙 a reindeer (単複同形).

どなた【何方】¶ ～でもいいですからやってください Please do it, if *anyone of you* wants to. ～に頼みましょうか *Who[m]* shall I ask? ～ですか *What*'s your name, please? / May I have your name?

どなべ【土鍋】an earthenware pot.

となり【隣】a next house. ¶ 彼は～に住んでいる He lives *next door to* me. 居間は～だ The sitting room is the *next.* / The sitting room *adjoins* this. ～の部屋 the *adjoining* (≒ *next*) room. ～に座っている婦人はおばです The woman sitting *side by side with* (≒ *next to*) *me* is my aunt. ～の犬がまた庭に入ってきた The *neighbor's* dog came into my garden again. 彼は1軒おいた～に住んでいる He lives *next door but one.* 彼の家の右～は花屋だ His *neighbor* on the right is a florist's. ～のよしみでとてもそんなまねはできない Our *neighborly* feeling never permits us to do so.

—合わせ ¶ ふたりは～合わせに住んでいる The two live *next door to* each other.

—近所 the neighborhood.

となりあ·う【隣り合う】¶ ～って座る sit *side by side with* (*a person*). ～った人と話す talk with those *next to* each other.

となりあわ·せる【隣り合わせる】¶ ふたりの机を～せて置く We *adjoin* both the desks. / We put their desks *side by side.*

どなりつ·ける【怒鳴りつける】¶ 彼はよく言うことを聞かぬ者を～ける He always *storms at* whoever doesn't do as he is told to.

どな·る【怒鳴る】cry aloud. ¶ 彼は～るような声で話す He speaks in a *roaring* voice. いたずらして彼に～られた He *scolded* me for my mischief. 彼は腹を立ててだれかれの見境なく～りちらしている He is so angry that he *is shouting* right and left.

とにかく【兎に角】at any rate. ¶ ～見に行こう Let's go and see, *anyhow.* ～腹ごしらえをする I'll take a meal *anyway.* ～きょうはだめだ *Be the matter what it may* (≒ *In any case*), we can't do it today. ～疲れた *At any rate,* I am tired.

トニック〘薬品·食料·化粧品〙 tonic.

ジン**—** a gin and tonic.

とねりこ【秦皮】〘植物〙 an ash tree.

どの what; which. ¶ あなたは～国においでになるのですか *Which* country are you going to visit? ～道を行ったら駅に行けますか *Which* way leads to the station? ～道を行っても彼の家に行ける *Whichever* way you take, you will come to his house. ～日ならご在宅ですか On *what* day will you be at home? ～学生もみなまじめだ *Each* of the students is diligent.

-どの【-殿】(男子) Esq. (≒ Esquire); Mr. (≒ Mr) (Mr. のあとのピリオドはつけないことがある); (女子) Mrs.; Miss. ¶ 佐藤太郎～ *Mr.* Taro Sato; Taro Sato, *Esq.* (Esq. は今あまり使わない).

どのう【土嚢】a sandbag.

どのくらい【どの位】(距離) how far; (量) how much; (数) how many; (時間) how long. ¶ 東京から横浜までは～ありますか *How far* is it from Tokyo to Yokohama? 名古屋までバスで～かかりますか *How long* does it take to go from here to Nagoya by bus? 北海道へ来て～になりますか *How long* have you been in Hokkaido? 彼の年齢は～だろう I wonder *how old* he is. 彼は～切手のコレクションがあるのだろう I wonder *how many* postage stamps he has collected. きょうは～まで読みましたか *How much* have you read today? その指輪は～しましたか *How much* did that ring cost you?

とのさま【殿様】a [feudal] lord; a prince. ¶ ～のような暮らしをする live like *a prince.*

とのさまがえる【殿様蛙】〘動物〙 a bullfrog.

どのへん【どの辺】¶ それを～に落としたのだろう I wonder *where* I dropped it. 自分はクラスの中で～にいるのだろう I don't know *how* I am getting on with my studies in the class. 今～かわからない (道が) I don't know *where* I stand.

どのみち【どの道】anyway; anyhow. ¶ ～一遍は行かねばなるまい I have to go once *sooner or later.* ～やっかいなことだ *In any case* it is troublesome.

どのように ¶ ～しましょうか *How* shall I do it? ～考えますか *What* do you think of it? ～して相手に納得させるか *How* do we win him to consent? ～してもだめだ *Everything* I do goes wrong.

-とは ¶ 美～いったいなんであるか What ever is beauty? 彼女は美人～いえない We cannot call her a beauty. 偶然～思えない It can't be a mere chance. タクシーで500円～かからない It does not cost *so much as* 500 yen to go by taxi. きみに会おう～思わなかった I least expected to meet you. / You were the last man I expected to see.

とば【賭場】a gambling-place; a gaming-house.

どば【駑馬】a hack; an inferior horse. ¶ ～にむち打って働きます I will work to the best of my *poor ability.*

トパーズ topaz.

とはいうものの【とは言うものの】but; however. ¶ ～そんなにうまくいくはずがない *For all that,* it cannot go on so smoothly. 病気～彼は気が

しっかりしていた *Though* ill, he was not depressed in spirits.

とはいえ【とは言え】although ; however. ¶ 春〜まだ寒い *Though* [it is] spring, it is still cold.

とばく【賭博】gambling. ¶ 〜をする gamble ; play for money. 彼は〜ですっかり金を失った He *gambled away* his whole money.
—者 a gambler.

どばし【土橋】an earthen bridge.

とば·す【飛ばす】¶ 伝書バトを〜した I *let loose* a carrier pigeon. 帽子を〜されないようにしなさい Be careful not to *have* your hat *blown off*. こっちに水を〜すな Don't *splash* water *on* me. すごい勢いで車を〜した He *drove* his car at full speed. 彼はどのくらいの速さで〜したのですか How *fast was* he *driving*? つまらないところは〜して読んだ I *skipped* the dull parts of the book.

と

どはずれた【度外れた】¶ 〜冗談はいけない You should not make an *extraordinary* joke.

どはつ【怒髪】¶ 〜天をつく boil with rage ; be in a towering rage.

とばっちり【迸り】a spray ; a splash. ¶ 泥水の〜がかかった I *was splashed* with muddy water. 事件の〜を食った I *was involved in* the affair.

とばり【帳·帷】a curtain ; a hanging. ¶ 夜の〜がおりた *Night* fell. その村はすっかり夜の〜につつまれた The village was covered with *a mantle of darkness*.

とび【鳶】〔鳥類〕a [black] kite ; (とびの者) a fireman. ¶ 〜がタカを生んだ It is a case of a black hen laying white eggs. / An ill cow may have a good calf.

どひ【土匪】bandits ; brigands.

とびあが·る【飛び上がる·跳び上がる】(空中へ) fly up ; (はねあがる) jump (≒ spring) up ; leap. ¶ 〜るほど痛かった I felt *intense* pain. 彼は合格の報せに〜らんばかりに喜んだ He *leaped* for joy at the news of his success.

とびある·く【飛び歩く】run about ; gad about. ¶ 彼は年中金策に〜いている He *is* always *bustling about* to raise money.

とびいし【飛び石】steppingstones.
—連休 off-and-on holidays.

とびいた【跳び板】〔水泳〕a springboard.

とびいり【飛び入り】(人) an adventitious player. ¶ 〜自由の open to *all-comers* ; open-for-all. 〜自由の試合 an *open* contest ; an *all-comers*' match.

とびいろ【鳶色】brown ; auburn.

とびうお【飛び魚】〔魚類〕a flying-fish.

とびうつ·る【飛び移る】¶ 花から花へ〜る *flutter* from flower to flower. 枝から枝へ〜る *fly* from branch to branch.

とびお·きる【飛び起きる】(寝床から) jump out of bed ; (寝床の上で) sit up in bed.

とびおり【飛び降り】**—自殺** ¶ 〜自殺する commit suicide by plunging (*from*).

とびお·りる【飛び降りる】jump down. ¶ 電車から〜りる *jump off* a train. 窓から〜りる *leap out* [*of*] a window.

とびかか·る【飛び掛かる】¶ 彼は賊に〜った He *sprang on* a robber. 犬が彼に〜った A dog *flew at* him.

とびきり【飛び切り】exceptionally ; extraordinarily. ¶ 〜うまい It tastes *best*. 彼は〜よく出来る He is bright *beyond comparison*. このペンは〜いい This pen is *by far* better than the rest.
—上等 ¶ 〜上等の品 an article *of the very best quality* ; a *choice* article.

とびこ·える【飛び越える】¶ 水たまりを〜える *jump over* a pool. へいを〜える *clear* a fence. 先輩を〜えて昇進する *walk over one's* senior into a superior post.

とびこ·す【飛び越す】¶ かきを〜す *leap over* a fence. みぞを〜す *jump* (≒ *vault*) *over* a ditch. 彼は私を〜して昇進した He *has been promoted over my head*.

とびこみ【跳び込み·跳込】〔水泳〕diving.
—自殺 suicide by throwing *one*self on a track. **—台** a diving board ; a spring board.

とびこ·む【跳び込む】¶ 跳込台から水中に〜む *dive* (≒ *jump* ; *plunge*) into the water from the spring board (≒ the diving board).

とびだしナイフ【飛び出しナイフ】a switchblade knife.

とびだ·す【飛び出す】¶ 子どもはよく路地から表通りへ〜す Children often *rush* (≒ *run*) *out* of a lane into the street. 彼は16のときに郷里を〜した He *ran away* from his home town at the age of 16. この魚は目が〜している This fish has *protruding* eyes. ベッドから〜す *jump out* of *one's* bed. 窓から〜す *leap out* [*of*] the window.

とびた·つ【飛び立つ】¶ ヒバリがぱっと〜った A lark *flew up* suddenly. ジェット機が〜った The jet plane *took off*.

とびち·る【飛び散る】¶ 水しぶきが〜った The water *splashed*. コップがこなごなに割れて〜った The glass crashed into pieces and *scattered* all around. 花びらが〜っている Petals *are scattering*.

とびつ·く【飛びつく】¶ 犬に〜かれた A dog *jumped* (≒ *flew*) *at* me. 彼は提案に〜くだろう He is sure to *jump at* the offer.

トピック a topic ; a subject.

とび·でる【飛び出る】¶ 眼玉が〜でるほど高い値段 a *ridiculously high* price ; an *exorbitant* (≒ *prohibitive*) price.

とびどうぐ【飛び道具】(総称) a missile ; weapon ; (火器) a firearm ; a gun ; a rifle.

とびとび【飛び飛び】¶ 本を〜に読む read a book *at random* ; read a book *skipping here and there*. 石が〜に置かれている Some stones are placed *at intervals*. / There are some stones placed *sporadically*.

とびぬけて【飛び抜けて】¶ 彼はクラスの中で〜成績がよい He is doing *outstandingly* well in his class. / He *distinguishes himself* in the class. 彼女の英語の発音は～うまい Her English pronunciation *outshines* (⇆ *stands out from*) others.

とびの·く【飛び退く】 jump back (⇆ aside) (*from* a car).

とびの·る【飛び乗る】 ¶ 電車に～る *jump onto* (⇆ *jump aboard*) a moving train. オートバイに～る *jump on* a motor bicycle.

とびばこ【跳び箱】〖競技〗 a box horse.

とびひ【飛び火】**1**〖火事・事件の〗 ¶ 火事は川向こうまで～した The fire *leaped* the river. 事件は意外なところまで～した The effect of the affair was felt in unexpected quarters.

2〖医学〗(ひふ病) pemphigus.

とびまわ·る【飛び回る】 fly about; (子どもが) romp about. ¶ 彼は商用で世界じゅうを～っている He *travels far and wide* all over the world on business. 彼は金策に～っている He *is* very *busy* raising money.

どひょう【土俵】 the 〔*sumo* wrestling〕 ring. ¶ ～際で right on (⇆ at) the edge of the ring; (比喩的に) at the last moment; at the eleventh hour.

—入り a ceremonial display of *sumo* wrestlers.

とびら【扉】(戸) a door; (本の) the title (⇆ front) page.

どびん【土瓶】 an earthen teapot; a teapot.

—敷 a teapot stand (⇆ mat).

とふ【塗布】 application. ¶ 薬を患部に～する *apply* an ointment to the affected part.

—剤 an ointment; unguent; salve.

と·ぶ【飛ぶ・跳ぶ】**1**〖空を〗 fly. ¶ 鳥が1羽空を～んでいる A bird *is flying* in the air. 彼は～んでいる鳥を撃ち落とした He shot a *flying* bird down.

彼ら一家は一昨日羽田からニューヨークへ～んだ Their family *flew* from Haneda to New York the day before yesterday.

2〖地上を〗 ¶ 幅跳びで8メートル以上～んだ人は何人いるだろうか How many persons *have jumped* over eight meters in the broad jump?

彼は三段跳びで17メートルを～んで優勝した He won the first prize in hop, step and jump with *a leap* of seventeen meters.

3〖比喩的に〗 ¶ この本は～ぶように売れている This book *is selling like hot cakes*.

すぐ現場に～んだ I *hastened to* the scene.

どぶ【溝】 a ditch; a drain; a gutter; a sewer. ¶ ～をさらう clear *a ditch*.

—板 a ditch plank. **—**さらい gutter-cleaning. **—**ネズミ a water rat.

とぶくろ【戸袋】 a sliding door receptacle.

とぶとり【飛ぶ鳥】 a flying bird. ¶ 彼は～も落とす勢いだ He is at the summit of his own power (⇆ prosperity). / His leadership is now unchallenged.

どぶろく【濁酒】 raw (⇆ unrefined) *sake*.

どぶん ¶ ～と水に跳び込む dive into the water *with a splash* (⇆ *with a plop*).

とべい【渡米】 a visit to America. ¶ ～する visit America; go over to America.

どべい【土塀】 an earthen wall.

とほ【徒歩】 going on foot; walking. ¶ 学校へ～で行く *walk* to school; go to school *on foot*.

—競走 a foot race. **—**者 a pedestrian.

—旅行 a walking tour.

とほう【途方】 ¶ 道に迷ったときはまったく～にくれた I *was at a loss* (⇆ I *was at my wits' end*) when I got lost. 彼はきのう～にくれた顔をしてやって来た He came to see me with a *puzzled* (⇆ *troubled*; *bewildered*) look. この絵には～もなく高い値段がついている This picture bears an *incredible* (⇆ *extraordinary*; *exorbitant*) price. 彼はときどき～もないことを言いだす He often talks about *ridiculous* things.

どぼく【土木】 engineering works; public works; civil engineering.

—技師 a civil engineer. **—**業者 a public works contractor. **—**工学 civil engineering. **—**工事 public (⇆ engineering) works.

とぼけ【惚け・恍け】 **—**顔 a vacant (⇆ blank) look. **—**者 a joker.

とぼ·ける【惚ける・恍ける】 ¶ ～けるな, これは私の物だ Don't *be silly*! This is mine, not yours. 彼は～けているのだ He *is pretending ignorance*. / He *is playing dumb*. 彼はよく～けて人を笑わせる He often *plays the fool* and creates the laughter of others.

とぼし·い【乏しい】 scanty; meager; poor; lacking. ¶ 彼は親切心に～い He *is lacking in* kindness. / He *lacks* kindness. 彼は勇気に～い He *has little* courage. 材料が～くなってきた We *have run short of* materials. 水が～くなりそうだ Water is likely to *run short*. 資金が～くなるかもしれぬ Our funds may *become scanty*.

とぼとぼ trudgingly; wearily. ¶ ～と歩く trudge along; plod *one's* way.

とま【苫】 a rush mat.

—屋 a rush-thatched hut.

どま【土間】 an earth (⇆ a dirt) floor; (劇場の) the pit.

とま·す【富ます】 enrich. ¶ 商業は国を～す Commerce *enriches* a nation.

トマト a tomato.

—ケチャップ tomato ketchup (⇆ catsup).

とまど·う【戸惑う】 ¶ なにを話していいのか～った I *was at a loss* (⇆ *was puzzled as to*) what to talk about.

とまり【泊まり】 ¶ 私は今夜～(宿直)だ I *am on duty* tonight. ～がけで遊びにいらっしゃい Come over and *stay a night* with us. ひと晩～で日光に行った I went to Nikko *for the night*.

—客(ホテルなどの) a paying guest; (家庭の) a house guest.

とまりぎ【止まり木】 a perch.

とま·る【止まる・停まる】**1**〖停止する〗 stop. ¶ 家の前に車が～った A car *stopped* in front of my house.

と

列車はその駅に〜らなかった The train did not *stop* at the station.
時計がいつの間にか〜っている The watch *has stopped* without my realizing it.
出血はまだ〜らない It has not *stopped* bleeding yet.
痛みはようやく〜った My pain *has gone* at last.
冷房が〜って暑くなった The air conditioning *went off* and it grew hot.
エンジンが急に〜った The engine *went dead*.
ついに彼の脈が〜った At last his pulse *ceased beating*.
水が〜った Water supply *failed*.
電気が〜った The electric current *failed*.
2 〚鳥などが〛 ¶ 鳥が１羽屋根の上に〜っている A bird *is perching* on the roof.
壁に〜っているのはハエだ It is a fly that *is* on the wall.
3 〚目に〛 ¶ 彼女の姿が目に〜った Her figure *attracted my attention*.

とま・る【泊まる】¶ 今夜は〜っていきなさい Why don't you *stay with* us tonight? 今友人の所に〜っている I *am staying with* my friend (≒ at my friend's). 京都に〜る予定だ I am going to *stay overnight* at Kyoto. ホテルに〜る *put up* at a hotel. そのホテルは何人ぐらい〜れますか How many guests can the hotel *accommodate*?

どまんじゅう【土饅頭】a grave mound.

とみ【富】wealth; riches; a fortune. ¶ 一代で巨万の〜を蓄える achieve (≒ gather) great *wealth* (≒ *riches*) in one generation. 健康は〜にまさる Health is above *wealth*. 〜の追求 the pursuit of *wealth*. 〜の分配 distribution of *wealth*.

とみくじ【富籤】a lottery; (１枚の) a lottery ticket. ¶〜を売り出す run *a lottery*. 〜を引く take a chance in *a lottery*. 〜に当たる win a prize in *a lottery*.

とみに【頓に】(急に) suddenly; (大いに) exceedingly. ¶ 風がやんで〜静かになった The wind has stopped and it has become quiet *suddenly* (≒ *all at once*).

とみん【都民】a citizen of Tokyo; (総称) people in Tokyo.

どみん【土民】the natives; the aborigines.

と・む【富む】¶ アメリカは天然資源に〜んでいる America *is rich in* (≒ *has ample*) natural resources. スイスは美しい景色に〜んでいる Switzerland *abounds with* (≒ *is full of*) beautiful sights. 常識に〜む have strong common sense. 機知に〜む会話 a witty conversation. 経験に〜む教師 an experienced teacher. 英知に〜む人 a man of wisdom.

とむらい【弔い】a funeral 〔service〕. ¶〜に参列する attend *a person's funeral service*. 〜を出す hold *a funeral* for *a person*.
—合戦 an avenging battle.

とむら・う【弔う】¶ 死者を〜う *pray* (≒ *mourn*) *for* the dead. 遺族を〜う *express one's sympathy with* the bereaved family. 彼の母が亡くなったので彼を〜った I *condoled with* him upon the death of his mother.

-どめ【-止め】せき**—** a cough-drop. 通行**—** (掲示) No Thoroughfare; Detour. ¶ ここは通行〜です The traffic *is shut off* here.

-どめ【-留め】¶ 局〜で電報を打つ send a telegram to general delivery; 英 send a telegram *poste-restante*.

とめお・く【留め置く】¶ 郵便物を局に〜く leave postal matter till called for.

とめがね【留め金】a clasp〔er〕; a hook.
¶ 〜を閉める(はずす) clasp (unclasp).

とめだて【留めだて】¶ いらぬ〜をすなる Don't try to *dissuade* (≒ Don't *keep*) me *from* doing it.

とめど【止めど】¶ 涙が彼女の目から〜なく流れた Tears streamed *endlessly* from her eyes. 彼は〜なくしゃべる He just doesn't know when to stop talking. / He talks on *incessantly*.

とめばり【留め針】a pin.

と・める【止める・停める・留める】**1** 〚停止させる〛
¶ 私たちは峠で車を〜めた We *pulled up* at the summit of the pass.
そこに車を〜めてはいけない You can't *park* your car over there.
警官は車を一台一台〜めて調べた The policemen *stopped* and checked each car.
デモ隊は銀座通りの交通を〜めた The demonstration parade *held up* the traffic on Ginza Street.
だれかの呼ぶ声に足を〜めて振り返った I *stopped* at somebody's call and looked back.
テレビを〜めてくれませんか Would you mind *switching off* the television set?
水道のせんをしっかり〜めなさい *Tighten* the faucet. / *Turn off* the water tightly.
山崩れの土砂が川の流れを〜めてしまった The stream *has been interrupted* by the earth and sand of the landslide.
出血を〜める応急手当をした They gave him first aid to *stop* bleeding.
私は息を〜めてその光景を見詰めた I *held my breath* and watched the scene.
2 〚抑止する〛 ¶ 彼はぼくの〜めるのも聞かずに部屋を出ていった He left the room in spite of my *dissuasion*.
ああ決心している以上〜めたってむだだ Once he is determined, there is no use trying to talk him out of it.
ぼくはふたりのけんかを〜めに入った I went between the two 〔men〕 to *stop* the fight.
痛みを〜める注射をしておきましょう I'll give you an injection to *stop* the pain.
三塁手は猛烈な打球を〜めそこねた The third baseman failed to *stop* the sharp batted ball.
3 〚禁止する〛 ¶ 私は医者から酒を〜められている I *am forbidden to* drink by the doctor.
彼は罰として１か月間外出を〜められた He *was prohibited from* going out for a month as punishment.
彼の発言を〜めるわけにはいかない It is impossible

to *prohibit* him *from* speak*ing*.

4 〚付ける〛 ¶ このピンナップ写真を壁に～めよう I'll *put* the pinup on the wall. / I'll *pin up* the picture on the wall.
門札は柱にくぎで～めてある The nameplate *is nailed* on the gate post.
この書類をクリップで～めてください Would you *fasten* these documents with a clip?

5 〚引き留める〛 ¶ お急ぎのところをお～めしてすみませんでした I am sorry to *have kept* you when you are in a hurry.
すぐ迎えに行くから彼女をそこに～めておいてください Would you *keep* her there, as I am coming to pick her up right away?
荷物は局に～めておいてください Please *hold* the parcel at the post office.

6 〚記憶・注意〛 ¶ そのことはまったく気にも～めなかった I did not *mind* it at all. / I did not *pay* any *attention to* it.
彼女はショーウインドーの赤いセーターに目を～めた A red sweater in a shopwindow *caught* her eye. / She *noticed* a red sweater in the window.

と・める 【泊める】 ¶ 1 晩～めてくれないか Will you *put* me *up* overnight?

とも 【友】 a friend. ¶ 彼は私の親しい～のひとりだ He is *a* great *friend* of mine. 彼は私の終生の～だ He is my lifelong *friend*. よい～と交わるのはたいせつなことだ It is important to keep good *company*. 彼は自然を～として暮らしている He lives with nature as *a friend*.

とも 【供】 (付き添い) an attendant; (従者) a retainer; (家来) a servant; (随員) a suite; a retinue.
¶ 喜んでお～します I shall be glad to *accompany* (≒ *come with*) *you*. 途中までお～しましょう I will *go* part of the way *with you*. A氏のお～に加わって in the *retinue* of Mr. A. ～も連れずに行く go *unattended*. 犬をお～に連れていく *go with one's* dog.

とも 【艫】 the stern. ¶ ～の方に astern.

-とも 【-共】 ¶ 交通費～1,000円 a thousand yen *including* transportation. 老若～に young and old *alike*. 彼は英語, フランス語～自由に話せる He talks freely *both* English *and* French.

-とも **1** 〚強意〛 certainly. ¶ そうです～ Yes, certainly.
そんなことは知らなく～いいことだ There's no need for you to know that sort of thing.
今後～よろしくお願いします Please do remember me. / I earnestly desire that you will do us a similar favor.

2 〚いえども〛 though; although. ¶ どんなに雨が降ろう～出かけるつもりです *However* hard it may rain, I will go out.
なにが起ころう～私は動じない *Whatever* may happen, I would not be surprised.
何回失敗しよう～私はあきらめない I will not give up *however* often I *may* fail.

3 〚いずれとも〛 whether...or.... ¶ そのうわさはほんとう～うそ～わからない We can't tell *whether* the rumor is true *or* not.
彼は行く～行かない～言わない He does not say *whether* he is going *or* not.

-ども ¶ 行け～行け～陸地は見えなかった They sailed *on and on* but no land came in sight. 押せ～引け～そのドアは開かなかった *For all* my pushing and pulling, the door would not open.

ともあれ ¶ なには～彼に会ってください *Anyway* would you come and see him? 理由は～戦争は文明の名折れだ *Whatever may be* the cause, war is a shame and a disgrace to civilization.

ともえ 【巴・鞆絵】 a whirl; an eddy.
三つ― ¶ 三つ～の争いがくりひろげられた There was *triangular* contest. まんじ― ¶ 雪はまんじ～と降りしきった The snow fell *in a whirl*.

ともかく 【兎も角】 at any rate; at all events.
¶ ～出発しよう Let's start *anyway*. ～もうすこしようすを見よう Why don't you wait and see *in any case*? ～その日がきっと来る The day is sure to come *at any rate*. ～お体をたいせつに Keep your health *before everything*. できるかできないか, ～やってみます I will try whether I shall succeed or not. 冗談は～として本題に入ろう *Apart from* joking (≒ Joking *apart*), shall we get to the point?

ともかせぎ 【共稼ぎ】 ¶ 夫婦は～をしている Both husband and wife are working to make a living.

ともぎれ 【共切れ】 ¶ ～でつぎをあてる patch up [a coat] with *the same cloth*.

ともぐい 【共食い】 ¶ ネズミは～をする Rats *feed* (≒ *prey*) *on each other*.

ともしび 【燈火・灯火】 a lamp; a lamplight.

ともしらが 【共白髪】 ¶ 夫婦は～まで添い遂げた The couple lived happily together till death parted them.

とも・す 【点す・燈す・灯す】 ¶ ランプを～す *light* a lamp. つめに火を～すようにして暮らす lead a stingy life.

ともすると ¶ ～人はこの事実を見逃してしまう People *are apt* (≒ *are liable*) *to* overlook this fact. このふたりは～けんかを始める These two boys *quite easily* (≒ *readily*) start a quarrel with each other.

ともだおれ 【共倒れ】 ¶ このままでは～になってしまう We might *be ruined together* (≒ *share the same fate*) the way we are.

ともだち 【友達】 a friend. ¶ 彼には真の～があまりいない He has few true *friends*. 彼はなかなか～ができなかった It was a long time before he made *a friend*. 彼は彼女と～づきあいをしている He is associating with her as *a friend*.
―がい ¶ 彼は～がいのない男だ He is not true to me as *a friend*.

ともづな 【艫綱・纜】 a hawser; a stern cable.
¶ ～を解く unmoor.

ともども 【共共】 together. ¶ 彼らは老いも若きも～にその勝利を祝った They celebrated their

と

victory young and old *alike*.
ともな·う【伴う】accompany ; go with.
¶この仕事には危険が〜う This work *involves* dangers. 彼の言うことと行動は相〜わない What he says does not *keep pace with* what he does. 理論と実際は相〜うとはいえない Theory and practice do not always *go together*. リーダーには責任が〜うものだ Leaders *are charged with* responsibilities. / Leadership *entails* responsibilities. 彼女は若い男を〜って出かけた She went out *accompanied by* a young man.
ともに【共に】**1**〖いっしょに〗¶彼は妻と〜現われた He appeared *with* his wife. われわれは〜昼食をとった We had lunch *together*. 母親は娘と喜びを〜した The mother *shared* her joy *with* her daughter.
このふたりの女性は〜独身だ These two girls are *both* unmarried.
彼はいつでも彼らと行動を〜している He always acts *in co-operation with* them.
彼は私と起居を〜している He lives *with* me.
彼は彼らと運命を〜した He *cast in his lot with* them.
英和辞書と〜和英辞書も持参するように Bring a Japanese-English dictionary *as well as* an English-Japanese one.
彼はテレビと〜家具も売った He has sold the furniture, *together with* the television set.
2〖につれて〗¶年と〜彼は背が伸びた He grew taller and taller *with* the years.
どもり【吃り】stammering ; (人) a stutterer.
どもり【度盛り】graduation.
とも·る【点る】¶ランプが明るく〜っている The lamp *is burning* brightly.
ども·る【吃る】¶彼は〜りながら答えた He answered *stammeringly* (≒ *stutteringly*).
彼はあわてると〜る He *falters in speaking* when he is in a hurry.
とや【鳥屋·塒】a hencoop. ¶めん鳥が〜につく (ねぐらにつく) A hen *goes to roost*. / (卵を抱く) A hen *sits on eggs*.
どやがい【どや街】slum quarters.
とやかく【兎や角】¶彼のことをあまり〜非難するな Don't criticize him *too harsh*. 他人のことに〜口を出すな Never *meddle in* others' affairs. 〜言わずに仕事に精を出せ Work hard without *making complaints*.
どやき【土焼き】unglazed pottery. ⇒すやき
どや·す ¶彼にしこたま〜された I *had a good scolding* from him. いきなり背中を〜された I *was given a* sudden *blow* on my back.
どやどや ¶大ぜいの人が〜と部屋に入ってきた Lots of people *noisily* thronged into the room. 暴徒は〜広間になだれ込んだ The mob poured into the hall in confusion.
どよう【土用】dog days ; midsummer.
—波 high waves in the dog days. —干し summer airing.
どようび【土曜日】Saturday.
どよめき ¶先頭のマラソン走者が姿を現わすと競技場にどっと〜が起こった As the first marathoner appeared, there was *a general stir* in the stadium.
どよめ·く ¶会場は拍手に〜いた The hall *resounded with* a storm of applause.
とら【虎】a tiger ; (雌) a tigress. ¶飲みすぎて〜になる get dead drunk. 〜の威をかるきつね an ass in the lion's skin.
どら【銅鑼】a gong. ¶出航の合図の〜が鳴り響いた The *gong* of departure sounded.
とらい【渡来】¶仏教の〜 *the introduction* of Buddhism *into* Japan. 鉄砲はポルトガルから〜した Guns *were introduced into* Japan from Portugal. まもなくロシアの提督も〜した Soon a Russian admiral also *visited* Japan (≒ *came over* [*the sea*] *to* Japan).
トライ a try. ¶まず彼が〜で4点をあげた First he scored four points on *a try*.
ドライ ¶あの男はなんでも〜に割り切って考えようとする He tries to *make everything clear*. 近ごろはなかなか〜な若者が多い Recently there are not a few young men rather *realistic* [*-minded*]. / Many young people do things in a *dry* mechanical way.
—アイス dry ice. —クリーニング dry cleaning. ¶これを〜クリーニングにしてください *Have* this *dry-cleaned*, please. —ミルク powdered milk.
トライアングル〘音楽〙a triangle.
ドライバー (運転者) a driver ; (ねじ回し) a screwdriver ; (ゴルフの) a driver.
ドライブ a drive. ¶いつか日光まで〜しましょう I hope we'll go for *a drive* to Nikko someday.
ドライブイン a drive-in.
ドライブウエー a driveway.
ドライヤー a drier ; a dryer.
とらえどころ【捕らえ所·捉え所】¶彼の話は〜がない There is *no point* in his talk. / He talks in a vague way.
とら·える【捕らえる·捉える】¶ネズミを〜える *catch* a rat. 〜えて捕虜にする capture (*a person*) ; take (*a person*) captive. 犯人を〜える *arrest* a culprit. 機会を〜える *seize* an opportunity. 意味を〜える *grasp* the meaning. 真相を〜える *see through* the matter ; *get* (≒ *come at*) a true knowledge of.
とらがり【虎刈り】¶彼の頭は〜だ His hair *is badly* (≒ *unevenly*) *cropped*.
トラクター a tractor.
どらごえ【どら声】a hoarse voice.
トラスト〘経済学〙a trust.
—禁止法 an antitrust law.
トラック **1**〖競走路〗a track.
—競技 track events.
2〖貨物車〗㊧ a truck ; ㊥ a lorry.
ドラッグストア ㊧ a drugstore.
とらねこ【虎猫】a tabby cat ; (山ねこ) a tiger (≒ wild) cat.
どらねこ【どら猫】a stray cat.
とらのこ【虎の子】(子トラ) a tiger kitten ; a tiger cub ; (貯金) precious savings. ¶彼は〜を盗まれた He was robbed of his *precious savings*.
とらのまき【虎の巻】a key (≒ crib) (*to* an

English reader).
トラピスト a Trappist.
—修道院 a Trappist monastery (≒ convent).
とらふ【虎斑】tiger's stripes. ¶ ～の猫 a *tabby* cat.
トラブル a trouble. ¶ よく～を起こす男だ He is *a troublemaker*./He often *makes trouble*.
トラホーム〔医学〕trachoma.
ドラマ a drama.
テレビ— a teleplay. ラジオ— a radio play.
ドラマー a drummer.
ドラマチック ¶ オリンピックの閉会式は～に行なわれた The closing ceremony of the Olympic Games *was dramatic* in performance.
ドラム a drum.
—かん a drum 〔can〕.
どらむすこ【どら息子】 a prodigal son; a spoiled child.
とらわれ【囚われ】¶ 彼はついに～の身となった He *was taken captive* (≒ *was taken prisoner*) at last. / He *was imprisoned* at last.
—人 a captive; a prisoner.
とらわ·れる【捉われる】 ¶ 彼のは感情に～れた意見だ His opinion *is influenced by* sentiment. 彼は因襲に～れている He *is tied down to* tradition. 因襲に～れるな Don't *be a slave to* tradition. 彼はあまりに目先のことに～れている He *is* too much *swayed by* the thought of immediate gains. 彼は恐怖に～れている He *is seized with* panic. 感情に～れすぎるのはよくない It is not advisable to *be* too much *swayed by* your feelings. 伝統に～れないのがこのグループの長所だ It is the merit of this group to *be free from* traditions.
トランキライザー〔医学〕a tranquilizer.
トランク (大型の) a trunk; (手さげの) 米 a suitcase; 英 a portmanteau (複 -s; -x); (自動車の) a trunk.
トランジスター a transistor.
—ラジオ a transistor radio.
トランス〔電気〕a transformer.
トランプ cards(日本でいうトランプは trump (切り札) のこと). ¶ ひと組の～ a pack of *cards*. ～を切る cut (≒ shuffle) *cards*. ～を配る deal *cards*. ～をする play *cards*.
—占い ¶ ～占いをする tell *one's* fortune from (≒ with) *cards*.
トランペット〔音楽〕a trumpet.
—奏者 a trumpeter.
トランポリン a trampolin.
とり【鳥】a bird. ¶ すべての～が飛べるとはかぎらない Not all *birds* can fly. あなたはどんな～を飼っていますか What kind of *birds* do you keep?
—屋 (小鳥商) a bird fancier; (鳥肉商) a poulterer.
とり【鶏】 chicken; (めんどり) a hen; (おんどり) 米 a rooster; 英 a cock; (ひなどり) a chicken; a chick.
とりあい【取り合い】¶ 乗客は席の～をした The passengers *scrambled for* seats.
とりあ·う【取り合う】¶ 子どもたちは一つのボールを～った The children *scrambled* (≒ *struggled*) *for* a ball. ふたりは手を～って泣いた The two *took each other's hand* and wept. 彼は笑って私の苦情などいっこうに～わない He laughs at me, *taking no notice of* my complaints. 今後はあの連中には～わないほうがいい You had better *have nothing to do with* them from now on.
とりあえず【取り敢えず】(第一に) first of all; (さしあたり) in the meantime; (急いで…する) hasten to (*do*). ¶ ～警察に知らせた *First of all* I informed the police of it. ～おわびします I *hasten to* crave your pardon. ～この薬を飲んでみてください Take this medicine *in the meantime*. 知らせを受けるや，取るものも～現場に急行した As soon as I heard the news, I *hastened* directly *to* the spot. / Hearing the news, I went to the spot *without a moment's delay*. ～10万円あればよい One hundred thousand yen will do *for the time being*.
とりあ·げる【取り上げる】1〖手に〗¶ 彼は新聞を～げた He *took up* a newspaper.
受話器を～げる *pick up* a receiver.
2〖奪う〗¶ どうして子どもの読んでいる本を～げたのですか Why did you *take away* the book the child was reading? 「task.
彼は仕事を～げられた He *was relieved of* his
彼は免許状を～げられた He *was deprived of* his license.
彼は調理師としての資格を～げられた He *was disqualified as* a cook.
犯罪を犯したため彼は全財産を～げられた All his property *was confiscated* because of his crime.
3〖考慮する〗¶ この問題はあす～げる This matter is to *be considered* (≒ *be taken up*) tomorrow.
彼の意見を～げてほしい I want his opinion to *be taken notice of*.
彼らは私の提案を～げなかった They did not *listen to* my proposal.
4〖赤ん坊を〗¶ 私はあの産婆さんに～げられた She was the midwife who *delivered* me.
とりあつかい【取り扱い】(人の) treatment; (物の) handling. ¶ このような子どもの～には細心の注意が必要だ Scrupulous care is necessary in *dealing with* these children. このホテルは客の～がよい The guests *are* well *served* in this hotel. 彼らは不公平な～を受けた They were given unfair *treatment*. この機械は～が難しい This machine is difficult to *handle*. ～注意 (掲示) *Handle* with care.
—時間 service hour. 校長事務— the acting principal. —人 an agent.
とりあつか·う【取り扱う】treat. ¶ この品物はこわれやすいから注意して～ってほしい Be careful in *handling* this article, since it is easily broken. ここでは電報は～わない Telegrams *are* not *accepted* here. この店では外国の商品は～わない They do not *deal in* foreign goods in this store.

と

とりあつ·める【取り集める】collect. ¶方々から関係書類を～めた I *collected* (⇆ *gathered*) the related documents from various quarters.
とりあみ【鳥網】a fowling net.
とりあわせ【取り合わせ·取合せ】an assortment; (配合) a combination; (配列) an arrangement.
¶そのブラウスはスカートと～がよい The blouse *matches well with* the skirt. 彼と彼女とは妙な～だ He and she make *a* strange *combination.*
とりい【鳥居】a *torii*; a Shinto shrine gate.
とりいそぎ【取り急ぎ】¶このことを～お知らせいたします I *hasten to* inform you of this.
とりい·る【取り入る】¶彼は町の有力者に～っている He *ingratiates himself with* the influential people of the town. 彼は上役に～るすべを心得ている He knows how to *curry favor with* his superiors. 彼は女に～るのがうまい He easily *wins a girl's heart.*
とりいれ【取り入れ】harvesting.
一時 the harvest time.
とりい·れる【取り入れる·採り入れる】¶洗たく物を～れる *take in* the washing. 稲を～れる *gather in* rice. 外国文化を～れる *introduce* foreign civilization. 学生たちの意見を～れる必要がある It is necessary to *accept* the students' opinions. 新計画には若い人たちの考えも～れてある Young men's views *have been incorporated in* the new plan.
とりうち【鳥撃ち·鳥打ち·鳥打】fowling.
一帽 (ハンチング) a sports cap; a tweed cap; a deerstalker (英語の a hunting cap は狩猟用帽子で，ふつう黒のビロード製で，競馬の騎手がかぶる型のもの).
トリウム〖化学〗thorium.
とりえ【取り柄】a merit; a good point.
¶彼はなんら～のない男だ He has nothing *to recommend* him. / He has no particular *merit.* / He is a *good-for-nothing* fellow. まじめなところが彼の～だ Steadiness is his *merit.* これは安いのが～だ That it is cheap is *a good point.*
トリオ a trio (複 -s); (三重唱) a vocal trio.
とりおこな·う【執り行なう】¶葬儀を～う *hold* a funeral. 除幕式を～う *perform* an unveiling ceremony.
とりおさ·える【取り押さえる】¶あばれ馬を～える *seize* a runaway horse. 犯行の現場を～える *arrest* (a criminal) in the act.
とりおと·す【取り落とす】¶うっかりペンを～してしまった I *let fall* my pen carelessly.
とりかえ【取り替え】exchange.
とりかえし【取り返し】¶～のつかない失敗をする make an *irreparable* error; commit a *fatal* mistake; take an *irrevocable* step. 済んだことは～がつかない What is done *cannot be undone.* 今更後悔しても～がつかない No repentance *will mend matters.* ～のつかない損失 an *irrecoverable* loss.
とりかえ·す【取り返す】¶今となっては遅れを～すのは難しい Now it is difficult to *make up for* lost time. その損失はもはや～すことができない The loss is no more to *be made up for.* なんとかして勉強不足を～さなければならぬ I must *catch up on* my studies. 盗まれた物を～すことは不可能に近い It is almost impossible to *get back* the stolen things.
とりか·える【取り替える】exchange. ¶このリンゴをそのバナナと～えよう Let me *exchange* this apple for that banana. 1万円札を1,000円札に～えた I *changed* a 10,000-yen note for ten 1,000-yen ones. 畳を～える時期だ Now it is time to *renew* the matting.
とりかか·る【取り掛かる】¶準備に～る *set about* getting ready. 仕事に～る *get to* work. すぐ勉強に～りなさい *Begin* your study at once.
とりかご【鳥籠】a 〔bird〕 cage; (鶏の) a hencoop.
とりかこ·む【取り囲む】¶群衆は彼を～んだ A crowd *surrounded* him. この国は四方を山で～まれている The country *is surrounded by* mountains on all sides. 彼らはマイクを～んで座っていた They were sitting *round* the microphone.
とりかじ【取り舵】(号令) Port 〔the helm〕!
とりかたづ·ける【取り片付ける】¶食事のあとを～ける *put* things *away* after the meal; *clear* the table. 古い建物を～ける *demolish* the old building.
とりかぶと【鳥兜】〖植物〗an aconite.
とりかわ·す【取り交わす】¶彼はその会社と契約を～した He *made a contract with* the company. われわれはその問題について意見を～した We *exchanged* views on the matter. 日本政府はアメリカ政府と覚書を～した The governments of Japan and the United States *sent* a note *to each other.*
とりきめ【取り決め】(決定) 〔a〕 decision; (約定) an agreement. ¶彼はその～に賛成するだろう (決定に) He will agree to the *decision.* 両者の間には～があった There was *an agreement* between the two. 彼の講演の日程についてはまだ～ができていない They *have* not yet *agreed on* the schedule of his lectures.
とりき·める【取り決める】¶彼らは雇主と賃金について協定を～めた They *made an agreement* with their employer about their wages. 出発の日時を～めた We *fixed* the date for our departure.
とりくず·す【取り崩す】¶石垣を～す *take down* the stone fence.
とりくち【取り口】¶横綱の～を研究する study the *style* of the champion *sumo* wrestler. 彼の～は充分研究されつくした A complete study has been made of his *trick* in *sumo* wrestling.
とりくみ【取り組み】(相撲などの) a match.
¶まったくいい～だ It is indeed *an* interesting *match* to look at.
とりく·む【取り組む】¶難問題と～んだ I *tackled* the difficult problem. AをBと～ませよう We will *match* A *with* B. 彼はその研究に10年一心不乱に～んできている He *has been engrossed in* the study these ten years.

とりけし【取り消し】cancellation. ¶ 予約の〜 *a withdrawal* of an appointment. 注文の〜 *cancellation* of an order. 免許の〜 *revocation* of a license.

とりけ·す【取り消す】¶ 注文の品を〜した I *canceled* the thing I had ordered. ホテルの予約を〜した I *canceled* my hotel reservation. 彼は簡単に約束を〜した He *withdrew* his promise lightly. 新聞は彼に関するその記事を〜した The newspaper *retracted* all the stories about him. 彼は自分のことばを〜した He *took back* what he had said before.

とりこ【虜】a prisoner; a captive. ¶ 〜にする take (*a person*) *prisoner*. 〜になる be captured. 彼はその女への恋の〜となった He *lost his heart to* the woman. そのとき以来彼は恋の〜となっている He *has been a slave to* love.

とりこしぐろう【取越苦労】worries about the future; (理由のない心配) unnecessary anxiety. ¶ そんなに〜をしてもしかたがない It is no use *worrying* so much *for the future*. そんなのは〜だ You *are borrowing trouble*. / You *are* just *meeting trouble halfway*. 〜をするな Don't cross the bridge before you come to it.

トリコット tricot.

とりこみ【取り込み】(混雑) confusion; (不幸) a misfortune; (もめごと) a trouble. ¶ 彼は家に〜があった (不幸) He had *a misfortune* in his family. / (もめごと) He had *a family trouble*.

—詐欺 a confidence game. **—詐欺師** a confidence man.

とりこ·む【取り込む】(いそがしい) be busy. ¶ 今は〜んでいますから, また来てください Sorry, I *am* too *busy*. Do you mind coming another time? きょうは〜んでいて都合がつかない Unfortunately I *am* too *busy* today.

とりごや【鳥小屋】a henhouse; (小さな) a hencoop.

とりころ·す【取り殺す】¶ 彼は亡霊に〜された He *was haunted* by a ghost *to death*.

とりこわ·す【取り壊す】¶ 老朽校舎を〜す *demolish* (≒ *pull down*) old school houses.

とりさげ【取り下げ】withdrawal. ¶ 訴訟を〜にした I *called off* the suit. その願い出は〜になった The request *was withdrawn*.

とりさ·げる【取り下げる】¶ 訴訟を〜げる *call off* a suit. その願いは〜げられた The request *was withdrawn*.

とりさし【鳥刺し】a bird catcher.

とりざた【取り沙汰】talk; [a] rumor. ¶ 世間ではいろいろ〜されている Various *rumors* are abroad (≒ are around; are in the air). 世間の〜など気にするな Never mind what people say of you.

とりさば·く【取り捌く】¶ 訴えを〜く *hear* a case. 雑事を一手に〜く *manage* miscellaneous affairs single-handed.

とりさ·る【取り去る】¶ 障害を〜る *remove* obstacles. 不純物を〜る *get rid of* impurities.

とりしき·る【取り仕切る】¶ あの店は彼がひとりで〜っている He *manages* the store by himself.

とりしず·める【取り鎮める】¶ 騒ぎを〜める *quiet* the trouble.

とりしまり【取り締まり·取締】control. ¶ 暴力に対して厳重な〜が行なわれた Strict *regulations* were enforced against violence. 選挙にはもっと〜を厳しくする必要がある Severer *control* is necessary in the election.

—規則 regulations. **—役** a director.

とりしま·る【取り締まる】¶ 暴力行為は厳重に〜るべきだ Strict *control* of violence is necessary. 酔っ払い運転は十分に〜られていない Drunken driving *has* not *been controlled* strictly enough.

とりしらべ【取り調べ】[an] investigation. ¶ その件は〜中だ The case *is under investigation*. 彼は警察の〜を受けた He *was examined* by the police. 彼は身元について徹底的な〜を受けた A thorough *investigation* was made into his background.

とりしら·べる【取り調べる】¶ 容疑者は〜べられた The suspect *was examined*. ⇒しらべる

とりすが·る【取り縋る】¶ 子どもは父親の首に〜った The child *hung on* his father's neck.

とりす·てる【取り捨てる】¶ いらないものは〜てなさい *Throw away* (≒ *Dump*) unnecessary things.

とりすま·す【取り澄ます】¶ 〜した顔 a *smug* face. あの人は人前では〜した顔をしている He *keeps a straight face* in company.

とりそこな·う【取り損なう】¶ ボールを〜った I *missed* a ball. 賞を〜った I *failed to get* the prize.

とりそろ·える【取り揃える】assort. ¶ あの店には各種のキャンデーが〜えてある They *have a* complete *assortment* of candies. いろいろ〜えてお客様をお待ちしています We have *a* large *assortment* of articles.

とりだ·す【取り出す】¶ 彼はポケットから財布を〜した He *took out* his wallet from his pocket. 引き出しからかぎを〜した He *fished out* a key from a drawer. 袋に手を入れてお金を一つかみ〜した He reached into the bag and *came out* with a handful of money.

とりたて【取り立て】**1**〖徴収〗collection. ¶ 貸した金の〜をする *collect* the money that was lent. 小切手は〜に回された The check was put through for *collection*.

2〖新鮮な〗¶ 〜の魚 *fresh* fish.

とりたてて【取り立てて】¶ 〜言うほどのことはない There is nothing *worth saying about*. 彼には〜いうほどの作品がない He has written no work *to speak of*. その絵については〜言うだけの価値はない The picture has no merit *worth mentioning*.

とりた·てる【取り立てる】¶ 税金を〜てる *collect* taxes. 彼はやがて課長に〜てられるだろう He will soon *be appointed to* the post of the section chief.

とりちが·える【取り違える】¶ 彼はしょっちゅう私

のことばを～える He *misunderstands* me too often. 文の意味を～えた I *misinterpreted* the sentence.

とりちら·す【取り散らす】¶ 部屋は～してある The room *is in disorder*. 紙くずが～してあった Pieces of wastepaper *were scattered about*.

とりつ【都立】¶ ～高校 a *municipal* high school. ～大学 *Metropolitan* University. ～病院 a *metropolitan* hospital.

とりつぎ【取り次ぎ】**1**〖仲介〗intermediation. ¶ だれも～に出てこなかった Nobody came out to *answer the door*.

お手伝いが～に出て行った The maid went to *answer the bell* (≒ *answer the door*).

名前の～を彼に頼んだ I asked him to *send in* my name.

2〖商業上の〗agency. ¶ 本の～をする act as *an agent for* books.

―店 an agent.

トリック a trick.

―映画 a trick film. ―写真 a trick picture. ―撮影 a trick shot.

とりつ·く【取りつく】¶ とんでもない考えに～かれた An extraordinary idea *took hold of* me. 熱病に～かれた I *was attacked* by fever. みんなに冷たくされて～く島もない I am treated in such a cold way that I *feel* utterly *helpless*.

とりつ·ぐ【取り次ぐ】¶ この伝言を彼に～いでほしい I want you to *convey* this message *to* him. 名刺を～いでもらうと応接間に通された On *sending in* my card I was shown into the drawing room.

とりつく·す【取り尽くす】¶ フィルムはもう～した This roll〔of film〕*has run out*. そこでは海洋の資源は～した All the sea resources *have been completely exploited* there.

とりつくろ·う【取り繕う】¶ 彼は貧しくなったが，なんとか体裁を～った He became poor, but he managed to *keep up* appearances. なんとか事を～った I managed to *smooth* things *over* in some way or other. 彼はその場の人の手前を～った He tried to *make it look all right to* those who were there. 彼は問い詰められてその場を～うのに懸命だった Pressed for an answer, he was doing his best to *temporize*.

とりつけ【取り付け】(銀行の) a run〔on a bank〕; (備えつけ) installment. ¶ 銀行が～になった There was *a run* on the bank. 電話の～が終わった The *installment* of a telephone was finished. ～の店 *one's usual* store.

とりつ·ける【取り付ける】¶ この部屋には水道が～けられている City water *is laid on* in this room. この建て物にはエレベーターが～けてある The building *is fitted up with* elevators.

とりで【砦】a fort; a stronghold. ¶ ～を築く build *a fort*.

とりどく【取り得】gain.

とりとめ【取り留め】¶ ～のない話〔a〕*rambling* talk. ～のない議論 (支離滅裂な) an *incoherent* argument. 彼は～のないことばかり言っている He is talking in a *rambling* way. ～のないことを考える indulge in *wandering* speculation.

とりと·める【取り留める】¶ 彼は危ないところで一命を～めた He narrowly escaped death. / He had a narrow escape from death.

とりどり【取り取り】¶ うわさは～だ There are *various* rumors in the air.

とりなお·す【取り直す】¶ 彼の話を聞いて私は気を～した I *took heart* (≒ *pulled myself together*) hearing his story. その相撲は～すことになった It was decided that the *sumo* wrestling match should be played once more.

とりなし【執り成し】(仲介) intercession; mediation; (尽力) good offices.

¶ 彼の～ですべては解決した The whole was settled through his *intercession*. 友人の～で彼は職を得ることができた He could find his job through his friend's *good offices*.

とりな·す【執り成す】intercede. ¶ 彼は私のため先生に～してくれた He *interceded with* the teacher *for* me. あのふたりを～して仲直りさせよう I will *make peace* between the two.

とりなべ【鳥鍋】(料理) chicken cooked in a pan.

とりにが·す【取り逃がす】¶ 好機を～した He *missed* an opportunity. とうとうどろぼうを～した I *failed to catch* the thief at last.

とりの·ける【取り除ける】¶ 机を～ける *take* a desk *away*. 自分の分は～けておく *put one's* share *aside*. 通路のじゃま物を～ける *clear* the passage *of* obstacles.

とりのこ【鳥の子】―紙 *torinoko* Japanese paper. ―もち a piece of oval rice-cake.

とりのこし【取り残し】¶ ごみの～ the *remaining* rubbish.

とりのこ·す【取り残す】¶ たったひとり～された I *was left* all alone. 彼は時代の進歩に～された感がある He seems to *have been left* behind the times.

とりのぞ·く【取り除く】¶ 障害物を～く *get rid of* the obstacles. 不純物をすべて～く *remove* all the impurities.

とりのぼ·せる【とり上せる】¶ ～せていたので何と言ったか覚えていない I *was* so〔much〕*excited* that I do not remember what I said.

とりはからい【取り計らい】management; discretion. ¶ 彼のすばらしい～で万事うまく運んだ Everything turned out well by his excellent *management*. 特別な～で受け付けてくれた It was accepted by *a special arrangement*.

とりはから·う【取り計らう】manage; arrange. ¶ それは私が～います I will *see to* it. それは彼がよろしく～ってくれることになっている It *is left to his discretion*. 適当に～ってください Please *arrange* it as you think fit.

とりはずし【取り外し】dismantling. ¶ この道具は～ができる This tool *is removable*. この機械の部品は～ができない Every part of this machine is fixed.

とりはず·す【取り外す】¶ この看板は簡単には～せない This signboard cannot *be taken down* easily.

とりはだ【鳥膚】goose flesh. ¶ 恐ろしさのため～が立った Fear gave me *goose flesh.* 全身に～が立った I was *goose flesh* all over.

とりはらい【取り払い】¶ この建物は今月末に～になる This building is to *be taken down* about the end of this month. この店は近く～になるらしい This store is likely to *be demolished* before long.

とりはら·う【取り払う】¶ 建物を～う *demolish* a building. 離れは～って新しく建て直した The detached house *was taken down* to be newly built.

とりひき【取引】business 〔relations〕; dealings. ¶ わが社はその会社と～がある Our company has *dealings* with that company. 当店はその会社と～はない We have no *business relations* with the firm. わが社はその商社と～を始めた We opened *business* with the firm. 彼らはその銀行と～を始めた They opened *an account* with the bank. 彼はその商社と多額の～をしている He is doing a lot of *business* with the firm. その会社との～は中止になった Our *connection* with the company was broken off. 彼はその会社との～をまとめた He *struck a bargain* with the company. ─関係 business relation. ─銀行 *one's* 〔own〕 bank. ─先（顧客）a customer;（取引関係者）a business connection. ─高 a turnover. 現金─ cash transactions. 信用─ dealings on credit.

とりひきじょ【取引所】an exchange. 株式─ the Stock Exchange. 株式─員 a member of the Stock Exchange. 穀物─ the Corn Exchange.

とりひし·ぐ【取り拉ぐ】¶ 彼は鬼も～ぐ大力の持ち主だ He is a man of *Herculean* strength.

とりひろ·げる【取り広げる】¶ 家を～げる *enlarge* a house. 道路を～げる *broaden* a road.

トリプシン〘生化学〙trypsin.

とりふだ【取り札】a *torifuda* (poem cards for playing と説明できる.「読み札」poem cards for reading に対する語).

トリプル ─クラウン〘野球〙a triple crown. ─プレー〘野球〙a triple play.

ドリブル〘球技〙a dribble.

とりぶん【取り分】*one's* share. ¶ わたしの～は利益の半分だ Half of the profits is my *share.* / Half of the profits falls to me.

とりほうだい【取り放題】¶ 盗賊が金品を～取っていった The burglar stole *as much* money and *many* valuables *as he could carry away.*

とりまき【取り巻き】*one's* followers. ¶ 彼もあの市長の～のひとりだ He is also one of that mayor's *adherents* (≒ *henchmen*). 彼は～を引き連れて飲みに行った He went for a drink with his *hangers-on* (≒ *satellites*). ─連 followers; attendants.

とりまぎ·れる【取り紛れる】¶ 多忙に～れてごぶさたしました I *have been too busy to* call on you. ほかの仕事に～れてすっかりそのことは忘れていた *Through pressure of* other business I have forgotten all about it.

とりま·く【取り巻く】surround. ¶ われわれはたちまち群集に～かれた All at once we *were surrounded by* a crowd. ファンが映画スターを～いた Fans *clustered* (≒ *thronged*) *around* the movie star. 彼は孫に～かれてにこにこしていた He was smiling *encircled* (≒ *ringed around*) *by* his grandchildren.

とりま·ぜる【取り混ぜる】mix. ¶ いろいろの見本を～ぜて送ります We will send you *an assortment* of samples.

とりまと·める【取りまとめる】collect. ¶ 急いで荷物を～めなさい *Pack up* your things in a hurry. 彼がわれわれの辞表を～めてくれることになっている He is to *gather* (≒ *collect*) our resignations.

とりみだ·す【取り乱す】¶ 子どもたちが部屋を～していった The children left the room *in disorder.* 彼女は～した服装で出てきた She came out *disheveled* (≒ *untidy*). その知らせに彼女は～した She *was upset by* the news. / She *lost her composure at* the news. 彼はその間ずっと～したようすを見せなかった He bore himself *calmly* all the while.

トリミング trimming. ¶ 写真の一部分を～する *trim away* a part of a picture.

とりむす·ぶ【取り結ぶ】¶ その会社と売買契約を～んだ We *made a contract for* sales *with* that company. 私が御両人の間を～んだ I *went between* (≒ *acted as a go-between of*) the two parties. たまには彼の御きげんでも～んでおこう I will *curry favor with* him once in a while.

とりめ【鳥目】night blindness; 〘医学〙nyctalopia.

とりもち【鳥黐】birdlime.

とりもち【取り持ち】treatment;（周旋）intermediation; good offices. ¶ 彼は客の～がじょうずだ He *treats* (≒ *entertains*) his guests very well. / われわれは彼の～で知り合った We got acquainted with each other *through his good offices.*

とりも·つ【取り持つ】treat; entertain. ¶ 彼らは私の両親を丁重に～ってくれた They *entertained* my parents with great consideration. / They *received* my parents hospitably. 山が～つ縁で親しくなった Mountain-climbing made us close friends.

とりもど·す【取り戻す】¶ われわれは優勝旗を～した We *won back* the championship flag. 彼は正気を～した He *recovered* (≒ *regained*) consciousness. 若さを～したいものだ I want to *be* young *again.*

とりもなおさず【取りも直さず】namely. ¶ あれは～きみの誤解だ That's *nothing but* (≒ *no better than*) your misunderstanding. きみが幸福になることは，～，ぼくが幸福になることである I hope you will be happy, *which means* that I will be also happy.

と

とりもの【捕り物・捕物】an arrest. ¶ 昨夜私の町で大～があった There was *a* large-scale *arrest* made in my town last night.

—帳 a detective story; the memoirs of a detective.

とりや【鳥屋】(鳥肉店) a poulterer; (小鳥屋) a bird fancier.

とりやめ【取り止め】¶ 遠足は雨天のため～になった The excursion *was called off* because of the rainy weather. / The rain *prevented* us *from going* on a picnic.

とりょう【塗料】paints.

発光(夜光)— a luminous paint.

どりょう【度量】¶ ～の広い人 a *generous* (≒ *broad-minded*) man. 彼は～が狭い He *is narrow*(≒ *small*)*-minded.*

どりょうこう【度量衡】weights and measures.

—学 metrology. **—**器 measuring instruments.

どりょく【努力】〔an〕effort. ¶ 彼の～は報いられて成功した His *efforts* were rewarded with success. 私は彼を理解しようと～した I made *an effort* to understand him. 彼はそれを土曜日までに仕上げようと,できるだけ～した He made every *effort* to finish it by Saturday. 彼は成功のために～を惜しまなかった He spared no *effort* for success. いま一息～すれば成功する One more *effort*, and we will succeed. 彼は名声を得んがために～した He *strove after* fame. 彼の成功は～の結晶だ His success is the result of his *exertions.* ～のかいなく失敗した In spite of my *efforts*, I failed. 彼は～型の人間だ He is a man of *effort* and diligence.

—家 a hard worker. ¶ 彼はたいへんな～家だ He is *an* exceedingly *hard worker.*

とりよせ【鳥寄せ】bird call. ¶ 彼は～の名人だ He is a great master of *luring birds by imitating their cries.* 彼は口笛を吹いて～をした He *called birds* by a whistle.

とりよ・せる【取り寄せる】¶ イギリスからその本を～せた I *ordered* the book *from* England. これらの品物を注文して～せた I *sent away for* these articles.

ドリル (道具) a drill; (練習) drills. ¶ 英文法の～がもっと必要だ You must have more *drills* in English grammar.

電気— an electric drill.

とりわけ【取り分け】above all things. ¶ スポーツ, ～野球が好きだ I am fond of sports, baseball *in particular.* 山が好きだが, ～夏山がいい I like mountain-climbing, *especially* in summer. きょうは～暑い It's hot today *in particular.* いつも忙しいが, ～年末は忙しい We are always busy, *particularly* at the end of the year.

とりわ・ける【取り分ける】¶ 料理を～けた We *served* food for them. / We *dished out* food. / We *helped* people *to* food. 鉱石の中から金属を～ける *separate* metal *from* ore.

と・る【取る・捕る・盗る・採る・執る・撮る】**1**〖手に持つ〗take. ¶ 彼はその写真を手に～ってよく見た He *took* the picture in his hand and looked at it carefully.

彼は相手の足を～って倒した He *took hold of* the opponent's leg and threw him down.

2〖持ってくる〗¶ たなの上の花びんを～ってくれませんか Please *hand* me the vase on the shelf.

病院に薬を～りに行ってきてください Will you go to the hospital for the medicine?

(食卓で) こしょうを～ってくださいませんか *Pass* me the pepper, please.

彼は私の手を～ってそこに座らせた He *took* me by the hand and let me sit down there.

彼らは武器を～って立ち上がった They rose *in arms.*

3〖受け取る・もらう〗obtain; win. ¶ 彼は3学期はよい成績を～った He *obtained* good results in the third term.

コンテストで1等賞を～った I *won* the first prize in the contest.

私が学位を～ったのは3年前だ I *took* the degree three years ago.

ずいぶん給料を～っているそうじゃないか I hear you *earn* a good salary.

彼は私がさし出した金を～ろうとはしなかった He would not *accept* the money I offered.

すこしだが当座の費用に～っておきなさい Though it's small I want you to *accept* the sum for temporary use.

4〖除く〗take off; take out. ¶ 室内では帽子とコートを～りなさい *Take off* your hat and coat in the room.

この洗剤はガラスの汚れがよく～れる This cleanser is effective for *cleaning* glass.

目ざわりだからこの木を～ってしまおう This tree spoils the view. Let's *get rid of* it.

私は手術をして胃を半分～ってもらった I *had* a half of my stomach *taken out* in an operation.

5〖奪う〗¶ 彼は弟のおもちゃを～ってしまった He *took away* the toy from his brother.

小売店は新しいデパートに客を～られてしまった The new department store *has taken* customers *away* from the retail stores.

戦争の結果領土の大半を敵に～られた Almost all the territory *was plundered* by the enemy as a result of the war.

6〖捕らえる・採取する・収穫する〗¶ 川へ魚を～りに行こう Let's go *fishing* to the river.

私たちは山へキノコを～りに出かけた We went mushroom-*gathering* to the hill.

これはゴマから～った油だ This oil *is extracted* from sesame.

耳から血を～って血液型を調べてもらった I had a blood classification test on the blood *taken* from my earlobe.

～らぬたぬきの皮算用 **(諺)** *Don't count your chickens before they are hatched.*

ことしは米がたくさん～れた We *have had* a nice crop of rice this year.

この鉱山からは良質の銅が～れる Copper of good quality *is produced* in this mine.

7〖人を採用する〗employ; hire. ¶ あの会社は

高校卒業生は～らない That company does not *hire* (≒ *employ*) high-school graduates.
50名の応募者から試験で５人を～った Five persons *were admitted* after the test from among fifty candidates.
8 〖採択・選択する〗 take ; choose. ¶ 名を捨てて実を～った I *preferred* profit *to* fame.
私はあのセーターよりもこちらを～る I'll *take* this sweater, not that one.
この二つの生地ではどちらをお～りになりますか Which of these two kinds of cloth would you *choose*?
私はその説は～らない I can't *support* the opinion.
政府は緊縮政策を～ることに決めた The Government has decided to *adopt* a retrenchment policy.
こうなっては最後の手段を～る以外に道はない There is nothing for it but to *take* the last measure at this stage.
9 〖予約する・確保する・しまっておく〗 reserve ; put aside. ¶ あなたのためにいい席を～ってあります We *have reserved* a good seat for you.
あなたのおやつはちゃんと～ってありますよ Don't worry about your refreshments. I'*ve put* them *aside* for you.
旅行の費用は別に～ってある I *have put aside* money for the traveling expenses.
10 〖食物・睡眠などを〗 take ; have. ¶ 昔は１日２食しか食事を～らなかった Long ago people *took* only two meals a day.
食事をたっぷり～ってもうすこし太りたまえ You must *eat* enough and gain a bit more weight.
睡眠を十分～らないといらいらしがちになる If you don't *have* enough sleep, you are apt to get irritated.
11 〖要する〗 ¶ 彼の仕事はていねいだが，時間を～りすぎる He works very carefully, but *spends* too much time.
このステレオは場所を～るから狭い部屋には不向きだ This stereo is not suitable for a narrow room, because it *takes up* too much space.
12 〖料金などを〗 ¶ 彼はスピード違反で罰金を～られた He *was fined* for speeding.
タクシーに乗ったら法外な料金を～られた The taxi driver *demanded* an unreasonable fare.
13 〖期間を決めて買う〗 take. ¶ お宅では何新聞を～っていますか What newspaper do you *take*?
私は雑誌を３種類～っている I *subscribe to* three kinds of magazines.
来月から牛乳を２本～ることにする I will *take* two bottles of milk from next month.
14 〖解する〗 take. ¶ 彼の沈黙を承諾と～った I *took* his silence as a sort of consent.
私のことばを悪く～らないでください I hope you will not *take* my words amiss.
親切に注意したのに非難と～られた I advised him out of kindness, but he *took* it ill.
15 〖引き受ける〗 ¶ 彼が両者間の仲介の労を～ってくれた He mediated for the two parties.
責任は私が～るから心配するな Don't worry yourself. I will *take* full responsibility.
16 〖事務を行なう・態度を保つ〗 ¶ 彼はその問題に対して適切な処置を～らなかった He did not *take* a measure appropriate to the matter.
この部屋ではたくさんの人が事務を～っている A lot of people *work* in this room.
きみが大掃除の指揮を～りなさい You may *take charge of* the general cleanup.
彼はあくまで断固とした態度を～った He *assumed* a firm and resolute attitude.
17 〖写真を写す・記録にとる〗 ¶ 父の誕生日に父母の写真を～ってあげた I *took* a photograph of my parents on my father's birthday.
胸のレントゲン写真を～ってもらった I *had* my chest *X-rayed*.
結婚ひろう宴のスピーチをテープに～っておこう I will *get* a tape recording of the speeches at the wedding reception.
私の言うことをノートに～ってください Please *write down* my words in your notebooks.
その試合はビデオテープに～ってある I *have recorded* the game on video tape.
18 〖注文して持って来させる〗 ¶ お昼はそばでも～りましょうか Shall we *get* noodles for lunch?
よさそうな商品だから見本を～ってみよう I'll *order* the sample, as this seems good.
19 〖残しておく・保存しておく〗 ¶ 不時の用意にすこしは金を～っておきなさい *Put by* (≒ *Put aside* ; *Lay up*) some money against a rainy day.
私は学生時代からの日記をぜんぶ～ってある I *have kept* all the diaries from my school days.
その話は最後の楽しみに～っておいてくれ *Put aside* that story for the last amusement.

ドル 【弗】 a dollar (記号 $).
—買い dollar purchase. —相場 the exchange rates of the dollar. —地域 a dollar area. —箱 a cash-box. —箱スター a box-office star.

トルコ Turkey.
—語 Turkish. —皇帝 the Sultan. —人 a Turk. —玉 a turquoise. —帽 a fez. —ぶろ a Turkish bath.

トルソー a torso (複 -s ; torsi).

とるにたりな・い 【取るに足りない】 insignificant; trifling ; trivial.

ドルフィンえいほう 【ドルフィン泳法】 a dolphin kick.

どれ 【何れ】 ¶ ～か一つください Please give me *one of them*. ～がいいですか *Which* do you like? ～がいちばん大きいですか *Which* is the biggest (one)?

どれでも 【何れでも】 ¶ ～欲しいのをとりなさい Take *whichever* you want. ～みな気に入った *All of them* took my fancy. ～いいから１冊貸してください Please lend me *any one* of the books.

どれい 【奴隷】 a slave. ¶ 彼はわれわれを～のようにこき使った He *made slaves of* us.
—解放 the emancipation of slaves. —制度 slavery.

トレーシングペーパー tracing paper.

と

トレース trace.
—工 a tracer.
トレード trade. ¶ 彼はA球団からB球団に〜された選手だ He is a player *traded* from A to B baseball team.
—マーク a trademark. —マネー transfer fee.
トレーナー a trainer.
トレーニング training. ¶ もう〜に励んでいる He has already gone into *training*. 彼はそのボクシング試合にそなえて〜に励んでいる He *is training for* the boxing match.
—キャンプ a training camp. —パンツ sweat pants (training pants は英米ではおしめがいらなくなったころの小児のための「小児用下着パンツ」をいう).
トレーラー a trailer.
—バス a trailer bus. —キャンプ a trailer camp.
ドレス a dress.
—メーカー a dressmaker. —メーキング dressmaking. —リハーサル a dress rehearsal.
トレパン sweat pants. ⇒トレーニングパンツ
とれだか【取れ高】(捕獲高) the catch; (収穫高) the crop; the yield.
ドレッシー ¶ 彼女は〜な服装で来た She came in *dressy* (≒ *stylish*) clothes.
ドレッシング〖服装〗〖ソース〗dressing.
フレンチ— French dressing.
どれほど【何れ程】**1**〖どのくらい〗¶ あれから〜たったろう *How long* is it since then?
あの人が〜偉い学者だったかわかりますか Do you have any idea of *what* a great scholar he was?
彼があなたのことを〜心配されていたことか *How* concerned he was about you!
〜かかりましたか(費用) *How much* did it cost?/ (時間) *How many hours* did it take?
2〖いくら〗¶ 〜金をもらってもこの仕事はごめんだ *However* much I *may* be given, I will reject this work.
〜がんばっても彼の成功は難しい *No matter how* hard he *may* work, it will be difficult for him to succeed.
きみが〜がんばっても彼には追いつけまい *However* hard you *may* work, you will not be able to catch up with him.
ドレミファ〖音楽〗*do, re, mi, fa* (イタリア語から).
トレモロ〖音楽〗a *tremolo*.
と·れる【取れる·撮れる】**1**〖獲得する〗catch.
¶ 魚はたくさん〜れた(あまり〜れなかった) I *made a good* (*poor*) *catch of* fish.
この地方ではジャガイモが多量に〜れる Plenty of potatoes *are produced* in this district.
2〖離れる〗¶ シャツのボタンが〜れた A button *has come off* my shirt.
ズボンのボタンが一つ〜れている One of the buttons on my trousers *is missing*.
この表紙の〜れた本はだれのですか Whose is this book with the cover *off*?
3〖なくなる〗¶ 痛みは〜れたか *Is* your pain *gone*?
歯の痛みはまだ〜れない I still have toothache.
4〖理解される〗¶ このことばはふた通りの意味に〜れる This remark can *be interpreted* in two ways.
彼の沈黙は承諾の意味に〜れる His silence can *be interpreted* as his consent.
5〖写真が〗¶ この写真はよく〜れたほうだ This photo seems to *have come out* rather well.
トレンチコート a trench coat.
とろ【瀞】a pool in a river. ¶ 〜を船で下った We sailed down *a slow and deep river*.
とろ【吐露】¶ 彼は私に本心を〜してくれた He *revealed* to me his real intention.
どろ【泥】**1** mud. ¶ 道は〜だった The road *was muddy*.
車に〜をかけられた A car splashed *mud* over me.
〜の深い沼 a *muddy* marshland.
2〖慣用的表現〗¶ 犯人は〜を吐いた The criminal *made a clean breast of* what he had done.
彼の顔に〜を塗るようなことはするな Never *disgrace* him.
どろあし【泥足】muddy feet.
トロイカ a troika.
とろう【徒労】lost labor. ¶ 彼のあらゆる努力も〜に終わった All his efforts *were in vain* (≒ *proved fruitless*). 〜と知りつつ, そうしないではいられなかった I couldn't help doing it, though I knew it would *come to nothing*.
どろうみ【泥海】a sea of muddy water; a (≒ the) muddy sea.
どろえのぐ【泥絵の具】distemper.
トロール —網 a trawl; a trawl net. —漁業 trawling. —漁船 a trawler.
どろくさ·い【泥臭い】¶ 彼は東京に来て10年にもなるのに, 〜さが抜けない He hasn't got urban refinement, though it's ten years since he came up to Tokyo.
どろぐつ【泥靴】muddy shoes (≒ boots).
とろ·ける【蕩ける·盪ける】¶ この暑さではバターが〜ける Butter *melts away* in this heat. その美しい音楽に〜けるような気持ちになった I *felt charmed with* the sweet music.
どろじあい【泥試合】mudslinging. ¶ 両市長候補は互いに相手の中傷をして〜を演じている Both candidates for the mayor *are throwing* (≒ *are slinging*) *mud at* each other.
どろだらけ【泥だらけ】¶ 彼は〜のズボンをはいていた He wore the pants *covered with mud*. 転んで〜になった I fell down and *got muddy*.
トロッコ a truck.
トロット (馬の速度) trot (walk, amble, trot, canter, gallop の順に速くなる); (ダンス) fox trot.
ドロップ (菓子) drops; 〖野球〗a drop.
とろとろ〔と〕¶ あめが〜になった Wheat gluten *was reduced to pulp*. いろりの火が〜燃えている The fire in the hearth is burning *low*.
彼は〜と居眠りをしていた He *was dozing off*./ He *was taking a nap*.
どろどろ ¶ くつが〜になった The shoes became *muddy*. 〜の道だった The roads were very *slushy*. スープは〜のが好きだ I like *thick* soup. 〜になるまで煮た I boiled it down *to pulp*

(≒ *to jelly*).

どろなわ【泥縄】 ―式 ¶～式の勉強ではよい成績はとれない You cannot expect to get a good mark in the examination by *the last-minute cramming*. 彼はいつでも～式に勉強したものだ He would often study at the last moment.

どろぬま【泥沼】 a bog. ¶彼は今や完全に政界の～に足を踏み入れてしまった He *has* completely *bogged down into* politics. ベトナム戦争でアメリカは～にはまってしまった The United States *was in a pretty fix* in Vietnam War.

とろび【とろ火】 a slow fire. ¶フライパンを～にかける place a frying pan over *a slow fire*.

トロフィー a trophy.

どろぼう【泥棒・泥坊】 a thief (複 thieves); (強盗) a robber; (夜盗) a burglar. ¶ゆうべ彼の家に～が入った *A thief* broke into his house last night. ～に追い銭(諺) To throw good money after bad. ～を見てなわをなう(諺) It is like shutting the stable door after the horse has bolted. 人を見たら～と思え(諺) Never trust a stranger.

どろまみれ【泥まみれ】 ¶服が～だった The dress *was covered with mud*. 彼らは～になって田植えをしていた They were planting rice, *getting muddy*.

どろみず【泥水】 muddy water.

どろよけ【泥除け】 a splashboard; a dasher.

どろり ¶～としたジャム *pasty* jam.

とろりと ¶つい,～居眠りしてしまった I took a short nap without meaning to.

トロリー a trolley.
―バス a trolley bus.

とろろ【薯蕷】 grated yam.
―いも a yam. ―こんぶ tangle flakes. ―汁 yam soup.

とろん ¶彼女は～とした目をしていた She *was heavy-eyed*.

どろん ¶彼は～をきめこんだ He *disappeared*. / He *made off*.

ドロンゲーム a drawn game. ¶日没のため～になった The game *was drawn* (≒ *was calld*) because of sunset.

どろんこ【泥んこ】 mud. ¶彼は～になって帰ってきた He came home *covered with mud*. ～の道だった It was a *muddy* road.

トロンボーン〔音楽〕a trombone.
―奏者 a trombonist.

とわ【永久】 ¶～に幸あれ May God bless you *forever*!

とわず【問わず】 ¶老若男女を～ *regardless* (≒ *irrespective*) *of* age or sex. 良否(遠近)を～ *irrespective of* the quality (distance). 値段のいかんを～ *at any cost*. 晴雨を～会は開かれる The party will be held *regardless of the weather* (≒ *rain or shine*). 事のいかんを～それはよろしくない *Whatever it may be*, it is not good.

とわずがたり【問わず語り】 ¶～に自分の過去を話す *tell one's* past life *without being asked*.

どわすれ【度忘れ】 ¶彼の名前を～した His name *has slipped* 〔*from*〕 *my memory*. / I *forgot* his name *for the moment*.

トン【噸・瓲・屯】 a ton; (容積トン数) tonnage. ¶砂糖2～ two *tons* of sugar. 6～積みダンプカー a six-*ton* dump truck. 10万～のタンカー a tanker of 100,000 *tons*.
重量― dead weight tonnage. 総(純; 登録; 積載; 排水)―数 gross (net; registered; freight; displacement) tonnage. 米(英)― a short (long) ton.

どん ¶人が私に～とぶつかった A man *bumped into* me. 彼はテーブルを～とたたいた He *banged* the table with his fist. ～と大砲の音がした We heard a cannon *boom*. よーい,～ Ready! *Go!* ～と来い Come on!

どん【鈍】 ¶～な子ども a *dull* (≒ *stupid*) child. 貧すれば～する(諺) Poverty *dulls* the wits. 運,～,根が成功の秘訣 Luck, *stolidity*, and perseverance are the essential factors of success.

どんか【鈍化】 ¶～する make (≒ become) dull.

どんかく【鈍角】〔数学〕an obtuse angle.
―三角形 an obtuse-angled triangle.

とんカツ a pork cutlet.

どんかん【鈍感】 dullness. ¶～な男 a *dull* (≒ *insensible*; *thick-skinned*) man. 騒音になれて耳が～になった I *am dull of* hearing, as I have got accustomed to noise.

どんき【鈍器】 a blunt weapon.

とんきょう【頓狂】 ¶～な声を出す give a *wild* (≒ *shrill*) cry.

どんぐり【団栗】 an acorn. ¶彼らはみな～の背くらべだ There's nothing to choose 〔from〕 among them. / They are all of a sort.
―眼 goggle eyes. ¶～眼の男 a *goggle-eyed* man.

どんこう【鈍行】 a local (≒ slow; 米 an accommodation) train.

とんざ【頓挫】 a setback. ¶運動は一～をきたした The movement *received* (≒ *suffered*) *a setback*. 商売は資金欠乏のため一～をきたしている The business *is at a standstill* (≒ *is at a deadlock*) for want of funds.

どんさい【鈍才】 dullness; stupidity; (人) a dull〔-witted〕(≒ slow-witted) person.

とんし【頓死】 a sudden death. ¶～する die suddenly.

とんじ【遁辞】 an excuse; an evasive answer. ¶～を弄(ろう)する give *an evasive answer* (≒ *a pretext*); make *an excuse*. ～に窮する be at a loss for *an excuse*.

とんじゃく【頓着】 ¶金銭に～しない *care nothing for* (≒ *be indifferent to*) money. 彼は服装に～しない He *pays no regard to* (≒ *is indifferent to*) his appearance. 彼はそんな細かいことには～しない He doesn't *care* (≒ *bother*) *about* such trifles. / He never *minds* such trifles. 他人がなんと言おうと～しない I'*m indifferent to* what others say of me. / I don't *mind* what others say.

とんしゅ【頓首】 (手紙の結びのことば) ～〔再拝〕

と

Yours〔very〕respectfully (≒ truly); Sincerely yours; Respectfully yours.

どんじゅう【鈍重】¶ ～な slow-witted; stolid; thick-headed.

どんす【緞子】¶ きんらん～の帯 a *damask* sash with *gold brocade*; a *gold brocaded* sash.

とんせい【遁世】escape from life. ¶ ～する retire (≒ seclude *oneself*) from the world; live secluded from the world.

とんそう【遁走】¶ ～する flee; run away.
　一曲〘音楽〙a fugue.

どんぞこ【どん底】the depths; the bottom. ¶ 彼は絶望の～にあった He *was in the depths of* despair. 戦争のため貿易は不況の～にある Owing to the war, trade *is in extreme depression.*

とんだ ¶ ～目に会う have a *terrible* experience; have a hard time of it. ～災難を受ける suffer〔an〕*unexpected* misfortune. ～ことをしてくれた See what you have done! / What *a pretty mess* you have made! ～ことをいたしまして申し訳ありません I'm very sorry for what I have done. これは～ことになったぞ Things have come to such *a pretty pass.* ～所で旧悪を暴露されたね *Little did I think* (≒ *Little did I dream*) my old sores would be opened here. そんなことをしたら～ことになるぞ It will *cost* you *dearly.* 昨夜は蚊に食われて～目に会った I suffered *untold* misery from mosquito bites last night.

とんち【頓智】wit; ready wit. ¶ ～のきく人 a man of *ready wit*; a *ready-* (≒ *quick-*) *witted* man. ～のきかない人 a dull-witted man. 彼は～のおかげで間一髪のところで死をまぬがれた He narrowly escaped death by his *ready wit.*

どんちゃんさわぎ【どんちゃん騒ぎ】merry-making; a racket. ¶ ～をする make *a racket*; make *a great noise.* 酒を飲んで～をした We *made merry* heavily drunk.

どんちょう【緞帳】a drop curtain. ¶ 芝居の～が上がる(下がる)ところだ The *drop curtain* is drawing up (down).

とんちんかん【頓珍漢】¶ ～な返事をする make an *irrelevant* answer; answer *irrelevantly.* ～なことを言う utter some *incoherent* remarks. 彼らの話はどうも～だ They are talking *at cross-purposes.*

どんつう【鈍痛】a dull pain.

どんづまり ¶ 日米間の交渉は～に来た The negotiations between Japan and the U.S. *have come to an end* (≒ *have come to the final stage*).

とんでもな·い ¶ ～い要求を出す make a *preposterous* demand. ～いまちがいをしでかす make a *fatal* mistake. ～い! Absurd! / What a thing to say! 彼が学者だなんて～い He is *no* scholar. ～い人に訪ねて来られた I had an *unexpected* visitor. 「お礼の申し上げようもありません」「～い」"I have no words to express my thanks." "*Don't mention it!*"

どんてん【曇天】dull weather. ¶ 本日は～だ It *is cloudy* today. / It *is dull* today.

どんでんがえし【どんでん返し】¶ 上告の結果判決は～となった An appeal resulted in *a reversal* of the decision. 第二試合では私と彼とは形勢は～となり私が優勢になった In the second match I *turned the tables on* him.

とんと【頓と】¶ そのことは～わからない I can't understand it *at all.* どんなものか～見当もつかない I have *no* idea (≒ I have *not the faintest* idea) of what it is like. それ以来彼から～便りがない I have heard *nothing* from him ever since. ⇒まったく; ぜんぜん

どんとう【鈍刀】a blunt sword.

とんとん 1〘打つ音〙a knock. ¶ ドアを～たたく音がした There was *a tap* (≒ *a knock*) on the door.
戸を～たたく *knock* (≒ *tap*) at a door.
彼女は私の肩を～たたいてくれた She *tapped* me on the shoulder.
2〘調子よく〙¶ すべては～拍子だった Everything went *smoothly and rapidly.*
彼は政界で～拍子に出世した He rose in the political world *by leaps and bounds.*
事は～と運んだ Things progressed *satisfactorily.*
3〘同等·同率·損得のないこと〙even. ¶ それで～だ Things become *even* then.
収支はこれで～だ We can *make*〔*both*〕*ends meet.*
利潤は前年度と～だ The profit *is about the same as* last year.
1,000部売れたら～だ If 1,000 copies are sold, we shall *break even.*

どんどん 1〘音〙bang. ¶ 太鼓を～たたく beat a drum *loudly*. 「*loudly.*
太鼓が～鳴っている The drum is beating
戸を～たたく *bang* (≒ *beat*) at a door.
2〘速やかに·自由に〙rapidly; quickly.
¶ その本は～売れている That book is selling *like hot cakes.*
～この道を歩いていきなさい Walk *right* along this road.
病状は～よくなっている He is getting *better and better.*
～先を読み続けなさい *Keep on* reading.
遠慮せずに～言ったほうがいい You had better *speak out* without reserve.
あっという間に人が～集まってきた People gathered *quickly* in a moment.

どんな 1〘疑問〙what. ¶ 彼は～人ですか *What sort of* man is he?
彼がこの場にいたら～ことにならないともわからない We cannot tell *what* might happen if he were here.
2〘いかなる…も〙¶ 彼は1枚の紙を～形にでもできる He can make *any kind of* form out of a sheet of paper.
100万円あれば～ことでもできると彼は言っている He says that a million yen would enable him to do any sort of thing.
その秘密を知るためなら～犠牲を払ってもいい I would *give anything* to know the secret.

〜ことがあっても彼には逆らうな Don't object to him *under any circumstances.*
〜ことがあってもここを離れるな Don't leave here *whatever* happens.
〜結果になろうと私はやめないぞ *Whatever* the results *may* be, I will not give up.

どんなに 1〖いかばかり〗¶ 彼は〜失望したことだろう *How* disappointed he must have been! / He couldn't have been *more* disappointed.
彼が〜喜んだかきみには想像もできまい You can hardly imagine *how* delighted he was.
2〖たとえ…でも〗¶ 〜一生懸命やっても彼は成功しそうにない *However* hard he *may* work, he is not likely to succeed.
〜速く走っても彼には追いつくまい *No matter how* fast you *may* run, you will be unable to overtake him.
〜仕事がたくさんあっても, きょうじゅうにぜひとも終えたい I want to finish all my work today, *however* much there *may* be.

トンネル【隧道】a tunnel. ¶ 〜を掘る *tunnel* (a mountain). 〜を通過する pass through *a tunnel*. 〜をする(野球で) let a grounder pass through *one's* legs; fail to catch a grounder.
—工事 tunneling work. —会社 a tunnel company. 海底— an undersea (≒ submarine) tunnel.

とんび【鳶】〖鳥類〗a kite. ¶ 〜が鷹を生む (諺) Black hens lay white eggs. 彼は〜に油揚げをさらわれた He lost his fortune to another. / He has his share taken by another.

どんぴしゃり ¶ 私の予想通り〜だ It is *just* as I expected. 予想が〜と当たった I guessed *just right*. / I hit the mark *right*.

ドンファン a Don Juan.

とんぷくやく【頓服薬】a dose 〔of medicine〕.

どんぶり【丼】a 〔porcelain〕 bowl.
—勘定 spending money at will without keeping accounts.

とんぼ【蜻蛉】a dragonfly.
—返り a somersault. ¶ 〜返りをする turn *a somersault*.

とんま【頓馬】an ass; a donkey; an idiot.
¶ 〜なことを言う(する) say (do) a *stupid* thing. 彼も〜なやつだ He is a *stupid* fellow. そんな〜なことはしない I know better than to do such a *silly* thing. / I know better than that.

とんや【問屋】(店) a wholesale store; (人) a wholesale dealer. ¶ 〜をする carry on *a wholesale trade*. 服地(呉服)〜 a *wholesale* draper. 電気器具〜 a *wholesale* electric goods store. そうは〜がおろさない You are expecting too much. / You are counting without your host.
—街 a wholesale district. —値段 a wholesale price.

どんよく【貪欲】greed; avarice. ¶ 彼は権力に対して〜である He *is avaricious of* power. 彼は金に対して〜だ He *is a miser*.

どんより ¶ 空が曇って〜とした天気 *dull* and overcast weather. 〜した空 the *dull* (≒ *leaden*) sky. 彼は〜した目をしている He has *fishy* (≒ *dull*; *vacant-looking*) eyes.

どんらん【貪婪】¶ 〜な avaricious.

な

な【名】1〖名まえ・姓名〗name. ¶ 彼は娘に花子という〜をつけた He *named* his daughter Hanako.
その子はおじいさんの〜をとって勇一と名づけられた The child *was named* Yuichi *after* his grandfather.
佐藤清という〜の人がご面会です A Mr. Kiyoshi Sato wants to see you. / A man *by the name of* Kiyoshi Sato is here to see you.
だれか私の〜を呼んでいる Somebody is calling my *name*. / Somebody is calling me.
私は彼の〜だけは知っている I know him only *by name*.
2〖名称〗¶ あれはなんという〜の鳥ですか What *is* that bird *called*? / What kind of bird is that?
彼はその曲に「春」という〜をつけた He *named* the tune "Spring."
彼は「カバ」という〜で通っていた He passed *by the name of* "Hippo".
「ちび」はその〜のとおり小さな犬だ "Tiny" is a small puppy, as the *name* shows.
春とは〜ばかりで, まだとても寒い It is too cold for spring. / Spring belies its *name* and it is still cold.
3〖名声・評判〗¶ 彼は〜のある先生について書道を学んでいる He is taking calligraphy lessons from a *noted* master.
彼は〜もない寒村に生まれた He was born in an *obscure* (≒ *rural*) out-of-the-way village.
彼は〜をとって実を捨てた He valued *fame* above profit. / He cared for his *honor* more than for his money. / He chose his *honor*, giving up his profit.
彼女はオペラ歌手として〜をあげた She *made a name for herself* as an opera singer.
彼はロケットの研究で〜をなした He *won fame* for the study of rockets.

親の～を汚すようなことだけはしてくれるな See that you do not disgrace the *name* of your family.

武士は死を軽んじて～を重んじた Warriors valued *honor* above life.

武士は～を惜しむ A *samurai* respects *honor*.

彼は功成り～とげて政界を引退した Having gained *fame and name*, he retired from the political world.

4 〖名目・口実〗 ¶ その国は正義の～のもとに侵略戦争を行なっている The country is waging an aggressive war *in the name of* justice.

彼らは革命の～を借りて略奪行為をする They plunder *in the name of* revolution.

地方自治の～において地域エゴが行なわれる *In the name of* autonomy, local interests are being pushed.

な 【菜】 (野菜) greens; vegetables; (菜種) rape. ¶ ～をつくる raise *greens*; grow *vegetables*. ～を漬ける (ゆでる) pickle (boil) *greens*.

-な **1** 〖否定〗 ¶ 行く～ Don't go. / You *must not* go.

彼に来る～と言え Tell him *not* to come.

2 〖命令〗 ¶ 早く行き～ Go at once.

3 〖感嘆〗 ¶ いい天気です～ It's fine, *isn't it?* / How fine it is!

彼は走るのがずいぶん速い～ *How* fast he runs!

-なあ **1** 〖願望〗 ¶ 100万円あったら～ 〔*How*〕 I *wish* I had one million yen.

彼が来てくれるといいのに～(見込みのあるとき) *I hope* he will come soon. / (見込みのないとき) *I wish* he would come.

2 〖感嘆〗 ¶ きれいだ～ *How* beautiful 〔it is〕!

なあて 【名宛】 an address.

—人 an addressee.

なあに ¶ ～かまうものか I don't care a bit! ～わけはないさ *Why,* nothing is easier. / *Why,* there is nothing to it. ～負けるものか *No,* I won't give in.

な・い 【無い】 **1** 〖在存しない〗 ¶ きょうは用事が～い I *am free* today.

そういう物は～い *There is no* such thing.

バケツには水が～い *There is no* water in the bucket.

迎えにきてくれた人は～かった *No one* came to see me.

雨のためピクニックは～かった On account of the rain our picnic *was called off*.

これを知らない人は～い *There is no* one who doesn't know this.

この池には水草がまったく～い This pond *is* entirely *free of* waterweeds.

この解答には誤りが～い This answer *is free from* error.

そういう遊びをする暇は～い I *have no* time for such amusements.

この部屋は人けが～い This room *is empty*.

あと３日しか～い *There are not more than* three days left.

これでも～いよりはまだましだ Even this is better than *nothing*.

2 〖持たない〗 ¶ 彼は借金が～い He *is free of* debts.

私は野球には興味が～い Baseball *is uninteresting to* me.

彼は常識が～い He *lacks* common sense.

彼には父も母も～い He *has neither* father *nor* mother.

-ない ¶ 彼は親切で～ He is *not* kind. 彼は政治家どころでは～ He is *no* statesman. 彼らが失敗したのも不思議は～ It is *no* wonder that they have failed. 彼はきみの言うことがわかってい～ He does *not* understand you. きょうという日は二度と来～ Today will *never* come again.

-ない 【-内】 ¶ 敷地～に *within* the fence. 収入のわく～で暮らす live *within one's* income. 視界～に現われる appear *in one's* sight. 車～で眠る sleep *on* a train. 船～にいる be *aboard* (≒ *on board*) a ship. 校～で遊ぶ play *in* the playground.

ないい 【内意】 (意中) *one's* intention; (私見) *one's* private opinion. ¶ ～を受けて by *secret order*. ～を漏らす reveal *one's intention*. その問題について彼の～を探ってくれ *Sound* him on the matter.

ナイアガラばくふ 【ナイアガラ瀑布】 Niagara Falls (動詞は単数で受ける, 冠詞不要).

ないえん 【内縁】 ¶ ～の妻 a *common-law* wife; a wife *not legally married*. ～関係を結ぶ contract a *common-law* marriage.

ないか 【内科】 〔医学〕 internal medicine.

¶ ～の治療を受ける be *internally* treated.

—医 a physician. **—**病棟 a medical ward.

ないかい 【内海】 an inland sea. ¶ 瀬戸～ the Seto *Inland Sea*.

ないがい 【内外】 (内と外) the inside and the outside; (およそ) about; around; or so.

¶ ～の学者が一堂に会している *Domestic and foreign* scholars are meeting in the auditorium. 彼は～の情勢に通じている He is well versed in *home and foreign* affairs. ２時間～で帰る予定だ I will return home in two hours *or so*.

ないかく 【内角】 〔数学〕 an interior angle. ¶ (野球で) ～低めにストライクがきまった The pitch *was* low and *close* but called strike.

ないかく 【内閣】 a cabinet (しばしばCは大文字); a ministry; the government. ¶ 現～ the present *Cabinet* (≒ *Government*). ～の更迭 a change of the *Cabinet*. ～の顔ぶれ the personnel (≒ line-up) of the *Cabinet*. 多数与党により～を組織する form *a Cabinet* based on a Parliamentary majority.

—改造 the Cabinet reshuffle (≒ reconstruction). **—**総辞職 a general resignation of the Cabinet; a resignation of the Cabinet *en bloc*. **—**官房長官 the Chief Cabinet Secretary. **—**総理大臣 the Premier; the Prime Minister. 政党**—** a party Cabinet. 超党派**—** a non-party Cabinet. 連立**—** a coalition Cabinet.

ないがしろ 【蔑ろ】 ¶ その研究は今まで～にされてきた The study of the subject *has been neglected* (≒ *has been made light of*). 彼はせ

っかくの私の意見を～にした He *ignored* my good advice.
ナイキ〔米軍〕(対空誘導弾) a Nike.
ないき【内規】a bylaw ; a private regulation.
ないきょく【内局】an intra-ministerial bureau (≒ office).
ないきん【内勤】office work ; indoor service. ¶ ～の警官 a *desk* policeman. ～の社員 an *indoor-service* employee. ～する work indoors.
ないこう【内攻】〔医学〕retrocession. ¶ ～性の病気 a *retrocessive* disease. 病気が～している The disease *is retroceding* (≒ *is striking inward*).
ないこう【内訌】internal troubles ; domestic discord.
ないこう【内項】〔数学〕internal terms.
ないこうせい【内向性】introversion. ¶ ～の強い人 an introvert.
ないごう【内剛】¶ 彼は外柔～の人だ He seems to be gentle, but *is very strong at heart*.
ないこきゅう【内呼吸】〔生理〕inner respiration.
ないこく【内国】—航路 domestic shipping lines. —貿易 home (≒ domestic) trade.
ないこっかく【内骨格】〔解剖学〕an endoskeleton.
ないさい【内妻】a common-law wife.
ないさい【内済】¶ この事件は～にしてほしいと彼から頼まれた He requested that the matter 〔should〕 *be settled out of court*.
ないさい【内債】a domestic loan.
ないざい【内在】〔哲学〕immanence. ¶ 神の～ the divine *immanence*.
ないし【乃至】¶ ペン～鉛筆で書きなさい You must write with a pen *or* a pencil. 日光に行くのに3,000円～4,000円ぐらいかかるだろう Our trip to Nikko will cost *between* three thousand *and* four thousand yen. 2,000円～3,000円のものをみせてください Please show me one which is *from* two thousand *to* three thousand yen.
ないじ【内示】an unofficial announcement. ¶ 支配人に昇進させるとの～があった I *was informally* (≒ *privately*) *told* that I would be promoted to a manager.
ないじ【内耳】〔解剖学〕the internal ear. —炎 inflammation of the internal ear.
ないじつ【内実】the fact. ¶ ～のところはどうなのだ What's *the true story* about it? あの会社は～のところ, 破産寸前なのだ *The fact is,* the company is just going to go bankrupt.
ないじゅ【内需】〔経済学〕domestic demand.
ないじゅうがいごう【内柔外剛】strong as a lion abroad, weak as a lamb at home.
ないしゅっけつ【内出血】〔医学〕internal bleeding ; internal hemorrhage.
ないしょ【内所・内証】a secret. ¶ この件は彼には～にしてほしい I want to *keep* this matter *secret from* him. この秘密はだれにも～にしてください Please *keep* this secret *to yourself*. これは私たち以外には～に願います *Keep* this secret *between us*. この事実は～にしておきます This fact shall *be kept unknown to* others. これはふたりだけの～だ This *is between ourselves.* / This *is between you and me*. きのう母に～で買い物に出た Yesterday I went out shopping *without* my mother's *knowledge*.
—事 a secret. —話 a whisper. ¶ ～話はやめなさい Don't *talk in whispers*. ふたりは～話ばかりしている The two *are* always *having confidential talks* together.
ないじょ【内助】¶ 彼の成功は夫人の～の功によるところが大きい He owed much of his success to his wife.
ないじょう【内情】the real state ; (内部事情) the inside affairs. ¶ 会社の～ *the inside* of a company. 国の～を探る inquire into *the real state of affairs* in a country. ～に詳しい者の犯行 an *inside* job.
ないしょく【内職】a side job. ¶ 彼は～に翻訳をした He translated books as *a side job*. 彼は妻に～をさせようとはしなかった He would not make his wife *take in work*.
ないしん【内心】*one's* mind ; 〔数学〕inner center. ¶ ああは言っているが～はうれしいのだ He is delighted *at heart* (≒ *in his heart*), though speaking that way. 彼は～ではその地位が欲しいのだ It is his *secret desire* to get the position. 彼は私に～を打ち明けた He *disclosed* (≒ *opened*) his *heart* to me. / He *unbosomed* (≒ *unburdened*) *himself* to me.
ないしん【内診】〔医学〕¶ ～する make *an internal examination*.
ないじん【内陣】the sanctuary ; the inner temple (≒ shrine).
ないしんしょ【内申書】a school report ; a report on a student's 〔school〕 record.
ないしんのう【内親王】an Imperial (≒ a Royal) princess.
ナイス nice. ¶ (サッカーなどで) ～シュート! What a *nice* shoot!
ないせい【内政】domestic administration. ¶ 他国の～に干渉することは慎むべきである We should avoid interfering in the *internal affairs* of another country.
ないせつ【内接】〔数学〕¶ ～する touch internally. —円 an inscribed circle.
ないせん【内戦】a civil war ; internal hostilities. ¶ あの国は～の絶え間がない There is always *an internal war* going on in that country.
ないせん【内線】(電話の) an extension ; (電気の配線の) interior wiring. ¶ ～の120番をお願いします 〔Give me〕 *extension* 120, please. / I want *extension* 120. (発音は [wʌ́n tú: zí:rou])
ないぞう【内蔵】¶ それが～している諸問題 the problems it *involves*. 組合は分裂の危険を～している The labor union is in danger of splitting into several factions.
ないぞう【内臓】the internal organs. —疾患 an internal disease (≒ disorder).

な

—神経 the splanchnic nerve. —逆位 heterotaxis.

ないそん【内孫】a grandchild; (特に) a child of *one's* daughter-in-law who lives together in the same house (欧米には内孫, 外孫を区別する習慣はなく, すべて孫という).

ナイター a night game.

ないだく【内諾】a private approval. ¶ 海外研修については彼の～は得てある He has already given me his *informal consent* to my study abroad. / I have his *private consent* to go abroad for my studies.

ないだん【内談】¶ ご子息のことで～があって参りました I have come to have *a private talk* with you about your son.

ないち【内地】the interior〔of a country〕; (島に対して) the home (⇔ main) land.
—勤務 home service. —産 home (⇔ domestic) products; home-made goods. —人 the people at home; (奥地人) an inlander. —米 home-grown rice.

ないつう【内通】¶ 彼は敵と～していた He *held secret communication with* the enemy. / He *betrayed his country to* the enemy.
—者 a betrayer.

ないてい【内定】informal decision. ¶ 彼は新大学の学長に～している He *has been informally designated* as president of the new university.

ないてい【内偵】¶ 敵の戦力を～する *make secret inquiries into* the war potential of the enemy.

ナイト (夜) night; (騎士) a knight.
—ガウン a nightgown; a nightdress. —キャップ a nightcap. —クラブ a nightclub. —ゲーム a night game.

ないない【内内】¶ この話は～にしておいてください Please *keep* this *secret*. / Please don't tell this to anybody else. ～でお話したいことがあります I'd like to *have a private talk with* you. 彼らは～で会合を持っている They are meeting *secretly*. 貴兄の無事を～案じていました I was anxious about your safety *at heart*.

ないねんきかん【内燃機関】an internal combustion engine.

ナイフ a knife (複 knives); (小さい鉛筆を削るもの) a penknife; a pocketknife. ¶ ～とフォーク a knife and fork (knife and fork はそろいのものであるからそれ全体に冠詞 a をつけるだけでよい).

ないぶ【内部】the interior; the inside. ¶ 家の～は美しく飾られていた *The interior* of the house was beautifully decorated. 彼はその会社の～事情に詳しい He is well acquainted with *the inside* of the company. この盗みは～の者の仕業だ The robbery is no doubt an *inside* job.

ないふく【内服】¶ この薬は1日3回～のこと This medicine is to *be taken* three times a day.
—薬 an internal medicine.

ないふん【内紛】an internal discord. ¶ 会社の～に巻き込まれてしまった I got involved in the *internal discord* of the company.

ないぶん【内分・内聞】¶ その問題は～にして済ました We settled the matter *privately* (⇔ *between ourselves*). このことは～にしておくほうがいいと私は思う I think we should *keep* this *to ourselves*.

ないぶんぴつ【内分泌】〘生理〙internal secretion.
—液 an internal secretion. —腺(せん) a ductless gland.

ないほう【内包】〘論理〙connotation.

ないみつ【内密】¶ 私の来たことは～にしてください Please *keep* my visit *secret*. / Please don't tell anybody that I came here.

ないむ【内務】—省 米 the Department of the Interior; 英 the Home Office; (昔の日本の) the Ministry of Home Affairs. —大臣 英 the Home Secretary (新設の省の大臣には Minister を使用するのが普通); (日本の) the Minister for Home Affairs. —長官 米 the Secretary of the Interior.

ないめい【内命】a secret order. ¶ その国の政治情勢を探るよう～を受けた I received *a secret order* to inquire into the political conditions of the country.

ないめん【内面】the interior; the inside. ¶ 事件の～も考える必要があろう We will have to think over *the inside* of that incident.
—生活〔*one's*〕inner life. —描写 inner description.

ないもの【無い物】¶ 彼はいつも～ねだりばかりしている He *is* always *crying for the moon*.

ないや【内野】〘野球〙the infield.
—安打 an infield hit. —手 an infielder. —フライ an infield fly.

ないやく【内約】¶ 彼らふたりの間にはなにか～がある There is some *private agreement* between the two. その件については彼と～がある He gave me his *personal word* on that matter.

ないゆう【内憂】¶ ～外患 troubles both at home and abroad.

ないよう【内用】¶ この薬は～に用いられる This medicine is used *internally*.

ないよう【内容】contents; substance. ¶ この手紙の～はまだだれも読んでいない No one has read the *contents* of this letter yet. 小包の～はなんですか What's in the package? 彼の講義の～はすばらしかった The *content* of his lecture was excellent. きみは芝居の～を誤解している You misunderstand the *meaning* of the play. ～のある話を聞きたい I want to hear a *suggestive* speech.
—証明郵便〔a〕contents-certified mail. —見本 (書物の) specimen pages.

ないらん【内乱】a civil war; (反乱) rebellion.

ないりく【内陸】inland. ¶ ～の気候はだいたい一定している The climate in the *interior* is rather stable.
—地方 an inland area. —国 a country which has no sea borders.

ナイロン nylon.

—ザイル a nylon rope. **—ストッキング** nylon stockings.

な·う【綯う】 ¶ なわを～う *twist* a rope. わらなわを～う *twist* straw *into rope*.

なうて【名うて】 ¶ ～の famous ; famed ; (悪名高い) ill-famed ; notorious.

なえ【苗】 a young plant ; a seedling.

なえぎ【苗木】 a young tree ; (種から育てたもの) a seedling ; (接ぎ木の苗) a graft.

なえどこ【苗床】 a nursery.

な·える【萎える】 (しおれる) wither ; (力がうせる) weaken. ¶ この暑さで草木がすっかり～えてしまった This hot weather *has withered up* flowers and plants.

なお【尚・猶】1 〖一層〗 ¶ その小説よりこの小説のほうが～難しい This novel is *still* harder than that one.
～いっそう勉強してほしい I want you to study *harder*.

2 〖その上〗 ¶ ～二っ三っ例をあげてください Please give a few *more* examples.
あすは8時に集合のこと, ～弁当を忘れぬように Meet at eight tomorrow, *and*, don't forget to bring your lunch with you.
～ひと言いいたいことがある I have something *more* to say.
彼は日本語は話せないし, 書くことは～できない He can't speak Japanese, *much less* write it.
まちがいないと思っても, ～もう一度見直したほうがいい Even if you think it all right, examine it *once more*.

なおかつ【尚且つ】 besides. ¶ 彼は頭がよい, ～思いやりがある He is *not only* intelligent *but* considerate to others.

なおさら【尚更】 all the more ; (否定) much less. ¶ 私は～神経質になった I got *all the more* nervous. 彼は欠点のある男だからこそ～好きなのだ I like him *all the better* because of his faults. うそをつくのも悪いが盗みを働くのは～悪い To tell a lie is bad, but to steal is *still* worse. 彼は英語が話せないのだから, ロシア語は～話せない He can't speak English, *much less* Russian. / He can't speak Russian, *to say nothing of* English. きみが来てくれれば～よい If you could come, *so much the better*.

なおざり【等閑】 negligence. ¶ 仕事を～にしてはいけません Don't *neglect* your work. この問題は～にできない This matter cannot *be left ignored* (≒ *be left untouched*).

なおし【直し】 (修理) repair ; (修正) [a] correction. ¶ その機械はもう～がきかない This machine is beyond *repair*. この校正は～が多い This proof is full of *corrections*. 簡単な車の～なら自分でできる I can do simple *repairs* on my car.
—物 ¶ 当店は～物専門です We do only *mending* work.

なお·す【直す・治す】1 〖修繕する〗 repair ; mend ; fix (自動車・テレビ・時計などの複雑なもの, また家などの修理には mend より repair を用いる. 囲 口語では repair, mend 代わりに fix〔up〕を用いる).
¶ この時計を～してください I would like to *have* this watch *repaired* (≒ *fixed*).
彼はこわれたドアを～した He *mended* a broken door.
冷蔵庫の故障を～すのに1万円もかかった It cost me ten thousand yen to *have* my refrigerator *fixed*.

2 〖訂正する〗 correct. ¶ 次の文に誤植があるから次のように～してください There are some printer's errors in the next sentence. *Correct* them as indicated.
この計画は無理があるから～さなければならない I think the plan is too ambitious. It needs some *modification*.

3 〖翻訳する・書きかえる〗 put ; translate. ¶ この手紙を英語に～してください Will you *put* the letter *into* English?
漢文を現代文に～す問題が出た In one of the questions in the exam, we were asked to *rewrite* a passage of classical Chinese in modern Japanese.

4 〖換算する〗 ¶ 1万円をドルに～すといくらになりますか How much can I get in dollars for ten thousand yen at the present exchange rate?

5 〖矯正する〗 correct. ¶ 悪い癖は若いうちに～さなければならない Bad habits must *be overcome* (≒ *be got rid of*) in youth.
私はアメリカ人について英語の発音を～してもらった I had an American teacher *correct* my English pronunciation.

6 〖整える〗 ¶ 彼は服装を～してからベルを押した He *straightened* his clothes before he rang the bell.
彼は話をするたびに眼鏡を～した He *adjusted* his glasses every time he spoke.

7 〖もとどおりにする〗 ¶ お菓子をあげるから, きげんを～してちょうだい Here, I will give you some cake. Now stop crying! (≒ Now give me a smile.)

8 〖治療する〗 cure. ¶ 風邪はひきはじめに～さないと長びく A cold must *be cured* before it gets serious. Otherwise, it will hang on and on.
この病気は～しようがないらしい There seems to be no *cure* (≒ *remedy*) for this disease.

なおまた【尚又】 besides ; moreover.

なおも【尚も】 ¶ 雨は～降りつづいている It is *still* raining.

なお·る【直る・治る】1 〖正しくなる〗 ¶ 一度悪い癖がつくとなかなか～らない Once you form a bad habit, it is very difficult to *stop* (≒ *get over* ; *get rid of*) it.
彼の曲がった根性はどうしても～らない His warped character will not *be corrected* (≒ *be remedied*).

2 〖訂正される〗 ¶ 再校でも～っていない (誤植が多い) There are still many typographical (≒ printer's) errors in the second proof.

3 〖修繕される〗 ¶ この時計の故障は～りますか Can this watch *be repaired*?
自動車の故障は1時間で～ります Your car trouble can *be fixed* in an hour.

4 〖復旧する〗 ¶ 鉄道の不通箇所が～るまで2日か

な

かる It will take two days to *reopen* the damaged part of the line.
ゴルフの話をすれば彼のきげんはすぐ～る His face brightens up when you talk about golf.
5 〚変わる・転位する〛 ¶ 一等席からボックス席に～りたいんだが I want to *change* from the first-class seat to the box seat.
6 〚病気・傷がよくなる〛 ¶ 彼の結核はやっと～った At last he *has been cured* of tuberculosis.
そのくらいの風邪は二, 三日で～るでしょう You will *get over* a slight cold like that in a few days.
この薬を飲めば頭痛はすぐ～る This medicine will soon *cure* you *of* the headache.
足の傷がすっかり～った The wound in the leg *has healed.*
ちょっとした切り傷でもとがめると～りにくいものだ A slight cut is hard to *heal* once it gets inflamed.

なおれ 【名折れ】 a disgrace. ¶ 家の～になるようなことはするな Don't *disgrace* our family name. このように廊下が汚れていては学校の～になるではないか These dirty passages are *a disgrace* (≒ *a shame*) to the school.

なか 【中】 **1** 〚内部〛 the inside. ¶ 家の～はうるさかった The house was noisy *inside.*
とびらは～からかぎがかかっていた The door was locked from *the inside.*
～は空っぽだった It was empty *inside.*
このリンゴは～が腐っている This apple is rotten *inside.*
2 〚あいだ〛 ¶ 5人の少年の～でいちばん活発なのは彼です It is he who is the most lively *of* the five boys.
この～からきみの好きなもの一つを選びなさい Choose anything you like *from among* these.
この二つの～できみの好きなのはどっちですか Which do you like better *of* these two?
人間の～にはきわめて貪欲(どんよく)な者もいる *Some* people are very, very greedy.
3 〚時間・場所〛 ¶ 豪雨の～を2時間歩いた I walked *in* the heavy rain for two hours.
林の～を歩くのは容易ではなかった It was no easy thing to walk *through* the forest.

なか 【仲】 relations. ¶ この兄弟は～がよい These brothers *are on good terms.* 私たちは～がよい We *are friendly* toward each other. この姉妹は～が悪い These sisters *are on bad terms.* 彼らとの～はうまくいっている We *get on well with* them. あるきっかけでふたりの～は割れた Something happened to sever *the friendship* between the two.

ながあめ 【長雨】 a long rain. ¶ 6月は～の季節だ There is usually *a long spell of rain* in June.

ながい 【長居】 ¶ ずいぶん～いたしました I'm afraid I'*ve overstayed my welcome.*

なが・い 【長い】 **1** 〚長さが〛 long. ¶ 象は鼻が～い An elephant has a *long* trunk.
この棒は2センチほど～い This pole *is* about two centimeters too *long.*
この鉛筆のほうがそれより1センチ～い This pencil *is* a centimeter *longer* than that.
2 〚時間が〛 long. ¶ 彼の話はいつも～い His talk *is* always *lengthy.*
その誤りを発見するには～い時間がかかった It took *a long time* to find the mistake.
彼は～い間アメリカに滞在していた He stayed in America *for a long time.*
ふたりは～い間の知り合いだ The two are acquaintances *of long standing.*
～いこと会わなかったね *It's quite a long time since* I saw you last, isn't it?
～い間には彼もわかってくれるだろう He will understand me *in the long run.*
～いことたって彼は現われた *It was a long time before* he appeared.
この問題はもっと～い目で見たほうがいい You must *take a longer view of* the matter.
あの病人はもう～いことない It will not *be long* before the patient dies.

ながいき 【長生き】 longevity. ¶ ～する live long. 一般に女は男よりも～だ In general women *live longer* than men. 彼はこの村いちばんの～だ He's *the oldest* man in this village. 摂生は～のもと An orderly life leads to *longevity.*

ながいす 【長椅子】 a sofa.

ながいも 【長芋・長薯】 〘植物〙 a yam.

なかおれぼうし 【中折れ帽子】 a soft hat.

なかがい 【仲買】 (行為) brokerage; (人) a broker; a commission merchant. ¶ 株の～ (株式取引所仲買人) をする act as a stockbroker. **—手数料** brokerage; commission. **—店** a brokerage house (≒ firm).

ながく 【長く】 long; for a long time (≒ while); (永久に) forever. ¶ スカートを3センチ～した I *lengthened* my skirt by three centimeters. だんだん日が～なる The days are getting *longer and longer.* 雨が～続く It has been raining *for a long time.* この議題は～かかりそうだ This discussion topic will take *a lot of time.* ぼくのランチまだですか, ずいぶん～かかるね Isn't my lunch ready yet? It's taking *a long time.* この生地は～もつ This cloth wears well. 広島・長崎の悲劇は～語り伝えられるだろう The tragedy of Hiroshima and Nagasaki will be told *from generation to generation.*

ながぐつ 【長靴】 米 boots; 英 high boots.

なかごろ 【中頃】 ¶ 10月の～ *about the middle of* October.

ながさ 【長さ】 length. ¶ あの橋の～はどれくらいですか How *long* is that bridge? / What is the *length* of that bridge? それは～が200メートルある It is two hundred meters *long* (≒ *in length*). この布は～が足りない This cloth is too short. ～1メートルに板を切る saw a board in *length* of a meter.

なかさ・れる 【泣かされる】 ¶ 巨額の負債に～れている I *am distressed with* a large debt. 学生時代は数学には～れたものだ I used to *have the worst difficulty with* mathematics in my school days.

ながさ·れる【流される】¶ 大水で橋が〜れた The bridge *was washed away* by the flood. 風船が風に〜れている A balloon *is floating* in the air driven by the wind. 1 そうの船が嵐のために航路から〜れた A ship *was driven off its course* by a storm.

ながし【流し】(台所の) a sink ; (ふろ場の) a draining floor ; (芸人の) a strolling musician. ¶ 〜のタクシーを拾う catch a [*cruising*] taxi.

ながしかく【長四角】a rectangle.

ながしめ【流し目】¶ 彼女は私を〜で見た She cast *a sidelong glance* at me.

なか·す【泣かす】¶ 彼は妹を〜せた He *made* his little sister *cry*. 金をせびって親を〜すな Don't *pester* (≒ *bother*) your parents for money.

なかす【中州】a holm.

なが·す【流す】 **1** 〖液体・物を〗 ¶ 隣の敷地に水を〜すな Don't let the water *flow* onto the neighbor's land.
水を〜しっぱなしにして野菜を洗う wash the greens *in running water*.
彼女はその悲しい知らせを聞いて涙を〜した She *shed* tears when she heard the sad news.
多くの人々が祖国の独立のために血を〜した A lot of people *shed* their blood for the independence of their country.
洪水は橋を〜した Flood waters *washed away* the bridge.
2 〖慣用的表現〗 ¶ 彼についてのいまわしいうわさを〜した者がある Somebody *started* a nasty rumor about him.
タクシーが繁華街を〜す Taxis *cruise* in the downtown area.
きみの過去の仕打ちは水に〜そう I will *forgive and forget* your past behavior toward me.

-なかせ【-泣かせ】¶ 乗客〜の交通ストはいやだ We are sick of the passenger-*hampering* strike. 彼は全く親〜だ He is a *regular pest* to his parents.

なか·せる【泣かせる】 ¶ 彼の話は〜せるじゃないか It's a *touching* (≒ *moving* ; *pathetic*) story that he told us.

ながそで【長袖】¶ 〜のセーター a *long-sleeved* sweater.

なかたがい【仲違い】an estrangement ; discord ; a quarrel. ¶ ふたりは完全に〜をしている There *is no love* between the two. 貿易交渉の断絶で両国は〜をした The breakdown of the trade talks *impaired the relations* between the two nations.

なかだち【仲立ち】(仲介) mediation ; (仲介人) a mediator ; (仲人) a go-between. ¶ その契約は彼に〜をしてもらった The contract has been concluded through his *mediation*.

ながたらし·い【長たらしい】¶ 彼の演説は〜くてたいくつだ His *long-winded* speech bores us.

なかだるみ【中弛み】¶ 市況は〜している The market *has fallen into a slump* (≒ *has slackened off*).

ながだんぎ【長談義】a long speech ; a rigmarole. ¶ 彼の〜にうんざりした We got sick of his *long talk*.

なかつぎ【中継ぎ】(売買などの) intermediary. —貿易 transit trade.

なかった〔な〕ら【無かった〔な〕ら】 ¶ あなたのご指導が〜, とても成功しなかったでしょう *If it had not been for* (≒ *But for* ; *Without*) your valuable guidance, I could not have succeeded. 水が〜どんな生物も長くは生きられないだろう *If there were no* (≒ *If it were not for* ; *Without*) water, no living thing could live long. 病気で〜その旅行に参加するのだが *If I were not ill*, I would take part in the trip.

ながっちり【長っ尻】¶ 彼は〜でこまる He *overstays his welcome*.

ながつづき【長続き】¶ この上天気は〜しないだろう This fine weather will not *last long*. 彼はなにをしても〜しない He does not do anything with patience. / He is not a man of patience.

なかなおり【仲直り】 reconciliation. ¶ 彼と〜をした I *have been reconciled with* him. / I *made peace with* him. ふたりは〜をした The two *have become reconciled*. もう〜しようじゃないか Let's shake hands and *be friends again*.

なかなか【中中】¶ 〜感じのよい青年だ He is a *very* agreeable young man. 彼は確かに〜の人物だ He is *somebody*, I assure you. この問題は〜難しい This problem is *rather* difficult. それをするには〜時間がかかる It takes *a great deal of* time to do that. 彼は〜よく本を読んでいる He reads *a lot*. / He is a *great* reader. 彼は〜の学者だ He is *no mean* scholar. この箱は〜開かない This box *will not* open. 彼は〜怒らない He *is slow to* anger. / He *is slow to* take offense. 彼女は彼の申し込みを〜受け入れなかった She did *not readily* accept his proposal. きみの文章はまだ〜完全とはいかない Your writing is far from perfect. 〜勝負がつかなかった It was a close game.

ながなが【長長】¶ 〜お世話になりました (長年の親切に感謝する) I really appreciate your kindnesses you have done for me *through these years*. / (長い滞在の親切に感謝する) I am much obliged to you for your kindness shown me *during my long stay*. 犬が〜と横になっている There is a dog lying *at full length*. 彼は自分の経験した苦労や不運のことを〜と話した He told *in detail* of the troubles and misfortunes he had experienced.

なかには【中には】¶ 彼らの大多数は優秀だが, 〜出来の悪い生徒もいる Most of them are very clever, but *some of them* are not.

なかにも【中にも】 ¶ このように, いつまでも存続するものは信仰と希望と愛と, この三つである. 〜もっとも大いなるものは愛である So faith, hope, love abide, these three ; but the greatest of these is love.

なかにわ【中庭】(邸宅・城・ホテルなどの囲まれている) a court ; a courtyard ; (大学などの) a quadrangle.

ながねん【長年】for a long time ; for many years. ¶ 彼らの〜の夢が実現した Their *long-*

な

cherished dream has come true. 彼のすばらしい腕前は～の練習によるものだ He obtained his astonishing skill by *long years of* practice.

ながの【長の】¶ それが彼との～別れになった It was the last time I saw him 〔alive〕. / We were never to meet each other again. 彼女は～患いでやつれて見えた She looked weak from her *lingering* illness.

なかば【半ば】**1**〖半分〗half. ¶ 9月も～は過ぎた September is *half* over.
その橋は～完成している The bridge is *half* finished.
会員の～は男性だ *Half* the members are men.
2〖中ほど〗halfway ; the middle. ¶ 彼は30代の～だ He is in *the middle* of his thirties.
2月の～ごろ about *the middle of* February.
来月～過ぎに in *the latter part* of next month.
3〖途中〗¶ 彼は話の～で席を立った He left his seat *while* the speech was being given. / He left his seat *before* the speech came to an end.
彼は学業～にして学校を去らねばならなかった He was obliged to leave school *half way.* / He failed to complete his education.
4〖一部分〗¶ ～好奇心から～必要もあってそうした *Partly from* curiosity *and partly from* necessity, I did it.
5〖ほとんど〗¶ 医者はその病人を～見放していた The doctor *almost* gave up the patient.
優勝は～あきらめていた We regarded it as *almost* hopeless that we would win the tournament.

ながばなし【長話】a long talk. ¶ 電話で～をする have *a long talk* (≒ *a long conversation*) on the telephone.

ながび・く【長引く】¶ 風邪が～いて困っている I'm being troubled with a *lingering* cold. 会議が～いて5時間もかかった The conference *dragged on* for five long hours. / The conference *took* as *long* as five hours. 話がはずんで食事が～いた A pleasant conversation *prolonged* the dinner.

なかほど【中程】¶ 坂の～に *halfway* uphill. 試合の～で *in the course of* the match.

なかま【仲間】(同僚) a colleague ; an associate ; a fellow worker ; (朋輩) a fellow ; (同志) a comrade ; (同業者) a fellow trader ; (共同経営者) a partner ; (連れ) a companion ; (集合的に) a company ; a party ; a set.
¶ 彼も彼の～もきらいだ I don't like him or his *crowd.* 人はつきあう～でわかる We know a person by the *company* he keeps. 彼はよい(悪い)～とつきあっている He keeps good (bad) *company.* ぼくたちのクラブの～になりませんか Won't you *join* our club? どうかぼくたちの運動の～に入ってください Please *join with* us in our campaign. / Please *take part in* our campaign. きみをその取引の～にしてあげよう We'll allow you to be *a party to* the deal.
—はずれ ¶ 彼はいつもけんかをするのでゲームで～はずれにしてやった He always fights, so we left him out of the game. **—割れ** ¶ 彼らはつまらぬことで～割れしている They are quarreling with each other about trifles. (3人以上は among themselves).

なかみ【中身】contents. ¶ この包みの～はなんだ What are the *contents of* this parcel? / What's in this parcel? 財布の～はからだ The purse is empty. / There is nothing in the purse. 彼の話は～がない He talks at random.

ながめ【眺め】a view. ¶ 山頂からの～はたとえようもなかった The *view* from the top of the mountain was wonderful. ホテルは海の～がすばらしい The hotel *has* (≒ *commands*) an excellent *view* of the sea.

ながめ【長め】¶ ～のズボン a *longish* pair of trousers.

なが・める【眺める】¶ 男は私をじろじろ～めていた The man *was staring at* me. 宿の部屋から美しい山が～められる We can *view* the beautiful mountains from the hotel room. / The hotel room *looks out on* the beautiful mountains. 秋の色とりどりの風景を飽かず～めた We *feasted our eyes on* the colors of the landscape in autumn. 彼は入ってくるなり部屋を～めまわした As soon as he came in, he *looked* around the room. 事柄を客観的に～めるべきだ We should *consider* the affair objectively.

ながもち【長持ち】¶ ずいぶん～するくつ下だ These socks *wear* quite *well.* このくつは～しなかった These shoes *wore badly.* このペンは～しない This pen will not *stand long use.* 木綿物は絹物よりも～する Cotton cloth *outlasts* silk cloth. 塩ザケは～する The salted salmon will *keep long.* この天気は～しないだろう This fine weather will not *hold* (≒ *last long*).

なかやすみ【中休み】a rest ; a recess ; a break. ¶ 仕事の～ a coffee (≒ tea) break. 梅雨の～ *a fine interval* during the rainy season. ～しよう Let's have *a rest.*

なかゆび【中指】a middle finger.

なかよく【仲よく】¶ 新しい友だちと～していますか *Are* you *getting along* (≒ *on*) *very well with* your new friends? 彼らはみな～暮らしている They are living together *in harmony.* ふたりはすぐ～なった The two *made friends with* each other soon.

なかよし【仲好し】¶ 彼とは大の～だ I *am great friends with* him. / I *am on* very *good terms with* him. 彼と～になった I *made friends with* him.

-ながら ¶ 残念～ご招待に応じられません *I am sorry, but* I cannot accept your invitation. 健康によくないと知り～よく夜更かしをしてしまう I often sit up late at night *though* I know it is not good for my health. 彼はラジオを聞き～勉強する He studies *as* he listens to the radio. お茶を飲み～おしゃべりをした We chatted *over* a cup of tea. 彼女は涙～に身の上話をした *In tears* she told her life story. 寝～本を読むのが彼の習慣だ It is his habit to read *in* bed. / He has a habit of reading *in bed.* 少女はほほ笑み～会釈した She bowed *with a smile.* いつも～お美しい You are *as* beautiful *as ever.* いつものこと～きみは遅刻だ You are late *as usual.*

ながら·える【長らえる】¶ 彼は80歳まで～えた He *lived* to be eighty. 彼女は夫の死後も～えた She *outlived* her husband.

ながらく【長らく】¶ ～ごぶさたしました(手紙で) I hope you will excuse me for my *long* silence.

-なかれ ¶ おどろく～, 彼は大どろぼうだった *To our surprise,* he proved to be a notorious burglar. ゆめゆめ油断する～ *Never* despise danger./*Be careful not to* be caught off your guard.

ながれ【流れ】a current ; a stream. ¶ ～を下る go down the *river.* ～に逆らって泳ぐ swim against the *stream.* 人の～が公園に向かう *A stream* of people goes toward the park. 自動車の～が渋滞した *A* long *line* of motorcars was delayed. 彼は時代の～に逆らおうとしたがだめだった He tried to fight against the *current* of the times in vain. あの家は徳川の～をくんでいる The family *is descended from* the Tokugawas. 彼はカントの～をくむ哲学者だ He is a philosopher belonging to the school of Kant.

—作業 an assembly line ; a conveyer system ; flow production. —星 a shooting star ; a meteor. —矢 a stray (≒ random) arrow. 質— a forfeited article.

ながれこ·む【流れ込む】¶ この川は東京湾に～む This river *flows* (≒ *pours*) *into* Tokyo Bay. 人々は会場に～んだ People *streamed into* the place.

ながれつ·く【流れ着く】¶ ヤシの実が海岸に～いた A coconut *drifted ashore.*

なが·れる【流れる】**1**〖液体·物体が〗¶ 川は海へゆっくりと～れた The river *flowed* slowly to the sea.
カヌーが川下へ～れていった The canoe *floated* downstream.
風船が風に～れてきた A balloon came *floating* on the wind.
傷口から血が～れていた Blood *was running* (≒ *was flowing*) from his wound.
体内を血が～れる Blood *circulates* (≒ *flows*) through the body.
涙が彼女のほおを～れた Tears *streamed* (≒ *trickled*) down her cheeks.
彼の顔には汗と涙が～れていた Sweat and tears *flowed down* his face.
数軒の家が洪水で～れた Several houses *were washed away* by the flood.
2〖中止になる〗¶ 委員会は～れて翌日になった The meeting of the committee *was adjourned to* the following day.
試合は雨で～れた The game *was rained out.*

ながわずらい【長煩い·長患い】lingering illness. ¶ 彼は～をしている He *has been ill in bed for a long time.* 彼女は～で弱っている She is weak from *lingering illness.*

なかんずく【就中】particularly ; above all ; especially. ¶ ～健康が第一だ Good health is *particularly* important. / Health is *above anything else.* ギリシア人は～美を愛した The Greeks loved beauty *above all things.*

なき【泣き】¶ 彼は私に～を入れた He *begged* me *for mercy.* あんなことをしていると彼はいまに～を見るぞ He will *be sorry for it* that way.

なき【亡き】¶ ～母 *one's dead* mother. ～A氏 *the late* Mr. A.

なぎ【凪】a calm ; a lull. ¶ 朝 (夕) ～ a morning (an evening) *calm.* ～になってから船を出す sail out when *the wind has dropped.*

なきあか·す【泣き明かす】¶ 一夜～す weep (≒ cry) all night ; weep a night away.

なきおとし【泣き落とし】¶ 彼女の～にかかって承知してしまった She wrung from me a slow consent *by force of tears.*

なきおと·す【泣き落とす】persuade *a person* ; win *a person* over by entreaties.

なきがお【泣き顔】a tearful face. ¶ ～をして with *a tearful face.* 彼女は顔をそむけて～を隠した She looked away to hide her tears.

なきがら【亡骸·亡軀】a dead body ; a corpse.

なきくず·れる【泣き崩れる】¶ その知らせを聞くと彼女は～れた She *burst into tears* when she heard the news.

なきくら·す【泣き暮らす】¶ 父の急死で彼女は三日三晩～した At the sudden death of her father she *spent* three days and three nights *in tears* (≒ *wept away* three days and three nights).

なきごえ【泣き声】a tearful voice. ¶ 彼女は～になって話した She talked in *a tearful voice.* 赤ん坊の～を聞いた I heard a baby *crying.*

なきごえ【鳴き声】a cry ; (鳥の) a song ; a chirp ; a note.

なきごと【泣き言】a complaint. ¶ 彼はいつも～ばかり言っている He *is* always *complaining* (≒ *grumbling*) *about* something.

なぎさ【渚·汀】a beach ; a shore.

なきさけ·ぶ【泣き叫ぶ】cry ; scream.

なきしき·る【鳴き頻る】¶ 草むらで虫が～っている Insects *are in full chirp* in the grass.

なきじゃく·る【泣きじゃくる】¶ 女は～りながら話した She spoke *between her sobs.* 女の子は母親の胸に抱かれて～りながら寝てしまった The girl *sobbed herself to sleep* on her mother's breast.

なきじょうご【泣き上戸】(酔うと泣く人) a crying drunkard ; (すぐ泣く人) a maudlin person.

なぎたお·す【薙ぎ倒す】¶ 草を～す *mow* (≒ *cut*) *down* the grass. 上位力士を～す *beat* the opponent *sumo* wrestlers of higher grades.

なきだ·す【泣き出す】¶ 彼はとうとう～した He *began to cry* at last. 彼女はわっと～した She *burst into tears.* / She *burst out crying.* 今にも～しそうな空もようだ The sky is overspread with raining clouds.

な

なきつ·く【泣きつく】¶ 彼はぼくに金を貸してくれと～いた He *implored* (≒ *entreated*) me *for* money.

なきつら【泣き面】¶ ～にはち(諺) *Misfortunes never come singly.*

なきどころ【泣き所】a weak point. ¶ いちばんの～を指摘された I was struck at my *weakest* (≒ *most vulnerable*) *point.* 弁慶の～ an Achilles heel.

なきなき【泣き泣き】¶ 彼女は～身の上話をした She told her story *between her sobs* (≒ *with tears*).

なぎなた【薙刀·長刀】a halberd ; a long handled sword.

なきぬ·れる【泣き濡れる】¶ ～れた顔 a *tear-stained* face.

なきねいり【泣き寝入り】¶ その子は～した The child *cried himself to sleep.* ～するよりしかたがない We just have to *swallow it.* ～するのはいやだ I'm not going to *let the matter drop.*

なきのなみだ【泣きの涙】¶ 彼女は彼を～で見送った She saw him off *in sorrow.*

なきはら·す【泣き腫らす】¶ 彼女は目を～していた Her eyes were swollen with crying. / (目もつぶれるほどに泣く) She *cried* (≒ *wept*) *her eyes out.*

なきひと【亡き人】¶ 彼も～の数に入った He *joined* (≒ *went over to*) *the majority.* / He *died.*

なきふ·す【泣き伏す】¶ 悲報を聞いて彼女は～した She *broke down* at the sad news.

なきべそ【泣きべそ】¶ しかられて子どもは～をかいた Having a good scold, the boy *nearly cried.* 子どもは～をかきながらついて来た The child followed me *nearly crying.* 子どもは～をかきながらもう二度としません, と言った The child *sobbed out* that he would never do it again.

なきまね【泣き真似】¶ 彼女は～がじょうずだ She *pretends to weep* quite well. / She is good at *feigning a crying.*

なきむし【泣き虫】a crybaby. ¶ この子は～で困る It is a pity that he is *a cryboy.*

なきもの【亡き者】¶ 人を～にする do away with *a person.*

なきや·む【泣きやむ】¶ 彼女に抱かれると赤ん坊はじきに～んだ Held in her arms, the baby *stopped crying* soon.

なきりぼうちょう【菜切り包丁】a kitchen knife.

なきわかれ【泣き別れ】¶ 母と娘はそこで～となった Mother and her daughter *parted in tears* there.

なきわらい【泣き笑い】¶ ～する smile between sobs ; smile tearfully.

な·く【泣く】(涙を流して) weep ; shed tears ; (声を出して) cry ; (すすり泣く) sob ; (嘆き悲しんで泣き叫ぶ) wail ; blubber.
¶ 赤ん坊が～きはじめた A baby began to *cry.* 子どもが母を求めて～き叫んでいる A child *is wailing for* his mother. その朗報を聞くと彼女はうれし泣きに～いた She *wept* (≒ *cried*) *for joy* when she heard the good news. どうしてよいやらわからず～きたくなった As I didn't know what to do, I felt like *crying.* この手紙を読んで～かない者はいない No one can read this letter with dry eyes. / Nobody can read this letter without *weeping.* ～いても笑ってもこれ限りだ This is the last chance for me.

な·く【鳴く】(犬) bark, (鼻を鳴らす) whine, (キャンキャンと鳴く) yelp ; (ネコ) mew, (ギャーギャー鳴く) caterwaul ; (牛) bellow, moo ; (馬) neigh, whinny ; (ロバ) bray ; (羊·ヤギ·子牛) bleat ; (豚) grunt ; (トラ·ライオン) growl, roar ; (象) trumpet ; (シカ) bell ; (オオカミ) howl ; (クマ) growl ; (キツネ) bark ; (サル) gibber, chatter ; (フクロウ) hoot ; (ネズミ) squeak ; (カエル) croak ; (おん鳥) crow ; (めん鳥) cluck, cackle ; (ひよこ) peep ; (コオロギ) chirr, chirrup, chirp ; (ガチョウ) cackle ; (アヒル) quack ; (七面鳥) gobble ; (虫·小鳥) chirp, sing, twitter, whistle ; (甲虫) drone ; (カラス) caw ; (ガン) honk ; (ヘビ) hiss ; (ハト) coo ; (ツバメ) twitter ; (スズメ) chirp ; (ワシ·タカ·カモメ) scream ; (ヒバリ·ウグイス) sing, warble.

な·ぐ【凪ぐ】(海·天候が) calm down ; (風が) die away ; drop. ¶ 海が～いでいる The sea *is calm.* 昼ごろになって風が～いできた The wind *dropped* (≒ *died away*) toward noon. 一瞬風が～いだ The gale *lulled* for a moment. (lull は一時的ななぎ)

なぐさみ【慰み】a pastime ; an amusement ; (気晴らし) a recreation. ¶ 彼の唯一の～は本を読むことだ His only *comfort* (≒ *consolation*) is to read books. 庭いじりが彼のおもな～だ Gardening is his chief *diversion* (≒ *recreation*). ～半分にやったまでだ I did it *just for fun.* みんなが彼を～ものにする All of them *make a plaything of* him. / He is *made sport of* by all.

なぐさ·む【慰む】¶ 花に心の～む日々を送っております I pass my days *diverted* by flowers.

なぐさめ【慰め】〔a〕comfort. ¶ 音楽が私の唯一の～だ Music is *a* sole *comfort* to me. 彼は彼女に～のことばをかけた He spoke *comforting* words to her. 彼はその後絵に～を求めた He sought for *consolation* (≒ *solace*) in painting later. 他人も同じように苦しんでいるのだといわれてもあまり～にならない It is *cold comfort* to be told that others suffer as much as we do.

なぐさ·める【慰める】¶ 彼らは互いに～め合った They *comforted* each other. それが彼女の悲しみを～めた It *consoled* (≒ *solaced*) her in her sorrow. 運命とあきらめて彼はみずから～めた He *consoled himself* with the thought that there is no striving against fate. 彼女はなにかと私を～めようとした She tried hard to *cheer* me *up.* 新緑が目を～める Fresh green leaves *gladden* (≒ *feast*) our eyes. 酒は心を～める Wine *makes* the heart *glad.*

なく·す【亡くす】¶ 彼は昨年ひとり息子を～した He *was deprived of* his only son last year. / He *lost* his only son last year. 彼は愛妻を～

な

してあきらめきれずにいる He cannot still get over *the loss* of his beloved wife.

なく·す【無くす】¶ 書類を～して困っている *Having lost* the papers, I am quite at a loss what to do. 彼はすっかり前途に希望を～してしまっている He *has been deprived of* all hopes for the future. 町から暴力団を～す *sweep away* (≒ *clear off*; *get rid of*) a band of gangsters of a town.

なくて【無くて】¶ 彼は彼女が～は生きていけない He cannot live *without* her. あなたの援助が～もやっていける We can do *without* your help. 勇気ある人で～だれがそんなことをできよう Who *but* a brave man could do such a thing? / None *but* the brave could do such a thing.

なくなく【泣く泣く】¶ その子は～帰っていった The child went home *weeping*. 彼女は～その身の上を語った She told her story *in tears*.

なくな·る【無くなる】¶ 財布が～った I *have lost* my purse. / My purse *is missing*. 机の引き出しの中の金が～っている The money in the drawer of the desk *is gone*. ケーキは早く～ったがパイはだれも平らげなかった The cake *went* fast, but no one finished the pie. 給料日前にいつも金が～りかけている I *am* always *running out of* money before payday. / My money *is* always *running out* before payday. 時間が～った Time *is up*. 水が～った We *have run out of* our water. 食欲が～った I *have lost* my appetite. / My appetite *has failed*. 熱は～った The fever *has left* me. 彼の人気は～った He *lost* his popularity.

なくな·る【亡くなる】die; pass away.

なくもがな【無くもがな】¶ その終幕はこの芝居には～の感がある I think this play *can be done without* the last act. / I think the last act *is rather needless* in this play.

なぐりあい【殴り合い】a fight. ¶ ついに～になった At last they *came to blows*. / Finally they *got into a fight*. ふたりの酔っ払いがなぐり合いのけんかをしているのを見た I saw *a fight* between two drunks.

なぐりあ·う【殴り合う】¶ 彼らは入り乱れて～った They *came to blows* in confusion. / They *exchanged blows* in confusion.

なぐりかえ·す【殴り返す】¶ 殴られたから～したのだ I *hit* him *back* because he hit me first.

なぐりがき【殴り書き】a scribble. ¶ 彼の～の字はだれにも読めない No one can read his *scribble*.

なぐりこみ【殴り込み】¶ 数名の暴力団員が彼の家に～をかけた Several gangsters *raided* (≒ *stormed*; *attacked*) his house.

なぐりころ·す【殴り殺す】strike (*a person*) dead.

なぐりたお·す【殴り倒す】knock (≒ strike) down (*a person*).

なぐりつ·ける【殴り付ける】¶ 初め彼が私の頭を～けたのです He *struck* me *on* the head first.

なぐりとば·す【殴り飛ばす】¶ 彼を物も言わず～してやった I *gave* him *a good thrashing* without saying a word.

なぐ·る【殴る】¶ ～るなら～ってみろ *Strike* me if you dare! 棒で～られた I *was hit* with a stick. 彼はめちゃくちゃに～られた He *was beaten* to a jelly. 彼はぼくのあごを～った He *punched* me *on* the chin. 彼の横面を～ってやった I *boxed* him *on* the ear. 初め顔を～ったのは彼のほうだ It was he that *struck* me *in* the face.

なげ【投げ】〘相撲〙 a throw; 〘株式〙 liquidation; 〘商業〙 a sacrifice sale.

なげあ·げる【投げ上げる】toss (*a thing*) up; throw up (*a thing*).

なげいれ【投げ入れ】〘生け花〙 free-style flower arrangement.

なげい·れる【投げ入れる】throw (*a thing*) into.

なげう·つ【擲つ·抛つ】¶ 彼は命を～って彼女を助けた He helped her *at the cost* (≒ *sacrifice*) *of* his life. / He *laid down his life* for her rescue. 彼はその運動のために牧師の職を～った He *threw* (≒ *gave*) *up* the ministry for the movement. 彼はすべてを～ってその著作に没頭した *Throwing* everything *away*, he devoted himself to writing it.

なげうり【投げ売り】a sacrifice sale; (蔵払い) a clearance sale; (特に海外市場へ) dumping. ¶ ～する sell (*goods*) at a sacrifice.
—商品 sacrifice goods.

なげかえ·す【投げ返す】throw back.

なげか·ける【投げかける】¶ それは彼らに深刻な問題を～けた It *caused* a great trouble *to* them.

なげかわし·い【嘆かわしい】¶ 彼のような高潔な人が若死にするとは～い It is a *lamentable* (≒ *sad*) thing that such a noble man as he died young. それは実に～いことだ It is indeed *a matter for regret*. 同じ失敗を繰り返すとは～い It *is deplorable* (≒ *is regrettable*) to make the same mistake twice.

なげき【嘆き】〔a〕sorrow; grief. ¶ この世は～に満ちている Life is full of *sorrows*. 彼女は～のあまり気がふれてしまった She was beside herself with *grief*. 家族の者たちは深い～に沈んだ The family were overwhelmed with *grief*.

なげ·く【嘆く】¶ 彼らは友の死を～いた They *grieved over* their friend's death. / They *lamented* the death of their friend. 彼女は自分の不幸を～いた She *lamented* 〔*over*〕 her misfortune. 彼は政界の腐敗を～いた He *deplored* the corruption of political circles. 夫に死なれてからは彼女はただ毎日を～き暮らした She *sighed away* her days after the death of her husband.

なげくび【投げ首】¶ みんな思案～の体である All *are sunk in thought*.

なげこ·む【投げ込む】throw (*a thing*) into.

なげす·てる【投げ捨てる】¶ 彼はそれをくずかごに～てた He *threw* (≒ *cast*) it *away* into the wastebasket.

なげだ·す【投げ出す】¶ 彼は荷物を窓から～した He *threw* his baggage *out* 〔*of*〕 the window. 彼は財産を～してわれわれの窮状を救った He *offered* his property and took us out of difficulty. 彼は自分から仕事を～した He *gave up* his work himself. 彼らは足を～して床の上に

座った They sat on the floor *stretching out* their legs. 命を〜して戦った We fought *at the risk* (≒ *cost*; *sacrifice*) *of* our lives.

なげつ·ける【投げ付ける】¶ 彼を力いっぱい〜けた I *threw* him *down* with all my might. 彼女はグラスを彼の顔に〜けた She *flung* the glass *in* his face. 彼は絵筆を床に〜けた He *cast* the brush down *to* the floor.

なけなし【無けなし】¶ 彼は〜の金をはたいてその本を手に入れた He paid *what* [*little*] *money he had* for the book.

なげもの【投げ物】〔商業〕sacrifice goods; 〔株式〕liquidation [shares].

なげやり【投げ槍】a javelin.

なげやり【投げ遣り】¶ 仕事を〜にするな Never *leave* your work *halfway*. / You shouldn't *neglect* your work. / Don't work *in a half-hearted manner*.

な·げる【投げる】¶ ここでボールを〜げるな Don't *pitch* balls here! ネコに石を〜げるな Don't *throw* stones *at* the cat! 彼のことばはその問題に新しい光を〜げた His words *shed* new light *on* the problem. 彼はけっして仕事を〜げるような男じゃない He never *scraps* his work.

なければ【無ければ】¶ 病気で〜自分でやるのだが I would do it myself *if* I *were* (≒ *was*) *not* sick. ペンが〜鉛筆でもいい *If* you *don't have* a pen, a pencil will do. それが〜どうにもならない *Without* it I am helpless. きょうで〜あすにしよう Let's do it tomorrow, *if not today*.

なげわざ【投げ技】¶ 彼は〜がとくいだ He is good at *throwing tricks*.

なこうど【仲人】a matchmaker; a go-between. ¶ 彼はよく人の〜をする He often *acts as go-between*. / He often *arranges a match*. (act as の次の名詞は冠詞が省略されることが多い).

なご·む【和む】¶ 孫の顔を見ると心が〜む My heart *softens* (≒ *is comforted*) at the sight of my grandchildren.

なごやか【和やか】¶ 〜な家庭 a *peaceful* home. 〜な会合 a *congenial* gathering. 〜なふんい気 a *harmonious* atmosphere. 〜な気分 a *placid* mood. 〜な生涯 a *placid* course of life. 〜な風 a *mild* (≒ *gentle*; *placid*) wind.

なごり【名残】¶ 彼が去るのは〜惜しい I *regret* he is leaving. お別れするのはなんともお〜惜しい I shall *miss* you when you are gone. / It is very sad you are going away. 別れに臨んで彼は〜惜しげだった He *was reluctant to* part from us. この世の〜にもう一度彼に会いたい I wish I could see him again *before I die*. 〜尽きないがここでお別れしましょう How I hate to see you go, but let's say good-bye now. それらは昔の栄華の〜だ They are *remnants* (≒ *reminders*) of the former glory.

なさけ【情け】(同情) sympathy; (哀れみ) pity; (親切) kindness; (慈悲) mercy; charity; (愛情) love.

¶ 〜深い sympathetic; merciful; kind; tender-(≒ kind-)hearted; charitable; generous; benevolent. 彼は〜を知らぬ独裁者だ He is a *pitiless* (≒ *merciless*) dictator. だれもが遺児に〜をかけた All of them felt *sympathy* (≒ *pity*; *compassion*) for the orphan. きみの〜が彼女のあだとなった Your *kindness* proved her ruin. お〜で先生から合格点をもらった The teacher gave me a passing mark *out of kindness*. 債権者は〜容赦なく借金を取り立てた The creditor dunned us for the payment of our debt *mercilessly* (≒ *without pity*).

なさけな·い【情けない】¶ 私たちが友だちになれないのは〜い *It's a pity* that we can't be friends. 彼は〜い境遇にある He is in *miserable* (≒ *pitiable*) circumstances. 〜いやつめ What a *wretched* fellow! / You *wretch*! 純真な子どもをだますとは〜い What *a shame* to deceive innocent children! なんと〜いことだ What *a pity*! / What *a shame*!

なざし【名指し】¶ 彼は〜で私にその仕事を頼んできた He *named* me to do the work. 〜で呼ばれた I was called *by name*.

なざ·す【名指す】name (*a person*); call (≒ mention) (*a person*) by name.

なさそう【無さそう】¶ もう時間も〜だ *There seems to be little* time *left*. 彼はもうよくなる見込みは〜だ *There seems to be no hope of* his recovery. 彼女はあまり知識は〜だ She *doesn't appear* to have much knowledge. 彼が私の意見を受け入れることはまず〜だ *It is most unlikely* that he will accept my opinion. / He will *hardly* accept my opinion.

なさぬなか【生さぬ仲】¶ あの子とは〜なのです He is not my *child by blood*. / He is my *stepchild*.

なし【梨】(実) a pear; (木) a pear tree. ¶ それきり彼は〜のつぶてだ Nothing has been heard from him since then.

なし【無し】¶ 彼は一文〜になった He became *penniless*. 若いころは休日も〜に働いた I worked *without* holidays when young. 彼〜ではやっていけない I cannot do *without* him. 文句〜 I have *no* complaint (≒ objection). / *No* complaint. / *No* objection. これだけやれば問題〜 You *have only to* do this.

なしくずし【済し崩し】¶ 〜にそれを払った I paid it *in* (≒ *by*) *installments*. / 米 I paid it *on an easy payment system*.

なしじ【梨地】aventurine lacquer.

なしと·げる【成し遂げる】¶ 彼はそれを必ず〜げるだろうと思う I am sure he will *carry* it *through*. 彼は仕事を〜げた He *accomplished* (≒ *completed*; *achieved*) his work.

なじみ【馴染み】¶ そこで彼と〜になった I *got acquainted with* him there. / I *made friends with* him there. 彼とは学生時代からの〜だ I *have known* him from our school days. 幼— an old playmate. 昔— ¶ 昔〜のよしみで助けてくれないか Will you help me *for old time's sake*?

なじ·む【馴染む】¶ 仕事を進めていくうちにだんだん〜んでくるだろう As you go ahead with the work, you will gradually *become used* (≒ *become accustomed*) *to it*. 新しい環境に〜むの

にかなり時間がかかった It took me quite a long time to *adapt myself to* the new surroundings. その国の風土に～めなかった I was unable to *become acclimated to* the climate of the country. 二, 三か月はいてようやくこのくつが～んできた These shoes *have* at last *got to fit* me after wearing them for a couple of months. ああいうタイプの女には子どもはなかなか～まない Children don't *take* easily *to* that type of women. 長い間～んだ土地を離れるのはつらいことだった It was painful for me to leave the place where I had lived for a long time.

なじ·る【詰る】¶ 市民はみな市長の怠慢を～った All the citizens *blamed* the mayor *for* his negligence. 彼女は彼の忘恩を～った She *rebuked* him *for* his ingratitude. 彼女は彼の所業を厳しく～った She *reproved* him sharply *for* what he had done.

なす【茄子】〘植物〙an eggplant.

な·す【成す】¶ 富を～す *make* a fortune. どの分野にせよ名を～すのは容易なことではない It is by no means easy to *win fame* (≒ *make a name for oneself*) in any sphere. この文は意味を～さない This sentence does not *make sense*. あの人は大事を～したことを誇りにしている He is proud of *accomplishing* a great task. あの山は天然の要塞(ようさい)を～している That mountain *forms* a natural fortress.

な·す【為す·作す】¶ 善(悪)を～す *do* good (wrong). 特に～すこともなくぶらぶらしている With nothing particular to *do*, I am idling away my time. 破損した船は波の～すままに漂った The damaged ship drifted *at the mercy of* the waves. 若い者の～すに任せておくわけにはいかない We cannot *let* the young *do* as they like.

なずな【薺】〘植物〙a shepherd's purse.

なす·る【擦る】¶ 皮膚に軟膏(なんこう)をたっぷり～ってお きなさい *Rub* an ointment in plenty *on* (≒ *in*) the skin. 人に責任を～りつけるのは卑劣だ It is mean to *put* (≒ *fix*) your responsibility *on* another.

なぜ【何故】why; for what reason (≒ purpose). ¶ 彼は～彼女が泣いているのか聞いたが, 彼女は～だか言えなかった He asked her *why* she was crying, but she could not tell him the *reason*. ～うれしいの *What* makes you so happy? 彼は病気かもしれない,～なら欠席しているから He may be ill, *since* he is absent. 彼は欠席している,～なら病気だから He is absent, *because* he is ill. ～だかわからないがきょうはきげんが悪い I don't know *why*, but he is in a bad humor today. 彼は～だか町を出ていった He left town *for some reason*.

なぜなら【何故なら】⇒ なぜ

なぞ【謎】a riddle; a puzzle; an enigma. ¶ それは科学者ががんについての～の一つを解明するのに役だつであろう That will help the scientist to solve one of the *unknown facts* of cancer. それは私にとって～だ It's *a mystery* (≒ *a riddle*) to me. 彼の失踪(しっそう)の～を解く手掛かりはなにもない We have no clue to the *mystery* of his disappearance. 彼は～の人物だ He is an *enigmatic* (≒ *a mysterious*) man. / He is *a riddle* (≒ *a mystery*). 彼女に～をかけた I put *a riddle* to her. / I gave (≒ asked) her *a riddle*. 彼に～をかけてみたが(それとなく言ったが)通じなかった I *dropped* him *a hint*, but he failed to take it. 彼の過去は～に包まれている His past life is shrouded in *mystery*.

なぞなぞ【謎謎】¶ ～〔ごっこ〕をしよう Let's play *riddles*. / Let's ask *riddles*.

なぞめ·く【謎めく】¶ それはどうも～いた話だ It is rather an *enigmatic* story. 彼は～いた笑いを浮かべた He had a *sphinx-like* smile. 彼にはどこか～いたところがある There is something *mysterious* (≒ *inscrutable*) about him.

なぞら·える【擬える·準える】¶ 人の一生はしばしば旅に～えられる Life *is* often *compared to* a journey. 心臓をポンプに～えることがある The heart *is likened to* a pump from time to time.

なぞ·る ¶ 彼は鉛筆のあとをインクで～った He *inked* the pencil. 彼は地図の上に薄い紙を置いて～った He *traced* the map by putting a sheet of thin paper on it.

なた【鉈】a hatchet.

なだ【灘】¶ 鹿島～ the *Sea* of Kashima.

なだい【名代】¶ ～のすき焼き屋 a *noted* (≒ *famous*) *sukiyaki* restaurant. ～の悪党 a *notorious* scoundrel.

なだか·い【名高い】¶ 彼は建築家として～い He *is famous* as an architect. この湖は白鳥で～い This lake *is noted* for its swans. この一帯は石油の生産によって世界に～い This district *is world-famous* for the production of petroleum.

なだたる【名だたる】¶ 彼の家はその地方での～旧家である His is a *well-known* family in that region.

なたね【菜種】rapeseed.
　—油 rape oil; rapeseed oil.

なたまめ【鉈豆】〘植物〙a horse bean.
　—ぎせる a flat-tubed pipe.

なだめすか·す【宥め賺す】¶ ～してやっと子どもに薬を飲ませた He *coaxed* his child *to* take the medicine.

なだ·める【宥める】appease; soothe; pacify. ¶ 怒っている人を～める *appease* an angry man. 泣く子を～める *calm down* (≒ *soothe*) a crying child. なんとかして彼の怒りを～めたい I will do my best to *pacify* his wrath.

なだらか ¶ ～な坂 a *gentle* slope. ～に傾斜する slope *gently*. 彼は～に話を進めた He continued to talk *fluently* (≒ *without a hitch*).

なだれ【雪崩】a snowslide; an avalanche. ¶ 聴衆は～を打って出口に殺到した The audience *surged forward* in crowds to the exit. 学生は会場に～込んだ The students *rushed* (≒ *crowded*) *into* the assembly hall.

ナチス the Nazis. ¶ ～化する Nazify.
　—党員 a Nazi.

ナチュラル natural. ¶ 彼の考え方は～なものだ

His way of thinking *is natural*.

なつ【夏】 summer. ¶ ～の日 a *summer* day. ～の初めに early in *summer*; in early *summer*. ～の盛りに in the height of *summer*; in *midsummer*. この～ this *summer*. 次の(前の)～ next (last) *summer*. 山や海で～を過ごす *summer* (≒ *spend the summer*) in the mountains or at the seaside. 飛んで火に入る～の虫(諺) That's a case of the moth flying into the flame. / The fool goes out to meet misfortune. 去年は～らしい～がなかった We had no real *summer* last year.

―時間 米 the daylight-saving time; 英 the summer time.

なついん【捺印】 ¶ この書類に～をお願いいたします Won't you please *affix* (≒ *put*) *your seal* to this document? (西洋ではふつう捺印がなくサインだけ).

なつかし・い【懐かしい】 ¶ ときどき～い故郷を思い出す I sometimes feel homesick for my *dear* old home. / I am sometimes reminded of my *dear* old home. この辺りの景色は～い The scenes around here *are familiar* to me. あなたに会ってほんとうに～い I am really very glad to see you. ～そうに後ろを振り返った He looked *longingly* back.

なつかしげ【懐かしげ】 ¶ 彼は～に昔を語った He talked of his old days *yearningly* (≒ *wistfully*).

なつかしさ【懐かしさ】 a dear feeling. ¶ 彼は～を隠しきれぬ表情だった He looked as if everything were indescribably dear to him.

なつかし・む【懐かしむ】 ¶ 過ぎた日々を～んだ We *longed for* our past days.

なつがれ【夏枯れ】 ¶ 今は～だ We are now in *the slack summer season*. ～でさっぱり売れない Business *slackens in summer*. / We *do very little business in summer*. 映画は今～だ The movies *are in the summer slackness*.

なつ・く【懐く】 ¶ 彼は親に～かない He does not *take to* his parents. 彼は部下の者たちに～かれている He *is beloved* by his men.

なつくさ【夏草】 summer grass.

ナックルボール 〘野球〙 a knuckle ball; a knuckler.

なつげ【夏毛】 summer fur.

なづけおや【名付け親】 a godparent; a godfather; a godmother. ¶ ～になる stand *godfather* (*to*).

なづ・ける【名づける】 ¶ 彼は子どもをドナルドと～けた He *named* the child Donald. タスマニアは発見者タスマンにちなんで～けられた Tasmania *was named for* (≒ *after*) its discoverer. (name for はアメリカ用法).

なつご【夏蚕】 summer silkworms; a summer crop of silkworms.

なっせん【捺染】 textile printing. ¶ ～する print.

―キャラコ cotton print. **―機** a printing machine. **―工場** a printing factory.

なっていない ¶ この絵は～ This picture *is no good*. 彼は司会者としては～ He *is* quite *a failure* as a master of ceremonies. こんなことが覚えられないなんて, 彼は全く～ Nothing is to be said of him, not to be able to remember such a thing.

ナット a nut. ¶ ～でとめる hold a bolt with *a nut*.

なっとう【納豆】 fermented soybean.

なっとく【納得】 (承諾) consent; assent; (了解) understanding. ¶ それは～ずくで決めたことだ We decided it *by common consent* (≒ *with mutual understanding*). 彼女は十分～のいくまで幾度も質問した She asked questions again and again till she *understood* well. その提案は～しかねる I can't *consent to* (≒ *give assent to*) the proposal. 私は彼らがまちがっていることを～させた I *persuaded* them that they were wrong. 私たちに～のいくように説明してください Please explain *to our satisfaction* (≒ *convincingly*).

なつば【夏場】 ¶ この湖のにぎわいは～だけだ This lake is popular only *in summer*. 浜は～はにぎわう The seaside is crowded *during the summertime*.

なっぱ【菜っ葉】 greens.

なつばしょ【夏場所】 〘相撲〙 the summer *sumo* tournament.

なつばて【夏ばて】 ¶ このところ～でなにもできない I *have been* too much *heat-stricken* to do anything these days.

なつふく【夏服】 a summer suit (≒ wear); summer clothes.

ナップザック a knapsack.

なつまけ【夏負け】 ¶ 私は毎年～する I *am susceptible to the heat* every summer.

なつみかん【夏蜜柑】 〘植物〙 a Chinese citron.

なつむき【夏向き】 ¶ この品は～になっている This article fits *for summer use*.

なつめ【棗】 a jujube; a nutmeg; (木) a jujube tree.

―やし a date palm.

なつもの【夏物】 summer wear. ¶ ～を着て行きなさい Go with *summer clothes* on. これは～としては不向きだ This is not suitable for *summer wear*.

なつやすみ【夏休み】 the summer vacation (英 では the summer holidays ともいう).
¶ ～の宿題はもう終わりましたか Have you finished doing your homework for *the summer holidays*? ～に旅行する予定だ I am going to make a trip during *the summer vacation*.

なつやせ【夏痩せ】 ¶ 私は～するたちだ I am likely to *lose weight in summer*.

なつやま【夏山】 (夏の山) summer mountains; (登山) summer mountaineering. ¶ ～のシーズンが来た The season of *summer mountaineering* has come.

なでおろ・す【撫で下ろす】 ¶ ほっと胸を～した I was greatly relieved. / I gave a sigh of relief.

なでがた【撫で肩】 ¶ 彼女は～だ She has *sloping shoulders*.

なでぎり【撫で斬り】¶ 片っぱしから敵兵を～にした They *made a clean sweep* of the enemy one after another.

なでしこ【撫子】〘植物〙 a pink.

なでつ·ける【撫で付ける】 ¶ 彼の髪はきちんと～けてある His hair *is* neatly *plastered down.* くしで髪を～けた I *combed* through my hair. 乱れた髪を～けた She *combed down* her disheveled hair.

なでまわ·す【撫で回す】 ¶ 彼は小犬の頭を～した He *passed his hand* over the puppy's head. / He *patted* the puppy on its head. 彼はあごを～した He *rubbed* his chin all over.

な·でる【撫でる】 ¶ 髪を～でる *smooth down one's* hair. 子どもの頭を～でる *pat* a child on the head. そよ風が彼のほおを～でた The breeze *touched* his cheeks. 彼女はひざの上のネコを～でていた She *was stroking* the cat in her lap.

-など【-等】¶ その店では果物～を売っている Fruits *and other things* are sold in that store. 部屋の中には机やいす～が置いてあった We found desks, chairs *and what not* in the room. 私～は演説はできない *As for me,* I am unable to make a speech. 日曜日～に家にいられるものではない How can I stay at home on Sunday? 魚釣り～に出かける暇はない I have no time to go out fishing and *such like.*

なとり【名取り】¶ 彼女は踊りの～だ She *has a professional name* in dancing. / She is *a mistress* of dancing.

ナトリウム〘化学〙 sodium (natrium は古い呼び名). 塩化── sodium chloride.

なないろ【七色】 seven colors; (物理) prismatic colors. ¶ ～のにじ a rainbow 〔of *seven colors*〕.

ななえ【七重】 sevenfold. ¶ ～のひざを八重に折って頼む implore (*a person*) on *one's* 〔bent〕 knees.

ななくさ【七草】(春の) seven spring herbs; (秋の) seven autumn flowers.
──がゆ rice porridge with seven herbs.

ななころびやおき【七転び八起き】¶ 人生は～だ Life is full of the *vicissitudes of fortune.*

ななし【名無し】¶ ～の権兵衛 a Mr. Unknown.

ななつ【七つ】 seven. ¶ ～めの the seventh. ～の海 the *seven* seas.
──道具 complete paraphernalia; an outfit.

ななひかり【七光り】¶ 親の～であそこまできた He has attained considerable success thanks to his parent's *prestige* (≒ *influence*).

ななふしぎ【七不思議】¶ 世界の～ 〔*the*〕 *seven wonders* of the world. この寄宿舎には～がある This dormitory has, so to speak, *seven mysterious things.*

ななまがり【七曲がり】 ¶ ～の道 a *tortuous* way.

ななめ【斜め】¶ この塔は～に傾いている This tower *is slanting.* 板を～に切る cut a plank *diagonally.* 太陽の光が～に室内にさしこんだ The sunlight *slanted* into the room. 彼はごきげん～だ He *is out of humor.* / He *is in a bad temper.*

なに【何】 **1** 〖感嘆詞〗 ¶ ～, かまいませんよ *Well,* that's all right. / *Why,* never mind.
～, 砂糖なしだって *What,* no sugar?
2 〖疑問〗 ¶ 彼のおとうさんは～をしている方ですか *What* is his father's occupation? / *What* is his father?
それは～かしら I wonder *what* it is.
～が起きたのですか *What* happened? / Tell me *what* happened.
3 〖慣用的表現〗 ¶ ～はさておき first of all; above all; before everything 〔else〕.
～はともあれ at all events; in any case; at any rate.
～を隠そう to be frank with you; to tell the truth.
～をするにも全力を尽くしなさい Do your best *whatever* you do.

なにか【何か】 **1** 〖肯定〗 some; something.
¶ ～召し上がりませんか Won't you have *something* to eat? / May I offer you *some* refreshments?
この電燈には～ぐあいの悪いところがある There is *something* the matter with this electric light.
シャベルか～貸してください Lend me a shovel *or something.*
～わけがあって彼女は夫と別れた She was separated from her husband for *some* reason.
あの人は～しら虫が好かない I don't like him, *somehow.*
～しら胸騒ぎがする *I don't know why,* but I feel uneasy.
2 〖否定·疑問〗 any; anything. ¶ (店員が客に向って) ～ご用ですか *What* can I do for you? / May (≒ Can) I help you?
～困ったことがあるのですか What is your trouble?
～読むものがありますか, なんでもかまいませんが Do you have *anything* to read? I don't mind what it is.

なにが【何が】 ¶ ～まじめなものか, あの男が How can he be a serious man? 彼はあんなこと言うけれど～忙しいもんか He is not busy at all, contrary to his words. ～なんだかさっぱりわからない I can't make out *what it is.* / I don't know *what's what.*

なにがし【某】¶ 山田～という人 *a certain man* named Yamada. ～かの金をつごうしてもらいたい Spare me *some* money. なんの～といわれるようになりたい I will be *somebody* in the future.

なにかと【何彼と】¶ ～忙しそうだ He seems to be busy *with one thing or another.* ～あの人には世話になっている I owe him *a great deal.* 彼は～親切にしてくれる He is kind to me *in various ways.* これをもっていると～都合がよい It is convenient to me *in various aspects* to have this with me.

なにくそ【何糞】 ¶ ～, 負けるものか *Damn it!* Let's see which of us is the stronger! ～, これしきのことに *Damn it!* This is not too much trouble to me.

なにくれ【何呉】 ¶ 彼は～とめんどうをみてくれた He looked after me 〔*in*〕 *every way.* 彼女はそばで～となく世話をしてくれた She took care of me *about everything.*

なにくわぬかお【何食わぬ顔】¶ 彼は～をしている He *looks innocent.* 彼は～をして私と話していた He was talking with me *as if nothing had happened.* 彼は～でいつものように勤めに出ていた He was working as usual, *pretending ignorance.*

なにげな·い【何気ない】casual; unconcerned. ¶ 彼は～いようすだった He *looked unconcerned.* 彼は～いふりをした He pretended *as if nothing had happened.* 彼は～いようすでたばこを吸った He smoked a cigarette in a *casual* manner.

なにげなく【何気無く】innocently; casually. ¶ ～彼に尋ねてみた I asked him *with an unconcerned air* (≒ *in a casual sort of way*). 彼が～言ったことばには味わうべきものが多い Many of his *casual* remarks are significant.

なにごころなく【何心なく】¶ ～彼にしゃべってしまった I *carelessly* talked to him about it. ～きみのいったことが社会問題にまで発展した Your *casual* remark developed into a social problem.

なにごと【何事】¶ ～ですか *What* is the matter? / *What* happened? ～が起こっても驚かないでください Don't be surprised *whatever* may happen. 彼は～にも熱心だ He is enthusiastic *in doing anything* (≒ *in everything*). 忘れたとは～か *What a shame* that you should have forgotten it! ～もなく月日がたった Time passed *quietly* (≒ *uneventfully*). / The days passed without *any incident* (≒ *a hitch*).

なにしおう【名にし負う】¶ ～美景 a beautiful scene *worthy of its name.* ここが～松島だ This is the *well-known* Matsushima.

なにしろ【何しろ】anyway; after all. ¶ ～今は非常時ですから This is an emergency, *you know.* ～彼らには食べ物がないのだ *At all events* (≒ *In any case*) they have nothing to eat. ～相手は名人だからとてもだめだ *Since* he is a master hand, I am no match for him.

なにせ【何せ】¶ ～彼は傑物 He is a great man *after all* (≒ *in any way*).

なにとぞ【何卒】¶ ～結果をご一報ください *Please* tell me about the result.

なになに【何何】¶ ～が必要か教えてください Tell me *what and what* are necessary.

なになに【何何】What? What's the matter 〔with you〕?

なにびと【何人】¶ それは～もわかっている *Everybody* is aware of it. ～もこの中には入れない *Nobody* is allowed to enter here. それをやった人は～といえども許さない *Anyone* who has done it is guilty.

なにひとつ【何一つ】¶ ～残っていない There is *nothing* left. きみは～やってくれないね You *don't* help me *at all*, do you?

なにぶん【何分】¶ ～よろしく I leave it to your discretion. ～のご寄付をお願いいたします Won't you donate some money? いずれ～のさたがあるはずだ You are to get an answer *one way or other* soon.

なにも【何も】¶ ～おかしいことはない There is *nothing* strange. 空腹も～忘れて仕事に没頭した I was absorbed in my work, forgetful of hunger and *any other thing.*

なにもかも【何もかも】¶ ～うまくいった *Everything* went well with me. ～終わった *All* is over. ～しゃべってしまった I have told you *all* I had to say.

なにもの【何者】¶ あの男はいったい～なのだ *Who* in the world is he? この部屋に～かが忍び込んだ *Someone* stole into this room. ～の仕業かわからない There is no telling *who* did it. その人は彼の父親以外の～でもなかった The gentleman was none other than his own father.

なにやかや【何や彼や】¶ ～と忙しい I am busy with *one thing or another.* ～することが残っている *All sorts of things* are yet to be done. 交通費や～で月５万はいる I need 50,000 yen a month for transportation *and what not.*

なにやら【何やら】¶ 昨晩～変な音がした I heard *some* strange sound last night.

なにより【何より】¶ 私はビフテキが～好きだ I like beefsteak *better than anything else.* 健康がまず～だ Health *is everything.* 無事で帰られた由～です *I'm very happy to learn* that you returned safe and sound. 寒いときには暖かい食物が～のごちそうだ Something hot is *the best* treat in cold weather. ～もまずその朝寝の癖を直さなければならない You must correct that habit of getting up late *before everything else.*

なぬし【名主】a village headman.

なのか【七日】the seventh day 〔of the month〕.

なのり【名乗り】¶ 彼は市長選挙に～をあげた He *announced* his candidacy for the mayoral election.

なの·る【名乗る】¶ 私たちはお互いに～り合った We *introduced ourselves to* each other. スミスと～る人があなたに会いたいと言っています A person *by the name* of Smith (≒ A person *named* Smith) wants to see you. 犯人は警察に～って出た The criminal *surrendered himself to* the police. 彼はその委員会の一員だと～った He *declared himself* to be a member of the committee.

なばかり【名ばかり】¶ 彼は社長とは～でまったく力がない He is only the *nominal* president of the company with no influence at all. 春とは～の寒さだ It is still too cold for (≒ to be) spring. / It's still so cold that spring belies its name. (文語的).

なびか·す【靡かす】¶ 権力で彼をどうにか～せた They managed to *win* him *over* by force. 彼はなんとしても彼女を～せようと思った He thought he would do everything to *win her love* (≒ *heart*). 騎兵隊は旗を風に～せて走り去った The cavalry rode away with their flag *streaming* in the wind.

なび·く【靡く】¶ アシが風に～いている The reed *is bending* (≒ *is swaying*) before the wind. 多くの者が彼の金力に～いた A lot of people *bowed to* his money.

ナプキン a table napkin.

なふだ【名札】(表札) a doorplate ; a name-plate ; (名刺) a [name] card ; (席の) a place card ; (荷物の) a tag.

ナフタリン〘化学〙naphthaline.

なぶりごろし【嬲り殺し】¶ かわいそうに男は～にされた They *tortured* the poor man *to death*. / The poor man *was battered to death.* / (ずたずたに切られたような場合) The poor man *was butchered by inches.*

なぶりもの【嬲り者】¶ 彼は村の～になった He became *a laughing-stock* in the village.

なぶ·る【嬲る】¶ 弱い者を～る *make a fool of* the weak.

なべ【鍋】(深い) a pot ; (浅い) a pan.
—ぶた a pot-lid. —物 a dish served in the pot.

なべかま【鍋釜】kitchen utensils ; pots and pans.

なべぞこ【鍋底】¶ ～景気だ Business (≒ Trade) *is dull* (≒ *is at its nadir*).

なべづる【鍋鶴】〘鳥類〙a white-headed crane.

なべて【並べて】¶ その島の住民は～性質がおとなしい *Speaking generally*, the inhabitants of the island are *all* gentle.

ナポレオン Napoleon Bonaparte.
—戦争 the Napoleonic Wars.

ナポリ Naples. ¶「～を見て死ね」"See Naples and then die." (「日光を見ずして結構というな」).

なま【生】¶ ～のニンジン a *raw* carrot. ～の肉 *raw* meat. ～の果物 *green* fruit. 野菜を～で食べるのは健康によい It is good for the health to eat vegetables *raw* (≒ *uncooked*). あの喫茶店では～の音楽を聞かせる We can listen to *live* music at the tea shop. / They present *live* music at the tea shop. 為政者は国民の～の声を聞くべきだ A statesman should listen to the *candid* voice of the people.
—放送 a live broadcast. —番組 a live program. —フィルム raw film. —クリーム fresh cream. —ゴム crude rubber. —魚 raw fish ; (塩物に対して) fresh fish. —卵 a raw egg. —ビール draught beer ; beer on draught. —水 unboiled water. —野菜 green vegetables. —ワクチン live vaccine. —乾き ¶ 洗たく物が～乾きだ The washing *is half-dry*.

なまあくび【生欠伸】¶ ～をかみころす stifle *one's yawning*.

なまあたたか·い【生暖かい】lukewarm.
¶ ～い風 a *warm* (≒ *tepid*) wind.

なまあたらし·い【生新しい】¶ ～い事件 a *quite recent* incident.

なまいき【生意気】¶ ～な態度 a *saucy* manner. ～ざかりの青年 a puppy. ～なことを言う say *a cheeky thing* ; have a *saucy* tongue. 彼は～にも私に口答えをした He *had the cheek to* talk back to me. / He *was cheeky* (≒ *was saucy* ; *was impudent*) *enough to* talk back to me. ～を言うな None of your cheek (≒ lip ; impudence)! 彼の～な態度にはまったくうんざりだ I'm really disgusted with his *impudence*.

なまえ【名前】a name. ¶ お～は？ May I have your *name*, please? / Your *name*, please. ～は知っているが彼にはまだ会ったことはない I know him *by name*, but I've never seen him yet. 私は～を出したくない I don't want my *name* mentioned.

なまかじり【生噛り】a superficial knowledge. ¶ 電子工学については～程度の知識だ I have only got *a smattering of* electronics. ～の学問をふりまわすのは危険なことだ *A little* learning is a dangerous thing.

なまき【生木】¶ そんな～を裂くようなまねはできない We can't be so cruel as to *force* them *to separate*.

なまきず【生傷】a bruise. ¶ 彼は～が絶えない He has always *a bruise* on his body.

なまぐさ·い【生臭い】¶ 風まで～い戦場 a *bloody* battlefield. きみの体は～い You *smell fishy*.

なまぐさぼうず【生臭坊主】a depraved (≒ corrupt) priest.

なまくら【鈍】(刀) a dull sword.

なまけぐせ【怠け癖】laziness. ¶ 彼は～がついている He has got into *an idle habit*.

なまけもの【怠け者】an idle person ; a sluggard. ¶ ～の節句働き He is a weekend (≒ a Sunday) farmer.

なまけもの【樹懶】〘動物〙a sloth.

なま·ける【怠ける】be lazy ; be idle. ¶ 仕事を～けてはいけない Don't *neglect* your work. 彼らは夏休みじゅう～けて過ごした They spent their whole summer vacation just *idling*.

なまこ【生子·海鼠】〘動物〙a trepang ; a sea cucumber.
—板 corrugated iron.

なまじっか ¶ ～彼を誘わなければよかった I'm sorry I ever asked him to join us. ～の遺産があったばっかりに彼は身を持ち崩してしまった A *small* inherited fortune ruined him.

なまじろ·い【なま白い】pale. ¶ ～い文学青年 an *anemic* literary youth.

なます【膾·鱠】raw fish salad. ¶ あつものに懲りて～を吹く(諺) *A burnt child dreads the fire.*

なまず【鯰】〘魚類〙a catfish.

なまず【癜】〘医学〙a white macula.

なまつば【生唾】¶ ケーキを見ると～が出てきた The cake *made my mouth water*.

なまづめ【生爪】¶ ～をはがす tear off a nail down to the quick.

なまなまし·い【生生しい】¶ ～い記憶 a *fresh* memory. ～い描写 a *vivid* description.

なまにえ【生煮え】¶ この魚は～だ This fish *is half-cooked* (≒ *is not well cooked*).

なまぬる·い【生温い】lukewarm. ¶ 彼に対しそんなやり方では～すぎる That's too *mild* a way of dealing with him. 乱暴な運転手に対する取り締まりはまだ～い We ought to be harder (≒ more strict) on reckless drivers.

なまはんか【生半可】¶ 物事を～にしてはいけない

な

Don't do things *by halves*. / Don't leave things done *half way*. 〜な知識をふりまわす parade *one's smattering* (≒ *superficial*) knowledge.

なまびょうほう【生兵法】 ¶ 〜は大けがのもと(諺) *A little learning is a dangerous thing.*

なまへんじ【生返事】 a vague answer. ¶ 〜ではなく，はっきりした返事が欲しい I'd like to have no *evasive* answer but a definite one.

なまみ【生身】 ¶ そのようなことは〜の人間としてとても耐えられない Such things are more than *flesh and blood* can bear.

なまめかし·い【艶かしい】 ¶ 〜い話 an *amorous* talk. 〜い目つき *coquettish* (≒ *amorous*) eyes. 彼女は〜い She *looks enticing* (≒ *looks seductive*).

なまもの【生物】 uncooked food.

なまやけ【生焼け】 ¶ 〜の肉 *underdone* roast.

なまやさし·い【生易しい】 ¶ 外国語をマスターするのは〜いことではない It's no *easy* task to master a foreign language.

なまり【鉛】 lead. ¶ 〜色の空 a *leaden* (≒ *gloomy*) sky.

な

なまり【訛り】 an accent ; (方言) a dialect.
¶ 彼の英語には外国〜がある He speaks English with *a* foreign *accent*.

なま·る【鈍る】 ¶ 斧が〜ってしまった The ax *has got blunted*. 運動不足で体が〜ってしまった The muscles *have got soft* through lack of exercise.

なま·る【訛る】 ¶ シャボンはサボンが〜った語である "Shabon" is *a corruption* of "savon."

なみ【波】 1 a wave ; (大波) a billow ; (さざなみ) a ripple.
¶ 〜が高い The *waves* are running high. / *The sea* is high.
〜が立つ *The sea* swells.
〜が静まる *The sea* subsides.
〜立つ海 a *chopping* sea.
湖は〜立っていた The lake *was choppy*.
〜が海岸線を洗っていた *Waves* lapped the shoreline.
難破船は〜のまにまに漂った The wrecked ship drifted about at the mercy of the *waves*.
2 〖慣用的表現〗 ¶ 彼は人の〜にまぎれて見えなくなった He disappeared in a crowd of people.
その候補者は人気の〜に乗って最高点で当選した Riding on the *wave* of popularity the candidate was returned to the head of the poll.
あの人は感情に〜がある He is a *capricious* man. / He is a man *of moods*.

なみ【並】 ¶ 彼は〜の人間だ He is an *average* (≒ *ordinary*) man. 私たちはありふれた〜の人間だ We are just *common* people.

なみあし【並み足】 ¶ 〜で行進する march *at a footpace*.

なみい·る【並み居る】 ¶ 彼はそう言いながら，〜る人々を見回した So saying, he looked around at *all present* (≒ *all assembled*).

なみうちぎわ【波打ち際】 a beach.

なみう·つ【波打つ】 ¶ その知らせに彼の胸は激しく〜った His heart *beat* fast at the news.

なみがしら【波頭】 the crest of a wave.
¶ 白い〜 whitecaps ; white horses ; (詩的) the foamy crests.

なみかぜ【波風】 ¶ 彼のところは〜の絶えたことがない His family *is in* constant *discord*. / There are constant *troubles* in his family. 彼は世間の〜にもまれてきた He has come through the worldly *troubles*.

なみき【並木】 a row of trees.
—道 an avenue ; a road lined with trees ; a road bordered by trees ; a tree-lined street.

なみだ【涙】 1 tears. ¶ 彼女はその悪い知らせを聞いて少し〜を流した She shed a few *tears* when she heard the bad news. / Hearing the bad news she *wept* a little.
その悲劇物語は私たちに〜を催させた The tale of tragedy moved us to *tears*.
彼は〜にむせんだ He was choked with *tears*.
彼の目に〜が浮かんだ *Tears* stood in his eyes.
彼の顔は〜にぬれていた His face was wet with *tears*.
目に〜があふれてきた *Tears* welled up in my eyes. / *Tears* welled from my eyes.
2 〖慣用的表現〗 ¶ 聞くも〜語るも〜の物語 We cannot hear nor tell the story with dry eyes.
すずめの〜ほどの退職金をもらった I was given *a pittance* (≒ *a modicum* ; *an atom*) of retirement allowance.
血も〜もない男だ He is a *hard-hearted* (≒ an *unfeeling*) man.
血も〜もある男だ He is a *sympathetic* (≒ *tender-hearted* ; *kind-hearted*) man.

なみたいてい【並大抵】 ¶ 彼を説得して計画をやめさせるのは〜のことではなかった It *was no easy thing* (≒ *task*) to persuade him out of his plan. その仕事は〜のものではない The task is *no easy* one.

なみだぐまし·い【涙ぐましい】 touching ; pathetic ; moving ; affecting. ¶ 〜い別れの場面だった It was a *touching* scene of farewell.

なみだぐ·む【涙ぐむ】 ¶ 彼女は手紙を読んで〜んだ The letter *moved* her *to tears*. / When she read the letter *her eyes dimmed* (≒ *her eyes glistened*) *with tears*. 〜んだ声 a *tearful* voice.

なみだながらに【涙ながらに】 tearfully ; in tears. ¶ 彼女は〜身の上話をしてくれた She told me her story *with tears in her eyes* (≒ *in tears* ; *tearfully*).

なみだもろ·い【涙もろい】 ¶ 彼は〜い He *is easily moved to tears*.

なみなみ【並並】 ¶ 彼の才能は〜ではない His talent *is far from ordinary* (≒ *is far from common*). これは彼の〜ならぬ努力による This is due to his *great* (≒ *unusual*) efforts. 彼は〜ならぬ腕前の職人だ He is an artisan of *exceptional* skill.

なみなみと ¶ コップに水を〜つぐ fill a glass *to the brim* with water.

なみのり【波乗り】surfing ; surf-riding. **—板** a surfboard.

なみはずれた【並外れた】¶ ～大男 an *unusually* big man. ～才能 an *extraordinary* talent. 彼は～才能がある He is an *extraordinarily* talented man. 彼にはどこか～ところがあった There was something *out of* 〔*the*〕 *common* (≒ *uncommon* ; *extraordinary*) about him.

なみひととおり【並み一通り】¶ ～の努力では勝てない We can't win by an *ordinary* effort.

なみま【波間】¶ 舟が～に漂う A boat is tossed about *in the waves.* / A boat is dancing *on the waves.*

なみよけ【波除け】(防波堤) a breakwater ; (船の) bulwarks.

なむあみだぶつ【南無阿弥陀仏】Lord have mercy upon me.

なめくじ【蛞蝓】〘動物〙a slug.

なめこ【滑子】〘植物〙a kind of mushroom.

なめしがわ【なめし皮・鞣し革】tanned leather.

なめ·す【鞣す】¶ 皮を～す *tan* hides.

なめらか【滑らか】¶ ～な海面 a *calm* sea. 板を～にする *smooth* a board. 彼は～な口調で話した He spoke *fluently*. 彼女はくしゃくしゃのハンカチをアイロンで～にした She *smoothed* the wrinkled handkerchief with an iron.

な·める【嘗める・舐める】¶ ネコはたちまちミルクをすっかり～めてしまった The cat quickly *lapped* up all her milk. はちみつを～めてみた I *tasted* the honey. 彼は世の中の辛酸を～めてきた He *has tasted* the sweet and bitter of life. / He *has gone through* the hardships of life. 火事は町の大半を～めつくした The fire *burned out* most of the city. ひとを～めるな Don't *despise* me so.

なや【納屋】a barn ; a shed.

なやまし·い【悩ましい】¶ 香水の薫りが～い The perfume smells *seductive*.

なやま·す【悩ます】¶ 今はつまらぬ不平を言って彼を～すな Don't *trouble* him with petty complaints now. 彼女はリューマチにひどく～されている Her rheumatism *troubles* her greatly. / She *is suffering from* bad rheumatism. 物価高に～されている We *are suffering from* high prices. / We *are troubled by* the rise in prices. 昨夜は一晩じゅう蚊に～された Mosquitoes kept *annoying* me all last night. 彼は将来の問題に～されている The question of his future *plagues* (≒ *troubles* ; *torments*) him. 公害問題の解決に頭を～した We *puzzled* (≒ *beat* ; *cudgeled* ; *racked*) *our brains* for a solution of environmental pollution.

なやみ【悩み】a distress; an agony ; trouble ; a worry ; a pain. ¶ 心の～ *anguish* of heart. 生活の～ *troubles* of life. 家庭の～ household *worries*. きみの～はなにか What is your *worry* (≒ *trouble*)? / What *is troubling* you? / What *are* you *worried about?* この子が～の種だ This child is *a distress* (≒ *a cause of trouble*) to me. その秘密が彼女の心の～になっていた The secret weighed heavily on her mind.

なや·む【悩む】¶ 彼はひとり暮らしの寂しさと不自由さに～んでいる He *is troubled with* the loneliness and inconvenience of living alone. われわれは住宅不足に～んでいる We *suffer from* the shortage of houses. 彼は恋に～んでいる He *is lovesick*. 中小企業では人手不足に～んでいる In medium or minor industry they *are suffering from* a lack of hands. 彼は近所の騒音に～んでいる He *is annoyed* (≒ *is disturbed*) *by* the noise in his neighborhood.

なよなよ【弱弱】¶ 彼女は見かけは～している She looks *slender* (≒ *feeble*).

なら【楢】〘植物〙a Japanese oak.

-なら ¶ もしお暇～うちへいらしてください *If* you have time to spare, please come to see me. 私～そんな申し出は断わる *If* I were you, I would decline such an offer. 給料がよい～その口を引き受けましょう I will accept the position *on condition that* I am well paid. 労働問題～彼がいちばん詳しい *As for* labor problems, he has the best knowledge.

ならい【習い】a custom ; a habit. ¶ それが世の～だ That is *the way* of the world. ～性となる(諺) *Habit is* 〔*a*〕 *second nature*.

なら·う【習う】learn. ¶ ぼくは8歳のときチェスのやり方を～った I *learned* to play chess when I was eight. 学生のときこの詩をA先生に～った I *was taught* this poem by Mr. A in school. フランス語を～いたい I should like to *learn* French. 彼女はピアノを～っている She *takes* piano *lessons*. その子は自転車を～った He *learned to* ride (≒ *learned how to* ride) a bicycle. ～うより慣れろ(諺) *Practice makes perfect*. / Custom makes all things easy.

なら·う【倣う】¶ 父に～って早起きをしている *Following* my father's custom I get up early. なんでも彼に～ってする I do everything that he does. / I do everything *as he has done*. 先例に～う *follow* the precedent.

ならく【奈落】(芝居の) a trap cellar ; (地獄) hell. ¶ ～の底に落ち込む fall into the *abyss* (≒ *bottomless pit*).

なら·す【鳴らす】¶ ベルを～す *ring* a bell. 指を～す snap *one's* fingers ; (指の関節を) crack *one's* finger joints. ゴングを～す *clang* a gong. 彼はポケットの中で硬貨をチャリンチャリン～した He *jingled* the coins in his pocket. 犬は散歩に行きたくて鼻を～している The dog *is whining* to be taken out for a walk. 彼はいつも食べ物のことで不平を～す He usually *complains* about the food. 彼は若いとき野球選手として～したものだ He was a famous baseball player when he was young. あの人は昔は～したものだ He has seen better days. 人の非を～すのはやさしい It is easy to *censure* others.

なら·す【慣らす】¶ 今の仕事に体を～しなさい *Accustom yourself to* (≒ Try to *get used to*) the present job. 映画を見て耳を～したい I want to *train* the ear by seeing movies. 体を寒さに～せられなかった I couldn't *accustom myself to* the cold.

な

なら·す【均す】¶～して月５万円の収入になる I get fifty thousand yen a month *on an average.*

なら·す【馴らす】¶ライオンを人に～す *tame* lions. 芸をするように犬を～す *train* a dog to do tricks.

ならずもの【ならず者】a rogue; a rascal.

-ならでは ¶この案は彼～の思いつきだ *Only* he is capable of thinking of this plan. きみ～できない仕事だ *Only* you could do it.

-ならない ¶男女は互いに協力しなければ～ Man and woman *should* cooperate with each other. 友だちを見送りに空港へ行かなければ～ I *must* go to the airport to see my friend off. ズボンにアイロンをかけなければ～ The trousers *need* ironing. 彼のわがままにはがまんが～ I *cannot* put up with his selfishness. カンニングをしては～ You *must not* (≒ *should not; ought not to*) cheat in the examination.

ならび【並び】¶川に沿ってひと～の木が生えている There is *a row of* trees along the river. その家はこの～にある The house stands *on this side.* 彼女はこの町では～ない美人だ She is the most beautiful woman in this city. A氏はB氏と～称せられる絵の大家だ Mr. A *ranks with* Mr. B as a great artist.

ならびに【並びに】both; and. ¶氏名，年齢，～職業 name, age *and* occupation.

なら·ぶ【並ぶ】¶映画館の入り口に大ぜいの人が～んでいた A lot of people *were lining* (≒ *were queuing*) *up* at the entrance of the movie theater. / A great number of people *were standing in* (≒ *were forming*) *a line* at the entrance of the movie house. 彼らはふたり～んで歩いた They walked *side by side* (≒ *two abreast*). 彼は教室で彼女と～んでいる He *sits next to* her in class. 大ぜいの人々がマラソン競走を見ようと歩道に～んだ Crowds of people *lined* the curb to see the marathon race. 通りには桜の木が～んでいる The street *is lined with* (≒ *is bordered by*) cherry trees. 仕事熱心にかけては彼に～ぶ者はいない No one can *rival* him in working hard.

ならべた·てる【並べ立てる】¶彼は彼女の長所を～てた He *gave a list of* her virtues.

なら·べる【並べる】(配列する) arrange; place (*things*) in a row; (陳列する) display; exhibit; lay out; (列挙する) enumerate; marshal (facts); (比較する) compare (*with*).
¶店頭に人目を引くような物を～べている They *display* attractive goods in the window. いすを１列に10個ずつ～べる *arrange* chairs ten in every row. 彼女は食事のために銀の食器を食卓に～べた She *placed* the silverware on the table for dinner. きみの計画の不備な点をいくつか～べてみよう Let me *enumerate* several flaws in your plan.

ならわし【習わし】a practice; a custom. ¶これがこの地方の～だ This is the *way* (≒ *custom*) in this part of the country. これはここでは昔からの～だ This is *an* old *practice* (≒ *custom*) here.

なり【鳴り】¶彼はこのごろ～をひそめている He *is not doing much* these days.

なり【形·態】size; personal appearance; dress. ¶彼は～は大きいが10歳だ He is big but only ten years old.

-なり ¶彼は部屋に入る～倒れた *As soon as* he entered the room, he fell down. ジュース～牛乳～好きなものを飲みなさい Drink whichever you like, milk *or* fruit juice. 私に～相談したらよかったのに You should have consulted somebody, —me, *for instance.* 子ども～に行儀よくした He behaved well *for* a child. 人にはその人～の考えがある Each man has his own way of thinking.

なりあがりもの【成り上がり者】an upstart.

なりあが·る【成り上がる】¶彼は労働者から社長に～った He *rose* from a worker *to* the president of a company.

なりかわ·る【成り代わる】¶父に～って一言申し上げます Let me say a word *for* (≒ *on behalf of*) my father.

なりき·る【成り切る】¶彼は役の人物に～っていた He believed (≒ was convinced) he was the very character he played.

なりきん【成金】a new rich. ¶戦争で彼は～になった He *profiteered* from the war. / War made him *a rich man.*
土地— a land profiteer; a landmade millionaire.

なりさが·る【成り下がる】¶彼はこじきまで～った He *was reduced to* begging. 人から借金をするとは彼も～ったものだ He *has fallen* so *low* that he is forced to borrow money from others.

なりすま·す【成り済ます】¶画家に～す *pose as* an artist.

なりそこ·ねる【成り損ねる】¶金持ちに～ねた I *missed becoming* a rich man.

なりたち【成り立ち】(歴史) a history; (由来) an origin; (構造) construction. ¶会社の～ *the organization* of a company. そのことの～を話すつもりです I'm going to talk about *the history* of the matter.

なりた·つ【成り立つ】¶きみの言い分は～たない Your claim does not *hold good.* 探検隊は10人のメンバーで～っている The expedition *consists of* ten members. 契約が～たなかった We couldn't *conclude* a contract. 私の会社はあなたの援助なしには～たない My company can't *exist* without your assistance.

なりたて【為りたて】¶彼は先生に～だ He has just become a teacher.

なりて【為り手】¶悪役に～がない There is no one to act the villain.

-なりと ¶なん～召し上がれ Please help yourself to *anything* you like. １時間～むだに使うな Don't waste *even* an hour. どこへ～消えうせろ Go away *anywhere* you want to.

なりは·てる【成り果てる】¶彼はどろぼうに～てた He *was reduced to* stealing.

なりひび·く【鳴り響く】¶彼の名は国じゅうに～いた His fame *resounded* (≒ *rang*) throughout the country. サイレンが真夜中に～いた A siren *went off* at midnight.

なりふり【形振り】¶ 彼は～かまわない He is careless about his *appearance* (≒ *dress*). 彼は～かまわず働く He works regardless of his *appearance*.

なりもの【鳴り物】¶ ～入りで宣伝する make an *elaborate* advertising campaign.

なりゆき【成り行き】¶ 自然の～に任せなさい Let things take their natural *course*. しばらく事の～を見守っていたい I want to watch *the course of events* for a time. ～しだいで計画を変える I'll change the plan according to *the development* of the situation.

なりわい【生業】an occupation.

な·る【成る·為る】**1**〖要素として持つ〗¶ 日本は主として四つの島から～っている Japan *consists* primarily *of* four islands.
水は水素と酸素から～る Water *consists of* hydrogen and oxygen. / Hydrogen and oxygen *make* water.
取締役会は12人のメンバーから～っている The board of directors *is composed of* twelve members.
この本は50枚の写真とその説明とから～っている This book *is made up of* fifty pictures and their descriptions.
2〖希望がかなう〗¶ 宿願の全国野球の優勝がついに～った Our long-cherished desire of winning the All Japan Baseball Championship *has* finally *materialized* (≒ *has been* finally *attained*).
3〖将棋で資格が変わる〗¶ 歩が金に～った A *fu* (≒ A pawn) *has been promoted* to a *kin* (≒ a bishop).
4〖…の状態·身分などに変わる〗¶ 金持ちに～りたいなあ How I'd like to *be* wealthy!
ああいう女性はいい細君に～るものだ A woman like her will *make* a good housewife.
早いもので私の娘も，もう３人の子の母親に～っている Time does fly. My daughter *is* now the mother of three children.
両親はぼくが医者に～ることを願っている My parents want me to *become* a medical doctor.
彼も偉く～ったものだ(出世した) He *has become* a very great man, indeed!
5〖変化して…になる〗¶ 水が氷に～った The water has frozen.
氷がとけて水に～った The ice has melted.
風邪から肺炎に～った My cold *developed into* pneumonia.
おたまじゃくしがみんなカエルに～った All the tadpoles *transformed* (≒ *metamorphosed*) *into* frogs.
彼女に対する同情がいつか愛情に～っていた My sympathy for her *turned into* love before I knew it.
知らせを聞いて彼は青く～った He *turned* pale at the news.
彼女はひとり息子を心配するあまり気が変に～った Her excessive worry about her only son has driven her mad.
肉を冷蔵庫に入れておかないと悪く～る Put the meat in the refrigerator, or it will *go* bad.
6〖時間·天候·季節·年齢などが〗¶ もうそろそろ５時に～る It will soon *be* five o'clock.
暗く～るまえに帰りなさい Go home before it *gets* dark.
９月の末になると，だいぶ涼しく～る It *gets* quite cool toward the end of September.
日ごとに寒く～ってきた It *is getting* colder and colder.
7〖数量が〗¶ ５たす３は８に～る Five and three *makes* (≒ *make*) eight.
５に５を掛けるといくらに～りますか How much *is* five times five?
代金は全部でいくらに～りますか How much does all that *come to*?
合計で３万円以上に～る It *totals* more than thirty thousand yen. / It *comes to* more than thirty thousand yen.
これで参加者は15名に～る This *makes* fifteen attendants.
8〖…しはじめる〗¶ ぼくは18のときから酒を飲むように～った I *began to* drink when I was eighteen 〔years old〕.
きみはいつからたばこを吸うように～りましたか When did you *start* smoking?
昼ごろから雪に～った It *began to* snow around noon.
9〖結果が〗¶ 労働条件は組合の要求どおりに～った The workmen's terms *have been met* (≒ *have been agreed to*) as demanded by the labor union.
その事件で彼の処分はどう～りましたか What *is* his punishment for the accident? / What punishment has been decided on for his part in the accident?
10〖役にたつ〗¶ あの失敗が彼には薬に～るだろう His failure will *be* a lesson to him. / He will learn a lesson from his failure.
酒は適量に飲めば薬に～る A moderate amount of drink *is* good for one.
この箱は机代わりに～るだろう This box will *serve as* (≒ *serve for*) a desk.
11〖妥当である〗¶ 彼のすることは～っていない What that fellow does *is improper* (≒ *is ridiculous*).
この成績はなんだ. まるで～ってない Look at your grades. Can't you do any better?

な·る【鳴る】**1**〖音〗sound; ring. ¶ 夜の10時におやすみのチャイムが～る The chime *sounds* good night at ten.
昨夜は雷がひどく～った It *thundered* hard last night. / The thunder *rolled* (≒ *roared*) last night.
遠くで太鼓が～っている A drum *is rolling* in the distance.
電話が～っている The telephone 〔bell〕 *is ringing*.
６時が～るとすぐ起きた On the stroke of six, I got up. / As soon as *it struck* six, I rose from my bed.
耳が～る My ears *ring* (≒ *are ringing*). / I *have a ringing* in my ears.

2 〖その他〗 ¶ 腕が～る I *am itching* (≒ *am burning*) *to* try my hand. / I *am burning* with *the desire to* do it.

な・る【生る】¶ このカキの木にはたくさん実が～る This persimmon tree *bears* a lot of fruit. ナシが鈴なりに～っている The tree *is covered* (≒ *is laden*) *with* pears.

なるこ【鳴子】a 〔bird〕 clapper.

なるたけ【成る丈】¶ ～早く来てください Please come *as* soon *as possible* (≒ *as* soon *as you can*).

なるべく【成る可く】¶ ～なら家にいたい I'd like to stay home *if permitted* (≒ *if possible*). ～早く寝なさい Go to bed *as* soon *as possible.* / You should go to bed at once.

なるほど【成る程】really ; indeed. ¶ ～すばらしい景色だ *Indeed,* a very beautiful view. ～, ～ Well, well. 彼の話を聞くと～と思う His story is convincing.

なれ【慣れ】¶ だれにも～がたいせつだ *Practice* is important for everybody.

なれあい【馴れ合い】conspiracy ; collusion. ¶ ～の試合 a *fixed* (≒ *put-up*) game. 彼らは～で人をだます They *work in collusion to* cheat others.

なれそめ【馴れ初め】¶ あなた方の～を聞かせてください Please tell me about *the beginning* of your love.

なれっこ【慣れっこ】¶ 満員電車には～になっている We *are accustomed to* crowded trains.

なれなれし・い【馴れ馴れしい】familiar. ¶ ～い態度をとるな Don't take too much for granted. / Don't take liberties with me.

なれのはて【なれの果て】¶ 彼は大金持ちの～だ He is a *ruined* millionaire. / He is *what's left of* a millionaire.

な・れる【慣れる】¶ 彼は重い荷物を持って歩くのに～れている He *is used to* carry*ing* heavy baggage with him. たいていの日本人はテーブルといすのある生活にすっかり～れてしまった Most of the Japanese *have become* quite *accustomed to* living with tables and chairs. 新しい職場に早く～れるようにしなさい You must try to *accustom yourself to* your new post. 新しい仕事に～れるのに２か月かかった It took me two months to *adjust myself to* my new work. 新しい環境にも～れた I *have acclimated* (≒ *have acclimatized*) *myself to* the new surroundings. 彼はまだその仕事には～れていない He *is* still *green at* the work. / He *is inexperienced in* the work. 習うより～れろ(諺) *Practice makes perfect.*

な・れる【馴れる】¶ その動物はよく～れやすい That animal *gets tame* easily. よく～れたクマですね You have a *tame* bear. 彼らは先生に～れてきた They *have got used to* their teacher.

な・れる【熟れる】¶ くつが足に～れた My feet *got used to* the shoes.

なわ【縄】a rope ; (細い) a cord. ¶ 入り口を～を張ってふさいだ We *roped off* the entrance. / We closed the entrance with *a rope*.

なわしろ【苗代】a bed for riceplants.

なわとび【縄跳び】rope skipping.

なわのれん【縄暖簾】a rope curtain ; (居酒屋) a tavern ; (飯屋) a chophouse.

なわばしご【縄梯子】a rope ladder.

なわばり【縄張り】¶ 土地の境目に～をした We *roped off* our land. ここは私の～だ This place is *my stamping ground.* / This place is *within my beat.* 人の～を荒らす tresspass upon *a person's territory*.

—争い ¶ それは彼らの～争いにすぎない It is nothing but a quarrel over their *sphere of interest.* 困ったことは官庁の～争いだ The trouble is *a dispute over the area of jurisdiction* 〔*of sectionalism*〕.

なわめ【縄目】¶ ～の恥を受ける be arrested ; be nabbed.

なん【難】¶ 彼は平然として～に当たる強い男だ He has the nerve to face *a difficulty*. 辛うじて～を免れた I just managed to escape *danger*. / I escaped narrowly. 強いて～をいえば彼女はちょっと恥ずかしがり屋だ *The only fault with* her is that she is a little bit too shy. 彼には～のつけどころがない He is free from *faults*. 彼は軽率だとの～を免れない He is open to the *charge* of rashness. 一～去ってまた一～ Out of the frying pan into the fire.

住宅**—** housing shortage. 食糧**—** food shortage. 生活**—** difficulty of living.

なん-【何-】¶ ～千万もの星 〔*tens of*〕 *millions of* stars. ～百万の軍人 *millions of* soldiers. ～万の人 〔*tens of*〕 *thousands of* people. ～千もの学生 *thousands of* students. ～十日 *dozens* (≒ *scores*) *of* days.

なんア【南ア】South Africa.

—連邦 the Union of South Africa.

なんい【南緯】the south latitude. ¶ その島は～40度20分に位置する The island is situated in lat. 40° 20′ S. (読み方は latitude 40 degrees 20 minutes south).

なんい【難易】¶ 報酬は仕事の～による The remuneration is according to the *difficulty* of the job. / The pay varies with the *relative difficulty* of the work. 事の～は問わない I don't care how *hard* the work *is*.

なんおう【南欧】Southern Europe.

なんか【南下】¶ ～する go south.

なんか【軟化】softening. ¶ 先方の態度もやや～した Their attitude *has got* a little *softened.* / They *have softened* their attitude a little. 市況はますます～している The market *is* decidedly *weaker*.

脳**—**症 softening of the brain.

なんが【南画】〖美術〗the southern school of Chinese painting.

なんかい【何回】⇒ いくど

なんかい【南海】the southern sea.

なんかい【難解】¶ この短編はなかなか～だ This short story *is* rather *hard to understand.* ここに一つ～な問題がある Here is a *difficult* problem to solve. / Here is *a difficulty.*

なんかん【難関】a difficulty ; a barrier. ¶ ～にぶつかる come to *a deadlock*. ～を切り抜ける

get over *a barrier*. ～突破の道はこれしかない This is the only way to get out of the *difficulty*. この～を越えれば勝利はこちらのものだ Once over these *obstacles*, victory will be ours.

なんぎ【難儀】difficulties ; (めんどう) trouble ; (苦痛) affliction ; suffering. ¶ 彼は金がなくて～している He *is distressed* (≒ *is hard up* ; *is pinched*) for money. / He *is suffering from* poverty. 彼は病気で～している He *is suffering from* illness. 親に～をかけるな Don't *get* your parents *into trouble*. 大雪で歩くのにそれは～だった We *had much trouble in* walking because of the heavy snow.

なんきつ【難詰】¶ その落ち度のために彼は彼女をひどく～した He *blamed* (≒ *censured*) her bitterly for her faults.

なんきゅう【難球】〖野球〗a difficult ball to catch. ¶ 彼はその～を軽くさばいた He handled *the hot shot* with ease.

なんきゅう【軟球】a soft ball.

なんぎょう【難行】¶ 彼は若いころ～苦行を重ねた He *practiced religious austerities* when young. / He *lived a life of penance* when young.

なんきょく【南極】(地球の) the South Pole ; the Antarctic Pole ; (磁石の) the south pole. ―海 the Antarctic Ocean. ―観測 an Antarctic exploration. ―圏 the Antarctic Circle. ―光 aurora australis ; the southern lights. ―星 the south pole star. ―帯 the Antarctic region (≒ zone). ―大陸 the Antarctic Continent.

なんきょく【難局】a crisis ; a difficult situation. ¶ 彼ならよくその～に処しうる He can deal with the *difficult situation* admirably. 政府は今～に立っている The Government is now in *a desperate situation*. ～を収拾する道はそれしかない It is the only way to save the *difficult situation*.

なんきん【軟禁】¶ 彼はどこかに～されている He *is confined informally* 〔in an unidentified place〕.

なんきん【南京】Nanking.
―錠 a padlock. ―豆 a peanut ; 英 a monkey nut. ―虫 a housebug ; 米 a bedbug.

なんく【難句】a difficult phrase (≒ passage).

なんくせ【難癖】¶ 彼はとかく人に～をつけたがる He is ready to *find fault with* others. 彼は私の計画を実行不可能といって～をつけた He *criticized* my plan as unworkable.

なんこう【軟鋼】mild steel.

なんこう【難航】¶ ソ連との交渉は～している *Difficulties are being encountered* in negotiation with USSR. 労使会議は～している The labor-management conference *is having a hard going*.

なんこう【軟膏】a salve ; an ointment ; an unguent.
水銀― a mercurial ointment. ペニシリン― a penicillin ointment.

なんこうがい【軟口蓋】〖解剖学〗the soft palate.

なんこうふらく【難攻不落】¶ ～の城 an *impregnable* fortress.

なんこつ【軟骨】〖解剖学〗a cartilage.
―魚 a cartilaginous fish. ―組織 a cartilage tissue.

なんざん【難産】a difficult delivery ; hard labor. ¶ 彼女は～だった She *had hard labor*./ She *had a difficult delivery*. 法案の成立は～だった The bill was approved *after much difficulty*.

なんじ【何時】¶ 今～ですか *What time* is it now? ～に出発しますか *When* will you start? ～の汽車にしましょうか *What* train shall we take? ～までにお帰りですか By *what time* will you come back? ～に会いに来ると彼女は言っていましたか *What time* did she say she would come to see me? あすは～ごろお見えになりますか *When* shall we expect you here tomorrow?

なんじ【難事】¶ それは～中の～だ It is *the most difficult of all things*. / It is *the hardest thing to do*. どんな～も慣れれば容易になる There is nothing so *hard* but becomes easy by practice.

なんじ【難治】¶ 癌が進むと～だ Advanced cancer *is hard to cure*. / Advanced cancer *is incurable* (≒ *is fatal*).

なんじ【爾・汝】¶ ～殺すなかれ *Thou* shalt not kill. ～自身を知れ Know *thyself*.

なんしき【軟式】―野球 soft-ball 〔baseball〕.
―庭球 soft-ball tennis (外国には soft-ball tennis はない).

なんじぎょう【難事業】a heavy task.

なんじゃく【軟弱】¶ ～な地盤 *soft* ground. ～な外交 *weak-kneed* diplomacy. ～な市況 a *weak* (≒ *bearish*) market. 近ごろ若い男は～に流れているという Recently young men *are growing effeminate*, they say.

なんじゅう【難渋】¶ 団体交渉は～している The collective bargaining *is proceeding with much difficulty*. 豪雨で歩行に～した We *had trouble in* walking because of the heavy rain.

なんしょ【難所】a dangerous place. ¶ 東海道の～ *the perilous passes* on the Tokaido highway.

なんしょく【難色】¶ 野党はみなこの法案に～を示している All the opposition parties *are opposed to* this bill. 彼は提案に～を示した He *showed* (≒ *expressed*) *disapproval of* the proposal.

なんしん【南進】¶ 探険隊は一路～している The expedition party *is marching* straight *southward*.

なんすい【軟水】〖化学〗soft water.
―剤 water softener.

なんせい【南西】the southwest. ¶ ～の風 the southwester.

なんせん【難船】(難破船) a wrecked vessel ; (遭難) shipwreck ; wreck. ¶ 鳥羽丸はインド洋で～した The Tobamaru *was wrecked* (≒ *was shipwrecked*) on the Indian Ocean.

な

—救助 salvage. **—現場** the scene of the wreck. **—信号** a distress signal; an S.O.S.

ナンセンス nonsense. ¶ そいつはまったく〜だ It *is* quite *nonsensical*! / Oh, *nonsense*!

なんだ【何だ】¶ 〜, きみか *What!* Is that you? 先生ぐらい〜 *What do I care if* it is the teacher? 〜ってそんなに遅くなったのか *What in the world* made you so late?

なんだい【難題】¶ 彼はときどき〜をふっかけてくる He sometimes *makes an unreasonable demand of* me. それは〜というものだ That's *asking too much*. / You *demand too much of* me.

なんたいどうぶつ【軟体動物】〘動物〙a mollusc.

なんだか【何だか】¶ なにが〜さっぱりわからない I don't know *what's what*. 今晩は〜寂しい *Somehow* I feel lonely this evening. 〜彼女のようすが変だった She looked *somewhat* unusual. (She was unusual. だけでもよい). 〜疲れた I am *kind* (≒ *sort*) *of* tired. あの男〜変だ There is *something* queer about him. 〜あいつは好きじゃない *I don't know why, but* I don't like him.

なんだかだ【何だかだ】¶ 〜と口実をこしらえて彼は会に出席しなかった *On some pretext or other* he did not come to the meeting. 〜と忙しい I am busy *with one thing and another*.

なんたる【何たる】¶ 〜ことだ *What* a shame! 〜あつかましさ *What* impudence!

なんたん【南端】the southern extremity. ¶ この島は日本の〜だ This island is *the southern extremity* (≒ *southernmost point*) of the Japanese dominion.

なんちゃくりく【軟着陸】〔a〕soft landing.

なんちょう【軟調】¶ 株式市場は〜ぎみだ The stock market *is* rather *weak*.

なんちょう【難聴】**—者** one who is hard of hearing. **—地域**(放送) a blanket area.

-なんて ¶ ぼく〜だめだ No, I'm of no use. あんな人〜問題じゃない I don't care such a man. A〜人知らないよ I don't know anybody called A. そんな話を真に受ける〜おかしいよ It is quite ridiculous to believe such a story.

なんてつ【軟鉄】〘冶金〙wrought iron.

なんでも【何でも】**1** 〘どんなことでも〙¶ きみは〜好きなことをしてよい You may do *anything* (≒ *whatever*) you like.
彼の命令なら〜従う I obey *whatever* orders he gives.
彼は彼女のためなら〜した He did *anything and everything* for her.
〜欠点のないものはない *Everything* has its drawbacks. / There is nothing that hasn't any drawbacks.
光るものが〜金とはかぎらない *All* is not gold that glitters.
彼は〜屋だがすぐれたものはない He is *Jack of all trades*, and master of none.
2 〘たいしたことでない〙¶ 富士山に登ることなんか, 彼女には〜ない It is *nothing* to her to climb Mt. Fuji.
彼は〜ないことを秘密にする He makes *the slightest* thing a mystery.
心配しなくてもいい, そんなことは〜ない Don't worry yourself about it; it is only *a trifle*.
そんな問題は〜ない, だれにだって容易に解ける It's an *easy* problem. Anybody can solve it easily.
3 〘ぜひ〙¶ 〜いいから8時までにここに来てくれ *No matter what*, come here by eight.
〜かでも借金を払わねばならない I must pay the debt *by all means*.
4 〘たぶん〙¶ 〜彼は来月の初めに来るらしい *Perhaps* he will come at the beginning of next month.
〜彼は退学するらしい *I understand* he is going to leave school.

なんてん【南天】〘植物〙a nandin.

なんてん【難点】a fault; a weakness.¶ 彼にはどこにも〜がない He is free from *faults*. 彼のいちばんの〜は約束を守らないということだ *The worst* of him is that he doesn't keep his words.

なんと【何と】**1** 〘感嘆〙¶ 〜美しい花だろう *What* a beautiful flower!
〜ご親切に *How* kind of you!
2 〘疑問・どんな〙¶ 日本語の花にあたる英語は〜いいますか *What* is the English equivalent for the Japanese word, "hana"?
彼らには〜でも好きなことを言わせておけ Let them say *what* (≒ *whatever*) they please.
〜懇願しても彼は私の言うことを聞こうとしなかった He would not listen to me *in spite of* all my pleading.

なんど【何度】⇒ いくど

なんど【納戸】a back room.

なんといっても【何といっても】¶ 〜彼は一流の文学者だ He is a first-class literary man *after all*. 他人が〜私は所信を述べるつもりだ *Whatever* others may say, I will speak my opinion.

なんとう【南東】the southeast. ¶ 〜の風 the southeaster.

なんとか【何とか】¶ 彼は〜言いましたか Did he say *anything*? 〜返事をしなければならない I must give *some* answer. 医者が〜してやらなければ彼は死んでしまうだろう If the doctor does not *do something* for him, he will die. 彼は〜事件が解決したのでとても喜んだ He was very glad when the matter was *somehow* settled. 〜赤字を出さぬようにしている We *managed to* make both ends meet. 彼は〜やっている He is getting along *somehow*. 彼は〜口実をつけて会に出席しない He is not going to attend the meeting *for some reason or other*. 世間の人は〜かんとか言うものだ People will talk. 〜いう方がご不在中に見えた *Mr. so and so* came to see you while you were away.

なんとかして【何とかして】¶ 〜それを取り戻したい I want to get it back *by some means or other*. 〜彼女を説得してほしいのだ I hope you will persuade her *somehow or other* (≒ *by all means*).

なんどき【何時】¶ いつ〜彼が現われるかわからない He is expected *every moment*. / I am afraid he will turn up *at any time*.

なんとしても【何としても】¶ ～やりぬくぞ I will carry it out *at any cost* (≒ *at any risk*; *at any sacrifice*). この仕事は～予定までにやりぬくぞ *I am sure to* finish this business by the expected date.

なんとなく【何と無く】 obscurely; in some way; vaguely. ¶ ～あの人はきらいだ I dislike him *without knowing why*. きょうは～うれしい I have a *vague* feeling of joy today. ～気味が悪い I have an *unaccountable* fear. 彼女には～人をひきつけるところがある There is *something* attractive about her. ～話したことが彼をすっかり怒らせてしまった What I said *unintentionally* made him quite angry.

なんとなれば【何となれば】because; for.

なんとも【何とも】¶ 彼が将来どうなるか～言えない Nobody can tell (≒ God knows) what will become of him in the future.
～返事ができなかった I could make no reply.
彼は自分の難儀を～思わない He *makes nothing of* his troubles.
～お礼の申し上げようもありません I have no words to thank you.
～申しわけありません I do not know how to apologize to you.
～いえぬが戦争が起きるかもしれない A war may break out *for all we know*.
彼女には～いえぬ魅力がある There is an *indefinable* charm about her.
困難に打ち勝つと～言えない喜びを感ずる The pleasure we feel when we have overcome a difficulty *is indescribable*.
痛くも～ない I *don't* feel *any* pain *at all*.
彼がいなくても～ない (寂しくない) I *don't* miss him *at all*.
悪口を言われても彼は～なかった He *was* quite *indifferent to* abuse.
診察してから医者は～ないと言った After examining me, the doctor said that *there was nothing the matter with* me.

なんなく【難なく】 without difficulty. ¶ われわれは～目的を果たした We *had no trouble* (≒ *difficulty*) *in* fulfilling our aim.

なんなら【何なら】¶ ～私から話そう I'm willing to tell him, *if you like*. ～あすまた参ります I'll call on you again tomorrow, *if necessary* (≒ *if you please*). ～二, 三日中にまた来てみてください Please come and see me again in a few days, *if you can*. ～連れていってください Please take me with you, *if possible*.

なんなりと【何なりと】¶ ～望みのものを差し上げる You may have *anything* you want. ご不満の点は～おっしゃってください Please tell me *anything* you have to complain of.

なんなんせい【南南西】the south-south-west.

なんなんとう【南南東】the south-south-east.

なんなんと・する【垂んとする】¶ 彼はもう90歳に～している He *is close* (≒*is hard*) *upon* ninety./ He *is near* ninety. 5万に～する大軍 a large force *close to* fifty thousand.

なんにち【何日】 ¶ 彼はもう～も寝たきりだ He has been lying in bed *for many days*. 会合の約束の日は～でしたか [*On*] *what day* [*of the month*] did we engage to meet? ～でもお待ちします I'll wait *any number of days*.

なんにも【何にも】¶ せっかくの苦労も～ならなかった All our efforts *were of no avail* (≒ *came to nothing*). 彼は～知らない人だ He is an *ignorant* man. / He knows *nothing whatever*.

なんにん【何人】¶ ～この会に出席するだろう *How many people* (≒ *How many persons*; *How many men*) will attend this meeting? ～でもけっこうです *Any number* will do. 敵が～来ようと恐れない No matter *how many* enemies may come, I don't fear to face them.

なんねん【何年】¶ 東京にいらして～になりますか *How many years* (≒ *How long*) have you lived in Tokyo? / *How many years* is it since you settled down in Tokyo? 彼は～生まれですか *What year* was he born in?

なんの【何の】**1** 〖疑問〗 ¶ ～ために外国へ行くのか *What* do you go abroad *for*?
～学科がいちばん好きですか *What* subject do you like best?
～因果でこんなに苦しまなければならないのだろう *What* have I done to deserve such misery?
2 〖否定〗 ¶ 彼は～役にもたたない He is good for nothing.
今更悔やんでも～役にもたたない It is no use crying over spilt milk.
～おかまいもしませんですみませんでした I am sorry I have not been much of a host to you.
3 〖その他〗 ¶ ～ことはない, ばかをみたのは私だ It didn't pay me, after all. / I was nothing but a fool.
～かのと言って彼は私に小づかいをせびる He importunately asks me for more pocket money *on some pretext or other*.

なんぱ【難破】wreck; shipwreck. ¶ 船は暗礁に乗り上げて～した The ship *was wrecked* on a rock.
—船 a wrecked ship.

なんぱ【軟派】(意見・主張) the moderate party; the moderate; (不良) a good-for-nothing.

ナンバー a number. ¶ 自動車の～ the *figure* on a car plate. ノートのページに～を打つ *number* the pages of a notebook; *paginate* (≒*page*) a notebook.

ナンバーワン (口語) number one; No. 1. ¶ 球界の～ *an ace* (≒ *a number one*) baseball player.

ナンバリング a numbering machine.

なんばん【何番】¶ (電話で) ～ですか *Number*, please? きみの成績は～か. 45名中2番だ *How do* you *stand* (≒ *rank*) in your class? I am second in a class of 45. 座席(登録; 受付) 番号は～ですか *What's* your seat (registration; reception) *number*? 右から～めがおとうさんですか *Which one* from the right is your father?

なんぴと【何人】¶ ～もそうすることは許されない *No*

one shall be allowed to do so. 言論の自由は～に対しても保障されなければならない Freedom of speech should be guaranteed to *all* (≒ *anybody*).

なんびょう【難病】a serious disease. ¶ ～を患う suffer from *an incurable disease*. ～と戦う combat *a malignant disease*. ～に打ち勝つ conquer *a deadly disease*.

なんぴょうよう【南氷洋】the Antarctic Ocean.

なんぶ【南部】the southern part; (アメリカの) the South. ¶ ～諸州 (アメリカの) the *Southern* States.

なんぷう【軟風】¶ 湖面をかすめて吹いてくる～を受ける enjoy the *breeze* that sweeps over the lake. ささやくとでも言いたいような～ *a soft breeze* that is little more than a whisper.

なんぶつ【難物】¶ 彼はなかなかの～だ He is *a difficult person* [*to do with*]. 第2問が～だった The second question *was most difficult* for me. 英語が～だ I'*m poor at* English.

なんぶんがく【軟文学】light (≒ amorous) literature.

なんべい【南米】South (≒ Latin) America. ―諸国 South (≒ Latin) American countries. ―大陸 the South American Continent.

なんべん【何遍】¶ ～言ったらわかるのか *How often* do I have to repeat the same thing before you can get it into your head?

なんべん【軟便】〘医学〙a loose bowel (≒ passage).

なんぼ ¶ これは～なんでもひどい仕打ちだ That's *too much*! / That's going *too far*!

なんぽう【南方】the south. ¶ 日本のはるか～に far [down] to the *south* of Japan. ～に行く go *south*.

なんぼく【南北】north and south. ¶ ～に走る run (≒ extend) *north and south*. ―両アメリカ North and South America. ―戦争 (アメリカの) the Civil War.

なんみん【難民】(貧困者) the destitute; (避難民・国外亡命者) refugees; (戦争で居住地を追い出された人々) displaced persons (DP; D.P.).

なんもん【難問】a hard question; a difficult problem. ¶ 数学の～を解く solve *a hard question* in mathematics. 人に～をふっかける put *a hard question* to *a person*. 日本外交の直面する～は山積している There are a lot of *hard problems* confronting Japanese diplomacy.

なんよう【南洋】the South Seas. ―群島 the South Sea Islands.

なんら【何等】¶ ～疑う余地はない There is no doubt *whatever*. ぼくはそんなことには～興味がない I'm not *at all* interested in it. ～かの理由で for *some* reason [*or other*]. ～かの処置をする take *some* action (*against*). ～の理由もなく without *any* reason; for no reason. 彼とは～の関係もない I *have nothing to do with* him.

なんろ【難路】¶ 人生の～ *the thorny path* of life. ～にさしかかる (でこぼこの) come to *a rugged pass*; (急な) come to *a steep pass*.

に

に【二】two; (第2) the second.

に【荷】**1**〘荷物〙a load; (船荷) a cargo; a burden. ¶ 船に～を積む *load* a ship. 馬から～をおろした I *unloaded* the horse. この～を解いてください Would you please *unpack* this?

2〘心の負担〙¶ 彼にはこの仕事は簡単だが, 私には～が重い This work is easy for him, but *is too heavy for* me. 農場での仕事は彼には～が重かった The farm work *was too much for* him. そのニュースで心の～がおりた The news took *a load* off my mind. 彼にはその仕事が～になっているにちがいない The work must be *a load* (≒ *a burden*) for him. 試験が終わって肩の～がおりた思いだった After the examination [was over], I felt as if *a load* had been taken off my shoulder.

ニ〘音楽〙D. ¶ ～長(短)調 *D* major (minor).

-に **1**〘場所・位置〙¶ 私は東京の新宿～住んでいる I live *in* Shinjuku, Tokyo. あすは家～いる予定だ I will be [*at*] home tomorrow. どこのホテル～お泊まりですか What hotel are you staying *at*? 彼女は今パリ～いる She lives (≒ is) *in* Paris now. 荷物を自動車～のせる put a package *in* a car. 教室の後ろ～いないで前へ来なさい Don't stay *at* the back of the room. Come to the front. 彼はクラスのトップ～いる He is *at* the top of his class. ポケット～両手を入れて歩く walk with *one's* hands *in one's* pockets.

2〘方向・目的地〙¶ 彼らは食堂～入っていった They went *into* the dining room. あすロンドン～向かう I am leaving *for* London tomorrow. 夕方東京～着く I will be arriving *in* Tokyo this evening.

そのいす～座ってください Please sit *on* the chair.
それを使ったあとは必ずもとの場所～戻してください Please put it back where it belongs, when you are through with it. (目的語が名詞でも語順は put back the book where... とはしない).

3 〖時〗 ¶ けさは5時～目が覚めた I woke up *at* five 〔o'clock〕 this morning.
私は1960年3月～大学を出た I graduated from college *in* March, 1960.
クラス会(卒業生の)は6月10日の月曜日～開かれる Our class reunion will be held *on* Monday, June 10.

4 〖行き着くところ〗 ¶ 彼は偉大な科学者～なった He became a great scientist. / He has grown *into* a great scientist.
私は医者～なるつもりだ I am planning to become a doctor.
彼女はいい奥さん～なるだろう She will make a good wife.

5 〖動作の目的〗 ¶ たばこを買い～行ってくれないか Will you go and get me a pack (≒ packet) of cigarettes?
プールへ泳ぎ～行こう Let's go swimming *in* the pool. (go to the pool for swimming は避ける).
彼は映画を見～出かけた He's gone *to* the movies.

6 〖よりどころ〗 ¶ けさの新聞～よると, きのうチリで大地震があったそうだ It is reported *in* the paper this morning that a strong earthquake shook Chile yesterday.
時計をラジオの時報～合わせた I set (≒ synchronized) my watch *by* the radio time signal.
この辞書～よって調べてみよう I will look it up *in* this dictionary. / I will consult this dictionary.

7 〖相手方・動作主〗 ¶ きのう彼女～会った I saw her yesterday.
その子ども～おもしろい話をしてやった I told an interesting story *to* the child.
彼女は赤ちゃん～ミルクを飲ませている She is feeding her baby.
彼～紹介してくれませんか Will you please introduce me *to* him?
小鳥～えさをやることを忘れないでください Remember to feed the bird.
弟～おもちゃを買ってやった I bought a toy *for* my brother.
私は忙しいからだれか～行かせてください As I am very busy, get somebody else to go there.

8 〖割合〗 ¶ 彼は月～2度は上京する He comes 〔up〕 to Tokyo at least twice *a* (≒ *every*) month.
彼は年～数回大阪へ行く He goes to Osaka a few times *a* year.
この紙をひとり～3枚ずつ配ってください Give them *each* three sheets of this paper.
月～3,000円の小づかいをもらう I get a monthly allowance of three thousand yen.
入学試験は6人～ひとりの競争率だった One *out of* six was successful in the examination.

にあい 【似合い】 ¶ ～の夫婦だ They make *an ideal* (≒ *a well-matched*) couple.

にあ・う 【似合う】 match; become; suit. ¶ その帽子はきみによく～う That hat *becomes* you. このネクタイはその紺色の服には～わない This tie doesn't *match* that dark blue suit. 紫色は彼女に～う Purple *suits* her. 彼女にはこの格好がいちばん～っている She *looks best* in this dress. そんなことをするとは彼に～わない Such conduct does not *become* him.

にあげ 【荷揚げ】 unloading. ¶ 貨物船から～する *unload* cargo from a freighter.
—船 a barge; a lighter. **—場** a landing place. **—料** landing charges (≒ rates).

にあわし・い 【似合わしい】 ¶ 彼は学長に～い人だ He is *an ideal person for* the presidency.

にいんせい 【二院制】 a bicameral (≒ two chamber) system.

にうけにん 【荷受人】 a consignee.

にうごき 【荷動き】〖商業〗 the flow (≒ movement) of goods. ¶ ～が活発だ There is a rapid trade in goods.

にえきらな・い 【煮え切らない】 ¶ ～い男 an *irresolute* (≒ *indecisive*) man. ～い態度をとる take a *lukewarm* (≒ an *irresolute*; a *cool*) attitude (*toward*). ～い返事をする make a *dubious* (≒ *vague*; *evasive*) answer (*to*).

にえ〔くり〕かえ・る 【煮え〔くり〕返る】 ¶ やかんが～っている The kettle *is boiling over*. やかんの湯が～っていた The water in the kettle *was boiling briskly*. ぼくの腹の中は～るようだった My blood *boiled* with indignation.

にえた・つ 【煮え立つ】 ¶ ～った湯 *boiling* water. (boiled water と言えば, いちど煮え立ち, また冷めていてもよい). やかんのお湯が～っている The water in the kettle *is boiling briskly*.

にえゆ 【煮え湯】 boiling water. ¶ ～を通す(ゆがく) scald (*a thing*) with *boiling water*. ～を飲まされる(裏切られる) be betrayed.

に・える 【煮える】 ¶ このジャガイモはよく～えてない These potatoes *are* not *boiled* (≒ *cooked*) enough. この魚はすぐ～える This fish *boils* (≒ *cooks*) easily.

におい 【匂い】 smell; (よい匂い) perfume; scent. ¶ すがすがしい若葉の～ the *fragrance* of fresh green leaves. この花はいい～がある This flower *smells* nice. なんといやな～だ What *a* horrible *smell*! この肉は悪い～がする This meat *stinks* (≒ *smells bad*). この部屋はガスの～がする This room *smells of* gas. なにかが燃える～がする I can *smell* something burning. それはバラの～がする It *smells like* roses. 彼は酒の～がする His breath *smells of* liquor.

におう 【二王・仁王】 the two Deva Kings (英語で説明すれば the two mythological strong kings).
¶ ～立ちになる stand firm on the ground.
—門 the Deva gate.

にお・う 【匂う・臭う】 ¶ ガスが～う I *smell* gas. この肉は～う This meat *stinks* (≒ *smells bad*). 彼女の服はじゃ香が～う Her clothes *smell of* musk. / She *scents* her clothes with musk. ライラックの薫りが辺りに～っていた The scent of lilacs *was drifting* in the neighborhood.

に

におくり【荷送り】consignment.
—人 a consignor.

におわ·す【匂わす】¶ハンカチにオーデコロンを～す *perfume* a handkerchief with eau de Cologne. 彼は前から辞職を～していた(ほのめかしていた) He *had hinted* (≒ *had implied*) that he would resign.

にかい【二回】twice; two times (two times より twice のほうがふつう). ¶１日(週)に～ *twice* (≒ *two times*) a day (a week). 月～の雑誌 a bimonthly; a bimonthly magazine. 年～の雑誌 a *biannually* published magazine. ～の表に(野球) in the first half of *the second inning*.

にかい【二階】米 the second floor; 英 the first floor (イギリスでは1階を the ground floor と言うため). ¶～に上がる go *upstairs*. ～からおりる come *downstairs*. (英語では朝起きてくるという意味もある).
—家 a two-storied (≒ two-story) house; a house of two stories. 中— a mezzanine.

にが·い【苦い】bitter. ¶～い薬 a *bitter* medicine. ～い経験をする have a *bitter* (≒ *hard*) experience. ～い顔をする make a *sour* face; look *sullen*.

にがお【似顔】¶～をかく draw (≒ paint) *a person's likeness* (≒ *semblance*); set down *the facial likeness* of *a person*.

にが·す【逃がす】¶鳥を～してやる *set* a bird *free*. (釣った)魚を～す *lose* a fish; *have* a fish *get away*. 好機会を～す *miss* a good opportunity. どろぼうを～す *let* a thief *escape*; *fail to catch* a thief.

にかた【煮方】¶この魚の～がわからない I don't know *how to cook* this fish.

にがつ【二月】February.

にがて【苦手】¶英語が～だ I *am poor at* (≒ *am weak in*) English./ English is my *weak point*. 泳ぎが～だ I'm a *poor* swimmer. 彼は～だ I *am no match for* him. / He is *an ugly customer for* me *to deal with*.

にがにがし·い【苦苦しい】bitter; disgusting. ¶～い事件 a *disgusting* (≒ *shameful; scandalous*) affair. 人の態度を～く思う *feel unpleasant* about (≒ *be disgusted* with) *a person's* attitude. ～い顔をして with *a displeased look*.

にがみ【苦味】bitterness; a bitter taste.
¶それは～がある It *is bitter*. / It tastes *bitter*. ～ばしったいい男 a *piquantly* handsome man.

にがむし【苦虫】¶彼は～をかみつぶしたような顔をしている He has a〔very〕sour face.

にがり【苦塩·苦汁】bittern; brine.

にがりき·る【苦り切る】¶～って with a sour face. 彼は１万円罰金を払わせられて～っていた He *looked sour* at being fined ten thousand yen.

にかわ【膠】glue. ¶～でつける fasten (*something*) with *glue*. ２枚の板を～でつける *glue* two boards together.

にがわせ【荷為替】¶～を組む draw *a documentary bill*.

にがわらい【苦笑い】a grim (≒ bitter) smile. ¶子どもにやりこめられて～をする *smile bitterly* (≒ *grimly*) after being bettered by a child.

にがん【二眼】¶～レフカメラ a *twin-lens* reflex〔camera〕.

にき【二季】¶～払い *semi-annual* clearance. 総会は春秋～に開かれる The general meeting is〔to be〕held *twice a year*, in spring and fall (≒ autumn). ～咲きのバラ a rose that blooms in two seasons a year.

にき【二期】¶～続けて for *two periods* in succession
—作 rice crop twice a year. —制 two-term system.

にぎてき【二義的】¶～な問題はあとまわしだ *Secondary* problems will be handled later.

にぎにぎし·い【賑賑しい】¶～くご来場くださいましてありがとうございます We'd like to present most cordial thanks for coming to see our play.

にきび【面皰】a pimple. ¶～だらけの顔 a *pimpled* face. 顔に～ができた *Pimples* came out in my face.

にぎやか【賑やか】¶～な笑い声 *merry* laughter. ～な人 a *merry* (≒ *lively; cheerful*) person. ～な所 a *bustling* quarter. ～な通り a *busy* street. この町は夏になると～だ This town becomes a *bustling* (≒ *busy*) quarter in summer. この辺りは最近すっかり～になった This neighborhood has become *prosperous* (≒ *flourishing*) lately.

にぎら·せる【握らせる】¶彼は彼らに金を～せて何も言わないようにさせた He *bribed* them *to* say nothing.

にぎり【握り】(ドアの) a knob; (取っ手) a handle. ¶ひと～の人 *a handful of* men. ひと～の砂 *a handful of* sand.
—ずし hand-rolled *sushi*. —めし a riceball.

にぎりこぶし【握り拳】a clenched fist.

にぎりし·める【握り締める】¶手にしっかり～める tightly *grasp* (*something*) in *one's* hand. 人の手を～める *grasp a person* by the hand.

にぎりつぶ·す【握り潰す】¶手で～す crush (an egg) in *one's* hand. 議案を～す *shelve* a bill; 米 *table* a bill (この句は英では議案を「上程する」の意). 人の計画を～す *abandon consideration* of *a person's* plan.

にぎ·る【握る】hold; grasp. ¶ふたりは互いに手を～った The two *took* each other's hands./ The two *shook* hands. 子どもは５円玉をしっかりと～っていた The boy *was clasping* a five-yen coin in his hand. 彼は彼女の秘密を～っている He *knows* her secret. 彼が政権を～った He *came into power*.

にぎわい【賑わい】(人出) a crowd; (繁盛) prosperity; (雑踏) bustle. ¶大通りはたいへんな～だった The main street *was thickly crowded* (≒ *was thronged; was bustling*) with people.

にぎわ·う【賑わう】¶この通りはどの店も～っている All the stores in this street *are doing well* (≒ *are prosperous; are flourishing*). 動

物園は子ども連れで～う The zoo *is crowded* (≒ *is thronged*) *with* people with their children.

にぎわし・い【賑わしい】¶祭で町が～い The town *is crowded for* the festival.

にぎわ・す【賑わす】¶そのことは最近の新聞紙上を大いに～している The matter *has been played up* (≒ *widely taken up*) in the newspapers lately.

にく【肉】meat; (人間などの) flesh; (鳥の) poultry. ¶私はよく焼いた (生ま焼けの) ～が大好きだ I like my *meat* well done (rare). この～は古いのではなかろうか This *meat* seems to have turned. 彼はよく食べるので～がついてきた He *has put on weight* probably because he eats enormously. (fat は避ける). ～の締まっている人 a *muscular* man. 彼は胸の～が落ちた He has *become thin* around the chest.

—色 flesh color. —切り包丁 a carving knife. —片 a piece of meat.

にく・い【憎い】hateful; spiteful. ¶～いやつ a *detestable* (≒ *hateful*) fellow. ～い仕打ち *spiteful* conduct. 彼が～い I *hate* him.

-にく・い【-難い】¶この文章はわかり～い This sentence *is difficult* (≒ *is hard*) to understand. つきあい～い男 a man *hard* to please. どうも打ち明け～い I find it *hard* to speak out my mind. この万年筆はどうも書き～い I find this pen *hard* to write with. この語の意味がわかり～い I *can hardly* make out this word.

にくが【肉芽】〘医学〙〘植物〙a granulation.

にくからず【憎からず】¶彼は彼女のことを～思っている He *has a fancy for* her. / He *loves* her.

にくがん【肉眼】the naked eye. ¶人工衛星はふつう～では見えない Man-made satellites are usually invisible to *the naked eye*.

にくぎゅう【肉牛】beef cattle.

にくげ【憎げ】¶彼女はときどき～なものの言い方をする She sometimes uses *malicious* language. 彼女はさも～に私をにらみつけた She glared *spitefully* (≒ *hatefully*) at me.

にくさ【憎さ】¶かわいさ余って～百倍 I have come to hate her as much as I loved.

にくしみ【憎しみ】hate; spite. ¶彼は私に対して～をいだいている He bears *hatred toward* (≒ *a grudge against*) me. 彼の死んだ今は，彼に対する～も消えた My *enmity against* him has disappeared now that he is dead.

にくしゅ【肉腫】〘医学〙malignant tumor.

にくしょく【肉食】(食物) animal food; (食事) a meat diet. ¶～する eat meat. 病気のために～を禁じられた I was told to abstain from *meat and flesh* because of illness.

—動物 a carnivorous (≒ flesh-eating) animal.

にくしん【肉親】blood relation. ¶あの人たちは彼の～だ They are his *immediate relatives*. 彼はまぎれもなく私の～です He is no doubt *my own flesh and blood*.

にくせい【肉声】a natural voice. ¶彼女の放送の声と～とではだいぶ違う Her voice on the air sounds quite different from her *natural voice*.

にくたい【肉体】the flesh; the body. ¶～の快楽 pleasures of *the flesh*. ～と精神 *body* and soul.

—美 physical beauty. —美人 a curvaceous beauty. —労働 manual (≒ physical) labor.

にくたらし・い【憎たらしい】¶彼はいつも～い言い方をする He always talks *provokingly*.

にくだん【肉弾】a human bullet.

—戦 a hand-to-hand struggle.

にくづき【肉づき】¶彼は～のよい体をしている He is of *fleshy* (≒ *stout*) build. この牛は～がよい This ox *is well-fed*.

にくづ・く【肉づく】get flesh. ¶彼女は急に～きはじめた She began to *gain* (≒ *put on*) *weight* rapidly.

にくづけ【肉づけ】¶作者は主人公にもう一つ～すべきだ The writer should describe the hero more concretely.

にくにくし・い【憎憎しい】¶彼は～げに私につばを吐きかけた He spat *spitefully* (≒ *maliciously*) at me. 彼は実に～い口をきく He uses quite *malicious* language.

にくはく【肉薄】¶わが軍は敵に～した Our troops *closed in upon* the enemy. / Our troops *pressed* the enemy *hard*. 彼は先頭に～しつつある He *is running* the head *hard* (≒ *close*).

にくひつ【肉筆】an autograph. ¶彼の～の手紙 a letter *in his own handwriting*; his *autograph* letter.

にくぶと【肉太】¶～の活字 a *bold-* (≒ *full-*) faced type. ～に書く write (*one's* name) *thick* (≒ *in bold characters*; *with bold strokes*).

にくまれぐち【憎まれ口】brickbat. ¶そんな～をきくものではありません Don't say such *a spiteful thing*. / Don't use *abusive language*.

にくまれっこ【憎まれっ子】a bad (≒ hated; naughty) child. ¶～世にはばかる (諺) *Ill weeds grow apace*.

にくまれもの【憎まれ者】a hated person. ¶ぼくが～になってやろう I am willing to be *an objective of hatred*.

にくまれやく【憎まれ役】¶彼が～を買って出た He offered to play *an ungracious* (≒ *a thankless*) *part*.

にくま・れる【憎まれる】¶彼は仲間から～れている He *is hated* (≒ *is detested*) by his fellows.

にく・む【憎む】hate. ¶そんなに～み合ってはいけない You must not *be hateful* to each other. 彼らは～みあっている They hate each other. / There is no love lost between them. (後者は慣用的表現). 罪を～んで人を～まず *Condemn* the offense, but pity the offender.

にくめな・い【憎めない】¶～いやつだ He is a man of *lovable* character.

にくや【肉屋】(人) a butcher; (店) a meat (≒ butcher's) store.

にくらし・い【憎らしい】¶～いことを言う say a

に

spiteful thing. 彼は～いほど落ち着いて見えた He looked *provokingly* calm.

にくるい【肉類】 meat.

にぐるま【荷車】 (手車) a cart ; (荷馬車) a wagon. ¶ ～1台分の荷物 *a cartload* of baggage.

ニグロ a Negro (複 Negroes) ; (女) a Negress (a colored lady のほうがよい).

ニクロム 〘化学〙 nichrome.
—線 nichrome wire.

にぐん【二軍】〘野球〙 a farm team. ¶ 彼は〔一軍から〕～にまわされた He was assigned to the *farm team*. / He *was farmed out*.

にげ【逃げ】 escape. ¶ 彼はうそをついて～を打った He tried to *get away from* (≒ *back out of*) it by telling a lie. そんな～をうってもだめだ Such *an excuse* won't do.

にげあし【逃げ足】 flight. ¶ ～の速いやつだ He is quick at *flight*.

にげう·せる【逃げ失せる】 ¶ 彼はとうとう～せてしまった He *fled* (≒ *ran away*) in the end.

にげおお·せる【逃げ果せる】 ¶ そうやすやすと～せられるものではない It is not easy for you to *escape*.

にげおく·れる【逃げ遅れる】 ¶ 彼らは～れて焼死した They *failed to escape* and were burnt to death.

にげかえ·る【逃げ帰る】 run back.

にげかくれ【逃げ隠れ】 ¶ われわれはけっして～しない We are willing to face justice.

にげぐち【逃げ口】 a way of escape.

にげこうじょう【逃げ口上】 an excuse. ¶ 彼の説明は単なる～にすぎなかった His explanation was only *a* mere *evasion* (≒ *excuse*).

にげごし【逃げ腰】 ¶ 彼らは～になった They *were ready to flee* (≒ *were ready to back out; were ready to run away*). ～になってはいけない Don't *take an evasive attitude*.

にげこ·む【逃げ込む】 ¶ 犬にほえられて人の家に～んだ Barked at by a dog, I *ran into* a house *for safety*. わが〔野球〕チームは1点差のまま，とうとう～んだ Our team won the game by a narrow margin of one run.

にげじたく【逃げ仕度】 ¶ 彼は～をしている He *is preparing for flight*.

にげそこ·なう【逃げ損う】 fail to escape.

にげだ·す【逃げ出す】 run away. ¶ あとも見ずに～した We *took to flight* without looking back. ひとりふたりとこそこそ～した They *sneaked* (≒ *slipped*) *away* one after another.

にげの·びる【逃げ延びる】 ¶ 運よく～びる have a lucky escape. かろうじて～びる have a narrow escape.

にげば【逃げ場】 ¶ 火事で～を失い焼け死んだ They *had their escape cut off* in the fire and were burnt to death. / They *were trapped* and were killed in the fire.

にげまど·う【逃げ惑う】 run about trying to escape.

にげまわ·る【逃げ回る】 ¶ さんざん～ったあげく，彼はついに逮捕された After *running from place to place*, he was arrested in the end. 彼は仕事がいやでいつも～っている He *is* always *shirking* work.

にげみず【逃げ水】 a kind of mirage on land; Monge's phenomenon (フランスの数学者 Gaspard Monge (1746–1819) が研究したので，この名がある).
¶ 武蔵野はかつて～で有名であった The Musashi plain was famous for its *mirage*.

にげみち【逃げ道】 a retreat ; a way of escape ; a way out. ¶ 前もって～を考えておくべきだ You should prepare your *escape* (≒ *excuse*) in advance. 万一の失敗に備えて～を作っておくべきだ You should provide for your *retreat* in case of your failure. ほかに～はない There is no other *way of escape*. / There is no other *way out*. 彼らの～を断った We cut off their *retreat*.

に·げる【逃げる】 run away ; escape. ¶ どうして～げたのだ Why did you *run away*? こそこそ～げていくのはだれだ Who *is sneaking away*? かごからオウムが～げた A parrot *flew* from the cage. どこか公害のないところに～げたい I want to *get away to* a place free from pollution. 彼は部屋から～げていちもくさんに走っていった He *escaped* from the room and ran away as fast as possible. またひとり捕虜が～げた A prisoner *has escaped* again. 犯人は捕まるのを恐れて村から～げた The criminal *fled* the village for fear of being arrested. 彼は会社の金を持って～げた He *absconded* with the office money.

にげん【二元】〘哲学〙 duality.
—放送 a simultaneous broadcast from two stations. —論 dualism. —論者 a dualist.

にけんだて【二軒建て】 ¶ ～の家 a *two-family* (≒ *double ; semi-detached*) house.

にこう【二項】 —式(方程式) 〘数学〙 a binomial expression (≒ equation). —定理 〘数学〙 binomial theorem. —分布〘統計〙 binomial distribution.

にごう【二号】 No. 2 ; (めかけ) a mistress. ¶ 雑誌の～を出した We published *the second issue* of the magazine. 彼女はA氏の～になった She became *a kept woman* of Mr. A. 彼は～をかこっている He keeps *a mistress*.

にこごり【煮凝り】 jelly ; congealed food.

にごしらえ【荷拵え】 packing.

にご·す【濁す】 make turbid (≒ muddy) ; muddle. ¶ ことばを～した He *said an ambiguous thing*. 彼はことばを～してはっきり答えなかった He *gave a vague* (≒ *an evasive*) *answer*. この程度のところでお茶を～しておこう Not enough, but thus much should be all right for the moment.

ニコチン 〘化学〙 nicotine.
—酸〘化学〙 nicotinic acid. —中毒 nicotinism ; nicotine poisoning.

にごった【濁った】 ¶ ～水 *muddy* (≒ *turbid*) water. ～空気 *foul* air. ～声 a *thick* voice. ～液体 *cloudy* liquid. ～血 *impure* blood.

にこにこ ¶ 彼はいつも～して話す He always

に

speaks *with a smile*. 彼女は私たちを見て～した She *smiled at* us.

—顔 a smiling (≒ beaming) face.

にこみ【煮込み】 a mixed stew; a kind of hotchpotch (≒ hodgepodge).

にこ·む【煮込む】 boil well; (混ぜて煮る) cook together.

にこやか ¶ 彼は来客を～に迎えた He received his guests *radiantly* (≒ *with a smile*). 彼は～な顔でわれわれにあいさつした He greeted us *with a smile on his face*.

ニコライどう【ニコライ堂】 the Greek Orthodox church.

にごり【濁り】 muddiness. ¶ かなに～を打つ *put a flat mark* (≒ *dot the mark of a voiced sound*) to the *kana* character.

—酒 crude (≒ unrefined) *sake*. —水 muddy water.

にご·る【濁る】 ¶ この川は～っている This river *is muddy*. この音は～っている This is a *flat* sound.

にごん【二言】 ¶ 私には～はない When I say "yes," I mean it.

にざかな【煮魚】 boild (≒ cooked) fish.

にさばき【荷捌き】 disposal of goods ¶ ～はかんばしくない The goods do not sell well.

にさん【二, 三】 ¶ 彼に～質問をしてみた I asked him *a few* questions. 会合には欠席者が～いた There were *a couple of* absentees at the meeting.

—回 two or three (≒ a few) times.

にさんか【二酸化】 —炭素 carbon dioxide. —物 a dioxide. —マンガン manganese dioxide.

にし【西】 the west. ¶ 日は～に沈む The sun sets *in the west*. コロンブスの一行は～へ～へと進んだ Columbus and his men sailed *west* and further *west*. 銀行は駅の～にある The bank stands *west of* the station. 町は名古屋から約50キロ～にある The town lies about fifty kilometers *to the west of* Nagoya. (離れていて距離が示されているときは, to the は省いてよい). 太陽は～に傾いていた The sun was low *in the west*. ポルトガルはヨーロッパの～にある Portugal is *in the west of* Europe. (内部にある場合). オーストリアはハンガリーの～に接している Austria lies *on the west of* Hungary. この家は～に向いている This house faces *west*.

—風 a west wind; (詩語) Zephyr. —半球 the western hemisphere.

にじ【虹】 a rainbow. ¶ ～色の *rainbow*-colored. 空に～がかかった *A rainbow* appeared in the sky.

—ます〘魚類〙a rainbow trout.

にじ【二次】 ¶ ～的な問題 a *secondary* problem.

—会 another party after a party. ¶ ～会をしよう Let's have *another feast* (≒ *spree*) *at another place* —方程式 a quadratic equation.

にしき【錦】 brocade. ¶ 彼は故郷に～を飾った He returned home *as a successful man* (≒ *loaded with honors*; *with flying colors*; *with colors flying*).

—絵 a color print. —へび a python.

にじき【二食】 ¶ きょうは～ですませた I *took only two meals* today. 私は～にしている I usually *eat twice a day*.

-にしては ¶ 年～彼女は若く見える She looks young *for* (≒ *considering*) her age. / She looks younger than she is. / She looks younger than her age. きみ～上出来だ We can expect nothing better of you.

-にしても ¶ それが事実～信じられない *Even if it is true*, (≒ *It may be true, and yet*) I cannot believe it. 問題は解決する～時間はかかろう *Granted* (≒ *Granting*) the matter will be settled, it may take some time. ある～少ない There are only a few, *if any*.

にしドイツ【西ドイツ】 West Germany.

にしはんきゅう【西半球】 the western hemisphere.

にしび【西日】 the westering sun. ¶ この部屋は～がさす This room is exposed to *the afternoon sun*.

にじみ·でる【滲み出る】 ¶ この暑さで額に汗が～出てくる This heat *brings* the sweat on my brow. この作品には彼の悲しみが～出ている His grief *is revealed* in this work. 血が～出る Blood *is oozing*.

にじ·む【滲む】 ¶ 彼は額に汗を～ませて働いた He worked *with a sweating brow*. 洗うと色が～む Colors *run* in washing. この紙はインクが～まない This paper *is never blotted* (≒ *blurred*) *with* ink. 包帯に血が～んでいる The bandage *is red with* blood.

にしめ【煮しめ】 [fish and] vegetables cooked hard with soy.

にし·める【煮しめる】 cook hard. ¶ ～めたような手ぬぐい a *horribly soiled* towel.

にしゃ【二者】 ¶ ～択一 an alternative. ～択一を迫られた I was urged to *choose between the two*.

にしゅ【二種】 ¶ 第～郵便物 *second-class* mail.

にじゅう【二十】 twenty; a score. ¶ ～代の女性 a woman in her twenties. ～年代 the twenties.

—世紀 the 20th century.

にじゅう【二重】 duplication. ¶ この窓は～になっている These windows are *double* ones. この仕事は～の利益がある This sort of job will be of *double* advantage. これは～に包んでください Please wrap this *double*. この金具は～の役をしている These metal fittings serve a *double* purpose. 飲みすぎてものが～に見える I have drunk so much *sake* that I see everything *double*. この表現には～の意味がある This expression has a *double* meaning. 不覚にも～に料金を払ってしまった I made the mistake of paying *twice* the amount of the charge. 戸に～錠をかけた I *double-locked* the door.

—写し a double image. —結婚 bigamy. —国籍 dual nationality. —唱[奏] a duet. —人格 a dual personality. —生活 a

に

double life. —橋(皇居の) the Double Bridge. —窓 a double window.

にじょう【二乗】〖数学〗 a square. ¶ 4の〜は 16 Four *squared* (≒ *multiplied by itself*) is sixteen.

—根 a square root.

にしょくずり【二色刷り】 two-color printing.

にしヨーロッパ【西ヨーロッパ】 Western Europe.

にじりよ・る【躙り寄る】 ¶ 彼らは徐々に私の方に〜ってきた They *edged* (≒ *sidled*) *nearer up to* me.

にしん【鯡・鰊】 a herring. ¶ 薫製〜 *a* red *herring*; *a* smoked (≒ kippered) *herring*; a kipper.

にしん【二伸】 a postscript (手紙では P.S. と略す). ¶ 〜別便にて上記の本を送りました P. S. I am sending you the above-mentioned book under separate cover.

にしん【二審】 the second instance. ¶ 彼は第〜で無罪となった He was found not guilty at *the second trial*.

にしんとう【二親等】〖法律〗 a relation of the second degree. ¶ きょうだいは〜である Brothers or sisters are *relations of the second degree to each other*.

ニス varnish. ¶ 〜を塗る *varnish* (a table).

にせ【偽・贋】 an imitation. ¶ あの絵は〜だ The painting is *a forgery*.

にせ【二世】〖仏教〗 this and the next world. ¶ 〜を契る pledge *one's* eternal love; be engaged to be married; become man and wife.

にせアカシア【偽アカシア】〖植物〗 a rose acacia; a locust tree; a false acacia.

にせい【二世】(2代目) the second generation; (日系二世) a Nisei; a second-generation Japanese-American.

¶ エリザベス〜 Elizabeth II (the second と読む). 高木〜 Takagi, *Jr.* (≒ *the Junior*); the *younger* Takagi; Takagi II.

にせがね【偽金】 counterfeit money; false coin; 米 bogus money.

—造り a counterfeiter.

にせさつ【偽札】 a counterfeit note; a false note.

にせもの【偽物・偽者】(偽物) an imitation; a counterfeit; (偽者) a pretender; an impostor. ¶ この店には〜がよくある There are so many *fakes* in this store.

に・せる【似せる】 ¶ この庭園は京都のある有名な庭園に〜せて造られてある This garden *is modeled after* (≒ *on*) a noted one in Kyoto. 彼は私の筆跡に〜せて署名した He *counterfeited* my signature.

にそう【尼僧】 a nun; (カトリック) a sister.

—院 a nunnery; a convent.

にそく【二足】 ¶ 〜のわらじをはく run after two entirely different things at the same time.

—動物 a biped (≒ two-footed) animal.

にそくさんもん【二束三文】 ¶ そんな物売ったって〜だ That would*n't fetch anything much.*/ It would *be dirt-cheap.* これは〜で買った I bought this *for a song* (≒ *for an old song*).

にだいせいとう【二大政党】 —主義 a two-party system.

にたき【煮炊き】 cooking. ¶ 自分で〜する do *one's* own cooking.

にだし【煮出し】 stock; broth.

—汁 stock; soup-stock.

にだ・す【煮出す】 take out the essence by boiling.

にた・つ【煮立つ】 ¶ やかんの湯が〜っている The water in the kettle *is boiling* [*up*].

にた・てる【煮立てる】 boil up. ¶ なべの湯を〜てる *boil up* the water in a pot.

にたにた ¶ 彼は私を見て〜笑った He *grinned broadly* at me. 彼はうれしくて〜笑った He *grinned* with delight.

にたもの【似た者】 ¶ 〜夫婦 Like husband, like wife.

にたりよったり【似たり寄ったり】 ¶ どちらも〜だ They *are both of a sort.* / There is little to choose between the two.

-にち【-日】 ¶ 12月12〜に on the twelfth of December (12 December と書いてもよい. December 12 とも書く. 前者は主としてイギリス式, 後者はアメリカ式). 二, 三〜内に within two or three *days*.

にちえい【日英】 Japan and England. ¶ 〜同盟 the *Anglo-Japanese* Alliance. 〜協会 the *Japan British* Society.

にちぎん【日銀】 the Bank of Japan.

—券 Bank of Japan notes. —総裁 the President of the Bank of Japan.

にちげん【日限】 ¶ 〜までに by *the date*. 〜どおりに in *time*. もう二, 三日で手形の〜が来る The bill *falls due* in a day or two.

にちじ【日時】 ¶ 会の〜をお知らせください Please let me know *the time and date* of the meeting.

にちじょう【日常】 everyday (1語なら形容詞, every day と離せばふつうは副詞). ¶ この時計は私には〜欠くべからざるものだ This watch is my *daily* "must." 〜の仕事をおろそかにしてはいけない Don't neglect your *routine* work.

—英語 daily English. —茶飯事 an everyday affair (≒ event); a chore (複数形で do *one's* chores (日常の仕事をする) のように用いるのがふつう). —生活 daily (≒ everyday) life.

にちどく【日独】 Japan and Germany.

にちぶ【日舞】 Japanese dancing. ¶ 〜の師匠 a master of *Japanese dancing*.

にちふつ【日仏】 Japan and France.

にちべい【日米】 Japan and America. ¶ 〜関係 Japanese-American relations.

—安全保障条約 the U.S.-Japan Security Treaty.

にちぼつ【日没】 sunset; 米 sundown. ¶ 日の出から〜まで from sunrise till *sunset*; 米 from sunup to *sundown*. 〜までは彼は帰らないだろう He won't be back before *sunset*. 〜の迫るころ風は凪いだ The wind died away toward *sunset*.

にちや【日夜】day and night; night and day. ¶ ～働く work *day and night*; work *around the clock*. 彼女は息子のため～心を砕いた She thought and thought of her son *constantly*.

にちよう【日曜】Sunday. ¶ 新聞の～版 a *Sunday* edition.
—画家 a Sunday painter. —学校 a Sunday school. —大工 a weekend carpenter.

にちようひん【日用品】daily necessaries; commodities.

にちりん【日輪】the sun.
—草〘植物〙a sunflower.

にちろ【日露】Japan and Russia.
—戦争 the Russo-Japanese War.

にっか【日貨】(商品) Japanese goods; (貨幣) Japanese money.

にっか【日課】(学業) a daily lesson; (仕事) a daily work (≒ task). ¶ 毎朝軽い運動をするのを～にしています I *make a point of* taking light exercises every morning. 自分の～を怠るようではだめだ You shouldn't neglect your own *routine*.

につかわし·い【似つかわしい】¶ それは彼のお土産にとても～い I think it very *suitable for* a souvenir to him. その帽子は彼女に～い The hat *becomes* her.

にっかん【日刊】daily issue.
—紙 a daily〔paper〕.

にっかん【肉感】¶ ～的な女 a *sensual* woman; a woman *with a sensual attraction*; a *sexy* woman.
—主義〘美学〙sensualism.

にっき【日記】a diary; a journal. ¶ 彼は～をつけている He keeps *a diary*. きのうは～をつけなかった I didn't write *a diary* yesterday.
—帳 a diary. 絵— a picture diary. ポケット— a pocket diary.

にっきゅう【日給】daily wages (通例複数形). ¶ ～で働く work *by the day*. ～は8,000円だ My *daily wage* is eight thousand yen. / They pay me eight thousand yen a day.

ニックネーム a nickname.

にづくり【荷造り】packing. ¶ ～する pack〔up〕. ～がしっかりしている It *is* well *packed*.

につけ【煮つけ】hard-boiled food. ¶ 野菜の～ *hard-boiled* greens.

にっけい【日系】—米人 a Japanese-American; an American of Japanese descent.
—三世 图 a Sansei.

にっけい【日計】a daily account; daily expenses.
—表 the daily trial balance.

にっけい【肉桂】〘植物〙a cinnamon; (桂皮) cassia bark.

ニッケル nickel.
—鋼 nickel steel. —クローム鋼 nickel chrome steel.

にっこう【日光】sunlight; sunbeam. ¶ この部屋は～が当たる This is a *sunny* room. ～を浴びながら散歩した I took a walk in the *sunshine*. この部屋は1日に1時間しか～が当たらない This room gets only about an hour of *sunshine* a day. ～を浴びよう I am going to take *a sun bath*. それは～で消毒した I *sunned* it to disinfect it. 窓を開けて～を中に入れる open a window and let in *the sun*.
—浴 ¶ ～浴をした I *sat in the sun*.

にっこり ¶ ～笑って with *a sweet smile*. 彼はうれしくて～笑った He *broke into a smile* with joy. 彼は満足げに～笑った His face *beamed* with satisfaction. 彼女は～笑って感謝した She *smiled* her thanks. / She *smiled* her thankful *smile*.

にっさん【日参】¶ 陳情に役所に～した We *visited* the office *frequently* for petition. お寺に～した I *paid a daily visit to* the temple.

にっさん【日産】daily output. ¶ その工場では～5,000台のテレビを生産する The factory can *produce* five thousand television sets *a day*.

にっし【日誌】a diary.
航海— a log〔-book〕. 臨床— a physician's diary.

にっしゃびょう【日射病】¶ ～にかかる have *sunstroke*.

にっしゅう【日収】¶ 彼は～3,000円とっている He has *an income of* three thousand *yen a day*.

にっしょう【日照】—権 the right to receive sunlight. —時間 the time from sunrise to sunset.

にっしょうき【日章旗】the flag of the Rising Sun; the national flag of Japan.

にっしょく【日食·日蝕】〘天文学〙an eclipse of the sun; a solar eclipse.
皆既(部分)— a total (partial) eclipse of the sun.

にっしんげっぽ【日進月歩】¶ この～の世に, あのような男は役にたたないだろう A man like him is of no use in this age of *rapid progress*. 科学は～だ Science *progresses day by day*.

にっすう【日数】〔the number of〕days. ¶ 彼が回復するまでにはまだまだ～がかかる *It will be long before* he recovers. 彼女を説得するのにはだいぶ～がかかる *Days* are required for my persuading her.
—表 a day table. —早見表 a dated ready-reckoner.

にっせき【日赤】(日本赤十字) the Japan Red Cross Society.
—看護婦 a Red Cross nurse. —病院 a Red Cross Hospital.

にっソ【日ソ】Japan and the Soviet Union.
¶ ～漁業条約 the *Japanese-Soviet* Fisheries Treaty.

にっちもさっちも ¶ 借金で～いかない I *am in a fix with* debts. いよいよ～いかなくなった At last *came the pinch*. / At last *it came to a deadlock*. 船が座礁して～いかなかった The ship *was stranded* on a reef.

にっちゅう【日中】the daytime. ¶ ～はなかなか暑いが夜は涼しい It is very hot *in the daytime* but cool at night. ～(日盛り)に仕事に出かける

のはつらい It is hard to go to work *during the heat of the day.* ～休んで夜歩いた We rested *by day* and walked by night. (ふつう日夜対照とするときは by day, by night を用いるが, 一方が省かれる場合もある).

にっちゅう【日中】 Japan and Communist China. ¶ ～の友好関係 the friendly relations between *Japan and China.*

にっちょく【日直】 day duty. ¶ きのうは～だった I *was on day duty* yesterday.

にってい【日程】 a day's program ; agenda. ¶ きょうの～は終わった We have completed today's *program.* ～がぎっしり詰まっていて彼に会えなかった My crowded *schedule* kept me from seeing him. われわれは～どおりに旅をした We traveled *as scheduled.* 議事～から事項を除く exclude an item from *the agenda.* それは～に上らなかった It wasn't mentioned in *the order of the day.*

—表 an order paper ; (旅の) itinerary.

にっとう【日当】 a daily allowance. ¶ ～3,000円払う *pay* three thousand yen *a day.*

にっぽう【日報】 a daily report.

にっぽん【日本】 Japan. ⇒にほん

にっぽんしき【日本式】 ¶ ～山水庭園 a *Japanese* landscape garden. ～に座る sit *in the Japanese style.* 彼らはアメリカで～に生活している They live *Japanese* in America.

につま·る【煮詰まる】 ¶ なべの中の果汁は～った The juice in the pot *has been boiled down.* 盛んに議論して問題が～ってきた The keen discussion *cleared up the obscure points.*

につ·める【煮詰める】 ¶ 肉汁を～める *boil down* the gravy. 大いに議論して問題を～めてくれ Discuss the matter fully and *bring out the point of importance.* われわれは問題を～めた We *boiled down* the problem.

にてひなる【似て非なる】 ¶ その二つは～ものだ The two *are alike only in appearance.* / The two *are as like as chalk and cheese.* 彼は～芸術家だ He is a *false* (≒ *pseudo*) artist.

にてもにつかぬ【似ても似つかぬ】 ¶ 彼女は母親とは～人だ She *doesn't bear the slightest resemblance* to her mother. / She *is quite different from* her mother.

にと【二兎】 ¶ ～を追う者は一兎をも得ず (諺) He who runs after *two hares* will catch neither. / *Between two stools you fall to the ground.*

にど【二度】 ¶ その婦人は彼の～めの妻だ The lady is his *second* wife. 今度で東京は～めだ This is my *second* visit to Tokyo. その話を聞いたのはこれが～めだ This is *the second time* [that] I've heard of the story. (現在完了形を用いることに注意). ～とそんなことはやるまい I will never do it *again.* ～同じことを言わせるな Never let me repeat the same thing. ～あることは三度ある (諺) Have it twice, and you will have it a third time.

にとう【二等】 the second class. ¶ 競走で～になった I was *a runner-up.* ～の席でその劇を見た I saw the play in a *second-class* seat.

—切符 a second-class ticket ; an economy-class ticket. **—国** a second-rate nation. **—賞** the second prize. **—船客** a second-class cabin passenger. **—品** second goods.

にとうぶん【二等分】 ¶ 線分を～する *divide* a line *into two equal parts.* 財産はふたりの息子に～された All the properties *were divided equally* between the two sons.

にとうへい【二等兵】 a second-class private ; a private second-class.

にとうへんさんかくけい【二等辺三角形】 an isosceles triangle.

にとうりゅう【二刀流】 ¶ 彼は～の名手だ He is a fighter with swords in both hands. 彼は～で酒も甘いものも好きだ He *has two sorts of tastes* ; he likes sweets as well as liquor.

ニトログリセリン 〖化学〗 nitroglycerine.

ニトロセルローズ nitrocellulose.

にないて【担い手】 ¶ 彼は一家の～だ He is *the supporter* (≒ *pillar*) of the whole family.

にな·う【担う】 ¶ 彼は責任を一身に～っている He *assumes* (≒ *undertakes ; takes up*) the responsibility [on his shoulders]. 彼は文化勲章受章の栄誉を～った He *was honored with* the Cultural Decoration (≒ Medal).

ににんさんきゃく【二人三脚】 a three-legged race.

ににんしょう【二人称】 〖文法〗 a second person.

—代名詞 〖文法〗 a personal pronoun of the second person.

にぬし【荷主】 a shipper ; a consignor.

にねん【二年】 two years. ¶ ～めごとに every two years ; every other year.

—級 the second-year class (≒ grade). **—生** a second-year boy (≒ girl) (3年制の high school の場合は a junior student という). ¶ 大学～生 a sophomore. 小学校～生 a second grader. 中学校～生 an eighth grader. 彼は中学～生だ He is in the eighth grade. **—生植物** a biennial.

にのあし【二の足】 ¶ その話には～を踏む I'll *be reluctant to* accept the proposal.

にのうで【二の腕】 the upper arm.

にのく【二の句】 ¶ 困りはてて～がつげなかった I was too much at a loss what to answer. あきれはてて～がつげなかった I was struck dumb with amazement.

にのつぎ【二の次】 ¶ そんなことは～だ Such a thing *is of secondary importance.* その問題は～にしよう Let's *put* the problem *aside.*

にのまい【二の舞】 ¶ 彼の～を演じてはならない Never *repeat* his failure. あの登山家の～を演じないよう, 注意が肝心だ Be careful not to *repeat* the folly of the alpinist.

-には ¶ きみ～難しい It is too difficult *for* you. 彼は彼女～親切だ He is kind *to* her. 雨の日～試合は行なわれない The match is not held *on* a rainy day. 庭～木が1本もない There is no tree *in* the garden.

にばい【二倍】 double ; twice. ¶ これはあれの～の長さがある This is *twice as* long *as* (≒ *as* long *again as*) that. 私の収入は10年前の～ある My income *is double* what it was ten years ago. 5の～は10だ *Twice* (≒ *Two times*) five is ten.

にばしゃ【荷馬車】a wagon; a cart.

にばん【二番】the second; number two. ¶ 彼は～で卒業した He graduated from the school *second on the list*. 彼は～で走った He was *a runner-up*. ～めの兄です This is my *second* oldest brother.

にばんせんじ【二番せんじ】 ¶ あれは～の映画だ That is *an imitation* of another moving picture.

にびいろ【鈍色】dark grey (≒ gray).

にびょうし【二拍子】〖音楽〗duple time.

ニヒル nihilism. ¶ ～な表情 a *nihilistic* look.

にぶ【二部】(ふたつの部分) two parts; (第二部) the second part.
¶ この物語は～に分かれている This story consists of *two parts*. これから～に移る Now *the second part* starts.
—音符〖音楽〗a minim. —合唱 a duet. —授業 the double session.

にぶ・い【鈍い】dull; (色) dim; (刃物) blunt. ¶ 切れ味の～いナイフ a *blunt* knife. ～い光 a *dim* light. ～い音がした A *dull* sound was heard. 彼女は頭が～い She *is slow in understanding*.

にふだ【荷札】a label; a tag. ¶ ～をつける attach *a tag* (*to*). トランクにはロンドン行きの～がはってあった The trunk *was labeled* for London.

にぶ・る【鈍る】¶ 決心が～った I *wavered* (≒ *was shaken*) in my resolution. このナイフは切れ味が～った This knife *has become blunt*. 勘が～った My intuition *doesn't work well*./ I'*m slow-witted*.

にぶん【二分】¶ ～の1 a (≒ one) half. 彼と私で利益を～した The gains *were divided into two* for him and me.

にべ【膠】¶ ～もない返事 a *curt* answer. ～もなく断わられた I was refused *bluntly*. / I was given a *flat* refusal.

にぼし【煮干し】dried small sardines.

にほん【日本】Japan. ¶ ～の風物 things *Japanese*. この機械は～製だ This machine is made in *Japan*. まさに～晴れの天気だ The weather *is really ideal*. / It is *ideal weather*.
—アルプス the Japan Alps. —海 the Sea of Japan. —海流 the Japan Current. —画 a Japanese painting. —学 Japanology. —学術会議 the Science Council of Japan. —学士院 the Japan Academy. —髪 Japanese coiffure. —銀行 the Bank of Japan. —芸術院 the Japan Art Academy. —犬 a Japanese dog. —語 Japanese; the Japanese language. —国憲法 the Constitution of Japan. —三景 the three fine views of Japan. —紙 Japanese paper. —酒 *sake*. —刀 a Japanese sword. —脳炎 Japanese encephalitis. —間 a Japanese-style room. —料理 Japanese food.

にほんだて【二本立て】(映画などの) a double feature (≒ bill).

にまいじた【二枚舌】equivocation. ¶ 彼は～を使う He *is double-tongued*. / He *tells a lie*.

にまいめ【二枚目】(役) a lover's part; (人) a handsome fellow.

にまめ【煮豆】boiled beans.

-にも ¶ 私～わからない I do not understand it, *either*. そんなことは子ども～できる *Even* a child can do that.

にもうさく【二毛作】 ¶ ～をする raise *two crops* a year. この辺一帯は～地帯だ This is a *two-crop* area.

にもかかわらず【にも拘らず】¶ 雨天～, 外出した I went out *in spite of* the rain. 努力した～, 結果は失敗だった I made every effort, *but* I failed. みんなそれに賛成している～, きみだけなぜ反対するのか All of us agree to the plan. *Nevertheless*, why are you opposed to it? あれほどの教養がある～, なぜあんなことをしたのだろう I wonder why he did such a thing *for all* his learning. それ～彼はだめだ *None the less* it is all over with him.

にもつ【荷物】a load; (旅客の) 米 baggage; 英 luggage. ¶ 二,三個の～ a few pieces of *luggage*. ～を預けたほうがいい It's better for you to have your *baggage* checked. ～はもうまとまったか Have you finished your *packing*? スーツケースはぎっしり～が詰まっている The suitcase *is* fully *packed*.
—一時預かり所 a baggage checking bureau. —電車 a goods car. —取扱所 a baggage (≒ luggage) office.

にもの【煮物】(食物) cooked food; (料理) cooking. ¶ この～はうまい This *boiled food* is delicious.

にゃあ ¶ ネコが～と鳴いた The cat *miaowed*.

にやけた【若気た】¶ ～男 a fop.

にや・ける【若気る】¶ 彼は～けている He *looks namby-pamby*.

にやっかい【荷厄介】¶ この土産物が～だ This packet is *a burden* to me. ぼくは彼から～にされた I was treated as *a nuisance*.

にやにや ¶ きみはなにを～しているのだ Why are you giving *a broad grin*? 私を見て彼は～笑った He *grinned at* me.

ニュアンス a nuance. ¶ このことばには微妙な～がある This word has *a* delicate *shade of meaning*. この表現の～は見落としてはならない You must not overlook *nuances* in this expression.

ニュー new.
—フェイス a new face. —モード a new mode. —ルック a new look.

にゅういん【入院】entrance to a hospital; hospitalization. ¶ ～する enter a hospital; go to hospital; be hospitalized. 彼は～させたほうがよさそうだ He needs to *be sent to* 〔*a*〕 *hospital*./ He requires *hospital treatment*. 彼はこの1週間～中だ He *has been in* 〔*the*〕 *hospital* for a week. (米 ではふつう the をつけ

に

る). すぐ〜を申し込んだ I applied for *admission to a hospital.* 彼はきのう〜した He *was hospitalized* yesterday.
—患者 an inpatient. —料 hospital charges.

にゅうえき【乳液】(化粧の) milky lotion.

にゅうえん【入園】¶ 幼稚園に〜する go to kindergarten.
—料 an admission fee.

にゅうか【入荷】receipt of goods. ¶ 野菜が〜した Fresh vegetables *have arrived.* カツオの〜は例年より少ない *A supply* of bonitoes on this occasion is less in amount than usual.

にゅうか【乳化】emulsification.

にゅうかい【入会】admission. ¶ 〜を申し込む apply for *admission to* (a society). クラブに〜する *become a member of* a club. ゴルフ部に〜する *join* a golf club. 手続きをとればだれでも〜できる Anyone who has gone through formalities can *enter* (≒ *join*) the society.
—金 an entrance (≒ admission) fee. —者 a member; an entrant.

にゅうかく【入閣】¶ 〜する enter (≒ join) the Cabinet; become a Cabinet Minister.

にゅうがく【入学】admission (≒ entrance) into a school. ¶ 彼はT大学に〜した He *was admitted* to T University. 彼女はY大学に〜を志望している She *has applied* to Y University *for admission.* 私は幸いにもX高校に〜した Fortunately I *entered* X senior high school.
—願書 an application for admission; an application form. —金 an entrance fee. —試験 an entrance examination. —式 an entrance ceremony.

にゅうがん【乳癌】breast cancer.

にゅうぎゅう【乳牛】a milch cow.

にゅうきょ【入渠】¶ 〜する go into a dock. この船は修理のため〜中だ This ship *is* now *in dock* for repair.

にゅうきょ【入居】¶ 彼はこのアパートに〜する He will *move into* this flat.
—者 a tenant.

にゅうきょう【入京】¶ 〜する come〔up〕to Tokyo; arrive in Tokyo.

にゅうぎょう【乳業】lactic manufacture.

にゅうきん【入金】money received; (受け取り) receipt of money; (支払い) payment; (受領金) receipts.
¶ 〜する receive (pay) (some money).
—伝票 a receipt slip; (銀行預金の) a paying-in (≒ 㒵deposit) slip.

にゅうこ【入庫】¶ その品はまだ〜していない The article *has* not *been stocked* yet.

にゅうこう【入坑】¶ 〜する enter a pit.

にゅうこう【入港】arrival〔in port〕. ¶ 横浜港に〜する *put in at* Yokohama. 船は〜中だ The ship *is in port.* 燃料を積むため〜する *put into port* to fuel.
—税 port dues. —手続き the clearance inward. —届 an entrance notice.

にゅうこく【入国】¶ 〜を許可する admit (*a person*) *into a country.* 〜を拒絶する refuse (*a person*) *entry into a country.*
—管理機関 the Immigration Service Division. —査証 a visa. —手続き entry formalities.

にゅうざい【乳剤】an emulsion.

にゅうさつ【入札】a tender. ¶ 〜する tender (*for*). 〜を募る call for *bids.* 〜に付する sell (*a thing*) by *tender.* 校舎建築の〜を募集している *Bids* are invited for a school building construction.
—者 米a bidder; 英a tenderer.

にゅうさん【乳酸】〘化学〙lactic acid.
—飲料 lactic acid drink. —菌 lactic acid bacilli.

にゅうし【入試】(入学試験) an entrance examination. ¶ 〜に通る (落ちる) pass (fail in) *an entrance examination.*

にゅうし【乳歯】a milk tooth.

にゅうじ【乳児】a suckling; a nursling; an infant.

ニュージーランド New Zealand.
—人 a New Zealander.

にゅうしゃ【入社】¶ 〜する enter a firm.
—試験 an entrance examination.

にゅうしゃ【入射】incidence.
—角 an incident angle; an angle of incidence. —光線 incident rays.

にゅうじゃく【柔弱】weakness. ¶ 彼は〜な体質だ He has a *weak* constitution. / He *is weak in* constitution. 彼は意外に〜な人物だ Unexpectedly he is a *weak-kneed* man.

にゅうしゅ【入手】¶ 原本の〜は難しい It is difficult to *get* the original. 資金を〜するには3日かかる It takes three days for capitals to *come to hand.* これは〜難だ The thing is difficult to *obtain.* その品物の〜径路を説明してください Please explain how you have come to *get* the article. この本はここで〜できる (できない) The book *is available* (*is unavailable*) here. この種のワインは日本では〜できない This kind of wine is not to *be had* in Japan.

にゅうしょう【入賞】¶ 展覧会で1等に〜した I *won* 〔the〕 first *prize* (≒ *was placed* first) at the exhibition. / I *was awarded* first prize.
—者 a prize winner.

にゅうじょう【入場】entrance; admission. ¶ この券では劇場に〜できない This ticket will not *admit* you *into* the theater. 私は無料で〜を許されている I am given free *admission.* この切符で何人〜できますか How many people can *get in* with this ticket? 10歳未満の子どもは〜できない They don't *let* children under ten years old *in.* 彼は館内に〜を許可された He *was admitted into* the building. 〜は無料だ *Admission* is free.
—券 an admission (≒ entrance) ticket. —式 an entrance ceremony. —者 a visitor; (総称的に) an attendance. —税 an admission tax. —無料 (掲示) Admission free.

にゅうじょう【乳状】¶ ～の液体 a *milky* (≒ *emulsified*) liquid.

にゅうしょく【入植】¶ 南米に～した We *settled in* (≒ *immigrated into*) South America.
—者 a settler; an immigrant.

にゅうしん【入信】¶ 彼はキリスト教に～した He *became a Christian.* / He *accepted Christianity.* / He *converted* (≒ *was converted*) *to* Christianity.

にゅうしん【入神】 ¶ 彼は鉄棒で～の技を見せた He displayed a *divine* skill in the iron bar [exercise].

ニュース news (単数扱い. 冠詞はつけない). ¶ よい～ a piece of good *news.*
—解説 news commentary. —解説者 a news commentator. —ソース the news source. —バリュー news value. —放送 newscasting. 電光— a sky sign.

にゅうせいひん【乳製品】dairy products.

にゅうせき【入籍】entry in a family register. ¶ ～する have *one's* name entered in the family register; become legally a new family member.

にゅうせん【入選】¶ 私の作文が～した My composition *was accepted* (≒ *was selected*).
—者 a winner. —作品 a winning work.

にゅうせん【乳腺】〘解剖学〙 the mammary gland.
—炎 mastitis.

にゅうたい【入隊】enlistment. ¶ ～する join (≒ enlist in) the army.

にゅうだん【入団】¶ 彼は巨人軍に～した He *joined* (≒ *became one of the players in*) the Giants.

にゅうちょう【入超】excess of imports.

にゅうてい【入廷】 ¶ 裁判官が～した The judges *entered the court room.*

ニューディール ¶ ～政策 the New Deal.

にゅうでん【入電】a telegram received. ¶ パリの特派員から～があった We *received a telegram from* a special correspondent in Paris. モスクワからの～によれば, 一行は市民から大歓迎されたとのことである *According to a telegram from* Moscow, (≒ *A telegram from* Moscow *reports that*) the party were warmly welcomed by Muscovites.

にゅうとう【入党】¶ 彼は共産党に～した He *joined* (≒ *became a member of*) the Communist party.

にゅうとう【乳頭】〘解剖学〙 a nipple; a teat.

にゅうとう【乳糖】〘化学〙 milk sugar; lactose.

にゅうどう【入道】a lay priest. ¶ 一つ目の～ a one-eyed *monster.*
—雲 gigantic columns of clouds; (積乱雲) a thunderhead. 大— a huge monster; a giant.

ニュートロン〘物理〙 neutron.

にゅうねん【入念】 ¶ ～な計画を立てる make *elaborate* (≒ *scrupulous*) plans. 車の点検を～にする inspect a car *carefully* (≒ *with great care*). 彼は～に投球をしている He is pitching *deliberately.*

にゅうばい【入梅】the rainy season. ¶ ～のころになるとぐあいが悪くなる I'm unwell when *the rainy* (≒ *wet*) *season* sets in.

にゅうはくしょく【乳白色】milk-white.

にゅうひ【入費】expenses. ¶ 家族の病気で～がかさんだ The illness of my family *cost* me a great deal. ～節約のこと We must cut down our *expenses.*

にゅうぶ 【入部】 ¶ 野球クラブに～をすすめられた I was invited to *join* the baseball *club.*

にゅうまく【入幕】〘相撲〙 rising to the first grade of *sumo.* ¶ 彼は無事～をはたした He succeeded in *becoming a first-grade sumo wrestler.*

にゅうもん 【入門】 ¶ さる書道家のところに～した I *became a disciple of* a certain calligrapher.
—書 a primer.

にゅうよう【入用】need. ⇒ひつよう

ニューヨーク New York. (州と区別するときは New York, N.Y. とするか, New York City とする).
—市民 a New Yorker.

にゅうようじ【乳幼児】an infant.

にゅうよく【入浴】bathing; bath. ¶ 赤ん坊を～させる give a baby *a bath.* ～する take (≒ have) *a bath.*

ニュールック a new look. (ふつう a をつけ, 時に the をつける). ¶ これが春の～です This is the *new look* (≒ *new fashion in dress*) this spring.

にゅうりょく【入力】〘機械〙 power input.

にゅうわ【柔和】tenderness; mildness.
¶ 彼は～な顔つきの人だ He has a *gentle* (≒ *tender*) look on his face. 象の目は～だ The elephant is a *meek-eyed* animal.

にゅっと ¶ 大蛇が～顔を出した *Suddenly* (≒ *Abruptly*) there appeared a big snake.

にょう【尿】urine (発音は [júərin]). ¶ ～を検査してもらった I had my *urine* examined (≒ tested).

にょう【二様】¶ このことばは～に解釈できる This word has a *double* (≒ *twofold*) meaning./ This word may be interpreted *in two ways.*

にょうさん【尿酸】〘化学〙 uric acid.

にょうそ【尿素】〘化学〙 urea.

にょうどう【尿道】〘解剖学〙 a urethra.
—炎 urethritio.

にょうどくしょう【尿毒症】〘医学〙 uremia; uremic poisoning.

にょうぼう【女房】a wife. ¶ 教頭は校長の～役だ A head teacher is *the right-hand man* of a principal.

にょきにょき〔と〕 ¶ キノコがあちこちから～顔を出している Mushrooms are coming out all over the place.

にょじつ【如実】¶ ～に realistically; in detail. 人生を～に描く depict life *just as it is.* このことは政界の現状を～に物語っている This gives us a *true* (≒ *vivid*) picture of the present

に

condition in political circles.

にょたい【女体】a female body. ¶ ～をスケッチする make a sketch of *a woman in the nude.* (her naked body はさける).

にょっきり ¶ タケノコが1本, ～裏庭にはえた A bamboo shoot *unexpectedly came out* in the back garden.

にょにん【女人】a woman; a female.
—禁制 no admittance to women.

にょらい【如来】〘仏教〙Buddha.

にら【韮】〘植物〙a leek; a scallion.

にらみ【睨み】a glare. ¶ 彼は町内では～がきく He *has a great influence* in the neighborhood. ボスが～をきかしている The boss *has much authority over* his followers.

にらみあい【睨み合い】¶ 両国とも～が続いている There is still *enmity* between the two countries.

にらみあ·う【睨み合う】glare at each other. ¶ 彼らはいまだに～っている They *are* still *at odds* (≒ *at variance*) *with* each other. 周囲の状況を～わせて行動する behave *oneself in consideration* (≒ *in the light*) *of* circumstances.

にらみかえ·す【睨み返す】¶ 彼女を～してやった I *glared* (≒ *stared*) *back at* her.

にらみつ·ける【睨み付ける】¶ 彼女は私をじっと～けた She *stared hard* (≒ *looked angrily*) *at* me. (look daggers at *a person* は言い古された表現 (cliché) だからさける).

にら·む【睨む】¶ 彼は私の顔を～んだ He *stared fixedly at* my face. 彼女にすごい目で～まれた I *was looked angrily* (≒ *was glared fiercely*) *at* by her. 君も社長に～まれたらおしまいだ It will be all over with you if you *incur the displeasure* of the president in your company. 彼のいたずらと～んだ I *suspect* that he worked mischief. 彼は殺人者と～まれている He *is suspected* as a murderer.

にらめっこ【睨めっこ】¶ ～をしよう Let's *play a staring game.*

にらんせいそうせいじ【二卵性双生児】a fraternal twin.

にりつはいはん【二律背反】antinomy.

にりゅう【二流】¶ ～の小説家 a *second-rate* (≒ *minor*) novelist. 彼は政治家としては～だ He is *the rank and file* of a political party.

にりゅうかたんそ【二硫化炭素】〘化学〙carbon disulfide.

にりん【二輪】—車 a two-wheeled vehicle; a two-wheeler. —咲き a double-flower; twin flowers.

にる【似る】¶ この二つの絵は似ている These two pictures *have a resemblance.* この形はなにに似ていますか What *is* this shape *like*? このふたりの兄弟は全然似ていない The two brothers *are* not at all *alike.* このふたりの女の子は似ている These two girls *look alike.* 彼は性格が父親にたいへん似ている There is *a great resemblance in* character between him and his father. この絵はほんものの彼によく似ている This painting is *a* good *likeness* of him. 彼は父親に似て勉勉だ He is diligent *like* his father. 彼女は母親に似ずおとなしい *Unlike* her mother, she is gentle. あなたの考えは私と似ている Your idea *is similar to* mine.

にる【煮る】boil; cook. ¶ 彼は煮ても焼いても食えない男だ He is quite a *crafty* fellow. / He *is too much for us* (≒ *more than we can manage*). 煮るなり焼くなり勝手にしろ You are free to do anything you like.

にるい【二塁】〘野球〙the second base.
—手 a second baseman. —打 a two-base hit.

にれ【楡】〘植物〙an elm.

にれつ【二列】two rows. ¶ ～に並ぶ form *two rows.* ～になって歩く walk *two abreast*; walk *in a double file.*
—縦隊 a double file (≒ column).

にれんぱつ【二連発】—銃 a double-barreled gun (≒ rifle).

にろくじちゅう【二六時中】always; at all times; day and night. ¶ ～働く work *round the clock.*

にわ【庭】a garden. ¶ ～の草むしりをする weed *a garden.* ～の手入れをする trim *a garden.*
—石 a garden stone. —木 a garden tree (≒ plant). —師 a gardener; a garden designer. 裏— a back garden. 中— a yard; a court.

にわか【俄】¶ ～に雨が降りだした *All of a sudden* (≒ *Suddenly*) it began to rain. この案は～に賛成はできない I cannot approve of this plan *readily.* ～づくりの案 an *improvised* (≒ a *hastily got-up*) plan. 試験の～勉強をする *cram* for an examination.
—雨 a shower. ¶ ～雨に会った I was caught in *a shower.*

にわさき【庭先】¶ 子どもたちが～で遊んでいる Children are playing *in the garden.*

にわづたい【庭伝い】¶ ～に隣家へ行った I went to the next door *from garden to garden.*

にわとり【鶏】〘鳥類〙a fowl; (雄) a cock; (雌) a hen; (ひな) a chicken; (肉) chicken. ¶ ～を飼う keep *hens*; raise *chickens.*
—小屋 a henhouse.

にん【任】¶ 彼は無事市長の～を果たした He fulfilled his *duties* as a mayor successfully. 私はその～ではない I *am* not *equal to the task.* / I *am unfit for the position.* ～に当たる undertake *the responsibility* (*of*).

にんい【任意】option. ¶ ～の optional; voluntary. ～に optionally; voluntarily. ～にやってみなさい Do it *at will* (≒ *of your free will*). ～な行動は慎みなさい Never do *as you please.* / Never act *at your option.* その件は諸君の～に任せることにしよう I will *leave* the matter *to your discretion.*
—出頭 voluntary appearance. —抽出法 the random sampling method.

にんか【認可】approval. ¶ デモをするには警察の～を得ねばならない You must get *a* police *permit* to hold a demonstration. 学校設置の～がおりた Our plan of founding a school *was authorized* (≒ *was received*) by the Ministry of Education.

—証 a certificate. —状 an exequatur.

にんかん【任官】appointment. ¶ 彼は国務次官に～した He *was appointed* [*to* the] Under-secretary of State.

—式 an inaugural ceremony.

にんき【人気】popularity. ¶ その歌手はたちまち～を得た The singer won immediate *popularity*. 彼は若者たちの間に～がある He *is popular among* young people. (小人数の場合は among の代わりに with を用いることが多い). その芝居はたいへんな～だ The play *is* highly *popular*. 目下～を集めている玩具(がんぐ)はこれだ This is the toy that *is catching on* now. 彼は～が落ちた He has lost *popularity*. 彼の～は急速に減退しつつある His *popularity* is declining rapidly.

—作家 a popular writer. —投票 a popularity vote. —取り政策 a claptrap policy.

—者 a popular person ; a favorite. ¶ パンダは動物園の～者だ Pandas are *favorites* in the zoo.

にんき【任期】a term of office (≒ service). ¶ 知事の～はこの4月に切れる The governor's *term of office* is to expire in this coming April. 市会議員の～は4年である The *term* of city councilors is four years. ～満了で at the expiration of *one's term of service* (≒ *office*).

にんぎょ【人魚】(女) a mermaid ; (男) a merman.

にんぎょう【人形】a doll ; (操り人形) a puppet ; a marionette.

—劇 a puppet show. —使い a puppet-show man ; a puppet operator.

にんげん【人間】a human being ; man (無冠詞). ¶ ～は偉大な創造力を持つ *Man* has great creative power.(無冠詞に注意). 彼は～がしっかりしている He has *a* steady *character*. 彼は～がまじめだ He is a sober man *by nature*. 彼は～味に乏しい He lacks *humane feelings*. ～ができている人だ He is indeed *a man of character*.

—関係 human relations. —ぎらい(人) a misanthrope. —性 human nature. —業 ¶ これはとても～業とは思えない This is certainly beyond *the reach* of *human power*.

にんさんぷ【妊産婦】pregnant women and nursing mothers.

にんしき【認識】recognition ; cognizance. ¶ ～する recognize ; understand. このことについて～を欠く人が多い Many people lack *proper knowledge* of this fact. 世界の情勢についての～が深まっている There has been *a* better *understanding* of the present world situation.

—論〘哲学〙epistemology ; the theory of knowledge. —不足 lack of understanding.

にんじゅう【忍従】endurance ; patience. ¶ 彼の生涯は～の生涯であった He has suffered a life of *submission*. 運命には～するほかはない We have to *endure* (≒ *submit to*) our fate.

にんじゅつ【忍術】¶ ～を使う practice *the art of invisibility*.

—使い a master of occult art.

にんしょう【人称】〘文法〙person.

—代名詞 a personal pronoun. 一(二 ; 三) — the first (second ; third) person.

にんしょう【認証】certification.

—官 an attestation official. —式 an attestation ceremony. —書 a certificate of attestation.

にんじょう【人情】human feelings ; humanity ; human nature. ¶ ～に厚い人だ What a *warm-hearted* man he is! そのような考え方をするのは～だ It *is only human* to think that way. ～はどこへ行っても同じだ *Human feelings* are the same everywhere. そういうことは～としてできない I can't find the heart to do that. 彼は～紙のごとしだ He has a cold heart. 彼は～の機微に通じている He understands *human nature*. 危険を逃れたいと思うのは～である It *is quite natural* to want to escape from danger.

にんじょう【刃傷】¶ 事件は～ざたに発展した The matter developed into *bloodshed*. 彼は～ざたを引き起こした He brought about *an affair of bloodshed*.

にん・じる【任じる】⇒にんずる

にんしん【妊娠】pregnancy ; conception. ¶ 彼女は～している She *is with child*. 彼女は～3か月である She is in the third month of *pregnancy*. ～3か月の女 a woman three months *gone*.

—中絶 suspension of conception ; abortion.

にんじん【人参】a carrot ; (薬用の) a ginseng. 朝鮮— a ginseng.

にんずう【人数】¶ 欠席者の～は何人でしたか *How many people* were absent? 出席者の～を数えてください Count the *number* of those present. 野球をするには～がじゅうぶんだ We have enough [*number of*] people here to play baseball. ～は100人だった They were 100 *in number*.

にん・ずる【任ずる】¶ 彼は文部大臣に～ぜられた He *was appointed* Minister of Education. 天才をもって～じている He *fancies himself to be* a genius. 責めに～ずる *bear* the responsibility.

にんそう【人相】a look ; features physiognomy. ¶ ～のよくない男 a man of forbidding *look* ; an evil-*looking* man. 彼の物欲しそうな～が気にいらない I don't like his hungry *look*.

—書き a description. —学 physiognomy.

—見 a physiognomist.

にんたい【忍耐】perseverance ; patience ; endurance. ¶ 子どもを教えることは多大の～を要する It requires a great deal of *perseverance* (≒ It requires the utmost *patience*) to teach children. ～によってのみそれは可能だ It can be done only by *perseverance*. それはもう～の限りではない It is [almost] beyond

(≒ past) *endurance.* / My *patience* is quite worn out. 彼は～強い He is a man *of patience.* / He *is very patient.*

—力 endurance; perseverance. ¶ 若い人はしばしば～力に欠けている Young people often lack *patience.*

にんち【任地】 ¶ ～に赴く proceed to *one's* new post. ～から帰る return from *the post.*

にんち【認知】 acknowledgment; recognition. ¶ 私生児を～する *acknowledge* (≒ *recognize*) an illegitimate child as *one's* own.

にんてい【認定】 recognition. ¶ 彼は無罪と～された He *was found* innocent. 文部省～の映画 a film *approved* by the Ministry of Education. その病気は最近まで伝染病と～されていなかった Until recently, the disease *was* not *recognized* as infectious. 資格～試験 a *qualification* examination.

にんにく【大蒜・葫】〘植物〙garlic.

にんぴ【認否】 ¶ その問題について～を問う *put* the question *to a vote.*

にんぴにん【人非人】 a brute; a man of brutal nature.

にんぷ【妊婦】 a pregnant woman; a woman with child; an expectant mother.

にんむ【任務】 duty. ¶ ～を果たす perform *one's duties*; accomplish *one's* 〔allotted〕 *task.* ～を怠る neglect *one's duties.* ～を引き受ける take over the *duties.* ～を負わせる place *a duty* on *a person*; assign *a task* to *a person.* ～を帯びて on *a mission.*

にんめい【任命】 an appointment. ¶ 彼は首席代表に～された He *was appointed* 〔*to*; *as*〕 chief negotiator. 彼は駐米大使に～された He *was appointed* 〔to the post of〕 Ambassador to the United States.

—権 the appointing power. **—式** the appointing ceremony.

にんめん【任免】 appointment and dismissal. ¶ 社員の～権は社長にある The president has the exclusive power of *appointing and removing* the employees.

ぬ

ぬいあが・る【縫い上がる】 ¶ そのドレスは今月中に～る予定です The dress is to *be finished* by the end of this month. あなたのドレスは今月中に～げましょう I am going to *finish* your dress by the end of this month.

ぬいいと【縫い糸】 a sewing thread; cotton; (ひと巻きの) a spool of thread.

ぬいぐるみ【縫いぐるみ】 ¶ ～のおもちゃ a stuffed animal. ～のクマ a Teddy bear.

ぬいしろ【縫い代】 an outlet seam.

ぬいつ・ける【縫い付ける】 ¶ ボタンを～ける *sew on* a button.

ぬいとり【縫い取り】 ¶ ハンカチにイニシアルの～をする *sew* (≒ *work*; *embroider*) *one's* initials on a handkerchief.

ぬいばり【縫い針】 a needle.

ぬいめ【縫い目】 a seam; (傷の) a suture. ¶ ～なしのくつ下 *seamless* stockings. ～がほころびた The *seam* has opened.

ぬいもの【縫い物】 sewing. ¶ ～をする sew; do *needlework.*

ぬ・う【縫う】1〘衣類・傷口などを〙 ¶ 着物を～う *sew* the clothes.

ズボンのほころびを～う *sew up* a rip on *one's* pants.

医師はその子の足の傷を3針～った The doctor *closed* the cut on the child's leg with three stitches.

2〘慣用的表現〙 ¶ 人波を～って進んだ I *threaded my way* through the crowd.

彼は公務の合間を～って小説を書いた He wrote his stories *in the intervals* of his official business.

川は町を～って流れている The river *meanders* through the city.

ぬえ【鵺・鵼】 ¶ 彼は～的人物であった He struck me as a *dubious* sort of person.

ぬか【糠】 rice bran. ¶ ～にくぎだ (諺) *It's like water off a duck's back.* / It's as useless as plowing (≒ sowing) the sand.

ヌガー a nougat.

ぬかあめ【糠雨】 a drizzle; a fine rain. ¶ ～が降っている It *is drizzling.*

ぬか・す【抜かす】 ¶ 1ページ～す *skip* a page. このひと幕は～してもよい This act may *be omitted.* 私はときどき朝食を～す I *do not take* breakfast from time to time.

ぬか・す【吐かす】 ¶ 生意気～すな None of your cheeks (≒ impudence)! よくも～したな How dare you say such a thing to me?

ぬが・す【脱がす】 ¶ 彼女は子どものくつを～せた She *took off* the shoes of her child. 彼は私に手を貸して外とうを～せた He *helped me off* my overcoat.

ぬかず・く【額突く】 ¶ 神前に～く *kneel* before the shrine.

ぬかみそ【糠味噌】 salted rice-bran paste 〔for pickling〕. ¶ きみが歌ったら～が腐る Don't bother us with your poor songs.

ぬかよろこび【糠喜び】 a fruitless (≒ premature) delight. ¶ 病気が回復したと思ったのも～だった I was glad I had recovered from illness, but it was *a transient delight*.

ぬかり【抜かり】¶ ～なくやれ Do it *well*. 準備に～はない The preparation *is complete*. 彼女はやることに～がない She *knows what she is about*.

ぬか・る【抜かる】¶ ～るな Look sharp! / Be on your guard.

ぬか・る【泥濘る】¶ 長雨のために道が～っていた The road *was muddy* (≒ *was heavy*) after a long rain.

ぬかるみ【泥濘】mire; mud. ¶ 車が～にはまった The car got stuck in the *mud*. 政局はA氏の死により～にはいった The political situation *got stuck* by the loss of Mr. A.

ぬき【抜き】¶ 朝飯はいつも～だ I usually *go without* breakfast. あいさつは～で本題に入ろう Let's get right down to business 〔*without* formalities〕. 冗談は～にして… joking *apart*; seriously speaking.

ぬきあし【抜き足】¶ 彼は～差し足で寝室に入った He *stole into* his bedroom.

ぬきうち【抜き打ち】¶ ～にテストをする give a *surprise* test. ～に国会を解散する dissolve the Diet *without notice*.

ぬきがき【抜き書き】an extract. ¶ 本の一節を～する *extract* a passage from a book.

ぬきさし【抜き差し】¶ ～ならぬ苦境に陥る be in a fix; be in a pinch.

ぬきずり【抜き刷り】an offprint.

ぬきだ・す【抜き出す】¶ 最優秀作品を～す *select* (≒ *pick out*) the best work.

ぬきて【抜き手】¶ ～を切って泳ぐ swim *with an overarm stroke*.

ぬきと・る【抜き取る】¶ くぎを～る *pull* (≒ *draw*) *out* a nail. 小包を～る *pilfer* (≒ *steal*) a parcel. 製品を～って検査する inspect goods *at random*. 財布を～る *pick* a pocketbook *of a person*.

ぬきみ【抜き身】¶ ～を持って with *a drawn* (≒ *naked*) *sword* in hand.

ぬきん・でる【抜きんでる】¶ 彼は数学ではクラスで～でている He *excels* (≒*outshines*) the others in his class *in* mathematics. / He *distinguishes himself* in the class *in* mathematics.

ぬ・く【抜く】**1**〚引き出す・取り出す〛pull out.
¶ 歯を～く *take out* a tooth.
刀を～く *draw* a sword.
だれかがタイヤの空気を～いた Someone *let* air *out of* the tire.
この中からいちばん好きなペンを～いてください Please *pick out* the pen you like best.
2〚慣用的表現〛¶ 彼はゴール前でひとり～いて優勝した He won the race by *overtaking* his opponent just in front of the finish line.
朝食を～いた I *skipped* breakfast.
彼は指導力では群を～いている He *towers above* the rest *in* leadership.
ビールを～きましょうか Shall I *open* a bottle of beer?
この仕事は手を～いている They *have skimped on* the work.

ぬ・ぐ【脱ぐ】¶ 上着は～いでいいです You may *take off* your coat. 外套(がいとう)は～がなくてもいい You may *keep* your overcoat *on*. この部屋で着物を～ぎなさい *Undress* in this room. 手伝ってコートを～がしてあげなさい *Help* him *get* his coat *off*. 彼のためにひと肌～いでやろう I will *offer* him *a helping hand*.

ぬぐ・う【拭う】¶ くつの泥を～う *scrape* dirt *off* (≒ *from*) the shoes. 涙をハンカチで～う *wipe one's* tears *away* (≒ *off*) with a handkerchief; *dry one's* eyes with a handkerchief. 口を～う *wipe one's* mouth; (知らぬふりをする) wear an air of innocence.

ぬくぬく〔と〕 ¶ ～暮らしている lead an *easy* life.

ぬくみ【温み】¶ 座布団にまだ～が残っている The cushion *is* still *warm* from the body of someone else.

ぬくもり【温もり】warmth.

ぬけあな【抜け穴】a secret 〔underground〕 passage; (比喩的に) a loophole. ¶ 彼は法の～をよく知っている He knows much about *a loophole* in the law.

ぬけがけ【抜け駆け】¶ 彼は～の功名を立てた He *forestalled* everybody *in* accomplishing it.

ぬけがら【抜け殻】a castoff skin (≒ shell); (ヘビの) a slough.

ぬけかわ・る【抜け替わる】¶ たいていの動物は毛が～る Most animals *shed* their coats. 鳥の羽が～った The bird *molted* its feathers.

ぬけげ【抜け毛】falling (≒ fallen) hair.

ぬけだ・す【抜け出す】¶ 途中で会場から～す leave 〔the place〕 before the meeting is over.

ぬけ・でる【抜け出る】¶ 彼は漫画の中から～でたような男だ He looks as if he had *come out of* a comic strip.

ぬけぬけ〔と〕 ¶ ～うそをつく *have no scruple about* lying. ～顔を出す show *oneself shamelessly*. よくも～そんなことが言えたものだ How *dare* you say such a thing to me?

ぬけみち【抜け道】(裏道) a by-pass; a bypath; (秘密の道) a secret path; (逃げ道) a loophole; a means of escape.
¶ ～を用意しておく be ready to offer *an excuse*.

ぬけめ【抜け目】¶ 彼は～がない He is a *shrewd* (≒ *smart*) fellow. / He knows what he is about. 彼は～なく立ちまわる He *is vigilant in* his own interests. 彼は商売に～がない He *is shrewd in* business. 彼は金もうけに～がない He *is smart* (≒ *shrewd*) *at* making money.

ぬ・ける【抜ける】**1**〚物が〛¶ 歯が～けた A tooth *came out*.
私はこのごろ髪の毛が～ける I *am* rapidly *losing* hair.
くぎが1本～けている A nail *is missing*. (すぐ前まであった場合ならば *has come out*).
このびんのせんが～けない The cork of this bottle won't *come out*.
ここが1ページ～けている One page *is missing* here.

ぬ

このしみは～ける This stain on the dress will *come out.*

2〖その他〗¶ 喫煙の習慣はなかなか～けない I can't *get rid of* the habit of smoking so easily. 林を～けると湖が見えてきた *Passing through* a forest we caught sight of the lake. 朝11時までは忙しくて～けられない I am too busy to *go out* till eleven in the morning. 風邪が～けない I can't *shake off* this cold. あの男は～けている He *is* a little *feather-brained.* / He is a sort of *featherbrain.* 気の～けたビールだ The beer *has become flat.* 全身の力が～けた感じだった I felt *drained of all strength.*

ぬ·げる【脱げる】¶ このくつは私の足に合わないのですぐ～げる These shoes do not fit me and so they readily *come* (≒ *slip*) *off.*

ぬし【主】¶ 氏は名実ともに会社の～だ He is *the proprietor* of the company both in name and reality. この神社はこの沼の～を祭ったものだ This shrine is dedicated to *the spirit* (≒ *the genius*) of this marsh.

ぬすびと【盗人】a thief; a robber. ¶ きみの行為はいわば～に追い銭というやつだ Your conduct is, as it were, *throwing good money after bad.*

ぬすみ【盗み】theft. ¶ あの男はたびたび～をしたあとでつかまった He was arrested after committing *theft* several times.

ぬすみぎき【盗み聞き】eavesdropping. ¶ 戸の外でだれかが～している Someone *is eavesdropping* at the door. ～するのはよくない It is no good thing to *overhear* others' talk.

ぬす·む【盗む】**1**〖物を〗steal. ¶ 人のものを～むのはよくない It is not good to *steal from* others.

電車の中で金を～まれた I *had* my money *stolen* in the train.

彼は家から5万円を～んで逃げた He ran away from his house *with* fifty thousand yen.

2〖その他〗¶ 彼らは人目を～んでしばしば集まっていた They *secretly* assembled.

彼は暇を～んでよくゴルフに出かける He often goes out playing golf *in his spare moments.*

ぬっと ¶ 岩陰からクマが～出てきた A bear *suddenly appeared* from behind the rock.

ぬの【布】cloth.

ぬのきれ【布切れ】a piece of cloth.

ぬのじ【布地】cloth.

ぬのめ【布目】¶ ～の細かい(粗い)布地 a cloth of fine (coarse) *texture.*

ぬま【沼】a marsh.

ぬまち【沼地】a marshy (≒ swampy) place.

ぬら·す【濡らす】¶ 不注意にも雨で服を～してしまった I was careless enough to *get* my suit *wet* with rain.

ぬらりくらり〔と〕¶ そのように～言い抜けるのはひきょうだ It's not fair *dodging* like that. 彼らの～した答弁にはすっかり飽きた We were quite tired of listening to their *evasive* answer.

ぬり【塗り】¶ 白～の壁 a white *painted* (≒ *washed*) wall. お盆の～ the *paint* (≒ *lacquering*) of a tray. この箱は～がいい This case *is* finely *lacquered.*

ぬりえ【塗り絵】a line drawing for coloring. ¶ あの子は～をしている The child *is coloring the pictures.*

ぬりか·える【塗り替える】¶ 壁を～える *repaint* a wall.

ぬりぐすり【塗り薬】〔an〕ointment. ¶ はれた部分に～をつける apply *ointment* to the swollen part.

ぬりたて【塗りたて】¶ ～の壁 *freshly* (≒ *newly*) *painted* wall. ペンキ～(掲示) *Wet* (≒ *Fresh*) Paint.

ぬりつ·ける【塗り付ける】¶ 暴徒たちは壁じゅうに赤ペンキを～けた All the walls *were smeared with* red paint by the mobs.

ぬりつぶ·す【塗り潰す】¶ 5月の村は野も山も緑一色に～される In May, the fields and hills of the village *are all in green.* この壁は青色で～してください Please *paint out* this wall *with* blue.

ぬりもの【塗り物】lacquer ware.

—師 a lacquerer; a japaner. **—商** a dealer in lacquer〔ware〕.

ぬ·る【塗る】paint. ¶ これにペンキを～ろう I will *paint* this. 彼女は地図に赤い色を～っていた She *was coloring* the map red. 壁は青く～った I *painted* the wall blue. その箱はうるしが～ってあった The box *was coated with* lacquer. ニスを薄く2度～る *give* (a desk) two thin *coats* of varnish. 軟膏(なんこう)を全身に～る *apply* ointment all over *one's* body. 彼は私の顔に泥を～った He *brought disgrace on* me. / He *disgraced* me. のどにヨードチンキを～ってもらった I had my throat *painted with* iodine. この傷はなにも～らないのがいちばんだ It is best not to *put* anything *on* this wound. パンにジャムを～る *spread* the bread *with* jam.

ぬる·い【温い】¶ ～いふろに入って風邪をひいた I caught cold because I took a *lukewarm* bath.

ぬるぬる【滑滑】¶ 彼の顔は汗と油で～している His face *is clammy with* greasy sweat.

ぬるまゆ【微温湯】¶ この汚れは～で洗うとよく落ちる This blot can be best removed in *tepid water.* 血気盛んな彼にはそのような～に浸ったような毎日には耐えられなかった He is a hot-blooded young man, so that such a *monotonous* life was unbearable.

ぬれぎぬ【濡れ衣】¶ 彼はまったく身に覚えのないのに～を着せられた He *was falsely* (≒ *unjustly*) *accused of* something of which he was entirely innocent.

ぬれて【濡れ手】a wet hand. ¶ ～で粟(あわ)をつかむ get rich quick; make easy money.

ぬれねずみ【濡れ鼠】¶ 川に落ちて～になった I fell into a river to *get as wet as a fish.*

ぬ·れる【濡れる】¶ かさを持っていなかったのでぐっしょり～れてしまった As I had no umbrella with me, I *was drenched* (≒ *was soaked*) *to the skin.*

ぬ

ね

ね【音】 a sound ;(鳴き声) a note ;(楽音) a tune. ¶ 鐘の～ the *sound* (≒ *toll*) of a bell. 虫の～ *chirps* of insects. さすがの彼もとうとう～をあげた(まいった) Tough as he was, he *gave in* at last.

ね【根】1〖草木の〗 a root. ¶ この草は～がついた This plant *took root*.
この～は地中に深く入り込んでいる This tree has deep *roots*.
2〖慣用的表現〗 ¶ 彼は3年前のことを今でも～に持っている He still *bears* me *a grudge* because of what happened three years ago.
彼が行方不明になったとは～も葉もないうわさだ The rumor that he is missing *is* quite *groundless*.
見かけは意地悪だが～は人がいい Although he looks perverse, he's good-natured *at heart*.
彼は～は善人だ It's his *nature* to be good.
犯罪の～を絶つ *root out* crimes.

ね【値】 a price. ¶ その本は～が上がった The book has risen in *price*. これはちょっと～が張る This *is* a little *expensive*. 土地はどんどん～が上がっている Land *prices* are going up at an extraordinary rate. このさらはいい～に売れそうだ This dish is likely to sell at *a* good *price*. この絵はどのくらいの～がつくだろう I wonder how much I can get for this painting.

ね【寝】〔a〕sleep ; sleeping. ¶ ～が足りない have *a* poor (≒ bad) *sleep*.

-ね ¶ 雨です～ It's raining, *isn't it?* あすきみを訪ねてもいい～ Is it all right if I call on you tomorrow? きのう電話をくれたのはきみだ～ It was you who phoned me yesterday, *wasn't it?* あなたは井上さんです～ You are Mr. Inoue, *aren't you?*

ねあがり【値上がり】 a rise in price. ¶ 昨年と比べると消費者物価は20パーセント～している Compared with last year, the consumer price *has risen* by twenty percent. 物価の～は世界的な傾向だ Prices show a *rising* tendency all over the world.

ねあげ【値上げ】 ¶ 物価の～ *a rise in* price. 運賃を～する *increase* (≒ *raise*) fare. 賃金の～を要求する demand *higher wages* (≒ *a rise of wages*).

ねあせ【寝汗】 night sweat. ¶ 毎晩～をかく I have *night sweat* every night.

ねいき【寝息】 ¶ 快い～をたてて眠る sleep soundly〔*with regular breathing*〕. その家族の者たちの～をうかがって making sure that the family are asleep.

ねいす【寝椅子】 a lounge ; a couch.

ねいりばな【寝入り端】 ¶ 昨夜～に電話で起こされた I was aroused by a telephone call last night *when I had just fallen asleep*.

ねい・る【寝入る】 ¶ 彼は目覚めるのも早いが～るのも早い He is quick in *falling asleep* as well as in waking up. 子どもたちはぐっすり～っている The children *are* fast *asleep* now.

ねいろ【音色】 a tone ; timbre.

ねうごき【値動き】 the price movement (*of*). ¶ この春は野菜の～が異常に激しかった This spring *the price movement of* vegetables has been unusually remarkable.

ねうち【値打ち】 worth. ¶ この石の～は私にはわからない I don't know how much this stone *is worth*. この日記は確かに一読の～がある This diary *is* certainly *worth* reading. この作品はほとんど～がない This work *is of little value*. ～のない本は売ろうと思っている I am thinking of disposing of those books which *are of no value* for me. これは大した～はあるまい I don't think it *is worth* much. この骨董(こっとう)品は50万円の～がある This curio *is worth* five hundred thousand yen. この切手がどのくらい～があるのかわからない I don't see how much this postage stamp *is worth*.

ねえさん【姉様】(姉) a sister ;(若い女) a young woman ;(料理屋の仲居) a waitress.

ネーブル〖植物〗 a navel orange.

ネーム a name.
—バリュー ¶ ～のある作家 a *name* (≒ *famous*) author. **—プレート** a nameplate.

ねおき【寝起き】 ¶ 先月以来駅の近くの下宿に～している Since last month I *have been staying* at a boarding house near the station. 彼とは学生時代いっしょに～した仲だ He is a close friend of mine with whom I *lived* under the same roof all through our school days. きみは～はいいほうですか Do you usually *wake in good humor?* 私は～が悪い I feel unwell when I wake up.

ネオン〖化学〗 neon.
—サイン a neon sign (≒ light).

ネガ〖写真〗 a negative.
—カラー a negative color film.

ねがい【願い】 a wish. ¶ 私の～はこれです This is my *wish*. ひとつお～があります I have *a favor* to ask of you. お～だから中に入れてください Please let me in *for God's sake!* あなたの～がかなうよう祈ります I hope your *wish* comes true. あなたの～をかなえてあげよう Your *request*

ね

will be granted. お～です，子どもたちのめんどうを見てやってください *Would you mind* looking after my children ?

ねがいごと【願い事】〔a〕wish. ¶ 彼女は～がかなった Her *request* has been fulfilled.

ねがいさげ【願い下げ】¶ そんなことは～だ I don't want to have anything to do with that sort of thing. / I *can't stand* such a matter.

ねがい·でる【願い出る】¶ 彼は1日の休暇を～出た He *asked for* a day's leave. 彼はお役の御免を～出た He *requested* his discharge from the position.

ねが·う【願う】 ask. ¶ 彼が現われることを心から～っている I sincerely *hope* he will come. 母親の姿をひと目見たいと～っている I *long to* see my mother. ぜひおいでくださるようお～いします I *should* (≒ *would*) *like you to* come by all means. 画家は死ぬまでパリにとどまりたいと～っている The painter *wishes* to stay in Paris as long as he lives. ご批判をお～いしたいと思いますが May I *ask* you *for* your comment? 彼が来るなんて～ってもないことだ Nothing would make me happier than if he came.

ねがえり【寝返り】¶ 蒸し暑くて眠れず一晩じゅう～を打った Unable to sleep due to sultry weather I *tossed about* (≒ *rolled over*) in bed all night. ～を打った拍子にベッドから落ちた While *turning* in my bed, I fell on the floor.

ねがえ·る【寝返る】¶ 保身のため～るものも少なからずいた Not a few *went over*, anxious for their own self-protection. 親友に～られて一時茫然(ぼうぜん)とした When I found my close friend *betrayed* me, I was struck dumb for a while.

ねがお【寝顔】 *one's* sleeping face.

ねがさ【値嵩】 a price level.
—株〖株式〗 high-priced articles (≒ stocks).

ねかしつ·ける【寝かし付ける】¶ 赤ちゃんを～けるには母の子守歌が一番だ Nothing is better than the mother's lullaby to *sing* (≒ *lull*) a baby *to sleep*.

ねか·す【寝かす】¶ 赤ん坊を～す *put* a baby *to bed*. 電柱を～す *lay down* an electric pole. 金を～しておくだけの余裕がない We cannot afford to *have* our money *lie idle*.

ねがったり【願ったり】¶ 彼が来てくれるとは～かなったりだ He is coming!—Well, *nothing suits us better*. これは～かなったりだ This is *just what I've wanted*. / This is *just the thing I have longed for*. (文語体).

ねがわくは【願わくは】¶ 神よ～われらの行く末を守りたまえ *May God* protect our future! / *May God* be with us! ～無事に帰国なされんことを I *heartily pray for* your safe returning home.

ねがわし·い【願わしい】¶ 率直に申せばそのようなことは～いことではありません Frankly speaking, such a thing is not to *be desired*. この際きみの出馬が最も～い Nothing *is* more *desirable* now than your standing as a candidate.

ねかん【寝棺】 a coffin.

ねぎ【葱】〖植物〗 a Welsh onion.

ねぎら·う【労う·犒う】¶ 市は彼を名誉市民にしてその功労を～った The city *rewarded* him by making him its honorary citizen. この会は彼の労を～うために催された This party was held to *thank for* his services. 社長は彼を重要な地位につけてその功を～った The president *rewarded* him *with* an important appointment.

ねぎ·る【値切る】¶ あまりしつこく～るのはいけない It is not good to *beat down the price* too excessively. ～れるだけ～ってみたらどうですか Why don't you *drive the hardest bargain*?

ネクタイ a tie; a necktie. ¶ ～を結ぶ tie *a necktie*. ～をつける wear *a tie*.
—ピン a scarfpin; a tiepin. チョウ— a bow tie.

ねくび【寝首】¶ その男の～をかく kill the man while he is asleep.

ねぐら【塒】 a roost. ¶ 夕方になるとカラスは～に急ぐ Toward evening I see crows flying home to *roost*.

ネグリジェ a négligé; a negligee.

ねぐるし·い【寝苦しい】¶ クーラーが故障したので昨晩は～かった The air-conditioner went wrong last night, so we *had a bad sleep*. 日本の夏の夜は～いことがよくある In Japan we often *pass a wakeful* summer *night*.

ねこ【猫】 **1** a cat; (雄) a tomcat; (雌) a female cat. ¶ ～がゴロゴロのどを鳴らしている The *cat* is purring.
どこかで～が鳴いている *A cat* is meowing somewhere.
2〖慣用的表現〗¶ このごろは～もしゃくしも英会話を習いたがる *All the world and his wife* want to learn English conversation these days.
～もしゃくしもいっしょくたにされてはかなわぬ It's foolish *to see things good and bad all alike*.
彼は～をかぶっている He *is feigning innocence*.
～に小判 (諺) *That's like casting pearls before swine*.

ねこいらず【猫要らず】 rat-poison.

ねこぎ【根扱ぎ】¶ きのうの風のため街路樹がほとんど～にされた Most of the street trees *were uprooted* by the wind of yesterday.

ねごこち【寝心地】¶ ベッドより布団のほうが私には～がいい To me *futon is* more *comfortable to sleep* 〔in〕 than a bed.

ねこじた【猫舌】¶ 私は～だ I can't eat anything very hot.

ねこぜ【猫背】 a stoop; round shoulders. ¶ 彼は～だ He *is round-shouldered*.

ねこそぎ【根こそぎ】 completely; entirely. ¶ 台風で街路樹を～にされた The street trees *were rooted up* by the typhoon.

ねごと【寝言】 a sleeper's talk; (愚言) nonsense. ¶ ～を言う talk in sleep. なにを～を言っているんだ Don't talk *nonsense*!

ねこなでごえ【猫撫で声】¶ ～で in *a coaxing voice.* 彼女は～で彼にその薬を飲ませた She *coaxed* him *to* take the medicine.

ねこのひたい【猫の額】¶ ～のような狭い庭 *a bit* (≒ *a strip*) of yard.

ねこのめ【猫の目】a cat's eye. ¶ ～のように気の変わりやすい人 a *fickle-minded* person. 彼の考えは～のように変わりやすい His thought *is as fickle as a weathercock.*

ねこばば【猫糞】¶ もうけを全部～する *pocket* all the profits.

ねこみ【寝込み】¶ 警察は犯人の～を襲った The police surprised the criminal *while* 〔*he was*〕 *asleep.*

ねこ·む【寝込む】¶ 彼はぐっすり～んでいる He *is* fast *asleep.* 彼はひと月も病気で～んでいる He *has been ill in bed* for a month. 彼は酔っぱらって～んでしまった He drank himself *to sleep.*

ねこやなぎ【猫柳】〘植物〙a pussy willow.

ねごろ【値頃】¶ これはちょうど～だ The *price is* just *reasonable.*

ねころ·ぶ【寝転ぶ】¶ 芝生に～ぶ *lie* on the grass.

ねさがり【値下がり】depreciation; a fall in price. ¶ 野菜は～しはじめた The price of green groceries is beginning to *fall.* / Green groceries are beginning to *fall in price.*

ねさげ【値下げ】cut in price. ¶ 思い切り～する make as great *a reduction* (≒ *discount*) *in price* as possible. 全商品1割～する *cut* (≒ *reduce*) *the prices* of all the goods by ten percent. 30ドルから20ドルに～になった *The price was lowered* from thirty to twenty dollars.

ねざけ【寝酒】a nightcap. ¶ ～をやる drink at bedtime; take *a nightcap.*

ねざ·す【根ざす】¶ 民主主義は日本の国土にしっかりと～さなかった Democracy didn't *take* firm *root* in Japanese soil.

ねざめ【寝覚め】¶ そんなことをすると～が悪いぞ You'll *be pursued by haunting remorse,* if you do it. / (後悔する) You'll *repent of* it (≒ Your *conscience* will *prick* you), if you do such a thing.

ねざや【値鞘】a margin. ¶ ～が薄い (多い; ない) have a narrow (a wide; no) *margin of profit.* ～を補償する meet the difference between cost price and selling price.

ねじ【捻子·捩子·螺子】a screw. ¶ 腕木を壁に～で取りつける *screw* a bracket to the wall. ～を回す turn *a screw.* ～を締める tighten up *a screw.* 一, 二回～を緩める loosen *a screw* one or two turns. 箱の側面は～で止めてあった The sides of the box *were screwed* together. 生徒の～を巻いてやろう I'll *encourage* the students a bit.

—せん a screw tap. **—**ぶた a screw cap. 雄(雌)**—** a male (female) screw. 止め**—** a nut.

ねじあ·ける【捩じ開ける】¶ 箱のふたを～ける *wrench open* the lid of a box.

ねじあ·げる【捩じ上げる】¶ 彼は私の腕を～げた He *wrenched* my arm.

ねじき·る【捩じ切る】¶ 錠前を～る *wrench* a lock *off* 〔a door〕.

ねじ·ける【拗ける】¶ 彼は心が～けている He *is perverse* in temper. / He is a man of a *crooked* (≒ *perverse*) disposition. 不幸が続くと人の性格は～けてしまうことがよくある Misfortunes often *perverts one's* character.

ねじこ·む【捩じ込む】¶ 週刊誌をポケットに～む *thrust* a weekly *into* the pocket. 彼らはわれわれのとった方策に対して強硬に～んできた They *made a* vigorous *protest against* the measures we had taken.

ねしずま·る【寝静まる】¶ 町はしんと～っている The town *is at rest.* その事件はみんなが～ったころ起こった The accident occurred when all the people *were fast asleep.*

ねしな【寝しな】¶ ～に薬を飲む take medicine *before sleep* (≒ *before going to bed*).

ねじふ·せる【捩じ伏せる】¶ 警官はどろぼうを～せた The policeman *held* the thief *down by wrenching his arms.*

ねじまわし【螺子回し】a screwdriver.

ねしょうがつ【寝正月】¶ 今年は～だった This year I *kept home for the first three days of the New Year.*

ねしょうべん【寝小便】bed-wetting. ¶ ～をする wet the bed.

ねじりはちまき【捩り鉢巻】¶ ～で high-spirited 〔with a twisted towel tightly tied around *one's* head〕.

ねじ·る【捩る】¶ 腕を～る *twist* (≒ *wrench*) *a person's* arm. ロープを1回～る *give* a rope *a twist.* 戸口の取っ手を～る *turn* at the door-knob. 水道のじゃ口を～る *turn* (≒ *tap*) *on* (締めるときは *off*) a faucet.

ねじ·れる【拗れる】¶ ネクタイが少し～れている You have your tie *awry* a little.

ねじろ【根城】the base of operations. ¶ 悪の～ *a den* of crime.

ねすご·す【寝過ごす】¶ けさは～した I *overslept* 〔*myself*〕 this morning.

ねずのばん【寝ずの番】¶ 見張りはその晩注意深く～をした The sentry kept *a* careful *vigil* all through the night.

ねずみ【鼠】1 a rat; a mouse (複 mice) (rat は大きく, mouse はふつう小さい). ¶ ～が鳴く *A rat* squeaks.
～が暴れている *Rats* are running about.
—取り (薬) ratsbane; rat poison; (器具) a rattrap.
2 〖慣用的表現〗¶ 敵は袋の～だ The enemy is like *a rat* in a trap.
彼はただの～ではない He is no common man.

ねずみいろ【鼠色】米 gray; 英 grey.

ねずみざん【鼠算】¶ ～的に増える increase in (≒ by) *geometrical progression.*

ねぞう【寝相】¶ ～が悪い toss about in *one's* sleep.

ねそび·れる【寝そびれる】¶ 階下の話し声が耳について～れた The chatterings downstairs *made* me *sleepless* (≒ 〔*lie*〕 *awake*).

ね

ねそべ・る【寝そべる】¶ 彼はソファーに〜って本を読んだ He *lay sprawled* on the sofa reading a book. 芝生に〜った I *stretched myself out* on the lawn.

ねた (証拠) evidence ; a proof ; (小説) a material ; (新聞) news. ¶ いくら隠したって〜は上がっているんだぞ We have enough *evidence* against you, however you may try to conceal it. どこでその〜を仕入れたのか Where did you get the *information*?

ねたまし・い【妬ましい・嫉ましい】be jealous ; be envious. ¶ 彼が成功を収めたと聞いても少しも〜く思わない I *feel* no *envy at* his success. 彼の名声が〜い I *am jealous of* his reputation. 友人が新しい車を持っているのを見て〜くてしかたがなかった I *was filled with envy* when I saw my friend's new car. 彼の成功が〜かった I *envied* his success.

ねたみ【妬み・嫉み】jealousy ; envy. ¶ 〜深い jealous ; envious. 〜深い女 a *jealous* woman. その問題の奥底には同業者間の〜があった There was professional *jealousy* at the bottom of the question.

ねた・む【妬む・嫉む】¶ 人の幸運を〜んでもしかたがない What's the use of *envying* others' good fortune? 概して貧乏人は金持ちを〜む The poor *are* generally *envious of* the rich.

ねだやし【根絶やし】¶ 雑草 (悪) を〜にする *root out* (≒ *up*) all weeds (evils). 害虫を〜にする *exterminate* vermin.

ねだ・る【強請る】¶ 金を母親に〜る *press one's* mother *for* money. 人にチップを〜る *ask a person for* a tip. その子は見るものがすべて欲しいと母親に〜った The child *teased* his mother *for* everything he saw.

ねだん【値段】a price. ¶ お〜はいくらですか How much [is this]? / What is the price? このごろはなんでも〜が高い Everything *is expensive* these days. (dear はさける). 〜はどんどん上がっていく *Prices* are rising rapidly. 手ごろな〜のサングラスを買いたい I want to buy some moderately *priced* sunglasses. その品でその〜では高い The article *is expensive* at that price. その〜はこれ以上下げられない I can't make it any cheaper. その品には3,000円の〜がついた Three thousand yen was offered for the article. その〜ならまあまあだ The *price* is reasonable.

ねちが・える【寝違える】¶ ゆうべ首を〜えたらしい I think I *had a twist in my neck while asleep* last night.

ねつ【熱】**1**〖物理的な〗heat. ¶ 銅は〜をよく伝える Copper conducts *heat* well.
水に〜を加えると水蒸気になる When water *is heated*, it turns into vapor.
太陽〜を最大限に活用するべきだ The *heat* of the sun ought to be utilized as much as possible.
2〖熱意・熱狂・流行〗enthusiasm ; craze.
¶ 彼はこの計画にはあまり〜がないようだ He does not seem to *be* very *enthusiastic* about this project.
どうもこの仕事に〜が入らない Somehow I cannot *concentrate* [*my attention*] *on* this work.
彼の〜のこもった演説に大いに感銘を受けた We were very much impressed by his *impassioned* speech.
もっと〜をこめてやらなければ成功しないよ You won't succeed unless you work with more *zeal*.
ふたりの恋も結婚2か月で〜がさめた After only two months of marriage, they cooled off.
彼は彼女に〜をあげている He *is infatuated with* her.
少年たちの間にサッカー〜が高まっている *Enthusiasm for* soccer is on the increase among the young boys.
日本人の野球〜も冷えかかっている The Japanese baseball *fever* is cooling down.
アメリカでは日本〜が盛んだ In America there is much *enthusiasm for* things Japanese.
彼はかってな〜を吹くだけだ He talks away as he likes, that's all.
3〖体温〗fever ; temperature. ¶ 〜をはかってみなさい Take your *temperature*.
別段〜はありません You don't have much *fever*. / You have no *temperature*.
少し〜がありますね (少し〜っぽい) You have *a* slight *fever*, don't you? / You seem to *be* a little *feverish*.
彼女は高い〜を出している She has *a* high *fever*. / She *is* very *feverish*.
もう〜はひいた The *fever* is gone now.
この薬を飲むと〜がすぐ下がる This medicine will soon bring down your *fever* (≒ *temperature*).
きょうは平〜になった My *temperature* is normal today.
子どもは〜に浮かされてうわごとを言っている The *fever* has made the child delirious. / The child is talking in delirium because of *a fever*.

ねつあい【熱愛】¶ 妻を〜する *love one's* wife *passionately* ; *adore one's* wife.

ねつい【熱意】enthusiasm ; zeal. ¶ 仕事に対する〜 *earnest devotion to one's* duty. きみは勉強に対して〜が足りない You lack *zeal for* studies. 彼の〜は冷めた His *enthusiasm* waned. / His *zeal* was chilled. 彼は仕事に〜を持っている He *is zealous* (≒ *is enthusiastic*) *in* his work. 彼は研究に並々ならぬ〜を示した He showed marked *enthusiasm for* his studies.

ねつえん【熱演】an enthusiastic performance. ¶ 彼の舞台はすごい〜だった He gave *a performance with zest* on the stage. そのバンドはたいへんな〜だった The band *played magnificently*.

ねつかくはんのう【熱核反応】〔物理〕thermonuclear reaction.

ネッカチーフ a neckerchief (複 -chiefs).

ねっから【根っから】¶ 彼は〜の好人物だ He is *quite* a good-natured man.

ねっき【熱気】heat ; hot air. ¶ 〜で乾く dry

by *heat*. 場内はしだいに～を帯びてきた There was growing *enthusiasm* (≒ *excitement*) in the hall.

ねつき【根つき】¶この木は～がよい This tree *sends out roots* easily. / This tree *roots* easily.

ねつき【寝つき】¶私は～のよいほうだ Usually I *fall asleep* easily.

ねつぎ【根接ぎ】¶バラの～をする *graft* a rose *at the root*.

ねつきかん【熱機関】a heat engine; a thermomotor.

ねっきょう【熱狂】wild enthusiasm. ¶彼は政治に～している He *is crazy about* politics. 試合は観衆の～のうちに終わった The match ended amid the *wild excitement* of the spectators. 彼の弁舌は集まった人たちを～させた His eloquent speech *made* the people gathering there *wild with enthusiasm*. ～的なファンが彼を取り巻いた *Ardent* fans surrounded him.

ねつ・く【寝つく】¶赤ん坊がやっと～いた I'm glad my baby *has got asleep*. / I've *put* my baby *to sleep*. 昨夜は～けなかった I couldn't *get to sleep* last night.

ネック（障害）a bottleneck. ¶土地不足が住宅問題解決の最大の～だ Land scarcity is the greatest *bottleneck* (≒ *obstruction*) *to* the solution of housing problems.

ねづ・く【根づく】¶その木は～いた The tree *has found root*. 民主主義は日本の国土にしっかり～かなかった Democracy didn't *take* firm *root* in Japanese soil.

ネックレス a necklace.

ねっけつかん【熱血漢】a hot-blooded man.

ねつげん【熱源】heat-source.

ねつこうりつ【熱効率】〔物理〕thermal efficiency.

ねつさまし【熱冷まし】an antifebrile.

ねつじき【熱磁気】〔物理〕thermomagnetism.

ねっしゃびょう【熱射病】heatstroke. ¶～にかかる suffer from (≒ be affected by) *heatstroke*.

ねつじょう【熱情】ardor; passion. ¶彼は愛国の～に燃えていた He *was burning with* patriotism.

ねっしん【熱心】zeal.

1〖熱心な〗¶彼はその政党の～な支持者だ He is an *ardent* supporter of that political party.

彼は～な学生だ He *is* very *studious*.

彼らは～なクリスチャンだ They are *devoted* Christians.

2〖熱心に〗¶彼はひとり～に祈っている He is praying *fervently* by himself.

彼は～に私のことばに耳を傾けていた He was listening *intently* to my words.

彼らは昼も夜も～に働いている They are working *hard* day and night.

3〖熱心さ〗¶彼のゴルフに対する～さはたいへんなものだ His *enthusiasm for* golf is obvious.

彼の～さは賞賛に値する His *eagerness* deserves praise.

4〖熱心だ〗¶このところ彼は切手収集に～だ He *is bent on* collecting stamps these days.

彼はフランス語の勉強に～だ He is *enthusiastically* studying French.

ねっ・する【熱する】日本人は～しやすく冷めやすい The Japanese are easy both to *get excited* and to cool down. 鉄は～すると赤くなる When *heated*, iron turns red.

ねっせい【熱誠】earnestness; zeal. ¶～あふれる手紙 an *earnest* letter. ～をこめた歓迎を受ける receive a *warm* welcome; be *heartily* welcomed. ～あふれる支援をする support *enthusiastically* (≒ *with enthusiasm*).

ねっせん【熱戦】a close game; a hot contest. ¶その賞をめぐって～が繰り広げられた The prize *was hotly contested*. A校グランドで両校の～が繰り広げられた *A close contest* between the two schools was staged on the A school grounds.

ねつぞう【捏造】invention; fabrication. ¶記事を～する *invent* (≒ *fabricate*) a report. そのうわさはすべて完全な～だった The whole report is *a* pure *invention* (≒ *fabrication*).

ねったい【熱帯】the tropics; the Torrid Zone.

—魚（植物）a tropical fish (plant). **—性低気圧** a tropical storm; tropical atmospheric pressure. **—病** a tropical disease.

ねっちゅう【熱中】¶仕事に～している *be absorbed in* business. チョウの研究に～する *devote oneself to* a study of butterflies. ドイツ語の勉強に～している *be bent on* learning German. 政治に～する *go in for* politics. 野球に～している *be mad* (≒ *be crazy*) *about* baseball.

ねつっぽ・い【熱っぽい】¶～いまなざしで with a *passionate* (≒ *serious*) look. ～い調子で話す speak *ardently* (≒ *enthusiastically*). ～い顔をしている，かぜをひいたにちがいない You *look feverish*. You must have caught cold.

ねつでんき【熱電気】〔物理〕thermoelectricity.

ネット a net. ¶～を張る put up *a net*.

—裏 the grandstand. **—プレー** a net play. **—ワーク**（テレビの）the TV networks.

ねつど【熱度】degrees of heat; (温度) temperature.

ねっとう【熱湯】boiling water. ¶彼女は～をひっくり返して手をやけどした She scalded her hand upsetting the *boiling water*. 哺乳(ほにゅう)びんを使う前に～消毒をしなさい *Scald* the baby's bottle before you fill it.

ねっとり ¶～したジャム *viscous* jam. ～汗ばむ feel *sticky*; feel uncomfortably sweaty.

ねつびょう【熱病】a fever.

ねっぷう【熱風】a hot wind; (アラビア・北アの砂漠の) a simoon; (サハラ砂漠の) a sirocco.

¶ふいごから～を送る send *a hot* (≒ *heated*) *wind* of the bellows.

ねつべん【熱弁】¶世界平和について～をふるう make *an impassioned* (≒ *passionate*) *speech on* world peace.

ねつぼう【熱望】an ardent wish. ¶ 彼女を妻にと〜する *Earnestly* (≒ *Strongly*) I *desire* her for my wife. もっと詳細を知りたいと〜している I *am desirous* (≒ *anxious*) *to* know further details. 世界平和を〜する I *long for* world peace. すぐにも助力が与えられることを〜する I *am anxious for* help to be offered promptly.

ねづもり【値積もり】¶ その古書の価値は〜不可能だ The value of the old book is not to *be estimated.* その土地の〜額は低い The land is low in *estimation.*

ねづよ·い【根強い】¶ 彼は黒人に対して〜い偏見を持っている He has a *deep-rooted* prejudice against negroes. / He is *deeply* prejudiced against colored people. 彼の反対する気持ちは〜かった His objection *was deeply rooted.*

ねつりきがく【熱力学】〘物理〙thermodynamics.

ねつりょう【熱量】heat capacity ; the quantity of heat ; (単位) calorie ; calory. ¶ 〜の多い(少ない) high (low) in *calorie* ; high (low) *caloried.* 1グラムの水の温度を1度上げるのに必要な〜 *the quantity of heat* necessary to raise the temperature of a gram of water one degree centigrade.

ねつるい【熱涙】hot tears. ¶ 〜にむせびつつ with *hot tears* in *one's* eyes. 〜が彼のほおを伝わって流れ落ちた *Hot tears* rolled down on his cheeks.

ねつれつ【熱烈】¶ 〜な調子で話す speak *with fervor.* 〜な愛国者 an *ardent* patriot. 美しい少女に〜な恋をした I fell in *passionate* love with a beautiful girl. 彼はその運動を〜に支持していた He was an *ardent* supporter of the movement.

ねてもさめても【寝ても覚めても】¶ このことは〜忘れない I can never forget the matter *waking or sleeping* (≒ *night and day*).

ねどこ【寝床】a bed. ¶ 〜に入る go to *bed.* 〜を離れる get out of *bed.* 〜を敷く(畳む) make (fold) *a bed.* 10時まで〜にもぐっている stay in *bed* till ten.

ねとまり【寝泊まり】¶ おじの家に〜している *stay* (≒ *live*) *with one's* uncle ; *stay at one's* uncle's. 学生たちはみな民家に〜した All the students were *lodged* in private houses.

ねなしぐさ【根無し草】a floating weed. ¶ 彼は〜のような生活をしている He leads a *vagrant* life. / He is a vagrant (≒ a rolling stone).

ネパール Nepal.
—語 Nepali. —人 a Nepalese.

ねばつ·く【粘つく】¶ ハエ取り紙は〜く Fly-paper *is sticky.*

ねばねば【粘粘】¶ この木の樹脂はたいへん〜する The resin of this tree *is very sticky.*

ねはば【値幅】¶ 〜の少ない株をお求めになることをお奨めします I advise you to buy shares which don't *fluctuate* much *in price.*

ねばり【粘り】stickiness. ¶ この米は〜がある The rice *is rich in gluten.* 〜気のある土 *sticky* (≒ *adhesive*) clay.

ねばりつ·く【粘り着く】¶ にかわが指に〜いた Glue *stuck to* my fingers. チューインガムがくつ底に〜いてとれなかった A piece of chewing-gum *stuck to* the sole of my shoe and wouldn't come off.

ねばりづよ·い【粘り強い】¶ 〜い男 a *tenacious* man ; 圏 a *tough* guy. 彼には〜さがない He lacks *tenacity.* きみは〜いのがとりえだ You have *persistence,* I'll say that for you.

ねば·る【粘る】¶ その仕事に最後まで〜れ *Stick to* the task to the last. 最後まで〜れ Don't give in to the last. コーヒー1杯で3時間も〜る学生がいる Some students *stay* as *long* as three hours over a cup of coffee.

ねはん【涅槃】〘仏教〙nirvana. ¶ 〜に入る enter (≒ pass into) *nirvana.*

ねびえ【寝冷え】¶ 昨夜〜してしまった I *caught cold while asleep* (≒ *while sleeping*) last night.

ねびき【値引き】¶ 当店は〜いたしません We never *make a reduction.* / We never *ask two prices.* それを少し〜いたしましょう We will *make* it a little *cheaper.* 1割〜しましょう We will *reduce the price* by ten percent.

ねぶか·い【根深い】deep-rooted. ¶ ヘビに対する〜い嫌悪(けんお) *deep-seated* dislike for snakes. その問題の原因は〜い The cause of the trouble *is deep-rooted.* それは〜い病気でなかなかなおらない It is a *deep-seated* (≒ *chronic*) disease and obstinate.

ねぶくろ【寝袋】a sleeping bag.

ねぶそく【寝不足】want of sleep. ¶ 〜で頭が痛い I have a headache from *want of sleep* (≒ *loss of sleep*). 〜は身体に毒だ *Lack of sleep* injures your health. きょうは〜だ I didn't get much sleep last night.

ねぶみ【値踏み】valuation ; estimation. ¶ 彼はその絵を5万円と〜した He *valued* the picture at fifty thousand yen. 古本の〜はそう簡単じゃない It is not so easy to *set a price on* secondhand books.

ねぼう【寝坊】oversleeping ; (朝寝坊の人) a late riser ; (眠たがる人) a sleepyhead. ¶ けさ〜して電車に乗り遅れた I *overslept myself* (≒ *rose late*) and missed the train this morning. 私はいつもよりも〜した I *got up later* than usual. この子は〜だ This child is *a sleepy-head.* ぼくは〜だ I'm *a late riser.*

ねぼ·ける【寝惚ける】¶ 彼はきっと〜けてそんなことを言ったのにちがいない He *must have been half-asleep* when he said it. 彼女は〜け顔で寝室から出てきた She came out of her bedroom *with a sleepy look.* 〜けたことを言うな Don't *talk nonsense* ! / Nonsense !

ねほりはほり【根掘り葉掘り】¶ 彼らは私に家族のことを〜尋ねた They questioned me *to the minutest details* of my family. そんなに〜聞くものじゃない Don't *be so inquisitive.*

ねま【寝間】a bedroom.

ねまき【寝巻き】night clothes ; pajamas ; 英 pyjamas ; (婦人, 子ども用) a nightgown ; a

ね

nightdress.

ねみだれがみ【寝乱れ髪】¶ 彼女は～をととのえた She arranged her *disheveled hair after sleep.*

ねみみ【寝耳】¶ その知らせは～に水だった The news was *a great surprise to* me. / The news *was like a bolt from the blue.* / I *was totally unprepared for* the news.

ねむ・い【眠い】 be (⇆ feel) sleepy. ¶ 彼は～そうだ He *looks sleepy* (⇆ *drowsy*). あの教授の講義は～かった That professor gave us *dull* lectures.

ねむくな・る【眠くなる】¶ 夕飯を食べるとすぐ～る I *feel* (⇆ *become*) *sleepy* soon after supper.

ねむけ【眠気】 sleepiness. ¶ ひどく～を催してきた I *felt* very *sleepy.* ～覚ましに茶を飲んだ I drank tea to *keep myself awake.*

ねむ〔た〕そう【眠〔た〕そう】¶ 彼は～な目をしていた He *was heavy-eyed.* / His eyes *looked heavy* (⇆ *looked sleepy ; looked drowsy*).

ねむのき【合歓の木】〖植物〗 a silk tree.

ねむら・せる【眠らせる】¶ 彼女は赤ん坊を～せた She *put* the baby *to sleep.*

ねむり【眠り】 sleep. ¶ 深い (浅い) ～ *a* sound (poor) *sleep.* 永の～ the last (⇆ eternal ; long) *sleep.* ～が足りない I am short of *sleep.* / I haven't slept enough.

ねむ・る【眠る】 sleep. ¶ ゆうべはよく～った I *slept* well last night. ゆうべはよく～れなかった I *slept* badly last night. この二, 三日よく～れない I *haven't slept* well these past few days. 薬を飲んだが～れなかった The medicine did not help me *go to sleep.* 赤ん坊はぐっすり～っている The baby *is* sound (⇆ fast) *asleep.* コーヒーを飲むと一晩じゅう～れない Coffee *keeps* me *awake* all night. 彼はぐっすり～らせておきなさい Let him *have* his *sleep* out. 疲れているだろうから, 一晩ぐっすり～りなさい Since you must be tired, *have* a good night's *sleep.* どれだけ～ればよいんだ How many hours' *sleep* do you need? ～っている子をおこすな (諺) *Let sleeping dogs lie.*

ねもと【根本・根元】 the root. ¶ 私は木の～に腰をおろした I sat down *at the root of* a tree. 彼女は髪を～から切った She cut off her hair *at the root.*

ねものがたり【寝物語】 a talk in bed 〔between husband and wife〕.

ねゆき【根雪】¶ 谷にはまだ～がある In the valley there still remains *unmelted snow.*

ねらい【狙い】 aim. ¶ この作者の～がわかりますか Can you tell what this writer *is trying to say* (⇆ *is getting at*)? 確かにそれはいい～だ That is really *a good idea.* 彼は空飛ぶ鳥に銃の～を定めた He *aimed* his gun *at* a flying bird. 弾丸は～がはずれた The bullet missed *the mark.* きみの～はよいのだが… Your *intentions* are good, but.... ～がはずれた I missed my *aim.*

ねら・う【狙う】 aim (*at*). ¶ よく～う *take* careful *aim.* あのカエルは虫を～っている That frog *has his eye on* a worm. 私は話の口を切る機会を～っていた I *was watching for* an opportunity to speak. 彼は議長のいすを～っている He *has an eye on* the office of chairman. 彼は父親の遺産を～っている He *is after* his father's inheritance. 彼の命をだれかが～っている Someone *is after* (⇆ *is seeking*) his life. 別にきみを～って言っているわけではない My remarks *are* not *aimed at* you.

ねりある・く【練り歩く】¶ 労働者は通りを～いた The working men *paraded* the streets.

ねりあわ・せる【練り合わせる】¶ ケーキを作るためにバター, 砂糖, ミルク, メリケン粉を～せる *mix* butter, sugar, milk, and flour for a cake.

ねりなお・す【練り直す】¶ 計画を～す *reconsider* (⇆ *polish up*) a plan.

ねりはみがき【練り歯磨き】 tooth-paste ; dental cream.

ネル flannel.

ね・る【練る】¶ パンを～る *knead* bread dough. 彼はもっと胆力を～らなければだめだ He should *develop* more backbone. 論文を書くに際してはまず構想を～ることだ In writing a thesis it is necessary first of all to *work over* your ideas. 深夜まで講義の草稿を～る *polish up* a draft of a lecture till late at night.

ねる【寝る】 **1**〖横になる・床につく〗¶ 草の上に寝るのは爽快(そうかい)だ It is refreshing to *lie down* on the grass.

ネコが日なたで長々と寝ている There is a cat *lying* at full length in the sun.

子どもはもう寝る時間です It is 〔high〕 time the children *went to bed.*

遅く寝るとあすの朝起きるのがつらい If you sit up late, you will find it hard to get up early tomorrow.

日曜日はたいてい一日じゅう寝ている On Sunday I usually *stay in bed* all day.

一日むだに寝て暮らした I *slept* the day *away.*

彼は病気で寝ている He *is* sick *in bed.*

医者から起きてもいいという許可が出るまでは寝ていなければいけない You should *stay in bed* until you get your doctor's permission to get out 〔of bed〕.

その問題は一晩寝て考えてみます I will *sleep on* the question.

2〖眠る〗¶ ゆうべはぐっすり寝た I *had a good sleep* last night. / I *slept like a log* last night.

こんな風邪は一晩よく寝れば治ってしまう A good night's *rest* will cure you of that sort of cold.

将来が心配で寝られない日が続いた I had a number of *sleepless* nights worrying about my future.

彼は寝る間も惜しんで勉強している He is studying long hours and cutting down on *sleep.*

3〖資金・商品などが〗¶ 寝ている商品を早急に処分する必要がある It is necessary to dispose of the *unsold* goods immediately.

その資金は寝かせておかないで活用すべきだ The capital should not be allowed to *lie idle* but utilized.

ねれた【練れた】¶ あの人はよく～人だ He is a man *of mellow character*. / He is a man *of the world*. / He is a *gentle and patient* person.

ねわけ【根分け】¶ 菊の～をする *part roots* of the chrysanthemums.

ねわざ【寝技】〖レスリング・柔道〗 ¶ 彼は～が得意だ He is skilled in *lying-down trick*.
―師 a political trickster.

ねん【年】a year. ¶ ～に2回九州に行く I go to Kyushu twice *a year*. その事件のあったのは昭和何～でしたか In what *year* of Showa did the accident take place? 彼は1890～に生まれた He was born *in 1890*. あなたは今何～ですか In what *grade* are you? 今1～です(小学校の場合) I am in the first *grade* (≒a first grader). / (中学の場合) I am in the first *year* of the junior high school (≒ in the seventh *grade*). / (高校の場合) I am a high school freshman. この貸付金には～3分の利子がつく This loan has an interest of (≒ at) three percent *perannum*. このウイスキーは30～ものだ This bottle of whisky is *thirty years old*.

ねん【念】**1**〖気持ち〗a sense. ¶ 彼は感謝の～に欠けている He has no *sense* of gratitude.
私は不安の～でいっぱいだった I was filled with [*a sense* of] uneasiness.
2〖心配〗¶ 御～には及びません You don't have to worry about it.
3〖入念〗¶ ～の入った御注意ありがたく存じます Thank you for your *scrupulous* care.
～を入れてやらないと失敗する You will make a mistake if you don't take *special care*.
～には～を入れなさい You cannot *be* too *careful*.
4〖注意〗¶ 途中でその店に寄るよう彼に～を押した I *reminded* him *to* drop in at the store on his way.
ぼくにそんなに～を押さなくてもいい I don't need to *be reminded about* it.
約束は守るねともう一度彼に～を押した Just to *make sure* I asked him again whether he would keep his promise.

ねんいり【念入り】¶ ゆっくり～にやりたまえ Take time and do it *well*. 彼は～に仕事をした He took *great pains* (≒ *much trouble*) *to* do his work. / He did his work *with great care* (≒ *with careful attention*). ～にやってほしい I want it done *thoroughly*. 彼女の化粧はいつも～だ Her toilet is always *elaborately* (≒ *carefully*) made.

ねんえき【粘液】viscous fluid. ¶ ～質の人 a *phlegmatic* person.

ねんが【年賀】¶ ～のあいさつをかわす exchange *New Year's greetings*.
―状 a New Year's card. **―**客 a New Year's visitor.

ねんがく【年額】an annual sum. ¶ 彼の収入は～300万円以上だ He earns more than three million yen a year. / His *annual* (≒ *yearly*) *income* amounts to more than three million yen.

ねんがっぴ【年月日】a date. ¶ 手紙に～を書き忘れる forget to *date* (≒ *put the date to*) a letter.

ねんがらねんじゅう【年がら年中】¶ あの男は～せわしなく働いている He is busy working *all the year round*. 彼は～ぴいぴいだ He remains *always* poor.

ねんかん【年間】¶ 輸入額は～300億ドルに達する The import amounts to thirty billion dollars *a year*. ～計画を立てる make *a program for the year*. 彼はその～の最優秀作品賞を与えられた He was given a prize for writing the best novel *in the year*. 明治～に二つの大きな戦争があった We had two great wars *during* (≒ *in*) *the Meiji era*. きょうの地震は過去数～(過去3～)でいちばんひどいものだ The earthquake today is the severest one we have had *for some years past* (*for the past* three *years*). 夏には引き続き10～札幌を訪れた I visited Sapporo in summer *for* ten successive *years*.
―収入 an annual income.

ねんかん【年鑑】a yearbook; an annual; an almanac.
経済**―** an economic yearbook.

ねんがん【念願】*one's* dearest wish; *one's* heart's desire. ¶ 多年の～がかなった My long-cherished *desire* has been fulfilled. ヨーロッパ旅行は私の多年の～だった It has been *in my thought* for many years to travel in Europe.

ねんき【年季】*one's* term. ¶ ～の入った者でなければできない仕事だ None but *long experienced* men can do it. / The job requires *long experience*.

ねんきゅう【年給】an annual (≒ yearly) salary.

ねんきゅう【年級】a year; a grade; 英 a form. ¶ 3～の生徒 a third-year student; a third grader. 彼は2～である He is *in the second-year class*. / He is *in the second grade*.

ねんきん【年金】annuity; a pension. ¶ ～を受ける receive *a pension*. 彼は～で暮らしている He lives on his *pension*.
―受領者 an annuitant; a pensioner. 終身**―** a life annuity. 厚生**―** a welfare annuity. 養老**―** an old age pension. 厚生**―**保険 the welfare pension insurance.

ねんぐ【年貢】a land tax. ¶ ～を納める pay *ground rent*. ～を取り立てる collect the *land tax*. 彼も～の納め時だ All is lost with him. / His time [of reckoning] has come. / It is the time for him to reap the harvest of crimes.

ねんげつ【年月】years. ¶ この本を書くのに長い～がかかった It took me [*a lot of*] *years* to write this book. 彼に最後に会ってから多くの～が過ぎ去った It is *years* since I saw him last. トンネル完成までにかなりの～を要するだろう It will *be long* before we can accomplish the tunnel. / It will take *a long time* to accomplish the tunnel. ～がたつにつれて彼には彼女の面影を思い出すのが困難になった *As the years went by* (≒ *With the lapse of time*), it became hard for him to be reminded of her image.

ねんげん【年限】a period ; a term. ¶ 市長の～は満了した The mayor's *term of office* has expired. ～が切れて彼は退いた He retired at the expiration of *the term*.

修業── the term of study. 服務── the term of office (≒ service).

ねんこう【年功】¶ 彼は～を積んだ He had *long experience*. / He is *an old timer* (≒ *a veteran*). 昇進は～による Promotion goes by *seniority*. ～が物をいう *Experience* will tell.

──序列制度 a seniority rule.

ねんごう【年号】the name of an era. ¶ ～は大正と改められた The new era was changed to (≒ was named) Taisho.

ねんごろ【懇ろ】**1**〖ていねいに〗¶ 彼は客を～にもてなす He entertains his guests *hospitably* (≒ *handsomely*).

彼はそれを～に説明してくれた He *took great pains* to explain it. / He explained it *in detail*.

彼は私に～に諭してくれた He talked to me *gently*. / He reasoned with me *earnestly*.

彼の遺骸(がい)を～に葬った We buried his body *with due ceremony*.

2〖むつまじい〗¶ われわれ一家は彼らと～になった Our family *became friends with* them.

3〖男女間について〗¶ 彼らは一目見て～になった They *fell in love with* each other at first sight.

ふたりはすでに～になっている They *have* already *become intimate with* each other.

ねんざ【捻挫】sprain. ¶ 彼は転んで足首を～した He *sprained* (≒ *wrenched* ; *twisted*) his ankle when he fell to the ground.

-ねんさい【-年祭】an anniversary. ¶ 100～ a centenary ; a centennial *anniversary*. 300～ a tercentenary. 400～ a quadricentennial. モーツアルト生誕200～ the *bicentenary* of the birth of Mozart.

ねんさん【年産】an annual (≒ a yearly) product (≒ output).

ねんし【年始】(元旦) the New Year's Day. ¶ ～回りをする make New Year's calls. ～のあいさつを言う wish a happy New Year. ～の客 a New Year's visitor (≒ caller).

ねんじ【年次】¶ 歴史上の出来事を～的に記録した We recorded the historic events *chronologically*.

──計画 a long term yearly plan. ──総会 an annual general meeting. ──報告 an annual report.

ねんしつ【粘質】viscosity.

ねんしつ【燃質】combustibility.

ねんしゅう【年収】an annual (≒ a yearly) income. ¶ 彼の～は500万円を超える His *income* is more than five million yen *a year*.

ねんじゅう【年中】all the year round. ¶ あの男は～ぶらぶらしている He idles away his time *year in and year out*. 彼は～金に困っている He is *always* hard up.

──無休 ¶ あの店は～無休だ That store is open *throughout the year*.

ねんしゅつ【捻出・拈出】¶ そこで彼は名案を～した Then he *contrived* (≒ *worked out*) a good plan. 新財源の～はほとんど不可能である It is almost impossible to *find out* a new source of revenue.

ねんしょう【年少】¶ ～気鋭の若者 a young man full of youthful ardor. 彼は～にして父母のもとを離れた He left his parents *in his tender age* (≒ *in his childhood*). 彼は～のゆえをもって許された He was pardoned in consideration of his *youth*.

──者 a youth ; a minor ; a person under age.

ねんしょう【燃焼】combustion.

──物 combustibles ; inflammable articles. 自然── spontaneous combustion. 不完全── imperfect combustion.

ねんすう【年数】¶ 絹は～がたつと光沢が出る Silk acquires a gloss *with* (≒ *from*) *age*.

ねん・ずる【念ずる】¶ 老母とともに彼女は夫の無事を～じて暮らしていた She lived with her old mother *praying for* the safety of her husband. 楽しいご旅行を～じます I *wish* you a pleasant journey. 国家の安泰を心に～じている I *have* the welfare of the country *at heart*.

ねんせい【粘性】viscosity.

ねんだい【年代】an epoch. ¶ ～を経た建物 a building which has seen *many years*. その木の高さは～を偲ばせる The height of the tree suggests its *age*. 彼は1930～にここに来た He came here in the 1930's. それは明治の～に起きた It took place in the Meiji *era*. その大詩人の出現は英文学史上に一つの新しい～を開いた The appearance of the great poet made a new *epoch* in English literature. その楽曲の創作～は正確にはきめられない We cannot fix the exact *date* of the composition.

──記 a chronicle. ──順 ¶ われわれは～順に歴史を読んだ We read the history *in chronological order*.

ねんちゃく【粘着】adhesion ; cohesion.

──力 *cohesive* (≒ *adhesive*) power ; viscosity.

ねんちゅうぎょうじ【年中行事】an annual event ; the year's celebration.

¶ それはスペイン人の～の一つである It is one of *the year's pageants* of Spanish life. オックスフォードとケンブリッジのボートレースは大きな～の一つだ The boat race (≒ The regatta) between Oxford and Cambridge is one of the chief *events of the year*.

ねんちょう【年長】seniority. ¶ 彼はぼくより三つ～だ He *is* my *senior by* three years. / He

ね

is three years *older than* I. / He *is* three years my *senior*.
—者 an elder; a senior. ¶ 彼は政界の最〜者だ He is *the oldest man* in the political world.

ねんど【年度】 the year; (会計年度) the fiscal year. ¶ 本〜は4月8日に学校が始まった Our *school year* began on the 8th of April. 昭和51〜の予算が成立した The budget for Showa 51 has been made.
—替わり the change of the fiscal year. **—始め(末)** the beginning (end) of the fiscal year.

ねんど【粘土】 clay. ¶ 〜質の clayey. 〜細工 *clay* works.

ねんとう【年頭】 the beginning of the year; New Year's Day.

ねんとう【念頭】 ¶ 彼は生涯そのことばを〜において忘れなかった He *kept* (≒ *bore*) the words *in mind* all his life. 自分のことは〜におかず彼は社会奉仕に専念した *Without a thought of* (≒ *Without thinking of*) himself he devoted himself to the social service. 母のことがいつも〜を離れない My mother *is ever in my mind.* / Mother always *haunts my mind.* すべての婦人の〜にあるものは衣服だ Every woman's *mind* is occupied with dress. 私は家族の健康ということをまず〜においている My first *thought* is the health of the family. 彼は彼女のことを〜から取り去ることができなかった He was not able to dismiss her from his *mind*.

ねんない【年内】 ¶ 家は〜に完成することになっている My new house is to be accomplished *before the end of the year* (≒ *before the year is out*). どうぞ〜に一度お出かけください I hope you will come to see me *within the year*.

ねんね ¶ さあ〜しなくてはだめよ Why not *go to sleep*, my dear? 彼女はまるきり〜です She is *a mere child*. 彼は世の中のことについては〜だ He *is quite ignorant of the world.* / He *knows little of the world.*

ねんねこ a nursery coat.

ねんねん【年年】 (毎年) every year; (年ごとに) from year to year. ¶ 議会は〜開かれる Diet is held *every year* (≒ *annually*). 〜物価が上がる Prices rise *from year to year* (≒ *year by year*).

ねんのため【念の為】 ¶ 〜証書を取り交わした We exchanged the notes *by way of precaution*. 万事異状はないか〜自分で行って調べたほうがよい You must go and see that all is right. 〜もう一度勘定してみた I went over the account *to make sure of it*. 〜この本を持っていってごらんなさい Take this book with you *just in case*. 〜懐中電燈を持っていったほうがいい You must take a flashlight with you *for safety's sake*. 彼は来ると思うが, 〜確かめたほうがよい I think he is coming, but had better *make sure*.

ねんぱい【年配】 ¶ 〜の人 an *elderly* person. 彼は私と同〜だ He *is as old as* I (≒ me). / He *is* [*about*] my *age*.

ねんばんがん【粘板岩】〔地質〕argillite.

ねんびゃくねんじゅう【年百年中】 always; all the year round.

ねんぴょう【年表】 a chronological table.

ねんぷ【年譜】 a chronological personal history.

ねんぷ【年賦】 a yearly instalment. ¶ 地代は5か年〜で払うことになっている The rent is to be paid by *yearly instalments* spread over five years.

ねんぶつ【念仏】 a Buddhist invocation. ¶ 彼は毎朝〜を唱える He *prays to Amida Buddha* every morning. 馬の耳に〜 (諺) *It is like water off a duck's back.*

ねんぽう【年報】 an annual report.

ねんぽう【年俸】 a yearly salary. ¶ 彼の〜は300万円だ His *annual* (≒ *yearly*) *salary* is three million yen. / He *earns* three million yen *a year*.

ねんまく【粘膜】〔解剖学〕the mucous membrane.

ねんまつ【年末】 the end of the year.
—大売り出し a year-end bargain sale. **—賞与** a year-end bonus.

ねんらい【年来】 these years; for years. ¶ 彼は30〜の親友だ He is my close friend of thirty years' standing. / He has been my close friend for thirty years. 10〜の大雪だ This is the heaviest snowfall we've had for the past ten years. 〜の望みがかなった His *long-cherished* dream has come true. 〜の懸案が解決して彼らは喜んでいる They are happy to have solved their *long-pending* problem at last.

ねんり【年利】 an annual interest. ¶ 〜1割で金を貸す lend money at *a yearly* (≒ *an annual*) *interest* of 10 percent.

ねんりき【念力】 psychokinesis. ¶ 思う〜岩をも通す (諺) *Where there's a will there's a way.*

ねんりょう【燃料】 fuel. ¶ 〜を補給するため飛行機は着陸した The plane came down to *refuel*.
—費 fuel expense. ¶ 〜費がばかにならない The *cost of fuel* is far from negligible. **—補給** refueling. **—補給所** a fueling station. 液(固; 気)体**—** liquid (solid; gaseous) fuel.

ねんりん【年輪】〔植物〕an annual ring [of a tree].

ねんれい【年齢】 age; years. ¶ この物語はあらゆる〜の人に読める People of all *ages* will enjoy this story. 30歳から60歳までの〜の人ならだれでもこのクラブに入れる Anyone between thirty and sixty can join this club.
結婚**—** marriageable age. 精神**—** mental age. 平均**—** the average age. **—層** age group. ¶ この〜層は最も虫歯になりやすい This *age group* is the most susceptible to tooth decay.

の

の【野】a field；(平原) a plain. ¶～の花 a *wild* (≒ *field*) flower. あとは～となれ山となれ (諺) *After me* (≒ *us*) *the deluge!* やはり～におけレンゲソウ Leave her where she is.

-の **1**〖所有・所属・同格〗¶私～家 *my* house. それはきみ～帽子ではなくぼく～だ That is not *your* hat, but *mine*.
この万年筆はだれ～か Whose pen is this?
きみはこの大学～学生ですか Are you a student *of* this college?
彼はハーヴァードの教授だ He is a professor *at* Harvard. (of にしない).
健康～ありがたみがよくわかった Now I understand how good it is to be healthy.
2〖主格〗¶あれは私～好きな曲だ That is my favorite piece (≒ melody).
彼～書いた小説はおもしろい *His* novels are interesting. / The novels he wrote are interesting. (後者は「彼」が故人になった感じを与える).
これは子ども～喜ぶおもちゃだ This is a toy which appeals to children.
3〖目的格〗¶子ども～教育には金がかかる It is costly (≒ expensive) to educate children.
4〖…についての〗¶英語～授業 an English lesson; a lesson *in* English.
経済学～研究 a study *of* economics; a work *on* economics.
数学～先生 a teacher *of* mathematics.
この図書館には歴史～本が多い This library has many books *on* history.
彼は脳外科～権威だ He is an authority *on* brain surgery.
5〖内容・材質〗¶ひとかご～ミカン a basket *of* tangerines.
ひと箱～鉛筆 a box *of* pencils.
3台～スキー three pairs *of* skis.
6〖場所〗¶東京～大学へ通う go to college *in* Tokyo.
神田～古本屋 second-hand bookstores *in* Kanda.
南米～国々 countries *in* South America; South American countries.
隣～家～人々 next-door neighbors; the people next door.
7〖…からの〗¶彼～手紙 a letter *from* him.
故郷～便りが着いた I heard *from* home.
これは友人〔から〕～贈り物です This is a gift *from* a friend of mine.
彼はシカゴ～人だ He is (≒ comes) *from* Chicago.
8〖…のための〗¶警察は事件解明～手がかりをつかんだ The police found a clue *to* the solution of the case.

ノア〔聖書〕Noah. ¶～の洪水 the Flood; the Deluge. ～の箱舟 *Noah's* ark.

ノイローゼ〔医学〕a neurosis (ノイローゼはドイツ語の Neurose から). ¶彼は～にかかっている He has been suffering from *a neurosis*. / He *is neurotic*.

のう【能】(能力) ability; (技能) skill; (能楽) a *no* play. ¶私には金もうけの～がない I have no *ability* to make money. 彼は野球しか～がない All that he can do is to play baseball. 金をためるばかりが～でない，じょうずに使うこともたいせつだ It is not everything to accumulate money; to spend it wisely is also important. ～ある鷹(たか)はつめを隠す (諺) *Still waters run deep*. ～をやる perform *no plays*.

のう【農】agriculture. 小作— a tenant farmer. 自作— a landed farmer.

のう【脳】the brain; (頭脳) brains. ¶彼は～のどこかが悪い He has *brain* trouble.
—外科 brain surgery. —作用 cerebration.
—性小児まひ cerebral polio. 小— cerebellum. 大— cerebrum.

のういっけつ【脳溢血】〔医学〕cerebral hemorrhage; cerebral apoplexy. ¶～の発作を起こす have a stroke of *apoplexy*; have an *apoplectic* fit (≒ stroke).

のうえん【脳炎】〔医学〕encephalitis. ¶日本～ Japanese *encephalitis*.

のうえん【農園】a plantation; a farm.

のうえん【濃艶】¶～な美人 a *voluptuous* beauty. ～な姿 a *charming* figure.

のうか【農家】(家) a farmhouse; a farm; (人) a farmer. ¶彼らは～で育った They were brought up *on the farms*.

のうか【濃化】〔薬学〕incrassation;〔化学〕concentrate.
—油 thickened oil.

のうか【農科】the agricultural department; (課程) a course in agriculture.
—大学 an agricultural college.

のうかい【納会】the last meeting of the year; (取引所の) the last session of the month. ¶5月の～相場は500ドルまで釣り上げられた The *closing price* for May was driven up to five hundred dollars.

のうがき【能書き】(薬の) a statement of virtues; (自己宣伝) self-advertisement. ¶～の半分も効く薬はない No drug is as good as its *puff* says. あの男はいつも～たくさんだ He *is* always *full of puffery*.

のうがく【能楽】a *no* play.

のうがく【農学】—校 an agricultural school. —士(博士) a Bachelor (Doctor) of Agriculture. —部 the department of agriculture.

のうかすいたい【脳下垂体】〘解剖学〙 the pituitary gland.

のうかん【納棺】¶ 1時に～の予定 The body is to *be put in a coffin* at one o'clock.

のうかんき【農閑期】the farmers' slack season.

のうき【納期】(物品の) the appointed date of delivery; (税の) the date of tax payment; (金銭の) the time for payment.

のうきぐ【農機具】farming machines and implements; (集合的) agricultural machinery.

のうぎょう【農業】agriculture. ¶ 集約(粗放)～ intensive (extensive) *agriculture*. 彼は～に従事している He is engaged in *farming* (≒ *agriculture*).

—試験場 an agricultural experiment station.

のうきん【納金】(納めた金) money paid; (納めるべき金) money due.

のうぐ【農具】a farming implement.

のうげい【農芸】agricultural technology.

のうこう【農耕】farming.

のうこう【濃厚】¶ ～な場面 a *hot* love scene. 彼の優勝の公算がますます～になった There is *stronger* possibility that he would win the championship.

のうこつ【納骨】¶ 彼女の遺骨を明日～するつもりだ We will *lay her ashes under the tomb* tomorrow.

—堂 a charnel house.

のうこん【濃紺】navy blue; dark blue.

のうさぎ【野兎】a hare (rabbit ほど穴居性がない).

のうさくぶつ【農作物】crops.

のうさつ【悩殺】¶ 彼は彼女に～された He *was captivated* (≒ *was fascinated*) by her.

のうさんぶつ【農産物】agricultural produce (≒ products).

のうじ【農事】agriculture.

—試験場 an agricultural experiment station.

のうしゅ【膿腫】〘医学〙 an abscess.

のうしゅく【濃縮】—ウラン concentrated (≒ enriched) uranium.

のうしゅっけつ【脳出血】〘医学〙 cerebral hemorrhage.

のうじょう【農場】a farm. ¶ ～を経営する run *a farm*.

—主 a farmer. —労働者 a farm hand. 共同— a collective farm.

のうしんけい【脳神経】〘解剖学〙 a cerebral nerve.

—細胞 a brain cell.

のうしんとう【脳震盪】〘医学〙 〔a〕 concussion of the brain.

のうずい【脳髄】the brain.

のうせい【農政】agricultural administration.

のうぜい【納税】payment of taxes. ¶ 国民は～の義務がある The people are under liability to *pay taxes*.

—額 the amount of *one's* taxes. —期限 the time-limit for tax payment. —組合 a taxpayers' union. —者 a taxpayer. —済み duty paid. —通知書 tax papers. —積立金 tax reserves. —申告用紙 a tax form.

のうせきずいまくえん【脳脊髄膜炎】〘医学〙 cerebrospinal meningitis.

のうそん【農村】a farm village.

—地帯 a rural district; a farm area. —問題 a rural problem.

のうたん【濃淡】light and shade. ¶ 絵の～ the *lights and shades* of a picture. 絵に～をつける *shade* a drawing.

—法(絵の) shading.

のうち【農地】farmland.

—委員会 a farmland committee. —改革 farmland reform. —開発 development of farmland.

のうちゅう【嚢中】¶ 彼は株の思惑買いをやって～無一文になった He gambled on the stock exchange and *became penniless*.

のうてん【脳天】the crown of the head.

のうど【濃度】density.

のうどう【能動】—態 〘文法〙 the active voice.

のうなし【能無し】a good-for-nothing.

のうなんかしょう【脳軟化症】〘医学〙 softening of the brain.

のうにゅう【納入】¶ 物品を～する *deliver* goods. 税金を～する *pay* tax.

のうのう ¶ 彼のように～と寝て暮らせる身分ではない I can't afford to *idle away my time* like him. 試験が済んだので～としている Now 〔that〕 the examination is over, I *feel much relieved* (≒ *relaxed*).

のうは【脳波】〘医学〙〘心理学〙 a brain wave.

のうはんき【農繁期】the busy farming season.

のうひつ【能筆】¶ 彼はなかなか～だ He writes a very good hand.

—家 a good penman.

のうひん【納品】delivery of goods.

—書 a bill of parcel.

のうひんけつ【脳貧血】〘医学〙 cerebral anemia. ¶ 彼女はあまりの暑さに～を起こして倒れてしまった It was so hot that she had a fit of *cerebral anemia* and fainted.

のうふ【農夫】a farmer; (小百姓) a peasant.

のうべん【能弁】eloquence. ¶ 彼は立て板に水を流すように～だ He is gifted with *a flowing eloquence*.

—家 an eloquent speaker.

のうほん【納本】¶ ～する deliver books (*to*); (当局へ見本を) present a specimen copy to the authorities.

のうまく【脳膜】〘解剖学〙 the meninx.

—炎 meningitis.

のうみそ【脳味噌】brains. ¶ 彼を救い出す方法に～を絞った We racked (≒ cudgeled) our *brains* to find a way of saving him. ～を使いたまえ Use your *brains*. 彼は～が足りない He is a simpleton (≒ a fool).

のうみん【農民】a farmer; (小百姓) a peasant. ―運動 a peasant movement. ―文学 peasant literature.

のうむ【濃霧】a dense fog. ¶ 〜のため航行不能になった The *dense fog* prevented us [from] making a voyage.

のうめん【能面】a *no*-mask. ¶ 〜のように無表情な顔 an *expressionless* (≒ *emotionless*) face like a *no*-mask.

のうやく【農薬】agricultural chemicals.

のうり【能吏】an able official.

のうり【脳裏】¶ 惨状が今でも〜に焼きついている The disastrous scene still haunts *my memory.* / The disastrous scene is present even now in *my mind.* 10年後の自分の姿を〜に描いてみた I *imagined* (≒ *pictured in my mind*) what I would be ten years from now.

のうりつ【能率】efficiency. ¶ 朝の涼しいうちに勉強の〜を上げておいた I have increased the *efficiency* of my study while it's cool in the morning. 〜的に仕事を進めた I got along with my work *efficiently.*
―給 efficiency wages; efficiency pay.

のうりょう【納涼】⇒すずむ
―客 a cool-breeze hunter. ―観光船 a summer pleasure boat.

のうりょく【能力】ability. ¶ 〜のある人物 a *competent* man. 彼は事務的な〜がある He has business *ability.* この種のパズルは考える〜を養う This sort of puzzle improves *one's* thinking *ability.* これは私の〜以上の仕事だ This work is beyond my *ability.* この工場は全〜をあげて操業している This factory is running *at full capacity.* これは人間の〜の限界だ This is the limit of human *ability.* この文章は私の〜では読めない This sentence *is beyond* me. この会社は〜給になっている In this firm they *are paid according to ability.*
―テスト a competence test.

のうりん【農林】―学校 an agricultural and forestry school. ―省 the Ministry of Agriculture and Forestry. ―大臣 the Minister of Agriculture and Forestry.

のうろう【膿漏】〚医学〛a purulent discharge. 歯槽― Riggs' disease; pyorrhea alveolaris.

ノーカウント〚競技〛no count.

ノーコメント no comment. ¶ それに関しては〜だ I will make *no comment* on it.

ノート a note. ¶ 〜しておきなさい *Note* (≒ *Write*) it down. あの講義は〜をとっておきなさい You should *take notes* of that lecture.

ノートブック a notebook.

ノーハウ know-how.

ノーヒットノーラン〚野球〛a no-hit, no-run game.

ノーベル Alfred Bernard Nobel.
―賞 a Nobel prize. ―賞受賞者 a Nobel prize winner; a Nobelist. ―医学 (化学; 物理; 文学; 平和) 賞 the Nobel prize for medicine (chemistry; physics; literature; peace).

ノーマル normal. ¶ それはほんとうに〜なケースだ It's really a *normal* case.

のが・れる【逃れる】escape. ¶ なんとか難を〜れた I managed to *escape* the difficulty. 彼は追手から〜れた He *escaped from* pursuers. 危険を〜れる *get out* of danger. 彼は責任を〜れようとした He tried to *shirk* responsibility. 生物は死を〜れられない Death *is inevitable to* all living things.

のき【軒】the eaves. ¶ 通りには本屋が〜を並べている Bookstores *stand side by side* (≒ *stand in a row*) in the street.

のぎく【野菊】a wild chrysanthemum.

のきさき【軒先】¶ 車の事故は私の家のすぐ〜で起こった There was a car accident just *in front of my house.*

ノギス calipers.

のきなみ【軒並】¶ 〜に寄付を集めて歩いた I called *from door to door* collecting contributions. / I made *house to house* calls to collect contributions. 不景気で問屋が〜に倒産した Owing to the business depression, wholesale stores became bankrupt *one after another.*

の・く【退く】¶ ちょっとそこを〜いてください Please *get out of my way.*

ノクターン〚音楽〛a nocturne.

のけぞ・る【仰け反る】¶ 彼は〜って近い投球をよけた He avoided the close throw by *bending himself back.*

のけもの【退け者】¶ 彼は〜にされた He *was boycotted.* / He *was excluded.* / He *was left out in the cold.*

の・ける【除ける】¶ じゃま物を〜けてください *Remove* (≒ *Get rid of*) the obstacles. / *Get* (≒ *Put*) those obstacles *out of the way.* いすを〜けてくれませんか Will you please *put* (≒ *move*) the chairs *away*?

のこぎり【鋸】a saw. ¶ 〜でひく saw [off]; cut with *a saw* (英米ののこぎりは引くのでなくて, 押すのが普通). 〜の目立てをする set [the teeth of] *a saw.*

のこくず【鋸屑】sawdust.

のこ・す【残す】leave. ¶ どうして私をひとりだけ〜すのですか Why do you *leave* me alone? 仕事を〜したまま彼は出かけていった He went out, *leaving* his work *unfinished.* 彼は息子たちにばく大な遺産を〜した He *left* a large fortune for his sons. 彼はきょう5時まで学校に〜された He *was kept* at school till five today. あの100万円を1円も〜さずに使ってしまった I *spent* that one million yen *to the last penny.* 彼は借金を〜して死んだ He *left* debts *behind* him.

のこのこ〔と〕(平気で) unconcernedly; (あつかましく) shamelessly. ¶ 今ごろ〜やってくるなんて How *shameless* you are to show up after so long a time!

のこらず【残らず】all; every. ¶ 彼は私に知っていることを〜教えてくれた He taught me *all* he knew. 借金は〜お返しします I'll pay off my debts. 兵士はひとり～死んだ The soldiers died *to the last man.* / *Every one of* the soldiers died. 彼はウイスキーを一本, 一滴～飲んでしまった He drank *up* a bottle of whisky. 彼女は身の上を～私に打ち明けてくれた She *made a clean breast of* her life story to me. / She told me *all about herself*. あの映画のシーンは～覚えている I remember *every* scene of that movie.

のこり【残り】the remainder ; the rest ; (少しの) a remnant. ¶ 三つナシをとって, ～はどこかにしまっておいてください Take three pears, and put *the rest* somewhere. 夕食の～は犬にやった I gave *the leftovers* from supper to the dog. 食糧は～少なくなった We *have run out of* food. 夏休みはもう～少ない The greater part of the summer vacation is over. 100から80を引くと～はいくつですか How much is eighty from one hundred?

のこりもの【残り物】leftovers ; remnants. ¶ ～には福がある *Leftovers* are the best of all.

のこ･る【残る】remain ; be left. ¶ 菓子が少し～った Some of the cakes *are left.* 金はたくさん～るだろう There will be plenty of money *left.* 10から3引くといくつ～りますか If you take three from ten, what *remains?* 財布には10円しか～っていない There is no more than ten yen *left* in my wallet. 本だなの本はみんな売ってしまってもうなにも～っていない Not a book *remains* on my bookshelf because I have sold them all. きみにはなに一つ～っていない Nothing *remains* for you.

のさば･る ¶ 彼はクラスで～っている He *is acting haughtily* in his class.

のざらし【野晒し】¶ ～の石地蔵 a *weather-beaten* stone image of *Jizo.* 車は～にされていた The car *was exposed to weather.*

のし【熨斗】¶ ～をつけてやろう I *am willing to give it to* you. / I will *make* you *a free present of it.*

のしあが･る【伸し上がる】¶ 彼は重役に～った He *was promoted to* a director.

のしかか･る【伸し掛かる】lean over. ¶ その力士は相手に～るようにして倒した The *sumo* wrestler *bent over* his opponent and threw him down to the ground.

のしもち【伸し餅】a flattened rice cake.

のじゅく【野宿】¶ ～する sleep in the open ; have a night out.

の･す【伸す･熨す】¶ 最近彼の勢力が～してきた He *has* lately *extended* his influence. 一撃で彼を～してしまった I *knocked* him *down* (≒ *out*) with a single blow.

ノスタルジア nostalgia.

ノズル a nozzle.

の･せる【乗せる･載せる】**1**〖上に置く〗put. ¶ 花びんをたなの上に～せる *place* (≒ *put*) a vase on a shelf.
さらを盆に～せて運ぶ carry plates *on* a tray.
この上にはなにも～せないようにしてください Don't *put* anything *on* this.

2〖乗り物に〗¶ 彼が車に～せてくれた He *gave* me *a ride* (≒ *gave* me *a lift* ; *picked* me *up*) in his car.
駅までぼくの車に～せていってあげようか Shall I *drive* you to the station?
牧場で馬に～せてもらった They let me *ride* a horse in the pasture.
ジェットコースターに～せてあげよう I will *give* you *a ride* on the roller coaster.
子どもは父親の肩車に～せてもらってごきげんだった The child was very pleased to *be taken about* his father's shoulders.
荷物はリヤカーに～せて運ぼう Let's carry the baggage in a cart, shall we?
彼女をタクシーに～せてやった I got a taxi for her.
彼女に手を貸してバスに～せてあげた I helped her [to] get on the bus.
その船は500人の乗客を～せていた The ship had five hundred passengers on board. / On board the ship were five hundred passengers.

3〖だます〗cheat. ¶ うかうかと彼のうそに～せられてしまった I *was* fairly *taken in* (≒ *was* fairly *cheated*) by his lies.
そんな手には～せられませんよ You cannot *cheat* me that way.

4〖参加させる〗¶ その事業に私も一口～せてください Let me *have a share* in that project.

5〖掲載する〗¶ きょうの新聞はその事故の記事を～せている Today's paper *carries* an account of the accident.
きみのあの論文をわれわれの雑誌に～せてあげよう I will *put in* that article of yours in our periodical.

6〖金額について〗¶ 株価は1,000円の大台に～せた Stock prices have reached the level as high as a thousand yen.

のぞき【覗き･覘き】a peep.
一穴 a peephole.

のぞ･く【除く】exclude. ¶ 障害を～く *remove* the obstacle. 彼はグループから～くべきだ We should *omit* him from our group. 日曜を～いて彼は毎日仕事場へ出かける He goes to his workshop every day *except* [on] Sundays.
この一節は二, 三の文法上のまちがいを～いては正しい This paragraph is all right *except for* a few mistakes in grammar.

のぞ･く【覗く･覘く】¶ だれかが家の中を～いている Someone *is peeping into* my house. 私の部屋を絶対に～くな Never *look into* my room. 彼女はしばしば鏡を～く She often *looks into* her mirror. 少なくとも週に1回は本屋を～く I *drop in at* a bookstore at least once a week. 今晩会場を～いてみよう I will *look in at* the hall this evening. 彼の上着のポケットには白いハンカチが～いている A white handkerchief *is showing* at his jacket pocket.

のそのそ slowly ; lazily. ¶ そんな所でなにを～しているのか What are you doing *idly* in such a place?

のぞまし･い【望ましい】¶ ～い(～くない) 人物 *a desirable* (*an undesirable*) person. みんなが

協力することが〜い *It is to be desired* (≒ *hoped*) that all the people should work together. 直接彼に話すほうが〜い I think it *advisable* for you to speak to him in person.

のぞみ【望み】**1**〖願い・志〗〔a〕wish. ¶ 私の〜は自分の店を持つことだ My *wish* is to have my own shop.

給料はきみの〜どおり出そう I will pay you whatever (≒ as much as) you *wish*.

彼は長年の〜がかなってイギリスに留学した In fulfillment of his long-standing *ambition*, he went to England for study.

彼は大きな〜をいだいて故郷を出た He left home with *a* great *aim* in life.

きみは〜が大きすぎる You *are aiming* too high. / You *are asking for* too much.

2〖見込み・期待〗〔a〕prospect ; 〔a〕hope. ¶ 彼の研究に成功の〜が出てきた *A prospect* of success is beginning to be seen in his research.

われわれが救助される〜はまだ残っている There is still the *possibility* of our being rescued.

彼の生存にはまだ一縷(いちる)の〜がある There is still a ray of *hope that* he is alive (≒ *hope of* his being alive).

この成績では合格の〜はない Your test scores are such that you can hardly *expect* to make the grade.

最後まで〜を捨てるな Don't give up *hope* to the last.

計画の実現は〜薄だ There is little *hope* that the plan will be realized.

彼は一家から大いに〜をかけられている His whole family *is expecting* much of him. / His whole family places high *hopes* on him.

彼は将来大いに〜が持てる He has a bright future 〔before him〕.

病人の回復の〜は失われた The patient's recovery *is* now *hopeless*. / There is no *hope* of the patient's recovery.

3〖選択〗¶ お〜の品をお取りください Take whatever you *like*.

お〜のときに伺います I will come and see you at your *convenience*.

料理に特にお〜がありましたらお申しつけください If you have any *preferences* in food, will you kindly tell us?

のぞ・む【望む】**1**〖願う・期待する〗hope ; want. ¶ 幸福を〜まない人はいない Who doesn't *hope* (≒ *wish*) *for* happiness?

私は富を〜んではいない I don't *care for* wealth.

彼は私が家業を継ぐことを〜んでいる He *wants* me *to* go into the family business.

彼は海外出張を〜んでいる He *is hoping* to make a business trip abroad.

よほど努力しなければ成功は〜めない You can't *expect* to be successful unless you work extra hard.

きみが来てくれることを〜みます I *hope* 〔*that*〕 you will come.

2〖選択する〗prefer. ¶ くつは黒と茶とどちらをお〜みですか Which do you *prefer*, black or brown shoes?

どこでもきみが〜む所へ案内しよう I will take you to any place of interest you *want* to visit.

3〖見渡す〗¶ 丘の上から市街が一望のもとに〜める From the top of the hill you can enjoy a panoramic view of the city.

この山頂から〜む富士はとても美しい The view of Mt. Fuji from the top of this mountain is extremely beautiful.

のぞ・む【臨む】¶ そのビルは海に〜んでいた The building *faced on* the sea. 別れに〜んでなにか言うことがありませんか Don't you have parting words to offer? 彼は落ち着いて死に〜んだ He *met* his death composedly. 危険に〜んでも彼は動じなかった He was unperturbed *in the face of* danger.

のそり ¶ 象が〜と立ちあがった The elephant staggered to its feet *heavily*.

のたう・つ ¶ 昨夜は腹痛で〜ちまわった Last night I *twisted and rolled about* with a stomachache. 彼は〜ちまわって苦しんだ He *writhed* in agony.

のたく・る (ヘビなどが) wriggle ; (苦痛などで) writhe ; (なぐり書きする) scrawl. ¶ ヘビが〜っていた The snake *was wriggling* (≒ *was squirming*).

のだて【野点】〖茶道〗an open-air tea ceremony.

のたれじに【野垂れ死に】¶ 〜する die on the road ; die by the roadside.

のち【後】after ; later. ¶ 1 週間〜にここでお会いしましょう We'll meet here *after a week* (≒ *a week from today*). あのビルは 1 か月〜に完成する That building will be finished a month *after* (≒ *afterward*). ひと月〜に帰る I'll be back *in* a month.

のちぞい【後添い】*one's* second wife. ¶ 彼は去年〜をもらった He *got married again* (≒ *got married second time*) last year.

のちのち【後後】forever ; 英 for ever. ¶ このことは〜まで忘れません I will never forget about this. 〜もよろしくお願いします Please remember me *forever*.

のちほど【後程】afterward ; later. ¶ また, 〜お会いしましょう Let's meet again *afterward*. / See you *later*. 〜, またうかがいます I will call on you again *later*.

ノック knock. ¶ ドアを〜する *knock at* (≒ *on*) a door.

ノックアウト〖野球〗〖ボクシング〗a knockout (K. O.). ¶ 〜する knock out.

ノックダウン〖ボクシング〗a knockdown. ¶ 〜する knock down.

のっけ・る【乗っける】¶ ぼくの自動車に〜てやろう I will *give* you *a ride* (≒ *a lift*) *in* my car.

のっけから from the start ; from the outset. ¶ 〜, しかられた I was scolded *from the start*.

のっしのっし ¶ 象が〜と歩きまわっていた An elephant was walking about *with heavy strides*.

のっそり ¶ 彼は〜した男だ He *is very slow in moving*. 大男は〜立ち上がった The big man rose to his feet *slowly* (≒ *sluggishly*).

ノット a knot. ¶ 30～の船 a vessel of 30 *knots.* 時速30～出す make 30 *knots* an hour.

のっと・る【乗っ取る】 ¶ 3人の男が船を～った Three men *seized* the ship. 最近飛行機を～る事件が続発している Recently *skyjackings* (≒ *airplane hijackings*) have happened in succession. 彼はその会社を～った He *took over* the company.

のっと・る【則る・法る】 ¶ われわれは万事先例に～って執り行なった We performed everything *following* (≒ *according to*) the precedents. われわれは規則に～って正々堂々と戦います We'll play games fairly *in conformity to* the rules. 古式に～って式を挙げる hold a ceremony with the traditional ritual.

のっぴきならない【退っ引きならない】 ¶ ～用事ができたのでお先に失礼します Please excuse my leaving earlier because I have *unavoidable* (≒ *urgent*) business. 事態は～ところまできた The situation *is desperate.* / At last *came the pinch.* ～立場に追い込まれた We *are in for it* now. / We *find ourselves in a fix* (≒ *a predicament*).

のっぺらぼう (化け物) a monster with no eyes and no nose. ¶ ～な顔 (人の顔) a flat, deadpan face; (化け物の顔) a face without eyes, a nose and a mouth.

のっぺりした ¶ ～顔 a *smooth, expressionless* (≒ *blank*) face.

のっぽ a very tall fellow.

-ので ¶ 彼は病気な～家に閉じこもっている He is staying at home *on account of* his illness. 雨が降りそうだった～かさを持っていった *Because* it was going to rain, I took an umbrella with me.

のてん【野天】 the open air.
—ぶろ an open-air (≒ outdoor) bath.

のど【喉・咽】 a throat. ¶ ～が渇いた I *feel thirsty.* ～が痛い I *have a sore throat.* 彼女はいい～をしている She *has a sweet voice.* ネコが～を鳴らしている The cat *is purring.* そのことばは～まで出かかっていた I *had* the word *on the tip of my tongue.* 心配のあまり食べ物が～を通らない I am so worried about it that I *have lost my appetite.* 彼のカメラが～から手が出るほど欲しい I *covet* his camera.
—ちんこ a uvula. **—笛** a windpipe. **—仏** an Adam's apple.

のどか【長閑】 ¶ ～な春の一日 a *peaceful* spring day. ～な天気 *serene* (≒ *genial*) weather.

のどくび【喉頸】 a neck. ¶ われわれはあの会社の～を押さえてある We *have a hold on* (≒ *over*) that company.

のどじまん【喉自慢】 ¶ 彼はたいへんな～だ He *is* very *proud of* his *voice.*
しろうと**—大会** an amateur singing contest.

のどもと【喉元】 ¶ ～過ぎれば熱さを忘れる(諺) *Danger past, God forgotten.*

-のに ¶ 忙しい～わざわざ来てくれた He took the trouble to see me, *though* he was very busy. 風が強い～彼らはピクニックに出かけた They went out on a picnic *in spite of* the strong wind. 知っている～どうして言わなかったのですか *Since* you knew about it, why didn't you say anything? 行けという～彼はどうしても行かない He won't go *though* I've told him to. 4月だという～まだ寒い It is still cold *though* we are already in April.

のねずみ【野鼠】 a field (≒ meadow) mouse.

ののし・る【罵る】 ¶ 彼は私のことを口ぎたなく～った He *abused* me. / He *called* me [*bad*] *names.*

のば・す【延ばす・伸ばす】 **1**〖時間を長くする・延期する〗¶ 会議は予定時間を1時間～して続行された The meeting *was extended* for one hour to continue the discussion.
ここでの滞在を1週間～した I *extended* my stay here for another week.
会合(の日取り)を10日ほど～そう Let's *postpone* the meeting for about ten days, shall we?
支払いを月末まで～したい I want to *postpone* paying the bill till the end of the month.
先方は返事を一日延ばしに～している The other party *is putting off* the answer from day to day.
契約期限をあと1年～していただきたい We want the term of the contract to *be extended* for another year.
きょうできることをあすに～すな Never *put off* till tomorrow what you can do today.
2〖まっすぐにする〗¶ 曲がったくぎを～して使おう Let's *straighten* the crooked nails and use them again.
ちょっと手を～して，たなの上の本をとってください *Reach out* your hand and get me the book from the shelf.
手足をゆっくり～した I *stretched* myself comfortably.
ズボンのしわを～す *press* trousers (smooth the wrinkles は手で伸ばす感じになる).
3〖長くする〗¶ バス路線をこの町まで～してほしい We want the bus service to *be extended* into this town.
近ごろ髪を長く～す青年が多くなった The number of young men who *wear* their hair *long* has increased these days.
あまりつめを～しているのは危険だ It is dangerous to *grow* your fingernails too *long.*
ズボンのたけを2センチ～してもらった I *had* my pants *lengthened* by two centimeters.
4〖薄める〗¶ ペンキをシンナーで～す *dilute* paint with thinner.
5〖成長させる〗¶ なんとかこの子の音楽の才能を～してやりたい I want this child to *develop* his musical talent one way or another.
彼はこの町で着々と勢力を～している He *is* steadily *increasing* (≒ *extending*) his influence in this town.
6〖たたきのめす〗¶ 彼は生意気だからこてんこてんに～してやった He was such a cheeky fellow that I *beat* him *up.*

のばなし【野放し】 ¶ 家畜を～にする *put* cattle *to pasture.* 犬は～にしてはいけない You must not *leave* your dog *free* (≒ *loose*).

のはら【野原】a field ; a plain.

のばら【野薔薇】a wild rose.

のび【伸び】¶ 疲れたので〜をした I was tired, so I *stretched myself*. 彼は技の〜が速い He *grows fast in* his art. 〜のよいおしろいだ This powder *spreads* well.

のび【野火】a field (≒ bush ; grass) fire.

のびあが·る【伸び上がる】¶ 一塁手は〜ってボールをつかんだ The first baseman caught the ball *on tiptoe*.

のびちぢみ【伸び縮み】expansion and contraction. ¶ 〜自在 elasticity. 〜自在の elastic.

のびなや·む【伸び悩む】¶ 彼は〜んでいる He hasn't progressed so much as was expected. / He is finding it hard to make as much progress as was expected. わが社の売り上げはことしは〜んでいる The sales of our company *are* so *slow in increase* this year.

のびのび【延び延び】¶ 彼の来日は〜になっている His visit to Japan *has long been delayed* (≒ *has been put off*) *from day to day*. 仕事を〜にならないようにしてください Don't *put off* your work *too long*.

のびのび【伸び伸び】¶ 芝生に〜と寝ていた I *stretched myself at ease* on the grass. 子どもたちは〜育っている The children have grown *free from all care*. この景色を見ると〜する I *feel relaxed* at this sight. 彼は〜した字を書く He writes *in free and easy style* (≒ *in a facile way*).

のびやか【伸びやか】¶ 〜な筆づかい a *facile* pen; *free and easy* style.

の·びる【延びる·伸びる】**1**〖長さ·距離〗¶ 彼は急に背が〜びた He *has* suddenly *grown taller*.
ゴムは引っぱれば簡単に〜びる Rubber *stretches* easily when it is pulled.
きみのつめは〜びすぎている You *have too long* nails. / Your nails *have grown too long*.
運動場は道路まで〜びている The playground *extends* as far as the road.
この道は港まで〜びている This road *goes* as far as the harbor.
アパラチア山脈はメーンからサウスカロライナまで〜びている The Appalachian Mountains *extend* from Maine to South Carolina.
2〖時間〗¶ このごろは日が〜びている The days *are getting longer* now.
夜はだんだん〜びる The night *is growing longer*.
人間の平均寿命はかなり〜びた The average span of human life *has been* considerably *prolonged*.
会合は日曜日に〜びた The meeting *has been put off* till Sunday.
3〖力·勢力が〗¶ 彼の学力はもっと〜びそうだ He will *make* more *progress in* his studies.
彼の勢力は党内で〜びている His influence *is increasing* in the party.
あの若い学者は将来〜びるだろう The young scholar *has a future before* him.
4〖まいる〗¶ 歩き疲れて〜びてしまった I *was* utterly *tired out* after the walk.
ほおを打たれて彼は〜びた A knock on the cheek *fell* him.
ぶどう酒1ぱいで彼は〜びた He *passed out* on a glass of wine.
そんなに働くと, 〜びるよ If you work so hard, you'll *be tired out*.

のべ【延べ】¶ その仕事に〜10日かかった The work took the *total number of* ten days. その家の〜坪数は25坪だ The *total* floor space of the house is 25 *tsubo*. ここ5日間での入場者は〜10万人であった The *total number of* visitors for these five days amounted to a hundred thousand 〔people〕. 〜人員1,000人の工事だった The work required a thousand *man-days*.

のべ【野辺】¶ 美しい〜の花 *a* pretty *wild flower*. 彼の〜の送りを済ませた I *buried* him.

のべつ ¶ 彼女たちは〜幕なしにしゃべっていた The women talked on *ceaselessly* (≒ *continuously ; all the time*).

のべばらい【延べ払い】deferred payment. ¶ 彼はその機械を〜で買った He bought the machine *on deferred payment*. 支払いは〜にされた The payment *was deferred*.

のべぼう【延べ棒】a bar. ¶ 金の〜 *a* gold *bar*.

の·べる【述べる】state. ¶ 自分の意見を〜べる *express one's* opinion. 真実を〜べることはたいせつだ It is necessary to *tell* the truth. 心からお礼を〜べたいと思います I would like to *express* my heartfelt gratitude. 前に〜べたように私はこの計画には賛成です As I *mentioned* before, I agree to this plan.

の·べる【延べる·伸べる】¶ われわれは彼に救いの手を〜べた We *offered* a helping hand to him. 彼女は床を〜べてくれた She *made* a bed for me.

のほうず【野放図】¶ 〜なやつだ He is a *wild* man. 彼は〜に金を使う He spends money *aimlessly*.

のぼ·せる【上せる】¶ 会議にその案を〜せた We *submitted* the plan to the conference. それを記録に〜せた We *put* it on record.

のぼ·せる【逆上せる】¶ 長湯して〜せた A long bath *made* me *dizzy*. 聴衆の前で〜せた I *lost my head* (≒ *was excited*) before the audience. 彼は彼女に〜せている He *is crazy* (≒ *is off his head*) *about* her. 彼はうれしくてすっかり〜せている He *is beside himself with* joy. 彼は暑さで〜せてしまった The heat *has gone to his head*.

のほほんと ¶ 彼は人の気も知らずに〜している He remains quite *indifferent* to others. 彼は人生を〜暮らした He spent his days *in a carefree way*. 彼は〜した男だ He is an *easy-going* (≒ *happy-go-lucky*) fellow.

のぼり【上り】¶ 〜はかなり急だった The *ascent* was fairly steep. 道は緩やかな〜だった The path *ran* gently *uphill*.
—坂 an uphill slope. **—線** an up line.

—列車 an up train.

のぼり【幟】a flag.

のぼ·る【上る·登る·昇る】**1** rise. ¶ 太陽は東から～る The sun *rises* in the east.
水銀柱は30度以上に～った The mercury *went up to* over thirty degrees.
この子どもはこの木のてっぺんまで～った This child *climbed* up to the top of the tree.
この山は高くないから，～るのになんの困難もなかろう Since this mountain is not high, you won't have any difficulty in *climbing* it.
川を～っていくと，やがてほこらがあった I *went up* the river and soon found a small shrine.
2 〖費用·地位など〗 ¶ 旅行の費用は５万円に～った The expenses of the trip *amounted to* fifty thousand yen.
彼は社長の地位にまで～った He *rose to* the office of president.

のま·せる【飲ませる】¶ 冷や水を一杯～せてください Please *give* me *a drink of* cold water. 運転手には酒を～せるな Don't *give a drink* to a driver. / Don't *treat* a driver *to liquor*. あとで一杯～せてあげるよ I'll *treat* you *to a drink* afterward. 母親は赤ん坊に乳を～せた The mother *suckled* her baby. 彼らは私に無理やりブランデーを～せた They *forced* some brandy *down my throat*. あの家ではいい酒を～せる They *serve* good *sake* at that house. 彼のことばで私は煮え湯を～された His words *wrung my heart*.

のま·れる【飲まれる】¶ そのボートは波に～れた The boat *was swallowed up* (≒ *was engulfed*) in the waves. そのふんい気に完全に～れてしまった I *was* completely *overcome* by the atmosphere. お偉方にすっかり～れた（圧倒された）I *was overawed* by the big men. 酒は飲んでも～れるな You may drink, but never be a slave to drinking.

のみ【蚤】a flea. ¶ ～に食われて眠れなかった I could not sleep because I was bitten by *fleas*. ～に食われた跡 a *fleabite*. 犬の～を取る *flea* a dog. 彼らは～の夫婦だ They are a little man with a big wife.
—取り a flea powder. —の市 a flea market.

のみ【鑿】a chisel. ¶ ～で像を彫る carve a statue with *a chisel*.

-のみ ¶ もう戦う～だ There is *nothing but* to fight. 人間～言語がある Man *alone* has language. / Man is *the only* creature that can speak. 波の音～聞こえる *Nothing but* waves can be heard here. あとどうなるかは神～ぞ知る *God* knows what will happen. 友としては書物ある～ Books are my *sole* (≒ *only*) companion.

のみあか·す【飲み明かす】¶ 彼らは夜通し～した They *drank all night long*. / They *drank away the night*.

のみかけ【飲みかけ】¶ 彼は～で席を立った He left the table with his glass *half-finished*. 灰ざらに～のたばこがある There are some *half-smoked* cigarettes on the ashtray.

のみくい【飲み食い】eating and drinking.

のみぐすり【飲み薬】〔a〕medicine. ¶ ～１服 a dose of *medicine*.

のみぐち【飲み口】a tap ; a cock.

のみこみ【呑み込み】¶ 彼は～が早い（遅い）He is quick (slow) of *understanding*. きみは早～しすぎる You *conclude too quickly*.

のみこ·む【飲み込む·呑み込む】swallow ; gulp. ¶ 大きな肉をひと切れ～んだ He *swallowed* a big piece of meat. 丸薬をぱくっと～んだ He quickly *swallowed* a pill. きみの言うことが～めない I can't *understand* (≒ *grasp*) what you mean. 彼は一目でその情勢を～んだ He *grasped* the situation at a glance. 彼は友人の長所をすぐ～んでしまう He quickly *takes in* the merits of his friends.

のみしろ【飲み代】drinking money.

のみたお·す【飲み倒す】¶ 彼はバーの勘定を～した He *did not pay his bill* at the bar.

のみち【野道】a field path.

のみつぶ·す【飲み潰す】¶ 彼は財産を～した He *drank away* his fortune. / He *drank himself out of* his fortune.

のみつぶ·れる【飲み潰れる】¶ 彼は～れた He *was dead drunk*. / He *drank himself down*.

のみなかま【飲み仲間】a boon companion. ¶ 彼とは～だ He is a companion of mine with whom I enjoy having a drink now and then.

のみならず ¶ 彼女は美人～親切だ She is *not only* pretty, *but* 〔*also*〕 kind. 彼は学者～教育者である He is a teacher *as well as* a scholar. 彼は小説家である～詩人でもあった *Besides* being a novelist, he was a poet.

のみにく·い【飲み難い·呑み難い】¶ それは～い薬だ It is a *bad-tasting* medicine. きみの要求は～い Your demand *is hard to accept*.

のみほ·す【飲み干す】¶ 彼は一気に～した He *drank up* at a gulp. 彼は一滴も残さずぶどう酒を～した He *drank* the wine *to the last drop*.

のみまわし【飲み回し】¶ お茶の～をする *pass round a cup of* tea.

のみみず【飲み水】drinking water ; water to drink.

のみもの【飲み物】〔a〕drink ; a beverage. ¶ 食べ物と～ food and *drink*. なにか冷たい～が欲しい I want *something* cold *to drink*. ～はいっさい出ません No *drink* is offered. ～はたくさんある We have plenty of *drinks*.

のみや【飲み屋】a public house ; a pub ; a bar ; a tavern. ¶ ～の主人 米 a saloon keeper ; 英 a publican.

のみよ·い【飲みよい】¶ この薬は～い This medicine *is pleasant* (≒ *is easy*) *to take*.

の·む【飲む·呑む】**1** 〖液体を〗 drink. ¶ 紅茶を１杯～んだ I *had* a cup of tea.
彼は薬を～むことがきらいだ He does not like *taking* medicine.
この川の水は～んでもいい It's safe to *drink* from this river.
なにか冷たいものを～みませんか Won't you *have* something cold to drink?

その晩は大いに～んだ We *drank* a lot that evening.
～もうか What about *a drink*?
2 〚たばこを〛 ¶ 日に何本たばこを～みますか How many cigarettes do you *smoke* a day?
3 〚要求を〛 ¶ この要求は私には～めない I cannot *accept* this request.
4 〚相手を〛 ¶ 彼は敵を～んでいる He *thinks nothing of* the enemy.
彼は完全に聴衆を～んでいる He *is not* at all *unnerved* by the audience.

のめのめ ¶ 今更～帰れない I can't return *shamelessly* now.

のめやうたえ【飲めや歌え】¶ 宴会で～の大騒ぎをした We *were drunk and had a spree* (≒ *an orgy*) at the party.

のめ·る ¶ 石につまずいて～った I stumbled over a stone and nearly *fell forward*.

のら【野良】a farm; a field.

のらいぬ【野良犬】an ownerless dog; a cur.

のらぎ【野良着】peasant costume.

のらくら ¶ ～と時を過ごしている I *idle* (≒ *loaf*) *away* my days. / I spend time *idly*. 彼はいつも～と言いわけをする He always makes excuses *somehow or other*. 彼女は～と暮らしていた She *was leading an idle life*. 私たちは～歩いた We walked along *aimlessly*.

のらしごと【野良仕事】¶ ～をする do *farm work*; work in the fields.

のらねこ【野良猫】an ownerless cat; a wild cat.

のり【乗り】¶ 4 人～の自動車 a *four-passenger* car. このおしろいは～がとてもいい This powder *spreads* very well.

のり【式·規·則·憲】a rule; a law. ¶ ～を越える break (≒ violate) the *rule*.

のり【糊】paste; (洗たく用の) starch. ¶ 彼は～でそのポスターを壁に張った He stuck the poster on the wall with *paste*. / He *pasted* the poster on the wall. このシャツは～がよくきいている This shirt *is* well *starched*. 彼の仕事は～とはさみの仕事にすぎない His work is merely a *scissors-paste* one.

のり【海苔】laver; a seaweed.
—巻き seasoned rice rolled in laver (≒ seaweed). 味つけ— seasoned laver.

のりあい【乗り合い】¶ ～の客 a fellow passenger.
—自動車 a bus; an omnibus. —馬車 an omnibus; a stagecoach.

のりあ·げる【乗り上げる】¶ 船が浅瀬に～げた A ship *ran aground*. 船は暗礁に～げた The ship *was stranded* on a reef. 彼の乗っているボートが岩に～げて転覆した His boat *ran on* a rock and turned over. 交渉は暗礁に～げた The negotiation *has come to a deadlock*.

のりあわ·せる【乗り合わせる】¶ 偶然彼とバスに～せた I *happened to ride* in the same bus with him.

のりいれ【乗り入れ】¶ この先～禁止 No *driving* beyond here.

のりい·れる【乗り入れる】¶ 車を構内に～れてはいけない You must not *drive* a car *into* the campus. バス路線は延びてその駅に～れた A bus service *was extended into* the station.

のりうつ·る【乗り移る】¶ 彼らはすばやく別のボートに～った They *transferred to* another boat quickly. 彼にキツネが～った He *is possessed by* a fox.

のりおく·れる【乗り遅れる】¶ 終電に～れる *miss* (≒ *fail to catch*) the last train.

のりおり【乗り降り】¶ 電車の～に注意しなさい Be careful in *getting on and off* the train. 東京駅は～の人が多い There are a lot of people *getting on and off* at Tokyo Station.

のりかえ【乗り換え·乗換】transfer; changing. ¶ そこへは～なしに行ける You can go there *without transfer* (≒ *without changing*). 上野で～だ We must *change* [cars] at Ueno. 奈良へ行くのに～が 3 回ある We have three *transfers* for Nara.
—切符 a transfer ticket. —駅 a transfer station.

のりか·える【乗り換える】¶ どこで～えたらいいでしょう. 渋谷で～えなさい Where shall I *change*? *Change* at Shibuya. 東海道線に～えた We *transferred* to the Tokaido line.

のりかか·る【乗りかかる】¶ ～った船だ Once we'*ve set out*, we can't turn back. / We have gone too far to retreat.

のりき【乗り気】enthusiasm; interest. ¶ 出版者はその本の出版に全然～でない The publishers *have* (≒ *show*) no *enthusiasm for* the publication [of the book]. その仕事にはあまり～がしない I *have* little *interest in* the work. 彼はその案にすっかり～になっている He *is enthusiastic about* the plan. 彼はその仕事にひじょうに～になっている He *is devoted to* the work.

のりき·る【乗り切る】¶ われわれには危機を～る自信がない We have no confidence to *tide over* (≒ *get over*) the crisis. そのボートはあらしを～った The boat *weathered* (≒ *rode out*) the storm. 船は大波を～った The ship *steered through* the high waves. スクーナーは日本海を～った This schooner *sailed across* the Japan Sea.

のりくみいん【乗組員】a crew. ¶ ～のひとりが死んだ One member of the *crew* was killed. ～はみんな疲れていた The *crew* were all tired.

のりく·む【乗り組む】¶ 彼は浅間丸に～んだ He *was on board* the Asamamaru.

のりこ·える【乗り越える】¶ どろぼうがへいを～えて逃げた A thief *climbed over* the fence and ran away. 彼はついに苦難を～えることができた At last he *has overcome* (≒ *has tided over*) the difficulties.

のりごこち【乗り心地】¶ この車は～がいい(悪い) This car *is comfortable* (*uncomfortable*) *to ride in*.

のりこし【乗り越し】—賃 an excess fare; an extra [fare].

のりこ·す【乗り越す】¶ 居眠りをして 2 駅～した While dozing I *was carried* two stations *beyond* my destination. 私は横浜から東京まで

〜した I *rode past* Yokohama to Tokyo.

のりこな·す【乗りこなす】¶ 車を〜すのには時間がかかる It takes quite a lot of time to *drive* a car *well*. 彼はその暴れ馬を〜すことができた He could *manage* the wild horse.

のりこ·む【乗り込む】¶ 神戸で船に〜んだ We *went on board* the ship at Kobe. 大ぜいの人がバスに〜んできた A lot of people *got into* the bus. われわれは敵地に〜んでいった We *marched into* the enemy's land. 代表団が次次に当地に〜んできた The delegates arrived here one after another.

のりすご·す【乗り過ごす】¶ うっかり〜した I happened to *ride past my destination.*

のりす·てる【乗り捨てる】¶ 自動車が道端に〜てであった There was a car *left* (≒ *abandoned*) on the roadside.

のりだ·す【乗り出す】¶ 新しい仕事に〜すことにした I decided to *begin* (≒ *set about*) a new business. 私は政界に〜すつもりだ I intend to *enter upon* a political career (≒ *go into* politics). それを見ようとして体を〜した I *leaned forward* to see it.

のりづけ【糊付け】¶ シャツを〜する *starch* a shirt. 壁にポスターを〜する *paste* a poster on a wall.

のりつ·ける【乗りつける】¶ 彼は玄関まで車を〜けた He *drove right up* to the door. 私は飛行機に〜けている I *am used to traveling* by air.

のりつぶ·す【乗り潰す】¶ 彼は車を〜した He drove his car to the extent of being beyond repair. 彼は馬を〜した He *rode down* his horse. / He *rode* his horse *to death.*

のりて【乗り手】a rider ; (客) a passenger. ¶ 彼はなかなかの〜だ He is *a* good *rider*. このローカル線にはあまり〜がない There is little *passenger traffic* on this local line.

のりと【祝詞】¶ 〜をあげる offer (≒ utter) *prayers*; read *an address to the gods.*

のりなら·す【乗り慣らす】¶ 馬を〜す *break in* a horse.

のりな·れる【乗り慣れる】¶ 私は新車に〜れた I *got used to driving* the new car.

のりにげ【乗り逃げ】¶ どろぼうは自転車を〜した The thief *rode away with* another person's bicycle. 彼はタクシーの〜をした He *bilked* the taxi driver *of his bill.*

のりば【乗り場】(待合所や出札所のある) a station ; (船なら) a landing-place. ¶ この辺にバス(電車)の〜がありますか Is there *a bus stop* (*a car-stop*) near here?

のりまわ·す【乗り回す】¶ オートバイを〜すのが彼の趣味だ His hobby is *riding about* on a motorcycle. 彼は最新型のベンツを〜している He boastfully *drives* a Mercedes-Benz of the latest model.

のりもの【乗り物】a conveyance. ¶ みさきに行くのになにか〜の便がありますか Is there any *conveyance* to take us to the cape? 東京は〜の便がいい Tokyo provides us with good *transportation facilities.*

の·る【乗る·載る】**1**〖物の上·乗り物などに〗¶ いすに〜って電球をはずしてください *Stand on* the chair and remove the bulb [for me]. その木箱の上に〜ってはいけない Don't *get on* that wooden box. きみは馬に〜れますか Can you *ride* a horse? 自転車に〜って学校へ通う I go to school *by* (≒ *on* a) bicycle. この車に6人は〜れないだろう I am afraid this car won't *take* six persons. 急いでいたのでタクシーに〜った As I was in a hurry, I *took* a taxi. 始発に〜るために早起きした I got up early enough to *take* the first train. 人工衛星はうまく軌道に〜った We succeeded in *putting* the man-made satellite in orbit. 彼女のあの歌は毎日電波に〜って流れている Her song *is on the air* every day. 街の騒音が風に〜って聞こえてきた The noises of the streets *were carried* to us *by the wind.*

2〖加わる〗¶ この話, きみも一口〜らないか Would you like to *join*, too? (take part でもよいが share はさける).
彼はその話には〜ってこなかった He didn't *show* any *interest in* it.
彼の相談に〜ってやってくれないか Won't you give some advice to him?

3〖だまされる〗¶ また彼の口車に〜ってしまった Again I *was taken in* by his pleasant words.
先方の計略に〜らないように用心したまえ Take care not to *fall into their trap.*

4〖調子が合う〗¶ リズムに〜って軽快に踊った We danced lightly and rhythmically.
彼の事業は今好調の波に〜っている His business *is* now *on the crest of the wave.*
彼の研究はようやく軌道に〜ったところだ At long last his research *is on the right track.*

5〖なじむ〗¶ おしろいのよく〜るお膚ですね Your skin *takes* powder well, doesn't it?
この紙はインクがよく〜らない This paper *blots.* / Ink *runs* on this paper.

6〖気乗りがする〗¶ この縁談にはどうも気が〜りません(女性が主語) I don't know why, but I don't *feel like* accepting this proposal.
きょうはどうも仕事に気分が〜らない Somehow I can't *concentrate on* my work today.

7〖掲載される〗¶ その調査の結果が新聞に〜る The result of the investigation will *be mentioned* (≒ *be recorded*) in the paper.
この語はどの辞書にも〜っていない This word *is* not *given* (≒ *is* not *listed*) in any dictionary.
きみの名前は名簿に〜っていない Your name *is* not *on the list.*
その町はこの地図に〜っている The town *is represented* in (≒ on) this map.

ノルウェー Norway. ¶ 〜の Norwegian. —人 a Norwegian.

のるかそるか【伸るか反るか】¶ 〜やってみよう *Sink or swim* (≒ *Win or lose*), I'll try. /

I'll *take a chance.* 彼は～あり金を全部その馬にかけてみた He *took the chance of* betting all the money he had on the horse. それは～の重大な事柄だ It is a matter of *life-or-death* (≒ *make-or-break*) importance. / It's a *make-or-break* situation.

ノルマ a norm. ¶ 彼らは従業員にきつい～を課した They set the workers *a* hard *norm.* われわれはすぐ～を果たした We filled (≒ did ; met ; fulfilled) our *norm* before long.

のれん【暖簾】 a shop-curtain ; (信用) credit ; the goodwill. ¶ あの店は～が古い That's an old shop. 彼は主人から～を分けてもらった He *was set up in business* by his master. / *The goodwill* was sold him with the business by the former owner. ～を汚すようなことはするな Don't do anything which will impair (≒ injure) the *credit* (≒ *good reputation*) of your shop. まるで～に腕押しだ It's useless like beating the air. / It's a waste of labor (≒ time).

のろい【呪い・詛い】 a curse. ¶ 魔女は王女に～をかけた The witch put *a curse* upon the princess. / The witch laid the princess under *a curse.*

のろ・い【鈍い】 slow. ¶ 彼はしゃべるのが～い He *is slow of* speech (≒ tongue). 彼女は計算が～い She *is slow* (≒ *is poor*) *at* figures (≒ accounts). 彼は仕事が～い He *is slow in* his work. / He is a *slow* worker.

のろ・う【呪う・詛う】 ¶ ～われた人生 *one's* cursed life. 彼は世を～いながら死んだ He died *cursing* the world. 人を～わば穴二つ（諺） *Curses, like chickens, come home to roost.* 彼は私を～っている He *wishes* me *evil.*

のろ・ける【惚気る】 ¶ 彼は細君のことをよく～ける He often *speaks amorously of* his wife. 彼は私に～た He *told* me *of* his *successful love affair.*

のろし【狼煙・烽火】 a signal fire ; a rocket ; the beacon[-fire]. ¶ 船舶は遭難の信号として～をあげる *Rockets* are fired by ships as signals of distress. ～が山の上にあがった *The beacon[-fire]* burnt on the hill-top. 彼らは女性解放の～をあげた They publicly *started a campaign for* the emancipation of women.

のろのろ[と] slowly. ¶ 車は急な山腹を～のぼっていった The car *crawled up* the steep hill. 深いやぶの中を～進んだ We *wormed our way* through the thick bushes. 時は～過ぎていった Time went by *sluggishly.*

のろま【鈍間】 a blockhead ; a dullard. ¶ あの男は～だ He is *a blockhead* (≒ *a dunce ; a slow coach*). この～め You *stupid donkey* !

のわき【野分き】 a wintry blast. ¶ ～が一晩じゅう吹き荒れた The *wintry blast* raged all night.

のんき【呑気】 ¶ 彼は～だ He is such *an easy-going fellow.* 彼は退職後～に暮らしている He lives a *carefree* life after his retirement. 試験を間近にしては～にしてもいられない I can't afford to *be easy and idle* when the examination is in sight. こんな難しい事態によくも～にしていられるものだ How can you *be* so *optimistic* when we are in such a difficulty? 彼らは心配がなくて～だ They *are free from care.*

ノンストップ nonstop. ¶ これは大阪行き～急行だ This is a *nonstop* express for Osaka.

のんだくれ a drunkard.

のんでかか・る【飲んでかかる】 ¶ 要は相手を～ることだ The point is to *face* your opponent *boldly.*

のんびり ¶ 仕事が済むと～する *It is a relief to* have my work off my hand. 彼は田舎で～と育った He grew up *free from all cares* in the country. 彼は二,三日休暇をとって～したかった He wanted to take a few days off and *relax.* 彼は都会の喧噪から逃れて,～と田舎で生活できたらと思った He wished he could escape from the hustle and bustle of the city and *enjoy a quiet life* in the country.

ノンフィクション nonfiction.

ノンプロ nonpro ; nonprofessional. —選手 a nonpro player. —野球 a nonpro baseball game.

のんべえ【飲んべえ】 a drunkard.

のんべんだらり idly. ¶ 彼は～と暮らしている He *leads an idle life.* / He *idles away* his time.

は

は【派】 (学派) a school ; (党派) a faction ; (宗派) a sect ; (派閥) a clique ; (団体) a group. ¶ プラトン学～ the *school* of Platonism. 党内の進歩～は彼を支持している The progressive *group* in the party supports him. その党は左右の２～に分かれた The party was divided into two *factions,* the right-wing and the left-wing ones.

は【刃】 an edge. ¶ ナイフの～はとても鋭かった（なまくらだった） The knife had a very sharp (dull) *edge.* 彼は刀に～をつけた He *gave an edge to* (≒ *put an edge on*) his sword. そんなものを切

ると〜がこぼれる If you try cutting such a thing, the *edge* of the sword will get nicked.

は【羽】 (はね) feathers. ¶ 鳥が２〜飛んでいった Two birds flew away.

は【葉】 (木の葉) a leaf (複 leaves); (針葉) a needle; (草の葉身) a blade; (シダの葉) frond; (集合的) foliage.
¶ 〜の落ちた枝 *bare* (≒ *naked*) branches. 〜の茂った枝 *leafy* branches. 〜がすっかり木から落ちてしまった The *leaves* have all gone off the trees. / The trees are bare of *leaves*. 落葉樹は今〜が出ている The deciduous trees *are* now *in leaf*. それは根も〜もない話だ It is a *groundless* story. 彼は根ほり〜ほりきく人だ He is an *inquisitive* person.

は【歯】 1 〖人間・動物の〗 a tooth (複 teeth).
¶ 彼はきれいな〜をしている He has good *teeth*. / His *teeth* are good.
彼は〜が悪いのでよく医者へ通っている He has bad *teeth* and often goes to the dentist's.
私は毎日〜の治療に通っている I go to the dentist's every day for treatment of my *teeth*.
寝る前に〜をみがきなさい Clean (≒ Brush) your *teeth* before you go to bed.
ゆうべから〜が痛い I have had *a toothache* since last night.
前〜が１本抜けた One of my front *teeth* came out.
奥〜が１本ぐらぐらしている One of my back *teeth* is loose.
子どもの〜が生えそろった The child has cut all its *teeth*.
その子はもう〜は抜けかわった The child has lost all his baby *teeth*.
人前で〜をほじるのは失礼だ It is impolite to pick your *teeth* in the presence of others.
〜が浮いてものがかめない My *teeth* are [set] on edge, so that I cannot chew my food.
〜を食いしばって痛いのをがまんした I *clenched my teeth* to bear the pain. / I *grinned* and bore the pain.
寒くて〜がガタガタいった My *teeth* chattered with the cold.
このパンは堅くて〜が立たない This bread is too hard for my *teeth*.
彼は〜をむき出してにたにた笑った He grinned. / He smiled, showing his *teeth*.
サルは〜をむき出して怒った The monkey became angry, showing (≒ baring) its *teeth*.
2 〖歯の形に似たもの〗 ¶ このくしは〜が細かすぎる This comb's *teeth* are too fine.
歯車の〜がすこし欠けた Some of *cogs* of this cogwheel have broken.
3 〖慣用的表現〗 ¶ 彼は〜の浮くようなお世辞ばかり言う He's always saying something that puts me on edge.
彼は〜に衣(きぬ)を着せずにものを言う He calls a spade a spade. / He is outspoken.
恐ろしくて〜の根が合わなかった My *teeth* chattered from fear.
われわれはあのチームにはとても〜が立たない We are no match for that team. / We cannot beat the team.
この問題は〜が立たない This problem is too hard for me. / This problem is beyond me.

は【覇】 ¶ 彼らは〜を争った They contended for *supremacy*. やがて天下に〜をとなえる英雄が現われるだろう There will soon appear a hero who will *get* (≒ *gain*) *the mastery of* (≒ *rule*; *hold sway over*) the world.

は【端】 the edge; (端物) odds. ¶ 月が山の〜にのぼった The moon is above the *edge* of the hill. 彼はアメリカに逃亡したということが人の口の〜にのぼるようになった It began to *be rumored* that he had escaped to America.

ハ ¶ 〜長調 (短調) *C* major (minor). 〜長調の曲だ a tune in *C* major.

ば【場】 1 〖場所〗 ¶ 彼はその〜を去ることはできなかった He was not able to leave *there* (≒ *the place*).
６時までには行くからよい〜をとっておいてください Please reserve *a* good *seat*, because I will be there by six.
彼は晴れの〜で演説した He made a speech on *a public occasion*.
それはすこし〜をとりすぎる That takes up (≒ occupies) too much *room* (≒ *space*).
私はたまたまその〜に居合わせた I happened to be *there* (≒ *on the scene*).
彼はその〜で決心した He made up his mind *then and there* (≒ *on the spot*).
私は目のやり〜に困った I was at a loss *whére to look*.
2 〖場合〗 ¶ 彼はその〜をごまかすためによく出任せを言う He often talks without thinking (≒ irresponsibly) to *save face*.
これはこの〜かぎりの(ないしょの)話だ This is *between ourselves*.
彼はその〜になって逃げだした He ran away *at the very critical* (≒ *last*) *moment*.
3 〖株の〗 ¶ 10時に〜が立つ The *session* is held at ten.

-ば ¶ あす雨が降れ〜行かない *If* it rains tomorrow, I won't go. 春がくれ〜花が咲く *When* spring comes, flowers come out. 彼は英語も話せ〜フランス語も話す He speaks *not only* English *but also* French.

はあ ¶「彼がぼくに来てほしいと言うんだね」「〜, そうなんです」 "He says he wants me to come?" "*Oh, yes.*"

ばあ bo[h].

バー a bar; (ホテルなどの) a barroom; (棒高跳びの) a bar. ¶ 〜の女 a barmaid.

パー 〔経済学〕〔ゴルフ〕 par.

ばあい【場合】 a case. ¶ その〜はこうしよう I will do it this way *in that case*. どんな〜でもしゃべるな Don't talk no matter what happens. 雨の〜は来るに及ばない You do not have to come *in case of* rain. 私が忘れた〜にはひと言いってください *In case* I forget, please tell me about it. そんな〜には質問するに限る *On such an occasion* nothing is better than to ask a question. 必要の〜には辞書を見てよろしい You may consult a dictionary, *if necessary*. 火事になった〜にはまずどうしますか What are you to do first of all *in the event of* a fire? どんな～にも落ち着いて行動しなさい Be composed *under all circumstances.* (文語). / Always take it easy. (口語). ～によっては according to *circumstances.* それは時と～による That (≒ It all) depends. (口語).

パーキング parking.
—エリア a parking lot (≒ 英 place). —メーター a parking meter.

はあく【把握】 ¶ 彼は実状をよく～している He *has a* good *grasp of* the situation. 彼はその文の意味を～できなかった He could not *grasp* (≒ *catch*; *understand*) the meaning of the sentence. 彼は100万の大軍をよく～していた He *kept* a great army of one million soldiers *under* perfect *control.*

バーゲンセール a bargain sale.

バースデー a birthday.
—ケーキ a birthday cake. —パーティー a birthday party. —プレゼント a birthday present (≒ gift).

パーセンテージ percentage. ¶ 在学生の大学進学者の～はどれくらいですか What *percentage* of the students are admitted to colleges?

パーセント percent. ¶ 現金払いなら10～の割引をいたします We make 10 *percent* discount for cash. / We make a reduction of 10 *percent* for cash. 米の収穫の約40～が今度の台風で被害を受けた Nearly 40 *percent* of the rice crop was damaged by the last typhoon.

バーター barter.
—制 barter system. —貿易 barter trade.

ばあたり【場当たり】 ¶ そんな～の政策ではきっと失敗するだろう Such a *haphazard* policy is sure to result in a failure. 彼は～なことばかり言う He always speaks *on the spur of the moment.* / His speeches are always *claptrap.* 現政府の政策は～だ The policies of the present government *are calculated for shortterm effect.* 彼は人気とりに～をねらっている He *is playing to the gallery* to make a name for himself.

パーティー a party. ¶ 今晩彼とダンス～に行く I'm going to the *dance* with him. (a dance party とは言わない).

バーテン〔ダー〕 a bartender; (とくに英) a barman.

ハート (心臓) the heart; (心) *one's* heart; (トランプの) a heart. ¶ 彼は彼女の～をとらえた He won her *heart.* ～型のキャンデーボックス a *heart*-shaped candy box.

パート part.
—タイマー a part-timer. —タイム part-time.

パートナー a partner.

ハードル〔競技〕hurdles; (ひとつの) a hurdle.
100メートル— a 100-meter hurdle race. —選手 a hurdler. —レース a hurdle race.

はあはあ ¶ 彼は～言って駆けてきた He came running *panting* (≒ *out of breath*; *breathlessly*). 「早く来い, 早く来い」と彼は～しながら言った "Come quick, come quick," *panted* he (≒ said he *panting*).

ハーフ half; (混血児) a half-breed. ⇒こんけつ
—コート a half coat. —タイム half time. —トーン halftone. —バック〔フットボール〕halfback.

ハープ〔音楽〕a harp.

ハープシコード〔音楽〕a harpsichord.

バーベキュー a barbecue.

バーベル a barbell.

パーマ〔ネント〕 permanent waves; a perm (口語). ¶ ～をかけに美容院に行ってきます I'm going to the hairdresser's for *a perm.* きのう～をかけた Yesterday I *had* my hair *permed.*

ハーモニカ〔音楽〕a harmonica; 英 a mouth organ ¶ 彼は～で「オールド ブラック ジョー」を吹いた He played "Old Black Joe" on his *harmonica.*

ばあや【婆や】 (乳母) a nurse; an old housekeeper.

パーラー a parlor (フルーツパーラーは和製英語. パーラーを一種の喫茶店の意味に使うのは日本独特の用法).

はあり【羽蟻】〔虫類〕a winged ant.

バール〔気象〕a bar.

パール a pearl.

はい【肺】〔解剖学〕the lungs. ¶ 彼は左の～が悪い His left *lung* is affected.
—結核〔医学〕tuberculosis〔of lungs〕.

はい【灰】 ash〔es〕. ¶ 彼はたばこの～をぽんと落とした He tapped the *ashes* from his cigarette (≒ pipe). 家も家財道具もすべて～になってしまった The house and its furniture *were* all *burned* (≒ *were* all *reduced*) *to ashes.* 彼は洗いざらいかまの下の～まで持っていってしまった He took *everything* to the last particle.

はい【胚】〔植物〕〔動物〕an embryo.
—乳〔植物〕an albumen.

はい (応答) yes; (出席の答え) Yes (≒ Present), sir (≒ ma'am); (人に物を渡すとき) Here it is./ Here you are. ¶「わかりましたか」「～」"Do you understand?" "*Yes,* I do." 「早く起きなさい」「～, おかあさん」"Get up at once!" "*All right,* Mother." 「～, それでは話をやめて聞きなさい」"*Now* (≒ *Well*), stop talking and listen to me." 「～, それでよい」"*Oh.* That's right." 「チョーク箱を持ってきてください」「～, かしこまりました」"Will you bring the chalkbox?" "*Yes,* sir. (≒ *Certainly,* sir.)" 彼はいつでも私には～～と言う He *is* always *at my beck and call.* 彼は決して私に～～と言わぬ He never *obeys me* at once.

-はい【-敗】 defeat. ¶ 3勝2～だ We've had three wins and two *losses.*

-はい【-杯】 ¶ 水を1～ください Give me a *glass* of water, will you? お茶を1～いかがですか Will you have a *cup* of tea? (a cup of tea は a tea-cup (お茶のコップ) とは別の語).

ばい【倍】 ¶ 彼は私の～の目方がある He is *twice as* heavy *as* I. 彼は私の～も本を持っている He has *twice as* many books *as* I. 物価は1年前の1～半だ Prices are *one and a half times* higher than a year ago.

パイ a pie. ¶ リンゴ入り～ *an* apple *pie.*

パイ【牌】 (マージャンの) a tile.

はいあが·る【這い上がる】¶ 虫が穴から～ってきた A worm *crawled* (≒ *crept*) *up* out of the hole. 彼は川の土手に～った He *clambered up* the bank.

はいあん【廃案】¶ その法律案は～になった The bill *has become null and void*. / The bill *has been dropped*.

はいいろ【灰色】㊎ gray; ㊖ grey. ¶ ～がかった服 a *grayish* suit. 私の学校生活は～だった My school days *were gloomy*.

はいいん【敗因】the cause of the defeat.

ばいう【梅雨】the rainy season.
—前線 a seasonal rain front.

ハイウエー a highway (国道·県道などを言う); (高速道路) a superhighway; an expressway.

はいえい【背泳】the backstroke. ¶ ～で泳ぐ swim the *backstroke*. ～の選手 a *backstroke* swimmer.

はいえき【廃液】factory waste. ¶ 工場の～を海に流す drain *waste water* from the factories into the sea.

はいえつ【拝謁】¶ 彼は天皇に～を仰せつかった He *had an audience of* His Imperial Majesty. / He *was received* (≒ *was admitted*) *in audience* by His Imperial Majesty. / The Emperor *granted* him *an audience*.

ハイエナ〘動物〙a hyena.

はいえん【肺炎】pneumonia. ¶ 風邪をこじらせて～になった My cold has developed into *pneumonia*.
急性— acute pneumonia.

ばいえん【梅園】a plum orchard (≒ garden).

ばいえん【煤煙】smoke; (すす) soot. ¶ ～の多い(ない)都市 a *smoky* (*smokeless*) city. その都市の建物はすべて～で汚れていた All the buildings in the city were stained with *soot and smoke* from the chimneys.

はいおく【廃屋】a dilapidated (≒ deserted) house.

パイオニア a pioneer.

バイオリニスト a violinist.

バイオリン a violin. ¶ ～をひく play *the violin*.
—協奏曲 a violin concerto.

バイオレット〘色〙violet; 〘植物〙a violet.

ばいおん【倍音】〘音楽〙a harmonic tone.

はいか【配下】*one's* man. ¶ 彼の～になって働いた I worked *under* him. 彼には10人の～がある He has ten men *under* him.

はいが【胚芽】〘植物〙a germ. ¶ ～米 rice with germs.

ばいか【倍加】¶ 鉄の産額が～した The product of iron *has been doubled*.

ばいか【梅花】plum-blossoms.

ハイカー a hiker.

はいかい【徘徊】¶ うさんくさい人がこの辺を～していた A suspicious fellow *was prowling about* here.

はいがい【排外】**—運動** an antiforeign movement. **—思想** antiforeign ideas.

ばいかい【媒介】(仲介) mediation; intermediation; (媒酌) matchmaking. ¶ 大統領の～によって争議は解決した The strike was settled by the *intervention* of the President. 彼は敵国間の～の労をとった He took the trouble of *mediating between* the hostile countries. 彼は二つの会社の合併の～をした He *intervened between* the two companies to arrange the merger. 日本脳炎は蚊によって～される Japanese encephalitis *is carried* (≒ *is conveyed*) by mosquitoes. / Mosquitoes are *carriers* of Japanese encephalitis. 病毒は空気か水の～によって伝播する Disease germs are disseminated *by the agency of* (≒ *through the medium of*) air or water.

ばいがく【倍額】double the amount. ¶ 不正乗車をすると運賃の～を要求される They demand *double* the usual passenger fares if we steal a ride on the train. 物価は昔の～になった Prices of commodities have become *double* what they were. / Prices of commodities have become *twice as* high *as* before. 日曜日に働いた場合には～の賃金をもらった When we worked on Sunday, we received *double* pay.

はいかつりょう【肺活量】breathing capacity. ¶ 私の～は3,000だ My *breathing capacity* is 3,000 cubic centimeters.
—計 a spirometer; a pulmometer.

ハイカラ ¶ 彼は～な(いきな)帽子をかぶっている He wears a *smart* (≒ *modish*; *dandiacal*; *stylish*) hat. 彼は～なりをしている He is *fashionably* (≒ *smartly*; *stylishly*) dressed. 彼は～な仕立ての服を着ている He wears a suit of *modish* cut. 彼女は～な(流行の)スカーフをしている She wears a *fashionable* (≒ *modish*) scarf. / She wears a scarf of *the latest fashion*.

はいかん【拝観】¶ その国宝を～に行った I went to *see* (≒ *look at*) the national treasure. 貴重な彫刻の～を許された I was allowed to *inspect* valuable sculptures.
—者 a visitor. **—料** an admission (≒ entrance) fee.

はいかん【廃刊】discontinuance (≒ discontinuation) of publication. ¶ 資金難で～のやむなきになった As we were in financial difficulties, we were forced to *discontinue* (≒ *cease publishing*) our magazine. A新聞が～になった The "A" Newspaper *went out of existence* (≒ *ceased to exist*). その雑誌はわずか半年で～になった The magazine *lived only for* (≒ *discontinued in*) half a year.

はいかん【配管】(集合的) piping. ¶ セントラルヒーティングの～をしている They *are laying pipes* for central heating. / They are constructing *piping* (≒ *plumbing*) for central heating.
—工 a plumber.

はいがん【拝顔】¶ ～の栄に浴しうれしく存じます I am glad to *have the honor* (≒ *the pleasure*) *of seeing you*.

はいがん【肺癌】〘医学〙cancer of the lung; lung cancer.

はいき【排気】exhaust; ventilation. ¶ 自動車の～ガスで空気が汚れる The air is polluted by automobile *exhaust*.

はいき【廃棄】 abolition; (条約) abrogation; (法律) repeal. ¶ 古い慣習の～ the *abolition* of an old custom. 不用家具の～ the *abandonment* of disused (≒ unnecessary) furniture. 平和条約の～ the *abrogation* of a peace treaty. ある法律の～ the *repeal* of a law. 条約は～された The treaty *was abrogated* (≒ *was annulled*). 政府は時代遅れの法律を～した The government *repealed* the out-of-date laws. 国鉄は蒸気機関車を～した The national railways *gave up using* (≒ *did away with*; *disused*) steam engines.

工場━物 factory waste. プラスチック━物 waste plastic material〔s〕.

ばいきゃく【売却】 disposal by sale. ¶ 彼は家屋を～した He *sold* his house. / He *disposed of* his house *by sale*.

━済み sold.

はいきゅう【配給】 (供給) supply; (配分) distribution. ¶ 戦争中には十分な米の～はなかった We had not *a* sufficient *supply* of rice during the war. 砂糖が～されたこともあった There was a time when sugar *was rationed*.

━米 rationed rice. ━所 a distributing station. ━制 ¶ 戦時中は生活物資はすべて～制だった All the essential commodities were on *a rationing system* during the war.

━会社 (映画などの) a distributing agency.

ばいきゅう【倍旧】 ¶ ～のお引き立てを請う We solicit your *increased* (≒ *further*; *redoubled*) patronage (≒ favor).

はいきょ【廃虚】 the remains; the ruins. ¶ ～となった大寺院 a *ruined* cathedral.

はいぎょ【肺魚】〘魚類〙a lungfish; a dipnoan 〔fish〕.

はいきょう【背教】 apostasy.

━徒 an apostate. ¶ 彼らはキリスト教から異教への～徒である They are *apostates* from Christianity to paganism.

はいぎょう【廃業】 ¶ 彼は旅館を1代で～した He *gave up* (≒ *discontinued*) his hotel business after the death of its founder. 彼は書店を～した He *closed down* his bookshop.

はいきん【拝金】 ━主義 mammonism. ━主義者 a money worshipper; a mammonist.

ばいきん【黴菌】 a bacterium (複 bacteria). ¶ その肉には～がついている The meat is infected by *microorganisms*. 傷口から～が入った The wound *became infected*.

ハイキング hiking. ¶ 家じゅうで～に行った The whole family *went on a hike*. 箱根へ～に行った We *went hiking* (≒ *hiked*; *walked*) *on* Hakone.

━コース a hiking course (≒ route).

バイキング 1〘8世紀～10世紀の北欧の海賊〙vikings; Vikings.
2〘セルフサービスの料理〙a smorgasbord.

はいく【俳句】 a *haiku*; a 〔Japanese〕 seventeen-syllabled poem.

ハイク 英 hike. ⇒ ハイキング

バイク (エンジンをつけた自転車) a motor-bicycle; a motorbike; a motorcycle; (モーターバイク) a motorbike; a lightweight motorcycle.

はいぐうしゃ【配偶者】 a wife; a husband; a spouse. ¶ 彼はよい～を得た He took *a* good *wife*. 彼女はよい～を得た She got *a* good *husband*.

ハイクラス highclass. ¶ ～(高級)なレストラン a *highclass* restaurant.

はいぐん【敗軍】 a defeated army. ¶ ～の将は兵を語らず A *defeated* (≒ *vanquished*) general has no right to talk of his defeat.

はいけい【拝啓】 1〘親族あての場合〙(a) (父母) My dear Father, / My dear Mother,
(b) (おじ・おば) My dear Uncle Thomas, / My dear Aunt Mary, (おじ・おばには Christian Name を添えることが多い).
(c) (兄弟・姉妹・いとこなど) My 〔dear〕 George, / My 〔dear〕 Kate, (受信者が女性の場合は dear の代わりに dearest あるいは darling とも書く).
2〘友人あての場合〙(a) (Family Name (姓)の前に Dear あるいは My dear をつける) Dear Smith, / My dear Smith, (または Dear Friend, / My dear Friend, とすることもある).
(b) (それほど親しくない友人あるいは目上の人の場合には Mr. をつける) Dear Mr. Johnson, / My dear Mr. Johnson,
3〘友人外で面識のない人とか身分の上の人などあての場合〙Dear Sir, / My dear Sir,
4〘女性あて〙(a) (既婚婦人あての場合) Dear Mrs. Smith, / My dear Mrs. Smith,
(b) (未婚婦人あての場合) Dear Miss Smith, / My dear Miss Smith,
(c) 形式ばった手紙には既婚・未婚どちらにも Mrs. あるいは Miss の代わりに Madam を用いる.
5〘非常に形式的な場合〙(a) (市長・大使などあての場合) Sir:
(b) (同夫人あての場合) Madam,
6〘商用の場合〙米 Gentlemen, / 英 Dear Sirs,
7〘相手のはっきりしないとき〙To Whom It May Concern.

はいけい【背景】 a background. ¶ ～には高い山がある There is a high mountain *in the background*. この絵の～は暗すぎる The *background* of this picture is too dark. 舞台の～は真に迫っている The *scenes* look quite real. / The *scenery* looks quite real. 京都は歴史的～に富んでいる Kyoto is rich in historical *background*. 彼は経済的～がない He has no economic *backing* (≒ *support*). 彼の～には有力な資本家がいた A great capitalist was supporting him *behind*. / He had an influential capitalist *behind* him.

はいげき【排撃】 rejection. ¶ 彼らは個人企業を～する They *reject* (≒ *denounce*; *condemn*) private industry.

はいけっかく【肺結核】〘医学〙pulmonary tuberculosis; consumption.

━患者 a consumptive 〔patient〕.

はいけつしょう【敗血症】〘医学〙septicemia; blood poisoning.

はいけん【拝見】 ¶ お写真を～したい Let me

have a look at your picture. / Let me *see* your photo. お手紙をただいま～しました Your letter *has been* just *received*. ちょっと脈を～しましょう Please let me *feel* your pulse. お手並～ I would like to *judge* your skill.

はいご【背後】the back. ¶ 彼らは敵の～を襲った They attacked the enemy *in the rear* (≒ *from behind*). 彼らは犯人の～関係を洗っている They are inquiring into the *background* of the criminal. 彼の～には有能なブレインがいる He has capable brains *behind him* (≒ *at his back*).

はいご【廃語】an obsolete word.

はいこう【廃坑】an unworked (≒ a disused) mine.

はいこう【廃校】¶ あの学校は経営難で～になった That school *has been closed* (≒ *has been abolished*) because of financial difficulty.

はいごう【配合】combination ; (調和) harmony. ¶ 白と黒との～がとてもよく似合う The *combination* of black and white is very becoming. 色の～によって花壇を作った I laid out my flower garden considering the *color scheme*. 部屋に使われている色彩は～がよい The colors used in the room *harmonize*. 薬局の人がこの薬を～した The man in the drug store *compounded* this medicine.

—飼料 mixed (≒ assorted) feed. —肥料 compound fertilizer.

はいごう【廃合】¶ 部課の～が行なわれるはずだ Some departments and sections are to *be reorganized* (≒ *be reshuffled*). / Some departments and sections are to *be abolished* and others *amalgamated* (≒ *combined*).

ばいこく【売国】—行為 a traitorous act (≒ a treacherous act ; a treachery) against *one's* country. —奴 a traitor to *one's* country ; a betrayer of *one's* country.

はいざい【配剤】dispensation. ¶ 彼は自分の不幸を天の～と考えた He regarded his misfortune as *an act of Providence* (≒ *a Divine dispensation* ; *a dispensation of Heaven*).

はいさつ【拝察】¶ ご胸中さぞかしと～いたします I can imagine what your feelings are and deeply sympathize with you. / Please accept my sincere sympathy.

はいざら【灰皿】an ashtray ; (スタンド式の) a smoking stand.

はいざん【敗残】¶ 彼は～の身を嘆いている He complains of his *failure* (≒ *ruin*).

—兵 the remnants of the defeated army (≒ scattered troops). —者 a failure. ¶ 彼は人生の～者だ He is *a failure* in life.

はいし【廃止】abolition ; discontinuance ; (法律) repeal. ¶ 虚礼は～すべきだ We should *do away with* formalities. 国鉄は赤字ローカル線を～した The National Railways *discontinued services* on the local line which had gone into the red. リンカーンは奴隷制～を決心した最初のアメリカの大統領だった Lincoln was the first American President to resolve the *abolition* of slavery. 労働者に不利な法律は～された The law unfavorable to the laborers *was repealed*.

はいジストマ【肺ジストマ】〘医学〙lung(-)distoma ; lung fluke.

ばいしつ【媒質】¶ 空気は音を伝える～である Air is *a medium* through which sounds are carried.

はいじつせい【背日性】〘植物〙negative heliotropism ; apheliotropism.

はいしゃ【配車】¶ 貨車を～する *operate* (≒ *allocate*) freight cars.

はいしゃ【敗者】a defeated person.

—復活戦 revival series ; revival round of a competition for teams eliminated in the preliminary rounds.

はいしゃ【歯医者】a dentist.

はいしゃく【拝借】¶ 私はこの一文をA氏の小説から～しました I *quoted* (≒ *borrowed*) this sentence from the novel by Mr. A. お知恵を～ I hope you will *help me* (≒ *give me some advice*). お電話を～したいのです May I *use* your telephone? (*borrow* a telephone とは言わない).

ばいしゃく【媒酌】¶ A氏夫妻は～の労をとった Mr. and Mrs. A took the trouble of *acting as go-between* (≒ *matchmaking*). われわれは社長の～で結婚式を挙げた We solemnized our marriage *through the good offices of* the president.

—人 a go-between ; a matchmaker.

ハイジャック hijacking ; highjacking. ¶ 飛行機が～にあった The airplane *was hijacked*.

ハイジャンプ〘競技〙the high jump.

はいしゅ【胚珠】〘植物〙an ovule.

ばいしゅう【買収】purchase ; (贈賄) bribery. ¶ アメリカ合衆国は1867年ロシアからアラスカを～した The United States of America *bought* (≒ *purchased*) Alaska from Russia in 1867. その新聞は政府に～されている The paper *is being bribed* by the government. 反対派を～した We *bribed* (≒ *bought off* ; *bought over*) the opposing party. 議員を～してその議案は通過させられた The bill was passed by *corrupting* the members. ～のできる(できない)人 a corruptible (an incorruptible) person.

—工作 a scheme of bribing.

はいしゅつ【排出】¶ この工場は汚水を～する They *discharge* filthy water from this factory.

—管 an exhaust (≒ a discharge) pipe. —口 an issue ; an outlet.

はいしゅつ【輩出】¶ わが校から年々大物選手が～した Our school *has produced*, year after year, a great many star players.

ばいしゅん【売春】prostitution.

—婦 a prostitute ; a harlot ; a street girl.

はいしょ【配所】¶ 彼は15年間～の月を眺めた He *lived in exile* for fifteen years.

はいじょ【排除】exclusion ; removal ; rejection. ¶ この町から暴力を～するよう努めている We

は

are making efforts to *exclude* (≒ *remove*) violence *from* this town. 警官は講堂を占拠した学生を〜した The policemen *evicted* students who had occupied the auditorium. ふたりはあらゆる障害を〜して結婚した They got married *in spite of* all obstacles.

ばいしょう【賠償】reparation; compensation; indemnity. ¶ 彼は損害〜として50万円を請求した He demanded 500,000 yen *in reparation of* (≒ *in compensation for*) the damage. 私は彼にけがに対する〜を請求した I claimed *compensation for* the injury from him. 彼は私の損失に対し〜の約束をした He promised me to *indemnify* for my losses. 現物(金銭)— reparation in kind (cash). 役務— service reparation.

はいしょく【敗色】signs of defeat. ¶ そのチェスは彼の〜が濃い He seems to *be losing* in the chess game. / He *shows signs of defeat* in the chess game. / *The odds have turned against him* in the chess game.

はいしょく【配色】coloring. ¶ 彼女は〜を考えてデザインする She designs with *a color scheme* in mind.

ばいしょく【陪食】¶ 私は〜を仰せつけられた I had the honor of *dining with the Emperor.* / I had the honor of *being present at the Imperial Court dinner*.

はいしん【背信】betrayal; breach of faith; bad faith. ¶ 彼の〜に私はひどく憤慨した I was very angry at his *betrayal* (≒ *breach of faith*). 彼は私に〜行為をした He *has broken faith with* me. / He *has betrayed my confidence*.

ばいしんいん【陪審員】(集合的に) the jury; (ひとり) a juror. ¶ 〜全員が法廷内に入った *The jury* have entered the court room. (ただし団体とみれば単数扱い). 〜はついに評決を下した *The jury* finally brought in its verdict. 〜はそれぞれ意見が分かれた *The jury* were divided in their opinions. (複数扱い). 彼は〜である He is (≒ sits; serves) on *a jury*.
—席 a jury box. —裁判 a trial by jury. —制度 the jury system (a jury は12名の jurymen からなる集合名詞).

はいしんじゅん【肺浸潤】〘医学〙infiltration of the lungs.

はいすい【排水】drainage; (下水) sewerage; sewage; (ポンプを用いて) pumping out. ¶ この土地は〜が悪い This land *drains* badly.
—管 a drainpipe. —溝(こう) a drain; a drainage ditch. —工事 drainage works. —トン数 displacement tonnage. —ポンプ a drain (≒ drainage) pump. —量 a displacement. ¶ その船は〜量5,000トンである The ship *displaces* 5,000 tons. / The ship has *a displacement* of 5,000 tons.

はいすいのじん【背水の陣】¶ 〜をしいて戦った We fought *desperately*. / We fought *with* our *backs to the wall*. 私は〜をしいて工場を再開した By reopening the factory, I *staked everything*.

ばいすう【倍数】〘数学〙a multiple. ¶ 6は2の〜である Six is *a multiple* of two. 4の〜は8 Twice four is eight. / Four *multiplied by* two, is eight.
最小公— the least (≒ lowest) common multiple.

はい・する【拝する】¶ 私は仏像を〜する I *worship* a Buddhist image. 私は聖母マリア像を〜する I *make an obeisance* (≒ *bow in veneration*) *to* an image of the Virgin Mary.

はい・する【排する】¶ 万難を〜して市民の福祉を確保した I *overcame* all difficulties to secure the welfare of the citizens. 万難を〜して工事を完成させよう We will complete the construction *in spite* (≒ *in defiance*) *of* all difficulties.

はい・する【配する】¶ 要所に多数の警官を〜した We *arranged* (≒ *placed*) many policemen at the important positions. 彼は白に黒を〜した He *combined* white *with* black. 庭の一隅に池を〜した One corner of the garden *was allotted* for a pond.

はい・する【廃する】¶ 人種差別を〜する *abolish* segregation. 旧体制を〜する *do away with* the old regime. 部を〜する *abolish* (≒ *put an end to*) a department. 古い法律を〜した We *repealed* (≒ *annulled*) the old law.

ばい・する【倍する】¶ 彼は以前に〜して勉強した He worked with *redoubled* efforts. その店は旧に〜するサービスをする They give *more service than ever* at that shop.

はいせき【排斥】rejection. ¶ 彼らは自由主義を〜した They *rejected* liberalism. 非協力な人は友だちから〜された The uncooperative person *was given the cold shoulder* [by his friends]. 日本の製品がその国で〜された Japanese goods *were boycotted* in that country. 知事の〜運動を起こす start *a movement against* a governor.

ばいせき【陪席】¶ 御歌会に〜の栄に浴した I had the honor of *attending the Poetry Party at the Imperial Court*.
—判事 an associate judge (≒ justice).

はいせつ【排泄】excretion. ¶ 運動は〜を促進する Exercise promotes *elimination* (≒ *evacuation*).
—器官 excretory organs. —作用 excretory process. —物 excrement; excreta; excretion; discharges; eliminations.

はいせん【配船】¶ 会社はアメリカ航路に新型船を〜した The company *placed* (≒ *put*) *a* new style *ship on* the American route (≒ line). / The company *allocated a* new style *ship to* the American route.

はいせん【配線】wiring. ¶ 電話を引くための〜をした They *wired* the house to have a telephone installed. この家は〜がまずい This house *is ill wired*.
—工事 wiring work. —図 a diagram of wiring.

はいせん【敗戦】a defeat.
—国 a defeated (≒ vanquished) country

は

(≒nation). ──投手 a losing pitcher.

はいせん【廃船】 a hulk ; a scrapped ship. ¶ ～する take a ship out of commission (≒service ; use) ; put a ship into dry dock.

はいせん【肺尖】〘解剖学〙the apex of a lung. ──カタル the catarrh of the apex of the lung.

はいぜん【配膳】 ¶ ～は6時です *Dinner is served* at six.
──係 a person in charge of serving food.

はいそ【敗訴】 a lost case. ¶ 彼は～した He *lost* his *lawsuit* (≒*courtcase*). 彼の訴訟は～となった His *suit* (≒*case ; action*) *was lost.* / He *failed in his suit* (≒*case ; action*). 原告側が～した *Judgment was passed against* the plaintiff. / The case *went against* the plaintiff.

はいそう【敗走】 ¶ 敵は算を乱して～した The enemy *retreated in disorder*.

はいぞう【肺臓】〘解剖学〙the lungs.
──ジストマ pulmonary distomiasis. ──がん lung cancer.

ばいぞう【倍増】 ¶ 所得を～する *double one's* income.

はいぞく【配属】 ¶ 彼は編集部に～された He *was assigned to* the editorial department. 彼は研究室に～されることを望んでいる He wants to *get an appointment to* the laboratory.

はいた【歯痛】〔a〕toothache. ¶ ひどい～に襲われた I was attacked by *a* severe *toothache*.

はいた【排他】 ¶ あのクラブは～的傾向がある That club tends to *be exclusive*.
──主義 exclusionism.

はいたい【敗退】 ¶ 初日に彼は～した He *lost his game* on the first day of the series of games.

はいたい【廃退】 decadence. ¶ 道義の～ぶりは目にあまるものがある The *decay of* morals is not to be overlooked.

はいたい【胚胎】 ¶ すべての禍根はそこに～している That is *the source of* all evils.

ばいたい【媒体】 a medium (複 media).
宣伝── the medium of propaganda.

はいだ・す【這い出す】 creep out.

はいたつ【配達】 delivery. ¶ その雑誌はまだ～されない The magazine *has* not *been delivered* yet. ここでは郵便は1日に1回の～だ Mail *is delivered* once a day here. 雷雨のため郵便の～が遅れている *Delivery* of mail will be delayed due to the thunderstorm. この手紙はまちがって～された This letter *has been* wrongly *delivered* (≒*was miscarried*). 新聞～をやってみませんか Will you *take a* newspaper *route*?

はいち【配置】 disposition ; arrangement. ¶ 十数名の警官が要所に～された More than ten policemen *were stationed* (≒*were posted*) at important positions. 社員の～転換を行なった *A reshuffle* (≒*A transfer*) of the personnel was made.

はいちゃく【廃嫡】 ¶ 彼は父親から～された He *was disinherited* by his father.

はいちょう【拝聴】 ¶ お話おもしろく～しました I *enjoyed* your talk very much.

はいてん【配点】 ¶ この問題の～は10点だ Ten points *are allotted to* this question.

はいでん【拝殿】 the front shrine.

はいでん【配電】 supply of electric power.
¶ 工事のため一時～を停止した On account of the construction work, *the electric supply* was cut off temporarily.
──所 a power distribution station. ──線 a service wire. ──盤 a switchboard.

ばいてん【売店】 a booth (複 booths) ; (とくに公園や街頭の) a kiosk. ¶ 学校の～ 米 *a* school *store* (≒*co-op*). 新聞の～ *a* news*stand*. 駅の～ *a* station *stall*.

はいとう【配当】 (株式への) a dividend. ¶ この株の～は4分だ The shares *pay* four percent. 普通株に年5分の～をした A *dividend* of 5 percent was paid on the ordinary shares.
──落ち ex dividend (ex div. と略す). ──金 a dividend. 無── ¶ 会社は無～のやむなきに至った The company was forced to pass *its dividend*.

はいとく【背徳】 immorality.
──行為 an immoral conduct. ──者 a man of immorality.

ばいどく【梅毒】〘医学〙syphilis. ¶ ～患者 a *syphilitic* person.

パイナップル〔a〕pineapple.

はいにち【排日】 ──運動 an anti-Japanese movement. ──感情 ¶ アメリカでは～感情が急速に高まりつつあった The *anti-Japanese* feeling was growing rapidly in America.

はいにゅう【胚乳】〘植物〙an albumen.

はいにょう【排尿】 urination.

はいにんざい【背任罪】 ¶ 彼は～に問われた He was charged with *breach of truth*.

はいのう【背嚢】 a knapsack.

ばいばい【売買】 trade ; buying and selling.
¶ 土地を～する *deal in* real estate. 彼はその商社と～契約をした He *struck a bargain* with the company. 約30万株の～があった About 300,000 shares *changed hands*.
──価格 sale price. 現物── a spot sale. 人身── human traffic.

バイバイ (小児語) bye-bye (いまでは大人も用いる. また電話を切るとき親しい間で Bye-bye now と言う). ¶ その子は私に～した The boy said *bye-bye* to me.

バイパス a by-pass.

はいび【配備】 arrangement. ¶ 警官の～が完了した The *stationing* of the police was finished. 軍隊が戦闘のために～された Troops *were arranged* for the battle.

ハイヒール high-heeled shoes.

はいびょう【肺病】 consumption ; tuberculosis〔of lungs〕.
──患者 a consumptive〔patient〕.

はいひん【廃品】 disused articles. ¶ ～を回収する collect *disused articles*.
──再生 recycling of articles.

ばいひん【売品】 an article for (≒on) sale.

¶ ～(掲示として) For Sale.

はいふ【配布・配付】 distribution. ¶ クラスにテキストを～する *distribute* textbooks among the class. 出席者のひとりひとりに記入用紙が～された A printed form *was distributed* to each of those present.

はいふ【肺腑】 ¶ ～をえぐるニュース *heart-breaking* news. 百万読者の～を突く名作だ This is such a superb novel that it will *deeply move* (≒ *touch*) *the heart* of a million readers.

パイプ (管) a pipe ; (刻み用の) a 〔tobacco〕 pipe ; (巻きたばこの) a cigarette holder. ¶ この～は詰まっている This *pipe* is stopped out. ～をふかす smoke *a pipe*. 両者の間に～(情報交換)がない There is no *communication* between the two.

—オルガン a pipe organ. ビニール— a vinyl pipe. マドロス— a seaman's pipe.

ハイファイ hi-fi ; high-fidelity.

はいぶつ【廃物】 rubbish. ¶ ～利用する utilize *refuse materials*.

バイブル the Bible. ¶ これは法律学の～と言われる書物だ This is called *the Bible* of law.

ハイフン a hyphen. ¶ 2語を～で結ぶ *hyphenate* two words. 2語の間に～を入れるのを忘れた I have forgotten to put *a hyphen* between the two words.

はいぶん【配分】 distribution. ¶ もうけは彼らに平等に～された The earned money *was* equally *distributed* among them.

ばいぶん【売文】 ¶ 彼は～を業としている He is engaged in *literary hack work*.

はいべん【排便】 evacuation.

ハイボール 米 〔a〕 highball ; 英 a whisky and soda.

はいぼく【敗北】 a defeat. ¶ 彼は自分の～を認めた He admitted his own *defeat*. わが軍は決定的な～を喫した Our army had suffered *a* decisive *defeat*. 日本チームはアメリカチームに大差で～を喫した The Japanese team *was beaten* by the American team by a large score. 1点差で～した We *lost the game* by one point.

はいほん【配本】 distribution of books. ¶ 漱石全集の第1回～ the first volume to *be distributed* of the complete works of Soseki.

はいまわ・る【這い回る】 ¶ 赤ん坊が部屋の中を～っている The baby *is crawling about* the room. つたが壁を～っている Ivies *are creeping over* the wall.

はいめい【拝命】 ¶ 彼は文部大臣を～した He *was appointed* Minister of Education.

ばいめい【売名】 self-advertisement. ¶ 彼は～のためにはなにごとをも辞さない He spares no efforts in *seeking publicity*. あの人はどう見ても～の徒だ He is *a publicity seeker* in every respect. 彼のあの～行為は許せない Those *publicity stunts* of his are not to be permitted. / We can never forgive him for his *self-advertisement*.

はいめん【背面】 ¶ 敵の～を襲う attack the enemy *in the rear*.

はいめんとび【背面跳び】 high jump with *one's* back down.

はいもん【肺門】 〘解剖学〙 the hilum of a lung.

—リンパ腺炎 tuberculous adenitis of the hilum.

ハイヤー a taxi (ハイヤーは和製英語). ¶ ～を呼んでくれ Call me *a taxi*.

バイヤー a buyer.

はいやく【配役】 the cast. ¶ ～を決める assign *a part* to (an actor). この映画は～がよい This picture *is* well *cast*. 劇の～が決まった The *cast* for the play has been chosen.

ばいやく【売約】 ¶ その戸だなには「～済み」の札がはられていた The closet was labeled *'Sold.'*

ばいやく【売薬】 a patent medicine ; a drug (drug は麻薬の意味に用いることがあるから注意).

バイヤス bias.

はいゆう【俳優】 a player ; (男) an actor ; (女) an actress. ¶ 彼は～になった He became *an actor*. / He *went on the stage*.

映画— a movie actor. 舞台— a stage actor.

ばいよう【培養】 cultivation. ¶ 細菌を～する *cultivate* bacteria.

—基 〘生物〙 a culture medium. —菌 cultured bacteria.

ハイライト highlight. ¶ 今週のニュース～ the news *highlight of* the week.

はいらん【排卵】 ovulation.

—日 the ovulation day.

はいりこ・む【入り込む】 ¶ ネコがへいの穴から～んだ A cat *crept* through the hole in the fence.

ばいりつ【倍率】 magnification. ¶ ～の高い(低い)レンズ a lens of high (low) *magnifying power*. ～8の双眼鏡 a field glass of eight *magnifications*. ～20の望遠鏡 a telescope of twenty *magnifications*. ～500の顕微鏡 a microscope of five hundred *magnifying power* (≒ *magnifications*). この大学の受験者～は年々高まっている Examinees for this university are increasing *in number* conspicuously year after year.

はいりょ【配慮】 consideration ; (気づかい) concern ; (ほねおり) trouble ; (心配) anxiety.

¶ ご～をわずらわし恐縮に存じます Thank you very much for your *trouble*. 病人が出ないようにご～をお願いしたい I want your kind *consideration* in case any one should fall sick.

ばいりん【梅林】 a plum orchard.

はい・る【入る】 1 〖中へ〗 ¶ どうぞこの部屋へお～りください Please *come into* this room.

どうぞお～りなさい Please *come on in*. (on を入れるのはアメリカ口語).

～っていいですか May I *come in*?

私の家にどろぼうが勝手口から～った A burglar *broke into* my house by the back door.

まもなく列車はトンネルに～ります The train will soon *be going into* a tunnel.

船はあすの朝港に～る The ship *enters* the harbor tomorrow morning. / The ship will *be in* tomorrow morning.

くつに水が～った Some water *got into* my shoes.

芝生に～るな（掲示）*Keep off* the grass.
私は彼のかさに～っていきます I will go with him under the same umbrella.
窓からさわやかな南風が～ってくる A fresh south breeze *comes in* through the window.
窓から朝日が部屋に～ってきた The morning sun *shone* (≒ *streamed*) through the window into the room.
早くふろに～りなさい Hurry and *take your bath.*
彼は病院に～っている He *is in* hospital.
彼について妙なうわさが耳に～ってきた A strange rumor about him *has reached* my ears.
目にごみが～った Some dirt *got in* my eye.

2 〚加入する・身を置く〛 ¶ この子は来年学校に～ります This child will *go to* school next year.
この会社に～って何年ですか How long is it since you *joined* this company?
彼は外務省に～った He *has joined* the Foreign Office.
きみも仲間に～らないか Won't you *join* us?
彼は政界を退いて実業界に～った He has retired from politics and *has gone into* business.
きみはどのクラブに～るつもりか What club are you going to *be enrolled in*? / What club are you going to *join*?

3 〚収容する・含む〛 ¶ このホールは3,000人～る This hall can *accommodate* three thousand people. / This hall *seats* three thousand.
この箱にリンゴがいくつ～るだろうか How many apples will this box *hold*?
このびんには劇薬が～っている This bottle *contains* a powerful drug.
この本はポケットに～る This book *goes in* my pocket.
この値段には税金も～っている The tax *is included in* the price.
部屋代はサービス料が～って4,500円です The room charge is 4,500 yen, service charge *included*.

4 〚始める・始まる〛 ¶ チームは来週から練習に～る予定だ Our team will *go into* training next week.
当地は今雨期に～っている We *are* now *in* the rainy season.
雨期に～った The rainy season *has* now *set in.*
世界は新しい時代に～ろうとしている The world is going to *enter* a new age.
すぐ討論に～りましょう Let's *begin* the debate right away.

5 〚手に入る・移入される〛 ¶ いい本が手に～った A good book *has come into* my hands. / A good book *has come into* my possession.
今～ったニュースによると旅客機が墜落したそうだ According to the news we *have* just *received*, a passenger plane has crashed.
世界のあらゆる産物がわが国に～ってくる Products from all over the world *are introduced into* our country.

6 〚収入がある〛 ¶ 月に15万しか～らない I *have an income of* only 150,000 yen a month.
あの店は１日に200万の現金が～る They *take in* two million yen in cash each day at that shop.

7 〚加えられる〛 ¶ この絵には彼の手が～っている This picture *was retouched* by him.
この子の作文にはおかあさんの知恵が～っている This child's composition has been corrected by his mother.

8 〚取りつけられる〛 ¶ 今度うちに電話が～った We *have* recently *installed* a telephone.
彼の別荘には電気が～っている Electricity *has been installed* in his cottage.

9 〚ある状態になる〛 ¶ コップにひびが～った There is a crack in the glass. / The glass is cracked.
こんな仕事には身が～らない I have no interest in such work.

はいれつ 【配列・排列】 arrangement. ¶ カードをＡＢＣ順に～する *arrange* the cards in alphabetical order. このことばを五十音順に～してほしい I want you to *arrange* these words according to the order of the Japanese syllabary.

パイロット a pilot.

は･う 【這う】 ¶ 赤ん坊は歩く前に～う Babies *crawl* (≒ *creep*) before they learn to walk. かたつむりが枝を～っている The snail *is crawling* along the branch. はたかれて彼は土俵の上に～った He was slapped on the back, and *was on all fours.*

バウンド bound; bounce. ¶ ボールが～してかきねの外へ出た The ball *bounced* out of the fence. 道の穴に車が～した The car *bounded* (≒ *bounced*) over the hole on the way. 遊撃手は球をワン～でつかんだ The shortstop caught the ball on the first *bounce.*

パウンドケーキ a pound cake.

はえ 【蠅】〚虫類〛 a fly. ¶ ～を追う fan *a fly* away. ～をたたく swat *a fly*. ～がうるさいなあ! What a nuisance these *flies* are!
━たたき a flyswatter. **━取り**（器具）a fly catcher;（紙の）a fly paper.

はえ 【栄え】 ¶ ～ある勝利 the *glorious* victory. ～ある賞を受けて彼はうれし涙にくれた Honored with the 〔*glorious*〕 prize, he shed tears of joy.

はえそろ･う 【生え揃う】 ¶ この赤ん坊は歯が～った This baby *has had all* the teeth *come out.*

はえなわ 【延縄】 stretching rope.
━漁法 rope-stretching fishing.

はえぬき 【生え抜き】 ¶ ～の江戸っ子 a Tokyo man *born and bred.* 彼は～のイギリス人だ He is English *to the backbone.*

は･える 【生える】 ¶ 庭に雑草が～えだした Weeds have started *growing* in the garden. 赤ん坊に歯が１本～えた The baby *has cut a tooth.*

は･える 【映える】 ¶ 朝日に～えて空が美しい The sky is beautiful in the morning sun. あの緑のドレスを着ると彼女は～える How *pretty* she *looks* in that green dress! 彼は在学中は～えなかった He did not *shine* as a college student.

はおと 【羽音】 ¶ ガが数羽～を立てて飛んでいる Several moths *are buzzing.* 大ワシが～も高

く飛び去った A big eagle *flapped* away.

はおり【羽織】a *haori.* ¶紋つきの～ *a* crested *haori.* この～は五つ紋だ This is *a haori* with five crests on it.

はお·る【羽織る】¶寒いからカーディガンを～った As it was cold, I *put on* my cardigan. コートを～るとあたふたと出かけた He *flinged* his overcoat *on,* and left in haste.

はか【墓】a grave; a tomb. ¶～を建てる set up *a tombstone.* 彼は～に眠っている He lies in his *grave.* 父の～参りに出かけた I visited the *grave* of my father.

—石 a tombstone. —場 a graveyard.

ばか【馬鹿】**1**〘愚かなこと・人〙a fool. ¶この～者め You *fool!*

～だねきみも,こんなことをするなんて How *foolish* you are to do such a thing! / It is *foolish* of you to do such a thing.

～の一つ覚えで彼はそればかり言っている He is always repeating it like the old dog that knows only one trick.

～につける薬はない There is no medicine for curing *a fool.* / No medicine can cure *folly.*

～とはさみは使いよう *Fools* and scissors require nice handling.

車なんて～でも運転できる Even *a fool* can drive a car.

彼の～さかげんにはあきれた I am amazed at his *foolishness.*

彼は～なことばかりしている He is always doing *foolish* things.

そんな～な話があるものか Can there be such an *absurd* story?

～を言うな Nonsense! / Don't *be absurd.*

彼に金を貸すなんて～だ It's a *silly* thing to lend him money.

～なまねをするな Don't *make yourself ridiculous.* / Don't *make a fool of yourself.*

2〘役にたたない〙¶このねじは～になっている This screw *won't work* any more.

3〘軽べつ·軽視〙¶すこしずつでも毎日のむだ使いは～にならない Even if the amount is small, money wasted every day will come to a considerable sum.

簡単な問題と思って～にしてはいけない You must not *make light of* even an easy question.

彼はみんなに～にされている He *is made a fool of* by everybody.

4〘損をする〙¶～をみたのはぼくではなく彼のほうだ It was not I but he that *was made a fool of.*

あんなことをして～をみた I *made a fool of myself* doing such a thing.

彼のことばを信用して～をみた I *regret* that I believed him.

はかい【破戒】transgression of a commandment.

—僧 a fallen priest.

はかい【破壊】destruction. ¶～は戦争にはつきものだ *Destruction* always goes with war. 建物は爆撃によって全部～された The building *was* totally *destroyed* by bombing. 酒は健康を～するものだ Drinking *is destructive of* health. ローマでは多くの建物が～されていた Many buildings *were in ruins* in Rome.

—力 destructive power. —主義 destructionism. —主義者 a destructionist.

はがいじめ【羽交い締め】¶～にして犯人を取り押さえた We *pinioned* and arrested the criminal.

はがき【葉書】a postcard; 米 a postal card (postcard はイギリスでは官製·私製, アメリカでは私製のものをさす).

¶彼に～を出した I sent *a postcard* to him. 彼に～でそのことを知らせよう I will inform him of it *by postcard.*

絵— a picture postcard. 往復— a return postal card.

はかく【破格】¶彼は～の待遇を受けた He was treated *exceptionally well.* 彼は～の昇進をした He obtained an *unprecedented* (≒ *exceptional*) promotion. ～の大安売りだった It was an *exceptionally* great bargain.

ばかげた【馬鹿げた】¶人の借金を払ってやるなんて～ことだ It *is absurd* that I should pay another's debts. そんな～ことはやめなさい Stop doing such a *silly* (≒ *foolish*) thing. ～まねをするな Don't *make an ass of yourself.* きみの年でそんな～ことをするものじゃない You *should know better* at your age. 彼は商売をやめるとは～ことをしたものだ He *should have known better than* to give up his business. 彼はそんなことをするような～男ではなかった He was not *foolish* to do such a thing.

ばかさわぎ【馬鹿騒ぎ】¶宴会で～をした We *abandoned ourselves to revelry and racket* (≒ *had a spree*) at the drinking party. 彼らは～をしている They *are on the spree.* / They *are having high jinks.*

ばかしょうじき【馬鹿正直】¶あの男は～だ He *is honest to the extent of absurdity.* / He *is too honest.* / He is a *naive* man.

はが·す【剥がす】¶はがきから切手を～した I *took* the postage stamp *off* the postcard. 強風で屋根が～された The roof *was torn off* by the strong wind. 彼は着物を～された He *was stripped of* his clothes.

ばか·す【化かす】¶タヌキはほんとうに人を～すのだろうか I wonder if a badger really *bewitches* us.

ばかず【場数】¶あの人は～を踏んでいる He *has various experiences.* / He *has a wide experience.* 彼は実戦の～を踏んだ軍人だ He *is a veteran of many battles.*

はかせ【博士】a doctor. ¶松本～ Doctor Matsumoto. (肩書きとしては男女とも Dr. を用いてよい).

—号 a doctor's degree. ¶～号をとる take a *doctor's* degree. ～号を授与する confer a *doctor's* degree. —論文 a thesis (≒ dissertation) for a doctor's degree.

ばかぢから【馬鹿力】¶あの男は～がある He *is exceedingly strong.* 彼は～を出してバットを折ってしまった *Putting forth enormous strength,* he has broken his bat.

ばかていねい【馬鹿丁寧】¶ 彼は～なところがある He *is excessively polite.* 彼は～にお辞儀をした He bowed *with overdone politeness.* 彼は仕事が～だ He *is excessively thorough* in his work. その医者は患者の診察に～だ The doctor *is excessively careful in* examining his patients.

はかど・る【捗る】¶ 道路工事はあまり～らない This construction work *makes* little *progress* (≒ *is progressing* little). きょうの仕事の～りぐあいはどうでしたか How much *have* you *got along* with your work today?

はかな・い【果敢無い・儚い】¶ 人生は～い夢にすぎない Life is but an *empty* dream. (詩的文体). 彼は～い最期を遂げた He died an *untimely* death. 家を建てるなんてわれわれにとっては～い望みだ It is but a *vain* hope to have our house built.

はかな・む【儚む】¶ 彼は世を～んで出家した He *was sick of* life and entered the priesthood. 彼は世を～んで自殺した He killed himself *in despair.*

ばかに【馬鹿に】¶ ～寒い It is *awfully* (≒ *mighty*) cold. 彼は～忙しそうだ He seems to be *extremely* busy. あの店はなんでも～安い Everything is *ridiculously* inexpensive at that store.

はがね【鋼】steel.

はかばかし・い【捗捗しい】¶ 商売は～くない Business *is at a standstill.* / Business *is* not doing very *well.* 仕事は～くいかない My work *has* not *made good* (≒ *satisfactory*) *progress.* 彼の病気は～くない His recovery *is slow.*

ばかばかし・い【馬鹿馬鹿しい】¶ ～い話 a *silly* talk. こんな～いことはない Nothing can *be* more *absurd* than this.

はかま【袴】(植物の) a sheath.

はかまいり【墓参り】¶ 一家で先祖の～に行った Our family *visited the grave* of our ancestors all together.

はがゆ・い【歯痒い】¶ 彼の仕事がのろいのを見てとても～かった I *felt very impatient at* the sight of his slow work.

はからい【計らい】 discretion. ¶ 私の～できみを雇いましょう I will employ you *on my own responsibility* (≒ *at my own discretion*). 氏の～で彼女は仕事につくことができた She could get a job *through* his *good offices.* 彼の～にまかせたい I am going to *leave it to his own discretion.*

はから・う【計らう】¶ 適当に～ってください Please *arrange* the matter as you think fit. その会社に就職できるよう～ってあげよう I will *see* (*to it*) *that* you can be employed in the firm. 私の一存では～いかねます I cannot decide *on my own judgment.*

ばからし・い【馬鹿らしい】¶ そんなことで仕事をやめるのは～いことだ How *absurd* (≒ *silly*) it is to quit because of such a thing.

はからずも【図らずも】¶ ～彼と出会った I *happened* (≒ *chanced*) *to* meet him. / I came upon him *by chance.* ～海外へ出張を命じられた *Unexpectedly* I have been ordered to go abroad.

はから・れる【謀られる】¶ 私はやすやすと彼らに～れた I was easily *imposed upon* by them. しまった. ～れた Oh! I *have been taken in*!

はかり【量り・計り・測り】¶ この店は～が悪い (いい) They give short (good) *measure* at this store.

―売り ¶ あの店ではなんでも～売りだ They sell everything *by measure* at the store.

はかり【秤・衡】a balance. ¶ ～のさお a *balance* beam. ～のさら a scale. ～にかける weigh (a thing) in the *balance.* この～は正確だ These *scales* are correct. ～に乗ってごらん Try to get on the *scale.*

ばかり【許り】**1**〖だいたい・およそ〗¶ 5万円～貸してくれないか Would you lend me 50,000 yen *or so*? (この例のような場合, 英米人は日本人のように about を用いない).

車は20メートル～走って止まった The car stopped after running *about* 20 meters.

15分～待っただけだ I waited only *about* fifteen minutes.

これは10日～前のことです It was *some* ten days ago.

2〖…だけ・わずか〗¶ 彼は自分のこと～考えている He thinks *only* of himself. / The *only* thing he does is to think of himself.

彼はうそ～言う He is *always* telling lies.

テレビ～見てないで早く寝なさい You should go to bed early and not stay up watching TV.

世間は悪い人～ではない *Not everyone* in the world is bad.

この子は泣いて～いる This child *does nothing but* cry. / This child is *always* crying.

悪いのは私～ではない It is not I *alone* who am wrong.

春とは名～でまだまだ寒い It is spring in name *only.* It is still cold.

それは会社とは名～で実は小さな事務所だ It is a company in name *only.* In reality it is a small office.

ぼくは社長とは名～だ I am president in name *only.* / I am a *mere* nominal president.

それ～のことで泣くやつがあるか Don't cry over *such a trifle.*

きみ～でなくぼくもつらいんだ It's hard on me as well as you.

彼は国内～でなく外国でも有名だ He is well-known *not only* at home but also abroad. / He is famous abroad *as well as* at home.

これ～の金では足しにもならない *Such a small* sum of money as this is not of any use.

3〖…してまもない〗¶ 今12時を打った～だ The clock has *just* struck twelve.

彼はさっき帰った～だ He returned *just* a little while ago.

会社に入った～でまだなにもわからない I have *just* entered the company and do not know what to do.

4〖ほとんど…しそう・用意ができて〗¶ 彼女は泣きださん～の顔だった Her face showed that she

was about to cry.
稲は刈る〜になっている The rice *is ready for* the harvest.
手紙は投函(とうかん)する〜になっている The letter *is ready to* be mailed.
5 〖さも…のように〗 ¶ 彼は私が悪いと言わん〜の口調だった His tone was *as much as* (≒ *as if*) to say that I was wrong.
それを任せておけと言わん〜に彼はうなずいた He nodded *as much as* (≒ *as if*) to say "Leave it to me."

はかりがた·い【測り難い】inscrutable. ¶ 彼の気持ちは〜い His mind *is inscrutable.* / His mind *is unfathomable.* 運命は〜い Fate *is mysterious.* 天道は〜い The ways of Heaven *are inscrutable.* 大地震がいつ起こるか〜い *We can never tell* (≒ *There is no saying*) when a great earthquake may happen.

はかりごと【謀·策】a plot; a trick; a stratagem. ¶ 彼らは国王殺害の〜をめぐらせた They formed *a plot* to kill the king. 〜が当たった(はずれた) The *stratagem* took (failed). 彼は〜に富む He is full of *resources.* 私は〜がつきた I *am at my wit's end.* 〜は密なるをよしとする *A stratagem* must be laid in secrecy.

はかりしれな·い【計り知れない】unfathomable; immeasurable; uncountable. ¶ 彼は〜い学識がある He has an *unfathomable* amount of scholarship. 〜い損害を被った I suffered an *immeasurable* amount of damage.

はか·る【図る】¶ 内閣は国家の平和と福祉を〜らなければならぬ The cabinet must *look to* the peace and welfare of the state. 彼は私利を〜った He *consulted* his own interests. 彼は自殺を〜った He *attempted* suicide. 相互の理解を〜ることが必要である It is necessary to *promote* mutual understanding of the people. 私はそのふたりの友人の和解を〜ろうとした I *tried* to bring about reconciliation between the two friends. いろいろ便宜を〜ってくれたことに彼には感謝している I am thankful to him for *having provided* me with every facility. 私は英語の上達を〜って非常な努力をした I worked very hard to improve myself in English. あに〜らんや, 私は敗れた *To my surprise,* I was defeated.

はか·る【計る·量る·測る】weigh; measure. ¶ 卵をはかりで〜る *weigh* eggs by means of a balance. 雨量を〜る *gauge* the rainfall. 海の深さを〜る *sound* the depth of the sea. オンスは重さを〜る単位である Ounce is a unit of *measuring* weight. その山は〜ってみると3,000メートルの高さがあった The mountain *measured* 3,000 meters *in height.* 定規で〜る *take measurements* with a rule. 患者の体温を〜る *take the temperature of* a patient.

はか·る【諮る】¶ この問題は委員会に〜ろう Let's *refer* this matter *to* the committee.

はが·れる【剝がれる】¶ 塗料が〜れた The paints *came off.*

ばかわらい【馬鹿笑い】¶ みっともないから〜はよせ Stop *laughing like an idiot.* It is inappropriate.

はがん【破顔】¶ 彼はその知らせを聞いて〜一笑した He *broke into a broad smile* at the news.

バカンス holidays; a vacation (バカンスはフランス語 vacances から).

はき【破棄】(条約など) abrogation; (約束など) breach; (判決) reversal. ¶ 判決は〜された The judgment *was reversed.* 条約は〜された The treaty *was abrogated.* 彼は約束を〜した He *broke* the promise.

はき【覇気】ambition; vigor. ¶ あの男は〜満々だ He *is full of ambition.* / He is an *ambitious* man. 彼は〜がない He lacks *spirit.*

はぎ【脛】a leg.
ふくら— the calf.

はぎ【萩】〖植物〗a bush clover.

はききよ·める【掃き清める】¶ 神社の境内を〜める *sweep* the precincts of a shrine.

はきけ【吐き気】nausea. ¶ 私は〜を催した I *felt sick.* そのにおいをかぐと〜を催す The smell *makes* me *sick.* / *My stomach turns* at the smell. その知らせを受けて〜を催した The news *was disgusting to* me.

はきごこち【履き心地】¶ 〜のよいくつだ The shoes are comfortable to wear. このくつの〜はどうですか How do you *feel with* these shoes *on*?

はぎしり【歯軋り】¶ 彼は眠っているとき〜をする He *grates his teeth* in his sleep. 彼は〜してくやしがった He was so much vexed that he *ground his teeth* (≒ *gnashed his teeth*). (grate (≒ grit) *one's* teeth は眠っているときに用い, grind (≒ gnash) *one's* teeth は起きているとき用いる).

はきす·てる【吐き捨てる】¶ 怒って彼は〜てるようにそう言った He *spit out* the words in anger.

はきそうじ【掃き掃除】¶ 〜する sweep and clean.

はきだ·す【吐き出す】spit out. ¶ あの火山は絶えず黒煙を〜している The volcano *is* constantly *emitting* clouds of black smoke. 廊下にガムを〜してはならない Never *spit out* chewing-gum on the corridor. 彼は私に〜すように言った He *spat* his words at me.

はきだ·す【掃き出す】¶ 庭にごみを〜す *sweep* the dust *out* into a garden.

はきだめ【掃き溜め】a rubbish heap. ¶ 〜に鶴(つる) (諺) A jewel in a dunghill.

はきちが·える【履き違える】¶ 人のくつを〜えた I *mistook* another's shoes *for* mine. 彼は自由と気ままとを〜えている He *takes* (≒ *mistakes*) license *for* liberty.

はぎと·る【剝ぎ取る】tear off; divest of; strip off. ¶ 彼は追いはぎに着物を〜られた He *had* his clothes *torn off* by a highwayman. / He *was stripped of* his clothes by a highwayman. 彼女は私のふとんを〜った She *took off* my bedcover. 彼は顧問の地位を〜られた He *was divested of* his position as an adviser. 彼はすべての権利を～られた He *was deprived of* all his rights. だれかが1ページ～った Someone *has torn* a page *off* the book.

はきはき〔と〕 briskly; promptly. ¶ ～した少年 a *lively* (≒ *brisk*) boy. あの子は～しない The child *is* somewhat *slow*. 彼は～返事した He answered *promptly*.

はきもの【履き物】 footwear (集合的に用いる).

ばきゃく【馬脚】 ¶ はたして彼は～をあらわした He *gave himself away* (≒ *betrayed himself*), just as I had expected.

はきゅう【波及】 spread; extend; influence. ¶ その運動は全国的に～した The movement *extended* (≒ *spread*) all over the country.

はきょく【破局】 collapse; catastrophe. ¶ 彼の発言は内閣の～を招いた His remark brought about the *collapse* of the cabinet. われわれは～に直面している We are in the face of *ruin*. それは～的な戦争だった It was a *catastrophic* war.

はぎれ【歯切れ】 ¶ 彼は～のよい調子で演説した He made a speech in a *clear* (≒ a *decisive*; an *articulate*) tone. 彼の英語は～がよい His English *is clean-cut*. 彼は～のよい文体で書く He writes in a *lively* style. 彼の話し方は～がよい(悪い) He has a *crisp and clear* (a *dull*) way of speaking.

は

はく【箔】 foil. ¶ 彼はその箱に金～をつけた He *gilt* the box. ～が落ちた The *gilt* has come off (≒ has fallen off). ～をつけるために彼はイギリスへ行った He went to England in order to *gain prestige*. 彼は学者としての～がついた He *gained reputation* as a scholar.

-はく【-泊】 ¶ 1～する stay overnight. 2～する make two nights' stay. 修善寺まで1～の旅行(3泊の旅行)をした We made an *overnight* trip to Shuzenji (a trip to Shuzenji requiring three *nights* away from home). その旅館では1～2食つきで7,000円だ The hotel charges are 7,000 yen *a night*, including (≒ with) two meals.

は·く【吐く】 ¶ 路上につばを～くな Don't *spit* on the road. 息を～く breathe out. 血を～く *spit* 〔*out*〕 blood. 煙を～く *emit* (≒ *puff out*) smoke. 意見を～く *give* (≒ *express*) *one's* opinion. ～きそうになったので窓を開けた As I *felt sick*, I opened the window. とうとう本音を～いた He *has told* the truth at last. 銃が火を～いた The gun *spat* fire.

は·く【掃く】 sweep; dust; clean. ¶ 庭のごみを～き寄せた I *swept* the litter in the garden into a heap. 部屋を～いた I *swept out* the room. 運転のできる者は～いて捨てるほどいる Those who can drive a car are to be found *by the cartload*.

は·く【履く·穿く】 put on (shoes, pants). ¶ ～いている wear (shoes); have (shoes) on. きみは新しいくつを～いているね You *have* new shoes *on*, don't you? 青いズボンを～いた少年 a boy *in* (≒ *wearing*) blue pants. 赤ん坊はくつを～いたまま眠っている The baby is sleeping *with* his (her) shoes *on*.

は·ぐ【剝ぐ】 ¶ 鳥の皮を～ぐ *skin* a bird; (獣などの生き皮を)～ぐ flay (a fox). 木の皮を～ぐ *bark* a tree.

ばく【貘】〔動物〕 a tapir.

ばぐ【馬具】 harness. ¶ ～一式 a set of *harness*. 馬に～をつける *harness* a horse.

はくあ【白亜】 chalk. ¶ ～の殿堂 a *white* hall. ～質の chalky.
—紀〔地質〕 the Cretaceous 〔period〕. **—層** a chalk bed.

はくあい【博愛】 philanthropy; charity. ¶ われわれは～に訴える We appeals to *philanthropy* (≒ *charity*). 彼は～を衆に及ぼした He *loved mankind*. / He *extended his benevolence to all*.
—事業 a philanthropic work. **—主義** philanthropism. **—主義者** a philanthropist.

はくい【白衣】 a white dress. ¶ ～の天使 an angel in white; a white-clad nurse (イギリスの看護婦は薄青だから白衣ではない).

ばくおん【爆音】 an explosion. ¶ 近くで～(爆発音)が聞こえた *An explosion* (≒ *An explosive sound*) was heard in the neighborhood. ジェット機の～がうるさくて一晩じゅう眠れなかった We could not sleep a wink all night because of the *noisy roars* (≒ *roaring sound*) of the jet planes.

ばくが【麦芽】 malt; wheat germ.
—酒 malt liquor. **—糖** maltose.

はくがい【迫害】 persecution. ¶ キリスト教徒はローマ皇帝に～された The Christians *were persecuted* by the Roman emperors. 人民は王に～された The people *were oppressed* by the king.
—者(宗教上の) a persecutor; an oppressor.

はくがく【博学】 erudition; great learning. ¶ このことは彼の～をもってしてもわからなかった He did not understand it in spite of his *extensive knowledge*. 彼は～の人だ He is *a learned man*. / He *is erudite*.

はくがんし【白眼視】 ¶ あの男は周囲の人から～されていた Everybody around him *looked coldly upon* him.

はぐき【歯茎】 the gums (通例複数で用いる).

はくぎん【白銀】 silver. ¶ ～のスロープをすべった We went skiing down a slope *covered with silver*〔*ly*〕 *white snow*.

はぐく·む【育む】 bring up; cherish. ¶ 彼は母の手ひとつで～まれた He *was brought up* exclusively by his mother. その事件が彼らの批判精神を～んだ The incident encouraged them to *develop* a critical mind.

ばくげき【爆撃】 bombing. ¶ 町は陸と空から～された The city *was bombed* from both land and air. ～は1週間も続いた The *bombing* lasted as long as a week.
じゅうたん**—** carpet bombing.

はくげきほう【迫撃砲】 a trench mortar.

はくさい【白菜】 a Chinese cabbage. ¶ ～を1たるつける pickle a tub of *Chinese cabbages*.

はくし【白紙】 a clean sheet of paper. ¶ ～の

答案を出した I handed in a *blank* paper. この問題は一応～に返そう Let's forget everything about this matter for the present.
—委任状 a blank letter of attorney.

ばくし【爆死】¶～する be killed by a bomb.

はくしき【博識】erudition. ¶ 彼は～だ He is *a learned* (≒ *erudite*; *well-informed*) *man*.

はくじつ【白日】daylight. ¶ いっさいが～のもとにさらされた Everything *was brought to light*.

はくしゃ【拍車】a spur. ¶ 馬に～をかける *spur* a horse. 車の増加が道路の悪化に～をかけた The increase of cars made the roads worse and worse.

はくしゃ【薄謝】a small token of [*one's*] gratitude. ¶～を呈上する offer *a reward* (*to*).

はくしゃく【伯爵】a count (英国以外の伯爵, 肩書きの場合には Ct. Gismond のごとく略すこともある); an earl (英国の伯爵). ¶ 彼は～に叙された He *was created count*.
—夫人 a countess (英国およびその他の国の伯爵夫人).

はくじゃく【薄弱】¶ 彼は意志～だ He *is weak* in character. / He has a *weak* will. それは～な理由だ It's a *superficial* (≒ *flimsy*) reason. きみの論拠は～だ Your argument is based on *flimsy* grounds.

はくしゅ【拍手】handclapping. ¶～する clap *one's* hands. 割れるような～ *a* thunderous *applause*. 彼の演奏に～を送った We *applauded* his performance. 満場の～をもって with *a* general *clapping of hands*. 賛同くださる方は～をお願いします If you agree with me, will you give me *a big hand* (≒ *a round of applause*)?

はくしょ【白書】a white paper.
経済— an economic white paper.

はくじょう【白状】confession. ¶ 事のいっさいを～した I *confessed* everything. / I *made a clean breast of* the whole affair. 容疑者はとうとう～しはじめた At last the suspect began to *own*. すっかり～しろ Own up! / Out with it!

はくじょう【薄情】cold-heartedness. ¶～な言葉 *cruel* (≒ *unkind*) words. ～な恋人 (移り気な) a *fickle* lover. きみは～だ You *are heartless* (≒ *unfeeling*; *cruel*). 彼は～な男だ He is a *cold-hearted* man. 彼のことばは～に聞こえた His words sounded *want of feeling*. 彼は友人に～な仕打ちをした He acted *cruelly* toward his friend. / He treated his friend *cruelly*.

ばくしょう【爆笑】¶ その光景を見て彼らは～した They *burst out laughing* (≒ *burst into laughter*; *roared with laughter*) at the sight. 先生の冗談でクラスの者の～が起きた The teacher's joke provoked *a boisterous laughter* (≒ *a roar of laughter*) of the class.

はくしょくじんしゅ【白色人種】the white race; the white people.

はくしん【迫真】¶～の演技 a *realistic* performance.
—性 truthfulness to life; verisimilitude.

はくじん【白人】a white man. 「whites.
—種 the white race (≒ people); the

はくじん【白刃】a drawn sword. ¶ 彼は～を頭上にふりかざした He held *a naked sword* aloft over his head. 彼は～の下をくぐってきた He *has crossed swords with* many swordsmen.

ばくしん【驀進】a dash. ¶ 戦車はわれわれに向かって～してきた The tank *made a dash at* us. そのとき戦車隊がわれわれの方に向かって～してきた Then the tank corps *charged down upon* us. 彼らは優勝街道を～した They *continued* to win victories.

ばくしんち【爆心地】a blast center; the center of explosion.

はく・する【博する】¶ 彼はこの本で名声を～した This book *won* him a reputation. 彼女はピアニストとして世界的名声を～した She *gained* (≒ *achieved*) a world-wide reputation as a pianist. 彼は会社の信用を～している He *is in high credit with* the firm.

はくせい【剥製】stuffing; a stuffed animal. ¶ 死んだ犬を～にする *stuff* a dead dog.
—標本 a stuffed specimen.

ばくぜん【漠然】¶～と vaguely; obscurely. 説明が～としている The explanation *is obscure* (≒ *indefinite*; *equivocal*). 彼女は～とヨーロッパへ行こうと考えている She has a *vague* idea of going to Europe.

ばくだい【莫大】vastness; immensity. ¶～な金 a *tremendous* (≒ *vast*; *huge*) sum of money. 彼は～な金を掛けて息子の教育をした He gave his son an education *at great expense*. 飛行機をつくるには～な費用がかかる Airplanes are made *at a great cost*.

はくだつ【剥奪】deprivation. ¶ 人民は王から権力を～した The people *deprived* the king *of* his power. 彼らは彼の位を～するだろう They will *strip* him *of* his honors.
公権— deprivation of civil rights.

ばくだん【爆弾】a bomb. ¶ 船へ～を投下する drop *bombs* on a ship. ～をかかえているように不安な状態だ We feel as uneasy as if we were sitting on *dynamite*.
—動議 a bombshell motion. 原子— an atomic bomb. 水素— a hydrogen bomb.

はくち【白痴】(人) an idiot; idiocy. ¶～の子 an *idiotic* (≒ *imbecile*) child.

ばくち【博打・博奕】gambling. ¶～を打つ *gamble*. 一かばちかの～を打った I took great risks. 彼は～で身代をつぶした He *has gambled away* his fortune.
—打ち a gambler.

ばくちく【爆竹】a [fire]cracker. ¶ 彼らは～を鳴らして浮かれ騒いだ They made merry, setting off *firecrackers*.

はくちゅう【白昼】¶ その事件は～起こった The event occurred *in broad daylight* (≒ *in the daytime*). 「dream.
—強盗 a daytime burglar. —夢 a day-

は

はくちゅう【伯仲】¶ 彼は技量の点で彼女と～している He *is equal to* her in skill. / He *is on a par with* her in skill. 両派の勢力は～している The two parties *are equally balanced*.
はくちょう【白鳥】〘鳥類〙a swan.
　―座〘天文学〙the Cygnus.
ばくちん【爆沈】¶ 軍艦が～した A battleship *sank by explosion*. 汽船が水雷のために～した A steamer *was blown up* by a mine.
ぱくつ・く ¶ 彼は菓子を～いていた He *was biting* a cake. 彼は堅いリンゴを～いた He *munched* 〔*at*〕 a hard apple. 彼は～くことばかり考えている He is bent on *feeding* (≒ *eating*).
バクテリア a bacterium (複 bacteria).
はくとう【白桃】a peach.
はくどう【白銅】nickel.
　―貨 a nickel〔coin〕.
はくないしょう【白内障】〘医学〙cataract.
はくねつ【白熱】incandescence. ¶ ～した議論がしばらく続いた A *heated* discussion continued for some time. 彼らは議論して～状態になった They *grew excited* in their discussion. 議論が～して彼らは昼食をとるのも忘れた *In the heat of* discussion they forgot to have lunch. この作品で彼の人気は～化した This work *marked the climax* of his popularity.
　―戦 ¶ 彼らは野球試合で～戦を演じた They played the baseball game *with a dead heat*. ―繊条 ¶ 電燈の明かりは～繊条から出てくる The light of an electric lamp comes from an *incandescent* filament. ―燈 an incandescent lamp.
ばくは【爆破】¶ 古い建物は～された The old building *was blasted*. 蒸気の圧力がボイラーを～した Steam pressure *exploded* the boiler. 建物は爆弾でこっぱみじんに～された The building *was blown* into fragments with a bomb.
ぱくぱく ¶ 彼は～菓子を食べた He *munched* 〔*at*〕 a cake. 彼はビフテキを～食べた He *ate* a beefsteak *with relish*. 彼女は録音に合わせて口を～させた She *moved her lips* to a recorded tape.
はくはつ【白髪】¶ ～の人 a *gray-haired* person. 彼は～になった His hair *has turned gray*.
ばくはつ【爆発】〔an〕explosion. ¶ 小屋はガス～で破壊された The cabin was wrecked by *a* gas *explosion*. ダイナマイトで岩石を～させた We *blasted away* a rock with a dynamite. 火薬庫が～した A powder magazine *blew up*. ついに彼の怒りが～した At last he *burst into a rage* (≒ *flew into a passion*).
　―物 an explosive. ―薬 an explosive compound. ―力 explosive power.
はくび【白眉】¶ この作品は本年度の～だ This is one of the best works this year.
はくひょう【白票】a blank (≒ an uncomitted) vote. ¶ ～を投じる cast *a blank vote*.
はくひょう【薄氷】¶ どうも～を踏む思いがする I feel as if 〔*I were*〕 *on thin ice*.
ばくふ【幕府】the *Shogunate*; Japan's feudal government.
ばくふう【爆風】a blast.
はくぶつがく【博物学】natural history.
　―者 a naturalist.
はくぶつかん【博物館】a museum.
　科学― a science museum. 大英― The British Museum.
はくぼ【薄暮】twilight; dusk (twilight は朝方, 夕方両方に用いられるが, dusk は夕暮れを言う).
　¶ ～になる Evening dusk gathers.
　―ゲーム a twilight game.
はくぼく【白墨】chalk. ¶ ～1本 a piece of *chalk* (口語では a chalk とも言う). ～で書く write *with* (≒ *in*) *chalk*.
はくまい【白米】polished rice.
ばくまつ【幕末】the closing days of the Tokugawa Government; the end of the Tokugawa regime.
はくめい【薄命】¶ ～な人々 the unfortunate. 彼は己の～に泣いた He grieved over his *bad luck* (≒ *misfortune*; *unhappiness*). 美人～(諺) Beauty and luck seldom go hand in hand. / Beautiful women are liable to misfortune.
ばくやく【爆薬】〔gun〕powder; (爆発物) an explosive. ¶ 敵は橋の近くに～をしかけた The enemy laid *an explosive* near the bridge.
はくらい【舶来】¶ ～のカメラ a *foreign-made* (≒ an *imported*) camera.
　―品 a foreign-made article; foreign (≒ imported) goods.
はぐらか・す ¶ 話の核心に触れると彼は必ず～してしまう When I touch the core, he never fails to *shuffle* (≒ *dodge about*).
はくらん【博覧】―強記 ¶ 彼は～強記の人だ He *is widely read and retentive*.
はくらんかい【博覧会】an exposition (an expo. と略す); 英 an exhibition; 米 a fair.
　万国― an international exposition.
はくり【薄利】small profit.
　―多売 quick sales at small profit.
ぱくりと ¶ 彼はお菓子を～食べてしまった He *has snapped up* a cake.
ばくりょう【幕僚】(総称) the staff; (ひとり) a staff-officer.
はくりょく【迫力】intensity; strength.
　¶ ～のある絵 an *impressive* picture. ～のある議論 a *forcible* discussion. 彼の演説は～がない His speech *appeals* little to the audience. / He lacks *power* in speaking. / His talk *is* not *convincing*.
はぐるま【歯車】a cogwheel. ¶ ～がかみ合わない The *cogwheels* are not in gear. 私の質問と彼の答えの～がかみ合わなかった My question and his answer did not directly meet (≒ cross).
はぐ・れる ¶ 連れの人々と～れた I *lost sight of* my companions. 私は森の中で～れた I *got lost* in the woods.
ばくろ【暴露】disclosure. ¶ 彼はそれを世間に～してやると言っておどした He threatened to make *a public disclosure* of it. 計画が～した The

plan *was disclosed.* 陰謀を～する *betray* a conspiracy; *lay* a conspiracy *open* (≒ *bare*). よけいなことを言って無知を～する He *shows* (≒ *reveals*; *exposes*) his ignorance through saying unnecessary things. 調査の結果，いくつかの秘密が～した On investigation some secrets *have come to light.*

はくろう【白蠟】white wax.

はけ【捌け】¶ このみぞは～が悪い This drainage does not *run* (≒ *flow*) well. これらの品物は～がいい These goods *sell* well (≒ *find a* good *market*).

はけ【刷毛・刷子】a brush. ¶ ～で払う *brush* off.

はげ【禿げ】baldness. ¶ 私は頭に～がある I have *a bald patch* on the head. 彼は～頭だ He is [*a*] *bald-headed* [*man*].

はげあが・る【禿げ上がる】¶ 彼は～っている His hair *retreats* (≒ *recedes*). 額の～った人 a man *with a broad brow.*

はげいとう【葉鶏頭】〘植物〙a Joseph's coat; an amaranth.

はけぐち【捌け口】¶ 彼はその商品の～を求めるのに躍起だ He is anxious to find *a market* for the goods. 彼に不満の～を与えねばならない We must *give vent to* his dissatisfaction. 運動は精力の～だ Exercise is an *outlet* for our energies.

はげし・い【激しい】¶ ～い寒さ *severe* (≒ *intense*) cold. ～い気性 a *violent* temper. ～い討論 a *heated* discussion; a *hot* argument. 風が～い It is blowing *hard.* ～い雨だった We had a *heavy* rain. ～い痛みを覚えた I had an *acute* (≒ a *severe*) pain. 知事選挙の競争が～く戦われている The election of the Governor is *sharply* contested. 暴風雨はいよいよ～くなった The gale *grew worse and worse.* 人々は彼を～く非難した People criticized him *severely.* ふたつの会社間に～い競争が起こった There occurred a *keen* competition between the two companies. 電話のベルが～く鳴った The telephone bell rang *violently.* 彼らは～い砲火を受けた They were subject to a *heavy* fire.

はげたか【禿鷹】〘鳥類〙a vulture; a condor.

バケツ a bucket; a pail. ¶ ～1杯の水 *a bucket* (≒ *bucketful*) *of* water.

ばけのかわ【化けの皮】¶ 彼の～をはいでやった I *unmasked* (≒ *uncovered*; *unveiled*) his character. / I *found* him *out.* 彼の～がはがれた His true character *came to light.* / He *betrayed himself.*

はげま・す【励ます】¶ 病人は～してやるべきだ We should *cheer up* an invalid. 彼を～してもう一度努力させた I *encouraged* him *to* make another effort. / I *spurred* him *into* making another effort. 彼のことばはその生徒を～した His words *animated* the student.

はげみ【励み】¶ 試験は生徒の勉強の～になる Examinations serve as *a stimulus* (≒ *an incentive*) *to* the study of the students. 彼のおほめのことばは私には一種の～となった His praise was a kind of *encouragement to* me. 彼のことばは私の～になった His remarks *were encouraging* (≒ *stimulating*) *to* me. 彼には一生けんめいに働く～になるものがない He has nothing *incentive* to work hard.

はげ・む【励む】¶ 彼は英会話に他人より優れようと～んでいた He *endeavored* to excel others in English conversation. 彼は学課に～む He *works hard at* his lessons. / He *applies himself to* his studies. 彼は自分の家業に～んでいた He *was closely occupied with* his business. / He *gave his attention* to his business. 彼は忠勤を～んでいる He *is zealous in* the discharge of his duties.

ばけもの【化け物】(怪物) a monster; (お化け) a ghost; an apparition. ¶ 彼女は～みたいだ She is *a fright.* ～が正体をあらわした The *ghost* (≒ *apparition*) revealed its true shape. その家は～が出る The house *is haunted.* ～みたいな犬 *a monster* of a dog.

—屋敷 a haunted house.

はげやま【禿げ山】a bare mountain.

は・ける【捌ける】¶ その品物はよく～ける The goods *sell* well.

は・げる【禿げる】¶ 私は頭が～げた I *have become bald-headed.* 彼はつるつるに～げている His head *is* as *bald* as an egg.

は・げる【剝げる】¶ ペンキが～げた The paint *has fallen off.* その色は～げやすい The color is easy to *fade.* 金ぱくが～げている The gilt *has come off.* つけ焼き刃は～げやすい False dye will not wash.

ば・ける【化ける】¶ タヌキが娘に～ける A badger *takes* (≒ *assumes*) *the form of* a girl. 死んだ人が～けて出る A dead man's spirit *haunts.* 彼は女に～けて庭にまぎれ込んだ He slipped into the garden *in the disguise of* a woman (≒ *disguised as* a woman). うまく～けたな Well transformed! / Your disguise is perfect.

はけん【派遣】¶ 出来事を知らせるため使者を～した I *dispatched* (≒ *despatched*) a messenger to tell what had happened. 現地に5隻の軍艦が～された Five warships *were ordered* to the spot.

はけん【覇権】hegemony. ¶ この2大勢力が今日の世界の～を争っている The two big forces are struggling for *the mastery* of the world today. 5チームで～を争う Five teams compete for *dominance.* / Five teams fight for *championship.* ついに彼が～を握った At last he won the *championship.*

ばけん【馬券】a pari-mutuel ticket; a betting-ticket. ¶ ～を買う buy *a ticket* (≒ *a betting-ticket*). 8番馬の～ *a ticket on* horse no. 8.

—売り場 a betting-ticket office.

はこ【箱】a box. ¶ ～にリンゴを詰める pack apples in *a box.* 本がいっぱい入った～ *a case* (≒ *a box*) full of books. リンゴを～で買う buy apples *by the case.*

本— a book case. 道具— a chest of tools. ごみ— a dust bin.

はごいた【羽子板】a battledore. ¶ ～をつく play *battledore and shuttlecock.*

はこいり【箱入り】 ―娘 *a person's* pet daughter; *a person's* beloved daughter.

はごたえ【歯応え】¶ するめは～がある Dried cuttlefish *is hard to chew.* これは～のある仕事だ This job *is tough.* その仕事はまったく～がない The work *is* mere *child's play.* 私は～のない人はきらいだ I don't like a *dull* fellow.

はこづめ【箱詰め】¶ ～の果物 fruit *packed in a box*; *cased* fruit. リンゴを～にする *pack* apples *in a box.*

はこにわ【箱庭】a miniature garden.

はこび【運び】¶ 学校は開校の～になっている Everything *is ready for* opening the school. 工事はまだ着手の～にも至っていない The work *is not yet started.* 彼らはことの～が速い They *settle* (≒ *arrange*) the matter promptly. 彼は筆の～が遅い He is slow in *writing.* 橋の建造は完成の～になった The construction of the bridge *has reached* the final stage. その小説の筋は～が遅い The plot of the novel *develops* slowly.

はこびこ・む【運び込む】¶ 家具を部屋に～んだ We *carried* the furniture *into* a room.

はこびさ・る【運び去る】¶ いつのまにか彼女が荷物を～った She *carried* a baggage *away* before I was aware of it.

はこ・ぶ【運ぶ】**1**〖物を〗¶「あの荷物をどこへ～びましょうか」「ここへ～んでください」 "Where shall I *carry* that baggage?" "*Bring* it here."

「荷物をあそこへ～んでください」 "*Take* the baggage over there."

その荷物を私の宿まで～ばせた I *had* the baggage *carried* to my hotel.

彼は家具を他の家に～んだ He *moved* (≒ *transferred*) his furniture into another house.

象を船でタイから日本に～んだ The ship *bore* the elephant from Thailand to Japan.

2〖来る〗¶ 彼はたびたび私の家に足を～んだ He often *came* to my house. / He *made* frequent *calls* at my house.(やや形式ばった文体).

3〖物事が進展する〗¶ その交渉は円滑に～んだ The negotiation *went on* smoothly.

工事は着々と～んだ The construction work *made* steady *progress.*

万事うまく～ぶようにと願っています I hope that things will *come all right.*

万事うまく～んでいる Everything *is going* well.

話がいっこうに～ばない The matter *makes* no *progress.*

はこぶね【箱舟】¶ ノアの～ Noah's *ark.*

はこべ【繁蔞】〘植物〙a chickweed.

はこぼれ【刃毀れ】¶ ～した刀 a *broken edged* sword.

はこやなぎ【箱柳】〘植物〙an aspen; a poplar.

はごろも【羽衣】a robe of feathers; a gossamer robe. ¶ 天女の～ the〔*celestial*〕*robe* of an angel.

はさい【破砕】smashing. ¶ 岩を～する *smash* a rock〔*into* (≒ *to*) *pieces*〕; *break* a rock *to pieces.*

バザー a bazaar. ¶ ～を開く hold *a bazaar.*

はざかいき【端境期】the between season; the off-crop season.

はざくら【葉桜】a cherry tree in leaf.

ばさばさ ¶ 木の葉が風に吹かれて～と鳴っている The leaves *are rustling* in the wind. 彼の髪は～だ His hair *is shaggy* (≒ *is dry*). 鳥が～と飛び立った Birds flew away *with a flutter.* / A bird took flight *with a rustle.* (文語).

はさま・る【挟まる】¶ 指がドアに～った My finger *was caught* in the door. 魚の骨が歯に～った A fish bone *got in between* the teeth. 本の間に絵はがきが1枚～っていた I found a picture postcard in the book. モンゴル人民共和国はロシアと中国二大国の間に～って存在する The Mongolian People's Republic *is sandwiched*〔*in*〕*between* the two great powers, Russia and China. 彼は奥歯に物が～ったような言い方をする He leaves things half-said. / He is not outspoken.

はさみ【鋏・螯】scissors; (大きな) shears; (切符切り) a punch; (カニの) claws. ¶ 私の～はよく切れる My *scissors* cut well. 机の上に～が2丁ある There are two pairs of *scissors* on the desk. 切符に～を入れる *punch* a ticket. 紙を～で切って穴をあけた I *snipped* a hole in a sheet of paper. 庭師が木に～を入れていた The gardener *was pruning* the tree.

はさみうち【挟み討ち】an attack on both sides. ¶ 警官が犯人を～にした The policemen *attacked* the criminal *from* (≒ *on*) *both sides.*

はさ・む【挟む】¶ 本のページの間に紙を～む *put* a piece of paper between the pages of a book. 川を～んで二つの家が相対している Two houses face each other *across* the river. とびらに指を～まないよう注意してください Be careful not to *catch* your fingers in the door. 彼はよく他人の話にことばを～む He has the habit of *interrupting* others.

ばさりと ¶ 彼女は髪を～きり落とした She cut her hair short *daringly.* 桐の花が～落ちた A big leaf fell off from a paulownia *with a rustle* (≒ *with a thud*). 教育予算を～けずられた The educational budget was cut down *drastically.*

はさん【破産】bankruptcy; failure. ¶ 事業の失敗のため彼は～した He *went bankrupt* because of his failure in business. 私の実家はとうに～した My parents' home *was financially ruined* long ago. 彼は～の宣告を受けた He was adjudicated to *be bankrupt.*

はし【端】an end. ¶ 板の～ *the end* of a board. 教会はこの通りの東の～にある The church is at the eastern *end* of this street. その家はこの通りの～にある The house stands at the *bottom* of this street. ページの～を折ってはいけない Don't make a dog-ear. 彼女はいすの～に腰かけた She sat down on the *edge* of a chair. 公園の～に小屋がある There is a cabin on the *edge* of the park. 私はいつも本を～から～まで読む I usually read a book *from cover to cover*. / I always read a book *through*. 彼は国内を～から～まで旅行した He traveled *throughout* the country.

はし【橋】 a bridge. ¶ 川に～をかける build (≒ span) *a bridge* over a river. この川に～をかけてもらいたいものだ I want *a bridge* over this river. ～を渡る cross *a bridge*. 川に～をかけた They spanned the river with *a bridge*.
—ぐい a bridge post. —げた a bridge girder. 石(つり)— a stone (suspension) bridge.

はし【箸】 ¶ ～1ぜん a pair of *chopsticks*. 彼は～の上げ下ろしにも文句を言う He is exacting *even in trifles*. 彼は～にも棒にもかからない He is *good for nothing*.

はじ【恥】 shame; (不面目) disgrace.
¶ 弱い者をいじめるなんて男の～だ It is *a disgrace* for a man to bully the weak.
また家の～をさらすようなことをしてくれたな You *have disgraced* our family again.
よくも～をかかせてくれたな How dare you *embarrass* me?
人前で大～をかいてしまった I *disgraced myself* (≒ *was disgraced*) in company.
知らないことを聞くのはけっして～ではない It *is* by no means *beneath our dignity* to ask what we do not know.
～を忍んで金を借りにいった I *stooped to* borrowing money.
そんなことをすれば～の上塗りだ It will *add to your shame*.
次の試合ではきっとこの～をすすいでみせる I will surely wipe away my *disgrace* in the next match.
彼はまったく～を知らない男だ He *is* quite *shameless*.
～を知れ, ～を For shame! Shame!
～も外聞もなくトイレへ走った I ran to the toilet, *caring not what others might think*.

はじい·る【恥じ入る】 ¶ ～った顔つきで with an *ashamed* look. 彼は深く～っている He *feels* quite *ashamed*.

はしか【麻疹】 the measles. ¶ ～にかかる catch the *measles*.

はしがき【端書き】 a preface; an introduction.

はじ·く【弾く】 ¶ おはじきを～く *flip* a marble. 油が水を～く Oil *repels* (≒ *draws away*) water. そろばんを～く *calculate* with an abacus; (自己の利益·損得を勘案する) act from selfish motives.

はしくれ【端くれ】 ¶ これでも男の～だ I am a man, humble though I am. ぼくも医者の～だ I am *a piece of* surgeon.

はしけ【艀】 a barge; a lighter.

はじ·ける【弾ける】 ¶ クリの実が～ける Chestnuts *burst open*. エンドウ豆のさやが～ける Pea-pods *split open*.

はしご【梯子】 a ladder. ¶ ～の1段 a step. ～を屋根にかける set up *a ladder* against the roof. ～を上る(下りる) go up (down) *a ladder*.
—〔自動〕車 a ladder truck. —段 a staircase. なわ— a rope ladder. 非常— an emergency ladder; a fire escape.

はしござけ【梯子酒】 pub-crawl. ¶ ～をする人 a pubcrawler. ～をする barhop; pub-crawl.

はじさらし【恥曝し】 ¶ この～め! *Shame* upon you!

はじしらず【恥知らず】 ¶ 彼は～だ He *is lost* (≒ *is dead; is past*) *to shame*.

はしたがね【端金】 an odd sum of money; a little money.

はしたな·い【端ない】 ¶ ～い口をきく use *vulgar* words. ～いことをする behave *shamefully* (≒ *shamelessly*).

はしっこ·い【敏い】 smart. ¶ 彼は～い男だ He is a *smart* fellow.

ばじとうふう【馬耳東風】 utter indifference.
¶ 彼はぼくがなんと言っても～だった He *turned a deaf ear* (≒ *paid no attention*) to my advice.

はしなくも【端無くも】 by chance; incidentally. ¶ ～彼の旧悪がばれてしまった *Unexpectedly* his past crime came to light.

はしばみ【榛】〔植物〕a hazel.

はじまり【始まり】 the beginning; the start.
¶ 争いの～はなにか What does the quarrel *arise from* (≒ *originate in*)?

はじま·る【始まる】 **1** begin; start. ¶ 授業はもう～った School *has* already *begun*.
梅雨は6月に～る The rainy season *sets in* in June.
会はまだ～らない The meeting *has* not *begun* yet.
映画は～っている The movie *has started*.
戦争が～りそうだ A war is likely to *break out*.
弁論大会は彼の開会の辞で～った The speech contest *opened with* his opening address.
英文のはじめの語は大文字で～る The first word in an English sentence *begins with* a capital letter.
2 〖さかのぼる〗 ¶ この衣装はビクトリア王朝に～る The *origin* of this costume *goes back to* the Victorian period.
この習慣は鎌倉時代に～る This custom *dates from* the Kamakura period.
3 〖その他〗 ¶ 今更話し合っても～らない *There is no sense in* our talking with each other.

はじめ【始め·初め】 **1** 〖発端·最初〗 the beginning; the start. ¶ 年の～ *the beginning* of the year.
～はよかった *The beginning* was good for me.
～が大事だ *The start* is important.
3月の～に伊豆に旅行した I made a journey to Izu *at the beginning of* March.
～の計画はどうだったのですか What was the *original* plan?
～にことばありき In *the beginning* was the Word. (ヨハネ伝).
すべて事は～が難しい Everything is difficult *at the start*.
彼は～は一生懸命勉強したがだんだんさぼりだした He

は

studied hard *at first*, but little by little he began goofing off.
〜はこの図書館には100冊しか本がなかった This library had no more than one hundred books *to start with*.
〜からそれはわかっていた I knew it *from the start*.
〜にそれをやった I did it *first thing*.
2 〖…を含んで〗 ¶ 彼を〜５人がやってきた Five men, *including* him, came to see me.

はじめて【初めて】¶ 私はここは〜だ I've never been here before. / I'm a stranger here. そのとき〜私は交通事故の恐ろしさを知った Then I realized *for the first time* how terrible a traffic accident was. 彼の死後〜われわれはその真相を知った We didn't know the truth until he died. 人は健康を失って〜そのありがたさを知る *It is not until* we lose our health that we realize its value. 〜お目にかかります How do you do?

はじめまして【始めまして・初めまして】¶ 〜, Aです. どうぞよろしく How do you do? My name is A. I'm glad to see you.

はじ・める【始める】begin; start. ¶ 勉強を〜めよう I will *begin to* study. / I will *start* study*ing*. 彼らは古い家を修繕し〜めた They *set about* repair*ing* the old house. この問題から〜めよう I will *begin with* this problem. きょうの授業は20ページから〜めることになっている We are to *begin* today's lesson at page 20. 彼は商売を〜めた He *went into* business.

はしゃ【覇者】the supreme ruler; (競技の) the champion.

ばしゃ【馬車】a carriage.
—馬 ¶ 〜馬のように働く work like a slave; toil and moil; work hard.

はしゃ・ぐ make merry; be cheerful. ¶ 子どもたちが庭で〜いでいる Children *are making merry* (≒ *are romping about*) in the yard. 子どもたちはゲームをやって〜ぎまわっている The children *are in jolly spirits* over the game.

パジャマ 米 pajamas; 英 pyjamas.

ばしゅ【馬主】a horse owner

はしゅつ【派出】—所 a branch office; (警官の) a police box. —婦 a visiting housekeeper.

ばじゅつ【馬術】horsemanship.

ばしょ【場所】a place. ¶ 集会の〜はどこですか Where will the meeting take place? ここが店のあった〜だ This is the *place* where the store was. 北海道は今ごろ暮らすにはいい〜だ Hokkaido is *a* good *place* to live in now. テレビを置くいい〜がない I cannot find *a* suitable *place* to fix the television set. その〜で彼は強盗に襲われた He was attacked by a robber *on the spot*. 座る〜は全然なかった There was no *place* (≒ *room*) to sit down. 机を置く〜はもうない There is no more *room* for the desk. この店は不便な〜にある This store *is* inconveniently *located*.
春— (すもうの) the spring *sumo* wrestling tournament.

はじょう【波状】—攻撃 an attack in waves. —スト a strike in waves; a piston strike.

ばしょう【芭蕉】〖植物〗a plantain; a banana plant.

はしょうふう【破傷風】〖医学〗tetanus. —菌 tetanus bacillus.

ばしょがら【場所柄】¶ 彼は〜も考えずにしゃべりつづけた He continued to talk regardless of *where he was*.

はしょ・る【端折る】¶ 難しいところを〜って読む *skip over* (≒ *skim through*) difficult passages. 説明を〜る *cut short* the explanation.

はしら【柱】a pillar; a post; (円柱) a column. ¶ 一家の〜 the *support* of *one's* family. 〜を立てる put (≒ set) up *a post*.
—時計 a wall clock. 火— a pillar of fire. 霜— ice columns. 水— a water column; a column of water. 大黒— (家の構造上の) the central pillar [of a house]; (一家の支えとなる人) the prop of *one's* family.

はしら・す【走らす】¶ 車を〜す *drive* a car. 敵を〜す *put* the enemy *to flight*.

はしり【走り】¶ 〜の果物 *early* fruits.

はしりがき【走り書き】a hurried note. ¶ 〜する write hurriedly; scribble (a few lines).

はしりたかとび【走り高跳び】〖競技〗a running high jump.

はしりづかい【走り使い】¶ 彼はわれわれの〜をしている He runs *errands* for us. 彼を〜に出した We rent him on *an errand*.

はしりはばとび【走り幅跳び】〖競技〗a running broad (≒ long) jump.

はしりまわ・る【走り回る】¶ 運動場を〜る *run about* in the playground. 金策に〜る *visit many acquaitances* for a loan of money. 慈善基金募集のため大いに〜る *make* an extensive *drive* to raise a charity fund.

はしりよみ【走り読み】¶ 手紙を〜する *read* a letter *hurriedly*; *skim over* a letter.

はし・る【走る】run. ¶ 〜らないで歩いた I did not *run* but walked. 駅には〜って５分だ It is a five minutes' *run* to the station. この道路は南北に〜っている This road *runs* from north to south. 彼は感情に〜る He is likely to *be carried away by* his feelings. 極端に〜るのはいけない You must not *go to extremes*. ペンがすらすらと〜った The pen *wrote* smoothly.

は・じる【恥じる】¶ 私は自分の過ちを〜じる I *am ashamed of* my faults. 〜じて赤面する blush with *shame*. その名に〜じない *be worthy of* (≒ *be true to*) its name.

はしわたし【橋渡し】¶ 労資間の〜(調停)をする *mediate* between labor and management. ふたりのために〜(仲人)をする act as *a go-between* for the two. 人の〜で結婚する marry through *the good offices* of *a person*.

ばしん【馬身】¶ 馬は半〜(２〜)の差で勝った The horse won by a half *length* (two *lengths*).

はす【斜】⇒ ななめ

はす【蓮】〖植物〗a lotus. ¶ 〜の花(葉) a *lotus* flower (leaf).

はず【筈】¶ 彼はやがてここへ来る～だ He *is to* come here before long. 一行は明朝出発の～だ The party *is supposed to* start tomorrow morning. 彼はきのうの会に出席の～だったが, 急病のため来られなくなった He *was supposed to* attend yesterday's meeting, but sudden sickness prevented him from coming. 彼はもう着いている～だ He *should* have already arrived. 彼が新聞記者である～がない He *cannot* be a journalist. もう彼は昼食を済ましている～だ He *ought to* have finished lunch.

バス a bus (複 bus[s]es); (2階つきの) a double decker. ¶ ～で行く go by *bus*. ～に乗り遅れる miss *a bus*; (比喩的に) miss the *bus*. ～に乗る(降りる) get on (off) *a bus*. ここからそこまで～の便がある There is *a bus service* from here to the place.
—停[留所] a bus stop. —路線 a bus line. 観光— a sightseeing bus. 長距離— a cross-country bus; a long-distance coach.

バス (ふろ) a bath.
—タオル a bath towel. —ルーム a bathroom.

バス〘音楽〙bass. ¶ ～で歌う sing in *bass*.

パス (定期券) a commutation (≒ 英 season) ticket; (無料入場(乗車)券) a [free] pass.
¶ 試験に～する *pass* (≒ *succeed in*) the examination. 球を～する *pass* a ball (*to a person*).

はすう【端数】a fraction; odds. ¶ ～を切り捨てる omit *fractions*.

バズーカほう【バズーカ砲】a bazooka.

バスーン〘音楽〙a bassoon.

ばすえ【場末】the outskirts. ¶ ～の飲み屋 a bar in *a poor quarter*.

はすかいに【斜交いに】aslant; obliquely. ¶ 板を柱に～にくぎで打ちつけよう I'll nail a board to a post *obliquely*.

はずかし·い【恥ずかしい】(きまりが悪い) shy.
¶ 彼女は～くて私たちと話ができなかった She *was* too *shy* to speak to us. こんな出来栄えで～い I *am ashamed of* such poor results. お～いかぎりです I *am ashamed of myself*. パーティーに出るのが～い I *am* too *embarrassed* (≒ *shy*; *scared*) to be present at the party. その行為を～く思いなさい You should *be ashamed of yourself*. 学生として～くない行動をとりなさい *Behave like* a student should. 彼は～くない服装でパーティーに出た He was present at the party in *decent* clothes.

はずかしがり【恥ずかしがり】¶ 彼はすごく～だ He *is* very *shy*. / He is a very *bashful* person.

はずかしが·る【恥ずかしがる】¶ 彼女は人前に出ると～ってろくに口もきけない She *is* too *shy* to speak in company. 彼女はなにをするにも～る She *is bashful in* doing anything. ～らずに言ってごらん Don't *be shy of* telling me. / Don't *hesitate* to tell me.

はずかしめ【辱め】insult. ¶ 人から～を受ける be insulted (≒ humiliated) by a person.

はずかし·める【辱める】¶ 人を～める put *a person* to shame; insult (≒ humiliate) *a person*.

バスケット a basket.
—ボール basketball.

はず·す【外す】¶ 眼鏡を～す *take off one's* glasses. 上着のボタンを～す *unbutton one's* coat. 腕時計を～す *take off one's* watch. 受話器を～す *take off* a receiver. 席を～す *leave one's* seat. 彼は席を～している He is not at his desk. ちょっとの間座を～したいのですが May I *be excused* for a moment?

パステル pastel.
—画 a pastel. —カラー a pastel color.

バスト (胸像·胸囲) a bust.

はずべき【恥ずべき】disgraceful; shameful.
¶ ～行為 a *disgraceful* (≒ *shameful*) conduct. 清貧はすこしも～ことではない Honest poverty is no *disgrace*. それは紳士として～行為だ Such a conduct *is not worthy* (≒ *unworthy*) *of* a gentleman.

はずま·せる【弾ませる】¶ 彼は心を(息を)～せて学校へ行く He goes to school *in high spirits* (*out of breath*; *panting for breath*).

はずみ【弾み】momentum. ¶ 時の～であんなことをやったのだ He did that *on the spur of the moment*. ものすごい勢いで転んだ～に右足をくじいた I fell with such force that I sprained my right foot. どうした～か彼は運よく私を訪ねてきた Happily he *happened to* call on me.

はず·む【弾む】bound. ¶ このボールはあまりよく～まない This ball does not *bounce* very well. 彼らは息を～ませている They *are panting*. 二, 三杯飲むと話は～んできた After a few drinks, the conversation became *lively*.

パズル a puzzle. ¶ ～を解く solve *a puzzle*.

はずれ【外れ】(町などの) the outskirts; (不作) failure; a poor harvest; (くじ) a blank.
¶ この通りの～に at *the end* of this street. 町の～に on *the outskirts* of a city. ことしの稲作は～だ The rice crop *has failed* this year. ～(くじ)を引いた I drew *a blank*.

はず·れる【外れる】come off. ¶ 窓が～れた The window *came off* (≒ *came out*). タイヤが～れた The tire *has come off*. この戸は取っ手が～れている The knob of this door *is off*. ボタンが一つ～れている One of the buttons *is undone*. 天気予報はこのところ～れてばかりいる The weather forecasts *have been unreliable* lately. すっかり当てが～れた I *am* utterly *disappointed in* my expectation.

はぜ【沙魚·鯊】〘魚類〙a goby.

はせい【派生】¶ ～的な出来事 a *secondary* matter; a matter *incidental to a main issue*. 思わぬ事態が～した An unexpected situation *developed* from it. これらの形容詞は固有名から～した These adjectives *are derived from* proper names.
—語 a derivative.

ばせい【罵声】abuse. ¶ 人に～を浴びせる boo (≒ hiss) *a person*; shower abuse upon *a person*.

はせさん·じる【馳せ参じる】¶ なにか危急なことが起こったときは～じます I'll *come* to help you *as quickly as possible* in an emergency. 彼を助け出すために～じた I *hurried* to his rescue.

バセドーしびょう【バセドー氏病】〔医学〕Basedow's disease.
パセリ〔植物〕parsley.
は・せる【馳せる】¶ 彼はたちまちのうちに名声を～せた He *won fame* (≒ *became well-known*) in a short time. 思いを遠い故郷の空に～せた I *thought of* my home town far away.
は・ぜる【爆ぜる】¶ 豆の～ぜる音がした We heard beans *pop* (≒ *burst*) *open*.
はせん【破線】an interrupted line.
ばぞく【馬賊】a mounted bandit.
ばそり【馬橇】a horse-sleigh.
はそん【破損】damage ; harm. ¶ その事故で両方の車ともたいした～を受けなかった The accident didn't do much *damage* to either of the cars. 陶器類の～が大きかった The china suffered heavy *damage*. / There was heavy *damage* done to the china. ～箇所をよく調べなさい Examine the *damaged* part carefully. 豪雨のため鉄道線路は～した The heavy rain *damaged* the railroad. 鉄管が～したのですぐ修理が必要だ The pipes *are out of order*, and require immediate repair.
はた【旗】**1** a flag. ¶ ～を掲揚する hoist (≒ set up ; erect ; display ; raise) *a flag*.
～をおろす lower *a flag*.
家ごとに～を立てて, 祝日を祝った *National flags* were set up at every door to celebrate the national holiday.
人々は～を振って一行を歓迎した People waved *flags* to welcome the party.
船は前マストに日本の～を掲げていた The ship displayed the Japanese *flag* at the fore.
2〖挙兵する〗¶ 頼朝が～をあげると源氏の残党が集まってきた When Yoritomo *raised his standard*, the remnants of the Genji forces flocked.
はた【端・側・傍】¶ それは池の～の閑静な宿屋だ That's a very quiet inn *by* 〔*the side of*〕 (≒ *at the edge of*) the pond. ～で見るほど楽ではない It's not so easy as *it may seem to others*.
はた【畑】a field. ⇒はたけ
はた【機】a loom. ¶ ～を織る weave.
はだ【膚・肌】**1**〖皮膚〗the skin. ¶ 彼女は～が荒れている Her *skin* is chapped.
～を刺すような寒さだった It was *biting* cold.
2〖気質〗¶ 彼は私とは～が合わない I can't *get along with* him.
彼は学者～のところがある He *has something of* the scholar in him.
3〖その他〗¶ 彼のために一～脱いでやろう I will *lend* him *a helping hand*.
バター butter. ¶ パンに～をぬる *butter* bread ; spread (≒ put) *butter* on bread. ～つきパン bread and *butter*. 彼の文体はちょっと～くさい His style is a little bit *outlandish*.
はだあい【肌合い】¶ 彼は私とは～が違う He is a man of different *stamp* from me. 彼はさっぱりした～の人だ He is a man of frank *disposition*. / He is an open-hearted fellow. 彼は学者のような～の男だ He is of *a* scholarly *turn of mind*. / He *is something of* a scholar.
はたあげ【旗揚げ】the levy of troops. ¶ ～する (挙兵する) rise in arms ; raise *one's* standard.
ばたあし【ばた足】the thrash. ¶ ～で泳ぐ swim with the thrash.
パターン a pattern. ¶ テレビのテスト～ *a* test *pattern*. 日本人には日本人独特の思考～がある Japanese people have their own *ways* of thinking.
センテンス── sentence patterns.
はたいろ【旗色】the tide 〔of war〕. ¶ 彼のほうが～がよくなりかかっていた The *tide* was turning to him. われわれのチームのほうが～が悪い(よい) *The chances* (≒ *odds*) are against us (are in our favor). しばらく～を見てどちらに味方するか決めよう Let's *wait and see* (≒ *sit on the fence*) for a while and decide which side to take.
はたおり【機織り】weaving ; (人) a weaver.
──工場 a weaving shop. ──虫 a grasshopper.
はだか【裸】nakedness ; nudity. ¶ ～の子どもたち *naked* children. (絵画で) ～の女 a woman *in the nude*. 彼は～だったが寒そうではなかった He *had nothing on* but he didn't seem to be cold. 彼は～になって水に跳び込んだ He *undressed* and jumped into the water. 彼は一年じゅう～で暮らす He *goes naked* all the year round.
──一貫 ¶ 彼は～一貫から大臣にまでなった He attained the post of minister, having begun his career with little capital to start with.
はたがしら【旗頭】¶ 彼は一方の～だ He is *the leader* of one of the parties.
はたき【叩き】a duster. ¶ ～をかける *dust* (a window).
はだぎ【肌着】an underwear ; (総称) underclothing.
はた・く【叩く】¶ 彼はオーバーのほこりを～いた He *dusted* his overcoat. 彼は財布の底を～いてその家具を買った He *spent every penny at his disposal* (≒ *emptied* his purse to the last penny) to buy the furniture.
はたけ【畑・畠】**1** a field ; a farm. ¶ ～を耕す till *the soil* (≒ *the ground*).
～に小麦の種をまく sow *the field* with wheat.
～仕事をする do *farm* work.
段々── a terraced field. お花── a flower garden. 小麦── a corn (≒ 英 wheat) field ; a field of wheat.
2〖分野〗¶ 彼は今～違いの仕事をしている He *is out of his element*.
彼は外交～に育った人だ He was brought up in diplomatic *circles*.
はたけ【疥・乾瘡】〔医学〕psoriasis.
はだ・ける ¶ 胸を～ける *expose one's* breast.
はたざお【旗竿】a flagpole.
はださむ・い【肌寒い】¶ 朝夕～くなった *We have* (≒ *It is*) *chilly* mornings and evenings now.
はだざわり【膚触り】the feel ; the touch.

は

¶ 彼は～のいい人だ He is a gentle-mannered person. このはだ着は～がいい This undershirt *feels* soft.

はだし【跣】 barefeet. ¶ ～で歩く walk *barefoot*[ed]; walk *with barefeet.*
玄人― ¶ 彼の料理は玄人～だ He *puts a professional to shame in* cooking.

はたしあい【果たし合い】 ⇒けっとう

はたしじょう【果たし状】 a letter of challenge.

はたして【果たして】 ¶ ～彼は成功した He succeeded *as expected.* 彼は～また失敗した He failed again *just as I feared he would.* このニュースは～事実であろうか *Can* this news be true? ～いつの日また会えるであろうか When *ever* shall we meet again? ～それが事実なら，死を覚悟せねばなるまい *If that is the case,* we must be prepared for death.

はたじるし【旗標】 ¶ 彼らは自由の～の下に集まった They gathered under the *slogan* of freedom.

はた・す【果たす】 ¶ きみは目的を～したか Did you *accomplish* your purpose? 彼はりっぱに約束を～した He *fulfilled* (≒ *carried out*) his promise to the letter. 私の使命は～された My mission *was accomplished* (≒ *was carried out*). 彼はついに長年の念願を～した At last he *realized* his long-cherished wishes.

はたせるかな【果たせる哉】 ¶ ～，大成功であった It turned out to be a great success *as expected.*

はたち【二十】 ¶ 私は～です I'm *twenty* [years old]. ～代に in *one's twenties.*

ばたつ・く ¶ テントが激しい風にあおられて～いていた The tent *was flapping* in the violent wind.

はたと【礑と】 ¶ 彼女がアメリカ人だという事実に～思い当たった *Suddenly* it occurred to me that she was an American. 彼は～ひざをたたいて「よい考えが思い浮んだ」と叫んだ He *suddenly* slapped his knee and cried, "I hit upon a good idea." 彼は～私をにらみつけた He *glared* (≒ *started a sharp glance*) *at* me. 彼をなんと慰めてよいか～思案にくれた I was *quite* (≒ *completely*) at a loss how to console him.

はたばこ【葉煙草】 leaf-tobacco.

はたはた ¶ 旗が～と風に鳴っている The flag *is fluttering* in the wind.

ばたばた ¶ 子どもたちは部屋の中を～走りまわった The children scampered *pitapat* about the room. その国では銀行が～倒れた Banks failed *one after another* in that country. 風のため雨戸が～鳴っている The sliding doors *are rattling* in the wind. 仕事を～片づけた I finished my business *with despatch.* / I *despatched* my business.

バタフライ 〘水泳〙 the butterfly stroke.
¶ ～で泳ぐ swim with *the butterfly stroke.*

はだみ【膚身】 ¶ 彼女はそのロケットを～離さず持っている She always carries the locket *next her skin* (≒ *on her body*). ～につける下着は清潔にしなさい Keep clean the undershirt which you *wear.*

はため【傍目】 ¶ 彼の悲しみは～にも明らかであった His grief was plain even *to others.* ～には彼は満足しているようだ He *seems* to be contented.

はためいわく【傍迷惑】 ¶ 彼はときどき～なことを言う He sometimes says what is embarrassing to others. 彼は～を考えず好きかってなことをする He will have his own way *regardless of other people's feelings.* きみにそんなことをされては～だ You do it *at the expense of others.*

はため・く ¶ 旗がそよ風に～いていた The flag *fluttered* in the breeze.

はたらか・す【働かす】 ¶ 頭を～したまえ *Use* your head. 彼は使用人を長時間～せる He *works* his men long hours. あなたの事務所で～してください Would you *employ* me in your office? / Please *let* me *work* in your office.

はたらき【働き】 work. ¶ 彼の～は高く評価されるべきだ His *work* ought to be valued highly. 彼は～のある商人だ He is an *able* merchant. 彼はなかなかの～をした He performed good *work.* 彼は際立った～を見せた He *distinguished himself.* どうもこのところ頭の～が悪い My brain *has not been working* well these days. 心臓の～ the *function* of the heart.
―ざかり ¶ 彼は今～ざかりだ He *is in the prime of life.* ―手 a worker. ―者 a hard worker.

はたらきか・ける【働き掛ける】 ¶ 彼に私たちの運動に参加するよう～けた We *asked* (≒ *appealed to*) him to take part in our movement. 彼はある方面から～けられた He *was pressured* from a certain quarter.

はたら・く【働く】 ¶ 彼は朝から晩まで～く He *works* from morning till night. このお手伝いはよく～いてくれる The maid *works* very well. 彼はもう10年以上もこの会社で～いている He *has been employed* in this firm over ten years. 彼は5年間銀行で～いた He *has been in the service of* the bank for five years. 私は～きすぎて病気になった I *worked* (≒ *overworked*) *myself sick.*

ばたり ¶ ～と倒れる fall *with a thud.*

ぱたり ¶ その妙な音は～とやんだ The strange sound stopped *suddenly.* 彼からの音信が～と止まった His letter ceased to come *suddenly.*

はたん【破綻】 [a] failure; (破産) bankruptcy.
¶ その計画は完全に～をきたした The plan *failed* completely. / The plan was *a complete failure.* その会社は資金繰りに～をきたした The company *went bankrupt.*

はだん【破談】 rejection; breaking off.
¶ 商談が～になった The negotiations *failed.* / The negotiations ended in *a rupture* (≒ *a failure*). 彼らとの契約を～にすべきではない We ought not to *break off* (≒ *cancel*) the contract with them. 縁談は～になった The engagement *was broken off.*

ばたん ¶ 彼はドアを～と閉めた He *banged* (≒ *slammed*) the door. / He shut the door

は

with a bang. ドアが～と閉まった The door *banged* shut.

ぱたん ¶ ～と本を閉じる close a book *with a flip*.

はたんきょう【巴旦杏】〖植物〗(木・実ともに) an almond.

はち【八】eight. ¶ 彼は怒ると額に～の字を寄せる He *frowns* (≒ *knits his brows*) when he gets angry. ～時間労働 *eight* hour labor.

はち【蜂】(ミツバチ) a bee ; (スズメバチ) a wasp. ¶ ～に腕を刺された I was stung on the arm by *a bee*.
―の巣 a beehive. ¶ 群衆はその知らせで～の巣をついたように騒ぎはじめた The news threw the crowd into *utter confusion*. 雄― a drone. 女王― a queen bee. 働き― a working bee.

はち【鉢】(植木ばち) a pot ; (水盤) a basin. ¶ バラの～ a *potted* rose. チューリップを～に植える *pot* a tulip.

ばち【撥】 a drum stick ; (マンドリンなどの) a plectrum.

ばち【罰】〔a〕punishment〔inflicted by Heaven〕. ¶ ざまあ見ろ, ～が当たったのだ It serves you right. そんなことをすると～が当たるだろう If you do such a thing, you will *be punished by Heaven*. そんなことを言うと～が当たるぞ *It is a blasphemy* to say such a thing. これも自堕落な生活をしてきた～だと思う This is, I think, *a punishment* for my loose living. / This is the *penalty* I must pay for loose living, I think.
―当たり ¶ この～当たりめが! Go to the hell! / Hang you!

はちあわせ【鉢合わせ】¶ 街角で見知らぬ人と～をした I *ran slap into* a stranger at the corner of the street. あるレストランで旧友と～した I *came across* an old friend of mine at a restaurant.

はちうえ【鉢植え】a potted plant.

ばちがい【場違い】¶ 彼はよく～なことを言う He often says what *is inadequate to the occasion*. / His remarks *are* often *out of place*.

はちがつ【八月】August.

はちき・れる ¶ 元気で～れそうな若者 a young man *full of vigor* ; a young man *bursting with vigor*. おなかが～れそうだ *I'm really fed up*. / I've had more than enough. 彼女は喜びで～れんばかりであった She *was beside herself* with joy.

はちく【破竹】¶ 彼らは～の勢いで進軍した They *carried everything before them*. 彼らは～の勢いであった They *were irresistible*.

ぱちくり ¶ 彼は驚いて目を～させた He *blinked his eyes* in surprise.

はちじゅう【八十】eighty. ¶ 彼は～代だ He is *in his eighties*. / He is *an octogenarian*.

ぱちっと ¶ ～とシャッターを切った I shuttered *with a click*.

ぱちぱち ¶ 彼女は突然ライトに照らされて目を～しばたいた She *blinked* at the sudden light. 彼は～その行列の写真を撮りまくった He took pictures of the procession *one after another*.

はちぶ【八分】eight-tenths. ¶ 仕事は～どおり終わった *Eight-tenths* of the work was completed. 腹～に医者要らず Temperance is better than medicine.
―音符〖音楽〗a quaver. ―曲〖音楽〗an octette. 村― ¶ 彼の家族は村～にあった His family *was ostracized* by the villagers.

はちまき【鉢巻き】 a frontlet ; a towel tied round the head. ¶ ねじり～で働く work very hard.

はちみつ【蜂蜜】honey.

はちミリ【八ミリ】(映写機) an eight mm. projector ; (フィルム) eight mm. film.

はちめんたい【八面体】an octahedron.

はちめんろっぴ【八面六臂】¶ 彼は～の人だ He is an *all-round* (≒ *versatile*) person. / He is *able all round*.

ばちゃばちゃ ¶ 赤ん坊がたらいの中で～水をはねかしていた The baby *was splashing* in the washtub.

ぱちゃぱちゃ ¶ 子どもたちが川で～水のかけっこをしている Children *are splashing* water〔over one another〕in the river.

はちゅうるい【爬虫類】〖動物〗the reptiles.

はちょう【波長】wave length. ¶ BBCの放送に～を合わせる *tune in to* the BBC program.

ぱちり ¶ 彼が落馬する瞬間を～と写真に撮った I *snapped* him falling off his horse.

ぱちん ¶ 彼女はバッグを～と締めた She *snapped down* her handbag. / She shut her handbag *with a snap*.

パチンコ pinball ; (Y字形の棒にゴムひもをつけた) a slingshot. ¶ ～の機械 a *pinball* machine.

はつ【初】¶ お～にお目にかかります I'm glad (≒ pleased) to meet (≒ know) you.
―顔合わせ meeting for the first time.

-はつ【-発】¶ 午後5時10分東京～大阪行きの急行に乗ります I'm going to take the express *leaving* Tokyo for Osaka at 5 : 10 p. m. 10時20分～に乗り遅れた I missed the 10 : 20〔train〕. ロンドン～の特電 *dispatches* from London.

ばつ【罰】punishment ; (ゲームの) penalty. ¶ 彼はいたずらして母から～を受けた He *was punished by* his mother for his naughtiness. 彼は窃盗した～として1年間投獄された His *punishment* for his theft was a year in prison. スピード違反は～として10ドルの罰金を支払わねばならない The *penalty* for speeding is a fine of ten dollars. 反則は多くのゲームで～が与えられる Fouls *are penalized* in many games. そんなことをすれば～を免れられない You could not do such a thing *without punishment*.

ばつ【閥】a faction ; a clique. ¶ この会社には出身校の～がない In this firm we have no academic *clique*.

ばつ ¶ 会議に遅刻したので～が悪かった I *felt embarrassed* (≒ *felt awkward*) to be late for the meeting.

はつあん【発案】a suggestion ; a proposal. ¶ ～する suggest ; propose. 彼の～で計画を進めた We proceeded with the plan *at his suggestion*.

—者 a proposer ; an originator.

はついく【発育】growth ; development. ¶この子は～がよい(悪い) This child *is well grown* (*is underdeveloped*). 雨が降らないので花の～が妨げられた The lack of rain checked the *growth* of flowers.

—ざかり ¶中学時代は～ざかりだ Children *grow* fast in their early teens. ～ざかりの子どもたち *growing* children.

はつえんとう【発煙筒】a smoke candle.

はつおん【発音】pronunciation ; articulation. ¶きみの英語の～はたいへんよい Your *pronunciation in* (≒ *of*) English is very good. 彼女の～は聞きとりにくい Her *pronunciation* is difficult to follow. この単語はどう～するのですか How do you *pronounce* this word?

—器官 a vocal (≒ speech) organ. —記号 a phonetic symbol (≒ sign).

はっか【発火】ignition ; (燃焼) combustion. ¶セルロイドは～しやすい Celluloid is very easy to *catch fire*.

—点 the ignition point. 自然— spontaneous combustion.

はっか【薄荷】peppermint ; mint. ¶～入りたばこ a *mentholated* cigarette.

はつが【発芽】germination. ¶豆が～する Beans *germinate* (≒ *sprout*).

はっかく【発覚】detection ; disclosure. ¶彼らの陰謀はついに～した Their plot *was finally brought to light*. 彼は犯行の～を恐れて逃亡した He ran away for fear of *detection* of his crime. 調査の結果驚くべき事実が～した The investigation *has revealed* an astonishing fact.

はっかくけい【八角形】an octagon.

はつかねずみ【二十日鼠】〘動物〙a mouse (複 mice).

はっかん【発刊】publication ; issue. ¶彼の本がついに～された At last his book *was published* (≒ *came out*).

はっかん【発汗】perspiration ; sweat.

はつがん【発癌】¶～性の cancer-developing ; carcinogenic. ～物質 a carcinogen.

はっき【発揮】¶この試合で彼は本領を～した He *demonstrated* his real ability in this game. 今がきみの実力を～する時だ This is the time when you should *make* full *use of* your real ability.

はつぎ【発議】a proposal ; a suggestion. ¶彼の～で会合を開いた We held a meeting at his *suggestion* (≒ *proposal* ; *initiative*).

はっきゅう【薄給】a small (≒ low) salary ; small pay. ¶彼は～に甘んじている He is satisfied with *small pay* (≒ *a low salary* ; *a meager salary*). こんな～ではやっていけない I can't get along on such *a small salary*.

はっきょう【発狂】¶～する go mad ; run mad. 彼女はそのショックで～した The shock *drove* her *mad*.

はっきり 1〘音・形などが明瞭な〙¶この単語を～発音してください Please pronounce this word *distinctly* (≒ *articulately*). 彼の来る姿が～見えた I could *plainly* see him coming toward us. 彼の話し声は～してよくとおる He speaks with a *clear* voice. 電話では彼の声が～きこえなかった His voice *was* not *clear* over the telephone.

2〘事柄・事物が確実な〙¶彼の考えはきわめて～したものだ He has very *decided* opinions. あの事件は～覚えている I remember that incident *clearly*. 彼が事業に失敗することは～している His enterprise *is certain to* fail. きのうのことは～記憶に残っている What happened yesterday still remains *vivid* in my memory. ～した数字を示していただけませんか Will you please *give* me an *exact* figure? ～したご返事をあすまでに頂けますか Shall I be able to have a *definite* answer by tomorrow? これだけは～申し上げられます I can say this much *clearly*. この点について私の考えを～申し上げたい I *want to make myself* quite *clear* on this point. どうして彼が自殺したかは～わからない We *cannot be sure* why he killed himself. 彼の出発時刻が～わからない I do not know the *exact* time of his departure. このところ天気は～しない The weather has been *unsettled* these days.

はっきん【白金】〘鉱物〙〘化学〙platinum.

はっきん【発禁】prohibition (≒ ban) of sale.

—本 a banned book.

ばっきん【罰金】a fine ; a penalty. ¶これをこわしたら～だ Anyone *is punished with a fine* for breaking this. 交通違反で5,000円の～をとられた The violation of traffic regulations imposed *a penalty* of 5,000 yen on me. 彼は～だけで済んだ He got off with *a fine*.

パッキング packing.

バック ¶富士山を～に写真をとってもらった I had my picture taken with Mt. Fuji for the *background*. この絵は～の色が薄すぎる The *ground* color of this picture is too light. 彼は資本家を～に立候補するだろう He will run for an election, *backed up* (≒ *supported*) by capitalists. 自動車を～させた I *backed* my car.

—アップ a backup. —ストレッチ a backstretch. —ストローク a backstroke. —ナンバー a back number. —ボーン backbone. —ミラー a rear-view mirror.

バックスキン buckskin.

はっくつ【発掘】excavation. ¶遺跡を～する *unearth* (≒ *dig up* ; *excavate*) the ruins. 死体を～する *exhume* a body.

—現場 the excavation scene.

はっくぶ【八九分】¶仕事は～どおり仕上がった We have *almost* finished the job.

ぱっくり ¶魚はえさに～食いついた The fish *snapped at* the bait.

バックル a buckle.

は

ばつぐん【抜群】¶ 彼は～の成績で高校を卒業した He graduated from the high school with an *unprecedented* record. 彼女は英語にかけては～だ She *excels others* (≒ *is unrivaled*) in English.

はっけ【八卦】prediction; fortune-telling; divination. ¶ 当たるも～, 当たらぬも～ The *prediction* may or may not come true. / *Divination* is a hit-or-miss sort of thing.

はっけいろじん【白系露人】a White Russian.

はっけっきゅう【白血球】〔解剖学〕a white blood corpuscle; a leucocyte.

はっけつびょう【白血病】〔医学〕leuk(a)emia.

はっけん【発見】discovery. ¶ コロンブスは新大陸を～した Columbus *discovered* the New World.

はつげん【発言】speaking; utterance. ¶ 彼はいつもいい～をする He always *expresses* his good opinions. きみの～を禁じる We prohibit you from *speaking*. 彼ははっきり～した He *spoke out* (≒ *up*).

—権 ¶ 私には～権がない I have no *voice*.

ばっこ【跋扈】¶ 暴力団の～が目だつ The gangster's *rampage* is remarkable.

はつこい【初恋】*one's* first love.

はっこう【発行】publication; issue. ¶ その新聞の～部数は約100万だ The newspaper has about one million *circulation*. 1万円札を～する *issue* 10,000-yen bank notes. その本はいつ～されますか When will the book *be published* (≒ *be out*)? 年4回(週1回; 年1回)～される雑誌 a quarterly (a weekly; an annual) magazine (≒ journal).

—所 a publishing office. **—停止** suspension (≒ prohibition) of publication. **—人** a publisher.

はっこう【発光】radiation.

—信号 a flash signal. **—体** a luminous body; a radiant. **—塗料** a luminous paint.

はっこう【発効】effectuation. ¶ この規則は8月1日から～する This regulation will *come into effect* (≒ *become effective*) on and after August 1.

はっこう【発酵】fermentation. ¶ ～する ferment.

—菌 a zymogen. **—素** yeast; leaven.

はっこう【薄幸】¶ 彼女は～だ She *is unlucky* (≒ *unfortunate; ill-starred; ill-fated*).

はっこつ【白骨】a bleached bone; a skeleton.

ばっさい【伐採】felling; lumbering. ¶ 山林を～する *deforest* a mountain; *cut down trees* on a mountain.

ばっさり ¶ 予算を～削る cut down a budget *drastically*.

はっさん【発散】exhalation; diffusion. ¶ 汗は体外に熱を～させる Sweat *gives forth* body heat outside. 彼らはスポーツで青春のエネルギーを～させた They *directed* their youthful energies to sports.

ばっし【抜糸】¶ 手術後1週間で～する The stitches will *be extracted* (≒ *be taken out*) in a week after the operation.

ばっし【抜歯】extraction of a tooth. ¶ 奥歯を～した I *had* a back tooth *pulled out*.

ばっし【末子】the youngest child.

バッジ a badge.

はっしと【発止と】¶ ～切りつける give a *quick* blow with a sword.

はつしも【初霜】the first frost of the year.

はっしゃ【発車】departure. ¶ ～まであと5分ある We have five minutes before *departure*. 列車は10分ごとに～する The train *leaves* every ten minutes. 東京行きは5番線から～する The train for Tokyo *starts* from Track No. 5.

はっしゃ【発射】firing; discharge. ¶ 彼はけんじゅうを～した He *discharged* (≒ *fired*) his revolver. 月ロケットを～する *launch* (≒ *shoot; blast-off*) a moon rocket.

—試験 proof firing. **—速度** rapidity of fire. **—台** a launching site.

はっしょう【発祥】¶ ナイル川流域は世界文明の～地だ The Nile basin is *the cradle* of the world's civilization.

はつじょう【発情】sexual excitement.

—期 the age of puberty; the mating season.

ばっしょう【跋渉】traveling. ¶ 彼は山野を～するのが好きだ He is interested in *roving over* hill and dale.

はっしん【発信】dispatch; transmission. ¶ 遭難船はSOSを～した The wrecked ship *sent* an SOS.

—人 an addresser; a sender. **—地** the place of dispatch. **—局** the sending office.

はっしん【発疹】〔医学〕eruption; rash.

—チフス eruptive typhus.

はっしんき【発振器】〔通信〕an oscillator.

ばっすい【抜粋】an extract; an excerpt. ¶ シェイクスピアの名文を～する *quote* (≒ *excerpt*) famous sentences *from* Shakespeare's works. それは芥川からの～だ It's *a selection* from Akutagawa's writings. 新聞記事の～ *a* newspaper *clipping*; *a clipping from* a newspaper.

はっ・する【発する】¶ この川はその湖に源を～している This river *rises from* the lake. トラブルは誤解から～することが多い The trouble *results* often *from* misunderstanding. / Misunderstanding often leads to trouble. 太陽は光と熱を～する The sun *sends out* (≒ *radiates*) light and heat. 内閣は声明を～した The government *issued* a statement.

ばっ・する【罰する】punish. ¶ 彼を裁判にかけて～する *bring* him *to justice*. 法律に背けば～せられる Anybody should *be punished* if he breaks the law. 先生はいたずらをした生徒を～した Our teacher *subjected to punishment* a pupil who had done mischief. 生徒は喫煙のかどで～せられた The student *got punished for* smoking. 彼は結局～せられなかった After all he *went unpunished* (≒ *got off scot-free; went scotfree; was acquitted*).

はっせい【発生】growth; generation. ¶ 事件が～した An event *happened* (≒ *occurred; took place*). / An affair *arose*. 害虫が～した Harmful insects *developed*. コレラがその市に～した Cholera *broke out* in the city. 文明の～ the *dawn* of civilization.
自然── spontaneous generation.

はっせい【発声】¶ 市長の～で万歳を三唱した We gave three cheers *at the call of* the Mayor.
──法 vocalization; elocution. ──器官 a vocal organ; a speech organ.

ばっせき【末席】¶ 私もその会の～を汚した I, too, was present at the party.

はっそう【発送】sending; dispatch. ¶ 駅で荷物を何個か～した I *sent out* several pieces of baggage at the station. その手紙は～済みです I *have mailed* the letter.
──係 a mailing clerk; a forwarding clerk.

はっそう【発想】conception. ¶ 両者の～が違う The *way of thinking* differs between the two. 小説の～ the *conception* of a novel.

はっそく【発足】¶ 会を～させる *start* (≒ *make a start of*) a club.

ばっそく【罰則】penal regulations.

ばった【飛蝗・蝗】〘虫類〙a grasshopper; a locust.

バッター〘野球〙a batter; a hitter. ¶ 右(左)～ *a* right(left)-handed *batter*.
──ボックス a batter's box.

はったつ【発達】development; growth. ¶ 彼は心身ともに～した He *has developed* mentally and physically. 低気圧が～して台風になった The low pressure *grew* into a typhoon. わが国の交通機関はすばらしい～を遂げた We have made remarkable *progress* in transportation in our country. (progressにはいつも冠詞をつけない). それは宇宙科学の～のたまものだ It is the result of the *advancement* of space science. 戦後の日本における都市の～は驚くべきものがある The *growth* of the cities in postwar Japan is remarkable.

はったり ¶ 彼はいつも～をきかす He *is* always *bluffing*.
──屋 a bluffer.

ばったり ¶ 道の途中で彼に～会った I *came* (≒ *ran*) *across* him on the way. 彼女からの音信がその後～とだえた She has stopped writing 〔to〕 me. 彼は貧血で～倒れた He *fell flat* because of his anemia. エンジンが～と止まった The engine *came to a dead stop*. / The engine *went dead*.

ぱったり ¶ 父の消息が～とだえた I have *no more* heard from my father. ⇒ばったり

はっちゃく【発着】arrival and departure. ¶ 日本の列車の～は正確だ Trains in Japan are always on schedule.

はっちゅう【発注】¶ その本を本屋に～した I *have ordered* the book *from* a bookstore.

ぱっちり ¶ 目が～した人形 a *bright-eyed* doll. 目を～と開けて with *one's* eyes *wide* open.

ばってき【抜擢】selection. ¶ 彼を～して係長にした We *selected* him to a chief clerk. 彼女を～して昇進させた We *chose* her for promotion.

バッテリー a battery. ¶ 彼と～を組む(野球で) I pair with him as *a battery*. (車の) ～があがってしまった The *battery* is dead.

はってん【発展】development; expansion. ¶ 都市の急速な～ the rapid *growth* of cities. 事業の～ *prosperity* of business. 文化が～する The culture *advances*. ～性のない議論はやめよう Let's stop discussing the matter of no *possibility*. 事態はわれわれに有利に～した The situation *developed* favorably for us. 日本は大規模な海外～をもくろんだ Japan aimed at a large-scale *expansion* abroad.

はつでん【発電】generation. ¶ 10万キロワット～する *generate* 100,000 kilowatts of power.
──機 a dynamo. ──所 a power plant (≒ station). 水(火)力──所 a hydro-electric (thermal) power plant. 原子力── atomic 〔power〕 generation.

ばってん【罰点】¶ こんどのテストで～をとった I was given *black marks* in this test.

はっと ¶ 忘れていたことを～思い出した I was *suddenly* reminded of what I had forgotten. 子どもが道に飛び出してきたので～した I *was surprised* (≒ *was startled*) to see a child running out into the street. ～してわれに返った I came to myself *with a start*.

バット〘野球〙a bat. ¶ ～を長く持つ hold *one's bat* long. 彼は思い切り～を振った He swung his *bat* with all his might.

パット (バスト用の) 〔a pair of〕 falsies; (ゴルフの) a putt.

ぱっと **1**〘一時に・突然〙¶ 桜の花が～開いた The cherry blossoms came out *all at once*.
電気が～消えた Electric light failed *suddenly*.
火が～燃え上がった The fire *burst into* flames.
うわさが町じゅうに～広がった The rumor spread *quickly* through the town.
彼女は～立ち上がった She *jumped to her feet*.
2〘かんばしくない〙¶ 彼はあまり～しない男だ He is a *dull* fellow.
あまり～しない成績だ It is an *unsatisfactory* result.

はつどう【発動】¶ 政府は災害救助法を～した The Government *invoked* the Disaster Relief Law.

はつどうき【発動機】a motor; an engine.

はっとうしん【八頭身・八等身】¶ ～の美人 a *well-formed* beauty.

はつに【初荷】the first cargo of the New Year.

はつねつ【発熱】〔a〕 fever. ¶ 風邪をひいて～している He has *a fever* with a cold.

はっぱ【発破】¶ ～をかける blast; blow up with dynamite. 彼に～をかけて仕事をさせよう I will *urge* (≒ *spur*) *on* him *to* work.

はつばい【発売】sale. ¶ その切手はあす～される The stamp will *be out* (≒ *be put on sale*) tomorrow. それは1,000円で～されている It *is on sale* at 1,000 yen.

—禁止 ¶ その本は～禁止になった The *sale* of the book *was prohibited.* / The book *was placed under a ban.* / The book *was banned.*

ぱっぱと ¶ 彼は～たばこを吸う He *puffs away* his cigarette. 彼女は～金を使う She spends money *extravagantly* (≒ *with a free hand*). / She throws away her money.

はつはる【初春】early spring.

はつひ【初日】the sunrise on New Year's Day.

はっぴ【法被・半被】a *happi* livery coat.

はつびょう【発病】an attack 〔of a disease〕. ¶ 彼は旅行中に～した He *fell ill* (≒ *was taken ill ; got sick*) while traveling. 彼は過労がもとで～した He *was broken down* through overwork.

はっぴょう【発表】〔an〕announcement. ¶ 試験の結果は１週間後に～される The result of the examination will *be announced* (≒ *be made known*) in a week. 政府は事件に関して見解を～した The Government *expressed* its view on the incident. 彼は学会で論文を～した He *read* the paper to the learned society. 調査の結果は委員会で～される The result of investigation is to *be presented* at the committee 〔meeting〕.

はっぷ【発布】promulgation ; proclamation. ¶ 憲法を～する *promulgate* (≒ *proclaim*) the constitution.

はつぶたい【初舞台】*one's* first appearance. ¶ 彼は13歳のときに～を踏んだ He *made his debut* (≒ *made his first appearance on the stage*) when he was thirteen.

はっぷん【発憤・発奮】¶ 私は彼の伝記を読んで～した I *was* greatly *inspired* (≒ *spurred ; stirred*) by his biography.

はっぽう【八方】¶ ～から集まる gather *from all quarters.* ～に逃げる run away *in all directions.* ヨーロッパでは鉄道が～に通じている The railways cross Europe *in every direction.* 警察は～手を尽くして犯人を追っている The police *are trying all possible means to* trace the criminal. 彼らは四方～から敵を攻めた They attacked the enemy *from all directions.*

—美人 ¶ あまり～美人になるな Don't try to please everybody. / Don't be all things to all men. / Don't be everybody's friend.

—ふさがり ¶ 私は～ふさがりだ I *am in a pretty fix.* / I *am hemmed.*

はっぽう【発砲】¶ 警官が賊に～した The policeman *fired* (≒ *discharged*) *his pistol at* the thief. 敵軍がわれわれに対し先に～した The enemy *opened fire on* us first.

はっぽうスチロール【発泡スチロール】styrofoam.

ばっぽんてき【抜本的】¶ ～改革 a *sweeping* (≒ *drastic*) reform.

はつまご【初孫】*one's* first grandchild.

はつみみ【初耳】¶ それは～だ That *is quite news to* me. / I *have heard* it *for the first time.*

はつめい【発明】invention. ¶ 必要は～の母である (諺) Necessity is the mother of *invention.* だれが飛行機を～したか Who *invented* the airplane? 彼は～の才を持っていた He was of *inventive* turn of mind.

—家 an inventor. —品 an invention.

はつもうで【初詣】¶ 家族そろって明治神宮に～した I *paid the first visit of the year to* the Meiji Shrine with all my family.

はつもの【初物】¶ このスイカは～だ This watermelon is *the first of the season.*

はつゆき【初雪】the first snow of the year.

はつゆめ【初夢】the first dream of the New Year.

はつよう【発揚】¶ 国威を～する *exalt* (≒ *enhance*) the national prestige.

はつらつ【溌剌】¶ ～とした少女 a *fresh* girl. ～とした表情 an *animated* expression. 彼はいつも～としている He *is* always *full of life.* / He *is* always *vivid with life.* 彼は才気～たる人だ He is *a man of acumen.* 彼女はいつも～としていた She *was* always *in the lovely bloom of health.*

はつれい【発令】〔an〕official announcement. ¶ 彼の任命は４月１日に～になる His appointment to the post is to *be announced* on April 1. 彼は４月１日の～で課長になった According to the *announcement of appointment* on April 1, he has become section chief.

はつろ【発露】an expression. ¶ それは彼らの友情の～だ It *results from* their friendship. / It is the *manifestation* (≒ *expression*) of their friendship.

はて【果て】¶ 彼は日本の～から～まで旅した He traveled Japan *from end to end.* 世界の～まで to *the uttermost end* of the earth. ここは本州の南の～だ This is *the southmost part* of the mainland. ～はどうなることやら There is no telling how it will *end.* ～は殴り合いのけんかとなった They came to blows *at last* (≒ *in the end ; at length ; finally*).

はて ¶ ～, それはなんだったろうか *Well,* what was it? ～, どうしたらよかろう *Now,* what shall I do? ～, どのくらいまえにそれは起きたっけね Let me see, how long ago did it happen? ～, それはなんだろう I wonder what it is.

はで【派手】¶ ～な色 a *gay* (≒ *bright*) color. ～な柄 a *pronounced* (≒ *gay*) pattern. ～な生活をする live a *gay* life. ～な宣伝をする advertise *in a big way.* この服はあなたには～すぎる This dress *is* too *young* (≒ *gay*) for you. 彼は金使いが～だ He spends money *lavishly.* 彼女は～好みだ She likes *display* (≒ *show*).

ばてい【馬蹄】a horse's hoof. ¶ ～形磁石 a *horseshoe* magnet.

はてし【果てし】¶ ～ない大海原 the *boundless* ocean. 議論が～なく続いた There was no *end* to their argument. / There was an *endless* argument among them.

はてな (驚き・疑い) Oh, my! / Oh, dear! / (考

えるとき) Well. / Let me see. (大てい Let's see. となる). / Wait a moment. ¶ ～どこかで見た人だが *Let me see*—where did I see him? / Where did I see him, *I wonder*? ～, 万年筆をどこへ置いたろう *Wait a minute*, where is my pen (≒ where did I put my pen)?

は·てる【果てる】¶ 議論はいつ～てるともしれなかった There seemed to be no *end to* their argument.

ば·てる ¶ 歩きすぎてすっかり～てた I walked so much that I *was* completely *worn* (≒ *tired*) *out*.

はてんこう【破天荒】¶ ～な出来事 a *record-breaking* (≒ an *unprecedented*) incident.

パテント a patent.

はと【鳩】a pigeon; a dove (pigeon のほうが一般的な語, また汚ない感じを与える. dove のほうが上品な語). ¶ ～が鳴く *A dove* coos. ～が豆鉄砲を食ったような顔をした He *looked amazed*.
—小屋 a pigeon house; a dovecote. —時計 a cuckoo clock. 伝書— a carrier pigeon.

はとう【波頭】the top of a wave.

はどう【波動】a wavy motion; undulation. ¶ 光はかつて～すると信じられた Light was once believed to *undulate*.

ばとう【罵倒】denunciation. ¶ 彼は私を人前で～した He *called* me *names* in public. 彼は政府を～するのが常であった He used to *heap abuse on* the Government.

はとば【波止場】a wharf (複 wharfs; wharves); (突堤) a pier; (岸壁) a quay.
—人足 米 a longshoreman; 英 a stevedore.

バドミントン badminton.

はとむぎ【鳩麦】〖植物〗pearl barley.

はとむね【鳩胸】pigeon-breast; chicken-breast.

はとめ【鳩目】an eyelet.

はどめ【歯止め】a brake. ¶ ～をかける (はずす) apply (release) the *brake*. 際限のない軍事費に～をつけなければならない We must put the *brakes* on unlimited defense spending.

パトロール patrol. ¶ 警官が日に2回～する The policeman *patrols* twice a day. ～中の警官 a *patroling* policeman; a paliceman *on patrol*; a patroller.
—カー a patrol car.

パトロン a patron; a supporter; (女性) a patroness.

ハトロンし【ハトロン紙】kraft〔paper〕.

バトン a baton. ¶ 彼は次の走者に～を渡した He passed the *baton* to the next runner. 彼らは～タッチが下手なので負けた They were defeated owing to their clumsy *baton pass*. 彼は校長としての任務の～タッチを受けた He *took over* the duties of the principal.
—ガール a drum majorette; a baton twirler.

はな【花·華】**1** 〖植物〗(草花) a flower; (果樹などの)〔a〕blossom.
¶ ～が咲いた The *flowers* have come out. 畑に一面に菜の～が咲いている The fields are covered with rape *flowers*.
なしの～が咲いている The pear-trees *are in blossom*.
桜の～はすっかり散ってしまった The cherry *blossoms* have all gone.
2 〖慣用的表現〗¶ ～の都パリ gay Paris (Merry England と同様に gay はパリにつく決まり文句).
きのうの事故のことで話に～が咲いた The talk *became heated over* yesterday's accident.
若いころの話に～が咲いた We *had a wonderful time reminiscing over* our younger days.
彼に～を持たせてやろう I will *let* him *have the credit* for our success.
若いうちが～だ Youth is *a treasure*.
彼女もそのころが～だった Those were *her best days*. / She *was in her prime then*.
言わぬが～ (諺) Better leave it unsaid.
～よりだんご (諺) Bread is better than the song of birds.

はな【鼻】**1** 〖人間·動物の〗a nose; (犬などの) a muzzle; (象の) a trunk. ¶ 高い～ a *long* nose (a high nose はさける).
犬は～がきく Dogs *have a keen sense of smell*.
風邪をひいて～が詰まっている I have caught cold and my *nose* is stopped up.
このにおいは～につく What a disgusting *odor* (≒ *smell*)!
彼は～にかかったしゃべり方をする He talks *through his nose*.
2 〖慣用的表現〗¶ 彼は息子が東大に入って～が高い He *has his nose in the air* because his son has entered Tokyo University.
彼女は彼に～であしらわれた She *has been snubbed by* him.
彼の～をあかしてやりたいと思っている I intend to *take the wind out of his sail*.
彼はいつも木で～をくくったような返事をする He always *gives a curt answer*.
彼の話はもう～についてきた I *am sick* (≒ *tired*) *of* his speech.

はな【洟】nasal mucus; snivel. ¶ ハンカチで～をかむ *blow one's nose* on (≒ into) a handkerchief. この子はいつも～をたらしている The child *is* always *sniveling*. 彼女は近ごろ私などには～もかけない She *makes nothing of* me these days.

はな【端】¶ ～から調子がよくなかった I was not in a good condition *from the start* (≒ *from the beginning*). ～のうちはすべてがうまくいった Everything went well *at first* (≒ *in the beginning*).

はないき【鼻息】¶ きょうは彼の～が荒い He *is* very *high-spirited* (≒ *high and mighty*) today. 売り手は～が荒い The sellers *won't come to terms*. 英語の教員はとても払底しているので～が荒い Teachers of English are so scarce that they *are unapproachable*. きみはいつも彼の～をうかがっている You *are* always *courting* him.

はなうた【鼻歌】¶ 私はひとりで～を歌っていた I

は

was humming a tune (≒ *a song*) to myself. 彼は～まじりに仕事をしていた He *hummed* while working. 彼は～まじりで仕事にとりかかった He set about his work *with a light heart.*

はなうりむすめ【花売り娘】a flower girl.

はなお【鼻緒】a clog thong.

はなかご【花籠】a flower basket.

はながさ【花笠】a flower-adorned hat ; a hat with flower decoration.

はなかぜ【鼻風邪】¶ ～をひいている I have *a cold in the nose* (≒ *head*).

はながた【花形】a star. ¶ コンピューターは時代の～だ The computer is *the lion of the day.* 彼は一座の～だ He is *the star* of the company.

—株 an active share (≒ stock). **—**作家 a popular writer. **—**選手 a star player.

はながみ【鼻紙】tissue [paper].

はなぐすり【鼻薬】a bribe. ¶ きみは～をかがされてそうした You *were bribed* to do so. ～が効いた The *bribe* had its effect.

はなくそ【鼻屎】nose wax (≒ dirt). ¶ ～をほじってはいけません Don't *pick your nose.*

はなぐもり【花曇り】a hazy flower season sky.

はなげ【鼻毛】¶ ～を抜く pull out *the hairs in the nostrils.* ～を読まれる be deceived by a [sweet-mouthed] woman.

はなごえ【鼻声】a nasal voice (≒ tone). ¶ 彼は～で話す He talks *through the nose.* / He has *a nasal twang.*

はなことば【花言葉・花詞】flower language. ¶ 白ユリは～では純潔を意味する A white lily means purity *in the language of flowers.*

はなざかり【花盛り】¶ 桜の～だ The cherry trees *are in full bloom.* / The cherry blossoms *are at their best.*

はなさき【鼻先】¶ 彼は私の忠告を～であしらった He *snubbed* my advice *away.* 彼女は彼を～であしらう She *turns up her nose at* him. その事件は警官の～で起こった The case was committed *under the nose of* a policeman. 春はもう～まで来ている Spring *is near at hand* (≒ *is just round the corner*).

はなし【話】**1**〖話すこと・談話〗a talk ; a conversation. ¶ あの人は～がじょうずだ He is great at *storytelling.* / He is *a good storyteller.*
たいへんおもしろいお～でした It was *a* very interesting *story.*
むだ～をやめて私の言うことをよく聞け Stop the idle *talk* and listen to me attentively.
友だちと気楽に～をするのは楽しい It is pleasant to *talk* with my friends in a familiar way.
私は～がへただ I'm not *a good talker.*
お～の途中ですが，そのことばの意味はなんでしょうか Excuse me for interrupting you, but what is the meaning of that word ?
彼は～の切れ目を見つけて席を立った He left his seat during a lull in the *conversation.*
彼がうまく私の～をつないでくれた He tactfully kept my *talk* going.
～がはずんでつい知らずに帰りが遅くなった The *conversation* became so lively that I was late getting home.
同級生が集まると学生時代の～に花が咲く When the classmates come together, they blossom out into reminiscences of their school days.
ここだけの～だが，彼はなかなか腹黒い男だ *Between ourselves* (≒ *Between you and me*), he is evil.
2〖うわさ・話題〗¶ 彼は～の種が豊富だ He never wants for *a subject to talk about.*
このへんで～を変えよう Let's change the *subject.*
彼の～によると近く人事異動があるらしい According to his *report,* there will be personnel changes before long.
税金の～で思い出したが今月は市民税の納期だ *Speaking of* taxes, this is the month when we have to pay the municipal tax.
よそうよ，そんな不愉快な～は Let's have done with such *an* unpleasant *subject.*
～の種にそれを食べてみた I tasted it *for my own experience.*
彼女が結婚するって～はほんとうか Is the *rumor* true that she is going to be married ?
彼は昨年の暮れに死んだという～だ *They say* that he died at the end of last year.
3〖物語〗a story. ¶ 子どものころピノキオの～を夢中で読んだ I was absorbed in reading the *story* of Pinocchio when I was a child.
この本にはいい～がたくさん載っている Many good *stories* are found in this book.
アイヌの～は悲しいものが多い Many of the *legends* of the Ainus are tragic.
私は子どもに自分の経験の～をしてやった I *related* my experience to my children.
4〖相談・約束・交渉〗¶ きみにもぜひ～に乗ってもらいたい I want you to *give* me *advice.*
損害の弁償について先方と～がついた As to the compensation for damages, I *have come to an agreement with* him.
折り入ってあなたに～がある I have *an* earnest *request* to make of you.
ちょっと～があるから今晩来てください Please come to my house this evening, because I have *something to talk over* with you.
それでは～が違うじゃないか That's not our understanding. / That's another *story.* / It's against our agreement.
縁談は～がこじれてしまった The marriage proposal has gone wrong.
その値段ではとても～にならない The price *is out of the question.*
3,000 円で泊めるという～だったじゃないか Didn't you *promise* that you would give me a night's lodging for 3,000 yen ?
～がうますぎてすこし心配だ I am afraid it is too good to be true.
5〖わけ・事情・問題〗¶ 彼ほど～のわからぬ者はない There is no one as dumb as he.
彼がもうすこし～がわかるといいんだが I wish [that] he *had* a little more *sense.*

は

はなしあい【話し合い】a consultation. ¶ 一応～が必要だ *A consultation* is necessary at any rate. これは～で決めよう Let's decide this by *common consent.* ふたりの間には～がついた The two persons *have come to an understanding* with each other. 直接の～で家を売ることになった We have decided to sell our house by personal *treaty.* われわれは～の結果結論に達した We *negotiated* to get at a conclusion.

はなしあいて【話し相手】a companion. ¶ 彼女は～がない She has no *one* she *can talk to.* この子はだれか～を欲しがっている This child wants to have *someone to talk to.*

はなしあ・う【話し合う】¶ どうして彼と～わないのですか Why don't you *consult with* him? みんなは旅行の計画を～っている They *are discussing* the plan of their trip.

はなしがい【放し飼い】¶ 牛を～にする (人を主語にして) We *leave* cattle *at large.* / (牛を主語にして) Cattle *are at grass.* / Cattle *are in pasture.*

はなしか・ける【話しかける】¶ 先方から～けられないかぎり, 口をきいてはいけない Don't speak unless you *are spoken to.* 彼は外国人に～けるのが好きだ He likes to *address* foreigners.

はなしごえ【話し声】a voice. ¶ 二, 三人の～が聞こえる We can hear a few persons *talking.*

はなしことば【話し言葉】speech.

はなしこ・む【話し込む】¶ 彼とすっかり～んでしまった I *had a* long *talk* with him. 久しぶりに会った友人と2時間以上～んだ I *talked* for more than two hours with a friend of mine whom I had not seen for a long time.

はなしずき【話し好き】¶ 彼はたいへん～だ He *likes talking.* なんと～な人だろう What a *talkative* person!

はなしはんぶん【話半分】¶ 彼は私の言うことを～に聞いている He does*n't take* what I say *seriously.* それは～に聞いておいたほうがいい You must *take the story at half its face value.*

はなしぶり【話し振り】*one's* way of talking. ¶ 彼はまるで知らないことはないという～だ He *talks as if* he knew everything. 彼の～では彼は真相がわかっていないらしい *By the way he talks,* he is ignorant of the real state of things. 彼の～は父親そっくりだ *The way he talks* resembles his father's.

はなしょうぶ【花菖蒲】〘植物〙 an iris (複 irises; irides); a flag.

はな・す【話す】**1**〚語る・しゃべる〛 ¶ お～ししたいことがあります I have something to *tell* you. / I'd like to *speak* with you.
先日～したのはこの本のことです This is the book 〔which〕 I *told* you *about* the other day.
彼女はスペイン語をじょうずに～す She *speaks* Spanish fluently.
マイクに向かって～す *speak into* a microphone.
電話で～す *speak through* (≒ *on*; *by*) the phone.
彼は世界平和について～した He *gave a speech* on world peace.
(電話で) Aさんに～したいのですが I'd like to *speak to* Mr. A. / May I *speak to* Mr. A?
2〚忠告する・相談する〛 ¶ もっと注意するように私から彼に～しておく I think I will *advise* (≒ *tell*) him to be more careful.
彼に～してみたらどうだろう How about consulting him? (consult with ならお互いに話し合うこと).
たばこをやめるように息子に～してください Would you *persuade* my son to stop smoking?
あの人だって～せばわかってくれるだろう I hope he will *understand* me.

はな・す【放す】¶ ～してください *Let* me *go.* そのスイッチから手を～せ *Get* your hands *off* the switch. 子どもは風船を～してしまった The child *let go* the balloon. 公園で犬を～さないでください Don't *let* your dog *loose* in the park. 今ちょっと手が～せません I *am busy* (≒ *am engaged*) just now. 彼はあの本をいつも～さぬ That book is *his constant companion.*

はな・す【離す】¶ 机を窓から～して置いた I *put* my desk *apart from* the window. もっと目を～してその絵を見てごらん Look at the picture *at a distance.* この子は目が～せない I can't *take my eyes off* this child. マラソンで2位を500メートル～して優勝した He won the marathon race running 500 meters *ahead of* the second 〔runner〕. 私はもう眼鏡を～せない I can't *do without* my glasses now.

はなすじ【鼻筋】the ridge of the nose. ¶ ～のとおった顔 a face with *a* high *bridge of the nose.*

はな・せる【話せる】 ¶ あれは～せる男だ He is a *sensible man* (≒ a man *of humor*). ～せないやつだ He *has no sense of humor.* / He is such *a bore.* きみも～せるようになった You *have become sensible.*

はなぞの【花園】a flower garden.

はなたば【花束】a nosegay; a bouquet (とくに手に持って人に捧げるようなものを言う.「花束贈呈」のような場合はこの語がよい); a bunch of flowers.

はなだより【花便り】the flower news.

はなたれこぞう【洟垂れ小僧】a sniveling child; an urchin; a naughty boy; (青二才) a fresh youngster; an upstart. ¶ ～がなにを言うか That's big talk for a young man like you.

はなぢ【鼻血】〔a〕 nosebleed; 〘医学〙 epistaxis. ¶ ～が出た I have *a nosebleed.*

はな・つ【放つ】¶ スパイを～つ *send out* a spy. 悪臭を～つ stink; *smell* bad; *give out* (≒ *give off*) a bad smell. 芳香を～つ *smell* sweet; *emit* (≒ *give out*) a sweet smell. 異彩を～つ cut a brilliant figure. 矢を～つ *shoot* an arrow. デマを～つ *spread* a false rumor.

はなっぱしら【鼻っ柱】¶ ～が強い (我が強い) self-assertive; (自信が強い) overconfident; (高慢な) arrogant; (反抗的) defiant. 彼は～の強い男だ He is a *haughty* (≒ *agressive*;

は

stubborn) man.

はなつまみ【鼻摘まみ】a nuisance; a disgusting fellow. ¶ 彼は学校じゅうの〜だ He is such *a nuisance* at school.

はなつみ【花摘み】flower picking.

はなでんしゃ【花電車】a streetcar decorated with flowers.

はなどき【花時】the flower-blossoming season.

バナナ a banana. ¶ 〜1房 a cluster of *bananas.*

はなはだ【甚だ】¶ 〜遺憾である It's a *great* pity. / (やや口語で) I am *awfully* sorry. (sorry for you は失礼な感じを与えるからさける) この知らせに人々は〜驚いた People were *greatly* (≒ *very much*) surprised at this news. この問題は〜難しい This problem is *extremely* difficult to solve. 彼の説は〜荒唐無稽なものであった His theory proved *highly* improbable. それは〜重要なことだ It is a matter of the *utmost* (≒ *greatest*) importance. こんなことが起こって〜おもしろくない We are *terribly* (≒ *awfully*) annoyed about this. 私は〜空腹であった I was *badly* (≒ *very*) hungry. それは〜迷惑だ It is a *great* nuisance for me.

はなばたけ【花畑】a flower garden (≒ bed).

はなはだし・い【甚だしい】excessive; intense; extreme. ¶ それは〜い誤解だ It is a *serious* misunderstanding. 赤インクで手紙を書くなんて非常識も〜い *How* thoughtless of you to write a letter in red ink! 信号を見ずに道を渡るなんて不注意も〜い It's *too* careless of you to cross the street without looking at the traffic sign.

はなばなし・い【花花しい・華華しい】brilliant; splendid. ¶ 彼は〜い出世をした He won a *brilliant* success in life. その町は〜い復興を遂げた The city made a *splendid* comeback. デパートがまたもや〜く開店した Another department store opened *in splendid style.* 彼は財界では〜い活躍を見せた He displayed *admirable* activities in the business circle. 将軍はその戦闘で〜い最期を遂げた The general died a *glorious* death in the battle. 彼女は〜く映画スターになった She *bloomed into* a movie star. 〜い競技は終わった The *spectacular* sports were concluded. 人々は彼の業績の〜さに驚嘆した People admired the *splendor* of his achievement.

はなび【花火】fireworks. ¶ 〜を上げる let off *fireworks.*

仕掛け— a set piece of fireworks. 線香— toy fireworks. —師 a fireworks manufacturer. —大会 ¶ 今夜〜大会がある There will be a show of *fireworks* tonight.

はなびら【花弁】a petal.

はなふだ【花札】Japanese playing cards (ふつう複数形. 1枚の札のときのみ単数形). ¶ 〜をやる play 'flower cards.'

パナマ Panama.

—運河 the Panama Canal. —帽 a Panama [hat].

はなまつり【花祭り】a floral fête; 〘仏教〙 Buddha's birthday festival.

はなみ【花見】flower-viewing. ¶ 毎年上野公園へお〜に行く We *go flower-viewing at* Ueno Park every year.

はなみず【鼻水】a watery discharge from the nose. ¶ 〜をたらした子どもがぼんやり空を眺めていた A child *with a running nose* (≒ *running at the nose*) was looking at the sky absentmindedly.

はなみずき【花水木】a [flowering] dogwood.

はなみち【花道】(すもうの) a passage leading to the *sumo* ring; (芝居の) a stage-passage. ¶ 役者が〜で見得をきる An actor makes a pose on *the stage-passage* (≒ *the passage leading to the stage*). 平和条約の締結は彼の引退の〜となった The conclusion of the peace treaty *paved the path* of his retreat *with flowers.*

はなむけ【餞】¶ 彼女には私も〜をするつもりです I am also going to *give her a parting present tribute* (≒ *make her a farewell present*).

はなむこ【花婿】a bridegroom.

はなめがね【鼻眼鏡】eyeglasses.

はなもじ【花文字】a capital letter. ¶ 〜で書く capitalize; write in *capital letters.*

はなもち【鼻持ち】¶ 彼は〜ならない He is a *detestable* (≒ *disgusting; stinking*) fellow.

はなや【花屋】(店) a flower shop; a florist's; (人) a florist.

はなやか【花やか・華やか】¶ 〜な衣装 a *gay* costume; a *showy* dress. 〜な色 a *gay* (≒ *gorgeous*) color. 〜な光景 a *spectacular* scene. 〜な文体 a *flowery* (≒ *florid*) style. 〜な政治生活 an *active* life as a statesman. 〜なりしころも一度はあった I have once seen better days.

はなやさい【花椰菜】a cauliflower.

はなよめ【花嫁】a bride.

—衣装 a bridal costume.

はならび【歯並び】a row of teeth. ¶ 彼女は〜がきれいだ She *has a regular row of teeth.*

ばなれ【場慣れ】¶ 〜した人 an *experienced* (≒ a *practiced*) man. 彼はこんなことには〜していて驚かない He doesn't get nervous as he *has got accustomed to* these things. あの俳優はまだ〜していない That actor *hasn't yet got over his stage fright.* あれは〜した女性だ She *has easy manners.*

はなれざしき【離れ座敷】an isolated room.

はなれじま【離れ島】a solitary island.

はなればなれ【離れ離れ】¶ 彼の一家はついに〜になった His family *broke up* at last. 街の雑踏で〜になった We *got separated from each other* in the crowded street. 彼は今妻子と〜に暮らしている Now he *lives apart from* his wife and children.

はなれや【離れ家】(一軒家) a solitary house.

はな・れる【離れる】**1** 〘場所について〙 ¶ 公園はここから遠く〜れている The park *is* a long way

from here. (far from はさける).
その島はかなり～れている The island *is a good way off*.
家を～れてもう10年になる It is ten years since I *left* home.
彼は故郷を～れて下宿している He lives in a lodging *away from* his home town.
突然彼は列を～れた Suddenly he *fell out of line*.
冬はなかなか寝床を～れられない It takes me a long time to *get out of bed* in winter.
彼らは5キロも～れた学校に通っている They attend school as much as five kilometers *away*.
2 〖その他の場合〗 ¶ その事件がかた時も私の心から～れない The incident is always on my mind.
彼は今仕事を～れている He *is* now *out of* work.
政治を～れてこの問題を考えることはできない It is impossible to consider this matter *apart from* politics.

はなれわざ【離れ業】 ¶ ～を演じる do *a stunt* (≒ *a feat*).

はなわ【鼻輪】 a nose ring.

はなわ【花輪】 a wreath. ¶ ～を作る wreathe flowers into *a garland*.

はにかみ【含羞み】 shyness.
—屋 a bashful (≒ shy) person.

はにか·む【含羞む】 ¶ 彼女は～んでひと言も口がきけなかった She *was* so *shy* that she couldn't utter a word. 彼は～んで彼女のそばへも寄れなかった He *was* too *bashful* to come near her.

ばにく【馬肉】 horseflesh.

バニシングクリーム vanishing cream.

パニック a panic. ¶ 1日に四つの銀行が破産したので実業家の間では～が起きた As four banks went bankrupt in a day, there was *a panic* among the businessmen.

バニラ vanilla.

はにわ【埴輪】 a clay figure.

はね【羽】(羽毛) a feather ; (装飾用の) a plume ; (総称) plumage ; (翼) a wing. ¶ ～を広げる(畳む) spread (fold) *the wings*. ～をはばたく flap *the wings*. ～で飛ぶ fly *on wings*. ～のように軽い as light as *a feather*. ～が生えたように売れる sell *like hot cakes*. 私の留守に彼らは～を伸ばしたことだろう Probably they *felt at ease* in my absence. その機会は彼に十分～を伸ばさせた The chance *gave ample scope to his talent*.
—布団 a feather quilt ; a quilt of down. **—**まくら a feather pillow. 赤い**—**募金運動 a 'Red Feather' campaign.

はね【羽根】 a shuttlecock. ¶ ～をつく play battledore and *shuttlecock*.

はね【跳ね】 splashes. ¶ ズボンに～がかかっていますよ You *have* your trousers *spattered with mud*. / Your trousers *are bespattered with mud*.

ばね【発条·撥条】 a spring. ¶ 彼は歩き方に～がある He has 〔*a*〕 *spring* to his step.
—仕掛け ¶ とびらは～仕掛けになっている The door works by *a spring*. 私は～仕掛けのおもちゃで遊んだ I played with a toy *worked by a spring*.

はねあが·る【跳ね上がる】 ¶ 相場はきのう～った The market *made a jump* yesterday. / The market *jumped* yesterday. 水害地の物価は～った The prices *rose suddenly* in the flooded district.

はねお·きる【跳ね起きる】 ¶ 悲鳴を聞いて寝床から～きた I *jumped* out of bed at the scream.

はねかえ·す【跳ね返す】 ¶ 壁が投げたボールを～してくれる The wall *bounces* the ball I throw. 敵の攻撃を～す力はない We haven't enough power to *repel* our enemy attack.

はねかえ·る【跳ね返る】 ¶ ボールは床に当たって～った The ball struck the floor and *rebounded*. 曲げられた枝が急に～った The bent branch *sprang back* suddenly. 賃銀値上げの物価への～り the *rebounding* of higher wages to higher prices.

はねか·ける【跳ね掛ける】 ¶ 通りすがりの車が泥水を私に～けた A car passing by *splashed* me *with* muddy water.

はねつ·ける【撥ねつける】 ¶ 彼の提案を私はきっぱりと～けた I *rejected* his proposal point-blank. / I *turned down* his proposal flatly. 私はけんもほろろに～けられた I *met with a* flat *refusal*. 彼はその申し出を～けた He *refused* the offer. 彼女は彼を～けた She *repulsed* him.

はねとば·す【跳ね飛ばす】 ¶ 彼は爆発で～されて死んだ The explosion *sent him flying* to death. トラックが私の全身に泥水を～した A truck *splashed* my whole body *with* muddy water.

はねの·ける【撥ね除ける】 ¶ 彼は私を～けて走り去った He ran away, *thrusting* me *aside*.

はねばし【跳ね橋】 a drawbridge.

はねまわ·る【跳ね回る】 ¶ 子どもたちは廊下で～っていた The children *were romping about* in the corridor. 庭は狭くて子どもたちが～ることもできない The garden is too narrow for the children *to jump about*. 3匹の子ネコが親ネコの近くで～っていた Three kittens *were frisking* near the mother cat.

ハネムーン a honeymoon. ¶ 彼らは～に出かけた They went for their *honeymoon*.

は·ねる【跳ねる】 (カエルなど) jump ; leap ; (バッタ) hop ; (馬) prance ; (花火) spark. ¶ 車が泥水を私に～ねた The car *splashed* muddy water *on* me. 芝居は午後9時に～ねた The play *was over* at 9 p.m.

は·ねる【撥ねる】 ¶ 身体検査で～ねられた I *was rejected* in the physical examination. 不良品を～ねる *eliminate* inferior goods. 彼は車に～ねられた He *was knocked down* by a car. 他人の賃銀の上前を～ねる *take off* a percentage from the others' wages.

は·ねる【刎ねる】 ¶ 彼らは彼の首を～ねた They *beheaded* him. / They *cut off* his head.

パネル a panel.

は

—ディスカッション a panel discussion.
パノラマ a panorama.
はは【母】a mother. ¶ ～の愛 *maternal* love; *one's mother's* affection. ～の日 *Mother's* Day (5月の第2日曜日). 必要は発明の～ Necessity is *the mother* of invention.
はば【幅】1 〖広さ〗 width; breadth. ¶ ～はどれだけあるか What is the *width* (≒ *breadth*)? 廊下の～を広げたい I want to *have* the corridor *wider*. この川の～は30メートルある This river is thirty meters *wide* (≒ *in width*).
2 〖勢力〗 ¶ 彼はこの市ではなかなか～をきかせている He *is* very *influential* (≒ *is* very *powerful*) in this city. この辺で～をきかせてみても始まらない It is useless to *exercise influence over* the people around here.
ばば【婆】(老婆) an old woman; (祖母) a grandmother; a grandmamma; a grandma; (小児語) a granny; (醜い老婆) a hag.
ばば【馬場】a riding ground; a racecourse; (競馬の) a race track.
パパ papa.
ははあ well; indeed; I see. ¶ ～, そうだったのか Well, I see. / Why, is that right?
パパイヤ a papaya.
ははかた【母方】¶ 彼は～のおじだ He is an uncle *on the mother's side*. / He is my *maternal* uncle.
はばかり【憚り】¶ ～ながら私はそんな男ではない Let me remind you that I am not a man of that sort. ～ながらこれでも画家だ *I flatter myself* that I am a painter. ～ながら私にお任せください Trust it to me, please. / Won't you trust me, if you please? ～ながら,あなたはまちがっておいでですよ *I beg your pardon* (≒ *Excuse me*), but you are mistaken.
はばか・る【憚る】¶ ～るところなくきみの考えを言ってくれたまえ Tell me your idea *without reserve*. / *Speak out* your thought, please. 世間を～って彼は家に閉じこもった He confined himself indoors *in diffidence to* others. 私にはなにも世間を～ることはない I can look the world in the face. これは他聞を～ります This is a *confidential* matter. 彼はいつも外聞を～ってばかりいる He *is* always *afraid of* what others may think. 過ちては改むるに～ることなかれ It is never too late to mend. / Never *hesitate* to correct your errors. 憎まれっ子世に～る(諺) *Ill weeds grow apace*. 彼は先生たちの前をも～らぬ He *is not awed in* the presence of the teachers. 断言して～らぬが日本は将来いろいろの問題があるだろう I *can safely say* that Japan will be confronted with many problems in future.
はばた・く【羽ばたく】¶ ワシが大空に～いて飛んでいる An eagle is flying by *flapping* (≒ *fluttering*) *the wings* in the sky.
はばつ【派閥】a faction. ¶ その政党は二つの～に分裂した The political party has split into two *factions* (≒ *cliques*). ～争いを解消することが先決だ What claims prior attention is the elimination of the *factional strife*.
はばとび【幅跳び】〖競技〗a broad jump.
はば・む【阻む】¶ その事件が彼の出世を～むこととなった The affair came to *prevent* (≒ *keep*; *hinder*) him 〔*from*〕 *rising* in the world. (from を省くのは口語). 山崩れがわれわれの行く手を～んだ A landslide *obstructed* our way.
はびこ・る【蔓延る】¶ 庭に雑草が～っている The garden *is thick* (≒ *is overgrown*) *with* grass. / Weeds *grow rank* (≒ *grow thick*) in the garden. 村には偏見と迷信が～った Prejudices and superstitions *were rampant* in the village. 大都会にはあらゆる悪が～っている All kinds of evils *thrive* in big cities. この地域には山賊が～っていた The bandits *grew in power* in this district.
パピルス papyrus.
バビロニア Babylonia.
—人 a Babylonian. —語 Babylonian.
はふ【破風】a gable. ¶ ～造りの家 a *gabled* house. 七つの～のある家 a house with seven *gables*.
—窓 a gable window.
パフ a 〔powder〕 puff.
はぶ・く【省く】¶ 詳しい説明は～きます Let me *omit* a detailed explanation. それは勘定から～いてくれ *Leave* it *out of* account. 生活のむだを～くべきだ We should *eliminate* the wastefulness of life. これでだいぶ手間が～ける This will *save* me a lot of trouble.
はぶたえ【羽二重】*habutae*; glossy silk.
バプテスト〖キリスト教〗a Baptist.
—教会 the Baptist Church.
バプテスマ〖キリスト教〗〔a〕 baptism.
はブラシ【歯ブラシ】a tooth-brush.
はぶり【羽振り】¶ 彼はなかなか～がいい He *is* very *powerful* (≒ *influential*). / He *is in the ascendant*.
ばふん【馬糞】horse manure (≒ dung); horse droppings.
はべ・る【侍る】¶ 彼女は酒宴に～った She *served at* the feast. / She *waited on* (≒ *at*) table.
バベルのとう【バベルの塔】the Tower of Babel.
はへん【破片】a broken piece; a shard (*of* glass). ¶ ガラスの～が床一面に飛び散った The *fragments* of glass were scattered all over the floor. 彼は手にガラスの～を刺した He got *a splinter* of glass in his hand.
はぼたん【葉牡丹】an ornamental cabbage.
はほん【端本】an odd volume.
はまき【葉巻】a cigar.
はまぐり【蛤】a clam. ¶ ～の殻 a clamshell.
はまだらか【羽斑蚊】an anopheles.
はまべ【浜辺】the beach; the seashore.
はまりやく【嵌まり役】¶ あなたはまさに～だ You *are the very man for the part*. / You *are very much suited for the part*.
はま・る【嵌まる・塡まる】¶ 戸が～らない The door doesn't *fit in*. 計略が思うつぼに～った The stratagem *hit it right*. この地位に～る人は少ない Few *are suited* (≒ *are fit*) *to* the post.

は

彼はわなに～ってしまった He *fell into* a snare. 彼は悪い道に～りこんでしまった He *has been given to evil ways.* 彼はすっかりその女に～りこんでいる He *is dead gone on* (≒ *is infatuated with*) the girl. 型に～った文句 a *stock* (≒ *stereotyped*) phrase. 型に～った結びで彼の演説は終わった His speech ended with a *conventional* conclusion.

はみがき【歯磨き】tooth powder; (練り歯磨き) tooth paste.

はみだ・す【食み出す】¶ ポケットからなにか～している Something *is sticking out of* (≒ *is protruding from*) your pocket. 2階が道路に～している The upper story *projects* over the street.

ハミング humming.

ハム (食料) ham.
—エッグズ ham and eggs. **—**サラダ ham and salad.

ハム (アマチュア無線士) a radio ham; a ham operator.

はむか・う【刃向かう・歯向かう】¶ 彼は命がけでその賊に～った He *struggled with* the robber for his life.

はむし【羽虫】a bird louse.

はめ【羽目】a pass; a fix. ¶ 彼は苦しい～に陥った He got himself in *a mess.* 困った～になった Things have come to *a* pretty *pass.* 彼は借金も返せない～に陥っている He is in *a* sad *plight* of being unable even to return his debt. たまには～をはずして騒ぐのもいいじゃないか Why don't you *go on a spree* (≒ *indulge in merrymaking*) once in a while?

はめこ・む【塡め込む・嵌め込む】¶ 指輪には大きなダイヤを～んであった A large piece of diamond *was inset* in the ring. この指輪には宝石が～んである A jewel *is inset* in this ring.

はめつ【破滅】ruin; [a] fall. ¶ 酒が彼の身の～を招いた Drinking brought about his *ruin.* あの人はみずから～を招いたようなものだ It may be said that he has brought *ruin* upon himself.

は・める【塡める・嵌める】¶ 手袋を～める *draw on one's* gloves. 指輪を～める *put* a ring *on one's* finger. ワイシャツのボタンを～める *button up one's* shirt. ガラスを障子に～める *fit* a pane *in* a sliding door. あの詐欺師にうまく～められた I *have been* cleverly *taken in* by that swindler.

ばめん【場面】¶ この小説の～はシカゴに置かれている The *scene* of this novel is laid in Chicago. (芝居で) ～が変わった The *scene* changed.

はもの【刃物】an edged tool; (総称) cutlery. ¶ 彼は～ざんまいに及んだ He resorted to *an edged tool.*

はもの【端物】an odd set. ¶ ～になる become *odd.* そうすれば～になるだろう That will *break the set.*

はもん【波紋】a ripple. ¶ 大臣の発言は政界に大きな～を投じた The statement of the minister brought about *a* big *sensation* in the political world.

はもん【破門】[an] expulsion; (宗教) [an] excommunication. ¶ 弟子を～する *expel one's* pupil. 背教のかどで彼は教会から～された He *was excommunicated* from the church because of his belief in heresy.

ハモンドオルガン a Hammond organ.

はや【鮠】〖魚類〗a dace (複数も同形).

はやあし【早足・速足】¶ 彼は～で家に帰った He walked home with *quick steps.* 馬が～で歩いている The horse *is trotting.* きみの～にはとてもついていけない I cannot keep pace with you because you *walk too fast.*

はや・い【早い・速い】**1**〖時間〗early. ¶ 彼は起きるのが～い He is an *early* (≒ *easy*) riser. まだ1時間～い It is still an hour too *early.* まだ夕食には～い It is too *early* to have supper.
明朝～い汽車で立つ予定です We are to leave by an *early* train tomorrow morning.
2〖速度〗¶ 自転車よりバスのほうが～い The bus *makes better time than* the bicycle.
月日のたつのはまったく～い Time [really] flies. (この後に like an arrow のごとき語句のある意味だが, ふつうはそれを言わない).
仕事が～いのが彼のとりえだ His forte is the speed with which he works.
彼が計算が～いのは定評がある His *being quick at* figures is proverbial. / He has a reputation for *being quick at* figures.
彼はのみこみが～い He *is quick in* the uptake.
3〖慣用的表現〗¶ ～い話が, 彼の言うことは信用できない *To make a long story short,* you shouldn't believe what he says.

はやおき【早起き】early rising. ¶ ～は健康によい It is good for the health to *get up early.* 彼はたいへん～だ He is *a* very *early riser.* 彼は～の習慣がついてる He *keeps early hours.* ～は三文の徳 (諺) *The early bird* catches the worm.

はやがてん【早合点】¶ ～する jump to a conclusion. きみは～の傾向がある You are apt to *be hasty in forming a conclusion.*

はやがね【早鐘】¶ 村人に危険を知らせるために～をついた I sounded *an alarm bell* to let the villagers know of the danger. 胸は～を打つようだった My heart was beating *like a hammer.*

はやがわり【早変わり】¶ 行商人はあっという間に強盗に～した The peddler *turned* into a robber *in a moment.*

はやく【破約】a breach of promise. ¶ 協定は～になった The agreement *was broken off.*

はやく【端役】a small (≒ minor) part. ¶ 彼はいつも～だ He always plays *a small part.*

はやく【早く】**1**〖時間〗early; soon. ¶ ～出発する start *early.*
出かけてもいいが～帰ってきなさい You may go out, but come back *early.*
一刻も～母に会いたい I want to see my mother *as soon as possible.*
彼は朝～から夜遅くまで働いている He is working from *early in the morning* till late at night.
きのうはいつもより～寝た Yesterday I went to

は

bed *earlier* than usual.
思ったほど～仕事は終えられなかった We were not able to finish the work *so soon as* we had expected.
彼女は～からピアノを習っている She began to play the piano *at an early age*.
2〚速度〛quickly. ¶ ～宿題を済ませたい I want to finish my homework *quickly*.
～行かないとまにあわない Unless you *hurry up*, you won't be in time.
言われたように～やりなさい Do it *immediately* as you are told to.

はやくち【早口】¶ 彼はずいぶん～だ He *talks* very *rapidly*.
―ことば a tongue-twister.

はやさ【速さ】swiftness. ¶ 彼の足の～は驚嘆に値する His *speed* of running is astonishing enough.

はやざき【早咲き】¶ ～のバラ *early* roses.

はやし【林】a forest (woods は町のはずれなどにある小さな林, a forest は森林を言う. 単数形 a wood よりも複数形のほうを多く用いるが, ひとつの森を woods (複数形) とした場合は複数扱いになる).
¶ 松の～ a pine *grove*. ぶなの～ *woods* of beech-trees.

はやじに【早死に】an early death. ¶ ～する die young.

はやじまい【早仕舞い】¶ 店は～にしよう Let's *close up* the store *early*. 仕事を～にする *knock off* work *early*.

はや･す【生やす】¶ 口ひげを～す *grow* a mustache. 彼はあごひげを～している He *wears* a beard.

はや･す【囃す】¶ 踊りに合わせて笛や太鼓で～した We *accompanied* the dances with flutes and drums. その役者が舞台に現われると観客はいっせいに～した When the actor appeared on the stage, the spectators *gave cheers* in a chorus.

はやだち【早立ち】¶ あすの朝は～にしよう Let's *start early* tomorrow morning.

はやて【疾風】a swift wind.

はやで【早出】¶ きょうは～だ Today we must *go to* the office *earlier*.

はやてまわし【早手回し】¶ 1か月前から準備するとはずいぶん～だ Your preparation a month prior to the event seems to *be early enough*.

はやね【早寝】¶ ～する go to bed early. ～早起きする keep early hours.

はやのみこみ【早呑み込み】¶ きみは～をしすぎる You are apt to *form too hasty a conclusion*.

はやばまい【早場米】an early crop of rice.

はやばや【早早】¶ ～お便りありがとう Many thanks for your writing to me *so early*.
～とおいでくださいまして恐縮です Thank you very much for your *immediate* visit to me.

はやびけ【早引け】¶ 学校を2時間～した I left school two hours *earlier than usual*. 仕事を2時間～した He left work two hours *before the closing time*.

はやぶさ【隼】〘鳥類〙a peregrine ; a falcon.

はやまき【早蒔き・早播き】early sowing.
¶ ～の early-sown.

はやま･る【早まる】¶ ～ったことをした I have done a *rash* thing. ～ってはいけない Don't *be too hasty*. ～ったことをしてくれた You should have been more considerate. 期日が1週間～った The date *was advanced* by a week.

はやみち【早道】¶ 雨が降りそうだ. ～をしよう It's going to rain at any moment. Let's *take a shortcut*.

はやみひょう【早見表】a chart.

はやみみ【早耳】¶ 彼は～だ He *is quick-eared*.

はやめ【早め】¶ ～に家を出た I left home *early*.
いつもより～に駅に着いた I arrived at the station *earlier than usual*. ～の昼食を済ませよう Let's have an *early* lunch. (朝飯を兼ねる場合は have brunch と言う).

はや･める【早める・速める】¶ 開会を～めた We *advanced* the opening of the meeting. 日どりを二, 三日～めた I *advanced* the date by a couple of days. それが彼の死期を～めた That *hastened* his end. 彼に追いつこうとして足を～めた I *quickened* my steps to catch up with him. バスはスピードを～めてやってきた The bus came, *gathering* speed.

はやり【流行】¶ ことしはこういう帽子が大～だ These hats *are all the go* this year. これは～すたりがない It is above changes *in the fashion*. ちょうネクタイが大～だった Bow ties *were* very much *in fashion*. このヘアスタイルが大～だ This hairstyle *is* now *the vogue*.
―ことば a word in vogue.

はや･る【逸る】¶ ～る心を抑えようと努力したがだめだった I tried to *restrain myself*, but I couldn't. 彼は～る心を静めて語りだした He began to speak, *controlling himself*.

はや･る【流行る】¶ 短いスカートが～っている Short skirts *are in fashion*. あの病院はよく～る The hospital *has a large practice*. コレラが～っている Cholera *is prevalent*. テレビはまたたく間に新しい歌を～らせる Television *makes* new songs *popular* in no time. そういう道具はもう～らない Such tools *have gone out of fashion*. あの店はかつては～ったものだ The store once *attracted a lot of customers*.

はやわざ【早業】¶ 彼は目にもとまらぬ～で相手を片づけた He dispatched (≒ killed) the opponent *like lightning*.

はら【原】a plain ; (大草原) a prairie.

はら【腹】**1**〚腹部〛the abdomen ; the belly (口語) ; the stomach.
¶ ～が痛い I have *a stomachache*.
～がくだっている I have *diarrhea*.
急に～がへった I *have* suddenly *become hungry*.
～が張ってしかたがない My *stomach* feels very heavy.
お菓子を～いっぱい食べてはいけない You mustn't *fill yourself with* sweets.
～がいっぱいで動けない I *am so full* 〔that〕 I cannot even move.
彼は～をかかえて笑った He roared with laughter.

～がへっては戦はできぬ You can't do anything *on an empty stomach.*
彼は私が～を痛めた子だ He is *my own child.*
彼女は大きな～(妊娠)をしている She *is in the family way.*
2 〖心〗 the heart. ¶ どうも彼の～の中はわからない I just cannot understand him.
～の中は煮えくり返っている I am boiling mad.
彼は泣いているが，～の中では笑っているのだ He is crying on the outside, but *inside* he is laughing.
彼の言は～にすえかねる What he said makes me boil.
彼は～に一物ある He *has an ax to grind.*
なんと～のすわった男だろう What a *resolute* man he is!
彼は息子に家業を継がせたい～だ He intends to let his son succeed him in his business.
今更～の探り合いをしても始まらない It is no use now trying to read each other's *thought.*
～を割って話したい I would like to have a *heart-to-heart* talk with you.
彼はそれで～を立てているのだ It has *made* him so *angry.*
3 〖食事〗 ¶ このへんで～をこしらえよう Let's *satisfy our appetite* now.

ばら 【散】 ¶ ～で売る sell (things) *loose.*

ばら 【薔薇】 a rose. ¶ ～の木 a *rose* tree. ～色の rosy.

バラード 〔詩学〕〔音楽〕 a ballade.

はらい 【払い】 ¶ ～が多い I have many bills to *pay.* ～は月末でけっこうです You may *pay* at the end of this month. 医者の～はまだ済んでいない I *have* not *paid* the doctor's bills.

はらいこみ 【払い込み】 〔a〕 payment. **―**金 subscription. **―**額 the amount paid-up. **―**資本 paid-up capital.

はらいこ·む 【払い込む】 ¶ 月に2,000円ずつ銀行に～んだ I *paid* two thousand yen *into* the bank every month. 毎月会費を～めば会員になれる Anyone can be a member if only he *pays* his due every month.

はらいさ·げる 【払い下げる】 ¶ この国有林はやがて～げられる The state forest is to *be disposed of* before long.

はらいすぎ 【払い過ぎ】 ¶ それは～だ You *have paid too much.* それでは100円の～だ You *have paid* 100 yen *in excess.*

はらいせ 【腹癒】 ¶ ～にやり返してやった I revenged myself upon him *out of spite.* それでいくらか～ができた That is some *consolation* to me.

はらいの·ける 【払いのける】 ¶ 彼はその手を～けた He *brushed* the hand *aside.* どうにか災難を～けた He managed to *drive* his misfortune *away.*

はらいもどし 【払い戻し】 〔a〕 refund. ¶ 支払った金額の～を要求した He requested *a* full *refund* of the amount paid. 切符の～をしてくれますか Could I get *a refund* on this ticket?

はらいもど·す 【払い戻す】 pay back; refund. ¶ 代金を～すことはできない We can't *refund* the price paid.

はら·う 【払う】 **1** 〖金を〗 pay. ¶ その金はあすまでに～ってください Please *pay* the money by tomorrow.
まだ本の代金を～ってない I *have* not *paid* for the book.
すぐ借金を～ってほしい I want you to *pay off* your debt immediately.
2 〖除く〗 ¶ 机のほこりを～う *dust* a desk.
ズボンのほこりを～う *brush one's* trousers.
この木の枝を五，六本～ってほしい I would like you to *cut* five or six branches *off* this tree.
3 〖注意・敬意を〗 ¶ みなこれから私の言うことに注意を～ってほしい All of you must *pay* attention to what I am going to say.
彼には大いに敬意を～ってしかるべきだ You should *pay* your respect for him.

はら·う 【祓う】 ¶ 神官に身の汚れを～ってもらった I got the *shinto* priest to *purify* myself.

バラエティー variety. ¶ この雑誌は～に富んでいる This magazine is rich in *variety.* **―**ショー a variety show.

はらおび 【腹帯】 (妊婦の) a maternity belt; (馬の) a saddle girth.

はらぐあい 【腹具合】 ¶ ～が悪い I have a *stomach* trouble. ～がおかしい My *bowels* are out of order.

はらくだし 【腹下し】 loose bowels; (下剤) laxative.

パラグラフ a paragraph. ¶ この～は大きく分けると二つに分けられる This *paragraph* is roughly divided into two parts.

はらぐろ·い 【腹黒い】 ¶ 彼は案外～い I am surprised that he is a *wicked* (≒ *crafty*) fellow.

はらげい 【腹芸】 ¶ 彼には～ができない He is a man of poor personality. ～でいってはどうか How about *taking a chance*?

はらごしらえ 【腹拵え】 ¶ 出発する前に～をしておきなさい *Eat amply* before you leave here. 今のうちに～しておこう I will *eat something* now.

はらごなし 【腹ごなし】 ¶ ～に運動しよう I will have exercise to *help digestion.*

パラシュート a parachute. ¶ ～で飛行機から降りる *parachute* 〔from an airplane〕. ～で食糧が投下された Food supplies were dropped by *parachute.*

はら·す 【晴らす】 ¶ 彼の無実の罪を～したい I want to *clear* him *of* the false charge. この恨みは必ず～してやる I shall never fail to *revenge myself on* him. / I will *be revenged* for this by all means.

はら·す 【腫らす】 ¶ 彼は泣いて目を赤く～していた He *had* his eyes *swollen* red with crying. くるぶしを～した I *have had* an ankle *swollen.*

ばら·す ¶ 子どもたちはおもちゃをみんな～してしまった The children *have taken* all the toys *to* *pieces.* 秘密をみんなに～してしまってもいいか May I *expose* the secret to all? 計画を～された I *had* my plan *laid bare.*

ばらせん【散銭】loose coins. ¶ ～の持ち合わせがない I have no *loose coins* with me./I don't have any 〔*small*〕 *change* about me.

パラソル a parasol.
ビーチ— a beach umbrella.

パラダイス paradise.

はらだたし·い【腹立たしい】¶ あのときの彼の言動はまったく～かった His behavior on that occasion *was* very *annoying.* きょうは～いことばかり起こる All sorts of *exasperating* things have been happening today. このごろの世の中は～いことばかりだ The world today is full of *provoking* events. 私がそう言うと彼は～そうな顔をした When I said so, he looked *irritated.*

はらだち【腹立ち】¶ お～もごもっともです No wonder you *get angry.* / It is natural that you 〔should〕 *get angry with* me. ～まぎれにネコをけとばした I kicked the cat in its side *in a fit of ill temper.*

はらちがい【腹違い】¶ ～の兄弟（姉妹）a half brother (half sister).

パラチフス〘医学〙paratyphoid fever.

バラック a barrack ; a temporary shelter.

はらのむし【腹の虫】¶ 彼は～をおさえた He *repressed his anger* (≒ *indignation*).

はらばい【腹這い】¶ ～になる lie on *one's* stomach.

はらば·う【腹這う】¶ ～ってかきねをくぐった I crept through the hedge *on my stomach.*
彼は～った He *lay on his stomach.*

はらはちぶ【腹八分】¶ ～に病なし *Temperance* is the best physic (≒ medicine).
～にしておきなさい Be temperate (≒ Be moderate) in eating.

はらはら 1〘涙など〙¶ 花びらが～と地面に散った The petals *fluttered down* to the ground.
涙が～と彼女のほおを伝わった Tears *streamed* (≒ *fell*) *down* her cheeks.
2〘不安に感ずる〙¶ きみたちにはまったく～したよ All of you *made* me *nervous* (≒ *uneasy*).
試合は～させるような場面の連続だった There were a series of *exciting* (≒ *thrilling*) scenes in the game.
その事件で私は～した The affair *made* me *tremble.*
まちがいはしないかと～した I *was very* 〔*much*〕 *afraid of* making mistakes.

ばらばら 1〘雨など〙¶ あられが～降ってきた It began to hail *noisily.*
節分には豆を～まく *scatter a shower of* beans on the day before the beginning of spring.
2〘別々に〙¶ 機械を～に分解した I *took* the machine *apart* (≒ *to pieces*).
戦争で私の一家は～になった The war caused my family to *be scattered* (≒ *be broken up*).
子どもたちが～と街角から飛び出してきた Children *suddenly* rushed out from the corner of the street.
群衆はちりぢり～に逃げた The crowd dispersed *in all directions.*
製本が悪いと本は～になる If the binding is defective, the sheets *fall apart.*
ヨーロッパへいっしょに行ったが，帰りは～だった We went to Europe together, but came home *separately.*
—事件 a mutilation murder case. —死体 a dismembered body.

ぱらぱら ¶ 雨が～降っている The rain *is pattering.* 本を～めくっていたらおもしろい文章にぶつかった *Riffling through* the leaves of the book, I found a very interesting passage. 会場には観客が～としかいない There is a small audience *scattering* here and there in the hall.

パラフィンし【パラフィン紙】paraffin paper.

パラボラアンテナ a parabola antenna.

はらまき【腹巻き】a stomach band.

ばらま·く【散蒔く】¶ 凍った歩道に灰を～く *scatter* ashes on an icy sidewalk. あの候補者は選挙で金を～いた That candidate *spent money recklessly* in the election.

はら·む【孕む】¶ 彼女は～んでいる She *is pregnant.* / She *is* 〔*big*〕 *with child.* 風が帆を～ませた The wind *filled* (≒ *swelled*) the sails.

バラライカ〘音楽〙a balalaika.

パラリンピック the Paralympics.

はらわた【腸】the intestines ; (内臓) the entrails. ¶ 彼は～の腐った人間だ He *is rotten* (≒ *is corrupt; is depraved*) utterly. それを聞いて～が煮えくり返った I *felt outraged at* the news.

はらん【波乱】¶ あの家庭には～が絶えぬ There are constant *troubles* in that family. ～が起きる *Troubles* arise. 彼は～に富んだ一生を送った He led an *eventful* life. 平地に～を巻き起こすようなことはするな Never raise *troubles.*

バランス balance. ¶ 体の～を失った I lost my *balance.* 体の～がよくとれている He is physically *well balanced.*
—シート a balance sheet.

はり【針】1 (縫い針) a needle ; (かぎ針) a hook ; (時計の) a hand ; (バラの) a thorn ; (ハチの) a sting ; (アザミの) a prickle ; (サボテンの) a spine.
¶ ～の目 the eye of *a needle.*
～に糸を通す thread *a needle.*
けが人は傷口を10～縫った The injured person had ten *stitches* in the wound.
2〘慣用的表現〙¶ 彼の～を含んだことばが私の胸に刺さった His *sharp* (≒ *biting*) words stung me to the quick.
～の落ちる音が聞こえるほどに静かだった A *pin* might have been heard to drop. (この英語の表現は後になにかが起こる緊迫感を表わすとき用いることが多い).
私は～のむしろに座る心地がした I felt as if *sitting on thorns.*

はり【張り】¶ ～のある声 a *steady* voice. これは～のある仕事だ This is *encouraging* work. 最近彼は勉強に～が出た He *has* recently *felt a strong inducement to* his studies.

はり【梁】a beam.

はり【鍼】¶～をする apply *acupuncture*.
—医 an acupuncturist.

ばり【罵詈】—雑言 ¶皆が彼に～雑言を浴びせた All the people *gave* him *much abuse.* / All the people *heaped abuse upon* him.

-ばり【-張り】¶左団次～の芸を見せた He acted *after the fashion of* Sadanji.

はりあい【張り合い】¶仕事に～がなくなった I have lost *interest* (≒ *enthusiasm*) *in* my work. これは～のある仕事だ This job *is worth the trouble.* 彼が帰ったので～が抜けた I *am discouraged* (≒ *am disappointed*), because he went back.

はりあ・う【張り合う】¶彼らは～っている They *are rivals.* その地位を得ようと～った We *contended* (≒ *vied*) with each other *for* the post.

はりあ・げる【張り上げる】¶彼女は声を～げて歌った She *raised* (≒ *lifted*) her voice and sang. 大声を～げて呼んだ I called out *at the top of my voice.*

バリウム〘化学〙barium.

バリエーション a variation.

はりかえ【張り替え】¶自分でふすまの～をした I *repapered* sliding doors myself.

はりか・える【張り替える】renew. ¶障子を～える時期だ It's time to *repair* paper screens.

はりがね【針金】wire. ¶～を張る stretch *a wire.* 彼は二つの板を～でしばった He *wired* the two boards together.
—細工 wirework.

はりがみ【貼り紙】a label; a tag. ¶びんには毒薬という～がついていた The bottle *was labeled* "Poison."

バリカン a barber's clippers.

ばりき【馬力】horsepower (h. p., hp., H. P., HP). ¶彼はなかなか～がある He is full of *energy.* さあ～をかけて仕事をしよう Let's work *hard* (≒ *with might and main*). 私の車は58～だ My car has a 58 *h. p.* engine. 100～のモーター a motor of 100 *h. p.*

はりき・る【張り切る】¶彼はすごく～っている He *is in high spirits.* みんな～って働いてください I hope you will work *with zeal* (≒ *at full strain*).

バリケード ¶～を築く set up *a barricade.*

ハリケーン a hurricane.

はりこ【張り子】¶～のトラ a *paper* tiger; a *papier-mâché* tiger.

はりこ・む【張り込む】¶上等の万年筆を～んだ I *treated myself to* a first-class pen. ふたりの警官が犯人を～んでいた Two policemen *were watching* (≒ *were on the lookout*) *for* the criminal.

はりさ・ける【張り裂ける】¶あの事件では胸も～けんばかりの思いをした My heart *was rent* (≒ *was near to breaking*) by that incident.

はりさし【針刺し】a pin-cushion; a needle-pad.

はりしごと【針仕事】¶彼女は～をして暮らしを立てた She made her living by *her needle* (≒ *needlework*).

はりたお・す【張り倒す】¶相手を～してやった I *knocked* (≒ *struck*) *down* my opponent.

はりだし【張り出し】〘建築〙(二階窓の) a balcony; (船尾の) the overhang.
—舞台 an apron stage. —窓 a bay window. —横綱 an extra grand champion *sumo* wrestler.

はりだ・す【張り出す・貼り出す】¶あすは授業がないという掲示が～されている A notice *is put up* saying that there is no school tomorrow.

はりつけ【磔】crucifixion. ¶～にする crucify *a person.*

はりつ・める【張り詰める】¶湖には氷が一面に～めていた The lake *was frozen all over.* 私は気を～めていた I *strained* my nerves (≒ mind). その知らせを聞いて私は～めた心が一時に緩んでしまった When I heard the news, my *strained* mind relaxed at once. われわれは全神経を～めて次の瞬間を待った We waited for the next moment *with all our nerves strung.*

パリティーけいさん【パリティー計算】a parity account (≒ computation).

バリトン〘音楽〙baritone; (歌手) a baritone.

はりねずみ【針鼠】〘動物〙a hedgehog.

はりばこ【針箱】a workbox; a needle case.

ばりばり ¶ポスターは～と引きはがされた The poster *was torn off.* 子どもがせんべいを～かじっていた The child *was crunching* a rice cracker. 彼はいつも仕事を～と片づけてしまう He always works *with might and main.*

ぱりぱり ¶彼は～の江戸っ子だ He's a *genuine Edokko.* / He's an *Edokko to the backbone.* 彼は音楽界では若手の～だ He is one of the *leading* young musicians.

はりばん【張り番】¶その犬は主人の家の～をする The dog *watches* the master's house. 彼が～に立っている He *is on the watch.* / He *is on the lookout.*

はりふだ【貼り札・張り札】a bill; a notice.

はる【春】spring. ¶もう～だ It is already *spring.* ～が来た *Spring* has come. 彼はことしの～大阪から東京に出て来た He came from Osaka to Tokyo *this spring.* 12月だというのに～のような陽気だ Although we are in December, the weather *is spring-like.* 彼女は17歳の～を迎えた She has just reached sweet seventeen. (sweet はふつう seventeen または sixteen に用いる).
—風 the spring breeze. —着 spring wear. —景色 spring landscape. —先 early spring. —作 a spring crop. —雨 a spring rain. —物 spring goods.

は・る【張る】**1**〚引っ張る・広がりのびる・広げのばす・いっぱいにする〛¶木と木の間にロープを～る *stretch* a rope between the trees.
警官たちは事故現場の周囲になわを～った The policemen *placed* a rope around the scene of the accident.
テントを～る *pitch* a tent.
皮を～った長いす a sofa *covered* with leather.
もっと胸を～って歩け Walk with your chest *puffed up.*

は

この木はよく枝が～っている The branches of this tree *spread* very far and wide.
バラが根を～って元気になった The rose *has spread* its roots and become healthy.
湖は一面に氷が～っている The lake *is frozen* over.
暴力団がこの町に勢力を～っている A tough gang *has influence over* this town.
2〖体·筋肉が〗¶ ビールを飲んだら腹が～った I had some beer, so my stomach *is full.*
一日じゅう書きものをしたら肩が～った I wrote all day long and my shoulders *are stiff.*
3〖引き締まる〗¶ 気が～っているから眠くない I'm so *worried* (≒ I'm so *concerned*) [that] I don't feel sleepy.
彼のお供は気が～る I'm *nervous* when I go with him.
4〖押し通す〗¶ そう強情を～るものではない Don't *be* so *obstinate* (≒ *be* so *positive*).
そう意地を～らずに人の意見も聞くものだ Listen to the opinions of others without *being* so *obstinate.*
5〖値段がかさむ〗 ¶ こちらの品はすこし値が～ります The price of this article *is* a little *high.*
欲しい本はみな値が～るので手が出せない The books I want *are* all *too expensive* for me.
6〖催す·構える〗 ¶ 銀座にりっぱに店を～っているのだからたいしたものだ He is very successful. He *has a* thriving *shop* on the Ginza.
新聞は政府批判の論陣を～った The newspapers criticized the Government.
7〖平手で打つ〗¶ 私は突然彼に横面を～られた He suddenly *boxed* my ears.
8〖番をする〗 ¶ 刑事があの家を～っていた A detective *staked out* the house.
きみはこの入り口を～ってくれ Please *keep an eye on* (≒ *watch over*) this entrance.
9〖対抗する〗 ¶ 彼の向こうを～ってスポーツカーを買った *Competing with* him, I bought a sports car. (文語体). / I bought a sports car *to keep up with* him. (口語体).

は·る【貼る】¶ 紙を～る *stick* (≒ *paste*) paper. 障子を～る *paper* a *shoji.* こうやくを～る *apply* a plaster. 広告を～る *post* a bill. この手紙にいくら[切手を]～ればいいですか What is the postage for this letter? 20円～りなさい *Put* a twenty-yen stamp *on* it.

はるか【遥か】 ¶ 海上～に白帆が見える We can see a white sail *far out* on the sea. ～かなたに富士山頂が見える The top of Mt. Fuji is seen *a long way off* (≒ *far away*). (この意味の far は疑問文,否定文に用いることが多い). 彼女らの中で彼女は～に美人だった She was *by far* the prettiest girl among them. このほうがあれより～にいい This is *far* (≒ *much*) better than that.

はるがすみ【春霞】 ¶ ～が山にかかっている The *spring haze* is hanging over the mountain.

はるばる【遥遥】 ¶ 彼は北海道から～上京した He came to Tokyo *all the way* from Hokkaido. 遠路～お越しくださいましてありがとうございました Thank you for coming *a great distance.*

バルブ a bulb; 〖機械〗 a valve.

パルプ pulp.
—材 pulpwood.

はるめ·く【春めく】 ¶ 日一日と～いてきた It *is getting springlike* day by day. / *Spring* seems to *be on its way* day by day.

はれ【晴れ】 fine (≒ nice; fair) weather (アメリカ口語では fine より nice を用いるほうがふつう). ¶ ～のち曇り *Fine,* later cloudy. 西の風～ West wind; *fair.* こんな～の場所で受賞できるなんて夢にも思わなかった Little did I dream that I could be awarded a prize in such a *public* place. (文語体). ～の舞台での彼の行動はりっぱなものであった His behavior was splendid *on the grand occasion.*

はれ【腫れ】 a swelling. ¶ 脚の～がひいた The *swelling* in the leg has gone away.

はれあが·る【晴れ上がる】 ¶ まもなく～った It *cleared up* soon. ～った秋空 a *cloudless* autumnal sky.

ばれいしょ【馬鈴薯】 a potato (複 potatoes).

バレエ a ballet.
—ダンサー a ballet dancer.

ハレーション〖写真〗 halation.

パレード a parade. ¶ 優勝～ *a* victory *parade.*

バレーボール volleyball. ¶ ～をする play *volleyball.*

はれがまし·い【晴れがましい】¶ そんな～い場所には出られません I am not suited for such a *formal* occassion.

はれぎ【晴れ着】¶ 娘たちは～を着飾っていた The girls wore *their best clothes.*

パレスチナ Palestine.

はれつ【破裂】explosion. ¶ 水道管が～した The water pipe *burst.* 爆弾が～した A bomb *exploded.*

パレット a palette.
—ナイフ a palette knife.

はれて【晴れて】¶ 彼らは～夫婦になった They were married *openly* (≒ *publicly*).

はればれ【晴れ晴れ】¶ 雨上がりは～とする It *is bright and clear* after a rain. 彼は～とした顔をしている He has a *bright* face. 気も～と in the best of spirits. どうも気分が～しない I *feel* somehow *depressed.* 海にでも行ったら気も～するだろうに If I were at the seaside, I would *feel cheerful* (≒ *feel refreshed*).

はればれし·い【晴れ晴れしい】¶ 彼女は～い微笑を浮かべた She had a *sunny* (≒ an *illuminating*) smile on her face. 彼らはみな～い顔つきをして現われた All of them appeared with *brightened* (≒ *cheerful*) looks.

はれぼった·い【腫れぼったい】¶ ～い目 *swollen* eyes. 彼女は～い顔をしている She has a *swollen* face.

はれま【晴れ間】a lull in the rain. ¶ ～を見て帰ろう I will return home *while it stops raining.*

は

はれもの【腫れ物】a swelling. ¶ 若い両親は～にさわるように赤ちゃんを扱った The young parents treated their baby *most tenderly* (≒ *with utmost care*).

はれやか【晴れやか】¶ 彼女はわれわれを見て～に微笑した She *beamed at* us. 心も～に cheerfully. 娘たちは～に装っていた Girls *were dressed up* (≒ *were gaily dressed*).

バレリーナ a ballerina (複 -s, ballerine).

は・れる【晴れる】**1**〘天気が〙 ¶ あすは～れるだろう It will *be fine* (≒ *be nice*) tomorrow. (fine より nice のほうがアメリカ口語的). / It will *clear up* tomorrow.
雨が～れて太陽が顔をのぞかせた The rain *has passed over* and the sun appeared from behind the clouds.
きょうは天気が～れそうだった The weather today showed signs of *clearing*.
2〘気分・疑いが〙 ¶ これで気が～れた This *made* me *refreshed*.
散歩でもすれば気が～れるよ Taking a walk will *cheer* you *up*.
嫌疑(けんぎ)が～れてよかったね I am glad to hear that you *are clear of suspicion* (≒ *are cleared of the charge*).

は・れる【腫れる】¶ 傷ついた足が～れた The injured leg *swelled* [*up*]. 歯痛で彼の顔は～れた Toothache *swelled up* his face. 足が～れている My foot *is swollen*.

バレル a barrel.

ば・れる ¶ 秘密が～れた The secret *has leaked* (≒ *has come*) *out*.

ハレルヤ hallelujah.

はれんち【破廉恥】¶ きみはそんな～なことをしてはまったく弁解の余地があるまい You have no excuse for having done such a *shameless* thing.
―罪 an infamous offense (≒ crime).

バロック baroque. ¶ ～風の邸宅 a baroque mansion (豪壮な感じを与える語句).

パロディー a parody.

バロメーター a barometer. ¶ 新聞は世論の～になることがしばしばある Newspapers are often *barometers* of public opinion.

ハワイ Hawaii. ¶ ～諸島 the *Hawaiian* Islands.

はわたり【刃渡り】blade length. ¶ ～3寸の短刀 a knife with a blade 3 inches long.

はん【煩】trouble. ¶ 資料を～をいとわず収集してくださいましてありがとうございます I very much appreciate your *trouble* of collecting the data. / Thank you very much for the *trouble* you have taken in collecting the data.

はん【判】a seal (西欧では封ろう・鉛・紙片に印で押してそれを文書に添え真正の証明とする. ふつうの場合には判を用いず署名だけ).
¶ 彼は契約書にサインして～を押した He signed and *sealed* the contract. 彼は～で押したように毎朝7時に仕事に出かける He goes to work at seven every morning *with clockwork regularity*. 彼は私の質問に～で押したような返事をした He made a *stereotyped* answer to my question.

はん【版】an edition. ¶ この本は～を重ねて10～になった This book has *gone through* ten *editions*.
改訂増補― ¶ この本の改訂増補～が近々出る A revised and enlarged *edition* of this book is soon coming out. 初(再)― the first (second) edition. 地方(市内)― the provincial (city) edition.

はん【班】(軍の) a squad ; (組) a group.

はん【範】a model ; an example. ¶ わが国の教育制度はアメリカの制度に～を採った The educational system of this country *is modeled upon* (≒ *after*) that of America.

はん【藩】a [feudal] clan.

-はん【-半】half. ¶ 5時～に集合のこと Gather at 5 : 30 (≒ *half* past five). 彼は2年～ぶりに故郷の町に戻った He came back to his home town after two and *a half* years' absence. ; 時間～ほど歩くと湖に出た An hour and *a half's* walk took us to a lake.

はん-【汎-】pan-.
―アメリカ主義 *Pan*-Americanism.

はん-【反-】anti-.
―軍国主義 anti-militarism. ―道徳行為 anti-moral conduct. ―日感情 anti-Japanese feeling.

ばん【万】¶ ～やむを得ず遅刻したのです I *was obliged to* be late. / I was late, but *this was unavoidable*. ～遺漏なきようにしなさい See that *everything will be all right*.

ばん【判】size. ¶ 大(小)～の紙 large-(small-)*sized* paper.
B 6― B 6 size. ¶ B 6～の本 a B 6-*sized* volume. 四つ折り― [a] quarto. 二つ折り― [a] folio.

ばん【番】**1**〘順番〙 turn. ¶ 今度はぼくの～だ Next, it's my *turn*.
次はだれが歌う～ですか Whose *turn* is it to sing?
ぼくの～がきたら教えてくれ When my *turn* comes, please let me know.
自分の～がくるまで待ちなさい Wait for your *turn*.
左から2～めが私の妹だ The second from the left is my [younger] sister.
それはここから何～めの停留所ですか How many stops is it from here?
きみは兄弟の何～めですか Where do you stand among your brothers and sisters? (「～番め」に当たる英語はないから, このように言いかえる).
ぼくが先に行って～をとっておこう I will go ahead and reserve *a place* for you.
ちょっとトイレへ行ってきますから, 私の～をとっておいてください Please keep my *place* for me, I'm just going out to wash my hands.
彼はいつも成績がクラスで1～だ He is always at the head of his class.
2〘番号〙 ¶ 受験番号は12～だ My examination seat number is *No.* 12.
もしもし, そちら123局の4567～ですか Hello, is this one two three—four five six seven? (電話ではこういうとき I am, you are はさける).

は

お宅の電話は何～ですか What is your telephone (≒ dial) *number*?
まもなく6～ホームに下り列車が到着します In a short time the down train will arrive at Platform *No.* 6.
3 〖見張り〗 ¶ ちょっとこの荷物の～をしていてください Please *keep watch over* the baggage just for a moment.
店の～は私がしますからゆっくり行ってらっしゃい Please take your time. I will *tend* the store for you.
弟はまだ小さいが電話の～ぐらいはできる My brother is still young, but he can answer the phone at least.
犯人のひとりは入り口で～をしていた One of the criminals *kept watch* at the entrance.
この犬はよく家の～をしてくれる This dog *watches* the house faithfully.
4 〖勝負の回数〗 ¶ きのう彼と碁を打って2～勝って1～負けた Yesterday I played *go* with him. I won twice; he beat me once.
将棋を1～差そうか Let me challenge you to *a game* of Japanese chess.
これより3～勝負を行ないます We are going to have a game *of three rounds.*
きょうの横綱どうしの一～は見ものだろう The wrestling *bout* which the fellow *sumo* champions are to have today will be quite a sight to see.

ばん 【晩】 an evening (evening はふつう夕方から夜半まで, 夜会うときのあいさつは good evening, 別れるときは good night).
¶ その～はテレビを見て過ごした We spent the *evening* watching television. (in watching と言う必要はない). 彼は～遅く帰ってきた He came back late *in the evening.* あすの～会いましょう See you tomorrow *evening.* 日曜日の～に遊びにきなさい Come and see me on 〔next〕 Sunday *evening.* (特定の日の～には前置詞は on を使う). 一～じゅう北風が吹き荒れていた The north wind roared *all through the night* (≒ *all night through*).

ばん 【盤】 (将棋などの) a board; (レコード) a record.

パン (食物) bread; 〖ギリシア神話〗 Pan. ¶ 1片 (1個; ひと巻き)の～ a slice (a piece; a roll) of *bread.* ～を焼く(つくる) bake *bread*; (食べるのに) toast *bread.* 人は～のみにて生くるものにあらず Man shall not live by *bread* alone. (キリストの「山上の垂訓」の中の名句).
―粉 flour. **―屋** (店) a bakery; (人) a baker.

バンアレンたい 【バンアレン帯】 〖天文学〗 Van Allen belt.

はんい 【範囲】 a scope; (制限) limits. ¶ 活動(勢力)～を広げる enlarge the *scope* (≒ *sphere*) of activity (influence). これは私の知る～ではもっともすばらしい発明だ This is the most wonderful invention *as far as* I know. 試験の～が広い The examination covers *a* wide *range.* / The examination is wide-*ranged.* この現象は人間の経験の～外のものだ This phenomenon is outside the *range* (≒ *scope*; *sphere*; *limits*) of human experience. 費用を10ドルの～内に抑えてほしい We want you to *limit* the expense *to* ten dollars.

はんいご 【反意語】 an antonym.

はんえい 【反映】 reflection. ¶ 時代精神を～した小説 a novel *reflecting* the spirit of the age.

はんえい 【繁栄】 prosperity. ¶ ～する prosper.

はんえいきゅうてき 【半永久的】 ¶ ～な建物 a *semi-permanent* building.

はんえん 【半円】 a semi-circle.

はんおん 【半音】 〖音楽〗 a chromatic semitone.
―階 a chromatic scale. **―符** a minim.

はんが 【版画】 a print. ¶ 木～ a woodcut.

ばんか 【晩夏】 late summer. ¶ ～に咲く花 flowers which come out *late in summer* (≒ *in late summer*).

ばんか 【挽歌】 an elegy.

ハンガー a hanger.

ハンガーストライキ a hunger strike.
¶ ～をやる go on 〔*a*〕 *hunger strike.*

はんかい 【半壊】 ¶ 台風によって～した家屋 houses 〔which *were*〕 *partially destroyed* by the typhoon.

ばんかい 【挽回】 retrieval; 〔a〕 recovery. ¶ 彼は勢力を～した He *regained* (≒ *retrieved*) his power. すぐ失った時間を～した We soon *recovered* lost time. 名誉を～する *retrieve* (≒ *redeem*) *one's* honor. この損害はとうてい～できるものではない This loss *is* quite *beyond* (≒ *past*) *retrieval.*

ばんがい 【番外】 ¶ ～の余興をする give an *extra* entertainment.

はんかがい 【繁華街】 busy quarters.

はんがく 【半額】 half the sum. ¶ 彼は～にしてくれた He reduced *the price by half* for us. あの店で～で買える You can get it *at half the price* at that store. 子どもの入場料は～だ Children are allowed *half rates.*

ばんがく 【晩学】 ¶ 彼は～だ He *began to study in* his *later years* (≒ *late in life*).

ハンカチ a handkerchief (複 -s).

はんかつう 【半可通】 superficial knowledge.
¶ 彼はなんでも～だ He *has only a smattering* (≒ *superficial knowledge*) *of* everything. / He *is half-learned* in everything. 彼は知ったかぶりの～だ He pretends to know everything, but he is nothing but *a smatterer.*

バンガロー a bungalow.

はんかん 【反感】 ill feeling. ¶ 彼女は彼に対して強い～を持っている She has a strong *antipathy* (≒ *ill feeling*) *against* (≒ *to*) him. この政策は国民の～を買った This policy roused the people's *antipathy.* 誇大広告は人々の～を買う The overdone advertisement arouses *resistance*〔*s*〕 in the public.

はんがん 【判官】 ¶ 日本人はだいたい～びいきだ The Japanese usually *take part with the weaker party.*

ばんかん【万感】¶ ～胸に迫った *A thousand emotions* crowded in on me. / I was overwhelmed with *a flood of emotions*.

はんかんはんみん【半官半民】¶ ～の鉄道会社 a *semi-governmental* railroad company.

はんき【半旗】¶ ～が家ごとに掲げられていた Flags were hung out *at half-mast* (≒ *half-mast high*) at every door.

はんき【反旗・叛旗】¶ 彼らは国王に～を翻した They *revolted* (≒ *rose in revolt*) *against* the king.

はんき【半期】¶ 決算は～ごとに行なう Accounts are to be settled *half-yearly*.
上(下)— the first (latter) half of the year. ¶ 本年の上～の営業成績は良好だ Our company has done a very good business during the first *half of the year*. 四— a quarter.

はんぎゃく【反逆・叛逆】 treason. ¶ 彼は主君に対して～した He *rebelled* (≒ *revolted*) *against* his lord. ～を企てる plot against (the government).
—罪 treason. —者 a traitor.

はんきゅう【半休】a half holiday.

はんきゅう【半球】a hemisphere.
東(西)— the Eastern (Western) Hemisphere.

はんきょう【反共】anti-Communism. ¶ ～政策 an *anti-Communist* policy.

はんきょう【反響】an echo ; 〔a〕 repercussion ; (応答) 〔a〕 response ; (影響) an influence ; 〔an〕 impact.
¶ 彼らが笑うと講堂が～した The auditorium *echoed* with their laughter. 問い合わせの手紙を書いたがなんの～もなかった My letter of inquiry brought no *response*. 政府の声明は大きな～を呼び起こした The statement of the government created *a* great *sensation*. 彼の論文に対して教育界からなにか～があったか Did his paper elicit any *comment* from the educational world?

パンク a puncture. ¶ ～する puncture. 自転車が～した My bicycle has got *a puncture* (≒ *a flat tire*).

ばんぐみ【番組】 a program〔me〕. ¶ 彼の演奏を～に入れた We put his performance on the *program*. テレビの～を見る see the television *program*. 特別～を放送する broadcast *a* special *program*.

ばんくるわせ【番狂わせ】a surprise. ¶ チャンピオンが負けて～となった The champion's defeat was *a* great *surprise to us*. 彼の敗北は～だった He suffered *an unexpected upset*.

はんぐん【反軍】—思想 anti-militarism.

はんけい【半径】 a radius. ¶ ～10センチの円 a circle with *a radius* of 10 centimeters. 東京から～20キロ以内に住む live within *a radius* of 20 kilometers from Tokyo.
行動— the radius of action.

はんげき【反撃】 a counterattack. ¶ わが軍は～した Our army made *a counterattack* upon the enemy. 敵の～に会った We *were attacked in return* by the enemy.

はんけつ【判決】 judgment. ¶ ついに～が下りた At last *judgment* (≒ *sentence*) was passed 〔on the case〕. 裁判官は被告に有利な(不利な) ～を下した The judge *decided* in favor of (against) the accused. ～に服す accept the *decision*. 彼は死刑の～を受けた He *was sentenced to* death. ～に不服を申し立てる protest against the *judgment*.
—文 the decision ; the written judgment.
—例 a leading case.

はんげつ【半月】a half moon. ¶ ～形の crescent.

はんけん【版権】a copyright. ¶ ～を持っている own (≒ hold) the *copyright* (*on* a book). ～を侵害する infringe *a copyright*. ～は昨年の1月10日に消滅した The *copyright* expired on January 10, last year.
—所有 (書籍に記載の標記) All rights reserved. —所有者 a copyright holder.

はんげん【半減】a reduction by half. ¶ この方法で交通事故が～するだろう This policy will *reduce* traffic accidents *by half*. 彼が出演しなかったのでショーのおもしろさが～した His absence *took off half* of the amusement of the show. / *Half* of the amusement of the show *was gone* (≒ *was lost*) because of his absence.

ばんけん【番犬】a watchdog.

はんご【反語】〔an〕 irony ; a rhetorical question.

はんこう【反抗】(抵抗) 〔a〕 resistance ; (反対) 〔an〕 opposition ; (不従順) disobedience ; (挑戦) defiance.
¶ その子どもは父親に～した The child *disobeyed* his father. 彼は私の厳格な規律に～した He *defied* (≒ *resisted boldly*) my strict rules. その～的な子どもたちをどう扱っていいのかわからなかった I did not know what to do with the *rebellious* children. 人々は侵入軍に果敢に～した The people *boldly resisted* (≒ *offered bold resistance to*) the invaders.
—期 ¶ あの子は今～期だ The boy is now at his *naughty* (≒ *rebellious*) age.

はんこう【犯行】a crime. ¶ ～を認める confess *one's crime*. ～を否認する deny *one's crime*.
—現場 the scene of a crime.

はんごう【飯盒】a canteen.

ばんごう【番号】a number. ¶ 若い～ *a low number*. 「～!」(号令) *Number!* 先生は生徒に～をかけた The teacher bade his students *number off*. この箱に～を1から20までつけよう Let's *number* (≒ give *a number* to) these boxes from 1 to 20. (電話で) ～が違います Sorry, 〔you have the〕 wrong *number*.
—札 a number ticket. 受験— an application seat number. —順 ¶ 本を～順に並べる put books in *numerical* order. 電話— a telephone (≒ dial) number. 電話—簿 a telephone directory. 通し— running numbers.

ばんこく【万国】—旗 the flags of all nations.

は

—博覧会 an international exposition. —標準時 the universal〔standard〕time.

ばんこつ【万骨】¶ 一将功成って～枯る *Thousands* die to raise one hero to fame. / A man's success is often built upon the sacrifice of *many*.

ばんごや【番小屋】a lodge.

はんごろし【半殺し】¶ あいつを～にしてやる I'll *beat* him *to a jelly*. 彼は彼らから～の目に会った He *was half-killed* (≒ *was nearly killed*) by them.

ばんこん【晩婚】late marriage. ¶ 彼は～だ He *got married late in life*.

はんさ【煩瑣】¶ ～な手続き a *troublesome* procedure ; (役所などの) a red tape.

はんざい【犯罪】a crime. ¶ 重大～を犯す commit *a* serious *crime*.

—学 criminology. —行為 criminal acts. ¶ 戦争は人間性に対する一つの～行為だ War is *a crime* against humanity. —心理学 criminal psychology. —捜査 criminal investigation. 少年— juvenile delinquency. 戦争—者 a war criminal.

ばんざい【万歳】cheers. ¶ 天皇陛下～! Long live the Emperor! ～を三唱する give three *cheers*.

ばんさく【万策】¶ ～尽きた We *are at the end of our resources*. / We *have exhausted every means*. ～尽きた. 私はもうだめだ *It's all over with* me.

はんざつ【煩雑】complexity. ¶ その道路地図の～なのに当惑した The *complexity* of the road map puzzled me. ～な手続きにはほとほと参った I was quite at a loss what to do with the *complicated* formalities. それは～な問題だ It is an *intricate* problem.

ハンサム handsome (男性について用いるのがふつう. 女性の場合には beautiful を用いる). ¶ 彼は～な青年だ He is a *handsome* young man.

はんさよう【反作用】reaction. ¶ AはBに～を及ぼす A *reacts upon* B. 作用があれば必ず～がある Where there is action, there is always *reaction*.

ばんさん【晩餐】supper ; (正餐) dinner. ¶ ～会を開く give *a dinner* (a dinner party と言わないでよい).

はんし【半死】—半生 ¶ 彼は～半生だった He *was more dead than alive*. / He *was on the verge of death*. ～半生のていたらくで逃げのびた I ran away *half-dead*.

はんし【半紙】common Japanese writing paper.

はんじ【判事】a judge.

—席 the bench. 首席— a presiding (≒ chief) judge. 陪席— an associate judge.

ばんし【万死】¶ その罪は～に値する The crime is sure to deserve *certain death*. ～に一生を得た He escaped *by a hair's-breadth*.

ばんじ【万事】all ; everything. ¶ ～金の世の中だ Money is *everything*. ～休す *All* is up with me. / *All hope* is gone. ～オーケーだ *All*'s well. ～あなたにお任せします I leave *everything* to you. 彼は～心得ている He knows what he is about. 一事が～ (諺) *One who steals an egg will steal an ox*. / *One instance shows all the rest*. 人間～塞翁が馬 (諺) Inscrutable are the ways of Heaven.

パンジー a pansy.

はんした【版下】a block copy.

—書き a block copy artist.

はんじもの【判じ物】a puzzle. ¶ なんだか～のような感じだ It seems something like *a riddle*.

はんしゃ【反射】reflection. ¶ 道路が暑い日には熱気を～する The street *reflects* heat on a hot day. 鏡に～している自分の顔を見るとがっかりだ The sight of my face *reflected* in the looking glass disappoints me.

—運動 reflex action. —鏡 a reflecting mirror. —望遠鏡 a reflecting telescope. —炉 a reverberatory furnace.

ばんしゃく【晩酌】a daily drink at dinner. ¶ きみは～しますか Do you *drink at supper*?

ばんじゃく【盤石】¶ 彼の地位は～のようにゆるがない His position *is as steadfast as the rock*.

はんしゅ【藩主】the lord of a clan ; a feudal lord.

はんしゅう【半周】a semicircle. ¶ トラックを～する *go halfway round* the track.

ばんしゅう【晩秋】late fall ; 英 late autumn. ¶ ～のある日 a day *late in autumn* (≒ *in late autumn*).

はんじゅく【半熟】¶ ～の卵 a *soft-boiled* egg. 卵を二つ～にしてほしい I want to *have* two eggs *boiled soft*.

はんしゅつ【搬出】¶ 絵を会場から～する *carry* (≒ *take*) a painting *out of* an exhibition hall.

ばんしゅん【晩春】¶ ～ののどかな一日 a peaceful day *in late spring*.

ばんしょ【板書】¶ ～する (黒板に書く) write on a blackboard (最近では greenboard と言うことが多い).

はんしょう【反証】counterevidence. ¶ ～をあげる produce *counterevidence* (≒ *contrary evidence*). それには～がたくさんあった There was a great deal of *evidence against* it.

はんしょう【半焼】¶ 昨夜の火事で1軒が～した By the fire which broke out last night, a house *was half destroyed* (≒ *was half burnt*).

はんしょう【半鐘】a fire bell. ¶ ～が鳴った The *fire bell* rang.

はんじょう【半畳】¶ 話の中途で～を入れないでほしい Don't *interrupt* me during my talk.

はんじょう【繁盛】prosperity. ¶ ご一家のご～をお祈り申し上げます I heartily wish for the *prosperity* of all your family. 事務所は～している The office *is flourishing*. 店が～するだろう The shop will *do a good business*. あの医者は～している The doctor *has a large practice*. ご～でけっこうです I am very glad you *are doing so well*.

ばんしょう【万障】¶ ～を排して行くべきだ You must go *by all means*. ～お繰り合わせのうえおいでください Please *do not fail to* come. (ふつ

は

うは Please *do* come. と言えばよい).

ばんしょう【晩鐘】the evening bell. ¶ ミレーの～(絵画) *the Angelus* by Millet.

はんしょく【繁殖】breeding. ¶ ウサギは～するのが早い Rabbits *breed* rapidly. 木は種子で～する Trees *propagate themselves* by seeds. バクテリアの～を止める stop the *propagation* of bacteria. ウナギは魚の中でもっとも～力が旺盛(おうせい)である The eels are the most *prolific* of all fishes.

—期 a breeding season. —力 propagative power.

はんしん【半身】half the body; (片側) one side of the body. ¶ 彼は～のり出して野球をみていた He was watching baseball *leaning forward*.

上(下)— the upper (lower) half of *one's* body. ¶ レントゲンをとるから, 上～はだかになりなさい Because you are to be X-rayed, strip yourself *to the waist*. 右— ¶ 彼は中風で右～がきかなくなっている He is paralyzed *on the right side*. / He has paralysis *on the right side* 〔*of his body*〕. —不随 ¶ 彼は～不随だ He is paralyzed *on one side*.

はんしんはんぎ【半信半疑】¶ 彼は～だった He *was half in doubt*. その悪いニュースに接して彼は～だった He *could not quite believe* the bad news. 彼は～のようすだった He *looked incredulous*. ～で引き下がっていった He went away *dubiously*.

はんしんろん【汎神論】〘哲学〙pantheism.

—者 a pantheist.

はんすう【反芻】rumination. ¶ 牛は食物を～する A cow *ruminates* its food.

—動物 a ruminant.

はんすう【半数】half the number. ¶ 合格者は～にも満たなかった Only less than *half* of the applicants have been successful.

—改選 re-election of half the members. 過— ¶ 彼は過～を得た He *gained a majority*.

はんズボン【半ズボン】shorts; knee breeches.

はん·する【反する】¶ 彼は言うこととやることが相～している What he says *is contradictory to* what he does. / His action *contradicts* his words. この記事は事実に～している This article *is opposed to* the fact. 彼の息子は意に～した結婚をした His son got married, *contrary to* his expectations. 彼女は規則に～した行動をした She acted *against* the rules. 兄はおとなしいのに～して, 彼は落ち着きがない His older brother is gentle, *while* he himself is restless. 彼は学校の規則に～した He *broke* the rule of his school.

はん·ずる【判ずる】¶ そのことの是非は～じがたい It is difficult to *judge* whether that is right or wrong. 彼の言ったことが～じかねた I could not *make out* what he said. この暗号が～じかねる I cannot *decipher* the countersign.

はんせい【反省】reflection. ¶ ～は人を賢明にする *Reflection* increases wisdom. 自分のやったことを～せよ *Reflect on* what you have done. われわれは政府の～を求めた We demanded the *reconsideration* of the government. 彼に～を促す必要がある We must urge him to *reconsider* the matter. ～してみると私の策はまちがっていた *On reflection*, I find that my method was wrong. (やや文語体).

—会 ¶ 彼らは～会を開いた They held a meeting for *reviewing* what they had done.

はんせい【半生】half *one's* life. ¶ 彼は～を身体障害者のためにささげた He devoted *half his life* to the welfare of the handicapped.

ばんせい【蛮声】¶ ～を張り上げて歌う sing in *a loud discordant voice*.

はんせいき【半世紀】half a century.

はんせつ【半切】¶ ～の写真 a *half-size* photo〔graph〕.

はんせん【反戦】—運動 an antiwar movement. —思想 antiwar ideas. —主義 pacifism. —主義者 a pacifist. —デモ an antiwar demonstration.

はんせん【帆船】a sailing ship (アメリカでは scooter という語を用いることがある).

はんぜん【判然】¶ 彼は～とした返事をしなかった He did not give a *definite* answer. これは～たる事実だ This is a *plain* fact. 彼の言うことの要旨が～としない The gist of what he says *is ambiguous* (⇆ *obscure*). そのことばの意味はまだ～としない The meaning of the word *is* not *clear* yet. A校とB校との学力差は～としている The difference of scholarship between A school and B school *is* quite *distinct*. その原因はまだ～としない The cause *is* not yet *ascertained*.

ばんぜん【万全】¶ ～を期するためにもう一度見直した We re-examined it to *make assurance doubly sure*. 準備には～を期した We paid a *prudential* attention to the preparation. ～の策を講じた *Every possible measure* was taken.

はんそ【反訴】recrimination. ¶ 彼は損害賠償の～をした He *brought a counterclaim for* the damages.

—状 a cross bill. —人 a counterclaimant.

はんそう【帆走】sailing; (グライダーの) gliding. ¶ 太平洋を～する *sail* across the Pacific.

ばんそう【伴奏】accompaniment. ¶ ピアノで人の～をする *accompany a person on* the piano. オルガンの～で歌った We sang *to the accompaniment of* the organ. 先生の～で歌いましょう Let's sing at the teacher's *accompaniment*. オーケストラの～はたいへんよかった The orchestral *accompaniment* sounded excellent to the ears.

—者 an accompanist.

ばんそうこう【絆創膏】〔a〕sticking plaster. ¶ その傷には～をはるといい You had better apply *a sticking plaster* to the wound.

はんそく【反則】(スポーツ) a foul play. ¶ それは～だ It *is against the rules*. 彼は～を犯した(スポーツで) He *played foul*. ～で5人が除外された(バスケットで) Five players *fouled out* of the game. ～で彼はフリースローを得た A free throw was given to him *on a foul.*

はんそで【半袖】a half-sleeve. ¶ ～のシャツ an undershirt with *half sleeves.* ～ワイシャツ a *half-sleeve* shirt.

はんだ【半田】solder. ¶ ～づけにする *solder* (a thing) to (some other thing).

パンダ a〔giant〕panda.

はんたい【反対】**1**〚逆〛 counter; opposite; reverse. ¶ 車は急に～の方向へ走りだした The car began to move suddenly in the *opposite* direction.

道の～側へ渡ろう Let us cross over the road to *the other* side.

彼の言っていることは事実と～だ What he says *is contrary* (≒ *is opposite*) *to* the fact.

今度は～側からバーを跳びなさい Jump over the bar from *the other* side this time.

ふたりの意見は正～だ The views of the two *are diametrically opposed to* each other.

彼をやりこめるつもりが～にやりこめられた I intended to put him to silence, but, *on the contrary,* I was driven into a corner.

票決したところ予想とは～の結果になった The decision by vote brought about a result *contrary to* our expectations.

2〚反抗・異議・不賛成〛〔an〕opposition. ¶ 彼らは道路建設に～だ They *are opposed to* (≒ *are against*) the establishment of the road.

この計画に～の人は手をあげてください Those who *are against* this plan, please indicate by raising their hands.

政府が新しい政策を実施するには強い～を覚悟せねばならない When the government carries out a new policy, it must be prepared for strong *opposition* (≒ it must be prepared to meet strong *opposition*).

彼らはわれわれの提案に～した They *countered* our proposal. / They *were contrary to* our proposal.

その法案は野党の猛烈な～を受けて不成立に終わった *Attacked strongly* by the Opposition Parties, the bill failed to pass.

彼らの～は押し切るつもりだ I will have my own way in spite of their *opposition.*

この結婚には彼の両親が～している His parents *are opposed to* his marriage.

投票の結果は賛成20票～15票であった This vote stood at twenty ayes and fifteen *nays.*

戦争～のデモが行なわれた They had an *anti-war* demonstration.

━運動 an opposition movement. ¶ 核実験～運動 a movement *against* nuclear tests. ━者 an opponent; an adversary. ━尋問〔a〕cross-examination. ¶ 被告側の証人に対する検事の～尋問が行なわれた The defense witness *was cross-examined* by the public prosecutor. ━勢力 a counterinfluence. ━提案 a counter proposal. ━党 an opposition party. ━投票 a negative vote. ¶ ～投票は少数だった There were few *negative votes.*

はんだくおん【半濁音】a semi-voiced sound.

パンタグラフ a pantograph.

バンタムきゅう【バンタム級】 the bantamweight〔class〕. ¶ ～のボクサー a bantamweight〔boxer〕.

はんだん【判断】judgment. ¶ 自分で～しなさい *Judge* for yourself. 彼の態度から彼はその案に賛成だと～される I *read* from his manner that he favors the plan. うわさから～すると彼は大うそつきだ *Judging by* (≒ *from*) the rumor, he seems to be a big liar. 私の～ではきみはすぐ行くべきだ *In my judgment* you should go at once. その問題に彼は独自の～を下した He formed (≒ passed) *an* independent *judgment* on the problem. 彼が正しいかどうか私には～がつかない I cannot *tell* whether he is right or not. ご～に任せます I leave it to your *discretion* (≒ *judgment*).

姓名━ onomancy. 身の上━ fortunetelling.

ばんたん【万端】¶ 用意～ととのった *Everything* is ready.

ばんち【番地】a house number; (所番地) *one's* address. ¶ A町5～ No. 5, A-cho. お宅は何～ですか What is the *street number* of your house? ～がまちがっていたのでその手紙は彼に届かなかった As the letter *was wrongly addressed,* it did not reach him.

パンチ a punch. ¶ 切符に～を入れる *punch* a ticket. 顔に～を食わせる land (≒ give) *a punch* on the face; *punch* (*a person*) on the face.

━カード a punch card; (コンピューターの) a punch〔ed〕card.

ばんちゃ【番茶】coarse tea.

はんちゅう【範疇】a category. ¶ それはこの～に入る That falls under this *category.* この～に属する項目はいくつあるか How many items belong to this *category?*

はんちょう【班長】a squad leader.

ハンチング a sports cap; a tweed cap.

パンツ pants; shorts; trunks.

運動━ athletic shorts. 海水━ bathing drawers. ショート━ shorts.

はんつき【半月】 half a month; a fortnight; two weeks. ¶ この雑誌は～ごとに出る This magazine *is semimonthly.* 彼はもう～近く会社を休んでいる He has been staying away from the firm *for nearly a fortnight.* ～分の給料 a *halfmonthly* pay.

ばんづけ【番付】a list. ¶ 芝居の～ a playbill. 相撲の～ *a list* of *sumo* wrestlers.

長者━ a list of millionaires.

ハンデ a handicap. ¶ 私は～18の腕前だ I play with handicap 18 in golf.

はんてい【判定】judgment; decision. ¶ 審判の～に従う obey the umpire's *decision.* 彼は～を誤った He *misjudged.* 彼は～で勝った He won *by a decision.*

━勝ち victory won by a decision. 写真━ ¶ 写真～は彼に有利だった The *photo finish* was to his advantage.

ハンディキャップ a handicap. ¶ ～をつける handicap *a person.* 彼はこの不利な～を克服し

た He overcame this disadvantageous *handicap*.

はんてん【斑点】a spot. ¶ この病気にかかると顔に〜ができる When a person is attacked by this disease, *spots* are formed on his face. まむしには〜がある A viper *is speckled*.

はんてん【反転】¶ 台風が〜して南下した The typhoon *turned its course* (≒ *made a U-turn*) and made its way southward.

バント〖野球〗a bunt. ¶ 〜する bunt. 〜で走者を二塁に送る advance a runner *on bunt* to second base. 〜の構えをする pose *one-self for bunting*. コーチはバッターに〜を命じた The coach instructed the batter to *bunt*. 彼は一塁側に〜した He *beat out a bunt* (≒ *bunted*) to first base.
犠牲— a sacrifice bunt. セーフティ— a safety bunt. ドラッグ— a drag bunt.

バンド 1〖洋服の〗a belt. ¶ 〜を締める tighten *one's belt*.
〜を緩める loosen *one's belt*.
〜を締め直す adjust the clasp of *one's belt*.
ズボンの〜通しがこわれた The *belt rungs* of my trousers have been broken.
2〖楽団〗a band. ¶ 〜は行進曲を二, 三奏した The *band* played a few marches.

はんとう【半島】a peninsula. ¶ 房総〜 the Boso *Peninsula*.

はんどう【反動】a reaction.
—思想 a reactionary idea. —主義者 a reactionary. —政府 a reactionary government. —内閣 a reactionary cabinet.

ばんとう【番頭】a clerk.

はんとうめい【半透明】semitransparency; translucency. ¶ すりガラスは〜だ Frosted glass *is translucent* (≒ *semitransparent*).

はんどく【判読】decipherment. ¶ ひどいなぐり書きを〜する *make out* so unintelligible a scrawl.

はんとし【半年】half a year; a half year. ¶ 〜ごとに half-yearly; semi-annually; once a half year; every half year.

ハンドバッグ a handbag.

ハンドブック a handbook.

ハンドボール〖球技〗handball.

パントマイム a pantomime. ¶ 〜を演じる pantomime.

ハンドル (自動車の) a [steering] wheel; (自転車の) handlebars; (ドアの取っ手) a handle (丸い取っ手は a knob). ¶ ドアの〜を右に回す turn the *handle* to the right. 車の〜を右(左)に切る *wheel* right (left).

ばんなん【万難】¶ 〜を排して at any cost; at all costs; in spite of *all difficulties*.

はんにえ【半煮え】¶ 〜の魚 a *half-boiled* (*half-cooked*; *half-done*) fish.

はんにち【半日】half a day; a half day.

はんにゅう【搬入】¶ 作品を会場へ〜する *carry one's* work *into* the hall.

はんにん【犯人】a criminal (容疑者の意味ではふつう a suspect).
¶ 〜を捕縛する(隠匿する; 追い詰める) apprehend (harbor; track down) *a criminal*.

ばんにん【万人】¶ 〜向きのデザイン a design for *all*. 彼がユニークな存在であるということは〜の認めるところだ It is *universally* acknowledged that he is unique.

ばんにん【番人】a keeper; a watch[man]. ¶ 倉庫には〜がつけてある The magazine *is under guard*.

はんね【半値】¶ 〜で品物を売る sell an article at *half the price* (≒ *half-price*). 〜にする reduce the *price by half*.

ばんねん【晩年】[*one's*] last years. ¶ 彼は〜はしあわせだった He lived a happy life *late in life*. 彼の〜は不遇だった He lived unknown *toward the end of his life*. / He outlived his fame. / His *last years* were unhappy.

はんのう【反応】a reaction; a response.
¶ 核連鎖〜を抑える control the nuclear chain *reaction*. 酸性〜を示す show *an* acid *reaction*. 〜がない have no *reactions* to (an offer). 相手の〜を打診する tap *a person's reaction*. 提案に対する彼の〜はどうでしたか What was his *reaction* to the proposal? その運動には熱心な〜があった The movement met *a* hearty *response*. / The campaign *was received* with enthusiasm.
核— a [nuclear] reaction. ツベルクリン— a tuberculin reaction.

ばんのう【万能】¶ 〜の神 the *Almighty* (≒ *Omnipotent*) [God].
—選手 an all-round player. —薬 a cure-all; a panacea.

はんのき【榛の木】〖植物〗a black alder.

はんば【飯場】laborers' quarters.

はんぱ【半端】(残り) the remnant; (端数) an odd sum; a fragment. ¶ 仕事を中途〜でやめる do things *half way*; leave things *half-done*. (セットまたは対になっている物を) 〜にする break the set (pair). 10円未満の〜な額は切り捨てる ignore any *fractional* sum less than ten yen.
—切れ odd cloth. —仕事 odd jobs. —者 a half-trained person. —物 an odd thing; odds and ends; (全集などの) an incomplete set.

バンパー 米 a bumper; 英 a buffer.

ハンバーグステーキ 米 a hamburg[er]; a Hamburg steak.

はんばい【販売】sale; selling. ¶ 予約〜する *sell* by subscription. 本を〜する店 a store *dealing in* books. 〜を禁止する ban (≒ prohibit) the *sale* of (something).
—員(係) (男) a salesman; (女) a saleswoman; a salesgirl. —店 米 a store; 英 a shop. —代理店 a selling agent. —網 a sales network. 委託— consignment sale; sale on consignment. 月賦— instalment sales; hire purchase. 入札— sale by sealed tender. 予約— sale by subscription. 割引— a reduction (≒ discount) sale.

はんばく【反駁】a retort; a rebuttal. ¶ 人の言に〜する *contradict* (≒ *refute*) *a person's* statement. 〜を受ける receive *contradiction*.

は

はんぱく【半白】¶～の紳士 a *gray-haired* gentleman.
はんぱつ【反発】a repulsion ; a resistance. ¶～を感じる feel *a repulsion* (*toward a person*). ～する repulse. 政府に～する *rebel against* the government.
—力〘物理〙repulsion ; repulsive force.
はんはん【半半】¶菓子を～に分ける divide a cake *in two*. 砂糖と塩を～に混ぜる mix sugar and salt *equally* (≒ *half-and-half*). 人と分け前を～にする go *fifty-and-fifty* with *a person*.
ばんばん【万万】¶そんなことは～承知のうえだ I know it *very well*. そんなことは～あるまい It's next to impossible. これは～かたじけない It is *most* (≒ *very*) kind of you. (形式ばった言い方). / [I am] *much* obliged [to you].
ぱんぱん ¶塵を～はたく *clear* dust. テーブルを～たたく *beat* a table. ふとんを～たたく *slap* a counterpane. ピストルを～撃つ *pop* a pistol.
はんびょうにん【半病人】a semi-invalid ; a half invalid.
はんびらき【半開き】¶～の戸 a *half-open* door. ～の窓 a window *ajar*.
はんぴれい【反比例】inverse proportion. ¶～する be in *inverse proportion* (*to*).
はんぷ【頒布】¶乗客に無料でパンフレットを～する *distribute* pamphlets *to* passengers free.
はんぷく【反復】[a] repetition. ¶～練習することは初学者にとってもっともたいせつだ *Repeated* practice is the most important to the beginners.
パンプス [a pair of] pumps.
ばんぶつ【万物】all things ; the whole creation. ¶人は～の霊長である Man is the lord of *creation*.
ハンブル〘野球〙fumble. ¶ボールを～する *fumble* a ball.
パンフレット a pamphlet.
はんぶん【半分】half. ¶仕事は～済んだ I have finished *half* of the work. コップに～入れる fill a glass *half-full*. 私は彼女の～しか本を持っていない I have only *half as* many books *as* she. 私は彼の～も英語を話せない I cannot speak English even *half as* well *as* he. 10万円あったらきみに～あげよう I would give *half* of 100,000 yen to you, if I had that much. これを～ずつ分けよう Let's *halve* it. 冗談～でもそんなことを言ってはいけない You should not say such a thing even *in fun*. 遊び～にそれをやった I did it *half in play*.
ばんぺい【番兵】a watch ; a guard. ¶入り口に～を置く place *a guard* at the door. ～に立つ go on *guard* ; stand *guard* (≒ *sentinel*).
はんべつ【判別】distinction. ¶敵味方(正邪)を～する *distinguish* (≒ *tell*) friend from foe (right from wrong).
—式〘数学〙a discriminant.
はんぺん【半片】steamed fishpaste.
はんぼいん【半母音】〘音声学〙a semi-vowel.
はんぼう【繁忙・煩忙】¶～をきわめる be very busy ; be busily engaged (*in doing*).

ハンマー a hammer.
—投げ hammer throwing ; throwing the hammer.
はんめい【判明】¶火事の原因は～しない The cause of the fire *is* not *cleared up*. そのうわさは誤りであると～した The report *proved* (≒ *turned out*) false. 死体はまだはっきりと身元が～していない The corpse *is* not clearly *identified* as yet. 彼の所在はいまだに～しない His whereabouts *is* still *unknown*.
ばんめし【晩飯】supper. ¶～のあとで after *supper*. ～を食う take (≒ have) *supper*. ～の最中である be at *supper*.
はんめん【半面】the other side ; one side. ¶顔の～ a *half* face. 月の～ the moon's *disc* (≒ *disk*). きみは彼の～を知らない You don't know *the other side* of his character. 問題の～だけを見る look upon only *one side* of a question. その～において on *the contrary* ; on *the other side*. 彼の言うことにも～の真理がある There is *some* truth in what he says.
ばんめん【盤面】¶～の推移を見守る watch the development of a *go* game.
はんも【繁茂】¶～した森 a *thick* (≒ *dense* ; *luxuriant* ; *rank*) forest. この辺りは雑草がよく～する Weeds *flourish* (≒ *grow thick*) around here.
はんもく【反目】antagonism. ¶～する両国 the two countries in *antagonism*. 互いに～し合う *be hostile* to each other. 2大国の～ the *antagonism* between the two powers.
ハンモック a hammock. ¶～をつる(たたむ) sling (lash) *a hammock*.
はんもと【版元】a publishing company.
はんもん【反問】cross-question. ¶～する ask *a person* in return ; ask back *a person*.
はんもん【煩悶】anguish. ¶罪の意識に～した The sense of guilt caused me *mental anguish*. / I *was agonized* by the sense of guilt.
パンや【パン屋】(人) a baker ; (製造所) a bakery.
はんやけ【半焼け】¶～の肉 *half-roasted* beef. 10軒以上の家が～になった More than ten houses *were partially destroyed* (≒ *were partially burnt*) *by fire*.
ばんゆう【蛮勇】¶～をふるって荒波の中に船を走らせた *With wild courage* we sailed our ship in the rough sea.
ばんゆういんりょく【万有引力】〘物理〙universal gravitation.
ばんらい【万雷】¶～の拍手のうちに amid the *wild applause* (*of* the audience). 聴衆は～の拍手をもって彼を迎えた The audience greeted him with *a storm of* applause.
はんら[たい]【半裸[体]】¶～でいる go *half-naked*. ～の女 a *semi-nude* woman.
はんらく【反落】〘株式〙a sharp (≒ reactionary) fall.
はんらん【反乱・叛乱】a revolt ; a rebellion. ¶～を鎮める quell (≒ put down) *a revolt* (≒ *a rebellion*). 国王に対し～する *revolt* (≒ *rebel*) against the king. ～を起こす raise *a rebellion* ; rise in *revolt* (≒ *rebellion*). ～

は

が起きる *A revolt* (≒ *A rebellion*) breaks out.

—軍 a rebel (≒ an insurrection) army; rebel forces.

はんらん【氾濫】overflowing; flood. ¶豪雨のため〜した河川 rivers *flooded* by heavy rainstorms. 川が〜して水が田畑へあふれている The river *is overflowing* its banks into fields. 道路は車の〜だった The road *was deluged* (≒ *was flooded; was overcrowded*) with cars.

ばんり【万里】¶〜の長城 the Great Wall of China. 〜の波濤を乗り越える cross (≒go over) *the vast ocean.*

はんりょ【伴侶】a companion. ¶一生の〜を得る get *a companion* for life; get a life *companion.*

はんれい【判例】a [judicial] precedent. ¶新しい〜を作る create *a* new *precedent.*

はんれい【凡例】introductory remarks; general explanations.

はんろ【販路】a market. ¶〜を拡張する extend (≒enlarge) *a market.* それらの製品の新しい〜を開拓する find *a* new *market* for those products. 外国の〜を拡張する develop *one's* foreign *market.* ヨーロッパにおける〜を開拓する cultivate *a market* in Europe.

はんろん【反論】[an] objection. ¶〜する make *objections (to)*; lodge (≒ utter) *an objection (against).*

はんろん【汎論】an introduction; an outline; a summary.

ひ

ひ【比】a ratio; a match; (比較) [a] comparison. ¶5対1の〜 *a ratio* of five to one. きみはとても彼の〜ではない You *are* no *match for* him. その発明はまったく他に〜を見ぬものだ The invention *is* absolutely *unique* in the world. 旭川の寒さは東京の〜ではない It is far colder in Asahikawa than in Tokyo. 東京に〜してロンドンは寒い London is cold *in comparison with* Tokyo.

ひ【否】no. ¶〜とするもの多数 The *noes* have it. 〜とするもの3 There are three *noes.* / There are three *votes against* it.

ひ【非】a fault; wrong. ¶彼の〜は責められなければならない He must be blamed for his *error* (≒*fault*). 形勢は彼に〜であった The situation *was to his disadvantage.* / The adds *are against* him. 彼は自分の〜を悟っていない He has not seen that he *is wrong.* あの俳優の演技は一点の〜の打ちどころもない His performance as an actor *is perpect* (≒ *leaves nothing to be desired*). 〜は〜として認めるべきだ We should condemn *wrong* as *wrong.*

ひ【妃】a princess; Her Imperial (≒ Royal) Highness.

ひ【碑】(墓碑) a tombstone; (記念碑) a monument. ¶墓に〜を建てる erect (≒ set up) *a tombstone* over a grave. 人を記念して〜を建てる erect (≒ set up) *a monument* to the memory of *a person.*

ひ【日】**1**〖太陽・日光・日照〗the sun; sunshine. ¶〜が水平線から上った *The sun* came up over the horizon.

今真っ赤な〜が沈むところだ *The* crimson *sun* is setting now.

真夏の〜がさんさんとふりそそいでいる *The* midsummer *sun* is shining brightly.

雨があがり〜が照りだした It has stopped raining and *the sun* has begun to shine.

〜が部屋いっぱいにさし込んでいる *The sun* is shining into every corner of the room. / *The sun* is filling the room.

彼の部屋はよく〜が当たる His room gets a lot of *sunshine.* / His room *is* very *sunny.*

セーターを洗ったら〜の当たらない所で乾かしなさい If you wash your sweater, be careful to dry it where there is no *sunshine.*

ネコが長くなって〜に当たっている A cat is stretching itself at ease, bathing in *the sun.*

〜の当たらない所でひと休みしよう Let's take a rest *in the shade.*

〜が陰って涼しくなった *The sun* went behind the clouds and it became cool.

〜のあるうちにその仕事をかたづけてしまおう Let us get through with the work before it is dark.

海へ行って真っ黒に〜に焼けてきた I went seabathing and came back, *sun-tanned* (≒ *burnt black by the sun*).

2〖昼間・日照時間〗¶冬は〜が短い The *days* are short in winter.

1月半ばになると少し〜が長くなったのを感じる We find that the *days* have got a little longer by the middle of January.

今ごろは〜が長い The *days* are long at this time of the year.

もうじき〜が暮れる In a short while night will fall. (文語体). / It will get dark very soon. (口語体).

3〖天気のようす〗¶日本晴れのすばらしい〜だった It was *a* splendidly nice *day.*

風がなくて穏やかな〜だ It is *a* calm, windless 「*day.*

登山には絶好の～だ It is *a* perfect (≒ capital) *day* for mountain climbing.
晴れた～にはここから富士山がよく見える This place commands a good view of Mt. Fuji *on a* fine *day*.
梅雨になると雨の～が続く In the wet season we have rainy *days* in succession.
寒くてあいにくな～になった It has become *a* cold unseasonable *day*.
4 〚一日・日時〛 ¶ ある～私は海へ釣りに出かけた *One day* I went fishing at the sea.
～を改めてまた出なおします I will come again *another day*.
彼は～に1度はこの店に現われる He drops in at this store once *a day*.
私は大学の入試に合格した～のことを今でも覚えている Even now I remember *the day* when I passed the entrance examination of the university.
このごろ新聞に火事の記事の出ていない～はない Not *a day* passes but there is some news of a fire in the paper. (文語体. 口語体なら Every day で始める).
赤ん坊は～に～に大きくなる Babies grow *day by day*.
彼らはその～その～の生活に追われている They barely manage to live on *from day to day*.
彼女はぶらぶら～を送っている She idles away her *time* (≒ *days*). / She leads an idle life.
彼にお願いしてレポート提出の～を2日延ばしてもらった We asked him to put off for two days *the date* for presenting our reports.
次の会合の～を決めよう Let us fix *the date* of the next meeting.
彼は夜を～について研究にいそしんだ He devoted himself to study *day and night*.
試験の～が迫ってきた *The date* of the examination is close at hand.
5 〚日数〛 ¶ 出発までもういくらも～がない We have only a few *days* before we start.
彼は入社してからまだ～が浅い It is only a short time since he entered the company.
～のたつにつれて仕事にも慣れてきた With every passing *day* I have been getting used to the work.
6 〚時・時代・場合〛 ¶ 若き～の思い出は忘れがたい We cannot forget the memories of our younger *days*.
彼にだって得意の～はあった Even he has seen good *days*.
7 〚比喩的に〛 ¶ ～のあたらぬ場所 *sunless* (≒ *cheerless*) quarters.

ひ【火】1 〚燃えること・炎・炭火・火事〛 a fire ; (大火) a conflagration. ¶ ～を貸していただけますか May I have *a light*, please?
彼はライターでたばこに～をつけた He *lighted* his cigarette with a lighter.
～のついたたばこを投げ捨てる throw away a cigarette without putting it out.
寒いから～をたいてあたろう It is cold ; let's *make a fire* to warm ourselves.
～をおこす light *a fire* ; make *a charcoal* (木炭を強調する場合).
枯れ枝を集めて～をつけた We gathered dead twigs and *set fire to* them.
ろうそくの～が風に揺れている A candle[*-flame*] is flickering in the wind.
この油は～がつきやすい The oil *is inflammable*.
衝突した車が～を吹いた The car which had crashed burst into *flames*.
辺りは～の海となった The neighborhood turned into a sea of *flames*.
その火事はたばこの～が原因だ The fire was caused by a lighted cigarette end.
～は目抜き通りをひとなめにした The *fire* burnt up the main street.
消防隊が～を消し止めた The fire brigade put out (≒ extinguished) the *fire*.
～は実験室から出た The *fire* started in the laboratory.
～は隣家に燃え移った The *fire* spread to the neighboring house. / The neighboring house caught *fire*.
～は四方に燃え広がった The *fire* spread on all sides (≒ in all directions).
～のまわりが早くひとり逃げ遅れた The *fire* spread so fast that a man failed to escape.
～はようやく下火になった The *fire* has burned down at last.
～の用心 Beware of *a fire*.
そんなことをすれば～に油を注ぐようなものだ To do such a thing is like pouring oil on *a fire*.
～のない所に煙は立たない (諺) *There is no smoke without fire*.
2 〚燈火〛 ¶ 丘の上から見下ろす町の～は美しい The *lights* of the town overlooked from the summit of the hill are beautiful.
街路にいっせいに～がともった The *lamps* were lighted along the streets at the same time.
部屋の～を消し忘れるな Don't forget to put out the *light* in your room.
夜空に飛行機の～が見えた I saw the *light* of an airplane flying in the night sky.
3 〚煮たきすること〛 ¶ この肉にもう一度～を通しなさい *Do* this meat thoroughly again.
この魚はよく～が通っていない This fish *is* not *done* enough.
4 〚慣用的表現〛 ¶ 彼になぐられて目から～が出た He struck me so hard that I *saw stars*.
9月になると避暑地は～の消えたように寂しくなる In September the summer resorts become still as death. / In September everything is dead in the summer resorts.
彼の潔白は～を見るよりも明らかだ His innocence *is as plain as a pikestaff*. / His innocence *is as clear as day*.
赤ん坊が～のついたように泣いている The baby is howling *frantically*.
彼女は～のような女だ She is a *fiery* woman.
顔から～が出るほど恥ずかしい思いだった I was quite ashamed. / I was flushed with shame.

ひ【緋】 scarlet. ¶ ～の衣 a *scarlet* robe.

ひー【非-】 un-. ¶ ～愛国的 *un*patriotic. ～アメリ

力的 *un*-American. ～学術的 *un*scientific.

び【美】 beauty. ¶ ～の探究 a study of *the beautiful*.

真善―― truth, good, and beauty. 均整―― the beauties of symmetry. 女性―― feminine beauty. ――的感覚 a sense of beauty.

び【微】 minuteness; a particle. ¶ ～に入り細にわたって説く give a *minute* explanation; explain *minutely*. ～に入り細をうがって論ずる discuss a matter *exhaustively* (≒ *in detail*).

ひあい【悲哀】 sorrow; grief. ¶ 人生の～を感じる suffer *sorrows* of life. 幻滅の～を感じる have a *sad* disillusionment. 酒に～を紛らす drown *grief* (≒ *sorrow*) in drink. 彼は～の淵に沈んでいる He is *in deep grief*.

ひあが・る【干上がる】 ¶ たんぼは日照り続きで～った The rice fields *dried* (≒ *parched*) *up* with dry weather. 彼は失業のためあごが～ってしまった He *lost his means of living* because of losing his job.

ひあし【日足】 ¶ ～が延びている The *days* are getting longer. 冬は～が短い The *days* are short in winter.

ひあし【火足】 ¶ 強風のため～が早かった The *fire* spread rapidly on account of a strong wind.

ヒアシンス a hyacinth.

ひあそび【火遊び】 ¶ ～をする play with fire (比喩的に言うときは fire または love).

ひあたり【日当たり】 ¶ ～のよい(悪い)部屋 a *sunny* (an *unsunny*) room.

ピアニスト a pianist.

ピアノ a piano. ¶ ～をひく play *the piano* (冠詞に注意). ～に合わせて歌う sing [a song] to *the piano*. ～を習う practice *the piano*; (レッスンを受ける) take *piano* lessons. ～で人の伴奏をする accompany a person on *the piano*. ～の調律をする tune *a piano*.

――線 piano wire. ――独奏 a piano solo. アップライト(グランド)―― an upright (a grand) piano.

びい【微意】 ¶ 感謝の～を表わすためなにかを送る send something as *a small token* of *one's* gratitude.

ピーアール P. R. (<public relations). ¶ 新政策を～する *publicize* (≒ *advertize*) a new policy.

ビーカー a beaker.

ひいき【贔屓】 [a] favor. ¶ 彼はその歌手のたいへんな～だ He *patronizes* that singer very much. 野球選手ではだれが～ですか To whom do you *give your custom*? (この To は省略しない). 彼の～しているチームがまた勝った The team he *supports* has won again. 彼は日本～だ He is *pro*-Japanese.

――客 a patron. ――役者 *one's* favorite actor. ――目 ¶ どう～目に見てもこっちが不利だ The situation is to our disadvantage, however we look at it.

ピーク peak. ¶ わが国の人口増加は本年が～だ This is the *peak* year for population growth in our country. / The increase in the population of our country is at its *peak* this year.

ビージー an office girl; a career girl.

びいしき【美意識】 a sense of beauty.

ビーズ beads.

ヒーター a heater. ¶ 電気～ *an* electric *heater*. ガス～ *a* gas *heater*.

ビーだま【ビー玉】 a bead.

ビーチパラソル a beach umbrella.

ピーティーエー a PTA (Parents and Teachers Association の略).

ひい・でる【秀でる】 ¶ 彼は数学に～でている He *excels in* mathematics. 彼は一芸に～でている He is *a master* of an art.

ビートぞく【ビート族】 (口語) a beat; a beatnik; (総称) the beat generation.

ビーナス〘ローマ神話〙 Venus. ¶ ミロの～ the *Venus* of Milo.

ピーナッツ a peanut.

ぴいぴい ¶ 小鳥が～鳴く A little bird *peeps* (≒ *chirps*). よく～泣く子だな What a *yelling* child! 私はいつも～して暮らしている I *am* always *hard up* [*for money*].

ビーフステーキ [a] beefsteak.

ひいまご【曾孫】 a great-grandchild; a great-grandson; a great-granddaughter.

ピーマン〘植物〙 a pimento; a pimiento.

ひいらぎ【柊】〘植物〙 a holly.

ビール ale; beer. ¶ 気の抜けた～ stale (≒ flat) *beer*. ～を飲もう Let's take *beer* (≒ a glass of *beer*).

生―― draught beer; beer on draught. びんづめ―― bottled beer. 黒―― dark beer; stout.

ビールス〘医学〙 a virus.

ヒーロー a hero (複 heroes).

ひうちいし【火打石】 a flint.

ひうん【非運】 bad (≒ ill) luck; [a] misfortune. ¶ わが身の～を嘆く complain of *one's misfortune* (≒ *bad luck*).

ひえ【稗】〘植物〙 a barnyard grass.

ひえいせい【非衛生】 ¶ あの店は～的だ The condition of the store *is insanitary* (≒ *is unwholesome*).

ひえいりてき【非営利的】 ¶ ～事業 a *nonprofit* (≒ *uncommercial*) undertaking.

ひえき【裨益】 benefit; profit. ¶ 彼の著書は教育に～すること大だ His books *benefit* (≒ *contribute to*) education.

ひえき・る【冷え切る】 ¶ 雪道を歩いて体が～ってしまった Walking along the snow-covered road, I *was chilled to the bone*.

ひえこ・む【冷え込む】 ¶ 朝晩～む It *gets cold* severely in the mornings and evenings.

ひえしょう【冷え症】 ¶ 私は～だ I have *a cold constitution*.

ひえびえ【冷え冷え】 ¶ ～する冬の夜 a *chilly* winter night. ～とした心 a *cold* [*and unfeeling*] heart.

ひ・える【冷える】 ¶ 夜は～えますね It *is* terribly *cold* at night, isn't it? ～えないうちにどうぞ Take it before it *gets cold*. 手が～えきっている My hands *are benumbed with cold*. / My hands *are as cold as ice*.

ピエロ a pierrot; a clown.

びえん【鼻炎】 nasal catarrh.
ひおい【日おい】 a sunshade ; a blind.
ビオラ a viola.
びおん【鼻音】〘音声学〙a nasal sound.
びおん【微温】 ¶ ～的政策をとる adopt a *luke-warm* policy.
ひか【皮下】 ―脂肪 subcutaneous fat. ―注射〔a〕hypodermic injection.
ひか【悲歌】 a song of lamentation ; an elegy.
ひが【彼我】 ¶ ～の力量の差ははっきりしている There is a distinct difference in ability between *this side and that*.
びか【美化】 beautification. ¶ 現実を～する *beautify* (≒ *idealize*) the realities of life. 街を～しよう *Keep* the street *clean*.
ひがい【被害】〔an〕injury ; damage (damage は法律用語「損害賠償」の意味のときのみ複数形となる).
¶ ～はどの程度でしたか How much was *the damage*? 台風のためこの辺り一帯は大きな～を受けた The typhoon did great *damage* to all this neighborhood. 作物に少なからぬ～があった Not a little *damage* was done to the crops. 不作のため農夫たちは～を被っている Farmers *are suffering losses from* the poor crops. 豪雨の～はかなり広範囲にわたっている Pretty extensive *damage* has been done by the heavy rain. 10人の中で彼ひとりが～を免れた Of all ten, he alone escaped *injury*.
―者 a sufferer. ―高 the amount of damage. ―地 the affected area. ―妄想(もうそう) persecution mania. ―妄想患者 a persecution maniac.
ぴかいち【ぴか一】 ¶ 彼はその劇団の～だ He is *the star* 〔*actor*〕 (≒ *No. 1*) of the theatrical troupe. 彼は絵では～だ He *is top in* painting.
ひかえ【控え】 a note ; a copy ; (手形などの) a counterfoil. ¶ 手帳にその～をとった I *made a note of* it (≒ *jotted* it *down*) in my memorandum. 書類の～をとった I *made a* 〔*duplicate*〕 *copy of* the papers.
―選手 ¶ ～選手の層があまりない There isn't too much *bench depth*. 彼は～選手だ He remained *in reserve*. ―力士 a *sumo* wrestler for the next bout. ―室 an anteroom.
ひかえめ【控え目】 moderation. ¶ 彼はいつも～に言う He always speaks *with reserve*. 彼は万事～な態度をとる He *is moderate in* everything. 彼は生来～だ He *is* naturally *reserved*. 食事を～にした I *was temperate in* eating.
ひがえり【日帰り】 a day's trip. ¶ ～の出張 *a day's* official trip. そこは～で往復できる We can get there and back *in a day*.
ひか·える【控える】 **1** 〘つつしむ〙 ¶ 人の中傷は～えなさい You should *refrain from* slander*ing* others.
食物は多少～えるよう医者に言われている I am advised by doctors to *eat moderately*.
2 〘書き留める〙 ¶ これから言うことを～えてください Would you *note down* (≒ *jot down*) what I am going to say?
3 〘その他〙 ¶ 彼は出発を2日後に～えている He *is waiting* to set off in two days.
試験を目の前に～えてろうばいしていた He was dismayed *with* the examination *before* him. 彼の後ろには有力なメンバーが～えていた There were influential members *behind* him.
ひかく【比較】 comparison. ¶ AとBを～する *compare* A *with* B. CとDは～にならない There is no *comparison* between C and D. この俳優と～すると彼は問題にならない *As compared with* this actor, he is by far inferior. この二つの方法を～すると，こちらのほうが～にならぬほどよい This method is so much better than the other that there's *no point in comparing* the two. 彼と～するときみはまだまだだ *Compared with* him, you are still not good enough. この戯曲は～的読みやすい This drama is *comparatively* readable. 彼は～的忙しい毎日を送っている He lives a *relatively* busy life every day.
―級〘文法〙the comparative degree. ―言語学 comparative linguistics. ―文学 comparative literature.
ひかく【皮革】 ―製品 a leather article.
びがく【美学】〔a〕esthetics.
ひかげ【日陰】 the shade. ¶ ～で休む take a rest *in the shade*.
―者 an obscure person ; a social outcast ; a person with a shady past.
ひがけ【日掛け】 a daily installment.
―貯金 daily savings.
ひかげん【火加減】 ¶ 天火の～を見よう I'll see if the oven is properly heating.
ひがさ【日傘】 a parasol.
ひかさ·れる【引かされる】 ¶ 日本人は人情に～れがちだ The Japanese are apt to *be touched with* humanity.
ひがし【東】 the east. ¶ 私たちは～に向かって歩いた We walked *east* (≒ *eastward*). ～の風が吹いている The *east* wind is blowing. / The wind is *in the east*. 太陽は～から出て西に沈む The sun rises *in the east* and sets in the west. 千葉県は東京都の～側にある Chiba Prefecture is *on the east of* Tokyo metropolis. 私の事務所は当市の～にある My office is *in the east of* this city. 彼の家は～に面している His house faces *east* (≒ *to the east*). そこは横浜の～5キロの所にある It is five kilometers 〔*to the*〕 *east of* Yokohama.
ひがし【干菓子】 dry confectionery.
ひかず【日数】 ¶ 旅の～を重ねる spend many *days* in traveling.
ひかぜい【非課税】 tax exemption.
―品 a no-tax (≒ tax free ; duty free) article.
ひがた【干潟】 a tideland.
びカタル【鼻カタル】〘医学〙nasal catarrh.
ぴかぴか ¶ くつを～にみがく put *a good shine on* shoes. 彼女の指輪のダイヤが～光った The diamond in her ring *sparkled*. 皿が～光っていた The dishes *were sparkling clean*.
ひがみ【僻み】〔a〕prejudice ;〔a〕bias. ¶ それは

ひ

きみの～だ It is your *jaundiced* view. / You *are prejudiced* (≒ *are biased*) *against* it. / You *are biased to* think so.

ひが·む【僻む】 ¶ 彼は～みやすい He very often *fancies himself wronged*. あまり出世すると～むぞ I'll *be jealous of* you if you make a remarkable success in life.

ひがめ【僻目】 a bias; prejudice; an error. ¶ そうだと思うのはきみの～だ It is *a bias* (≒ *a prejudice*) on your part to think so.

ひから·びる【干からびる】 ¶ ～びた井戸 a *dried-up* well. ～びたリンゴ a *shriveled* apple.

ひかり【光】 light; (光線) a ray. ¶ 太陽は～と熱を与える The sun gives us *light* and heat. 月の～がさし込む *The moonlight* streams in. くつをみがいて～を出す put *a* good *shine* on shoes. 彼の前途には一筋の希望の～もなかった There was not *a ray* of hope before him. この結果は問題の解明に～を投じるかもしれない This result may throw *light* on the problem.

ぴかりと ¶ いなずまが～光った The lightning *flashed* (≒ *gave out a flash*).

ひか·る【光る】 **1** 〖光を発する〗 ¶ 夜空に星が～っている Stars *are twinkling* in the night sky. ネコの目が暗やみで～っていた The cat's eyes *gleamed* in the darkness.
芝生に露がきらきら～っていた Dewdrops *were sparkling* on the lawn.
彼の目は喜びに～っていた His eyes *shone* with delight.
～るもの必ずしも金ではない (諺) *All is not gold that glitters.*
このズボンはすれて～っている These trousers *are shiny* from wear.
2 〖目立つ〗 ¶ 彼はグループの中でも～っている He *is outstanding* among his group.

ひかん【悲観】 pessimism. ¶ 彼は前途を～した He *took a pessimistic view of* the future. / He *was despondent over* the future. 彼女は極度に～していた She was in the depths of *despair*. なにも～する理由はない There is no reason whatever for *pessimism*.
—論 pessimism. —論者 a pessimist.

ひがん【彼岸】 (春·秋の) the equinoctial week. ¶ ～の中日 *the* spring (autumnal) *equinox*. 暑さ寒さも～まで No heat or cold lasts over *the equinox*.
—桜 an early flowering cherry tree. —花〖植物〗Lycoris radiata.

ひがん【悲願】 ¶ 彼の～がかなった His *long-cherished hope* has been realized.

びかん【美感】 ¶ その絵は彼の～に訴えた The picture appealed to his *sense of beauty*.

びかん【美観】 ¶ あの広告塔は当市の～を損ねる The advertisement tower spoils *the beauty* (≒ *appearance*) of this city.

びがんじゅつ【美顔術】 facial[s].

ひき【引き】 [a] favor; (縁故) support; backing. ¶ 彼は重役のよい～がある He *is well-connected with* a director. / He *has a good pull with* a director. 彼はおじの～で職を得た He got the job through his uncle's *influence*. あの店は定価の2割～で売る They sell at 20 percent *discount* [on the price] at the store.

ひき【悲喜】 ¶ ～こもごもである I have *joy and sorrow* by turns.

びぎ【美技】 a brilliant performance; (野球·テニスなどの) a fine play; a beautiful feat.

ひきあい【引き合い】 a reference. ¶ それを～に出した I *mentioned* it. / I *referred to* it. / I *cited* it *as an example*. 当社は外国からカメラの～を受けた We received *inquiries for* our cameras from abroad.

ひきあ·う【引き合う】 ¶ その仕事はぼくには～わない It won't *pay* me to take the job. それは～う商売だ It is a *paying* (≒ *profitable*) business. あんなに努力したのに責められては～わない It *is too much* to be blamed after all my efforts.

ひきあげ【引き上げ·引き揚げ】 (船の) salvage. ¶ 賃金の～ *a* wage *increase* (≒ *raise*). われわれは外地からの～だ We *were repatriated from* the foreign countries.
—者 a repatriate.

ひきあ·げる【引き上げる·引き揚げる】 ¶ 船を～げる *salvage* a ship. 外地から～げる *withdraw from* a foreign country. 彼らはその地区から～げた They *evacuated* the place. 値段を～げる *raise* the price. 軍は大陸から～げた The armies *withdrew from* the continent.

ひきあみ【引き網】 a seine.

ひきあわせ【引き合わせ】 introduction. ¶ 父にお～いたします *Meet* my father. / Let me *introduce* you *to* my father. 原稿と～をする *check* it *with* the manuscript. ここでお互いに会えたのは神さまのお～です It is *by God's providence* that we have been able to meet each other.

ひき·いる【率いる】 ¶ 彼は大軍を～いている He *commands* (≒ *leads*) a great army. 彼は人を～いる器だ He *has leadership*.

ひきい·れる【引き入れる】 ¶ それはイギリスを戦争に～れた It *dragged* England *into* a war. 彼のがわに～れられた I *was won over to* his side. つい彼の話に～れられた I *was enticed into* talk*ing* with him in spite of myself.

ひきう·ける【引き受ける】 ¶ 責任を～ける *assume* responsibility. 商売を～ける *take over* the business. 注文を～ける *take up* an order. 私がその事件を～けます I will *take* the matter *in hand*. すべての損害は私が～けます I will *hold myself responsible for* all damage. 返済は彼が～けた He *guaranteed* payment. 彼は私の要求を快く～けた He readily *complied with* my request. 私は手形を～けた I *accepted* a bill. 私は50株～けた I *subscribed for* fifty shares. 私がその仕事を～けます I will *undertake* (≒ *commit myself to*) the work. 彼は重任を～けた He *took* the important trust *on himself*. 彼の身元は私が～ける I will *vouch for* him. 彼の成功は私が～ける I will *answer for* his success.

ひきうす【挽き臼】 a hand mill.

ひきうつ·す【引き写す】 ¶ 薄い紙を地図の上に置いて, それを～した By putting thin paper over

ひ

the map, I *traced* it. 参考書を～してレポートをつくった I made my report by *copying* from a reference book.

ひきおこ·す【引き起こす】¶ 彼は倒れた人を～した He *raised* a man who had fallen down. その事件が戦争を～した The incident *caused* (≒ *brought about*) the war.

ひきおろ·す【引き下ろす·引き降ろす】¶ たこを～す *pull down* a kite. 旗を～す *haul down* a flag. 聴衆は弁士を演壇から～した The audience *dragged down* the speaker from the platform.

ひきかえ【引き換え】exchange. ¶ 現金と～に品物を受け取る receive goods *in exchange for* cash. 代金～で品物を送る send goods *C.O.D.* (C.O.D. は cash on delivery の略).

ひきかえ·す【引き返す】¶ 途中から～す *turn back* halfway. もと来た道をすぐ学校へ～した I *retraced my steps to* the school immediately. 船は暴風雨のため余儀なく～した The ship was compelled by the storm to *put back*.

ひきか·える【引き換える】¶ 小切手を現金に～える *cash* a check. 姉はしっかりしているが, それに～えて妹のほうはだらしがない The older sister is steady, *while* the younger is untidy.

ひきがえる【蟇蛙】a toad.

ひきがね【引き金】a trigger. ¶ ピストルの～を引く pull the *trigger* of the pistol.

ひ

ひきげき【悲喜劇】a tragicomedy.

ひきこみせん【引込線】(鉄道の) a railway siding; (アンテナの) a lead-in; (電燈の) indoor wiring.

ひきこ·む【引き込む】¶ 田に水を～む They *draw* water *into* the rice fields. 彼を味方に～みたい I want to *win* him *over* to my side. その国はアメリカを戦争に～んだ The country *dragged* America *into* the war.

ひきこも·る【引き籠る】¶ 彼はいつも家に～っている He always *keeps* (≒ *stays*) *indoors*. 彼はひどい風邪をひいて～っている He *has been laid up* with a bad cold.

ひきころ·す【轢き殺す】¶ 彼はトラックに～された He *was run over and killed* by a truck. (run over だけなら「轢き殺す」の意味は含まない).

ひきさが·る【引き下がる】¶ しかられて部屋から～った I was scolded and *withdrew* from the room. きみはこのへんで～ったほうがいい Now you had better *leave* the place. (かなりきびしい口調).

ひきさ·く【引き裂く】¶ 彼女は手紙をずたずたに～いてしまった She *tore* the letter *to pieces*. ふたりの仲は一時～かれた The two persons *were separated* for a time.

ひきさげ【引き下げ】〔a〕reduction; a cut. ¶ 物価の～ the *reduction* of prices.

ひきさ·げる【引き下げる】¶ 旗を～げる *pull down* a flag. 野菜の値段を～げる *reduce* the price of vegetables. 近く賃銀を～げるというわさだ It is rumored that wages will *be cut* before long. 試験問題の質を～げる *deteriorate* (≒ *debase*) the quality of examination questions.

ひきざん【引き算】subtraction. ¶ 10から 3 を～するといくつになるか *Subtract* 3 from 10, and what number will you get?

ひきしお【引き潮】an ebb tide. ¶ 今～だ The tide *is ebbing* (≒ *is on the ebb*). 5 時過ぎに～になる The tide will begin to *ebb* after five.

ひきしぼ·る【引き絞る】¶ 弓を～る *draw* a bow *to the full*. 幕を～る *draw aside* the curtain.

ひきしま·る【引き締まる】¶ ～った顔 *firm* features. 身が～るような空気だ The air *is bracing*. 彼は～った体をしている He *is firm-fleshed*. ～った口もと a *compressed* mouth.

ひきし·める【引き締める】¶ 気を～める *brace oneself up*. 気を～めて仕事にとりかかりなさい Begin your work *with your socks pulled up*. 家計を～める *tighten one's* household economy.

ひぎしゃ【被疑者】a suspect.

ひきずりこ·む【引き摺り込む】¶ その男を部屋に～んだ He *pulled* (≒ *dragged*) the man *into* his own room.

ひきずりだ·す【引き摺り出す】¶ その男を部屋から～せ *Pull* (≒ *Drag*) the man *out of* the room.

ひきずりまわ·す【引き摺り回す】¶ 子どもがおもちゃを部屋じゅう～している The child *is pulling* a toy here and there about the room.

ひきず·る【引き摺る】¶ 彼は疲れた足を～っている He *is dragging* his weary legs. 彼女はスカートを地に～っていった Her skirt *trailed* on the ground.

ひきたお·す【引き倒す】¶ 柱を～す *pull down* a pole.

ひきだし【引き出し】a drawer. ¶ ～に手紙を入れておいた I kept the letters in the *drawer*.

ひきだ·す【引き出す】¶ 車庫から車を～す *pull* (≒ *drive*) a car *out of* the garage. 銀行から預金を～した I *drew* my money *from* the bank. 被告を法廷へ～した They *brought* the accused *into* court.

ひきた·つ【引き立つ】¶ あの服を着ると彼女は～つ She *looks better* in that dress. 庭石一つで庭が～った A stone *set off* the garden *to advantage*. / A single stone *added to the beauty* of the garden.

ひきたて【引き立て】¶ いっそうお～のほど願います I hope to receive further *favor* from you. —役 a setoff.

ひきた·てる【引き立てる】¶ 罪人を～てていった They *marched* the criminal *off* to the police. 彼は後進を～てるのに懸命だ He is eager to *look after* his juniors. 帽子が彼をいちだんと～てた The hat *set* him *off to advantage*. そのニュースはわれわれの気を～てた The news *cheered* us *up*.

ひきちぎ·る【引き千切る】¶ 子どもは絵を～った The children *tore* the picture *to pieces*.

ひきつぎ【引き継ぎ】(渡し) handing over; (受け) taking over. ¶ 彼は事務の～をした His official duties *have been taken over* by his successors.

ひきつ·ぐ【引き継ぐ】¶ 事務を～ぐ *take over* the official duties. 父の商売を～ぐつもりはない I have no intention to *succeed to* my father's business. 仕事をだれに～がせようか To whom shall I *hand over* the work?

ひきつけ【引き付け】¶ 子どもが急に～を起こした The child had *a* sudden *convulsive fit*.

ひきつ·ける【引き付ける】¶ 彼の話は人を～ける His way of talking *is attractive*. 彼女は人を～けるところがある She *is attractive* (≒ *is fascinating*). 彼はいつも私をそばに～けておきたい He always wants to *keep* me *close to* him.

ひきつづき【引き続き】¶ 10年間～この仕事をやっている I have been engaged in this work for the last ten years. 私は三度～勝った I won three times *running* (≒ *in succession*). あれから～ここに住んでいる I have been living here *ever since*. 戦争があるとそれに～いろいろの悪いことが生まれるものだ Many evils will *follow in the train of* war. 彼は1970年以来～代議士だ He is an M. P. *without a break* from 1970.

ひきつづ·く【引き続く】¶ ～く雨 *a long spell of* rainy weather; a *continuous* rain. 彼には不幸が～いていた Misfortunes befell him *one after another*.

ひきつ·る【引き攣る】¶ 水泳中に足が～った I *had a cramp in* the leg while swimming. / My leg *was cramped* while I was swimming. 彼の顔が～っている His face *is drawn*. 私の横腹が～った I *had a twitch* in the side.

ひきつ·れる【引き連れる】¶ 彼らを～れてピクニックに行った I went on a picnic *with* them. / I *took* them out for a picnic.

ひきて【弾き手】¶ 彼はすばらしいハープの～だ He is *an* excellent harp *player*.

ひきて【引き手】a handle; (とびら) a knob. ¶ ハンマーにも手桶にも～がある Both hammers and pails have *handles*. あの男はどこに行っても～がある He *is sought after* wherever he goes.

ひきでもの【引き出物】a gift; a present. ¶ この時計が宴会での～だった This watch was the *present* made at the banquet.

ひきど【引き戸】a sliding door.

ひきと·める【引き止める】¶ あの男をもう1時間～めておけ *Detain* the man an hour longer.

ひきとりにん【引取人】a claimant. ¶ 遺体の～がない No one *claims* the body.

ひきと·る【引き取る】¶ その子は私が～る I will *take over* the child. / I will *take care of* the child. その品物を～った We *took back* the articles. 彼は息を～った He *breathed* his *last*. (形式ばった文体). / He *passed away*.

ビキニ a bikini.

ひきにく【挽き肉】minced meat.

ひきにげ【轢き逃げ】¶ ～する hit and run.
—事件 a hit-and-run accident.

ひきぬき【引き抜き】(ひっぱって抜くこと) pulling out; (選びとること) picking out.

ひきぬ·く【引き抜く】¶ ゴボウを～く *pull out* a burdock. あのスターは～かれた The star *was hired away*.

ひきのばし【引き延ばし·引き伸ばし】¶ 会期の～を要求した We requested the session to *be prolonged* (≒ *be extended*).
—機〔写真〕an enlarger. —作戦 a delay move; (米議会) a filibustering. —写真 an enlarged photo (≒ photograph).

ひきのば·す【引き延ばす·引き伸ばす】¶ 議事を～す *delay* the proceedings. 写真を～す *enlarge* a photo. 金属を～す *draw out* metals.

ひきはな·す【引き離す】¶ 走者は見る間に彼を5メートル～した The runner *outdistanced* him by five meters in a moment. 取っ組み合っている子どもを～した I *pulled apart* the wrestling children.

ひきはら·う【引き払う】¶ 東京を～った I *removed from* Tokyo. 5年住み慣れた家を～った I *vacated* the house in which I had lived for five years.

ひきふね【引き船】a tug; a tugboat. ¶ ～で引く tow (a ship).

ひきまく【引き幕】a [drawing] curtain.

ひきまわ·す【引き回す】¶ 幕を～す *draw* a curtain *around*.

ひきもきらずに【引きも切らずに】continually; constantly. ¶ きのうは～来客があった We had *a continuous stream of* callers yesterday.

ひきもど·す【引き戻す】(人を連れ帰る) bring *a person* back; (人をうしろに引っぱる) pull back *a person*.

ひきゃく【飛脚】¶ 昔は急用の場合には～をたてた In olden times *an express messenger* was sent on an urgent business.

ひきゅう【飛球】〔野球〕a fly [ball]. ¶ ～をとる catch *a fly ball* (この場合は ball を略すと「ハエをとらえる」と誤解される).

びきょ【美挙】¶ それはすばらしい～というべきだ It may be said to be *an undertaking worthy of praise*.

ひきょう【秘境】¶ アマゾンの～ the *mysterious regions* around the Amazon.

ひきょう【悲境】adverse circumstances; (悲しみ) distress. ¶ ～に陥る fall into *adverse circumstances*. 彼は～にあったとき私を助けてくれた He helped me when I *was in adversity*. ～にある人にそんなことを言うのは残酷だ How cruel it is to say such a thing to a person *in distress*!

ひきょう【卑怯】cowardice. ¶ それは～だ That *is unfair* (≒ *is not fair*). ～なふるまいはよせ Never act *cowardly*. / Do not *act the coward*. ～なことに彼はそのことをだれにも知らせないでおいた He *was* so *mean* that he kept the news to himself.
—者 a coward.

ひぎょう【罷業】a strike. ¶ その会社は～中である The firm is *on a strike*.

ひきよ·せる【引き寄せる】¶ 彼らはいすをストーブのそばへ～せた They *drew* their chairs *near* the stove. いすを壁の方に～せた He *drew up*

ひ

his chair *toward* the wall.

ひきわけ【引き分け】a tie〔game〕; a draw. ¶ 試合は～となった The game ended in *a draw.*

ひきわ·ける【引き分ける】¶ 延長戦で～けた The match went into extra innings and *ended in a draw.* 1回は彼が勝ち2回めは～けた He won the first game and *drew* the second.

ひきわた·す【引き渡す】¶ 死体は親戚(しんせき)の者に～される The dead body will *be delivered to* the relatives. 迷子を親に～す *hand over* a stray child *to* his parents. 彼は財産を息子に～して引退した He *transferred* his property *to* his son and retired from active life. 彼は現地から～され当市で裁判されるだろう He will *be extradited* from there for trial here.

ひきわり【碾き割り】ground barley.
—麦 ground barley.

ひきん【卑近】¶ ～な例をあげよう I will give a *familiar* example.

ひきんぞく【非金属】a nonmetal.
—元素 a nonmetallic element.

ひ·く【引く】**1**〚引っぱる〛pull. ¶ ひもを～く *pull* a string.
カーテンを～く *draw* a curtain.
2匹のトナカイがサンタクロースの乗っているそりを～いていた Two reindeer〔s〕*were hauling* the sled Santa Claus was in.
2〚敷設する〛¶ この家にはガスは～いてあるが, 水道は～いてない We *have* gas in this house but water *is* not *laid on.*
3〚注意を〛¶ 彼は私の注意を～いた He *attracted* my attention.
4〚辞書を〛consult (a dictionary). ¶ この単語の意味は辞書を～けばすぐわかる You will find the meaning of this word soon if you *look* it *up in* a dictionary.
5〚数·値段を〛¶ 9から5を～くと4残る Five *from* nine leaves four.
100から30を～くといくつ残りますか If you *subtract* 30 *from* 100, what remains?
いくらか～いてもらえませんか Will you *cut down* the price a little?
私はもう1円も～けない I can't *take* a yen *less.*
給料から税金を～かれていた The taxes *were deducted* from my salary.
6〚油を〛¶ 床に油を～く *oil* a floor.
この階段にはろうが～いてある This staircase *is waxed.*
7〚風邪を〛¶ 風邪を～かないようにしなさい Be careful not to *catch cold.*
彼はよく風邪を～く He *takes cold* often.
8〚引用する〛¶ このことばはどこから～いたものですか From what *is* this word *quoted*?
これは聖書から～いた一節だ This is a passage *from* the Bible.
9〚線を〛¶ 紙に横線を～く *draw* a line from left to right on a sheet of paper.
10〚手を〛¶ この子の手を～いて公園まで行った I *took* this child *by the hand* to the park.

ひ·く【退く】¶ 彼は政界から身を～いた He *has retired* from the political world. 洪水はやがて～くだろう The floods will *subside* before long. 潮が～いた The tide *has ebbed.* 彼は熱が～いた The fever *has left* him. はれが～いた The swelling *has gone down.* 彼は一歩も～かない He won't *yield* an inch. もう～くに～かれない Now he has gone too far to *retreat.*/ It is *a point of no return.* いったん言いだしたら彼はけっしてあとへ～かぬ He never *swerves* his resolution. その問題からはすぐ手を～いた I *washed* my *hands of* the matter.

ひ·く【挽く】¶ 板を～く *saw* a board.

ひ·く【弾く】¶ ギターを～く *play* 〔*on*〕 the guitar (会話では on を省く). ピアノで1曲～いた I *played* a piece *on* the piano. 彼女はバイオリンを～くのがうまい She is *a good violinist.*

ひ·く【碾く】¶ トウモロコシを～いて粗粉にする *grind* corn into meal.

ひ·く【轢く】¶ トラックが子どもを～いた A truck *ran over* a child.

びく【魚籠】a creel.

ひく·い【低い】low. ¶ この学校は程度が～い This school *is of a low grade.* 彼は～い地位についていた He held a *humble* position. 彼は腰が～い He *is polite* (≒ *is condescending*). (ただし condescending はいんぎん無礼の感じを与えるときに用いる). 彼の～い声は聞きとれない I can hardly hear his *low* voice. 彼女は鼻が～い She has a *flat* nose. あの人は背が～い He *is short of stature.* ～い山 a *low* hill.

ひくく【低く】¶ 頭を～してください *Lower* your head. ラジオの音を～する *turn down* the radio. 枝が～垂れている The branches hang *low.* 声を～してくれ *Lower* (≒ *Drop*) your voice. その商品を～見積もりすぎた I made a too *low* estimation of the article.

びくしょう【微苦笑】a forced smile.

ひくつ【卑屈】¶ 彼は～な男だ He is an *unmanly* fellow. / He *has no spirit.* 彼の～な根性は直す必要がある His *servile* spirit is to be remedied. ～な態度をとるな Never assume such a *sneaking* attitude.

びくつ·く ¶ こんなことで～くな Never *be afraid of* such a thing. / Don't *wince under* such a thing. / Never *flinch from* such a matter.

びくっと ¶ 私は自分の名前を呼ばれて～した I *was frightened at* my name being called.

ひくて【引く手】¶ 彼女は～あまただ She has a number of suitors. / She is much sought after. / (就職など) She has many invitations.

びくとも ¶ 彼はその知らせに接して～しなかった He *was unperturbed* (≒ *was unmoved*) *at* the news. ～せず相手に立ち向かった *Nothing daunted,* I fought against the opponent. そんな出来事に～する彼ではなかった He was not a man *to be daunted* by such an incident. この家はどんな台風にも～しないだろう This house will *stand* any typhoon.

ピクニック a picnic. ¶ きのう家族で～に行った All our family went out on *a picnic* yesterday.

びくびく ¶ 私は～しながらこれをやった I did this

with fear and tremble. しかられはしないかと～した I *was afraid of* being scolded. そんなに～することはない You need not *be* so *nervous.*

ぴくぴく ¶ 馬は耳を～動かした The horse *twitched* its ears. 魚が～動く The fish *wriggles.*

ひぐらし【蜩】〘虫類〙 a clear-toned cicada.

ピクルス pickles.

ひぐれ【日暮れ】 ¶ ～に京都に着いた I reached Kyoto *toward[s] evening* (≒ *at nightfall; at sunset*). (この用法では英でも towards とすることが多い). ～前に仕事を済ませなさい Finish your work *before it gets dark* (≒ *before dark*).

ひけ【引け】(弱点) a weak point; (劣勢) a defeat. ¶ 日本人は勤勉さでは他のどの国民にも～をとらぬ The Japanese *are* in no way *inferior to* any other nation in industry. 彼はテニスではだれにも～をとらない Nobody can beat him at tnnis. (口語的). / He *yields to none in* tennis. (文語的). / He *is behind none in* tennis. (文語的).

ひげ【髭】(口ひげ) a mustache; (あごひげ) a beard; (ほおひげ) whiskers. ¶ ～のある男 a bearded man. ～のない顔 a beardless face. ～を生やす grow *a beard.* 彼は～を生やしている He wears *a beard.* ～をそる get a shave; shave *oneself.* 私は～をそらせた I *got* myself *shaved.* ～をそり落とす shave off *one's mustache.* ～をひねって考えこんだ He was lost in thought, *twirling his mustache.* 彼は～をよくそっている He *is clean-shaven* (≒ *well-shaven*).

ひげ【卑下】¶ やたらに～するな Never *depreciate yourself* (≒ *humble yourself*) too much.

ピケ a picket [line]. ¶ 彼らはストライキの間～を張った They *posted a picket* (≒ *placed a picket*) during the strike. / They *picketed* during the strike. ～ラインを破った I broke through *a picket line.*

ひげき【悲劇】[a] tragedy. ¶ その問題は～に終わった The matter ended *tragically.*

ひけし【火消し】a fireman; (消火器) a fire extinguisher.
―役 (事件の) a trouble shooter.

ひけつ【否決】rejection. ¶ 議案は～された The bill *was voted down.* その提案は45票対38票で～された The proposal *was rejected* by a vote of 45 to 38.

ひけつ【秘訣】 a secret. ¶ 努力することは成功の～だ It is the *secret* of success to make efforts.

ひけどき【引け時】¶ ～なので電車はたいへんな混雑だ As it is *the closing time,* the cars are overcrowded. 普通～は5時だ The regular *closing hour* is at five o'clock.

ひけめ【引け目】¶ 彼はクラスの者たちに～を感じている He *feels inferior to* his classmates. 偉い学者の前へ出ると～を感じる I *feel small* in the presence of a great scholar.

ひけやす 【引け安】 〘株式〙 ¶ 相場は～だった Prices closed lower.

ひけらか・す ¶ 能力を～す *parade* (≒ *make a parade of*) *one's* abilities.

ひ・ける【引ける】¶ 会社は5時に～ける The office *closes* at five. / We *knock off* at five at the company. 学校が～けたらいらっしゃい Come to see me *after school is over* (≒ *after school*). こんな格好では気が～ける I *feel shy* (≒ *feel awkward; feel ill at ease*) to be seen in a dress like this.

ひけん【比肩】¶ ピアニストとして彼に～する人はいない He *is unrivaled* as a pianist. この点ではこの町もパリに～することができる In this respect this town can *compare with* Paris.

ひけん【卑見】¶ ～をのべます I will express *my* [*humble*] *point of view.* ～をもってすれば, それには反対です I, *for me,* object to that. (英語では対立していることをなるべく婉曲的に I have a diffent opinion. または My opinion is different. などとしたほうがよい. 少なくとも I'm afraid I can't agree with you. などと言うにとどめる).

ひげんぎょういん 【非現業員】 a clerical worker; a desk worker.

ひげんじつてき【非現実的】¶ ～な計画 an *impracticable* plan. ～な考え a *fantastic* idea.

ひご【卑語】slang; a vulgarism.

ひご【庇護】protection; patronage. ¶ 彼の～のもとにその計画に加わった I participated in the plan *under his patronage.* 神の～によって病人は救われた The patient was rescued *under the aegis of* God.

ひごい【緋鯉】a gold carp.

ひこう【非行】[a] delinquency; misconduct.
―少年 a juvenile delinquent.

ひこう【飛行】 a flight. ¶ この天候で～は可能だろうか Is *flying* possible in this weather?
―家 a flier. ―雲 a vapor trail. ―場 an airfield; an airport; a flying-field. ―船 an airship. ―服 a flying suit. 試験― a test flight. 単独― a solo flight. 低空― a low flight. 無着陸― a nonstop flight. 夜間― a night flight.

ひごう【非業】¶ 彼は～の最期を遂げた He died a *violent* (≒ an *untimely*; an *unnatural*) death.

びこう【尾行】¶ だれかに～されているらしい I seem to *be shadowed* (≒ *be followed; be trailed*) by somebody.
―者 a shadow. ¶ ～者をうまくまいた I shook off *a shadow* successfully.

びこう【微光】a faint light.

びこう【微行】¶ 女王は～にて博覧会へおいでになった The queen *made a private visit to* the exhibition.

びこう【備考】a note.
―欄 a remarks column.

びこう【鼻孔】a nostril.

ひこうかい【非公開】¶ その会議は～で行なわれた The meeting was held *privately* (≒ *behind closed doors*).

ひこうき【飛行機】an airplane. ¶ ～に乗ったことがありますか Have you ever been in *an air-*

ひ

plane? 彼は大阪から～で東京にやってきた He *flew* from Osaka to Tokyo. 彼は～で来日した He came over to Japan *by air.* ～で北海道へ行く I will *fly to* Hokkaido. 私は～に酔った I *got airsick.*

ひこうしき【非公式】¶ ～の会合 an *informal* meeting. ～の記者会見を行なった We held an *unofficial* press interview.

ひごうほう【非合法】illegality. ¶ 彼の行動は～である His conduct *is illegal.*
—活動 unlawful activities.

ひこく【被告】(民事) a defendant ; (刑事) the accused.
—弁護人 the counsel for the defence (≒ accused). —席 the dock.

ひこくみん【非国民】an unpatriotic person.

びこつ【尾骨】the coccyx (複 coccyges).

ひごと【日毎】day by day ; daily. ¶ ～に寒くなってきた It is getting colder *day by day.*

ひごろ【日頃】¶ 彼は～はあんなふうではなかった That is not *what he used to be.* ～の望みがついにかなった My *long-cherished* desire has been realized at last. 彼の～の行動がよくなかった His *everyday* conduct was not good.

ひざ【膝】a knee. ¶ 彼女は～に子どもを抱いている She is with a child *on* her *lap.* ～を組んで座る sit *cross-legged* ; sit with *one's* legs crossed. 雪は～まであった The snow *was knee-deep.* その辺は～まで雑草が生えていた The weeds *were knee-high* in that neighborhood. ふたりは～を交えて語り合った The two talked with each other *knee to knee.* どうぞ～をくずしてください Please *sit at ease.* そのズボンは～が切れている Those trousers are worn out *at the knees.*
—掛け a lap robe. —頭 a kneecap.

ビザ a visa. ¶ ～をとらなければならない I must *have* my passport *visaed.* 私の5年の～は期限が切れた My five-year *visa* gave out.

ひさい【非才】incapacity ; incompetence.
¶ ～を顧みずこの任にあたることになりました I am to undertake the responsibility of the post, *though I am incapable* (≒ *in spite of my poor ability*).

ひさい【被災】¶ 地震で彼の一家は～した All his family *suffered from* the earthquake.

びさい【微細】¶ ～な説明が行なわれた Explanation was made *in full detail.* / A *minute* explanation was given.

びざい【微罪】〘法律〙 a minor offence. ¶ ～で送検をまぬがれた It was found *a petty* (≒ *minor*) *offence* and escaped prosecution.

ひざかり【日盛り】high noon ; (夏) the heat of the day. ¶ ～には1時間休む We take a rest for one hour *in the heat of the day.*

ひさく【秘策】¶ ～を授ける give *secret measures.* ふたりはいかなる～をとるべきか話しあった The two talked together as to what *secret measures* (≒ *tactics*) to take.

ひざくりげ【膝栗毛】a walking tour ; travel on foot. ¶ 東海道を～で行った We *went on a walking tour* along the Tokaido highway.

ひさし【庇・廂】(家の) [the] eaves ; (帽子の) a peak.

ひざし【日射し】the sunlight. ¶ ～で見ると3時ごろだろう Judging from *the height of the sun,* it must be about three. 夏の～は強い The *sunbeams* glare in summer.

ひさし·い【久しい】long. ¶ われわれの交際は～い Our intercourse *is of long standing.* 彼には～くごぶさたしている I have not seen [anything of] him *for a long time* (≒ *for an age*).

ひさしぶり【久しぶり】¶ ～ですね I haven't seen you *for a long time* (≒ *for an age*). ～に先日山登りをした The other day I climbed the mountain *after a long interval.* ～にクラス会に出た I presented myself at the class meeting *after a long absence.* 私たちは～で対面した We met *after a long separation.*

ひざづめ【膝詰め】¶ われわれは彼らと～談判をした We entered into *direct negotiations with* them.

ひさびさ【久久】¶ 親子は～に対面した The parent and the child met *after a long separation.* ～の雨にみんな喜んだ Everybody was delighted to have rain *after a long time* (≒ *after a long interval*).

ひざまくら【膝枕】¶ 子どもは母親の～で眠っている The child is sleeping *with his head on his mother's lap.*

ひざまず·く【跪く】kneel. ¶ ～く kneel down ; go down on *one's* knees. ～いて on *one's* knees. ～いて祈る *kneel* in prayer.

ひざもと【膝元·膝下】¶ 彼女は親の～で育った She grew up *under her parents' care.*

ひさん【飛散】¶ ガラスの破片が～した The broken pieces of the glass *were dispersed* in all directions.

ひさん【悲惨】misery ; disaster. ¶ 家庭も友人もない～さを考えてみよ Think of the *misery* of having no home or friends. ～な物語 a *pathetic* story. なんという～な出来事だろう What a *tragic* incident! ～な最期を遂げた He died a *tragic* death.

ひし【秘史】¶ 昭和外交～ the *secret* diplomatic *history* of the Showa era.

ひじ【肘·肱·臂】an elbow. ¶ ～を張る spread out *one's elbows.* 机の上に～をつく rest *one's elbow*[*s*] on the desk. ～で隣の人を突いた I *nudged* the person next to me. ～をまくらにして横になった I rested my head on my *elbow.* このシャツは～が擦り切れている This shirt is torn out *at the elbow.*

ひじ【秘事】a secret. ¶ 人の～をもらす reveal another's *secret* (≒ *secret affairs*).

びじ【美辞】—麗句 ¶ ～麗句を並べる use all sorts of *flowery words.*

ひじかけいす【肘掛け椅子】an armchair.

ひしがた【菱形】a lozenge.

ひし·ぐ【拉ぐ】¶ 彼は鬼をも～ぐ力の持ち主だ He is so strong as to *beat* even a fiend. (日常会話では He is very strong. でじゅうぶん).

ひじでっぽう【肘鉄砲】¶ ～を食う get (≒

meet with) *a snub.* ～を食わす give *a rebuff* to *a person.*

ひしと【犇と】tightly ; firmly. ¶ 彼はその子を～抱き締めた He clasped the child *in a tight embrace* (≒ *close to his bosom*).

ビジネス business.
—マン a businessman.

ひしひし〔と〕【犇犇〔と〕】¶ 彼の話が～身にこたえた His talk *came home to my heart.*

びしびし severely. ¶ 今度の選挙では～取り締まりが行なわれた *Strict* regulations were enforced in the recent election. 反則者は～処分する We shall deal *severely* with the offenders.

ひしめ·く【犇めく】jostle ; throng. ¶ 入り口で観衆が～いていた The spectators *were thronging* (≒ *were jostling*) at the entrance. プラットホームで群衆が～きあっていた The crowd on the platform *were pushing and jostling.*

ひしゃく【柄杓】a dipper ; a ladle. ¶ ～で水をくむ *ladle* (≒ *dip up*) water.

びじゃく【微弱】¶ 昨夜～な地震があった There was a *slight* earthquake last night.

ひしゃ·げる ¶ ～げた汚ない帽子 a dirty *flattened* (≒ *squashed*) hat.

ひしゃたい【被写体】a 〔camera〕 subject.

びしゃびしゃ ¶ 雪が解けて道が～になった Snow melting, the streets turned *slushy* (≒ *sloppy*).

ぴしゃり〔と〕¶ ～戸を閉める *slam* the door. 本を～閉じる shut the book *with a snap.* 不当な要求を～断わる refuse an unreasonable demand *flatly.*

びしゅ【美酒】a good drink ; a delicious wine.

ひじゅう【比重】specific gravity. ¶ 鉄の～は7.86だ The *specific gravity* of iron is 7.86. 予算全体に対して人件費の占める～が大きい The personnel expenditure *is given much weight* in the total estimate.
—計 a 〔standard〕 hydrometer.

ひじゅつ【秘術】a secret art ; the mysteries. ¶ 双方互いに～を尽くして戦った Both of them fought *to the best of their skill.*

びじゅつ【美術】art ; 〔the〕 fine arts. ¶ ～を鑑賞する appreciate *art.* ～に趣味をもっている have taste for *art.* ～的 artistic. ～と工芸 *arts* and crafts.
—家 an artist (英語では画家を指すことが多い). —学校 an art school ; a school of fine arts. —館 an art museum. —工芸 artistic handicrafts. —商 a fine art dealer. —展覧会 an art exhibition. —評論家 an art critic. —品 a work of art ; an object of art. 造形— plastic arts ; formative arts.

ひじゅん【批准】ratification. ¶ 国会が正式に条約を～する The diet *ratifies* a treaty formally.

ひしょ【秘書】(役) a 〔private〕 secretary ; (人) a confidential clerk.

ひしょ【避暑】summering. ¶ 軽井沢で～をする I *summer* at Karuizawa.
—客 a summer visitor. —地 a summer resort.

ひじょう【非情】¶ ～の世界 the *inanimate* world.

ひじょう【非常】**1**〘異常〙an emergency. ¶ ～に備える prepare for *an emergency.* ～の際はこのベルを押してください Please push this bell in case of *emergency.* ～呼集を受けた警官はすぐ現場に赴いた The policemen rushed to the spot immediately after they *were called out.* 政府は～事態を宣言した The government proclaimed *a state of emergency.*
2〘極度〙¶ 現在は～な危機だ The present time is *a time of crisis.* きのうは～な暑さだった It was *terribly* hot yesterday. その知らせを聞いて彼らは～な喜びようだった They were *not a little* delighted at the news. ～な高齢にもかかわらず彼はその会合に出席した He presented himself at the meeting in spite of his *extremely* old age.

びしょう【微笑】a smile. ¶ 彼女はとてもかわいい～をもらす She *smiles a* very lovely *smile.* ～を浮かべて話す speak *with a smile.*

びしょう【微小】¶ ～な分子 *minute* particles. ～な有機体 a *microscopic* organism.

びしょう【微少】¶ ～な損害 *slight* damage.

びじょう【尾錠】a buckle ; a clasp.

ひじょうきん【非常勤】—講師 a part-time teacher.

ひじょうしき【非常識】lack of common sense. ¶ 彼の行動は～もはなはだしい What he does *is* quite *ridiculous* (≒ *absurd*). 彼は～な男だ He *lacks common sense.* / He *is* utterly *senseless.*

ひじょうせん【非常線】a cordon ; (火事場の) a fire line. ¶ ～を張る post *a cordon.* ～を突破する break through *a cordon.*

ひじょうに【非常に】very ; much. ¶ この仕事は～やさしい This work is *very* easy. その知らせを聞いて～驚いた I was *much* surprised at the news. このところこの町の人口は～増大している The population of this town has been increasing *remarkably.*

びしょうねん【美少年】a handsome (≒ comely) young man.

びしょく【美食】¶ ～する live on *dainty food.*
—家 an epicure ; a gourmet.

ひじょすう【被除数】〘数学〙a dividend.

びしょぬれ【びしょ濡れ】¶ 夕立に会って～だ Being caught in a shower, I *have been drenched to the skin.* ズボンのすそが～だ The bottoms of my trousers *are dripping wet.* ～の着物を火でかわかす dry *dripping* clothes over the fire.

びしょびしょ ¶ 毎日雨が～降る It *drizzles* every day. シャツが汗で～だ My shirt *is dripping wet* with sweat.

びしん【微震】a slight shock 〔of an earthquake〕.

びじん【美人】a beautiful (≒ good-looking ;

an attractive; a pretty) woman (≒girl).
—コンテスト a beauty contest.

ひすい【翡翠】〔宝石〕green jadeite; jade.

ビスケット 米 a cracker; 英 a biscuit.

ヒステリー hysteria; hysterics. ¶～の女 a *hysteric* woman. 彼女はなにかというと～を起こす She will *go into hysterics* in everything.

ピストル a pistol; (連発銃) a revolver; 米 a gun. ¶ 賊は私に～を突きつけた The robber pointed his *pistol* at me. 賊に～を突きつけられて金を渡した I had to give up money *at* the burglar's *gun point*.
—強盗 a burglar armed with a revolver; 米 a gunman.

ピストン〔機械〕a piston.

ひずみ【歪み】distortion; warp; bias. ¶床に～ができた The floor *has warped*.

びせい【美声】a sweet (≒melodious; beautiful) voice.

ひせいさんてき【非生産的】unproductive; nonproductive.

びせいぶつ【微生物】〔生物学〕a microbe.

びせきぶん【微積分】〔数学〕infinitesimal calculus; differential and integral calculus.

ひぜに【日銭】¶ 彼は商売をしているから～が入る He has *a daily income* through his business.

ひせん【卑賤】humbleness; lowliness.
¶～の身 a man *of low birth*. 彼は～から身を起こした He rose from *obscurity*. / He started life *in humble circumstances*.

ひせんきょけん【被選挙権】eligibility for election. ¶ 彼には代議士の～がない He *is* not *eligible for* an M. P.

ひせんきょにん【被選挙人】an eligible person.

ひせんとういん【非戦闘員】a noncombatant.

ひそ【砒素】〔化学〕arsenic.
—中毒 arsenical poisoning.

ひそう【皮相】¶～な議論 a *shallow* argument.

ひそう【悲壮】¶～な決意で with a *grim* resolution. ～な光景はいたく彼の心を動かした The *pathetic* scene moved him much.

ひぞう【脾臓】〔解剖学〕the spleen.

ひぞう【秘蔵】¶ 美術品を～する *keep* works of fine arts *under lock and key*; *treasure* objects of fine arts.
—っ子 *one's* beloved son (≒daughter).
—弟子 *one's* favorite disciple.

ひそかに【密かに・窃かに】secretly; in secret. ¶ 式は～行なわれた The ceremony took place *in strict privacy*. 彼は～日本を去った He left Japan *secretly*. 彼はその夜～家に忍び込んだ He slipped into the house *stealthily* that night. 彼は～彼女を息子の嫁にしようと決めていた He resolved to make her his son's bride *inwardly*. ～その問題を調べた I looked into the affair *privately*.

ひぞく【卑俗】vulgarity; coarseness. ¶～な vulgar; coarse; low. ～な映画が流行している *Vulgar* films are in vogue.

ひそひそ ¶～と話す talk *secretly* (≒*softly*); talk *in whispers* (≒*in an undertone*).
—話 a whispering talk.

ひそ・む【潜む】¶この事件の裏には女が～んでいる There is a lady in this case. 彼のにわかの退陣にはきっとなにかが～んでいる Something must *lie behind* his sudden resignation. 彼は一晩じゅう納屋に～んでいた He *hid* (≒*concealed*) *himself* in the barn all through the night.

ひそ・める【潜める】¶そこで急に彼女は声を～めた Then suddenly she *dropped* (≒*lowered*) her voice. 声を～めて語り合った We talked each other *in whispers* (≒*in a subdued tone*). 彼は物置に身を～めた He *hid himself* in the storeroom. 一同鳴りを～めて彼を見守った We watched him *with breathless attention*.

ひそ・める【顰める】¶ 彼の粗野な態度に彼女はまゆを～めた She *frowned* (≒*contracted her eyebrows*) *to* see his rough manners. / She *frowned at* him for his vulgar manners.

ひだ【襞】a plait; (遠山などの) creases. ¶スカートの～がとれている The *pleats* (≒*plaits; folds*) on your skirt have come out.

ひたい【額】the forehead; the brow. ¶ 彼は～に八の字を寄せた He *knitted his brow*. / He *frowned*. 彼の～は玉の汗だ Beads of sweat stand on his *brow*. 彼は～の汗をふいた He mopped his *brow*. 彼は～に数か所の傷を負った He received several wounds on his *forehead*. 彼らは～を集めて談合した They *laid* (≒*put*) *their heads together*. ～に汗して働く earn with the sweat of *one's brow*. ネコの～ほどの土地 a strip of land; a bit of ground.

ひだい【肥大】obesity; fleshiness; corpulence. ¶ 心臓が～している The heart *is enlarged*.
へんとうせん— an enlarged tonsil.

びたい【媚態】coquetry. ¶ 彼女は～をつくって彼ににじり寄った She edged closer up to him *coquettishly* (≒*playing the coquet*).

びたいちもん【鐚一文】¶～もない I *am utterly penniless*. / I *haven't a penny in the world*.

ひたおし【直押し】¶ 彼らは城に～に押し寄せた They marched *steadily* on the castle.

ピタゴラス Pythagoras. ¶～の定理 *Pythagorean* theorem.

ひた・す【浸す】¶ 冷たい水に足を～した I *dipped* my feet in the cold water. 乾燥野菜を水に～す *soak* (≒*steep*) the dehydrated vegetables in water well.

ひたすら【只管】earnestly. ¶ ただ～謝罪する以外にない We can do nothing but *humbly* apologize. 彼は～謝罪した He *earnestly* prayed for pardon. ご回復の早からんことを～祈念いたします I *sincerely* wish you a speedy recovery. 若いころは～文学に専念した I *devoted myself to* (≒*was intent on; was absorbed in*) literature when young. それからはただもう～仕事のみであった I *have confined myself exclusively to* work since then. ～神の慈悲を祈った I prayed to god for mercy *fervently*.

ひだち【肥立ち】recovery. ¶ 彼女は産後の～が

よい She *is doing well* after her delivery (≒ childbirth).

ひだね【火種】a live coal. ¶ 火鉢の中に～がない There is no *embers* left in the charcoal burner *hibachi*.

ひたばしり【ひた走り】¶ ゴールを目指して彼は～に走った He *ran and ran* (≒ *ran for his life*) for the goal.

ひたひた ¶ 大軍が～と押し寄せてくる The great army *is pressing hard on* us. 波が～と岸に打ち寄せる The waves *lap* the shore.

ひだまり【日溜まり】¶ 子どもたちが～で遊んでいる Children are playing in *a sunny place*.

ビタミン vitamin. ¶ 彼は～の不足で病気になった He got ill through *vitamin deficiency*.
—B vitamin B. 総合— multivitamin.
—剤 a vitamin compound.

ひたむき【直向き】¶ その後彼は～に働きつづけた He worked on *earnestly* (≒ *single-mindedly*) ever after.

ひだり【左】the left. ¶ 銀行の所を～に曲がりなさい Turn 〔*to the*〕 *left* at the bank. 彼はむしろ～のほうだ (左派だ) He is rather *pink* (≒ *radical*). / He is rather *a leftist*. ～向け～ (号令) *Left turn!*

ぴたりと ¶ 車が店のまん前に～止まった A car *stopped short* just in front of the shop. ～体をへいにすりつけてやっと車をよけた I managed to make the car pass *holding* my body *close to* the wall. きみの想像は～当たった You've guessed *right*.

ひだりうちわ【左団扇】¶ 彼は今は～で暮らしている He now *lives at ease* (≒ *lives in comfort*).

ひだりがわ【左側】the left side. ¶ この道の～に学校がある There stands a school *on the left*〔*-hand*〕〔*side*〕 *of* this road.
—通行 (掲示) Keep to the left.

ひだりきき【左利き】a left-handed person; 〘野球〙 囲 a southpaw; (酒を飲む人) a drinker.

ひだりて【左手】the left hand; (左側) the left side (≒ hand).

ひだりまえ【左前】¶ 着物を～に着る *fold one's* clothes *to the left*. 彼のところは～になってきた He *is in straitened circumstances*. / His family *is going downhill*.

ひだりまき【左巻き】¶ ～の機械 a *counterclockwise* machine. ～の巻き貝 a *sinistral* shell. あの人は～だ He *is crazy*. / He *is an eccentric*.

ひた·る【浸る】¶ 田畑が水に～ってしまった The fields *have been flooded with* water. ブロンズ像が月光に～っている The bronze statue *is bathed in* the moonlight. 庭草が露に～っている The grass in the garden *is moist with* dew.

ひだるま【火達磨】¶ 全身～になった The whole body *was covered with flames*.

ひたん【悲嘆】grief; sorrow. ¶ 父を失って彼女は～にくれている She *has been heartbroken at* her father's death. / She *has greatly grieved over* her father's death. 彼女は～のあまり自殺した She committed suicide *in sorrow*.

びだん【美談】a moving (≒ beautiful) story; a fine anecdote.

びだんし【美男子】a handsome man.

ぴちぴち ¶ ～した娘 a *young and lively* girl; a girl *of early youth*.

びちゃびちゃ ¶ 水の中を～音をたてて歩いた I *splashed* through the water. 波は～海岸を洗った The waves *lapped* the shore.

ぴちゃぴちゃ ¶ 彼はぬかるみの中を～歩いた He *went sloshing* through the mud.

ひつ【櫃】a chest; (御飯入れ) a rice tub.

ひつう【悲痛】sorrow; grief. ¶ ～なおももち a *sad* countenance. ～な出来事 a *touching* incident. ～な光景 a *pathetic* scene. ～な経験 a *bitter* experience. ～な思い a *bitter* grief. ～な話 a *sorrowful* talk; a *pathetic* story.

ひっか【筆禍】¶ 彼は新聞に載せた論文で～を招いた He *had the misfortune of being prosecuted for his article* in the newspaper.

ひっかかり【引っ掛かり】¶ それには少し～がある(関係がある) I *have something to do with* it. 彼女の家は私のところと多少～がある (縁戚関係がある) Her family *is* in some way *related to* ours.

ひっかか·る【引っ掛かる】¶ このペンは～るので書けない I cannot write with this pen, as it *scratches* so. この錠前はどこかで～って動かない This lock *catches* somewhere and will not work. オーバーのすそがくぎに～った The nail *caught* the bottom of my overcoat. たこが電柱に～った The kite *was caught in* an electric pole. 彼がその事件に～っている He *is involved in* the affair. 彼は悪い女に～っている He *has got entangled with* a bad woman. そうたやすく～らない I *am not taken in* so easily. / They can never *cheat* me so easily.

ひっかきまわ·す【引っ掻き回す】¶ 机の引き出しの中を～して古い手紙を捜す *ransack* a drawer *for* an old letter. 彼の妻がひとりで家の中を～している His wife *carries matters with a high hand*.

ひっか·く【引っ掻く】¶ つめで人の顔を～く *scratch a person's* face with *one's* nails.

ひっか·ける【引っ掛ける】¶ 酒を一杯～ける *have* (≒ *take*) a drink. くぎに物を～ける *hang* a thing *on* a nail. 上着を～ける (さっと着る) *slip on one's* coat. のどへ骨を～けた A bone *stuck in* my throat.

ひっかぶ·る【引っ被る】¶ 頭からふとんを～る *pull* the bedclothes *over one's* head. 全責任を～る *assume* entire (≒ full) responsibility (*for*).

ひっき【筆記】a note; a transcript. ¶ 先生の言うことを～する *take notes of* (≒ *write down*) what a teacher says.
—試験 a written examination. —者 a copyist. —体 regular handwriting.

ひつき【火付き】¶ この炭は～がいい The charcoal *takes* (≒ *catches*) *fire* easily.

ひつぎ【棺·柩】a coffin.

ひっきょう【畢竟】⇒つまり

ひっきりなしに【引っ切りなしに】continually; incessantly. ¶ ～電話がかかってきた I had telephone calls *without a break.* 自動車が～通る There is *a constant stream of* cars. 雨が～降る It rains *continuously.* (断続的なら *continually* あるいは *incessantly*).

ピックアップ (ステレオ・テレビなどの) a pickup.

ひっくりかえ·す【ひっくり返す】¶ カードを～す *turn up* a card. リバーシブルコートを～す *turn* 〔*over*〕 a reversible coat *inside out.* 花びんを～す *overturn* a vase. ランプを～す *overturn* a lamp. 彼は炉で焼いている菓子をときどき～した He *turned over* the cakes baking over the fire from time to time.

ひっくりかえ·る【ひっくり返る】¶ あおむけに～る fall on *one's* back. 彼は～った He *overturned* (≒ *toppled down*). このびんはすぐ～る This bottle *tumbles* easily. ボートが湖で～った A boat *capsized* (≒ *turned upside down*) in the lake.

びっくり·する【吃驚する】¶ 彼が健在だと聞いて～した I *was surprised to* hear that he is well. 深夜の電話に～した I *was startled to* hear the telephone bell ringing late at night. 妙な所で彼女に会って～した I *was astonished to* see her in a strange place. 彼はときどき～するようなことを言う He often makes *surprising* remarks.

ひっくる·める【引っ包める】¶ 全部～めて3,000円かかる It costs 3,000 yen *in all.* みんな～めていくらですか What do you ask *all together*?

ひづけ【日付】a date. ¶ ～のない手紙 an *undated* letter. 5月3日の～のある手紙 a letter *dated* (≒ *of*) May 3.

—変更線 the date line.

ひっけい【必携】a handbook. ¶ 初学者～の書 a book *indispensable to* beginners. 英文法～ *a handbook to* English grammar.

ひつけやく【火付け役】a troublemaker. ¶ 彼はその事件の～だった He was the chief *instigator* (≒ *agitator*) of the event.

びっこ【跛】lameness. ¶ ～の男 a cripple; a *lame* (≒ *crippled*) man. ～をひく walk *lame.* ～になる go (≒ fall) *lame.* 彼女は左足が～だ She *is lame in* the left leg. あの子は片足が～だ The child *is lame of* one leg. このテーブルは足が～だ This table has *uneven* legs.

ひっこう【筆耕】copying; (人) a copyist. ¶ 内職に～する *copy* as a side-line.

ひっこし【引っ越し】removal; moving. ¶ もっと便利な場所への～を決心する determine *one's removal* to more convenient quarters. ～の費用を払う pay the *removal* expenses. いつお～ですか When are you going to *move*?

ひっこ·す【引っ越す】¶ 新しい家に～す *move out* into a new house. 現在の家を～す *move* from *one's* present house. 私どもは大阪の郊外へ～しました We *have moved* into the suburbs of Osaka. 彼は東京から仙台へ～した He *moved* from Tokyo to Sendai.

ひっこみ【引っ込み】¶ 家に～がちの人 a *home-keeping* person. ～思案の人々 *reserved* (≒ *shy*; *conservative*) people. 彼は～がつかなくなった He *has gone too far to retreat.* こうなったのでアメリカは今～がつかない Under these circumstances America *can't retreat with a good grace.*

ひっこ·む【引っ込む】¶ 家に～む *keep one's* house; *stay at* home. すみの方へ～む *withdraw* into a corner. 田舎に～む *retire* into the country. 店は通りから少し～んだ所にある The store stands a little way *back* from the street. だまって～んでいろ! Hold your tongue! / That's none of your business.

ひっこ·める【引っ込める】¶ 辞表を～める *withdraw one's* resignation. 提案を～める *drop* (≒ *withdraw*) a proposal.

ピッコロ a piccolo. ¶ ～を吹く play 〔on〕 *the piccolo.*

ひっさ·げる【提げる】¶ 白刃を～げて死地におもむく go into the jaws of death *with* a naked blade *in one's hand.* 彼はこの質問を～げて政府に肉薄した He *took up* this question in his attack on the Government.

ひっさん【筆算】calculation with figures. ¶ ～する do sums on paper.

ひっし【必死】¶ ～の努力をする make *desperate* efforts. ～になって逃げる run away *for one's life.* ～に敵を食い止める check the enemy *desperately* (≒ *with desperation*). こんな～の場合には手段を選んではいられない We cannot afford to be scrupulous about the means under such *desperate* circumstances.

ひっし【筆紙】¶ その渓谷の美は～に尽くしがたい The beauty of the valley *is beyond description* (≒ *is indescribable*; *is beyond expression*).

ひっし【必至】¶ 国会の解散は～である The dissolution of the Diet *is inevitable* (≒ *is unavoidable*).

ひつじ【羊】a sheep (単複同形); (子羊) a lamb. ¶ ～が草を食っている *Sheep* are grazing.

—飼い a shepherd.

ひっしゃ【筆写】¶ 本から～する *copy* out of a book.

ひっしゃ【筆者】a writer; an author. ¶ ～が考えるように as *the present writer* ventures to think. 一流の～ *a writer* of the first class.

ひっしゅう【必修】¶ 数学や歴史は～〔課目〕だ Mathematics and history are *required* (≒*compulsory*) subjects.

ひつじゅひん【必需品】necessaries; requisites.

生活— the necessaries (≒ necessities) of life. 日用— daily necessities. 家庭— household necessities.

ひっしょう【必勝】¶ ～を期して戦う fight with a firm conviction of victory.

びっしょり ¶ きみは汗～だ You'*re all in a sweat*! ワイシャツが汗～だ The shirt *is sweat-*

ed through. 彼は汗を〜かいていた He was covered with sweat.

ひっす【必須】 ¶〜条件にかなう meet an *indispensable* condition. 〜科目をとる take a *required* subject. 能力は成功の〜条件の一つだ Ability is one of the *conditions* of success.

ひっせい【筆勢】 [the power of] the stroke of the pen (≒ brush).

ひっせい【畢生】 ¶ある問題の研究を〜の大事業とする make the study of a question *one's lifework*. 〜の努力をする strive *to the utmost*.

ひっせき【筆跡】 calligraphy; handwriting. ¶肉太の〜 *a* thick *hand*. 非常に読みにくい〜 *a* very illegible *hand*. ぼくは彼の〜をよく知っている I know his *hand* very well.
 —鑑定 handwriting analysis.

ひつぜつ【筆舌】 ¶その景色の美しさは〜に尽くしがたい The scenery is beautiful *beyond description*. / The beauty of the scenery *is beyond description*.

ひつぜん【必然】 ¶〜的に inevitably; necessarily.
 —性 necessity; inevitability.

ひっそり ¶彼は〜余生を送るためその地に腰を落ち着けた He settled down there to end his days *in quiet*. 船内は〜と静まりかえった *A hush* fell over the ship. 夜のその時刻に通りは〜閑としていた The street *was* completely *deserted* at that time of night.

ひったくり【引っ手繰り】 snatch; (人) a snatcher.

ひったく·る【引っ手繰る】 ¶男は彼女の手からハンドバッグを〜って逃げた. The man *snatched* the handbag from her hand and ran away.

ひった·てる【引っ立てる】 ¶警官は男を〜ていった The policeman *walked* a man *off*.

ぴったり ¶戸を〜閉める close the door *tightly*. 〜くっついて座る sit *closely together*. 概念に〜合うことばを求める search for the words that *fit close* to the thoughts. 勘定が〜合っている The accounts are *perfectly* correct. この上着は私に〜だ This coat fits me *perfectly* (≒ *to a nicety*). / This coat is *a perfect fit* (≒ *an excellent fit*). きみはその仕事に〜の人だ You are *the right man for* the job. 〜当てた You guessed *right*!

ひつだん【筆談】 ¶われわれは〜で話をした Our *conversation* was carried on *in writing*. / I *talked* with him *in writing*.

ひっち【筆致】 ¶軽妙な〜で書く write with agile *pen*.

ピッチ ¶〜をあげる quicken the *pace* (≒ *speed*). 〜をあげて at *a* faster *pace*. 急〜で at *a* great (≒ fast) *pace*. クルーは30の〜を出した The crew put in 30 *strokes* a minute.

ヒッチハイク hitchhike. ¶〜をして東京まで行く *hitchhike* to Tokyo.

ピッチャー 〘野球〙〘ゴルフ〙 a pitcher.

ひっちゅう【必中】 一発— ¶一発〜である be infallible; never miss the target.

ひっちゅう【筆誅】 ¶〜を加える denounce (≒ criticize) *a person* in writing.

ピッチング pitching.

ひってき【匹敵】 ¶現存作家で彼に〜する者はほとんどない He has few *equals* among living authors. その大学はヨーロッパの一流大学に〜しうる The college *ranks with* the best universities in Europe. この大学は本邦で〜するものがない The college *is second to none* in this country.

ヒット a hit. **1** 〘野球〙 ¶〜を放つ hit; make *a* base *hit*.
 ノー〜に抑える allow no *hits*.
 2 〘大当たり〙 ¶記録破りの大〜 *a* record-breaking *hit*.
 その歌は大〜だった The song was *a* great *hit*.

ひっとう【筆頭】 the first on the list. ¶彼が長者番付の〜だ He *is at the head of* the list of millionaires.

ひつどく【必読】 ¶この本は学生〜の書だ This is a book every student *should read*. / This is a book *to be read by* all students.

ひっぱく【逼迫】 pressure. ¶財政が〜している The financial conditions *are tight* (≒ *are stiffened*). 金融が〜している Money *is tight*.

ひっぱりこ·む【引っ張り込む】 ¶家の中に人を〜む *pull* (≒ *draw*) *a person into* the house. ある国を戦争に〜む *drag* a country *into* war. 人をみなの話の中に〜む *entice a person into* the general talk. 人を悪事に〜む *entice a person* to do something wrong.

ひっぱりだこ【引っ張り凧】 ¶彼は各会社から〜だ He *is eagerly sought after* by firms.

ひっぱ·る【引っ張る】 ¶人の手を〜る *pull a person by* the hand. 毛布をあごのところまで〜る *pull* a blanket under *one's* chin. ぐいと綱を〜る *pull* a rope with a jerk. 人をわきに〜ってくる *draw a person* aside. どろぼうを警察へ〜っていく *drag* (≒ *take*) a thief *off* to the police station. 自分の得意な話題へ〜っていく *lead up to one's* favorite topic. 支払いを〜る *put off* payment. 彼を〜ってこい *Bring* him with you! ゴムは〜るとすぐのびる Rubber *stretches* easily.

ヒッピー a hippie.

ヒップ *one's* hips.

ひっぷ【匹夫】 ¶〜の勇 foolhardiness.

ひっぽう【筆法】 a style of writing; (方法) a method. ¶人の〜をまねる imitate *a person's style of writing*.

ひづめ【蹄】 a hoof (複 -s).

ひつめい【筆名】 a pen name. ¶…の〜で書く write under the *pen name* of....

ひつよう【必要】 necessity. **1** 〘必要だ〙 ¶彼には休養が〜だ He *needs* to take a rest. / It *is necessary* for him to take a rest.
 この子には今親の愛情が最も〜だ What *is* now most *necessary* for this child (≒ What this child *needs* most now) is his parents' love.
 健康を保つには十分な睡眠が絶対〜だ Sufficient sleep *is* absolutely *necessary* to keep one's

health.

銀行から借り入れるには保証人が～だ You *must* find surety (≒ give security) to borrow money from the bank.

植物の生長には空気と水と日光が～だ Air, water and sunshine *are needed for* the growth of vegetation.

事業にはまず資金が～だ In the first place you *must* have capital to undertake an enterprise. / Capital *is needed* to undertake an enterprise, to begin with.

このクラブに入会するには会員の推薦が～だ You *must* be recommended by a member to join this club. / The recommendation of a member *is required* to join this club.

2〖必要を〗 ¶わが社は有能な技術者の～を痛感している We *are in* great *need of* able technical experts in the company. / The *need* for able technical experts is keenly felt in our company.

3〖必要がある〗 ¶きみは医者にみてもらう～がある You *must* see the doctor. / It *is necessary* for you to take medical advice.

この仕事は急ぐ～がありますか Does this work *need* to be finished quickly? / Is there any *need* for this work to be done in a hurry?

きみはもっと努力する～がある You *must* work harder. / It *is necessary* for you to make more efforts.

4〖必要はない〗 ¶まだあわてる～はない You *need* not make haste yet. / There is no *need* to hurry yet.

それを彼に任せておけば心配する～はない If you entrust it to him, you *need* not worry about it.

彼女がそれをする～はなかったのだ She *need* not have done it.

5〖必要な〗 ¶これで～な品は全部そろった Here all *the necessaries* are gathered.

6〖必要なら〗 ¶～なら資金はいくらでも出そう *If necessary* I will furnish you with whatever funds you need.

～ならぼくが保証人になってあげる *In case of need* (≒ *When occasion requires it*) I will stand surety for you.

7〖必要に〗 ¶～に迫られれば彼も働くだろう He will work, if *necessity* compels him to.

この資金は～に応じて引き出せるようにしてある The funds can be drawn, *as occasion demands* (≒ *according to the need*).

それが～にして十分な条件だ It is a *necessary* and sufficient condition.

8〖必要は〗 ¶「～は発明の母」ということわざがある There is a proverb which says "*Necessity* is the mother of invention."

9〖その他〗 ¶金はいくら～なのか How much money do you *want*?

彼らは経済的な援助を～としている They *are in need of* financial support.

～以上の金を持ってきてはいけない You must not bring with you more money than *is necessary*.

──悪 a necessary evil. ──経費 a legitimate reducible expense. ──条件 a necessary condition; a sine qua non.

ひつりょく【筆力】the power of the brush (≒ pen); the brush stroke.

ひてい【否定】¶～しがたい事実 an *undeniable* fact. 彼は躍起になってその事実を～した He vehemently *denied* the fact. 彼がひとりでそれをしたという事実を～することはできない There is no *denying* (≒ It is impossible to *deny*) the fact that he did it alone.

──文〖文法〗a negative sentence. 二重──〖文法〗double negatives.

びていこつ【尾骶骨】〖解剖学〗the coccyx.

ビデオ video.

びてき【美的】¶～感覚 a sense of beauty; an aesthetic sense.

ひてつきんぞく【非鉄金属】nonferrous metals.

ひでり【日照り】a drought; dry weather.

──続き a long drought; a spell of dry weather.

ひでん【秘伝】¶～を伝授する initiate (*a person*) into the *secrets*.

びてん【美点】¶その器具の～は簡単なところである The *merit* (≒ *worth*) of the apparatus is its simplicity.

ひでんか【妃殿下】Her 〔Imperial; Royal〕 Highness.

ひと【人】**1**〖人間・個人〗(人類) man; (個人) a man (複 men).

¶あの～を知っているか Do you know *him* (≒ that *man*)?

彼はどんな～ですか What kind of *person* is he?

田中さんという～からお電話です A Mr. Tanaka (≒ *A man* named Tanaka) wants you on the phone.

駅前はたいへんな～だ There are lots of *people* outside the station.

若い～たちは元気だ Young *people* are full of vitality.

わからない～もあった There were some who could not understand.

この意味のわかる～はありませんか Can anyone of you understand what this means?

彼は正直な～だ He is *an* honest *man*.

努力する～でなければ成功しない You do not succeed without working hard. / Only *those* who work hard will succeed.

～の運命なんてわからないものだ No *one* can foretell his destiny.

～はみな死ぬものだ *Man* is mortal. / All *men* must die.

2〖世間の人・他人〗people. ¶～がなんと言おうと気にすることはない Do not mind whatever *others* (≒ *people*) may say.

～のまねばかりしていては進歩がない You will make no progress if you always imitate *others*.

彼は～あしらいがとてもいい He receives *others* very warmly. / He has an easy gift of making *people* at home.

ひ

～の口に戸は立てられない(諺) We cannot stop gossip. / *People* will talk.

～の話だと彼は会社を辞めるそうだ According to what *people* say, he will leave the company.

彼の～を～とも思わない態度は不愉快だ I am displeased with the way he tramples on *people's* feelings.

～の上に立つと気苦労が多い If you take a leading position (≒ If you lead *others*), you will worry yourself very much.

彼は～を食ったことを言う He says *insolent* things.

少しは～の言うことも聞くもんだ You must give heed a little to what *others* say.

まったく～をばかにした話だ It's really insulting!

～をなんだと思っているんだ Who do you think you are? (Who do you think I am? と言えばこれは単に自分の身分に言及することになる).

彼は自分のことばかり考えて～のことを少しも考えない He thinks of himself only and not of *others* at all.

～の気も知らないで，あんなことをするとはまったく情けない I am sorry that he should have done such a thing without knowing my good intention.

3 〘人材・人柄〙 ¶ 彼は近ごろ得がたい～だ He is a kind of *man* not to be met with these days.

わが国の政界には～がいない Our political world is suffering from a dearth of *talent*. / Our political world is wanting in *able men*.

彼はこの上なく～がいい He *is* extremely *good-natured*.

彼はなかなか～を見る目がある He is a very good judge of *character*.

最近彼は～が変わったようによく働く Nowadays he works so hard that you'd think he was *a* different *man*.

外見で～を判断してはいけない You must not judge *a person* by his appearance.

～は見かけによらない *A man* is not to be judged by his appearance.

きみも～が悪い How *ill-natured* you *are*!

4 〘成人〙 ¶ 私は物の乏しい時代に～となった I *grew up* in days of great scarcity.

5 〘人手〙 ¶ ～が足りなくて困っている We are troubled with the shortage of *labor*.

6 〘訪問者・使いの者〙 ¶ 彼女は～を招いてごちそうするのが好きだ She likes to invite *visitors* and give them dinner.

家にはよく田舎から～が来る We often have *callers* from the country.

病院に～をやって薬を受け取らせてくれ Send *somebody* to the hospital for the medicine.

～をやって駅まで出迎えさせます I will send *somebody* to meet you at the station.

ひとあし【一足】 ¶ ～お先に失礼します Let me precede you *a minute*. ～違いで彼に会えなかった I missed him *by a second*. きみが出かけると～違いで彼が来た He came *just after* you went out. ～ごとに水が深くなった The water became deeper *at every step*.

ひとあせ【一汗】 ¶ ～かく be sweated all over.

ひとあたり【一当たり】 ¶ ～当たってみる ask *one by one* (≒ *one after another*).

ひとあたり【人当たり】 ¶ 彼はだれにも～のいい人だ He *is affable to* everybody.

ひとあめ【一雨】 ¶ ～欲しい *Rain* is much needed. / We all want *a shower* to come.

～ごとに暖かくなる It is getting warmer *with each rainfall*. 今にも～来そうだ It threatens to *rain*.

ひとあれ【一荒れ】 ¶ ～来そうだ (比喩的に) The situation *is getting serious*.

ひとあわ【一泡】 ¶ 彼に～吹かせる *give* (≒ *deal*) *a blow* to him.

ひど・い【酷い】 ¶ ～い暑さだった It was *terribly* hot. ～い風邪をひいている I have caught a *bad* cold. この辺は夏蚊が～い The mosquitoes *are terrible* in this neighborhood. なんと～いことを言う人だ Doesn't he say some *dreadful* things! 彼は～い男だ He is *a beast of* a man. 笑うなんて～い Your laughing at me *is unbearable*. 彼は～い目に会わせたほうがいい He had better *be treated harshly*. ～い目に会った I *have had a hard time of it*. こんな～い点数は初めてだ This is *the worst mark* that I have ever got.

ひといき【一息】 ¶ ～ついてから after [taking] *a breath*. ～つく take *a rest*; make *a pause*.

～にビールを飲み干す empty a glass of beer *at a gulp* (≒ *at a draught*). 仕事を～にやってしまう do something *at a stroke*. もう～で仕事が終わる *Another effort*, and the work will be over. ほっと～ついたところだ I*'ve given a sigh of relief*. 彼の仕事には今～というところがある His work leaves something to be desired.

ひといきれ【人いきれ】 ¶ その電車の中はこんでいて～でむんむんしていた I felt *stuffy* in the crowded train.

ひといちばい【人一倍】 ¶ ～努力をする work *harder than others*; make a *redoubled* effort.

ひどう【非道】 ¶ ～な行為 a *cruel* deed; an *inhuman* act.

極悪―― infernal cruelty.

びとう【尾燈・尾灯】 (自動車などの) a taillight; a tail lamp.

びどう【微動】 ¶ その会社は不況にも～だもしなかった The company *was not affected at all* by depression. その岩は～だもしない The rock *won't budge*.

ひとうち【一打ち】 ¶ 人を～で倒す knock *a person* down *at a blow*.

ひとえ【一重】 ¶ われわれは壁～隔てて住んでいる We are neighbors living with a wall between. それらは紙～の違いだ There is only *a slight difference* between them.

ひとえ【単衣】 ¶ ～の着物 *unlined* clothes; a summer gown.

ひとえに【一重に・偏に】 ¶ ～あなたのご親切のおかげです I owe *a great deal* to your kindness.

ひ

ご配慮のほど～お願い申し上げます I *earnestly* ask a favor of you.

ひとおじ【人怖じ】¶ 彼は～しない He *is* not *afraid* (⇆ *is* not *shy*) *of* strangers.

ひとおもいに【一思いに】¶ いっそ～死にたい I wish I could kill myself *once* [*and*] *for all*. 彼は～屋根から飛び降りた He *dared to* jump down from the roof.

ひとかかえ【一抱え】¶ ～もある木 a tree as thick as one can pass one's arms around. ～の本 *an armful of* books.

ひとがき【人垣】¶ 沿道に～ができた The street *was lined with people*.

ひとかげ【人影】¶ 通りには～ひとつなかった There was *not a soul* on the street. / There was *no sign of life* on the street.

ひとかせぎ【一稼ぎ】¶ 彼は東京へ～に出かけた He went to Tokyo *to earn some money*.

ひとかた【一方】¶ あの人には～ならず世話になった He did me *many* kindnesses. / I owe *a great deal* to him. 彼は～ならず喜んだ He was *very much* (⇆ *immensely*; *more than*) pleased. これは彼を～ならず当惑させた This puzzled him *a great deal*.

ひとかたまり【一塊】¶ ～のさとう *a lump of* sugar. ～の土 *a clod of* earth.

ひとかど【一廉】¶ 彼は～の人間になった He has become [*a*] *somebody*. / He has become *a person of importance*. ～の役にたつ人間が欲しい I need a man who can *be of some help*. 彼も～の学者だ He is *quite* a scholar.

ひとがら【人柄】personality. ¶ あの人の話しぶりには～があらわれている His way of speaking showed his *personality*. どんな～の人ですか What kind of *person* (⇆ *man*) is he?

ひとかわ【一皮】¶ ～むけば彼はぺてん師だ *Unmask* him and you will find a swindler.

ひとぎき【人聞き】¶ そんな～の悪いことを言うな Don't say such *an indecent thing*.

ひときれ【一切れ】¶ ～のパン *a piece of* bread.

ひときわ【一際】¶ 彼はクラスでは～背が高い He is *by far* the tallest boy in his class. 彼の勇敢な行為が～目だっている His brave deed stands out *conspicuously*.

ひどく ¶ 私は～忙しい I am *badly* busy. 彼は～困っている He is suffering *badly*. ～けがをしたね You've injured yourself *badly*, haven't you? ～しかられた I was *severely* scolded. ～腹がすいた I am *terribly* hungry. ～疲れている I am *dead* tired. あんまり～子どもを打つな Don't beat your child *too hard*. ～腹痛がする I have a *severe* stomachache.

びとく【美徳】¶ 正直は～である Honesty is *a virtue*.

ひとくいじんしゅ【人食い人種】cannibals.

ひとくくり【一括り】¶ 荷物を～にする tie things up *in a package*. 大根は人参と～にされた The radishes *were bundled with* the carrots.

ひとくさり【一くさり】¶ 彼は話を～したところだ He has just told a piece of story.

ひとくせ【一癖】¶ 彼は～ある男だ He is a man *of extraordinary character*. / He is *a tough customer*. 彼は～ありそうな顔をしている He has *a sinister look*.

ひとくち【一口】**1**〖飲食〗¶ ～いかがですか Won't you have some? / (飲み物) Won't you have a drink?

コーヒーを～で飲んだ He emptied a cup of coffee *at one gulp*.

彼はそれを～で飲み込んだ He swallowed it *at a mouthful*.

けさから～も食べていない I haven't had *a morsel of food* since this morning.

きみは～食べたほうがよい You had better eat *a bit*.

2〖寄付などの〗¶ ～100円で寄付を集めた I collected contributions at 100 yen *a share*.

きみも～乗らないか Won't you have *a share*?

ひとくふう【一工夫】¶ きみの絵はもう～欲しい You have to do something more for your picture.

ひとくろう【一苦労】¶ 彼が大学に入るのは～だ He *has some difficulty in* entering the university.

ひとけ【人気】¶ 通りには全然～がなかった There was *no sign of life* on the street.

ひどけい【日時計】a sundial.

ひとごえ【人声】¶ どこかで～がした I heard *a voice* somewhere.

ひとごこち【人心地】¶ 彼女は1時間して～がついた She *came to herself* (⇆ *regained consciousness*) in an hour. 温かいコーヒーを飲んで～がついた Drinking hot coffee, I *felt quite myself*.

ひとこと【一言】¶ ～言いたいことがある I have *something to say*. / I would like to *have a word*. きみはいつも～多い You always say more than you have to. 彼は日本語は～も話せない He can't speak *a word* of Japanese. ～で言えば失敗だ *In a word* (⇆ *In short*) it is a failure.

ひとごと【人事】¶ 彼はまるで～のように言う He says as if it were none of his business. ～とは思えなかった I felt as if it were my own affair. / We couldn't be onlookers.

ひとこま【一齣】¶ 映画の～ *a shot* of the movie.

ひとごみ【人込み】a crowd. ¶ ～を押し分けて通った I elbowed my way through the *crowd*. 彼は～で見えなくなった He was lost in the *crowd*.

ひところ【一頃】¶ 彼は～よりずっと元気になった He has got much better than he was *some time ago*. その町も～の町とは違ってきている The town is not what it *once* was. その服装は～はやった The dress was *once* in vogue.

ひとごろし【人殺し】(事件) a murder; (人) a murderer; a killer.

ひとさしゆび【人指し指】the index finger; the forefinger.

ひとざと【人里】¶ 彼らは～離れた山の中に住んでいる They live in the mountain far away from the inhabited localities.

ひとさらい【人攫い】kidnapping; (人) a kid-

ひ

napper.

ひとさわがせ【人騒がせ】¶ありもしないことを言いふらして～な男だ He is *a scaremonger*. / He is *an alarmist*. 銀行の破綻(たん)は～だった The failure of the bank *caused a scare*.

ひとし·い【等しい】¶ XとYは～い X *is equal to* Y. PとQは長さが～い P *equals* Q in length. この表現とその表現は～い意味だ This expression *is equivalent to* that in meaning. 彼の声は脅迫にも～かった His voice was *almost* a threat. 彼は死んだも～かった He was *as good as* dead.

ひとしく【等しく】 ¶彼も彼女も～人間である Both he and she are human beings. みんな～彼に同情した Everybody was *alike* sympathetic toward him.

ひとしお【一入】¶末っ子だけに～彼がかわいい We love him *all the more* because he is the youngest of our children. ここから見た富士のながめは～美しい The view of Mt. Fuji is *especially* fine when seen from this place.

ひとしきり【一頻り】¶その歌も～はやった The song was popular *for some time*. ～大雨が降った It rained in torrents *for a while*.

ひとしごと【一仕事】¶これを仕上げるのは～だ It is quite *a job* to finish this.

ひとじち【人質】¶彼らは彼を～にした They *took* him *in hostage*.

ひとしれず【人知れず】¶～そのことに悩むことが多かった I often worried about it *in secret*.

ひとしれぬ【人知れぬ】¶彼は～努力によりそれを完成した He completed it by efforts *unknown to others*.

ひとずき【人好き】¶彼女は～のする顔をしている She has an *attractive* (≒ a *pleasing*) look. 彼は～のする男だ He is an *affable* man.

ひとすじ【一筋】¶～の光 *a ray of* light. 彼はこの道～に生きた He devoted himself all his life to this job alone.

ひとすじなわ【一筋縄】¶彼は～ではいかない男だ He is very difficult to deal with. / He is a tough customer.

ひとずれ【人擦れ】¶～のした worldly-wise; sophisticated. ～のしてない naive.

ひとそろい【一揃い】¶洋服～ *a suit of* clothes. ゴルフ道具～ a golf *set*; *a set of* golf clubs.

ひとだかり【人だかり】¶その店頭に～がしていた *A crowd* gathered in front of the store.

ひとだすけ【人助け】¶これも～というものだ This will *be of some help to other people*.

ひとだのみ【人頼み】¶～はあてにならない *Others* can't *be relied on*. / You can't *rely upon others*.

ひとたび【一度】once; one time.

ひとだま【人魂】a will-o'-the-wisp; an *ignis fatuus*.

ひとたまり【一溜まり】¶彼のチームは～もなく負かされた His team was *very easily* defeated. 彼らは近代兵器の前では～もなかった They *could no way* resist modern weapons.

ひとちがい【人違い】¶彼は太って～されることがある He has become so fat that he *is* sometimes *taken for another*.

ひとつ【一つ】**1**〖数〗one. ¶～バナナをあげよう I will give you *a* banana.
このスイカは～いくらですか How much are these water melons *each*?
～は兄ので，～は私のです *One* is my older brother's, and *the other* mine.
この中の～はあなたにあげます You shall have *one* of these.
2〖同じ〗¶ふたりは～部屋に暮らしていた The two lived in *the same* room.
きみもぼくも考えることは～だ What you have in your mind is *the same as* what I have in my mind.
彼らは～穴のむじなだ They are all of a gang.
3〖慣用的表現〗¶～やってみよう Let's have *a try*.
何事も努力～だ Everything depends on *entirely* our efforts.
皆が～になってこの仕事をしなければだめだ Everyone of us should *be united* to do this work.
パンツ～になって涼む cool *oneself* by *stripping oneself down to one's* shirts.
彼は今は手紙～書けない忙しさだ He is now so busy that he cannot even write a letter.
～には病気のため，～には多忙のため，彼は会に欠席した He stayed away from the meeting *partly because* he was sick and *partly because* he was busy.

ひとつおき【一つ置き】¶ここに並んでいる石を～に取りなさい Take *every other one* out of this line of stones. 白いカードと黒いカードが～に並んでいた White and black cards were arranged *alternately*.

ひとつおぼえ【一つ覚え】¶また彼の～が始まった Now he has started repeating the same old thing over again.

ひとづかい【人使い】¶彼は～が荒い He *works* his men hard. / He is a hard master.

ひとつかみ【一摑み】¶～の塩 *a handful of* salt.

ひとづきあい【人付き合い】¶～のよい人 an *affable* (≒ a *sociable*) man. ～の悪い人 an *unsociable* man.

ひとっこ【人っ子】¶通りには～ひとりいない *Not a soul* is to be seen on the street. / *No sign of life* is on the street. / The street *is deserted*.

ひとづて【人伝】¶これは～に聞いた This is what I knew *by hearsay* (≒ *at second-hand*).

ひとっぱしり【一っ走り】¶駅まで～行ってくる I'll run to the station and be back. 駅まではここから～だ It's *a run* from here to the station.

ひとつばなし【一つ話】¶それは今でも～だ That story is still *common talk* among us.

ひとつぶ【一粒】¶～の米 *a grain of* rice. 涙が～彼女のほおを流れ落ちた *A* 〔*single*〕 *tear* ran down her cheek.
─種 the only child.

ひとづま【人妻】a married woman.

ひとつまみ【一つまみ】¶ 彼女は菓子を～した She *picked at* sweets. ～の塩 *a pinch of* salt.

ひとて【一手】¶ 私はそれを～に引き受けた I undertook it *single-handed.* 彼らは敵を～に引き受けた They fought the enemy *all by themselves.* 私は～で勝った（将棋）I won the game *by a move.*

ひとで【海星】〘動物〙a starfish.

ひとで【人手】¶ ～が足りない We *are short-handed.* その店はついに～に渡った The store *has passed into other hands* after all. ～を借りず完成した I completed it *without help* (≒ *unassisted*).

ひとで【人出】¶ 上野公園はたいへんな～だった Ueno Park *was crowded with people.*

ひとでなし【人でなし】a brute; a beast; a brutal person.

ひととおり【一通り】¶ 彼は息子たちには～の教育を受けさせた He gave his sons an *average* (≒ *ordinary*) education. 彼に～のことを話した I told him *an outline of the matter.* 試験前にノートに～目を通した I *glanced through* my notes before the examination. ～の努力では偉人にはなれない One can't become a great man by an *ordinary* effort. 彼女は日本語を～知っている She has *a general knowledge of* Japanese.

ひとどおり【人通り】¶ この通りは～は多くない There is not much *traffic* on this street. / This street *is* not much *frequented.* この通りは～がない This street *is deserted.* 4時にはこの通りには～がある At four this street *is active* (≒ *is stirring*).

ひととき【一時】¶ 家族と楽しい～を過ごした I *had a good time* 〔*of it*〕 with my family.

ひとところ【一所】¶ 彼はいつまでも～に勤めていない He never continues to work *at one place.* / He never sticks to *one place.*

ひととなり【人となり】¶ これは彼の～をよく表わしている This shows well *what he is.* / This is characteristic of his *personality.*

ひとなか【人中】¶ 彼女は～に出るのをいやがる She avoids *society.* 彼は～で恥をかかされた He was insulted *in public.*

ひとなかせ【人泣かせ】¶ 彼はいつも～なことをしてくれる He *is annoying* (≒ *is nuisance*) always.

ひとなつ【一夏】¶ この～軽井沢で過ごした I spent *this summer* in Karuizawa.

ひとなつかし·い【人懐かしい】¶ 山中に住んでいたので～い I *want company* (≒ I *yearn toward people*), for I've lived alone in the mountain.

ひとなつ〔っ〕こ·い【人懐〔っ〕こい】¶ その子は～い The child *is friendly* (≒ *is affable*). その犬は～い The dog *takes kindly to men.*

ひとなみ【人並】¶ 彼は～の子どもだった He was an *average* boy. 彼は～以上の能力を持っている His ability *is above the average* (≒ *is more than average*). ～はずれた大男 an *uncommonly* big man. たいていのことは～にできる I can do most things as well as other people can. 彼は今～に暮らせるようになった He can now *make a decent living.*

ひとなみ【人波】¶ われわれは～にもまれていた We were jostled by the *crowd.* ～が押し寄せてきた *A crowd* surged toward us.

ひとにぎり【一握り】¶ ～の砂 *a handful of* sand. 彼らは～の人間に抑えられている They are dominated by *a handful of* people.

ひとねむり【一眠り】¶ 電車の中で～した I *had a nap* in the train.

ひとのみ【一飲み】a gulp. ¶ 彼女はお茶を～した She *gulped down* her tea. / She *drank* her tea *at a draught* (≒ *at a gulp*).

ひとばしら【人柱】a human sacrifice. ¶ ～に立つ be made *a victim* (*of*).

ひとはしり【一走り】¶ 酒屋まで～行ってこよう I'll run to the wine shop for a bottle.

ひとはた【一旗】¶ ～揚げる start a new business; make a name in the world.

ひとはだ【一膚·一肌】¶ 友人のために～脱ぐ lend a helping hand to *one's* friend; give *one's* friend a lift.

ひとはだ【人膚·人肌】the skin of a human being. ¶ ～が恋しい feel lonely. 酒は～がよい *Sake* is best when it is heated lukewarm. / *Sake* should be warmed skin-warm.

ひとはな【一花】¶ もう～咲かせようとがんばる work hard to have *one's* days again.

ひとばらい【人払い】¶ ～をして話す talk *in private.* ～を願います I wish *the room to be cleared.*

ひとばん【一晩】¶ ～じゅう all night 〔through〕. ～休めば治るよ *A night's* rest will set you right.

ひとびと【人人】people.

ひとひねり【一捻り】a crush. ¶ 彼なんか～さ I can *beat* him *easily.* ～ひねった説 a *sophisticated* opinion.

ひとふさ【一房】¶ ～のブドウ *a bunch of* grapes.

ひとふで【一筆】a stroke of the pen; (手紙など) a few words. ¶ 馬を～で書く draw a horse *with one stroke of the brush.*

ひとふゆ【一冬】a winter. ¶ ～越す pass *the winter*; (もちこたえる) keep over *the winter.*

ひとまえ【人前】¶ ～に出せる作品ではない The work *is not worth seeing.* ～もはばからず泣き叫ぶ cry *openly.* 私は～で恥をかいた I was put to shame *in company* (≒ *in public*). 私は～をはばかって泣かずにいた I refrained from tears *for the sake of decency.* 彼らは～にも出せない They *are not fit to be seen.*

ひとまかせ【人任せ】¶ 仕事を～にする *leave one's* job *to another.*

ひとまく【一幕】¶ 親子げんかの～が終わったところだ The quarrel between father and son is just finished.

—物 a one-act play.

ひとまず【一先ず】for the present. ¶ ～帰国することにした I'm going back to my home town *first thing.* これで～安心だ *Now* I'm relieved. それだけお金があれば～じゅうぶんだろう The sum of money will be enough *for the present* (≒ *for the time being*).

ひとまちがお【人待ち顔】¶ 彼は～で駅に立っていた He was standing at the station, maybe *waiting for someone to come*.

ひとまとめ【一纏め】¶ 本を～にして送る send books *in a pack*.

ひとまね【人真似】mimicry. ¶ サルは人間の～をする Monkeys *mimic* (≒ *imitate*) man. ～するオウム a parrot that *talks*. 子どもはすぐ～する Children are quick to *follow another's example*.

ひとまわり【一回り】a turn; a round. ¶ 彼は私より～若い He is *twelve years* younger than I. 彼は私たちより～大きい He is *a size* bigger than we. 工場内を～する *make a round of* the factory. 公園を～散歩する *take a walk* in the park. 池を～する *walk round* the pond. お得意さんを～してくる I'll *make my round* among our customers.

ひとみ【眸・瞳】the pupil of the eye. ¶ ～を凝らす gaze steadily.

ひとみごくう【人身御供】a human sacrifice. ¶ ～にされる be made a victim (*of*).

ひとみしり【人見知り】¶ この子はよく～する This child *is* often *afraid of strangers*. 彼はだれにも～しない He *takes to everybody*.

ひとむかし【一昔】an age. ¶ ～前の話 an *age-old* story.

ひとむれ【一群れ】a group. ¶ 野牛の～ *a herd of* bisons. イルカの～ *a school of* dolphins.

ひとめ【一目】a glance. ¶ 彼女に～会いたい How I wish to *have a sight of* her! この絵は～見て気に入った I began to like this picture *at first sight*. 教師は～見ればそれとわかる I can tell a teacher *on sight*. ここから全市が～で見える Here you can see the whole city *at a glance*.

—ぼれ love at first sight.

ひとめ【人目】attention; notice. ¶ ～をはばかる feel *the eyes of people*; be afraid of *being observed by other people*. ～をはばからず泣く cry *without reserve*. ～がうるさい People like to find fault with others. 彼女の着物は～を引く Her dress attracts *the attention of other people*. ～を忍んで会う have a *secret* meeting. ～につかぬ所に物を隠す hide a thing to a *secret* place. ～につかぬようにする avoid *notice*. ここは～が多すぎる This place *is* too *public*.

ひとめぐり【一巡り】¶ 名所を～する *make a tour of* famous places.

ひともうけ【一儲け】¶ 株で～する *make money* on the stock market.

ひとやく【一役】¶ 仕事に～買う *take part in* the work.

ひとやすみ【一休み】¶ ～する have *a break*.

ひとやま【一山】a lot. ¶ ～50円 50 yen *a lot*. 商売で～当てた He *made a hit* in business.

ひとり【一人・独り】one person. ¶ 友人の～がきのうアメリカに発った *A* friend of mine left for America yesterday. (ふつうは a friend だけでよい). 彼は評議員の～だ He is *one* of the councillors. あたりには人～いなかった *Nobody* could be seen around here. 会で彼女～が欠席だった She *alone* was absent from the meeting. ～のときは彼女はいつも推理小説を読む She always reads detective stories when she is *alone*. この問題に答えられた者は～もいなかった *None* of them were able to answer this question. (口語では none は複数扱い). この本を～に1冊ずつ配りなさい Give *each* of them one of these books. こんな仕事は～でできる You can do this sort of work *for yourself*.

ひどり【日取り】the date. ¶ 結婚の～を決める fix *the date* for *one's* wedding.

ひとりあたり【一人当たり】for each person; per capita. ¶ ～の作付面積 the cultivated acreage *a head*.

ひとりあるき【独り歩き】¶ 夜の～は危ない It's not safe to *go out alone* after dark. 彼も商売で～している He *is* now *standing on his own legs* in business. 彼は～できる年ごろだ He is old enough to *look out for himself*.

ひとりがてん【独り合点】¶ それがきみの～だ You *take too much for granted*. 彼は万事うまくいっていると～している He *takes it for granted* that all is well. (口語では it を省くこともある).

ひとりぎめ【独り決め】⇒ひとりがてん

ひとりぐらし【一人暮らし】¶ ～はのんきでいい I'm happy in *a* carefree *single life*.

ひとりごと【独り言】¶ ～を言う talk to *one*self; think aloud (say to *one*self は think と同じ意味になることが多く,独り言を言うなら say to *one*self aloud となる). 彼はぶつぶつ～を言う He *mutters to himself*.

ひとりじめ【独り占め】¶ よい部屋を～する *have* a nice room *all to oneself*.

ひとりずもう【独り相撲】¶ だれも相手にしないので彼の～に終わった He just *beat the air* with nobody listening to him.

ひとりだち【独り立ち】¶ 赤ん坊が～できるようになった The baby is beginning to *stand on its own legs*. 学校を出てすぐ～は難しい It's hard to *make one's own living* just after leaving school. 彼は～で理髪店をはじめた He *set up on his own account* as a barber.

ひとりたび【独り旅】¶ ～をする travel alone.

ひとりっこ【一人っ子】an (≒ the) only child.

ひとりでに automatically; of itself. ¶ 窓が～開いた The window opened *of itself*.

ひとりのこらず【一人残らず】¶ ～集まれ *Everybody* fall in! 彼らは～処罰された They were punished *to the last man*.

ひとりのみこみ【独りのみこみ】hasty judgment. ¶ 彼は～で使いに出た He went on an errand as if he knew what to do.

ひとりひとり【一人一人】¶ 彼らは～部屋に入っていった They entered the room *one after another*.

ひとりぶたい【独り舞台】¶ 野球の話なら彼の～だ When it comes to baseball he *monopolizes* the conversation.

ひ

ひとりぼっち【独りぼっち】¶ 彼は～の身の上だ He is *all alone in the world*.

ひとりもの【独り者】(男) a single man; a bachelor; (女) a single woman; a spinster. ¶ 彼はまだ～だ He *is not married* yet. / He *is single* (≒ *is unmarried*) yet.

ひとりよがり【独りよがり】¶ これは彼の～な考えだ It is his *self-conceited* view.

ひとわたり【一亙り】¶ 書類に～目を通す look over papers. 会場を～見渡す take *a glance over* the meeting place.

ひな【雛】(小鳥) a young bird; (鶏) a chicken. ¶ 鶏の～をかえす hatch *chickens*. ～から育てる raise fowls from *chickens*.

ひなが【日長・日永】a long day. ¶ 春の～にまりをついて遊ぶ enjoy *a long* spring *day* bouncing a ball. しだいに～になる The days *grow* (≒ *get*) *longer*.

ひながた【雛型】a model; a specimen. ¶ 届け書きの～ the *form* of notification.

ひなぎく【雛菊】〔植物〕a daisy.

ひなげし【雛罌粟】〔植物〕a 〔corn〕 poppy.

ひなた【日向】a sunny place. ¶ ふとんを～に干す air the bedclothes *in the sun*.
—水 water warmed in the sun. **—ぼっこ** ¶ ～ぼっこをする bask *in the sun*.

ひなだん【雛壇】(人形の) a tier stand for dolls; (国会) the Cabinet members gallery.

ひなどり【雛鳥】a young bird; a chicken; (一かえり全部) a brood.

ひなにんぎょう【雛人形】a doll 〔displayed on the Girls' Festival〕.

ひなびた【鄙びた】¶ ～景色 *rural* (≒ *rustic*) scenery.

ひなまつり【雛祭り】the Doll's Festival; the Girls' Festival 〔on March 3〕.

ひならず【日ならず】¶ 彼は～して全快した He got quite well *before long*.

ひなわじゅう【火縄銃】a matchlock.

ひなん【非難】criticism. ¶ 皆は彼の行動を激しく～した Everybody *censured* his behavior severely. 彼の言動に～すべき点はなかった His words and behavior *were above reproach*. 彼のその行動は世間の～を免れまい That conduct of his will be open to public *reproach*. 人から～されそうなことはするな Never do what is likely to *be blamed* by others. 彼の演説はひどく～された His speech met with severe *criticism*. 彼に～の声が高まった He *was criticized* loudly.

ひなん【避難】¶ 洪水のため高台に～する *take refuge from* the flood onto the hilltop. 彼らの大部分はスイスへ～した Most of them *found shelter in* Switzerland. 彼らはこの森に～した They *came* to this wood *for safety*.
—所 a shelter; a refuge. **—民** a refugee.

びなん【美男】a handsome man (≒ boy).

ビニール〔化学〕vinyl.

ひにく【皮肉】sarcasm; cynicism; irony. ¶ 彼はよく～を言う He *is* often *sarcastic*. / He *speaks* often *with his tongue in his cheek*. ～な笑い方をする He has a *sardonic* smile. 彼は辛らつな～を言う He is bitter *in irony*. ～にも ironically.
—屋 a cynic; a sarcastic person.

ひにく【髀肉・脾肉】¶ ～の嘆をかこつ *One's* fingers itch 〔*to* do〕.

ひにく・る【皮肉る】be cynical (*about*); make a cynical remark. ¶ ～る mock (*a person*).

ひにち【日にち】¶ 会の～を決める fix *the date* of the meeting. この仕事は完成するまでに～がかかる It will take 〔me〕 *many days* to finish my job.

ひにひに【日に日に】day by day; day after day. ¶ ～彼の病状が悪化する He is getting worse *day by day* (≒ *day after day*).

ひにょうき【泌尿器】the urinary organs.
—科 urology. **—病** a urinary disease.

ひにん【否認】denial; disapproval. ¶ 彼は犯行を～した He *refused to admit* the committal of the crime. 彼は公然と社会主義を～した He *made a* public *denial of* socialism. 彼の自分の言ったことを～した He *denied* his words. 彼は自分の行為を～した He *disowned* his own action. 西洋道徳では自殺を～する Western ethics *disapproves of* suicide.

ひにん【避妊】birth control; contraception. ¶ ～する control birth; prevent conception.
—器具 a contraceptive appliance. **—薬** a **contraceptive.** 経口**—薬** the Pill (ふつう大文字); an oral contraceptive.

ひにんじょう【非人情】¶ 自然は～だ Nature doesn't concern human feelings. 彼は～な人だ He is a *heartless* (≒ *unfeeling*) person. 不人情じゃありません, ～です It is not inhuman, but *non-human*. 小説も～で読むから筋なんかどうでもよい We read novels with a *non-human*, objective approach, so we don't care about the plot.

ひねくりまわ・す ¶ おもちゃを～す *play with* a toy. ひげを～す *twirl one's* mustache. いくら頭を～してもよい考えは出てこない No matter how hard I *rack my brains*, I can't hit upon a good idea.

ひねく・る ¶ ペンを～りながら考える think *playing with* a pen. 理屈を～る quibble; chop logic. 彼は俳句を～る He *is an amateur haiku poet*.

ひねく・れる ¶ 彼は～れた性質だ He has a *crooked* disposition. 彼は考えが～れている He has *distorted* views. 私はこの上もなく～れた女性と結婚した I married the most *perverse* woman in the world.

ひねつ【比熱】〔物理〕specific heat.

びねつ【微熱】a slight fever. ¶ 私は～がある I *feel a little feverish*.

ひねりだ・す【捻り出す】¶ 折衷案を～す *work out* a compromise. 旅費を～す *raise* traveling expenses.

ひねりつぶ・す【捻り潰す】crush (*a thing*) with *one's* fingers. ¶ 法案を～す *kill* a bill.

ひねりまわ・す【捻り回す】¶ おもちゃを～す *play with* a toy. 文章をあれこれ～す *improve* (≒ *polish*) a sentence.

ひね·る【拈る·捻る】¶ ひげを〜る *twirl one's* mustache. 電燈のスイッチを〜ってつける(消す) *switch on* (*off*) an electric light. ガス〔栓〕を〜ってつける(消す) *turn on* (*off*) the gas. 彼は首を〜って考えていた He stood thinking *with his head on one side.* これを見るとだれでも首を〜るだろう If anyone sees it, he will *fall to thinking.* 体を〜る *twist one's* body. この問題は〜ってある It's a *tricky* problem. —首(一句)〜る compose a *tanka* (a *haiku*). 彼は苦手の相手に〜られた He *was easily beaten* by the tough opponent.

ひ·ねる【陳ねる】なんと〜ねた少年だろう What a *precocious* boy he is! あの子どもは〜ねている That child *has an old head on young shoulders.*

ひのうみ【火の海】a sea of flames. ¶ 街は〜となった The whole street *was covered with flames.*

ひのき【檜】〘植物〙a *hinoki*; a Japanese cypress.

ひのきぶたい【檜舞台】¶ 〜を踏む appear on the big stage; stand in the limelight. 甲子園は高校野球の〜だ The Koshien Stadium is *the coveted* (≒ *craved*) *arena* for high school baseball players.

ひのくるま【火の車】¶ 物価の値上がりで〜だ We *are hard up* as prices are going up.

ひのけ【火の気】fire. ¶ 〜のない部屋 an *unheated* room.

ひのこ【火の粉】sparks. ¶ 降りかかった〜は払わにゃならぬ We cannot avoid a quarrel sought by another.

ひのたま【火の玉】a fireball; (鬼火) a will-o'-the-wisp. ¶ 彼は〜のようになって怒った He *became red with anger.* / He *fell into a violent rage.*

ひのて【火の手】a fire; the flames. ¶ 東の方に〜が上がった *A fire* broke out in the eastern direction. 政府糾弾の〜がますます強くなってきた The campaign against the Government has been growing more and more fierce.

ひので【日の出】sunrise. ¶ この地域では〜が早い(遅い) *The sun rises* early (late) in this district. われわれは手をたたいて〜をおがんだ We clapped our hands and worshiped *the rising sun.* 元日に〜をおがんだ I greeted *the sunrise* on New Year's Day. 彼は今〜の勢いだ He *is at the zenith of his power.* / His power *is at its zenith.*

ひのべ【日延べ】postponement; (期間延長) extension. ¶ 会は次の日曜日まで〜になった The meeting *was postponed* (≒ *was put off*) until the next Sunday. 会議を3日間〜することにした We decided to *extend* the term of the conference for three days.

ひのまる【日の丸】the rising-sun flag; a sun flag.

ひのみやぐら【火の見櫓】a fire lookout; (通例森林の) a watch tower.

ひのめ【日の目】¶ 彼の本はまもなく〜を見ることになる His book will *see the light* 〔*of day*〕(≒ *be published*) before long. 法案は結局〜を見なかった The bill *was shelved* after all.

ひばいどうめい【非買同盟】a boycott. ¶ 主婦たちはその会社のすべての製品に対して〜を結んだ The housewives *boycotted* all of the company's products.

ひばいひん【非売品】an article not for sale; (掲示) Not for Sale. ¶ この雑誌は会員に無料頒布されるもので〜になっている This magazine, which is distributed free to the members, *is not for sale.*

ひばく【被爆】—地 a bombed area. 原爆—者 an atomic bomb victim.

ひばし【火箸】a pair of tongs.

ひばしら【火柱】a pillar (≒ column) of flames. ¶ 夜空に〜が立つのが見えた I saw *a pillar of flames* shooting up into the night sky.

ひばち【火鉢】a brazier.

ひばな【火花】a spark. ¶ 薪が〜を発して燃えた The firewood burned throwing off *sparks.* 戦争の正義に関する論議に〜を散らした We had a *hot* (≒ *heated*) argument about the justice of war.

ひばり【雲雀】a skylark.

ひはん【批判】criticism. ¶ 友だちのことをそんなに〜するものではない Don't *be* so *critical* of your friends. 彼女は人のことを絶えず〜ばかりしている She always *finds fault with* others. 音楽は〜する資格がない I *am* no *judge of* music. / I have no ability to *comment on* music. —者 a critic. —力 critical power. 自己—〔a〕self-criticism.

ひばん【非番】off duty. ¶ 〜の警官 a policeman *off duty.* 彼はきょうは〜だ He *is off duty* today.

ひひ【狒狒】〘動物〙a baboon.

ひび【皹】a chap. ¶ 寒くなるとよく手に〜が切れる My hands often *chap* in cold weather.

ひび【罅】a crack. ¶ 壁に二, 三か所〜が入っている There are a couple of *cracks* in the wall. コップに〜が入った The glass *cracked.* 根も葉もないうわさのためにふたりの愛情に〜が入った That groundless rumor caused *a crack* in their love.

ひび【日日】¶ 〜の出来事 *daily* happenings. 〜に寒さがつのる It's getting colder *day by day.*

びび【微微】¶ 損害は〜たるものだ We've had only a *small* loss.

ひびか·せる【響かせる】¶ 彼は名を天下に〜せている He *is famous* throughout the world.

ひびき【響き】a sound; an explosion. ¶ 太鼓の〜が遠くに聞こえた We heard the *sound* of drums in the distance. 巨木はすさまじい〜をたてて倒れた The big tree fell down *with a* terrific *crash.*

ひび·く【響く】1〘鳴る〙sound. ¶ ホールに拍手のあらしが〜き渡った The hall *resounded* with a storm of applause.
鐘はクリスマスの祝いの調べを〜かせた The bells *pealed forth* the message of Christmas joy.

ひ

2 〖影響する〗 ¶ 働きすぎると体に～く Overwork will *tell on* you soon. / Working too much will soon *ruin your health*. 家で勉強していたので長い間学校を休んでいても成績には～かなかった Because he studied at home, his long absence from school did not *effect* his school records. 米の値上がりは生活へ大きく～く The rise in the price of rice *has a* serious *influence* (≒ *impact*) upon our daily life.

ひひょう【批評】〔a〕criticism. ¶ 彼は私の研究に対して～をしてくれた He *gave a criticism on* my studies. 彼はその案は実行不可能と～した He *criticized* the plan as unworkable. 彼はタイム誌の新刊書の～を担当している He *reviews* new books for *Time*. 私にはあの人が語学者としての素質があるかどうかを～するだけの資格はない I am not competent enough (≒ I am not qualified) to *comment on* his aptitude as a linguist.
—家 a critic. ¶ 彼は～家として一家をなしている He is recognized as one of the outstanding *critics* of the day. —眼 ¶ 彼は鋭い～眼で物事を観察する He observes things with *a* sharp *critical eye*.

ひびわれ【罅割れ】 ¶ ちゃわんが～した The cup *cracked* and broke.

びひん【備品】 fixtures ; (設備) equipment. ¶ 実験室に～一式を備えた The laboratory was equipped with a complete set of *fixtures*.

ひふ【皮膚】 the skin. ¶ ぼくは～が弱い (強い) I have *a* delicate (strong) *skin*. 彼女は～が荒れている She has *a* rough *skin*. 彼女は～がきれいだ(汚い) She has fair (coarse) *skin*. (fair はふつう金髪・色白・へき眼の意味になるから,「美しい」とは別の判断になることが多い).
—科 dermatology. —病 a skin disease.

ひぶ【日歩】 interest per diem. ¶ ～5銭 interest of 5 sen *per diem*. 利子は～で計算される Interest is calculated *by the day*.

びぶ【尾部】 the tail (*of* a plane).

びふう【美風】 a good custom.

びふう【微風】 a breeze. ¶ こころよい～が吹いていた There was *a* pleasant *breeze*.

ひふきだけ【火吹き竹】 a bamboo blowpipe.

ひふく【被服】 clothing.
—費 clothing expenses.

びふく【美服】 a fine dress. ¶ ～で身を飾る be gorgeously dressed.

ひぶくれ【火膨れ】 a blister. ¶ 腕のやけどしたところが大きな～になっている I *have got* my arm *blistered* from a burn. 背中を日に焼きすぎて～になってしまった Too much exposure to the sun *has blistered* my back.

ひぶそう【非武装】 demilitarization.
—地帯 a demilitarized zone.

ひぶた【火蓋】 ¶ 彼が政府攻撃の～を切った He *was the first to start an attack against* the Government.

ビフテキ〔a〕beefsteak. ¶ 私は～は生焼き(よく焼けたの, 中間の)が好きだ I like my *beefsteak* rare (well-done, medium). 「～の焼き具合は？」「生焼きにお願いします」"How do you like your *beefsteak*?" "Rare, please." (ただしイギリスでは rare の代わりに underdone を用いる).

ひふん【悲憤】 indignation. ¶ 今日の政界の腐敗ぶりに～慷慨(こうがい)しない人はあるまい Who does not *deplore* the corruption of the political world today?

ひぶん【碑文】 an epitaph.

びぶん【美文】 flowery language.

びぶん【微分】〖数学〗 differential calculus.
—方程式 a differential equation.

びぶんし【微分子】 a molecule.

ひぶんめいこく【非文明国】 ¶ われわれの生活は～の人たちとあまり変わらないと思うことがよくある I often think that our way of living is little different from that of *uncivilized* people. (今日では非文明国ということばは避けて「発展途上国」a developing country と言う).

ひへい【疲弊】 exhaustion ; impoverishment. ¶ 不作続きで農村が～した A series of poor crops *impoverished* the villages.

ひほう【秘宝】 a treasure.

ひほう【秘法】 a secret ; a secret method. ¶ 不老長寿の～のようなものがあるのなら教えてもらいたいものだ I want you to teach me the *secret* of longevity if there is such a thing at all in the world.

ひほう【悲報】 sad news. ¶ その～に接して家族の者は悲しみのどん底につき落とされた When they heard *the sad news*, the family were thrown into the depth of misery.

ひぼう【誹謗】 slander. ¶ 彼は敵からひどく～された He *was* basely *slandered* by his rival. 彼は私を市の公金を不正に使用したと～した He *slandered* me for a dishonest use of city fund. 彼はむやみに人を～する He *abuses* others without any proper reasons.

びほう【弥縫】 ¶ 政府は～策でこの難局をなんとか乗り切ろうとしている The Government is determined to tide over the present critical situation *by taking a temporizing measure* (≒ *by resorting to a makeshift*).

びぼう【美貌】 good looks. ¶ ～の good-looking. 彼は彼女の～に迷わされた He was captured by her *beauty*.

びぼうろく【備忘録】 a memorandum (複 memoranda ; -s). ¶ 彼に会う約束の時間を～に書き入れた I *made a memo*〔*randum*〕*of* my appointment with him. / I put down my appointment with him in my *notebook*.

ひほけんしゃ【被保険者】 the insured ; (おもに米) the assured.

ひほごしゃ【被保護者】 (おもに未成年の) a ward ; (男) a protégé ; (女) a protégée.

ひぼし【干乾し】 ¶ 腹がへって～になりそうだ I'm *simply starving*. / I'm *dying of hunger*.

ひぼし【日干し・日乾し】 drying in the sun. ¶ 魚を～にする *dry* fish *in the sun*.

ひぼん【非凡】 ¶ 彼は音楽に対して～な才能を持っている He has an *extraordinary* talent for music. / He has *a genius* for music. 彼にはどことなく～なところがある There is something *out of the common* about him.

ひま【暇】1〖時間〗time. ¶ 汽車の時間まで一杯やって～をつぶそう Let's go and have a drink to pass *time* while we're waiting for the train.

朝は忙しくて新聞を読む～もない I am too busy to read the paper in the morning. / I am so busy in the morning that I have scarcely any *time* to read the paper.

私がテレビを見ている～に彼は仕事を全部やってしまった He finished all his work *while* I was watching television.

お～はとらせませんからちょっとお寄りください Please drop in, as I will not keep you long.

彼は少しの～も惜しんで仕事する He gives every *spare moment* to his work.

彼女は化粧に～どるのでいつも遅れてくる She takes so much *time* in making up that she always comes late.

こう～がかかっては仕事はきょうじゅうに終わらない As the work takes so much *time*, it will not be finished before the day is out.

2〖余暇〗leisure. ¶ 彼は～さえあればレコードを聴いている All his *spare time* is spent in listening to records.

土曜日なら～がある I *am free* on Saturdays.

私は今～だ I *am at leisure* now.

～なときに遊びにきなさい Come and see me *when you have time to spare* (≒ *when you are free*).

～になったら遊びにきてください Come and see me, *when you have done your work* (≒ *if you can find time to spare*).

きょうはお～ですか *Are* you *free* today?

彼は～を持て余している *Time* hangs heavy on his hands. / He does not know what to do with himself.

3〖休暇〗¶ 1週間～をもらって山へ行ってきた He *took* a week *off* (≒ *got* a week's *leave*) to go to the mountains.

3日～を頂けませんか Would you give me a three days' *leave*?

～をあげるからしばらく静養しなさい I will give you *leave*, so take a rest for some time.

4〖解雇〗¶ まじめに働かないので彼には～を出した I *dismissed* him (≒ *gave* him *the sack*; *fired* him (口語)), as he did not work hard.

彼女は店の主人から～をとって国に帰った She *gave in her notice to* the storekeeper and returned to her home town.

5〖閑散〗¶ 雨の日はどの店も～だ On rainy days business *is dull* at every store.

こう商売が～では会社はつぶれてしまう As business *is* so *slack*, the firm will fail.

ひまご【曾孫】 a great-grandchild; (男) a great-grandson; (女) a great-grand daughter.

ひまし【日増し】 ¶ 赤ん坊が～にかわいくなる The baby is growing lovelier *day by day*.

ひましゆ【蓖麻子油】 castor oil.

ひまじん【暇人・閑人】 a man of leisure; a leisured person. ¶ ぼくは彼のような～ではない I can't afford to *enjoy leisure* as he does.

ひまつぶし【暇潰し】 ¶ ～にテレビを見る watch TV just *to kill time*. 夕食までの～に将棋をさした We played Japanese chess by way of *passing the time* until dinner.

ひまつり【火祭り】〔a〕fire festival.

ヒマラヤ ―山脈 the Himalaya Mountains; the Himalayas. ―杉 a Himalayan cedar.

ひまわり【向日葵】〖植物〗a sunflower.

ひまんたい【肥満体】 ¶ ～の人 a *corpulent* (≒ *fat*) man. 運動不足のためこのごろの子どもには～が多い Many children today *are morbidly obese* (≒ *chubby*) because of lack of exercise. (chubby のほうがよい感じを与える).

びまん【瀰漫】 ¶ 反戦思想が全国に～していた The antiwar sentiment *pervaded* the whole country.

びみ【美味】 deliciousness; (食物) a dainty.

ひみつ【秘密】 a secret; secrecy.

1〖秘密だ〗¶ これはきみとぼくだけの～だ This is *between you and me* (≒ *between ourselves*).

このことはもはや公然の～だ This has already become *an open secret*.

2〖秘密に〗¶ 彼は彼女との婚約を～にしている He *keeps* his engagement with her *secret*.

この話は当分～にしておいてくれ Please *keep* this matter *private* for some time.

彼は自分の病気を同僚に～にしていた He *kept* his illness *from* his fellow workers.

3〖秘密を〗¶ きみは～を守れるか Can you *keep a secret*?

だれがわれわれの～を彼に漏らしたのか Who let out our *secret* to him?

彼はぼくにだけその重大な～を明かしてくれた He confided the great *secret* only to me. / He let only me into the great *secret*.

ぼくは彼の～を握っている I hold his *secret* in my hands. / I am privy to his *secret*.

興信所に頼んで彼の出生の～を探ってもらった I asked a private detective agency to find out the *mystery* of his origin.

信書の～を侵すことは禁じられている It is prohibited to violate the *privacy* of correspondence.

だれもこの～を知らない Nobody has found out the *secret*.

4〖秘密の〗¶ 計画は～のうちに進められた The scheme was carried forward *in secret*.

5〖秘密は〗¶ 彼の健康の～は摂生にある The *key* to his good health lies in temperance.

彼に話したら～はすぐに漏れてしまう The *secret* will leak out at once, if I tell it to him.

ぼくたち夫婦の間に～はないはずだ There should be no *secret* between my wife and me.

―会議 a secret meeting. ―外交 secret diplomacy. ―結社 a secret society. ―情報 secret information. ―条約 a secret treaty. ―探偵 a secret service agent; an undercover agent. ―文書 a confidential document.

びみょう【微妙】 ¶ ふたりの意見は～な点で食い違

ひ

っている There is a *subtle* difference between their opinions. 政局の〜な動き the *subtle* shifting of the political situation. 国際関係が〜になった The world situation has become *delicate*.

ひめ【姫】 a princess. ¶ 諺に「一〜二太郎」と言う "First a girl, then a boy," goes an old saying.
—ユリ a red starlily.

ひめい【悲鳴】 a scream. ¶ 隣の部屋から女の〜が聞こえた A woman's *scream* came from the next room. / We heard a woman *scream* in the adjoining room. 彼はあまりの痛さに〜をあげた He *screamed* with pain. 難問ばかりなので〜をあげた The problems were all so difficult that we gave *a cry of despair*.

ひめい【碑銘】 an epitaph.

びめい【美名】 ¶ 彼は友情という〜のもとに卑劣なことをした He did mean deeds *under the cloak of* friendship. 恐ろしい残虐行為や犯罪行為が宗教という〜に隠れて行なわれた Horrible cruelties and frightful crimes were committed *in the name of* religion.

ひめごと【秘め事】 a secret. ⇒ひみつ

ひ·める【秘める】 ¶ 彼女はその事件をひとり胸に〜めていた She *kept* the incident *all to herself*. 彼女は彼に対する思いを胸に〜めていた She tried to *hide* her love for him from anyone.

ひ

ひめん【罷免】 dismissal. ¶ 彼は収賄で〜された He *was dismissed* (⇆ *was discharged*) for bribery.

ひも【紐】 a string; (索) a cord; (組みひも) a braid; (皮ひも) a strap. ¶ くつの〜を結ぶ(ほどく) *tie* (*untie*) *one's* shoes. 新聞紙を〜で縛って束ねておく tie newspapers together with *string* (無冠詞に注意).

びもく【眉目】 ¶ 〜秀麗な若者 a *handsome* (⇆ *good-looking*) young man.

ひもじ·い【饑じい】 hungry. ¶ 子どもには〜い思いはさせたくない My children shan't *go hungry*.

ひもち【火持ち·火保ち】 ¶ この炭は〜がよい This charcoal fire *lasts long*.

ひもつき【紐付き】 ¶ 〜の女 a bad girl *with a pander*. 〜の援助はごめんだ We can't accept offers of help *with conditions* (⇆ *with strings*) *attached*.

ひもと【火元】 the origin of a fire. ¶ 〜は彼の家であった *The fire started* (⇆ *originated*) in his house. 〜に用心せよ Look out for *fire*!

ひもと·く【繙く】 ¶ 古典を〜く *read* the classics.

ひもの【干物·乾物】 dried fish. ¶ アジを〜にする *dry* horse mackerel.

ひや【冷や】 (酒) cold *sake*; (水) cold water. ¶ 酒を〜で飲む drink *sake cold*.

ひやあせ【冷や汗】 a cold sweat. ¶ 〜をかく be in *a cold sweat*.

ひやかし【冷やかし】 mere inspection; (冷笑) chaff. ¶ 〜の客が二, 三人入った A few customers have come in merely to look at things.

ひやか·す【冷やかす】 ¶ ちょっと〜してやった (店などを) I went in just to *have a look at things*. 彼女は彼に〜された She *was made fun of* (⇆ *was jeered at*) by him.

ひゃく【百】 one hundred. ¶ 〜番目 the hundredth. 何〜人という人が並んだ *Hundreds of* people lined up. そんなことは〜も承知だ I only know that too well.

ひやく【秘薬】 a secret (⇆ magic) remedy.

ひやく【飛躍】 a leap; activity. ¶ 彼は政界で〜が期待される He is expected to *play an active part* in political affairs. 論理に〜が見られる *A leap* is noticed in argument. 科学技術は〜的発展を遂げた Scientific technique has made great progress.

びやく【媚薬】 an aphrodisiac; a philter.

ひゃくがい【百害】 ¶ 〜あって一利なし Far from being beneficial, it is harmful.

ひゃくしゅつ【百出】 ¶ その問題をめぐって議論〜した There were a variety of discussions on the matter. 5時間にわたり議論〜した The matter was made a subject of heated discussion for a period of five hours.

ひゃくしょう【百姓】 a farmer; (小農) a peasant. ¶ 彼は〜をしている He is *a farmer*. / He is engaged in farming (⇆ doing farm work). (動詞 farm は「農場を経営する」, 名詞 farmer は「農場経営者」の意味になることが多い).
—一揆(いっき) a peasants' uprising (⇆ revolt). **—仕事** farmwork. **—家** a farmhouse; a peasant's cottage.

ひゃくせん【百戦】 ¶ 〜百勝のつわものだ He is invincible. 〜錬磨(れんま)のつわものぞろいだ All the members are old veterans.

ひゃくてん【百点】 ¶ 〜満点 a full mark. 評価は〜満点による The grading is on a *one-hundred-point* basis.

ひゃくにちぜき【百日咳】〘医学〙 whooping cough.

ひゃくにちそう【百日草】〘植物〙 a zinnia.

ひゃくにんいっしゅ【百人一首】 the Hundred Celebrated Poems.

ひゃくねん【百年】 one hundred years.
¶ 〜の計を立てる make a *far-sighted* policy.
—祭 the centenary. **—目** ¶ 見つかったが〜目 You're doomed now that I've caught you.

ひゃくパーセント【百パーセント】 one hundred percent. ¶ 効果〜だ It is *one hundred percent* efficacious. 投票率は〜だった The voting average was *one hundred percent*.

ひゃくばい【百倍】 ¶ 〜する increase hundredfold. 勇気〜して出発した We started *with redoubled courage*.

ひゃくぶん【百分】 ¶ 〜の1 one hundredth.
—率 percentage.

ひゃくぶん【百聞】 ¶ 〜は一見にしかず (諺) *Seeing is believing*.

ひゃくまん【百万】 one million. ¶ 〜の味方を得たという感じだ I feel as if I had *a number of* supporters.

ひゃくめんそう【百面相】 comic-faces making.

ひゃくようばこ【百葉箱】〘気象〙a screen.
ひゃくらい【百雷】¶〜のようなものすごい音だった It was a *thunderous* sound.
ひやけ【日焼け】sunburn; suntan; tan. ¶〜する be sunburnt; be tanned; tan (tan がいちばんよい意味で用いられる). 〜した顔 a *tanned* face; a *sunburnt* face (sunburnt は痛みを感じたり醜い感じを与えたりする). その〜はスキーのためですか Is it from skiing that you *have got* so much *sunburnt*? 私はすぐ〜する I *get sunburnt* easily.
ヒヤシンス〘植物〙a hyacinth.
ひや·す【冷やす】(水で) cool; (氷で) ice. ¶〜した水 *cooled* water. これを〜さないようにしなさい Keep this warm. スイカが冷蔵庫に〜してある You can find a watermelon *cooled* in the refrigerator. 頭を〜して考えなさい You must *cool* your head.
ビヤだる【ビヤ樽】a beer barrel. ¶彼は〜のような腹をしている He *is potbellied*.
ひゃっか【百花】¶この庭園はまさに〜撩乱(りょうらん)だ The garden is indeed adorned with every variety of flowers.
ひゃっかじてん【百科事典】an encyclopedia. ¶〜で調べる consult *an encyclopedia*; look up (*something*) in *an encyclopedia*.
ひゃっかぜんしょ【百科全書】an encyclopedia; a cyclopedia. ¶〜的知識 *encyclopedic* knowledge.
ひゃっかてん【百貨店】㊅ a department store; ㊆ the stores.
ひゃっきやこう【百鬼夜行】¶〜のありさまだった It was a hell of sight.
ひゃっぱつひゃくちゅう【百発百中】¶彼の射撃は〜だ His shot never misses the mark. / He is a marksman that never misses.
ひゃっぽう【百方】¶〜手を尽くしたがだめだった I tried every means possible in vain. / I left no stone unturned but in vain.
ひやとい【日雇い】(仕事) daily work; (人) a day laborer. ¶彼は〜で働いている He *is working by the day*.
ひやひや【冷や冷や】¶けさは〜する It *is chilly* this morning. あんなに〜したことはない I *have* never *been* so much *frightened*. 曲芸を見て〜した I *felt thrilled* to see the acrobatic feat.
ビヤホール a beer hall; a beer house.
ひやみず【冷や水】cold water. ¶年寄りの〜 Old men often forget their own age and do what young men generally do.
ひやむぎ【冷や麦】iced noodles.
ひやめし【冷や飯】¶〜を食わされた(冷遇された) I was treated coldly.
ひややか【冷ややか】¶〜に coldly; (態度が) indifferently. 風は〜だ The wind *is chilly*. 彼の態度は私には〜に見えた His manners impressed me *cold*.
ひやり【冷やり】¶〜とする feel chilled. 暗やみで声をかけられて〜とした When I was called in the dark, *a cold shiver ran through me* (≒ *I felt a shiver in the spine*).

ひゆ【比喩】a figure of speech; (a) simile. ¶〜的に言うとこうなる *Figuratively* speaking, it is like this. 〜的に言ったにすぎない I only said it by way of *a metaphor*.
ヒューズ a fuse. ¶〜が切れた The *fuse* got blown out. 〜が飛んでいる The *fuse* is burnt out. 〜を取り替える replace the *fuse*.
ひゅうひゅう ¶風が〜吹いている The wind is blowing *with a whistle*. / The wind *is whistling*.
ぴゅうぴゅう ¶風が〜吹いている The wind *is whistling*. 弾丸が〜飛んでいた Bullets *were whizzing*.
ヒューマニスト a humanist.
ヒューマニズム humanism.
ビュッフェ a buffet.
びゅん ¶〜と飛ぶ zip. 〜と飛ばす send (*a thing*) *zipping*. 〜と石が飛んできた A stone came *zipping*. 矢は〜と音を立てて飛んでいった An arrow flew away *zipping*.
ひょいと ¶〜小川を跳び越えた I leaped *lightly* across the brook. 〜外をながめた I looked out of doors *in spite of myself*. 名案が〜頭をかすめた A splendid idea *flashed* across my mind. 彼が〜頭をのぞかせた He *popped his head* out of the room.
ひょいひょい (ときどき) now and then; (軽々と) lightly. ¶彼は〜跳ぶように走っていった He went away jumping (≒ skipping) *lightly*. 彼は足場の上を〜渡っていった He went away *nimbly* on the scaffold.
ひょう【表】a list. ¶項目を〜にする make *a list* of items. 彼は〜に載っている He is on the *list* (≒ *roster*). それを〜に書き入れた I noted it down in the *table*.
一覧— a catalog. 時間— a timetable; a schedule. 成績— a report card. 統計— a stational table.
ひょう【俵】¶米百〜 one hundred *bags* of rice. 綿10〜 ten *bales* of cotton.
ひょう【票】a vote. ¶〜を集める gather *votes*. 〜をとる win *a vote*. 彼に1〜を投じた I cast *a vote for* him. その法案は150〜対92〜で可決された The bill was passed *by a vote of* 150 to 92.
固定— fixed votes. 浮動— floating votes.
ひょう【評】criticism; reputation. ¶作品は傑作との〜を得た The work *was reputed* to be a masterpiece. 彼は皮肉屋との〜がある He *is spoken of as* a cynic.
ひょう【豹】a leopard; a panther.
ひょう【雹】hail. ¶〜が降っている It *is hailing*.
ひよう【費用】expenses. ¶〜はどのくらいですか How much will it *cost*? 〜は少なくとも5万円はかかる The *expenses* will amount to 50,000 yen at least. 〜にかまわず買ってよろしい You may buy it regardless of *expense*. 〜ならいくらでも出そう I will *go to any expense*. もっと〜を切り詰めなさい Cut down your *expenses* more. 会社の〜でそんなことはできない I can never do it *at the cost of* the company.
びょう【秒】a second. ¶5分20〜 five min-

utes twenty *seconds.* タイムを〜まではかる clock the time *to the second.*

—針 the second hand. —読み [a] countdown.

びょう【鋲】a rivet; (画鋲) a take; a thumbtack; (くつの底の) a hobnail. ¶ カレンダーを〜でとめる *tack* a calendar on to the wall.

びょう【廟】a mausoleum (複 mausolea).

びよう【美容】beauty. ¶ 彼女は〜に注意する She is careful in *cosmetics.*

—院 a beauty parlor. —師 a beauty artist; a beautician. —体操 beauty exercise; calisthenics.

ひょういつ【飄逸】¶ 〜な男 a *happy-go-lucky* man.

ひょういもじ【表意文字】an ideograph; an ideogram.

びょういん【病院】a hospital. ¶ 〜に入る enter [the] *hospital*; be hospitalized. 〜へ通う attend *hospital.* 彼は〜に入っている He *is in* [the] *hospital.* 彼は〜へ入れるべきだ He should be sent to [the] *hospital.* (米 では the を用いることが多い).

—船 a hospital ship. 小児科— a children's hospital. 精神— a mental hospital. 総合— a general hospital.

ひょうおんもじ【表音文字】a phonogram.

ひょうか【評価】valuation; (成績の) evaluation. ¶ 人物を〜する *judge* a person. 品物を高く(低く)〜する *rate* an article high (low). きみは事を過大に〜しすぎる You *overestimate* everything. 過小〜するのが彼の癖だ He habitually *underestimates* everything. 詩人としては彼より彼女を高く〜する I put her above him as a poet. 彼の本は国の内外で高く〜されている His book *is valued* highly both at home and abroad.

ひょうが【氷河】a glacier.

—期 the glacial period. —時代 the glacial age.

びょうが【病臥】¶ 〜する be sick (≒ ill) in bed. 長く〜中の母親が気の毒だ I feel sorry for my *bedridden* mother.

ひょうかい【氷解】¶ 疑問は〜した The doubts *were cleared.* これですっかり心配が〜した This *has dispelled* all my fears.

ひょうかい【氷海】a frozen sea.

ひょうかん【剽悍】¶ 〜な fearless; ferocious.

ひょうき【表記】¶ 〜のあて名 the address *mentioned on the face.*

ひょうぎ【評議】discussion; conference. ¶ その問題を〜した We *counseled* together about the matter. 〜一決した The *conference* has come to a decision. 目下〜中である The problem is under *discussion.*

—員 a councilor. —会 a council.

びょうき【病気】sickness; illness. ¶ 彼は〜だ He *is sick.* (sick は米語で, イギリスでは ill を用いる. イギリスで sick と言うと,「胸が悪い・吐き気がする」の意味). 彼は〜で寝ている He *is sick* in bed. 息子さんのご〜はいかがですか *How* is your son? あなたの〜は過労からきている Your *sickness* comes of overwork. 彼は〜にかかりやすい He soon *gets sick.* 彼の〜は完全には回復していない He has not completely recovered from his *sickness.* 彼は〜がちだ He *is sickly.* 彼は心臓に〜がある He has heart *trouble.* この辺りに妙な〜が発生した A strange *disease* broke out in this neighborhood. 彼の〜を見舞いに行きたい I want to inquire after his *health.*

ひょうきん【剽軽】¶ 彼はよく〜なことを言う He often says *funny* things. 〜なまねはよせ Never *play the fool.*

—者 a jovial person.

びょうきん【病菌】a [disease] germ; a virus.

ひょうぐ【表具】mounting. ¶ 〜する mount.

—師 a mounter; a paper hanger.

びょうく【病苦】the pain of sickness (≒ illness). ¶ 彼は〜に苦しんでいる He is suffering from *sickness.* 彼の〜を慰めたい I am going to relieve his *pain of sickness.*

びょうく【病軀】¶ 彼は〜をおして働いている He is working hard in spite of his sickness.

ひょうけつ【氷結】¶ 港が〜している The harbor *is icebound.* この港は冬じゅう〜しない This harbor *is ice-free* throughout the winter.

ひょうけつ【票決】decision by voting. ¶ その件を〜する *vote* (≒ *take a vote*) on the matter.

—権 a vote.

ひょうけつ【評決】[a] decision; (陪審官などの) a verdict.

びょうけつ【病欠】absence because of sickness. ¶ きのう彼は〜した Yesterday he *was absent because he was sick.* その日の欠席は〜ではなかった He absented himself that day, but he was not sick.

ひょうげん【氷原】an ice field.

ひょうげん【表現】[an] expression. ¶ 彼は適切な〜を用いている He uses *a* proper *expression.* 自分の思うことを〜する *express* what *one* thinks. この音楽は春の情景を〜している This music *represents* a scene of the spring.

—力 *one's* power of expression.

びょうげん【病原】—学 etiology. —菌 a germ; a virus. —体 a pathogenic organ.

ひょうご【標語】a motto; a slogan; a watchword.

びょうご【病後】convalescence. ¶ 〜の老人 a *convalescent* old man. 彼女は〜でまだ体が弱っている She is still weak *after her sickness.*

ひょうこう【標高】⇒かいばつ

びょうこん【病根】¶ 〜は深い The *disease* is deeply rooted. 〜をたつ(残す) stamp out (leave) the *seeds of disease* (≒ *trouble*).

ひょうさつ【表札】a name plate; a door plate. ¶ 〜を出す put up *a name plate* (欧米では表札はあまりなくかわりに house number (家の番号) をつけるが, ひとつの番号は1軒だけ).

ひょうざん【氷山】an iceberg. ¶ 今回の事件はほんの〜の一角にすぎない The latest incident is only the tip of *the iceberg.*

ひょうし【拍子】time; rhythm; measure; beat; (はずみ) chance. ¶ 音楽に〜を合わせて踊る dance *to* the music. みんなは手足で〜をとりながら大声で歌った We sang loudly *keeping* (≒

beating) *time* with our hands and feet. コーラスは〜がそろっている(いない) The chorus *is in* (*is out of*) *beat*. 子どもはくしゃみをした〜にコップをとり落とした The child let fall his glass *when* he sneezed. なにかの〜で電流が切れた The electric current failed *by some chance*.

二(三)── 〘音楽〙 binary (triple) time. とんとん── ¶計画はとんとん〜に進んでいる The scheme is in active (≒ gratifying) progress. / Steady progress is being made with the scheme.

ひょうし【表紙】a cover. ¶その本の〜は紙(皮;布)だ The book is bound in paper (leather; cloth). 〜のカバー a 〔book〕 jacket.

表── a front cover. 裏── a back cover.

ひょうじ【表示】indication; 〔an〕 expression. ¶その件に関し彼はなんら意志〜はしていない He *has* not yet *expressed* his opinion about the matter. 価格の〜がない場合はしばしば高いことがある Where prices *are* not *posted*, they are often high.

びょうし【病死】death from sickness; (事故死に対して) a natural death. ¶彼はパリで〜した He died of sickness in Paris.

ひょうしき【標識】a sign; a mark.

航空── a radio beacon. 交通── a traffic sign. 航路── a buoy. 水深── a depth marker. 里程── a mileage marker. 地上── a ground mark.

ひょうしぎ【拍子木】〔wooden〕 clappers.

びょうしつ【病室】a sickroom; (病院の) a 〔sick〕 ward.

隔離── an isolation ward.

ひょうしぬけ【拍子抜け】¶工場が移転を決定したので公害防止運動は〜となってしまった As the factory decided to move out, the anti-pollution campaign *lost momentum*.

ひょうしゃ【評者】a critic; a reviewer; a commenter; a commentator.

びょうしゃ【描写】description; depiction. ¶新聞記事はその試合の息詰まるようなクライマックスを生き生きと〜している The newspaper report gives *a* vivid *description* of the exciting climax of the match. その小説家は人物〜ばかりでなく心理〜も得意としている The novelist is a master hand at psycological *description* as well as character *portrayal*.

ひょうしゃく【評釈】〔critical〕 notes; annotation. ¶〜つきのリア王の新版 a new edition of *King Lear* with *notes*.

びょうじゃく【病弱】¶私は生まれつき〜だ I *am weak* (≒ *am delicate*) by nature. 〜な少年 a *sickly* boy.

びょうしゅつ【描出】¶おびえた表情を〜する *portray* (≒ *describe*) the coward look.

ひょうじゅん【標準】a standard. ¶この子どもの身長は〜だ This child is of *average* stature. この国は生活〜が高い The *standard* of living is high in this country. 彼女のバイオリンの能力は〜に達しない Her violin playing ability does not *come up to the standard*. 彼のやることは〜以下だ What he does *is below the standard*. 金持ちであることは人間の価値を決める〜にはならない Wealth is not *a criterion* of the merit of a man. 彼の言うことは〜的な見解だ What he says is a *standard* opinion.

──語 the standard language. ──時 the standard time. 万国──時 the universal time.

ひょうしょう【表象】〘哲学〙 an idea; 〘心理学〙 a representation; (象徴) an emblem; a symbol.

¶ハトは平和の〜とされている A dove is considered to be *a symbol* (≒ *an emblem*) of peace. 白は純潔を〜する White *stands for* purity.

ひょうしょう【表彰】〔official〕 commendation. ¶彼はおぼれかけた子どもを救って〜された He *was officially commended* (≒ *won official commendation*) for rescuing a child from drowning.

──式 a commendation. ──状 a citation; a testimonial. ──台 an honor platform.

ひょうじょう【表情】〔an〕 expression; a look. ¶彼はにわかに怒りの〜を見せた Suddenly he showed *an* angry *look*. /*An expression* of rage suddenly came into his face. 新聞がその事件に対する現地の人たちの〜を伝えている The paper reports the *reaction* to the incident on the part of the residents there. 〜のゆたかな俳優 an *expressive* actor.

ひょうじょう【評定】a conference.

小田原── an inconclusive conference.

びょうしょう【病床】a sickbed. ¶彼は〜についている He *is sick in* (≒ *is confined to*) *bed*. / He *is laid up*.

びょうじょう【病状】the condition of a patient. ¶〜はいかがですか(医師に) How is his *condition*? 患者の〜に変化はない There has been no change in the *condition* of the patient.

びょうしん【秒針】the second hand (*of* a watch).

びょうしん【病身】¶彼は〜だ He *is sickly*. / He *is of a delicate constitution*.

ひょう·する【表する】¶敬意を〜する *pay one's* respects (*to*). 謝意を〜する *show* (≒ *express*) *one's* gratitude. 祝意を〜する *offer one's* congratulations. 弔意を〜する *present one's* condolences. 満足の意を〜する *express* a satisfaction (*at*). 首相は閣僚が関係した汚職事件に遺憾の意を〜した The premier *expressed* his regret at the graft case in which some cabinet ministers were involved.

ひょうせつ【氷雪】ice and snow. ¶この港は冬季は〜に閉ざされる This port *is icebound* during the winter.

ひょうせつ【剽窃】plagiarism; 〔literary〕 piracy. ¶〜する pirate. 著者は〜を認めた The author admitted his *piracy*.

ひょうぜん【飄然】¶〜と casually; (あてもなく) aimlessly. 〜と旅に出る go on an *aimless* trip; go on a trip *aimlessly*.

ひょうそ【瘭疽】〘医学〙 whitlow; felon.

ひ

ひょうそう【表装】(絵の) mounting ; (本などの) binding ; (商品の) makeup. ¶ 本を～する *bind* a book (in a paper). 絵を～する *mount* a picture.

びょうそう【病巣】〘医学〙a focus (複 focuses, foci). ¶ ～を摘出する extract *a focus.*

びょうそく【秒速】the speed per second. ¶ ～1マイルで at a speed of one mile a second.

ひょうだい【表題・標題】(本の) a title ; (新聞記事などの) a headline ; a head ; 米 a caption.

ひょうたん【氷炭】¶ ～相いれず They are contradictory to each other.

ひょうたん【瓢箪】〘植物〙a gourd. ¶ ～から駒(こま) Unexpected things often happen. / Things will happen.

ひょうちゃく【漂着】¶ 女性の死体が岸に～した The body of a woman *was washed ashore.*

ひょうちゅう【氷柱】an ice pillar ; (つらら) an icicle.

ひょうちゅう【評注】¶ ～のついた本 an *annotated* book. シェイクスピア劇～ *notes and comments* on Shakespeare's plays.

ひょうてい【評定】rating ; evaluation. 勤務— efficiency rating system.

ひょうてき【標的】a target ; a mark. ¶ ～の黒星 a bull's eye. ～にむかって銃を発射した We fired (≒ shot) our guns at the *target.* —船 a target vessel.

びょうてき【病的】¶ ～な心理 *abnormal* psychology. あんなことをするのは～な性格のためだ It is because of his *abnormal* character that he does things like that.

ひょうてん【氷点】the freezing point. ¶ けさ寒暖計は～下5度だった This morning the thermometer stood five degrees *below zero.* この地方では冬でも気温が～下に下がることはめったにない In this region, the temperature rarely falls *below zero* (≒ *below the freezing point*) even in winter.

ひょうてん【評点】examination marks ; a grade. ¶ あの先生は私の作文によい～をつけてくれない That teacher does not give high *marks* to my composition.

ひょうでん【評伝】a critical biography (*of* Samuel Johnson).

びょうとう【病棟】a ward. 隔離— an isolation ward. 外科— a surgical ward.

びょうどう【平等】equality. ¶ すべての人は生まれながらにして～である All men are created *equal.* すべての人は法の前には～である All men *are* absolutely *equal* before the law. 彼の息子たちは遺産を～に分けた His sons divided his fortune *equally* among them. 教師は生徒たちを～に取り扱わねばならぬ Teachers must treat their students *impartially* (≒ *without discrimination*).

びょうどく【病毒】disease germs. ¶ ハエがその～を運んでくる Flies bring *disease germs.*

びょうにん【病人】a sick person ; (患者) a patient ; a case ; (総称) the sick. ¶ 彼はまるで～みたいな顔をしている He looks as if he *were sick.*

ひょうのう【氷嚢】an ice bag.

ひょうはく【漂白】bleaching. ¶ シャツを～する *bleach* a shirt. —粉 bleaching powder. —剤 a bleaching agent ; a decolorant.

ひょうはく【漂泊】wandering ; roaming. ¶ ～の旅に出る go on *aimless wanderings.*

ひょうばん【評判】(名声) reputation ; fame ; (人気) popularity.

1〚評判が〛¶ 彼は同僚に～がいい He *is popular* among his fellow workers. / He *is well spoken of* by his fellow workers. 彼女は同性の間では～が悪い She *is ill spoken of* by her own sex. / She *is unpopular* among her own sex.

2〚評判の〛¶ あれが～の詐欺師だ He is a *notorious* swindler. あれが天才だという～の高い少年だ That is the gifted boy who *is much talked of.* これが今アメリカで～の小説で, 映画になった This is a novel *much talked of* in America now and it has been made into a film. 彼女はこの会社で～の美人だ She is the toast of this firm.

3〚評判を〛¶ この作家はその小説によって～を得た The novel gained this writer great *popularity.* この作品は彼の～を高めた The work added to his *reputation.* この事件でその店は～を落とした The store has lost its *good reputation* because of this affair.

4〚評判に〛¶ ふたりの恋愛は社内で～になっている The whole firm *is talking about* the love affair of the two. この村では小さなことがすぐ～になる A trifling thing is apt to create *a sensation* in this village. この映画は昔大～になったものだ This picture was very *popular* in former days.

5〚評判など・評判ほど〛¶ 彼は世間の～など全然気にしない He never minds *what the world says* about him. 彼の演奏は～ほどのものではなかった His musical performance was not so good as it *was reported* to be.

6〚評判だ〛¶ 彼女は名女優だというもっぱらの～だ She *is widely talked about as* a great actress.

7〚評判する〛¶ 近所の人たちは彼を名医だと～している He has the *reputation* of an excellent physician among his neighbors.

ひょうひ【表皮】the outer skin ; 〘解剖学〙the cuticle ; (木の) bark.

ひょうひょう【飄飄】¶ ～たる aimless ; roaming ; wandering. ～として(ふわふわと) buoyantly ; floatingly ; (人に関して) lighthearted. 彼は～としている He is aloof from the world.

びょうびょう【渺渺】¶ ～たる大海 the *bound-*

less ocean.

びょうぶ【屏風】a folding screen. ¶ ～を立てる set up *a screen*. ～で仕切る screen off.

—岩 a screen crag.

ひょうへん【豹変】¶ ～する change suddenly. 君子は～する The wise are quick to correct their mistakes.

ひょうぼう【標榜】¶ この新聞は自由主義を～する This newspaper *stands for* liberalism.

びょうぼつ【病没・病歿】¶ ～する die of a disease (≒ sickness).

ひょうほん【標本】a specimen ; a type ; (見本) a sample. ¶ 動物(植物)の～ *a* zoological (botanical) *specimen*. こん虫の～を作る make *specimens* of insects. あの人は日本人の～みたいなものだ He is a *typical* Japanese.

びょうま【病魔】¶ 彼女は結婚後まもなく～に冒されるところとなった She *became sick* soon after she got married.

ひょうめい【表明】declaration. ¶ 大統領は日本が提案を受け入れたことに対して感謝の意を～した The president *expressed* (≒ *showed*) his appreciation of Japan's acceptance of the suggestion. 私はその案に対して反対 (賛成) の意を～した I *declared against* (*for*) the proposal. 彼は理事会に辞意を～した He *tendered* his resignation to the board of directors.

びょうめい【病名】the name of a disease. (disease は illness や sickness よりはっきりした病名を予想させる. かぜや頭痛は illness, sickness にはいるが disease ではない).

¶ 彼の～はまだはっきりしない His disease *has* not *been identified* yet.

ひょうめん【表面】the surface. ¶ この土地の～はでこぼこだ This land has *a* rough *surface*. 地球の～の4分の3は水だ Three-fourths of the *surface* of the earth is water. ～だけで物事を判断するのは当たらない It is not right to judge things merely by *appearances*. 彼は～はまじめを装っている He has a *superficial* seriousness. ～を見ただけで本質はわからない We cannot understand the essence of anything merely by seeing its *appearance*. 事件は～化した The affair came to *be noticed by the public*. 首相と閣僚との間の意見の違いが～化した A difference in opinion between the prime minister and the other cabinet ministers *came to light*.

ひょうめんせき【表面積】surface (≒ superficial) area.

ひょうよみ【票読み】¶ 私の～は当たった My *estimation of the votes* was accurate. 各候補者は～に忙しい All the candidates are busy guessing how many votes they can poll (≒ get) in the coming elections.

びょうよみ【秒読み】countdown (*for* the launch of a missile). ¶ 仕事もいよいよ～の段階に入った We are now in *the final stage* of the work. ～が終わって発射ボタンが押された The *countdown* concluded, and the firing button was pushed.

ひょうり【表裏】the face and the back.

¶ すべて物には～がある There are *two sides* to everything. 物には～のあることを知らねばならぬ You must know 〔*the*〕 *both sides* of the shield.

びょうりがく【病理学】pathology.

—者 a pathologist.

ひょうりゅう【漂流】drifting. ¶ 船はあらしのために破損し1週間～した The ship was disabled in a terrible storm, and *drifted* (≒ *was adrift*) for a week. 彼らは～中を救助された They were rescued while *drifting*.

—船 a drifting ship. **—物** a drift.

びょうれき【病歴】a man's clinical history. ¶ あの人には結核の～がある That man has *a history* of tuberculosis.

ひょうろう【兵糧】provisions ; food. ¶ 敵は～が尽きた The enemy has come to the end of their *food supplies*. 敵を～攻めにした We took the tactics of *starving out* the enemy.

ひょうろん【評論】criticism ; comment. ¶ 時事問題の～をする *comment on* current events.

—家 a critic ; a commenter. 映画**—** a movie review. 経済**—** comments on economics. 人物**—** character-sketch. 文芸**—** literary criticism.

ひよく【肥沃】¶ ～な土地 *fertile* (≒ *rich* ; *productive*) soil.

びよく【尾翼】the tail (*of* an airplane).

ひよけ【日除け】a sunshade ; a sunscreen ; (窓の) a blind ; (ズックの) an awning.

¶ この部屋は西日があたりすぎる. ～をおろしておこう This room gets too much afternoon sun. Let's draw down the *blind*.

ひよこ【雛子】a chick ; a chicken.

ひょこひょこ ¶ ～歩く waddle ; (子どもが) toddle ; (けがをして) walk with a slight limp.

ぴょこん ¶ 街で会ったら彼は～と頭を下げた When I met him on the street, he made a slight bow to me.

ひょっこり ¶ 電車の中で～友人に会った I met a friend *by chance* (≒ *by accident*) in the train. (by chance, by accident を用いるより I *happened to* meet…のほうが口語的). 彼は3年ぶりでアメリカから～帰ってきた He came home from America *quite unexpectedly* after three years' absence.

ひょっと ¶ ～して彼の居所をご存じないでしょうか Do you know *by chance* where he is living? / Do you *happen* to know where he lives? ～すると彼は遅れてくるかもしれない He may *possibly* come later.

ひょっとこ a clown ; an ugly fellow.

ぴよぴよ ¶ ひよこが～鳴いている The chickens *are peeping* (≒ *are cheeping*).

ひよどり【鵯】a bulbul.

ひより【日和】(天気) weather ; (快晴) fine weather. ¶ よいお～ですね It's *a nice day*, isn't it? きょうはピクニックには絶好の～だ The *weather* today is ideal for a picnic.

ひよりみ【日和見】¶ この場合～をすることは許されない You are not allowed to *sit on the fence* at this juncture.

ひ

—主義 opportunism; a wait-and-see policy. —主義者 an opportunist; a timeserver.

ひょろなが·い【ひょろ長い】tall and slender. ¶ ～い男 a *tall, lank* man.

ひょろひょろ ¶ 酔って足もとが～していた I was drunk and *walked staggeringly* (≒ *with unsteady steps*). 重い荷物を負っていたので～した I *staggered* under a heavy burden.

ひよわ【ひ弱】¶ 過保護であるせいか最近の子どもは概して～だ Probably protected too much by their parents, children today *are*, on the whole, very *delicate*.

ぴょん ¶ 彼は身軽にかきねを～と飛び越えた He *jumped* (≒ *went*) *over* the fence lightly.

ぴょんぴょん ¶ 鳥は止まり木から止まり木へ～と飛んだ The bird *hopped* from one perch to another.

ひら【平】(手のひら) the palm; the flat of a hand.
—社員 a mere clerk. —教員 a common teacher.

ビラ (広告) a [hand]bill; a leaflet; (はり札) a placard; a poster; an advertisement.
¶ ～をまく distribute *handbills*. 選挙の～を壁にはる post election *placards* on the walls.

ひらあやまり【平謝り】¶ あんなに～に謝っているのだから, 今度だけは許してやろう Since he *makes such a humble apology* (≒ *apologizes so humbly*), I'll pardon him for this once.

ひらい【飛来】¶ 春になるとツバメが南から群れをなして～する In spring swallows *come flying* in groups from the south.

ひらいしん【避雷針】a lightning rod (≒ guard; conductor). ¶ 家の屋根に～をつける install *a lightning rod* on the roof of a house.

ひらおよぎ【平泳ぎ】the breast stroke [swim]. ¶ ～で泳ぐ swim with (≒ do) *the breast stroke*. ～の選手 a breast stroker.

ひらおり【平織り】plain fabrics.

ひらがな【平仮名】the Japanese cursive syllabary; *hiragana*. ¶ ～で書く write in *hiragana*.

ひらき【開き】¶ 両者間には大きな～がある There is *a* great *difference* between the two. 彼らの年齢の～が問題になるだろう The *disparity* in age between them will become a problem.
—戸 a hinged door; (庭へすぐ出られる両開きの戸) a French window. —封 an unsealed letter.

ひらきなお·る【開き直る】¶ そんな扱いをされるとだれだって～る Such treatment would make anyone *turn upon you* (≒ *take a defiant attitude toward you*).

ひら·く【開く】**1**〚あく・あける〛¶ 桜の花が～いている The cherry blossoms *have come out* (≒ *are out*). / The cherry trees *are in bloom*. (cherry blossoms が主語の場合は bloom を用いない).
この戸は通りに面して～く This door *opens* on the street.
包を～く *unpack* a parcel.
本の51ページを～きなさい *Open* your books to page fifty-one. (主として to は㊍, at は㊌).
彼は口を～けば必ず説教だ He never *opens* his mouth without lecturing.
われわれは胸襟を～いて語った We *opened* our hearts to each other.
彼は駅の近くに店を～いている He *has* a store near the railroad station.
彼らは道を～いてわれわれを通した They made way for us.
(体操で) もう少し右へ～きなさい *Spread out* a little to the right.
彼は後進に道を～くために引退した He retired in order to *give* place to his juniors.
2〚会・法廷を〛¶ 会は来週～かれる The meeting will *be held* next week. / The meeting will *take place* next week.
彼らは娘の誕生日にダンスパーティーを～いた They *gave* a dance on their daughter's birthday.
あすは法廷が～かれる The case is to be heard tomorrow.
3〚開拓する〛¶ 森林を～く *clear* forest land.

ひら·ける【開ける】¶ その国は今ではすっかり～けている It is now quite a *civilized* country. ジャングルを抜けると大草原が眼前に～けた When we passed through the jungle, a great prairie *spread* out before us.

ひらぞこ【平底】¶ ～の flat-bottomed.
—船 a flatboat.

ひらた·い【平たい】¶ ～い顔 a *flat* face. ～く言えば in *plain* language.

ひらて【平手】¶ 彼女は彼の顔を～打ちした She *gave* him *a slap* on the face. / She *slapped* him *on* the face.

ひらに【平に】earnestly; humbly. ¶ ～ご容赦願います I *humbly* (≒ *earnestly*) ask for your pardon.

ひらひら ¶ 風で帆が～とひらめいていた The wind *was flapping* the sails. 枯れ葉が風に吹かれて～と飛んだ The dead leaves *fluttered* about in the wind.

ピラミッド a pyramid.

ひらめ【平目・鮃】〘魚類〙a flatfish; a plaice.

ひらめか·す【閃かす】¶ 燈台では合図を2回～した The lighthouse *flashed* signals twice. 彼は刀を～して敵に突撃した He *brandished* his sword and rushed at the enemy.

ひらめき【閃き】a flash; a gleam. ¶ 電光の～ *a flash* of lightning. 彼女には音楽に関しては天才の～がある She shows *flashes* (≒ *sparks*) of genius in music.

ひらめ·く【閃く】¶ いなずまが夜のやみに～いた The lightning *flashed* through the darkness of the night. その考えがぱっと頭に～いた The idea *flashed into* my mind.

ひらや【平屋】a one-story house; a house of one story.

ひらりと quickly. ¶ 彼は馬に～またがると走り去った He *sprang* (≒ *jumped*) *on* his horse and rode away. 彼は～身をかわした He *nimbly* dodged the blow.

びり ¶ 彼はいつもクラスの～だ He *is* always *at*

the bottom of his class. / He *is* always *the lowest boy* of his class. 彼は～で卒業した He graduated *last on the list*.

ひりつ【比率】 percentage ; ratio. ¶ 3対2の～だ They are *in the ratio of* three to two. ～が高い(低い) The *ratio* is high (low).

ひりひり ¶ 切り傷がまだ～する The cut still *smarts*. けがしたところが～痛んで彼は眠れなかった The *smart* of the hurt kept him awake. 口の中が～する My mouth *is burning*. からしをなめると舌が～する Mustard *bites* the tongue.

びりびり ¶ 彼は手紙を～引き裂いてしまった He *tore up* the letter. そのコードにさわったら～ときた I *received a succession of shocks* when I touched the cord.

ぴりぴり ¶ 口の中が～する My mouth *is burning*. すり傷が～痛む The scratch *smarts*.

びりゅうし【微粒子】〔物理〕 a corpuscle.

ひりょう【肥料】 manure ; fertilizer. ¶ 土地がやせているときは～をやらねばならない If the land is sterile, it must *be fertilized*.
化学── a chemical fertilizer.

びりょう【微量】 a very small amount (*of* salt).

びりょく【微力】 ¶ 会議を成功させるために私も～を尽くすぞ I'll *do what I can* (≒ *do my bit*) to make the conference successful.

ひりろんてき【非理論的】 illogical.

ひる【昼】(日中) day ; 正午(noon) ; (昼食) lunch. ¶ コウモリは～寝て, 夜飛びまわって果物や虫を食べる Bats sleep *in the daytime* and fly about at night, feeding on fruit and insects. ～は歩き, 夜は眠った I walked *by day*, and slept by night. (昼と夜を対照して言うときはこのように by day ... by night としてもよい). ～を欺くような電燈だ The electric lights *are as bright as day*. お～はもう済ませましたか Have you had *lunch* yet? お～ごろおいでください Come and see me about *noon*.

ひる【蛭】〔虫類〕 a leech.

ビル (手形) a bill ; (建物) a building.

ひるあんどん【昼行燈】 ¶ 彼は～のようだ He is as useless as *a lamp in broad daylight*.

ひるい【比類】 ¶ ヘレン＝ケラーの人生における大成功はおそらく世界歴史に～がないものだろう The complete success of Helen Keller's life *is* perhaps *without*〔*a*〕 *parallel* (≒ *is unparalleled*) in the history of the world. これはわが国の史上に～のないことだ This *is unexampled* (≒ *is unprecedented*) in our history.

ひるがえ·す【翻す】 ¶ 彼はいよいよになって決心を～した He *changed* his mind at the last moment. 犯人は前の告白を～した The criminal *reversed* (≒ *took back*) his former confessions. 彼は身を～して逃げた He *turned* (≒ *swung*) *round* and ran away. 日本の国旗を～している船 a ship *flying* the Japanese flag.

ひるがえって【翻って】 ¶ ～考えてみるに on second thoughts ; on reflection.

ひるがえ·る【翻る】 ¶ 優勝旗が空高くメーンポールに～っていた The championship flag *was floating* (≒ *was flying* ; *was fluttering*) high from the main pole.

ひるがお【昼顔】〔植物〕 a bindweed.

ひるさがり【昼下がり】 early afternoon.
¶ ～に early in the afternoon.

ひるすぎ【昼過ぎ】 afternoon. ¶ ～に in the afternoon ; a little past midday.

ビルディング a building.

ひるね【昼寝】 a nap. ¶ ～する take a nap ; take a siesta.

ひるひなか【昼日中】 ¶ それは～行なわれた犯罪だ It is a crime committed *in full* (≒ *open*) *daylight*.

ひるま【昼間】 daytime ; day. ¶ 彼は～働いて夜学校に行く He works *by day* and attends school by night. ～のうちに仕事を済ませた I finished my work *before it gets dark* (≒ *in the daytime*).

ひるまえ【昼前】 morning. ¶ ～にしておかなければならない仕事がある I have some work to do *in the morning*. 彼は～に出かけた He left *just before noon*.

ひる·む【怯む】 ¶ 彼は少しも～まずにその難局に立ち向かった He faced the difficult situation without *flinching*. 困難な仕事だからといって～むな You mustn't *flinch from* (≒ *shrink from*) a difficult task./ You mustn't allow yourself to *be discouraged* (≒ *be daunted*) by a difficult task. われわれは敵の大軍に～んだ We *gave way to* the great enemy.

ひるめし【昼飯】 lunch. ¶ ～を食べる have (≒ take ; eat) *lunch*.

ひるやすみ【昼休み】 ¶ 私たちの事務所ではお昼に1時間の～をとる In our office we have an hour's *recess at noon*. ～に散歩しよう Let's go for a walk in the *noon recess*.

ひれ【鰭】 a fin. ¶ 背(腹 ; 尾)～ a dorsal (ventral ; caudal) fin.

ひれい【比例】 proportion. ¶ この戸は高さに～して狭い This door is narrow *in proportion to* its height. 販売が増加するのに～して収益も上がる *In proportion as* the sale increases, the profit will rise. (as のあとには節が続くことに注意). 出費を収入に～させる *proportion one's* expenditure *to one's* income. 3対5と30対50と6対10の～は同じだ The *ratios* 3 to 5, 30 to 50, and 6 to 10 are the same.
──式 a proportion. ──代表 proportional representation. ──配分 proportional allotment. 単(複)── simple (compound) proportion. 正(反)── ¶ …に正(反)～する be directly (inversely) proportional to (*something*).

ひれい【非礼】 impoliteness ; rudeness. ¶ 彼がそんなことを言うのは～きわまる It *is* very *rude of* him to say such a thing.

びれい【美麗】 beauty. ¶ ～な beautiful. 装飾は～をきわめている The decorations *are gorgeous*.

ひれき【披瀝】 ¶ 胸中を～する *unbosom oneself* ; *open one's* heart. 彼は考えていたことを～した He *revealed* what was in his mind.

ひれつ【卑劣】 ¶ 彼は～な手段を用いてわれわれを欺いた He deceived us by a *mean* (≒ *dirty*)

ひ

trick. 彼はまさかそんな〜なことはすまい Surely he is above such *baseness* (≒ *meanness; wretchedness*).

ひれふ·す【ひれ伏す】¶ 捕虜たちは征服者の前に〜した The captives *prostrated themselves before* the conqueror. 彼女は王の足下に〜して夫の釈放を懇願した She *threw herself at* the king's feet and begged him to set her husband free.

ひれん【悲恋】heartbroken love. ¶ 彼らの恋は〜に終わった Their love ended in tragedy. / Their love bore no fruit after all.

ひろ【尋】a fathom.

ひろ·い【広い】**1**〖広がり・幅などが〗wide; broad (wide, broad はしばしば同義に用いられるが, 両端の間の距離に力点を置いて言われるときには wide が用いられる; a wide street (river). 一方, 表面の広がり, 幅の広さを強調するときは broad が用いられる; the broad ocean; broad shoulders).
¶ 〜い世界 a *wide* world.
〜い通り a *broad* street.
〜い家 a *large* (≒ *roomy*) house.
〜い部屋 a *large* (≒ *spacious*) room.
〜い野原 an *open* field.
テキサスは〜い州だ Texas is a *vast* state.
〜い額 a *high* brow (≒ forehead).
彼は肩幅が〜い He is a *broad-shouldered* fellow.
川は河口で〜くなっている The river *widens* (≒ *broadens*) at its mouth.
2〖心・趣味などが〗¶ 〜い見解 *wide* views.
彼は趣味の〜い人だ He is a man with *wide* interests.
彼女は心の〜い人だ She is a *broad-minded* (≒ *generous*) woman.
3〖その他〗¶ この品物は販路が〜い There is *a good market* for these goods.
彼は顔が〜い He has a *wide* circle of acquaintance.
〜い意味において in a *broad* sense.

ひろいあ·げる【拾い上げる】pick up.

ひろいぬし【拾い主】the finder.

ひろいもの【拾い物】a found article. ¶ 〜は落とし主へ返せ Return the *lost property* to its owner. それは〜だ It's *a windfall*.

ひろいよみ【拾い読み】¶ 私は数ページ〜した I *read* several pages *at random*.

ヒロイン a heroine.

ひろう【疲労】fatigue; exhaustion. ¶ 〜困憊(ぱい)その極に達していた I *was dead tired*./ I was *tired out* (≒ *was fatigued; was exhausted*). 彼は徹夜したがまったく〜の色を見せなかった He sat up all night, but showed no signs of *fatigue*.

ひろう【披露】(紹介) introduction; (告知) announcement. ¶ 結婚の〜宴を張る give a wedding dinner. 結婚〜案内状 a wedding card.

ひろ·う【拾う】¶ 活字を〜う *pick out* types. 道端で万年筆を〜った I *found* a〔fountain〕pen on the road. 通りで財布を〜った I *picked up* a wallet on the street. 危ういところで命を〜った I had a narrow escape. 駅前でタクシーを〜った I *took* a taxi in front of the〔railroad〕station. 床に散らばっている豆を〜う *gather* beans scattered on the floor. 農夫は麦畑の落ち穂を〜った The farmer *gleaned* the wheat field.

びろう【尾籠】indecency. ¶ 〜なお話で恐縮ですが… It is an *indecent* matter to mention, but.... 〜な話 a *bawdy* (≒ *obscene*) talk.

ビロード velvet. ¶ 彼女は青い〜を着ている She is in blue *velvet*.

ひろがり【広がり】an expanse. ¶ 松の林の〜 *a stretch of* pine trees. 大洋の果てしなき〜 the boundless *expanse* of the ocean.

ひろが·る【広がる】¶ その事故のうわさはすぐにすみずみまで〜った News of the accident soon *spread* far and wide. 平原ははるか海まで〜っている The plains *extend* (≒ *stretch; reach*) as far as the sea. 太平洋は果てしなく〜っている The Pacific Ocean *expands* boundlessly.

ひろく【広く】¶ その本は実は彼が書いたものだということは〜知られている It is *widely* known that he was the real author of the book. 彼は〜世界を旅行している He has traveled *far and wide* in the world. / He has *widely* traveled. 彼は和漢の書に〜通じている He is *widely* read in Chinese and Japanese classics.

ひろく【秘録】a memoir; private papers.

ひろ·げる【広げる】¶ ワシは翼を〜げると飛び去った The eagle *spread* its wings and flew away. テーブルの上にクロースを〜げる *spread*〔out〕a cloth over (≒ on) a table. かさを〜げる *open* (≒ *unfold; unfurl*) an umbrella. 事業を〜げる *expand* (≒ *extend*) *one's* business. 領土を〜げる *extend* (≒ *enlarge*) *one's* domains. 家を〜げる *build an extension to* a house; *extend* a house. 彼は私を両手を〜げて出迎えた He welcomed me *with open arms*. 彼はその地位についてから交際の範囲を〜げた He *has enlarged* his circle of acquaintance since he got the position. 彼は大ぶろしきを〜げる He *talks big*.

ひろさ【広さ】an extent; an area. ¶ この野原は長さ約7マイル, 〜約5マイルある This field is about 7 miles in length and 5 miles *in breadth* (≒ *in width*). アメリカの〜はどれだけありますか What is the *extent* of America? 彼の知識の〜は相当なものだ The *range* of his information is considerable.

ひろば【広場】an open space; (通りの集まっている四角の) a square; (通りの集まっている丸い) a circus.

ひろびろ【広広】¶ 〜とした家 a *large* (≒ *roomy*) house. 〜とした部屋 a *spacious* room. 〜とした野原が西の方へ何マイルも続いていた An *open* field stretched for miles westward.

ひろま【広間】a hall; (船などの) a saloon.

ひろま·る【広まる】¶ 若者の間には長髪が〜った It *has become popular* among young people to wear their hairs long. 彼の英雄的な行為のうわさはたちまち国じゅうに〜った The report of his heroic deed *spread* quickly throughout the country. ゴルフ熱が国じゅうに〜った The enthusiasm for golf *has pervaded*

(≒ *is prevailing in*) the whole country. 彼の説がだんだん～ってきた His theory *is gaining ground.* 科学の知識が一般に～っている Scientific knowledge *has been diffused* among the people.

ひろ·める 【広める】 ¶ 彼らがそのうわさを～めた They *spread* the rumor. 彼は学問を～めるのに努力した He made efforts to *diffuse* learning. 彼はキリスト教を～めた He *propagated* Christianity.

ひろんりてき 【非論理的】 illogical.

ひわ 【秘話】 a secret story.

びわ 【枇杷】〔植物〕 a loquat.

びわ 【琵琶】 a lute; a *biwa.* ¶ ～法師 a *lute* player.

ひわい 【卑猥】 ¶ ～な話 an *obscene* (≒ a *bawdy*) story.

ひわり 【日割り】 daily rate; (日程) a program; a schedule. ¶ ～で支払う pay *(a person) by the day.* 試験の～が決定した The examination *schedule* has been made (≒ formed).

ひん 【品】 **1** 〖品格〗 dignity; grace. ¶ ～のよい人 a person *of refined character* (≒ *of dignity*).

～のよい住宅 an *elegant* residence.

～のよい文章 a *dignified* style.

彼女は～のよい顔をしている She has *delicate* features.

そんな～の悪いことばは使わないでください Don't use such *vulgar* language!

彼女は～のよい装いであった She was *gracefully* dressed.

2 〖品目〗 an article. ¶ 昨夜レストランで 3 ～料理を食べた We had a three course dinner at a restaurant.

衣類 3 ～ three *articles* of clothing. (ズボン·シャツ·上着などをばく然と衣類と称するときは an article of clothing と言う).

ひん 【貧】 poverty. ¶ ～すれば鈍する(諺) *Want dulls the wit.* 彼は～に甘んじていた He suffered himself to live *in poverty.* / He lived *in contented poverty.*

びん 【便】(郵便) 米 mail; 英 post. ¶ 私は次の～を待つ I'll wait for the next *ship* (≒ *train*). あの島へ行く～がない There is no means of going to the island. その本を航空～で送ってあげます I'll send you the book *by air mail.*

びん 【敏】 ¶ 彼は機をみるに～な男だ He *is quick to* seize the opportunity. 彼は利をみるに～だ He *has a quick eye* for the main chance.

びん 【瓶】 a bottle; (薬) a vial. ¶ 彼はウイスキーを 1 ～あけてしまった He emptied *a* 〔*whole*〕 *bottle* of whisky. ウイスキーの～ *a flask* of whisky. この～にはいくら入るか How much does this *bottle* hold?

ピン a pin; (ヘアピン) a hairpin; (安全ピン) a safety pin. ¶ 掲示板に～で掲示をはる *pin* up a notice on a notice board. コートに～でバラの花をつける *pin* a rose on a coat. お茶といっても～からキリまである There are all sorts of tea, from the *choicest one* to the coarsest one.

—アップ a pinup. **—**カール a pin curl.

ひんい 【品位】 dignity. ¶ ～のある老紳士 a *dignified* (≒ *noble*) old man. 良書を読んで～を高める elevate *one's character* by reading good books. 学問は～を高める Study *ennobles* a man. そんなことをすると～を落とすことになる That would *be a disgrace to* you. / That would *be beneath the dignity of* a gentleman.

ひんかく 【品格】 character; dignity.

びんかつ 【敏活】 promptitude; quickness; activity. ¶ その仕事は～に行なわれた The work was done *with expedition.* ～な処置をとらねばならない A *prompt* action (≒ measure) must be taken. 行政事務の～を図る必要がある There is a need to *promote* (≒ *increase; raise*) *efficiency* in the prosecution of administrative affairs. 彼は～かつ慎重に行動した He acted *swiftly* and with calm deliberation.

びんかん 【敏感】 sensibility; susceptibility. ¶ 彼は寒さに非常に～だ He *is* very *sensitive to* cold. 大ていの人はへつらいに対して～だ Most people *are susceptible to* flattery.

ひんきゅう 【貧窮】 ⇒ひんこん

ひんく 【貧苦】 poverty 〔and hardship〕. ¶ 彼の家庭は～に打ちひしがれていた His family *was poverty-stricken.* 彼は～のうちに成人した He grew up *in poverty.*

ひんけつ 【貧血】 anemia; 英 anaemia. ¶ ～する become *anemic.* ～で倒れる break down from *anemia.* ～を起こす have an attack of *anemia.* ～性の人 an *anemic* person.

ひんこう 【品行】 conduct; behavior. ¶ ～のよい人 a man of good *conduct.* ～の悪い人 a man of loose *morals.* ～を慎む be prudent in *conduct.*

—方正 ¶ 彼は～方正だ His *conduct* is perfect (≒ above reproach).

ひんこん 【貧困】 (貧乏) poverty; (欠乏) lack. ¶ ～な家庭 a *poor* family. ～の中に育つ be brought up in *poverty.* ～に陥る be reduced to *poverty.* 政治の～ political *poverty.*

ひんし 【品詞】〖文法〗 a part of speech.

ひんし 【瀕死】 ¶ ～の病人 a *dying* patient (patient は医者のみが用いる); a *critical* case. 彼は～の状態にある He *is dying.* / He *is in critical condition.* 彼は～の重傷を負った He was *fatally* injured (≒ wounded).

ひんしつ 【品質】 quality. ¶ ～を改良する improve *(a thing) in quality*; improve *the quality of (a thing).* ～をよく調べる check up *quality.* この品は～がよい(悪い) The goods are of good (inferior) *quality.*

—管理 quality control.

ひんじゃ 【貧者】 a poor man; (総称) the poor. ¶ ～の一燈〖聖書〗 the widow's mite.

ひんじゃく 【貧弱】 ¶ ～な体格 a *poor* physique. ～な食事 a *meager* meal. 彼は～な服装をしていた He was *poorly* (≒ *shabbily*) dressed. 彼の演説は内容が～だった His speech *lacked substance.* / His speech *sounded hollow.* 彼の英語の知識は～だ He has only a

ひ

scanty (≒ *poor*) knowledge of English. / He knows *little* English. 彼の～な知識ではどうにもならぬ He knows too *little* to do anything about it.

ひんしゅ【品種】(種類) a kind ; (変種) a variety ; (品等) a grade ; (家畜の) a breed.
¶ それらは同じ (違う) ～だ They are of the same *kind* (of different *kinds*).
―改良 (家畜の) breed improvement ; (植物の) plant breeding.

ひんしゅく【顰蹙】¶ ～すべき despicable ; outrageous. 人の～を買う be frowned upon (≒ at). 彼の行動はみんなの～を買った His conduct *disgusted* everyone.

ひんしゅつ【頻出】¶ これらは～する単語だ These are very *common* words./ These are words we *frequently come across*.

びんしょう【敏捷】¶ ～な quick ; sharp. 彼はたいへん～だ He *is* very *nimble*. ～な行動が要求される *Quick* action is required.

びんじょう【便乗】¶ 彼の車に～させてもらった I got a lift in his car. 彼は時勢に～して成功した He succeeded by *making the most of* the trend of the times.

ひん・する【瀕する】¶ 彼は死に～している He *is on the brink of* death. その会社は破産に～している The firm *is on the verge of* bankruptcy.

ひんせい【品性】character. ¶ ～を養う build *one's character*. ～のりっぱ (下劣) な人 a man of fine (base) *character*. ～の陶冶(とうや) development of *moral character*.

ピンセット〔a pair of〕tweezers ; a *pincette*.
¶ 彼は～でとげを引き抜いた He pulled out the thorn with *tweezers*.

びんせん【便箋】letter paper ; (つづり) a writing pad. ¶ 彼は～に欠席届を書いた He wrote out the notice of absence on *a piece of letter paper*.

ひんそう【貧相】¶ ～な男 a *poor-looking* man. 彼は～ななりをしている He is *poorly* dressed.

びんそく【敏速】¶ ～に処置する take a *prompt* action.

びんた¶ ～を張る slap (*a person*) on the cheek. ～をくう get slapped on the cheek.

ピンチa pinch. ¶ ～に陥る be thrown into *a pinch*. ～を切り抜ける get out of *a pinch* ; tide over *a difficulty*.
―ヒッター〔野球〕a pinch hitter.

びんづめ【瓶詰め】¶ ～にする *bottle* (wine). ～の酒 (ビール) *bottled* wine (beer). ～ですか生ですか *Bottled* or draft?

ヒントa hint. ¶ ～を与える give (*a person*) *a hint*. ～を得る get (≒ take) *a hint* (*from*).

ひんど【頻度】frequency. ¶ ～の高い (低い) 語 a word of high (low) *frequency*. これらの語の～数を調べてみよう Let's check the *frequency* in use of these words. / Let's see how *frequently* these words are used.

ぴんと¶ なわを～張る strain (≒ tighten) a rope. 指先で～はじく snap (*a thing*) with fingers. 花びんが～音をたてて割れた The vase broke with a crack. なにを言おうとしているのか～こなかった I could not make out what he was driving at. 変だということが～きた It struck me as odd.

ピントfocus. ¶ ～を合わせる focus (the lense); bring (*something*) into focus. この写真は～が合っている (いない) This picture *is in* (*out of*) *focus*. 彼のことばは～がはずれている What he says *is off the point*.

ひんぱつ【頻発】frequent occurrence. ¶ ～する occur frequently. ここは交通事故の～地点だ Traffic accidents *frequently happen* here.

ひんぱん【頻繁】¶ 往来の～な通り a *busy* street. ～に起こる火事 *frequent* fires. 最近は地震が～に起こる Earthquakes *are frequent* these days. 彼女は～にあの店に出入りする She *frequently* visits that store./She is a *regular* customer of that store.

ひんぴょう【品評】comment ; criticism.
¶ ～する criticize ; comment.
―会 a competitive show (≒ exhibition) ; a competition ; a contest ; 米 a fair.

ひんぴん【頻頻】¶ ～と frequently. 冬になると火事が～と起こる Fires *are frequent* in winter.

ぴんぴん¶ ～した (元気がいい) full of life ; (達者である) in good health ; (生きがいい) fresh. 彼はまだ～している He *is hale and hearty*.

ひんぷ【貧富】wealth and poverty. ¶ ～の差が大きい The gulf between *rich and poor* is great.

びんぼう【貧乏】poverty. ¶ 彼はきわめて～だ He *is* very *poor*. ～暇なし *The poor* have no leisure.
―神 a god of poverty. ―くじ ¶ ～くじを引いた I happened to be most unlucky of all. ―性〔be〕unlucky by nature. ―人 a poor man. ―揺すり ¶ 彼は～揺すりする He has a nervous habit of shaking.

ピンぼけ¶ ～の out of focus. ～の写真 a picture *out of focus* ; a photograph *not properly taken*. 彼の発言は少々～だ What he said *was* somewhat *off the point*.

ピンポンping-pong ; table tennis (ふつうは table tennis のほうが多く聞かれる). ¶ ～をする play *ping-pong*. ～の試合 a game of *ping-pong* (≒ *table tennis*).

ひんみん【貧民】the poor ; the needy.
―救済 the relief of the poor. ―窟(くつ) the slums ; poor quarters.

ひんもく【品目】(一品) an item ; (品目表) a list of items. ¶ ～別に by items.

ひんやり¶ 外気は～と感じられた It *was chilly* outside.

びんらん【紊乱】官紀― slackness of official discipline. 風紀― an offense against public decency.

びんわん【敏腕】ability ; competence. ¶ 彼は大いに～をふるった He gave full play to his ability.
―家 an able person ; a man of ability ; a competent man.

ふ

ふ【府】(行政区) a prefecture ; an urban prefecture. ¶ 京都～ Kyoto Prefecture. ～〔立 ; 営〕の prefectural ; metropolitan. 大阪～庁 the Osaka Prefectural Office. 学問の～ a *seat* of learning. 文教の～ the *fountainhead* of culture.
―会〔議員〕〔a member of〕a prefectural assembly. **―**知事 a〔prefectural〕governor. 都道**―**県 urban and rural prefectures.

ふ【負】〘数学〙¶ ～の negative ; minus. ～の数 a negative number. 〘物理〙～の電子 a negatron.

ふ【譜】(楽譜) a music ; (音符) a musical note ; (総譜) a score ; (系譜) a family record ; (図表) a table.
¶ 歌詞に～をつける set a poem to *music*. ～を読む read *notes*. ～を見て曲をひく refer to the *score* while playing a piece.

ふ【斑】 a spot ; a speck. ¶ ～のある spotted ; speckled.

ふ【腑】 ¶ 彼の言うことは～に落ちない I cannot quite understand what he says. / His explanation is hard to swallow. / His story does not go down with me.

ふ【麩】 *fu* (英語で説明すれば a kind of gluten bread).

ぶ【分】(割合) rate ; (百分比) percent ; (厚み) thickness. ¶ 8～の利子 8 percent interest. ～がいい(悪い) be at an advantage (a disadvantage). 工事は九～どおり完成した The work is almost finished. こちらに～がない(ある) The odds are against us (in our favor).

ぶ【武】(武勇) military prowess ; (軍事) military affairs. ¶ ～をきそう struggle for military supremacy. 文と～をかねる be both a fine scholar and a gallant warrior ; excel in the arts of both pen and sword.

ぶ【歩】(割合) rate ; (歩合) a commission ; a percentage.

ぶ【部】(部分) a part ; a portion ; (部門) a section ; a department ; (書物の) a copy ; a volume ; (…部) a division.
¶ 三～作の小説 a trilogy ; a novel in three *parts*. それは哲学研究の～に属する It belongs under the study of philosophy. 彼は営業～にいる He is with the business *department*. 野球～に入るつもりだ I will join the baseball *club*. そんなことでは～の統制がとれない That will disturb the order in the *department*. その本を100～まとめて買った I bought 100 *copies* of the book at a time.

ファースト〘野球〙(一塁)〔the〕first base ; (一塁手) a first baseman. ¶ 彼のポジションは～だ He is *a first baseman*.
―レディー the first lady (困 大統領夫人を the first lady of the land, 州知事夫人を the first lady of the state と言う). レディー**―** lady first.

ぶあい【歩合】(割合) rate ; (手数料) a commission. ¶ 利子の～ the *rate* of interest. 割引～ the discount *rate*. 彼は固定給のほかに売り上げの1割の～ももらっている He receives *a commission* of ten percent on sales as well as a salary.

ぶあいそう【無愛想】 unsociability. ¶ ～な態度 a *cold* manner. ～な返事をする give a *curt* answer. ～にふるまう behave *coldly* ; be short with (*a person*). 彼女は～な人だ She is an *unfriendly* person. / She *is hard to make friends with*. / She *is unaffable*. / She *is uncourteous*.

ファイト(闘志) fight ; fighting spirit. ¶ ～を燃やして仕事をする work *with fervor*. 彼は大いに～がある He has plenty of *fight*. / He has *guts*.

ファイル(書類とじ) a file. ¶ ～する file. ～にとじ込んでおく keep (*something*) on *file*.

ファインダー〘写真〙a finder. ¶ ～からのぞく look through *a finder*.

ファインプレー a fine play. ¶ ～をする give *a fine performance*.

ファウル〘競技〙〘野球〙a foul. ¶ ～する foul. ～を打つ foul.

ファシスト a fascist.

ファシズム fascism.

ファスナー a fastener ; a zipper. ¶ ～を締める fasten up ; zip up.

ぶあつ・い【分厚い】 thick. ¶ ～い本 a *thick* volume. 1インチもの～い書類 *an inch-thick* document.

ファッショ(主義) fascism ; (人) a fascist.
¶ ～化する fascistize ; go fascist.
―思想 fascistic ideas.

ファッション a fashion.
―ショー a fashion show. ニュー**―** a new fashion ; the latest fashion.

ファン a fan. ¶ 映画(野球)の～ a movie (baseball) fan. 彼の～は多い He has many *fans* (≒ *admirers*).

ふあん【不安】(心配) uneasiness ; anxiety ; (不安定) instability ; uncertainty. ¶ 社会～ social *unrest*. ～の時代 an age of *anxiety*. ～を感じる feel *uneasy* (*about*). ～な顔つきをする look *anxious*. ～の色を隠せない betray

ふ

one's feeling of *anxiety*. ～な一夜を明かす pass an *uneasy* night. どうなるのかと～でならない I *tremble to think* (≒*feel anxious*) how it will end.

ファンタジー fantasy.

ふあんてい【不安定】 instability. ¶ ～な気持ち an *uneasy* feeling. ～な立場 a *precarious* position. ～な天候 *unsettled* weather. ～な政局 an *unstable* situation in politics.

ふあんない【不案内】 (不慣れ) unfamiliarity; (未知) ignorance. ¶ ～な土地 a *strange* place. 土地に～な人 a stranger (*in*). 私はその町については～だ I *am unfamiliar with* (≒ *am a stranger in*) the town.

ファンファーレ a fanfare. ¶ 高らかに～が鳴り響いた There was a loud flourish of *fanfare*.

ふい ¶ まる1日を～にした I *wasted* a whole day. 彼の努力も～になった All his efforts *were in vain*.

ふい【不意】 ¶ ～に unexpectedly. ～の来客 an *unexpected* visitor. ～の出来事 an *unforeseen* event. ～を打つ take (*a person*) by surprise. ～を打たれる be taken by surprise. 彼の死はまったく～だった His death *was quite unexpected*. その知らせはまったく～にやってきた The news came *as a* complete *surprise* to us. 天気が～に変わった The weather changed *suddenly*. あの先生はよく～に試験をする That teacher often gives us an examination *without previous warning* (≒ *without previous notice*). ～にそう言われてまったく困った *Taken by surprise*, I did not know what to say to that.

ブイ a buoy.

フィアンセ (男) *one's* fiancé; (女) *one's* fiancée. ¶ 彼には～がある He is engaged. / He has his *fiancée*.

フィート feet (圏 a foot) (単数形 foot を複数に用いる場合がある). ¶ 3～6インチ three *feet* six inches; three *foot* six.

フィールド〔競技〕the field. ¶ あの選手は～に強い That athlete is good at *field* sports.
—競技 the field sports. **—種目** a field event.

ふいうち【不意打ち】 a surprise attack. ¶ ～を食ってさんざんに負けた *Taken by surprise*, we suffered a crushing defeat.

フィギュア〔スケート〕 figure skating. ¶ ～をする skate figures. ～の選手 a figurer.

フィクション fiction. ¶ 彼の話はある程度～だ His story *is* partly *fictitious*.

ふいご【鞴】 〔a pair of〕 bellows. ¶ ～で吹く blow with the *bellows*. ～を使う work the *bellows*.

ふいちょう【吹聴】 ¶ 彼は金持ちだと～しているHe *gives himself out* for a millionaire. / He *makes out* that he is a rich man. これを～されては困る Do not *tell* this to anybody. この書物をお知り合いにご～くださいPlease *recommend* this book to your friends.

ふいっち【不一致】 disagreement; discord. ¶ 言行～ the *discrepancy* between what *one* says and what *one* does. 性格の～ *incompatibility* of temperament.

ふいと (突然) suddenly; (なにげなく) casually. ¶ 彼は～立ち上がっていった He *suddenly* stood up and went out.

ぷいと (怒って) angrily; sulkily. ¶ 注意された彼は～横を向いた He *got sulky* at my words of admonition and looked away.

フィナーレ〘音楽〙a finale. ¶ 華やかな～で幕がおりた The curtain fell amid the fine music (≒ on the splendid scene) of the *finale*.

フィニッシュ (仕上げ) a finish; (決勝線) the finish line; the goal.

フィヨルド a fiord; a fjord.

フィラメント a filament.

ふいり【不入り】 a small audience; a poor (≒ an empty) house. ¶ 近ごろの映画館は～だ Movie theaters *draw small audiences* (≒ *draw poor houses*) nowadays.

フィリピン the Philippines.
—共和国 the Republic of the Philippines.
—諸島 the Philippine Islands. **—人** a Filipino (圏 Filipinos). **—〔人〕の** Philippine; Filipino.

フィルター a filter. ¶ ～つきたばこ a *filter-tipped* cigarette. レンズに～をかける fix *a filter* to a camera lens.

フィルム a film. ¶ ～1巻 a reel of *film*. ～におさめる *film* (≒ *shoot*) (a scene). ～を現像する develop *a film*. ～をカメラに入れる load a camera.
生— a raw film.

フィンランド Finland.
—人 a Finn. **—語** Finnish. **—〔人〕の** Finnish.

ふう【風】 **1**〘ようす・姿〙a look; an appearance. ¶ 彼はみじめな～をして町に戻ってきた He came back to the town *looking* miserable.
ぜいたくな～はしているが内情は苦しいらしい He *pretends* to live in luxury, but in reality he seems to be hard up.
彼女は私を知らない～を装った She *pretended* not to know me.
それはどんな～の人でしたか What did he *look like*?
教師～の人 a man who *looked like* a teacher.
彼は偉そうな～をするからきらいだ I don't like him, because he *puts on airs*. (on は副詞).
2 〘様式〙 ¶ 西洋～の家 a Western-*style* house; a house in the Western *style*.
北欧～の装い a dress *in* (≒ *after*) the North European *fashion*.
ペトラルカ～(シェイクスピア～)のソネット a Petrarchan (a Shakespearean) sonnet.
漱石～の小説 A novel *after* (≒ *in*) the *manner* of Soseki.
3〘方法〙 ¶ こんな～にするとうまくいく If you do it *thus* (≒ *in this way*; *like this*), you will be all right.
どんな～に彼に説明しようか *How* shall I explain

it to him?
こんな～にしたまえ Do it *in this way.*
4 〖傾向〗¶ あんな ～ だから彼は女にもてない Because he acts *that way* (≒ *like that*), he is not popular with women.
ふう【封】a seal. ¶ ～をする seal; close (an envelope). ～を切る break (≒open) the seal (≒ an envelope); cut (a letter) open. ～のしてある封筒 a *sealed* envelope.
ふうあつ【風圧】wind pressure. ¶ ～に耐える endure *wind pressure.*
―計 an anemometer.
ふういん【封印】sealing. ¶ ～が破られていた The *seal* was broken. その書類は厳重に～してあった The document *was* kept tightly *sealed.*
ふうう【風雨】wind and rain; a storm. ¶ 廃虚は何百年か～にさらされてきた The ruins have been exposed to *the weather* (≒ *wind and rain*) for several centuries. 救援隊は～を冒して出動した The rescue party went out through *the storm.* 昨夜関東地方は激しい～に見舞われた Last night there was *a* heavy *rainstorm* in the Kanto districts.
―注意報 a storm warning.
ふううん【風雲】¶ 世界情勢はいまや～急を告げている The situation of the world *is* now *threatening* (≒ *critical*). 彼は～に乗じてみごとに成功した He successfully *took advantage of troubled times.*
―児 a man of fortune.
ふうか【風化】weathering. ¶ 岩が～する The rocks *are weathered by wind and water.*
ふうが【風雅】¶ ～な人だ a man *of refined taste.* 彼はまるで～を解しない He has no sense for *the elegant and tasteful.*
フーガ〖音楽〗a fugue.
ふうがい【風害】damage from a wind (≒ storm). ¶ ～に見舞われて作物に大損害を受けた *The wind caused* great *damage* to the crops.
ふうかく【風格】a personality; a style. ¶ ～のある人だ He is a man *of noble style* (≒ *of noble appearance*). 彼は彼独自の～を持っている He has *a personality* of his own.
ふうがわり【風変わり】eccentricity. ¶ ～な男 a *queer* character; a *peculiar* man. あの男はどことなく～だ There is something *eccentric* (≒ *odd*) about him. ～な家 a *quaint* house.
ふうかん【封緘】a seal.
―はがき a letter card.
ふうき【風紀】public morals. ¶ 連中の行動は社会の～を乱すものだ Their behavior is injurious to *public morals.* 最近は～が乱れている *Public decency* has recently been corrupt (≒ loose). 学校の～を取り締まる enforce school *discipline.*
ふうき【富貴】¶ 彼は～の生まれだ He was born *rich.* / He was born *with a silver spoon in his mouth.*
ふうぎ【風儀】manners. ¶ ～のよい(悪い)人たちだ How *good-* (*ill-*)*mannered* they are! あそこは～の悪い所だ That is a place of lax *morals.* / *Manners* are corrupt there.
ふうきり【封切り】〖映画〗release. ¶ この映画は世界初めての～だ This is the world *première* of the film.
―映画 a newly released (≒ first-run) film. **―**館 a first-run theater; a first-runner.
ふうけい【風景】the scenery; a sight. ¶ 絵のように美しい～だった *The scenery* was just picturesque. あの丘からながめた町の～はすばらしい That hill commands *a* fine *view* of the town. その川ぞいにはすばらしい～の所がたくさんある There are many lovely *scenes* (≒ *views*) along the river. スイスは～の美しさで有名だ Switzerland is famous for its *scenic* beauty.
―画 a landscape. **―**画家 a landscape painter.
ふうげつ【風月】the beauties of nature; the natural beauty. ¶ 彼は～を友としている He leads a life enjoying nature.
ふうこう【風光】scenery. ¶ 当地は～明媚(めいび)だ We have great *scenic* (≒ *natural*) beauty here.
ふうさ【封鎖】a blockade (*of* a harbor). ¶ 港が～された The port *was blockaded.* 出入口を～すべし The doorway must *be blocked up.* ～を解いた We *lifted* (≒ *broke*; *raised*) *the blockade.*
ふうさい【風采】presence; appearance. ¶ 彼は堂々たる～の人だ He is a man of commanding *presence.* 彼は～のあがらない人だ He is a *plain-looking* man. 彼は～があがらない He is unattractive in *appearance.* / He *cuts a poor figure.*
ふうさつ【封殺】〖野球〗a force-out. ¶ ランナーを～する *force* a runner *out.*
ふうし【風刺・諷刺】〔a〕satire. ¶ イソップ物語の中のあるものは～である Some of Aesop's Fables are *satires.* その小説は世相を痛烈に～している The social conditions *are* severely *satirized* in the novel. / The novel *satirizes* the social conditions severely.
―家(作家) a satirist. **―**画 a caricature. **―**画家 a caricaturist. **―**小説 a satirical novel.
ふうじこ・む【封じ込む】enclose; contain. ¶ お金が手紙の中に～んであった Some money *was enclosed* in the letter. われわれは敵を陣地に～めた We *enclosed* the enemy in their position. ～め作戦 containment.
ふうしゃ【風車】a windmill.
―小屋 a windmill shed.
ふうしゅう【風習】〔manners and〕customs. ¶ ～に従う(を破る) observe (break) *a custom.* 以前には50歳になると引退するのが～だった Formerly it *was customary* for men and women to retire at fifty.
ふうしょ【封書】a sealed letter.
ふうしん【風疹】〖医学〗rubella. ¶ 子どもが～

にかかった My child had (≒ contracted) *German measles.*

ふうすいがい【風水害】damage from (≒ by) the storm and flood. ¶ 毎年〜の痛手を受けている We *are damaged* severely *by storms and floods* every year.

ふう·ずる【封ずる】¶ のりで手紙を〜ずる *seal* a letter with a wafer. 彼の口を〜じておいた(口止め) We *sealed up* his lips.

ふうせつ【風雪】wind and snow. ¶ 彼らは〜をおかして出発した They started in the teeth of (≒ in spite of) the *snowstorm.* 彼はこの20年間世の〜にひとりで耐えてきた He has gone through many *hardships* these twenty years by himself.

ふうせつ【風説】a rumor. ¶ ふたりは生きているとの〜がある *There is a rumor* (≒ *It is rumored*) that the two are alive.

ふうせん【風船】a balloon. ¶ 〜をふくらます inflate *a balloon.* 〜を飛ばす fly *a balloon.*
—ガム a bubble gum. —玉 a toy balloon. 紙— a paper balloon.

ふうぜん【風前】¶ 〜のともしび a candle flickering *before the wind.* 彼の運命もいまや〜のともしびだ His life now *hangs by a thread* (≒ *hair*). / His life *is precarious.*

ふうそく【風速】the velocity of the wind. ¶ 〜1時間90マイルに達した The wind attained *a velocity* of ninety miles an hour. 〜30メートルの暴風だった The wind blew at thirty meters a second.
—計 an anemometer.

ふうぞく【風俗】manners. ¶ 彼らは世の〜を乱している They are against *good manners.*
—習慣 manners and customs. —小説 a genre novel. —喜劇 a comedy of manners.

ふうたい【風袋】(包装) packing ;〘商業〙tare. ¶ 〜こみ(ぬき)で5ポンドあった It weighed five pounds *gross* (*net*).

ふうち【風致】¶ あの建物がこの辺りの〜をすっかり害してしまった That building entirely spoilt *the beauty* around here. チューリップやその他の草花が〜を添えた Tulips and other flowers made *artistic effect.*
—地区 a scenic zone. —林 an ornamental forest.

ふうちょう【風潮】tide ; currency ; (傾向) tendency. ¶ 現代生活の〜は昔の風習から遠ざかっている The *trend* of modern living is away from the old customs. たいていの人は世の〜に従う Most people go with *the current of the times.* 世間の〜に逆らう者はほとんどない Few people swim against *the stream of the times.*

ふうてい【風体】¶ 怪しい〜の男 a suspicious-*looking* man. 見すぼらしい〜をして彼は私に会いにきた He came to see me, poorly *dressed.*

ふうてん【瘋癲】lunacy ; insanity.
—病人 a lunatic ; an insane person. —病院 a lunatic (≒ an insane) asylum.

ふうど【風土】climate ; natural features. ¶ できるだけ早く日本の〜に慣れますように I hope you will *get acclimatized* to Japan as soon as possible.
—病 an endemic ; a local disease.

ふうとう【封筒】an envelope. ¶ 〜にあて名を書く address *an envelope*; write an address on *an envelope.* 手紙を〜に入れる put a letter in *an envelope.* 〜には50円切手をはる put a fifty-yen stamp on *an envelope.*

ふうどう【風洞】a wind tunnel.

プードル (犬) a poodle.

ふうにゅう【封入】enclosure. ¶ 手紙に私の写真を〜した I *enclosed* my photograph in my letter. 1万円の小切手を〜しましたからお受け取りください We are pleased to *enclose* a check for 10,000 yen. / We *are enclosing* a check for 10,000 yen.

ふうは【風波】wind and waves. ¶ 〜が高い *The sea* is rough. / *The wind and waves* are high. 〜をおかして出かけた I went out *in the face* (≒ *teeth*) *of a storm.* あの家庭には〜が絶えない There are endless *troubles* in that family.

ふうばいか【風媒花】an anemophilous flower.

ふうび【風靡】¶ 彼の権威は一世を〜した His authority *took the world by storm.* / His authority *swayed the public at large.*

ふうひょう【風評】a rumor. ¶ そんな根も葉もない〜は気にするな Never mind such a groundless *rumor.* それは一般の〜だ It is *common talk.*

ふうふ【夫婦】a married couple ; man and wife. ¶ きのう小田君〜が来た *Mr. and Mrs.* Oda came to see us yesterday. 彼らは〜になった They *were* (≒ *got*) *married.* / She *was married to* him. / They became *man and wife.* 似合いの〜だ They are *a* well-matched *couple.* 似た者〜 *Like man, like wife.*
—げんか a quarrel between husband and wife. ¶ 〜げんかは犬も食わない One should not interfere in *lovers' quarrels.* —気どり ¶ ふたりとも〜気どりでいる Both of them behave *just like man and wife.* —仲 ¶ 彼らは〜仲がよい They live happily together as *man and wife.* —約束 ¶ ふたりは〜約束をした The two promised to *marry.*

ふうふう ¶ 彼は〜言いながらゴールインした He reached the goal *out of breath.* 彼は〜言ってスープを飲んだ He ate soup *blowing on* it.

ぶうぶう ¶ 彼はいつもなにか〜言っている He *is* always *grumbling.* / He *is complaining of* something. 自動車が警笛を〜鳴らして通った A car passed *honking.*

ふうぶつ【風物】¶ 日本の〜 *things* Japanese. 私はイギリスの〜を楽しみながら旅行した I traveled in England, enjoying *the scenery* there.

ふうぼう【風貌】features. ¶ 彼は堂々たる〜の持ち主だ He is a grand-*looking* man. / He is a man of commanding *presence.* 彼には大家(たいか)の〜がある He has *the look* of a great master. 彼は美しい〜の人だ He is a man of

handsome *features.*
ふうみ【風味】 flavor ; taste. ¶ ～のある(のよい)お茶だ This tea has *a delicious taste.* / This tea *tastes delicate.* ～のないことおびただしい It *tastes* too bad. こしょうで～をつけてある This food *is seasoned* with pepper.
ブーム a boom. ¶ 近ごろ漫画～は大学生にまで及んでいる Nowadays there is *a* comic strip *boom* even among university students. 土地が今～を起こしている Land is now stirring (≒ creating) *a boom* in speculation (≒ prices). テニスが今～だ Tennis playing *is booming* at present.
ブーメラン a boomerang.
ふうらいぼう【風来坊】 a wanderer ; a vagabond. ¶ 困った～だ What *a whimsical person* he is!
ふうりゅう【風流】 elegance. ¶ ～な人だ He is a man *of* [*refined*] *taste.* 彼は～の道にいそしんでいる He is devoting himself to *cultured tastes.* ～な生活をする live *elegantly.* ～なお住まいをお持ちですね You have a *tasteful* residence.
ふうりょく【風力】 the force (≒ velocity) of the wind.
—計 an anemometer.
ふうりん【風鈴】 a wind (≒ hanging) bell.
プール 1 〘水泳〙 a swimming pool.
2 〘共同出資〙 ¶ 金を～する *pool* money.
ふうろう【封蠟】 sealing wax. ¶ ～で封じる seal with *wax.*
ふうん【不運】 misfortune ; ill luck. ¶ 彼は男らしく～に耐えた He met his *misfortune* like a man. ～にも決勝で負けた *Unfortunately* (≒ *Unluckily*) I lost the final match. 彼はわが身の～を嘆いた He lamented his *hard fate* (≒ *hard lot*). 彼は～な一生を送った He had an *ill-fated* life.
ぶうん【武運】 ¶ ～を祈ります I pray for your *victory in war.* ～つたなく敗れ去った *Fortune being against us,* we were defeated.
ふえ【笛】 a flute ; a pipe. ¶ ～を吹く play *a flute* (≒ *on the flute*).
フェア 〘野球〙 fair. ¶ ライナーは～だった The liner *was fair.*
—プレー a fair play. **—ボール** a fair ball.
ふえいせい【不衛生】 ¶ ～な生活 an *unwholesome* way of living. 多くの捕虜は～のため死んだ Many captives died from *unsanitary* conditions.
フェイント feinting ; a feint.
フェーンげんしょう【フェーン現象】 a Föhn phenomenon.
ふえき【賦役】 forced labor.
フェザーきゅう【フェザー級】 〘ボクシング〙 the featherweight.
ふえて【不得手】 ¶ 野球は～だ I *am a poor hand at* baseball. 理科が～だ I *am poor* (≒ *am weak*) *in* science. 計算が～だ I *am bad at* figures. / I *have no head for* figures. 父は商売が～だ Business is *not in my father's line.*
フェニックス 〘エジプト神話〙 ph[o]enix.
フェミニスト a feminist (英語では婦権論者の意味).
フェリーボート a ferryboat.
ふ･える【増える･殖える】 increase ; multiply. ¶ この花は毎年～えるだろう These flowers will *increase* every year. 目方が3キロ～えた I *gained* three kilograms *in weight.* / I *put on weight* by three kilograms. 東京の人口は～える一方だ The population of Tokyo *goes on increasing.* 川の水が急に～えた The river *has risen* fast. 不注意な運転で事故が～える Careless driving *breeds* accidents. 木は種子によって～える Trees *propagate themselves* by seeds.
フェルト felt. ¶ ～のスリッパ *felt* slippers.
—帽 a felt hat.
ふえん【敷衍】 enlargement. ¶ さらに～して説明する *amplify* (≒ *enlarge*) *on one's* explanation.
フェンシング 〘競技〙 fencing. ¶ ～の選手 a fencer.
ぶえんりょ【無遠慮】 unreservedness. ¶ きみはあまりに～すぎる You *are* too *forward* (≒ *outspoken*). ～なものの言い方をしないように気をつけなさい Be careful not to speak *without reserve.* 彼に対して～にすぎたのではないかと心配だ I am afraid of *having been* too *free with* him. 彼が～に客間へ飛び込んできた He dashed into the parlor *without ceremony.*
フォアボール 〘野球〙 four balls. ¶ ～で打者を3人も歩かせた He *has walked* three batters *on four balls.* ～で出塁した He went to first *on four balls.*
フォークソング a folk song.
フォークダンス a folk dance.
フォークボール 〘野球〙 a fork ball.
フォースアウト 〘野球〙 force-out.
フォーム form. ¶ 彼の泳ぐときの～はいい His *form* in swimming is excellent.
フォックステリア (犬) a fox terrier.
フォックストロット 〘音楽〙 a fox trot.
ぶおとこ【醜男】 an ugly man; an ill-favored man.
フォルテ 〘音楽〙 *forte* (イタリア語から).
フォワード 〘球技〙 a forward (F.W.).
フォン 〘物理〙 phon.
ふおん【不穏】 unrest ; sedition. ¶ 目下の情勢は～だ The present situation *is threatening* (≒ *is critical*). 彼らが～な行動に出る恐れもある It is feared that they will *disturb the peace* of society.
—分子 disturbing elements. **—文書** seditious documents.
ふおんとう【不穏当】 impropriety. ¶ それは～な処置だ It is an *improper* (≒ *unfair*) dealing. きみはことば遣いが～だ You use *improper* language.
ふか【鱶】 a shark.
ふか【不可】 ¶ この作品は可もなく～もなしだ This work *is neither good nor bad.* 彼らはその案を～として, 彼に新計画の作成を命じた They *disapproved of* the plan and ordered him to make a new one. それを彼は断じて～とする

ふ

He is absolutely *against* it. 可とする者15名, ～とする者 6 名 The yeses were 15 and *noes* 6. / Fifteen are in favor of the plan, while six are *against* it. 彼は物理で～をとった He *failed in* physics.

ふか【付加】addition ; supplement. ¶ それらの報告書は当然その文献に～すべきだ You should *add* those reports *to* the literature of the subject.

—税 an additional tax ; a supertax ; 米 a surtax. **—物** an addition.

ふか【賦課】levy ; imposition. ¶ 所得税を～する *levy* an income tax (*on*). 土地には固定資産税が～される A fixed assets tax *is imposed on* land.

ふか【孵化】hatching. ¶ ひなを～する *hatch out* chickens ; *incubate* chickens.

人工**—** artificial incubation. 人工**—器** an 〔artificial〕 incubator.

ぶか【部下】a subordinate ; *one's* man ; a follower ; (従者) a retainer. ¶ ～の兵 soldiers (≒ men) *under one's command.* あの人には有能な～がいる He *has* some able *men under him.* あの男をきみの～にしよう I will *place him under your orders.* あの人の～となって働くくらいなら会社をやめたほうがいい I would rather leave the firm than *work under him.*

ふかい【不快】(不愉快) unpleasantness ; (病気) sickness ; discomfort. ¶ ～なにおい an *unpleasant* smell. ～な音 a *jarring* sound. 彼は私を見ると～な顔をした He *looked displeased* to see me. 彼のぶしつけなことばは彼らを～にさせた His blunt speech *hurt their feelings.* / They *were offended by* his blunt speech.

—指数 a discomfort index (DI).

ふか・い【深い】deep ; profound. ¶ ～い海 a *deep* sea. ～い考え a *deep* thought. ～い配慮 a *thoughtful* consideration. ～い意義 a *profound* significance. ～い学問 *profound* learning. ～い眠り a *sound* (≒ *deep; heavy*) sleep. ～い悲しみ *deep* sorrow. ～い憎しみ *intense* hatred. ～い感謝 *deep* gratitude. ～い印象 a *deep* impression. ～い霧 a *dense* (≒ *thick ; heavy*) fog. ～い森 a *dense* (≒ *thick*) forest. ～い交わり *close* relations. 彼は彼女と～い仲だ He *is deeply in love with* her.

ぶかい【部会】a sectional meeting.

ぶがい【部外】**—者** outsiders. **—秘** Restricted ; Confidential.

ふがいな・い【腑甲斐ない】(意気地のない) pluckless ; unmanly ; cowardly ; poor-spirited ; (働きのない) good-for-nothing ; (頼みがいのない) untrustworthy ; unreliable. ¶ われながら～いと思う I *am ashamed of myself.*

ふかいり【深入り】¶ そのことにあまり～しないほうがいい You had better not *go too far* in the affair. 政治には～するな You shouldn't *get mixed up in* politics.

ふかおい【深追い】¶ ～は危ない It is dangerous to *go too far.* 敵を～するのは賢明でない I think it unwise to *chase* our enemy *too far.*

ふかかい【不可解】¶ ～なこと a mystery ; a riddle. ～な男 a *mystery* man ; a sphinx ; an enigma. まったく～だ (理解できない) It *is beyond comprehension.* / (不思議である) It *is* quite *mysterious.* ときに女は男にとって～である Sometimes women *are ununderstandable* (≒ *are inscrutable*) to men.

ふかく【不覚】(敗北) a defeat ; (失敗) a failure ; (過失) a mistake. ¶ 残念ながら～をとった I *was defeated* to my great regret. 筆記試験に～をとった I *failed in* the written examination. 彼に頼ったのは～だった I *made a blunder in* relying on him. / *It was careless of me to* rely upon him. 彼は思わず～の涙を流した He shed tears *involuntarily* (≒ *in spite of himself*). 酔っ払って彼は前後～となった He was very drunk and *knew no more.*

ふかく【俯角】〘数学〙an angle of depression.

ふかく【深く】¶ もっと～考えなさい Think of it more *deeply.* みんな～感動した All were *deeply* moved. ～みなさんにおわびいたします I *profoundly* (≒ *heartily*) apologize to all of you. ～感謝いたします I thank you *from the depth of my heart* (≒ *very much*). そのためにふたりの感情のみぞがいっそう～なった The gap between the two *widened* for it. この本を読んで音楽に対する興味が～なった My interest in music *deepened* by reading this book. それから彼との関係が～なった Then I began to have *closer* contacts with him. 雪が～積もった The snow lay *deep.* ～掘る dig *deep.* 秋もようやく～なった Autumn *is far advanced* now.

ふかくじつ【不確実】uncertainty. ¶ その真相はまだ～だ The truth *is* still *uncertain.* 方法が～だ The method *is doubtful.* ～な約束はしない I never make *unreliable* promises.

ふかくだい【不拡大】**—方針** ¶ 政府は～方針をとった The government adopted *a policy of localizing the affair.* / The government took *a non-expansion policy* (≒ *localization policy*).

ふかくてい【不確定】¶ ～なこと *uncertain* things. ～な問題 an *unsettled* (≒ *undecided*) matter. ～な命題 an *indefinite* proposition.

—性原理〘物理〙uncertainty principle.

ふかけつ【不可欠】¶ 新鮮な空気は健康に～だ Fresh air *is indispensable to* health. 公平無私の精神は裁判官に～だ Impartiality *is essential to* a judge.

ふかこうりょく【不可抗力】an act of god. ¶ その惨事は～だった The miserable accident *was inevitable* (≒ *was beyond control*). なにか～のものがわれわれを遅らせた Something *beyond our control* delayed us.

ふかさ【深さ】depth. ¶ ～を測る sound *the depth* (*of*). ～8フィート It is eight feet *deep* (≒ *in depth*). ～の知れない深淵(しんえん) a *bottomless* (≒ *fathomless*) abyss.

ふかざけ【深酒】heavy drinking. ¶ あまり～

ふ

するな Don't *drink too much.* / You must not *overdrink yourself.*

ふかしぎ【不可思議】a mystery ; (なぞ) a riddle ; an enigma ; (奇跡) a miracle. ¶ ～な微笑 a *mysterious* smile.

ふかしん【不可侵】nonaggression.
—権 an inviolable right. —条約 a nonaggression pact.

ふか·す【吹かす】¶ たばこを～す *smoke* (tabacco). パイプを～す *smoke* a pipe. エンジンを～す *rev up* the motor. 先輩風を～す *give oneself airs* as a senior.

ふか·す【蒸かす】¶ ジャガイモを～す *steam* potatoes.

ふかち【不可知】—論 〖哲学〗 agnosticism. —論者 an agnostic.

ぶかっこう【不格好】¶ ～な男 an *awkward-looking* man. ～な服 an *ill-cut* coat. ～な手つきで in an *awkward* manner ; with a *clumsy* hand. ～な鼻 an *ill-shaped* (≒ *unshapely*) nose. ～な歩き方 an *awkward* gait (≒ way of walking). 彼女は～な身なりをしている She is *awkwardly* dressed.

ふかっぱつ【不活発】¶ ～な子ども a *spiritless* child. ～な性質 a *sluggish* temperament. 彼は動作が～だ He *is slow in* motion. この季節は取引が～である Business *is slack in* this season. / The market *is stagnant* (≒ *is slow*) *in* this season. 小麦の市況は～である The trade for wheat *is inactive.*

ふかづめ【深爪】¶ ～しないように Take care not to *cut your nail to the quick.*

ふかで【深手】a serious wound ; (致命的) a mortal wound. ¶ 激しく争って両者とも～を負った Both *were seriously wounded* in their furious fight.

ふかのう【不可能】impossibility. ¶ その計画は実現～だ It *is impossible* to realize the plan. 彼は～を可能にする男だ He is a man to make *the impossible* possible. それは明らかに履行～な約束だ It is a promise obviously *impossible* to keep.

ふかひ【不可避】¶ 交渉決裂は～と思われる The breakdown of the negotiations seems *unavoidable.* 死は～である Death *is inevitable.*

ぶかぶか ¶ ～のズボン *baggy* trousers. ～の上着 a coat *too large for a person.*

ぷかぷか ¶ たばこを～吹かす *puff away at one's* cigarette.

ふかぶかと【深深と】¶ ～頭を下げる make a *deep* bow. 彼はいすに～腰掛けてくつろいだ He made himself at ease *with his body deep in* the chair.

ふかぶん【不可分】¶ それとこれとは～の関係にある This *is inseparable from* that. 両国は～の関係にある The two countries *are inseparably related to* each other.

ふかま·る【深まる】¶ 美術に対する興味が～る The interest in art *deepens.* 秋が～った Autumn *is far advanced.* 経験が～るにつれて彼は自信がついてきた He came to have confidence in himself *with growing experience.* 夜が～るにつれてとても寒くなった As night *wore on,* it got very cold.

ふかみ【深み】a depth. ¶ 少年は～にはまった The boy *got into deep waters.* 彼の書くものには～がない His writings have no *depth.* あまり～にはまりこんではいけない(深く関係する) You must not *go too far.*

ふか·める【深める】¶ 印象を～める *deepen one's* impression. 経験を～める *enrich one's* experience. 理解を～める *promote* a better understanding. 憎しみを～める *intensify one's* hatred. 懸念を～める *heighten one's* anxiety. 関係を～める *make* the connection *closer.*

ふかん【俯瞰】¶ これは飛行機から～撮影した写真だ This is a *bird's-eye view* photo taken from an airplane.
—図 a bird's-eye view ; (飛行機からの) an air view.

ぶかん【武官】大使館付き— a military (≒ naval) attaché (to the embassy).

ふかんしへい【不換紙幣】inconvertible notes (≒ paper money) ; 米 fiat money.

ふかんしょう【不干渉】nonintervention ; noninterference.

ふかんしょう【不感症】〖医学〗 frigidity. ¶ 彼らは不正な取引に対して～になっている *Their conscience is benumbed to* unlawful trades. いまや市民の大半は交通事故の惨事に～になっている Most of the citizens *are* now *unmoved* (≒ *immune*) *to* the misery of traffic accidents. あの女は～だ She *is frigid.*

ふかんぜん【不完全】imperfection ; incompleteness ; (欠陥) defectiveness. ¶ ～な点 a defect ; a fault. 人間は～なものだ Man *is imperfect.* 彼の英語は～だ His English *is far from perfect.* この車には構造に～なところがある This car *is defective in* construction.
—動詞 〖文法〗 an incomplete verb. —燃焼 imperfect combustion.

ふき【蕗】〖植物〗 a butterbur(r).

ふき【付記】an addition. ¶ 彼女はその手紙に新しい車を手に入れたことを～した She *added* (≒ *mentioned in addition*) in the letter that she had got a new car.

ふぎ【不義】adultery ; (不道徳) immorality ; (不正) injustice ; (密通) illicit intercourse.

ぶき【武器】arms ; a weapon ; (総称) weaponry. ¶ ～をとる take up *arms* ; rise in *arms.* ～を捨てる give up *one's arms.* 人から～を取り上げる disarm (*a person*) of his *weapons.* 涙は女の～ Tears are *a* woman's *weapon.*

ふきあ·げる【吹き上げる】¶ シャボン玉を～げる *blow up* a soap balloon. 鯨が潮を～げる The whale *spouts* water.

ふきあ·れる【吹き荒れる】¶ 風が一晩じゅう～れた It *blew hard and strong* all through the night.

ふきおく·る【吹き送る】¶ 芳香が果樹園から～られてくる A fragrance *comes wafted* from

ふ

the orchard.

ふきおと·す【拭き落とす】¶ 机の上のしみを～す *wipe out* a stain on the desk. 窓ガラスの汚れを～す *wipe* a windowpane *clean.* 彼はほおから血を～した He *wiped* the blood *off* his cheek.

ふきおろ·す【吹き下ろす】¶ 山から～す風が冷たい The wind *blowing down* over the mountain is cold.

ふきかえ【吹き替え】(代役)〘映画〙a stand-in; 〘演劇〙 a substitute actor; (フィルムの再録音)〘映画〙dubbing.

ふきかえ·す【吹き返す】¶ まもなく彼は息を～した He *came to life again* (≒ *came to himself*) before long. 冷たい風に当たって彼は息を～した The cool air *brought him to himself.*

ふきか·える【葺き替える】reroof; (かわらを) retile; (わら屋根を) rethatch.

ふきか·ける【吹き掛ける】¶ 指に息を～ける *blow* (≒ *breathe*) *on one's* fingers. ズボンに霧を～ける *spray upon* the trousers. 無理難題を～ける *ask* too much *of (a person).* 高い値段を～ける *ask* a fancy price. けんかを～ける *pick* (≒ *seek*) a quarrel *with (a person).* 風が窓に雨を～けた The wind *blew* the rain *against* the window.

ふきけ·す【吹き消す】¶ マッチの火を～す *blow out* a lighted match.

ふ

ふきげん【不機嫌】displeasure; bad (≒ ill) humor. ¶ きょうは彼は～な顔をしている He *looks displeased* (≒ *looks sullen; looks ill-humored*) today. きょうは彼は～だ He *is in bad humor* (≒ *is out of humor*) today.

ふきこぼ·れる【吹きこぼれる】¶ なべが～れている The pot *is boiling over.*

ふきこ·む【吹き込む】¶ 雨が部屋に～む It *rains into* the room. 風が透き間から部屋に～む It *blows into* the room through the crevices. / The draft (≒ draught) *blows into* the room. 彼女は新曲をレコードに～んだ She *had* a new song *recorded.* 彼は青年たちに向学心を～んだ He *inspired* young men *with* a love for learning.

ふきさらし【吹き曝し】¶ 会場は～だ The meeting place *is exposed to the wind.* 彼女は～の駅で2時間彼を待った She waited for him two hours at the *wind-swept* station.

ふきすさ·ぶ【吹き荒ぶ】¶ その夜は風が～んでいた It *was blowing violently* (≒ *furiously*) that night. / That night the storm *was raging.*

ふきそ【不起訴】non-prosecution. ¶ 彼は～になった He *was acquitted.* 検事たちはその件を～処分にすることに決めた The public prosecutors decided to *drop the case.*

ふきそうじ【拭き掃除】¶ 彼は毎朝自分の部屋の～をする He *sweeps and dusts* his room every morning.

ふきそく【不規則】irregularity. ¶ 彼は生活が～だ He lives an *irregular* life. / He *is irregular* in his life. 彼は仕事ぶりが～だ He works *by fits and starts.* 彼は出席状況が～だ He *is irregular in* his attendance. 彼の勉強方法は～だ He studies *unsystematically.*

ふきたお·す【吹き倒す】¶ かきねが風で～された The fence *was blown down.* / The wind *blew* the fence *down.*

ふきだ·す【吹き出す】(風が) begin to blow; (息を) breathe out; (水や血が) spout (≒ spurt) out; (ガスや火を) blow out; (煙を) send out; (はれものが) erupt; break out; (笑いだす) burst out laughing; burst (≒ break) into laughter.

ふきだまり【吹き溜り】a snowdrift. ¶ 運動場の片すみに雪が～になっている The snow in a corner of the playground *is piled into drifts.*

ふきちら·す【吹き散らす】scatter about; blow about (≒ away).

ふきつ【不吉】¶ ～な日 an *evil* (≒ *ominous*) day. ～な前兆 an *ill* omen. ～な鳥 a bird *of ill omen.* ～な夢 an *unlucky* dream. ～な星 an *inauspicious* (≒ *unlucky*) star. ～な予感 a foreboding; an *ominous* presentiment.

ふきつ·ける【吹き付ける】¶ 風が雨戸にあられを～けた The wind *blew* hailstones *against* the shutters. 船はとうとう岸に～けられた The ship *was* at last *blown ashore.* 壁を二度～けてもらった I *had* the wall *sprayed* twice.

ふきでもの【吹き出物】an eruption; a boil; a carbuncle; (にきび) a pimple. ¶ 首に～ができている I have *eruptions* on my neck.

ふきとば·す【吹き飛ばす】blow away. ¶ 風で家の屋根が～された The wind *blew* the roof *away from* the house. 私は帽子を～された I *had* my hat *blown off.*

ふきと·る【拭き取る】wipe out. ¶ 彼女はこぼれたテーブルのミルクを～った She *wiped out* the spilt milk on the table. 壁の汚れを～った I *wiped* the wall *clean.*

ふきながし【吹き流し】a streamer. ¶ すんだ空に鯉の～がみえる I see *a set of carp pennants* fluttering in the clear sky.

ふきのとう【蕗の薹】a butterbur flower.

ふきはら·う【吹き払う】blow away; drive away. ¶ 風が霧を～った The wind *has driven away* the fog.

ふきぶり【吹き降り】a driving rain. ¶ 一日じゅう～だった We have had *a driving rain* all day. / It *has been raining and blowing* all day. ひどい～の中を彼は飛び出していった He ran away in *the heavy storm.*

ふきほんぽう【不羈奔放】¶ 彼は～な男だ He *has a free and independent spirit.* / He is a man *impatient of control.* / He *lives a free and wild life.*

ふきまく·る【吹きまくる】¶ 木枯らしが街を～っていた The cold blasts *were sweeping along* the streets. あまり自分の才能を～るのは感心しない It is not good to *brag* (≒ *talk big*) about your gifts.

ふきまわし【吹き回し】¶ どういう風の～でここへ来

たのだ What good wind has blown you here? / What stroke of fortune has brought you here?

ぶきみ【無気味】¶ ～な静寂 an *ominous* silence. ～な容貌(ぼう) an *unearthly* (≒ a *ghastly*) look. ～なようす an *uncanny* (≒ a *weird* [wiəd]; an *eerie* [iəri]) appearance. ～な殺人の話 a *gruesome* tale of murder. 暗夜にフクロウの鳴き声は～だ The hooting of an owl in the dark night *makes our blood run cold.*

ふきや【吹き矢】a blowpipe; a blowgun.

ふきや·む【吹き止む】¶ 風が～んだ The wind *dropped* (≒ *lulled; blew over; died away; went down*). / It *ceased to blow.*

ふきゅう【不朽】immortality. ¶ ～の名作 an *immortal* work. ～の名声 an *eternal* fame. その作品が彼の名を～のものとした The work *immortalized* his name.

ふきゅう【普及】spread; diffusion. ¶ 英語は全国に～した English *has spread* all over the country. 教育の～が目下の急務だ Our urgent business now is to *promote the spread* (≒ *diffusion*) *of* education. カラーテレビが～している Color television *has come into wide use.* これは視聴覚教育の～に役だつ This aids (≒ is useful) in *popularizing* audio-visual education. キリスト教は全国に～している Christianity *is widely spread.*
—版 a popular edition.

ふきょう【不況】recession. ¶ 市場は～である The market *is slack* (≒ *is inactive; is bad*). 鉄鋼業界の～は深刻である The iron and steel industry *is in* extreme *depression.* ～時代が近づいている *Depression* (≒ *Recession*) *days* are coming near.

ふきょう【不興】displeasure; ill humor. ¶ 私は彼の～を買った I incurred his *displeasure.* / He *fell into disgrace with* me. 彼女は彼の言を聞いて，いかにも～げであった She *was* quite *ill-humored* to hear his words./ She listened to him *with a very displeased look.*

ふきょう【布教】propagation. ¶ モルモン教を～する *propagate* (≒ *preach*) Mormonism. 彼は～に従事した He was engaged in *missionary work.*

ふきょう【富強】prosperity and power. ¶ 国家の～を図る strive for national *wealth and power.* ～な国 a *prosperous and powerful* country.

ぶきよう【不器用】unskillfulness; inaptness. ¶ 彼は～だ He *is awkward* (≒ *is clumsy*)./ He is *a bungler* (≒ *a botcher*). 彼女はやることなすこと～だ She does everything *in an awkward manner.* 彼はのこぎりの使いかたが～だ He handles a saw *unskillfully* (≒ *awkwardly; with a clumsy hand*).

ぶぎょう【奉行】a magistrate; an administrator.
—所 a magistrate's office.

ふぎょうせき【不行跡】misconduct; evil way. ¶ 彼の～は困ったものだ His *misconduct* is annoying.

ふきょうわおん【不協和音】〘音楽〙a discord; a dissonance.

ぶきょく【部局】a department.
—制度 a departmental system.

ぶきょく【舞曲】a dancing music.

ふきよせ【吹き寄せ】¶ 雪の～ a snowdrift. 砂の～ a dune; a sand drift.
音曲— a variety of entertainments.

ふぎり【不義理】default; ingratitude; dishonesty. ¶ 彼は～な人だ He *is dishonest* (≒ *is unjust*). 彼は人に～をしても目的を果たす He will *do* others *a wrong* in order to gain his end. あのような～をしては世間で許さぬ Such *an act of injustice* will not pass. きみに～がある I *owe* you *a debt.* 彼に～をしてしまった I *broke faith with* him. ～な人 an *ungrateful* person.

ぶきりょう【不器量】¶ 彼女は～だからもらい手がない She *is so plain* that nobody will marry her. その娘は～だが親切だ The girl has a *homely* countenance, but a kind heart.

ふきわ·ける【吹き分ける】blow away by fanning. ¶ もみがらを～ける *winnow* chaff *from* grain. 鉱石から鉄を～ける *smelt* iron *from* the ore.

ふきわた·る【吹き渡る】¶ そよ風が野原を～っている A gentle breeze *is blowing* over the fields.

ふきん【付近】neighborhood; vicinity. ¶ ～の町 a *neighboring* town. 彼はこの～に住んでいる He lives somewhere *near here* (≒ *in this neighborhood*). ～に家がなかった There was no house *around.* 東京～に雪が降った They had snow *in and around* Tokyo (≒ *in* Tokyo *and its vicinity*).

ふきん【布巾】a dishcloth; a napkin; a wiping cloth.

ふきんこう【不均衡】imbalance; disparity. ¶ ～な給与 *unequal* (≒ *disproportioned*) wages. それを～でないように配分した It was distributed *equally* (≒ *evenly*). 1週間の労働に対して10ドルはあまりにも～だ Ten dollars would *be* too *disproportionate for* a week's work. 貧富の間の～ the *inequality* between the rich and the poor.

ふきんしん【不謹慎】indiscretion; imprudence. ¶ 彼は～にもそんなことをした He had the *imprudence* to do such a thing. 彼女はいつも～だ She always *lacks prudence.* 彼は～にもそんなことを言った He *was imprudent* enough to say such a thing. ～なことば *immodest* remarks.

ふく【服】a dress; clothes; a suit. ¶ 彼女は～を着た She put on *a dress.* 彼は～を着替えた He changed his *clothes.* 彼はイギリスの士官～を着ていた He wore *the uniform* of a British officer. 彼女は白い～を着ていた She *was dressed* in white. きのう～を新調した Yesterday I had *a* new *suit* made.

ふく【福】fortune; a blessing. ¶ ～は内，鬼は

外 Let *fortune* in and the devil out. / In with *fortune*! Out with the demon!

ふく【副】（控え）a duplicate;（写し）a copy. ¶正～2通の文書 two copies of a document; an original and *a copy*.
―議長 a vice-chairman. ―支配人 an assistant manager. ―大統領 a vice-president.

-ふく【-服】 ¶薬2～ two *doses of* medicine. 茶一～ *a cup of* tea. たばこを一～する have (≒ take) a smoke (≒ a puff); smoke a pipe. 彼は葉巻きを二, 三～吸った He *took* two or three *puffs at* his cigar. お茶を一～いかがですか Do you care for *a cup of* tea?

ふ・く【吹く・噴く】 ¶風がひどく～く It *blows* hard. ろうそくを～いて消す *blow out* a candle. 柳が芽を～く A willow *puts forth* buds. 御飯が～いている The rice *is boiling over*. 火山が火を～いている A volcano *is emitting* fire. 笛を～く *play* the flute. 牛乳を口で～いて冷やす *blow* milk to cool it. 風がそよとも～かぬ There is not *a breath of air*. 彼は口から泡を～いた He *foamed* at the mouth. 彼女は私の服に霧を～いた She *sprayed on* my dress. 彼はほらを～く He *talks big*. / He *blows his own trumpet*.

ふ・く【拭く】 ¶私はぞうきんで机を～いた I *wiped* the desk with a floorcloth. ふきんでさらを～く *dry* dishes with a cloth. タオルで体を～く *dry oneself* with a towel. 彼女はエプロンで涙を～いた She *dried* her tears *on* her apron. 彼は額の汗を～いた He *wiped* the perspiration *off* his forehead.

ふ・く【葺く】 ¶その家はわらで～いてある The house *is thatched* (≒ *is covered*) *with* straw. かわら～きの家 a *tiled* house. 板～き屋根 a shingle roof. わら～きの家 a *thatched* cottage.

ふぐ【河豚】 a globefish; a swellfish.
―中毒 swellfish poisoning. ―汁 swellfish soup.

ふぐ【不具】 deformity; malformation. ¶彼は交通事故で～になった He *was deformed* (≒ *was crippled*) in a traffic accident.

ぶぐ【武具】 arms; weapons of war;（よろい）armor. ¶私は～に身を固めた I *armed* (≒ *armored*) *myself*.

ふくあん【腹案】 a plan; a design. ¶～はできている I have *a plan* ready. 私はなんの～もなく演壇に立った I stood on the platform without any *preparation*.

ふくいく【馥郁】 ¶～たる花 a *sweet-smelling* flower. ～たる梅の香が漂った The *fragrance* (≒ *scent*) of the plum blossoms filled the air. 彼は窓を開いて新鮮な～たる香の空気を入れた Throwing open the window, he let in the fresh *fragrant* air.

ふくいん【復員】 demobilization; deactivation. ¶彼はベトナムから～した He *was demobilized* (≒ *was discharged*; *was demobbed*) from Vietnam.
―軍人 a demobilized serviceman.

ふくいん【福音】 gospel. ¶この薬はがんの患者にとって～かもしれない This medicine may be *a boon* to the cancer patient. それはサラリーマンには～だ It is *good news* for salaried men.
―会 a gospel society. ―教会 the Evangelical Church. ―書 the Gospels.

ふぐう【不遇】 misfortune; adversity. ¶彼は～を冷静に耐え忍んだ He bore *misfortune* calmly. 彼は一生～で終わった He lived *in obscurity* all his life. 彼女は～をかこつ She complains of her *ill fate*. 私は～の地位にある I *am in adverse circumstances*.

ふくえき【服役】 ¶私は～(兵役)したことがない I *have* never *served* in the army. 彼は5年間～した He served *a prison term* for five years. 彼女は刑期～中だ She *is serving her time* (≒ *her sentence*).
―期間（兵役）a term of service;（懲役）a term of sentence. ―者 a convict.

ふくえん【復縁】 reconciliation. ¶彼は彼女に～を迫った He urged her to *be reinstated* as his wife.

ふくがく【復学】 ¶彼は2年後～した He *was re-enrolled* two years later. / He *returned to school* two years later.

ふくがん【複眼】 a compound eye.

ふくぎょう【副業】 a side job (≒ work); subsidiary work. ¶～として喫茶店を経営した I managed a tea house *on the side* (≒ *as a sideline*). 生活難の緩和策として～が奨励された *Subsidiary industry* was encouraged as a means of lightening the difficulty of living.

ふくげん【復元】〔a〕reconstruction. ¶金閣寺を～した We *restored* the Kinkakuji Temple *to the former* (≒ *original*) *state*.
―力 dynamical stability; force of restitution.

ふくごう【複合】 compositeness.
―概念 a complex concept. ―語 a compound word. ―体 a complex. ―文 a compound sentence. ―汚染 multiple contamination.

ふくさ【袱紗】 a small crape wrapper.

ふくざい【伏在】 ¶彼の失職にはなにかが裏面に～している Something *lies behind* his unemployment.

ふくざい【服罪】 submission. ¶彼は判決に潔く～した He *submitted to* a decision with resignation. / He *entered a plea of guilty* with resignation. 犯人は～した The suspect *pleaded guilty*.

ふくざつ【複雑】 complexity; intricacy; complication. ¶人生は～だ Life *is complex* (≒ *is complicated*). それは～な文章だ It is an *involved* style. 彼は～な表情だった He had an expression of *mixed* feelings. これには～な事情がある There are *intricate* circumstances behind this matter. 彼の論証はかなり～だ His proof *is rather involved*. / His proof *is hard to understand*. それは構造が～だ It *is complicated* in structure. 彼女

ふ

は～な笑い方をした She smiled a *mystic* smile. 日本では親戚(しんせき)関係は非常に～だ There is a great deal of *complexity* about relationship in Japan.

ふくさよう【副作用】reaction; a secondary effect; a side effect. ¶ その薬は胃に～を起こす The medicine produces *harmful effects on* the stomach. この薬は～がない This medicine is free from *harmful aftereffects.* / This medicine produces no *ill effects.* 抗ヒスタミン剤の～で眠くなった *A side effect* of antihistamines made me drowsy.

ふくさんぶつ【副産物】a by-product.

ふくし【副詞】〔文法〕an adverb. ¶ ～的用法 an *adverbial* use.
—句 an adverbial phrase.

ふくし【福祉】welfare; well-being. ¶ その政策は社会の～を促進する The policy promotes social *welfare.* それは国民の～を増進する It makes for the *welfare* (≒ *well-being*) of the people.
—国家 a welfare state. —事務所 a welfare office. 社会—事業 social welfare service.

ふくじ【服地】dress material; cloth.

ふくしき【複式】—火山 a double volcano. —記帳法 double entry. —投票 plural voting. —簿記 double entry bookkeeping.

ふくしきこきゅう【腹式呼吸】abdominal breathing; the abdominal type of respiration.

ふくじてき【副次的】secondary; subsidiary; supplementary; auxiliary. ¶ それは～なことだ It is a *secondary* thing.

ふくしゃ【複写】duplication; (複写したもの) a duplicate; a copy; a reproduction.
¶ カーボン紙で～する *duplicate* (*a thing*) through a sheet of carbon paper. さし絵は写真を～したものである The illustration *is reproduced from* the photograph. 原稿を～しておく I'll *make a copy of* (≒ *copy; reproduce*) my manuscript. ラファエルの～ *a copy from* Raphael.
—機 a duplicator; a copying press; a duplicating apparatus. —紙 copying paper. —用インク copying ink. —用カメラ a duplicating camera.

ふくしゃ【輻射】〔物理〕radiation. ¶ ～する radiate.
—光 radiant light. —線 a radiant ray. —体 a radiator. —熱 radiant heat.

ふくしゅ【副手】a sub-assistant.

ふくしゅう【復習】review. ¶ きょうの英語の～は終わったか *Have* you already *reviewed* today's English *lesson*? / Did you *go over* today's English *lesson*?

ふくしゅう【復讐】avenge; revenge (他人のために復讐するときは avenge を用い, 自分のために復讐するときは revenge を用いる).
¶ 彼は～の念に燃えた He burnt with *revengeful* thought. 彼は敵に～した He *revenged himself on* the enemy. / He *was revenged on* the enemy. 彼女は殺された主人のために～した She *avenged* her master *on* his murderer. ～を企てたが失敗だった We sought *vengeance upon* our enemy in vain. 彼女は～に彼を殺した She killed him *in vengeance.* その国はドイツに対し～的手段をとった The nation adopted *retaliatory* measures against Germany.
—劇 a revenge tragedy. —者 a revenger. —心 revengeful thought. —戦 a revenge; a return match.

ふくじゅう【服従】obedience. ¶ どの子どもも～ということを教えられるべきだ Every child should be taught *obedience.* われわれは両親の言うことに～する We *obey* our parents. / We *are obedient to* our parents. 会員は会則に～する All the members of the society *are subjected to* its rules. 彼は目上には～し, 目下には親切だ He *is submissive to* the superiors and kind to the inferiors.

ふくじゅそう【福寿草】〔植物〕an adonis; a pheasant's-eye.

ふくしょう【副賞】an extra prize; a supplementary prize.

ふくしょう【復唱】repetition. ¶ 私の命令を～せよ *Repeat* my orders.

ふくしょく【服飾】dress and its ornaments.
—学校 a dressmaking school. —品 accessories; ladies' accessories.

ふくしょく【復職】reinstatement; reappointment. ¶ 私は先月～した I *was reinstated in the service* last month. 学生は女教師の～を求めてストライキをしている The students are on strike for the *return* of the school mistress.

ふくしょく〔ぶつ〕【副食〔物〕】a side dish; a subsidiary food.

ふくしん【腹心】a confidant (女性の場合は confidante). ¶ ～の友 a *bosom* friend. ～の部下 one of *one's confidential* (≒ *trusted*) men; a *devoted* follower. 首相は彼を～の部下とした The prime minister *admitted* him *into his confidence.* / He was *the confidant* of the premier.

ふくじん【副腎】〔解剖学〕adrenal glands.
—ホルモン adrenalin〔e〕.

ふくじんづけ【福神漬】sliced vegetables preserved in soy sauce.

ふく・す【服す】⇒ふくする

ふくすい【腹水】〔医学〕ascites; dropsy of the belly.

ふくすい【覆水】¶ ～盆に返らず(諺) *It is no use crying over spilt milk.*

ふくすう【複数】〔文法〕the plural number.
—形 ¶ 'ox' の～形はなにか What is the *plural form* of 'ox'? それは～形で用いられる It is used *in the plural.*

ふく・する【服する】¶ われわれは命令に～する We *obey* the orders. 彼女は罪に～した She *submitted to* (≒ *pleaded guilty to*) the sentence. 彼は1年間喪に～することになる He is supposed to *be in mourning* (≒ *observe mourning*) for one year. 兵役に〜する *serve* in the army. 彼は道理に〜する(〜さない) He is *amenable* (*deaf*) to reason.

ふく·する【復する】¶かくて平常の状態に〜した Normal conditions *were* thus *restored*.

ふくせい【複製】reproduction ; reprinting. ¶そのさし絵は珍しい版画から〜された The illustrations *are reproduced* (≒ *are reprinted*) from rare prints.

—品 a reproduction ; a duplicate. 不許— All rights reserved.

ふくせき【復籍】¶昨年〜した I *returned to the original domicile* last year.

ふくせん【伏線】¶これは本筋の〜だ This is *an underplot* (≒ *a preparation*) of the main plot.

ふくせん【複線】〔鉄道〕a double track ; a two-track line. ¶この線は1975年に〜になった This road *was double-tracked* in 1975.

—工事 double tracking.

ふくそう【服装】dress ; clothes. ¶平安時代の〜 the *costume* of the Heian era. 彼は〜にむとんじゃくだ He is careless about his *dress*. 彼は〜がりっぱだ(みすぼらしい) He *is* well (poorly) *dressed*. 彼女はいつも〜がこざっぱりしている She *is* always neatly *dressed*. 〜はご随意に(招待状などで) *Dress* optional. 彼女はどんな〜でしたか What *was* she *dressed* like?

—検査 a dress inspection.

ふくそう【福相】a happy look ; a radiant face.

ふくそう【輻湊】a congestion ; overcrowding. ¶貨物が〜する Goods *accumulate*. / There is *a congestion* of goods. 駅は貨物で〜していた The station *was congested with* goods. 港は船が〜している The harbor *is crowded with* shipping.

ふくぞう【腹蔵】¶〜なく話してほしい I'd like you to speak *freely* (≒ *frankly*). / Please *speak out your mind*. / Please *speak what is in your mind*. 〜なく批判し合った We criticized each other *unreservedly* (≒ *plainly*; *without reserve*). 私はあなたに〜なく申し上げます I will *be* quite *frank* with you.

ふくそくるい【腹足類】〔動物〕a gastropod.

ふくだい【副題】a subtitle.

ふぐたいてん【不倶戴天】¶〜の敵 a *mortal* foe ; a *sworn* enemy. 彼と彼女は〜の敵だ He *is at feud with* her. 〜の間柄だ There is *a deadly feud* between them.

ふくつ【不屈】fortitude ; indomitability. ¶〜の精神 an *indomitable* (≒ *dauntless*) spirit. 人間〜の精神 man's *unconquerable* mind ; man's mind *never to be conquered*.

ふくつう【腹痛】a stomachache ; a bellyache. ¶〜がする I have *a stomachache*. ひどく〜がする My *stomach aches* very badly.

ふくとう【復党】¶彼は２年ぶりに〜した He *rejoined* (≒ *returned to*; *was reinstated in*) the party after two years' interval.

ふくどく【服毒】¶彼女は〜した She *took poison*. 彼は〜自殺をした He killed himself by *taking poison*. / He *poisoned himself* to death.

ふくどくほん【副読本】a supplementary reader.

ふくのかみ【福の神】the God of Wealth.

ふくはい【腹背】the back and front. ¶〜に敵を受けた We were attacked *both in front and rear*. / We found ourselves *between two fires*.

ふくびき【福引き】a lottery. ¶〜に当たった I drew a prize *in a lottery*. 〜でテレビが当たった I got a TV set *in a lottery*.

—景品 premiums by lottery. —券 a lottery ticket.

ふくぶ【腹部】the abdomen ; the abdominal region ; the belly.

ぶくぶく ¶〜あわが立っている It's *foamy*. / It *bubbles up*. ボートが〜沈んだ A boat sank *bubbling*. 彼は〜太っている He's a *fat* (≒ *plump*) man.

ふくぶくし·い【福福しい】happy-looking ; radiant. ¶〜い顔つき a *fat and well-looking* face ; a *full* face. あの娘のほおが〜い She has *plump* cheeks.

ふくふくせん【複複線】a four-track line.

ふくぶん【複文】〔文法〕a complex sentence.

ふくへい【伏兵】an ambush. ¶〜を置く make (≒ lay ; plant) *an ambush*.

ふくぼく【副木】a splint. ¶骨折した腕に〜を当てる put *a splint* on the broken arm.

ふくほん【副本】a duplicate.

ふくまく【腹膜】〔解剖学〕the peritoneum (覆 peritonea).

—炎 peritonitis.

ふくま·せる【含ませる】¶布切れにベンジンを〜せる *soak* a piece of cloth *with* benzine. 病人に錠剤を〜せる *make* a patient *hold* a pill *in the mouth*. 赤ん坊に乳房を〜せる *give the breast to* her baby ; *suckle* a baby.

ふくまでん【伏魔殿】a pandemonium. ¶政界の〜 a political intrigue hotbed.

ふくみ【含み】an implication. ¶〜のあることばは明言よりたいせつだ *An implication* is more important than the direct statement. 首相は〜のある答弁をした The premier gave an *equivocal* reply. 代表たちは再開の〜を残して会談を一時中止した The negotiators suspended the talks for the time being, *leaving some room for* further negotiations.

—資産 undeclared assets. —笑い a suppressed laugh ; a chuckle.

ふくみみ【福耳】ears suggestive of wealth ; a rich man's ears.

ふくむ【服務】¶彼らは３年間〜した They *remained in* 〔*public*〕 *service* for three years. 〜中である be in 〔public〕 service; be on duty.

—規定 the service regulations. —時間 office (≒ business ; working) hours. —年

限 the term of service.

ふく·む【含む】1〘含有する〙contain. ¶ビールにはどのくらいアルコールが～まれていますか How much alcohol *is there* in beer?

この中に税金は～まれていない This does not *include* tax.

郵送料を～んで200円お送りください Please send 200 yen, which *includes* postage.

2〘心に〙¶私の言うことを～んでおいてください I hope you will fully *understand* what I am going to say.

3〘口に〙¶なにを口に～んでいるのですか What *have* you *got* in your mouth?

4〘意味する〙¶彼のことばは深い意味を～んでいる His words *imply* a deeper meaning.

ふくめい【復命】¶彼はイタリアの経済事情について～するために帰国した He returned to his country to *report* on the economic conditions in Italy.

ふく·める【含める】¶旅費は宿泊費を～めて2万円かかる The trip will cost 20,000 yen *including* (≒ *inclusive of*) the hotel bill. 乗組員は彼を～めて10人だった The crew consisted of ten men *with* him.

ふくめん【覆面】a mask. ¶～の強盗 a *masked* robber. ～の筆者 an *anonymous* writer. ～をかぶる assume (≒ put on) *a mask*.

ふくも【服喪】mourning. ¶～中である be in *mourning* for (*a person*).

ふくよう【服用】¶薬を食前に～する *take* medicine (≒ a drug) before meals.

ふくよう【複葉】a compound leaf.

—飛行機 a biplane.

ふくよか ¶赤ん坊は～な顔をしている The baby has *round* (≒ *chubby*) cheeks. 彼女の胸は～だ She *is full-breasted*. / She has an *ample* (≒ a *well-developed*) breast.

ふくらしこ【膨らし粉】baking powder.

ふくら·す【脹らす】⇒ふくらます

ふくらはぎ【膨ら脛】〘解剖学〙the calf (複 calves).

ふくらま·す【膨らます】¶風がヨットの帆を～せた The wind *filled* (≒ *swelled*) the sail of the yacht. 彼はよくほおを～せる He often *puffs out* his cheeks. 彼は風船を～せた He *inflated* a balloon. パンをイーストで～せた I *raised* bread with yeast. ポケットを～す *bulge* (≒ *swell out*) *one's* pocket with (cookies). タイヤを～す *pump up* a tire. 息を吸って胸を～せてください(医者などが) *Expand* your chest by inspiration. 彼らは希望に胸～せて学校を卒業していった They graduated from their school *full of hope*.

ふくらみ【膨らみ】a swell; a bulge; a rising. ¶たるにはまん中に～がある A cask *swells* in the middle.

ふくら·む【膨らむ】¶バラのつぼみは春～む The rose buds *swell* in spring. 希望で彼女の胸は～んだ Her breast *swelled* with hope. 彼のポケットはリンゴで～んだ His pocket *bulged* with apples. 彼の顔は赤く～んでいた His face *was* red and *puffy*. 軽気球はガスで～む A balloon *swells out* with gas.

ふくり【福利】welfare. ¶その政策は国の～を増進した The policy promoted the *welfare* of the country.

—事業 welfare enterprise. **—施設** welfare facilities.

ふくり【複利】compound interest. ¶貸し金を～で計算する calculate the loan at *compound interest*.

ふくれっつら【膨れっ面】a sulky face (≒ look). ¶～をするな Don't *become* (≒ *look*) *sulky*.

ふく·れる【膨れる】¶風船が～れた The balloon *got inflated* (≒ *was big*). パンが～れる Bread *rises*. 彼女は～れてばかりいる She always *looks sulky*. / She *pouts* very easily. 腹が～れた I *am full*. / I *have eaten enough*.

ふくろ【袋】a sack; a bag; (小物入れ) a pouch (sack は粗布で作られ穀物·粉·ジャガイモ·石炭などを入れるのに用いられる. bag は紙·布などで作られ sack より小さい).

¶これでもう彼は～の中のねずみだ Now he is caught like *a mouse in a trap*. おなかの～に赤ちゃんを入れているおかあさんカンガルー a mother kangaroo with a little one in her *pouch*.

—小路 a blind (≒ dead) alley. **—物** pouches. **—物商** a dealer in pouches. **—だたき** ¶彼らは彼を～だたきにした They ganged up on him and beat him up.

ふくろう【梟】an owl (発音は [aul]). ¶～が鳴いている *An owl* is hooting.

ふくわじゅつ【腹話術】ventriloquism; a ventriloquial art.

—者 a ventriloquist.

ふくん【夫君】*a person's* husband.

ぶくん【武勲】a distinguished military service. ¶彼は～を立てて叙勲された He was decorated for his *distinguished military service*.

ふけ【雲脂】dandruff; scurf. ¶～をとる(払う) remove (brush off) *dandruff*. ～だらけの scurfy.

—性 a dandruff forming head by nature.

—取り香水 hair lotion (≒ tonic).

ぶけ【武家】(総称) a military family; (武士) a warrior.

—時代 the age of military ascendancy; the feudal times. **—政治** military government.

ふけい【父兄】*one's* parents and older brothers; (保護者) guardians.

—会(組織としての) a parents' association. ¶来週〔高校〕2年の～会(父兄の集まり)がある There will be *a meeting of the parents* of the second grade students next week.

ふけい【父系】the paternal line; the father's (≒ spear) side. ¶～のおば an aunt on *one's father's side*.

ふけい【不敬】disrespect; (神に対する) blasphemy; profanity.

ぶげい【武芸】¶～の達人 a man of *martial* accomplishments. ～のたしなみ *military* ac-

complishments. 〜を修める practice *military arts.* 〜に秀でる be skilled in *military arts.*
—者 a master of military arts.

ふけいき【不景気】(世間一般の) hard (≒ bad) times; (商業の) a business depression.
¶この店は〜だ There is not much business in this store. ことしは〜だ Times *are bad* (≒ *are hard*) this year. この業界の〜は1年は続くだろう The present *business depression* will go on for at least a year. 戦争が終わると産業界は非常に〜になる When the war is over, severe *industrial recession* (≒ *depression*) will follow. 市況は〜だ The market *is inactive* (≒ *is dull*; *is slow*). / Trade *is* rather *depressed.* 鉄鋼業界は深刻な〜に見舞われている Steel industry is suffering from *a* serious *slump.* 〜を理由として一社だけが配当を切り下げた Only one firm cut its rate because of *poor business* (≒ *business recession*). 〜な顔をするな Don't look *gloomy* (≒ *cheerless*). / Look happy.

ふけいざい【不経済】¶それは時間の〜だ That is *waste of time.* 〜な買い物はやめなさい Don't *waste* your money on trifles. 彼は〜な生活をしている He *is extravagant* (≒ *is uneconomical*) *in* his way of living. / He lives an *extravagant* life. ホテル生活は〜だ Hotel life *is uneconomical.*

ふ

ふけつ【不潔】dirtiness. ¶手を〜にしておいてはいけない Don't leave your hands *dirty.* 都会人は〜な空気を吸わされている City people are obliged to breathe *unclean* air.

ふけつだん【不決断】indecision. ¶彼の〜な態度にはいつも困ってしまう I am always perplexed with his *indecision.* 彼は〜な男だ He *lacks decision.*

ふけやく【老け役】¶彼女は〜をやった She played *the part of an old woman.* 彼は〜がうまい He is good at playing *the part of an old man.*

ふけ・る【耽る】¶彼は飲酒に〜っている He *is given to* drinking. 彼はばくちに〜っている He *indulges in* (≒ *gives himself up to*) gambling. 彼は読書に〜っている He *is absorbed in* reading. 彼は瞑想(めいそう)に〜っている He *is lost in* meditation. 彼は思案に〜っている He *is deep in* thought. 彼と酒を飲みながら雑談に〜った I *enjoyed* chatting with him over wine.

ふ・ける【老ける】¶彼は年よりも〜けて見える He *looks older than* (≒ *looks old for*) his age. 家庭にごたごたがあって以来彼は急に〜けた He *has aged* rapidly since family trouble.

ふ・ける【更ける】¶夜が〜けるにつれて寒くなる As the night *advances,* it becomes colder. 夜が〜けるまで話し込んだ We continued to enjoy chatting till *late* at night. 夜が〜けた *It was late* at night. / The night *is advanced.*

ふけん【夫権】marital authority; the husband's rights.

ふけん【父権】paternal authority (≒ rights).

ふけん【府県】a prefecture. ¶〜の prefectural.

ふげん【付言】an additional remark. ¶先程の私の意見にひと言〜します Let me *add one word* (≒ *make an additional remark*) *to* what I have said before. 彼はこのことを〜した He *added this remark.*

ふけんこう【不健康】unhealthiness. ¶彼は〜な生活をしている He is leading an *unhealthy* life. 当地は〜な土地だ This is an *unwholesome* (≒ *unhealthful*) place to live in.

ふけんしき【不見識】¶彼の発言は〜だ His remark betrayed his *lack of broad vision.* そんなことをするのは〜だ Such an act would *be below your dignity.*

ふげんじっこう【不言実行】action rather than words. ¶彼は〜の人だ He is a man of *action rather than words.* 〜が私の信条だ *Work before talk* is my principle in life.

ふけんぜん【不健全】¶〜な遊びはやめなさい Keep away from *unsound* (≒ *unhealthy*) pastime. 青年のなかに〜な考えがはびこっている An *unwholesome* (≒ *morbid*) idea is prevailing among the young people today.

ふこう【不孝】undutifulness [to *one's* parents]; lack of filial duty.
—者 an undutiful (≒ unfilial) son (daughter).

ふこう【不幸】 **1** unhappiness; (不運) misfortune. ¶〜が次々と彼の身にふりかかった *Misfortunes* befell him one after another. 彼は〜な一生を送った He led an *unhappy* life. 彼は人生のもろもろの〜を味わってきた He has experienced various *miseries* in life. 彼は〜にも事故で死んだ *Unfortunately* he died in an accident. ことしは彼らの一家にとって〜な年だった This has been an *unlucky* year for his family. 彼の家が焼けたのは〜なことだった It *was unlucky* that his house burnt down.
2〖家族の死去〗¶家に〜があって彼はきのう学校を休んだ He was absent from school yesterday on account of *a death* in his family. ご〜なんとも申し上げようがありません I cannot find words to express my feelings at your *sad bereavement.*

ふごう【符号】a sign; a mark; a symbol. ¶Hは水素の〜だ H is the *symbol* of hydrogen. 〜をつける mark; affix *a mark.* 商品の値段を〜で書く write the prices *in cipher* (≒ *in code*). この〜はなんですか What does this *mark* stand for? 〜を解読する decipher. プラス(マイナス)— 〖数学〗 the plus (minus) sign.

ふごう【符合】correspondence; coincidence. ¶彼の陳述はきみの陳述と〜する His statement *agrees with* (≒ *corresponds to*) yours. その男の風体は手配書と〜している The appearance of the man *answers* the description. この事実は目撃者の証言と〜する This fact *is coincident with* the testimony of the witness of the scene.

ふごう【富豪】a rich (≒ wealthy) man; a man of wealth; a millionaire; a billionaire.

ふごうかく【不合格】failure. ¶ 彼は試験に～となった He *failed in* the examination. その品は出来が悪くて～になった The article *was rejected* because of its insufficient workmanship.

—者 an unsuccessful candidate (≒ applicant); a failure. **—品** a rejected article.

ふこうそく【不拘束】nonrestraint. ¶ 彼の身柄は依然として～のままである He remains *undetained.*

ふこうへい【不公平】partiality; unfairness. ¶ それは～だ That's *unfair.* 政府は外国人に対する～な処置を避けている The government avoids *partial* measures toward foreigners.

ふごうり【不合理】irrationality; absurdity; unreasonableness. ¶ ～な価格 an *unreasonable* price. ～な制度を廃止する abolish *irrational* (≒ *illogical*) systems. 社会的～を是正する remove social *absurdities.*

ふこく【布告】proclamation; declaration; announcement; notification. ¶ フランスはドイツに対して宣戦を～した France *declared* war on (≒ against) Germany. (政令などを)～する proclaim; announce. ～を出す issue *a proclamation.*

—文 a decree; an ordinance. 宣戦**—** a declaration of war.

ふこくきょうへい【富国強兵】¶ ～を図る promote *the national prosperity and strength* policy.

ふこころえ【不心得】indiscretion; imprudence. ¶ そんなことをするとは～なことだ It *is imprudent* (≒ *indiscreet*) of you to do such a thing. 彼は～にも私にこんな手紙をよこした He *had the imprudence* (≒ *was imprudent enough*) *to* send me such a letter. 彼を説得して～を改めさせた I persuaded him out of the *misconduct.*

—者 an indiscreet person.

ぶこつ【武骨】¶ ～な blunt; rough; (素朴な) rustic; unrefined; (ぎごちない) clumsy. 彼は口のきき方が～だ He *is blunt in* his speech.

—者 a blunt person; a rustic.

ふさ【房】(装飾の) a tuft; a tassel; (縁飾り) a fringe; (植物の) a bunch; a cluster. ¶ フジは～になって咲く Wisterias bloom *in clusters.* ブドウの～ *a bunch* of grapes. ～のついたカーテン a *fringed* curtain. ～のついた帽子 a cap with *a tuft.*

ブザー a buzzer (発音は [bʌ́zə]). ¶ ～を鳴らす sound *a buzzer.* そこで～が鳴る Then goes the *buzzer.*

ふさい【夫妻】husband and wife. ¶ A氏～ *Mr. and Mrs.* A. ～とも無事に大阪に着いた *Both husband and wife* arrived in Osaka safe and sound.

ふさい【負債】liabilities; (借金) a debt. ¶ 彼には～の支払い能力がない He cannot meet his *liabilities.* きみは～はどれだけあるか How much do you *owe*? / What is the extent of your *liabilities*? 彼は巨額の～がある He has a large *debt.* 彼は私に100万円の～がある He *owes* (≒ *is indebted to*) me 1,000,000 yen. ～で首が回らない He is deeply (≒ over head and ears) *in debt.* 月割りで～を払う pay off *one's debt* on monthly payment. ～を残す leave *debts* behind.

ふざい【不在】absence. ¶ 主人は～です My husband *is not at home* (≒ *is away from home*). 事務所を訪ねたが彼は～だった I called on him at his office and found him *absent.* ～中に電話がありましたか Did anyone call *in* (≒ *during*) *my absence*?

—証明 an alibi. **—地主** an absentee [landlord]. **—投票** absentee ballot. **—投票者** an absentee voter.

ぶさいく【不細工】(ぶきりょうな) plain; (無器用な) awkward. ¶ ～な娘 a *plain* (≒ *homely*) girl. ～な家 a house *of bad* (≒ *defective*) *workmanship.* 彼のこぎ舟は～なものだった. 彼が自分でこしらえたものだったから His rowboat was *a clumsy affair,* for he had made it himself. 彼は～な職人だ He is an *awkward* workman.

ふさが·る【塞がる】**1**〚物など〛¶ 管が泥で～っている The water-pipe *is blocked* (≒ *is choked*) *with* mud.

国道が車で～っている The highway *is clogged* (≒ *is jammed*) *with* swarming cars.

どの部屋も～っていた Every room *was occupied* (≒ *was engaged*).

このテーブルは～っています (予約済み) This table *is reserved.*

あしたは～っている I *am engaged* (≒ *have an appointment*) tomorrow.

今手が～っている I *have my hands full* now./ I *am engaged* (≒ *am busy*) right now.

電話線が～っている The line *is busy.*

2〚感情など〛¶ 悲しみに胸が～っている My heart *is full of* (≒ *is filled with*) grief. / My heart *is breaking.*

その知らせを聞いてみんなは開いた口が～らなかった At the news, their *jaws dropped.* / They *were dumbfounded at* the news.

ふさぎこ·む【鬱ぎ込む】¶ 彼は母にしかられて一日～んでいた Scolded by his mother, he *felt gloomy* (≒ *felt melancholy*) all day. 彼はいつも～んでいる He *is* always *in low spirits.*

ふさく【不作】a bad crop; a poor harvest. ¶ ～の年 a *lean* (≒ *bad*) year. ことしは米が～だった We have had *a poor* (≒ *bad*; *short*) *rice crop* this year. 天候不良のためことしは～だった Owing to the unfavorable weather, the crops *have failed* (≒ *have turned out to be a failure*).

ふさ·ぐ【塞ぐ】¶ へいの穴をモルタルで～ぐ *stop up* the hole in the wall with mortar. 口を～ぐ *put one's hand over one's* mouth. 医師は傷口を縫って～いだ The doctor *closed* the wound with stitches. こわれた窓ガラスが紙で～いであった The broken window *was covered with* a piece of paper. このテーブルは場所を～

ふ

ぐ This table *takes up* much room. 落石が国道を～いだ Some fallen rocks *obstructed* (≒ *blocked*) the highway. 彼は私の忠告に耳を～いでいる He *rejects* (≒ *disregards; is deaf to*) my advice.

ふさ・ぐ【鬱ぐ】 ¶ 彼女は～いだ顔をしている She puts on a *melancholy* (≒ *downcast*) look. なにを～いでいるのだ What makes you so *sad* (≒ *gloomy*)?

ふさくい【不作為】〖法律〗forbearance.

ふざ・ける ¶ 本気にするな, 彼は～て言ったのだ Don't take it serious. He *is* just *joking* (≒ *kidding*). 子どもたちは～けるのが好きだ Children are fond of *frisking* (≒ *frolicking*). 彼は～けて後ろから私の目をふさいだ He covered my eyes from behind *in fun* (≒ *for a joke*). ～けた話じゃないか They are making a fool of me. ～けたことを言うな Don't be a fool. ～けたまねはよせ None of your nonsense.

ぶさた【無沙汰】 ¶ 久しくご～をしました I owe you an apology for my long *silence*. / Excuse me for not writing so long. / (会ってのあいさつ) It's a long time since I saw you last. 病気のため長い間ご～しました Illness *kept* me *silent* so long.

ふさふさ ¶ ～とした髪の少女 a girl with *abundant* hair. ブドウが～となる Grapes grow *in* [*big*] *bunches*. あなたの髪はずいぶん～している You've got *so much* hair.

ふ

ぶさほう【無作法】 bad manners. ¶ ～な人 an *ill-mannered* (≒ *ill-bred*) man; a *rude* person. ～な子だね (直接本人に) Where are your manners?/ (第三者に) He wants manners. 人前であくびをするのは～だ It *is rude* (≒ *is bad manners*) to yawn before other people. ～なふるまいは許せません I won't have you *behave* so *badly* (≒ *rudely*).

ぶざま【無様】 ¶ こわれたトラックが道端に～な姿をさらしている The crushed truck still presents a *poor* (≒ *sorry*) appearance on the roadside. それは～な細工だ It is of *clumsy* workmanship. 彼女は～な服装をしていた She was clad in *objectionable* attire.

ふさわし・い【相応しい】 suitable; appropriate. ¶ きみに～い仕事が見つかってよかった I am glad you have found a *suitable* job. 彼のような慎重な人に～くないやり方だ That is the way quite *unbecoming to* a cautious man like him. 彼こそは教育者たるに～い人だ He is the *right* man to be a teacher. この景色はその名に～くない This view *is unworthy of* its name. 収入に～い生活をすべきだ You should live *according to* your income. / You should not live beyond your income. / (諺) *Cut your coat according to your cloth*. 時と所と場合に～い服装をすべきだ We should be *properly* dressed for time, place, and occasion. 草は牛に～い食物だ Grass is a *fit* food for cows.

ふさんせい【不賛成】 disagreement; disapproval; objection. ¶ この点についてきみの意見に～だ I *don't agree with* you on this point. きみは原案に賛成か～か *Are* you for or *against* the original plan? みんなが～を唱えたらどうしよう What if other people *disagree* (≒ *disapprove*)? ～が多数を占めた *The noes* were in the majority. 彼らはその案に～だった They *disapproved of* the plan. 彼の父はその結婚に～だ His father *does not approve of* the match.

—者 a dissenter.

ふし【節】 **1**〖関節〗a joint; (指などの) a knuckle; (結節) a knot; a knob.

¶ 木の～ a gnarl; a knob.

竹の～ a bamboo *joint*.

～の多い(ない)材木 a *knotty* (*clean*) board.

指の～が痛む I have a pain in the *knuckle*.

2〖歌の節〗a tune; a tone. ¶ 歌に～をつける *set* a song *to music*.

～をつけて本を読む read a book in *a* musical *tone*.

歌詞を忘れたが～だけは覚えている I forgot the song except for the *tune*.

3〖箇所〗a point. ¶ 彼の話には疑わしい～がある There are some doubtful *points* in what he says.

ふし【父子】 father and son. ¶ ～相伝の秘法 a secret inherited *from father to son*. ～ともに政治家だ Both *father and son* are politicians.

ふじ【藤】 a wisteria; a wistaria. ¶ ～の花 a *wisteria* flower.

—色 light purple; mauve. **—だな** a wisteria trellis. **—づる** wisteria vine. **—紫** dark lilac; (絵の具の) smalt.

ふじ【不治】 ¶ 彼は～の病に冒された He was attacked with an *incurable* (≒ a *fatal*) disease. ～のガン a *terminal* cancer.

ふじ【不時】 ¶ ～の場合に in time of need; in an emergency; in case of accidents. ～の出費に備える provide against an *unforeseen* expense. ～の来客 an *unexpected* (≒ *untimely; uninvited*) visitor.

ぶし【武士】 a *samurai*; a warrior. ¶ ～は食わねど高楊枝(ようじ) The *samurai* glories in honorable poverty. ～に二言なし The *samurai* never tells a lie. ～の面目にかけて upon the honor of *a warrior*. 花は桜木, 人は～ The cherry blossoms among flowers, the *samurai* among men.

—道 *Bushido*; chivalry.

ぶじ【無事】 (安全) safety; (平穏) peace; (健康) good health. ¶ 私は～に帰宅した I returned home *safe and sound* (≒ *in safety*). きょうも～に済んだ It has been a *peaceful* (≒ *quiet*) day. 彼は銀行で20年を～に勤め上げた He has worked for the bank for 20 years *without accident* (≒ 20 *uneventful* years). 私も～に暮らしています I *am doing well* (≒ *am living in peace*). ～にお帰りでおめでとう I am glad to see you *safe* home again. 台風が～に通過した The typhoon has passed *without* serious *damage*. 小包が～に届いた The parcel arrived *in good condition* (≒ *all right*). ～な顔を見てうれしい I am glad to see you *in good health*. そのほうが～だろう That will be *safer* (≒ *better*). 事件はかくて～解決をみた The matter was thus settled *peacefully*.

ふしあな【節穴】a knothole. ¶ ～からのぞく peep through *a knothole*. 彼の目は～同然だ His eyes are nothing but glass beads.

ふしあわせ【不幸せ・不仕合わせ】unhappiness; misfortune. ¶ 彼女は～な境遇だ She is leading an *unhappy* life. / She is living *in adversity*. ～は重なってくるものだ *Misfortune* never comes single.

ふしおが・む【伏し拝む】¶ 仏像を～む *kneel down and worship* a statue of Buddha.

ふしぎ【不思議】〔a〕wonder; 〔a〕mystery. ¶ 世界の七～ the seven *wonders* of the world. 彼がそんなことを言うとは～だ It *is strange* that he should say such a thing. 彼が失敗するのも～はない It *is no wonder* (≒ *natural*) that he should fail in the attempt. これは～なランプのお話です This is a story of a *miraculous* (≒ *magical*) lamp. これは世にも～な物語だ This is a very *wonderful* story. ～なこともあればあるものだ The world is indeed full of *mysteries* (≒ *marvels*). 生命の～のかずかずはいまだに解明されていない Many of the *miracles* (≒ *hidden processes*) of life still remain unexplained.

ふしくれだった【節くれだった】¶ 農民の～指 *bony* fingers of a farmer. ～木 a *gnarled* tree.

ふしぜん【不自然】¶ ～な態度 *one's unnatural* bearing. 彼の態度は～だ (気どっている) He has an *affected* manner. 私が話しかけると彼は～な笑い方をした He *forced a smile* (≒ *smiled awkwardly*) when I spoke to him.

ふしだら ¶ ～な男 a *dissolute* man. ～な女 a *loose* woman. 彼は若いころは～な生活をしていた He used to lead a *loose* life when he was young.

ふじちゃく〔りく〕【不時着〔陸〕】a forced landing. ¶ われわれはアフリカのジャングルに～した We made *a forced* (≒*an emergency*) *landing* in a jungle in Africa.

ふしちょう【不死鳥】a phoenix. ¶ ～のようによみがえる rise again like *a phoenix*.

ふじつ【不実】insincerity. ¶ ～な友 a *false* (≒ *faithless*) friend. 彼は友人に対して～なことをした He *was false to* his friends. / He *broke faith with* his friends. だれにも～なことをしたことがないから彼は信頼されている He is trusted because he *has* never *betrayed* a single man. そりゃあまりに～だ That's too *unkind* of you.

ぶしつけ【不躾】bad manners; (厚顔) impudence. ¶ 人の顔をじろじろ見るのは～だ It is *bad manners* to stare at people. ～ですみませんがお年はいくつですか *Excuse me,* but may I ask you how old you are? ～にそんなことを尋ねるものではない Don't *be* so *impudent* as to ask such a question.

ふじつぼ【富士壺・藤壺】〘動物〙a barnacle.

ふして【伏して】¶ 息子の命を助けてくださるようお願いする I *implore* you (≒ *beg* you *humbly*) *to* spare my son's life.

ふしまつ【不始末】(不品行) misconduct; (やりそこない) mismanagement; (浪費) unthriftiness.
¶ 彼は～をしでかして首になった He was dismissed for his *misconduct*. 火の～から大火になった They *did not take enough care in* dispos*ing* the embers, which led to the big fire. 度重なる事務取り扱いの～がその会社の命取りになった The repeated *mismanagement* of the affairs was a fatal blow to the company. 親の身の～は子供に悪影響を与える A parent's *laxity* of morals exerts a bad influence on the children.

ふしまわし【節回し】a melody. ¶ これは～が実によい歌だ This song *is very melodious*.

ふじみ【不死身】¶ 彼は～の男だ He *has nine lives*. / He *has a charmed life*.

ふしめ【伏し目】¶ ～がちに dropping *one's* eyes; with downcast eyes.

ふじゆう【不自由】**1** 〖不便〗〔an〕inconvenience. ¶ 水不足で～だった Because of a water shortage it *was inconvenient*.
母がいないと～でしかたない It's extremely *inconvenient* when my mother is away.
なにかとご～をおかけしました I am sorry I have caused you a lot of *inconveniences*.
2 〖窮乏〗poverty. ¶ 彼は金に～している He *is short of* money. / He *is badly off*.
彼女は～なく暮らしている She *is well off*.
彼には～はさせないつもりだ He shall *want for nothing*.
金に～するのはもうこりごりだ I cannot put up with *being hard up* for money any more.
彼は～な生活をしている He lives *in poverty*.
3 〖身体の〗¶ 彼は体が～らしい He seems to *be disabled*.
彼は急に左足が～になった He suddenly *lost the use* of his left leg.

ふじゅうぶん【不十分】insufficiency; (不完全) imperfection. ¶ 彼の英語は～だ His English *is far from perfect* (≒ *is inadequate; is incomplete*). 証拠～のため釈放された He was acquitted for *want* of evidence (≒ *weak* evidence). 年金では生活費としてさえも～だ The pension *is insufficient* (≒ *is not sufficient*) even for living expenses. 彼の説明では～だ We *are not satisfied with* his explanation. / His explanation *is unsatisfactory*. 彼の研究はまだ～なところがある His studies *leave something to be desired*. 彼は新しい事業を始めるには資金が～であった He did *not* have *enough* (≒ *sufficient*) money to start a new business. この仕事にはぼくの能力は～だ My ability *is inadequate to* the task. この本は荷造りが～だ These books are *badly* packed.

ぶじゅつ【武術】military arts; the use of arms.

ふしゅび【不首尾】failure. ¶ 首脳会談は～に終わった The top conference *failed* (≒ ended in *failure*).

ふじゅん【不純】 impurity. ¶ガソリンの中の～物を取り除く get rid of *impurities* in gasoline. 彼は～な動機から彼女を救ったのではなかった No *base* (≒ *impure; interested*) motive prompted him to help her.

ふじゅん【不順】 ¶春は天候が～だ The weather *is changeable* (≒ *is unfavorable*) in spring. ～な天候のため農作物の被害が大きかった The *unseasonable* weather has done serious damage to the crops.

ふじょ【扶助】 support. ¶私はまだ両親の～を受けている I'm still dependent on my parents for *support*. 彼のところは県の～を受けた His family received *an allowance* (≒ *a subsidy*) from the prefectural government.
—料 an allowance in aid. 遺族—料 an allowance to a bereaved family. 相互— mutual aid.

ぶしょ【部署】 *one's* post. ¶～を守る(離れる) keep (desert) *one's post*. 火災報知機が鳴るとそれぞれがいっせいに～についた When the fire alarm sounded, each man rushed to his *post*. 彼は最後まで～に踏みとどまって死んだ He died *at his post*. 水兵たちは～についた The sailors went to *quarters*. ～につけ(海軍の号令) To *quarters*!

ふしょう【不肖】 ¶彼はいわゆる～の子である He is what is called *a son unworthy of his father*. ～ながら全力を尽くす所存です *Unworthy as I am*, I'll do my best.

ふしょう【不詳】 ¶被害者の身元はまだ～だ The victim *is not identified* yet. 作者～(注などで) The author *unknown*. / *Anonymous*.

ふしょう【負傷】 a wound. ¶その男は腕に～した The man *had a wound* (≒ *was injured; was wounded*) in the arm. 石で彼は左足をひどく～した The stone *hurt* his left foot badly. 彼は～で死んだ He died from *a wound*.
—者 a wounded person; (総称) the wounded (≒ injured); (戦争の) the war wounded. ¶その戦闘で約1,000名の～者が出た About one thousand *got wounded* in the battle.

ふじょう【不浄】 uncleanness; impurity. ¶冷水に浸って彼は身の～を清めた Bathing in cold water, he *purified* (≒ *cleansed*) *himself*. ～の金 *ill-gotton* (≒ *tainted*) money.

ふじょう【浮上】 ¶潜水艦が東京湾に～した A submarine *surfaced* in Tokyo Bay.

ぶしょう【無精・不精】 laziness. ¶きょうは～をきめこんで家に引っ込んでいる I *feel too lazy* to go out today.
—ひげ ¶～ひげを生やした男 an *unshaven* fellow. 出— ¶彼はどちらかといえば出～のほうだ He is rather *a stay-at-home*. 筆— ¶私は筆～だ I am *a bad correspondent*.

ふしょうか【不消化】 indigestion; 〖医学〗 apepsy. ¶よくかまないと～が起こる *Bad indigestion* comes from lack of mastication. ～な食べもの *indigestible* food. 知識の～ intellectual *indigestion*.

ふしょうじ【不祥事】 ¶市の収入役が税金の使い込みをするという～が起こった There took place *a scandal* (≒ *a disgraceful affair*) that the city treasurer took (≒ embezzled) tax money for his own use.

ふしょうじき【不正直】 dishonesty. ¶～な男 a *dishonest* man.

ふしょうち【不承知】 (不賛成) disapproval. ¶私はその計画には～だ I'*m against* (≒ *don't approve of; disapprove of; object to; can never consent to*) the plan.

ふしょうにん【不承認】 disapproval. ¶その協定の～はもっともであった The *disapproval* of the treaty was reasonable. 参議院ではその協定は～であった The treaty *was disapproved by* the House of Councilors.

ふしょうぶしょう【不承不承】 unwillingly. ¶彼は～私のアメリカ行きを認めた He *unwillingly* (≒ *reluctantly*) consented to my leaving for America.

ふしょうふずい【夫唱婦随】 ¶彼らの家庭は～の家庭だった Theirs was a home where *the wife was willing to follow the husband's opinion*.

ふじょうり【不条理】 irrationality; absurdity. ¶～な irrational.

ふしょく【腐食】 corrosion. ¶鉄は～しやすい Iron *corrodes* easily. / Iron is easy to *corrode*. 酸は金属を～する Acid *erodes* (≒ *corrodes; eats away*) metal. 風雨で橋が～した Rain and wind *have rotted* the bridge. ほとんどの酸は～性のものだ Most acids *are corrosive*.
—剤 a corrosive. —作用 corrosion. —止め an anticorrosive.

ふしょく【扶植】 ¶ギリシアはしだいに西海岸に勢力を～した Greece gradually *established* (≒ *extended*) *its influence* on the west coast.

ぶじょく【侮辱】 an insult; a contempt. ¶ぼくはそんな～には耐えられない I can't put up with such *an insult*. 彼は隣人からひどい～を受けた He *was* badly *insulted* by his neighbor. 彼は法廷～のため退廷を命ぜられた He was ordered to leave the court on the charge of his *contempt* of it. ギリシア人にとってはローマ帝国の存在は耐えられない～であった For the Greeks the existence of the Roman Empire was *an* intolerable *affront*.

ふしょくど【腐植土】 mold.

ふじょし【婦女子】 women 〔and children〕; (総称) the fair sex.

ふしん【不信】 (疑惑) distrust; (不誠実) insincerity. ¶彼は友人の～を責めた He reproached his friend for his *insincerity* (≒ *treachery*). 彼は～の目でその見知らぬ人を見詰めた He looked at the stranger *with distrust*. 彼は執行部に対する～の念を表明した He declared that he could *not trust* the executive any longer.

ふしん【不振】 dullness. ¶商売はきわめて～である Business *is* very *dull* (≒ *is in a* very *bad condition*). わがチームは～であった Our team *did* very *badly*. / Our team *made a poor*

ふ

showing. 食欲〜で困っている I have trouble with *a decrease of appetite*.

ふしん【不審】(疑惑) suspicion. ¶ 挙動〜の男 a *suspicious-looking* man. そんなことをするときみの動機に関して〜の念を起こされる That would excite *suspicion* about your motive. なにか〜な点がありましたら説明します Let me explain *doubtful* points if there are any. 彼が来ないのはどうも〜に思えてならぬ I think it *is* really *strange* that he doesn't come. 彼の話がほんとうかどうか〜に思う I *doubt* (≒ *question*) the truth of his story. 請求書に〜な点がある I see *a* certain *discrepancy* in the bill.

—尋問 ¶ 彼は帰宅の途中, 警官より〜尋問を受けた He *was questioned* by a policeman on his way home.

ふしん【普請】 building; construction. ¶ 私の家は今〜中だ My house *is under construction*. / My house *is under building*. 御〜はいつだったのですか When did you *have* your house *built*? / When *was* your house *built*?

道— road construction. **安—** ¶ 私の家は安〜だ My house *is jerry-built*.

ふしん【腐心】 ¶ その運動の資金集めに大いに〜した We *took great pains* (≒ *were at great pains*) to raise money for the campaign.

ふじん【夫人】 a wife; (敬称) Mrs. ¶ 佐藤〜 *Mrs*. Sato. 彼は〜を同伴していた He was accompanied by his *wife*. 佐藤氏は〜同伴で出席した He attended the party *with Mrs*. Sato.

ふじん【婦人】 a woman.

—科 gyn(a)ecology. **—科医** a gyn(a)ecologist. **—警官** a policewoman. **—記者** a lady reporter. **—客** a lady visitor. **—雑誌** a ladies' magazine. **—参政権** women's suffrage. **—席** a ladies' seat. **—病** a women's disease. **—問題** the problem of woman.

ふしんじん【不信心】 unbelief. ¶ 〜な unbelieving; impious.

ふしんせつ【不親切】 unkindness. ¶ 今彼に〜にしたくない I hate to *be unkind* to him now.

ふしんにん【不信任】 nonconfidence. ¶ 彼は〜の動議を出した He moved a vote of *nonconfidence*.

—案 ¶ 彼らは〜案を票決に付した They put *a nonconfidence bill* to the vote. 国会は内閣〜案を決議(否決)した The Parliament passed (rejected) *a nonconfidence bill* in the Cabinet.

ふしんばん【不寝番】 night watch; (人) a night watch. ¶ 〜をする keep watch during the night; keep vigil.

ふ·す【付す】 ¶ この問題は委員会の審議に〜すほうがいいだろう It would be better to *refer* this problem *to* (≒ *bring* this problem *before*) the committee meeting. 彼が収賄したことは不問に〜すべきではない We should not *overlook* (≒ *shut our eyes to*) the fact that he committed bribery. 彼のアメリカ行きには3年たったら帰国するという条件が〜せられた He was permitted to go to the United States *on condition that* he should return at the end of three years.

ふ·す【伏す】 ¶ 彼女は先月の終わりごろから病床に〜している She has been ill in bed since the end of last month.

ふず【付図】 an attached chart.

ふずい【不随】 paralysis. ¶ 彼は半身〜になった He *was* partially *paralyzed*. 半身〜の患者 a case of *paralysis* on one side.

ふずい【付随】 ¶ 契約に〜する条件 conditions *annexed to* the contract. そういったものが外交官の生活に〜している社会的義務だ Those are the social obligations *incident to* (≒ *attaching to*) the life of the diplomatic service.

ぶすい【無粋·不粋】 ¶ 彼は〜な人だ He is an *inelegant* person. / He is a man *with no sense of refinement*.

ふずいいきん【不随意筋】〖解剖学〗 an involuntary muscle.

ふすう【負数】〖数学〗 a negative (number).

ぶすう【部数】 the number of copies. ¶ この雑誌は発行〜が多い(少ない) This magazine has *a* large (small) *circulation*.

ぶすっと ¶ 彼は思うようにできなくて〜していた He *looked glum* (≒ *looked sullen*; *looked sulky*) because he could not have his own way.

ふすま【麩·麸】 wheat bran.

ふすま【襖】 a sliding door (≒ screen).

ぶすりと ¶ 彼は敵の胸に〜短刀を突き刺した He thrust (≒ plunged) a dagger *home* into his enemy's breast.

ふ·する【付する】 ⇒ふす(付す)

ふせ【布施】 a monetary offering. ¶ お寺にお〜を上げる make *a monetary offering* to the temple.

ふせい【不正】(不当なしうち) injustice; (不正直) dishonesty; (違法) illegality. ¶ 〜なことはしてはならない Never *do wrong*. 彼は〜な手段で金をかせいだ He earned some money by a *dishonest* means. この〜は当然とがめられるべきだ This *unjust* act should naturally be blamed.

—行為(不正直な) a dishonest act; (卑劣な) a dirty trick; (カンニング) cheating. **—所得** illicit gains. **—乗車** ¶ 彼はよく〜乗車をする He often *steals a ride* on a train. **—取引** an illegal transaction. **—品** a fraudulent article.

ふせい【父性】 paternity.

—愛 paternal love.

ふぜい【風情】 **1**〖趣〗 taste. ¶ 彼女はどことなく捨てがたい〜がある She has *a* certain *charm* about her.

この庭にはなんともいえない〜がある There is something very *appealing* about this garden. / This garden is very *tastefully* laid out.

2〖身分〗 ¶ そのような大仕事は私〜の者にはとてもできない Such a big task is just beyond *a man like me*. / *A man like me* is not at all

ふ

equal to such a big task.

3 〘もてなし〙 ¶ なんの～もありません I am sorry I have nothing to entertain you with.

ぶぜい【無勢】 ¶ 多勢に～ではとてもかなわない There is no contending against such heavy odds. / *The few* cannot fight the many successfully.

ふせいかく【不正確】 inaccuracy. ¶ ～に英語の単語を覚えてもなんにもならない It's no use memorizing English words *inaccurately* (≒ *incorrectly*).

ふせいこう【不成功】 failure ; unsuccess. ¶ 彼の試みはすべて～に終わった All his attempts *failed* (≒ *ended in failure*). 彼は教師としては～だった He was *a failure* as a teacher.

ふせいじつ【不誠実】 insincerity. ¶ ～な insincere.

ふせいしゅつ【不世出】 ¶ ～の天才 a genius *with few parallels* ; an *unparalleled* genius. 彼は～の大詩人である He is the greatest poet that has ever lived.

ふせいせき【不成績】 poor results. ¶ 彼は～の学科が多かった He *did* very *badly* in many subjects. ことしの沿岸漁業は～に終わった The inshore fishery this year *has proved unsuccessful* (≒ *has produced poor results*).

ふせいりつ【不成立】 failure. ¶ 予算案は～に終わった The budget *failed to pass* (≒ *fell through* ; *miscarried*). 会議は～となった The conference *fell through*.

ふ

ふせ・ぐ【防ぐ】 ¶ 敵(寒さ)を～ぐ *keep off* the enemy (the cold). 彼らは勇敢に彼らの町を敵の侵略から～いだ They *defended* their city bravely *against* the invaders. 天然痘の流行はなんとしても～がねばならない We must *prevent* the spread of smallpox by all means. 蚊を～ぐのにかやをつる We hang up a 〔mosquito〕 net to *keep off* mosquitoes. 食塩は野菜の腐敗を～ぐ Salt *preserves* vegetables *from* decay. 風を～ぐものはなにもなかった There was no *protection* at all *from* the wind.

ふせじ【伏せ字】 a cipher.

ふせつ【敷設】 ¶ 二つの市を結ぶ鉄道が～された A railroad *was constructed* (≒ *was built*) between the two cities. 海底電線を～する *lay* a cable.

ふせつ【符節】 a tally. ¶ 彼らの話はまるで～を合わせたようであった Their stories *tallied with one another*.

ふせっせい【不摂生】 intemperance. ¶ 彼は～な生活をした He led a way of *unwholesome* living. / He lived *intemperate*.

ふせっせい【不節制】 intemperance. ¶ ～な生活をする lead an *intemperate* life. 彼は～して体をこわしてしまった He injured his health by *intemperance* (≒ *excesses*).

ふせ・る【臥せる】 ¶ 彼は先週の月曜日から体をこわして～っている He *has been ill in bed* since last Monday.

ふ・せる【伏せる】 **1** 〘物・体を〙 ¶ きれいなコップはたなの上に～せておきなさい *Turn* the clean glasses *upside down* on the shelves. 彼は身を～せた He *lay down*. / He *prostrated himself*. 彼女は目を～せた She *dropped* (≒ *lowered*) her eyes. ～せ！(号令) Lie down !

2 〘秘密にする〙 ¶ このことはだれにも～せておいてください Please *don't tell* anybody about this. / Please *keep* this *to yourself*. / This is just *between you and me*. / Please *keep* this *secret*. 私の名前は～せておいてください Please *keep* my name *unmentioned*.

ふせん【付箋】 a slip ; a tag. ¶ 手紙は～をつけて彼のところに回してやった I forwarded the letter to him with *a* redirection *tag* attached to it.

ふぜん【不善】 evil ; vice. ¶ 他人に～をなすなかれ Don't do *evil* to others. 小人閑居して～をなす (諺) Idleness is the root of all evils.

ぶぜん【憮然】 ¶ ～として gloomily ; discontentedly ; disconsolately.

ふせんしょう【不戦勝】 an unearned win. ¶ 1回戦は～であった We *got a win without playing* in the first game.

ふせんじょうやく【不戦条約】 an antiwar treaty. ¶ その国はアメリカと～を結んだ The country concluded (≒ entered into) *an antiwar treaty* with the United States.

ふせんめい【不鮮明】 ¶ その絵は～であった The picture *was indistinct*.

ふそ【父祖】 ancestors ; forefathers.

―伝来 ¶ これは～伝来の屋敷だ This is our *ancestral* (≒ *hereditary*) seat. ～伝来の土地 the land inherited from *ancestors* (≒ *forefathers*).

ぶそう【武装】 arms ; (軍備) armament. ¶ 人々は全部～した All the people *bore arms*. その国の～は世界平和にとって一大脅威となった The *armament* of the country became a great menace to the world peace. 彼はピストルで～した He *armed himself with* a gun.

―解除 disarmament. ¶ 砲艦は～解除された The gun-boats *were disarmed*. **―警官〔隊〕** armed police. **―中立** armed neutrality.

ふそうおう【不相応】 ¶ その仕事は私には～だった I *was unfitted* (≒ *was unsuitable*) *for* the task. / I *was unequal to* the task. このコートは品質に～な値段がついている The price of this coat *is out of proportion* to its quality.

分― ¶ 彼は分～な生活をしている He lives *above* (≒ *beyond*) *his means*.

ふそく【不足】 **1** 〘欠乏〙 lack ; shortage. ¶ 水～ *lack* of water. 紙～は本の値上げの原因となる *Lack* of paper results in a rise in the price of books. 食糧がだんだん～してきた We *have* gradually *run short of* food. ガソリンが～している We *are running short of* gas. 睡眠～で困っている We are suffering from *lack* of sleep.

ビタミンが～するとどうなりますか What will happen if we *are short of* vitamins?

2 〖窮乏〗 want. ¶ 彼ら一家は～のない暮らしをしている His family live *in comfort.*

彼は息子に～ない生活をさせている He has provided *sufficiently* for his son.

3 〖不満〗 dissatisfaction. ¶ 私はなに一つ～はない I have *nothing to be desired.*

なにか～がありますか Do you have *anything to complain of?*

彼なら仕事仲間として～はない He is a *good* match for me as a business companion.

ふそく【不測】 ¶ ～の出来事 a contingency; an accident; an *unforeseen* event. あらゆる～の事故に備える be prepared for every *contingency.* ～の事態が生じたらしい It seems that something *unexpected* happened.

ふそく【付則】 a supplementary rule.

ふぞく【付属】 ¶ A大学～高等学校 the Senior High School *attached to* A University. A大学～病院 the A University Hospital.

—品 accessories. —物 belongings.

ぶぞく【部族】 a tribe.

ふそくふり【不即不離】 ¶ ～の態度を堅持するのが望ましい It is desirable that a *neutral* attitude should be maintained. わが社はその会社と～の関係にある Our company *is rather closely connected* (≒ *associated*) *with* the company.

ふぞろい【不揃い】 ¶ 彼らは背の高さが～だった They *were not uniform in* height. 生徒は学力が～だ The students *are unequal in* scholarship. 彼女は歯並びが～だ She has *irregular* (≒ *uneven*) teeth.

ふそん【不遜】 ¶ ～な態度 insolence; insolent manner. 彼は～にも私に向かって「黙れ」と言った "Shut up," he said to me *insolently* (≒ *with arrogance*).

ふた【蓋】 (箱の) a lid; (おおい) a cover. ¶ 箱の～をあける(する) lift (put on) the *lid* of a box; open (shut) a box. 国会は昨日～をあけた The Diet *opened* yesterday. 人は臭いものには～をしがちである One is apt to *hush up* unfavorable matters. 結果は～をあけてみないとわからない. No one can predict the results.

ふだ【札】 (ラベル・はり札) a label; a tag; (合い札) a check. ¶ 本は箱に入れてその上に～がはられた The books were packed in a box with *a label* on it. それには劇薬という～がはってある It *is labeled* as poison. 成田山のお～を身につけている I have on *a talisman* from Naritasan Temple.

名— a name plate. 番号— a number check. 荷— a baggage label (≒ tag). はり—無用 Stick No Bills. / Post No Bills.

ぶた【豚】 a pig; (肉) pork. ¶ ～のように太った女だ She is *a* fat *pig.* / She is as fat as *a pig.* ～に真珠だ It's like *casting pearls before swine.*

焼き— roast pork.

ふたい【付帯】 —事項 a supplementary item. —条件 an incidental (≒ a collateral) condition. —設備 attached facilities.

ぶたい【部隊】 a force; a unit; a corps (発音は [kɔː]). ¶ 敵の大～を攻撃した We attacked *a* large enemy *force.*

—長 the commanding officer (C. O. と略記する). 外人— a foreign legion.

ぶたい【舞台】 the stage. ¶ 彼女はまだいちども～に立ったことがない She has never appeared on *the stage.* この脚本を～にのせてほしい I want this play *staged.* ～は変わって寺の庭の場面となった The *scene* changed and now it was the garden of the temple. この小説の～は小豆島だ The *scene* of this novel is Shodoshima Island. 彼の活動の～はあまりに広い His *sphere* of activity is too large.

—裏 ¶ ～裏の取引 a *backdoor* dealing. ～裏で活躍する maneuver *behind the scenes.* —監督 a stage manager. —げいこ a dress rehearsal. —劇 a stage play. —照明 stage lighting. —装置 stage setting. —中継 a stage relay. —生活 a stage career.

ふたいてん【不退転】 ¶ ～の決意をする make an *unyielding* (≒ *indomitable*) determination.

ふたいとこ【二従兄弟・二従姉妹】 a second cousin.

ふたえ【二重】 ¶ 紙を～に折る *double* the paper; fold the paper *in two.*

—まぶた a double eyelid.

ふたおや【二親】 *one's* parents.

ふたく【付託】 reference; submission. ¶ 予算案を委員会に～する *refer* (≒ *submit*) the budget bill *to* the committee.

ふたご【双子】 twins; twin brothers (≒ sisters); (ふたごの一人) a twin. ¶ 彼女は私と～だ She is my *twin.*

—座 the Twins.

ふたごころ【二心】 double-heartedness; duplicity. ¶ 彼は主君に～のないことを誓った He swore to *be loyal to* his lord. / He pledged *loyalty* (≒ *allegiance*) to his lord. 彼は～を懐いている He *is playing a double game.*

ふたことめ【二言目】 ¶ 彼女は～には勉強しなさいと言う She never opens her mouth without telling me to work harder. / She is always telling me to work hard. 彼は～には死ぬと言う He *constantly talks of* dying.

ぶたごや【豚小屋】 a pigpen; a pigsty.

ふたしか【不確か】 ¶ ～な情報 *uncertain* (≒ *unreliable; unauthorized*) information. 私の成功は～だ I *am uncertain of* success.

ふたたび【再び】 again; once more. ¶ ～戦争を繰り返すな No more war! 二度と～同じまちがいをするな Never *repeat* the same error. / Never make the same mistake *again.* 彼は戦争に行ったまま二度と～わが家にもどらなかった He went to the war *never to* return home.

ふたつ【二つ】 two. ¶ リンゴを～に切る cut an apple *in two.* 紙を～に折る *double* the paper; fold paper *in two.* こんな品は～とない This article *is matchless.* / This article *has no match* (≒ *has no equal*). ～ともよろしい

Both of them will do. 酔っ払いには物が～に見える A drunken man *sees double*.

―返事 ¶ 彼は～返事でそれを受け入れた He accepted it most willingly. うり― ¶ 彼らはうり～だ They are exactly alike. / They are *as like as two peas*.

ふだつき【札付き】 ¶ ～の悪人 a *notorious* scoundrel. 彼はこの町で～だ He is a *marked man* in this town.

ふたて【二手】 two groups. ¶ 彼らは～に分かれて進んだ They marched *in two groups*. 彼らを～に分けた I divided them *into two groups*.

ふたとおり【二通り】 two ways. ¶ これには～の解き方がある There are *two ways* of solving this. / This has *two ways* of solving. 書類を正副～作った I drew the documents *in duplicate*.

ふだどめ【札止め】 ¶ 連日興行は～の盛況であった The performance *drew a full house* every day.

ふたば【二葉・双葉】 (芽) a bud. ¶ 悪を～のうちに摘み取る nip an evil *in the bud*. せんだんは～より芳し Genius always shows itself early in life.

ぶたばこ【豚箱】 a police cell. ¶ 彼は～に入っている He is detained in the *police cell*.

ふたまた【二股】 ¶ その木は～になっていた The tree *was forked*. 道路は～に分かれていた The road *divided into two branches*. / The road *forked in two*. ～をかける have it both ways; sit on the fence.

―こうやく double-dealing; (人の場合) a double-dealer. **―ダイコン** a forked radish.

ふため【二目】 ¶ 彼は～と見られぬ姿となった He was *horribly* disfigured. / He was too dreadful to be seen twice.

ふたもの【蓋物】 a lidded food container.

ふたり【二人】 ¶ 彼らは～とも私に親切だ They are *both* kind to me. / *Both* of them are kind to me. 彼女は～の子どもがいる She has *two* children. 彼女と～で公園を散歩した I walked in the park with her. 兄弟～で身代を使いつぶした The *two* brothers squandered the fortune *between them*. 彼女は～とない美人だ Nobody is so beautiful as she. / She is a *matchless* beauty. 私の両親は～とも生きている *Both* my parents are alive. これはあなたと私と～きりの話だ It is *between you and me*. 私が～の仲を取り持った I *went between the lovers*. なにかが～の友の仲を割いた Something *came between the two friends*. この仕事を～きりでしよう Let us finish this work *between us*.

ふたん【負担】 a burden; (支払い) a charge; (責任) responsibility. ¶ その～に耐えられない I can't bear the *burden*. 政府は国民に税を～させる The government *imposes* a tax *on* the people. その費用は国庫～だった The charges *were borne by* the National Treasury. その借金はきみに～させる I will *make* you *liable for* the debt. 私が費用を～する I will *pay* the expenses.

ふだん【不断】 ¶ ～のとおり8時に家を出た I left home at eight *as usual*. ～より早く帰宅した I got home *earlier than usual*. 日曜日は～なにをしていますか How do you *usually* spend Sundays? 彼は～注意を怠らなかった He was *always* watchful. これは～に使うにはもったいない This is too good for *everyday* use. 彼には～とちっとも違うところはなかった There was *nothing unusual* about him. ～の努力を怠るな You must make a *ceaseless* effort.

ふだんぎ【不断着】 casual wear. ¶ このスーツは～だ This suit is for *everyday wear*. / This is a suit for *casual wear*.

ふち【縁】 (帽子・コップなどの) a brim; (眼鏡の) a rim; (布の) a hem; (庭の) the borders; (川の) a bank.

¶ がけの～にある家 a house on the *edge* of a precipice. 金～の本 a book with gilt *edges*. 金～の額 *a* gilt *frame*. 金～の眼鏡の男 a man with a gold-*rimmed* spectacles.

ふち【淵】 a deep water; the depths. ¶ 老人が川の～に身を投げた An old man threw himself into the *depths* of the river. 彼は絶望の～に立っている He *is in the depths of* despair. 彼女は悲しみの～に沈んでいる She *is lost* (≒ *is sunk*) *in* grief.

ぶち【斑】 spots; specks. ¶ 白黒の～の犬 a dog *spotted with* black and white.

ぶちこ・む【打ち込む】 ¶ その男を監獄へ～んだ We *threw* the man *into* prison. / We *imprisoned* him. 私はこわれたいすを物置へ～んだ I *put* broken chairs *into* the warehouse.

ぶちこわし【打ち壊し】 ¶ われわれの計画は～になった Our plan *was destroyed*. これで彼の計画は～になった This *baffled* him *out of* his *design*. へたをやってその縁談は～になってしまった The match *has been broken off* through want of tact.

ぶちこわ・す【打ち壊す】 ¶ その箱をばらばらに～した I *broke* that box *to pieces*. その大きな建物は一瞬のうちにダイナマイトで～された The big building *was destroyed* with dynamite in a moment. 彼らは古家を～した They *demolished* (≒ *pulled down*) the old house.

ふちど・る【縁どる】 ¶ テーブル掛けに花模様が～られている The tablecloth *is bordered with* flower patterns.

ぶちぬ・く【打ち抜く】 ¶ 弾丸が壁を～いた The bullet *pierced* the wall 〔*through*〕. 仕切りを～いて臨時の講堂をつくった We *removed* the partitions to make a temporary auditorium.

ぶちのめ・す【打ちのめす】 knock down (*a person*).

プチブル (人) a petit bourgeois; (階級) petty bourgeoisie (フランス語から).

ぶちま・ける【打ちまける】 ¶ 彼はバケツ1杯の水を～けた He *threw out* a bucketful of water. 彼は袋の中にある物をみな～けた He *shook out* all the contents of his bag. 私はその事実を彼に～けた I *told* him the fact *frankly*. 私の思って

いることを〜けて話した I *spoke out* what I had in mind. 彼は自分の怒りを〜けた He *gave vent to* his anger.

ふちゃく【付着】¶コケが岩に〜している Moss *grows on* the rocks. ズボンに血痕(けっこん)が付着していた There were some blood stains *on* the trousers. 雪の砕片がつえに〜していた The fragments of snow *adhered* (≒ *stuck*) *to* the staff.

ふちゅうい【不注意】carelessness. ¶その事故は〜のために起こった The accident took place through *carelessness.* きみは試験で〜なまちがいをよくする You often make *careless* mistakes in an examination. 彼は自分の体に〜だ He *neglects* his health. きみはいつも授業中に〜だ You *are* always *inattentive* in class.

ふちゅうじつ【不忠実】¶彼は自分の職務に〜だ He *does not stick to* his duty. / He *neglects* his duty.

ふちょう【不調】¶彼は体が〜であった He *was in a bad condition.* / He *was out of form.* われわれの話し合いは〜に終わった We *failed to agree.* / Our negotiation *ended in failure.*

ふちょう【符丁・符牒】(しるし) a sign; a mark; (暗号の) a code; a cipher. ¶その商品に〜で値段を書く put the price of the article by *a mark.*

ふちょう【婦長】a head (≒ chief) nurse; a matron.

ぶちょう【部長】the head (≒ chief) of a department.

ぶちょうほう【無調法・不調法】¶とんだ〜をしてすみません I'm sorry for having been so *rude* (≒ *careless*). とんだ〜いたしました How *awkward of* me! 酒は〜なほうです I don't drink. 口— ¶口〜の者です I am *a poor speaker.*

ふちょうわ【不調和】disharmony; discordance. ¶その着物にこの帯は〜だ This *obi* doesn't *go with* the *kimono.* その語の音と意味とが〜だ The sound of the word *does not harmonize with* its sense.

ふちん【浮沈】¶それは彼の生涯の〜に関する大事だった It was an important matter *affecting* his whole career. 彼は〜の多い一生を送った He led a life *of ups and downs.* / He had a life *of vicissitudes.*

ぶ・つ【打つ】¶一席〜つ *give* a lecture; *make* a speech.

ふつう【不通】¶雪のために列車が〜になった The railroad service *was suspended* because of the snow. 彼とは2年間音信〜だ I *have heard nothing from* him for two years. 電話は〜だ The telephone service *is interrupted* (≒ *is suspended*).

ふつう【普通】usually. ¶彼はごく〜の人だ He is a quite *ordinary* man. 私は〜8時に家を出る I *usually* leave home at eight. 彼は〜1日に10時間働く He *generally* works ten hours a day. きみの論文の出来栄えは〜以下だ Your thesis is below *the average.* 彼女の才能は〜以上だ She is more than *average* in her talent. 〜そういう言い方はしない That is not the *usual* way of expression. あなたのは〜のかぜだ You have a *common* cold. この暑さは〜ではない It is *unusually* hot. 彼の服装は〜ではない There is something *eccentric* in his dress. 体の調子は〜ではない I do not *feel up to par.*
—科 the regular course. —急行 an ordinary express. —教育 common education. —高校 a liberal high school. —人 the average person. —選挙 universal suffrage. —名詞〔文法〕a common noun. —郵便 ordinary mail. —預金 an ordinary deposit. —料金 ordinary rate. —列車 a slow train.

ふつか【二日】two days. ¶〜めごとに彼から便りがある I receive a letter from him *every two days.*

ぶっか【物価】prices (おもに複数形で使う). ¶〜は上がりっぱなしだ *Prices* go on rising. 都会では〜は高い(安い) *Prices* are high (low) in cities. 〜の上がり下がりが激しい *Prices* fluctuate very widely. / *Prices* jump and slump.
—指数 a price index. —政策 a price policy. —統制 price control. —値下げ price cut; price reduction.

ぶっかき【打っ欠き】(氷) cracked ice.

ふっか・ける【吹っ掛ける】¶彼は値段を〜けてきた He *charged* me an unreasonable price. 彼はこんなものに1万円も〜けた He *asked* 10,000 yen *for* such a worthless article. 彼らはけんかを〜けてきた They *picked* a quarrel *with* me. 手に息を〜けた I *blew* breath to my hand.

ぶっか・ける【打っ掛ける】¶彼の頭に水を〜けた I *dashed* water over his head.

ふっかつ【復活】revival; (キリストの) the Resurrection. ¶祭りを〜するのを決めた We decided to *revive* the festival. 失われた名誉を〜するのは困難だ It is difficult to *restore* lost honor. キリストは十字架上で死に，3日めに〜した Christ died on the cross and *rose again* on the third day.
—祭 Easter.

ふつかよい【二日酔い】unpleasant aftereffects of excessive drinking; a hangover. ¶〜だ I am suffering from *a hangover.*

ぶつか・る ¶彼は急いでいたので知らない人に〜った He *ran* (≒ *knocked*) *against* a stranger, as he was in a hurry. 彼はドアにひどく〜った He *bumped against* the door. ボールが私に〜った A ball *hit* (≒ *struck*) me. バスとタクシーが〜った A bus *collided with* a taxi. 今度の祭日は日曜と〜る The next national holiday *falls on* Sunday. われわれはその問題に〜っていく覚悟はできている We are ready to *face* the problem.

ふっかん【副官】an adjutant.

ふっかん【復刊】reissue. ¶〜第1号 the first number of *reissue.* その雑誌は〜した The magazine *was reissued.*

ふっき【復帰】return. ¶彼はもとの仕事に〜するだろう He will *return to* the former job. 沖

ふ

縄は日本に～した The Okinawa Islands *have reverted to* Japan.

ぶつぎ【物議】¶ 彼の演説は大きな～をかもした His speech *caused* (≒ *gave rise to*) much *discussion*. その決定は大なる～をかもした The decision *evoked* a great deal of *comment and criticism*.

ふっきゅう【復旧】restoration. ¶ 鉄道は～した The railroad *has been reopened*. 二, 三年すれば町は～するだろう The town will *be restored* [*to the former state*] in a few years.
—工事 a repair work.

ぶっきょう【仏教】Buddhism.
—徒 a Buddhist.

ぶっきらぼう ¶ 彼は～な話し方をする He has a *curt* (≒ *blunt*) way of speaking. / He speaks *curtly* (≒ *bluntly*). 彼は～に話を切り出した He began to speak *abruptly*. 彼は～だ He is an *uncouth* fellow.

ぶつぎり【ぶつ切り】¶ ～の肉 *chopped* meat. 魚を～にする *cut* a fish *into small lumps*; *chop* a fish.

ふっきん【腹筋】the abdominal muscles.

フック a hook. ¶ 彼は左～を相手のあごにきめた He landed *a* left *hook* to the chin of the opponent.

ブック a book.
—エンド book ends. —カバー a [book] jacket. —レビュー a book review.

ぶつぐ【仏具】Buddhist altar fittings.

ふっくら ¶ その赤ん坊はほおが～している The baby has *plump* cheeks. 彼女は～したくちびるをしている She has *full* lips.

ぶつ・ける【打付ける】¶ 壁に頭を～けた I *knocked* my head *against* the wall. 犬に石を～けた I *threw* a stone *at* a dog. 私の意見を彼に～けた I *challenged* him *with* my opinion.

ぶっけん【物件】a thing; an article.
—費 the cost of supplies. 証拠— material evidence.

ふっこ【復古】restoration; revival. ¶ 明治時代に王政が～した The Imperial regime *was restored* in the Era of Meiji.
—主義 reactionism. —調 a reactionary tendency; a tendency to revival. 王政—〖歴史〗the Restoration.

ぶっこ【物故】¶ ～された王は非常に民主的な方だった *The late* king was very democratic.
—者 the dead persons; the deceased.

ふっこう【復校】¶ 彼は～が許された He was allowed to *return to school*. / He *was readmitted into school*.

ふっこう【復興】reconstruction. ¶ わが国は完全に～した Our country *has been* completely *reconstructed*. 当時東京は～中であった Then Tokyo *was under reconstruction* (≒ *was reconstructing*).
文芸—〖歴史〗the Renaissance.

ふつごう【不都合】(不便) inconvenience; (不正) wrong; misconduct. ¶ その日は私には～だ The day *is inconvenient to* me. 彼は～なことをして首になった He was fired for his *misconduct*. それに背くとは～だ Your disobedience *is unpardonable* (≒ *is inexcusable*). 私は～なことはなにもしなかった I have done nothing *wrong*. きみにはなんの～もない You *are above reproach*. この計画に～はありませんか Have you no *objection* to the plan? その計画にはすこし～な点がある There are some *objectionable* points in the plan.

ふっこく【復刻・覆刻】reproduction. ¶ 原本を～する *reproduce* the original book.

ぶっさん【物産】a product; (総称) produce. ¶ 主要な～ staple *products*.
—会社 a products company.

ぶっし【物資】goods; commodities. ¶ わが国は～が豊かである Our country is rich in *resources*. ～が不足しはじめた We began to run short of *goods*. 紙をつくる～が日本には十分にない Japan lacks *raw materials* to make paper. 急いで彼らに～を補給した We supplied *goods* to them in a hurry.

ぶっしき【仏式】Buddhist rites.

ぶっしつ【物質】material. ¶ この液はたいていの～を溶かす This liquid will dissolve almost every sort of *material*. 彼らは～的快楽に満足していない They are not contented with *physical* comforts.
—界 the material world. —主義 materialism. —文明 material civilization. —名詞〖文法〗a material noun.

ぶっしゃり【仏舎利】Buddha's ashes.

ぶつじょう【物情】¶ ～騒然としている *Public feelings* are excited.

ぶっしょく【物色】¶ あとがまを～中だ I *am looking for* the successor.

ぶっしん【物心】¶ 彼は私を～両面から援助してくれた He supported me *both materially and morally*.

ぶつぜん【仏前】¶ ～に花を供える offer flowers *before the tablet of the deceased*.

ふっそ【弗素】〖化学〗fluorine.

ぶっそう【物騒】¶ 女の夜道のひとり歩きは～だ It *is dangerous* for a woman to go out alone at night. 彼は～な顔つきの男だ He is an *evil-looking* man. いまはなんて～な世の中なんだ What *troubled* times we live in!

ぶつぞう【仏像】an image of Buddha; a Buddha statue.

ぶったい【物体】an object; a body. ¶ なぞの～ *a* mysterious *object*.

ぶつだん【仏壇】a family altar.

ぶっちょうづら【仏頂面】a sour face. ¶ 彼は～をしている He *is* (≒ *looks*) *sullen* (≒ *sulky*). / He is making *a sour face*. 彼はそれに～で答えた He answered it *sulkily* (≒ *with a sulky look*).

ふつつか【不束】¶ ～ながら私が彼の役を果たしましょう *Incompetent as I am*, I will act his part.

ぶっつけ【打っ付け】(突然) abruptly; (直接に) directly; (ざっくばらんに) flatly.
—本番 acting (≒ performance) without rehearsal.

ぶっつづけ【ぶっ続け】¶ 6時間〜に雨が降った It rained six hours *running.* (running の前に複数名詞がくる). 昼夜〜に働く work all day and all night. 私は8時から12時まで〜に働いた I worked from 8 to 12 *at a stretch.*

ぷっつり entirely; once for all. ¶ 彼はそのことを〜忘れた He forgot it *entirely.* 酒とは〜縁を切った I gave up drinking *once for all.* 彼らと〜手を切った I *have nothing more to do with* them. 綱が〜切れた The rope *snapped.* 先方との無電連絡が〜とだえた We lost radio contact with the other party *once for all.* ダイアモンドのことは〜思い切った I never gave the diamond another thought. 彼女はその男との結婚の望みを〜思い切った She *gave up all hope of* marrying the man.

ふってい【払底】〔a〕shortage. ¶ 最近はどこへ行っても住宅が〜して困るだろう Nowadays you will be troubled with *a* housing *shortage* wherever you go. 当時は砂糖は〜していた Sugar *was scarce* in those days.

ぶってき【物的】material; physical.
—資源 material resources. —証拠 material evidence.

ふってん【沸点】the boiling point.

ぶってん【仏典】the Buddhist scriptures; the sutras.

ふっと ¶ ろうそくを〜吹き消す *blow* (≒ *puff*) *out* a candle.

ふっとう【沸騰】boiling. ¶ 水は摂氏100度で〜する Water *boils* at 100°C. 〜した湯 *boiling* water. スープを3分間〜させる *give* three minutes' *boil* to the soup; *boil* the soup for three minutes. 委員会では議論が〜した The committee *became heated with* argument. 首都は知事選挙で〜している The metropolis *is seething with* the gubernatorial election.

ぶっとおし【ぶっ通し】¶ 一晩〜に *all through* the night; *all* night *through.* 10時間〜に働く work for ten hours *running* (≒ *at a stretch*). 映画は3か月間〜に上映された The film had a run of three months. 3日間〜に雨が降っている It has been raining three days *without a stop* (≒ *without a break*).

ふっと・ぶ【吹っ飛ぶ】¶ 台風で家の屋根が〜んだ The roof of the house *was blown off* by the typhoon. 彼の顔を見たとたん心配が〜んだ The moment I saw him, my cares *were gone.*

フットボール football; soccer. ¶ 〜をやる play *football.*

フットライト footlights. ¶ 〜を浴びる appear before the *footlights.*

フットワーク footwork.

ぶつのう【物納】payment in kind. ¶ 昔は税金を〜したものだった In former days people used to *pay taxes in kind.*

ぶっぴん【物品】an article. ¶ 〜を管理する take care of (≒ take charge of) the *articles and fixtures.*
—税 a commodity tax; (売り上げ税) a sales tax.

ぶつぶつ ¶ 彼はいつも〜文句を言っている He *is* always *grumbling* (≒ *complaining*). 〜ひとりごとを言ってないで, はっきりものを言え Stop (≒ Quit) your *muttering* (≒ *mumbling*) to yourself and speak out what is in your mind. 顔に〜ができて困る I am troubled with the *rashes* (≒ *pimples; blisters*) in my face.

ぶつぶつこうかん【物物交換】barter. ¶ 戦時中は衣類と米の〜をしたものだ During the war we would *barter* clothing *for* rice. 戦後も農家との〜は日常茶飯事だった Even after the war it was an everyday occurrence to *barter with* farmers.

ぶっぽうそう【仏法僧】〘鳥類〙a broad-billed roller.

ぶつもん【仏門】¶ 〜に入る enter the Buddhist priesthood; be converted to Buddhism.

ぶつよく【物欲】worldly desires. ¶ 彼は〜にとらわれている He *is worldly-minded.*

ぶつり【物理】—学 physics. —学者 a physicist. —現象 a physical phenomenon. —療法 physical therapy. 理論(応用)—学 theoretical (applied) physics.

ぷつり ¶ 糸が〜と切れた The string *snapped off.*

ふつりあい【不釣り合い】unbalance; imbalance. ¶ 〜な unbalanced. きみの支出は収入に〜だ Your expenses *are out of keeping with* (≒ *are out of proportion to*) your income. 彼女の帽子は服に〜だ Her bonnet *does not match* her dress. 彼らは〜の夫婦だ They are an *ill-matched* couple. それは〜な縁組だ It is an *unequal* match. その家の門は〜に大きい The gate of the house is *disproportionately* big.

ぶつりょう【物量】the amount (≒ quantity) of materials (≒ resources). ¶ 〜にものを言わせて on the strength of *material* superiority.

ふつわ【仏和】—辞典 a French-Japanese dictionary.

ふで【筆】a writing brush. ¶ 彼は小説の〜をとった He started writing a novel. 彼は執筆の途中で〜をおいた He laid down his *pen* in the course of writing his story. 彼は〜が立つのでよく原稿を頼まれる Since he is *a good writer,* he is often asked to write articles.

ふてい【不定】¶ 彼は住所〜だ He has *no fixed* abode. / He *is a vagabond.* 収入が〜だ My income *is irregular.* / I have *no regular* income. このごろは天候が〜だ We've had *changeable* (≒ *unsettled*) weather these days.
—冠詞(代名詞)〘文法〙an indefinite article (pronoun). —詞〘文法〙an infinitive.

ふてい【不貞】unfaithfulness. ¶ 〜の妻 an *unfaithful* wife; a wife *false* to her husband. 彼の妻は彼に〜を働いた His wife *was unfaithful* (≒ *was false*) to him.

ふてい【不逞】¶ 〜のやから *lawless* (≒ *rebellious; unruly*) people; outlaws.

ふていき【不定期】—貨物船 a tramp〔steamer]; a tramper. —便 an irregular service. —列車 an extra train.

ふていけいし【不定型詩】free verse.

ふていさい【不体裁】awkwardness. ¶ 成績不良で親が学校に呼ばれるなんて〜なことだ It *is ungainly* (≒ *embarrassing*) to have *one's* parent summoned to school because of *one's* bad school work. こんな格好では〜で人前に出られない As I *am in a slovenly dress,* I am not fit to be seen.

ふでいれ【筆入れ】a writing-brush case; (万年筆など) a pen case.

プディング〔a〕pudding.

ふてき【不敵】¶ 〜なふるまい a *fearless* conduct; a *daring* act. 大胆〜な面魂だ He has a *bold and daredevil* look. / He looks *bold and daredevil.*

ふでき【不出来】¶ この作品は〜だ This work *is unsatisfactory* (≒ *is poorly done*). / This *is a bungled work* (≒ *is a failure*). ことしは稲作が〜だった The rice crop *has failed* (≒ *is poor; has turned out badly*) this year. 彼は〜な息子だ He is an *unsatisfactory* son to his father. 学科の出来〜にあまりくよくよするな Don't worry too much about the result of your school work.

ふてきとう【不適当】¶ そのことばはこの場合〜だ That diction *is unsuitable* (≒ *is inadequate; is inappropriate*) in this case. その服装は改まった席には〜だ That dress *is out of place* on a formal occasion. この引用はこの場合には〜だ The quotation *is improper to* the occasion.

ふてきにん【不適任】inaptitude. ¶ 彼はその仕事(地位)には〜だ He *is not fit for* (≒ *is unfit for; is unequal to*) the task (the post). / He *is not suited for* the task (the post). 彼は〜のため解雇された He was discharged for *inaptitude.*
—者 a misfit; an unqualified person.

ふてぎわ【不手際】clumsiness; awkwardness. ¶ 〜な作品 a *clumsy* work.

ふてくさ·れる【不貞腐れる】¶ 〜れるな Don't *be sulky* (≒ *be sullen*). / Don't *sulk.* 彼は〜れてものを言わなかった He was in *sulky* silence.

ふでたて【筆立て】a writing-brush stand (≒ receptacle).

ふてってい【不徹底】¶ 〜な指示 *not thoroughgoing* directions. 〜な論旨 the *inconsistent* point of argument. 〜な手段 *half-way* measures. 物事を〜にしておくのはよくない It is not good to *leave* things *half done.* 私の言うことは〜であった I have made myself very *imperfectly* understood.

ふてね【不貞寝】¶ 〜をする stay in bed out of spite.

ふでばこ【筆箱】a pencil case.

ふでぶしょう【筆無精】¶ 彼は〜だ He *is a lazy* (≒ *bad; poor*) *correspondent.*

ふてぶてし·い【太太しい】¶ 彼は態度が〜い He has an *impudent* (≒ *insolent*) manner.

ふでまめ【筆まめ】¶ 〜な人だ He *is a ready writer.* / He *is a good correspondent.* / He *writes readily.*

ふと【不図】¶ 〜目を覚ますと6時だった I woke up *by chance* to find it was six o'clock. 3日前のことが〜思い浮かんだ What happened three days ago occurred to me *suddenly.* 〜名案を思いついた I *hit upon* a good idea. 〜したことでふたりは仲よくなった The two became friends *from a mere trifle.* 〜したことから彼はアメリカへ旅立った It was *by chance* that he started on a trip to America.

ぶと【蚋】〘虫類〙a gnat (発音は [næt]).

ふと·い【太い】¶ 〜い腕 a *big* arm. 〜い足 a *thick* (≒ *stocky*) leg. 〜い幹 a *thick* trunk. 〜い声 a *deep* voice. 〜い線 a *bold* line. 〜い柱 a *massive* pillar. 肝玉の〜い男 a *bold* man. 彼は〜いためいきをついた He *drew a deep breath.* それは〜く書いてあった It was written *in bold strokes.* 彼は〜く短く世を渡った He lived a short life and a merry one. なんて〜いやつだ What an *insolent* (≒ an *impudent; a shameless*) fellow!

ふとう【不当】¶ その処置は〜だ You *have done wrong.* / It is *an act of injustice.* 〜な差別に反対する We are against an *unjust* discrimination. 〜な解雇 *unfair* dismissal. 〜な値段 an *unreasonable* price. 〜な要求 an *excessive* demand.

ふとう【不撓】¶ 彼はまったく〜不屈の精神を持っていた He had a simply *indomitable* spirit. 彼は〜不屈の闘士である He is an *unyielding* fighter.

ふとう【埠頭】a quay; a wharf (複 wharfs; wharves).

ふどう【不同】(差異) difference; (不規則) irregularity; (不平均) unevenness. ¶ 順序〜 No special order is observed. どの家も高さが〜だ All the houses *vary* in height.

ふどう【不動】¶ 〜の信念 *firm* belief. 彼は〜の姿勢で立った He *stood at attention.* 革新勢力の前進は〜だろう The development of the progressive camp will *be unshakable.*

ふどう【浮動】¶ 〜する物価 *fluctuating* prices. 〜する市況 an *unsteady* market.
—株 floating stocks. —人口 floating population. —投票者 floating voters. —票 floating votes.

ぶとう【舞踏】—会 a ball; a dancing party; a dance. —曲 a dance music. —ぐつ dancing shoes. —室 a ball (≒ dancing) room. —場 a dancing hall.

ぶどう【葡萄】〘植物〙a grape; (木) a 〔grape〕 vine. ¶ 〜1房 a cluster (≒ bunch) of *grapes.* 〜の豊作 (不作) an abundant (a poor) *vintage.* 〜の豊作の年 a *vintage* year.
—色 dark purple. —液 grape juice. —園 (畑) a vineyard. —酒 wine. —酒商 a vintner. —状菌〘医学〙a staphylococcus (複 staphylococci). 干し— raisins.

ふどうい【不同意】disagreement; disapproval. ¶ 出席者の多くがその提案に〜だった Many of those present *did not agree to*

ふ

(≒ *did not approve of*) the proposal.
ふとういつ【不統一】¶ 組織の～ *lack of unity* in the organization. 色彩の～ the *disharmoney* of colors.
ふとうこう【不凍港】an ice-free port.
ふとうごう【不等号】〔数学〕a sign of inequality.
ふどうさん【不動産】immovables; real estate; real property. ¶ 彼は1億円の～を持っている He has *real property* worth one hundred million yen. 彼は～で5,000万円持っている He has fifty million yen *in reality* (≒ *in real estate*).
ふとうしき【不等式】〔数学〕an inequality.
ふどうたい【不導体】〔電気〕a nonconductor.
ふどうとく【不道徳】immorality. ¶ ～な行ない an *immoral* conduct.
ふとうめい【不透明】opacity.
—ガラス an opaque glass. —体 an opaque body.
ふどき【風土記】a topography; a local history.
ふとく【不徳】lack (≒ want) of virtue; immorality. ¶ これはみな私の～のいたすところです I *am* solely *to blame for* it. / It is all my *fault*.
ふとくい【不得意】¶ 私は話が～だ I *am a poor* talker. 彼はスポーツが～だ He *is bad at* athletic sports. / He *is poor* (≒ *is weak*) *in* athletic sports. 私は店の経営は～だ Storekeeping *is not in my line*.
ふとくさく【不得策】a poor (≒ bad) policy. ¶ 今彼に反対するのは～だ It *is unwise* for us to oppose him now. その協定は双方にとって～なものだった The agreement *was disadvantageous* to both parties.
ふとくようりょう【不得要領】¶ ～な返事をする give an *evasive* answer. 彼の議論は～だ His argument *is not to the point*. / He does *not* argue *to the point*. 彼の言うことは～だ His statement *is vague* (≒ *is ambiguous*).
ふところ【懐】the bosom. ¶ 赤ん坊は母親の～に抱かれている The baby is *in* her mother's *arms*. 彼はいつも～が暖かい He always *has plenty of cash*. このところ～が寂しい I *am short of money* these days. 彼は～を痛めるのを恐れている He is afraid of *paying out of his own pocket*. 彼は～を肥やしているという評判だ It is reputed that he *has feathered his own nest*. 私の～を当てにするな Please don't expect me to pay for it.
ふところがたな【懐刀】(腹心の者) *one's* right hand; *one's* right-handed man.
ふとさ【太さ】¶ この丸太は～が15センチある This log *is* 15 centimeters *thick*. / This log has *a thickness of* 15 centimeters.
ふとじ【太字】a thick character; (活字) a bold〔-faced〕type; a boldface. ¶ 次の文を～に注意して読みなさい Read the following sentences, paying attention to *Gothic letters*.
ふとっぱら【太っ腹】¶ ～な男だ He *is large-* (≒*broad-*) *minded*. / He is a *generous* man.
ふとどき【不届き】¶ ～なふるまい(やつ) an *insolent* (≒ *outrageous*) behavior (fellow).
プトマイン ptomain〔e〕.
—中毒 ptomaine poisoning.
ふともも【太股】a thigh.
ふと・る【太る】¶ 彼はたばこをやめてから～った He *has gained flesh* (≒ *has put on weight*) since he quit smoking. 彼女は～ってきた She *is getting fat*. その娘はまるまると～っている The girl *is plump*. 彼女は～りぎみだ She *is on the stout side*. きみはちょっと～りすぎだ You *have put on a little too much flesh*. / You *are a little too fat*. ～ったのでこの洋服が着られなくなった I *have outgrown* this suit of mine.
ふとん【布団】(夜具) bedclothes; bedding; (掛けぶとん) a quilt; a coverlet; (座ぶとん) a cushion.
¶ ～2組 two sets of *bedding*. ～を敷く make a bed; lay out the *bedclothes*. ～をあげる put away the *bedclothes*.
—掛け a counterpane; a bedspread.
ふな【鮒】〔魚類〕a crucian〔carp〕.
ぶな【橅・山毛欅】〔植物〕a beech〔tree〕.
ふなあし【船足】(喫水) 米 draft; 英 draught; (速力) speed. ¶ ～の速い(遅い)船 a fast (slow) boat.
ふなあそび【船遊び】boating; rowing. ¶ ～に出かける go *for a row*; go *boating* (≒ *rowing*).
ぶない【部内】¶ 彼は～のベテランだ He is a veteran *in the department*. 彼は～のいろいろな困難な問題を解決した He solved various *departmental* difficulties.
政府— government circles.
ふなうた【船歌】(ゴンドラの) a barcarole. ¶ ボルガの～ the Song of the Volga Haulers.
ふながいしゃ【船会社】a shipping (≒ steamship) company.
ふなかじ【船火事】a fire at sea; a fire on a ship; a ship-fire. ¶ ～があった A fire broke out on a ship. 英国船に～が起こっている The British steamer *is afire at sea*.
ふなぐ【船具】rigging; tackle. ¶ ～をつける(取りはずす) rig up (down) a boat.
—商 a ship chandler.
ふなぞこ【船底】the bottom of a ship; the bilge.
ふなだいく【船大工】a ship carpenter; a ship builder; a shipwright.
ふなたび【船旅】a voyage; a sea trip. ¶ ～を楽しむ enjoy *a sea trip*. 楽しい～だった It was a pleasant *voyage*.
ふなちん【船賃】passage money; a fare; (貨物の) freight; freightage. ¶ 別府までの～はいくらですか How much is the *fare* to Beppu?
ふなつきば【船着き場】(港) a port; a harbor; (上陸地) a landing place; (波止場) a wharf.
ふなづみ【船積み】loading; (発送) shipment; shipping. ¶ ～する load (a boat); ship (goods).

ふ

—送り状 a shipping invoice. —係 a shipping clerk. —港 a shipping port. —指図書 a shipping order. —書類 shipping documents.

ふなで【船出】departure〔of a ship〕; sailing. ¶ サンフランシスコに向けて〜する *set sail* (≒ *sail out*) for San Francisco.

ふなどんや【船問屋】a shipping agent.

ふなに【船荷】a cargo (複 cargo(e)s); freight. ¶ ばら積みの〜 *a* bulk *cargo*.

—証券 a bill of lading (B/L).

ふなのり【船乗り】a seaman (複 seamen); a sailor. ¶ 私は〜になりたかった I wanted to *go to sea.* / I wanted to be *a sailor.*

—生活 a sailor's life; a seafaring life (文語).

ふなびん【船便】shipping service; (郵便物) surface mail. ¶ 〜で荷物を送る send goods *by ship* (≒ *by water*). 次の〜で *by* the next *boat.*

ふなべり【船縁】boatsides. ¶ 〜から身を乗り出して海中を見る look overboard into the sea.

ふなむし【船虫】〘虫類〙a shipworm.

ふなやど【船宿】(回漕店) a shipping agent; (貸し船屋) a pleasure-boat keeper.

ふなよい【船酔い】seasickness. ¶ 〜する get seasick. 私は〜をしやすい(しない) I am a poor (good) sailor.

ふなれ【不慣れ】unfamiliarity; inexperience. ¶ 〜な仕事 *unaccustomed* (≒ *unfamiliar*) work. 〜な土地 a *strange* land. 〜な人 an *inexperienced* (≒ *untrained*) person. まだこの仕事に〜だ I *am not* yet *experienced in* this job. / I am *not* yet *accustomed to* this job.

ぶなん【無難】(安全) safety; (完全) faultlessness. ¶ 彼は〜な道を選んだ He chose a *safer* (≒ *easier*) way. 彼は試験で〜な成績をおさめた He obtained *good* (≒ *high*) marks in the examination. そのいすは〜な出来だ The chair is of *good* (≒ *satisfactory*) workmanship. 彼は〜な値段でその土地を手放した He sold the land at a *reasonable* price. これなら〜な答案といえる This will turn out a *passable* (≒ *tolerable*) answer. 彼なら〜な人選といえる He may be competent to the post. / He may have been *properly* chosen for the post.

ふにあい【不似合い】¶ 〜な夫婦 an *ill-matched* couple. それはきみに〜な仕事ではないかと思う I fear it is an *unsuitable* (≒ *unfit*) job for you. その本は内容に〜な題がついている The book *is unworthy of* (≒ *does not deserve*) its title. 彼女はきみには〜だ She *is not for* you. 彼のような慎重な人には〜なやり方だ That's the way quite *unbecoming* (≒ *unfitted*) to a cautious man like him. 収入に〜な生活をすべきではない We should not live *beyond* (≒ *above*) *our income.*

ふにおちな・い【腑に落ちない】¶ どうもそれには〜いことがある Still there is something *incomprehensible* in it. / I still *fail to understand* something in it. 彼の説明は〜かった His explanation *did not convince* (≒ *was not satisfactory to*) me. きみはぼくの説明では〜いという顔をしている You look as if you *are not satisfied with* my explanation.

ふにょい【不如意】¶ 手元〜だ I *am hard up* (≒ *am in needy circumstances*). 万事〜だった Everything *went wrong with* me.

ふにん【不妊】sterility; barrenness.

—手術 sterilization.

ふにん【赴任】¶ 彼は転勤で任地へ単身〜した He *left for* his new post by himself. 新任の先生が近く〜してくる A newly appointed teacher is to *arrive here* shortly.

—地 *one's* new post; the place of appointment. —旅費 traveling expenses to *one's* post.

ふにんき【不人気】unpopularity. ¶ 彼は女の子の間で〜だ He *is unpopular among* (≒ *with*) girls. 日本製品は当地では〜だ Japan-made goods *are in poor demand* here.

ふにんしょう【不妊症】sterility. ¶ 彼女は〜だ She *is sterile.*

ふにんじょう【不人情】unkindness; heartlessness. ¶ あなたはなんて〜なのでしょう How *unfeeling* you are! 〜な仕打ちはがまんがならない I cannot tolerate such a *cruel* (≒ an *unkind*) treatment. 〜なことをするな Don't behave in a *heartless* manner. そう〜な断わり方もできない I can't bear to give him a flat refusal.

ふぬけ【腑抜け】(愚か者) a fool; an idiot; an imbecile; (おくびょう者) a coward. ¶ 彼は精神的ショックで〜のようになった He *was stupefied* from a mental shock.

ふね【船・舟】a ship; a boat (ship は大きく美しい船. boat は小型な特殊の船, 一般的にも使う).

¶ 〜に乗る take *a ship.* 〜を降りる get off *a ship.* 〜でヨーロッパに行く go to Europe *by boat.* この荷物は〜で送る We send this package *by ship.* 私は〜に強い(弱い) I *am a good* (*bad*) *sailor.* 乗りかかった〜だ(途中でやめられない) There's no turning back.

ふねっしん【不熱心】(怠惰) laziness; (無関心) indifference. ¶ 彼は仕事に〜だ He *takes* (≒ *has*) *no interest in* his work. きみの〜にも困ったものだ I am ashamed of your *laziness.* 彼らはそのプランに〜だった There was *little enthusiasm* for the plan among them. 彼らはその企てに〜だった They *were indifferent to* the enterprise. 彼は〜がたたって職を失った He paid for his *negligence* by losing his job.

ふねんせい【不燃性】incombustibility; uninflammability. ¶ 〜の incombustible; uninflammable; fireproof.

—住宅 a fireproof house. —物 incombustibles.

ふのう【不能】(不可能) impossibility; (無能) incapacity; inability; (性的) impotence.

¶ 〜な impossible; incapable; unable; impotent. 自動車は修理〜なほど破損した The car was smashed *beyond repair.* 船はあらしのため破損して航行〜となった The ship *was dis-*

ふ

abled by the storm. 回収〜の貸し *bad* debts.

ふのり【布海苔】〘植物〙〔gloiopeltis〕glue.

ふはい【不敗】invincibility. ¶〜を誇るチーム an *ever-victorious* team.

ふはい【腐敗】(物質について) rotting; spoiling; decomposition; (精神的に) corruption; decay.

¶この魚は〜している This fish *is rotten.* 肉は〜しやすい Meat is likely to *go bad.* 梅雨時はなんでも〜しやすい Everything is apt to *rot* during the rainy season. 政治の〜 the political *corruption.*

ふばいどうめい【不買同盟】a boycott; a buyers' strike. ¶電化製品の〜を結ぶ *boycott* electric appliances.

ふはつ【不発】misfire. ¶この銃は〜のことはない This gun never *misses fire.* その企ては〜に終わった(不達成) The attempt *was without definite result.*

—弾 a blind shell.

ふばつ【不抜】¶〜の精神を養う nourish an *indomitable* (≒ *unconquerable*) spirit.

ふばらい【不払い】nonpayment. ¶賃銀の〜が続いている The workers' wages remain *unpaid.*

ふび【不備】defect; deficiency. ¶この書類には〜がある These papers *are defective* (≒ *are incomplete*). 法案には修正を要する〜な点が若干ある The bill has some *defects* to amend. 日本の工場は一般に公害防止の設備が〜である Most Japanese factories *have imperfect* (≒ *lack proper*) equipment to prevent industrial pollution. 証文には〜の点がある The bond *is not all right.* 形式上の〜 *improper* form. 法の〜を悪用する abuse *a loophole* in the law; abuse *a* legal *loophole.* 調査の〜のため owing to *insufficient* investigation.

ふひつよう【不必要】¶日本ではチップは〜だ Tipping *is unnecessary* (≒ *is needless*) in Japan. 季節外れならホテルの予約は〜だ During the "off" season, *no* reservations for accommodation at hotels *are necessary* (≒ *are needed*). もはや議論は〜だ *There is no need for* debate now. 私はこの金は当分〜だ I *can do without* this money for the time being. 入試に〜な科目 *unrequired* subjects in the entrance examination.

ふひょう【不評】a poor reputation. ¶日本の移民は昔は〜であった Long ago the Japanese immigrants *were not well spoken of* (≒ *gave rise to evil reports*). 施政方針演説は世間では〜だった The policy speech *was received unfavorably* by the general public. 彼の不法な行為は周囲の〜を買った He *lost his popularity* (≒ *became unpopular*) by the illegal act. / His illegal act was the target of criticism. 彼は生徒に〜になった He *became unpopular with* (≒ *among*) the students.

ふひょう【浮氷】floating (≒ drift) ice.

ふひょう【浮標】a buoy; a marker.

ふひょう【譜表】〘音楽〙a score; (五線紙) a staff (複 staves).

ふびょうどう【不平等】inequality; (不公平) unfairness. ¶〜な unequal; unfair. 富の〜 *inequalities* of wealth. 人種や宗教による〜な扱いは不当である Discrimination by race or religion *is unjustifiable.*

—条約 an unequal treaty.

ふびん【不便・不憫・不愍】¶〜な子だ What a *poor* child〔he is〕! 身寄りのない老人を〜に思う I *take pity on* (≒ *feel pity for*) a helpless old man. 〜と思って助けてくれ *For pity's sake,* save me. 彼らはその子どもを〜に思った They *regarded* the child *with pity.* 彼は〜な人々を助けた He helped *the unfortunate.*

ぶひん【部品】parts. ¶自動車の〜 *parts* of an automobile. エンジンのスペア〜 spare *parts* of the engine.

ふひんこう【不品行】loose morals; a misconduct. ¶〜な男 a man *of loose morals.* 〜がもとで地位を失った He paid for his *misconduct* (≒ *immoral act*) by losing his situation. / He lost his job because of his *misconduct.* 〜をする act *immorally*; *misconduct oneself.* 彼を説得して〜をやめさせた I persuaded him out of *misdeed.*

ぶふうりゅう【無風流】tastelessness. ¶〜な inelegant; ungraceful. 〜なことで恐縮です I am ashamed of my *tastelessness.* その部屋の具合は〜だ The arrangement of the room *is out of taste.*

ふぶき【吹雪】a snowstorm; 米 a blizzard. ¶大〜で汽車が立ち往生している The train has been snowbound (≒ has been stalled in the snow) by *a* heavy *snowstorm.*

ふふく【不服】dissatisfaction; discontent; (不平) a complaint; a grievance; (異議) an objection; (不同意) disagreement.

¶〜があるのですか *Are* you *dissatisfied* (≒ *Aren't* you *satisfied*) *with* this? / Do you have any *complaint* to make about this? 〜があったらはっきり言いなさい In case you have *an objection,* speak out. 〜な顔をするな Don't *look dissatisfied.* / Remove *that look* from your face. 今の生活に〜はない I *am* perfectly *contented* (≒ *satisfied*) *with* my present life. 彼は何事にも〜を言う He *finds fault with* everything. その計画に私はなにも〜はない I *have no objection to* the plan.

ふぶ・く【吹雪く】¶山岳地帯は朝から〜いている *There has been a blinding snowstorm* (≒ *A snowstorm has been blowing*) among the hills since morning.

ふふん(軽べつ・不快) pooh; pshaw; (疑惑・不満) humph. ¶彼はぼくをばかにしきって〜という顔をした He looked at me *with undisguised contempt.*

ぶぶん【部分】〔a〕part; a portion; a section. ¶〜的に partially; in part. その詩は最後の〜が失われている The last *part* of the poem has been lost. 町は二つの〜に分けられる The city is divided into two *sections.* 彼の計画は〜的な成功をみた His attempt made *partial*

ふ

success. その車には～的に欠陥があった The automobile had *minor* defects. 彼のことばのほんの一～だけが真実だ Only *a fraction* of his statement is true. それは理由の一～にすぎない It is only *one* of the reasons. 彼は父の遺産のほんの一～を相続したにすぎない He inherited only *a* small *portion* of the fortune of his father.

—軍縮 partial disarmament. —蝕 a partial eclipse. —スト a partial strike. —調査 sample survey; random sampling.

ぶぶんひん【部分品】 parts; (予備の) spare parts. ¶機械の～ *parts* of a machine. この機械は～に分解して輸入された This machine was imported in *sections*.

ふぶんりつ【不文律】 an unwritten law.

ふへい【不平】 dissatisfaction; discontent; grievance. ¶彼女は夫のことでめったに～を言わない She seldom *complains of* her husband. 税金に対して～を言う人は多い Many people *grumble about* (≒ *murmur against*) the taxes. 彼は父親に対して～を抱いている He *is dissatisfied with* his father. 学生たちは学校当局に対して～を並べ立てた The students made a variety of bitter *complaints* to the school authorities. なにか～がありますか Do you have any *complaint* to make? 別に～はありません I have no *complaints* to make. / I have *nothing to complain of*. 彼女は～も言わずに手つだってくれた She helped me *without a murmur*.

ぶべつ【侮蔑】 contempt. ¶彼女ははっきり～の色を浮かべて彼の顔を見た She looked at him with undisguised *contempt*.

ふへん【不変】 ¶～の自然法則 *immutable* (≒ *immovable; invariable*) law of nature. ～の科学的真理 *everlasting* (≒ *unalterable; unchangeable*) scientific truth. ～の愛 *steadfast* love.

—色 a lasting color. —数 a constant. —性 invariability; inalterability.

ふへん【普遍】 ¶～的 universal; general. ～妥当性 *universal* validity. ～的真理 *universal* truth.

ふへん【不偏】 ¶私はまったく～不党の立場からそれを観察した I observed it from altogether *non-partisan* (≒ *impartial; fair; unprejudiced; unbiassed*) standpoint. ～不党の新聞 an *independent* (≒ a *nonpartisan*) newspaper.

ふべん【不便】 inconvenience. ¶ここは～な所だ This is an *inconvenient* place. 郵便局は～な所にあった The post office was *inconveniently* situated. 夜着いたのでたいへん～だった As I arrived there at night, it *was* very *inconvenient*. 彼がいないのでたいへん～な思いをした I *suffered* great *inconvenience from* his absence. これは持ち運びに～だ This *is* too *bulky* for us to carry. 電話がないと～なことだろう If it were not for telephones, we would *be* much *inconvenienced*. ～を忍ぶ put up with *inconveniences*.

ふべんきょう【不勉強】 ¶彼は～だ He is a *lazy* boy. / He *is not diligent enough*. / He *is inattentive to* his studies. ～でそういうことはよくわかりません I am ashamed of my ignorance on that subject.

ふぼ【父母】 father and mother; parents. ¶～の愛 *parental* love. ～のもとでくらす live *under one's parental care*; live *with one's parents*. 彼は早く～を失った He lost his *parents* at a very early age.

ふほう【不法】 unlawfulness; illegality; (不正) wrong; injustice. ¶人種差別は～である Racial discrimination *is* utterly *wrong* (≒ *unjustified*). 学生たちは～な手段に訴えた The students took *illegal* (≒ *unlawful*) means. その船は～に拿捕(だほ)された The ship was detained quite *unlawfully*. その船は～な攻撃を受けた The ship was attacked *without justification*.

—監禁 illegal confinement. —行為 an unlawful act; an illegality. —出(入)国 illegal exit (entry). —所持 illegal possession (*of* weapons). —侵入 trespass. —占拠 illegal occupation. —入国者 an illegal (≒ unlawful) entrant.

ふほう【訃報】 the news of *a person's* death. ¶私はパリで彼の～に接した I *heard of his death* (≒ *received the news of his death*) in Paris.

ふほんい【不本意】 reluctance. ¶～ながら賛成した I gave a *reluctant* consent to it. / I consented to it *reluctantly* (≒ *unwillingly; against my will*). ～ながらご招待をご辞退いたします *To my regret* I must decline your invitation. ～ながらこの手段をとりました I have had to take this step *with great reluctance*. 新しい方法は～な成績だった The new method brought about only *unsatisfactory* results.

ふま・える【踏まえる】 ¶事実を～えた立論 argument *based upon* a fact.

ふまじめ【不真面目】 ¶～な学生 a *lazy* student. ～な友人 an *unfaithful* friend. ～な恋 *frivolous* love. 彼は～な男だ He *lacks sincerity*. 彼は仕事に～だ He *takes no serious interest in* his work.

ふまん【不満】 dissatisfaction; discontent. ¶なにが～なのか What *displeases* you? 私は自分の現在の仕事に～である I *am dissatisfied* (≒ *am discontented; am not satisfied*) *with* my [present] job. 彼の顔には～の色があった I saw a *discontented* look on his face. 私にはなんの～もない I *am* completely *contented with* my life. 科学者は実験の結果に～だった The scientists *were not pleased* (≒ *satisfied*) *with* the result. 民衆の間には政府に対する～の声が高まっている There are loud *complaints* among the people against the government. 大統領は日本の対案に対して～の意を表明した The president expressed *disapproval* of the Japanese counterproposal.

ふまんぞく【不満足】discontent ; dissatisfaction. ¶ ～な設備 *insufficient* (≒ *unsatisfactory*) equipment. これらの工場は公害防止のためには～な設備しか持っていない These factories have only *incomplete* (≒ *insufficient ; unsatisfactory*) equipment to prevent public pollution.

ふみあら・す【踏み荒らす】¶ 畠を～す *trample* the field *underfoot.*

ふみいし【踏み石】(飛び石) a stepping stone ; a series of stepping stones ; (上り段の) a stepstone.

ふみい・れる【踏み入れる】¶ あんな場所に二度と足を～れてはいけない Don't *tread on* (≒ *step in ; set* your *foot in*) such a place again.

ふみえ【踏み絵】a tablet with a crucifix.
¶ ～を踏ませる make *a person* tread on the *tablet of crucifix* to see his commitment.

ふみかた・める【踏み固める】¶ 雪を～める *stamp down* the snow. 雪を～めて道をつける *beat* a path across the snow.

ふみきり【踏切・踏み切り】(鉄道の) a〔railroad〕crossing ; (運動競技の) a takeoff. ¶ 無人～で子どもがひかれて死んだ A child was killed on the ungated (≒ unattended) *crossing.* ～を横切る pass through *a crossing.*
—線(板) a take-off line (≒ plank). —番 困 a flagman ; 困 a watchman ; a gateman.

ふみき・る【踏み切る】**1**〖始める・決断する〗¶ 彼は新しい事業に～った He *ventured on* the new enterprise.
彼らは原油の値上げに～った They *decided* at last to raise the price of crude oil.
政府はやっと公害対策法に～った At last the government *took action* by instituting anti-pollution law.
私鉄の組合は半日ストに～った The unionists of the private railroad company *entered into* (≒ *launched out*) a half-day strike.
2〖外に出る〗¶ 横綱がついに土俵を～った The grand *sumo* champion *was pushed out of* (≒ *stepped out of*) the ring at last.

ふみこ・える【踏み越える】¶ 国境を～えてカナダへ入る *cross* the borders into Canada. 難関を～える *overcome* difficulties.

ふみこ・む【踏み込む】¶ 警官隊は未明に彼の隠れがに～んだ The policeman *made a raid on* (≒ *rushed into*) his hiding place just before dawn. 消防士は子どもを救うために窓から家に～んだ The fireman *entered* the house through a window to rescue the little child.

ふみし・める【踏み締める】¶ 大地を～めて立つ(歩く) stand firmly (walk steadily) on the ground.

ふみだい【踏み台】a footstool. ¶ ～に上がって棚の物を取る stand on *a footstool* to reach for the thing on a shelf. 人を～にして出世する *make a stepping stone of* another to success and fame.

ふみたお・す【踏み倒す】¶ 子どもたちがかきねを～した Children *trampled down* the fence. 借金を～す *repudiate* (≒ *bilk*) the debt. 彼は借金を～して姿を消した He disappeared *without paying his debt.*

ふみだ・す【踏み出す】step forward ; advance. ¶ 再建に向かって一歩～す *take a step* toward reconstruction.

ふみだん【踏み段】a step; (一続きの) a flight of stairs; (車の) a footboard. ¶ ～を上がる(下りる) go up (down) the stairs.

ふみつ・ける【踏みつける】¶ たばこの吸いがらを～ける *trample* (≒ *stamp*) *on* a cigaret-end.

ふみつぶ・す【踏みつぶす】¶ カエルを～す *crush* a frog under *one's* foot.

ふみどころ【踏み所】¶ 部屋は足の～もないほど散らかっていた The room was in such a confusion that I could not find *a place to stand in.*

ふみとどま・る【踏みとどまる】¶ 最後まで～って戦った They made a desperate stand against the enemy. 彼は終戦まで首相の職に～った He *held out* premiership till the war was over. 船長は沈没する船に最後まで～った The captain *was the last man to leave* the sinking ship.

ふみなら・す【踏み均らす】¶ 道を～す *level* the path *by treading down ; beat* the path. ～した道 a *well-trodden* (≒ *beaten*) path.

ふみにじ・る【踏み躙る】¶ 花壇を～る *trample* (≒ *tread*) a flowerbed *underfoot.* 人の好意を～る *trample upon* (≒ *completely ignore*) *a person's* favor.

ふみぬ・く【踏み抜く】¶ くぎで足の裏を～く *tread* (≒ *run*) a nail *into*〔the sole of〕*one's* foot. 床を～く *tread through* the floor.

ふみば【踏み場】⇒ふみどころ

ふみはず・す【踏み外す】¶ 階段を～す *slip* (≒ *make a false step*) on the stairs. 絶壁を～して転落する *stumble* down a precipice. 彼は足を～した He *lost his footing.*

ふみわ・ける【踏み分ける】¶ 彼らは山道を～けてふもとに着いた They *found* (≒ *made*) *their way* down to the foot of the mountain.

ふみん【不眠】¶ ～不休でがんばる work *with no sleep* and rest.

ふみんしょう【不眠症】〖医学〗insomnia ; sleeplessness. ¶ ～に悩む suffer from *insomnia.*
—患者 an insomniac.

ふ・む【踏む】**1**〖足で〗step. ¶ 電車の中で誤って婦人の足を～んだ I *stepped on* a woman's foot in the train by mistake.
昨年初めてヨーロッパの地を～んだ I went to Europe for the first time last year. / I *set foot on* European soil for the first time last year.
2〖見積もる〗estimate. ¶ この花びんは安く～んで5万円だ This vase *is* easily *worth* 50,000 yen.
このつぼの値段をどのくらいに～みますか How much do you *estimate* the value of this jug?
3〖手続きを〗¶ 彼は正式の手続きを～んでいない He *has* not *gone through* the formalities.

ふ

4 〖韻を〗 ¶ この2語は韻を～んでいる These two words *rhyme with* each other.

ふむき【不向き】¶ 彼女はきみには～だ She *is unsuitable for* you. きみには～なくつだ These shoes *don't suit* you. 彼は議長には～だ He *is incompetent to* act as chairman. 彼はそういう仕事には～だ He *is not cut out for* that kind of work.

ふめい【不明】obscurity; uncertainty. ¶ 遭難船の正確な位置は依然として～だ The exact location of the ill-fated ship *is* still *uncertain*. その病気の原因は～である The cause of the disease *is unknown*. 今のところ真偽のほどは～である *No one knows* so far whether it is true or not. / We *are not sure of* its reliability. 首相の病状は～である The condition of the premier *has not been disclosed*. 身の～を恥じるばかりだ I am heartily ashamed of my *ignorance* (≒ *incompetence*). 文意の～な箇所がある Some passages *are obscure* in meaning.
原因── ¶ 原因～の火事があった There was a fire of *unknown* (≒ *obscure*) origin. 国籍── ¶ 国籍～の飛行機 a plane of *unidentified* (≒ *dubious*) nationality. 身元── ¶ 身元～の死体 an *unidentified* body. 行方── ¶ 数人の人が行方～になっている A few people *are missing*.

ふ

ふめいよ【不名誉】dishonor; disgrace. ¶ まったく～な話だ It is quite a *shameful* story. / What *a shame*! きみの行ないは家族全体の～になるだろう Your behavior will *disgrace* (≒ *be to the discredit of*) the whole family. そんなことをすると学校の～になる Such an act will bring *disgrace* (≒ *dishonor*) to your school. 清貧は～ではない Honest poverty is no *disgrace*. / Noble poverty causes no *shame*. ビクトリア朝では働くことは～な習慣とされた During the reign of Queen Victoria, work was considered a rather *disgraceful* habit.

ふめいりょう【不明瞭】¶ ～な音 *inarticulate* sound. ～なことば *indistinct* speech. 印刷が～だ The print *is illegible*. テレビの映像が～だ The television *is out of focus*. その政策は目的が～だThe policy *lacks a defined purpose*.

ふめつ【不滅】immortality. ¶ 霊魂の～ *immortality* of the soul. 物質～は真理である The *indestructibility* of matter is a truth. ～の名作 a *monumental* work.

ふめん【譜面】music. ¶ ～を読む read *music*. ～を見て歌う (歌詞でなく音階で) sol-fa.
──台 a music stand (≒ rack).

ふめんぼく【不面目】¶ まったく～な次第だ I *am* heartily *ashamed of* myself. ～なことをしてくれたな *Shame on* you! / I *am ashamed of* you. ～なことをした I *disgraced* myself. / I *fell into* disgrace.

ふもう【不毛】barrenness; sterility. ¶ ～の土地 *barren* (≒ *waste*; *sterile*) land. ～の論争 a *fruitless* (≒ *profitless*) controversy.

ふもと【麓】the foot; the base. ¶ 山の～に住む live at the *foot* (≒ *base*) of a mountain.

ふもん【不問】¶ きみの失策は～に付されるであろう Your fault will *be ignored* (≒ *be overlooked*). / People will *take no notice* (≒ *heed*) *of* your fault.

ぶもん【武門】(総称) military stock. ¶ 彼は由緒ある～の出だ He comes of a good *military family*.

ぶもん【部門】a class; a department. ¶ その花はそれだけで一～をなしている The flowers form *a class* by themselves. 算数は学問の一～だ Arithmetic is *a department* of learning. 各～に分かれて協議する hold minor assemblies.

ふやか・す ¶ 大豆を水につけて～す *soak* (≒ *sodden*; *steep*) beans in the water.

ふや・ける ¶ 湯につかって手が～けた My hands *have swollen up* (≒ *have become sodden*) in the hot water.

ふやじょう【不夜城】a nightless city; an all-night city.

ふや・す【増やす・殖やす】add; increase. ¶ 仕事の人数を～す *get more* people to work. 月給を10万円に～す *raise* (≒ *increase*) *a person's* salary *to* 100,000 yen. 財産を～す *add to one's* wealth. 語彙(ごい)を～す *extend* (≒ *enlarge*) *one's* vocabulary. 知識を～す *enrich one's* knowledge.

ふゆ【冬】winter; the winter season. ¶ ～が間近だ *Winter* is drawing near. ～が忍び寄る *Winter* creeps on. 当地では11月から～になる *Winter* comes in November up here. この～は寒さがきびしかった (きびしくなかった) We have had *a* hard (*a* mild) *winter*. 私は～のさなかにローマに着いた I arrived in Rome *in midwinter* (≒ *in the depth of winter*).
──支度 ¶ ～支度に忙しい We are busy preparing for *the winter*.

ふゆう【浮遊】¶ ちりが空中に～している Dust *is floating* in the air.
──機雷 a floating mine. ──生物 plankton. ──選鉱 flo[a]tation. ──船渠 a floating dock. ──物 a floating matter.

ふゆう【富裕】wealth; prosperity. ¶ ～な家に生まれる be born of (≒ into) a rich family; be born *with a silver spoon in one's mouth*; be born *under a lucky star*. ～な家柄の生まれである come of a *wealthy* family.

ぶゆう【武勇】valor; 英 valour; bravery; courage; prowess. ¶ 彼は～のほまれが高い He is famed for his *valor* (≒ *bravery*).
──談 a tale of heroism. ──伝 a heroic episode.

ふゆかい【不愉快】unpleasantness; disagreeableness; displeasure. ¶ 彼は～な男だ He is an *unpleasant* man. 私は～だ I *am displeased*. / I *am not pleased* at all. 彼は～そうだった He looked *displeased*. / He wore a *frowning* look. それはだれにも～に聞こえる It sounds *disagreeable* to anybody. ときには～な仕事もある Sometimes I have to do a *disagreeable* (≒ an *unpleasant*) work.

彼の自慢話でみな～になった His brag *displeased* everyone. / Everyone *was disgusted with* (≒ *by*) his big talk.

ふゆがれ【冬枯れ】¶ ～の野 a *wintry* scene.

ふゆきとどき【不行き届き】negligence. ¶ ～で相すみません I'm sorry I *was careless.* / (物をこわした時など) I'm sorry I *was awkward.* その事故は警察の～から起こった The accident happened through *negligence* of the police. 親の監督が～だった The parents *lacked proper care* of their child. 支配人は～だ The manager *is neglectful.* 庭の掃除が～だった The garden *was ill-kept.* 家の手入れが～でこわれている The house *is out of repair.*

ふゆげしき【冬景色】a bleak (≒ desolate) winter (≒ wintry) scene.

ふゆごもり【冬籠り】wintering. ¶ 雪国では冬の間は～だ In a snow country, people must *keep indoors in winter.*

ふゆしょうぐん【冬将軍】the rigors of winter; (擬人的に) Jack Frost; General Winter. ¶ ～の訪れ the advent of General Winter; the coming of winter.

ふゆふく【冬服】winter clothes (≒ clothing); winter wear.

ふゆもの【冬物】winter clothes; winter wear.

ふゆやすみ【冬休み】a winter vacation. ¶ 学校は～になった School is over for the *Christmas* (≒ *winter*) *vacation.*

ふゆやま【冬山】¶ ～では遭難が多い A lot of people meet with disasters *in the mountains during the winter months.*

ふよ【付与・賦与】grant; bestowal; investment; conferment. ¶ 大学は彼に博士の学位を～した The university *conferred* a doctorate *on* him. 彼は詩の才能を～されている He *is endowed* (≒ *is gifted*) *with* poetic talent.

ぶよ【蚋】〔虫類〕a gnat.

ふよう【不用・不要】¶ ～な useless; unnecessary. 申告は～だ *No* report *is necessary* (≒ *is needed*). この本は～になった I *don't need* this book any more. / I can *spare* this book.

—品 a discarded article. **—不急融資** non-urgent loan.

ふよう【扶養】support; maintenance. ¶ 人は親を～する義務がある We are expected to *support* (≒ *maintain*) our parents.

—家族 a dependent. **—家族手当** a family allowance. **—義務** supporting duty. **—控除** allowance for dependents. **—者** a supporter; a sustainer; the breadwinners.

ふよう【浮揚】¶ 潜水艦が～してきた A submarine *emerged* from the water. 座礁した船が～した A stranded steamer *floated off.*

—力 buoyancy.

ふよう【芙蓉】〔植物〕a kind of rose mallow.

ぶよう【舞踊】dancing; a dance.

郷土**—** a folk dance. 日本**—** Japanese dancing.

ふようい【不用意】carelessness; want of preparation. ¶ 大臣は～な発言をした The minister made a *careless* (≒ *thoughtless*) remark. ～なところをつかれた I was caught *unawares.* ～に試験に臨んだ I took the examination quite *unprepared.* 彼は～なことを言ってしまったと後悔している He regrets *the rashness* of his speech.

ふようじょう【不養生】neglect of *one's* health; intemperance. ¶ 若いときは～をしがちだ Young people are apt to *be careless of their health.* 医者の～ (諺) It is a good doctor who follows his own directions.

ぶようじん【無用心・不用心】¶ 娘がひとりで夜間外出するのは～だ It *is unsafe* for a girl to go out unaccompanied at night. ドアにかぎをかけないのは～だ It *is careless* (≒ *is imprudent*) to leave the door unlocked.

ふようど【腐葉土】leaf mold; humus.

ぶよぶよ ¶ 水につかった菓子が～になった The cake became *sodden* in the water. 桃が～に熟している The peaches *are soft* and mellow.

フライ **1**〚野球〛a fly. ¶ 浅いライト～ *a fly* to short right field.

彼は～を打ちあげた He *flew out.*

2〚料理〛a fry. ¶ 彼は～が好きだ He likes *fries.*

エビの～があがりかけている The lobsters *are frying* (≒ *are being fried*).

小エビの～ *fried* shrimps.

—パン a frying pan. カキ**—** fried oysters.

フライイング ¶ ～をする jump the gun.

ぶらいかん【無頼漢】a rogue; a rascal; a ruffian.

フライきゅう【フライ級】flyweight. ¶ ～のボクサー a flyweight boxer.

フライスばん【フライス盤】a fraise; a milling machine.

プライバシー privacy. ¶ 人の～を侵害する disturb the *privacy* of people.

プライベート private. ¶ ～なことで相談したい I'd like to have a talk with you on some *private* affairs.

ブラインド 米 a shade; 英 a blind. ¶ ～を上げる (下ろす) draw up (draw down) *a blind.*

ブラウス a blouse.

ブラウンかん【ブラウン管】a Braun tube.

プラカード a placard. ¶ ～を掲げて行進する march with *placards* lifted up.

ぶらく【部落】a village; a tribe. ¶ 山間の～ *a village* among the mountains.

—会 a village meeting. 漁業**—** a fishing village (≒ community).

プラグ a plug. ¶ トースターの～をコンセントに差し込む *plug in* a toaster.

プラグマチズム〔哲学〕pragmatism.

ぶらさが・る【ぶら下がる】¶ 鳥かごがくぎに～っている There is a bird cage *hanging* (≒ *dangling*) from the nail. 熟したなしが木に～っている Ripe pears *are dangling on* the tree. つららが屋根から～っている Some icicles *are hanging* from the roof. 社長のいすが彼の目

の前に～っている He *is next in line to* presidency.

ぶらさ·げる【ぶら下げる】¶ 天井からランプを～げる *hang* (≒ *suspend*) a lamp *from* the ceiling. 彼は知識を鼻の先に～げている He *parades* his knowledge.

ブラシ a brush. ¶ 服に～をかける *brush* 〔*up*〕 (≒ *give a brush to*) clothes.

歯— a toothbrush.

ブラジャー a brassiere.

ブラジル Brazil ; (正式名) the United States of Brazil.

—人 a Brazilian.

ふら·す【降らす】¶ 不連続線が雨を～す A line of discontinuity *causes a rain.*

プラス plus. ¶ あともう1,000円～してください Give me 1,000 *more* yen. 差し引き500円の～になる That means 500 yen gain for me after all. そうすればきみの～になる If you do that, it will help you. きみが来てくれれば会社の～になる You will *be a great asset to* our firm. 学問で社会に～したい I wish to *benefit* (≒ *do good to*) the world through my major. そんなことをしてもなんの～にもならない That will *add nothing* to the situation. 2～3は5 Two *and* (≒ *plus*) three is (≒ are) five.

—アルファ plus something.

フラスコ a flask.

プラスチック plastic〔s〕. ¶ ～製品 *plastic* goods.

ブラスバンド a brass band.

ふら·せる【降らせる】⇒ふらす

プラタナス〔植物〕a plane 〔tree〕. ¶ ～の並木道 an avenue lined on both sides with *plane trees.*

フラダンス hula〔-hula〕. ¶ ～を踊る dance the hula.

ふらち【不埒】(無法な) lawless ; outrageous ; (無礼な) rude ; impolite. ¶ ～なやつだ How *shameless* you are ! ～な行ないをする misbehave *oneself* ; do wrong. ～なことを言う make an *unpardonable* remark.

プラチナ platinum.

ふらつ·く ¶ 高熱で足が～いた I *staggered* because of violent fever. それを聞いて彼の決心は～いた *It shook* his resolution. その辺を～いてきたところです I *have been for a little walk.* 彼女は～いてもう動けなかった She *became giddy* and could'nt walk any farther. 酒に酔って足が～く The drink made my legs *unsteady.* 頭が～いた My head *swam.*

ブラック **1** 〔黒〕 black. ¶ コーヒーを～で飲む drink *coffee black.*

「クリーム入れますか」「～にしてください」"Cream ?" "No ; *black,* please."

2 〔印刷〕(肉太活字) boldface 〔type〕.

ぶらつ·く ¶ その辺を～いてくる I'll *go out for a little walk.* ひとりで海岸を～いた I *took a* solitary *stroll* along the beach. 森の中を～く *walk leisurely* (≒ *aimlessly*) through the woods.

ブラックリスト a blacklist. ¶ 彼の名は～にのっている His name is on the *blacklist.* / He *is black-listed.*

フラッシュ〔映画〕flash. ¶ ～をたく light *a flash bulb* ; snap *a flashlight.*

—ガン〔写真〕a flashgun. —バック a flashback ; a cutback. ニュース— a flash.

フラット〔音楽〕a flat (♭) ;〔競技〕flat. ¶ 11秒～で in 11 seconds *flat.*

プラットホーム a platform.

プラネタリウム a planetarium (複 planetaria).

フラノ flannel. ¶ ～のズボン *flannel* trousers.

ふらふら **1** 〔足·体が〕¶ 酔って～と歩いた I was drunk and walked *with my unsteady legs.*

疲れて足が～した I was too tired to walk steadily.

彼は～と立ち上がった He *staggered* (≒ *tottered*) to his feet. / (なにげなく) He stood up *unintentionally.*

熱で頭が～する My head *swims with* a high fever.

空腹で～する I *am faint with* hunger.

私は～と後ろへよろめいた I *staggered* back.

頭を打たれて～する I *feel dizzy* because of the blow on my head.

2 〔心·決心が〕¶ 彼は～と迷って就職がきまらない He *is wavering* in the choice of jobs.

つい～と秘密を漏らしてしまった I betrayed the secret *in spite of myself* (≒ *before I thought*).

ぶらぶら ¶ ヘチマが～と揺れている Some sponge gourds *are swinging* in the breeze. 公園の辺りを～歩いてきた I *have been loitering about* the park. 夕飯を済まして～出かけよう Let us *go out for a stroll* after supper. 大学を出たというのにまだ～しているのか *Are* you still *idling away* at home when you have finished the college? 彼は職を離れて～している He is *at a loose end.*

ブラボー bravo (複 bravo〔e〕s). ¶ ～と叫ぶ shout bravo〔s〕.

プラモデル a plastic model.

ふらりと ¶ ～彼の家に立ち寄った I *dropped in on* him./I *dropped in at* his house./ I called on him *unexpectedly* (≒ *without notice*). インドへ行く途中彼は～日本へ立ち寄った He paid a *casual* visit to Japan on his way to India. ～旅に出た I went on a trip *aimlessly.*

ぶらり ¶ ヘチマが～と下がっている A sponge gourd *is dangling.* 彼は～と散歩に出た He went out for a *casual* walk.

ふら·れる【振られる】¶ 彼はあの女に～れた He *was rejected* (≒ *was jilted*) by that girl.

ふらん【腐乱】(死体の) decomposition ; (はれもの) ulceration. ¶ ～する decompose ; ulcerate ; putrefy. ～した rotten ; corrupt.

—死体 a decomposed (≒ putrefied) body.

フラン (フランス·ベルギー·スイスの貨幣) franc.

プラン a plan. ¶ 夏休みの～を立てる make (≒ form ; lay out) *a plan* for the summer vacation.

ふ

ブランク a blank. ¶ ノートの〜を埋める fill in the *blanks* of a notebook. 彼は野球選手として1年間の〜がある He has *a blank* of a year as a baseball player. 彼は答案を〜のまま提出した He handed in *a blank paper*.
プランクトン 〘生物〙 plankton.
ぶらんこ a swing. ¶ 〜に乗る get on *a swing*.
フランス France. ¶ 〜の French.
—革命 the French Revolution. —語 French; the French language. —国歌 the French national anthem. —国旗 the national flag of France. —人 a Frenchman; (女) a Frenchwoman; (総称) the French. —パン French bread. —料理 French dishes.
フランチャイズ 〘野球〙 a franchise.
—制 the franchise system.
ブランデー brandy.
プラント a plant.
—輸出 plant exports.
ふり 【振り】 ¶ 〜の客 a *chance* customer. ひと〜の剣 a sword. 彼はバットの〜がいい He *swings* his bat nicely.
ふり 【降り】 rainfall. ¶ ひどい〜 *a* heavy *rain*. ひどい〜だ How heavily *it rains*! ひと〜ありそうだ We may have *a rainfall*. ひと〜ほしい We are thirsty for *a rainfall*. 大した〜にもなるまい It won't be much of *a fall*.
ふり 【不利】 disadvantage. ¶ きみは〜な立場にある You are in a *disadvantageous* position. 形勢はますます味方に〜になった The situation became more and more *unfavorable* to our side. 裁判では〜な証拠が出された An evidence was shown in the court *against* me. 選挙の結果は政府に〜だった The election *went against* the Government. この点は彼に〜だ He *is at a disadvantage* in this respect. 形勢〜だ The odds *are against* us.
ふり 【風】 show; pretense. ¶ 聞こえぬ〜をするな Never *pretend* not to hear. 彼は眠った〜をするのが得意だ He is a good hand at *pretending* to be asleep. 見て見ぬ〜をするのはよくない It is not good to *turn a blind eye to* something done. 彼は私に会って知らぬ〜をした He *cut* me *dead*. 彼はなんでもない〜を装った He *feigned* that nothing was the matter with him. 人の〜見てわが〜直せ (諺) One man's fault is another's lesson. / Correct your manners by seeing others' faults. 彼は逃げる〜をした He *made as if* he were going to run away. 彼は親切そうな〜をして私をだました He cheated me *under pretence of* friendship. 彼はこわがる〜をした He *dissembled* fear.
ぶり 【鰤】 〘魚類〙 a yellowtail.
-ぶり 【-振り】 ¶ 話し〜 a *way* of speaking. 彼の歩き〜はおかしい His *manner* of walking is strange. 彼の仕事〜はまじめだ He is a diligent worker. ここ20年〜の寒さだ This is the coldest winter in twenty years (≒ that we have had for these twenty years). 5年〜で彼に会った I met him whom I had not seen for five years. / I met him *after* five years' *interval*. / It is (≒ (口語) has been) five years since I saw him last.
ふりあい 【振り合い】 comparison. ¶ ほかとの〜を考える take other things into consideration.
ふりあ·げる 【振り上げる】 ¶ げんこつを〜げる *shake one's* fist. 彼は刀を〜げた He *swung up* his sword over his head.
ふりあ·てる 【振り当てる】 ¶ その仕事は私に〜てられた The work *was assigned to* me. ひとりひとりの弁士は3分間を〜てられた Each speaker *was allotted* three minutes.
フリー free. ¶ 〜の時間がもっとほしい I want to have more *time to spare*. 彼は今は〜になっている He is now a *free* lance.
—スタイル 〘水泳〙 a free style; 〘レスリング〙 catch-as-catch-can. —スロー 〘バスケット〙 a free throw. —パス 〘バスケット〙 a free pass. —バッティング 〘野球〙 free batting.
フリーザー an icecream freezer.
フリージア 〘植物〙 a freesia.
プリーツ a pleat. ¶ スカートの〜 *pleats* on the skirt.
—スカート a pleated skirt.
フリーメーソン a Freemason.
ふりえき 【不利益】 disadvantage. ¶ 彼の発言はわれわれには〜だった His remark *was disadvantageous* (≒ *was derogatory*) *to* us.
ふりおと·す 【振り落とす】 ¶ 彼は車から〜された He *was thrown off* (≒ *was shaken off*) the car. 10人以上が試験で〜された More than ten *failed* the examination.
ふりかえ 【振替】 transfer. ¶ 〜で金を送る send money *by postal transfer*. 〜で雑誌代を払う pay for a magazine *by postal transfer*.
—貯金 transfer savings. ¶ 〜貯金口座東京12番 postal transfer account No. 12. Tokyo.
ぶりかえ·す 【ぶり返す】 ¶ 暑さが〜した Hot weather *has returned*. 彼の病気が〜した He *has had* (≒ *has suffered*) *a relapse*.
ふりかえ·る 【振り返る】 ¶ 二, 三歩行って彼は〜った He walked two or three steps, and *turned about* (≒ *turned round*). 彼は〜って私のほうを見た He *looked back toward* me. 昔を〜るといろいろ思い出がある When I *look back on* my past, I am reminded of a variety of things.
ふりかえ·る 【振り替える】 ¶ 普通預金を定期預金に〜た He *changed* his ordinary deposit to a fixed one.
ふりかか·る 【降り懸かる】 ¶ 災難が彼に〜った A misfortune *befell* him. / He *was overtaken by* a misfortune. 身に〜る危険を感じた I felt an *impending* danger. 〜る火の粉は払わねばならぬ We cannot sit idle when we *are exposed to danger*.
ふりか·ける 【振り掛ける】 ¶ 肉に塩を〜ける *sprinkle* salt *on* (≒ *over*) meat. いちごに砂糖を〜ける *sprinkle* sugar *over* strawberries.
ふりかざ·す 【振りかざす】 ¶ 彼は刀を〜した He

brandished his sword *over* his head. 彼らは国威を～している They *are showing off* the national prestige.

ふりかた【振り方】¶ きみは身の～を決めるのが第一だ You must first of all make up *a plan for your future.* / You must first of all decide *how to dispose of yourself.*

ふりがな【振り仮名】*kana* pronouncing letters〔given to a Chinese ideograph〕. ¶ 名前に～をつけなさい Give the reading of your name in *kana.* この漢字に～をつけてほしい I want you to give *kana* to this Chinese character.

ふりかぶ・る【振りかぶる】¶ 彼は刀を大上段に～った He *held* his sword *aloft* overhead.

ブリキ tin plate.
—かん a tin; 英 a can. —細工 tinware.
—屋 a tinsmith.

ふりき・る【振り切る】¶ つかみかかってくる手を～って逃げた I *tore myself away* from the man's grasp. すがりついてくる彼を～ることはできなかった I could not *refuse* him asking for my help desperately.

ふりこ【振り子】a pendulum.

ふりこう【不履行】nonfulfillment.
契約— nonfulfillment of a contract. 約束— a breach of promise.

ふりこ・む【降り込む】¶ 雨が室内に～んだ It *rained into* the room. 雨が～んだ The rain *swept in.*

ふりこ・む【振り込む】¶ 小切手を銀行に～む *pay* a check *into* a bank.

ふりこめら・れる【降り込められる】¶ 雨に～れた I *was kept indoors by rain.* 雪に～れた I *was snow-bound.* / I *was snowed in.* 大雨に～れて家に帰れなかった *Because of the heavy rain* I was unable to come back home.

ふりしき・る【降り頻る】¶ 雨が～っている It *is raining in torrents.* / It *is raining incessantly* (≒ *heavily*). ～る雨の中を急いだ I made haste *in a downpour.*

ふりしぼ・る【振り絞る】¶ 力を～って戦った I fought out *to the utmost of* my power.

ふりす・てる【振り捨てる】¶ 彼は家族を～てて東京へ出た He went to Tokyo, *leaving* his family *behind.* 彼は彼女を～てて他の女に走った He *discarded* her *for* another girl.

プリズム a prism. ¶ ～式の prismatic.

ふりそそ・ぐ【降り注ぐ】¶ 雨が～いでいる It *is raining heavily.* 日光が～いでいる The sun *is shining on.* 屋根に雨が～ぐ Rain *is pattering* on the roof.

ふりそで【振り袖】a long-sleeved *kimono.*
¶ ～姿の少女 a girl *in long sleeves.*

ふりだし【振り出し・振出】(始め) the starting point; beginning; (薬) infusion. ¶ 日本を～に世界を一周した I *started* from Japan on a trip round the world.
—手形 a bill payable. —人 a drawer.
—日 the date of issue. —地 the place of issue.

ふりだ・す【振り出す】¶ 小切手を～す *issue* a check. 為替を～す *issue* a money order.

ふりだ・す【降り出す】¶ 雨が～した It *has begun to rain.* / It *has started raining.* 今にも～しそうだ *It threatens to rain* at any moment. 雪が～している It *is beginning to snow.*

ふりた・てる【振り立てる】¶ 首を～てる *perk up one's* head. しっぽを～てる *wag one's* tail. 子どもたちは旗を～てて歩いている The children are walking, *waving their flags* overhead.

ふりつ【府立】¶ ～学校 a *prefectural* school.

ふりつけ【振り付け】dance composition; (バレー) choreography. ¶ ～をする *arrange* dances. バレーの～をする *compose* a ballet.
—師 a dance composer; a choreographer.

ブリッジ 1〖トランプ〗¶ ～をする (トランプ) play *bridge.*
オークション— auction bridge.
2〖歯の〗¶ 歯に～を入れる *bridge* a tooth.

ふりつづ・く【降り続く】¶ まだ～いている It *is* still *raining.* 雨が5日間～いた *The rain continued* for five days *on end.* ～く長雨には飽き飽きした *A long spell of rainy weather* has been tiring to me. 3日前から雪が～いている It *has been snowing* for three days.

ふりつも・る【降り積もる】¶ 雪が50センチも～った Snow *lay* half a meter *deep.* だいぶ～りそうだ It is likely to *lie pretty deep.*

ふりはな・す【振り放す】¶ 手を～す shake *oneself* free from *a person's* grasp. 彼は私の手を～した He *shook off* my hand.

ぷりぷり ¶ 彼は～怒っている He *is in a huff.* 彼は～怒って行ってしまった He went away *steaming* (≒ *red*) *with anger.*

ふりま・く【振り撒く】¶ 彼女はあいきょうを～いている She *is all smiles*〔*to everybody*〕. 彼はさかんにお世辞を～いている He is trying to *please* (≒ *make himself agreeable to*) *everybody.*

プリマドンナ a prima donna (主としてオペラ. イタリア語から). ¶ 彼女はこの5年ずっとその歌劇団の～である She has been the *prima donna* of the operatic company these five years.

ふりまわ・す【振り回す】¶ 彼は刀を～して敵に向かって突進した He rushed at the enemy *brandishing* (≒ *flourishing*) his sword. つえを～す *swing* a cane. 知識を～す *show off one's* knowledge. やたらに権力を～す *display* authority too much.

ふりみだ・す【振り乱す】¶ 髪を～して *with disheveled hair.*

ふりむ・く【振り向く】¶ 思わず後ろを～いた I *turned round* (≒ *turned back*) in spite of myself. 彼は私を～きもしなかった He did not *take notice of* me at all.

ふりむ・ける【振り向ける】¶ 報酬をそのまま本代に～けた He *appropriated* (≒ *applied*) all the pay *to* books.

ふりや・む【降り止む】¶ 雨がようやく～んだ It *has stopped raining* at last. すぐ雪は～むだろう The snow will *stop falling* soon.

ふりょ【不慮】¶ ～の出来事 an *unforeseen*

ふ

(≒ *unexpected*) event. 彼は交通事故で～の死をとげた He met an *untimely* (≒ a *sudden*) death in a traffic accident.

ふりょ【俘虜】a prisoner.
戦争― a prisoner of war (P.O.W.).

ふりょう【不良】¶ 稲作～ a *poor* rice crop; a *bad* rice harvest. 成績～ *poor* results. 発育～ *poor* development. 天候～のため遠足は延期された The picnic was postponed owing to the *bad* weather. 彼は～になった He *has gone to the bad.* / He *has become a bad boy.*
―化 degradation. ―少年 (少女) a delinquent boy (girl); a juvenile delinquent. ―青年 a young ruffian. ―品 an inferior article.

ふりょう【不漁】a poor catch.

ふりょう【不猟】a poor bag.

ぶりょう【無聊】tedium; wearisomeness; ennui. ¶ 彼は～に苦しんでいる He *is feeling bored.*

ふりょうけん【不料簡】¶ ～を起こすな Never think of *doing wrong.* こんなことになったのはおまえの～からだ It was because of your *indiscretion* that such a thing happened to you. きみはどうしてそんな～なことをしたのか What made you think of committing such a *rash* act?

ふりょうどうたい【不良導体】〔電気〕a non-conductor.

ふりょく【浮力】buoyancy. ¶ この金属板は～がある This metal plate *is buoyant.*

ぶりょく【武力】military power. ¶ ～に訴える resort to *arms.* 彼らはあくまでも～で解決しようとしている They are going to settle the problem *by force* by all means.
―干渉 an armed intervention. ―政治 power politics. ―戦 an armed conflict.

ふりわけ【振り分け】¶ ～荷物 a strapped pair of bundles 〔slung over *one's* shoulder〕. 彼は荷物を～にして運んだ He *carried packages before and behind* him 〔with straps over his shoulder〕.

ふりん【不倫】immorality; adultery. ¶ ～の恋 an *illicit* love. 彼らは～の関係にある They are in an *immoral* relation to each other.

プリン pudding.

プリンス a prince.

プリンセス a princess.

プリント a print. ¶ ～する print. 講義の～ *printed sheets* of the synopsis of a lecture.

ふる【古】¶ 父のお～のズボン trousers *handed down* from my father.
―物 ¶ ～物の家具だが, しっかりしていたので買った I bought this article of furniture *second-hand,* which was very strong.

フル ¶ 機械は～に動いている *All* the machines are in motion *to the full.* きょうも彼は一日じゅう～に働いた He has worked *all through the day without rest.* 設備は～に活用すべきだ We should *make full use of* the facilities.

ふ・る【振る】**1** shake; wave. ¶ 手を～る *wave one's* hand.
びんを～る *shake* a bottle.
バットを～る *swing* a bat.
しっぽを～る *wag* the tail.
手を～って別れた I *waved* goodbye to him.
首を縦に～る *nod* assent.
首を横に～る *shake one's* head.
2 〖ふりかける〗 ¶ 塩を～る *sprinkle* salt (*on*).
3 〖きらう〗 ¶ 彼女は私を～って彼に走った She *jilted* me *for* him.

ふ・る【降る】¶ 雨が～る It *rains.* 雪が～る It *snows.* 雨に～られた I *was caught in the rain.* この1週間～り続いている It *has been raining* for a week. これで2週間雨が～らない We *have had no rain* these two weeks. / It *has not rained* these two weeks. 一日じゅう～ったりやんだりしている It *has been raining* on and off all day. 雨が～りそうだ It *looks like rain.* いつ～るかもしれない It may *rain* at any moment. ～っても照っても出かける予定だ We are to go out *rain or shine.* 満天～るほどの星空だった The sky *was full of* shining stars. まさに～ってわいた幸運だった It was quite *a windfall.*

-ぶ・る【-振る】¶ 彼は学者～るところがある He *assumes the air of* a scholar. 彼は上品～っていていやみだ He *is* too *genteel* to be liked by others. あまりにもおとな～った子どもだ The child *is* too *precocious.* 彼はもったい～っている He *puts on airs.* 彼は紳士～っている He *affects* a gentleman.

ふるい【篩】a sieve. ¶ ～にかける sieve. 砂を～にかける *pass* sand *through a sieve.* 砂と砂金を～い分ける *sift* gravel *from* sand.

ふる・い【古い】old. ¶ ～い友だち an *old* friend. ～い魚 *stale* fishes. ～いしゃれ a *worn-out* joke. ～い切手 a *used* postage stamp. ～くからの伝統 an *old* tradition. この店で私は～いほうだ I am one of the *old-timers* in this store. そんな衣服はもう～い Such sort of clothes *are old-fashioned.* 彼は頭が～い He *is old-fashioned.* 彼らの国語は非常に～い Their language *is of great antiquity.* きみはこの雑誌の～いのをお持ちですか Have you *the back numbers* of this magazine?

ぶるい【部類】a class. ¶ 鯨は動物と同じ～に属する A whale belongs in the same *class* with the animals. ～に分ける classify. それは魚の～に入る It *comes under the head* of fish.

ふるいおこ・す【奮い起こす】¶ 勇気を～しなさい *Summon up* your courage. 満身の力を～した I *put forth* all the strength in my power.

ふるいおと・す【篩い落とす】¶ 試験の結果数名の志願者を～した We *screened* a few candidates through the test. / A few candidates *were rejected* after the test.

ふるいけ【古池】an old pond.

ふるいた・つ【奮い立つ】¶ 彼らは勝報に～った They *roused themselves up* at the victorious news. その成功で彼は～った He *was encouraged with* the success.

ふる・う【振るう・奮う・揮う】**1**〖力を発揮する〗¶ 彼はその方面ではかなりの手腕を～った He *showed* considerable ability in that direction.
彼は手腕を～う余地がない He has no scope for his abilities.
彼は非常な権力を～うことができる He can *wield* (≒ *exercise*) enormous power.
彼はわれわれに暴力を～った He *used* violence toward us.
彼は熱弁を～った He *made* a passionate speech.
2〖栄える〗¶ このところ商売は～わない Business *has been slack* (≒ *has been dull*; *has been slow*) these days.
彼女の人気は～わない Her popularity *is at a low ebb* (≒ *is at the ebb*).
3〖奇抜な〗¶ 彼女の言うことは～っている What she says *is impressive* (≒ *is strange and original*).
まったく～った答えだ It's a quite *queer* (≒ *unexpected*) answer.
彼はときどき～ったことを言う He sometimes says what we don't expect at all.

ふる・う【篩う】sift. ¶ 労務者たちがじゃりを～っていた The workmen *were sifting* the gravel. 多くの男たちが川でじゃりと砂金を～っていた A lot of men *were sifting out* gravel from the gold dust. 彼女はパンを焼く前に小麦粉を～った She *sifted* (≒ *sieved*) the flour before baking. 志願者を～った We *screened* the candidates.

ブルース〖音楽〗blues. ¶ ～を歌う sing *blues*.
—歌手 a blues singer.

フルーツケーキ fruit cake; fruitcake.

フルーツパーラー a soda fountain; a soda parlor.

フルート a flute. ¶ ～を吹く play on *a flute*.
—奏者 a flutist.

ふるえ【震え】shivering; shudder; tremble. ¶ ～がきた I was attacked by *a fit of shivering*. / *A shudder* passed over me. 恐ろしさで～がとまらなかった I was so frightened that I could not stop *shivering*.

ふるえあが・る【震え上がる】tremble; shudder; shiver. ¶ 寒さで～った I *trembled* (≒ *shivered*) *with* cold. オオカミの遠ぼえで羊は～った The long howls of wolves *struck terror into* (≒ *completely frightened*) the sheep.

ふるえごえ【震え声】¶ ～で in *a trembling* (≒ *quivering*; *shaking*) *voice*.

ふる・える【震える】shake; tremble. ¶ 手足が～える My hands and legs *tremble*. 子犬はぶるぶる～えていた The puppy *was trembling*. 彼の声は恐ろしさのあまり～えていた His voice *trembled* (≒ *shook*) *with* fear. 彼は体を～わして笑った His body *shook with* laughter.

ふるがお【古顔】an old-timer; a familiar face. ¶ この道では彼は～だ He is *a veteran* (≒ *an old-timer*) in this line.

ふるかぶ【古株】an old stump; (古顔) an old-timer.

ブルガリア Bulgaria.
—語 Bulgarian; the Bulgarian language.
—人 a Bulgarian.

ふるぎ【古着】old clothes.
—屋 (店) a secondhand clothing store; (人) an old-clothes dealer.

ふるきず【古傷】an old wound. ¶ 彼の～を暴くようなことは言うな Don't say anything to open up his *old sore* (≒ *old wound*). 雨が降ると左脚の～がひどくうずく The *old wound* (≒ *old hurt*) in my left leg aches very much when it rains.

ふるくさ・い【古臭い】old. ¶ ～い冗談 *stale* jokes. そんな～い話はやめろ Don't tell such an *antiquated* (≒ *old*) story. そのような表現はもう～くなった Such expressions have become *trite* (≒ *commonplace*; *hackneyed*).

ふるさと【古里・故郷】⇒こきょう

ブルジョア bourgeois.
—階級 the bourgeoisie. **—趣味** bourgeois taste.

ふるす【古巣】an old nest. ¶ ～に帰ることに決めた I have decided to return to my *old place*. ～の学校を訪ねた I visited the school where I served as a teacher formerly.

フルスピード full speed. ¶ 車は～で走っていた The car was going *at full speed*.

ふるだぬき【古狸】(悪賢い人) an old fox. ¶ 彼はたいへんな～だ He is such *an old fox*. / He is *an old stager* (≒ *an old bird*; *an old hand*).

ふるって【奮って】¶ ～ご参加ください You *are cordially invited to* take part in the meeting. ～ご意見をお寄せください I hope you will give your straightforward opinions.

ふるつわもの【古つわもの】a veteran. ¶ 彼は名うての～だ He is reputed as *an old campaigner*.

ふるて【古手】an old-timer; an oldster.
¶ ～の教師 an *experienced* teacher.

ふるどうぐ【古道具】a secondhand article.
—屋 (人) a dealer in secondhand articles; a junk dealer; (店) a secondhand store; a junk shop.

ブルドーザー a bulldozer. ¶ ～で建て物を取り払う *bulldoze out* a building.

ブルドッグ a bulldog.

プルトニウム〖化学〗plutonium.

ふるなじみ【古馴染】¶ 彼とは～だ He is my *old friend*. / We've been friends since we were small children.

ふる・びる【古びる】grow old. ¶ ～びた服 *worn-out* clothes. ～びたオーバー an overcoat *that has seen long service*; an overcoat *that has been long used*. 書類は～びて黄色くなっている The documents have yellowed *with age*.

ぶるぶる ¶ 寒さで～震える *shiver with* cold. 手が～して書けない I can not write because my hands *shake* (≒ *tremble*). くちびるが～震えた His lips *quivered*. 恐ろしさで～震える

shake (≒ *tremble*) *with* fear.

フルベース〔野球〕¶～になっている The bases are full. これで～になった Now this fills the bases. ～でホームランを打った I whacked out a homer with *the bases full*.

ブルペン〔野球〕a bull pen.

ふるぼ・けた【古ぼけた】¶～けたかばん a *worn-out* briefcase.

ふるほん【古本】a secondhand (≒ used) book (old books は時代的に古い本など). ¶本を～で買う buy a book *at secondhand*.

―屋 (人) a secondhand bookseller; (店) a secondhand bookstore.

ふるまい【振る舞い】behavior. ¶粗暴な～ rude *behavior*. けしからぬ～ misconduct. 彼から夕食の～を受けた He *treated* me to dinner.

ふるま・う【振る舞う】behave. ¶彼はりっぱに～った He *behaved* 〔*himself*〕(≒ *conducted himself*) well. 男らしく～いなさい Behave 〔yourself〕like a man. 彼に昼食を～われた I *was entertained* by him at lunch.

ふるめかし・い【古めかしい】⇒ふるくさい

ふれ【触れ】an official notice. ¶その地区の樹木は伐採してはならないという～が出された The *official notices* that no trees should be cut down in that area were sent out.

ふれあい【触れ合い】心の～が大切だ It is important for us to *be brought into contact with* other minds.

ふれあ・う【触れ合う】come in touch (*with*). ¶ふたりは心と心が～った The two *sympathized with* each other.

フレアスカート a flared skirt.

ふれある・く【触れ歩く】¶彼がうわさを～いている He *is circulating* the rumor.

ぶれい【無礼】rudeness; (失礼) impoliteness. ¶目上に～なことをするな Don't *be rude* to your superiors. 彼は～なことを言う人だ What a *rude* thing he says! / What a *rude* fellow he is! 彼は～にもさよならも言わず出ていってしまった He *was rude* enough to go away without saying goodbye. こんな手紙をよこすとはなんと～な How *impertinent* he *is* to write such a letter to me!

―講 ¶～講にしよう Let's throw away all formality and enjoy ourselves.

フレー Hooray!

プレーガイド a theater ticket agency.

ブレーキ a brake. ¶～をかける apply (≒ put on) the *brakes*. ～を緩める take off the *brakes*. ～をかけて車を止める *brake* a car to a stop. ～がきかない The *brakes* won't work. 信号機が赤に変わるのを見て彼は強く～を踏んだ He stepped on the *brakes* strongly when he saw the traffic sign (≒ light) turn red.

空気― an air brake. 手動― a hand brake. 非常― an emergency brake.

プレート〔野球〕a pitcher's plate. ¶きょう～に立つのはだれかな Who is going to *be on the mound* (≒ *take the mound*) today?

プレーボーイ a playboy.

プレーボール Play ball!

フレーム a frame.

プレーヤー (レコードの) a record player; (選手) a player.

ブレーントラスト a brain trust. ¶企業の～をつとめる *brain-trust* a company.

ふれこみ【触れ込み】announcement. ¶彼は一徹者という～だった *It was given out* that he was of a stubborn character. 彼は電子工学の専門家という～だった He *announced himself as* an expert in electronics.

ブレザーコート a blazer.

プレス press. ¶アイロンでズボンを～する *press* trousers with an iron; *iron* trousers. ズボンを～してもらった I *had* my pants *pressed*.

プレスキャンペーン 〔a〕press campaign. ¶汚職問題で一大～を展開している They are waging *a* big *press campaign* against official corruption.

ブレスト (水泳) the breast stroke. ¶～で泳ぐ swim with *the breast stroke*.

プレスハム pressed ham.

プレゼント a present. ¶～する give *a present* (*to*). われわれは彼の50歳の誕生日に時計を～した We gave him a watch as *a present* on his fiftieth birthday. / We *presented* him *with* a watch on his fiftieth birthday.

プレハブじゅうたく【プレハブ住宅】a prefab; a prefabricated house.

ふれまわ・る【触れ回る】¶彼はその話をクラスじゅうに～った He *trumpeted* the story among all the classmates.

プレミアショー a premier show.

プレミアム a premium. ¶入場券は～つきで売られた The admission tickets were sold *at a premium*.

プレリュード〔音楽〕a prelude.

ふ・れる【振れる】shake. ¶カメラが～れた The camera *moved* (≒ *shook*). 磁石が3度西に～れた The magnet *has moved* west by three degrees.

ふ・れる【触れる】touch. ¶だれかが私の背中に手を～れたように感じた I felt someone *touch* me on the back. 手を～れるな (掲示) Hands Off! 彼らの乗ったジープが地雷に～れて爆発した Their jeep *hit* a mine and exploded. 彼女は無断で欠席したために彼の怒りに～れた Her absence without his permission *offended* him. 彼のその行動は法律に～れる That conduct of his *is contrary to* (≒ *against*) the law. / That conduct of his *infringes* the law. この問題にはもう～れないと彼は約束した He promised never to *refer to* this matter again.

ふ・れる【狂れる】¶彼は気が～れた He *has gone* (≒ *has run*) *mad*.

ふれんぞくせん【不連続線】〔気象〕a line of discontinuity. ¶～のいたずらでここのところ雨天が続いている On account of *a line of discontinuity* it has been raining these days.

フレンチドレッシング French dressing.

フレンチホルン a French horn.

ふろ【風呂】a bath. ¶～をたててくれましたか Did

ふ

you get the *bath* ready? 赤ん坊を〜に入れるのは母親の仕事だ It is the mother's job to *give a bath to* the baby. 〜が沸きました Your *bath* is ready. 私は1週に3回〜に入る I *take* (≒ *have*) *a bath* three times a week. 彼はたいへん〜好きだ He is very fond of *bath*. 〜に行こう Let's go to *a public bath*. 〜の具合はどうですか How do you like the *bath*? 〜のかげんを見てください See how hot the *bath* is.

—おけ a bathtub. —銭 a bath fee. —場 a bathroom. —屋 a bathhouse; a public bath.

プロ a professional.

—野球 professional baseball. —選手 a professional player. —野球選手 a professional baseball player.

ふろう【不老】 eternal youth. ¶ 〜不死の霊薬 the elixir of life.

ふろう【浮浪】 vagrancy.

—児 a juvenile vagrant; a street Arab.

—者 a vagrant; a tramp.

ふろうしょとく【不労所得】 unearned income.

ブローカー a broker. ¶ 〜の手数料 brokerage. 彼は株の〜だ He is *a* stock *broker*.

ブロークン broken. ¶ 彼の英語は〜だ His English *is broken*.

ブローチ a brooch. ¶ 〜をつける wear *a brooch*.

ブロード broadcloth.

ブロードウェイ Broadway.

ブローニー a brownie.

ブローニング a Browning〔pistol〕.

ふろく【付録】 a supplement. ¶ 雑誌の〜 *a supplement to* a magazine. きょうの新聞には〜がない Today's paper has no *supplement* to it.

日曜— a Sunday supplement.

プログラマー a programer; 英 programmer.

プログラム a program. ¶ 〜を作る make *a program*. そのコーラスは〜に載っていない The chorus is not on the *program*. 彼に〜の進行を頼んだ I asked him to run off the events. すべては〜どおりに進行した Everything went on as〔*had been*〕*scheduled before*.

ふろしき【風呂敷】 a cloth wrapper; a wrapping cloth. ¶ 〜に本を包む wrap up books in *a cloth wrapper*.

—包み a bundle. 大— ¶ 彼は大〜を広げる He tends to *talk big*.

プロセス a process.

プロダクション〘映画〙a film studio.

フロック〘玉突き〙a fluke. ¶ 彼は幸運にも〜で勝った He was lucky enough to win *by a fluke*.

ブロック **1**〘地区・建築用〙a block.

—建築 a bloc (≒ block) building. —経済 bloc economy.

2〘競技〙¶ 〜する *block* an opponent.

フロックコート a frock coat (アメリカには a prince Albert という言い方がある).

プロテクター a protector.

プロテスタント a Protestant.

プロデューサー a producer.

プロパガンダ propaganda.

プロパンガス propane gas.

プロフィ〔ー〕ル a profile. ¶ 彼ほどりっぱな〜を持っている人はそうざらにはいない Few have *a* finer *profile* than he.

プロペラ a propeller.

プロポーズ proposal. ¶ 彼女は彼の〜をすなおに受けた She gently accepted his *proposal of marriage*.

ブロマイド〘化学〙bromide. ¶ 〜写真 a still (ブロマイドは和製英語).

プロムナード a promenade.

—コンサート a promenade concert.

プロモーター a promoter.

プロレス ¶ 彼はテレビで〜を見るのが好きだ He is fond of watching *professional wrestling* on TV.

プロレタリア a proletarian;〔階級〕the proletariat.

—革命〔a〕proletarian revolution. —文学 proletarian literature.

プロレタリアート the proletariat.

プロローグ a prologue.

ブロンズ bronze. ¶ 〜の立像 a *bronze* statue.

フロント front; (ホテルなどの) reception desk.

—グラス a windshield; a windscreen.

ブロンド blond (女性の場合は blonde).

ふわ【不和】 discord. ¶ 彼がぐれたのは家庭の〜が原因だ The cause of his delinquent behavior can be traced to his family *trouble*. 両国は当分〜の関係が続くだろう The two countries will remain *on bad terms with* each other for a while. ふたりは昔は仲よしだったのに最近〜になった Once they were close friends to each other, but of late they *have become estranged* (≒ *have fallen away*) *from* each other.

ふわく【不惑】 ¶ 彼も〜の年を過ぎたにしてはばかなことをやったものだ Considering he *is past* (≒ *is on the wrong side of*; *turned*) *forty*, he has really acted quite foolishly!

ふわたり【不渡り・不渡】 nonpayment; dishonor. ¶ 彼の手形は一夜にして〜になった His check *was dishonored* overnight.

—手形 a dishonored check.

ふわふわ ¶ 白い雲が青い空に〜浮かんでいる Some white clouds are floating *lightly* in the blue sky. よく干したふとんは〜して気持ちがいい The bedclothes well dried (≒ aired) in the sun feel *soft* and comfortable. そんな〜した気持ちではなにをやってもだめだ Don't *be* so *unsteady* (≒ *wavering*), or you will fail in whatever you may do.

ふわらいどう【付和雷同】 ¶ 自主性がないと，とかく〜するものだ One is apt to *follow others blindly* without the spirit of independence.

ふわり ¶ 風に乗って風船が〜〜飛んでいる I see a

balloon *floating* [up high] in the wind.

ふん【分】 a minute. ¶ 3時15～です It is fifteen *minutes* past (≒ after) three. 30～待った I waited half an hour. / I waited thirty *minutes*. 5～もすれば雨もやむでしょう It will stop raining *in five minutes* or so. 外国語で5～間しゃべることは初学者にはたいへんだ It is no easy matter for a beginner to speak in a foreign language *for five minutes*. 10～後にまた電話します I will phone you again *after* (≒ *in*) *ten minutes* (≒ *ten minutes later*). 北緯20度20～ 20 degrees 20 *minutes* north latitude (20° 20′ N. Lat. と記す).

ふん【糞】 excrements; night soil; (動物の) dung. ¶ 鳥の～ the *droppings* of fowls.

—づまり ¶ この薬は～づまりによく効く This medicine works very well to *constipation*.

ふん Hum! / Humph! / Pshaw. ¶ 彼女は気位が高くいつでも人を鼻先で～とあしらう Being a proud (≒ haughty) girl, she is apt to turn up her nose at others.

ぶん【分】 1 〖部分〗 a part. ¶ 行列していた人たちの4～の1が切符を買えた One-fourth (≒ A quarter) of those who were standing in line could buy tickets.

ぼくの月給は彼の3～の2だ My salary is two-thirds of his.

5万～の1の地図 a map on the scale of 1 : 50,000 (one-fifty thousands と読む).

足りない～はあす買ってくる Whatever is lacking I will buy tomorrow.

ボーナスは必要なものだけ買って残った～は貯金しなさい With your bonus, buy only necessities and put the rest in the bank.

2 〖分け前・割り当て〗 a part; a share. ¶ これがきみの～だ This is for you. / This is your *share*.

彼の～は残しておきなさい Put his *share* aside.

きみの～も払っておいた I have paid your *share*. / I have paid for you.

今月～の小づかいをまだもらってない I have not got my allowance *for* this month yet.

きみの～までしかられた I got your *share* of the scolding.

3 〖分量〗 ¶ 食糧はまだ3日～残っている Rations *for* three days are still left.

5人～の昼食を注文してくれ Please order lunch *for* five.

医者は3日～の薬をくれた The doctor gave [enough] medicine *for* three days.

彼らは秋に一冬～の燃料を買う In autumn they buy enough fuel *for* the whole winter.

彼はふたり～の仕事ができる He can do the work *of* two men. / He can work *for* two.

このウイスキーはアルコール～が多い This whisky contains a high percentage of alcohol.

4 〖本分〗 duty. ¶ おのれの～を尽くす do *one's duty*.

各自が～を尽くせば仕事はうまくいく If everyone does his own *part*, the work will go well.

学生としての～を尽くせ Do your *bit* as a student.

5 〖身分・資力〗 standing; means. ¶ 各自～に応じて寄付金を出した Each of us contributed according to his *means*.

彼は～不相応の生活をしている He lives *above* (≒ *beyond*) *his means*.

～に過ぎたお祝いを頂き恐縮に存じます I most cordially thank you for your kind congratulations which I am afraid I don't deserve.

人はおのれの～を知ることがたいせつだ It is important [for one] to know one's own *place*.

6 〖状態〗 ¶ この～だと仕事は予定どおり終わりそうにない *Judging from the present state of things* (≒ *If things go on at this rate*), we will not be able to finish the work according to schedule.

この～ではあすは雪になりそうだ *Judging from* [the look of] the sky, we will have snow tomorrow.

ぶん【文】 writings ; a sentence ; (作文) a composition. ¶ ～は人なり *The style* is the man. ～は武にまさる *The pen* is mightier than the sword.

散— prose. 韻— verse. 単(複; 重; 混)— 〖文法〗 a simple (complex ; compound ; mixed) sentence.

ぶんあん【文案】 a draft. ¶ 今晩はあすの講演の～作りに忙しい He will be busy tonight making *a draft* of his speech for tomorrow. ～はほとんどできた The *draft* has been almost completed.

ぶんい【文意】 the meaning of a passage. ¶ くりかえして読めば～はおのずからはっきりする If you read it again and again, you will make out *what it means*.

ふんいき【雰囲気】 an atmosphere. ¶ あのホテルにはなんとなく家庭的な～がある There is something of *a* 'home' *atmosphere* in the hotel. 普通の人ではそのような殺風景な～には耐えられない An ordinary man can't stand such monotonous *atmosphere*. 彼の話で出席者の間に打ちとけた～がかもしだされた His speech produced (≒ created) *a* congenial *atmosphere* among those present.

ぶんいん【分院】 a branch hospital.

ふんえん【噴煙】 ¶ その火山の～は遠くからでも見える The *smoke shot up from the volcano* is visible even from far away.

ふんか【噴火】 an eruption. ¶ ～する erupt ; burst into eruption. 彼らは無謀にも～中の火山に登ろうとした They were reckless enough to plan a climbing of a volcano that *was in eruption*. 浅間登山者は常に～の備えが必要だ Those who want to climb Mt. Asama must be always prepared against *a* possible *eruption*.

—口 a crater. —山 an active volcano (複 volcanoes, -s).

ぶんか【文化】 [a] culture. ¶ その民族は優れた～を生み出した The race produced *a* superior *culture*. ～の高い国もあれば低い国もある Some nations are of high *culture*; some are

ふ

of low *culture.* 二つの～ two *cultures.* ―勲章 A Culture Medal. ―交流 cultural exchange. ―功労者 a person of cultural merits. ―国家 a cultured nation. ―祭 a school festival. ―財 cultural assets. ―史 cultural history. ―水準 ¶ 日本の～水準は高い Japan is at *a* high *cultural level.* ―施設 cultural facilities. ―生活 a civilized life. ―の日 Culture Day.

ぶんか【文科】 the literary course. ¶ 彼は～の学生だ He is a student in *the department of literature.*
―大学 a college of literature (≒ liberal arts).

ぶんか【分化】 specialization; division. ¶ 文化が進めば進むほど, 学問は～する The more advanced a culture, the more *specialized* learning *becomes.*

ぶんか【分科】 a department; a division. ¶ 文化が進めば進むほど学問の～は多くなる The more advanced a culture [is], the more *branches* of learning we have. 量子力学は物理学の一～である Quantum mechanics is *a branch* of physics.
―会 a sectional meeting; a subcommittee.

ふんがい【憤慨】 indignation. ¶ そのような侮辱を受ければ～するのはあたりまえだ It's natural that one should *get indignant at* such insult. 彼の無責任な放言にみんなはひどく～している They *are mad with anger* (≒ *rage*) *at* his irresponsible statement. つまらぬことにいちいち～していてはきりがない Don't *be in resentment at* each trifle; there is no end to it. / There's no use *getting angered at* trifles.

ぶんかい【分会】 a branch.

ぶんかい【分解】 ¶ この物質をこれ以上～することはできない This matter can't *be analyzed* (≒ *be dissolved; be resolved*) any further.
―作用 disintegration. ―写真 a photographic playback. ―掃除 ¶ この時計は～掃除が必要だ This watch has to *be taken all to pieces* for cleaning. 因数― factorization.

ぶんがく【文学】 literature; letters. ¶ 大学では～を専攻した I majored in *literature* in the university. 今学期は19世紀フランスの～作品を読む We are to read some *literary works* of 19th century France in the coming term. 彼には～の素養がある He has *literary culture.* 彼は若いころ～に志した He aspired to *literary honors* in youth. / He hoped to *be a man of letters* when young.
―運動 a literary movement. ―科 a literary course. ―界 the literary world; literary circles. ―概論 an introduction to literature. ―作品 a literary work. ―雑誌 a literary magazine. ―士 a Bachelor of Arts (B. A. または A. B. と略す). ―史 a history of literature. ―者 a man of letters; a literary man; a writer; an author. ―趣味 literary taste. ―青年 a literary youth. ―博士 Doctor of Literature (Lit. D. と略す). ―部 the Faculty (≒ Department) of Literature. ―部長 the Chairman (≒ Dean) of the Faculty of Literature. ―論 comments on literature. 国民― national literature. 純― polite literature. 大衆― popular literature.

ぶんかつ【分割】 division. ¶ ドイツは今大戦後東と西に～されている Germany *has been divided* into East and West [section] since the last war.
―払い ¶ ～払いは結局高くつく After all, *easy payment* (≒ *payment by* (≒ *in*) *installments*) will turn out expensive.

ぶんかん【文官】 a civil officer (≒ servant); (総称) the civil service. ¶ ～のほうが武官よりも偉いとは限らない It does not follow that *civil service* is more important than military service.

ふんき【奮起】 ¶ 全員の～がなければ挽回(ばんかい)は不可能だ Unless everyone *is stirred up* (≒ *exerts himself; does what he can*), there will be no restoration. ついに彼の～しなければならないときが来た At last the time has come when he must *brace himself up.*

ぶんき【分岐】 ¶ この道はまもなく本道から～する This road *diverges* from the main road before long. ここがこの道が五つに～している地点だ This is the place where the road *branches off* in five directions.
―点 〔鉄道〕 a junction. ¶ この事件は彼の人生の～点になった This incident proved to be *the turning-point* (≒ *the dividing line*) in his life.

ふんきゅう【紛糾】 complication. ¶ 国会はその議案をめぐって～している The Diet *is in confusion* (≒ *is in tangle*) about the bill. ～に巻き込まれぬよう注意しなさい Be careful not to be involved in that *complication.* きみのあの発言が事態を～させた That remark of yours *complicated* the matters.

ぶんきょう【文教】 education. ¶ ～地区 a *school* zone.

ぶんぎょう【分業】 assembly work. ¶ ～でやる divide the work.

ぶんきょうじょう【分教場】 a branch school.

ふんぎり【踏ん切り】 ¶ 彼は優柔不断だから, いざというときに～がつかない Being an irresolute man, he *can never make up his mind* in case of emergency. きみはどうしてそんなに～が悪いのか Why do you *hesitate* so much at doing anything?

ぶんぐ【文具】 ⇒ぶんぼうぐ

ぶんけ【分家】 a branch family. ¶ ～する set up a new family.

ぶんけい【文型】 sentence pattern.

ぶんげい【文芸】 literary arts. ¶ 彼の関心はいつでも～にある He is always interested in *literary arts.* 彼は～に造詣が深い He has a profound knowledge of *art and literature.*
―学部 the faculty (≒ department) of art

and literature. ―雑誌 a literary magazine. ―批評 literary criticism. ―批評家 a literary critic. ―復興 the Renaissance; the Revival of Learning.

ふんげき【憤激】 indignation. ¶ 彼らの冷たい仕打ちに対し彼の～は最高潮に達した He was just beside himself with *indignation over* their coldest treatment. そのような不当な非難を受けたのだから～するのも無理はない It is natural that he should *be* so *indignant at* such unreasonable criticism. 彼はその冷酷な人間に～している He *is indignant with* the cruel man.

ふんげき【奮激】 ¶ ～する be inspired (by); be stirred into action.

ぶんけん【文献】 literature; books to be consulted; books to be referred to. ¶ この問題に関する～はあまり多くはない There is not much *literature* about this matter. 参考― literature cited; (目録) a bibliography. ―学 philology.

ぶんけん【分権】 decentralization of authority (≒ power). ¶ 権力が過度に集中するのを防止するために～が必要となることもある *Decentralization* often becomes necessary to prevent overcentralization of authority. 地方― decentralization.

ぶんけんたい【分遣隊】 a detachment.

ぶんこ【文庫】 a library; (蔵書) a collection of books. ―本 a pocket edition. 金沢― Kanazawa Library.

ぶんご【文語】 written (≒ literary) language. ―体 ¶ その本は典型的な～体で書かれている The book is written in a typically *literary* (≒ *classical*) *style*.

ぶんこう【分光】 spectrum (複 spectra; -s). ―器 a spectroscope.

ぶんこう【分校】 a branch school.

ぶんごう【文豪】 a great man of letters; a great (≒ distinguished) writer. ¶ 夏目漱石は近代日本を代表する～の名に値する作家だ Soseki Natsume deserves to be called *the master writer* representing modern Japan.

ぶんこつ【分骨】 part of *a person's* remains (≒ ashes).

ふんこつさいしん【粉骨砕身】 ¶ ～するつもりです I will *do* my *very best*.

ふんさい【粉砕】 ¶ 敵を～するまでは断じて戦いをやめない We shall never stop fighting until we *smash* (≒ *annihilate*) our enemy.

ぶんさい【文才】 literary talent (≒ ability). ¶ 彼は子どものときから～があった He showed *literary talent* even when he was a boy.

ぶんざい【分際】 *one's* social position (≒ standing). ¶ 私の～ではぜいたく品だ It is a luxury to a poor man *in my position*. きみは学生の～で生意気だ None of your cheek (≒ impudence); you are a mere student.

ぶんさつ【分冊】 a separate volume. ¶ その小説は～で出版された The novel was published *in parts* (≒ *in separate volumes*).

ぶんさん【分散】 dispersion. ¶ 大都市の工場を地方へ～させることが急務である It is an urgent need to *decentralize* industries in cities into the country. 公害の～を防止することが先決問題だ It's a matter of prior decision to prevent the *dispersion* of public nuisance.

ふんし【憤死】 ¶ 彼は潔白を訴え続けながら獄中に～した He *died of indignation* (≒ *died of resentment*) in a prison, appealing all the time to the court for his innocence.

ぶんし【分子】〔物理・化学〕a molecule;〔数学〕a numerator. ¶ ～は原子からできている A *molecule* consists of atoms. 2/3という分数の～は2である The *numerator* of the fraction two-thirds is two. ―式 a molecular formula. ―量 molecular weight. 不平― ¶ どんな時代にも不平～はいるものだ In any age there are always some *malcontent elements*. 反動― ¶ 今度の政変は反動～の一掃をねらいにしたものだ The present political change aimed at wiping out the *reactionary elements*.

ぶんし【分詞】〔文法〕a participle. ―構文 a participial construction. 現在― a present participle. 過去― a past participle.

ぶんし【文士】 a literary man; a man of letters. ¶ 彼は今では押しも押されもしないりっぱな～となった He has come to be universally recognized as *a* fine *literary man*. 三文― ¶ 彼は依然として三文～だ He still remains to be *a hack writer*.

ふんしつ【紛失】 loss. ¶ どんな物でも～した際は届けることだ Whatever you *have lost*, you had better report. 展覧中の名画が～して大騒ぎになった The gallery was thrown into a great confusion with the *disappearance* of the famous picture on exhibition. ―届 a report of the loss of an article. ―物 a lost (≒ missing) article.

ぶんしつ【分室】 a branch office. ¶ 彼は～に勤めています He works in *a branch* (≒ *a detached*) *office*.

ふんしゃ【噴射】 jet. ¶ ～する jet. ―推進機関 a jet engine. ―推進飛行機 a jet (air)plane.

ぶんじゃく【文弱】 effeminacy. ¶ 彼は子どもの時から～だった He *was effeminate* from his childhood.

ぶんしゅう【文集】 a collection of works; an anthology. ¶ ～を作りますので奮ってご寄稿ください As we are going to make our *anthology*, everybody is cordially asked to write for it.

ふんしゅつ【噴出】 spouting. ¶ 新建材は火災時に有毒ガスを～する Plastic building material *shoots up* poisonous gas when it catches fire. この岩の下から冷たい水が勢いよく～する Cold water *spouts* (≒ *gushes out*) from under this rock.

ふんしょ【焚書】 ¶ 王は～で有名であった The

king was infamous for *burning of books*.

ぶんしょ【文書】(書類) a document;(通信) correspondence;(記録) a record. ¶ 回答は～でお願いします You are requested to answer in *written form*. ～にしないと正式な書類にはならない We can make it a formal document only by *committing* it *to writing*.

—課 the section of archives. —偽造 ¶ 彼は～偽造で捕まった He was arrested for *forgery of documents*. 公— official documents.

ふんじょう【粉状】 ¶ ～の雪 *powdery* snow.

ぶんしょう【文章】 a sentence; a composition. ¶ ～は苦手だ I am not good at *writing* (≒ *composition*). この～の意味はあいまいだ The meaning of this *sentence* is ambiguous. 彼は話はへただが～がじょうずだ Though a poor speaker, he is *a good writer*. ～のうまさでは彼の右に出る者はいない He is second to none as *an accomplished writer*. / He is second to none in *writing*. / Nobody is superior to him as *a stylist*.

—家 a good (≒ fine) writer; a stylist.

ぶんしょう【文相】 the Minister of Education; the Education Minister.

ぶんしょう【分掌】 division of duties.

ぶんじょう【分乗】 ¶ 5 台のバスに～して出発した We started in five buses.

ぶんじょう【分譲】 ¶ 土地を～する *sell* land *in lots*.

—地 land for sale in lots.

ふんしょく【粉食】 powdered food.

ふんしょく【粉飾】 embellishment. ¶ その話は～もはなはだしい There is too much *embellishment* in that story.

—決算 fraudulent (≒ hole-and-corner; rigged) accounts.

ふんしん【分針】 the minute (≒ long) hand.

ぶんしん【分身】 the other self. ¶ この小説はいわば作者の～だ This novel is so to speak *the other self* (≒ *persona*) of the writer.

ぶんじん【文人】 a literary man; a man of letters.

—画 a painting in literary artist's style.

ふんすい【噴水】 a fountain. ¶ ～が吹き上げているのが見える The *fountain* can be seen playing.

ぶんすいれい【分水嶺】 a divide; 困 a watershed. ¶ この山脈は～の役割りをしている This mountain range plays the part of a *divide* (≒ *watershed*).

ぶんすう【分数】〔数学〕 a fraction.

—式 a fractional expression. —方程式 a fractional equation.

ふん·する【扮する】 ¶ 彼が今度の上演ではロミオに～することになっている He is supposed to *play* (≒ *act*) *the part* (≒ *role*) of Romeo in the forthcoming production.

ぶんせき【分析】 analysis;(文学作品の) explication. ¶ 論文の内容を～する *analyze* the contents of the thesis. 元素に～する *analyze* something into elements.

—学 analytics. —者 an analyst. —表 an analysis table. 精神— psychoanalysis. 定量(定性)— quantitative (qualitative) analysis.

ぶんせき【文責】 ¶ ～記者にあり The editor is responsible for the wording of this article.

ぶんせつ【文節】 a paragraph. ¶ 文章を～に切る *paragraph* a sentence.

ふんせん【奮戦】 a hard fighting; a desperate fighting. ¶ 敵と～する *have a severe fight with* the enemy. 兵士たちは最後まで～して死んだ The soldiers *fought desperately* to the death.

ふんぜん【憤然】 in anger (≒ a fury). ¶ 彼は～として席を立った He went away *in indignation* (≒ *in a rage*). 彼は彼らの卑劣な行為に～としていた He *was indignant at* their mean actions.

ふんぜん【奮然】 courageously; resolutely. ¶ 少数ながら～として敵に立ち向かった Although greatly outnumbered, we *courageously* (≒ *boldly*) faced the enemy.

ぶんせん【文選】 type picking. ¶ ～する pick types.

—工 a type picker.

ふんそう【紛争】 a trouble; a strife; a dispute. ¶ ～を解決する settle *a dispute*. 両者間の～を調停する役を買って出た I offered to take the trouble of adjusting the *dispute* between the two parties. 両国間に～を起こす stir up *trouble* between the two countries. 外国と～を起こさないようにする keep out of *trouble* with foreign countries.

学園— a campus riot; a campus dispute. 国際— an international dispute.

ふんそう【扮装】 disguise; make-up. ¶ 女の姿に～する *disguise oneself* as a woman.

ぶんそうおう【分相応】 ¶ ～に暮らす live *according to one's means*. ～の寄付をする contribute *according to one's means*.

ふんぞりかえ·る【踏ん反り返る】(文字どおり) throw *one's* head back with legs outstretched;(威張る) lord it over; assume a lordly attitude.

ぶんたい【文体】 a style. ¶ 簡潔な～で書かれた小説 a novel written in *a* concise (≒ crisp) *style*. 彼はいつも彼一流の～でものを書く He always writes in *a style* of his own.

—論 stylistics.

ぶんたい【分隊】(陸軍) a squad;(海軍) a division.

—長 a squad commander. 射撃— a firing squad. 特別—(白バイなどの) a flying squad.

ふんだく·る ¶ 人相の悪い男が女の手からハンドバッグを～った An evil-looking man *snatched* the handbag *from* (≒ *out of*) the hand of the girl. 彼らは私の金をみんな～ってしまった They *have done me out of* all my money.

ふんだりけったり【踏んだり蹴ったり】 ¶ ～の目に会わせる heap *insults* upon *a person*. ～の目に会った I *had a very hard time of it*. これじゃまるで～だ This is very much like *add-*

ふ

ing insult to injury.

ふんたん【粉炭】powdered coal.

ぶんたん【分担】allotment ; assignment. ¶ その仕事を4人で～してやることにした We decided to *divide* the work *among* us four. 同じ割合で費用を～しよう Let's *bear* an equal *share* of the expenses. 責任を～する *bear*(≒ *have*; *take*) *one's share in* responsibility.

―金 a share of the expenses ; allotted charges.

ぶんだん【分断】⇒すんだん

ぶんだん【文壇】the literary world (≒ circles). ¶ ～に出る start a literary career. 彼は30代なかばにして～に名を成した He *won literary fame* (≒ *became a famous writer*) in his mid-thirties. ～の寵児 a popular writer.

ふんだんに in plenty ; in abundance ; fully ; generously.

¶ 金を～使う use *a lot of* money.

ぶんちょう【文鳥】〘鳥類〙a paddybird.

ぶんちん【文鎮】a 〔paper〕 weight. ¶ 書類がばらばらにならないように～で押さえる use *a weight* to keep the loose papers from being displaced.

ぶんつう【文通】correspondence. ¶ 彼女はボーイフレンドと～を始めた She has begun to *exchange letters* with a boy friend. 彼とはまだ～を続けている I *have been in correspondence* (≒ *have been keeping up a correspondence*) *with* him.

ふんづまり【糞詰まり】⇒ふん

ふんど【憤怒】anger ; wrath ; rage ; fury.

¶ ～の形相ものすごく like a fury.

ぷんと ¶ 私がそう言うと彼女は～そっぽを向いた When I said so, she looked the other way *angrily*. 彼の息は～酒臭い His breath smells of *sake strongly*.

ふんとう【奮闘】a struggle. ¶ 最後まで自由のために～する決心だ We are resolved to *fight* for liberty to the last. ～したまえ You might as well *exert yourself to the utmost*. / You must *try what you can*.

ふんどう【分銅】a weight.

―ばかり a balance.

ぶんとう【文頭】¶ 句を～に置く put a phrase *at the beginning of the sentence*.

ぶんどき【分度器】a graduator ; a protractor.

ふんどし【褌】a loincloth. ¶ ～を引き締めてがんばらないとまた失敗する You will fail again unless you *brace yourself up*. 他人の～ですもうを取るな Don't benefit yourself (≒ get a free ride) *at the expense of another* !

ぶんど・る【分捕る】¶ 敵から武器弾薬を～る *capture* arms and ammunition from the enemy.

ぶんどりひん【分捕品】spoils. ¶ 兵士たちは～を分配した The soldiers divided the *spoils* among themselves.

ふんにゅう【粉乳】powdered (≒ dry) milk.

ふんにょう【糞尿】excreta. ¶ ～をくみ取る scoop *excreta*.

ぶんのう【分納】¶ 授業料は2回に～することになっている We are supposed to *pay* school fees *in two installments*.

ぶんぱ【分派】a branch ; (宗教上などの)a sect.

¶ ～活動を始める start *factional* activities.

ぶんぱい【分配】division ; distribution. ¶ 彼は財産を平等に子どもたちに～した He *divided* his property equally among the children. 利益は株主に～される Profits *are divided* among the shareholders. 利益の～を受ける資格がある We are entitled to *have a share* in the profits. / We are entitled to *share* in the profits.

ふんぱつ【奮発】exertion. ¶ 客はボーイにチップを～した The customer tipped the waiter *generously*. もう1,000円～しよう *I'm willing to pay* another thousand yen. ～してダイヤの指輪を買った I *treated myself to* a diamond ring.

ふんば・る【踏ん張る】¶ もう一息～ってもらいたい I want you to *make* another *effort*. ～り通す hold out to the last ; hold fast to the end. ～りがきかない, ぼくも年だ I *give in easily*. I am already old.

ふんぱんもの【噴飯物】¶ きみの要求はまったく～だ Your claim *is* quite *absurd* (≒ *ridiculous* ; *ludicrous*). …とは～だ It is *absurd* (≒ *ridiculous*) that….

ぶんぴ【分泌】⇒ぶんぴつ

ぶんぴつ【分泌】secretion. ¶ ～する secrete.

―器官 a secretory 〔organ〕. ―作用 secretion. ―腺 a secretory ; a secretor. ―物 a secretion. ―薬 a secretory drug. 内― internal secretion.

ぶんぴつ【文筆】literary pursuits. ¶ ～によって立つ His profession is *writing*.

―家 a writer ; a journalist. ―業 journalism ; literary profession.

ふんびょう【分秒】¶ これは～を争う問題だ It's urgent. / It's a matter of great urgency.

ぶんぶ【文武】civil and military arts ; the pen and 〔the〕 sword. ¶ ～両道の達人 a man endowed with 〔*a matter of*〕 *civil and military arts*. ～兼備の名将と言えばアレキサンダー大王だ Talking of the greatest commander equally 〔*as*〕 *distinguished as a soldier and a scholar*, Alexander the Great is the very man.

ぶんぷ【分布】distribution. ¶ この植物はわが国には広く～している This plant *is* widely *distributed* throughout our country.

―図 a distributional map.

ぶんぶつ【文物】culture. ¶ 日本の～ *things* Japanese ; the Japanese *culture*. 明治時代に日本人は西洋の～を採り入れた In the Meiji era the Japanese people adopted Occidental *civilization* (≒ *things* Western).

ふんぷん【紛紛】¶ この点に関しては諸説～としている *Opinion is divided* on this point. / They *are divided in opinion* as to this point.

ふ

ぶんぶん ¶ 蚊が〜いう Mosquitoes *buzz*. ミツバチが花から花へ〜飛びまわっている Bees *are humming* around from flower to flower.

ぷんぷん 1〖怒って〗¶ 〜怒って彼は部屋を出た He left the room *in an angry mood*. 彼は〜怒ってそっぽを向いた He *angrily* looked the other way.
2〖においが〗¶ 彼の息はいつも酒のにおいが〜している His breath always *smells* of *strong* liquor. この肉は変なにおいが〜する This meat *smells very bad*. / This meat *stinks*. 彼女の服はじゃこうのにおいが〜していた Her dress *was scented with strong* musk.

ふんべつ【分別】discretion ; prudence. ¶ 〜くさい顔をした男 a *prudent-looking* man. 〜ざかりの男 a man of *good sense* (≒ *great discretion*). 〜ざかりの年齢 age (≒ years) of *discretion*. それくらいの〜はあってほしいものだ You should *know better than that*.

ぶんべん【分娩】delivery ; parturition. ¶ 彼女は女の子を〜した She *gave birth to* a girl. / She *was delivered of* a girl.
—室 a delivery room. 無痛— painless delivery.

ふんぼ【墳墓】a grave. ¶ 彼らの〜の地には青々と草がおい茂っていた The grass was green upon their *graves*.

ぶんぼ【分母】a denominator. ¶ 〜を払う cancel *a denominator*.

ぶんぽう【文法】grammar. ¶ 〜上の誤りをおかさないで英語を書くことはなかなか容易なことではない It is no easy task to write English without making *grammatical* mistakes.
—学者 a grammarian. —書 a grammar.

ぶんぼうぐ【文房具】stationery ; writing materials.
—屋 (店) a stationer's ; (人) a stationer.

ふんまつ【粉末】powder ; dust. ¶ 大理石を砕いて〜にする grind marble to *powder*.
—剤 powdered medicine.

ぶんまつ【文末】¶ 〜の言い回しに注意せよ Take care of the expression of *the end of sentence* (≒ *the closing sentence*).

ふんまん【憤懣・忿懣】anger ; indignation ; resentment. ¶ 彼はそのことについてぼくに〜を漏らした He strongly *complained to* me *of* (≒ *about*) that matter. ぼくは〜やるかたなかった I was burning with *indignation*.

ぶんみゃく【文脈】the context. ¶ この部分の意味を〜から読み取ることはそう困難ではあるまい I don't think it is very difficult to understand this passage from the *context*.

ふんむき【噴霧器】a spray. ¶ 植物に〜で駆虫剤をかける *spray* plants with an insecticide ; *spray* an insecticide over plants.

ぶんめい【文名】literary fame (≒ renown). ¶ 彼は20代なかばにして〜を上げた He *won literary fame* (≒ *became a famous writer*) in his mid-twenties. / He *was renowned as a writer* (≒ *was a renowned writer*) by his mid-twenties.

ぶんめい【文明】civilization. ¶ 〜が進むにつれてわれわれの生活が便利になる As *civilization* advances our life becomes convenient.
—国 a civilized country. —社会 civilized society. 機械 (物質)— mechanical (material) civilization.

ぶんめん【文面】the contents of a letter. ¶ 彼からきた手紙の〜からするとわれわれの提案に不賛成のようだ According to his *letter*, he seems to be against our proposal. 手紙の〜にはこう書いてある The *letter* reads as follows.

ぶんや【分野】a sphere ; a field ; a realm ; a department. ¶ 産業界の各〜 various *fields* of industry. 院内の新しい勢力〜 *a* new *line-up* of the parties in the House of the Diet. 彼の研究は科学の新しい一〜を開いた His research opened a new *field* (≒ *sphere*) of science. 私の得意の〜は詩だ My *speciality* is poetry.

ぶんよ【分与】distribution. ¶ 彼は息子たちに財産を〜した He *distributed* the property among his sons.

ぶんり【分離】separation. ¶ 政治と宗教を〜する *separate* politics from religion.
—器 a separator. 遠心—機 a centrifugal separator.

ぶんり【文理】literature and science.
—学部 the faculty of liberal arts (≒ literature) and sciences.

ぶんりつ【分立】〔a〕separation ; independence. ¶ 立法・行政・司法の〜 the *independence* of the legislative, executive, and judicial branches. この憲法の著しい特徴は三権の〜である A distinctive feature of the constitution is the *separation* of the three powers. 都議会は5党〜の状態にある The metropolitan assembly *is divided into* the five parties.

ぶんりょう【分量】a quantity ; an amount. ¶ 多い(少ない)〜 a large (small) *quantity*. かなりの〜の… an amount of .... 〜が減る(増す) diminish (gain) in *quantity*. 牛乳の〜を2倍にする double the *quantity* of milk. ある一定の〜のサケを取る catch *a* fixed *quantity* of salmon. 薬の〜を誤る give *a* wrong *dose* of medicine. このクッキーは砂糖の〜がすこし多すぎた There is a little too much sugar in these cookies. 私は毎晩〜を決めて酒を飲む I drink in fixed *quantities* every evening.

ぶんるい【分類】classification. ¶ これらの本は題目によって〜されている These books *are classified* by subjects. 年齢(国籍)によって〜する *classify* by age (nationality).
—表 a classified table (≒ list). —法 classification system. —目録 a classified catalog.

ふんれい【奮励】endeavor ; effort. ¶ 〜努力してこの危機を乗り切ってもらいたい I want all of you to *do your best* to tide over the present crisis. 〜努力してやりとげよ *Make every effort* to carry it out.

ぶんれい【文例】an example. ¶ 〜をあげる give *an example* ; show *a model sentence*.

ふ

ぶんれつ【分裂】division; (宗教などの) schism; split; (核などの) fission. ¶ 彼らは幾派にも〜している They *are divided* into many sects. 社会党はその問題で2派に〜した The Socialist Party *split* over the problem into two groups.
—生殖〖生物〗schizogenesis. 核—〖物理〗nuclear fission; 〖生物〗nuclear division. 精神—症〖医学〗schizophrenia.

ぶんれつ【分列】a split; a division.
—行進 ¶ 〜行進を行なう march past; have a march past. —飛行 fly past.

ふんわり softly. ¶ 飛行機は〜と着陸した The plane landed *softly*.

へ

へ【屁】wind. ¶ 〜をする break *wind*. 彼はすこしぐらい誤りをおかすことは〜とも思わない He *makes nothing of* making a few mistakes.

-へ to; for; in; into; at; on; toward.

ヘアクリーム hair cream.

ヘアスタイル hairstyle. ¶ 最近の若者の〜はどうも気にいらない I don't like *the way young men today do their hair*.

ヘアスプレー a hair spray.

ヘアトニック hair tonic.

ヘアピン a hairpin.

ヘアブラシ a hairbrush.

ベアリング bearing.
ボール— ball bearing.

ヘアローション hair lotion.

へい【兵】(兵卒) a soldier; a private; an enlistee; (総称) enlisted men. ¶ 〜となる become *a soldier*. 〜を募る raise *an army*; recruit (≒ draft) *soldiers*. ラオスから〜を引き揚げた They withdrew *troops* from Laos. 〜は迅速をとおとぶ Celerity is the soul of *warfare*. 敗軍の将〜を語らず A defeated general should not talk of war.
二等— a private second class (p.s.c.). 一等— a private first class (p.f.c.).

へい【弊】an abuse; an evil. ¶ 彼は長年の〜を正すよう努めた He attempted to remove (≒ counteract) the *evil* of long standing. 青年はややもするとこの〜に落ち入りやすい Young men are apt to fall into this *evil*.

へい【屛・塀】(石がき; 土塀) a wall; (かき) a fence. ¶ 家の周囲に〜を巡らした We surrounded our house with *a wall*. 〜を巡らした家 a *fenced-in* house. 高い〜のある庭 a *high-walled* garden. 〜を越える climb over *a wall*. 〜越しに見る look over *a wall*.

へい【丙】(程度で) a third class; C; (第三の人) a third.

へいあん【平安】peace; quiet. ¶ 〜な毎日 a *quiet* (≒ *peaceful*; *calm*) everyday life. 彼は〜に暮らしている He lives *in peace*.

へいい【平易】simplicity. ¶ 彼は難しい事柄を〜に説明した He explained the difficult matter *in easy language*. 〜な文体 a *plain* (≒ *simple*) style.

へいいん【兵員】strength of an army; army personnel.
—名簿 a muster roll; an army list. —削減 a troop cut.

へいいん【閉院】the closing of the Diet.

へいえい【兵営】barracks (通常複数).

べいえい【米英】England and America.

へいえき【兵役】military service. ¶ 彼は〜を済ました He *has served his time* in the army. 私は来年は〜に服する I shall serve in *the army* next year. / I shall be drafted for *military service* next year. 彼は〜を免除された He was exempted from *military service*. あの学校へ入ると〜猶予になる The school temporarily exempts you from *military service*. 〜は国民の義務であった *Military service* was one of the duties of people.
—義務 compulsory military service. —免除 exemption from military service. —年限 the term of military service.

へいおん【平穏】calmness; quietness. ¶ 〜無事な生活 a *peaceful* (≒ *quiet*) life; an *uneventful* life. その日は〜無事に過ぎた The day passed *uneventfully*. 学生運動も〜になった The student power has become *quiet*. 程なく〜に復した It was not long before *peace* was restored. 首謀者たちが逮捕されたので〜にもどった The ringleaders having been caught, *tranquillity* was restored.

へいか【平価】par; parity. ¶ それは〜以上 (以下) である It is above (below) *par*. それは〜で買える It is purchasable *at par*. 〜の切り下げをする devalue (≒ lower) *the legal exchange value*.
—切り下げ devaluation. 法定— mint par; par of exchange.

へいか【陛下】His (Her) Majesty (H.M.); Your Majesty. ¶ 天皇〜 His Majesty the Emperor; H.M. the Emperor. 皇后〜 Her Majesty the Empress; H.M. the Empress. 両〜 Their Majesties. 女王〜 Her Royal Highness the Queen.

べいか【米価】the price of rice. ¶ ～を据え置くことになった They have decided to leave *the price of rice* as it is.
—審議会 a 〔deliberative〕 council of rice 「price.
へいかい【閉会】the closing ; a close. ¶ 彼が～の辞を述べた He gave the *closing* address. 国会は～中である The Diet *is out of session.* 会議は12時15分～する The conference will *adjourn* (≒ *come to a close*) at 12 : 15. 会議はイギリス国歌をうたって～した The meeting *ended* (≒ *was closed*) with the singing of "God Save the Queen."
へいがい【弊害】an evil ; an ill effect. ¶ 酒の～ the *ill effects* of liquor. 喫煙は～を伴う Smoking is attended by many *evils.* 体重の超過は健康に～を及ぼす Overweight exerts *an evil influence* upon the health. 共和政治にも～はある A republic too is subject to *abuses.*
へいかん【閉館】¶ 博物館は日曜は～する The museum *closes* on Sundays.
へいき【平気】coolness ; indifference ; nonchalance. ¶ 彼は～な顔をしてみせた He pretended to *be calm* (≒ *be unmoved*).
彼は～な顔をして戻ってきた He came back *as if nothing had happened.*
彼らがなんと言おうと～だ I *don't care* whatever they may say.
彼女は～でうそをつく She tells lies *without shame.*
雨なんか～だ I *don't mind* the rain.
彼は徹夜しても～だ He *makes nothing of* sitting up all night.
彼はどんなことでも～でやる He *dares* anything.
彼は失敗しても～だ He *takes* his failure *quite easy.*
失敗なんか～だ I *think nothing of* my fail- 「ure.
その報に接しても彼は～だった He heard it *unmoved.*
彼は～で判決を受けた He took the verdict 「*coolly.*
彼は驚いたが, ～を装っていた He was surprised, but he *kept his countenance.*
彼はどんな危険にあっても～だ He *is* perfectly *calm and serene* in the presence of any danger.
若者は暴飲暴食しても～だ Young men commit all sorts of excesses *with impunity.*
彼はどんな恥をかいても～だ *Nothing can abash* him.
へいき【兵器】weapons of war ; arms ; (総合) weaponry.
—庫 an armory ; an arsenal.
へいきん【平均】**1** 〖ならし〗 an average. ¶ この湖の深さは～20メートルだ The *average* depth of this lake is 20 meters.
4と8と9の～はいくつか What is the *average* of 4, 8 and 9?
この赤ん坊の体重は～よりはるか上だ This baby's weight is far above the *average.*
あなたは1日～どのくらい歩きますか How much *on an average* do you walk a day?
彼の能力は～以上だ His ability is more than the *average.*
～60点に及ばない者は不合格だ A student whose *average* mark is below 60 fails.
私の収入は～より悪い My income is lower than the *average.*
このチームの選手の～身長は190センチだ The *average* stature of the players of this team is 190 centimeters.
～寿命は延びつつある The *average* life span is getting longer.
このグループの～年齢は30歳だ The *average* age of the members of this group is 30.
2 〖釣り合い〗 balance. ¶ 彼女は～のとれた体をしている She *is* well *balanced.*
～台の上で～をとる *balance* on *a balance* beam.
曲芸師が～を失った The acrobat lost his *balance.*
べいぐん【米軍】the United States Armed Forces ; the U.S. Armed Forces.
へいげい【睥睨】¶ ～する glare at ; look down upon. 天下を～する *reign over* the world as a conqueror.
へいげん【平原】a plain ; 米 a prairie.
べいご【米語】American English ; an Americanism.
へいこう【平行】¶ その道は川と～している The street *runs parallel* to the river. この線はあの線と～だ This line *is parallel* to that.
—四辺形〖数学〗 a parallelogram. —線〖数学〗 parallel lines. —棒 parallel bars.
へいこう【並行】¶ 消費が生産と～する Consumption *keeps pace with* production. 世の中の動きと～して歩むつもりだ I'll go *abreast of* the times. ふたりは～して走っていた The two were running *side by side.*
へいこう【平衡】equilibrium ; balance. ¶ 彼は身体の～を保っている（失ってしまった） He is keeping (has lost) his *balance.* 軽業師は張り綱の上で～を保っていた The acrobat maintained *equilibrium* on a tightrope. 同じ重さの物が両側にあるとはかりは～状態になっている Scales *are in equilibrium* when equal weights are on each side.
—感覚 the sense of equilibrium. —交付金 an equalization grant 〔to a local government〕. —水準器 a balance level. —力 counterbalance. —負荷 a balanced load. —輪（時計の） a balance wheel.
へいこう【閉口】¶ 彼の無作法なのには～した His bad manners *was embarrassing* (≒ *embarrassed* me). 彼がいると～する I *feel uneasy* (≒ *feel abashed*) in his presence. 彼女には～だ She *is too much for* me. この暑さには～している I *can't stand* the heat. この仕事に～している I *am annoyed with* this work. あの子には～している The boy *is a nuisance.* 私は～している I *am stuck* (≒ *am in a fix ; am stumped*).
へいこう【閉校】¶ この学校は～することになる This school is expected to *be closed.*
へいごう【併合】incorporation ; annexation ;

merger. ¶ その会社は私の会社に〜されるだろう The firm will *be amalgamated into* (≒ *be absorbed in*; *be merged into*) ours. ハワイは1898年合衆国に〜された The Hawaiian Islands *were annexed* to the United States in 1898.

べいこく【米国】 the United States of America; the U.S.A.; the U.S.; America. **—**旗 the American flag; the Stars and Stripes. **—**政府 the U.S. Government (≒ Administration). **—**ドル U.S. dollar. **—**民 the Americans.

べいこく【米穀】 rice; (穀類) grain; cereals. **—**商 a rice dealer. **—**通帳 a rice-ration book. **—**問屋 a wholesale grain merchant.

へいさ【閉鎖】 closing. ¶ その銀行は〜した The Bank *closed its doors*. その銀行は支店を〜した The Bank *closed* its branch. 入り口を〜する *stop* (≒ *obstruct*) the entrances. 経営者は工場を〜した (ストライキのため) The manager of the factory *locked out* the workers.

べいさく【米作】 rice crop; rice harvest.

へいさつ【併殺】〔野球〕 a double play. ¶ 〜する make two put-outs.

へいざん【閉山】 ¶ 炭鉱を〜する *shut down* a mine.

べいさんち【米産地】 a rice-producing district.

へいし【兵士】 a soldier; a private.

へいじ【平時】 ordinary times; peacetime. ¶ 〜は in *time of peace*; in *peacetime*; ordinarily.

へいじつ【平日】 a weekday. ¶ 〜は on *weekdays*; on *ordinary days*; usually. 〜どおり授業があった We had school *as usual*. 〜の休み a weekday off. 事務〜どおり Bussiness *as usual*.

へいしゃ【兵舎】 barracks.

べいじゅ【米寿】 ¶ 彼の〜を祝った We had his *eighty-eighth birthday* celebration.

へいしゅう【弊習】 an evil practice; abuses. ¶ 〜を打破する do away with *an evil practice*.

へいしょう【併称】 ¶ 〜される be ranked with.

へいじょう【平常】 usually; ordinarily. ¶ 1月の〜の天候 the *usual* January weather. あすは〜どおり出勤することになっている We are to come to our office tomorrow *as usual*. 鉄道が〜に復した The railroad service *was restored to normal*. その船は〜300名を収容する *In the ordinary way* the ship has accommodation for 300 passengers. 〜のやり方 business *as usual*.

へいじょう【閉場】 closing. ¶ 〜する close.

べいしょく【米食】 rice diet. **—**国民 a rice-eating (≒ rice-diet) nation.

へいじょぶん【平叙文】 a declarative sentence.

へいしんていとう【平身低頭】 ¶ 彼が私に〜して謝った He begged my pardon *on his knees*.

へいせい【平静】 calmness; composure; serenity of mind. ¶ 彼女は〜を装った She pretended to *be calm* (≒ *be serene*; *be cool*). 彼はついに〜を失った At last he *lost his head* (≒ *was perturbed*; *got agitated*). 再び私は〜に戻った I *recovered composure*. 20年間わが国は〜であった For twenty years our country *enjoyed peace*.

へいぜい【平生】 usually; ordinarily. ¶ 〜より早く帰った I came home earlier than *usual*. 授業は〜どおりあった We had school *as usual*. もし〜もっと勉強すれば, 徹夜する必要なんかないだろうに If you worked harder *at other times*, it would be unnecessary to sit up all night.

へいせき【兵籍】 a military register. ¶ 彼は〜に入った He *enlisted* [*himself*] *in the army*. / He *was taken by draft for military service*.

へいぜん【平然】 ¶ 彼女は〜としていた She *remained calm*. / She *kept her composure*. 彼の〜とした態度は心憎いばかりだ His *calm attitude* is simply unnerving. 彼はその判決を〜として受けた He took the verdict *lightly* (≒ *calmly*; *composedly*).

へいそ【平素】 ¶ 〜の行ない *one's routine* (≒ *daily*) conduct. 〜のごぶさたをお許しください Please pardon me for my long silence. 彼は〜よく働く男だ He is *usually* a hard worker.

へいそく【閉塞】 blockade; stoppage. ¶ 港口を〜する *block up* (≒ *blockade*; *bottle up*) the harbor. **—**船 a blockader. 腸**—** intestinal obstruction.

へいたい【兵隊】 a soldier; (海軍) a sailor. **—**ごっこ ¶ 〜ごっこをする play at soldiers. **—**あがり ¶ あの人は〜あがりだ He is an *ex-soldier*. / He *has served in the army*.

へいたん【平坦】 ¶ 以前はこの道は〜でなかった Formerly this road *was* not *smooth*. オランダの地勢はおおむね〜だ Holland *is* generally *flat*.

へいたん【兵站】 communications; supply trains; logistics (単数扱い). **—**基地 a base for supplies; a supply base. **—**学 logistics.

へいだん【兵団】 an army corps.

へいち【平地】 level ground. ¶ 〜では積雪15センチだった The snowfall measured 15 centimeters *on the level* (≒ *on the level ground*; *on the flat*). 〜に波乱を起こす create an unnecessitated disturbance; create a disturbance unnecessarily; create a disturbance where there is no cause.

へいてい【平定】 suppression. ¶ 天下を〜する *subjugate* the whole county; *restore peace* in the country; *reduce* the country *to subjection*. 彼は内乱を〜した He *suppressed* civil war.

へいてい【閉廷】 the rising of the court. ¶ 5分ほどで〜になった The court *rose* (≒ *adjourned*) in five minutes or so. 判事は水曜日まで〜を宣した The judge *adjourned court* until Wednesday.

へいてん【閉店】 ¶ まもなく〜だ Presently the

へ

shop will *close*. / Shortly the shop will *be closed* (≒ *be shut up*). その店は数日中に～するだろう(廃業) The shop will *close its doors* (≒ *put up its shutters*) within a few days. 私は不況のため店は～せざるをえなかった(廃業) My shop could not help *discontinuing* business because of the depression. ～(店の前などにかける掲示) Closed.

—時間 the closing hour.

へいどん【併呑】 annexation. ¶小国を～する *swallow up* a smaller country.

へいねつ【平熱】 a normal temperature. ¶薬のおかげで～になった The medicine made the temperature fall to normal.

へいねん【平年】 a normal year ; a common year. ～以上 above the average.

—作 a normal (≒ an average) crop. **—並** ¶昨年度のわが国の収穫は～並であった The crop of our country last year was *an average crop*.

へいはつ【併発】 concurrence ; complication. ¶風邪をひいて肺炎を～した I caught a cold from which pneumonia *developed*. 余病が～した Complications have set in.

へいばん【平板】 ¶～な話 a *monotonous* story. ～な人 a *dull* person.

へいふく【平伏】 ¶彼は～した He *prostrated himself before* me. / He *fell down on his knees*.

へいふく【平服】 an ordinary (≒ everyday) dress ; plain clothes. ¶～の巡査が彼らのあとをつけた A constable *in plain clothes* (≒ *in everyday dress*) followed them. その士官は～を着ていた The officer *was in civilian dress*.

へいへい ¶彼は上司にいつも～している He *courts* (≒ *is* always *servile to*) his superiors. / He always *fawns upon* (≒ *flatters*) his superiors.

べいへい【米兵】 an American soldier.

ぺいぺい an inferior ; a novice.

へいへいぼんぼん【平平凡凡】 common ; commonplace ; ordinary ; dull ; stereotyped.

へいほう【平方】 a square. ¶2～メートル two *square* meters. 2メートル～ a two-meter *square*. 4の～は16である The *square* of 4 is 16. 100を～に開く extract the *square root* of 100.

—根 a square root. **—数** a square number.

へいほう【兵法】 (戦略) strategy ; (戦術) tactics.

—家 a tactician ; a strategist.

へいぼん【平凡】 commonplaceness. ¶～な出来事 a *commonplace* event. ～な人たち *ordinary* (≒ *average*) people. ～な暮らし a *humdrum* (≒ *uneventful*) life. ～な日々 *uneventful* days. ～な才 *mediocre* talents. 彼の言うことはみな～な説だ All he says are *platitudes*.

へいまく【閉幕】 the curtainfall. ¶9時に～となる The performance *closes* at nine. / The *curtain falls* at nine.

へいみん【平民】 a commoner ; the common people. ¶女王は非常に～的であった The queen *was* very *democratic*.

へいめい【平明】 ¶～な文章 a *plain* (≒ *clear* ; *simple*) style.

へいめん【平面】 a plane ; a level.

—幾何 plane geometry. **—鏡** a plane mirror. **—図** a plan figure.

へいや【平野】 a plain ; an open field. 関東— the Kanto plains.

へいゆ【平癒】 recovery. ¶彼の～を祈ってやみません I earnestly pray for his *recovery*. 彼は～した He *has got well*. / He *has recovered health*.

へいよう【併用】 joint use. ¶水薬と粉薬を～する *take* a liquid medicine *together with* a powder one.

へいりつ【並立】 ¶自由と軍国主義とは～することはできない Freedom and militarism cannot *go together*.

へいりょく【兵力】 military power. ¶～によって問題を解決する settle a question by *force of arms*. ～に訴える resort to *force* ; appeal to *arms*. 敵はわれわれより～優勢である The enemy is superior to us *in numbers*.

へいれつ【並列】 ¶～の線 *parallel* lines.

へいわ【平和】 peace ; tranquil[l]ity. ¶世界の～ world *peace*. 家族の～ domestic *peace*. 心の～ *peace* of mind. ～を愛する国民 a *peace*-loving nation. 永遠の～を確立する establish *a* permanent (≒ *an* everlasting) *peace*. 彼が家族の～を乱した He disturbed domestic *harmony* (≒ *peace*). 彼らは～に暮らした They enjoyed a *peaceful* life. 彼はことを～的に解決した He brought the matter to an *amicable* settlement.

—運動 a peace movement. **—攻勢** a peace offensive. **—産業** a peacetime industry. **—論者** a pacifist.

へえ Dear me! / Indeed! ¶～, まさかそんなこと You don't mean to say so! ～, なんですって *Well!* What did you say? ～, だれがそんなことを言ったんだ *What!* Who the devil said such a thing?

ベーカリー a bakery.

ベーキングパウダー baking powder.

ベークライト bakelite.

—製品 bakelite manufactures.

ベーコン bacon.

—エッグ bacon and eggs.

ページ a page. ¶～をめくる turn over the *pages* (≒ *leaves*). 15～を開く open the book *to* (≒ *at*) *page* 15. ～を折り返しておいた I quit reading and doubled over (≒ turned down) the *leaf*. この本は何～か落丁がある There are some *pages* missing from this book. 12～にもどって最初の行を見なさい Turn back to *page* 12 and look at the first line. ノートに～をつけるとよい Why don't you *page* your notebooks? 30～に続く(雑誌などで) Continued to *page* 30.

へ

ページェント a pageant. ¶ 大～を繰り広げる march in *a* colorful *pageant.*
ベージュ (生地のままの毛織物, またその色) beige.
ベース 〔野球〕a base ; (ベース板) a base bag ; (基準) a base ; a basis (複 bases) ; 〔音楽〕basetone. ¶ 走者が～を離れている The runner is off *the base.*
—ライン a base line. 賃金— the wage level (≒ base) ; the basic pay rate.
ペース a pace. ¶ 自分の～で勉強する I work *at my* 〔*own*〕 *pace.* きみも自分の～を守るべきだ You should keep your *pace.* 彼の～に巻き込まれた I was led by the nose by him. 外交は相手国よりアメリカの～で進められた America was more than their match in diplomatic shrewdness. 早い(おそい)～で at a rapid (slow) *pace.* 人とペースを合わせる *keep pace with* others. 1時間に3マイルの～で *at a pace* of 3 miles an hour.
—メーカー a pacemaker.
ベースアップ pay rate raise. ¶ 組合は～を要求している The union is demanding *a raise of the wage level* (≒ *higher wages ; wage hike*).
ペースト paste. ¶ ペーストをパンに塗る smear the bread with *paste.*
レバー— liver paste.
ベースボール baseball.
ペーソス pathos. ¶ 彼の物語は～にあふれている His story is full of *pathos.*
ペーパー paper.
—ナイフ a paper knife. —バック 〔a〕 paperback. —プラン a paper plan.
ベール a veil. ¶ その起源は神秘の～に包まれている Its origin *is veiled* in mystery. ～をはいだ日本 a Japan *unmasked.*
ペガサス 〔神話〕Pegasus.
-べからざる 【-可らざる】¶ その国の軍備はあなどる～ものがある The military power of the nation *is not negligible.* 彼は当たる～勢いだった He *could not possibly* be stopped. それは許す～不法行為だ It is an *unpardonable* lawless act. その成果はたんげいす～ものがある The result *is beyond conjecture.* 塩は日常生活に欠く～食品だ Salt is an *indispensable* (≒ *essential*) item of food to our daily life.
-べからず 【-可らず】¶ 喫煙(駐車)する～(掲示) No Smoking (Parking). 手をふれる～(掲示) Hands Off. 芝生に入る～(掲示) Keep off the Grass. / Keep to the Path. 私道につき立ち入る～(掲示) Private Drive ; No Trespassing. 部外者立ち入る～(掲示) Authorized Personnel Only. / No Admittance except Authorized Personnel. 授業中話をす～(掲示) No Talking in Class. 壁にらく書きす～(掲示) No Scribbling on the Walls.
べき 【冪】〔数学〕a power. ¶ 3の3乗～ 3 to the third *power.*
-べき 【-可き】¶ 両親の意見に従う～だ You *should* (≒ *have to*) obey your parents. 人には親切にす～だ You *must* (≒ *are to*) be kind to others. 彼は住む～家もなかった He had no house *to* live in. 前から知りたかったのですが聞いてみる～かどうか迷っていました I have always wanted to know why, but I have hesitated if I *should* ask.
へきえき 【辟易】¶ 彼の忘れっぽさには～する I *am bewildered with* his forgetfulness. 彼の長談義には～する I *am bored by* (≒ *am sick of*) his tedious talk. / His tedious talk *bores* me *to death.* 騒音に～している I *am plagued to death* by the disturbing noise. その難題に～した I *flinched* (≒ *shrank back*) *from* the difficulties.
へきが 【壁画】a murál painting ; a fresco (複 frescoes ; -s).
へきがん 【碧眼】¶ ～の少女 a *blue-eyed* girl ; a girl *with blue eyes.*
—紅毛 blue-eyed and red-haired.
へきぎょく 【碧玉】〔鉱物〕jade ; jadeite.
へきそん 【僻村】a secluded village.
へきち 【僻地】a remote place ; an out-of-the-way place ; an isolated district. ¶ ～に暮らす live *remote from cities.*
へきとう 【劈頭】the outset ; the start. ¶ ～から激しい議論になった There was a heated argument *at the outset.* ～から彼はあやまった *The first thing* he apologized.
へきれき 【霹靂】¶ 青天の～ a bolt from the blue. 青天の～のごとく戦争が勃発(ぼっ)した The war broke out as *a thunderbolt from a clear sky.*
ペキンげんじん 【ペキン原人】〔人類〕a Peking man.
ヘクタール (面積の単位) a hectare.
ベクトル 〔数学〕vector.
ペケ ¶ すべて～になった Everything *came to nothing.* 私のプランは～になった (拒否された) My plan *was rejected.*
ヘゲモニー hegemony. ¶ ～をにぎる hold the *hegemony* (*in*).
へこた·れる ¶ すこしぐらいの失敗に～れてはいけない Don't *lose heart* (≒ *be discouraged ; be daunted*) *at* such a minor failure. ～れんぞ Nothing would stop me. / I won't let anything stop me.
ベゴニア 〔植物〕a begonia.
ぺこぺこ ¶ おなかが～だ I *am starved.* / I *faint with hunger.* 彼は上の人には～している He *cringes submissively to* a superior.
へこま·す 【凹ます】(くぼみを生じる) dent ; make hollow ; (屈服させる) put down ; stump.
¶ 彼の車は他の車とぶつかってフェンダーを～してしまった His car hit another 〔car〕 and *made a dent* in the fender. 反対者を～せようと一生懸命だった I was eager to *corner* (≒ *silence*) the opponent in argument. 彼はそんなことでは～されなかった He *was* not *stumped* (≒ *was* not *floored ; was* not *silenced*) by that. 彼はたまには～されるほうが身のためだ It will do him a lot of good to *be taken down a peg or two.* / *A* wholesome *snubbing* will do him good.
へこ·む 【凹む】¶ 彼の車はあちこちが～んでいる His

car *is dented* at many places. 壁が～んだ The wall *caved in.* 私の足はかっけでふくれているから押すと～む My legs are swollen with beriberi and *yield to pressure.*

へさき【舳先】a bow; the prow.

へしお·る【圧し折る】¶ 枝を～る *break off* a branch. 彼の高慢の鼻を～ってやりたい I wish to *take* him *down a peg or two.*

ペシミスト a pessimist.

ペシミズム pessimism.

ぺしゃんこ ¶ 車が事故で～になった The car *was crushed* in the accident. 彼は議論に負けて～になった He *was cornered* (≒ *was silenced*) in argument. それでは私の商売は～になる It will *ruin* my business.

ベスト best. ¶ ～を尽くします I will do my *best.* / I will do *what I can* (≒ *all I can*).
―セラー a best seller. ―テン the best ten. ―ドレッサー a best dresser.

ベスト a vest.

ペスト the black plague; pest.
―菌 pest-bacilli (單 -bacillus). 腺― bubonic plague.

へそ【臍】a navel; an umbilicus. ¶ ～で茶を沸かす· be extremely ridiculous. ～を曲げる get out of (≒ lose) temper.

べそ ¶ ～をかく make a wry face. 彼は～をかきながらなにか言った He *blubbered out* something.

へそくり【臍繰り】*one's* secret fund (≒ savings); *one's* pin money. ¶ ～でそれを買った I paid for it with my own *pocket money.*

へそのお【臍の緒】a navel string; an umbilical cord.

へそまがり【臍曲がり】perverseness. ¶ あの人は～で人の言うことに反対ばかりする He *is perverse* enough to do just what others advise him not to.

へた【下手】**1**〖まずい〗¶ 彼は字が～だ He *writes a bad* (≒ *clumsy*) *hand.*
彼は絵が～だ He *is poor* (≒ *not good*) *at* painting.
私は泳ぎが～だ I *don't* swim *well.* / I am a *poor* swimmer.
彼は英語を話すのが～だ He speaks English *terribly* (≒ *badly*).
彼は事務が～だ He *is awkward* at his business.
彼は計算が～だ He *is unskillful* (≒ *not skillful*) *at* accounts.
きみはナイフの使い方が～だ You are *a bad hand with* the knife.
私のテニスは～の横好きだ I like tennis, though I am but *a poor player.*
私は推量が～だ I *am not good at* guessing something.
2〖へたをすると·へたに〗¶ ～をすると遅れますよ You won't be in time *if you are unlucky* (≒ *if you are not lucky enough*).
～をすると患者は助からないかもしれない The patient might lose his life *unless properly treated.*
～をするとチャンスを逃がしますよ You'll miss the chance *if you are not careful enough.*
これは～には口を出せないことだ It is a delicate matter.

ベターハーフ *one's* better half.

へたくそ【下手糞】¶ 彼は字が～だ He is *a bad hand at* handwriting. ⇒へた

べたぐみ【べた組み】〘印刷〙solid printing (≒ typesetting).

へだたり【隔たり】**1**〖差〗a disparity. ¶ 日本とアメリカでは習慣に大きな～がある There is *a* great *difference* between Japanese and American customs.
彼と私の意見には～がある His opinion and mine *are worlds apart.* / His opinion *differs* entirely *from* mine.
本物とは～があるががまんしよう I know it's *a far cry* from the real thing, but I have to forbear.
むかしは科学と一般人との間には越えられない～があるように思われた The *distance* between science and the ordinary man once seemed impossible to cross.
この事件について人々の意見にはまだ～があるPeople still *don't agree* in opinion as to this incident.
離れていたためにわれわれの間に～ができた Absence *estranged* us.
貧富の～ the *gulf* between the rich and the poor.
ふたりの年齢には～がある There is *a disparity* of age between the two.
2〖距離〗〔a〕distance. ¶ ふたりの住んでいる村と村は4マイルの～がある The villages in which each lives *are* four miles *apart.*

へだた·る【隔たる】¶ 首府は海岸から50マイル～っている The capital *is* fifty miles *distant from* the coast. (be distant from は distant の前に必ず距離を表わす語句を入れて用いる). 村と村は5マイル～っている The villages *are* five miles *apart.* 町なかから～るにつれて家がまばらになった *Toward the edge of the town* (≒ *Farther down from the down-town*), the houses thinned out.

べたつ·く ¶ 汗で手が～く My hands *are sticky with* sweat.

へだて【隔て】¶ 彼はだれとでも～なく話す He talks to anyone without *reserve* (≒ *distinction*). あの医師は貧富の～なくだれにでも親切だ That doctor is kind to all patients, *rich or poor.* われわれは～のない交際をしている We *are on good terms* with each other.

へだ·てる【隔てる】¶ イギリスはイギリス海峡によってフランスから～てられている England *is separated* (≒ *is parted*) *from* France by the English Channel. / England and France *have* the English Channel *between* them. ふたりはテーブルを～てて座っていた They were sitting *with* a table *between* them. 彼の家は道路を～ててすぐ向こうだ His house is just across the street. われわれは2千年の歳月で彼らと～てられている We and they *are separated* in time by

2,000 years. 雲に～てられて景色が見えなかった The view *was blotted out* by the clouds. 何がふたりの仲を～てたのか What *has estranged* him from her (⇆ them from each other)? 電柱は30メートルずつ～ててある The poles stand *at intervals of* thirty meters.

へたば・る ¶もう～った I *am exhausted.* / I *am worn out.* / I *am tired out.* 彼は腹がへって～った He *dropped* with hunger.

へたへたと ¶彼は～座り込んだ He *sank into* the chair.

べたべた[と] ¶手が～する My hands *are sticky.* ビラを～へいにはる stick posters *all over* the fence; cover the fence *all over* with posters. 東京の夏は暑くて湿度が高くて～する Summer in Tokyo *is* hot, humid, and *sticky.* 彼はよく彼女と～する He often *dallies with* her.

ぺたぺた ¶こうやくを肩に～はる *put on* plasters *all over* the shoulder. 赤ん坊のほおを～たたく *give* the baby *affectionate little pats* on its cheek.

べたぼめ【べた褒め】 ¶彼女は息子を～する She *is generous in praise of* her son. 新聞の新刊批評は彼の新作を～している The book review in the paper *gives enthusiastic praise to* (⇆ *praises highly*) his new book.

べたりと ¶机の前に～座る *drop down* at the desk. 何かが顔に～ついた Something stuck *fast* right on my face.

ぺたりと ¶切手を～はる stick a postage stamp *fast* (*on*).

ペダル a pedal. ¶自転車の～を踏む *pedal* a bicycle.

ペダンティック ¶～な pedantic.

ぺたんと ¶～腰をおろす sit down *with a flop.*

ペチコート a petticoat.

へちま【糸瓜】〔植物〕 a snake (⇆ towel) gourd.

べちゃべちゃ ¶～しゃべる chatter.

ぺちゃぺちゃ ¶小犬が～牛乳を飲んでいる A puppy *is lapping* milk. ～音をたてて食べるな Don't *slurp.*

ぺちゃんこ ¶お菓子が～になった The cake *was crushed* (⇆ *was flattened*). 私の自転車は～になった My bicycle *was badly crushed.*

へちょう【へ調】〔音楽〕 F.

べつ【別】 **1** 〚区別・分類〛 distinction; classification. ¶男女の～なく受験できる Men and women alike can take the examination. / Anybody can sit for the examination without *distinction* of sex.
競技は年齢～に行なわれる The competition is to be separated *according to* our age. / We will take part in the competition *according to* age.
催しには年齢の～なく参加できる Anybody can join the entertainment no matter what the age may be.
われわれは品目～に在庫調べをした We checked the goods in stock *item by item.*
先生はクラス～に平均点を出した Our teacher worked out the average mark of each class. / Our teacher figured out the average mark *class by class.*
合格者を出身校～に分類した一覧表 the list of the successful candidates classified *according to* their Alma Maters.
2 〚別個〛 ¶それとこれとは問題が～だ That is one thing and this is another. / They are entirely *different* things.
彼にそれを断わられたらだれか～の人に頼もう If he refuses, I will ask *somebody else* (⇆ *another person*).
彼と同じ下宿にいるが，部屋は～だ We are living in the same lodging house, but we have *different* rooms.
彼は彼の父とは～の建物に住んでいる He is living in one house and his father in *another.*
きょうは忙しいから～の日にしてくれ I am busy today, so could you please come on *another* day?
3 〚除外〛 ¶傷のあるリンゴは～にしておきなさい Please *set aside* the bruised apples.
よい桃と悪い桃は～にしてください Please *separate* the good peaches *from* the bad ones.
家を買う費用は～に貯金している I have been saving money to buy the house *in a separate account.*
費用は～として，今は旅行する暇がない *Apart from* the expense, I have no spare time to travel now.
彼を～にすればあとの生徒はどんぐりの背比べだ *Except for* him the rest of the students are all about the same.
酒癖の悪いのを～にすればいい男だ He is a good-natured man, *except* when he is drunk. / *Except for* the fact that he gets mean when he is drunk, he is a good-natured man. (形式ばった文体).
冗談は～としてほんとうに冬山に登る気か *Joking apart,* do you really intend to climb mountain in the winter?
4 〚余分〛 ¶宿泊料とは～に税とサービス料を取られる *In addition to* the hotel fee, they put tax and a service charge on the bill.
配達料は～にして3万円頂きます It will be 30,000 yen *exclusive of* the delivery charge.
(メニューなどで)税金は～に頂戴します Tax not included. / (ヨーロッパで) Service non comprise.
5 〚特別〛 ¶きょうは～に予定はない I have nothing *particular* to do today. / I haven't planned anything *in particular* for today.
～に急ぐ必要はない There is no real reason to hurry.
それは～に重要なことではない It is nothing important. / It is of no *particular* importance.
留守中～に変わったことはなかったか Did anything *special* happen while I was gone?
～に理由はないがなんとなく気が進まない I don't know why, but for some reason I am in no mood for it.
彼の言うことなど～に気にはしていない I do not

mind what he says at all.
いつもは忙しいがきょうは～だ I am always busy, but today is *an exception.*

べつあつらえ【別誂え】special order.

べついん【別院】a branch (≒ separate; detached; independent) temple; an annexed part of the temple.

べっか【別科】a special course. ¶ ～に入る take *a special course.*
—生 a special student.

べっかく【別格】¶ 彼は～だ He *is exceptional.*

べっかん【別館】an annex[e] (*to* a hotel).

べつかんじょう【別勘定】a separate account (≒ bill); (別払い) extra charge. ¶ ～にしよう (割り勘) Let's go Dutch.

べっき【別記】¶ ～のとおり as *stated* (≒ *mentioned*) *elsewhere* (≒ *above; below*).

べっきょ【別居】separation. ¶ 夫婦は目下～中だ The married couple *are* now *living separately* (≒ *apart*). 彼女は夫と～するだろう She will *live apart from* her husband.

べつくち【別口】¶ それは～だ It belongs to *another lot.* / It's quite *different.*

べっけん【瞥見】¶ ～する glance at; catch a hurried glimpse of. 私はその雑誌を～した I *glanced through* the magazine.

べっこ【別個】¶ それは～の問題だ That is *another* (≒ *a different*) question.

べっこう【別項】a separate paragraph (≒ clause).

べっこう【鼈甲】tortoise shell.
—色 amber color. —細工 tortoise-shell work.

べっこん【別懇】¶ 彼とは～の間柄だ I *am on good terms with* him. / He *is a close* (≒ *bosom*) *friend with* me. / He and I *are very good friends.* (good の代わりに intimate を使うことはさける). 彼らは～の間からであった They *were on the best of terms with* one another.

べっさつ【別冊】a separate volume; (雑誌の) an extra number (≒ issue).
—付録 a [separate] supplement (*to* a magazine).

べっし【別紙】an annexed (≒ accompanying) paper; an attached sheet. ¶ 両国政府は～のとおりの同意に達した Both Governments reached an agreement *as stated in the accompanying document.*

べっし【蔑視】¶ 白人は有色人種を～する傾きがある Some white people *look down upon* (≒ *make light of*) colored people.

べっしつ【別室】another room; a separate room.

べっして【別して】¶ 彼は～スキーが得意だ He is *especially* (≒ *particularly*) good at skiing. 彼女は～バラが好きだ She loves roses *in particular* (≒ *above all*).

べつじょう【別状】¶ 乗客に～はなかった The passengers *are all safe and sound* (≒ *are out of danger; are unharmed; are unhurt*). 彼の健康に～はない He *is well enough.* / He *is in good health.* / Nothing is wrong with his health. 小包は～なく届いた The parcel arrived *in good shape* (≒ *without accident*). 船荷に～はない *No damage* has been caused to the cargo.

べつじん【別人】a different person; another man. ¶ 今日では彼はまったく～の観がある He looks quite *different* (≒ *another person*) from what he was. / He is not what he was.

べつずり【別刷り】an excerpt.

べっせかい【別世界】another (≒ a different) world. ¶ まったく～の観がある It looks like quite *a different world.*

べっそう【別荘】困 a country house (≒ cottage); a cottage; 困 a villa; (避暑地にある) 困 a summer cottage (≒ house).

べったく【別宅】¶ ～を構える keep *a separate house.*

べったり ¶ 草の上に～腰を下ろす *flop down* on the grass. ～くっついて離れない stick *fast* like a wax. のりが指に～つく Paste sticks *fast* to the finger. 彼は体制に～だ He *always sticks to* (≒ *is always for*) the Establishment.

べつだん【別段】¶ 私は～用事もない I have nothing *particular* to do. 彼らは～言うことはなかった They had nothing *special* to say. 私は～用事はしていない I am not *particularly* engaged.

へっつい【竈】a kitchen furnace; a hearth.

べってい【別邸】a detached residence; a villa.

ペッティング petting. ¶ ～をする pet.

べってんち【別天地】¶ ここはまるで～の感がある It is *a world in itself.* / This is *another world.* / The place makes *a world of its own.*

ヘット fat.

べっと【別途】¶ ～の支出をする make a *special* outlay. ～の収入がある have a *special* (≒ *casual*) income. 彼の待遇については～考慮した His treatment was considered *apart from this.*
—積立金 a special reserve fund. —預金 a special deposit.

ベッド a bed. ¶ ～につく go to *bed.* 子どもを～に寝かせる put a child to *bed.* ～から飛び起きる jump out of *bed.* ～を作る(ベッドを整える) make *a bed.*
—カバー a bedcover. —タウン a bedroom town (≒ community). —ルーム a bedroom. シングル(ダブル)— a single (double) bed.

ペット a pet. ¶ ～を飼う keep *a pet.*

べつどうたい【別動隊】a flying column; a detachment.

ヘッドコーチ a head coach.

ヘッドライト a headlight; a headlamp.

べっとり ¶ 床には～血がついていた There was blood *all over* the floor. 転んだ拍子に手に～泥がついた The moment I stumbled, I got mud on my hand.

へ

べつに【別に】⇒べつ

べつのう【別納】料金— charge separately paid. 料金—郵便 postpaid.

べっぱ【別派】another sect; another school.

べっぴょう【別表】¶～を参照する refer to *an attached table.*

へっぴりごし【へっぴり腰】¶～で with *one's* back bent. ～で試合をやる play games with (*a person*) *cowardly* (≒ *in great fear*).

べつびん【別便】¶～でパンフレットを送る send a pamphlet *by separate post* (≒ *under another cover; separately*).

べっぷう【別封】¶～の手紙 a letter *under separate cover.*

べつべつ【別別】¶～の家に住む live in *separate* houses. ～の行動をする act *in one's own way.* ～に歩く walk *apart from one another.* 物を～にしまっておく keep things *apart.* 家族と～に住む live *separate* from *one's* family. 品物を～に包む wrap up articles *separately.* ～にやってくる come *one by one.*

べつむね【別棟】¶～に住む live in *an outhouse* (≒ *an outbuilding*).

べつめい【別名】another name; a byname. ¶ X～Y X *alias* Y.

べつめい【別命】¶～あるまで待て Wait till you receive *another order.*

べつもんだい【別問題】a different matter; another question. ¶それは～だ It's *a different story.* / That is *aside from the subject.* / It's *another question.* それとこれとは～だ They are *two different questions.* 知っていることと教えることとは～だ To know is one thing, to teach *another.*

へつらい【諂い】flattery. ¶見えすいた～ coarse *flattery.* ～を真に受ける swallow *flattery.*
—者 a flatterer.

へつら・う【諂う】¶上役に～う *flatter* (≒ *curry favor with; court*) *one's* superior. 彼は～ってもだめだ He is above *flattery.* / He is proof against *flattery.*

べつり【別離】¶～の悲しみ the sorrow of *parting.* ～の涙を流す shed *parting* tears. ～の握手を交わす shake hands with *a person at parting.*

ヘディング〘フットボール〙a heading. ¶～をする make *a heading.*

ベテラン a veteran (日本語でいうベテランは expert に当たることが多い).

ぺてん fraud; trickery. ¶人を～にかける play *a trick* on *a person.* 人を～にかけて金を取る *trick* (≒ *swindle*) *a person* out of money.
—師 a swindler.

へど【反吐】a vomit. ¶～を吐く vomit (≒ spew) what *one* has eaten. 彼の顔は見ただけでも～が出そうだ His very sight *is quite disgusting.* / His very sight *made* me *sick.*

べとつ・く ¶汗で体が～く feel sticky.

ベトナム Vietnam; Viet Nam.
—人 a Vietnamese.

へとへと ¶終日働いたので～だ I'*m tired out* (≒ *am exhausted*) from working all day.

べとべと ¶ここにいると汗で～する I *feel* rather *sticky* here. 壁にペンキを～に塗った I *bedaubed* the walls *with* paint. ペンキはまだ～している The paint *is* still *wet and smeary.*

へどもど ¶～して返答できない *be at a loss* how to answer. 自分のしでかした過ちで～する *be confused at one's* error. 人の顔を見て～する *be bewildered at* the sight of *a person.*

ペナルティー〘競技〙penalty.
—キック a penalty kick.

ペナント a pennant. ¶～を争う compete for *the pennant.* ～を握る win *the pennant.* ～レースに勝つ win *the pennant race.*

べに【紅】rouge. ¶～をつけたほお cheeks touched with *rouge*; *rouged* cheeks.
—色 red; crimson.

ペニー a penny. ¶自動販売機に1～銅貨を入れる drop *a penny* into the slot.

べにしょうが【紅生姜】red pickled ginger.

ペニシリン penicillin. ¶臀部(でんぶ)に～注射をする make an *penicillin* injection (≒ shot) in the hip.

ベニス Venice.
—人 a Venetian.

べにます【紅鱒】〘魚類〙a red trout; a rainbow trout.

ベニヤ a plywood; a veneer. ¶壁に～を張る *veneer* a wall.

へのかっぱ【屁の河童】¶そんなことは～だ Nothing *is easier* (≒ *simpler*) 〔*than that*〕. なにを言われようと～だ I *don't care a pin* what people say. 1日に20キロ歩くぐらい～だ I *make nothing of* walking twenty kilometers a day.

へのじ【への字】¶口を～に結んで with a firmly-set mouth; with a wry look. 口を～に結ぶ make a wry face.

へばりつ・く ¶地面に～く *lie flat* on the ground. 地位に～く *cling to one's* position. 机に～いて勉強する sit (≒ work) at *one's* desk for hours without stopping. 自分の仕事に～く *stick at* (≒ *to*) *one's* work.

へば・る ¶猛練習で～る *be* (≒*feel*) *much exhausted from* (≒ *with*) intensive exercise.

へび【蛇】a snake; (大蛇) a serpent. ¶～のように執念深い be as spiteful as *a viper.* ～に見込まれたカエルのような like a frog fascinated by *a snake.* ～の抜けがら the slough of *a snake.*
毒— a poisonous (≒ venomous) snake.

ベビー a baby.
—だんす a small-sized chest of drawers.
—用品 baby's ware.

ヘビーきゅう【ヘビー級】the heavyweight.

ヘブライ Hebrew.
—語 Hebrew. —人 a Hebrew.

へべれけ ¶～に酔っている be dead (≒ beastly) drunk.

へぼ ¶～医者 a *quack* 〔doctor〕. ～画家 a dauber; a *wretched* painter. ～将棋 a *poor* Japanese chess.

ヘボンしき【ヘボン式】the Hepburn system.

へ

¶ ～ローマ字 Romanized Japanese *according to* Hepburn; the *Hepburn system* Romanization.

へま (大失策) a blunder; (不手際) a bungle. ¶ ～なやつ a bungler; a stupid fellow. とんでもない～をやる make *an* astounding *blunder*; make *an* awful *mess* of it. きょうはなにをやっても～ばかりだ Everything *went wrong* today.

へや【部屋】 a room. ¶ ホテルに～を取る engage (≒ take) *a room* in a hotel. 6畳の～に住む live in *a* six-mat *room*. 私の家は3～ある My house has three *rooms*. / There are three *rooms* in my house. 明るく風通しのよい～ *a* bright airy *room*. 風通しの悪い～ *an* ill-ventilated *room*. 南向きの～ *a* southward (≒ *a* south aspect) *room*. ～に風を通す air *a room*. ～を掃除する (片付ける) clean (clear up) *a room*. 勉強── a study room.

へら【篦】 a spatula.

へら·す【減らす】 ¶ 腹を～す be hungry. くつのかかとを～す *wear out* the heels of *one's* boots. 出費を～す *cut down* the expenses. 不必要の人員を～す *cut down* unnecessary personnel. 肉を～して野菜をたくさん食べるようにしなさい Try to eat *less* meat and more vegetables.

へらずぐち【減らず口】 ¶ ～をたたく talk back to *a person*; talk impudently. ～をたたくな Hold your tongue! / Shut up!

べらべら ⇒ぺらぺら

ぺらぺら ¶ あることについて～しゃべる *chatter* about (≒of) a matter. 英語を～しゃべる speak English *fluently*. ～の紙ではなをかむ blow the nose with *thin* paper. ページを～めくる turn the pages *one after another*.

べらぼう【箆棒】 ¶ 彼はその品物に～な値段をふっかけた He charged me an *exorbitant* price for the article. そんな～な話があるか Your claim is *quite absurd*!

ベランダ a veranda(h).

へり【縁】 ¶ 帽子の～ the *brim* of a hat. 川の～ a river*side*; *an edge* of a river. 川の～にある be *by the side* of a river. 畳の～ a mat-*border*. 畳に～をつける sew *a border* on a mat.

へり【減り】 a decrease; (損失) a loss; (摩滅) wear. ¶ 人口の～ *a* population *decrease*. 生産の～ *decrease* in production.

ヘリウム 〘化学〙 helium.

ペリカン 〘鳥類〙 a pelican.

へりくだ·る【謙る·遜る】 ¶ 目上の人の前で～る *abase one*self before a superior. ～った言い方をする talk *in a modest way* (≒ *with modesty*). 彼は～った態度の人だ He is a man *of modesty*.

へりくつ【屁理屈】 a quibble; a cavil. ¶ 彼はなんにでも～を言う He *cavils at* everything. 彼は～をつけられて財産を奪われた He *was quibbled* out of his property. そのような行為を弁明するのは～にすぎない It is nothing but *sophistry* to justify such acts.

──屋 a quibbler; a sophist; stickler.

ヘリコプター a helicopter. ¶ ～の発着場 a heliport.

ヘリポート a heliport.

へ·る【減る】 **1** 〚人数などが〛 ¶ この数年その国は人口が～っている The population of that nation *is decreasing* in number. 集まっていた群衆はしだいに～ってきた The crowd gathered there *has* gradually *diminished*.

2 〚量などが〛 run short. ¶ タンクの水が～ってきた The water in the tank *is running short*. 貯水池の水は5メートルほど～った The water in the reservoir *has fallen* about five meters. 輸入がいくらか～った The imports *have shown* a little *decrease*. 販売高が10パーセント～った There has been *a* ten percent *decrease* in sales. 彼は病気のため目方がだいぶ～った Because of sickness he *has lost* a lot of weight. 腹が～ってきた I *am getting hungry*. くつが～るほど歩いた I walked so much that my shoes *were worn out*.

へる【経る】 ¶ アンカレッジを経てロンドンに飛ぶ fly to London *via* (≒ *by way of*) Anchorage. 正規の手続きを経てから after *going through* due formalities. 幾多の変遷 (困難) を経る *go through* many changes (hardships). 試験を経てから (経ずに) 許可証を発行する issue a license *on* (*without*) examination. 数年間の準備期間を経て試験を受ける take an examination *after* years of preparation. 友人の手を経てその金を受け取った I received the money *by the hand of* a friend.

ベル a bell. ¶ 玄関の～ a door*bell*. 非常用～ *an* emergency *bell*. ～を押す push a *bell* button. ～を鳴らす ring *a bell*. 電話の～が鳴っている The telephone *is ringing*. 玄関の～が鳴った There was *a ring* at the door. / *A ring* came to my door. ～とともに教室に入った I entered the classroom with the *bell*. ～が鳴った. 休み時間だ The *bell* has gone; it's time to cease work. そら, ～が鳴っている There goes the *bell*!

ペルー Peru.

──人 a Peruvian.

ベルギー Belgium.

──人 a Belgian.

ベルサイユ Versailles.

──宮殿 (条約) the Versailles Palace (Treaty).

ペルシァ Persia.

──語 Persian. ──ネコ a Persian cat. ──じゅうたん Persian carpet.

ベルト a belt. ¶ 腰に～をしめる wear *a belt* round *one's* waist.

グリーン── a green belt.

ベルトコンベア a belt conveyer.

──システム a belt conveyer system; an assembly line system.

ヘルニア 〘医学〙 hernia.

ヘルメット a helmet.

ベルモット (酒) vermouth.

ベルリン Berlin.

東 (西)── East (West) Berlin. ──市民 a

Berliner.
ベレー〔ぼう〕【ベレー〔帽〕】a beret.
ヘレニズム Hellenism.
ヘロイン〖薬〗heroin. ¶ ～常用による中毒 poisoning by habitual use of *heroin*; *heroin* addiction poisoning.
べろべろ ¶ ～に酔っ払う get *beastly* (≒ *dead*) drunk.
ぺろり ¶ ～と舌を出す stick out *one's* tongue. ～となめる lick up with the tongue. ケーキを全部～と平らげる eat up the whole cake in a flash.
へん【辺】**1**〖地方〗¶ 郵便局はどの～ですか *Where* is the post office?
彼は川越～に住んでいる He lives *somewhere* Kawagoe way.
この～はよく知っている I know this *neighborhood* well.
この～は静かだ It's quiet *around here*.
この～はジャガイモの産地だ Potatoes are produced in this *district*.
この～で休んではどうですか What do you say to having a rest *about here*?
2〖程度〗¶ 今晩はこの～にしておこう That's enough for this evening./ So much for this evening.
その～のことはよくわからない I don't know about it for certain.
3〖幾何学の〗a side. ¶ 正方形の四つの～の長さは同じだ The four *sides* of a square are equal in length.
へん【変】**1**〖奇異な〗¶ 彼はようすが～だ There is something *queer* about him.
きょうは調子が～だ I *feel unwell* today.
あの人がそんなことをするなんて～だ *It is strange* that he should do such a thing.
～な物音を聞いた I heard a *strange* noise.
～なことを言う人だ What *queer* things he says!
彼は頭が～なのだ I think he must *be mad*.
彼は～な目つきでこっちを見ている He is glancing at me *suspiciously*.
～な男が庭に立っている There is a *suspicious-looking* man standing in the garden.
彼の行動には～なところがある There is *a strangeness* about his behavior.
ゆうべ～な夢を見た I had a *strange* dream last night.
～なまちがいをしたものだ What a *curious* mistake I have made!
2〖変事〗a disaster. ¶ 承久の～ the *upheaval* of the Jokyu Period.
桜田門外の～ the *disturbance* outside the Sakurada Gate.
へん【編】(章) a chapter; (節) a section; (巻) a volume. ¶ 一～の詩 *a* poem. (本の) 第1～ the first *chapter* (≒ *section*). A氏～の教科書 a textbook *edited* (≒ *compiled*) by Mr. A.
-へん【-遍】¶ 2～ twice; two *times* (twiceのほうを多く用いる). 幾～も many *times*; again and again. 読書百～意おのずから通ず Read a hundred *times* over, and the meaning will become clear of itself.
べん【弁】(花弁) a petal; (機械の) a valve. ¶ ボイラーの～ *a valve* on a boiler.
安全― a safety valve. ¶ 安全～を締める lock up *a* safety *valve*. 空気― an air valve.
べん【弁】¶ ～が立つ be fluent. ～の立つ人 a good speaker. 関西～で話す speak with *a* Kansai *accent*.
べん【便】**1**〖便利〗convenience. ¶ 私の家は交通の～が悪い所にある My house *is inconveniently located* for the traffic.
この辺りは交通の～が悪い This neighborhood is lacking in *traffic facilities*.
この村にはバスの～がある There is *a bus service* in this village.
この地域は地下鉄の～がよい This district *is convenient for* the subway.
このかばんは携帯に～である This briefcase *is handy* to carry.
2〖便通〗motions. ¶ 軟らかい～だった The *feces* were soft.
～を検査してもらった I had my *feces* examined.
ペン a pen (もとペン先. 現在英語の pen は万年筆もボールペンもふくむ). ¶ ～とインクで書く write with *pen* and ink.
―画 a pen[-and-ink] sketch. ―先 a nib; a point. ―軸 a penholder. ―習字 penmanship.
へんあい【偏愛】partiality. ¶ 私は長男を～してはいない I *am* not *partial to* my oldest son. 両親の～が彼をわがままにした The *partiality* (≒ *fondness*; *partial favor*) of his parents made him selfish.
へんあつ【変圧】〔電気〕transformation.
―器 a transformer. ―所 a [transformer] substation.
へんい【変位】〔物理〕displacement.
―電流 a displacement current.
へんい【変異】〔生物〕variation; (突然の) mutation.
―説 variation theory. 突然―(変異した動植物) a sport. 突然―説 mutation theory.
べんい【便意】a desire to evacuate (≒ relieve) the bowels. ¶ ～を催す have a call of nature; be going to have a motion of bowels.
べんえき【便益】(利益) benefit; (便宜) convenience. ¶ 会員にはさまざまの～がある The members of the society have various *advantages and conveniences.* / The society *benefits* (≒ *is benefited to*; *is beneficial to*) the members in many ways. 市民の～をはかるのが彼らの義務ではないか Isn't it their duty to administer to the *convenience* of the citizens?
へんか【変化】change;〖文法〗(動詞の) conjugation; (格の) declension; (語尾の) inflection.
¶ ～しやすい天候 *changeable* weather. 山の気温の～ははげしい Temperature in the mountains *changes* (≒ *alters*) quickly. この景色は

〜があっておもしろい This scenery *is* impressively *diversified.* 彼は〜に富んだ生涯を送った He lived a life *full of variety.* / He had a *dramatic* (≒ an *eventful*; a *colorful*; a *varied*; a *checkered*) career. 気候の〜は健康を増進する *Variations* of climate improve health. 彼女は〜のない生活に飽きていた She was tired of her *uneventful* (≒ *changeless*; *monotonous*) life. 情勢に〜はない The situation *remains unchanged.* 次の動詞の〜を示せ *Conjugate* the following verbs.

—球 a ball thrown for a change of pace; a screwball; (カーブ) a curve.

べんかい【弁解】(言いわけ) an excuse; (わび) an apology. ¶ 〜の要はすこしもない It requires no *apology.* 〜の余地はまったくない It admits (≒ allows) of no *defense* (≒ *excuse*). / It *is* quite *inexcusable.* その〜は聞きあきた I have had enough of that *excuse.* 知らなかったということは〜にならない Ignorance is no *excuse.* 今更〜してもなんにもならない It is [of] no use trying to *excuse yourself* now. あまり〜がましいことを言うな Don't *be* so *apologetic.* へたな〜を聞くとかえっていらいらする *A* poor *excuse* only makes me irritate. 彼はいつも〜ばかりしている He *is* always *making excuses.* 彼はいろいろ私のために〜してくれた He *said much for* me. 彼は自分のしたことをなんと言って〜したか What did he say *in explanation of* (≒ *to explain*) his conduct?

へんかく【変革】 a change. ¶ 自動車がわれわれの生活様式をすっかり〜した Automobiles *have* completely *changed* our way of life. / Cars have brought about *a* large *reform* in our whole way of life. それは人間の考え方に大〜をもたらした It worked (≒ brought about) *a revolution* in our way of thinking. / It *revolutionized* our way of thinking.

べんがく【勉学】 study. ¶ 彼はその大学で3年の間〜にいそしんだ He *studied* hard in college for three years. / He *pursued his studies* in the university for three years. (文語体).

ベンガラ red ocher.

へんかん【返還】 return. ¶ 王は彼らに政権の〜を求めた The king demanded them to *return* the political powers. 彼は王位の〜を強く望んだ He strongly desired the *restoration* of the throne.

べんき【便器】 a chamber pot; a stool.

べんぎ【便宜】(便利) convenience; (融通) accommodation; (利益) benefit. ¶ 〜上そう呼んでいる We call it so *for convenience* (≒ *for convenience' sake*). 彼は私のためにあらゆる〜をはかってくれた He offered (≒ provided) every *convenience* possible for me. 彼のあっせんでわれわれはたいへんな〜を得た His kind offices afforded us great *facilities.* われわれはなんら財政上の〜は受けていない We obtained no *accommodation* financially. 一時の〜のためにそれを採用した We adopted it as *a* temporary *expedient.* 〜なこと必ずしも正しくはない What *is expedient* is not always right. こちらのほうが〜がよろしい This one *is handier* (≒ *is more convenient*) for me. 彼が持ち場の変更を希望したが,〜をはかってやれなかった He wanted change for the position of duty, but I could not *accommodate* him. 当市は商業に〜の地位を占めている This city holds an *advantageous* position for commerce. 鉄の船は軽くて強いという二つの〜がある An iron ship has the double *advantages* of lightness and strength.

—主義 opportunism.

ペンキ paint. ¶ 〜で犬小屋を白く塗った I *painted* the dog's house white. 〜がはげているThe *paint* has worn off. 家を〜で塗りかえなければいけない My house needs *repainting.* 〜塗りたて (掲示) Wet (≒ Fresh) Paint.

—屋 a painter.

へんきゃく【返却】 return; repayment. ¶ 本の〜が遅れてすみません I am sorry I have delayed *returning* (≒ *giving back*) the books. 金の〜に苦慮している I am quite at a loss how to *repay* (≒ *pay back*) money.

へんきょう【辺境】 a frontier; a border; the border districts.

へんきょう【偏狭】 bigotry. ¶ 彼は〜だ He *is narrow-minded* (≒ *is bigoted*). その考えは青年の心を〜にする The idea will make *less flexible* the minds of the rising generation.

べんきょう【勉強】 1〖勉学〗 study. ¶ 熱心に〜する *study* hard.

こつこつ〜する dig at (a subject).
がりがり〜する cram up (a subject).
〜しすぎる overwork [*oneself*].
〜を怠ける neglect *one's study.*
彼は〜がよくできる (できない) He *gets good* (*bad*) *marks at school.*
彼は〜不足だ He *doesn't work hard enough.*

—部屋 a study [room]. **—家** a hard worker; a studious (≒ diligent) person.

2〖値段を〗¶ あの店は〜する (安い) They *sell at a low* (≒ *reasonable*) *price.* / *Things are cheaper* at that store. / (まける) They *reduce the price* (≒ *give a discount*) at that store. できるだけ〜しますからお買いください We will *sell as cheap as we can,* so please give us your custom.

へんきょく【編曲】 arrangement. ¶ これはピアノ曲に〜されたものだ This piece *is arranged for* the piano.

へんきん【返金】 repayment; refund. ¶ 彼から〜を迫られている He urges me to *repay.* / He presses me for *repayment.* 〜は済ませた I *have returned* (≒ *have paid back*; *have paid off*) my debt.

ペンギン a penguin.

へんくつ【偏屈】(風変わり) eccentricity; (がんこ) obstinacy. ¶ あの男にはちょっと〜なところがある He is rather an *eccentric* person. / He is *a crank.* / There is something *eccentric* about him. 彼は〜で手に負えない He *is* too *obstinate* to control.

ペンクラブ the P. E. N. (<International Association of Poets, Playwrights, Editors, Essayists and Novelists).

へんげ【変化】 a ghost; a specter; a goblin; an apparition.

へんけい【変形】 transformation; variation; (動物の) metamorphosis; (変形物) a variety. ¶ おたまじゃくしがカエルに～する Tadpoles *transform into* frogs.
—文法 transformational grammar.

べんけい【弁慶】 ¶ ～の泣きどころ *one's* Achilles' heel (≒ tendon).
内— ¶ 彼は内～だ He is a lion at home, but a mouse abroad. 陰— ¶ 彼は陰～だ A cock is valiant on his dunghill. —縞 checks; checkers (≒ chequers); a checkered pattern.

へんけん【偏見】 a prejudice. ¶ まず～を捨てよ Cast away all your *prejudiced views* first. ～にとらわれぬ人 a man *free from bias*; an *unbiased* man. 彼らはなんら人種的～をいだいていない They have no racial *prejudice*. それは～だ It is *a partial view*. 彼は～がある He *is prejudiced*.

へんげん【変幻】 ¶ 夢の中でさまざまなイメージが～自在に出没する Various images appear and disappear *like phantoms* in my dream. ～きわまりない幻想 a *phantasmagoric* (≒ *kaleidoscopic*) illusion.

べんご【弁護】 defense; pleading; (主張) advocacy. ¶ その事件は～の余地がない The case admits (≒ allows) of no *defense.* / The case *is indefensible*. 喜んで被告人の～を引き受けましょう I am willing to *plead for* the defendant. すぐ～を依頼すべきだ You must *consult a lawyer* promptly. 私は一言も自己～しなかった I said nothing *in self-defense*. 新聞は彼の行動を～した The newspaper *defended* his action. 彼は熱弁をふるって社会的平等を～した He *advocated* social equality with passionate eloquence.
—人 a defender; a lawyer; a pleader; an advocate.

へんこう【変更】 a change. ¶ この法律は～を必要とする This law requires *modification*. 計画にすこしく～を加えたい We want to make *a* slight *alteration* in the plan. ある程度計画の～は避けられない It is inevitable to *change* (≒ *alter*) the plan to some extent. 生産計画に～はない The production schedules remain *unchanged* (≒ *unaltered*). 再び～することのない確たる目標を打ち立てなければならない We must set up an *unchangeable* (≒ *unalterable*) firm purpose. その計画は～すべきではない You should not *depart from* the plan.

へんこう【偏向】 an inclination; a tendency. ¶ それは極端に左翼～の団体だ It is an organization with extreme leftwing *leanings*. / The organization *inclines too much to* communism. / The body *is* left *leaning* extremely.
—教育 a deflected education; ideologically prejudiced education.

へんこう【偏光】〔物理〕 polarized light.
—板 a polarizing plate. —プリズム a polarizer..

べんごし【弁護士】 (一般的) a lawyer. ¶ ～になる enter the law. ～の免許をとる be admitted (≒ be called) to the bar. ～を開業する practice law. ～を依頼する consult *a lawyer*.
—会 a bar association. —試験 the bar examination. —事務所 a law office. 顧問— a legal adviser.

へんさ【偏差】〔物理〕 deflection; variation.
標準— standard deviation.

へんさい【返済】 repayment. ¶ 彼は借金の～を迫ってきた He urged me to *pay back* (≒ *repay*) my debt. / He pressed me for *repayment* of the money. 彼は～を求めなかった He did not *ask* it *back*. 借金の～期限になる The debt *falls due*. 借金の～の期限が過ぎている The debt is overdue.

へんざい【偏在】 maldistribution. ¶ 資源が～している Resources *are maldistributed* (≒ *are unevenly distributed*).

へんざい【遍在】 omnipresence. ¶ 神は宇宙に～する God *is omnipresent* (≒ *is ubiquitous*).

べんさい【弁才】 eloquence. ¶ 彼には～がない He is awkward in speaking. / He doesn't have *an oratorical talent*. (文語調).

べんさい【弁済】 payment; repayment.

へんさん【編纂】 compilation; editing.
¶ 彼は「現代のアメリカ」という本を～した He *compiled* a book of "Contemporary America."
—者 a compiler; an editor.

へんし【変死】 an unnatural death. ¶ 彼女の～のいきさつは知るすべもない There is no knowing why and how she *died an unnatural* (≒ *untimely*) *death*. 彼はきのう～した He *died accidentally* yesterday. (殺害された意味なら died の代わりに was killed を用いる).
—人 a person who had met an unnatural death; (殺された人) a person accidentally killed.

へんじ【変事】 an accident; (大惨事) a disaster; a calamity; a mishap. ¶ 彼は～に出くわした He met with *an accident*. 何か彼に～が起こったにちがいない *Something must have happened to* him. われわれは地震と火事という二大～にあった We have had two great *disasters* (≒ *calamities*) in the shape of earthquake and fire.

へんじ【返事】 an answer. ¶ すぐ～が欲しい I want your *answer* at once. 手紙の～がまだ来ない I have not received *an answer* to my letter. 電話で～する *answer* by phone. 手紙に～する *reply to* a letter. ベルを押しても～がなかった No one *answered* when I rang the bell. お～いただきました Your *answer* should be appreciated.
ふたつ— ¶ 彼がふたつ～で承知してくれてありがたい I am grateful to him for *consenting so readily*.

へ

べんし【弁士】a speaker ; an orator.

へんしつ【変質】change of quality ; (悪変) deterioration ; degeneration ; perversity. ¶ 加熱すると~するものもある Heating *changes* some things *in quality*. 暖かくて湿気のある気候は革を~させる A hot damp climate *deteriorates* leather.

—者 a degenerate ; a pervert.

へんしゃ【編者】an editor ; a compiler.

へんしゅ【変種】〘生物〙 a variety ; (突然変異による) a mutation ; a sport. ¶ チューリップの~ *a variety* of the tulip.

人工— an artificial variety.

へんしゅう【偏執】—狂 monomania ; (人) a monomaniac. —病 paranoia.

へんしゅう【編集】compilation ; editing. ¶ 教科書を~する *edit* (≒ *compile*) a textbook. その雑誌の~はなかなか気がきいている The magazine *is* cleverly *edited*.

—員〔a member of〕the editorial staff ; a staff member. ¶ 彼はその本の~員だ He *is on the staff of* the book. —会議 an editorial conference. —者 an editor. —長 the chief (≒ managing) editor ; the editor in chief. —部 the editorial department.

べんじょ【便所】a lavatory ; a water closet (ヨーロッパ諸国, とくにフランスでW. C. という掲示を用いる) ; 困 a toilet [room] ; a rest room ; (工場などの) a latrine ; (屋外の) a privy ; (男子用) gentlemen ; men ; men's room ; (女子用) ladies ; women ; a women's room.

¶ ~へ行く go to the toilet (≒ closet) ; go to stool ; (えん曲に) go to the back ; wash *one's* hands. ~に入っている be at stool. ~はふさがっている(あいている) The closet is now engaged (vacant). ~はどこですか Where can I wash my hands? / Where is the *men's* (*women's*) *room*? (便所の場所は必ず同性に聞くのがエチケット).

公衆— a public lavatory ; a street latrine. 水洗— a flush toilet.

へんじょう【返上】¶ みんな休暇を~して懸命に働いた All of us worked hard, *giving up* our vacation. 彼はその通知をあえて~した He dared to *send back* the notice.

べんしょう【弁償】payment ; compensation. ¶ 損失の~としてこれを受け取ってください Please accept this *in compensation for* the loss. あなたの損害は私が~します I will *pay* (≒ *make good*) *for* your loss. 私が持ち主に破損の~をする I will *compensate* (≒ *indemnify*) the owners *for* damages. お気の毒です, 全部~いたしましょう I am sorry, and will *make* complete *restitution*.

—金 an indemnity ; a compensation.

べんしょうほう【弁証法】〘哲学〙 dialectic.

—的唯物論 dialectical materialism.

へんしょく【変色】discoloration. ¶ ~したスカーフ a *discolored* scarf. ~した花 *faded* flowers. その布は~しない The cloth *has fast colors*. / The cloth does not *change color*.

へんしょく【偏食】an unbalanced diet. ¶ そうすると子どもは~しなくなる It keeps a child from *having an unbalanced diet*. 私はとても~です I have too many likes and dislikes in what I eat.

べん・ずる【弁ずる】¶ 一席~ずる tell a story ; make a speech. 彼は友のために大いに~じた He *said much for* his friend.

へんしん【返信】a reply ; an answer.

—用はがき a reply card. —料 return postage.

へんしん【変心】a change of mind (≒heart) ; (不実) infidelity ; inconstancy ; (裏切り) treachery.

¶ ~して彼は敵方に走った *Changing his mind*, he went over to his enemy. 彼は~したのだ He *played* us *false*! / He *betrayed* us! 彼は彼女の~をなじった He blamed her for her *inconstancy*.

へんしん【変身】metamorphosis (覆 metamorphoses).

へんじん【変人】an eccentric (≒ an odd) person ; an oddity ; a crazy person ; 困 a crank.

ベンジン〘化学〙 benzine.

へんずつう【偏頭痛】〘医学〙 megrim ; migraine.

へん・する【偏する】¶ 彼の説は一方に~している He has a *partial* view. / His view *is one-sided* (≒ *is unfair*). / He *is prejudiced*.

へん・ずる【変ずる】change ; alter ; turn (*to* ; *into*). ¶ 一晩のうちに街は廃墟と~じた The town *turned into* a ruin in one night. 突如針路を~じて, 船は西に向かった *Changing* (≒ *Altering*) the course suddenly, the ship sailed west.

へんせい【編成】organization ; formation. ¶ クラスは45人で~する We *organize* a class with 45 pupils. 10両~の列車が山手線を走っている Trains *made up of* 10 carriages run on the Yamanote Line. 今月10日までに予算を~する We are to *make up* the budget by the 10th of this month.

へんせい【編制】formation. ¶ 軍隊は戦闘の~であった The troops were in battle *formation*. すべて戦時~になっている They are all on *a war footing*.

へんせいがん【変成岩】〘鉱物〙 metamorphic rocks.

へんせつ【変節】apostasy ; treachery. ¶ ~したのは彼だ It was he that *changed* (≒ *turned*) *his coat*. 彼は~して保守党に移った He *turned over* to the conservative party.

—漢 an apostate ; a traitor ; a renegade.

べんぜつ【弁舌】speech ; eloquence. ¶ 彼は~がさわやかである He *speaks fluently*. / He *speaks eloquently*. / He *has a silver* (≒ *fluent*) *tongue*. 彼は~の力によって名声を得た His *oratorical powers* secured him a good reputation.

—家 an eloquent (≒ a fluent ; a good) speaker.

へんせん【変遷】change ; transition. ¶ 人生

の～ the *vicissitudes* (≒ *ups and downs*) of life. 風俗の～ the *changes* of manners and customs. 幾多の～を経る undergo many *changes*. 彼の政治的生涯は～が多かった His political life *was varied*. 世の～は常なきものだ Human things *are mutable*. あらゆるものが常に～している All things *are in a state of flux*.

へんそう【返送】¶ 手紙はあて名不明で～されてきた The letter *was sent back* labeled 'blind.'

へんそう【変装】 disguise. ¶ 彼は僧侶(そうりょ)に～して旅をした He traveled *in* (≒ *under*) *the disguise of* a priest. / He made a trip *disguising himself as* a priest. 彼はつけひげで～した He *was disguised by* a false beard.

へんぞう【変造】 forgery. ¶ 1万円を～する *falsify* (≒ *forge*) 10,000 yen notes.
—小切手 an altered (≒ a forged) check.
—紙幣 a forged (≒ counterfeit) note.

へんそうきょく【変奏曲】〚音楽〛a variation.

へんそく【変則】 irregularity. ¶ ～的な発音 *incorrect* pronunciation. ～的な教育 a *picked-up* education. ～的な方法 an *irregular* method. 彼の精神生活にはなにか～的なものがある There is *a* strange *anomaly* in his mental life.

へんたい【変態】〚生物〛 metamorphosis; transformation; (異常) abnormality; anomaly; perversion; perversity.
¶ 大多数の動物は～しない The great majority of animals do not go through *metamorphosis* (≒ *transformation*). ～的状態 *abnormal* (≒ *anomalous*) conditions.
—心理 abnormal psychology. **—**性欲 abnormal sexuality.

へんたい【編隊】 a formation. ¶ ～で飛ぶ fly in *formation*. 6機～で in *a* six-plane *formation*.
—飛行 a formation flight.

ペンタゴン the Pentagon.

べんたつ【鞭撻】 ¶ よりいっそうご支援とご～をお願いいたします I beg for your further help and *encouragement*. 彼は勉強するように～された He *was spurred* (≒ *was whipped up his enthusiasm*) *to* study. 彼は部下を～して事務をはかどらせた He *urged* his men to dispatch business.

ペンダント a pendant.

へんち【辺地】 a remote (≒ secluded) place.

ベンチ a bench; 〚野球〛a dugout.

ペンチ cutting pliers.

へんちくりんな odd; queer; funny.

へんちょ【編著】 ¶ ベンスン～ *compiled* (≒ *edited*) *by* Benson.

へんちょう【変調】 (調子の変化) a change of tone; (不規則) irregularity; (異常) abnormality.
¶ このテープレコーダーは音が～をきたしている The sound of this tape recorder has become *irregular* (≒ *abnormal*). 病人が急に～をきたした The patient *has* suddenly *changed* (≒ *has taken a turn*) *for the worse*. 穀物市場は土曜日は～だった The corn market *was irregular* on Saturday.

へんちょう【偏重】 ¶ 学歴の～は好ましくない It is not desirable to *make too much of a person's* academic career.

ベンチレーター a ventilator. ¶ 部屋には～をつけるべきだ We should install (≒ furnish) the room with *a ventilator*. / The room must *be* well *ventilated*. (後者は必ずしも設備・機械としてのベンチレーターは意味せず，窓を開けるなどの操作で空気の入れ替えを行なうことをも意味する).

べんつう【便通】 evacuation; the action (≒ movement; motion) of the bowels (このような表現にはえん曲的な語法がよく使われるが, evacuation はどちらかというと「排便」というような感じの直接的な表現である. しかし実際には a motion とか the action of the bowels という表現よりも使われる頻度が多い).
¶ 毎日1回～がある I *evacuate* once every day. / I *have a* (≒ *one*) *motion* every day. / My *bowels act* once every day. この薬は～をうながす This medicine quickens *the action of the bowels*. / This medicine is good for *constipation*. きのうから～がない I have no *evacuation* (≒ *motion*) since yesterday.
—剤 laxative.

へんてこ〔りん〕【変梃〔りん〕】1 〚妙な〛 strange; queer; quaint; odd (「見聞きしたこともないような」という意味では strange を,「怪しげな」という意味では queer を,「古ぼけておかしな」という意味では quaint を,「正常ではなく, どちらかというと気まぐれで空想的な」という意味では odd を用いる).
¶ 彼は～な服装をしていた He was dressed in *strange* clothes. / He wore *queer* clothes. / He was *quaintly* dressed.
ずいぶん～なおたずねですね Your question sounds quite *strange* to me.
2 〚人間関係において〛 ¶ ふたりの仲が～になった(不和) They *are* now *at odds* with each other. / They *are not getting along well*. / (恋仲になった) They *are on intimate terms* now. (intimate は男女の仲について用いる).

へんてつ【変哲】 ¶ それはなんの～もない考えだ The idea is not worthy of serious consideration.

へんてん【変転】 ¶ 彼は～きわまりない人生を送った His life was full of *ups and downs*. その国は数多くの～を経てきた The nation has known many *vicissitudes* in the course of its history.

へんでん【返電】 a reply telegram. ¶ すぐに～を打った We *telegraphed on reply* immediately.

べんてん【弁天】 Saraswati; an Indian goddess of music, eloquence, and wealth; (美人) a beauty.

へんでんしょ【変電所】 a transformer substation.

へんとう【返答】 ⇒へんじ

へんどう【変動】 a change; alteration; (相場の) fluctuation. ¶ 野菜の価格は～がはげしい The prices of vegetables *fluctuate* very widely. 相場は先週来～がない The quotation *remains unchanged* since last week. この事件で内閣の顔ぶれに～をきたしそうだ The incident will possibly bring about *a change* in the cabinet (≒ *a reshuffle* of the cabinet). 社会の～に応じる meet the possible *change* in society. 西ドイツはマルクの～制を採用した Bonn *floated* mark. ～のない為替相場が切に望まれている *Steady* exchange rate is eagerly sought after.

べんとう【弁当】a lunch; a box lunch. ¶きょうは～を持っていきなさい Take *a lunch* along today. ～はいりません. 駅で～を買いますから I don't need *a box lunch*, because I'm going to buy *a box lunch* at the station. このあたりで～を開きましょう(ピクニックなどで) How about having *lunch* around here? / Let's have open-air *lunch* around here. / Let's take a rest and unpack our *lunches* here.

手── ¶彼は手～で働いてくれる He works for us *on his own*.

へんとうせん【扁桃腺】〘解剖学〙the tonsils. ¶～がはれて熱が出た I was feverish because my *tonsils* were swollen. / I was feverish because I had swollen *tonsils*.

へんにゅう【編入】(学生など) admission; (合併) incorporation. ¶彼はその大学の2年生に～された He *was admitted* into the college as a sophomore. ここは新たに市に～された This place *has been* newly *incorporated into* the city.

──試験 an examination for admission for transfer students.

ペンネーム a pen name; a nom de plume [nɔ́:mdəplú:m]; a pseudonym [sú:dənim] (「偽名」という一般的な語が pseudonym で作家の pseudonym を pen name または nom de plume(フランス語からの借用語)と言う. このほかに犯罪人などの偽名を alias, 有名人が身の上をかくすために使うものを incognito と言う).

へんねんたい【編年体】¶多くの歴史書は～で書かれている Most books on history are written *chronologically* (≒ *in chronological order*).

──史 a chronicle; annals.

へんのう【返納】return; restoration. ¶その本はもう図書館へ～した I *returned* (≒ *gave back*) the book to the library already. この本は来週の火曜日までに～しなくてはならない This book *is due* next Tuesday. この奨学金は卒業後～しなくてはならない This scholarship must *be paid back* after graduation.

へんのうゆ【片脳油】camphor oil.

へんぱ【偏頗】¶彼には～なところがない He *is* always *fair and impartial*. 人種による～な扱いは不当である *Discrimination* by race is unjustified. 教師は生徒に対して～なところがあってはならぬ Teachers should *be impartial to* his students.

ペンパル a pen pal; a pen friend. ¶私は3人の～と文通している I exchange letters with three *pen pals*.

へんぴ【辺鄙】¶～な場所 a *remote* (≒ *out-of-the-way*) place. 彼は～な村に住んでいる He lives in a village *remote from cities* (≒ *life*).

べんぴ【便秘】constipation. ¶～で悩む suffer from *constipation*. この通じ薬は～に効く This laxative is good for *constipation*.

へんぴん【返品】returned goods. ¶書店は売れない雑誌を出版元に～する Booksellers *return* the unsold magazines *to* the publishers.

ペンフレンド a pen pal; a pen friend.

へんぺい【偏平・扁平】¶ひらめは～な魚だからその名がついた A flatfish is so named because it *is flat*.

──足 a flatfoot.

べんべつ【弁別】¶きみの年齢になればもう善悪を～することができるはずだ You are old enough to *know* (≒ *tell*) good *from* bad.

べんべん【便便】¶彼は～として暮らしている He leads a lazy life. ～としてはいられない I can't waste (≒ idle away) my time. / There is not time to lose. (後者はすこしさし迫った状況で「ぐずぐずしていられない」という意味を表わす). 彼は～たるたいこ腹をしている He has a potbelly.

ぺんぺんぐさ【ぺんぺん草】a shepherd's purse.

へんぼう【変貌】transfiguration. ¶近郊農村の～は目覚ましい The villages near the city have undergone *a* remarkable *change*.

へんぽう【返報】an answer; a reply; (復讐) retaliation. ¶空軍は～として対空陣地に爆撃を加えた The air force bombed the antiaircraft position *in retaliation*. / The air force made a *retaliatory* bombing on the antiaircraft position. われわれは彼らの～を恐れない We are not afraid of their *revenge*. 私は彼が受けたひどい仕打ちに～をした I *avenged* the cruel treatment that had been given to him. これこそ彼に～するチャンスだ This is a good (≒ capital) chance to *get even with* him.

べんぽう【便法】an expedient 〔means〕. ¶これは一時の～にすぎない This is only *a* temporary *expedient*. / This will help only for a while. なにか～を講じよう Let's adopt (≒ work out) *expedient*.

へんぽん【翩翻】¶旗が1本～と風に翻っていた A flag *was flying* (≒ *was fluttering*) in the wind.

べんまく【弁膜】〘解剖学〙a valve.

心臓──症〘医学〙〔a〕heart valvular disease.

べんむかん【弁務官】a commissioner.

高等── the High Commissioner.

へんめい【変名】a false (≒ an assumed) name; a pseudonym; an alias; an incognito (犯罪人などの変名を alias, 有名人が身の上を隠すのに使うものを incognito と言う).

¶～を使う use *a false name*. ～で旅館に泊まる stay at a hotel *under a false name* (≒ *under an alias*).

べんめい【弁明】explanation. ¶彼は一身上の

～をした He *explained* (≒*excused*) *himself*. 彼のために～に努めた I did my best to *explain* his delicate situation. 彼らは私に～の機会を与えた They let me have my *say*.

べんもう【鞭毛】〘生物〙a flagellum (複 flagella; flagellums).
―虫 a flagellate.

べんらん【便覧】a handbook; a manual; (案内書) a guide.

べんり【便利】convenience. ¶学校は～な所にある Our school is *conveniently* located. 今ではこれよりもはるかに～な機械をつくることができる We can make far more *convenient* (≒*useful*) machines today. そこへ行くにはバスが～だ Taking a bus is an *easy* way to get there. どちらがご～ですか Which will *suit* you better? / Which *is* more *convenient* to (≒for) you?

べんりし【弁理士】a patent attorney (≒lawyer).

へんりん【片鱗】a glimpse; a part. ¶この詩に彼の天才の～をうかがうことができる We can *get a glimpse of* his genius for poetry from this poem.

へんれい【返礼】return. ¶スミスさん一家を招待の～に招いた We invited the Smiths *in return* for their invitation.

へんれき【遍歴】travels. ¶彼はヨーロッパ諸国を～した He *traveled through* Europe. / He *visited* various places in Europe.

べんろん【弁論】(法廷) pleading; (演説) public speaking. ¶弁護人は法廷で被告のために～する A defense council *pleads* (≒*argues*) for the defendant in court. 彼は～に長じている He *is a good* (≒*an eloquent*) *public speaker*. / He *is an orator*.
―家 an orator; a debater. ―大会 a speech (≒an oratorical) contest. ―部 a debating club (≒society). 口頭― (法廷の) oral proceedings.

ほ

ほ【歩】a step; a pace. ¶駅が近くなったので～を速めた(緩めた) As we got near the station, we quickened (slowed down) our *pace*. 彼らは成功に向かって着実に～を進めている They *are making* steady *progress toward* success.

ほ【帆】a sail; a canvas. ¶～を揚げる hoist (≒put up; spread) *a sail*. ～を下ろす lower (≒take down) *a sail*.

ほ【穂】¶稲(トウモロコシ)の～ *an ear* of a rice plant (a corn). 稲の～が出た Rice plants have come into *ear*[*s*]. やりの～が日光に輝いている The *tip* (≒*point*) of the spear is glistening in the sun. 彼はうまく話の～を継いだ He tactfully took up the *thread* of a story.

ホ〘音楽〙E. ¶～長(短)調 E major (minor). ～長調のソナタ a sonata *in E* major.

ほあん【保安】the preservation of public peace.
―官 米 a sheriff. ―要員 the maintenance personnel. ―林 a forest reserve. 海上―庁 Maritime Safety Agency.

ボア (婦人用のえり巻き) a boa; (大蛇) a boa.

ほい【補遺】a supplement; an addendum (複 addenda).

ほいく【保育】nurture. ¶子どもの～ childcare; taking care of children; (教育) children's education.
―園(所) a nursery school; 米 a day nursery. ―器 (未熟児用) an incubator.

ボイコット boycotting; a boycott. ¶主婦たちはその会社の製品の～運動を始めた Housewives launched *a boycott* of the products of the company. / Housewives began to *boycott* the firm's products.

ホイッスル a whistle. ¶～が鳴った *A whistle* was blown. / (ホイッスルが鳴っているとき) There goes the *whistle*.

ボイラー a boiler.
―係 a boiler man; an engineer in charge of a boiler.

ぼいん【母音】〘音声学〙a vowel [sound].
―字 a vowel [letter]. 半― a semivowel.

ぼいん【拇印】a thumbmark. ¶日本では書類に署名または印鑑の代わりに～を押すことがある In Japan we sometimes imprint (≒impress; seal) *a thumbmark* on a paper instead of a signature or a stamp.

ポインター (犬) a pointer.

ポイント (小数点) a [decimal] point; (鉄道の) 米 a switch; 英 points; 〘印刷〙a point; a dot; (要点) the [main] point; a gist; (試合などの得点) a point.
¶彼は第1ラウンドで2～かせいだ He gained two *points* in the first round.

ほう【方】**1** 〘方向〙a direction. ¶彼がこっちの～を見ている He is looking *this way*.
彼は反対の～に歩いていった He walked *in the* opposite *direction*. (誤って to the direction としがちである).
彼もわれわれの行く～へ行くそうだ He is going *our way*, I hear.
まっすぐ左の～へ行きなさい Go straight on *to the left*.
その町は大阪の西の～にある The town lies *to*

the west of Osaka.

彼は鳥取の～に住んでいる He lives somewhere *around* Tottori.

風はどっちの～から吹いているか From which *direction* is the wind blowing?

2 〖側〗 a side. ¶ その店は通りの右の～にある The store is on the right-hand *side* of the street.

3 〖対比〗 ¶ こっちの～があっちの箱より大きい This box is larger than that.

私の～が正しいと信じる I believe I am right. / I am sure I am in the right.

彼の～が悪い He is in the wrong.

ほう【法】**1** 〖法則〗 a law. ¶ 人はみな～の前には平等である Everybody is equal before the *law.*

だれでも～を守るべきだ Everyone should obey the *law.*

彼の行動は～にかなっている His action *is lawful.*

この際～に訴えるつもりだ I am going to appeal to the *law* on this occasion.

だれでも～を犯すと罰を受ける Anybody is punished when he has broken the *law.*

これは自然の～にかなっている This conforms to natural *law.*

イギリス── English law.

2 〖道理〗 reason. ¶ そんな～はない It *is* quite *unreasonable.*

盗みをしていいという～などはない There can be no *reason* for theft to be right.

3 〖教義〗 a doctrine. ¶ 人を見て～を説けという It is said that we should suit our speech to the audience.

～を説く preach *the truth.*

ほう【報】a news; a report. ¶ 事故の～に接して急いで帰郷した I hurried to my hometown at the *news* of the accident.

ほう'（驚き・感嘆など） oh; well; why. ¶ ～, これはおいしい *Why,* this is delicious.

ぼう【暴】violence; (不法) outrage. ¶ ～に報いるに～をもってす meet *violence* with *violence*; an eye for an eye and a tooth for a tooth.

ぼう【棒】(柱) a pole; (さお) a rod; (つえ) a stick; (こん棒) a club; a cudgel; (横棒) a bar; (線) a line; a dash.

¶ 一日足を～にして歩いた I walked all day till my legs gave way. あなたのために一生を～に振りたくはない I don't want to *waste* (≒ *ruin; sacrifice*) the best years of my life. 100万円を～に振る気か Are you trying to *spend* 1,000,000 yen *for nothing?*

ぼう-【某-】one; a certain. ¶ ～氏 Mr. *So-and-so*; Mr. —. ～月～日 (*on*) *a certain* date. 佐藤～ *a* (≒ *one*) Mr. Sato. (日本語と同様, 英語でもあまりていねいな感じを与えないから, 当人の聞こえるところでは言わないほうがよい).

ほうあん【法案】a bill; a measure. ¶ ～を議会に提出する introduce *a bill* in the Diet; submit *a bill* to the Diet. ～を可決(否決)する pass (reject) *a bill.* その～は衆議院を通過した The *bill* passed the House of Representatives.

ぼうあんき【棒暗記】¶ 何事もただ～ではだめだ Don't *learn* anything *by rote.* (*rote* はなにかを機械的にすることを言う. したがって *learn by rote* は意味もわからずに暗記することを言う.これに対して,一般的に「暗記する」という表現は *memorize, learn by heart* が用いられる).

ほうい【方位】the point of the compass; a bearing. ¶ 磁石で～を確かめる make sure the *direction* with the compass. 船の～を知る get (≒ take) *one's bearings.* 英詩の新～ new *bearings* in English poetry.

ほうい【包囲】siege; encirclement. ¶ 敵を～する *close in upon* (≒ *lay siege to*) the enemy. 敵の～を突破した We broke through the *besieging* enemy forces. われわれは～されている We *are penned.* / We *are besieged.*

ほうい【法衣】a clerical (≒ canonical) robe; (複数形で) clericals.

ぼうい【暴威】tyranny; great violence. ¶ 日本では毎年台風が～をふるう Typhoons *rage* in Japan every year. 流感が全国に～をふるっている The flu *is rampant* (≒ *is raging*) across the country.

ほういがく【法医学】legal (≒ forensic) medicine.

ほういつ【放逸】¶ ～な生活を送る lead a *licentious* (≒ *dissolute; riotous*) life.

ぼういん【暴飲】excessive drinking.

──暴食 ¶ ～暴食を慎め Don't *drink* or *eat too much.* / You should not *overdrink* or *overeat yourself.* (口語では yourself を省くのがふつう).

ほうえ【法会】〘仏教〙 a Buddhist memorial service. ¶ 亡父の追悼～を行なった We observed *a memorial service* for our late father.

ぼうえい【防衛】defense. ¶ 自衛隊は国土を～することができるか Are the Self Defense Forces strong enough to *defend* our land? 彼は選手権の～に成功した He succeeded in *defending* his title.

──海域 a sea defense zone. ──官 a defense officer. ──強化 a defense build-up. ──大学 the Defense Academy. ──庁 the Defense Agency.

ぼうえき【防疫】〘医学〙 the prevention of epidemics.

──官 a health officer.

ぼうえき【貿易】trade; commerce. ¶ 日本の中国～は近ごろ著しく伸びた Japan's *trade with* China has remarkably increased lately. ～する trade (*with*).

──外収支 invisible trade. ──額 the amount of trade. ──業界 trading circles. ──港 a trade port. ──自由化 liberalization of trade. ──商 a foreign trader; (輸出商) an exporter; (輸入商) an importer. ──商社 a trading firm (≒ company). ──尻 the balance of trade. ──手形 a trade bill. ──風 the trade wind. 外国── foreign trade. 自由── free trade; laissez-faire (フランス語から).

ほ

中継― transit trade. 保護― protective trade. 保護―主義 protectionism. 保護―主義者 a protectionist.

ほうえつ【法悦】ecstasy ; rapture ; transport. ¶ 彼はしばし～に浸った He was immersed in *ecstasy* for a while.

ぼうえんきょう【望遠鏡】a telescope ; (双眼鏡) field glasses ; binoculars. ¶ ～で月を見る look at the moon through *a telescope*.
天体(反射; 電波)― an astronomical (a reflecting ; a radio) telescope.

ぼうえんレンズ【望遠レンズ】a telephoto lens. ¶ ～で遠くの物を撮影する telephotograph a distant object.

ほうおう【法王】a pope ; (ローマ法王) the Pope ; the 〔Supreme〕 Pontiff.
―庁 the Vatican.

ほうおん【報恩】gratitude. ¶ 彼は主人への～のために尽くした He did what he could in order to *return* his master's *kindness*.

ぼうおん【忘恩】ingratitude. ¶ ～の徒 an ungrateful person ; an ingrate. ～の行為 an act of *ingratitude*.

ぼうおん【防音】¶ この部屋は～になっている This room *is soundproof*.
―室 a soundproof room. ―装置 soundproofing ; a soundproof equipment ; (銃の発砲音などを消す消音装置) a silencer ; a sound arrester.

ほうか【邦貨】Japanese currency (≒ money) ; (貨物) Japanese goods. ¶ 空港の両替所でドルを～に換えた I exchanged dollar into *yen* (≒ *Japanese money*) at the exchange office in the airport.

ほうか【放火】arson (法律用語) ; (行為) incendiarism ; (火) an incendiary fire. ¶ その火事は～とわかった The fire has been caused by *arson*. その男は保険金をとるために自分の家に～した The man *set fire to* his own house (≒ *set* his own house *on fire*) in order to collect insurance.
―罪〔法律〕arson. ―犯人 an incendiary.

ほうか【法科】a law department ; a law school (この school は大学の学部のこと).
¶ ～の学生 a *law* student. 彼は～出身だ He is a graduate of *the law department*.

ほうか【砲火】gunfire. ¶ ～を浴びる be under fire. ～を交える exchange fire.

ほうが【邦画】(映画) a Japanese film (≒ movie).

ほうが【萌芽】a sprout ; a bud. ¶ そのころから彼の才能の～が見えた His talent was germinating about that time.

ぼうか【防火】fire prevention. ¶ この建物には～の設備がある This building is safe from fire.
―訓練 a fire drill. ―週間 Fire Prevention Week. ―線 a fire-arresting line. ―装置 fire protection. ―壁 a fireproof shutter. ―幕 (劇場の) safety curtain.

ぼうが【忘我】¶ 彼は～の境地にある He *is in ecstasies*. (歓喜しているなら in an ecstasy of delight と言う).

ほうかい【崩壊】collapse. ¶ 堤防が～した The embankment *has broken*. 内閣が～した The cabinet *fell down*. 壁が～した The wall *gave way*.

ほうがい【法外】¶ ～な要求 an *excessive* demand. ～な値段 an *exorbitant* price.

ぼうがい【妨害】obstruction. ¶ 私の勉強の～にならないよう気をつけてほしい I want you never to *interfere with* my studies. 安眠を～するな Never *disturb* my sleep. 暴徒が営業を～した The mob *has interrupted* the conduct of business. 公務執行～で逮捕する arrest (*a person*) because of *interference* with a government official in the performance of his duties.
―物 an obstacle.

ぼうがい【望外】¶ ～の成功だった It was an *unlooked-for* success. / It was an *unexpected* windfall.

ほうかいせき【方解石】〔鉱物〕calcite.

ほうがく【方角】a direction ; a bearing.
¶ ～を見失う lose *one's bearings*. ～をよくまちがえることがある It often happens that I lose my sense of *directions*. お宅はどっちの～ですか Which *way* is your house? ～がわからない I cannot find my *way*.

ほうがく【邦楽】Japanese music.

ほうがく【法学】law ; (法理学) jurisprudence.
―士 a bachelor of laws (B. LL. または LL. B. と略す). ―者 a jurist. ―博士 a doctor of laws (LL. D. と略す). ―部 a law department (≒ school).

ほうかご【放課後】after school. ¶ ～1時間ばかりテニスをした *After school* 〔*was over*〕, we played tennis 〔together〕 for about an hour.

ほうかつ【包括】inclusion ; comprehension.
¶ この問題はあらゆる事項を～している The problem *embraces* every item. その提案に対して～的に意見を述べた I gave a *general* opinion of that proposal. ～的な記述 a *comprehensive* description.

ほうがん【包含】inclusion ; implication.
¶ この政策は疑問点を～している This policy *contains* some doubts. このひと言にはあらゆる意味が～されている This single remark *implies* a variety of meaning.

ほうがん【砲丸】a shot.
―投げ shot-putting. ¶ ～投げの選手 a shot-putter.

ぼうかん【防寒】protection against cold.
―具 ¶ 私は～具に身を固めた I protected myself *against cold*. ―服 clothes for cold weather.

ぼうかん【傍観】looking on. ¶ 彼はなにかにつけて～的態度をとる He takes an *indifferent* attitude in everything. ただ～するだけでじっと立っていた I merely *looked on* and did nothing.
―者 a looker-on (複 lookers-on).

ぼうかん【暴漢】a rowdy ; a ruffian. ¶ 夜道で～に襲われた I was assaulted by *a ruffian*

ほ

while walking on the road during the night.

ほうがんし【方眼紙】section paper.

ほうき【箒・帚】a broom. ¶ 庭を～で掃く sweep a garden with *a broom.* ああいうタイプの人間は～で掃くほどいる Persons of such a type are to be found by the dozen.

—草〖植物〗a broom cypress. —星〖天文学〗a comet.

ほうき【芳紀】¶ 彼女は～まさに17歳 She is '*sweet seventeen.*'

ほうき【放棄】abandonment. ¶ 計画を～する *give up* a plan. 彼らは職場を～した They *walked off* the job. 日本は戦争を～することを誓った The Japanese have sworn to *renounce* war.

ほうき【法規】the law. ¶ ～を無視する ignore *the rule.* 犯人を～に照らして処罰する punish criminals according to *the law.* ～上の手続きを済ませた He went through the *legal formalities.*

ほうき【蜂起】uprising. ¶ ～する rise in revolt. 暴徒の～があった There was *an uprising* of mobs.

ぼうぎ【謀議】〔a〕conference;〔a〕conspiracy. ¶ ～をこらす conspire together.

共同— joint conspiracy.

ぼうきゃく【忘却】oblivion.

ぼうぎゃく【暴虐】tyranny; atrocity. ¶ ネロは～の限りを尽くした Nero committed all sorts of *atrocities.*

ほうきゅう【俸給】a salary; pay. ¶ 彼は月10万円の～をとっている He draws (≒ gets) *a salary* of 100,000 yen a month. ～があがった I had my *salary* raised. / I got a raise in my *salary.* きみの～をあげよう Your *salary* shall be raised. ～で生活する live on *one's salary.* 彼は～が高い(安い) He is *high-salaried* (≒ *low-salaried*).

—生活者 a salaried man. —日 a payday (文の中ではしばしば無冠詞). —袋 a pay envelope.

ほうぎょ【崩御】demise.

ぼうきょ【暴挙】violence. ¶ ～に出る resort to *violence.* 彼のそのような～は戒められるべきだ He is to be warned against such *an outrage.*

ぼうぎょ【防御】defense. ¶ ～する defend. ～のない攻撃はだめだ Offense without *defense* is of no use. ～型のボクサー a *defensive* fighter.

—工事 defensive works. —戦 a defensive war.

ぼうきょう【望郷】homesickness. ¶ ～の念にかられた I felt *homesick.*

ぼうぐい【棒杭】a stake. ¶ ～を打ち込む drive in *a stake.*

ぼうくう【防空】air defence.

—演習 anti-air-raid drills. —壕 an air-raid shelter. —施設 air defenses.

ぼうぐみ【棒組】〖印刷〗a galley proof. ¶ ～にする set up in *a galley.*

ぼうグラフ【棒グラフ】a bar chart.

ぼうくん【暴君】a tyrant. ¶ 家庭では彼は～だ He *is despotic* at home. ～ネロ Nero, *the tyrant.*

ほうけい【方形】a square. ¶ ～の square.

ぼうけい【傍系】¶ ～の親族 a *collateral* relative. この研究所は～の出身者が多い In this research institute a lot of *collateral* members are engaged.

—会社 a subsidiary company.

ぼうけい【亡兄】*one's* dead brother.

ほうげき【砲撃】bombardment. ¶ 味方の陣地は～を受けた Our position *was bombarded* by the enemy.

ほうけん【封建】¶ 彼は～的だ He *is* too *old-fashioned.*

—国家 a feudal state. —思想 feudal ideas. —時代 the feudal age. —社会 a feudal society. —制度 feudalism; the feudal system.

ほうげん【方言】a dialect.

—地図 a dialect atlas. 階級— a class dialect. 地域— a local dialect.

ほうげん【放言】a random remark. ¶ 大臣の～は世間を騒がせた The *careless remarks* made by the minister brought about no small response among the people.

ぼうけん【冒険】adventure. ¶ 彼は～好きだ He is an *adventurous* man. それはすこしも～ではない(危険でない) There is no *risk* in it. それはたいへんな～だ(成功が不確実な時など) I am afraid such a thing is too *hazardous.* ある程度の～はむしろ必要だ(思いきったことをする時など) You must run a certain amount of *risk.*

—心 an adventurous spirit.

ぼうげん【暴言】violent language. ¶ ～を吐く use *violent language.* 彼の～はとがめられるべきだ His *abusive use of language* is to be criticized.

ほうこ【宝庫】a treasure house. ¶ この百科事典は知識の～だ This encyclopedia is *a treasure house* of knowledge.

ほうこう【方向】a direction. ¶ この～に行くとどこに出ますか Where do we get if we go *this way?* ここから東京の～に行きたいのですが,どっちへ行ったらいいですか I want to go *in the direction of* Tokyo. Which way should I go? 声のする～を見た I looked *in the direction of* the voice. 富士山はどっちの～に見えますか In what *direction* is Mt. Fuji to be seen? ～を誤って目的地に着けなかった As I went the wrong *way,* I could not get to my destination.

—感覚 a sense of direction. —舵(だ) a rudder. —探知機 a radar. —転換 ¶ ここで～転換が必要だ We should change our *course* here. —音痴 ¶ 彼の～音痴は有名だ He is well-known for *having no sense of direction.*

ほうこう【放校】expulsion from school. ¶ 彼は品行が悪いので～になった He *was expelled from school* because of his bad behavior.

ほうこう【芳香】fragrance. ¶ クチナシが～を放っている The gardenias are giving out *fra-*

grance. / The gardenias *smell sweet.*
―剤 an aromatic.

ほうこう【奉公】service. ¶彼は娘を～に出した He sent out his daughter into *domestic service.*
―先 *one's* employer's house. ―人 an employee.

ほうこう【彷徨】roaming 〔about〕. ¶彼はあちこちを～している He *is wandering* up and down. いなかを～するのは心地よいものだ It is comfortable to *roam about* the country.

ほうこう【咆哮】roar. ¶～する roar.

ほうごう【縫合】stitch. ¶～する stitch. 切り口を～する *stitch* the cut. 傷口を～する *suture* the wound.

ぼうこう【暴行】violence. ¶婦女に～を加える attack (≒rape) a woman. 酔っぱらって～をはたらくとは何事か What a shame it is that you should commit *outrage* after getting drunk!

ぼうこう【膀胱】〘解剖学〙the bladder.
―炎〘医学〙inflammation of the bladder.
―結石〘医学〙a bladder stone.

ほうこく【報国】¶～の patriotic. ～精神にあふれた人 a man full of *patriotism*; a patriotic man.

ほうこく【報告】a report. ¶学長は事件の経過を教員に～した The president *reported* the course of the events to the faculty. 問題の要点を～せよ Give *a report* of the gist of the problem.
―者 a reporter. ―書 a 〔written〕 report. 中間― an interim report. 年次― an annual report. 最終― the final report.

ぼうこく【亡国】¶～の民 a *ruined* (≒ *homeless*) people.

ぼうこん【亡魂】a spirit; a ghost. ¶～をとむらう mourn for *the spirit* of the deceased person. ～この世にとどまる *A departed soul* lingers in this world.

ぼうさい【防災】protection against calamities. ¶～に手抜かりがあった There was a slip in the methods of *preventing disasters.*
―計画 a plan for preventing disasters. ―対策 a countermeasure for preventing disasters.

ほうさく【方策】a plan; a policy; a scheme. ¶盛んに生活を立て直す～をめぐらしている He *is thinking out* a plan to start his life anew. もう～が尽きた Now we *are at our wits' end.* 不景気を乗り切るための万全の～を立てよう Let us adopt *a* prudential *policy* to tide over the current business depression.

ほうさく【豊作】a good harvest; a bumper crops; a bumper harvest. ¶ことしは米が～だった We have had *a rich crop* of rice this year. ブドウの～の年 a vintage year.

ぼうさつ【忙殺】¶彼は旅行の準備に～されている He *is kept busy* preparing for the trip. 彼女は家事に～されている She *is busying herself about* the house. / She *is extremely busy with* her housework.

ぼうさつ【謀殺】〔willful〕 murder. ¶～する murder (*a person*).

ぼうさりん【防砂林】a forest for preventing sand shifting.

ほうさん【硼酸】〘化学〙boric acid.

ほうさん【放散】(光熱の) radiation; (蒸発) evaporation; (拡散) diffusion. ¶～する radiate; evaporate.

ほうし【奉仕】service. ¶社会に～する *serve* the community.
―事業 public welfare service. ―品 a bargain. 社会― social service.

ほうし【芳志】kindness; kind thought; considerateness. ¶御～に感謝いたします Many thanks for *your kindness.* 御～かたじけなく存じます Allow me to express my gratitude for *your good wishes.* (文語体).

ほうし【法師】a Buddhist priest.

ほうし【放恣】licence. ¶～な licentious. ～な生活を送る live a *licentious* life.

ほうし【胞子】〘植物〙a spore.
―植物 sporophyte. ―生殖 spore reproduction.

ほうじ【法事】a Buddhist 〔memorial〕 service. ¶～を営む hold *a Buddhist service.* 亡父の～を営んだ I held *a memorial service* for my dead father.

ぼうし【防止】prevention. ¶伝染病の蔓延(まんえん)を～する *prevent* the spread of the infectious disease.

ぼうし【帽子】(縁つき) a hat; (ひさしつき) a cap; (婦人用) a bonnet. ¶～をかぶる put on *one's hat.* ～をとる take off *a hat.* 彼は～をかぶっている He has *a hat* on. / He wears *a hat.* (put on のあとでは one's, wear のあとでは不定冠詞を付けて a hat のようにすることが多い). 彼女は～をかぶっていない She *is bareheaded.* だれかが～を振っている Someone is waving his *hat.*
―かけ a hatrack. ―屋 (人) a hatter; (店) a hat shop; (女性の帽子などの) a milliner.

ほうしき【方式】a form. ¶この証書の～は正しい This deed is drawn up in due *form.* この～で文書を作ってほしい I want you to make the document according to this *form.* 会議は一定の～に従って行なわれた The conference was given in *a* prescribed *form.*

ほうじちゃ【ほうじ茶】fired (≒roasted) tea.

ぼうしつざい【防湿剤】a desiccant; a desiccating agent.

ほうしゃ【硼砂】〘化学〙borax.

ほうしゃ【放射】radiation. ¶六つの道路が～状に走っている Six streets *radiate* from here. この物体は熱を四方に～している This material *is radiating* heat on all sides.

ぼうじゃくぶじん【傍若無人】impudence; audacity; shamelessness. ¶彼は～のふるまいをしている He is behaving *outrageously.* なんという～な男だ What an *insolent* (≒ *impudent; audacious*) fellow he is!

ほうしゃせい【放射性】―元素 a radioactive element. ―物質 the radioactive substance.

ほうしゃせん【放射線】radiant rays.

ほうしゃのう【放射能】radioactivity. ¶ ～のちり *radioactive* dust. あの人たちは～にさらされた They were exposed to *radioactivity*. 彼は～によるやけどを負った He was burned because of *radioactivity*.
—汚染 radioactive contamination.

ほうしゅ【砲手】an artillery man.

ぼうじゅ【傍受】interception. ¶ 無線を～する *intercept* a radio message. ペキンのラジオ放送を～した We *picked up* Radio Peking.

ほうしゅう【報酬】a reward. ¶ 彼は～を受けていない He *is* not *paid*. 彼は相当の～を受けている He *is* well *paid*. 彼は～をもらって働いている He works *for a consideration*. ～なしでもかまわない I don't mind working *for nothing*. 仕事に対してよい～を受けた I *was* well *rewarded* for my work.
無— ¶ 彼は無～でそのやっかいな仕事を買って出た He offered to do such a troublesome task *without pay*.

ぼうしゅうざい【防臭剤】a deodorant.

ぼうしゅく【防縮】¶ ～加工のしてある毛布 a *shrinkproof* blanket. ワイシャツに～加工をする *shrinkproof* a shirt.

ほうしゅつ【放出】[a] release. ¶ 非常食糧が～された Emergency food supplies *were released*.

ほうじゅつ【砲術】gunnery.
—長 a gunnery lieutenant. —練習艦 a gunnery ship.

ほうじゅん【芳醇】mellowness. ¶ ～な酒 *mellow* wine.

ほうしょ【奉書】thick Japanese paper.

ほうじょ【幇助】¶ 友人の犯罪の～をした He *abetted* his friend in a crime.
—者(犯罪の) an abetter.

ぼうしょ【某所】a certain place.

ほうしょう【法相】(法務大臣) the Minister of Justice.

ほうしょう【報奨】a bonus. ¶ 特別～金を出して農家に出荷を促す encourage farmers to market their products by paying them special *bonuses* (≒ *bounties*).

ほうしょう【報償】compensation; a consideration; remuneration. ¶ かけた損害についてその会社に～金を支払う *compensate* the firm for its damage.

ほうしょう【褒章】藍綬(らんじゅ)— a Blue Ribbon. 紫綬— a Purple Ribbon.

ほうしょう【褒賞】a prize; a reward. ¶ ～を与える award (≒ bestow) *a prize*. ～を受ける win (≒ be awarded) *a prize* (win first prize という語法にも注意).

ほうじょう【豊饒】fertility; fruitfulness. ¶ ～な土地 *fertile* (≒ *rich*; *productive*) land.

ほうじょう【褒状】a certificate of merit.

ぼうしょう【傍証】¶ その件については明確な～がある There is conclusive *circumstantial evidence* about it.

ぼうじょう【棒状】¶ ～の cylindric[al]. ～のワックス *a stick of* wax.

ほうしょく【奉職】¶ 本校に～して10年になる I *have been teaching* at this school for ten years. 彼は教師として～した He *had a job* as a teacher. / He *got a position* as a teacher.

ぼうしょく【暴食】gluttony. ¶ ～する overeat [*oneself*]; eat too much.
—家 a glutton; a heavy eater.

ほう・じる【奉じる】(従う) obey; follow; (信じる) believe in; embrace; profess. ¶ …の命を～じて *in obedience to* (≒ *in pursuance of*) *a person's* orders. 仏教を～じる *embrace* (≒ *believe in*) Buddhism. 職を～じる *hold* a post; *hold* an appointment; serve.

ほう・じる【焙じる】heat; roast. ¶ 茶を～じる *heat* tea leaves.

ほうじる【報じる】⇒ ほうずる

ほうしん【方針】a policy; lines. ¶ 国家の～ *a* national *policy*. ～を定める decide on *a policy* (≒ *a course of action*). ～を誤る take *a* wrong *policy*. 一定の～に従って進む proceed on *a* definite *line*. どういう～にしますか What *lines* are you going to take?

ほうしん【放心】absent-mindedness. ¶ ～状態で absent-mindedly; with an air of *abstraction*. 被害者の家族は～状態でその場に立ちつくした The family of the victim stood *aghast* on the spot (≒ stood there with *an air of abstraction*).

ほうしん【砲身】a gun barrel.

ほうじん【邦人】a Japanese. ¶ 在外～ *Japanese nationals* abroad. 在留～ *Japanese* residents.

ほうじん【法人】a juridical (≒ legal) person; a corporation; a corporate body. ¶ 会社を～組織にする *incorporate* a firm.
—税 the corporation tax. 公共— a public corporation. 財団— a juridical foundation. 社団— a corporation.

ぼうず【坊主】(僧) a Buddhist priest; a monk; a bonze; (子どもに対する呼びかけ) my boy. ¶ ～になる(僧になる) become *a priest*; enter the priesthood; (頭をそる) have *one's* head shaved; (短く刈り込む) have *one's* hair clipped close.
—頭 a shaven head; a close-cropped head.

ほうすい【放水】drainage. ¶ ～する drain water off; (水を浴びせる) pour water (*on* a fire).
—管 a drainpipe. —路 a drain; a flood control channel.

ぼうすい【防水】waterproof. ¶ ～のコート a *waterproof* coat. 布に～する *make* cloth *watertight* (≒ *waterproof*); *waterproof* cloth.
—加工 waterproof. ¶ ～加工する *waterproof* (cloth). —剤 waterproof stuff. —布 waterproof cloth.

ほう・ずる【報ずる】report; (放送で) broadcast. ¶ そのニュースはすぐにテレビで～じられた The news *was televised* (≒ *was reported* on television) at once. 新聞の～じるところによればフランスの核実験は今月末まで延期されたということである *According to* the newspaper, (≒ The newspaper *says* that) the nuclear test by the French has been put off until the end of this month. その男が出火を～じたのはそれから10分後であった It was ten minutes later that the man *gave* (≒ *raised*) *an alarm of* fire.

ほうすん【方寸】(心) *one's* mind. ¶ 万事は彼の～にある Everything depends upon his *decision* (≒ *discretion*).

ほうせい【法制】 laws; (立法) legislation. 内閣―局 the Cabinet Legislation Bureau.

ほうせい【砲声】 the sound of firing; the roaring (≒ boom) of a gun; the report of a gun. ¶ ～がとどろく The guns *roar*.

ぼうせい【暴政】 tyranny.

ほうせき【宝石】 a gem; a jewel; (総称) jewelry (gem はカットされ磨かれたものでそれを貴金属にはめ込むと jewel と呼ばれる).
¶ ～を身につける wear *jewelry*; put on *jewels*. 王冠は～がちりばめてある The crown is bedecked with *jewels*.
―商 a jeweler. ―類 jewelry.

ぼうせき【紡績】 spinning.
―会社 a cotton spinning company. ―機械 a spinning machine. ―業 the spinning industry. ―業者 a cotton spinner. ―工 a cotton-mill hand. ―工場 a cotton mill.

ぼうせつりん【防雪林】 a snow forest (≒ wood).

ぼうせん【防戦】 a defensive battle (≒ struggle). ¶ ～する defend; fight in defense.

ぼうせん【傍線】 a side line. ¶ 重要な箇所に～を引く draw *a side line* along an important passage.

ぼうぜん【呆然】 blank surprise. ¶ ～と in dumb (≒ blank) surprise. われわれはその知らせを聞いて～として物が言えなかった We *were struck dumb with surprise* (≒ *were left speechless*) to hear the news.

ぼうぜん【茫然】 abstraction. ¶ ～と vacantly; blankly; absent-mindedly. 遺族の人たちは～として事故の現場に立ち尽くした The bereaved family stood *aghast* on the spot of the accident. ～自失する be completely at a loss what to do; be at *one's* wit's end.

ほうせんか【鳳仙花】〖植物〗 a balsam; a touch-me-not.

ほうそう【包装】 packing. ¶ ～する pack; wrap 〔up〕. ～がよい *be* properly *packed*.
―紙 packing (≒ wrapping) paper. ―料 packing charge. ―物 a package.

ほうそう【放送】 broadcasting; (個々の) a broadcast; (ラジオの) radiobroadcast; radiocast; (テレビの) a television broadcast; a telecast.
¶ ～する broadcast; send (≒ put) (news) on the air; (人が主語) speak over (≒ through) the radio (≒ 圏 wireless). テレビで～する telecast; televise; (人が主語) go on television. ～を聴く (ラジオ) listen to a program over the *radio*. ～を見る (テレビ) watch the TV program. その出来事はすぐにテレビで～された The incident *was* immediately *televised*.
―記者 a radio (≒ TV) newsman. ―局 a radio (≒ broadcasting) station. ―時間 (局の) broadcasting hours; air time; (ある番組の) the time for a program. ―室 a radio studio. ―番組 a radio (≒ TV) program. ―網 radio (≒ TV) network. 海外― overseas radio service. 試験― a test broadcast. 全国― a nation-wide broadcast. 中継― relay broadcasting; hook-up. ¶ 試合のもようは全国に中継～される The game is to *be broadcast* over a nation-wide *hook-up*. ニュース― a newscast. ¶ 7時のニュース～でそれを聞いた I heard about it on the seven o'clock *newscast*.

ほうそう【疱瘡】〖医学〗 smallpox; (種痘) vaccination. ¶ ～がついた The *vaccination* has taken in me.

ぼうそう【暴走】(車) reckless driving. ¶ 列車が～した A train *ran away*. 車を～させた He *drove* a car *recklessly*.
―者 a reckless driver.

ほうそうかい【法曹界】 legal circles; the bench and bar; the Bar. ¶ ～に入る (弁護士になる) go to the *bar*.

ほうそく【法則】 a law; a rule. ¶ 科学者は～を発見しそれを応用しようと努める Scientists try to discover and apply the *law*. 適者生存はさけられぬ自然の～だ The survival of the fittest is the inevitable *law* of nature.

ほうたい【包帯】 bandage; dressing. ¶ 腕に～する *bandage* an arm. 傷に～する *dress* (≒ *bind up*) a wound. 彼は頭に～をしている He *has* his head *bandaged*. / He wears *a bandage* around his head.

ほうだい【砲台】 a battery.

-ほうだい【-放題】 ¶ したい～のことができると思ったら大まちがいだ It is a serious mistake to think that you can *do everything as you please* (≒ *like*). 若いころはわがままのしたい～だった When young, I used to *have my own way*. 彼は言いたい～のことを言う He speaks *without reserve*. 食べ～食べた We ate *to our hearts' content*. 髪を伸ばし～にする若者が多い Many young people nowadays *leave their hair uncut* (≒ *are long-locked*).

ぼうだい【膨大】 bulk. ¶ ～な bulky; big; huge. ～な予算 a *huge* budget. ～な金額 an *enormous* amount (≒ a *vast* sum) of money. この本には～な知識が集積されている There is a *vast* accumulation of knowledge in this book.

ぼうたかとび【棒高跳び】 pole jump〔ing〕; pole vault.

ぼうだち【棒立ち】 ¶ ～になる stand upright (≒ erect). みんなはその恐ろしい光景を見て～となった They *stood aghast at* the dreadful sight.

ほうたん【放胆】 ¶ ～な bold; daring.

ほうだん【放談】 a random (≒ tall) talk; random remarks (複数形が多い). ¶ ～する have *a random talk*.

ほ

ほうだん【砲弾】a shell; a cannonball. ¶敵に～を浴びせる rain *shells* upon the enemy. ～が雨と降った *Cannonballs* were showered on us. / We were showered with *cannonballs*.

ぼうだん【防弾】―ガラス bulletproof glass. ―チョッキ a bulletproof jacket.

ほうち【放置】¶路上に車を～する *leave* a car on the street. 事態は～できない The situation cannot *be left as it is*.

ほうちこく【法治国】a constitutional state; a law-governed country.

ぼうちゅう【忙中】¶～閑あり A busy man will snatch a moment of leisure.

ぼうちゅう【傍注】marginal notes.

ぼうちゅうざい【防虫剤】an insect repellent.

ほうちょう【包丁・庖丁】a kitchen knife.

ぼうちょう【傍聴】attendance (at a lecture, etc.). ¶国会を～する *attend* a session of the Diet. 裁判を～する *attend* a trial. 会議は～が許されていない(いる) The conference is closed (is open) to the public.
―券 an admission ticket. ―者 a hearer; (集合的に) an audience. ―席 the visitors' gallery. ―無料(掲示) Admission free. ―料 an admission fee.

ぼうちょう【膨張・膨脹】(通貨などの) inflation; expansion; swelling. ¶通貨の～ *inflation* of currency. 人口の～ *increase* (≒ *growth*) of population. 都市の～ *growth* of a city. 水は凍ると～する Water *expands* as it freezes. 来年度の予算は～する見込みである The budget plan for next year is to *be expansive*. 世界の人口は年ごとに～を続けている The population of the world goes on *increasing* year by year.
―係数 the rate of expansion.

ほうっており・く【放って置く】¶あんな人は～きなさい *Leave* such a man *alone*. ぼくのことは～いてくれ *Leave* (≒ *Let*) me *alone*. / *Let* me *be alone*. 仕事をやりかけで～いてはいけない You should not *leave* your work *unfinished*. こんなわがままを言う子を～けない I can't *allow* such disobedience *to go uncorrected*. 泣く子を～けない I can't *leave* a crying baby *unattended*.

ぼうっと **1**〖不明瞭に〗¶ガラス越しに彼の姿が～見えた He was seen *faintly* through the glass.
その島は沖合はるかに～かすんで見える The island is seen *dimly* (≒ *faintly*) far off the coast. 黒い影が～先に見えた The dark outline *loomed* ahead.
2〖頭・記憶などが〗¶きょうは頭がなんとなく～している I *feel* somehow *dazed* today.
彼は～空の一点を見詰めていた He was *blankly* looking at a spot in the sky.
子どものころの記憶は～している I have only *wandering* (≒ *uncertain*; *unreliable*) memories of my childhood.
3〖火が〗¶紙くずが～燃えだした Waste paper *blazed up*.
枯れ草は～燃え上がった The dry grass *flamed up* (≒ *blazed up*).

ぽうっと ¶～体にぬくもりを感じた I *felt a warm glow* all over. 彼女は～顔を赤らめた Her face *went red*. 彼女は私を見て～顔を赤らめた She noticed me and *blushed*. 彼女は恥ずかしくて～ほおを染めた She felt so ashamed that her cheeks gradually *became flushed*. 彼は彼女に～なっている He *is fascinated by* her. 彼はその若い娘に～なった He *was charmed by* the young girl.

ほうてい【法定】―価格 the legal price. ―金利 the legal rate. ―準備金 a legal reserve. ―選挙費用 legal campaign expenditure. ―相続人 an heir-at-law (複 heirs-at-law). ―推定相続人 an heir apparent (複 heirs apparent). ―伝染病 a legal infectious disease.

ほうてい【法廷】〔a〕court; a court of law. ¶～に出る appear in *court* (at court は「宮中で」, in court は「法廷で」). ～で争う go to law with (*a person*) (go to court は拝謁のため宮中に行くこと). ～に持ち出す bring an affair into *court*. その件は今も～で争われている The case is still pending in *court*.
―秩序維持法 the Law for Maintenance of Court Order. ―闘争 struggle at the court. ―侮辱 contempt of court.

ほうていしき【方程式】〖数学〗an equation. ¶～を立てる set up *an equation*. ～を解く solve *an equation*.
一次(二次; 三次)― a simple (quadratic; cubic) equation. 化学― a chemical equation. 微分― a differential equation. 連立― simultaneous equations.

ほうてき【法的】legal. ¶それには～な根拠はなにもない It has no *legal* grounds. 彼は事故に対する補償を要求する～な権利がある He has a *legal* right to demand a compensation for the accident. それは～に認められている It is *legally* recognized.

ほうてん【宝典】a thesaurus (複 thesauruses; thesauri); a treasury; a handbook.

ほうてん【法典】a code of laws; a statute; 〖宗教〗a canon.

ほうでん【放電】〖物理〗electric discharge. ¶～する discharge electricity.
空中(真空)― atmospheric (vacuum) discharge.

ほうと【方途】a step; a measure. ¶これ以上改善の～がない There is no *measure* to be taken for further improvement. 必要な～を講ずる take the necessary *measures*. 予防の～を論議する discuss preventive *measures*.

ぼうと【暴徒】a mob; rioters. ¶～の一群 a mob of *rioters*. ～を鎮圧する put down *rioters*.

ほうとう【宝刀】a treasured sword. ¶伝家の～ a heirloom *sword*. 伝家の～を抜く(最後の手段をとる) play *one's* trump card.

ほうとう【放蕩】dissipation; prodigality. ¶彼は～三昧(ざんまい)のあげく親の遺産を使い果たした

He came to the end of his inheritance through his *prodigality*. 彼は～にふけっている He has abandoned himself to *dissipation*.

—息子 a prodigal (≒ an extravagant) son.

ほうとう【砲塔】a turret.

ほうどう【報道】news; a report; information. ¶ 最新の～ hot *news*; the latest *news*. 恐ろしい(満足すべき; 有望な)～ a horrible (satisfactory; hopeful) *news*. ～を抑える control *news*. ～を差し止める suppress *news*. ～を曲げる distort (≒ twist) *news*. 片寄った～をする give *a* biased *report* (*of*). 新聞は毎日の出来事を～する The newspaper *reports* (≒ *informs us of*) daily events. その～は誤りであることがわかった The *report* turned out false.

—員 a reporter. (新聞の)—停止 a newspaper blackout. —機関 the press; an information medium. —写真 a news photo.

ぼうとう【冒頭】the beginning; the start; the outset. ¶ ～の陳述 the *opening* statement. 20世紀の～から since the *opening* (≒ *beginning*) of the 20th century. 議事の～に at *the outset* of the proceedings. ～から from [at] *the outset*; from *the start*.

ぼうとう【暴投】〖野球〗a wild pitch. ¶ ～する pitch (≒ throw) wild.

ぼうとう【暴騰】an abnormal rise; a jump. ¶ 物価が～する Prices *are rising suddenly*. / Prices *take a jump*. 株価がここしばらく～している Stock prices *have been skyrocketing* for some time.

ぼうどう【暴動】a riot. ¶ ～を起こす raise (≒ start) *a riot*. ～を鎮める put down (≒ suppress) *a riot*. ～が起きた *A riot* broke out.

ぼうとく【冒瀆】blasphemy. ¶ 神を～する *blaspheme* against God. 国旗を～する *profane* the national flag.

ぼうどく【防毒】—マスク a gas mask.

ほうにち【訪日】¶ ～アメリカ使節団 an American mission to Japan. ～する visit Japan.

ほうにょう【放尿】¶ ～する urinate; discharge urine; make (≒ pass) water.

ほうにん【放任】non-interference. ¶ 人を～する let (≒ leave) *a person* alone.

—主義 (政治) the laissez-faire principle. ¶ 子どもを育てるのに～主義をとる adopt *a let-alone* (≒ *a non-interference*) *policy* in bringing up *one's* children.

ほうねつ【放熱】radiation. ¶ 発光体から～する *radiate heat* from luminous bodies.

—器 a radiator.

ほうねん【放念】¶ なにとぞ, ご～ください Please *be at ease* (≒ *feel easy*). / Forget it.

ほうねん【豊年】a fruitful year; a good crop; a bumper harvest; bumper crops; a bumper year.

¶ ことしは米は～だった The rice crop bore *a plentiful harvest* this year. / We had *a bumper rice crop* this year.

ぼうねんかい【忘年会】a year-end party.

ほうのう【奉納】[an] offering. ¶ 神社にささやかな供え物を～する *present* some little offering to [the spirit of] a shrine; *offer* (≒ *dedicate*) *something* to the god.

—者 an offerer; a dedicator. —物 an offering [to God].

ほうばい【傍輩・朋輩】a friend; a companion.

ぼうはく【傍白】an aside.

ぼうばく【茫漠】vastness. ¶ 見渡すかぎり～たる大海原が広がっていた A *vast* expanse of water spread as far as the eye could reach.

ぼうはつ【暴発】an accidental discharge. ¶ ピストルの～ *an accidental firing* of a pistol. その男のライフルが～した His rifle *went off accidentally*.

ぼうはてい【防波堤】a breakwater.

ぼうはん【防犯】prevention of crimes.

—週間 Crime Prevention Week. —ベル a burglar alarm.

ほうひ【包皮】〖解剖学〗the foreskin; the prepuce.

ほうひ【放屁】fart. ¶ ～する break wind.

ほうび【褒美】a reward; a prize. ¶ お使いに行ってくれたからなにか～をあげよう I will give you *something nice* for having done an errand for me.

ぼうび【防備】defense. ¶ 国の～ national *defense*. 攻撃に備える～ *a defense against* an attack. ～のない都市 an *open* city. ～を強化する strengthen the *defenses*. 敵に備えて都市の～を強化する *fortify* a town *against* the enemy.

ぼうびき【棒引き】cancellation. ¶ 借金を～にする *cancel* a debt. 勘定を～にする consider an account *as settled*.

ぼうひょう【妄評】an outspoken (≒ frank; straightforward) comment. ¶ ～多謝 Many apologies for my *frank criticism* (≒ *outspoken comment*).

ほうふ【抱負】an aspiration; an ambition. ¶ 彼は会社の発展についての～を語った He expressed his *ambitious plan* for the future development of his company. 若い人は大きな～を持つべきだ Young people should have *a* great *ambition*. / Young people should *aspire after a great thing*.

ほうふ【豊富】abundance. ¶ ～な資源 *an abundance of* material resources. ～な知識 *a wealth of* knowledge. ～な語彙 an *abundant* vocabulary. 経験(知識; 語彙)を～にする *enrich one's* experiences (knowledge; vocabulary). 教育の内容を～にする *enrich* the content of education. 語彙が～である *be rich in* vocabulary. その国は天然資源が～だ The country *is abundant in* natural resources. あの店は～に品物を取りそろえている They have *a variety* (≒ *a copious supply*) *of* goods in stock at the store.

ぼうふ【亡父】*one's* deceased father.

ぼうふ【亡夫】*one's* deceased husband.

ぼうふ【防腐】prevention against putrefaction. ¶ ～の処置を施す apply *antiseptic* treatment; (死体に) embalm.

ほ

—剤 an antiseptic.

ぼうふう【暴風】a storm; a typhoon; a tempest.

ぼうふうう【暴風雨】a storm; a rainstorm. ¶はげしい～ *a* heavy *storm.* ～に会う(襲われる) be overtaken by *a storm*; be caught in *a storm.*

—警報 a storm warning. —圏 a storm zone. —信号 a storm signal.

ぼうふうりん【防風林】a windbreak.

ほうふく【法服】a 〔judge's〕 robe; a gown.

ほうふく【報復】retaliation; revenge. ¶人に～する have (≒ take) *one's revenge* (≒ *revenge oneself*) on *a person.*

—手段 a retaliatory (≒ vindictive) measure.

ほうふくぜっとう【抱腹絶倒】convulsive laughter. ¶彼は満座の人々を～させた He *threw* all present *into convulsions.* 聴衆はほとんど～の有様だった The audience almost *went into convulsions of merriment.* / The audience *was convulsed with mirth.* われわれは彼の珍芸を見て～した We *were* all *convulsed with laughter* at his strange performance.

ほうふつ【彷彿・髣髴】¶あの子は死んだ母親を～させる The child *reminds* me *of* her dead mother. / The child *resembles* her deceased mother *closely.*

ほうぶつせん【放物線】a parabola. ¶～を描いて飛ぶ pass describing *a parabola.*

ぼうふら【孑孑】a mosquito larva (複 larvae). ¶～がわいた *Mosquito larvae* were hatched.

ほうぶん【邦文】Japanese; the Japanese language.

—タイプ a Japanese typewriter. —タイピスト a typist for the Japanese typewriter.

ほうぶん【法文】the text of the law. ¶公害対策を～化する enact an anti-environment pollution policy into *a law.*

—学部 Faculty of Law and Literature.

ほうへい【砲兵】(隊) artillery; (人) an artillery man.

ほうべい【訪米】¶～する visit America. 彼の～は成功だった His *visit to* America proved successful.

ぼうへき【防壁】a protective wall; a barrier. ¶～を築く build *a protective* (≒ *defensive*) *wall* (*against*). 思想的～ an ideologic *barrier.* 一般民衆の自由を保障する～ the *bulwark* of public liberty. 帝国主義への～となる form *a bulwark against* imperialism.

ほうべん【方便】an expedient; expediency. ¶一時の～としてそうせざるをえなかった We could not help doing so as *a* temporary *expedient.* うそも～ (諺) *The end justifies the means.*

ほうほう【方法】a way; a manner; a method (way は一般的な意味での方法で, 広範囲な語. 時としてばく然としたものにもなる. manner は個人・機関などに独特の方法・流儀. method は整然と組み立てられた方法). ¶これをやる適当な～が思いつかない I cannot think of *a* good *way* to do it. 英語の単語を覚える特別の～はない There is no special *method* for learning English words. だれかしかるべき～を講じてくれる人はいないだろうか I hope there will be someone who will take the proper *measure* for it. この計画を実行する～を知りたい I want to know *how to* put this plan into practice. とにかくどんな～でもいいから, あすまでにこの仕事を完成してほしい I want this work completed by tomorrow, in whatever *way* it may be done.

ほうぼう【方方】everywhere. ¶彼の家を捜そうとして～歩きまわった I walked about *from place to place* trying to find his house. きみを～捜した We have looked for you *everywhere.* ぼくは～に借金がある I have many debts.

ほうぼう【魴鮄】〘魚類〙a gurnard; a gurnet.

ぼうぼう ¶ひげ～の男 a man with a *shaggy* beard. 庭には草が～生えている The garden *is overgrown with* weeds. 家が～燃えあがった The house *burst into flames* (≒ *burnt with a bright flame*).

ほうほうのてい【這這の体】¶～で逃げ出す run away *with the tail between the legs*; beat a hasty retreat. 彼は～であった(しょげていた) He *was crestfallen.*

ほうぼく【放牧】pasturage; grazing. ¶原野に牛馬を～する *send* the cows and horses *to graze* upon the wild fields; *put* (≒ *turn; send*) the cows and horses *out to grass.* 牛は～中だ Cows *are grazing.* / Cows *are at grass.*

ほうまつ【泡沫】a bubble.

—会社 a bubble company. —候補 a fringy candidate.

ほうまん【放漫】recklessness. ¶彼は～な経営のため事業に失敗した He failed in his business by *reckless* management.

ほうまん【豊満】¶われわれはすべてその女優の～な肉体美に魅せられた We were all charmed with the *plump and voluptuous* (≒ *rounded and plump*) beauty of the actress.

ほうむ【法務】—省 (大臣) the Ministry (Minister) of Justice.

ほうむ・る【葬る】bury. ¶死者を～る *bury* the dead. 事件をうやむやのうちに～る *hush up* a matter. 世間から～られる(忘れられる) fall (≒ sink) into oblivion. 議案を～る 米 *table* a bill (この英語は英では上程するの意となる); *kill* a bill.

ほうめい【芳名】your 〔honored〕 name. ¶ご～はかねがね伺っていました I have often heard of *you* (≒ *your name*).

—録 a list of names; a visitors' register.

ぼうめい【亡命】running away; desertion. ¶アメリカに～する *abscond* (≒ *seek refuge*) in America. 故国を離れてイギリスへ～する *flee from one's own country to* England. アメリカで～生活を送る live in *exile* in America.

—者 an exile; a refugee; a fugitive; an

ほ

absconder. ―政権 the government in exile.

ほうめん【方面】1 〖方向〗 a direction. ¶ 犯人は北海道～に逃げた The criminal has fled *toward* Hokkaido.

上野～に出たいのですが，この道を行っていいでしょうか I want to go *in the direction of* Ueno. Will this road take me there?

2 〖分野〗 a field. ¶ 彼はこの～での権威だ He is an authority *in this line* (≒ *in this field*). あなたは物理学のどんな～をご専攻ですか What *line* of physics are you majorng in?

どんな～をご研究ですか What is *the field* of your research?

彼はいろいろの～に仲間を持っている He has companions in various *fields*.

ほうめん【放免】 release. ¶ 人を無罪～にする *acquit a person of* the charge. 彼は無罪～になった He *was acquitted of* the crime. ～された He *was released from prison*.

ほうもう【法網】 the meshes of the law.

¶ ～をくぐる evade *the law*; escape *the meshes of the law*. ～にかかる fall into *the meshes of the law*.

ほうもつ【宝物】 a treasure.

―館 a treasure house.

ほうもん【訪問】 a call; a visit (㊥ では call を visit より口語的に多く用いる). ¶ 首相は目下ヨーロッパを～中だ The Prime Minister *is* now *on a visit to* Europe. きのう彼を自宅に～した I *visited* him at his home yesterday. 日曜日は人を～すべき日ではない Sunday is not the proper day for *making calls* (≒ *paying visits*). これからすこし～するところがある I have a few *visits* to make.

―着 a visiting dress. ―客 a caller; a visitor.

ぼうや【坊や】 (呼びかけ) My boy!; Sonny! ¶ うちの～ my little son; my dear boy. ねえ，～ Listen, *sonny*. ～こっちへいらっしゃい Come on, *my boy*!

ぼうゆう【亡友】 a deceased friend.

ほうよう【包容】 inclusion; tolerance. ¶ 彼には人を～する雅量がある He has *a capacity for tolerance*.

―力 ¶ あの人は～力の大きい人だ He is a *broad-minded* man.

ほうよう【抱擁】 embrace. ¶ 夫と妻は互いにしっかりと～した The man and his wife *embraced* each other tightly.

ほうよう【法要】 a Buddhist service. ¶ ～を営む hold *a Buddhist service*. 亡父の三回忌の～をする hold *a memorial service* at the third anniversary of *one's* deceased father.

ぼうよう【茫洋・芒洋】 vastness; boundlessness. ¶ ～たる海原 the *boundless* of the sea.

ぼうよみ【棒読み】 ¶ 彼はただ祝辞を～するだけであった He only *read* his congratulatory message *without accentuation* (≒ *in a sing-song manner*; *monotonously*).

ほうらく【崩落】 ⇒ ほうかい；ぼうらく

ぼうらく【暴落】 a sudden fall; 〖株式〗 a heavy decline (≒ fall). ¶ アメリカの経済政策は株価の大～をもたらした The U. S. economic policy brought about *a* heavy (≒ severe) *slump* in stock prices. 玉ネギの値段はキロ当り50円に～した The price of onions *has slumped to* 50 yen by the kilogram.

ほうらつ【放埒】 propligacy. ¶ ～な生活をする lead a *loose* (≒ *propligate*; *immoral*) life.

ぼうり【暴利】 an excessive profit. ¶ 彼は土地の売買で～を得ている He *is making excessive* (≒ *undue*) *profits* by dealing in real estate.

ほうりあ・げる【放り上げる】 ¶ ボールを空中に～げる *throw* (≒ *toss*) *up* a ball in the air.

ほうりこ・む【放り込む】 throw in〔to〕. ¶ 容疑者は留置場に～まれた The suspect *was thrown into* the lockup. 彼は手当たりしだいくずかごの中へ物を～んだ He *threw into* the wastepaper basket whatever he could get his hands on.

ほうりだ・す【放り出す】 throw out. ¶ ネコを窓から外へ～す *throw* a cat *out* 〔*of*〕 the window. 今会社から～されたら生活に困ってしまう If I *am dismissed* (≒ *am fired*) *from* my company, I will find it difficult to make a living. 彼は素行不良のため学校から～された He *was expelled from* his school because of his delinquent behavior. 彼はどたんばになって旅行計画を～した He *gave up* his travel plan at the last moment.

ほうりつ【法律】 〔a〕 law. ¶ ～を守るのはわれわれの義務だ It is our duty to obey the *law*. ～は人のすべきことを示している *Law* teaches us what to do. 私は～に暗い I am *a poor lawyer*. この行為は～で禁じられている This act is forbidden by the *law*. ～を犯すとだれでも処分される Anyone is punished if he breaks *a law*. これは～に規定してある This is specified in the *law*. 彼は～に照らして処分すべきだ He ought to be dealt with *according to law*. ～から見れば彼の行為が正しいはずがない *In the eyes of the law* his behavior cannot be correct.

―案 a bill. ―違反 breach of the law. ―学 jurisprudence. ―行為 a legal act. ―顧問 a legal adviser. ―事務所 a law office.

ほうりな・げる【放り投げる】 ⇒ ほうりあげる；ほうりこむ

ぼうりゃく【謀略】 a stratagem. ¶ ～をめぐらす frame (≒ work out) *a plot*; devise *stratagems*. 彼は反対派の～にかかった He fell a prey to the *trap* (≒ *snare*) of the rival group.

ほうりゅう【放流】 discharge. ¶ 水を～する *discharge* water. 魚を川に～する *release* fish in a river; *stock* a river *with* fish.

ほうりょう【豊漁】 ¶ きょうは～だった We made *a good* (≒ *a big*; *a heavy*) *catch* today.

ぼうりょく【暴力】 force; violence. ¶ ～に訴える use *force*; resort (≒ appeal) to *violence*. ～で人の金を奪う take *a person's* money by *violence* (≒ *force*).

―行為 an act of violence; terrorism. ―団 a gang of racketeers.

ほ

ほう·る【放る】throw. ¶列車の窓から空きかんを～るな Don't *throw* an empty can out of the train window. 少年は犬に大きな石を～った The boy *threw* a big stone at a dog. (hit という動詞がなければ当たったかどうかは不明).

ほうれい【法令】laws and ordinances. ¶～によって定めてある be provided for (≒ specified) in the *law*.

ほうれい【法例】rules for the application of laws. ¶～の定むるところに従って according to *the rules concerning the application of the law*.

ぼうれい【亡霊】a ghost; a spirit. ¶ハムレットだけが父の～を見た Hamlet alone saw his father's *spirit* (≒ *ghost*).

ほうれつ【放列】a battery. ¶～をしく form (≒ build; arrange) *a battery*; place guns in position. 彼女はカメラの～の前でポーズをとった She posed before *a battery* (≒ *a forest; a barrage*) of cameras. 彼らはカメラの～をしいた They made *a barrage* of cameras. / They arranged *a battery* of cameras.

ほうれんそう【菠薐草】〖植物〗spinach; spinage.

ほうろう【放浪】wandering. ¶彼は世界じゅうを～した He *wandered* all over the earth. / He *roamed about* the world. ～の旅に出る start on *wanderings* (≒ *a wandering journey*).

—生活 ¶私は若いころ～生活をした I *led a wandering* (≒ *vagrant*) *life* while young. **—**者 a wanderer; a vagabond. **—**癖 wanderlust; vagrant habits.

ほうろう【琺瑯】enamel. ¶～引きのなべ an *enameled* pan.

—質 enamel.

ぼうろん【暴論】a groundless argument. ¶～をはく make *a wild argument*; made *absurd remarks*. 彼はその～に抗議し, 取り消させた He made a protest against *the outrageous statement* and had it withdrawn.

ほうわ【法話】a sermon. ¶あの寺の坊さんがきのうすばらしい～をした The priest of the temple preached *a* fine *sermon* yesterday.

ほうわ【飽和】〖化学〗saturation.

—溶液 saturated solution. **—**点 ¶モータリゼーションが大都市では～点に達した In big cities motorization has reached *the saturation point*. **—**状態 ¶東京の人口は～状態にある Tokyo has an *overflowing* population.

ほえごえ【吠え声】(犬の) a bark; (ライオンなどの) a roar; (オオカミなどの) a howl.

ほえづら【吠え面】a tearful face. ¶～かくな You shall smart for this.

ほ·える【吠える】(犬が) bark (*at*). ¶犬は知らない人に～える A dog *barks at* a stranger. ライオンが～える Lions *roar*. オオカミが～える Wolves *howl*. ～える犬はめったにかまない (諺) *A barking dog seldom bites*. 遠くで犬が～えている I hear a dog *barking* in the distance.

ほお【頬】a cheek. ¶彼女はすぐに～をふくらませる She easily puffs out her *cheeks*. / She is quick to be sulky. あの子は赤い～をしている The child has rosy *cheeks*. / The child is rosy-*cheeked*. 彼女は私を見て～を赤らめた When she saw me, she *blushed* [*her cheeks*]. このリンゴは～が落ちるほどおいしい This apple *is very delicious*.

ボーイ a boy; (飲食店の) a waiter; (事務所の) an office boy; (汽船の) a steward; a cabin boy; (ホテルの) a bellboy; a porter.

—頭 a head waiter (≒ porter); (ホテルの) a bell captain.

ボーイスカウト (団) the Boy Scouts; (団員) a boy scout.

ボーイフレンド a boy friend; a boyfriend (girl friend は2語に分けて書くのがふつう).

ポーカー (トランプの) poker.

—フェイス a poker face.

ほおかぶり【頬被り】¶その男は～をしていた I found him *covering* (≒ *wrapping*) *his cheeks with a towel*. その政治家が世間の非難に～したのはけしからぬ It is inexcusable that the politician should *have been deaf to* public censure.

ボーカル vocal.

—ミュージック vocal music.

ボーキサイト〖鉱物〗bauxite.

ボーク a balk. ¶7回裏に味方のピッチャーが～をおかした The pitcher of our team *balked* (≒ *made a balk*) in the second half of the seventh inning.

ボーグ vogue.

ポークカツ a pork cutlet.

ほおじろ【頬白】〖鳥類〗a Japanese bunting.

ホース a hose (発音は [houz]). ¶～で庭に水をまいた I watered the garden with *a hose*.

ポーズ a pose. ¶彼はカメラの前で気どった～をとった He *posed* (≒ *made an* affected *pose*) before the camera. 彼の同情なんか単なる～に過ぎない His sympathetic attitude is *a* mere *pose*.

ほおずき【酸漿·鬼頭】〖植物〗a ground cherry. ¶～を鳴らす blow *a ground cherry*.

ほおずり【頬摺り】¶彼女は赤ん坊に～した She *nestled* (≒ *laid; pressed*) *her cheek* against the baby's.

ポーター a porter.

ボーダーライン a border line.

—ケース a borderline case.

ポータブル portable (a をつけて名詞としても用いる).

—テレビ a portable television set. **—**ラジオ a portable radio (≒ 英 wireless).

ポーチ a porch.

ほおづえ【頬杖】¶～をつく rest *one's* chin on *one's* hand[s].

ボート a boat; a row[ing] boat. ¶～をこぎに行こう Let's go *boating* (≒ *for a row; rowing*). ふたりで～をこいだ We two rowed *a boat* together. ～で湖を一周した We *rowed* round the lake.

—レース a boat race; (競漕会) a regatta.

ポートワイン port (英語では port wine とはほと

んど言わないで, ただ port と言う).
ボーナス a bonus. ¶ 年末の〜を要求する demand *a* year-end *bonus.* きょう月給 3.5 か月分の〜が出た Today we got *a bonus* equivalent to three and a half months' pay.
ほおばる【頰張る】 ¶ 食べ物を〜る *fill* (≒ *cram*) *one's* mouth. 子どもがケーキを〜っている The child *has his mouth full of* cake. 物を〜ったままでしゃべってはいけません Don't speak *with your mouth full.*
ほおひげ【頰髭】 whiskers(ふつう複数形). ¶ 彼は〜を生やしている He grows (≒ wears) *whiskers.*
ほおべに【頰紅】 rouge. ¶ 彼女は薄く〜をつけた She slightly *rouged* her cheeks. / She lightly put *rouge* on her cheeks.
ほおぼね【頰骨】 a cheekbone. ¶ あの人は〜が高い He has high (≒ broad) *cheekbones.*
ホーマー 〖野球〗 a homer ; a home run.
ホーム (家) [a] home (家庭の意味では不定冠詞 a をつけず, 療養所の意味では a をつける) ; (駅の) a platform (platform は 囲 では列車の乗降段を指すこともある) ; 〖野球〗 the home [base ; plate]. ¶ 彼は勇躍〜を踏んだ He crossed the *home plate* in high spirits.
老人— an old people's home.
ホームイン 〖野球〗 ¶ 〜する score a run ; get (≒ go) home ; cross the home plate.
ホームグラ[ウ]ンド a home-ground.
ホームシック homesickness. ¶ 彼女は海外旅行中〜にかかった She *got* (≒*felt*) *homesick* during her travel abroad. 彼女は美しい高い山山を見て故郷の山々を思い起こし〜にかかった The beautiful lofty mountains reminded her of the mountains of her country and *made* her *homesick.*
ホームストレッチ the homestretch. ¶ 選手たちは〜でスピードを上げた The runners spurted (≒ made a spurt) in *the homestretch.*
ホームスパン homespun [cloth].
ホームソング a home song.
ホームラン 〖野球〗 a home run ; a homer.
¶ 彼は6回に走者ひとりおいて〜を打った He *homered* (≒ *hit a home run*) in the sixth inning with one on base.
満塁— a bases-loaded homer. 場外— an out-of-the park homer. ソロ— a solo homer. —王 a home-run king.
ホームドラマ a drama of domestic situation.
ホームルーム a homeroom.
—委員 a member of a homeroom committee. —活動 a homeroom activity.
ポーランド Poland.
—語 Polish. —人 a Pole ; (国民) the Poles ; the Polish.
ボーリング 1 〚せん孔〛 boring.
—マシン a boring machine.
2 〚球戯〛 bowling. ¶ 〜をやろうか Let's *bowl,* shall we?
彼は〜で200出した He *bowled* a 200 game.
—場 a bowling alley.
ホール 1 〚大広間〛 a hall ; (ダンスの) a dancing (≒ dance) hall.
2 〚ゴルフ〛 a hole ; a cup. ¶ 〜インワンする make *a hole in one.*
ボール (球) a ball. ¶ 〜を投げる throw *a ball.*
ボール (容器) a bowl.
サラダ— a bowl of salad ; a salad bowl. フィンガー— a finger bowl.
ボールがみ【ボール紙】 cardboard ; pasteboard.
ホールディング 〖球技〗 holding. ¶ 〜をとられた It was announced as *holding.*
ボールばこ【ボール箱】 a cardboard (≒ pasteboard) box ; a carton.
ボールペン a ball-point pen ; a ball pen.
ほおん【保温】 heating. ¶ 部屋の〜と換気に注意しなさい Take care of *keeping* the room *warm* and ventilating it.
ぼおん【母音】 ⇒ぼいん
ほか【外・他】 1 〚他のもの〛 another ; else ; [the] other[s]. ¶ 〜の子どもたちはどこへ行ったのか Where did *the other* children go?
なにか〜の話をしよう Let's talk about something *else.* / Let's change the topic of conversation.
そこまでで結構だ, 〜の人に頼むから That will be enough, thank you. I will ask somebody *else* to do it.
きょうは忙しいから, 〜の日に来てください I am awfully busy today. Could you come *some other* day?
この時計は気に入らないから〜のを見せてください I don't like this watch ; please show me *another.*
今度は〜の方法でやってみよう I will try it *another* way this time.
〜に仕事がなかったら手伝ってください I would like you to help me, if you have nothing *else* to do.
〜に好きな女性がいるのか Do you have any *other* sweetheart?
〜になにか質問は? Do you have any *other* questions to ask [me]?
このペンはぼくのではない. だれか〜の人のです This pen is not mine, it is somebody *else's.*
そのニュースは〜の新聞にはみんな出ている The news is in all the *other* papers.
山本氏〜4名の一行がけさ羽田を立ってロンドンへ向かった Mr. Yamamoto with a party of four *others* left Haneda for London this morning.
2 〚よそ〛 ¶ 〜ではこのお値段では手に入りません You can't buy it at this price anywhere *else.*
彼はこの会社をやめて〜へ移るつもりらしい It seems that he is going to leave this firm for *another.*
3 〚…を除いて・…以外〛 ¶ きみの〜にこんないたずらをする者はいない No one *but* you would do such a naughty thing.
あなたの〜に好きな人はいません I love no one *but* you.
ぼくはきみの〜には親友はいない I have no friends

besides (≒ *other than*) you.
彼の命令に従うより～しかたがない There is nothing to do *but* to obey him. / We have no choice *but* to obey him.
これより～に方法はないのか Is there no *other* way *than* (≒ *besides*) this?
彼のばかさかげんにはあきれる～ない I *cannot help* being amazed at his stupidity.
彼は釣りの～に趣味はない He has *no other* hobby *than* angling. / Fishing is the only hobby he has.
手を擦りむいた～は異常ありません I have skinned my hand, but nothing *else* is wrong with me.
田中さんの～に, 佐藤さんも出席した *Besides* Tanaka, Sato was also present.
きみはメロンの～果物はなにが好きですか What other fruit do you like *besides* melons?
彼は小説の～に絵もかく *Not only* does he write novels, *but also* he paints. (形式ばった言い方). / He writes novels and paints *as well.*
給料の～に収入がある I have something *besides* my pay.
給料の～に収入はない I have nothing *but* my pay.
4 〖外部〗 ¶ このうわさは～から耳に入った The rumor has come to my ears *from the outside* (≒ *from an outside source*).
～でこの話を聞くとは意外だった It was a surprise to me to hear of this *from an outsider.*
彼は最近～から来た人だ He is new here.

ほかく【捕獲】 capture. ¶ 捕鯨船はおびただしい数の鯨を～した The whaling ship *caught* a great number of whales. 敵船を２隻～した We *captured* two enemy ships.

ほかげ【火影・灯影】 a 〔flicker of〕 light. ¶ 遠くに港の～を見つけた We sighted *a light* of a harbor in the distance.

ほかけぶね【帆掛け船】 a sailing boat (≒ vessle); a sailboat.

ぼかし【暈し】 shading off; gradation. ¶ その写真は～にしてください Finish the photograph in the manner of *a vignette.*

ぼか·す【暈す】 **1** 〖色を〗 shade off; gradate. ¶ その木炭画を擦筆で～した I *shaded off* the charcoal drawing with a stump.
一つの色をしだいに～して別の色にした I *gradated* one color into the other.
2 〖態度を〗 ¶ 返事を～した I gave a *vague* (≒ *evasive*) answer.
彼はことばを～した He used *ambiguous* language.
彼はその問題については態度を～してしまった He *did not commit himself to* the problem.

ほかならぬ【他ならぬ】 ¶ ～きみの頼みだからやってみよう Since the request comes from you *and none other,* I will try it. 彼女こそ私の求めていた理想の女性に～ She is *the only one* who can ever fit my ideal of a woman. / She is *the very* woman that I have been seeking as my ideal. ～ならぬきみの頼みなら断わるわけにいかない All right, but I wouldn't do it for anybody *else* but you.

ほかほか ¶ 昼間日に干したのでこのふとんは～としている This mattress *feels warm* as it has been sunned in the daytime. ～のさつまいも *steaming* potatoes.

ぽかぽか **1** 〖暖かい〗 ¶ だんだん～した陽気になってきている It (≒ The weather) is getting (≒ growing) *warmer and warmer.*
足早に歩いたので体が～している I *feel warm* from walking quickly.
2 〖続けて〗 ¶ 父親はわんぱく息子を～なぐりつけた The father *gave* 〔*several*〕 *smart blows to* his naughty son.

ほがらか【朗らか】 ¶ ～に晴れている It's *bright* and clear. 彼女は～な娘だ She is a *cheerful* girl. 彼は～に笑う He laughs *merrily.*

ぽかり ¶ 彼は弟の頭を～となぐった He *gave* his brother *a whack on* the head.

ほかん【保管】 custody; charge; safekeeping. ¶ それは私が～している I *keep* it. / It *is in* my *keeping* (≒ *custody*). / I have it *in* my *keeping* (≒ *custody*). 宝石は安全に～してある The jewels *are in safekeeping.* 重要書類は彼が～している The important papers *are in* his *custody.* / He *is in charge* (≒ *has charge*) *of* the important articles.
このかぎの～をお願いします I ask you to *keep* this key.
―人 a custodian; a keeper. ―品 an article in custody. ―料 charges for custody; (倉庫料) storage; a storage fee.

ぼかん【母艦】 a tender; a depot ship.
航空― an aircraft carrier. 潜水― a submarine tender.

ぽかんと **1** 〖音〗 ¶ 彼はこん棒で犬を～なぐった He *whacked* the dog with a club.
2 〖ぼんやり〗 ¶ 彼は～した顔をしている He has a *blank* (≒ *vacant*) look. / He looks *blank* (≒ *vacant*). / He looks *like a fool.*
彼は～水面を見つめていた He looked *absent-mindedly* (≒ *vacantly*) on the surface of the water.
彼は～彼女に見とれていた He stared at her *stupidly.*

ぼき【簿記】 bookkeeping. ¶ ～をつける keep books; keep accounts.
―係 a bookkeeper. ―帳 an account book. 商業― commercial bookkeeping.

ぽきぽき ¶ 彼は小枝を～折りながら歩いていった He walked along *snapping off* some twigs. 彼は指を～鳴らす He has the habit of *cracking* his finger joints.

ほきゅう【補給】 a supply. ¶ あらしのために食糧の～がとだえた The storm cut off the *supply* of food. タンクに水を～する *replenish* a tank with water.
―基地 a supply base (≒ depot). ―路 a supply route. 栄養― nutrition.

ほきょう【補強】 reinforcement. ¶ 堤防は～工事が必要だ The bank needs *reinforcement work.* メンバーを増やしてわれわれのチームをもっと～しなければならない We must *strengthen* our

ほ

team by increasing its members.

ぼきん【募金】 fund-raising. ¶ 彼は原爆被爆者救援の～運動に参加した He took part in a *fund-raising* campaign to rescue the victims of the atomic air raids. その孤児のため～をしよう Let's *collect* some *money* for the orphan. 新しい図書館の建築のため～している We *are raising money* for the building of a new library. (fund-raising は collecting money よりかなり大がかりな場合に用いることが多い). 東パキスタンの地震の被災者のために～をした We *collected contributions* in behalf of the sufferers from the earthquake in East Pakistan.
街頭— a street collection of subscriptions. 共同— the community chest.

ほきんしゃ【保菌者】 a 〔germ〕 carrier.

ぽきんと ¶ 枝が～折れた The branch broke *with a snap.* 小枝を～折った I *snapped off* a twig. 指を～鳴らした I *cracked* my fingers.

ぼく【僕】 I. ¶ ～の my. ～に(を) me. ～のもの mine.

ほくい【北緯】 the north latitude (N.L. と略記する). ¶ 日本は～24度から46度の間にある Japan extends from 24 degrees 〔*North*〕 to 46 degrees *North* 〔*latitude*〕.

ほくおう【北欧】 North〔ern〕 Europe.
—人 a Scandinavian ; a Northman. —神話 the Norse mythology.

ぼくぎゅう【牧牛】 cattle at pasture ; cattle at grass ; pasturing (≒ grazing) cattle.

ボクサー a boxer ; a pugilist (特にプロボクサー).

ぼくさつ【撲殺】 slaughter. ¶ 野良犬を～する *beat* a cur *to death.* 食用に獣を～する *slaughter* animals for food.

ぼくし【牧師】 a clergyman ; a minister ; a pastor ; (教区の) a parson ; a rector ; a vicar ; a curate ; (旧教) a father ; (総称) the clergy (clergyman は一般的な語で, 殊にイギリス国教会の牧師に言う. pastor, parson は俗語的. rector は教区 (parish) の管理をする教区牧師. vicar は rector の代務者で curate の上位. curate は rector または vicar の手助けをする下級牧師. minister は非国教会の牧師).
¶ ～になる enter the ministry ; take 〔holy〕 orders.

ぼくしゃ【牧舎】 (牛舎) a cowshed ; a cowhouse ; (羊小屋) 圏 a sheepfold ; a fold ; 米 a sheepcote.
¶ 羊の群れが～に帰った Flocks of sheep have returned to their *folds.*

ぼくしゅ【墨守】 adherence. ¶ 旧習を～する *adhere* (≒ *cling; stick*) *to* the old custom.

ぼくじゅう【墨汁】 India (≒ China) ink.

ほくじょう【北上】 ¶ 台風が～する The typhoon *goes* (≒ *moves ; proceeds*) *north* (≒ *northward*).

ぼくじょう【牧場】 a stock farm ; 米 a ranch ; (放牧場) a pasture. ¶ 彼はケンタッキーで～を経営している He runs *a ranch* (≒ *a stock farm*) in Kentucky. 春になると村人たちは牛を山の～へ連れていく In spring, the villagers take their cattle to the mountain *pastures.* スイス高原の～はたいてい酪農場だ Most of the *farms* on the Swiss Plateau are dairy farms.

ぼくしん【牧神】 〖ギリシア神話〗 a satyr ; Pan ; 〖ローマ神話〗 a faun. ¶ ～は田野の神だ *Pan* is a rural deity.

ほぐ·す【解す】 loosen ; disentangle. ¶ 肩の凝りを～す *ease* (≒ *relieve*) the stiffness of the shoulder. もつれたたこ糸を～す *disentangle* a thread of a kite. 髪を～す *loosen* the hair. 旅に出て気分を～す go on a trip *for a change* (≒ *to relax ; for relaxation*).

ぼく·する【卜する】 ¶未来を～する(占う) *tell* (≒ *read ; foretell ; predict*) the future. この地に居を～して10年になる(定める) It is (≒ (口語) has been) ten years since I *came to live* (≒ *settled down*) here.

ほくせい【北西】 northwest (NW または N.W. と略記する). ¶ ～の風曇り cloudy with *northwesterly* wind. ～に向かって移動する move toward the *northwest.*

ぼくせき【木石】 stocks and stones ; (生命のないもの) inaminate objects. ¶ 無感動で～のような顔つきの男 a man with an impassive, rather *wooden* face. 彼のにこやかな愛想のよさは～をも動かすほどであった His charming geniality would have had its effect on *a stone.*
—漢 an unfeeling fellow ; an impassive person.

ぼくそう【牧草】 grass. ¶ 牛が数頭～を食べている There are some cows *grazing* on the pasture (≒ in the fields).
—地 a pasture ; a meadow ; grass.

ほくそえ·む【北叟笑む】 ¶ その知らせを聞いて彼はひとり～んだ He *chuckled to himself* (≒ *chuckled with delight*) at the news. 彼は～んでそう言った He said so *with a chuckle.*

ほくたん【北端】 the northern end (≒ extremity).

ぼくちく【牧畜】 cattle breeding ; stock farming ; stock raising. ¶ 彼は～を営んでいる He *is a stock farmer.* / He *is a stock raiser.* この国土の大きな部分が～に充てられている A large proportion of the land is devoted to *cattle breeding* (≒ *stock farming ; stock raising*). その町の周辺の土地は農業や～には適さない The land around the city is not fit for farming or *the keeping of cows and sheep.*

ほくちょう【北朝】 〖日本歴史〗 the Northern Dynasty.

ほくとう【北東】 northeast (NE または N.E. と略記する). ¶ ～の風 a *northeasterly* wind. 町の～に学校がある In the *northeast* of the city stands a school.

ぼくとう【木刀】 a wooden sword.

ぼくどう【牧童】 a herdboy. ¶ ～が羊の群れの番をする *A shepherd boy* tends a flock. ～が牛を扱う *A cowboy* handles cattle.

ほくとしちせい【北斗七星】 〖天文〗 Ursa Major ; the Great Bear (ほかに the Plough,

ほ

the Wagon, the Big (≒ Great) Dipper, Charles's Wain などとも言う).

ぼくとつ【木訥・朴訥】 simplicity; honesty. ¶ 彼の～さが私の心を打った His *simplicity* (≒ *naivety*) touched me.

ぼくねんじん【朴念仁】 a blockhead; a dunce. ¶ 彼はまったくの～だ He is *a* hopeless *blockhead.* / He is *a regular stick.* / He is *not a smart mixer.*

ほくぶ【北部】 the north; the northern part.

ほくべい【北米】 North America.
—合衆国 the United States of America; the States (とくに外国にいるアメリカ人が故国アメリカをさしていうとき用いる); U.S.A.; the U.S. —大陸 the North American Continent.

ほくほく ¶ 売れ行きがよくて彼らは～だ They *are in glee* (≒ *are in high delight*) because of their thriving business.

ほくほくせい【北北西】 north-northwest (NNW または N.N.W. と略記する).

ほくほくとう【北北東】 north-northeast (NNE または N.N.E. と略記する).

ぼくめつ【撲滅】 extermination. ¶ がん～運動を開始する inaugurate a movement *against* cancer; start *anti*-cancer campaign. 農薬が害虫を～した Agricultural chemicals *have exterminated* (≒ *have extirpated; have eradicated*) harmful insects. あらゆる悪を～しなくてはならない We must *root out* (≒ *stamp out*) all the evils.

ほくよう【北洋】 the northern ocean (≒ seas).
—漁業 northern-seas fisheries.

ほぐ·れる【解れる】 ¶ 糸が～れた The thread *got loose.* / The thread *became disentangled.* 肩の凝りが～れた The stiffness of the shoulders *was gone* (≒ *was eased; was relieved*). 仕事の疲れが～れた The fatigue of the work *was banished* (≒ *was relieved*). 眠ったら疲れが～れた I *slept off* the fatigue. / I *was refreshed from* fatigue by sleep. 謎が～れた The riddle *was solved.* ふたりの感情のもつれが～れた The ill feeling between the two *was subdued* (≒ *was pacified; was subsided; was shed off*).

ほくろ【黒子】 a mole.
つけ— an artificial mole.

ぼけ【木瓜】〘植物〙a Japan[ese] quince.

ほげい【捕鯨】 whaling; whale fishing.
—会社 a whaling company. —業 the whaling industry. —水域 a whale catch quarter. —船 a whaler; a whaleship. —用キャッチャーボート a whale catcher. 国際—取締条約 the International Whale Fishing Control Treaty. 南氷洋—期間 the Antarctic Whaling season.

ぼけい【母系】 the maternal line.

ぼけい【母型】〘印刷〙a matrix.

ほけつ【補欠】 (人) a substitude; (事) filling a vacancy. ¶ ～で入学を認める admit students into a college *to fill vacancies.* 彼はその大学の～合格候補のひとりだ He *is placed on the wait[ing] list* by the college. 彼が病気のときは私が彼の～ということになっている When he is sick, I *substitute for* him (≒ *take his place*). 彼は～で野球の試合に出た He took part in the ball game *to replace* one of the regular players.
—選挙 a by-election. ¶ ～選挙が行なわれた *A by-election* (≒ 米 *A special election*) was held *to fill up the vacancy.* —選手 a substitute player; a bench warmer.

ぼけつ【墓穴】(墓) a grave. ¶ 彼はみずから～を掘った He worked his own ruin. きみは自分の方針だけに固執していたら～を掘ることになる To persist in your own line will *be disastrous* to you.

ポケット a pocket; (上着の胸の) a breast pocket; (上着の内側の) an inside-pocket; (上着の横の) a side-pocket; (小ぜに用の) a change pocket; (ズボンの両脇の) a trouser-pocket; (ズボンのうしろの) a hip pocket.
¶ ～に両手をつっこんで歩く walk with *one's* hands *in one's pockets.* 彼は定期券を胸の～に入れた He put his commutation ticket in his breast *pocket.* 彼は自分の～をふくらますことばかり考えている (私腹を肥やす) He is always busy *feathering his nest.*
—版 a pocket edition. —マネー pocket money. ¶ 毎週いくらかの～マネーをもらうことになっている I am allowed some *pocket money* every week.

ぼ·ける【惚ける】 dote; become senile. ¶ 彼は年をとって～けてしまった He *has grown senile* (≒ *has grown siily; has grown weak-headed*) with age. / He *is* old and *hazy.*

ぼ·ける【暈ける】 ¶ この色は～けやすい This color *fades* rapidly. 色の～けるのがだんだん広がっていった The *discoloration* spread gradually. 青のカーテンが～けて灰色になりかけている The blue curtain *is shading away* (≒ *off*) into gray. この写真は～けている This picture *is out of focus.* 霧で山が～けている Mists *blur* the mountains.

ほけん【保健】 hygiene; sanitation. ¶ 学童の～に心を配る try to *preserve* (≒ *protect*) *the health* of school children. 環境の～衛生に力を向ける direct *one's* effort to the *sanitation* of the environment. 喫煙は～上有害である Smoking is bad to your *health.*
—医 a public health doctor. —事業 a public health service. —所 a public health center. —体育 health and physical education. —婦 a public health nurse. 学校—婦 a school nurse. 世界—機構 the World Health Organization (WHO と略記する).

ほけん【保険】 insurance. ¶ ～を契約する effect *insurance.* この家屋は300万円の～がついている This house *is secured for* three million yen.
—会社 an insurance company. —勧誘員 an insurance salesman. —期間 the term insured. —代理店 an insurance agent.

ほ

―金 insurance 〔money〕. ¶ その損害は～金で償われる The damage is covered by *insurance.* ―金受取人 the beneficiary. ―契約 an insurance contract. ―契約者 a policy holder. ―証書 an insurance policy. ―料 an insurance premium. 生命― life insurance. ¶ 私は2000万円の生命～に入っている I *am insured for* twenty million yen. 生命～料を払った I have paid the *insurance upon* my life. 健康(生命; 火災; 失業; 傷害) ― health (life; fire; unemployment; accident) insurance.

ほこ【矛・鉾】a halberd; (武器) arms. ¶ 両者は～を収めて和解した They've agreed to bury *the hatchet.*

ほご【保護】protection. ¶ 彼は私の～のもとに暮らしていた He lived under my *protection.* 彼はすぐ警察に～を求めた He immediately applied for police *protection.* この浮浪児たちは～を必要とする These homeless children must *be looked after.* 彼は日光から目を～するため黒っぽいめがねをかけていた He was wearing dark glasses to *protect* his eyes *from* the sun.

―者 a protector; a guardian. ―色 protective coloring. ―鳥 a protected bird. ―貿易 protective trade. ―貿易主義 protectionism. ―貿易主義者 a protectionist.

ほご【補語】〘文法〙a complement. ¶ たいていの自動詞は～をとる Most intransitive verbs require *a complement* (≒ *complements*).

ほご【反故】wastepaper. ¶ 原稿用紙をたくさん～にする *waste* a lot of copypaper. 約束を～にしてはいけません You must not *break* your promise. / You should be true to your words.

―紙 waste paper.

ほこう【歩行】walking. ¶ ～はよい運動である *Walking* is a good exercise. 患者は～困難である The patient has some difficulty in *walking.* 雪で～不能だ There is no *walking* in the snow.

―者 a walker; a pedestrian. ¶ ～者は車よりも優先されるべきだ *Walkers* (≒ *Pedestrians*) should have priority over vehicle traffic.

ほこう【補講】a supplementary lecture. ¶ 長く欠席したので～を受ける take *supplementary lessons* after a long absence.

ぼこう【母校】*one's* old school; *one's* Alma Mater. ¶ 私の～はハーバードだ Harvard is my *old school* (≒ *Alma Mater*). / I *finished* (≒ *graduated from*) Harvard University.

ぼこう【母港】the home port.

ぼこく【母国】*one's* mother country; the homeland. ¶ 彼は～日本に帰ってきた He has come home to Japan.

―語 *one's* mother tongue. ¶ 彼はまるで～語のように英語を流暢にしゃべる He speaks English fluently as if it were his *mother tongue.*

ほこさき【矛先】¶ やりの～ a spear *point.* 敵に向かって～鋭く切り込む make *a* sharp *thrust at* an enemy. ～をかわす parry *a thrust.* 彼らはわれわれに～を向けた(攻撃を始めた) They *rose in arms* against us. 非難の～を政府に向ける *cast reproaches upon* the government.

ほこら【祠】a small shrine.

ほこらか【誇らか】¶ ～に語る speak *proudly* (≒ *in high pride*). ～なようすで with an air of *ostentatious pride*; very proudly. ～な笑みを浮かべて with a *triumphant* smile.

ほこらし・い【誇らしい】proud. ¶ 優勝チームは～げに町を練り歩いた The winning team paraded *proudly* (≒ *triumphantly; in high pride*) through the street.

ほこり【誇り】pride. ¶ 彼は国の～だ He is *a credit* (≒ *an honor*) to the country. 彼は学校の～を傷つけた He stained the *honor* of our school. 人はすべて自分の職業に～を持つべきだ Everyone should *take pride in* (≒ *be proud of*) his work. 私は日本人であることを～に思っている I *am proud of* (≒ *take pride in*) being a Japanese. 彼女は記憶力がいいのを～にしている She *prides herself on* her good memory. 彼にお金を無心するなんて私の～が許さない I *am too proud to* ask him for money. / *Pride* stands in the way of my asking him for money. 彼女の～は傷つけられた Her *pride* was hurt.

ほこり【埃】dust. ¶ 上着の～を払う *dust* a jacket. はたきでいすの～を払う *dust* a chair with a duster. 体の～を払う *dust oneself.* もうもうと～を巻き上げる raise a cloud of *dust.* 水で～を静める lay the *dust* with water. 古ぐつが～だらけになっていた My old shoes *were dusty* all over. 田舎道を歩きどおしですっかり～を浴びてしまった I *got dusty* all over after a long walk along the country road. 風で～が立つ *Dust* rises in the wind.

ほこ・る【誇る】¶ 彼は貴族の出であることを～っている He *is proud of* (≒ *takes pride in; shows pride in*) his noble birth. 彼は学校の成績のよいことを～っている He *is proud of* his success in school. そのダムは空前の規模を～っている The dam *is famous* (≒ *is noted*) *for* a scale of unprecedented immensity. 当時フランスは栄華を～っていた France *was* then *at the zenith* (≒ *in the acme*) *of* its prosperity. 彼の成功は偶然であり～るに足らない His success is accidental and deserves no *praise.*

ほころび【綻び】a rip; a rent; an open seam. ¶ ～をつくろう sew up (≒ mend) *a rip* (≒ *a rent*). 縫い目の～をつくろう stitch (≒ sew up) *an open seam.* 縫い目に～ができた A seam *gaped.*

ほころ・びる【綻びる】¶ この生地はすぐ～びる This cloth *rips* easily. そでの縫い目が～びた A seam *opened* on the sleeve. 桜の花が～びはじめた The cherry blossoms began to *open* (≒ *bloom*). 合格の知らせに思わず顔が～びた I *could not check my smile* at the news of my success in the examination.

ほさ【補佐】assistance. ¶ 校長を～する *assist* the principal. 彼には助言を与え～する人が必要だ

He needs someone to *counsel* (≒ *advise*) him.

大統領―官 a presidential aid.

ほさき【穂先】(稲などの) an ear ; (やりの) a spearhead. ¶ 稲の～が出そろっている The rice plants *are* all *in the ear*.

ほざ·く ¶ 生意気なことを～くな None of your impudence! / Shut up! くだらんことを～くな Stuff and nonsense! / Nonsense!

ぼさつ【菩薩】〖仏教〗 a Bodhisattva ; a Buddhist saint.

ぼさん【墓参】 a visit to a grave. ¶ 先祖の～をする *visit the graves* of *one's* ancestors.

ほし【星】 **1** 〖空の〗 a star. ¶ 空に～が輝いている *Stars* are twinkling in the sky.

～の明るい夜だった It was a *starlit* night.

一面に～のある夜 a *starry* night.

2 〖運勢〗 fortune. ¶ 私は悪い～の下に生まれた I was born *under an* unlucky *star*.

3 〖しるし·点〗 an asterisk ; a point ; a mark. ¶ 知らない単語には～じるしをつけなさい *Asterisk* the words you don't know.

難解な語には～じるしが二重についている Difficult words are marked with two *asterisks*.

4 〖容疑者〗 a suspect. ¶ ～はまだあがらない No *suspect* has been found yet.

5 〖斑点〗 a spot. ¶ 目に～が出た I had *a white speck* in my eye.

ほじ【保持】 maintenance. ¶ 友好関係を～する *maintain* friendly relations. 健康を～する *preserve* (≒ *keep*) *one's* health. 世界選手権を～する *hold* the world championship.

記録―者 a record holder. 選手権―者 a titleholder.

ぼし【母子】 ―家庭 a fatherless family. ―手帳 a maternity passbook.

ポジ positive.

ほし·い【欲しい】 **1** 〖欲する〗 ¶ もうすこし時間が～い I *want* (≒ *wish I had*) a little more time.

なにが～いですか. コーヒーが～い What do you *want* to take? I *would like* some coffee.

古い靴がだめになったので新しいのが～い I *need* a new pair of shoes since the old ones are worn out.

今の子どもは～いものはなんでも買ってもらえる Children today get everything they *like*.

酒なんか～くない I don't *care for* a drink.

2 〖…してほしい〗 ¶ 早く春が来て～い I *wish* spring would come soon.

もうすこし気をつけて～い I *wish* you to be more careful.

水を取りに行って～い I *want* (≒ *would like*) you to go and get some water for me.

私になにをして～いというのか What do you *expect* me to do?

3 〖望ましい〗 ¶ 彼に～いものは自信だ What he *needs* (≒ *lacks*) is confidence 〔in himself〕.

政府にもっと国民感情に対する配慮が～い The Government *needs* more consideration on national feelings.

ほしいまま【縦·恣】 ¶ 彼女はいつも～にふるまう She always *has her own way*. 彼は空想を～にした He *gave free play to* his fancy. 彼は権勢を～にしている He *is at the summit of* his power. 彼は名選手の名を～にした He *enjoyed* a high reputation as a distinguished player. 彼は～に使える多額の金を持っている He has a lot of money *at his disposal*.

ほしがき【干し柿】 a dried persimmon.

ほしかげ【星影】 ¶ ～がさやかに光っている The *stars* are shining brilliantly. ～のまばゆいほどの夜空を背景に木々はくろぐろと美しく立ちならんでいた The trees stood out, dark and beautiful against the *starry* sky.

ほしが·る【欲しがる】 ¶ この子はアイスクリームばかり～ってきりがない This boy *craves* ice cream and never seems to get enough of it. 彼女は新しい上着に合う帽子を～っている She *wants* a hat to match her new coat. 名声を～る人は多い Many people *long for* (≒ *are eager to win*) fame. 彼はみなが～っていた賞を手に入れた He won the prize they all *coveted*.

ほしくさ【干し草】 hay.

ほじく·る ¶ 鼻(耳)を～るのはやめなさい Don't *pick* your nose (ears). 彼は人のあらを～るのが好きだ He is fond of *finding fault with* others. 以前この問題を～ってみたことがある I once *made inquiries into* (≒ *looked into*) this matter.

ほしづきよ【星月夜】 a starry night. ¶ 冬の～ *a starry* (≒ *a starlight*) winter *night*.

ほしぶどう【干し葡萄】 raisins.

ほしまつり【星祭り】 the star festival ; the love-star festival.

ほしまわり【星回り】 ¶ 私は～がよい I was born *under a lucky star*. 私～はが悪い I was born *under an unlucky* (≒ *an evil*) *star*. あの男は～が悪い He *is ill-starred* (≒ *is ill-fated ; is unlucky*).

ほしもの【干し物】 clothes for drying. ¶ 物干し綱に～をつるす pin the *laundry* on the clothesline.

―ばさみ 英 a clothes peg ; 米 a clothespin.

―場 a drying place.

ほしゃく【保釈】 bail. ¶ 被告を～する *bail* the accused. 彼の～を許す *grant* (≒ *allow*) him *bail* ; admit him to *bail*. ～を認めない refuse *bail*. ～の願いを出す make an application for *bail*. 彼は～で出所している He *is out on bail*.

―金 bail. ¶ ～金を積む furnish *bail*. 彼は100万円の～金を積んで～された He was released *on bail* of a million yen. / He was released of a million yen *bail*.

ほしゅ【保守】 conservation.

―主義 conservatism. ―主義者 a conservative. ―陣営 the conservative camp. ―勢力 the conservative force. ―党 a conservative party. ¶ 与党の～党はその法案に反対した The ruling *Conservative Party* was against the bill. その選挙で～党が勝った *The Conservatives* won the election. ―反動 ¶ 彼は～反動だ He is *a reactionary conservative*.

ほしゅ【捕手】〘野球〙a catcher.
ほしゅう【補修】repair. ¶ その古城は～が行き届いている The old castle *is in good repair*. その道路は～工事中だ The road *is under repairs*.
ほしゅう【補習】a supplementary lesson. ¶ ～を受ける take *supplementary lessons*.
—科 a supplementary course.
ほじゅう【補充】supplement; replacement. ¶ 欠員を～する *fill* 〔*up*〕a vacancy. 兵員を～する *recruit* an army. 水槽(すいそう)に水を～する *replenish* a tank *with* water. 壊れたいすの～をした The broken chairs *were replaced by* new ones.
—者名簿 a wait〔ing〕list. —兵 a recruit. —問題 a supplementary exercise.
ぼしゅう【募集】¶ この隊は兵を～している They *are recruiting* troops for this army. 今年度はこの幼稚園は入園者の～をしない This kindergarten will not *take applications for admission* this year. この会社では数名の社員を～中だ The company *is looking for* some new employees. 数学科の～人員は50名だ The students *to be admitted to* the Mathematics Department are fifty in number. 寄付金は今～中だ Subscriptions *are being raised*.
ほじょ【補助】assistance; help; aid. ¶ 18歳のとき彼は両親の～なしで自活できた At eighteen he could manage to make his living without any *help* of his parents. 彼は息子の～にたよっている He lives *in dependence on* his son. 彼はおじから学資の～を受けている He *owes* school expenses *to* his uncle. 一家には金銭的～が必要だった The family needed pecuniary *assistance*. 鉄道は政府の財政的～を得て敷設された The railroad was laid with the financial *aid* of the government. 事業は国庫の～を受けている The enterprise *is subsidized by* the government. 人から～を受けたくない I want to be independent. それは～的な役割を果たすにすぎない It plays only a *minor* role.
—いす a spare chair. —員 an assistant. —貨幣 a subsidiary coin. —金 subsidy. 政府— government grant.
ぼしょ【墓所】a graveyard.
ほしょう【保証】guarantee; security; assurance. ¶ 彼の人物は私が～する I *assure* you that he is a reliable man. この時計は1年間の～付きだ This watch *is guaranteed* for one year. アメリカは日本に事前協議を～した America *assured* Japan *of* prior consultations. 事の真偽は～しかねる I can't *answer for* the truth of the matter.
—金 security; (株式売買の) margins; (手付け) a deposit. —書 a written guarantee. —人〘法律〙a guarantor; (連帯の) a surety. ¶ 私は彼の～人になった I *stood surety* (≒ *security*) *for* him. 支払—小切手 a certified cheque. 政府—債 Government guaranteed bond. 身元—人 a reference.
ほしょう【保障】guarantee. ¶ その権利は憲法に～されている The right *is guaranteed* in the constitution. 会社員は生活を～されている Office workers lead a *secure* life. 彼らは～された生活よりチャンスを求めている They are looking for opportunity, not for *security*.
安全—理事会 the Security Council. 日米安全—条約 the U. S.-Japan Security Treaty. 社会— social security.
ほしょう【補償】compensation. ¶ 人に損失に対して～する *compensate* (≒ *indemnify*) *a person* for his loss. その損失に対する～を受けた I received *compensation* (≒ *indemnity*) for the loss.
—金 an indemnity. ¶ 彼は私に100万円の～金を払った He paid me *an indemnity* of a million yen. —法案 a compensation bill. —融資 compensation finance. 損害—請求 a claim for damages.
ほしょう【歩哨】a sentinel. ¶ 見張りのため～を配置する post *a sentinel* in order to keep guard. ～が立っている *A sentinel* is on guard. 彼は～に出ている He is〔standing〕on *sentry*. / He is standing *sentinel*.
ぼじょう【慕情】longing. ¶ 彼はふるさとへはげしい～をいだいている He has *a great longing* (≒ *yearning*) for home. この映画には母と子の～が美しく描かれている The *affection* of mother and child is prettily expressed in this movie.
ほしょく【補色】complementary color. ¶ この二つの色は～になっている These two colors *are complementary*.
ぼしょく【暮色】twilight. ¶ ～が迫っている The *dusk* is gathering.
ほじ・る【穿る】⇒ ほじくる
ほしん【保身】self-protection. ¶ 彼は～の術にたけている He is skillful in *defending his own interest*.
ほ・す【干す】**1**〖乾かす〗dry. ¶ ひなたで(たき火で)ぬれたシャツを～した I *dried* my wet shirt in the sun (over a bonfire).
洗たく物はまだ～していない We *have* not *hung out* the washing *to dry*.
この季節には衣類を～す We *air* clothes in this season.
2〖飲み干す〗¶ ブドウ酒のグラスを～した I *emptied* (≒ *drank up*) a glass of wine. さあ, 杯を～してください Oh, *bottom up*, please.
3〖仕事を与えない〗¶ 彼女は映画界から～されて仕事がない She is now out of work, for she *has been shut out* from the cinema world.
ボス a boss. ¶ 彼は町内の～だ He is the *boss* of the town.
ほすうけい【歩数計】a pedometer.
ポスター a poster. ¶ 芝居の～ *a* theatrical *poster*. バザーの～をはる put up bazaar *posters*. その運動は～の宣伝がきいている The campaign *is* well *postered*.
—カラー a poster color.
ホステス a hostess. ¶ 彼女が会の～をつとめた She acted as *hostess* in the meeting.

ホステル a hostel. ¶ ～は安く泊まれる It does not cost much to stay at *a hostel*.
ユース— a youth hostel.
ポスト 米 a mailbox; 英 a pillar box; (地位) a post. ¶ ～に手紙を投函(ﾄｳｶﾝ)する *mail* (≒ *post*) a letter. 彼は大蔵大臣の～についた He was appointed to the *post* of Finance Minister.
ボストンバッグ a Boston bag.
ほ·する【補する】¶ 彼は会計課長に～された He *was appointed to* the post of chief accountant.
ほせい【補正】correction; revision. ¶ ～する correct; revise.
—予算 a revised budget.
ほぜい【保税】bond.
—貨物 bonded goods. —倉庫 a bonded warehouse. ¶ これは～倉庫に入れることになっている This is to be stored in *a bonded warehouse*.
ぼせい【母性】motherhood. ¶ 彼女の行為は～愛の現われだった Her behavior was a sign of *motherly* love.
—本能 maternal instinct. —保護 protection of motherhood.
ほせん【保線】maintenance of railway tracks.
—区 track maintenance section. —工事 track maintenance work. —工夫 a lineman.
ほぜん【保全】preservation. ¶ 領土の～に意を用いるべきだ We should be considerate in *preserving* the territorial integrity. 政府は文化財の～に努めるべきだ The government should do its utmost for the *preservation* of cultural properties.
ぼせん【母船】a mother ship.
捕鯨— a whaling mother ship.
ぼぜん【墓前】¶ 彼の～に花を捧げた We offered up flowers *before his tomb*. ～で式があった There was a service *at the grave*.
—祭 ¶ ～祭を営んだ We held a memorial service *in front of the tomb* (≒ *before the tomb*).
ほぞ【臍】¶ われわれは観念の～を固めた We *have made up our minds at last*.
ほそ·い【細い】slender; fine; (やせた) spare-built; (狭い) narrow. ¶ 彼女は首が～い She has a *slender* neck. ～い糸 a *fine* thread. ～い道が山頂まで通じている There is a *narrow* path leading to the mountaintop. ～い線を引いてそれを示しなさい Show it by drawing a *fine* line. 彼は～い声でしゃべっている He is talking in a *thin* voice. 彼は食が～い He is a *light* eater.
ほそう【舗装】pavement. ¶ この道路はアスファルトで～してある This road *is surfaced* with asphalt. 道路はコンクリートで～された The road *was paved* with concrete.
—道路 a pavement; a paved road.
ほそうで【細腕】¶ 彼女は女の～で子ども3人を育てた *Woman as she is*, she has brought up her three children alone (≒by herself). こんな少女の～でそんな大家族を養うことはできない It is impossible for *this girl* to support such a large family.
ほそおび【細帯】an under sash.
ほそおもて【細面】a slender face. ¶ 彼女は～の美人だ She is a beautiful woman with *a slender face*.
ほそく【補足】a supplement; a complement. (complement は, 互いに補って完全なものにして「補足」すること, supplement は加えて「補足」すること).
¶ この作品には索引を～する必要がある This work must *be supplemented by* an index. 正義と愛は相互に～し合うものだ Justice and love *complement* each other. 彼がものを書いてかせぐ金は, 教師としてもらうサラリーを～するものであった The money earned from his writings *was supplementary to* his salary as a teacher.
ほそく【捕捉】¶ 彼は～しがたい人物だ He is an *elusive* person. あなたの発言の主旨は～しがたい The gist of what you have said is hard to *grasp*. この文の意味は～しがたい We can hardly *grasp* the meaning of this sentence.
ほそく【細く】thinly. ¶ 鉛筆を～削る sharpen a pencil *to a fine point*. 彼女は目を～して彼の顔を見た She, *narrowing* her eyes, looked at him. / (笑顔を作って) She looked at him *with a smile spreading over her face*. 彼女は～長く生きた She lived a *long and temperate* life.
ほそなが·い【細長い】long and slender.
¶ ～い顔 a *slender* face. 紙を～く切る cut paper *into long slips*.
ほそびき【細引き】(a) cord. ¶ 包みに～をかける *cord up* (≒ *put a cord*) round a package.
ほそぼそ【細細】¶ 彼は～と暮らしている He is making a *poor* living. 彼らは～ながら商売を続けている They have been carrying on a *scanty* business.
ぼそぼそ ¶ なにか～話している They are talking *in a subdued voice*. このパンは～している This bread *is dry and crumbles easily*.
ほそみち【細道】a narrow path; a lane.
ほそめ【細目】narrow eyes. ¶ 窓を～に開けた He opened the window *a little*. 彼女は～で新聞を読んでいる She is reading a newspaper *with her eyes narrowed*. ニンジンを～に切る cut carrot *fine*. このズボンはやや～だ These trousers look rather *narrow*.
ほそ·める【細める】narrow. ¶ 彼は目を～めた He *narrowed his* eyes. 彼女は目を～めてこちらを見ていた She was looking at me *with her eyes half-closed*.
ほそ·る【細る】¶ 食が～ってきた I *have lost my appetite*. 商売がだんだん～ってきた Business *is dwindling* (≒ *is shrinking; is declining*). 心配で身も～る思いだ I *am oppressed* (≒ *am racked*) with anxieties.
ほぞん【保存】preservation. ¶ この証明書はたいせつに～しておいてほしい I want you to *keep* (≒ *preserve*) this certificate. このハムはいつまで～

がききますか How long can this piece of ham *be preserved*?

ポタージュ *potage* (フランス語). ¶ これは〜スープだ This is *potage*.

ぼたい【母体】 a mother's body. ¶ 労働組合が彼の選挙の〜だ The labor union is his *electorate*.

ぼたい【母胎】 the mother's womb.

ぼだい【菩提】 ¶ 彼の〜を弔った I *prayed for the repose of his soul*.

—寺 a family temple. —樹 a linden [tree].

ほださ・れる【絆される】 ¶ 母の情に〜れた I *was moved* (≒ *was overcome*) by maternal affection. 彼の親切に〜れた I *was moved* (≒ *was touched*) by his kindness.

ほたてがい【帆立貝】〘貝類〙 a scallop.

ぽたぽた ¶ 血が〜腕から流れてきた Blood *trickled* down from my arm.

ぽたぽた ¶ 〜と水が落ちてきた Water fell down *in drops*. 顔から汗が〜落ちてきた Sweat *trickled down* from my forehead.

ぼたもち【牡丹餅】 bean paste covered rice cake. ¶ まったくたなから〜だ It's quite *a windfall*.

ぼたやま【ぼた山】 a dirt heap; a slag heap.

ぽたり ¶ カキが一つ〜と落ちた A persimmon fell *with a thud*. しずくが〜と天井から落ちてきた A drop of water *fell down* from the ceiling.

ほたる【蛍】〘虫類〙 a firefly. ¶ 〜の光 a firefly glow. 「〜の光」を全員で歌った All those present sang '*Auld Lang Syne*' together.

—狩り firefly-catching.

ほたるぐさ【螢草】〘植物〙 a hare's-ear.

ぼたん【牡丹】〘植物〙 a [shrub] peony.

—雪 large snowflakes. ¶ 〜雪が降ってきた Snow has begun to fall *in large flakes*.

ボタン a button. ¶ 上着の〜をかける *button up one's* coat. シャツの〜を外す *unbutton one's* shirt. 〜が一つ取れている *A button* is missing. ズボンの〜が一つ取れた *A button* has come off my trousers. この〜は取れそうだ This *button* is loose. 〜が外れている The *button* is undone.

—穴 a buttonhole.

ぼち【墓地】 a graveyard (教会に付属した共同墓地は a churchyard, 教会に付属しない共同墓地は a cemetery).

外人— a foreigners' cemetery.

ホチキス a stapler; a [Hotchkiss] paper fastener (商標名). ¶ 〜で書類をとじた I *stapled* the papers together.

ぼちゃぼちゃ ¶ 子どもが水の中で〜やっている Children *are splashing about* in the water.

ぽちゃぽちゃ ¶ 小さい子どもが〜水遊びをしている Little children *are splashing* in the water. その子は〜と太っている The child *looks plump*.

ぼちゃんと ¶ カエルが池に〜飛び込んだ A frog *splashed* into the pond. 海へ〜石を投げた I threw a stone into the sea *with a splash*.

ほちゅうあみ【捕虫網】 an insect net.

ほちょう【歩調】 pace. ¶ 〜を合わせなさい *Keep in step with* others. もうすこし〜を早め(緩め)よう Let's quicken (slacken) our *pace*. 〜をそろえて行進した We marched *in step*.

ホちょう【ホ調】〘音楽〙 the tone E. ¶ 〜長調 E major. 〜短調 E minor.

ほちょうき【補聴器】 an acousticon.

ぼつ【没】 ¶ きみの作品は〜だ Your work shall *be discarded*. 1950年〜 He *died in* 1950.

ぼっか【牧歌】 a pastoral [song]. ¶ この辺りの〜的風景が大好きだ I like the *pastoral* scenery around here very much.

ぼつが【没我】 self-effacement. ¶ 彼は〜の境地に達した He *has risen above self*. / He *has got to the self-effacing way of living*.

ほっかい【北海】 a northern sea; (イギリス北方の海) the North Sea.

ぽっかり ¶ 道路に〜穴があいた A hole *has broken open* on the road. 空に雲が一つ〜浮かんでいる A cloud is floating *lightly* in the sky.

ほっき【発起】 (事業・新会社の創始) promotion; (提案) proposal; (率先) initiation. ¶ 彼はその案の〜人だ He *has proposed* the plan. T氏の〜でA氏昇進の祝賀パーティーが催された A party was held in celebration of Mr. A's promotion at the *suggestion* of Mr. T. 一念〜して独力で道を切り開こうと思った I *have resolved* to find a way for myself.

—人 a promoter; a proposer; an initiator. —人会 a meeting of promoters.

ぼっき【勃起】 erection. ¶ 〜する erect; stand erect.

ぼっきゃく【没却】 disregard; ignoring. ¶ 自我を〜することが必要だ One must *efface oneself*.

ほっきょく【北極】 the North Pole.

—海 the Arctic Ocean. —グマ a polar bear. —圏 the Arctic Circle. —星 the polestar. —地方 the Arctic regions. —横断飛行 a flight across the North Pole. ¶ 〜横断飛行をした We made a flight across *the North Pole*. —回り ¶ 〜回りでヨーロッパへ飛んだ He flew over to Europe by way of *the North Pole*. —探検 an Arctic expedition. ¶ 一行は〜探検旅行に出かけた The party started on their *Arctic* expedition.

ぽっきり ¶ 1,000円〜しかくれなかった He gave me *neither more nor less than* (≒ *only*; *no more than*) 1,000 yen.

ほっく【発句】 a *hokku*; a *haiku* poem; a seventeen syllable Japanese poem.

ホック a hook. ¶ 服の〜を止める(外す) *hook up* (*unhook*) *one's* dress.

ボックス (席) a box; 〘野球〙 the box. ¶ 彼は〜に立っている He is standing in the *box*. / He *is at bat*.

ぽっくり【木履】 wooden clogs.

ぽっくり ¶ 彼は〜死んだ He died *suddenly*. / He *died a sudden death*.

ホッケー 〘競技〙 hockey.

アイス— ice hockey.

ぼっけん【木剣】 a wooden sword.

ほ

ぼつご【没後】¶ その作家は～人気が出た It was *after his death* that the writer became popular among people. ～有名になる人もいるようだ It seems that some persons do not win a reputation *until they are dead.* 彼は～５年だ It is five years *since he died* (≒ *since he passed away*).

ぼっこう【勃興】rise. ¶ 民族国家の～ the *rise* of racial nations. 戦後のアフリカ諸国の～はめざましいものがある The *rise* of some countries in Africa after the war is really wonderful. / Some countries in Africa *have* rapidly *risen to great power* after the war.

ぼっこうしょう【没交渉】¶ このごろ彼とは～だ I *have nothing to do with* him of late.

ほっこく【北国】the northern provinces.
—人 a northerner.

ぼっこん【墨痕】¶ 彼は～鮮やかに書き上げた He wrote it *in bold strokes.*

ほっさ【発作】a fit. ¶ ～が起こった I had *a fit.* この子どもは～的に泣く The child is in the habit of crying *hysterically.* 彼は～的に勉強をする He studies *by fits and starts.* 卒中の～に襲われた I was seized with *a fit* of apoplexy.

ぼっしゅう【没収】confiscation. ¶ 彼は全財産を～された He *had* all his properties *confiscated.* 彼は反逆によって土地を～された He *forfeited* his estate because of treason. / His estate *was confiscated* because of treason.

ぼっしゅみ【没趣味】tastelessness. ¶ 彼は～な生活をしている He lives a *tasteless* life.

ほっしん【発心】spiritual awakening. ¶ 彼は～して出家した *Having spiritual awakening,* he became a priest.

ほっ·する【欲する】desire ; wish ; want. ¶ だれでも長生きすることを～する Every man *desires* to live long. 彼は自分の～するがままに行動している He behaves as he *pleases.* 私たちはみな平和を～する We all *wish for* peace. それは私の～するところではない That is against my *wish* (≒ *will*). 救いを～する者は来れ Those who *want* to be saved, come to me. おのれの～するところを人に施せ Do to others as you *would* be done by. 将を射んと～すればまず馬を射よ He that *would* the daughter win must with the mother first begin.

ぼっ·する【没する】sink ; (死ぬ) die. ¶ 太陽は西に～した The sun *has set* in the west. 彼は水中に～して二度と浮かばなかった He *sank* under the water, never to appear above the surface. 満潮時には岩は水中に～した The rocks *were submerged* at high tide. 雪はひざを～するほどに積もっていた The snow lay knee-deep. 1616年シェイクスピア～する Shakespeare *died* in 1616.

ぼつぜん【勃然】¶ ～と騒動が起こった A riot has broken out *suddenly.* 彼は～と怒りだした He *got into a rage.*

ほっそく【発足】starting. ¶ この会は来月から～する This society is to *start* next month.

ほっそり ¶ ～した slender ; slim ; slight ; thin.

ほったてごや【掘っ立て小屋】a hut ; a cabin.

ポツダムせんげん【ポツダム宣言】the Potsdam Declaration. ¶ 日本は～を無条件で受諾した Japan accepted *the Potsdam Declaration* without reservation.

ほったらか·す neglect. ¶ 彼女は子どもを～しておいた She *neglected* her children. 仕事を～しておいてはいけない Never *leave* your work *undone.* 背中の痛みを～しておいてはいけません You must not *leave* the pain on your back *untreated* (≒ *untended*).

ほったん【発端】the origin. ¶ それが事件の～となった That was *the origin* of the affair. そもそもの～から話すことにしたい I am going to tell the story from the very *beginning.* ～にまでさかのぼろう Let's trace it to its *origin.*

ぼっちゃん【坊ちゃん】a boy ; a son ; (世間知らず) a greenhorn. ¶ 彼はほんとにお～だ (世間知らずだ) He *knows nothing of the world.* すぐむきになるところはまだまだ～だ He may well be called *a greenhorn,* for he flies into a passion so easily. この人は～育ちだ (世間知らずだ) He *is ignorant of the world.*

ぽっちり a little ; a bit. ⇒すこし

ぽってり ¶ ～としたかわいい少女 a pretty *plump* girl. ～としたほっぺの赤ちゃん a baby with *plump* cheeks. ～として健康そうな若い女性 a *buxom* young lady. ～とした丸いびん a *big-bellied* bottle.

ほっと ¶ ～して with relief. それで彼は～ひと安心した It *reassured* him. それを聞いて～した I *was relieved* to hear that. 彼はいくらか～した He *felt* a certain *relief.* 彼は～ため息をついた He *gave* (≒ *breathed*) *a sigh of relief.* 彼女は～ひと呼吸した She *drew a breath of relief.* 一同は～安どのため息をもらした *A sigh of relief* went round. ここに着いて～した *We have* all *felt at home* here.

ぽっと ¶ 彼はすぐ～顔を赤らめる He *blushes* (≒ *colors up*) easily. 彼女のほおが～紅潮した Her cheeks *blushed.* 彼女の顔に～赤みがさした *A tinge of color* came into her face. 彼は～赤くなって何事か小さな声で言った He *reddened* and muttered something.

ポット a pot. ¶ 彼女は～でお茶を入れた She made tea in *a pot.*
コーヒー— a coffee pot.

ぼっとう【没頭】¶ 彼は詩作に～している He *devotes himself to* (≒ *is engrossed in ; gives himself up to ; is absorbed in*) composing poems. 彼は仕事に～した He *threw himself into* work. 彼はその研究に～していた *His whole mind was intent on* the study.

ホットケーキ a hot cake ; a pancake ; a griddlecake.

ぽっとで【ぽっと出】¶ 田舎から～の学生 a student *fresh from the country.*

ホットドッグ a hot dog.

ホットパンツ hot-pants.

ぼつにゅう【没入】¶ 彼は研究に～している He *is*

immersed (≒ *immerses himself*; *is involved*; *is absorbed*) *in* research (≒ study). 彼は思索に～している He *is lost* (≒ *is deep*) *in* thought. 彼は思索に～した He *gave himself up to* thought.

ぼつねん【没年】¶～78歳 He *died at the age of* seventy-eight. ～は1970年 He *died in* 1970.

ぽつねんと ¶彼女は～座っていた I found her sitting *all alone*. 彼は皆から離れてひとり～窓辺に立っていた He was standing *aloof* by the window.

ぼっぱつ【勃発】an outbreak. ¶戦争の～のとき at the *outbreak* of war. 戦争が～した A war *broke out*.

ホップ〘植物〙a hop. ¶～を摘む pick *hops*.
—乾燥所 a hop kiln; an oasthouse. —畑 a hop field.

ホップ（跳躍）hop.
—ステップアンドジャンプ hop, step and jump; the triple jump.

ほっぺ(た)【頬っぺ(た)】a cheek. ¶リンゴのような(まっかな)～の少女 a little *apple-cheeked* (≒ *rosy cheeked*) girl. 人の～をぶつ slap *a person* on the *cheek*. このお菓子は～が落ちるほどおいしい This cake *tastes very delicious*.

ぽっぽ ¶～と湯気を立てている湯 *steaming* water. やかんが～と湯気を立てている The kettle *is puffing*. 汽車はきれいな空に～と白い煙をはいていた The *puffs* of train smoke were white in the clear air.

ほっぽう【北方】¶彼らはさらに～に進んだ They went farther *north*. 飛行機は～に向かって飛んだ The airplane flew *toward the north*. 仙台は東京の～に位する Sendai is *to the north* of Tokyo. ～領土問題 the *northern* territories problem.

ぼつぼつ ¶さて～出かけましょう Well, let's be getting along. 仕事はまあ～だ My business *has been only so-so*. / My business *has been neither very good nor very bad*.

ぼつぼつ（吹出物）rash; eruption. ¶彼は顔じゅうに～がある He has *rashes* all over his face.

ぽつぽつ（すこしずつ）bit by bit;（はん点）a spot. ¶雨が～降りだした The rain began to fall in drops. 雨は降っていたが～だった Rain was falling, but only *very slightly*. 彼はすこしずつ～と証拠を集めた *Piece by piece* he assembled the evidence. そのテーブル掛けには～と小さな丸いしみがついていた On the tablecloth there were small round *stains*.

ぼつらく【没落】fall. ¶ローマ帝国の～ the *fall* of the Roman Empire. 王国の～ the *downfall* of a kingdom. 一家の～ the *ruin* of a family. 一家は～した The family *was reduced* (≒ *was brought*) *to ruin*. / The family *was ruined*.

ぽつりぽつり ¶彼女は～と自分の家族のことを話しはじめた *Little by little* she began to talk of her family.

ほつれ【解れ】a fray.
—毛 stray hairs.

ほつ・れる【解れる】fray. ¶～れたそで口 a *frayed* sleeve-opening. ～れた糸 a *loose* thread. へりが～れないようにする prevent the hem from *raveling out*. 髪が～れた My hair *has become loose*.

ボディーガード a guard; a bodyguard. ¶彼は～として常に大統領と行動を共にする He always goes with the president as *a bodyguard*.

ボディービル body-building. ¶彼は～にいっしょうけんめいだ He is keen on *body-building*.

ほてり【火照り】heat; glow. ¶火の～で彼女のほおは上気していた The *heat* made her cheeks look flushed.

ホテル a hotel. ¶～のボーイ a page; 米 a bellboy. ～に泊まる put up (≒ register) at *a hotel*; 米 check in at *a hotel*. ～を出る leave *a hotel*; 米 check out of *a hotel*. 彼はその～に滞在している He is staying at the *hotel*. この～に泊めてもらえますか Can I have an accommodation in this *hotel*? この～には300人泊まれる The *hotel* has accommodations for three hundred.

ほて・る【火照る】¶そのことを考えると彼女の顔は～った Her face *flushed* at the thought. 彼の顔は暑さで赤く～っていた His face *was red* with the heat.

ほてん【補塡】¶損害を～する *make up* [*for*] (≒ *make good*) a loss. 不足分を～する *supply* (≒ *fill up*) a deficiency. これで費用が～できるだろう This will *cover* the expenses.

ほど【程】**1**〚程度〛¶彼はひとりで歩けない～弱っている He is *so* weak *that* he cannot walk by himself. / He is *too* weak *to* walk by himself.
あのとき～困ったことはない I have never been *so* troubled *as* I was then.
きのうは足が痛くなる～歩いた Yesterday I walked till my feet were sore.
さっきからこれ～言っているのに，私の言うことがわからないのか After all I have said, you still don't understand?
あれ～言ったのに本を忘れてきたのか Even after speaking to you as I did, did you forget to bring the book?
自慢できる～のことをしたことはない I have done nothing worth boasting of.
今は忙しいという～でもない I am not *so* (≒ *very*) busy now.
それはそうくやしがる～のことでもない It is nothing to get *so* upset about.
心配する～のけがではない The injury is nothing to be anxious about.
彼女に失恋したからといって，死ぬ～のことはない It *is* not *worth* killing yourself just because you cannot have her.
私のなど別荘といえる～のものではない Mine is no villa *worth* mentioning. / Mine is no villa to speak of.
私には財産といえる～の財産はない I have no property *worth* mentioning. / I have no

property to speak of.

あの人はそばにいてもよく聞こえない～小さい声で話す He speaks in *so* small a voice 〔*that*〕 it is difficult to hear him even if you are at his side.

花びんが倒れる～の激しい地震だった The earthquake was *so* strong *that* the flower vase fell over.

2 〖比較〗 ¶ 彼は私～成績がよくない He does not do *so* (≒ *as*) well at school *as* I.

彼は私～背が高くない He is not *so* (≒ *as*) tall *as* I.

この仕事ははたで見る～簡単ではない This work is not *so* (≒ *as*) simple *as* it might seem 〔to someone who is not familiar with it〕.

その仕事は思った～たいへんではなかった The work was not *so* (≒ *as*) difficult *as* I had thought it would be.

彼～速く走れる者はいない Nobody 〔else〕 can run *so* (≒ *as*) fast *as* he.

ことしの冬は去年の冬～寒くない It is not *so* (≒ *as*) cold this winter *as* it was last winter.

故郷～よい所はない There is no place *like one's* hometown.

健康～ありがたいものはない There is no blessing *like* health. / Nothing is more important *than* health.

久しぶりで親友に会ったとき～楽しいことはない Nothing is nicer *than* meeting a close friend after a long time.

その問題は考えれば考える～難しい *The more* I think about the problem, *the more* difficult it becomes.

返事は早ければ早い～よい *The sooner* you can give me an answer, *the better*.

スポーツは練習すればする～じょうずになる In sports, *the more* you practice, *the better* you become.

値段が高ければ高い～, 品がよいとはかぎらない It does not necessarily follow that *the higher* an article is in price, *the better* it is (≒ *the higher* the price, *the better* the article).

3 〖限度・適度〗 a limit ; a degree. ¶ 酒も～を過ごすと毒になる Too much liquor is bad for the health.

ものには～というものがある There are *limits* to everything.

彼はあつかましいにも～がある His impudence *goes to extremes*. / He is *awfully* impudent.

4 〖分際〗 ¶ 彼は身の～を知らない He does not know his *place*.

彼に身の～を思い知らせてやろう I will put him in his *place*.

5 〖時間・距離など〗 ¶ 京都まであとどれ～かかりますか *How much longer* will it take to Kyoto?

ここから学校までどれ～ありますか *How far* is it from here to the school?

6 〖およそ・約〗 ¶ この道を300メートル～行くと駅に出る If you go along this road *about* 300 meters, you will come to the station.

返事は3日～待ってください Please wait three days *or so* for my answer.

列車は15分～遅れた The train was *about* fifteen minutes late.

5,000円～貸してくれないか Would you lend me *about* 5,000 yen?

地滑りで15人～がけがをした *Some* fifteen people were injured in the landslide.

ほどあい 【程合い】 ¶ それが～だろう It may *be moderate*. 彼は～をよくわきまえた人間だ He is a very *moderate* man.

ほどう 【歩道】 英 a footway ; a footpath ; 米 (おもに舗装した歩道) a sidewalk ; 英 (舗装した歩道) a pavement.

横断― a crosswalk.

ほどう 【舗道】 英 (舗装した歩道) a pavement ; 米 (舗装した歩道) a sidewalk ; 米 (舗装した車道) a pavement.

ほどう 【補導】 guidance. ¶ ～によって非行を少なくする reduce delinquency by *guidance*. 職業～の担当者 a man in charge of vocational *guidance* ; a vocational counselor.

ほど・く 【解く】 ¶ 結び目(なわ)を～く *untie* (≒ *loosen*) knots (ropes). 包みを～く *unwrap* a package. その荷を～く *unpack* the baggage.

ほとけ 【仏】 the Buddha ; (死んだ人) the dead ; the deceased. ¶ 彼はまるで～のような人だ He is *a perfect angel*. その男はベッドで～になっていた We found him *dead* in his bed. ～が運ばれてきた The *dead body* has been brought in. 地獄に～とはこのことだ It's just the mercy of heaven you're here. 皆がかげで笑っていても彼は知らぬが～だった He *was blissfully unaware* that everybody laughed at him behind his back.

ほど・ける 【解ける】 ¶ 彼の体を縛っているひもが～けた His bonds *were loosened* (≒ *came loose* ; *got untied*).

ほどこし 【施し】 almsgiving.

ほどこ・す 【施す】 ¶ 彼はばく大な金を貧者に～した He *gave* (≒ *donated*) a great deal of money to the poor. 彼は私に恩恵を～してくれた He *has done* me a favor. 彼はあらゆる手段を～した He *took* every possible means. 彼が善政を～したおかげでその国は一時平和で栄えた Owing to his good government the land enjoyed a period of peace and prosperity.

ほどちか・い 【程近い】 ¶ ～い所にある公園 a *near-by* park ; a park *near by*. ～い所に教会がある There is a church in the neighborhood.

ほどとお・い 【程遠い】 ¶ 満足というには～い It *is far from* satisfactory.

ほととぎす 【時鳥・不如帰】 〖鳥類〗 a cuckoo.

ほどなく 【程無く】 ¶ ～目的地に着いた *Soon* (≒ *Before long*) we arrived at the destination. 彼は～来るだろう He will come *soon* (≒ *before long*). / *It will not be long before* he comes. / He will be here *in one moment*. ～彼はもどってきた *Presently* he returned. 私が着いてから～彼は家を出た He left home *shortly* after I arrived. 冬は～やってくる

Winter *is near at hand.* / Winter *is round the corner.* / Winter *is on its way.*

ほとばし·る【迸る】 ¶ 血が～り出た Blood *gushed out* (≒ *spurted out*). 彼女の口からどっとことばが～り出た Words *rushed* from her. / *A torrent* of words *poured* from her mouth.

ほとほと completely ; quite ; entirely. ¶ 彼はそのことが～いやになった He was *completely* disgusted with that. それを思うと～いやになる It makes me *quite* sick to think of it. こういう生活が～いやになった I am *quite* tired of this life. あの連中が～いやになった *I'm fed up with* them.

ほどほど【程程】 ¶ 飲むのは～にしなくてはいけません You must not drink more than is good for you. 冗談も～にしなさい You carry your joke too far.

ぽとぽと ¶ 水が～と流れ落ちていた A stream of water *was trickling.* 彼は～水滴をたらしながら水の中から上がってきた He came *dripping* out of the water. しずくが枝から～と落ちた Drops of water *fell* from the branches. 血が地面に～と落ちた Drops of blood *fell* on the ground.

ほとぼり ¶ 興奮の～はまださめていない The excitement *has* not yet *cooled down.* 事件の～がさめた The affair *has blown* (≒ *is*) *over.*

ほどよ·い【程よい】 ¶ 部屋は～く暖房がきいていた The room was *properly* heated. 運動は～いのがたいせつだ You must take exercise *in moderation.* 彼は彼らを～くあしらった He dealt with them *tactfully.* / He *was very tactful with* them. ちょうど～く煮えている It is *perfectly* boiled. / It is done *to a turn.* ～く塩味がついている It is *well* seasoned.

ほとり【辺り】 ¶ 池の～に家がある There is a house *by* (≒ *near*) the pond.

ほとんど【殆ど】 almost ; nearly ; (否定) little ; hardly ; (およそ) about.

¶ もう～暗い It is *almost* dusky (≒ dark). ～同じサイズだ It is *about* the same size. 昨夜は～一睡もしなかった I *hardly* slept a wink last night. 彼には～会ったことがない I saw *very little* of him. この10年間彼は～日本にいたことがない For the last ten years he has been *little* in Japan. 彼がそこに行くことは～ない It is *seldom* that he goes there. 私に会いに来る人は～いない *Very few* people come to see me. 食物は～残っていない There is *scarcely* any food left. 現金は～尽きてしまった Cash is *nearly* out. それは～奇跡ともいうべきだ It is *little short of* a miracle.

ボナンザグラム a bonanzagram (bonanza は「大当たり」「大福運」の意味).

ほにゅう【哺乳】 ━動物 a mammal. ━類〘動物〙 Mammalia. ━びん a [nursing] bottle.

ぼにゅう【母乳】 breast milk. ¶ 赤ちゃんを～で育てる feed a baby on *mother's milk.*

ほね【骨】 1〘動物の〙 a bone. ¶ 犬は牛の～をしゃぶるのが好きだ Dogs like to gnaw on beef *bones.* この魚は～が多い This fish *is bony.* 魚の～がのどに刺さって痛い A fish *bone* is stuck in my throat and it hurts. 魚の～を取る *bone* a fish. 彼は～ばった顔をしている He has a *bony* face. 彼の体は～太だ He is stoutly built. / He has large *bones.* 彼はスキーで足の～を折った He broke his leg when he was skiing. 医者に～を接いでもらった I had *a* broken *bone* set by the doctor. 寒くて～の髄まで冷えきった I am chilled to the *bone.* 彼女は～と皮ばかりにやつれてしまった She has been reduced to *a mere skeleton.* / She has become all skin and *bones.* 交通事故でももに～まで達する傷を負った In the traffic accident my thigh was cut to the *bone.*

2〘骨に似たもの·中心·支え〙 ¶ かさの～が2本折れている Two of my umbrella *ribs* are broken. 子どもたちが暴れて障子の～を折ってしまった The children ran wild and broke the *frames* of the paper-covered sliding door. 計画の～だけはできた I have worked out *an outline* for the plan.

3〘気骨〙 ¶ 彼はなかなか～のある人物だ He is a man of *fortitude.* / He has *fortitude.* 男がそんな～なしでどうするのだ How can you call yourself a man with so little *backbone?*

4〘苦労·努力·世話〙 ¶ この仕事を3日でやるのはちょっと～だ It will take some doing to finish the work in three days. 彼は～のおれる仕事を進んでする He is willing to do hard work. この件では彼もたいへん～をおってくれた He *took* great *pains in* this matter for me. 彼を説得するのに～をおった It took some doing for me to persuade him. / I had a hard time persuading him. ときどき～を休めながらやってください *Take a rest* sometimes while working on it.

5〘慣用的表現〙 ¶ 彼らはブラジルに～を埋める覚悟で移民した They emigrated into Brazil to make it their last home. こんな店で働いていては～までしゃぶられてしまう If we continue to work at this store, we will be worked to death. ぼくには～を拾ってくれる子どもがいない I have no child to take care of my *remains.* 彼もとうとう～になってしまった He has passed away. / He has finally been called to Heaven.

ほねおしみ【骨惜しみ】 ¶ ～してはいけない Spare no pains. 4年間～せずその仕事をやってきた For four years he *has labored at* the task. 彼は～せず働く He *keeps* (≒ *has*) *his nose to the grindstone.* ～しては何事も上達しない You cannot make progress in anything without some *efforts.*

ほねおり【骨折り】 trouble ; an effort ; exertion. ¶ あなたのお～でこの会を開くことができまし

ほ

た Thanks to your good offices it was possible to hold this meeting.

ほねおりがい【骨折りがい】¶ ～があった My efforts *were crowned* (≒ *were rewarded*) *with success.* 彼はその～のない仕事にうんざりしている He is fed up with the *thankless* task.

ほねおりぞん【骨折り損】¶ まったく～だった All my labor *was thrown away* (≒ *was lost*). それを捜したが～だった I searched for it *vainly* (≒ *in vain*). ～のくたびれもうけだった I only got laughed at for my *pains.* / All my *efforts* were for nothing.

ほねぐみ【骨組み】frame. ¶ 計画の～ the *outline* of a plan. 建物の～ the *frame* of a building. ～のがっちりした男 a *strongly-built* man. ～のがっちりした体 a *sturdy* body. この家は～ががっちりしている This house *is solidly built.*

ほねつぎ【骨接ぎ】bone setting. ¶ ～をする set broken bones.
—医 a bonesetter.

ほねっぽ･い【骨っぽい】¶ ～い男 (気骨のある男) a man *of spirit.* ～い魚 a *bony* fish.

ほねぬき【骨抜き】¶ ～になった法案 a *mutilated* (≒ *watered-down*) bill.

ほねみ【骨身】¶ 北風が～にしみた The north wind *was severe.* その教訓は私の～にしみた The lesson *came deeply home to me.* / The lesson *came deeply to my heart.*

ほねやすめ【骨休め】a rest; relaxation. ¶ きみには仕事の～が必要だ You need some *rest* from business. ～して苦労を忘れた I *relaxed* and forgot all my troubles. ～にどこかに行きましょう Let's go somewhere for *relaxation.* 毎日がいそがしくて～はほとんどできない My days are so full that I have little *leisure.*

ほのお【炎】a flame. ¶ 階段は～に包まれていた The stairs were *in flame.*

ほのか【仄か】¶ 彼らの間には～な愛情が通っているようだった There was apparently a *warm* note of affection between them. 彼はそのことを～に覚えていた He remembered it *vaguely* (≒ *in a vague sort of way*). 彼女のことばには～に不満の調べがあった There was a *slight* note of disapproval in her voice. 遠くに～な光が見えた There was a *faint* (≒ *dim*) light in the distance. ～な笑みが彼女の口もとに浮かんだ A *faint* smile crossed her lips.

ほのぐら･い【仄暗い】dim; dusky. ¶ ～いホール a *dimly-lighted* hall. ～い光 a *dim* light. ～い空 the *pale gray* sky.

ほのじろ･い【仄白い】dimly white.

ほのぼの【仄仄】¶ やっと夜が～と明けはじめた At last came the *glimmer* of dawn.

ほのめか･す【仄めかす】¶ 彼はそのことを暗に～した He *referred vaguely to* the matter. 医者は病人はもうだめかもしれないと～した The doctor *hinted* (≒ *dropped a hint*) that the end might come any time. 彼はそのことについてなにも～そうとしなかった He *kept me* completely *in the dark* as to that. 彼はなにをしてきたのかなにも～さなかった He *gave no hint of* what he had been doing.

ほのめ･く【仄めく】glimmer. ¶ ろうそくの光が～いていた The candle *glimmered.*

ほばく【捕縛】¶ 警官はその泥棒を～した The policeman *apprehended* (≒ *arrested*) the thief. 彼らはその犯罪者を～して凶器を取り上げた They *seized* the criminal and disarmed him.

ほばしら【帆柱】a mast. ¶ 2本の～の船 a two-*masted* vessel; a schooner with two *masts.*

ぼひ【墓碑】a tombstone; a gravestone.
—銘 an epitaph.

ポピュラー popular.
—ソング a popular song. —ミュージック popular music; pop music; pop.

ぼひょう【墓標】a grave-post; a headstone. ¶ ～の前にぬかずく bow (≒ kneel; prostrate) *oneself* before *a headstone.*

ほふく【匍匐】creeping. ¶ ～で進む *crawl* along.

ボブスレー a bobsleigh; a bobsled. ¶ 疾走する～ *a* fast running *bobsleigh.*

ポプラ a poplar; an aspen. ¶ 背の高い～が2列にずっと並んでいる道 a road with double lines of high *poplars.* ～並木の道 an avenue of *poplars.*

ポプリン poplin. ¶ ～の織物 a *poplin* fabric.

ほふ･る【屠る】¶ 牛を～る *slaughter* (≒ *butcher*) cows. 全員を～る *massacre* (≒ *slaughter*) all of them. 敵を～る *defeat* the enemy.

ほへい【歩兵】an infantryman; a foot soldier.
—師団 an infantry division. —銃 a rifle. —隊 an infantry corps. —連隊 an infantry regiment.

ぼへい【募兵】¶ ～によって兵を補強する *recruit* an army (徴兵 (強制的募兵) は conscription; 米 draft).

ほぼ【保母】a nurse.

ほぼ【略･粗】about; (大部分) for the most part. ¶ 彼は～それを完成した He has *nearly* (≒ *almost*) finished it.

ほほえまし･い【頬笑ましい】pleasant; cheerful. ¶ ～い光景であった It was a *cheerful* (≒ *comforting*) scene.

ほほえみ【頬笑み】a smile. ¶ 彼は愛想のよい～を浮かべた He gave me *a* friendly *smile.* 彼の顔から～が消えていった The *smile* faded from his face.

ほほえ･む【頬笑む】¶ 彼は彼女を見てにこやかに～んだ He *smiled* blandly *at* her.

ほまえせん【帆前船】a sailing ship; a sailing vessel.

ポマード pomade. ¶ ～をつける apply *pomade* to hair.

ほまれ【誉れ】an honor. ¶ 美人の～高い女性 a *noted* beauty. 一国の～となる人物 *an honor to* a country.

ほめたた･える【褒め称える】¶ 聴衆は彼を～えた The audience *applauded* him. 受賞者は熱烈に～えられた There was hearty *applause* at the winner. われわれはその光景を～えた We *admired* the view. 彼は心からそれを～えた He *gave* it *his highest praise*.

ほめちぎ·る【褒めちぎる】¶ 彼らは口をきわめて彼を～った They *praised* him *to the skies*. 彼は彼女の音楽の才能を～った He *spoke very highly of* her talent for music.

ほめ·る【賞める·誉める·褒める】praise. ¶ 大いに～る speak highly(*of*); praise to the skies. 彼をだれもが～た Everyone *spoke well of* him. / Everyone *praised* him. われわれは彼のがんばり精神を～る We *admire* his fortitude. 彼の勇気は～きれない His courage is beyond all *praise*. / We cannot *overpraise* him for his courage. 人は彼女の責任感を～た People *praised* her for her responsibility.

ホモ homosexuality. ¶ ～の人 a homosexual; a homo. ～の傾向 homosexual tendency.

ホモサピエンス Homo sapiens.

ほや【火屋】a lamp chimney. ¶ ランプの～を掃除する clean *a lamp chimney*.

ぼや【小火】a small fire.

ぼや·く complain. ¶ あの男はいつも～いてばかりいる That fellow *is* always *grumbling*. 彼は給料が低いと～いている He *complains* that his salary is too small. なにをぶつぶつ～いているのか What *are* you *grumbling about*?

ぼや·ける grow dim. ¶ この眼鏡をかけると～けて見える I can only see *dimly* with these glasses on. 涙で彼の顔が～けて見えた Tears *blurred* his countenance.

ほやほや steaming; hot. ¶ 焼きたての～のイモ a potato *steaming hot from the fire*. この料理はできたての～だ This dish *is fresh from the oven*. 彼は大学出の～だ He *is fresh from college*. ふたりは新婚～だ They are a *newly wedded* couple. / The couple has been married only for a short time.

ぼやぼや ¶ ～するな Look out! ～して電車を乗りすごした I *was* so *careless* (≒ *absent-minded*) that I rode past my stop. もう～してはいられない We have no time to *lose*. / We have no time to *fool around* like this.

ほゆう【保有】possession.
—者 a possessor. —地 a holding. —米 rice holdings.

ほよう【保養】recuperation. ¶ 目の～には美しい自然に接するのがいちばんいい Nothing is better *for the health* of your eyes than to see beautiful scenery. きのう上野へ行ったら桜が満開で, 思いがけず目の～になった Yesterday when I went to Ueno Park, I found the cherry blossoms at their best, and I could unexpectedly *feast my eyes* on the beautiful scene. 伊豆で病後の～をしている He *is recuperating* in Izu.
—地 a health resort.

ほら【洞】a cave.

ほら【法螺】a big talk; (俗語) hot air. ¶ ～を吹く talk big. あの男の言うことは～ばかりだ What he says is a lot of *hot air*. / He is full of *hot air*.
—貝 a trumpet shell. —話 a tall story. —吹き a braggart. 大— a big talk.

ほら Look! ¶ ～, ごらん Look there! ～, 犬がやってくる *Look!* There comes a dog! ～, 鳥が鳴いている *Listen!* Birds are singing. ～, その機械に触っちゃいけないって言っただろう I told you not to touch the machine, *you know*. ～, だからそう言ったのに *Oh,* I've told you, haven't I?

ぼら【鯔】a gray mullet.

ほらあな【洞穴】a cave.

ほらがとうげ【洞が峠】¶ 彼は～をきめこんで動こうともしない He won't move an inch, *sitting on the fence*.

ほり【堀】(城の) a moat; (掘り割り) a canal. ¶ ～を掘る dig *a moat*. ～を埋める fill up *a moat*.

ほり【彫り】engraving. ¶ これは～がよい This *is* well *carved*. 彼は～の深い顔をしている He has a *clear-cut* face. / He has a face with *clear-cut* features.

ほりあ·てる【掘り当てる】¶ 油田を～てる *strike* oil. 彼はついに大金鉱を～てた At last he *struck* a big gold mine.

ポリエチレン polyethylene.

ほりおこ·す【掘り起こす】¶ 土を～す *turn up* the soil. 埋もれた真実を～そうとしている They are trying to *bring to light* the buried truth.

ほりかえ·す【掘り返す】¶ 土を～す *turn* (≒ *dig*) *up* the soil. 水道工事で道路を～している They *are digging* the road for waterway construction.

ほりさ·げる【掘り下げる】dig down. ¶ 真相をもっと～げる必要がある It is necessary to *look* deeper *into* the matter.

ほりだしもの【掘り出し物】a find. ¶ ～をする make *a great find*. あの店にはよく～がある We often find *a bargain* in that store.

ほりだ·す【掘り出す】¶ 地下に埋められた宝物を～す *dig out* the treasure buried under the ground.

ほりぬきいど【掘り抜き井戸】an artesian well.

ほりぬ·く【掘り抜く】dig through; bore. ¶ 山を～いてトンネルをつくった We *dug* a tunnel *through* the mountain.

ほりばた【堀端】the side of the moat; the moat embankment.

ぼりぼり ¶ あまり～かくな Don't *scratch* so violently. 歯が痛くてピーナッツを～かじれない I can't *crunch* peanuts as I have a toothache.

ほりもの【彫り物】(彫刻) carving; (いれずみ) tattoo. ¶ ～をする tattoo. あの男は背中一面にヘビの～をしている The man has serpents *tattooed* all over his back.

ほりゅう【保留】reservation. ¶ 返事はあすまで～させてください Let me *defer* my answer till tomorrow. その問題はもうすこし～にしておいてほしい The problem shall *be reserved* till a little while later. 反対する権利を～する We *reserve* the right to disagree. ～つきで

with *reservations.* 〜なしで without *reservations.*

—事項 a reddendum (複 reddenda). —条件 a reserve.

ほりゅう【蒲柳】(かわ柳) a purple willow ; (弱い体質) delicate health. ¶ 生まれつき彼女は〜の質だ She is *of delicate health* by nature.

ボリューム volume. ¶ 〜の豊かな声 a voice of great *volume.* 〜が増す gain in *quantity.*

ほりょ【捕虜】 a prisoner. ¶ 〜にする take *a person prisoner.*

—収容所 a prisoners camp (POW Camp と略記する).

ほりわり【掘り割り】 a canal.

ほ・る【彫る】 carve. ¶ いすとテーブルの脚にカシの葉の模様が〜ってあった The legs of chairs and table *were carved with* oak leaves. 大理石に馬が〜ってある The image of a horse *is carved* (≒ *is engraved*) in the marble. 碑に彼の名前が〜られている His name *is inscribed* on the monument. 指輪に彼女の名を〜ってプレゼントした I presented her with a ring *inscribed with* her name.

ほ・る【掘る】 dig. ¶ 穴を〜る *dig* a hole. 地面を〜る *dig* the ground. 石炭を〜る *cut* coal. イモを〜る *dig up* potatoes. 深さ5メートルの穴を〜る *dig* the ground five meters deep. 海底トンネルを〜る *make* (≒ *cut*) a tunnel under the sea. モグラは地中にトンネルを〜って進む The mole goes *tunneling* in the ground.

ぼ・る make undue profits (*on*). ¶ あの店はばかに〜る That store *overcharges.*

ポルカ〘音楽〙 polka.

ボルシェビキ a Bolshevik.

ホルスタイン a Holstein.

ボルト〘電気〙 volt ; (ねじ) a bolt. ¶ 100〜の電流 a 100-*volt* current. 〜を締める screw *a bolt.*

ボルドー (ブドウ酒) Bordeaux. ¶ 〜の赤がこの料理によく合う The red *Bordeaux* goes well with this food.

—液 Bordeaux mixture.

ホルマリン〘化学〙 formalin. ¶ 〜につける preserve (*something*) in *formalin.*

ホルモン hormone. ¶ 彼は〜の分泌が異常だ He suffers from a disorder in the secretion of *hormone.* 彼女は〜欠乏症だ She has a *hormone* deficiency.

男性(女性)— the male (female) hormone.

ホルン〘音楽〙 a horn. ¶ 〜を演奏する play *the horn.*

イングリッシュ— an English horn. フレンチ— a French horn.

ほれこ・む【惚れ込む】¶ 彼らは彼女の人柄に〜んだ Her sweet nature *gripped* their hearts. 彼女は彼の勇敢さに〜んだ She *was carried away by* his bravery.

ほれぼれ【惚れ惚れ】¶ 〜するような声だ What a *fascinating* voice! 彼は着飾った美しい娘の姿を〜とながめた He looked *fondly* at his daughter beautifully dressed up. 彼女は〜するような微笑を浮かべてわれわれにあいさつをした She greeted us *with a* most charming *smile* on her face. 彼は彼女の〜とする姿に見とれた He was enchanted by her *beauty.* 彼女は美しい音楽に〜と聴き入っていた *In rapture* (≒ *In ecstasy*) she listened to the beautiful music.

ほ・れる【惚れる】¶ 女に〜れる *fall in love with* a woman. 彼らは〜れ合った仲だ The two *are in love with* each other.

ボレロ (婦人の上着) a bolero (複 boleros) ; (舞踊) bolero.

ほろ【幌】 a hood. ¶ 〜をかける(おろす) pull up (let down) *the top.*

—馬車 a caravan.

ぼろ【襤褸】 **1** rags.

—会社 a shaky firm. —きれ a rag. —ぐつ worn-out shoes. —自転車 a shabby bicycle.

2〖失敗する〗¶ 彼は味方のふりをしてかえって〜を出した He *betrayed himself* when he tried to pretend to be our friend.

彼はけっして〜を出さない He never fails to *put his best foot forward.*

ぼろ・い ¶ 〜いもうけだ What an *easy* gain! 〜い商売だ What a *lucrative* job!

ぼろくそ【襤褸糞】¶ 人を〜に言う speak very ill of *a person* ; speak most disparagingly of *a person.*

ポロシャツ a polo shirt.

ほろにが・い【ほろ苦い】 ¶ 〜い人生 a *bitter-sweet* life. 人生は〜い Life *is sweet as well as bitter.*

ポロネーズ〘音楽〙 polonaise.

ほろ・びる【滅びる】 be destroyed. ¶ この風習は〜びてしまっている The custom *has died out.* その民族は3,000年前に〜びた The race *perished* 3,000 years ago. 原子爆弾を用いる戦争がもう一度起こったなら，人類は〜びてしまうかもしれない If another atomic war should break out, mankind may *be* completely *destroyed.*

ほろぼ・す【滅ぼす】 destroy. ¶ 国を〜す *ruin* the country. 彼は酒で身を〜した He *ruined himself* through drinking.

ぼろぼろ ¶ あの人は〜の着物を着ている The man wears *worn-out* (≒ *ragged*) clothes. 壁は〜にくずれている The walls *are crumbling.* 着物は着古して〜になった My clothes *have worn to shreds.* くつははき古して〜になっている My shoes *have* quite *worn out.* 本を〜になるまで使う use a book *until it falls apart.* 彼は涙を〜流した He *shed big drops of tears.*

ぽろぽろ ¶ 涙が〜こぼれた Tears *streamed down* my cheeks. 彼女は涙を〜こぼした She *shed* tears copiously.

ほろほろちょう【ほろほろ鳥】〘鳥類〙 a guinea fowl (「めす」は a guinea hen と言う).

ほろよい【ほろ酔い】¶ 彼は〜きげんだった He *was mellow* (≒ *was merry* ; *was tipsy*) *from a drink.*

ほろり ¶ 彼は思わず〜とした He *was moved to tears* in spite of himself. まったく〜とさせる話

だ It is indeed a *touching* story.

ぽろり ¶ 彼は～と球を落とした The ball *slipped* from his hand.

ホワイト white.
—カラー white collar. —ソース white sauce. —ハウス the White House.

ほん【本】 a book. ¶ 彼はよく～を読む He reads very much. あの人はよく～を読んでいる He *is well read.* 彼女は子どもに毎晩眠る前に～を読んできかせた She *read to* her children every night before they went to bed. 彼の随筆が～になって出た His essays were published in *book* form. 彼は～の虫だ He is, so to speak, *a bookworm.*

ほん-【本-】 (この) this; (主な) head. ¶ ～年 *this* year. ～月 *this* month. ～研究所 *this* laboratory. ～会員 a *regular* member.

ぼん【盆】 a tray. ¶ ～をくつがえすような雨だった It *was raining in a torrent.* 覆水～にかえらず (諺) What is done cannot be undone.

ほんあん【翻案】 an adaptation. ¶ その映画はシェイクスピアの劇から～した The motion picture *was adapted from* a play by Shakespeare. これはフランスの戯曲の～だ This is *an adaptation* from a French drama. / This is an *adapted* French play.

ぼんおどり【盆踊り】 the *Bon* Festival dance.

ほんい【本位】 standard. ¶ 彼女は子ども～だ Her first object of consideration is the child. この店は品質～だ "Quality first" is the motto of this store. 当社では人物～で採用する *Stress is laid on* character in the employment of our new staff. 彼は自己～だ He *is egoistic.* きみの考え方は自己～だ Your way of thinking *is self-centered.*
—貨幣 standard coin. 金— the gold standard. 銀— the silver standard.

ほんい【本意】 a true (≒ real) intention; an original desire. ¶ それは私の～ではなかった It was far from *my real intention.* ～をとげて彼は満足そうだ After having attained his *purpose,* he looks contented.

ほんい【翻意】 ¶ 彼の～を促したい I want to urge him to *change his decision* (≒ *change his mind*). 彼にはまったく～のけはいも見られない Not a sign of *reconsideration* is to be found in him.

ほんか【本科】 the regular course.
—生 a regular student. ¶ 彼は～生, 私は大学院学生である He is *an undergraduate* and I am a (post) graduate student.

ほんかい【本懐】 ¶ ～の至りだ It gives me the *greatest pleasure.* その計画が首尾よく実行されて～だ It is indeed *a great satisfaction* to us that the plan has been successfully carried out. 彼は～をとげて感涙にむせんだ Having attained his *long-cherished object,* he shed tears of gratitude.

ほんかいぎ【本会議】 (議会の) a plenary session; (会議の) a full session. ¶ (国会の)～に議案を上程した A bill was introduced into the Diet.

ほんかくてき【本格的】 ¶ ～な暑さになった The *real* summer heat has come. きみのゴルフは～だ You are almost as good as a professional golfer. / Your way of playing golf is as good as professional. ～に英会話を学ぶつもりだ I intend to study English conversation *in good earnest.* ～な梅雨になった The *real* (≒ *proper*) rainy season has set in.

ほんかん【本官】 the present official; I. ¶ それは～の責任です That's *my* fault. / *I'm* responsible for that. / The responsibility *is on my part.*

ほんかん【本管】 a main pipe. ¶ 水道の～が破裂した The water *main* has burst. ガスの～工事中だ The gas *main* is under construction.

ほんかん【本館】 the main building.

ほんがん【本願】 a long-cherished desire.
¶ ～成就 the realization of *one's* long-cherished desire. 彼は～を成就した He fulfilled his *long-cherished desire.*

ポンカン〘植物〙 a "pon-kan" (ポンカンという名称は中国語の pong-kam からきたもの).

ほんき【本気】 seriousness; truth; sanity.
¶ ～にする take for *truth.* ～で言う talk *seriously.* 私は彼の言うことを～にしなかった I didn't take what he said *seriously.* 彼は～で言っている He *means what he says.* / He *is serious.* もっと～になって仕事をしなさい *Be* more *serious* in your work.

ほんぎ【本義】 the real meaning; the fundamental meaning. ¶ 憲法の～がなにか知っていますか Do you know what the *fundamental principle* of the constitution is?

ほんぎまり【本決まり】 ¶ ふたりの結婚は～になった It *has been decided definitely* (≒ *has been decided at last*) for the two to be married. 彼の渡仏は～になった His going over to France *has been definitely decided.*

ほんきゅう【本給】 *one's* regular pay. ¶ 彼の～は年額500万円だ His annual *pay* is five million yen.

ほんきょ【本拠】 a base. ¶ 敵の～地はどこか Where is the *headquarters* of the enemy?

ほんきょく【本局】 the main office. ¶ 電話で～を呼び出した I called up *the Central.* ～と連絡を取りたいのだが I want to contact the *head office.*

ぼんくら a blockhead.

ぼんくれ【盆暮れ】 the *Bon* festival and the year end. ¶ 彼は～のつけ届けを忘れない He never fails to make the *Bon and year-end* presents. ～のボーナスはサラリーマンにはありがたい Nothing is so satisfying to salaried men as *biannual* bonuses.

ほんけ【本家】 the head house. ¶ この国は共産主義の～として知られている This country is known as the *birthplace* of communism.

ぼんけい【盆景】 a tray landscape.

ほんけがえり【本卦帰り・本卦還り】 dotage.
¶ 彼は～だ He is in his second childhood.
⇒かんれき

ほんけん【本件】¶～は未解決のままである *This case* [*lying before us*] remains unsolved.
ほんけん【本絹】pure silk. ¶このハンカチは～だ This handkerchief is [made] of *pure silk.*
ぼんご【梵語】Sanskrit. ¶～の Sanskritic.
—学者 a Sanskritist.
ほんこう【本校】(この学校) this school; (分校に対して) the principal school. ¶これが～の校章だ This is the badge of *this school.*
ほんこく【翻刻】reprinting; (書) a reprint. ¶絶版の本が～された A book out of print *was reprinted.*
—者 a reprinter. —書 a reprint.
ほんごく【本国】*one's* own country; home. ¶彼は3年ぶりに～へ帰った He returned to *his home country* after three years' absence. 戦いが終わると, 捕虜たちは～へ送還された After the war was over, prisoners *were repatriated.*
—政府 the home government.
ほんごし【本腰】¶～を入れてやりなさい Do it *seriously.* もっと～を入れて勉強しなさい You must study *harder.*
ほんさい【本妻】*one's* legal wife; *one's* lawful wife.
ぼんさい【凡才】(才能) ordinary ability; (人) a man of mediocre ability. ⇒ぼんじん
ぼんさい【盆栽】a potted plant. ¶松の～ *a dwarf* pine *tree.* 彼は～をつくるのを楽しみにしている He enjoys growing *a dwarf tree.* ～つくりが私の趣味だ *Dwarf-tree culture* is my hobby.
ほんざん【本山】the head temple (*of*); (この寺) this temple. ¶この寺は真宗大谷派の～だ This temple is *the headquarters of* the Otani sect of the Shinshu.
ほんし【本旨】the principal object; the object in view; the true aim.
ほんし【本紙】this paper. ¶～は内容を一新したいと考えている *This paper* is going to be refreshed in substance. ～は値上げはしない *This paper* shall not rise in price.
ほんし【本誌】¶～の購読料はさほどではない The subscription to *this magazine* (≒ *this journal*) is not so expensive.
ほんじ【本字】a Chinese character.
ぼんじ【梵字】a Sanskrit character.
ほんしき【本式】¶～の食事 a *regular* dinner. これが～のコーラスだ This is a chorus *in orthodox style.* そうするのが～だ That's the *regular way.* 彼はバイオリンを～にはやっていない He has not taken *regular* violin lessons. ～に英会話を習った I studied English conversation *in a systematic way.*
ほんしつ【本質】essence. ¶学問の～ *the essence of* learning. この二つの意見は～的に同じものだ These two opinions are *essentially* of the same nature. ～が問題なのだ What matters is its *true nature.*
ほんじつ【本日】today. ¶～休業(掲示) Closed *today.* 特売は～かぎりです The special bargain sale is to be over *today.*
ほんしゃ【本社】(支社に対して) the head office; (この会社) our firm. ¶～特派員 *our* special correspondent.
ほんしゅう【本州】the Main Island; Japan proper. ¶～を北から南へ縦断旅行した I traveled through *the Main Island* from north to south.
ほんしょ【本書】this book.
ほんしょ【本署】the police station; the headquarters. ¶容疑者は～へ連行された The suspect was taken to *the police station.*
ほんしょう【本性】(生まれつきの性質) nature; real character; (正気) sense. ¶とうとう彼は～をあらわした He *betrayed himself* at last. / He showed *his real character* at last. ことばはその人の～をあらわす Words often betray *the real character* of the utterer. 彼は酔って～を失っている He is drunk *out of his senses.*
ほんしょう【本省】(本部) the home office; (この省) this ministry; this department.
ぼんしょう【梵鐘】a Buddhist temple bell.
ほんしょく【本職】principal occupation. ¶彼の～は音楽家だ He is a musician *by profession.*
—はだし ¶彼女のピアノの演奏は～はだしだ Her piano performance would give credit to a professional pianist. / She plays as well as a professional pianist.
ほんしん【本心】*one's* real intention; (本来の正しい心) conscience; (正気) right mind. ¶彼は～は怒っている He is angry *at heart.* 彼は～を明らかにすべきだ He should speak *his mind.* / He should tell *what he really thinks.* 彼はようやく～に返った He *has come to his senses* after all. 彼もいずれ～をあらわすときが来るだろう He will reveal *his real intention* sooner or later.
ぼんじん【凡人】an ordinary (≒ a common) man. ¶それは～にはとうていできない芸当だ That would be beyond the power of *an ordinary person.*
ほんすじ【本筋】the main line. ¶～に入ろう Let's go into *the main issue.* それは～からはずれることになる That would digress from *the main subject.* 議論を～にもどさねばならない We must *resume the thread of our talk.*
ほんせい【本性】the original nature. ¶人間の～ *the original nature* of man.
ほんせき【本籍】*one's* domicile. ¶～を東京に移したいと思っている I think I will transfer *my domicile to* Tokyo. 私の～地は神戸市だ I *am domiciled at* Kobe City.
ほんせん【本船】(この船) this ship; (親船) the mother ship.
—渡し free on board (F.O.B.; f.o.b.).
ほんせん【本線】the main line. ¶東北～ the Tohoku *Main Line.*
ほんぜん【翻然】¶～として自己の非を悟った I *suddenly* realized that I was wrong.
ほんそう【奔走】(努力) efforts; exertion; (世話) good offices. ¶彼は国事に～している He *is*

ほ

taking an active part in the affairs of state. 息子の就職のことで彼は～している He *is busying himself about* finding employment for his son. 彼の～のおかげで私は首尾よく就職できた I could find my job *through his good offices*.

ぼんぞく【凡俗】vulgarity. ¶ 彼の趣味は～の域を出ない His taste does not go beyond *the line of vulgarity* (≒ *that of the average man*). 彼は～を超越している He rises above *the common crowd*.

ほんぞん【本尊】**1**〖仏教〗the object of worship. ¶ 浅草寺の～はなんですか What *is* the Sensoji Temple *sacred to*?
2〖本人〗the very man. ¶ ご～がまだ姿を見せない He *himself* has not arrived yet.

ほんたい【本体】(本尊) the object of worship; (真の姿) the real form; 〖哲学〗(実体) substance.

ほんたい【本隊】the main body.

ほんだい【本題】the main subject. ¶ これから話の～に入る Now we are going into *the very subject* of our story.

ほんだい【本代】payment for books. ¶ ～を払った I *paid for the books*. ～がだいぶかさんだ My *book bills* have run up to a large sum.

ぼんたい【凡退】¶ ピッチャーは連続５人を～にうちとった The pitcher *put out* five batters at a stretch. 三者～となった The three *went out* one after another.

ほんたく【本宅】*one's* home; *one's* principal residence.

ほんたて【本立て】a bookstand; bookends.

ほんだな【本棚】a bookshelf. ¶ 作りつけの～ a built-in *bookshelf*.

ぼんち【盆地】a basin. ¶ この一帯は～になっている This district forms *a basin*. この山間の～は避暑地になっている This *basin* among the mountains forms a summer resort.

ほんちょうし【本調子】(三味線の) normal note; (本格的) regular way. ¶ どうも～でない Somehow I *am not my usual self*. / I *am not in my form*. このごろようやく～が出てきた I *have got into my stride* these days. なかなか～がもどらない *My real self* has not been regained so easily.

ほんてん【本店】the head (≒ main) office; (この店) this store.

ほんでん【本殿】the main (≒ inner) shrine.

ほんど【本土】the mainland. ¶ 日本～ Japan proper.

ぽんと (たたく音) pop; (物を投げ出すさま) throw to. ¶ だれかが私の背中を～たたいた Somebody *tapped* me on the back. 彼は100万円を～寄付した He donated a million yen *on the spot*.

ポンド (貨幣) a pound (£); (重量) a pound (lb.). ¶ 10～ 10 *pounds* (£ 10). 5～紙幣 a five-*pound* note. イギリスは～の危機を乗り越えた Britain overcame *the pound sterling* crisis.
——地域 the sterling area.

ほんとう【奔騰】soar in price. ¶ このところ豚肉は～している Pork *has jumped in price* these days.

ほんとう【本当】the truth. ¶ ～の true; real. ～に really; quite. その話は～ですか *Is* that story *true*? 彼はどうしても～のことを言わない He won't tell me *the truth*. あの人の～の年はわからない I don't know how old he *really* is. これは～のダイヤモンドではあるまい I doubt if this is a *genuine* diamond. きみは～にそこに行ったのか Did you *really* go there? ～らしく聞こえるが, 実はうそだ It may sound *plausible*, but in reality it is a lie. あの人の言うことはもう～にはできない I cannot believe him any longer. ～を言うと彼が犯人なのだ *To tell the truth*, he is the very criminal.

ほんどう【本堂】the main (≒ inner) temple; the main hall (*of* a temple).

ほんどう【本道】the main road; a highway; (正しい道) the proper way. ¶ ここが～から分かれる地点だ This is the point where the road branches off from *the highway*. これが英語を勉強する～だ This is *the proper way* to learn English.

ほんどおり【本通り】the main street; 英 the high street. ¶ ～は商店が並んでいる Stores stand on both sides of *the main street*. / Both sides of *the high street* are lined with shops.

ほんにん【本人】the person himself (≒ herself); (問題のその人) the said person. ¶ 彼女は～みずから来た She came *in person*. 私が～です I am *the very man* (≒ *the very woman*).

ほんね【本音】¶ ついに彼は～をはいた At last he disclosed *his real intention*. / At last he *gave himself away*.

ボンネット (車の) a hood; 英 a bonnet; (婦人帽子) a bonnet.

ほんねん【本年】this year. ¶ ～は梅雨が例年より短いということだ *This year* the rainy season is shorter than in the average year, we are told.

ほんの only; mere; just. ¶ ～すこししか時間がない We have *only* a little time left. ～すこし待っただけだ We have been waiting *just* for a while. 彼は～すこししかくれなかった He gave me *only* a bit. その本は～数ページ読んだだけだ I have read *only* a few pages of the book. 彼は～５分前に来たところだ He came here *only* five minutes ago. 歩いて～二, 三分だ It is *only* [a] two or three minutes' walk from here. ～一瞬の出来事だった It *only* occurred in a fraction of a second. 彼は～子どもだ He is a *mere* child.

ほんのう【本能】instinct. ¶ ～で行動する act *on instinct*. 鳥は～で飛べるようになる Birds learn to fly *by instinct*. 動物は～的に火を恐れる Animals have an *instinctive* fear of fire. リスは～的に食べ物を集めるものだ Squirrels *instinctively* gather their food.

ぼんのう【煩悩】worldly desires; passions.

¶～に悩まされる be harassed by *passions.*

ほんのり faintly. ¶～空が明るくなってきた A *faint* glow of light has come out into the sky. 彼女の顔が～[と]赤らんだ Her face has become *slightly* flushed.

ほんば【本場】 the best place; the home. ¶山梨県はブドウの～だ Yamanashi Prefecture is *the best place for* grapes. これは～のスコッチウイスキーだ This is a *genuine* Scotch whisky.

―仕込み ¶彼は～仕込みのフランス語で私を驚かした I was surprised at his French he had learned during his stay in France.

ほんばこ【本箱】 a bookcase.

ほんばしょ【本場所】(すもうの) a regular *sumo* tournament. ¶こんどの～は福岡だ The next *regular sumo tournament* is to be held in Fukuoka.

ほんばん【本番】〔映画〕¶撮影はぶっつけ～で行なわれた Film-making was carried on *without rehearsal.*

ぽんびき【ぽん引き】(客引き) a tout; (売春の) a pander.

ほんぶ【本部】 the headquarters. ¶この建物は大学～だ This is *the administrative building* of the university.

ぼんぷ【凡夫】 an ordinary person.

ポンプ a pump. ¶～で井戸から水をくみ上げた I *pumped up* water from the well. 水たまりの水を～でくみ出した I *pumped* water *out of* the pool.

蒸気― a steam pump. 手押し― a hand pump.

ほんぶしん【本普請】 ¶～の家 a *strongly-built* house.

ほんぶり【本降り】 a downpour. ¶雨は～になってきた It began to *rain in real earnest.*

ほんぶん【本文】 the text. ¶手紙の～ *the body* of a letter. 協定書の～ *the text* of the agreement. その本は～が230ページで, 注が40ページだ The book contains 230 pages of *text* and 40 pages of notes.

ほんぶん【本分】 duty. ¶彼は～を尽くした He did his *duty.* 彼女は学生としての～をおろそかにした She neglected *her duty* as a student. それはスポーツマンとしての～を忘れた行為だ Such conduct *is unworthy of* a sportsman. 学生としての～をわきまえてやることがたいせつだ It is important to behave yourself *in a way worthy of* a student.

ボンベ a gas cylinder.

酸素― an oxygen cylinder.

ほんぽう【本邦】 this (≒ our) country. ¶このオペラは～初演だ This is the first time this opera has been staged in *this country.*

ほんぽう【奔放】¶彼は自由～な生活をしている He lives a free and *unrestrained* life.

ほんぽう【本俸】 *one's* regular salary. ⇒ほんきゅう

ぼんぼり【雪洞】 a hand lamp; a paper lantern.

ボンボン (菓子) a bonbon.

ぽんぽん **1**〖音〗¶手を～鳴らす *clap one's* hands.

遠くで花火が～鳴り続けた Fireworks kept *banging* in the distance.

ぽんぽん蒸気が～音を立てて通っている A steam launch is passing with the sound '*pop, pop.*'

2〖遠慮なく〗¶彼はなんでも～言う He says anything *without reserve.*

3〖腹〗(小児語で) the tummy.

ほんまつ【本末】 cause and effect.

―転倒 ¶それは～転倒だ That would be *putting the cart before the horse.* まさに～転倒の発言だ That remark *is* certainly *preposterous.*

ほんみょう【本名】(雅号や俗名に対して) *one's* real name.

ほんめい【本命】(競馬の) the favorite; (選挙の) a prospective winner. ¶彼はいつも～にかける He always plays *the favorite.*

ほんめい【奔命】 ceaseless activity. ¶彼は～に疲れている He is quite tired from too much *bustling about.*

ほんもう【本望】 satisfaction; a long-cherished desire. ¶これで私は～だ I *am quite satisfied with* this. この土地で死ねれば～だ I shall *be satisfied* if I can die in this place. 喜んでいただければ～です I *shall be happy* if only you can be delighted with it. 彼は～を遂げたというべきだ We should say that he has attained *his long-cherished desire.*

ほんもと【本元】 the source; the original maker.

本家― ¶この商売の本家～は彼だ He is *the very originator* of this business.

ほんもの【本物】 a genuine thing; (本格的な技芸など) genuine art.

¶～のダイヤ a *genuine* diamond. ～そっくりの肖像 a *lifelike* portrait. ～そっくりの造花 artificial flowers which *look just like natural ones.* この浮世絵は～だ This *ukiyoe* print *is original.* これと～とを見分けることは難しい It is difficult to distinguish this from *the genuine* (≒ *real*) *thing.* 彼の絵は～だ(しろうとばなれしている) His painting *is far from amateurish.* きみの英語は～だ You speak English as if you were a native speaker. 彼の学問は～だ His learning *is genuine* in every respect.

ほんもん【本文】 the body (*of* a letter); the text. ⇒ほんぶん

―研究 the textual criticism.

ほんや【本屋】(店) 米 a bookstore; 英 a bookshop; (人) a bookseller. ¶彼は～をやっている He keeps *a bookstore.*

ほんやく【翻訳】 translation. ¶彼はそのフランス語の小説を日本語に～した He *translated* the French novel *into* Japanese. 彼は～がうまい He is *a good translator.* 彼の小説は～してもうまくいかない His novel does not *translate* well. ハムレットを～で読んだ I read 'Hamlet' *in translation.* この日本語は英語に～できない This

Japanese word does not bear English *translation*. この語はなんと～したらよいだろうか How shall I *translate* this word?
―権 the translation right. ¶ その出版社がその本の～権を持っている The publisher has *the translation right* of the book. **―者** a translator. **―書** a translation.

ぼんやり 1 〖人〗 a blockhead. ¶ きみはなんと～なのだ What *a stupid person* you are!
2 〖呆然とした〗 absent-mindedly. ¶ 彼は～している He *is absent-minded.*
彼は～空を見ていた He was looking up at the sky *with a vacant expression.*
彼は書斎から～外をながめている He is looking *vacantly* out of the window in his study.
3 〖不注意・無為〗 ¶ ～していてあなたの言うことがわからなかった I *was* so *careless* that I could not catch what you said.
車にひかれるから～するな *Be careful,* or you may get run over by a car.
～している暇はない There is no time for *being idle.*
4 〖不明瞭〗 ¶ スモッグのため山々が～見える Because of the smog, the mountains are only *faintly* to be seen.
きょうは頭が～している My head *is dull and heavy* today.
10年前の自分のことは～しか覚えていない I have only a *faint* recollection of what I was ten years ago.

ぼんよう【凡庸】 mediocrity. ¶ ～な人 a mediocrity; a person *of mediocre abitity.* この本は～の域を出ない This book *is* quite *commonplace.*

ほんよみ【本読み】(演劇の) reading. ¶ ～をする have *a* [*scenario*] *reading.*

ほんらい【本来】(本質的) essentially; (元来) originally. ¶ 彼は～学者ではない He is not *essentially* (≒ *by nature; properly speaking*) a man of learning. ～よい物が用い方しだいで悪くもなる A thing good *in itself* may become harmful in use. このお堂は～は大名の離れ座敷であった This temple was *originally* a *daimyo's* detached room.

ほんりゅう【本流】 the main course. ¶ 信濃川の～ *the main course* (≒ *the main stream*) of the Shinano River. アメリカ史の～ *the main currents* in American history. 時の～に逆らう go against *the stream.* 時の～に従う swim with *the stream.*

ほんりゅう【奔流】 a torrent; rapids. ¶ 彼は～を泳いで渡った He swam across *a rushing* (≒ *rapid*) *stream.* 橋は～に押し流された The bridge was swept away in *the rushing torrents.*

ほんりょう【本領】(特性) a characteristic; (本分) *one's* line. ¶ 彼は商売で彼の～を発揮した He showed (≒ displayed) *his own ability in* business.

ほんるい【本塁】〘野球〙 the home base; the home plate. ¶ 彼は～を踏んだ He *homed in.* / He *got home.*
―打 a home run; a homer. ¶ ～打を打つ hit *a home run.* 彼は逆点～打を打った He smacked *a pinch homer.*

ほんろう【翻弄】 ¶ ボートは波に～された The boat *was tossed about* in (≒ by) the waves.

ほんろん【本論】 the main subject; (この論) this thesis. ¶ それから彼は～に入った He then took up (≒ proceeded to) *the main issue.* それはいささか～からはずれている It is a little aside from *our subject.* それはさておき～にもどろう Let us return to *our subject.*

ま

ま【真】 ¶ 冗談を～に受けるな Don't take a joke *seriously.* 彼女のことばを～に受けるな Don't *believe* her. (believe *in* her と言えば一時的でなく,いつも信用していること) / Don't take her *seriously.*

ま【魔】 ¶ 彼がそんなことをしたなんて～がさしたにちがいない He must have been possessed by some *evil spirit* to have done such a thing. きょうもまた～の踏切で事故が起きた Another accident happened today at the *fatal* railroad crossing. 好事～多し (諺) *There's many a slip 'twixt the cup and the lip.*

ま【間】 1 〖部屋〗 a room. ¶ この家は3～だ This house has three *rooms.*
2 〖時間〗 time. ¶ ここへ移ってまだ～がない It has *not* been *long* since I moved to this place.
彼は眠る～もないくらいだ He *hardly has time to* sleep.
私は少しの～でも眠ることにしている I make it a practice to sleep even *for a moment.* (口語なら I usually sleep...でよい).
あの人は30に～もない He is *nearly* thirty.
～に合いそうだ We are likely to *be in time.*
3 〖面目〗 ¶ ちょっと～が悪かった I *was* a bit *puzzled* (≒ *was awkward; was embarrassed*).
4 〖役に立つ〗 ¶ 万年筆はこれで～に合いそうだ This pen *will do.*
この本では～に合わない This book *won't do.*
この箱で～に合うだろうか I wonder if this box

serves the purpose. (間に合いそうもない気持ちを表わす).

まあ ¶ ～, これなにかしら *Oh, my!* What's this? ～, いったいなんの音でしょう *Good Heavens!* What can that noise be? ～そんなところだ *Well,* it's something like that. ～だいじょうぶだろう *Probably* it will be all right. ～ちょっと着てごらんなさい *Just* put (≒ try) it on.

まあい【間合い】 ¶ いる～をはかって彼を訪問した I visited him expecting him to be at home.

マーガリン margarine.

マーガレット 〔植物〕 a marguerit.

マーキュロ〔クローム〕 mercurochrome. ¶ 傷口に～をぬる apply *mercurochrome* to a wound.

マーク a mark. ¶ ～されている人物 a *marked* man; a person *on the blacklist.* 彼を注意人物として～した We *put* him *on a blacklist.* その箱に～をつけなさい *Mark* (≒ *Put a mark on*) the box. 重要な語に星の～をつけた We put (≒ set) *an asterisk* against important words.

クエスチョン― a question mark.

マーケット a market. ¶ ～に行く go to *market.* ブラジルに新しい～を開拓せねばならない We must exploit (≒ cultivate) new *markets* in Brazil. 海外の～を調査する study overseas *markets.*

―リサーチ market research. スーパー― a supermarket.

マーケティング marketing.

―リサーチ marketing research; market research.

マージャン mahjong. ¶ ～のパイ a 〔*mahjong*〕 tile. ～をする play *mahjong.*

―屋 a mahjong saloon.

マージン 〔a〕 margin. ¶ これらの品は～が多い (少ない) These goods have *a* wide (narrow) *margin of profit.* その値段では～が薄くなる The price leaves *a* narrow *margin of profit.* 堅い商売は～も少ないのが普通だ Sound business usually allows one *a* narrow *margin of profit.*

まあたらし·い【真新しい】 brand-new. ¶ ～い帽子 a *quite* (≒ *brand-*) *new* hat.

マーチ a march. ¶ ウエディング～を奏する play *a* wedding *march.*

マーブル marble. ¶ ～の像 a statue in *marble*; a *marble* statue.

まあまあ ¶ ～というところだ (どうやら満足) It's *barely satisfactory.* / (健康状態) I'*m not so good in health.* ～, そうあわてるな *Now, now,* don't be in such a hurry! ～, そんな口のきき方をするものではありません *Come, come,* you shouldn't speak like that!

マーマレード marmalade.

まい【舞】 a dance. ¶ ～を舞う dance; perform *a dance.*

まい-【毎-】 every; each. ¶ ～週 *every* week.

-まい【-枚】 ¶ 15円切手 3 ～ three fifteen-yen stamps. さら 5 ～ five plates. イチョウの葉 5 ～ five gingko leaves. 3 ～の紙 three *sheets* (≒ *pieces*) of paper (piece は不規則の紙片でもよい). 大阪まで往復 1 ～ください Please 〔give me〕 a round-trip ticket to Osaka.

-まい ¶ ぼくは行く～ I'll never go there. あすは雨は降る～ I don't think it will rain tomorrow. たぶんそうではある～ I don't think so. / I suppose not. / I'm afraid not. / I hope not.

まいあが·る【舞い上がる】 ¶ 空高く～ったヒバリ a lark *soaring* high into the sky. 木の葉が風でひらひらと～った The leaves *were whirled up* by the wind. 風が吹くたびにほこりが～った Every gust of wind *stirred up* the dust. 車が通るときほこりが～る A car *raises* dust as it passes.

まいあさ【毎朝】 every morning. ¶ ～6 時に起きる I get up at six *every morning.*

マイカーぞく【マイカー族】 owner-drivers.

まいかい【毎回】 ¶ ～ごめんどうをかけてすみません I'm sorry to trouble you *so often.* わがチームは～ランナーを出した Our team had a base runner *at every inning.* 彼は～帰郷するたびに私のところへやってきた *Every time* he returned to his home town, he came to see me.

まいきょ【枚挙】 enumeration. ¶ そのような例は～にいとまもない Such examples are too numerous to *mention* (≒ *count*).

マイクロウエーブ 〔電気〕 a microwave.

マイクロフィルム a microfilm. ¶ 文献を～にとる *microfilm* some documents.

―シート a microfiche; a sheet of microfilm.

マイク〔ロホン〕 a microphone; a mike. ¶ ～に向かって話す speak *at a mike.* 彼は～を通じて聴衆に呼びかけた He addressed his audience *through a mike.*

隠し― a concealed mike (≒ microphone).

マイクロメーター a micrometer.

マイクロリーダー a microfilm reader.

まいご【迷子】 a lost child. ¶ ～の女の子 a *lost* (≒ *missing*) girl. その子はデパートで～になった The child *was lost* in the department store. 彼女は森の中で～になった She *lost her way* in the woods.

―札 a child's identification tag.

まいこ·む【舞い込む】 ¶ 木の葉が窓から～んだ Leaves *came in fluttering* at the window. 不幸が彼の家に～んだ A misfortune *befell* (≒ *happened to*) his family. 変な手紙が～んだ I *had* a strange letter. 妙な客が～んだ I *had* an unwelcome visitor.

まいじ【毎時】 ¶ 台風は～20キロの速さで北上中だ The typhoon is going up north at a speed of twenty kilometers *an hour.* ～80マイルのスピードで車を運転した I drove a car *at* 80 *M.P.H.* (≒ *at* 〔*a speed of*〕 80 *miles per hour*).

まいしゅう【毎週】 weekly; every week. ¶ ～2 回 twice 〔in〕 *every week*; twice *a week.* ～水曜日にテストがある We have a test *every* Wednesday. ～～*week* in *week* out.

まいしん【邁進】 ¶ 自己の目的貫徹のため～せよ *Strive hard* to carry out your aim. 彼は研

ま

究に〜した He *vigorously pushed on with* the study.

まいすう【枚数】¶ この紙束の〜はどのくらいですか How many *sheets* are there in this bundle? 〜を数える count *the number of sheets.* 〜がちがっている The *number* you counted is not correct. この厚さなら100枚はある〜だ Judging from the thickness of this bundle of papers, there must be at least a hundred *sheets* contained in it.

まいせつ【埋設】¶ ガス管を〜する *lay* a gas pipe. 地下ケーブルを〜する *lay* electric-telegraph cables. 海底電線を〜する *lay* (≒ *build*) a submarine cable.

まいそう【埋葬】burial. ¶ 彼は故郷の町に〜された He *was buried* in his home town. **—**許可証 a burial permit (≒ certificate). **—**式 the burial service. **—**地 a graveyard; (共同墓地) a cemetery. **—**届 report of a burial. **—**料 funeral expenses.

まいぞう【埋蔵】**—**金 the buried gold (≒ treasures). **—**量 reserves; an estimated amount. ¶ 石炭の〜量 coal *reserves*; *an estimated amount* of coal.

まいちもんじ【真一文字】¶ 〜に突進する go *straight* ahead.

まいど【毎度】(たびたび) often; (そのつど) every time. ¶ 〜ありがとうございます Thank you very much [for your patronage]. 〜お手数をかけて申しわけありません I'm sorry to trouble you *so often.*

マイナス minus. ¶ 〜の数量 a *minus* (≒ *negative*) quantity. 〜の電気 *minus* (≒ *negative*) electricity. 〜の符号 a *minus* (≒ *negative*) sign. 7〜3は4 Seven *minus* three leaves four. けさの気温は〜4度だった The temperature was *minus* four degrees this morning.

まいにち【毎日】daily; every day. ¶ 〜の勤め *daily* (≒ *everyday*) duties. 〜の出来事 *everyday* occurrences (everyday が1語なら形容詞). ほとんど〜[のように] almost *every day.* 〜散歩する I go for a walk *every day.*

まいねん【毎年】annually; every year. ¶ 〜の行事 an *annual* event. 〜1度は once *a year.* 〜夏になると海辺の保養地に行く I go to the seaside health resort *every* summer. 〜今ごろになると彼が水泳が好きだったことを思い出す I remember about this time of *the year* that he loved swimming.

まいばん【毎晩】every evening.

まいぼつ【埋没】¶ 家は土砂に〜した The house *was buried* in earth and sand.

まいもど・る【舞い戻る】¶ 彼は凶行現場に〜るだろう He will *come back* (≒ *return*) to the scene of murder. 彼は元の地位に〜った He *has come back* (≒ *has returned*) to his former position.

マイル a mile. ¶ 2〜半 two *miles* and a half; two and a half *miles.* 彼は1,000〜旅行した He traveled [for] a thousand *miles.* 公園は駅から1〜の所にある The park is within *a mile* of the station. 車は時速60〜で走った The car made sixty *miles* an hour.

まい・る【参る】**1**〖行く〗go. ¶ 5分後にそこに〜ります I will *go* there in five minutes. (話し相手の所へ行くなら go のかわりに come を用いる). 彼はあとから〜ります He will *arrive* here later. まにあうように〜れると思います I think I will be able to *come* in time.
こんどの日曜日に御いっしょに映画に〜りましょうか Won't you *go* with me to see the movies next Sunday?
2〖負ける〗¶ 彼は〜ったとは言わないだろう He will not *admit his defeat.*
彼は〜ったと言った He *admitted that he was beaten.*
この暑さには〜った I *cannot stand* this heat.
3〖困る〗¶ あの仕事にはまったく〜る I *am* quite *at a loss* what to do about that work.
あんまり歩いて〜った I walked so much I'*m* all *tired out.*
仕事の途中で〜ったと言うな Don't *say die* during your work.
4〖死ぬ〗die. ¶ 彼は急病のため〜った He *died* of a sudden disease.

ま・う【舞う】¶ 舞を〜う dance; *perform* a dance. 枯れ葉が風に〜う The dead leaves *whirl* in the wind. トビが数羽われわれの頭上を〜っていた Several kites *were circling* over our heads.

まうえ【真上】¶ 飛行機が頭の〜を飛んだ An airplane flew *right over my head* (≒ *directly overhead*).

まうしろ【真後ろ】¶ 彼の〜に立った I stood *right behind* him.

マウンド〖野球〗the mound. ¶ 〜上のピッチャー the pitcher on *the mound.* 〜に立つ take *the mound.*

まえ【前】**1**〖時〗¶ 今5時10分〜だ It is ten [minutes] *to* (≒ *before*) five now. (口語ではあまり minute[s] を用いない). / It's ten *of* five now. (米語法).
ぼくは11時〜には寝ない I don't go to bed *before* eleven at night.
彼は1時間〜に出かけた He left an hour *ago.*
彼は3年〜に亡くなった He died three years *ago.* / He has been dead for three years.
彼は1週間〜から入院している He has been in [the] hospital *since* a week *ago.* / He has been hospitalized for a week.
ほんのちょっと〜に帰ってきたところだ I came back just a little while *ago.*
二，三日〜にその事件を知った I heard of the event a few days *ago.*
1週間〜の新聞を見せてください I want to have a look at last week's newspaper.
きみは3日〜のことも覚えていないのか Don't you remember what happened three days *ago*?
これはだいぶ〜に撮った写真ですね This picture was taken long *ago,* wasn't it?
私は集合時刻より30分も〜に駅に着いた I got to the station thirty minutes *early* for the meeting.

ま

私が着くより15分～に彼は家を出ていた He had left home fifteen minutes *before* I arrived.
暗くなる～にかならず帰りなさい Be sure to come back *before* dark.
その話は～に聞いたことがある I have heard the story *before*.
～はニンジンがきらいだったが, 今は違う I was *once* a hater of carrots, but not now.
きみは～にこの絵を見たことがありますね You have seen this picture *before*, haven't you?
この～来たときとは町のようすがすっかり変わっている The town has changed completely since I visited it *last*.
この～会ったのは何年～だろう I wonder how many years it has been since we met *last*. (文法では it *is* だが, 口語では完了形も用いる).
この～会ったときはきみはまだ小学生だった *The last time* I met you, you were still a primary schoolboy.
この～の話だが, あれはなかったことにしてくれ As for the matter I told you about *last time*, I want you to forget it.
この～の日曜はひどい雨降りだった It rained heavily *last* Sunday.
～にはこの川でフナがたくさん釣れたものだ We *used to* catch a lot of crucians in this river.
～に1度お目にかかったことがあると思います I remember seeing you *once*.
きのう～の担任の先生に会った I met my *former* class teacher yesterday.
私たちが帰国する～の日にパーティーを開いてもらった We were given a party on the *eve* of our return.
彼女の～の住所を知っていますか Do you happen to know her *former* address?
彼は吉田さんの～の首相だ He was the prime minister *prior to* Mr. Yoshida.
彼はもう～のバスで先に行った He left on the *previous* bus.
彼はこの会社に入る～は先生をしていた He used to be a teacher *before* entering this company.
～は静かな農村だったのに, 今ではこんな騒々しい町になってしまった This *once* quiet rural village has turned into such a noisy town.
そのうわさなら～にも聞いたことがある I have *once* heard of that rumor.
彼には～からああいう癖がある It is habitual with him./He always did have such a tendency.
今週はテスト～だから遊んではいられない I cannot afford to be idle, as I have a test this week.
彼女はまだ50～だ She isn't fifty yet.
2 〖場所〗 ¶ 私の家の～に小さな公園がある There is a small park *across from* (≒ *opposite*) my house.
駅～からバスに乗ってください Take the bus *in front of* the station.
その子は母親の目の～で車にはねられた The child was knocked down by a car *in front of* his mother's eyes.
彼は先生の～に出ると急におとなしくなる He suddenly becomes well behaved *in the presence of* his teacher.
人さまの～でそんなことを言うものではありません Don't say such a thing *in the presence of others* (≒ *in public; in company*).
彼女は彼の～ではなんにも言えなくなる She is too shy to say anything *in* his *presence*.
あなたの～ですがどうも彼が好きになれない I regret telling you, but I just can't like him.
賛成の人は1歩～に出てください All those in favor take a step *forward*.
ぼくは～から3列めの席に着いた I took seat in the third row from *the front*.
ぼくの～の席にはアメリカ人が座った An American sat down *in front of* my seat (≒ me).
もっと～のほうの席はありませんか Can I have a more *forward* seat?
まっすぐ～を見て歩きなさい Look straight *to the front* when you walk.
もう一度～のページにもどりましょう Let's return to the *previous* page.
この語は3ページほど～にも出ていた You learned this word already about three pages *back*.
3 〖…分〗 ¶ 彼はゆうに3人～の仕事をする He can easily do the work of *three men*.
彼は食欲旺盛(おうせい)だから食事は1人～ではとても足りない He has such a hearty appetite that one *portion* is not sufficient for him.
昼食を6人～注文してください Please order lunch *for* six.

まえあし【前足】forefeet; forelegs; paws.

まえいわい【前祝い】celebration in advance. ¶ ～をする celebrate beforehand. 成功の～に一杯やろう Let's have a drink *in anticipation of* our success.

まえうり【前売り】¶ 切符の～ *an advance sale* of tickets. 切符を～する sell tickets *in advance*.
―券 an advance ticket.

まえおき【前置き】an introduction; a preface; preliminaries. ¶ ～する make *introductory remarks*. 彼は～ばかり長くて時間をむだにした He wasted time in *a* lengthy *introduction*.

まえかがみ【前かがみ】¶ ～になる bend forward; slouch.

まえがき【前書き】a preface; a foreword; an introduction. ¶ 手紙の～ *a preface* to a letter.

まえかけ【前掛け】an apron; (子ども用の) a pinafore.

まえがし【前貸し】¶ 賃銀の～ *an advance on* wages. 彼に1万円だけ月給の～をした I *advanced* him ten thousand yen *on* his salary. 5,000円だけ月給から～してもらった I obtained *an advance* of five thousand yen *on* my salary.

まえがり【前借り】¶ 1か月の給料を～した I *borrowed* one month's salary *in advance*. 月給から5,000円～した I *had* five thousand yen *advanced* on my salary. 5,000円月給から～できませんか Could you *advance* me five thousand yen *on* my salary?

まえきん【前金】advance payment. ¶ ～で家賃を払った I paid the rent *in advance.* 雑誌の購読料を～で払った I *advanced* subscriptions to the magazine.

まえげいき【前景気】a prospect; an outlook. ¶ ～は上々だ The *prospects* are encouraging.

まえこうじょう【前口上】¶ ～を述べる make *introductory remarks.*

まえば【前歯】a front tooth. ¶ ～で物をかむ bite things with the *front teeth.*

まえばらい【前払い】advance payment. ¶ 地代を～する *pay* the land rent *in advance.* 電報の返信料を～する *prepay* a reply to the telegram. 運賃～で彼に小荷物を送った I sent him a parcel *freight paid.*

まえぶれ【前触れ】¶ 彼は～もなしに来た He came *without notice.* 道徳の退廃は国民衰亡の～である Moral corruption is the *forerunner* (≒ *omen*) of national decline. カッコウは春の～である The cuckoo is the *harbinger* of spring. あの黒い雲は雨の～だ Those black clouds are *a sign* of coming rain.

まえむき【前向き】¶ ～の姿勢でその問題に取り組もう We will handle the problem *positively.*

まえもって【前以って】¶ ～到着の時間を知らせてください Please let me know *beforehand* (≒ *in advance*) when you will arrive.

まおう【魔王】Satan; the Devil.

まがい〔もの〕【紛い〔物〕】¶ ～のダイヤ an *imitation* (≒ *fake*) diamond. その真珠は～だった The pearl was *an imitation* (≒ *a sham*).

まが・う【紛う】¶ これは～うかたなく彼の初期の作品の一つだ This is one of his early works *beyond doubt.* 彼が自分ひとりでやったことは～うかたなき事実だ It is *indisputably* evident that he did it by himself. 彼が私の後継者になることは～うかたなきことだ It is *absolutely* certain that he will succeed me.

まがお【真顔】¶ 彼は急に～になった He suddenly *looked serious* (≒ *looked grave*). 彼はよく～でうそをつく He often tells a lie *with a straight face.*

まがし【間貸し】¶ 月に１万円で学生に～する *rent* (≒ 英 *let*) *a room* to a student for ten thousand yen a month.

まか・す【負かす】¶ 議論で相手を～す *beat a person* in argument. 競走で相手を～す *beat a person* in a race. 値段を～す *cut* the price; *have* the price *reduced.* 私はテニスの試合で彼を～した I *beat* him in a tennis match. わがチームは大差をつけて相手方を～した Our team *beat* theirs by a large score.

まかず【間数】¶ その家は～はいくつありますか How many *rooms* does the house have? その家は～が三つ(たくさん)ある The house has three (≒ a large number of) *rooms.*

まか・せる【任せる】¶ 力に～せて with might and main. 金に～せて regardless of expense. 彼は足に～せて一日じゅう市中を歩きまわった He walked about the city all day *as his legs led him.* 仕事を彼に～せることはできない I cannot *entrust* the work *to* him. 運を天に～せた I *trusted* to chance. 万事運に～せた I *left* everything *to* chance. 彼は仕事を～されている He *is charged with* the task. 決定はきみに～せる I *leave* you *to* decide. 彼はその判断を私に～せた He *left* it *to* my judgment. その家の管理を彼に～せた I *left* the house *in* his charge. 彼は子どもの教育を妻に～せている He *leaves* the education of his children *to* his wife.

まがった【曲がった】¶ ～線 a *curved* line. ～道 a *winding* road. 腰の～老人 an old man with a *bent* back. ～行ない a *crooked* deed. ～行為をするな Don't do *wrong.* 私は～ことは大きらいだ I hate anything *wrong.*

まかない【賄い】fare; board. ¶ ～つき下宿 *board* and lodging. ～料を毎月15,000円払う I pay fifteen thousand yen for *board* every month. この部屋は～つき１か月いくらですか How much do you charge a month for room and *board*? この部屋は～つき１か月20,000円です We charge twenty thousand yen for this room *with board* a month. / The room rent is twenty thousand yen *with board* a month.

まかな・う【賄う】¶ 40人分の食事を半月以上～った We *furnished* (≒ *supplied; provided*) forty persons *with* meals for more than half a month. いくらで～ってくれますか How much will you *board* me for? 月８万円で一家を～うのは楽ではない It is not easy for us to *live* (≒ *maintain our family*) *on* eighty thousand yen a month. これだけあれば旅費は～えるだろう This will be enough *to pay* (≒ *cover; meet*) your traveling expenses.

まがり【間借り】¶ いまだに～生活をしている I *am* still *living in a rooming house.* 人の家に月決めで～する *rent a room from a person* by the month.

―人 ¶ 彼の所では～人に学生を置いている He *rents a room to* a student.

まがりかど【曲がり角】(町の) a corner; (川・道の) a bend; a turning. ¶ この先に急な～があるから注意して運転してください Drive carefully, because there is *a* sharp *bend* ahead. 二番目の～を右に曲がれば左手に教会が見える Turn right at the second *corner,* and you will see the church on your left. 日本経済もついに～にきた The economy of Japan has reached *a turning point* (≒ *a crisis*) at last.

まがりくね・る【曲がりくねる】¶ ～った道 a *winding* road. ～った枝 a *crooked* branch. ～ったコース a *zigzag* course. 川が峡谷を～って流れていた There was a river *winding* (≒ *meandering*) through the valleys. 道はかなり～っている The road *turns and twists* a good deal.

まかりとお・る【罷り通る】¶ あんな作品がほんもの

ま

として～っていることを考えてみたまえ Just imagine that such works *pass as* genuine. 無法者が～るのを黙って見過ごすわけにはいかない We cannot allow outlaws to *push their way*.

まがりなりにも【曲がりなりにも】¶ ～彼は仕事をやり終えた He *somehow* [*or other*] managed to finish the work. / He has done the work, *though not satisfactorily*.

まかりまちがえば【罷り間違えば】¶ ～倒産だ The company will go bankrupt *if the worst comes to the worst*. ～それはえらい騒ぎになる *If things go wrong*, they will make a big fuss about it.

まが·る【曲がる】¶ 道は川に沿って～っている The road *curves* along the river. そこの角を右に～りなさい *Turn* [to the] right at the corner. 彼女はよる年波で腰が～っている She *is* now *bent* with age. ネクタイがちょっと～っています Your tie *is* a little *crooked* (≒ *askew*). 雪の重みで竹が～っている The bamboos *are bending* under the weight of the snow.

まき【巻き·巻】(書物) a book; a volume; a roll. ¶ 1の～ the first book; Book I; the first volume; Vol. I. 8日～の時計 an eight-day clock. 右～(左～)のばね a clockwise (counterclockwise) spring.

まき【槇】〘植物〙a black pine.

まき【薪】firewood. ¶ ～を割る chop *wood*.
—割り an ax[e].

まきあ·げる【巻き上げる】¶ すだれを～げる *roll up* a screen. 彼女は毛糸を糸巻きに～げていた She *was winding* [*up*] wool into a ball. 彼は多くの善良な市民の金を～げた He *cheated* many good citizens *of* their money. 風がほこりを～げる The wind *flings up* dust.

まきえ【蒔き絵】gold lacquer; silver lacquer.
—師 a worker in [gold] lacquer.

まきおこ·す【巻き起こす】¶ 彼の作品は画壇に一大センセーションを～した His work *created* (≒ *produced*) a great sensation in the artists' world. 彼もかつては風雲を～した男だ He is the man who once *brought about* a crisis.

まきかえしせいさく【巻き返し政策】¶ 野党が～をとった The opposition turned to *a roll-back policy*.

まきがみ【巻紙】rolled letter paper.

まきこ·む【巻き込む】¶ 彼は右腕を機械に～まれた He *had* his right arm *caught in* a machine. 彼は波に～まれて死んだ He *was caught* (≒ *was engulfed*) *in* the waves and drowned. 彼はある事件に～まれている He *has been involved* (≒ *has been entangled*) *in* a certain case. 二度と戦争に～まれるのはごめんだ We will never *be dragged into* a war again.

マキシ a maxi dress; a maxi.

まきじた【巻き舌】¶ あの男は～で話す He speaks *rolling his tongue*. / He *trills* (≒ *rolls*) *his r*'s.

まきじゃく【巻尺】a tape measure; a tape-line.

まきぞえ【巻き添え】¶ 彼はけんかの～で死んだ He was killed *through getting mixed up in* a quarrel. けっして暴動の～を食うな Never *get entangled* (≒ *get involved*) *in* a riot.

まきたばこ【巻き煙草】a cigarette (米 でも cigaret より cigarette のほうがふつう).
—入れ a cigarette case.

まきちら·す【撒き散らす】¶ 彼らは道路に砂利を～した They *scattered* gravel on the road. 床に灰を～すな Don't *sprinkle* ashes on the floor. 部屋にはバラの花が～してあった The room *was strewn with* roses.

まきつ·く【巻き付く】¶ 古木にツタが～いている The old tree *is entwined with* an ivy. / An ivy *has coiled itself around* the old tree.

まきつ·ける【巻き付ける】¶ 彼女はスカーフを首に～けていた She *twisted* her scarf *around* her neck.

まきとりがみ【巻き取り紙】rolled paper.
新聞用**—** a roll of newsprint.

まきなおし【蒔き直し】¶ 新規～だ I will make a fresh start. / I'll do it all over again. (この again には強勢がはいる). もう遅すぎて種の～はできない It is too late to *reseed* (≒ *resow*; *replant*).

まきば【牧場】a pasture; a meadow; (アメリカ西部・カナダで) a ranch.

まきもど·す【巻き戻す】roll back. ¶ ぐるぐる巻かれたロープを～した I *unwound* the coiled rope.

まきもの【巻き物】a roll; a scroll.

まぎら·す【紛らす】¶ 彼は本を読んでたいくつを～している He *is beguiling* the time (≒ tedium) *with* a book. 彼女はよく歌をうたって気を～している She often *diverts* (≒ *distracts*) *herself by* singing. 彼はそれを冗談に～そうとした He tried to *turn* it *off* with a joke. 話を～すな You must not *change the subject* [of conversation]. / You must not *evade the point*. 彼は酒に悲しみを～した He *drowned* his sorrows *in* drink. 彼女は悲しみを笑いに～した She *laughed away* her tears. / She *concealed* her grief *in* smiles.

まぎらわし·い【紛らわしい】(混同されやすい) confusing; misleading; (意味のあいまいな) ambiguous; equivocal.
¶ ～い広告が多すぎる There are too many *misleading* advertisements. 彼女は私に～い答えをした She gave me an *ambiguous* (≒ *equivocal*) answer. この文は意味が二通りにとれて～い This sentence *is ambiguous* in two ways. この複製はほんものと～い This replica tends to *be confused with* the original.

まぎれこ·む【紛れ込む】¶ われわれは森の中へ～んでしまった We *strayed into* the woods. すりは群衆の中に～んでしまった The pickpocket *has been lost among* (≒ *has disappeared into*) the crowd. 重要書類がどこかに～んでしまった The important documents *have mixed up with* other papers.

-まぎれに【-紛れに】¶ 苦し～彼はうそを言った He told a lie *in despair* (≒ *in despera-*

tion; as a last resort). うれし～彼女は秘密をもらしてしまった She let out her secret *in the excess of her joy.* 彼は腹立ち～上役に暴言を吐いた He made a wild remark to his boss *in a fit of anger.*

まぎれもな·い【紛れもない】¶ それは～い事実だ It is a *plain* (≒ an *obvious*; an *indisputable*) fact. それは～く彼の仕業だ It is *unmistakably* (≒ *no doubt*) his doing.

まぎ·れる【紛れる】¶ 読書で私の悲しみは～れる Reading *distracts* me *from* grief. / I *am diverted from* sorrow with reading. 彼らは闇に～れて逃亡した They escaped *under the cover of* night (≒ darkness). このところ忙しさに～れて彼女とデートもできない I have been *too busy to* date her these days. たいせつな書類が他のいろいろな書類の中に～れてしまった The important papers *got mixed up* (≒ *were lost*) among various other papers.

まぎわ【間際】the last moment. ¶ 彼は発車～に駅に着いた He arrived at the station when the train *was on the point of* starting (≒ *was about to* start). ～になってそれは延期と決まった They decided to put it off *at the last moment.*

まく【幕】**1**〖演劇·とばり〗a curtain; a tent.
¶ ～を上げる raise the *curtain.*
～をおろす drop the *curtain.*
～を引く draw the *curtain.*
紅白の～が張りめぐらされていた The *curtain* in red and white stripes was stretched around.
第1～の～が開く The *curtain* rises (≒ goes up) on the first *act.*
～がおりる The *curtain* drops (≒ falls).
2～4場の芝居 a play in two *acts* and four scenes.
第1～第2場 *Act* One, scene two. (省略形は Act I, sc. ii.).
それは2～物だ It is a two-*act* play.
2 ¶ 彼が死んで事件は～になった The affair *ended with* his death.
これでこの事件も～だ This concludes the case./ This brings us to *the end* of the case.
きみの出る～じゃない It's none of your business.
いよいよきみの出る～だ Now it's your *turn* 〔to act〕.

まく【膜】a film; 〖解剖学〗a membrane.

ま·く【巻く】¶ 手に包帯を～く *bind* (≒ *tie up*) the hand with bandage; *bandage* the hand. 毛糸を～いて球にする *roll* wool into a ball. 時計のねじを～く *wind* 〔*up*〕 a watch. 彼女は首にスカーフを～いていた She *had* a scarf around her neck. 彼は彼女の腕に包帯を～いた He *bandaged* her arm.

ま·く【蒔く·播く】¶ 春～く草花 spring-*sown* flowers. 畑に小麦を～く季節だ It is the season to *sow* (≒ *seed*) wheat in the field (≒ to *sow* the field *with* wheat). ～かぬ種は生えぬ (諺) *Out of nothing, nothing comes.* / *You must sow before you reap.* 自分で～いた種だ (自分で刈れ) *As a man sows, so shall he reap.*

ま·く【撒く】**1**〖まき散らす〗¶ 砂を～く *strew* sands. 水を～く *sprinkle* water.
2〖人を〗¶ 彼は刑事を～いた He *gave* the detective *the slip.* / He *dodged* (≒ *shook off*) the detective.
彼は追っ手を～いて姿をくらました He *threw* the pursuers *off the scent* and disappeared.

まくあい【幕間】an interval; 米 an intermission. ¶ 20分の～に軽い食事をとりましょう Let's have a light meal during a twenty minutes' *interval* (≒ *intermission*).

まくぎれ【幕切れ】¶ あっけない～だった (芝居が) *The curtain fell* abruptly when it wasn't expected to. / (結末が) It came to *an* abrupt *end.* 交渉も～に近づいた The negotiation is nearing (≒ approaching) its *end.*

まぐさ【秣】fodder; hay.
—おけ a manger.

まくした·てる【捲し立てる】¶ 彼女は1時間もべらべら～てた She *rattled on* for an hour. 彼はとうとうと～てた He *kept talking* with torrential eloquence.

まぐそ【馬糞】horse-manure.

まぐち【間口】a frontage; a width. ¶ 私の家は～6間に奥行き4間ある My house is 6 *ken wide* and 4 *ken* deep. / My house has a *frontage* of 6 *ken* and a depth of 4 *ken.* 彼の話は～は広いが奥行きがない His talk *covers a wide range,* but lacks depth. われわれは事業の～を広げたい We want to widen our *range* of business.

マグニチュード magnitude. ¶ きのうの地震は～2だった The earthquake we had yesterday was of *magnitude* 2.

まくら【枕】**1**〖寝具〗a pillow; (長まくら) a bolster.
¶ 彼はよくひじ～をして寝る He often *pillows* his arm (≒ elbow). / He often *lies with his head pillowed* (≒ *resting*) *on his arms.*
—掛け a pillowcase. **—**もと ¶ 手紙は～もとにあるじゃないか Can't you see that the letter is *by* (≒ *at*) *your bedside*? 空気**—** an air cushion.
2〖慣用的表現〗¶ 借金を返すまでは私は～を高くして眠れない I can never *sleep in peace* before I am free from debts.
彼らは～を並べて討ち死にした They fell fighting *side by side.*
彼の話の～はいつも長い His *preliminary remarks* are always lengthy.

まくらぎ【枕木】a sleeper; a 〔cross-〕tie.

まくらことば【枕詞】〖修辞〗a conventional (≒ customary) epithet.

まく·る【捲る】¶ 彼女はそでを～ってさらを洗いはじめた She *rolled up* her sleeves and began to do the dishes. 彼女はすそを～って流れを渡った She went across the stream with her dress *tucked up.*

まぐれあたり【紛れ当たり】¶ ～で合格した I passed the examinations *by a lucky fluke* (≒ *by a freak of chance*). もちろん～だ Of course, it is only *a hit by chance* (≒ *a chance hit*). / It is nothing but *a fluke*, no doubt.

まく・れる【捲れる】 ¶ 彼女のすそが少し～れている She *has* her skirt *rolled up* a little.

まぐろ【鮪】〘魚類〙a tunny ; tuna ; (種類をいう場合) tunas. ¶ ～の刺身 slices of raw *tuna* fish.

まくわうり【真桑瓜・甜瓜】〘植物〙a musk-melon.

まけ【負け】 a defeat ; a loss. ¶ その戦闘はドイツ軍の～となった The battle ended in the *defeat* of the German forces. 訴訟は彼の～だろう He will *lose* the case. この勝負は私の～だ I'*ve lost* this game. / You've won this game.

まけおしみ【負け惜しみ】 ¶ この子は～の強い子だ This child is *a bad* (≒ *poor*) *loser*. / This child *hardly ever admits his defeat*. ～を言うな Don't *say anything in a sour-grape humor*. 彼女は私の新しいカメラはきらいだと言ったが, それは明らかに～だった She said she didn't like my brand-new camera, but it was obviously 〔*a case of*〕 *sour grapes*.

まけこ・す【負け越す】 ¶ 彼は春場所 (相撲) で～した He *lost the majority* of his matches in the spring *sumo* tournament. 結局私は彼に～した In the end he led me in games won.

まけじだましい【負けじ魂】 ¶ 彼は～の塊だ He is an *indomitable* (≒ *unyielding*) man. / He *is very competitive*.

まけずおとらず【負けず劣らず】 equally ; neck and neck. ¶ 両チームとも～の強豪だ Both of the teams are *equally* strong. 弟も兄に～のがんばり屋だ The brothers work *equally* hard. 両馬とも～で決勝点に向かってきた The two horses were coming toward the finish line *neck and neck*.

まけずぎらい【負けず嫌い】 ¶ あんな～な男は見たことがない I have never come across such a *stubborn* (≒ *competitive*) man. / He is the most *unyielding* spirit that I have ever met.

まげて【枉げて】 ¶ 彼に～承諾してもらった We *obtained his reluctant* consent. / *Unwillingly* (≒ *Reluctant* as he was,) he gave us his consent. (形式ばった文体). 私のために推薦状を書いてくださるよう～お願いします *Would you be kind enough to* write a letter of recommendation on my behalf? ～お越しくださいませんか *Couldn't you oblige* me by coming?

ま・ける【負ける】 **1**〘敗れる〙 ¶ 野球の試合で～けた We *were beaten* in baseball.
わがチームはアメリカチームにバスケットボールの試合で～けた Our team *was beaten* by the American team in basketball.
ゴルフで彼に～けた He beat me in golf.
彼の馬はレースに～けた His horse *lost* the race.
2〘譲る〙 yield (*to*). ¶ 感情に～ける *give way to one's* feelings.
運命に～けて彼は都会を離れていった *Bowing to fate*, he left the metropolis.
私はすぐ誘惑に～ける I *yield to* temptation easily.
彼は誘惑に～けて悪事を働いた *Giving way to* temptation, he committed a crime.
3〘劣る〙 be inferior (*to*). ¶ 彼は英会話にかけてはクラスのだれにも～けない He *is second to none* in his class in English conversation.
議論好きだという点ではだれにも～けない I *give way to* none in my love for discussion.
4〘値引きする〙 reduce (the price). ¶ いくらか～けてもらえますか Would you *take* anything *off* 〔the price〕?
100円～けましょう I will *take off* one hundred yen.
1,000円に～けてください Please *lower* the price to a thousand yen.
もっと～けてほしい I'd like you to *allow* me *more reduction*. (形式ばった言い方). / *Reduce* more, please.
5〘かぶれる〙 be poisoned (*with*). ¶ うるしに～ける人もある Some people *are poisoned with* lacquer.

ま・げる【曲げる】 **1**〘屈折〙 ¶ 背を～げる *bend one's* back.
鉄棒を～げる *curve* (≒ *bend*) an iron bar.
口を～げる *twist one's* mouth.
指を～げる *crook* a finger.
2〘主義・意味などを〙 ¶ 主義を～げる *depart* (≒ *deviate*) *from one's* principle.
自説を～げない *stick to* (≒ *maintain*) *one's* own views.
事実を～げる *deviate from* the truth.
意味を～げて解釈する *distort* (≒ *twist*) the meaning.
法を～げる *pervert* the law.
彼女はいつも自分のつごうのいいように人のことばを～げてとる She always *twists* (≒ *distorts*) others' words to suit herself.

まご【孫】 a grandchild ; (男) a grandson ; (女) a granddaughter.
—子 ¶ そんなことをすると～子の代までたたるぞ That would bring a misfortune *to your children and children's children* (≒ *to all posterity*).

まごい【真鯉】〘魚類〙carp (複 carp).

まごころ【真心】 faith ; sincerity. ¶ 彼から～のこもった手紙をもらった He wrote me a *sincere* letter. ～こめて自分の仕事をせよ Do your work *devotedly* (≒ *with devotion* ; *with your whole heart and soul*). / *Devote yourself to* your work. ～こめて彼は私に禁酒を説いた He preached me temperance *with his whole heart and soul*. 肝心なのは彼に～があるかないかだ It is whether he has *a true heart* or not that matters. (形式ばった言い方).

まごつ・く **1**〘混乱する〙 ¶ 彼女の思いがけない質問に彼は～いた He *felt embarrassed* (≒ *felt puzzled*) *at* her unexpected question.
彼は～いて電話をまちがえてかけた He dialed a

ま

wrong number *in confusion.*

2 〘うろうろする〙 ¶ 彼はたぶん公園の辺りを〜いている Perhaps he *is hanging* around the park. 彼はこの初めての町で〜いているにちがいない He must *be getting lost* in this strange town.

まこと【誠】(誠実) sincerity; (真実) the truth; the reality; a fact. ¶ 〜のある人とない人ではそこが違う Here is the difference between a *sincere* (≒ *faithful*) man and an *insincere* (≒ a *false*) man.

まことしやか【誠しやか】¶ 〜なうそをつくな Don't tell a *plausible* lie〔to me〕. 彼はいかにも〜にそう言った He said so *as if he knew the truth.* 〜な涙を流す必要はない There is no need for you to shed *crocodile tears.* 〜に plausibly; seemingly.

まことに【誠に・真に】indeed. ¶ あなたのおっしゃることは〜ごもっともです You are *really* right in saying so. 出席できなくて〜残念です I am *very* sorry I will not be able to attend the party. 〜おっしゃるとおりだ You are *absolutely* right. 〜に幸運なことに私は成功した It was a *great* luck for me to be successful. / *Very* luckily I succeeded. (このほうが口語的). 彼は〜すばらしい人物だ He is *truly* a great man.

まごびき【孫引き】requotation. ¶ 〜はあまりするな Don't *quote at second hand* too often.

まごまご ¶そんなに〜するな Don't *be* so *upset.* 今は〜している時ではない We have no time to lose now. / There is not a moment to lose. / Not a moment is to be lost. 〜しているとだまされるぞ *Be careful, or* you will get fooled. 連中はまだあんな所で〜している They *are* still *hanging around* over there. 彼はきっと今ごろ駅で〜しているだろう I am sure he *is* now *at a loss what to do* at the station.

まさか【真逆】by no means; surely not. ¶〜 You don't say so! / Well, I never! / That can not be! / Impossible! 〜彼が来るとは思わなかった I had *least* expected him. 〜彼じゃあるまいね *Surely* it is not he? 〜の時のために貯金するようにしなさい Save money *against a rainy day.* 〜の時は頼むよ I expect you to stand by me *in time of need* (≒ *in an emergency*). (「まさか」は次のように文脈により大きな違いがある.「きみ, 結婚してるの」「まさか」 "Are you married?" "*Of course not.*" /「ぼく1等賞をもらったよ」「まさか」 "I got the first prize." "*Impossible!*").

まさかり【鉞】a broadax〔e〕.

まさしく【正しく】certainly; surely. ¶ それは〜彼の仕業だ It is *surely* (≒ *no doubt*; *undoubtedly*) his doing. / *There is no doubt* that it is his doing. これこそ〜彼の本心だ *Evidently* (≒ *Obviously*) this is his real intention. この指輪は〜私のものだ *No doubt* this ring is mine.

まさつ【摩擦】friction. ¶ 〜すると熱が生じる Heat is produced by *friction.* 土人は木片を〜して火を起こす The aborigines make fire by *rubbing* together two pieces of wood. 中近東でずいぶん〜が起こっている There is a lot of *trouble*〔*s*〕 in the Middle East. 両者の〜を少なくするのが先決だ We should first ease the *tension* between the two.

—音〘音声学〙a fricative〔sound〕. 冷水**—** a rubdown with a cold wet towel. ¶ 冷水〜をする have *a rubdown with a cold towel.*

まさに【正に】¶ 〜きみの言うとおりだ You are *perfectly* right. これこそ〜ぼくが捜していた本だ This is *the very* book that I have been looking for. 〜きみが行くべきだ Nobody but you should go. 〜社会改造の時だ Now is the time for social reorganization. 日は〜西に沈もうとしている The sun is *just* setting in the west.

まざまざと clearly; distinctly; vividly. ¶ その光景を〜思い浮かべることができる I can recall the scene *clearly* (≒ *vividly*).

まさめ【正目・柾目】the straight grain〔of wood〕. ¶ 〜の通った板 a *straight-grained* board.

まさゆめ【正夢】a prophetic dream. ¶ あれは〜だった The dream came true.

まさ・る【勝る・優る】excel. ¶ 彼は彼の兄に〜るとも劣らない実力がある He *is not less* able *than* his brother. 米は去年に〜る豊作だ The rice crop this year *is even better than* the last year's rich harvest. 彼は英語では私よりも, はるかに〜っている He *is* much *superior to* me in English.

まざ・る【混ざる・交ざる】⇒まじる

まし【増し】increase; addition. ¶ 彼らは給料の1割5分〜を要求した They demanded a fifteen percent salary *increase.* 休日の観客は平日の2割〜だ The number of the audience on holidays *increases* by twenty percent over weekdays. こんな苦しい目に会うくらいなら死んだほうが〜だ I *would rather* die *than* have such a hard time. もっと〜な話をしなさい Say something *better.*

まじ・える【交える】¶ 敵と砲火を〜えた We *exchanged* fire *with* the enemy. 彼とひざを〜えて話した I *had a heart-to-heart talk with* him.

ましかく【真四角】a perfect square.

ました【真下】¶ 東京タワーを〜から見上げた I looked up at the Tokyo Tower *right from its bottom.* 地下鉄がこの通りの〜を走っている The subway runs *just under* this street. 山の〜に温泉町がある There is a spa *right at the foot of* the mountain.

マジック magic.

—アイ a magic eye.

まして【況して】¶ ぼくにだってそのくらいのことはできる.〜きみにできないはずはない I can do that much; *still more* it must be possible for you to do that. きみがだめなのに〜ぼくにやれるものか You can't do it; *still less* is it possible for me to do it. (文語的. it is still less possible とすれば口語的になる). 英語を知らない彼女が〜スペイン語のできるわけがない She doesn't know English

ま

well, *not to speak of* (≒ *to say nothing of*) Spanish.

まじない【呪い】a spell; magic words. ¶ お～で病気を治す cure *one's* sickness by *a charm*; *charm away one's* sickness.

まじまじと ¶ 彼女は～私の顔を見た She *looked* (≒ *stared*) me *in the face*. / She *looked in my face*. / She *stared at* me.

まじめ【真面目】¶ ～な人 an *honest* (≒ a *serious*) person. ～な顔をする look *serious*. ～になる(行ないを改める) mend *one's* way. ～に勉強する study *earnestly*. ～に話す speak *in earnest*. ～に暮らす live *honestly*. 彼は私の冗談を～にとった He took my joke *seriously*. ～に言っているんだ I'*m serious*. / I *mean what I say*.

ましゃく【間尺】¶ これは～に合わない仕事だ This work does not *pay*.

まじゅつ【魔術】(奇術の類) a conjuring; a jugglery; (悪魔の魔術) black magic; black art.

¶ ～を使う use (≒ practice) *magic*. ことばの～にかかる be bound by the *spell* of the words.

―師 a magician.

まじょ【魔女】a witch.

―狩り a witch-hunt.

ましょうめん【真正面】¶ 建物の～に立つ stand *right in front of* the building. ～から問題に取り組む tackle the problem *squarely*. 私の～に彼が座った He sat down *just opposite to* me.

まじり【混じり】a mixture. ¶ 雨～の雪が降っていた It was snowing *mixed with* rain. / It was sleeting.

―物 a mixture; (不純物) an impurity.

まじりけ【混じり気】an impurity. ¶ ～のない情熱 *genuine* enthusiasm.

まじ・る【交じる】¶ 油と水は～らない Oil and water will not *mix*. これは毛とレーヨンが～っている This is *a mixture* of wool and rayon. 彼の頭に白いものが～ってきた His hair is beginning to *be shot* (≒ *be streaked*) *with* gray.

まじわり【交わり】(面識) acquaintance; (親交) friendship. ¶ 彼女との～をやっと断つことができた I was finally able to *break with* her. 彼とは浅からぬ～がある He and I are *close friends*.

まじわ・る【交わる】**1**〖交際する〗¶ 悪友と～るな *Keep away from* bad company.

人は～る友を見ればわかる A man is known by the company he *keeps*.

彼と友人として深く～っている I *am great friends with* him. / He and I are great friends. / He is a great friend of mine.

朱に～れば赤くなる(諺) *You can't touch pitch without being defiled*.

彼らは親しく～っている They are good friends. (good のかわりに intimate を用いると異性との深交を暗示することが多い).

2〖交差する〗¶ そこで道路と線路が～る There the road and the railroad *cross each other*.

マシン a machine.

―ガン a machine gun.

ます【升】a measure. ¶ 1升～ではかる measure with *a one-sho measure*.

―席 a box seat. ¶ ～席に座る sit in *a box seat*.

ます【鱒】〖魚類〗a trout (複 trout).

ま・す【増す】increase; add; gain. ¶ 修養は威厳を～す Mental training *adds to one's* dignity. 彼女は体重が～した She *put on* weight. 連日の雨で水かさが～した The river *rose* owing to the long rain. 列車はしだいに速さを～していった The train *was picking* (≒ *was speeding*) *up*. / The train *was increasing* its speed.

まず【先ず】¶ ～彼が帰った He was *the first to* leave. ～きょうはそれまでにしよう *Well*, that'll be all for today. 私の言えることは～こんなところだ This is *about* all I can say. ～行ってみよう Let's go *anyway*. ～それでいいとして，そのあとどうしよう *So far* so good; what shall we do next?

ますい【麻酔】anesthesia. ¶ 手術のため～をかける *anesthetize a person* for an operation. 彼は～をして手術を受けた He *was given an anesthesia* and operated on.

―薬 an anesthetic. 全身(局部)― general (local) anesthesia.

まず・い【不味い】**1**〖味が〗poor. ¶ このリンゴは～い This apple *does not taste good*.

このカキ(果物)は～いですね This persimmon *is unpalatable*, isn't it?

この料理は～そうだ This dish does *not* look *tasty*.

2〖へたな〗poor. ¶ ～いやり方だ What a *poor* method!

その手紙は～い英語で書かれていた The letter was written in *poor* English.

彼の話はなんとも～いものだった His speech *was* very *poor*.

彼女はたいへん字が～い Her handwriting *is* very *bad*. / She *is* very *poor* in handwriting. / She writes a very *bad* hand.

3〖不適当・不都合〗unfavorable. ¶ ～いことを言ってしまった What I said was*n't* very *good*.

これをやらないと～い It *is unwise* not to do this.

きみはこの要求を断わっては～い You *shouldn't* decline this request.

仕事を途中でやめては～い It *is not advisable* to stop your work halfway.

ここにいるところを見られては～い It's *awkward* (≒ *embarrassing*) *for* me to be seen here.

彼にこの仕事をやらせては～い I don't want him to do this work.

居留守をつかったのは～かった I *should not* have pretended to be away from home.

4〖みにくい〗ugly. ¶ 彼女は～い顔だちだ She is *poor*-looking. (人の顔だちに対して ugly はなるべく用いないほうがよい).

マスク **1**〖顔だち〗look. ¶ 彼女は彫りの深い～をしている She has *a face* with clear-cut features. (顔の目や鼻や口はそれぞれ a feature だから，まとめて言えば必ず複数形となる) / She is a

pretty woman.
2〖面〗a mask. ¶ キャッチャーが～をつけた The catcher put on the *mask*.
デス―― a death mask.

マスゲーム〘体育〙a mass game. ¶ ～をやる play *a mass game*.

マスコット a mascot.

マスコミ〔ュニケーション〕 mass communication. ¶ 彼女は～で騒ぎ立てられた She was given much publicity by *journalism*. ～の世界 the world of *mass communication*.

まずし・い【貧しい】 poor; needy. ¶ 彼は～い家に生まれた He was born *poor*. / He was born of a *poor* family. わが家は～い Our family *is badly off*. / Our family *lives in poverty*. 私の～い経験から言えばきみの言っていることは違う Judging from my *little* experience, you are wrong.

マスター (料理店などの主人) a proprietor; an owner; (修士号) a Master's degree. ¶ 英会話を～する *become proficient in* English; *master* English conversation. 彼は大学院の英語の～コースを修了した He completed his *Master's* program in English.

マスト a mast. ¶ 3本～の船 a three-masted ship; a three-master.

マスプロ〔ダクション〕 mass production. ¶ ～教育 education conducted on *a mass-production* basis.

ますます【益】 more and more; (減少) less and less. ¶ 風が～激しくなる The wind blows *harder and harder*. 日本を訪れる外国人は～増えてきた The number of foreigners who visit Japan has become *increasingly* large. ～深刻になりつつある住宅事情になにか思い切った手を打たなければならない Something drastic has to be done about the *increasingly* desperate housing situation. 事態は～悪化した The matter went *from bad to worse*.

まずまず【先ず先ず】 ¶ 今度のテストは～の結果だ I have done *fairly* (≒ *pretty*; *passably*) *well* in this test.

マスメディア mass media; the means of communication.

まぜかえ・す【混ぜ返す】 ¶ 人の話を～すな Don't *break in on* me. (in に強勢がある) / Don't *interrupt* me. / (冷やかす) Don't *make fun of* me.

まぜこぜ【混ぜこぜ】 a jumble. ¶ いいものも悪いものも～になっている Both good and bad *are all mixed up* (≒ *are jumbled together*).

ませた ¶ 彼女は～子だ She is a *precocious* child. / She *is too smart for her age*.

まぜもの【混ぜ物】 an impurity (ふつう複数形で用いる). ¶ この酒は～はない This *sake* does not contain any *admixture* (≒ *impurities*).

ま・ぜる【混ぜる】 mix; blend. ¶ 赤と青を～ぜると何色になるか What color will you get if you *mix* (≒ *blend*) the red paint *with* the blue? 彼らはセメントとじゃりを～ぜた They *mingled* cement and gravel.

また【又・復・亦】 **1**〖別・次〗¶ 話の続きは～の日にしよう I'll tell you the rest of this story *some other* day.
大阪, ～の名は水の都 Osaka is *also* known as the 'City of Water.'
今回はあきらめて～の機会を待とう I'll give up this time and wait for *another* opportunity.
2〖再び・あとで〗¶ いずれ～ご連絡します I'll inform you of it *later*.
近いうちに～お出かけください Please come *again* soon. / Please drop in soon *again*.
彼はあした～来ると言った He told me that he would come *again* tomorrow.
では～明日お目にかかりましょう Then I'll see you *again* tomorrow. (会話ではしばしば See you tomorrow. となる).
午後から～雨になった It began raining *again* in the afternoon.
きみは～うそをついたね You told *another* lie, didn't you?
～とない機会だから見送る手はない We should take advantage of it now since we may not have *another* chance.
3〖同じく・そのうえ・やはり〗¶ 姉に劣らず妹も～美しい The younger sister is *as* beautiful *as* the older one.
彼は学者であり, ～詩人でもある He is *not only* a scholar *but* a poet *as well*.
彼の話はおもしろく, ～参考にもなった His speech was instructive *as well as* interesting.
これも～美しい曲ですね This is a beautiful tune, *too*, isn't it?
父はあわて者だが, 母も～たいへんなあわて者だ My father is a careless man, but my mother is just *as* careless.
私はそこへ行かなかった, ～行きたいとも思わなかった I *neither* went there, *nor* did I wish to.
彼はそんなことは言わなかったし, ぼくも～言わなかった He didn't say such a thing, *nor* did I.
4〖強調〗¶ 彼は1歩～1歩と怪しい人影に近づいた *Step by step* he approached the suspicious-looking figure.
同志はひとり～ひとりと彼のもとを去った His comrades left him *one after another*.
1匹～1匹とアリが寄ってきた The ants began to gather *one after another*.
そこは山～山の山の中であった The place was surrounded with *range upon range* of mountains.
行けども行けども水～水だった I went on and on, but I saw nothing but water.
その知らせが～彼女の不安をかきたてた The news made her *more and more* anxious.
～ひどい仕打ちをしたものだ What an act of outrage this is!

また【叉】 a fork. ¶ ～になっている道 a *forked* road. あそこで川が～になっている That is the place where the river *forks*.

また【股】 the thigh. ¶ 世界じゅうを～にかける travel all over the world. 彼は元気よく大～に歩いた He walked with vigorous *strides*.

まだ【未だ】 **1**〖いまだ〗¶ 彼は～現われない He has

ま

not appeared *yet*.
～完成したとはいえない This is *still* far from complete.
もう入浴はすみましたか—いや，～です Have you finished taking a bath yet? — No, not *yet*.
2 〚今なお〛 still. ¶ ～雪はやまない It is *still* snowing.
～時間はある There is *still* enough time.
試合は～続行中だ The game is *still* going on.
～もう一つ欲しいものがある I have one *more* thing I want.
～なにか質問がありますか Do you have anything *more* to ask me?
3 〚やっと〛 only. ¶ ここへ来て～1か月にしかならない It is *only* a month since I came here. (米口語では It has *only* been a month.... ともいう).
この子は～小学生だ This child is a *mere* elementary schoolboy.
～8時なので，帰るには早い It is *only* eight; it is too early for me to go home.
4 〚その上〛 still. ¶ ～2時間ある We *still* have two *more* hours.
～5キロある I have *still* five kilometers to go.
お話しすることは～たくさんある I *still* have a lot more to tell you.

まだい【真鯛】〘魚類〙 a reddish sea bream.

まだい【間代】〔a〕 room rent. ¶ 高い～を払う pay *a* high *rent for the room*. 彼の～は3か月滞っている He is three months behind *the rent for his room*.

またいとこ【又従兄弟・又従姉妹】 a second cousin.

またがし【又貸し】 sublease. ¶ 家を～する *sublet* a house. 本の～はだめだ Don't lend somebody else's (≒ a borrowed) book to another. 旅行中アパートを3か月～した I *subleased* my apartment for three months while I traveled.

またがり【又借り】 ¶ 本を～する borrow a book secondhand.

またが・る【跨る】 ¶ 馬に～る *ride* on horseback; *mount* (≒ *stride*) a horse. その山は2か国に～る The mountain *extends* over two countries. 隅田川に～る橋は多い There are a number of bridges *spanning* (≒ *lying across*) the River Sumida. / The River Sumida *is spanned with* lots of bridges. この仕事は来年に～るだろう The work will *spread over* (≒ *extend*) *to* next year.

またぎき【又聞き】 secondhand (≒ indirect) information; hearsay. ¶ この話は～だ I *heard* about it 〔*at*〕 *secondhand*.

また・ぐ【跨ぐ】 ¶ 小川を～ぐ *stride over* (≒ *across*) a stream. 敷居を～ぐ *step over* (≒ *cross*) the threshold.

まだしも【未だしも】 rather; preferably. ¶ 恥をさらすよりも～死んだほうがいい I *would rather* die than disgrace myself. これだけなら～，まだその次がある It would be better if this were all, but there's still more coming.

また・せる【待たせる】 ¶ 外に友人を～せてある I *have* a friend *waiting* outside. 彼をあまり～せるな Don't *keep* him *waiting* long. 長い間～された I *was kept waiting* for a long time. (上例二つの文については long を副詞に用いるほうが for a long time よりも文語的).

またたき【瞬き】 a wink; (星の) twinkling; (明かりの) flickering.

またた・く【瞬く】 twinkle; flicker. ¶ 星が～いていた The stars *were twinkling*. ろうそくがゆらゆらと～いていた The candle *was flickering*. 彼は～く間に仕事を仕上げた He finished his work *in an instant*. ～くうちに点差がついた We got a long lead on them *in the twinkling of an eye*.

またとない【又とない】 ¶ ～チャンス a chance of my life; a *golden* opportunity. ～楽しさだった We had never been so happy before.

またのな【又の名】 another name; an alias. ¶ 巌窟(がんくつ)王～はエドモン=ダンテス Count of Monte Cristo *alias* (≒ *also known as*) Edmond Dantès.

またのひ【又の日】 another (≒ some other) day. ¶ ～を期そう Let's look forward to *another chance*.

または【又は】 or; (言い換えると) in other words. ¶ 母～父が伺うはずです 〔Either〕 my mother *or* father is coming. (or で結ばれた語が主語の場合，動詞は次のように or の次に来る語に支配される．〔Either〕 he or his parents *are* to be invited).

またまた【又又】 again; once again.

まだまだ【未だ未だ】 still; still more. ¶ ～日は暮れない It will be *still* long before it gets dark. ～このほうがよい This is *much* better. きみは～勉強が足りない You must work *still* harder.

マダム a madam; (料理屋などの) a proprietress.

まだら【斑】 spots; patches; speckles. ¶ 白と茶の～の犬 a dog *spotted with* white and brown; a white and brown dog. 雪が谷間に～に残っていた *Patches* of snow remained in the valley.

まだるこ・い【間怠こい】 ¶ きみの話し方は～い You *drawl out* your words. / You speak *with a drawl*. 彼の仕事は～い He is a *slow* worker.

まち【町】 a town; a city; (街路) a street. ¶ あの山を越えると～に出る There's *a town* beyond the mountain. 彼は～へ買い物に行った He went shopping to *town*. (go to town は無冠詞; go to town for shopping は避ける). 神奈川県葉山～ Hayama *Town*, Kanagawa Prefecture.

まちあい【待合】 a *geisha* restaurant.
—政治 behind-the-scenes political dealings.

まちあいしつ【待合室】 a waiting room.

まちあわ・せる【待ち合わせる】 ¶ 友人と4時に駅で～せるはずだった I was to *meet* my friend at the station at four.

まちう·ける【待ち受ける】¶ 返事をいまや遅しと～けた We *waited for* the answer impatiently. / We *looked forward to* 〔receiving〕 the answer.

まぢか【間近】¶ 目的地も～だ The end of our trip *is close* (≒ *is near*) *at hand*. 締め切りも～に迫った The deadline *is drawing near*.

まちがい【間違い】**1** 〖誤り〗a mistake. ¶ きみの答えは～だ Your answer *is incorrect*.
彼は自分の～を認めない He won't acknowledge his *error*.
同じ～を２度繰り返すな Never make the same *mistake* twice.
この英文は～だらけだ This English sentence is full of *mistakes*.
だれでもこの仕事ができると思ったら～だ It *is wrong* (≒ *is a mistake*) to think that everyone is able to do this work.
彼が成功するのは～ない He *is sure to* succeed.
彼なら絶対～がない He is indeed to *be trusted*.
彼に親切心が欠けていたことは～のない事実だ It is an *undeniable* fact that he was lacking in kindness.
(電話で) 番号がお～ですよ Sorry, you have the *wrong* number.
2 〖事故〗an accident. ¶ 彼が来るのが遅い. ～がなければいいが He is late in coming. I hope *nothing is the matter with* him.
～を起こしたのはだれだ Who committed *an indiscreet conduct*!
3 〖紛争〗¶ 誤解が～のもとになる *Trouble* often results from misunderstanding.

まちがいなく【間違いなく】without fail; (正しく) correctly. ¶ 彼は～試験に合格するだろう He will *surely* pass the test. / He *is sure to* pass the test. (He *is sure of* passing the test. は「彼は自分の合格を確信している」). 彼は～来る *I'm sure* he will come.

まちが·う【間違う】make a mistake. ¶ 計算を～う *make an error in* calculation. ～っても盗みはするな You must never steal. ～って風邪薬を飲んだ I took a remedy for colds *by mistake* (≒ *by accident*).

まちが·える【間違える】err. ¶ 人を別人と～える *take* (≒ *mistake*) *a person for* another. 部屋を～える come to a *wrong* room. 計算を～える *make an error* (≒ *a mistake*) *in* calculation; make *a miscalculation*.

まちがった【間違った】incorrect; mistaken. ¶ ～答えをする give (≒ make) a *wrong* answer.

まちかど【町角】a street corner. ¶ ～の店 a store *on the street corner*. ふたりは～で話し合った The two talked with each other *at a street corner*. (町角で話すのは at, 町角の店は on のほうがよい).

まちか·ねる【待ち兼ねる】wait impatiently (*for*). ¶ 彼は母親に会える日を～ねている He *can hardly wait for* the day when he will meet his mother. 出発の日を～ねている We *are looking forward to* the day of departure. (look forward to は進行形で用いることが多い).

まちかま·える【待ち構える】wait eagerly (*for*). ¶ チャンスを～えている They *are awaiting* a good chance. (他動詞 await はチャンスや命令をいまかいまかと待ち構えるときに用いるが, wait for より形式ばった表わし方). 子どもたちは夏休みを～えていた The children *were looking forward to* summer vacation. 選手は笛の合図を～えていた The players *were ready for* the signal of the whistle.

まちくたび·れる【待ちくたびれる】¶ 彼の帰宅を～れた I *got weary of waiting for* him to return home.

まちくら·す【待ち暮らす】¶ 彼からの電話を待って一日～した I spent the whole day waiting impatiently for the telephone from him. (waiting を文頭に出せば文語的になる).

まちこが·れる【待ち焦がれる】long for. ¶ 夏休みを～れている He *is* eagerly *looking forward to* summer vacation. (long for を用いれば形式ばった形になる). 彼の帰りを～れている I *can hardly wait for* him to be back.

まちじゅう【町中】the whole town. ¶ ～が彼を出迎えた *The whole town* greeted him heartily. ～がその火事のうわさをしていた *The townspeople* were talking about the fire.

まちどおし·い【待ち遠しい】¶ 日曜日が～い Sunday *seems long* 〔*in*〕 *coming*. (in のないほうが口語的). 彼の帰りが～い I *am looking forward to* his return.

まちなみ【町並み】the row of houses. ¶ ～がきれいだ *The street* is beautiful.

まちはずれ【町外れ】the outskirts of a town. ¶ 彼の家は～にある His house is *on the outskirts of the town*. (in the suburbs は町の外郭にある住宅地をさすから, 必ずしも「郊外」ではなく,「町外れ」にあたることもある).

まちばり【待ち針】a marking pin.

まちぶせ【待ち伏せ】¶ ～する lie in wait (*for*); ambush. 先回りして彼を～した I anticipated him, *lying in ambush*. / I *waylaid* him, going ahead of him.

まちぼうけ【待ちぼうけ】¶ ３時間も～を食った I *was kept waiting for* him three hours *in vain*. 彼はまた～を食わせた He *kept me waiting in vain* again.

まちまち ¶ ～の diverse. ～に severally. 彼らの意見は～だった They *were divided in* opinion. うわさは～だ Rumors *are conflicting*. 同じことが新聞によって～だ The same event is reported *differently* (≒ *in different ways*) in a variety of papers.

まつ【松】a pine. ¶ この～は枝ぶりがいい This *pine* has graceful branches. (欧米では樹木はまっすぐ生えているものと思っているからまがりくねった松の枝やその根はきわめて日本的な風景と考えられる. したがって graceful は日本と欧米とではイメージが違う).

ま·つ【待つ・俟つ】**1** 〖待ち受ける〗wait. ¶ だれを～っているのですか Who〔m〕 *are* you *waiting for*?

ま

30分以上バスを〜った I *waited for* a bus for more than half an hour.
ちょっと〜ってください Please *wait* a moment.
もうどのくらい〜っているのですか How long *have* you *been waiting*?
〜っても〜っても彼は来なかった I *waited and waited* but he did not come (≒ he never showed up).
2 〘期待する〙 expect. ¶ 彼の来るのを今やおそしと〜っていた We *were expecting* him to come immediately. (expect のかわりに wait for を使うと待たされる感じになる).
いいご返事を〜っています I *am expecting* a favorable reply.
3 〘頼る〙 depend (*upon*). ¶ 彼の援助に〜つばかりだ I *depend upon* him only *for* help.
私たちが成功するか否かは彼の努力に〜つところが大きい We *depend* a great deal *upon* his efforts *for* our success.
彼らの活躍に〜つところが大きい We *rely* very much *on* them.

まつえい【末裔】a descendant.

まっか【真っ赤】deep red. ¶ 〜な deep red. 〜になる turn *red*. 恥ずかしさのあまり〜になった She was so shy that she *flushed up*. 彼は〜になって怒った He *turned red* with rage. 男たちは〜になって議論している They are *getting hot* over an argument. それは〜なうそだった It was a *downright* lie.

まつかさ【松かさ】a pine cone.

まつかざり【松飾り】the New Year's pine decorations. ¶ もう〜をする時期だ It is the time we put *the New Year's pine decorations* at the gate. (この場合の put は過去形).

まつかぜ【松風】the wind among the pines.

まっき【末期】the last stage. ¶ この機械は15世紀の〜に発明された This machine was invented *at the close of* the fifteenth century. それは戦国時代〜の出来事だった It happened in the *late* Sengoku era. 資本主義は〜的症状を呈している Capitalism is heading for a collapse.

まっくら【真っ暗】¶ 〜な pitch-dark. 表は〜だった It *was pitch-dark* (≒ *was dark as pitch*) outdoors. 〜な所をなにかが動いている Something is stirring *in utter darkness*. 廊下は〜だった It *was utterly dark* along the corridor. お先〜だ The future seems to *be dark and uncertain*. / I have no foresight at all.

まっくろ【真っ黒】¶ このネコは〜だ This cat has a *coal-black* fur. この布地は〜だ The color of the cloth *is deep-black*. 日に焼けて〜だった He *was tanned deeply*. (tanned はよい感じを与えるが sunburnt を用いると痛々しい感じになる). 〜な顔になって(日焼けして)帰ってきた He came back with a *sunburnt* (≒ *tanned*) face. 手はすすで〜に汚れていた My hands *were smudged* with soot.

まつげ【睫】eyelashes. ¶ 彼女は〜が濃い She has thick *eyelashes*. 彼女は〜が長い She has *long-lashed eyes*. (まつげの長いのは美人の条件). 逆さ── trichiasis. つけ── false eyelashes.

まつご【末期】death. ¶ 私は父の〜の水をとった I attended the *deathbed* of my father. 彼の〜が近づいている His *end* is near. これが彼の〜のことばだった Such were his *last* words.

まっこう【抹香】incense. ¶ あの部屋は〜臭い That room *is monkish*. 彼は〜臭いことを言う He says something that sounds *religious*.

まっこう【真っ向】¶ 船は〜から風を受けて進んでいった The ship advanced with the wind *in her face*. 新聞は彼の行動を〜から非難した The newspapers *made a front attack upon* his conduct. 彼は私の申し出を〜から拒否した He refused my offer *flatly*.

まっこうくじら【抹香鯨】〘動物〙 a sperm whale.

マッサージ massage. ¶ 〜をする massage. 人の背中を〜する *massage a person* on the back. 顔を〜する apply facial *massages*.
──師 a massagist; (女) a masseuse.

まっさいちゅう【真っ最中】¶ あらしの〜に出かけていった He started *in the midst of* a storm. 今会議の〜だ The conference *is in full swing*. 彼らは訓練の〜だった They were then undergoing training. 日本は戦争の〜だった Japan *was at the height of* the war.

まっさお【真っ青】¶ 空は〜だった The sky *looked quite blue*. 彼はあまりのショックに〜になった Such was his shock that he *turned white*. (white は血の気のうせた状態をいう). 彼は〜になって怒った He was *whitely* angry.

まっさかさま【真っ逆様】¶ 〜に headlong. 彼はがけから〜に落ちた He fell *head over heels* from the cliff. 飛行機は〜に墜落した The plane crashed *end over end* to the ground.

まっさかり【真っ盛り】¶ 桜は今や〜だ The cherry-blossoms *are at their best*.

まっさき【真っ先】¶ 〜に first of all. 彼が〜にやってきた He *was the first to* come. (この不定詞 (to come) はいつも過去を表わす). 彼が一行の〜に立った He stood *at the head of* the party. 〜に彼に会いにいった *First thing*, I went to see him.

まっさつ【抹殺】erasure. ¶ 〜する erase. この原稿から５行ほど〜してほしい I want about five lines to *be crossed out* form the manuscript.

まつじ【末寺】a branch temple.

まっしぐら【驀地】¶ 〜に at full speed. 彼らは劇場の入り口を目指して〜に突進した They *dashed for* the door of the theater. 彼は川ぞいを〜に車を駆っていった He drove his car along the river *at full speed*.

まつじつ【末日】the last day.

マッシュ mash.
──ポテト mashed potatoes (イギリスでは俗に mash とだけ言う).

マッシュルーム〘植物〙 a mushroom.

まっしょう【末梢】¶ 〜的な話 *trivial* matters.
──神経 the peripheral nervous system.

まっしょうじき【真っ正直】honesty itself.

¶〜な straightforward. 〜に straightforwardly. 彼は〜すぎる He *is* too *straightforward.* そんな〜なやり方ではだめだ Such a *straightforward* method won't do.

まっしろ【真っ白】 pure-white. ¶屋根という屋根は雪で〜だ All the roofs *are white* with snow. 彼の答案は〜でなにも書いてなかった His examination paper *was all blank.* 彼女は〜な肌をしている Her skin *is white and pure.*

まっすぐ【真っ直ぐ】1〖一直線に・直立して〗¶〜な straight.
〜な線を引く draw a *straight* line.
〜200メートル行きなさい Go *straight* ahead about two hundred meters.
風がないので煙は〜立ちのぼっている There is no wind blowing, and the smoke is rising *straight* up.
〜に並ぶ make a *straight* line.
〜家路についた I came *direct* back home.
2〖正直〗¶あの人は〜な人柄で，皆に信頼されている Because he is a man of *upright* character, he is trusted by everybody.
〜に世を渡るべきだ You should live *straight.*

まっせ【末世】 a degenerate age.

まっせき【末席】 the lowest seat. ¶私も〜を汚した I had the honor of presenting myself at the meeting. 委員の〜を汚しているひとりとして申し上げます I am going to speak as a member of the committee.

まった【待った】 wait. ¶〜をする(囲碁・将棋) retract a move; (相撲) be not ready. 〜なしだ(勝負で) "*Not ready*" is never allowed. 〜をかけてはならない Never call "*not ready.*"

まつだい【末代】 all ages to come. ¶この栄誉は〜まで残したい We hope this honor will remain *forever.* 彼の名は〜に伝えるべきだ His name must *be perpetuated.*

まったく【全く】 entirely. ¶〜そのとおりだ That's *quite* right.
〜消耗した I am *utterly* exhausted.
彼は〜途方にくれている He doesn't know *utterly* what to do. / He is *wholly* at a loss what to do. (文語体).
それは〜時間のむだだ It is *sheer* waste of time.
〜突然の出来事だった It happened suddenly.
〜時間が正確だ He is *quite* punctual.
それは〜知らない I know nothing about it *at all.*
〜予想どおりになった It has turned out *just* as I expected.
この辺は〜不案内です I am *quite* a stranger around here myself.
〜幸運というほかはない It is due to *nothing but* good luck.
ふたりは〜似ていない The two are *in no way* alike.
あの人は親切心など〜ない He has *not a particle of* kindness in him.
彼は〜うそつきだ He is a *great* (≒*perfect*) liar.

まつたけ【松茸】〘植物〙 a mushroom. ¶〜狩りに行った We went *mushrooming.*

まっただなか【真っ只中】 ¶あらしの〜を突っ走った I dashed on *in the midst of* the storm.

まったん【末端】 the end. ¶その思想は社会の〜にまで浸透している The ideas are diffusing to every inch of the community.
—機構 a terminal organization.

マッチ 1〖発火の〗 a match. ¶〜をする strike *a match.*
この〜はつかない This *match* won't strike.
〜を吹いて消す blow out *a match.*
〜を一箱買った I bought a box of *matches.*
—箱 a matchbox. ¶彼は〜箱のような家に住んでいる He lives in a very small house. / He lives in *a matchbox of* a house. (文語体).
2〖試合〗 a match.
—ポイント a match point. チャレンジ**—** a challenge match.
3〖調和〗 a match. ¶新しい帽子は衣装とよく〜している The new hat *is a match for* her dress.

まっちゃ【抹茶】 powdered tea. ¶〜をたてる make *powdered tea.*

マット a mat. ¶床に〜を敷く spread *a mat* on the floor.

まっとう・する【全うする】 complete. ¶首尾よく本分を〜した I *have accomplished* my duty. ついに使命を〜した I *fulfilled* my mission after all. 一度やりかけたことは最後まで〜するようにしなさい Once you have set about a thing, try to *bring* it *to perfection.* 彼は天寿を〜した He *died a natural death.*

マットレス a mattress.

まつのうち【松の内】 the first seven days of the New Year.

マッハ Mach. ¶あのジェット機は〜1の速力で飛ぶ That jet plane flies at [the speed of] *Mach* 1.

まつば【松葉】 a pine needle.

まっぱだか【真っ裸】 stark-nakedness. ¶彼は〜だった He *was stark-naked.* 子どもたちは〜になって遊んでいた The children were playing *stark-naked.* 子どもは〜になった The child *stripped himself bare.* 赤ん坊は〜で立っていた The baby stood *with no clothes* on.

まつばづえ【松葉杖】 a crutch; (一組(2本)の松葉杖) a pair of crutches. ¶彼は〜をついて歩いている He is walking *on crutches.*

まつばぼたん【松葉牡丹】〘植物〙 a sunplant.

まつばやし【松林】 a pine wood.

まつばら【松原】 a pine grove.

まつび【末尾】 the end. ¶〜1の電話番号 the telephone number of which the first order is 1.

まっぴつ【末筆】 ¶〜ながらみなさまによろしく With best wishes for you and your family.

まっぴら【真っ平】 ¶それは〜だ I *wouldn't* have it, *for the life of me.* ぶどう酒は〜だ *No* wine for me. ああいう人は〜だ I *won't* see such a kind of man. もうあそこに行くのは〜だ I *never* hope to go there.

まっぴるま【真っ昼間】 ¶〜に in *broad daylight.*

まっぷたつ【真っ二つ】 ¶彼はそれを〜に切った He cut it *right in two.* 彼らの意見が〜に割れた

They were split *in two* groups in opinion.

まつむし【松虫】〘虫類〙a cricket. ¶ ～が鳴いている *A cricket* is chirping. (ヨーロッパ人は日本人ほど虫の音の違いを聞き分けることができないから，松虫か鈴虫かなどの区別はほとんど無視する).

まつやに【松脂】pine resin.
 一油 rosin oil.

まつよう【末葉】¶ 20世紀の～に toward the end of the 20th century.

まつり【祭り】a festival. ¶ なんの～ですか What *festival* is going on? 神社では今お～の最中だ They are celebrating (⇆ having) *a festival* at the shrine. 彼らはお～気分でさわいでいる They are making merry *in a holiday mood.* / They *are making a fuss about it.*

まつりあ·げる【祭り上げる】¶ 彼は委員長に～げられた He *was exalted as* the head of the committee. 彼は議長に～げられたようなものだ He may be said to *have been set up as* chairman.

まつりごと【政】administration. ¶ ～を執り行なう conduct *the affairs of the state.*

まつりゅう【末流】(支流) a tributary; (末裔) a descendant.

まつ·る【祭る】(神として) deify; (神社に) enshrine. ¶ 東照宮には徳川家康が～ってある The Toshogu Shrine *is dedicated to* Ieyasu Tokugawa. お盆は先祖の霊を～る行事だ The *Bon* Festival is a festival of *worshipping* our ancestors.

まつろ【末路】the last days. ¶ 彼の～はあわれだった His *last days* were miserable. 彼の一家の～はあわれだった *The end* of his family was miserable. 英雄の～は時としてあわれだ Heroes sometimes have miserable *ends.* / Heroes sometimes *end* in misery.

まつわ·る【纏わる】¶ 子どもたちはその親切な人に～りついた The children *hung about* the kind man. ファンは女優に～りついて離れない The fans *are dangling about* the actress. この湖に～る伝説は多い There are a lot of legends *attending* this lake.

まで【迄】**1** 〘時〙 ¶ 日曜には10時～寝ることにしている I make it a rule to sleep *till* ten o'clock on Sundays. (make it a rule to はないほうが口語的).

彼ならさっき～ここにいた He was here *till* just a few minutes ago.

雨はあすの朝～降りつづくでしょう The rain will probably continue *until* tomorrow morning.

約束の3時～待ったが彼は来なかった Though I waited for him *until* three o'clock as we promised, he did not show up.

子どもが夜遅く～起きていてはいけません Children should not sit up [*till*] late at night. (till のないほうが口語的).

店は午前10時から午後6時～営業しています Our shop is open from 10 a.m. *to* 6 p.m. (米では to のかわりにしばしば through を用いる).

全員そろう～待とう Let's wait *until* all the members are here.

この映画は金曜日～上映している This film will be shown (⇆ showing) *till* Friday.

彼らは最後～あきらめずに戦った They fought *to* the last without giving up.

いま～のところまだ先方から返事がない *So far* I have received no answer from him.

会合～まだ1週間ある There is still a week *till* the meeting.

今ごろ～どこへ行っていたんですか Where have you been *all this while*?

今～のところ事故の原因はわかっていない The cause of the accident is *still* unknown.

先月～私は福岡に住んでいた I was living in Fukuoka *till* last month.

きょう～の努力が水のあわになってしまった I have done my best *till* today, but all in vain.

これ～彼があんなに怒ったのを見たことがない I have never seen him get so angry.

いつ～待っても彼はお金を返してくれない I *have waited and waited,* but he has not paid the money back yet.

あすは8時～に出勤しなさい Be at the office *by* eight o'clock tomorrow.

正午～に彼の家に行く約束だ I have an appointment to call on him *by* noon.

夕食～にはもどります I'll be back *before* supper.

月曜～にこの報告書を書き上げなければならない I must finish writing this report *by* Monday.

私が外遊から帰るころ～には，この家も完成しているだろう *By the time* I come home from abroad, this house will have been completed.

工事はいつ～かかりますか *How long* will it take to do the work?

2 〘場所〙 ¶ ちょっと駅前～行ってきます I'm just going *near* the station.

彼は商用で仙台～行った He went *to* Sendai on business.

暗いからお宅～お送りしましょう I'll take you home, because it is dark.

友人に駅～車で迎えにきてもらった I had my friend pick me up *at* the station.

急いで東京駅～やってくれ Take me *to* Tokyo Station quickly.

家から駅～約2キロある It is about two kilometers from my house *to* the station.

彼に私のところ～来るように伝えてください Will you please tell him to come and see me?

公園～散歩しましょうか Shall we take a walk *as far as* the park? (公園が目的地なら as far as のかわりに to を用いる).

あまり遠く～行ってはいけません Don't go too far.

3 〘範囲·程度〙 ¶ 彼の言うことはどこ～信用できるだろうか *How far* can we believe what he says?

そこ～は私にもわからない That's beyond my knowledge.

川の水は胸～あった The water of the river came up *to* my chest.

きょうはここ～にしておこう Let's call it a day. / (教室などで) So much for today.

ま

そこ〜言っては言いすぎだ You shouldn't be that blunt.
仕事は終わり〜きちんとしなさい Do your work carefully *to* the last.
最近はさっぱり運動をしなくなった. 好きなテニス〜やっていない I have lately taken no exercise, *including* my favorite tennis.
きみがそんなに〜彼に親切にするのは, かえって彼のためにならない If you show him *too much* kindness, it will be all the worse for him.
彼〜ぼくの言うことを信じてくれない *Even* he does not believe me.
そんなこと〜きみがしなくてもいいだろうに You will not have to do such a trifling thing.
言う〜もないが, 試合は正々堂々とやりなさい *Needless to say*, you must play fair.
彼の意見もある程度〜正しい His opinion is partially right.
念のためにご注意した〜です I am *only* giving you this piece of advice by way of precaution.
勉強がいやなら学校をやめる〜だ I'll advise you to give up school, if you dislike to study.

まてんろう【摩天楼】a skyscraper (skyscraper はふつうビジネス街にある高い建物をさす).

まと【的】**1**〚射撃の〛the target; the mark. ¶弾は〜に当たった The bullet hit *the mark*.
矢は〜をはずれた The arrow missed *the mark*.
彼は〜をねらった He aimed at *the mark*.
2〚対象〛¶彼は衆人の攻撃の〜となった He became *the target* of attack of the people.
私は衆人注視の〜となった I became *the cynosure of all eyes*.
彼の一家の生活は私たちの羨望(せんぼう)の〜だった The life of all his family was *the object* of our envy.
政治家はいつも批判の〜になっている A statesman is always *a target* of criticism.
—はずれ ¶きみの答えは〜はずれだ Your answer *is wide of the mark* (≒ *is beside the mark*).

まど【窓】a window (window は壁にあいている空間をさすこともあり, またその空間を閉じる戸をさすこともあり, 窓ガラス1枚をさすこともある).
¶〜を開ける open *a window*.
〜を閉める shut *a window*.
〜を上に(下に)開ける raise (lower) *a window*.
だれかが〜からのぞいている Somebody is peeping in at *the window*.
ぼんやりとバスの〜から外を見ていた I was looking out 〔of〕 *the window* of the bus absent-mindedly. (of を省くのは米語法).
〜から顔を出してはいけない You must not put your head out 〔of〕 *the window*.
〜を開けると広場だ *The window* gives on an open space.
〜に明かりのついた家が私たちの泊まる宿屋だ The house with lights in *the windows* is the inn we are going to stay at.
—敷居 a window sill. 二重**—** a double window.

まと・う【纏う】¶身にぼろを〜う *wear* rags.

まど・う【惑う】be puzzled. ¶四十にして〜わず (論語のことば) At the age of forty I *had no doubts*.

まどガラス【窓ガラス】a windowpane.

まどぐち【窓口】a window. ¶〜の係の人が親切にしてくれた The person at the *counter* (≒ *front desk*) was very kind to me.

まとまった【纏まった】¶〜金があればなあ If only I had *a round sum of* money. 今月は各方面から〜注文を受けた We got *large* orders from all directions this month. それについて私にはまだ〜考えはない I have no *definite* idea about it yet. あなたの論文を読みましたが, よく〜ものと思います I read your essay, and thought it *well-arranged*.

まとまり【纏まり】〔a〕 settlement. ¶その件についてはできるだけ早く〜をつけたい I want to *bring* the matter *to a settlement* (≒ *a conclusion*) as soon as possible. 彼の話は〜のないものだった His speech *was rambling*.

まとま・る【纏まる】**1**〚落ち着く〛¶紛争はようやく〜った The dispute *was settled* at last.
交渉はまだ〜らない The negotiation *has* not *been concluded* yet.
ふたりの話し合いは〜った The two *have come to an agreement*.
値段は〜らない The price *has not been agreed upon*.
先方と最終的に話が〜った We *reached* the final *agreement with* the other party.
おだやかに〜ればいいのだが I wish the matter would *be arranged* amicably. (希望があれば I *hope* the matter will.... とする).
交渉はどうしても〜らない The treaty *has fallen through* after all.
2〚集まる・統一される〛be collected. ¶彼の随筆はこのほど1巻に〜った His essays *have* recently *been collected together* in a volume.
3人ずつ〜って出かけなさい Go out *in a group of* three.
クラスが〜ってその案に賛成した The whole class *was united* for the proposal.
きみのこの作文はよく〜っている This composition of yours *is* systematically *constructed*.
この絵の構図はよく〜っている This picture *is* well *composed*.

まと・める【纏める】**1**〚落ち着ける〛¶私が紛争を〜めよう I will *settle* the dispute.
この問題は彼なら首尾よく〜められるだろう He will be able to *bring* this affair *to a* successful *conclusion*.
チームを〜めるのは彼をおいていない Only he can *get* the team *together*.
これは簡単には〜められない問題だ This is a matter that cannot *be settled* simply.
彼がこの縁談を〜めた He *arranged* the couple's marriage.
2〚集める〛collect. ¶彼は自分の短篇小説を〜めて本にした He *gathered* his short stories *together* into one volume.

ま

私がこの取り引きを～めよう I will *get* this deal *closed.*

ことしじゅうにこの研究を～めたい I am going to *complete* my study before the end of the year.

この辺で私たちの考えを～めておこう Let's *shape up* our ideas now.

3〘整頓する〙arrange. ¶ まず考えを～めてから話をしてください *Collect* your thoughts before you make a speech.

この書類を～めてください Please *arrange* these papers.

まとも【真面】1〘正面〙¶ 彼は～に私の顔を見た He looked me *full* (≒ *straight*) in the face. / He looked *straight* at me. / He faced me *full.*

風を～に受けながらも進んだ We went on *in the teeth of* the wind.

～にあごをやられた I was hit *directly* (≒ *square*) on the jaw.

2〘まじめ・まっとう〙¶ 最近彼は～に暮らしている He lives *straight* (≒ *honestly*) these days.

～な人間だったらそんなことをやるはずがない An *honest* man could not do such a thing.

彼女はそのことをあまり～に受けとらなかった She did not take the matter too *seriously.*

あんなことを言うなんて，彼は～じゃない Judging from what he said, he *is out of senses.*

マドモアゼル a *mademoiselle.* (複 *mesdemoiselles*) (フランス語．英語の Miss に当たる．略 Mlle., 複 Mlles.).

まどり【間取り】 the plan of a house. ¶ この家は～がいい This house *is* well *planned.*

マドロス a sailor ; a seaman (マドロスはオランダ語 *matroos* から).

―パイプ a〔tobacco〕pipe.

まどろ･む【微睡む】 doze〔off〕. ¶ あまりに天気がよかったので読書中つい～んでしまった It was such a nice day that I *fell into a doze* (≒ *dropped off to sleep*) while reading a book.

まどわく【窓枠】 a window frame (≒ sash).

まどわ･す【惑わす】 ⇒まよわす

マドンナ（聖母）the Madonna. ¶ ～の像（絵）a Madonna.

マナー manner〔s〕. ¶ 彼は～のよい（悪い）男だ He is a *well-mannered* (*ill-mannered*) man.

まないた【まな板・俎】 a chopping board. ¶ 彼は～の上のコイのようなものだ（一般的に）He *is entirely left to his fate.* /（われわれにとって）He *is at our mercy.*

まなざし【眼差し】 a look. ¶ 彼は私に鋭い～を向けた He gave me *a* sharp *look* (≒ *glance*).

まなつ【真夏】 midsummer. ¶ あそこは～でも涼しい It's very cool there even *at the height of summer.*

まなづる【真鶴】〘鳥類〙a white-naped crane.

まなでし【愛弟子】 *one's* favorite pupil.

まな･ぶ【学ぶ】 learn ; study (learn は「習う」「覚える」で努力が必ずしも伴わない．study は努力が必ず伴うので「学習・研究する」の意味になる).

¶ 私はあの人からフランス語を～んだ I *learned* French *from* him.

私は大学ではA教授のもとで哲学を～んだ I *studied* philosophy under Prof. A at college.

彼は若いころケンブリッジ大学で～んだ He *was educated* at Cambridge University when young.

彼には物理を～んだ I *was taught* physics by him.

大学ではなにを～びましたか What did you *major* (≒ *specialize*) *in* at college? (major in は米語法). / What subject did you *make a special study of* at the university?

５年間の海外生活で大いに～ぶところがあった I *have learned* a great deal through five years' experience of living abroad.

よく～びよく遊べ（諺）*All work and no play makes Jack a dull boy.*

まなむすめ【愛娘】 *one's* beloved daughter.

マニア a mania. ¶ 彼は切手～だ He is a *passionate* stamp collector.

まにあわせ【間に合わせ】 ¶ ～の応接間 a *makeshift* drawing room. ～にこれを使ってみてください Please use this *for a shift.* テーブルの～にその箱を使っていた We used the box as *a makeshift for* a table. それを一時の～にしておこうと思う I will *make it do* for the present. 一時の～に私が彼のかわりをする I will take his place *temporarily.*

マニキュア a manicure. ¶ 彼女の～をしたつめ her *manicured* nails. 私は～をしてもらった I had *a manicure.*

まにまに【随に】 ¶ 船が２隻波の～漂っているのが見えた Two ships were seen to drift about *at the mercy of* the waves.

マニラ Manil〔l〕a.

―麻(紙) Manila hemp (≒ paper).

まにんげん【真人間】 ¶ 彼は私に～になると誓った He promised me to *turn over a new leaf.*

まぬか･れる【免れる】 ¶ 彼は危険を～れた He *escaped* danger. 彼の家は類焼を～れた His house *escaped* the fire. かろうじて難を～れた I *had a narrow escape.* 別の列車に乗っていたので事故を～れた Since I was not in the train, I *escaped* the accident. 幸いにも彼の船は沈没を～れた Luckily his ship *was saved from* sinking.

まぬけ【間抜け】 stupidity. ¶ そんなことをするなんてなんて彼は～なんだろう What a *stupid* (≒ *silly ; foolish*) man he is to do such a thing! ふたりは～なことをした The two *have made fools of* themselves. ～なやつめ! What *a fool* (≒ *an ass*) you are!

まね【真似】 imitation. ¶ 人の～をする *imitate* another ; *follow* another's example. 彼は～がうまい He is a good *mimic.* 彼女は他人の声の～ができる She can *copy* people's voices. それは～のできない考えだ That's a *unique* idea. 私のような者には彼の～はできない I cannot *do just as* he does. 子どもたちは海賊の～をして遊んでいた The children were playing pirates. ばかな～はよしなさい Don't *act* (≒ *play*) *the fool*! / Don't *make a fool of yourself.*

マネージャー a manager.

まねき【招き】an invitation. ¶ ～に応じる(を断わる) accept (decline) *an invitation.* お～ありがとう I thank you (≒ Thank you; Many thanks) for your *invitation.*

マネキン a mannequin; a manikin; a dummy.

まね・く【招く】**1**〖招待する・呼び入れる〗¶ ふたりは私を結婚式に～いてくれた The couple *invited* (≒ *asked*) me *to* their wedding ceremony. 誕生日には友だちを数人～くつもりだ I will *have* some of my friends to dinner on my birthday.
彼は国務省から～かれて渡米した He visited America *at the invitation of* the State Department.
彼は私に中に入るようにと手で～いた He *beckoned* me to come in.
2〖原因となる〗¶ 不注意がその火事を～いた The cause of the fire was carelessness. / Carelessness *caused* (≒ *incurred*) the fire.
ばくちが彼の破滅を～いた Gambling *brought about* his ruin.
きみの最近の行動は誤解を～くおそれがある Your recent behavior is liable to *cause* misunderstanding.

ま・ねる【真似る】¶ 子どもは親を～ねる Children *imitate* their parents. 彼のよいところを～ねなさい You must *copy* his good points.

まのあたり【目の当たり】¶ こんな大きな交通事故を～にしたのはこれが初めてだ This is the first time that I *saw* such a big traffic accident as this *actually* (≒ *with my own eyes*). 彼の話は真にせまっていたので, その場面を～に見る心地がした His talk made me feel as if I were on the scene.

まのび【間延び】¶ 彼は～のした顔つきをしている He has a *stupid-looking* (≒ an *expressionless*; an *impassive*; a *stolid*) face.

まばたき【瞬き】a wink. ¶ ～でわかったと合図してよこした He *winked* knowingly at me. / He gave me *a* knowing *wink.* ～もせずに私を見詰めた He looked *steadily* (≒ *unblinkingly*) at me.

まばた・く【瞬く】blink; wink.

まばゆ・い【目映い・眩い】¶ ～いばかりの白色 *dazzling* whiteness. 日の光が～いばかりにふりそそいだ The sun *glared* down on us.

まばら【疎ら】¶ 人影～な通りを歩いた We walked along the *deserted* street. その村は人口も～だった The village was *thinly* peopled. / The village was *thinly* populated. 講演会は聴衆も～だった It was a *thin* lecture meeting. / The lecture meeting was *poorly* attended. / The attendance at the lecture meeting *was thin.*

まひ【麻痺】paralysis. ¶ 彼は両脚が～している He *is paralyzed* in both legs. 私の指は寒さで～している My fingers *are numb* (≒ *are numbed; are benumbed*) with cold. 国鉄のストで東京の交通機関は～状態になった The National Railways strike *paralyzed* Tokyo traffic facilities. 彼の良心は～している His conscience *never troubles* him. / He has *unfeeling* conscience.
心臓── heart failure. ¶ 彼は心臓～で急死した He suddenly died of *heart failure.*

まびき【間引き】thinning out. ¶ 組合は5パーセントの～運転を実施した The union carried out a five-percent *slowdown in train runs.*

まび・く【間引く】¶ ダイコンを～く *thin out* radishes.

まひる【真昼】noon; midday; highnoon.
¶ その建物の中は～でも暗い It's dark inside the building even *in broad daylight.*

まぶか【目深】¶ 彼は帽子を～にかぶっていた He was wearing a hat *low* (≒ *pulled down*) *over his eyes.*

まぶし・い【眩しい】dazzling; blinding. ¶ 真夏の太陽が～かった The midsummer sun *was very dazzling.* 明かりが～くて, 一瞬目が見えなくなった The light *blinded my eyes* (≒ *dazzled me*) for a moment. ～いばかりのフットライトを浴びて, 彼は舞台に登場した He appeared on the stage *in the glare of* the footlights.

まぶ・す【塗す】¶ それはメリケン粉に～された It *was dusted* (≒ *was sprinkled*) *with* flour. / It *was floured.*

まぶた【目蓋・瞼】an eyelid. ¶ ～の母 the mother who lives in the memory of *one's* childhood; the mother kept in memory; the old mom (最後は口語的. もっともふつうな言い方). ときどき故郷のことが～に浮かぶ Sometimes my home town comes *in my memory.*
一重(二重)── a single (double)-edged eyelid. 上(下)── an upper (a lower) eyelid.

まふゆ【真冬】midwinter. ¶ ～に in *the depth of* (≒ *dead*) *winter.*

マフラー a muffler. ¶ ～を巻く(とる) wind (unwind) *a muffler.*

まほう【魔法】magic; black art; witchcraft.
¶ まるで～でもかけられたかのように私は動けなかった I stood unable to move as if *spellbound.*
──使い a magician; (男の) a wizard; a sorcerer; (女の) a witch; a sorceress. ──びん a vacuum bottle; a thermos.

マホガニー (色・材) mahogany. ¶ ～材の食卓 a *mahogany* dining-table. ～色の *mahogany*-colored.

マホメットきょう【マホメット教】Mohammedanism; Islamism; Islam; Moslem religion.
¶ ～の寺院 a mosque.
──徒 a Mohammedan; a Moslem.

まぼろし【幻】a vision. ¶ ～の女 a *phantom* lady. ～にでさえ彼の顔が見られたらいいのに How I wish I could see his face even *in a vision*! ～の大選手 an *ideal* great champion.

まま【儘】**1**〖その状態のまま〗¶ 部屋はその～にしておいてください Please *leave* the room *as it is.* 彼は机の上をその～にして出ていった He went out of the room, *leaving* the things on the desk *as they were.*
くつをはいた～家の中へ入ってはいけない Don't

enter the house *with* your shoes *on*. (欧米の習慣との違いに注意しないとわかりにくい内容になる).
帽子はかぶった～でよい You may *keep* your hat *on*.
東京から京都までずっと立った～だった I *was kept standing* all the way from Tokyo to Kyoto. (これを I stood とすると自発的に立っていたことにもなる).
2〖…のとおり〗¶思う～にやっていい You may do *as you like*.
彼にやりたい～やらせていい It's all right to *let* him *have his way*.
私のいう～にやってほしい I want you to do *as* I tell you.

ママ (小児語) mam〔m〕a ; mummy ; 米 mom ; 英 mum.

ままこ【継子】a stepchild ; (男の) a stepson ; (女の) a stepdaughter. ¶彼は両親から～扱いされた He was treated like *a stepchild* by his parents. / His parents left him out in the cold.

ままごと【飯事】¶子どもたちは～をして遊んでいた The children *were playing house*. まるで～のような生活だった Our life was like *playing at housekeeping*.

ままならぬ【儘ならぬ】¶～のは人の世の定め (諺) *If wishes were horses, beggars might ride*.

ままはは【継母】a stepmother.

まみ·える【見える】¶貞婦は二夫に～えず A faithful wife would not marry again. ついに決勝戦で両雄相～えた At last the two great men *met* in the finals.

まみず【真水】fresh water.

-まみれ【-塗れ】¶レスラーは血～になった The wrestler *got covered with* blood. 子どもたちは泥～だった The children *were muddy all over*.

まみ·れる【塗れる】¶新調したばかりのくつが泥に～れてしまった My newly-made shoes *became muddy all over*. 残念ながら, われわれはその戦いで一敗地に～れた To our great regret, we *suffered a complete defeat* (≒ *were defeated completely*) in the battle.

まむかい【真向かい】just in front of. ¶彼は私の～に座った He sat down *just in front of* me. 彼の家はうちの～にある His house is *right opposite* us.

まむし【蝮】a viper ; an adder. ¶あの男は～のような人間だ He is *a viper* (≒ *a malignant person*).

まめ【豆】〖植物〗a bean ; (エンドウ) a pea. ¶～科の植物 a leguminous plant ; a legume.
—類 pulse. インゲン**—** a string (≒ French) bean. ソラ**—** a kidney (≒ broad) bean.

まめ【肉刺】a blister. ¶手のひらに～ができた I got *a blister* on my palm. ～がつぶれてひりひりする The *blister* has broken and hurts. 足に底～ができた I got *a corn* on my foot.

まめ【忠実】¶両親は～で暮らしています (元気だ) My parents *are healthy* (≒ *are quite well*). お宅のご主人はなんて～な人なのでしょう (まめまめしい) How *diligent* (≒ *industrious* ; *hardworking*) your husband *is*!

まめ-【豆-】**—**自動車 a baby car ; a mini-car. **—**電球 a midget lamp. **—**本 a very small book.

まめがら【豆幹】a beanstalk.

まめつ【摩滅】wear. ¶あなたの印鑑は文字が～している The inscription on your seal impression *has been worn out*.

まめつぶ【豆粒】¶～ほどの時計 a small watch like *a fingertip*.

まめでっぽう【豆鉄砲】a popgun. ¶彼はハトが～を食ったような顔をしていた He stood *amazed with a stupid* (≒ *puzzled*) *look*.

まもなく【間も無く】before long ; soon ; presently. ¶～彼はもどってきた He *soon* (≒ *before long*) returned home. 彼女は～現われます She will appear *presently* (≒ *before long* ; *in no time*). ～彼は帰国するでしょう He will be back〔from abroad〕*very soon*. 彼は～渡米の予定です He is *shortly* to leave for America. ～おじゃまします I will call on you *in a short time* (≒ *in a little while*). (「近日中に」の意味なら one of these days と言う). 彼女は去年高校を卒業したが, その後～結婚した She graduated from a high school last year, and *soon* (≒ *shortly*) *after* she got married.

まもの【魔物】¶女は～だ, 気をつけろ You must keep yourself from women, *bewitching* as they are.

まもり【守り】defense ; 英 defence ; (お守り) a charm ; a talisman (charm は幸運を呼ぶため, または災難よけのため時計の鎖や腕輪などにつける小さい飾り. talisman は指輪や石に文字や像をきざんだもの).
¶～を固めねばならぬ We must strengthen our *defenses*. 味方が～についた (野球などで) Our team *took the field*.

まもりがみ【守り神】a guardian deity (≒ god).

まも·る【守る】**1**〖防ぐ〗defend. ¶彼は祖国を敵の侵略から～った He *defended* (≒ *protected*) his own country *against* the enemy's invasion.
彼は勇敢に私を危険から～ってくれた He *defended* (≒ *guarded*) me *from* danger bravely.
毛布が寒さから～ってくれた The blanket *kept* (≒ *protected*) me *from* the cold.
このコートでは寒さから身を～れない This coat does not *keep* the cold *out*.
2〖結束·平和·規則などを〗. ¶平和を～ることがわれわれの第一のつとめだ It is our first duty to *keep* (≒ *maintain*) peace.
諸君は学校の規則を～らねばならない You must *keep* (≒ *follow*) the rules of your school.
交通法規はしっかり～るべきだ You should *observe* traffic regulations strictly.
彼は約束は～る He always *keeps* his word. /

He *never breaks* his promise. / He is a man of his word.
彼は相変わらず中立を〜っている He *is* still *on neutral ground.* / He still *stands* neutral.
彼ひとりが沈黙を〜った He alone *kept* (≒ *observed*) silence.

まやかし deception. ¶ その指輪は〜物だ The ring is *a fake* (≒ (米俗語) *a phon[e]y*). あの男の言うことは〜だ His words *are deceptive.*

まやく【麻薬】 a narcotic; a drug. ¶ 〜常用者 a confirmed *drug*-taker; a *drug* addict; a *dope* fiend.

まゆ【繭】 a cocoon. ¶ 蚕が〜をつくる The silkworm spins *a cocoon.*

まゆ【眉】 an eyebrow. ¶ 私の話を聞きながら彼は〜をひそめた Hearing my story, he *frowned* (≒ *knitted his brows; drew his brows together*).

まゆげ【眉毛】 an eyebrow.

まゆずみ【眉墨・黛】 an eyebrow pencil.

まゆつばもの【眉唾物】 ¶ その話は〜だ The story *must have been faked up.* / It must be *a faked story.* 彼の言うことは〜だ His story *is quite unbelievable.* / We must *take* his story *with a grain of salt.*

まよい【迷い】 delusion. ¶ それはすべて心の〜だった That was all *a delusion* (≒ *an illusion*). それは気の〜だ That's a *mere fancy.* 彼の〜をさましてやろう I'll *disillusion* him./ I'll *bring* him *to his senses.*

まよ・う【迷う】 **1**〖道に〗 lose *one's* way. ¶ 道に〜わないようにしなさい Be careful not to *lose your way.*
彼がいなかったら道に〜ったろう Without him, I would *have gotten* (≒ 英 *have got*) *lost.*
2〖当惑する〗 be perplexed. ¶ どうしたらいいか〜った I *was at a loss* what to do.
私はどれを選ぶべきか選択に〜っている I *am perplexed* as to which to choose.
彼は彼女を叱るべきかどうか〜っている He *is in two minds* whether he should punish her or not.
3〖邪道にそれる〗 ¶ 彼らは悪の道に〜い込んだ They *were led into* error.
4〖ためらう〗 hesitate. ¶ 彼は絶えず〜っている He *is* always *wavering in his mind.* 「so.
そうするのに〜うことはない Never *hesitate* to do
行くべきかとどまるべきか〜った We *hesitated* between going or (≒ and) staying.
私は会うべきか否か〜った I *was undecided* whether to meet him or not.

まよけ【魔除け】 an amulet; a charm against evil. ¶ これは〜になる This will protect you from evil. / This is *a charm against bad luck.* ⇒まもり(守り)

まよなか【真夜中】 midnight. ¶ 〜の出来事だった It happened *at midnight* (≒ *in the middle of the night*). 〜になろうとしている It's getting on for *midnight.* きのうは〜まで勉強した Yesterday I worked *far into the night.*

マヨネーズ mayonnaise. ¶ サラダに〜をかける dress salad with *mayonnaise.*

まよわ・す【迷わす】 **1**〖当惑させる〗 ¶ その事件は彼を〜せた The event *bewildered* (≒ *confused; puzzled*) him.
彼の話は子どもたちを〜すだけだ What he says only serves to *perplex* children.
彼らはその考え方に〜された They *were led astray* by that way of thinking.
彼の話に〜されないように Be careful not to *be misled by* his words.
2〖誘惑する〗 tempt. ¶ 彼女の魅力は皆の心を〜せた Her charm fascinated everyone.

マラソン〘競技〙 a marathon [race]. ¶ 〜をやる run *a marathon race.*
—選手 a marathon runner.

マラヤ Malay.
—語 Malay[an]. **—人** a Malay[an]. **—半島** the Malay Peninsula.

マラリア〘医学〙 malaria. ¶ 彼は〜にかかった He was ill with *malaria.*

まり【毬・鞠】 a ball. ¶ 〜つきをする *play* [*at*] *hand-ball.* あの子は〜投げをするのが好きだ The child likes to *play ball* (≒ *play catch*).

マリア ¶ 聖母〜 the Blessed Virgin [Mary]; Saint Mary.

マリオネット a marionette. ¶ 〜を操る work *a marionette.*

まりも【毬藻】 an aegagropila.

まりょく【魔力】 charm. ¶ それは数字の〜だ It is the *magic* of numbers.

マリンバ〘音楽〙 a marimba.

まる【丸・円】 a circle. ¶ 鉛筆で〜をかく draw *a circle* with a pencil. 正しいと思う語の番号を〜で囲め Enclose with *a circle* (≒ Put *a circle* around) the number of the word you think right.

まる-【丸-】 ¶ それを仕上げるのに〜1時間かかった It took *a whole* (≒ *one full*) hour to finish it. 〜5分とたたないうちに彼が現われた I had not waited for *full* five minutes before he appeared.

まるあんき【丸暗記】 ¶ その長い詩を〜した I *learned* the long poem *by heart* (≒ *by rote*).

まる・い【丸い・円い】 round; circular. ¶ 〜いテーブル a *round* table. 〜い顔 a *round* face. 〜い(球状の)種子 a *spherical* seed. 〜い屋根 a dome.

まるおび【丸帯】 a one-piece sash.

まるがお【丸顔】 a round face. ¶ 〜の少女 a *round-faced* girl.

まるがり【丸刈り】 close clipping. ¶ 〜の少年 a boy with *close-cropped* hair. 頭を〜にした I *had my hair cut close.*

まるき【丸木】 a log.
—橋 a log bridge. **—舟** a canoe.

まるく【丸く・円く】 **1**〖円形に〗 ¶ 紙を〜切る cut a sheet of paper *round.*
彼らは〜なって座った They sat *in a circle.*
彼は毛布にくるまって体を〜して寝た He *curled himself up* in a blanket.
口をもっと〜しなさい *Round* your lips more closely.

彼女はその知らせを聞いて目を～した She *rounded* her eyes on hearing the news. / She heard the news *with her eyes wide open.*

ネコは犬を見て背を～した The cat *humped* (≒ *hunched*) its back when it saw a dog.

角を削って～した I *planed off* the corners.

2 〖おだやかに〗 ¶ 彼は人間が～なった The rough edges of his character *have been rounded off.*

紛争を～おさめた I *made up* (≒ *smoothed over*) the dispute.

事件は～おさまった The trouble *came to an amicable conclusion.* / The trouble *was peacefully settled.*

マルク a mark (ドイツの貨幣).

マルクス Karl Marx.

—主義 Marxism. **—**主義者 a Marxist. **—**・レーニン主義 Marxism-Leninism.

まるくびシャツ【丸首シャツ】a T-shirt; a tee-shirt.

まるごし【丸腰】¶ ロンドンの警官は～だ Policemen in London *go unarmed.*

まるごと【丸ごと】entirely; wholly. ¶ リンゴを～かじる eat an apple *rind and all.* その一節を～暗記した I learned the *whole* passage by heart.

マルサス Malthus.

—主義 Malthusianism.

まるぞん【丸損】a total loss. ¶ 彼の事業は～になった His business turned out [to be] *a dead loss.*

まるた【丸太】a log.

—小屋 a log cabin.

まるだし【丸出し】¶ 彼女は肩を～にして歩いていた She was walking with her shoulders *exposed* (≒ *bare*). 彼は田舎ことば～で話す He speaks with a *broad* provincial accent.

まるつぶれ【丸潰れ】¶ 私の面目は～だ My face *is utterly lost.* 会議で半日～だった The conference *took up* a half day.

まるで【丸で】**1** 〖あたかも〗 as if; just like. ¶ 彼は～子どものようなことをする He acts *like* (≒ *as if he were*) a child.

彼女は～幽霊のようだ She looks *as if* (≒ *as though*) she were a ghost.

～未知の国にでもいるような気がした I felt *as if* I were in a strange land.

～私が悪いことをしたみたいだ It seems *as if* I had done wrong.

彼は～ぼくをなぐろうとするかのように立ち上がった He stood up *as if* to strike me.

彼は～生き字引だ He is, *as it were* (≒ *so to speak*), a walking dictionary.

2 〖全然〗 ¶ ～それを覚えていない I don't remember it *at all.*

彼の意見は～ばかげている His opinion is *perfectly* absurd.

私はこの土地は～不案内だ I am *quite* a stranger here.

まるてんじょう【丸天井】a dome.

まるのみ【丸呑み】¶ 彼はその話を～した He *swallowed* the story.

まるはだか【丸裸】¶ 彼は～になった He *stripped himself bare.* 彼は火事で～になった He *got penniless* because of the fire. / He *had all his property burnt up* in the fire. あの山は～だ The hill *is bare of trees.*

まるばつしき【丸ばつ式】**—**テスト a multiple choice test. **—**問題 a multiple choice question.

まるぼうず【丸坊主】¶ 彼は～だ He has *a close-cropped head.* / He is a man with *a close-cut hair.*

まるぼし【丸干し】¶ ダイコンの～ a radish *dried whole.* イワシの～ a *dried* sardine.

まるぽちゃ【丸ぽちゃ】¶ ～の顔 a *plump* (≒ *chubby*) face. ～のほおをした赤ちゃん a baby with *plump* cheeks. ～の女 a *plump* woman.

まるまど【丸窓・円窓】a round window.

まるまる【丸丸】¶ ～と太った顔 a *full, round* face. ～1か月 a *whole* month. 私は1万円～もうけた I *got a clear profit of* ten thousand yen. / I *cleaned up* ten thousand yen. (くだけた言い方). それは～損にはならない That won't prove a *dead* loss.

まるまる【○○】¶ ～事件 a *certain* affair. 6時～分の列車 the six *something* train. 19～年 nineteen hundred *something.*

まるみ【丸み】roundness. ¶ それは～がある It *is roundish.* それに少し～をつけた I made it a little *round.*

まるみえ【丸見え】¶ この室は外から～だ The interior of this room *is fully exposed to view* from the outside.

まるめこ・む【丸め込む】¶ 彼は彼女を～んで1万円巻き上げた He *wheedled* (≒ *cajoled*) her *out of* ten thousand yen. / He *wheedled* (≒ *coaxed*) ten thousand yen *out of* her.

彼女は彼をすっかり～んだ She *had* (≒ *carried*) him *in her pocket.*

まる・める【丸める】¶ 角を削って～めた I *rounded off* the edges. 手紙を～めて捨てた I *crumpled* the letter *into a ball* and threw it away. 体を～めて寝た I *curled myself up* in bed. 彼は頭を～めて僧になった He *shaved his head* and became a Buddhist monk.

まるもうけ【丸儲け】¶ 1万円～した I *got a clear gain of* ten thousand yen. / I *made* ten thousand yen *clear profit.*

まるやき【丸焼き】a barbecue. ¶ ～の豚 a *roast* (≒ *roasted*) pig. 豚を～にする *roast* (≒ *barbecue*) a hog *whole over* on open fire.

まるやけ【丸焼け】¶ 彼の家は～になった His house *was totally destroyed by fire.* / His house *was completely burnt* [*down*]. / His house *was completely reduced to ashes.*

まれ【希・稀】¶ 彼が約束の時間に遅れるのは～だ He is *seldom* (≒ *rarely*) late for the appointed time. こんなにうまくいくことは～だ Such a success is *a rarity.* 彼は上京することがあっても～だ He *seldom,* if ever, comes up to Tokyo. 読む価値のある本はあるにしても～である

Few books, if any, are worth reading. 彼は～にみる手腕家だ He is a man of *rare* (≒ *exceptional*) ability. これは～にみる例だ This is a *rare* instance.

マロニエ 〘植物〙 a horse chestnut tree (フランス語で *marronnier*). ¶ ～の並木道 a street lined with *horse chestnut trees* on both sides.

まわしもの 【回し者】 a spy ; a secret agent.

まわ·す 【回す】 **1** 〘回転さす〙 ¶ 車のハンドルを～した I *turned* the steering wheel.

ノックの音に彼女は頭を～した She *turned* her head at the knock.

ねじを～す *drive* a screw.

自動車を玄関へ～してください Please *send* the car *round* to the door.

2 〘回付する〙 ¶ (食卓で) 私に塩を～してください *Pass* me the salt, please.

彼はその本を友だちに～してやった He *handed on* (≒ *passed on*) the book to his friends.

この手紙を彼の新住所に～してください Please *forward* this letter *to* his new address.

書類を係へ～した I *sent round* the papers *to* the man in charge.

彼は会計課に～された He *was transferred to* the account section.

まわた 【真綿】 floss-silk ; silk-wadding. ¶ ～で首を締めるようなものだ It seems that you give a gentle reproof. / Soft words are hard arguments.

まわり 【回り·周り】 **1** 〘周囲〙 circumference. ¶ たき火の～に座る sit *around* a fire.

月は地球の～を回る The moon turns *around* the earth.

その木の幹の～は5メートルあった The trunk was five meters *in circumference*.

地球はひと～約25,000マイルある The *circumference* of the earth is about twenty-five thousand miles.

2 〘付近〙 neighborhood. ¶ ～にはだれもいなかった No one was *around*.

～には物音一つ聞こえなかった Not a sound was heard *in the neighborhood*.

3 〘経由〙 ¶ 新宿～で渋谷に出た I went to Shibuya *by way of* Shinjuku.

北極～で飛ぶ fly 〔by〕 the North Pole *route* ; fly by the *route* across the 〔North〕 Pole.

どちら～で行ったらいいですか *Which way* am I to go?

4 〘巡回〙 ¶ 彼はヨーロッパをひと～した He *made an extended tour around* Europe.

彼は得意先～をしているところだ He *is making the rounds of* his customers.

まわりあわせ 【回り合わせ】 fate ; fortune ; luck. ¶ こんなに～が悪いことは今までになかった Never have I had such bad *luck*. 不思議な～で彼と友だちになった I made friends with him *by a strange coincidence*. ～だとあきらめた I resigned myself to my *fate*. 運命の～で九死に一生を得た *As luck would have it*, I had a narrow escape.

まわりくど·い 【回りくどい】 ¶ 彼の話は～い He talks in a *round-about* way. ～ことを言うな Don't *beat about* (≒ 米 *beat around*) *the bush*. ～い議論はきらいだ I don't like a *circuitous* argument.

まわりぶたい 【回り舞台】 a revolving stage.

まわりみち 【回り道】 a detour. ¶ ～をした I took *a circuitous route*. / I came by *a roundabout route*. 5マイル～した I made *a detour* of five miles. / I went five miles *out of my way*.

まわりもち 【回り持ち】 ¶ 当番は～にしよう Let's be on duty *by turns*. 金は天下の～ (諺) Money *changes hands*.

まわ·る 【回る】 **1** 〘回転する〙 ¶ 地球はみずから～りながら太陽のまわりを～る The earth, *rotating* on its own axis, *goes* 〔a〕*round* the sun.

こまが静かに～っている The top *is spinning* silently.

飛行機は空港の上空を3回～った The airplane *circled* above the airport three times.

モーターがものすごい勢いで～っている The engine *is rotating* (≒ *is turning*) at full speed.

バレリーナがスカートを翻して美しく～った The ballerina *turned round* beautifully with her skirt waving about her.

世界が自分を中心に～ると考えてはいけない You should not think that the world *goes round* you alone.

ぼくは最近目が～るほど忙しい I have been *as busy as a bee*.

2 〘巡回する〙 ¶ このホテルではガードマンが絶えず構内を～っている Security guards constantly *patrol* this hotel.

私は毎日農場を見て～る Every day I *make a round of* the farm.

彼はセールスに東北地方を～っている He *is on a* sales *trip* in the Northeast area of Japan.

巡査が毎日1度は～ってくる The policeman *comes round* here once a day.

この秋は一月ほどヨーロッパを～ってくる予定だ This autumn I am going to *tour* Europe for a month or so.

近所をあいさつに～った I *paid a courtesy visit* in the neighborhood.

ついに私があいさつする番が～ってきた Finally, my turn to greet *came*.

3 〘循環する〙 ¶ (野球で) 打順が1番まで～れば1点が取れる If the batting order *comes round* to the first, we can perhaps score a run.

酒が～っていい気持ちになった I felt good as the wine *took hold*.

ヘビの毒が彼の体に～った The snake's poison *passed into* his system.

4 〘曲がる〙 ¶ たばこ屋について左に～るとその病院がある *Turn* to the left along the cigar store, and you will find the hospital.

こっちへ来るのかと思ったら, 彼は四つ角を右に～ってしまった I thought he would come this way, but he *turned* right at the corner.

5 〘回り道する·経由する〙 ¶ 会社の帰りに歯医者へ～る I'll *drop in at* the dentist's on my way home from the office.

急がば～れ (諺) *The more haste, the less speed.*

電車の事故で, 新宿を～って家に帰った Owing to the railroad accident, I went home *by way of* Shinjuku.

モスクワを～ってロンドンへ行く予定だ I intend to go to London *via* (≒ *by way of*) Moscow.

勝手口へ～ってください *Come round* to the kitchen.

船はみさきを～って沖に出た The ship *went round* the cape and headed toward the open sea.

6 〖及ぶ〗 ¶ そこまでは手が～らない I am unable to *get around to* it.

忙しくて掃除までは手が～らない I am *too* busy *to* sweep the room.

子どものことだから, そこまで知恵が～らなかったのだろう As he is only a child, I think he was incapable of realizing it.

7 〖過ぎる〗 ¶ 12時をちょっと～ったところだ It *is* a little *after* twelve now.

まわれみぎ 【回れ右】 ¶ (号令) ～! Right about turn! ～をする *turn completely around.*

まん 【万】 ten thousand. ¶ 幾～の人々 *tens of thousands* of people. 幾十～の人々 *hundreds of thousands* of people. そんなことは～に一つも起こるまい It is one in *ten thousand* that such a thing will happen. ～が一列車に乗り遅れたらどうしよう If I *should* miss the train 〔*by any chance*〕, what should I do? 5～分の1の地図 a map on the scale of one-*fifty-thousandth.*

まん 【満】 ¶ 彼は～20歳だ He's *full* twenty years old. 私たちが当地に来てから～3年になる It is *full* three years since we came to live here. 私は～を持していた I *watched* (≒ *was in full readiness*) *for* an opportunity.

まんいち 【万一】 ¶ ～の場合に備えておくべきだ We should be prepared *for the worst.* ～の場合の行動の仕方を教えてください Tell me how to act *in case of emergency* (≒ *in an emergency*). ～だれか訪ねてきたら, 不在だと言ってください If anyone *should* call on me, tell him I am out. ～の用意に金をとっておくべきだ We should reserve money *against a rainy day* (≒ *for an emergency*).

まんいん 【満員】 ¶ (掲示) ～ House Full. / Sold Out. 劇場は大入り～だ The theater *is filled to capacity.* 興行のたびに～だった They had *a crowded house* (≒ *a full house*) at every performance. ～札止めだった They put up a *soldout* notice. 列車は～だった The train *was full* (≒ *was jammed full*).

まんえつ 【満悦】 ¶ 彼は至極ご～のていだった He *looked* very much *delighted* (≒ *pleased*).

まんえん 【蔓延】 ¶ インフルエンザが日本に～している The flu *is about* (≒ *is prevalent*) in Japan. / The flu *is sweeping* 〔*over*〕 Japan. その港町にはコレラ～の兆がある There are signs of cholera *spreading* in the port town.

まんが 【漫画】 a caricature; a comic. ¶ それは～になる It *is caricaturable.* / We can make *a caricature* of it.

—映画 a movie cartoon; a cartoon film. **—**家 a cartoonist. **—**雑誌 a comic magazine.

まんかい 【満開】 ¶ 桜が～だ The cherry trees *are in full bloom.* / The cherry blossoms *are at their best.*

マンガン 〖化学〗 manganese.

まんかんしょく 【満艦飾】 ¶ あの船は～だ The ship *is fully dressed.* 彼女は～だ (気飾っている) She *is dressed up.*

まんき 【満期】 expiration. ¶ 契約があと1か月で～になる The contract *expires* in a month. この手形は2か月で～だ This bill *is due* (≒ *falls due*) in two months. この家屋の保険は～になった The insurance on this house *has run out.* この債券は10年～だ This bond *matures* in ten years.

まんきつ 【満喫】 ¶ その美しい景色を～した We *enjoyed* the beautiful sight *to the full.*

まんげきょう 【万華鏡】 a kaleidoscope.

まんげつ 【満月】 a full moon. ¶ 今夜は～だ *The moon is* 〔*at its*〕 *full* tonight.

まんこう 【満腔】 ¶ ～の謝意を表します I tender my *full gratitude.*

マンゴー 〖植物〗 a mango.

まんざ 【満座】 ¶ ～の中で恥をかかされた I was put to shame *before the whole company* (≒ *in public*).

まんさい 【満載】 ¶ トラックが家具を～していた The truck *was loaded to capacity* (≒ *was fully loaded*) with furniture. 船は貨物を～していた The ship *was carrying a full cargo.* この雑誌はその事件の記事を～している This magazine *is full of* the news of the affair.

まんざい 【漫才】 a cross-talk comedy.

—師 a cross-talk comedian.

まんざら 【満更】 ¶ ～悪くもない It is *not altogether* 〔*too*〕 bad. ～不満でもないらしい He does *not* seem to be *wholly* dissatisfied with it. 彼とは～知らない仲ではない He is *not* an *entire* stranger to me.

まんじ 【卍】 a fylfot; a swastika. ¶ ～の模様 a *fylfot* pattern.

—どもえ ¶ 雪は～どもえと降った Snow fell *in whirls.*

まんしゅう 【満州】 Manchuria.

—人 a Manchurian. **—**族 the Manchus. **—**文字 Manchu.

まんじゅう 【饅頭】 a bun.

—がさ a round wicker hat. **—**屋 a bun store.

まんじょう 【満場】 the whole audience. ¶ そのすばらしい音楽に～うっとりと聞き入っていた *The entire audience* was fascinated by the wonderful music. ～黙して語る者はなかった A dead silence fell over *the whole assembly.* ～騒然たるものがあった *The whole house* was thrown into an uproar. ～一致でその議案は可決された The bill was passed *unanimously*

(≒ *by common consent*).

マンション a condominium.

まんじり ¶ 昨夜は～ともしなかった I could *not sleep a wink* last night.

まんしん【満身】 ¶ ～の力をこめて綱を引っ張った I pulled at the rope *with all my strength.* 彼は～創痍(そうい)だった He was covered *all over* with wounds.

まんしん【慢心】 pride ; self-conceit. ¶ 彼は～している He *is self-conceited.* / He *is inflated with conceit* (≒ *pride*). 彼は成功して～している He *is puffed up with* (≒ *is too proud of ; is swollen with*) his success. 彼の～ぶりは目に余る His *conceit* is intolerable.

まんせい【慢性】 ¶ あの人は～の病人だ He is a *chronic* invalid. / He is suffering from a *chronic* disease. 彼は～盲腸炎で悩んでいる He is suffering from *chronic* appendicitis. ～インフレは今日世界共通の問題だ The *creeping* (≒ *lingering*) inflation is the common problem of the world today.

まんぜん【漫然】 ¶ 本を～と読む read books *at random.*

まんぞく【満足】 **1** contentment. ¶ ～は富にまさる *Contentment* is better than riches.

あなたは今の生活に～していますか *Are* you *contented with* your present life?

われわれは今持っているもので～している We *content ourselves with* what we have.

彼はどんなに努力しても成績表で母を～させることができなかった He could not *satisfy* (≒ *please*) his mother with his report card, no matter how hard he tried.

科学者たちはその実験の結果に～した The scientists *were gratified* (≒ *were satisfied ; were pleased*) *with* the result of the experiment.

大統領は宇宙飛行士たちの成功に～の意を表明した The President expressed his *gratification with* the success of the astronauts.

このｘの値はその方程式を～する This value of x *satisfies* the requirements of the formula.

2 〚まともな〛 ¶ 組合はまだ～な回答を受け取っていない The unionists have not received a *satisfactory* answer yet.

日本の工場のほとんどは公害防止のための～な設備を持っていない Most factories in Japan have only *insufficient* (≒ *imperfect*) equipment to prevent industrial pollution.

彼は子どものころ～な教育を受けられなかった He could not receive *much* (≒ *regular ; satisfactory*) education in his childhood.

きのうから～に食事をしていない I haven't eaten *enough* since yesterday.

まんだん【漫談】 a gossip ; (寄席の) a comic chat. ¶ 彼は授業中にときどき～をやる He sometimes *goes into a friendly chat* (≒ *makes a digression*) during the lesson.

まんちょう【満潮】 the high (≒ full) tide ; the high water. ¶ 4時に～になる The tide *rises* at four. 今～だ The tide *is at the full.* ～時に at *full* (≒ *high*) *tide.*

まんてん【満点】 **1** 〚得点〛 full marks. ¶ 英語〔の試験〕で～の成績をとった I won *full marks* for English.

2 〚申し分ないこと〛 ¶ 卵は栄養～の食品だ Eggs are an *ideal* article of food.

彼女の演奏は～の出来ばえだった Her performance *was flawless* (≒ *was perpect*). / Her performance *left nothing to be desired.*

照明効果は～だった The lighting *proved completely effective.* / The lighting brought about a *quite satisfactory* effect.

まんてんか【満天下】 ¶ こうしてスキャンダルは～の人々に知れ渡った Thus the scandal was known to *the whole world.* その運動は～の同情を得た The movement won the sympathy of *the world* (≒ *the public in general*).

マント a mantle ; a cloak.

—ヒヒ〘動物〙a sacred baboon.

まんどう【満堂】 the entire hall ; (聴衆) the whole audience. ¶ ～立錐(りっすい)の余地なし *The whole house* is packed to suffocation (≒ capacity).

マンドリン a mandolin〔e〕.

—奏者 a mandolinist.

マントルピース a mantel ; a mantelpiece.

まんなか【真ん中】 the center. ¶ 町の～に高い塔が建っている There is a tall tower *in the center of* the city. 彼女はお菓子を～から分けた She divided the piece of cake right *in the middle.* 私はみんなの～に座った I sat *in the midst of* the group. 彼は町の～に住んでいて歩いて通勤する He lives *in the heart of* the city and walks to work. 仙台は東京と青森の～にある Sendai lies *halfway between* Tokyo and Aomori. 水曜日は週の～だ Wednesday is *the middle* of the week.

マンネリ〔ズム〕 a mannerism. ¶ その雑誌は当初の精神を失って～に陥った The magazine has lost its original spirit and *has become a mere form.*

まんねん【万年】 an eternity. ¶ つるは千年，かめは～ A crane lives a thousand years, and a tortoise〔lives〕ten thousand years.〔Both are symbols of long life〕.

—景気 permanent prosperity. **—**候補 a permanent candidate. **—**暦 a perpetual almanac (≒ calendar).

まんねんどこ【万年床】 ¶ 彼は～でだらしがない He is a lazy person leaving his bed unmade from week to week.

まんねんひつ【万年筆】 a〔fountain〕pen (通常は pen だけでよい). ¶ ～にインクを入れる fill *a pen.* この～はインクが漏る This *pen* has a bad leak. この～はインクの出がよい（悪い）This *pen* has a smooth (an uneven) ink flow. この～はもうインクがない This *pen* is dry. この～はとても書きよい This *pen* writes smoothly.

まんねんゆき【万年雪】 eternal snow. ¶ 山の頂は～に閉ざされている The mountain top is capped (≒ is enveloped) with *eternal* (≒

ま

perpetual) *snow*.

まんびき【万引】shoplifting ; (人) a shoplifter. ¶ 彼はデパートでなにか～するところを見つかった He was caught in the act of *lifting* something from (≒ at) a counter of a department store.

まんびょう【万病】¶ ～に効く薬 a cure-all ; a panacea. 風邪は～のもと Cold may lead to *all kinds of diseases*.

まんぷく【満腹】a full (≒ loaded) stomach. ¶ もう～だ I *have had enough*. / I *have eaten my fill*. / I *have eaten to my heart's content*. もう～で頂けません No more, thank you. I *have had enough*.

まんべんなく【万遍なく】evenly ; (一律に) uniformly ; (公平に) impartially ; equally ; (残らず) without exception ; (全体に) all over. ¶ さくに～ペンキを塗った I painted the fence *evenly*. どの科目も～学ぶのは難しい It is hard to learn every subject *equally well*.

マンボ〘音楽〙a mambo. ¶ ～を踊る mambo. —ズボン drainpipe trousers (≒ pants).

まんぽ【漫歩】a ramble ; an amble. ¶ ～する ramble.

まんぼう【翻車魚】〘魚類〙a sunfish.

マンホール a manhole.

まんまく【幔幕】a curtain ; a drapery.

まんまと successfully ; completely ; nicely. ¶ ～一杯食わされた I was *completely* (≒ *nicely*) taken in. 彼は～ライバルを追い出した He got rid of his rival *successfully* (≒ *with success*). 犯人は～逃走した The criminal *made good* his *escape*.

まんまん【満満】¶ 貯水池は～と水をたたえていた The reservoir was filled with water *to the brim*. 彼は自信～で試験に臨んだ He took the examination *in full confidence*. 彼は闘志～だった He *was full of* (≒ *was brimming with*) fighting spirit.

まんめん【満面】the whole face. ¶ 彼女は～に笑みをたたえてステージに立った She stood on the stage with her *face* beaming.

まんもく【満目】the whole view. ¶ ～荒涼の原野であった It was a bleak view of a wilderness *as far as one could see* (≒ *as far as the eye could reach*).

マンモス〘動物〙a mammoth. —企業 a mammoth enterprise. —タンカー a monster tanker. —都市 a megalopolis ; a huge city.

まんゆう【漫遊】¶ 彼は先月世界～の旅に出た He started on *a tour* (≒ *a pleasure trip*) of the world last month. 昨年アメリカ各地を～した I made *a trip* of America last year.

まんりき【万力】㊎ a vice ; ㊍ a vise ; a jack.

まんりょう【満了】expiration. ¶ 彼は任期～を待たずに辞任した He resigned before his term of office *expired* (≒ *came to an end*). 契約の期限はあと数週間で～する The contract *expires* (≒ *terminates*) in a few weeks.

まんるい【満塁】〘野球〙loaded bases. ¶ ～だ The bases *are filled* (≒ *are loaded*). 二死～だ The bases *are filled* and there are two out. ～でホーマーを打つ hit a grand slam home run ; hit a home run *with the bases loaded*.

み

み【身】**1**〘体〙*one's* body. ¶ 彼は～をかがめてくつのひもを結んだ He *stooped* (≒ *bent himself*) to tie his shoestring.

彼女は～のこなしが上品だ She has *a* graceful *carriage*.

三塁手は～を挺(てい)してゴロを止めた The third-baseman stopped the grounder with his *body*.

彼女はいつも高価な物を～につけている She is always expensively dressed.

大金を～につけて歩くのは危険だ It is dangerous to go out with a lot of money *on your person*.

外は～を切るような寒風が吹いていた A *cutting* (≒ *biting*) wind was blowing outside.

年をとって近ごろは寒さが～にしみる The cold seems more *piercing* (≒ *biting*) recently because I have grown old.

「わが子の苦しみは～を切られるよりつらい」と母は言った "When I see my child in agony, I feel more pain than any injury to myself," said my mother.

好きな食べ物は～になる To eat your favorite food does you good.

新しい服がだんだん～についてきた The new suit is becoming better fitting.

彼は～を粉にして主人に仕えた He worked *hard* to serve his master.

彼女は～も心も音楽に打ち込んでいる She *is entirely devoted to* music. / She devoted herself, *body* and soul, to music. (body and soul は副詞句,「身も心も打ち込んで」として用いる).

彼は～も心も清めて神に祈った He prayed to God after he purified his *body* and soul.

2〘自分・自己〙*oneself*. ¶ 若いうちに技術を～につけるべきだ You ought to acquire some skill while you are young.

彼の誘いに乗らないほうが～のためだ It is for your good not to be tempted by him.

マラソンの苦しさを～をもって体験した I have *actually* experienced the agony of a marathon race.

彼は酒で～を持ちくずした(～を滅ぼした) *Sake* was his ruin. / He ruined himself by *sake*.

あまりの恥ずかしさに～の置きどころもなかった I was overwhelmed with shame.

残された子どもたちの～の振り方を考えてやらなければならない We must consider the future for the bereaved children.

きみの失敗は～から出たさびだ You have no one to blame but *yourself* for your failure.

彼は～をもって手本を示してくれた He *personally* set a good example.

～を捨ててこそ浮かぶ瀬もあれ Risk all and you will have a chance.

～にふりかかる火の粉は払わなければならない We must try to avoid the impending danger.

～も世もなく泣きくずれた She cried her heart out, overwhelmed with grief. (文語体).

3 〚身分・立場〛 *one's* place ; *one's* standing. ¶ おほめを頂いて～に余る光栄です Your compliment is an honor greater *than I deserve* (≒ *than my due*).

彼は作家としてりっぱに～を立てている He *has established himself* as a writer.

ぼくの～にもなってごらん Put yourself in my *place*.

彼はあまりにも～の程を知らなすぎる He pays too little regard for his social *standing*. / He knows *himself* too little.

彼は貧しい百姓の息子から～を起こした He rose from a son of a poor peasant. / Though born a son of a poor peasant, he became a great success.

それは親の～になってみれば，もっとたいへんだ *In the case af* your parents, it is more troublesome.

きみももう30になったのだからそろそろ結婚して～を固めたほうがいい I hope you will marry and *settle down*, because you are thirty now.

4 〚心〛 ¶ 近ごろ勉強に～が入らない I *lack interest in* study recently.

もっと～を入れて練習しろ *Put more heart into* your exercise. / *Throw yourself into* your exercise with more ardor.

彼らの友情がしみじみ～にしみた Their friendship *struck* me *deeply*. / Their friendship *touched* me *to the heart*.

彼は今恋に～を焦がしている He is burning with love now.

5 〚中身・肉〛 ¶ そう言ってしまっては～もふたもない You are altogether too outspoken. / That's too frank a criticism.

この魚は～が柔らかくておいしい This fish is tender and delicious.

この魚は骨が多くて～が少ない This fish is full of fine bones with little *meat*.

6 〚ふたのある容器について〛 ¶ この入れ物はふたと～が合わない The lid does not fit well.

み【実】(果実) fruit ; (クリなど) a nut ; (イチゴなど) a berry ; (草などの) 〔a〕 seed ; (実質) substance ; (汁の) ingredients.

¶ この木はよい～がなる This tree bears fine *fruit*. このスイカは～がいっている(いない) This watermelon *is ripe* (*is green*). 彼らの努力は～を結んだ Their efforts *proved fruitful*. / Their efforts *were crowned with success*. (文語体).

み【箕】 a winnow. ¶ ～でもみがらをふるい分ける *winnow* the chaff *from* the grain.

-み【-味】〔a〕 taste ; 〔a〕 flavor ; 〔a〕 savor ; 〔a〕 tinge. ¶ 赤(黄色；青)～を帯びた reddish (yellowish ; bluish). それは甘～がある It has *a* sweet *taste* (≒ *flavor*).

みあい【見合い】 an interview (≒ an arranged meeting) with a view to matrimony (≒ marriage).

¶ あすお～があるのです I have a meeting arranged for me with a prospective bride (≒ bridegroom) tomorrow.

―結婚 an arranged marriage.

みあ・う【見合う】 ¶ 生活費の値上がりに～う給料を要求している We demand salaries *commensurate with* increased living costs. 収入に～った暮らしをしなさい You should live *within your income* (≒ *means*).

みあ・きる【見飽きる】 ¶ テレビドラマは～きた I *am tired of watching* TV dramas. / I *have seen enough of* those television plays. この景色を～きることはないだろう I shall never *be weary of seeing* this view.

みあ・げる【見上げる】 look up. ¶ 少年は私を～げた The boy *looked up at* me. 男の前に立って彼女はその顔を～げた As she stood before him, she *looked up into* his face. ～げるばかりの大男 a *towering* man ; a giant. 実に～げた精神だ I *admire* your spirit.

みあた・る【見当たる】 ¶ 適当な場所が～らなかった We failed to *find* a suitable place. 財布が～らない My wallet *is missing*.

みあやま・る【見誤る】 ¶ 敵を味方と～る *take* a foe *for* a friend.

みあわ・せる【見合わせる】 ¶ ふたりは顔を～せて笑った They *looked at each other* with a smile. / They exchanged smiling glances. 高速道路の建設は来年まで～される The construction of the turnpike is to *be postponed* (≒ *be put off* ; *be deferred*) until next year.

みいだ・す【見出す】 ¶ 報告書に二，三の誤りが～された A few mistakes *were found* (≒ *were detected*) in the report.

ミーティング a meeting. ¶ ～を開く hold *a meeting* (受動態で用いることが多い).

ミイラ a mummy. ¶ ～にする mummify. ～とりが～になることが多い Many *go for wool and come back shorn*.

みいり【実入り】 (収入) an income ; (利得) profit. ¶ 彼は～が多い(少ない) He earns *a* large (small) *income*. / He *is* well-*paid* (*is* under*paid*). この職業は～がよい This profession *pays well* (≒ *is profitable* ; *is remunerative*).

みい·る【見入る】¶ 彼女はじっと鏡の中の自分の姿に～った She *gazed at* (≒ *watched*) herself intently in the mirror.

みい·る【魅入る】¶ 悪魔に～られる *be possessed by* a devil. 彼女の美しさに～られる *be fascinated* by her beauty.

みう·ける【見受ける】¶ お～けしたところあなたは学校の先生のようですね I think you are a school teacher. / To me you *look like* (≒ *have the appearance of*) a teacher. 駅でよくあの人を～ける I often *see* him at the station.

みうごき【身動き】¶ みんなは～もせずに彼の話を聞いた They listened to him *motionlessly* (≒ *quite still*). 電車は満員で～もできなかった The train was so crowded that I could not *move* (≒ *stir*) an inch.

みうしな·う【見失う】¶ 人ごみで彼を～った I *lost sight* (≒ *track*) *of* him in the crowd. この編集者は雑誌の精神を～っている The editor *has lost* the original spirit of the magazine.

みうち【身内】(親族) *one's* relatives. ¶ ～の者だけで結婚式を済ませた We had a quiet wedding within our *family circle*. 彼は～が多い He has many *relations*. / (子分の意味) He has *a* large *following* (≒ many *followers*). その光景に接して～の引き締まるのを覚えた I *felt myself strained* (≒ *tense*) *with emotion* at the sight.

みうり【身売り】¶ 工場を～する *sell* a factory *away*.

みえ【見え】show ; display ; good appearance ; (虚栄) vanity. ¶ 彼は～を張るのが好きだ He is fond of *display*. もう～も外聞もない I can't afford to mind what people think. 大～を切ってしまった手前, 引っ込みがつかない Since I *have made a grand gesture*, I am in an embarrassing position to retreat. 役者が舞台で～を切る The actor puts up *a spectacular pose* on the stage.

みえがくれ【見え隠れ】¶ 刑事は～にその男のあとをつけた The detective *shadowed* the man. 月が雲間に～している The moon is shining *on and off* through the scattered clouds.

みえす·く【見え透く】¶ 彼は～いたうそをつく He tells *hollow* (≒ *transparent* ; *obvious*) lies. 忙しいからというのは～いた口実だ It's a *lame* (≒ *clumsy*) excuse that he is too busy. 彼の本心は～いている His true aim *is transparent*.

みえっぱり【見えっぱり】a vain person ; a fop.

み·える【見える】**1** 〖目に見える〗 see. ¶ ここから富士山が～える Mt. Fuji can *be seen* from here.

遠くに子どもたちが遊んでいるのが～える We can *see* children playing in the distance.

私たちはやがて湖の～える所に来た We soon *came in sight of* the lake.

細菌は肉眼では～えない Germs *are invisible to* the naked eye.

2 〖来る〗 come. ¶ そのうちだれか～えるでしょう Someone will *appear* before long.

3 〖らしく見える〗 look. ¶ 彼は年のわりに若く～える He *looks* young for his age.

彼女はなんでも知っているように～える She *seems* to know everything.

この企てはうまくいきそうに～える This scheme *is likely* (≒ *appears* ; *seems*) *to* succeed.

みおくり【見送り】a send-off ; seeing off ; (人) a well-wisher ; a sender-off. ¶ 彼の～に空港へ行ってきた I have been to the airport to *see* him *off*. 彼は多数の～の人たちに囲まれた He was surrounded by a lot of *senders-off*.

みおく·る【見送る】¶ 数人の友人が彼を～るために集まった Some of his friends gathered to *send* him *off* (≒ *give* him *a send-off*). 彼を空港まで～るつもりだ I'll go as far as the airport to *see* him *off*. 彼はなにかわけがあってその機会を～った He *let go* (≒ *passed up*) the opportunity for some reason or other. この案の決定は～る The decision of the proposal should *be postponed*.

みおさめ【見納め】¶ それが彼の～だった That was *the last* that I saw him. この世の～にもう一度故郷が見たい I am dying to see my home town once again *for the last time in my life* (≒ *before I die*).

みおとし【見落とし】an oversight ; an omission. ¶ それには少し～がある There are a few *omissions* in it. 彼は重大な～をした He committed *a* grave *oversight*. 彼は～がないように答案用紙を見直した He reread his paper so as not to *overlook* a mistake. (否定の目的を表わす不定詞(副詞用法)は必ず so as not to または in order not to とする). / He reread his paper in case there was an *oversight*.

みおと·す【見落とす】¶ うっかり掲示を～した I happened to *overlook* (≒ *miss seeing*) the bulletin. / The bulletin *escaped my notice* by chance. 彼らは現代の学校制度の重大な欠陥を～している They *fail to notice* grave defects in the present school system.

みおとり【見劣り】¶ 一般に日本人の体格は西洋人に比べて～がする Generally speaking, the Japanese people *can't stand* (≒ *bear* ; *sustain*) *comparison with* the Western people in their physique.

みおぼえ【見覚え】remembrance ; recognition ; recollection. ¶ この辺りには～がある (ない) This place *is familiar* (*is unfamiliar* ; *is strange*) *to* me. これは確かに～のある写真だ I do *remember* (≒ *recognize*) this picture.

みおも【身重】pregnancy. ¶ 彼女は～だ She *is pregnant* (≒ *is with child*).

みおろ·す【見下ろす】¶ 彼は窓から街路を～した He *looked down on* the street out of (≒ through) the window. エッフェル塔はパリ全市を～している Eiffel Tower *overlooks* (≒ *commands*) the whole city of Paris.

みかい【未開】¶ ～の地域 *barbaric* (≒ *uncivilized*) regions.

みかいけつ【未解決】¶ 政府は幾多の～課題をかかえている The cabinet is confronted with a number of *pending* (≒ *outstanding* ; *un-*

み

solved) problems. 国の内外に～の政治問題が山積している There are a heap of political issues 〔which *remain*〕 *unsettled* both at home and abroad. 事件は～のままだ The matter *is* still *pending*. 殺人事件は～のままになっている The police *is* still *in the dark* about the murder case.

みかいこん【未開墾】**―**地 the land out of cultivation; uncultured land; virgin soil.

みかえし【見返し】a flyleaf.

みかえ・す【見返す】¶ 驚いて彼を～した I *looked* (≒ *stared*) *back at* him in surprise. 彼を～してやりたくてたまらない I am dying to *look down on* (≒ *avenge myself upon*) him. 彼は注意深く何度も書類を～した He carefully *looked over* the papers again and again.

みかえり【見返り】**―**資金 a counterpart fund; collateral money. **―**担保 a collateral security. **―**品 a collateral article. **―**物資 collateral goods.

みかえ・る【見返る】¶ 彼は手を振りながら何度もこちらを～った He *looked back* toward us again and again, waving his hand in farewell.

みがき【磨き】polishing; burnishing. ¶ 彼女はヨーロッパでピアノの腕に～をかけてきた She received her *final polishing* on the piano in Europe. 彼はその床に～をかけた He *polished* the floor.

みがきあ・げる【磨きあげる】¶ ～げた芸だ It is a *highly polished* talent.

みかぎ・る【見限る】¶ 彼は会社を～った He *gave up* (≒ *abandoned*) his firm. ずいぶんお～りですね You are quite a stranger. / It's ages since I saw you last. ～られたものだ How they *turn the cold shoulder toward* me!

みかく【味覚】taste; the palate; the sense of taste.

みが・く【磨く】¶ 毎日くつを～く I *shine* (≒ *polish*) my shoes every day. 寝る前に歯を～きなさい *Brush* (≒ *Clean*) your teeth before you go to bed. ナイフを～く *sharpen* a knife. 腕を～く *improve one's* skill. 肌を～く *clean one's* skin.

みかけ【見かけ】appearance; looks. ¶ 人は～によらぬもの You can't judge a man by his *appearance* (≒ *looks*). このいすは～より重い This chair is heavier than it *looks*. 彼の親切は～だけだ His kindness *is all on the surface*. ～では彼は正直だ *In appearance*, he is honest.

みかげいし【御影石】granite.

みかけだおし【見かけ倒し】deceptive appearance. ¶ このペンは～だった This pen *was not as good as it looked*. 彼は～だ He is not what he is cracked up to be.

みか・ける【見かける】¶ 町でよく～ける風景だ It is a *familiar* sight on the street. この地方でよく～ける病気だ It is a *common* disease to the people of this region. あの人はときどき会で～ける I sometimes *see* him at the meeting. あまりこの辺で～けない人だ He is quite a stranger here. こんな品はめったに～けぬ I seldom *come across* such articles. / Such a thing is not to *be had* so often.

みかた【見方】a point of view; an outlook. ¶ 人によって～は違う Different people have different *viewpoints*. きみの～はおもしろい I think your *point of view* is interesting. 別な～をしてみたまえ Why not take another *way of looking at* it? / Why not *look at* it from a different angle? 金持ちと貧乏人ではものの～が違う People *see* things differently according to whether they are rich or poor. ～によってはきみも正しい *In a sense*, you are also right. きみの人生の～は狭い Your *outlook* on life is limited.

みかた【味方】a friend; an ally. ¶ あなたの～をします I will *support* you. / I will *be on your side*. 医師は病める者の～でなければならない A doctor should *be a friend* (≒ *be on the side*) of the sick. 私としてはどちらの～もできない As for me, I can *take* neither *side* (≒ I can *side with* neither of them). / I remain neutral. きみがやり方を改めないならだれも～をしないだろう No one will *stand by* you unless you amend your way. オーストリアはドイツの～だった Austria was *an ally* of Germany.

みかづき【三日月】the crescent; a new moon; the horned moon.

みがって【身勝手】selfishness. ¶ 彼は～だ He *is selfish*. それはあなたの～というものだ It *is selfish* of you. / You *are asking too much*.

みか・ねる【見兼ねる】¶ ～ねて手を貸した *Being unable to remain indifferent*, he offered a helping hand.

みがまえ【身構え】a posture. ¶ 走りだす～をした He *assumed a posture of* starting to run. / He *was ready to* start.

みがま・える【身構える】¶ さあこいと～えた He *pulled himself up* for a fighting posture. / He threw himself into a defensive attitude. 強盗をやっつけようと～えた I *stood in readiness* to attack the thief. 弁慶は牛若丸にとびかかろうと～えた Benkei *held himself ready* to strike at Ushiwakamaru.

みがら【身柄】*one's* person. ¶ 彼は息子の～を引き取りに出かけた He went out to claim his son. ～は遺族に引き渡された The *body* was handed over to the bereaved family. われわれは彼の～を預かった We took charge of him.

みがる【身軽】sprightly; light. ¶ 彼は～な服装をしていた He was *lightly* dressed. ～に旅行した We traveled *light*. 彼らは～にダンスする They are *agile* dancers. 彼はいかにも～だ He is quite *sprightly*. 重荷がなくなって～になった I *was relieved of* my burden.

みかわ・す【見交わす】¶ 私たちは互いに顔を～した We *looked at each other*. / We *exchanged glances*. 互いに～す顔と顔 Our eyes *met*.

みがわり【身代わり】a substitute. ¶ 私は校長の～になった I *took the place of* the principal. 氏は彼らの～になって死んだ He died *for* (≒ *in place of*) them. 父は息子の～にその責任を負っ

た The father took the responsibility *instead of* (≒ *in place of*) his son. 親は子どものためには～になるものだ Parents will *sacrifice themselves for* their children.

みかん【未刊】¶ ～の unpublished.

みかん【未完】To be continued (「次号完結」の意味では To be concluded. を用いる). ¶ ～の物語 an *unfinished* story. 彼は～の大器といわれる He is said to be a great promising talent.

みかん【蜜柑】a tangerine〔orange〕; (温州みかん) a mandarin orange. ¶ その本の表紙は～色だ The cover of the book is *tangerine*-colored. ～の皮 an *orange* peel.

—箱 a box of tangerines. —畑 an orange orchard.

みかんせい【未完成】incompletion. ¶ ～の incomplete ; unfinished. 小説を～のまま彼は世を去った *Leaving* the novel *unfinished*, he died. ～の仕事を今週中に終えるつもりだ I intend to accomplish my *unfinished* work before the end of this week.

みき【幹】a trunk. ¶ この木の～は周囲5メートルある This *trunk* is five meters round.

みぎ【右】the right. ¶ その十字路を～へ曲がりなさい Turn the crossroads *to the right*. ～へならえ (号令) Right, dress! ～向け～ (号令) Right turn! やがて～に塔が見えるでしょう You will see the tower *on your right*. 弁舌にかけては彼の～に出る者はいない He *is second to none in* eloquence. ～のとおり相違ありません I affirm the *above* statement to be true in every particular. 彼は～寄りの政治家だ He is a *right*-leaning (≒ *rightist*) statesman.

みぎうで【右腕】the right arm. ¶ 彼は社長の～となって働いている He is working as *the right-hand man* of the president of his company.

みぎがわ【右側】the right side. ¶ ～通行 (掲示) Keep to *the right*. 神社は～にある You will find the shrine *on your right*.

みきき【見聞き】¶ 当地では実に多くのことを～した We *have seen and heard* quite a lot of things here.

みぎきき【右利き】¶ ～の right-handed. 彼は～だ He *is right-handed*.

ミキサー a mixer.

コンクリート— a concrete mixer.

みぎて【右手】*one's* right hand. ¶ ～に見える山が高尾山だ The mountain you see *to the right* is Mt. Takao.

みぎひだり【右左】¶ 道路を横断するときは～をよく見なさい Look *right and left* carefully when you cross the street.

みきょういく【未教育】¶ ～の uneducated.

—者 uneducated people.

みきり【見切り】abandonment. ¶ 幾度やってもだめだから, もう～をつけた All my attempts have been in vain, and I *give* it *up* as a bad job. あの男には～をつけた I *have done with* him. / I *have given* him *up* as hopeless.

—売り a sacrifice sale ; a bargain sale ; a clearance sale. —品 a bargain ; clearance goods.

みぎり【砌】¶ 酷暑の～ *in this season of* severe heat. 厳寒の～ *in this season of* severe cold.

みき・る【見切る】¶ 彼はその考えはずっと前に～っている He *gave up* the idea long ago. もう旅行の計画は～るほかなくなった We have found no other way than to *abandon* our plan for the journey. ぼくはその件を全く～ってしまった I *have washed my hands of* the whole business.

みぎれい【身綺麗】¶ 彼女はいつも～にしている She *is* always *neatly dressed*.

みぎわ【汀】the water's edge ; the beach.

みきわ・める【見極める】¶ それが正しいかどうか～めなければならない We must *ascertain* whether it is right or wrong. 彼が不在であることを～めた We *made sure* that he was out. 事の真相を～めたい I want to *probe* (≒ *explore*) the matter〔*to the bottom*〕.

ミグ a MIG (ソ連製のジェット戦闘機).

みくだ・す【見下す】¶ 彼はどんな人をも～す He *looks down upon* (≒ *despises*) any sort of person. それは人を～した言い方だ Such words show that you *are despising* others.

みくだりはん【三下り半・三行半】a letter of divorce.

みくび・る【見くびる】¶ 彼は病気を～って, 手おくれになった He *made light of* his sickness, till it was too late. 相手を～ったのが失敗のもとだった It was because I *despised* him that I failed at last. きみの才能を～っていた I *have underestimated* your abilities.

みくら・べる【見比べる】¶ この二つを～べてみなさい *Compare* these two *with the eye*. よく～べて判断しなさい Judge after *looking one from the other*.

みぐるし・い【見苦しい】(服装) shabby ; (恥ずべき) disgraceful ; awkward ; mean. ¶ なんと～い服装だろう How *shabbily* dressed he is! 彼のふるまいは～い His behavior *is* too *unbecoming*. 彼がそんな考え方をするのは～いことだ It *is mean* of him to think like that. 彼の態度は～くて見ていられない His attitude *looks* so *awkward* that I can hardly watch him.

みぐるみ【身ぐるみ】¶ ～はぎとられた I was robbed of *all I had*. ～置いていけと言われた I was told to leave *all I had on* there.

ミクロ micro. ¶ ～の世界 the *microscopic* world.

—コスモス a microcosm.

ミクロン a micron (複 microns ; micra).

ミリ— a millimicron.

みけいけん【未経験】inexperience. ¶ このようなことは彼は～だ He *is inexperienced in* this sort of thing.

—者 an inexperienced person.

みけつ【未決】¶ この罪人は～だ This criminal *is unconvicted*. その問題は依然～のままだ The question *remains unsettled* (≒ *is undicided*). 彼は～で1年も刑務所に入っている He

has been in prison for a year, *pending trial.*
—拘留 detention pending trial. —囚 an unconvicted prisoner. —書類 pending documents.

みけっさん【未決算】 —勘定 unsettled (≒ outstanding) account. —手形 an unsettled bill.

みけねこ【三毛猫】 a tortoise-shell cat.

みけん【未見】 ¶ 〜の unacquainted. 〜の書 an *unread* book.

みけん【眉間】 brow; forehead; the middle of the forehead. ¶ 〜に傷がある He has got a cut *between the brows.* 〜を割られた I got a cut across my *forehead.* 彼は〜にしわを寄せている He *is knitting his brows.*

みこ【巫女】 a maiden in the service of a shrine.

みこし【御輿・神輿】 a portable shrine. ¶ 子どもらは〜をかついだ The children carried about *a portable shrine.* そろそろ〜を上げよう(出かけよう) Well, I must *take my leave* now. / We must *be leaving* now. / It is about time we *left.* われわれは彼の家に〜をすえて長居した We *settled down* at his house too long.

みごしらえ【身拵え】 getting dressed; outfit. ¶ 私は急いで〜した I *got dressed* (≒ *dressed myself*) in haste. 彼女は〜ができてしまうと, 階下へ行った After having completed her *toilet* she went downstairs.

みこ・す【見越す】 ¶ 雨を〜してかさを持っていった I brought an umbrella with me *just in case of* rain (≒ *against* rain; *in case* it might rain). 試験を〜して準備をした I prepared myself *in anticipation of* the examination. 彼の来るのを〜してへやをきれいにしておいた I made a clean sweep of the room *in expectation of* his visit.

みごたえ【見応え】 ¶ この映画は〜がある This movie *is worth seeing.* なかなか〜のある芝居だった The play *was* quite *enjoyable.*

みごと【見事】 ¶ 〜な splendid; excellent; admirable. 実に〜だった It *was fine* indeed. バラが〜に咲いている The roses *are in their glory* (≒ *are at their best*). あの人の英語は〜なものだ He is a *splendid* speaker of English. 彼は〜な成功をおさめた He was a *great* success. / He won an *admirable* success. / He succeeded *admirably.* 〜に失敗した It ended in a *complete* failure. 〜なホームランだった It was a *wonderful* home run. 敵の計画は〜に敗られた The enemy's plan was *entirely* (≒ *fairly*) defeated.

みこみ【見込み】 **1** 〖望み〗 hope; prospect. ¶ きみは〜がある You *are promising.* 彼は〜がない He *is unpromising.* もはや彼の将来は〜がない His future *is* not *hopeful* any more. 〜がないと知りながら彼は努力している He is making efforts, though he knows that it *is hopeless.* / He makes efforts *hoping against hope.*

2 〖予想〗 expectation. ¶ 彼は来月帰国する〜だ He will be back next month. / He *is expected to* come back next month. 彼の作品の出来栄えは〜どおりだった The results of his work *met* (≒ *came up to*) our *expectations.* ことしの米の収穫の〜はよい The *prospects* for the rice crops this year are good. 私の〜は当たった (はずれた) I *guessed right* (*wrong*). 医者の〜によると彼は心配ない According to the doctor he is out of danger.

3 〖可能性〗 probability. ¶ 彼の病気は回復の〜がない He has no *chance* of recovering. 彼の病気は回復の〜がないと私は思う I have no *hope* of his recovery. / I see little *prospect* of his recovery. 彼がきょうじゅうに帰宅する〜はほとんどない It *is* hardly *probable* that he will come back today. 彼の助かる〜はない There is no *likelihood* of his being rescued.

4 〖見積もり〗 estimation. ¶ 損害は約5万円の〜だ The damage *is estimated at* about fifty thousand yen. それは私の〜違いだと思う I think it was a miscalculation on my part.

みこ・む【見込む】 ¶ 彼は私を〜んでいる He *is putting confidence in* me. 彼は上役に〜まれた He *won the confidence of* his superiors. 費用は全部で100万円と〜んだ He *estimated* the expense at a million yen in all. 彼女は将来を〜まれている She *is marked as a promising figure.* 国家の援助を〜んで彼は探検旅行に出ることに決めた He decided to make a trip of expedition *in anticipation of* the Government's aid.

みごろ【見頃】 ¶ 今が梅の〜だ The plum-blossoms *are* now *at their best.*

みごろし【見殺し】 ¶ 彼らは彼を〜にした They *left him to his fate.* きみを〜にはしない I will not *leave* you *to your fate.*

みこん【未婚】 ¶ 〜の unmarried; single. 〜の男子 a bachelor. 〜の女子 an old maid (口語的); a spinster (主に法律用語). 彼女は〜だ She *is unmarried* (≒ *is single*). 彼女はずっと〜のままだ She is *a* confirmed *spinster.* 彼は生涯〜で通した He *remained single* all his life.
—者 a single person; an unmarried person.

ミサ a Mass; a mass. ¶ 〜を行なう say *mass.*

みさい【未済】 ¶ 決算の〜がある There are some *unsettled* accounts.

ミサイル a missile.
—関係者 missilemen. —基地 a missile base. —兵器 a missile weapon. 空対空— an air-to-air missile (A. A. M.). 空対地— an air-to-surface missile (A. S. M.). 地対空— a ground-to-air missile.

みさお【操】 chastity; virtue. ¶ 彼女は亡夫に〜をたてた She *was true* (≒ *faithful*) *to* the memory of her deceased husband. 彼女は

〜の正しい女だ She is a woman *of virtue.* / She is a *virtuous* woman. 彼女は〜のない女だ She is a woman *of easy virtue.* 彼女は最後まで〜をたて通した She *remained chaste* to the end.

みさかい【見境】discrimination. ¶ 彼は善悪の〜がつかない He cannot *discriminate* (≒ *tell*) good from evil. 前後の〜もなく騒いだ We made merry, *forgetting ourselves.* 彼は〜なくどんなことでもやる He sets about any sort of thing *indiscriminately.* 彼はだれかれの〜がない He *makes no distinction of* persons.

みさき【岬】a cape; a promontory. ¶ 足摺〜 Ashizuri *Promontory.* コッド〜 *Cape* of Cod.

みさげは・てる【見下げ果てる】¶ なんという〜てたやつだ What a *contemptible* fellow he is! まったく〜てた根性だ What a *mean* nature he has!

みさ・げる【見下げる】¶ 〜げた根性だ What a *mean* (≒ *despicable*) nature he has! 彼らは彼を居候のように〜げた They *looked down upon* him as a sort of dependent.

みさだ・める【見定める】¶ 彼は敵の隠れている所を〜めた He *ascertained* the enemy's hiding place. ここでコースを〜めよう We will *make sure of* our course here.

みじか・い【短い】short; brief. ¶ 〜い命 a *short* life. 〜い期間 a *short* (≒ *brief*) period of time. この鉛筆はあの鉛筆より５センチ〜い This pencil *is* five centimeters *shorter* than that one. このドレスはそでが〜い This dress *is short*-sleeved. このドレスは彼女に〜すぎる This dress *is* too *short* for her. 彼は気が〜い He *is short*-tempered. ことしの梅雨は〜そうだ The rainy season is expected to *be short* this year.

みじかく【短く】short; briefly. ¶ 日が〜なってきた The days are getting *shorter.* 説明はできるだけ〜お願いします Please explain as *briefly* as possible. 髪を〜切ったね You have cut your hair *short,* haven't you?

みじたく【身支度】equipment. ¶ すぐ〜しなさい *Dress yourself* at once. 急いで〜した I *got dressed* in haste. 旅の〜をする *fit* oneself *up* for a trip.

みじまい【身仕舞い】dressing. ¶ 彼女は〜をしている She is at her *toilet.* 彼女は〜に１時間以上かかる She spends more than an hour at her *toilet.*

みしみし ¶ 天井が〜鳴っている The ceiling *is creaking.* この床は歩くと〜鳴る This floor *creaks* under our feet.

みじめ【惨め】misery. ¶ 彼らは〜な生活をしている They lead a *miserable* life. 少女は〜な服装をしていた The girl was *poorly* dressed. すっかり〜な気持ちになった We *felt* very *wretched.* 事業に失敗して〜な気持ちを味わっている I *feel wretched* because of my failure in the enterprise. 資金不足のため計画は〜な結果に終わった Because of the shortage of funds, the plan came to an *unhappy* end. 〜な光景だった It was a *piteous* spectacle.

みしゅうにゅう【未収入】—金 an account outstanding.

みじゅく【未熟】unripeness; inexperience. ¶ 〜な役者 an *unskilled* actor. 〜な思想 an *immature* thought. 彼は〜だ He *is not yet skillful enough.* 〜ながらもまとまった作品だ This work is coherent though it *is immature.* 〜な運転が事故を招くことはよくある *Unskillful* driving often brings about an accident. 彼の話す英語は〜だ His English *is poor.* / The English he speaks is far from perfect.

—児 a premature baby.

みしょう【未詳】作者— anonymous. ¶ この詩は作者〜だ The writer of this poem *is not known* (≒ *is unknown; is unidentified*).

みしょう【実生】¶ この木は〜のものだ This tree *is grown from the seed.* カシの木を〜で育てた We *grew* an oak *from the seed.*

みし・る【見知る】meet; get acquainted with. ¶ あなたをお〜り申しております I *know you by sight.* 〜らぬ人 a stranger. 彼とは〜らぬ仲だ He *is a stranger to* me. どうぞお〜りおきください I am very glad to *meet* you. / I am happy to *make your acquaintance.*

みじろぎ【身動ぎ】stirring. ¶ 彼は〜もしなかった He would not *stir* an inch. 彼は〜もせず立っていた He was standing *as firm as a rock.*

ミシン a sewing machine. ¶ ズボンに〜をかける sew trousers with *a sewing machine.* これは〜縫いですか Was this sewing done by *machine?*

電気— an electric sewing machine.

みじん【微塵】an atom; a bit; a piece. ¶ かびんは〜に砕け散った The vase was broken *to pieces* (≒ *to bits*). 茶わんは〜に砕けていた The cup *was in bits.* 彼は〜も驚く様子はなかった He did *not* seem to be surprised *at all.* 彼は感謝の気持ちなど〜もないようだ He *does not show even a spark of* gratitude.

ミス（失敗）a mistake. ¶ 〜をする make *a mistake.*

ミス（未婚の婦人）¶ 彼女はいまだに〜だ She *is unmarried* yet.

—日本 Miss Japan. ¶ 彼女は〜日本に選ばれた She was chosen *Miss* Japan. オールド— an old maid.

みず【水】**1**〖液体〗water. ¶ 〜を１杯ください Please give me a glass of *water.*

この〜は飲めない This *water* is not good to drink.

〜は低きにつく（諺）*Water* seeks its own level. / *Water* always flows down.

〜清ければ魚棲まず（諺）A clear stream is avoided by fish.

2〖比喩的に〗¶ 〜を打ったように静かになった A hush has fallen over the place.

これまでのことは〜に流そう Let bygones be bygones. / Let's forget the past.

彼は立て板に〜を流すようにしゃべった He talked very fluently.

彼は彼らの熱意に～をさした He *threw cold water on* their zeal.
～もしたたるような美人だ She is an outstandingly beautiful woman.
彼は～を得た魚のようだ He *is in his element*.
3 〖すもうで〗 ¶ すもうに～がはいった The *sumo* match had an interruption for rest.
4 〖洪水〗 ¶ この辺に～が出た This neighborhood *has been flooded*.

みずあか【水垢】fur. ¶ ～がたまった *Fur* has formed. やかんに～がついた The inside of the kettle is covered with a crust (≒ deposit) of minerals.

みずあげ【水揚げ】unloading. ¶ 彼らはサンマの～で忙しい They are busy catching mackerel pike〔s〕. タクシーの１日の～はどのくらいですか How much are the *takings* of a taxi in a day? この花は～がいい This flower *draws water* well (≒ satisfactorily).

みずあたり【水中り】water-poisoning. ¶ 旅行で～した *The water disagreed with* me during my trip.

みずあび【水浴び】bathing. ¶ 川に～に行こう Let's go *bathing* in the river. 池で～をした We *had a bathe* in the pond. (have a bath は「入浴する」の意味となる).

みずあめ【水飴】millet jelly.

みすい【未遂】an abortive attempt. ¶ 彼の企ては～に終わった He *failed in the attempt*.
—罪 an attempted crime. 殺人**—** an attempted murder. 自殺**—** an attempted suicide. ¶ 彼は自殺～に終わった He *failed at suicide*.

みずいらず【水入らず】¶ 夫婦～で暮らしている The couple live *by themselves in undisturbed peace*. 一家～で集まった All our family members gathered *by themselves*.

みずいれ【水入れ】a water-holder; a pitcher; a jug.

みずいろ【水色】light blue; aquamarine.

みずうみ【湖】a lake; a pond.

みす・える【見据える】stare fixedly (*at*); look hard (*at*). ¶ 彼は私を～えた He *looked straight into* my eyes.

みずおち【鳩尾】the pit of the stomach; the solar plexus.

みずおと【水音】a splash. ¶ 彼は～も高く跳び込んだ He jumped into the water *with a* great *splash*. ～をたてる make *a splash*.

みずかがみ【水鏡】¶ 彼は自分を～に映して見た He looked at *his reflection in the water*. ナーシサスは～に映った自分の姿に恋をした Narcissus fell in love with his own image *reflected in the water*.

みずかき【水掻き】a web. ¶ たいていの水鳥には～がある Nearly all aquatic birds *are web-footed* (≒ *have webbed feet*).

みずかけろん【水掛け論】an endless (≒ fruitless) dispute. ¶ ～はやめないか Stop this *fruitless argument*. それは結局～だ That's *a matter of opinion* after all.

みずかさ【水嵩】the〔volume of〕water.
¶ 川の～が増した(減った) The river has risen (has fallen).

みすか・す【見透かす】see through; penetrate into. ¶ 彼らの魂胆を～した I *saw through* (≒ *penetrated into*) their motives. 彼らは私の足もとを～した They *took mean advantage of* me.

みずから【自ら】self; *one*self. ¶ 彼～電話に出た He *himself* answered the phone. / He answered the phone *personally* (≒ *in person*). 彼は～進んで責任をとった He assumed the responsibility *of his own accord* (≒ *of his own free will*; *of his own choice*). ～をかえりみるがよい Reflect upon *yourself*. 彼は～の危険をかえりみずその子を救った He saved the child at the risk of his *own* life. 天は～助くる者を助く (諺) *Heaven helps those who help themselves*.

みずぎ【水着】a swimming (≒ bathing) suit; (男子のパンツ)〔a pair of〕swimming trunks.

みずききん【水飢饉・水饑饉】shortage of water supply; a water famine (≒ shortage).

みずきり【水切り】(遊戯) ducks and drakes. ¶ ～をして遊ぶ play *ducks and drakes*.

みずぎわ【水際】the water's edge. ¶ コレラの侵入を～で防ぐことができた We were able to keep the epidemic of cholera off *the shores*.

みずぎわだ・つ【水際立つ】¶ 彼の演奏は～っていた His performance *was splendid* (≒ *was excellent*; *was superb*; *was flawless*). きのうのバスケットの試合では～ったプレーがたくさん見られた There were a lot of *fine* (≒ *good*; *striking*) plays in the basketball game yesterday.

みずぐき【水茎】(筆跡) handwriting. ¶ ～の跡もうるわしい手紙だった The letter *was written in a beautiful hand*.

みずくさ【水草】a water plant (≒ weed); an aquatic plant.

みずくさ・い【水臭い】too reserved; cold; evasive; lacking in frankness. ¶ ～いじゃないか You *are not frank* with me. そんな～いことをするな Acting that way *is too reserved*. / It's *acting like a stranger*. / Don't *be so reserved* (≒ *be like a stranger*) doing that way.

みずぐすり【水薬】a liquid medicine.

みずけ【水気】(湿気) moisture; (液) juice. ¶ 豆に～を加えて柔らかにする soften beans by *moisture*. このリンゴは～が多い (少ない) This apple *is juicy* (*is dry*). ～の多い watery; moist; sodden.

みずけむり【水煙】spray. ¶ 飛行機は～をあげて着水した The plane made a landing on the water, raising a huge cloud of *spray*.

みずごけ【水苔】〖植物〗 a sphagnum (複 sphagna); (水あか) incrustation.

みすご・す【見過ごす】overlook; miss. ¶ 人はこのことを～しがちだ People are apt to *overlook* this fact. そんな不正を～すことはできない I can't *connive at* such an injustice.

みずごり【水垢離】purification by ablution; cold-water ablutions. ¶ ～をとる purify by *ablution*; perform *cold-water ablutions.*

みずさいばい【水栽培】tank cultivation; water culture. ¶ 球根の～ the *tank cultivation* of a bulb.

みずさかずき【水杯】¶ ～をして別れる exchange farewell cups of water.

みずさきあんない【水先案内】piloting; (人) a pilot. ¶ 船の～をする *pilot* a boat.

みずさし【水差し】㊍ a pitcher; ㊋ a jug; (寝室の) an ewer.

みずしごと【水仕事】washing; kitchen work.

みずしょうばい【水商売】a gay trade; a profession of entertainment. ¶ ～の女 a girl *of a certain character*; a girl *of gay life*; a woman *of pleasure*. ～をする follow *a gay trade.*

みずしらず【見ず知らず】¶ ～の男 a *strange* man. 彼はまったく～の人だ He is *a* perfect *stranger* to me.

みずすまし【水澄まし】〘虫類〙a water beetle.

みずぜめ【水攻め】flooding. ¶ 城を～にする (洪水で) *flood* the enemy's castle; (飲み水を断っ) cut off the water supply.

みずぜめ【水責め】¶ ～にする torture by water; put (*a person*) to water torture.

みずた【水田】a paddy field; a rice field.

ミスター Mr.; Mister (㊇ Messrs.).

みずたま【水玉】(水滴) a drop of water; a water drop; (露) a dewdrop. ¶ クモの巣に～が光っている Several *beads of water* are sparkling on the web. ハスの葉の上を～が風でころがっていた *Drops of water* rolled in the wind on the lotus leaf.

—模様 polka dots. ¶ ～模様の着物 a *polka-dot* dress.

みずたまり【水溜まり】a pool; a puddle.

みずため【水溜め】(おけ) a cistern; a water tank; (貯水池) a reservoir.

みずっぱな【水っ洟】snivel; running mucus. ¶ ～が出ている His nose is running. その子は～を垂らしている The child *is running at the nose* (≒ *has a running nose*).

みずっぽ・い【水っぽい】watery; washy; thin. ¶ ～い酒 *watery sake.*

みずでっぽう【水鉄砲】a squirt〔gun〕; a syringe.

ミステリー mystery.

—小説 a mystery; a mystery story.

みす・てる【見捨てる・見棄てる】¶ 私を～てないでくれ Don't *forsake* (≒ *desert*) me. 彼らは運に～てられた Their luck *failed* them. 彼は故郷を～てて新天地を求めて去った He *abandoned* his home and went for a new place to settle in. / He *left* his home town to find a new place to live. (口語的. この場合最後を live in とする必要はない). そう～てたものでもない (物) You can't *neglect* it completely. / It is not without its good points. / (人) He is not so hopeless as you think. / He may not be altogether worthless.

みずどけい【水時計】a water clock.

みずとり【水鳥】〘鳥類〙a waterfowl; a water bird.

みずな【水菜】a Japanese cabbage.

みずに【水煮】boiling in water.

みずのあわ【水の泡】fruitlessness. ¶ すべての努力は～となった All the efforts *were in vain* (≒ *were wasted; were fruitless*). 長年の努力も～だった Years of efforts *ended in a failure* (≒ *came to naught*).

みずのみ【水飲み・水呑み】(茶わん) a cup; (グラス) a tumbler; a glass.

みずはけ【水捌け】drainage. ¶ そこは～がよい(悪い) *The water drains* well (badly) there. / The place *is* well (ill) *drained.*

みずばしょう【水芭蕉】〘植物〙a skunk cabbage; Lysichiton camtschatcense.

みずばしら【水柱】a column of water. ¶ 砲弾は～を立てて海に落ちた The shell fell into the sea, throwing up *a* tall *column of water.*

みずひき【水引】a ceremonial red (black) and white paper cord. ¶ 進物に～をかける tie a present with *a ceremonial paper cord.*

みずびたし【水浸し】¶ 数千戸の家が～になった Thousands of houses *were flooded* (≒ *got under water*).

みずぶくれ【水腫れ】a〔water〕blister. ¶ やけどで手が～になった I burnt myself by mistake and raised *a blister* on my palm.

みずぶね【水船】(給水船) a water boat; (水浸しの) a water-logged boat.

ミスプリント a misprint. ¶ ～を訂正する correct *errors in printing.*

みずぼうそう【水疱瘡】〘医学〙the chicken pox.

みすぼらし・い【見窄らしい】poor-looking; shabby; seedy. ¶ 彼は～い身なりをしている He is *poorly* (≒ *shabbily*) dressed.

みずまき【水撒き】watering; sprinkling. ¶ 道路に～をする *water* the street; *sprinkle* the street with *water; sprinkle water* on a dusty street.

—器 a sprinkler. —車 a watering cart.

みずまくら【水枕】a〔rubber〕water pillow (≒ cushion). ¶ 病人に～をさせた I placed *a water pillow* under the patient's head.

みずまし【水増し】watering; dilution. ¶ 彼は～して請求した He *padded* the bill. 酒を～した I *diluted sake with water*. この酒は～されている This *sake is watered down.*

—資産 watered assets. —請求 a padded demand. —請求書 a padded bill. —入学 more than capacity enrollment (≒ admission).

みすま・す【見澄ます】observe carefully; (確かめる) make sure; ascertain. ¶ 他の人がみんな眠り込んだのを～して彼はそっとベッドを抜け出した *Making sure* that all the others had gone to sleep, he slipped out of bed.

みすみす【見す見す】¶ ～犯人を取り逃がした We let the criminal escape *in our sight*. ～機会

を失った I missed the opportunity *before my eyes.* ～損をした I couldn't help the loss *though I was aware of it.*

みずみずし·い【瑞瑞しい】young; fresh; unspoiled. ¶ ～い果物 a *fresh* (≒ *juicy*) fruit. あの子は～い娘だ She *is fresh and attractive.* / She is in the first bloom of youth.

みずむし【水虫】〘虫類〙 a water insect; 〘医学〙 water eczema.

みずもの【水物】an uncertain affair; a gamble. ¶ 選挙は～だ Election has an element of *uncertainty* in it.

みずもり【水盛り】a water level. ¶ ～する take *a level*; level.

み·する【魅する】charm; bewitch; fascinate. ¶ 満堂の聴衆は彼のすばらしい演奏に～せられた The packed audience *were fascinated* (≒ *were charmed*) by his flawless performance.

みずわり【水割り】¶ ウイスキーの～ *watered* whisky; 英 whisky *and water.*

みせ【店】米 a store; a shop; 英 a shop; (露店) a stall; (事務所) an office (イギリスでは商店を一般に shop と言うが, アメリカでは品物を売る店は store で, サービスを売る店は shop. Cf. a bookstore; a barbershop).
¶ ～を開く open *a store* (≒ *shop*); set up *in business.* ～を閉める close (≒ shut) *a shop.* ～を畳む shut up *one's shop*; wind (≒ give) up *one's business.* ～を張る keep *shop*; run *a store.* 大道に～を出す keep *a stall* in the street. 近ごろではリンゴは一年じゅう～に出ている Recently apples *are on sale* all the year round. 彼は10年前にその～を始めた He founded the *business* ten years ago. あの～は老舗だ That is *a shop* with an old established name.

みせいねん【未成年】minority; juvenility. ¶ 彼は～だ He *is under age.* / He *is not yet of age.*
—者 a minor; a juvenile (「～者お断わり」の掲示はふつう "Adult Entertainment" とする).
—者禁酒(禁煙)法 the Law for Prohibiting Minors from Drinking (Smoking). —犯罪 juvenile delinquency. —犯罪者 a juvenile delinquent.

みせかけ【見せかけ】(外観) appearance; a look; (偽装) a pretense; a sham; make-believe.
¶ ～は当てにならないことが多い *Appearances* are often deceitful. / *Appearances* often prove false. 彼のていねいは～だけだ His politeness is all *on the surface.* / His politeness is *a* mere *pretense* (≒ only *a sham*). ～で人を判断してはならない Don't judge a person by *outer appearance.* 彼らの協力は～にすぎない Their cooperation is *a* mere *show.*

みせか·ける【見せかける】pretend; feign; sham; assume a false appearance. ¶ 病気と～けて寝たまま彼に会った I received him in bed *pretending* to be sick (≒ *feigning* sickness). 彼女は若く～けているがもう40歳以上だ Though she *tries to look* young (≒ *assumes* a young *appearance*), she is already over forty. (後半はユーモラスに She will never see forty again とも言う). 彼はさも金があるかのように～ける He *makes a great show of* wealth.

みせかざり【店飾り】shop dressing; window dressing (≒ decoration). ¶ ～をする dress the window.

みせがね【見せ金】show money.

みせがまえ【店構え】the appearance of a shop (≒ store). ¶ はでな～ a flaming *shop-front.*

みせさき【店先】the shop-front; the shop; the store. ¶ 一日じゅう彼は～にいる All day, he stays right *behind the counter.* ～に駐車しないでください Don't park your car *at the entrance of the store.*

みせじまい【店仕舞い】¶ ～をする(廃業する) shut up the shop; give up business. きょうはこれで～だ We *are closing* [*the door*] for the day.

みせしめ【見せしめ】a warning; a lesson; an example. ¶ ほかの者の～に彼を処罰すべきだ We should punish him as *a warning* to the others. これでいい～になったろう I hope he *has learned a lesson* from this.

ミセス Mrs. (複 Mmes.; Mesdames).
¶ ロングヘアが若い～の間で人気がある Long hair is popular with young *mistresses* (≒ *married women*).

みせつ·ける【見せつける】show off; make a display. ¶ 彼の指導力をまざまざと～けられた I fully *realized* his unchallenged leadership. 彼は金のあることを～けたいのだ His intention is to *make an ostentatious display of* wealth. あまり～けるな Don't flirt before me.

ミゼット midget.
—カメラ a midget camera.

みぜに【身銭】¶ ～を切ってその代を払った I paid for it *out of my own pocket.*

みせば【見せ場】a highlight; a climax. ¶ この劇は～がない This play lacks *a dramatic climax.*

みせばん【店番】a shop tending; (人) a salesman; (女) a salesgirl; a shop assistant. ¶ ～をする tend (≒ mind) the shop.

みせびらか·す【見せびらかす】¶ 新しい帽子を～す *show off* a new hat. 学問を～す *make a show of one's* learning.

みせびらき【店開き】the opening of a shop (≒ store). ¶ 彼は近ごろ～をしたばかりだ He *has started* (≒ *has founded*) *the business* only recently. そこで～した He *set* [*himself*] *up in business* there.

みせもの【見世物】a show; an exhibition; (博覧会·祭りなどの) a side show; an attraction. ¶ だれだって～にされたくはない No one likes to *make a show* (≒ *spectacle*) *of himself* before strangers. / No one wants to be *an object of mockery.* ～ではないぞ This is not meant for *a show.*

—小屋 a show tent; a show booth. **—師** a showman.

み·せる【見せる】1 show; let (*a person*) see; (陳列して) exhibit. ¶ その本をちょっと〜せてください Let me have a look at the book. 身分証明書を〜せてください *Show* me your identification card. そのくつを〜せてください (商店で) I'd like to *see* those shoes. 彼はきょうの試合で何回か妙技を〜せた He *made some good plays* in the game today. 彼はけっしていやな顔を〜せない He never *looks* displeased. / He is a happy and smiling person. 彼女は私に笑顔を〜せた She *gave* me a friendly smile. 目にものを〜せてやろう I will *teach* them *a lesson.* / I will crop their feathers. 弱みを〜せてはいけない Try not to *show* the white feather. / Try not to *betray* weakness.
2〚医者に〛¶ 医者に〜せましたか (本人に) Did you *see* (≒ *consult*) a doctor? / Did you *have* yourself *examined* by a doctor? / (第三者に) Did you *have* him *examined* by a doctor (≒ *take* him *to* a doctor)?

みぜん【未然】 beforehand; in advance. ¶ 災害を〜に防ぐ prevent (≒ stem off) a disaster. 陰謀を〜に防ぐ *nip* a plot *in the bud.*

みそ【味噌】 bean paste; *miso*; (比喩的) a mess; a failure. ¶ 〜をする mash the *miso.* すっかり〜をつけてしまった I *made a* fine *mess of it.* そこが彼の〜だ That's *the point* he wants to make. そんなに彼のことをくそ〜に言うな Don't *speak so meanly of* (≒ *abuse*) him. 彼らは〜もくそもいっしょにしている They are mixing up *good things and bad.*

みぞ【溝】 (堀) a ditch; (下水) a drain; a gutter; (敷居などの) a groove; (隔たり) a gulf; a gap. ¶ 〜を掘る dig *a ditch.* ふたりの間に〜ができた They *were estranged* from each other. その結果両国の間に深い〜ができた As a result, *a* deep *gulf* was formed between the two nations.

みぞう【未曾有】 ¶ 50年前関東地方は〜の大地震に見舞われた Fifty years ago, a *record* earthquake shook the Kanto districts. (この record は名詞からの転用だからアクセントは第1音節にある). (第2次) 大戦後の日本は歴史上〜の変貌(へんぼう)を遂げた The postwar Japan has undergone a transfiguration *unprecedented* (≒ *unparalleled*) in her history.

みぞおち【鳩尾】 ⇒みずおち

みそか【三十日】 the last day of the month.

みそぎ【禊】 a purification ceremony; a ceremonial ablution.

みそこない【見損い】 a mistake; misjudgment. ¶ 〜もはなはだしい You have made too glaring *a misjudgment.*

みそこな·う【見損なう】 misjudge; make a mistake. ¶ その映画は〜った To my regret I *missed* 〔*seeing*〕 the movie. きみを〜っていた I have *made a mistake* in my estimate of you. / I *am disappointed* in you.

みそさざい【鷦鷯】〖鳥類〗a Japanese wren.

みそしき【未組織】 ¶ 〜の unorganized. 〜労働者 *unorganized* (≒ *non-unionized*) workers (≒ labor).

みそしる【味噌汁】 *miso* soup.

みそっかす【味噌っ滓】 a useless person; a greenhorn.

みそっぱ【味噌っ歯】 a decayed tooth.

みそ·める【見初める】 ¶ 彼が彼女をどのようにして〜めたかはだれも知らない Nobody knows how he *fell in love with* her 〔at first sight〕.

みぞれ【霙】 sleet. ¶ 〜が降る It *sleets.*

みそ·れる【見それる】 ¶ あわてていてついお〜れしてしまいました Pardon me for *not recognizing you*; I have been in such a hurry.

-みたい ¶ 1月だというのにきょうはまるで春〜だ It's really spring-*like* today, though it's still January. あんなことをしている彼を見るとほんとうに気違い〜だ Should you see him doing such a thing, you would think him crazy. (文語体). / He *looks like* mad, doing such a thing. 夢〜な話でとても信じられない It's such a dream*like* story that I can't believe it.

みだし【見出し】 a title; (新聞の) a headline. ¶ 書物の〜 a caption. 本に〜をつける *index* a book. **—語** a head word.

みだしなみ【身嗜み】 ¶ 一般にイギリス人は〜がいい Generally speaking, an Englishman is careful about his *personal appearance.* 年ごろの娘は〜に注意すること Young and nubile girls should *keep themselves neat.*

みた·す【満たす】 ¶ その地位は彼の名誉心を〜してくれた That post *gratified* (≒ *satiated*) his love of honor. グラスにウイスキーを〜した I *filled* a glass with whisky.

みだ·す【乱す】 disturb; stir; (心を) distract. ¶ 平和を〜す者は社会の敵だ Those who *disturb* the peace of society are our enemy. 子どもたちに絶対に列を〜さないように注意すること See 〔to it〕 that the children don't *break* the line. そんなものに心を〜されるようではまだ修業が足りない You are not sufficiently trained yet to *have* your mind *distracted* by such a thing. 彼女は髪を〜して飛び込んできた She rushed in with *disheveled* hair.

みたて【見立て】 (鑑定) judgment; (選択) selection; choice; (診断) a diagnosis. ¶ 画家だけにさすがに彼はネクタイの〜がいい Artist as he is, his *choice* of ties is excellent. 医者の〜では五分五分だ According to the doctor's *diagnosis,* the chances are even (≒ fifty-fifty). 医者が〜違いをした The doctor made *a* wrong *diagnosis.*

みた·てる【見立てる】 ¶ 医者は彼の病気を全治2か月と〜てた The doctor *diagnosed* that he would be recovered completely in two months. 彼は服装には気難しいから人の〜てた柄はたいてい気に入らない He is very particular about his dress, so he is usually dissatisfied with a pattern *selected* by others.

みたところ【見たところ】apparently ; seemingly. ¶ ～彼は疲れきっていた He was *apparently* tired out. ちょっと～では川魚だ *At first glance* it is a river fish. 彼は～その結果に満足していた He was *seemingly* satisfied with the result.

みたま【御霊】the spirit of the dead ; *one's* departed soul.

みため【見た目】¶ 彼は～には人づきあいが悪そうだが,実際は社交的だ He does not *look* sociable, but in reality he is 〔sociable〕.

みだら【淫ら・猥ら】¶ ～な女 a *loose* (≒ *wanton ; lewd*) woman. ～な物語 a *bawdy* (≒ *obscene*) story. 彼はいつも～なことばかり言う He always says *improper* (≒ *indecent*) things.

みだりに【妄りに・濫りに】(むやみに) at random ; (無許可で) without permission. ¶ ～他人のことに干渉するな Don't interfere with others *unreasonably* (≒ *without good reasons*).

みだれ【乱れ】disorder. ¶ 世の～は悪い政治から生まれる Public *disturbance* results from irresponsible government. 服装の～は心の～だといえよう It may be said that *disorder* of one's dress is that of one's mind.

みだれがみ【乱れ髪】unkempt hair ; disheveled hair.

みだ・れる【乱れる】¶ 心の～れているときはなにをやってもだめだ One is sure to fail in anything when *disturbed* in mind. 彼の部屋はいつでも～れている His room *is* always *in disorder* (≒ *is* always *in confusion*). 夫婦仲が悪ければ家庭はおのずから～れる Man and wife who don't love each other find their home *demoralized*. ～れた国家財政を立て直すことが彼の仕事だった His duty was to re-establish the national economy which *was in bad shape*. 盛り場はとかく風紀が～れる Public morals of amusement quarters are apt to *be lax* (≒ *be sadly decayed ; be corrupt*). 髪が～れないようにヘアネットを使う use a hairnet so that *one's* hair *is* not *disheveled*.

みち【道・路・途】**1**〖道路〗a road ; a way ; a street. ¶ 駅へ行く～を聞かれた I was asked the *way* to the station.

この～をまっすぐ行くと公園に出る Go straight along this *street*, and you will find the park.

途中～が込んで思わぬ時間がかかった It took more time than I expected, because the *road* was crowded on the way.

どうやら～をまちがえたらしい I am afraid I have taken the *wrong way*.

山で～に迷うとたいへんなことになる It will be dangerous if you *lose your way* in the mountains.

彼らは～なき～を進んでいった They went along the trackless *path*.

すべての～はローマに通ず(諺) *All roads lead to Rome*.

2〖距離・道程〗¶ 1日に50キロの～を歩くのは楽ではない It is not easy to *cover* (≒ *walk*) fifty kilometers in a day.

きのうは～がはかどらなかった I couldn't make a good going yesterday.

3〖途中〗¶ 家へ帰る～で彼に出会った *On my way home* I happened to meet him.

学校へ行く～で万年筆を落としたらしい I'm afraid I lost my pen *on my way to* school.

4〖進路・方法〗¶ 彼は最も安全な～を選んだ He chose the safest *course* (≒ *way*).

彼は後進に～を開くため勇退した He retired voluntarily to *make way for* younger people (≒ to *give* younger people *chances*).

成功への～は険しい The *path* to success is steep.

われわれに残された～は一つだけだ There is only one *way* left to us.

5〖正道〗¶ 彼は～ならぬ恋に夢中だ He is infatuated with *illicit* love.

私はきみに～を説く資格はない I am not qualified to preach about *the right way of life* to you.

どうしてそんな～にはずれたことをしたのか Why did you do such a crooked thing?

6〖専門・分野〗¶ 彼はその～ではかなり有名だ He is quite a famous man *in that field*.

その～の人に聞いてみなさい Go and seek *expert* views on the matter.

みち【未知】¶ ～の世界 the *unknown* world. ～の人 a stranger ; an *unknown* person.

みちあんない【道案内】guidance ; (人) a guide.

¶ 人に～をする show *a person* the way. 彼の～のおかげで楽しい旅行をした Thanks to his *guidance*, we could enjoy our trip.

みぢか【身近】¶ その事件以来彼を～な人と感じるようになった Since the event I have come to feel him to *be close* (≒ *be familiar*) *to* me. 危険が～に迫らないと人は立てないものだ One will not be up and doing unless the danger *is imminent* (≒ *is impending*).

みちが・える【見違える】¶ 彼を弟さんと～えた I *took* him *for* his brother. 10年にわたるヨーロッパ滞在で彼は～えるほど変わった His ten-year staying in Europe has changed him *beyond recognition*. 彼女は～えるほどきれいになった I can hardly recognize her ; she has become so beautiful. 高層ビルの出現で駅前もすっかり～えるようになった The appearance of high-rise buildings has given *quite a different* air to the depot street.

みちくさ【道草】¶ ～を食う loiter on the way ; hang about. ～を食わずに帰る go straight home.

みちしお【満ち潮】the high tide.

みちじゅん【道順】a route ; a road. ¶ 美術館までの～を教えてあげましょうか Shall I tell you the *way* to the museum? どんな～がいいでしょうか Which *route* shall we follow?

みちしるべ【道標】a guidepost ; a signpost ; (手引き) a guide.

みちすう【未知数】〖数学〗an unknown quantity. ¶ 新内閣の実力は～だ The ability of the New Cabinet *is yet to be known*.

みちすじ【道筋】a route ; a course. ¶ 大小の旅館が～にひしめいて建っている Hotels of various sizes are crowded together along the *route*. / Hotels of various sizes line the *street*.

みちた·りる【満ち足りる】¶ 物質的にはどうにか～りた生活をしている Materially I manage to live a *full* (≒ *satisfying*) life.

みちづれ【道連れ】a fellow traveler. ¶ 彼のようなすばらしい～はそうざらにはいない Such *a* good *traveling companion* as he is quite rare. 旅は～世は情け (諺) In traveling good company, in life good will.

みちならし【道均し】road leveling. ¶ ブルドーザーで～をすればわけはない With a bulldozer, *road-leveling* is quite easy.

みちのり【道程】〔a〕distance. ¶ ～はたいしたことはない It's not *a* great *distance*. 東京から大阪までの～はいかほどか *How far* is it from Tokyo to Osaka?

みちばた【道端】a roadside.

みちひ【満ち干】ebb and flow ; rise and fall.

みちびき【導き】guidance.

みちび·く【導く】¶ 私は応接間に～かれた I *was shown* (≒ *was ushered*) *into* the drawing room. 生徒を～くということはなまやさしいことではない It's no easy matter to *guide* students. 頑迷(がんめい)な指導者は民族を破滅に～く Bigoted leaders are liable to *lead* the country to destruction.

みちぶしん【道普請】road repair.

みちみち【道道】all the way ; on the way. ¶ ～彼女が聞かせてくれた話はまことにあわれな物語だった The story she told me *as we went along* was so sad. ～話しましょう Let me tell you *as we go* 〔*along*〕.

みちゃく【未着】¶ 品物は～だ The goods *are not delivered yet*.

み·ちる【満ちる】**1**〖月や潮が〗¶ 潮が～ちてくるまで待ちましょう Let's wait till the tide *rises*. 月は～ちたり欠けたりする The moon becomes *full* and wanes.

2〖充満する〗¶ だれもがロマンの香りに～ちたメロディーに魅せられた Everybody was fascinated by the melody *imbued with* romantic flavor. / Everybody was fascinated by the romantic melody.

夏山の登山は依然として危険に～ちている Mountain climbing in summer *is* still *full of* danger.

みつ【密】¶ 今後彼との連絡をますます～にする必要がある It is necessary to *get in closer touch with* him. はかりごとは～なるをもってよしとする *Secrecy* is essential to strategy. 人口の～な地方 a *densely populated* district.

みつ【蜜】honey ; (花の) nectar. ¶ ミツバチは～を吸うために花から花へ飛ぶ Bees fly from flower to flower to suck *honey*. 新婚のふたりには毎日が～のごとく甘い Being newly married, they find every day sweet like *honey*.

みつうん【密雲】dense (≒ thick) clouds.

みっか【三日】¶ 彼は～にあげず彼女の家に来る He comes to see her *at frequent intervals* (≒ *frequently*).

—天下 a three-day reign. **—**坊主 ¶ ～坊主では成功は望めぬ One who can stick to nothing succeeds in nothing. (形式ばった文体).

みっかい【密会】a secret meeting. ¶ ～する have *a secret meeting*.

みつか·る【見つかる】¶ なにか変わったものが～りましたか Did you *find* anything strange? 彼は先週酔っ払い運転しているところを～った Last week he *was caught* in the act of drunken driving. だれにも～らずに裏門から出た I passed the back door *unnoticed* (≒ *unobserved*). じょうずに変装すれば簡単には～らないでしょう With a good disguise, you may not *be recognized* so easily. なくなった傘が1週間後に～った I *found* my lost umbrella a week afterward.

みつぎ【密議】a private (≒ secret) conference.

みつぎもの【貢ぎ物】a tribute.

みっきょう【密教】〖仏教〗esoteric Buddhism.

みつ·ぐ【貢ぐ】¶ 彼が学生時代に生活費と学費を～いでくれた He *supplied* me *with* my living and school expenses during my school life.

ミックス mixture. ¶ ～する mix.

みつくち【三つ口·兎唇】a harelip.

みづくろい【身繕い】dressing.

みつくろ·う【見繕う】¶ なにか新家庭にふさわしいものを～ってください Please *select* something suitable for a newly-married couple.

みっけい【密計】an intrigue ; a plot. ¶ ～をめぐらす plot *secretly*.

みつげつ【蜜月】a honeymoon.

—旅行 a honeymoon trip.

みつ·ける【見つける】¶ 警官は人ごみの中に犯人を～けた(発見した) The policeman *detected* the criminal in the crowd. 彼女は人の欠点を～けるのが早い She is quick in *finding fault with* others. ふだん～けている (見なれている) から別段すばらしいとは思わない I do not think it particularly wonderful, because I *am accustomed to seeing* it.

みつご【三つ子】**1**〖三生児〗triplets.

2〖3歳の子·幼い子〗¶ そんな簡単なことは～でも知っている Even *a child* knows such a simple thing.

～の魂百まで (諺) *The child is father of the man.*

みっこう【密航】a secret passage. ¶ 彼は～を決行したが失敗した He *stowed away to escape the country*, but in vain.

—者 a stowaway. **—**船 a smuggler.

みっこく【密告】〔secret〕information (information に直接不定冠詞がつくことはない). ¶ 警察への～がなかったらそう簡単にはつかまらなかっただろう Without *secret information against* him, the police could not have caught him so easily. 警察に～する *inform* the police *se-*

cretly. 友人を～する *inform against one's* friend.

—者 an informant ; a betrayer.

みっし【密使】an emissary ; a confidential agent.

みっしつ【密室】a secret room. ¶ ～での会議は夜通し続けられた The meeting held *behind closed doors* continued throughout the night.

—恐怖 claustrophobia.

みっしゅう【密集】¶ この辺りには大小さまざまの家が～している In this neighborhood houses of varying sizes *stand close together.* 汚染は人の～する所にはつきものだ Pollution is inseparable from the place where people *crowd* (≒ *swarm ; cluster*).

みっしょ【密書】a secret letter.

ミッションスクール a Christian school ; a mission school ; a school run by Christians.

みっしり〔と〕(熱心に) hard ; earnestly ; (きびしく) severely. ¶ 練習を～やらないと実力はつかない We can cultivate our ability only through a *severe* training. 子どもを～しかることもときには薬になる It will sometimes do your children good to give them a *good* scolding. 庭には雑草が～茂っていた Weeds grew *rank* all over the garden.

みっせい【密生】¶ このあたりは樹木が～している Trees *have grown thick* (≒ *have grown in cluster*) in this region.

みっせつ【密接】¶ 英米はいろいろな点で互いに～な関係がある In many respects Britain and America *are closely related* (≒ *bound up ; connected*) *with* each other. 日本はアメリカと戦後特に～な関係を結ぶに至った Japan has come into *close* relation with America especially since the end of the war.

みつぞう【密造】illicit manufacture. ¶ 酒を～する brew *sake* secretly (≒ illicitly).

—者 a moonshiner ; a home-brewer. —酒 moonshine.

みつぞろい【三つ揃い】¶ 洋服の～ a suit of clothes (a coat, vest and trousers (上着とチョッキとズボン) を三つ揃いと言う).

みつだん【密談】a secret conversation ; a confidential talk. ¶ ～する talk privately ; have a confidential talk.

みっちゃく【密着】¶ よく～しているので, はがすことはできない They *have stuck together* too well to be torn off.

—焼き付け〔写真〕contact printing.

みっちり ⇒ みっしり

みっつう【密通】adultery ; misconduct.

みってい【密偵】a spy ; a secret agent. ¶ 情報を得るため～が放たれた Some *spies* were sent out for getting informations.

ミット a mitt.

みつど【密度】density. ¶ 人口～では日本は世界有数である As to the population *density* Japan occupies a very high place in the world.

—計 a densimeter.

みつどもえ【三つ巴】¶ ～の混戦からだれがリードするかはまったく予測できない There is no forecasting who will take the lead of the present *triangular* (≒ *triple*) *struggle.*

みっともな･い ¶ なんという～いふるまいだ What an *indecent* (≒ a *scandalous* ; a *shameful* ; an *outrageous*) behavior ! その服は流行おくれで～い The dress *is* too outmoded and *shabby.*

みつにゅうこく【密入国】smuggling. ¶ 彼らは～を企てて失敗した They plotted *smuggling* but failed.

—者 a stowaway ; a smuggler.

みつば【三つ葉】〘植物〙a trefoil.

みつばい【密売】an illicit sale (≒ trade). ¶ 麻薬を～する *deal secretly in* drugs ; *sell* drugs *in secret.*

—者 a secret trader. —品 smuggled goods.

みつばち【蜜蜂】〘虫類〙a 〔honey〕bee. ¶ ～の巣 (箱) a beehive.

みっぷう【密封】¶ 手紙を～する *seal*〔*up*〕a letter. ジャムのびんを～する *seal* a jar of jam ; *make* a jar of jam *airtight.*

みっぺい【密閉】¶ ～した容器 an *airtight* vessel. ～した部屋 a *tightly-closed* room. せんべいが長く保存できるようにかんを～しておきなさい *Leave* the tin box *closed* so that the rice-cake will keep long.

みつぼう【密謀】an intrigue. ¶ 政治の～ political *intrigues.*

みつぼう【蜜房】a cell.

みつぼうえき【密貿易】smuggling. ¶ ～で金を日本に入れる *smuggle* gold *into* Japan.

みつまた【三つ叉】a three-pronged fork ; a trident. ¶ ～の道 a *three-pronged* road.

みつ･める【見詰める】¶ 彼女は私の顔をじっと～めた She *watched* my face intently. / She *stared* intently (≒ *gazed* intently ; *looked* hard) *at* me. 彼は彼女の顔を～めつづけていた He *kept his eye on* her face. 彼は彼女をしげしげと～めた He *studied* her closely.

みつもり【見積もり･見積】an estimate (*for*).

—書 an estimate ; a written estimate.

みつも･る【見積もる】¶ その会社は新築家屋を500万円と～った The firm *estimated* (≒ *calculated*) the cost of the new house at five million yen. 売り上げを過大に (過小に) ～った We *overestimated* (*underestimated*) the takings. / We *estimated* (≒ *rated*) the takings high (low). どんなに安く～っても100万円はかかる It will cost a million yen *at the lowest estimate.*

みつやく【密約】a secret treaty. ¶ 政府はその国と～を結んだ The Government entered into *a secret treaty* with the country. 両者には～がある They have *a secret understanding* with each other.

みつゆしゅつ【密輸出】smuggling abroad. ¶ 大麻を～する *smuggle* hemp *abroad* ; *smuggle out* hemp ; *smuggle* hemp *out of* *the country.*

みつゆにゅう【密輸入】smuggling. ¶マリファナを～する *smuggle* marijuana *into the country*; *smuggle in* marijuana; *import* marijuana *secretly into the country.*

―品 smuggled goods.

みつりょう【密猟・密漁】poaching. ¶保護鳥を～する *poach* protected birds. サケを～する *poach* salmon.

―者 a poacher. ―船 a poaching boat.

みつりん【密林】a dense (≒ thick) forest; a jungle.

みてい【未定】¶計画は～だ The plan *is unsettled.* / The plan *remains to be seen.* / The plan *is* yet *to be decided.* 会議の日取りは～だ The date of the conference *is not yet fixed.*

みてくれ【見てくれ】¶～のよくない女 a *plain* (≒ a *bad-looking*; an *ill-favored*) woman (a homely woman は醜い容貌を婉曲に表わしたもの). この家具は～がいい This furniture *looks nice.*

みてと・る【見て取る】¶彼はなにが起こったかをすぐ～った He at once *realized* what had happened. 彼女はすぐ相手の言わんとする趣旨を～った She at once *saw* his drift.

みとう【未踏】¶人跡～のジャングル an *untrodden* jungle. 前人～の森林 a *virgin* forest.

みとおし【見通し】(視野) visibility; (予見) a prospect; (洞察) 〔an〕 insight. ¶～のきく(悪い)場所 a place where *visibility* is good (bad). 塔に上れば村の～がきく From the tower we *have an unobstructed view of* (≒ *can command*) the village. 将来の～が立たない I cannot *forecast* the future. 成功の～はまったく立たない There is no *prospect* of success. 将来の～は明るかった The *prospects* all seemed good. 明るい～はまったく立たなかった We saw no hope anywhere.

みとお・す【見通す】¶彼の部屋の窓がここからはっきり～せる The window of his room *is* plainly *visible* from here.

みとが・める【見咎める】¶～められずに逃げる escape *undetected.* ～められずに家を出る get out of a house *unobserved* (≒ *unnoticed*).

みどく【味読】¶古典を～する *read* classics *with appreciation*; *enjoy* classics.

みどころ【見所】(取り柄) a good point; (興味のある点) the high light. ¶～のある若者 a *promising* (≒ *likely*) young man. 最後の場面は一つの～だ The last scene is a point *worthy of note.*

みとど・ける【見届ける】¶なにも起こらなかったかどうか～けに行った I went there to *ascertain* (≒ *make sure*) that nothing had happened. 彼がその部屋に忍び込むのを私はこの目で～けた I *saw* him steal into the room with my own eyes.

みとめ【認め】(認め印) a private seal; a signet.

みと・める【認める】**1**〖見る〗¶彼の姿はどこにも～められなかった He was nowhere to *be seen.* 彼の顔にかすかに皮肉な表情が浮かぶのを私は～めた I *perceived* a faintly cynical expression on his face.

2〖承認する・認定する〗¶彼はその計画が不適当であることを～めた He *admitted* that the plan was unsuitable. 彼は敗北を～めた He *accepted* defeat. 彼はその計画を～めない He does not *approve of* the plan. 彼女はすぐれた画家として～められている She *is recognized* as a good artist. 彼らは彼の仕事を～めるようになった They have come to *appreciate* his work. それを事実として～めなくてはならない We have to *acknowledge* it as a fact. 彼はきみが～めているよりもっと独創性に富んでいる He has more ingenuity than you *give* him *credit for.* 医者は彼女に異常は～められないと言った The doctor told her that she was all right. 彼は有罪を～めた He *pleaded* guilty. / He *admitted* that he was guilty.

みどり【緑】green. ¶～がかった黄色 *greenish* yellow. 山々は～の草木でおおわれている The mountains are covered with *green* (≒ *verdure*). ～の週間 Arbor Week. ～したたる山々 the mountains in fresh *verdure.*

みとりず【見取り図】a sketch.

みと・る【看取る】¶病人を～る(看護する) *nurse* (≒ *take care of*) a patient.

ミドルきゅう【ミドル級】the middleweight.

―選手 a middleweight. ―選手権 a middleweight championship.

みと・れる【見とれる】¶彼女の美しさに～れた I *was fascinated* (≒ *was charmed*) by her beauty. / I *was lost in admiration of* her beauty. 私はその景色に～れた I *admired* (≒ *gazed at*) the scenery *in rapture.*

みな【皆】all; everybody. ¶彼らは～同意した They *all* agreed. ～が車を持っているわけではない Not *everybody* has a car. ～で100名の出席者があった There were a hundred attendants *in all* (≒ *all told*). ～で1万円払った *Altogether* I paid ten thousand yen. ～で一団となってそこに行った They went there *in a body.* ～私が悪いのです It's *only* I who am to blame.

みなお・す【見直す】¶彼は辺りを～した He *looked* round him *again* (≒ *twice*). そのリストを～した I *looked over* the list *again.* 彼の行為で彼を～した His conduct *led* me to *have a better opinion of* him.

みなかみ【水上】(川の上流) the upper 〔reaches of the〕 stream; (川の源流・上流) headwaters; (川の源) the source of a river.

みなぎ・る【漲る】¶彼には活力が～っている He *is full of* vitality. 彼の目には歓喜の光が～っていた His eyes *were suffused with* rapture. 部屋には不穏な空気が～っていた The air of unrest *pervaded* the room.

みなげ【身投げ】drowning *oneself*; (人) a drowned person. ¶湖に～する *drown one-*

self in a lake ; *throw oneself into* a lake.

みなごろし【皆殺し】 extermination. ¶ 彼らは〜になった They *were all killed* (⇆ *were murdered* ; *were wiped out*). 軍隊は〜になった The army *was annihilated*. ネズミは〜になった The rats *were exterminated*.

みなしご【孤児】 an orphan. ¶ 彼女は5歳のとき〜になった She was left *an orphan* when she was five.

みな·す【見做す】 ¶ 彼は財政の権威と〜されている He *is looked upon as* (⇆ *is regarded as* ; *is considered to be*) an authority on finance. 彼は権利を放棄したものと〜された He *was considered to* have renounced his right.

みなと【港】 a harbor ; a port. ¶ 2隻の客船が〜に着いた(停泊している) Two passenger boats reached *port* (are at anchor in the *harbor*). その観光船は20の〜に寄港する The sightseeing boat calls at twenty *ports*.

—町 a port town. ¶ 〜町神戸 the *port* of Kobe.

みなみ【南】 the south. ¶ 東京から約30マイル〜 some thirty miles *south* of Tokyo. 家の〜側 the *southern* side (⇆ aspect) of a house. 〜の方向に進む proceed *south* ; proceed in the *souther*[*n*]*ly* direction. 横浜は東京の〜にある Yokohama is *to the south of* Tokyo. (両者が離れている場合に限る ; 距離を示せば to the を省き第1例のようになる). 〜の方に航海する sail *southward*. 船は真〜に向かって航行している The ship is sailing due *south*. 〜向きの日当たりのよい部屋 a sunny room facing *south*.

—アメリカ South America. **—風** a south wind. **—十字星** the Southern Cross. **—太平洋** the South Pacific.

みなもと【源】 (水源) the source ; the fountainhead ; (根源) the origin ; the source.
¶ 川の〜 *the source* of a river ; the headspring. この川の〜はあの山脈の中にある This river *rises* (⇆ *has its source*) among the mountains. 事件の〜にさかのぼる trace an event to *the origin*.

みならい【見習い】 apprenticeship ; (徒弟) an apprentice. ¶ 彼は3年間〜として働いた He served as *an apprentice* for three years. 彼は床屋の〜となった He *apprenticed himself* (⇆ *was apprenticed*) *to* a barber. 彼は〜を終えた He has served his full *apprenticeship*. 彼は〜中だ He *is on probation*.

—期間 the period of apprenticeship. **—工** an apprentice. **—士官** a cadet. **—生** a trainee ; an apprentice student.

みなら·う【見習う】 ¶ 先生を〜う *follow the example of one's* teacher ; *take example by one's* teacher. 商売を〜う *learn* a trade.

みなり【身なり】 appearance ; clothing. ¶ 〜のよい若者 a *well dressed* young man. 彼は〜がよい He *is well dressed*. 彼はいつも〜がきちんとしている He *is* always *neatly dressed*. 彼女はスマートなスーツを着て, 〜がよくあかぬけしていた She was *neat* and chic in her smart suit. 彼女は〜をかまわない She is careless about her *appearance*.

みな·れる【見慣れる】 ¶ 〜れた顔 a *familiar* face. 私がまったく〜れてない顔 a face entirely *strange to* me. 〜れない人が何人かいる There are a few *strangers* here. その光景は子どものときから〜れている I *have been accustomed to* the scenery since I was a child.

ミニアチュア a miniature. ¶ ジェット機の〜 *a miniature* jet plane.

ミニカー a minicar.

みにく·い【見悪い】 ¶ 〜い筆跡 *illegible* handwriting. その木はわが家からは〜い It is *difficult to see* the tree from my house. この鏡は〜い This mirror *is dull*.

みにく·い【醜い】 (容貌が) plain ; ugly ; (不名誉な) ignominious. ¶ 〜い顔 an *ugly* face (会話では ugly はなるべく避けて homely-looking などとする). 眼鏡を取れば彼女はそんなに〜くない Without spectacles she *is* not so *plain*. 私は〜い争いに巻き込まれたくない I don't like to be dragged into a *scandalous* (⇆ an *unpleasant*) quarrel.

ミニスカート a mini-skirt.

みぬ·く【見抜く】 ¶ すばやく計略を〜いた I *saw through* the trick at once. 彼女は賢い女性でじきに私の人物を〜いた She was a shrewd girl and soon *took my measure*.

みね【峰】 the ridge ; a peak. ¶ 山の〜 a peak ; a summit. 〜をきわめる get to the *top* of a mountain. 刀の〜 *the back* [of a sword].

みねうち【峰打ち】 ¶ 〜にする strike (*a person*) with the back of *one's* sword.

ミネラル a mineral.

—ウオーター mineral water.

みの【蓑】 a straw raincoat.

みのう【未納】 ¶ 〜の税金(家賃) *arrears* of taxes (rent). 彼は授業料〜だ He *has not yet paid* his tuition fees. 彼は税金〜だ His taxes *are in arrears*.

—額 the amount in arrears. **—者** a person in arrears ; a defaulter.

みのうえ【身の上】 **1**〚運勢〛 *one's* fortune.
¶ 占い師に〜を判断してもらう have *one's fortune* told by a fortuneteller.

2〚境遇〛 ¶ カウンセラーに〜相談をする consult with a counselor about *one's personal affairs*.

安楽な〜の人間 a man in easy (⇆ good) *circumstances*.

今の〜ではやりたいこともできない *In my present condition*, I can't do what[ever] I want to do.

3〚閲歴〛 ¶ 彼女は〜いっさいを私に語った She told the whole story of her *life* to me. / She told me all about *herself*.

彼のこれまでの〜について私はほとんどなにも知らない I know very little of his previous *history*.

—相談欄 a home council column. **—話** the story of *one's* life.

みのが·す【見逃す】 **1**〚見落とす〛 ¶ 彼女はその事

み

実を～した She *let escape* the fact. 彼女はそのドラマを～した She *missed* the drama. そんなチャンスを～してはならない We must not *overlook* (≒ *pass over*) such a chance. 彼の姿を雑沓の中に～した I *lost sight of* his figure in the crowd. 誤植を～した I *overlooked* some printer's errors.

2 〖黙認する〗 ¶ 悪徳警官はその犯罪に目をつぶって～した The corrupted policeman *connived at* the crime.

3 〖野球〗 ¶ 好球を～す *miss* a nice ball.

みのけ 【身の毛】 ¶ ～のよだつような話 a *hair-raising* (≒ *blood-curdling*) story. 恐ろしさのあまり～がよだった My *hair stood on end* with fright. それは～がよだつような光景だった The horrible sight *made my hair stand on end.*

みのこ･す 【見残す】 ¶ 最後のイニングを～して野球場を出た I left the stadium *without seeing* the last inning.

みのしろきん 【身の代金】 a ransom 〔money〕. ¶ 彼は5,000万円の～を要求された He had *a* fifty-million-yen *ransom* demand.

みのたけ 【身の丈】 height. ¶ 彼は～が6フィートある He *is* six feet *tall* (≒ *in height*). / He *stands* six feet.

みのほど 【身の程】 ¶ ～を知りなさい You must know your *place*. 彼に～を知らせよう We must keep him in his *place*. 彼は～をわきまえずに振る舞う He acts with no regard for his *social standing*.

みのまわり 【身の回り】 ¶ ～の物 *one's* belongings. 彼には～の世話をやいてくれる人間が必要だ He needs someone who *takes care of* him. あの政治家は～が清潔だ That statesman is pure and honest.

みのむし 【蓑虫】 〖虫類〗 a bagworm.

みのり 【実り】 a crop ; a harvest. ¶ ～の秋 the *harvest* season. ことしの～は悪かった We have had *a* bad *harvest* this year.

みの･る 【実る】 (熟す) ripen ; (実がなる) bear fruit. ¶ 稲が～りはじめた The rice began to *ripen*. 桃の木が～りはじめた The tree began to *bear* peaches. 彼の努力がやっと～った At last his efforts *bore fruit* (≒ *were crowned with success*).

みば 【見ば】 ¶ ～が悪い It's bad *in appearance*. / It doesn't *look* well. / It *looks* awkward.

みばえ 【見栄え】 ¶ ～のする attractive ; nice-looking. ～のしない unattractive ; poor-looking. 彼女は絹のドレスを着ると～がする She *looks well* in a silk dress. / A silk dress *sets off her charm* (≒ *sets her figure off to advantage*).

みはからい 【見計らい】 discretion ; judgment. ¶ ～でやってください I leave it to your *discretion*. / It is within your *discretion*. / It is left to your *judgment*.

みはから･う 【見計らう】 ¶ ～って土産品を買ってください Buy some souvenirs *at your own discretion*. 彼はころあいを～って出ていった He went out *at the proper time*.

みはつ 【未発】 ¶ 暴動を～に防ぐ *prevent* a riot ; *nip* a riot *in the bud*.

みはっぴょう 【未発表】 ¶ ～の作品 a work *not yet published* ; an *unpublished* work.

みはてぬ 【見果てぬ】 ¶ ～夢 an *unfinished* dream.

みはな･す 【見放す】 ¶ 彼女は医者に～された The doctor *has given* her *up*. 彼は多くの友に～された Many friends *turned their back on* him. 私はついに両親に～された At last I *was abandoned* (≒ *was forsaken* ; *was deserted*) by my parents.

みはば 【身幅】 the width of a dress.

みはらい 【未払い】 ¶ 勘定を～のままで with *one's* bill *unpaid* (≒ *unsettled*).

—勘定 an outstanding account. **—金** an amount not yet paid.

みはらし 【見晴らし】 a view ; a prospect. ¶ 丘の上からの海の～はすばらしい From the top of the hill we *have a* splendid *view of* the sea. / The hill *has a* fine *lookout over* the sea. / The hill *commands a* fine *view of* the sea. / The *prospect* from the hill top is striking. ～のよい部屋 a room with *a* beautiful *outlook*.

みはら･す 【見晴らす】 ¶ その部屋から海を～すことができる The room *overlooks* the sea. その窓から入り江を～すことができる The window *opens out upon* the inlet. 丘の上から町のすばらしい景色を～すことができる The hill *commands* a fine view of the city.

みはり 【見張り】 watch ; lookout ; (人) a guard ; a watchman. ¶ 入り口に～を立てた We placed *a guard* at the entrance. あの男に～をつけなくてはならない We must set *a watch* on him. 強盗に対する～をおこたるな Keep *a* sharp *lookout* for robbers. たえず～を続けるつもりだ We are going to *be on the watch* all the time.

—所 a lookout ; a watch house.

みは･る 【見張る】 ¶ 荷物を～っていてください Will you *watch* my baggage? 敵を～っていなくてはならぬ We must *keep watch over* the enemy. 彼は驚いて目を～った He *stared* in wonder. / His eyes *opened wide* in wonder.

みびいき 【身贔屓】 favoritism to *one's* relatives ; nepotism. ¶ 縁者に～する *be partial* (≒ *show favoritism*) *to one's* relatives.

みひらき 【見開き】 ¶ ～のグラビアページ a gravure picture *on two facing pages*.

みひら･く 【見開く】 ¶ 彼はびっくりして目を～いた He *opened* his eyes wide in surprise. / His eyes *opened wide* in surprise.

みぶり 【身振り】 a gesture ; gesticulation. ¶ 彼は絶望の～をした He made *a gesture* of despair. / He *gestured* in despair. 彼女は彼に～でついてらっしゃいといった She *motioned* him *to* follow. 彼らの会話は～たっぷりで行なわれた

Their conversation was carried on with much *gesticulation*.

みぶるい【身震い】a shudder; a shiver. ¶ 彼はその恐ろしい光景を見て～した He *shuddered at* the horrible sight. 彼は寒さで～した He *shivered* (≒ *shuddered*) *with* cold. ～がした *A shiver* went through me. 夜の寒い空気の中で～した I *trembled* in the cold night air. ～するような(恐ろしい)光景 a *frightful* (≒ *terrible*; *horrible*; *shocking*) sight.

みぶん【身分】(地位) a position; a station; (資力) means; (素姓) birth; origin. ¶ ～のある人 a man *of position*; a man *of high standing*. 彼は～のよい家の出だ He comes from a *good* family. 彼はきみよりずっと～が高い(低い) He is much above (below) you in *station*. ここではきみの～を保証する We guarantee your *status* here. 彼がどんな～の人か私はよく知らない I am uncertain of his *status*. ～相応に暮らしなさい You must live within your *means*. 彼は～を隠して旅をした He traveled *incognito*. (文語体).

―証明書 an identification card.

みぼうじん【未亡人】a widow. ¶ A氏の～ the wife of late Mr. A. 彼女は～になった She *lost her husband*. / She *was bereaved of her husband*. (文語体).

戦争**―** a war widow.

みほん【見本】(商品の) a sample; (本の) a sample copy. ¶ これは～どおりだ This is up to (≒ corresponds with) the *samples*. 彼は勤勉さの～だ He is *a model* of industry. これは現代詩のよい～だ This is *a* good *example* of modern poetry.

―市 a trade fair. **―**帳 a sample book; a pattern book. **―**売買 sale by sample.

みまい【見舞い・見舞】(病気の) an inquiry after a sick person; (事故・死亡の) an expression of *one's* sympathy.

¶ 彼を病院に～に行くところだ I am going to *visit* him at the hospital. 彼は罹災(りさい)者に心からの～のことばを述べた He expressed his hearty *sympathy* to the sufferers.

―客 a visitor; an inquirer. **―**金(慰謝料) a solatium; a present of money. ¶ 罹災者のための～金を募った We collected *money for the victims*. **―**状 a letter of inquiry; a letter of sympathy. **―**品 a present; a relief goods. 火事**―** an inquiry on the occasion of a fire. 暑中**―** (の手紙) a letter of inquiry in the hot season (この習慣は英米にはないからわかりにくい).

みま・う【見舞う】**1** 〚病気を〛 visit (a sick person). ¶ 病人を～った We went to *visit* (≒ *call on*) the patient.

2 〚襲う〛 ¶ その船はあらしに～われた The ship *was struck* by a storm.

一家は災難に～われた Disaster *overtook* the family.

みまちがい【見間違い】misperception. ¶ それは彼の筆跡であることに～はない It is *unmistakably* his handwriting.

みまちが・える【見間違える】¶ 雲を山と～えた I *mistook* clouds for mountains.

みまわ・す【見回す】¶ きょろきょろ～すな Don't *look* curiously *around*. 一座を～したが, 知った顔が見えなかった I *looked around* the company, but saw no face I knew.

みまわり【見回り】(動作) patrol; (人) a watchman. ¶ 彼は1週1回工場の～をする He *makes a visit of inspection to* the factory once a week.

みまわ・る【見回る】¶ 校舎を～った We *went round* the school building.

みまん【未満】less than; under. ¶ 7歳～の子ども children *under* seven years of age. 100円～は切り捨てる ignore fractions *smaller than* (≒ *less than*; *under*) one hundred yen.

みみ【耳】**1** 〚体の器官〛 an ear. ¶ 彼は～の後ろに手を当てて聞いていた He listened with his hand cupped to his *ear*.

うちの犬は～が垂れている Ours is a flap-*eared* dog.

隣の部屋のラジオがうるさいので～をふさいだ I covered my *ears*, because the radio next door was too noisy.

2 〚聞くこと・聞く力〛 ¶ 祖母はとても～が遠い My grandmother is very hard of *hearing*. / My grandmother's *hearing* is very weak.

彼女のよからぬうわさが～に入ってきた A scandal about her has reached my *ears*.

このことが彼の～に入ったらたいへんだ If this reaches (≒ comes to) his *ears*, it will complicate matters.

ご参考までにお～に入れておきます I'll tell this to you for your information.

ちょっと～を貸してください I want to speak to you in private. / Just a word for your *ear*.

彼は人の意見に～を貸そうとしない He *has no ear for* others' opinions. / He *shuts his ears to* others.

彼は～を澄ましてその足音を聞いていた He was listening to the steps with strained *ears*.

彼女の音楽の～はなかなか肥えている She *has a* nice *ear for* music. / She *has a* fine musical *ear*.

英会話の練習では～を慣らすことがたいせつだ In practicing English conversation it is important to develop your *aural* comprehension.

そのお説教なら～にたこができるほど聞かされた I am sick and tired of hearing that lecture.

彼のことばがまだ～に残っている His words are still ringing in my *ears*.

風の音が～について眠れなかった Disturbed by the sound of the wind, I could not get to sleep.

それを言われると実に～が痛い I *feel a prick of conscience* when you say so. / I *am ashamed to* hear you say so.

大砲の音は～を聾(ろう)するばかりだった The boom of guns *was deafening*.

そんな言いわけなど聞く～持たぬ I will never *lis-*

ten to such an excuse.

3 〖端・縁〗 ¶ 本の～を折る *dog-ear* a book. パンの～を落とす cut away the *edges* from slices of bread.

4 〖その他〗 ¶ 貸したお金は約束の日までに～をそろえて返してもらいたい I want you to pay off the money I lent you by the promised time (≒ day).

みみあか【耳垢】earwax. ¶ ～をとる clean off *one's* earwax.

みみあたらし・い【耳新しい】¶ その話は私には～い That story *is new* (≒ *is news*) *to* me.

みみうち【耳打ち】¶ 彼はなにか警官に～していた He *was whispering* something *into* the policeman's *ear*.

みみかき【耳掻き】an earpick.

みみがくもん【耳学問】learning by the ear; picked-up knowledge. ¶ 彼は～でいろいろ知っている He has learned a lot of things by listening to others.

みみかざり【耳飾り】an earring (複数形で用いることが多い).

みみくそ【耳屎】earwax.

みみざわり【耳障り】¶ 車の音が～で眠れなかった The sound of cars *was* so *offensive to the ear* that I could hardly sleep.

みみず【蚯蚓】an earthworm.

—ばれ ¶ 足をネコにひっかかれたあとが～ばれになった A cat scratched me, raising *furrows* on my leg.

みみずく【木菟】〘鳥類〙 a horned owl.

みみたぶ【耳朶】an ear-lobe.

みみだれ【耳垂れ】discharge from the ears.

みみっち・い ¶ なんという～いことを言う人だ What a *stingy* thing he utters! そんな～い考えは捨てなさい Give up such a *mean* idea.

みみなり【耳鳴り】a ringing in the ears. ¶ ～がする I have *a ringing in* my *ears*. ～がとまらない My *ears are ringing* continually.

みみより【耳寄り】¶ ～な話だ That's *welcome* (≒ *good*) news.

みみわ【耳輪】an earring.

みむき【見向き】¶ 彼は私を～もしなかった He *did not even look at* me. 彼は甘いものは～もしない He *has no taste at all for* sweet things to eat.

みめ【見目】¶ ～麗しい乙女 a pretty girl. ～より心 (諺) *Handsome is that handsome does.*

みめい【未明】¶ ～に before dawn; before daybreak.

みもだえ【身悶え】a writhe. ¶ 負傷した男は痛さのため～した The wounded (≒ injured) man *writhed* with pain.

みもち【身持ち】conduct; behavior. ¶ ～がよい be well-behaved. ～が悪い be of loose morals. 彼はあまり～がよくなかった He *has been leading a* somewhat *dissipated life*.

みもと【身元・身許】*one's* identity. ¶ 彼の～は証明された He *has been identified*. / His *identity* has been established. 彼の～を調査しよう Let us look into his *background* (≒ *past*; *history*). 彼の～は確かだ He is a man with *a* good *record*. ～不明の死体が発見された A body of an *unidentified* person has been discovered.

—引受人 a guarantee. **—保証人** a surety.

みもの【見物】a sight. ¶ なかなかの～だった It was *a great sight to see*. 彼の踊りはたいした～だった His dance *was worth watching*. 当日の彼はさぞ～だろう It will *be worth while to watch* how he will act on that day.

みゃく【脈】**1** 〖脈はく〗 pulse. ¶ ～が打つ The *pulse* beats. もう～がない The *pulse* beats no longer. ～は普通になった His *pulse* returned to the normal condition. この子どもは～が速い (遅い) This child's *pulse* is quick (slow). 彼の心臓はまだ～を打っていた His heart *was* still *throbbing*.

2 〖望み〗 ¶ あの話はまだ～がある There is still some *hope* from what he has said. もう～がない There is no *hope*.

みゃくどう【脈動】pulsation. ¶ 心臓は～する The heart *pulsates*. 彼の演説には新思想が～していた The *pulsation* of new ideas was in his speech.

みゃくはく【脈搏】pulse.

みゃくみゃく【脈脈】¶ 民族の精神が～と続いている The racial spirit has been flowing *incessantly*.

みゃくらく【脈絡】logical connection; (文脈) context. ¶ 両者の間にはなんの～もない There is no *connection* between the two. 彼の議論には～がない His argument *is incoherent*.

みやけ【宮家】the house of a prince of the blood.

みやげ【土産】(贈り物) a present; (旅の) a souvenir. ¶ 彼はいつも～を買ってきてくれる He always brings us some *presents*. 駅ビルで家に～を買った I bought some *souvenirs* to take home at the "station building."

—話 ¶ 彼はいろいろ～話をしてくれた He gave us a variety of accounts of his travel.

みやこ【都】a capital; (大都会) a metropolis; a city. ¶ 住めば～ (諺) *There is no place like home*. (この英文は主として故郷のよいことを表わすもの). ～育ちの bred in *a city* (bred を brought up とすればいっそう口語的になる). ～落ちする leave town; leave Tokyo.

みやこどり【都鳥】〘鳥類〙 an oyster catcher.

みやす・い【見易い】¶ 掲示板を～い所に出す put a signboard up at a *conspicuous* place. この本は～い This book *is easy to read*. 彼のは～い筆跡だ His is a *legible* hand. / His handwriting *is legible*. (legible を readable (内容がよい) としてはいけない).

みやづかえ【宮仕え】the court service. ¶ すまじきものは～ Wretched is the lot of a government official!

みやびた【雅びた】elegant; graceful; refined. ¶ 彼女の～ことば遣いは人々を魅了した Her *graceful* manner of speech charmed the people. 彼は～暮らしをしている He lives an *elegant* life.

みやぶ·る【見破る】¶彼らのたくらみは～られた Their scheme *was seen through.* 私たちはその秘密をたちまち～った We *penetrated into* the secret at once.

みやまいり【宮参り】a new-born baby's first visit to the shrine.

みや·る【見遣る】¶窓越しに景色を～った I *glanced* (≒ *looked*) *at* the scenery through the window.

ミュージカル a musical.
―コメディ a musical comedy.

みよ【御代】the reign. ¶明治の～に in *the reign* of Meiji.

みょう【妙】**1**〖奇妙〗¶彼は～なことを言った He said *strange* things.
彼の言うことは～に聞こえる What he says sounds *strange.*
～なことに彼は自転車に乗れない *Strange to say,* he cannot ride a bicycle.
きょうは～に暑い日だ It is *extremely* hot today.
彼は～な笑い方をする He laughs *strangely.*
一瞬彼は～な顔をした He made a *queer* face for a moment.
子どものことが～に気にかかる I am *unusually* anxious about my children.
2〖巧妙〗skill. ¶彼は話術に～を得ている He *is good at* speak*ing.*
彼は日本式泳法に～を得ている He *is good at* swimm*ing* Japanese style.
彼のこの描写は言いえて～である This description of his *is excellent* (≒ *is admirable*).

みよう【見様】¶～見まねで following another's example. 彼女は～見まねで踊りを覚えた She learned dancing, 〔*by*〕 *watching and following others' examples.*

みょうあん【妙案】an excellent plan. ¶ふと～を思いついた I hit upon *a happy idea.*

みょうが【茗荷】〘植物〙Zingiber Mioga.

みょうが【冥加】divine protection. ¶～の至り a great blessing. これは～に余る This is too good for me. / This is a blessing that I do not deserve.

みょうぎ【妙技】an exquisite performance. ¶彼らの～に見とれた We were enchanted by their *fine* (≒ *wonderful*) *performance.* 彼の空中の～は観客を驚かした His aerial *feats* (≒ *stunts*) were surprising to the spectators.

みょうごにち【明後日】the day after tomorrow.

みょうごねん【明後年】the year after next.

みょうじ【名字·苗字】a surname ; a family name. ¶今は彼女の～は中田でなく,変わっているだろう She will not be Nakada but something else now.

みょうしゅ【妙手】an excellent hand. ¶彼はバイオリンの～として知られる He is known as *an expert in* playing the violin. / He is known as an *expert* violin-player. この一手は～というべきだろう(将棋で) It might be called *a capital move.*

みょうしゅん【明春】next spring.

みょうじょう【明星】Venus. ¶明けの～ the morning star. 宵の～ the evening star. 彼は詩壇の～だ He is *a* poetical *star.*

みょうだい【名代】(代理人) a deputy ; (代表者) a representative. ¶父の～として式に参列することとなった I was to present myself at the ceremony *on behalf of* my father. 彼は首相の～をつとめた He *acted for* the prime minister. 彼は天皇の～として訪英した He *represented* the Emperor in visiting England.

みょうちょう【明朝】tomorrow morning.

みょうにち【明日】tomorrow.

みょうねん【明年】next year.

みょうばん【明晩】tomorrow evening ; tomorrow night.

みょうばん【明礬】〘化学〙alum.

みょうみ【妙味】a charm ; a beauty ; a nice point. ¶茶の湯の～はきみにはわかるまい I am afraid you cannot appreciate the *delicacies* of tea ceremony. 音楽の～はどこにあるのか What is the *charm* of music? この遊びは～にとぼしい This game lacks *charm.* 彼の文章のスタイルにはなんともいえない～がある There is *an* indescribable *nice point* in the style of his writings. 彼にはこの詩の～がわからない He cannot appreciate the *exquisite beauty* of this poem.

みょうやく【妙薬】a specific. ¶これは胃痛の～だ This is *a golden remedy for* (≒ *a specific against*) stomachache. インフレ防止の～はない There is no *excellent remedy for* prevent*ing* inflation.

みょうれい【妙齢】youth. ¶～の女性 a *young* girl ; a girl *in the flower of maidenhood* (文語的表現). ～の婦人が家をたずねてきた A woman *of marriageable age* (≒ A *young* lady) came to see me. (marriageable age は少し大げさな言い方).

みよし【舳·船首】the bow. ¶船は～から沈んでいった The ship sank down from *the bow.*

みより【身寄り】a relative. ¶彼には～がない He has no *one to depend on.* / He has no *kith and kin.*

みらい【未来】future. ¶～のある promising. ～に in the future (in future (今後は) と区別すること). 彼は～の総理大臣と言われている He is rumored to be a *future* prime minister. 彼女は作家として大いに～がある She has *a* great *future* as a writer. 日本の～はどうなると思いますか What do you think the *future* of Japan will be? 彼は～のある青年だ He is a *promising* young man. この国の～はきみたちの双肩にある The *future* of this country rests on your shoulders. ～にどんなことが起こるかだれにもわからない No one knows what will happen *in the future.* 人は～に希望を持つべきだ We should keep hope for the *future.* きみは～を信じるか(来世を) Do you believe in *the life after death*?
―学 futurology. ―派 futurism.

み

ミリグラム a milligram. ¶ このはかりはなんでも～の単位まで測ることができる This balance can weigh anything to the unit of *milligram.*

ミリバール a millibar.

ミリ〔メートル〕 a millimeter.

みりょう【未了】 ¶ この法案は審議～になった This bill *has been shelved.*

みりょう【魅了】 ¶ オーケストラのすばらしい演奏は聴衆を～した The wonderful performance of the orchestra *enchanted* (≒ *fascinated*; *captivated*) the audience.

みりょく【魅力】 〔a〕 charm; 〔a〕 fascination. ¶ 彼女は～がある She *is charming.* ゴルフはぼくに特別な～がある Golf has *a* special *attraction* for me. 彼の小説はスタイルに～がある There is *a charm* of style in his novels. その女優はたいへんな～をふりまいている The actress exercises *a* fearful *attraction.* 釣りにはあまり～がない Fishing does not *appeal to* me very much.

ミリリットル a milliliter.

みりん【味醂】 a sweet sort of *sake.* ¶ ～につけたサケ a salmon preserved in *mirin.* イワシの～干し a dried sardine seasoned with *mirin.*

みる【見る】 1 〘目で〙 see; look. ¶ みんなこちらを見なさい *Look* this way, everybody.

こんな美しい景色は見たことがない I *have* never *seen* such a fine view.

飛行機が山に墜落するのを見た I *saw* an airplane crash on to the mountain.

左右をよく見てから道路を横断しなさい *Look* in both directions before crossing the street.

彼の顔を見るのも不愉快だ I cannot bear the *sight* of him. / I hate the very *sight* of him.

彼はそれを見て見ぬふりをした He pretended not to *have seen* it. / He *connived at* it.

今度だけは大目に見ておこう I'll *overlook* it this once.

彼はじっと私の顔を見た He *stared* fixedly *at* my face. / He *looked* hard *at* my face. / He *fixed* his *eyes on* my face.

彼女は彼の顔をちらっと見た She *glanced at* his face.

見る人が見れば偽物とわかるだろう A *discerning* person would find that it is an imitation.

見れば見るほどすばらしい絵だ The more closely I *look at* the picture, the better I find it to be.

2 〘見物する〙 ¶ 京都は見る所がたくさんある There are lots of sights to *see* in Kyoto.

1日で東京を見てまわるのは無理だ It is impossible to *do* all *the sights* of Tokyo in a day.

彼女は芝居を見るのがなによりも好きだ She likes *theater-going* better than anything else.

映画を見にいこうか Shall we *go to the movies?* (go to see と言わないでよい).

うちの子どもはテレビばかり見ている Our children *are* always *watching* television.

3 〘視察する・観察する〙 ¶ あすは工場を見にいってくる I'll *visit* (≒ *inspect*) the factory tomorrow.

彼はアメリカの教育施設を見に出かけている He has gone to America to *inspect* educational facilities.

4 〘考察する・判断する〙 ¶ 私の見たところ, 先方は信頼できる会社だ *In my judgment,* it is a reliable company.

どう見てもこの計画は実行不可能だ It is *by no means* possible to carry out this plan.

どう見ても彼女は40すぎだ She will never see forty again. (この言い方は若い年齢の場合には避ける).

まだ現われないところを見ると, 彼は不参加らしい *Seeing* that he has not arrived yet, I guess he is not going to participate.

彼には人を見る目がある He is *a good judge of* people. / He is *a shrewd reader of* character.

空もようから見るとあすも天気だ *From* the look of the sky, it will be nice tomorrow, too.

大局的に見て, この政策は当を得たものだ *From a* broad *perspective,* this policy is right.

この小説を彼の代表作と見る人が多い Many people *regard* this novel as his most important work.

5 〘読む・調べる〙 ¶ 先日提出した報告書を見てくださいましたか *Have* you *read* the report I handed in yesterday?

わからない語があったら辞書を見なさい *Consult* (≒ *Look up*) a dictionary when you come across a word you do not understand.

先生が宿題を見て返してくださった The teacher returned the homework to us after *going through* them.

彼は今新聞を見ている He *is reading* a newspaper now.

ガスが切ってあるかどうか見てきてください Go and *see* if the gas is turned off (≒ out).

ちょっとこのスープの味をみてください Will you *taste* this soup?

6 〘世話する・監督する〙 ¶ しばらくこの子を見ていてください Please *look after* (≒ *watch over*) this child for a while.

部長は営業全般を見ている The head of the department *is in charge of* the business as a whole.

大学生に子どもの勉強を見てもらっている I am having a university student tutor my child.

7 〘その他〙 ¶ 費用は5,000円も見ておけば十分だ Five thousand yen should be sufficient.

それ見たことか I told you so! / It serves you right.

ざまを見ろ Serves you right.

いまに見ていろ You shall smart for this. / You will regret it someday.

彼女は見る影もなく老け込んでしまった She has grown old and is a mere shadow of her former self.

見るに見かねてこの子を家に引き取った Being unable to remain a mere spectator, I have adopted the child.

みる【診る】 ¶ きみはすぐ医者にみてもらいなさい You

み

must *see* a doctor at once. きょう医者にみてもらうことになっている I *am seeing* the doctor today. 私は耳をみてもらった I *had* my ears *examined*.

みるからに【見るからに】 ¶ このケーキは～うまそうだ This cake *looks* tempting. 彼は～学者だ He is *every inch* a scholar. / *To all appearance*, he is a scholar.

ミルク milk. ¶ この赤ん坊は～で育った This baby has been brought up *on the bottle*.
—セーキ milk shake. 粉— dried milk. コンデンス— condensed milk.

みるみる【見る見る】 ¶ ～うちにその船は沈んで姿を消した The vessel went down *while we were watching*. ～相手に追いついた He caught up with his opponent *in an instant*. その花は～しぼんでいった The flower withered *before our eyes*. ～うちに山は霧に包まれてしまった The mountain was veiled in mist *in an instant*.

みるめ【見る目】 ¶ 彼は骨董(こっとう)品を～のある人だ He is *a good connoisseur* of curios. 私は絵を～がない I have no *eye for* pictures.

みれん【未練】 (遺憾) regret; (愛着) attachment. ¶ 東京に～はない I feel no *regret* for Tokyo. 彼女はまだ舞台に～がある Her heart *is still on* the stage. 彼は別れた妻に～がある He *is still attached to* (≒ *has a lingering love for*) his divorced wife. もう彼女に～はない I *have done with* her. このピアノには～がある I *feel attached to* this piano.

みわく【魅惑】 fascination. ¶ 美しい風景に～された We *were captivated* (≒ *were fascinated*) by the beauty of the scenery. なんとなく～的な話しぶりだ There is a sort of *charm* in his way of talking.

みわけ【見分け】 distinction. ¶ 英米人の～がつきますか Can you *tell* an Englishman *from* an American? 彼は善悪の～がつかない He does not *know* good *from* evil. このふたりのきょうだいはうりふたつで～もつかない The two brothers look so much alike that we cannot *tell one from the other*.

みわ·ける【見分ける】 ¶ 赤とだいだいを～けることができない I cannot *tell* red *from* orange. 暗かったのでふたりを～けられなかった It was so dark that I could not *distinguish* the two *from* each other.

みわす·れる【見忘れる】 ¶ 友人の顔を～れた I *have failed to recognize* (≒ *have forgotten*) the face of a friend.

みわた·す【見渡す】 ¶ 山頂から平野を～した We *took an extensive view of* (≒ *looked out over*) the plain from the top of the mountain. この丘からは周囲の山々がよく～せる This hill *commands* a fine view of the surrounding mountains. (動詞 command は人間·場所のいずれも主語になる). 両側には～すかぎり平野が広がっていた On either side the plain stretched *as far as the eye could reach*.

みんえい【民営】 private management. ¶ この遊園地は～だ This amusement park *is under private management*.

みんか【民家】 a private house.

みんかん【民間】 —事業 a private enterprise. —人 a civilian. —治療 home treatment. —伝承 a folklore; a legend. —貿易 private foreign trade. —放送 commercial broadcasting.

ミンク a mink. ¶ ～のコート a *mink* coat.

みんげい【民芸】 folk art.
—品 a folk-art object.

みんけん【民権】 the civil rights. ¶ ～を主張する assert the *civil rights*.
—伸張 extention of the civil rights. —擁護 defense of the people's rights.

みんじ【民事】 a civil case.
—裁判 a civil trial. —裁判所 a civil court. —事件 a civil case. —訴訟 a civil action. —訴訟法 the Code of Civil Procedure.

みんしゅ【民主】 democracy. ¶ ～的 democratic. ～的に democratically. 教育の～化 democratization of education. その国は～化された The country *has been democratized*.
—国家 a democratic country. —主義 democracy. —主義者 a democrat. —政体 democracy. —党(アメリカの) the Democratic Party. —党員 a Democrat. 議会制—主義 parliamentary democracy.

みんじゅ【民需】 private demands. ¶ この品は～用にふりむけられることになっている These goods are to be turned into *civilian consumption*.
—産業 civilian industry. —品 civilian goods.

みんしゅう【民衆】 the people. ¶ この建物は～のためのものだ This building is erected for *people in general*. ～的詩人 a poet *for the people*.
—運動 a popular movement. —駅 a [railway] station for the people (station だけでは必ずしも鉄道駅の意味にはならない). —化 popularization. ¶ 政治の～化 the *popularization* of politics. —芸術 popular arts. —心理 popular psychology. —大会 a mass meeting. 一般— the masses of the population.

みんしゅく【民宿】 a private lodging house.

みんじょう【民情】 ¶ 彼は～に通じていた He was well acquainted with *the conditions of the people*.

みんしん【民心】 popular feeling; popular sentiment. ¶ ～を失う lose *the goodwill of the people*. ～を得る win *the confidence of the people*.

みんせい【民生】 public welfare.
—委員 public welfare commissioner. —局 the Public Welfare Bureau.

みんせい【民政】 civil administration.
¶ 新生国には～が敷かれた *A civil government* was established in the new-born country.

みんぞく【民俗】 folkways.
—音楽 folk music. —学 folklore. —学者 a folklorist. —舞踊 folk dance.

みんぞく【民族】 a race.

み

—意識 racial consciousness. —移動 a racial migration. —運動 the racial movement. —学 ethnology. —学者 an ethnologist. —国家 a racial nation. —自決 racial self-determination. —資本 the racial capital. —主義 racialism. —心理学 folk psychology. —性 racial traits. —精神 the racial spirit. —文化 racial culture. 日本— the Japanese race. ヨーロッパ諸— the peoples of Europe.

みんど【民度】the cultural standard. ¶ この国は〜が高い The *cultural standard* of the people of this country is high.

みんぺい【民兵】(人) a militiaman; (隊) a militia.

みんぽう【民放】(民間放送) commercial broadcasting.

みんぽう【民法】civil law; (法典) the civil code.

—学者 a civilian; a scholar of the civil law.

みんよう【民謡】a folk song.

みんりょく【民力】national strength (≒ resources).

みんわ【民話】a folk story.

—劇 a folk-story play.

む

む【無】nothing. ¶ 私のせっかくの努力が〜になった My efforts *came to nothing.* / My efforts *were for nothing.* 彼の好意を〜にしてはいけない You must not *bring* his favor *to naught.* / You should not *set* his kindness *aside.* / You should not *abuse* his kindness. 私は彼の親切を〜にしてしまった I *could not avail myself of* his kindness. 〜から有は生じない(諺) *Nothing comes out of nothing.* 彼には親切にしても〜になる Kindness *is thrown away upon* him.

むい【無為】idleness; inactivity. ¶ 彼は〜に暮らしている He lives an *idle* life. 彼は〜徒食の徒だ He is *an idler.*

むいぎ【無意義】insignificance. ¶ 〜な生活 a *meaningless* life.

むいしき【無意識】unconsciousness. ¶ 〜に unconsciously; involuntarily. 彼は自分の行動にほとんど〜だ He *is* almost *unaware of* his conduct. 〜のうちにそれをやっていた I did it *involuntarily.*

むいそん【無医村】a doctorless village.

むいちぶつ【無一物】¶ 私はまったく〜になった I *became* utterly *penniless.* 懐は〜だ I *have not a penny* in my purse.

むいちもん【無一文】¶ 〜の penniless. 彼はまったく〜だ He *is* utterly *penniless.*

むいみ【無意味】¶ 〜なことを言う talk *nonsense.* 彼らの言うことはまったく〜だ *There is no meaning* at all *in* what they say. 私は25年教師をしていたが, 〜ではなかった I had not been a teacher for twenty-five years *for nothing.*

むいん【無韻】¶ 〜の unrhymed; rhymeless. 絵画は〜の詩と言われる Painting is said to be poetry *without sound.*

—詩 a blank verse.

ムード mood. ¶ 私は冗談を言うような〜になっていなかった I *was in* no *mood for* joking. 悲観的〜が強かった Pessimism was high.

むえき【無益】¶ そんな本を読んでも〜だ It *is* [*of*] *no use* reading such a book. このうえ待っていても〜だ It *is useless* (≒ *is of no use*) to wait any longer. なぜ〜な議論を続けるのか Why do you continue a *futile* argument? 金を遊ばしておくのは〜だ It *is unadvisable* to have your money lying idle.

むえん【無煙】smokelessness.

—火薬 smokeless powder. —炭 anthracite. —地帯 a smokeless zone.

むえん【無縁】¶ それとこれとは〜ではない It has a certain degree of connection with that. 彼は私には〜の人だ He *has nothing to do with* me. 〜の墓 an *unidentified* person's grave (≒ gravestone).

—仏 a person who died leaving no relatives behind.

むが【無我】self-effacement. ¶ 〜の愛 *selfless* love. 〜の境に入る attain a state of *perfect selflessness.*

—夢中 ¶ 〜夢中になって走った I ran *with all my might and main.*

むかい【向かい】¶ 私の家は郵便局の〜だ My house stands *opposite* the post office. 彼ら一家はちょうどその道の〜に住んでいる His family lives just *across the street* (≒ *over the way*). 〜の家 the house *opposite.* 銀行はちょうど駅の〜にある The bank *is* just *across from* the station.

むがい【無害】¶ この虫は〜有益だ This worm *is* not only *harmless* but also useful. この殺虫剤は人間には〜だ This insecticide *does not harm* human beings. 酒は少量なら〜だ Liquor *produces no ill effects* if only a small amount of it is taken.

むがい【無蓋】without covering; non-covered.

—貨車 an open wagon; a truck. —燈 an open light.

むかいあ・う【向かい合う】face each other. ¶彼と～って座った I sat *face to face with* him. 彼と私は～ってテーブルについた He and I sat *facing each other* with a table between. 床屋と花屋は～っている The barber's and the florist's *stand opposite to each other*.

むかいあわせ【向かい合わせ】¶ふたりは～に座った The couple sat *facing each other*.

むかいかぜ【向かい風】an adverse wind; a head wind. ¶風は～だ The wind *is against us*.

むか・う【向かう】**1**〚面する〛¶彼は毎晩遅くまで机に～っている He *sits at* his desk till late every night.

彼女はさっきから鏡に～っている She has been looking in the glass for some time.

大統領は大群衆に～って演説した The president made a speech *before* a large crowd.

駅の～って右側に新しいデパートが開店した A new department store has opened on the right side of the station〔as you face it〕.

写真の～って右から３人めが妹です The third person from the right in the photograph is my younger sister.

面と～ってそんなことを彼に言われたのか Did he say such a thing *to your face*?

2〚目指す〛¶彼はあすロンドンに～って羽田を立つ He leaves Haneda *for* London tomorrow.

彼は車で名古屋へ～った He left (≒ started) *for* Nagoya by car.

台風が関東地方へ～っている The typhoon *is approaching* (≒ *is coming nearer to*) the Kanto district.

さあ勝利に～ってがんばろう Let's strive *for* victory.

船がどこに～っているのかわからなかった I couldn't tell where the ship *was bound* (≒ *was headed*) *for*.

3〚対する・逆らう〛¶先生に～ってそんなことを言ってはいけません You must not say such a thing *to* your teacher.

今シーズンのわがチームは～うところ敵なしだ Our team is invincible wherever it goes this season.

船は強い南風に～って進んだ The ship sailed *against* (≒ *in the teeth of*) the strong south wind.

4〚赴く〛¶彼の病気はようやく快方に～った At last he has taken a favorable turn.

あすは天気も回復に～うでしょう The weather will improve tomorrow.

むかえ【迎え】¶羽田にアメリカ帰りの友人を～に行った I went to Haneda to *meet* a friend of mine returning from America. 医者を～にやった I *sent for* a doctor.

むかえい・れる【迎え入れる】¶客を部屋へ～れた We *invited* the guest *into* the room. / We *showed* (≒ *ushered*) the guest into the room. 彼はヒットを打って二塁のランナーをホームに～れた He *drove in* a runner from second base.

むかえう・つ【迎え撃つ】¶敵を～つ *fight against* the attack of the enemy.

むかえざけ【迎え酒】¶～をやった I took a hair of the dog that bit me.（かみついた犬の毛でその傷がなおるという昔話から）. 二日酔には～ Like cures like.（毒をもって毒を制すのことわざ）.

むかえび【迎え火】a welcome fire for a departed soul. ¶～をたく burn *a welcome fire for the departed spirits*.

むか・える【迎える】¶一行は暖かく～えられた The party *was welcomed* warmly. もう１週間でクリスマスを～える We are going to *greet* Christmas Day in a week. / Christmas will come in a week. 彼はあす75回めの誕生日を～える He is to *celebrate* his 75th birthday tomorrow. 講師はかっさいをもって演壇に～えられた The lecturer *was greeted to* the platform with cheers. 彼は２度めの妻を～えた He *took* a second wife.

むがく【無学】illiteracy. ¶彼は～だが常識は持っている Though he *is ignorant* (≒ *is illiterate*), he is a man of common sense. 彼は～で自分の名前も書けない He *is* so *uneducated* that he cannot even write his own name.

むかし【昔】ancient times. ¶～～ once upon a time; many years ago. ～はこの辺は村だった *Formerly* this neighborhood was a village. ～は地球が丸いということを人は知らなかった *In old[en] times* people did not know that the earth is round. ～この山のふもとに大きな松の木があった There *used to* be a big pine tree at the foot of the mountain. ～の人は月に人間が行くなど夢にも思わなかった *Ancient* people never dreamed of visiting the moon. ～の遊び友だちに会った I met an *old* playmate of mine.

むかしかたぎ【昔気質】the old-time spirit. ¶彼は～でがんこだ He *sticks to old-time ideas*. 彼は～なところがある He *has something old-fashioned* in him.

むかしなじみ【昔馴染み】（友人）an old acquaintance. ¶～の彼と話に花が咲いた I had a lively chat with him, *an old friend of mine*. ～の顔もいくつか見えた We could see some *old familiar* faces.

むかしばなし【昔話】an old story. ¶日本の～ Japanese *old legends*. ～に花が咲いた We had *a happy chat of reminiscences*.

むかつ・く ¶なんとなく胸が～いた I *felt* somewhat *sick*. 彼の顔を見ると胸が～く The sight of his face *makes* me *sick* (≒ *sickens* me). 彼の話を聞くと胸が～く I *feel offended* (≒ *feel irritated*) *at* his words.

むかっぱら【むかっ腹】¶～を立てる burst into *a fit of anger*.

むかで【百足】〚虫類〛a centipede.

むかむか ¶～する feel sick. それを見るたびに～した Every time I saw it, I *became sick*. 不愉快で～する I feel so disagreeable that I *am irritated*.

むかん【無冠】¶～の帝王 an *uncrowned* king.

むかんかく【無感覚】insensibility. ¶手の指が～になっている My fingers *are numb*. 寒さのた

む

め足先が〜になっている My toes *are benumbed with* cold. 彼は恥に対して〜だ He *is insensible to* shame.

むかんけい【無関係】¶ 〜の unrelated. ふたりはお互いに〜だ The two persons *have nothing to do with* each other. それとこれとは〜だ That *has no connection with* this. 彼の演説はこの問題には〜だ His speech *has no bearing on* this subject. その評判はほんとうであろうとうそであろうと私には〜だ Whether it is true or false, the report *does not concern* me. どちらが勝とうと私には〜だ It *does not matter* to me which side will win.

むかんしん【無関心】indifference. ¶ そんなことには彼は〜だ He *is indifferent to* such sort of thing. 私は政治には〜でいられない Politics cannot be a matter of *indifference* to me. 私は宗教にはまったく〜だ I *have not* the least *interest in* religion. 彼は〜を装って黙っていた He remained silent, assuming the air of *indifference*.

むき【向き】**1**〘方向〙direction. ¶ 煙突から出る煙は風の〜を示す The smoke from the chimney shows the *direction* of the wind.
風の〜が南に変わった The wind *veered* to the south.
机の〜がよろしくない The *position* of the desk is not right.
テーブルの〜を窓の方へ変えてください Turn the table to the window.
できるなら家は北〜でないほうがいい If possible a house should not be built *facing* north.
私どもの家は南〜だから冬でも暖かい Since our house *faces* south (≒ *faces to* the south), it is warm even in winter.
2〘適合〙suitability. ¶ 彼は政治家〜でない He *is* not *suited for* a statesman.
これは事務所〜の家だ This house can also *serve as* an office.
彼らは輸出〜のくつをつくっている They make shoes *for* exportation.
この柄は女性万人〜だ This pattern *is suitable for* any woman.
3〘人〙¶ その意見には反対する〜もある *Some people* are against the opinion.
きみのためにしかるべき〜に運動してあげましょう I will make interest with the proper *quarter* on your behalf.

むき【無期】¶ 〜の indefinite. 会は〜延期になった The meeting was *indefinitely* postponed.
—懲役 imprisonment for life. ¶ 彼は〜懲役に処せられた He was imprisoned *for life*.

むき【無機】¶ 〜の〘化学〙inorganic.
—化学 inorganic chemistry. —化合物 an inorganic compound. —物 inorganic substance.

むき ¶ 〜になる become serious. そう〜になるな Don't *be* so *serious*. 彼は〜になってわめいた He shouted *with a vengeance*. 彼は〜になって怒った He flew into a passion. 彼はなだめるとかえって〜になる He *gets* all the more *angry* when you try to pacify him.

むぎ【麦】(小麦) wheat; (大麦) barley; (カラスムギ) oat.
—茶 barley tea. —畑 a wheat (≒ barley) field. —飯 boiled rice and barley. —わら [a] straw. —わら細工 a strawwork. —わら帽子 a straw hat.

むきあ·う【向き合う】¶ ふたりは〜ってテーブルについた The two persons sat at the table *face to face*.

むきげん【無期限】¶ 〜の limitless. 会は〜の延期となった The meeting was to be postponed *indefinitely*. 組合は〜ストに入った The union went into a strike *for an indefinite period*.

むきず【無傷】¶ 〜の faultless. 彼は〜で逃げおおせた He managed to escape *unhurt* (≒ *uninjured*). 事件に関係した者で〜なのは彼ひとりだ Of those who had a connection with the matter, none but him *were free from blemish*. この品物はみな〜だ All these articles *are in perfect condition* (≒ *are free from blemish*).

むきだし【剝き出し】¶ 〜の open; bare. 子どもはひざを〜にしていた The child *left* his knees *bare*. 彼はなんでも〜に言う He speaks any sort of thing *plainly*.

むきだ·す【剝き出す】¶ 犬が歯を〜している The dog *is showing* its teeth. 歯を〜してわっと笑った He *broke into a grin*.

むきどう【無軌道】¶ 〜な生活 a *dissipated* life. 彼の〜ぶりにはあきれた I was astonished at his *reckless* behavior.

むきなお·る【向き直る】¶ 声のする方に〜った I *turned round toward* where the voice was being heard.

むぎふみ【麦踏み】treading barley-plants (≒ wheat-plants). ¶ 〜をする tread barley-plants.

むきみ【剝き身】stripped shellfish. ¶ カキの〜 stripped oysters.

むきむき【向き向き】¶ 人によって〜がある Everyone has his own taste. / Tastes differ. めいめい〜があるものだ Each man has his forte.

むきめい【無記名】—株 an uninscribed share. —公債 a bearer bond. —投票 secret ballot. —預金 an uninscribed deposit.

むきゅう【無休】¶ この日刊新聞は年じゅう〜だ This daily newspaper is issued throughout the year. この会社は〜だ This firm *has no holiday*. 年じゅう〜(掲示) Open throughout the year.

むきゅう【無給】¶ 〜の unpaid; (名誉職の) honorary. 〜助手 an *unpaid* assistant. 彼は〜で働いている He is working *without pay* (≒ *for nothing*).

むきょういく【無教育】¶ 〜な人 an *uneducated* person. まだ読書のできない〜な民族がいる There are still some peoples in the world who *are illiterate* and are incapable of reading.

むきょうそう【無競争】¶ 彼は〜で市長に当選し

む

た He was elected mayor *unopposed.*

むきりょく【無気力】¶～な spiritless. なんと～な負け方だろう How *spiritlessly* he lost the game. 彼は～だ He *has no spirit.* / He *has no backbone.*

むきん【無菌】asepsis. ¶～の牛乳 *pasteurized* (≒ *sterilized*) milk. このびんの中は～状態になっている The inside of this bottle is in a *germless* condition.

むく【無垢】¶～の pure; innocent. ～の処女 a virgin. ～の少女 an *innocent* girl.

む・く【向く】**1**〖向かう〗¶彼はこちらを～いて笑った He *looked* this way and smiled.
赤ん坊は私のほうを～いて泣きだした The baby *turned to* me and began to cry.
絶対後ろを～くな Never *look* back.
2〖面する〗¶私の部屋は南に～いている My room *looks* (≒ *faces*) south.
別荘は湖の方に～いている The villa *faces* 〔*on*〕 the lake.
3〖適する〗¶私はそのような仕事には～いていない I *am* not *fit for* such work.
彼は牧師のような職業に～いている He *is suited for* a profession such as pastorate.
この海岸は水泳に～いている This seaside *is suitable for* swimming.
この天候は山登りには～いていない This weather *is* not *good for* climbing.
4〖気が〗¶彼は気が～かないことはけっしてやろうとしない He never tries to do what he does not *like* to do.
気が～かなくとも彼の言うことには従いなさい Obey him whether you *feel inclined to* or not.

む・く【剝く】¶バナナの皮を～く *peel* a banana. ナイフでカキの皮を～く *pare* a persimmon. 木の皮を～く *bark* a tree. 獣の皮を～く *skin* an animal.

むくい【報い】return. ¶悪事を働けば必ず～がある You have to *pay for* your evil deed. 怠けたため～を受けた I *suffered for* my idleness. / I *paid penalty for* my idleness. 善行には～がある A good deed is sure to *be rewarded* fairly.

むくいぬ【尨犬】a shaggy dog.

むく・いる【報いる】¶悪に～いるに善をもってする *Return* good for evil. 会社側は私の損失に十分～いてくれた The company *compensated* sufficiently *for* my loss. 親切にすれば好意はいつかは～いられる Be kind, and you will *be rewarded* some day.

むくげ【木槿】〖植物〗a rose of Sharon.

むくげ【尨毛】down.

むくち【無口】reticence. ¶～な男 a *silent* (≒ *reticent*) man. 彼は～だ He is a man *of few words.* / He *is silent.*

むくどり【椋鳥】〖鳥類〗a starling.

むくみ【浮腫】dropsy. ¶足に～がきている My legs *are swollen.* ～がひいた The *dropsical swelling* has gone down.

むく・む【浮腫む】¶かっけで足が～んだ My legs *have swollen* with beriberi.

むくむく ¶彼は～してきた（太ってきた）He has grown *plump.* 空に入道雲が～出てきた A *towering* mass of clouds has appeared in the sky.

-むけ【-向け】¶アメリカ～の絹製品 silk goods exported to America. 子ども～テレビ番組 a television program *for* children.

むげ【無下】¶～に断わるわけにもいかなかった I could not have the heart to give him a *flat* refusal.

むけい【無形】¶私は彼から有形～の援助を受けた I have received assistance, both material and *moral*, at his hands. 有形～の財産 material and *immaterial* property.
—文化財 intangible cultural properties.

むげい【無芸】¶あの男は～だ He *has no accomplishment.* 彼は～大食だ He is a *good-for-nothing* fellow. 多芸は～（諺）*Jack of all trades, and master of none.*

むけいかく【無計画】¶それはあまりにも～なやり方だ It is too *reckless* a way of doing. ～な登山は禁物だ You must avoid *unplanned* mountain climbing. ～な勉強方針 a *planless* course of study.

むけいけん【無経験】lack of experience; inexperience. ¶彼は商売は～だ He *is inexperienced in* business. ピンポンは～だ I *have no experience in* table tennis.

むけいこく【無警告】¶船は～で魚雷攻撃をうけた The ship was torpedoed *without warning.* 彼は～で解雇された He was dismissed *without notice.*

むけいさつ【無警察】lawlessness. ¶全市は目下～状態にある The whole city *is in a lawless condition.*

むけつ【無血】¶～の bloodless.
—革命 a bloodless revolution.

むげっしゃ【無月謝】free tuition. ¶彼は～で英語を教える He teaches English *free of tuition fee.* 彼は～の特典を与えられた He was granted the license of *free tuition.*

むけっせき【無欠席】regular attendance.
¶3年間～だった I *did not absent myself* even a single day for three years. / I *did not miss* a day for three years.

む・ける【向ける】¶顔をこちらに～けてください Please *turn* your face *toward* me. 走っているトラに銃口を～けた I *pointed* my gun *at* a running tiger. 聴衆はみな講師の話に注意を～けた The audience *turned* their attention *to* the lecturer's speech. 彼は収入を学費に～けた He *applied* his earnings *to* his school expenses.

む・ける【剝ける】¶右手の皮が～けた The skin of my right hand *has peeled* (≒ *has come*) *off.*

むげん【無限】infinity. ¶日本は～の海産物を持っている Japan has an *inexhaustible* supply of marine products. 宇宙は～に大きい The universe is *immeasurably* vast. しなければならないことが～にある What we have to do *is* indeed *unlimited.* 彼の精力は～ともいえるほどだ His energy seems almost *boundless.*

む

—軌道 an endless track. **—級数**〔数学〕 an infinite series. **—空間** infinite space. **—責任** unlimited responsibility. **—大** infinity. ¶ ～大の infinite.

むげん【夢幻】〔a〕fantasy. ¶ ～の境〔a〕dreamland; a world of phantasm. 私は～の境をさまよっていた My mind was in *a dreamland*.

むこ【婿】 a son-in-law (複 sons-in-law). ¶ 彼女は～をとるだろう She will *take a husband*. 彼は～に行った He *has married an heiress*.

むご·い【惨い】 cruel; pitiless. ¶ 彼らはわれわれに～い取り扱いをした They gave us *hard-hearted* treatment. そんな幼い子をいじめるなんて彼らは～い It *is cruel* of them to bully such small children. 彼は～い扱いを受けた He *was ill-treated* (≒ *was badly used*). ～いことを言う人だ What a *merciless* thing he says!

むこいり【婿入り】 ¶ ～する marry an heiress.

むこう【向こう】 **1**〖向こう側·先の方〗¶ 彼は駅の～側に住んでいる He lives *on the other* (≒ *opposite*) *side of* the station.

彼はテーブルの～から立ち上がって私にあいさつした He stood up and greeted me *from behind* the table.

あの山の～は新潟県だ *Beyond* that mountain is Niigata Prefecture.

～に見えるのが白根山だ The mountain which you see *over there* is Mt. Shirane.

～から来るのは山本さんじゃないか The man approaching us is Mr. Yamamoto, isn't he?

子どもは～へ行っていなさい You children must go *away* (≒ *there*).

大通りから～に行ってはいけません Don't go *across* the main street.

2〖行き先〗¶ ～に着いたらすぐ電話します I'll phone you as soon as I arrive *there*.

10時に～から迎えの車が来ることになっている They are to send a car to meet us at ten.

3〖今後〗¶ ～1週間外出を禁止する You must not go out for one week *from now* (≒ *the next* one week).

～5年のうちにマンションを買おうと思う I am thinking of buying an apartment *within* five years.

4〖相手〗¶ こちらは乗り気だが～が契約を渋っている We are willing to make the contract, but *the other party* is reluctant.

費用～持ちで試合をしようといってきた They challenged us to the match at *their* expense.

～が先に手を出したから, 相手になったまでだ I did nothing but defend myself, since *the other fellow* attacked me first.

チャンピオンを～にまわし彼は互角に戦った He put up a good fight *against* the champion.

5〖対抗〗¶ 相手チームの～をはって, はでな応援をした We cheered vigorously *against* the other team.

むこう【無効】 invalidity. ¶ ～になる become *void*; become *invalid*. ～にする make *void*; make *invalid*. この契約は～だ The contract *is invalid* (≒ *is of no effect*). あれだけやったものがすべて～になった All my efforts *came to nothing*. もうこの切符は～だ This ticket *is not available* any more. 議長はこの投票は～と宣言した The chairman declared the vote to *be null and void*.

—小切手 an invalid check. **—投票** an invalid vote.

むこうき【向こう気】 ¶ ～の強い人 an *aggressive* (≒ *a determined*) man.

むこうぎし【向こう岸】 the other side〔of〕the river.

むこうきず【向こう傷】 a frontal wound. ¶ あの男には～がある He bears a scar on the forehead.

むこうずね【向こう脛】 a shin.

むこうはちまき【向こう鉢巻き】 ¶ ～をする tie a rolled towel round *one's* head. 私は～をして(いっしょうけんめい)試験勉強した I *girded up my loins to* prepare for the examination.

むこうみず【向こう見ず】 recklessness. ¶ それは～な行為だ It is a *reckless* (≒ *rash*) act. ～に rashly; recklessly.

むごたらし·い【惨たらしい】 ¶ なんと～い死にざまだろう What a *cruel* death he died!

むこん【無根】 ¶ このニュースは事実～だ The news *is unfounded* (≒ *is groundless*). まったく事実～の記事だ That account is indeed *a fabrication*.

むごん【無言】 silence. ¶ 彼は～で聞いていた He listened *in silence*. / He was a *silent* listener. ～の行 ascetic practice of *silence*. 彼は～のまま立ち去った He left *without a word*. 彼女は～で絵をながめた She looked at the picture, *speechless*.

—劇 a dumb show; a pantomime.

むざい【無罪】 innocence. ¶ 彼は～になった He was found *innocent*. 彼らは～を主張した They pleaded that they *were not guilty*. / They protested their *innocence*. 彼は～を宣告された He was declared *not guilty*.

—放免 acquittal. ¶ 殺人犯に問われたが彼は～放免となった He *was acquitted of* the murder.

むさく【無策】 lack of policy. ¶ 物価問題について政府は無為～である As regards the prices of commodities, the government *lacks* (≒ *has no*) *policy* at all.

むさくい【無作為】 ¶ ～の unintentional. ～に5人を選んだ We selected five persons *unintentionally* (≒ *at random*).

—抽出法 a random sampling method.

むさくるし·い【むさ苦しい】 foul; sordid. ¶ 彼は～い身なりをしている He is *shabbily* dressed. ～い小屋に泊まった We stayed at a *filthy* (≒ *squalid; uncomfortable*) hut. ここは～いから庭へ出ましょう Let's go out to the garden, as it *is unpleasant* here.

むさべつ【無差別】 indiscrimination. ¶ ～に indiscriminately. 男女～にそれをやらせた I made them try *without distinction of* sex.

—爆撃 indiscriminate bombing. 平等—

equality and indiscrimination.

むさぼ·る【貪る】 ¶ ～り食う eat (≒devour) greedily. 暴利を～る make excessive profits. その小説を～るように読んだ I *pored over* the novel.

むざむざ(と) ¶ ～彼に一杯食わされた I was deceived *easily* by him. ～引きさがる彼ではなかった He was not a man to retire *helplessly*.

むさん【無産】 ¶ ～の propertyless; unpropertied.

—階級 the proletariat. **—者** a proletarian. **—党** a proletarian party.

むざん【無残·無惨】 ¶ 彼は～な最期を遂げた He *died a tragic death*. 見るも～な光景だった It was indeed a *horrible* scene to look at. ～にも彼の夢は破れた *To his sorrow and disappointment*, his dream did not come true.

むし【虫】 1 〘虫類〙 an insect. ¶ 子どもは～をとるのが好きだ Children like to catch *insects*. 秋の夜はいろいろな～が鳴く Various kinds of *insects* chirp at night in autumn. ナフタリンを入れ忘れたので, セーターが～に食われてしまった Since I forgot to put naphthaline in, my sweater was eaten by *moths*. ～に食われて体じゅうがかゆい I feel itchy all over, as I was bitten by *insects*. このチーズには～がついている This cheese is *worm*-eaten. あの子は～がわいたらしく, このごろ顔色が悪い The child looks pale, perhaps because he has got *worms*.
2 〘慣用的表現〙 ¶ 彼はきょうは～のいどころが悪い He *is out of humor* (≒*is in ill humor; is in a cross mood*) today. どうもああいう男は～が好かない I *dislike* such a man. / I *have an aversion to* such a man. 私が駆けつけたときは彼はもう～の息だった When I hastened to the spot, he was but faintly breathing. ～の知らせできみのところへ寄ってみたんだ Something told me to drop in at your house. / Some instinct brought me to your house. こんな仕事をぼくに押しつけようなんて～がよすぎる It *is selfish* of you to force such work upon me. そんなことを言われては腹の～がおさまらない I cannot *put up with* such an insulting remark. 彼はまったく仕事の～みたいな男だ He *devotes himself exclusively to* his work. / He is *a demon for* work. この子はよく～を起こして困る To my annoyance, this child often *gets nervous* (≒*fretful*). 一寸の～にも五分の魂 (諺) *Even a worm will turn. / Even a fly has its spleen.*

むし【無私】 unselfishness. ¶ 彼は～の精神をモットーとしている He makes it his motto to *be impartial*.

むし【無視】 ¶ われわれはこの事実を～することはできない We cannot *ignore* (≒*shut our eyes to*) this fact. きみは世論を～している You *disregard* public opinion. 彼は信号を～して道路を横断した He crossed the street *against* the traffic signal. だれもなにも言ってくれないので～されたと思った Since nobody told anything to me, I felt myself *left out in the cold*. 他人を～してものを言う人はきらわれる Those who talk *without regard for* (≒*to*) others are disliked.

むじ【無地】 ¶ ～の色 *plain* color. ～の衣服 a dress *of plain color*.

むしあつ·い【蒸し暑い】 sultry. ¶ きょうは～い It *is sultry* today. この部屋はなんと～いことだろう How *hot and stuffy* this room *is*!

むしかえ·す【蒸し返す】 ¶ 事件を～しては困る I don't want the affair to *be revived*. 彼はよく古い話を～す He often *rehashes* old stories.

むしかく【無資格】 disqualification. ¶ ～の教師 an *unqualified* teacher. ～のドライバー an *unlicensed* driver.

—者 a disqualified person.

むじかく【無自覚】 unconsciousness. ¶ ～に unconsciously. 彼は～な行動を非難されるだろう He will be blamed for his *thoughtless* behavior.

むしかご【虫籠】 an insect cage.

むしくい【虫食い】 ¶ このクリは～が多い Many of the chestnuts *are worm-eaten* (≒*are wormy*).

むしくだし【虫下し】 a vermifuge.

むしけら【虫螻】 ¶ 彼は人を～のように扱う He deals with men *like mere worms*. 彼はわれわれを～のように思っている We are beneath his notice.

むしけん【無試験】 ¶ 彼は～で入学が決まった He was admitted *without examination*. 高等学校卒業者は～とする *No examination is required of* those who have graduated from the upper secondary school.

—検定 getting a certificate without examination. **—入学** admission to a school without examination.

むじこ【無事故】 ¶ 彼は3年間～で運転しているHe has been driving his car *without causing any traffic accident* these three years.

むしず【虫酸】 ¶ 彼は見ただけで～が走る His very sight *makes* me *sick*. 彼は～が走るようなやつだ He is a *disgusting* fellow. / He's a skunk —a bad chap about the heart. (口語).

むしタオル【蒸しタオル】 a steamed towel.

むじつ【無実】 ¶ ～の罪 a *false* charge; an *unjust* accusation. 彼は～の罪に問われた He was charged with a *false* accusation. 彼は自己の～を主張した He insisted upon his *innocence*.

むじな【狢·貉】 〘動物〙 a badger. ¶ 彼らは一つ穴の～だ They *are of a feather*. / They *are of a gang*.

むしば【虫歯】 a decayed tooth; (状態) decay of teeth. ¶ ～を1本抜いてもらった I had *a decayed tooth* pulled out. ～が痛くてしかたがない I have a severe ache in my *decayed tooth*.

むしば·む【蝕む】 ¶ 心ない行為が童心を～むことは

む

よくあることだ It often happens that thoughtless conduct *spoils* children's minds. あわれにも彼の体は麻薬に～まれていった He *was* miserably *undermining himself* by drug addiction.

むじひ【無慈悲】mercilessness. ¶～な merciless; heartless.

むしぶろ【蒸し風呂】a vapor (≒ steam) bath.

むしぼし【虫干し】airing. ¶衣服の～をした We *gave* our clothes *an airing.* / We *aired* our clothes.

むしまんるい【無死満塁】(野球) No down, full bases. ¶～だ The bases are full with no outs.

むしむし【蒸し蒸し】¶～していやな気持ちだ It *is sultry* and uncomfortable.

むしめがね【虫眼鏡】a magnifying glass. ¶～で見る see through *a magnifying glass.* ～で見るように小さい字だ It is written in such small letters that they are to be read through *a magnifying glass.*

むしゃ【武者】a warrior. **—修行** knight-errantry. ¶彼は～修行に出ていった He *went out on knight-errantry.* **—修行者** a knight-errant. **—人形** a doll warrior. **—ぶり** ¶彼は戦場であっぱれな～ぶりを見せた He *distinguished himself on the battlefield.*

むしやき【蒸し焼き】¶鶏を～にする *steam* a chicken. まつたけの～ a *baked* mushroom.

むじゃき【無邪気】innocence. ¶彼は年のわりに～だ He *is innocent for* his age. 彼女は～そのもののように見える She looks like *innocence* itself. その子どもの～なしぐさに一同は見とれた All those present looked admiringly at the *naive* behavior of the child.

むしゃくしゃ ¶なんとなく～する I *am* somehow *irritated* (≒ *out of humor*).

むしゃぶりつ·く【武者ぶりつく】¶その子どもは幾度投げられても私に～いてきた However often that child was thrown away, he *grappled with* (≒ *seized violent hold of*) me.

むしゃぶるい【武者震い】¶ボクサーは試合を前に～した The boxer *quivered with excitement* before the fight began.

むしゃむしゃ ¶彼は出されたものを～食べた He *devoured* the food served to him.

むしゅう【無臭】¶このガスは～だ This gas *is odorless.* 無色～のガス colorless and *scentless* gas.

むしゅうきょう【無宗教】irreligion. ¶彼は～だ He is an *irreligious* man. 日本人の多くは～だ Most Japanese *have no religion.*

むしゅく【無宿】¶彼は～の放浪者だ He is a *homeless* wanderer.
—者 a vagabond.

むしゅみ【無趣味】lack of taste. ¶～な装飾 a *tasteless* decoration. 彼は～な男だ He is a man *of no tastes.* 私はスポーツには～だ I *have no taste for* (≒ *no interest in*) sports.

むじゅん【矛盾】inconsistency. ¶世の中は～がいっぱいだ The world is full of *contradictions.* 彼はしばしば～したことを言う He often *contradicts himself.* 今あなたの言ったことはきのうあなたが言ったことと～している What you have said *is inconsistent with* what you said yesterday. 彼の理論には大きな～がある There is *a* big *conflict* in his theory. それは彼らの因襲的思想とは～する It *conflicts with* their conventional idea.

むしょう【無償】no compensation. ¶この品は～で交付される This article is to be delivered *free of charge.*

むじょう【無上】¶～の光栄です It is *the supreme* honor to me. / I considered it *the highest* honor.

むじょう【無情】heartlessness. ¶彼は～な人だ He *is merciless* (≒ *is heartless*). 彼は～な仕打ちを受けた He received a *cruel* treatment. 世の～を痛感した I keenly felt the *hardness* of the world. 私を～なやつだと思わないでください Don't think me *unfeeling.* ～にも雨が降りだした It started raining *heartlessly.*

むじょう【無常】uncertainty. ¶人生は～だ Nothing is certain in this world. 世の～を感じないではいられない I cannot but feel *the vanity of life.*

むじょうけん【無条件】¶彼は～で私の申し出を受け入れてくれた He accepted my offer *without any condition.* ～で引き受けさせられた I was obliged to undertake the work *unconditionally.* 敵は～降伏を要求した They demanded an *unconditional* surrender.

むしょうに【無性に】¶～腹が立った I got *excessively* angry. 彼に～会いたくなった I *was impatient to* see him. ～彼と話したくなった I felt an *irresistible* desire to talk with him.

むしょく【無色】¶水は～だ Water *is colorless.* ～透明の液体 a *colorless* and transparent liquid.

むしょく【無職】¶彼は～だ He *has no occupation.* / (失業した) He *is jobless* (≒ *is out of work*).

むしよけ【虫除け】an insect repellent; (衣類などの) a moth ball; an insecticide.

むしょぞく【無所属】¶彼は～だ He *is not affiliated to any political party.* 彼は～で立候補した He ran as a candidate, *independent of any party.* ～の代議士 an *independent* 〔member of the Diet〕.

むしりと·る【毟り取る】¶彼は本のカバーを～った He *tore off* the jacket of the book. 彼は草を～った He *plucked up* the weeds. 鶏はきれいに毛を～ってある The chicken *has been plucked* clean.

むしりょ【無思慮】thoughtlessness. ¶そんなことを言うとは彼も～な男だ It *is imprudent of* him to say so. 彼は～にも目上の人に対して失礼なことを言った He *had the indiscretion to* say rude things to his superior.

むしりょく【無資力】¶～で企業をはじめるとは彼はあまりにも無謀だ It is rash of him to try to begin his enterprise *without any capital* (≒ *without funds*).

むし·る【毟る】¶庭の草を～った I *weeded* the

む

garden. 草花の葉を～ってはいけない Never *pick* leaves of the plant. 彼は髪の毛をかき～って悔しがった He *tore* his hair with vexation.

むしろ【筵・蓆】a straw mat.

むしろ【寧ろ】better; rather. ¶ 彼は作家というより～評論家だ He is *not so much* a writer *as* a critic. この小説はおもしろいというより～有益だ This novel is instructive *rather* than interesting. そんなことをするくらいなら～死んだほうがいい I *would rather* die *than* do such a thing.

むしん【無心】innocence. ¶ わが子の～の寝顔をじっとながめた I watched the *innocent* sleeping face of my child. 彼は金の～を言ってきた He came to see me to *ask for* a loan of money. ～の手紙 a *begging* letter.

むじん【無人】¶ 彼は～の境を行くようだった He *carried everything before him.*

—スタンド a self-service stand. —電車 an unmanned electric train. —島 a desert island; an uninhabited island. —飛行機 a pilotless plane. —踏切 an unattended crossing.

むじん【無尽】a mutual financial association. ¶ ～に当たった I drew a winning number in *a loan lottery.*

むしんけい【無神経】¶ 彼は～で, その酷評をも意にとめなかった He *was* too *thick-skinned* to mind the severe criticism. / He had the *insensibility* not to mind the severe criticism. どんな苦痛にも彼は～だ He *is insensible to* any pain. (痛がらない意). 彼はなにが起こっても～だ He *is insensible of* anything that happens around him. (insensible of... は, …に気づかぬ意).

むしんじん【無信心】¶ ～な irreligious; unbelieving. ～な人 an unbeliever; an irreligious person.

むじんぞう【無尽蔵】¶ ～の limitless; unlimited. アメリカの資源は～だ America's resources *are inexhaustible.* 彼の話の種は～だった His supply of stories *was endless.*

むしんろん【無神論】atheism.
—者 an atheist.

む・す【蒸す】¶ きょうはばかに～す It *is* awfully *close* (≒ *sultry*) today. ジャガイモを～す *steam* potatoes.

む・す【生す・産す】¶ 岩にコケが～している Moss *has grown* over a rock.

むすう【無数】¶ 空には～の星がある There are *innumerable* stars in the sky. バクテリアの種類は～にある There are *numberless* varieties of bacteria.

むずかし・い【難しい】**1**〖困難な〗difficult; hard. ¶ この問題は～い This problem *is difficult to* solve.

彼の成功は～い It *is difficult* for him to succeed.

この作品は文章が～くて私には読めない The style of this work *is* too *difficult* for me. / The style of this book makes the book too *difficult* for me to read.

～しくてうまく言えなかった It *was* too *hard* for me to express well.

事態はますます～くなってきた The situation became more and more *difficult.*

彼は～い立場にある He is in a *delicate* position.

～い試験が控えている We have a *difficult* examination ahead of us.

彼の回復は～い His recovery *is doubtful.*

あまり～く考えないほうがいい It is better not to *take* this too *seriously.*

2〖その他〗¶ 彼は細かいことに～い He *is particular about* trifling things.

彼女のあつかいは～くて私の手に負えない She *is* so *hard to please* that I cannot see how to deal with her.

彼はいつも～い顔をしている He always *looks serious.*

むずがゆ・い【むず痒い】¶ 霜焼けが～い My frostbite *feels creepy* (≒ *feels itchy*).

むずか・る ¶ この子はよく～る This child is easy to *become fretful.*

むすこ【息子】a son.

ひとり— *one's* only son. 跡取り— an heir.

むずと ¶ 彼は～私に組みついた He *grappled* (≒ *closed*) *with* me. 彼は～私の腕をつかんだ He *grabbed* my arm.

むすび【結び】(結末) an end; a conclusion; a close. ¶ ～の一番 (相撲で) the *final sumo* match.

むすび【結飯】a rice ball.

むすびあわ・せる【結び合わせる】¶ ひもを～せる *tie* strings *together.* 二つの糸を～せる *join* two threads *together.*

むすびつ・く【結び付く】¶ この二つの事柄は密接に～く These two events *are* closely *linked with* each other. あのような行動と彼の姿とは～かない Such conduct *is inconsistent with* my image of him.

むすびつ・ける【結び付ける】¶ この二つは～けて考えるべきだ These two things should be considered *in connection with* each other. 彼は綱で犬を木に～けた He *tied* his dog *to* a tree with a rope (≒ with its leash).

むすびめ【結び目】a knot. ¶ ～を解く untie *a knot.*

むす・ぶ【結ぶ】**1**〖ひもなどを〗tie. ¶ この包みを堅く～んでほしい I want this package *tied* securely.

2〖つなげる〗¶ ふたりは友情で～ばれた仲だ The two *are bound* together by friendship.

この二つの事実は密接に～ばれている These two facts *are* closely *connected with* each other.

この町と名古屋を～ぶ電車がありますか Is there any railroad *linking* this town *with* Nagoya?

この二つの国は運河で～ばれている These two countries *are connected* (≒ *are linked*) by a canal.

3〖実を〗¶ 彼の研究はようやく実を～んだ His studies *bore fruit* at last.

4 〖くちびるを〗 ¶ 彼は堅くくちびるを～んでいた He *had* his lips tightly *closed*.

5 〖終える〗 ¶ 私は自分の好きなことばで論文を～んだ I *concluded* my thesis with my favorite words.

むずむず ¶ 背筋が～する *A tingle* races (≒ runs) up and down my spine. / I feel *a tingle* in my spine. / My spine *tingles*. 彼は彼らの秘密を知りたくて～していた He *itched to* find out their secret. / He *had an itching for* finding out their secret. 彼はあの話をしたくて～していた He *was dying to* tell the story.

むすめ【娘】 (娘) a girl; (息女) a daughter. ¶ ～らしい girlish.

—心 a girlish innocence. —ざかり ¶ 彼女は～ざかりだ She *is in the bloom of girlhood*. —婿 a son-in-law.

むせい【無声】 —映画 a silent film. —音〖音声学〗a voiceless sound.

むせい【無性】 ¶ ～の sexless; 〖植物〗asexual; 〖文法〗neuter.

むぜい【無税】 exemption from duty. ¶ 年収100万円以下の人は～だ Those who earn less than a million yen a year *are duty-free* (≒ *are free of duty*).

—港 a free port. —輸入品 duty-free goods.

むせいげん【無制限】 ¶ 年齢は～だ There are *no restrictions* as to age. だれでも～に入ってよろしい Anyone is admitted *free*.

むせいふ【無政府】 anarchy. ¶ この国は～状態にある This country is in a state of *anarchy*.

—主義 anarchism. —主義者 an anarchist. —党 the anarchist party.

むせいぶつ【無生物】 an inanimate object.

むせいらん【無精卵】 a wind egg.

むせかえ･る【噎せ返る】 ¶ ～るような雑踏 a *choking* crowd.

むせきついどうぶつ【無脊椎動物】 an invertebrate animal.

むせきにん【無責任】 irresponsibility. ¶ 彼の～な行動はとがめられるべきだ His *irresponsible* conduct should be blamed. 彼は～にそんな約束をした He has promised it *without a due sense of responsibility*.

むせっそう【無節操】 (無定見) inconstancy; (無貞操) unchastity. ¶ ～な女 a *wanton* woman. ～な政治家 an *unprincipled* (≒ *inconstant*) politician.

むせびな･く【咽び泣く】 sob; mourn.

むせ･ぶ【咽ぶ･噎ぶ】 ¶ 少女は涙に～んだ The girl *was choked with* tears.

む･せる【噎る】 ¶ 食べ物がつっかえて～せた His food *choked* him. たばこの煙に～せた I *was choked with* tobacco smoke. ～せるような煙 *choking* fume.

むせん【無銭】 ¶ 彼は～飲食をした He *jumped* a restaurant bill. 彼らは毎年～旅行で全国を歩いている They make a trip all over the world *without money* every year.

むせん【無線】 —自動車 a radio car. —操縦 wireless control. —電信 wireless. —電報 a wireless 〔telegram〕. —電話 a wireless telephone. —放送 broadcasting by wireless.

むそう【夢想】 a dream; a vision. ¶ ～だにしなかった事件だった It was an event never *dreamt of*.

むぞうさ【無造作】 ¶ 彼は～に友人をつくる He makes friends *with ease* (≒ *with facility*). 彼は仕事を～にかたづけてしまう He accomplishes his task *with ease* (≒ *offhand*). 彼女は～に髪を束ねている She is doing up her hair *simply*.

むだ【無駄】 1 〖浪費〗waste. ¶ それはまさに時間の～だ It *is* indeed *a waste of* time. いっときも～にはできない There is no time to *lose*.

2 〖役に立たない･かいがない〗 ¶ この箱にふたをしても～だ It *is useless* to put a lid on this box. そんなことを彼に言っても～だ *It is no use* saying such things to him.

いろいろやってみたが～だった I tried everything but it was all *in vain*.

その計画をきみがしようとしても～だろう It will *do no good* for you to try to plan it.

彼に対する忠告はいっさい～になった My advice *was* entirely *wasted on* him.

彼にそれを頼んでも～だ *It is no good* asking him for it.

あの男は言い聞かしても～だ You can't make him listen.

努力してもまず～だろう No matter what you do, it will be *no use*.

逃れようとして～なことをやった He made a *futile* attempt to escape.

彼の献身的な働きも～だった His devoted efforts proved *fruitless*.

むだあし【無駄足】 ¶ 彼を駅に迎えにいったが，まったくの～だった I went to the station to meet him, but it was *a fool's errand*.

むだい【無題】 no title. ¶ ～の詩 a poem *without a title*.

むだぐち【無駄口】 ¶ そんな～をたたくものじゃない Never *say* such *useless things*. / Never *waste your breath*.

むだづかい【無駄遣い】 ¶ あまり金を～するな Don't *waste too much money*. 彼は雑誌に～をする He *squanders money on* magazines. 子どもに～させないようにしなさい Tell children to *spare their money*. そんなものは～と言ってよい That may be said to be *an utter waste*.

むだばなし【無駄話】 an idle talk. ¶ ～で一日終わってしまった I spent a whole day in *an idle talk*.

むだぼね【無駄骨】 vain efforts. ¶ まったく～をおった What *vain efforts* I have made! / I *labored in vain*. すべては～だった All my efforts *were in vain*.

むだめし【無駄飯】 ¶ 彼は～を食っているわけではない Not that he *lives a useless life*.

むだん【無断】 ¶ 彼は～で家を飛び出した He left

む

home *without the knowledge of* the people. ～で学校を休んではいけない You must not stay away from school *without leave* (≒ *unless you give us notice*). 彼は～で私の本を持っていった He took my book away *without my permission*.
—欠勤 (欠席) absence without leave (A.W.O.L.; AWOL と略記する). ¶ 彼は～欠席した He *played truant*.

むたんぽ【無担保】 ¶ 私は彼に～で100万円を貸した I granted him a loan of a million yen *without security*.

むち【鞭】 a whip; a rod. ¶ ～を当てて馬を走らせた I *whipped* my horse and made it run.

むち【無知】 ignorance; (無学) illiteracy. ¶ 電気製品については私はまったく～だ I *am* quite *ignorant of* electric appliances. この国には～蒙昧(もうまい)な人がたくさんいる Many inhabitants of this country are in an *uncivilized* state.

むち【無恥】 shamelessness. ¶ なんという～なやつだ What a *shameless* fellow he is!

むちうちしょう【鞭打ち症】 whiplash. ¶ 追突されて彼は～にかかった *Whiplash* resulted when his car was struck from behind.

むちつじょ【無秩序】 disorder. ¶ 世界はいまや～の状態にある The world *is* now *in chaos* (≒ *is* now *in disorder*). この寮生活はまったく～だ The life in this dormitory *is lawless*.

むちゃ【無茶】 ¶ ～を言うな Don't *be unreasonable*. ～をやる人は意外に多い There are unexpectedly many people who do *reckless things*. なんといってもそれは～だ It *is* absolute *nonsense*, in every respect. 全部私がやらなければならないなんて～だ It's *too much for* me to do all that.

むちゃくちゃ【無茶苦茶】 ¶ 部屋の中はなにもかも～だ Everything in the room *is in a mess* (≒ *in disorder*). 彼は机の上に本を～に置いた He put the books on the desk *in a disorderly fashion*. 電車は～に込んでいた The train was *excessively* crowded. 彼の運転は～だ He drives *like mad*.

むちゃくりく【無着陸】 ¶ ～飛行する make a *nonstop flight* (*to*).

むちゅう【夢中】 **1**〚有頂天〛¶ 彼はうれしくて～になっていた He *was beside himself with* joy.
2〚熱中する〛¶ 弟はジャズに～だ My younger brother *is crazy about* jazz.
彼はその少女に～だ He *is crazy about* the girl.
子どもたちはおもちゃに～になっている The children *are lost with* their toys.
少年たちはトランプに～だった The boys *were absorbed in* a game of cards.
2時間以上読書に～だった I *was engrossed in* reading for more than two hours.
話に～だったので帰るのを忘れた We *were so deep in* conversation that we forgot to go home.
3〚必死に〛¶ ～で走った I ran *for my life*. ～で逃げた I ran away *for all I was worth*. ～になって大声で叫んだ I cried out in a loud voice *in spite of myself*.

むつう【無痛】 ¶ ～分娩(ぶんべん) *painless* delivery.

むっくり ¶ ～起き上がる *spring to one's feet*; *get up suddenly*.

むっちり ¶ 健康な赤ん坊は～したほおをしている A healthy baby has *plump* cheeks. ～した小犬 a *chubby* dog.

むっつり ¶ 彼は～した人だ He is a *morose* (≒ *grim-looking*) man. 彼は～黙りこんで口をきかなかった He remained silent *sullenly* and would never utter words. 彼は～していて近寄りがたい He *looks* so *sullen* that he is difficult to approach.
—屋 a taciturn fellow.

むっと **1**〚おこった〛¶ ～したような顔つきをしている He *looks sullen*. / He has a *sullen* (≒ *grim*) look.
私は彼の発言に～した I *was offended* (≒ *got angry*) *at* his remark.
彼は～して立ち去った He went away *in a huff* (≒ *in a rage*).
2〚息づまる〛¶ ホールは～する人いきれだった The hall *was stuffy* (≒ *was suffocating*) because of the crowd.

むつまじ・い【睦まじい】 (和合した) harmonious; (親密な) friendly; intimate. ¶ そのふたりは～い The two *are on friendly terms*. 夫婦は～く暮らしている The man and wife are living *happily* (≒ *in harmony*). 一家は～く暮らしている The family live *in concord*.

むていけい【無定形】 ¶ ～の amorphous.
—状態 an amorphous state. **—**金属 an amorphous metal.

むていけい【無定型】 ¶ ～の formless.
—短歌 a free (≒ formless) *tanka* poem.

むていけん【無定見】 ¶ そんな～なことでは救いがたい There is no help for such *fickleness* of yours. 彼らは政府の～を攻撃した They attacked *the lack of a fixed policy* on the part of the government.

むていこう【無抵抗】 nonresistance. ¶ ～で without offering any resistance.

むてき【無敵】 ¶ 彼の強さはまさに天下～だ His strength *is unequaled* (≒ *is matchless*; *is peerless*).

むてき【霧笛】 a fog siren.

むてっぽう【無鉄砲】 rashness; recklessness. ¶ 両側を見ないで街を横切るのは～だ It *is rash* to cross the street without looking both ways. なんという～なことをするやつだ What a *reckless* fellow he is!

むでん【無電】 wireless; radio. ¶ ～で彼に無事を知らせた I told him *by wireless* (≒ *by radio*) that I was safe.
—技師 a radio operator. **—**室 a radio-room; a wirelessroom. **—**装置 wireless apparatus.

むとうせい【無統制】 lack of control. ¶ 彼のやり方は～だ His method *is unsystematic*.

むとうひょう【無投票】 ¶ 彼は～で議長に選ばれた He was elected chairman *without voting*. 彼は～で当選した He was returned *without voting*.

む

むどく【無毒】¶この薬品は～だ This medicine *is innocuous* (≒ *is not poisonous*).

むとくてん【無得点】¶投手は相手チームを～に封じた The pitcher *shut out* the opposing team. わがチームは～に終わった Our team ended *scoreless*.

むとどけ【無届け】¶～で休む stay away *without notice*.

—欠席 absence without notice. **—**デモ an unsanctioned demonstration.

むとんじゃく【無頓着】indifference. ¶彼は金には～だ He *is careless of* money matters. 彼女は身なりにはまったく～だ She *is* quite *unconcerned about* her appearance. 彼は政治にも経済にも～だ He *is indifferent* both *to* politics and *to* economics.

むないた【胸板】the chest. ¶彼は厚い～をしている He *is thick-chested*.

むなぎ【棟木】the ridge beam of a roof.

むなくそ【胸糞】¶～が悪い I *feel disgusted*. 彼の傲慢(ごう)な態度には～が悪くなる I *am disgusted at* his insolent attitude.

むなぐら【胸倉】¶彼は私の～をつかんだ He seized me by *the breast of my coat*.

むなぐるし・い【胸苦しい】¶なんとなく～い I *feel* somehow *heavy* (≒ *oppressed*) *in my breast*.

むなげ【胸毛】chest hair. ¶彼は～が濃い He has thick *hair* matted *on his chest*.

むなさわぎ【胸騒ぎ】(不安) uneasiness; (虫の知らせ) a presentiment. ¶ちょっと～がする I *have a* little *presentiment*. / I *feel* a little *uneasy*.

むなざんよう【胸算用】mental arithmetic. ¶～をする do *a mental calculation*.

むなし・い【空しい・虚しい】(無効) futile; vain; fruitless; (空虚) vacant; empty.

¶われわれの祈りは～かった Our prayer *was ineffective*. それは～い望みにすぎない It is but a *vain* hope. 彼らの努力は～かった Their efforts *were in vain*. やるだけやってみたが, ～かった I did my best but it *was in vain*. 彼は～い希望をいだいている He *hopes against hope*. 学生時代を～く過ごしたことを後悔している I regret having spent my school days *in idleness*. 軍隊生活の～さはなんともいいがたいものだった The *emptiness* of army life was indescribable.

むなはば【胸幅】the breadth of the chest. ¶～が広い be *broad*-chested.

むなもと【胸元】the chest; the breast. ¶球は打者の～をかすめた The ball brushed the batter's *breast*.

むに【無二】¶天下～の美人 *a peerless* (≒ *matchless*) beauty. ～の友 *one's bosom* friend.

むにゃむにゃ ¶～とひとりごとを言う *mumble* to *oneself*. ～と寝言を言う *mumble* in sleep.

むにんしょ【無任所】**—**大使 an ambassador at large. **—**大臣 a minister without portfolio.

むね【旨】**1**〖主旨〗¶その～彼に手紙で知らせよう I will write〔to〕him *to that effect*. 二, 三日中に上京する～きのう彼から連絡があった He *wrote* to me yesterday *that* he would come up to Tokyo in a few days.

2〖主義〗¶彼は親切を～とする He makes it *a principle* to be kind. ここでは食事は質素を～としている Plain food is *the essential point* here.

むね【胸】**1**〖胸部〗the chest; the breast. ¶彼は～の病で静養している He is recuperating on account of *consumption*. ～を大胆にあけたドレスが流行だ Extremely *low-necked* dresses are now in fashion. さつまいもを食べたら～がやけた I ate sweet potatoes and now *have a heartburn*. もっと～を張って歩きなさい Walk with your head held higher. この～で決勝のテープを切った I *finished first*. / I broke the top with my *chest*. 彼に～一つの差で敗れた I lost the race to him *by a narrow margin*.

2〖乳房〗the breasts. ¶彼女は豊かな～をしている She *is* full-*breasted*.

3〖心〗the heart. ¶私は喜びで～がいっぱいになった My *heart* was full of joy. この子の将来を考えると～が痛む I *pity* (≒ *feel sorry for*) this child when I think of his future. スタートを切る前は～がどきどきした My *heart* was beating quickly until I started. 希望に～をふくらませて彼らは卒業していった They graduated with their *hearts* full of hope. 成績表を見て～をなでおろした I *felt relieved* when I saw the report-card. 子どもが～をはずませて帰ってきた The child came back *with his eyes sparkling*. 悲しみに～も張り裂けんばかりだった My *heart* almost burst with grief. このことは私ひとりの～にたたんでおきましょう I will *keep* the matter *only to myself*. 彼の勇敢な行為に～を打たれた I *was impressed with* (≒ *by*) his brave act. きみの話を聞いて～がすっとした I *felt* much *relieved* when I heard your story. 彼の苦言がぐっと～にこたえた His frank advice *came home to my heart*. 彼はなにか～に一物あるようすだ He looks as if he *had his own axe to grind* (≒ *had an ulterior motive*).

むね【棟】(むな木) the ridge beam of a roof. ¶火は平屋1～を焼いた The fire burned a onestoried house.

—割り長屋 a tenement house.

むねやけ【胸焼け】a heartburn. ¶さつまいもを食べたらひどく～がする I ate sweet potatoes and now I have *a* bad *heartburn*.

むねん【無念】(口惜しさ) mortification. ¶体力がないのを～に思う I *feel a deep regret for* my lacking physical strength. 彼はいまや～無想の境地にある He *is* now *free from all worldly thoughts*.

むのう【無能】lack of ability; incapacity.

¶ 彼らは政府の～を攻撃した They attacked the government for its *inefficiency*. その失敗で彼は～ぶりを露呈した He betrayed his *incapacity* by the failure. そういうことにかけては彼は～だ He *is incompetent to* do such a matter.

むのうりょく【無能力】 lack of ability; 〖法律〗 incompetence; incapacity. ¶ ～な incompetent; incapable.

—者 an incompetent person.

むはいとう【無配当】 non-dividend.

—株 a non-dividend stock.

むひ【無比】 ¶ 日本の列車の運行は正確～である Japan maintains the *unrivaled* (≒ *unequaled*) punctuality of trains. 彼の指導力は当代～だ His leadership *is unchallenged* (≒ *is unsurpassed*).

むひはん【無批判】 ¶ ～に人の意見に従う accept another's opinion *uncritically* (≒ *indiscriminately*).

むびょう【無病】 ¶ 一家じゅう～息災でおります All my family *are in good health* (≒ *are quite well*).

むひょうじょう【無表情】 ¶ 彼女はまるで～だった I read *no* distinct *expression* in her face. 彼は～に私を見た He looked at me *without expression*.

むふう【無風】 ¶ あらしのあとに～状態がやってきた After the storm came *a* great *calm*. その日は快晴～であった On that day the weather was perfect, and there was *not a breath of wind*. 政局は今のところまったく～状態である The political situation is in a perfectly *settled* state at present. / The political situation *is* now *in the doldrums*.

むふんべつ【無分別】 thoughtlessness; (軽率) rashness. ¶ それは～というものだ You should know better. / You don't know what you are doing. ～にもほどがある How *thoughtless* (≒ *indiscreet*) you *are*!

むほう【無法】 unlawful; illegal; (わがまま) arbitrary. ¶ そのような～な要求には応じられない We can't meet such an *unreasonable* demand. この結果隣国から～な干渉を招くにいたった This led to the *arbitrary* intervention of the neighboring country.

—地帯 a disturbed area. —者 an outlaw; an outrageous fellow.

むぼう【無謀】 ¶ 風の強い日に海へ泳ぎにいくなんて～だ It *is rash* (≒ *is imprudent*) to go swimming in the sea on a windy day.

むほうしゅう【無報酬】 ¶ その医師は貧しい患者は～で診療する The doctor treats his poor patients *for nothing*. / The doctor *asks* his poor patients *no fee for* his cures. 彼らは～で社会奉仕をした They worked for the public benefit *without reward* (≒ *without recompense*).

むほうしん【無方針】 planless. ¶ 当局は事実上～だ The authorities *have* virtually *no fixed policy*.

むぼうび【無防備】 ¶ その町は～だ The city *is unfortified* (≒ *is defenseless*).

—都市 an open city.

むほん【謀反】 revolt; insurrection; rebellion (この順で規模が大きくなる. mutiny は軍隊などの謀反をいう); (陰謀) conspiracy; (反逆) treason.

¶ 政府に対して～を起こす *rise in revolt against* the government.

むみ【無味】 ¶ 彼の演説は～乾燥だった His speech *was dull* (≒ *was insipid*). (新鮮味がない意味では *stale* または *cut and dried* という表現がある).

むめい【無名】 ¶ 当時彼は～の弁護士だった At that time he was an *obscure* lawyer. その本は～の作家のものだ The book is by an *unknown* author. 彼は終生～であった He remained *unknown* (≒ *undistinguished*) all his life.

—氏 an anonymous person; a nobody. —戦士の墓 the tomb of the unknown soldier.

むめい【無銘】 ¶ ～の名刀 a celebrated sword with *no signature* (≒ *no name*) on it.

むめんきょ【無免許】 ¶ ～で運転する drive (an automobile) *without a license*.

むやみ【無暗】 ¶ 彼は～に酒を飲む He drinks *too much* (≒ *to excess*; *excessively*). 彼は～に子どもをかわいがる He is *immoderately* fond of his children. 彼は人の言うことを～に信ずる He *is too ready to* believe others. ～に人を非難するものではない Don't blame others *unreasonably* (≒ *without due cause*).

むゆうびょう【夢遊病】 somnambulism; sleepwalking.

—者 a somnambulist; a sleepwalker.

むよう【無用】 **1** 〖不必要・無益〗 ¶ ～の摩擦は避けたい I wish to avoid *needless* (≒ *unnecessary*) friction.

それは～の長物だ It *is a good-for-nothing*. / It *is worse than useless*. / It *is a white elephant*.

弁解は～だ Make no more excuse. / Don't "Yes, but" me.

心配は～です *There is no need for* anxiety. / You *have no cause to* worry.

商売に情けは～だ *There is no place for* sentiment in business dealings.

2 〖してはならない〗 ¶ このことについてはくれぐれも他言は～に願います Be sure not to let anyone know anything about this.

御意見— No coaching. 天地— (包装表記) This side up. / Do not turn over. 通り抜け— (掲示) No thoroughfare. 問答— This is no time for arguing. / Stop arguing. 落書き— (掲示) No scribbling on the walls. 小便— (掲示) Commit no nuisance.

むよく【無欲】 freedom from avarice; generosity. ¶ ～な generous; unselfish.

むら【村】 a village; (小部落) a hamlet. ¶ ～はずれに on the outskirts of *a village*.

—人 a villager. —役場 the village office.

むら【斑】unevenness; irregularity. ¶ 彼は壁にペンキを塗ったが～がある He painted the wall *unevenly.* この布は～なく染まる This cloth takes dye *well.* あの人の仕事には～がない He works *uniformly* well. 彼は気分に～がある He *is capricious.*

むらが·る【群がる】¶ 多勢の人が広場に～っていた A lot of people *crowded* the square. 娘たちは人気歌手のまわりに～った The young girls *clustered* (≒ *thronged*; *crowded*) around the well-known singer. ハチが花のまわりに～っていた The bees *swarmed* about the flowers. / The bees flitted about the flowers *in swarms.* 鳥が～る The brids *flock* together.

むらき【斑気】caprice; fickleness. ¶ 彼は～でなにをしても長続きしない He *is* too *fickle* (≒ *capricious*; *whimsical*) to stick to one thing.

むらさき【紫】violet; purple. ¶ ～色の purple; purple-colored. ～がかった purplish.

むらさきずいしょう【紫水晶】〘鉱物〙amethyst.

むらさめ【村雨·叢雨】a shower; a passing rain.

むらはちぶ【村八分】boycott; ostracism. ¶ 彼は～にされた He *was ostracized* (≒ *was boycotted*) by the villagers.

むらむらと ¶ 怒りが～こみ上げてきた I was seized with a *sudden* anger. / A *sudden* anger seized me.

むり【無理】**1**〘不条理·不可能·困難〙unreasonableness; impossibility. ¶そんな～を言われても困る I cannot meet such an *unreasonable* demand.

この仕事を今週いっぱいに仕上げるのはとても～だ It *is impossible* to finish this work by the end of this week.

ご～でしょうが, まげてご承諾いただきたい I know I am asking a lot of you, but I hope you will oblige me.

～を承知できみに頼んでいるのだ I allow that it is an *unreasonable* demand, but I should like you to do it.

彼が腹を立てるのも～はない It *is natural* (≒ *is no wonder*) that he should get angry.

子どもにじっとしていろというのは～だ It *is too much* to expect children to keep still.

人間～がきくのは若いうちだけだ Only young people can *strain themselves to the limit of endurance.*

その気にならない子どもを～に勉強させようとするのはよくない It is not good to make children study *against their will.*

2〘強引·強制〙¶ そんな重要な問題を～押しに決めてしまうのはよくないことだ It is not good to *force* a decision on such an important problem.

3〘過労·過度〙overwork; overstrain. ¶ いくら忙しいからって, あまり～するな Don't *overwork* even though you are very busy.

疲れたら～しないで寝たほうがいい If you get tired, go to bed without *overstraining yourself.*

あまり～をして体をこわしたら元も子もなくなる If you *work yourself sick,* you will lose everything.

～な運動はかえって体によくない *Too much* exercise will do more harm than good to your health.

むりかい【無理解】lack of understanding. ¶ 両国民相互の～から戦争になった *Lack of* mutual *understanding* between the two nations caused the war.

むりじい【無理強い】compulsion; coercion. ¶ 彼に酒を～するな Don't *force* him to (≒ *make* him) drink much.

むりしき【無理式】〘数学〙an irrational expression.

むりすう【無理数】〘数学〙an irrational number; a surd〔number〕.

むりそく【無利息】no interest. ¶ ～で金を貸す lend money *without interest.*

むりなんだい【無理難題】¶ ～を言う make *an unreasonable demand.*

むりょう【無料】¶お茶は～サービスだ The tea is served *free* (≒ *for nothing*). 避難民は～で衣食の供給を受けた The refugees received *free* food and clothing.

むりょく【無力】powerlessness; incapacity. ¶彼はそのことで自分の～を悟った He realized his *incapacity* (≒ *powerlessness*) in the matter. 事の起こるごとに政府の～が暴露された Every accident betrayed the *impotence* of the government. 私は～でなにもできない I *am powerless* (≒ *am helpless*) to do anything. われわれは政治的には～だ We *are not* politically *influential* enough.

むるい【無類】¶ 彼は～の記憶力を持っている He enjoys a *matchless* (≒ an *unequaled*; an *unusually powerful*) memory.

むれ【群れ】a group; (人) a crowd; a band; a host; (悪人) a gang; a mob; (牛·馬·豚など大型の家畜) a herd; a drove; (鳥·羊·ウサギなど温順な動物) a flock; (魚類·イルカ·鯨など) a school; (魚類) a shoal; (こん虫類) a swarm; (星など) a cluster (以上の分類は厳密なものではなく, 共通に用いられるものも多い).

¶ 春になると人々は～をなして桜を見に行く In spring people go to see the cherry blossoms *in crowds.*

む·れる【蒸れる】¶ 草を生のまま蓄えると～れる Grass *heats* if stored green. 御飯が柔らかく～れた The rice *has been steamed* soft. (くつ下が) go stinking.

むろん【無論】of course; needless to say. ¶ それは～のことだ It is *a matter of course.* ～だ Of course. / Why not? ～それには法的根拠はない *Needless to say,* (≒ *It goes without saying*〔that〕) it is legally groundless.

むんむん ¶ そこは人いきれで～していた The place *was* terribly *stuffy* (≒ *close*). 部屋の中は暑さで～していた The room was *oppressively* hot.

む

め

め【目】 an eye. **1**〚目〛¶ 彼女はすごくチャーミングな～をしている She has truly charming *eyes.*
彼は～を閉じてじっと考え込んで坐っていた He sat deep in meditation with his *eyes* closed.
彼は～をさらのようにして遭難者名簿を見た He stared at the list of the victims with *saucer eyes* (≒ *eyes* as big as saucers).
せっけんが～にしみて痛い My *eyes* are smarting from soap.
午前10時ごろ訪ねたのに彼は眠そうな～をして出てきた I went to see him at about ten in the morning but he came out with sleepy *eyes.*
酔うにつれて彼の～がすわってきた As he continued to drink his *eyes* became dull.
子どもが母親の～の前で車にはねられた The child was hit right in front of its mother's *eyes* by a car.
華やかな舞台を見て～の保養になった The gorgeous stage was a feast for my *eyes.*
2〚視力・視線〛 sight; eyesight. ¶ 彼は若いころから～が悪かったが, ついにまったく～が見えなくなった His *sight* has been weak since boyhood, but now he is totally blind.
～の届く限り水また水であった An endless stretch of water lay before me as far as I could *see.*
彼は毎朝通勤電車の中で新聞に～を通す He *scans* the newspaper on the train on his way to work every morning.
～は口ほどに物を言う The *eyes* are as eloquent as the tongue.
彼女の大胆な服装が人々の～をひいた Her loud dress attracted people's *attention.*
ちょっと～を離している間に, 荷物を盗まれた The suitcase was stolen *while I looked aside* for a minute.
彼のまじめなプレーが私の～にとまった His earnest performance *caught my attention.*
四方に～を配りながら森の中を進んだ They made their way through the forest, *casting* observant *eyes* in all directions.
親の～を盗んで彼はよく遊びに出かけた Eluding his parents, he often slipped out to play.
ふたりは人の～を忍ぶ仲だった The two were secretly in love.
3〚見地・判断〛 ¶ アメリカ人の～から見た日本の社会機構はわれわれ日本人には大いに参考になる American *views* of Japanese social structure are highly valuable for us Japanese.
冷静な～で見ればどちらが悪いかはすぐわかるはずだ If you look at the situation with an impartial *eye,* you will understand at once which side is to blame.
4〚眼識〛 ¶ 彼には人を見る～がない He is *a* poor *judge of* a man's character.
彼は絵を見る～がだんだん肥えてきた He has gradually gained *discrimination* in his appreciation of painting.
ぼくの～に狂いはなかった I was right in my *judgment.*
5〚親切・世話〛 ¶ 彼はわれわれ若い者によく～をかけてくれる He looks after the younger members very well.
6〚経験〛 ¶ きのうはひどい～に会った I *had* a terrible experience yesterday.
若いころはずいぶんつらい～に会った I *went through* many hardships when I was young.
7〚面会〛 ¶ ご主人にお～にかかりたいのですが I should like to *see* your husband.
お初にお～にかかります It is a great pleasure to *meet* you.
いいものをお～にかけましょう Let me *show* you something good.
8〚自覚・意識〛 ¶ これにこりて彼も～が覚めるだろう He will *come to his senses* (≒ *realize the facts*) after this experience.
夜中に大きな音で～が覚めた A loud noise *woke* me *up* in the night.
9〚好み〛 ¶ 彼女はチョコレートに～がない She *has a fancy for* chocolates.
彼は酒となるとまったく～がない He *loves* drinking *more than anything else.*
10〚縦横に交わるものの間隙〛 ¶ こんなに粗い～の網では小さい魚は逃げてしまう The *meshes* of this net are too large for small fish.
このセーターは～がつんでいるから暖かい The sweater is very warm, because it is knit with small stiches.
11〚慣用的表現〛 ¶ その悲報を聞いて～の前が真っ暗になった Everything went black when I heard the sad news.
人を疑いの～で見てはいけない You must not look at people with suspicious *eyes.*
映画やテレビには～もくれないで, 彼は受験勉強に励んだ He studied hard for the examination, *giving* no *attention to* films and television programs.
あの店は忙しいので, すべての店員にまで主人の～が届かない The shop is so busy that it is impossible for the master to *keep* all the shop-assistants *under his direct control* (≒ *keep* all the shop-assistants *within the*

reach of his eyes).

ボールが顔に当たって～から火が出た I saw stars when the ball hit me in the face.

マットの上で前方回転を繰り返したら～が回った I tumbled head over heels on the mat and my *eyes swam.*

彼はひとり娘を～の中に入れても痛くないほどかわいがっていた He regarded his only daughter *as the apple of his eye.*

彼は～から鼻へ抜けるような切れ者だ He is a man of keen intelligence.

このところ忙しくて～が回りそうだ I'm so busy these days *my head's in a spin.*

～が飛び出るほどの代金を請求された My *eyes* popped out when I saw the bill. / They charged me an *astonishingly* high price.

彼はここから～と鼻の所に住んでいる He lives *only a few steps away from here.*

特売場は～の色を変えた主婦たちでいっぱいだった The bargain department was packed with *frenzied* housewives.

このごろ～に見えて体力が衰えてきた I am *noticeably* losing my strength these days.

今度こそ彼に～に物見せてやる Next time, I will hit (≒ strike) him hard to teach him a lesson.

彼女は目前の利益に～がくらんだ She was blinded by the hope of *immediate* gain.

今度だけは～をつぶって許してあげよう I will shut my *eyes* and let you go just this time.

彼はその会社の将来性に～をつけて株を買った He *noticed* the bright prospect of the company, and bought shares in it.

彼女の最近の言動は～に余る Her recent words and actions are objectionable in our *eyes.*

め【芽】**1**〖若芽·つぼみが〗a bud; (芽の枝) a sprout; a shoot; (幼芽) a germ.

¶～が出る bud; shoot; sprout; germinate.

柳はすでに～をふいている The willow tree *is* already *budding.*

2〖運が〗¶商売が～を出しかけてきた The business has begun to *prosper.*

彼はどうも～が出ない He doesn't seem to *get on* in the world.

彼はやっと～が出てきた The *luck* has turned to him. / The *luck* has turned in his favor. / *Fortune* has begun to smile upon him.

悪の～は早く摘まねばならぬ Crime must be nipped in the *bud.*

-め【-目】**1**〖順序〗¶銀行は角から5軒～だ The bank is the fifth building from the corner.

彼はハワイに着いて7日～に発病した He fell sick *on the seventh* day after he arrived in Hawaii.

彼は5番～に会場に現われた He was *the fifth to* appear in the hall.

いちばん向こうの列の前から3人～がうちの息子です The *third person from* the front in the farthest row is our son.

上から10枚～のカードを1枚取ってください Please take out *the tenth* card *from* the top.

右から5冊～の本を本棚から取ってくれませんか Will you please get me *the fifth* book *from* the right in the bookshelf?

2〖程度〗¶粒の大き～のイチゴが欲しい I want *rather* large strawberries.

パンを薄～に切る slice bread (≒ loaf) *a bit* thin.

早～に目的地に着くようにしなさい Try to arrive at your destination *earlier.*

めあたらし·い【目新しい】new; original.

¶見るものがみな私には～い Every sight *is strange* (≒ *new*) *to* me. それは～くなくなった It had ceased to *be novel* (≒ *be a novelty*).

めあて【目当て】(目的) an object; (目標) a guide. ¶なにを～にこれをするのですか What is your *purpose* in doing this? 教会の塔を～に歩いた We walked on with the church tower as our *guide.*

めい-【名-】¶～選手 a *star* (≒ an *excellent*) player. ～ピアニスト a *celebrated* (≒ an *excellent*) pianist.

めい【命】(命令) order; command; instructions; (天命) destiny; fate; providence; (生命) life.

¶～を受ける receive *orders* (*from a person*); *be ordered* (*by a person*). ～に従う (そむく) obey (disobey) *a person's orders.* ～旦夕に迫る be on the verge of death.

めい【明】¶彼は人を見る～がある He *is a good judge of* (≒ *has an eye for*) character. 彼は先見の～がある He has *foresight.*

めい【銘】(記念碑の) an inscription; (墓の) an epitaph; (刀剣の) a signature; (座右の) a motto; (メダルやコインの) a legend.

めい【姪】a niece.

めいあん【名案】a good (≒ brilliant; capital; splendid) idea (≒ plan). ¶そのときふと～が浮かんだ Then *an idea* came to me. / Then I hit upon *a good* (≒ *splendid*) *plan.*

めいあん【明暗】light and shade. ¶人生の～両面を見るべきだ You should look on the *bright side* as well as the *dark side* of life.

めいい【名医】a noted (≒ skilled) physician.

めいおうせい【冥王星】〖天文学〗Pluto.

めいが【名画】a famous (≒ notable) painting; a masterpiece; (映画) a good (≒ celebrated) film.

めいかい【明快】¶彼は～に答弁した He gave a *clear-cut* answer. 彼は～に説明した He gave a *lucid* explanation. / He explained *lucidly.*

めいかい【明解】a clear explanation.

めいかく【明確】clearness; precision; accuracy; exactness. ¶彼の指示は～で疑問の余地を残さなかった His *definite* directions left no room for doubt. この点をもっと～にすべきだ This point should *be clarified.*

めいがら【銘柄】(商標) a brand; a trademark; 〖株式〗a name; an isue.

—売買 a sale on description. 株式— a

name [of the stock].

めいき【明記】¶それは条文に～されている It *is specified* in the article. / The article *specifies* it.

めいき【銘記】¶きみはこれらのことを心に～すべきだ You should *bear* these facts *in mind*. 私は彼のことばは心に～している His words *are impressed* (≒ *are engraved*) *on* my memory.

めいぎ【名義】*one's* name. ¶彼は～だけの編集者だ He is an editor *in name only*. / He is *a mere nominal* editor. 彼は不動産の一部を妻の～に書き換えた He transferred a part of his estate to his wife. 彼は他人～でその土地を買った He bought the lot *under the name of* another person. この家は私の～になっている This house *is in my name*.

—人 a nominal person.

めいきゅう【迷宮】a labyrinth ; a maze. ¶事件は～入りだ The authorities *are* still *in the dark about* the case. / The case *is unsolved*.

めいきょく【名曲】a famous music.

めいく【名句】(名言) a wise saying ; (詩) a beautiful verse.

めいくん【名君】a wise ruler (≒ lord).

めいげつ【名月】a bright (≒ clear) moon ; (満月) a full moon. ¶中秋の～ the harvest moon.

めいげん【名言】a wise saying. ¶千古の～ an immortal (≒ historic) saying. それは～だね Well said!

めいげん【明言】declaration. ¶きみのほうが悪いのだと～できる I can *declare* (≒ *assert*) that you are in the wrong. それが真実であるかどうか～できない I can't *say for certain* (≒ *say definitely*) whether it is true or not.

めいさい【明細】details ; particulars. ¶～に説明する explain *in detail*. ～をつけて請求する ask for payment with *an account*.

—書 a detailed account.

めいさい【迷彩】camouflage. ¶～を施した家 a *camouflaged* house.

めいさく【名作】a masterpiece.

めいさつ【明察】insight. ¶事情ご～のほどをお願いします I hope you'll *understand* the situation well.

めいさん【名産】a special product ; a speciality. ¶マツタケが私たちの村の～だ Our village is famous for its mushrooms. 北海道は～が多い Hokkaido is rich in *noted products*.

めいし【名士】a man of note ; a celebrity ; a notable. ¶彼は～気どりだ He poses as *a noted* (≒ *distinguished*) *man*. 彼はいまや学界の～だ He is now *a prominent figure* in the academic world.

めいし【名刺】a card ; a visiting card. ¶彼に～を取り次いでもらった I sent my *card* in to him. ～を出す give (≒ present) *one's card*. ～を交換する exchange *cards*.

—入れ a card-case. —受け a visiting-card tray.

めいし【名詞】〖文法〗a noun ; a substantive.

めいじ【明示】¶契約は細かい点まで～すべきだ The contract should *specify* the details.

めいじつ【名実】¶彼は～ともに最も優れた政治家だ He is *nominally and virtually* the greatest statesman. / He is the greatest statesman *in fact as well as in name*.

めいしゃ【目医者】an oculist ; an eye doctor.

めいしゅ【名手】an expert. ¶射撃の～ an *expert* in shooting ; an *excellent* (≒ *expert*) shot.

めいしょ【名所】a noted place ; a place of interest. ¶東京の～を見物する *do the sights of* Tokyo. ～を案内する show (*a person*) round *places of note*. その庭園はユリの～だ The garden *is famous for* its lilies.

—旧跡 ¶～旧跡のバス巡りをした I took a bus trip (≒ tour) round *places of scenic and historical interest*.

めいしょう【名称】a name. ¶われわれはそれに「みどり会」という～をつけた We *called* (≒ *named*) it "Midori Association."

めいじょう【名状】¶その美しさは～しがたい Its beauty *is beyond description*.

めいしん【迷信】a superstition. ¶～を打破する get rid of (≒ do away with) all *superstitions*.

—家 a superstitious person.

めいじん【名人】a master ; an expert. ¶彼女はピアノの～だ She is an *excellent* (≒ *accomplished*) pianist. 彼は料理の～だ He is *an expert in* cooking.

—芸 ¶彼は～芸を見せてくれた He showed us *a master performance*. —はだ ¶彼の仕事には～はだのところがある He *has something of a master hand* in his work.

めい·する【瞑する】¶もって～せられんことを May your soul rest in peace!

めい·ずる【命ずる】¶隊長は部下に突撃を～じた The captain *ordered* (≒ *commanded*) his men to charge at the enemy. 良心の～ずるところに従え Do what your conscience *tells* you to do. / Follow the *dictates* of your conscience. 彼に即刻退場を～じた I *ordered* him out of the room at once. 彼は部長に～じられた He *was appointed* head of the department.

めい·ずる【銘ずる】¶あなたのご忠告を肝に～じておきます I'll *keep* (≒ *bear*) your advice *in mind*. / I'll *take* your advice *to heart*.

めいせい【名声】[a] fame. ¶彼はその小説で一躍～を得た He leapt into *fame* by the novel. 彼の演奏は大いに～を博した His performance won him *a* great *fame*. 彼女の～は内外に響いている Her *name* is known both at home and abroad. 彼女は世界的～のあるピアニストだ She is a pianist *of world-wide fame*.

めいせき【明晰】clearness ; plainness ; distinctness. ¶彼は頭脳～だ He has a *clear* head. / He is a *clear*-headed man. 彼のことばは～さを欠く His words *are* not *plain* (≒ *are* not *clear*). / His words *are indistinct*.

め

めいそう【瞑想】meditation. ¶ ～にふける be lost in *meditation.*

めいそうしんけい【迷走神経】〘解剖学〙the vagus (複 vagi) ; the pneumogastric nerves.

めいだい【命題】〘論理〙a proposition. ¶ ～を解明する make *a proposition* clear.

めいちゃ【銘茶】tea of a well-known brand ; choice tea.

めいちゅう【命中】a hit. ¶ 弾が目標に～した A bullet *hit* the mark (≒ target). 石が彼の頭に～した A stone *hit* (≒ *struck*) him on the head. ―弾 a hit.

めいちょ【名著】a famous book ; a masterpiece.

めいてい【酩酊】intoxication ; drunkenness. ¶ 彼はすっかり～していた He *was dead drunk.*

めいてん【名店】a well-known store. ―街 a street (≒ an arcade ; a quarter) of speciality (≒ well-known) stores.

めいど【冥土・冥途】Hades. ¶ ～の旅に出る go (≒ start on a journey) to *the other* (≒ *the nether*) *world.*

めいとう【名刀】a noted (≒ an excellent) sword.

めいとう【名答】a right answer. ¶ ご～ You are quite right. / That's right.

めいどう【鳴動】rumbling. ¶ 大地が～する The earth *rumbles.* 大山～してねずみ一匹 (諺) *Much cry and little wool.*

めいにち【命日】the anniversary of *a person's* death. ¶ きょうは彼の～です This is the *anniversary of* his *death.*

めいば【名馬】a fine horse.

めいはく【明白】clearness ; obviousness. ¶ ～な clear ; obvious ; evident. 事実を～にする *make* the fact *clear.* その意味は子どもにさえ～だ The meaning *is obvious* (≒ *is clear*) even *to* children. 彼がそれをしたことは～だ It *is evident* that he has done it. / *Evidently* he has done it.

めいび【明媚】¶ 風光～の地 a place of scenic beauty.

めいひつ【名筆】(書) an excellent handwriting ; (画) an excellent painting.

めいびん【明敏】sagacity. ¶ 彼は頭脳～な政治家だ He is a *quick-witted* (≒ *very intelligent*) politician.

めいふく【冥福】¶ 彼の～を祈る May he rest in peace !

めいぶつ【名物】(産物) a special product. ¶ 彼はこの大学の～教授だ He is a *popular* professor of this university. リンゴは青森の～だ Aomori is famous for its apples. / Apples are *a special product* of Aomori. この店はてんぷらが～だ *Tempura* is *a feature* of this shop.

めいぶん【名文】a beautiful composition ; a masterpiece ; (1節) a beautiful passage. ¶ 彼は～を書く He is a fine writer. ―家 a stylist.

めいぶん【明文】a provision. ¶ この問題に関しては法律に～がない There is no *provision* in the law on this subject.

めいぼ【名簿】a list. ¶ ～を作成する make *a list.* 彼の名前が～に載っている His name *is on the list.* 名前を～に記入しなさい Put your name *on the list* (≒ *on the roll*). 先生が出欠の～を呼んだ The teacher called *the roll.* 会員― a membership list. 学生― a register of students. 参観人― a visitors' list. 職員― a staff list. 選挙人― a pollbook.

めいぼう【名望】high reputation. ¶ ～を得る gain *one's fame* (≒ *popularity*). ―家 a popular figure.

めいぼく【名木】a fine old (≒ historic) tree ; (香木) fine incense wood.

めいみゃく【命脈】life. ¶ ～を保つ survive ; keep alive. 現内閣の～は尽きかけている The *existence* of the present Cabinet is precarious.

めいむ【迷夢】an illusion. ¶ その政治家は民衆の～をさました The statesman *disillusionized* the common people.

めいめい【命名】christening ; naming. ¶ その列車をコダマと～した They *named* the train 'Kodama.' その子どもはジョンと～された The child *was christened* John. ―式 the christening ceremony.

めいめい【銘銘】everyone. ¶ ～自分の持ち物に注意しなさい *Each of you* must be careful of your own things. ～に部屋がある *Each one* has his own room. 私はそのことについて彼ら～に意見を打診した I sounded them out on the matter *individually.* 彼らは～の家に帰った They went to their *several* homes.

めいめいはくはく【明明白白】¶ それは～な事実だ The fact *is as clear as day.*

めいめつ【明滅】¶ 明かりが遠くで～している Lights *are blinking* (≒ *are flickering*) in the distance. ―信号 a blinking signal.

めいもく【名目】a title ; a name. ¶ 彼は～だけの社長だ He is the *nominal* president of the company. 病気という～で会社に行っていない I've been absent from company *under the pretext* (≒ *excuse*) *of* sickness. ―賃金 nominal wages.

めいもく【瞑目】¶ ～する (目を閉じる) close *one's* eyes ; (死ぬ) die ; pass away.

めいもん【名門】a noted family ; (貴族) a noble family. ¶ 彼女は～の出だ She comes of *a noble family.* / She comes from *good stock.* わが校は野球の～校だ Our school *is distinguished for* its history of baseball games.

めいもんく【名文句】wise words ; a fine expression ; a happy phrase.

めいやく【名訳】an excellent translation ; (語句の適訳) a happy translation.

めいゆう【名優】a great actor (≒ (女の) actress) ; a distinguished actor (≒ actress).

めいよ【名誉】honor. ¶ この賞は私にとってたいへん～だ This prize is *a great honor* to me.

彼は母校の～だ He is *a credit* to his Alma Mater. 彼は～を重んじる人物だ He is a man of *honor*. 彼はその行ないによって～を回復した He restored his *honor* by that act. 彼は～の戦死を遂げた He died a *glorious* death on the battlefield. この不祥事は会社の～にかかわる This scandal affects the *honor* of the firm. 彼がこの分野での先駆者としての～を受けた He was given *credit* for being the pioneer in this line. 彼の行為は国の～を汚す His behavior stains the *honor* of his country. 人の～を傷つけてはならない Never injure another's *reputation*. きみは～にかけてそれをすべきだ You should do that as a point of *honor*.

—会員 an honorary member. —毀損 defamation of character; 〔a〕 libel. ¶ 彼は～毀損で訴えられた He was sued for *libel*. —教授 a professor emeritus; an emeritus professor. —心 desire for fame.

めいり【名利】 face and profit; riches and honor. ¶ 彼は～にきゅうきゅうとしている He is striving after *fame and profit*. 彼は～に超然としている He is above *riches and honor*.

めいりょう【明瞭】 clearness; plainness; obviousness. ¶ ～な clear; plain; distinct. ～に clearly; plainly; distinctly. 事実を～にする *make* the fact *clear*. きみの発音は～だ Your pronunciation *is clear* (≒ *is distinct*). 彼が一言も信じないことは～だった It *was plain* that he did not believe a word.

めい·る【滅入る】 ¶ 雨天続きで気が～る A long spell of rainy days *made* me *feel gloomy* (≒ *depressed*).

めいれい【命令】 an order; a command; (指令) an instruction. ¶ 私がきみたちに～を出す I give you my *order*. 当局の～によって劇場は閉鎖された By *order* of the authorities the theater was closed. ～どおりにしなさい Do as you *are told* (≒ *are ordered*). 私の～に背いてはならぬ You must not disobey (≒ violate) my *order*. 絶対安静にするように医者から～を受けている I *am ordered* by my doctor to take a complete rest in bed. 彼はいつも～口調で話す He always speaks *in a commanding* (≒ *in an imperative*) *tone*.

—文 〘文法〙 an imperative sentence. —法 〘文法〙 the imperative mood.

めいろ【目色】 ¶ 彼は～を変えてどなっていた He was shouting *with a fiery look* (≒ *with fiery eyes*).

めいろ【迷路】 a maze; a labyrinth.

めいろう【明朗】 ¶ ～な女性 a *cheerful* woman. ～な政治 *clean* politics. ～さを欠く報告 an *dishonest* report. ～化する make bright; brighten.

めいろん【名論】 an excellent opinion; a sound argument.

—卓説 excellent arguments and opinions.

めいわく【迷惑】 (面倒) trouble; (うるさいこと) annoyance; (不便) inconvenience. ¶ ～をおかけしてすみません I'm sorry to *trouble* you. この出来事で彼は非常に～した He *was* much *annoyed at* what happened. 人の～になることをけっしてするな Never do what gives others *trouble* (≒ *inconvenience*; *nuisance*). ～でなければあなたのお供をさせてください Let me accompany you *if you don't mind* (≒ *if it is not inconvenient to you*). なんと～千万なこと What *a nuisance*! / How *annoying* it *is*! 彼は他人に～をかけて金もうけをした He enriched himself *at the cost of other people*.

めうえ【目上】 *one's* superiors; *one's* betters.

めうし【雌牛】 a cow.

めうつり【目移り】 ¶ 見本をあまりたくさん見せてくれたので，～してどれにしてよいかわからなかった They showed me so many samples that I *was quite puzzled which one to take*. 美人ぞろいで～する Each one looks more beautiful than the others.

メーカー a manufacturer.

—品 an article produced by a big manufacturer.

メーキャップ a make-up. ¶ 彼女の～は自然に見えた Her *make-up* had a natural look.

メーター (長さ) a meter; (計量器) a meter. ¶ 50～のプール a 50 *meter* swimming pool. ～を調べる read the *meter*.

ガス(水道)— a gas (water) meter. タクシー— a taxi meter.

メーデー May Day. ¶ ～のパレード a May Day parade.

メード a maid; a maid-servant; a house-maid.

メートル a meter. ¶ 高さ(深さ)が10～ある be ten *meters* high (deep). 一杯飲んで～を上げる *be in high spirits* (≒ *be on the spree*) over *one's* cups.

—法 the metric system.

メーン —エベント a main event. —スタンド the main stand. —ストリート the main street. —テーブル the main table. —マスト the mainmast.

めがお【目顔】 ¶ ～で知らせる make a sign with *one's* eye; give (*a person*) a wink; wink at (*a person*).

めかくし【目隠し】 a blind; (遊戯) blindman's buff; (馬の) blinders; blinkers. ¶ 窓に～をつける set *a blind* on the window. 人に～をする bandage *a person's* eyes; put a bandage over *a person's* eyes. 木が～になって彼の家は道路からは見えない A screen of trees hides his house from the street.

めかけ【妾】 a mistress. ¶ ～を置く(囲う) keep a concubine.

めが·ける【目がける】 ¶ 人を～けてピストルをうつ fire a pistol at *a person*. 彼らは敵を～けて突撃した They *charged at* the enemy. クマは獲物を～けて突進した The bear *rushed at* its prey.

メガサイクル 〘電気〙 megacycle (mc, mc., m.c.).

めがしら【目頭】 ¶ ～の熱くなるような光景 a *heart-warming* sight; a *moving* spectacle. ～を押さえる keep back *one's* tears. 思わず～が熱くなった I *was moved to tears in*

め

spite of myself.

めか・す dress *oneself* up. ¶～して出かける go out *stylishly dressed* (≒ *in one's best*).

-めか・す ¶彼は冗談～してそう言った He said it *half in joke*. 冗談～して言ったことをまともにとられた What I meant *for a joke* was seriously taken.

めかた【目方】 weight. ¶正しい～ honest *weight*. ～不足 short *weight*. ～が重い(軽い) be heavy (light) in *weight*. パンの～を計る *weigh* bread. きみの～はどのくらいありますか How much do you *weigh*? 彼女の～は45キロだ She *weighs* 45 kilograms. ぼくは最近～が減った I have lost much *weight* of late.

—売り ¶～売りする sell *by weight*.

メガトン ¶1～爆弾 a *megaton* bomb.

メカニズム mechanism. ¶電子計算機の～ the *mechanism* of an electronic computer.

めがね【眼鏡】1〖眼鏡〗glasses;〔a pair of〕spectacles (glasses のほうがよく用いられる).

¶～をかける(はずす) put on (take off) *one's glasses*.

～をふく wipe (≒ polish) *one's glasses*.

～をかけた人 a person *in spectacles*.

～越しに見る look over *one's spectacles*.

～なしでは読めない I can't read without *glasses*.

—入れ a spectacle-case. **—ザル** a tarsier; a specter lemur. **—屋** an optician. 色(黒)— colored (smoked) glasses. 遠(近)視用— glasses for a long (short)-sighted person. 金縁— gold-rimmed glasses. 鼻— eyeglasses; a pince-nez. 縁なし— rimless glasses.

2〖鑑識〗judgment; discernment. ¶彼は社長のお～にかなった He gained the president's *confidence*. / He won the president's *credit*.

メガホン a megaphone.

めがみ【女神】 a goddess. ¶愛(月;知恵)の～ the *goddess* of love (the moon; wisdom).

メガロポリス a megalopolis.

めきき【目利き】 judging; connoisseurship; (人) a judge; a critic; a connoisseur.

¶刀剣類の優れた～ *a* good *judge* of swords. 絵画の～ *a connoisseur of* (≒ *in*) pictures. 彼は絵の～がうまい He is a good judge of pictures.

メキシコ Mexico.

—人 a Mexican.

めきめき rapidly; remarkably. ¶英会話が～うまくなる make *remarkable* progress in English conversation; become *more and more* proficient in English conversation. 彼の病気は～よくなった His health improved *perceptibly*.

-め・く become like; look like. ¶春～いてきた It *has become like* spring. 逆説～くかもしれないが… It may *sound* paradoxical, but....

めくぎ【目釘】 ¶～を打つ drive *a rivet*.

めくじら【目くじら】 ¶～を立てて言う talk *with an angry glare* (≒ *with glaring eyes*).

めぐすり【目薬】 eyewater; eye lotion.

¶～をさす apply *eyewater* (≒ *eye lotion*). 二階から～ (諺) *Fanning the sun with a peacock's feather*.

めくそ【目屎】 eye mucus; eye wax.

めくばせ【目配せ】 ¶互いに～する exchange glances. 彼に警察へ連絡するよう～した I *made* him *a sign with the eyes* to call the police.

めぐま・れる【恵まれる】 ¶～れた生活を送る lead a *happy* (≒ *blessed; comfortable*) life. 彼は文才に～れている He *is endowed with* literary talent. 私はよい息子(健康)に～れている I *am blessed with* a good son (good health). 日本は気候の点で～れている Japan *is favored* climatically. わが国は天然資源に～れていない Our country *is* not *blessed with* natural resources.

めぐみ【恵み】 mercy; (神の) blessing; (慈善) charity; (施し物) alms. ¶～深い人 a *merciful* (*benevolent; charitable*) person. 神の～により by the *grace* of God; with God's *blessing*. 神の～に浴する receive *a blessing* from God. 人の～を受ける receive *a favor* from another. 人の～を受けて生活する live on *charity*; live by *alms*. 人に～をたれる *be merciful* to a person; show *a person kindness* (≒ *mercy*).

めぐ・む【恵む】 ¶こじきに金を～む *give* money *to* a beggar. 神よわれわれを～みたまえ God *bless* us!

めぐ・む【芽ぐむ】 ¶(木々が)春になって青々と～む The trees *put forth* (≒ *send out; shoot out*) *their* green *leaves* in spring.

めくら【盲】 blindness; (人) a blind person.

¶～になる become (≒ go) blind; lose *one's* sight. 彼は生まれつき～だ He is born *blind*. その事故で片目が～になった He *went blind* in one eye by the accident.

めぐら・す【巡らす】1〖囲いを〗¶彼は自分の家のまわりにへいを～した He *surrounded* his house *with* walls.

2〖思いを〗¶きのう一日のことに思いを～した I *let my thoughts wander over* the events of yesterday. / I *thought of* what happened yesterday.

ひとり少年時代に思いを～した I *looked back on* the days of my boyhood.

3〖策を〗¶なにか策を～す必要がある It is necessary for us to *devise* a scheme.

4〖回転させる〗turn. ¶くびすを～して立ち去った He *turned on* his heels and left.

めぐり【巡り】 ¶四国88か所寺～ *a pilgrimage* to the eighty-eight famous temples in Shikoku. 佐渡の島～をする *make a tour of* Sado Island. 美術館～をする *make* the *rounds of* art museums. 彼は血の～が悪い He has *a* poor *circulation* of the blood. / (比喩的に) He *is dull-witted*. 彼は血の～が良い (比喩的に) He *is quick-witted* (≒ *is intelligent*).

めぐりあい【巡り合い】 an unexpected (≒ accidental) meeting.

めく･る【捲る】¶ 本を二, 三ページ〜る *turn over* two or three pages of the book. トランプを〜る *turn up* a card. カレンダーを〜る *turn over* the calendar. 布団を〜る *take off* the bedding. ワイシャツのそでを〜る *roll* (≒ *turn*) *up* the sleeves of *one's* shirt.

めぐ･る【巡る】¶ その問題を〜って論じ合った We discussed the matter. / We had a discussion *about* the matter. ロンドンの名所を〜る see (≒ do) the sights of London. 春が〜ってくる Spring *comes round*. 〜る因果 the inevitable retribution.

め･げる ¶ 小さな障害に〜げぬように Don't *be disheartened* (≒ *be discouraged*) by small obstacles. 困難にあっても〜げることなく without *being discouraged* by difficulties.

めさき【目先】¶ 〜がきく be far-sighted. 〜がきかない be near (≒ short)-sighted. 〜の利益を求める seek *immediate* gain. 〜のことばかり考える think only of *the present*. それは彼の〜で起きた It happened *under* his *nose*[*s*]. 子どもたちの顔が〜にちらついて離れない My children's faces haunt me.

めざし【目刺し】dried sardines.

めざ･す【目指す】¶ 〜す敵 *one's* enemy. 〜す物 the object. 〜す所 *one's* destination. 特に生産増強を〜して *with a* special *view to* increasing the output. 山頂を〜して登る climb *toward* the mountaintop. 世界平和の維持を〜す *aim at* the maintenance of world peace.

めざと･い【目敏い】¶ 彼はちょっとしたまちがいも〜く見つける He *has a keen* (≒ *quick*) *eye for* a slight mistake. / He *is keen-eyed* enough to find a slight mistake.

めざまし〔どけい〕【目覚まし〔時計〕】an alarm clock. ¶ 〜を6時に鳴るようにしておく set the *alarm* 〔*clock*〕 for six 〔o'clock〕; set the *alarm* to go off at six.

めざまし･い【目覚ましい】¶ 英語が〜く進歩する make *remarkable* progress in English. 〜い成功をおさめる achieve a *remarkable* (≒ *brilliant*) success. 〜い仕事をする do *splendid* (≒ *excellent*) work. 〜い発展を遂げる achieve a *remarkable* (≒ *brilliant*; *striking*) development.

めざめ【目覚め】awakening. ¶ 大衆の知識への〜 intellectual *awakening* of the masses. 彼も春の〜の年頃になった He has attained the age of *puberty*.

めざ･める【目覚める】awake; wake up; (非を悟る) come to *one's* senses. ¶ 彼は7時に〜めた He *woke* at seven. 本分に〜める *awake to one's* duty. 真実に〜めさせる *open a person's eye* to the truth. 新時代の要求に〜める *be awakened* to new needs. 性に〜める *experience the awakening* of the erotic impulse.

めざわり【目障り】an eyesore. ¶ あの煙突は〜だ That chimney is *an eyesore*. 彼は〜だ He is *an offense to the eye*. 〜なやつだ, あっちへ行け You'*re in the way*. Go away!

めし【飯】**1**〖米飯〗boiled rice. ¶ 〜をたく boil *rice*.
彼は毎朝〜を3杯食べる He eats three bowls of *rice* every morning.
2〖食事〗¶ 〜はもう済ませたか Have you finished your *meal*?
彼はジャズが〜より好きだ He prefers jazz to *eating*.
3〖生計〗¶ 彼は筆で〜を食っている He *makes his living* by the pen.
この商売だけではとても〜は食えない I can't possibly *make a living* in this business.
このままいったら〜の食い上げだ If things go on at this rate, I will *starve* (≒ *lose my means of livelihood*).

メシア〖宗教〗Messiah.

めしあが･る【召し上がる】¶ なにを〜りますか What *would* you *like to have*? 〜り物はなんにいたしましょうか (レストランで) *Your order*, please. なにか〜りませんか May I offer you some refreshment? お菓子をもっと〜れ Please *help yourself to* some more sweets.

めしあ･げる【召し上げる】¶ 彼は財産を政府に〜げられた His property *was forfeited* to the Government. / His possessions *were confiscated* by the Government.

めじか【牝鹿】a doe; a hind.

めしかか･える【召し抱える】¶ 適当な者を〜える *employ* some suitable men; *take* some suitable men *into one's service*.

めじし【牝獅子】a lioness.

めした【目下】*one's* inferior〔s〕; (部下) *one's* subordinate〔s〕. ¶ 以前はイギリスは他のヨーロッパ諸国を〜のごとく見ていた Formerly England looked down upon the rest of the European countries.

めしだ･す【召し出す】¶ 王の御前に〜される *be summoned* into the presence of the king.

めしと･る【召し捕る】¶ 警官は3人の賊を〜った The policemen *arrested* (≒ *took up*; *apprehended*) three thieves. 彼は窃盗のかどで〜られた He *was arrested* on the charge of theft.

めしべ【雌蕊】〖植物〗a pistil.

メジャー (計器) a measure.

めじり【目尻】the corner of the eye. ¶ 〜のしわ crow's feet. 〜の上(下)がった人 a person with eyes slanting up (down). 女を見て〜を下げる *make eyes* (≒ *cast sheep's eyes*) *at* a woman.

めじるし【目印】a sign; a mark. ¶ 〜をつける mark; put *a mark* (*on*). この〜で敵か味方かを見分けた We told friend from foe by this *sign*. その山を〜にして道をたどった We followed the path with the mountain as *a guide*. 塔がその寺の〜だ The temple can easily be located by its pagoda.

めじろ【目白】〖鳥類〗a white eye.

めじろおし【目白押し】¶ 廊下には人々が〜に並んでいた The corridor *was jammed* with people. (jammed with はその間を通れないくらいにひしめき合っているような場合. crowded with はそれほ

め

どまででなくても群がっている場合).

めす【雌】 a female. ¶ ～犬 a bitch ; a *she*-dog. ～ネコ a *she*-cat. ～のトラ a tigress. ～のヤギ a *she*-goat.

メス a surgical knife ; a scalpel (メスはオランダ語のmes から). ¶ 事件に～を入れる *get to the bottom* (≒ *heart*) *of* the case ; *probe* the case *to the core*.

め·す【召す】 ¶ お～しでしたか (呼ぶ) Did you *call* me? お気に～したら if you *please*. これ, お気に～しましたか *Are* you *pleased with* this? どれもお気に～しませんか Do none of these *suit* you? 服を～す *put on one's* suit. かぜを～す *catch* cold.

めずらし·い【珍しい】 (まれな) rare ; uncommon ; (奇異な) curious ; (新奇な) original. ¶ ～い出来事 an *extraordinary* event. ～い例 a *rare* example. ～いデザイン a *novel* design. ～い光景 a *curious* (≒ *strange* ; *novel*) sight. ～くない風景 a *common* (≒ *familiar*) sight. ～い物を土産に買う buy *novelties* for gifts. ～くなくなる lose its *novelty*. 見るもの, 聞くもの, みな私には～かった Everything I saw and heard *was new to* me. やあ, ～いじゃないか Hello! I haven't seen you for ages. / You are quite a stranger. 彼が家にいるのは～い We *seldom* find him at home. ～い品をありがとう Thank you for your *nice* present. きょうは～い客が来た Today I had a visitor I haven't seen for a long time. ～く暖かい be *unusually* (≒ *exceptionally*) warm.

めずらしが·る【珍しがる】 ¶ なんでも～る *look* at everything *with curiosity*. 原住民たちは時計をとても～った My watch *excited* (≒ *piqued*) intense *curiosity* of the natives. 彼らは～って私にいろいろ質問した They asked me a lot of questions *out of curiosity*.

めずらしそうに【珍しそうに】 ¶ 彼は～箱の中をのぞいた He looked *curiously* into the box. / He looked into the box *with curiosity*.

メゾソプラノ 〘音楽〙 mezzo-soprano.

メソッド a method. ¶ オーラル～を採用 (導入) する adopt (introduce) the oral *method*.

メソポタミア Mesopotamia.

めそめそ ¶ ひとりで～泣く *sob* to *oneself*.

めだか【目高】 〘魚類〙 a killifish (複 killifish ; killifishes).

めだけ【雌竹】 〘植物〙 a reed-grass ; the *medake* bamboo.

めだ·つ【目立つ】 ¶ ～つ色 a *gay* (≒ *striking*) color. ～たない色 a *quiet* (≒ *subdued*) color. 絵を～つ場所に掛ける hang a picture in a *prominent* position (≒ *conspicuous* place). 実業界において～つ地位を占める occupy a *prominent* position in the business world. ～って美しい女 a woman of *striking* beauty. あの建物は～つ That building *stands out*. 白いワイシャツは汚れが～つ A white shirt easily *shows* dirt. 交通事故が～って増えてきた Traffic accidents have *remarkably* increased in number.

めたて【目立て】 setting. ¶ そののこぎりは～の要がある The saw needs to *be sharpened*.

メタフィジック metaphysics (単数扱い).

めだま【目玉】 an eyeball. ¶ ～をぎょろぎょろさせる roll (≒ goggle) *one's eyes*. 私の～の黒いうちは as long as I live. ～の飛び出るほど高い be *extremely* expensive. 彼からお～をちょうだいした I *got a lecture* from him. お～を食うぞ You will catch it.

一商品 a loss leader ; a tempting bargain.

めだまやき【目玉焼き】 fried eggs ; a sunny-side up. ¶ ～にする fry eggs *sunny-side up*.

メダリスト a medalist. ¶ ゴールド～ *a* gold *medalist*.

メダル a medal. ¶ (賞に) 金 (銀 ; 銅) ～をもらう be awarded *a* gold (silver ; copper) *medal*.

メタン〔ガス〕 〘化学〙 methane. ¶ ～ガスは沼から生じる *Methane* comes from marshes.

めちゃくちゃ【滅茶苦茶】 ¶ ～な議論 *incoherent* argument. ～な計画を立てる make plans *completely contrary to common sense*. ～なことを言う talk *nonsense* ; say *unreasonable* things. ～に高い (値段) be *ridiculously* dear. ～に並べる put (*things*) all *muddled up*.

めちゃめちゃ【滅茶滅茶】 ¶ 彼の身代は～になった His fortune *has gone to wreck*. 船は岩に当たって～になった The boat *was dashed to pieces* on the rocks. 本が～に破れている The book *is torn to tatters*. 事業がまったく～になった The whole business *went to pieces*. 雨のためぼくたちの修学旅行は～になった The rain utterly *spoiled* our school excursion.

メチルアルコール 〘化学〙 methyl alcohol.

メッカ Mecca. ¶ パリは世界じゅうの芸術愛好者の～だ Paris is *the Mecca* of the world's art lovers.

めっき【鍍金】 plating ; gilt. ¶ 銀～したスプーン a silver-*plated* spoon. 銅に金(銀)～する *plate* copper with gold (silver). ～がはげた The *gilt* came off. / (比喩的) He showed his true colors.

めつき【目付き】 a look. ¶ 彼は恐ろしい～で私をにらんだ He glared at me with *an* angry *look*. リスはかわいい～をしていた The squirrel had *a* charming *look* in its eye. 彼はどうも～が怪しい He has something questionable in his *look*. 彼は～が悪い He has *a* sinister *look*.

めっきり considerably ; noticeably. ¶ ここ数日～暖かくなった It has got *very* warm these past few days. 彼は～やせた He has become *remarkably* lean recently.

メッセージ a message. ¶ ～を送る send *a message*.

めっそう【滅相】 ¶ ～もない Absurd! ～な, それはうそだ God forbid! It's false. 私が犯人だなんて～な I am a criminal? *Impossible!*

めった【滅多】 ¶ 彼が学校を遅刻することは～にない He *seldom* comes late to school. ～なことをいうな You must be careful about what you say. ここには来客は～にない We *rarely* have visitors here. こんな美しい景色は～にない Such a beautiful scene is *rarely* to be seen. あんなだらしのない男は～にない There are *very few* who are so untidy as he. この病気で死ぬ人は～にない *Few* people die of this disease.

めったうち【滅多打ち】¶敵を～にした We showered *blows* on the enemy. 男は～にされた The man *was beaten black-and-blue*.

めったやたら ¶人を～に叱りつける scold *a person* too severely. 彼は～に本を読む He reads *at random*. 彼は～に遅刻する He is *too often* late.

めつぶし【目潰し】¶彼に～を食わしてやった I threw dust into his eyes.

めつぼう【滅亡】downfall. ¶ローマ帝国が～したのはいつか When *was* the Roman Empire *ruined*? 戦争は人類を～させる War will bring about the *destruction* of mankind.

めっぽう【滅法】¶～暑い It is *awfully* hot. このごろ～背が高くなった He has lately become *conspicuously* tall. ～おもしろい本だ This is an *exceedingly* interesting book.

めでた·い【目出度い】¶それは～いことだ It is *a matter for congratulation*. 去年わが家には～いことがいくつかあった There were several *joyous* events in our family last year. ～く試験に合格した He has *successfully* passed the examination. お～いやつだ He is *a simpleton*.

めど【目処】(目標) an aim. ¶仕事の～がつかない The business has not yet been put in a smooth, ordinary order. ようやく～がついた Now we have a promising future before us at last.

めど【針孔】the eye of a needle. ¶～へ糸を通す run a thread through *an eye*.

めどおり【目通り】¶王にお～を許された I was admitted to the presence to the lord.

めと·る【娶る】¶彼は妻を～った He *got married*.

メドレー a medley〔race〕.
—リレー a medley relay. 個人**—** the individual medley. 400メートル個人**—** the individual 400-meter medley〔race〕.

メトロノーム a metronome.

メトロポリス a metropolis.

メニュー a menu. ¶～を見せてください Will you please show me the *menu*?

メヌエット〘音楽〙a minuet.

めぬき【目抜き】¶ここは市内の～の場所だ This is one of *the busiest quarters* in the city. ～通りはいつも自動車でいっぱいだ *The main street* is always crowded with cars.

めねじ【雌捻子】a female screw.

めのう【瑪瑙】〘鉱物〙agate.
しま**—** onyx.

めのかたき【目の敵】¶あの男は私を～にしている He regards me with hatred.

めのこざん【目の子算】¶参加者の数を～で数える *count* the number of the participants *with one's eyes*. ～では正確といえない *Rough estimation* is not accurate enough.

めのした【目の下】¶～1尺の鯛 a bream a foot long from eye to tail.

めのたま【目の玉】¶食料品が～が飛び出るほど高いのに驚いた I was astonished at the *exorbitant* prices of food.

めのまえ【目の前】¶彼は息子を～でほめた He praised his son *to his face*. 本はすぐ～にある The book is just *in front of* you. 入試は～に迫っている The entrance examination *is close at hand*. / The examination *is just around the corner*.

めばえ【芽生え】a sprout. ¶ふたりの間に恋の～があった There was *the awakening of love* (≒ *the awakened love*) between the two.

めば·える【芽生える】¶草花が～えはじめた Plants *have sprung up*. ふたりの間には愛が～えた Love *budded out* between the two.

めはし【目端】¶～のきく人 a *quick-witted* person. 彼は～がきかない He *is dull-witted*.

めはな【目鼻】¶仕事に～がついた My job *has taken shape*. その問題は依然として～がつかない The matter *remains unsettled*.

めばな【雌花】a female flower.

めはなだち【目鼻立ち】features. ¶彼女は～が整っている She *is well-featured*. / She *has regular features*. 彼女は～が美しい She has a beautiful *look*.

めばり【目張り】¶窓に全部～をした We *weather-stripped* all the windows against drafts. 風がはいらないよう戸のすき間に紙で～をした I closed the chinks in the door with paper.

めぶんりょう【目分量】measurement by the eye. ¶～で測る measure *at a guess*. 薬を～で測ってはいけない You must not measure medicine *by your eye*.

めべり【目減り】loss in weight. ¶～を見込んで荷をつくった I packed my things counting on the *ullage*.

めぼし【目星】an aim. ¶警察では犯人の～がついたようだ The police seem to *have spotted* the suspect.

めぼし·い valuable ; important. ¶この会社には～い人物は少ない There are only a few men *of ability* on the staff of this company. ～い絵はみな売れた *Valuable* pictures have been all sold.

めまい【眩暈】dizziness ; giddiness. ¶～がする I *feel giddy*.

めまぐるし·い【目紛しい】bewildering ; dizzy. ¶なんという～い世の中だ What a *fast-moving* world this is! 政局は～く変わっている The political situation is changing *at a giddy speed*.

めめし·い【女女しい】effeminate ; womanish. ¶～いやつだ What an *effeminate* man! そんな～いことを言うな Don't say such a *womanish* thing.

メモ a memo. ¶電話番号を～してください *Make a note of* the telephone number, please. 彼のことばを～した I *noted down* (≒ *took*

down) what he said.
—帳 a memorandum pad; a memo pad.
—用紙 memo paper.

めもと【目許】eyes. ¶ 彼女は～がぱっちりしている She has bright *eyes*. 彼は～がおとうさんにそっくりだ He is like his father especially *around his eyes*.

めもり【目盛り】graduation. ¶ この物指はセンチの～になっている This measure *is graduated* in centimeters.

めやす【目安】(標準) a standard. ¶ この仕事にどのくらいの日数がかかるか～が立たない I can't *guess* how many days it will take me to finish this work.

めやに【目脂】eye mucus; eye wax. ¶ ～がたまっている Your eyes *are rheumy*.

メラニン〖化学〗melanine.

めらめら ¶ 小屋はあっという間に～燃えあがった The cottage *burst into flames* in a moment.

めりこ·む【めり込む】¶ 車輪が泥の中に～んだ The wheels *stuck* in the mud. 建物の重みで地面が10センチ～んだ The ground *has sunk* 10 centimeters under the weight of the building.

メリット a merit. ¶ このプランの～をひとことでいってください Please give a short remark of the *merit* of this plan.

めりはり ¶ ～のきいたせりふ a speech *with modulated intonation.*

めりめり ¶ 古い家は大風で～と音をたてた The old house *creaked* with the strong wind.

メリヤス knit goods. ¶ ～のシャツ a *knit* shirt. ～の下着 *knit* underwear.
—工場 a knitting mill. —商 a hosier.

メロディー a melody. ¶ 甘い～ *a* sweet *melody*.

メロドラマ a melodrama.

メロン a melon.

めん【面】**1**〖顔·マスク〗a face; a mask. ¶ お～をかぶる put *a mask* on.
お～のような顔をしている He has a *poker* face.
ふたりは～と向かって座った The two sat *face to face* with each other.
彼は私に～と向かって文句を言った He complained *to my face*.
2〖側面〗¶ あらゆる～からこの問題を考えた We considered this problem in every *aspect*.
彼は社会の暗い～ばかり見る He looks on the dark *side* of society only.
彼にはおかしな～がある He has *an* eccentric *side*.

めん【綿】cotton. ¶ ～のシャツ a *cotton* shirt.

めんえき【免疫】immunity. ¶ 種痘をすると天然痘に対して～になる Vaccination *makes* you *immune from* smallpox. 一度この病気になった人は～になる Those who have had this disease *are immune from* it. 彼は世評には～になっている He *is immune to* public criticism.
—性 immunity. —注射 protective inoculation.

めんおりもの【綿織物】cotton; cotton fabrics.

めんか【綿花】raw cotton.
—栽培 cotton growing.

めんかい【面会】an interview; a meeting. ¶ 校長に～した I *met* the principal. 彼に～を求めた I asked him for *an interview*. きょうはだれにも～は遠慮したい I am not seeing any visitors today. / I am not at home for anyone. 病人は～謝絶だ The patient is not allowed to see anyone.
—時間 the visiting hours. —人 a caller; a visitor. —日 a receiving day; a visiting day

めんかやく【綿火薬】guncotton.

めんかん【免官】dismissal. ¶ 彼は依願～となった He *was relieved of his post* at his own request.

めんきつ【面詰】reproof. ¶ 先生は生徒の非行を～した The teacher *reproved* the pupil for his misconduct.

めんきょ【免許】a license. ¶ ～をとった I obtained *a license*. ～のある licensed. ～のない unlicensed. ～を没収された I had my *license* forfeited.
—状 a license. —料 a license fee. 運転—証 a driving license. 仮—証 a learner's license.

めんくい【面食い】¶ 彼は相当の～だ He emphasizes good looks in the choice of a woman.

めんくら·う【面食らう】¶ その知らせを聞いて～った I *was confused at* the news. 知らない人に道であいさつをされて～ってしまった I *felt* quite *embarrassed* when a total stranger greeted me on the street. 「火事だ」と言われて～った I *was taken aback to* hear people crying "Fire!"

めんざい【免罪】acquittal.
—符 an indulgence.

めんし【綿糸】cotton thread.

めんしき【面識】acquaintance. ¶ 彼とは～がある I *am acquainted with* him. 彼女とは～がない She *is a stranger to* me. ～もない人から話しかけられて当惑した Addressed by *an utter stranger*, I was embarrassed. その人とは一～もない He is *an utter stranger to* me.

めんじて【免じて】¶ 私に～彼を許してやってほしい Won't you please forgive him *for my sake*? 若いのに～男は解放された The man was released *in consideration of* his youth.

めんじょ【免除】exemption. ¶ 彼は授業料を～された He was given *free* instruction. 彼は近視のために兵役を～された He *was exempted from* military service on account of shortsightedness. 収入の少ない人は税金を～される Low-income people *are not required to* pay taxes.

めんじょう【免状】a diploma. ¶ ～をとる obtain *a license*. ～を交付する grant *a license* to (*a person*). 彼は教員の～を持っている He holds *a* teacher's *certificate*.

めんしょく【免職】dismissal. ¶ 彼は職務怠慢のため～になった He *was dismissed from*

め

the service for neglect of duty. 彼は教員を～になった He *was relieved of* his post as a teacher.

めん·する【面する】¶ ホテルは海に～している The hotel *faces* (≒ *looks out on*) the sea. この家は南に～している The house *has a* south *aspect.* 私の部屋は南に～している My room *faces* south. 太平洋に～した国 countries *bordering on* the Pacific. 彼は危機に～して平然としていた He remained calm even *in the face of* a crisis.

めん·ずる【免ずる】¶ 人の職を～ずる *dismiss a person from* his job. 授業料を～ぜられた He was given free instruction. 税を～ずる *exempt* taxation.

めんぜい【免税】tax exemption. ¶ この商品は～になっている This article *is exempt from taxation.* / This article *is tax-free.* これらの品は～にすべきだ These goods should *be exempted from* taxation.

—点 the tax exemption point. **—品** tax-free goods.

めんせき【面積】area. ¶ この体育館の床の～は500平方メートルある The *area* of this gymnasium is five hundred square meters. この土地の～は1,000平方マイルだ The land has *an area* of a thousand square miles.

めんせき【面責】¶ その学生は～された The student *was reproved to his face.* 彼は私が不注意だといって～した He *reproved* me for my carelessness.

めんせつ【面接】an interview. ¶ 彼に～していろいろ話し合った We *had an interview with* him and talked over a variety of topics.

—試験 an oral test; an interview. ¶ ～試験を受けた We underwent *an oral test.* **—試験委員** an interviewer.

めんぜん【面前】¶ 彼は人々の～で私の悪口を言った He spoke bad things about me *before* other people (≒ *in the presence of* others).

めんそ【免訴】acquittal. ¶ 彼は～になった He *was acquitted of a charge.* 彼は証拠不十分のため～になった He *was acquitted* for lack of evidence.

メンタルテスト a mental test. ¶ 新入生全員を対象に～が行なわれた *A mental test* was carried out on (≒ was administered to) all the new students.

めんだん【面談】an interview. ¶ この問題については彼と～した I *talked* this matter *over with* him. 彼と個人的に～することになっている We are going to *have a* personal *interview with* him.

めんちょう【面疔】〖医学〗 a carbuncle on the face.

メンツ【面子】reputation. ¶ ～を保つ(失う) save (lose) *one's face.* ～にかかわる問題だ It's a matter of *honor* (≒ *face*). こんなことでは～にかかわる That will affect my *honor.* 彼は一家の～にかかわるような者だった He was *a disgrace* to his family.

めんてい【面体】looks; a face. ¶ 怪しい～の男 a man of suspicious *looks.* 一癖ありそうな～の男 an evil-*looking* man.

メンデル ¶ ～の法則 〖生物〗 Mendel's laws; Mendelism.

めんどう【面倒】**1**〖やっかいごと·手数〗trouble. ¶ 来客にいちいち面会するのは～だ It *is troublesome* to see all the callers.

～な問題が起こった Something *unpleasant* has happened.

事が～になってきた The thing *is getting to be difficult to handle.* / The matter *has become complicated.*

～なことになりそうだ I smell (≒ sense) *trouble* coming.

ご～でもご一報ください I am sorry to *trouble* you, but please drop me a line.

そうすればだいぶ～が省ける That'll save us a lot of *trouble.*

彼の弁護は事をいっそう～にするばかりだ His defense only *makes* the matter *worse.*

毎日同じことをしているのが～になった I *am tired of* doing the same thing day after day.

2〖世話〗¶ 子どもの～はだれが見るのか Who *looks after* the children?

彼は～見のいい男だ He *takes a kindly interest in* others.

もう彼の～は見きれない I won't *take care of* him any longer.

めんどうくさ·い【面倒臭い】troublesome. ¶ ～がらずに辞書をよく引く *spare no pains* and make full use of a dictionary.

めんどおし【面通し】¶ ～でその男は容疑者と確認された The man was identified as the suspect. (アメリカでは, 一列に並べられた人たちのなかから選ぶので He is a suspect identified in a police line-up. と言う).

めんどり【雌鳥】a hen. ¶ ～が卵を暖めている The *hen* is sitting on the eggs.

めんば【面罵】an open insult. ¶ 彼は私を～した He *abused* me *to my face.*

メンバー a member. ¶ ～が変わったら仕事の成績がよくなった With *a* changed *line-up* better work was done. きみもわれわれの～になれ Why don't you *join us*? ～がそろいそうもない (たとえば9人で1組になる場合など) I am afraid we cannot *make up a nine.*

めんぷ【綿布】cotton cloth.

めんぼう【麺棒】a rolling pin.

めんぼく【面目】**1**〖体面〗honor. ¶ このようなことをしでかして～次第もない *I am very sorry to* have done such a folly.

そんなことでは～にかかわる That would affect my *reputation.*

～丸つぶれだ My *good name* is ruined.

われわれはみな～を失った We *have* all *disgraced ourselves.*

失敗をして彼は～を失った His *reputation* suffered by his failure.

～なげに彼女は首をうなだれていた *Shame-facedly* she hung her head.

危うく～は保てた I barely managed to *save my face*.

今度の働きで彼は大いに～をほどこした His recent exploit *added* much *to his credit*. / His recent exploit *reflected* great *credit on* him.

2 〖様相〗 appearance. ¶ 改装により店は～を一新した The store was remodeled into a completely new one. / The store underwent a complete transformation.

めんみつ 【綿密】 ¶ ～な観察 *minute* observation. ～な調査 *close* (≒ *thorough*) investigation. ～な計画 a *careful* plan. ～な報告 a *detailed* report. ～な計算 *accurate* calculation. ～な人 a *thoroughgoing* man. ～な細工 *elaborate* workmanship. ～に仕上げをする put a finishing touch *with minute care*.

めんめん 【面面】 ¶ 関係者の～が顔をそろえた *All concerned* were present. 彼は一座の～におじぎをした He bowed to *every one* of those present.

めんめん 【綿綿】 ¶ その伝統は～として今日まで続いている The tradition has come down *unbroken* to this day. 彼女は～たる情緒で訴えた She gave vent to *a flood of* emotion. 彼の話は～として尽きなかった His story *was endless*. / His story continued *endlessly*.

めんよう 【綿羊】 a sheep (単複同形).

めんるい 【麺類】 noodles.

も

も 【喪】 mourning. ¶ ～中である be in *mourning* (*for a person*). ～を秘する conceal *a person's death*. ～が明けた The *mourning* is over. / We are out of *mourning*. 彼女は彼の～に服している She *has gone into mourning for* him.

―章 a mourning band ; a weed.

も 【藻】 waterweed ; (海草) seaweed ; (アオウキクサ) duckweed.

-も **1** 〖どちらも・全部〗 ¶ 父～母～出かけて留守です *Both* my father *and* my mother are away.

彼女は成績～いいし運動～得意だ She is *not only* a good student *but also* a good athlete.

この家は庭～狭いし，日当たり～よくない The house has a small garden, *besides* it doesn't get much sunshine.

ゴルフをやりたいが，そんな金～暇～ない I wish I could enjoy golfing. But unfortunately, I have *neither* money *nor* time to do so.

2 〖…もまた〗 ¶ きょう～また雪だ It is snowing *again* today. / *Another* day of snow!

ぼく～連れていってくれ Can you take me, *too*?

ついでにこの本～買いましょう I have decided to buy this book *as well*.

きみ～あの映画を見たのか Did you *also* see that film?

「ぼくは映画が好きだ」「ぼく～だ」 "I am fond of movies." "*So* am I."

「ぼくは泳げない」「ぼく～そうだ」 "I cannot swim." "*Neither* can I."

3 〖程度〗 ¶ 彼は40度～熱がある He has a temperature of *no less than* forty degrees.

駅からぼくの家までは歩いて３分～かかりません It is *less than* a three-minute walk from the station to my house.

もう１時間～彼を待っている I have been waiting for him for a *whole* hour.

パーティーには50人～の人が集まった *As many as* fifty people came to the party.

まちがえてチップに５ドル～やってしまった I tipped *all of* five dollars by mistake.

３日～あればこの仕事はかたづくでしょう I can finish the work in *less than* three days.

4 〖…さえも〗 ¶ 彼女は振り向いて～くれないで立ち去った She went away *without so much as* looking back.

私が話しかけても彼は返事～してくれなかった He did not *even* take the trouble to answer me when I spoke to him.

きみにはこんな簡単なこと～わからないのか Don't you understand such a smiple thing as that?

疲れはててもの～言えなかった He was so tired that he could not speak a single word.

まだ一度～飛行機に乗ったことがない I have never been on an airplane.

5 〖…のに・…ところで〗 ¶ 彼女は手紙を出して～返事をくれない She does not even answer my letters.

急いで行って～まにあわないだろう You will be late, *no matter how* fast you go.

彼と試合して～勝つ見込みは全然ない I have no chance of winning, *if ever* I fight him.

6 〖どちらでも〗 ¶ あすは来て～来なくて～よろしい Tomorrow you may *either* come here *or* not.

降って～照って～ラクビーの試合は日曜日に行なわれる Rain *or* shine, the Rugby game will be held on Sunday.

7 〖たとえ…でも〗 ¶ 彼は暇があって～その利用法を知らない *Admitting that* he has leisure time, I am sure he does not know how to use it.

少しくらい波があって～船は予定通り出る The boat will leave as scheduled *even if* the sea is a little rough.

いくら待って～彼は来ないよ He won't come *no matter how* long you wait for him.

もう-【猛-】 ¶ ～打 a *heavy* hit. ～毒 a *deadly* poison. ～勉強 *hard* work；(詰め込み勉強) cramming. ～練習 *intensive* training.

-もう【-網】 a net. ¶ 通信～ a *communication* network；a system of *newsgathering*. 鉄道～ a network of *railways.* 放送～ a *broadcasting* network.

もう【蒙】 ignorance. ¶ 人の～をひらく *enlighten* a person.

もう **1**〖今〗¶ ～彼はここに来ている He is here *now*.
～春だ Spring is *now* with us.
～出かけなければならない I must be going *now*.
2〖既に〗¶ 会は～始まっている The meeting has *already* begun.
～準備が終わったのですか (ずいぶん早いなあ) Have you *already* finished your preparation?
～夕食はすんでいるかもしれない He may *have finished* his dinner.
3〖もう…でない〗¶ ～これ以上黙ってはいられない I cannot remain silent *any longer*.
足が痛くて～これ以上歩けない My foot hurts so much that I can't walk *any farther*.
4〖さらに〗¶ ～二，三日ここにいる予定だ I will stay here for a few *more* days.
～1杯お茶をいかがですか Won't you have *another* cup of tea?
～1回読んでくれますか Would you please read it *once more*?
～1度数えたほうがよい You had better count them *once again*.
～2か月で帰国することになっている He is to come back in *another* two months.
宿題は～少しで終わる My homework is *almost* completed.
～少し行くと図書館があります If you go *a little farther* you will find the library.
～たくさんです No more, thank you.
5〖やがて〗¶ 彼は～来るだろう He will come *before long*.
～日も暮れるだろう It will *soon* grow dark.

もうあい【盲愛】 blind love. ¶ 彼は息子を～している He *dotes on* his son. 彼はその少女を～している He *is infatuated with* the girl.

もうい【猛威】 fury. ¶ 風波は～をたくましくした Both wind and sea increased *in violence*.
疫病が～をふるった The pestilence *raged in all its fury.*

もうか【猛火】 roaring (≒ raging) flames；a conflagration.

もうがっこう【盲学校】 a school for the blind.

もうか･る【儲かる】**1**〖金銭的に〗¶ ～る(～らない)商売 a *profitable* (an *unprofitable*) business.
その株は～らない *There is* no *money* in that stock (≒ those stocks).
～るといってもたいしたことはない *There isn't* much *money* in it after all.
この取引で正味200ドル～った The transaction *netted* me two hundred dollars.
～る話を逃がす男ではない He won't let pass a chance to *make money.* / He has an eye to the main chance.
それでいくら～ったか How much did you *get* out of it? / How much did it *bring in*?
3割～った We *had a* thirty percent *profit* on that.
これからはなんの商売がいちばん～るだろうか What line of business would *be* most *profitable* in future?
2〖得をする〗¶ 掃除をしなくてすんだので～った We *were lucky* that we did not have to do the cleaning.

もうかん【毛管】 a capillary；a capillary tube.
―現象 a capillary action.

もうけ【儲け】 profit；gain；earning. ¶ この仕事は～が多い(少ない) This is a *profitable* (an *unprofitable*) job. / *There is* much (not much) *money* in this job. その取引で100ドルの～だ I *earned* 100 dollars out of the deal. / I *gained* a hundred dollars by the transaction. ～を折半した We divided the *gains* into halves. 彼は株でうまい～をした He *has done a good thing in* shares.
―話 ¶ ぼろい～話だ There's easy money in it.

もうげき【猛撃】 a vigorous attack. ¶ ～を加える deal (*a person*) a severe blow；hit (*a person*) hard. ～によって要塞(ようさい)を奪った We took the fortress by *storm*.

もうけもの【儲けもの】 a good bargain.

もう･ける【設ける】**1**〖設備・規定など〗¶ 大学に芸術の講座を～ける *create* a chair of arts in a college.
その建物に新しい彼の事務所が～けられた His new office *was established* in the building.
その銀行は新しい支店を～けた The bank *opened* a new branch office.
その会議はこの点に関し特別の規定を～けた The meeting *laid down* a special rule on this point.
2〖その他〗¶ その会には口実を～けて欠席した I *made an excuse* and absented myself from the meeting.
お祝いに一席～けねばならない We must *give* (≒ *have*) a party to celebrate this.
最初の妻で彼は3児を～けた He *had* three children by his first wife.

もう･ける【儲ける】¶ きみは月いくら～けるか What do you *make* in a month? / How much do you *earn* in a month? この取引で100万円～けた I *gained* a million yen by this transaction. その土地を売って純益5割～けた I *netted* a fifty percent profit by selling the land.
休みを1日～けた I *had an unexpected additional* holiday.

もうけん【猛犬】 a fierce dog. ¶ ～に注意(掲示) Beware of the dog!

もうこ【蒙古】 Mongolia.
―語 Mongolian. **―人** a Mongol；a Mongolian. **―人種** the Mongolian race. 外

も

(内)― Outer (Inner) Mongolia.

もうこう【猛攻】¶〜を加える deliver *a violent attack* (*on* an enemy). 要塞(ようさい)はわが軍の〜の前についに陥落した The fortress finally fell under our *violent attack.*

もうこん【毛根】the root of hair.

もうさいかん【毛細管】⇒もうかん

もうさいけっかん【毛細血管】a capillary.

もうしあ·げる【申し上げる】¶事件のあらましを〜げましょう Let me *summarize* what happened. 後ほど〜げます I will *let you know* later. 厚く御礼〜げます I beg to tender my cordial thanks. 確たることは〜げられませんが… I cannot *say* for certain, but....

もうしあわせ【申し合わせ】agreement. ¶当事者の間で次の〜がとりきめられた The following *agreement* was reached by the parties concerned. 〜により市民は新年祝賀の礼をやめた *By mutual consent* there was no wishing of Happy New Years among the citizens.
―事項 terms of agreement.

もうしあわ·せる【申し合わせる】¶みな〜せたように同じ本を持ってきた Everyone brought a copy of the same book *as if by some prearrangement.* 全員〜せた時間に集合した Everyone was there at the *appointed* time.

もうしいれ【申し入れ】(要求) a request; (発議) a proposal; (抗議) a protest.

もうしい·れる【申し入れる】¶この問題について至急善処を〜れた We *requested* that the matter should be promptly and properly dealt with.

もうしう·ける【申し受ける】¶紛失·破損の際には実費を〜けます Cost price will *be charged* in case of loss or damage.

もうしおく·る【申し送る】¶後任の人に仕事を〜った I *handed over* my business to my successor. / I *transferred* my duties *to* my successor.

もうしおく·れる【申し遅れる】¶〜れてすみません I am sorry *not to have said* this *before.* / I apologize for *not having said* this *before.* 〜れましたが私が青木です I *ought to have said before* that my name is Aoki.

もうしか·ねる【申し兼ねる】¶〜ねますが二,三日待ってください *I am sorry to inconvenience you,* but please wait a few days.

もうしご【申し子】a heaven-sent child. ¶この子は氏神様の〜だ This child is a gift from our guardian god.

もうしこし【申し越し】¶お〜の件, すぐに調べてみます *In reference to your suggestion,* we will look into the matter promptly.

もうしこみ【申し込み·申込】(出願) an application; (依頼) a request; (提議) a proposal; (提供) an offer; (購読の) subscription.
¶男子200メートルバタフライに参加〜が30人あった There were thirty *entries for* men's 200-meter butterfly. 就職の〜 *an application for* employment. 結婚の〜 *a* marriage *proposal.* 試合の〜 *a challenge to* a game. 〜ありしだい upon receipt of *a request.* 〜順に in the order of *application.* 予約のお〜はお早めに願います Early *reservations* are advised. 座席の〜が殺到した *Applications for* the seats poured in. 遺憾ながら〜には応じられません We regret we are unable to comply with your *request.* 〜の受付は10月1日からだ *Applications* will be accepted starting October 1.
―期限 a time limit for application. ―金 application money. ―書 a written application. ―人 an applicant; (購読の) a subscriber. ―用紙 an application form.

もうしこ·む【申し込む】(部屋などを予約する) reserve (a room); (結婚を) propose (marriage *to* a girl).
¶会見を〜む *ask for* an interview. 受験を〜む *enter oneself for* an examination. 入学を〜む *apply for* admission into a school. 入会を〜む *apply for* membership. 当局に苦情を〜む *lodge* a complaint *with* the authorities. その会社の株1,000株を〜んだ I *subscribed for* 1,000 shares in the company. A高校はB高校に野球試合を〜んだ A High School *challenged* B High School *to* a baseball game. 慈善基金に5万円の寄付を〜んだ I *subscribed* fifty thousand yen *for* the charity fund.

もうしたて【申し立て】a statement; a declaration; (証言) testimony. ¶正当防衛の〜 *a plea* of self-defense. 彼女は陳述に異議の〜をした She objected to the *statement.* 証人は虚偽の〜をした The witness *gave a* false *testimony.*

もうした·てる【申し立てる】¶彼は新聞の記事は虚偽だと〜てた He *declared* that the newspaper account was false. 事実を〜てる *state* the fact. 異議を〜てる *raise* an objection (*to*). 無罪を〜てる *plead* not guilty. 彼は判決に対して不服を〜てた He *appealed against* the decision of the court.

もうしつけ【申し付け】an order. ¶お〜に従いお届けしました Here is what you *have ordered.* お〜に従います I will do *as you wish.*

もうしつ·ける【申し付ける】¶食事の用意をするよう家人に〜けました I *have told* my people *to* prepare a dinner. きょう伺うよう主人から〜かりました I *was ordered* by my master *to* call on you today.

もうしで【申し出】(届け出) a notice; (申し込み) application. ¶お〜ありしだい upon [receipt of your] *request.* お〜のこと, よく検討してみます I promise to give your *proposal* a careful consideration.

もうしで·る【申し出る】¶詳細については, 事務所まで〜られたし Those who want to know the details should *apply to* the office. 彼らは彼女の援助を〜た They *offered* to assist her. だれも彼の企てに加わろうと〜る者はなかった No one *proposed* to join him in his undertaking.

もうしひらき【申し開き】explanation. ¶〜す

る explain *one*self; defend *one*self. 自分の行為に対して〜する *account for one's* conduct. これではなんとも〜ができない This allows of no *excuse*. / This is quite inexcusable.

もうしぶん【申し分】¶ こちらにも〜がある I have my *say*. その議論には〜がある There are *objections* to the argument. この服なら彼女に〜ないだろう This dress would suit her *to perfection*. 〜のない天気だった The weather *was perfect*. 彼の答えは〜なかった His answer *was satisfactory*. 彼女は妻として〜ない She is all that a wife should be. これは〜のない贈り物になる This will make a *most suitable* gift. 彼の行ないはまったく〜がない His conduct leaves nothing to be desired. 彼は〜のない学生だ He is an *exemplary* student.

もうじゃ【亡者】the dead; a ghost. ¶ 彼は権力の〜だ He *is possessed by a lust for* power.

がりがり— the greedy.

もうじゅう【盲従】blind obedience. ¶ 上役に〜するだけではだめだ You must not be content with *following* your superiors *blindly*.

もうじゅう【猛獣】a fierce animal; a beast of prey.

—狩り big game hunting. —使い a tamer (≒ trainer) of wild animals.

もうしょ【猛暑】intense heat; a heat wave.

もうしよう【申し様】¶ なんともお礼の〜もありません I cannot thank you enough. / I don't know how to thank you. なんともおわびの〜がありません I don't know what to say by way of apology.

もうしわけ【申し訳】(謝罪) an apology; (弁明) an excuse. ¶〜不用です There is no *apology* needed. 彼の〜は役に立たなかった His *excuse* was of no avail. 彼女は息子の不品行に対し〜した She *apologized for* her son's misconduct. まことに〜ありません I don't know what *excuse* to make. 約束を忘れてなんとも〜ありません I *am* really *sorry for* forgetting my promise. 〜ないでは済まされない It is no use *apologizing*. 私は〜ない気持ちでいっぱいだった I *felt* very *guilty*. 彼はほんの〜に手伝ってくれた He helped me but *only half-heartedly*. 彼は〜程度のお粗末な小説家だ He is *a sorry apology for* a novelist.

もうしわたし【申し渡し】(判決) a sentence. ¶ 判事は彼に死刑の〜をした The judge *passed a sentence* of death on him. 彼に対する判決〜は来週の月曜日に決まった The time for *sentencing* him is set for next Monday.

もうしわた·す【申し渡す】¶ 彼らは本部へ出頭するように〜された They *were instructed to* report at the headquarters. 彼は死刑を〜された He *was sentenced to* death. 彼は退学の旨を〜された He *was ordered to* leave school.

もうしん【盲信】blind belief; credulity. ¶ 彼は易者の言うことを〜する He *believes everything* a fortuneteller tells him.

もうじん【盲人】a blind person; (総称) the blind.

もう·す【申す】¶ 〜すまでもなく needless to say. 彼は英語は〜すまでもなくドイツ語，フランス語も自由だ He has a good command of both German and French, *to say nothing of* English.

もうすこし【もう少し】(量) a little more; (数) a few more; (時間) a little longer. ¶ お茶を〜ください Give me *some more* tea, please. 〜勉強しなさい Work *a little harder*. 〜おとどまりください Please stay *a little longer*. 〜遅ければ汽車に乗り遅れるところだった *A few minutes* later, and I would have missed the train. 〜ゆっくり話してください Speak *a little more* slowly, please. 〜で車にはねられるところだった I got *nearly* knocked down by a car.

もうせい【猛省】serious reflection. ¶ 今回のことについてきみの〜を促したい I must urge you to *reconsider seriously* what you have done lately.

もうせん【毛氈】a carpet; a rug. ¶ 〜を敷く spread *a rug*; lay *a carpet*.

もうぜん【猛然】furiously. ¶ ライオンはハンターに〜と襲いかかった The lion attacked the hunter *savagely*. 彼は〜と反撃してきた He struck back *furiously*.

もうせんごけ【毛氈苔】〘植物〙a sundew.

もうそう【妄想】a wild fancy; fantasy; a delusion. ¶ 〜をいだく nurse *delusions*. 彼は〜にふけっていた He was lost in *wild fancies*. / He was rapt in *daydreams*.

もうそうちく【孟宗竹】〘植物〙a *moso* bamboo.

もうだ【猛打】a hard blow; 〘野球〙slugging. ¶ われわれは相手チームに連続〜を浴びせた We slammed out a shower of *heavy hits* on the opponent team.

もうちょう【盲腸】〘解剖学〙the caecum (複 caeca); the blind gut; (虫垂) the vermiform appendix (複 appendices).

—炎〘医学〙appendicitis; caecitis. —炎手術 appendectomy.

もう·でる【詣でる】visit (a temple).

もうてん【盲点】(網膜の) a scotoma (複 scotomata); (不用意な点) a blind spot. ¶ 法の〜 *a blind point* of law. 捜査の〜をつく take advantage of *the blind spot* of the police investigation. そのことが議論の〜になっている That makes *a blind point* in the argument.

もうとう【毛頭】¶ 私は〜異存はない I have *no* objection *at all*. 私は不平は〜ありません I have *nothing whatever* to complain of. そうする考えは〜ない I haven't *the least* desire to do so. 私はそんなことを〜恐れはしない I am not *in the least* afraid of it. そんなことを言うつもりは〜ない I haven't *the slightest* intention of saying such things. 彼と私の間には悪感情は〜ない *There is not a trace of* ill feeling between him and me.

もうどうけん【盲導犬】a guide dog.

もうどく【猛毒】a deadly poison.

もうはつ【毛髪】hair.
もうひつ【毛筆】a writing brush.
もうふ【毛布】a blanket. ¶ ～をもう１枚かけてください Lay another *blanket* over me, please.
もうまく【網膜】〘解剖〙the retina (複 -s, retinae).
—剝離(はくり) detachment of retina.
もうもう【濛濛】¶ ～たる砂塵(さじん)が空に舞っていた *Clouds of dust* were swirling in the air. 湯げが～と部屋に立ち込めている The room *is bursting with* white steam. 工場の煙突から～たる煙が吹き出ている The factory chimneys are giving forth *columns of black smoke*.
もうら【網羅】¶ 報告書はあらゆる重要問題を～している The report *covers* (≒ *comprises*) all important questions. ひとりの作家の手紙や日記も～した全集 the complete works of an author *including* (≒ *containing*) letters and diaries.
もうれつ【猛烈】¶ ～な風が吹いている There is a *severe* wind blowing now. きのう～な雨が降った It rained very *heavily* yesterday. 関東地方は～な嵐に襲われた The Kanto district was hit by a *violent* storm. 新聞は政府の政策に対して～な攻撃を加えた The press made a *furious* attack on the Government's policy. ～な暑さだ It is *terribly* hot. ～に腹がへった I am *awfully* hungry. 彼は～に怒っている He is in *great* anger. 彼らは朝から晩まで～に働いている They are working *very hard* from morning till night.
—社員 an aggressive office man.
もうろう【朦朧】¶ 暑さで彼女は意識が～となった She *grew faint* from the heat. 記憶が～としてなにも思い出せない My memory *is* so *indistinct* that I can remember nothing.
もうろく【耄碌】dotage. ¶ 彼女は～している She *is in her dotage* (≒ *is in her second childhood; is senile*). 彼はまだ～するのは早すぎる He is too young to *dote* (≒ *fall into dotage*).
もえあが·る【燃え上がる】¶ ふすまはみるみるうちに～った The sliding doors *blazed up* (≒ *burst into flames*) in an instant.
もえうつ·る【燃え移る】¶ 火が隣の家に～った The flames *spread to* the next house.
もえがら【燃え殻】cinders; embers.
もえぎいろ【萌黄色】light green.
もえさし【燃えさし】embers. ¶ ～の薪 a *half-burned* log.
もえだ·す【燃え出す】¶ とうとう隣の家も～した The next door *caught fire* (≒ *began to burn*) at last.
もえつ·く【燃えつく】¶ 干し草はすぐ～く Dry grass is quick to *catch fire*.
もえ·でる【萌え出る】¶ 春になると若芽が～出る In spring tender shoots *come out*. / When spring comes, trees *put forth* young shoots.
もえにく·い【燃えにくい】slow to catch fire.
もえのこり【燃え残り】embers.
もえやす·い【燃えやすい】easy (≒ quick) to burn; inflammable; combustible.
も·える【燃える】**1**〘火が〙burn. ¶ ～えている船 a *burning* ship; a ship *on fire*. 赤々と～えているストーブ a *red-glowing* stove. 薪が湿っていてなかなか～えない The wood is so damp that it will not *burn*. 火が盛んに～えている Fire *is blazing* briskly.
2〘比喩的に〙¶ ～えるような太陽 a *blazing* (≒ *glaring*) sun. ～えるような緑 *fresh* green. 山は深紅の紅葉に～えている The mountains *are ablaze with* crimson tints. 彼は怒りに～えている He *is in great rage*. 彼は向学心に～えている He *is burning with* a desire to learn.
も·える【萌える】⇒もえでる
モーション a motion. ¶ ピッチャー振りかぶって第１球の～ The pitcher winds up for the first pitch. 彼は彼女に～をかけた He *made a pass at* her.
モーター a motor.
—バイク a motorbike; a motor bicycle.
—プール a motor pool. **—ボート** a motorboat.
モード〔a〕mode.
モーニング（礼服の一種）a morning coat.
モールス ¶ ～電信符号 Morse code. ～符号で送信する send *Morse code*.
もが·く【踠く】¶ 今更～いたって始まらない It is useless to *struggle* now. トラは～いて立ち上がろうとした The tiger *struggled* (≒ *wriggled*) to his feet.
もぎ【模擬】**—試験** a sham examination.
—店 a booth.
もぎと·る【捥ぎ取る】¶ 少女は人形の腕を～った The girl *tore* (≒ *broke*) *off* the arm of the doll. リンゴを木から～る *pluck* apples *from* a tree.
もく【目】（項目）an item;（生物分類項目）an order;〘囲碁〙（碁石）a piece;（盤の目）a cross. ¶ ３～勝つ（負ける）win (lose) by three *crosses*.
も·ぐ【捥ぐ】⇒もぎとる
もくあみ【木阿弥】¶ もとの～だ *I am no better than before*. / I *have lost all I gained*.
もくぎょ【木魚】a wooden gong (≒ drum).
もくげき【目撃】¶ 多くの人がその事件を～した Many people *witnessed* the incident. 犯行は何者かに～されていた The crime *was observed* by somebody. 現にこの目で～した I *saw it with my own eyes*.
—者 an eyewitness; a witness.
もぐさ【艾】moxa.
もくざい【木材】wood; 米 lumber; 英 timber.
もくさく【木柵】a wooden fence (≒ barricade).
もくさつ【黙殺】¶ 私の提案は～された They *ignored* (≒ *took no notice of*) my proposal.
もくし【黙視】¶ 彼の苦境は～するに忍びない It's intolerable for me to *remain indifferent to* his difficulties. / I cannot *remain a mere spectator of* him in great distress.

もくじ【目次】〔a table of〕contents.

もくじゅう【黙従】passive obedience; acquiescence. ¶～する obey passively; acquiesce in.

もくしろく【黙示録】〖聖書〗the Revelations; the Apocalypse.

もくず【藻屑】seaweeds. ¶多くの兵士たちが海底の～と消えた Many soldiers *were drowned at sea* (≒ *were sent to the bottom*).

もく·する【目する】¶彼は陰謀の張本人と～されている He *is regarded as* the author of the plot.

もく·する【黙する】¶彼は問題の核心については～して語らない He *is silent on* the main point of the issue. / He *holds his tongue about* the heart of the matter.

もくせい【木星】〖天文学〗Jupiter.

もくせい【木製】¶～のスプーン a *wooden* spoon.

—品 wooden ware (≒ articles); woodwork.

もくせい【木犀】〖植物〗a fragrant olive.

もくぜん【目前】¶惨事は見物人の～で起こった The miserable affair happened *in full view of* the spectators. 彼の逮捕は～に迫っている His arrest *is near at hand* (≒ *is just ahead*). 夏休みは～に迫っている The summer vacation *is just around the corner*.

もくそう【目送】¶彼らは彼を～した They *gazed after* him. / They *followed* him *with their eyes*.

もくそう【黙想】meditation. ¶彼はひとり座して～していた He sat alone *in meditation* (≒ *in reverie*). 静かに己れの運命について～する *meditate on one's* fate calmly.

もくぞう【木造】¶家は～です The house *is* 〔*built*〕 *of wood*. (That is a wooden house. はよいが, The house is wooden. とはしない).

—家屋 a wooden house; a frame house.

—船 a wooden vessel.

もくぞう【木像】a wooden image (≒ statue).

もくそく【目測】eye-measurement. ¶距離を～する *measure* the distance *with the eye*.

もくたん【木炭】charcoal.

—画 a charcoal drawing. —紙 charcoal paper.

もくちょう【木彫】wood carving.

もくてき【目的】an object; an aim. ¶当初の～を達成するまではあきらめるな Don't give up until you attain the original *object*. 利己的な～を追求する follow selfish *ends*. 確固たる～もなしに外国へ行くのはよくない It is wrong for you to go abroad without any fixed *purpose*. どんなことがあっても～を変えてはいけない Whatever may happen, you must stick to your *purpose*. この措置は世界平和の維持を～とする The *aim* of this measure is the maintenance of world peace. 政治の～は国民の幸福でなければならない The *object* of politics must be national welfare. 彼が足しげくここに来るにはなにか～がある He has some *intention* in coming here so often. 私は日本の事物を学ぶ～で来た I have come here *for the purpose of* study*ing* things Japanese. 彼を雇った～は彼の手腕を買ったからだ We employed him *with the intention of* using his ability. 彼女はなにを買う～もなく店に入った She went into the store *with no intention to* buy.

—格〖文法〗the objective case. 直接(間接)—語 the direct (indirect) object. —地 the destination.

もくとう【黙祷】¶戦死者の冥福(めいふく)を祈って1分間の～をささげる offer a one-minute *silent prayer* for the souls of the war dead.

もくどく【黙読】¶本を～する *read* a book *silently*.

もくにん【黙認】connivance; tacit consent. ¶ふたりの結婚は～されている Their marriage *is admitted tacitly*.

もくねじ【木捻子】a wood screw.

もくば【木馬】a wooden horse; (小児の) a rocking horse; (体操の) a vaulting horse.

もくはん【木版】wooden engraving; block printing.

—画 a wood engraving; a woodcut.

もくひけん【黙秘権】the right of silence. ¶彼は～を使った He used *the right of silence*.

もくひょう【目標】a mark; (目じるし) a sign; (道しるべ) a guide; (標的) a target; (目的) an aim; a goal.

¶わが社は生産～を既に突破した We have already passed our production *goal* (≒ *target*). ～は高いところにおけ Keep your *purpose* high. まだとても～に達しない We are far from the *goal*. お宅に行くのになにか～がありますか Is there any *guide* to your house?

もくへん【木片】a piece of wood; (大きな) a block; (小さな) a chip.

もくめ【木目】the grain of wood. ¶～の粗い(細かい)材木 timber of coarse (fine) *grain*.

もくもく【黙黙】¶彼らはみな～と働いていた They were working *without saying anything*. 彼はいつも～としていた He *remained silent*. / He *was* always *quiet*.

もぐもぐ ¶口の中で～言っていてはだれにもわかりませんよ Nobody will understand you if you *mumble* your words.

もくやく【黙約】a tacit agreement.

もくようび【木曜日】Thursday.

もぐら【土竜】a mole.

—塚 a mole hill.

もぐり【潜り】**1**〖潜水〗diving.

2〖無資格〗¶～の歯医者 an *unlicensed* dentist. ～のタクシー運転手 an *unregistered* taxi driver. あの男は～で商売している He trades *without a license*.

もぐりこ·む【潜り込む】¶彼は家に帰るとすぐにベッドに～んだ He *got* (≒ *crept*) *into* bed as soon as he came home. 彼はすばやく人ごみに～んだ He *slipped* away *into* the crowd. 子どもがテーブルの下に～んだ The child *concealed* (≒ *hid*) *himself* under the table.

もぐ·る【潜る】¶2分間水中に～っていられる I

can *remain under water* for two minutes. 彼はナイフを持って水中に〜った He *dived into the water* with a knife. 戦争中彼らは地下に〜って政治活動を続けた During the war they *went underground* in order to continue their political activities.

もくれい【目礼】¶ 彼は部屋に入ってきたとき私に〜した He *gave* me *a nod* when he came into the room.

もくれい【黙礼】¶ 〜をかわす exchange nods; make a bow to each other in silence; exchange salutes in silence.

もくれん【木蓮】〘植物〙 a magnolia.

もくろく【目録】a catalog[ue]; a list; (目次) the contents. ¶ 新刊書〜 *a list* of new publications. カード式〜 *a* card *catalog*. 蔵書の〜を作る *catalog* (≒ *make a list of*) *one's* library. 結納の〜 *a list* of betrothal presents.

もくろみ【目論み】(計画) a plan; a project; (意図) an intention; (予定) a program.
¶ 〜がはずれた My *plans* have gone wrong. 彼にはなにか別の〜があるにちがいない He must have some other *design* in his mind.

もくろ·む【目論む】¶ 彼はなにを〜んでいるのかわからない I can't make out what he *is driving at* (≒ *is going to do*). / What *plan* is in his hand, I wonder? 彼はまた事業を〜んでいる He *is projecting* another undertaking. 彼らはなにか悪いことを〜んでいる They *are* apparently *planning* to do something evil.

もけい【模型】a model; (機械など) a pattern.
—飛行機 a model airplane.

も·げる【捥げる】¶ 人形の右腕が〜げてしまった The right arm of the doll *has come off*.

もさ【猛者】a stalwart person. ¶ 彼はその道の〜だ He is *a veteran* in that line. 彼は柔道の〜だ He is *an expert judo man*.

モザイク [a] mosaic.
—細工 mosaic work. —模様 mosaic.

もさく【模索】¶ 私はその問題の解決策を〜した I *groped for* a means of solving the problem.

もさっと ¶ なにをそんなに〜しているのだ Why is it you *look stupefied* like that?

もし if. ¶ 〜雨なら外出はやめよう *If* it rains, I will give up going out. 〜天気が悪ければ家にいるつもりだ *Unless* it is fine, I will stay at home.

もじ【文字】a letter; a character. ¶ 彼は〜を知らない He *is illiterate*.
—どおり ¶ 彼は〜どおり骨と皮ばかりになった *It is no exaggeration to say* that he has lost all his flesh. 道路は〜どおりの大混雑だった The street was *really* crowded. 和文英訳をあまり〜どおりにやろうとしてはいけない You must not try to translate Japanese into English *word for word* (≒ *too literally*).

もしかすると ¶ 〜家にいるかもしれないと思って彼を訪ねてみた I went to his house *on the chance of* finding him at home. 〜あの人がその金を用立ててくれるかもしれない He may lend us the money, *though I'm not sure*.

もしくは ¶ 手紙〜電話でお知らせします I'll let you know it *either* by letter *or* by phone. 私〜彼がお会いします *Either* I *or* he will meet you.

もじばん【文字盤】a dial plate.

もしも ¶ 〜のことがあったら知らせてください Please let me know *when something unexpected has turned up*. 彼に〜のことが起こったらどうしよう What shall I do, *if anything should happen to him*?

もしもし ¶ (電話で) 〜, こちらはAです *Hello*, this is A speaking. 〜, Bさんですか *Hello*, is that you, Mr. B? 〜, お嬢さん, 定期券が落ちましたよ *I say*, Miss, you've dropped your commutation (≒ season) ticket.

もじもじ ¶ 少女は〜しながらしゃべった The girl talked *hesitatingly*. 〜しないで返事をしなさい Don't *hesitate* to answer.

もしゃ【模写】a copy. ¶ ゴッホの〜 *a copy* of Gogh. 壁画を〜する *copy* a wall painting.

もしや ¶ 成功するとは思わなかったが, 〜と思ってやってみた I did not expect success, but I only took a chance. 〜ご存じなら教えてくれませんか *If by any chance* you know, would you please let me know?

もじゃもじゃ ¶ 彼は〜の髪をしている He has *disheveled* hair. 彼は眉毛が〜している His eyebrows *are hairy*.

もしゅ【喪主】a chief mourner.

もしょう【喪章】a mourning band; a mourning badge.

もじ·る【捩る】¶ これはなにかを〜った歌だ This is a sort of *parody*. これはバーンズの詩を〜ったものだ This is *a parody* of a poem of Burns.

もず【鵙·百舌】〘鳥類〙 a shrike.

もぞう【模造】imitation. ¶ このつぼは〜だ This jar is *an imitation*. このネックレスは〜だ This necklace is *a fake*.
—皮 imitation leather. —品 an imitation.

もぞもぞ ¶ なにを〜しているのですか Why *are* you so *hesitating*?

もだ·える【悶える】¶ 彼はそんな罪を犯して, 今ごろは精神的に〜え苦しんでいるにちがいない Having committed such a crime, he must now *be suffering from* remorse.

もた·げる【擡げる】¶ ヘビが鎌首を〜げた The snake *raised* its head.

もたざる【持たざる】¶ 持てる者と〜者との差があまりにも多すぎる The differences between *the* haves and *have-nots* are too great.

もだしがた·い【黙し難い】¶ 彼らの懇望〜く, 提案に同意した I agreed to the plan at their earnest request.

もたせか·ける【凭せ掛ける】¶ 背中を壁に〜ける *lean one's* back *against* a wall. モップをドアに〜ける *put* a mop *against* a door.

もた·せる【持たせる】¶ 返事は彼に〜せましょう He *shall carry* my answer to you. 費用は私に〜せてください Please let me pay for it. / This is on me. (後者は口語).

もたら·す【齎す】¶ 吉報を〜す *bring* good

news. 豪雨は関東一帯に大きな被害を〜した The heavy rain *caused* a lot of damage all over the Kanto district.

もた·れる【凭れる】¶いすに〜れる *lean against* a chair. 脂っこい食べ物が胃に〜れた The greasy food *lay heavy on* my *stomach*.

モダン modern. ¶あの家は〜な建築だ That house is of a *modern* style. 〜なデザイン an *up-to-date* design.

もち【持ち】durability; wear. ¶この服は〜が悪い This dress *wears ill*. このくつは〜がよいだろう These shoes will *go a long way*. 概して高い物のほうが〜がよい Generally speaking, the dearer a thing is, the more *durable* it *is*.

もち【餅】rice cake. ¶〜をつく make *rice cake*. 〜は〜屋 (諺) *Every man for his own trade*.

もち【黐】birdlime. ¶さおに〜を塗る *lime* a pole.

もちあが·る【持ち上がる】¶彼らの間に一騒動〜った A trouble *arose* between them. もう一つ新たな問題が〜った A new problem *has cropped up*. 事件が〜った An incident *took place* (≒ *turned up*).

もちあ·げる【持ち上げる】¶この石を〜げてごらん Try to *raise* (≒ *lift up*) this stone. 彼は人に〜げられて(おだてられて)有頂天になった He went into ecstasies through *being flattered*.

もちあじ【持ち味】a characteristic; (味) a peculiar flavor. ¶そのものの〜を生かすべきだ You should make the most of its *peculiar characteristics*. 彼の〜を十分に生かした話しぶりだった His way of speaking reflected his *distinctive personality*.

もちある·く【持ち歩く】¶そんな大金を〜くのは危険だ It is dangerous to *carry* such a large amount of money *about with* (≒ *on*) you.

もちあわせ【持ち合わせ】¶金の〜がありますか Do you have any money *with* (≒ *on*) you?

もちあわ·せる【持ち合わせる】¶金を〜せていない I *have no* money *with* (≒ *on*) me.

モチーフ a motif.

もち·いる【用いる】¶ペンを〜いる *use* a pen. これはなにに〜いるのか What *is* this *used* for? ブラジルでは何語が〜いられているか What language do they *speak* in Brazil? もっと違った方法を〜いたほうがいい We must *adopt* a different method. この機械はもう〜いられなくなっている This machine *has gone out of use*. これからはもっと健康に意を〜いるべきだ You should *take* more care of your health from now on.

もちかえ·る【持ち帰る】¶これらの資料は家に〜ってけっこうです You may *take* these data *home*.

もちか·える【持ち替える】¶かばんを左手から右手に〜える pass a bag from the left hand to the right.

もちか·ける【持ちかける】¶彼がそのプランを私に〜けた He *approached* me *with* the plan. その会の席上彼は二つの問題を〜けてきた In the meeting he *broached* (≒ *suggested*) two subjects to us.

もちがし【餅菓子】bean jam cake (西洋には餅菓子の類は見られない).

もちかた【持ち方】¶彼にラケットの〜を教えた I told him *how to hold* a racket. 非常の際の心の〜はたいせつである *A frame of mind* in case of emergency is important.

もちかぶ【持ち株】*one's* holdings.
—会社 a holding company.

もちきり【持ち切り】¶ゴルフの話で〜だった We *talked about nothing but* golf. 町じゅうがその男のうわさで〜だ His name *is* now much *on the lips of people* in the town. 新聞は島に20年間独りで暮らしたその男のことで〜だった The newspapers *were full of stories about* the man who had lived alone in the island for twenty years.

もちぐされ【持ち腐れ】¶これは私には宝の〜だ This *is of little use to* me.

もちくず·す【持ち崩す】¶彼は競馬で身を〜した He *ruined himself* by playing the horses. 放蕩で身を〜した He *went wrong* through dissipation.

もちこ·す【持ち越す】¶これは前年度から〜された問題だ This is the problem *brought over from* the previous year. あとはあすに〜すことにしよう Let's *carry* the work *to* tomorrow.

もちこた·える【持ち堪える】¶その病人は今月いっぱいは〜えるだろう The invalid will be able to *go* as far as the end of this month. / The man who is ill in bed will *live* throughout this month.

もちこ·む【持ち込む】¶犬をバスに〜んではならない You must not *take* a dog *into* the bus. その筋に苦情を〜んではどうか What about *lodging* a complaint *with* the authorities?

もちごめ【糯米】glutinous rice.

もちさ·る【持ち去る】¶知らぬ間に自転車を〜られた I *had* my bicycle *carried* (≒ *taken*) *away* without my knowledge.

もちだし【持ち出し】¶これらの本は〜は禁じられている You must not *take* these books *away*. 会社から出張費はもらったが1万円も〜になった I received traveling expenses from the company, but I had to *pay* ten thousand yen *out of my own pocket*.

もちだ·す【持ち出す】¶いすを庭に〜す *take* a chair *out* into a garden. 火事のときにはまずこのかばんを〜さなければならない This bag is the first thing we have to *save* in case of fire. 彼は会議の席上で人員削減の話を〜した At the conference he *broached* the subject *of* cutting personnel.

もちつもたれつ【持ちつ持たれつ】¶世の中は〜だ Mutual aid is what makes the world an agreeable place to live in.

もちなお·す【持ち直す】¶患者は〜した The patient *has rallied*. 天気は〜した The weather *has improved*. 景気は〜しつつある Business *is picking up*. / Business *is on* *the brighter side.*

もちにげ【持ち逃げ】 ¶ だれかが私の旅行かばんを～した Someone *has carried off* (≒ *has taken away*) my trunk.

もちぬし【持ち主】 the owner. ¶ この車の～はだれですか Who *owns* this car? 彼がこの店の～だ He is *the proprietor* of this store. この荷物は～がわからない This baggage *is unclaimed.* / This is an *unclaimed* baggage.

もちば【持ち場】 *one's* post. ¶ ～を守るようにつとめる try to be faithful to *one's post.* それぞれ～が違っている Each one has his particular *field.*

もちはこび【持ち運び】 carrying; conveyance. ¶ このタイプライターは～のできるのが利点だ The typewriter *is portable* and very useful. / This typewriter has the advantage of being handy to *carry.*

もちはこ・ぶ【持ち運ぶ】 ¶ 本はこの箱に入れて～ぶといい *Carry* your books in this box.

もちふだ【持ち札】 the card in *one's* hand. ¶ きみの～が知りたい I want to know what *cards are in your hands.*

もちまえ【持ち前】 ¶ 彼の～の親切が人々の共感を呼んだ People were impressed by his *natural* kindness. ～の話術で聴衆を魅了した He charmed the audience with his *natural* eloquence.

もちまわり【持ち回り】 ¶ その問題は～閣議に付された The matter was submitted for individual consideration of the Cabinet members.

もちまわ・る【持ち回る】 ¶ 原稿を携えて出版社を～った I submitted my manuscript to several publishing companies.

も

もちもの【持ち物】 *one's* property. ¶ これは私の～だ This *belongs to* me. この土地は彼の～だ This land is his *property.*

もちゅう【喪中】 ¶ 彼は父の～だ He *is in mourning for* his father.

もちより【持ち寄り】 ¶ ～で会をしよう Let's have a party *all sharing the expense.*

もちよ・る【持ち寄る】 ¶ めいめいがビールかなにか～って忘年会をやろうじゃないか How about giving a year-end party, *each bringing* beer or something?

もちろん【勿論】 of course. ¶ ～そのとおりだ *Of course,* it is right. うそをつくのが悪いのは～だ *Needless to say,* telling lies is wrong. 英語は～ロシア語も話せる I can speak Russian, *not to mention* English. 彼は～成功するだろう *I am sure of* his success. ～あなたはアメリカへ行ったことがあるだろうと思った I *took it for granted* that you had been to America before.「ぼくとスキーに行くかね」「～」"Will you come skiing with me?" "*Sure!*"

も・つ【持つ】 1 〖手に〗 ¶ 彼は雑誌を～っている He *has* a magazine in his hand.

2 〖携帯〗 ¶ いつも時計は～って歩くことにしている I always *carry* a watch *with* me.

今は金を～っていない I *have got* no money *on* me.

このスーツケースを～ってくれませんか Won't you *hold* this suitcase for me?

雨が降りそうだから, かさは～っていきなさい It looks like rain, *take* an umbrella.

返事は彼に～たせようと思っている I will *send* him *with* my answer.

3 〖所有〗 ¶ 彼は良い万年筆を～っている He *has* a good pen.

彼は喫茶店を～っている He *runs* a tea shop.

このカメラを～っているのはだれですか Who *keeps* (≒ *owns*) this camera?

彼は伊豆に土地を～っている He *has* (≒ *is in possession of*) a piece of land in Izu.

この国はばく大な石油資源を～っている This country *possesses* an immense supply of oil resources.

4 〖気持ちを持つ〗 ¶ 彼はブラジルへ行く希望を～っている He *hopes to* visit Brazil.

5 〖持ちこたえる〗 ¶ このケーキは二, 三日は～つだろう These cakes will *keep well* for two or three days.

この服は1年は～つ This suit will *last* for at least a year.

この金魚は何日ぐらい～つだろうか I wonder how long this goldfish will *live.*

6 〖負担〗 ¶ 私が費用を～とう I will *pay* the expenses.

彼が勘定を～ってくれた He *paid* my bill.

7 〖担当〗 ¶ 彼は2年を～っている He *is in charge of* the second-year class.

もっか【目下】 now. ¶ ～のところは物価は安定している Prices are stable *at present* (≒ *for the moment; for the present*). ～の状態では危険だ It is critical, *as things stand now.* ～のところ彼の消息はない I have heard nothing of him *till now.*

もっかん【木管】 ―楽器 a woodwind instrument.

もっきん【木琴】 a xylophone.
―奏者 a xylophonist.

もっけ【勿怪】 ¶ 主人が留守なのを～の幸いに彼らは午後の仕事を休んだ *Taking advantage of* their master's absence, they stopped work for the afternoon.

もっこ【畚】 a straw basket.

もっこう【木工】 (人) a woodworker; (木工細工) wood-working.

もっこう【黙考】 meditation. ¶ 彼は沈思～している He is absorbed in *contemplation.* / He is lost in *thought.*

もったい【勿体】 ¶ ～をつける assume an air of importance. 彼はいつでも～をつけて話す He always speaks *pompously* (≒ *like a prig*).

もったいな・い【勿体ない】 ¶ この万年筆は私には～い This pen *is too good for* me. まったく時間が～い It is *an* utter *waste* of time. それでは労力が～い That is *a* mere *waste* of labor. このまま引退して世間に忘れられるのは～い He *is too useful to* retire in oblivion. これはぼくには～い I don't *deserve* this.

もったいぶ・る【勿体ぶる】 ¶ ～るな Never *put on airs.* 私は彼の～らないところが好きだ I like him for not *being pompous.* 彼はいつも〜って話す He always speaks *pompously* (≒ *with an air of importance*).

もって 【以て】 ¶ 書面を〜ご返事します I will answer *by* letter. 多忙の理由を〜出席を断わった I declined to be present at the meeting *by reason of* being busy. 彼は天才を〜世間に聞こえが高い He is well known all over the world *for* his genius. 競技会は２月10日を〜閉会の予定です The athletic meet is to close *on* February 10. 展覧会は次の日曜日を〜おしまいです The exhibition will be closed *through* next Sunday.

もってい・く 【持って行く】 ¶ この手紙を彼のところに〜きなさい *Take* this letter *to* him. 彼が私の本を〜ったにちがいない He must *have walked off with* my book. 外出するならかさを〜きなさい *Take* your umbrella *with* you when you go out.

もって・くる 【持って来る】 ¶ 茶を〜きてください *Bring* me a cup of tea, will you? きょうは弁当を〜こなかった I *have brought* no lunch from home today. 隣の部屋からいすをひとつ〜きてください *Fetch* a chair from the next room, please.

もってこい 【持って来い】 ¶ その仕事は彼女に〜だ The job *is just the thing for* her. 彼はこの役にはまさに〜の人物だ He *is just the right person for* this role. 遠足には〜の天気だ This is indeed *the ideal* weather for a picnic.

もってのほか 【以ての外】 ¶ そんなことを考えるとは〜だ It *is quite absurd* to think of such a thing. そんな質問をするとは〜だ How *unreasonable* it *is* of him to ask such a question! 黙って欠席するなどとは〜だ You *must never think of* staying away without making any excuse.

もっと more. ¶ 彼も悪いが彼女のほうが〜悪い Indeed he is bad, but she is *worse.* 〜バナナが欲しい I want *more* bananas. なにか〜言うことがあるようだね You have something *more* to say, haven't you?

モットー a motto. ¶ 不言実行を〜としている I make it my *motto* to act before words.

もっとも 【尤も】 **1** 〚当然〛 ¶ ご〜です You *are quite right.*
彼は確かに〜なことを言う It is certain that he *talks sense.*
そうするのは親として〜なことだ It *is quite natural* for parents to do so.
彼女がきみに対して怒るのも〜だ She *may well* get angry with you.
まことに〜らしい言いわけだ The excuse he made seems *plausible.*
彼は〜らしい顔で冗談を言う He makes jokes with a *serious* look.
2 〚ただし〛 ¶ そうすればうまくいく, 〜例外はあるが You can be successful by doing so, *though* there can be some exceptions.

もっとも 【最も】 〔the〕 most. ¶ 今までに読んだあらゆる小説の中で私はこれが〜好きだ Of all the novels I have so far read, I like this *best.* これが〜私を困らせる問題だ This is the problem which puzzles me *most.* 自分に〜適した職業を選ぶべきだ You should choose a job *most* suitable for you.

もっぱら 【専ら】 ¶ この車は〜彼が使っている This car is *exclusively* for his use. 彼は余暇は〜スポーツに打ち込んだ He *devoted* his spare time *to* sport. 休日は〜家で過ごす I spend holidays *chiefly* at home. あのふたりは仲がいいと〜のうわさだ *Everybody talks* of those two being lovers.

もつら・す 【縺らす】 tangle. ¶ 糸を〜せてしまった I *entangled* the threads. / I *got* the threads *into a tangle.*

もつれ 【縺れ】 a tangle; (紛糾) difficulty; trouble. ¶ 糸の〜 *a tangle* of threads. 仲間の間に感情の〜が生じた There was *a mixture* of feelings among ourselves. / We *quarreled* among ourselves.

もつ・れる 【縺れる】 ¶ 糸が〜れた The thread *got tangled.* 話が〜れた The matter *became complicated.* / The matter *got entangled* (≒ *got embarrassed*). 話すとき舌が〜れる He speaks *with a lisp* (≒ *inarticulately*).

もてあそ・ぶ 【玩ぶ・弄ぶ】 ¶ ナイフを〜ぶ *play* (≒ *toy*) *with* a knife. 彼女は数奇な運命に〜ばれた She *was at the mercy of* (≒ *was the sport of*) a strange fate. 彼女は彼の愛情を〜んでいる She *plays* (≒ *trifles*) *with* his affections.

もてあま・す 【持て余す】 ¶ 私は数学を〜している Mathematics *is too much for* me. 先生もそのいたずらっ子を〜している Even the teacher *does not know what to do with* the naughty boy. 時間を〜した *There was too much time* for me *to kill.* ケーキが甘すぎて〜した The cake *was too sweet* for me *to finish.* 彼は近所の〜し者だ He is *a regular pest* of the neighborhood.

もてなし 【持て成し】 reception; service; (歓待) hospitality. ¶ 私は彼の家で暖かい〜を受けた I received *a* warm *welcome* at his home. / I was given *a* hearty *welcome* at his home. 茶菓の〜を受けた We *were entertained* (≒ *were served*) with refreshments. お〜に感謝いたします Thank you very much for your *hospitality.*

もてな・す 【持て成す】 ¶ 彼女は客を手厚く〜す She *treats* her guests hospitably. 彼女は客を手料理で〜す She *entertains* her guests with dishes prepared by herself.

もてはや・す 【持て囃す】 ¶ 彼女はスター歌手として〜されている She *is made much of* as a star singer. この雑誌は子どもたちに〜されている This magazine *is very popular among* children.

も・てる 【持てる】 **1** 〚人気がある〛 ¶ 彼女はクラスの中でたいへん〜てる She *is very popular* in her class.
彼はどこに行っても女に〜てる Wherever he goes he *is popular* (≒ *is a great favorite*)

with girls.
2 〖富んでいる〗 ¶ アメリカは世界で有数の〜てる国だ America is one of *the foremost "haves"* (≒ *the richest countries*) in the world.

モデル a model. ¶ 彼女は画家の〜になった She *posed for* an artist. / She acted as *an* artist's *model*. 彼らは〜を写生している They are painting from *a model*. この小説の〜はAさんだ *The living model* of this novel is Mr. A. / The hero of this novel *is modeled after* Mr. A. (女性の場合は The heroine...Miss (Mrs.) となる).
—ケース a model case. **—スクール** a model school. **—チェンジ** a model change.

もと 【元・本】 **1** 〖起源・原因〗 the origin; the cause. ¶ ふたりの不和の〜はどこにあるのか What is *the cause* of discord between the two? 〜はといえばきみが彼の悪口を言ったのが悪いのだ All this *has resulted from* the abusive language you used against him.
彼は過労が〜で健康を害した He ruined his health *from* (≒ *on account of*) overwork.
風邪は万病の〜 All diseases *originate in* a cold.
口は災いの〜 (諺) *Out of the mouth comes evil.* / The tongue *is responsible for* many a misfortune.
失敗は成功の〜 (諺) Failure is a stepping stone to success. / Failure is but a gate to success.
2 〖土台・根本〗 the basis; the foundation. ¶ 昔は農は国の〜であるとされていた Formerly, agriculture was regarded as *the basis* (≒ *the foundation*) of a nation's economy.
柱が〜から倒れてしまった The column fell together with its *foundation*.
3 〖原料・材料〗 material. ¶ スープの〜 *a* soup *base*.
これは薬草を〜にして作った薬だ This medicine is made (≒ is extracted) from medicinal herbs.
この映画は史実を〜にして作られている The film *is based on* a true story.
4 〖資本〗 capital. ¶ この商売を始めるにはずいぶん〜がかかった The business required a large amount of *capital*.
あまり欲を出すと〜も子もなくしてしまう If you are too enterprising, you will lose both *the principal* and the interest.
うまくいけば5年で〜がとれるだろう If everything goes well, you will be able to recover the *cost* (≒ *capital*) in five years.
5 〖原価〗 ¶ 1,000円でこれだけ楽しめれば〜がとれたというものだ You cannot complain if you have got so much out of a thousand yen.
6 〖以前〗 ¶ この壊れたつぼをなんとか〜の姿に返したい I hope to put back the broken vase into its *original* shape at all cost.
彼は〜は高校の先生をしていた He was *formerly* (≒ He *used to* be) a senior high school teacher.
これが〜私が住んでいた家だ This is the house I *used to* live in.
部屋を〜どおりに整とんしておきなさい Put the room in order *as it was before*.
この本を〜の場所にもどしておいてください Put the book back to its *former* place.
夫婦は結局〜のさやに収まった Eventually, the man and his wife were reconciled with each other.

もと 【下・許】 with; at; under. ¶ 結婚するまで両親の〜で暮らした I lived *with* my parents till I got married. 彼を一撃の〜に倒した I knocked him down *at* a blow.

もとい 【基】 basis. ¶ その国は農業を国の〜とする The nation *is based on* agriculture. / Agriculture is *the basic industry* of the nation.

もどかし・い impatient. ¶ 思うように表現できなくて〜い I *am irritated* as I cannot express myself satisfactorily. 彼は〜そうに子どもの動作を見ていた He *impatiently* watched the child's behavior. 彼女は〜がって自分でやりだした She *grew impatient* and began to do it herself.

-もどき 【-擬き】 ¶ 彼は芝居〜にしゃべる He speaks *dramatically* (≒ *in a dramatic way*).

もときん 【元金】 the principal. ¶ 〜は保証されている *The principal* is guaranteed.

もとじめ 【元締め】 a manager. ¶ 彼がこの仕事の〜をしている He *manages* the business. / He is the *manager* of the business.

もど・す 【戻す】 return. ¶ 余ったプリントは〜してください Please *return* (≒ *give back*) the rest of the printed papers *to* me. 使ったら箱の中に〜しておきなさい *Put* it *back* in the box when you have finished using it. 時計を30分〜した I *turned back* the watch by 30 minutes. 彼からカメラを〜してもらった I *got* the camera *back* from him. 彼は食べたものを〜した He *vomited* (≒ (口語) *threw up*) what he had eaten.

もとちょう 【元帳】 a ledger.

もとづ・く 【基づく】 ¶ 経験に〜く(根拠とする)判断 a judgment *based on* experience. 事実に〜いた物語 a story *founded on* facts. 誤解に〜く(起因する)不和 a quarrel *caused by* misunderstanding. 迷信に〜く習慣 a custom *originated from* a superstition. 実績に〜いて評価される You are estimated *according to* your accomplishments. 彼の言動は信仰に〜いている His belief *is the base of* his word and deed. / His word and deed *is based on* his belief.

もとで 【元手】 capital; funds. ¶ なにをやるにも〜がかかる Whatever we may undertake we need *funds* for it. それを実行に移すだけの〜があるのか Do you have the *funds* enough to carry it out? からだだけが〜だ Health is the only *capital* that I have.

もとどおり 【元通り】 as before; as it was before. ¶ 彼女は〜元気になった Now she is *as* healthy *as before*. このおもちゃを〜に直すの

は難しい It is difficult to *fix* (≒ *mend*) the toy *as it was.*

もとね【元値】the cost. ¶ あの店では～で(～以下で)売っている They sell *at cost* (≒ *below cost; at less than cost*) at that shop.

もとめ【求め】a claim; a demand; a request. ¶ 聴取者の～に応じて番組を作る We make programs in compliance with the audience's *request* (≒ *wish*). お～によりもう1曲歌いましょう I am going to sing one more song *at your request.*

もと·める【求める】**1**〖買う〗¶ 6,000円で時計を～めた I *bought* a watch for six thousand yen.

2〖要求する〗¶ 彼は首相自身の説明を～めた He *called for* an explanation from the prime minister himself.

彼が私に出席を～めた He *requested* my attendance.

だれか学者に援助を～めなければならない We must *depend upon* some scholar *for* help.

～めよ, さらば与えられん (聖書) *Ask,* and it shall be given you.

3〖ほしがる〗¶ 地位を～めるから彼はきらわれるのだ It is because he *seeks after* a good position that he is disliked.

彼は職を～めている He *is looking for* a job.

もともと【元元】(元来) originally; (生来) by nature. ¶ これは～彼のものだった This *originally* belonged to him. その仕事は～私には無理だった The work was too much for me *from the first.* ～やる気はないのだ He has been unwilling to do it *from the beginning* (≒ *from the start*). 彼は～体が弱い He is *by nature* in delicate health. 失敗したって～だ We *are to lose nothing* if we fail. / We *will be none the worse for* failure.

もとより【固より·素より】¶ ～決心はついていた I was determined *from the first* (≒ *from the start*). ～そんなことがあるわけがない *Of course* it cannot be true. 英語は～フランス語も話せる I can speak French *as well as* (≒ *to say nothing of*) English. / I can speak *not only* English *but also* French.

もどり【戻り】¶ ～がけに彼に会った I met him *on the way back.*

もと·る【悖る】¶ そのような行動は学生の本分に～る Such a behavior *is contrary to* (≒ *is against; conflicts with*) the duty of a student. 泣き言をいうのは私の主義に～る It's *against* my principle to make a complaint.

もど·る【戻る】return. ¶ 彼が出張から～ってきた He *has come back* from his business trip. 自分の席に～りなさい *Go back* (≒ *Return*) to your seat. さて本論に～ろう Let's *return* to the main subject. 彼はまた元の地位に～った He *was restored to* his former position. 彼らのよりが～った They *have got reconciled.*

もなか【最中】a wafer stuffed with bean jam.

モニター a monitor. ¶ 放送局の～ *a monitor* to a broadcasting company.

もぬけ【裳抜け·蛻】¶ ベッドは～のからだった The bed *was* [*found*] *empty.* 刑事が彼の家に踏み込んだときには既に～のからだった When the policemen broke into his house, *nobody was found there.*

もの【物】**1**〖物質·物体·品物〗matter; a thing. ¶ 背中になにか白い～がついていますよ I see *something* white on your back.

なにか食べる～はありませんか Do you have *anything* to eat?

～の値段が高くなった *Prices* have risen.

2〖所有物〗¶ これは私の～だ This is *mine.*

人の～を無断で使ってはいけない You must not make free use of another's *possessions.*

月賦が終わって自動車がようやく自分の～になった Now that I have paid the last instalment money, the car *is in my possession* (≒ *belongs to me*).

3〖品質〗¶ あの店の品は安いが～がよくない That shop sells cheap but inferior *goods.*

もっと～のいいのを見せてください Show me an article of better *quality.*

4〖存在·物事〗¶ 親切という～はけっして金で買える～ではない Kindness can never be bought with money.

彼は～に動じない He is not shaken easily.

彼は実に～をよく知っている He is well-informed, indeed.

疲れて～を言うのもおっくうだった I was too tired to *speak.*

～には順序という～がある There is a proper order in doing *everything.*

～は試しだ, やってみよう Let us have a try and see what will happen.

5〖成功·ひとかどのもの·習得·獲得〗¶ 彼のテニスは～になりそうだ Most likely, he will make a good tennis player.

この試合だけは～にしたい I want to *win* this game at least.

彼は渡米前に英会話を～にしようと猛勉強中だ He is doing his best to *master* spoken English before he leaves for America.

彼はなにをやらせても～にならない He *is good at nothing.*

6〖道理〗¶ 彼は～のわかる(わからない)人だ He is a man *of deep* (*little*) *understanding.*

7〖効力·価値〗¶ 日本の政界は金が～をいう世界だ Money still *talks* in the political world of Japan.

きみの実力が～をいうときが必ず来る Your real ability will lead you to success some day.

敵は数に～をいわせて猛攻してきた The enemy fell on us with the full strength of their number.

8〖その他〗¶ 彼は急流を～ともせずに川を泳ぎ渡った He swam across the river, not at all frightened by the rapids.

彼は～の役にたつ男だ He is a *useful* man in many ways.

～の本で読んだことがある I remember reading

も

about it in *some book or other.*
こんな障害くらいは～の数ではない An obstacle like this *does not matter* in the least.

もの【者】 a person ; one. ¶山田という～ *one* (≒ *a*) Yamada ; *a person* named Yamada. 18歳未満の～ *persons* under 18 〔years old〕. 遅れてきた～ *those* who arrived late. 私は大阪の～だ I *come from* Osaka. 彼を知らない～はいない *Everybody* knows him. その問いに答えられる～はだれもいなかった There wasn't *anyone* who could answer that question. / *Nobody* could answer the question. きみともあろう～がそんなことをするなんて *You, of all people,* should do such a thing !

もの- (接頭辞として) ¶～悲しい歌声が聞こえてきた I heard a sorrowful voice singing.

-もの ¶年寄りは敬うべき～だ You *should* respect the old. 子どもは親のまねをする～だ Children *naturally* imitate what their parents do. いつか外国に行ってみたい～だ I *would* (≒ *should*) *like to* go abroad some time. 少しは私の言うことも聞く～だ Sometimes listen to what I say. さすがに超音速ジェット機は速い～だ It is amazing how fast the supersonic jet can fly.

ものいい【物言い】 ¶審判の判定に～がついた *A protest* was made against the umpire's decision.

ものいり【物いり】 expenses. ¶今月は～だった I had to *spend a lot of money* this month. / My *expenses* have considerably run this month.

ものう・い【物憂い】 melancholy ; lazy. ¶なにをするにも～い I *am weary of* doing. ～い気分だ I *feel languid* (≒ *feel dull*).

ものおき【物置】 a storeroom ; a lumber room ; a barn.

ものおじ【物怖じ】 ¶この子は～しない This child *is not timid.* 彼は～せずにはきはき答えた He answered clearly *without hesitation.*

ものおしみ【物惜しみ】 niggardliness. ¶彼は金持ちのくせに～する Though he is rich, he *is stingy* (≒ *is closefisted ; is ungenerous*).

ものおと【物音】 a noise ; a sound.

ものおぼえ【物覚え】 **1** 〚記憶力〛〔a〕memory. ¶彼は～がよい（悪い） He has *a* good (bad ; poor) *memory.*
最近～が悪くなった（忘れる） I am getting *forgetful* these days. / My *memory* is failing.
2 〚理解力〛 ¶彼女は～が早い（遅い） She *learns* fast (slowly). / She is quick (slow) at *learning.*

ものおもい【物思い】 meditation ; reflection. ¶彼女は～にふけっている She is deep (≒ is lost) in *thought* (≒ *meditation*).

ものかげ【物陰】 ¶足音を聞いて彼は～に隠れた Hearing footsteps he *hid himself.*

ものがた・い【物堅い】 ¶～い人物 a *conscientious* (≒ *scrupulous*) person.

ものがたり【物語】 a story ; a tale ; (寓話) a fable ; (伝説) a legend ; (小説) a novel ; a fiction ; (伝奇物語) a romance.
¶「イソップ～」 "Aesop's *Fables.*" 「源氏～」の主人公 the hero of "The *Tale* of Genji."

ものがた・る【物語る】 ¶彼の経歴は彼が多才な男であることを～る His record *is indicative of* his manifold abilities. このことは彼女の世間知らずを～る This *shows* that she knows nothing of the world. 彼のふるえる指は内心の興奮を～っていた His trembling fingers *told of* his inner excitement.

ものぐさ【物臭】 laziness. ¶～な人 a *lazy* (≒ an *indolent*) person. このごろ～になって手紙も書かない I *am* recently very *lazy* (≒ *indolent*) and seldom write letters.

モノクローム a monochrome.

ものごころ【物心】 ¶～がついて以来ずっとここに住んでいる We have lived in this place *ever since I could remember.* 彼は～もつかないころ母親に死に別れた His mother died *in his earliest childhood.*

ものごし【物腰】 bearing. ¶彼は～がやわらかい He has *a* gentle *manner.* / He is gentle-*mannered.* 彼女は優しい～で話す She speaks *gracefully.*

ものごと【物事】 things. ¶彼は～を苦にしすぎる He takes *things* too seriously. 彼は～をきちんと始末する He puts *everything* in order. 彼は～のけじめをわきまえている He knows *where to draw the line.*

ものさし【物指】 a ruler ; a measure ; (1フィート差し) a foot rule ; (大工の用いる折り尺) a carpenter's rule.
¶～で布をはかる measure the cloth with *a ruler.* 彼は自分の～でしかものをみない He always takes his own narrow view of everything. / He judges a matter only from his own *point of view.*

ものしずか【物静か】 ¶～な女性 a *quiet* (≒ *gentle-natured*) lady. ～な態度 *gentle* manners. 彼女は～に話しかけた She spoke to me *gently.*

ものしり【物知り】 a man of wide information. ¶彼は～だ He *is well-informed* (≒ *is well-learned*). 彼はいつも～顔にしゃべる He usually speaks *knowingly.*

ものずき【物好き】 curiosity. ¶なんと～なやつだろう What a *curious* fellow he is ! ～にもこんな雨の中を出歩くとは You *must be crazy to* go out in such a heavy rain. 私は～でこんなことをしているのではない It is not *for fun* that I do this.

ものすご・い【物凄い】 terrible. ¶～い音 a *terrible* noise. ～いあらし a *violent* storm ; a *furious* wind. 彼は～い形相で敵に襲いかかった With a *fierce* look on his face he flung to the enemy.

ものたりな・い【物足りない】 ¶この仕事は私には～い This job *is unsatisfactory for* me. / I *am unsatisfied with* this job. せっかく集まったのにこれで終わりとは～い We *feel unsatisfied* that our meeting should come to an end so soon. 彼は課長としてはちょっと～い He *is not good enough as* the chief of our section.

ものなれた【物慣れた】experienced. ¶ 彼女は～手つきでその仕事をさばく She does the task with a *practiced* (≒ *skilled*) hand. 彼は～態度で会の司会役をつとめた He presided at the meeting in an *easy* manner.

ものの 1 〖たった〗¶ 駅まで歩いても～5分だ It is *only* five minutes' walk from here to the station.

～1分とたたないうちに彼はもどってきた He came back in less than a minute.

～100メートルと歩かないうちに海岸に出た We had *hardly* (≒ *scarcely*) walked a hundred meters when we came to the seashore.

2 〖…とはいえ〗 ¶ 引き受けてはみた～気が進まない *Though* I accepted the job, I am unwilling to do it.

もののあわれ 【物の哀れ】 ¶ 彼は～を知る人だ He *is sensitive to beauty.* ～は秋こそまされ Autumn is a time of *pathos.*

ものほし【物干し】―綱 a clothesline. ―場 a drying place.

ものまね【物真似】mimicry. ¶ 彼は～がうまい He is *a good mimic.* 彼は非常にじょうずに人気歌手の～をした He *imitated* the popular singer's voice and gestures very cleverly.

ものみ【物見】(物見やぐら) a watch tower.

―遊山 ¶ 彼らは～遊山に出かけた They went *sightseeing.*

ものみだか・い【物見高い】curious. ¶ 彼らは～い近所の人たちの目を避けようとした They tried to avoid the *curious* (≒ *inquisitive*) eyes of their neighbors.

ものめずらし・い【物珍しい】¶ 人々が～そうにぞろぞろ集まってくる One after another people, *full of curiosity,* are gathering.

ものもち【物持ち】¶ 彼はこの村いちばんの～だ He is *the richest man* in this village. 彼女はたいへん～がいい (物を大事にする) She takes good care of her things.

ものものし・い【物物しい】pompous ; pretentious ; imposing. ¶ 彼女は～いいでたちでやってきた She turned up in a *pompous* dress. その町には～い警戒が敷かれた The town was put under a *strict* watch.

ものもらい【物貰い】(こじき) begging ; (人) a beggar ; (眼病) a sty(e). ¶ 目に～ができて困っている I am suffering from *a sty* in my eye.

ものやわらか 【物柔らか】 ¶ ～な物腰で応対する behave *gently* toward others. 彼のしゃべり方は～だ He speaks *in soft tones* (≒ *softly; gently*).

ものわかり【物分かり】¶ ～のよい人 a *sensible* person ; (理解の早い人) an *intelligent* person. ～の悪い人 (頭のにぶい人) a *dull-witted* person. ～がよい have a good understanding (*of*).

ものわかれ【物別れ】¶ 交渉は～に終わった The negotiations *were broken off.*

ものわすれ【物忘れ】¶ 近ごろ～がひどくなった I *am* very *forgetful* these days.

ものわらい【物笑い】 ¶ ～の種 a laughingstock. 彼は近所の～〔の種〕となった He became *a laughingstock* in his neighborhood. / He *was laughed at* by his neighbors.

もはや【最早】(既に) already ; (もはや…でない) no longer. ¶ 梅が咲いて～春だ The plum trees are now in blossom and it is *already* spring. 今となっては～あきらめるよりしかたあるまい *Now* there will be nothing for us but to give it up. 彼は～彼女を愛していない He *no longer* loves her. / He does *not* love her *any longer.* ～これまで It is all over *now.*

もはん【模範】an example. ¶ ～的な行為 an *exemplary* conduct. ～的な妻 a *pattern* (≒ *model*) wife. 上級生は下級生の～にならねばならぬ Seniors should give (≒ set) *a good example* to their juniors.

―生 a model student. ―答案 a model paper. ―試合 an exhibition game. ―演技 ¶ 彼はフィギュアスケートの～演技を行なった He gave *a demonstration* of figure skating.

もふく【喪服】a mourning dress.

もほう【模倣】imitation.

―者 an imitator.

もま・れる【揉まれる】¶ 満員電車で人に～れるのには慣れた I got used to *being jostled* in a crowded train. 小さな船は荒波に～れた The small ship *was tossed* 〔*about*〕 by the 〔rough〕 waves. 彼は子どものころから世の荒波に～れてきた He *has gone through* many hardships of life ever since he was a boy.

もみ【籾】〖植物〗paddy.

―がら chaff.

もみ【樅】〖植物〗a fir.

もみあ・う【揉み合う】¶ 入口で群衆が～った People *jostled one another* at the gate. デモ隊と警官隊とが～った There was *a struggle* between the demonstrators and the police.

もみあげ【揉み上げ】sideburns. ¶ 彼は～を長くしている He wears long *sideburns.*

もみけ・す【揉み消す】¶ 火を～す *rub out* (≒ *smother*) a fire. 事件を～す *hush up* (≒ *suppress*) an affair.

もみじ【紅葉】〖植物〗(カエデ) a maple ; (紅葉) red leaves. ¶ あの子は～のような手をしている She has pretty little hands like *maple* leaves.

もみで【揉み手】¶ ～する rub *one's* hands.

もみりょうじ【揉み療治】a massage. ¶ ～を受ける be massaged.

も・む【揉む】¶ 腰を～んでもらった I *had* my waist *massaged.* 気を～むな Don't *worry.* / Take it easy. 彼女はいつも息子のことで気を～んでいる She *is* always *worried about* her son. 国会はその法案で～みに～んだ There was a hot dispute about the bill in the Diet. キュウリを塩で～む *rub* sliced cucumber in salt. 新人を～んでやった I *gave a training to* my new pupils.

もめごと【揉め事】a quarrel ; 〔a〕 discord.

¶ 彼はなにかうちわの～がある He has some family *problems.*

も・める【揉める】(紛糾する) get into trouble.

¶ 実験の成否に気が～める I *am anxious about* the result of the experiment. 電車が遅れて気が～める I *am impatient* because the train is late. それの扱いで～めている We *are having a dispute* (≒ *are having trouble*) as to how to deal with it.

もめん【木綿】cotton〔cloth〕.
—糸(縫い糸) cotton thread; (編み・織り糸) cotton yarn. **—**物 cotton stuff.

もも【桃】《植物》a peach〔tree〕. ¶ ～の節句 the Doll's Festival; the Feast of Peach Blossoms on March 3rd.

もも【股】a thigh. ¶ ～の付け根 the groin.

ももいろ【桃色】pink; rose color. ¶ ～色の rosy; pink. ～遊戯にふける play at *love-making*.

もや【靄】a haze; a mist.

もや·う【舫う】moor. ¶ 港に船が数隻～ってある There are a few boats *moored* in the harbor.

もやし【萌やし】malt; (豆もやし) bean sprouts.

もや·す【燃やす】burn. ¶ ろうそくを～す *light* a candle. 彼は革命運動に情熱を～している He *is burning with* the passion for a revolutionary movement.

もやもや ¶ ～した春の日 a *misty* spring day. ～した(憂うつな) 気分になる feel *gloomy*; become *gloomy*.

もよう【模様】**1**〖布などの〗a pattern; a design. ¶ 花の～のついた服 a dress with *a pattern* of flowers.
ハンカチに花の～をつける *pattern* a handkerchief with flowers.
2〖様子〗¶ 目撃者が当時の～を語った The eyewitnesses related *how it happened*.
計画は失敗した～だ It *seems* that the plan has failed.

もようがえ【模様替え】¶ 計画を～する *make changes* in the plan. 部屋の～をする(一部改造する) *rearrange* the room; (机の置き場所を変えたり) *remodel* the room; *redecorate* the room; *do over* the room.

もよおし【催し】(集会) a meeting; (式など) a function; a ceremony; (余興) an entertainment.
¶ 市の～で今夜音楽会がある There will be a concert this evening *under the auspices of* the city.

もよお·す【催す】**1**〖開催する〗¶ 旧師の送別会を～した We *had* (≒ *held*) a farewell party for our old teacher.
オリンピック大会は4年ごとに～される The Olympic Games *are held* (≒ *take place*) every four years.
2〖感じる〗¶ 吐き気を～す feel sick.
涙を～す be moved to tears; feel like crying.

もより【最寄り】¶ ～の駅 *the nearest* station.

もらい【貰い】¶ あのこじきは～が少ない The beggar gets little *alms*.

もらいて【貰い手】(受取人) a recipient; a receiver; (求婚者) a suitor. ¶ この子ネコには～がない Nobody asks for this kitten. 嫁の～がなくなるよ Nobody will want to marry you.

もらいなき【貰い泣き】¶ 私はその女の話を聞いて～をした I *cried* (≒ *wept*) *in sympathy with* the woman when I heard her story.

もらいもの【貰い物】a gift; a present. ¶ 彼から～をした I *got something* (≒ *got a present*) from him. これは～です Somebody gave it to me.

もら·う【貰う】**1**〖受ける〗get; (子どもなどを) adopt. ¶ 月に10万円～っている I *get* (≒ *make*) a hundred thousand yen a month.
これは～ったものです Somebody *gave* it *to me*.
彼は妻を～った He *got married*.
養女を～った We *adopted* a girl as our heiress.
2〖…してもらう〗¶ 彼に来て～いたい I *want* him *to* come.
彼に頼んで英語の手紙を書いて～った I *asked* him *to* write a letter in English. / I *had* him *write* a letter in English.

もら·す【漏らす】¶ これを人に～すな *Keep* it *to yourself*. 言い～したことがある I *forgot to say* one thing. 彼は辞意を～した He *hinted at* his resignation. 思わず～したことばを聞きのがさなかった I didn't miss the words he *let fall* unconsciously. この子はまたおしっこを～した He'*s wetted his pants* (≒ *bed*) again.

モラル morals; moral sense. ¶ 彼は～に欠けている He is lacking in *moral sense*.

もり【盛り】¶ 御飯の～がよい The rice is heaped up in the bowl.

もり【森】a wood; 圏 woods (森は grove—wood—forest の順に大きくなる).

もり【守り】¶ 子どもの～をする *take care of* (≒ *look after*) a child; 圏 baby-sit.

もり【銛】a harpoon. ¶ 鯨に～を打つ *harpoon* a whale.

もりあがり【盛り上がり】an uprush (*of* emotion); a climax. ¶ 世論の～が足りなかった Public opinion *was* not *strong* enough.

もりあが·る【盛り上がる】¶ 世論が～った Public opinion *was roused*.

もりかえ·す【盛り返す】rally. ¶ 敵は勢いを～して反撃してきた The enemy *regained* their strength and made a counterattack.

もりだくさん【盛り沢山】¶ ～のごちそう *lots of* fine dishes. ～の行事 a *crowded* (≒ *tight*) program.

もりた·てる【守り立てる】(支持する) support; back (*a person*) up. ¶ 社運を～てる *bring* a company *to prosperity*.

もりばな【盛り花】flowers arranged in a basin (≒ basket).

モリブデン《化学》molybdenum.
—鉱 molybdenite.

もりもり ¶ ～食べる eat *like a wolf*; wolf〔down〕*one's* food. ～勉強する study *hard as anything*.

も·る【盛る】(食物を) serve; (薬を) prescribe; (土を) heap up. ¶ 自分で御飯を～って食べなさい Help yourself to rice.

も·る【漏る】(水・ガスなどが) leak. ¶ 屋根が～る

も

The roof *leaks.* この万年筆は～る This pen *leaks.* 雨が～る The rain *comes through* the roof. このやかんは二, 三か所～る This kettle *leaks* at a few spots. / *There are* several *leaks* in this kettle. 水(ガス; 空気)の～らぬ管 a water (gas; air)-*tight* pipe.

モルタル mortar. ¶ ～塗りの家 a *mortared* frame house.

モルヒネ 〘薬品〙 morphia; morphine.
—中毒患者 a morphinomaniac.

モルモット 〘動物〙 a guinea pig (marmot とは別種の動物だがオランダ人が誤伝した).

もれ 【漏れ】 a leak; leakage. ¶ 記載～ [an] omission.

もれき・く 【漏れ聞く】 overhear. ¶ ～くところでは according to what I [have] heard....

もれなく 【漏れなく】 without exception (≒ omission). ¶ 全員～会に参加した *Everyone of them* (≒ *Every member*) joined the meeting.

も・れる 【漏れる】 (水・ガスが) leak out; escape. ¶ ガスが～れる Gas *escapes.* このパイプはガスが～れる This pipe *leaks* gas. ドアの下から明かりが～れている The light *is coming out* from under the door. 秘密が～れた The secret *leaked* (≒ *slipped*) *out.* 彼の絵は選に～れた His picture *was left out of* selection.

もろ・い 【脆い】 (金属など) brittle; (弱い) fragile. ¶ 彼はとても情に～いたちだ He is quite a *susceptible* type.

もろく 【脆く】 easily. ¶ 敵は～も敗れた The enemy were beaten *without difficulty.*

もろこし 【唐黍・蜀黍】 〘植物〙 Indian (≒ African) millet.

モロッコ Morocco.
—皮 morocco [leather].

もろて 【諸手】 ¶ ～をあげてご意見に賛成します I *completely* agree with you. / I support your idea *wholeheartedly.*

もろとも 【諸共】 ¶ 死なば～ Let's die *together.*

もろはだ 【もろ膚・諸肌】 ¶ 彼は～を脱いでいた He *was stripped to the waist.*

もろみ 【諸味】 unrefined *sake.*

もろもろ 【諸・庶】 ¶ ～の関係者がその会談に出席した *All sorts of* interested parties attended the conference. / *All* the people concerned attended the conference.

もん 【門】 a gate; a gateway; 〘解剖学〙 (内臓などの) hilum (複 hila); (生物分類の) 〘動物〙 phylum (複 phyla); 〘植物〙 division.
¶ 狭き～ *a* strait *gate* (聖書 *Matt.* 7: 13). 彼は山田先生の～に入った He *became a pupil of* Mr. Yamada.

もん 【紋】 (衣服の) a family crest; (盾形の) a coat of arms.

もんえい 【門衛】 a gatekeeper; a porter.

もんがい 【門外】 ¶ ～に車がおいてある A car is parked *outside the gate.*
—不出 ¶ この書物は～不出だ This book *is not to be loaned out.*

もんがいかん 【門外漢】 (局外者) an outsider; (素人) a layman; an amateur. ¶ 音楽については～だ I am *an amateur in* music.

もんかせい 【門下生】 ¶ 佐藤先生の～ *a pupil* (≒ *a student*) *under* Mr. Sato.

もんがまえ 【門構え】 ¶ ～の家 a house *with a gate.*

もんきりがた 【紋切り型】 ¶ ～のテーブルスピーチ a *stereotyped* (≒ *cut and dried*) after-dinner speech.

もんく 【文句】 (文章・歌の) words; (不平) a complaint; an objection. ¶ 手紙の～を直す improve the *wording* of the letter. ～なしの傑作 a *perfect* masterpiece. 彼はいつもなにか～を言っている He *is* always *grumbling about* something. 彼女は私のすることにいちいち～をつける She always *finds fault with* what I do.

もんげん 【門限】 closing time; lockup.
¶ ～に遅れないでください Be sure to come back by the *closing time.*

もんこ 【門戸】 a door. ¶ すべての国に～を開放する *open the door to* all nations.

もんさつ 【門札】 a doorplate; a name plate on the gate.

もんし 【門歯】 an incisor; a front tooth.

もんじゅ 【文殊】 〘宗教〙 Manjusri. ¶ 三人寄れば～の知恵 (諺) *Two heads are better than one.* / *As many heads, so many wits.*

もんしょう 【紋章】 a crest; a coat of arms.
—学 heraldry.

もんしろちょう 【紋白蝶】 〘虫類〙 a cabbage butterfly.

もんじん 【門人】 a pupil; a disciple.

モンスーン a monsoon.
—地帯 a monsoon climate.

もんせき 【問責】 censure; reproof. ¶ 大臣の失言を～した We *censured* the Minister *for* his slip of the tongue.

もんぜつ 【悶絶】 ¶ ～する fall unconscious from agony; become faint with agony.

もんぜん 【門前】 ¶ ～市をなす Visitors call on him incessantly. / His home is crowded with callers. ～の小僧習わぬ経を読む (諺) *A saint's maid quotes Latin.* / *The sparrow near a school sings the primer.*
—払い ¶ 彼は客に～払いを食わせた He refused to see the visitor. —町 a cathedral (≒ temple) town.

モンタージュ [a] montage.
—写真 a montage photograph.

もんだい 【問題】 **1** 〖テストなどの問題・議題〗 a question; a problem; (事項) a matter.
¶ 英語の～はやさしかった We had relatively easy *questions* in the English exam.
数学の～が一つ解けなかった In the mathematics exam, there was one *problem* I could not solve.
議会でこの～が討議されている The *problem* is under discussion in the parliament.
この～はとても私の手には負えません The *problem* is beyond my ability.
2 〖中心点・関心事・疑問〗 ¶ 値段よりも品質が～

も

だ Quality *counts* more than the price. 〜はいつそれを実行するかだ The *question* is when to put it into practice. 彼を課長にするなんて〜だね If he is promoted to chief of the section, I think it will *create a stir* (≒ *raise a problem*). どの方法を選ぶかが〜になっている There is *a controversy* about which method to choose. 彼が会議に出席するかどうかが〜だ The *question* is whether or not he is coming to the meeting. 事件の解決はもはや時間の〜だ The case will be settled before long. 彼が新聞をにぎわしている〜の人物だ He is the very person we read about in papers. これは金の〜ではなくて, 誠意の〜だ What *matters* here is not money but good faith. それは単なる好みの〜だ I think it is merely *a question* (≒ *a matter*) of taste. 私にとってこの程度の損失は〜ではない A loss of this extent *is* not *serious to* me. この相手ではとても〜にならない The opponent *is* too *insignificant* to notice. 彼女はきみなど〜にしていない She *leaves* you *out of her consideration.* 彼の意見など〜外だ I am determined not to listen to his advice. これが〜の本だ This is the book *in question.* 彼が〜の人だ He is the man *in question.* **3** 〖事件〗 ¶ また彼が〜を起こした He has started *trouble* again.

—集 a collection of problems. **外交—** diplomatic issues. **政治—** political problems. **人口—** the population problem. **社会—** a social problem. ¶ ごみ戦争は大きな社会〜となっていた The so-called garbage war has become *a* social *problem.* **死活—** ¶ 物価上昇はわれわれの死活〜だ Rising prices are *a matter of life and death* for us. **人種—** ¶ 人種〜を解決する妙案はないのだろうか I wonder if there isn't any quick remedy for racial discrimination.

もんちゃく【悶着】 trouble; complications; (論争) a quarrel. ¶ また一〜起こりそうだ *Difficulties* may arise again.

もんちゅう【門柱】 a gatepost.

もんつき【紋付き】 a *kimono* with the family crest.

もんてい【門弟】 a pupil; a disciple.

もんとう【門燈】 a gate lamp.

もんどう【問答】 questions and answers; (対話) a dialog[ue]; conversation. ¶ 〜無用 There's no use in *talking.* (おだやかな言い方). / Shut your mouth! (粗暴な言い方). / Keep quiet. (中間的な言い方).

もんどり a somersault. ¶ 〜打って倒れる fall *head over heels* [to the ground].

もんなし【文なし】 ¶ 彼は〜だ He *is penniless.* 〜でどうしようというのだ What are you going to do *without a farthing?*

もんばつ【門閥】 noble lineage. ¶ 〜の出だから彼女はなかなか気位が高い *Coming of a distinguished family,* she is rather proud. 実力より〜と金だ *Birth* and money count for more than real ability.

もんばん【門番】 a gatekeeper; a doorkeeper; a janitor; a porter. ¶ 〜をする keep the gate.

もんぶしょう【文部省】 the Ministry of Education.

もんぶだいじん【文部大臣】 the Minister of Education; the Education Minister.

もんもん【悶悶】 ¶ 彼は〜として不遇の日を送った He lived his dark days *discontentedly.* 彼は〜の情を訴えた He gave vent to the *anguish of his heart.*

や

や【矢】 an arrow. ¶ 〜を射る shoot *an arrow.* 〜をつがえる fix *an arrow* to the bow. 彼に会いたくて彼女は〜も盾もたまらなかった She *was dying to* see him. また息子から金送れと〜の催促だ My son *presses me hard* for remittance as usual.

や【野】 ¶ 彼は潔く〜に下った He *left the government service* without reluctance. 彼は〜に在ることすでに久しい He *has remained out of office* for a long time.

-や and; or. ¶ もっと野菜〜果物をとりなさい Eat more vegetables *and* fruit. あれ〜これ〜ですっかり参った I am exhausted with one thing *or* another. / What with this *and* that, I am dead tired.

やあ (感嘆) Oh! / Ah! / Dear me! / Oh my! / Good Heavens! (呼びかけ) Hello! (Hallo という綴りはいまあまり用いない).

ヤード a yard (yd.). ¶ 〜ポンド法 the yard-pound system.

ヤール a yard (yd.).

やい Hi! / Hey! / (ののしり) Bah! / Fie!

やいば【刃】 (刀身) a blade; (刀) a sword. ¶ 氷の〜 *a* burnished *blade.* いつかは彼と〜を交えなければならない I am destined to cross *swords* with him some day. (気どった言い方).

やいやい (呼びかけ) Hi! / Hey! ¶ ～言ってもいっこうにらちがあかない Though we *press* them *hard*, it makes no satisfactory progress. ～言ってやっと彼にそうさせた We *urged* him *on to* do so. 彼は私に～金を催促した He *pressed* me *hard for* money. あんまり～言うな Don't *annoy* (≒ *molest*) me so much.

やいん【夜陰】¶ 彼らは～に乗じて越境した They crossed the border *under cover of darkness* (≒ *under cover of night*).

やえ【八重】━桜 double cherry blossoms.

やえい【野営】a camp; (行為) camping.
¶ ～する camp out; make camp.
━地 a camping ground.

やえば【八重歯】a double tooth.

やおちょう【八百長】a put-up job; a cross.
¶ あれは明らかに～だ That's evidently *a sold game* (≒ *a put-up match; a fixed fight*).
～をやるボクサーがいないわけではない There may be some boxers who would *fix a fight*.

やおもて【矢面】¶ 彼は臆せず世の非難の～に立った He *faced* the public censures bravely.
私が質問の～に立った I *bore the brunt of* questions.

やおや【八百屋】(店) 英 a greengrocer's; 米 a vegetable store; (人) a greengrocer; (業) greengrocery.

やおよろず【八百万】¶ ～の神々 *myriads of* gods and deities (形式ばった言い方); *all* the gods of heaven and earth.

やおら (ゆっくり) slowly; (静かに) gently; quietly. ¶ 彼は～いすに身を沈めた He *slowly* (≒ *gently; heavily*) sank into the chair.
彼女は～自席から立ち上がった She rose from her seat *without haste*.

やかい【夜会】an evening party; (舞踏会) a ball (大規模なもの). ¶ ～を催す give *a ball*.
━服 (男女とも) an evening dress.

やがい【野外】(原野) the field; (屋外) the open air. ¶ ～で out of doors; in the open air.
━運動 outdoor sports. ━演習 field exercises; field work. ━研究 field research.
━研究旅行 a field trip (学校の「遠足」も school excursion よりこの英語のほうがよい).

やがく【夜学】an evening (≒ a night) school.
¶ ～に通う go to (≒ attend) *an evening* (≒ *a night*) *school*.

やかた【屋形・館】(貴人の邸宅) a mansion; a residence; (居城) a castle; (荘園領主の邸宅) a manor house.
━船 a houseboat; (遊覧船) a pleasure boat.

やがて【軈て】(まもなく) soon; (ほとんど) almost.
¶ ～彼が到着した He arrived *soon* 〔*after*〕(≒ *presently*). ～晴れるでしょう It will *soon* clear off. 彼女は～やってきた *Before long* she came to see me. ～負債をかたづけなければならない We must settle the debt *in due time*. ～なにもかも明らかになろう Everything will be clear *in time*. ～は彼も本心に立ち返ろう He will come to his senses *some day*. この道に入って～4年になる It is *almost* (≒ *nearly*) four years since I engaged in this business.

やかまし・い【喧しい】**1**〘騒々しい〙noisy. ¶ 大通りは～い The main street *is noisy*.
彼はなんて～いやつだ What a *boisterous* (≒ *noisy*) fellow he is!
～いぞ, きみら! *Keep quiet*, boys!
赤ん坊が眠っているんだから, そんなに～くするな Don't *make such a noise*. Baby is sleeping.
2〘世評〙¶ 公害は～い問題になった Environmental pollution has become a *much discussed* problem (≒ has become a subject *of much discussion*).
世間は政府の政策に～く反対した The public *loudly* protested against the policy of the government.
3〘厳しい〙¶ 規則は以前より～くなった The rule has become more *stringent* than before.
彼はあまり～いのでわれわれに人気がない He *is* so *strict* that he is not popular with us.
彼は～い校長に仕えた He served a *hard* principal.
彼は私たちの服装に～い He *is particular about* our clothes.
彼は私がすることになんでも～く言う He *finds fault with* everything I do.
あの人は～い She is a *faultfinding* person.
彼は時間にとても～い He is *a* great *stickler for* punctuality.
4〘その他〙¶ お～ゅうございます I am sorry to *have disturbed* you.
あんなに～く言ってもまだだめだ All my talk has been in vain.

やかましや【喧し屋】(気難し屋) a particular (≒ meticulous) person; a man hard to please; (些事にこだわる人) a stickler; (規律に厳格な人) an exacting person.

やから【族・輩】(仲間) fellows; a set; (一族) a family; kinsmen. ¶ ああいう～とかかわり合いを持つな Don't have anything to do with *those fellows*.

やかん【夜間】at night; by night (by day と相関的に用いられることが多い).
━勤務 night duty. ━飛行 a night flight.
━部 the evening session of a school.

やかん【薬罐】a kettle.

やき【焼き】**1**〘火による〙¶ 信楽～ *Shigaraki ware*.
この刀は～が甘い This blade *is* not well *tempered*.
2〘慣用的表現〙¶ むちで～を入れてやれ *Chastise* him with a whip.
とうとう彼も～が回ってきた He *has got dull* at last.

やぎ【山羊】a goat; (雄) a he-goat; (雌) a she-goat; (子ヤギ) a kid. ¶ ～が鳴く *A goat* bleats (≒ baas).
━皮 goatskin. ━ひげ a goatee.

やきいも【焼き芋】roast (≒ baked) sweet potatoes.

やきいん【焼き印】a brand; (器具) a brand iron. ¶ 牛に～を押す *brand* cows with a mark.

や

やきうち【焼き討ち】attacking and burning. ¶ 近ごろ当地で交番ー事件が頻発(ひんぱつ)する Recently, there have often been cases here of police box *burning*. 昨夜日比谷のレストランが暴徒に〜された A restaurant at Hibiya *was set on fire* by the mob last night.

やきぐし【焼き串】a skewer; a spit. ¶ 魚を〜に刺す *spit* fish.

やきころ·す【焼き殺す】¶ 無残にも犬は〜された The dog *was* horribly *burnt alive* (≒ *burnt to death*).

やきざかな【焼き魚】〔a〕broiled fish.

やきしお【焼き塩】baked salt.

やきす·ぎる【焼き過ぎる】(食物を) overdo; overbake; overroast; overbroil; (写真を) overprint.

¶ 〜ぎるとまずくなる If it's *overdone*, it becomes tasteless.

やきす·てる【焼き捨てる】¶ 不要な書類を〜てる *burn up* waste papers.

やきたて【焼きたて】¶ 〜のパン *fresh baked* bread; bread *hot from the oven*.

やきだま【焼き玉】—エンジン a hot-bulb engine; 米 a hot-rod engine.

やきつ·く【焼き付く】¶ 〜くようなのどのかわき a *burning* thirst. 彼女の悲しそうな顔が私の心に〜いて離れない Her sad face *is branded on* my memory.

やきつく·す【焼き尽くす】¶ 火事は近隣の家もすべて〜した The fire *burned out* all the adjoining houses, too.

やきつけ【焼き付け】(写真の) printing; (陶器の) glazing; enameling. ¶ 写真の〜をする *print* photographs.

やきつ·ける【焼き付ける】¶ 彼は自分で現像し〜ける He develops films and *prints photographs* for himself. 彼女の寂しげな表情が私の心に〜けられた Her lonely expression *was branded on* my memory.

やきとり【焼き鳥】roast fowl; broiled chicken; grilled chicken.

やきなおし【焼き直し】(食物の) rebaking; reroasting; (著作など) a rehash; an adaptation.

¶ これはスコットの作品の〜だ This is *an adaptation from* one of Scott's works.

やきば【焼き場】a crematory; a crematorium (複 crematoria).

やきはら·う【焼き払う】¶ その辺りの家はすべて〜われた All the houses around there *were reduced* (≒ *were burned*) *to ashes*.

やきばん【焼き判】a brand; (器具) a brand iron. ¶ 木材に〜を押す *brand* timbers.

やきぶた【焼き豚】roast pork; (丸焼きの) roast pig (丸焼きでも食用と考えれば冠詞不要).

やきまし【焼き増し】extra printing. ¶ 何枚〜してもらいましょうか How many *extra copies* do you want?

やきめし【焼き飯】frizzled boiled rice.

やきもき ¶ そんなことに〜したって始まらない It's no use *worrying yourself about* such a thing. なにをいったい〜しているのだ What on earth *are* you *nervous about*?

やきもち【焼き餅】jealousy. ¶ ときどき彼は妻に〜を焼いた At times he *was jealous of* his wife.

—焼き ¶ 彼の妻は〜焼きだ His wife is *a jealous woman*.

やきもの【焼き物】(陶磁器) ceramic ware; pottery; porcelain; china; chinaware; earthenware; (日本料理の) a broiled fish.

やきゅう【野球】baseball. ¶ 〜の試合をする have *a baseball game* (baseball match とは言わない).

—界 baseball circles. —場 a baseball field (≒ ground). —選手 a baseball player; (選手全体) the nine. —チーム a baseball team. —ファン a baseball fan. 職業—選手 a professional baseball player.

やぎゅう【野牛】〔動物〕a wild ox (複 oxen); a buffalo.

やきょく【夜曲】〔音楽〕a nocturne; a serenade.

やきん【冶金】metallurgy.

—学(術) metallurgy. —学者 a metallurgist.

やきん【夜勤】night duty; (夜業) night work (≒ shift). ¶ 月に数回は〜をする I take *night duty*(≒ *night shift*) several times a month. 彼は今夜は〜だ He *is on duty* tonight.

—手当 night(-)work (≒ night(-)shift) allowance.

やく【役】**1** 〘地位·官職〙a post; an office.

¶ 彼は議長の〜に選ばれた He was voted into the *office* of chairman.

今度彼は社長の〜を退くことになった He will soon retire from the *office* of president of the company.

このいすは彼には〜不足だ His present position is beneath his capabilities.

2 〘任務·役割〙¶ 彼を説得するのがきみの〜だ It is your *duty* to persuade him.

この計画にはあなたも一〜買っていただきたい I hope you will *take an active part in* the project.

きみにはお客さんの案内〜をやってほしい I hope you will help us *in the capacity of* guide for our visitors.

この〜は私にはいささか重荷だ I am afraid I am not equal to the *task*.

3 〘芝居の役割〙¶ 彼女にオフェリアの〜がついた She was given the *role* of Ophelia.

彼には織田信長の〜が最適だ He is best suited for the *part* of Oda Nobunaga.

この舞台では彼はひとりふた〜をつとめている He performs *a* double *role* (≒ *part*) in the play.

4 〘効用〙 ¶ 彼はなかなか〜にたつ He is a *helpful* person. / He *is helpful* in many ways.

この参考書はとても〜にたつ This reference book *is useful* (≒ *is very helpful*; *is full of information*).

〜にたたない物を整理する throw away things that have become *useless*.

お〜にたてて幸いです I am glad to *have been*

や

of help to you.

こんな本を読んでいったいなんの～にたつのか What is the *use* of reading such a book?

こんな本がお～にたちますか Could you find *use* for such a book?

技術を身につけておけばいつかは～にたつものだ If you master a skill, it will *help* you some day.

やく【約】 about; around; approximately. ¶ ～4フィート *some* (≒ *about*) four feet. ～2時間 *about* two hours; two hours *or so.* それは～100万ドルと評価されている It is estimated *roughly* at one million dollars. 総収入は～2億ドルだ The total income is *approximately* two hundred million dollars.

やく【訳】 [a] translation. ¶ 彼の～はうまい（まずい）His *translation* is well (poorly) done. / He is a good (poor) translator. これの日本語～はありますか Has *a Japanese version of it* been published? 谷崎～源氏物語 "The Tale of Genji" *translated by* Tanizaki.

やく【厄】 evil; calamity. ¶ それは～をよけるための年中行事の一つだ It is one of the annual events to drive away *evils.*

や·く【焼く】 **1**〘物·食物を〙¶ 狂人は自分の家を～いた The mad man *burned* (≒ *set fire to*) his own house.

最近の火事で彼は家を～いた（～かれた） He *had* his house *burned down* (≒ *reduced to ashes*) in the recent fire.

炭を～く *make* charcoal.

死体を～く *cremate* a body.

肉を～く *roast* meat.

魚を～いて食べる eat fish *broiled.*

写真を～く（焼きつける） *print* a photograph.

パンを～く（こしらえる） *bake* bread; (火を通す) *toast* bread.

イモを～く *bake* a potato.

2〘世話を〙¶ 彼は弟の世話で手を～いている He *has burned his fingers in* trying to help his brother.

彼はなにくれと私の世話を～いてくれた He *helped* me in every way.

私は自分のことで世話を～いてもらいたくない I don't like people *meddling in* my affairs.

3〘嫉妬する〙¶ 彼女は私を～いている She *is jealous* (≒ *is envious*) *of* me.

やぐ【夜具】 bedclothes; bed clothing; bedding.

やくいん【役員】 an officer; 米 an executive; (総称) the board; the staff.

—会 a meeting of officers. —室 an executive office.

やくがく【薬学】 pharmacy; pharmacology.

—科 a pharmaceutical department. —士(博士) a bachelor (doctor) of pharmacology. —者 a pharmacologist.

やくがら【役柄】 ¶ ～上やむをえない It can't be helped, for it is *a matter of duty.* 彼女にはその～がのみこめない（演劇などの）She can't make out *the nature of her part.*

やくご【訳語】 words used in translation. ¶ それの適切な英語の～を教えてください Will you tell me the proper *English* [*equivalent; counterpart*] *for* it?

やくざ (ろくでなし) a good-for-nothing fellow; a desperado; (ばくち打ち) a gambler. ¶ どれもこれも～な物ばかりだ（物がりっぱでない） They are all *rubbishes* (≒ *worthless articles*). あれが～のなれの果てだ He is the wreck of *a gambler.*

やくざい【薬剤】 drugs; chemicals; medicine.

—師 a pharmacist.

やくさつ【扼殺】 strangulation. ¶ 彼は～された He *was strangled to death.*

やくしゃ【役者】 a player; an actor; (女) an actress. ¶ ～になる go on the stage. ～をやめる retire from the stage. きみより彼のほうが～が一枚上だ He *is superior to* (≒ *has some advantage over*) you *in ability.*

大根— a poor actor. 千両— a star actor. 花形— a star actor. 旅— a strolling actor. 人気— a popular actor.

やくしゃ【訳者】 a translator.

やくしょ【役所】 a government (≒ public) office. ¶ ～に勤める work for the [*government*] *office.* ～の用事で on *official* business.

やくしょ【訳書】 a translation.

やくじょ【躍如】 ¶ この仕事には彼の面目～たるものがある This work *is quite characteristic of* (≒ *is just like*) him. それには彼の風貌(ふう)が～として描かれている It *vividly* depicts his appearance. / It *gives a graphic picture of* him. / We see *a life-like portrait* of him in it.

やくしん【躍進】 progress; strides. ¶ ことしは～の年と確信する I am sure we'll *make rapid progress* (≒ *make great strides*) this year. 今こそ～すべきときだ This is the time for us to *make a dash* (≒ *take a bold leap*).

やく·す【約す】 ¶ 彼らは再会を～して別れた They *promised* to meet again and parted. このクラスでは分数の～し方を習っている The boys and girls in this class are learning *how to reduce* a fraction. この分数は～せる（せない） This fraction *is reducible* (*is irreducible*).

やく·す【訳す】 translate (日常会話では translate (翻訳する) よりも put ... into Japanese のように言うほうがよい). ¶ 次の文を日本語に～しなさい *Put* the following [passage] *into* Japanese. 彼はハムレットを日本語に～した He *translated* "Hamlet" *into* Japanese. この表現は英語に正確には～せまい I am afraid that this expression can not *be* exactly *rendered* in English. 彼は源氏物語を現代語に～した He *produced a modern version of* "The Tale of Genji."

やくすう【約数】〘数学〙a measure.

公— a common measure (≒ divisor). 最大公— the greatest common measure (G.C.M. と略す).

やくせき【薬石】 medicine. ¶ 彼は～効なく死去した He died in spite of all the *medical treatments.*

やくそう【薬草】 a [medicinal] herb.

や

—園 a herb garden. —医 a herb doctor.

やくそく【約束】(一般に) a promise; (面会·会食·出演など) an engagement; an appointment; a date; (取引きなどの) a bargain. ¶ ～をする make *one's promise* (≒ *one's word*). ～を果たす fulfill *one's promise*. 彼はりっぱに～を果たしている He is *as good as his word*. ～を破る break *one's promise* (≒ *one's word*). ～を取り消す call off *one's engagement*. ～を守る人 a man *of his word*. ～している be under promise. ～どおりに true to *one's* word; according to *one's* promise. 今晩6時に彼に会う～がある I have *an engagement* (≒ *an appointment*) *to* see him at six this evening. (大げさな言い方. 若い人同士では appointment や engagement はあまり使わない. I am going to see... でよい). 3時に～がある I have *an appointment* [to keep] at three. いったん～したのだからしかたがない A bargain is a bargain. 彼女は～の時間に来た She came at the *appointed* time. 私は月末に金を払うと～した I *promised to* pay the money at the end of the month. 彼女は彼と結婚の～をしている She *is engaged to* him. 酒をやめるという～で彼を雇った I employed him *on the condition* that he would quit drink. それは前世の～だ It *is decreed by predestination*. そんな～はしなかった I didn't *bargain for* that.

やくそくてがた【約束手形】a promissory note. ¶ 彼は銀行あてに100万円の～を振り出した He *drew a promissory note* on a bank for a million yen.

やくづき【役付き】¶ 彼は会社で～になった He got *a responsible post* in the company. —手当 an allowance for the post.

やくどう【躍動】¶ 高校野球を見ると青春の血が～する Inter-highschool baseball games *stir* the blood of youth. 春になると万物が～する Everything *moves lively* in spring.

やくとく【役得】a perquisite. ¶ 彼は～のある仕事についた He got a job with some *perquisites* (≒ *official privileges*).

やくどく【訳読】[literal] translation. ¶ 生徒たちはその英文を～するように言われた The students were told to *translate* the English passage *into* Japanese.

やくどし【厄年】an unlucky age.

やくにん【役人】an official; (公務員) a public officer; 英 a civil servant; (官吏) a government official; (高官) a high official. ¶ 彼は市の～になった He *entered into the city office*. 彼はやたらに～風を吹かす He always *behaves arrogantly toward* others.

やくば【役場】an office. ¶ 町(村)～ a town (village) *office*.

やくび【厄日】¶ きょうはさんざんな目に会ってとんだ～だった What *an evil* (≒ *an unlucky*) *day* it has been to have such a hard time!

やくびょう【疫病】a plague. —神 a god of plague; a pest. ¶ 彼は～神のようにきらわれている People avoid him as if he had *the plague*.

やくひん【薬品】(一般に) drugs; (おもに内服薬) medicines. 化学— chemicals.

やくぶつ【薬物】medicines; medicament. —検査 examination by medicine. —療法 (処理) medication.

やくぶん【約分】〔数学〕reduction. ¶ 3/9を1/3に～する *reduce* 3/9 to 1/3.

やくぶん【訳文】a translation. ¶ よくこなれた～ *an* idiomatic *translation*.

やくほん【訳本】a translation.

やくみ【薬味】spices. ¶ ～をきかした料理 a *spiced* (≒ *spicy*) dish. そばに～を入れる *spice* the Japanese buckwheat vermicelli.

やくめ【役目】a duty. ¶ 彼はりっぱに大使としての～を果たした He performed his *office* well as an ambassador. 家事を切り盛りするのは妻の～だ It is a wife's *duty* to keep house. 彼女は弟たちに対して母親の～をしている She *is playing the role of* mother to her little brothers. —柄 ¶ 彼は～柄寡黙だ *The nature of his office* makes him reticent.

やくよう【薬用】—アルコール medicinal alcohol. —植物 a medicinal herb (≒ plant) (薬用を主に考えるときの植物を herb と言う). —せっけん medicated soap.

やくよけ【厄除け】a talisman. ¶ ～のお守り a talisman. ¶ ～に車にお守りをぶらさげた I hung a talisman in my car to *keep off evils*.

やぐら【櫓】a tower; (城の) a castle turret. —太鼓 the drum announcing the day's *sumo* matches. 物見— a watchtower. 火の見— a fire tower.

やぐるまそう【矢車草】〔植物〕a cornflower.

やくろう【薬籠】a medical container. ¶ 彼は英語を自家～中のものとした He *got a complete mastery of* English. / He *mastered* English.

やくわり【役割】a part; a role. ¶ 彼は両国の平和のために大きな～を演じた He played *a* great *part* for the peace between the two countries. 彼は委員長としての～を果たした He did his *part* (≒ *duties*) as a chairman. 女性の社会的～が向上した Women have come to play *a* more important *part* than ever in [the] society.

やけ【自棄】desperation. ¶ 彼は～になって家を飛び出した *In desperation* he ran away from home. ～を起こすな Don't *be* (≒ *become*) *desperate*. 彼は近ごろ～ぎみだ He *is* a little *desperate* these days. ～に腹が立つ I am *terribly* irritated. ～に雨が降る It rains *violently*.

やけあと【焼け跡】the ruins of (≒ after) a fire.

やけい【夜景】a night view.

やけい【夜警】night watch; (人) a night watchman. ¶ 彼らは交替で～をした They *kept night watch* by turns.

やけいし【焼け石】a hot stone. ¶ こんなことでは～に水だ It's *like throwing water on the* *parched land.*

やけお·ちる【焼け落ちる】be burned down. ¶家は20分で～ちた The house [*was*] *burned down* in twenty minutes.

やけくそ【自棄糞】¶えい, もう～だ It's *all or nothing*! / It's go for broke now!

やけこげ【焼け焦げ】¶たばこで服に～をつくった The cigarette *burned a hole* in my clothes.

やけざけ【自棄酒】¶～を飲む drink out of desperation.

やけし·ぬ【焼け死ぬ】¶その火事で3人が～んだ Three people *were burned to death* by the fire.

やけださ·れる【焼け出される】¶その火事でたくさんの人が～れた Many people *were burned out* (≒ *lost their houses*) by the fire.

やけただ·れる【焼け爛れる】¶広島市中は原爆で～れた The whole city of Hiroshima *was* miserably *burned down* by the atomic bomb.

やけつ·く【焼け付く】scorch. ¶～くような暑さだった The weather *was* simply *baking*. / It was *baking* (≒ *burning*; *scorching*) hot.

やけど【火傷】(火によるやけど) a burn; (熱湯·湯げによるやけど) a scald. ¶～の跡 a scar of *a burn*. ストーブで～をした I *burned myself* on the stove. 熱湯で手を～した I *scalded* my hand with hot water. 指に～した I *got burnt* at the finger.

やけのこ·る【焼け残る】¶幸いにもわが家は～った Fortunately my house *escaped the fire*.

やけのはら【焼け野原】a burnt field. ¶町は～となった The town *was reduced to ashes*.

やけぼっくい【焼けぼっくい】charred stump. ¶あのふたりは～に火がついた *The passion once lost flared up afresh* between them.

や·ける【焼ける】1〖焼失〗¶彼の家は昨夜～けた His house *was burned* (≒ *was reduced to ashes*) last night.

市の3分の1が～けた One-third of the city *was destroyed by the fire* (≒ *was burned to the ground*).

2〖食物〗¶(肉などが)もう～けたか *Is it done*? 肉(魚)が～ける Meat (Fish) *broils*. パンが～けた The bread *toasted*.

3〖日焼け〗¶日に～けた顔 a *sunburnt* (≒ *tanned*) face.

4〖空〗¶夕空が～ける(～けている) The evening sky *glows* (*is glowing*).

5〖胸やけ〗¶私は胸が～ける I *have a heartburn*.

6〖世話〗¶おまえは世話の～ける子どもだ You are a *troublesome* child.

彼らは私にずいぶん世話を～かせた They *gave* me a lot of *trouble*.

7〖変色〗¶日なたに置くと紙は～ける Paper *gets discolored* in the sun.

や·ける【妬ける】¶彼女の幸福が～ける I *am jealous of* her happiness.

やけん【野犬】an ownerless dog. ¶～狩りをする hunt *ownerless* (≒ *stray*) *dogs*.

やこう【夜光】—時計 a watch with luminous hands. —虫 noctiluca (複 noctilucae). —塗料 luminous paint.

やこう【夜行】¶～性の鳥 a *nocturnal* bird.
—列車 a night train.

やごう【屋号】a store name; (かぶきの) a stage title.

やさい【野菜】vegetables; (英口語) greens. ¶農園で～を作っている We grow (≒ raise) *vegetables* on the farm.

—サラダ vegetable salad. —スープ vegetable soup. —畑 a vegetable (≒ kitchen) garden. —料理 a vegetable dish.

やさがし【家捜し】a house searching. ¶～したが書類は見つからなかった We *searched the house for* papers in vain.

やさき【矢先】¶出ようとした～に雨が降りだした It began to rain *just when* I was going out./ I *was on the point of* going out, when it began to rain.

やさし·い【優しい】(柔和な) gentle; tender; (親切な) kind; kindly; (愛情深い) affectionate. ¶～い女性 a *sweet* woman. 気だての～い娘 a *gentle*-(≒ *kind*-)*hearted* girl. 目つきの～い人 a *gentle*-eyed person. ～い声 a *sweet* (≒ *soft*) voice. 彼女は～い物腰で応対する She behaves toward others in a *gentle* manner. 年寄りには～くすべきだ We should *be kind* to old people. 母親は子どもに～いことばをかけた The mother spoke *kindly* (≒ *tenderly*) to her child. ～さ tenderness; gentleness; kindness.

やさし·い【易しい】easy. ¶～い仕事 an *easy* task (easy work とすれば不定冠詞不要). ～い文章で書かれた小説 a novel written in a *simple* style. その問題を解くのは私には～かった It *was easy* for me to solve the problem.

やし【香具師】a mountebank; a quack; a charlatan; (見世物師) a showman.

やし【椰子】〖植物〗(実) a coconut; (木) a coconut palm.
—油 coconut oil.

やじ【野次】hooting; jeering. ¶観衆の～で彼の声は消された *Hoots* of the audience made his voice inaudible. ～を飛ばさないでください Don't *interrupt* the speaker.

—うま ¶火事場の～うまは消火のじゃまだ *A curious crowd* at a fire disturbs the fire-fighting.

やしき【屋敷】(大邸宅) a mansion; (建物と土地) the premises.
—町 a residential quarter.

やしな·う【養う】1〖扶養する〗bring up; nurture; (食物を与える) feed. ¶彼は5人の子どもを男手一つで～った He *brought up* the five children entirely by himself.

彼は大家族を～わねばならぬ He has a large family to *support* (≒ *provide for*). / He has a large family *dependent on* him.

100万の金があれば孤児ひとりを1年間～えるだろう The sum of one million yen will *maintain* an orphan for a year.

や

家畜を～う *feed* cattle.

2〚その他〛¶ 彼は大磯で病後を～っている He *is recuperating* at Oiso.

よい習慣を～うのはけっして容易なことではない It is by no means easy to *form* (≒ *cultivate*) a good habit.

病人を～う *foster* a sick person.

やしゅ【野手】〘野球〙a fielder.

外― an outfielder. 内― an infielder.

やしゅ【野趣】 rural beauty; rusticity. ¶ ～に富んだ風景 *pastoral* scenery; scenery rich in *rustic beauty*. ～あふれる人物 a person with *unsophisticated charms*.

やしゅう【夜襲】 a night attack. ¶ 敵に～をかけた We *made an attack on* the enemy *under cover of the night*.

やじゅう【野獣】 a wild animal. ¶ ～のような男 a *brutal* (≒ *beastly*) man; a beast. ～狩りをする hunt *wild animals* (≒ *beasts*).

―派〘美術〙Fauvism.

やしょく【夜食】(夕食) supper; (深夜食) a midnight meal.

やじり【矢尻・鏃】 an arrowhead.

やじ・る【野次る】 ¶ 彼らは盛んに演説を～った They *hooted* the speaker violently. / They often *interrupted* the speech. 候補者を～り倒して演壇から追い出した We *hooted* (≒ *heckled*) the candidate out of the platform.

やじるし【矢印】 an arrow. ¶ ～の方向に進んだ We made our way directed by *arrows*.

やしろ【社】 a shrine; a temple.

やしん【野心】 ambition. ¶ 女優になるのが彼女の～だった It was her *ambition* to be an actress. 彼は有名になりたいという～をいだいている He has *an ambition to* become famous. / He *is ambitious for* fame. 彼は会長に(なりたい)～をいだいた He had *designs on* the president. / The presidency was his *ambition*. 彼女は流行歌手として～満々だ She *is* highly *ambitious* as a popular singer. わが国は領土的～を持たない Our country has no territorial *ambition*.

―家 an ambitious man. ¶ 彼は～家だ He *is ambitious*. / He is *an ambitious man*. / He has great *ambition*. / He is full of *ambition*. ―作 an ambitious work.

やじん【野人】(田舎者) a rustic; (粗野な人) a boor; (民間人) a civilian. ¶ 退官後は一介の～として暮らした After retirement he lived as *a private citizen*.

やす【簎】 a fish spear; a gig. ¶ ～で魚を突く *spear* a fish.

やす【安】〘株式〙down. ¶ 株価は５円～ The stock price is five yen *lower* (≒ *down* five yen).

やすあがり【安上がり】 economical; inexpensive. ¶ 自分の家で食べるほうが～だ It *is cheaper* to dine at home than out.

やす・い【安い】 1〘金額が〙cheap. ¶ その古本は～い The secondhand book *is inexpensive*. (㊥ では cheap より inexpensive が普通. cheap には「安っぽい」の感じが加わる).

これは～いです This *is reasonable*. (とくに売る立場で).

その家を～い家賃で借りた We hired the house *at a low rent*.

それは～い買い物だ It is *a good bargain*.

～かろう悪かろう *Cheap* and nasty.

2〘その他〛¶ 彼らはお～くない仲だ They *are in love with each other*. / They are *intimate* friends. (intimate は男女間の親しさを意味することが多い).

そんなことはお～いことだ It is *no trouble at all*.

お～いことです (頼まれたとき) Sure. / Certainly. / (礼を言われたとき) You are welcome. / Not at all. (いまは Don't mention it. とはあまり言わない). / With pleasure.

-やす・い【-易い】(容易な) easy; (…しやすい; …しがちな) be apt to (*do*); (可能性の強いとき) liable to.

¶ こわれ～い花びん a *fragile* vase. 使い～い道具 *convenient* tools. 感じ～い人 a *susceptible* (≒ *sensitive*) person. 傷つき～い心 a *sensitive* heart. これは書き～いペンだ This pen *is easy to* write with. 彼の話はわかり～い His speech *is easy to* understand. きみはだまされ～い You *are credulous* (≒ *are easily cheated*). 私は風邪をひき～い I *am liable to* catch cold.

やすうけあい【安請け合い】 ¶ 彼は～ばかりして実行しない He *is* always *too ready to make promises* and seldom carries them out. そんなに～しないほうがいい You should not *undertake it so lightly*.

やすうり【安売り】 a [bargain] sale. ¶ あの店では毎週月曜に～する They *sell* every article *cheap* (≒ *at a bargain*) on Mondays.

―日 a bargain day. 大―(掲示) Sale. ¶ 大～で買った I bought this *at a bargain sale*.

やすく【安く】 cheap[ly]. ¶ この本を～買った I bought this book *cheap*. 米が～なった The price of rice *has gone down*. もう少し～しなさい Can't you *make* it *cheaper*? テレビを定価より１割～買った I bought the television set *at a discount* of ten percent on the fixed price. 生活費は～ない The cost of living *is* not *low*.

やすげっきゅう【安月給】 low wages. ¶ ～取り a *low-salaried* man. ～で働く work *on a small* (≒ *low*) *salary*.

やすっぽ・い【安っぽい】 cheap. ¶ ～いネックレス a *tawdry* necklace. ～い品物 *cheap-looking* goods. そんな笑い方をすると～く見える The way you laugh makes you look *frivolous*.

やすで【安手】 ¶ ～の品 *cheap* goods.

やすね【安値】 a low price. ¶ 法外な～で売る sell at an excessively *cheap price*. 3か月来の～だ The price is the record *low* for three months.

やすぶしん【安普請】 a jerry-building. ¶ ～の家 a *jerry-built* house; a *flimsily-built* house.

やすま・せる【休ませる】 ¶ しばらくの間体を～せた I *rested myself* for a while. その知らせは彼の

気持ちを～せた The news *set* his mind *at rest* (≒ *at ease*). 彼は部下を1日たっぷり～せた He *gave* his men a good day's *rest*.

やすま·る【休まる】¶ この部屋に入ると心が～る In this room I *feel at rest* (≒ *feel at ease*). / In this room I *get relaxed*. 心が～ることが一時もない We have no moment of *ease*. 悪いことをしても, それを他人に話せば気が～る If we have done wrong, it *relieves* us to tell others what we have done.

やすみ【休み】**1**〖休息〗rest. ¶ ひと～して, 一服しよう Let's *take a rest* and have a smoke. 私たちは12時から1時まで1時間の～がある We have an hour's *recess* from twelve to (≒ 米 through) one.

2〖休暇〗a holiday; a vacation. ¶ きょうは学校は～だ We *have no school* today.

学校は先週末から～だ The school *has been closed* since the end of last week.

今はとても忙しいので, 1日の～もとれない Because we are very busy now, we cannot take *a holiday* (≒ *a day off*).

彼はきょう～だ He *is absent* today.

あすは授業は～だ We shall *have no classes* (≒ *have no lessons*) tomorrow. (no lessons は大学ではあまり使わない).

3〖中断〗¶ 昨夜から～なく雨が降りつづいている It *hasn't stopped* raining since last night.

兵隊は夜まで～なく歩いた The soldiers walked till night *without a break*.

やす·む【休む】**1**〖仕事·学校を〗rest. ¶ ちょっと～みましょう Let's *rest* (≒ *take a rest*) for a while.

ちょっと仕事をやめ, ～もう Let's stop working a little while and *relax*.

彼は仕事を2時間～んだ He *rested from* his work for two hours.

私は月曜日に1日～む I will *take a day off* on Monday.

彼は仕事を2週間～んだ He *was away from* work for two weeks.

流感のため～んだ小学校もあった Some primary schools *closed* (≒ *were closed*) on account of influenza.

建築中商売を～みます We shall *stop business* during construction.

彼は30時間～まずに勤務した He took thirty hours' duty *on end*.

彼は2日学校を～んだ He *stayed away from* school for two days. / He *was absent from* school for two days.

私は英語は一度も～んだことがない I *have* never *cut* English. (とくにくだけた言い方).

～め(号令) Stand at ease!

われわれは～み～みその高山に登った We climbed up the high mountain *with frequent stops to rest*.

2〖眠る〗¶ 私は昨夜はよく～んだ I *slept* well last night.

早く～んで早く起きなさい *Go to bed* early and get up early.

彼女はよく～んでいる(眠っている) She *is* fast *asleep*.

お～みなさい Good night!

3〖その他〗¶ 機械が～んでいる The machinery *is at rest* (≒ *is standing idle*).

冗談も～み～み言え You *are too constantly joking*. / 米 No kidding!

やす·める【休める】¶ 疲れを十分～めなさい *Have* a good *rest* from your work. 散歩に出て頭を～めた I went out for a walk to *rest* my brain. 彼らはしばらく手を～めた They *rested from* labor for a while. 彼は機械を～めた He *stopped* the machine. 3年間土地を～めた We *allowed the land to lie fallow* for three years.

やすもの【安物】a cheap article. ¶ ～をあさる look (≒ hunt) for *a bargain*. ～でけっこうまにあう *Cheap things* will do for me. ～買いの銭失い(諺) *Penny wise and pound foolish*.

やすやす〔と〕easily; with ease. ¶ 彼はどんな問題も～解くことができる He can solve any problem *easily* (≒ *without difficulty; with ease*). そう～引き受けられません We can't undertake it so *readily*. そう～だまされない Nobody can deceive me so *easily*.

やすやど【安宿】a cheap inn.

やすらか【安らか】¶ ～に眠れ Rest *in peace*! 彼は～に死んだ He died a *calm* death. ～な日日を送っている We are living *a peaceful life* (≒ *in peace*). その光景を見て心～でなかった I *felt uneasy at* the scene.

やすらぎ【安らぎ】¶ 心の～ *tranquility* of mind. 心の～を感じる feel at ease.

やすら·ぐ【安らぐ】¶ 慰められても心の～ぐことはない Though solaced, I have not come to *feel at ease*.

やすり【鑢】a file; (紙やすり) sandpaper. ¶ ～をかける file.

やすん·ずる【安んずる】¶ 小成に～じてはならない Never *be contented* (≒ *be satisfied*) *with* a small success. 意を～じて彼の返事を待ちなさい *Rest assured* and wait for his reply. その知らせを聞いて心を～じた The news made me easy.

やせい【野生】wildness. ¶ このユリは～だ This lily *grows wild*. ～のサルを飼い慣らす tame a *wild* monkey.

—植物 a wild plant. **—**動植物 wild life.

やせい【野性】wild nature. ¶ そのライオンは～味をなくしてきた The lion has lost its *wild nature*. 彼らは相変わらず～的だ They remain *naive* (≒ *unsophisticated*).

やせうで【痩せ腕】¶ 女の～で家族を養った She supported the family *on her small means*.

やせおとろ·える【痩せ衰える】¶ 彼は長い病気で～えた He *has grown thin* (≒ *lean*) *and worn* on account of a long sickness. / He *is emaciated* by long sickness.

やせがまん【痩せ我慢】strained endurance. ¶ 彼は疲れているのに～している He *is straining* not to show his fatigue. 私はとうていできないと思ったが～してみた I *tried to be a sport*, though I knew that I was unequal to it.

やせぎす【痩せぎす】spare; lean; thin. ¶ 彼女は〜だ She *is slightly built.* 彼は背が高く〜だ He *is* tall and *spare in build.*

やせぐすり【痩せ薬】a fat-reducer.

やせこ·ける【痩せこける】¶ 彼女は病気で〜けた She *has lost much weight* on account of sickness.(become thinner とはあまり言わない).
彼は〜けて骨と皮ばかりだ He *is very thin,* nothing but skin and bone. / He is *a living skeleton.*

やせち【痩せ地】barren (≒sterile; poor) land (≒soil).

やせっぽち【痩せっぽち】a skinny person.

やせほそ·る【痩せ細る】¶ いろいろな悩みで彼女は〜った She *has lost flesh* from her troubles.

や·せる【痩せる】**1**〘からだが〙lose weight. ¶ なんとかして〜せたいと思っている I'd like to *reduce flesh* somehow or other.
彼があんなに〜せたのに驚いている I'm surprised that he *has lost flesh* like that.
彼女はここ数か月間〜せるために食餌療法している She has been dieting (≒has been on a diet) to *reduce her weight* for the past few months. (かんたんに be on a reducing diet と言うほうが口語的).
2〘土地が〙become sterile. ¶ あの土地は〜せていて耕作には適さない The land *is* too *barren* to cultivate.
3〘比喩的に〙¶ 〜せても枯れても彼は紳士だ *However reduced his circumstances may be,* he is still a gentleman.

やせん【野戦】a field battle.
—病院 a field hospital.

やせん【夜戦】a night battle; a night operation.

やそう【野草】wild grass.

やそうきょく【夜想曲】〘音楽〙a nocturne.

やたい【屋台】(店) a stall; stand; (山車) a float. ¶ 踊りの〜 *a stage* for dancing.
—骨 ¶ 彼は一家の〜骨となっている He *supports his family.* その失敗で彼の一家の〜骨が傾いた The fortune of his family declined on account of the failure.

やたらに【矢鱈に】¶ 彼女は〜英語を使う She speaks English *too much.* 彼は〜金を使う He spends money *freely* (≒*lavishly*). 彼は〜株を買った He bought stocks *blindly.* 彼は〜人をほめる He praises others *excessively* (≒*lavishly*).(回数が多い場合は too often).

やちゅう【夜中】at night; in the night.

やちょう【野鳥】a wild bird.

やちん【家賃】rent. ¶ 私は毎月4万円の〜を払っている I *pay* forty thousand yen *for the house* every month. 〜を滞らせている The *rent* is overdue.

やつ【奴】a fellow; a guy. ¶ すばらしい〜 *a* swell *guy.* なんてあわれな〜だ What *a* poor *fellow!*

やつあたり【八つ当たり】¶ うまくいかないといつも彼は〜する Whenever he fails, he *gets angry* (≒*gets cross*) *with* everybody that comes his way.

やつおりばん【八つ折り判】octavo (8 vo.).

やっか【薬価】the price of medicine.

やっか【薬科】—大学 a college of pharmacy.

やっかい【厄介】**1**〘めんどう〙trouble. ¶ 彼は私にいろいろと〜をかけた He gave me a lot of *trouble.*
彼は警察の〜になったこともある He *has been in trouble with* the police.
ご〜をかけてすみませんでした I am sorry to *have troubled* you.
彼は自分の仕事を〜がっている He finds his work *troublesome.*
この道具は取り扱いが〜だ This is an *awkward* tool.
2〘世話〙care. ¶ 他人の〜になるな Don't *depend on* others.
まだきみは両親の〜になっているのか *Are* you still *dependent on* your parents?
私は子どもの〜にはなりたくない I want to *be* no *burden on* my children. / I don't want to *be looked after* by my children.
私は彼のところに長い間〜になった (滞在) I *stayed with* him for a long time. / (居候) I *lived on* him for a long time.
私はときどき医者のご〜になる I sometimes *go to see the doctor.*
ご〜になりました Thank you for your kindness.
—払い ¶ 彼は〜払いをして喜んでいる He is glad to *have got rid of a nuisance.*

やつがしら【八つ頭】〘植物〙a taro (複 taros).

やっかん【約款】(条項) a clause; an agreement; a stipulation.

やっき【躍起】¶ 彼らは〜になって助けを求めた They cried for help *frantically.* 彼女は逃げ出そうと〜になった She tried to run off *desperately.* 彼は〜になって言いわけをした He *was mad with* excusing himself.

やつぎばや【矢継早】¶ 〜に rapidly; in rapid succession. 記者はその問題に〜に質問を浴びせた The pressmen *showered questions on* the problem.

やっきょう【薬莢】a cartridge.

やっきょく【薬局】a pharmacy; 米 a drugstore; 英 a chemist; (病院の) a pharmacist office.
—方 pharmacopoeia.

やつぎり【八つ切り】〘写真〙an octavo.

やっこ【奴】¶ 〜さんなにしに来たんだ What has the *chap* (≒*fellow; guy*) come to do?
—だこ a *yakko-* (≒footman-)shaped kite.

やつざき【八つ裂き】¶ 〜にしたいくらい彼が憎い I hate him so much that I wish I could *tear* him *to pieces.*

やつ·す【窶す】¶ 彼は道楽に憂き身を〜している He *is given to* debauchery. 彼女は化粧に憂き身を〜した She *spent much time* 〔*in*〕 mak*ing* a toilet.

やっつけしごと【遣っ付け仕事】a rough and hasty work; a make-shift work.

や

やっつ·ける【遣っ付ける】¶ ついに敵を～けた At last we *have beaten* the enemy. 討論で相手方を徹底的に～けてやった I *vanquished* the adversary in the debate. 彼を～けろ *Down with* him! / Let us *be rid of* him! 来週までにその仕事を～けるつもりだ I'm going to *finish* the work by next week.

やつで【八つ手】〘植物〙 a Japanese fatsia.

やってい·く【やって行く】¶ 現在の給料ではとても～けない I can never *manage* (≒ *get along; live*) on the present salary. お金がなくてもなんとか～くほかはないでしょう We shall have to *manage* without money. 彼とはうまく～ける I can *get along quite well with* him.

やって·くる【やって来る】¶ 彼はいつも同じ時刻に～くる He always *appears* at the same time. 彼ははるばる北海道から～きた He *came* all the way from Hokkaido.

やっての·ける【遣って退ける】¶ 彼はみごとにその仕事を～けた He *accomplished* the work successfully. / He *succeeded in* the work splendidly. 私は同じ方法でそれを～けた I *disposed of* the matter in the same way.

やって·みる【やって見る】try; attempt. ¶ もう一度それを～みる I'm going to *try* it once more. / I'll *have a try* once again. 私にできるか～みよう I will see if I can. ～みてもだめだ It is no use *trying*. 一かばちか～みよう I will *take my chance*.

やっと (かろうじて) only just; barely; (ついに) at last; at length. ¶ ～汽車にまにあった I was *just* in time for the train. ～のことで山頂にたどりついた I got to the top of the mountain *with great difficulty*. ～その仕事を完成した *At last* (≒ *At length*) we've accomplished the work. 彼女は～読み書きができる She can *barely* read and write. 彼は～死を免れた He *narrowly* escaped death.

やっとこ【鋏】 pincers.

やつめうなぎ【八つ目鰻】 a lamprey; a lamper eel.

やつ·れる【窶れる】¶ 彼は睡眠不足で～れた顔をしている He *looks haggard* for lack of sleep. 長い病気で彼女は～れてしまった She *is emaciated* on account of a long illness. 彼女は見る影もなく～れた She *is worn* to a shadow. / She *is worn* to a mere shadow of her former self.

やど【宿】 an inn; a (≒ an) hotel. ¶ 駅の近くに～をとっている I *am staying* (≒ *am putting up*) *at a hotel* near the railroad station. / I *have taken up my quarters* close to the station.

やとい【雇い】 employment.
臨時— a temporary employee. 日—人夫 a day laborer.

やといいれ【雇い入れ】 employment.

やといい·れる【雇い入れる】 employ; hire.

やといにん【雇い人】 an employe[e].

やといぬし【雇い主】 an employer.

やとう【野党】 the Opposition [party]; the party out of office. ¶ ～連合 combination of *the Opposition parties*. ～の党主 the leader of *the Opposition*.

やと·う【雇う】 employ; hire. ¶ タイピストを～う *employ* a typist. タクシーを～う *take* a taxi. 彼を通訳として～った I *employed* (≒ *engaged*) him as [an] interpreter. われわれは彼に～われている We *are in his service*.

やどかり【宿借り】〘動物〙 a hermit crab.

やど·す【宿す】¶ 彼女は彼の子を～している She *is with child by* him.

やどちょう【宿帳】 a hotel (≒ an inn) register; a hotel (≒ an inn) book.

やどちん【宿賃】 hotel charges. ¶ その旅館の～はひと晩いくらですか What is the charge for a night at the inn?

やどなし【宿なし】 a homeless person; (浮浪者) a vagabond; a tramp. ¶ 洪水で多くの人が～になった A lot of people *have lost their houses* (≒ *have become homeless*) by the flood.

やどや【宿屋】 an inn; a hotel. ¶ ～の主人(男) a landlord; an innkeeper.

やどりぎ【宿り木】〘植物〙 a mistletoe; a parasite.

やど·る【宿る】 lodge; stop; dwell. ¶ 正直の頭に神～る God *dwells* in an honest heart. 健全な精神は健全な身体に～る A sound mind in a sound body. (英語では「健全な身体に健全な精神を」(教育の理想) の意).

やどろく【宿六】¶ うちの～ my husband; my old man.

やどわり【宿割り】 assignment of lodgings. ¶ ～をする *allot lodgings* (*of* the students).

やな【梁·簗】 a weir.

やなぎ【柳】 a willow. ¶ 彼はそれを～に風と受け流した He *gave no heed to* the remark. ～の下にいつもどじょうはいない Good luck does not always repeat itself. ～に雪折れなし(諺) Oaks may break when reeds stand the storm.
—腰 a slim waist. ¶ ～腰の女 a woman *of slim waist*. —ごうり a willow trunk. ネコ— a pussy willow.

やなみ【家並み】 a row of houses.

やに【脂】(たばこの) nicotine; (木の) resin; gum. ¶ パイプが～でつまっている The pipe is stopped up with *nicotine*.
松— pine resin. 目— eye discharges; rheum.

やにさが·る【脂下がる】¶ 彼は美人を前にして～っている He *looks pleased* (≒ *looks* [*self*-]*satisfied*) *with* a beautiful girl near at hand.

やにょうしょう【夜尿症】〘医学〙 night enuresis; bed-wetting.

やにわに【矢庭に】 suddenly; abruptly. ¶ われわれを見ると彼は～逃げ出した He ran away *the moment* he saw us.

やぬし【家主】 a landlord; the owner of a house.

やね【屋根】 a roof. ¶ ～をかわら(わら)でふく cover the *roof* with tiles (thatch). きみとは同じ～の下で暮らしたくない I don't want to live with you under the same *roof*.

や

—板 a shingle. —裏部屋 an attic. —屋 a roofer. —伝い ¶ 彼は～伝いに逃げた He ran away along *the roofs.*

やば【矢場】(屋外の) an archery ground ; (屋内の) an archery gallery.

やはり【矢張り】all the same ; nonetheless ; yet ; still. ¶ 私も～彼がきらいだ I don't like him, *either.* 彼は～うそをついていた He had told a lie, *as was expected.* 彼女は病気でも～勉強を続けている She *still* keeps studying in spite of her illness. / She is ill, but she is studying *all the same.* 今でも～横浜にお住みですか Are you *still* living in Yokohama? 大きなことを言っても～ばかはばかだ Even if he talks big, a fool is *still* a fool.

やはん【夜半】¶ ～に at *midnight*; in *the middle of the night.* ～来の雨だ It has been raining since *midnight.*

やばん【野蛮】barbarism. ¶ ～な savage ; rude. 戦争はどんなによくみても～だ War at best is *barbarism.* ～な行為はするな Never do anything *barbarous.*

—人 a barbarian ; a savage.

やひ【野卑】rudeness ; vulgarity ; coarseness. ¶ ～な rude ; coarse ; vulgar ; mean ; repulsive (行儀が悪くまた粗暴なふるまいの形容には rude, coarse (coarse のほうが粗暴な意味が強い), 育ちが悪くて下品な意味には vulgar, 態度などが人道にもとるようないやしさのある場合には mean, 嫌悪(けんお)を催させる意味では repulsive を用いる).

¶ ～な人 a person *without manners*; a *vulgar* person. ～なことば *coarse* (≒ *bad*) language.

やぶ【藪】a bush ; a thicket. ¶ 彼は～から棒に私を首にすると言った He told me *all of a sudden* (≒ *on a sudden ; point-blank*) that I was fired. ～から棒になんだね, おちついて話してごらん You surprise me with these *unexpected things.* Calm down and tell me what's on.

やぶいしゃ【藪医者】a quack 〔doctor〕.

やぶいり【藪入り】the servants' holiday.

やぶか【藪蚊】a striped mosquito.

やぶさか【吝か】¶ みんながそう言うなら私もそれに同意するに～でない Since I am in the minority, I *don't hesitate to* agree to the proposal.

やぶにらみ【藪睨み】a squint 〔eye〕. ¶ 彼は少し～だ He has *a* slight *squint.* / He *is* slightly *squint-eyed* (≒ *cross-eyed*).

やぶへび【藪蛇】¶ ～になるといけないからおよしなさい Better stay away from it, since it might *wake up a sleeping dog.* よけいなことを言って～になってしまった I wish I had left it unsaid. It *boomeranged.*

やぶ・る【破る】**1**〖物を〗break. ¶ 彼は着物を～った He *tore* his clothes.

彼はノートブックから1枚紙を～り取った He *tore* a sheet *out of* the notebook.

犬がかきを～って入った A dog *broke through* the fence.

2〖その他〗¶ 彼は約束を～った He *broke* (≒ *did not keep*) his promise.

彼は法を～ったので罰せられた As he *broke* (≒ *infringed*) the law, he was punished.

その事件がヨーロッパの平和を～るにいたった The incident came to *disturb* the peace of Europe.

彼らは戦うたびに敵を～った They *defeated* the enemy at every battle.

新しいチャンピオンは今までの記録を全部～った The new champion *has broken* all the previous records.

やぶれ【破れ】(裂け目) a tear ; a rent ; a rip ; a split ; (破損) a break ; (穴) a hole ; a gap (布・紙などを力で引き裂いた破れは tear, さらに大きな力で引き裂いた裂け目は rent と言う. rip は継ぎ目・縫い目などに沿って強い力で引き裂いた破れ目, split は長い一直線の裂け目, break はテーブル・いすなどの固い物の場合は一部がもぎとれた状態, 布・紙などでは一部が破れて穴があいた状態を言う. 小さな穴は hole).

¶ 彼女は彼の服の～を繕った She mended (≒ repaired ; darned) *a tear* (≒ *a rent ;* (穴) *a hole*) in his clothes. くつ下の～を繕ってもらった I had my socks mended (≒ repaired ; darned). 障子の～からのぞいた I peeped through *a hole* in the sliding screen. 犬が生垣の～からはいってきた A dog came in through *a gap* (≒ *a break*) in the hedge.

～やすい fragile ; easily broken.

—がさ a broken umbrella. —ぐつ (擦り切れた) worn-out shoes ; (底がとれたり, 部分がばらばらになった) broken shoes. —服 (糸が見えるほど着古した) threadbare clothes ; (ぼろぼろになった) tattered clothes.

やぶれかぶれ【破れかぶれ】¶ もうそのときは私も～だった I *was driven to desperation* (≒ *became desperate*) then. 彼は～でそんなことをしたのだ He has done such a thing *desperately* (≒ *in desperation*).

やぶれた【破れた】(裂けた) torn ; (使い古してぼろぼろの服など) ragged ; tattered ; (擦り切れた) wornout ; (一部がとれたり破れたりして壊れた) broken. ¶ ひじの～上着 a coat *out* at elbows. ～くつ下 *worn-out* socks.

やぶれめ【破れ目】(裂け目) a rip ; a tear ; a split ; a crack ; (穴) a hole ; a gap ; a worn spot ; a rent.

やぶ・れる【破れる】tear ; rip. ¶ その本はとびらのページが下半分～れている The title page of the book *is torn* half way down. くぎにひっかけてそでが～れた My sleeve caught on a nail and *was torn* (≒ *was ripped*). 彼の夢は～れた His dream *did not come true* (≒ *failed* him). / His dream *was not fulfilled* (≒ *was not realized*). 両者の均衡が～れた The balance between the two *was lost.* うすい紙片はすぐ～れる A thin piece of paper *tears* easily.

やぶ・れる【敗れる】¶ わが校のチームは惜しくも決勝戦で～れた It's a pity that our team *lost* the final game.

やぶん【夜分】night ; the evening (一般に人が寝ている時間は night, 夕食後起きてだんらんをしている時間は evening と言う. ただし, 起きて楽しんでいても夕食後かなりの時間が経過していれば night と

や

言うことが多い).
¶ ～におじゃまして申しわけありません I am sorry to disturb you so late *at night.* ～は涼しい *In the evening* it is cool.

やぼ【野暮】boorishness. ¶ 彼は～な身なりをしている He is *not well* dressed. / His dress *is not stylish.* / He looks *far from refined* (≒*far from stylish*). 彼は～な男だ He *is corny* and *clumsy.* / He *is boorish.* / He is *a boor.* それは～というものだ You *are lacking in delicacy* to do (≒say) such a thing. ～なことを言うな How *thoughtless* you *are* to say such a thing! / Don't *be inconsiderate.* / Don't *spoil the fun.* 健康が富にまさるなどと言うだけ～だ It *is needless* to say that health is above wealth.

やほう【野砲】a fieldpiece; a field gun; (移動可能な砲の総称として) field artillery.

やぼう【野望】ambition; aspiration (ambition は個人的な欲望を含む野望, aspiration はふつう崇高な目的を伴う大望を言う).

やま【山】**1** a mountain; a hill (筑波山くらいは hill).
¶ 夏には～へ行くつもりだ I intend to go to *the mountains* in summer.
～(の中)で暮らす live in *the mountains.*
2〖堆積〗¶ 私は読みたい本が～とある I have *lots of* (≒ *a heap of*) books to read.
～と金を積まれても, そんなことはまっぴらごめんだ I would not do such a thing *for all the gold* in the world.
～のような借金 *a mountain of* debts.
～のように高い波 *mountain*-high waves.
～のような大波だ The waves are *mountain*〔*s*〕high.
3〖投機〗¶ ～が当たった(はずれた) The *speculation* has turned out well (has failed).
試験に～をかけた I *took my chance in* the examination.
4〖最高潮〗¶ 戦争の勃発(ぼっ)がその話の～だ The outbreak of the war is *the climax* of the story.

やまあい【山間】(中央に川のあるゆるやかな傾斜の間の谷間) a valley; (険しいがけの間の谷間) a gorge; a ravine.
¶ ～の村 a village *among the mountains.*

やまあらし【豪猪】〘動物〙a porcupine.

やまい【病】sickness; illness; a disease.
¶ ～に倒れる get sick; become (≒fall) ill; be taken ill. それがあの人の～だ(悪い性癖) That is his *bad habit.* / That is what he is hated for.

やまいぬ【山犬】〘動物〙a wild dog; a Japanese wolf; 米 a coyote.

やまいも【山芋】〘植物〙a yam.

やまおく【山奥】the heart (≒depth) of a mountain.

やまおとこ【山男】(森林に住む男; 森林で働く男) a hillman; a wood〔s〕man; 米 a hillbilly; (登山家; 山中に住む男) a mountaineer; (登山家) a mountain climber; an alpinist.

やまかじ【山火事】a forest fire.

やまがら【山雀】〘鳥類〙a Japanese titmouse.

やまがらす【山烏】〘鳥類〙a Japanese raven.

やまがり【山狩り】¶ 容疑者が逃げ込んだので警察は～をした The police made *a sweeping search for* the suspect who had taken refuge *in the mountains.*

やまかん【山勘】speculation; venture.
¶ ～で数を言いあてる *guess* the number 〔*at a venture* (≒ *on speculation*)〕.

やまくずれ【山崩れ】米 a landslide; 英 a landslip.

やまぐに【山国】a mountainous province (≒ country; region). ¶ ～の人 a mountaineer.

やまけ【山気】speculative disposition. ¶ あの人は～がある He *is speculative* (≒ *is ambitious*). / He has *a speculative mind.* ～を出してはいけない Don't be tempted to take the *pecuniary risk.*

やまごえ【山越え】¶ ～する cross (≒ pass over; go across; travel across) a mountain.

やまごや【山小屋】a hut; a mountain hut; (避暑のための小別荘など) a cottage.

やまざくら【山桜】〘植物〙(花) wild cherry blossoms; (木) a wild cherry tree.

やまざと【山里】a mountain village; a village (≒ hamlet) among (≒ in) the mountains.

やまざる【山猿】a wild monkey; (田舎者) a rustic; a country person.

やまし【山師】(鉱山業者) a miner; (探鉱師) a mine operator; 米 a prospector; (山林業者) a lumber-dealer; (投機師) a speculator; (自己の地位・職業などを偽って詐欺をするぺてん師) an impostor; (まがい物を売りつける商人) a mountebank; (詐欺師) a swindler.

やまじ【山路】a mountain path.

やまし・い【疚しい】¶ ～い行ない a *shameful* act. 私に～いところはない I *have a clear conscience.* / I *have nothing to be ashamed of.* / I *am innocent.* 彼は～いことはしない His conduct *is* entirely *above board.* / He is an *honorable* person. それはきみに～い気持ちがあるからだ That's because you *have a guilty conscience.*

やまたかぼうし【山高帽子】米 a derby; 英 a bowler 〔hat〕.

やまつつじ【山躑躅】〘植物〙a (≒ an Indian) rhododendron.

やまつなみ【山津波】a landslide.

やまでら【山寺】a mountain temple.

やまと【大和】〔ancient〕Japan.
—ことば the 〔classical〕 Japanese language. —魂 the Japanese spirit. —ナデシコ〘植物〙pink; (人) a Japanese woman. —民族 the Yamato (≒ Japanese) race.

やまなみ【山並】mountain ranges.

やまなり【山鳴り】the rumbling of a mountain.

やまねこ【山猫】〘動物〙a wildcat.
—スト a wildcat strike.

やまのかみ【山の神】(妻) *one's* wife.

やまのて【山の手】(丘陵地域) the hilly section 〔of a city〕; (住宅地) the residential section (≒district) 〔of a city〕; the uptown; (横浜・神戸の) the Bluff. ¶ ～に住む live *uptown*.
—線 the Yamanote 〔loop〕 line.

やまのぼり 【山登り】 mountain climbing; mountaineering. ¶ ～に行く climb 〔up〕 a mountain; go mountaineering.

やまばと【山鳩】〘鳥類〙 a turtledove; 米 a mourning dove.

やまばん【山番】(森林の管理者) a ranger; a forester.

やまびこ【山彦】an echo (複 echoes).

やまびらき【山開き】the 〔formal〕 opening of a mountain to climbers; the beginning of mountaineering season.
¶ 7月1日は富士山の～だ The mountaineering season begins on July 1 at Mt. Fuji.

やまぶき【山吹】〘植物〙 a yellow rose.
—色 bright yellow.

やまぶし【山伏】a Buddhist hermit; a traveling Buddhist monk.

やまふところ【山懐】a mountain recess; the bosom of a mountain.

やまみち【山道】 a mountain path (≒road) (path は小道, road は自動車道など).

やまもり 【山盛り】 ¶ 彼女は御飯を茶わんに～につ いだ She *heaped* the bowl with 〔boiled〕 rice.
茶さじに～の砂糖 *a teaspoonful of* sugar.

やまやま【山山】very much; a great deal.
¶ 会いたいのは～だが時間がない *I really wish to* (≒*I wish I could*) go and see him, but I have no time. それを欲しいのは～だ I want it *very much*.

やまゆり【山百合】〘植物〙 a goldband lily; a golden-banded lily; a tiger lily.

やまわけ【山分け】an equal division. ¶ 彼らは獲物を～にした They divided the profit *equally* between the two (≒them). / They *went halves with* each other in the profits. / They *had an equal division* each of the profit. ～にしよう Let's *go halves* (≒*go shares*). / Let's *go fifty-fifty*. (go halves や go fifty-fifty はふたりの場合. go shares や share (動詞) はふたり以上何人の間でも使える).

やみ【闇】**1** 〘暗黒〙 darkness. ¶ 犯人は～にまぎれて逃亡した The culprit fled *under cover of darkness*.
われわれは～の中をさまよい歩いた We wandered about in the *dark*.
真の～(の) pitch-dark.
その事件は～から～へ葬られた The matter *was hushed up*.
一寸先は～だ Who knows what tomorrow may have in store for us?
2 〘不正取引〙 ¶ 彼は多量の砂糖を～に流した He *channeled* a great quantity of sugar *into the black market*.
～で (不法に) 売る (買う) black-market.
—値 a black market price. —物資 black market goods. —屋 a black marketeer.

やみあがり【病み上がり】¶ きみの～の体に無理は禁物だ You must stay away from hard work *until you recover* 〔*your health*〕 *completely* (≒*during your convalescence*). ～の人 a convalescent.

やみくも【闇雲】¶ 彼は～に成功を焦っている He *is so crazy to* win a success.

やみつき【病みつき】¶ 彼は競馬が～になった He *is* now *crazy about* the horse races. / He *is so infatuated with* horse races.

やみとりひき 【闇取引】 (市場・制度) black market; (行為) black-marketing; black-marketeering.
¶ 政治上の～ *secret dealings on* political matters. 入学試験に～があるといううわさがある There is a rumor of *back-door admissions* to some school.

やみよ【闇夜】a dark (≒moonless) night.

や・む【病む】(病気になる) get sick (主として米); fall ill (主として英); (心配する) be worried.
¶ 彼は試験の失敗を気に～んでいる He *is fretting about* his failure in the examination.
きみは小さなことを気に～みすぎる You *worry* too much *over* (≒You *make too much of*) trifles. 気に～むのはからだによくない *Worrying* is bad for the health.

や・む【止む・已む】**1** 〘止まる・なくなる〙 ¶ 雨が～んだ The rain *has stopped*. / It *has stopped raining*.
雨がなかなか～まない It goes on raining. / The rain shows no sign of *leaving off*.
風(物音)が～んだ The wind (noise) *has died down*.
あらしが～んだ The storm *is over* (≒*has passed off*).
幕がおりて拍手が～んだ The applause *ceased* when the curtain fell (≒came down).
痛みは夕方になって～んだ The pain *left me* (≒*was gone*) toward evening.
2 〘その他〙 ¶ ご多幸を祈って～みません I *really* wish you a good luck (≒every happiness).
～むに～まれぬ事情があったのでしょう There must have been some *unavoidable* (≒*inevitable*) cause.

やむをえず【已むを得ず】¶ 彼は～(強制されて)犯行を認めた He admitted his crime *under compulsion*. / (法廷で) He *was forced to* plead guilty. 私は～(いやいや)家にとどまった I stayed at home *reluctantly* (≒*against my will*). 私は～うそをついた I *had to* tell a lie. / I *was compelled* (≒*was forced*) *to* tell a lie.

やむをえない【已むを得ない】¶ ～事情で彼は遅刻した He was late owing to *unavoidable* (≒*uncontrollable*) circumstances. 実質的な回答がないかぎりストライキも～ We *are* now *ready to* stage a strike unless some tangible offers are presented. 多少の混乱は～ A little confusion *can't be helped*. ～こととしてあきらめなければなるまい We shall have to accept it as *unavoidable*.

や

やめ【止め】¶ 雨のため試合は～になった The game *was cancelled* on account of rain. / The game *was rained* (≒ *was washed*) *out*. もう議論は～にしよう Let's *stop* our discussion here. / Let's not discuss it any further.

やめさ·せる【止めさせる】stop. ¶ 医者は彼にたばこを～せた (やめるように命じた) The doctor *told* him to *quit* (≒ *give up*; *refrain from*; *abstain from*) smoking. / (実際にやめさせた) The doctor *made* him *give up* smoking. 彼は非行のため学校を～せられた He *was expelled* (≒ *was dismissed*) *from* school because of delinquency. 彼は背任行為で職を～せられた He *was dismissed* (≒ *was fired*) *from* office for misconduct.

や·める【止める】stop; cease; (職などを) resign. ¶ 彼は酒を～めた He *stopped* (≒ *gave up*; *quit*) drinking. 彼は途中で学校を～めた He *left* (≒ *quit*) school halfway. 彼は公務員を～めて実業界に入った He *retired from* government service and went into business. 彼は社長の職を～めた He *resigned* the post of the president. 私はアメリカ行きの旅行を～めた I *gave up* my trip to America. 彼は医業を～めて小説を書きだした He *abandoned* the medical profession *for* novel-writing. 私はしばらくフランス語の勉強を～めている I *have discontinued* the study of French for a time. これで～めることにしよう Let's call it a day. / (学校の授業などで) So much for today.

やもうしょう【夜盲症】〘医学〙 night blindness; nyctalopia.

やもめ【寡婦】a widow; the bereaved wife. ¶ 彼女は～になった She *was widowed*. / She *lost her husband*. / She *was bereaved of her husband*. 彼女は夫の死後ずっと～で暮らした After her husband's death she remained *a widow* all her life.

やもめ【寡夫】a widower.

やもり【守宮】〘動物〙 a gecko (複 gecko〔e〕s); a wall lizard.

やや (少し) a little; a bit; rather; (多少) somewhat; slightly; more or less; in a measure; to some extent; in a way (a bit は口語的, a little と somewhat はほぼ同じ意だが, somewhat のほうが少し堅苦しい. rather は「どちらかというと」が原意だが,「かなり」「だいぶ」の意味も含む. more or less は「多少なりとも」の意. in a measure, to some extent は抽象的な事柄にのみ用いる. in a way は「ある意味では」の意味を持つ).

¶ こちらの問題のほうが～難しい This problem is *a little* (≒ *a bit*) more difficult. 死亡率は昨年より～増加している The death rate shows a *slight* increase over last year. 新聞の論調は～好意的である The press comments are *comparatively* favorable.

ややこし·い complicated; tangled; intricate; complex; involved; confusing; troublesome; difficult (理解・説明が困難なほどややこしいのは complicated, 事件などが入り組んでややこしいのは tangled, 物の構造, 状況, 製造の過程などが複雑なのは intricate, 多種類の部分から成り立っていてややこしいのは complex, 議論・事件・社会状況などが複雑で部分を個別に切り離して論じられないのが involved, 考えを混乱させて判断に苦しむようなのは confusing と言う. troublesome はややこしいので「めんどうな」ことを表わし, difficult は単に「困難な」という意味なので, あとに difficult to *solve* のように別のことばが補われることが多い).

¶ ～いんですね It certainly *is confusing*, isn't it? 問題は～かった The problems *were hard* (≒ *were difficult*) to solve. これは～いことになった The affairs *are in a tangle*. 彼が外国人だったので事件はよけい～くなった The fact that he was a foreigner made the matter more *complicated*.

ややもすれば【動もすれば】¶ 人はみな～怠りがちになる We *are apt* (≒ *are liable*; *are inclined*) *to* become lazy and unwilling to work.

やゆ【揶揄】ridicule; banter. ¶ 人を～する(からかう) make fun of (≒ tease; banter) *a person*; (嘲笑する) ridicule *a person*.

-やら ¶ 野菜～肉～卵～, いろいろな食物をとる eat a variety of foods, such as vegetables, meat, eggs, etc. (such vegetables as...とするよりもよい). 泣く～わめく～たいへんな騒ぎだった There was a great deal of yelling, crying, and screaming. 雨～風～で遠足はだいなしだった *What with* the wind *and* 〔*what with*〕 the rain, our picnic was completely spoiled.

やらい【夜来】throughout the whole night. ¶ ～の雨がなおも降りやむようすがない The rain that has been falling *since last night* still shows no sign of leaving off.

やら·れる ¶ その家は台風で～れた The house *was destroyed* (≒ *was damaged*) by the typhoon. 彼は頭を～れた He *was shot* in the head. 財布を～れた I *had* my wallet *stolen*. / My wallet *was stolen* (≒ *was gone*). 決勝戦で～れた We *were beaten* (≒ *were defeated*) in the final match. / We *lost* the final match. 流感に～れて2日休んだ I *had* the flu and took two days off.

やり【槍】a spear; (騎兵の) a lance; (投げ槍) a javelin. ¶ ～を構える lower *a spear* for attack. ～で突く thrust *a spear*.

やりあ·う【遣り合う】¶ 先日彼と～った (議論をたたかわせた) I *argued* (≒ *had a heated discussion*) *with* him the other day. / (口げんかをした) I *quarreled* (≒ *had a quarrel*) *with* him a few days ago.

やりかえ·す【遣り返す】retort; answer back. ¶「それがなぜ悪い」と私は～した "What's wrong with that?" I *talked back* in protest. / "So what?" I *retorted*.

やりかけ【遣り掛け】¶ ～の仕事をやってしまいなさい Finish the work *in hand*. 彼は仕事を～で外出してしまった He went out *leaving* the work *half-done* (≒ *unfinished*).

やりかた【遣り方】a way. ¶ 彼は彼一流の～でその問題を解決した He solved the problem *in his own way*. 人にはそれぞれ～がある Everybody *has his own way* 〔*of doing things*〕.

や

やりきれな·い【遣り切れない】¶ 仕事が多くてあすまでにはとうてい～い We have so much work that we shall *never finish* it by tomorrow. 年じゅうお説教では～い I *can hardly stand* his habitual scolding. / I *cannot stand* being continually scolded.

やりくり【遣り繰り】¶ 少ない収入で～して暮らしている I am getting along by *making shift* with a small income. あるだけでなんとか～しよう I will *manage* (≒ *make do*) with what I have. 彼女は～がうまい(まずい) She is *a good* (*a poor*) *manager*. 時間の～をして会に出席した I *managed* to find time to attend the meeting.

やりこ·める【遣り込める】¶ 彼にかかってはだれでも～められる He *puts* everyone *to silence*. / Everyone *is talked down* by him.

やりす·ぎる【遣り過ぎる】¶ きみは仕事を～ぎる You *overdo* your work. / You *are overworking*. 仕事熱心なのはけっこうだが, 彼は～ぎる It is all very well to be diligent, but he *goes too far*. きみは彼に対して～ぎる You *are too sharp upon* him.

やりすご·す【遣り過ごす】¶ 途中大型トラックを何台も～した While we were driving to this place we *let* large-sized trucks *go past*.

やりそこな·う【遣り損う】¶ ～うことを恐れてはいけない Don't be afraid of *failure*. ～ったら, またやる If I should *fail* I would try again.

やりだま【槍玉】a victim; a sacrifice. ¶ 彼がまっ先に～にあがった He *was* (≒ *fell*) the first *victim*. / They *made* the first *victim of* him.

やりつ·ける【遣り付ける】¶ ～けない仕事をするとすっかり疲れてしまう The work I *am not used to* doing makes me tired out. 彼はその仕事を～けている He *is familiar with* the business.

やりっぱなし【遣りっ放し】¶ 彼は仕事を～にして出かけてしまった He went out *without finishing* his work. 彼には物事を～にする He often *leaves* a thing *unfinished* (≒ *half-done*).

やりて【遣り手】a shrewd person. ¶ 彼はなかなかの～だ(敏腕家だ) He is *a man of ability*. / He is *a man of action*. / He *is* quite *able* (≒ *clever*). 割りが悪くてその仕事の～がない *No one* is willing to do the job, because it does not pay.

やりとお·す【遣り通す】¶ 彼はその仕事を最後まで～した He *carried out* (≒ *carried through*) the task.

やりと·げる【遣り遂げる】¶ 彼はそれを独力で～げた He *carried* it *through* by himself. / He *went through* with it by himself. / He *did* it all by himself.

やりとり【遣り取り】¶ われわれは手紙の～をした *We exchanged* letters. 激しいことばの～があった *We bandied words with each other*.

やりなお·す【遣り直す】start (≒ begin) over again. ¶ 設計をもう一度～した I *drew* the plan *all over again*.

やりなげ【槍投げ】〘競技〙 the javelin 〔throw〕. ¶ ～をする throw a javelin. ～の選手 a javelin thrower.

やりにく·い【遣り難い】¶ この作業は～い This work *is hard to* do. なんて～い仕事だ What an *awkward* job! 反応がないクラスは授業が～い It *is difficult to* teach in a class not so responsive. 彼女は～い立場にいる She is in a *delicate* position.

やりば【遣り場】¶ 彼は怒りの～がなかった He did not know how to *vent* (≒ *give vent to*) his anger. 身の～のない思いをした I did not know *what to do with myself*. 目の～に困った I did not know *which way to look*.

や·る【遣る】**1** 〖送る〗 send. ¶ 私は彼に手紙を～った I *sent a letter to* him. (Christmas card は send を用いるのが普通). / I *wrote* 〔*to*〕 him. (to の省略はとくに米).

彼は私を映画に～るのを好まなかった He did not like me to go to the movies.

2 〖与える〗 give. ¶ 私は彼に多額の金を～った I *gave* him a large sum of money.

少ないが, これをきみに～るよ Here is something for you.

ほねおり賃をいくら彼に～ろうか What shall I *pay for* his trouble?

3 〖行なう〗 do; perform. ¶ 私は彼のために戸を開けて～った I opened the door *for* him.

彼はなんでも～る He can *do* anything.

そのやり方を教えて～ろう I will tell you how to do it.

今帝劇でなにを～っていますか What *is on* now at the Imperial Theater? (on は映画・劇に用いるが showing は映画にのみ用いる. たとえば, 今おもしろい映画をやっている An exciting movie *is* now *showing*.).

彼はハムレットを～った He *played* 〔*the part of*〕 *Hamlet*.

野球を～ろう Let's *play* baseball.

きみはドイツ語を～ったことがあるか *Have* you ever *studied* (≒ *learned*) German?

日曜日にはお茶会を～る We *give* a tea ceremony on Sunday.

われわれもどうにかこうにか～っている We *are getting along* somehow or other.

できるだけ早く～ってしまってください *Finish* it as soon as possible.

彼はあの町で洗たく屋を～っている He *keeps* (≒ *runs*) a laundry in that town.

一杯～ろう Let's *have* a drink. / *What about* a drink?

やるせな·い【遣る瀬ない】miserable; disconsolate. ¶ 彼は～い胸のうちを打ち明けた He confessed *how miserable he felt* at heart. 金もなし, 暇もなし, まったく～い How *dreary* it is having no money and no time to spare.

やれ ¶ ～宿題だ, ～テストだと追いかけられる *What with* homework *and what with* tests, we hardly have a day to idle away.

やれやれ ¶ ～, それを聞いてほっとした *Well, well,* (≒ *Oh, my!*) I am relieved to hear that. ～やっと終わった *Thank Heaven,* we have done it at last.

やろう【野郎】 a fellow ; a rascal. ¶ この～ You rascal! / Damn you! ばか～ You fool (≒ blockhead)!

やわらか・い【柔らかい・軟らかい】 ¶ ～い春の日ざし the *gentle* (≒ *soft*) sunbeam in spring. ～い肉 *tender* meat. 絹は手触りが～い Silk *is soft* to the touch. / Silk *feels soft*. 土を～くする till and *soften* the earth.

やわら・ぐ【和らぐ】 ¶ 暑さ(寒さ)が～ぐ The heat (cold) *moderates*. 風が～いだ The wind *abated* (≒ *went down*). 痛みもかなり～いだ The pain *has been eased*. 彼の怒りが～いだ His anger *is softened* (≒ *is appeased* ; *is mitigated*). 彼らの対立感情は～いだ Their antagonism *was pacified*.

やわら・げる【和らげる】 ¶ 声を～げる *soften one's* voice ; *speak gently* ; *modify one's* tone 〔of voice〕. 表現を～げる *moderate* the sharpness of *one's* expressions. 彼女のことばは彼の怒りを～げた Her words *appeased* (≒ *softened* ; *pacified*) his anger.

ヤンキー a Yankee. ¶ ～気質 Yankeeism.

やんごとな・い【止ん事無い】 ¶ ～いお方 a *royal* personage ; a personage *of noble birth* (≒ *of noble blood*).

やんちゃ ¶ ～な子 a *mischievous* (≒ *naughty*) child. そんな～をしちゃだめ Don't *be* so *naughty*.

—坊主 an imp (≒ urchin). **—娘** a tomboy ; a tomboyish girl.

やんま〖虫類〗 a large dragonfly.

やんや ¶ 彼の演説にみな～とかっさいした Everybody applauded him *loudly* (≒ *enthusiastically*) for his speech.

やんわり ¶ 彼女は彼を～とたしなめた She *gently* (≒ *softly*) reproved him.

ゆ

ゆ【湯】 hot water ; (ふろ) a bath. ¶ ～を沸かしてお茶をいれる *boil water* and make tea. 夏は毎日～を沸かして入る In summer I *have a bath* (≒ *get the bath ready*) every day. ～の町 a spa ; *a hot spring* resort. 赤ちゃんに～を使わせる *give* a baby *a bath*.

—加減 ¶ ～加減はいかがですか How do you find *the bath*?

ゆあか【湯垢】 fur ; scale. ¶ やかんに～がついた The kettle is covered with *fur*. ～を取る get rid of the *fur*.

ゆあがり【湯上がり】 ¶ ～に一杯やる have a drink of *sake after a bath*.

—タオル a bath towel.

ゆいいつ【唯一】 ¶ ～の方法 *the only* way. ～無二の友 *one's sole* (≒ *only*) friend. ～の例外 a *solitary* (≒ *the only*) exception. ～の例 a *single* (≒ *the only*) example.

ゆいごん【遺言】 a will ; a testament ; (口頭の) *one's* last words. ¶ 彼女は全財産を心身障害児の施設へ贈ると～した She *willed* all her estate *to* the homes for mentally and physically handicapped children. ～により葬儀は内輪で行なわれた The funeral was held privately by the *will* of the deceased.

—執行者 an executor. **—状** a will.

ゆいしょ【由緒】 a history. ¶ あの寺には～ある鐘がある There is a bell with *a history* in that temple. 彼は～ある家の生まれだ He is of *noble* (≒ *high* ; *good*) birth.

ゆいしんろん【唯心論】〖哲学〗 idealism ; spiritualism.

—者 an idealist ; a spiritualist.

ゆいのう【結納】 a betrothal present (≒ gift). ¶ ～を取り交わす exchange *betrothal gifts*.

—金 betrothal money.

ゆいび【唯美】 ¶ ～的 〔a〕esthetic.

—主義 〔a〕estheticism. **—主義者** an 〔a〕esthete. **—論者** an 〔a〕esthetician.

ゆいぶつ【唯物】 **—史観**(史的唯物論) historical materialism. **—論** materialism. **—論者** a materialist.

ゆう【勇】 courage ; bravery. ¶ 彼は～を鼓して立ち上がり意見を述べた He *dared* (≒ *took courage* ; *summoned up his courage*) *to* stand up and tell his opinion.

ゆう【雄】 ¶ 彼は一方の～だ He is *the leader* of his group. 彼は言論界の～だ He is one of *the greatest men* of the press.

ゆう【優】 (成績の) excellent ; A.

全**—** ¶ 彼は全～というりっぱな成績をおさめた He had a good school record of straight A's.

ゆう【夕】 an evening. ¶ 朝に～に彼のために祈った *Day in and day out* I prayed for him.

ゆ・う【結う】 ¶ 髪を～う *dress* (≒ *do* 〔*up*〕; *arrange*) *one's* hair. 彼女は母に髪を～ってもらった She *had* her hair *dressed* (≒ *done* ; *arranged*) by her mother. 家の周囲にかきねを～う *make* a fence around a house.

ゆうあい【友愛】 friendship ; fellowship ; fraternity.

ゆうい【有為】 ¶ 前途～の青年 a *promising* young man.

ゆうい【優位】 predominance ; superiority. ¶ 金持ちのほうが貧乏人より～に立っている The rich *are predominant over* the poor. 体力のおかげで彼は相手より～を占めた His physical strength *gave* him *an advantage over* his opponent. / Thanks to his health and strength, he *had the advantage of* the opponent.

ゆういぎ【有意義】significance; usefulness. ¶ ～な学校生活を送る lead a *useful* school life. ～にこの休みを過ごした I spent this vacation *to some* (≒ *good*) *purpose*.

ゆういん【誘因】an occasion; a cause.

ゆううつ【憂鬱】melancholy; gloom; dejection; depression; low spirits; despondency; the blues (米口語. 単数あつかいが多い).

¶ ～な天気が続く We have had *gloomy* weather. また試験かと思うと～だ I *feel gloomy* when I think of another examination. / The mere thought of another examination *drives me into a melancholy mood* (≒ *gives me a melancholy feeling*; *makes me dejected*). それを考えると～になる The idea *gives* me *the blues*. ～になった I fell into *despondency*. / I became *despondent*. ～な気持ちで一日じゅう家にとじこもっていた I *moped myself* at home all day. 彼女は～な顔をしている She looks *blue* (≒ *gloomy*). / She *pulls a long face*.

—症 melancholia; hypochondria. —症患者 a hypochondriac.

ゆうえい【遊泳】swimming. ¶ 彼は人生～術がうまい He is wise in the way of life. / He knows well how to get along in the world.

—禁止 (掲示) No Swimming Here.

ゆうえき【有益】¶ ～な (有利な) profitable; (ためになる) instructive; (有用な) useful. 時間と金をできるだけ～に使いなさい *Make the best* (≒ *Make the most*) *of* your time and money. あの講演は～だった That lecture *was instructive* (≒ *was profitable*). / I *profited* (≒ *benefited*) by the lecture. この本は初心者に～だ This book *is useful* (≒ *is of great use*) to the beginners. 朝の軽い運動は健康に～だ Light exercise in the morning *is good for* (≒ *is beneficial to*) the health. 彼のことばはいつも私にとって～だ His comments *are* always *helpful* to me.

ゆうえつ【優越】superiority; supremacy; predominance. ¶ 憲法はあらゆる法令に～する The Constitution is *the supreme* law of all laws and ordinances.

—感 a sense of superiority; a superiority complex.

ゆうえんたん【有煙炭】〔鉱物〕bituminous coal; soft coal.

ゆうえんち【遊園地】an amusement park; a recreation ground; a [public] pleasure ground.

ゆうか【有価】—証券 a negotiable instrument [paper]; securities. —物 valuables.

ゆうが【優雅】elegance; grace. ¶ 彼女は物腰の～な人だ She has a *graceful* manner. / She *is graceful in* manner. 少女たちは～に踊った The girls danced *with a grace* (≒ *gracefully*). ～な生活 an *elegant* life.

ゆうかい【融解】melting; (溶解) dissolution; (金属などの) fusion. ¶ 銑鉄は鋼よりたやすく～する Pig iron *is* more easily *fused* than steel.

—点 (融点) the melting point; the point of fusion. —熱 the melting heat; the heat of fusion.

ゆうかい【誘拐】kidnap[p]ing; abduction. ¶ 彼は子どもを～し身の代金を要求した He *kidnaped* (≒ *abducted*; *carried off*; *lured away*) the child for ransom.

—罪 abduction. —者 a kidnap[p]er; an abductor.

ゆうがい【有害】¶ ～な harmful; injurious; pernicious. たばこは体に～だ Smoking *is bad for* (≒ *is injurious to*) health. アルコールにふけることは恐ろしく～な習慣である Alcoholic addiction is a *pernicious* habit. 青少年に～な週刊誌やテレビ番組も少なくない Not a few weeklies and TV programs are found *harmful* (≒ *injurious*) to young people.

ゆうがい【有蓋】—貨車 米 a boxcar; 英 a covered (≒ box) waggon.

ゆうがお【夕顔】〔植物〕a bottle gourd.

ゆうかぜ【夕風】an evening breeze.

ゆうがた【夕方】evening. ¶ ～に in the *evening*. 土曜日の～に on Saturday *evening* (特定の日の夕方のときは, 前置詞は on). 彼はいつも～帰宅する He usually returns home *in the evening*. ～近く大きな地震があった There was a strong earthquake *toward evening*.

ゆうがとう【誘蛾燈】a light trap.

ユーカリ〔植物〕a eucalyptus.

ゆうかん【夕刊】(夕刊専門紙) an evening paper; (朝刊に対して) an evening edition.

ゆうかん【勇敢】bravery; audacity; boldness. ¶ ～な人 a *brave* (≒ *courageous*) man. ～な民族 a *heroic* people. 彼の～な行為が皆に賞賛された His *gallant* (≒ *brave*; *heroic*) deed was applauded by everybody. ～に戦う fight *bravely*.

ゆうき【有期】¶ 彼は～刑を宣告された He was sentenced to imprisonment *for a definite term*.

ゆうき【有機】¶ 二つの概念は～的に中心課題に結びついている Both ideas are *organically* connected with the central theme.

—化学 organic chemistry. —体 an organic body; organism. —物 organic matter.

ゆうき【勇気】courage. ¶ 彼は～のある男だ He is a *courageous* man. / He is a man *of courage*. ～を出せ Don't *be discouraged*! / Take (≒ Pluck up) *courage*! ～を失った I have lost *heart* (≒ *courage*). / I *was discouraged*. 二度とやる～を失った I *am discouraged from* trying again. 彼はけっして～を失わなかった His *courage* never failed him. その失敗を彼に話す～がない I have no *courage to* (≒ I *dare not*) tell the failure to him. 彼は友だちにほめられて～づいた He *was encouraged* by the praise of his friends. 彼の励ましでチームは～百倍した His advice gave the

ゆ

team a lot of *courage.* / His advice *bolstered* 〔*up*〕 the team greatly. 私たちは～を奮い起こした We mustered 〔up〕 all our *courage.*

ゆうぎ【遊戯・遊技】a play ; (勝負) a game ; (競技) a sport ; (娯楽) a pastime. ¶ きみの言っているのはことばの～にすぎない What you say is only *a play* of words.

—場 (運動場) a playground ; (娯楽場) a place of amusement. **—**施設 recreation facilities.

ゆうぎ【友誼】friendship ; friendly relations. ¶ 彼は～に厚い男だ He *is true* (≒ *is very kind ; is faithful*) *to* his friends. 何人かの幼友だちが昔の～から私に手を貸してくれた Some friends from my childhood helped me out of old *friendship.* 長年仲のわるかった両者間に～が成立した *Friendly relations* were formed between the two who had been on bad terms for years.

ゆうきゅう【有給】**—**休暇 a paid holiday.

ゆうきゅう【遊休】**—**資金 unemployed (≒ idle) capital. **—**施設 idle facilities (≒ equipment).

ゆうきゅう【悠久】eternity. ¶ 彼は～の大義に生きんと欲した He wished to devote his life to the *everlasting* (≒ *eternal*) cause. この国には～二千年の歴史がある This country has a *very long* history of two thousand years.

ゆうきょう【遊興】pleasure ; merrymaking. ¶ ～にふける pursue (≒ indulge in) *pleasure.*

—税 the amusement tax. **—**費 the expense for pleasures.

ゆうぎり【夕霧】an evening mist.

ゆうぐう【優遇】good treatment. ¶ 行く先々で～された We *were received favorably* (≒ *were treated with hospitality ; were entertained greatly*) everywhere we went. 経験者を～します We'll *pay a good salary* to experienced hands. 心身障害者は法律上～措置をされるべきだ The handicapped should *be treated considerately* at law.

ゆうぐれ【夕暮れ】evening. ⇒ゆうがた

ゆうぐん【友軍】friendly forces ; (連合軍) an allied army.

ゆうぐん【遊軍】a flying column ; reserve forces.

ゆうげ【夕餉】supper ; (正餐) dinner.

ゆうけい【有形】materiality. ¶ 彼から～無形の援助を受けた I received support, both *material* and moral, from him.

—財産〘法律〙corporeal property.

ゆうげい【遊芸】elegant accomplishments. ¶ 彼は～のたしなみがある He enjoys *artistic things.* 彼女は子女に～を仕込んだ She gave her children *artistic training.*

ゆうげき【遊撃】a raid ; a diversion.

—手〘野球〙a shortstop. **—**戦 guerilla warfare. **—**隊 (陸軍) a flying column ; (海軍) a flying squadron.

ゆうげしき【夕景色】an evening view. ¶ 琵琶湖の～は美しい Lake Biwa is beautiful in the evening.

ゆうけん【郵券】a postage stamp.

ゆうげん【有限】limitedness.

—会社 ㊐a corporation ; ㊧a limited liability company. **—**数 a finite number. **—**級数 a finite series.

ゆうげん【幽玄】profundity ; mystery. ¶ 彼の芸術は～だ His art strikes one with its *mystic quality.* / *Subtlety* is the soul of his art.

ゆうけんしゃ【有権者】a voter ; ㊧ an elector ; (総称) the electorate.

ゆうこう【友好】friendship ; amity. ¶ 日本はアメリカと～関係を維持している Japan maintains *friendly relations with* the United States. / Japan *is on friendly terms with* the United States. 話し合いは～的に進められている Negotiations are under way *in an amicable and cordial atmosphere.*

—国 a friendly nation.

ゆうこう【有効】(法規など) validity ; (薬など) efficacy. ¶ ～である hold good ; be in effect. ～になる take effect ; come into force. もっと～な手段をとるべきだ We should take more *effective* measures. この保証書の～期間は１か年だ This guarantee *is effective* for one year. 時間をできるだけ～に用いなさい Spend your time *to the best advantage.* この切符は７日間 (当日限り)～だ This ticket *is good* (≒ *is effective*) for seven days (on the day of issue only). この条約は10年～だ The treaty *remains in force* for ten years. 法廷はその契約を～と裁定した The court ruled the contract *valid.* この規定は依然～だ The regulation still *stands.* この薬はこのような病症には～だ This medicine *is effective* in such cases.

—期間 term of validity. **—**距離 effective range (*of* a gun). **—**数字〘数学〙a significant figure. **—**投票 a valid ballot.

ゆうごう【融合】fusion ; union. ¶ 両民族が～して一国民となった The two races *united* (≒ *merged*) *into* one nation. たがいの心が～するように感じた We felt as if our hearts *united into one.*

核**—**反応〘物理〙nuclear fusion.

ゆうこく【夕刻】evening ; the evening hour.

ゆうこく【憂国】¶ ～の志士 a patriot. ～の情 patriotism ; a patriotic sentiment.

ゆうこん【雄渾】grandeur ; sublimity ; magnificence. ¶ ～な筆致 a *bold* stroke of the pen. ～な文体 a *vigorous* (≒ *pithy*) style.

ゆうざい【有罪】guilt. ¶ 彼は～の宣告を受けた He *was found guilty.* / He *was convicted.* 彼の～が確定した His *guilt* was confirmed (≒ was proved). 彼は殺人事件で～を宣告された He *was convicted of* murder.

ゆうさんかいきゅう【有産階級】the propertied (≒ moneyed) classes ; the bourgeoisie.

ゆうし【有史】¶ それは～以来初めての出来事だった The event was the first of its kind *in history.*

ゆうし【有志】an interested person ; a volunteer ; a supporter. ¶ ～の者が集まった

ゆ

Volunteers (≒ *Those interested*) got together. これは～一同からの贈り物です This is a gift from *all concerned*. ～の方は参加してください If you *are interested*, please join us.

ゆうし【勇士】 a brave man (≒ soldier); a hero. ¶ 第2次大戦の～ *a* World War II *veteran*.

ゆうし【雄姿】 a gallant (≒ majestic) figure. ¶ 彼は人前にさっそうとその～を現わした He *made a gallant appearance* before the public. 富士山の～を遠くに望むことができる This place enjoys *a majestic view* of Mt. Fuji in the distance.

ゆうし【融資】 (貸し付け) financing; (貸付金) a loan; (資金) funds; money. ¶ 銀行から～を受けた He *borrowed money* from the bank. 銀行は会社に～を行なった The bank *furnished* the company *with funds*.

ゆうしかいひこう【有視界飛行】 visual flying.

ゆうしかく【有資格】 —者 a qualified person. 教員—者 a certificated teacher.

ゆうしきしゃ【有識者】 a well-informed person.

ゆうしゃ【勇者】 a brave man.

ゆうしゅう【有終】 perfection. ¶ ～の美を飾る bring (*a thing*) to perfection. この発見は彼の長い研究生活に～の美を飾った This discovery was a final triumph that *brought* his years of research *to perfection*.

ゆうしゅう【憂愁】 melancholy; gloom. ¶ 事故の報に家族たちは～にとざされている His relatives *are grief-stricken at* the news of the accident.

ゆうしゅう【優秀】 excellence; superiority. ¶ ～な技術者 a technical expert *of superior ability*. ～な学者 a *brilliant* scholar. 学力～ *excellence* (≒ *distinction*) *in* scholarship. 最～選手 the most *valuable* player. 彼は～な成績をあげた He *did very well*. / He *distinguished himself in* his work. / He *made a fine record*.

ゆうじゅうふだん【優柔不断】 indecision; irresolution; vacillation. ¶ 彼は～な男だ He is an *irresolute* person. 彼は～でどうも煮え切らない He can never make up his mind.

ゆうしょう【有償】 ¶ 地所を～で払いさげる make transference of property *for payment*.
—契約 a contract made for a consideration.

ゆうしょう【勇将】 a brave general. ¶ ～のもとに弱卒なし (諺) There are no cowards under a brave general. / *Like master, like men*.

ゆうしょう【優勝】 (勝利) a victory; (選手権) championship. ¶ そのチームは初～を飾った The team *won* its first *championship*. ～の行方は混沌(こんとん)としている There is no telling who will *win the championship*.
—旗 a championship banner; a penant. —者 a winner; a champion. —チーム a champion team. —杯 a championship cup; a trophy; a cup.

ゆうじょう【友情】 〔a〕 friendship. ¶ 彼の～に打たれた I was struck with the sincerity of his *friendship*. ふたりの間に暖かい～が芽生えた *A* warm *friendship* sprang up between the two. 彼は～に厚い He is a *friendly* person.

ゆうしょく【夕食】 supper; an evening meal.

ゆうしょく【有色】 —人種 a colored race.

ゆうしょく【憂色】 a worried look; gloom. ¶ 悲報に家族は～にとざされていた The family *were in a state of deep anxiety* on hearing the sad news.

ゆうじん【友人】 a friend. ¶ 彼は私の～だ He is *a friend* of mine. 私の～のジャックはアメリカ人だ My *friend* Jack is an American. (my friend は特定の友人の場合に用いる). 私は～が多い I have a lot of *friends*. 彼と～になった I *made friends with* him. ～代表としてあいさつする speak a few words on behalf of *friends*.

ゆうしんろん【有神論】 theism.
—者 a theist; one who believes in God.

ゆうすい【幽邃】 ¶ ～の境に住む live in a *secluded* place.

ゆうすう【有数】 ¶ 彼はわが国～の外科医だ He is an *eminent* surgeon of this county. / He is one of *the foremost* surgeons of this country. ～の輸出国 a *leading* export country.

ゆうずう【融通】 (金融) accommodation; finance; (順応性) adaptability; flexibility. ¶ 100万円ばかり～してください Please *lend* me a million yen. 計画の資金は～しましょう I will undertake to *finance* the project. 彼が求めている金を～することはできない I cannot *lend* him the money he wants. 彼は～のきかない男だ He lacks *flexibility*. / He is an *obstinate* man. 彼は～のきく男だ He is an *adaptable* person. 規則を適用するにもときに～をきかせることが必要だ It is sometimes necessary to *make allowances* for circumstances in applying rules.
—手形 an accommodation bill; a negotiable paper.

ゆうすずみ【夕涼み】 ¶ ～に公園まで行く go to a park to *enjoy the evening cool*.

ユースホステル a youth hostel.

ゆう·する【有する】 possess; own. ⇒もつ(持つ)

ゆうせい【有声】 —音 a voiced sound.

ゆうせい【有性】 —生殖 〖生物〗 sexual reproduction.

ゆうせい【郵政】 —省 the Ministry of Postal Services. —大臣 the Minister of Postal Services.

ゆうせい【遊星】 〖天文学〗 a planet.
小— a planetoid.

ゆうせい【優生】 —学 eugenics. —結婚 a eugenic marriage. —保護法 the Eugenic Protection Act.

ゆうせい【優性】 〖生物〗 dominance.
—遺伝 prepotence.

ゆうせい【優勢】 superiority; ascendancy. ¶ わが軍は数において敵より～だった We *were* *superior* in number *to* the enemy. / We *outnumbered* the enemy. 圧倒的に～な敵に包囲された We were surrounded by an overwhelmingly *powerful* enemy unit. はじめは相手チームのほうが～だった At first the opponent team *was ahead of* us (≒ *was doing better*). わが党は依然として～を保っている Our party *is* still *in the lead.*

ゆうぜい【郵税】 postage. ¶ この手紙の～はいくらですか What is the *postage on* this letter? ～40円不足だ There is 40 yen *postage due.*
—不要 post-free; free of postal charge. —前払い postage prepaid; postpaid. —不足 postage due.

ゆうぜい【遊説】 electioneering; canvassing; stumping. ¶ 彼は全国を選挙～してまわった He made *an electioneering tour* of the whole country. 彼は～のため西下した He went to the western part of the country to *make a series of campaign speeches.*

ゆうせん【有線】 —電信（電話）telegraph (telephone). —放送 a broadcasting system; (テレビ) closed-circuit television.

ゆうせん【優先】 priority. ¶ ～順位 the order of *priority.* 安全がすべてに～するべきだ Safety should be *the first consideration.* 国民の福祉を他のなによりも～させている The welfare of the people is given *the highest* (≒ *a top*) *priority.* 本校卒業生の子弟は～的に入学させる *Priority* is given to the children of the graduates of this school in deciding admission.
—権 the preference; the priority. ¶ 会員には施設使用の～権がある Members *have the preference in* the use of the facilities. だれに～権を与えるかが問題だ The question is whom to give *priority.*

ゆうぜん【悠然】 calmly; leisurely. ¶ なにが起こっても彼は～としている Whatever happens, he *remains unperturbed.*

ゆうそう【勇壮】 ¶ ～な働き a *brave* deed. ～活発な行進曲 a *heroic* march.

ゆうそう【郵送】 mailing; sending by mail. ¶ その本を1部～してください *Send* me a copy of the book *by mail* (≒ 英 *by post*).
—料 postage. —無料 postage free.

ゆうだ【遊惰】 laziness. ¶ 彼は～な毎日を過ごしている He *idles his days away.* / He lives an *idle* life from day to day.

ユーターン a U-turn. ¶ ～禁止（掲示）No U-turn.

ゆうたい【有体】 —資産 tangible assets. —動産 corporeal property.

ゆうたい【勇退】 voluntary retirement (≒ resignation). ¶ 彼は政界から～した He *retired from* the political world. 彼は定年を前にして～した He *retired* just before reaching the age limit.

ゆうたい【優待】 preferential treatment; welcome; hospitality; generous treatment. ¶ ～する give preferential treatment (*to a person*); welcome; receive (*a person*) warmly.
—券 a complimentary ticket.

ゆうだい【雄大】 grandeur; magnificence; sublimity. ¶ ～ながめ a *magnificent* (≒ *sublime*) view. ～な山脈 a *majestic* range of mountains. 計画の規模が～だ This plan *is on a grand scale.*

ゆうだち【夕立】 a [summer] shower. ¶ 私は～に会った I was caught in *a shower.*
—雲 a shower cloud.

ゆうだん【勇断】 a resolute decision. ¶ 関係当局の～が期待される The authorities concerned are expected to *take drastic measures.*

ゆうだんしゃ【有段者】 a person who holds a [certain] rank.

ゆうち【誘致】 a lure; attraction; enticement. ¶ 観光客を～する *attract* tourists. 町に工場を～する *invite* factories *to* the town.

ゆうちょう【悠長】 ¶ 彼はなにをするにも～だ He *takes his time in* whatever he does. / He is always *a slow worker.*

ゆうてん【融点】〘物理〙 the melting point; the fusing point.

ゆうでん【誘電】〘電気〙 induced electricity.
—子 an inductor. —体 a dielectric. —率 a dielectric constant.

ゆうと【雄図】 an ambitious design (≒ plan); a daring undertaking. ¶ ～むなしく引き返さざるをえなかった We had to turn back without realizing our *ambition.* 彼の～もむなしく潰えた His *ambitious plan* failed.

ゆうとう【優等】 excellence; honors. ¶ 彼は大学を～で卒業した He graduated from the university *with honors.*
—生 an honor student. —賞 ¶ 彼は～賞を受けた He was awarded *an honor* prize.

ゆうとう【遊蕩】 dissipation. ¶ ～にふける live a life of *dissipation.*
—児 a libertine; a prodigal person.

ゆうどう【誘導】 inducement;〘電気〙 induction. ¶ 飛行機は管制塔の～によって着陸した The plane landed following the *instructions* of the control tower. 船長は難破船を港に～した The captain *led* the damaged ship to the port.
—コイル an induction coil. —者 a guide; a conductor. —尋問 ¶ 彼は被告に～尋問した He asked the defendant *a leading question.* —体 a conductor. —弾 a guided missile. —電気 induced electricity.

ゆうとく【有徳】 ¶ ～の人 a man of virtue.

ゆうどく【有毒】 —ガス poisonous gas.

ユートピア a Utopia.

ゆうなぎ【夕凪ぎ】 an evening calm.

ゆうに【優に】 ¶ 彼の月収は～100万をこえる His monthly income is *well* over a million. 彼が出てから～2時間はたつ It is a *good* two hours since he left. 彼の背は～180センチはある He stands more than 180 centimeters. その部屋は～50人入る The room can hold 50 people *easily.*

ゆ

ゆうのう【有能】ability; competence. ¶ ～の士 a man *of ability*; an *able* man; a *competent* man.

ゆうばえ【夕映え】the evening glow. ¶ ～の空が美しい *The evening glow* is beautiful.

ゆうはつ【誘発】¶ 大火は地震によって～された The big fire *was caused* by the earthquake. 米価のつり上げは諸物価の高騰を～する A rise in the price of rice will *result in* a rise in the prices of commodities.

ゆうばれ【夕晴れ】a fine evening sky.

ゆうはん【夕飯】supper; an evening meal; dinner (一日の主要な食事を dinner と言い, ふつう夕食が dinner だが, 日曜などの昼に dinner をとれば, 夕食は supper と言う).

ゆうひ【夕日】the setting (≒ evening; declining) sun. ¶ ～が部屋にさしこむ *The setting sun* shines into the room. ～が長い影をおとしていた *The evening sun* cast (≒ threw) long shadows.

ゆうひ【雄飛】¶ 彼は海外に～する夢をいだいている He dreams that he will *go overseas* (≒ *go abroad*) *to do something great.*

ゆうび【優美】grace; elegance. ¶ 彼は彼女の～な姿に引かれた He was attracted by her *graceful* figure.

ゆうびん【郵便】㊍ mail; ㊇ post; (手紙) a letter.

1〖郵便は〗¶ きょうの～はまだ来ませんか Hasn't today's *mail* come yet?

アメリカまで～は何日かかりますか How many days does it take for *mail* to reach America?

～は1日に何回配達されますか How many times each day is the *mail* delivered? / How many *deliveries* are there every day?

2〖郵便が〗¶ 全逓のストで～が大幅に遅れている The *mail* is delayed on a large scale because of the strike of the All Communication Employees' Union.

先週出した～がもどってきてしまった The *letter* I sent last week was returned.

3〖郵便で〗¶ けさの～でこの手紙が来ました This letter came in the morning *mail.*

この荷物を～で送ったらいつ着きますか If this package is sent by parcel *post,* when will it arrive?

入学願書は～で受け付けてくれる Applications for admission are accepted by *mail.*

4〖郵便を〗¶ ～を投函(とうかん)する *mail* (≒ ㊇ *post*) a letter.

けさはまだ～を集めに来ない They haven't come to collect the *mail* yet this morning. / The *mail* (≒ ㊇ *post*) hasn't been collected this morning yet.

5〖郵便に〗¶ ～による問い合わせが殺到している *Letters* of inquiry are pouring in.

申し込みは必ず～によること Applications should be made by *mail.*

―受け ㊍ a mailbox; ㊇ a letter box; a mail drop. ―為替 ㊍ a postal (≒ post) money order (p.m.o.); ㊇ a post-office order (p.o.o.). ―切手 a postage stamp. ―業務 mail service; postal service; mail business. ―局 a post office; ㊇ a post. ―局員 ㊍ a mail clerk; ㊇ a post clerk. ―局長 a postmaster. ―小包〔small〕parcel; package. ―私書箱 a post-office box (P.O.B., POB., P.O. Box). ―制度 postal system. ―船 a mail boat; a mail steamer; ㊇ a post boat. ―貯金 postal (≒ post-office) savings. ―貯金通帳 a postal savings passbook; a post-office savings bankbook. ―年金 a post-office (≒ postal) annuity; the mail pension system. ―配達 mail delivery. ―配達人 ㊍ a mailman; ㊇ a postman. ―はがき ㊍ a postal card; ㊇ a postcard. ―番号 ㊍ zip code; Zip code; ZIP code. ―物 postal (≒ mail) matter. ―ポスト ㊍ a mailbox; ㊇ a postbox; a letter box; a post. ―料金 postage; postal charges. 外国― foreign mail. 書留― registered mail (≒ ㊇ post). 局留め― general delivery; (封筒上の指示文句) poste restante. 軍事― ㊍ military mail (≒ ㊇ post). 航空― air mail. 国内― domestic mail (≒ ㊇ post). 集配―局 a distributing post office. 速達― special delivery; express mail (≒ ㊇ post). 第1種―物 first-class mail. 第3種―物 third-class mail. 中央―局 the Central Post Office.

ゆうふく【裕福】affluence; prosperity. ¶ 彼は～だ He *is well*[-]*off* (≒ *well-to-do*). 彼は～な家に生まれた He was born *rich.* ～に暮らす live in *affluence* (≒ *easy circumstances*).

ゆうべ【夕べ】an evening. ¶ 秋の～に on *an* autumn *evening.* 音楽の～を催す have *a* musical *evening.*

ゆうべ【昨夜】last night (≒ evening).

ゆうへい【幽閉】confinement. ¶ 彼はロンドン塔に～されていた He *was confined* (≒ *was imprisoned*) in the Tower of London.

ゆうべん【雄弁】eloquence; fluency. ¶ 彼は～をふるった He spoke *eloquently* (≒ *with eloquence*). / He made *a powerful speech.*

ゆうほう【友邦】a friendly nation.

ゆうぼう【有望】¶ ～な青年 a *promising* young man; a young man *of promise.* 彼の商売は前途～だ His business has *bright prospects* for the future. 彼女は前途～だ She has a *bright* (≒ *rosy*) future.

ゆうぼく【遊牧】nomadism. ¶ ～生活を送る live a *nomadic* life.

―民族 a nomadic tribe.

ゆうほどう【遊歩道】a promenade.

ゆうめい【有名】¶ ～な famous; (悪名高い) notorious. ～な歴史家 a *famous* historian. ～な詐欺師 a *notorious* swindler. 彼は詩人として～だ He *is famous* (≒ *is famed*) as a poet. 日本の労働者は勤勉さで～だ Workers of Japan *are famous* (≒ *are well-known*) *for* diligence. 世界的に～な物理学者 a physicist *of* world-wide *fame*; a *world-famous* physicist. この店はコーヒーがうまいので～

ゆ

だ This shop *is noted for* its good coffee. 彼は教育の分野では～な人物だ He is *a big name* in education.

―校 a big-name school. ―人 a big name; a celebrity.

ゆうめい【勇名】 ¶ その戦闘で彼は～をとどろかせた He *was famous for* his brave act in the battle.

ゆうめいむじつ【有名無実】 ¶ それは～の委員会だ It is a *nominal* committee. その協定は今や～だ The treaty *is* now *little more than a name.*

ユーモア humor; 英 humour. ¶ きみは～を解するね You have a sense of *humor.* 彼女は～を解さない She has no sense of *humor.* 彼は～たっぷりに話した He told *with much humor.* 彼は～のある人だ He is a *humorous* person.

―作家 a humorous writer. ―小説 a humorous novel.

ゆうもう【勇猛】 bravery. ¶ ～果敢な探検家 a *fearless* explorer.

―心. ¶ ～心を奮い起こして戦う *summon up courage* to fight.

ゆうもや【夕靄】 evening dusk.

ユーモラス humorous. ¶ 人生の～な面 the *humorous* side of life.

ゆうやく【勇躍】 ¶ ～して in high spirits.

ゆうやけ【夕焼け】 the sunset (≒ evening) glow; the glow at sunset.

ゆうやみ【夕闇】 dusk; 〔evening〕 twilight. ¶ ～迫るころ彼らは家路を急いだ At *dusk* (≒ *nightfall*) they hurried home. ～になった *Evening dusk* is gathering.

ゆうゆう【悠悠】 ¶ ～とたばこを吸う smoke *serenely* (≒ *at ease*). 雨が降りはじめたが彼は～と歩きつづけた He walked on *calmly* though it began to rain. 彼は～1着になった He won the first place *without difficulty.* ～自適する live in comfort.

ゆうよ【猶予】 (遅延) 〔a〕 delay; (延期) 〔a〕 postponement; (支払いなどの) grace; (刑の) a respite; a reprieve.

¶ 準備のためしばらくの～をください Give me *some time* to prepare for it. 2時間の～をあげよう I will give you two hours' *grace.* 一刻の～もすべき場合でない There is no time to *lose* (≒ *be lost*). / The situation admits of no *delay.* 彼は刑の執行を3か月～された He *was reprieved* for three months. 彼らは3か月の～期間の後解雇された They were dismissed after three months' *grace.*

執行― a stay of execution; probation. 徴兵― temporary exemption from conscription (≒ military service).

ゆうよう【有用】 ¶ ～な useful. 社会の～な一員 a *useful* member of the society. それがきみにとって～だ That *is helpful* to you.

ゆうよう【悠揚】 ¶ ～せまらぬ態度で with an air *of perfect composure*; with a *serene* air. ～せまらず calmly; complacently; self-composediy.

ユーラシア Eurasia.

―大陸 the Eurasian Continent.

ゆうらん【遊覧】 sightseeing. ¶ 彼は1か月のヨーロッパ～旅行をした He made a month's *sightseeing* trip through Europe. 彼は用事と～を兼ねてアメリカへ行った He went over to America on business and *for pleasure.*

―船 a pleasure boat. ―地 a pleasure (≒ holiday) resort. ―バス a sightseeing bus (≒ 英 coach).

ゆうり【有利】 ¶ ～な profitable. ～な取引 a *profitable* deal. ～な条件 *advantageous* (≒ *profitable*; *favorable*) conditions. きみは～な立場にいる You are in an *advantageous* position. 彼は人より～な位置を占めた He got (≒ gained; had) *an advantage* (≒ *the upper hand*) *over* the others. 局面がわれわれに～に展開した The state of affairs turned to our *advantage.* / The situation turned out *favorable* to us. ～な条件を生かしきれば成功する If you make the most of the *advantageous* (≒ *profitable*; *favorable*) conditions, you are sure to succeed.

ゆうり【有理】 〖数学〗 ―式 a rational expression. ―数 a rational number.

ゆうり【遊離】 isolation; separation; alienation. ¶ きみのは現実から～した計画だ Your plan *is far from* realistic. あの作家は社会から～している That writer *is alienated from* society.

ゆうりょ【憂慮】 anxiety. ¶ われわれは国家の前途を～する We *are* (≒ *feel*) deeply *concerned about* the future of our country. 彼女は息子の健康を～した She *was anxious about* her son's health. 公害の及ぼす影響は～すべき程度に達している Pollution has affected us to a *serious* degree. その大学は～すべき事態にある The college is in a *grave* (≒ *critical*) situation.

ゆうりょう【有料】 ¶ その講演会は～だ The admission *is charged* for the lecture meeting. 天気予報を電話で聞くのは～だ Asking weather forecast by telephone *is charged.*

―道路 a toll road. ―便所 a pay toilet. ―電話 a pay telephone. ―試写会 a charged preview.

ゆうりょう【遊猟】 hunting; shooting.

¶ ～に出かける go 〔out〕 *hunting.*

―家 a sportsman; a hunter; a huntsman. ―期 the shooting season. ―禁止期 the close season.

ゆうりょう【優良】 superiority; excellence. ¶ ～な品 *superior* goods.

ゆうりょく【有力】 influence; power. ¶ ～な相手 a *powerful* rival. ～な証拠 a *strong* evidence. ～な新聞 a *leading* newspaper. 軍備縮小の～な賛成論 a *strong* (≒ *convincing*) argument for disarmament. われわれの中に悲観的な見方が～になってきた A pessimistic outlook *has been prevailing* among us. 彼はもっとも～な優勝候補だ He is *the likeliest* winner. その問題に関する～な情報を入手した We

ゆ

have received *reliable* information on the subject.

—者 an influential man. ¶ 町の～者たち *influential* men in the town.

ゆうれい【幽霊】a ghost ; an apparition ; a specter. ¶ あそこには～が出るというううわさだ They say that place is haunted by *ghosts*.

—会社 a bogus company. —船 a phantom ship. —屋敷 a haunted house.

ゆうれつ【優劣】superiority or (≒ and) inferiority. ¶ これら3者の間ではほとんど～がつけがたい There is little to choose among these three. 両者の意見の～を論じる discuss the *merits and demerits* of the opinions of the both parties. 腕に覚えのある面々が～を争った Those who were confident of their ability struggled for mastery.

ゆうわ【融和】(調和) harmony ; (和解) reconciliation. ¶ 家具の色が部屋に～している The colors of furniture *harmonize with* the room. 彼は他人と～して働く性質だ He has a disposition to work *harmonizing* (≒ *in harmony*) *with* others. この国はアメリカと～した The country *got reconciled with* America.

ゆうわく【誘惑】temptation ; seduction. ¶ 彼は悪への～に抵抗した He resisted *temptation* to evil. ～なんかされるものか I would not fall before *temptation* for anything. 彼らは金で彼を～した They *allured* him with money. 男は少女を甘言で～した The man *seduced* the girl with honeyed words.

ゆえ【故】(理由) a reason ; (原因) a cause ; (事情) circumstances. ¶ ～あって夫と別れた I divorced my husband *for a certain reason* (≒ *under the inevitable circumstances*). 彼は～なくして侮辱された He was insulted *for nothing* (≒ *without cause*). 彼が不平を言うのも～なきことではない He complains *with reason*. / He complains, *and with reason*.

ゆえん【所以】reason ; ground ; cause. ¶ これが私が彼を推す～だ This is [*the reason*] *why* I recommend him. これが人の人たる～だ This is *why* man is what he is.

ゆえん【油煙】lampblack ; lamp soot.

ゆか【床】a floor. ¶ 家の～を張る *floor* a house.

—板 floorboards. —運動 floor exercise (≒ gymnastics). —張り flooring.

ゆかい【愉快】pleasure ; delight. ¶ そいつは～だ That's *fun*. / What *fun*! 先日は実に～でした I *had a* very *good time* the other day. / I *enjoyed myself* very much the other day. 彼はとても～な人だ He *is* great *fun*. (無冠詞に注意). 気楽な旅をするのは私には実に～だ It gives me *a* great *pleasure* to travel easily. 彼女は～な性質だ She has a *pleasant* (≒ *cheerful*) disposition. それは～な驚きだ It is a *delightful* surprise.

ゆかうえ【床上】¶ 多くの家が～浸水した A lot of houses were flooded *above the floor level*.

ゆかし・い【床しい】(りっぱな) admirable ; (なつかしい) charming ; sweet ; (上品な) refined. ¶ ～い行為 an *admirable* deed. ～い人たち *refined* (≒ *graceful*) people.

ゆかした【床下】¶ 何百軒もの家が～浸水した Hundreds of houses were flooded *below the floor level*.

ゆかた【浴衣】a light summer *kimono*.

ゆがみ【歪み】distortion ; contortion ; a warp. ¶ ここ20年の間にこの家は～が生じた This house *has been warped* in the past twenty years.

ゆが・む【歪む】¶ 彼の～んだ心が気にくわない I don't like his *crooked* mind. 彼は苦痛に～んだ顔をしていた He had a face *distorted* (≒ *twisted*) with pain.

ゆが・める【歪める】¶ 新聞記者は記事を書くときに事実を～めてはならない A journalist should not *pervert* (≒ *distort*) the facts in making a report. 彼は痛さで顔を～めた He *distorted* his face in his pain.

ゆかり【縁】connection ; relation ; acquaintance. ¶ 鎌倉は頼朝～の地だ Kamakura is a place *noted in connection with* Yoritomo. 彼には縁も～もない He is *a perfect stranger to* me. / I don't have any *connection* whatever *with* him.

ゆかん【湯灌】¶ ～をする wash a dead body for burial.

ゆき【雪】snow. ¶ ～の日 a *snowy* day. ～深い山々 *snow-covered* mountains. ～が降る It *snows*. ～が降りそうだ It looks like *snow*. 今夜は～だろう It will *snow* tonight. / We shall have *snow* tonight. この冬は～がほとんど降らなかった We have had little *snow* this winter. ～が降りしきる It *is snowing* heavily (≒ hard ; thick and fast). ～が2メートル積もっている The *snow* lies two meters deep. 10年来の大～だ It is the heaviest *snowfall* we have had in the last ten years. / We have never seen such *a* heavy *snowfall* as this for the last ten years. 列車は～で立ち往生した The train *was snowed under*. われわれは汽車の中で～に閉じこめられた We *were snowed in*, in a railway train. 村は冬じゅう～に閉じ込められる The village *is snowed in* (≒ *is snow-bound*) through[out] winter.

粉— fine (≒ powdery) snow. 初— the first snow [of the season]. ぼたん— snow in large flakes. 万年— perpetual (≒ eternal ; everlasting) snow.

ゆき【行き】¶ 東京～[直通]列車 a [through] train *for* Tokyo. ～は船で帰りは飛行機で沖縄へ行ってきた I went to Okinawa by ship and came back home by plane. この列車はどこ～ですか Where is this train *for*?

ゆき【裄】the length of the sleeve. ¶ その服は私には～が足りない The dress is short for me *in the sleeves*.

ゆきあ・う【行き会う】encounter. ¶ 町で友人にぱったり～った I *met* [*with*] (≒ *came across* ; *encountered*) a friend on the street.

ゆきあたりばったり【行き当たりばったり】¶ ～のことば a *casual* remark. 彼は～の暮らし方をしている He lives *in a happy-go-lucky fashion.* ～に本を選ぶ choose books *in a haphazard way* (≒ *at random*).

ゆきあた・る【行き当たる】¶ まっすぐに行くと学校に～ります Go straight on, and you will *find* a school *at the end* (≒ *at the bottom*) of the street.

ゆきおとこ【雪男】 an Abominable Snowman; a Snowman.

ゆきおれ【雪折れ】¶ 庭の樹木が～した The snow has broken some of the plants in the garden. / Some branches of the trees in the garden were broken by snow. 柳の枝に～なし(諺) *Oaks may fall when reeds brave the storm.*

ゆきか・う【行き交う】 come and go. ¶ 広場は～う人の波で埋まった The square was filled with streams of people *coming and going.*

ゆきかえり【行き帰り】¶ ～とも列車は込んでいた The trains were crowded *both ways.*

ゆきがかり【行き掛かり】¶ ひとつ～を捨てて前向きに話し合いましょう Let's forget what has passed and talk about for the mutual benefit. ～上やらざるをえない *By* 〔*force of*〕 *circumstances,* I have to do it. / *Circumstances* force (≒ compell) me to do it.

ゆきかき【雪掻き】 snow shoveling; snow removal; (道具) snow shovel (≒ rake). ¶ 通路の～をする *shovel* (≒ *rake*; *sweep*) *away snow* from the footpath.

ゆきがけ【行き掛け】¶ 学校への～にこの手紙をポストに入れてくれ Post this letter *on your way to* school.

ゆきがっせん【雪合戦】 snowballing. ¶ ～をやる play 〔at〕 *snowballs*; have *a game of snowballing.*

ゆきき【行き来】 going and coming; traffic; (交際) intercourse. ¶ 通りは人の～も絶えていた There was no one to be seen on the street. / The street *was deserted.* 都会は人や車の～が激しい There is quite a lot of *traffic* in big cities. 彼とはあれから～がない I *have* never *exchanged visits with* him since then. 彼はだれとも～しない He does not *associate with* any one.

ゆきぐに【雪国】 a snow〔y〕 province (≒ country).

ゆきぐも【雪雲】 a snow cloud.

ゆきく・れる【行き暮れる】 be overtaken by darkness; be benighted.

ゆきげしき【雪景色】 a snow scene.

ゆきげしょう【雪化粧】¶ 野原も山も新雪で～している Both the fields and mountains *are dressed up with freshly fallen snow.*

ゆきけむり【雪煙】¶ ～を立ててスキーヤーはすべり降りていく The skiers are going downhill *with the spray of snow* (≒ *in a cloud of snow spray*).

ゆきさき【行き先】 *one's* destination. ¶ 彼の～がわからない I don't know where he has gone.

ゆきすぎ【行き過ぎ】¶ それはちょっときみの～だ You have gone a little too far there.

ゆきす・ぎる【行き過ぎる】¶ 何事も～ぎるのはよくない It is no good that you should *go too far* (≒ *go to extremes*) in anything.

ゆきずり【行きずり】¶ ～の人 a casual passer-by (複 passers-by).

ゆきぞら【雪空】 a snowy sky.

ゆきだおれ【行き倒れ】 a person dying (≒ dead) on the street.

ゆきだまり【雪だまり】 a snowdrift.

ゆきだるま【雪だるま】 a snowman. ¶ ～を作る make *a snowman.* ～式に小さな商売を大企業にする *snowball* a small business *into* a great enterprise.

ゆきちがい【行き違い】 (すれちがい) crossing; (誤解) misunderstanding; (不和) disagreement; estrangement.
¶ われわれの手紙は～になった Our letters *have crossed.* / Your letter *has crossed* mine. ふたりの間になにか～が生じた Some *misunderstanding* arose between the two. 彼は細君と～があった He had *a disagreement* with his wife. ふたりの間に～が生じた Some *estrangement* arose between them. / Something *estranged* them.

ゆきちが・う【行き違う】 cross. ¶ 私たちは道で～った We *crossed* each other on the road.

ゆきつ・く【行き着く】¶ 村に～いたのは夜中だった It was midnight when we *reached* the village. ～くところまでこの仕事をやる I will do the work *to the finish.*

ゆきつけ【行きつけ】¶ ～の食堂 *one's favorite* restaurant.

ゆきづまり【行き詰まり】 a deadlock; an impasse; a stalemate. ¶ ～を打開する break the *deadlock* (≒ *stalemate*).

ゆきづま・る【行き詰まる】¶ われわれの研究は資金不足のために～っている Our research *is at a standstill* for want of funds. 会は賃銀問題で～った The meeting *deadlocked* (≒ *came to a deadlock*) over the wage issue.

ゆきどけ【雪解け】 a thaw; 〔a〕 thawing. ¶ ～している It *is thawing.* ～の道 a *slushy* road. ～の国際関係 a *thawing* international scene.

ゆきどころ【行き所】¶ 彼の～がわからない Nobody knows about his *whereabouts.* / No one knows *where he is.* 私は～がない I don't have any *place to go.* (文尾にふつう to は付けない).

ゆきとど・く【行き届く】 be perfect; be complete. ¶ われわれは～いたもてなしを受けた We were treated with *great* (≒ *lavish*; *perfect*) hospitality. この部屋は掃除が～いている This room *is quite clean and tidy.* 彼の車は手入れが～いている His car *is in good running condition.* 当方に～かない点があったのは遺憾です We must apologize for our *neglect.*

ゆきどまり【行き止まり】 the dead end 〔of a

road (≒street)]; (袋小路) a blind alley.
¶ この道は～だ This is *a blind alley.*

ゆきなやみ【行き悩み】a deadlock. ¶ 交渉は～の状態だ The negotiation is at *a deadlock* (≒*a standstill*). / The negotiation has come to *a deadlock.* / The negotiation has been brought to *an impasse.*

ゆきなや·む【行き悩む】¶ 調査が～んでいる The investigation *has come to a deadlock.*

ゆきのした【雪の下】〖植物〗a creeping (≒strawberry) saxifrage.

ゆきみち【雪道】a snow-covered road.

ゆきもよう【雪模様】¶ 今夜は～だ It *is going to snow* tonight.

ゆきやけ【雪焼け】¶ スキーで～した I *got snow-tanned* while skiing.

ゆきやなぎ【雪柳】〖植物〗a spir[a]ea.

ゆきわた·る【行き渡る】prevail. ¶ お茶が～った Tea *went around.* 知らせはすぐ町じゅうに～った Soon the news *spread* all over the town. テレビは全国に～った (受像機が) Almost every home in this country has a television set. その風習がこの国で～っている The custom *prevails* in this country.

ゆきわりそう【雪割草】〖植物〗a mealy primrose; a hepatica.

ゆ·く【行く】**1**〖行く·通う〗go; (相手のところへ行く; 相手の行く方へ行く) come.
¶ 毎朝8時に学校へ～く I *go* to school at eight every morning.
来週パリへ～く予定だ I am to *leave for* Paris next week.
次の日曜日にきみのところへ～きます I will *come* and see you next Sunday. / I will *call on* you next Sunday.
今度の同窓会には～きますか *Are* you *coming* to the next alumni meeting? / Are you going to *attend* the next class reunion?
今ごろまでどこへ～っていたのです Where *have* you *been* all this while?
ヨーロッパへ～ったことがありますか *Have* you ever *been to* Europe?
このバスは日比谷へ～きますか Does this bus *go* to Hibiya?
私は毎日電車で会社へ～く I *go* (≒*commute*) to my office by train every day.
～きつもどりつした I walked to and fro.
2〖進行する·事が運ぶ〗go. ¶ 万事うまく～くといいが I hope everything *goes* well!
物事はそう思うようには～かないものだ Things don't always *go* as smoothly as you might expect.
計画はそう簡単には～かないだろう The plan won't *work* so easily.
あの夫婦はうまく～かない He *is* not *getting on well with* his wife. / They *are* not *getting on well* with each other.
3〖…してゆく〗¶ 軽く食事をして～こうか Shall we *start* after a light meal?
子どもの日だからケーキでも買って～こう Since it is Children's Day, I think I'll buy some cakes to take home.
どうだい, 映画でも見て～かないか How would you like to see a movie?
4〖その他〗¶ きょうの試合はこの作戦で～こう Let's take up this strategy for today's game.
それで納得が～った. That satisfied me.
いまになっては事業を投げ出すわけには～かない It is impossible for me to give up the business now.

ゆくえ【行方】*one's* whereabouts. ¶ 彼の～はわからない No one knows his *whereabouts.* / Nobody knows *where he is.* 警察は彼の～を捜している The police *are searching* (≒*are looking*) *for* him. 彼はその金を持って～をくらました He *disappeared* with the money. 誘拐(ゆうかい)された子どもの～はまだわからない There is still no *trace* of the kidnapped child.
—不明 ¶ 彼は～不明だ He *is missing.*

ゆくさき【行く先】a destination; (行方) whereabouts. ¶ 出かけるときは～を言って出かけなさい Tell us *where you are going* before you go out.

ゆくすえ【行く末】future. ¶ 親はみな子どもの～を案じる Parents are all anxious about their children's *future.*

ゆくて【行く手】*one's* way. ¶ われわれの～は多難だ We will be faced with a lot of difficulties *in future.*

ゆくゆく【行く行く】in the future; in due course.

ゆくりなくも unexpectedly; by chance.
¶ ～旧友に会った I *happened to* meet an old friend.

ゆげ【湯気】steam; vapor. ¶ やかんから～が立っている The kettle *is steaming* [hot]. / *Steam* is getting up (≒is rising) from the kettle. 紅茶から～があがっている The cup of tea *is steaming.*

ゆけつ【輸血】a blood transfusion. ¶ けが人は～をほどこされた The injured man was given *a blood transfusion.* 彼は弟のために～を申し出た He offered to *transfuse* his blood *into* his brother.

ゆさぶ·る【揺さ振る】¶ 政界を～った大事件があった There was a very notable incident which *gave a serious shock to* the political circles.

ゆざまし【湯冷まし】[cooled] boiled water.

ゆざめ【湯冷め】a chill after a bath. ¶ ～した I felt cold after a bath.

ゆし【油脂】oils and fats.

ゆし【諭旨】an official suggestion; a request; an admonition. ¶ 彼は～退学になった He withdrew from the school at the *advice* of the school authorities. 彼は～免官となった He resigned office at the *official suggestion.*

ゆしゅつ【輸出】export; exportation.
¶ 政府は石油の～を禁じた The government prohibited the *export* of petroleum. 現在～は輸入を超過している Our *exports* now exceed our imports. わが国は車をアメリカに～する We *export* automobiles to America.

ゆ

彼らは武器の～禁止を解いた They *lifted the embargo on* arms. ～を奨励する encourage *exports.*

—業 the export trade. **—業者** an exporter. **—港** an export port. **—税** an export duty. **—超過** an excess of exports over imports. **—手続き** customs formalities for export. **—品** an export; an article for export.

ゆしゅつにゅう【輸出入】exportation and importation; export and import. ¶ ～のバランスをとる adjust the balance of *trade.*

—貿易 export-import trade.

ゆず【柚・柚子】〖植物〗a citron.

ゆす·ぐ【濯ぐ】¶ 口を～ぐ *wash out one's* mouth. 洗たく物を～ぐ *rinse out* the wash. ハンカチを水で～ぐ *rinse* a handkerchief in water.

ゆすり【強請】extortion; blackmail; (人) an extortioner; a blackmailer.

-ゆずり【-譲り】¶ 彼の短気は父親～だ His hot temper *was handed down from* his father.

ゆずりあ·う【譲り合う】¶ 彼らは互いに席を～った Each of the two asked the other to take the seat. ～いで解決しようではないか Why not settle the matter by *compromising* (≒ *meeting each other half way*)?

ゆずりう·ける【譲り受ける】be transferred; receive. ¶ その車は私が～けましょう I'll *buy* the car. 彼は父から財産を～けた He *inherited* the property *from* his father. / He *succeeded to* his father's estate.

ゆずりわた·す【譲り渡す】transfer; hand over. ¶ 私は彼に店を～した I *handed* (≒ *made*) *over* my store *to* him.

ゆす·る【揺する】shake; sway; rock (shake は前後・左右・上下にすばやく揺すること, sway は前後・左右に振るように揺すること, rock は揺りかご・いすなどを静かにゆっくり揺すること. ただし rock-'n-roll のときの rock は電気ギターに合わせてはげしく体を揺り動かすこと).

¶ 彼は身を～って大笑いした He laughed himself into *convulsions.*

ゆす·る【強請る】¶ 彼はぼくから金を～りとった He *extorted* money *from* me by the use of threats. / He *blackmailed* me.

ゆず·る【譲る】**1**〖譲渡〗hand over; transfer. ¶ 私は商売を息子に～るつもりだ I will *hand over* (≒ *make over*) my business *to* my son.

彼はその権利を私に～った He *transferred* the rights *to* me.

その本を私に～ってくれないか Can you *spare* me the book?

彼は私に店を安く～ってくれた He *sold* me the shop cheap.

バスの中で老人に席を～った I *gave* my seat *to* an old man in the bus.

彼は後進のために地位を～った He *resigned* his post in favor of his juniors.

2〖譲歩〗¶ 彼は一歩も～れぬと拒否した He refused to *budge an inch.*

ふたりは互いに一歩も～らなかった The two did not *yield* an inch to each other.

学問では彼は彼女にはるかに～っている He *is* far *inferior to* her *in* scholarship.

私は彼女を愛する点ではだれにも～らない I am *no man's second in* my love of her.

ゆせいかん【輸精管】〖解剖学〗the deferent duct.

ゆそう【油送】**—管** a feeding (≒ an oil) pipe; a pipe-line. **—船** a tanker.

ゆそう【油層】a pool of oil; an oil stratum.

ゆそう【輸送】transportation; conveyance. ¶ 汽車は人や貨物を～する A train *carries* (≒ *transports*) passengers and goods.

—機 a transport [plane]. **—機関** a means of transportation. **—船** a transport [ship].

ゆたか【豊か】(豊富) abundance; richness; (裕福) affluence; wealth. ¶ ～な人 a *rich* (≒ *wealthy*) man. ～な社会 the *affluent* society. 収穫の～な年 a *good* year; (ブドウの) a *vintage* year. ～でない人 a man *of small means.* その国は鉱物が～だ The country *is rich* (≒ *is abundant*) *in* minerals. 彼は～な生活をしている(いない) He *is well off* (≒ *is badly off*). 彼は財政～だ He *is in good circumstances* financially. 彼は資本が～だ He has *ample* capital. 彼は才能～な人だ He is a *gifted* man. 彼は6尺～だ He *stands full* six feet. 彼女の想像力はきわめて～だ She *is* very *imaginative.* 彼は趣味の～な人だ He has a highly *cultivated* taste.

ゆだ·ねる【委ねる】¶ 私はその仕事を彼に～ねた I *entrusted* the task *to* him. / I *entrusted* him *with* the task. その件はきみの手に～ねられている The matter is now in your hand. 私の身のふり方はすべて彼に～ねてある I asked him to direct me what to do in the future.

ユダヤ Judea (現在のユダヤ人の国, すなわちイスラエルは Israel と言う).

—教 Judaism. **—人** a Jew; a Hebrew (現在のイスラエル人は an Israeli と言う).

ゆだ·る【茹る】¶ 卵が～っている The eggs *are boiling.* 卵が固く～った The eggs *were boild* hard. ～るような暑さだ It's *boiling* hot.

ゆだん【油断】(不注意) carelessness; inattention; (怠慢) negligence; (不用意) unpreparedness.

¶ われわれは敵に～させた We *threw* the enemy *off their guard.* わが軍は敵の～に乗じてやっつけた Our troops took advantage of the enemy's *unguarded moment.* 彼らはいつも～がない They *are* always *on their guard.* ～ならぬやつ a *cunning* (≒ *sly*) fellow. ～のならぬ世の中だ We *cannot be too careful* in this world. ～をするとけがをするよ You will get hurt if you *don't take care.* ～大敵 *There's many a slip 'twixt the cup and the lip.* / *Security is the greatest enemy.* ～するな Look sharp about you! 彼は挙動が怪しい, ～なく見はれ His movements are suspicious. *Keep a watchful eye on* him.

ゆたんぽ【湯たんぽ】a hot-water bottle (陶器製・ゴム製のものあり).

ゆちゃく【癒着】healing up ;〖医学〗adhesion. ¶ 傷口が～した The wound *healed up.* / The wound *has closed* 〔*up*〕.

ゆっくり slowly ; (気長に) leisurely. ¶ 彼は～歩いた He walked *slowly.* ～お眠りください Have a *good* sleep. その事はもっと～した時話しあいましょう Let us talk over the matter *when I have more time.* 彼は～答えた He *took his time in* answering. そこに座って～してください Please be seated there and *take it easy.* 議長は～自席から立ち上がった The chairman rose from his seat *without haste.* いずれ～おじゃまします I shall come again *for a longer visit.* 私は～していられない I cannot *stay so long.* ～したまえ Stay *as long as you like.* 私は自分の部屋で～した I *felt at ease* (≒ *felt relaxed*) in my room. ～ふろに入った I took a *long* bath. ～でいいのだよ Take your time ! / Don't be in a hurry.

ゆったり ¶ ～した上着 a *loose* jacket. ～いすに腰をかける sit *comfortably* in a chair. ～した気分になる feel *at home* ; feel *relaxed.*

ゆ・でる【茹でる】boil. ¶ ～でた卵 a *boiled* egg.

ゆでん【油田】an oil field.

ゆとり reserve ; (余剰) surplus ; (余地) room ; scope ; (時間) time. ¶ ぼくは今時間に～がない I have no time *to spare* now. 彼らは生活に～がある(ない)ようだ They seem to *be well* (*badly*) *off.* 彼は心に～がある He *is broad-minded.* スケジュールに～がない We are on a *tight* schedule. 車を買う～がない I can't *afford to* buy a car.

ユニーク unique. ¶ 彼は～な画法で知られている He is well-known for his *unique* (≒ *unusual ; extraordinary*) style of painting.

ユニホーム a uniform.

ゆにゅう【輸入】import ; importation. ¶ 外国車の～ the *import* of foreign cars. わが国は石油を中東諸国から～する We *import* oil *from* some middle eastern countries. 戦前はイタリアの～は輸出を超過していた Before the war Italian *imports* exceeded exports. わが国は～と輸出の均衡を保っている Our country maintains the balance of *imports* and exports.

—業者 an importer. —許可証 an import license. —港 a port of entry. —税 an import duty. —超過 an excess of imports over exports. —手続き import procedure. —品 an import ; an imported article. —貿易 import trade. 密— smuggling. ¶ ヘロインを日本に密～する *smuggle* heroin into Japan.

ゆにょうかん【輸尿管】〖解剖学〗the ureter.

ユネスコ UNESCO (the *U*nited *N*ations *E*ducational, *S*cientific and *C*ultural *O*rganization (国際連合教育科学文化機構)).

ゆのみ【湯飲み】a mug ; a cup.

ゆび【指】**1** (手の) a finger (ふつう親指 (thumb) を除く) ; (足の) a toe.

¶ ～を鳴らす snap *one's fingers.*

2 〖慣用的表現〗 ¶ 彼は彼女の時計を～をくわえて見ていた (うらやましそうに見ていた) He *was looking enviously at* her watch.

彼女に～一本でもさそうものなら, ただではおかぬ If you *lay a finger on* her, you shall smart for it.

当選した候補者は5本の～で数えるほどしかなかった The successful candidates could *be counted on the fingers of one hand.*

ゆびあと【指痕】a finger mark.

ゆびおり【指折り】¶ 彼は日本でも～の銀行家だ He is one of *the leading* (≒ *the prominent*) bankers in Japan. 彼らは彼の帰国を～数えて待っている They *are eagerly waiting for* his return home.

ゆびきり【指切り】 ¶ 私たちは～して誓った We made a pledge by *hooking and crossing our little fingers.* / We pledged ourselves to each other.

ゆびさき【指先】a finger tip. ¶ 彼は～が器用だ He is a *deft* person.

ゆびさ・す【指差す】 ¶ 人を～すのは失礼だ It is rude to *point at* another. 彼は地図を～して説明した He explained it *pointing to* the map.

ゆびぬき【指貫き】a thimble.

ゆびわ【指輪】a ring. ¶ ダイヤの～ *a ring* set with a diamond ; *a* diamond *ring.* ～をはめる put *a ring* on *one's* finger. 彼女は金の～をはめている She wears *a* gold *ring* on her finger.

婚約— an engagement ring. 結婚— a wedding ring.

ゆぶね【湯船】a bathtub ; a bath.

ゆみ【弓】a bow. ¶ ～を射る shoot an arrow. ～の名人 a very good archer. 彼は主君に～を引いた (反抗した) He *revolted* (≒ *rose*) *against* his lord.

ゆみがた【弓形】¶ ～の木の枝 a *bow-shaped* branch of a tree.

ゆみず【湯水】¶ 彼は金を～のように使う He *spends* (≒ *squanders*) money *like water.*/ He *muddles away* money.

ゆみなり【弓形】¶ 体を～に反らせる bend backword.

ゆみや【弓矢】bow and arrow.

ゆめ【夢】**1** 〖睡眠中の〗a dream. ¶ 私は幸福な～を見た I had *a* happy *dream.* / I *dreamt* (≒ *dreamed*) *a* happy *dream.*

私は突然～を破られた I *was* suddenly *awaked from a sound sleep.*

～ともなくうつつともなく亡父の呼ぶのを聞いた *Half asleep and half awake,* I heard my dead father's call.

逆— ¶ 心配するな, 逆～ということもあるからな Never fear ; *dreams* sometimes *go by contraries.* 正— ¶ それは正～だった *The dream came true.*

2 〖慣用的表現〗 ¶ ～かとばかり喜んだ I was so glad that I could hardly believe my senses.

平家は20年栄華の～を見た The Tairas *reveled*

ゆ

in prosperity for twenty years.

あの放蕩(ほうとう)息子も～がさめた The prodigal son *came to his senses.*

人生の現実がロマンチックな青年の～をさますのだ The realities of life *disillusion* romantic young people.

彼はそんなことをしようと～にも思わなかった He never *dreamed of* doing such a thing.

きみにここで会おうなどと～にも思わなかった Little did I *dream* that I should meet you here. (形式ばった表わし方).

その報を聞いて私は～見る心地がした When I heard the news, I *felt as if I were in a dream.*

これは～かうつつか Is this *a dream* or reality?

ゆめうつつ【夢現】¶私は～だった I *was half asleep and half awake.* / I *was between asleep and awake.* ～に物音を聞いた I heard some noise *in my dream.* 彼の話を～に聞いていた I was listening to him *dreamily* (≒ *half dreaming*).

ゆめうらない【夢占い】oneiromancy. ¶～をしてもらった I had my fortune told by *oneiromancy.*

―師 an oneirocritic.

ゆめごこち【夢心地】¶私は～でその朗報を聞いた I felt as if I *were dreaming* (≒ *were in a dream*) when I heard the lucky news.

ゆめじ【夢路】¶赤ん坊は安らかに～をたどっている The baby *is sleeping* in peace (≒ peacefully).

ゆめまくら【夢枕】¶ある晩母が私の～に立った One night I *had a dream of* my [late] mother. / One night my mother *appeared in my dream.*

ゆめみ【夢見】¶～が悪い have a bad dream.

ゆめものがたり【夢物語】a fantastic story. ¶きみの計画はまるで～だ Your plan *is* entirely *unrealistic.*

ゆめゆめ【努努】never. ¶見張りは～怠るべからず *Never* neglect to keep a good look-out. ～人に頼るべからず *Do not* depend on others *under any circumstances.*

ゆもと【湯元】the source of a hot spring.

ゆゆし·い【由由しい】serious. ¶これはほうっておくには～い問題だ This is too *serious* a problem to ignore.

ゆらい【由来】(起源) an origin; a source; (来歴) a history. ¶私はあの寺の～を知っている I know the *origin* (≒ *history*) of that temple. この句の～を彼に教えてもらった He told me about the *origin* of this phrase. この習慣は江戸時代に～する This custom *dates back to* the Edo period.

―書 a history; a memoir.

ゆら·ぐ【揺らぐ】shake. ¶透き間風でろうそくの炎が～いでいる The draft is making the flame of the candles *sway* (≒ *swing*; *flicker*).

ゆらゆら ¶遠くにかげろうが～と立ちのぼっている Heat waves are seen *wavering* in the distance. 木のこずえが～揺れている The treetops *are swaying.*

ゆり【百合】〔植物〕a lily.

―科 Liliaceae.

ゆりおこ·す【揺り起こす】¶昨夜は近くの火事のため真夜中に～された I *was shaken out of my sleep* at midnight by a fire near my house.

ゆりかえし【揺り返し】an aftershock. ¶～が来るかも知れないから油断するな Don't be off your guard since *an aftershock* may come.

ゆりかご【揺り籠】a cradle. ¶～から墓場まで from the *cradle* to the grave.

ゆる·い【緩い】slow; loose. ¶～いこう配の坂 a *gentle* slope. ～いこう配の屋根 a *gently sloping* roof. そのズボンは彼には～い The trousers *are too big for* him. 帯が～い The *obi is loose.* 結び目が～い The knot *is loose.* 投手は～いカーブを投げた The pitcher threw a *slow* curve. わが校の規律は～くない The discipline of our school *is* not *lax.*

ゆるが·す【揺るがす】¶猛爆撃は天地を～すばかりだった The bombing was fierce enough to *shake* heaven and earth.

ゆるがせ【忽せ】negligence. ¶研究は一日も～にできない Our study cannot *be neglected* even a day. 毎日の勤めを～にしないことが最もたいせつだ It is most important never to *slight* (≒ *make light of*) your daily work.

ゆるし【許し】(許可) permission; (容赦) pardon. ¶講堂を使用する～は得られなかった We *were* not *allowed to* use the hall. 当局の～を受けるのが先決だ First of all we must get *permission* from the authorities. 彼はひたすら神の～を求めた He earnestly prayed to God to *forgive* his sins.

ゆる·す【許す】**1**〖許可する·許容する〗allow; permit. ¶午後10時まで外出を～す You *may* stay out until 10 p.m.

彼は3年へ編入学を～された He *was permitted to* enroll in the third year class.

どうか彼女との結婚を～してください Please *permit* me *to* marry her.

彼は私の登山を～すまい He won't *allow* me *to* go mountain-climbing.

発言を～していただきたい Please *allow* me *to* speak. / May I have your *permission to* speak?

時間の～すかぎり私も手伝います I'll help you as far as time *permits.*

代理人を立てることは法律で～されている The law *permits* that you make someone your proxy.

天候が～せば,われわれはあす出発します We'll start tomorrow, if weather *permits* (≒ weather *permitting*).

2〖容赦する·免除する〗forgive. ¶彼の暴言は～しがたい His violent language *is unforgivable.* / His rude speech *is unpardonable.*

今度だけは彼の失敗を～してやろう I'll *overlook* his mistake for [this] once.

本心から後悔しているなら～してやる I'll *forgive* you if you are really sorry for what you've done.

ゆ

出席はしますがあいさつをするのだけは～してください I'll attend the meeting, but *excuse* me *from* making a speech.
どんな小さなうそも～さない I won't *forgive* a lie, however small it is.
いっさい弁解は～されない No excuse *is accepted*.
3 〖認める〗 acknowledge. ¶ 彼はわが国最高の画家として自他ともに～している He *is acknowledged as* the greatest painter of our country.
彼は自他ともに～す文壇の長老だ He is *admittedly* the most prominent figure in the literary world.
4 〖心などを〗 ¶ 私には心を～せる友だちが何人かいる I have several *trustworthy* friends. / I have several *confidants*.
知らない人に心を～してはいけませんよ Don't *trust* a stranger.
5 〖放免する〗 ¶ 微罪だったのでその日のうちに～されて家に帰った Since it was a minor offense, he *was released* in the course of the day and he returned home.

ゆるみ【緩み】 slackness ; relaxation.
¶ 気の～ほどこわいものはない Nothing is more dreadful than mental *slackness* (≒ *relaxation*).

ゆる·む【緩む】 slacken ; get loose.
¶ 歩いているうちにくつのひもが～んだ My shoestring *got loose* while I was walking. 寒さがだいぶ～んできた The cold *has abated* remarkably. 転んだのはつい気が～んだからだ I fell down because I *was off guard*. 遺憾なことに社内の規律は～んでいる To our great regret, discipline in our company *is lax* (≒ *is loose ; is slack*).

ゆる·める【緩める】 ¶ 食べすぎてベルトを～めなければならなかった Overeating, I had to *unfasten* the belt. 雨の日はスピードは～めなさい You must *slow down* (≒ *reduce your speed*) on a rainy day. まだ警戒を～めるわけにはいかない We cannot afford to *relax* our guard yet. 気を～めると風邪をひくぞ Don't *relax* too much or you'll catch [a] cold.

ゆるやか【緩やか】 ¶ ～な坂 a *gentle* slope. 川は平原を～に流れている The river flows through the plain *gently* (≒ *slowly*).

ゆるゆる ¶ 道は込んでいるので車は～としか動けない Because the roads are congested, the cars can only move *slowly*. ぬるま湯に～とつかると疲労がとれる Take a *long leisurely* bath in tepid water, and your fatigue will be relieved.

ゆれ【揺れ】 a shake ; a sway. ¶ 熟睡していたので家の～など感じなかった Because I was sound asleep, I did not feel the house *shake*. 波が高かったので船の～はひどかった Because of the high waves, our ship *pitched* (≒ *rolled*) badly.

ゆ·れる【揺れる】 sway ; swing. ¶ 庭の大木が風に～れている The big trees in the garden *are swaying* in the wind. のぼりが風に～れている The banners *are flowing* in the wind. 船はひどく～れた Our ship *rolled* badly. このバスはひどく～れる How this bus *joggles*! 地震で家が～れるのを感じた I felt the house *shake* in the earthquake.

ゆわかし【湯沸かし】 a kettle ;.

よ

よ【余】 more than ; odd ; upward.
¶ 学校まではまだ５マイル～ある It is still *over* (≒ *more than*) five miles [to go] to the school. この会社に勤めてから20年～になる It is twenty *odd* years since I began to work for the company. (㊟ 口語では It has been... とも言う).

よ【世·代】 **1** 〖世の中·世間·人世〗 the world ; society ; life.
¶ あの大地震に会ったときはこの～の終わりかと思った When that big earthquake occurred, I felt as if my end had come.
彼はりっぱな科学者として広く～に知られている He is well known as a distinguished scientist.
彼女は小説家として中年になって～に出た She made her name as a novelist in her middle age.
彼はもう～に忘れられた存在だ He is now a forgotten man.
～のため人のためになる仕事をしたい I want to work for *the public* good.
彼女は～にもまれな語学の天才だ She is a rare linguistic genius.
彼女は～をはかなんで自殺した She killed herself out of despair.
彼は今わが～の春を謳歌(おうか)している He is now at the height of his prosperity.
2 〖現世·来世·前世〗 ¶ 彼は75歳で～を去った He *died* (≒ *passed away*) at the age of 75.
この～の別れにきみに会いたい I would like to see you before I die.
ぼくはあの～など信じない I do not believe in *the next* (≒ *the other*) *world*. / I do not believe *the after world* (≒ *the life after*

death).

3 〖時勢〗 the times. ¶ ～が～なら彼は今ごろ大臣くらいにはなっていたろうに *In better times* he would now be a cabinet minister.

～に逆らって生きる swim (≒go) against *the current.*

～におくれないように努力する make an effort to keep up with *the times.*

4 〖時代・治世〗 an age. ¶ 明治のみ～が懐かしい I miss the good old *days* of Meiji.

昭和の～に日本は大きく変わった Japan has undergone dramatic changes since the beginning of Showa.

よ 【夜】 night; (よいのうち) evening.

¶ 土曜日の～7時ごろにお訪ねしたいのですが May I call on you 〔at〕 about seven on Saturday *evening?* ～が明けるまでここで休みましょう Let's rest here till daybreak. 私は～にまぎれて脱走した I ran away *under cover of the night.* あらしに会い小屋で～を明かした I was caught in a storm, and had to spend *the night* in a hut. 彼らは～が更けるまで歌ったり踊ったりした They kept singing and dancing *till late at night.* 工事は～を日についで行なわれた The work proceeded day and *night.*

よあかし 【夜明かし】 ¶ マージャンで～する *sit up all night* playing mah-jong〔g〕.

よあけ 【夜明け】 daybreak; dawn. ¶ ～は少し冷える It's rather chilly at *daybreak.* 出発は～前だ We start before *dawn.*

よあそび 【夜遊び】 ¶ 彼は～ばかりしている He *goes out in the evening for pleasure.*

よあるき 【夜歩き】 ¶ ひとりで～する *go out* alone *at night.*

よい 【酔い】 drunkenness. ¶ いつのまにかすっかり～がまわった I *was* quite *drunk* before I was aware of it. 家に帰りつくまでにはすっかり～がさめた I *was* completely *sober* (≒*sobered down*) by the time I got back home.

よ・い 【良い・善い】 1 〖良好な・優れている・適当な〗 good; fine; nice.

¶ これは～い本だ This is a *good* book.

～いお宅にお住みですね Your house *is* very *splendid,* isn't it? / You live in a *wonderful* house.

彼女は英語の成績はクラスでいちばん～い She is *the best* student of English in her class.

彼女のきょうのピアノの演奏はとても～かった She played the piano very *well* today.

この薬は頭痛に～い This medicine *is good for* headaches.

この1年間～くないことばかり続いた I have had a series of misfortunes in the past year.

きょうは～い天気だ Today is a very *nice* day.

ちょうど～いところへ来てくれた You've come at the *right* moment.

あなたの都合の～い日を教えてください Tell me when it will *suit* (≒*be convenient to*) you.

このジャケットの大きさはきみにちょうど～い This jacket *fits* you perfectly.

風邪ぎみならすぐ寝るのがいちばん～い You *had best* go to bed right away, if you have a touch of cold.

きみが～いと信じることをやりなさい Do what you believe *right.*

きのうは日が～かったのでたくさん結婚式があった Yesterday happened to be a *lucky* (≒an *auspicious*) day, and many weddings took place.

母親の留守を～いことにして，子どもたちは友だちを連れてきて騒いだ *Taking advantage of* their mother's absence, the children brought their friends home and indulged in merrymaking.

2 〖…すべきだ・正しい〗 ¶ 学生時代にもっと勉強しておけば～かった *I wish I had studied* harder when I was a student.

心配しているのだから結果くらい知らせてくれれば～いのに Because I have been anxious about you, you *might at least* have let me know the result.

もう少し早く来てくれれば～かったのに You *should have come* here a little earlier.

わからないときはあとで私に聞けば～い You *should* ask me later whenever you don't understand.

3 〖十分な〗 ¶ 家での復習は毎日2時間で～い It will *be sufficient* if you go over your lessons for two hours every day.

4 〖気分・容態などが〗 ¶ 少し飲んだだけで～い気持ちになった I *felt slightly intoxicated* although I drank only a little.

秋晴れの空は気持ちが～い The fine autumn sky *is very delightful.*

5 〖ためになる〗 ¶ 適度な運動は健康に～い Moderate exercise *is good for* the health.

6 〖許可・かまわない〗 ¶ 用が済んだら帰っても～い You *may* go home when you are through with your job.

都合が悪かったら無理に来なくても～い You *don't have to* come if it is inconvenient for you.

時間はまだ十分あるから，そんなに急がなくても～い *There is no need to* hurry. We have plenty of time left.

7 〖好む・選ぶ〗 ¶ どちらでも～いほうをお持ちなさい You may take whichever you *like.*

～かったらいっしょに行きませんか Would you like to go with me?

彼の言うことを聞くくらいなら死んだほうが～い *I would rather* (≒*would sooner*) die *than* obey him.

～かったらもう1杯どうぞ Please have another cup.

8 〖うれしい・安心な〗 ¶ 彼の病気が早く治ってほんとうに～かった *I feel relieved* that he recovered so soon.

あす晴れれば～いが *I hope* tomorrow will be a nice day.

ああ～かった Thank heaven! That's a relief.

けががなくてほんとうに～かった *I am glad* 〔*to* see that〕 you were not injured.

よ

9 〖上等な・高価な〗 ¶ このかばんは革も～いが値段も～い This suitcase, made of *superior* quality leather, *is* rather *expensive*.

彼は役所では～い地位にいる He holds a *superior* (≒ *high*) post at the government office.

10 〖…しよい〗 ¶ これは飲み～い薬だ This medicine *is easy to* take.

この計算機は使い～い This calculator *is easy to* use.

これは書き～いペンだ The pen writes *well* (≒ *smoothly*).

もっと見～い席へ移ろう Let's move to a seat where we can have a *better* view.

よいざめ【酔い覚め】 ¶ ～の水の味はまた格別だ Water is awfully good for *sobering up*.

よいしょ (かけ声) Heave-ho!

よいっぱり【宵っぱり】 ¶ 私は～の朝寝坊だ I *keep late hours.* / I *am late to bed and late to rise*. (bed は自動詞). 最近～ばかりしている These days I *sit up late at night*. (till late とする必要はない).

よいつぶ・れる【酔い潰れる】 ¶ さすがの酒豪も～れた Heavy drinker as he was, he *was dead* (≒ *helplessly*) *drunk*.

よいどれ【酔いどれ】 a drunkard.

よいのくち【宵の口】¶ 火事が起きたのはまだ～だった It was still *early in the evening* (≒ *at the beginning of the night*) when the fire broke out.

よいのみょうじょう【宵の明星】 the evening star (この遊星に star (恒星) を用いることは例外); Venus.

よいまちぐさ【宵待ち草】〘植物〙 an evening primrose.

よいまつり【宵祭り】 the festival eve.

よいやみ【宵闇】 the dusk; the twilight.
¶ 辺りはすっかり～に包まれた *Evening darkness* has already fallen around me. / *Evening dusk* has gathered.

よ

よいん【余韻】suggestiveness; (音) reverberations. ¶ ～嫋々(じょうじょう)たる寺の鐘の音はいつ聞いてもすばらしい The *trailing note* (≒ *lingering sound*) of the temple bell always fascinates me. きみにこの詩の～がわかるだろうか I doubt whether you appreciate what this poem *suggests*.

よう【用】 **1** 〖用事〗 business. ¶ 私は～がある I *have something to do.* / I *am engaged*. (後者は形式ばった言い方).

～があって行かれなかった *Business* prevented me from going.

～があって上京した I have come to Tokyo *on business*.

～があって彼を彼らのところへやった I sent him to them *on an errand*.

彼はあなたに～がありますよ He *wants* you.

私は英語で～がたせる I can *make myself understood* in English.

2 〖使用〗 ¶ 婦人～手袋 ladies' gloves.

家庭～せっけん soap *for* family use.

3 〖関係〗 ¶ きみには～はない I *have nothing to do with* you.

この本にはもう～はない I *have done with* this book.

4 〖注文〗 ¶ なにかご～はありませんか Have you any *order* for me?

5 〖用便〗 ¶ ～(便所) に行く go to the toilet; wash *one's* hands.

よう【洋】 the ocean; the sea. ¶ 子を愛する親の愛は～の東西を問わず同じだ Love of *one's* children is the same *whether in the West or in the East* (≒ *everywhere in the world*).

よう【要】 ¶ 彼の話は常に簡にして～を得ている His speech *is* always brief and *to the point*. ～は本人の意欲しだいだ *The essential thing* is whether he really desires it [or not]. 当分彼女は絶対安静の～あり For the time being she *needs* absolute rest.

よう【陽】 the positive. ¶ 彼は陰に～に後輩のめんどうをみている He is looking after his juniors both *publicly* and privately.

よう【様】 **1** 〖ようす・格好〗 ¶ 赤ん坊はやっと眠った～だ The baby *appears* to have fallen asleep at last.

われわれの考えがまちがっていた～だ What we thought *seems* to have been wrong.

彼はなんでも知っている～な顔をする He *looks as if* he knew everything. (口語では knows とも言う).

2 〖仕方・方法〗 ¶ この～にしてボールをけりなさい Kick the ball *like this* (≒ [*in*] *this way*).

この文はどの～に日本語に訳したらいいのでしょうか *How* should I put this sentence into Japanese?

きみの捜し～が悪いから見つからないのだ You won't be able to find it, because *the way* you are looking for it is wrong.

きみの好きな～にしてよい You can (≒ may) do *as* you like (≒ please; choose).

3 〖種類・程度〗 ¶ その～な品は当店にはございません We don't carry things *like* that (≒ article of that *kind*) in this store.

彼はぼくを裏切る～な男ではない He is not *the sort of* man to betray me. / He won't betray me.

ぼくは音楽や図工の～な学科が好きだ I like *such* subjects *as* music and art.

この～なつぼは珍しい *Such* a pot is very rare. (such a pot as this とはあまり言わない).

4 〖同様〗 ¶ それは春の～に暖かい冬の一日だった It was a very mild day for winter, *almost like* spring.

いつもの～に8時に家を出た I left home at eight *as usual*.

ぼくも彼の～に背が高くなりたい I wish I were *as* tall *as* he is.

近ごろ男の～な服装をした女性が多くなった Recently the number of women who dress *like* men is increasing.

5 〖目的〗 ¶ バスにまにあう～に急いで歩いた I hurried *in order to* catch the bus.

皆によくわかる～に詳しくそれについて説明しなさい

Explain it in detail *so that* we can understand it well. (㊟ 口語では so または that を省くこともある).
交通事故に会わない〜に十分注意しなさい Be very careful not *to* have a traffic accident.
彼と顔を合わせない〜に横道へそれた I turned into a side street *to* avoid meeting him.
6〖趣旨〗¶ 彼の話はそんな〜な内容だった He said something *to that effect* (≒ *like that*).
彼女は東京の生活がいやになったという〜なことを手紙に書いてきた She wrote me a letter *to the effect* (≒ *saying* (口語的)) that she was getting tired of living in Tokyo.

よう【幼】¶ 彼は〜にして人の上に立つ素質があった He was gifted with the talent for leadership even *in his childhood* (≒ *as a mere child; in his early life*). (形式ばった言い方).

よ・う【酔う】**1**〖酒に〗 get drunk. ¶ 彼はウイスキーで〜った He *has got drunk on* whisky.
〜った勢いで, 彼は戸を壊した He broke the door *under the influence of liquor*.
2〖船などに〗¶ 船(飛行機)に〜う get seasick (airsick).
汽車(車)に〜う get train-sick (car-sick).
船に〜う人 a poor sailor.
船に〜わぬ人 a good sailor.
3〖夢中〗¶ 彼は自分の成功に〜った His success *intoxicated* him.
彼らは勝利に〜っている They *are elated with* victory.

よう (呼びかけ) Hello! (いまはあまり Hallo, Hullo とは綴らない). / Hi!

ようい【用意】(準備) preparation; readiness; arrangements; (予備) provision; (用心) precaution.
¶ 私は試験の〜をした I *prepared for* the examination.
すぐ夕食の〜をしなさい *Get* supper *ready* at once.
旅行の〜は万事ととのえた I *had* everything *ready* for the trip.
〜万端ととのっている All *is ready*.
なんの〜もなく私は演壇に立った I stood on the platform without any *preparation*.
会合の〜をしてください Will you please *arrange* (≒ *make arrangements for*) the meeting?
まさかのときの〜をしなければならぬ We must *provide against* a rainy day (≒ a time of need).
私は少しばかり〜(金)があります I *have provided myself with* some money.
これは妻の〜してくれた弁当だ This is a lunch my wife *prepared for* me.
〜! (号令) Ready!

ようい【容易】ease; easiness. ¶ それは大人にも〜なことではない It's no *easy* matter even to a grown-up. ぼやぼやしているうちに〜ならぬ事態になってしまった The situation turned *serious* while I was off my guard. その紛争は〜に解決しなかった *It was quite long before* the dispute was settled. 市民の協力がありさえすれば万事〜になるのだが If only we could have the people's cooperation, everything would *be simplified*.

よういく【養育】¶ 彼は田舎の祖父母に〜された He *was brought up* (≒ *was reared*) in the country by his grandparents.
—院 an asylum; a workhouse. **—費** the expense of bringing up children.

よういん【要因】a cause. ¶ 今回の騒動の〜は権力争いだ The *cause* of the present trouble lies in the struggle for power.

よういん【要員】needed personnel (personnel はふつう無冠詞単数形で複数扱い); an employee.
保安**—** workers required for security.

ようえき【溶液】a solution.

ようえん【妖艶】¶ 〜な美しさでは彼女の右に出る者はない As a *fascinating* (≒ *bewitching*) beauty, she is second to none.

ようおん【拗音】a contracted sound.

ようか【養家】an adoptive family. ¶ 彼の〜先の両親はどちらも達者だ Both of his *adoptive* parents are well.

ようが【洋画】an oil (≒ a Western) painting; (映画) a foreign film.
—家 an oil painter.

ようが【陽画】〖写真〗a positive picture.

ようかい【溶解】solution; melting. ¶ 一般に金属は水中では〜不能だ Generally speaking, metals cannot *be dissolved* in water.
—液 a solution. **—点** the melting point.

ようかい【妖怪】a ghost; an apparition.

ようかい【容喙】interference. ¶ 彼はとかく他人のことに〜したがる He is apt to *meddle with* (≒ *interfere in*) others' affairs. そのような言動はいらざる〜だ Such comments are uncalled-for *interference*.

ようがい【要害】a stronghold.

ようかぐ【洋家具】Western style furniture.

ようがく【洋学】European (≒ Western) learning.

ようがく【洋楽】Western (≒ European) music.
—家 a player of European music.

ようがし【洋菓子】Western cakes.

ようかん【洋館】a Western style building; a building in a foreign style.

ようかん【羊羹】sweet jelly of beans.
—色 a rusty color; a faded color.

ようがん【溶岩】lava. ¶ あの火山からはときどき〜が流れ出る Sometimes *lava* flows out from that volcano.
—流 a lava stream (≒ flow).

ようき【容器】a vessel; a receptacle.

ようき【陽気】**1**〖時候〗a season; 〔the〕 weather (weather に形容詞がつくとふつう warm weather のように the はつけない).
¶ いい〜ですね What a fine day!
腰が痛いのはたぶん〜のせいですよ I'm afraid your backache has something to do with *the weather*. (この場合は必ず定冠詞をつける).
2〖活気〗cheerfulness; liveliness. ¶ 彼女は

よ

〜だからだれにも人気がある As she *is cheerful* (≒ *is merry; is jolly*), she is popular with everybody.

彼がいると職場がいつも〜になる His presence always *brightens* his work place.

ウイスキーを飲むと彼は必ず〜になる He never fails to *become jolly* when he drinks whiskey.

ようき【妖気】 ¶ 夕暮れになるとその寺にはなんとなく〜が漂ってくる Whenever evening approaches I feel *something ghostly* about that temple.

ようぎ【容疑】 suspicion. ¶ 彼の〜はまもなく晴れた His *suspicion* was cleared away before long. 彼は殺人〜で逮捕された He was arrested *on* 〔*the*〕 *suspicion of* murder.

—者 a suspect; a suspect person. ¶ 殺人の〜 *a suspect in* a murder.

ようきが【用器画】 instrumental drawing; mechanical drawing.

ようきゅう【要求】 a demand; (請求) a request; (必要) a need. ¶ 彼らの損害賠償の〜はまったく不当だ Their *claim* for damages is quite unreasonable. 労働者は賃上げを〜してストに入った The workers went on a strike, *demanding* a wage increase. この出版は時代の〜にこたえるものだ This publication will meet the *requirements* of the age. 彼は彼らの〜に応じた He yielded to their *request*. 地主から立ち退きを〜された I *was told to* move out by my landowner.

ようきゅう【洋弓】 Western archery.

ようぎょ【養魚】 fish breeding.

—場 a fish farm.

ようきょう【容共】 —政策 a pro-communist policy. —派 the pro-communist faction.

ようぎょう【窯業】 ceramics; ceramic industry.

—家 a ceramist.

ようきょく【陽極】〔電気〕 the anode; the positive pole.

—線 the anode ray.

ようきょく【謡曲】 *no* recitation (≒ singing).

ようぐ【用具】 a tool; an instrument; (一式) an outfit; a kit. ¶ 運動〜 sport〔ing〕 *goods* (goods は数詞で修飾されないが複数扱い). 筆記〜を必ずご持参ください Please be sure to bring something to write with.

ようけい【養鶏】 poultry farming (≒ raising). ¶ 〜をやる raise poultry.

—家 a poultry raiser (≒ farmer). —業 poultry raising. —場 a poultry farm.

ようげき【要撃】 an ambush. ¶ ここは敵を〜する絶好の場所である This is the best place *to ambush* (≒ *lie in wait for*) the enemy.

ようけん【用件】 business. ¶ 急な〜で彼は出かけた He is out *on* urgent *business*. どんなご〜でしょう *What can I do for you?* 〜のみ言いなさい *Come to the point*, please.

ようけん【要件】 (必要条件) an essential condition; (重大要件) an important business. ¶ これで入学資格の〜は満たされる This will satisfy all *the necessary conditions* for admission. あの人は重要な〜があって来た He came *on* important *business*.

ようけん【洋犬】 a foreign dog.

ようご【用語】 (ことば遣い) wording; diction; phraseology; (術語) a term; (総称) terminology; (語彙) vocabulary.

¶ 専門〜 technical *terms*. 哲学〜 metaphysical *terms*. 彼はいつも〜に注意している He is always careful about his *wording* (≒ *choice of words*).

ようご【養護】 protection; nursing.

—学級 a class for the handicapped 〔children〕. —施設 a protective institution.

ようご【擁護】 (保護) protection; (援助) support. ¶ 彼らは民衆を暴政から〜するために立ち上がった They rose to *defend* (≒ *protect*) the public *against* tyranny. われわれは物心両面から彼らの運動を〜した We *supported* their movement both materially and spiritually.

—者 a protector; a supporter.

ようこう【洋行】 ¶ もし〜するならイギリスへ行く If I were to *go abroad*, I would go to England. 一度も〜したことはない I *have* never *been abroad*. 彼は先週〜から帰った He returned from *abroad* last week.

ようこう【要港】 a strategic port; an important harbor.

ようこう【要項】 essential points. ¶ 今の話の〜を書き留めておいてくれ Write down *the point* of what we've just discussed.

ようこう【要綱】 the outline; a summary.

ようこう【陽光】 sunshine; sunlight.

ようこうろ【溶鉱炉】 a smelting furnace; a blast furnace.

ようこそ ¶ これは〜 I am very glad you have come! / I am glad to see you! / How good of you to come and see me!

ようさい【洋裁】 dressmaking. ¶ 彼女は〜がうまい She is a good dressmaker.

—学校 a dressmaking school.

ようさい【要塞】 a fortress; a stronghold.

—地帯 a fortified zone.

ようざい【用材】 material; (材木) timber.

¶ 建築〜 building materials.

ようざい【溶剤】 a solvent.

ようさん【養蚕】 sericulture; silk raising.

¶ 〜をやる raise the silkworm.

—家 a silk raiser. —業 the silkworm raising industry. —所 a cocoonery. —地 a silkworm raising district.

ようし【用紙】 a 〔blank〕 form; 図 a blank; paper. ¶ 所定の〜に書き込んでください Fill out *the printed form*, please.

答案— an examination paper (米大学では青い表紙のついたノートになっているので a blue book と言う). 投票— a ballot 〔paper〕. 申込— an application form. 注文— an order form.

ようし【洋紙】 〔foreign〕 paper.

ようし【要旨】 the point; the gist; (趣旨) the purport. ¶ 議論の〜を述べる tell *the essential points* (≒ *the gist*; *the substance*; *the*

よ

summary) of *one's* argument.

ようし【容姿】a figure ; an appearance. ¶ 彼は〜がりっぱだ He has *a* handsome *appearance.*

ようし【養子】an adopted child ; a son-in-law. ¶ 彼は裕福な家庭へ〜に行った He *was adopted into* a wealthy family. 彼は兄の子を〜にした He *adopted* his brother's child. 子どもを〜にやる give *one's* child to another. —縁組み adoption.

ようし【陽子】〘物理〙a proton.

ようじ【用事】business ; (仕事) an engagement. ¶ 彼女は母の〜で町へ出かけた She went to town *on an errand for* her mother. きょうはあまり〜がない I don't *have much to do* today. あすはこれという〜がない I *have nothing* particular *to do* tomorrow. ほかに〜がありますから, これで失礼します I must excuse myself now, because I *have another engagement* (≒ *have something more to do*).(形式ばった言い方で特に目上の人に言う). / I must say goodby, because I am busy. (口語的で, 同僚などに言う).

ようじ【幼児】an infant ; a baby. —教育 infant education.

ようじ【幼時】childhood. ¶ 彼は〜に母を失った He lost his mother *in his childhood.*(in *one's* childhood は when *one* was a child よりはるかに文語的).

ようじ【楊枝】(小ようじ) a toothpick ; (歯みがき用) a toothbrush. ¶ 〜を使う use *a toothpick.*

ようしき【洋式】¶ 彼の生活はすべて〜だ He is living entirely *in Western style.* ⇒ようふう

ようしき【様式】a style ; a form. ¶ ロマネスク〜(建築) the Romanesque *style.* 〜化されたデザイン a *conventionalized* design. 法令諸〜 legal *forms.* それが彼らの普通の生活〜だ It is *a* proper *way* (≒ *mode*) of their life. / It is their proper life-*style.*

ようしし【養嗣子】an adopted heir.

ようしゃ【容赦】(ゆるし) pardon ; forgiveness ; (しんしゃく) consideration ; allowance. ¶ 不行き届きの点はご〜ください *I beg your pardon* (≒ *I hope you will pardon us*) *for* our poor service. 違反者は〜なく処罰する punish violators *mercilessly* (≒ *without mercy*). 彼は〜なく彼らの腐敗を責めた He accused them of their corruption *without reserve.*

ようしゅ【洋酒】foreign wine (≒ liquors).

ようしゅん【陽春】spring ; springtime.

ようしょ【要所】an important point ; an important position. ¶ 〜を把握(はあく)する grasp *the main points.* 〜〜に警官が配置された Policemen were posted *at important* (≒ *strategic*) *places.*

ようしょ【洋書】a foreign (≒ Western) book.

ようじょ【幼女】a baby girl ; a little girl.

ようじょ【養女】a foster daughter ; an adopted daughter. ¶ 彼女は幼いころからめいを〜にして育てている She *has fostered* her niece *as her daughter* from the cradle.

ようしょう【幼少】¶ 〜のころ in *one's infancy* ; in *early life.* 彼はまだ〜のころの面影をとどめている He still retains traces of his *infantile* features.

ようしょう【要衝】an important place ; a strategic point.

ようじょう【洋上】¶ 〜に浮かぶ2隻の船 two vessels *on the ocean.*

ようじょう【養生】(保健) care of health ; (保養) recuperation. ¶ 〜して長生きしてください *Be careful of your health* and enjoy long life. 〜第一と心掛けてください I hope you'll *take care of health* above all things.

ようしょく【洋食】Western food ; European dishes. ¶ 〜の食べ方 Western table manners. —店 a 〔Western〕 restaurant.

ようしょく【要職】an important post (≒ office). ¶ 彼は中央政府の〜にある He holds *a responsible post* (≒ *office*) in the central government. 彼は会社の〜についた He was appointed to *an important position* in the company.

ようしょく【容色】looks. ¶ 彼女の〜もいつかは衰える Her *personal beauty* (≒ *charming features*) will fade sooner or later. 彼女は〜は十人並だ She is an average-*looking* girl.

ようしょく【養殖】raising ; culture. ¶ カキの〜 oyster-*farming.* ニジマスを〜する *raise* (≒ *farm ; cultivate*) rainbow trout. —場 a nursery ; a farm. —真珠 a cultured pearl.

ようじん【用心】(注意) care ; carefulness ; heed ; (慎重) prudence ; (警戒) caution ; precaution ; guard.

¶ 転ばぬように〜しなさい *Take care not to* fall down. 〜して歩く walk *with care.* 彼にだまされないように〜しなさい *Be careful not to* let him cheat you. われわれは敵に対して〜していた We *were on* our *guard against* the enemy. そのベルはどろぼうの〜のためだ The bell is *a precaution against* burglars. 足もとに〜(掲示) *Watch* your step! 懐中物に〜(掲示) *Beware of* pickpockets. 彼は〜して秘密を漏らさない He *is cautious of* tell*ing* secrets. 〜してものを言いなさい Speak *guardedly* (≒ *cautiously*). あき家は〜が悪い An empty house *is unsafe.* —棒 a bodyguard ; (旅館・酒場などの) (米俗) a bouncer.

ようじん【要人】a very important person (米口語では VIP または V.I.P. と略すことがある) ; a leading person.

ようじんぶか・い【用心深い】careful ; cautious ; prudent. ¶ 彼の運転は〜い He is a *cautious* driver. 彼女は男性とのつきあいには〜い She *is prudent in* seek*ing* a man's friendship.

ようす【様子】1 〖状態〗the state of affairs. ¶ 初めてあの町へ行ったので〜がわからなくて困った Since it was the first time I'd ever been to that town, I didn't know *anything about*

よ

it and had a hard time of it.
ここ数年の間に駅前の～が一変してしまった The *appearance* of the area in front of the station has completely changed in the last few years.
もう少し経済界の～を見よう Let's watch the economic *outlook* for a while.
今はひどい雨だ. もう少し～を見よう It is raining hard now. Let's wait for a little longer.
空の～ではあすも天気はもちそうだ *The way the sky looks* (≒ *Judging from the look of the sky*) we will have another fine day tomorrow.
だれか門のところからこの家の～をうかがっている Someone is at the gate *looking over* this house.
2 〖外観・態度〗 an appearance ; a look.
¶ 彼はどうもきょうは～が変だ He *looks* a little strange today. / I notice something unusual in his *manner* today.
彼女はひどく疲れた～だ She *looks* (≒ *appears* to be) extremely tired.
彼はだいぶ酔っている～だ He *seems* to be quite drunk.
けさから病人の～がおかしい There has been something wrong in the *condition* of the patient since this morning.
家のまわりを～のおかしな男がうろついている A suspicious-*looking* man is hanging around the house.
彼は私の話を聞いて驚いた～だった He listened to me with *a look* of surprise.
3 〖兆候〗 a sign. ¶ 雪にでもなりそうな～だ It *looks like* snow.
彼女の病気はいっこうによくなる～が見えない She shows no *sign* (≒ *symptom* ; *indication*) of getting better.
4 〖ふり〗 ¶ 彼は私に気づかない～をした He *pretended* not *to* notice me.

よ

ようすい 【用水】 (水道の) service water.
—池 a reservoir. **—おけ** a rainwater barrel.

ようずみ 【用済み】 ¶ ではきみはもう～というわけだね Then you'*re no longer wanted,* is that right? それはもう～だ We *don't need it any more.*

よう･する 【要する】 ¶ その家は修理を～する The house *needs* (≒ *wants*) repairing. その仕事には忍耐を～する The work *requires* patience. 取り扱いには注意を～する It *wants* careful handling. それは細心の注意を～する問題だ The matter *demands* (≒ *calls for*) close attention. 仕上げには日数を～する It *takes* us long to get it done. (long を a long time とするほうが口語的). これは急を～する問題だ This is an *urgent* matter. / This is a matter which *needs* immediate attention.

よう･する 【擁する】 ¶ 大資本を～する会社には太刀打ちできない We cannot compete with the firm *possessing* (≒ *with*) a big capital. ふたりは相～して泣いた They wept *embracing each other.*

ようするに 【要するに】 in short ; in a word ; in sum. ¶ ～彼女は信用できない *In short* (≒ *In a word* ; *In brief*) she is not to be trusted. ～こうなのだ *To make a long story short,* it's like this. / I'll tell you what. (ふつうよいことを伝えるのに用いる). ～彼は敵だ *After all* (≒ *To sum up*), he is our enemy.

ようせい 【要請】 request. ¶ 政府の～で彼は式典に参列した He attended the ceremony *at the request of* the Government. 彼は機動隊の出動を～した He *requested* that the riot police 〔should〕 be called in. その法律は時代の～に応じている The law meets the *needs* of the times. 平和は時代の～だ Our own time *demands* (≒ *claims*) peace.

ようせい 【陽性】 positivity. ¶ ～反応 *positive* reaction. ツベルクリン反応では～に転換しています Your tuberculin test shows a change to the *positive.*

ようせい 【養成】 (訓練) training ; (教育) education. ¶ オリンピックにそなえて選手を～している We *are training* athletes for the Olympics. 音楽の正しい鑑賞力を～する *educate* (≒ *develop*) a correct ear for music. その研究所ではいろいろな専門家を～している They *are training* various specialists in that institute.
教員**—**大学 a teachers 〔training〕 college.

ようせい 【妖精】 a fairy ; a sprite ; an elf (複 elves).

ようせい 【夭逝】 young death.

ようせき 【容積】 (容量) capacity ; (体積) volume ; (かさ) bulk. ¶ びんの～を測定する measure the *capacity* of a bottle. このびんの～は1.6リットルだ This is a bottle with *a capacity* of 1.6 liters.

ようせつ 【溶接】 welding. ¶ 電気～ electric *welding.* 鉄板を～する *weld* the sheets of iron.
—機 a welding machine. **—工** a welder. **—剤** a welding flux.

ようせつ 【夭折】 a premature (≒ an early) death. ¶ ～する die young ; suffer an early death ; die an untimely death.

ようせん 【用船】 chartering ; (船) a chartered vessel. ¶ その船は～契約が結んである It is *a chartered vessel.* / The ship *is under charter.* 船を～する *charter* a ship.
—業 chartering business. **—料** charterage.

ようせん 【用箋】 stationery ; (便箋) letter paper ; a writing pad.

ようそ 【沃素】 〖化学〗 iodine.

ようそ 【要素】 a factor. ¶ それには悲劇的～が含まれている It contains tragic *elements.* 幾多の～が結合して彼の詩的美をつくっている Various *factors* have combined to make his poetic beauty.

ようそう 【洋装】 ¶ 彼女は～だった She *was dressed in foreign style.* / She *wore Western dress* (≒ *Western clothes*).

ようそう【様相】a phase; an aspect. ¶アイルランドでは事態はただならぬ～を呈している Things are assuming *a* serious *aspect* in Ireland. それは発展途上の一時的～にすぎない It is nothing but *a* passing *phase* in the development.

ようだい【容体・容態】condition. ¶昨夜突然患者の～が悪化した The *condition* of the patient took a sudden change for the worse last night. 彼の～が思わしくない He is not well. / He is in *a* bad *condition.*

ようたし【用達し】¶～に行く go on an errand; go out on business.

ようだ・てる【用立てる】¶彼は好意からその金を～ててくれた Out of kindness he *lent* me the money. / He had the kindness to *lend* me the money. 彼に2万円～ててやった I *accommodated* him *with* a sum of twenty thousand yen.

ようだん【用談】a business talk. ¶午後バイヤーと～がある I'll have *a talk on business* with a buyer this afternoon.

ようだん【要談】an important talk. ¶～する have a talk on an important matter (*with*); have an important business talk (*with*).

ようだんす【用簞笥】a chest of drawers; a cabinet.

ようち【用地】a lot; a site.
建築— a building lot (≒site). 鉄道— a railway land.

ようち【要地】a strategic point.

ようち【幼稚】¶～な考え a *childish* idea. ～な意見 a *crude* opinion. ～なふるまい an *infantile* behavior. ～な思想 an *immature* thought. ～な方法 a *primitive* method. ～なしゃれ a *raw* joke.

ようちえん【幼稚園】a kindergarten. ¶来春から息子を～にやる I'll send my son to *a kindergarten* next spring.

ようちゅう【幼虫】a larva (複 larvae). ¶ハエの～ a maggot. 甲虫の～ a grub.

ようつい【腰椎】〘解剖学〙the lumbar vertebra.

ようつう【腰痛】〘医学〙lumbago.

ようてい【要諦】¶成功の～ the secret of success; the key to success.

ようてん【要点】the point. ¶論争の～がつかめない I can't grasp *the essential point* at issue. 彼の話は～にふれなかった He didn't *come to the point.* 彼の話の～はなんだったのか What was *the gist* of his speech? 彼の話の～を聞きもらした I missed *the point* of what he said.

ようてん【陽転】〘医学〙change to positive. ¶ツベルクリン反応が～した My tuberculin reaction *changed to positive.*

ようでんき【陽電気】positive (≒plus) electricity.

ようと【用途】〔a〕use; service. ¶石油の～は広い Oil has various *uses.* / Oil *is used* for many purposes. / Oil *is useful* in various ways.

ようど【用度】expenses; expenditure.

ようとう【羊頭】¶～を掲げて狗肉(くにく)を売る(諺) Cry up wine and sell vinegar.

ようとして【杳として】¶彼の行方は～わからない His whereabouts is *completely* (≒*utterly*) unknown. / Nobody knows where he has gone. (口語的).

ようとん【養豚】hog raising.
—業者 a hog raiser. —場 a hoggery.

ようなし【用なし】¶あんなやつにはもう～だ I *have nothing* more *to do with* such a man.

ようにん【容認】¶彼の行動はとても～できない I cannot *allow* his conduct.

ようねん【幼年】childhood; infancy. ¶彼は～時代に父親に死別した His father died *when he was a mere child.* / He lost his father *in his infancy* (≒*in his childhood*). (文語的). 私は～時代を外国で過ごした I spent *my childhood* 〔staying〕 abroad.

ようばい【溶媒】〘化学〙a solvent; a menstruum (複 -s, menstrua).

ようび【曜日】a day of the week. ¶きょうは何～ですか What *day of the week* is 〔it〕 today? (of the week がなくても day だけで曜日の意味になる).

ようひし【羊皮紙】parchment.

ようひん【用品】家庭— domestic articles. 旅行— traveling requisites. スポーツ— sports requisites. 台所— kitchen utensils.

ようひん【洋品】foreign articles.
—雑貨 haberdashery; hosiery. —店 a haberdasher's 〔shop〕; hosier's 〔shop〕 (おもに紳士用品について言う).

ようふ【養父】a foster father.

ようふ【妖婦】a vampire; an enchantress.
¶彼女はよく～役を演じる She often plays the role of *a vamp.*

ようぶ【腰部】the waist; the hips.

ようふう【洋風】¶～の家 a *foreign-style* house; a house *in Western style.* ～の生活 *Western style* (≒*Western fashion*) living.

ようふく【洋服】clothes of Western (European) style; European clothes. ¶このごろ三つぞろいの～を注文する人が少なくない Not a few people order *a* three-piece *suit* these days.
—掛け a coat hanger. —だんす a wardrobe. —屋(人) a tailor (紳士服); a dressmaker (婦人服); (店) a tailor's (a dressmaker's) shop.

ようぶん【養分】nourishment.

ようへい【用兵】—術 tactics.

ようへい【葉柄】〘植物〙a leafstalk; a petiole.

ようへい【傭兵】a mercenary 〔soldier〕.
—制 mercenary system. —隊 mercenary (≒hired) troops.

ようべん【用便】¶～する go to the lavatory; relieve *one*self (≒nature); wash *one's* hands.

ようぼ【養母】a foster mother; an adoptive mother.

ようほう【用法】〔a〕use; 〔a〕usage; the way to use.

よ

¶ 彼はそのことばの〜を誤った He *misused* the word.

ようほう【養蜂】 beekeeping; apiculture. —家 a beekeeper; an apiarist. —場 an apiary.

ようぼう【要望】 a demand. ¶ 政府はただちに国民の〜に応じた The Government complied at once with the *wishes* of the people.

ようぼう【容貌】 looks. ¶ 〜魁偉(かいい)な男 a man with *an* impressive *face*.

ようま【洋間】 a Western style room; a room furnished in Western style.

ようむ【要務】 important business. ¶ 彼は〜を帯びて出発した He started *on important business*.

ようむいん【用務員】 a janitor.

ようむき【用向き】 *one's* business; an errand. ¶ 〜はなんですか What is your *business* here? 私はいやな〜で来た I have come *on a* disagreeable *errand*.

ようめい【用命】 command; order. ¶ これがご〜の品です This is what you *have ordered*. なんなりとご〜に応じます I am ready to comply with any *request* of yours.(形式ばった表現)./ I *am at your service*.

ようもう【羊毛】 wool. —製品 woolen goods.

ようもうざい【養毛剤】 hair tonic.

ようもく【要目】 principal items. 教授— a syllabus (複 syllabuses, syllabi). —索引 an index of principal topics.

ようやく【要約】 a summary. ¶ 会議の内容は〜すると次のとおり The details of the conference can *be summed up* as follows.

ようやく【漸く】 (ついに) at last; (かろうじて) barely. ¶ 話に夢中になっているうちに, 〜辺りが暗くなりはじめた(しだいに) While we were absorbed in talking it was *gradually* getting dark. 思案の末〜決心した(ついに) After much thinking I *finally* made up my mind. 〜目的地に着いた *At last* we got to our destination. 〜時間にまにあった(かろうじて) He arrived *barely* in time.

ようよう【洋洋】 ¶ 〜たる大海原 the *vast* ocean. 前途〜たる青年 a young man *with a bright* (≒ *rosy*) *future*; a *promising* young man. きみの前途は〜たるものだ The world is all before you. / You have *a bright future before you*.

ようらん【揺籃】 a cradle; (比喩的) the beginning. ¶ 〜時代 the cradle; infancy. 日本の民主主義は当時まだ〜期にあった Japanese democracy was still *in the cradle* then.

ようらん【洋蘭】 a foreign orchid; a European orchid.

ようりょう【用量】 dosage.

ようりょう【容量】 capacity. ¶ 〜2リットルのびん a bottle with *the capacity* of two liters.

ようりょう【要領】 (要点) the point; (やり方) the knack. ¶ 彼の演説は〜を得ていた His speech *was to the point*. 彼は〜を得た演説をした He made a *pointed* speech. 彼の言うことは〜を得ていない His remarks *are* not *to the point* (≒ *are beside the mark*). 「そうかもしれない」というのは〜を得ない答えだ "Maybe" is an *indefinite* answer. いろいろと質問したが, 〜を得なかった I asked many questions, but I *was* not *satisfied*. 〜のいい男 a man *of sense*; (気転のきくまたは抜けめのない人) a *sharp* (≒ *shrewd*) fellow. 〜を飲み込む get *the knack* (*of* doing something).

ようりょく【揚力】〘機械〙〘物理〙 lift.

ようりょくそ【葉緑素】〘植物〙 chlorophyl〔l〕.

ようれい【用例】 an example. ¶ 〜をいくつか挙げて説明した He explained by giving *examples*.

ようろ【要路】 **1** 〘道路〙 a main road; a highway. ¶ 交通の〜 *the artery* of traffic. **2** 〘権威〙 ¶ 〜にある人々 those *in authority*. 〜に立つ hold *an important position*. 〜の大官 a *high* official.

ようろう【養老】 —院 an asylum (≒ a home) for the aged. —年金 an old-age pension. —保険 an endowment insurance.

ヨーグルト yog〔h〕urt.

ヨーデル a yodle; a yodel. ¶ 〜で歌う yodel (a song).

ヨード 〘化学〙 iodine. —剤 iodine preparation. —チンキ tincture of iodine; (口語) iodine. —ホルム iodoform.

ヨーロッパ Europe. ¶ 〜の European. —人 a European. —大陸 the 〔European〕 Continent.

よか【予科】 a preparatory course (≒ department).

よか【余暇】 leisure. ¶ 〜に絵をかくのが楽しみだ I enjoy painting *in my spare time* (≒ *in my leisure hours*).

ヨガ yoga (ヒンズー教の修行法). —行者 a yogi.

よかく【余角】 〘数学〙 the complementary angle.

よかぜ【夜風】 ¶ 〜が身にしみる *The night wind* makes me shiver.

よからぬ【良からぬ】 ¶ 彼はなにか〜ことをたくらんでいる He is up to something *evil*. 彼らは〜相談をしているらしい They seem to *be conspiring*.

よかれあしかれ【善かれ悪しかれ】 ¶ 〜まもなく決定が下される *Whether for good or for evil* (≒ *For better or for worse*), the decision will soon be made. 〜事は終わった *Right or wrong*, all is over now.

よかん【予感】 a presentiment. ¶ ばく然とした(不吉な)〜 *a* vague (sinister) *presentiment*. この実験には危険が起こりそうな〜がする I have *a presentiment* (≒ *a premonition*) *of* danger for the experiment. / I *forebode* danger for the experiment. 私の〜が的中した My *presentiment* came true.

よかん【余寒】 lingering cold 〔after the coldest season〕.

よき【予期】 (期待) expectation; anticipation; (希望) hope. ¶ 私は成功を〜していた I *expected* to succeed. 彼は～どおり成功した He succeeded as it *had been expected.* 彼はわれわれの～に反して失敗した He failed contrary to *our expectation.* 私の年収は～以上だった My yearly income exceeded my *expectations.* / My yearly income was beyond my *expectations.* 展覧会の成功は～したとおりだった The success of the exhibition proved to *be up to expectations.* 戦争は～しない結果を生み出した The war has produced *unexpected* (≒ *unlooked-for*) results.

よぎ【余技】 a hobby.

よぎしゃ【夜汽車】 a night train.

よぎな·い【余儀ない】 ¶ ～く辞めさせられた I *was forced* (≒ *was compelled*) *to* resign. 当局は～く断固たる処置をとった Necessity *compelled* the authorities to take a drastic measure. ～い事情で under *unavoidable* circumstances.

よきょう【余興】 an entertainment. ¶ 彼女は～にピアノをひいた She played the piano by way of *entertainment.* それでは～を始めましょう Now let us have some *entertainments.*

よきん【預金】 a deposit. ¶ 私は1万円～した I *placed* (≒ *deposited*) ten thousand yen *in the bank.* 私は100万円の銀行～がある I have *a deposit* of a million yen in a bank. / I have *a bank account* of a million yen. 彼は～から５万円引き出した He drew (≒ withdrew) fifty thousand yen from the bank. ―者 a depositor. ―通帳 a bankbook. 信託― a deposit in trust. 定期― a fixed deposit. 当座― a current deposit.

よく【欲】（貪欲）avarice ; greed ; covetousness ;（欲望）desire ; want ; appetite.
¶ 彼は～が深い He *is greedy* (≒ *is avaricious ; is grasping*). 彼は～で目がくらんでいる He is blind with *avarice.* 彼は～の少ない人だ He is a man *of few wants.* ～を言えば家がもう少し駅に近いといい *I wish* my house *were* a little nearer to the railroad station. 彼女は～を離れて彼の世話をした She took care of him *with no hope of gain* (≒ *from a disinterested motive*). 人生に～がなくなった I have lost *interest in* life.
知識― desire for knowledge. 金銭― love of money. 所有― possessive instinct. 権勢― power lust.

よく【翼】（飛行機・建築・軍隊などの）a wing.
¶ 敵の左～を攻めた We attacked *the left wing* of the enemy.

よく【良く】 **1**〘じょうずに・十分に・りっぱに〙
¶ たいへん～できました Very *well* done! / *Good* for you!
みんなきょうはほんとに～働いてくれた I am grateful to you all for your *hard* work today.
～考えさせてください Let me think it over.
ゆうべは～眠れた I slept *well* last night. / I slept a *sound* sleep last night.
ステーキは～焼いてください I'd like my steak *well* done, please.
ぼくの言うことを～注意して聞きなさい Listen to me *carefully.*
彼は父親にとても～似ている He is very *much* like his father.
問題を～読んでから答えを書きなさい Read the questions *carefully* before you answer them.
あなたのおっしゃる意味が～わかりません I don't understand *exactly* what you mean. (I cannot... とすれば「あなたの言うことは支離滅裂だ」のように解される恐れがある).
彼はまったく～しゃべるやつだ He is *really* talkative. / He *really* talks a lot.
悪銭身につかずとは～いったものだ It is *well* said that easy come, easy go.
彼のことを～いう人はひとりもいない Not a soul speaks *well* of him. / Everybody speaks ill of him.
体の不自由な人には～してあげなさい *Be good to* the physically handicapped.
2〘天候・健康など〙¶ あすは天気も～なるでしょう I hope the weather will *clear up* tomorrow.
病気はすっかり～なりましたか *Have* you completely *recovered* from your sickness?
3〘しばしば・普通に〙¶ それは～あることだ It is just one of those things〔that happen〕. / It is an *everyday* affair.
彼は～学校に遅刻する He is *often* late for (≒ to) school.
この子は～うそを言う He *habitually* tells lies.
子どものころは～この小川で遊んだものだ I used to (≒ would *often*) play in this stream when I was a child.
それは今日の社会に～見られる現象だ It is a phenomenon which is *frequently* observed in society today.
4〘せいぜい〙¶ 集まるのは～て10人ぐらいだろう *At*〔*the*〕*most* (≒ *At*〔*the*〕*best*), ten of us will get together.
売り上げは～いって目標の８割というところかな *If* sales *go well,* we can make about eighty percent of our goal.
5〘驚き・感嘆・非難〙¶ ～こんなに早く来られましたね I wonder how you were able to come so early.
お忙しいのに～ご出席くださいました It is nice of you to have come when you are so busy.
～まあ無事に逃げてこられましたね It is〔really〕wonder that you were able to escape.
彼のあんなに少ない月収で～家族５人が暮らせるものだ I wonder how a family of five can manage to live on a small salary like his.

よく-【翌-】 the next ; the following.
¶ ～３月10日に on *the next day,* the 10th of March.

よくあつ【抑圧】 suppression. ¶ 軍隊が暴動を～した The army *suppressed* (≒ *repressed*) the revolt. 戦時中は言論の自由が～されていた Freedom of speech *was*〔*being*〕*restrained* during the war.

よくげつ【翌月】 the next (≒ following) month.

よ

よくし【抑止】control ; restraint.
よくしつ【浴室】a bathroom.
よくじつ【翌日】the next (≒following) day. ¶雪の日の～は道が悪い The road becomes muddy〔on〕*the day after*〔a〕snow.
よくしゅう【翌週】the next (≒following) week.
よくじょう【浴場】a bathhouse. 公衆— a〔public〕bathhouse.
よく·する【浴する】(湯や水をあびる) bathe ; (恩恵を受ける) be favored. ¶多くの人がその発明の恩恵に～している Many people *enjoy the benefits of* the invention.
よくせい【抑制】control ; restraint ; repression. ¶彼は怒りのあまり感情を～できなかった He was so angry that he could not *control himself*.
よくそう【浴槽】a bathtub.
よくちょう【翌朝】the next (≒following) morning (文脈によっては in the morning でもよい).
よくど【沃土】rich soil ; fertile land.
よくとく【欲得】¶彼は～ずくで彼女と結婚した He married her *for a purely self-interested reason* (≒ *for the sake of gain*). ～抜きの立場から彼は忠告を与えた He advised them from a *disinterested* position.
よくねん【翌年】the next year.
よくばり【欲張り】greed ; avarice. ¶なんと～なやつだ What a *greedy* (≒ *avaricious*) fellow he is! / He is quite *a miser*!
よくば·る【欲張る】¶そんなに～るな Don't *be so greedy* (≒ *avaricious*). / You should not *want so much*. その本をどれもこれも読もうというのは～っている It is too much to wish to read every one of the books.
よくばん【翌晩】the following evening (≒ night) ; the next evening (≒ night).
よくふか·い【欲深い】greedy.
よくぼう【欲望】desire. ¶金銭的～ *desire* for money. 肉体的～ carnal (≒ sexual) *desire* (≒ *appetite*). 常に～を満足させるわけにはいかない We cannot always gratify our *wishes*.
よくめ【欲目】partiality. ¶われわれは親の～で子どもを見がちだ We are apt to regard our children *with partial eyes*.
よくも【克くも·能くも】¶私に向かって～そんなことが言えるな *How dare* you say such a thing to me? ～も殴ったな *How dared* you hit me? / *You are a fine one to* hit me! ～ぼくの悪口を言ったな *How dare* you call me bad names?
よくや【沃野】fertile plains.
よくよう【抑揚】intonation ; modulation. ¶彼は～をつけて詩を朗読した He recited a poem *with a certain intonation*.
よくよう【浴用】—せっけん bath soap.
よくよく (非常に) exceedingly ; (注意して) very carefully. ¶彼は～のお人よしだ He is a *perfect* dupe. ～困ったときはよろしく頼みます Please help me when I am *badly* in need of help. ～の事情がなければそんなことはしなかったろうに There must have been some *compelling* reasons for his doing so.
よくよく【翌翌】—日 (月) two days (months) later ; the next day (month) but one.
よくりゅう【抑留】detention ; internment. ¶彼はシベリアに～されていた He *was detained* in Siberia. / He was a detainee in Siberia. —漁船員 a detained fisherman. —所 a detention camp.
-よけ【-除け】¶弾～ *a protection against* bullets. 泥～ a mudguard ; (自動車の) a fender. 日～ a sunshade ; a blind.
よけい【余慶】influence ; prosperity resulting from a good deed. ¶積善の家に～あり (諺) Good deeds are rewarded by happiness.
よけい【余計】(余分) extra ; (過剰) an excess ; a surplus ; superfluity ; (大量) abundance. ¶私は100円～に払いすぎた I paid a hundred yen *too much*. 彼がひとり～だった He was one *too many*. 私は～な金は持っていない I do not have a single penny *to spare*. ～な世話を焼くな Mind your own business. ～なことに出しゃばるな Don't interfere in *other people's affairs*. 人のことで～な心配をすることはない You need not worry yourself about other *people's affairs*. ～な(頼まれもしない)発言 an *uncalled-for* remark. 人は金持ちになればなるほど, ～に金が欲しくなる The richer a man becomes, *the more* money he wants.
よ·ける【避ける】¶水たまりを～けて行く go *stepping aside* from the puddle. バスを危うく～けた I barely *got out of the way of* the bus. 木にむしろをかぶせて霜を～ける *protect* trees *from* frost by covering them with straw-mats.
よけん【予見】foresight. ¶10年先を～することはできない We cannot *foresee* (≒ *predict*) what will happen ten years hence.
よげん【予言】a prophecy ; a prediction. ¶～する prophesy ; foretell ; predict. 彼の～は的中した(はずれた) His *prophecy* came true (failed). 彼は戦争を～していた He *had predicted* the war.
—者 a prophet ; (女) a prophetess.
よげん【余弦】〖数学〗a cosine.
よこ【横】**1**〖物の〗(横側) the side ; (幅) the width.
¶縦32センチ～21センチの紙 a sheet of paper〔which is〕32 by 21 centimeters.
板を縦～25センチに切る cut a board 25 by 25 centimeters.
15センチの線を～に引く draw a 15 centimeter *horizontal* line ; draw a *horizontal* line of 15 centimeters.
彼女は私の～に座った She sat *by* (≒ *beside* ; *next to*) me.
新聞ならあなたの～にあります If you are looking for the newspaper, it is *beside* you.
彼は不服そうに～を向いてしまった He *looked away* (≒ *turned his face aside*) discon-

よ

tentedly.

彼らは～に２列に整列した They lined up in two *rows*.

額が少し～に曲がっている The picture frame is [hung] a little *askew*.

箱は重ねないで～に並べなさい Don't stack (≒ pile) up the boxes; put them *side by side*.

ぬれた道路は車が～に滑りやすい The car is apt to *skid* on the wet road.

彼はベレー帽を～にかぶって澄ましている He wears his beret *on one side* with affectation.

2 〖慣用的表現〗 ¶ 彼ときたら縦の物を～にもしない He won't lift a finger to help.

～から口を出さないでくれ Don't interfere (≒ meddle) in my affairs. / Mind your own business.

うちの会社では～の連絡がよくとれていない No good *horizontal* contact exists in our company. / Our company does not have good *horizontal* communications.

また話が～にそれたようだ I'm afraid I'*m digressing* again.

なん回頼んでも彼は首を～に振りつづけた No matter how often we begged him, he kept shaking his head.

失礼して～にならせてもらいます Excuse me, but I would like to *lie down* to rest.

ネコは日なたで長々と～になっている A cat is lying at full length in the sun.

よご【予後】〖医学〗 prognosis; (回復までの経過) convalescence.

¶ 彼の手術の～は良好だ He is doing well *after* the operation.

よこあい【横合い】 ¶ ～から口を出すのは無作法だ It is rude to *interrupt a person* when he is speaking.

よこあな【横穴】 a cave; a tunnel; 〖鉱山〗 a drift.

よこいと【横糸】 the weft; the woof.

よこう【予行】 **──演習** [a] rehearsal. ¶ 式の～演習をする *rehearse* the ceremony.

よこがお【横顔】 a profile. ¶ ～の写真 a portrait *in profile*. 新大臣の～が新聞に紹介されている The *profile* (≒ *personal aspect*) of the new minister is described in the newspapers.

よこがき【横書き】 ¶ ～にする write *sideways*; write *from left to right*.

よこがみやぶり【横紙破り】 ¶ 彼は～だ He doesn't hesitate to do what an ordinary person would not dream of doing. / He is capable of any extremities.

よこぎ【横木】 a bar.

よこぎ・る【横切る】 ¶ 通りを～る *cross* the street. 川が原野を～っている A river *flows across* the plain.

よこく【予告】 [previous] notice; warning. ¶ ～どおり as *already announced*. 1か月前に解雇を～する give (*a person*) a month's *notice* of dismissal. それについてはなんの～もなかった We got no *notice* about the matter. 彼は～なしに解雇された He was dismissed without [*previous*] *notice*.

──編(映画の) a preview. 新刊**──** the announcement of books to be published.

よこぐるま【横車】 ¶ 彼に～を押させるな Don't let him *interfere with* our plans.

よこしま【邪】 ¶ ～な人間 a *dishonest* (≒ *wicked*) person. ～な考え an *evil* thought.

よこじま【横縞】 lateral stripes; horizontal stripes.

よこ・す【寄越す】 ¶ 彼はこのごろさっぱり手紙を～さない He seldom *writes* me of late. 彼は手紙ですぐ来るといって～した He *wrote* me that he was coming soon. 新聞をこっちへ～してくれ *Pass* me the newspaper.

よご・す【汚す】 ¶ 服を～す *soil one's* clothes. 工場の排水で川を～す *pollute* a river with the drainage from the factory. ほうれん草をゆでてごまで～す(あえる) boil spinach and *dress* it with ground sesame.

よこずき【横好き】 ¶ へたの～でゴルフをやります I like to play golf, although I'm not good at it.

よこすべり【横滑り】 a sideslip. ¶ 彼は蔵相から通産相に～した He *switched* (≒ *was shifted*) *from* the post of the Minister of Finance *to* that of the Minister of International Trade and Industry.

よこせん【横線】 a horizontal line. ⇒おうせん

よこた・える【横たえる】 ¶ 体をベッドに～える *lay oneself* on a bed.

よこたおし【横倒し】 ¶ 自転車が～になった The bicycle *fell* (≒ *was turned over*) *sidelong*.

よこたわ・る【横たわる】 ¶ 寝床に～る *lie* on the bed. 多くの困難がわれわれの前途に～っている Many difficulties *lie* ahead of us.

よこちょう【横町】 a by-street; 米 an alleyway; 英 an alley.

¶ 二つめの～を右に折れなさい Take the second turning to the right.

よこづけ【横付け】 ¶ 車が入り口に～になった A car *pulled up* at the entrance. 船を岸壁に～にする *bring* a ship *alongside* the pier.

よこっつら【横っ面】 a cheek. ¶ ～を張りとばす slap *a person on the cheek*; box *a person's* ears. ～を張られる get slapped *on the cheek*.

よこっとび【横っ飛び】 ¶ ～に車を避ける *jump aside* from a car; *jump out of* the way of a car. ～に飛んで行く dash off.

よこづな【横綱】〖相撲〗 a grand champion [*sumo*] wrestler. ¶ 彼は繊維界の～だ He is *the tycoon* in the textile business circles.

よこて【横手】 ¶ 公園の～に at *the side* of a park. 私の家は教会の～にある My house stands *next to* the church.

よごと【夜毎】 ¶ ～に every night.

よこどり【横取り】 ¶ 人の分け前のお菓子を～する *snatch away a person's* share of sweets. 彼は私の恋人を～した He *won away* my sweetheart. / He *stole* my girl friend.

よこなが【横長】 ¶ ～の oblong.

よこながし【横流し】¶ 塩を～する *sell* salt *in the black market*; *sell* salt *illegally*.

よこなぐり【横殴り】a side blow. ¶ ～の雨 a *slanting* rain. ～に雨が降ってきた The rain came down *aslant, beating me sideways*.

よこなみ【横波】a side wave; 〘物理〙 a transverse wave. ¶ ボートが～をくらって転覆した The boat was hit by *side waves* and was turned over.

よこばい【横這い】¶ 物価は～状態を続けている Prices *show no fluctuations.* / Prices *remain stable.* / Prices *keep the present level.*

よこはば【横幅】breadth. ¶ ～2メートルの運河 a canal two meters *wide*.

よこばら【横腹】the side. ¶ ～が痛い I have a pain *in the side*.

よこぶえ【横笛】a flute. ¶ ～を吹く play 〔on〕 the *flute*.

よこみち【横道】a side road; (誤った方向) a wrong way. ¶ 話が～にそれた The conversation *wandered from the subject*. ～にはいる fall into *wrong ways*.

よこむき【横向き】¶ ～に座る sit *sideways*.

よこめ【横目】a side glance. ¶ ～で見て通る pass *with a side glance* (*at*). 人を～で見る look at *a person sideways*. 人を～でにらむ give a sharp glance at *a person out of the corner of one's eyes*.

よこもじ【横文字】a European (≒ Western) language. ¶ それは～で書いてある It is written *in Roman letters*.

よこやり【横槍】¶ 他人のやることに～を入れるな Mind your own business. / Don't *interrupt* others.

よこゆれ【横揺れ】rolling. ¶ 船がひどく～した The ship *rolled* a great deal.

よごれ【汚れ】a stain; a spot; a blot. ¶ 体の～を取る *clean one's* body. 衣服の～をふき取る wipe (≒ remove) the *stains* off *one's* clothes.
—物 soiled things; (洗たく物) the washing.

よご・れる【汚れる】¶ 汗でシャツが～れている My undershirt *is soiled* (≒ *is smudged*) with sweat. 手が泥で～れている My hands *are muddy*. スモッグで空気が～れている The air *is tainted* (≒ *is polluted*) by smog.

よこれんぼ【横恋慕】illicit love. ¶ ～する love *another's* mate.

よざい【余罪】other crimes. ¶ ～を追及する question *a person* of his *other crimes*. 彼には～がある He is suspected of *some other crimes*.

よざい【余財】money to spare; surplus funds. ¶ ～を蓄える save up *money to spare*.

よざくら【夜桜】¶ ～を見物する view *the cherry blossoms at night*.

よさん【予算】a budget. ¶ 政府は～を作成し, これを議会に提出する The government makes *a budget* and presents it to the Diet. ～は議会で削減された The *budget* was cut down by the Diet. それは～に計上されている It is included in the *budget*. 建築費は～を5000万円超過している The cost of building exceeds the *estimate* by fifty million yen. その建築物は2000万円の～だ The cost of the building *is estimated at* twenty million yen. ～がない We have no *budget* for it.
—案 a budget. ¶ ～案は通過した (否決された) *The budget* has been passed (has been rejected). **—委員** a member of budget committee. **—委員会** the budget committee. 総**—** the general budget. 暫定**—** a provisional budget. 追加**—** a supplementary budget. 歳出**—案** an appropriation bill.

よし【由】¶ 彼の消息は知る～もない *There is no knowing* how he is getting along. お元気の～なによりと存じます I am glad to hear you are fine.

よし **1** 〖よろしい〗 Good. / Very well. / All right. ¶ 帰って～ You *may* go home now.
2 〖決意〗 ¶ ～, やろう *All right.* I will try to do it.

よし【葦】〘植物〙 a reed.

よじ【余事】other things. ¶ ～はさておき本論にはいろう Leaving aside *other things*, let's get down to the main subject. 話が～にわたりはじめた The conversation wandered off the main subject. / He started to digress from the main subject.

よしあし【善し悪し】good or bad. ¶ 事の～に迷う can't easily tell whether it is *good or bad*. 天気の～にかかわらず出かける We are going *in all weather* (≒ *regardless of weather*). それも～だ It has its own disadvantages.

よじげん【四次元】four dimensions. ¶ ～の世界 a world *in four dimensions*.

よしず【葭簀・葦簾】a reed screen. ¶ ～張りの小屋 a shack sheltered with *reed screens*.

よじのぼ・る【攀じ登る】¶ へいに～る *climb on to* the top of a fence. 険しい山道を～る *clamber up* a steep mountain path.

よしみ【好しみ・誼】¶ 友人の～で世話をした I helped him *for friendship's sake* (≒ *out of friendship*).

よしゅう【予習】preparation of lessons.
¶ あすの～をする *prepare* tomorrow's lessons. あすの～がまだだ I'm not *ready for* tomorrow's lesson.

よじょう【余剰】a surplus.
—価値 〖経済学〗 surplus value. **—農産物** farm surpluses. **—物資** surplus articles. **—労働力** surplus labor.

よしょく【余色】〘物理〙 a complementary color.

よじ・る【捩る】twist. ¶ 体を～って笑う *writhe* with laughter.

よじ・れる【捩れる】¶ 糸が～れている The thread *is kinked*. 腹の皮が～れるほど笑った I was convulsed with laughter.

よしん【予審】〘法律〙 a preliminary hearing

(≒ trial; examination).
—廷 the preliminary court of inquiry.
—判事 a preliminary court judge.

よしん【余震】an aftershock. ¶ ～が続いた *The aftershocks* continued. / There were repeated *aftershocks*.

よじん【余人】other people. ¶ ～は知らず私は承知できぬ *For my own part*, I will not agree to it.

よしんば【縦んば】¶ ～彼が謝っても私は許さない I will not forgive him *even if* he apologizes.

よ·す【止す】¶ 会社を～す (やめる) *quit one's* job; *leave* office. マッチのいたずらは～せ (禁じる) *Don't* play with the matches. そんなことは～せ *Don't* do that. / Cut that out! もう～せ That's enough.

よすが【縁】(手段) a means. ¶ それを知る～もない There is no knowing it.

よすてびと【世捨て人】(隠者) a hermit; (僧侶) a priest.

よすみ【四隅】the four corners.

よせ【寄席】㊎ a vaudeville house; ㊇ a music hall; a variety theatre.
—芸人 a vaudevillian; ㊇ a variety show entertainer.

よせあつめ【寄せ集め】a medley. ¶ ～のチーム a *scratch* team. ～の軍隊 a *medley* army.

よせあつ·める【寄せ集める】gather together; collect. ¶ 木の葉を～める *sweep* dead leaves *into a heap*. 部品を～めて車を作る build a car out of a jumble of parts.

よせい【余生】the rest of *one's* life. ¶ 彼は～を故郷で送った He spent his *remaining years* in his native place. / He lived in his home town *for the rest of his life*.

よせい【余勢】¶ ～を駆って敵を攻めたてた *Following up the victory*, we made another attack on the enemy. / *Encouraged by the success*, we delivered a further attack against the enemy.

よせがき【寄せ書き】a collection of autographs. ¶ 皆で入院中の友人に～をして送った We sent a letter to our friend in the hospital, each contributing a few words.

よせぎ【寄せ木】a parquet.
—細工 parquetry; wooden mosaic.

よせつ【余接·余切】〘数学〙a cotangent.

よせつ·ける【寄せつける】¶ 彼のような人を～けるな *Keep away from* such a person. 彼は他人をめったに～けない男だ He *keeps* others *off*. / He *keeps himself to himself*. / He *keeps his own company*.

よせて【寄せ手】an attacking force; the enemy.

よせなべ【寄せ鍋】chowder.

よ·せる【寄せる】**1**〘接近〙¶ 彼は机を窓の近くに～せた He *drew up* his desk *close to* the window.
彼はほおを彼女のほおに～せた He *touched* his cheek *against* hers.
2〘加算〙¶ 全部～せるといくらですか What is *the sum total*?
3〘身·心を〙¶ 私は身を～せる所がなかった I *had* no *place to go to*. / I had no *person to live with*.
彼は彼女に思いを～せている He *is in love with* her.
私はその気の毒な子どもに同情を～せた I *felt sympathy for* the poor child. / I *sympathized with* the poor child.
4〘訪問〙¶ また近いうちに～せていただきます I will *drop in* again one of these days.
5〘その他〙¶ 白波が岸に～せては返している The white waves *surge back and forth* against the shore.
彼は額に八の字を～せた He *knitted his brow*.

よせん【予選】(競技) preliminary heats; elimination matches. ¶ 100メートル～ *a* 100-meter *preliminary*. 彼は～で落ちた He was eliminated from the tournament. / He failed to qualify *in the heats*. 彼女は～を通過した She qualified *in the heats races*. / She passed the *preliminary heats*.

よそ【余所·他所】¶ それはどこか～に忘れてきたにちがいない I must have left it *somewhere else*.
～の場所で遊びなさい You should play *at some other place*. ～でもっと安く買える You can buy them cheaper *at some other stores*. そんなことをすると～の人に笑われますよ If you do such a thing, you will be laughed at. 家族を～に彼は酒に浸っていた He was drowned in wine *neglecting* his family. 彼女はよく～で食事をする (外食する) She often eats *out*.

よそいき【余所行き】⇒よそゆき

よそう【予想】(予期) expectation; anticipation; (予測) forecast; foresight; (推断) presumption; (予想·見積もり) estimate; (想像) imagination; supposition.
¶ 物価騰貴を～して私はたくさん買い込んだ As I *expected* (≒ *anticipated*) a rise in prices, I laid in a large stock.
われわれは近い将来すら～できない We can never *forecast* (≒ *foresee*) even the immediate future.
私は彼がそれを断わるだろうと～する I *presume* that he will refuse it.
米の収穫～ rice crop *prospects*.
志願者の数ははるか～以上だった The number of the applicants *was beyond* (≒ *far ahead*) *expectations*. / The number of the applicants far exceeded *expectations*.
～に反して彼は失敗した *Contrary to expectations* (≒ *Unexpectedly*), he failed.
～どおりの豊作だった We had a rich harvest, *as we had expected* (≒ *as was expected*).
結果は～どおりだった The result came up to my *expectations*.
われわれはその国に反動の起きることを～した We *anticipated* a reaction in the country.
—外 ¶ ～外の成功 an *unexpected* success.

よ

—屋(競馬などの) a tipster ; (俗語) a [racing] prophet.

よそ･う【装う】 dish up ; serve. ¶ 彼に御飯を〜ってあげてください *Help* him *to* rice, will you? 御飯は軽く〜ってください Would you *dish* [*up*] a little rice for me? / Would you *give* me a little rice?

よそおい【装い】 attire ; dress. ¶ 夏の〜 the summer *dress.* 〜も新たなホテル a newly *furnished* hotel. 〜も華やかな婦人たち ladies arrayed in gorgeous *clothes.*

よそお･う【装う】 **1** 〖身づくろいをする･着飾る〗 ¶ 彼女はいつも地味に〜っている She *is* always *dressed* plainly.
彼女ははでに〜っていた She *was* gaily *dressed.* 彼女は宝石などで華やかに〜う She *adorns herself with* jewels and other ornaments.
2 〖ふりをする〗 ¶ 彼は作り笑いを浮かべて平気を〜った He put on a forced smile *with assumed calmness.*
彼はつんぼを〜って急場を切り抜けた He found his way out of the difficulty *feigning* deafness (≒ *feigning himself* deaf).
彼女は病気を〜った She *pretended* to be sick.

よそく【予測】 prediction ; (見積もり) estimation. ¶ それはとても〜できない It can hardly *be foreseen.* 彼の〜したとおりだった It was just as he *had predicted.* / His *prediction* came true. われわれの〜ははずれた We made *a* wrong *estimate.* 彼は〜できない言動をとる He *is unpredictable.*

よそごと【余所事】 ¶ まるで〜みたいな話しぶりだ He talks as if it were *none of his concern.* 彼の失敗は私たちにとって〜ではない His failure is *a matter of great concern to* us. / His failure *concerns* us.

よそながら【余所ながら】 ¶ 〜ご成功を祈っています I wish you success *in my heart.* 〜彼に別れを告げた I took leave of him *casually.*

よそみ【余所見】 ¶ 〜しないで読みなさい Never *look away from* (≒ *take your eyes off*) your book. / Keep your eyes on your book. 〜しながら歩く walk along *looking around one.*

よそめ【余所目】 ¶ 彼らは〜にもうらやましい仲だ Their love is quite enviable *even to a casual observer.* 彼女の狂乱は〜にも哀れであった Her frenzy was *a most pitiable* (≒ *touching*) *sight to see.*

よそゆき【余所行き】 ¶ 彼女は〜の着物を着ていた She *was in her best clothes.* 彼女は〜の顔をしていた She *was* (≒ *looked*) *prim and proper.* 彼女は〜のことばで返事をした Her answer *was unnaturally formal.*

よそよそし･い【余所余所しい】 ¶ 彼は私に〜い He *is cold and distant to* me. / He *is short with* me. / He *treats* me *coldly.* 彼女は私に〜い態度をとった She *gave* me *the cold shoulder.* / She *was unconcerned with* (≒ *was indifferent to*) me. 彼のあいさつはていねいではあったが〜かった His greeting *was* polite but *frigid.*

よぞら【夜空】 a night sky. ¶ 〜に星が輝いていた Stars were shining *in a nocturnal sky.* / At the night, the stars were shining *in the sky.*

よた【与太】 ¶ 彼は〜ばかり飛ばしている He always talks *nonsense.* / He talks nothing but *silly things.*

よたか【夜鷹】 〖鳥類〗 a nighthawk ; a goatsucker.

よたく【余沢】 ¶ 先祖の〜 the *blessings* of *one's* ancestors. 近代文明の〜を受ける receive the *benefits* of modern civilization.

よだ･つ【彌立つ】 ¶ 身の毛も〜つような話だ It is a *bloodcurdling* story. / The story *makes my hair stand on end.* / The story *makes my blood run cold.*

よたもの【与太者】 (ならず者) a hooligan ; a hoodlum ; a ruffian ; a street gangster.

よたよた ¶ 老婆が〜した歩どりで出ていった An old woman walked out *unsteadily* (≒ *totteringly ; with faltering steps*).

よだれ【涎】 slaver ; slobber. ¶ 赤ちゃんが〜を流している The baby *is slavering* (≒ *is slobbering*). 見ただけで〜の出そうなごちそうだ The mere sight of the dish *makes my mouth water.* それは〜の出そうなケーキだった It was a *mouth-watering* cake.
—掛け a bib.

よだん【予断】 prediction. ¶ 目下のところ次になにが起こるか〜を許さない As things stand now, *there is no knowing* what will happen next. 彼らの行動は〜を許さない Their conduct admits of no *prediction.* / We can make no *guess* about their conduct.

よだん【余談】 a digression. ¶ 〜はさておき to return from the *digression.* 〜にわたって恐縮ですが if you allow me to *make a digression.* 〜ですが in this connection I may add that....

よち【予知】 foreknowledge ; foresight. ¶ 地震は〜できないものか Is it impossible to *foretell* (≒ *forecast*) an earthquake? それは〜しない結果だった It was an *unexpected* result.

よち【余地】 room ; (活動の) a scope ; (余白) a blank. ¶ もう1台も入る〜はない There is no *room* for another car. それには弁解の〜はない You have no excuse for it. これには妥協の〜はまったくない This *admits of* no compromise. まだ議論の〜がある It *calls for* further discussion. この仕事には改善の〜がかなりある There is much *room* for improvement in this work. これにはまだまだ研究の〜がある This requires much more study. これには疑いをはさむ〜がない This leaves no *room* for doubt. その仕事はきみが自由に腕をふるう〜がある The work has free *scope* for your activities.

よちよち ¶ 赤ちゃんが〜歩きを始めた The baby began to walk *totteringly* (≒ *with un-*

よ

steady steps). / The baby began to *toddle*.

よつ【四つ】(数) four; (年齢) four years of age;〖相撲〗cross-grips. ¶ 彼は難問と〜に取り組んでいた He *was squarely tackling with* a difficult task. / He *was wrestling with* a hard work.

よつあし【四つ足】(四足獣) a quadruped; a four-footed animal.

よつおり【四つ折り】(四つ折り本) a quarto.

よつかど【四つ角】(街路の角) a street corner; (十字路) a crossroad〔s〕. ¶ 〜を左へ曲がる turn *the corner* to the left.

よつぎ【世継ぎ】an heir; (女の) an heiress.

よっきゅう【欲求】〔a〕desire. ¶ 知的〜 the *desire* to learn. 金銭的〜 the *desire* after riches. 性的〜 sexual *desire*. 生きんとする〜 the *will* to live. 〜を満たす satisfy *one's wants*; gratify *one's desire*.

—不満〖心理学〗frustration.

よつぎり【四つ切り】〖写真〗a quarter.

よつご【四つ子】quadruplets.

よつつじ【四つ辻】(街路) a street corner; (道の) a crossroad〔s〕. ⇒よつかど

よって【因って】(故に) consequently; therefore; (…に従って) according to; in accordance with; (…に応じて) in compliance with; (…の理由で) because of; by reason of; on account of; owing to; (手段で) by dint of; by means of; through; (…の結果として) in consequence of; as a result of.

¶ 〜くだんのごとし Such is the purpose of this document. (証書の文句).

よつであみ【四つ手網】a fishing net with crossed bamboo supports.

ヨット a yacht; a sailboat. ¶ 〜を操る sail (≒ manage) *a yacht*; yacht (動詞).

—クラブ a yacht club. **—所有者** (男) a yachtsman; (女) a yachtswoman. **—レース** a yachting race. 競走用**—** a racing yacht.

よっぱらい【酔っ払い】a drunken man; a drunk; a drunkard.

—運転 ¶ 〜運転をする drive while *intoxicated*; drive *under the influence of alcohol*. 彼は〜運転の常習だ He is a habitual *drunk*〔*en*〕driver.

よっぱら·う【酔っ払う】¶ 彼は〜っている He *is drunk*. / He *has got drunk*.

よつゆ【夜露】the night dew. ¶ ゆうべは〜がひどく下りた It *dewed* heavily last night. 〜に当たると体に毒だ It is bad for the health to expose yourself to *the night dew*.

よづり【夜釣り】night fishing; fishing at night. ¶ 〜に行く go *fishing at night*.

よつわり【四つ割】a quarter. ¶ スイカを〜にする *divide* a watermelon *into four*.

よつんばい【四つん這い】¶ みな狭いほら穴から〜になって出て来た They came out of the narrow cave *on hands and knees* (≒ *on all fours*).

よてい【予定】**1**〖あらかじめ決めること・計画〗a program; a previous arrangement.

¶ あすのご〜は What are your *plans* for tomorrow? / What *are* you *planning* to do tomorrow?

今晩は別に〜はない I have nothing in particular to do this eveninig.

急行列車は10時5分着の〜だ The express *is due*〔*to arrive*〕at 10:05 (≒ ten five).

夏休みの〜はもう立てましたか Have you already made *plans* for the summer vacation?

列車は〜どおりですか *Is* the train *on time* (≒ *on schedule*)?

飛行機は〜より30分遅れて羽田を飛び立った The plane took off from Haneda Airport thirty minutes behind *schedule*.

〜した歌手が病気で出場できなくなった The singer who *was scheduled to perform* could not come because of sickness.

今月のわが家の家計は〜外の支出が多かった Our living costs far exceeded the *estimated* amount this month.

サイクリングの〜を変更しゴルフをした We changed our *plan* to go on a cycling trip and played golf.

この新製品の宣伝には500万円を〜している We *intend* to spend five million yen on advertising this new product.

彼がこの会合に出てこないのは〜の行動だろう It may have been his *intention from the beginning* not to attend this meeting.

長雨が続いたために工事の〜がすっかり狂った A long spell of rainy weather upset our entire construction *schedule*.

新工場の〜地はどこでしょうか Where is the *proposed* site for the new plant?

2〖予期・予想〗expectation. ¶ あすのパーティーには8人のお客さんを〜している We invited eight guests to the party tomorrow.

彼女は来年3月出産の〜だ She *is expecting* a baby next March.

〜よりだいぶ早く目的地に着いた We got to our destination a lot earlier than *expected*.

よとう【与党】a party in power; a ruling party; the Government party; 米 the Administration party.

¶ 〜側議員 the ministerialists.

よどおし【夜通し】all night; throughout the night. ¶ 彼女は〜寝ずに看護した She was up with the sick *all night* (≒ *all through the night*).

よとく【余得】an extra pofit; (役得) a perquisite.

よとく【余徳】¶ わが家族はみなご先祖の〜をこうむっている All my family *are under the influence of our ancestors*. / All my family *have received the benefits* (≒ *blessings*) *of our forefathers*.

よどみ【淀み・澱み】(停滞) stagnation; (沈澱) sediment; (ことばの渋滞) hesitation.

¶ 彼は〜なく意見を述べた He expressed his opinion *fluently*. / He delivered his opinion *without hesitation* (≒ *without faltering*; *without pause*).

よど·む【淀む・澱む】(停滞する) stagnate; (沈澱

する) settle; deposit. ¶ 〜んだ水 *stagnant* water.

よなか【夜中】midnight. ¶ 〜に *in the middle of the night*; at *midnight.* 息子は〜の2時3時まで勉強している My son studies hard *till the small hours* 〔*of the morning*〕.

よなが【夜長】¶ 秋の〜を読書で過ごすほど楽しいことはない Nothing is more pleasant than to read in the *long* autumn *nights.*

よなき【夜泣き】¶ 赤ん坊が〜する Our baby *cries at night.*

よなべ【夜なべ】night work. ¶ 〜をする do *night work*; work at night.

よなよな【夜な夜な】night after night; nightly; every night.

よな·れる【世慣れる】¶ いかにも彼は〜れた人だ He is quite *a man of the world.* / He *knows much of the world.* 彼女はまだ〜れない少女にすぎない She is only an *unsophisticated* girl. 彼の応対ぶりはいかにも〜れている He meets people in a very *sophisticated* manner.

よにげ【夜逃げ】flight by night. ¶ 〜する flee by night.

よねつ【余熱】¶ それにはアイロンの〜を使うとよい Use the *remaining* (≒ *retained*; *waste*) *heat* of the iron for it.

よねん【余念】¶ 彼は読書に〜がない He *is absorbed in* reading. 彼は研究に〜がない He studies *with his whole heart.* / He *devotes himself to* his studies.

よのなか【世の中】(世間) the world; (人生) life; (時勢) times; an age. ¶ せちがらい〜だ This is *a* hard *world.* 〜がいやになった I am sick and tired of *life.* 広いようで狭いのがこの〜だ This is *a* small *world* after all. 〜とはそうしたものだ That's the way of *the world.* / Such is *life.* / They are facts of *life.* 〜はそういうわけにはいかない That's not the way *the world* is run. 〜が変わった *Times* have changed.

よは【余波】an aftereffect; an aftermath; (暴風雨の) a trail. ¶ 戦争の〜 the *aftermath* (≒ *aftereffect*) of the war.

よはく【余白】〔a〕 space; a blank; (欄外の) a margin. ¶ 〜を埋めよ Fill in the *spaces* (≒ *blanks*). (問題の文句). 各文のあとに〜を残しておくこと Leave *a blank space* after each sentence.

よばなし【夜話】a night tale; a tale by the fireside.

よば·れる【呼ばれる】¶ この花はヒヤシンスと〜れる This flower *is called* (≒ *is named*) a hyacinth. 大声で〜れる *be hailed* in a loud voice. 警察へ〜れる *be summoned to* a police station. 夕食に〜れる *be invited to* a dinner.

よばわり【呼ばわり】¶ どろぼう〜するとはけしからん It is inexcusable to *brand* me *as* a thief.

よばん【夜番】night watch; (番人) a night watchman; a night guard. ¶ 〜をする keep *night watch.*

よび【予備】reserve. ¶ 旅行するときには少し〜の金を持つがよい It is wise to have some money *in reserve* when you travel. 〜の食料 a *reserve* of food. 〜に金をとっておく I have some money *in reserve.*
　—資金 a reserve fund. ¶ 彼は〜資金に食い込んだ He drew on his *reserve fund.* **—校** ¶ 彼は〜校で大学受験の準備をした He prepared for the entrance examination for college *at the "preparatory school."* (アメリカ・イギリスではこのような制度がない. アメリカの prep school とはちがう). **—交渉** a preliminary talk (≒ negotiation). ¶ 彼が私のために〜交渉してくれた He arranged the *preliminary talks* for me. **—試験** a preliminary examination. **—会議** a preliminary conference. **—室** a spare room. **—知識** a previous knowledge. **—費** a reserve fund. **—役** the Reserve.

よびあ·げる【呼び上げる】¶ 学生たちの名前を〜げる *call out* (≒ *call up*) the students' names. 名簿を〜げる *call* a roll.

よびあつ·める【呼び集める】call together. ¶ 子どもたちを〜める *call* children *together.* 聴衆を〜める *assemble* an audience. 関係者一同を〜める *summon together* all the parties concerned.

よびい·れる【呼び入れる】call (*a person*) in.

よびおこ·す【呼び起こす】remind; recall; recollect; arouse. ¶ それが過ぎし昔を〜した It *reminded* me *of* the days gone by. その光景が今でもありありと〜される I *recall* the scene vividly even now.

よびか·ける【呼び掛ける】call to; accost. ¶ 見知らぬ人が私に〜けてきた A stranger *hailed* (≒ *called to*) me. / I *was accosted* by a stranger. 彼は力強く聴衆に〜けた He forcibly *appealed to* the audience.

よびこ【呼び子】a whistle. ¶ 〜を鳴らす blow *a whistle.*

よびごえ【呼び声】¶ 彼は次期社長の〜が高い He *is much talked about as* the next president.

よびこ·む【呼び込む】¶ 彼は私を家へ〜んだ He *called* me *into* his house.

よびすて【呼び捨て】¶ どうか私を〜にしてください Call me by my last name only. / Don't call me with "mister." / Don't mister me.

よびだし【呼び出し】a call; (召喚) a summons; (すもうの) a crier. ¶ 彼は警察署の〜に応じなかった He ignored (≒ did not answer) *the summons* from the police.

よびだ·す【呼び出す】¶ 彼は先生の前に〜された He *was called to* (≒ *was called before* (叱られるとき)) his teacher. 彼は裁判所に〜された He *was summoned to* the court. 彼女を電話口に〜しなさい *Call* her *up to* the phone. 電話で会社に〜された I *was called up to* the company by telephone.

よびた·てる【呼び立てる】¶ お〜てして恐縮です I'm sorry, but I had to *ask you to come over.*

よびつ·ける【呼びつける】¶ ふたりとも先生に〜けら

れた Both *were called before* their teacher.

よびと·める【呼び止める】¶ 彼女は通りがかりの人を～めて助けを求めた She *called to* a passer-by *to stop* for help. 彼女はタクシーを～めた She *called and stopped* a taxi.

よびな【呼び名】a given name; the first name; (別名) an alias.

よびにい·く【呼びに行く】¶ すぐにあの人を～ってくれ *Go and fetch* him right away.

よびに·くる【呼びに来る】¶ 彼が来たら～来てくれ If he calls, *come for* me.

よびにや·る【呼びに遣る】¶ 医者を～る *send for* a doctor.

よびね【呼び値】(名目相場) a nominal price; (言い値) the price asked.

よびみず【呼び水】priming water. ¶ ポンプに～をやる *prime* a pump. 彼の発言が～となって討論が活発になった His comment worked as a sort of *prime mover* for the discussion.

よびもど·す【呼び戻す】call back; (家に) call (*a person*) home. ¶ 私は突然急用で～された I *was* suddenly *called home* on urgent business.

よびもの【呼び物】a chief attraction. ¶ 私たちの劇は文化祭の～だった Our show was the *highlight* (≒ the *chief attraction*) on the program of our annual school festival.

よびょう【余病】a complication. ¶ ～を併発する develop *a complication.*

よびよ·せる【呼び寄せる】call; summon; (呼び集める) call together; (呼びにやる) send for. ¶ 彼は彼女を～せてひと言ふた言ささやいた *Calling* her *near* him, he whispered a word or two into her ear.

よびりん【呼び鈴】a buzzer; a doorbell. ¶ ～を鳴らして人を呼ぶ ring for *a person.* ～を押す press *a buzzer* (≒ *a doorbell*).

よ·ぶ【呼ぶ】**1**〖声を出して〗call. ¶ 彼がきみを～んでいる He *is calling* you.

「太郎」と彼は私を～んだ "Taro" he *called to* me.

私は後ろから大声で彼女を～んだ I *called after* her in a loud voice.

名前を～んだら「はい」と答えなさい Answer "Present," when your name *is called.*

2〖呼び寄せる〗¶ 医者をすぐ～んでください Please *send for* the doctor at once.

われわれは電報(手紙)で彼を～んだ We *telegraphed* (*wrote*) *for* him.

列車にまにあうように車を～んだ I *ordered* a car *for* the train.

彼らをここへ～んできなさい *Bring* them here!

3〖称する〗¶ われわれはその花を桜草と～ぶ We *call* that flower a primrose.

彼は祖父の名にちなんで太郎と～ばれる He *is named* Taro *after* his grandfather.

彼を国賊と～ぶことはできない We cannot *brand* (≒ *denounce*) him *as* a traitor.

4〖招待〗¶ 私はダンスパーティーに～ばれた I *was invited to* the dance.

今晩人を～ぶことになっている We are going to *give a party* this evening.

私は結婚式に～ばれていった I *was a guest at* the wedding ceremony.

よふかし【夜更かし】¶ ～は健康に悪い *Sitting* (≒ *Staying*) *up late at night* is harmful to the health.

よふけ【夜更け】¶ ～の町は静かだ The streets are quiet *at late hours.* 彼は～まで働く He works *till late* (≒ *far into the night*). / He *burns the midnight oil.*

よぶん【余分】extra; excess. ¶ ～な物を買うような金はない I have no money for *superfluities.* ～の金をお持ちですか Do you have some *extra* money (≒ money *to spare*) with you? 彼は人より～に働いた He worked *more than* others. ～の仕事をすることはない You don't have to do any *extra* work.

よほう【予報】a forecast. ¶ きょうは天気～がはずれた The 〔weather〕 *forecast* proved wrong today.

よぼう【予防】(防止) prevention; (予防策) a precaution. ¶ チフスの伝染の～をする *take precautions against* a typhoid epidemic. 洪水のあとで伝染病に対する～策を講じた We *took preventive measures against* epidemics after the flood.

―接種 vaccination. **―注射** inoculation. ¶ 私はチフスの～注射をした I *was inoculated against* typhoid. / I had *a* typhoid *inoculation.* **―線** ¶ 彼は世間から非難されぬよう～線を張った He *forestalled* public censure. **―医学** preventive medicine.

よほど【余程】¶ ～の金持ち a *very* rich man. ～の学者 a *pretty good* scholar. 彼はきみより～よく働く He works *far* (≒ *much*) better than you. 学校は～先だ The school is *a long way* ahead. 彼は～遠方から来たらしい He seems to have come from *quite* a distant place. 私は～前に彼に会った I met him *quite* a long while ago. ～そう言ってやろうと思った I *had a good mind* to say so. 彼の自殺には～のことがあるのだ Circumstances must have been *very bad* to force him to commit suicide.

よぼよぼ ¶ 老人が～と歩いていく An old man *is tottering* on (≒ is walking *unsteadily*). ～の老人 an old man *feeble* with age.

よまいごと【世迷い言】¶ ～を言うな Don't talk *nonsense*!

よま·せる【読ませる】¶ これはなかなか～せる小説だ This novel *reads* fairly *well.*

よみ【読み】(判断) judgment; (読むこと) reading. ¶ ～の深い人 a man *of insight*; a man *of sound judgment.* ～の浅い人 a *short-sighted* man. 漢字の～をまちがえた I *misread* the *kanji.*

よみあ·げる【読み上げる】¶ 先生は名簿を～げた The teacher *called* the roll. 私はこの本を1日で～げた I *read through* (≒ *finished reading*) this book in a day.

よみあやま·る【読み誤る】¶ どうも質問を～ったらしい I am afraid I *have misread* (≒ *misinterpreted*) the question.

よ

よみあわせ【読み合わせ】¶校正の～をする do the *proofreading.* 俳優たちは脚本の～をしている The actors are engaged in scenario *reading.*

よみあわ·せる【読み合わせる】collate; read and compare (≒ verify). ¶本文と書き写しとを～せる *collate* a copy *with* the text.

よみおと·す【読み落とす】¶そのページの数行を～した I *omitted reading* a few lines on the page. / I *missed* a few lines *in reading* the page.

よみおわ·る【読み終わる】¶あの本はもう～った I *have finished* 〔*reading*〕 the book.

よみかえ·す【読み返す】reread. ¶彼女は息子からの手紙を何度も～した She *read* her son's letter *over and over again.*

よみがえ·る【蘇る·甦る】resurrect. ¶イエス=キリストは～った Jesus Christ *resurrected* (≒ *rose from the dead*). 古いアルバムから幼年時代の記憶が～った The old album *refreshed* (≒ *waked*) the memories of my childhood. 雨で草木はみな～った All the plants *freshened up* after the rain. ああ涼しい,～った心地がする It's so cool here. I *feel refreshed.* / It is *refreshingly* cool.

よみかき【読み書き】reading and writing. ¶彼が私に～を教えてくれた He taught me *how to read and write.* 彼は～ができない He *can neither read nor write.* / He *is illiterate.* ―そろばん the three R's (reading, writing and arithmetic から).

よみかた【読み方】reading; (解釈) a reading. ¶～を練習する practice *reading.* 彼は英語の～がへただ He *reads* (≒ *pronounces*) English badly. この文はいろいろな～ができる(解釈できる) This sentence can *be interpreted* in various ways. / This sentence has various *readings.*

よみきり【読み切り】―小説 a complete story.

よみき·る【読み切る】¶本を一気に～る *read through* a book at (≒ on) a stretch.

よみこな·す【読みこなす】¶彼は難しい哲学書でも～した He even *digested* difficult books on philosophy. 彼はドイツ語を～す He *is able to read* German well.

よみこ·む【読み込む】¶詩人は感動を歌に～んだ The poet *expressed* his emotion *in* his poem.

よみさし【読みさし】¶彼は本を～にして遊びに行った He went out to play *leaving* his book *unfinished* (≒ *half-read*).

よみせ【夜店】a night stall. ¶～を出す open (≒ set up) *a night stall.*

よみち【夜道】¶～は危ない It is dangerous to *walk at night.*

よみて【読み手】(詩歌の作者) a poet; an author; (詩の朗読者) a reciter. ¶この詩の～は不明だ The *author* of this poem is anonymous.

よみで【読みで】¶～のある本 a *voluminous* book; a book *not easy to read through.*

よみと·る【読み取る】¶彼はたやすく人の心を～る He easily *reads* what other people are thinking. 言外の意味を～る *read* between the lines.

よみなお·す【読み直す】¶答案を提出する前に～しなさい *Read* your 〔examination〕 paper *over again* before you hand it in.

よみにく·い【読みにくい】hard to read; (筆跡の) illegible. ¶この本は～かった I found this book *hard* (≒ *difficult*) *to read.* 彼女の字は～い Her handwriting *is unreadable* (≒ *is illegible; is undecipherable*).

よみびと【読み人】¶～知らずの anonymous.

よみふけ·る【読み耽る】¶明けがたまで書物を～った I *have been absorbed* (≒ *have been lost*) *in* a book till dawn.

よみもの【読み物】reading; a book. ¶子ども向けの～ *books* for children; children's *books.*

よ·む【読む】**1**〘本などを〙read. ¶私は毎朝新聞を～む I *read* the newspaper every morning.

この新聞にはあまり～むところがない There is little *reading matter* in this paper.

この本は始めから終わりまで～む価値がある This book is worth *reading* thoroughly.

彼はその短編小説をむさぼるように(ざっと)～んだ He *devoured* (*scanned*) the short story.

彼は2章飛ばして～んだ He *skipped over* two chapters.

私はその本を～んでしまった I *have read through* (≒ *have finished*) the book.

彼女はその話を私に～んでくれた She *read* the story *to* me.

手紙を～むと次のようだ The letter *reads* as follows.

2〘その他〙¶私は彼の心(顔)を～んだ I *read* his thoughts (≒ his face).

その暗号を～むのは難しい It is difficult to *decipher* the code.

彼の手が～めた(将棋で) I could *guess* his move.

よ·む【詠む】¶彼女は和歌を～む She *composes* (≒ *writes*) Japanese 〔*tanka*〕 poems.

よめ【嫁】(妻) a wife; (花嫁) a bride; (息子の嫁) a daughter-in-law. ¶彼は彼女を～にもらった He *took* her *for his wife* (≒ *to wife*). / He *married* her. そろそろ～をもらったらどうだ It's about time that you *got married* (≒ *had a wife*). 彼女は農家に～に行った She *married* a farmer. / She *is married to* a farmer. 彼は娘を音楽家に～にやった He *married* his daughter *to* a musician. 彼は酒飲みなので～の来てがない He drinks so much that no girl is going to *marry* him.

よめ【夜目】¶山は～にもはっきり見えた The mountain was clearly seen even *in the dark.* ～,遠目,笠の内 A woman looks prettier *at night,* at a distance, or under an umbrella.

よめい【余命】*one's* remaining days. ¶彼の～はいくばくもない His *days* (≒ *years*) are numbered. / He will not be long for this world.

よめいり【嫁入り】a marriage; a wedding. ¶彼女は良家に～した She *married into* a distinguished family.

—支度 a trousseau (発音は [trú:sou]) (覆 -s; -x); (結婚式の衣装) a wedding dress. **—前** ¶うちには～前の娘がふたりいる We have two daughters *of marriageable age.*

よ·める【読める】¶彼の字は乱暴でどうも～めない His writing is so rough that I can hardly *make* it *out.* / He writes a rough and *illegible* hand. この小説はちょっと～める(楽しい) This novel *reads* quite *well.* この一節は幾通りにも～める(解釈できる) This passage *can be interpreted* in various ways. それできみの心は～めた(判断できる) Now I *can see* what you are thinking about.

よも【四方】¶～の海 the sea *all around* (≒ *on all sides*). 展望台に登って～の景色をめでた We enjoyed a *complete* view on the observatory.

よもぎ【蓬】〘植物〙a mugwort.

よもすがら【夜もすがら】all through the night. ¶～病人を看病した I cared for the patient *all through the night.* 昼はひねもす夜は～ all day long and *all night through.*

よもや surely...not. ¶～私を忘れはしまいね *Surely* you have *not* forgotten me! ～あんなことが起ころうとは思わなかった I *never expected* that such a thing *would* happen.

よもやま【四方山】¶～の話が尽きなかった We talked on and on *about one thing after another.* / We chatted on *various topics* (≒ *all sorts of things*).

よやく【予約】(新聞·雑誌の) [a] subscription; (ホテル·座席などの) a reservation; (人に会う約束) an appointment.

¶私は10部～した I *subscribed for* ten copies. 私は歌舞伎座の席を二つ～した I *booked* two seats (≒I *had* two seats *reserved*) *for* the Kabuki Theater. ホテルの部屋を～する *reserve* a room at a hotel. ホテルの～をする make *a* hotel *reservation.* ～を受け付ける take *reservations.* ～を取り消す cancel *a reservation.* 歯医者との～ *a* dental *appointment.*

—期間 ¶～期間は終わった *The term of subscription* has closed. **—金** a deposit. **—購読者** a subscriber (*to* a magazine). **—出版** publication by subscription. **—席** a reserved seat. **—代価** the subscription price. **—募集** an invitation for subscription. **—販売** ¶この本は～販売だ This book is sold by *subscription.* **—済み** ¶本日はどの部屋も～済みです All the rooms *are reserved* today.

よゆう【余裕】(余地) room; (時間) time [to spare]. ¶私は車を持つ～がない I cannot *afford to* keep a car. 私は1円の～もなかった I could not *spare* one yen. 車は4人乗れる～がある There is *room enough for* four persons in the car. 私はありあまるほどお金の～がある I have money *enough and to spare.* 彼は読書するのにじゅうぶん時間の～がある He has *plenty of* time to read.

—しゃくしゃく ¶彼は～しゃくしゃくとしている(体力) He *has a great reserve of energy.* / (平然として) He *is calm and composed.* 彼は～しゃくしゃくたる態度で大統領と語った He talked with the president *in a free and easy manner.*

よよと ¶彼女は父の死に～泣き伏した She *broke down crying* (≒ *burst into tears*) at her father's death.

より【縒り·撚り】¶あのふたりは～がもどった Those two *have become reconciled.* 彼女は客のために腕に～をかけて料理をした She cooked for her guests *to the best of her ability.*

より **1** 〘時間·場所〙¶学校は月曜～始まる School begins *on* Monday.

講義は2時～始まる The lecture begins *at* two.

1時～3時まで講義がなかった We had no lecture *from* one *to* three (≒ 米 *from* one *through* three).

来月1日～新郵便制度が行なわれる The new postal service is to be inaugurated *on* the 1st of next month.

友遠方～来たる A friend has come *from* afar.

2 〘比較〙¶私は紅茶～コーヒーが好きだ I *prefer* coffee *to* tea.

彼は学識では私～優れている He *is superior to* me in scholarship.

彼は私～金持ちだ He *is richer than* I.

私は命～も名誉を重んずる I value honor *above* life.

より【因り·依り】(原因) on account of; owing to; by. ¶彼は不勉強に～落第した He failed the examination *on account of* (≒ because of) his laziness. 命令に～着任した I arrived at my post *by* order.

-より【-寄り】¶東～の風が吹いている An *easterly* wind is blowing. 南～に隣家ができた They built a house *to the south of* our house.

よりあい【寄り合い】a gathering; a meeting. ¶きょう町内の～がある The town *meeting* is going to be held today.

—世帯 ¶このチームの弱点は～世帯である点だ The disadvantage of this team is that it is *a mixed up group.*

よりあ·う【寄り合う】¶1年に1度～うのが楽しみだ We look forward to *meeting together* once a year.

よりあつま·る【寄り集まる】¶同好の士が～る People of similar tastes *flock together.*

よりあわ·せる【縒り合わせる】¶赤糸と白糸を～せてひもを作った I *twisted* red and white threads [*together*] *into* a string.

よりかか·る【寄り掛かる】¶壁に～る *lean against* a wall. 手すりに～る *lean over* a banisters. いつまでも親に～ってはいられない You can not *rely* (≒ *depend*; *lean*) *on* (≒

よ

upon) your parents indefinitely.

よりきり【寄り切り】〘相撲〙 pushing (*a person*) out of the ring.

よりごのみ【選り好み】¶ 彼女は着る物に～がはげしい She *is very particular* (≒ *fastidious*) *about* her clothes. 彼は招待客の～がやかましい He *is very select in* the people he invites.

よりすぐ·る【選りすぐる】select. ¶ ～った選手 *selected* players.

よりそ·う【寄り添う】¶ 彼らは～って歩いた They walked *side by side*.

よりつき【寄り付き·寄付】〘商業〙 the opening. ─値段 the opening price; the opening quotation.

よりつ·く【寄り付く】¶ 彼にはだれも～かなかった Nobody *approached* him. / Everybody *kept away from* him.

よりどころ【拠り所】(根拠) the ground; the authority; (出典) the source. ¶ 彼が有罪だと考えるには十分～がある(ない) I have good (no) *ground*[*s*] for thinking that he is guilty. マルクスを～にして彼は自説を展開させた He developed his theory *on the authority of* Marx. 多くの人が心の～を求めている Many people are seeking after their spiritual *anchor*.

よりどり【選り取り】¶ どの品でも～見取り100円です You may *pick and choose* (≒ You may *take your choice*) for a hundred yen.

よりによって ¶ ～あんな男と結婚するなんて Fancy her marrying such a man of all men!

よりぬき【選り抜き】the choice. ¶ クラスの～の選手 *picked* (≒ *select*) players of our class. ～の品々 *select* goods. ～の人々 the elite; *choice* people.

よりみち【寄り道】¶ ～しないでまっすぐ帰ってきなさい Come straight home without *stopping on the way*. 彼はわざわざ～して私に会いにきた He took the trouble to *make a detour* (≒ *go out of his way*) to visit me.

よりめ【寄り目】cross-eye. ¶ 彼は～だ He *is cross-eyed*.

よりめ【縒り目·撚り目】(糸などの) a ply; (なわの) a lay.

よりょく【余力】reserve power. ¶ まだ走りつづける～がある I still have *the energy left* to keep on running. うちには寄付する～はない We have no *money to spare* for making a contribution.

よりより【寄り寄り】¶ ～集まって協議した We assembled *now and then* (≒ *from time to time*) and consulted together.

よりわ·ける【選り分ける】¶ 小さいミカンを～ける *sort out* small tangerines. 良いのと悪いのと～ける *separate* the good *from* the bad ones.

よる【夜】**1** night; (晩) evening. ¶ ～になる *Night* falls.
～が明ける Day breaks.
～が更けた *The night* is advanced.
～遅くまで(夜じゅう)起きていた I sat up *till late at night* (*all night*).
～が長くなっている *The nights* are getting longer.
彼には10日の～に会った I met him *on the night of* the 10th.
彼らは～も昼も戦った They fought day and *night*.
彼は昼働き～勉強する He works by day and studies *by night*.
～にならないうちにお帰りなさい Go back *before dark*.
うちの犬は～じゅうほえる Our dog howls *at all hours of the night*.
敵は～に紛れてわれわれを襲った The enemy attacked us *under cover of darkness*.
～の銀座 the Ginza *at night*.
2〘慣用的表現〙¶ 彼は酒がなくては～も日もあけぬ *Sake* is as dear as life to him.

よ·る【寄る】**1**〘近くに·ある場所に〙¶ もっと火の近くに～ってください Please *come nearer to* the fire.
少し～って彼らを通してやれ *Make room for* them.
帰りにちょっと～ってください Please *drop in* on your way home.
彼らは私のまわりに～ってきた They *crowded about* me.
その船は神戸に～る The steamer *calls at* (≒ *stops at*; *touches at*) Kobe.
2〘慣用的表現〙¶ 彼らは～ってたかって私を殴った They *got together* (≒ *ganged up*) and beat me.
～ると触ると彼のうわさだ He is one of the topics of conversation *everywhere*. / He is spoken of *on all sides*.

よ·る【因る·由る·依る】**1**〘原因する〙¶ 事故は運転者の前方不注意に～るものだった The accident *was due to* the fact that the driver failed to look ahead carefully.
この地域には水銀中毒に～る病人が多い Many people are sick *because of* (≒ *on account of*) mercury poisoning in this area.
試合は彼のホームランに～って決まった His home run gave a decisive turn to the ball game.
流感に～る欠席者が激増している The number of flu absentees is showing a sudden increase.
2〘基づく〙¶ 未成年者の喫煙は法律に～って禁じられている It is against the law for minors to smoke.
1学期の成績に～ってクラスの編成替えが行なわれた *According to* their grades of the first term, their class was regrouped.
彼の小説は中国の伝説に～って書かれている His novel *is based on* a Chinese legend.
あなたのご要請に～って計画を変更した The plan was modified *in accordance with* your request.
けさの新聞に～れば南米で大地震があったそうだ *According to* the newspaper this morning, there was a strong earthquake in South America.
大きさに～って値段が異なる The price *depends on* (≒ *depends upon*) the size.

よ

人をその地位や富に〜って判断してはならない We should not judge people *by* their status or wealth.

聞くところに〜ると彼女はイギリスへ留学するそうだ *From* what I have heard of her, she is going to go to England for study.

3 〖手段・方法〗 ¶ 作者はこの小説に〜ってなにを語ろうとしているのだろうか What does the author try to express *in* this novel?

政府は警察力に〜って暴動を抑えようとした The government *resorted to* police force to suppress the riot.

労働者はストライキに〜って会社に抗議した The company workers protested *by* striking.

この問題の解決は話し合いに〜ったほうがいい It would be better for us to settle this problem *by* common consent. / We should talk out this problem before settling it.

4 〖依存する・応ずる〗 ¶ 彼女は夫の遺産に〜って生活している She lives *on* her husband's inheritance.

文筆に〜って身を立てるのは難しい It is hard to establish oneself as a professional writer.

場合に〜っては今晩は帰れないかもしれない It may happen that I can't come home this evening. / I may not come home this evening, if something happens.

人に〜って考え方はいろいろだ(十人十色) So many men, so many minds. / What people think varies from one person to another.

そんな話を聞けば, 人に〜っては怒るかもしれない That kind of talk may hurt someone. / Some people may get angry if they hear such a thing.

人を信用するのも相手に〜りけりだ You should not trust everybody indiscriminately. / There are some people who should not be trusted.

5 〖行為の主体〗 ¶ この曲もベートーベンに〜って書かれたものだ This piece was also composed *by* Beethoven.

よ・る 【選る】 ¶ よいリンゴを〜る *pick out* (≒ *choose; select*) good apples.

よ・る 【縒る・撚る】 ¶ 3本の糸を〜ってひもを作る *twist* (≒ *twine*) three threads *into* a string.

よるひる 【夜昼】 night and day; day and night. ¶ 〜なしに働く work *day and night.*

よるべ 【寄る辺】 ¶ 〜のない老人 an old man *with no relative to depend upon.*

よれよれ ¶ 〜のワイシャツ(着古した) a *worn-out* shirt; (しわくちゃの) a *crumpled* shirt. この服地はじきに〜になる(しわくちゃになる) This cloth *crumples* easily.

よ・れる 【縒れる・撚れる】 (もつれる) be tangled.

よろい 【鎧】 armor.

—武者 an armored (≒ armor-clad) warrior.

よろいど 【鎧戸】 shutters.

よろく 【余禄】 an extra (≒ additional) profit.

よろ・ける ¶ 石につまずいて〜けた I stumbled over a stone and *staggered.*

よろこばし・い 【喜ばしい】 happy; pleasant. ¶ 〜いニュース *happy* news. 〜い結果 a *good* result.

よろこば・す 【喜ばす】 please; delight; satisfy. ¶ 彼女の話は私を〜せた Her story *made* me *happy.* 美しい景色は目を〜せる The beautiful scenery *delights* (≒ *pleases*) the eye.

よろこび 【喜び】 joy; pleasure. ¶ 彼女は〜のあまり泣いた She cried for *joy.* 私は心から〜を申し述べた I expressed my *joy* heartily. 少年は贈り物を見て〜の色を浮かべた The boy showed *pleasure* at the gift. 私は彼の結婚に〜を述べた I offered my *congratulations on* his marriage. / I *congratulated* him *on* his marriage.

—事 a happy event; (めでたい) a matter for joy; (祝すべき) a matter for congratulation.

よろこびいさ・む 【喜び勇む】 ¶ 彼らは〜んで出かけた They left home *with great joy.*

よろこ・ぶ 【喜ぶ】 ¶ その知らせを聞いて〜んでいる I *am glad* (≒ *am pleased; am delighted*) *to* hear the news. きみの成功を〜んでいる I *am* very *happy about* your success. / I *am pleased with* your success. / I *am glad of* your success. / I *am glad that* you have succeeded. 彼はその知らせを聞いて跳び上がって〜んだ He *jumped for joy* to hear the news. 〜んでお教えします I will teach you *with pleasure.* 〜んでお手伝いいたします I will *be glad* (≒ *be delighted*) *to* help you. / I will *gladly* (≒ *willingly*) help you. われわれは彼を〜んで迎えた We received him *with joy.* ご結婚お〜び申し上げます I *congratulate* you *on* your marriage.

よろし・い 【宜しい】 ¶ 〜い, やってみましょう *Very well,* I'll try. ええ, 〜いとも Yes, *all right.* もう〜いです. じゅうぶん頂戴しました *No more, thanks,* I have had plenty. 帰宅しても〜い You *may* go home. それで〜い That's *right.* / That *will do.* 私はコーヒーより紅茶のほうが〜い I *prefer* tea *to* coffee. きみが望むなら教えてやっても〜い If you want, I *don't mind* telling you.

よろしく 【宜しく】 **1** 〖適当に〗 ¶ その件〜取り計らってください Please *manage* the matter *as you think fit.*

それを〜ご判断ください I *leave* it *to your judgment.*

2 〖あいさつ〗 ¶ 今後とも〜お願いします I *beg a continuance of your favor.* (会話ではこの英語は用いない. ただ Good-bye. でじゅうぶん).

息子のこと〜お願いします I hope you will look after my son.

みなみなさまに〜お伝えください *Remember me kindly to* your family. / *Give my best regards to* your family. (give *one's* love は親戚(しんせき)間, あるいは婦人の親友間で用いる. 親しい間では Say hello for me to your family. と言うのが普通).

彼から〜とのことでした He *sends* you *his best regards.* / He *sent* you *his greeting.*

よ

よろず【万】all.
—屋 a Jack-of-all-trades.
よろめ·く ¶ 彼は〜く足どりで帰ってきた He came back home with *unsteady* (≒ *faltering*) steps. 彼は酔っ払いのように〜いた He *staggered* (≒ *reeled*) like a drunken man. 彼女は〜きそうだ (浮気しそうだ) She is liable to have an affair [with *a person*].
よろよろ totteringly. ¶ 彼は〜歩いた He walked *unsteadily.* / He *staggered* (≒ *reeled*) along. 彼女は〜と道を横切った She crossed the road *totteringly* (≒ *with faltering steps*).
よろん【輿論】public opinion. ¶ 〜を喚起する arouse (≒ stir up) *public opinion.* 彼は〜を無視した He defied *public opinion.* 政府は〜を反映してほしい We would like the Government to act in accordance with *public opinion.* / It is desirous that *public opinion* [should] be reflected in the Governmental policy. 彼の発言は〜を刺激した His remarks gave an impetus to *public sentiment.*
—調査 a public opinion poll; a survey of public opinion.
よわい【齢·歯】[an] age. ¶ 〜80に近い私の母 my mother, *aged* nearly eighty; my mother, about eighty years *of age.*
よわ·い【弱い】weak; frail. ¶ 〜い酒 a *mild* (≒ *weak*) *sake.* 〜い風 a *gentle* wind. 〜い光 *feeble* (≒ *faint*) light. 〜い震動 a *slight* shock. 〜い熱 *low* heat. 女は〜い Woman *is weak.* 彼は体が〜い He *is weak* (≒ *is delicate*). / He has a *frail* constitution. 彼は気が〜い He *is timid.* / He is a person of *weak* character. 彼は意志が〜い He is a person *of weak will.* 彼は頭が〜い He *is soft* (≒ *is weak*) *in* the head. 彼は胃が〜い He has a *poor* digestion. 私はテニスが〜い I am *a poor hand at* tennis. / I'm a *poor* tennis player. 私は船に〜い I am a *poor* (≒ *bad*) sailor. 私は酒に〜い I am a *poor* drinker. 私は英語に〜い I *am poor at* (≒ *am weak in*) English. 既製品のくつは〜い Ready-made shoes *do not wear well.*
よわいもの【弱い者】a weak person.
¶ 彼は〜いじめだ He is *a bully.*
よわき【弱気】timidness. ¶ 〜な男 a *timid* (≒ *timorous; cowardly; faint-hearted*) man. 〜になるな Don't *be discouraged.*
—市場 a bear[ish] market.
よわく【弱く】weakly; softly. ¶ そんなに強く引っ張るな. もう少し〜引っ張ってくれ Don't pull it quite so strongly. Pull it *less strongly,* please. 彼は病気で体を〜した He *became weak* after the illness. / The illness *has weakened* him. / After the illness he *has declined* (≒ *has deteriorated*) *in health.* 光を〜してくれませんか Would you please *turn down* (≒ *turn dim*) the light? 酒に〜なった I *soon get drunk* nowadays.
よわごし【弱腰】¶ そんなに〜ではだめだ You shouldn't *be* so *timid* (≒ *weak-kneed; faint-hearted*).
よわ·せる【酔わせる】make drunk; intoxicate. ¶ 今夜は彼を〜せよう Let's *make* (≒ *get*) him *drunk* this evening. 聴衆は彼の弁舌に〜された The audience *were fascinated* (≒ *were charmed; were enraptured; were intoxicated*) with his fluent speech.
よわたり【世渡り】¶ 〜の道 the art of living. 彼は〜がじょうずだ He knows *how to get on in the world* (≒ *how to make his way in life*). / He *is wise in worldly affairs.* / He *is worldly-wise.*
よわね【弱音】¶ 彼らは訓練は厳し過ぎると〜をはいた They *complained about* the hardness of the training. 〜をはいてはいかん You must persevere courageously. / Never *say die.*
よわみ【弱味】weakness; (弱点) a weak point; a weakness.
¶ 私は〜につけこまれた He took advantage of my *weakness.* 彼女は絶対に〜を見せない She never betrays her *weak point* (≒ *weakness*). ついに彼の〜を握った At last I *gained an advantage over* him. 敵に〜を見せてはだめだ You must not show *a weak attitude to* your rivals.
よわむし【弱虫】a coward; a weakling.
¶ 彼はなんて〜だ How *cowardly* (≒ *chicken-hearted*) he is!
よわ·める【弱める】weaken; enfeeble.
¶ 病は心身ともに人を〜める Illness *weakens* (≒ *enfeebles*) us both mentally and physically. ガスの火を〜める *turn down* the gas; *lower* the flame of the gas. それは労組の勢力を〜めた It *decreased* the influence of the labor union. 湿っぽい気候は消化器官を〜める Dampness *dulls* our digestive organs.
よわよわし·い【弱弱しい】feeble; frail.
¶ 彼女は〜い体つきの人だ She looks *feeble* (≒ *weak*). / She is a woman of *delicate* (≒ *fragile*) constitution. 彼女はいつも〜い声で話す She always speaks in a *feeble* (≒ *faint*) voice.
よわら·せる【弱らせる】weaken; enfeeble.
¶ その質問には〜せられた I *was embarrassed* (≒ *was perplexed; was harassed*) *with* the question. 消化不良が彼の体力を〜せた Dyspepsia *has weakened* him.
よわりは·てる【弱り果てる】¶ 彼の愚痴に〜てた I *was fed up with* (≒ *was annoyed by*) his complaints. 長い旅ですっかり〜てた He *was* utterly *exhausted from* his long trip. / He *was* quite *tired* after his long trip. 彼は〜てていた (途方にくれていた) He *was at his wits'* (≒ *wit's*) *end.*
よわりめ【弱り目】¶ 〜にたたり目 (諺) Misfortunes never come *alone* (≒ *singly*). / *It never rains but it pours.* まったく当時の私は〜にたたり目だった I *had been having a run of bad luck* then.
よわ·る【弱る】**1**〖弱くなる〗weaken; become weak. ¶ 彼の健康は2年前から〜っている His

よ

health *has been failing* for two years.
彼は少し体が～っている He *is* a little *out of health.*
私は～ってしまった I *have grown weak.*
2 〖困る〗 ¶ その失敗で彼は心中～り切っている He *is depressed* in mind at the failure.
すりに会って,彼は～って帰って来た As he had his pocket picked, he came home *crestfallen.*
どう扱ったらよいかあの男には～っている I *do not know what to do with him.*
なんと返事をしてよいか～った I *was at a loss* (≒ *was perplexed*) what answer to make. (形式ばった言い方. ふつうは I didn't know...).
あらゆる試みに失敗して彼は～っていた(途方にくれていた) He failed in every attempt and *was at his wits'* (≒ *wit's*) *end.*
ひどい暑さで～った The unbearable heat *has knocked* me *up.*

よんどころな・い【拠ん所ない】inevitable; unavoidable. ¶ ～い事情で欠席します I'll be absent because of *unavoidable* circumstances. ～く私が行かざるをえない I *am compelled* (≒ *am forced*) *to* go myself. 彼は～く「はい」と言った "Yes," he said rather *reluctantly.* それは～いことだ It *can't be helped.*

ら

-ら 【-等】 ¶ きみ～のでる幕でない That is no business of *yours.* / The matter does not concern *you.* 子供～はどこにいるのか Where are the *children*? それ～は狂っている *They* (≒ *Those*) are out of order. 高橋～5人のメンバーがその山に登った Takahashi *and* four other members climbed the mountain.

ラード lard.

ラーメン Chinese noodles.

らい-【来-】¶ ～学期 *next* term; the *coming* term.

-らい【-来】¶ 昨年～ *since* last year. 10年～の友人 a friend of ten *years' standing.* 5年～の大雪 the heaviest snowfall *in* five years.

らいい【来意】the object of a visit. ¶ ～を聞いてみなさい Will you ask him *what he has come for*? / Will you ask him *what it is he wants to see me about*?

らいう【雷雨】a thunderstorm.

らいうん【雷雲】a thundercloud.

らいえん【来援】¶ 村民は自衛隊の～を求めた Villagers asked the Self Defense Forces to *come and help* them (≒ *come to* their *assistance*).

らいえん【来演】¶ 彼女が当地に～する She is to *come and perform* here.

ライオン a lion; (雌) a lioness; (子) a cub.

らいかい【来会】**―者** those present at the meeting. ¶ 多数の～者があった There was *a* large *audience.* / A lot of people *attended.*

らいかん【来観】a visit; attendance. ¶ その博物館は～する者が多い The museum is largely visited.
―者 a visitor.

らいかん【雷管】a percussion (≒ detonating) cap; a detonator.
―撃発装置 a percussion lock.

らいきゃく【来客】a visitor. ¶ きょうは～が多いだろう Today I'll have a good many *visitors.* / I expect plenty of *company* today. ～はお断りだ I am not at home to anyone.

らいげつ【来月】next month. ¶ 彼は～20日に上京する He'll come up to Tokyo on the 20th *proximo* (≒ *prox*; *of next month*). ～のきょう this day 〔*next*〕 *month.*

らいこう【来航】¶ ペリーは1853年に浦賀に～した Perry *visited* Uraga in 1853.

らいさん【礼賛】glorification; adoration. ¶ 科学の進歩を～する *glorify* the progress of science. 美の～ the *cult* of beauty. 科学～ the *glorification* of science.

らいしゅう【来週】next week; the coming week. ¶ ～の金曜日 *next* Friday; Friday *next week* (next Friday ではその週の月曜・火曜などでも言うから誤解の起こりそうな時). ～のきょう this day 〔*next*〕 *week.*

らいしゅん【来春】next spring; the coming spring.

らいしん【来信】¶ 彼から～があった I *received a letter from* him. ここしばらく彼から～がない I *have* not *heard from* him for some time.

らいしんし【頼信紙】a telegram (≒ telegraph) form (≒ 米 blank).

ライスカレー curry and rice; curried rice.

らいせ【来世】a (≒ the) future life; the life after death.

ライセンス a license.

ライター **1** a lighter. ¶ ～の石 a *lighter* flint.
2 〖作者〗 a writer.
シナリオ― a scenarist.

らいだん【来談】¶ ご～の程, 御願い致します Would you please *come and see* me? 本人～あれ *Apply personally* (≒ *in person*).

らいちょう【来朝】¶イギリスの外相が～する The Foreign Minister of the United Kingdom will *visit* (≒ *come to*) *Japan*.

らいちょう【来聴】━者 ¶～者は多かった (少なかった) There was *a* large (small) *audience*.

らいちょう【雷鳥】〘鳥類〙 a grouse (単複同形); a ptarmigan.

らいでん【来電】¶パリからの～によれば according to *a dispatch* from Paris. ロンドンから～があった We have received *a telegram* from London.

ライト (あかり) a light. ¶水面に～が照らし出されている *A light* is being thrown on the surface of the water.
━ブルー light blue. ━級選手 a light-weight. ━ヘビー級選手 a light heavy-weight. ヘッド━ headlights. ¶自動車のヘッド～がまぶしい The *headlights* dazzle my eyes.

ライト (右) right. ¶(野球で) 彼は～を守る He is *a right fielder*. ～のスタンドにホームランを打ち込んだ He drove a home run into the *right-field* stands.

ライナー a liner. ¶(野球で) 彼はレフトの奥深くにすごい～を打った He hit *a* tremendous *drive* (≒ *liner*) deep to the left field.

らいにん【来任】¶新校長がきょう～した The new principal *arrived at his post* today.

らいねん【来年】next year. ¶～の夏 *next* summer; summer *next year*. ～4月 *next* April. ～の今ごろは日本にいない I won't be here in Japan about this time *next year*. ～のことを言うと鬼が笑う(諺) *Don't count your chickens before they are hatched*.

ライノタイプ a linotype.

ライバル a rival.

らいびょう【癩病】leprosy; Hansen's disease.
━患者 a leper. ━病院 a leper house.

らいひん【来賓】a guest; a visitor.
━室 a reception room. ━席 the guests' seats.

ライフ [a] life.
━ボート a lifeboat. ━ワーク *one's* lifework.

ライフルじゅう【ライフル銃】a rifle.

らいほう【来訪】a visit. ¶3時にご～ください Please *come* at 3. あすご～をお待ちしています I am expecting you tomorrow. / I am looking forward to seeing you tomorrow.
━者 a visitor. ━者名簿 the visitors' book.

ライむぎ【ライ麦】〘植物〙 rye.

らいめい【雷名】¶彼は映画界に～をとどろかせている監督だ He is a director who *has won wide fame* (≒ *is famous*; *is widely known*) in the film world.

らいめい【雷鳴】a thunder. ¶ものすごい～を伴って激しい雨が降った It rained heavily with a lot of *thunder*.

らいらく【磊落】¶～な人 an *open-hearted* (≒ a *jolly*; a *frank*) man.

ライラック〘植物〙 a lilac.

らいれき【来歴】*one's* career. ¶彼女にはおもしろい～がある She has had *an interesting life* (≒ *an interesting experience*).

ライン a line.
━アップ a line-up. ━ダンス a line dance. ━ドライブ a line drive.

ラウドスピーカー a loud speaker.

ラウンド a round; (ゴルフ) a round of golf.
━テーブル a round table. ━ナンバー ¶～ナンバーで (概数で) in round numbers (≒ figures).

らく【楽】**1**〘安楽〙¶私は10万円で1か月～に暮らせる I can live *in comfort* on a hundred thousand yen a month.
彼は～な暮らしをしている He *is in easy circumstances*.
彼は実業界を退いて～な暮らしをしている He has retired from business and is living *at his ease*.
私は両親に～をさせたい I wish to *make* my parents *comfortable*.
どうぞお～にしてください Please *make yourself at home* (≒ *comfortable*).
その薬で痛みが～になった The medicine *relieved* me *of* the pain.
(堅くならずに) ～にしてください Take it *easy*.
～あれば苦あり After *pleasure*, pain.
2〘容易〙¶それはけっして～な仕事でない It is no *easy* (≒ *light*) task.
彼は英語を～に話す He speaks English *with ease* (≒ *with fluency*; *without difficulty*).
私は1日に10時間～に働く I *make nothing of* work*ing* ten hours a day.
教科書があると先生がとても～だ The textbook *saves* the teacher *much trouble*.

らくいん【烙印】a brand mark. ¶彼は落伍(らくご)者の～を押された He *was branded* (≒ *was stigmatized*) as a dropout.

らくいんきょ【楽隠居】¶彼は～の身だ He *lives in comfortable retirement*. / He *leads an easy life in retirement*.

らくえん【楽園】a paradise; an Eden. ¶地上の～ a paradise; an earthly paradise. 日本は子供の～だ Japan is *a paradise* for children.

らくがき【落書き】a scrawl; [a] scribbling. ¶壁に～をする *scribble* on the wall. 壁じゅうに～をする *scrawl* all over the wall. ～を禁ず (掲示) No *Scribbling*.

らくご【落語】a comic story.
━家 a professional comic storyteller.

らくご【落伍】¶隊から～する *fall* (≒ *drop*) *out* of the ranks (≒ *out* of line). マラソンで～する *drop behind* in the marathon race.
━者 a straggler; a failure.

らくさ【落差】(水の) a head. ¶40フィートの～のある水 forty feet *head* of water.

らくさつ【落札】¶彼に～した The *contract was awarded to* him. その品は最初の入札者に～した The article *was knocked down to* the first bidder.
━者 a successful bidder. ━値 a contract price.

らくじつ【落日】the setting sun. ¶～の金色の光 the golden rays of the *sunset*.

らくしゅ【落手】¶(チェスで)～をする make a bad move. 4月3日づけのお手紙たぢいま～しました I *received* (≒ *am in receipt of*) your letter dated (≒ of) the 3rd of April.

らくしゅ【落首】a satire; a satirical poem; a lampoon.

らくしょう【楽勝】an easy win. ¶私は～した I *won* (≒ *had; got*) *an easy victory.* / I *had a walkover* (≒ *had a walkaway*).

らくじょう【落城】the fall of a castle. ¶遂に彼らの城も～した They at last *surrendered the castle to* the enemy.

らくせい【落成】completion. ¶校舎が～した The school buildings *have been completed* (≒ *have been finished*).
—式 an inauguration ceremony.

らくせき【落石】¶～注意(掲示) Watch out for *falling rocks.*

らくせん【落選】(選挙の) failure (≒ defeat) in an election; (展覧会の) rejection. ¶彼は選挙で～した He *was defeated* in the election. この絵は～した This picture *was rejected.* / The picture *was not accepted.*
—候補 a defeated candidate.

らくだ【駱駝】a camel; a dromedary (アラビア産の乗用ラクダ). ¶～のこぶ a hump.
—織り ¶～織りの布 camel's-hair cloth.

らくだい【落第】failure. ¶私は試験に～した I *failed* [*in*] an examination. (米 では fail the examination が普通). そんな作品は～だ Such a work should *be rejected.*
—生 a failure; a plucked student. —点 a failing mark.

らくたん【落胆】disappointment; discouragement; despondency. ¶彼の言動には～した I *was disappointed at* his words and deeds. 彼は試験に落ちて～している He *is disappointed* (≒ *is depressed; is downcast*) because he failed the examination.

らくちゃく【落着】[a] settlement. ¶難事件もやっと～した The difficult matter *was* finally *settled.*

らくちょう【落丁】a missing page. ¶1ページ～がある There is *a page missing.* / There is *a missing page.*

らくてん【楽天】optimism. ¶彼女は～的な人生観を持っている She has an *optimistic* view of life.
—家 an optimist.

らくのう【酪農】dairy [farming]. ¶彼は北海道で～を営んでいる He *is a dairy farmer* in Hokkaido. / He *runs a dairy farm* in Hokkaido.
—家 a dairy farmer. —場 a dairy farm. —製品 dairy products (≒ produce).

らくば【落馬】falling from a horse. ¶～する fall from (≒ be thrown by) *one's* horse.

らくばん【落盤】a cave-in.

ラグビー Rugby [football]. ¶～をする play *Rugby.*
—選手 a Rugby (≒ football) player.

らくめい【落命】death. ¶彼は飛行機事故で～した He *died* (≒ *lost his life*) in an airplane accident.

らくよう【落葉】a fallen leaf (複 leaves). ¶秋の夜には新しい～の乾いた音がする Autumn evenings are whispering with the crisp rustle of newly *fallen leaves.*
—樹 a deciduous tree. —松 a larch.

らくよう【洛陽】an old capital of China. ¶彼の本は～の紙価を高めた His book sold like hot cakes. / His book had a tremendous reception.

らくらい【落雷】¶どこかに～があったにちがいない *Lightning* must have struck somewhere.

らくらく【楽楽】¶あの人たちは年金で～と暮らしている They live *in comfort* on a pension. ～と試合に勝った We *easily* won the game. 座席は広いので3人が～座れた The seat was wide enough for three people to sit *at ease.*

ラグラン a raglan.
—袖 raglan sleeves.

らくるい【落涙】¶その話を聞いて思わず～した Hearing the story I *shed tears* in spite of myself. / The story *moved* me *to tears.* / I *was moved to tears* by the story.

ラケット a racket.

-らし·い ¶男(紳士; 女)～い man*ly* (gentleman*ly*; woman*ly*). 婦人～い lady*like*. フランス人～い French-*looking*. 彼は賢い青年～い He *looks like* a bright young man. その評判はほんとう～い The report *seems* to be true. そのリンゴは腐っている～い The apple *appears* rotten. 雨～い It *is likely to* rain. / It *looks like* rain. それなら英語～い That's *something like* English. 彼は少しも学者～いところがない He *is nothing of* a scholar. その行為は紳士～くない His conduct *is unworthy of* a gentleman. / His conduct *is* not *becoming* a gentleman. 彼は学生～くふるまった He behaved *as becomes* a student.

ラジウム〘化学〙radium.
—鉱泉 a radium spring. —療法 a radium therapy.

ラジエーター〘電気〙〘機械〙a radiator.

ラジオ 米 radio; 英 wireless; (機械) a radio; a radio (≒ wireless) set. ¶～をかける(止める) turn on (turn off) *the radio.* ～を聴く listen to *the radio*; 英 listen in to *the radio.* ～の音を大きく(小さく)する turn up (down) *the radio.* この～でB.B.C.が聞ける We can get B.B.C. *on this set.* 私は～をB.B.C.に合わせた I tuned in to B.B.C. / I tuned my *radio* to B.B.C. 彼は～で講演をした He spoke on *the radio.*
—解説者 a radio commentator. —受信機 a [radio] receiver. —体操 radio gymnastics. —聴取者 a radio listener. —ドラマ a radio drama. —ニュース the news on the radio. —放送 broadcasting. —放送局 a radio station. トランジスター— a transistor radio [set]. ポータブル— a portable radio.

ラシャ【羅紗】wool[l]en cloth.
綾— twilled cloth. 縞— tweed. 平—

broadcloth.

らしんばん【羅針盤】a [mariner's] compass.

ラスク a rusk.

ラスト the last. ¶ 彼はマラソンで〜になった He *was the last to finish* (≒ *finished last in*) the long-distance race.

—イニング the last inning. —シーン the last scene. —スパート the last spurt. ¶ 〜スパートをかけた I made *the last spurt*.

らせん【螺旋】(ねじ) a screw; (うずまき) a spiral.

—階段 a spiral staircase. —形(状) spiral (adj.) —ばかり a spiral balance.

らぞう【裸像】a nude; a nude stature (≒ figure).

らたい【裸体】a naked (≒ nude) body.

—画 a nude [picture]. —主義 nudism. —主義者 a nudist. —美 physical beauty.

らち【埒】¶ その問題もやっと〜があいた(まだ〜があかない) The problem *has been settled* at last (*remains* still *unsettled*).

—外 ¶ このチームは優勝の〜外にある This team is *outside* the competition for the championship.

ラッカー lacquer. ¶ 箱に〜をぬって仕上げた I *lacquered* the box as a finish.

らっかさん【落下傘】a parachute. ¶ 〜で降りた I descended by *parachute*. / I made a *parachute* descent.

—部隊 a parachute troop; a paratroop battalion. —兵 a paratrooper.

らっかせい【落花生】a peanut; a groundnut.

らっかん【落款】a writer's (≒ painter's) signature and seal. ¶ 絵に〜をした I *signed and sealed* my picture.

らっかん【楽観】optimism. ¶ だれもが前途を〜していた Everybody *was optimistic about* the future. 事態の推移は〜を許さない The situation does not warrant optimism. / We cannot hold an optimistic view about the situation. 彼は物事を〜的にみる He *takes an optimistic view of* things. / He *looks at the bright side of* things. / He *is an optimist*.

—論 optimism. —論者 an optimist.

ラッキー lucky.

—セブン the lucky seventh inning. —ゾーン the lucky zone.

らっきょう【辣韮】a shallot.

らっこ【猟虎】〔動物〕a sea otter.

ラッシュアワー the rush hour.

ラッセル〔医学〕a murmur (ラッセルはドイツ語の Rasselgeräusch (水泡音) から). ¶ 心臓の〜音 *a* heart *murmur*.

ラッセルしゃ【ラッセル車】a [Russel] snowplow (≒ 英 snowplough).

らっぱ【喇叭】(軍隊用) a bugle; a trumpet. ¶ 〜を吹く blow (≒ sound) *a bugle*.

—手 a bugler; a trumpeter. —ズボン bell-bottom[ed] trousers. —飲み ¶ ビールを〜飲みした I *drank* some beer *from the bottle*.

進軍(起床)— ¶ 進軍(起床)〜を吹く *sound* the advance (the reveille).

ラップ a lap.

—タイム a lap time. ¶ 500メートルの〜タイム the five hundred meter *lap time*.

らつわん【辣腕】shrewdness. ¶ 彼は外交官として〜をふるった He showed his *unusual brilliance and adeptness* as a diplomat.

—家 a man of ability; an efficient man; a shrewd person.

ラテン Latin.

—アメリカ Latin America. —音楽 Latin American Music. —語 Latin. —民族 the Latin races (≒ peoples).

らでん【螺鈿】nacre; mother-of-pearl.

¶ 〜の宝石箱 a jewel case inlaid with *nacre* (≒ *mother-of-pearl*).

ラドン〔化学〕radon.

ラノリン〔化学〕lanolin[e].

らば【騾馬】a mule.

らふ【裸婦】a woman in the nude.

—像 the nude.

ラフ rough. ¶ 〜な生地 *rough* cloth. 〜な態度 a *rough* (≒ *rude*) manner. 〜な服装 an *informal* dress.

ラブ 1 〖恋〗love.

—シーン a love scene. —レター a love letter.

2 〖テニス〗¶ 15対〜 fifteen-*love*.

—ゲーム a love game.

ラプソディー a rhapsody.

ラベル a label (発音は [léibl]).

ラマ —教 Lamaism. —教徒 a Lamaist; a Lamaite. —僧 a lama. —寺 a lamasery.

ダライ— Dalai Lama.

ラム (酒) rum.

ラムネ lemonade.

ラリー a rally; (車の) a rally of sport cars.

¶ 激しい〜の応酬があった(テニスで) The *rally* was quite fierce.

られつ【羅列】[an] enumeration. ¶ それは単なる事実の〜にすぎない It is just *a* simple *enumeration* of facts. 演説の始めに彼は自分の肩書きを〜した At the beginning of his speech, he *listed up* his titles.

ラワン〔植物〕lauan.

らん【乱】(戦乱) a war; (反乱) a revolt; a rebellion; (蜂起) [an] insurrection. ¶ 応仁の〜 *The* [*Civil*] *War* of the Onin Era.

らん【欄】a column. ¶ 読者からの投書のための〜を設けた We provided *a column* for letters from the readers.

広告— the advertisement (≒ ad) column. スポーツ— the sporting column. 文芸— the literary column.

らん【蘭】〔植物〕an orchid.

らんうん【乱雲】〔気象〕a nimbus (複 -es; nimbi).

らんおう【卵黄】the yolk.

らんがい【欄外】the margin. ¶ 〜の注 a note on *the margin*; a *marginal* note.

らんかく【乱獲・濫獲】indiscriminate fishing (≒ hunting).

ら

らんがく【蘭学】the study of the Dutch language; the Dutch studies.
—者 a Dutch scholar.

らんかん【欄干】a rail; a railing; (階段の) a balustrade; banisters.

らんぎょう【乱行】misconduct. ¶ 彼は若いころ～にふけっていた While young, he led a wild life. / While young, he gave himself up to *debauchery* (≒ *profligacy*). / He sowed his wild oats.

らんきりゅう【乱気流】turbulence.

ランキング ranking. ¶ 彼はいつも～第1位を占めている He is always the first in *the ranking*. / He always *takes the first rank*.

ランク rank. ¶ 彼女はことしの新人歌手第1位に～された She *was given* (≒ *was placed in*) *the first rank* among the new singers of this year.

らんぐいば【乱杭歯】an irregular set of teeth.

らんさく【乱作・濫作】overproduction. ¶ あの小説家はどちらかといえば～する The novelist *writes* rather *excessively*.

らんざつ【乱雑】disorder. ¶ 彼の部屋はいつも～だ His room *is* always *in disorder*. 机の上が～だ Everything *is in a mess* on the desk. 本が～に積んである Books are piled up *in a disorderly manner*.

らんし【乱視】〖医学〗astigmatism. ¶ ～になった I have got affected by *astigmatism*.
—眼 astigmatic eyes. —用眼鏡 astigmatic lenses.

らんし【卵子】〖生物〗an egg cell; an ovum (㊫ ova).

らんしゃ【乱射】random shots. ¶ ピストルを～する *fire* a pistol *blindly* (≒ *at random*).

らんじゅく【爛熟】ripeness; full maturity.
¶ 19世紀末フランス文学は～期を迎えた At the end of the nineteenth century French literature reached *the full maturity* (≒ *the stage of overripeness*; *the era of decadence*). 文化は～した The culture *is full-grown* (≒ *is full-fledged*).

らんしん【乱心】insanity. ¶ 彼は心労のあまり～した Too much grief *drove* him *mad*. / He was so distressed that he *lost his mind* (≒ *went mad*).
—者 a madman; a lunatic.

らんせい【乱世】〔the〕troubled (≒ disturbed) times; a civil war period. ¶ そのころ日本は～だった Japan was then in *a state of anarchy*.

らんせい【卵生】〖生物〗oviparity. ¶ 一～の monovular. 二～の biovular.
—動物 an oviparous animal; ovipara (複数形).

らんせん【乱戦】a confused fight; a dogfight; a melee. ¶ 敵味方入り乱れ～となった Both sides *fought in utter confusion*. / Both sides *engaged in a free-for-all*. 試合は～気味だった The game was rather *a confused one*.

らんそう【卵巣】〖解剖学〗an ovary.
—炎 ovaritis. —切除 ovariotomy. —ホルモン ovarian hormones.

らんぞう【乱造・濫造】overproduction.
¶ 粗製～ *excessive production* of inferior (≒ poor) articles.

らんだ【乱打】¶ 警鐘を～する *ring* (≒ *sound*) an alarm bell *violently*. 投手は敵の～を浴びて降板した The pitcher was knocked out by *successive hits* of the opponent team.

ランタン a lantern.

ランチ **1**〖食事〗lunch; (正式に) luncheon.
¶ ～を食べる have lunch. 彼は～を食べていた He *was at lunch*. あそこはいい～だった They *lunched* us decently there.
—タイム lunchtime. お子様— an assorted dish for children.
2〖はしけ〗a launch.

らんちきさわぎ【乱痴気騒ぎ】a revel; an orgy (しばしば複数). ¶ ～をした We *had an orgy* of merrymaking. 酒を飲んで～をした We got drunk and *went on a spree* (≒ *made a racket*). 彼らの～がまた始まった They *are raising hell* again.

らんちょう【乱丁】¶ この本には～がある There *are* several *pages out of place* (≒ *disarranged pages*) in this book.

ランデブー a rendezvous. ¶ 今夜彼女と～がある I have *a date* with her tonight. / I will *rendezvous* with her tonight. そのレストランがわれわれの～の場所だ The restaurant is our *rendezvous*. (宇宙船が)～する rendezvous (*with*).

らんとう【乱闘】a free fight; a dogfight.
¶ 警官隊とデモ隊との間に～があった There was *a struggle* between the police and the demonstrators.

らんどく【乱読・濫読】¶ 小説を～する *read* every novel that comes in *one's* way *indiscriminately*.

ランドセル a knapsack; a satchel.

ランドリー a laundry.

ランナー a runner.

らんにゅう【乱入】trespassing; 〔an〕intrusion. ¶ 暴徒がへやに～した A gang of ruffians *intruded* (≒ *broke*) *into* the room.

ランニング running.
—シャツ a sleeveless undershirt. —ホーマー an inside-the-park homer.

らんばい【乱売】underselling.

らんぱく【卵白】the white of an egg; albumen.

らんばつ【乱伐・濫伐】indiscriminate deforestation. ¶ 森林を～する *fell* trees *indiscriminately*.

らんぱつ【乱発・濫発】an overissue; an excessive issue. ¶ 公債を～する *overissue* bonds.

らんはんしゃ【乱反射】〖物理〗diffused (≒ irregular) reflection.

らんぴ【乱費・濫費】waste; extravagance.
¶ 公費を～する *waste* public money.

らんぴつ【乱筆】 a scribble; careless writing. ¶ ～ごめんください Excuse me for my *hasty writing*.

らんぶ【乱舞】 ¶ 狂喜～する dance for joy.

ランプ a lamp. ¶ ～のかさ a *lamp* shade. ～のしんを切る clip the wick of the *lamp*. ～をつける(消す) light (put out) *a lamp*.

石油― an oil lamp; a petroleum (≒ kerosene) lamp.

ランプ (高速道路の) a ramp.

らんぼう【乱暴】 violence; excess; disorderly conduct. ¶ ～な言動 *rude* speech and behavior. ～に運転する drive *recklessly*. 彼のことばは～だ His language *is violent*. そんなに～するな Don't *be* so *rude*. 若者は～だ Young men *are wild*. 金もなしで旅行に出かけるとはきみも～だ It *is reckless* of you to start on a trip without money.

―者 a rascal.

らんま【欄間】〔建築〕 a transom.

らんまん【爛漫】 ¶ 子どもは天真～だ Children *are frank and open-hearted*. 桜が～と咲き乱れる The cherry trees *are in full bloom*./The cherry blossoms ... *at their best*.

らんみゃく【乱脈】 disorder; confusion. ¶ ～な経理(人事) *disorderly* accounting (personnel affairs).

らんよう【濫用・乱用】 misuse; abuse. ¶ 統治者は権力を～してはならない The ruler must not *abuse* his power.

らんらん【爛爛】 ¶ ～たるトラの目 the *glaring* eyes of a tiger. ～としたまなざし *piercing* eyes.

らんりつ【乱立・濫立】 ¶ 会長の候補者が～している Too many candidates are running for presidency. 道路に沿って看板が～している Standing signboards *bristle* along the road.

り

り【利】 advantage; profit. ¶ ～が～を生む *Interest* bears *interest*. 味方は地の～を得ている Our side has geographical *advantage*. 彼は～にさとい He *is* extremely *profit-centered*.

り【理】 reason. ¶ きみの意見は～にかなわぬ Your opinion is contrary to *reason*. 彼のエッセーは～に落ちる His essays *are* too *serious*. 彼がそう言うのは～の当然だ It's only *natural* for him to say so. 彼の言にも～はある There's some *truth* in what he says.

リアリズム realism. ¶ ～文学 *realistic* literature.

リーグ a league.

―戦 the league series. ¶ 六大学野球～戦 the Big Six Varsity Baseball League Tournament.

リーダー (読本) a reader.

リーダー (指導者) a leader. ¶ クラブの～になる *take the lead in* the club.

リード a lead. ¶ 相手を～しながら踊る *lead one's* partner. 8対3で～する have an 8 to 3 *lead*. 2馬身(艇身)～する *lead* by two lengths.

りえき【利益】 1 〖もうけ〗 [a] profit. ¶ 私は1万円～を得た I *made a profit of* ten thousand yen.

この商売は大きな～がありそうだ This business will *yield large returns*.

そのマンションを売って50万の～を得た The mansion was sold *at a profit of* five hundred thousand yen.

彼は～のためにはなんでもする He will do anything for the sake of *gain*.

―配当 a dividend. 純― a net profit. 総― a gross profit.

2 〖益〗 profit; advantage. ¶ 私はこの本を読んで～を得た I *have profited* reading this book.

ヨーロッパ旅行はとてもきみの～になるだろう The travel in Europe will do you a world of *good*.

それを勉強してなんの～になるか What is *the good of* studying it?

彼と結婚するのは彼女の～だ It is *to her advantage* to marry him.

公共の～のために for *the benefit* of the public; for the public *good*.

相互の～のために for mutual *advantage*.

りえん【離縁】 [a] divorce. ¶ 妻を～する *divorce one's* wife. 養子を～する *disown one's* adopted son.

りおち【利落ち】 (市場) ex interest; interest off. ¶ ～の債券 an *ex dividend* bond.

りか【理科】 science. ¶ ～の学生 a student studying *science*. 大学は～へ行きたい I'd like to take *the science course* in the university.

―大学 a college of science.

りかい【理解】 understanding. ¶ その文章は～しやすい(しがたい) The sentence is easy (hard) to *understand*. その問題は私には～しがたい The question *is incomprehensible to me*./The question *is above my comprehension*./I cannot *understand* the question. 彼らふた

り

りの間には～がない There is no *understanding* between them. 彼は妻に～がない He does not *sympathize with* his wife. 彼は音楽を～する He *appreciates* music. 彼は～が早い He is quick to *comprehend*.

相互(共通)── a mutual (common) understanding.

りがい【利害】 interests. ¶ 私はそれに大きな～関係がある I have *a* great *interest in* the matter. 銀行家と実業家の～は一致している The *interests* of the bankers are in harmony with those of business men. ～の衝突 a conflict (≒ clash) of *interests*. ～の一致 identity of *interests*.

──関係者 the parties interested (≒ concerned). ──得失 ¶ その政策の～得失はなにか What are the *advantages* and disadvantages (≒ *pros* and cons) of the policy?

りかがく【理化学】 physics and chemistry.

りがく【理学】 physical science.

──士 a bachelor of science (B. Sc.). ──的療法 physiotherapy. ──博士 a doctor of science (D. Sc.). ──部 the faculty of science.

りかん【離間】 ¶ 両国の～をはかる try to drive a wedge between the two nations. 南と北を～する *alienate* (≒ *separate*) the South from the North.

──策 a scheme of alienation.

りき【利器】 (道具) a device; (武器) a weapon. ¶ 文明の～ *a* modern *convenience*.

りきがく【力学】〘物理〙 dynamics (単数扱い). 応用── applied mechanics. 空気(航空)── aerodynamics. 静── statics. 動── kinetics. 熱── thermodynamics. 量子── quantum mechanics.

りきさく【力作】 a labored work; a great work; a major work. ¶ この展覧会は～ぞろいだ The works displayed at this exhibition are all equally fine.

りきし【力士】 a *sumo* wrestler.

りきせつ【力説】 ¶ 英語の必要性を～する *emphasize* the need for English.

りきせん【力戦】 a good (≒ hard) fight. ¶～むなしく試合に敗れた We lost the game though we *fought desperately*.

りきそう【力走】 ¶ 全コースを～する *run hard* (≒ *run as fast as one can*) all through the course.

りきそう【力漕】 ¶ 両チームとも～した Both crews *rowed* (≒ *pulled*) *hard*.

りきてん【力点】 emphasis. ¶ 語学に～をおく *emphasize* (≒ *put stress on*) language study.

りきとう【力投】〘野球〙 ¶ 最後まで～する *pitch with all one's might* to the end of the game.

りき・む【力む】 strain *oneself*. ¶ 力いっぱい～んで岩を動かそうとした He *exerted all his strength in* trying to move the rock.

りきゅう【離宮】 a detached palace. ¶ 桂～ the Katsura *Detached Palace*.

リキュール liqueur.

りきりょう【力量】 ability; capacity. ¶ ～ある人 a man *of ability*; an *able* (≒ *capable*) man. 指導者としての～を示す show (≒ exhibit) the *capacity* for leadership. 絵の～を試す機会 a good opportunity to test *one's talent* for painting.

りく【陸】 land. ¶ 横浜で～に上がる *go ashore* at Yokohama.

りくあげ【陸揚げ・陸上げ】 unloading. ¶ マグロの～をする(船が) A ship *discharges* (≒ *unloads*) tunnies. / (人が) They *discharge* (≒ *land; unload*) tunnies *from* the ship.

──場 a landing place.

りぐい【利食い】〘株式〙 profit taking. ¶ ～する take a profit.

──売り ¶ ～売りに出る be on the *profit-taking* sale.

りくうん【陸運】 transportation by land.

──局 Regional Land Transportation Bureau.

リクエスト 〔a〕 request. ¶ ～番組 a *request* program.

りくかいくう【陸海空】 land, sea and air. ¶ ～三軍 the land, sea and air forces.

りくぐん【陸軍】 the army; the military service.

──士官学校 the Military Academy. ──大学 the Military Staff College. ──大臣 英 the Secretary of State for War. ──長官 米 the Secretary of the Army.

りくじょう【陸上】 ──競技 athletic sports; field-and-track events. ──勤務 ¶ ～勤務につく(船上に対して) be on *shore* duty; (航空に対して) be on *ground* duty. ──自衛隊 the Ground Self-Defense Force. ──輸送 land carriage (≒ transportation).

りくち【陸地】 land.

りくつ【理屈】 (理論) 〔a〕 theory; (理由) 〔a〕 reason. ¶ きみの言うことには少し～がある There is some *sense* in what you say. それは～にかなわぬ That's against *reason*. / That's *unreasonable*. ～と実際とは一致しない *Theory* and practice do not go hand in hand. 彼の学説は～に合っている His theory *is logical*. 彼はなんとか～をつけて行かなかった *For some reason or other* he did not go. そんな～があるものか That is impossible. 彼はよく～をこねる He's always *splitting hairs*. ～のわかる人 a man of sense.

──ずく ¶ ～ずくで彼を謝らせてやった I *reasoned* him *into* apologizing. ──屋 an argumentative man. 小──屋 a hair-splitter.

りくとう【陸稲】 upland rice.

りくろ【陸路】 a land route. ¶ ～をとる go (≒ travel) *by land*. ～モスクワへ向かう head (≒ leave) for Moscow *overland*.

りけん【利権】 a right (rights ともいう); (官許の) a concession. ¶ ～をあさる hunt for *rights*. ～を獲得する acquire *rights*.

──屋 a concession hunter; 米 a grafter.

りこ【利己】 selfishness; self-interest. ¶ ～的

り

な態度 *selfish* behavior. ～的で人のことは考えない世相 the *egoistic* tendency of the present world.

—主義 egoism (egotism は自己中心癖). —主義者 an egoist.

りこう【利口】clever; wise. ¶ ～な子 a bright child (bright は子どもの場合のみ). 彼は～ぶる He tries to appear *intelligent* (≒ *sharp*). / He *acts knowingly*. 黙っているほうが～だ It is *wise* to keep *one's* mouth shut. 彼は～に立ち回る He acts *tactfully* (≒ *smartly*). / He is a *smart* boy. きみのおかげでひとつ～になった Thanks to you, I have learned a lesson.

—者 a clever person (clever は「抜け目のない」という悪い意味に用いることがある); a smart fellow.

りこう【履行】fulfillment; performance. ¶ 約束を～する *keep one's* promise. 義務を忠実に～する be faithful in *doing* (≒ *discharging*) *one's* duties.

りごう【離合】—集散 ¶ 政党の～集散 changing the alignments of political parties.

リコール〘政治〙图〔a〕recall. ¶ 市長を～する *recall* the mayor.

—制 the recall system.

りこん【離婚】〔a〕divorce. ¶ 妻と～する *divorce one's* wife. ～の訴訟を起こす sue for *a divorce*.

—手続き divorce procedure. —届 a divorce notice.

りさい【罹災】affliction; suffering. ¶ 地震で～する *suffer from* an earthquake.

—者 a victim; a sufferer. —地 the afflicted area.

リサイタル a recital. ¶ ～を開く give *a recital*.

りさげ【利下げ】a reduction of interest. ¶ 銀行が～をした Bank rates *were reduced*.

りざや【利鞘】a profit margin. ¶ ～をかせぐ make *a small profit*; 〘株式〙scalp.

りさん【離散】separation. ¶ 一家～した The family *was broken up*.

りし【利子】interest. ¶ 5分の～で金を貸す loan (≒ lend) money at 5 percent *interest*. 6分の～がつく carry (≒ draw) 6 percent *interest*. ～をとる(払う) charge (pay) *interest*.

—率 a rate of interest.

りじ【理事】a director; (大学などの) a trustee.

—会 a board of directors (≒ trustees). —者側 the management. —長 the chief director; the chairman of the board of directors (≒ trustees).

りしゅう【履修】¶ ～する科目 subjects to *study*. 全教科を～する *finish* all the subjects.

りじゅん【利潤】〔a〕profit. ¶ ～をあげる(追求する) produce (pursue) *a profit*.

りしょう【離礁】¶ 船が～する The ship *gets off the rock*.

りしょく【利殖】moneymaking.

—法 the secret of making a fortune.

りしょく【離職】—者(総称) the unemployed; (個人) an unemployed person.

りす【栗鼠】〘動物〙a squirrel.

りすい【利水】irrigation. ¶ 利根川の～工事 the River Tone *irrigation* project.

リスト a list. ¶ 輸出品目の～を作る *list up* the items of export. 彼の名前が～に載っている He is *on the list*.

リズミカル ¶ ～な音楽 *rhythmical* music.

リズム〔a〕rhythm. ¶ 彼女は足で音楽に合わせて～をとった She tapped her foot *in time to* the music.

り・する【利する】profit. ¶ その仕事は私に～するところが多かった The work *was of* much *benefit to* me. 敵を～する行為 an action to *favor one's* enemy. 彼は長身を～してバーを跳んだ He *made use of* his height to jump over the bar.

りせい【理性】reason. ¶ ～的な人間 a man *of reason*; a *rational* type of man. ～に従って行動する act with (≒ according to) *reason*.

りそう【理想】an ideal. ¶ ～の女性 an *ideal* woman; a woman *after one's own heart*. ～的な家庭生活 an *ideal* home life. ～的な設備の整った家 an *ideally*-equipped house; a house with *ideal* equipment. 世界平和の～に燃える hold *a* lofty *ideal* of world peace. そうできれば～的だ It would be *ideal* if you could do it that way.

りそうか【理想化】¶ 彼は女性を～して観音像にあらわした He *idealized* (≒ *imagined the ideal of*) woman and expressed it in an image of *Kannon*. 彼は現実に背を向けて将来ばかり～している He turns his back on reality and only dreams of the *idealized* future.

りそうきょう【理想郷】a Utopia.

りそうしゅぎ【理想主義】idealism.

—者 an idealist.

りそうろん【理想論】idealism. ¶ ～としてはそのとおりだ *Idealistically* it's quite all right.

りそく【利息】⇒りし

リターンマッチ a return match.

りだつ【離脱】¶ 国籍～ the *renunciation* of *one's* nationality. 彼は党籍を～した He *left* the party.

りち【理知】intellect. ¶ ～的な人 an *intellectual* man; a man of *intellect* (≒ *intelligence*). ～的な顔 an *intelligent* (≒ *intellectual*) face.

りちぎ【律儀・律義】honesty; faithfulness. ¶ ～な人 an *honest* (≒ a *faithful*) person. 彼は～に働く He works *faithfully*.

りつ【律】(法) law; (戒律) a commandment.

りつ【率】a rate. ¶ とても～が悪い The *percentage* (≒ *rate*) is very poor.

死亡(出生)— a death (birth) rate. 投票— a vote rate.

りつあん【立案】¶ それはだれの～になるものですか Who *planned* (≒ *framed; originated*) it? 規約を～する *draft* an agreement. 新産業政策を～する *design* (≒ *devise*) a new industrial policy.

—者 a planner; a designer; a framer.

りつき【利付き】—債券 an interest-bearing

り

bond.

りっきゃく【立脚】¶事実に〜した議論 arguments *based* (≒ *grounded*) *on* facts.

りっきょう【陸橋】a viaduct; a girder bridge.

りっけん【立憲】—君主 a constitutional sovereign. —君主国 a constitutional monarchy. —政治 constitutional government.

りっこうほ【立候補】candidacy; candidature. ¶彼は次の選挙に〜する He will *run for* the next election. / 英 He will *stand for* the next election. 〜を宣言する announce *one's candidacy* (*for*). 〜を届け出る(取り下げる) file (withdraw) *one's candidacy* (*for*). 彼は総裁選に〜するだろう He will *be a candidate for* the presidency. 彼は共産党公認で衆院選に〜した He *ran for election* to the House of Representatives on the Communist ticket.

—者 a candidate.

りっしでん【立志伝】a biography (≒ life) of a self-made man. ¶〜中の人 a *self-made* man.

りっしゅう【立秋】the setting-in of autumn; the first day of autumn.

りっしゅん【立春】the setting-in of spring; the first day of spring.

りっしょう【立証】proof. ¶事実によって〜する *prove* (*something*) by the fact. 法廷で彼の無罪を〜できるか Can you *prove* (≒ *establish*) his innocence in court? 検事は彼の有罪を〜した The prosecutor *presented proof of* the man's guilt.

りっしん【立身】—出世 success in life. ¶〜出世する rise in the world.

りっすい【立錐】¶会場は〜の余地もなかった There wasn't even standing room in the hall.

りっ·する【律する】¶おのれをもって他人を〜するな Don't *judge* others by yourself. / You must not *measure* others by your own standard.

りつぜん【慄然】¶彼はその光景に〜とした He *was terrified* (≒ *was horrified*) *at* the sight. そのニュースに一同〜とした All *were horror-stricken at* the news.

りつぞう【立像】a statue.

りったい【立体】〔数学〕a solid〔body〕.

—映画 a three-dimensional film; a 3-D picture. —音響 stereophonic sound. —画法 stereography. —感 cubic effect. —幾何学 solid geometry. —交差 a two-level crossing. —交差道路 a freeway. —派〔美学〕cubism. —放送 a stereophonic broadcast.

りったいてき【立体的】¶〜調査 survey *from all angles.* 事件を〜にとらえる必要がある We are required to examine the case *from all viewpoints.* / We should consider *various sides of* the case.

りっちじょうけん【立地条件】conditions of location. ¶彼の店は〜がよい(悪い) His shop *is conveniently* (*inconveniently*) *located.* / He has his shop *in a favorable* (*an unfavorable*) *location.*

りっとう【立冬】the first day of winter.

りつどう【律動】rhythm; rhythmic movement.

リットル a liter; a 英 litre (記号 *l.*).

りっぱ【立派】¶〜な家 a *fine* house. 〜な宮殿 a *splendid* (≒ *magnificent*) palace. 〜な紳士 a *perfect* gentleman; (風采) a *distinguished-looking* gentleman. 〜な人格 a *noble* character. 〜な行為 *praiseworthy* conduct. 〜な服装をした人 a *well-dressed* man; a *finely dressed* man. 〜な顔 a *handsome* face. 〜な手際 an *admirable* performance. 〜な人 a *respectable* man. 彼は〜な口をきく He talks *like a man of virtue*. 教師は〜な職業だ Teaching is a *respectable* profession. 彼はそれを〜にやってのけた He did it *very well*. 彼は〜に英語を話す He speaks English *perfectly* (≒ *fluently*). 彼は息子を〜に教育した He educated his son *properly*.

りっぷく【立腹】anger; offense; rage; wrath; indignation. ¶ご〜はもっともですがなにとぞご辛抱を Be patient, please, though you have good reason to *be* (≒ *get*) *angry*.

りっぽう【立方】〔数学〕cube. ¶5メートル〜 five meters *cube*. 5〜メートル five *cube* meters.

—根 the cube root. —積 cube contents. —体 a cube.

りっぽう【立法】legislation.

—機関 a legislative organ. —権 legislative power. —者 a legislator; a lawmaker. —府 the legislature.

りづめ【理詰め】¶彼の〜のことばに彼らも納得した His *convincing* words won them over. 彼らの〜の戦法には手をやいた Their *theoretical* tactics were a bitter experience to us.

りつろん【立論】argument. ¶〜の過程がたいせつだ The point is the manner in which the *argument* is made.

りてい【里程】mileage; 〔a〕 distance.

—標 a milestone; a milepost.

りてき【利敵】¶それは〜行為だ It *is profitable* (≒ *does good*) *only to the enemy.*

りてん【利点】an advantage.

りとう【離党】¶〜する leave the party.

りとく【利得】〔a〕 profit; gain〔s〕.

リトマス〔化学〕litmus.

—試験紙 litmus paper.

りにゅう【離乳】weaning. ¶〜する *wean* a child.

—期 the weaning period. —食 baby food.

りにょう【利尿】—剤 a diuretic.

りねん【理念】an idea.

リノリウム linoleum.

リハーサル a rehearsal.

リバイバル revival.

りはつ【理髪】haircutting; hairdressing.

—師 a barber; a hairdresser. —店 a bar-

り

ber's〔shop〕; a barbershop.

りはん【離反】(むほん) revolt; a rebellion; (疎隔) estrangement; alienation. ¶ 人心は既に政府から～している The government *has* already *lost the support of* the public.

りひ【理非】rights and wrongs. ¶ ただちに～曲直を明らかにするつもりだ I intend to make clear *the rights and wrongs* of the case.

リビングキッチン a living room with kitchenette attached (living kitchen は和製英語).

りふじん【理不尽】¶ ～な要求 an *unreasonable* demand.

リフト〔スキー〕a lift.

リベート a rebate; 困 a rake-off.

りべつ【離別】parting; separation; (離婚)〔a〕divorce. ¶ 3年前夫と～した I *divorced* my husband three years ago.

リベット a rivet. ¶ ～を打つ beat *a rivet.*

りほう【理法】〔a〕law. ¶ 自然の～ the *order* of nature; Nature's *laws.*

リポーター a reporter.

リポート a report.

リボン a ribbon.

りまわり【利回り】〔経済学〕a yield;〔a〕return. ¶ ～率 a rate of *yield.* その債券は～が悪い The bonds bear (≒ yield) *a* bad *return.* その債券は6分5厘の～になる The bond *yields* 6.5%.

りめん【裏面】¶ 政界の～ *the dark side* of the political world. きっと～になにかある I am sure something lies *behind it.* / There must be something *at the bottom of it.* ～でだれかが動いている Someone is playing an active part *in the background.*

リモートコントロール remote control.

りゃく 【略】(語句の) abbreviation; (書物の) abridg〔e〕ment; (省略) omission; (略字) an abbreviation. ¶ liter という語は l. または lit. と～す The word "liter" *is abbreviated to* "l." or "lit." エリザベスを～してリズと呼ぶ We call Elizabeth Liz *for short.* 堅苦しいあいさつは～しましょう Let formalities *be cast aside.* 以下～ The rest *is omitted.*

りゃくが【略画】a sketch.

りゃくご【略語】an abbreviation.

りゃくごう【略号】a code address.

りゃくじ【略字】an abbreviation.

りゃくしき【略式】informality. ¶ 結婚式は～でやるつもりだ We plan to have a rather *informal* wedding.

りゃくしょう【略称】an abbreviation.

りゃくず【略図】a sketch; (地図) a rough map.

りゃくだつ【略奪】plunder. ¶ 都市の～ *pillage* (≒ *loot; sack*) of a town. 町を～する *plunder* a town.

りゃくでん【略伝】a short biography; a brief life.

りゃくふく【略服】an ordinary dress.

りゃくれき【略歴】a brief personal record.

りゃっき【略記】¶ ～する give a brief sketch (*of*).

りゅう【竜】a dragon.

-りゅう【-流】¶ ドイツ～の考え方 the German *way* of thinking. (華道などの)草月～ the *Sogetsu school.* まったく自己～です I *am* completely *self-taught.* 一～の画家 a first-*rate* painter; an artist of the first *order.* 三～の旅館 a third-*class* inn.

りゆう【理由】a reason; a cause. ¶ 私がそんなことをしなければならぬ～はない There is no *reason* why I should do such a thing. これが私が辞職したい～だ This is *the reason why* I wish to resign. 彼を信じうる十分な～がある There is every *reason* to believe him. この～で私は彼を解雇した *On this ground* I dismissed him. いかなる～があっても彼に金を借りてはいけない *On no account* should you borrow money from him. 彼の欠席は～がたつ(たたぬ) His absence *is excusable* (*inexcusable*). それは～にならぬ It is *a* poor *excuse.* 深い～もないのに彼らは折り合いが悪い There is no *reason,* but they are not on good terms. なんとかかんとか～をつけて彼は顔を出さない *On some pretext or other* he does not show up.

りゅうあん【硫安】〔化学〕ammonium sulfate.

りゅうい【留意】¶ その点十分ご～のほどを I hope you will *give* it *serious consideration.*

りゅういき【流域】a basin; a watershed. ¶ 信濃川～ the *basin* of the River Shinano.

りゅういん【溜飲】¶ 彼が呆然(ぼう)とするのを見て～が下がった I *was satisfied to* see him struck dumb with surprise. / I *was keenly delighted at* his bewildered face.

りゅうか【硫化】〔化学〕sulfuration. **―**ゴム vulcanized rubber. **―**水素 hydrogen sulfide. **―**鉄 iron sulfide. **―**物 a sulfide.

りゅうかい【流会】adjournment. ¶ 株主総会は～となった The general meeting of shareholders *was adjourned.* 出席者少数で～した The meeting *didn't come off* (≒ *was not held; was cancelled*) because only a few came (≒ appeared).

りゅうがく【留学】studying abroad. ¶ 彼は近くアメリカに～する He'll *go to* America *for study* in the near future. 彼は演劇研究のためパリに～中だ He *is now in* Paris *to study* theatrical performances.

―生 a student studying abroad. ¶ 在日インド～生 an Indian student in Japan.

りゅうかん【流感】⇒りゅうこうせいかんぼう

りゅうき【隆起】upheaving. ¶ 地震で地盤が～した The earthquake *upheaved* (≒ *caused the upheaval of*) the ground.

りゅうぎ【流儀】a way; a style. ¶ 彼はなんでも自分の～でやる He does everything *in his own way* (≒ *in his own fashion*). これがわが家の～だ This is *our way of doing things* at home.

りゅうきゅう【琉球】the Loochoo (≒ Ryukyu) Islands.

りゅうぐう【竜宮】the Dragon's Palace.
りゅうけつ【流血】¶ ～の惨事 a *bloodshedding* accident. 革命は～を見ずに達成された The revolution was achieved without *bloodshed.* / The *bloodless* revolution was realized.
りゅうげん【流言】a rumor.
—飛語 ¶ ～飛語を飛ばして人心を惑わせた They circulated (≒ spread) *false news* (≒ *wild rumors*) and made people feel uneasy.
りゅうこ【竜虎】¶ ～相打つ争い a fight between the two great rivals ; a dragon-and-tiger fight.
りゅうこう【流行】fashion. ¶ あの帽子は最新～だ That hat *is of the latest fashion.* あの種の帽子が～している(していない) That sort of hat *is in fashion* (*is out of fashion*). あの種の帽子が～してきた(しなくなった) That sort of hat *has come into fashion* (*has gone out of fashion*). ゴルフが～してきた(しなくなった) Golf *has come into vogue* (*has gone out of vogue*). クイズゲームは大～だ Quiz games *are all the rage.* 彼女は～のあとを追う She follows the *fashions.* 流感が～している Influenza *is prevalent.*
—歌 a popular song. —歌手 a singer of popular songs. —作家 a popular writer.
りゅうこうせいかんぼう【流行性感冒】〖医学〗influenza ; (口語) [the] flu[e]. ¶ ～にかかる(かかっている) get (be suffering from) *influenza.*
りゅうこうせいのうえん【流行性脳炎】〖医学〗epidemic encephalitis.
りゅうこつ【竜骨】the keel.
—座〖天文学〗the Carina. —台 the keel blocks.
りゅうさ【流砂】quicksand.
りゅうさん【硫酸】〖化学〗sulfuric acid.
—アンモニウム ammonium sulfate. —塩 a sulfate. —カルシウム calcium sulfate. —紙 sulfated paper. —銅 copper sulfate.
りゅうざん【流産】[a] miscarriage. ¶ 彼女は～した She had *a miscarriage* (≒ *an abortion*). 計画はすべて～した All our plans *failed* (≒ *miscarried*).
りゅうし【粒子】a particle.
りゅうしつ【流失】¶ 多くの橋が洪水で～した A number of bridges *were washed*(≒ *were carried*) *away* by the flood.
—家屋 houses washed away by the flood.
りゅうしゅつ【流出】an outflow. ¶ 金の～the *outflow* (≒ *drain*) of gold. 金が海外へ～した The gold *flowed* out of the country. 頭脳の海外～を止めなくてはならない We must stop the brain *drain.*
りゅうじょう【粒状】¶ ～の薬 *granular* (≒ *granulated*) medicine.
りゅうず【竜頭】the stem of a watch.
—巻き ¶ ～巻きの時計 a stem-winder ; a stem-winding watch.
りゅうすい【流水】running water.
りゅうせい【流星】a falling (≒ shooting) star ; a meteor.
—群 a meteoric shower.
りゅうせい【隆盛】prosperity. ¶ 国家の～national *prosperity.* 国運が～に赴いている The nation is growing *in prosperity.* 彼の事業は～をきわめている His business *is flourishing* (≒ *is prosperous* ; *is thriving*).
りゅうぜつらん【竜舌蘭】〖植物〗an agave.
りゅうせんけい【流線型】a streamline shape.
¶ ～の列車 a *streamline[d]* train ; a streamliner.
りゅうたい【流体】〖物理〗[a] fluid.
—静力学 hydrostatics. —動力学 hydrodynamics.
りゅうだん【流弾】¶ ～が彼の足に当たった *A stray bullet* struck (≒ hit) him in the leg.
りゅうだん【榴弾】a shell.
—砲 a howitzer.
りゅうち【留置】detention. ¶ 彼は容疑者として～されている He *is detained* (≒ *is locked up*) as a suspect.
—場 a detention ward. ¶ 彼は～場で一夜を明かした He *was kept in custody* overnight.
りゅうちょう【流暢】fluency. ¶ 彼は～な英語を話す He speaks English *fluently* (≒ *with fluency*). / He speaks *fluent* English.
りゅうつう【流通】circulation. ¶ 貨幣の～*the circulation* (≒ *currency*) of money. 空気の～ *the circulation* of air ; *ventilation.* 政府は新貨幣を～させた The government *put* new coins *into circulation.* 私の部屋は空気の～がよい(悪い) My room *is* well (ill ; poorly) *ventilated.*
—革命 distribution revolution. —貨幣 currency ; current money. —紙幣 paper currency. —資本 circulating (≒ floating) capital. —証券 a negotiable bond.
りゅうでんち【流電池】a voltaic battery (≒ cell).
りゅうどう【流動】a flow.
—資本 circulating (≒ floating) capital. —食 liquid food ; a liquid diet. —性 fluidity ; liquidity. —体 a fluid ; a liquid. —物 fluid substances.
りゅうとうだび【竜頭蛇尾】¶ 彼の演説は～に終わった His speech *started well and ended in a fiasco.* / His speech *fizzled out.* / His speech *failed miserably after a good start.*
りゅうにん【留任】¶ 彼は社長に～するだろう He will *continue to serve* as the president. / He will *stay on the president's job.*
りゅうねん【留年】¶ 彼は1年～することになった He is to *stay in the same class* for another year.
りゅうは【流派】a school. ¶ 日本舞踊にはいろいろの～がある Japanese dancing has many *schools.*
りゅうびじゅつ【隆鼻術】〖医学〗nasal plastic surgery.
りゅうひょう【流氷】drift ice ; an ice floe.

りゅうほ【留保】〔法律〕reservation. ¶ われわれの発言権が～ された Our right to speak *was reserved.*

りゅうぼく【流木】driftwood.

リューマチ〘医学〙rheumatism. ¶ ～が起こる have an attack of *rheumatism.*

—患者 a rheumatic. **関節—** articular rheumatism. **筋肉—** muscular rheumatism.

りゅうよう【流用】diversion. ¶ 研究費を旅費に～した They *diverted* research funds to traveling expenses. 彼は公金を～した He *misapplied* (≒ *misappropriated*) public money.

りゅうりゅう【粒粒】¶ 彼は～辛苦の末，やっとその仕事を完成した His *long, patient efforts* enabled him to do the work.

りゅうりゅう【隆隆】¶ ～たる運勢 a *successful* fortune. ～たる筋肉 *well-developed* muscles. 国家は～と栄えている The nation *is in full prosperity.*

りゅうりょう【流量】flux〔per second〕.

りゅうれい【流麗】¶ ～な筆致で描かれた随筆 an essay written in an *elegant* (≒ a *refined*) style.

リュックサック a rucksack.

りょう【良】good. ¶ 優～可 Excellent, *Good,* Fair ; A, B, C.

りょう【量】quantity ; amount. ¶ 多(少)～の水 a large (small) *quantity* (≒ *amount*) of water. ～より質がたいせつだ Quality matters more than *quantity.* 酒の～が多くなってきた My *capacity* for alcohol is getting larger. 食事の～を減らしたほうがいい You had better reduce the *amount* of your meal.

りょう【漁】fishing. ¶ 朝早く～に出た We went *fishing* early in the morning. きょうは～が多そうだ We will make *a* good *catch* 〔*of fish*〕 today.

りょう【涼】¶ 夏休みに～を求めて軽井沢に旅行した We took a trip to Karuizawa to *enjoy the cool and fresh air* during summer vacation.

りょう【猟】¶ 彼らは～に出かけた They went *hunting* (≒ *shooting*). きょうは～が多い We made *a* big *bag* today. / We had a lot of *game* today.

りょう【寮】a dormitory ; a dorm.

—母 a housemother. **独身—** apartments for bachelors. **母子—** a house for mother and children.

りょう【諒】¶ 彼は快くわれわれの申し出を～とした He readily *appreciated* (≒ *understood*) our offer.

りょう【領】(領有) possession ; (領土) a territory ; a dominion.

-りょう【-料】¶ 入場～ *an* admission *fee.* 手数～ *a charge* for trouble ; a commission. 授業～ *a* tuition *fee* ; *a* school *fee.* 受験～ *an* examination *fee.* 調味～ seasonings.

-りょう【-領】¶ この島は日本～だ This island is *a possession* (≒ *a territory*) of Japan. / This island *belongs to* Japan.

りよう【利用】use ; utilization. ¶ われわれは自分の才能を最もよく～すべきだ We should *use* our talents to the best advantage. 彼はその機会を～してロンドン見物をした He *improved* (≒ *availed himself of*) the opportunity to see (≒ take in) the sights of London. 時間を～しなければならぬ We must *economize* (≒ *make the most of*) our time. 彼はささいなことをも～した He *turned* every trifling circumstance *to account.* 彼らはその小川を灌漑(かんがい)に～した They *utilized* the brook for irrigation. 支配者は民衆を～して私利をはかった The ruler *exploited* the masses for selfish purposes.

—価値 utility value. **—者** a user ; (図書館) a visitor. **—率** utilization rate.

りよう【里謡】a folksong ; a ballad.

りょういき【領域】a territory. ¶ それはわれわれの～を犯す行為だ The act is an invasion upon our *territory.* それは科学の～に属する It is in the *domain* (≒ *field* ; *realm*) of science. その学問は人間生活のあらゆる～にまたがる The discipline covers all *areas* of human life. その仕事は私の～ではない That kind of work is not in my *line* (≒ *province*). / That kind of work is not of my *domain* (≒ *sphere*).

りょういん【両院】¶ 法案は～を通過した The bill passed *both Houses.*

—議員 members of both Houses. **—協議会** a conference of the two Houses.

りょうえん【良縁】a good match. ¶ 彼女は～を得た She has made *a good match.*

りょうか【良家】a good family. ¶ ～の子女 a daughter of *a good family.* 彼は～の出だ He is (≒ comes) of *a respectable family.*

りょうか【良貨】good money. ¶ 悪貨は～を駆逐する Bad money drives out *good.*

りょうか【寮歌】a dormitory song ; (校歌) a school (≒ a college) song.

りょうが【陵駕・凌駕】¶ 彼は力では兄を～している He *excels* (≒ *surpasses* ; *exceeds*) his brother in strength.

りょうかい【了解・領会・領解】consent ; understanding. ¶ 私の真意を～してほしい I would like you to *understand* what I really mean. 私の～するところでは会合は延期になる I *understand* that (≒ As I *understand* it,) the meeting is to be postponed. その問題について彼の～を求めなければならない We should ask for his *consent* to the matter. / We should seek *an understanding* with him about the matter. そのような意見は私には～できない Such an opinion is above (≒ beyond) my *comprehension.* 彼は私の～なしにそれをした He did it without my *consent.* みなさん同意と～していいですか Do (≒ May) I *take it* that you all agree?

—事項 agreed items. **—済み** ¶ それはもう～済みだ That's already *been understood.* / We *have* already *come to an agreement* about it. —点 ¶ やっと～点に達した We have finally reached *the point of understanding.*

りょうかい【領海】territorial waters (≒ seas). ¶ 彼ら(漁夫)は日本の～内で操業している They are engaged in fishing within the *territorial waters* of Japan.

りょうがえ【両替】exchange. ¶ この1万円札を～していただけませんか Could you *break* (≒ *change*) this ten thousand-yen bill? 銀行で5万円をアメリカドルに～した I *exchanged* (≒ *changed*) fifty thousand yen for the U. S. dollars at the bank.
—機(屋；商) a money changer.

りょうがわ【両側】¶ 道の～に on *both sides* of the road; on *either side* of the road.

りょうかん【量感】¶ ～のある絵 a *massive* painting. ～のある書物 a *voluminous* book.

りょうがん【両岸】¶ ～に on *the banks*; on *both banks*; on *either bank.*

りょうがん【両眼】both eyes.

りょうき【猟奇】¶ ～的な bizarre.
—小説 a bizarre story.

りょうき【猟期】an open season; a shooting season. ¶ ～が始まった The *hunting* (≒ *shooting*) *season* has opened.

りょうき【漁期】¶ サケ・マスの～になった The *fishing season* has begun for salmon and trout.

りょうきょく【両極】the two poles. ¶ 両家の教育・家柄は～に立っている In education and background the two families are *poles apart.*

りょうきん【料金】a fee; a charge; (有料道路・橋などの) a toll. ¶ この部屋の～はいくらか How much do you *charge* for this room? 海外への航空郵便～はいくらですか What are the *rates* for overseas airmail? 往復～は100ドルです The *rate* for a round trip is a hundred dollars.
—箱 a fare box. —表 a price list. 水道— a water rate. タクシー(バス)— a taxi (bus) fare.

りょうくう【領空】territorial air. ¶ 日本の～を飛行する fly over Japanese *territory.* 日本の～侵犯 the invasion of Japan's *territorial air.*

りょうくん【両君】¶ 市川, 佐藤両君 *both* Ichikawa *and* Sato.

りょうけん【猟犬】a hound; a hunting dog; a bird dog; a gun dog.

りょうけん【了見・料簡・了簡】(意図) intention; (考え) an idea. ¶ いったいどういう～なのだ What in the world is your *intention*? 彼は悪い～を起こした He entertained *an* evil *design.* 彼は～の狭い人間だ He *is narrow-minded.* それは～違いだ You *are mistaken* (≒ *wrong*). それはあなたの～しだいだ That is up to you.

りょうげん【燎原】¶ そのニュースは～の火のごとくひろがった The news spread (≒ ran) *like wildfire.*

りょうこう【良好】¶ 彼は成績～だ His records *are excellent.* 病人の経過は～だ The patient is recovering *satisfactorily.*

りょうさい【良妻】a good wife.
—賢母 a good wife and worthy mother.

りょうさん【量産】mass production. ¶ あの工場ではカメラを～している They *mass-produce* cameras at the factory.
—車 mass-produced cars.

りょうさん-【両三-】¶ ～度 *two or three* times. ～日 *two or three* days; a few days.

りょうし【猟師】a hunter; a huntsman.

りょうし【漁師】a fisherman.

りょうし【量子】quantum.
—物理学 quantum physics. —力学 quantum mechanics. —論 the quantum theory.

りようし【理容師】a barber; (おもに婦人の) a hairdresser; (美容師) a beautician.

りょうじ【領事】a consul. ¶ 駐日イギリス～ *a* British *consul* [stationed] in Japan.
—館 a consulate. —館員 a consular attaché. 総— a consul general. 副— a viceconsul.

りょうじ【療治】treatment. ¶ 彼は温泉でリューマチを～している He *is under* spa-*treatment* for rheumatism.
荒— a rough treatment.

りょうしき【良識】good sense. ¶ ～ある人 a man *of good sense* (≒ *of sound judgment*); a *sensible* man. 彼の行動は～に反する His conduct is against *good sense.* ～を働かせなさい Use *good sense.*

りょうしつ【良質】¶ ～の紙 paper *of good* (≒ *superior*) *quality.*

りょうしゃ【両者】¶ ～互角の試合だった *The two* were evenly matched.

りょうしゅ【領主】a lord; a feudal superior; the proprietor of a manor.

りょうしゅう【領収】receipt. ¶ 金10万円まさに～しました Duly *received* the sum of a hundred thousand yen.
—者 a receiver. —証 a receipt. —済み "received"; "paid."

りょうしゅう【領袖】¶ 自民党の～ *a leader* of the Liberal-Democratic Party.

りょうじゅう【猟銃】a hunting gun; a shotgun.

りょうしょう【了承】acknowledgment.
¶ お話の件～しました I *acknowledge* (≒ *understand*) this matter you've spoken of.

りょうしょく【糧食】food; provisions.
¶ 3日分の～ three days' *provisions.* 非常時用の～ the *provision* of food for emergencies.

りょうじょく【陵辱・凌辱】offense; insult; (婦女を) violation. ¶ ～する offend (≒ insult) *a person*; (婦女を) rape (≒ violate) a woman.

りょうしん【両親】parents (形容詞は parental).

りょうしん【良心】conscience. ¶ 私は～にやましいことはない(がある) I have *a* clear (guilty) *conscience.* 私は～に従って行動する I act according to the dictates of *conscience*. 私は〜に従った(背いた) I followed (ran counter to) the dictates of *conscience*. 〜に恥じずにそんなことができますか Can you do such a thing *with a clear conscience*? 彼にうそを言ったので,〜の呵責(かしゃく)を感じた As I told him a lie, I *felt* a prick of *conscience*. / My *conscience* pricked me because I told him a lie. それをきみの〜に任せる I will leave it to your *conscience*. 〜的な(〜的でない)人 a *conscientious* (an *unconscientious*) man.

りょうせい【両性】 both sexes.
—花 a bisexual flower. —生殖 digenesis.

りょうせい【寮生】 a boarding student ; a boarder.

りょうせい【両棲】〔動物〕 —動物 an amphibious animal ; an amphibian. —類 the amphibia.

りょうせいばい【両成敗】 ¶けんか〜 Both sides are to blame in a quarrel.

りょうせん【稜線】 an edge of a mountain.

りょうぜん【瞭然】 obvious ; evident. ¶一目〜としている It *is obvious* (⇔ *is plain* ; *is as clear as day*).

りょうぞく【良俗】 good manners ; proper morals. ¶〜を乱す行為 an action which corrupts *good manners*.

りょうたん【両端】 both ends.

りょうち【領地】 a territory ; a domain.

りょうて【両手】 both hands. ¶〜に花とはうらやましい(女性を) I envy you *sitting between two beautiful ladies*.

りょうてい【料亭】 a restaurant.

りょうてき【量的】 ¶きみのほうが私より〜に恵まれている *Substantively,* you have more than I.

りょうてんびん【両天秤】 ¶〜をかけると失敗する You're bound to miss if you *aim at two objects at once*.

りょうど【領土】 a territory ; a domain ; territorial possessions. ¶日本の〜 Japanese *territory* ; the *land* belonging to Japan. 〜的野心を持つ have (⇔ hold) *territorial* ambitions.
—権 territorial rights. —主義 territorialism.

りょうとう【両刀】 two swords. ¶あの人は酒と菓子の〜使いだ He *has wide-ranging tastes*. 武蔵は〜使いで有名だ Musashi is well-known as a swordsman who brandished *two swords* at once.

りょうどう【糧道】 ¶空爆で敵の〜を断った We cut the enemy's *supply of provisions* by raiding.

りょうどうたい【良導体】〔物理〕 a good conductor.

りょうば【両刃】 ¶〜の剣 a *two-edged* sword.

りょうはし【両端】 both ends. ¶なわの〜を結ぶ tie ropes at *both ends*.

りょうひ【良否】 quality. ¶物の〜を判定する estimate the *quality* of something. 彼には物の〜がわからない He can't tell whether it *is good or bad*.

りょうびらき【両開き】 ¶〜の戸 a pair of swinging doors.

りょうふう【涼風】 a cool (⇔ a refreshing) breeze. ¶〜がそよそよと吹く *A refreshing breeze* comes in gently. / *A gentle wind* feels soft.

りょうふう【良風】 a good custom.
—美俗 a good and beautiful custom.

りょうぶん【領分】 a territory ; a sphere. ¶他国の〜を侵す invade the *territory* of another country. それは科学の〜ではない It's out of the *sphere* of science. その仕事はきみの〜ではない That sort of business is out of your *territory*.

りょうほう【両方】 both. ¶きみたち〜とも悪い *Both* of you are wrong. その双子が〜ともやってきた *Both* the twins came to see me. / The twins *both* came here. 彼らの〜とも知りません I don't know *either* of them. 〜とも私のではない *Neither* 〔of them〕 is mine. 〜とも欲しくない I want *neither*. / I don't want *either*.

りょうほう【療法】 a remedy ; a cure. ¶化学的〜 a chemical *remedy*.
精神— a mental treatment.

りょうみん【良民】 law-abiding citizens.

りょうめ【量目】 weight. ¶〜をごまかす give short *weight*. これは〜が不足だ This is short of *weight*.

りょうめん【両面】 both sides. ¶貨幣の〜 *both sides* of the coin. 事の表裏〜を考えよ Consider *both sides* of the matter. 物事には〜がある There are *two sides* to every question.

りょうやく【良薬】 good medicine (drug は麻薬の意味があるから避ける). ¶〜は口に苦し (諺) *A good medicine* tastes bitter.

りょうゆう【両雄】 two great men. ¶〜並び立たず *A great man* cannot brook a rival. / *Two cocks* in one yard will fight.

りょうゆう【領有】 occupation ; possession. ¶その島は日本の〜になるはずだ The land is expected to *be annexed to* Japan.

りょうゆう【僚友】 a colleague ; a co-worker ; a comrade.

りょうよう【両様】 ¶〜ともこの場合適切だ In this case *either way* is adequate.
和戦— ¶その国は和戦〜の構えだ The country is prepared for *both* war *and* peace.

りょうよう【療養】 recuperation ; medical treatment. ¶彼は目下自宅〜中だ He is now under *treatment* at home. 私は盲腸炎後〜に努めている I'm *recuperating* from appendicitis.
—所 a sanatorium. —費 medical expenses. 転地— ¶彼女は転地〜の必要がある She needs *a change of air*.

りょうよく【両翼】 both wings ; two wings.

りょうり【料理】 1〖食事の〗 cooking ; (料理品) a dish.
¶魚を〜する *dress* fish.
肉を〜する *cook* meat.

り

〜をこしらえる prepare *dinner.*
この〜は私の口に合う This *food* pleases me.
彼は〜がじょうずだ He is good at *cooking.* / He is a good cook.
この店の〜はうまい They serve good *food* here.
—学校 a cooking school. —人 a cook. —法 the art of cooking. —屋 a restaurant. 一品— a one-course dinner. 日本— Japanese dishes (≒ food).
2 〖処理〗¶ この問題はなかなか〜しにくい It is not easy to *dispose of* this matter.
この難局を〜するのは難しい The situation is not easy to *deal with.*

りょうりつ【両立】¶ 彼女の仕事は家庭と〜する(しない) Her job *is compatible* (*is incompatible*) *with* housekeeping. ふたりの意見は〜する Their two opinions are capable of *coexistence.*

りょうりょう【両両】¶ 努力と才能が〜相まって彼は成功した He succeeded with ability and effort *going hand in hand.* / Ability and effort *together* brought success to him.

りょうりょう【寥寥】¶ 賛成者は〜たるものだった There were *only a few* supporters.

りょかく【旅客】a traveler; a passenger.
—案内所 an R.T.O.; a ticket and information office. —運賃 passengers' fares. —機 a passenger plane; an airliner. —列車 a passenger train.

りょかん【旅館】a(n) hotel; (旧式な) an inn. ¶ 〜に泊まる put up (≒ stay) at *a hotel.* 〜を営む run (≒ keep) *a hotel.*
—業 hotel business.

りよく【利欲】greed; avarice. ¶ 彼女は〜に目がくらんだ She was blind with *greed.*

りょくいん【緑陰】the shade of trees.

りょくか【緑化】tree planting. ¶ 公害をなくし〜を進める計画である We are going to *plant trees* to combat pollution.

りょくち【緑地】a green tract of land.
—帯 a green belt.

りょくちゃ【緑茶】green tea.

りょくないしょう【緑内障】〖医学〗glaucoma.

りょくひ【緑肥】〖農業〗green manure.

りょくべん【緑便】〖医学〗green stool.

りょけん【旅券】a passport. ¶ 〜を申請する apply for *a passport.* 〜を交付する issue *a passport* (*to*). 〜の査証を受けた I had my *passport* stamped with a visa.

りょこう【旅行】travel; (小旅行) a trip; (巡歴) a tour. ⇒たび(旅) ¶ 世界〜をする *travel* (≒ *make a trip*) around the world. イギリスを〜する *travel* in England. イギリスへ〜する *travel* to England. 彼は〜中だ He is *on a trip.*
—案内 a travelers' handbook. —案内所 a tourist bureau. —かばん a traveling bag. —記 an account of a travel. —業者 a tour agent. —者 a traveler; a tourist. 海外— a foreign travel. ¶ 海外〜をする *travel* abroad. 視察— ¶ 視察〜に出かける set out on *an inspection tour* (*to*). 修学— an educational tour. 新婚— a wedding tour; a honeymoon.

りょしゅう【旅愁】loneliness on a trip. ¶ 〜を覚える feel melancholy (≒ lonely; depressed).

りょじょう【旅情】¶ 〜を慰めるものがたくさんあった There were many attractions to entice tourists.

りょそう【旅装】a traveling outfit. ¶ 〜をととのえる prepare for a trip.

りょだん【旅団】〖軍事〗a brigade.

りょてい【旅程】an itinerary.

りょひ【旅費】traveling expenses.

リラ〖植物〗a lilac; (イタリアの貨幣) a lira (発音は [liərə]) (複 lire (発音は [liəri])).

リリーフ〖野球〗relief. ¶ 〜投手 a *relief* pitcher. ぼくが彼を〜した I *relieved* him [at the mound]. / I went in as *relief* [*pitcher*] for him.

りりく【離陸】a take-off. ¶ 〜する take off (*from* an airport).

りりし·い【凛凛しい】manly; valiant. ¶ 〜い顔つき *imposing* (≒ *dignified*; *majestic*) looks.

リリシズム lyricism.

りりつ【利率】the rate of interest. ¶ 〜を上げる(下げる) increase (decrease) *interest rates.* 年8分7厘の〜で at *the rate* of 8.7 percent per annum.
法定— the legal rate of interest.

リレー〖競技〗a relay.
—競走 a relay race. ¶ 400メートル〜 *a* four hundred meter *relay.*

りれき【履歴】a personal history. ¶ 彼の〜はりっぱだ He is a man of good *background.* 彼は大学出の〜を持っている He has *a* college *background.* 彼はどんな〜の人か What is his *career?*
—書 a personal history; a curriculum vitae (履歴書の冒頭には My Personal History または Curriculum Vitae と書く).

りろ【理路】¶ 〜整然とした主張をする express *logical* (≒ *cogent*; *reasonable*) opinions.

りろん【理論】a theory. ¶ 彼の〜体系はしっかりしている His *theory* is well systematized. 物事はそう〜どおりにはいかない We can hardly settle things by *theory* alone.
—家 a theorist. —闘争 a theoretical dispute. —物理学 theoretical physics. 相対性— the theory of relativity.

りん【燐】〖化学〗phosphorus.

りん【鈴】a bell. ¶ 〜を鳴らす ring *a bell.* 〜が鳴っている The *bell* is ringing. / There goes the *bell.*
呼び— a call bell; a buzzer.

-りん【-輪】¶ 一〜の花 a flower. 二〜車 a two-*wheeled* vehicle.

りんか【隣家】a neighboring house; the next door.

りんか【輪禍】a traffic accident. ¶ 〜に会う be injured in *a traffic accident.*

り

りんかい【臨界】 ―温度〘化学〙the critical temperature. ―角 the critical angle.
りんかい【臨海】 ―学校 a seaside school. ―実験所 a marine biological laboratory.
りんかいせき【燐灰石】〘鉱物〙apatite.
りんかく【輪郭】 an outline. ¶ 花びらの～を描く draw the *outline* of a flower. 話の～がつかめた I could grasp the *outline* of the plan.
りんがく【林学】 forestry.
りんかすいそ【燐化水素】〘化学〙hydrogen phosphate.
りんかん【林間】 ―学校 a camping school; a school in the woods; an open-air school.
りんきおうへん【臨機応変】 ¶ ～の処置をとる resort to a *temporary* expedient; adapt *one*self to circumstances; take whatever measure the occasion demands.
りんぎょう【林業】 forestry.
リンク (鎖の輪) a link; (ゴルフ場) 〔a〕 golf links; (スケートの) a skating rink.
―制〘経済学〙a link system.
リング (指輪) a ring; (ボクシングの) the ring.
―サイド the ringside; (座席) a ringside seat.
りんげつ【臨月】 the month of parturition; the last month of pregnancy. ¶ ～の婦人 a woman *who is going to have a baby soon*. 彼女は～が近い *Her time* 〔*of childbirth*〕 is near. / She *is near her time*.
リンゲル ―〔氏〕液 Ringer's solution (≒ fluid). ―注射 injection of Ringer's solution.
りんけん【臨検】 an 〔official〕 inspection; (捜査) a search; investigation; (急襲による捜査) a raid; (船の) boarding.
¶ 税官吏が外国船を～した The customs officers *inspected* (≒ *made an inspection of*) a foreign ship.
りんご【林檎】 an apple. ¶ ～の木 an *apple* tree. ～のような頬 *rosy* cheeks.
―園 an apple orchard. ―酒 cider (わが国のサイダーとは別物).
りんこう【輪講】 ¶ われわれは週1回集まって「平家物語」を～した We met once a week and studied *Heike Monogatari*, each person *lecturing a part of it in turn*.
りんこう【燐光】 phosphorescence. ¶ ～を発する give off (≒ out) *phosphorescence*.
りんこう【燐鉱】〘鉱物〙phosphate ore.
りんこう【臨港】 ―列車 a boat-train.
りんごく【隣国】 a neighboring country; a neighbor. ¶ 日本と中国は互いに～だ China and Japan are *neighbors* 〔to each other〕.
りんさく【輪作】〘農業〙crop rotation.
―作物 rotating crops.
りんさん【燐酸】〘化学〙phosphoric acid.
―カリ potassium phosphate. ―カルシウム(石灰) phosphate-lime. ―肥料 phosphatic manure (≒ fertilizer).
りんじ【臨時】 ¶ 彼は～に雇われた He was engaged *temporarily*. きょう議会が～に開かれた The Diet assembled in special session today.
―休業 a special holiday. ¶ 1月7日まで～休業します (掲示) Closed *temporarily* till January 7. ―試験 a special examination. ―仕事 an extra (≒ odd) job. ―政府 a provisional government. ―総会 an extraordinary general meeting. ―増刊 a special supplement. ―ニュース news special. ―配当 an interim dividend. ―費 incidental expenses. ―雇人 a temporary employee. ―予算 a provisional budget. ―列車 a special train.
りんしつ【隣室】 the next (≒ an adjoining) room.
りんじゅう【臨終】 *one's* dying hour; *one's* last moment; *one's* deathbed. ¶ ～のことば *one's* last (≒ dying) words. 私は彼の～の席に連なった I was with him *at his death*. / I saw him *on his deathbed*. ～が迫っている The *end* is near. ご～です He *is dying*.
りんしょう【輪唱】〘音楽〙a round; a troll.
¶ ～する troll.
りんしょう【臨床】〘医学〙clinic.
―医学 clinics. ―講義 clinical instruction. ―実験(実習) bedside and clinical demonstration (training). ―心理学 clinical psychology.
りんじょう【臨場】 ¶ 皇太子ご～の栄を賜わった We were honored by the *attendance* of the Crown Prince.
りんしょく【吝嗇】 stinginess; parsimony; niggardliness; miserliness. ¶ 彼は～だ He *is stingy* (≒ *is parsimonious*). / He is *a miser*. (stingy は何事についてもしぶしぶ金を出すこと, persimonious は非常識なほどけちけちしていること, miser は金のために金をためる人).
りんじん【隣人】 a neighbor; (総称) the 〔whole〕 neighborhood. ¶ ～のよしみで言ってあげたのだ I told it to you as *a* good *neighbor*. おのれのごとく汝の～を愛せよ〘聖書〙Love your *neighbor* as yourself.
―愛 love of *one's* fellowmen.
りんず【綸子】 figured satin.
りんせき【隣席】 the next seat. ¶ われわれは食卓で～に座りあわせた We happend to sit *side by side* at the table. トラックの運転手の～にいた人はその事故で即死した In that accident, the person sitting *beside* the truck driver was killed instantly.
りんせき【臨席】 attendance; presence; company.
―者 those present; (集合的に用いて) attendance. ¶ ～者は予想外に多数であった *Attendance* was unexpectedly good.
りんせつ【隣接】 ¶ 彼の土地と私の土地とは～している His land and mine *adjoin*. 都市に～する農村の変貌(ぼう)は著しい The villages *near* the city have undergone a complete change.
―家屋 the adjoining house. ―諸国 the neighboring countries. ―地 adjoining land.
りんせん【臨戦】 ¶ ～態勢はととのっている We

り

are ready for fight at any moment.

リンチ lynch. ¶ ～を加える lynch *a person.*

りんてん【輪転】 rotation.

—機〘印刷〙 a rotary press; a cylinder press. —謄写機 a multigraph. 超高速度—機 a super-high speed rotary press.

りんどう【竜胆】〘植物〙 a gentian.

りんどく【輪読】 ¶ 毎月１回集まって万葉集を～している We meet once a month and *read* Manyoshu, each person *lecturing a part of it in turn.*

りんね【輪廻】 the cycles of life; the transmigration of souls.

リンネル linen.

リンパせん【リンパ腺】〘解剖学〙 a lymph node; a lymph gland (前者のほうが新しい言い方).

¶ ～がはれている You have *a* swollen *lymph node.*

—炎 inflammation of a lymph node (≒ gland).

りんばん【輪番】 ¶ ～で夜警をする stand on night watch *by turns* (≒ *in turn*; *alternately*) (by turns; alternately は「交替で」, in turn は「順序だって次々に」の意).

—制 a rotation system.

りんびょう【淋病】〘医学〙 gonorrh〔o〕ea.

りんぶ【輪舞】 a round dance.

りんや【林野】 forests and fields (≒ plains).

—庁 the Forestry Agency.

りんらく【淪落】 fall; ruin. ¶ ～の女 a *fallen* (≒ *ruined*) woman; a *delinquent* girl.

りんり【倫理】 ethics; morals. ¶ 彼らは～的判断が欠けている They are lacking in *moral sense* (≒ *a sense of morality*).

—学 ethics; moral philosophy. 実践— practical ethics.

りんり【淋漓】 ¶ 流汗～たり I *sweat a great deal.* / I *was dripping* (≒ *was covered*) with perspiration (≒ sweat) all over.

りんりつ【林立】 ¶ その一帯は煙突が～している The area *bristles with* chimneys. 港にはヨットのマストが～していた There were *a forest of* masts in the harbor.

りんりん ¶ ～と鈴が鳴る The bell *rings* (≒ *jingles*; *tinkles*). (鈴などが「鳴る」ことをあらわす最も一般的な語は ring. jingle は小さな鐘がジャランジャランと鳴ること. tinkle は小さなベルが鳴るときのようにかなり高い断続的な音(チリンチリンなど)をあらわす).

りんりん【凛凛】 ¶ 勇気～たる青年 a *high spirited* youth; a youth *in a full* (≒ *great*) *spirit*; a young man *full of spirits.* 勇気～として出発した We started *in high* (≒ *full*) *spirits.*

る

るい【類】（種類）a kind; a sort;（分類）a class;（動植物の）a family; a genus (複 genera; genuses);（特徴の同じグループ）a type;（範疇）a category;（生物の種）a species.

¶ ～のない文体 a *unique* style of writing. 彼は～のない記憶力を持っている His memory *is extraordinary.* / He has an *extraordinarily* (≒ *exceptionally*) good memory. ～は友を呼ぶ（諺）*Birds of a feather flock together.*

るい【累】 a trouble. ¶ 他人に～を及ぼす *get* (≒ *involve*) others *in trouble*; *cause troubles to* others.

るい【塁】〘野球〙 a base. ¶ ランナーがふたり～に出ている There are two runners *on* 〔*base*〕. / Two of the *bases* are loaded.

るいか【累加】 acceleration; accumulation; increase. ¶ 州の数は～して50に達した The number of the States *has increased* to fifty. 疲労は～する Weariness *is cumulative.*

るいかん【涙管】〘解剖学〙 the lachrymal duct.

るいく【類句】 a synonymous phrase (≒ expression).

るいけい【累計】 the 〔sum; grand〕 total; the aggregate. ¶ 必要経費の～は100万円にのぼる The *total* expense amounts to a million yen. / The expenditure *in the aggregate* amounts to a million yen. / The *sum* (≒ *grand*) *total* of the cost amounts to a milllion yen. 交通事故の死者の～はすでに１万人に達した The *death toll* of traffic accidents has already reached ten thousand.

るいけい【類型】 a type; a group; a pattern (type は他とはっきり区別できる共通の特徴を持った種類をいい, pattern をこれに近い意味で用いるときには, 各類に特有の共通・不変な思考・行動などの様式, 型をいう);（文学など）genre.

¶ ～的（型にはまった）stereotyped. 英語のイントネーションにはいくつかの～がある There are a certain number of *patterns* in English intonation. / The intonation of English can be classified into several *patterns.*

るいご【類語】 a synonym. ¶ 怠惰は怠慢の～である 'Idleness' is *a synonym of* (≒ is *synonymous with*) 'laziness.'

るいじ【類似】 similarity. ¶ アメリカンフットボールはイギリスのラグビーと～した競技だ American

る

football is a game *similar to* (≒ which *resembles*) Rugby. ヨーロッパ諸国は文化的背景が～している European nations *are* much *alike* in their cultural background.

—点 a similarity; a point of similarity; a similar point. **—品** an imitation.

るいしょ【類書】 similar books (≒ works); books of the same kind (≒ purpose).

るいしょう【類焼】 ¶ 昨夜火事があって多くの家が～した A fire broke out last night and a number of houses were burnt down [by the spreading fire]. 私の家は幸いに～を免れた Fortunately my house escaped the fire.

るいしん【累進】 successive promotion.
¶ 彼は～して社長になった He became president after *successive promotion*.
—税 a progressive tax [rate].

るいしん【塁審】〘野球〙a base (≒ field) umpire; an umpire on a base.

るいじんえん【類人猿】〘動物〙an anthropoid [ape].

るいすい【類推】 analogy; (類推による推理) analogical inference. ¶ ～する analogize. 手紙から～すると, 彼はきちょうめんな人らしい *Judging from* his letter, he seems to be a punctilious man. …からの～で考えてみると If we reason by the *analogy* of ....
—法 analogy.

るいせき【累積】 accumulation; cumulation.
¶ ～する accumulate; cumulate.
—赤字 accumulated deficit.
¶ その会社は～赤字に悩んでいる The firm is suffering an *increasing* loss in business.

るいせん【涙腺】〘解剖学〙the lachrymal gland.

るいだ【塁打】〘野球〙a base-hit.
—数 total bases. **二—** a double; a two-base hit; a two-bagger (≒ baser). ¶ 二～を打つ make a *two-base* hit; hit a *two-bagger*. **三—** a triple; a three-base hit; a three-bagger. ¶ 打者は左中間に三～を飛ばした The batter sent *a triple* (≒ *a three-base hit*) between center and left. **本—** a home run [hit]; a homer.

るいだい【累代】 successive generations; generation after generation.

るいべつ【類別】 classification. ¶ 図書館では本が題目別に～されている In a library books *are classified* according to subjects.

るいらん【累卵】 ¶ 世界の平和は～の危うきにある Peace of the world *is now in a great* (≒ *grave; serious*) *crisis*. その国は～の危うさだ *The Sword of Damocles is hanging over* the nation.

るいるい【累累】 in heaps. ¶ 辺りは～たる死体の山だった [Dead] bodies lay *in piles* (≒ *in heaps*) all around.

るいれい【類例】 an example; a similar case (≒ instance). ¶ ～のない unexampled; unparalleled; unprecedented; unique. 日本の造船界はこの1世紀の間に～のない発展をとげた The ship-building industry of Japan has attained a *unique* (≒ an *unprecedented*) development during this century.

るいれき【瘰癧】〘医学〙scrofula; the king's evil.

ルーキー 〔米〕 a rookie.

ルージュ rouge (フランス語から). ¶ ～をぬる put on *rouge*; *paint* (≒ *rouge*) *one's* lips.

ルーズ loose (英語では [lu:s] と発音する). ¶ 彼は～な人間だ(だらしがない) He is a *slovenly* (≒ an *untidy*) man. 彼は時間が～だ He *is not punctual*. 彼は金使いが～だ He *wastes* his money. / He *spends* money *carelessly and wastefully*. / He is *a spendthrift* (≒ *a squanderer*). 彼は～な生活をしている He leads a *loose* life. あの女は～だ(身持ちが悪い) The woman *is loose*.

ルーズリーフ loose-leaf (形容詞として使い, ふつう名詞としては使わない); (ノート) a loose-leaf notebook.

ルート **1** a route; a channel (日本語の「ルート」は多くの場合 channel と訳すべきであることに注意. 英語の route は定まった経路, 特に highway とか旅行・交通のための経路などに用い, 比喩的な意味に用いられることは少ない).
¶ 外交～を通して through diplomatic *channels*.
正規の～で物資を買う buy goods through *a* legal *channel*.
青少年の間に販売～を開拓する procure larger *sales* among youngsters.
情報入手の～を探る trace the *source* of the information.
2〘数学〙root.

ループ a loop.
—アンテナ a loop antenna.

ルーブル (ソ連の貨幣) a rouble; (パリの博物館) the Louvre.

ルーマニア Rumania; Romania.
—語 Rumanian; Romanian. **—人** a Rumanian; a Romanian.

ルーム a room.
—サービス room service. **—メート** *one's* roommate.

ルール a rule; a regulation. ¶ ～を決める set down *a rule*. ～を守る keep *a rule* (≒ *a regulation*). ～を破る violate *a rule* (≒ *a regulation*). ～に従って競技を行なう play according to the *rules* of the game.
—違反 violation (≒ infraction; infringement) of a rule (≒ a regulation); (スポーツ) (反則) a foul; violation of a rule. ¶ きみは～違反だ You're against the *rules*.

ルーレット roulette.

ルクス〘物理〙a lux (複 luxes; lux).

るざい【流罪】 exile. ¶ 謀反人は～に処せられた The rebels *were exiled* (≒ *were banished*) from the land.

るす【留守】 absence. ¶ だれか私の～中にお見えになりましたか Did anyone come to see me *in* (≒ *during*) *my absence*? / Did anyone come to see me *while I was away*? 商用で一日じゅう～をした Business *kept* me *out*

all day. 彼は勉強がお～になっている He *has neglected* his studies.
—番 a caretaker. ¶ ～番をする look after the house in another's absence.

るつぼ【坩堝】a crucible ; a melting pot. ¶ 彼が壇上に現われると満場は興奮の～と化した The packed capacity went into a state of feverish excitement at the sight of him on the stage. アメリカはしばしば人種の～と呼ばれる America is often called the *melting pot* of races.

るてん【流転】¶ 万物は～する Everything *changes*. / All things *flow* (≒ *transmigrate*). 彼らはあてもなく～の旅を続けた They *traveled* (≒ *wandered*; *roamed*) from place to place without any particular destination in mind.

ルネッサンス the Renaissance.
—建築 Renaissance architecture. —様式 Renaissance style.

ルビ *kana* printed alongside Chinese characters [to show the pronunciation]; 〖印刷〗 英 a ruby; 米 an agate.
¶ 漢字に～をつける print small *kana* alongside *kanji* (≒ Chinese characters) to show the pronunciation.

ルビー〖鉱物〗a ruby.

ルピー (インド・パキスタン・スリランカなどの貨幣) a rupee.

るふ【流布】circulation ; spread. ¶ この説は広く～している This theory *has obtained* [a] wide *circulation*. さまざまの風説が～している There are a number of rumors *going around* (≒ *getting about*). / A number of rumors *are on the lips of people*.

ルポルタージュ reportage (フランス語から); a report.

るり【瑠璃】〖鉱物〗lapis lazuli.

るる【縷縷】¶ 彼は事件の顛末(てんまつ)を～と述べた He gave all the *detailed* (≒ *minute*) *particulars* of the incident.

るろう【流浪】roaming ; roving ; nomadism ; vagrancy ; vagabondage ; wandering.
¶ ジプシーは各地を～して暮らす Gypsies *roam* (≒ *rove*) from place to place. ～の民 a *nomadic* people.

ルンバ〖音楽〗rumba.

ルンペン (浮浪者) a loafer ; a tramp ; (失業者) a jobless (≒ an unemployed) man ; (放浪者) a vagabond.

れ

れい【令】(命令) an order ; a command ; (政府・教会などの) a decree ; an edict ; (法令) a law ; a statute ; (法令・政令) an act ; (市条例) an ordinance ; municipal regulations.

れい【礼】**1**〖礼儀〗etiquette. ¶ 彼は先輩に対する～を知っている (知っていない) He *is polite* (*is impolite*) to his seniors.
彼は後輩にさえも～を尽くす He *behaves respectfully* even toward his juniors.
2〖会釈〗a bow ; salutation ; greeting. ¶ 私は彼に～をした I *bowed to* him.
彼は帽子をとって私に～をした He *took his hat off to* me.
兵士は上官に～をした The soldier *saluted* to the senior officer.
3〖謝礼〗a fee. ¶ 彼は私に１万円お～を出した He *offered* me ten thousand yen.
私は親切にしてやって厚くお～をされた I *was* handsomely *rewarded for* my kindness.
ここでは医者のお～はいくらですか What is the doctor's *fee* here?
4〖返礼〗¶ あの人から贈り物をもらったのでなにかお～をしたい I want to *give something in return for* his present.
5〖待遇〗¶ 彼は私を～を尽くして遇してくれた He treated me *with all honor*.
6〖感謝〗thanks. ¶ なんとお～申し上げてよいのかわかりません I don't know *how* (≒ *in what words*) *to thank you*.

れい【例】**1**〖実例〗an example ; an instance.
¶ 彼は先輩の～にならった He followed *the example* of his senior.
ひとつ～を挙げましょう Let me give you *an example*.
～を挙げれば (人と物) for example ; (事柄) for instance.
こんな大火は～のないことだ Such a big fire is without *precedent*. / Such a big fire *is unprecedented*. / This is the biggest fire that we have ever had.
よい～を作る create *a* good *precedent*.
2〖場合〗a case. ¶ これは珍しい～だ This is *a* singular *case*.
ここに適当な～がある Here is *a case* in point.
3〖慣例〗a custom. ¶ 私は毎朝散歩をするのが～だ It is *a habit* with me to take a walk every morning.
～のごとく彼はけさ遅刻した *As is his habit* (≒ *As is usual with him*; *As usual*), he was late this morning.
4〖問題の・いつもの〗¶ これが～の小説だ This is the novel *in question*.
～の件はどうなりましたか What has become of *that* matter?

〜の所できのう彼に会った I met him at the *usual* place yesterday.

れい【零】zero; nought; cipher. ¶ 101 (棒読みの場合は one O [ou] (≒ zero) one). 001 (棒読みの場合は double O [ou] one; O [ou] O [ou] one; zero zero one).

れい【霊】the spirit; the soul; (文語) a shade; (集合的に用いて, 死者の霊) the shades. ¶ 〜の世界 the world of *spirit*; the *spiritual* world; (死者の世界) Hades; the shades. 〜と肉 [the] *spirit* and [the] flesh. 祖先の〜を祭る(あがめる) worship *the spirits* of *one's* ancestry.

レイ (ハワイの花輪) a lei.

レイアウト the layout. ¶ 雑誌写真の〜 the *layout* of magazine pictures. 〜する lay out.

れいか【零下】below zero. ¶ 〜3度 three degrees *below zero.*

れいかい【例会】a regular meeting.

れいかい【例解】an illustration. ¶ 図と図表で〜する *illustrate* by charts and diagrams.

れいかい【霊界】(精神界) the spiritual world; (宗教界) the religious world. ¶ 彼は〜の名士である He is one of the eminent leaders of *the religious world.*

れいがい【冷害】cold-weather damage.
¶ 関東地方はひどい〜に見舞われた The Kanto district *was* badly *damaged by cold weather.*

れいがい【例外】an exception. ¶ 〜的事件 an *exceptional* case. 〜なく without *exception.* 〜のない法則はない There is no rule without *exceptions.* そういう場合は〜を認める *Exceptions* are made in such cases. ことしの寒さは〜だ It is *unusually* cold this winter.

れいかん【霊感】inspiration. ¶ ワーズワースは自然から〜を受けた Wordsworth *was inspired by* nature. / Wordsworth drew his *inspiration* from nature.

れいき【冷気】(涼気) cool weather; coolness; (寒気) cold weather.

れいぎ【礼儀】courtesy; politeness; civility; (作法) manners; etiquette.
¶ 彼女は〜正しい She *is polite* (≒ *is civil*; *is courteous*) *to* others. / She *has good manners.* 彼は〜をわきまえない He is an *impolite* (≒ *ill-mannered*; *ill-bred*) fellow. 彼にそんなことを頼むのは〜はずれだ It's *impolite to* ask him to do such a thing. 〜上言ったのに真に受けるやつがあるか What a fool [you are] to swallow what he said *out of courtesy*!

れいきゃく【冷却】refrigeration; cooling.
¶ 液体を〜する *refrigerate* the liquid. エンジンを〜する *cool down* an engine.
—器 a cooler; a refrigerator. **—**装置 a cooling device. **—**期間 a cooling-off period.

れいきゅう【霊柩】a coffin; 困 a casket.
—車 a motor hearse; a funeral carriage.

れいきん【礼金】a recompense; a reward; remuneration.

れいぐう【冷遇】a cold treatment. ¶ 私は〜に甘んじる男ではない I am the last man to submit to *inhospitality.* 彼を〜するつもりはなかった I had no intention to *treat* him *coldly.*

れいけつ【冷血】cold blood.
—漢 a cold-hearted (≒ merciless; heartless) fellow; a man with a heart of stone.
—動物 a cold-blooded animal.

れいげん【冷厳】austerity. ¶ 〜な態度 a *stern* attitude. 〜な現実 *hard* facts; *grim* realities.

れいげん【霊験】a miracle. ¶ この寺の観音さまは〜あらたかだということだ They say *Kannon* enshrined in this temple *is highly responsive to prayers.*

れいこう【励行】strict enforcement. ¶ みな早起きを〜しなければいけない Early rising should *be enforced* (≒ *be carried out strictly*) by everybody. 毎朝私は冷水摩擦を〜している Every morning I *never fail to* rub myself with a wet towel.

れいこく【冷酷】cruelty; heartlessness.
¶ 〜な仕打ち a *cold-hearted* (≒ *cold-blooded*) action. 〜な男 a *cruel* man. 〜な処分 a *merciless* (≒ *heartless*) punishment. 〜な心 a *pitiless* heart. 彼は〜きわまりない男だ He *is cruelty itself.* / He *is* unusually *cold.*

れいこん【霊魂】a soul. ¶ 〜不滅 the immortality of *the soul.*

れいさい【零細】¶ 〜な金 a *trifling* sum. 〜な預金 *petty* deposits.
—企業 small-scale enterprises. **—**農業 petty farming.

れいじ【零時】twelve o'clock; (午後) noon; (午前) midnight. ¶ 列車は午前〜10分発です The train starts *at ten past midnight.*

れいしき【礼式】(作法) etiquette; manners; (儀式) a ceremony; a rite.

れいしょう【冷笑】a sneer; a cold smile; a sardonic smile. ¶ われわれははじめ彼の努力を〜していた We *mocked at* his efforts at first. 彼は私の作品を〜した He *sneered at* my works.

れいしょう【例証】an illustration; an instance; an example. ¶ あなたの理論を〜できますか Can you *demonstrate* (≒ *give any examples to verify*) your theory?

れいじょう【令状】a warrant; a writ. ¶ 〜を発する issue *a warrant.* 〜を執行する serve *a writ* on *a person.* 彼の〜は出ているのか Is *a warrant* out against him?
捜査**—** a search warrant.

れいじょう【礼状】a letter of thanks.

れいじょう【令嬢】a daughter; a young lady.
¶ A氏〜 Mr. A's daughter; Miss A.

れいすい【冷水】cold water.
—摩擦 a rubdown with a wet towel. **—**浴 a cold bath.

れいせい【冷静】calmness; composure.
¶ 〜な判断 [a] *cool* judgment. 〜な態度 a *calm* attitude. 〜な人 a *cool* head. やがて彼女

れ

も〜になるだろう She will *calm herself* soon. けっして〜さを失うな Never lose *your presence of mind* [at any time]. 常に〜を保つように心がけよ Try to *keep cool* at all times. あとで〜に考えてみるがいい Try to think it over *calmly* afterward.

れいせい【霊性】divine nature.

れいせつ【礼節】propriety. ¶ 中国人は〜を重んじる The Chinese make much of *courtesy* (≒ *courteousness*). ⇒れいぎ

れいせん【冷戦】a cold war.

れいぜん【霊前】¶ 〜に花輪を捧げた I offered a wreath to *the spirit of the departed*. 〜にぬかずく bow before *the deceased*.

れいぜん【冷然】¶ 〜たる態度 a *cold* attitude. 〜と *coldly*; *icily*; *indifferently*.

れいそう【礼装】a ceremonial dress.

れいぞう【冷蔵】refrigeration. ¶ 魚は2か月〜される The fishes are to *be kept in cold storage* for two months.

—庫 an icebox; 困 a refrigerator. **—車** a refrigerator car. 電気**—庫** an electric refrigerator (≒ fridge).

れいぞく【隷属】¶ 彼らは当時フランスに〜していた They *were subordinate* (≒ *were subject*) *to* France in those days. / They *were* then *under the control of* France.

れいだい【例題】(練習問題) an exercise; (範例) an example. ¶ 〜を課す give *exercises*.

れいたん【冷淡】coolness; coldness; cold-heartedness. ¶ 〜な態度 a *cold* attitude. 〜な仕打ち a *cold-hearted* treatment. 〜なもてなし a *cool* reception. 彼女は彼の〜な返事に失望した She was disappointed with his *indifferent* answer. 彼は昔の級友に〜だ He *is indifferent to* his old classmates.

れいちょう【霊長】¶ 人間は万物の〜だ Man is *the lord* of creation.

れいてつ【冷徹】¶ 彼は〜な人で感情におぼれない He *is* so *cool-headed* that he isn't swayed by passion. 彼は〜な人でロマンチストではない He *is realistic*, not a romanticist.

れいてん【零点】zero. ¶ 試験で〜をとった I got *zero* in the examination. / I was not able to answer any questions. / (数学などで) I was not able to solve any problems.

れいど【零度】zero; the freezing point. ¶ 今夜は〜以下に下がるだろう It (≒ The temperature) will fall below *zero* tonight.

れいとう【冷凍】refrigeration. ¶ 魚ばかりかソラマメや大豆も〜にされる Beans and soy beans as well as fish *are kept in cold storage*.

—魚 frozen fish. **—食品** frozen food. **—船** a refrigerator boat.

れいにく【冷肉】cold meat.

れいにく【霊肉】¶ 彼は〜の一致を唱えた He advocated the unity of *body and soul*.

れいねん【例年】(平年) an average (≒ normal; ordinary) year; (毎年) every year. ¶ 〜の大会 an *annual* mass meeting. 〜のように as usual. ことしの夏は〜になく涼しい It is *unusually* cool this summer.

れいはい【礼拝】worship; (教会の) service. ¶ 朝の〜に出る attend morning *service*. 彼らは熱心に神を〜する They *worship* God in earnest.

—者 a worshiper. **—堂** a church; a chapel.

れいはい【零敗】¶ 残念ながらわがチームは〜を喫した I am sorry that our team *was shut out*.

れいばい【霊媒】a medium.

れいひょう【冷評】a sarcastic remark. ¶ 批評家は彼のドラマを〜した The critics *sneered at* (≒ *made cold remarks on*) his drama.

れいふく【礼服】a ceremonial dress. ¶ 結婚式にはみな〜を着用する All *are in full dress* at a wedding.

れいふじん【令夫人】*a person's* wife. ¶ ホワイト氏〜 *Mrs.* White.

れいぶん【例文】an illustrative sentence. ¶ 〜をひとつ挙げる give one *sentence as an example*.

れいほう【礼砲】a [gun] salute. ¶ 21発の〜が放たれた *A salute of* 21 *guns* was fired.

れいぼう【冷房】air-cooling; air-conditioning. ¶ 〜のきいた部屋 an *air-conditioned* room.

—車 an air-conditioned car. **—装置** air-conditioning apparatus.

れいまいり【礼参り】¶ お〜に行く visit a shrine for thanksgiving.

れいまわり【礼回り】¶ お〜をする go round to return thanks.

れいみょう【霊妙】¶ 〜な力 *miraculous* power. 〜な美しさ *ethereal* beauty. 〜な音楽 an *exquisite* piece of music.

れいめい【令名】¶ 彼の〜は大いに上がった He won *a* high *reputation*. 彼の〜は高まるばかりだ He enjoys *an* ever-increasing *fame*.

れいめい【黎明】dawn; daybreak. ¶ 新美術の〜期 the *dawn* of a new art.

れいやく【霊薬】a miraculous remedy; 困 a wonder drug. ¶ 不老長寿の〜 *an elixir* of life.

れいらく【零落】¶ 彼は〜した貴族だ He is one of the *ruined* nobles. 彼は今すっかり〜している He *is* now *in* unutterably *needy* (≒ *reduced*) *circumstances*. 2年とたたないうちに彼は〜してしまった He *has come to ruin* in less than two years.

れいり【怜悧】¶ 〜な少年 a *bright* (≒ *clever*) boy (bright のほうが相手の喜ぶ表現). 〜な若者 a *bright* (≒ *smart*) young man.

れいれいし・い【麗麗しい】¶ 大きな看板が門のところに〜く出ている A big signboard is *conspicuously* displayed at the gate. 彼は自分の業績を〜く書きたてた He wrote up about his own works *boldly*. あまり〜く自分の経歴を述べたてるものではない You shouldn't relate the story of your life so *pretentiously*.

れいろう【玲瓏】¶ 〜たる月影 the *brilliant* moonlight. 〜たる声 a *bright and clear*

れ

voice. 八面～の霊峰 a sacred mountain *graceful* in all its aspects.
レインジャー (森林警備隊員) a ranger; (アメリカ特別遊撃隊員) a U.S. Army Ranger.
レーサー a racer.
レース 1 〖競走〗 a race.
ボート―― a boat race. ヨット―― a yacht race.
2 〖編み物〗 a lace. ¶ ～のついたブラウス a *laced* blouse.
～のついたドレス a dress trimmed with *lace*.
～の縁どりをする *lace up* a dress.
レーダー a radar.
レート a rate. ¶ ～を上げる(下げる) advance (lower) *the rate*.
レーヨン rayon.
レール a rail. ¶ ～を敷く lay *rails*.
レーンコート a raincoat.
れきさつ【轢殺】 ¶ 子どもがトラックに～された A child *was run over and killed* by a truck.
れきし【歴史】 history; (編年史) a chronicle. ¶ ～的発明 a *historic* invention. ～的偉業 a great *historic* achievement. ～上の出来事 a *historical* event. ～上の人物 a *historical* figure. 日本の～ the Japanese *history*. 彼の名は永久に～にとどまるだろう His name will go down in *history* forever.
――家 a historian. ――学 historical science. ――観 a historical view. ――劇 a historical play. ――小説 a historical novel.
れきし【轢死】 ¶ 彼は3年前～した He *was run over and killed* three years ago.
れきせい【瀝青】 〘鉱物〙 pitch.
――岩 pitchstone. ――炭 pitch coal.
れきせん【歴戦】 ¶ ～の勇士 a veteran; a warrior who has fought many battles.
れきぜん【歴然】 ¶ ～たる事実 an *obvious* (≒ a *plain*) fact. ～たる相違 a *distinct* (≒ *clear*) difference. ～たる証拠 an *unmistakable* evidence; a *positive* proof.
れきだい【歴代】 successive generations.
¶ ～の内閣 *successive* cabinets.
れきにん【歴任】 ¶ 彼は要職を～した He *has filled* important *posts successively*.
れきほう【歴訪】 ¶ 首相はヨーロッパ諸国を～の予定だ The prime minister is expected to *make a tour of various countries* in Europe.
レギュラー 〔a〕 regular. ¶ 私はラグビー部の～だ I am *a regular* 〔*member*〕 of the Rugby team. 彼女はテレビ番組の～メンバーのひとりだ She is a *regular* member of a television program.
れきれき【歴歴】 ¶ 政界のお～ *prominent* (≒ *eminent; distinguished; leading*) *figures* in the political world.
レグホン (鶏) a leghorn. ¶ 白色～ *a* white *leghorn*.
レクリエーション recreation.
レコーダー a recorder.
タイム―― a time recorder. テープ―― a tape recorder.
レコード 1 〖音楽〗 a record. ¶ ～をかける play *a record*.
～に歌を吹き込む *record* a song.
2 〖記録〗 a record. ¶ ～をつくる establish *a* new *record*.
～を破る break *a record*.
――保持者 a record holder.
レシート (受取) a receipt.
レシーバー a receiver.
レシーブ 〘球技〙 receiving. ¶ ～する receive.
レジ〔スター〕 a register; (人) a cash register.
レジスタンス resistance. ¶ ～の闘士 a fighter of the resistance.
レジャー leisure. ¶ 今は～ブームだ There are many people now who enjoy *leisure hours* (≒ *recreation time*). / Now everyone tries to enjoy his *leisure*.
レストハウス a resthouse.
レストラン a restaurant.
レスビアン a Lesbian; a Les; a female homosexual.
レスラー a wrestler.
レスリング wrestling.
レター a letter.
――ペーパー letter paper; (1冊の) a writing pad.
レタス 〘植物〙 lettuce; a head of lettuce.
れつ【列】 (一般に) a row; a rank; (横列) a line; (縦列) a file; a column; (行列) a procession; (順番列) a queue.
¶ ～をなして進む march *in a line*. ～をつくる form *a row* (≒ *a line; a file; a queue*). ～を整える(解く) dress (break up) *the ranks*. ～に遅れる drop behind. ～に入る stand in *a queue*. ～から先に出る jump the *queue*. ～(行列)を横切る cross *a procession*. 2～縦(横)隊 *a* double *file* (*line*). 4～になって進む march four abreast. 4～に整列する be drawn up four deep. 彼は～を離れた He dropped out of 〔*the*〕 *line*.
前(後)―― a front (back) row.
れつあく【劣悪】 ¶ ～な品 an article *of poor quality*; *inferior* goods.
れっか【烈火】 ¶ 彼はその知らせを聞いて～のごとく怒った He *was infuriated at* the news. / The news made him *boil* (≒ *burn*) *with anger*.
れっきと【歴と】 ¶ ～した事実 an *obvious* fact. ～した妻 *one's legal* wife; a *legally* married woman. ～した紳士 a *respectable* (≒ *decent*) gentleman. ～した身分の人 a man *of position*.
れっきょ【列挙】 ¶ 考えられる原因をすべて～してみた We *enumerated* (≒ *counted up; made a list of*) all the possible causes.
れっきょう【列強】 the Great Powers.
れっこく【列国】 the powers; the nations of the world.
れっしゃ【列車】 a train. ¶ 午前9時30分東京発の～で行く I am leaving Tokyo by the 9:30 a.m. 〔*train*〕. この町と港の間は～の便がよい There is a good service of *train* between this city and the harbor. / We have good *train* service between this city and the

port. 〜のダイヤが乱れている The *trains* are not running on schedule.
—事故 a train accident. —時刻表 a train schedule; a timetable. —妨害(労働争議中の) a railway sabotage. 貨物— 英 a goods train; 米 a freight train. 急行— an express [train]. スキー— a skiers' special. 準急— 米 a local express. 超特急— a bullet train. 直通— a through train. 東京行き(発)— a train for (from) Tokyo. 特急— a special express. 上り(下り)— an up (a down) train. 普通— a slow (≒ local) train; 米 an accommodation train. 夜行— a night train. 臨時— a special [train].

れっしょう【裂傷】 a cut; a laceration. ¶ 頭部に〜を負った I *had* my head *lacerated* (≒ *cut*). / I had *a laceration* on the head.

れつじょう【劣情】 low passions; carnal desire; lust. ¶ この映画は男の〜を刺激する This film excites *low passions* in men.

れっ·する【列する】 ¶ 式に〜した人々 those who *attended* (≒ *were present at*) the ceremony. フランスはヨーロッパの大国に〜する France *ranks among* (≒ *with*) the European Powers.

レッスン a lesson. ¶ ピアノの〜を受ける take (≒ have) piano *lessons*.

れっせい【劣性】 inferiority.
—形質(遺伝) a recessive character. —遺伝 recessive heredity.

れっせい【劣勢】 ¶ われわれのほうが数において〜だ We *are inferior to* them in number. / We *are outnumbered*.

れっせき【列席】 attendance. ¶ 祝賀会に〜した I *attended* (≒ *was present at*) the celebration. パーティーにご〜を賜わりたくお願い申し上げます We request the pleasure (≒ honor) of your *company* at the party. / Your *presence* is requested at the party.
—者 ¶ 多数の〜者があった There was *a* large *attendance*.

レッテル a label. ¶ そのびんには毒薬の〜がはってある The bottle *is labeled* poison. 彼は不良の〜をはられた He *was labeled* (≒ *was branded; was categorized*) as a bad boy.

れつでん【列伝】 ¶ アメリカ大統領〜 the *lives* of the Presidents of the United States of America.

れっとう【列島】 a chain of islands. ¶ 日本〜 *the Islands* of Japan.

れっとう【劣等】 inferiority. ¶ 品性〜な人 a man of *low* character.
—生 a poor (≒ backward) student. —感(複合) inferiority complex. ¶ 彼は常に〜感に悩まされている He always suffers from *inferiority complex*.

れっぷう【烈風】 a violent wind; a gale.

レディ a lady. ¶ 〜ファーストです *Ladies*, first.

レディーメード ¶ 〜の服 a *ready-made* dress.

レニューム〘化学〙 rhenium.

レバー (肝臓) the liver; 〘機械〙 a lever.

レパートリー a repertory. ¶ 彼女は歌の〜が広い She has *a* wide *repertory* (≒ *repertoire*) of songs.

レビュー a revue; (書評) a [book] review.
—ガール a revue girl. ブック— a book review.

レフ a reflex.
一眼(二眼)— a single- (twin-)lens reflex.

レフェリー a referee.
—ストップ ¶ 〜ストップで勝った He won the match by the *referee* stop.

レフト〘野球〙 the left field; (人) a left fielder.

レプラ〘病理〙 lepra; leprosy.

レベル a level. ¶ この国は文化の〜が高い The culture in this country is on *a* high *level*. / The cultural *level* of this country is high. わが国の産業が先進国の〜に達した The industry of our country has reached the *level* of advanced nations of the world. きみと彼とでは〜が違う You are on *a* different *level* from his. 給料の〜をあげた They made our pay *level* up.
—アップ level up. —ダウン level down.

レポート a report.

レモネード lemonade.

レモン a lemon.
—ジュース lemon juice. —水 lemonade. —スカッシュ lemon squash. —ティー lemon tea.

レリーフ relief.

-れん【-連】 ¶ 文士〜 *a* literary *set*; literary *people*. 悪童〜 *a gang* of bad boys.

れんあい【恋愛】 love. ¶ 彼は〜している He *is falling in love* [with her]. あのふたりは〜中だ Those two *are in love* [*with each other*].
—結婚 a love marriage. ¶ 彼らは〜結婚をした They married for *love*.

れんか【廉価】 ¶ あの店では中古品を〜で売っている They sell secondhand articles *cheap* (≒ *at low prices*).
—版 a cheap (≒ popular) edition. —品 low- (≒ popular-) priced goods.

れんが【煉瓦】 a brick. ¶ 〜を積んでいるところだ We are laying *bricks*.
—造り ¶ 〜造りの建物 a *brick* building. 私の家は〜造りだ My house is built of *brick*.

れんき【連記】 ¶ 投票は２名〜にする write two names on a ballot.
—制 the plural ballot system.

れんきゅう【連休】 consecutive (≒ straight) holidays. ¶ 飛び石２日〜 two *holidays* with a working day in between.

れんきんじゅつ【錬金術】 alchemy.

れんけい【連係】 connection; contact. ¶ 隣国と〜を保つことが望ましい It is desirable to *keep in contact* (≒ *touch*) *with* our neighboring countries. 当社はA社と緊密な〜がある We *are* closely *connected* (≒ *associated; cooperated*) *with* A company.
—動作 a conjoint action; a combination.

れんげそう【蓮華草】〘植物〙 the Chinese milk vetch.

れんけつ【連結】 connection; joining. ¶ これ

れ

は10両～の列車だ This is a ten-car (≒ -carriage) train. / This is ten cars long. この駅で車両を～する They *couple* (≒ *connect*) cars at this station. この汽車には食堂車が～されている A dining car *is attached to* this train.

—器 a connection; a coupling.

れんけつ【廉潔】 integrity; honesty. ¶ ～の士 a man of *integrity*; an *upright* man.

れんこ【連呼】 ¶ われわれは彼の名前を～した We *called* (≒ *cried*; *shouted*) his name *repeatedly*.

れんご【連語】 (複合語) a compound word; (句) a phrase.

れんこう【連行】 ¶ 彼らは容疑者を署に～した They *took* the suspect to the police station.

れんごう【連合】 alliance; confederation. ¶ 2国間の～ *a union* between the two countries. 野党が～して与党を攻撃した The Opposition parties *combined together* and attacked the government. / The opposition parties attacked the government *in concert*.

—軍 (第1・第2次大戦の) the Allied Forces. —国 the Allies; the Allied Powers. —政権 a coalition government. 国際— the United Nations.

れんさ【連鎖】 a chain; a connection.

—店 a chain store; 英 a multiple store. —反応〘物理〙〔a〕 chain reaction.

れんざ【連座】 involvement; implication. ¶ 彼はその汚職事件に～した He *was involved* (≒ *was implicated*) *in* the bribery case.

れんさい【連載】 serialization. ¶ ～する serialize. 彼は新聞に小説を～している He *is writing* a novel *serially* (≒ a *serial* novel) in a newspaper. この小説は雑誌に～された This novel *was published serially* (≒ *in serial form*) in a magazine.

—小説 a serial story.

れんさく【連作】 ¶ この畑ではジャガイモを～している They *crop* (≒ *plant*) this field *with* potatoes *every year*.

れんざん【連山】 a chain of mountains.

れんじつ【連日】 day after day. ¶ 彼は～仕事に追われている His work keeps him busy *every day*. ～連夜彼から電話がかかってくる 〔*Every*〕 *Day and night* he calls me up. ～の雨で川が氾濫(はんらん)した Owing to a *long* rain the river overflowed its banks.

れんじゅ【連珠】 goban〔g〕.

れんしゅう【練習】 practice; exercise. ¶ 毎日のヴァイオリンの～ daily violin *practice*; daily *practice at* the violin. 何事も～が第一 *Practice* makes perfect. 少し～すればじょうずにピアノが弾けるでしょう You will be able to play the piano well *with a little practice*. 私はバッティングの～をしていない I *am out of practice at* batting. 私はアメリカ人について英会話の～をした I *practiced* English conversation *on* an American. われわれは学校劇をするので役の～をした We *rehearsed* our parts for the school play. 彼らの劇の～を見ましょう Let's see their *rehearsal*. 彼は水泳の～をつんでいる He *is* well *trained in* swimming.

—機 a training airplane. —試合 a practice game; (ボクシング) a workout. —航海 a training cruise. —航海船 a practice ship. —問題 an exercise. —問題集 an exercise book; a drill book.

れんしょ【連署】 joint signature. ¶ この書類には保証人の～が必要だ The *joint signature* of guarantors is required for the papers. / The papers should *be countersigned* (≒ *be signed jointly*) by guarantors.

—人 joint signers.

れんしょう【連勝】 a series of victories; victory after victory. ¶ 巨人軍は4～した The Giants won four games *straight* (≒ *consecutively*; *in a row*).

レンズ a lens. ¶ ～の焦点 a focus. ～を門に向ける direct *the lens* to the gate. ～を f 11に絞る stop down 〔*a lens*〕 to f 11.

凹(おう)— a concave lens. 凸(とつ)— a convex lens. 拡大— a magnifying lens. 合成— a compound lens. 望遠— a telephoto lens.

れんせん【連戦】 ¶ 巨人阪神3～ three *consecutive games* between the Giants and the Tigers. 味方は～連勝(連敗)した Our side *won a series of victories* (*suffered a series of defeats*). / Our side *won battle after battle* (*lost battle after battle*).

れんそう【連想】 association 〔of ideas〕. ¶ ナイチンゲールといえば赤十字を～する The name of Nightingale *is associated with* the Red Cross. この音楽は田園交響曲を～させる This music *suggests* (≒ *is suggestive of*) the "Pastoral" Symphony.

—テスト(ゲーム) an association test (game).

れんぞく【連続】 continuation. ¶ 3日～して雨が降っている It has been raining for three days *without a break* (≒ *in succession*; *running*). その後～して数回の地震があった After that there *succeeded* several earthquake shocks. 裁判は～10日間続いた The trial lasted for ten days *together* (≒ *on end*).

—講演 a series of lectures. —殺人 successive murders; murders in succession. —放送劇 a serial radio drama. —漫画 a comic strip.

れんたい【連帯】 ¶ われわれは～責任で20万円借りた We borrowed two hundred thousand yen *on joint responsibility*. 私は彼と～責任を負うつもりだ I will *share the liability with* him. ～責任は無責任(諺) *Everybody's business is nobody's business*.

—債務 joint obligation (≒ debt). —債務者 a joint debtor. —保証人 a joint surety. —証書 a joint note. —感(意識) the feeling of togetherness.

れんたい【連隊】 a regiment.

—旗(長) a regimental colors (commander).

れんたつ【練達】 mastery. ¶ ～の士 an ex-

れ

pert; a veteran.

れんたん【練炭】a briquet(te).

れんだん【連弾】〔音楽〕a four-hand(ed) playing (on the piano).

—曲 a piece for four hands.

れんち【廉恥】honor. ¶ 彼は～を重んじる男だ He is a man of *honor*.

—心 a sense of honor. ¶ 彼には～心がない He has no *sense of honor*.

れんちゅう【連中】a company; a lot. ¶ 会社の～と旅行した I made a trip with my *colleagues* in the firm (≒ my *fellow workers*). ～の言うことはあてにならない We cannot trust what *they* say.

れんちょく【廉直】¶ ～の士 a man of *integrity*; an *honest* man.

れんどう【連動】¶ この機械は～している These machines *synchronize*.

—装置(器) an inter locking device.

レントゲン ¶ 肺の～写真を撮った I *had* my lungs *X-rayed* (≒ *radiographed*).

—検査 a Röntgen (≒ an X-ray) examination. —撮影 X-raying. —写真 a Röntgen (≒ an X-ray) photograph; a radiograph. —線 Röntgen rays; X-rays.

れんにゅう【練乳】condensed milk.

れんぱ【連破】¶ ジャイアンツはタイガースを３～した The Giants *won* three *successive victories* over the Tigers.

れんぱ【連覇】¶ プロ野球日本選手権の３～を成し遂げる *win* three *successive* Japanese pro-baseball *championships*.

れんばい【廉売】a bargain sale. ¶ あの店は大量に仕入れるので～ができる As they stock in large quantities they can *sell cheap* (≒ *at low prices; at a bargain rate*).

れんぱい【連敗】successive defeats. ¶連戦～の憂き目に会った We suffered *a series of defeats*. / We *lost game after game*. われわれのチームは３～を喫した Our team *lost three games straight* (≒ *in succession; in a row*).

れんぱつ【連発】¶ ２～銃 *a double barreled* gun; (拳銃) *a revolver*. 生徒たちは先生に質問を～した The students *fired* questions at their teacher. 彼女は「うれしい」を～した She *said over and over again*, "I am so happy."

れんぱんじょう【連判状】a pledge (≒ compact) under joint signature.

れんびん【憐憫・憐愍】pity. ¶ 貧しい人々に対し～の情をいだく We *feel pity for* (≒ *take pity on; take compassion on; show mercy to*) the poor.

れんぺいじょう【練兵場】〔軍事〕a parade ground.

れんぼ【恋慕】attachment. ¶ 彼女への～の情断ちがたし I *am* deeply *attached to* her. / I *am* deeply *in love with* her. / I *have* completely *lost my heart to* her.

れんぽう【連邦】commonwealth; dominion; federation.

イギリス— the British Commonwealth of Nations. ソビエト— the Union of Soviet Socialist Republics (U.S.S.R.). カナダ— the Dominion of Canada. —裁判所(特にアメリカの) a federal court. —制度 a federal system; a federation. —政府 a federal government.

れんぽう【連峰】a chain (≒ range) of mountains. ¶ アルプスの～ the Alpine *range*; the Alps.

れんま【練磨・錬磨】training; practice. ¶ 精神を～することはたいせつだ It is important to *train* (≒ *improve*) our mind.

れんめい【連名】joint signature. ¶ 500名～の請願書 a petition *signed by* five hundred persons. われわれは～で質問状を彼に出した We sent him a letter of questions *in our joint names*.

れんめい【連盟】league; federation; union; association.

国際— the League of Nations. 陸上競技— the Federation of Athletic Associations. 大学野球— the League of Intercollegiate Baseball.

れんめん【連綿】¶ ～たる家系 an *old, uninterrupted* family tree. 彼は～たる医者の家系の５代目だ He is the fifth *in a line* of doctors.

れんらく【連絡】**1**〖交通の〗(a) connection. ¶ 私は大阪で新幹線に～しそこねた I missed (≒ could not get) *a connection at* Osaka *with* the New Tokaido Line.

—駅 a junction. —切符 a combination ticket. —船 a ferryboat. ¶ 青函(せいかん)～船が本州と北海道を～する The Aomori-Hakodate ferryboat *connects* Japan proper *with* Hokkaido. 徒歩— ¶ 徒歩～する *make a connection* on foot.

2〖当事者間の〗¶ 高等学校は大学と～がなければいけない The upper secondary schools should *be in connection with* the universities.

ふたつのクラブは会員は別だが互いに～がとれていた The two clubs did not have the same members, but they *were affiliated with* each other.

彼らの政府はアメリカ政府と～がついている(～を失った) Their government *is keeping touch with* (*has lost contact with*) the government of the U.S.A.

—会議 a liaison conference. —事務所 a liaison office.

3〖通信〗¶ その船は出帆後３日で～を絶った The ship ceased *communication* three days after its departure.

それを電話で～してください *Let me know* (it) by telephone.

れんりつ【連立】—内閣 a coalition cabinet. —方程式 simultaneous equations.

れんれん【恋恋】¶ 彼は自分の地位にいつまでも～としている He *is* still *reluctant to give up* his position. / He still *clings to* his position.

ろ

ろ【炉】(家庭などの) a hearth ; a fireplace.
原子── a〔nuclear〕reactor. 溶鉱── a blast furnace.

ろ【櫓】a scull ; an oar. ¶彼はじょうずに～をこいだ He pulled *a* good *oar.* / He skillfully worked at the *oar.*

ロ〘音楽〙B. ¶～長(短)調 *B* major (minor).

ロイター Reuters.
──通信社 Reuters ; the Reuter's News Agency. ──電報 a Reuter dispatch.

ロイドめがね【ロイド眼鏡】glasses with thick rims ; celluloid (≒ plastic) glasses.

ろう【労】labor ; effort. ¶～多くして功少なし You will get little profit for your *pains.* 彼は昇進のためには～を惜しまない男だ He spares no *pains* for his promotion. 彼の～は十分に報いられた He was amply repaid for his *trouble* (≒ *pains*). 彼が媒酌の～をとった He *took the trouble to* arrange the marriage.

ろう【蠟】wax. ¶～を引いた床 a *waxed* floor. ～のような白い顔 a *waxen* (≒ *pallid*) complexion.
──紙 wax paper. ──細工 a waxwork. ──人形 a wax doll.

ろう【牢】a prison ; a jail(㊖では gaol とつづる). ¶彼は～に入れられた He *was imprisoned.* 彼は～に入っている He is in *prison.* ～を出た I was released from *prison.*

ろうあ【聾唖】──学校 a deaf and dumb school.
──者 a deaf and dumb person ; a deaf-mute.

ろうえい【漏洩】leakage. ¶わが国の機密が～した Our national secrets *leaked out.*

ろうえき【労役】labor ; toil. ¶彼は3年間の～に服することになった He was sentenced to three years at *hard labor.*

ろうか【老化】senility. ¶読書は精神の～を防ぐ Reading prevents our mind from *growing old.* 働きすぎは～を早める Too much work makes you *age* rapidly.
──現象 a symptom of age (≒ senility). ¶それは～現象のひとつだった It was part of *the aging process.*

ろうか【廊下】a corridor ; ㊖ a hall ; a hallway.

ろうかい【老獪】¶～な男 a *crafty* (≒ *cunning* ; *sly* ; *foxy*) man. 彼は～な手段で人を陥れる男だ He traps others with his *cunning.*

ろうかく【楼閣】a castle.
空中── a castle in the air.

ろうがん【老眼】〘医学〙presbyopia. ¶～になった My eyes have become *dim with age.*
──鏡 glasses for the aged ; farsighted glasses.

ろうきゅう【老朽】superannuation. ¶～教授をふたりやめさせた We *superannuated* two professors. この会社では～者が多い *Superannuated* people are many in the firm.
──官吏 a superannuated official. ──車 a decrepit car.

ろうきゅう【籠球】〘競技〙basketball.

ろうきょう【老境】old age. ¶彼も～に入った He *is* now *advanced in age.*

ろうく【労苦】labor. ¶彼の多年の～が報いられた Many years of his *efforts* are now rewarded.

ろうく【老軀】¶彼は～をひっさげて社会福祉に尽くした In spite of his *old age* he worked for social welfare.

ろうけつぞめ【蠟纈染め・臈纈染め】batik.

ろうこ【牢乎】¶～たる自信 *firm* (≒ *strong*) confidence.

ろうご【老後】*one's* old age. ¶～のために蓄えをすることが必要だ It is necessary to provide for our *old age.* 彼は平和に～を送った He spent his *last days* in peace.

ろうこう【老巧】¶～な政治家 a *veteran* (≒ an *experienced*) politician ; an *elder* statesman.

ろうさいほけん【労災保険】the Workers' Accident Compensation Insurance. ¶彼は～で治療費を支払った His doctor's fee was covered by *the Workers' Accident Compensation Insurance.*

ろうさく【労作】a fruit (≒ product) of *one's* labor. ¶これは彼の10年間の～だ This is the *fruit* (≒ *product*) of his ten years' labor.

ろうし【労使】labor and management.

ろうし【労資】labor and capital.
──協調 cooperation between labor and capital. ──関係 labor-management (≒ employer-employee) relations.

ろうしゅう【陋習】convention. ¶～にとらわれないで考えてほしい I wish you to be free from *conventionalisms* and think about it.

ろうしゅう【老醜】ugliness of old age.
¶～をさらしたくない I don't want to show my *senility* (≒ *senile decay*).

ろうじゅく【老熟】mature experience.
¶～した腕前 *mature* (≒ *experienced*) skill. 彼の演技は～の域に達した His performance has come to *full maturity.*

ろうじょう【籠城】¶敵に囲まれてどのくらい～でき

ろ

るだろうか How long can we *stand a siege?* 1か月ホテルに～してその小説を書き上げた I *shut myself up* in a hotel room for a month to finish the novel.

ろうじん【老人】an old man.
—病 the diseases of the aged; the infirmities of [old] age. —ホーム an old people's home; a home for the aged.

ろうすい【老衰】senile decay; the infirmity of [old] age; decrepitude. ¶ 彼は～している He *is senile* (≒ *is old and infirm; is infirm with age*). 彼は～で死んだ He died of *old age* (≒ *decrepitude*).

ろうすい【漏水】leakage. ¶ ～する Water *leaks out.* ～を防いだ I stopped *a leak of water.* 船が～した The boat *had sprung a leak.*

ろう·する【労する】labor. ¶ ～して功なしだった All my *efforts* were wasted. 心身を～する仕事だ This task *requires a lot of energy* (≒ *labor*).

ろう·する【弄する】¶ 彼はよく詭弁(きべん)を～する He often *uses* sophistry. / He often *tries to reason out the unreasonable.* 彼は私に対して卑劣な手段を～した He *played* a dirty trick on me. 彼はあれこれ策を～した He *used* one trick after another.

ろう·する【聾する】deafen. ¶ 耳を～する歓声が聞こえた *Deafening* shouts were heard.

ろうせい【老成】¶ ～した人物 a *mature* person; a person *of ripe age.* 彼は年齢のわりには～している(大人びている) He *is precocious* for his age.

ろうせき【蠟石】〖鉱物〗agalmatolite.

ろうぜき【狼藉】¶ 彼は家族に対して〔乱暴〕～を働いた He *beat* (≒ *attacked*) his family violently. 部屋の中は～をきわめていた The room *was in a mess* (≒ *was messy*).
—者 a rascal; an outlaw.

ろうそく【蠟燭】a candle. ¶～の心 a *candle* wick. ～をともす(消す) light (put out) *a candle.* ～が消えた The *candle* went out. ～が揺らいでいた *A candle* was flickering.
—立て a candlestick.

ろうたい【老体】old age; an aged person. ¶～にむち打って働いた In spite of his *old age* he worked hard. ご～だから無理はなさらぬように As you *are old*, you must take a good care of yourself.

ろうたいか【老大家】a veteran authority (on); a grand old man.
¶ 英文学の～ *an old authority* on English literature.

ろうちん【労賃】wages. ¶ ～が安い(高い) I *am under-paid* (*am highly paid*).

ろうでん【漏電】a short circuit; short.
¶ 火事の原因は～だった The fire was caused by *a short circuit* (≒ *leakage of electricity*).

ろうどう【労働】labor; work. ¶ ～する work; labor. われわれは～によって生活する We live by *work.*
—運動 labor movement. —管理 labor management. —基準局 the Labor Standards Bureau. —基準法 the Labor Standards Law. —貴族 a labor aristocrat. —組合 a labor union. —組合員 a member of a labor union. —省 the Ministry of Labor. —戦線 labor front. —争議 a strike. ¶ ～争議をする go on *a strike.* この会社は独自の方法で～争議を解決した The concern solved the *labor* problem in its own way. —対策 a labor policy. —大臣 the Minister of Labor. —党 the Labor Party. —党員 a Labor member. 強制— compulsory labor. 肉体(精神)— physical (mental) labor. 1日8時間— an eight-hour working day. ¶ 1日8時間～する We *work* eight hours a day.

ろうどうしゃ【労働者】a laborer; a working man. ¶ ～と資本家 *labor* and capital.
—階級 the working classes. 頭脳(筋肉)— a brain (manual) worker. 日雇い(季節)— a day (seasonal) laborer.

ろうどく【朗読】reading. ¶ 詩の～ *recitation* of a poem. 彼はシェイクスピアの作品を～した He gave *a reading from* Shakespeare. 彼はワーズワースの詩を～した He *recited* a poem by Wordsworth.

ろうにゃく【老若】young and old. ¶ ～男女を問わず黒山のような参拝者があった Crowds of people, without distinction of *age* or sex, visited the shrine. / Crowds of people, *young and old* of both sexes, visited the shrine.

ろうにん【浪人】(さむらい) a *ronin*; a lordless *samurai*; (失業者) an unemployed. ¶ 彼は今～している(失業中) He *is out of employment* (≒ *job*) now. / He *is jobless* now. / (受験準備中) He is a high school graduate waiting for another chance to be admitted to a college.

ろうねん【老年】old age.

ろうば【老婆】an old woman.
—心 〔excessive〕 kindness; considerateness. ¶ ～心から彼にこう言った I told him this *for his good* (≒ *out of kindness*).

ろうばい【狼狽】confusion. ¶ 不意の客に彼女は～した The unexpected visitor *upset* (≒ *embarrassed*) her. 本の盗みの現場を押さえられて彼は～した Being caught in the act of stealing a book he got *panic-stricken* (≒ *panicky*). 彼らは周章～して逃げていった They fled *in confusion* (≒ *in a panic*). 彼女はその質問で周章～した She *was confused* (≒ *was nonplused*) by the question.

ろうはいぶつ【老廃物】waste matter; wastes.

ろうひ【浪費】waste; (ぜいたくの) extravagance. ¶ そんなことをするのは時間(金)の～だ It is *a waste* of time (money) to do such a thing. / You *are wasting* your time (money) to do such a thing. 彼女は～するから借金する羽目になる Her *extravagance* puts her

in debt. われわれは天然資源を～している We *are wasteful with* natural resources.
—家 a waster. —癖 a wasteful habit.

ろうほう【朗報】 happy (≒ good) news; a happy piece (≒ bit; item) of news.

ろうむ【労務】 labor; work.
—管理 personnel management. —者 a 〔day〕 laborer; a worker. 季節—者 a seasonal worker. —担当重役 a personnel manager.

ろうや【牢屋】 a prison.

ろうらく【籠絡】 ¶ 彼を～するのはわけない He can easily *be taken in.* 彼は彼女を～して同意させた He *cajoled* her *into* consent. セールスマンは彼を～して車を買わせた The salesman *inveigled* him *into* buying the car.

ろうりょく【労力】 (労働) labor; (骨折り) efforts. ¶ ～のいる仕事 a *laborious* work. ～を惜しまないで働いてほしい I want you to work *unsparingly.* / Don't *spare yourself in* your work. ～を省く方法を考える try to find out a *labor-saving* device. 人間の～には限度がある Human *energy* is not infinite.

ろうれい【老齢】 old age. ¶ 彼は相当の～だ He *is* well *advanced in age* (≒ *years*). いつの間にか～に達した I *have become a senior citizen* without knowing it. / I *am getting old* now without knowing it.
—年金 retirement (≒ old age) pension.

ろうれつ【陋劣】 meanness. ¶ ～な人格の持ち主 a man of *mean* (≒ *base*) character. 彼は友人に対して～な手段を弄した He played a *dirty* trick on his friend.

ろうれん【老練】 ¶ ～な外科医 a *skilled* surgeon. ～な教師 an *experienced* (≒ *expert*) teacher.

ろうろう【朗朗】 ¶ 彼は音吐～と詩を朗読した He recited a poem in a *clear, resonant* voice.

ろえい【露営】 encampment. ¶ ～する encamp; camp out; pitch a camp.

ローカル local.
—カラー a local color. —線 a local line. —ニュース local news. —版(新聞) a local edition. —放送 a local broadcast.

ローション lotion.
アフターシェーブ— after-shave lotion. ハンド— hand lotion. ヘアー— hair lotion.

ロース (牛肉の) sirloin.

ロースト roast (「(肉を) 火にかけて焼く」という動詞と「焼き肉」という名詞の両方に用いる).
—チキン roast chicken. —ビーフ roast beef.

ローズもの【ローズ物】 (売れ残り商品) a shopworn article.

ロータリー (交差点の) a rotary; a traffic circle; 英 a roundabout.
—エンジン a rotary engine. —クラブ the Rotary Club.

ローティーン (10歳から15歳までの年齢) the ages 10 to 15; the ages between 10 and 15; (13歳から15歳までの年齢) *one's* early teens (英語の teens は 13 から 19 までを意味する).
¶ ～の少年 a boy *in his early teens.*

ロードショー a road show; a roadshow.

ロードレース (自動車競走などの) road racing; (1回の競走) a road race.

ロープ a rope.
—ウエー a ropeway.

ローマ Rome. ¶ ～は1日にして成らず(諺) *Rome was not built in a day.* すべての道は～に通ず(諺) *All roads lead to Rome.*
—カトリック教 Roman Catholicism. —カトリック教会 the Roman Catholic Church. —カトリック教徒 a Roman Catholic. —人 a Roman. —数字 Roman numerals. —法王 the Pope.

ローマじ【ローマ字】 Roman letters. ¶ ～でつづる spell *in Roman letters.*

ローラー a roller.
—カナリア a roller. —コースター a roller coaster. —ベアリング a roller bearing. —スケート(くつ) 〔a pair of〕 roller skates. ¶ ～スケートをする roller skate.

ローリング rolling. ¶ しけのときこの船は～がひどい The ship *rolls* heavily when the sea is rough.

ロール —キャベツ a cabbage roll. —パン a roll 〔of bread〕.

ろか【濾過】 filtration. ¶ 砂で水を～する *filter* water through the sand.
—液 filtrate. —器 a filter. —紙 filter paper. —性 filterability. —性病原体 a filterable virus.

ろかた【路肩】 a shoulder. ¶ ～注意 (道路標識) Soft Shoulders.

ろく【六】 six; (第6) the sixth.
—角形〔の〕 hexagon〔al〕. —・3・3・4 制教育 a 6-3-3-4 system of education. —年生 a sixth grader; (総称) the sixth graders. —面体 a hexahedron. —連発銃 a six-chambered revolver.

ろく【禄】 ¶ 500石の～をはむ hold *a fief* of five hundred *koku.* A社の～をはんでいる I *work for* A company. / I receive *a salary* from A company.

ろく【碌】 ¶ きょうは～なことがない Everything *goes wrong* with me today. ここでは～な暮らしはできない We can't live *decently* here. / We can't make a *decent* living here. 彼は～な者にはなるまい He won't 〔turn out to〕 be *a respectable person.* そんなことをすると～なことはないぞ If you do that, you will *be sorry for it.* 近くには～な病院もなかった There were no *decent* hospitals around there.

ろくおん【録音】 recording. ¶ 詩の朗読を～にとる *record* the recitation of a poem.
—機(者) a recorder. —技師 a recording engineer; (調整装置担当者) a sound mixer; (フィルムに録音を入れる人) a recordist. —室 a recording room. —テープ a magnetic tape. —放送(番組) a transcribed program; (録音による放送) broadcast by 〔electrical〕 transcription.

ろくが【録画】 〘テレビ〙 telerecording. ¶ 試合を～する *record* the match *on video tape.*

ろ

ろくがつ【六月】June (Jun. と略す).
ろくじゅう【六十】sixty; threescore. ¶ 〜代の半ばに in the middle of *one's sixties.* 〜の手習いでゴルフを始めた I have recently begun to learn how to play golf, for it is never too late to learn.
ろくしょう【緑青】verdigris; copper (≒ green) rust. ¶ 銅器は〜が出やすい *Verdigris* is very apt to form on the surface of copperware.
ろくぶんぎ【六分儀】a sextant.
ろくぼく【肋木】wall bars; Swedish bars; gymnastics ladder.
ろくまく【肋膜】〘解剖学〙 the pleura (複 pleurae).
—炎 pleurisy.
ろくろ【轆轤】(旋盤) a lathe; (陶器用の) a potter's wheel; (滑車) a pully; (巻き上げ機) windlass. ¶ (材料を) 〜にかける place (≒ turn) the material on *a* [*potter's*] *wheel.*
ロケーション〘映画〙 location. ¶ この映画はハワイに〜をした They went over to Hawaii to make this film *on location.* その映画は今〜中だ The picture *is now on location.*
ロケット a rocket; (ネックレスの) a locket. ¶ 〜を打ち上げる launch *a rocket.*
—エンジン a rocket engine. —学 rocketry. —機 a rocket plane. 3段式— a three-stage rocket. 多段式— a multistage rocket (各段ごとのロケットは the first (second,...) stage rocket のように呼び, 最終のものを the final stage rocket と呼ぶ).
ろけん【露見】exposure. ¶ 彼の旧悪が〜した His past crime *was found out* (≒ *was detected; was exposed; was laid bare*).
ろこつ【露骨】**1**〘あからさまな〙 ¶ 〜に言えば to be *frank* (≒ *plain*) with you.
彼は〜にものを言う He *is outspoken.* / He speaks *frankly* (≒ *plainly; bluntly; candidly; openly*). (社会慣習にとらわれず真実や意見を率直に述べる態度を表わすのが frankly, 思ったとおり明快に言うのが plainly, 他人の感情などにかまわずずばずばものを言う態度が bluntly, 包み隠しなく正直にものを言うのが candidly, あけっぴろげで率直な態度が openly).
われわれの努力は〜な政治干渉によって水泡と帰した Our efforts were rendered futile on account of *undisguised* interference in politics.
2〘性的な〙 ¶ 〜な話 an *obscene* talk.
この小説は〜な描写があるので非難されている This novel is blamed for its *obscenity* (≒ *indecency; bawdiness*) in expression.
ろじ【路地】an alley; a lane.
ロシア Russia.
—語 Russian. —人 a Russian; (総称) the Russians.
ろしゅつ【露出】exposure; disclosure.
¶ 鉱脈が〜している The mineral vein *crops out.* この写真は〜不足(過度)だ This picture *is underexposed* (*is overexposed*).
—計 a photometer. —時間〘写真〙 time of exposure. —電線 a bare wire.
ろせん【路線】(バスなどの) route; (方針) lines.
ロッカー a locker.
ろっかクローム【六価クローム】hexavalent chromium.
ろっかん【肋間】—神経〘解剖学〙 the intercostal nerve. —神経痛〘医学〙 intercostal neuralgia.
ろっかん【六感】the sixth sense. ¶ 第〜でそれがわかった My *sixth sense* told it to me. / I knew it *by intuition* (≒ *intuitively*).
ロックアウト a lockout. ¶ 〜する lock out.
ロッククライミング rock-climbing.
ろっこつ【肋骨】〘解剖学〙 a rib; 〘医学〙 a costa (複 costae); (総称) the ribs.
ろっぽうぜんしょ【六法全書】a compendium of laws; the statute book.
ろてい【露呈】exposure; disclosure; discovery. ¶ 彼はとうとう弱点を〜した His weak point *revealed itself* (≒ *was exposed; was betrayed*) at last.
ろてん【露天】¶ 〜で夜を明かす spend a night *in the open* (≒ *out of doors*).
—ぶろ an open-air bath. —掘り strip mining.
ろてん【露店】a street stall; a booth.
—商 a stall keeper; a street trader (≒ vendor).
ろとう【路頭】¶ 彼を失って一家は〜に迷った All the family *were left without support* because of his death.
ろば【驢馬】a donkey; an ass.
ろばた【炉端】the fireside.
ロビー a lobby; a lounge.
ろへん【炉辺】a fireside; a hearth.
—談話 a fireside chat.
ろぼう【路傍】the roadside; the wayside.
¶ 〜の人 a stranger.
ロボット a robot.
—雨量計 a robot rain gauge. —学 robotology. —工学 robotics.
ロマン *roman* (フランス語. 英語では a novel).
—主義 romanticism. —派 the romantic school; (人) a romanticist; (特に複) romantics.
ロマンス a romance; a love affair. ¶ こうしてふたりの間に〜が芽生えた Thus *a romantic* (≒ *love*) *relationship* was formed between the two people.
—グレー fine silver-gray hair. —カー 米 a deluxe reserved coach. —語 a Romance language. —シート 米 a love seat.
ロマンチシズム romanticism.
ロマンチスト a romanticist (ロマンチストはフランス語 romantiste にならった言い方).
ロマンチック romantic. ¶ 〜な物語 a *romantic* story.
ろめい【露命】a miserable life. ¶ 内職で〜をつないでいた I had a hard time earning a scanty living by doing odd jobs.
ろめん【路面】a road surface.
—電車 米 a streetcar; 英 a tram; a tramcar.
ろれつ【呂律】¶ 彼は酔って〜が回らなかった He

ろ

was drunk and *could not speak distinctly.*

ろん【論】 an argument. ¶～より証拠(諺) *The proof of the pudding is in the eating.* 円の切り上げが好ましくないことは～をまたない *It goes without saying* (≒*It is beyond dispute*) that the revaluation of yen is undesirable. 同日の～ではない It is beyond all comparison. / It defies all comparison.

ろんがい【論外】 ¶彼の言うことは～だ What he says *is out of the question.* / His opinion *has gone to an extreme.*

ろんかく【論客】 a controversialist; a debater.

ろんぎ【論議】 discussion; argument; debate (discussion はある問題についていろいろの建設的意見を出し合って和気あいあいのうちに話し合うこと, argument は意見の不一致を論理またはデータによって解決しようとする論争, debate は主として正式な討論).

¶きょうの授業は日米文化の相違について～します We will *discuss* the cultural differences between America and Japan. ～の最中だ It's under *discussion.* ～をつくして方針を考えよう Let's *discuss fully* what should be done.

ろんきゅう【論及】 ¶彼は政府の外交政策に～した He *referred to* the diplomatic policy of the Government.

ろんきょ【論拠】 the ground of argument.

¶その意見は～が薄弱だ It is *a* flimsy *argument.* きみの言うことは～がはっきりしない Your argument is lacking in obvious *grounds.* 彼らの主張には～がない Their claims *are groundless.* そういう強い～がある I have *a* strong *case* to say so.

ロングラン〔映画・演劇〕a long run. ¶あの映画は3か月も～を続けている The movie has made *a long run* of three months.

ろんこく【論告】 a prosecution. ¶検事の～が行なわれた The *final speech* of the prosecutor was made.

ろんし【論旨】 the point of an argument; the purport; the drift. ¶彼の演説は～が明快だ The *point* of his speech is quite clear.

ろんじゅつ【論述】 a statement.

ろんしょう【論証】 proof; demonstration.

¶彼はあらゆる資料によって自説を～した He *proved* his argument using every evidence available.

ろんじん【論陣】 an essay; a treatise.

¶堂々の～を張る argue forcibly; make a persuasive argument.

ろん·ずる【論ずる】 argue; discuss; debate (argue は意見の不一致を理論もしくは事実を用いて解決しようと論じること, discuss はいろいろの意見について友好的に論じ合うこと, debate はある問題について相反する意見を正式にたたかわせること); (論争する) dispute; (論評する) comment on; (主題とする) treat (*of*); deal with; (考慮する) consider.

¶彼はその本で今日のさまざまの問題を～じている He *discusses* (≒*comments on*) various problems of the day in the book.

ろんせつ【論説】 (新聞の社説) an editorial; 英 a leading article; a leader. ¶きょうの新聞は交通問題についての～を載せている Today's paper *carries an editorial on* (≒*devotes the leader to*) the traffic problem.

—委員 an editorial writer.

ろんせん【論戦】 a controversy; a debate; an argument; a dispute. ¶総会では激しい論戦がかわされた *A* very heated *argument* arose at the general meeting.

ろんそう【論争】 a controversy; a dispute.

¶このことについてはまだ激しい～が続いている There is still *a* heated *controversy* 〔raging〕 on this subject.

ろんだい【論題】 a subject of discussion; a theme; a topic.

ろんだん【論断】 conclusion. ¶彼はそれは誤りであると～した He *concluded* (≒*came to a conclusion*) that it was wrong.

ろんちょう【論調】 the tone of argument.

¶新聞の～は政府に批判的だ The press *comments* are critical of the Government.

ろんてき【論敵】 an opponent; an adversary.

ろんてん【論点】 the point of (≒at) issue.

¶きみの意見は～をはずれている Your opinion *is beside* (≒*off*) *the point.* ～が明らかでない The *point at issue* (≒*in question*) is out of focus.

ロンドン London.

—子 a Londoner; a cockney. **—塔** the Tower of London. **—なまり** cockney.

ろんなん【論難】 adverse criticism; confutation. ¶彼は他の宗教を激しく～した He bitterly *denounced* (≒severely *criticized*) other denominations.

ろんぱ【論破】 refutation; confutation. ¶彼は彼らを～できる He can *refute* (≒*argue away*) their opinion. / He can *confute* them *to silence.*

ろんばく【論駁】 refutation; confutation.

¶彼は巧みに相手を～した He skillfully *confuted* his opponent. / He *attacked* his opponent by his skillful argument.

ろんぴょう【論評】 a comment; criticism.

¶新聞はその問題について好意的～を下した The newspapers *commented* favorably upon the problem.

ろんぶん【論文】 (文学などの) an essay; (学位の) a thesis; a treatise; a dissertation; (報告的なもの) a paper; (新聞・雑誌の) an article; (社説) a leading article; an editorial.

¶(学会などで)～を発表する read *a paper* (*at*). 卒業— a graduation thesis. 博士— a doctor's (≒doctorial; doctoral) thesis.

ろんぽう【論法】 argument; logic. ¶同じ～がこれにも当てはまる The same *reasoning* applies to this.

三段— a syllogism.

ろんぽう【論鋒】 ¶彼の鋭利な～にはだれもどうしようもなかった Nobody could refute his *pow-*

ろ

erful (⇋*keen*) *argument.*
ろんり【論理】logic. ¶そこには〜の飛躍がある I see a leap of *logic* there. 〜的には間違いない It is correct *logically.* 〜的だが現実感に乏しい It *is logical* but not realistic.
—学 logic. **—**学者 a logician.

わ

わ【和】(平和) peace ; (和合) harmony ; (合計) the sum ; the total. ¶ …と〜を結ぶ (仲直りする) make *peace* with.... 〜を請う seek *peace.* 人の〜 *harmonious* personal relations. 人の〜に欠けていたから彼らは敗れた The lack of *unity* among themselves caused their defeat. 3と5の〜は8 Three and five are (⇋is ; make[s]) eight.
わ【輪】(図形としての円形) a circle ; (金属その他の物で作った環) a ring ; (糸・なわ・針金などで作った輪) a loop ; (車輪) a wheel ; (たが) a hoop. ¶針金を〜にする make (⇋form) *a loop* with a wire. 彼らは手をつないで〜になった They formed *a ring* hand in hand. / They joined hands and formed *a ring.* 彼はコンパスを使わずに〜をかいた He described (⇋drew) *a circle* without using compasses.
-わ【-羽】¶2〜のツバメ two swallows.
-わ【-把】a bundle. ¶ 2〜のまき two *bundles* of firewood.
ワークブック a workbook.
ワールドシリーズ〘野球〙the World Series.
わあわあ ¶〜言うだけでなにもまとまらなかった *The noisy talk* resulted in nothing. 子どもたちが〜泣いていた The children were crying *loudly.* / The children *were blubbering.*
ワイ エム シー エー Y. M. C. A. ; YMCA (Young Men's Christian Associationから).
わいきょく【歪曲】distortion. ¶事実を故意に〜する *distort* the facts on purpose.
わいざつ【猥雑】¶〜な小説 an *indecent* (⇋a *vulgar and obscene*) novel.
ワイシャツ a shirt (日本語のシャツは undershirt).
わいせつ【猥褻】indecency ; obscenity.
¶〜な本 an *obscene* book. 〜な行為 an *indecent* act ; an indecency.
ワイ ダブリュー シー エー Y. W. C. A. ; YWCA (Young Women's Christian Association から).
わいだん【猥談】an indecent (⇋an obscene ; a nasty) talk. ¶〜をする have *an indecent talk* ; tell *dirty* (⇋*nasty*) *stories.*
ワイパー a wiper.
ワイヤ wire.
—ガラス a wire glass. **—**レスマイク a wireless microphone. **—**ロープ a wire rope.
ワイルドピッチ〘野球〙a wild pitch. ¶わがチームは彼の〜で1点を得た Our team scored one point on his *wild pitch.*
わいろ【賄賂】(贈収賄) bribery ; (物) a bribe.
¶彼は役人たちに〜を贈った He offered *a bribe* to the officials. / He *oiled* (⇋*greased*) the officials' *palm.* 彼は〜を受け取った He took *a bribe.* 彼は役人に〜を使って認可してもらった He *bribed* the officials *into* approving it. 彼は〜がきかない He cannot *be bribed.*
わいわい ¶なにを連中は〜言っているのだ What *are* they *shouting* (⇋*clamoring*) for? / What *are* they *making such a fuss* about? 彼らは〜騒ぐだけでなにもできなかった They could do nothing but *making* (⇋*raising*) *a clamor.*
ワイン wine.
—グラス a wineglass.
わえい【和英】¶〜両文で in *Japanese and English.*
—辞典 a Japanese-English dictionary.
わおん【和音】〘音楽〙a chord.
わか【和歌】*tanka* poetry ; a *tanka* (英語で説明すれば a 31-syllable Japanese poem).
わが【我が・吾が】*one's* ; my ; our. ¶〜国 *our* country. 〜子 *one's* own child.
わかい【和解】reconciliation ; compromise (reconciliationは争い・論争などを両者の満足のいくようにうまくおさめること. compromise は対立している両者が, 要求・主張などの一部を放棄することによって和解すること).
¶彼らを〜させる方法はない There is no way of *reconciling* them. 両者間に〜が成立した *A reconciliation* has been effected between the two. 彼らは互いに歩み寄って〜した They made *a compromise* by their mutual concession.
わか・い【若い】**1**〚年齢が〛young ; (年下の) younger. ¶〜いころぼくはジャズが好きだった When I *was young* I loved jazz.
彼は年のわりに〜く見える He looks *young* for his age.
彼女はあのスーツを着ると若く見える She looks *young* in that suit.
彼は私より五つ〜い He *is* five years *younger* than I. / He *is younger* than I by five years.
私は年はとっても気は〜い Though old in years, I *am young* in spirit.

彼はいくつになっても～い He *has kept his youth* very well. / He *is well-preserved*.
年より～い女 a *well-preserved* woman.
2 〘未熟な〙 green. ¶ それを信ずるほどぼくは～くない I *am* not so *green* as to believe that.
3 〘数が〙 low. ¶ 番号の～いほうがよい A *low* number is preferable.

わがい【我が意】¶ 彼の見解は～を得たものだ His views *are quite satisfactory*. / I *heartily* (≒ *quite*) *agree to* his views.

わかいもの【若い者】(青少年) young people; the youth; (若い従業員) a young employe〔e〕; (若い社員・店員) a young clerk; (子分) a young follower; a henchman.
¶ ～たち the young; youngsters.

わかがえり【若返り】restoration of youth (≒ youthful strength); rejuvenation.
¶ これが私の～法だ This is my secret to *look younger*.

わかがえ・る【若返る】¶ ゴルフをすればあなたも～る I recommend you to play golf. It'll make you *look and feel young*. その服を着ると10歳ほど～って見える You *look* ten years *younger than your age* in the dress. / The dress *takes* ten years *off your age*.

わかぎ【若木】a sapling; a young tree.

わかくさ【若草】green grass.

わかげ【若気】youthful spirit. ¶ ～のいたりだ, 許しておやりなさい You should forgive him. He must have been urged to do that by *his youthful passion*. / Forgive him. He must have been carried away by *youthful ardor*. あんなことをして, ～のいたりと思っている I am regretful for what I have done; it was *a youthful folly*.

わがこと【我が事】¶ 彼女は私の悩み事を～のように気づかってくれている She is worried about my trouble *as if it were her own*〔*concern*〕.

わかさ【若さ】youth. ¶ 彼の強みは～だ His strength lies in his *youth* (≒ *youthfulness*).

わかさぎ【若鷺】〘魚類〙 a pond smelt.

わかじに【若死に】early death. ¶ 残念なことに彼は～した To my great regret he *died young*.

わかしらが【若白髪】premature gray〔hair〕.
¶ 彼は～だ He has gray hair though he is still young.

わか・す【沸かす】¶ 湯を～す *make* hot water; (沸騰させる) *boil* water. 茶を～す *make* tea. ふろを～す *heat* (≒ *prepare*) the bath. 彼のファインプレーが観衆を～せた His fine play *excited* all the fans in the ball park.

わかぞう【若造】a〔young〕lad; a youngster; a stripling; a junior.

わかだんな【若旦那】a young master.

わかちがき【わかち書き・分かち書き】writing in parts.

わか・つ【分かつ】(分割する) divide; (分配する) share. ¶ 生涯彼らは彼と苦しみを～ち合った They *shared* their sufferings with him all their life. 彼は昼夜を～たず仕事に励んだ He devoted himself to the work *night and day*.

わかづくり【若作り】¶ (化粧) 彼女は～だ She *is youthfully made up*. / (衣服) She *dresses herself up younger*.

わかて【若手】a young man. ¶ ～を起用する employ *young people*.

わかな【若菜】young greens.

わかば【若葉】young leaves; (新緑) fresh green. ¶ ～のころに in the season of *fresh green*.

わかはげ【若禿げ】a premature baldhead.
¶ ～の人 a *prematurely bald* man.

わかふうふ【若夫婦】a young couple.

わがまま【我が儘】(我欲) selfishness; egoism; (気まま) wilfullness; (気まぐれ) caprice.
¶ ～な (利己的な) 要求 a *selfish* demand. それじゃあんまり～がすぎる That's too *selfish*. ～な子 (わがままに育てられた子) a *spoilt* child; (我の強い子) a *willful* (≒ *wayward*) child. 子どもを～に育ててはならない We must not *pamper* our children. ～を通させてください Let me *have my own way*, please. / Please let me *do what I like*. / Please let me *do it as I like*.

わがみ【我が身】*one*self. ¶ ～をつねって人の痛さを知れ Judge〔of〕others' feelings by *your own*. その話を聞くと～につまされる When I hear the story I *deeply* (≒ *heartily*) *sympathize with* the man. ～を省みて物を言え Reflect on *yourself* before you speak ill of others.

わかめ【若芽】sprouts;〔young〕buds; fresh shoots.

わかめ【若布・和布】*wakame* seaweed.

わかもの【若者】a young man; a lad; a youth; a youngster. ¶ ～たち the young.

わがもの【我が物】*one's* own. ¶ 彼は公有地を～にした He *appropriated* the public land *for his own use*. / He *took* the public land *to himself*. 読んだものを～にするよう心掛けよ Try to *make use of* the knowledge you have gotten from the book.

わがものがお【我が物顔】¶ 彼は～にふるまっている He is doing just *as he pleases* (≒ *as he likes*). / He *has everything his own way*.

わかや・ぐ【若やぐ】¶ 彼女はいつになく～いだ気分になった She *felt herself younger than ever*.

わがよ【我が世】¶ 彼らは～の春を謳歌(おうか)している (最盛期だ) They are more prosperous than ever. / (繁栄に思いあがっている) They are puffed up with their prosperity.

わからずや【分からず屋】(がんこ者) an obstinate person; (ばか) a blockhead.

わかり【分かり】comprehension. ¶ 彼は～が早い He is quick of *understanding*. / He is a *quick-witted* man. / (よく気がつく) He is a *sensible* person. あんな～の遅い人は見たことがない I've never seen such a *slow-witted* fellow.

わかりきった【分かり切った】plain; (明白な) obvious; evident. ¶ それは初めから～ことだ It is a *foregone* conclusion. ～こと a *plain*

わ

(≒ an *evident*) fact. きみは〜ことばかり言う You talk only *a matter of course*.

わかりにく·い【分かり難い】incomprehensible; vague. ¶ 彼の文体は〜い His style of writing *is hard to understand*. あの人の講義は〜い His lecture *is unintelligible*.

わかりやす·い【分かり易い】¶ 彼の書くものは〜い His writings *are easy to understand* (≒ *are easy to comprehend*). なるべく〜く言ってください Please use as *plain* language as possible. 〜く言えばそうです It is so, to speak in *plain* language.

わか·る【分かる·判る·解る】**1**〖理解する·了解する〗understand. ¶ 私の言っていることが〜りますか Do you *understand* me?

おっしゃることはよく〜りました I've got your point. / I *follow* you.

彼の理屈はちっとも〜らない I can't *follow* his reasoning.

(会話で) おっしゃることがよく〜りませんが I beg your pardon? (文尾を上げる).

話し合えば彼も事情を〜ってくれるだろう I think he will *understand* the circumstances after we talk.

彼は絵が〜らない He is not *a connoisseur of* paintings.

彼女は音楽が〜る She *has an ear for music*.

あの男には文学は〜らない He cannot *appreciate* literature.

私には骨董(こっとう)品は〜らない I *am* no *judge of* antiques.

政治というものがどうやら〜った I *have a* vague *idea of* politics.

彼には冗談が〜らない He *has* no *sense of* humor.

2〖判断する·知る〗¶ きみにはしてよいことと悪いことの区別が〜らない You don't *know* the right thing to do *from* wrong.

あの姉妹はよく似ていて, どちらが姉でどちらが妹か私には〜らない Those two sisters resemble each other, and I cannot *tell* one *from* the other.

これからどうしたらいいか〜らない I don't *know* what to do from now on.

後ろ姿ですぐきみだと〜った I *recognized* you at once when I saw your back.

声を聞いただけですぐ彼だと〜った I *knew* him at once by his voice.

地震はいつなんどき起こるか〜らない There might be an earthquake at any moment.

たばこ屋で聞けば彼の家はすぐ〜ります Ask at the tobacconist's, and you will *find* his house easily.

3〖判明する〗¶ 選挙の結果はあすの午前中に〜る The result of the election will *be declared* by tomorrow noon.

試験の成績はいつ〜りますか When are the results of the examination to *be published*?

これで彼がうそをついていたことが〜った This *shows* that he told a lie.

それで〜った (なるほど) That accounts for it.

いまに〜る (時がたてば) Time will *show*.

自殺した人の身もとはまだ〜らない The suicide *has* not *been identified* yet.

彼が誠実な人間であることがだんだん〜ってきた I've begun to *understand* that he is a man of sincerity.

4〖道理などが〗¶ 彼はものの〜った人だ He certainly is an *understanding* person.

ものの〜らない人 a *senseless* person.

彼はもっと話の〜る人かと思った I gave him credit for more sense.

(子どもに)そんな〜らないことを言うと, 置いていきますよ If you *are difficult*, I'll abandon you here.

わかれ【別れ】(離別) parting; separation; a farewell. ¶ 〜のことば a farewell; a *farewell* speech. 〜の杯 a *parting* cup. 〜のつらさ the sorrow of *parting*. 私は彼と〜の握手をした I shook hands with him and *said good-bye*. 彼は彼らに〜を告げた He *said good-bye to* them. 彼は彼女の家族たちと〜を惜しんだ He was loath to *part from* her family. それが彼女とのこの世の〜となった It was *the last I saw of* her. / I *parted from* her never to meet again.

わかればなし【別れ話】(離婚) divorce (一つ一つの離婚事件は a divorce). ¶ ふたりの間に〜がもちあがったことがある Once they thought of *getting divorced* (≒ *dissolving their marriage*).

わかれみち【分かれ道】a forked road; (道の分岐点) a fork [of a road]; (枝道) a branch road; (十字路) a crossroads (crossroads は複数形でも不定冠詞をつける. なお, 十字に交わるいずれか一方の道は単数形にして a crossroad と言う).

わかれめ【分かれ目】(転機) a turning point; (道の) a fork of a road. ¶ それは彼の人生の〜であった It was *a turning point* of his life.

わか·れる【別れる·分かれる】**1**〖人と〗¶ われわれは駅前で〜れた We *parted* (≒ *separated*) in front of the station.

京都で彼と〜れた I *parted from* him in Kyoto.

彼は両親と〜れて暮らしている He lives *separated from* his parents.

彼女は夫と〜れた (離婚した) She *divorced* her husband.

2〖意見·川などが〗¶ 委員会は意見が〜れている The committee *are divided in* opinion.

川はそこで二つに〜れる The river *divides into* two branches there.

この本は項目別に〜れている These books *are classified* by subjects.

わかれわかれ【別れ別れ】¶ 彼らは各自〜に帰宅した They went home *one by one* (≒ *separately*). そこで彼らは〜になった They *parted* (≒ *separated*) then and there.

わかわかし·い【若若しい】youthful. ¶ この写真では彼はいかにも〜い He certainly *looks young* (≒ *looks youthful*) in this photograph. 彼女はいまでも〜さを失わない She keeps her *youth* (≒ *youthfulness*) even now.

わかん【和漢】¶ 彼は〜の学に通じている He has

a thorough knowledge of *Japanese and Chinese classics.*

わき【脇・腋】1〖かたわら〗the side. ¶ 彼らはテーブルを〜に動かした They moved the table *aside.*

彼は私を〜に押しのけた He pushed me *away.*

彼らを通すために〜に寄った I stepped *aside* to let them go by.

彼はわれわれの話に突然〜から口を出した He suddenly *interrupted* our conversation.

2〖よそ〗¶ どこか〜に行ってゆっくり話しましょう Let's go away from here to talk leisurely.

話を〜にそらすな Don't turn the subject *in another direction.*

彼の話は〜にそれがちだ His speech is apt to *stray from* the subject.

3〖わきの下〗the armpit. ¶ 〜に1冊の本をかかえる carry a book *under one's arm.*

4〖能の〗a *waki*; a support.

わき【和気】harmony. ¶ 〜あいあいのうちに会談が行なわれた The conference proceeded *in a most friendly atmosphere.*

わぎ【和議】(講和) negotiation for peace; a peace conference (≒talk); (債権者との) a composition. ¶ 債権者と〜が成立した We made *a composition* with the creditors.

わきおこ·る【沸き起こる】¶ 広間で割れるような拍手が〜った A storm of hand clapping *arose* in the hall.

わきが【腋臭・狐臭】the smell of the armpit. ¶ あの人は〜がひどい He has *a* strong *body* (≒*armpit*) *odor.*

わきかえ·る【沸き返る】¶ やかんの湯が〜っている The water of kettle *is boiling up* (≒*is boiling over*). (boil over は「煮えこぼれる」). / (音をたてて沸いている) The kettle *is singing.* 町じゅうが〜るような騒ぎだった The whole town *was in an uproar* (≒*was in a ferment*).

わきげ【腋毛】hair of the armpit.

わきた·つ【沸き立つ】¶ 彼が優勝して町じゅうが〜った The whole town *was in an uproar* at his victory.

わきで·る【涌き出る・湧き出る】¶ 泉から冷たい水がこんこんと〜る Cold water *gushes out* from the spring.

わきのした【腋の下】the armpit. ¶ 〜から冷や汗が出た I broke out in a cold sweat. (armpit という語は避けるほうがよい). 人の〜をくすぐる tickle *a person under his arm.*

わきばら【脇腹】¶ 〜が痛い I feel pain *in the side.*

わきぼね【わき骨】a rib.

わきまえ【弁え】discretion. ¶ 〜のある男 a *discreet* man; (行儀のよい) a *well-mannered* man. 〜のない人 an *indiscreet* (≒a *thoughtless*) man; (行儀の悪い) an *ill-mannered* man. 彼は前後の〜もなくわめいた He shouted *thoughtlessly* (≒*without knowing what he was doing*). 彼女はお茶の〜がある She *has a knowledge of* tea ceremoney.

わきま·える【弁える】¶ 彼は善悪を〜えている He *knows* right from wrong. / He *can discern* between good and evil. 彼は物事(礼儀・進退)を〜えていない He doesn't *know* a hawk from a handsaw (how to behave; how to retire).

わきみ【脇見】¶ 勉強中〜をしてはいけません Keep your eyes on your book. ちょっと〜をしただけなのにかばんがなくなっていた I *looked away* for just a moment, but the briefcase had disappeared.

—運転 ¶ 〜運転は危険だ It is dangerous to *take your eyes off the road* while you are driving a car.

わきみず【湧き水】spring water.

わきみち【脇道】a side road; a by-road. ¶ 車は〜にそれた The car turned off [from the main street]. 話が〜にそれたようだ We seem to *have wandered* (≒*have digressed*) *from the subject.*

わきめ【脇目】¶ 彼は〜もふらずに仕事をした He *devoted himself* (≒*gave himself up*) *solely to* his work. 〜もふらずにせっせと歩いた We walked and walked without *looking aside.*

わきやく【脇役】a supporting role; a secondary part; (人) a supporting player.

わぎり【輪切り】round slices. ¶ ダイコンの〜 *a slice* of radish. トマトを〜にする *cut* tomatoes *in round slices.*

わく【枠】1〖ふち〗a frame. ¶ 窓の〜 *a* window *frame.*

木の〜(荷造り用) a crate.

2〖範囲〗a limit. ¶ 予算の〜 the *framework* of the budget.

収入の〜内で暮らす live *within* [*the limit* of] *one's* income.

彼の行動はしばしば常識の〜を越える His conduct often goes beyond *the bounds* of common sense.

わ·く【沸く】boil. ¶ 湯が〜いている The water *is boiling.* 〜いた湯 *boiled* water (boiling water はまだ熱い状態のときに限る). ふろが〜いた The bath *is ready.* 新チャンピオン誕生に観衆はどっと〜いた The spectators *broke into an uproar* at the creation of a new champion.

わ·く【涌く・湧く】¶ 岩陰から清水が〜いている Clear water *is springing* (≒*is gushing*) *out* (≒*forth*) from between the rocks. あなたのお話を聞いて希望が〜いてきた Your words have filled me with hope. 夏にはすぐウジが〜く Maggots *breed* (≒*grow*) rapidly in summer. チーズに虫が〜いた The cheese *is full of* worms.

わくせい【惑星】〖天文学〗a planet. ¶ 政界の〜 *a dark horse* in the political world.

ワクチン〖医学〗vaccine (発音は [vǽksin]). ¶ 流感の予防に〜を注射した I *was vaccinated against* influenza.

—注射 vaccine injection; vaccination. ソーク— Salk vaccine. 生— live-virus vaccine.

わくでき【惑溺】¶ 彼は酒色に〜している He *has*

わ

given himself up to woman and alcohol.

わくらん【惑乱】¶彼の演説は人心を～した His speech *troubled* (≒ *disturbed*) the public feeling.

わくわく ¶期待で胸が～した I *got nervous* with expectation. / My heart *throbbed* (≒ *fluttered*) with expectation. ～しながら手紙を開いた I opened the letter *in a flutter*.

わけ【訳】**1**〖理由・原因〗a reason. ¶どういう～できのう欠席したか *Why* (≒ *For what reason*) were you absent yesterday?
～があって彼と別れた I parted from him with good *reason*.
どういう～か彼女はパーティーに来なかった She did not come to the party *for some reason or other* (≒ *somehow or other*).
そういう～で私はそこへ行かなかった *Such being the case* (≒ *Under these circumstances*), I did not go there.
2〖意味〗meaning. ¶それで～がわかるでしょう That will *account for* it.
彼の言うことはさっぱり～がわからぬ I can *make nothing of* what he says.
3〖道理〗reason. ¶彼は～のわかった人だ (わからぬ人だ) He is *a man of sense* (≒ *is devoid of reason*).
なるほどきみがそう考える～だ It *is* quite *natural* that you *should* think so. / You *have good reason* to think so.
4〖事情・次第〗circumstances. ¶私はきみを待つ～にはいかぬ I cannot wait for you.
私は笑わないでいる～にはいかなかった I *could not help* laughing.
それはどういう～ですか What do you *mean by* ⌈*that*?
それとこれとは～が違う That is *one thing*; this is *another*.

わけあ・う【分け合う】¶彼は家族と苦楽を～った He *shared* his joys and sorrows *with* his family.

わけい・る【分け入る】¶人ごみの中へ～った I *pushed my way through* the crowd. 深山へ～った We *went deep into* the mountains.

わけて【別けて】particularly. ¶私は果物が好きだが～もメロンが好きだ I like fruits, *especially* melons (≒ melons *in particular*).

わけな・い【訳ない】easy. ¶～い仕事 a *simple* task. それは～い It *is* quite *easy*. そうするのは～い It *is easy* to do that. こんな英文は～く訳せる I can *easily* translate such an English passage.

わけへだて【分け隔て】discrimination.
¶彼はだれにも～なく接する He treats everyone *impartially* (≒ *without discrimination*).
上役から～された My boss *was unjust* (≒ *unfair*) *to* me.

わけまえ【分け前】a share. ¶当然の～ *a* fair *share*. これがきみの～だ This is your *share* 〔of it〕. 彼は財産の～を要求した He claimed his *portion* of the property.

わけめ【分け目】the parting; a dividing line.
¶髪の～ *the part* in the hair; *the parting* of the hair. 天下～の合戦 a *decisive* battle.

わ・ける【分ける】**1**〖分割する〗divide. ¶先生はクラスを三つに～けた The teacher *divided* the class into three groups.
彼は髪をまん中で～けている He wears his hair *parted* in the middle.
2〖分配する〗share. ¶皆で利益を～けた We *shared* the profits among ourselves.
このケーキをふたり (3人) で～けなさい *Divide* this cake *between* the two of you (*among* the three of you). (ふつう「ふたりで」は between, 「3人以上の間で」は among を用いる).
弁当を友だちに～けてやった I *shared* my lunch *with* my friend.
たばこを1本～けてくださいませんか Can you *spare* me a cigarette?
3〖分離〗separate. ¶彼女はけんかしている子どもたちを～けた She *separated* (≒ *parted*) the fighting children.
4〖分類〗classify. ¶これらの本を作家別に～けた I *classified* (≒ *sorted*) these books according to their authors.

わごう【和合】concord. ¶一家は～して暮らしている The family live *in harmony*.

わこうど【若人】a young man; a youth; (総称) the young.

わゴム【輪ゴム】a rubber band.

わざ【業・技・術】(行為) work; (技術) an art.
¶それは容易な～ではない It is no simple *task*.
それは人間～ではない It is beyond human *power*. 彼はA氏の指導で～をみがいた He improved his *art* under the guidance of Mr. A.

わさい【和裁】Japanese dressmaking.

わざと【態と】on purpose. ¶～やったな You did it *on purpose*, didn't you! 彼は～本を読み違えた He *intentionally* (≒ *deliberately*) misread the book. 彼女は～らしい微笑を浮かべた She wore a *forced* (≒ an *artificial*) smile. / She *forced* a smile. 彼の態度は～らしい He has an *unnatural* (≒ *affected*) manner. ～したこととしか思えない It must have been an *intentional* (≒ *intended*) act.

わさび【山葵】〖植物〗Japanese horse-radish; *wasabi*. ¶これは～がきいている This is seasoned with enough *wasabi*.
—づけ *wasabi* preserved in *sake* lees.

わざもの【業物】(刀物) a fine sword.

わざわい【災い】(災難) a disaster; (不幸) a misfortune. ¶なにか～がふりかかりそうだ I feel *something bad* is going to happen to me. / I fear some *evil* will befall me. (この文は形式ばった言い方). 彼は～を転じて福となした He turned *a misfortune* into a blessing. 口は～のもと (諺) *Out of mouth comes evil.*

わざわざ【態態】(とくに) especially; (故意に) on purpose. ¶彼は～私に会いにきてくれた He *especially* came by to see me. / He came all the way to see me *purposely* (≒ *expressly*). ～おいでいただき, ありがとうございます Thank you for *taking the trouble to* come by.

わ

わし【鷲】an eagle. ¶ ～の子 an eaglet. ～の巣 an aerie.
—鼻 a hooked (≒ an aquiline) nose.
わし【和紙】Japanese paper.
わしつ【和室】a Japanese-style room.
わしづかみ【鷲掴み】¶ 男は札を～にして逃げた The man *clutched* (≒ *snatched* ; *grabbed*) banknotes and ran away.
わじゅつ【話術】the art of conversation (≒ talking). ¶ 彼の～はすばらしい He is *a* remarkable *conversationalist.* セールスマンは～がたいせつだ A salesman should be tactful in his *speech.*
わしょ【和書】a Japanese book.
わしん【和親】amity.
—条約 a treaty of peace and amity.
わずか【僅か・纔か】(数が) a few ; (量が) a little. ¶ ～の金 *a little* money ; *a small sum of* money. ～の家具 *a few* pieces of furniture. ～の収入 a *small* income. ～100円 *only* one hundred yen. ～の時間 *a little* (≒ *a short*) time. ～な違い a *slight* difference. ～ばかりの人が会に出席した Only *a few* (≒ *a handful of*) people attended the meeting. フランス語を～ばかり話します I speak *a little* French. ～なことで言い争った We quarreled over *some trifle* (≒ *nothing at all*). 駅まではほんの～だ It is *only a step* (≒ *a little way* ; *a minute*) to the station. / The station is just around the corner. 彼だけが～に難を免れた Only he was able to make a *narrow* escape. / Only he *narrowly* escaped.
わずらい【煩い】illness ; disease.
長— a long illness. ¶ 彼は長～で寝ている He *has been ill in bed* 〔*for*〕 *a long time.*
わずら・う【患う・煩う】**1**〖病気である〗be ill.
¶ 彼は肺を～っている He *is suffering from* lung disease. / He *has* lung *trouble.*
彼は大病を～っている He *is* seriously *ill.*
彼女は子どものころ大病を～った She *had a* serious *illness* in her childhood.
2〖心配する〗be worried. ¶ 小さなことを思い～うな Don't *be worried* (≒ Don't *worry yourself*) over such a little thing.
わずらわし・い【煩わしい】(めんどうな) troublesome ; (複雑な) complicated. ¶ ～い問題 a *troublesome* problem. ～い手続き *complicated* formalities. 客を呼ぶのは～い It *is troublesome* to have visitors. なにをやるのも～い I *don't feel like* doing anything.
わずらわ・す【煩わす】(めんどうをかける) trouble ; (悩ます) worry. ¶ お手を～せてすみません I am sorry to *trouble* you. / Thank you very much for *giving* me *a hand.* このことでは彼を～した I *troubled* him *about* (≒ *with*) this matter. そんなつまらぬことで心を～したくない I don't want to *be bothered with* such trivial matters. 彼女は息子のことで心を～している She *is anxious about* her son. つまらぬ質問で～さないでくれ Don't *bother* me with foolish questions.
わ・する【和する】harmonize. ¶ 夫婦相～して暮らしている The couple live *in* 〔*perfect*〕 *harmony.* 君子は～して同ぜず A gentleman *makes friends with* others but does not blindly follow them.
わすれがたみ【忘れ形見】(記念の品) a keepsake ; a memento (複 -s, -es) ; (遺児) a posthumous child. ¶ この子は彼の～だ This is *the child* he *left behind.*
わすれがち【忘れ勝ち】¶ 病気がすこし良くなるとつい薬を飲むのを～だ People *are apt to forget* to take medicine when they get a little better. 急いでいるとつい戸締まりを～だ People *easily forget* to lock the door when they are in a hurry.
わすれっぽ・い【忘れっぽい】forgetful. ¶ ～い人 a *forgetful* person. 近ごろ～くなった I *have become forgetful* these days.
わすれなぐさ【勿忘草】〖植物〗a forget-me-not.
わすれもの【忘れ物】a thing left behind.
¶ ～はないか *Have* you *left* anything *behind?* 電車内に～をした I *left* something in the train. (場所が示されれば forget は用いない).
—取扱所 the Lost and Found.
わすれら・れる【忘れられる】be forgotten.
¶ 彼の名は世間から～れてしまった His name *was* quite *forgotten* by the world. / His name *was buried in* (≒ *sank into*) *oblivion.* 彼のことが～れない I cannot *get* him *out of my mind.* / He is never to *be forgotten.*
わす・れる【忘れる】**1**〖失念する〗forget.
¶ 彼の名前を～れてしまった I *have forgotten* his name. / His name *has escaped my memory.* / I *don't remember* his name.
彼のあの恐ろしい顔がつきまとって～れられぬ That frightful face of his *haunts my memory* (≒ *haunts me*).
～れないで6時に起こしてください Don't *forget* to wake me at six. / Wake me at six *without fail.*
私は翌日の学課の予習を～れた I *neglected* the preparation for the next day's lessons.
彼は寝食を～れて読書した He was so absorbed in reading that he *forgot* to eat and sleep.
彼は酒で憂苦を～れようとした He tried to *drown* his cares and troubles *in wine.*
彼は彼女のことをかたときも～れなかった He *kept* her *in his mind* all the time. (keep...in *one's* mind は比較的長期間の場合).
そんなことは～れてしまいなさい *Forget* it. / *Think no more of* the matter.
彼は書物のことを～れることがなかった He never *took his mind off* his books.
彼はその損失をほどなく～れた He *got over* the loss in no time.
～れえぬ思い出 a *lasting* memory.
～れることのできない日 a *never-to-be-forgotten* day ; a day *to remember.*
～れられない出来事 a *memorable* happening.
2〖置き忘れる〗¶ 急いだので本を～れてきた In my haste I *forgot* the book.
私は財布を机の上に～れてきた I *left* my purse

わ

on my desk.(「置き忘れる」は場所を示す副詞がつくと leave を用い, forget は用いない).

わせ【早生・早稲】 an early rice crop; early rice. ¶ ～のミカン *early* oranges.

わせい【和声】〘音楽〙harmony.

わせい【和製】 Japanese make. ¶ この玩具は～だ This toy *is made in Japan.* / This toy *is of Japanese make.*

—品 homemade products.

ワセリン〘化学〙vaseline (発音は [væsili:n]).

わせん【和船】 a boat of Japanese style.

わせん【和戦】 war and peace. ¶ ～を決する会議 a conference on which hangs the prospect of *war or peace.* 政府は～両様の備えをしている The government is prepared for *both war and peace.*

わそう【和装】 Japanese clothes. ¶ ～の婦人 a woman in *kimono.* ～の本 a book of *Japanese binding.*

わた【綿】 cotton. ¶ ～の木 a *cotton* plant. ～のような雲 *fleecy* clouds. 座布団に～を入れた I stuffed the cushion with *cotton.* ～のように疲れた I *am tired out* (≒ *am worn out; am exhausted*).

—入れ wadded clothes. **—打ち** cotton beating. **—繰り機** a cotton gin. **—菓子** cotton candy; a candy floss. **—摘み** cotton picking. **生—** raw cotton.

わだい【話題】 a topic 〔of conversation〕. ¶ 時の～ current *topics.* 彼は～の豊富な人だ He always has an ample store of *topics.* 政治問題が～に上った The problem of politics was (≒ became) *the topic* (≒ *the subject*) of our conversation. / We *talked about* the problem of politics. ～を変えよう Let's change *the subject.*

わだかまり【蟠り】(悪感情) grudge; ill feeling; animosity; (屈託) troubles; (気兼ね) reserve.

¶ 彼女は私に対して～をいだいている She has *a feeling of animosity toward* me. 彼らの間にはなにか～がある There is some *reserve* (≒ *restraint*) between them. 彼らは～を捨てて協力し合った Putting all *ill feeling* aside, they co-operated with each other. 彼女はなにか心に～がある *Something is troubling* her.

わだかま・る【蟠る】 ¶ 両家の間にはなにか～る悪感情がある There is a *deep-rooted* antagonism between the two families.

わたくし【私】1〘自分・一人称単数〙I.

¶ ～は日本人です *I* am a Japanese.

これは～の弟です This is *my* brother.

彼のかばんは～のより重い His bag is heavier than *mine.*

～にこの本を貸してくださいませんか Would you lend *me* this book?

～を信じてください Please believe *me.*

～自身でやった I did it *myself.*

～です It's *me.*

～としてはその計画に反対です *As for me* (≒ *For my part*) I am against the plan.

2〘個人〙¶ 公のことと～のこととは区別しなければならない A strict line must be drawn between official life and *private* life.

公の施設を～してはいけない Public office must not be put to *personal* use.

彼は他人の物を～した He *appropriated* the belongings of another.

—事 a private affair; a personal matter.

—立の学校 a private school.

わたげ【綿毛】 fluff; down. ¶ タンポポの～ a piece of dandelion *fuzz.* ～におおわれた桃 *fluffy* (≒ *downy*) peaches.

わたし【渡し】1〘受け渡し〙delivery.

着荷— delivery on arrival. 本船— free on board (F. O. B.). 鉄道— free on rail (F. O. R.).

2〘渡し船〙a ferry 〔boat〕. ¶ 向こう岸まで～に乗った I crossed the river by *ferry.*

—賃 ferriage. **—場** a ferry. **—守り** a ferryman.

わたし【私】 ⇒ わたくし

わた・す【渡す】1〘かける〙¶ 川に橋を～す *build* (≒ *span*) a bridge *over* a river.

家の前のみぞに板を～した I *laid* a plank *across* the ditch in front of my house.

2〘手渡す・引き渡す〙¶ 給料は毎月5日に～される Our wages *are paid* on the fifth of every month.

彼は自分の全財産を息子に～した He *transferred* all his property to his son.

彼はお金を少し私に～してくれた He *gave* (≒ *handed over*) some money to me.

現金引き換えにこの小包をお～しします We will *deliver* this parcel in exchange for cash.

彼は私に1通の手紙を～してくれた He *handed* me a letter.

3〘船で〙¶ 彼らはわれわれを渡し船で川を～してくれた They *ferried* us *across* the river. / They *carried* us in a ferry-boat *across* the river.

わだち【轍】 a rut; a wheel track. ¶ 道には深い～がついている The road *is rutted* deeply.

わたり【渡り】 ¶ 彼はその提案を～に船と引き受けた He *readily* accepted the proposal. / He *jumped at* the proposition. どうやって彼に～をつけたのか How did you establish *contact* (≒ *connections*) with him?

わたりあ・う【渡り合う】 ¶ ふたりの好敵手は堂々と～った (戦った) With great dignity the two rivals *crossed swords*(≒ *faced each other in a duel*). 仕事のことで上役と～った I *argued* (≒ *had words; quarreled*) *with* my chief about the work.

わたりある・く【渡り歩く】 ¶ 彼は方々～いた He *wandered* from place to place.

わたりぞめ【渡り初め】 the opening of a new bridge.

わたりどり【渡り鳥】 a migrant; a migratory bird; a bird of passage.

わたりもの【渡り者】(放浪者) a vagabond; a tramp; (移動労働者) a traveling laborer; (よそ者) a stranger.

わたりろうか【渡り廊下】 a roofed passage

〔connecting two buildings〕; a connecting corridor.

わた·る【渡る】**1**〚越える〛cross. ¶川(橋)を～れば川崎だ *Cross* the river (bridge), and you will come to Kawasaki.

冬になるとほとんどの小鳥は暖かい国に～ってゆく Most birds *migrate* to warmer countries in winter.

2〚渡来する〛¶ガラスは海外から～ってきた Glass *was imported* from abroad.

仏教は中国から日本に～ってきた Buddhism *was introduced* to Japan from China.

3〚人手に〛¶彼の財産は人手に～ってしまった His property *has passed into* strange hands.

4〚慣用的表現〛¶～る世間に鬼はない There is kindness to be found everywhere.

彼は危ない橋を～った(投機など) He *ran a risk.* 彼は石橋をたたいて～るHe *is far too prudent.* / He *is very cautious.* / He never *takes* (≒ *runs*) *a risk.*

わた·る【亙る·亘る】¶彼の土地は数マイルに～る His estate *extends* (≒ *spreads*) *over* several miles. イギリスは数世紀に～ってこの国を支配した Britain ruled the country *for* centuries. / British rule of the country *extended over* centuries. 彼の研究は広範囲に～っている His studies *cover* a wide field. 私事に～ってすみません Excuse me for *mentioning* a personal matter.

ワックス wax. ¶床に～を塗る *wax* a floor.

ワッセルマンはんのう【ワッセルマン反応】Wassermann reaction.

ワット a watt. ¶100～の電球 a 100-*watt* bulb.

—時 watt-hour.

ワッフル〔菓子〕a waffle.

わとじ【和綴じ】binding in Japanese style.

¶～の本 a book *bound in Japanese style.*

わどめ【輪留め】a linchpin.

わな【罠】a trap. ¶ウサギをとろうと～をしかけた I set (≒ laid) *a trap* (≒ *a snare*) for the rabbit. キツネを～にかけた I *trapped* (≒ *entrapped; ensnared*) a fox. キツネは～にかかった The fox was caught in (≒ fell into) *a trap.* / The fox *was trapped.* 彼はやすやすと敵の～に落ちた He walked straight into the enemy's *trap.* 彼女の甘いことばにまんまと～にかけられた I *was* fairly *taken in* by her sweet words.

わなげ【輪投げ】quoits. ¶～をする play *quoits.*

わなな·く【戦く】tremble. ¶彼女は恐怖に～いた She *trembled for* (≒ *with*) fear.

わなわな ¶彼女は～震えていた She *was trembling all over.* / She *was all of a tremble.*

わに【鰐】(アフリカ·アジア産の) a crocodile; (アメリカ産の) an alligator. ¶～皮のハンドバッグ a *crocodile* (≒ an *alligator*) handbag.

わにぐち【鰐口】a splay-mouth.

ワニス varnish (発音は [vá:niʃ]). ¶仕上げに～を塗った I gave it a finish of *varnish.* / I *varnished* it.

わび【侘び】quiet refinement; sobriety.

¶この寺の建築には～が感じられる There is an air of *quiet elegance* (≒ *quiet refinement*) in the construction of this temple.

わび【詫び】an apology. ¶この件ではお～の申し上げようもございません I cannot *apologize* enough for this matter. あなたにお～をしなければなりません I owe you *an apology.* あの方に無礼のお～を言いなさい *Apologize* to the gentleman for your rudeness. 彼は私たちの～を聞き入れてくれた He accepted our *words of apology.* これはほんのお～のしるしです This is just a token of *apology.*

—言 words of apology. **—**状 a written apology; a letter of apology.

わびし·い【侘しい】(寂しい) lonely; (みじめな) miserable. ¶～い山村の景色 the *dreary* scene of a mountain village. ～い暮らし a *miserable* life; a *lonely* life.

わびずまい【侘び住まい】(住居) a shanty; (生活) a lonely life. ¶彼は田舎に～している He *leads a simple* country *life.* / He *lives very simply* in the country. ぼくは下宿の～だ I *lead a lonely life* in a boarding house. / I am a *lonely* boarder.

わ·びる【詫びる】apologize. ¶彼にごぶさたを～びた I *apologized* to him for my long silence. 彼女は息子の不行跡を～びた She *apologized* (≒ *made an apology*) for her son's misbehavior.

わふう【和風】Japanese style. ¶～の庭園 a *Japanese-style* garden. ～の料理 *Japanese* dishes.

わふく【和服】Japanese clothes; 〔a〕*kimono.*

わぶん【和文】Japanese; Japanese writing.

—英訳 translation from Japanese into English. **—**タイプ〔ライター〕a Japanese tipewriter.

わへい【和平】peace. ¶～を提唱する強力な第三者がいない No powerful neutral party is advocating *peace.* これまでのところ～の申し出はいずれの側からも出ていない So far there have been no overtures for *peace* from either side.

—会談 a peace conference. **—**交渉 a peace negotiation.

わほう【話法】〚文法〛narration.

間接**—** indirect narration. 直接**—** direct narration.

わぼく【和睦】(講和) peace; (和解) reconciliation. ¶彼らは快く～の条件に応じた They willingly consented to the terms of *peace settlement.* ついに両国は～した At last the two countries *became reconciled* to each other.

わめきごえ【喚き声】a shout; a yell; a scream; a shriek.

わめ·く【喚く】cry; shout; yell; shriek; scream.

わやく【和訳】translation into Japanese.

¶英文を～する *translate* English *into Japanese.*

英文**—** translation from English into Japanese.

わ

わよう【和洋】―折衷 a combination (≒ compromise) of (≒ between) Japanese and European styles.

わら【藁・稈】a straw (西洋の藁は麦. 日本のは米). ¶おぼれる者～をもつかむ(諺) *A drowning man will catch at a straw.* (at を落とさぬこと).

―ぐつ straw boots. ―細工 straw work. ―灰 straw ashes. ―半紙 straw writing paper. ―布団 a straw mattress.

わらい【笑い】a laugh; laughter; (くすくす笑い) a chuckle; a giggle; (微笑) a smile.

¶～を抑えるのにほんとうに苦労した I *suppressed my laughter* (≒ *swallowed a laugh*) with great difficulty. 人様の～を買うようなまねはするな Don't *make yourself a laughingstock.* / Don't do anything that will *make* people *laugh at* you. 彼女のしぐさが彼らに～を催させた Her action *made* them *laugh.* もうかって彼は～がとまらない He cannot stop *chuckling over* the large profit.

大― a hearty laugh. せせら― derisive laughter. ばか― a horse laugh.

わらいがお【笑い顔】a smiling face. ¶あの娘の～を見るといつも心が和む My heart melts whenever I see her *smiling face.*

わらいぐさ【笑い草】a laughingstock.

¶彼女は人々の～となった She *made herself a laughingstock* to the others. まったくお～だ It's really *a farce.* / It's really *a caricature.*

わらいごえ【笑い声】laughter. ¶隣の部屋から～が聞こえた *A laughing voice* came from the next room.

わらいごと【笑い事】¶～じゃないぞ, ほんとうに It is no *laughing matter,* I tell you.

わらいじょうご【笑い上戸】an easy laugher.

¶彼女は～だ She *laughs easily.* / She *is always laughing for nothing at all.* 彼は～だ (飲酒の) He is *a merry drinker.*

わらいだ・す【笑い出す】¶彼らはくすくす～した They *began to giggle* under their breath. 聴衆はどっと～した The audience *burst out laughing.*

わらいとば・す【笑い飛ばす】¶彼はそのうわさを～した He *laughed* the rumor *off.*

わらいばなし【笑い話】a laugh; a funny story. ¶～のようだけれどほんとうだ It sounds like *a joke,* but it's quite true.

わら・う【笑う】**1**〖声を出して〗laugh; (ほほ笑む) smile; (くすくす) chuckle; (大きく口をあけて, にやりと笑う) grin.

¶私は～わずにはいられなかった I could not help *laughing.*

思わず～った I *laughed* in spite of myself.

これは～って済ませることでない This is no matter to *be laughed away.*

彼らはどっと～った They *burst into a roar of laughter.*

私は涙の出るほど～った I *laughed myself into tears.*

その冗談を聞いて腹を抱えて～った At the joke we *split our sides with laughter.*

私は彼のおどし文句を～ってあしらった I *smiled at his threats.*

～う門には福きたる(諺) Fortune comes in by a merry gate. / Laugh and grow fat.

来年のことを言うと鬼が～う(諺) Next year is the devil's joke. / Talk about next year, and the devil will laugh.

2〖あざける〗¶～うべき laughable; ridiculous.

彼らは私の失敗を～った They *laughed at* (≒ *ridiculed*) my failure.

彼は腹の中で彼らを～った He *laughed up his sleeves at* them. / He *laughed at* them behind their backs.

わらじ【草鞋】straw sandals. ¶二足の～をはく be engaged in two trades at the same time.

―虫 a woodlouse.

わらび【蕨】〘植物〙a bracken.

わらぶき【藁葺き】¶～の家 a *straw-thatched* cottage.

わらべ【童】a child.

―歌 an ancient children's song; nursery rhyme.

わらわ・せる【笑わせる】¶彼は巧みな司会で聴衆を～せた He *set* the audience *to laughing* with his witty remarks. 彼が芸術家だって? ～せるな He is an artist? *Don't make me laugh!* (≒ *Don't be silly!*)

わり【割】**1**〖比率〗percentage. ¶日用品が3～上がった Daily necessities have gone up (≒ 㘝 have advanced) 30 *percent.*

2〖利害〗an advantage; a profit. ¶彼は～のよい取引をする He makes an *advantageous* transaction.

この商売は～に合わない This business does not *pay.* / This business *is not profitable.*

3〖割合〗rate. ¶大工の賃金は1日10,000円の～で支払われる The wages of a carpenter are paid *at the rate of* 10,000 yen a day.

わりあい【割合】**1**〖割〗proportion; (a) rate; ratio; (比較) comparison.

¶3対2の～で混ぜてください Mix them *at the ratio of* 3 to 2, please.

男女の～は2対3だ The *proportion* of males to females has *a ratio of* 2 to 3.

そういう人が1,000人にひとりくらいの～で存在する A man like that is about one in a thousand.

それはどんな～になっていますか What is the *ratio*?

2〖比較的〗¶この問題は～解きやすい This problem is *comparatively* easy to solve.

きょうは～涼しい It is *rather* cool today.

それは文化価値が～に高い It has a *relatively* high cultural value.

わりあて【割り当て・割当】allotment; assignment; a quota.

―制 the quota system. ―配給 quota delivery; rationing. ―量 an allotted amount; an allotment; a quota.

わりあ・てる【割り当てる】assign; allot; give a quota. ¶株を～てる *allot* shares. ～てられた仕事 *allotted* work. 班ごとに部屋を～てるのがほ

わ

くの仕事だった It was my part to *assign* each group to a room. その役をほかの役者に〜てた I *assigned* the part to another actor.

わりいん【割り印】a tally seal; a seal over two edges. ¶書類に〜を押す *affix one's seal simultaneously over* the edges of the two papers.

わりかん【割り勘】an equal split. ¶費用は〜にした We *split the expense.* / We *went fifty-fifty.* われわれは昼食は〜でいくことに決めた We decided to *go Dutch on* the luncheon.

わりき・る【割り切る】¶彼は旧友によくもそんな〜った態度がとれたものだ I'm surprised to hear that he *took such a businesslike attitude toward* his own friend. むしろ〜った見方をしてもらいたい I want you to *have a less sentimental view.* なんでも〜って考えるというわけにはいかない You cannot *be* so *positive about* everything.

わりき・れる【割り切れる】**1**〖数が〗¶それは7で〜れるか. いいえ〜れません Can it *be divided* by 7? No, it can't.

2〖気持ち・事情などが〗¶彼の態度はどうもぼくには〜れない His attitude *is quite incomprehensible* to me.

彼の説明にはなんだか〜れないものがある His explanation *doesn't convince me.* / I still *feel something lacking in* his explanation.

彼の措置に対して〜れない感情をいだいている人もある Some *remain unconvinced of* the sincerity of his actions.

判決後も〜れないものが残った *There was some room for doubt* left after the sentence.

わりこ・む【割り込む】¶列の間に〜む *break into* a line. 車が1台〜んできた A car *cut in.* 彼らは混んだ会場に無理に〜んだ They *forced their way into* the crowded meeting hall. 私は電車の中央に〜んで彼に近づいた *Squeezing* (≒ *Wedging*) *my way* into the middle of the railway car, I came up to him. 話の中に〜むのは失礼だ It's rude to *interrupt* others while they are talking.

わりざん【割り算】〖数学〗division. ¶〜する divide.

わりだか【割高】¶それでは〜になる It's *rather expensive* in that case. / That will *cost* you *much.* ばらでは〜になる If you buy them loose, they *are comparatively dear.*

わりだ・す【割り出す】¶なにから結論を〜したのか How could you *figure* it *out*? / What *is* it *based on*? / How did you *come to* that conclusion?

わりつけ【割り付け】layout. ¶雑誌写真の〜 *the layout* of magazine pictures. もう〜して印刷に出した I'*ve* already *laid* it *out* and sent it to press.

わりに【割に】¶彼は〜金持ちだ (比較的に) He is *comparatively* rich. 彼は今は〜のん気に暮らしている (前にくらべて) He lives in *comparative* comfort. きのうは〜疲れた (かなり) I felt *rather* tired yesterday. このスイカは〜甘い (思ったより) This watermelon is sweeter *than I expected.* 彼は年の〜身長が低い (…を考えると) He is short *for* his age. 彼は体の〜頭が大きい His head is big *in proportion to* his body.

わりばし【割り箸】splittable chopsticks.

わりびき【割り引き】a discount; a reduction. ¶古本は4〜で売られた The secondhand books were sold *at a discount* (≒ *reduction*) *of* 40 percent. 現金で買えば〜しますか Do you allow any *discount* for cash? 大量にお買いあげくださるなら, 1割〜します If you buy it in quantity, we give you 10 percent *discount.* 彼は定価の2〜した He *knocked* 20 percent *off* the price. 彼女の話は〜して聞かねばならぬ We must *discount* her talk. / We must take what she says *with a grain of salt.* / We can't believe everything she says.

—券 a discount ticket. —債券 a discount bond. —乗車券 a reduced fare ticket. —手形 a bill discounted. 銀行— bank discount. 現金— discount for cash. 手形—率 the discount rate. 団体—料金 a group rate.

わりふ【割り符】a tally; a check.

わりまえ【割り前】(割り当て) allotment; (割り当額) a quota; (分け前) a share. ¶各自〜を出してください I want each of you to *pay your own share.* 〜はどのくらいもらったか How much is your *share*? / How much did you get?

わりまし【割り増し】extra pay; a premium. ¶タクシー料金は夜間は〜になる We have to *pay extra* for a taxi at night. / Taxi fares increase proportionally at night.

—金 a premium; a bonus. —賃銀 extra wages; extra pay. —配当金 an extra dividend; a premium. —料金 an extra charge.

わりもどし【割り戻し】〖商業〗a rebate; a drawback. ¶〜がきく We can get *a rebate.*

わりもど・す【割り戻す】rebate. ¶即時払いには1割〜します We will *give a* 10 percent *rebate* for immediate payment. そういう際は5%〜します We will *allow a* 5 percent *drawback* in that case.

わりやす【割安】¶まとめて買えば〜になる If you buy them by the lot, it *is economical.* こちらの品は〜になっている The goods over here *are bargain-priced* (≒ are *moderate in price*). / We *can sell* the goods over here *at a low price.*

わ・る【割る】**1**〖壊す・裂く〗break. ¶クルミを〜る *crack* a nut.

石を〜る *break* a stone.

窓ガラスを〜る *smash* a windowpane.

彼は木を〜って燃料にした He *split up* the wood for fuel.

さらをこなごなに〜る *break* a dish *to pieces.*

リンゴを二つに〜る *halve* an apple; *cut* (≒ *divide*) an apple in two.

2〖割り算する〗divide. ¶10を2で〜ると5 *Divide* 10 by 2 and you get 5.

3〖薄める〗¶ウイスキーを水で〜る *mix* whisky

with water.

4 〘下回る〙 ¶ ドルは300円を～った The dollar *broke below* (≒ *got lower than*) 300 yen.

5 〘その他〙 ¶ 刑事はおどして犯人に口を～らせた The detective threatened the suspect into *making a confession*.

わる·い【悪い】 **1** 〘不道徳・邪悪〙 bad; wrong. ¶ 約束を破るのは～い Breaking a promise *is wrong*. / It *is not good* to break your promise.

うそをつくのは～い It *is wrong* to tell a lie. / Lying *is wrong*.

～い仲間とつきあうな Don't get into *bad* company.

彼らはなにか～いことをたくらんでいる They are up to *no good*. / They are planning something *wrong*.

～いと思ったらすぐに謝りなさい You must apologize soon if you realize you have done *wrong*.

すぐけんか腰になるのは彼の～い癖だ Hot-headedness is his *weakness*.

2 〘悪意〙 ill; malicious. ¶ 意地の～い子 an *ill-natured* boy.

きみは口が～い You *are foul-mouthed*.

ぼくをかつぐなんて，きみも人が～い It *is malicious* (≒ *is unkind*) of you to trick me [like that].

彼は人柄が～いからだれにも好かれない Nobody likes him, because he *is unpleasant*.

知らずにしたことだから～く思わないでくれ No hard feelings; I didn't mean to do it.

彼女は人の言うことを～くとる She takes what other say *amiss*.

3 〘責任がある〙 wrong. ¶ 私が～かったのだ. どうか許してくれ Pardon me; I *was wrong*.

～いのはあなたではなく私だ It is not you but I who *am in the wrong*.

きみが言いつけどおりにしなかったから～いのだ It's *wrong* of you, because you didn't do as you were told to.

私が～かった It was my *fault*.

4 〘有害な〙 bad. ¶ 夜ふかしは健康に～い It *is not good* to keep late hours.

子どもにこんな本を読ませるのは教育上～い It *is not good* for children's education to allow them to read such books.

すき腹に強い酒を飲むのは胃に～い To drink strong *sake* when you are hungry *is bad* for your stomach.

5 〘体が〙 ill. ¶ 彼はこのところぐあいが～くて休んでいる He *is ill* in bed these days.

彼は胃がだいぶ～い He *has problems with* his stomach.

顔色がよくない，どこか～いんじゃないか You look pale. *Is anything the matter* [*with* you]?

ぼくは歯が～くて困る I *am having trouble with* my teeth.

気分が～いので少し休ませてください Please let me rest for a while. I *feel sick*.

6 〘品質・調子など〙 bad; poor. ¶ 値段は安いけれど品が～い This is inexpensive, but *poor* in quality.

この机は出来が～い This desk is *poorly* made.

～いものでも食べたのか，腹のぐあいが変だ I am afraid I ate something *bad*. I have a stomach trouble.

この牛乳は～くなっている This milk has gone *bad* (≒ *sour*).

この機械は調子が～い This machine *doesn't work well*.

7 〘頭などが〙 ¶ うちの子どもは頭が～いので進学には苦労している My son *is slow*, so he is having a hard time getting into high school.

だれでも年をとると記憶力が～くなる When we get older, our memory *declines*.

彼女はことば遣いが～い She *is rough-spoken*.

私は物覚えが～くて困る I am plagued by a *bad* memory.

あの娘は器量は～いが性質はこのうえなくよい The girl *is not good-looking*, but has a very good character.

見てくれは～いがなかなか利口な犬だ This dog *is ugly*, but very smart.

ほんとに行儀の～い子どもたちだ How *badly* they behave!

8 〘天候など〙 bad. ¶ あいにく～い天気になってしまった Unfortunately, the weather has turned *bad*.

天気が～かったらあすのハイキングは中止しよう If we have *bad* weather tomorrow, we will give up going hiking.

9 〘道が〙 bad. ¶ この辺はひと雨降ると道が非常に～くなる When it rains the roads *are terrible* around here.

～い道を走ると車にガタがくる If we drive on *bad* roads, the car will become creaky.

10 〘不快・迷惑・気の毒〙 ¶ 待たせて～かったね *I'm sorry* to have kept you waiting.

生暖かい風が吹いて気味の～い夜だった The wind was lukewarm and the neighborhood *was scary* in the night.

～いけれどきょうは忙しくてきみに話をしてあげられない I *am afraid* I am too busy to talk to you today.

人にほめられて～い気持ちはしないものだ No one *is displeased* by praise.

きみに～い知らせがある I have *bad* news for [you.

それを聞いて彼は気を～くして部屋を出ていってしまった On hearing that, he *was displeased* and left the room.

11 〘評判が〙 bad. ¶ このごろ彼女は同僚の間で評判が～い She has a *bad* reputation among her colleagues these days.

彼の今度の小説は受けが～い His latest novel has a *cool* reception.

12 〘その他〙 ¶ そのうえ～いことに彼が病気で倒れた *What is worse*, he became ill.

皆で一杯やるのも～くないね It's not half *bad* to have a drink together.

～いときに彼が現われたものだ He came at an *unfortunate* moment.

手伝わせて～いね Thank you for your help.

そんな人聞きの～いことを言うなよ Don't talk of

such *scandalous* things. / That doesn't sound nice. (穏やかな言い方).

わるがしこ·い【悪賢い】 cunning ; crafty ; sly.

わるぎ【悪気】 malice. ¶ 〜があってやったのではない I meant no *harm*. 彼の言うことに〜は感じられない I find no *malice* (≒ *ill will*) in his remarks.

わるくすると【悪くすると】 ¶ 〜あすは雪だ *I fear* it will snow tomorrow. 〜たいへんなことになるかもしれない *I am afraid* it might cause a lot of trouble. 〜計画は中止になるかもしれない *If* [*the*] *worst comes to* [*the*] *worst*, the plan will be dropped.

わるくち【悪口】 slander ; abuse. ¶ 陰で人の〜を言う *speak ill of* others behind their backs. 人の〜を言う *say bad thing about* others. みんなひどく彼の〜を言った All of them *spoke* very *badly of* him (≒ *said terrible things about* him). 候補者はお互いの〜を言い合った The candidates *have been slandering* each other.

わるだくみ【悪巧み】 a mean plot ; an intrigue. ¶ 彼らは集まって〜をこらした They gathered to form *a mean* (≒ *an evil*) *plot*. 彼はとてもそんな恐ろしい〜に加わるような男ではない He is the last man to take part in such *a dreadful scheme*. 彼の〜にひっかかった I fell a victim to his *schemes*.

わるぢえ【悪知恵】 cunning ; craft. ¶ 〜にたけた男 a *crafty* (≒ *cunning* ; *wily*) man. 彼はだれかに〜をつけられたのだ He *was evilly influenced* by someone. / Someone *put bad ideas into his head*.

ワルツ 〔音楽〕 a waltz. ¶ 〜を踊る dance *a waltz*.

わるび·れる【悪びれる】 ¶ 彼は少しも〜れずまともに私の顔を見た He looked me in the face *without fear*. 彼は〜れず自説を主張した He stood by his opinion *without flinching* (≒ *with calm composure*). 彼は〜れることなく自分の過ちを認めた He admitted his mistake *with good grace*. うそが露見してもあの男にはいっこうに〜れたようすがない That man never *looks abashed* even when his lie has been detected.

わるふざけ【悪ふざけ】 ¶ 私に〜をするな Don't *play a trick on* me. 彼らは〜をしていて窓ガラスを割った They *mischievously* broke the windowpane.

わるもの【悪者】 a bad fellow ; a rascal ; a rogue ; a villain. ¶ 彼らはすっかり彼女を〜にした (罪を着せた) They *laid all the blame on* her. 彼は自分が〜になって彼らを救った He saved them by *taking all the blame on himself*.

わるよい【悪酔い】 ¶ このぶどう酒は上等だから〜はしない This wine is of the best quality, so it never *gives you nasty aftereffects*.

われ【我】 oneself ; self. ¶ 学者というものは〜を忘れて研究に熱中するものだ Scholars *lose themselves* in their studies. 息子がもどったうれしさに彼女は〜を忘れている She *is beside herself* with joy because of her son's return. 〜ながらうまくやれたと思う It is well-done, *if I may say so myself*. 〜ながら恥ずかしい I am ashamed of *myself*. 〜に返ると彼は不思議そうに辺りを見回した *Recovering his senses* (≒ *Coming to himself*), he looked around suspiciously. 〜と思わん者はやってみろ *If there is a man among you*, have a try!

われがち【我勝ち】 ¶ ものすごい火の手に〜に逃げた We saw the furious flames and ran away *for dear life*.

われがね【割れ鐘】 ¶ 彼は〜のような声でどなった He shouted *in a thunderous voice*.

われかんせず【我関せず】 ¶ 〜と彼は黙っていた He uttered no word *looking quite uninterested* (≒ *looking quite indifferent*). / He kept silent *showing no interest in it*.

われさきに【我先に】 ¶ 乗客は〜席を争った The passengers *scrambled for* seats. 彼らは人を押しのけて〜出口に急いだ They rushed to the exit *pushing others aside*.

われしらず【我知らず】 ¶ 彼女のことばに彼は〜微笑した He smiled at her words *unconsciously* (≒ *in spite of himself*).

われなべ【破れ鍋】 a cracked pot. ¶ 〜にとじぶた (諺) *Every Jack has his Jill.*

われめ【割れ目】 a crack ; a split. ¶ 壁の〜 *a crack* in the wall. 板の〜 *a split* in the board. 地面の〜 *a chasm* in the earth ; *a fissure* in the ground. 岩の〜 *a crevice* in the rock. 壁に〜ができた The wall *cracked* (≒ *split*).

われもの【割れ物】 (割れやすい物) a fragile article ; an easily broken thing ; a thing easy to break. ¶ 〜注意 (標記) Fragile.

わ·れる【割れる】 ¶ 氷が〜れる Ice *breaks*. 地面が〜れた The ground *was cracked*. 岩石が〜れた A rock *split*. 党が二つに〜れる A party *splits* into two. 労働者仲間が〜れた Labor's ranks *were split*. 頭が〜れるように痛む I have a *splitting* headache. 〜れるようなかっさいが起こった *A storm of applause* arose from all sides. とうとうしりが〜れた At last he was found out.

われわれ【我我·吾吾】 we. ¶ 〜は〜をよく理解してもらおうと思って〜の最善を尽くしている *We* are doing *our* best to have *us* understood well.

わん【湾】 (小さい) a bay ; (大きい) a gulf. ¶ 大阪〜 Osaka *Bay* ; the *Bay* of Osaka. メキシコ〜 the *Gulf* of Mexico.

わん【椀】 a wooden bowl.

わんきょく【湾曲】 a curve ; a bend. ¶ 〜する bend ; curve. 足が〜した男 a *bandy-legged* (≒ *bow-legged*) man. ボートは流れの急に〜した所にさしかかった The boat came to *a* sharp *curve* (≒ *bend*) in the stream.

わんさと ¶ 若者たちが〜押し寄せた Young men and women came *in swarms* (≒ *in crowds ; in great numbers*). 志願者は〜いる We have *a great many* (≒ *a plenty of*) applicants.

ワンサイドゲーム 〔競技〕 a one-sided game.

わんしょう【腕章】an arm band.
ワンダーフォーゲル *Wandervogel* (ドイツ語から) ; a hiking club.
わんにゅう【湾入】¶ そこで海は深く～している There an arm of the sea penetrates far into the land.
わんぱく【腕白】naughtiness. ¶ うちの子は～ざかりで手に負えない We cannot do anything with our boy now that he *is at a mischievous age*.
―小僧 a naughty boy ; an urchin ; an imp.
ワンピース a one-piece dress.
ワンマン (独裁者) an autocrat. ¶ うちの社長は～だ Our president is *a dictator*. / Our president *runs a one-man show*.
―カー a one-man car. **―ショー** a one-man show (女性の場合にも用いる).
わんりょく【腕力】force ; physical strength ; (暴力) violence ; brutal force. ¶ ～に訴える appeal to *force* ; resort to *force*. 学校で～をふるうのを許してはならない We shouldn't allow boys to use *force* at school. 彼らは～で彼の同意を得た They obtained his consent *by force* (≒ *by violence*).
―ざた ¶ とうとう～ざたになった They *came to blows* in the end.
わんわん (幼児語で犬) a doggy ; a doggie ; a bowwow (発音は [báuwáu]) ; (なき声) bowwow. ¶ 犬が～ほえる A dog *says* (≒ *barks*) *bowwow*.

英文手紙の書き方

I. 形　式

英文手紙は次の順で書く.

(1) 頭書(Heading)——差出人の住所と日付け.

(2) 序部(Introduction)——名宛人の名前と住所(親しい間では省く).

(3) 敬辞 (Salutation) ——Dear Mr. Brown など.

(4) 本文 (Body)

(5) 結辞 (Complimentary Close) ——Yours sincerely など.

(6) 署名 (Signature)——署名は必ず自分で書く.

(7) 本文に書きもらしたことは追伸(Postscript——P. S. と略す)として書きそえてもよいが, 正式の手紙のときは, なるべく避ける.

次にその位置を示す.

(1) Correspondent's Address
Date

Name
Address (2)

(3) Salutation

(4) Body

(5) Complimentary Close

(6) Signature

(7) P. S.

次にその実例を示す.

〠112 東京都文京区音羽2—12—21

上田花子が昭和51年7月17日にハワイのメリー・ブラウン嬢に出した手紙である.

12—21, Otowa 2 chome
Bunkyo-ku , Tokyo
112 Japan
July 17 , 1976

Miss Mary Brown
1727 Pali Highway
Honolulu, Hawaii 96813

Dear Mary,

I have just learned of your graduation from Bennington College, and your plans to go on to Columbia for your master's degree.

May I express my pride in your accomplishment, and extend to you my wish for your continued success and happiness?

Sincerely,
Hanako Ueda

P.S. Would you please send me a picture of your pet dog?

(1) 頭書 (Heading)
差出人の住所と日付けである．頭書の書き方には次のふた通りがある．

(a) 垂直式 (Block Form)
各行の初めをそろえ，各行の終わりにコンマやフルストップを打たない．アメリカ人がよく用いる．

〔例〕〒112 東京都文京区音羽2-12-21
昭和51年7月17日は
12—21, Otowa 2 chome
Bunkyo-ku, Tokyo
112 Japan
July 17, 1976

(b) 斜線式 (Indented Form)
行を改めるごとに少し右へずらして書き，各行の終わりにコンマを，最後の行の終わりにフルストップを打つ．イギリス人がよく用いる．

〔例〕 12—21, Otowa 2 chome,
Bunkyo-ku, Tokyo,
112 Japan,
17th July, 1976.

(2) 序部 (Introduction)
名宛人の名前と住所であるが，親しい友人間ではふつう省かれる．主として商業文や公用文に用いられ，最後の左下のすみに書くこともある．

(3) 敬辞 (Salutation)
一般に男性には Dear George または Dear Mr. Brown, 既婚女性には Dear Mrs. Brown, 未婚女性には Dear Mary または Dear Miss Brown のように書く． また名前のあとにはコンマを用い Dear Mr. Brown, のようにする．
商業文や公用文では男性には Dear Sir, 女性には Dear Madam とし，複数の相手，会社名などには Gentlemen または Dear Sirs とする．語の終わりにはコロンを用いる．名前のわからぬときは To Whom It May Concern などとすることもある．

(4) 本文 (Body)
日本ではふつう時候の挨拶から書き始め，要件はあとまわしになるが，英文手紙では初めから用件を書き，時候の挨拶などはあとまわしになるか省かれる．

(5) 結辞 (Complimentary Close)
敬辞が Dear Mr. ～ であれば結辞は Yours sincerely, Sincerely yours, Sincerely などとする． また Truly yours, Yours truly, Your friend なども用いる． 結辞のあとは Yours sincerely, のようにコンマを打つ．
（敬辞が Dear Sir のときは， 結辞は

商業文では Yours truly を，公用文では Yours respectfully を用いることが多い)

(6) 署名 (Signature)

上田太郎（男性）は Taro Ueda とし，上田花子（女性）は親しい友人間では Hanako だけでよい．親しい友人間でないとき，または商業文などでは未婚なら Miss Hanako Ueda，または Miss をかっこに入れて (Miss) Hanako Ueda とする．上田太郎夫人の上田花子ならば Hanako Ueda (Mrs. Taro Ueda)，または Mrs. Taro Ueda とする．Mrs. Hanako Ueda とすると「職業婦人の上田花子」か「未亡人の上田花子」となる．また未亡人の上田花子は Mrs. をかっこに入れて (Mrs.) Hanako Ueda とすることが多い．

II．封筒の書き方

名宛人の名前と住所は封筒のほぼ中央から書き始める．頭書 (Heading) と同じく各行の左端をそろえる垂直式 (Block Form) と各行を右へ少しずらして書く斜線式 (Indented Form) とある．垂直式はアメリカ人がよく用い，斜線式はイギリス人が多く用いる．

差出人の名前と住所は封筒の表の左上方に書く書き方と，封筒の裏の折り返しのところに書く書き方とがある．

名宛人および差出人の名前と住所の書き方は垂直式または斜線式に統一すること．

(1) 垂直式 (Block Form)

Taro Ueda
12—21, Otowa 2 chome
Bunkyo-ku, Tokyo
112 Japan

Stamp

Mr. John Brown
1727 Pali Highway
Honolulu, Hawaii 96813
U. S. A.

By Air Mail

(2) 斜線式 (Indented Form)

Hanako Ueda,
  12—21, Otowa 2 chome,
    Bunkyo-ku, Tokyo,
      112 Japan.

Stamp

Miss Mary Smith,
  65 Davies Street,
    London W 1 Y 2 AA,
      ENGLAND.

By Air Mail

(3) 封筒の裏の折り返しに差出人の名前と住所を書く書き方．(垂直式の例)

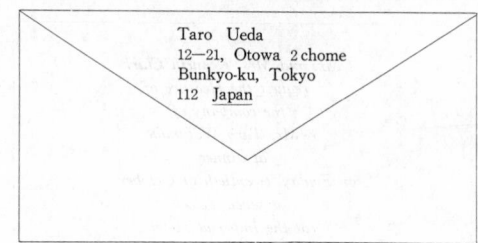

Taro Ueda
12—21, Otowa 2 chome
Bunkyo-ku, Tokyo
112 Japan

(4) 封筒の書き方に関する注意

(a) 名宛人の住所の最後の国名は全部大文字の活字体で書くことが多い．最近は下線を引いて国名を明確にするのがふつう，差出人の住所の場合も同じ．

(b) 名宛人が男性のときは，ふつう Mr. John Brown である．博士号を有する人には Dr. Thomas Wright とし，大学教授には Professor Lawrence Evans とする．名宛人が未婚女性のときは，Miss Mary Brown とする．また John Brown 夫人なら Mrs. John Brown とする．(Mrs. Mary Brown とすると，職業婦人メアリー・ブラウンか，未亡人メアリー・ブラウンとなる)

(c) 封筒に差出人の住所と名前を書かないこともあるが，外国あての郵便の場合は，なるべく書くことが望ましい．

(d) 名宛人の住居が下宿，アパートなどで，「～方」と書くときは，名宛人の住所の前に c/o Mr. Tanaka (田中様方) と書く．c/o は care of の略．

(e) 航空便は Air Mail, 速達は (米では) Special Delivery, (英では) Express Delivery, 書留は (米では) Registered Mail, (英では) Registered Post として封筒の表の左下に書き，郵便局でそれぞれ特別料金を払う．

Ⅲ. はがきの書き方

(1) はがきの表書きの書き方は封書と同じ形式でよい．

(2) 明瞭な場合は主語のIを省いてもよい．

(3) 絵はがきはスペースが少ないため，月名や年号は Nov. 10, '76 のように短縮形を用いてもよい．

〔例〕

Aug. 25, '76

Dear Hanako,
Visited Westminster Abbey today. It was magnificent. Met Miss Tanaka there. Will tell you all about our trip soon.

Your friend, Mary

Stamp

Miss Hanako Ueda
12—21, Otowa 2 chome
Bunkyo-ku, Tokyo
112 JAPAN

IV. 招待状の書き方

Mr. and Mrs. Kenneth Clark
request the pleasure of
the company of
Mr. Taro Watanabe
at dinner
on Friday, twentieth of October
at seven o'clock
at the Imperial Hotel

英文履歴書の書き方

PERSONAL HISTORY

Name in Full : Hanako Ueda
Date of Birth : November 30, 1950.
Present Address : 12—21, Otowa 2 chome, Bunkyo-ku, Tokyo.
Description　Age : 25　Height : 5′2″　Weight : 135 lbs.　Single.
Education : 1968—1972 Tokyo University of Arts.
　Degree : Bachelor of Arts, 1972.
　Major : Theory of Music.
Activities in University : English Speaking Society, 3 years.
Occupation : 1972 to date : Secretary to the president of Japan Musical Instruments Co., Ltd.
Special Acquirements : Typewriting, 40 words per minute.
　Driver's licence.
References : Mr. Ichiro Tanaka, chief of the Personnel Section Musical Instruments Co., Ltd.
　13—1, Ojihoncho, 1 chome Kita-ku, Tokyo.

注意　その他 Publications（著書・論文の類）とか，Awards（奨学金・研究助成金の類）など必要に応じて加えることがある．

英文日記の書き方

英文日記は「日付け」,「天候」,「本文」の順に書く.

(1)日付け

日付けは曜日，月，日の順に書く.「4月15日，土曜日」は Saturday, April 15.

曜日，月名は略語を用いてもよい.

曜日の略語は，日 Sun.，月 Mon.，火 Tues.，水 Wed.，木 Thurs.，金 Fri.，土 Sat.

月名の略語は，1月 Jan.，2月 Feb.，3月 Mar.，4月 Apr.，6月 Jun.，7月 Jul.，8月 Aug.，9月 Sept.，10月 Oct.，11月 Nov.，12月 Dec.

また祝祭日を書くときは「5月3日，月曜日，憲法記念日」は Mon.，May 3，Constitution Day. 滞在地を書くときは「8月25日，ロンドンにて」は Aug. 25, London. または London, Aug. 25.

(2)天候

天候は日付けの次に書く.

「晴れ」fine, fair, sunny ;「くもり」cloudy ;「風」windy ;「雨」rainy, wet ;「雪」snowy ;「霧」foggy ;「暴風雨」stormy ;「晴れ，のちくもり」fair, later cloudy ;「くもり，のち晴れ」cloudy first, later fine;「晴れ，ときどきくもり」fair, occasionally cloudy ;「きょうもまた雨」another rainy day.

「暖い」warm ;「暑い」hot ;「涼しい」cool ;「寒い」cold ;「晴れ，非常に寒い」fine but pretty cold.

(3)省略

主語の私（I）や，わかりきった語は省いてもよい.

「7時起床」は Got up 7. (I の省略).「10時就寝」は Bed at 10. (I went to の省略).「映画を見に行った」Went to the movies. (I の省略).「9時に帰宅」Back home at 9. (I came の省略)。

(4)実例

11月13日　火曜　くもりのち晴れ

英語の試験あり，放課後次郎とテニスをした．ロンドンの叔父から絵はがきをもらった.

Tues., Nov. 13. Cloudy, later fine.

Had a quiz in English. Played tennis with Jiro after school. Got a picture post card from Uncle in London.

ローマ字つづり方

（ローマ字を用いる場合，本書は下記の方式によった）

あ a	い i	う u	え e	お o	は ha	ひ hi	ふ fu	へ he	ほ ho
か ka	き ki	く ku	け ke	こ ko	ま ma	み mi	む mu	め me	も mo
さ sa	し shi	す su	せ se	そ so	や ya	い i	ゆ yu	え e	よ yo
た ta	ち chi	つ tsu	て te	と to	ら ra	り ri	る ru	れ re	ろ ro
な na	に ni	ぬ nu	ね ne	の no	わ wa	い i	う u	え e	を o

が ga	ぎ gi	ぐ gu	げ ge	ご go	だ da	ぢ ji	づ zu	で de	ど do
ざ za	じ ji	ず zu	ぜ ze	ぞ zo	ば ba	び bi	ぶ bu	べ be	ぼ bo

ぱ pa	ぴ pi	ぷ pu	ぺ pe	ぽ po

きゃ kya		きゅ kyu	きょ kyo	ひゃ hya	ひゅ hyu	ひょ hyo
ぎゃ gya		ぎゅ gyu	ぎょ gyo	びゃ bya	びゅ byu	びょ byo
しゃ sha	しゅ shu	しぇ she	しょ sho	ぴゃ pya	ぴゅ pyu	ぴょ pyo
じゃ ja	じゅ ju	じぇ je	じょ jo	みゃ mya	みゅ myu	みょ myo
ちゃ cha	ちゅ chu	ちぇ che	ちょ cho	りゃ rya	りゅ ryu	りょ ryo
にゃ nya		にゅ nyu	にょ nyo			

本書では「ン」はすべてｎで表わし，ｂ，ｍ，ｐの直前の「ン」もｎで示した。

米英つづり字の相違

1	《米》	-or	col*or*	fav*or*	lab*or*	neighb*or*
	《英》	-our	col*our*	fav*our*	lab*our*	neighb*our*
2	《米》	-er	cent*er*	lust*er*	met*er*	theat*er*
	《英》	-re	cent*re*	lust*re*	met*re*	theat*re*
3	《米》	-er	pedl*er*	bri*er*		
	《英》	-ar	pedl*ar*	bri*ar*		
4	《米》	in-	*in*close	*in*dorse	*in*quiry	
	《英》	en-	*en*close	*en*dorse	*en*quiry	
5	《米》	-i-	c*i*der	fl*i*er	t*i*re	
	《英》	-y-	c*y*der	fl*y*er	t*y*re	
6	《米》	-y-	sh*y*er	dr*y*ly	ga*y*ety	
	《英》	-i-	sh*i*er	dr*i*ly	ga*i*ety	
7	《米》	l	disti*l*	jewe*l*er	trave*l*er	woo*l*en
	《英》	ll	disti*ll*	jewe*ll*er	trave*ll*er	woo*ll*en
8	《米》	-g-	wagon	fagot		
	《英》	-gg-	waggon	faggot		
9	《米》	-se	defen*se*	licen*se*	offen*se*	preten*se*
	《英》	-ce	defen*ce*	licen*ce*	offen*ce*	preten*ce*
	［注］	次の名詞は米英共通.	advice	device	practice	
10	《米》	-ize	real*ize*	civil*ize*	organ*ize*	
	《英》	-ize	real*ize*	civil*ize*	organ*ize*	
		-ise	real*ise*	civil*ise*	organ*ise*	
11	《米》	-ization	real*ization*	civil*ization*	organ*ization*	
	《英》	-ization	real*ization*	civil*ization*	organ*ization*	
		-isation	real*isation*	civil*isation*	organ*isation*	
12	《米》	-ction	connec*tion*	inflec*tion*		
	《英》	-ction	connec*tion*	inflec*tion*		
		-xion	conne*xion*	infle*xion*		
13	《米》	-m	gra*m*	progra*m*		
	《英》	-mme	gra*mme*	progra*mme*		
14	《米》	-g	catalo*g*	dialo*g*	prolo*g*	
	《英》	-gue	catalo*gue*	dialo*gue*	prolo*gue*	
15	その他					
	《米》	dis*k*	*sk*eptic	chec*k*	ma*nik*in	
	《英》	dis*c*	*sc*eptic	che*que*	man*nequ*in	
	《米》	co*z*y	veranda	judgment		
	《英》	co*s*y	veranda*h*	judg*e*ment		
	《米》	encyclop*e*dia	medi*e*val			
	《英》	encyclop*ae*dia	medi*ae*val			
	《米》	dr*aft*	pl*ow*			
	《英》	dr*augh*t	pl*ough*			
	《米》	today	goodby	nearby		
	《英》	today	good-bye	near-by		
		to-day				
	《米》	jail	gray	mustache	pajamas	
	《英》	gaol	grey	moustache	pyjamas	

不規則動詞表

現在形	過去形	過去分詞
abide	abode, abided	abode, abided
arise	arose	arisen
awake	awoke	awoke, awaked
be (am, is; are)	was, were	been
bear	bore	borne, born
beat	beat	beaten
become	became	become
befall	befell	befallen
beget	begot	begotten, begot
begin	began	begun
behold	beheld	beheld
bend	bent	bent
bereave	bereaved, bereft	bereaved, bereft
beseech	besought	besought
beset	beset	best
bespeak	bespoke	bespoken
bespread	bespread	bespread
bestrew	bestrewed	bestrewed, bestrewn
bestride	bestrode, bestrid	bestridden, bestrid
bet	bet, betted	bet, betted
betake	betook	betaken
bethink	bethought	bethought
bid	bade, bid	bidden, bid
bide	bode, bided	bided
bind	bound	bound
bite	bit	bitten, bit
bleed	bled	bled
blend	blended, blent	blended, blent
bless	blessed, blest	blessed, blest
blow	blew	blown
break	broke	broken
breed	bred	bred
bring	brought	brought
broadcast	broadcast, broadcasted	broadcast, broadcasted
build	built	built
burn	burned, burnt	burned, burnt
burst	burst	burst
buy	bought	bought
can	could	——
cast	cast	cast
catch	caught	caught
chide	chided, chid	chided, chid, chidden
choose	chose	chosen
cleave	cleft, cleaved, clove	cleft, cleaved, cloven
cling	clung	clung
come	came	come
cost	cost	cost
creep	crept	crept
crow	crowed, crew	crowed
curse	cursed, curst	cursed, curst
cut	cut	cut

現在形	過去形	過去分詞
deal	dealt	dealt
dig	dug	dug
dive	dived, dove	dived
do, does	did	done
draw	drew	drawn
dream	dreamed, dreamt	dreamed, dreamt
drink	drank	drunk
drip	dripped, dript	dripped, dript
drive	drove	driven
drop	dropped, dropt	dropped, dropt
dwell	dwelt, dwelled	dwelt, dwelled
eat	ate	eaten
fall	fell	fallen
feed	fed	fed
feel	felt	felt
fight	fought	fought
find	found	found
flee	fled	fled
fling	flung	flung
fly	flew	flown
forbear	forbore	forborne
forbid	forbade, forbad	forbidden
fordo	fordid	fordone
forecast	forecast, forecasted	forecast, forecasted
forego	forewent	foregone
foreknow	foreknew	foreknown
forerun	foreran	forerun
foresee	foresaw	foreseen
foreshow	foreshowed	foreshown
foretell	foretold	foretold
forget	forgot	forgotten, forgot
forgive	forgave	forgiven
forsake	forsook	forsaken
forswear	forswore	forsworn
freeze	froze	frozen
gainsay	gainsaid	gainsaid
geld	gelded, gelt	gelded, gelt
get	got,	got, gotten
gild	gilded, gilt	gilded, gilt
gird	girt, girded	girt, girded
give	gave	given
gnaw	gnawed	gnawed, gnawn
go	went	gone
grave	graved	graven, graved
grind	ground	ground
grow	grew	grown
hang	hung, hanged	hung, hanged
have, has	had	had
hear	heard	heard
heave	heaved, hove	heaved, hove
hew	hewed	hewn, hewed
hide	hid	hidden, hid
hit	hit	hit
hold	held	held
hurt	hurt	hurt

現在形	過去形	過去分詞
inlay	inlaid	inlaid
inset	inset	inset
interbreed	interbred	interbred
interweave	interwove, interweaved	interwoven, interwove, interweaved
keep	kept	kept
kneel	knelt, kneeled	knelt, kneeled
knit	knit, knitted	knit, knitted
know	knew	known
lade	laded, laden	laden
lay	laid	laid
lead	led	led
lean	leaned, leant	leaned, leant
leap	leaped, leapt	leaped, leapt
learn	learned, learnt	learned, learnt
leave	left	left
lend	lent	lent
let	let	let
lie	lay	lain
light	lighted, lit	lighted, lit
lose	lost	lost
make	made	made
may	might	—
mean	meant	meant
meet	met	met
melt	melted	melted, molten
misgive	misgave	misgiven
mislay	mislaid	mislaid
mislead	misled	misled
misread	misread	misread
misspell	misspelled, misspelt	misspelled, misspelt
misspend	misspent	misspent
mistake	mistook	mistaken
misunderstand	misunderstood	misunderstood
mow	mowed	mowed, mown
must	must	—
offset	offset	offset
ought	—	—
outbid	outbid, outbade	outbid, outbidden
outdo	outdid	outdone
outgo	outwent	outgone
outgrow	outgrew	outgrown
outride	outrode	outridden
outrun	outran	outrun
outsell	outsold	outsold
outshine	outshone	outshone
outwear	outwore	outworn
overbear	overbore	overborne
overcast	overcast	overcast
overcome	overcame	overcome
overdo	overdid	overdone
overdraw	overdrew	overdrawn
overdrink	overdrank	overdrunk
overdrive	overdrove	overdriven
overeat	overate	overeaten
overfeed	overfed	overfed

現在形	過去形	過去分詞
overgrow	overgrew	overgrown
overhang	overhung	overhung
overhear	overheard	overheard
overlay	overlaid	overlaid
overleap	overleaped, overleapt	overleaped, overleapt
overlie	overlay	overlain
overpay	overpaid	overpaid
override	overrode	overridden
overrun	overran	overrun
oversee	oversaw	overseen
overshoot	overshot	overshot
oversleep	overslept	overslept
overspend	overspent	overspent
overspread	overspread	overspread
overtake	overtook	overtaken
overthrow	overthrew	overthrown
overwork	overworked, overwrought	overworked, overwrought
partake	partook	partaken
pay	paid	paid
pen	penned, pent	penned, pent
plead	pleaded, ple(a)d	pleaded, ple(a)d
prepay	prepaid	prepaid
proofread	proofread	proofread
prove	proved	proved, proven
put	put	put
quit	quitted, quit	quitted, quit
read	read	read
rebuild	rebuilt	rebuilt
recast	recast	recast
re-lay	re-laid	re-laid
remake	remade	remade
rend	rent	rent
repay	repaid	repaid
reread	reread	reread
rerun	reran	rerun
resell	resold	resold
reset	reset	reset
retell	retold	retold
rewrite	rewrote	rewritten
rid	rid, ridded	rid, ridded
ride	rode	ridden
ring	rang	rung
rise	rose	risen
rive	rived	riven, rived
roughcast	roughcast	roughcast
run	ran	run
saw	sawed	sawn, sawed
say	said	said
see	saw	seen
seek	sought	sought
sell	sold	sold
send	sent	sent
set	set	set
sew	sewed	sewed, sewn
shake	shook	shaken
shall	should	—
shave	shave	shaved shaven
shear	sheared	sheared, shorn

現在形	過去形	過去分詞
shed	shed	shed
shine	shone	shone
shoe	shod	shod
shoot	shot	shot
show	showed	shown, showed
shrink	shrank, shrunk	shrunk, shrunken
shrive	shrived, shrove	shriven, shrived
shut	shut	shut
sing	sang	sung
sink	sank	sunk, sunken
sit	sat	sat
slay	slew	slain
sleep	slept	slept
slide	slid	slid, slidden
sling	slung	slung
slink	slunk	slunk
slit	slit	slit
smell	smelled, smelt	smelt, smelled
smite	smote	smitten, smit
sow	sowed	sowed, sown
speak	spoke	spoken
speed	sped, speeded	sped, speeded
spell	spelled, spelt	spelled, spelt
spellbind	spellbound	spellbound
spend	spent	spent
spill	spilled, spilt	spilled, spilt
spin	spun	spun
spit	spat, spit	spat, spit
split	split	split
spoil	spoiled, spoilt	spoiled, spoilt
spread	spread	spread
spring	sprang, sprung	sprung
stand	stood	stood
steal	stole	stolen
stick	stuck	stuck
sting	stung	stung
stink	stank, stunk	stunk
strew	strewed	strewed, strewn
stride	strode	stridden
strike	struck	struck, stricken
string	strung	strung
strive	strove	striven
sunburn	sunburned, sunburnt	sunburned, sunburnt
swear	swore	sworn
sweat	sweat, sweated	sweat, sweated

現在形	過去形	過去分詞
sweep	swept	swept
swell	swelled	swelled, swollen
swim	swam	swum
swing	swung	swung
take	took	taken
teach	taught	taught
tear	tore	torn
tell	told	told
think	thought	thought
thrive	throve, thrived	thriven,thrived
throw	threw	thrown
thrust	thrust	thrust
tread	trod	trodden, trod
typewrite	typewrote	typewritten
unbend	unbent	unbent
unbind	unbound	unbound
underbid	underbid	underbid
undergo	underwent	undergone
underlay	underlaid	underlaid
underlie	underlay	underlain
underpay	underpaid	underpaid
undersell	undersold	undersold
understand	understood	understood
undertake	undertook	undertaken
underwrite	underwrote	underwritten
undo	undid	undone
unstring	unstrung	unstrung
unwind	unwound	unwound
uphold	upheld	upheld
upset	upset	upset
wake	waked, woke	waked, woken
wear	wore	worn
weave	wove	woven, wove
wed	wedded	wedded
weep	wept	wept
wet	wet, wetted	wet, wetted
will	would	——
win	won	won
wind	wound	wound
withdraw	withdrew	withdrawn
withhold	withheld	withheld
withstand	withstood	withstood
work	worked, wrought	worked, wrought
wrap	wrapped, wrapt	wrapped, wrapt
wring	wrung	wrung
write	wrote	written

編集主幹

清水　護（しみず　まもる）

1908年大分県生まれ。1931年東京大学文学部卒。成蹊大学，ICU教授を経て東京女子大学教授，ELEC研修所所長。英語学・英文学専攻。

成田成寿（なりた　しげひさ）

1907年新潟県生まれ。1932年東京文理大文学部卒。東京教育大学名誉教授。英米批評文学・現代英米文学専攻。

講談社学術文庫

定価　1200円

和英辞典

編集主幹　清水　護・成田成寿

昭和54年２月10日　第１刷発行
昭和58年３月５日　第５刷発行

発行者　加藤勝久

発行所　株式会社講談社

東京都文京区音羽２－12－21　〒112
電話・東京(03)945－1111(大代表)
振替・東京８－3930

装　幀　蟹江征治

レイアウト　志賀紀子

印　刷　共同印刷株式会社

製　本　共同印刷株式会社

ISBN4-06-158364-6（1）　（術E）

「講談社学術文庫」の刊行に当たって

これは、学術をポケットに入れることをモットーとして生まれた文庫である。学術は少年の心を養い、成年の心を満たす。その学術がポケットにはいる形で、万人のものになることは、生涯教育をうたう現代の理想である。

こうした考え方は、学術を巨大な城のように見る世間の常識に反するかもしれない。また、一部の人たちからは、学術の権威をおとすものと非難されるかもしれない。しかし、それはいずれも学術の新しい在り方を解しないものといわざるをえない。

学術は、まず魔術への挑戦から始まった。やがて、いわゆる常識をつぎつぎに改めていった。学術の権威は、幾百年、幾千年にわたる、苦しい戦いの成果である。こうしてきずきあげられた城が、一見して近づきがたいものにうつるのは、そのためである。しかし、学術の権威を、その形の上だけで判断してはならない。その生成のあとをかえりみれば、その根は常に人々の生活の中にあった。学術が大きな力たりうるのはそのためであって、生活をはなれた学術は、どこにもない。

開かれた社会といわれる現代にとって、これはまったく自明である。生活と学術との間に、もし距離があるとすれば、何をおいてもこれを埋めねばならない。もしこの距離が形の上の迷信からきているとすれば、その迷信をうち破らねばならぬ。

学術文庫は、内外の迷信を打破し、学術のために新しい天地をひらく意図をもって生まれた。文庫という小さい形と、学術という壮大な城とが、完全に両立するためには、なおいくらかの時を必要とするであろう。しかし、学術をポケットにした社会が、人間の生活にとってより豊かな社会であることは、たしかである。そうした社会の実現のために、文庫の世界に新しいジャンルを加えることができれば幸いである。

一九七六年六月　　野間省一

辞典・事典

国語辞典
監修・久松潜一、林大、阪倉篤義
日本最初の文庫版国語辞典。学習と社会生活に必要な七万三千語を収録。故事・成語・慣用句も豊富に採録。同義語・類義語・対語・語源なども収める。基準表記や慣用表記などを明示した用字用語辞典の決定版。
363

和英辞典
編集主幹・清水護、成田成寿
日本ではじめての文庫版による和英辞典。和英辞典中最高の文例六万、見やすく引きやすい五十音順ひらがな見出し、日常の必要語五万を完全網羅等々の特色により、評価の高い「講談社和英辞典」の文庫版。
364

英和辞典
編集主幹・川本茂雄
語数九万、適切な訳語、周到な語法・用法の注意。機能語の重点解説などで定評ある『講談社英和辞典』の文庫版。学習に実務に、高校・大学から社会人、研究家まで、ひろく活用できる全内容を文庫に収録。
365

古語辞典
佐伯梅友、馬淵和夫編
日本古典の学習・研究に必備の文庫判古典語辞典。主要古典を通読できる四万五千の豊富な語彙、正確でわかりやすい解説・解釈・用例など古典をより深く、より正しく理解できる、本格的な古語辞典である。
366

英和基本語小辞典
監修・成田成寿　編集・吉田正俊、中村義勝
中学生から大学生・一般社会人に必要な重要基本英単語一万三千語を厳選。重要語には星印、英会話に役立つ例文、英語の背景知識、カナ発音、関連語など、基本単語の知識と活用・日常会話は本書で十分。
367

実用辞典　和英併用
講談社編
職場や家庭での日常生活に便利な万能実用辞典。国語辞典・漢字辞典・外来語辞典、さらに和英辞典・ペン字辞典を兼ね、付録として手紙の書き方・難読語一覧などを収録する。コンパクトな文庫判で新登場。
368

現代フランス文学作家作品事典
佐藤朔　白井浩司　若林真　編
現代芸術の精華、20世紀フランス文学の全容を明らかにする。ジッド、プルーストからサルトル、カミュを経てロブグリエ、ルクレジオまで、現代文化をリードするフランス文学の作家評伝と作品梗概の集大成。
390

《講談社学術文庫　既刊より》

ことば・考える・書く・話す

論文の書き方
澤田昭夫著
論文を書くためには、ものごとを論理的にとらえて、それを正確に、説得力ある言葉で表現することが必要である。論文が書けずに悩む人人のために、自らの体験を踏まえてその方法を具体的に説いた力作。
153

日本語を考える
岩淵悦太郎著（解説・大石初太郎）
日本語に関心をもつすべての人々にとって、正しい言葉遣いと文章を知るための恰好の書。日本語の問題点を指摘し、言葉としての働きを高めるため、日本語をどのように発展させるべきかを論じた名著。
159

日本語横丁
板坂　元著（解説・浅井　清）
本書は従来の日本語研究の表通りでは取扱われにくい言葉や用法を積極的に取り上げ、これを学問の対象とした。日本語についての尽きない興味を語りながら日本人の考え方や価値観までをも考察した好著。
257

レポート・小論文・卒論の書き方
保坂弘司著
レポート・論文作成の実際過程を懇切に説く書き下ろし。テーマの捉え方、資料の探し方、構成の組立て方など、論文の書き方のコツを豊富な具体例を引きながら詳述。実際的で即効的な指針に満ちている。
297

文字の書き方
藤原宏・氷田光風
毛筆と硬筆による美しい文字の書き方の基本が身につく。用具の選び方や姿勢に始まり、筆づかいから字形まで、日常使用の基本文字についてきめ細かに実例指導をほどこし、自由自在な応用が可能である。
436

日本語のしゃれ
鈴木棠三著（解説・小池章太郎）
著者はことば遊び研究の第一人者。しゃれことば、だじゃれ、地口、語路あわせ、もじり、なぞなぞ、和歌の掛詞……これら言語技術のすべてを紹介解説し、日本人の言語伝統やシャレ的思考を明らかにする。
445

なぞの研究
鈴木棠三著
わが国の「なぞなぞ」の歴史、なぞと文芸との関連性、古典なぞの解き方、なぞの種類、なぞの名人たち、なぞの興行、なぞ本の板行、民間伝承のなぞ等々、なぞの史的実態は本書により始めて解明された。
492

《講談社学術文庫　既刊より》

政治・経済・社会

向坊 隆著	エネルギー問題についての基礎知識	ますます深刻さを増す資源・エネルギー問題に対して、我々は今後どのように対処していったらいいのだろうか。明日のために学界の第一人者が、その基本的な見方、考え方を説き明かした必読の書下ろし。	30
小泉信三著（解説・気賀健三）	共産主義批判の常識	自由主義の立場から「共産主義とはなにか」を分析、解説した歴史的名著。いまだ占領下の昭和二十四年に刊行、圧倒的な話題をよんだ本書は、再び激動と混迷の状況下にある今日、大きな意味をもつ。	44
伊東光晴著	生活のなかの経済学	日常生活のなかに累積する経済問題を解決すべく、著者が現実との格闘を通して創出した、市民の経済学としての本書は、新しい公共料金政策の提示など、市民のための政策科学を前進させた好著である。	58
ダニエル・ベル著／林雄二郎訳	資本主義の文化的矛盾(上)(中)(下)	マルクスもウェーバーも社会を単一と見る誤りを犯していた。ベル教授は本書で「経済・文化・政治の分裂」の理論を展開し、解決策として、「宗教の復興」「公共家族の建設」を提唱する。話題の新著の本邦初訳。	84〜86
宇野弘蔵著（解説・桜井 毅）	資本論入門	宇野理論の名でよばれる著者の業績は、日本のマルクス経済学研究の最高峰に位置するが、このマルクス経済学の泰斗の手になる本書は、『資本論』を深く学ぼうとするひとにとって、不可欠の名著である。	146
内野達郎著	戦後日本経済史	戦後三十年余、敗戦の痛手から奇跡の発展をとげた日本経済は今日その真価がとわれている。本書はその渦中にいた著者が文化史、世相史の視点も織りまぜ、立体的・巨視的に展開した戦後日本経済史の必読書。	339
正村公宏著	経済学の学び方	「近代経済学」「マルクス経済学」の両方に通じた著者によって書き下ろされた最もわかりやすい経済学入門書。とくに限界効用説や需要・供給曲線の意味など、経済学の基本的な考え方が充分説明されている。	401

《講談社学術文庫　既刊より》